TO:

FROM:

ON:

trueidentity

THE BIBLE FOR WOMEN

becoming
who you are
in Christ

ZONDERVAN™

GRAND RAPIDS, MICHIGAN 49530 USA
www.zondervan.com

table of contents

The Old Testament

The New Testament

iii

feature contents

Ask Me Anything

Myths

more myths

welcome to True Identity

Who are you?

> "I'm a senior analyst at Rolls-Royce."
> "I'm Joe's wife."
> "I'm the mother of three amazing children."
> "I'm a seventh grade teacher."
> "I'm Senator Philip's daughter."

How do you answer that simple question: *Who are you?*

As women, we often define ourselves by our accomplishments or our relationships. But those things do not last. When we lose the job, or our husbands fail us or leave us, or we feel like our lives are falling apart, then our identities crumble. But if we define our true identity by who we are in Christ, by who God tells us we are, then we are unshakeable. Then no matter what happens in life, we know who we are, and we can face whatever comes our way.

The purpose of this Bible, *True Identity*, is to help women deal with life issues by defining their true identity in Christ through his Word. Once we as women understand who we are in God's eyes, who we are because of what Jesus did for us on the cross, we can begin to see ourselves and our lives differently. And when we root our identities in Christ, we have the freedom, security and confidence to deal with the issues in our lives and not be overcome by them.

Relevant to Your Life

The core value for this Bible is *relevancy*. God wrote a timeless Book that's relevant to your life today, even though it was written thousands of years ago. You'll discover that the features in this Bible are both intellectually stimulating and relevant to everyday life. You won't find dry study notes that don't tie to life or feel-good devotions that don't tie to the Bible. You'll find personal, sophisticated, honest, practical advice. You'll find relevance, redefined.

Created for Women

True Identity was written for Christian women in their twenties and thirties, with an emphasis on the issues women face during these years, such as career, dating, marriage, children, changing friendships, moving, etc. This is a time of transition for women. Other women outside this demographic will also relate to the issues and decide that this is the Bible for them.

Features

TNIV Bible Text—

Women have known, loved and trusted the NIV for decades. The TNIV continues the NIV's legacy of communicating the Bible's timeless truth in today's language. For more information on the TNIV, read "a word to the reader" on p. x.

introduction

100 Myths—

"We should live together before we get married to make sure we're compatible."

"I am what I do."

"If I were a good Christian, I wouldn't struggle with this."

Everyday you hear (and subconsciously believe) myths that the world tells you. Satan's tried-and-true weapon against you is lies. In *True Identity*, 100 of the most common myths are exposed. For each "Myth," you'll read a story (based on true stories of women's lives) about how believing that myth affected the woman's life. Then you'll explore what God's Word says so that the next time you hear the myth, you can name the lie and replace it with the truth.

30 Ask Me Anything—

Hannah struggled with infertility. Leah lived in a loveless marriage. Deborah found a way to be a leader in a man's world.

If you could sit down with the women of the Bible and have a one-on-one conversation, what would you ask them? The dates they lived? The historical context of their stories? Wouldn't you rather know how they dealt with the issues in their lives and what God taught them? The "Ask Me Anything" profiles are intimate interviews with the women of Scripture, as if they're your own friend or mentor.

200 Conversations—

Do you ever find yourself skimming over the top of a familiar passage of Scripture and wondering what you're missing? "Conversations" give you penetrating questions to reflect on, either alone as you read the Bible or as you discuss Scripture with a friend, group or mentor.

200 He Is...—

If your identity is rooted in God, then it's important to know who he is. The first part of each "He Is" note introduces you to God as he reveals himself in Scripture. The second part of the note teaches how that attribute of God affects who you are and how you think and live.

300 At Issue—

What does the Bible say about _____ (money, friendships, gossip, shopping, dating, etc.)? These short, hard-hitting notes on life topics bring you the Bible's teaching on the varied and sundry issues of life.

66 Book Introductions—

For each of the 66 Bible books, you'll find quick facts that help you put the book in context (author, audience, date, setting, verse to remember and theme to consider). You'll also find in-depth questions to consider as you read the book—which will add depth to your Bible study and help you remember what you're reading.

Articles—

Have you tried to have a consistent quiet time . . . and failed?

Do you long to have, or to be, a mentor?

Do you wonder how to share your faith in a more natural way?

Do you need ideas for what to read in the Bible?

In the back of your Bible are a topical index and suggested Bible reading plans to help you get the most out of your time with God.

contributors

Developed for Zondervan by Livingstone

General Editor
Paige Drygas

Development Team
Mary Horner Collins
Paige Drygas
Betsy Todt Schmitt
Linda Taylor

Writers
Katherine Cloyd
Mary Ann Lackland
Amber Rae
Penny Pierce Rose
Betsy Todt Schmitt
Linda Washington

Reviewers
Tiffnie Jackson
(B.A. Psychology, M.S. Criminology),
Director of Women's Ministry

Sally Marcey (C.P.C., L.M.F.T.),
counselor

Graphic Design
Jeff James
Kirk Luttrell

Production Team
Joel Bartlett
Ann Luttrell
Kathleen Ristow
Tom Ristow
Ashley Taylor

ix

a word to the reader

Today's New International Version (TNIV) is a revision of the New International Version (NIV). Among the many English versions of the Bible that appeared in the twentieth century, the NIV (1973, 1978, 1984) has gained the widest readership in all parts of the English-speaking world. It was a completely new translation made by over a hundred scholars working directly from the best available Hebrew, Aramaic and Greek texts. The fact that participants from the United States, Great Britain, Canada, Australia and New Zealand worked together gave the project its international scope. That they were from many denominations—including Anglican, Assemblies of God, Baptist, Brethren, Christian Reformed, Church of Christ, Evangelical Covenant, Evangelical Free, Lutheran, Mennonite, Methodist, Nazarene, Presbyterian, Wesleyan and other churches—helped to safeguard the translation from sectarian bias. Responsibility for the NIV text, and now also for the text of the TNIV, is held by a self-governing body, the Committee on Bible Translation (CBT), composed of biblical scholars from colleges, universities and seminaries. During the revision process, many of the original members of CBT have been replaced by other scholars owing to retirement and other causes, but a similar geographical and denominational mix has been maintained.

From the beginning the translators have been united in their commitment to the authority and infallibility of the Bible as God's Word in written form. For them, the Bible contains the divine answer to the deepest needs of humanity, sheds unique light on our path in a dark world and sets forth the way to our eternal well-being. Out of this deep conviction, the Committee has held to certain goals for the NIV and for the present revision: that it would be an accurate translation and one that would have clarity and literary quality and so prove suitable for public and private reading, teaching, preaching, memorizing and liturgical use. The Committee has also sought to preserve a measure of continuity with the long tradition of translating the Scriptures into English.

There is a sense in which the work of translating the Bible is never finished. This very fact has prompted the Committee to engage in an ongoing review of the text of the NIV with the assistance of many other scholars. The chief goal of this review has always been to bring the text of the NIV abreast of contemporary biblical scholarship and of shifts in English idiom and usage. Already in 1978 and again in 1984 various corrections and revisions to the NIV text were made. In the TNIV the Committee offers to the reading public the latest fruits of its review.

The first concern of the translators has continued to be the accuracy of the translation and its faithfulness to the intended meaning of the biblical writers. This has moved the translators to go beyond a formal word-for-word rendering of the original texts. Because thought patterns and syntax differ from language to language, accurate communication of the meaning of the biblical authors demands constant regard for varied contextual uses of words and idioms and for frequent modifications in sentence structures.

To achieve clarity the translators have sometimes supplied words not in the original texts but required by the context. In a few instances, where some uncertainty about such material remained, it is enclosed in corner brackets. As an aid to the reader, italicized sectional headings have been inserted. They are not to be regarded as part of the biblical text and are not intended for oral reading. It is the Committee's hope that these headings may prove more helpful to the reader than the traditional chapter divisions (which were introduced in the thirteenth century).

For the Old Testament the standard Hebrew text, the Masoretic Text as published in the latest editions of *Biblia Hebraica*, has been used throughout. The Masoretic Text tradition contains marginal notations that offer variant readings. These have sometimes been followed instead of the text itself.

Because such instances involve variants within the Masoretic tradition, they have not been indicated in the textual notes. In a few cases, words in the basic consonantal text have been divided differently than in the Masoretic Text. Such cases are usually indicated in the textual footnotes. The Dead Sea Scrolls contain biblical texts that represent an earlier stage of the transmission of the Hebrew text. They have been consulted, as have been the Samaritan Pentateuch and the ancient scribal traditions concerning deliberate textual changes. The translators also consulted the more important early versions—the Greek Septuagint, Aquila, Symmachus and Theodotion, the Latin Vulgate, the Syriac Peshitta, the Aramaic Targums, and for the Psalms the *Juxta Hebraica* of Jerome. Readings from the Dead Sea Scrolls, the scribal traditions and these versions were occasionally followed where the Masoretic Text seemed doubtful and where accepted principles of textual criticism showed that one or more of these textual witnesses appeared to provide the correct reading. In rare cases, the translators have emended the Hebrew text where it appears to have become corrupted at an even earlier stage of its transmission. These departures from the Masoretic Text are also indicated in the textual footnotes. Sometimes the vowel indicators (which are later additions to the basic consonantal text) found in the Masoretic Text did not, in the judgment of the translators, represent the correct vowels for the original text. Accordingly, some words have been read with a different set of vowels. These instances are usually not indicated in the footnotes.

The Greek text used in translating the New Testament has been an eclectic one, based on the latest editions of the Nestle-Aland / United Bible Societies' Greek New Testament. The translators have made their choices among the variant readings in accordance with widely accepted principles of New Testament textual criticism. Footnotes call attention to places where uncertainty remains.

The New Testament authors, writing in Greek, often quote the Old Testament from its ancient Greek version, the Septuagint. This is one reason why some of the Old Testament quotations in the TNIV New Testament are not identical to the corresponding passages in the TNIV Old Testament. Such quotations in the New Testament are indicated with the footnote "(see Septuagint)."

Other footnotes in this version are of several kinds, most of which need no explanation. Those giving alternative translations begin with "Or" and generally introduce the alternative with the last word preceding it in the text, except when it is a single-word alternative. In poetry quoted in a footnote a slash mark indicates a line division.

It should be noted that references to diseases, minerals, flora and fauna, architectural details, clothing, jewelry, musical instruments and other articles cannot always be identified with precision. Also, linear measurements and measures of capacity can only be approximated (see Appendix I). The manner in which Hebrew proper names are to be represented in English has not become fully standardized. In the TNIV the spelling of many names has been revised to conform more closely to current scholarly practice and to the phonetics of the Hebrew originals. A list of such changes can be found in Appendix II, following the biblical text. A parallel list provides the spelling of these names in the NIV. Although *Selah,* used mainly in the Psalms, is probably a musical term, its meaning is uncertain. Since it may interrupt reading and distract the reader, this word has not been kept in the English text, but every occurrence has been signaled by a footnote.

Three changes of special note in the TNIV are the frequent substitution of "Messiah" for the more traditional "Christ," the replacement of "saints" in most cases with alternative renderings, and a greater sensitivity to shifts in English idiom. A word about each is in order.

While "Messiah" (from the Hebrew) and "Christ" (from the Greek) both mean "Anointed One," what began as a title full of meaning to the early Jewish hearers of the gospel tended in the later Greek-speaking churches to become just another name for Jesus. So where the term is clearly used to designate the God-sent deliverer of Jewish expectations (primarily in the Gospels and Acts), it was judged more appropriate to use "Messiah." However, where this sense seems less prominent (primarily in the Epistles), the transliteration of the Greek word ("Christ") has been retained.

Concerning "saints," current usage (as reflected in major dictionaries of the English language) burdens it with meanings that lie outside the sense of the original-language words. The main Old Testament term that has traditionally been rendered "saints" refers to those who are faithful to God. The New

a word to the reader

Testament term primarily designates those who have become followers of the Christian Way as people consecrated to God and thus belonging to the Lord in a special sense.

Although a basic core of the English language remains relatively stable, many diverse and complex cultural forces continue to bring about subtle shifts in the meanings and/or connotations of even old, well-established words and phrases. Among the more programmatic changes in the TNIV are the removal of nearly all vocative "O"s and the elimination of most instances of the generic use of masculine nouns and pronouns. Relative to the second of these, the so-called singular "they/their/them," which has been gaining acceptance among careful writers and which actually has a venerable place in English idiom, has been employed to fill in the vocabulary gap in generic nouns and pronouns referring to human beings. Where an individual emphasis is deemed to be present, "anyone" or "everyone" or some other equivalent is generally used as the antecedent of such pronouns.

Sometimes the chapter and/or verse numbering in English translations of the Old Testament differs from that found in published Hebrew texts. This is particularly the case in the Psalms, where the traditional titles are included in the Hebrew verse numbering. Such differences are marked by asterisks (*) in the text and informative footnotes set off in a separate line (or lines) at the bottom of the page. In the New Testament, verse numbers that marked off portions of the traditional English text not supported by the best Greek manuscripts are now set alongside the immediately preceding verse numbers and placed in brackets (see, for example, Matthew 17:20[21]).

Mark 16:9-20 and John 7:53—8:11, although long accorded virtually equal status with the rest of the Gospels in which they stand, have a very questionable—and confused—standing in the textual history of the New Testament, as noted in the bracketed annotations with which they are set off. A different typeface has now been chosen for these passages to indicate even more clearly their uncertain status.

Basic formatting of the text, such as lining the poetry, paragraphing (both prose and poetry), setting up of (administrative-like) lists, indenting letters and lengthy prayers within narratives and the insertion of sectional headings, has been the work of the Committee. However, the choice between single-column and double-column formats has been left to the publishers. Also the issuing of "red-letter" editions is a publisher's choice—one that the Committee does not endorse.

The Committee has again been reminded that every human effort is flawed—including this revision of the NIV. We trust, however, that many will find in it an improved representation of the Word of God, through which they hear his call to faith in our Lord Jesus Christ and to service in his kingdom. We offer this version of the Bible to him in whose name and for whose glory it has been made.

The Committee on Bible Translation
August 2003

The Old Testament

4 **GENESIS** 74 **EXODUS** 129 **LEVITICUS**

165 **NUMBERS** 220 **DEUTERONOMY**

the bo

of mo

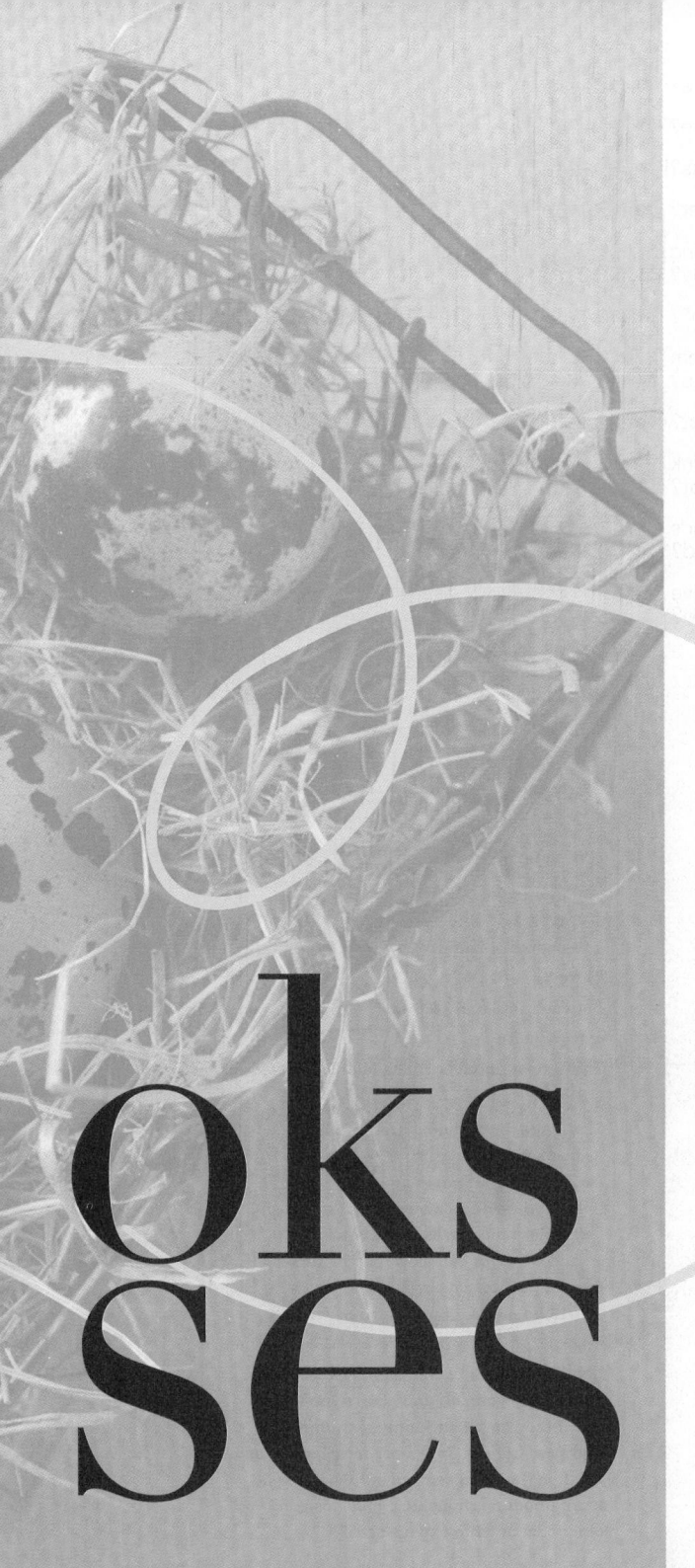

The five books of Moses are accounts of the history of God's people, the people of Israel. Beginning with Genesis, the narrative moves from a broad view of the universe and all of creation to human beings and their role in the world. From this general view of humankind, the account narrows down—from a focus on "all nations" to "one nation," the chosen people of Israel.

Also called the *Pentateuch* (from the Greek words for "five books"), the five books of Moses comprise the first major section in the Old Testament. This section is also referred to as the *Torah*, or Law, referring especially to the latter four books in which God's covenant with his people is described and confirmed.

oks
ses

4

genesis

AUTHOR
Moses.

AUDIENCE
The people of Israel.

DATE
Between 1446 and 1406 B.C.

SETTING
The area we would call the Middle East today.

VERSES TO REMEMBER
"I will make you into a great nation,
    and I will bless you;
I will make your name great,
    and you will be a blessing.
I will bless those who bless you,
    and whoever curses you I will curse;
and all peoples on earth
    will be blessed through you." (12:2–3)

THEME TO CONSIDER
Read the stories in Genesis to learn about
people like yourself and others you know.
See if they aren't strikingly similar to you
and your friends. Your story may have a new
twist on time and setting, but what do you
learn about relationships, love, loss and
other common life experiences?

The Beginning

1 In the beginning God created the heavens and the earth. ²Now the earth was formless and empty, darkness was over the surface of the deep, and the Spirit of God was hovering over the waters.

³And God said, "Let there be light," and there was light. ⁴God saw that the light was good, and he separated the light from the darkness. ⁵God called the light "day," and the darkness he called "night." And there was evening, and there was morning—the first day.

⁶And God said, "Let there be a vault between the waters to separate water from water." ⁷So God made the vault and separated the water under the vault from the water above it. And it was so. ⁸God called the vault "sky." And there was evening, and there was morning—the second day.

⁹And God said, "Let the water under the sky be gathered to one place, and let dry ground appear." And it was so. ¹⁰God called the dry ground "land," and the gathered waters he called "seas." And God saw that it was good.

¹¹Then God said, "Let the land produce vegetation: seed-bearing plants and trees on the land that bear fruit with seed in it, according to their various kinds." And it was so. ¹²The land produced vegetation: plants bearing seed according to their kinds and trees bearing fruit with seed in it according to their kinds. And God saw that it was good. ¹³And there was evening, and there was morning—the third day.

¹⁴And God said, "Let there be lights in the vault of the sky to separate the day from the night, and let them serve as signs to mark seasons and days and years, ¹⁵and let them be lights in the vault of the sky to give light on the earth." And it was so. ¹⁶God made two great lights—the greater light to govern the day and the lesser light to govern the night. He also made the stars. ¹⁷God set them in the vault of the sky to give light on the earth, ¹⁸to govern the day and the night, and to separate light from darkness. And God saw that it was good. ¹⁹And there was evening, and there was morning—the fourth day.

HE IS: creator

1:1 Meet God, the *creator* of everything. He who decided that things should be and they were. He who set the hands of time in motion. The One whose imagination *created* the heavens and the earth and all they contain: stars, plants, seasons, trees . . . penguins. When he reviewed his creation, God saw that "it was very good" (v. 31).

God, who *created* everything, created everyone—including you. You may look in the mirror and see flaws. But God designed every freckle, every wrinkle, every crinkle and even numbered the hairs on your head (see Luke 12:7). When he created you, he considered it "very good." Do you?

For the next He Is, go to p. 18.

²⁰And God said, "Let the water teem with living creatures, and let birds fly above the earth across the vault of the sky." ²¹So God created the great creatures of the sea and every living and moving thing with which the water teems, according to their kinds, and every winged bird according to its kind. And God saw that it was good. ²²God blessed them and said, "Be fruitful and increase in number and fill the water in the seas, and let the birds increase on the earth." ²³And there was evening, and there was morning—the fifth day.

²⁴And God said, "Let the land produce living creatures according to their kinds: livestock, creatures that move along the ground, and wild animals, each according to its kind." And it was so. ²⁵God made the wild animals according to their kinds, the livestock according to their kinds, and all the creatures that move along the ground according to their kinds. And God saw that it was good.

²⁶Then God said, "Let us make human beings in our image, in our likeness, so that they may rule over the fish in the sea and the birds in the sky, over the livestock and all the wild animals,ᵃ and over all the creatures that move along the ground."

²⁷So God created human beings in his own image,
in the image of God he created them;
male and female he created them.

²⁸God blessed them and said to them, "Be fruitful and increase in number; fill the earth and subdue it. Rule over the fish in the sea and the birds in the sky and over every living creature that moves on the ground."

²⁹Then God said, "I give you every seed-bearing plant on the face of the whole earth and every tree that has fruit with seed in it. They will be yours for food. ³⁰And to all the beasts of the earth and all the birds in the sky and all the creatures that move on the ground—everything that has the breath of life in it—I give every green plant for food." And it was so.

³¹God saw all that he had made, and it was very good. And there was evening, and there was morning—the sixth day.

2 Thus the heavens and the earth were completed in all their vast array.

²By the seventh day God had finished the work he had been doing; so on the seventh day he rested from all his work. ³Then God blessed the seventh day and made it holy, because on it he rested from all the work of creating that he had done.

Adam and Eve

⁴This is the account of the heavens and the earth when they were created, when the LORD God made the earth and the heavens.

⁵Now no shrub had yet appeared on the earthᵇ and no plant had yet sprung up, for the LORD God had not sent rain on the earth and there was no one to work the ground, ⁶but streamsᶜ came up from the earth and watered the whole surface of the ground. ⁷Then the LORD God formed a manᵈ from the dust of the ground and breathed into his nostrils the breath of life, and the man became a living being.

⁸Now the LORD God had planted a garden in the east, in Eden; and there he put the man he had formed. ⁹The LORD God made all kinds of trees grow out of the ground—trees that were pleasing to the eye and good for food. In the middle of the garden were the tree of life and the tree of the knowledge of good and evil.

¹⁰A river watering the garden flowed from Eden; from there it was separated into four headwaters. ¹¹The name of the first is the Pishon; it winds through the entire land of Havilah, where there is gold. ¹²(The gold of that land is good; aromatic resinᵉ and onyx are also there.) ¹³The name of the second river is the Gihon; it winds through the entire land of Cush.ᶠ ¹⁴The name of the third river is the Tigris; it runs along the east side of Ashur. And the fourth river is the Euphrates.

¹⁵The LORD God took the man and put him in the Garden of Eden to work it and take care of it. ¹⁶And the LORD God commanded the man, "You are free to eat from any tree in the garden; ¹⁷but you must not eat from the tree of the knowledge of good and evil, for when you eat of it you will certainly die."

¹⁸The LORD God said, "It is not good for the man to be alone. I will make a helper suitable for him."

¹⁹Now the LORD God had formed out of the ground all the wild animals and all the birds in the sky. He brought them to the man to see what he would name them; and whatever the man called each living creature, that was its name. ²⁰So the man gave names to all the livestock, the birds in the sky and all the wild animals.

But for Adamᵍ no suitable helper was found. ²¹So the LORD God caused the man to fall into a deep

---

ᵃ 26 Probable reading of the original Hebrew text (see Syriac); Masoretic Text *the earth*   ᵇ 5 Or *land*; also in verse 6   ᶜ 6 Or *mist*   ᵈ 7 The Hebrew for *man (adam)* sounds like and may be related to the Hebrew for *ground (adamah)*; it is also the name *Adam* (see Gen. 2:20).   ᵉ 12 Or *good; pearls*   ᶠ 13 Possibly southeast Mesopotamia   ᵍ 20 Or *the man* sleep; and while he was sleeping, he took one of the man's ribs^a and then closed up the place with flesh. ²²Then the Lord God made a woman from the rib^b he had taken out of the man, and he brought her to the man.

²³The man said,

> "This is now bone of my bones
> and flesh of my flesh;
> she shall be called 'woman,'
> for she was taken out of man."

²⁴For this reason a man will leave his father and mother and be united to his wife, and they will become one flesh.

²⁵The man and his wife were both naked, and they felt no shame.

The Fall

3 Now the serpent was more crafty than any of the wild animals the Lord God had made. He said to the woman, "Did God really say, 'You must not eat from any tree in the garden'?"

²The woman said to the serpent, "We may eat fruit from the trees in the garden, ³but God did say, 'You must not eat fruit from the tree that is in the middle of the garden, and you must not touch it, or you will die.'"

⁴"You will not certainly die," the serpent said to the woman. ⁵"For God knows that when you eat of it your eyes will be opened, and you will be like God, knowing good and evil."

⁶When the woman saw that the fruit of the tree was good for food and pleasing to the eye, and also desirable for gaining wisdom, she took some and ate it. She also gave some to her husband, who was with her, and he ate it. ⁷Then the eyes of both of them were opened, and they realized they were naked; so they sewed fig leaves together and made coverings for themselves.

⁸Then the man and his wife heard the sound of the Lord God as he was walking in the garden in the cool of the day, and they hid from the Lord God among the trees of the garden. ⁹But the Lord God called to the man, "Where are you?"

¹⁰He answered, "I heard you in the garden, and I was afraid because I was naked; so I hid."

¹¹And he said, "Who told you that you were naked? Have you eaten from the tree that I commanded you not to eat from?"

¹²The man said, "The woman you put here with me—she gave me some fruit from the tree, and I ate it."

¹³Then the Lord God said to the woman, "What is this you have done?"

The woman said, "The serpent deceived me, and I ate."

¹⁴So the Lord God said to the serpent, "Because you have done this,

> "Cursed are you above all livestock
> and all wild animals!
> You will crawl on your belly
> and you will eat dust
> all the days of your life.
> ¹⁵And I will put enmity

7

---

^a 21 Or took part of the man's side ^b 22 Or part

myth# 01 "I'LL NEVER BE FREE FROM MY PAST."

I feel as if I've lived two or three different lives. And if any one of those past lives ever catches up with me, then everything I can safely call my own today is gone—my reputation as a leader at work, a successful marriage, loving family—my past threatens all of it. I fear someone, somewhere will claim to know what I'm "really like." Only I'm not that person anymore. Not perfect, but thank God not what I used to be. I truly believe I've changed and am growing into the person Christ wants me to be.

But that person still carries a secret burden. As bright as her future is, she's never free from her past.

I'm never free from the haunting accusations surrounding yesterday's mistakes that may ambush me today. Imaginary scenarios and entire conversations play out in my head. They sneak into my thoughts with crafty subtlety. Sometimes when I tuck my baby girl under the covers for the night and she whispers, "I love you, Mommy," I want so much to enjoy the moment and soak in her affection. But a faint, persistent voice inside tells me, "You don't deserve her, you know. Not after what you've done . . ."

And when I meet someone that I genuinely like, whose friendship I really enjoy, the thought inevitably traipses through my head that if she knew my past, she wouldn't think so highly of me.

When my boss compliments me at a meeting for my "innovative leadership," I beam with a sense of accomplishment. Until I begin to remember all my failures.

It sounds hypocritical to say I believe Jesus has forgiven my past. I do believe. I just want to know, will I ever be free from it?

—Karen

HAVE YOU EVER felt like you're

the only one with something to hide? That sense of isolation magnifies your feelings of guilt. Satan wants you to feel alone, crippled by a false sense of guilt. Yet the truth is that every person on earth has a "past"—even those we consider "Mother Teresa" types who seemingly never did anything wrong. The book of Genesis describes how we inherited a sinful nature. Adam and Eve instilled a sinful nature into the entire human race (see Romans 5:12,17).

However, we must understand and accept that we are free from the **penalty of our past** because we trust Christ's sacrifice as the ultimate and final payment for sin (see Hebrews 7:27). Even so, sometimes the **pain of our past** comes calling. Many women have an emotional disposition or personality type that lends itself to dwelling on bitter memories. Our adversary, the devil, often misuses this sensitivity to accuse and discourage us. He tempts our thoughts with guilt over past deeds. He calls into question the penalty of our past as if it is somehow unpaid— an outstanding debt he convinces us we must pay ourselves. We respond to his perverse persuasion by feeling as if we don't deserve the love of family or friends, much less God's love. *After what you've done? Who are you kidding?* This is the language of lies—a familiar tongue to anyone who longs to be free from a shameful past.

Satan tries to slip the chains of guilt back on our shoulders. And sometimes we again pick up those old familiar chains—our guilt feels so comfortable that we revert to it out of habit. But Christ has set us free! He paid the FULL penalty for our sins. Every wrong thought, word or action—all paid for.

Don't believe the lie. God set you free; Christ died that you would be free—but you must choose to live that way.

"Sometimes it takes time to forgive ourselves for our past. About 80 percent of adults ages 45 and older said they knew that God forgave them for their sins and that this knowledge gave them the strength to face their faults and be a better person, compared to 69 percent of those ages 18 to 44."

—University of Michigan, Institute for Social Research

"SO IF THE SON SETS YOU FREE, YOU WILL BE FREE INDEED."

JOHN 8:36

SEE ALSO

Romans 8:1–4

2 Corinthians 5:17

Galatians 5:1

For more on **Forgiveness**, check the index.

between you and the woman,
and between your offspring*a* and hers;
he will crush*b* your head,
and you will strike his heel."

¹⁶To the woman he said,

"I will make your pains in childbearing very severe;
with pain you will give birth to children.
Your desire will be for your husband,
and he will rule over you."

¹⁷To Adam he said, "Because you listened to your wife and ate from the tree about which I commanded you, 'You must not eat of it,'

"Cursed is the ground because of you;
through painful toil you will eat of it
all the days of your life.
¹⁸It will produce thorns and thistles for you,
and you will eat the plants of the field.
¹⁹By the sweat of your brow
you will eat your food
until you return to the ground,
since from it you were taken;
for dust you are
and to dust you will return."

²⁰Adam*c* named his wife Eve,*d* because she would become the mother of all the living.
²¹The Lᴏʀᴅ God made garments of skin for Adam and his wife and clothed them. ²²And the Lᴏʀᴅ God said, "The man has now become like one of us, knowing good and evil. He must not be allowed to reach out his hand and take also from the tree of life and eat, and live forever." ²³So the Lᴏʀᴅ God banished him from the Garden of Eden to work the ground from which he had been taken. ²⁴After he drove them out, he placed on the east side*e* of the Garden of Eden cherubim and a flaming sword flashing back and forth to guard the way to the tree of life.

conversations

competition «» 4:1–11

1» What is God's view of competition?

2» Do you see Christians compete for God's acceptance? In what ways?

3» If we compete with others for God's approval, what are the results?

For more on competition, check the index.
For the next Conversations, go to p. 16.

Cain and Abel

4 Adam*f* made love to his wife Eve, and she became pregnant and gave birth to Cain.*g* She said, "With the help of the Lᴏʀᴅ I have brought forth*h* a man." ²Later she gave birth to his brother Abel.

Now Abel kept flocks, and Cain worked the soil. ³In the course of time Cain brought some of the fruits of the soil as an offering to the Lᴏʀᴅ. ⁴And Abel also brought an offering— fat portions from some of the firstborn of his flock. The Lᴏʀᴅ looked with favor on Abel and his offering, ⁵but on Cain and his offering he did not look with favor. So Cain was very angry, and his face was downcast.

⁶Then the Lᴏʀᴅ said to Cain, "Why are you angry? Why is your face downcast? ⁷If you do what is right, will you not be accepted? But if you do not do what is right, sin is crouching at your door; it desires to have you, but you must rule over it."

a 15 Or *seed* *b* 15 Or *strike* *c* 20 Or *The man* *d* 20 *Eve* probably means *living.* *e* 24 Or *placed in front* *f* 1 Or *The man* *g* 1 *Cain* sounds like the Hebrew for *brought forth* or *acquired.* *h* 1 Or *have acquired*

⁸Now Cain said to his brother Abel, "Let's go out to the field."ᵃ While they were in the field, Cain attacked his brother Abel and killed him.

⁹Then the Lᴏʀᴅ said to Cain, "Where is your brother Abel?"

"I don't know," he replied. "Am I my brother's keeper?"

¹⁰The Lᴏʀᴅ said, "What have you done? Listen! Your brother's blood cries out to me from the ground. ¹¹Now you are under a curse and driven from the ground, which opened its mouth to receive your brother's blood from your hand. ¹²When you work the ground, it will no longer yield its crops for you. You will be a restless wanderer on the earth."

ᵃ 8 Samaritan Pentateuch, Septuagint, Vulgate and Syriac; Masoretic Text does not have "Let's go out to the field."

ASKmeanyTHING

eve

Genesis 2:19 – 4:2

You had it all—a great husband, a terrific place to live, friendship with God. What happened?

You're right. I *did* have it all. Living in the garden with Adam and having God for company was perfect. Paradise, really. But when that serpent came along and pointed out the one thing that I *didn't* have—well, that's all I could think about. And oh, that snake was clever. Once he planted the seed, the thoughts kept running through my mind: *How could I possibly be happy when I wasn't allowed to eat from that tree? Why wouldn't God want me to be just like him? Why couldn't I have that one thing?* I was consumed with it. Nothing would satisfy me until I had it. Or so I thought.

What would you say to women who struggle with discontentment?

First, ask yourself, *What is driving my discontentment?* Often we try to fill up our lives with everything but what will really satisfy us.

Second, guard yourself against that "got to have it all" feeling. Don't act on your impulses. Check with God first. Tell him what it is that you've "got to have," and let him guide you. Confide in a friend. Find someone who can offer you an objective, rational opinion. Just think what might have been if I had asked God first, or even Adam, about taking that one piece of fruit! And if you're longing for something that you are too embarrassed to share with another person, then that should be a red flag.

Third, focus on what you do have. Make a list, share it with someone, recite it to yourself—whatever you have to do to keep in mind *all* that God has given you. Thank God for everything you have been given. Focus on what you have rather than what you don't have. The truth is that God had given me everything I needed to be completely happy in this world. He has done the same for you. Don't waste your time on anything less.

FOR MORE INSIGHT: Is discontentment a struggle for you? Take a look at what Solomon (the king of having it all) had to say about finding contentment in Ecclesiastes 5:18–20. Read Paul's secret to contentment in Philippians 4:10–13; and 1 Timothy 6:6–8.

¹³Cain said to the Lord, "My punishment is more than I can bear. ¹⁴Today you are driving me from the land, and I will be hidden from your presence; I will be a restless wanderer on the earth, and whoever finds me will kill me."

¹⁵But the Lord said to him, "Not so^a; anyone who kills Cain will suffer vengeance seven times over." Then the Lord put a mark on Cain so that no one who found him would kill him. ¹⁶So Cain went out from the Lord's presence and lived in the land of Nod,^b east of Eden.

¹⁷Cain made love to his wife, and she became pregnant and gave birth to Enoch. Cain was then building a city, and he named it after his son Enoch. ¹⁸To Enoch was born Irad, and Irad was the father of Mehujael, and Mehujael was the father of Methushael, and Methushael was the father of Lamech.

¹⁹Lamech married two women, one named Adah and the other Zillah. ²⁰Adah gave birth to Jabal; he was the father of those who live in tents and raise livestock. ²¹His brother's name was Jubal; he was the father of all who play stringed instruments and pipes. ²²Zillah also had a son, Tubal-Cain, who forged all kinds of tools out of^c bronze and iron. Tubal-Cain's sister was Naamah.

²³Lamech said to his wives,

> "Adah and Zillah, listen to me;
> wives of Lamech, hear my words.
> I have killed a man for wounding me,
> a young man for injuring me.
> ²⁴If Cain is avenged seven times,
> then Lamech seventy-seven times."

²⁵Adam made love to his wife again, and she gave birth to a son and named him Seth,^d saying, "God has granted me another child in place of Abel, since Cain killed him." ²⁶Seth also had a son, and he named him Enosh.

At that time people began to call on^e the name of the Lord.

From Adam to Noah

5 This is the written account of Adam's family line.

When God created human beings, he made them in the likeness of God. ²He created them male and female and blessed them. And when they were created, he called them "human beings."

³When Adam had lived 130 years, he had a son in his own likeness, in his own image; and he named him Seth. ⁴After Seth was born, Adam lived 800 years and had other sons and daughters. ⁵Altogether, Adam lived a total of 930 years, and then he died.

⁶When Seth had lived 105 years, he became the father^f of Enosh. ⁷After he became the father of Enosh, Seth lived 807 years and had other sons and daughters. ⁸Altogether, Seth lived a total of 912 years, and then he died.

⁹When Enosh had lived 90 years, he became the father of Kenan. ¹⁰After he became the father of Kenan, Enosh lived 815 years and had other sons and daughters. ¹¹Altogether, Enosh lived a total of 905 years, and then he died.

¹²When Kenan had lived 70 years, he became the father of Mahalalel. ¹³After he became the father of Mahalalel, Kenan lived 840 years and had other sons and daughters. ¹⁴Altogether, Kenan lived a total of 910 years, and then he died.

¹⁵When Mahalalel had lived 65 years, he became the father of Jared. ¹⁶After he became the father of Jared, Mahalalel lived 830 years and had other sons and daughters. ¹⁷Altogether, Mahalalel lived a total of 895 years, and then he died.

¹⁸When Jared had lived 162 years, he became the father of Enoch. ¹⁹After he became the father of Enoch, Jared lived 800 years and had other sons and daughters. ²⁰Altogether, Jared lived a total of 962 years, and then he died.

²¹When Enoch had lived 65 years, he became the father of Methuselah. ²²After he became the father

---

^a *15* Septuagint, Vulgate and Syriac; Hebrew *Very well*   ^b *16 Nod* means *wandering* (see verses 12 and 14).   ^c *22* Or *who instructed all who work in*   ^d *25 Seth* probably means *granted.*   ^e *26* Or *to proclaim*   ^f *6 Father* may mean *ancestor*; also in verses 7-26.

of Methuselah, Enoch walked faithfully with God 300 years and had other sons and daughters. ²³Altogether, Enoch lived a total of 365 years. ²⁴Enoch walked faithfully with God; then he was no more, because God took him away.

²⁵When Methuselah had lived 187 years, he became the father of Lamech. ²⁶After he became the father of Lamech, Methuselah lived 782 years and had other sons and daughters. ²⁷Altogether, Methuselah lived a total of 969 years, and then he died.

²⁸When Lamech had lived 182 years, he had a son. ²⁹He named him Noah*a* and said, "He will comfort us in the labor and painful toil of our hands caused by the ground the Lᴏʀᴅ has cursed." ³⁰After Noah was born, Lamech lived 595 years and had other sons and daughters. ³¹Altogether, Lamech lived a total of 777 years, and then he died.

³²After Noah was 500 years old, he became the father of Shem, Ham and Japheth.

Wickedness in the World

6 When human beings began to increase in number on the earth and daughters were born to them, ²the sons of God saw that these daughters were beautiful, and they married any of them they chose. ³Then the Lᴏʀᴅ said, "My Spirit will not contend with*b* human beings forever, for they are mortal*c*; their days will be a hundred and twenty years."

⁴The Nephilim were on the earth in those days—and also afterward—when the sons of God went to the daughters of the human beings and had children by them. They were the heroes of old, men of renown.

⁵The Lᴏʀᴅ saw how great the wickedness of the human race had become on the earth, and that every inclination of the thoughts of the human heart was only evil all the time. ⁶The Lᴏʀᴅ regretted that he had made human beings on the earth, and his heart was deeply troubled. ⁷So the Lᴏʀᴅ said, "I will wipe from the face of the earth the human race I have created—and with them the animals, the birds and the creatures that move along the ground—for I regret that I have made them." ⁸But Noah found favor in the eyes of the Lᴏʀᴅ.

Noah and the Flood

⁹This is the account of Noah and his family.

Noah was a righteous man, blameless among the people of his time, and he walked faithfully with God. ¹⁰Noah had three sons: Shem, Ham and Japheth.

¹¹Now the earth was corrupt in God's sight and was full of violence. ¹²God saw how corrupt the earth had become, for all the people on earth had corrupted their ways. ¹³So God said to Noah, "I am going to put an end to all people, for the earth is filled with violence because of them. I am surely going to destroy both them and the earth. ¹⁴So make yourself an ark of cypress*d* wood; make rooms in it and coat it with pitch inside and out. ¹⁵This is how you are to build it: The ark is to be three hundred cubits long, fifty cubits wide and thirty cubits high.*e* ¹⁶Make a roof for it, leaving below the roof an opening one cubit*f* high all around.*g* Put a door in the side of the ark and make lower, middle and upper decks. ¹⁷I am going to bring floodwaters on the earth to destroy all life under the heavens, every creature that has the breath of life in it. Everything on earth will perish. ¹⁸But I will establish my covenant with you, and you will enter the ark—you and your sons and your wife and your sons' wives with you. ¹⁹You are to bring into the ark two of all living creatures, male and female, to keep them alive with you. ²⁰Two of every kind of bird, of every kind of animal and of every kind of creature that moves along the ground will come to you to be kept alive. ²¹You are to take every kind of food that is to be eaten and store it away as food for you and for them."

²²Noah did everything just as God commanded him.

7 The Lᴏʀᴅ then said to Noah, "Go into the ark, you and your whole family, because I have found you righteous in this generation. ²Take with you seven pairs of every kind of clean animal, a male and its mate, and one pair of every kind of unclean animal, a male and its mate, ³and also seven pairs of every

---

a 29 Noah sounds like the Hebrew for *comfort.*   *b 3* Or *My spirit will not remain in*   *c 3* Or *corrupt*   *d 14* The meaning of the Hebrew for this word is uncertain.
e 15 That is, about 450 feet long, 75 feet wide and 45 feet high or about 135 meters long, 22.5 meters wide and 13.5 meters high   *f 16* That is, about 18 inches or about 45 centimeters   *g 16* The meaning of the Hebrew for this clause is uncertain.

kind of bird, male and female, to keep their various kinds alive throughout the earth. ⁴Seven days from now I will send rain on the earth for forty days and forty nights, and I will wipe from the face of the earth every living creature I have made."

⁵And Noah did all that the Lord commanded him.

⁶Noah was six hundred years old when the floodwaters came on the earth. ⁷And Noah and his sons and his wife and his sons' wives entered the ark to escape the waters of the flood. ⁸Pairs of clean and unclean animals, of birds and of all creatures that move along the ground, ⁹male and female, came to Noah and entered the ark, as God had commanded Noah. ¹⁰And after the seven days the floodwaters came on the earth.

¹¹In the six hundredth year of Noah's life, on the seventeenth day of the second month—on that day all the springs of the great deep burst forth, and the floodgates of the heavens were opened. ¹²And rain fell on the earth forty days and forty nights.

¹³On that very day Noah and his sons, Shem, Ham and Japheth, together with his wife and the wives of his three sons, entered the ark. ¹⁴They had with them every wild animal according to its kind, all livestock according to their kinds, every creature that moves along the ground according to its kind and every bird according to its kind, everything with wings. ¹⁵Pairs of all creatures that have the breath of life in them came to Noah and entered the ark. ¹⁶The animals going in were male and female of every living thing, as God had commanded Noah. Then the Lord shut him in.

¹⁷For forty days the flood kept coming on the earth, and as the waters increased they lifted the ark high above the earth. ¹⁸The waters rose and increased greatly on the earth, and the ark floated on the surface of the water. ¹⁹They rose greatly on the earth, and all the high mountains under the entire heavens were covered. ²⁰The waters rose and covered the mountains to a depth of more than fifteen cubits.ᵃ, ᵇ ²¹Every living thing that moved on the earth perished—birds, livestock, wild animals, all the creatures that swarm over the earth, and the entire human race. ²²Everything on dry land that had the breath of life in its nostrils died. ²³Every living thing on the face of the earth was wiped out; human beings and animals and the creatures that move along the ground and the birds were wiped from the earth. Only Noah was left, and those with him in the ark.

²⁴The waters flooded the earth for a hundred and fifty days.

8 But God remembered Noah and all the wild animals and the livestock that were with him in the ark, and he sent a wind over the earth, and the waters receded. ²Now the springs of the deep and the floodgates of the heavens had been closed, and the rain had stopped falling from the sky. ³The water receded steadily from the earth. At the end of the hundred and fifty days the water had gone down, ⁴and on the seventeenth day of the seventh month the ark came to rest on the mountains of Ararat. ⁵The waters continued to recede until the tenth month, and on the first day of the tenth month the tops of the mountains became visible.

⁶After forty days Noah opened a window he had made in the ark ⁷and sent out a raven, and it kept flying back and forth until the water had dried up from the earth. ⁸Then he sent out a dove to see if the water had receded from the surface of the ground. ⁹But the dove could find nowhere to perch because there was water over all the surface of the earth; so it returned to Noah in the ark. He reached out his

atissue:obedience

6:22 Noah did *everything* exactly the way God told him. Can the same be said of you? If you're honest . . . probably not. But do you want it to be true? Do you love and respect God enough that you genuinely want to obey him 100 percent? Let's assume that you do—but you find it's easier said than done. Don't get discouraged. Remember that God has an endless supply of mercy and forgiveness. Confess your failure to him, and know that he will forgive you and give you the grace to try again . . . and again . . . and again. Just don't give up!

ᵃ *20 That is, about 22 feet or about 6.8 meters* ᵇ *20 Or rose more than fifteen cubits, and the mountains were covered* hand and took the dove and brought it back to himself in the ark. [10]He waited seven more days and again sent out the dove from the ark. [11]When the dove returned to him in the evening, there in its beak was a freshly plucked olive leaf! Then Noah knew that the water had receded from the earth. [12]He waited seven more days and sent the dove out again, but this time it did not return to him.

[13]By the first day of the first month of Noah's six hundred and first year, the water had dried up from the earth. Noah then removed the covering from the ark and saw that the surface of the ground was dry. [14]By the twenty-seventh day of the second month the earth was completely dry.

[15]Then God said to Noah, [16]"Come out of the ark, you and your wife and your sons and their wives. [17]Bring out every kind of living creature that is with you—the birds, the animals, and all the creatures that move along the ground—so they can multiply on the earth and be fruitful and increase in number on it."

[18]So Noah came out, together with his sons and his wife and his sons' wives. [19]All the animals and all the creatures that move along the ground and all the birds—everything that moves on the earth—came out of the ark, one kind after another.

[20]Then Noah built an altar to the LORD and, taking some of all the clean animals and clean birds, he sacrificed burnt offerings on it. [21]The LORD smelled the pleasing aroma and said in his heart: "Never again will I curse the ground because of human beings, even though[a] every inclination of the human heart is evil from childhood. And never again will I destroy all living creatures, as I have done.

> [22]"As long as the earth endures,
> seedtime and harvest,
> cold and heat,
> summer and winter,
> day and night
> will never cease."

God's Covenant With Noah

9 Then God blessed Noah and his sons, saying to them, "Be fruitful and increase in number and fill the earth. [2]The fear and dread of you will fall on all the beasts of the earth and all the birds in the sky, on every creature that moves along the ground, and on all the fish in the sea; they are given into your hands. [3]Everything that lives and moves will be food for you. Just as I gave you the green plants, I now give you everything.

[4]"But you must not eat meat that has its lifeblood still in it. [5]And for your lifeblood I will surely demand an accounting. I will demand an accounting from every animal. And from each human being, too, I will demand an accounting for the life of another human being.

> [6]"Whoever sheds human blood,
> by human beings shall their blood be shed;
> for in the image of God
> has God made humankind.

[7]As for you, be fruitful and increase in number; multiply on the earth and increase upon it."

[8]Then God said to Noah and to his sons with him: [9]"I now establish my covenant with you and with your descendants after you [10]and with every living creature that was with you—the birds, the livestock and all the wild animals, all those that came out of the ark with you—every living creature on earth. [11]I establish my covenant with you: Never again will all life be destroyed by the waters of a flood; never again will there be a flood to destroy the earth."

[12]And God said, "This is the sign of the covenant I am making between me and you and every living creature with you, a covenant for all generations to come: [13]I have set my rainbow in the clouds, and it will be the sign of the covenant between me and the earth. [14]Whenever I bring clouds over the earth and the rainbow appears in the clouds, [15]I will remember my covenant between me and you and all living creatures of every kind. Never again will the waters become a flood to destroy all life. [16]Whenever the

15

---

rainbow appears in the clouds, I will see it and remember the everlasting covenant between God and all living creatures of every kind on the earth."

¹⁷So God said to Noah, "This is the sign of the covenant I have established between me and all life on the earth."

The Sons of Noah

¹⁸The sons of Noah who came out of the ark were Shem, Ham and Japheth. (Ham was the father of Canaan.) ¹⁹These were the three sons of Noah, and from them came the people who were scattered over the whole earth.

²⁰Noah, a man of the soil, proceeded[a] to plant a vineyard. ²¹When he drank some of its wine, he became drunk and lay uncovered inside his tent. ²²Ham, the father of Canaan, saw his father's nakedness and told his two brothers outside. ²³But Shem and Japheth took a garment and laid it across their shoulders; then they walked in backward and covered their father's nakedness. Their faces were turned the other way so that they would not see their father's nakedness.

²⁴When Noah awoke from his wine and found out what his youngest son had done to him, ²⁵he said,

> "Cursed be Canaan!
>   The lowest of slaves
>   will he be to his brothers."

²⁶He also said,

> "Praise be to the LORD, the God of Shem!
>   May Canaan be the slave of Shem.
> ²⁷May God extend Japheth's[b] territory;
>   may Japheth live in the tents of Shem,
>   and may Canaan be the slave of Japheth."

²⁸After the flood Noah lived 350 years. ²⁹Noah lived a total of 950 years, and then he died.

conversations

alcohol «» 9:20–27

1 What are the results of alcohol abuse in a family?

2 Was Noah's sin drinking too much or drinking at all? Why?

3 How should you respond to someone who's making poor choices?

For more on **alcohol**, check the index.
For the next Conversations, go to p. 19.

The Table of Nations

10 This is the account of Shem, Ham and Japheth, Noah's sons, who themselves had sons after the flood.

The Japhethites

²The sons[c] of Japheth:

Gomer, Magog, Madai, Javan, Tubal, Meshek and Tiras.
³The sons of Gomer:

Ashkenaz, Riphath and Togarmah.
⁴The sons of Javan:

Elishah, Tarshish, the Kittites and the Rodanites.[d] ⁵(From these the maritime peoples spread out into their territories by their clans within their nations, each with its own language.)

16

---

^a 20 Or soil, was the first   ^b 27 Japheth sounds like the Hebrew for extend.   ^c 2 Sons may mean descendants or successors or nations; also in verses 3, 4, 6, 7, 20-23, 29 and 31.   ^d 4 Some manuscripts of the Masoretic Text and Samaritan Pentateuch (see also Septuagint and 1 Chron. 1:7); most manuscripts of the Masoretic Text Dodanites

The Hamites

⁶ The sons of Ham:

Cush, Egypt, Put and Canaan.

⁷ The sons of Cush:

Seba, Havilah, Sabtah, Raamah and Sabteka.

The sons of Raamah:

Sheba and Dedan.

⁸Cush was the father*a* of Nimrod, who became a mighty warrior on the earth. ⁹He was a mighty hunter before the LORD; that is why it is said, "Like Nimrod, a mighty hunter before the LORD." ¹⁰The first centers of his kingdom were Babylon, Uruk, Akkad and Kalneh, in*b* Shinar.*c* ¹¹From that land he went to Assyria, where he built Nineveh, Rehoboth Ir,*d* Calah ¹²and Resen, which is between Nineveh and Calah—which is the great city.

¹³ Egypt was the father of

the Ludites, Anamites, Lehabites, Naphtuhites, ¹⁴Pathrusites, Kasluhites (from whom the Philistines came) and Caphtorites.

¹⁵ Canaan was the father of

Sidon his firstborn,*e* and of the Hittites, ¹⁶Jebusites, Amorites, Girgashites, ¹⁷Hivites, Arkites, Sinites, ¹⁸Arvadites, Zemarites and Hamathites.

Later the Canaanite clans scattered ¹⁹and the borders of Canaan reached from Sidon toward Gerar as far as Gaza, and then toward Sodom, Gomorrah, Admah and Zeboyim, as far as Lasha.

²⁰These are the sons of Ham by their clans and languages, in their territories and nations.

The Semites

²¹Sons were also born to Shem, whose older brother was*f* Japheth; Shem was the ancestor of all the sons of Eber.

²² The sons of Shem:

Elam, Ashur, Arphaxad, Lud and Aram.

²³ The sons of Aram:

Uz, Hul, Gether and Meshek.*g*

²⁴ Arphaxad was the father of*h* Shelah,

and Shelah the father of Eber.

²⁵ Two sons were born to Eber:

One was named Peleg,*i* because in his time the earth was divided; his brother was named Joktan.

²⁶ Joktan was the father of

Almodad, Sheleph, Hazarmaveth, Jerah, ²⁷Hadoram, Uzal, Diklah, ²⁸Obal, Abimael, Sheba, ²⁹Ophir, Havilah and Jobab. All these were sons of Joktan.

³⁰The region where they lived stretched from Mesha toward Sephar, in the eastern hill country.

³¹These are the sons of Shem by their clans and languages, in their territories and nations.

³²These are the clans of Noah's sons, according to their lines of descent, within their nations. From these the nations spread out over the earth after the flood.

The Tower of Babel

11 Now the whole world had one language and a common speech. ²As people moved eastward,*j* they found a plain in Shinar*k* and settled there.

³They said to each other, "Come, let's make bricks and bake them thoroughly." They used brick instead of stone, and tar for mortar. ⁴Then they said, "Come, let us build ourselves a city, with a tower that reaches

---

a 8 Father may mean *ancestor* or *predecessor* or *founder*; also in verses 13, 15, 24 and 26.   *b 10* Or *Uruk and Akkad—all of them in*   *c 10* That is, Babylonia
d 11 Or *Nineveh with its city squares*   *e 15* Or *of the Sidonians, the foremost*   *f 21* Or *Shem, the older brother of*   *g 23* See Septuagint and 1 Chron. 1:17;
Hebrew *Mash.*   *h 24* Hebrew; Septuagint *father of Cainan, and Cainan was the father of*   *i 25 Peleg* means *division.*   *j 2* Or *from the east;* or *in the east*
k 2 That is, Babylonia

to the heavens, so that we may make a name for ourselves and not be scattered over the face of the whole earth."

HE IS: God alone

11:1–9 The people of Shinar made elaborate plans to build a high tower to reach the heavens. They were confused enough to believe they could bridge the gap between heaven and earth. "But the LORD came down" (v. 5) to foil their prideful plans. *God alone* paves the way between divinity and humanity.

Are you striving to build a tower to reach God? Don't be confused thinking your passions, possessions or positions will get you to heaven. "The LORD came down" and died on a cross so that you don't have to build anything but a personal relationship with him.

For the next He Is, go to p. 21.

⁵But the LORD came down to see the city and the tower that they were building. ⁶The LORD said, "If as one people speaking the same language they have begun to do this, then nothing they plan to do will be impossible for them. ⁷Come, let us go down and confuse their language so they will not understand each other."

⁸So the LORD scattered them from there over all the earth, and they stopped building the city. ⁹That is why it was called Babel ᵃ—because there the LORD confused the language of the whole world. From there the LORD scattered them over the face of the whole earth.

From Shem to Abram

¹⁰This is the account of Shem's family line.

Two years after the flood, when Shem was 100 years old, he became the father ᵇ of Arphaxad. ¹¹And after he became the father of Arphaxad, Shem lived 500 years and had other sons and daughters.

¹²When Arphaxad had lived 35 years, he became the father of Shelah. ¹³And after he became the father of Shelah, Arphaxad lived 403 years and had other sons and daughters. ᶜ

¹⁴When Shelah had lived 30 years, he became the father of Eber. ¹⁵And after he became the father of Eber, Shelah lived 403 years and had other sons and daughters.

¹⁶When Eber had lived 34 years, he became the father of Peleg. ¹⁷And after he became the father of Peleg, Eber lived 430 years and had other sons and daughters.

¹⁸When Peleg had lived 30 years, he became the father of Reu. ¹⁹And after he became the father of Reu, Peleg lived 209 years and had other sons and daughters.

²⁰When Reu had lived 32 years, he became the father of Serug. ²¹And after he became the father of Serug, Reu lived 207 years and had other sons and daughters.

²²When Serug had lived 30 years, he became the father of Nahor. ²³And after he became the father of Nahor, Serug lived 200 years and had other sons and daughters.

²⁴When Nahor had lived 29 years, he became the father of Terah. ²⁵And after he became the father of Terah, Nahor lived 119 years and had other sons and daughters.

²⁶After Terah had lived 70 years, he became the father of Abram, Nahor and Haran.

Abram's Family

²⁷This is the account of Terah's family line.

Terah became the father of Abram, Nahor and Haran. And Haran became the father of Lot. ²⁸While his father Terah was still alive, Haran died in Ur of the Chaldeans, in the land of his birth. ²⁹Abram and Nahor both married. The name of Abram's wife was Sarai, and the name of Nahor's wife was Milkah; she

---

ᵃ *9* That is, Babylon; *Babel* sounds like the Hebrew for *confused.* ᵇ *10 Father* may mean *ancestor*; also in verses 11-25. ᶜ *12,13* Hebrew; Septuagint (see also Luke 3:35, 36 and note at Gen. 10:24) *35 years, he became the father of Cainan.* ¹³*And after he became the father of Cainan, Arphaxad lived 430 years and had other sons and daughters, and then he died. When Cainan had lived 130 years, he became the father of Shelah. And after he became the father of Shelah, Cainan lived 330 years and had other sons and daughters* was the daughter of Haran, the father of both Milkah and Iskah. ³⁰Now Sarai was childless because she was not able to conceive.

³¹Terah took his son Abram, his grandson Lot son of Haran, and his daughter-in-law Sarai, the wife of his son Abram, and together they set out from Ur of the Chaldeans to go to Canaan. But when they came to Harran, they settled there.

³²Terah lived 205 years, and he died in Harran.

The Call of Abram

12 The Lord had said to Abram, "Go from your country, your people and your father's household to the land I will show you.

> ²"I will make you into a great nation,
> and I will bless you;
> I will make your name great,
> and you will be a blessing.*ᵃ*
> ³I will bless those who bless you,
> and whoever curses you I will curse;
> and all peoples on earth
> will be blessed through you."*ᵇ*

⁴So Abram went, as the Lord had told him; and Lot went with him. Abram was seventy-five years old when he set out from Harran. ⁵He took his wife Sarai, his nephew Lot, all the possessions they had accumulated and the people they had acquired in Harran, and they set out for the land of Canaan, and they arrived there.

⁶Abram traveled through the land as far as the site of the great tree of Moreh at Shechem. At that time the Canaanites were in the land. ⁷The Lord appeared to Abram and said, "To your offspringᶜ I will give this land." So he built an altar there to the Lord, who had appeared to him.

⁸From there he went on toward the hills east of Bethel and pitched his tent, with Bethel on the west and Ai on the east. There he built an altar to the Lord and called on the name of the Lord.

⁹Then Abram set out and continued toward the Negev.

Abram in Egypt

¹⁰Now there was a famine in the land, and Abram went down to Egypt to live there for a while because the famine was severe. ¹¹As he was about to enter Egypt, he said to his wife Sarai, "I know what a beautiful woman you are. ¹²When the Egyptians see you, they will say, 'This is his wife.' Then they will kill me but will let you live. ¹³Say you are my sister, so that I will be treated well for your sake and my life will be spared because of you."

¹⁴When Abram came to Egypt, the Egyptians saw that Sarai was a very beautiful woman. ¹⁵And when Pharaoh's officials saw her, they praised her to Pharaoh, and she was taken into his palace. ¹⁶He treated Abram well for her sake, and Abram acquired sheep and cattle, male and female donkeys, male and female servants, and camels.

¹⁷But the Lord inflicted serious diseases on Pharaoh and his household because of Abram's wife Sarai. ¹⁸So Pharaoh summoned Abram. "What have you done to me?" he said. "Why didn't you tell me she was your wife? ¹⁹Why did you say, 'She is my sister,' so that I took her to be my wife? Now then, here is your wife. Take her and go!" ²⁰Then Pharaoh gave orders about Abram to his men, and they sent him on his way, with his wife and everything he had.

"conversations"

trusting your husband «» 12:1–9

1» How do you think Sarah felt when Abraham decided to move their family?

2» If a wife trusts her husband's decisions, how does that affect him?

3» What does it do to a husband if his wife *doesn't* trust his decisions?

For more on **trusting your husband**, check the index.
For the next Conversations, go to p. 27.

ᵃ *2* Or *great, / and you will be seen as blessed*   ᵇ *3* Or *earth / will use your name in blessings* (see Gen. 48:20)   ᶜ *7* Or *seed*

Abram and Lot Separate

13 So Abram went up from Egypt to the Negev, with his wife and everything he had, and Lot went with him. ²Abram had become very wealthy in livestock and in silver and gold.

³From the Negev he went from place to place until he came to Bethel, to the place between Bethel and Ai where his tent had been earlier ⁴and where he had first built an altar. There Abram called on the name of the LORD.

⁵Now Lot, who was moving about with Abram, also had flocks and herds and tents. ⁶But the land could not support them while they stayed together, for their possessions were so great that they were not able to stay together. ⁷And quarreling arose between Abram's herders and the herders of Lot. The Canaanites and Perizzites were also living in the land at that time.

⁸So Abram said to Lot, "Let's not have any quarreling between you and me, or between your herders and mine, for we are close relatives. ⁹Is not the whole land before you? Let's part company. If you go to the left, I'll go to the right; if you go to the right, I'll go to the left."

¹⁰Lot looked around and saw that the whole plain of the Jordan was well watered, like the garden of the LORD, like the land of Egypt, toward Zoar. (This was before the LORD destroyed Sodom and Gomorrah.) ¹¹So Lot chose for himself the whole plain of the Jordan and set out toward the east. The two men parted company: ¹²Abram lived in the land of Canaan, while Lot lived among the cities of the plain and pitched his tents near Sodom. ¹³Now the people of Sodom were wicked and were sinning greatly against the LORD.

¹⁴The LORD said to Abram after Lot had parted from him, "Look around from where you are, to the north and south, to the east and west. ¹⁵All the land that you see I will give to you and your offspring*a* forever. ¹⁶I will make your offspring like the dust of the earth, so that if anyone could count the dust, then your offspring could be counted. ¹⁷Go, walk through the length and breadth of the land, for I am giving it to you."

¹⁸So Abram went to live near the great trees of Mamre at Hebron, where he pitched his tents. There he built an altar to the LORD.

> *at issue: conflict*
>
> **13:1–12** What do you do when you find yourself going head-to-head with a coworker, a friend or your husband? Some would advise: "Fight to get what's yours, to get what you *deserve*." But Abram demonstrates another way. It's the way of peace. This way involves looking out for the other person's interests and not just your own. It forces you to remember that everything in this world belongs to God. He'll make sure you get all that you need and more, so you can quit fighting for your "rightful" share.

Abram Rescues Lot

14 At the time when Amraphel was king of Shinar,*b* Arioch king of Ellasar, Kedorlaomer king of Elam and Tidal king of Goyim, ²these kings went to war against Bera king of Sodom, Birsha king of Gomorrah, Shinab king of Admah, Shemeber king of Zeboyim, and the king of Bela (that is, Zoar). ³All these latter kings joined forces in the Valley of Siddim (that is, the Dead Sea Valley). ⁴For twelve years they had been subject to Kedorlaomer, but in the thirteenth year they rebelled.

⁵In the fourteenth year, Kedorlaomer and the kings allied with him went out and defeated the Rephaites in Ashteroth Karnaim, the Zuzites in Ham, the Emites in Shaveh Kiriathaim ⁶and the Horites in the hill country of Seir, as far as El Paran near the desert. ⁷Then they turned back and went to En Mishpat (that is, Kadesh), and they conquered the whole territory of the Amalekites, as well as the Amorites who were living in Hazezon Tamar.

⁸Then the king of Sodom, the king of Gomorrah, the king of Admah, the king of Zeboyim and the king of Bela (that is, Zoar) marched out and drew up their battle lines in the Valley of Siddim ⁹against

---

a 15 Or seed; also in verse 16   *b 1 That is, Babylonia*; also in verse 9

Kedorlaomer king of Elam, Tidal king of Goyim, Amraphel king of Shinar and Arioch king of Ellasar—four kings against five. ¹⁰Now the Valley of Siddim was full of tar pits, and when the kings of Sodom and Gomorrah fled, some of the men fell into them and the rest fled to the hills. ¹¹The four kings seized all the goods of Sodom and Gomorrah and all their food; then they went away. ¹²They also carried off Abram's nephew Lot and his possessions, since he was living in Sodom.

¹³A man who had escaped came and reported this to Abram the Hebrew. Now Abram was living near the great trees of Mamre the Amorite, a brother*ᵃ* of Eshkol and Aner, all of whom were allied with Abram. ¹⁴When Abram heard that his relative had been taken captive, he called out the 318 trained men born in his household and went in pursuit as far as Dan. ¹⁵During the night Abram divided his men to attack them and he routed them, pursuing them as far as Hobah, north of Damascus. ¹⁶He recovered all the goods and brought back his relative Lot and his possessions, together with the women and the other people.

¹⁷After Abram returned from defeating Kedorlaomer and the kings allied with him, the king of Sodom came out to meet him in the Valley of Shaveh (that is, the King's Valley).

¹⁸Then Melchizedek king of Salem brought out bread and wine. He was priest of God Most High, ¹⁹and he blessed Abram, saying,

> "Blessed be Abram by God Most High,
>   Creator of heaven and earth.
> ²⁰And praise be to God Most High,
>   who delivered your enemies into your hand."

Then Abram gave him a tenth of everything.

²¹The king of Sodom said to Abram, "Give me the people and keep the goods for yourself."

²²But Abram said to the king of Sodom, "With raised hand I have sworn an oath to the Lᴏʀᴅ, God Most High, Creator of heaven and earth, ²³that I will accept nothing belonging to you, not even a thread or the thong of a sandal, so that you will never be able to say, 'I made Abram rich.' ²⁴I will accept nothing but what my men have eaten and the share that belongs to the men who went with me—to Aner, Eshkol and Mamre. Let them have their share."

God's Covenant With Abram

15 After this, the word of the Lᴏʀᴅ came to Abram in a vision:

> "Do not be afraid, Abram.
>   I am your shield,*ᵇ*
>   your very great reward.*ᶜ*"

²But Abram said, "Sovereign Lᴏʀᴅ, what can you give me since I remain childless and the one who will inherit*ᵈ* my estate is Eliezer of Damascus?" ³And Abram said, "You have given me no children; so a servant in my household will be my heir."

HE IS: enough

15:1 Abram rescued Lot from four marauding kings but refused to accept a reward from the king of Sodom. Rather than settling for temporal treasures, he looked to God for his reward. And God offered the gift of himself. "I am your shield, your very great reward." To Abram, God was *enough*.

God is a shield from the enemies of your soul: the pressures of the world, your own selfish desires and the schemes of the devil. He himself is your great reward. Don't get so busy fighting your personal battles and seeking the world's goods that you forget that all you need is God. He is *enough*.

For the next He Is, go to p. 26.

ᵃ 13 Or *a relative; or an ally* *ᵇ 1* Or *sovereign* *ᶜ 1* Or *shield; I your reward will be very great* *ᵈ 2* The meaning of the Hebrew for this phrase is uncertain.

⁴Then the word of the LORD came to him: "This man will not be your heir, but a son coming from your own body will be your heir." ⁵He took him outside and said, "Look up at the heavens and count the stars—if indeed you can count them." Then he said to him, "So shall your offspring*ᵃ* be."

⁶Abram believed the LORD, and he credited it to him as righteousness.

⁷He also said to him, "I am the LORD, who brought you out of Ur of the Chaldeans to give you this land to take possession of it."

⁸But Abram said, "Sovereign LORD, how can I know that I will gain possession of it?"

⁹So the LORD said to him, "Bring me a heifer, a goat and a ram, each three years old, along with a dove and a young pigeon."

¹⁰Abram brought all these to him, cut them in two and arranged the halves opposite each other; the birds, however, he did not cut in half. ¹¹Then birds of prey came down on the carcasses, but Abram drove them away.

¹²As the sun was setting, Abram fell into a deep sleep, and a thick and dreadful darkness came over him. ¹³Then the LORD said to him, "Know for certain that for four hundred years your descendants will be strangers in a country not their own and that they will be enslaved and mistreated there. ¹⁴But I will punish the nation they serve as slaves, and afterward they will come out with great possessions. ¹⁵You, however, will go to your ancestors in peace and be buried at a good old age. ¹⁶In the fourth generation your descendants will come back here, for the sin of the Amorites has not yet reached its full measure."

¹⁷When the sun had set and darkness had fallen, a smoking firepot with a blazing torch appeared and passed between the pieces. ¹⁸On that day the LORD made a covenant with Abram and said, "To your descendants I give this land, from the Wadi*ᵇ* of Egypt to the great river, the Euphrates— ¹⁹the land of the Kenites, Kenizzites, Kadmonites, ²⁰Hittites, Perizzites, Rephaites, ²¹Amorites, Canaanites, Girgashites and Jebusites."

Hagar and Ishmael

16 Now Sarai, Abram's wife, had borne him no children. But she had an Egyptian servant named Hagar; ²so she said to Abram, "The LORD has kept me from having children. Go, sleep with my servant; perhaps I can build a family through her."

Abram agreed to what Sarai said. ³So after Abram had been living in Canaan ten years, Sarai his wife took her Egyptian servant Hagar and gave her to her husband to be his wife. ⁴He slept with Hagar, and she conceived.

When she knew she was pregnant, she began to despise her mistress. ⁵Then Sarai said to Abram, "You are responsible for the wrong I am suffering. I put my servant in your arms, and now that she knows she is pregnant, she despises me. May the LORD judge between you and me."

⁶"Your servant is in your hands," Abram said. "Do with her whatever you think best." Then Sarai mistreated Hagar; so she fled from her.

⁷The angel of the LORD found Hagar near a spring in the desert; it was the spring that is beside the road to Shur. ⁸And he said, "Hagar, servant of Sarai, where have you come from, and where are you going?"

"I'm running away from my mistress Sarai," she answered.

---

atissue:patience

16:1–6 *Wait.* When you're asking God for something you really want, W-A-I-T can feel like a nasty, four-letter word. So, like Sarai, you adopt the motto: "God helps those who help themselves." Despite the cost to your kids, you take the job with the higher pay—and the later hours and added stress—so you can buy that gigantic house. Or you charm Mr. Available-But-Not-So-Great into marrying you, instead of waiting for God to bring Mr. Right-For-You into your life. Was it really worth it? Could it be you need a new motto: "God helps those who wait on him"?

---

⁹Then the angel of the LORD told her, "Go back to your mistress and submit to her." ¹⁰The angel added, "I will increase your descendants so much that they will be too numerous to count."

¹¹The angel of the LORD also said to her:

> "You are now pregnant
>   and you will give birth to a son.
> You shall name him Ishmael,ᵃ
>   for the LORD has heard of your misery.
> ¹²He will be a wild donkey of a man;
>   his hand will be against everyone
>   and everyone's hand against him,
> and he will live in hostility
>   towardᵇ all his brothers."

¹³She gave this name to the LORD who spoke to her: "You are the God who sees me," for she said, "I have now seenᶜ the One who sees me." ¹⁴That is why the well was called Beer Lahai Roiᵈ; it is still there, between Kadesh and Bered.

¹⁵So Hagar bore Abram a son, and Abram gave the name Ishmael to the son she had borne. ¹⁶Abram was eighty-six years old when Hagar bore him Ishmael.

The Covenant of Circumcision

17 When Abram was ninety-nine years old, the LORD appeared to him and said, "I am God Almightyᵉ; walk before me faithfully and be blameless. ²Then I will make my covenant between me and you and will greatly increase your numbers."

³Abram fell facedown, and God said to him, ⁴"As for me, this is my covenant with you: You will be the father of many nations. ⁵No longer will you be called Abramᶠ; your name will be Abraham,ᵍ for I have made you a father of many nations. ⁶I will make you very fruitful; I will make nations of you, and kings will come from you. ⁷I will establish my covenant as an everlasting covenant between me and you and your descendants after you for the generations to come, to be your God and the God of your descendants after you. ⁸The whole land of Canaan, where you now reside as a foreigner, I will give as an everlasting possession to you and your descendants after you; and I will be their God."

⁹Then God said to Abraham, "As for you, you must keep my covenant, you and your descendants after you for the generations to come. ¹⁰This is my covenant with you and your descendants after you, the covenant you are to keep: Every male among you shall be circumcised. ¹¹You are to undergo circumcision, and it will be the sign of the covenant between me and you. ¹²For the generations to come every male among you who is eight days old must be circumcised, including those born in your household or bought with money from a foreigner—those who are not your offspring. ¹³Whether born in your household or bought with your money, they must be circumcised. My covenant in your flesh is to be an everlasting covenant. ¹⁴Any uncircumcised male, who has not been circumcised in the flesh, will be cut off from his people; he has broken my covenant."

¹⁵God also said to Abraham, "As for Sarai your wife, you are no longer to call her Sarai; her name will be Sarah. ¹⁶I will bless her and will surely give you a son by her. I will bless her so that she will be the mother of nations; kings of peoples will come from her."

¹⁷Abraham fell facedown; he laughed and said to himself, "Will a son be born to a man a hundred years old? Will Sarah bear a child at the age of ninety?" ¹⁸And Abraham said to God, "If only Ishmael might live under your blessing!"

¹⁹Then God said, "Yes, but your wife Sarah will bear you a son, and you will call him Isaac.ʰ I will establish my covenant with him as an everlasting covenant for his descendants after him. ²⁰And as for Ishmael, I have heard you: I will surely bless him; I will make him fruitful and will greatly increase his numbers. He will be the father of twelve rulers, and I will make him into a great nation. ²¹But my

ᵃ 11 Ishmael means God hears.   ᵇ 12 Or live to the east / of   ᶜ 13 Or seen the back of   ᵈ 14 Beer Lahai Roi means well of the Living One who sees me.
ᵉ 1 Hebrew El-Shaddai   ᶠ 5 Abram means exalted father.   ᵍ 5 Abraham probably means father of many.   ʰ 19 Isaac means he laughs.

myth#02 "HAVING A CHILD WILL MAKE ME HAPPY."

My other friends couldn't believe I went for it. But why not? The professional single-mom-by-choice is hardly the pariah anymore. We live in an age of technological wonders that give women options they never had before. I have a successful business, a large home with room for a child, good friends and stability. I'm at a good place in my life for the "next" thing, and a baby just seemed to fit the need.

I'm the same as most any other woman. God gave me this nesting urge, so do I just ignore it until I find the right man? Set my sights on other goals? I deserve to be happy as much as the next person. Unfortunately, contentment seems to always be on the next horizon. When I bought my new home, I thought that would satisfy me. It did for a while, and then I resumed the search and focused on a baby. This nagging feeling of incompleteness is undeniable. I'm tired of waiting for all the circumstances to be "right."

I was talking with some other moms at Lamaze class last week, and they asked me why I decided to have a baby as a single mom. Sure, I think it would be ideal if I were married and decided to start a family. But I can't see why experiencing the next best thing is a bad idea if it makes me happy. I told them I wanted to hear the sound of a baby's laughter in the house at Christmas. I wanted some central pleasure to bring my family together and build our unity around. I wanted to give a baby all the things I never experienced when I was a child.

I'm bringing life into this world—a baby I can love and one who will love me back unconditionally. I'll be there for him and build my life around him. He will never know what it's like to be lonely. What could possibly be wrong with that?

—Leslie

THE SEARCH FOR happiness

and significance is central to what it means to be alive. As long as we're breathing, we will deeply desire happiness and meaning in our lives. God created us to crave significance and to know with certainty that we matter, so that he could provide himself as our heart's one, true fulfillment. However, we tend to fill in the blanks with any number of pursuits. "Having _____ will make me happy." More money. Success. A relationship. A home.

So we try everything to bring closure to the idea that if we only had that one thing, *then* we would be ultimately and finally happy. And we'll get that one thing any way we can. It's why Sarah pushed for her maidservant, Hagar, to carry Abraham's baby instead of waiting on God.

Mind you, it's not that having a child won't make a person happy. It certainly will! God's pleasures and blessings, such as the precious gift of a baby, do bring our lives a measure of happiness—some extraordinarily so. However, only God's love will satisfy us for a lifetime of joy, which surpasses mere happiness (see Nehemiah 8:10). Depending on him to satisfy the elusive search for happiness enables us to enjoy life's pleasures and enhances our ability to be happy. Otherwise, we may expect a baby, a job or a relationship to meet a level of satisfaction that created things were never designed to bring to us. Then, we soon find we are disappointed with our unmet expectations, and the desire for a second child or a new job or a new relationship becomes the only feasible antidote. And the cycle begins again.

"The Bible talks plentifully about joy, but it nowhere talks about a 'happy Christian.' Happiness depends on what happens; joy does not. Remember, Jesus Christ had joy, and he prayed 'that they might have my joy fulfilled in themselves.' "

—Oswald Chambers

"I Have come THaT THEY may Have LIFE, anD Have IT TO THE FULL."

JOHN 10:10

SEE ALSO

For more on **Happiness**, check the index.

covenant I will establish with Isaac, whom Sarah will bear to you by this time next year." ²²When he had finished speaking with Abraham, God went up from him.

²³On that very day Abraham took his son Ishmael and all those born in his household or bought with his money, every male in his household, and circumcised them, as God told him. ²⁴Abraham was ninety-nine years old when he was circumcised, ²⁵and his son Ishmael was thirteen; ²⁶Abraham and his son Ishmael were both circumcised on that same day. ²⁷And every male in Abraham's household, including those born in his household or bought from a foreigner, was circumcised with him.

The Three Visitors

18 The LORD appeared to Abraham near the great trees of Mamre while he was sitting at the entrance to his tent in the heat of the day. ²Abraham looked up and saw three men standing nearby. When he saw them, he hurried from the entrance of his tent to meet them and bowed low to the ground.

³He said, "If I have found favor in your eyes, my lord,ᵃ do not pass your servant by. ⁴Let a little water be brought, and then you may all wash your feet and rest under this tree. ⁵Let me get you something to eat, so you can be refreshed and then go on your way—now that you have come to your servant."

"Very well," they answered, "do as you say."

⁶So Abraham hurried into the tent to Sarah. "Quick," he said, "get three seahsᵇ of the finest flour and knead it and bake some bread."

⁷Then he ran to the herd and selected a choice, tender calf and gave it to a servant, who hurried to prepare it. ⁸He then brought some curds and milk and the calf that had been prepared, and set these before them. While they ate, he stood near them under a tree.

⁹"Where is your wife Sarah?" they asked him.

"There, in the tent," he said.

¹⁰Then the LORDᶜ said, "I will surely return to you about this time next year, and Sarah your wife will have a son."

Now Sarah was listening at the entrance to the tent, which was behind him. ¹¹Abraham and Sarah were already very old, and Sarah was past the age of childbearing. ¹²So Sarah laughed to herself as she thought, "After I am worn out and my lord is old, will I now have this pleasure?"

¹³Then the LORD said to Abraham, "Why did Sarah laugh and say, 'Will I really have a child, now that I am old?' ¹⁴Is anything too hard for the LORD? I will return to you at the appointed time next year and Sarah will have a son."

HE IS: always on time

18:14 Picture Abraham and Sarah. They're old—really old. Yet God still planned to keep his promise to give them a child, right on time. The Lord would come "at the appointed time" and supernaturally enable Sarah to conceive. Too hard? Not for the God who created the universe! Too late? Not God.

Sometimes to us a few months seem like a lifetime; years feel like an eternity. But God has a divine daytimer that's tailor-made for you. At just the right time, he'll bring his perfect plan to pass. Nothing is too hard for him. You can trust him. He is *always on time*.

For the next He Is, go to p. 30.

¹⁵Sarah was afraid, so she lied and said, "I did not laugh."

But he said, "Yes, you did laugh."

Abraham Pleads for Sodom

¹⁶When the men got up to leave, they looked down toward Sodom, and Abraham walked along with them to see them on their way. ¹⁷Then the LORD said, "Shall I hide from Abraham what I am about to do?

ᵃ *3 Or eyes, Lord*   ᵇ *6 That is, probably about 36 pounds or about 16 kilograms*   ᶜ *10 Hebrew Then he*

[18]Abraham will surely become a great and powerful nation, and all nations on earth will be blessed through him.[a] [19]For I have chosen him, so that he will direct his children and his household after him to keep the way of the LORD by doing what is right and just, so that the LORD will bring about for Abraham what he has promised him."

[20]Then the LORD said, "The outcry against Sodom and Gomorrah is so great and their sin so grievous [21]that I will go down and see if what they have done is as bad as the outcry that has reached me. If not, I will know."

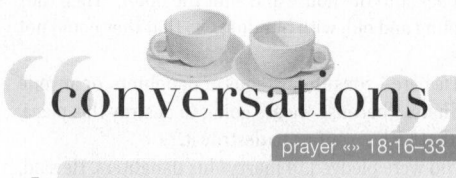

conversations

prayer «» 18:16–33

1 » Does prayer change God's mind?

2 » How does your attitude affect the outcome of your prayers?

3 » How have you seen God answer prayer in your life or for those around you?

For more on **prayer**, check the index.
For the next Conversations, go to p. 29.

[22]The men turned away and went toward Sodom, but Abraham remained standing before the LORD.[b] [23]Then Abraham approached him and said: "Will you sweep away the righteous with the wicked? [24]What if there are fifty righteous people in the city? Will you really sweep it away and not spare[c] the place for the sake of the fifty righteous people in it? [25]Far be it from you to do such a thing—to kill the righteous with the wicked, treating the righteous and the wicked alike. Far be it from you! Will not the Judge of all the earth do right?"

[26]The LORD said, "If I find fifty righteous people in the city of Sodom, I will spare the whole place for their sake."

[27]Then Abraham spoke up again: "Now that I have been so bold as to speak to the Lord, though I am nothing but dust and ashes, [28]what if the number of the righteous is five less than fifty? Will you destroy the whole city for lack of five people?"

"If I find forty-five there," he said, "I will not destroy it."

[29]Once again he spoke to him, "What if only forty are found there?"

He said, "For the sake of forty, I will not do it."

[30]Then he said, "May the Lord not be angry, but let me speak. What if only thirty can be found there?"

He answered, "I will not do it if I find thirty there."

[31]Abraham said, "Now that I have been so bold as to speak to the Lord, what if only twenty can be found there?"

He said, "For the sake of twenty, I will not destroy it."

[32]Then he said, "May the Lord not be angry, but let me speak just once more. What if only ten can be found there?"

He answered, "For the sake of ten, I will not destroy it."

[33]When the LORD had finished speaking with Abraham, he left, and Abraham returned home.

Sodom and Gomorrah Destroyed

19 The two angels arrived at Sodom in the evening, and Lot was sitting in the gateway of the city. When he saw them, he got up to meet them and bowed down with his face to the ground. [2]"My lords," he said, "please turn aside to your servant's house. You can wash your feet and spend the night and then go on your way early in the morning."

"No," they answered, "we will spend the night in the square."

[3]But he insisted so strongly that they did go with him and entered his house. He prepared a meal for them, baking bread without yeast, and they ate. [4]Before they had gone to bed, all the men from every part of the city of Sodom—both young and old—surrounded the house. [5]They called to Lot, "Where are the men who came to you tonight? Bring them out to us so that we can have sex with them."

---

[a] 18 Or will use his name in blessings (see Gen. 48:20)   [b] 22 Masoretic Text; an ancient Hebrew scribal tradition but the LORD remained standing before Abraham   [c] 24 Or forgive; also in verse 26

28

⁶Lot went outside to meet them and shut the door behind him ⁷and said, "No, my friends. Don't do this wicked thing. ⁸Look, I have two daughters who have never slept with a man. Let me bring them out to you, and you can do what you like with them. But don't do anything to these men, for they have come under the protection of my roof."

⁹"Get out of our way," they replied. "This fellow came here as a foreigner, and now he wants to play the judge! We'll treat you worse than them." They kept bringing pressure on Lot and moved forward to break down the door.

¹⁰But the men inside reached out and pulled Lot back into the house and shut the door. ¹¹Then they struck the men who were at the door of the house, young and old, with blindness so that they could not find the door.

¹²The two men said to Lot, "Do you have anyone else here—sons-in-law, sons or daughters, or anyone else in the city who belongs to you? Get them out of here, ¹³because we are going to destroy this place. The outcry to the Lord against its people is so great that he has sent us to destroy it."

¹⁴So Lot went out and spoke to his sons-in-law, who were pledged to marry*a* his daughters. He said, "Hurry and get out of this place, because the Lord is about to destroy the city!" But his sons-in-law thought he was joking.

¹⁵With the coming of dawn, the angels urged Lot, saying, "Hurry! Take your wife and your two daughters who are here, or you will be swept away when the city is punished."

¹⁶When he hesitated, the men grasped his hand and the hands of his wife and of his two daughters and led them safely out of the city, for the Lord was merciful to them. ¹⁷As soon as they had brought them out, one of them said, "Flee for your lives! Don't look back, and don't stop anywhere in the plain! Flee to the mountains or you will be swept away!"

¹⁸But Lot said to them, "No, my lords,*b* please! ¹⁹Your*c* servant has found favor in your*c* eyes, and you*c* have shown great kindness to me in sparing my life. But I can't flee to the mountains; this disaster will overtake me, and I'll die. ²⁰Look, here is a town near enough to run to, and it is small. Let me flee to it— it is very small, isn't it? Then my life will be spared."

²¹He said to him, "Very well, I will grant this request too; I will not overthrow the town you speak of. ²²But flee there quickly, because I cannot do anything until you reach it." (That is why the town was called Zoar.*d*)

²³By the time Lot reached Zoar, the sun had risen over the land. ²⁴Then the Lord rained down burning sulfur on Sodom and Gomorrah—from the Lord out of the heavens. ²⁵Thus he overthrew those cities and the entire plain, destroying all those living in the cities—and also the vegetation in the land. ²⁶But Lot's wife looked back, and she became a pillar of salt.

²⁷Early the next morning Abraham got up and returned to the place where he had stood before the Lord. ²⁸He looked down toward Sodom and Gomorrah, toward all the land of the plain, and he saw dense smoke rising from the land, like smoke from a furnace.

²⁹So when God destroyed the cities of the plain, he remembered Abraham, and he brought Lot out of the catastrophe that overthrew the cities where Lot had lived.

Lot and His Daughters

³⁰Lot and his two daughters left Zoar and settled in the mountains, for he was afraid to stay in Zoar. He and his two daughters lived in a cave. ³¹One day the older daughter said to the younger, "Our father is old, and there is no man around here to give us children—as is the custom all over the earth. ³²Let's get our father to drink wine and then sleep with him and preserve our family line through our father."

³³That night they got their father to drink wine, and the older daughter went in and slept with him. He was not aware of it when she lay down or when she got up.

³⁴The next day the older daughter said to the younger, "Last night I slept with my father. Let's get him to drink wine again tonight, and you go in and sleep with him so we can preserve our family line through our father." ³⁵So they got their father to drink wine that night also, and the younger daughter went in and slept with him. Again he was not aware of it when she lay down or when she got up.

---

a 14 Or *were married to*   *b 18* Or *No, Lord*; or *No, my lord*   *c 19* The Hebrew is singular.   *d 22 Zoar* means *small.*

³⁶So both of Lot's daughters became pregnant by their father. ³⁷The older daughter had a son, and she named him Moab*ᵃ*; he is the father of the Moabites of today. ³⁸The younger daughter also had a son, and she named him Ben-Ammi*ᵇ*; he is the father of the Ammonites*ᶜ* of today.

Abraham and Abimelek

20 Now Abraham moved on from there into the region of the Negev and lived between Kadesh and Shur. For a while he stayed in Gerar, ²and there Abraham said of his wife Sarah, "She is my sister." Then Abimelek king of Gerar sent for Sarah and took her.

³But God came to Abimelek in a dream one night and said to him, "You are as good as dead because of the woman you have taken; she is a married woman."

⁴Now Abimelek had not gone near her, so he said, "Lord, will you destroy an innocent nation? ⁵Did he not say to me, 'She is my sister,' and didn't she also say, 'He is my brother'? I have done this with a clear conscience and clean hands."

⁶Then God said to him in the dream, "Yes, I know you did this with a clear conscience, and so I have kept you from sinning against me. That is why I did not let you touch her. ⁷Now return the man's wife, for he is a prophet, and he will pray for you and you will live. But if you do not return her, you may be sure that you and all who belong to you will die."

⁸Early the next morning Abimelek summoned all his officials, and when he told them all that had happened, they were very much afraid. ⁹Then Abimelek called Abraham in and said, "What have you done to us? How have I wronged you that you have brought such great guilt upon me and my kingdom? You have done things to me that should never be done." ¹⁰And Abimelek asked Abraham, "What was your reason for doing this?"

¹¹Abraham replied, "I said to myself, 'There is surely no fear of God in this place, and they will kill me because of my wife.' ¹²Besides, she really is my sister, the daughter of my father though not of my mother; and she became my wife. ¹³And when God had me wander from my father's household, I said to her, 'This is how you can show your love to me: Everywhere we go, say of me, "He is my brother."'"

¹⁴Then Abimelek brought sheep and cattle and male and female slaves and gave them to Abraham, and he returned Sarah his wife to him. ¹⁵And Abimelek said, "My land is before you; live wherever you like."

¹⁶To Sarah he said, "I am giving your brother a thousand shekels*ᵈ* of silver. This is to cover the offense against you before all who are with you; you are completely vindicated."

¹⁷Then Abraham prayed to God, and God healed Abimelek, his wife and his female slaves so they could have children again, ¹⁸for the LORD had kept all the women in Abimelek's household from conceiving because of Abraham's wife Sarah.

The Birth of Isaac

21 Now the LORD was gracious to Sarah as he had said, and the LORD did for Sarah what he had promised. ²Sarah became pregnant and bore a son to Abraham in his old age, at the very time God had promised him. ³Abraham gave the name Isaac*ᵉ* to the son Sarah bore him. ⁴When his son Isaac was eight days old, Abraham circumcised him, as God commanded him. ⁵Abraham was a hundred years old when his son Isaac was born to him.

⁶Sarah said, "God has brought me laughter, and everyone who hears about this will laugh with me." ⁷And she added, "Who would have said to Abraham that Sarah would nurse children? Yet I have borne him a son in his old age."

"conversations"

pregnancy «» 21:1–6

1» Is God somehow involved in conception and pregnancy? Support your opinion.

2» In what ways do some women have a false sense of control with family planning?

3» How is pregnancy a gift from God?

For more on **pregnancy**, check the index.
For the next Conversations, go to p. 40.

ᵃ 37 Moab sounds like the Hebrew for *from father.*   *ᵇ 38 Ben-Ammi* means *son of my father's people.*   *ᶜ 38* Hebrew *Bene-Ammon*   *ᵈ 16* That is, about 25 pounds or about 11.5 kilograms   *ᵉ 3 Isaac* means *he laughs.*

HE IS: the bringer of laughter

21:6 Is God a serious, stone-faced, unsmiling deity? Actually, God invented laughter, and he gives us reason to laugh. Sarah laughed in disbelief when God said she'd have a child—then she laughed with joy after giving birth to her newborn son. And she gave all the credit to God: "[He] has brought me laughter."

Perhaps you are in a season of tears. For so long you've been waiting for a husband, a child or a job. Take heart—he is *the bringer of laughter*. He can provide a way so that you can laugh—and invite others to laugh along with you.

For the next He Is, go to p. 44.

30

Hagar and Ishmael Sent Away

⁸The child grew and was weaned, and on the day Isaac was weaned Abraham held a great feast. ⁹But Sarah saw that the son whom Hagar the Egyptian had borne to Abraham was mocking, ¹⁰and she said to Abraham, "Get rid of that slave woman and her son, for that slave woman's son will never share in the inheritance with my son Isaac."

¹¹The matter distressed Abraham greatly because it concerned his son. ¹²But God said to him, "Do not be so distressed about the boy and your servant. Listen to whatever Sarah tells you, because it is through Isaac that your offspring^{*a*} will be reckoned. ¹³I will make the son of the servant into a nation also, because he is your offspring."

¹⁴Early the next morning Abraham took some food and a skin of water and gave them to Hagar. He set them on her shoulders and then sent her off with the boy. She went on her way and wandered in the Desert of Beersheba.

¹⁵When the water in the skin was gone, she put the boy under one of the bushes. ¹⁶Then she went off and sat down about a bowshot away, for she thought, "I cannot watch the boy die." And as she sat there, she^{*b*} began to sob.

¹⁷God heard the boy crying, and the angel of God called to Hagar from heaven and said to her, "What is the matter, Hagar? Do not be afraid; God has heard the boy crying as he lies there. ¹⁸Lift the boy up and take him by the hand, for I will make him into a great nation."

¹⁹Then God opened her eyes and she saw a well of water. So she went and filled the skin with water and gave the boy a drink.

²⁰God was with the boy as he grew up. He lived in the desert and became an archer. ²¹While he was living in the Desert of Paran, his mother got a wife for him from Egypt.

The Treaty at Beersheba

²²At that time Abimelek and Phicol the commander of his forces said to Abraham, "God is with you in everything you do. ²³Now swear to me here before God that you will not deal falsely with me or my children or my descendants. Show to me and the country where you now reside as a foreigner the same kindness I have shown to you."

²⁴Abraham said, "I swear it."

²⁵Then Abraham complained to Abimelek about a well of water that Abimelek's servants had seized. ²⁶But Abimelek said, "I don't know who has done this. You did not tell me, and I heard about it only today."

²⁷So Abraham brought sheep and cattle and gave them to Abimelek, and the two men made a treaty. ²⁸Abraham set apart seven ewe lambs from the flock, ²⁹and Abimelek asked Abraham, "What is the meaning of these seven ewe lambs you have set apart by themselves?"

³⁰He replied, "Accept these seven lambs from my hand as a witness that I dug this well."

³¹So that place was called Beersheba,^{*c*} because the two men swore an oath there.

---

^{*a*} **12** Or *seed*   ^{*b*} **16** Hebrew; Septuagint *the child*   ^{*c*} **31** *Beersheba* can mean *well of seven* or *well of the oath*.

[32]After the treaty had been made at Beersheba, Abimelek and Phicol the commander of his forces returned to the land of the Philistines. [33]Abraham planted a tamarisk tree in Beersheba, and there he called on the name of the LORD, the Eternal God. [34]And Abraham stayed in the land of the Philistines for a long time.

Abraham Tested

22 Some time later God tested Abraham. He said to him, "Abraham!"

"Here I am," he replied.

[2]Then God said, "Take your son, your only son, whom you love—Isaac—and go to the region of Moriah. Sacrifice him there as a burnt offering on a mountain I will show you."

[3]Early the next morning Abraham got up and loaded his donkey. He took with him two of his servants and his son Isaac. When he had cut enough wood for the burnt offering, he set out for the place God had told him about. [4]On the third day Abraham looked up and saw the place in the distance. [5]He said to his servants, "Stay here with the donkey while I and the boy go over there. We will worship and then we will come back to you."

[6]Abraham took the wood for the burnt offering and placed it on his son Isaac, and he himself carried the fire and the knife. As the two of them went on together, [7]Isaac spoke up and said to his father Abraham, "Father?"

"Yes, my son?" Abraham replied.

"The fire and wood are here," Isaac said, "but where is the lamb for the burnt offering?"

[8]Abraham answered, "God himself will provide the lamb for the burnt offering, my son." And the two of them went on together.

[9]When they reached the place God had told him about, Abraham built an altar there and arranged the wood on it. He bound his son Isaac and laid him on the altar, on top of the wood. [10]Then he reached out his hand and took the knife to slay his son. [11]But the angel of the LORD called out to him from heaven, "Abraham! Abraham!"

"Here I am," he replied.

[12]"Do not lay a hand on the boy," he said. "Do not do anything to him. Now I know that you fear God, because you have not withheld from me your son, your only son."

[13]Abraham looked up and there in a thicket he saw a ram[a] caught by its horns. He went over and took the ram and sacrificed it as a burnt offering instead of his son. [14]So Abraham called that place The LORD Will Provide. And to this day it is said, "On the mountain of the LORD it will be provided."

[15]The angel of the LORD called to Abraham from heaven a second time [16]and said, "I swear by myself, declares the LORD, that because you have done this and have not withheld your son, your only son, [17]I will surely bless you and make your descendants as numerous as the stars in the sky and as the sand on the seashore. Your descendants will take possession of the cities of their enemies, [18]and through your offspring[b] all nations on earth will be blessed,[c] because you have obeyed me."

[19]Then Abraham returned to his servants, and they set off together for Beersheba. And Abraham stayed in Beersheba.

---

atissue:obedience

22:1–19 Obeying God can come at a high price. Often it means making choices you don't want to make, choices between doing what *you* want and what *God* wants. At that point you've got to decide: Does God mean more to you than anything else? More than your dream job? More than your boyfriend, fiancé or spouse? More than your children? Your parents? Your friends? Is it worth it to obey him at any cost? Just look at what you get in exchange—God himself. And he is so much greater than anything you might be called to give up.

---

[a] *13* Many manuscripts of the Masoretic Text, Samaritan Pentateuch, Septuagint and Syriac; most manuscripts of the Masoretic Text *a ram behind ⌞him⌟*
[b] *18* Or *seed* [c] *18* Or *and all nations on earth will use the name of your offspring in blessings* (see Gen. 48:20)

myth# 03

"IF I COMMIT MY LIFE TO GOD, HE'LL MAKE ME A MISSIONARY TO AFRICA."

I had the dream again last night. I'm walking down the aisle of my church, but there's no wedding march playing (sigh), just the off-tune ramblings of the church organist struggling through another verse of "Just As I Am." A preacher is there waiting for me, and so is my mother, sister and third-grade teacher, Mrs. Boulter. (Remember, this is a dream.) It's at the end of a revival service. The preacher asks those who want to "commit themselves wholeheartedly to God's purposes for their lives" to come to the front of the church. In my dream, I tell the preacher I am ready to do whatever God wants me to do. Everyone is so happy. Mrs. Boulter is happy. I'm happy. The organist is happy.

The next scene, however, is something altogether different. It's nighttime. And I'm stumbling around inside this primitive hut with a mosquito net wrapped around my head and body, blindly swiping at insects with a gigantic King James Bible. I try to scream, but it's useless. A small town girl from Ohio has turned into an unwitting missionary. In the middle of Africa. And I'm miserable. I wake up the same way every time—drenched in sweat, with the sheets twisted around my head, clutching the phonebook.

I know it's only a dream. Still, I've heard the stories. If you "give it all up to God," something terrible will happen to you to test your faith and see if you're really a good Christian. It would be just my luck to have to quit my job and leave my family so God can ship me off to Africa to be a missionary. And I've never even been outside Ohio.

I'm a Christian. I want to be totally, unapologetically obedient to God. But if I give God my entire life, I'm afraid he'll do something extreme to prove a point. He might take away my boyfriend to see which one I love more—"him or Him"? Worse yet, what if something happens to my family because I said God could "have it all"? My mom will get cancer. Or my best friend will be killed in a car wreck. (You know, those things you never say around the donut table in Sunday school, but they're legitimate fears.)

I love God. And sometimes I'm this close to giving him everything. But in order to prove my love for God, I feel like I have to do something drastic. And I'm not ready for that yet.

—Kate

LET'S BE HONEST —most of us are afraid of God. And we should be. He's the all-powerful King of the universe. In comparison, we are helplessly powerless. But because we fear him, we hold back from him a few things we feel we can't live without, afraid that he'll strip them from us. *A relationship. A job. A standard of living. Health. Dreams.* It's scary to know that God wants what's best for us—because it may come at a price.

Anyone who's familiar with the story of Abraham and Isaac knows that sometimes God asks us to give him what we're clutching protectively to our chests. What if God asked you to give up what's most dear to you? What would you do? How would you react? The danger is camping out in that line of thinking. If you continually live in fear of God and what he will do if you surrender your life to him, you likely won't surrender. The Bible teaches, "There is no fear in love. But perfect love drives out fear, because fear has to do with punishment. The one who fears is not made perfect in love" (1 John 4:18).

God's will is always tied to *who he is.* (Read that again.) The rumor that God is a sadist in the sky, waiting for some unsuspecting woman to give her life to him just so he can toy with her, is a twisted myth. That's not who the Bible describes God to be. It's not his nature. Instead, if we believe he is a loving God, we will be convinced all his plans for us will be full of love and for our good. If we trust the Father, we will trust his plans for us . . . even if they take us through difficult times, down roads we wouldn't otherwise choose or even to the "Africas" we fear the most. Life with God may not always be "safe," as we'd define it; but he will always, always be good to us. Our lives are in good hands.

"The real issue in life is not the search for God's will; it is the search for God. The issue in faith is not knowing what God is doing, rather it is knowing that God knows what he is doing. The issue of faith is seeking God's presence, not God's plan for my life, because there is no plan outside of my knowing him."

—Mike Yaconelli

33

"FOR I KNOW THE PLANS I HAVE FOR YOU," DECLARES THE LORD, "PLANS TO PROSPER YOU AND NOT TO HARM YOU, PLANS TO GIVE YOU HOPE AND A FUTURE."

JEREMIAH 29:11

SEE ALSO

Psalm 34:8

Psalm 84:11

Philippians 1:6

For more on **God's Will**, check the index.

Nahor's Sons

²⁰Some time later Abraham was told, "Milkah is also a mother; she has borne sons to your brother Nahor: ²¹Uz the firstborn, Buz his brother, Kemuel (the father of Aram), ²²Kesed, Hazo, Pildash, Jidlaph and Bethuel." ²³Bethuel became the father of Rebekah. Milkah bore these eight sons to Abraham's brother Nahor. ²⁴His concubine, whose name was Reumah, also had sons: Tebah, Gaham, Tahash and Maakah.

The Death of Sarah

23 Sarah lived to be a hundred and twenty-seven years old. ²She died at Kiriath Arba (that is, Hebron) in the land of Canaan, and Abraham went to mourn for Sarah and to weep over her.

³Then Abraham rose from beside his dead wife and spoke to the Hittites.ᵃ He said, ⁴"I am a foreigner and stranger among you. Sell me some property for a burial site here so I can bury my dead."

⁵The Hittites replied to Abraham, ⁶"Sir, listen to us. You are a mighty prince among us. Bury your dead in the choicest of our tombs. None of us will refuse you his tomb for burying your dead."

⁷Then Abraham rose and bowed down before the people of the land, the Hittites. ⁸He said to them, "If you are willing to let me bury my dead, then listen to me and intercede with Ephron son of Zohar on my behalf ⁹so he will sell me the cave of Machpelah, which belongs to him and is at the end of his field. Ask him to sell it to me for the full price as a burial site among you."

¹⁰Ephron the Hittite was sitting among his people and he replied to Abraham in the hearing of all the Hittites who had come to the gate of his city. ¹¹"No, my lord," he said. "Listen to me; I giveᵇ you the field, and I giveᵇ you the cave that is in it. I giveᵇ it to you in the presence of my people. Bury your dead."

¹²Again Abraham bowed down before the people of the land ¹³and he said to Ephron in their hearing, "Listen to me, if you will. I will pay the price of the field. Accept it from me so I can bury my dead there."

¹⁴Ephron answered Abraham, ¹⁵"Listen to me, my lord; the land is worth four hundred shekelsᶜ of silver, but what is that between me and you? Bury your dead."

¹⁶Abraham agreed to Ephron's terms and weighed out for him the price he had named in the hearing of the Hittites: four hundred shekels of silver, according to the weight current among the merchants.

¹⁷So Ephron's field in Machpelah near Mamre—both the field and the cave in it, and all the trees within the borders of the field—was deeded ¹⁸to Abraham as his property in the presence of all the Hittites who had come to the gate of the city. ¹⁹Afterward Abraham buried his wife Sarah in the cave in the field of Machpelah near Mamre (which is at Hebron) in the land of Canaan. ²⁰So the field and the cave in it were deeded to Abraham by the Hittites as a burial site.

Isaac and Rebekah

24 Abraham was now very old, and the LORD had blessed him in every way. ²He said to the senior servant in his household, the one in charge of all that he had, "Put your hand under my thigh. ³I want you to swear by the LORD, the God of heaven and the God of earth, that you will not get a wife for my son from the daughters of the Canaanites, among whom I am living, ⁴but will go to my country and my own relatives and get a wife for my son Isaac."

⁵The servant asked him, "What if the woman is unwilling to come back with me to this land? Shall I then take your son back to the country you came from?"

⁶"Make sure that you do not take my son back there," Abraham said. ⁷"The LORD, the God of heaven, who brought me out of my father's household and my native land and who spoke to me and promised me on oath, saying, 'To your offspringᵈ I will give this land'—he will send his angel before you so that you can get a wife for my son from there. ⁸If the woman is unwilling to come back with you, then you will be released from this oath of mine. Only do not take my son back there." ⁹So the servant put his hand under the thigh of his master Abraham and swore an oath to him concerning this matter.

¹⁰Then the servant left, taking with him ten of his master's camels loaded with all kinds of good things from his master. He set out for Aram Naharaimᵉ and made his way to the town of Nahor. ¹¹He had the camels kneel down near the well outside the town; it was toward evening, the time the women go out to draw water.

ᵃ 3 Or *the descendants of Heth*; also in verses 5, 7, 10, 16, 18 and 20   ᵇ 11 Or *sell*   ᶜ 15 That is, about 10 pounds or about 4.6 kilograms   ᵈ 7 Or *seed*
ᵉ 10 That is, Northwest Mesopotamia

¹²Then he prayed, "LORD, God of my master Abraham, make me successful today, and show kindness to my master Abraham. ¹³See, I am standing beside this spring, and the daughters of the townspeople are coming out to draw water. ¹⁴May it be that when I say to a girl, 'Please let down your jar that I may have a drink,' and she says, 'Drink, and I'll water your camels too'—let her be the one you have chosen for your servant Isaac. By this I will know that you have shown kindness to my master."

¹⁵Before he had finished praying, Rebekah came out with her jar on her shoulder. She was the daughter of Bethuel son of Milkah, who was the wife of Abraham's brother Nahor. ¹⁶The girl was very beautiful, a virgin; no man had ever slept with her. She went down to the spring, filled her jar and came up again.

¹⁷The servant hurried to meet her and said, "Please give me a little water from your jar."

¹⁸"Drink, my lord," she said, and quickly lowered the jar to her hands and gave him a drink.

¹⁹After she had given him a drink, she said, "I'll draw water for your camels too, until they have had enough to drink." ²⁰So she quickly emptied her jar into the trough, ran back to the well to draw more water, and drew enough for all his camels. ²¹Without saying a word, the man watched her closely to learn whether or not the LORD had made his journey successful.

²²When the camels had finished drinking, the man took out a gold nose ring weighing a beka*a* and two gold bracelets weighing ten shekels.*b* ²³Then he asked, "Whose daughter are you? Please tell me, is there room in your father's house for us to spend the night?"

²⁴She answered him, "I am the daughter of Bethuel, the son that Milkah bore to Nahor." ²⁵And she added, "We have plenty of straw and fodder, as well as room for you to spend the night."

²⁶Then the man bowed down and worshiped the LORD, ²⁷saying, "Praise be to the LORD, the God of my master Abraham, who has not abandoned his kindness and faithfulness to my master. As for me, the LORD has led me on the journey to the house of my master's relatives."

²⁸The girl ran and told her mother's household about these things. ²⁹Now Rebekah had a brother named Laban, and he hurried out to the man at the spring. ³⁰As soon as he had seen the nose ring, and the bracelets on his sister's arms, and had heard Rebekah tell what the man said to her, he went out to the man and found him standing by the camels near the spring. ³¹"Come, you who are blessed by the LORD," he said. "Why are you standing out here? I have prepared the house and a place for the camels."

³²So the man went to the house, and the camels were unloaded. Straw and fodder were brought for the camels, and water for him and his men to wash their feet. ³³Then food was set before him, but he said, "I will not eat until I have told you what I have to say."

"Then tell us," Laban said.

³⁴So he said, "I am Abraham's servant. ³⁵The LORD has blessed my master abundantly, and he has become wealthy. He has given him sheep and cattle, silver and gold, male and female servants, and camels and donkeys. ³⁶My master's wife Sarah has borne him a son in her old age, and he has given him everything he owns. ³⁷And my master made me swear an oath, and said, 'You must not get a wife for my son from the daughters of the Canaanites, in whose land I live, ³⁸but go to my father's family and to my own clan, and get a wife for my son.' ³⁹"Then I asked my master, 'What if the woman will not come back with me?'

35

at|issue:character

24:18–21 You can learn a lot about another person just by watching how she lives everyday life. That's because actions speak volumes about the heart that's motivating them. Rebekah's actions spoke of her heart of service and humility, of her kind and hard-working spirit. What do your actions say about you? Do the people at the grocery store, the gas station or the gym see a woman of integrity and character? Do your family, friends and co-workers see a woman who's living for Christ in the little things? And if they don't— why not?

---

a 22 That is, about 1/5 ounce or about 5.7 grams   *b 22* That is, about 4 ounces or about 115 grams

⁴⁰"He replied, 'The LORD, before whom I have walked faithfully, will send his angel with you and make your journey a success, so that you can get a wife for my son from my own clan and from my father's family. ⁴¹Then, when you go to my clan, you will be released from my oath even if they refuse to give her to you—you will be released from my oath.'

⁴²"When I came to the spring today, I said, 'LORD, God of my master Abraham, if you will, please grant success to the journey on which I have come. ⁴³See, I am standing beside this spring. If a young woman comes out to draw water and I say to her, "Please let me drink a little water from your jar," ⁴⁴and if she says to me, "Drink, and I'll draw water for your camels too," let her be the one the LORD has chosen for my master's son.'

⁴⁵"Before I finished praying in my heart, Rebekah came out, with her jar on her shoulder. She went down to the spring and drew water, and I said to her, 'Please give me a drink.'

⁴⁶"She quickly lowered her jar from her shoulder and said, 'Drink, and I'll water your camels too.' So I drank, and she watered the camels also.

⁴⁷"I asked her, 'Whose daughter are you?'

"She said, 'The daughter of Bethuel son of Nahor, whom Milkah bore to him.'

"Then I put the ring in her nose and the bracelets on her arms, ⁴⁸and I bowed down and worshiped the LORD. I praised the LORD, the God of my master Abraham, who had led me on the right road to get the granddaughter of my master's brother for his son. ⁴⁹Now if you will show kindness and faithfulness to my master, tell me; and if not, tell me, so I may know which way to turn."

⁵⁰Laban and Bethuel answered, "This is from the LORD; we can say nothing to you one way or the other. ⁵¹Here is Rebekah; take her and go, and let her become the wife of your master's son, as the LORD has directed."

⁵²When Abraham's servant heard what they said, he bowed down to the ground before the LORD. ⁵³Then the servant brought out gold and silver jewelry and articles of clothing and gave them to Rebekah; he also gave costly gifts to her brother and to her mother. ⁵⁴Then he and the men who were with him ate and drank and spent the night there.

When they got up the next morning, he said, "Send me on my way to my master."

⁵⁵But her brother and her mother replied, "Let the girl remain with us ten days or so; then you*a* may go."

⁵⁶But he said to them, "Do not detain me, now that the LORD has granted success to my journey. Send me on my way so I may go to my master."

⁵⁷Then they said, "Let's call the girl and ask her about it." ⁵⁸So they called Rebekah and asked her, "Will you go with this man?"

"I will go," she said.

⁵⁹So they sent their sister Rebekah on her way, along with her nurse and Abraham's servant and his men. ⁶⁰And they blessed Rebekah and said to her,

> "Our sister, may you increase
>   to thousands upon thousands;
> may your offspring possess
>   the cities of their enemies."

⁶¹Then Rebekah and her attendants got ready and mounted their camels and went back with the man. So the servant took Rebekah and left.

⁶²Now Isaac had come from Beer Lahai Roi, for he was living in the Negev. ⁶³He went out to the field one evening to meditate,*b* and as he looked up, he saw camels approaching. ⁶⁴Rebekah also looked up and saw Isaac. She got down from her camel ⁶⁵and asked the servant, "Who is that man in the field coming to meet us?"

"He is my master," the servant answered. So she took her veil and covered herself.

⁶⁶Then the servant told Isaac all he had done. ⁶⁷Isaac brought her into the tent of his mother Sarah, and he married Rebekah. So she became his wife, and he loved her; and Isaac was comforted after his mother's death.

a 55 Or *she*   *b 63* The meaning of the Hebrew for this word is uncertain.

The Death of Abraham

25 Abraham had taken another wife, whose name was Keturah. [2]She bore him Zimran, Jokshan, Medan, Midian, Ishbak and Shuah. [3]Jokshan was the father of Sheba and Dedan; the descendants of Dedan were the Ashurites, the Letushites and the Leummites. [4]The sons of Midian were Ephah, Epher, Hanok, Abida and Eldaah. All these were descendants of Keturah.

[5]Abraham left everything he owned to Isaac. [6]But while he was still living, he gave gifts to the sons of his concubines and sent them away from his son Isaac to the land of the east.

[7]Abraham lived a hundred and seventy-five years. [8]Then Abraham breathed his last and died at a good old age, an old man and full of years; and he was gathered to his people. [9]His sons Isaac and Ishmael buried him in the cave of Machpelah near Mamre, in the field of Ephron son of Zohar the Hittite, [10]the field Abraham had bought from the Hittites.[a] There Abraham was buried with his wife Sarah. [11]After Abraham's death, God blessed his son Isaac, who then lived near Beer Lahai Roi.

Ishmael's Sons

[12]This is the account of the family line of Abraham's son Ishmael, whom Sarah's servant, Hagar the Egyptian, bore to Abraham.

[13]These are the names of the sons of Ishmael, listed in the order of their birth: Nebaioth the firstborn of Ishmael, Kedar, Adbeel, Mibsam, [14]Mishma, Dumah, Massa, [15]Hadad, Tema, Jetur, Naphish and Kedemah. [16]These were the sons of Ishmael, and these are the names of the twelve tribal rulers according to their settlements and camps. [17]Ishmael lived a hundred and thirty-seven years. He breathed his last and died, and he was gathered to his people. [18]His descendants settled in the area from Havilah to Shur, near the eastern border of Egypt, as you go toward Ashur. And they lived in hostility toward[b] all the tribes related to them.

Jacob and Esau

[19]This is the account of the family line of Abraham's son Isaac.

Abraham became the father of Isaac, [20]and Isaac was forty years old when he married Rebekah daughter of Bethuel the Aramean from Paddan Aram[c] and sister of Laban the Aramean.

[21]Isaac prayed to the LORD on behalf of his wife, because she was childless. The LORD answered his prayer, and his wife Rebekah became pregnant. [22]The babies jostled each other within her, and she said, "Why is this happening to me?" So she went to inquire of the LORD.

[23]The LORD said to her,

> "Two nations are in your womb,
>   and two peoples from within you will be separated;
> one people will be stronger than the other,
>   and the older will serve the younger."

[24]When the time came for her to give birth, there were twin boys in her womb. [25]The first to come out

---

atissue:remarriage

25:1 Today, remarriage is a reality. But a second marriage brings added complications, especially when children are involved. Abraham remarried after Sarah died, and he and Keturah had six children together. Then and now, the universal fact is that kids sometimes have difficulty adjusting to major changes in a family. They may be confused by all the changes and want their old life back. Family relationships and inheritances in Abraham's time were more strictly defined by culture, which eliminated some of the uncertainty and insecurity. Today, *we* must identify each person's role in a blended family—which takes hard work, love and forgiveness.

37

---

myth# 04 "HE'S NOT A CHRISTIAN, BUT HE'S A GREAT GUY."

I didn't know what to say when Richard asked the question. Does Kevin go to church? Hello, I thought you were going to be happy for me! I remember thinking, I've finally found someone I really like, and things are going great.

Still, Richard is my partner at work, and he and his wife know everything there is to know about me. They know I grew up in church. And they also know I tried to make the church singles group thing work. But there just wasn't anyone I was remotely attracted to there. I had always dreamed that God would have the perfect person picked out for me and deliver him right to my door. However, I was fast approaching the big 3-0, and it still hadn't happened. In fact, I had almost given up, figuring I was destined to be single for the rest of my life, and then Kevin came along. We met at the gym. I would have married him on the spot for his calves alone. However, it was his smile that really got to me. We kept running into each other in the mornings before work, and he finally asked me to go out one weekend. We talked for hours that first night, as if we'd known each other forever. He was wonderful.

Over the next few weeks, as my relationship with Kevin grew, Richard started to ask me more questions. "Does Kevin know you're a Christian? Have you told him about your faith?" I fended him off with a few cursory answers. "Kevin didn't grow up in church like you and I did," I told him. "But I think he gets it, or at least he's pretty close." Richard didn't seem satisfied with my answer. Truthfully, something inside of me cringed when I said it. But I'm not going to let anything or anyone spoil my happiness. Who's to say Kevin isn't the man I dreamed of all along? He'll probably become a Christian at some point in our relationship, and then everything will be perfect.

—Christy

DO YOU BELIEVE love stories

like Isaac and Rebekah's can happen? Two people who aren't even from the same country brought together by God's hand. But oh, the things we're willing to believe in the midst of a man-drought. When the phone isn't ringing because no one's calling. When we spend another Valentine's Day with the cat. There's a "certain age," you know, past which all of our mothers' friends believe the odds for us finding the man of our dreams plummet. Add to the mix the complication of a Christian woman looking for a Christian man—and the situation becomes even more discouraging. We begin to convince ourselves that we somehow missed God's best. Maybe that's the problem. We just weren't *open* before—our standards were too high. And so, now we're not being *desperate*; we're being *open*. Unfortunately, that's when we begin to rationalize whatever we want to fit the ideal.

He's not super-spiritual, but show me a man who is.

He has such great potential—he needs someone like me to encourage him.

It's important to note that we won't change God's mind, even though we can list all sorts of factors in favor of our decision to marry outside of our convictions. The Bible's warning not to marry a non-Christian is very clear (see 2 Corinthians 6:14). Think about it. How will you celebrate Christmas and Easter? Or discipline your children? Will your husband understand wanting to tithe from your joint account? Will he mind if you're gone for part of every Sunday? How do you feel about having a quiet time alone? The issues range from minor to major.

If you're single and lonely, God knows it. If you're approaching a certain age, God knows how old you are. And he is not worried. The important thing is not to *be married* . . . it's to *be married to the right person*. And God can bring that person unexpectedly, just as he did for Isaac and Rebekah. Feelings and emotions can be disastrously misleading in this area. That's why we have to hold onto God's Word, not a wish list, and let God dictate our decision whether or not to marry someone.

"About one out of four (26 percent) born-again Christians believe that it doesn't matter what faith you follow because they all teach the same lessons, a belief held by 56 percent of non-Christians."

—Barna Research Group (2000)

39

"DO NOT BE YOKED TOGETHER WITH UNBELIEVERS. FOR WHAT DO RIGHTEOUSNESS AND WICKEDNESS HAVE IN COMMON? OR WHAT FELLOWSHIP CAN LIGHT HAVE WITH DARKNESS?"

2 CORINTHIANS 6:14

SEE ALSO

Genesis 2:24
Proverbs 4:23
Jeremiah 17:9
1 Corinthians 2:14

For more on **Dating**, check the index.

was red, and his whole body was like a hairy garment; so they named him Esau.*a* 26 After this, his brother came out, with his hand grasping Esau's heel; so he was named Jacob.*b* Isaac was sixty years old when Rebekah gave birth to them.

27 The boys grew up, and Esau became a skillful hunter, a man of the open country, while Jacob was content to stay at home among the tents. 28 Isaac, who had a taste for wild game, loved Esau, but Rebekah loved Jacob.

29 Once when Jacob was cooking some stew, Esau came in from the open country, famished. 30 He said to Jacob, "Quick, let me have some of that red stew! I'm famished!" (That is why he was also called Edom.*c*)

31 Jacob replied, "First sell me your birthright."

32 "Look, I am about to die," Esau said. "What good is the birthright to me?"

33 But Jacob said, "Swear to me first." So he swore an oath to him, selling his birthright to Jacob.

34 Then Jacob gave Esau some bread and some lentil stew. He ate and drank, and then got up and left. So Esau despised his birthright.

Isaac and Abimelek

26 Now there was a famine in the land—besides the previous famine in Abraham's time—and Isaac went to Abimelek king of the Philistines in Gerar. 2 The LORD appeared to Isaac and said, "Do not go down to Egypt; live in the land where I tell you to live. 3 Stay in this land for a while, and I will be with you and will bless you. For to you and your descendants I will give all these lands and will confirm the oath I swore to your father Abraham. 4 I will make your descendants as numerous as the stars in the sky and will give them all these lands, and through your offspring*d* all nations on earth will be blessed,*e* 5 because Abraham obeyed me and did everything I required of him, keeping my commands, my decrees and my instructions." 6 So Isaac stayed in Gerar.

7 When the men of that place asked him about his wife, he said, "She is my sister," because he was afraid to say, "She is my wife." He thought, "The men of this place might kill me on account of Rebekah, because she is beautiful."

conversations

parenting «» 25:26

1 » What causes parents to favor one child over others?

2 » What does that favoritism do to children?

3 » How can parents avoid favoritism?

For more on **parenting**, check the index. For the next Conversations, go to p. 43.

8 When Isaac had been there a long time, Abimelek king of the Philistines looked down from a window and saw Isaac caressing his wife Rebekah. 9 So Abimelek summoned Isaac and said, "She is really your wife! Why did you say, 'She is my sister'?"

Isaac answered him, "Because I thought I might lose my life on account of her."

10 Then Abimelek said, "What is this you have done to us? One of the men might well have slept with your wife, and you would have brought guilt upon us."

11 So Abimelek gave orders to all the people: "Anyone who harms this man or his wife shall surely be put to death."

12 Isaac planted crops in that land and the same year reaped a hundredfold, because the LORD blessed him. 13 The man became rich, and his wealth continued to grow until he became very wealthy. 14 He had so many flocks and herds and servants that the Philistines envied him. 15 So all the wells that his father's servants had dug in the time of his father Abraham, the Philistines stopped up, filling them with earth.

16 Then Abimelek said to Isaac, "Move away from us; you have become too powerful for us."

17 So Isaac moved away from there and encamped in the Valley of Gerar, where he settled. 18 Isaac reopened the wells that had been dug in the time of his father Abraham, which the Philistines had stopped up after Abraham died, and he gave them the same names his father had given them.

---

a 25 Esau may mean hairy. b 26 Jacob means he grasps the heel, a Hebrew idiom for he deceives. c 30 Edom means red. d 4 Or seed e 4 Or and all nations on earth will use the name of your offspring in blessings (see Gen. 48:20)

¹⁹Isaac's servants dug in the valley and discovered a well of fresh water there. ²⁰But the herders of Gerar quarreled with those of Isaac and said, "The water is ours!" So he named the well Esek,ᵃ because they disputed with him. ²¹Then they dug another well, but they quarreled over that one also; so he named it Sitnah.ᵇ ²²He moved on from there and dug another well, and no one quarreled over it. He named it Rehoboth,ᶜ saying, "Now the Lord has given us room and we will flourish in the land."

²³From there he went up to Beersheba. ²⁴That night the Lord appeared to him and said, "I am the God of your father Abraham. Do not be afraid, for I am with you; I will bless you and will increase the number of your descendants for the sake of my servant Abraham."

²⁵Isaac built an altar there and called on the name of the Lord. There he pitched his tent, and there his servants dug a well.

²⁶Meanwhile, Abimelek had come to him from Gerar, with Ahuzzath his personal adviser and Phicol the commander of his forces. ²⁷Isaac asked them, "Why have you come to me, since you were hostile to me and sent me away?"

²⁸They answered, "We saw clearly that the Lord was with you; so we said, 'There ought to be a sworn agreement between us'—between us and you. Let us make a treaty with you ²⁹that you will do us no harm, just as we did not harm you but always treated you well and sent you away peacefully. And now you are blessed by the Lord."

³⁰Isaac then made a feast for them, and they ate and drank. ³¹Early the next morning the men swore an oath to each other. Then Isaac sent them on their way, and they went away peacefully.

³²That day Isaac's servants came and told him about the well they had dug. They said, "We've found water!" ³³He called it Shibah,ᵈ and to this day the name of the town has been Beersheba.ᵉ

Jacob Takes Esau's Blessing

³⁴When Esau was forty years old, he married Judith daughter of Beeri the Hittite, and also Basemath daughter of Elon the Hittite. ³⁵They were a source of grief to Isaac and Rebekah.

27 When Isaac was old and his eyes were so weak that he could no longer see, he called for Esau his older son and said to him, "My son."

"Here I am," he answered.

²Isaac said, "I am now an old man and don't know the day of my death. ³Now then, get your equipment—your quiver and bow—and go out to the open country to hunt some wild game for me. ⁴Prepare me the kind of tasty food I like and bring it to me to eat, so that I may give you my blessing before I die."

⁵Now Rebekah was listening as Isaac spoke to his son Esau. When Esau left for the open country to hunt game and bring it back, ⁶Rebekah said to her son Jacob, "Look, I overheard your father say to your brother Esau, ⁷'Bring me some game and prepare me some tasty food to eat, so that I may give you my blessing in the presence of the Lord before I die.' ⁸Now, my son, listen carefully and do what I tell you: ⁹Go out to the flock and bring me two choice young goats, so I can prepare some tasty food for your father, just the way he likes it. ¹⁰Then take it to your father to eat, so that he may give you his blessing before he dies."

¹¹Jacob said to Rebekah his mother, "But my brother Esau is a hairy man while I have smooth skin. ¹²What if my father touches me? I would appear to be tricking him and would bring down a curse on myself rather than a blessing."

¹³His mother said to him, "My son, let the curse fall on me. Just do what I say; go and get them for me."

¹⁴So he went and got them and brought them to his mother, and she prepared some tasty food, just the way his father liked it. ¹⁵Then Rebekah took the best clothes of Esau her older son, which she had in the house, and put them on her younger son Jacob. ¹⁶She also covered his hands and the smooth part of his neck with the goatskins. ¹⁷Then she handed to her son Jacob the tasty food and the bread she had made.

¹⁸He went to his father and said, "My father."

"Yes, my son," he answered. "Who is it?"

41

ᵃ 20 Esek means dispute.   ᵇ 21 Sitnah means opposition.   ᶜ 22 Rehoboth means room.   ᵈ 33 Shibah can mean oath or seven.   ᵉ 33 Beersheba can mean well of the oath or well of seven.

¹⁹Jacob said to his father, "I am Esau your firstborn. I have done as you told me. Please sit up and eat some of my game, so that you may give me your blessing."

²⁰Isaac asked his son, "How did you find it so quickly, my son?"

"The LORD your God gave me success," he replied.

²¹Then Isaac said to Jacob, "Come near so I can touch you, my son, to know whether you really are my son Esau or not."

²²Jacob went close to his father Isaac, who touched him and said, "The voice is the voice of Jacob, but the hands are the hands of Esau." ²³He did not recognize him, for his hands were hairy like those of his brother Esau; so he proceeded to bless him. ²⁴"Are you really my son Esau?" he asked.

"I am," he replied.

²⁵Then he said, "My son, bring me some of your game to eat, so that I may give you my blessing."

Jacob brought it to him and he ate; and he brought some wine and he drank. ²⁶Then his father Isaac said to him, "Come here, my son, and kiss me."

²⁷So he went to him and kissed him. When Isaac caught the smell of his clothes, he blessed him and said,

> "Ah, the smell of my son
>   is like the smell of a field
>   that the LORD has blessed.
> ²⁸May God give you of heaven's dew
>   and of earth's richness—
>   an abundance of grain and new wine.
> ²⁹May nations serve you
>   and peoples bow down to you.
> Be lord over your brothers,
>   and may the sons of your mother bow down to you.
> May those who curse you be cursed
>   and those who bless you be blessed."

³⁰After Isaac finished blessing him, and Jacob had scarcely left his father's presence, his brother Esau came in from hunting. ³¹He too prepared some tasty food and brought it to his father. Then he said to him, "My father, please sit up and eat some of my game, so that you may give me your blessing."

³²His father Isaac asked him, "Who are you?"

"I am your son," he answered, "your firstborn, Esau."

³³Isaac trembled violently and said, "Who was it, then, that hunted game and brought it to me? I ate it just before you came and I blessed him—and indeed he will be blessed!"

³⁴When Esau heard his father's words, he burst out with a loud and bitter cry and said to his father, "Bless me—me too, my father!"

³⁵But he said, "Your brother came deceitfully and took your blessing."

³⁶Esau said, "Isn't he rightly named Jacob*? This is the second time he has taken advantage of me: He took my birthright, and now he's taken my blessing!" Then he asked, "Haven't you reserved any blessing for me?"

³⁷Isaac answered Esau, "I have made him lord over you and have made all his relatives his servants, and I have sustained him with grain and new wine. So what can I possibly do for you, my son?"

³⁸Esau said to his father, "Do you have only one blessing, my father? Bless me too, my father!" Then Esau wept aloud.

³⁹His father Isaac answered him,

> "Your dwelling will be
>   away from the earth's richness,
>   away from the dew of heaven above.

ᵃ 36 Jacob *means* he grasps the heel, *a Hebrew idiom for* he takes advantage of *or* he deceives.

⁴⁰"You will live by the sword
    and you will serve your brother.
But when you grow restless,
    you will throw his yoke
    from off your neck."

⁴¹Esau held a grudge against Jacob because of the blessing his father had given him. He said to himself, "The days of mourning for my father are near; then I will kill my brother Jacob."

⁴²When Rebekah was told what her older son Esau had said, she sent for her younger son Jacob and said to him, "Your brother Esau is planning to avenge himself by killing you. ⁴³Now then, my son, do what I say: Flee at once to my brother Laban in Harran. ⁴⁴Stay with him for a while until your brother's fury subsides. ⁴⁵When your brother is no longer angry with you and forgets what you did to him, I'll send word for you to come back from there. Why should I lose both of you in one day?"

⁴⁶Then Rebekah said to Isaac, "I'm disgusted with living because of these Hittite women. If Jacob takes a wife from among the women of this land, from Hittite women like these, my life will not be worth living."

28 So Isaac called for Jacob and blessed him. Then he commanded him: "Do not marry a Canaanite woman. ²Go at once to Paddan Aram,ᵃ to the house of your mother's father Bethuel. Take a wife for yourself there, from among the daughters of Laban, your mother's brother. ³May God Almightyᵇ bless you and make you fruitful and increase your numbers until you become a community of peoples. ⁴May he give you and your descendants the blessing given to Abraham, so that you may take possession of the land where you now reside as a foreigner, the land God gave to Abraham." ⁵Then Isaac sent Jacob on his way, and he went to Paddan Aram, to Laban son of Bethuel the Aramean, the brother of Rebekah, who was the mother of Jacob and Esau.

⁶Now Esau learned that Isaac had blessed Jacob and had sent him to Paddan Aram to take a wife from there, and that when he blessed him he commanded him, "Do not marry a Canaanite woman," ⁷and that Jacob had obeyed his father and mother and had gone to Paddan Aram. ⁸Esau then realized how displeasing the Canaanite women were to his father Isaac; ⁹so he went to Ishmael and married Mahalath, the sister of Nebaioth and daughter of Ishmael son of Abraham, in addition to the wives he already had.

Jacob's Dream at Bethel

¹⁰Jacob left Beersheba and set out for Harran. ¹¹When he reached a certain place, he stopped for the night because the sun had set. Taking one of the stones there, he put it under his head and lay down to sleep. ¹²He had a dream in which he saw a stairwayᶜ resting on the earth, with its top reaching to heaven, and the angels of God were ascending and descending on it. ¹³There above itᵈ stood the Lord, and he said: "I am the Lord, the God of your father Abraham and the God of Isaac. I will give you and your descendants the land on which you are lying. ¹⁴Your descendants will be like the dust of the earth, and you will spread out to the west and to the east, to the north and to the south. All peoples on earth will be blessed through you and your offspring.ᵉ ¹⁵I am with you and will watch over you wherever you go, and I will bring you back to this land. I will not leave you until I have done what I have promised you."

¹⁶When Jacob awoke from his sleep, he thought, "Surely the Lord is in this place, and I was not aware of it." ¹⁷He was afraid and said, "How awesome is this place! This is none other than the house of God; this is the gate of heaven."

"conversations"

dating ◊ 28:1–2

1 Where should Christian women look for their future husbands?

2 What issues arise in cross-cultural dating (not inter-racial dating, which God allows, or inter-faith dating, which God forbids)?

3 How does a man's background shape who he is?

For more on **dating**, check the index.
For the next Conversations, go to p. 58.

ᵃ *2* That is, Northwest Mesopotamia; also in verses 5, 6 and 7   ᵇ *3* Hebrew *El-Shaddai*   ᶜ *12* Or *ladder*   ᵈ *13* Or *There beside him*   ᵉ *14* Or *will use your name and the name of your offspring in blessings* (see Gen. 48:20)

HE IS: watching

28:15 Jacob left his home and family and found himself in unfamiliar territory. In those days, people believed that leaving their homeland meant leaving behind their gods. But God inhabited Jacob's dream to remind him that he couldn't venture anywhere without God *watching* over him.

Are you moving into uncharted waters: a new job, city or relationship? Know that God is with you and will keep you. He is *watching* no matter what may happen. You may have left your comfort zone, but the Comforter goes with you night and day.

For the next He Is, go to p. 51.

44

¹⁸Early the next morning Jacob took the stone he had placed under his head and set it up as a pillar and poured oil on top of it. ¹⁹He called that place Bethel,ᵃ though the city used to be called Luz.

²⁰Then Jacob made a vow, saying, "If God will be with me and will watch over me on this journey I am taking and will give me food to eat and clothes to wear ²¹so that I return safely to my father's household, then the LORDᵇ will be my God ²²andᶜ this stone that I have set up as a pillar will be God's house, and of all that you give me I will give you a tenth."

Jacob Arrives in Paddan Aram

29 Then Jacob continued on his journey and came to the land of the eastern peoples. ²There he saw a well in the open country, with three flocks of sheep lying near it because the flocks were watered from that well. The stone over the mouth of the well was large. ³When all the flocks were gathered there, the shepherds would roll the stone away from the well's mouth and water the sheep. Then they would return the stone to its place over the mouth of the well.

⁴Jacob asked the shepherds, "My brothers, where are you from?"

"We're from Harran," they replied.

⁵He said to them, "Do you know Laban, Nahor's grandson?"

"Yes, we know him," they answered.

⁶Then Jacob asked them, "Is he well?"

"Yes, he is," they said, "and here comes his daughter Rachel with the sheep."

⁷"Look," he said, "the sun is still high; it is not time for the flocks to be gathered. Water the sheep and take them back to pasture."

⁸"We can't," they replied, "until all the flocks are gathered and the stone has been rolled away from the mouth of the well. Then we will water the sheep."

⁹While he was still talking with them, Rachel came with her father's sheep, for she was their shepherd. ¹⁰When Jacob saw Rachel daughter of Laban, his mother's brother, and Laban's sheep, he went over and rolled the stone away from the mouth of the well and watered his uncle's sheep. ¹¹Then Jacob kissed Rachel and began to weep aloud. ¹²He had told Rachel that he was a relative of her father and a son of Rebekah. So she ran and told her father.

¹³As soon as Laban heard the news about Jacob, his sister's son, he hurried to meet him. He embraced him and kissed him and brought him to his home, and there Jacob told him all these things. ¹⁴Then Laban said to him, "You are my own flesh and blood."

Jacob Marries Leah and Rachel

After Jacob had stayed with him for a whole month, ¹⁵Laban said to him, "Just because you are a relative of mine, should you work for me for nothing? Tell me what your wages should be."

¹⁶Now Laban had two daughters; the name of the older was Leah, and the name of the younger was

---

ᵃ *19 Bethel means house of God.* ᵇ *20,21 Or Since God…father's household, the LORD* ᶜ *21,22 Or household, and the LORD will be my God, ²²then*

Rachel. [17]Leah had weak[a] eyes, but Rachel had a lovely figure and was beautiful. [18]Jacob was in love with Rachel and said, "I'll work for you seven years in return for your younger daughter Rachel."

[19]Laban said, "It's better that I give her to you than to some other man. Stay here with me." [20]So Jacob served seven years to get Rachel, but they seemed like only a few days to him because of his love for her.

[21]Then Jacob said to Laban, "Give me my wife. My time is completed, and I want to make love to her."

[22]So Laban brought together all the people of the place and gave a feast. [23]But when evening came, he took his daughter Leah and brought her to Jacob, and Jacob made love to her. [24]And Laban gave his servant Zilpah to his daughter as her attendant.

[25]When morning came, there was Leah! So Jacob said to Laban, "What is this you have done to me? I served you for Rachel, didn't I? Why have you deceived me?"

[26]Laban replied, "It is not our custom here to give the younger daughter in marriage before the older one. [27]Finish this daughter's bridal week; then we will give you the younger one also, in return for another seven years of work."

[28]And Jacob did so. He finished the week with Leah, and then Laban gave him his daughter Rachel to be his wife. [29]Laban gave his servant Bilhah to his daughter Rachel as her attendant. [30]Jacob made love to Rachel also, and his love for Rachel was greater than his love for Leah. And he worked for Laban another seven years.

Jacob's Children

[31]When the LORD saw that Leah was not loved, he enabled her to conceive, but Rachel remained childless. [32]Leah became pregnant and gave birth to a son. She named him Reuben,[b] for she said, "It is because the LORD has seen my misery. Surely my husband will love me now."

[33]She conceived again, and when she gave birth to a son she said, "Because the LORD heard that I am not loved, he gave me this one too." So she named him Simeon.[c]

[34]Again she conceived, and when she gave birth to a son she said, "Now at last my husband will become attached to me, because I have borne him three sons." So he was named Levi.[d]

[35]She conceived again, and when she gave birth to a son she said, "This time I will praise the LORD." So she named him Judah.[e] Then she stopped having children.

30 When Rachel saw that she was not bearing Jacob any children, she became jealous of her sister. So she said to Jacob, "Give me children, or I'll die!"

[2]Jacob became angry with her and said, "Am I in the place of God, who has kept you from having children?"

[3]Then she said, "Here is Bilhah, my servant. Sleep with her so that she can bear children for me and I too can build a family through her."

[4]So she gave him her servant Bilhah as a wife. Jacob slept with her, [5]and she became pregnant and bore him a son. [6]Then Rachel said, "God has vindicated me; he has listened to my plea and given me a son." Because of this she named him Dan.[f]

[7]Rachel's servant Bilhah conceived again and bore Jacob a second son. [8]Then Rachel said, "I have had a great struggle with my sister, and I have won." So she named him Naphtali.[g]

[9]When Leah saw that she had stopped having children, she took her servant Zilpah and gave her to Jacob as a wife. [10]Leah's servant Zilpah bore Jacob a son. [11]Then Leah said, "What good fortune!"[h] So she named him Gad.[i]

[12]Leah's servant Zilpah bore Jacob a second son. [13]Then Leah said, "How happy I am! The women will call me happy." So she named him Asher.[j]

[14]During wheat harvest, Reuben went out into the fields and found some mandrake plants, which he brought to his mother Leah. Rachel said to Leah, "Please give me some of your son's mandrakes."

[15]But she said to her, "Wasn't it enough that you took away my husband? Will you take my son's mandrakes too?"

---

[a] 17 Or delicate [b] 32 Reuben sounds like the Hebrew for he has seen my misery; the name means see, a son. [c] 33 Simeon probably means one who hears. [d] 34 Levi sounds like and may be derived from the Hebrew for attached. [e] 35 Judah sounds like and may be derived from the Hebrew for praise. [f] 6 Dan here means he has vindicated. [g] 8 Naphtali means my struggle. [h] 11 Or "A troop is coming!" [i] 11 Gad can mean good fortune or a troop. [j] 13 Asher means happy.

"Very well," Rachel said, "he can sleep with you tonight in return for your son's mandrakes."

¹⁶ So when Jacob came in from the fields that evening, Leah went out to meet him. "You must sleep with me," she said. "I have hired you with my son's mandrakes." So he slept with her that night.

¹⁷ God listened to Leah, and she became pregnant and bore Jacob a fifth son. ¹⁸ Then Leah said, "God has rewarded me for giving my servant to my husband." So she named him Issachar.ᵃ

¹⁹ Leah conceived again and bore Jacob a sixth son. ²⁰ Then Leah said, "God has presented me with a precious gift. This time my husband will treat me with honor, because I have borne him six sons." So she named him Zebulun.ᵇ

²¹ Some time later she gave birth to a daughter and named her Dinah.

²² Then God remembered Rachel; he listened to her and enabled her to conceive. ²³ She became pregnant and gave birth to a son and said, "God has taken away my disgrace." ²⁴ She named him Joseph,ᶜ and said, "May the LORD add to me another son."

Jacob's Flocks Increase

²⁵ After Rachel gave birth to Joseph, Jacob said to Laban, "Send me on my way so I can go back to my own homeland. ²⁶ Give me my wives and children, for whom I have served you, and I will be on my way. You know how much work I've done for you."

²⁷ But Laban said to him, "If I have found favor in your eyes, please stay. I have learned by divination that the LORD has blessed me because of you." ²⁸ He added, "Name your wages, and I will pay them."

²⁹ Jacob said to him, "You know how I have worked for you and how your livestock has fared under my care. ³⁰ The little you had before I came has increased greatly, and the LORD has blessed you wherever I have been. But now, when may I do something for my own household?"

³¹ "What shall I give you?" he asked.

"Don't give me anything," Jacob replied. "But if you will do this one thing for me, I will go on tending your flocks and watching over them: ³² Let me go through all your flocks today and remove from them every speckled or spotted sheep, every dark-colored lamb and every spotted or speckled goat. They will be my wages. ³³ And my honesty will testify for me in the future, whenever you check on the wages you have paid me. Any goat in my possession that is not speckled or spotted, or any lamb that is not dark-colored, will be considered stolen."

³⁴ "Agreed," said Laban. "Let it be as you have said." ³⁵ That same day he removed all the male goats that were streaked or spotted, and all the speckled or spotted female goats (all that had white on them) and all the dark-colored lambs, and he placed them in the care of his sons. ³⁶ Then he put a three-day journey between himself and Jacob, while Jacob continued to tend the rest of Laban's flocks.

³⁷ Jacob, however, took fresh-cut branches from poplar, almond and plane trees and made white stripes on them by peeling the bark and exposing the white inner wood of the branches. ³⁸ Then he placed the peeled branches in all the watering troughs, so that they would be directly in front of the flocks when they came to drink. When the flocks were in heat and came to drink, ³⁹ they mated in front of the branches. And they bore young that were streaked or speckled or spotted. ⁴⁰ Jacob set apart the young of the flock by themselves, but made the rest face the streaked and dark-colored animals that belonged to Laban. Thus he made separate flocks for himself and did not put them with Laban's animals. ⁴¹ Whenever the stronger females were in heat, Jacob would place the branches in the troughs in front of the animals so they would mate near the branches, ⁴² but if the animals were weak, he would not place them there. So the weak animals went to Laban and the strong ones to Jacob. ⁴³ In this way the man grew exceedingly prosperous and came to own large flocks, and female and male servants, and camels and donkeys.

Jacob Flees From Laban

31 Jacob heard that Laban's sons were saying, "Jacob has taken everything our father owned and has gained all this wealth from what belonged to our father." ² And Jacob noticed that Laban's attitude toward him was not what it had been.

³ Then the LORD said to Jacob, "Go back to the land of your fathers and to your relatives, and I will be with you."

ᵃ 18 *Issachar* sounds like the Hebrew for *reward.*　ᵇ 20 *Zebulun* probably means *honor.*　ᶜ 24 *Joseph* means *may he add.*

⁴So Jacob sent word to Rachel and Leah to come out to the fields where his flocks were. ⁵He said to them, "I see that your father's attitude toward me is not what it was before, but the God of my father has been with me. ⁶You know that I've worked for your father with all my strength, ⁷yet your father has cheated me by changing my wages ten times. However, God has not allowed him to harm me. ⁸If he said, 'The speckled ones will be your wages,' then all the flocks gave birth to speckled young; and if he said, 'The streaked ones will be your wages,' then all the flocks bore streaked young. ⁹So God has taken away your father's livestock and has given them to me.

¹⁰"In breeding season I once had a dream in which I looked up and saw that the male goats mating with the flock were streaked, speckled or spotted. ¹¹The angel of God said to me in the dream, 'Jacob.' I answered, 'Here I am.' ¹²And he said, 'Look up and see that all the male goats mating with the flock are streaked, speckled or spotted, for I have seen all that Laban has been doing to you. ¹³I am the God of Bethel, where you anointed a pillar and where you made a vow to me. Now leave this land at once and go back to your native land.'"

¹⁴Then Rachel and Leah replied, "Do we still have any share in the inheritance of our father's estate? ¹⁵Does he not regard us as foreigners? Not only has he sold us, but he has used up what was paid for us. ¹⁶Surely all the wealth that God took away from our father belongs to us and our children. So do whatever God has told you."

¹⁷Then Jacob put his children and his wives on camels, ¹⁸and he drove all his livestock ahead of him, along with all the goods he had accumulated in Paddan Aram,^a to go to his father Isaac in the land of Canaan.

¹⁹When Laban had gone to shear his sheep, Rachel stole her father's household gods. ²⁰Moreover, Jacob deceived Laban the Aramean by not telling him he was running away. ²¹So he fled with all he had, crossed the Euphrates River, and headed for the hill country of Gilead.

Laban Pursues Jacob

²²On the third day Laban was told that Jacob had fled. ²³Taking his relatives with him, he pursued Jacob for seven days and caught up with him in the hill country of Gilead. ²⁴Then God came to Laban the Aramean in a dream at night and said to him, "Be careful not to say anything to Jacob, either good or bad."

²⁵Jacob had pitched his tent in the hill country of Gilead when Laban overtook him, and Laban and his relatives camped there too. ²⁶Then Laban said to Jacob, "What have you done? You've deceived me, and you've carried off my daughters like captives in war. ²⁷Why did you run off secretly and deceive me? Why didn't you tell me, so I could send you away with joy and singing to the music of timbrels and harps? ²⁸You didn't even let me kiss my grandchildren and my daughters good-by. You have done a foolish thing. ²⁹I have the power to harm you; but last night the God of your father said to me, 'Be careful not to say anything to Jacob, either good or bad.' ³⁰Now you have gone off because you longed to return to your father's household. But why did you steal my gods?"

³¹Jacob answered Laban, "I was afraid, because I thought you would take your daughters away from me by force. ³²But if you find anyone who has your gods, that one shall not live. In the presence of our relatives, see for yourself whether there is anything of yours here with me; and if so, take it." Now Jacob did not know that Rachel had stolen the gods.

³³So Laban went into Jacob's tent and into Leah's tent and into the tent of the two female servants, but he found nothing. After he came out of Leah's tent, he entered Rachel's tent. ³⁴Now Rachel had taken the household gods and put them inside her camel's saddle and was sitting on them. Laban searched through everything in the tent but found nothing.

³⁵Rachel said to her father, "Don't be angry, my lord, that I cannot stand up in your presence; I'm having my period." So he searched but could not find the household gods.

³⁶Jacob was angry and took Laban to task. "What is my crime?" he asked Laban. "How have I wronged you that you hunt me down? ³⁷Now that you have searched through all my goods, what have you found that belongs to your household? Put it here in front of your relatives and mine, and let them judge between the two of us.

---

^a *18* That is, Northwest Mesopotamia

[38]"I have been with you for twenty years now. Your sheep and goats have not miscarried, nor have I eaten rams from your flocks. [39]I did not bring you animals torn by wild beasts; I bore the loss myself. And you demanded payment from me for whatever was stolen by day or night. [40]This was my situation: The heat consumed me in the daytime and the cold at night, and sleep fled from my eyes. [41]It was like this for the twenty years I was in your household. I worked for you fourteen years for your two daughters and six years for your flocks, and you changed my wages ten times. [42]If the God of my father, the God of Abraham and the Fear of Isaac, had not been with me, you would surely have sent me away empty-handed. But God has seen my hardship and the toil of my hands, and last night he rebuked you."

[43]Laban answered Jacob, "The women are my daughters, the children are my children, and the flocks are my flocks. All you see is mine. Yet what can I do today about these daughters of mine, or about the children they have borne? [44]Come now, let's make a covenant, you and I, and let it serve as a witness between us."

[45]So Jacob took a stone and set it up as a pillar. [46]He said to his relatives, "Gather some stones." So they took stones and piled them in a heap, and they ate there by the heap. [47]Laban called it Jegar Sahadutha, and Jacob called it Galeed.[a]

[48]Laban said, "This heap is a witness between you and me today." That is why it was called Galeed. [49]It was also called Mizpah,[b] because he said, "May the LORD keep watch between you and me when we are away from each other. [50]If you mistreat my daughters or if you take any wives besides my daughters, even though no one is with us, remember that God is a witness between you and me."

[51]Laban also said to Jacob, "Here is this heap, and here is this pillar I have set up between you and me. [52]This heap is a witness, and this pillar is a witness, that I will not go past this heap to your side to harm you and that you will not go past this heap and pillar to my side to harm me. [53]May the God of Abraham and the God of Nahor, the God of their father, judge between us."

So Jacob took an oath in the name of the Fear of his father Isaac. [54]He offered a sacrifice there in the hill country and invited his relatives to a meal. After they had eaten, they spent the night there.

*[55]Early the next morning Laban kissed his grandchildren and his daughters and blessed them. Then he left and returned home.

Jacob Prepares to Meet Esau

32 *[1]Jacob also went on his way, and the angels of God met him. [2]When Jacob saw them, he said, "This is the camp of God!" So he named that place Mahanaim.[c]

[3]Jacob sent messengers ahead of him to his brother Esau in the land of Seir, the country of Edom. [4]He instructed them: "This is what you are to say to my lord Esau: 'Your servant Jacob says, I have been staying with Laban and have remained there till now. [5]I have cattle and donkeys, sheep and goats, male and female servants. Now I am sending this message to my lord, that I may find favor in your eyes.'"

[6]When the messengers returned to Jacob, they said, "We went to your brother Esau, and now he is coming to meet you, and four hundred men are with him."

[7]In great fear and distress Jacob divided the people who were with him into two groups,[d] and the flocks and herds and camels as well. [8]He thought, "If Esau comes and attacks one group,[e] the group[e] that is left may escape."

[9]Then Jacob prayed, "O God of my father Abraham, God of my father Isaac, LORD, you who said to me, 'Go back to your country and your relatives, and I will make you prosper,' [10]I am unworthy of all the kindness and faithfulness you have shown your servant. I had only my staff when I crossed this Jordan, but now I have become two camps. [11]Save me, I pray, from the hand of my brother Esau, for I am afraid he will come and attack me, and also the mothers with their children. [12]But you have said, 'I will surely make you prosper and will make your descendants like the sand of the sea, which cannot be counted.'"

[13]He spent the night there, and from what he had with him he selected a gift for his brother Esau: [14]two hundred female goats and twenty male goats, two hundred ewes and twenty rams, [15]thirty female camels with their young, forty cows and ten bulls, and twenty female donkeys and ten male donkeys.

---

[a] 47 The Aramaic Jegar Sahadutha and the Hebrew Galeed both mean witness heap.   [b] 49 Mizpah means watchtower.   [c] 2 Mahanaim means two camps.
[d] 7 Or camps   [e] 8 Or camp

* 31:55 is numbered 32:1 in Hebrew texts.   * 32:1-32 is numbered 32:2-33 in Hebrew texts.

¹⁶He put them in the care of his servants, each herd by itself, and said to his servants, "Go ahead of me, and keep some space between the herds."

¹⁷He instructed the one in the lead: "When my brother Esau meets you and asks, 'Who do you belong to, and where are you going, and who owns all these animals in front of you?' ¹⁸then you are to say, 'They belong to your servant Jacob. They are a gift sent to my lord Esau, and he is coming behind us.'"

¹⁹He also instructed the second, the third and all the others who followed the herds: "You are to say the same thing to Esau when you meet him. ²⁰And be sure to say, 'Your servant Jacob is coming behind us.'" For he thought, "I will pacify him with these gifts I am sending on ahead; later, when I see him, perhaps he will receive me." ²¹So Jacob's gifts went on ahead of him, but he himself spent the night in the camp.

Jacob Wrestles With God

²²That night Jacob got up and took his two wives, his two female servants and his eleven sons and crossed the ford of the Jabbok. ²³After he had sent them across the stream, he sent over all his possessions. ²⁴So Jacob was left alone, and a man wrestled with him till daybreak. ²⁵When the man saw that he could not overpower him, he touched the socket of Jacob's hip so that his hip was wrenched as he wrestled with the man. ²⁶Then the man said, "Let me go, for it is daybreak."

But Jacob replied, "I will not let you go unless you bless me."

²⁷The man asked him, "What is your name?"

"Jacob," he answered.

²⁸Then the man said, "Your name will no longer be Jacob, but Israel,^a because you have struggled with God and with human beings and have overcome."

²⁹Jacob said, "Please tell me your name."

But he replied, "Why do you ask my name?" Then he blessed him there.

³⁰So Jacob called the place Peniel,^b saying, "It is because I saw God face to face, and yet my life was spared."

³¹The sun rose above him as he passed Peniel,^c and he was limping because of his hip. ³²Therefore to this day the Israelites do not eat the tendon attached to the socket of the hip, because the socket of Jacob's hip was touched near the tendon.

Jacob Meets Esau

33 Jacob looked up and there was Esau, coming with his four hundred men; so he divided the children among Leah, Rachel and the two female servants. ²He put the female servants and their children in front, Leah and her children next, and Rachel and Joseph in the rear. ³He himself went on ahead and bowed down to the ground seven times as he approached his brother.

⁴But Esau ran to meet Jacob and embraced him; he threw his arms around his neck and kissed him. And they wept. ⁵Then Esau looked up and saw the women and children. "Who are these with you?" he asked.

Jacob answered, "They are the children God has graciously given your servant."

⁶Then the female servants and their children approached and bowed down. ⁷Next, Leah and her children came and bowed down. Last of all came Joseph and Rachel, and they too bowed down.

⁸Esau asked, "What do you mean by all these flocks and herds I met?"

"To find favor in your eyes, my lord," he said.

⁹But Esau said, "I already have plenty, my brother. Keep what you have for yourself."

¹⁰"No, please!" said Jacob. "If I have found favor in your eyes, accept this gift from me. For to see your face is like seeing the face of God, now that you have received me favorably. ¹¹Please accept the present that was brought to you, for God has been gracious to me and I have all I need." And because Jacob insisted, Esau accepted it.

¹²Then Esau said, "Let us be on our way; I'll accompany you."

¹³But Jacob said to him, "My lord knows that the children are tender and that I must care for the ewes and cows that are nursing their young. If they are driven hard just one day, all the animals will die.

---

^a 28 Israel probably means he struggles with God.   ^b 30 Peniel means face of God.   ^c 31 Hebrew Penuel, a variant of Peniel

¹⁴So let my lord go on ahead of his servant, while I move along slowly at the pace of the flocks and herds before me and the pace of the children, until I come to my lord in Seir."

¹⁵Esau said, "Then let me leave some of my men with you."

"But why do that?" Jacob asked. "Just let me find favor in the eyes of my lord."

¹⁶So that day Esau started on his way back to Seir. ¹⁷Jacob, however, went to Sukkoth, where he built a place for himself and made shelters for his livestock. That is why the place is called Sukkoth.^a

¹⁸After Jacob came from Paddan Aram,^b he arrived safely at the^c city of Shechem in Canaan and camped within sight of the city. ¹⁹For a hundred pieces of silver,^d he bought from the sons of Hamor, the father of Shechem, the plot of ground where he pitched his tent. ²⁰There he set up an altar and called it El Elohe Israel.^e

Dinah and the Shechemites

34 Now Dinah, the daughter Leah had borne to Jacob, went out to visit the women of the land. ²When Shechem son of Hamor the Hivite, the ruler of that area, saw her, he took her and raped her. ³His heart was drawn to Dinah daughter of Jacob; he loved the young woman and spoke tenderly to her. ⁴And Shechem said to his father Hamor, "Get me this young woman as my wife."

⁵When Jacob heard that his daughter Dinah had been defiled, his sons were in the fields with his livestock; so he did nothing about it until they came home.

⁶Then Shechem's father Hamor went out to talk with Jacob. ⁷Meanwhile, Jacob's sons had come in from the fields as soon as they heard what had happened. They were shocked and furious, because Shechem had done an outrageous thing in^f Israel by sleeping with Jacob's daughter—a thing that should not be done.

⁸But Hamor said to them, "My son Shechem has his heart set on your daughter. Please give her to him as his wife. ⁹Intermarry with us; give us your daughters and take our daughters for yourselves. ¹⁰You can settle among us; the land is open to you. Live in it, trade^g in it, and acquire property in it."

¹¹Then Shechem said to Dinah's father and brothers, "Let me find favor in your eyes, and I will give you whatever you ask. ¹²Make the price for the bride and the gift I am to bring as great as you like, and I'll pay whatever you ask me. Only give me the young woman as my wife."

¹³Because their sister Dinah had been defiled, Jacob's sons replied deceitfully as they spoke to Shechem and his father Hamor. ¹⁴They said to them, "We can't do such a thing; we can't give our sister to a man who is not circumcised. That would be a disgrace to us. ¹⁵We will enter into an agreement with you on one condition only: that you become like us by circumcising all your males. ¹⁶Then we will give you our daughters and take your daughters for ourselves. We'll settle among you and become one people with you. ¹⁷But if you will not agree to be circumcised, we'll take our sister and go."

atissue:rape

34:1–29 Dinah's brothers took the law into their own hands and exacted an even greater punishment than the law required for the crime of rape. Sometimes a woman's family and friends are supportive while she's working through the emotional, physical and legal effects of rape. At other times, a woman feels isolated, as if she were partly to blame for the attack. Rape is a crime not only of sex but also of rage and the abuse of power. Women dealing with the aftermath of rape need the support of caring family, friends and church.

¹⁸Their proposal seemed good to Hamor and his son Shechem. ¹⁹The young man, who was the most honored of all his father's family, lost no time in doing what they said, because he was delighted with Jacob's daughter. ²⁰So Hamor and his son Shechem went to the gate of their city to speak to the men of their city. ²¹"These men are friendly toward us," they said. "Let them live in our land and trade in it; the land has plenty of room for them. We can marry their daughters and they can marry ours. ²²But the men

---

^a *17 Sukkoth means shelters.* ^b *18 That is, Northwest Mesopotamia* ^c *18 Or arrived at Shalem, a* ^d *19 Hebrew hundred kesitahs; a kesitah was a unit of money of unknown weight and value.* ^e *20 El Elohe Israel can mean El is the God of Israel or mighty is the God of Israel.* ^f *7 Or against* ^g *10 Or move about freely; also in verse 21*

will agree to live with us as one people only on the condition that our males be circumcised, as they themselves are. ²³Won't their livestock, their property and all their other animals become ours? So let us agree to their terms, and they will settle among us."

²⁴All the men who went out of the city gate agreed with Hamor and his son Shechem, and every male in the city was circumcised.

²⁵Three days later, while all of them were still in pain, two of Jacob's sons, Simeon and Levi, Dinah's brothers, took their swords and attacked the unsuspecting city, killing every male. ²⁶They put Hamor and his son Shechem to the sword and took Dinah from Shechem's house and left. ²⁷The sons of Jacob came upon the dead bodies and looted the city where*ᵃ* their sister had been defiled. ²⁸They seized their flocks and herds and donkeys and everything else of theirs in the city and out in the fields. ²⁹They carried off all their wealth and all their women and children, taking as plunder everything in the houses.

³⁰Then Jacob said to Simeon and Levi, "You have brought trouble on me by making me obnoxious to the Canaanites and Perizzites, the people living in this land. We are few in number, and if they join forces against me and attack me, I and my household will be destroyed."

³¹But they replied, "Should he have treated our sister like a prostitute?"

Jacob Returns to Bethel

35 Then God said to Jacob, "Go up to Bethel and settle there, and build an altar there to God, who appeared to you when you were fleeing from your brother Esau."

²So Jacob said to his household and to all who were with him, "Get rid of the foreign gods you have with you, and purify yourselves and change your clothes. ³Then come, let us go up to Bethel, where I will build an altar to God, who answered me in the day of my distress and who has been with me wherever I have gone." ⁴So they gave Jacob all the foreign gods they had and the rings in their ears, and Jacob buried them under the oak at Shechem. ⁵Then they set out, and the terror of God fell on the towns all around them so that no one pursued them.

⁶Jacob and all the people with him came to Luz (that is, Bethel) in the land of Canaan. ⁷There he built an altar, and he called the place El Bethel,*ᵇ* because it was there that God revealed himself to him when he was fleeing from his brother.

⁸Now Deborah, Rebekah's nurse, died and was buried under the oak below Bethel. So it was named Allon Bakuth.*ᶜ*

⁹After Jacob returned from Paddan Aram,*ᵈ* God appeared to him again and blessed him. ¹⁰God said to him, "Your name is Jacob,*ᵉ* but you will no longer be called Jacob; your name will be Israel.*ᶠ*" So he named him Israel.

¹¹And God said to him, "I am God Almighty*ᵍ*; be fruitful and increase in number. A nation and a community of nations will come from you, and kings will come from your body. ¹²The land I gave to Abraham and Isaac I also give to you, and I will give this land to your descendants after you." ¹³Then God went up from him at the place where he had talked with him.

HE IS: God Almighty

35:11 *God Almighty* redirected Jacob to a new home, the promised land. Jacob reacted by encouraging all in his household to purify themselves and destroy their pagan gods (see v. 2). Jacob had to change some things, but consider what he received in return—a royal heritage for his children and a place in the line of Christ.

God Almighty wants you to enter the "promised land," but that may feel like a risk to you. Step out in faith when he asks you to bury your other gods—those things that rival his rightful place in your heart. He has the power to give you better things in exchange.

For the next He Is, go to p. 61.

ᵃ 27 Or *because*   *ᵇ 7 El Bethel* means *God of Bethel.*   *ᶜ 8 Allon Bakuth* means *oak of weeping.*   *ᵈ 9* That is, Northwest Mesopotamia; also in verse 26
ᵉ 10 Jacob means *he grasps the heel,* a Hebrew idiom for *he deceives.*   *ᶠ 10 Israel* probably means *he struggles with God.*   *ᵍ 11* Hebrew *El-Shaddai*

[14]Jacob set up a stone pillar at the place where God had talked with him, and he poured out a drink offering on it; he also poured oil on it. [15]Jacob called the place where God had talked with him Bethel.[a]

The Deaths of Rachel and Isaac

[16]Then they moved on from Bethel. While they were still some distance from Ephrath, Rachel began to give birth and had great difficulty. [17]And as she was having great difficulty in childbirth, the midwife said to her, "Don't despair, for you have another son." [18]As she breathed her last—for she was dying—she named her son Ben-Oni.[b] But his father named him Benjamin.[c]

[19]So Rachel died and was buried on the way to Ephrath (that is, Bethlehem). [20]Over her tomb Jacob set up a pillar, and to this day that pillar marks Rachel's tomb.

[21]Israel moved on again and pitched his tent beyond Migdal Eder. [22]While Israel was living in that region, Reuben went in and slept with his father's concubine Bilhah, and Israel heard of it.

Jacob had twelve sons:

[23]The sons of Leah:

Reuben the firstborn of Jacob,

Simeon, Levi, Judah, Issachar and Zebulun.

[24]The sons of Rachel:

Joseph and Benjamin.

[25]The sons of Rachel's servant Bilhah:

Dan and Naphtali.

[26]The sons of Leah's servant Zilpah:

Gad and Asher.

These were the sons of Jacob, who were born to him in Paddan Aram.

[27]Jacob came home to his father Isaac in Mamre, near Kiriath Arba (that is, Hebron), where Abraham and Isaac had stayed. [28]Isaac lived a hundred and eighty years. [29]Then he breathed his last and died and was gathered to his people, old and full of years. And his sons Esau and Jacob buried him.

Esau's Descendants

36 This is the account of the family line of Esau (that is, Edom).

[2]Esau took his wives from the women of Canaan: Adah daughter of Elon the Hittite, and Oholibamah daughter of Anah and granddaughter of Zibeon the Hivite— [3]also Basemath daughter of Ishmael and sister of Nebaioth.

[4]Adah bore Eliphaz to Esau, Basemath bore Reuel, [5]and Oholibamah bore Jeush, Jalam and Korah. These were the sons of Esau, who were born to him in Canaan.

[6]Esau took his wives and sons and daughters and all the members of his household, as well as his livestock and all his other animals and all the goods he had acquired in Canaan, and moved to a land some distance from his brother Jacob. [7]Their possessions were too great for them to remain together; the land where they were staying could not support them both because of their livestock. [8]So Esau (that is, Edom) settled in the hill country of Seir.

[9]This is the account of the family line of Esau the father of the Edomites in the hill country of Seir.

[10]These are the names of Esau's sons:

Eliphaz, the son of Esau's wife Adah, and Reuel, the son of Esau's wife Basemath.

[11]The sons of Eliphaz:

Teman, Omar, Zepho, Gatam and Kenaz.

[12]Esau's son Eliphaz also had a concubine named Timna, who bore him Amalek. These were grandsons of Esau's wife Adah.

[13]The sons of Reuel:

Nahath, Zerah, Shammah and Mizzah. These were grandsons of Esau's wife Basemath.

---

[a] 15 Bethel means house of God.   [b] 18 Ben-Oni means son of my trouble.   [c] 18 Benjamin means son of my right hand.

¹⁴ The sons of Esau's wife Oholibamah daughter of Anah and granddaughter of Zibeon, whom she bore to Esau:

Jeush, Jalam and Korah.

¹⁵ These were the chiefs among Esau's descendants:

The sons of Eliphaz the firstborn of Esau:

Chiefs Teman, Omar, Zepho, Kenaz, ¹⁶Korah,*ᵃ* Gatam and Amalek. These were the chiefs descended from Eliphaz in Edom; they were grandsons of Adah.

¹⁷ The sons of Esau's son Reuel:

Chiefs Nahath, Zerah, Shammah and Mizzah. These were the chiefs descended from Reuel in Edom; they were grandsons of Esau's wife Basemath.

¹⁸ The sons of Esau's wife Oholibamah:

Chiefs Jeush, Jalam and Korah. These were the chiefs descended from Esau's wife Oholibamah daughter of Anah.

¹⁹ These were the sons of Esau (that is, Edom), and these were their chiefs.

²⁰ These were the sons of Seir the Horite, who were living in the region:

Lotan, Shobal, Zibeon, Anah, ²¹Dishon, Ezer and Dishan. These sons of Seir in Edom were Horite chiefs.

²² The sons of Lotan:

Hori and Homam.*ᵇ* Timna was Lotan's sister.

²³ The sons of Shobal:

Alvan, Manahath, Ebal, Shepho and Onam.

²⁴ The sons of Zibeon:

Aiah and Anah. This is the Anah who discovered the hot springs*ᶜ* in the desert while he was grazing the donkeys of his father Zibeon.

²⁵ The children of Anah:

Dishon and Oholibamah daughter of Anah.

²⁶ The sons of Dishon*ᵈ*:

Hemdan, Eshban, Ithran and Keran.

²⁷ The sons of Ezer:

Bilhan, Zaavan and Akan.

²⁸ The sons of Dishan:

Uz and Aran.

²⁹ These were the Horite chiefs:

Lotan, Shobal, Zibeon, Anah, ³⁰Dishon, Ezer and Dishan. These were the Horite chiefs, according to their divisions, in the land of Seir.

The Rulers of Edom

³¹ These were the kings who reigned in Edom before any Israelite king reigned:

³² Bela son of Beor became king of Edom. His city was named Dinhabah.

³³ When Bela died, Jobab son of Zerah from Bozrah succeeded him as king.

³⁴ When Jobab died, Husham from the land of the Temanites succeeded him as king.

³⁵ When Husham died, Hadad son of Bedad, who defeated Midian in the country of Moab, succeeded him as king. His city was named Avith.

³⁶ When Hadad died, Samlah from Masrekah succeeded him as king.

³⁷ When Samlah died, Shaul from Rehoboth on the river succeeded him as king.

³⁸ When Shaul died, Baal-Hanan son of Akbor succeeded him as king.

³⁹ When Baal-Hanan son of Akbor died, Hadad*ᵉ* succeeded him as king. His city was named Pau, and his wife's name was Mehetabel daughter of Matred, the daughter of Me-Zahab.

ᵃ 16 Masoretic Text; Samaritan Pentateuch (see also Gen. 36:11 and 1 Chron. 1:36) does not have *Korah.*   *ᵇ 22* Hebrew *Hemam,* a variant of *Homam* (see 1 Chron. 1:39)   *ᶜ 24* Vulgate; Syriac *discovered water;* the meaning of the Hebrew for this word is uncertain.   *ᵈ 26* Hebrew *Dishan,* a variant of *Dishon*
ᵉ 39 Many manuscripts of the Masoretic Text, Samaritan Pentateuch and Syriac (see also 1 Chron. 1:50); most manuscripts of the Masoretic Text *Hadar*

53

⁴⁰These were the chiefs descended from Esau, by name, according to their clans and regions:
Timna, Alvah, Jetheth, ⁴¹Oholibamah, Elah, Pinon, ⁴²Kenaz, Teman, Mibzar, ⁴³Magdiel and Iram.
These were the chiefs of Edom, according to their settlements in the land they occupied.

This was Esau the father of the Edomites.

Joseph's Dreams

3 7 Jacob lived in the land where his father had stayed, the land of Canaan.

²This is the account of Jacob's family line.

Joseph, a young man of seventeen, was tending the flocks with his brothers, the sons of Bilhah and the sons of Zilpah, his father's wives, and he brought their father a bad report about them.
³Now Israel loved Joseph more than any of his other sons, because he had been born to him in his old age; and he made a richly ornamented *a* robe for him. ⁴When his brothers saw that their father loved him more than any of them, they hated him and could not speak a kind word to him.

⁵Joseph had a dream, and when he told it to his brothers, they hated him all the more. ⁶He said to them, "Listen to this dream I had: ⁷We were binding sheaves of grain out in the field when suddenly my sheaf rose and stood upright, while your sheaves gathered around mine and bowed down to it."

⁸His brothers said to him, "Do you intend to reign over us? Will you actually rule us?" And they hated him all the more because of his dream and what he had said.

⁹Then he had another dream, and he told it to his brothers. "Listen," he said, "I had another dream, and this time the sun and moon and eleven stars were bowing down to me."

¹⁰When he told his father as well as his brothers, his father rebuked him and said, "What is this dream you had? Will your mother and I and your brothers actually come and bow down to the ground before you?" ¹¹His brothers were jealous of him, but his father kept the matter in mind.

Joseph Sold by His Brothers

¹²Now his brothers had gone to graze their father's flocks near Shechem, ¹³and Israel said to Joseph, "As you know, your brothers are grazing the flocks near Shechem. Come, I am going to send you to them."

"Very well," he replied.

¹⁴So he said to him, "Go and see if all is well with your brothers and with the flocks, and bring word back to me." Then he sent him off from the Valley of Hebron.

When Joseph arrived at Shechem, ¹⁵a man found him wandering around in the fields and asked him, "What are you looking for?"

¹⁶He replied, "I'm looking for my brothers. Can you tell me where they are grazing their flocks?"

¹⁷"They have moved on from here," the man answered. "I heard them say, 'Let's go to Dothan.'"

So Joseph went after his brothers and found them near Dothan. ¹⁸But they saw him in the distance, and before he reached them, they plotted to kill him.

¹⁹"Here comes that dreamer!" they said to each other. ²⁰"Come now, let's kill him and throw him into

atissue:abandonment

37:25–28 When we feel abandoned, our instincts often tell us to project those feelings onto all our relationships. "My loved one rejected me. *Everyone* rejects me. *God* rejects me." Sold as a slave by his own brothers, Joseph had to deal with complete abandonment by his family. This trial in his life was all part of God's plan, however, to preserve Joseph's family from a future drought (see Genesis 45:9–11). We all face feelings of abandonment in some way at some time in life. But no matter how our human relationships fail us, God has promised to *never* leave us (see Deuteronomy 31:6).

---

a 3 The meaning of the Hebrew for *richly ornamented* is uncertain; also in verses 23 and 32.

one of these cisterns and say that a ferocious animal devoured him. Then we'll see what comes of his dreams."

²¹When Reuben heard this, he tried to rescue him from their hands. "Let's not take his life," he said. ²²"Don't shed any blood. Throw him into this cistern here in the wilderness, but don't lay a hand on him." Reuben said this to rescue him from them and take him back to his father.

²³So when Joseph came to his brothers, they stripped him of his robe—the richly ornamented robe he was wearing— ²⁴and they took him and threw him into the cistern. The cistern was empty; there was no water in it.

²⁵As they sat down to eat their meal, they looked up and saw a caravan of Ishmaelites coming from Gilead. Their camels were loaded with spices, balm and myrrh, and they were on their way to take them down to Egypt.

²⁶Judah said to his brothers, "What will we gain if we kill our brother and cover up his blood? ²⁷Come, let's sell him to the Ishmaelites and not lay our hands on him; after all, he is our brother, our own flesh and blood." His brothers agreed.

²⁸So when the Midianite merchants came by, his brothers pulled Joseph up out of the cistern and sold him for twenty shekels*a* of silver to the Ishmaelites, who took him to Egypt.

²⁹When Reuben returned to the cistern and saw that Joseph was not there, he tore his clothes. ³⁰He went back to his brothers and said, "The boy isn't there! Where can I turn now?"

³¹Then they got Joseph's robe, slaughtered a goat and dipped the robe in the blood. ³²They took the ornamented robe back to their father and said, "We found this. Examine it to see whether it is your son's robe."

³³He recognized it and said, "It is my son's robe! Some ferocious animal has devoured him. Joseph has surely been torn to pieces."

³⁴Then Jacob tore his clothes, put on sackcloth and mourned for his son many days. ³⁵All his sons and daughters came to comfort him, but he refused to be comforted. "No," he said, "in mourning will I go down to the grave to my son." So his father wept for him.

³⁶Meanwhile, the Midianites*b* sold Joseph in Egypt to Potiphar, one of Pharaoh's officials, the captain of the guard.

Judah and Tamar

38 At that time, Judah left his brothers and went down to stay with a man of Adullam named Hirah. ²There Judah met the daughter of a Canaanite man named Shua. He married her and made love to her; ³she became pregnant and gave birth to a son, who was named Er. ⁴She conceived again and gave birth to a son and named him Onan. ⁵She gave birth to still another son and named him Shelah. It was at Kezib that she gave birth to him.

⁶Judah got a wife for Er, his firstborn, and her name was Tamar. ⁷But Er, Judah's firstborn, was wicked in the LORD's sight; so the LORD put him to death.

⁸Then Judah said to Onan, "Sleep with your brother's wife and fulfill your duty to her as a brother-in-law to raise up offspring for your brother." ⁹But Onan knew that the child would not be his; so whenever he slept with his brother's wife, he spilled his semen on the ground to keep from providing offspring for his brother. ¹⁰What he did was wicked in the LORD's sight; so he put him to death also.

¹¹Judah then said to his daughter-in-law Tamar, "Live as a widow in your father's household until my son Shelah grows up." For he thought, "He may die too, just like his brothers." So Tamar went to live in her father's household.

¹²After a long time Judah's wife, the daughter of Shua, died. When Judah had recovered from his grief, he went up to Timnah, to the men who were shearing his sheep, and his friend Hirah the Adullamite went with him.

¹³When Tamar was told, "Your father-in-law is on his way to Timnah to shear his sheep," ¹⁴she took off her widow's clothes, covered herself with a veil to disguise herself, and then sat down at the entrance to Enaim, which is on the road to Timnah. For she saw that, though Shelah had now grown up, she had not been given to him as his wife.

a 28 That is, about 8 ounces or about 230 grams   *b 36* Samaritan Pentateuch, Septuagint, Vulgate and Syriac (see also verse 28); Masoretic Text *Medanites*

myth# 05 "IF I'M A GOOD CHRISTIAN, THEN NOTHING BAD WILL HAPPEN TO ME."

This isn't what I asked for, thank you. I want my old life back.

The one where my parents were the perfect couple. Where I was the only one among my friends whose parents were still together. And seemingly still in love.

The one where I was voted most likely to succeed and everyone, right or wrong, envied my life because it seemed so perfect. And I believed it was.

I want to go back to the times when I knew you were involved in my life. The ones where I prayed and you answered. I talked to you, and you listened. The times when I knew you were alive. Loving. And on my side.

I want the life where all I had to do was show up for class, and I got good grades. Name a job opening, and I landed it squarely. Speak my needs, and my husband moved heaven and earth to meet them.

That . . . that's what I want.

This . . . that I have right now . . . You can take this all away.

This split in my perfect family that I didn't ask for, and this side of my parents' relationship I never knew.

This embarrassment of being a college graduate and yet unemployed. The shame of being "let go" from my first real job—the one I e-mailed everyone about and was so confident I'd be successful in.

This heaviness of heart from knowing that I can't make my husband love me. This crushing realization that he may leave me for someone else someday. This fear of being divorced before I'm 30 years old.

This stagnant spirituality that barely gets me by. And makes me question all I've known up to this point.

This can all go. Because this isn't what I asked for when I first came to you. I want life the way it was supposed to be.

—Teresa

IF WE BELIEVE a true Christian ought not to experience adversity, then the moment our lives fall apart, so does our faith. We begin to question a fundamental issue: "Am I really a Christian? After all, if I were really following God, then this wouldn't happen to me."

Following this line of false thinking, we perceive adversity as God's punishment for unknown sin. As if God is dropping hints from heaven with every tragedy or that he has deserted us somewhere along the way. How easy it would have been for Joseph to question his belief in God and to assume God was punishing him with every misfortune (see Genesis 37; 39–40). Instead, the Bible records his remarkably opposite attitude of faith.

Similarly, we can look to Jesus as the ultimate example to debunk the idea that bad things do not happen to good people. Isaiah prophesied centuries before that the Messiah would be "despised" and "rejected" and well-acquainted with sorrows (Isaiah 53:3). If Jesus' life is the Christian ideal, an example in every way, then we must accept Jesus' suffering as a part of God's divine impartiality and learn how Jesus handled it. If we were to believe the claims that adversity is unfitting for a believer, then we must discount the examples of Moses, Hannah, Naomi, David, Job, Hosea, Jeremiah, Paul, Mary, John and countless others who experienced great adversity as believers.

The Bible is, above all, *realistic* in its approach to life. Life sometimes hurts and threatens to crush us beneath its weight. But life in the Spirit is about perseverance and peace in the midst of struggle, not the absence of struggle. To believe otherwise is to join the disillusioned throng who encounter life on its own terms and are unprepared for the blow.

> "The deepest level of worship is praising God in spite of pain, thanking God during a trial, trusting him when tempted, surrendering while suffering, and loving him when he seems distant."
>
> —Rick Warren

57

"YOU INTENDED TO HARM ME, BUT GOD INTENDED IT FOR GOOD TO ACCOMPLISH WHAT IS NOW BEING DONE, THE SAVING OF MANY LIVES."

GENESIS 50:20

SEE ALSO

Isaiah 53:3
Romans 8:28
2 Corinthians 12:9

For more on **Trusting God**,
check the index.

¹⁵When Judah saw her, he thought she was a prostitute, for she had covered her face. ¹⁶Not realizing that she was his daughter-in-law, he went over to her by the roadside and said, "Come now, let me sleep with you."

"And what will you give me to sleep with you?" she asked.

¹⁷"I'll send you a young goat from my flock," he said.

"Will you give me something as a pledge until you send it?" she asked.

¹⁸He said, "What pledge should I give you?"

"Your seal and its cord, and the staff in your hand," she answered. So he gave them to her and slept with her, and she became pregnant by him. ¹⁹After she left, she took off her veil and put on her widow's clothes again.

²⁰Meanwhile Judah sent the young goat by his friend the Adullamite in order to get his pledge back from the woman, but he did not find her. ²¹He asked the men who lived there, "Where is the shrine prostitute who was beside the road at Enaim?"

"There hasn't been any shrine prostitute here," they said.

²²So he went back to Judah and said, "I didn't find her. Besides, the men who lived there said, 'There hasn't been any shrine prostitute here.'"

²³Then Judah said, "Let her keep what she has, or we will become a laughingstock. After all, I did send her this young goat, but you didn't find her."

²⁴About three months later Judah was told, "Your daughter-in-law Tamar is guilty of prostitution, and as a result she is now pregnant."

Judah said, "Bring her out and have her burned to death!"

²⁵As she was being brought out, she sent a message to her father-in-law. "I am pregnant by the man who owns these," she said. And she added, "See if you recognize whose seal and cord and staff these are."

²⁶Judah recognized them and said, "She is more righteous than I, since I wouldn't give her to my son Shelah." And he did not sleep with her again.

²⁷When the time came for her to give birth, there were twin boys in her womb. ²⁸As she was giving birth, one of them put out his hand; so the midwife took a scarlet thread and tied it on his wrist and said, "This one came out first." ²⁹But when he drew back his hand, his brother came out, and she said, "So this is how you have broken out!" And he was named Perez.^a ³⁰Then his brother, who had the scarlet thread on his wrist, came out and he was given the name Zerah.^b

Joseph and Potiphar's Wife

39 Now Joseph had been taken down to Egypt. Potiphar, an Egyptian who was one of Pharaoh's officials, the captain of the guard, bought him from the Ishmaelites who had taken him there.

²The LORD was with Joseph so that he prospered, and he lived in the house of his Egyptian master. ³When his master saw that the LORD was with him and that the LORD gave him success in everything he did, ⁴Joseph found favor in his eyes and became his attendant. Potiphar put him in charge of his household, and he entrusted to his care everything he owned. ⁵From the time he put him in charge of his household and of all that he owned, the LORD blessed the household of the Egyptian because of Joseph. The blessing of the LORD was on everything Potiphar had, both in the house and in the field. ⁶So Potiphar left everything he had in Joseph's care; with Joseph in charge, he did not concern himself with anything except the food he ate.

conversations

sex «» 39:6–12

1» Why are some women drawn to men with power (such as Joseph)?

2» How can you avoid situations where you'll be tempted to sin sexually?

3» What's the difference between sexual temptation and sexual sin?

For more on **sex**, check the index.
For the next Conversations, go to p. 78.

---

^a *29 Perez means breaking out.* ^b *30 Zerah can mean scarlet or brightness.*

Now Joseph was well-built and handsome, ⁷and after a while his master's wife took notice of Joseph and said, "Come to bed with me!"

⁸But he refused. "With me in charge," he told her, "my master does not concern himself with anything in the house; everything he owns he has entrusted to my care. ⁹No one is greater in this house than I am. My master has withheld nothing from me except you, because you are his wife. How then could I do such a wicked thing and sin against God?" ¹⁰And though she spoke to Joseph day after day, he refused to go to bed with her or even be with her.

¹¹One day he went into the house to attend to his duties, and none of the household servants was inside. ¹²She caught him by his cloak and said, "Come to bed with me!" But he left his cloak in her hand and ran out of the house.

¹³When she saw that he had left his cloak in her hand and had run out of the house, ¹⁴she called her household servants. "Look," she said to them, "this Hebrew has been brought to us to make sport of us! He came in here to sleep with me, but I screamed. ¹⁵When he heard me scream for help, he left his cloak beside me and ran out of the house."

¹⁶She kept his cloak beside her until his master came home. ¹⁷Then she told him this story: "That Hebrew slave you brought us came to me to make sport of me. ¹⁸But as soon as I screamed for help, he left his cloak beside me and ran out of the house."

¹⁹When his master heard the story his wife told him, saying, "This is how your slave treated me," he burned with anger. ²⁰Joseph's master took him and put him in prison, the place where the king's prisoners were confined.

But while Joseph was there in the prison, ²¹the LORD was with him; he showed him kindness and granted him favor in the eyes of the prison warden. ²²So the warden put Joseph in charge of all those held in the prison, and he was made responsible for all that was done there. ²³The warden paid no attention to anything under Joseph's care, because the LORD was with Joseph and gave him success in whatever he did.

at issue: work

39:21–23 Whether or not you've chosen to climb the corporate ladder, society tells you that your work defines who you are. Naturally you hate the feeling of being stuck in a nowhere job. As a result, you may feel tempted to do as little as possible in unwanted jobs, all the while waiting for your big break. Joseph's work philosophy turns this thinking on its head. He didn't bide his time until he was recognized. Joseph worked responsibly—even under the worst conditions. And God rewarded his diligence. Don't wait—work for God where you are now.

59

The Cupbearer and the Baker

40 Some time later, the cupbearer and the baker of the king of Egypt offended their master, the king of Egypt. ²Pharaoh was angry with his two officials, the chief cupbearer and the chief baker, ³and put them in custody in the house of the captain of the guard, in the same prison where Joseph was confined. ⁴The captain of the guard assigned them to Joseph, and he attended them.

After they had been in custody for some time, ⁵each of the two men—the cupbearer and the baker of the king of Egypt, who were being held in prison—had a dream the same night, and each dream had a meaning of its own.

⁶When Joseph came to them the next morning, he saw that they were dejected. ⁷So he asked Pharaoh's officials who were in custody with him in his master's house, "Why do you look so sad today?"

⁸"We both had dreams," they answered, "but there is no one to interpret them."

Then Joseph said to them, "Do not interpretations belong to God? Tell me your dreams."

⁹So the chief cupbearer told Joseph his dream. He said to him, "In my dream I saw a vine in front of me, ¹⁰and on the vine were three branches. As soon as it budded, it blossomed, and its clusters ripened into grapes. ¹¹Pharaoh's cup was in my hand, and I took the grapes, squeezed them into Pharaoh's cup and put the cup in his hand."

¹²"This is what it means," Joseph said to him. "The three branches are three days. ¹³Within three days

Pharaoh will lift up your head and restore you to your position, and you will put Pharaoh's cup in his hand, just as you used to do when you were his cupbearer. ¹⁴But when all goes well with you, remember me and show me kindness; mention me to Pharaoh and get me out of this prison. ¹⁵I was forcibly carried off from the land of the Hebrews, and even here I have done nothing to deserve being put in a dungeon."

¹⁶When the chief baker saw that Joseph had given a favorable interpretation, he said to Joseph, "I too had a dream: On my head were three baskets of bread.ᵃ ¹⁷In the top basket were all kinds of baked goods for Pharaoh, but the birds were eating them out of the basket on my head."

¹⁸"This is what it means," Joseph said. "The three baskets are three days. ¹⁹Within three days Pharaoh will lift off your head and impale your body on a pole. And the birds will eat away your flesh."

²⁰Now the third day was Pharaoh's birthday, and he gave a feast for all his officials. He lifted up the heads of the chief cupbearer and the chief baker in the presence of his officials: ²¹He restored the chief cupbearer to his position, so that he once again put the cup into Pharaoh's hand— ²²but he impaled the chief baker, just as Joseph had said to them in his interpretation.

²³The chief cupbearer, however, did not remember Joseph; he forgot him.

Pharaoh's Dreams

41 When two full years had passed, Pharaoh had a dream: He was standing by the Nile, ²when out of the river there came up seven cows, sleek and fat, and they grazed among the reeds. ³After them, seven other cows, ugly and gaunt, came up out of the Nile and stood beside those on the riverbank. ⁴And the cows that were ugly and gaunt ate up the seven sleek, fat cows. Then Pharaoh woke up.

⁵He fell asleep again and had a second dream: Seven heads of grain, healthy and good, were growing on a single stalk. ⁶After them, seven other heads of grain sprouted—thin and scorched by the east wind. ⁷The thin heads of grain swallowed up the seven healthy, full heads. Then Pharaoh woke up; it had been a dream.

⁸In the morning his mind was troubled, so he sent for all the magicians and wise men of Egypt. Pharaoh told them his dreams, but no one could interpret them for him.

⁹Then the chief cupbearer said to Pharaoh, "Today I am reminded of my shortcomings. ¹⁰Pharaoh was once angry with his servants, and he imprisoned me and the chief baker in the house of the captain of the guard. ¹¹Each of us had a dream the same night, and each dream had a meaning of its own. ¹²Now a young Hebrew was there with us, a servant of the captain of the guard. We told him our dreams, and he interpreted them for us, giving each man the interpretation of his dream. ¹³And things turned out exactly as he interpreted them to us: I was restored to my position, and the other man was impaled."

¹⁴So Pharaoh sent for Joseph, and he was quickly brought from the dungeon. When he had shaved and changed his clothes, he came before Pharaoh.

¹⁵Pharaoh said to Joseph, "I had a dream, and no one can interpret it. But I have heard it said of you that when you hear a dream you can interpret it."

¹⁶"I cannot do it," Joseph replied to Pharaoh, "but God will give Pharaoh the answer he desires."

¹⁷Then Pharaoh said to Joseph, "In my dream I was standing on the bank of the Nile, ¹⁸when out of the river there came up seven cows, fat and sleek, and they grazed among the reeds. ¹⁹After them, seven other cows came up—scrawny and very ugly and lean. I had never seen such ugly cows in all the land of Egypt. ²⁰The lean, ugly cows ate up the seven fat cows that came up first. ²¹But even after they ate them, no one could tell that they had done so; they looked just as ugly as before. Then I woke up.

²²"In my dream I saw seven heads of grain, full and good, growing on a single stalk. ²³After them, seven other heads sprouted—withered and thin and scorched by the east wind. ²⁴The thin heads of grain swallowed up the seven good heads. I told this to the magicians, but none of them could explain it to me."

²⁵Then Joseph said to Pharaoh, "The dreams of Pharaoh are one and the same. God has revealed to Pharaoh what he is about to do. ²⁶The seven good cows are seven years, and the seven good heads of grain are seven years; it is one and the same dream. ²⁷The seven lean, ugly cows that came up afterward are seven years, and so are the seven worthless heads of grain scorched by the east wind: They are seven years of famine.

ᵃ 16 Or three wicker baskets

[28]"It is just as I said to Pharaoh: God has shown Pharaoh what he is about to do. [29]Seven years of great abundance are coming throughout the land of Egypt, [30]but seven years of famine will follow them. Then all the abundance in Egypt will be forgotten, and the famine will ravage the land. [31]The abundance in the land will not be remembered, because the famine that follows it will be so severe. [32]The reason the dream was given to Pharaoh in two forms is that the matter has been firmly decided by God, and God will do it soon.

HE IS: the interpreter

45:15–16 The ancient Egyptians believed astrology, magic and interpretation of dreams provided the answers for their lives. But Pharaoh's forecasters had no idea what his dream meant. Only Joseph knew the truth: *God* would give Pharaoh the answer. Only with God's help could Joseph interpret the dream.

Have you been looking for truth in all the wrong places? Whether it's astrology, psychics, talk show hosts or even your friends—they can't tell you what's ahead. God is *the interpreter*, the one with all the answers. If you want your mysteries solved, there's only one place to go.

For the next He Is, go to p. 69.

61

[33]"And now let Pharaoh look for a discerning and wise man and put him in charge of the land of Egypt. [34]Let Pharaoh appoint commissioners over the land to take a fifth of the harvest of Egypt during the seven years of abundance. [35]They should collect all the food of these good years that are coming and store up the grain under the authority of Pharaoh, to be kept in the cities for food. [36]This food should be held in reserve for the country, to be used during the seven years of famine that will come upon Egypt, so that the country may not be ruined by the famine."

[37]The plan seemed good to Pharaoh and to all his officials. [38]So Pharaoh asked them, "Can we find anyone like this man, one in whom is the spirit of God[a]?"

[39]Then Pharaoh said to Joseph, "Since God has made all this known to you, there is no one so discerning and wise as you. [40]You shall be in charge of my palace, and all my people are to submit to your orders. Only with respect to the throne will I be greater than you."

Joseph in Charge of Egypt

[41]So Pharaoh said to Joseph, "I hereby put you in charge of the whole land of Egypt." [42]Then Pharaoh took his signet ring from his finger and put it on Joseph's finger. He dressed him in robes of fine linen and put a gold chain around his neck. [43]He had him ride in a chariot as his second-in-command,[b] and people shouted before him, "Make way[c]!" Thus he put him in charge of the whole land of Egypt.

[44]Then Pharaoh said to Joseph, "I am Pharaoh, but without your word no one will lift hand or foot in all Egypt." [45]Pharaoh gave Joseph the name Zaphenath-Paneah and gave him Asenath daughter of Potiphera, priest of On,[d] to be his wife. And Joseph went throughout the land of Egypt.

[46]Joseph was thirty years old when he entered the service of Pharaoh king of Egypt. And Joseph went out from Pharaoh's presence and traveled throughout Egypt. [47]During the seven years of abundance the land produced plentifully. [48]Joseph collected all the food produced in those seven years of abundance in Egypt and stored it in the cities. In each city he put the food grown in the fields surrounding it. [49]Joseph stored up huge quantities of grain, like the sand of the sea; it was so much that he stopped keeping records because it was beyond measure.

[50]Before the years of famine came, two sons were born to Joseph by Asenath daughter of Potiphera, priest of On. [51]Joseph named his firstborn Manasseh[e] and said, "It is because God has made me forget all my trouble and all my father's household." [52]The second son he named Ephraim[f] and said, "It is because God has made me fruitful in the land of my suffering."

---

[a] *38* Or *of the gods*   [b] *43* Or *in the chariot of his second-in-command*; or *in his second chariot*   [c] *43* Or *Bow down*   [d] *45* That is, Heliopolis; also in verse 50
[e] *51 Manasseh* sounds like and may be derived from the Hebrew for *forget*.   [f] *52 Ephraim* sounds like the Hebrew for *twice fruitful*.

[53]The seven years of abundance in Egypt came to an end, [54]and the seven years of famine began, just as Joseph had said. There was famine in all the other lands, but in the whole land of Egypt there was food. [55]When all Egypt began to feel the famine, the people cried to Pharaoh for food. Then Pharaoh told all the Egyptians, "Go to Joseph and do what he tells you."

[56]When the famine had spread over the whole country, Joseph opened all the storehouses and sold grain to the Egyptians, for the famine was severe throughout Egypt. [57]And all the world came to Egypt to buy grain from Joseph, because the famine was severe everywhere.

Joseph's Brothers Go to Egypt

42 When Jacob learned that there was grain in Egypt, he said to his sons, "Why do you just keep looking at each other?" [2]He continued, "I have heard that there is grain in Egypt. Go down there and buy some for us, so that we may live and not die."

[3]Then ten of Joseph's brothers went down to buy grain from Egypt. [4]But Jacob did not send Benjamin, Joseph's brother, with the others, because he was afraid that harm might come to him. [5]So Israel's sons were among those who went to buy grain, for the famine was in the land of Canaan also.

[6]Now Joseph was the governor of the land, the person who sold grain to all its people. So when Joseph's brothers arrived, they bowed down to him with their faces to the ground. [7]As soon as Joseph saw his brothers, he recognized them, but he pretended to be a stranger and spoke harshly to them. "Where do you come from?" he asked.

"From the land of Canaan," they replied, "to buy food."

[8]Although Joseph recognized his brothers, they did not recognize him. [9]Then he remembered his dreams about them and said to them, "You are spies! You have come to see where our land is unprotected."

[10]"No, my lord," they answered. "Your servants have come to buy food. [11]We are all the sons of one man. Your servants are honest men, not spies."

[12]"No!" he said to them. "You have come to see where our land is unprotected."

[13]But they replied, "Your servants were twelve brothers, the sons of one man, who lives in the land of Canaan. The youngest is now with our father, and one is no more."

[14]Joseph said to them, "It is just as I told you: You are spies! [15]And this is how you will be tested: As surely as Pharaoh lives, you will not leave this place unless your youngest brother comes here. [16]Send one of your number to get your brother; the rest of you will be kept in prison, so that your words may be tested to see if you are telling the truth. If you are not, then as surely as Pharaoh lives, you are spies!" [17]And he put them all in custody for three days.

[18]On the third day, Joseph said to them, "Do this and you will live, for I fear God: [19]If you are honest men, let one of your brothers stay here in prison, while the rest of you go and take grain back for your starving households. [20]But you must bring your youngest brother to me, so that your words may be verified and that you may not die." This they proceeded to do.

[21]They said to one another, "Surely we are being punished because of our brother. We saw how distressed he was when he pleaded with us for his life, but we would not listen; that's why this distress has come on us."

[22]Reuben replied, "Didn't I tell you not to sin against the boy? But you wouldn't listen! Now we must give an accounting for his blood." [23]They did not realize that Joseph could understand them, since he was using an interpreter.

[24]He turned away from them and began to weep, but then came back and spoke to them again. He had Simeon taken from them and bound before their eyes.

[25]Joseph gave orders to fill their bags with grain, to put each man's silver back in his sack, and to give them provisions for their journey. After this was done for them, [26]they loaded their grain on their donkeys and left.

[27]At the place where they stopped for the night one of them opened his sack to get feed for his donkey, and he saw his silver in the mouth of his sack. [28]"My silver has been returned," he said to his brothers. "Here it is in my sack."

Their hearts sank and they turned to each other trembling and said, "What is this that God has done to us?"

²⁹When they came to their father Jacob in the land of Canaan, they told him all that had happened to them. They said, ³⁰"The man who is lord over the land spoke harshly to us and treated us as though we were spying on the land. ³¹But we said to him, 'We are honest men; we are not spies. ³²We were twelve brothers, sons of one father. One is no more, and the youngest is now with our father in Canaan.'

³³"Then the man who is lord over the land said to us, 'This is how I will know whether you are honest men: Leave one of your brothers here with me, and take food for your starving households and go. ³⁴But bring your youngest brother to me so I will know that you are not spies but honest men. Then I will give your brother back to you, and you can trade^a in the land.'"

³⁵As they were emptying their sacks, there in each man's sack was his pouch of silver! When they and their father saw the money pouches, they were frightened. ³⁶Their father Jacob said to them, "You have deprived me of my children. Joseph is no more and Simeon is no more, and now you want to take Benjamin. Everything is against me!"

³⁷Then Reuben said to his father, "You may put both of my sons to death if I do not bring him back to you. Entrust him to my care, and I will bring him back."

³⁸But Jacob said, "My son will not go down there with you; his brother is dead and he is the only one left. If harm comes to him on the journey you are taking, you will bring my gray head down to the grave in sorrow."

The Second Journey to Egypt

43 Now the famine was still severe in the land. ²So when they had eaten all the grain they had brought from Egypt, their father said to them, "Go back and buy us a little more food."

³But Judah said to him, "The man warned us solemnly, 'You will not see my face again unless your brother is with you.' ⁴If you will send our brother along with us, we will go down and buy food for you. ⁵But if you will not send him, we will not go down, because the man said to us, 'You will not see my face again unless your brother is with you.'"

⁶Israel asked, "Why did you bring this trouble on me by telling the man you had another brother?"

⁷They replied, "The man questioned us closely about ourselves and our family. 'Is your father still living?' he asked us. 'Do you have another brother?' We simply answered his questions. How were we to know he would say, 'Bring your brother down here'?"

⁸Then Judah said to Israel his father, "Send the boy along with me and we will go at once, so that we and you and our children may live and not die. ⁹I myself will guarantee his safety; you can hold me personally responsible for him. If I do not bring him back to you and set him here before you, I will bear the blame before you all my life. ¹⁰As it is, if we had not delayed, we could have gone and returned twice."

¹¹Then their father Israel said to them, "If it must be, then do this: Put some of the best products of the land in your bags and take them down to the man as a gift—a little balm and a little honey, some spices and myrrh, some pistachio nuts and almonds. ¹²Take double the amount of silver with you, for you must return the silver that was put back into the mouths of your sacks. Perhaps it was a mistake. ¹³Take your brother also and go back to the man at once. ¹⁴And may God Almighty^b grant you mercy before the man so that he will let your other brother and Benjamin come back with you. As for me, if I am bereaved, I am bereaved."

¹⁵So the men took the gifts and double the amount of silver, and Benjamin also. They hurried down to Egypt and presented themselves to Joseph. ¹⁶When Joseph saw Benjamin with them, he said to the steward of his house, "Take these men to my house, slaughter an animal and prepare a meal; they are to eat with me at noon."

¹⁷The man did as Joseph told him and took the men to Joseph's house. ¹⁸Now the men were frightened when they were taken to his house. They thought, "We were brought here because of the silver that was put back into our sacks the first time. He wants to attack us and overpower us and seize us as slaves and take our donkeys."

¹⁹So they went up to Joseph's steward and spoke to him at the entrance to the house. ²⁰"We beg your pardon, our lord," they said, "we came down here the first time to buy food. ²¹But at the place where we

---

^a 34 Or move about freely   ^b 14 Hebrew El-Shaddai

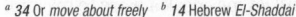

stopped for the night we opened our sacks and each of us found his silver—the exact weight—in the mouth of his sack. So we have brought it back with us. ²²We have also brought additional silver with us to buy food. We don't know who put our silver in our sacks."

²³"It's all right," he said. "Don't be afraid. Your God, the God of your father, has given you treasure in your sacks; I received your silver." Then he brought Simeon out to them.

²⁴The steward took the men into Joseph's house, gave them water to wash their feet and provided fodder for their donkeys. ²⁵They prepared their gifts for Joseph's arrival at noon, because they had heard that they were to eat there.

²⁶When Joseph came home, they presented to him the gifts they had brought into the house, and they bowed down before him to the ground. ²⁷He asked them how they were, and then he said, "How is your aged father you told me about? Is he still living?"

²⁸They replied, "Your servant our father is still alive and well." And they bowed down, prostrating themselves before him.

²⁹As he looked about and saw his brother Benjamin, his own mother's son, he asked, "Is this your youngest brother, the one you told me about?" And he said, "God be gracious to you, my son." ³⁰Deeply moved at the sight of his brother, Joseph hurried out and looked for a place to weep. He went into his private room and wept there.

³¹After he had washed his face, he came out and, controlling himself, said, "Serve the food."

³²They served him by himself, the brothers by themselves, and the Egyptians who ate with him by themselves, because Egyptians could not eat with Hebrews, for that is detestable to Egyptians. ³³The men had been seated before him in the order of their ages, from the firstborn to the youngest; and they looked at each other in astonishment. ³⁴When portions were served to them from Joseph's table, Benjamin's portion was five times as much as anyone else's. So they feasted and drank freely with him.

A Silver Cup in a Sack

44 Now Joseph gave these instructions to the steward of his house: "Fill the men's sacks with as much food as they can carry, and put each man's silver in the mouth of his sack. ²Then put my cup, the silver one, in the mouth of the youngest one's sack, along with the silver for his grain." And he did as Joseph said.

³As morning dawned, the men were sent on their way with their donkeys. ⁴They had not gone far from the city when Joseph said to his steward, "Go after those men at once, and when you catch up with them, say to them, 'Why have you repaid good with evil? ⁵Isn't this the cup my master drinks from and also uses for divination? This is a wicked thing you have done.'"

⁶When he caught up with them, he repeated these words to them. ⁷But they said to him, "Why does my lord say such things? Far be it from your servants to do anything like that! ⁸We even brought back to you from the land of Canaan the silver we found inside the mouths of our sacks. So why would we steal silver or gold from your master's house? ⁹If any of your servants is found to have it, he will die; and the rest of us will become my lord's slaves."

¹⁰"Very well, then," he said, "let it be as you say. Whoever is found to have it will become my slave; the rest of you will be free from blame."

¹¹Each of them quickly lowered his sack to the ground and opened it. ¹²Then the steward proceeded to search, beginning with the oldest and ending with the youngest. And the cup was found in Benjamin's sack. ¹³At this, they tore their clothes. Then they all loaded their donkeys and returned to the city.

¹⁴Joseph was still in the house when Judah and his brothers came in, and they threw themselves to the ground before him. ¹⁵Joseph said to them, "What is this you have done? Don't you know that a man like me can find things out by divination?"

¹⁶"What can we say to my lord?" Judah replied. "What can we say? How can we prove our innocence? God has uncovered your servants' guilt. We are now my lord's slaves—we ourselves and the one who was found to have the cup."

¹⁷But Joseph said, "Far be it from me to do such a thing! Only the man who was found to have the cup will become my slave. The rest of you, go back to your father in peace."

¹⁸Then Judah went up to him and said: "Pardon your servant, my lord, let me speak a word to my lord.

Do not be angry with your servant, though you are equal to Pharaoh himself. [19]My lord asked his servants, 'Do you have a father or a brother?' [20]And we answered, 'We have an aged father, and there is a young son born to him in his old age. His brother is dead, and he is the only one of his mother's sons left, and his father loves him.'

[21]"Then you said to your servants, 'Bring him down to me so I can see him for myself.' [22]And we said to my lord, 'The boy cannot leave his father; if he leaves him, his father will die.' [23]But you told your servants, 'Unless your youngest brother comes down with you, you will not see my face again.' [24]When we went back to your servant my father, we told him what my lord had said.

[25]"Then our father said, 'Go back and buy a little more food.' [26]But we said, 'We cannot go down. Only if our youngest brother is with us will we go. We cannot see the man's face unless our youngest brother is with us.'

[27]"Your servant my father said to us, 'You know that my wife bore me two sons. [28]One of them went away from me, and I said, "He has surely been torn to pieces." And I have not seen him since. [29]If you take this one from me too and harm comes to him, you will bring my gray head down to the grave in misery.'

[30]"So now, if the boy is not with us when I go back to your servant my father, and if my father, whose life is closely bound up with the boy's life, [31]sees that the boy isn't there, he will die. Your servants will bring the gray head of our father down to the grave in sorrow. [32]Your servant guaranteed the boy's safety to my father. I said, 'If I do not bring him back to you, I will bear the blame before you, my father, all my life!'

[33]"Now then, please let your servant remain here as my lord's slave in place of the boy, and let the boy return with his brothers. [34]How can I go back to my father if the boy is not with me? No! Do not let me see the misery that would come on my father."

> ## aussue:dysfunctional family
>
> **44:18–34** No family is perfect. But what exactly makes a home dysfunctional? A *dysfunction* is simply something that ceases to function correctly. When families stop protecting, loving and sharing with each other, they've lost their original function. Family members turn against each other, and a mountain of bitterness forms. The good news is that this process is reversible. Joseph's family was a model of dysfunction, but after many years God transformed each member's heart. What is your role in your family? Do you work to benefit others or tear them down? Ask God to help your family function his way.

65

Joseph Makes Himself Known

45 Then Joseph could no longer control himself before all his attendants, and he cried out, "Have everyone leave my presence!" So there was no one with Joseph when he made himself known to his brothers. [2]And he wept so loudly that the Egyptians heard him, and Pharaoh's household heard about it.

[3]Joseph said to his brothers, "I am Joseph! Is my father still living?" But his brothers were not able to answer him, because they were terrified at his presence.

[4]Then Joseph said to his brothers, "Come close to me." When they had done so, he said, "I am your brother Joseph, the one you sold into Egypt! [5]And now, do not be distressed and do not be angry with yourselves for selling me here, because it was to save lives that God sent me ahead of you. [6]For two years now there has been famine in the land, and for the next five years there will be no plowing and reaping. [7]But God sent me ahead of you to preserve for you a remnant on earth and to save your lives by a great deliverance.[a]

[8]"So then, it was not you who sent me here, but God. He made me father to Pharaoh, lord of his entire household and ruler of all Egypt. [9]Now hurry back to my father and say to him, 'This is what your son Joseph says: God has made me lord of all Egypt. Come down to me; don't delay. [10]You shall live in the

---

[a] 7 Or *save you as a great band of survivors*

region of Goshen and be near me—you, your children and grandchildren, your flocks and herds, and all you have. ¹¹I will provide for you there, because five years of famine are still to come. Otherwise you and your household and all who belong to you will become destitute.'

¹²"You can see for yourselves, and so can my brother Benjamin, that it is really I who am speaking to you. ¹³Tell my father about all the honor accorded me in Egypt and about everything you have seen. And bring my father down here quickly."

¹⁴Then he threw his arms around his brother Benjamin and wept, and Benjamin embraced him, weeping. ¹⁵And he kissed all his brothers and wept over them. Afterward his brothers talked with him.

¹⁶When the news reached Pharaoh's palace that Joseph's brothers had come, Pharaoh and all his officials were pleased. ¹⁷Pharaoh said to Joseph, "Tell your brothers, 'Do this: Load your animals and return to the land of Canaan, ¹⁸and bring your father and your families back to me. I will give you the best of the land of Egypt and you can enjoy the fat of the land.'

¹⁹"You are also directed to tell them, 'Do this: Take some carts from Egypt for your children and your wives, and get your father and come. ²⁰Never mind about your belongings, because the best of all Egypt will be yours.'"

²¹So the sons of Israel did this. Joseph gave them carts, as Pharaoh had commanded, and he also gave them provisions for their journey. ²²To each of them he gave new clothing, but to Benjamin he gave three hundred shekels*a* of silver and five sets of clothes. ²³And this is what he sent to his father: ten donkeys loaded with the best things of Egypt, and ten female donkeys loaded with grain and bread and other provisions for his journey. ²⁴Then he sent his brothers away, and as they were leaving he said to them, "Don't quarrel on the way!"

²⁵So they went up out of Egypt and came to their father Jacob in the land of Canaan. ²⁶They told him, "Joseph is still alive! In fact, he is ruler of all Egypt." Jacob was stunned; he did not believe them. ²⁷But when they told him everything Joseph had said to them, and when he saw the carts Joseph had sent to carry him back, the spirit of their father Jacob revived. ²⁸And Israel said, "I'm convinced! My son Joseph is still alive. I will go and see him before I die."

Jacob Goes to Egypt

46 So Israel set out with all that was his, and when he reached Beersheba, he offered sacrifices to the God of his father Isaac.

²And God spoke to Israel in a vision at night and said, "Jacob! Jacob!"

"Here I am," he replied.

³"I am God, the God of your father," he said. "Do not be afraid to go down to Egypt, for I will make you into a great nation there. ⁴I will go down to Egypt with you, and I will surely bring you back again. And Joseph's own hand will close your eyes."

⁵Then Jacob left Beersheba, and Israel's sons took their father Jacob and their children and their wives in the carts that Pharaoh had sent to transport him. ⁶So Jacob and all his offspring went to Egypt, taking with them their livestock and the possessions they had acquired in Canaan. ⁷Jacob brought with him to Egypt his sons and grandsons and his daughters and granddaughters—all his offspring.

⁸These are the names of the sons of Israel (Jacob and his descendants) who went to Egypt:

Reuben the firstborn of Jacob.
⁹The sons of Reuben:
Hanok, Pallu, Hezron and Karmi.
¹⁰The sons of Simeon:
Jemuel, Jamin, Ohad, Jakin, Zohar and Shaul the son of a Canaanite woman.
¹¹The sons of Levi:
Gershon, Kohath and Merari.
¹²The sons of Judah:
Er, Onan, Shelah, Perez and Zerah (but Er and Onan had died in the land of Canaan).

---

a 22 That is, about 7 1/2 pounds or about 3.5 kilograms

The sons of Perez:

Hezron and Hamul.

¹³ The sons of Issachar:

Tola, Puah,ᵃ Jashubᵇ and Shimron.

¹⁴ The sons of Zebulun:

Sered, Elon and Jahleel.

¹⁵ These were the sons Leah bore to Jacob in Paddan Aram,ᶜ besides his daughter Dinah. These sons and daughters of his were thirty-three in all.

¹⁶ The sons of Gad:

Zephon,ᵈ Haggi, Shuni, Ezbon, Eri, Arodi and Areli.

¹⁷ The sons of Asher:

Imnah, Ishvah, Ishvi and Beriah.

Their sister was Serah.

The sons of Beriah:

Heber and Malkiel.

¹⁸ These were the children born to Jacob by Zilpah, whom Laban had given to his daughter Leah—sixteen in all.

¹⁹ The sons of Jacob's wife Rachel:

Joseph and Benjamin. ²⁰ In Egypt, Manasseh and Ephraim were born to Joseph by Asenath daughter of Potiphera, priest of On.ᵉ

²¹ The sons of Benjamin:

Bela, Beker, Ashbel, Gera, Naaman, Ehi, Rosh, Muppim, Huppim and Ard.

²² These were the sons of Rachel who were born to Jacob—fourteen in all.

²³ The son of Dan:

Hushim.

²⁴ The sons of Naphtali:

Jahziel, Guni, Jezer and Shillem.

²⁵ These were the sons born to Jacob by Bilhah, whom Laban had given to his daughter Rachel—seven in all.

²⁶ All those who went to Egypt with Jacob—those who were his direct descendants, not counting his sons' wives—numbered sixty-six persons. ²⁷ With the two sonsᶠ who had been born to Joseph in Egypt, the members of Jacob's family, which went to Egypt, were seventyᵍ in all.

²⁸ Now Jacob sent Judah ahead of him to Joseph to get directions to Goshen. When they arrived in the region of Goshen, ²⁹ Joseph had his chariot made ready and went to Goshen to meet his father Israel. As soon as Joseph appeared before him, he threw his arms around his fatherʰ and wept for a long time.

³⁰ Israel said to Joseph, "Now I am ready to die, since I have seen for myself that you are still alive."

³¹ Then Joseph said to his brothers and to his father's household, "I will go up and speak to Pharaoh and will say to him, 'My brothers and my father's household, who were living in the land of Canaan, have

67

atissue:change

46:3–4 It seems that just when we've perfected our survival routine, life changes. Our plans get altered. We change jobs. A family member dies. We have a child. The reality is that change is always stressful; even good changes can be scary. When God revealed huge changes in store for Jacob and his descendants, the Bible doesn't tell us Jacob's immediate reaction. Instead we see something more important—Jacob's obedience in embracing the change. Feeling anxiety during change is normal, but don't allow your emotions to cripple you. Your life *will* change, but God's protection is steady.

ᵃ 13 Samaritan Pentateuch and Syriac (see also 1 Chron. 7:1); Masoretic Text *Puvah*   ᵇ 13 Samaritan Pentateuch and some Septuagint manuscripts (see also Num. 26:24 and 1 Chron. 7:1); Masoretic Text *Iob*   ᶜ 15 That is, Northwest Mesopotamia   ᵈ 16 Samaritan Pentateuch and Septuagint (see also Num. 26:15); Masoretic Text *Ziphion*   ᵉ 20 That is, Heliopolis   ᶠ 27 Hebrew; Septuagint *the nine children*   ᵍ 27 Hebrew (see also Exodus 1:5 and footnote); Septuagint (see also Acts 7:14) *seventy-five*   ʰ 29 Hebrew *around him* come to me. ³²The men are shepherds; they tend livestock, and they have brought along their flocks and herds and everything they own.' ³³When Pharaoh calls you in and asks, 'What is your occupation?' ³⁴you should answer, 'Your servants have tended livestock from our boyhood on, just as our fathers did.' Then you will be allowed to settle in the region of Goshen, for all shepherds are detestable to the Egyptians."

47 Joseph went and told Pharaoh, "My father and brothers, with their flocks and herds and everything they own, have come from the land of Canaan and are now in Goshen." ²He chose five of his brothers and presented them before Pharaoh.

³Pharaoh asked the brothers, "What is your occupation?"

"Your servants are shepherds," they replied to Pharaoh, "just as our fathers were." ⁴They also said to him, "We have come to live here for a while, because the famine is severe in Canaan and your servants' flocks have no pasture. So now, please let your servants settle in Goshen."

⁵Pharaoh said to Joseph, "Your father and your brothers have come to you, ⁶and the land of Egypt is before you; settle your father and your brothers in the best part of the land. Let them live in Goshen. And if you know of any among them with special ability, put them in charge of my own livestock."

⁷Then Joseph brought his father Jacob in and presented him before Pharaoh. After Jacob blessed^a Pharaoh, ⁸Pharaoh asked him, "How old are you?"

⁹And Jacob said to Pharaoh, "The years of my pilgrimage are a hundred and thirty. My years have been few and difficult, and they do not equal the years of the pilgrimage of my fathers." ¹⁰Then Jacob blessed^b Pharaoh and went out from his presence.

¹¹So Joseph settled his father and his brothers in Egypt and gave them property in the best part of the land, the district of Rameses, as Pharaoh directed. ¹²Joseph also provided his father and his brothers and all his father's household with food, according to the number of their children.

Joseph and the Famine

¹³There was no food, however, in the whole region because the famine was severe; both Egypt and Canaan wasted away because of the famine. ¹⁴Joseph collected all the money that was to be found in Egypt and Canaan in payment for the grain they were buying, and he brought it to Pharaoh's palace. ¹⁵When the money of the people of Egypt and Canaan was gone, all Egypt came to Joseph and said, "Give us food. Why should we die before your eyes? Our money is all gone."

¹⁶"Then bring your livestock," said Joseph. "I will sell you food in exchange for your livestock, since your money is gone." ¹⁷So they brought their livestock to Joseph, and he gave them food in exchange for their horses, their sheep and goats, their cattle and donkeys. And he brought them through that year with food in exchange for all their livestock.

¹⁸When that year was over, they came to him the following year and said, "We cannot hide from our lord the fact that since our money is gone and our livestock belongs to you, there is nothing left for our lord except our bodies and our land. ¹⁹Why should we perish before your eyes—we and our land as well? Buy us and our land in exchange for food, and we with our land will be in bondage to Pharaoh. Give us seed so that we may live and not die, and that the land may not become desolate."

²⁰So Joseph bought all the land in Egypt for Pharaoh. The Egyptians, one and all, sold their fields, because the famine was too severe for them. The land became Pharaoh's, ²¹and Joseph reduced the people to servitude,^c from one end of Egypt to the other. ²²However, he did not buy the land of the priests, because they received a regular allotment from Pharaoh and had food enough from the allotment Pharaoh gave them. That is why they did not sell their land.

²³Joseph said to the people, "Now that I have bought you and your land today for Pharaoh, here is seed for you so you can plant the ground. ²⁴But when the crop comes in, give a fifth of it to Pharaoh. The other four-fifths you may keep as seed for the fields and as food for yourselves and your households and your children."

²⁵"You have saved our lives," they said. "May we find favor in the eyes of our lord; we will be in bondage to Pharaoh."

²⁶So Joseph established it as a law concerning land in Egypt—still in force today—that a fifth of the

^a 7 Or greeted ^b 10 Or said farewell to ^c 21 Samaritan Pentateuch and Septuagint (see also Vulgate); Masoretic Text and he moved the people into the cities

produce belongs to Pharaoh. It was only the land of the priests that did not become Pharaoh's.

²⁷ Now the Israelites settled in Egypt in the region of Goshen. They acquired property there and were fruitful and increased greatly in number.

²⁸ Jacob lived in Egypt seventeen years, and the years of his life were a hundred and forty-seven. ²⁹ When the time drew near for Israel to die, he called for his son Joseph and said to him, "If I have found favor in your eyes, put your hand under my thigh and promise that you will show me kindness and faithfulness. Do not bury me in Egypt, ³⁰ but when I rest with my fathers, carry me out of Egypt and bury me where they are buried."

"I will do as you say," he said.

³¹ "Swear to me," he said. Then Joseph swore to him, and Israel worshiped as he leaned on the top of his staff.ᵃ

Manasseh and Ephraim

48 Some time later Joseph was told, "Your father is ill." So he took his two sons Manasseh and Ephraim along with him. ² When Jacob was told, "Your son Joseph has come to you," Israel rallied his strength and sat up on the bed.

³ Jacob said to Joseph, "God Almightyᵇ appeared to me at Luz in the land of Canaan, and there he blessed me ⁴ and said to me, 'I am going to make you fruitful and increase your numbers. I will make you a community of peoples, and I will give this land as an everlasting possession to your descendants after you.'

⁵ "Now then, your two sons born to you in Egypt before I came to you here will be reckoned as mine; Ephraim and Manasseh will be mine, just as Reuben and Simeon are mine. ⁶ Any children born to you after them will be yours; in the territory they inherit they will be reckoned under the names of their brothers. ⁷ As I was returning from Paddan,ᶜ to my sorrow Rachel died in the land of Canaan while we were still on the way, a little distance from Ephrath. So I buried her there beside the road to Ephrath" (that is, Bethlehem).

HE IS: the blesser

48:3-4 "Blessing" is such an old-fashioned word, but it's such a right-now need. *To bless* means to wish God's care for another person. God blessed Jacob by giving him life, love and land. God is still *the blesser* today. God gives everyone unconditional love and offers everyone eternal life and a spiritual inheritance

May God bless you with everything you need to live a rich and full life! May *the blesser* give you every good thing, starting with eternal life in Jesus Christ. And because you know *the blesser*, may you in turn declare God's favor on someone else.

For the next He Is, go to p. 82.

⁸ When Israel saw the sons of Joseph, he asked, "Who are these?"

⁹ "They are the sons God has given me here," Joseph said to his father.

Then Israel said, "Bring them to me so I may bless them."

¹⁰ Now Israel's eyes were failing because of old age, and he could hardly see. So Joseph brought his sons close to him, and his father kissed them and embraced them.

¹¹ Israel said to Joseph, "I never expected to see your face again, and now God has allowed me to see your children too."

¹² Then Joseph removed them from Israel's knees and bowed down with his face to the ground. ¹³ And Joseph took both of them, Ephraim on his right toward Israel's left hand and Manasseh on his left toward Israel's right hand, and brought them close to him. ¹⁴ But Israel reached out his right hand and put it on

---

ᵃ 31 Or *Israel bowed down at the head of his bed* ᵇ 3 Hebrew *El-Shaddai* ᶜ 7 That is, Northwest Mesopotamia

Ephraim's head, though he was the younger, and crossing his arms, he put his left hand on Manasseh's head, even though Manasseh was the firstborn.

[15] Then he blessed Joseph and said,

> "May the God before whom my fathers
> Abraham and Isaac walked faithfully,
> the God who has been my shepherd
> all my life to this day,
> [16] the Angel who has delivered me from all harm
> —may he bless these boys.
> May they be called by my name
> and the names of my fathers Abraham and Isaac,
> and may they increase greatly
> on the earth."

[17] When Joseph saw his father placing his right hand on Ephraim's head he was displeased; so he took hold of his father's hand to move it from Ephraim's head to Manasseh's head. [18] Joseph said to him, "No, my father, this one is the firstborn; put your right hand on his head."

[19] But his father refused and said, "I know, my son, I know. He too will become a people, and he too will become great. Nevertheless, his younger brother will be greater than he, and his descendants will become a group of nations." [20] He blessed them that day and said,

> "In your[a] name will Israel pronounce this blessing:
> 'May God make you like Ephraim and Manasseh.'"

So he put Ephraim ahead of Manasseh.

[21] Then Israel said to Joseph, "I am about to die, but God will be with you[b] and take you[b] back to the land of your[b] fathers. [22] And to you I give one more ridge of land[c] than to your brothers, the ridge I took from the Amorites with my sword and my bow."

Jacob Blesses His Sons

49 Then Jacob called for his sons and said: "Gather around so I can tell you what will happen to you in days to come.

> [2] "Assemble and listen, sons of Jacob;
> listen to your father Israel.

> [3] "Reuben, you are my firstborn,
> my might, the first sign of my strength,
> excelling in honor, excelling in power.
> [4] Turbulent as the waters, you will no longer excel,
> for you went up onto your father's bed,
> onto my couch and defiled it.

> [5] "Simeon and Levi are brothers—
> their swords[d] are weapons of violence.
> [6] Let me not enter their council,
> let me not join their assembly,
> for they have killed men in their anger
> and hamstrung oxen as they pleased.
> [7] Cursed be their anger, so fierce,
> and their fury, so cruel!
> I will scatter them in Jacob
> and disperse them in Israel.

---

a 20 The Hebrew is singular.   *b 21* The Hebrew is plural.   *c 22* The Hebrew for *ridge of land* is identical with the place name Shechem.   *d 5* The meaning of the Hebrew for this word is uncertain.

⁸"Judah,ᵃ your brothers will praise you;
    your hand will be on the neck of your enemies;
    your father's sons will bow down to you.
⁹You are a lion's cub, Judah;
    you return from the prey, my son.
Like a lion he crouches and lies down,
    like a lioness—who dares to rouse him?
¹⁰The scepter will not depart from Judah,
    nor the ruler's staff from between his feet,ᵇ
until he to whom it belongsᶜ shall come
    and the obedience of the nations be his.
¹¹He will tether his donkey to a vine,
    his colt to the choicest branch;
he will wash his garments in wine,
    his robes in the blood of grapes.
¹²His eyes will be darker than wine,
    his teeth whiter than milk.ᵈ

¹³"Zebulun will live by the seashore
    and become a haven for ships;
    his border will extend toward Sidon.

¹⁴"Issachar is a rawbonedᵉ donkey
    lying down among the sheep pens.ᶠ
¹⁵When he sees how good is his resting place
    and how pleasant is his land,
he will bend his shoulder to the burden
    and submit to forced labor.

¹⁶"Danᵍ will provide justice for his people
    as one of the tribes of Israel.
¹⁷Dan will be a snake by the roadside,
    a viper along the path,
that bites the horse's heels
    so that its rider tumbles backward.

¹⁸"I look for your deliverance, Lᴏʀᴅ.

¹⁹"Gadʰ will be attacked by a band of raiders,
    but he will attack them at their heels.

²⁰"Asher's food will be rich;
    he will provide delicacies fit for a king.

²¹"Naphtali is a doe set free
    that bears beautiful fawns.ⁱ

²²"Joseph is a fruitful vine,
    a fruitful vine near a spring,
    whose branches climb over a wall.ʲ
²³With bitterness archers attacked him;
    they shot at him with hostility.

71

ᵃ 8 Judah sounds like and may be derived from the Hebrew for praise.   ᵇ 10 Or from his descendants   ᶜ 10 Or to whom tribute belongs; the meaning of the
Hebrew for this phrase is uncertain.   ᵈ 12 Or will be dull from wine, / his teeth white from milk   ᵉ 14 Or strong   ᶠ 14 Or the campfires; or the saddlebags
ᵍ 16 Dan here means he provides justice.   ʰ 19 Gad sounds like the Hebrew for attack and also for band of raiders.   ⁱ 21 Or free; / he utters beautiful words
ʲ 22 Or Joseph is a wild colt, / a wild colt near a spring, / a wild donkey on a terraced hill

²⁴But his bow remained steady,
  his strong arms stayed*ᵃ* limber,
because of the hand of the Mighty One of Jacob,
  because of the Shepherd, the Rock of Israel,
²⁵because of your father's God, who helps you,
  because of the Almighty,*ᵇ* who blesses you
with blessings of the heavens above,
  blessings of the deep that lies below,
  blessings of the breast and womb.
²⁶Your father's blessings are greater
  than the blessings of the ancient mountains,
  than*ᶜ* the bounty of the age-old hills.
Let all these rest on the head of Joseph,
  on the brow of the prince among*ᵈ* his brothers.

²⁷"Benjamin is a ravenous wolf;
  in the morning he devours the prey,
  in the evening he divides the plunder."

²⁸All these are the twelve tribes of Israel, and this is what their father said to them when he blessed them, giving each the blessing appropriate to him.

The Death of Jacob

²⁹Then he gave them these instructions: "I am about to be gathered to my people. Bury me with my fathers in the cave in the field of Ephron the Hittite, ³⁰the cave in the field of Machpelah, near Mamre in Canaan, which Abraham bought along with the field as a burial place from Ephron the Hittite. ³¹There Abraham and his wife Sarah were buried, there Isaac and his wife Rebekah were buried, and there I buried Leah. ³²The field and the cave in it were bought from the Hittites.*ᵉ*"

³³When Jacob had finished giving instructions to his sons, he drew his feet up into the bed, breathed his last and was gathered to his people.

50 Joseph threw himself on his father and wept over him and kissed him. ²Then Joseph directed the physicians in his service to embalm his father Israel. So the physicians embalmed him, ³taking a full forty days, for that was the time required for embalming. And the Egyptians mourned for him seventy days.

⁴When the days of mourning had passed, Joseph said to Pharaoh's court, "If I have found favor in your eyes, speak to Pharaoh for me. Tell him, ⁵'My father made me swear an oath and said, "I am about to die; bury me in the tomb I dug for myself in the land of Canaan." Now let me go up and bury my father; then I will return.'"

⁶Pharaoh said, "Go up and bury your father, as he made you swear to do."

⁷So Joseph went up to bury his father. All Pharaoh's officials accompanied him—the dignitaries of his court and all the dignitaries of Egypt— ⁸besides all the members of Joseph's household and his brothers

---

atissue:death of a parent

49:33—50:3 When a parent dies, we need to grieve. The only wrong way to grieve is to not grieve at all. Let out your feelings of sadness or loss, anger or fear, resentment or regret. Your grief will be different from everyone else's. God promises to be there for you in your grief: "A father to the fatherless, a defender of widows, is God in his holy dwelling. God sets the lonely in families" (Psalm 68:5–6). If you have lost your earthly parents, you still have Someone to comfort you. As a Christian, you are part of a family that cannot be destroyed by death.

ᵃ 23,24 Or archers will attack…will shoot…will remain…will stay   ᵇ 25 Hebrew Shaddai   ᶜ 26 Or of my progenitors, / as great as   ᵈ 26 Or of the one separated from   ᵉ 32 Or the descendants of Heth and those belonging to his father's household. Only their children and their flocks and herds were left in Goshen. [9]Chariots and horsemen[a] also went up with him. It was a very large company.

[10]When they reached the threshing floor of Atad, near the Jordan, they lamented loudly and bitterly; and there Joseph observed a seven-day period of mourning for his father. [11]When the Canaanites who lived there saw the mourning at the threshing floor of Atad, they said, "The Egyptians are holding a solemn ceremony of mourning." That is why that place near the Jordan is called Abel Mizraim.[b]

[12]So Jacob's sons did as he had commanded them: [13]They carried him to the land of Canaan and buried him in the cave in the field of Machpelah, near Mamre, which Abraham had bought along with the field as a burial place from Ephron the Hittite. [14]After burying his father, Joseph returned to Egypt, together with his brothers and all the others who had gone with him to bury his father.

Joseph Reassures His Brothers

[15]When Joseph's brothers saw that their father was dead, they said, "What if Joseph holds a grudge against us and pays us back for all the wrongs we did to him?" [16]So they sent word to Joseph, saying, "Your father left these instructions before he died: [17]'This is what you are to say to Joseph: I ask you to forgive your brothers the sins and the wrongs they committed in treating you so badly.' Now please forgive the sins of the servants of the God of your father." When their message came to him, Joseph wept.

[18]His brothers then came and threw themselves down before him. "We are your slaves," they said.

[19]But Joseph said to them, "Don't be afraid. Am I in the place of God? [20]You intended to harm me, but God intended it for good to accomplish what is now being done, the saving of many lives. [21]So then, don't be afraid. I will provide for you and your children." And he reassured them and spoke kindly to them.

The Death of Joseph

[22]Joseph stayed in Egypt, along with all his father's family. He lived a hundred and ten years [23]and saw the third generation of Ephraim's children. Also the children of Makir son of Manasseh were placed at birth on Joseph's knees.[c]

[24]Then Joseph said to his brother Israelites, "I am about to die. But God will surely come to your aid and take you up out of this land to the land he promised on oath to Abraham, Isaac and Jacob." [25]And Joseph made the Israelites swear an oath and said, "God will surely come to your aid, and then you must carry my bones up from this place."

[26]So Joseph died at the age of a hundred and ten. And after they embalmed him, he was placed in a coffin in Egypt.

73

[a] 9 Or charioteers   [b] 11 Abel Mizraim means mourning of the Egyptians.   [c] 23 That is, were counted as his

exodus

AUTHOR
Moses.

AUDIENCE
The people of Israel.

DATE
Between 1450 and 1410 B.C.

SETTING
God miraculously liberates the Israelites
from slavery in Egypt and then establishes
his covenant with them in the desert.

VERSES TO REMEMBER
"God heard their groaning and he remem-
bered his covenant with Abraham, with
Isaac and with Jacob. So God looked on the
Israelites and was concerned about them."
(2:24–25)

THEME TO CONSIDER
Who is God? And does he truly care about
his people? Those are the questions the book
of Exodus answers in the story of the Israelites' miraculous rescue from Egypt and the
start of their new life.

The Israelites Oppressed

1 These are the names of the sons of Israel who went to Egypt with Jacob, each with his family: ²Reuben, Simeon, Levi and Judah; ³Issachar, Zebulun and Benjamin; ⁴Dan and Naphtali; Gad and Asher. ⁵The descendants of Jacob numbered seventy*a* in all; Joseph was already in Egypt.

⁶Now Joseph and all his brothers and all that generation died, ⁷but the Israelites were exceedingly fruitful; they multiplied greatly, increased in numbers and became so numerous that the land was filled with them.

⁸Then a new king, to whom Joseph meant nothing, came to power in Egypt. ⁹"Look," he said to his people, "the Israelites have become far too numerous for us. ¹⁰Come, we must deal shrewdly with them or they will become even more numerous and, if war breaks out, will join our enemies, fight against us and leave the country."

¹¹So they put slave masters over them to oppress them with forced labor, and they built Pithom and Rameses as store cities for Pharaoh. ¹²But the more they were oppressed, the more they multiplied and spread; so the Egyptians came to dread the Israelites ¹³and worked them ruthlessly. ¹⁴They made their lives bitter with harsh labor in brick and mortar and with all kinds of work in the fields; in all their harsh labor the Egyptians used them ruthlessly.

¹⁵The king of Egypt said to the Hebrew midwives, whose names were Shiphrah and Puah, ¹⁶"When you help the Hebrew women in childbirth and observe them on the delivery stool, if it is a boy, kill him; but if it is a girl, let her live." ¹⁷The midwives, however, feared God and did not do what the king of Egypt had told them to do; they let the boys live. ¹⁸Then the king of Egypt summoned the midwives and asked them, "Why have you done this? Why have you let the boys live?"

¹⁹The midwives answered Pharaoh, "Hebrew women are not like Egyptian women; they are vigorous and give birth before the midwives arrive."

²⁰So God was kind to the midwives and the people increased and became even more numerous. ²¹And because the midwives feared God, he gave them families of their own.

²²Then Pharaoh gave this order to all his people: "Every Hebrew boy that is born you must throw into the Nile, but let every girl live."

at issue: identity

1:15–21 "Hi, my name is _____. I work as a _____." Meeting anyone new requires this exchange of information. Our society tells us that our identities are wrapped up in our jobs. Essentially, we are what we do. There are two dangers in this thinking: 1) At some point you're going to fail at what you do—and then who are you? 2) At some point who you truly are (God's child) is going to conflict with what you do—and then what do you do? Because the midwives knew who they really were, they feared the Boss more than the king. In any job, remember who you are.

75

The Birth of Moses

2 Now a man of the house of Levi married a Levite woman, ²and she became pregnant and gave birth to a son. When she saw that he was a fine child, she hid him for three months. ³But when she could hide him no longer, she got a papyrus basket*b* for him and coated it with tar and pitch. Then she placed the child in it and put it among the reeds along the bank of the Nile. ⁴His sister stood at a distance to see what would happen to him.

⁵Then Pharaoh's daughter went down to the Nile to bathe, and her attendants were walking along the riverbank. She saw the basket among the reeds and sent her female slave to get it. ⁶She opened it and saw the baby. He was crying, and she felt sorry for him. "This is one of the Hebrew babies," she said.

⁷Then his sister asked Pharaoh's daughter, "Shall I go and get one of the Hebrew women to nurse the baby for you?"

⁸"Yes, go," she answered. And the girl went and got the baby's mother. ⁹Pharaoh's daughter said to her,

"Take this baby and nurse him for me, and I will pay you." So the woman took the baby and nursed him. [10]When the child grew older, she took him to Pharaoh's daughter and he became her son. She named him Moses,[a] saying, "I drew him out of the water."

Moses Flees to Midian

[11]One day, after Moses had grown up, he went out to where his own people were and watched them at their hard labor. He saw an Egyptian beating a Hebrew, one of his own people. [12]Glancing this way and that and seeing no one, he killed the Egyptian and hid him in the sand. [13]The next day he went out and saw two Hebrews fighting. He asked the one in the wrong, "Why are you hitting your fellow Hebrew?"

[14]The man said, "Who made you ruler and judge over us? Are you thinking of killing me as you killed the Egyptian?" Then Moses was afraid and thought, "What I did must have become known."

[15]When Pharaoh heard of this, he tried to kill Moses, but Moses fled from Pharaoh and went to live in Midian, where he sat down by a well. [16]Now a priest of Midian had seven daughters, and they came to draw water and fill the troughs to water their father's flock. [17]Some shepherds came along and drove them away, but Moses got up and came to their rescue and watered their flock.

[18]When the girls returned to Reuel their father, he asked them, "Why have you returned so early today?"

[19]They answered, "An Egyptian rescued us from the shepherds. He even drew water for us and watered the flock."

[20]"And where is he?" he asked his daughters. "Why did you leave him? Invite him to have something to eat."

[21]Moses agreed to stay with the man, who gave his daughter Zipporah to Moses in marriage. [22]Zipporah gave birth to a son, and Moses named him Gershom,[b] saying, "I have become a foreigner in a foreign land."

[23]During that long period, the king of Egypt died. The Israelites groaned in their slavery and cried out, and their cry for help because of their slavery went up to God. [24]God heard their groaning and he remembered his covenant with Abraham, with Isaac and with Jacob. [25]So God looked on the Israelites and was concerned about them.

Moses and the Burning Bush

3 Now Moses was tending the flock of Jethro his father-in-law, the priest of Midian, and he led the flock to the far side of the wilderness and came to Horeb, the mountain of God. [2]There the angel of the LORD appeared to him in flames of fire from within a bush. Moses saw that though the bush was on fire it did not burn up. [3]So Moses thought, "I will go over and see this strange sight—why the bush does not burn up."

[4]When the LORD saw that he had gone over to look, God called to him from within the bush, "Moses! Moses!"

And Moses said, "Here I am."

[5]"Do not come any closer," God said. "Take off your sandals, for the place where you are standing is holy ground." [6]Then he said, "I am the God of your father,[c] the God of Abraham, the God of Isaac and the God of Jacob." At this, Moses hid his face, because he was afraid to look at God.

[7]The LORD said, "I have indeed seen the misery of my people in Egypt. I have heard them crying out because of their slave drivers, and I am concerned about their suffering. [8]So I have come down to rescue them from the hand of the Egyptians and to bring them up out of that land into a good and spacious land, a land flowing with milk and honey—the home of the Canaanites, Hittites, Amorites, Perizzites, Hivites and Jebusites. [9]And now the cry of the Israelites has reached me, and I have seen the way the Egyptians are oppressing them. [10]So now, go. I am sending you to Pharaoh to bring my people the Israelites out of Egypt."

[11]But Moses said to God, "Who am I that I should go to Pharaoh and bring the Israelites out of Egypt?"

---

a 10 Moses *sounds like the Hebrew for* draw out.   *b 22* Gershom *sounds like the Hebrew for* a foreigner there.   *c 6* Masoretic Text; Samaritan Pentateuch (see Acts 7:32) *fathers*

[12] And God said, "I will be with you. And this will be the sign to you that it is I who have sent you: When you have brought the people out of Egypt, you[a] will worship God on this mountain."

[13] Moses said to God, "Suppose I go to the Israelites and say to them, 'The God of your fathers has sent me to you,' and they ask me, 'What is his name?' Then what shall I tell them?"

[14] God said to Moses, "I AM WHO I AM.[b] This is what you are to say to the Israelites: 'I AM has sent me to you.'"

[15] God also said to Moses, "Say to the Israelites, 'The LORD,[c] the God of your fathers—the God of Abraham, the God of Isaac and the God of Jacob—has sent me to you.'

> "This is my name forever,
> the name you shall call me
> from generation to generation.

[16] "Go, assemble the elders of Israel and say to them, 'The LORD, the God of your fathers—the God of Abraham, Isaac and Jacob—appeared to me and said: I have watched over you and have seen what has been done to you in Egypt. [17] And I have promised to bring you up out of your misery in Egypt into the land of the Canaanites, Hittites, Amorites, Perizzites, Hivites and Jebusites—a land flowing with milk and honey.'

[18] "The elders of Israel will listen to you. Then you and the elders are to go to the king of Egypt and say to him, 'The LORD, the God of the Hebrews, has met with us. Let us take a three-day journey into the wilderness to offer sacrifices to the LORD our God.' [19] But I know that the king of Egypt will not let you go unless a mighty hand compels him. [20] So I will stretch out my hand and strike the Egyptians with all the wonders that I will perform among them. After that, he will let you go.

[21] "And I will make the Egyptians favorably disposed toward this people, so that when you leave you will not go empty-handed. [22] Every woman is to ask her neighbor and any woman living in her house for articles of silver and gold and for clothing, which you will put on your sons and daughters. And so you will plunder the Egyptians."

Signs for Moses

4 Moses answered, "What if they do not believe me or listen to me and say, 'The LORD did not appear to you'?"

[2] Then the LORD said to him, "What is that in your hand?"

"A staff," he replied.

[3] The LORD said, "Throw it on the ground."

Moses threw it on the ground and it became a snake, and he ran from it. [4] Then the LORD said to him, "Reach out your hand and take it by the tail." So Moses reached out and took hold of the snake and it turned back into a staff in his hand. [5] "This," said the LORD, "is so that they may believe that the LORD, the God of their fathers—the God of Abraham, the God of Isaac and the God of Jacob—has appeared to you."

[6] Then the LORD said, "Put your hand inside your cloak." So Moses put his hand into his cloak, and when he took it out, the skin was leprous[d]—it had become as white as snow.

[7] "Now put it back into your cloak," he said. So Moses put his hand back into his cloak, and when he took it out, it was restored, like the rest of his flesh.

[8] Then the LORD said, "If they do not believe you or pay attention to the first sign, they may believe the

---

atissue:purpose

3:7–12 When we really want to do something, we come up with a million reasons why we should. We become the world's greatest saleswoman, convincing God why our plans are so rational. But when we don't want to do something God's asked us to do, we reverse the process. We criticize. We nitpick. We search for the irrational or the impossible in God's plan. Our own weaknesses loom large in our vision. When Moses heard God's plan, he immediately started the excuses. And God immediately shut him down. God doesn't want your excuses—he wants your open heart.

77

---

[a] 12 The Hebrew is plural.   [b] 14 Or *I WILL BE WHAT I WILL BE*   [c] 15 The Hebrew for *LORD* sounds like and may be related to the Hebrew for *I AM* in verse 14.
[d] 6 The Hebrew word for *leprous* was used for various diseases affecting the skin.

second. ⁹But if they do not believe these two signs or listen to you, take some water from the Nile and pour it on the dry ground. The water you take from the river will become blood on the ground."

¹⁰Moses said to the LORD, "Pardon your servant, Lord. I have never been eloquent, neither in the past nor since you have spoken to your servant. I am slow of speech and tongue."

¹¹The LORD said to him, "Who gave human beings their mouths? Who makes them deaf or mute? Who gives them sight or makes them blind? Is it not I, the LORD? ¹²Now go; I will help you speak and will teach you what to say."

¹³But Moses said, "Pardon your servant, Lord. Please send someone else."

¹⁴Then the LORD's anger burned against Moses and he said, "What about your brother, Aaron the Levite? I know he can speak well. He is already on his way to meet you, and his heart will be glad when he sees you. ¹⁵You shall speak to him and put words in his mouth; I will help both of you speak and will teach you what to do. ¹⁶He will speak to the people for you, and it will be as if he were your mouth and as if you were God to him. ¹⁷But take this staff in your hand so you can perform the signs with it."

conversations

shyness ‹›› 4:10–17

1 ›› Is shyness a positive or negative character trait?

2 ›› Has shyness ever held you back from saying something God wanted you to say?

3 ›› If you are uncomfortably shy, how can you allow God to help you overcome this?

For more on **shyness**, check the index. For the next Conversations, go to p. 81.

Moses Returns to Egypt

¹⁸Then Moses went back to Jethro his father-in-law and said to him, "Let me return to my own people in Egypt to see if any of them are still alive."

Jethro said, "Go, and I wish you well."

¹⁹Now the LORD had said to Moses in Midian, "Go back to Egypt, for all those who wanted to kill you are dead." ²⁰So Moses took his wife and sons, put them on a donkey and started back to Egypt. And he took the staff of God in his hand.

²¹The LORD said to Moses, "When you return to Egypt, see that you perform before Pharaoh all the wonders I have given you the power to do. But I will harden his heart so that he will not let the people go. ²²Then say to Pharaoh, 'This is what the LORD says: Israel is my firstborn son, ²³and I told you, "Let my son go, so he may worship me." But you refused to let him go; so I will kill your firstborn son.'"

²⁴At a lodging place on the way, the LORD met Moses[a] and was about to kill him. ²⁵But Zipporah took a flint knife, cut off her son's foreskin and touched Moses' feet with it.[b] "Surely you are a bridegroom of blood to me," she said. ²⁶So the LORD let him alone. (At that time she said "bridegroom of blood," referring to circumcision.)

²⁷The LORD said to Aaron, "Go into the wilderness to meet Moses." So he met Moses at the mountain of God and kissed him. ²⁸Then Moses told Aaron everything the LORD had sent him to say, and also about all the signs he had commanded him to perform.

²⁹Moses and Aaron brought together all the elders of the Israelites, ³⁰and Aaron told them everything the LORD had said to Moses. He also performed the signs before the people, ³¹and they believed. And when they heard that the LORD was concerned about them and had seen their misery, they bowed down and worshiped.

Bricks Without Straw

5 Afterward Moses and Aaron went to Pharaoh and said, "This is what the LORD, the God of Israel, says: 'Let my people go, so that they may hold a festival to me in the wilderness.'"

²Pharaoh said, "Who is the LORD, that I should obey him and let Israel go? I do not know the LORD and I will not let Israel go."

---

[a] 24 Hebrew *him*   [b] 25 The meaning of the Hebrew for this clause is uncertain.

³Then they said, "The God of the Hebrews has met with us. Now let us take a three-day journey into the wilderness to offer sacrifices to the LORD our God, or he may strike us with plagues or with the sword."

⁴But the king of Egypt said, "Moses and Aaron, why are you taking the people away from their labor? Get back to your work!" ⁵Then Pharaoh said, "Look, the people of the land are now numerous, and you are stopping them from working."

⁶That same day Pharaoh gave this order to the slave drivers and overseers in charge of the people: ⁷"You are no longer to supply the people with straw for making bricks; let them go and gather their own straw. ⁸But require them to make the same number of bricks as before; don't reduce the quota. They are lazy; that is why they are crying out, 'Let us go and sacrifice to our God.' ⁹Make the work harder for them so that they keep working and pay no attention to lies."

¹⁰Then the slave drivers and the overseers went out and said to the people, "This is what Pharaoh says: 'I will not give you any more straw. ¹¹Go and get your own straw wherever you can find it, but your work will not be reduced at all.'" ¹²So the people scattered all over Egypt to gather stubble to use for straw. ¹³The slave drivers kept pressing them, saying, "Complete the work required of you for each day, just as when you had straw." ¹⁴And Pharaoh's slave drivers beat the Israelite overseers they had appointed, demanding, "Why haven't you met your quota of bricks yesterday or today, as before?"

¹⁵Then the Israelite overseers went and appealed to Pharaoh: "Why have you treated your servants this way? ¹⁶Your servants are given no straw, yet we are told, 'Make bricks!' Your servants are being beaten, but the fault is with your own people."

¹⁷Pharaoh said, "Lazy, that's what you are—lazy! That is why you keep saying, 'Let us go and sacrifice to the LORD.' ¹⁸Now get to work. You will not be given any straw, yet you must produce your full quota of bricks."

¹⁹The Israelite overseers realized they were in trouble when they were told, "You are not to reduce the number of bricks required of you for each day." ²⁰When they left Pharaoh, they found Moses and Aaron waiting to meet them, ²¹and they said, "May the LORD look on you and judge you! You have made us obnoxious to Pharaoh and his officials and have put a sword in their hand to kill us."

God Promises Deliverance

²²Moses returned to the LORD and said, "Why, Lord, why have you brought trouble on this people? Is this why you sent me? ²³Ever since I went to Pharaoh to speak in your name, he has brought trouble on this people, and you have not rescued your people at all."

6 Then the LORD said to Moses, "Now you will see what I will do to Pharaoh: Because of my mighty hand he will let them go; because of my mighty hand he will drive them out of his country."

²God also said to Moses, "I am the LORD. ³I appeared to Abraham, to Isaac and to Jacob as God Almighty,ᵃ but by my name the LORDᵇ I did not make myself known to them.ᶜ ⁴I also established my covenant with them to give them the land of Canaan, where they resided as foreigners. ⁵Moreover, I have heard the groaning of the Israelites, whom the Egyptians are enslaving, and I have remembered my covenant.

aiissue:doubting God

5:22–23 Shouldn't a goal or ministry, if it's truly from God, be achieved without problems or setbacks? We've done exactly what's expected of us—why are things *still* going wrong? It's normal to feel frustrated and confused in moments like these. Moses did. He wasn't afraid to share his true feelings with God. Our doubts do not anger God. In fact, God uses roadblocks in our lives to make us doubt our own plans and rely on him. You may have the perfect skills for the job, but your true strength will always come when you're resting in God's arms.

79

ᵃ *3* Hebrew *El-Shaddai*   ᵇ *3* See note at Exodus 3:15.   ᶜ *3* Or *Almighty, and by my name the* LORD *did I not let myself be known to them?*

⁶"Therefore, say to the Israelites: 'I am the LORD, and I will bring you out from under the yoke of the Egyptians. I will free you from being slaves to them, and I will redeem you with an outstretched arm and with mighty acts of judgment. ⁷I will take you as my own people, and I will be your God. Then you will know that I am the LORD your God, who brought you out from under the yoke of the Egyptians. ⁸And I will bring you to the land I swore with uplifted hand to give to Abraham, to Isaac and to Jacob. I will give it to you as a possession. I am the LORD.'"

⁹Moses reported this to the Israelites, but they did not listen to him because of their discouragement and harsh labor.

¹⁰Then the LORD said to Moses, ¹¹"Go, tell Pharaoh king of Egypt to let the Israelites go out of his country."

¹²But Moses said to the LORD, "If the Israelites will not listen to me, why would Pharaoh listen to me, since I speak with faltering lips^a?"

Family Record of Moses and Aaron

¹³Now the LORD spoke to Moses and Aaron about the Israelites and Pharaoh king of Egypt, and he commanded them to bring the Israelites out of Egypt.

¹⁴These were the heads of their families^b:

The sons of Reuben the firstborn son of Israel were Hanok and Pallu, Hezron and Karmi. These were the clans of Reuben.

¹⁵The sons of Simeon were Jemuel, Jamin, Ohad, Jakin, Zohar and Shaul the son of a Canaanite woman. These were the clans of Simeon.

¹⁶These were the names of the sons of Levi according to their records: Gershon, Kohath and Merari. Levi lived 137 years.

¹⁷The sons of Gershon, by clans, were Libni and Shimei.

¹⁸The sons of Kohath were Amram, Izhar, Hebron and Uzziel. Kohath lived 133 years.

¹⁹The sons of Merari were Mahli and Mushi.

These were the clans of Levi according to their records.

²⁰Amram married his father's sister Jochebed, who bore him Aaron and Moses. Amram lived 137 years.

²¹The sons of Izhar were Korah, Nepheg and Zikri.

²²The sons of Uzziel were Mishael, Elzaphan and Sithri.

²³Aaron married Elisheba, daughter of Amminadab and sister of Nahshon, and she bore him Nadab and Abihu, Eleazar and Ithamar.

²⁴The sons of Korah were Assir, Elkanah and Abiasaph. These were the Korahite clans.

²⁵Eleazar son of Aaron married one of the daughters of Putiel, and she bore him Phinehas.

These were the heads of the Levite families, clan by clan.

²⁶It was this Aaron and Moses to whom the LORD said, "Bring the Israelites out of Egypt by their divisions." ²⁷They were the ones who spoke to Pharaoh king of Egypt about bringing the Israelites out of Egypt—this same Moses and Aaron.

Aaron to Speak for Moses

²⁸Now when the LORD spoke to Moses in Egypt, ²⁹he said to him, "I am the LORD. Tell Pharaoh king of Egypt everything I tell you."

³⁰But Moses said to the LORD, "Since I speak with faltering lips, why would Pharaoh listen to me?"

⁷ Then the LORD said to Moses, "See, I have made you like God to Pharaoh, and your brother Aaron will be your prophet. ²You are to say everything I command you, and your brother Aaron is to tell Pharaoh to let the Israelites go out of his country. ³But I will harden Pharaoh's heart, and though I multiply my signs and wonders in Egypt, ⁴he will not listen to you. Then I will lay my hand on Egypt and with

---

^a 12 Hebrew *I am uncircumcised of lips*; also in verse 30   ^b 14 The Hebrew for *families* here and in verse 25 refers to units larger than clans.

mighty acts of judgment I will bring out my divisions, my people the Israelites. [5]And the Egyptians will know that I am the LORD when I stretch out my hand against Egypt and bring the Israelites out of it."

conversations

aging «» 7:6-7

1 » Does wisdom truly come with age? Why or why not?

2 » What effect does aging have on a Christian's ministry?

3 » Is there an age when someone becomes ineffective in ministry?

For more on **aging**, check the index.
For the next Conversations, go to p. 84.

[6]Moses and Aaron did just as the LORD commanded them. [7]Moses was eighty years old and Aaron eighty-three when they spoke to Pharaoh.

Aaron's Staff Becomes a Snake

[8]The LORD said to Moses and Aaron, [9]"When Pharaoh says to you, 'Perform a miracle,' then say to Aaron, 'Take your staff and throw it down before Pharaoh,' and it will become a snake."

[10]So Moses and Aaron went to Pharaoh and did just as the LORD commanded. Aaron threw his staff down in front of Pharaoh and his officials, and it became a snake. [11]Pharaoh then summoned wise men and sorcerers, and the Egyptian magicians also did the same things by their secret arts: [12]Each one threw down his staff and it became a snake. But Aaron's staff swallowed up their staffs. [13]Yet Pharaoh's heart became hard and he would not listen to them, just as the LORD had said.

The Plague of Blood

[14]Then the LORD said to Moses, "Pharaoh's heart is unyielding; he refuses to let the people go. [15]Go to Pharaoh in the morning as he goes out to the river. Wait on the bank of the Nile to meet him, and take in your hand the staff that was changed into a snake. [16]Then say to him, 'The LORD, the God of the Hebrews, has sent me to say to you: Let my people go, so that they may worship me in the wilderness. But until now you have not listened. [17]This is what the LORD says: By this you will know that I am the LORD: With the staff that is in my hand I will strike the water of the Nile, and it will be changed into blood. [18]The fish in the Nile will die, and the river will stink; the Egyptians will not be able to drink its water.'"

[19]The LORD said to Moses, "Tell Aaron, 'Take your staff and stretch out your hand over the waters of Egypt—over the streams and canals, over the ponds and all the reservoirs—and they will turn to blood.' Blood will be everywhere in Egypt, even in the wooden buckets and stone jars."

[20]Moses and Aaron did just as the LORD had commanded. He raised his staff in the presence of Pharaoh and his officials and struck the water of the Nile, and all the water was changed into blood. [21]The fish in the Nile died, and the river smelled so bad that the Egyptians could not drink its water. Blood was everywhere in Egypt.

[22]But the Egyptian magicians did the same things by their secret arts, and Pharaoh's heart became hard; he would not listen to Moses and Aaron, just as the LORD had said. [23]Instead, he turned and went into his palace, and did not take even this to heart. [24]And all the Egyptians dug along the Nile to get drinking water, because they could not drink the water of the river.

The Plague of Frogs

8 [25]Seven days passed after the LORD struck the Nile. *[1]Then the LORD said to Moses, "Go to Pharaoh and say to him, 'This is what the LORD says: Let my people go, so that they may worship me. [2]If you refuse to let them go, I will send a plague of frogs on your whole country. [3]The Nile will teem with frogs. They will come up into your palace and your bedroom and onto your bed, into the houses of your officials and on your people, and into your ovens and kneading troughs. [4]The frogs will come up on you and your people and all your officials.'"

*[5]Then the LORD said to Moses, "Tell Aaron, 'Stretch out your hand with your staff over the streams and canals and ponds, and make frogs come up on the land of Egypt.'"

* 8:1-4 is numbered 7:26-29 in Hebrew texts.   * 8:5-32 is numbered 8:1-28 in Hebrew texts.

82

⁶So Aaron stretched out his hand over the waters of Egypt, and the frogs came up and covered the land. ⁷But the magicians did the same things by their secret arts; they also made frogs come up on the land of Egypt.

⁸Pharaoh summoned Moses and Aaron and said, "Pray to the LORD to take the frogs away from me and my people, and I will let your people go to offer sacrifices to the LORD."

⁹Moses said to Pharaoh, "I leave to you the honor of setting the time for me to pray for you and your officials and your people that you and your houses may be rid of the frogs, except for those that remain in the Nile."

¹⁰"Tomorrow," Pharaoh said.

Moses replied, "It will be as you say, so that you may know there is no one like the LORD our God. ¹¹The frogs will leave you and your houses, your officials and your people; they will remain only in the Nile."

¹²After Moses and Aaron left Pharaoh, Moses cried out to the LORD about the frogs he had brought on Pharaoh. ¹³And the LORD did what Moses asked. The frogs died in the houses, in the courtyards and in the fields. ¹⁴They were piled into heaps, and the land reeked of them. ¹⁵But when Pharaoh saw that there was relief, he hardened his heart and would not listen to Moses and Aaron, just as the LORD had said.

The Plague of Gnats

¹⁶Then the LORD said to Moses, "Tell Aaron, 'Stretch out your staff and strike the dust of the ground,' and throughout the land of Egypt the dust will become gnats." ¹⁷They did this, and when Aaron stretched out his hand with the staff and struck the dust of the ground, gnats came on people and animals. All the dust throughout the land of Egypt became gnats. ¹⁸But when the magicians tried to produce gnats by their secret arts, they could not.

Since the gnats were on people and animals everywhere, ¹⁹the magicians said to Pharaoh, "This is the finger of God." But Pharaoh's heart was hard and he would not listen, just as the LORD had said.

The Plague of Flies

²⁰Then the LORD said to Moses, "Get up early in the morning and confront Pharaoh as he goes to the river and say to him, 'This is what the LORD says: Let my people go, so that they may worship me. ²¹If you do not let my people go, I will send swarms of flies on you and your officials, on your people and into your houses. The houses of the Egyptians will be full of flies; even the ground will be covered with them.

²²"'But on that day I will deal differently with the land of Goshen, where my people live; no swarms of flies will be there, so that you will know that I, the LORD, am in this land. ²³I will make a distinction*a* between my people and your people. This sign will occur tomorrow.'"

²⁴And the LORD did this. Dense swarms of flies poured into Pharaoh's palace and into the houses of his officials; throughout Egypt the land was ruined by the flies.

²⁵Then Pharaoh summoned Moses and Aaron and said, "Go, sacrifice to your God here in the land."

²⁶But Moses said, "That would not be right. The sacrifices we offer the LORD our God would be

---

a 23 Septuagint and Vulgate; Hebrew will put a deliverance

HE IS: all-powerful

8:19 Water turning to blood and frogs infesting the land plagued the Egyptians. Pharaoh's magicians were able to duplicate these annoyances. However, when the dust became a swarm of gnats, the magicians recognized a power far greater than their own—*the finger of God.*

If things are plaguing you, don't become hardhearted like Pharaoh. Open your eyes to see the finger of God at work in your life. Recognize his power. He works miracles, he fights your hardheartedness, he breaks your addiction to having everything your own way. He is *all-powerful,* and he may be lovingly pointing his finger at you.

For the next He Is, go to p. 89.

detestable to the Egyptians. And if we offer sacrifices that are detestable in their eyes, will they not stone us? ²⁷We must take a three-day journey into the wilderness to offer sacrifices to the LORD our God, as he commands us."

²⁸Pharaoh said, "I will let you go to offer sacrifices to the LORD your God in the wilderness, but you must not go very far. Now pray for me."

²⁹Moses answered, "As soon as I leave you, I will pray to the LORD, and tomorrow the flies will leave Pharaoh and his officials and his people. Only let Pharaoh be sure that he does not act deceitfully again by not letting the people go to offer sacrifices to the LORD."

³⁰Then Moses left Pharaoh and prayed to the LORD, ³¹and the LORD did what Moses asked. The flies left Pharaoh and his officials and his people; not a fly remained. ³²But this time also Pharaoh hardened his heart and would not let the people go.

The Plague on Livestock

9 Then the LORD said to Moses, "Go to Pharaoh and say to him, 'This is what the LORD, the God of the Hebrews, says: "Let my people go, so that they may worship me." ²If you refuse to let them go and continue to hold them back, ³the hand of the LORD will bring a terrible plague on your livestock in the field—on your horses, donkeys and camels and on your cattle, sheep and goats. ⁴But the LORD will make a distinction between the livestock of Israel and that of Egypt, so that no animal belonging to the Israelites will die.'"

⁵The LORD set a time and said, "Tomorrow the LORD will do this in the land." ⁶And the next day the LORD did it: All the livestock of the Egyptians died, but not one animal belonging to the Israelites died. ⁷Pharaoh investigated and found that not even one of the animals of the Israelites had died. Yet his heart was unyielding and he would not let the people go.

The Plague of Boils

⁸Then the LORD said to Moses and Aaron, "Take handfuls of soot from a furnace and have Moses toss it into the air in the presence of Pharaoh. ⁹It will become fine dust over the whole land of Egypt, and festering boils will break out on people and animals throughout the land."

¹⁰So they took soot from a furnace and stood before Pharaoh. Moses tossed it into the air, and festering boils broke out on people and animals. ¹¹The magicians could not stand before Moses because of the boils that were on them and on all the Egyptians. ¹²But the LORD hardened Pharaoh's heart and he would not listen to Moses and Aaron, just as the LORD had said to Moses.

The Plague of Hail

¹³Then the LORD said to Moses, "Get up early in the morning, confront Pharaoh and say to him, 'This is what the LORD, the God of the Hebrews, says: Let my people go, so that they may worship me, ¹⁴or this time I will send the full force of my plagues against you and against your officials and your people, so you may know that there is no one like me in all the earth. ¹⁵For by now I could have stretched out my hand and struck you and your people with a plague that would have wiped you off the earth. ¹⁶But I have raised you up*a* for this very purpose, that I might show you my power and that my name might be proclaimed in all the earth. ¹⁷You still set yourself against my people and will not let them go. ¹⁸Therefore, at this time tomorrow I will send the worst hailstorm that has ever fallen on Egypt, from the day it was founded till now. ¹⁹Give an order now to bring your livestock and everything you have in the field to a place of shelter, because the hail will fall on every person and animal that has not been brought in and is still out in the field, and they will die.'"

²⁰Those officials of Pharaoh who feared the word of the LORD hurried to bring their slaves and their livestock inside. ²¹But those who ignored the word of the LORD left their slaves and livestock in the field.

²²Then the LORD said to Moses, "Stretch out your hand toward the sky so that hail will fall all over Egypt—on people and animals and on everything growing in the fields of Egypt." ²³When Moses stretched out his staff toward the sky, the LORD sent thunder and hail, and lightning flashed down to the ground. So the LORD rained hail on the land of Egypt; ²⁴hail fell and lightning flashed back and forth.

It was the worst storm in all the land of Egypt since it had become a nation. ²⁵Throughout Egypt hail struck everything in the fields—both people and animals; it beat down everything growing in the fields and stripped every tree. ²⁶The only place it did not hail was the land of Goshen, where the Israelites were.

²⁷Then Pharaoh summoned Moses and Aaron. "This time I have sinned," he said to them. "The LORD is in the right, and I and my people are in the wrong. ²⁸Pray to the LORD, for we have had enough thunder and hail. I will let you go; you don't have to stay any longer."

²⁹Moses replied, "When I have gone out of the city, I will spread out my hands in prayer to the LORD. The thunder will stop and there will be no more hail, so you may know that the earth is the LORD's. ³⁰But I know that you and your officials still do not fear the LORD God."

³¹(The flax and barley were destroyed, since the barley had headed and the flax was in bloom. ³²The wheat and spelt, however, were not destroyed, because they ripen later.)

³³Then Moses left Pharaoh and went out of the city. He spread out his hands toward the LORD; the thunder and hail stopped, and the rain no longer poured down on the land. ³⁴When Pharaoh saw that the rain and hail and thunder had stopped, he sinned again: He and his officials hardened their hearts. ³⁵So Pharaoh's heart was hard and he would not let the Israelites go, just as the LORD had said through Moses.

The Plague of Locusts

10 Then the LORD said to Moses, "Go to Pharaoh, for I have hardened his heart and the hearts of his officials so that I may perform these signs of mine among them ²that you may tell your children and grandchildren how I dealt harshly with the Egyptians and how I performed my signs among them, and that you may know that I am the LORD."

³So Moses and Aaron went to Pharaoh and said to him, "This is what the LORD, the God of the Hebrews, says: 'How long will you refuse to humble yourself before me? Let my people go, so that they may worship me. ⁴If you refuse to let them go, I will bring locusts into your country tomorrow. ⁵They will cover the face of the ground so that it cannot be seen. They will devour what little you have left after the hail, including every tree that is growing in your fields. ⁶They will fill your houses and those of all your officials and all the Egyptians—something neither your parents nor your ancestors have ever seen from the day they settled in this land till now.'" Then Moses turned and left Pharaoh.

⁷Pharaoh's officials said to him, "How long will this man be a snare to us? Let the people go, so that they may worship the LORD their God. Do you not yet realize that Egypt is ruined?"

⁸Then Moses and Aaron were brought back to Pharaoh. "Go, worship the LORD your God," he said. "But tell me who will be going."

⁹Moses answered, "We will go with our young and our old, with our sons and our daughters, and with our flocks and herds, because we are to celebrate a festival to the LORD."

¹⁰Pharaoh said, "The LORD be with you—if I let you go, along with your women and children! Clearly you are bent on evil.ᵃ ¹¹No! Have only the men go and worship the LORD, since that's what you have been asking for." Then Moses and Aaron were driven out of Pharaoh's presence.

¹²And the LORD said to Moses, "Stretch out your hand over Egypt so that locusts swarm over the land and devour everything growing in the fields, everything left by the hail."

¹³So Moses stretched out his staff over Egypt, and the LORD made an east wind blow across the land all that day and all that night. By morning the wind had brought the locusts; ¹⁴they invaded all Egypt and

conversations

attitude «» 10:1

1 Did Pharaoh choose his own attitude, or did God give it to him?

2 Do you think God ever hardens people's hearts today?

3 What are the dangers of having a hard heart?

For more on **attitude**, check the index. For the next Conversations, go to p. 93.

ᵃ 10 Or Be careful, trouble is in store for you!

settled down in every area of the country in great numbers. Never before had there been such a plague of locusts, nor will there ever be again. [15]They covered all the ground until it was black. They devoured all that was left after the hail—everything growing in the fields and the fruit on the trees. Nothing green remained on tree or plant in all the land of Egypt.

[16]Pharaoh quickly summoned Moses and Aaron and said, "I have sinned against the LORD your God and against you. [17]Now forgive my sin once more and pray to the LORD your God to take this deadly plague away from me."

[18]Moses then left Pharaoh and prayed to the LORD. [19]And the LORD changed the wind to a very strong west wind, which caught up the locusts and carried them into the Red Sea.[a] Not a locust was left anywhere in Egypt. [20]But the LORD hardened Pharaoh's heart, and he would not let the Israelites go.

The Plague of Darkness

[21]Then the LORD said to Moses, "Stretch out your hand toward the sky so that darkness spreads over Egypt—darkness that can be felt." [22]So Moses stretched out his hand toward the sky, and total darkness covered all Egypt for three days. [23]No one could see anyone else or move about for three days. Yet all the Israelites had light in the places where they lived.

[24]Then Pharaoh summoned Moses and said, "Go, worship the LORD. Even your women and children may go with you; only leave your flocks and herds behind."

[25]But Moses said, "You must allow us to have sacrifices and burnt offerings to present to the LORD our God. [26]Our livestock too must go with us; not a hoof is to be left behind. We have to use some of them in worshiping the LORD our God, and until we get there we will not know what we are to use to worship the LORD."

[27]But the LORD hardened Pharaoh's heart, and he was not willing to let them go. [28]Pharaoh said to Moses, "Get out of my sight! Make sure you do not appear before me again! The day you see my face you will die."

[29]"Just as you say," Moses replied. "I will never appear before you again."

The Plague on the Firstborn

11 Now the LORD had said to Moses, "I will bring one more plague on Pharaoh and on Egypt. After that, he will let you go from here, and when he does, he will drive you out completely. [2]Tell the people that men and women alike are to ask their neighbors for articles of silver and gold." [3](The LORD made the Egyptians favorably disposed toward the people, and Moses himself was highly regarded in Egypt by Pharaoh's officials and by the people.)

[4]So Moses said, "This is what the LORD says: 'About midnight I will go throughout Egypt. [5]Every firstborn son in Egypt will die, from the firstborn son of Pharaoh, who sits on the throne, to the firstborn son of the female slave, who is at her hand mill, and all the firstborn of the cattle as well. [6]There will be loud wailing throughout Egypt—worse than there has ever been or ever will be again. [7]But among the Israelites not a dog will bark at any person or animal.' Then you will know that the LORD makes a distinction between Egypt and Israel. [8]All these officials of yours will come to me, bowing down before me and saying, 'Go, you and all the people who follow you!' After that I will leave." Then Moses, hot with anger, left Pharaoh.

[9]The LORD had said to Moses, "Pharaoh will refuse to listen to you—so that my wonders may be multiplied in Egypt." [10]Moses and Aaron performed all these wonders before Pharaoh, but the LORD hardened Pharaoh's heart, and he would not let the Israelites go out of his country.

The Passover and the Festival of Unleavened Bread

12 The LORD said to Moses and Aaron in Egypt, [2]"This month is to be for you the first month, the first month of your year. [3]Tell the whole community of Israel that on the tenth day of this month each man is to take a lamb[b] for his family, one for each household. [4]If any household is too small for a whole lamb, they must share one with their nearest neighbor, having taken into account the number of people there are. You are to determine the amount of lamb needed in accordance with what each

---

[a] 19 Or the Sea of Reeds   [b] 3 The Hebrew word can mean lamb or kid; also in verse 4.

person will eat. [5]The animals you choose must be year-old males without defect, and you may take them from the sheep or the goats. [6]Take care of them until the fourteenth day of the month, when all the members of the community of Israel must slaughter them at twilight. [7]Then they are to take some of the blood and put it on the sides and tops of the doorframes of the houses where they eat the lambs. [8]That same night they are to eat the meat roasted over the fire, along with bitter herbs, and bread made without yeast. [9]Do not eat the meat raw or boiled in water, but roast it over a fire—with the head, legs and internal organs. [10]Do not leave any of it till morning; if some is left till morning, you must burn it. [11]This is how you are to eat it: with your cloak tucked into your belt, your sandals on your feet and your staff in your hand. Eat it in haste; it is the LORD's Passover.

[12]"On that same night I will pass through Egypt and strike down every firstborn of both people and animals, and I will bring judgment on all the gods of Egypt. I am the LORD. [13]The blood will be a sign for you on the houses where you are, and when I see the blood, I will pass over you. No destructive plague will touch you when I strike Egypt.

[14]"This is a day you are to commemorate; for the generations to come you shall celebrate it as a festival to the LORD—a lasting ordinance. [15]For seven days you are to eat bread made without yeast. On the first day remove the yeast from your houses, for whoever eats anything with yeast in it from the first day through the seventh must be cut off from Israel. [16]On the first day hold a sacred assembly, and another one on the seventh day. Do no work at all on these days, except to prepare food for everyone to eat; that is all you may do.

[17]"Celebrate the Festival of Unleavened Bread, because it was on this very day that I brought your divisions out of Egypt. Celebrate this day as a lasting ordinance for the generations to come. [18]In the first month you are to eat bread made without yeast, from the evening of the fourteenth day until the evening of the twenty-first day. [19]For seven days no yeast is to be found in your houses. And anyone, whether foreigner or native-born, who eats anything with yeast in it must be cut off from the community of Israel. [20]Eat nothing made with yeast. Wherever you live, you must eat unleavened bread."

[21]Then Moses summoned all the elders of Israel and said to them, "Go at once and select the animals for your families and slaughter the Passover lamb. [22]Take a bunch of hyssop, dip it into the blood in the basin and put some of the blood on the top and on both sides of the doorframe. None of you shall go out of the door of your house until morning. [23]When the LORD goes through the land to strike down the Egyptians, he will see the blood on the top and sides of the doorframe and will pass over that doorway, and he will not permit the destroyer to enter your houses and strike you down.

[24]"Obey these instructions as a lasting ordinance for you and your descendants. [25]When you enter the land that the LORD will give you as he promised, observe this ceremony. [26]And when your children ask you, 'What does this ceremony mean to you?' [27]then tell them, 'It is the Passover sacrifice to the LORD, who passed over the houses of the Israelites in Egypt and spared our homes when he struck down the Egyptians.'" Then the people bowed down and worshiped. [28]The Israelites did just what the LORD commanded Moses and Aaron.

[29]At midnight the LORD struck down all the firstborn in Egypt, from the firstborn of Pharaoh, who sat on the throne, to the firstborn of the prisoner, who was in the dungeon, and the firstborn of all the live-

---

atissue:salvation

12:13 For an Israelite, blood wasn't just a symbol of salvation—it *was* salvation. The Hebrew law commanded that when an Israelite committed a sin, blood had to be shed in the form of a sacrifice. Blood was always required because life is in the blood (see Leviticus 17:11). Today we don't participate in the bloody sacrifice of an animal to pay for our sins because our payment was made long ago—and it was just as bloody and even more costly. We may imagine the crucifixion as a pristine scene, but the fact is that Christ's blood flowed out of his body to pay for our sins. The perfect sacrifice has been made, once for all time.

stock as well. ³⁰Pharaoh and all his officials and all the Egyptians got up during the night, and there was loud wailing in Egypt, for there was not a house without someone dead.

The Exodus

³¹During the night Pharaoh summoned Moses and Aaron and said, "Up! Leave my people, you and the Israelites! Go, worship the LORD as you have requested. ³²Take your flocks and herds, as you have said, and go. And also bless me."

³³The Egyptians urged the people to hurry and leave the country. "For otherwise," they said, "we will all die!" ³⁴So the people took their dough before the yeast was added, and carried it on their shoulders in kneading troughs wrapped in clothing. ³⁵The Israelites did as Moses instructed and asked the Egyptians for articles of silver and gold and for clothing. ³⁶The LORD had made the Egyptians favorably disposed toward the people, and they gave them what they asked for; so they plundered the Egyptians.

³⁷The Israelites journeyed from Rameses to Sukkoth. There were about six hundred thousand men on foot, besides women and children. ³⁸Many other people went up with them, and also large droves of live-stock, both flocks and herds. ³⁹With the dough the Israelites had brought from Egypt, they baked loaves of unleavened bread. The dough was without yeast because they had been driven out of Egypt and did not have time to prepare food for themselves.

⁴⁰Now the length of time the Israelite people lived in Egypt*ᵃ* was 430 years. ⁴¹At the end of the 430 years, to the very day, all the LORD's divisions left Egypt. ⁴²Because the LORD kept vigil that night to bring them out of Egypt, on this night all the Israelites are to keep vigil to honor the LORD for the generations to come.

Passover Restrictions

⁴³The LORD said to Moses and Aaron, "These are the regulations for the Passover:

"No foreigner is to eat of it. ⁴⁴Any slave you have bought may eat of it after you have circumcised him, ⁴⁵but a temporary resident or a hired worker may not eat of it.

⁴⁶"It must be eaten inside one house; take none of the meat outside the house. Do not break any of the bones. ⁴⁷The whole community of Israel must celebrate it.

⁴⁸"A foreigner residing among you who wants to celebrate the LORD's Passover must have all the males in his household circumcised; then he may take part like one born in the land. No uncircumcised male may eat of it. ⁴⁹The same law applies both to the native-born and to the foreigner residing among you."

⁵⁰All the Israelites did just what the LORD had commanded Moses and Aaron. ⁵¹And on that very day the LORD brought the Israelites out of Egypt by their divisions.

Consecration of the Firstborn

13 The LORD said to Moses, ²"Consecrate to me every firstborn male. The first offspring of every womb among the Israelites belongs to me, whether human or animal."

³Then Moses said to the people, "Commemorate this day, the day you came out of Egypt, out of the land of slavery, because the LORD brought you out of it with a mighty hand. Eat nothing containing yeast. ⁴Today, in the month of Aviv, you are leaving. ⁵When the LORD brings you into the land of the Canaanites, Hittites, Amorites, Hivites and Jebusites—the land he swore to your ancestors to give you, a land flow-ing with milk and honey—you are to observe this ceremony in this month: ⁶For seven days eat bread made without yeast and on the seventh day hold a festival to the LORD. ⁷Eat unleavened bread during those seven days; nothing with yeast in it is to be seen among you, nor shall any yeast be seen anywhere within your borders. ⁸On that day tell your children, 'I do this because of what the LORD did for me when I came out of Egypt.' ⁹This observance will be for you like a sign on your hand and a reminder on your forehead that this law of the LORD is to be on your lips. For the LORD brought you out of Egypt with his mighty hand. ¹⁰You must keep this ordinance at the appointed time year after year.

¹¹"After the LORD brings you into the land of the Canaanites and gives it to you, as he promised on oath to you and your ancestors, ¹²you are to give over to the LORD the first offspring of every womb. All the

---

ᵃ 40 Masoretic Text; Samaritan Pentateuch and Septuagint *Egypt and Canaan* firstborn males of your livestock belong to the LORD. ¹³Redeem with a lamb every firstborn donkey, but if you do not redeem it, break its neck. Redeem every firstborn among your sons.

¹⁴"In days to come, when your children ask you, 'What does this mean?' say to them, 'With a mighty hand the LORD brought us out of Egypt, out of the land of slavery. ¹⁵When Pharaoh stubbornly refused to let us go, the LORD killed the firstborn of both people and animals in Egypt. This is why I sacrifice to the LORD the first male offspring of every womb and redeem each of my firstborn sons.' ¹⁶And it will be like a sign on your hand and a symbol on your forehead that the LORD brought us out of Egypt with his mighty hand."

Crossing the Sea

¹⁷When Pharaoh let the people go, God did not lead them on the road through the Philistine country, though that was shorter. For God said, "If they face war, they might change their minds and return to Egypt." ¹⁸So God led the people around by the desert road toward the Red Sea.ᵃ The Israelites went up out of Egypt ready for battle.

¹⁹Moses took the bones of Joseph with him because Joseph had made the Israelites swear an oath. He had said, "God will surely come to your aid, and then you must carry my bones up with you from this place."ᵇ

²⁰After leaving Sukkoth they camped at Etham on the edge of the desert. ²¹By day the LORD went ahead of them in a pillar of cloud to guide them on their way and by night in a pillar of fire to give them light, so that they could travel by day or night. ²²Neither the pillar of cloud by day nor the pillar of fire by night left its place in front of the people.

14 Then the LORD said to Moses, ²"Tell the Israelites to turn back and encamp near Pi Hahiroth, between Migdol and the sea. They are to encamp by the sea, directly opposite Baal Zephon. ³Pharaoh will think, 'The Israelites are wandering around the land in confusion, hemmed in by the desert.' ⁴And I will harden Pharaoh's heart, and he will pursue them. But I will gain glory for myself through Pharaoh and all his army, and the Egyptians will know that I am the LORD." So the Israelites did this.

⁵When the king of Egypt was told that the people had fled, Pharaoh and his officials changed their minds about them and said, "What have we done? We have let the Israelites go and have lost their services!" ⁶So he had his chariot made ready and took his army with him. ⁷He took six hundred of the best chariots, along with all the other chariots of Egypt, with officers over all of them. ⁸The LORD hardened the heart of Pharaoh king of Egypt, so that he pursued the Israelites, who were marching out boldly. ⁹The Egyptians—all Pharaoh's horses and chariots, horsemenᶜ and troops—pursued the Israelites and overtook them as they camped by the sea near Pi Hahiroth, opposite Baal Zephon.

¹⁰As Pharaoh approached, the Israelites looked up, and there were the Egyptians, marching after them. They were terrified and cried out to the LORD. ¹¹They said to Moses, "Was it because there were no graves in Egypt that you brought us to the desert to die? What have you done to us by bringing us out of Egypt? ¹²Didn't we say to you in Egypt, 'Leave us alone; let us serve the Egyptians'? It would have been better for us to serve the Egyptians than to die in the desert!"

¹³Moses answered the people, "Do not be afraid. Stand firm and you will see the deliverance the LORD will bring you today. The Egyptians you see today you will never see again. ¹⁴The LORD will fight for you; you need only to be still."

¹⁵Then the LORD said to Moses, "Why are you crying out to me? Tell the Israelites to move on. ¹⁶Raise your staff and stretch out your hand over the sea to divide the water so that the Israelites can go through the sea on dry ground. ¹⁷I will harden the hearts of the Egyptians so that they will go in after them. And I will gain glory through Pharaoh and all his army, through his chariots and his horsemen. ¹⁸The Egyptians will know that I am the LORD when I gain glory through Pharaoh, his chariots and his horsemen."

¹⁹Then the angel of God, who had been traveling in front of Israel's army, withdrew and went behind them. The pillar of cloud also moved from in front and stood behind them, ²⁰coming between the armies

ᵃ 18 Or the Sea of Reeds   ᵇ 19 See Gen. 50:25.   ᶜ 9 Or charioteers; also in verses 17, 18, 23, 26 and 28

HE IS: a fighter

14:14 God foretold that Pharaoh would regret releasing the Israelites. Sure enough, the Egyptians followed the fleeing Hebrews with a vengeance. Though the Hebrews were quaking in their sandals, Moses understood that the best offense was a good defender. He promised: *The LORD will fight for you.*

Do you feel like the enemy is hot on your heels, roaring accusations, threatening destruction? God knows the enemy's tactics. He is not a passive deity; he's a ferocious fighter. You have the ultimate defender on your side. Be brave enough to be still. He is *a fighter*.

For the next He Is, go to p. 99.

of Egypt and Israel. Throughout the night the cloud brought darkness to the one side and light to the other side; so neither went near the other all night long.

²¹ Then Moses stretched out his hand over the sea, and all that night the LORD drove the sea back with a strong east wind and turned it into dry land. The waters were divided, ²² and the Israelites went through the sea on dry ground, with a wall of water on their right and on their left.

²³ The Egyptians pursued them, and all Pharaoh's horses and chariots and horsemen followed them into the sea. ²⁴ During the last watch of the night the LORD looked down from the pillar of fire and cloud at the Egyptian army and threw it into confusion. ²⁵ He jammed*ᵃ* the wheels of their chariots so that they had difficulty driving. And the Egyptians said, "Let's get away from the Israelites! The LORD is fighting for them against Egypt."

²⁶ Then the LORD said to Moses, "Stretch out your hand over the sea so that the waters may flow back over the Egyptians and their chariots and horsemen." ²⁷ Moses stretched out his hand over the sea, and at daybreak the sea went back to its place. The Egyptians were fleeing toward*ᵇ* it, and the LORD swept them into the sea. ²⁸ The water flowed back and covered the chariots and horsemen—the entire army of Pharaoh that had followed the Israelites into the sea. Not one of them survived.

²⁹ But the Israelites went through the sea on dry ground, with a wall of water on their right and on their left. ³⁰ That day the LORD saved Israel from the hands of the Egyptians, and Israel saw the Egyptians lying dead on the shore. ³¹ And when the Israelites saw the great power the LORD displayed against the Egyptians, the people feared the LORD and put their trust in him and in Moses his servant.

The Song of Moses and Miriam

15 Then Moses and the Israelites sang this song to the LORD:

> "I will sing to the LORD,
>   for he is highly exalted.
> Both horse and driver
>   he has hurled into the sea.

> ² "The LORD is my strength and my defense*ᶜ*;
>   he has become my salvation.
> He is my God, and I will praise him,
>   my father's God, and I will exalt him.
> ³ The LORD is a warrior;
>   the LORD is his name.
> ⁴ Pharaoh's chariots and his army
>   he has hurled into the sea.
> The best of Pharaoh's officers

89

ᵃ 25 See Samaritan Pentateuch, Septuagint and Syriac; Masoretic Text *removed*   *ᵇ 27* Or *from*   *ᶜ 2* Or *song*

myth# 06

"TRUE SUCCESS MEANS ALWAYS REACHING FOR THE NEXT RUNG ON THE CORPORATE LADDER."

I've achieved a level of success my parents only dreamed of. I was a National Merit Scholar and the valedictorian of my high school class with a perfect 4.0 GPA. I earned four academic scholarships (a full-ride) to college, and I was the first in my family to graduate from law school. I'm one of only a few attorneys in my firm who passed the Bar on my first attempt. And I'm on track to be a partner in five years. The workload is enormous. I'm working 17 hours a day, especially when I'm studying for a case. And for an African-American woman, the pressure to succeed is even greater.

So why am I frightened by what lies ahead? Why doesn't the idea of becoming senior partner in the firm excite me more? I own my own home and drive a sweet car. I'm dating a wonderful man who supports me in my career and is my undisputed biggest fan. Yet when I think about how I'm spending my life, I feel empty. When I dream about where I'll be in 10 years, I don't see myself as a power-hitter for Pryor and Schmitt. I picture myself as a mom. I see myself staying home with my kids, just like my mom did for my brothers and me.

I know my parents would support me in anything I choose to do, but I sense I would be letting them down if I didn't take advantage of all the opportunities they never had. They worked so hard so that I could be here. I don't want to be known as "The Woman Who Walked." I want them to be proud of me. I just don't know if I'm comfortable with the price of that success. I feel torn between being the person everyone else wants me to be and making the sacrifices I'm not yet willing to make.

—Toya

THE REFUTATION OF this

myth is not based on the premise that something is inherently wrong with a woman who's climbing the corporate ladder. Look at Miriam, who was a significant leader in the book of Exodus. It's worth celebrating that we live in an era where women have executive-level positions in many Fortune 500 companies. It wasn't always that way.

Rather, the idea that women should *always* reach for that next rung is dangerously misleading. Some women feel that in today's era of liberation they are somehow letting down their gender if they decide to step down from high-ranking corporate positions. They feel enormous pressure to stay.

Most women will agree that to continue enjoying the perks of a top-level position requires tradeoffs. Family vacations cut short by pressing deadlines. Early hours and late nights. Travel. Missed baseball games and dance recitals. Broken promises. These are inevitable components of the often-stressful juggle of career and family—for both women and men, though the price is often higher for women. At some point, we must ask ourselves, "Are these tradeoffs that I'm willing to make?"

God has a specific plan for you that will maximize your talents and gifts, bring maximum glory to himself and provide for your maximum good. Ask yourself:

- Is God able to carry out that plan where I am now?
- Is God nudging me to make a change in my priorities?

Women in the workforce must take a good hard look at the price of corporate success. They have at least two valid choices. Some may decide that career advancement is not worth the price. They may continue to work and contribute but without the intention of climbing the ladder. Other Christian women may feel called to rise higher in the corporate world, and they equally deserve our support so that they can represent Christ in spheres of great influence (see 2 Corinthians 5:20).

"No matter how much they make, most Americans believe twice as much income is required to 'live well' ... Americans seem programmed to deny that they are well-off, which only detracts from our ability to appreciate what's going well in our lives ... If there was ever doubt, modern American life proves that money cannot buy happiness."

—Gregg Easterbrook

91

"BUT GODLINESS WITH CONTENTMENT IS GREAT GAIN. FOR WE BROUGHT NOTHING INTO THE WORLD, AND WE CAN TAKE NOTHING OUT OF IT."

1 TIMOTHY 6:6–7

SEE ALSO

Matthew 16:26
1 Corinthians 10:31
1 Timothy 6:8–10

For more on **Success**, check the index.

are drowned in the Red Sea.^a

[5] The deep waters have covered them;
  they sank to the depths like a stone.
[6] Your right hand, LORD,
  was majestic in power.
Your right hand, LORD,
  shattered the enemy.

[7] "In the greatness of your majesty
  you threw down those who opposed you.
You unleashed your burning anger;
  it consumed them like stubble.
[8] By the blast of your nostrils
  the waters piled up.
The surging waters stood up like a wall;
  the deep waters congealed in the heart of the sea.
[9] The enemy boasted,
  'I will pursue, I will overtake them.
I will divide the spoils;
  I will gorge myself on them.
I will draw my sword
  and my hand will destroy them.'
[10] But you blew with your breath,
  and the sea covered them.
They sank like lead
  in the mighty waters.
[11] Who among the gods
  is like you, LORD?
Who is like you—
  majestic in holiness,
awesome in glory,
  working wonders?

[12] "You stretch out your right hand,
  and the earth swallows your enemies.
[13] In your unfailing love you will lead
  the people you have redeemed.
In your strength you will guide them
  to your holy dwelling.
[14] The nations will hear and tremble;
  anguish will grip the people of Philistia.
[15] The chiefs of Edom will be terrified,
  the leaders of Moab will be seized with trembling,
the people^b of Canaan will melt away;
[16] terror and dread will fall on them.
By the power of your arm
  they will be as still as a stone—
until your people pass by, LORD,
  until the people you bought^c pass by.
[17] You will bring them in and plant them
  on the mountain of your inheritance—

---

^a 4 Or the Sea of Reeds; also in verse 22 ^b 15 Or rulers ^c 16 Or created

the place, Lord, you made for your dwelling,
    the sanctuary, Lord, your hands established.

¹⁸"The Lord reigns
    for ever and ever."

¹⁹When Pharaoh's horses, chariots and horsemen*^a went into the sea, the Lord brought the waters of the sea back over them, but the Israelites walked through the sea on dry ground. ²⁰Then Miriam the prophet, Aaron's sister, took a timbrel in her hand, and all the women followed her, with timbrels and dancing. ²¹Miriam sang to them:

"Sing to the Lord,
    for he is highly exalted.
Both horse and driver
    he has hurled into the sea."

The Waters of Marah and Elim

²²Then Moses led Israel from the Red Sea and they went into the Desert of Shur. For three days they traveled in the desert without finding water. ²³When they came to Marah, they could not drink its water because it was bitter. (That is why the place is called Marah.*^b) ²⁴So the people grumbled against Moses, saying, "What are we to drink?"

²⁵Then Moses cried out to the Lord, and the Lord showed him a piece of wood. He threw it into the water, and the water became sweet.

There the Lord issued a ruling and instruction for them and put them to the test. ²⁶He said, "If you listen carefully to the Lord your God and do what is right in his eyes, if you pay attention to his commands and keep all his decrees, I will not bring on you any of the diseases I brought on the Egyptians, for I am the Lord, who heals you."

²⁷Then they came to Elim, where there were twelve springs and seventy palm trees, and they camped there near the water.

Manna and Quail

16 The whole Israelite community set out from Elim and came to the Desert of Sin, which is between Elim and Sinai, on the fifteenth day of the second month after they had come out of Egypt. ²In the desert the whole community grumbled against Moses and Aaron. ³The Israelites said to them, "If only we had died by the Lord's hand in Egypt! There we sat around pots of meat and ate all the food we wanted, but you have brought us out into this desert to starve this entire assembly to death."

⁴Then the Lord said to Moses, "I will rain down bread from heaven for you. The people are to go out each day and gather enough for that day. In this way I will test them and see whether they will follow my instructions. ⁵On the sixth day they are to prepare what they bring in, and that is to be twice as much as they gather on the other days."

conversations

complaining «» 16:1–8

1 » Is it ever OK to complain?

2 » Is your everyday complaining the same as "grumbling against God"?

3 » How does complaining affect you and those around you?

For more on **complaining**, check the index.
For the next Conversations, go to p. 111.

⁶So Moses and Aaron said to all the Israelites, "In the evening you will know that it was the Lord who brought you out of Egypt, ⁷and in the morning you will see the glory of the Lord, because he has heard your grumbling against him. Who are we, that you should grumble against us?" ⁸Moses also said, "You will know that it was the Lord when he gives you meat to eat in the evening and all the bread you want in the morning, because he has heard your grumbling against him. Who are we? You are not grumbling against us, but against the Lord."

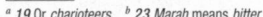

^a 19 Or *charioteers*   *^b 23 Marah* means *bitter.*

93

myth# 07 "IF WE DON'T LOVE EACH OTHER ANYMORE, WE SHOULD GO OUR SEPARATE WAYS."

My parents stopped loving each other years ago. It's as if they're strangers living together in the same house. Mom says divorce is not an option, no matter what. And Dad refuses to talk with me about it. But it's obvious to everyone that they're unhappy.

It hasn't always been this way. I remember my dad taking my mom out for romantic dinner dates for Valentine's or their anniversary. But over the past few years, it seems like they've simply fallen out of love. Aside from being devoted parents to my brother and me, I wonder what they still have in common with each other.

I would never come right out and say that I want my parents to get divorced. But I wonder if they could find happiness with someone else. It seems to me that people change. Things change. That's just life. So why stay trapped in a relationship that isn't working anymore? Just so the neighbors won't talk? So you can go to Bermuda with your "couple friends"? It seems to me that if you no longer love each other, then going your separate ways is something you have to consider—for both of your sakes.

Which is why I'm taking my time when it comes to getting married. I've heard the statistics. They say one out of every two marriages ends in divorce. That means divorce is basically inevitable for half of all couples. It's a fact. With any luck, I'll be in the 50 percent whose marriage doesn't self-destruct. But I know one thing. I'm not following my mother's example. I refuse to endure a relationship God meant for me to enjoy.

—Allison

SOME WOMEN JUSTIFY

walking out on their marriages after the love dies. *Well,* they reason, *we had a 50 percent chance of failure anyway.* But that's not true. The one-in-two statistic originated from mis-interpreting the research originally released by the National Center for Health Statistics during the late 1970s when the introduction of the no-fault divorce contributed to a skyrocketing incidence of divorces. The research stated that the number of divorces in one year was precisely half the number of marriages. The media helped deduce the one-in-two theory, and the rest is history. However, what about the millions of existing marriages (more than 50 million at the time) who neither married nor divorced that year? Those who propagated the 50-percent headline "forgot" to account for this second category. The result was a skewed repre-sentation of research that still makes its way into articles and news reports (and even well-meaning pastors' sermons), bemoaning the "inevitability" of divorce in the U.S.

It's no wonder that many women who sense a pall wash over the passion in their marriages assume it's the beginning of the end. They conclude with fatalistic resolve that they must have wound up on the other side of the one-in-two dividing line—just the luck of the draw.

So, what do you do when your marriage seems to be waning? When you don't feel in love any-more? When you wonder if you made a mis-take?

Beyond the fact that this statistic simply isn't true, the reality is that "going our separate ways" is not as easy as it initially sounds. Divorce court is no picnic—alimony, custody battles, division of property. Any divorce is a life-altering deci-sion with lasting effects. Women and men may heal from the emotional damage divorce causes, but the scars remain for a lifetime.

The Bible endorses a mature marriage commit-ment based on love. It's a *choice* we make—whether we *feel* like being loving or not

(see Colossians 3:12–14). In every relationship, we will face times when we feel as if the love is lacking. Like the Israelites who didn't feel like they could go on, we may desperately want to give up during difficult seasons. While fluctuat-ing feelings are a reality in marriage, they are not a loophole in the marriage vows.

95

> "50 percent of all marriages do not end in divorce. While any divorce is tragic, recent research suggests that one marriage in four is closer to the true divorce rate."
>
> —Rich Bulher and Jim Killan

"ABOVE ALL, LOVE EACH OTHER DEEPLY, BECAUSE LOVE COVERS OVER A MULTITUDE OF SINS."

1 PETER 4:8

SEE ALSO

1 Corinthians 13:4–7

1 John 3:11

For more on **Divorce**, check the index.

⁹Then Moses told Aaron, "Say to the entire Israelite community, 'Come before the LORD, for he has heard your grumbling.'"

¹⁰While Aaron was speaking to the whole Israelite community, they looked toward the desert, and there was the glory of the LORD appearing in the cloud.

¹¹The LORD said to Moses, ¹²"I have heard the grumbling of the Israelites. Tell them, 'At twilight you will eat meat, and in the morning you will be filled with bread. Then you will know that I am the LORD your God.'"

¹³That evening quail came and covered the camp, and in the morning there was a layer of dew around the camp. ¹⁴When the dew was gone, thin flakes like frost on the ground appeared on the desert floor. ¹⁵When the Israelites saw it, they said to each other, "What is it?" For they did not know what it was.

Moses said to them, "It is the bread the LORD has given you to eat. ¹⁶This is what the LORD has commanded: 'Each one is to gather as much as they need. Take an omer ᵃ for each person you have in your tent.'"

¹⁷The Israelites did as they were told; some gathered much, some little. ¹⁸And when they measured it by the omer, the one who gathered much did not have too much, and the one who gathered little did not have too little. Each one had gathered just as much as they needed.

¹⁹Then Moses said to them, "No one is to keep any of it until morning."

²⁰However, some of them paid no attention to Moses; they kept part of it until morning, but it was full of maggots and began to smell. So Moses was angry with them.

²¹Each morning everyone gathered as much as they needed, and when the sun grew hot, it melted away. ²²On the sixth day, they gathered twice as much—two omers ᵇ for each person—and the leaders of the community came and reported this to Moses. ²³He said to them, "This is what the LORD commanded: 'Tomorrow is to be a day of sabbath rest, a holy sabbath to the LORD. So bake what you want to bake and boil what you want to boil. Save whatever is left and keep it until morning.'"

²⁴So they saved it until morning, as Moses commanded, and it did not stink or get maggots in it. ²⁵"Eat it today," Moses said, "because today is a sabbath to the LORD. You will not find any of it on the ground today. ²⁶Six days you are to gather it, but on the seventh day, the Sabbath, there will not be any."

²⁷Nevertheless, some of the people went out on the seventh day to gather it, but they found none. ²⁸Then the LORD said to Moses, "How long will you ᶜ refuse to keep my commands and my instructions? ²⁹Bear in mind that the LORD has given you the Sabbath; that is why on the sixth day he gives you bread for two days. Everyone is to stay where they are on the seventh day; no one is to go out." ³⁰So the people rested on the seventh day.

³¹The people of Israel called the bread manna. ᵈ It was white like coriander seed and tasted like wafers made with honey. ³²Moses said, "This is what the LORD has commanded: 'Take an omer of manna and keep it for the generations to come, so they can see the bread I gave you to eat in the wilderness when I brought you out of Egypt.'"

³³So Moses said to Aaron, "Take a jar and put an omer of manna in it. Then place it before the LORD to be kept for the generations to come."

³⁴As the LORD commanded Moses, Aaron put the manna with the tablets of the covenant law, so that it might be preserved. ³⁵The Israelites ate manna forty years, until they came to a land that was settled; they ate manna until they reached the border of Canaan.

³⁶(An omer is one-tenth of an ephah.)

Water From the Rock

17 The whole Israelite community set out from the Desert of Sin, traveling from place to place as the LORD commanded. They camped at Rephidim, but there was no water for the people to drink. ²So they quarreled with Moses and said, "Give us water to drink."

Moses replied, "Why do you quarrel with me? Why do you put the LORD to the test?"

³But the people were thirsty for water there, and they grumbled against Moses. They said, "Why did you bring us up out of Egypt to make us and our children and livestock die of thirst?"

ᵃ 16 That is, possibly about 3 pounds or about 1 1/3 kilograms; also in verses 18, 32, 33 and 36   ᵇ 22 That is, possibly about 6 pounds or about 2 2/3 kilograms   ᶜ 28 The Hebrew is plural.   ᵈ 31 Manna means What is it? (see verse 15).

[4]Then Moses cried out to the LORD, "What am I to do with these people? They are almost ready to stone me."

[5]The LORD answered Moses, "Go out in front of the people. Take with you some of the elders of Israel and take in your hand the staff with which you struck the Nile, and go. [6]I will stand there before you by the rock at Horeb. Strike the rock, and water will come out of it for the people to drink." So Moses did this in the sight of the elders of Israel. [7]And he called the place Massah[a] and Meribah[b] because the Israelites quarreled and because they tested the LORD saying, "Is the LORD among us or not?"

The Amalekites Defeated

[8]The Amalekites came and attacked the Israelites at Rephidim. [9]Moses said to Joshua, "Choose some of our men and go out to fight the Amalekites. Tomorrow I will stand on top of the hill with the staff of God in my hands."

[10]So Joshua fought the Amalekites as Moses had ordered, and Moses, Aaron and Hur went to the top of the hill. [11]As long as Moses held up his hands, the Israelites were winning, but whenever he lowered his hands, the Amalekites were winning. [12]When Moses' hands grew tired, they took a stone and put it under him and he sat on it. Aaron and Hur held his hands up—one on one side, one on the other—so that his hands remained steady till sunset. [13]So Joshua overcame the Amalekite army with the sword.

[14]Then the LORD said to Moses, "Write this on a scroll as something to be remembered and make sure that Joshua hears it, because I will completely blot out the name of Amalek from under heaven."

[15]Moses built an altar and called it The LORD is my Banner. [16]He said, "Because hands were lifted up against[c] the throne of the LORD,[d] the LORD will be at war against the Amalekites from generation to generation."

Jethro Visits Moses

18 Now Jethro, the priest of Midian and father-in-law of Moses, heard of everything God had done for Moses and for his people Israel, and how the LORD had brought Israel out of Egypt.

[2]After Moses had sent away his wife Zipporah, his father-in-law Jethro received her [3]and her two sons. One son was named Gershom,[e] for Moses said, "I have become a foreigner in a foreign land"; [4]and the other was named Eliezer,[f] for he said, "My father's God was my helper; he saved me from the sword of Pharaoh."

[5]Jethro, Moses' father-in-law, together with Moses' sons and wife, came to him in the wilderness, where he was camped near the mountain of God. [6]Jethro had sent word to him, "I, your father-in-law Jethro, am coming to you with your wife and her two sons."

[7]So Moses went out to meet his father-in-law and bowed down and kissed him. They greeted each other and then went into the tent. [8]Moses told his father-in-law about everything the LORD had done to Pharaoh and the Egyptians for Israel's sake and about all the hardships they had met along the way and how the LORD had saved them.

[9]Jethro was delighted to hear about all the good things the LORD had done for Israel in rescuing them from the hand of the Egyptians. [10]He said, "Praise be to the LORD, who rescued you from the hand of the Egyptians and of Pharaoh, and who rescued the people from the hand of the Egyptians. [11]Now I know that the LORD is greater than all other gods, for he did this to those who had treated Israel arrogantly." [12]Then Jethro, Moses' father-in-law, brought a burnt offering and other sacrifices to God, and Aaron came with all the elders of Israel to eat bread with Moses' father-in-law in the presence of God.

[13]The next day Moses took his seat to serve as judge for the people, and they stood around him from morning till evening. [14]When his father-in-law saw all that Moses was doing for the people, he said, "What is this you are doing for the people? Why do you alone sit as judge, while all these people stand around you from morning till evening?"

[15]Moses answered him, "Because the people come to me to seek God's will. [16]Whenever they have a dispute, it is brought to me, and I decide between the parties and inform them of God's decrees and instructions."

---

[a] 7 Massah means testing.   [b] 7 Meribah means quarreling.   [c] 16 Or to   [d] 16 The meaning of the Hebrew for this clause is uncertain.   [e] 3 Gershom sounds like the Hebrew for a foreigner there.   [f] 4 Eliezer means my God is helper.

[17]Moses' father-in-law replied, "What you are doing is not good. [18]You and these people who come to you will only wear yourselves out. The work is too heavy for you; you cannot handle it alone. [19]Listen now to me and I will give you some advice, and may God be with you. You must be the people's representative before God and bring their disputes to him. [20]Teach them his decrees and instructions, and show them the way they are to live and how they are to behave. [21]But select capable men from all the people—men who fear God, trustworthy men who hate dishonest gain—and appoint them as officials over thousands, hundreds, fifties and tens. [22]Have them serve as judges for the people at all times, but have them bring every difficult case to you; the simple cases they can decide themselves. That will make your load lighter, because they will share it with you. [23]If you do this and God so commands, you will be able to stand the strain, and all these people will go home satisfied."

[24]Moses listened to his father-in-law and did everything he said. [25]He chose capable men from all Israel and made them leaders of the people, officials over thousands, hundreds, fifties and tens. [26]They served as judges for the people at all times. The difficult cases they brought to Moses, but the simple ones they decided themselves.

[27]Then Moses sent his father-in-law on his way, and Jethro returned to his own country.

98

lot's wife

Genesis 18:16 – 19:29

ASKmeanyTHING

What made you stop to look back?

I felt like I just had to. I couldn't resist looking at what was happening. Fire was falling from the sky on the place I had called home. It was awful, terrible destruction, but I needed to look. I needed to see my home one last time.

Didn't God give you clear instructions not to look back?

Yes, he did. But I was frightened and unsure of what was ahead. My security and identity were tied up in that one place. I was so unsure of where God was taking us that I looked back to the only certainty I'd known. I couldn't let go of my past, and it cost me my life.

What advice would you give to women who are facing uncertainty ahead in their lives?

Let go of the past. Don't allow your fears of the future to hold you back when God is trying to lead you in a new direction. God certainly had something new and better planned for my family when he led us out of Sodom that awful day, but I just couldn't see it. I was too scared. When your future looks uncertain, keep your eyes focused on God. You will never be sorry that you did.

FOR MORE INSIGHT: Do you fear what's ahead? Do you look back to your comfortable past rather than following God into the future? God is always doing something new (see Isaiah 43:19). Read Luke 17:20–33 to see what Jesus had to say about being prepared for what's to come.

At Mount Sinai

19 On the first day of the third month after the Israelites left Egypt—on that very day—they came to the Desert of Sinai. [2]After they set out from Rephidim, they entered the Desert of Sinai, and Israel camped there in the desert in front of the mountain.

[3]Then Moses went up to God, and the Lord called to him from the mountain and said, "This is what you are to say to the house of Jacob and what you are to tell the people of Israel: [4]'You yourselves have seen what I did to Egypt, and how I carried you on eagles' wings and brought you to myself. [5]Now if you obey me fully and keep my covenant, then out of all nations you will be my treasured possession. Although the whole earth is mine, [6]you[a] will be for me a kingdom of priests and a holy nation.' These are the words you are to speak to the Israelites."

HE IS: treasure keeper

19:5–6 The whole earth is God's. He owns the cattle on the hills, the fish that swim, the birds that fly, the water that flows, the oil and gas and the precious gold and minerals buried underground. But of all God's resources, he values his people most—they are his treasured possession.

In God's kingdom, you are his princess. He considers you a priceless treasure, of far more value than diamonds or rubies. What he asks of you is obedience. That's a small price to pay the *treasure keeper* for cherishing you above all things.

99

For the next He Is, go to p. 115.

[7]So Moses went back and summoned the elders of the people and set before them all the words the Lord had commanded him to speak. [8]The people all responded together, "We will do everything the Lord has said." So Moses brought their answer back to the Lord.

[9]The Lord said to Moses, "I am going to come to you in a dense cloud, so that the people will hear me speaking with you and will always put their trust in you." Then Moses told the Lord what the people had said.

[10]And the Lord said to Moses, "Go to the people and consecrate them today and tomorrow. Have them wash their clothes [11]and be ready by the third day, because on that day the Lord will come down on Mount Sinai in the sight of all the people. [12]Put limits for the people around the mountain and tell them, 'Be careful that you do not approach the mountain or touch the foot of it. Whoever touches the mountain is to be put to death. [13]They are to be stoned or shot with arrows; not a hand is to be laid on them. Whether people or animals, they shall not be permitted to live.' Only when the ram's horn sounds a long blast may they approach the mountain."

[14]After Moses had gone down the mountain to the people, he consecrated them, and they washed their clothes. [15]Then he said to the people, "Prepare yourselves for the third day. Abstain from sexual relations."

[16]On the morning of the third day there was thunder and lightning, with a thick cloud over the mountain, and a very loud trumpet blast. Everyone in the camp trembled. [17]Then Moses led the people out of the camp to meet with God, and they stood at the foot of the mountain. [18]Mount Sinai was covered with smoke, because the Lord descended on it in fire. The smoke billowed up from it like smoke from a furnace, and the whole mountain[b] trembled violently. [19]As the sound of the trumpet grew louder and louder, Moses spoke and the voice of God answered him.[c]

[20]The Lord descended to the top of Mount Sinai and called Moses to the top of the mountain. So Moses went up [21]and the Lord said to him, "Go down and warn the people so they do not force their way through to see the Lord and many of them perish. [22]Even the priests, who approach the Lord, must consecrate themselves, or the Lord will break out against them."

---

[a] *5,6* Or *possession, for the whole earth is mine.* [6]*You*   [b] *18* Most Hebrew manuscripts; a few Hebrew manuscripts and Septuagint *and all the people*
[c] *19* Or *and God answered him with thunder*

²³Moses said to the LORD, "The people cannot come up Mount Sinai, because you yourself warned us, 'Put limits around the mountain and set it apart as holy.'"

²⁴The LORD replied, "Go down and bring Aaron up with you. But the priests and the people must not force their way through to come up to the LORD, or he will break out against them."

²⁵So Moses went down to the people and told them.

The Ten Commandments

20 And God spoke all these words:

² "I am the LORD your God, who brought you out of Egypt, out of the land of slavery.

³ "You shall have no other gods before^a me.

⁴ "You shall not make for yourself an image in the form of anything in heaven above or on the earth beneath or in the waters below. ⁵You shall not bow down to them or worship them; for I, the LORD your God, am a jealous God, punishing the children for the sin of the parents to the third and fourth generation of those who hate me, ⁶but showing love to a thousand generations of those who love me and keep my commandments.

⁷ "You shall not misuse the name of the LORD your God, for the LORD will not hold anyone guiltless who misuses his name.

⁸ "Remember the Sabbath day by keeping it holy. ⁹Six days you shall labor and do all your work, ¹⁰but the seventh day is a sabbath to the LORD your God. On it you shall not do any work, neither you, nor your son or daughter, nor your male or female servant, nor your animals, nor any foreigner residing in your towns. ¹¹For in six days the LORD made the heavens and the earth, the sea, and all that is in them, but he rested on the seventh day. Therefore the LORD blessed the Sabbath day and made it holy.

¹² "Honor your father and your mother, so that you may live long in the land the LORD your God is giving you.

¹³ "You shall not murder.

¹⁴ "You shall not commit adultery.

¹⁵ "You shall not steal.

¹⁶ "You shall not give false testimony against your neighbor.

¹⁷ "You shall not covet your neighbor's house. You shall not covet your neighbor's wife, or his male or female servant, his ox or donkey, or anything that belongs to your neighbor."

a tissue: infidelity

20:14,17 The word *adultery* usually brings to mind a sexual act. So if you're not actually sleeping with a married man (who's not married to *you*), then you think you're in the clear. You haven't broken any commandments, right? Actually, infidelity, as the tenth commandment clarifies, begins long before the bedroom. Adultery starts with coveting something that's not yours, whether it's emotional stability, love or the kindness or touch of a man who doesn't belong to you. While such needs are natural, seeking to get those needs met by a man who's involved with another woman crosses the line. Don't fool yourself. Emotional unfaithfulness destroys marriages too.

¹⁸When the people saw the thunder and lightning and heard the trumpet and saw the mountain in smoke, they trembled with fear. They stayed at a distance ¹⁹and said to Moses, "Speak to us yourself and we will listen. But do not have God speak to us or we will die."

²⁰Moses said to the people, "Do not be afraid. God has come to test you, so that the fear of God will be with you to keep you from sinning."

²¹The people remained at a distance, while Moses approached the thick darkness where God was.

---

a 3 Or besides

Idols and Altars

²²Then the LORD said to Moses, "Tell the Israelites this: 'You have seen for yourselves that I have spoken to you from heaven: ²³Do not make any gods to be alongside me; do not make for yourselves gods of silver or gods of gold.

²⁴"'Make an altar of earth for me and sacrifice on it your burnt offerings and fellowship offerings, your sheep and goats and your cattle. Wherever I cause my name to be honored, I will come to you and bless you. ²⁵If you make an altar of stones for me, do not build it with dressed stones, for you will defile it if you use a tool on it. ²⁶And do not go up to my altar on steps, lest your nakedness be exposed on it.'

21 "These are the laws you are to set before them:

Hebrew Servants

²"If you buy a Hebrew servant, he is to serve you for six years. But in the seventh year, he shall go free, without paying anything. ³If he comes alone, he is to go free alone; but if he has a wife when he comes, she is to go with him. ⁴If his master gives him a wife and she bears him sons or daughters, the woman and her children shall belong to her master, and only the man shall go free.

⁵"But if the servant declares, 'I love my master and my wife and children and do not want to go free,' ⁶then his master must take him before the judges.ᵃ He shall take him to the door or the doorpost and pierce his ear with an awl. Then he will be his servant for life.

⁷"If a man sells his daughter as a servant, she is not to go free as male servants do. ⁸If she does not please the master who has selected her for himself,ᵇ he must let her be redeemed. He has no right to sell her to foreigners, because he has broken faith with her. ⁹If he selects her for his son, he must grant her the rights of a daughter. ¹⁰If he marries another woman, he must not deprive the first one of her food, clothing and marital rights. ¹¹If he does not provide her with these three things, she is to go free, without any payment of money.

Personal Injuries

¹²"Anyone who strikes someone a fatal blow is to be put to death. ¹³However, if it is not done intentionally, but God lets it happen, they are to flee to a place I will designate. ¹⁴But if anyone schemes and kills someone deliberately, that person is to be taken from my altar and put to death.

¹⁵"Anyone who attacksᶜ their father or mother is to be put to death.

¹⁶"Anyone who kidnaps someone is to be put to death, whether the victim has been sold or is still in the kidnapper's possession.

¹⁷"Anyone who curses their father or mother is to be put to death.

¹⁸"If two people quarrel and one hits the other with a stone or with a fistᵈ and the victim does not die but is confined to bed, ¹⁹the one who struck the blow will not be held liable if the other can get up and walk around outside with a staff; however, the guilty party must pay the injured person for any loss of time and see that the victim is completely healed.

²⁰"Anyone who beats their male or female slave with a rod must be punished if the slave dies as a direct result, ²¹but they are not to be punished if the slave recovers after a day or two, since the slave is their property.

²²"If people are fighting and a pregnant woman is hit and gives birth prematurelyᵉ but there is no serious injury, the offender must be fined whatever the woman's husband demands and the court allows. ²³But if there is serious injury, you are to take life for life, ²⁴eye for eye, tooth for tooth, hand for hand, foot for foot, ²⁵burn for burn, wound for wound, bruise for bruise.

²⁶"An owner who hits a male or female slave in the eye and destroys it must let the slave go free to compensate for the eye. ²⁷And an owner who knocks out the tooth of a male or female slave must let the slave go free to compensate for the tooth.

ᵃ 6 Or before God   ᵇ 8 Or master so that he does not choose her   ᶜ 15 Or kills   ᵈ 18 Or with a tool   ᵉ 22 Or and has a miscarriage

myth# 08 "GOD DOESN'T WANT ME TO HAVE ANY FUN."

Growing up in a strict fundamentalist home, I wondered why God let the devil have all the good music. But I would never tell my parents that— they didn't even let us go to school dances, much less listen to pop music. Our church's summer camp had strict rules about PDA (public displays of affection). Mild flirting was tolerated, but there was absolutely no hand-holding. We had to sneak off in the woods with the boys just to kiss, and we often came home with mysterious patches of poison ivy.

When I got older, I guess I rebelled against my conservative upbringing. So much had been "off-limits" for so long that I kind of went wild once I was out on my own. I smoked pot with some friends in college and started drinking pretty heavily. For the first time in my life, I was popular with the right people. I was free and enjoying every minute of it.

I thought about God from time to time, especially when I would come home for school breaks. I knew he wouldn't approve of my new lifestyle (or my new boyfriend), but I did not intend to give up either. My boyfriend and I moved in together right after we graduated so we could both look for jobs in Boston, but that turned out to be a disaster. The job and the boyfriend. Now, five years after college, I hardly talk with any of my college friends, though the girls from work and I hit the bars after work every weekend.

I suppose it's time to grow up and settle into the routine of being a devout religious person again. I just keep putting it off. Maybe I'll wait till I have a real career and start a family. Even then, I'm not sure I'll be ready for high-maintenance Christianity again. There's a lot on God's list I'm not ready to forego just yet.

—Kim

WHY DO WE think God's rules are designed to strip all the fun out of life? Perhaps for the same reason that kids think their parents' job is to make their lives miserable. We don't like to think of ourselves as children, but from God's perspective, that's exactly what we are (see John 1:12). Why is an indignant attitude toward God's commands childish?

- We see what looks like fun—temptation has a beautiful face—but God sees the misery it would bring us.

- We don't fully trust God. We suspect that he's holding out on us.

- When God draws the line, we manipulate and stretch the rules to place a single toe over it.

- We think God is trying to rein us in from experiencing all of life when in reality he is lovingly protecting us from dangers we're not smart enough to avoid.

If only we could see. If only we could see the suffering that our choices bring. If only we could see the lifelong consequences we'll face. If only we would take God's commands to heart. If only we'd take him at his word.

God wants us to respond to him with obedience, but not out of a sense of duty, resentment or compliance (see Isaiah 29:13). Not because he is a cosmic control freak. And not because keeping rules can earn his approval. God wants us to obey him for the love of him (see 1 John 5:3). Once we move from rule-keeping to a relationship with God based on love, we'll see his commands in a different light.

"God's will is what you would choose for your own life, if you had sense enough to choose it."

—Anonymous

103

"MY YOKE IS EASY AND MY BURDEN IS LIGHT."

MATTHEW 11:30

SEE ALSO
Deuteronomy 28:2
John 14:15
Hebrews 12:10–11

For more on **Obedience**,
check the index.

²⁸"If a bull gores a man or a woman to death, the bull is to be stoned to death, and its meat must not be eaten. But the owner of the bull will not be held responsible. ²⁹If, however, the bull has had the habit of goring and the owner has been warned but has not kept it penned up and it kills a man or woman, the bull is to be stoned and its owner also is to be put to death. ³⁰However, if payment is demanded, the owner's life may be redeemed by the payment of whatever is demanded. ³¹This law also applies if the bull

ASKmeanyTHING

sarah

Genesis 12:1–9; 15:1 – 17:22; 21:1-21

104

Why did you ask your husband to sleep with your maid?

Please understand that was a very difficult decision. I was desperate. Here I was, an old woman, way past my childbearing years, not getting any younger, and still I had no children. God had promised Abraham that we would have many heirs—as many as the stars, if you can believe that—and that this son would come from Abraham's own body. What was I supposed to think? We had waited more than ten years for God to make good on his word, and *nothing* had happened. It didn't seem like it could be God's plan for me to carry Abraham's son. And I so deeply wanted a child, as did Abraham. So I decided to do something about it. Having Abraham sleep with my maidservant (which, by the way, wasn't all that uncommon) seemed like my best option.

And was it?

No, not at all. You know the story. Hagar conceived, and as soon as she was pregnant, she hated me. And how do you think I felt every time I saw her belly, with Abraham's child growing inside? I couldn't stand being around her, so I mistreated her and she ran away. God sent her back to me and told her to be obedient, which she was. But our relationship was strained. The damage had been done. After Isaac was born, I finally sent her away for good. I didn't want Ishmael sharing Isaac's inheritance. It was an awful situation.

What advice would you give to women who have been waiting for God to act?

Look at my life. Look at the mess I made because I tried to work things out on my own. I hurt so many people. And then look at how God took the terrible mess I'd made and turned it around for good. Even after all the conniving I'd done, God still allowed me to conceive and carry a child! Remember that there is no situation, no circumstance, that is outside of God's control. And there's no mess that God can't somehow turn around for good. But think about how much simpler my life would have been if I'd just waited on God.

FOR MORE INSIGHT: Do you ever doubt that God will keep his promises? Check out the following verses on God's guarantee to keep his Word: Isaiah 55:10–11; Titus 1:2–3; and Hebrews 10:23.

gores a son or daughter. [32]If the bull gores a male or female slave, the owner must pay thirty shekels[a] of silver to the master of the slave, and the bull is to be stoned to death.

[33]"If anyone uncovers a pit or digs one and fails to cover it and an ox or a donkey falls into it, [34]the one who opened the pit must pay the owner for the loss and take the dead animal in exchange.

[35]"If anyone's bull injures the bull of another and it dies, the two parties are to sell the live one and divide both the money and the dead animal equally. [36]However, if it was known that the bull had the habit of goring, yet the owner did not keep it penned up, the owner must pay, animal for animal, and take the dead animal in exchange.

Protection of Property

22 *[1]"Whoever[d] steals an ox or a sheep and slaughters it or sells it must pay back five head of cattle for the ox and four sheep for the sheep.

*[2]"If a thief is caught breaking in and is struck a fatal blow, the defender is not guilty of bloodshed; [3]but if it happens[b] after sunrise, the defender is guilty of bloodshed.

"Anyone who steals must certainly make restitution, but if they have nothing, they must be sold to pay for their theft. [4]If the stolen animal is found alive in their possession—whether ox or donkey or sheep—they must pay back double.

[5]"If anyone grazes their livestock in a field or vineyard and lets them stray and they graze in another person's field, restitution must be made from the best of the livestock owner's field or vineyard.

[6]"If a fire breaks out and spreads into thornbushes so that it burns shocks of grain or standing grain or the whole field, the one who started the fire must make restitution.

[7]"If anyone gives a neighbor silver or goods for safekeeping and they are stolen from the neighbor's house, the thief, if caught, must pay back double. [8]But if the thief is not found, the owner of the house must appear before the judges, and they must[c] determine whether the owner of the house has laid hands on the other person's property. [9]In all cases of illegal possession of an ox, a donkey, a sheep, a garment, or any other lost property about which somebody says, 'This is mine,' both parties are to bring their cases before the judges.[d] The one whom the judges declare[e] guilty must pay back double to the other.

[10]"If anyone gives a donkey, an ox, a sheep or any other animal to a neighbor for safekeeping and it dies or is injured or is taken away while no one is looking, [11]the issue between them will be settled by the taking of an oath before the Lord that the neighbor did not lay hands on the other person's property. The owner is to accept this, and no restitution is required. [12]But if the animal was stolen from the neighbor, restitution must be made to the owner. [13]If it was torn to pieces by a wild animal, the neighbor shall bring in the remains as evidence and shall not be required to pay for the torn animal.

[14]"If anyone borrows an animal from a neighbor and it is injured or dies while the owner is not present, restitution must be made. [15]But if the owner is with the animal, the borrower will not have to pay. If the animal was hired, the money paid for the hire covers the loss.

Social Responsibility

[16]"If a man seduces a virgin who is not pledged to be married and sleeps with her, he must pay the bride-price, and she

---

alissue:cohabitation

22:16–17 In today's society, "shacking up" has moved from scandalous to socially acceptable. Living together before marriage has somehow become the "responsible thing to do." Besides, who goes to a movie without checking the preview first? Sadly, the preview you get from living together does not accurately depict a committed marriage. It doesn't come close. In fact, any benefits of living together get short-circuited because real security is only found in real commitment. When you move in together, you have everything to lose and nothing to gain. Ask yourself: What's stopping me from making a lifetime commitment?

---

[a] 32 That is, about 12 ounces or about 345 grams   [b] 3 Or if the defender kills the thief   [c] 8 Or before God, and he will   [d] 9 Or before God   [e] 9 Or whom God declares

* 22:1 is numbered 21:37 in Hebrew texts.   * 22:2-31 is numbered 22:1-30 in Hebrew texts.

shall be his wife. ¹⁷If her father absolutely refuses to give her to him, he must still pay the bride-price for virgins.

¹⁸"Do not allow a sorceress to live.

¹⁹"Anyone who has sexual relations with an animal is to be put to death.

²⁰"Whoever sacrifices to any god other than the Lord must be destroyed.^a

²¹"Do not mistreat or oppress a foreigner, for you were foreigners in Egypt.

²²"Do not take advantage of a widow or an orphan. ²³If you do and they cry out to me, I will certainly hear their cry. ²⁴My anger will be aroused, and I will kill you with the sword; your wives will become widows and your children fatherless.

²⁵"If you lend money to one of my people among you who is needy, do not treat it like a business deal; charge no interest. ²⁶If you take your neighbor's cloak as a pledge, return it by sunset, ²⁷because that cloak is the only covering your neighbor has. What else can your neighbor sleep in? When he cries out to me, I will hear, for I am compassionate.

²⁸"Do not blaspheme God^b or curse the ruler of your people.

²⁹"Do not hold back offerings from your granaries or your vats.^c

"You must give me the firstborn of your sons. ³⁰Do the same with your cattle and your sheep. Let them stay with their mothers for seven days, but give them to me on the eighth day.

³¹"You are to be my holy people. So do not eat the meat of an animal torn by wild beasts; throw it to the dogs.

Laws of Justice and Mercy

23 "Do not spread false reports. Do not help a guilty person by being a malicious witness. ²"Do not follow the crowd in doing wrong. When you give testimony in a lawsuit, do not pervert justice by siding with the crowd, ³and do not show favoritism to the poor in a lawsuit.

⁴"If you come across your enemy's ox or donkey wandering off, be sure to return it. ⁵If you see the donkey of someone who hates you fallen down under its load, do not leave it there; be sure you help your enemy with it.

⁶"Do not deny justice to your poor people in their lawsuits. ⁷Have nothing to do with a false charge and do not put an innocent or honest person to death, for I will not acquit the guilty.

⁸"Do not accept a bribe, for a bribe blinds those who see and twists the words of the righteous.

⁹"Do not oppress a foreigner; you yourselves know how it feels to be foreigners, because you were foreigners in Egypt.

Sabbath Laws

¹⁰"For six years you are to sow your fields and harvest the crops, ¹¹but during the seventh year let the land lie unplowed and unused. Then the poor among your people may get food from it, and the wild animals may eat what they leave. Do the same with your vineyard and your olive grove.

¹²"Six days do your work, but on the seventh day do not work, so that your ox and your donkey may rest and the slave born in your household, and the foreigner among you as well, may be refreshed.

¹³"Be careful to do everything I have said to you. Do not invoke the names of other gods; do not let them be heard on your lips.

The Three Annual Festivals

¹⁴"Three times a year you are to celebrate a festival to me.

¹⁵"Celebrate the Festival of Unleavened Bread; for seven days eat bread made without yeast, as I commanded you. Do this at the appointed time in the month of Aviv, for in that month you came out of Egypt.

"No one is to appear before me empty-handed.

¹⁶"Celebrate the Festival of Harvest with the firstfruits of the crops you sow in your field.

---

^a *20* The Hebrew term refers to the irrevocable giving over of things or persons to the Lord, often by totally destroying them.   ^b *28* Or *Do not revile the judges*   ^c *29* The meaning of the Hebrew for this phrase is uncertain.

"Celebrate the Festival of Ingathering at the end of the year, when you gather in your crops from the field.

[17] "Three times a year all the men are to appear before the Sovereign Lord.

[18] "Do not offer the blood of a sacrifice to me along with anything containing yeast.

"The fat of my festival offerings must not be kept until morning.

[19] "Bring the best of the firstfruits of your soil to the house of the Lord your God.

"Do not cook a young goat in its mother's milk.

God's Angel to Prepare the Way

[20] "See, I am sending an angel ahead of you to guard you along the way and to bring you to the place I have prepared. [21] Pay attention to him and listen to what he says. Do not rebel against him; he will not forgive your rebellion, since my Name is in him. [22] If you listen carefully to what he says and do all that I say, I will be an enemy to your enemies and will oppose those who oppose you. [23] My angel will go ahead of you and bring you into the land of the Amorites, Hittites, Perizzites, Canaanites, Hivites and Jebusites, and I will wipe them out. [24] Do not bow down before their gods or worship them or follow their practices. You must demolish them and break their sacred stones to pieces. [25] Worship the Lord your God, and his blessing will be on your food and water. I will take away sickness from among you, [26] and none will miscarry or be barren in your land. I will give you a full life span.

[27] "I will send my terror ahead of you and throw into confusion every nation you encounter. I will make all your enemies turn their backs and run. [28] I will send the hornet ahead of you to drive the Hivites, Canaanites and Hittites out of your way. [29] But I will not drive them out in a single year, because the land would become desolate and the wild animals too numerous for you. [30] Little by little I will drive them out before you, until you have increased enough to take possession of the land.

[31] "I will establish your borders from the Red Sea[a] to the Mediterranean Sea,[b] and from the desert to the Euphrates River. I will give into your hands the people who live in the land, and you will drive them out before you. [32] Do not make a covenant with them or with their gods. [33] Do not let them live in your land or they will cause you to sin against me, because the worship of their gods will certainly be a snare to you."

The Covenant Confirmed

24 Then he said to Moses, "Come up to the Lord, you and Aaron, Nadab and Abihu, and seventy of the elders of Israel. You are to worship at a distance, [2] but Moses alone is to approach the Lord; the others must not come near. And the people may not come up with him."

[3] When Moses went and told the people all the Lord's words and laws, they responded with one voice, "Everything the Lord has said we will do." [4] Moses then wrote down everything the Lord had said.

He got up early the next morning and built an altar at the foot of the mountain and set up twelve stone pillars representing the twelve tribes of Israel. [5] Then he sent young Israelite men, and they offered burnt offerings and sacrificed young bulls as fellowship offerings to the Lord. [6] Moses took half of the blood and

---

aissue:impatience

23:27–33 If only God would always give us such clear explanations for his timing! What Israelite would have considered wild animal control as an important factor in the military plan for conquering the Promised Land? But God looked ahead and saw all the complications and roadblocks, and he adjusted his plan accordingly. We believe we're great managers of our lives, but God knows better. He doesn't always tell us the reasons for his timing. But he asks us to trust him. If you charge ahead of God in your plans, you may achieve initial success, but you may soon realize several significant problems you overlooked. So relax. Wait on his master plan.

107

---

myth#09 "I'M ACCOUNTABLE ONLY TO MYSELF."

They said to bring a Bible, something I must have packed in the same box with my old Billy Joel cassettes that I haven't seen since my last move, so I had to buy one. Honestly, I was the last person who wanted to go on a singles retreat—people I figured were such losers they had to form their own club. But I was desperate for something new. I didn't want to fall back to old habits and old relationships. So, I reluctantly signed up for the weekend retreat.

That first night, we split into small groups after the speaker talked. The leader asked if we wanted to share something that was going on in our lives so the group could pray for us. I panicked and began scrambling for something I could say. Somehow I thought that "Please pray for me because I really, really want a drink right now" probably wouldn't go over well.

As people started opening up to each other, I was shocked. They weren't asking for prayer about trivial items. These people were real. Some of them were going through almost the exact same things I was experiencing. One guy shared that he and his girlfriend were struggling with sexual temptation. Another girl asked us to pray about some old friends from the party scene who were calling her again. When another person shared about being a recovering alcoholic, I was floored. When it came my turn, I eked out something lame about my job. I wasn't ready to open up just yet, but I believed them when they said they'd pray for me.

I've tried to live my life on my own, but I found out that I wasn't able to hold myself to much of anything for very long. The only person I had been answering to was myself. If I wanted to party until 3:00 A.M. and go to work hung over the next day, I did. If I saw a pair of stilettos, and it wasn't even close to payday, I charged them and wore them home from the store. I swore a million times that I was going to get out of debt, stop drinking so much, get to bed at a decent hour and maybe even go to church this Easter.

In reality, I couldn't even talk myself out of eating half a box of chocolate éclairs. I was out of control.

At this retreat, I realized that answering to myself just wasn't working. I was on course to self-destruct. Being accountable to other Christians was my first step on a long journey back to God.

—Carla

THINKING YOU CAN

be accountable to yourself is like trying to kiss your own elbow. It's impossible to do. (Tried it, didn't you?) We may try calling the shots, but we aren't equipped to handle the responsibility of running our own lives. Life is not designed to work that way.

Accountable to God

Giving control over to God is to work ourselves out of a job. It means we begin to operate with one simple understanding: God is God; we are not. As the Israelites had to learn (and relearn), deciding to be accountable to God and answer to him makes life much less complicated. The Creator made us and even wrote the owner's manual for how our lives "run" best.

Accountable to Each Other

Knowing there will be many times when we want to squirm back onto the throne of our lives, our Creator also made us accountable to each other to help us do the right things. It's called *community*. Christians are instructed to "carry each other's burdens" and, by doing that, to build one another's resolve to remain under Christ's control (see Galatians 6:2).

"Only 14 percent of women are involved in a discipleship process at a church, and 20 percent of women are involved in a small group that meets regularly for Bible study, prayer, and fellowship."

——Barna Research Group (2000)

109

"THOUGH one may Be overpowered, two can Defend themselves. A Cord of three strands is not Quickly Broken."

ECCLESIASTES 4:12

SEE ALSO

Ecclesiastes 4:10
Ephesians 4:14–16
Hebrews 10:24–25

For more on **Accountability**, check the index.

put it in bowls, and the other half he splashed against the altar. [7] Then he took the Book of the Covenant and read it to the people. They responded, "We will do everything the LORD has said; we will obey."

[8] Moses then took the blood, sprinkled it on the people and said, "This is the blood of the covenant that the LORD has made with you in accordance with all these words."

[9] Moses and Aaron, Nadab and Abihu, and the seventy elders of Israel went up [10] and saw the God of Israel. Under his feet was something like a pavement made of lapis lazuli, as bright blue as the sky. [11] But God did not raise his hand against these leaders of the Israelites; they saw God, and they ate and drank.

[12] The LORD said to Moses, "Come up to me on the mountain and stay here, and I will give you the tablets of stone with the law and commandments I have written for their instruction."

[13] Then Moses set out with Joshua his aide, and Moses went up on the mountain of God. [14] He said to the elders, "Wait here for us until we come back to you. Aaron and Hur are with you, and anyone involved in a dispute can go to them."

[15] When Moses went up on the mountain, the cloud covered it, [16] and the glory of the LORD settled on Mount Sinai. For six days the cloud covered the mountain, and on the seventh day the LORD called to Moses from within the cloud. [17] To the Israelites the glory of the LORD looked like a consuming fire on top of the mountain. [18] Then Moses entered the cloud as he went on up the mountain. And he stayed on the mountain forty days and forty nights.

Offerings for the Tabernacle

25 The LORD said to Moses, [2] "Tell the Israelites to bring me an offering. You are to receive the offering for me from everyone whose heart prompts them to give. [3] These are the offerings you are to receive from them: gold, silver and bronze; [4] blue, purple and scarlet yarn and fine linen; goat hair; [5] ram skins dyed red and another durable leather[a]; acacia wood; [6] olive oil for the light; spices for the anointing oil and for the fragrant incense; [7] and onyx stones and other gems to be mounted on the ephod and breastpiece.

[8] "Then have them make a sanctuary for me, and I will dwell among them. [9] Make this tabernacle and all its furnishings exactly like the pattern I will show you.

The Ark

[10] "Have them make an ark[b] of acacia wood—two and a half cubits long, a cubit and a half wide, and a cubit and a half high.[c] [11] Overlay it with pure gold, both inside and out, and make a gold molding around it. [12] Cast four gold rings for it and fasten them to its four feet, with two rings on one side and two rings on the other. [13] Then make poles of acacia wood and overlay them with gold. [14] Insert the poles into the rings on the sides of the ark to carry it. [15] The poles are to remain in the rings of this ark; they are not to be removed. [16] Then put in the ark the tablets of the covenant law, which I will give you.

[17] "Make an atonement cover of pure gold—two and a half cubits long and a cubit and a half wide. [18] And make two cherubim out of hammered gold at the ends of the cover. [19] Make one cherub on one end and the second cherub on the other; make the cherubim of one piece with the cover, at the two ends. [20] The cherubim are to have their wings spread upward, overshadowing the cover with them. The cheru-

---

at issue: failure

24:9–11 After you see God work in an amazing way, it's easy to let your guard down. You've been to the spiritual mountain and stood on its tallest peak. Who would have guessed a steep slope lay before you? The truth is that no one spiritual experience in life protects you from future failure. Shortly after supping with the Almighty himself, Aaron, Nadab and Abihu all committed deeply disrespectful acts against God (see Exodus 32:1–8; Leviticus 10:1–2). Don't become complacent in your relationship with God. Intentional, daily growth will keep you steady on your path.

---

[a] 5 Possibly the hides of dugongs   [b] 10 That is, a chest   [c] 10 That is, about 3 3/4 feet long and 2 1/4 feet wide and high or about 1.1 meters long and 67 centimeters wide and high; also in verse 17

bim are to face each other, looking toward the cover. [21]Place the cover on top of the ark and put in the ark the tablets of the covenant law that I will give you. [22]There, above the cover between the two cherubim that are over the ark of the covenant law, I will meet with you and give you all my commands for the Israelites.

The Table

[23]"Make a table of acacia wood—two cubits long, a cubit wide and a cubit and a half high.[a] [24]Overlay it with pure gold and make a gold molding around it. [25]Also make around it a rim a handbreadth[b] wide and put a gold molding on the rim. [26]Make four gold rings for the table and fasten them to the four corners, where the four legs are. [27]The rings are to be close to the rim to hold the poles used in carrying the table. [28]Make the poles of acacia wood, overlay them with gold and carry the table with them. [29]And make its plates and dishes of pure gold, as well as its pitchers and bowls for the pouring out of offerings. [30]Put the bread of the Presence on this table to be before me at all times.

The Lampstand

[31]"Make a lampstand of pure gold. Hammer out its base and shaft, and make its flowerlike cups, buds and blossoms of one piece with them. [32]Six branches are to extend from the sides of the lampstand—three on one side and three on the other. [33]Three cups shaped like almond flowers with buds and blossoms are to be on one branch, three on the next branch, and the same for all six branches extending from the lampstand. [34]And on the lampstand there are to be four cups shaped like almond flowers with buds and blossoms. [35]One bud shall be under the first pair of branches extending from the lampstand, a second bud under the second pair, and a third bud under the third pair—six branches in all. [36]The buds and branches shall all be of one piece with the lampstand, hammered out of pure gold.

[37]"Then make its seven lamps and set them up on it so that they light the space in front of it. [38]Its wick trimmers and trays are to be of pure gold. [39]A talent[c] of pure gold is to be used for the lampstand and all these accessories. [40]See that you make them according to the pattern shown you on the mountain.

The Tabernacle

26 "Make the tabernacle with ten curtains of finely twisted linen and blue, purple and scarlet yarn, with cherubim worked into them by skilled hands. [2]All the curtains are to be the same size—twenty-eight cubits long and four cubits wide.[d] [3]Join five of the curtains together, and do the same with the other five. [4]Make loops of blue material along the edge of the end curtain in one set, and do the same with the end curtain in the other set. [5]Make fifty loops on one curtain and fifty loops on the end curtain of the other set, with the loops opposite each other. [6]Then make fifty gold clasps and use them to fasten the curtains together so that the tabernacle is a unit.

[7]"Make curtains of goat hair for the tent over the tabernacle—eleven altogether. [8]All eleven curtains are to be the same size—thirty cubits long and four cubits wide.[e] [9]Join five of the curtains together into one set and the other six into another set. Fold the sixth curtain double at the front of the tent. [10]Make fifty loops along the edge of the end curtain in one set and also along the edge of the end curtain in the other set. [11]Then make fifty bronze clasps and put them in the loops to fasten the tent together as a unit. [12]As for the additional length of the tent curtains, the half curtain that is left over is to hang down at the rear of the tabernacle. [13]The tent curtains will be a cubit[f] longer on both sides; what is left will hang over the sides of the tabernacle so as to cover it. [14]Make for the tent a covering of ram skins dyed red, and over that a covering of the other durable leather.[g]

conversations

church «» 25:1–9

1 Does God value outward beauty and artistry in church buildings?

2 Does the appearance of a church building send a message to the congregation and community?

3 Does God want our church buildings to look a certain way?

For more on church, check the index.
For the next Conversations, go to p. 119.

111

---

[a] 23 That is, about 3 feet long, 1 1/2 feet wide and 2 1/4 feet high or about 90 centimeters long, 45 centimeters wide and 67 centimeters high   [b] 25 That is, about 3 inches or about 7.5 centimeters   [c] 39 That is, about 75 pounds or about 34 kilograms   [d] 2 That is, about 42 feet long and 6 feet wide or about 13 meters long and 1.8 meters wide   [e] 8 That is, about 45 feet long and 6 feet wide or 13.5 meters long and 1.8 meters wide   [f] 13 That is, about 18 inches or about 45 centimeters   [g] 14 Possibly the hides of dugongs

112

¹⁵"Make upright frames of acacia wood for the tabernacle. ¹⁶Each frame is to be ten cubits long and a cubit and a half wide,ᵃ ¹⁷with two projections set parallel to each other. Make all the frames of the tabernacle in this way. ¹⁸Make twenty frames for the south side of the tabernacle ¹⁹and make forty silver bases to go under them—two bases for each frame, one under each projection. ²⁰For the other side, the north side of the tabernacle, make twenty frames ²¹and forty silver bases—two under each frame. ²²Make six frames for the far end, that is, the west end of the tabernacle, ²³and make two frames for the corners at the far end. ²⁴At these two corners they must be double from the bottom all the way to the top and fitted into a single ring; both shall be like that. ²⁵So there will be eight frames and sixteen silver bases—two under each frame.

²⁶"Also make crossbars of acacia wood: five for the frames on one side of the tabernacle, ²⁷five for those on the other side, and five for the frames on the west, at the far end of the tabernacle. ²⁸The center crossbar is to extend from end to end at the middle of the frames. ²⁹Overlay the frames with gold and make gold rings to hold the crossbars. Also overlay the crossbars with gold.

³⁰"Set up the tabernacle according to the plan shown you on the mountain.

³¹"Make a curtain of blue, purple and scarlet yarn and finely twisted linen, with cherubim worked into it by skilled hands. ³²Hang it with gold hooks on four posts of acacia wood overlaid with gold and standing on four silver bases. ³³Hang the curtain from the clasps and place the ark of the covenant law behind the curtain. The curtain will separate the Holy Place from the Most Holy Place. ³⁴Put the atonement cover on the ark of the covenant law in the Most Holy Place. ³⁵Place the table outside the curtain on the north side of the tabernacle and put the lampstand opposite it on the south side.

³⁶"For the entrance to the tent make a curtain of blue, purple and scarlet yarn and finely twisted linen—the work of an embroiderer. ³⁷Make gold hooks for this curtain and five posts of acacia wood overlaid with gold. And cast five bronze bases for them.

The Altar of Burnt Offering

27 "Build an altar of acacia wood, three cubitsᵇ high; it is to be square, five cubits long and five cubits wide.ᶜ ²Make a horn at each of the four corners, so that the horns and the altar are of one piece, and overlay the altar with bronze. ³Make all its utensils of bronze—its pots to remove the ashes, and its shovels, sprinkling bowls, meat forks and firepans. ⁴Make a grating for it, a bronze network, and make a bronze ring at each of the four corners of the network. ⁵Put it under the ledge of the altar so that it is halfway up the altar. ⁶Make poles of acacia wood for the altar and overlay them with bronze. ⁷The poles are to be inserted into the rings so they will be on two sides of the altar when it is carried. ⁸Make the altar hollow, out of boards. It is to be made just as you were shown on the mountain.

The Courtyard

⁹"Make a courtyard for the tabernacle. The south side shall be a hundred cubitsᵈ long and is to have curtains of finely twisted linen, ¹⁰with twenty posts and twenty bronze bases and with silver hooks and bands on the posts. ¹¹The north side shall also be a hundred cubits long and is to have curtains, with twenty posts and twenty bronze bases and with silver hooks and bands on the posts.

¹²"The west end of the courtyard shall be fifty cubitsᵉ wide and have curtains, with ten posts and ten bases. ¹³On the east end, toward the sunrise, the courtyard shall also be fifty cubits wide. ¹⁴Curtains fifteen cubitsᶠ long are to be on one side of the entrance, with three posts and three bases, ¹⁵and curtains fifteen cubits long are to be on the other side, with three posts and three bases.

¹⁶"For the entrance to the courtyard, provide a curtain twenty cubitsᵍ long, of blue, purple and scarlet yarn and finely twisted linen—the work of an embroiderer—with four posts and four bases. ¹⁷All the posts around the courtyard are to have silver bands and hooks, and bronze bases. ¹⁸The courtyard shall be a hundred cubits long and fifty cubits wide,ʰ with curtains of finely twisted linen five cubitsⁱ high, and with bronze bases. ¹⁹All the other articles used in the service of the tabernacle, whatever their function, including all the tent pegs for it and those for the courtyard, are to be of bronze.

ᵃ *16* That is, about 15 feet long and 2 1/4 feet wide or about 4.5 meters long and 67 centimeters wide   ᵇ *1* That is, about 4 1/2 feet or about 1.4 meters
ᶜ *1* That is, about 7 1/2 feet or about 2.3 meters long and wide   ᵈ *9* That is, about 150 feet or about 45 meters; also in verse 11   ᵉ *12* That is, about 75 feet or about 22.5 meters; also in verse 13   ᶠ *14* That is, about 22 feet or about 6.8 meters; also in verse 15   ᵍ *16* That is, about 30 feet or about 9 meters   ʰ *18* That is, about 150 feet long and 75 feet wide or about 45 meters long and 22.5 meters wide   ⁱ *18* That is, about 7 1/2 feet or about 2.3 meters

Oil for the Lampstand

[20]"Command the Israelites to bring you clear oil of pressed olives for the light so that the lamps may be kept burning. [21]In the tent of meeting, outside the curtain that shields the ark of the covenant law, Aaron and his sons are to keep the lamps burning before the LORD from evening till morning. This is to be a lasting ordinance among the Israelites for the generations to come.

The Priestly Garments

28 "Have Aaron your brother brought to you from among the Israelites, along with his sons Nadab and Abihu, Eleazar and Ithamar, so they may serve me as priests. [2]Make sacred garments for your brother Aaron to give him dignity and honor. [3]Tell all the skilled workers to whom I have given wisdom in such matters that they are to make garments for Aaron, for his consecration, so he may serve me as priest. [4]These are the garments they are to make: a breastpiece, an ephod, a robe, a woven tunic, a turban and a sash. They are to make these sacred garments for your brother Aaron and his sons, so they may serve me as priests. [5]Have them use gold, and blue, purple and scarlet yarn, and fine linen.

The Ephod

[6]"Make the ephod of gold, and of blue, purple and scarlet yarn, and of finely twisted linen—the work of skilled hands. [7]It is to have two shoulder pieces attached to two of its corners, so it can be fastened. [8]Its skillfully woven waistband is to be like it—of one piece with the ephod and made with gold, and with blue, purple and scarlet yarn, and with finely twisted linen.

[9]"Take two onyx stones and engrave on them the names of the sons of Israel [10]in the order of their birth—six names on one stone and the remaining six on the other. [11]Engrave the names of the sons of Israel on the two stones the way a gem cutter engraves a seal. Then mount the stones in gold filigree settings [12]and fasten them on the shoulder pieces of the ephod as memorial stones for the sons of Israel. Aaron is to bear the names on his shoulders as a memorial before the LORD. [13]Make gold filigree settings [14]and two braided chains of pure gold, like a rope, and attach the chains to the settings.

113

The Breastpiece

[15]"Fashion a breastpiece for making decisions—the work of skilled hands. Make it like the ephod: of gold, and of blue, purple and scarlet yarn, and of finely twisted linen. [16]It is to be square—a span[a] long and a span wide—and folded double. [17]Then mount four rows of precious stones on it. The first row shall be carnelian, chrysolite and beryl; [18]the second row shall be turquoise, lapis lazuli and emerald; [19]the third row shall be jacinth, agate and amethyst; [20]the fourth row shall be topaz, onyx and jasper.[b] Mount them in gold filigree settings. [21]There are to be twelve stones, one for each of the names of the sons of Israel, each engraved like a seal with the name of one of the twelve tribes.

[22]"For the breastpiece make braided chains of pure gold, like a rope. [23]Make two gold rings for it and fasten them to two corners of the breastpiece. [24]Fasten the two gold chains to the rings at the corners of the breastpiece, [25]and the other ends of the chains to the two settings, attaching them to the shoulder pieces of the ephod at the front. [26]Make two gold rings and attach them to the other two corners of the breastpiece on the inside edge next to the ephod. [27]Make two more gold rings and attach them to the bottom of the shoulder pieces on the front of the ephod, close to the seam just above the waistband of the ephod. [28]The rings of the breastpiece are to be tied to the rings of the ephod with blue cord, connecting it to the waistband, so that the breastpiece will not swing out from the ephod.

[29]"Whenever Aaron enters the Holy Place, he will bear the names of the sons of Israel over his heart on the breastpiece of decision as a continuing memorial before the LORD. [30]Also put the Urim and the Thummim in the breastpiece, so they may be over Aaron's heart whenever he enters the presence of the LORD. Thus Aaron will always bear the means of making decisions for the Israelites over his heart before the LORD.

---

[a] 16 That is, about 9 inches or about 22.5 centimeters   [b] 20 The precise identification of some of these precious stones is uncertain.

Other Priestly Garments

[31]"Make the robe of the ephod entirely of blue cloth, [32]with an opening for the head in its center. There shall be a woven edge like a collar[a] around this opening, so that it will not tear. [33]Make pomegranates of blue, purple and scarlet yarn around the hem of the robe, with gold bells between them. [34]The gold bells and the pomegranates are to alternate around the hem of the robe. [35]Aaron must wear it when he ministers. The sound of the bells will be heard when he enters the Holy Place before the LORD and when he comes out, so that he will not die.

[36]"Make a plate of pure gold and engrave on it as on a seal: HOLY TO THE LORD. [37]Fasten a blue cord to it to attach it to the turban; it is to be on the front of the turban. [38]It will be on Aaron's forehead, and he will bear the guilt involved in the sacred gifts the Israelites consecrate, whatever their gifts may be. It will be on Aaron's forehead continually so that they will be acceptable to the LORD.

[39]"Weave the tunic of fine linen and make the turban of fine linen. The sash is to be the work of an embroiderer. [40]Make tunics, sashes and caps for Aaron's sons to give them dignity and honor. [41]After you put these clothes on your brother Aaron and his sons, anoint and ordain them. Consecrate them so they may serve me as priests.

[42]"Make linen undergarments as a covering for the body, reaching from the waist to the thigh. [43]Aaron and his sons must wear them whenever they enter the tent of meeting or approach the altar to minister in the Holy Place, so that they will not incur guilt and die.

"This is to be a lasting ordinance for Aaron and his descendants.

Consecration of the Priests

29 "This is what you are to do to consecrate them, so they may serve me as priests: Take a young bull and two rams without defect. [2]And from the finest wheat flour make round loaves without yeast, thick loaves without yeast and with olive oil mixed in, and thin loaves without yeast and brushed with olive oil. [3]Put them in a basket and present them in it—along with the bull and the two rams. [4]Then bring Aaron and his sons to the entrance to the tent of meeting and wash them with water. [5]Take the garments and dress Aaron with the tunic, the robe of the ephod, the ephod itself and the breastpiece. Fasten the ephod on him by its skillfully woven waistband. [6]Put the turban on his head and attach the sacred emblem to the turban. [7]Take the anointing oil and anoint him by pouring it on his head. [8]Bring his sons and dress them in tunics [9]and fasten caps on them. Then tie sashes on Aaron and his sons.[b] The priesthood is theirs by a lasting ordinance. Then you shall ordain Aaron and his sons.

[10]"Bring the bull to the front of the tent of meeting, and Aaron and his sons shall lay their hands on its head. [11]Slaughter it in the LORD's presence at the entrance to the tent of meeting. [12]Take some of the bull's blood and put it on the horns of the altar with your finger, and pour out the rest of it at the base of the altar. [13]Then take all the fat on the internal organs, the long lobe of the liver, and both kidneys with the fat on them, and burn them on the altar. [14]But burn the bull's flesh and its hide and its intestines outside the camp. It is a sin offering.[c]

[15]"Take one of the rams, and Aaron and his sons shall lay their hands on its head. [16]Slaughter it and take the blood and splash it against the sides of the altar. [17]Cut the ram into pieces and wash the internal organs and the legs, putting them with the head and the other pieces. [18]Then burn the entire ram on the altar. It is a burnt offering to the LORD, a pleasing aroma, a food offering presented to the LORD.

[19]"Take the other ram, and Aaron and his sons shall lay their hands on its head. [20]Slaughter it, take some of its blood and put it on the lobes of the right ears of Aaron and his sons, on the thumbs of their right hands, and on the big toes of their right feet. Then splash blood against the sides of the altar. [21]And take some of the blood on the altar and some of the anointing oil and sprinkle it on Aaron and his garments and on his sons and their garments. Then he and his sons and their garments will be consecrated.

[22]"Take from this ram the fat, the fat tail, the fat on the internal organs, the long lobe of the liver, both kidneys with the fat on them, and the right thigh. (This is the ram for the ordination.) [23]From the basket of bread made without yeast, which is before the LORD, take one round loaf, one thick loaf with olive oil mixed in, and one thin loaf. [24]Put all these in the hands of Aaron and his sons and have them wave them before

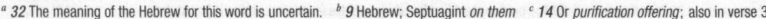

[a] 32 The meaning of the Hebrew for this word is uncertain.   [b] 9 Hebrew; Septuagint on them   [c] 14 Or purification offering; also in verse 36

the Lord as a wave offering. [25]Then take them from their hands and burn them on the altar along with the burnt offering for a pleasing aroma to the Lord, a food offering presented to the Lord. [26]After you take the breast of the ram for Aaron's ordination, wave it before the Lord as a wave offering, and it will be your share.

[27]"Consecrate those parts of the ordination ram that belong to Aaron and his sons: the breast that was waved and the thigh that was presented. [28]This is always to be the perpetual share from the Israelites for Aaron and his sons. It is the contribution the Israelites are to make to the Lord from their fellowship offerings.

[29]"Aaron's sacred garments will belong to his descendants so that they can be anointed and ordained in them. [30]The son who succeeds him as priest and comes to the tent of meeting to minister in the Holy Place is to wear them seven days.

[31]"Take the ram for the ordination and cook the meat in a sacred place. [32]At the entrance to the tent of meeting, Aaron and his sons are to eat the meat of the ram and the bread that is in the basket. [33]They are to eat these offerings by which atonement was made for their ordination and consecration. But no one else may eat them, because they are sacred. [34]And if any of the meat of the ordination ram or any bread is left over till morning, burn it up. It must not be eaten, because it is sacred.

[35]"Do for Aaron and his sons everything I have commanded you, taking seven days to ordain them. [36]Sacrifice a bull each day as a sin offering to make atonement. Purify the altar by making atonement for it, and anoint it to consecrate it. [37]For seven days make atonement for the altar and consecrate it. Then the altar will be most holy, and whatever touches it will be holy.

[38]"This is what you are to offer on the altar regularly each day: two lambs a year old. [39]Offer one in the morning and the other at twilight. [40]With the first lamb offer a tenth of an ephah[a] of the finest flour mixed with a quarter of a hin[b] of oil from pressed olives, and a quarter of a hin of wine as a drink offering. [41]Sacrifice the other lamb at twilight with the same grain offering and its drink offering as in the morning—a pleasing aroma, a food offering presented to the Lord.

[42]"For the generations to come this burnt offering is to be made regularly at the entrance to the tent of meeting before the Lord. There I will meet you and speak to you; [43]there also I will meet with the Israelites, and the place will be consecrated by my glory.

[44]"So I will consecrate the tent of meeting and the altar and will consecrate Aaron and his sons to serve me as priests. [45]Then I will dwell among the Israelites and be their God. [46]They will know that I am the Lord their God, who brought them out of Egypt so that I might dwell among them. I am the Lord their God.

115

HE IS: among us

29:44–46 God isn't some distant being watching his creation from afar. He chose to be in the midst of his people, so they could know him personally. He reminded Moses of his goal in freeing the Israelites and establishing them as a nation: *That I might dwell among them.*

Today, God doesn't dwell in a building, a temple or a palace; he lives in the hearts of his people. Through Christ's death and resurrection, he performed a mighty miracle of freeing us from sin so he could send to us his indwelling Holy Spirit. Wherever we roam, he is with us. Wherever believers gather, he is *among us.*

For the next He Is, go to p. 120.

The Altar of Incense

30 "Make an altar of acacia wood for burning incense. [2]It is to be square, a cubit long and a cubit wide, and two cubits high[c]—its horns of one piece with it. [3]Overlay the top and all the sides and the horns with pure gold, and make a gold molding around it. [4]Make two gold rings for the altar below

---

[a] *40* That is, probably about 3 1/2 pounds or about 1.5 kilograms   [b] *40* That is, probably about 1 quart or about 0.9 liter   [c] *2* That is, about 1 1/2 feet long and wide and 3 feet high or about 45 centimeters long and wide and 90 centimeters high

the molding—two on each of the opposite sides—to hold the poles used to carry it. ⁵Make the poles of acacia wood and overlay them with gold. ⁶Put the altar in front of the curtain that shields the ark of the covenant law—before the atonement cover that is over the tablets of the covenant law—where I will meet with you.

⁷"Aaron must burn fragrant incense on the altar every morning when he tends the lamps. ⁸He must burn incense again when he lights the lamps at twilight so incense will burn regularly before the Lord for the generations to come. ⁹Do not offer on this altar any other incense or any burnt offering or grain offering, and do not pour a drink offering on it. ¹⁰Once a year Aaron shall make atonement on its horns. This annual atonement must be made with the blood of the atoning sin offering*ᵃ* for the generations to come. It is most holy to the Lord."

Atonement Money

¹¹Then the Lord said to Moses, ¹²"When you take a census of the Israelites to count them, each one must pay the Lord a ransom for his life at the time he is counted. Then no plague will come on them when you number them. ¹³Each one who crosses over to those already counted is to give a half shekel,*ᵇ* according to the sanctuary shekel, which weighs twenty gerahs. This half shekel is an offering to the Lord. ¹⁴All who cross over, those twenty years old or more, are to give an offering to the Lord. ¹⁵The rich are not to give more than a half shekel and the poor are not to give less when you make the offering to the Lord to atone for your lives. ¹⁶Receive the atonement money from the Israelites and use it for the service of the tent of meeting. It will be a memorial for the Israelites before the Lord, making atonement for your lives."

Basin for Washing

¹⁷Then the Lord said to Moses, ¹⁸"Make a bronze basin, with its bronze stand, for washing. Place it between the tent of meeting and the altar, and put water in it. ¹⁹Aaron and his sons are to wash their hands and feet with water from it. ²⁰Whenever they enter the tent of meeting, they shall wash with water so that they will not die. Also, when they approach the altar to minister by presenting a food offering to the Lord, ²¹they shall wash their hands and feet so that they will not die. This is to be a lasting ordinance for Aaron and his descendants for the generations to come."

Anointing Oil

²²Then the Lord said to Moses, ²³"Take the following fine spices: 500 shekels*ᶜ* of liquid myrrh, half as much (that is, 250 shekels) of fragrant cinnamon, 250 shekels*ᵈ* of fragrant calamus, ²⁴500 shekels of cassia—all according to the sanctuary shekel—and a hin*ᵉ* of olive oil. ²⁵Make these into a sacred anointing oil, a fragrant blend, the work of a perfumer. It will be the sacred anointing oil. ²⁶Then use it to anoint the tent of meeting, the ark of the covenant law, ²⁷the table and all its articles, the lampstand and its accessories, the altar of incense, ²⁸the altar of burnt offering and all its utensils, and the basin with its stand. ²⁹You shall consecrate them so they will be most holy, and whatever touches them will be holy.

³⁰"Anoint Aaron and his sons and consecrate them so they may serve me as priests. ³¹Say to the Israelites, 'This is to be my sacred anointing oil for the generations to come. ³²Do not pour it on anyone else's body and do not make any other oil using the same formula. It is sacred, and you are to consider it sacred. ³³Whoever makes perfume like it and puts it on anyone other than a priest must be cut off from their people.'"

Incense

³⁴Then the Lord said to Moses, "Take fragrant spices—gum resin, onycha and galbanum—and pure frankincense, all in equal amounts, ³⁵and make a fragrant blend of incense, the work of a perfumer. It is to be salted and pure and sacred. ³⁶Grind some of it to powder and place it in front of the ark of the covenant law in the tent of meeting, where I will meet with you. It shall be most holy to you. ³⁷Do not make any incense with this formula for yourselves; consider it holy to the Lord. ³⁸Whoever makes incense like it to enjoy its fragrance must be cut off from their people."

116

ᵃ 10 Or *purification offering*   *ᵇ 13* That is, about 1/5 ounce or about 5.7 grams; also in verse 15   *ᶜ 23* That is, about 12 1/2 pounds or about 5.8 kilograms; also in verse 24   *ᵈ 23* That is, about 6 1/4 pounds or about 2.9 kilograms   *ᵉ 24* That is, probably about 1 gallon or about 3.6 liters

Bezalel and Oholiab

31 Then the LORD said to Moses, [2]"See, I have chosen Bezalel son of Uri, the son of Hur, of the tribe of Judah, [3]and I have filled him with the Spirit of God, with wisdom, with understanding, with knowledge and with all kinds of skills— [4]to make artistic designs for work in gold, silver and bronze, [5]to cut and set stones, to work in wood, and to engage in all kinds of crafts. [6]Moreover, I have appointed Oholiab son of Ahisamak, of the tribe of Dan, to help him. Also I have given ability to all the skilled workers to make everything I have commanded you: [7]the tent of meeting, the ark of the covenant law with the atonement cover on it, and all the other furnishings of the tent— [8]the table and its articles, the pure gold lampstand and all its accessories, the altar of incense, [9]the altar of burnt offering and all its utensils, the basin with its stand— [10]and also the woven garments, both the sacred garments for Aaron the priest and the garments for his sons when they serve as priests, [11]and the anointing oil and fragrant incense for the Holy Place. They are to make them just as I commanded you."

The Sabbath

[12]Then the LORD said to Moses, [13]"Say to the Israelites, 'You must observe my Sabbaths. This will be a sign between me and you for the generations to come, so you may know that I am the LORD, who makes you holy.

[14]"'Observe the Sabbath, because it is holy to you. Anyone who desecrates it is to be put to death; those who do any work on that day must be cut off from their people. [15]For six days work is to be done, but the seventh day is a day of sabbath rest, holy to the LORD. Whoever does any work on the Sabbath day is to be put to death. [16]The Israelites are to observe the Sabbath, celebrating it for the generations to come as a lasting covenant. [17]It will be a sign between me and the Israelites forever, for in six days the LORD made the heavens and the earth, and on the seventh day he abstained from work and rested.'"

[18]When the LORD finished speaking to Moses on Mount Sinai, he gave him the two tablets of the covenant law, the tablets of stone inscribed by the finger of God.

The Golden Calf

32 When the people saw that Moses was so long in coming down from the mountain, they gathered around Aaron and said, "Come, make us gods[a] who will go before us. As for this fellow Moses who brought us up out of Egypt, we don't know what has happened to him."

[2]Aaron answered them, "Take off the gold earrings that your wives, your sons and your daughters are wearing, and bring them to me." [3]So all the people took off their earrings and brought them to Aaron. [4]He took what they handed him and made it into an idol cast in the shape of a calf, fashioning it with a tool. Then they said, "These are your gods,[b] Israel, who brought you up out of Egypt."

[5]When Aaron saw this, he built an altar in front of the calf and announced, "Tomorrow there will be a festival to the LORD." [6]So the next day the people rose early and sacrificed burnt offerings and presented fellowship offerings. Afterward they sat down to eat and drink and got up to indulge in revelry.

[7]Then the LORD said to Moses, "Go down, because your people, whom you brought up out of Egypt, have become corrupt. [8]They have been quick to turn away from what I commanded them and have made themselves an idol cast in the shape of a calf. They have bowed down to it and sacrificed to it and have said, 'These are your gods, Israel, who brought you up out of Egypt.'

---

a 1 Or a god; also in verses 23 and 31   b 4 Or This is your god; also in verse 8

atissue:giftedness

31:1–6 In a day when many church buildings are functional (read: spare, efficient, unadorned), many of us have lost an eye for beauty in the church. We may admire the engineers and accountants, those left-brained thinkers who make the church functional, all the while forgetting the artists and creative right-brained thinkers who make the church beautiful. Isn't it refreshing to read how God handpicked talented artists and then gave them an extra dose of his Spirit's creativity to design his home? If you have the gift of creativity and an eye for design, make the Master Artist proud. Use your gifts for him.

117

⁹"I have seen these people," the LORD said to Moses, "and they are a stiff-necked people. ¹⁰Now leave me alone so that my anger may burn against them and that I may destroy them. Then I will make you into a great nation."

¹¹But Moses sought the favor of the LORD his God. "LORD," he said, "why should your anger burn against your people, whom you brought out of Egypt with great power and a mighty hand? ¹²Why should the Egyptians say, 'It was with evil intent that he brought them out, to kill them in the mountains and to wipe them off the face of the earth'? Turn from your fierce anger; relent and do not bring disaster on your people. ¹³Remember your servants Abraham, Isaac and Israel, to whom you swore by your own self: 'I will make your descendants as numerous as the stars in the sky and I will give your descendants all this land I promised them, and it will be their inheritance forever.'" ¹⁴Then the LORD relented and did not bring on his people the disaster he had threatened.

¹⁵Moses turned and went down the mountain with the two tablets of the covenant law in his hands. They were inscribed on both sides, front and back. ¹⁶The tablets were the work of God; the writing was the writing of God, engraved on the tablets.

¹⁷When Joshua heard the noise of the people shouting, he said to Moses, "There is the sound of war in the camp."

¹⁸Moses replied:

> "It is not the sound of victory,
>   it is not the sound of defeat;
>   it is the sound of singing that I hear."

¹⁹When Moses approached the camp and saw the calf and the dancing, his anger burned and he threw the tablets out of his hands, breaking them to pieces at the foot of the mountain. ²⁰And he took the calf they had made and burned it in the fire; then he ground it to powder, scattered it on the water and made the Israelites drink it.

²¹He said to Aaron, "What did these people do to you, that you led them into such great sin?"

²²"Do not be angry, my lord," Aaron answered. "You know how prone these people are to evil. ²³They said to me, 'Make us gods who will go before us. As for this fellow Moses who brought us up out of Egypt, we don't know what has happened to him.' ²⁴So I told them, 'Whoever has any gold jewelry, take it off.' Then they gave me the gold, and I threw it into the fire, and out came this calf!"

²⁵Moses saw that the people were running wild and that Aaron had let them get out of control and so become a laughingstock to their enemies. ²⁶So he stood at the entrance to the camp and said, "Whoever is for the LORD, come to me." And all the Levites rallied to him.

²⁷Then he said to them, "This is what the LORD, the God of Israel, says: 'Each man strap a sword to his side. Go back and forth through the camp from one end to the other, each killing his brother and friend and neighbor.'" ²⁸The Levites did as Moses commanded, and that day about three thousand of the people died. ²⁹Then Moses said, "You have been set apart to the LORD today, for you were against your own sons and brothers, and he has blessed you this day."

³⁰The next day Moses said to the people, "You have committed a great sin. But now I will go up to the LORD; perhaps I can make atonement for your sin."

³¹So Moses went back to the LORD and said, "Oh, what a great sin these people have committed! They have made themselves gods of gold. ³²But now, please forgive their sin—but if not, then blot me out of the book you have written."

a tissue: prayer

32:11–14 Whether it was years ago on the playground or just yesterday in the office, standing up for another person is a heroic act. The act of intercession is essentially the same thing—when we intercede for someone in prayer, we stand up for her in God's presence. We ask God to exercise his great mercy on someone who, like us, doesn't deserve it. God is perfectly just in his judgments—the Israelites who made the golden calf deserved his wrath. Yet he gives us the chance to intercede for others, just as Moses begged for mercy for his people. Who could you intercede for today?

³³The LORD replied to Moses, "Whoever has sinned against me I will blot out of my book. ³⁴Now go, lead the people to the place I spoke of, and my angel will go before you. However, when the time comes for me to punish, I will punish them for their sin."

³⁵And the LORD struck the people with a plague because of what they did with the calf Aaron had made.

33

Then the LORD said to Moses, "Leave this place, you and the people you brought up out of Egypt, and go up to the land I promised on oath to Abraham, Isaac and Jacob, saying, 'I will give it to your descendants.' ²I will send an angel before you and drive out the Canaanites, Amorites, Hittites, Perizzites, Hivites and Jebusites. ³Go up to the land flowing with milk and honey. But I will not go with you, because you are a stiff-necked people and I might destroy you on the way."

⁴When the people heard these distressing words, they began to mourn and no one put on any ornaments. ⁵For the LORD had said to Moses, "Tell the Israelites, 'You are a stiff-necked people. If I were to go with you even for a moment, I might destroy you. Now take off your ornaments and I will decide what to do with you.'" ⁶So the Israelites stripped off their ornaments at Mount Horeb.

The Tent of Meeting

⁷Now Moses used to take a tent and pitch it outside the camp some distance away, calling it the "tent of meeting." Anyone inquiring of the LORD would go to the tent of meeting outside the camp. ⁸And whenever Moses went out to the tent, all the people rose and stood at the entrances to their tents, watching Moses until he entered the tent. ⁹As Moses went into the tent, the pillar of cloud would come down and stay at the entrance, while the LORD spoke with Moses. ¹⁰Whenever the people saw the pillar of cloud standing at the entrance to the tent, they all stood and worshiped at the entrances to their tents. ¹¹The LORD would speak to Moses face to face, as one speaks to a friend. Then Moses would return to the camp, but his young aide Joshua son of Nun did not leave the tent.

Moses and the Glory of the LORD

¹²Moses said to the LORD, "You have been telling me, 'Lead these people,' but you have not let me know whom you will send with me. You have said, 'I know you by name and you have found favor with me.' ¹³If you are pleased with me, teach me your ways so I may know you and continue to find favor with you. Remember that this nation is your people."

¹⁴The LORD replied, "My Presence will go with you, and I will give you rest."

¹⁵Then Moses said to him, "If your Presence does not go with us, do not send us up from here. ¹⁶How will anyone know that you are pleased with me and with your people unless you go with us? What else will distinguish me and your people from all the other people on the face of the earth?"

¹⁷And the LORD said to Moses, "I will do the very thing you have asked, because I am pleased with you and I know you by name."

¹⁸Then Moses said, "Now show me your glory."

¹⁹And the LORD said, "I will cause all my goodness to pass in front of you, and I will proclaim my name, the LORD, in your presence. I will have mercy on whom I will have mercy, and I will have compassion on whom I will have compassion. ²⁰But," he said, "you cannot see my face, for no one may see me and live."

²¹Then the LORD said, "There is a place near me where you may stand on a rock. ²²When my glory passes by, I will put you in a cleft in the rock and cover you with my hand until I have passed by. ²³Then I will remove my hand and you will see my back; but my face must not be seen."

conversations

talking to God «» 33:11

1» How do you speak with your closest friends?

2» How do you speak with God?

3» When you talk with God, how can you balance respect and intimacy?

For more on talking to God, check the index. For the next Conversations, go to p. 122.

119

HE IS: all that

33:18—34:7 Moses yearned to see God in his fullness. But no one can see God and live. So God told his faithful servant, "I can't show you my face, but I'll show you my goodness." Then the Lord passed by Moses, proclaiming his character traits: compassionate, gracious, patient, loving, faithful, forgiving and just.

What do you need God to be? He is *all that* and more. Need sympathy? He's *compassion-ate*. Craving mercy? He's *gracious* and *forgiving*. Are you quick-tempered? He's *slow to anger*. Longing for love? He is *abounding in love*. Been mistreated? He is *just*. God is all that is good and nothing that is bad.

For the next He Is, go to p. 121.

The New Stone Tablets

34 The LORD said to Moses, "Chisel out two stone tablets like the first ones, and I will write on them the words that were on the first tablets, which you broke. [2]Be ready in the morning, and then come up on Mount Sinai. Present yourself to me there on top of the mountain. [3]No one is to come with you or be seen anywhere on the mountain; not even the flocks and herds may graze in front of the mountain."

[4]So Moses chiseled out two stone tablets like the first ones and went up Mount Sinai early in the morning, as the LORD had commanded him; and he carried the two stone tablets in his hands. [5]Then the LORD came down in the cloud and stood there with him and proclaimed his name, the LORD. [6]And he passed in front of Moses, proclaiming, "The LORD, the LORD, the compassionate and gracious God, slow to anger, abounding in love and faithfulness, [7]maintaining love to thousands, and forgiving wickedness, rebellion and sin. Yet he does not leave the guilty unpunished; he punishes the children and their children for the sin of the parents to the third and fourth generation."

[8]Moses bowed to the ground at once and worshiped. [9]"Lord," he said, "if I have found favor in your eyes, then let the Lord go with us. Although this is a stiff-necked people, forgive our wickedness and our sin, and take us as your inheritance."

[10]Then the LORD said: "I am making a covenant with you. Before all your people I will do wonders never before done in any nation in all the world. The people you live among will see how awesome is the work that I, the LORD, will do for you. [11]Obey what I command you today. I will drive out before you the Amorites, Canaanites, Hittites, Perizzites, Hivites and Jebusites. [12]Be careful not to make a treaty with those who live in the land where you are going, or they will be a snare among you. [13]Break down their altars, smash their sacred stones and cut down their Asherah poles.[a] [14]Do not worship any other god, for the LORD, whose name is Jealous, is a jealous God.

[15]"Be careful not to make a treaty with those who live in the land; for when they prostitute themselves to their gods and sacrifice to them, they will invite you and you will eat their sacrifices. [16]And when you choose some of their daughters as wives for your sons and those daughters prostitute themselves to their gods, they will lead your sons to do the same.

[17]"Do not make any idols.

[18]"Celebrate the Festival of Unleavened Bread. For seven days eat bread made without yeast, as I commanded you. Do this at the appointed time in the month of Aviv, for in that month you came out of Egypt.

[19]"The first offspring of every womb belongs to me, including all the firstborn males of your livestock, whether from herd or flock. [20]Redeem the firstborn donkey with a lamb, but if you do not redeem it, break its neck. Redeem all your firstborn sons.

"No one is to appear before me empty-handed.

---

[a] *13 That is, wooden symbols of the goddess Asherah*

HE IS: jealous

34:14 God's names reflect his personality. One of his names might surprise you—*jealous*. But God is red-hot in his affections toward his people and yearns for them when they stray. The word *jealous* in the Hebrew can also be translated "zealous."

When your affections wander from the Lord, he will zealously, jealously pursue you. He loves you so much that he is hot on your trail, seeking to woo you back to himself, his Word and his ways. And he expects you to be jealous where he's concerned. Determine to follow him wholeheartedly and safeguard his reputation.

For the next He Is, go to p. 127.

²¹ "Six days you shall labor, but on the seventh day you shall rest; even during the plowing season and harvest you must rest.

²² "Celebrate the Festival of Weeks with the firstfruits of the wheat harvest, and the Festival of Ingathering at the turn of the year.ᵃ ²³ Three times a year all your men are to appear before the Sovereign Lord, the God of Israel. ²⁴ I will drive out nations before you and enlarge your territory, and no one will covet your land when you go up three times each year to appear before the Lord your God.

²⁵ "Do not offer the blood of a sacrifice to me along with anything containing yeast, and do not let any of the sacrifice from the Passover Festival remain until morning.

²⁶ "Bring the best of the firstfruits of your soil to the house of the Lord your God.

"Do not cook a young goat in its mother's milk."

²⁷ Then the Lord said to Moses, "Write down these words, for in accordance with these words I have made a covenant with you and with Israel." ²⁸ Moses was there with the Lord forty days and forty nights without eating bread or drinking water. And he wrote on the tablets the words of the covenant—the Ten Commandments.

The Radiant Face of Moses

²⁹ When Moses came down from Mount Sinai with the two tablets of the covenant law in his hands, he was not aware that his face was radiant because he had spoken with the Lord. ³⁰ When Aaron and all the Israelites saw Moses, his face was radiant, and they were afraid to come near him. ³¹ But Moses called to them; so Aaron and all the leaders of the community came back to him, and he spoke to them. ³² Afterward all the Israelites came near him, and he gave them all the commands the Lord had given him on Mount Sinai.

³³ When Moses finished speaking to them, he put a veil over his face. ³⁴ But whenever he entered the Lord's presence to speak with him, he removed the veil until he came out. And when he came out and told the Israelites what he had been commanded, ³⁵ they saw that his face was radiant. Then Moses would put the veil back over his face until he went in to speak with the Lord.

Sabbath Regulations

35 Moses assembled the whole Israelite community and said to them, "These are the things the Lord has commanded you to do: ² For six days, work is to be done, but the seventh day shall be your holy day, a day of sabbath rest to the Lord. Whoever does any work on it is to be put to death. ³ Do not light a fire in any of your dwellings on the Sabbath day."

Materials for the Tabernacle

⁴ Moses said to the whole Israelite community, "This is what the Lord has commanded: ⁵ From what you have, take an offering for the Lord. Everyone who is willing is to bring to the Lord an offering of gold, silver and bronze; ⁶ blue, purple and scarlet yarn and fine linen; goat hair; ⁷ ram skins dyed red and

---

ᵃ *22 That is, in the autumn*

another durable leather[a]; acacia wood; [8]olive oil for the light; spices for the anointing oil and for the fragrant incense; [9]and onyx stones and other gems to be mounted on the ephod and breastpiece.

[10]"All who are skilled among you are to come and make everything the LORD has commanded: [11]the tabernacle with its tent and its covering, clasps, frames, crossbars, posts and bases; [12]the ark with its poles and the atonement cover and the curtain that shields it; [13]the table with its poles and all its articles and the bread of the Presence; [14]the lampstand that is for light with its accessories, lamps and oil for the light; [15]the altar of incense with its poles, the anointing oil and the fragrant incense; the curtain for the doorway at the entrance to the tabernacle; [16]the altar of burnt offering with its bronze grating, its poles and all its utensils; the bronze basin with its stand; [17]the curtains of the courtyard with its posts and bases, and the curtain for the entrance to the courtyard; [18]the tent pegs for the tabernacle and for the courtyard, and their ropes; [19]the woven garments worn for ministering in the sanctuary—both the sacred garments for Aaron the priest and the garments for his sons when they serve as priests."

[20]Then the whole Israelite community withdrew from Moses' presence, [21]and everyone who was willing and whose heart moved them came and brought an offering to the LORD for the work on the tent of meeting, for all its service, and for the sacred garments. [22]All who were willing, men and women alike, came and brought gold jewelry of all kinds: brooches, earrings, rings and ornaments. They all presented their gold as a wave offering to the LORD. [23]Everyone who had blue, purple or scarlet yarn or fine linen, or goat hair, ram skins dyed red or the other durable leather brought them. [24]Those presenting an offering of silver or bronze brought it as an offering to the LORD, and everyone who had acacia wood for any part of the work brought it. [25]Every skilled woman spun with her hands and brought what she had spun—blue, purple or scarlet yarn or fine linen. [26]And all the women who were willing and had the skill spun the goat hair. [27]The leaders brought onyx stones and other gems to be mounted on the ephod and breastpiece. [28]They also brought spices and olive oil for the light and for the anointing oil and for the fragrant incense. [29]All the Israelite men and women who were willing brought to the LORD freewill offerings for all the work the LORD through Moses had commanded them to do.

Bezalel and Oholiab

[30]Then Moses said to the Israelites, "See, the LORD has chosen Bezalel son of Uri, the son of Hur, of the tribe of Judah, [31]and he has filled him with the Spirit of God, with wisdom, with understanding, with knowledge and with all kinds of skills— [32]to make artistic designs for work in gold, silver and bronze, [33]to cut and set stones, to work in wood and to engage in all kinds of artistic crafts. [34]And he has given both him and Oholiab son of Ahisamak, of the tribe of Dan, the ability to teach others. [35]He has filled them with skill to do all kinds of work as engravers, designers, embroiderers in blue, purple and scarlet yarn and fine linen, and weavers—all of them skilled workers and

66 **conversations** 99

giftedness «» 35:30—36:3

1» What is the relationship between natural talent and discipline?

2» Are certain gifts better than others?

3» In what ways are you using your gifts for the Giver of gifts?

For more on **giftedness**, check the index.
For the next Conversations, go to p. 134.

36 designers. [1]So Bezalel, Oholiab and every skilled person to whom the LORD has given skill and ability to know how to carry out all the work of constructing the sanctuary are to do the work just as the LORD has commanded."

[2]Then Moses summoned Bezalel and Oholiab and every skilled person to whom the LORD had given ability and who was willing to come and do the work. [3]They received from Moses all the offerings the Israelites had brought to carry out the work of constructing the sanctuary. And the people continued to bring freewill offerings morning after morning. [4]So all the skilled workers who were doing all the work

122

---

[a] 7 Possibly the hides of dugongs; also in verse 23

on the sanctuary left what they were doing [5]and said to Moses, "The people are bringing more than enough for doing the work the LORD commanded to be done."

[6]Then Moses gave an order and they sent this word throughout the camp: "No man or woman is to make anything else as an offering for the sanctuary." And so the people were restrained from bringing more, [7]because what they already had was more than enough to do all the work.

The Tabernacle

[8]All those who were skilled among the workers made the tabernacle with ten curtains of finely twisted linen and blue, purple and scarlet yarn, with cherubim worked into them by expert hands. [9]All the curtains were the same size—twenty-eight cubits long and four cubits wide.[a] [10]They joined five of the curtains together and did the same with the other five. [11]Then they made loops of blue material along the edge of the end curtain in one set, and the same was done with the end curtain in the other set. [12]They also made fifty loops on one curtain and fifty loops on the end curtain of the other set, with the loops opposite each other. [13]Then they made fifty gold clasps and used them to fasten the two sets of curtains together so that the tabernacle was a unit.

[14]They made curtains of goat hair for the tent over the tabernacle—eleven altogether. [15]All eleven curtains were the same size—thirty cubits long and four cubits wide.[b] [16]They joined five of the curtains into one set and the other six into another set. [17]Then they made fifty loops along the edge of the end curtain in one set and also along the edge of the end curtain in the other set. [18]They made fifty bronze clasps to fasten the tent together as a unit. [19]Then they made for the tent a covering of ram skins dyed red, and over that a covering of the other durable leather.[c]

[20]They made upright frames of acacia wood for the tabernacle. [21]Each frame was ten cubits long and a cubit and a half wide,[d] [22]with two projections set parallel to each other. They made all the frames of the tabernacle in this way. [23]They made twenty frames for the south side of the tabernacle [24]and made forty silver bases to go under them—two bases for each frame, one under each projection. [25]For the other side, the north side of the tabernacle, they made twenty frames [26]and forty silver bases—two under each frame. [27]They made six frames for the far end, that is, the west end of the tabernacle, [28]and two frames were made for the corners of the tabernacle at the far end. [29]At these two corners the frames were double from the bottom all the way to the top and fitted into a single ring; both were made alike. [30]So there were eight frames and sixteen silver bases—two under each frame.

[31]They also made crossbars of acacia wood: five for the frames on one side of the tabernacle, [32]five for those on the other side, and five for the frames on the west, at the far end of the tabernacle. [33]They made the center crossbar so that it extended from end to end at the middle of the frames. [34]They overlaid the frames with gold and made gold rings to hold the crossbars. They also overlaid the crossbars with gold.

[35]They made the curtain of blue, purple and scarlet yarn and finely twisted linen, with cherubim worked into it by expert hands. [36]They made four posts of acacia wood for it and overlaid them with gold. They made gold hooks for them and cast their four silver bases. [37]For the entrance to the tent they made a curtain of blue, purple and scarlet yarn and finely twisted linen—the work of an embroiderer; [38]and they made five posts with hooks for them. They overlaid the tops of the posts and their bands with gold and made their five bases of bronze.

The Ark

37 Bezalel made the ark of acacia wood—two and a half cubits long, a cubit and a half wide, and a cubit and a half high.[e] [2]He overlaid it with pure gold, both inside and out, and made a gold molding around it. [3]He cast four gold rings for it and fastened them to its four feet, with two rings on one side and two rings on the other. [4]Then he made poles of acacia wood and overlaid them with gold. [5]And he inserted the poles into the rings on the sides of the ark to carry it.

[6]He made the atonement cover of pure gold—two and a half cubits long and a cubit and a half wide. [7]Then he made two cherubim out of hammered gold at the ends of the cover. [8]He made one cherub on one end and the second cherub on the other; at the two ends he made them of one piece with the cover.

⁹The cherubim had their wings spread upward, overshadowing the cover with them. The cherubim faced each other, looking toward the cover.

The Table

¹⁰They^a made the table of acacia wood—two cubits long, a cubit wide and a cubit and a half high.^b ¹¹Then they overlaid it with pure gold and made a gold molding around it. ¹²They also made around it a rim a handbreadth^c wide and put a gold molding on the rim. ¹³They cast four gold rings for the table and fastened them to the four corners, where the four legs were. ¹⁴The rings were put close to the rim to hold the poles used in carrying the table. ¹⁵The poles for carrying the table were made of acacia wood and were overlaid with gold. ¹⁶And they made from pure gold the articles for the table—its plates and dishes and bowls and its pitchers for the pouring out of drink offerings.

The Lampstand

¹⁷They made the lampstand of pure gold. They hammered out its base and shaft, and made its flower-like cups, buds and blossoms of one piece with them. ¹⁸Six branches extended from the sides of the lampstand—three on one side and three on the other. ¹⁹Three cups shaped like almond flowers with buds and blossoms were on one branch, three on the next branch and the same for all six branches extending from the lampstand. ²⁰And on the lampstand were four cups shaped like almond flowers with buds and blossoms. ²¹One bud was under the first pair of branches extending from the lampstand, a second bud under the second pair, and a third bud under the third pair—six branches in all. ²²The buds and the branches were all of one piece with the lampstand, hammered out of pure gold.

²³They made its seven lamps, as well as its wick trimmers and trays, of pure gold. ²⁴They made the lampstand and all its accessories from one talent^d of pure gold.

The Altar of Incense

²⁵They made the altar of incense out of acacia wood. It was square, a cubit long and a cubit wide and two cubits high^e—its horns of one piece with it. ²⁶They overlaid the top and all the sides and the horns with pure gold, and made a gold molding around it. ²⁷They made two gold rings below the molding—two on each of the opposite sides—to hold the poles used to carry it. ²⁸They made the poles of acacia wood and overlaid them with gold.

²⁹They also made the sacred anointing oil and the pure, fragrant incense—the work of a perfumer.

The Altar of Burnt Offering

38 They^f built the altar of burnt offering of acacia wood, three cubits^g high; it was square, five cubits long and five cubits wide.^h ²They made a horn at each of the four corners, so that the horns and the altar were of one piece, and they overlaid the altar with bronze. ³They made all its utensils of bronze—its pots, shovels, sprinkling bowls, meat forks and firepans. ⁴They made a grating for the altar, a bronze network, to be under its ledge, halfway up the altar. ⁵They cast bronze rings to hold the poles for the four corners of the bronze grating. ⁶They made the poles of acacia wood and overlaid them with bronze. ⁷They inserted the poles into the rings so they would be on the sides of the altar for carrying it. They made it hollow, out of boards.

The Basin for Washing

⁸They made the bronze basin and its bronze stand from the mirrors of the women who served at the entrance to the tent of meeting.

The Courtyard

⁹Next they made the courtyard. The south side was a hundred cubitsⁱ long and had curtains of finely twisted linen, ¹⁰with twenty posts and twenty bronze bases, and with silver hooks and bands on the

124

^a 10 Or He; also in verses 11-29   ^b 10 That is, about 3 feet long, 1 1/2 feet wide and 2 1/4 feet high or about 90 centimeters long, 45 centimeters wide and 67 centimeters high   ^c 12 That is, about 3 inches or about 7.5 centimeters   ^d 24 That is, about 75 pounds or about 34 kilograms   ^e 25 That is, about 1 1/2 feet long and wide and 3 feet high or about 45 centimeters long and wide and 90 centimeters high   ^f 1 Or He; also in verses 2-9   ^g 1 That is, about 4 1/2 feet or about 1.4 meters   ^h 1 That is, about 7 1/2 feet or about 2.3 meters long and wide   ⁱ 9 That is, about 150 feet or about 45 meters

posts. ¹¹The north side was also a hundred cubits long and had twenty posts and twenty bronze bases, with silver hooks and bands on the posts.

¹²The west end was fifty cubits*a* wide and had curtains, with ten posts and ten bases, with silver hooks and bands on the posts. ¹³The east end, toward the sunrise, was also fifty cubits wide. ¹⁴Curtains fifteen cubits*b* long were on one side of the entrance, with three posts and three bases, ¹⁵and curtains fifteen cubits long were on the other side of the entrance to the courtyard, with three posts and three bases. ¹⁶All the curtains around the courtyard were of finely twisted linen. ¹⁷The bases for the posts were bronze. The hooks and bands on the posts were silver, and their tops were overlaid with silver; so all the posts of the courtyard had silver bands.

¹⁸The curtain for the entrance to the courtyard was of blue, purple and scarlet yarn and finely twisted linen—the work of an embroiderer. It was twenty cubits*c* long and, like the curtains of the courtyard, five cubits*d* high, ¹⁹with four posts and four bronze bases. Their hooks and bands were silver, and their tops were overlaid with silver. ²⁰All the tent pegs of the tabernacle and of the surrounding courtyard were bronze.

The Materials Used

²¹These are the amounts of the materials used for the tabernacle, the tabernacle of the covenant law, which were recorded at Moses' command by the Levites under the direction of Ithamar son of Aaron, the priest. ²²(Bezalel son of Uri, the son of Hur, of the tribe of Judah, made everything the Lord commanded Moses; ²³with him was Oholiab son of Ahisamak, of the tribe of Dan—an engraver and designer, and an embroiderer in blue, purple and scarlet yarn and fine linen.) ²⁴The total amount of the gold from the wave offering used for all the work on the sanctuary was 29 talents and 730 shekels,*e* according to the sanctuary shekel.

²⁵The silver obtained from those of the community who were counted in the census was 100 talents*f* and 1,775 shekels,*g* according to the sanctuary shekel— ²⁶one beka per person, that is, half a shekel,*h* according to the sanctuary shekel, from everyone who had crossed over to those counted, twenty years old or more, a total of 603,550 men. ²⁷The 100 talents of silver were used to cast the bases for the sanctuary and for the curtain—100 bases from the 100 talents, one talent for each base. ²⁸They used the 1,775 shekels to make the hooks for the posts, to overlay the tops of the posts, and to make their bands.

²⁹The bronze from the wave offering was 70 talents and 2,400 shekels.*i* ³⁰They used it to make the bases for the entrance to the tent of meeting, the bronze altar with its bronze grating and all its utensils, ³¹the bases for the surrounding courtyard and those for its entrance and all the tent pegs for the tabernacle and those for the surrounding courtyard.

The Priestly Garments

39 From the blue, purple and scarlet yarn they made woven garments for ministering in the sanctuary. They also made sacred garments for Aaron, as the Lord commanded Moses.

The Ephod

²They*j* made the ephod of gold, and of blue, purple and scarlet yarn, and of finely twisted linen. ³They hammered out thin sheets of gold and cut strands to be worked into the blue, purple and scarlet yarn and fine linen—the work of skilled hands. ⁴They made shoulder pieces for the ephod, which were attached to two of its corners, so it could be fastened. ⁵Its skillfully woven waistband was like it—of one piece with the ephod and made with gold, and with blue, purple and scarlet yarn, and with finely twisted linen, as the Lord commanded Moses.

⁶They mounted the onyx stones in gold filigree settings and engraved them like a seal with the names of the sons of Israel. ⁷Then they fastened them on the shoulder pieces of the ephod as memorial stones for the sons of Israel, as the Lord commanded Moses.

125

---

a 12 That is, about 75 feet or about 22.5 meters *b 14* That is, about 22 feet or about 6.8 meters *c 18* That is, about 30 feet or about 9 meters *d 18* That is, about 7 1/2 feet or about 2.3 meters *e 24* The weight of the gold was a little over a ton or about 1 metric ton. *f 25* That is, about 3 3/4 tons or about 3.4 metric tons; also in verse 27 *g 25* That is, about 45 pounds or about 20 kilograms; also in verse 28 *h 26* That is, about 1/5 ounce or about 5.7 grams *i 29* The weight of the bronze was about 2 1/2 tons or about 2.4 metric tons. *j 2* Or *He;* also in verses 7, 8 and 22

The Breastpiece

⁸They fashioned the breastpiece—the work of a skilled craftsman. They made it like the ephod: of gold, and of blue, purple and scarlet yarn, and of finely twisted linen. ⁹It was square—a span*ᵃ* long and a span wide—and folded double. ¹⁰Then they mounted four rows of precious stones on it. The first row was carnelian, chrysolite and beryl; ¹¹the second row was turquoise, lapis lazuli and emerald; ¹²the third row was jacinth, agate and amethyst; ¹³the fourth row was topaz, onyx and jasper.*ᵇ* They were mounted in gold filigree settings. ¹⁴There were twelve stones, one for each of the names of the sons of Israel, each engraved like a seal with the name of one of the twelve tribes.

¹⁵For the breastpiece they made braided chains of pure gold, like a rope. ¹⁶They made two gold filigree settings and two gold rings, and fastened the rings to two of the corners of the breastpiece. ¹⁷They fastened the two gold chains to the rings at the corners of the breastpiece, ¹⁸and the other ends of the chains to the two settings, attaching them to the shoulder pieces of the ephod at the front. ¹⁹They made two gold rings and attached them to the other two corners of the breastpiece on the inside edge next to the ephod. ²⁰Then they made two more gold rings and attached them to the bottom of the shoulder pieces on the front of the ephod, close to the seam just above the waistband of the ephod. ²¹They tied the rings of the breastpiece to the rings of the ephod with blue cord, connecting it to the waistband so that the breastpiece would not swing out from the ephod—as the Lord commanded Moses.

Other Priestly Garments

²²They made the robe of the ephod entirely of blue cloth—the work of a weaver— ²³with an opening in the center of the robe like the opening of a collar,*ᶜ* and a band around this opening, so that it would not tear. ²⁴They made pomegranates of blue, purple and scarlet yarn and finely twisted linen around the hem of the robe. ²⁵And they made bells of pure gold and attached them around the hem between the pomegranates. ²⁶The bells and pomegranates alternated around the hem of the robe to be worn for ministering, as the Lord commanded Moses.

²⁷For Aaron and his sons, they made tunics of fine linen—the work of a weaver— ²⁸and the turban of fine linen, the linen caps and the undergarments of finely twisted linen. ²⁹The sash was of finely twisted linen and blue, purple and scarlet yarn—the work of an embroiderer—as the Lord commanded Moses.

³⁰They made the plate, the sacred emblem, out of pure gold and engraved on it, like an inscription on a seal: HOLY TO THE LORD. ³¹Then they fastened a blue cord to it to attach it to the turban, as the Lord commanded Moses.

Moses Inspects the Tabernacle

³²So all the work on the tabernacle, the tent of meeting, was completed. The Israelites did everything just as the Lord commanded Moses. ³³Then they brought the tabernacle to Moses: the tent and all its furnishings, its clasps, frames, crossbars, posts and bases; ³⁴the covering of ram skins dyed red and the covering of another durable leather*ᵈ* and the shielding curtain; ³⁵the ark of the covenant law with its poles and the atonement cover; ³⁶the table with all its articles and the bread of the Presence; ³⁷the pure gold lampstand with its row of lamps and all its accessories, and the oil for the light; ³⁸the gold altar, the anointing oil, the fragrant incense, and the curtain for the entrance to the tent; ³⁹the bronze altar with its bronze grating, its poles and all its utensils; the basin with its stand; ⁴⁰the curtains of the courtyard with its posts and bases, and the curtain for the entrance to the courtyard; the ropes and tent pegs for the courtyard; all the furnishings for the tabernacle, the tent of meeting; ⁴¹and the woven garments worn for ministering in the sanctuary, both the sacred garments for Aaron the priest and the garments for his sons when serving as priests.

⁴²The Israelites had done all the work just as the Lord had commanded Moses. ⁴³Moses inspected the work and saw that they had done it just as the Lord had commanded. So Moses blessed them.

ᵃ 9 That is, about 9 inches or about 22.5 centimeters   *ᵇ 13* The precise identification of some of these precious stones is uncertain.   *ᶜ 23* The meaning of the Hebrew for this word is uncertain.   *ᵈ 34* Possibly the hides of dugongs

Setting Up the Tabernacle

40 Then the LORD said to Moses: ²"Set up the tabernacle, the tent of meeting, on the first day of the first month. ³Place the ark of the covenant law in it and shield the ark with the curtain. ⁴Bring in the table and set out what belongs on it. Then bring in the lampstand and set up its lamps. ⁵Place the gold altar of incense in front of the ark of the covenant law and put the curtain at the entrance to the tabernacle.

⁶"Place the altar of burnt offering in front of the entrance to the tabernacle, the tent of meeting; ⁷place the basin between the tent of meeting and the altar and put water in it. ⁸Set up the courtyard around it and put the curtain at the entrance to the courtyard.

⁹"Take the anointing oil and anoint the tabernacle and everything in it; consecrate it and all its furnishings, and it will be holy. ¹⁰Then anoint the altar of burnt offering and all its utensils; consecrate the altar, and it will be most holy. ¹¹Anoint the basin and its stand and consecrate them.

¹²"Bring Aaron and his sons to the entrance to the tent of meeting and wash them with water. ¹³Then dress Aaron in the sacred garments, anoint him and consecrate him so he may serve me as priest. ¹⁴Bring his sons and dress them in tunics. ¹⁵Anoint them just as you anointed their father, so they may serve me as priests. Their anointing will be to a priesthood that will continue throughout their generations." ¹⁶Moses did everything just as the LORD commanded him.

¹⁷So the tabernacle was set up on the first day of the first month in the second year. ¹⁸When Moses set up the tabernacle, he put the bases in place, erected the frames, inserted the crossbars and set up the posts. ¹⁹Then he spread the tent over the tabernacle and put the covering over the tent, as the LORD commanded him.

²⁰He took the tablets of the covenant law and placed them in the ark, attached the poles to the ark and put the atonement cover over it. ²¹Then he brought the ark into the tabernacle and hung the shielding curtain and shielded the ark of the covenant law, as the LORD commanded him.

²²Moses placed the table in the tent of meeting on the north side of the tabernacle outside the curtain ²³and set out the bread on it before the LORD, as the LORD commanded him.

²⁴He placed the lampstand in the tent of meeting opposite the table on the south side of the tabernacle ²⁵and set up the lamps before the LORD, as the LORD commanded him.

²⁶Moses placed the gold altar in the tent of meeting in front of the curtain ²⁷and burned fragrant incense on it, as the LORD commanded him.

²⁸Then he put up the curtain at the entrance to the tabernacle. ²⁹He set the altar of burnt offering near the entrance to the tabernacle, the tent of meeting, and offered on it burnt offerings and grain offerings, as the LORD commanded him.

³⁰He placed the basin between the tent of meeting and the altar and put water in it for washing, ³¹and Moses and Aaron and his sons used it to wash their hands and feet. ³²They washed whenever they entered the tent of meeting or approached the altar, as the LORD commanded Moses.

HE IS: glorious

40:34–38 God designed the tent of meeting (the tabernacle) in exact detail. When it was completed, the cloud of his presence settled upon it and his glory filled it. God's glory rested on an earthly building for all to see.

Before time began, God planned for Jesus to "tabernacle" among humans (see John 1:14). God's glory filled a human body when Jesus was born. Just as the Israelites fixed their eyes on God's glory cloud for their cues of when to stay and when to go, so we should fix our eyes on Jesus to guide us through the wilderness of this world. He is *glorious*, and he'll shine through our darkness.

For the next He Is, go to p. 139.

127

³³Then Moses set up the courtyard around the tabernacle and altar and put up the curtain at the entrance to the courtyard. And so Moses finished the work.

The Glory of the LORD

³⁴Then the cloud covered the tent of meeting, and the glory of the LORD filled the tabernacle. ³⁵Moses could not enter the tent of meeting because the cloud had settled on it, and the glory of the LORD filled the tabernacle.

³⁶In all the travels of the Israelites, whenever the cloud lifted from above the tabernacle, they would set out; ³⁷but if the cloud did not lift, they did not set out—until the day it lifted. ³⁸So the cloud of the LORD was over the tabernacle by day, and fire was in the cloud by night, in the sight of all the house of Israel during all their travels.

Instead of bringing their checkbooks to church, what did the Israelites put in the offering plate? »» (1:2–3)

Does God count the sins we unintentionally commit? »» (4:1–3,13–14,22–23,27–28)

What if your pastor had this job description? »» (8:1 – 9:24)

Why is God so serious about holiness? »» (10:1–7)

What did each of the goats on the Day of Atonement represent? »» (16:1–34)

Why all the blood? Why not require something less messy as a sacrifice for sins? »» (17:1–12)

How was this mega-church of more than two million people to worship together? »» (23:1–44)

How did Israel essentially "tear up their credit cards" once every 50 years? »» (25:8–10,25–28,39–41)

leviticus

129

AUTHOR
Moses.

AUDIENCE
The people of Israel.

DATE
During the 1400s B.C., while the Israelites were traveling in the desert.

SETTING
At the foot of Mount Sinai God introduces laws for living.

VERSE TO REMEMBER
"I am the LORD, who brought you up out of Egypt to be your God; therefore be holy, because I am holy." (11:45)

THEME TO CONSIDER
Holiness is a forgotten virtue in our culture. This book reminds us of the important fact that those who belong to God must be different. Although we may not be obligated to keep the rituals and rules listed in Leviticus, we still must be holy.

The Burnt Offering

1 The LORD called to Moses and spoke to him from the tent of meeting. He said, [2]"Speak to the Israelites and say to them: 'When you bring an offering to the LORD, bring as your offering an animal from either the herd or the flock.

[3]"'If the offering is a burnt offering from the herd, you are to offer a male without defect. You must present it at the entrance to the tent of meeting so that you may be acceptable to the LORD. [4]You are to lay your hand on the head of the burnt offering, and it will be accepted on your behalf to make atonement for you. [5]You are to slaughter the young bull before the LORD, and then Aaron's sons the priests shall bring the blood and splash it against the sides of the altar at the entrance to the tent of meeting. [6]You are to skin the burnt offering and cut it into pieces. [7]The sons of Aaron the priest are to put fire on the altar and arrange wood on the fire. [8]Then Aaron's sons the priests shall arrange the pieces, including the head and the fat, on the wood that is burning on the altar. [9]You are to wash the internal organs and the legs with water, and the priest is to burn all of it on the altar. It is a burnt offering, a food offering, an aroma pleasing to the LORD.

[10]"'If the offering is a burnt offering from the flock, from either the sheep or the goats, you are to offer a male without defect. [11]You are to slaughter it at the north side of the altar before the LORD, and Aaron's sons the priests shall splash its blood against the sides of the altar. [12]You are to cut it into pieces, and the priest shall arrange them, including the head and the fat, on the wood that is burning on the altar. [13]You are to wash the internal organs and the legs with water, and the priest is to bring all of them and burn them on the altar. It is a burnt offering, a food offering, an aroma pleasing to the LORD.

[14]"'If the offering to the LORD is a burnt offering of birds, you are to offer a dove or a young pigeon. [15]The priest shall bring it to the altar, wring off the head and burn it on the altar; its blood shall be drained out on the side of the altar. [16]He is to remove the crop and the feathers[a] and throw them down east of the altar where the ashes are. [17]He shall tear it open by the wings, not dividing it completely, and then the priest shall burn it on the wood that is burning on the altar. It is a burnt offering, a food offering, an aroma pleasing to the LORD.

The Grain Offering

2 "'When anyone brings a grain offering to the LORD, your offering is to be of the finest flour. You are to pour olive oil on it, put incense on it [2]and take it to Aaron's sons the priests. The priest shall take a handful of the flour and oil, together with all the incense, and burn this as a memorial[b] portion on the altar, a food offering, an aroma pleasing to the LORD. [3]The rest of the grain offering belongs to Aaron and his sons; it is a most holy part of the food offering presented to the LORD.

[4]"'If you bring a grain offering baked in an oven, it is to consist of the finest flour: either thick loaves made without yeast and with olive oil mixed in or thin loaves made without yeast and brushed with olive oil. [5]If your grain offering is prepared on a griddle, it is to be made of the finest flour mixed with oil, and without yeast. [6]Crumble it and pour oil on it; it is a grain offering. [7]If your grain offering is cooked in a pan, it is to be made of the finest flour and some olive oil. [8]Bring the grain offering made of these things

---

aussie:God's forgiveness

1:3–9 God's forgiveness is freely offered to us. However, God's forgiveness is not free. For the Israelites, the penalty for sin required an animal to be killed in a person's place. To symbolize the transfer of blame, the offender laid a hand on the animal's head just before taking its life. What a visual reminder of the cost of forgiveness! Because we don't have this kind of reminder, we may forget the agonizing price of our forgiveness— the sinless Lamb killed in our place (Jesus). This is why Jesus admonished us to *remember* him (see Luke 22:19–20). *Remember* the price of your forgiveness. *Remember* him.

---

[a] 16 Or *crop with its contents*; the meaning of the Hebrew for this word is uncertain.   [b] 2 Or *representative*; also in verses 9 and 16

to the Lord; present it to the priest, who shall take it to the altar. ⁹He shall take out the memorial por-tion from the grain offering and burn it on the altar as a food offering, an aroma pleasing to the Lord. ¹⁰The rest of the grain offering belongs to Aaron and his sons; it is a most holy part of the food offerings presented to the Lord.

¹¹"'Every grain offering you bring to the Lord must be made without yeast, for you are not to burn any yeast or honey in a food offering presented to the Lord. ¹²You may bring them to the Lord as an offering of the firstfruits, but they are not to be offered on the altar as a pleasing aroma. ¹³Season all your grain offerings with salt. Do not leave the salt of the covenant of your God out of your grain offerings; add salt to all your offerings.

¹⁴"'If you bring a grain offering of firstfruits to the Lord, offer crushed heads of new grain roasted in the fire. ¹⁵Put oil and incense on it; it is a grain offering. ¹⁶The priest shall burn the memorial portion of the crushed grain and the oil, together with all the incense, as a food offering presented to the Lord.

The Fellowship Offering

3 "'If your offering is a fellowship offering, and you offer an animal from the herd, whether male or female, you are to present before the Lord an animal without defect. ²You are to lay your hand on the head of your offering and slaughter it at the entrance to the tent of meeting. Then Aaron's sons the priests shall splash the blood against the sides of the altar. ³From the fellowship offering you are to bring a food offering to the Lord: the internal organs and all the fat that is connected to them, ⁴both kidneys with the fat on them near the loins, and the long lobe of the liver, which you will remove with the kid-neys. ⁵Then Aaron's sons are to burn it on the altar on top of the burnt offering that is lying on the burn-ing wood; it is a food offering, an aroma pleasing to the Lord.

⁶"'If you offer an animal from the flock as a fellowship offering to the Lord, you are to offer a male or female without defect. ⁷If you offer a lamb, you are to present it before the Lord, ⁸lay your hand on its head and slaughter it in front of the tent of meeting. Then Aaron's sons shall splash its blood against the sides of the altar. ⁹From the fellowship offering you are to bring a food offering to the Lord: its fat, the entire fat tail cut off close to the backbone, the internal organs and all the fat that is connected to them, ¹⁰both kidneys with the fat on them near the loins, and the long lobe of the liver, which you will remove with the kidneys. ¹¹The priest shall burn them on the altar as a food offering presented to the Lord.

¹²"'If your offering is a goat, you are to present it before the Lord, ¹³lay your hand on its head and slaughter it in front of the tent of meeting. Then Aaron's sons shall splash its blood against the sides of the altar. ¹⁴From what you offer you are to present this food offering to the Lord: the internal organs and all the fat that is connected to them, ¹⁵both kidneys with the fat on them near the loins, and the long lobe of the liver, which you will remove with the kidneys. ¹⁶The priest shall burn them on the altar as a food offering, a pleasing aroma. All the fat is the Lord's.

¹⁷"'This is a lasting ordinance for the generations to come, wherever you live: You must not eat any fat or any blood.'"

The Sin Offering

4 The Lord said to Moses, ²"Say to the Israelites: 'When anyone sins unintentionally and does what is forbidden in any of the Lord's commands—

³"'If the anointed priest sins, bringing guilt on the people, he must bring to the Lord a young bull without defect as a sin offering*ᵃ* for the sin he has committed. ⁴He is to present the bull at the entrance to the tent of meeting before the Lord. He is to lay his hand on its head and slaughter it there before the Lord. ⁵Then the anointed priest shall take some of the bull's blood and carry it into the tent of meeting. ⁶He is to dip his finger into the blood and sprinkle some of it seven times before the Lord, in front of the curtain of the sanctuary. ⁷The priest shall then put some of the blood on the horns of the altar of fragrant incense that is before the Lord in the tent of meeting. The rest of the bull's blood he shall pour out at the base of the altar of burnt offering at the entrance to the tent of meeting. ⁸He shall remove all the fat from the bull of the sin offering—all the fat that is connected to the internal organs, ⁹both kidneys with the

ᵃ 3 Or purification offering; here and throughout this chapter

myth# 10

"MY MONEY IS MY MONEY."

4—*That's the number of credit cards I maxed out by the time I turned thirty.*

18—*That's the average annual percentage rate I never bothered to check when I applied for credit.*

441—*That's the number of payments it would take to pay off what I owe in unsecured debt.*

36—*Believe it or not—is 441 months translated into years.*

And 26,615.17—*That's the total additional interest I'd owe at the end of that time, assuming I wasn't already in jail for credit fraud, hiding as a fugitive in France or on the streets panhandling for money to make my minimum payments! Oh, I believed my money was my money alright. And so was my debt—I had only myself to blame.*

As a pharmaceutical sales rep, I was amazed when I received my first commission check. After a few more checks rolled in, I signed a lease on a fully loaded SUV. I don't know why. My husband earns a good living as an engineer, so my money became the family's play-money. We took a trip to Hawaii for the honeymoon we'd never had. The kids enjoyed the best Christmas ever. I'd never had so much fun spending money—in fact, I'd never had so much money to spend. Eventually, however, the money I was spending was no longer my money. It actually belonged to creditors.

Soon, every penny that came through my hands was going out the door to keep the bills at bay. At one point, I was tossing the credit bills in the air each month—whichever ones landed face-up got paid. I ignored the rest and used Caller ID to block calls from creditors threatening to sue. I didn't tell my husband how bad it really was. I wanted him to think I could handle it. I believed if I manipulated, juggled and plotted enough, eventually I could.

—*Elise*

THIS ISN'T JUST another reminder that "it's all God's money." Of course, money does originate from God's hand. However, practically speaking, he has put you in charge of a certain amount of it. In that sense, your money *is* your money to manage. And God expects you to use it well and not to abuse it. The Old Testament tells how the Israelites gave offerings to God out of the abundance he'd given them. In one of Jesus' parables in the New Testament, he likened spiritual faithfulness to being a responsible manager or steward of funds (see Matthew 25:14–30). In this story, only two of three managers graduated from God's Business School with their MBAs. (The other flunked out.)

One of the prerequisite "courses" in this prestigious university underlines the principle that money is for managing first and spending second. The difference between the two is the difference between the financially foolish and financially confident woman.

- The foolish woman hears only the mythical qualities behind the idea of having her own money. She imagines it means fine living and gratifying her indulgences.

So, she lives beyond her means.

She confuses desires with needs.

She loses sleep over unpaid debts.

She wonders where all the fun associated with having her own money has gone.

- In contrast, the financially confident woman recognizes God as the source of her money.

She has a sound plan for the amount divinely allotted to her.

She knows she cannot afford to keep all her money, so she gives generously.

Out of what is left, she pays herself first, saving aggressively.

Then, she is free to spend her money within the boundaries she has established.

She knows the secret to enjoying life's pleasures is not living on credit, paycheck to paycheck. Rather,

she is in control of her money, not the other way around. The financially confident woman foregoes temptations to spend her money today, and by doing so she manages to be good to herself tomorrow.

When we graduate from God's Business School, we will have our MBA in Biblical financial principles—rules to live by that honor us as intelligent women who are respected managers of God's money.

133

"Approximately two-thirds of Jesus' parables are about money and financial management."

"SO THEN, WE WILL ALL GIVE an account of OURSELVES TO GOD."

ROMANS 14:12

SEE ALSO

Deuteronomy 8:10–18

1 Chronicles 29:10–14

Romans 13:8

For more on **Money**, check the index.

fat on them near the loins, and the long lobe of the liver, which he will remove with the kidneys— [10]just as the fat is removed from the ox[a] sacrificed as a fellowship offering. Then the priest shall burn them on the altar of burnt offering. [11]But the hide of the bull and all its flesh, as well as the head and legs, the internal organs and the intestines— [12]that is, all the rest of the bull—he must take outside the camp to a place ceremonially clean, where the ashes are thrown, and burn it there in a wood fire on the ash heap.

[13]"'If the whole Israelite community sins unintentionally and does what is forbidden in any of the Lord's commands, even though the community is unaware of the matter, when they realize their guilt [14]and the sin they committed becomes known, the assembly must bring a young bull as a sin offering and present it before the tent of meeting. [15]The elders of the community are to lay their hands on the bull's head before the Lord, and the bull shall be slaughtered before the Lord. [16]Then the anointed priest is to take some of the bull's blood into the tent of meeting. [17]He shall dip his finger into the blood and sprinkle it before the Lord seven times in front of the curtain. [18]He is to put some of the blood on the horns of the altar that is before the Lord in the tent of meeting. The rest of the blood he shall pour out at the base of the altar of burnt offering at the entrance to the tent of meeting. [19]He shall remove all the fat from it and burn it on the altar, [20]and do with this bull just as he did with the bull for the sin offering. In this way the priest will make atonement for them, and they will be forgiven. [21]Then he shall take the bull outside the camp and burn it as he burned the first bull. This is the sin offering for the community.

[22]"'When a leader sins unintentionally and does what is forbidden in any of the commands of the Lord his God, when he realizes his guilt [23]and the sin he has committed becomes known, he must bring as his offering a male goat without defect. [24]He is to lay his hand on the goat's head and slaughter it at the place where the burnt offering is slaughtered before the Lord. It is a sin offering. [25]Then the priest shall take some of the blood of the sin offering with his finger and put it on the horns of the altar of burnt offering and pour out the rest of the blood at the base of the altar. [26]He shall burn all the fat on the altar as he burned the fat of the fellowship offering. In this way the priest will make atonement for the leader's sin, and he will be forgiven.

[27]"'If any member of the community sins unintentionally and does what is forbidden in any of the Lord's commands, when they realize their guilt [28]and the sin they have committed becomes known, they must bring as their offering for the sin they committed a female goat without defect. [29]They are to lay their hand on the head of the sin offering and slaughter it at the place of the burnt offering. [30]Then the priest is to take some of the blood with his finger and put it on the horns of the altar of burnt offering and pour out the rest of the blood at the base of the altar. [31]They shall remove all the fat, just as the fat is removed from the fellowship offering, and the priest shall burn it on the altar as an aroma pleasing to the Lord. In this way the priest will make atonement for them, and they will be forgiven.

[32]"'If they bring a lamb as their sin offering, they are to bring a female without defect. [33]They are to lay their hand on its head and slaughter it for a sin offering at the place where the burnt offering is slaughtered. [34]Then the priest shall take some of the blood of the sin offering with his finger and put it on the horns of the altar of burnt offering and pour out the rest of the blood at the base of the altar. [35]They shall remove all the fat, just as the fat is removed from the lamb of the fellowship offering, and the priest shall burn it on the altar on top of the food offerings presented to the Lord. In this way the priest will make atonement for them for the sin they have committed, and they will be forgiven.

conversations

forgiveness of sins «» 4:27–31; 5:1–6

1» What would fall into the category of an "unintentional sin" today?

2» Are the rules for dealing with unintentional sin in Leviticus applicable today?

3» What does God expect you to do about your sins, intentional and unintentional?

For more on forgiveness of sins, check the index.
For the next Conversations, go to p. 152

134

---

[a] 10 The Hebrew word can refer to either male or female.

5 "'If anyone sins because they do not speak up when they hear a public charge to testify regarding something they have seen or learned about, they will be held responsible. ²Or if anyone unwittingly touches anything ceremonially unclean—whether the carcass of an unclean animal, wild or domestic, or of any unclean creature that moves along the ground—and they are unaware that they have become unclean, but then they come to realize their guilt; ³or if they touch human uncleanness—anything that would make them unclean—even though they are unaware of it, but then they learn of it and realize their guilt; ⁴or if anyone thoughtlessly takes an oath to do anything, whether good or evil—in any matter one might carelessly swear about—even though they are unaware of it, but then they learn of it and realize their guilt— ⁵when anyone realizes their guilt in any of these matters, they must confess in what way they have sinned ⁶and, as a penalty for the sin they have committed, they must bring to the Lord a female lamb or goat from the flock as a sin offering*ᵃ; and the priest shall make atonement for them for their sin.

⁷"'Anyone who cannot afford a lamb is to bring two doves or two young pigeons to the Lord as a penalty for their sin— one for a sin offering and the other for a burnt offering. ⁸They are to bring them to the priest, who shall first offer the one for the sin offering. He is to wring its head from its neck, not dividing it completely, ⁹and is to splash some of the blood of the sin offering against the side of the altar; the rest of the blood must be drained out at the base of the altar. It is a sin offering. ¹⁰The priest shall then offer the other as a burnt offering in the prescribed way and make atonement for them for the sin they have committed, and they will be forgiven.

¹¹"'If, however, they cannot afford two doves or two young pigeons, they are to bring as an offering for their sin a tenth of an ephah*ᵇ of the finest flour for a sin offering. They must not put oil or incense on it, because it is a sin offering. ¹²They are to bring it to the priest, who shall take a handful of it as a memorial*ᶜ portion and burn it on the altar on top of the food offerings presented to the Lord. It is a sin offering. ¹³In this way the priest will make atonement for them for any of these sins they have committed, and they will be forgiven. The rest of the offering will belong to the priest, as in the case of the grain offering.'"

The Guilt Offering

¹⁴The Lord said to Moses: ¹⁵"When anyone is unfaithful to the Lord by sinning unintentionally in regard to any of the Lord's holy things, they are to bring to the Lord as a penalty a ram from the flock, one without defect and of the proper value in silver, according to the sanctuary shekel.*ᵈ It is a guilt offering. ¹⁶They must make restitution for what they have failed to do in regard to the holy things, pay an additional penalty of a fifth of its value and give it all to the priest. The priest will make atonement for them with the ram as a guilt offering, and they will be forgiven.

¹⁷"If anyone sins and does what is forbidden in any of the Lord's commands, even though they do not know it, they are guilty and will be held responsible. ¹⁸They are to bring to the priest as a guilt offering a ram from the flock, one without defect and of the proper value. In this way the priest will make atonement for them for the wrong they have committed unintentionally, and they will be forgiven. ¹⁹It is a guilt offering; they have been guilty of*ᵉ wrongdoing against the Lord."

135

at issue: trustworthiness

5:1 Giving a testimony in court requires a promise to tell the truth. However, we're also sworn to tell the *whole* truth and nothing but the truth. Maybe that seems like semantics, but the words of this oath reveal a lot about trustworthiness. A trustworthy person doesn't need to have information prompted and prodded from her. She loves the truth and openly shares it because she has nothing to hide. By withholding information in public testimony, you set yourself up for punishment. Don't fool yourself—*not* saying something you know to be true is a form of lying.

ᵃ *6* Or *purification offering*; here and throughout this chapter   ᵇ *11* That is, probably about 3 1/2 pounds or about 1.5 kilograms   ᶜ *12* Or *representative*
ᵈ *15* That is, about 2/5 ounce or about 11.5 grams   ᵉ *19* Or *have made full expiation for their*

6 *The LORD said to Moses: [2]"If anyone sins and is unfaithful to the LORD by deceiving a neighbor about something entrusted to them or left in their care or about something stolen, or if they cheat a neighbor, [3]or if they find lost property and lie about it, or if they swear falsely about any such sin that people may commit— [4]when they thus sin and realize their guilt, they must return what they have stolen or taken by extortion, or what was entrusted to them, or the lost property they found, [5]or whatever it was they swore falsely about. They must make restitution in full, add a fifth of the value to it and give it all to the owner on the day they present their guilt offering. [6]And as a penalty they must bring to the priest, that is, to the LORD, their guilt offering, a ram from the flock, one without defect and of the proper value. [7]In this way the priest will make atonement for them before the LORD, and they will be forgiven for any of the things they did that made them guilty."

The Burnt Offering

*[8]The LORD said to Moses: [9]"Give Aaron and his sons this command: 'These are the regulations for the burnt offering: The burnt offering is to remain on the altar hearth throughout the night, till morning, and the fire must be kept burning on the altar. [10]The priest shall then put on his linen clothes, with linen undergarments next to his body, and shall remove the ashes of the burnt offering that the fire has consumed on the altar and place them beside the altar. [11]Then he is to take off these clothes and put on others, and carry the ashes outside the camp to a place that is ceremonially clean. [12]The fire on the altar must be kept burning; it must not go out. Every morning the priest is to add firewood and arrange the burnt offering on the fire and burn the fat of the fellowship offerings on it. [13]The fire must be kept burning on the altar continuously; it must not go out.

The Grain Offering

[14]"'These are the regulations for the grain offering: Aaron's sons are to bring it before the LORD, in front of the altar. [15]The priest is to take a handful of the finest flour and some olive oil, together with all the incense on the grain offering, and burn the memorial[a] portion on the altar as an aroma pleasing to the LORD. [16]Aaron and his sons shall eat the rest of it, but it is to be eaten without yeast in the sanctuary area; they are to eat it in the courtyard of the tent of meeting. [17]It must not be baked with yeast; I have given it as their share of the food offerings presented to me. Like the sin offering[b] and the guilt offering, it is most holy. [18]Any male descendant of Aaron may eat it. For all generations to come it is his perpetual share of the food offerings presented to the LORD. Whatever touches them will become holy.[c]'"

[19]The LORD also said to Moses, [20]"This is the offering Aaron and his sons are to bring to the LORD on the day he[d] is anointed: a tenth of an ephah[e] of the finest flour as a regular grain offering, half of it in the morning and half in the evening. [21]It must be prepared with oil on a griddle; bring it well-mixed and present the grain offering broken[f] in pieces as an aroma pleasing to the LORD. [22]The son who is to succeed him as anointed priest shall prepare it. It is the LORD's perpetual share and is to be burned completely. [23]Every grain offering of a priest shall be burned completely; it must not be eaten."

atissue:cheating

6:1–7 Tax time's coming, and you happen to have found a few loopholes in the system. *So what*, you think, *cheating is only cheating if you get caught, right?* Actually, the Bible doesn't focus on getting caught in the act. Instead, God tells us what to do personally after we've cheated—regardless of whether or not we've been found out. The penalty not only includes proper compensation but added interest as well. If you have a history of dishonest dealings, making it right may seem like a long, hard road. However, God's forgiveness and a clear conscience are worth the effort.

---

[a] *15* Or *representative*   [b] *17* Or *purification offering*; also in verses 25 and 30   [c] *18* Or *Whoever touches them must be holy*; similarly in verse 27
[d] *20* Or *each*   [e] *20* That is, probably about 3 1/2 pounds or about 1.5 kilograms   [f] *21* The meaning of the Hebrew for this word is uncertain.

* 6:1-7 is numbered 5:20-26 in Hebrew texts.   * 6:8-30 is numbered 6:1-23 in Hebrew texts.

The Sin Offering

²⁴The LORD said to Moses, ²⁵"Say to Aaron and his sons: 'These are the regulations for the sin offering: The sin offering is to be slaughtered before the LORD in the place the burnt offering is slaughtered; it is most holy. ²⁶The priest who offers it shall eat it; it is to be eaten in the sanctuary area, in the courtyard of the tent of meeting. ²⁷Whatever touches any of the flesh will become holy, and if any of the blood is spattered on a garment, you must wash it in the sanctuary area. ²⁸The clay pot the meat is cooked in must be broken; but if it is cooked in a bronze pot, the pot is to be scoured and rinsed with water. ²⁹Any male in a priest's family may eat it; it is most holy. ³⁰But any sin offering whose blood is brought into the tent of meeting to make atonement in the Holy Place must not be eaten; it must be burned up.

The Guilt Offering

7 ¹"'These are the regulations for the guilt offering, which is most holy: ²The guilt offering is to be slaughtered in the place where the burnt offering is slaughtered, and its blood is to be splashed against the sides of the altar. ³All its fat shall be offered: the fat tail and the fat that covers the internal organs, ⁴both kidneys with the fat on them near the loins, and the long lobe of the liver, which is to be removed with the kidneys. ⁵The priest shall burn them on the altar as a food offering presented to the LORD. It is a guilt offering. ⁶Any male in a priest's family may eat it, but it must be eaten in the sanctuary area; it is most holy.

⁷"'The same law applies to both the sin offering[a] and the guilt offering: They belong to the priest who makes atonement with them. ⁸The priest who offers a burnt offering for anyone may keep its hide for himself. ⁹Every grain offering baked in an oven or cooked in a pan or on a griddle belongs to the priest who offers it, ¹⁰and every grain offering, whether mixed with oil or dry, belongs equally to all the sons of Aaron.

The Fellowship Offering

¹¹"'These are the regulations for the fellowship offering anyone may present to the LORD:

¹²"'If they offer it as an expression of thankfulness, then along with this thank offering they are to offer thick loaves made without yeast and with olive oil mixed in, thin loaves made without yeast and brushed with olive oil, and thick loaves of the finest flour well-kneaded and with olive oil mixed in. ¹³Along with their fellowship offering of thanksgiving they are to present an offering with thick loaves of bread made with yeast. ¹⁴They are to bring one of each kind as an offering, a contribution to the LORD; it belongs to the priest who splashes the blood of the fellowship offering against the altar. ¹⁵The meat of their fellowship offering of thanksgiving must be eaten on the day it is offered; they must leave none of it till morning.

¹⁶"'If, however, their offering is the result of a vow or is a freewill offering, the sacrifice shall be eaten on the day they offer it, but anything left over may be eaten on the next day. ¹⁷Any meat of the sacrifice left over till the third day must be burned up. ¹⁸If any meat of the fellowship offering is eaten on the third day, the one who offered it will not be accepted. It will not be reckoned to their credit, for it has become impure; the person who eats any of it will be held responsible.

¹⁹"'Meat that touches anything ceremonially unclean must not be eaten; it must be burned up. As for other meat, anyone ceremonially clean may eat it. ²⁰But if anyone who is unclean eats any meat of the fellowship offering belonging to the LORD, they must be cut off from their people. ²¹Anyone who touches something unclean—whether human uncleanness or an unclean animal or any unclean creature that moves along the ground[b]—and then eats any of the meat of the fellowship offering belonging to the LORD must be cut off from their people.'"

Eating Fat and Blood Forbidden

²²The LORD said to Moses, ²³"Say to the Israelites: 'Do not eat any of the fat of cattle, sheep or goats. ²⁴The fat of an animal found dead or torn by wild animals may be used for any other purpose, but you must not eat it. ²⁵Anyone who eats the fat of an animal from which a food offering may be[c] presented to the LORD must be cut off from their people. ²⁶And wherever you live, you must not eat the blood of any bird or animal. ²⁷Anyone who eats blood must be cut off from their people.'"

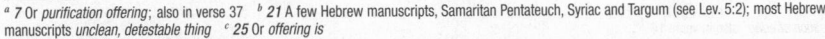

---

a 7 Or *purification offering*; also in verse 37   *b* 21 A few Hebrew manuscripts, Samaritan Pentateuch, Syriac and Targum (see Lev. 5:2); most Hebrew manuscripts *unclean, detestable thing*   *c* 25 Or *offering is*

The Priests' Share

²⁸The Lord said to Moses, ²⁹"Say to the Israelites: 'Anyone who brings a fellowship offering to the Lord is to bring part of it as their sacrifice to the Lord. ³⁰With their own hands they are to present the food offering to the Lord; they are to bring the fat, together with the breast, and wave the breast before the Lord as a wave offering. ³¹The priest shall burn the fat on the altar, but the breast belongs to Aaron and his sons. ³²You are to give the right thigh of your fellowship offerings to the priest as a contribution. ³³The son of Aaron who offers the blood and the fat of the fellowship offering shall have the right thigh as his share. ³⁴From the fellowship offerings of the Israelites, I have taken the breast that is waved and the thigh that is presented and have given them to Aaron the priest and his sons as their perpetual share from the Israelites.'"

³⁵This is the portion of the food offerings presented to the Lord that were allotted to Aaron and his sons on the day they were presented to serve the Lord as priests. ³⁶On the day they were anointed, the Lord commanded that the Israelites give this to them as their perpetual share for the generations to come.

³⁷These, then, are the regulations for the burnt offering, the grain offering, the sin offering, the guilt offering, the ordination offering and the fellowship offering, ³⁸which the Lord gave Moses on Mount Sinai in the Desert of Sinai on the day he commanded the Israelites to bring their offerings to the Lord.

138

The Ordination of Aaron and His Sons

8 The Lord said to Moses, ²"Bring Aaron and his sons, their garments, the anointing oil, the bull for the sin offering,ᵃ the two rams and the basket containing bread made without yeast, ³and gather the entire assembly at the entrance to the tent of meeting." ⁴Moses did as the Lord commanded him, and the assembly gathered at the entrance to the tent of meeting.

⁵Moses said to the assembly, "This is what the Lord has commanded to be done." ⁶Then Moses brought Aaron and his sons forward and washed them with water. ⁷He put the tunic on Aaron, tied the sash around him, clothed him with the robe and put the ephod on him. He also fastened the ephod with a decorative waistband, which he tied around him. ⁸He placed the breastpiece on him and put the Urim and Thummim in the breastpiece. ⁹Then he placed the turban on Aaron's head and set the gold plate, the sacred emblem, on the front of it, as the Lord commanded Moses.

¹⁰Then Moses took the anointing oil and anointed the tabernacle and everything in it, and so consecrated them. ¹¹He sprinkled some of the oil on the altar seven times, anointing the altar and all its utensils and the basin with its stand, to consecrate them. ¹²He poured some of the anointing oil on Aaron's head and anointed him to consecrate him. ¹³Then he brought Aaron's sons forward, put tunics on them, tied sashes around them and fastened caps on them, as the Lord commanded Moses.

¹⁴He then presented the bull for the sin offering, and Aaron and his sons laid their hands on its head. ¹⁵Moses slaughtered the bull and took some of the blood, and with his finger he put it on all the horns of the altar to purify the altar. He poured out the rest of the blood at the base of the altar. So he consecrated it to make atonement for it. ¹⁶Moses also took all the fat around the internal organs, the long lobe of the liver, and both kidneys and their fat, and burned it on the altar. ¹⁷But the bull with its hide and its flesh and its intestines he burned up outside the camp, as the Lord commanded Moses.

¹⁸He then presented the ram for the burnt offering, and Aaron and his sons laid their hands on its head. ¹⁹Then Moses slaughtered the ram and splashed the blood against the sides of the altar. ²⁰He cut the ram into pieces and burned the head, the pieces and the fat. ²¹He washed the internal organs and the legs with water and burned the whole ram on the altar. It was a burnt offering, a pleasing aroma, a food offering presented to the Lord, as the Lord commanded Moses.

²²He then presented the other ram, the ram for the ordination, and Aaron and his sons laid their hands on its head. ²³Moses slaughtered the ram and took some of its blood and put it on the lobe of Aaron's right ear, on the thumb of his right hand and on the big toe of his right foot. ²⁴Moses also brought Aaron's sons forward and put some of the blood on the lobes of their right ears, on the thumbs of their right hands and on the big toes of their right feet. Then he splashed blood against the sides of the altar.

ᵃ 2 Or *purification offering*; also in verse 14

²⁵After that, he took the fat, the fat tail, all the fat around the internal organs, the long lobe of the liver, both kidneys and their fat and the right thigh. ²⁶And from the basket of bread made without yeast, which was before the Lᴏʀᴅ, he took one thick loaf, one thick loaf with olive oil mixed in, and one thin loaf, and he put these on the fat portions and on the right thigh. ²⁷He put all these in the hands of Aaron and his sons, and they waved them before the Lᴏʀᴅ as a wave offering. ²⁸Then Moses took them from their hands and burned them on the altar on top of the burnt offering as an ordination offering, a pleasing aroma, a food offering presented to the Lᴏʀᴅ. ²⁹Moses also took the breast, which was his share of the ordination ram, and waved it before the Lᴏʀᴅ as a wave offering, as the Lᴏʀᴅ commanded Moses.

³⁰Then Moses took some of the anointing oil and some of the blood from the altar and sprinkled them on Aaron and his garments and on his sons and their garments. So he consecrated Aaron and his garments and his sons and their garments.

³¹Moses then said to Aaron and his sons, "Cook the meat at the entrance to the tent of meeting and eat it there with the bread from the basket of ordination offerings, as I was commanded: 'Aaron and his sons are to eat it.' ³²Then burn up the rest of the meat and the bread. ³³Do not leave the entrance to the tent of meeting for seven days, until the days of your ordination are completed, for your ordination will last seven days. ³⁴What has been done today was commanded by the Lᴏʀᴅ to make atonement for you. ³⁵You must stay at the entrance to the tent of meeting day and night for seven days and do what the Lᴏʀᴅ requires, so you will not die; for that is what I have been commanded." ³⁶So Aaron and his sons did everything the Lᴏʀᴅ commanded through Moses.

The Priests Begin Their Ministry

9 On the eighth day Moses summoned Aaron and his sons and the elders of Israel. ²He said to Aaron, "Take a bull calf for your sin offering*ᵃ* and a ram for your burnt offering, both without defect, and present them before the Lᴏʀᴅ. ³Then say to the Israelites: 'Take a male goat for a sin offering, a calf and a lamb—both a year old and without defect—for a burnt offering, ⁴and an ox*ᵇ* and a ram for a fellowship offering to sacrifice before the Lᴏʀᴅ, together with a grain offering mixed with olive oil. For today the Lᴏʀᴅ will appear to you.'"

⁵They took the things Moses commanded to the front of the tent of meeting, and the entire assembly came near and stood before the Lᴏʀᴅ. ⁶Then Moses said, "This is what the Lᴏʀᴅ has commanded you to do, so that the glory of the Lᴏʀᴅ may appear to you."

⁷Moses said to Aaron, "Come to the altar and sacrifice your sin offering and your burnt offering and make atonement for yourself and the people; sacrifice the offering that is for the people and make atonement for them, as the Lᴏʀᴅ has commanded."

HE IS: the atonement

9:7 Eve's bite of forbidden fruit (followed by Adam's) separated the human race from God. So God instituted the sacrificial system to make atonement for sin, allowing sin's price to be paid via a blood offering. When blood was shed, God could restore "at-one-ment" with his people . . . until the next sin required sacrifice.

We've all tasted the forbidden fruit of sin—it's part of our nature. Thankfully, Jesus offered his blood once and for all, so no other sacrifice is needed. Because he is *the atonement*, you can be "at one" with him forever when you accept his precious offering.

For the next He Is, go to p. 150.

⁸So Aaron came to the altar and slaughtered the calf as a sin offering for himself. ⁹His sons brought the blood to him, and he dipped his finger into the blood and put it on the horns of the altar; the rest of the blood he poured out at the base of the altar. ¹⁰On the altar he burned the fat, the kidneys and the

ᵃ 2 Or purification offering; here and throughout this chapter ᵇ *4 The Hebrew word can refer to either male or female; also in verses 18 and 19.*

long lobe of the liver from the sin offering, as the Lord commanded Moses; ¹¹the flesh and the hide he burned up outside the camp.

¹²Then he slaughtered the burnt offering. His sons handed him the blood, and he splashed it against the sides of the altar. ¹³They handed him the burnt offering piece by piece, including the head, and he burned them on the altar. ¹⁴He washed the internal organs and the legs and burned them on top of the burnt offering on the altar.

¹⁵Aaron then brought the offering that was for the people. He took the goat for the people's sin offering and slaughtered it and offered it for a sin offering as he did with the first one.

¹⁶He brought the burnt offering and offered it in the prescribed way. ¹⁷He also brought the grain offering, took a handful of it and burned it on the altar in addition to the morning's burnt offering.

¹⁸He slaughtered the ox and the ram as the fellowship offering for the people. His sons handed him the blood, and he splashed it against the sides of the altar. ¹⁹But the fat portions of the ox and the ram—the fat tail, the layer of fat, the kidneys and the long lobe of the liver— ²⁰these they laid on the breasts, and then Aaron burned the fat on the altar. ²¹Aaron waved the breasts and the right thigh before the Lord as a wave offering, as Moses commanded.

²²Then Aaron lifted his hands toward the people and blessed them. And having sacrificed the sin offering, the burnt offering and the fellowship offering, he stepped down.

²³Moses and Aaron then went into the tent of meeting. When they came out, they blessed the people; and the glory of the Lord appeared to all the people. ²⁴Fire came out from the presence of the Lord and consumed the burnt offering and the fat portions on the altar. And when all the people saw it, they shouted for joy and fell facedown.

The Death of Nadab and Abihu

10 Aaron's sons Nadab and Abihu took their censers, put fire in them and added incense; and they offered unauthorized fire before the Lord, contrary to his command. ²So fire came out from the presence of the Lord and consumed them, and they died before the Lord. ³Moses then said to Aaron, "This is what the Lord spoke of when he said:

"'Among those who approach me
I will be proved holy;
in the sight of all the people
I will be honored.'"

Aaron remained silent.

⁴Moses summoned Mishael and Elzaphan, sons of Aaron's uncle Uzziel, and said to them, "Come here; carry your cousins outside the camp, away from the front of the sanctuary." ⁵So they came and carried them, still in their tunics, outside the camp, as Moses ordered.

⁶Then Moses said to Aaron and his sons Eleazar and Ithamar, "Do not let your hair become unkempt[a] and do not tear your clothes, or you will die and the Lord will be angry with the whole community. But your relatives, all the house of Israel, may mourn for those the Lord has destroyed by fire. ⁷Do not leave the entrance to the tent of meeting or you will die, because the Lord's anointing oil is on you." So they did as Moses said.

⁸Then the Lord said to Aaron, ⁹"You and your sons are not to drink wine or other fermented drink whenever you go into the tent of meeting, or you will die. This is a lasting ordinance for the generations

atissue:obedience

10:1–2 *Maybe God's not serious about that rule. Maybe he hasn't thought through it fully. Surely he didn't consider my situation.* Have you ever felt tempted to take God's law into your own hands? To try to bend the rules in your favor and rationalize why you should be exempt from his rules? Our motives for doing so are less than honorable. We elevate our own logic and downplay God's. Yet his instructions are for our good. Outside the protection of his rules, we set ourselves up for tragic consequences, like Nadab and Abihu. In the end, our pride will be our downfall.

ᵃ 6 Or Do not uncover your heads

to come, ¹⁰so that you can distinguish between the holy and the common, between the unclean and the clean, ¹¹and so you can teach the Israelites all the decrees the LORD has given them through Moses."

¹²Moses said to Aaron and his remaining sons, Eleazar and Ithamar, "Take the grain offering left over from the food offerings prepared without yeast and presented to the LORD and eat it beside the altar, for it is most holy. ¹³Eat it in the sanctuary area, because it is your share and your sons' share of the food offerings presented to the LORD; for so I have been commanded. ¹⁴But you and your sons and your daughters may eat the breast that was waved and the thigh that was presented. Eat them in a ceremonially clean place; they have been given to you and your children as your share of the Israelites' fellowship offerings. ¹⁵The thigh that was presented and the breast that was waved must be brought with the fat portions of the food offerings, to be waved before the LORD as a wave offering. This will be the perpetual share for you and your children, as the LORD has commanded."

¹⁶When Moses inquired about the goat of the sin offering*a* and found that it had been burned up, he was angry with Eleazar and Ithamar, Aaron's remaining sons, and asked, ¹⁷"Why didn't you eat the sin offering in the sanctuary area? It is most holy; it was given to you to take away the guilt of the community by making atonement for them before the LORD. ¹⁸Since its blood was not taken into the Holy Place, you should have eaten the goat in the sanctuary area, as I commanded."

¹⁹Aaron replied to Moses, "Today they sacrificed their sin offering and their burnt offering before the LORD, but such things as this have happened to me. Would the LORD have been pleased if I had eaten the sin offering today?" ²⁰When Moses heard this, he was satisfied.

Clean and Unclean Food

11 The LORD said to Moses and Aaron, ²"Say to the Israelites: 'Of all the animals that live on land, these are the ones you may eat: ³You may eat any animal that has a divided hoof and that chews the cud.

⁴"'There are some that only chew the cud or only have a divided hoof, but you must not eat them. The camel, though it chews the cud, does not have a divided hoof; it is ceremonially unclean for you. ⁵The hyrax, though it chews the cud, does not have a divided hoof; it is unclean for you. ⁶The rabbit, though it chews the cud, does not have a divided hoof; it is unclean for you. ⁷And the pig, though it has a divided hoof, does not chew the cud; it is unclean for you. ⁸You must not eat their meat or touch their carcasses; they are unclean for you.

⁹"'Of all the creatures living in the water of the seas and the streams you may eat any that have fins and scales. ¹⁰But all creatures in the seas or streams that do not have fins and scales—whether among all the swarming things or among all the other living creatures in the water—you are to regard as unclean. ¹¹And since you are to regard them as unclean, you must not eat their meat; you must regard their carcasses as unclean. ¹²Anything living in the water that does not have fins and scales is to be regarded as unclean by you.

¹³"'These are the birds you are to regard as unclean and not eat because they are unclean: the eagle,*b* the vulture, the black vulture, ¹⁴the red kite, any kind of black kite, ¹⁵any kind of raven, ¹⁶the horned owl, the screech owl, the gull, any kind of hawk, ¹⁷the little owl, the cormorant, the great owl, ¹⁸the white owl, the desert owl, the osprey, ¹⁹the stork, any kind of heron, the hoopoe and the bat.

²⁰"'All flying insects that walk on all fours are to be regarded as unclean by you. ²¹There are, however, some flying insects that walk on all fours that you may eat: those that have jointed legs for hopping on the ground. ²²Of these you may eat any kind of locust, katydid, cricket or grasshopper. ²³But all other flying insects that have four legs you are to regard as unclean.

²⁴"'You will make yourselves unclean by these; whoever touches their carcasses will be unclean till evening. ²⁵Whoever picks up one of their carcasses must wash their clothes, and they will be unclean till evening.

²⁶"'Every animal that does not have a divided hoof or that does not chew the cud is unclean for you; whoever touches the carcass of any of them will be unclean. ²⁷Of all the animals that walk on all fours, those that walk on their paws are unclean for you; whoever touches their carcasses will be unclean till

141

---

a 16 Or *purification offering;* also in verses 17 and 19   *b 13* The precise identification of some of the birds, insects and animals in this chapter is uncertain.

myth# 11 "GOOD PARENTS ALWAYS HAVE GOOD CHILDREN."

How could two children raised in the same home turn out so different from each other? Our son is popular at school, gets decent grades and loves the church youth group. Micah has his days, of course, but overall he wants to please us and make us proud of him.

Our daughter, Kayla, is a different child altogether.

Two years younger than Micah, but with a temperament twice as fiery, it's as if she's determined to be the opposite of her brother in every way. I've already been up to the school to meet with her teachers four times this semester, but she doesn't respond to discipline. If we try to talk to her about our concerns, she becomes belligerent, taking our remarks way out of context and throwing them back in our faces. Even when she was a child, her flashpoint temper erupted over the slightest thing.

My heart aches for her. I love my daughter very much. After her latest outburst at home, I realized something I hadn't dared admit to anyone. Somehow I must have failed as a mother, and Kayla is now paying for my mistakes.

Though they would never say it to my face, I know people believe that all rebellious children, including Kayla, come from dysfunctional homes. And looking back, I know my husband and I weren't the perfect parents. But we tried to do everything we could for our children to make sure they grew up in a stable home environment. I gave up my career to stay home with them. We took family vacations together. We went to their piano recitals, choir concerts and basketball games. We tried.

I know a lot of parents who haven't invested nearly as much attention in their kids as we have, and their children turned out fine. I thought if I did everything right, if I loved my children enough, they would turn out OK. Where did I go wrong?

—Ranjita

WE HEAR OF healthy, successful children who somehow survive dysfunctional homes. But, as illustrated by Aaron's sons Nadab and Abihu, it's also possible to have a dysfunctional child despite a healthy home environment (see Leviticus 10). The assumption that good parents always raise good children is unrealistic, and the harsh judgments that come from that assumption have devastated many good parents whose child rebelled. Parents rehearse the past, trying to pin the blame on themselves for how their children rebelled against them and their values.

Because God has lovingly created us with free will, no amount of good parenting, fervent prayer and the best of intentions can *control* an individual's choices. The Bible reminds us that the potential for disobedience is within each child (see Proverbs 22:15). Most Christian psychologists will agree that the reason why some children who are raised in a healthy, Christian family grow up to be compliant, decent citizens and others rebel against a Christian upbringing is a mystery. It just happens.

If you have a prodigal child, remember this:

- It's normal to grieve the sense of loss you experience as a mother—this isn't the family you'd envisioned.

- If necessary, seek professional help for you and your family. Don't suffer alone.

- Lean on Christian friends who will pray with you and give you insight.

- Recognizing how your own faults may have contributed to the family dynamics is not the same as weighing yourself down with irrational blame.

- Don't give up. It may take years, and there's no guarantee that your child will change, but with Jesus there's always hope.

- Remember that God loves prodigal children—even more so than their parents do. Ultimately, the best thing good parents can do for their rebellious children is to release them to their heavenly Father through prayer.

"Let's be candid. All of us Christian parents, no matter what our background, parenting style or level of spiritual maturity, share a common fear—that a child will become a prodigal child. There is no jolt of agony to compare to the child who says with his words and his behavior, 'I reject you, your values, your lifestyle, your God.' We desperately desire that this will never happen in our homes. But it can and does."

—Dennis Rainey

143

"THE SON OF MAN CAME TO SEEK AND TO SAVE WHAT WAS LOST."

LUKE 19:10

SEE ALSO

1 Kings 11:4–6
Matthew 18:12–14
Luke 15:11–32

For more on **Parenting**, check the index.

evening. ²⁸Anyone who picks up their carcasses must wash their clothes, and they will be unclean till evening. These animals are unclean for you.

²⁹"'Of the animals that move about on the ground, these are unclean for you: the weasel, the rat, any kind of great lizard, ³⁰the gecko, the monitor lizard, the wall lizard, the skink and the chameleon. ³¹Of all those that move along the ground, these are unclean for you. Whoever touches them when they are dead will be unclean till evening. ³²When one of them dies and falls on something, that article, whatever its use, will be unclean, whether it is made of wood, cloth, hide or sackcloth. Put it in water; it will be unclean till evening, and then it will be clean. ³³If one of them falls into a clay pot, everything in it will be unclean, and you must break the pot. ³⁴Any food you are allowed to eat that has come into contact with water from any such pot is unclean, and any liquid that is drunk from such a pot is unclean. ³⁵Anything that one of their carcasses falls on becomes unclean; an oven or cooking pot must be broken up. They are unclean, and you are to regard them as unclean. ³⁶A spring, however, or a cistern for collecting water remains clean, but anyone who touches one of these carcasses is unclean. ³⁷If a carcass falls on any seeds that are to be planted, they remain clean. ³⁸But if water has been put on the seed and a carcass falls on it, it is unclean for you.

³⁹"'If an animal that you are allowed to eat dies, anyone who touches its carcass will be unclean till evening. ⁴⁰Anyone who eats some of its carcass must wash their clothes, and they will be unclean till evening. Anyone who picks up the carcass must wash their clothes, and they will be unclean till evening.

⁴¹"'Every creature that moves about on the ground is to be regarded as unclean; it is not to be eaten. ⁴²You are not to eat any creature that moves about on the ground, whether it moves on its belly or walks on all fours or on many feet; it is unclean. ⁴³Do not defile yourselves by any of these creatures. Do not make yourselves unclean by means of them or be made unclean by them. ⁴⁴I am the LORD your God; consecrate yourselves and be holy, because I am holy. Do not make yourselves unclean by any creature that moves about on the ground. ⁴⁵I am the LORD, who brought you up out of Egypt to be your God; therefore be holy, because I am holy.

⁴⁶"'These are the regulations concerning animals, birds, every living thing that moves in the water and every creature that moves about on the ground. ⁴⁷You must distinguish between the unclean and the clean, between living creatures that may be eaten and those that may not be eaten.'"

Purification After Childbirth

12 The LORD said to Moses, ²"Say to the Israelites: 'A woman who becomes pregnant and gives birth to a son will be ceremonially unclean for seven days, just as she is unclean during her monthly period. ³On the eighth day the boy is to be circumcised. ⁴Then the woman must wait thirty-three days to be purified from her bleeding. She must not touch anything sacred or go to the sanctuary until the days of her purification are over. ⁵If she gives birth to a daughter, for two weeks the woman will be unclean, as during her period. Then she must wait sixty-six days to be purified from her bleeding.

⁶"'When the days of her purification for a son or daughter are over, she is to bring to the priest at the entrance to the tent of meeting a year-old lamb for a burnt offering and a young pigeon or a dove for a sin offering.ᵃ ⁷He shall offer them before the LORD to make atonement for her, and then she will be ceremonially clean from her flow of blood.

"'These are the regulations for the woman who gives birth to a boy or a girl. ⁸If she cannot afford a lamb, she is to bring two doves or two young pigeons, one for a burnt offering and the other for a sin offering. In this way the priest will make atonement for her, and she will be clean.'"

Regulations About Defiling Skin Diseases

13 The LORD said to Moses and Aaron, ²"When anyone has a swelling or a rash or a shiny spot on their skin that may be a defiling skin disease,ᵇ they must be brought to Aaron the priest or to one of his sonsᶜ who is a priest. ³The priest is to examine the sore on the skin, and if the hair in the sore has turned white and the sore appears to be more than skin deep, it is a defiling skin disease. When the priest examines them, he shall pronounce them ceremonially unclean. ⁴If the shiny spot on the skin is

---

ᵃ 6 Or purification offering; also in verse 8   ᵇ 2 The Hebrew word for defiling skin disease, traditionally translated "leprosy," was used for various diseases affecting the skin; here and throughout verses 3–46.   ᶜ 2 Or descendants white but does not appear to be more than skin deep and the hair in it has not turned white, the priest is to isolate the affected person for seven days. [5]On the seventh day the priest is to examine them, and if he sees that the sore is unchanged and has not spread in the skin, he is to isolate them for another seven days. [6]On the seventh day the priest is to examine them again, and if the sore has faded and has not spread in the skin, the priest shall pronounce them clean; it is only a rash. They must wash their clothes, and they will be clean. [7]But if the rash does spread in their skin after they have shown themselves to the priest to be pronounced clean, they must appear before the priest again. [8]The priest is to examine them, and if the rash has spread in the skin, he shall pronounce them unclean; it is a defiling skin disease.

[9]"When anyone has a defiling skin disease, they must be brought to the priest. [10]The priest is to examine them, and if there is a white swelling in the skin that has turned the hair white and if there is raw flesh in the swelling, [11]it is a chronic skin disease and the priest shall pronounce them unclean. He is not to isolate them, because they are already unclean.

[12]"If the disease breaks out all over their skin and, so far as the priest can see, it covers all the skin of the affected person from head to foot, [13]the priest is to examine them, and if the disease has covered their whole body, he shall pronounce them clean. Since it has all turned white, they are clean. [14]But whenever raw flesh appears on them, they will be unclean. [15]When the priest sees the raw flesh, he shall pronounce them unclean. The raw flesh is unclean; they have a defiling disease. [16]If the raw flesh changes and turns white, they must go to the priest. [17]The priest is to examine them, and if the sores have turned white, the priest shall pronounce the affected person clean; then they will be clean.

[18]"When someone has a boil on their skin and it heals, [19]and in the place where the boil was, a white swelling or reddish-white spot appears, they must present themselves to the priest. [20]The priest is to examine it, and if it appears to be more than skin deep and the hair in it has turned white, the priest shall pronounce them unclean. It is a defiling skin disease that has broken out where the boil was. [21]But if, when the priest examines it, there is no white hair in it and it is not more than skin deep and has faded, then the priest is to isolate them for seven days. [22]If it is spreading in the skin, the priest shall pronounce them unclean; it is a defiling disease. [23]But if the spot is unchanged and has not spread, it is only a scar from the boil, and the priest shall pronounce them clean.

[24]"When someone has a burn on their skin and a reddish-white or white spot appears in the raw flesh of the burn, [25]the priest is to examine the spot, and if the hair in it has turned white, and it appears to be more than skin deep, it is a defiling disease that has broken out in the burn. The priest shall pronounce them unclean; it is a defiling skin disease. [26]But if the priest examines it and there is no white hair in the spot and if it is not more than skin deep and has faded, then the priest is to isolate them for seven days. [27]On the seventh day the priest is to examine them, and if it is spreading in the skin, the priest shall pronounce them unclean; it is a defiling skin disease. [28]If, however, the spot is unchanged and has not spread in the skin but has faded, it is a swelling from the burn, and the priest shall pronounce them clean; it is only a scar from the burn.

[29]"If a man or woman has a sore on their head or chin, [30]the priest is to examine the sore, and if it appears to be more than skin deep and the hair in it is yellow and thin, the priest shall pronounce them unclean; it is a defiling skin disease on the head or chin. [31]But if, when the priest examines the sore, it does not seem to be more than skin deep and there is no black hair in it, then the priest is to isolate the affected person for seven days. [32]On the seventh day the priest is to examine the sore, and if it has not spread and there is no yellow hair in it and it does not appear to be more than skin deep, [33]then the man or woman must shave themselves, except for the affected area, and the priest is to keep them isolated another seven days. [34]On the seventh day the priest is to examine the sore, and if it has not spread in the skin and appears to be no more than skin deep, the priest shall pronounce the man or woman clean. They must wash their clothes, and they will be clean. [35]But if the sore does spread in the skin after they are pronounced clean, [36]the priest is to examine them, and if he finds that the sore has spread in the skin, he does not need to look for yellow hair; they are unclean. [37]If, however, the sore is unchanged so far as the priest can see, and if black hair has grown in it, the affected person is healed. They are clean, and the priest shall pronounce them clean.

145

³⁸"When a man or woman has white spots on the skin, ³⁹the priest is to examine them, and if the spots are dull white, it is a harmless rash that has broken out on the skin; they are clean.

⁴⁰"A man who has lost his hair and is bald is clean. ⁴¹If he has lost his hair from the front of his scalp and has a bald forehead, he is clean. ⁴²But if he has a reddish-white sore on his bald head or forehead, it is a defiling disease breaking out on his head or forehead. ⁴³The priest is to examine him, and if the swollen sore on his head or forehead is reddish-white like a defiling skin disease, ⁴⁴the man is diseased and is unclean. The priest shall pronounce him unclean because of the sore on his head.

⁴⁵"Anyone with such a defiling disease must wear torn clothes, let their hair be unkempt,ᵃ cover the lower part of their face and cry out, 'Unclean! Unclean!' ⁴⁶As long as they have the disease they remain unclean. They must live alone; they must live outside the camp.

Regulations About Defiling Molds

⁴⁷"As for any fabric that is spoiled with a defiling mold—any woolen or linen clothing, ⁴⁸any woven or knitted material of linen or wool, any leather or anything made of leather— ⁴⁹if the affected area in the fabric, the leather, the woven or knitted material, or any leather article, is greenish or reddish, it is a defiling mold and must be shown to the priest. ⁵⁰The priest is to examine the affected area and isolate the article for seven days. ⁵¹On the seventh day he is to examine it, and if the mold has spread in the fabric, the woven or knitted material, or the leather, whatever its use, it is a persistent defiling mold; the article is unclean. ⁵²He must burn the fabric, the woven or knitted material of wool or linen, or any leather article that has been spoiled; because the defiling mold is persistent, the article must be burned.

⁵³"But if, when the priest examines it, the mold has not spread in the fabric, the woven or knitted material, or the leather article, ⁵⁴he shall order that the spoiled article be washed. Then he is to isolate it for another seven days. ⁵⁵After the article has been washed, the priest is to examine it again, and if the mold has not changed its appearance, even though it has not spread, it is unclean. Burn it, no matter which side of the fabric has been spoiled. ⁵⁶If, when the priest examines it, the mold has faded after the article has been washed, he is to tear the spoiled part out of the fabric, the leather, or the woven or knitted material. ⁵⁷But if it reappears in the fabric, in the woven or knitted material, or in the leather article, it is a spreading mold; whatever has the mold must be burned. ⁵⁸Any fabric, woven or knitted material, or any leather article that has been washed and is rid of the mold, must be washed again. Then it will be clean."

⁵⁹These are the regulations concerning defiling molds in woolen or linen clothing, woven or knitted material, or any leather article, for pronouncing them clean or unclean.

Cleansing From Defiling Skin Diseases

14 The LORD said to Moses, ²"These are the regulations for any diseased person at the time of their ceremonial cleansing, when they are brought to the priest: ³The priest is to go outside the camp and examine them. If they have been healed of their defiling skin disease,ᵇ ⁴the priest shall order that two live clean birds and some cedar wood, scarlet yarn and hyssop be brought for the person to be cleansed. ⁵Then the priest shall order that one of the birds be killed over fresh water in a clay pot. ⁶He is then to take the live

---

atissue:cleanliness

13–14 We humans judge each other by our exteriors, while asserting that God looks at our hearts (see 1 Samuel 16:7). God's law in Leviticus may surprise us, though. These chapters concerning God's explicit cleanliness guidelines for his people might make OSHA look tame. These health standards stood right alongside God's spiritual laws. The Israelites understood God's desire for a balance between physical and spiritual health. Caring for your physical body is not vanity, nor is it a waste of time. Maintaining your physical health allows your spiritual life to flourish.

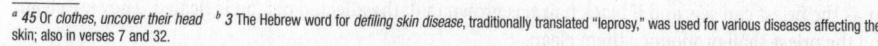

ᵃ 45 Or clothes, uncover their head   ᵇ 3 The Hebrew word for *defiling skin disease*, traditionally translated "leprosy," was used for various diseases affecting the skin; also in verses 7 and 32.

bird and dip it, together with the cedar wood, the scarlet yarn and the hyssop, into the blood of the bird that was killed over the fresh water. ⁷Seven times he shall sprinkle the one to be cleansed of the defiling disease, and then pronounce them clean. After that, he is to release the live bird in the open fields.

⁸"The person to be cleansed must wash their clothes, shave off all their hair and bathe with water; then they will be ceremonially clean. After this they may come into the camp, but they must stay outside their tent for seven days. ⁹On the seventh day they must shave off all their hair; they must shave their head, their beard, their eyebrows and the rest of their hair. They must wash their clothes and bathe themselves with water, and they will be clean.

¹⁰"On the eighth day they must bring two male lambs and one ewe lamb a year old, each without defect, along with three-tenths of an ephah *ᵃ* of the finest flour mixed with olive oil for a grain offering, and one log *ᵇ* of oil. ¹¹The priest who pronounces them clean shall present both the one to be cleansed and their offerings before the Lᴏʀᴅ at the entrance to the tent of meeting.

¹²"Then the priest is to take one of the male lambs and offer it as a guilt offering, along with the log of oil; he shall wave them before the Lᴏʀᴅ as a wave offering. ¹³He is to slaughter the lamb in the sanctuary area where the sin offering *ᶜ* and the burnt offering are slaughtered. Like the sin offering, the guilt offering belongs to the priest; it is most holy. ¹⁴The priest is to take some of the blood of the guilt offering and put it on the lobe of the right ear of the one to be cleansed, on the thumb of their right hand and on the big toe of their right foot. ¹⁵The priest shall then take some of the log of oil, pour it in the palm of his own left hand, ¹⁶dip his right forefinger into the oil in his palm, and with his finger sprinkle some of it before the Lᴏʀᴅ seven times. ¹⁷The priest is to put some of the oil remaining in his palm on the lobe of the right ear of the one to be cleansed, on the thumb of their right hand and on the big toe of their right foot, on top of the blood of the guilt offering. ¹⁸The rest of the oil in his palm the priest shall put on the head of the one to be cleansed and make atonement for them before the Lᴏʀᴅ.

¹⁹"Then the priest is to sacrifice the sin offering and make atonement for the one to be cleansed from their uncleanness. After that, the priest shall slaughter the burnt offering ²⁰and offer it on the altar, together with the grain offering, and make atonement for them, and they will be clean.

²¹"If, however, they are poor and cannot afford these, they must take one male lamb as a guilt offering to be waved to make atonement for them, together with a tenth of an ephah *ᵈ* of the finest flour mixed with olive oil for a grain offering, a log of oil, ²²and two doves or two young pigeons, such as they can afford, one for a sin offering and the other for a burnt offering.

²³"On the eighth day they must bring them for their cleansing to the priest at the entrance to the tent of meeting, before the Lᴏʀᴅ. ²⁴The priest is to take the lamb for the guilt offering, together with the log of oil, and wave them before the Lᴏʀᴅ as a wave offering. ²⁵He shall slaughter the lamb for the guilt offering and take some of its blood and put it on the lobe of the right ear of the one to be cleansed, on the thumb of their right hand and on the big toe of their right foot. ²⁶The priest is to pour some of the oil into the palm of his own left hand, ²⁷and with his right forefinger sprinkle some of the oil from his palm seven times before the Lᴏʀᴅ. ²⁸Some of the oil in his palm he is to put on the same places he put the blood of the guilt offering—on the lobe of the right ear of the one to be cleansed, on the thumb of their right hand and on the big toe of their right foot. ²⁹The rest of the oil in his palm the priest shall put on the head of the one to be cleansed, to make atonement for them before the Lᴏʀᴅ. ³⁰Then he shall sacrifice the doves or the young pigeons, such as the person can afford, ³¹one as a sin offering and the other as a burnt offering, together with the grain offering. In this way the priest will make atonement before the Lᴏʀᴅ on behalf of the one to be cleansed."

³²These are the regulations for anyone who has a defiling skin disease and who cannot afford the regular offerings for their cleansing.

Cleansing From Defiling Molds

³³The Lᴏʀᴅ said to Moses and Aaron, ³⁴"When you enter the land of Canaan, which I am giving you as your possession, and I put a spreading mold in a house in that land, ³⁵the owner of the house must go and tell the priest, 'I have seen something that looks like a defiling mold in my house.' ³⁶The priest is to

---

ᵃ 10 That is, probably about 11 pounds or about 5 kilograms   *ᵇ 10* That is, about 1/2 pint or about 0.3 liter; also in verses 12, 15, 21 and 24
ᶜ 13 Or *purification offering*; also in verses 19, 22 and 31   *ᵈ 21* That is, probably about 3 1/2 pounds or about 1.5 kilograms

order the house to be emptied before he goes in to examine the mold, so that nothing in the house will be pronounced unclean. After this the priest is to go in and inspect the house. ³⁷He is to examine the mold on the walls, and if it has greenish or reddish depressions that appear to be deeper than the surface of the wall, ³⁸the priest shall go out the doorway of the house and close it up for seven days. ³⁹On the seventh day the priest shall return to inspect the house. If the mold has spread on the walls, ⁴⁰he is to order that the contaminated stones be torn out and thrown into an unclean place outside the town. ⁴¹He must have all the inside walls of the house scraped and the material that is scraped off dumped into an unclean place outside the town. ⁴²Then they are to take other stones to replace these and take new clay and plaster the house.

⁴³"If the defiling mold reappears in the house after the stones have been torn out and the house scraped and plastered, ⁴⁴the priest is to go and examine it and, if the mold has spread in the house, it is a persistent defiling mold; the house is unclean. ⁴⁵It must be torn down—its stones, timbers and all the plaster—and taken out of the town to an unclean place.

⁴⁶"Anyone who goes into the house while it is closed up will be unclean till evening. ⁴⁷Anyone who sleeps or eats in the house must wash their clothes.

⁴⁸"But if the priest comes to examine it and the mold has not spread after the house has been plastered, he shall pronounce the house clean, because the defiling mold is gone. ⁴⁹To purify the house he is to take two birds and some cedar wood, scarlet yarn and hyssop. ⁵⁰He shall kill one of the birds over fresh water in a clay pot. ⁵¹Then he is to take the cedar wood, the hyssop, the scarlet yarn and the live bird, dip them into the blood of the dead bird and the fresh water, and sprinkle the house seven times. ⁵²He shall purify the house with the bird's blood, the fresh water, the live bird, the cedar wood, the hyssop and the scarlet yarn. ⁵³Then he is to release the live bird in the open fields outside the town. In this way he will make atonement for the house, and it will be clean."

⁵⁴These are the regulations for any defiling skin disease, for a sore, ⁵⁵for defiling molds in fabric or in a house, ⁵⁶and for a swelling, a rash or a shiny spot, ⁵⁷to determine when something is clean or unclean.

These are the regulations for defiling skin diseases and defiling molds.

Discharges Causing Uncleanness

15 The Lord said to Moses and Aaron, ²"Speak to the Israelites and say to them: 'When any man has an unusual bodily discharge, such a discharge is unclean. ³Whether it continues flowing from his body or is blocked, it will make him unclean. This is how his discharge will bring about uncleanness:

⁴"'Any bed the man with a discharge lies on will be unclean, and anything he sits on will be unclean. ⁵Anyone who touches his bed must wash their clothes and bathe with water, and they will be unclean till evening. ⁶Whoever sits on anything that the man with a discharge sat on must wash their clothes and bathe with water, and they will be unclean till evening.

⁷"'Whoever touches the man who has a discharge must wash their clothes and bathe with water, and they will be unclean till evening.

⁸"'If the man with the discharge spits on anyone who is clean, they must wash their clothes and bathe with water, and they will be unclean till evening.

⁹"'Everything the man sits on when riding will be unclean, ¹⁰and whoever touches any of the things that were under him will be unclean till evening; whoever picks up those things must wash their clothes and bathe with water, and they will be unclean till evening.

¹¹"'Anyone the man with a discharge touches without rinsing his hands with water must wash their clothes and bathe with water, and they will be unclean till evening.

¹²"'A clay pot that the man touches must be broken, and any wooden article is to be rinsed with water.

¹³"'When a man is cleansed from his discharge, he is to count off seven days for his ceremonial cleansing; he must wash his clothes and bathe himself with fresh water, and he will be clean. ¹⁴On the eighth day he must take two doves or two young pigeons and come before the Lord to the entrance to the tent of meeting and give them to the priest. ¹⁵The priest is to sacrifice them, the one for a sin offering[a] and

---

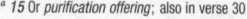

ᵃ 15 Or purification offering; also in verse 30

the other for a burnt offering. In this way he will make atonement before the Lord for the man because of his discharge.

¹⁶"When a man has an emission of semen, he must bathe his whole body with water, and he will be unclean till evening. ¹⁷Any clothing or leather that has semen on it must be washed with water, and it will be unclean till evening. ¹⁸When a man has sexual relations with a woman and there is an emission of semen, both of them must bathe with water, and they will be unclean till evening.

¹⁹"When a woman has her regular flow of blood, the impurity of her monthly period will last seven days, and anyone who touches her will be unclean till evening.

²⁰"Anything she lies on during her period will be unclean, and anything she sits on will be unclean. ²¹Anyone who touches her bed will be unclean; they must wash their clothes and bathe with water, and they will be unclean till evening. ²²Anyone who touches anything she sits on will be unclean; they must wash their clothes and bathe with water, and they will be unclean till evening. ²³Whether it is the bed or anything she was sitting on, anyone who touches it will be unclean till evening.

²⁴"If a man has sexual relations with her and her monthly flow touches him, he will be unclean for seven days; any bed he lies on will be unclean.

²⁵"When a woman has a discharge of blood for many days at a time other than her monthly period or has a discharge that continues beyond her period, she will be unclean as long as she has the discharge, just as in the days of her period. ²⁶Any bed she lies on while her discharge continues will be unclean, as is her bed during her monthly period, and anything she sits on will be unclean, as during her period. ²⁷Anyone who touches them will be unclean; they must wash their clothes and bathe with water, and they will be unclean till evening.

²⁸"When she is cleansed from her discharge, she must count off seven days, and after that she will be ceremonially clean. ²⁹On the eighth day she must take two doves or two young pigeons and bring them to the priest at the entrance to the tent of meeting. ³⁰The priest is to sacrifice one for a sin offering and the other for a burnt offering. In this way he will make atonement for her before the Lord for the uncleanness of her discharge.

³¹"You must keep the Israelites separate from things that make them unclean, so they will not die in their uncleanness for defiling my dwelling place,ᵃ which is among them.'"

³²These are the regulations for a man with a discharge, for anyone made unclean by an emission of semen, ³³for a woman in her monthly period, for a man or a woman with a discharge, and for a man who has sexual relations with a woman who is ceremonially unclean.

The Day of Atonement

16 The Lord spoke to Moses after the death of the two sons of Aaron who died when they approached the Lord. ²The Lord said to Moses: "Tell your brother Aaron that he is not to come whenever he chooses into the Most Holy Place behind the curtain in front of the atonement cover on the ark, or else he will die. For I will appear in the cloud over the atonement cover.

³"This is how Aaron is to enter the Most Holy Place: He must first bring a young bull for a sin offeringᵇ and a ram for a burnt offering. ⁴He is to put on the sacred linen tunic, with linen undergarments next to his body; he is to tie the linen sash around him and put on the linen turban. These are sacred garments; so he must bathe himself with water before he puts them on. ⁵From the Israelite community he is to take two male goats for a sin offering and a ram for a burnt offering.

⁶"Aaron is to offer the bull for his own sin offering to make atonement for himself and his household. ⁷Then he is to take the two goats and present them before the Lord at the entrance to the tent of meeting. ⁸He is to cast lots for the two goats—one lot for the Lord and the other for the scapegoat.ᶜ ⁹Aaron shall bring the goat whose lot falls to the Lord and sacrifice it for a sin offering. ¹⁰But the goat chosen by lot as the scapegoat shall be presented alive before the Lord to be used for making atonement by sending it into the wilderness as a scapegoat.

¹¹"Aaron shall bring the bull for his own sin offering to make atonement for himself and his household, and he is to slaughter the bull for his own sin offering. ¹²He is to take a censer full of burning coals

149

from the altar before the LORD and two handfuls of finely ground fragrant incense and take them behind the curtain. ¹³He is to put the incense on the fire before the LORD, and the smoke of the incense will conceal the atonement cover above the tablets of the covenant law, so that he will not die. ¹⁴He is to take some of the bull's blood and with his finger sprinkle it on the front of the atonement cover; then he shall sprinkle some of it with his finger seven times before the atonement cover.

¹⁵"He shall then slaughter the goat for the sin offering for the people and take its blood behind the curtain and do with it as he did with the bull's blood: He shall sprinkle it on the atonement cover and in front of it. ¹⁶In this way he will make atonement for the Most Holy Place because of the uncleanness and rebellion of the Israelites, whatever their sins have been. He is to do the same for the tent of meeting, which is among them in the midst of their uncleanness. ¹⁷No one is to be in the tent of meeting from the time Aaron goes in to make atonement in the Most Holy Place until he comes out, having made atonement for himself, his household and the whole community of Israel.

¹⁸"Then he shall come out to the altar that is before the LORD and make atonement for it. He shall take some of the bull's blood and some of the goat's blood and put it on all the horns of the altar. ¹⁹He shall sprinkle some of the blood on it with his finger seven times to cleanse it and to consecrate it from the uncleanness of the Israelites.

²⁰"When Aaron has finished making atonement for the Most Holy Place, the tent of meeting and the altar, he shall bring forward the live goat. ²¹He is to lay both hands on the head of the live goat and confess over it all the wickedness and rebellion of the Israelites—all their sins—and put them on the goat's head. He shall send the goat away into the wilderness in the care of someone appointed for the task. ²²The goat will carry on itself all their sins to a remote place; and the man shall release it in the wilderness.

²³"Then Aaron is to go into the tent of meeting and take off the linen garments he put on before he entered the Most Holy Place, and he is to leave them there. ²⁴He shall bathe himself with water in the sanctuary area and put on his regular garments. Then he shall come out and sacrifice the burnt offering for himself and the burnt offering for the people, to make atonement for himself and for the people. ²⁵He shall also burn the fat of the sin offering on the altar.

²⁶"The one who releases the goat as a scapegoat must wash his clothes and bathe himself with water; afterward he may come into the camp. ²⁷The bull and the goat for the sin offerings, whose blood was brought into the Most Holy Place to make atonement, must be taken outside the camp; their hides, flesh and intestines are to be burned up. ²⁸The man who burns them must wash his clothes and bathe himself with water; afterward he may come into the camp.

²⁹"This is to be a lasting ordinance for you: On the tenth day of the seventh month you must deny yourselvesᵃ and not do any work—whether native-born or a foreigner residing among you— ³⁰because on this day atonement will be made for you, to cleanse you. Then, before the LORD, you will be clean from all your sins. ³¹It is a day of sabbath rest, and you must deny yourselves; it is a lasting ordinance. ³²The

_____
ᵃ 29 Or *must fast*; also in verse 31

HE IS: the purifier

16:29–30 The Day of Atonement was the holiest day on the Israelite calendar. After bathing and putting on special clothing, the high priest entered the Most Holy Place with burning incense. He then sprinkled sacrificial blood on the atonement cover of the ark of the covenant. When this happened, God promised the people, *You will be clean from all your sins.*

Christ became both the sacrifice and the high priest who intercedes for you (see Hebrews 9:11–14). Now you can enter God's presence and ask for forgiveness any time, night or day, no elaborate rituals needed. Simply pray, and you will be clean.

For the next He Is, go to p. 153.

priest who is anointed and ordained to succeed his father as high priest is to make atonement. He is to put on the sacred linen garments ³³and make atonement for the Most Holy Place, for the tent of meeting and the altar, and for the priests and all the members of the community.

³⁴"This is to be a lasting ordinance for you: Atonement is to be made once a year for all the sins of the Israelites."

And it was done, as the LORD commanded Moses.

Eating Blood Forbidden

17 The LORD said to Moses, ²"Speak to Aaron and his sons and to all the Israelites and say to them: 'This is what the LORD has commanded: ³Any Israelite who sacrifices an ox,ᵃ a lamb or a goat in the camp or outside of it ⁴instead of bringing it to the entrance to the tent of meeting to present it as an offering to the LORD in front of the tabernacle of the LORD—such persons shall be considered guilty of bloodshed; they have shed blood and must be cut off from their people. ⁵This is so the Israelites will bring to the LORD the sacrifices they are now making in the open fields. They must bring them to the priest, that is, to the LORD, at the entrance to the tent of meeting and sacrifice them as fellowship offerings. ⁶The priest is to splash the blood against the altar of the LORD at the entrance to the tent of meeting and burn the fat as an aroma pleasing to the LORD. ⁷They must no longer offer any of their sacrifices to the goat idolsᵇ to whom they prostitute themselves. This is to be a lasting ordinance for them and for the generations to come.'

⁸"Say to them: 'Any Israelite or any foreigner residing among them who offers a burnt offering or sacrifice ⁹and does not bring it to the entrance to the tent of meeting to sacrifice it to the LORD must be cut off from their people.

¹⁰"'I will set my face against any Israelite or any foreigner residing among them who eats blood, and I will cut them off from their people. ¹¹For the life of a creature is in the blood, and I have given it to you to make atonement for yourselves on the altar; it is the blood that makes atonement for one's life.ᶜ ¹²Therefore I say to the Israelites, "None of you may eat blood, nor may any foreigner residing among you eat blood."

¹³"'Any Israelite or any foreigner residing among you who hunts any animal or bird that may be eaten must drain out the blood and cover it with earth, ¹⁴because the life of every creature is its blood. That is why I have said to the Israelites, "You must not eat the blood of any creature, because the life of every creature is its blood; anyone who eats it must be cut off."

¹⁵"'Anyone, whether native-born or foreigner, who eats anything found dead or torn by wild animals must wash their clothes and bathe with water, and they will be ceremonially unclean till evening; then they will be clean. ¹⁶But if they do not wash their clothes and bathe themselves, they will be held responsible.'"

Unlawful Sexual Relations

18 The LORD said to Moses, ²"Speak to the Israelites and say to them: 'I am the LORD your God. ³You must not do as they do in Egypt, where you used to live, and you must not do as they do in the land of Canaan, where I am bringing you. Do not follow their practices. ⁴You must obey my laws and be careful to follow my decrees. I am the LORD your God. ⁵Keep my decrees and laws, for whoever obeys them will live by them. I am the LORD.

⁶"'No one is to approach any close relative to have sexual relations. I am the LORD.

⁷"'Do not dishonor your father by having sexual relations with your mother. She is your mother; do not have relations with her.

⁸"'Do not have sexual relations with your father's wife; that would dishonor your father.

⁹"'Do not have sexual relations with your sister, either your father's daughter or your mother's daughter, whether she was born in the same home or elsewhere.

¹⁰"'Do not have sexual relations with your son's daughter or your daughter's daughter; that would dishonor you.

ᵃ *3* The Hebrew word can refer to either male or female.　ᵇ *7* Or *the demons*　ᶜ *11* Or *atonement by the life in the blood*

¹¹"Do not have sexual relations with the daughter of your father's wife, born to your father; she is your sister.

¹²"Do not have sexual relations with your father's sister; she is your father's close relative.

¹³"Do not have sexual relations with your mother's sister, because she is your mother's close relative.

¹⁴"Do not dishonor your father's brother by approaching his wife to have sexual relations; she is your aunt.

¹⁵"Do not have sexual relations with your daughter-in-law. She is your son's wife; do not have relations with her.

¹⁶"Do not have sexual relations with your brother's wife; that would dishonor your brother.

¹⁷"Do not have sexual relations with both a woman and her daughter. Do not have sexual relations with either her son's daughter or her daughter's daughter; they are her close relatives. That is wickedness.

¹⁸"Do not take your wife's sister as a rival wife and have sexual relations with her while your wife is living.

¹⁹"Do not approach a woman to have sexual relations during the uncleanness of her monthly period.

²⁰"Do not have sexual relations with your neighbor's wife and defile yourself with her.

²¹"Do not give any of your children to be sacrificed to Molek, for you must not profane the name of your God. I am the LORD.

²²"Do not have sexual relations with a man as one does with a woman; that is detestable.

²³"Do not have sexual relations with an animal and defile yourself with it. A woman must not present herself to an animal to have sexual relations with it; that is a perversion.

²⁴"Do not defile yourselves in any of these ways, because this is how the nations that I am going to drive out before you became defiled. ²⁵Even the land was defiled; so I punished it for its sin, and the land vomited out its inhabitants. ²⁶But you must keep my decrees and my laws. The native-born and the foreigners residing among you must not do any of these detestable things, ²⁷for all these things were done by the people who lived in the land before you, and the land became defiled. ²⁸And if you defile the land, it will vomit you out as it vomited out the nations that were before you.

²⁹"Everyone who does any of these detestable things—such persons must be cut off from their people. ³⁰Keep my requirements and do not follow any of the detestable customs that were practiced before you came and do not defile yourselves with them. I am the LORD your God.'"

conversations

homosexuality «» 18:22

1» Why do many people view homosexuality as a "worse" sin than other sins?

2» What should be your reaction to a person you know is a homosexual?

3» Are homosexual feelings as sinful as the actual practice of homosexuality?

For more on homosexuality, check the index.
For the next Conversations, go to p. 154.

Various Laws

19 The LORD said to Moses, ²"Speak to the entire assembly of Israel and say to them: 'Be holy because I, the LORD your God, am holy.

³"'Each of you must respect your mother and father, and you must observe my Sabbaths. I am the LORD your God.

⁴"'Do not turn to idols or make metal gods for yourselves. I am the LORD your God.

⁵"'When you sacrifice a fellowship offering to the LORD, sacrifice it in such a way that it will be accepted on your behalf. ⁶It shall be eaten on the day you sacrifice it or on the next day; anything left over until the third day must be burned up. ⁷If any of it is eaten on the third day, it is impure and will not be accepted. ⁸Whoever eats it will be held responsible because they have desecrated what is holy to the LORD; they must be cut off from their people.

⁹"'When you reap the harvest of your land, do not reap to the very edges of your field or gather the

HE IS: holy

19:2 God describes himself as holy. *Holy* means perfect, set apart, free from evil. And God wants us to follow his example. The only way to holiness is through spiritual transformation, becoming like the only perfect human—Jesus Christ.

Because God is holy, we *should* be and *can* be holy. We could never do this on our own— only through Christ's work in us. If holiness seems too lofty a goal, think of it as a process. You became holy when you accepted Christ's sacrifice on the cross. You are becoming more holy as you follow him. And you will become completely holy when you reach heaven.

For the next He Is, go to p. 155.

gleanings of your harvest. ¹⁰Do not go over your vineyard a second time or pick up the grapes that have fallen. Leave them for the poor and the foreigner. I am the LORD your God.

¹¹"Do not steal.

"Do not lie.

"Do not deceive one another.

¹²"Do not swear falsely by my name and so profane the name of your God. I am the LORD.

¹³"Do not defraud your neighbors or rob them.

"Do not hold back the wages of a hired worker overnight.

¹⁴"Do not curse the deaf or put a stumbling block in front of the blind, but fear your God. I am the LORD.

¹⁵"Do not pervert justice; do not show partiality to the poor or favoritism to the great, but judge your neighbor fairly.

¹⁶"Do not go about spreading slander among your people.

"Do not do anything that endangers your neighbor's life. I am the LORD.

¹⁷"Do not hate a fellow Israelite in your heart. Rebuke your neighbor frankly so you will not share in their guilt.

¹⁸"Do not seek revenge or bear a grudge against anyone among your people, but love your neighbor as yourself. I am the LORD.

¹⁹"Keep my decrees.

"Do not mate different kinds of animals.

"Do not plant your field with two kinds of seed.

"Do not wear clothing woven of two kinds of material.

²⁰"If a man sleeps with a female slave who is promised to another man but who has not been ransomed or given her freedom, there must be due punishment.ᵃ Yet they are not to be put to death, because she had not been freed. ²¹The man, however, must bring a ram to the entrance to the tent of meeting for a guilt offering to the LORD. ²²With the ram of the guilt offering the priest is to make atonement for him before the LORD for the sin he has committed, and his sin will be forgiven.

²³"When you enter the land and plant any kind of fruit tree, regard its fruit as forbidden.ᵇ For three years you are to consider it forbiddenᵇ; it must not be eaten. ²⁴In the fourth year all its fruit will be holy,

aussie:stealing

19:9–11 We define *stealing* as taking someone else's property. However, stealing also means keeping something that isn't ours. God commanded the Israelite farmers to leave some of their harvest in the fields for the poor. The harvest belonged to the farmers, but to gather all of it would have been to rob those who needed it most. Maybe you've never taken something that wasn't yours, but have you kept something that wasn't yours to keep? Perhaps you're hoarding your talents or squirreling away your possessions or money to hide them from God. What things are you still holding onto that God has asked you to give up?

153

ᵃ **20** Or *be an inquiry*   ᵇ **23** Hebrew *uncircumcised* an offering of praise to the LORD. ²⁵But in the fifth year you may eat its fruit. In this way your harvest will be increased. I am the LORD your God.

²⁶"'Do not eat any meat with the blood still in it.

"'Do not practice divination or seek omens.

²⁷"'Do not cut the hair at the sides of your head or clip off the edges of your beard.

²⁸"'Do not cut your bodies for the dead or put tattoo marks on yourselves. I am the LORD.

²⁹"'Do not degrade your daughter by making her a prostitute, or the land will turn to prostitution and be filled with wickedness.

³⁰"'Observe my Sabbaths and have reverence for my sanctuary. I am the LORD.

³¹"'Do not turn to mediums or seek out spiritists, for you will be defiled by them. I am the LORD your God.

³²"'Stand up in the presence of the aged, show respect for the elderly and revere your God. I am the LORD.

³³"'When foreigners reside among you in your land, do not mistreat them. ³⁴The foreigners residing among you must be treated as your native-born. Love them as yourself, for you were foreigners in Egypt. I am the LORD your God.

³⁵"'Do not use dishonest standards when measuring length, weight or quantity. ³⁶Use honest scales and honest weights, an honest ephah*ᵃ* and an honest hin.*ᵇ* I am the LORD your God, who brought you out of Egypt.

³⁷"'Keep all my decrees and all my laws and follow them. I am the LORD.'"

Punishments for Sin

20 The LORD said to Moses, ²"Say to the Israelites: 'Any Israelite or any foreigner residing in Israel who sacrifices any of his children to Molek is to be put to death. The members of the community are to stone him. ³I myself will set my face against him and will cut him off from his people; for by sacrificing his children to Molek, he has defiled my sanctuary and profaned my holy name. ⁴If the members of the community close their eyes when that man sacrifices one of his children to Molek and if they fail to put him to death, ⁵I myself will set my face against him and his family and will cut them off from their people together with all who follow him in prostituting themselves to Molek.

⁶"'I will set my face against anyone who turns to mediums and spiritists to prostitute themselves by following them, and I will cut them off from their people.

⁷"'Consecrate yourselves and be holy, because I am the LORD your God. ⁸Keep my decrees and follow them. I am the LORD, who makes you holy.

⁹"'Anyone who curses their father or mother is to be put to death. Because they have cursed their father or mother, their blood will be on their own head.

¹⁰"'If a man commits adultery with another man's wife—with the wife of his neighbor—both the adulterer and the adulteress are to be put to death.

¹¹"'If a man has sexual relations with his father's wife, he has dishonored his father. Both the man and the woman are to be put to death; their blood will be on their own heads.

¹²"'If a man has sexual relations with his daughter-in-law, both of them are to be put to death. What they have done is a perversion; their blood will be on their own heads.

¹³"'If a man has sexual relations with a man as one does with a woman, both of them have done what is detestable. They are to be put to death; their blood will be on their own heads.

conversations

infidelity «» 20:10

1 » What actions constitute cheating on your spouse?

2 » How does infidelity begin, and how can you guard against the beginnings of an affair?

3 » Can a marriage survive adultery? How?

For more on **infidelity**, check the index. For the next Conversations, go to p. 157.

ᵃ 36 An ephah was a dry measure having the capacity of about 3/5 of a bushel or about 22 liters.   *ᵇ 36* A hin was a liquid measure having the capacity of about 1 gallon or about 3.6 liters.

¹⁴"'If a man marries both a woman and her mother, it is wicked. Both he and they must be burned in the fire, so that no wickedness will be among you.

¹⁵"'If a man has sexual relations with an animal, he is to be put to death, and you must kill the animal.

¹⁶"'If a woman approaches an animal to have sexual relations with it, kill both the woman and the animal. They are to be put to death; their blood will be on their own heads.

¹⁷"'If a man marries his sister, the daughter of either his father or his mother, and they have sexual relations, it is a disgrace. They are to be publicly removed from their people. He has dishonored his sister and will be held responsible.

¹⁸"'If a man has sexual relations with a woman during her monthly period, he has exposed the source of her flow, and she has also uncovered it. Both of them are to be cut off from their people.

¹⁹"'Do not have sexual relations with the sister of either your mother or your father, for that would dishonor a close relative; both of you would be held responsible.

²⁰"'If a man has sexual relations with his aunt, he has dishonored his uncle. They will be held responsible; they will die childless.

²¹"'If a man marries his brother's wife, it is an act of impurity; he has dishonored his brother. They will be childless.

²²"'Keep all my decrees and laws and follow them, so that the land where I am bringing you to live may not vomit you out. ²³You must not live according to the customs of the nations I am going to drive out before you. Because they did all these things, I abhorred them. ²⁴But I said to you, "You will possess their land; I will give it to you as an inheritance, a land flowing with milk and honey." I am the LORD your God, who has set you apart from the nations.

155

HE IS: just

20:22–24 God condemned the sexual sins practiced by the inhabitants of Canaan: adultery, incest, homosexuality and bestiality. In contrast he promised blessing if his people would avoid sinful behavior: *You will possess their land; I will give it to you as an inheritance.*

He is *just.* God will dole out either divine punishment or divine blessing. The choice is up to you. On the one hand, you can stubbornly disobey God's laws and risk his displeasure. On the other hand, you can choose the blessings of obedience by staying sexually pure. The just judge sees your choices and will reward you accordingly.

For the next He Is, go to p. 163.

²⁵"'You must therefore make a distinction between clean and unclean animals and between unclean and clean birds. Do not defile yourselves by any animal or bird or anything that moves along the ground—those which I have set apart as unclean for you. ²⁶You are to be holy to me because I, the LORD, am holy, and I have set you apart from the nations to be my own.

²⁷"'A man or woman who is a medium or spiritist among you must be put to death. You are to stone them; their blood will be on their own heads.'"

Rules for Priests

21 The LORD said to Moses, "Speak to the priests, the sons of Aaron, and say to them: 'A priest must not make himself ceremonially unclean for any of his people who die, ²except for a close relative, such as his mother or father, his son or daughter, his brother, ³or an unmarried sister who is dependent on him since she has no husband—for her he may make himself unclean. ⁴He must not make himself unclean for people related to him by marriage,ᵃ and so defile himself.

⁵"'Priests must not shave their heads or shave off the edges of their beards or cut their bodies. ⁶They

---

ᵃ *4 Or unclean as a leader among his people*

must be holy to their God and must not profane the name of their God. Because they present the food offerings to the LORD, the food of their God, they are to be holy.

⁷"They must not marry women defiled by prostitution or divorced from their husbands, because priests are holy to their God. ⁸Regard them as holy, because they offer up the food of your God. Consider them holy, because I the LORD am holy—I who make you holy.

⁹"If a priest's daughter defiles herself by becoming a prostitute, she disgraces her father; she must be burned in the fire.

¹⁰"The high priest, the one among his brothers who has had the anointing oil poured on his head and who has been ordained to wear the priestly garments, must not let his hair become unkempt[ᵃ] or tear his clothes. ¹¹He must not enter a place where there is a dead body. He must not make himself unclean, even for his father or mother, ¹²nor leave the sanctuary of his God or desecrate it, because he has been dedicated by the anointing oil of his God. I am the LORD.

¹³"The woman he marries must be a virgin. ¹⁴He must not marry a widow, a divorced woman, or a woman defiled by prostitution, but only a virgin from his own people, ¹⁵so that he will not defile his offspring among his people. I am the LORD, who makes him holy.'"

¹⁶The LORD said to Moses, ¹⁷"Say to Aaron: 'For the generations to come none of your descendants who has a defect may come near to offer the food of his God. ¹⁸No man who has any defect may come near: no man who is blind or lame, disfigured or deformed; ¹⁹no man with a crippled foot or hand, ²⁰or who is a hunchback or a dwarf, or who has any eye defect, or who has festering or running sores or damaged testicles. ²¹No descendant of Aaron the priest who has any defect is to come near to present the food offerings to the LORD. He has a defect; he must not come near to offer the food of his God. ²²He may eat the most holy food of his God, as well as the holy food; ²³yet because of his defect, he must not go near the curtain or approach the altar, and so desecrate my sanctuary. I am the LORD, who makes them holy.'"

²⁴So Moses told this to Aaron and his sons and to all the Israelites.

22 The LORD said to Moses, ²"Tell Aaron and his sons to treat with respect the sacred offerings the Israelites consecrate to me, so they will not profane my holy name. I am the LORD.

³"Say to them: 'For the generations to come, if any of your descendants is ceremonially unclean and yet comes near the sacred offerings that the Israelites consecrate to the LORD, that person must be cut off from my presence. I am the LORD.

⁴"'If a descendant of Aaron has a defiling skin disease[ᵇ] or a bodily discharge, he may not eat the sacred offerings until he is cleansed. He will also be unclean if he touches something defiled by a corpse or by anyone who has an emission of semen, ⁵or if he touches any crawling thing that makes him unclean, or any person who makes him unclean, whatever the uncleanness may be. ⁶The one who touches any such thing will be unclean till evening. He must not eat any of the sacred offerings unless he has bathed himself with water. ⁷When the sun goes down, he will be clean, and after that he may eat the sacred offerings, for they are his food. ⁸He must not eat anything found dead or torn by wild animals, and so become unclean through it. I am the LORD.

⁹"'The priests are to perform my service in such a way that they do not become guilty and die for treating it with contempt. I am the LORD, who makes them holy.

¹⁰"'No one outside a priest's family may eat the sacred offering, nor may the guest of a priest or his hired worker eat it. ¹¹But if a priest buys a slave with money, or if slaves are born in his household, they may eat his food. ¹²If a priest's daughter marries anyone other than a priest, she may not eat any of the sacred contributions. ¹³But if a priest's daughter becomes a widow or is divorced, yet has no children, and she returns to live in her father's household as in her youth, she may eat of her father's food. No unauthorized person, however, may eat any of it.

¹⁴"'Anyone who eats a sacred offering by mistake must make restitution to the priest for the offering and add a fifth of the value to it. ¹⁵The priests must not desecrate the sacred offerings the Israelites present to the LORD ¹⁶by allowing them to eat the sacred offerings and so bring upon them guilt requiring payment. I am the LORD, who makes them holy.'"

ᵃ 10 Or not uncover his head ᵇ 4 The Hebrew word for defiling skin disease, traditionally translated "leprosy," was used for various diseases affecting the skin.

Unacceptable Sacrifices

¹⁷The Lord said to Moses, ¹⁸"Speak to Aaron and his sons and to all the Israelites and say to them: 'If any of you—whether an Israelite or a foreigner residing in Israel—presents a gift for a burnt offering to the Lord, either to fulfill a vow or as a freewill offering, ¹⁹you must present a male without defect from the cattle, sheep or goats in order that it may be accepted on your behalf. ²⁰Do not bring anything with a defect, because it will not be accepted on your behalf. ²¹When anyone brings from the herd or flock a fellowship offering to the Lord to fulfill a special vow or as a freewill offering, it must be without defect or blemish to be acceptable. ²²Do not offer to the Lord the blind, the injured or the maimed, or anything with warts or festering or running sores. Do not place any of these on the altar as a food offering presented to the Lord. ²³You may, however, present as a freewill offering an ox ᵃ or a sheep that is deformed or stunted, but it will not be accepted in fulfillment of a vow. ²⁴You must not offer to the Lord an animal whose testicles are bruised, crushed, torn or cut. You must not do this in your own land, ²⁵and you must not accept such animals from the hand of a foreigner and offer them as the food of your God. They will not be accepted on your behalf, because they are deformed and have defects.'"

²⁶The Lord said to Moses, ²⁷"When a calf, a lamb or a goat is born, it is to remain with its mother for seven days. From the eighth day on, it will be acceptable as a food offering presented to the Lord. ²⁸Do not slaughter a cow or a sheep and its young on the same day.

²⁹"When you sacrifice a thank offering to the Lord, sacrifice it in such a way that it will be accepted on your behalf. ³⁰It must be eaten that same day; leave none of it till morning. I am the Lord.

³¹"Keep my commands and follow them. I am the Lord. ³²Do not profane my holy name, for I must be acknowledged as holy by the Israelites. I am the Lord, who made you holy ³³and who brought you out of Egypt to be your God. I am the Lord."

157

23

The Lord said to Moses, ²"Speak to the Israelites and say to them: 'These are my appointed festivals, the appointed festivals of the Lord, which you are to proclaim as sacred assemblies.

The Sabbath

³"'There are six days when you may work, but the seventh day is a day of sabbath rest, a day of sacred assembly. You are not to do any work; wherever you live, it is a sabbath to the Lord.

The Passover and the Festival of Unleavened Bread

⁴"'These are the Lord's appointed festivals, the sacred assemblies you are to proclaim at their appointed times: ⁵The Lord's Passover begins at twilight on the fourteenth day of the first month. ⁶On the fifteenth day of that month the Lord's Festival of Unleavened Bread begins; for seven days you must eat bread made without yeast. ⁷On the first day hold a sacred assembly and do no regular work. ⁸For seven days present a food offering to the Lord. And on the seventh day hold a sacred assembly and do no regular work.'"

conversations

rest «» 23:3

1 » What is true *rest*?

2 » How do you practice Sabbath rest?

3 » Are you good at resting? If not, why not?

For more on rest, check the index.
For the next Conversations, go to p. 161.

Offering the Firstfruits

⁹The Lord said to Moses, ¹⁰"Speak to the Israelites and say to them: 'When you enter the land I am going to give you and you reap its harvest, bring to the priest a sheaf of the first grain you harvest. ¹¹He is to wave the sheaf before the Lord so it will be accepted on your behalf; the priest is to wave it on the day after the Sabbath. ¹²On the day you wave the sheaf, you must sacrifice as a burnt offering to the Lord a lamb a year old without defect, ¹³together with its grain offering of two-tenths of an ephah ᵇ of the

ᵃ 23 The Hebrew word can refer to either male or female.   ᵇ 13 That is, probably about 7 pounds or about 3 1/4 kilograms; also in verse 17 finest flour mixed with olive oil—a food offering presented to the Lord, a pleasing aroma—and its drink offering of a quarter of a hin*a* of wine. [14]You must not eat any bread, or roasted or new grain, until the very day you bring this offering to your God. This is to be a lasting ordinance for the generations to come, wherever you live.

The Festival of Weeks

[15]"'From the day after the Sabbath, the day you brought the sheaf of the wave offering, count off seven full weeks. [16]Count off fifty days up to the day after the seventh Sabbath, and then present an offering of new grain to the Lord. [17]From wherever you live, bring two loaves made of two-tenths of an ephah of the finest flour, baked with yeast, as a wave offering of firstfruits to the Lord. [18]Present with this bread seven male lambs, each a year old and without defect, one young bull and two rams. They will be a burnt offering to the Lord, together with their grain offerings and drink offerings—a food offering, an aroma pleasing to the Lord. [19]Then sacrifice one male goat for a sin offering*b* and two lambs, each a year old, for a fellowship offering. [20]The priest is to wave the two lambs before the Lord as a wave offering, together with the bread of the firstfruits. They are a sacred offering to the Lord for the priest. [21]On that same day you are to proclaim a sacred assembly and do no regular work. This is to be a lasting ordinance for the generations to come, wherever you live.

[22]"'When you reap the harvest of your land, do not reap to the very edges of your field or gather the gleanings of your harvest. Leave them for the poor and for the foreigner residing among you. I am the Lord your God.'"

The Festival of Trumpets

[23]The Lord said to Moses, [24]"Say to the Israelites: 'On the first day of the seventh month you are to have a day of sabbath rest, a sacred assembly commemorated with trumpet blasts. [25]Do no regular work, but present a food offering to the Lord.'"

The Day of Atonement

[26]The Lord said to Moses, [27]"The tenth day of this seventh month is the Day of Atonement. Hold a sacred assembly and deny yourselves,*c* and present a food offering to the Lord. [28]Do not do any work on that day, because it is the Day of Atonement, when atonement is made for you before the Lord your God. [29]Those who do not deny themselves on that day must be cut off from their people. [30]I will destroy from among their people anyone who does any work on that day. [31]You shall do no work at all. This is to be a lasting ordinance for the generations to come, wherever you live. [32]It is a day of sabbath rest for you, and you must deny yourselves. From the evening of the ninth day of the month until the following evening you are to observe your sabbath."

The Festival of Tabernacles

[33]The Lord said to Moses, [34]"Say to the Israelites: 'On the fifteenth day of the seventh month the Lord's Festival of Tabernacles begins, and it lasts for seven days. [35]The first day is a sacred assembly; do no regular work. [36]For seven days present food offerings to the Lord, and on the eighth day hold a sacred assembly and present a food offering to the Lord. It is the closing special assembly; do no regular work.

[37]("'These are the Lord's appointed festivals, which you are to proclaim as sacred assemblies for bringing food offerings to the Lord—the burnt offerings and grain offerings, sacrifices and drink offerings required for each day. [38]These offerings are in addition to those for the Lord's Sabbaths and*d* in addition to your gifts and whatever you have vowed and all the freewill offerings you give to the Lord.)

[39]"'So beginning with the fifteenth day of the seventh month, after you have gathered the crops of the land, celebrate the festival to the Lord for seven days; the first day is a day of sabbath rest, and the eighth day also is a day of sabbath rest. [40]On the first day you are to take branches from luxuriant trees—from palms, willows and other leafy trees—and rejoice before the Lord your God for seven days. [41]Celebrate this as a festival to the Lord for seven days each year. This is to be a lasting ordinance for the generations to come; celebrate it in the seventh month. [42]Live in temporary shelters for seven days: All native-born

---

a 13 That is, about 1 quart or about 0.9 liter   b 19 Or purification offering   c 27 Or and fast; also in verses 29 and 32   d 38 Or These festivals are in addition to the Lord's Sabbaths, and these offerings are

Israelites are to live in such shelters ⁴³so your descendants will know that I had the Israelites live in temporary shelters when I brought them out of Egypt. I am the LORD your God.'"

⁴⁴So Moses announced to the Israelites the appointed festivals of the LORD.

Oil and Bread Set Before the LORD

24 The LORD said to Moses, ²"Command the Israelites to bring you clear oil of pressed olives for the light so that the lamps may be kept burning continually. ³Outside the curtain that shields the ark of the covenant law in the tent of meeting, Aaron is to tend the lamps before the LORD from evening till morning, continually. This is to be a lasting ordinance for the generations to come. ⁴The lamps on the pure gold lampstand before the LORD must be tended continually.

⁵"Take the finest flour and bake twelve loaves of bread, using two-tenths of an ephah*a* for each loaf. ⁶Arrange them in two stacks, six in each stack, on the table of pure gold before the LORD. ⁷By each stack put some pure incense as a memorial*b* portion to represent the bread and to be a food offering presented to the LORD. ⁸This bread is to be set out before the LORD regularly, Sabbath after Sabbath, on behalf of the Israelites, as a lasting covenant. ⁹It belongs to Aaron and his sons, who are to eat it in the sanctuary area, because it is a most holy part of their perpetual share of the food offerings presented to the LORD."

A Blasphemer Stoned

¹⁰Now the son of an Israelite mother and an Egyptian father went out among the Israelites, and a fight broke out in the camp between him and an Israelite. ¹¹The son of the Israelite woman blasphemed the Name with a curse; so they brought him to Moses. (His mother's name was Shelomith, the daughter of Dibri the Danite.) ¹²They put him in custody until the will of the LORD should be made clear to them.

¹³Then the LORD said to Moses: ¹⁴"Take the blasphemer outside the camp. All those who heard him are to lay their hands on his head, and the entire assembly is to stone him. ¹⁵Say to the Israelites: 'Anyone who curses their God will be held responsible; ¹⁶anyone who blasphemes the name of the LORD is to be put to death. The entire assembly must stone them. Whether foreigner or native-born, when they blaspheme the Name they are to be put to death.

¹⁷"'Anyone who takes the life of a human being is to be put to death. ¹⁸Anyone who takes the life of someone's animal must make restitution—life for life. ¹⁹Anyone who injures a neighbor is to be injured in the same manner: ²⁰fracture for fracture, eye for eye, tooth for tooth. The one who has inflicted the injury must suffer the same injury. ²¹Whoever kills an animal must make restitution, but whoever kills a human being is to be put to death. ²²You are to have the same law for the foreigner and the native-born. I am the LORD your God.'"

²³Then Moses spoke to the Israelites, and they took the blasphemer outside the camp and stoned him. The Israelites did as the LORD commanded Moses.

The Sabbath Year

25 The LORD said to Moses on Mount Sinai, ²"Speak to the Israelites and say to them: 'When you enter the land I am going to give you, the land itself must observe a sabbath to the LORD. ³For six years sow your fields, and for six years prune your vineyards and gather their crops. ⁴But in the seventh year the land is to have a year of sabbath rest, a sabbath to the LORD. Do not sow your fields or prune your vineyards. ⁵Do not reap what grows of itself or harvest the grapes of your untended vines. The land is to have a year of rest. ⁶Whatever the land yields during the sabbath year will be food for you—for yourself, your male and female servants, and the hired worker and temporary resident who live among you, ⁷as well as for your livestock and the wild animals in your land. Whatever the land produces may be eaten.

The Year of Jubilee

⁸"'Count off seven sabbath years—seven times seven years—so that the seven sabbath years amount to a period of forty-nine years. ⁹Then have the trumpet sounded everywhere on the tenth day of the

a 5 That is, probably about 7 pounds or about 3 1/4 kilograms   *b 7 Or representative* seventh month; on the Day of Atonement sound the trumpet throughout your land. ¹⁰Consecrate the fiftieth year and proclaim liberty throughout the land to all its inhabitants. It shall be a jubilee for you; each of you is to return to your family property and to your own clan. ¹¹The fiftieth year shall be a jubilee for you; do not sow and do not reap what grows of itself or harvest the untended vines. ¹²For it is a jubilee and is to be holy for you; eat only what is taken directly from the fields.

¹³"'In this Year of Jubilee everyone is to return to their own property.

¹⁴"'If you sell land to any of your own people or buy land from them, do not take advantage of each other. ¹⁵You are to buy from your own people on the basis of the number of years since the Jubilee. And they are to sell to you on the basis of the number of years left for harvesting crops. ¹⁶When the years are many, you are to increase the price, and when the years are few, you are to decrease the price, because what is really being sold to you is the number of crops. ¹⁷Do not take advantage of each other, but fear your God. I am the LORD your God.

¹⁸"'Follow my decrees and be careful to obey my laws, and you will live safely in the land. ¹⁹Then the land will yield its fruit, and you will eat your fill and live there in safety. ²⁰You may ask, "What will we eat in the seventh year if we do not plant or harvest our crops?" ²¹I will send you such a blessing in the sixth year that the land will yield enough for three years. ²²While you plant during the eighth year, you will eat from the old crop and will continue to eat from it until the harvest of the ninth year comes in.

²³"'The land must not be sold permanently, because the land is mine and you reside in my land as foreigners and strangers. ²⁴Throughout the land that you hold as a possession, you must provide for the redemption of the land.

²⁵"'If anyone among you becomes poor and sells some of their property, their nearest relative is to come and redeem what they have sold. ²⁶If, however, there is no one to redeem it for them but later on they prosper and acquire sufficient means to redeem it themselves, ²⁷they are to determine the value for the years since they sold it and refund the balance to the one to whom they sold it; they can then go back to their own property. ²⁸But if they do not acquire the means to repay, what was sold will remain in the possession of the buyer until the Year of Jubilee. It will be returned in the Jubilee, and they can then go back to their property.

²⁹"'Anyone who sells a house in a walled city retains the right of redemption a full year after its sale. During that time the seller may redeem it. ³⁰If it is not redeemed before a full year has passed, the house in the walled city shall belong permanently to the buyer and the buyer's descendants. It is not to be returned in the Jubilee. ³¹But houses in villages without walls around them are to be considered as belonging to the open country. They can be redeemed, and they are to be returned in the Jubilee.

³²"'The Levites always have the right to redeem their houses in the Levitical towns, which they possess. ³³So the property of the Levites is redeemable—that is, a house sold in any town they hold—and is to be returned in the Jubilee, because the houses in the towns of the Levites are their property among the Israelites. ³⁴But the pastureland belonging to their towns must not be sold; it is their permanent possession.

³⁵"'If any of your own people become poor and are unable to support themselves among you, help them as you would a foreigner and stranger, so they can continue to live among you. ³⁶Do not take interest or any profit from them, but fear your God, so that your poor neighbors may continue to live among you. ³⁷You must not lend them money at interest or sell them food at a profit. ³⁸I am the LORD your God, who brought you out of Egypt to give you the land of Canaan and to be your God.

³⁹"'If any of your own people become poor and sell themselves to you, do not make them work as slaves. ⁴⁰They are to be treated as hired workers or temporary residents among you; they are to work for you until the Year of Jubilee. ⁴¹Then they and their children are to be released, and they will go back to their own clans and to the property of their ancestors. ⁴²Because the Israelites are my servants, whom I brought out of Egypt, they must not be sold as slaves. ⁴³Do not rule over them ruthlessly, but fear your God.

⁴⁴"'Your male and female slaves are to come from the nations around you; from them you may buy slaves. ⁴⁵You may also buy some of the temporary residents living among you and members of their clans born in your country, and they will become your property. ⁴⁶You can bequeath them to your children as

inherited property and can make them slaves for life, but you must not rule over your fellow Israelites ruthlessly.

⁴⁷"'If a foreigner residing among you becomes rich and any of your own people become poor and sell themselves to the foreigner or to a member of the foreigner's clan, ⁴⁸they retain the right of redemption after they have sold themselves. One of their relatives may redeem them: ⁴⁹An uncle or a cousin or any blood relative in their clan may redeem them. Or if any of them prosper, they may redeem themselves. ⁵⁰They and their buyer are to count the time from the year they sold themselves up to the Year of Jubilee. The price for their release is to be based on the rate paid to a hired worker for that number of years. ⁵¹If many years remain, they must pay for their redemption a larger share of the price paid for them. ⁵²If only a few years remain until the Year of Jubilee, they are to compute that and pay for their redemption accordingly. ⁵³They are to be treated as hired workers from year to year; you must see to it that those to whom they owe service do not rule over them ruthlessly.

⁵⁴"'Even if they are not redeemed in any of these ways, they and their children are to be released in the Year of Jubilee, ⁵⁵for the Israelites belong to me as servants. They are my servants, whom I brought out of Egypt. I am the LORD your God.

Reward for Obedience

26 "'Do not make idols or set up an image or a sacred stone for yourselves, and do not place a carved stone in your land to bow down before it. I am the LORD your God.

² "'Observe my Sabbaths and have reverence for my sanctuary. I am the LORD.

³ "'If you follow my decrees and are careful to obey my commands, ⁴I will send you rain in its season, and the ground will yield its crops and the trees their fruit. ⁵Your threshing will continue until grape harvest and the grape harvest will continue until planting, and you will eat all the food you want and live in safety in your land.

⁶ "'I will grant peace in the land, and you will lie down and no one will make you afraid. I will remove wild beasts from the land, and the sword will not pass through your country. ⁷You will pursue your enemies, and they will fall by the sword before you. ⁸Five of you will chase a hundred, and a hundred of you will chase ten thousand, and your enemies will fall by the sword before you.

⁹ "'I will look on you with favor and make you fruitful and increase your numbers, and I will keep my covenant with you. ¹⁰You will still be eating last year's harvest when you will have to move it out to make room for the new. ¹¹I will put my dwelling place*a* among you, and I will not abhor you. ¹²I will walk among you and be your God, and you will be my people. ¹³I am the LORD your God, who brought you out of Egypt so that you would no longer be slaves to the Egyptians; I broke the bars of your yoke and enabled you to walk with heads held high.

" conversations "

obedience «» 26:1–13

1» What are some of the ways that God says he'll reward obedience?

2» Are there other benefits for following God's rules?

3» Which motivation is more effective for you —fear of punishment or desire for reward?

For more on **obedience**, check the index.
For the next Conversations, go to p. 172.

Punishment for Disobedience

¹⁴ "'But if you will not listen to me and carry out all these commands, ¹⁵and if you reject my decrees and abhor my laws and fail to carry out all my commands and so violate my covenant, ¹⁶then I will do this to you: I will bring on you sudden terror, wasting diseases and fever that will destroy your sight and sap your strength. You will plant seed in vain, because your enemies will eat it. ¹⁷I will set my face against you so that you will be defeated by your enemies; those who hate you will rule over you, and you will flee even when no one is pursuing you.

¹⁸ "'If after all this you will not listen to me, I will punish you for your sins seven times over. ¹⁹I will

---

a 11 Or my tabernacle

break down your stubborn pride and make the sky above you like iron and the ground beneath you like bronze. ²⁰Your strength will be spent in vain, because your soil will not yield its crops, nor will the trees of your land yield their fruit.

²¹"'If you remain hostile toward me and refuse to listen to me, I will multiply your afflictions seven times over, as your sins deserve. ²²I will send wild animals against you, and they will rob you of your children, destroy your cattle and make you so few in number that your roads will be deserted.

²³"'If in spite of these things you do not accept my correction but continue to be hostile toward me, ²⁴I myself will be hostile toward you and will afflict you for your sins seven times over. ²⁵And I will bring the sword on you to avenge the breaking of the covenant. When you withdraw into your cities, I will send a plague among you, and you will be given into enemy hands. ²⁶When I cut off your supply of bread, ten women will be able to bake your bread in one oven, and they will dole out the bread by weight. You will eat, but you will not be satisfied.

²⁷"'If in spite of this you still do not listen to me but continue to be hostile toward me, ²⁸then in my anger I will be hostile toward you, and I myself will punish you for your sins seven times over. ²⁹You will eat the flesh of your sons and the flesh of your daughters. ³⁰I will destroy your high places, cut down your incense altars and pile your dead bodies*a* on the lifeless forms of your idols, and I will abhor you. ³¹I will turn your cities into ruins and lay waste your sanctuaries, and I will take no delight in the pleasing aroma of your offerings. ³²I myself will lay waste the land, so that your enemies who live there will be appalled. ³³I will scatter you among the nations and will draw out my sword and pursue you. Your land will be laid waste, and your cities will lie in ruins. ³⁴Then the land will enjoy its sabbath years all the time that it lies desolate and you are in the country of your enemies; then the land will rest and enjoy its sabbaths. ³⁵All the time that it lies desolate, the land will have the rest it did not have during the sabbaths you lived in it.

³⁶"'As for those of you who are left, I will make their hearts so fearful in the lands of their enemies that the sound of a windblown leaf will put them to flight. They will run as though fleeing from the sword, and they will fall, even though no one is pursuing them. ³⁷They will stumble over one another as though fleeing from the sword, even though no one is pursuing them. So you will not be able to stand before your enemies. ³⁸You will perish among the nations; the land of your enemies will devour you. ³⁹Those of you who are left will waste away in the lands of their enemies because of their sins; also because of their ancestors' sins they will waste away.

⁴⁰"'But if they will confess their sins and the sins of their ancestors—their unfaithfulness and their hostility toward me, ⁴¹which made me hostile toward them so that I sent them into the land of their enemies—then when their uncircumcised hearts are humbled and they pay for their sin, ⁴²I will remember my covenant with Jacob and my covenant with Isaac and my covenant with Abraham, and I will remember the land. ⁴³For the land will be deserted by them and will enjoy its sabbaths while it lies desolate without them. They will pay for their sins because they rejected my laws and abhorred my decrees. ⁴⁴Yet in spite of this, when they are in the land of their enemies, I will not reject them or abhor them so as to destroy them completely, breaking my covenant with them. I am the Lᴏʀᴅ their God. ⁴⁵But for their sake I will remember the covenant with their ancestors whom I brought out of Egypt in the sight of the nations to be their God. I am the Lᴏʀᴅ.'"

⁴⁶These are the decrees, the laws and the regulations that the Lᴏʀᴅ established on Mount Sinai between himself and the Israelites through Moses.

Redeeming What Is the Lᴏʀᴅ's

27 The Lᴏʀᴅ said to Moses, ²"Speak to the Israelites and say to them: 'If anyone makes a special vow to dedicate a person to the Lᴏʀᴅ by giving the equivalent value, ³set the value of a male between the ages of twenty and sixty at fifty shekels*b* of silver, according to the sanctuary shekel*c*; ⁴for a female, set her value at thirty shekels*d*; ⁵for a person between the ages of five and twenty, set the value of a male at twenty shekels*e* and of a female at ten shekels*f*; ⁶for a person between one month and five years, set

---

ᵃ 30 Or your funeral offerings ᵇ 3 That is, about 1 1/4 pounds or about 575 grams; also in verse 16 ᶜ 3 That is, about 2/5 ounce or about 11.5 grams; also in verse 25 ᵈ 4 That is, about 12 ounces or about 345 grams ᵉ 5 That is, about 8 ounces or about 230 grams ᶠ 5 That is, about 4 ounces or about 115 grams; also in verse 7

HE IS: the rememberer

26:44–45 God could have nullified his covenant when the Israelites disobeyed his commands. He could have forgotten his promise to be the Lord their God when they turned to other gods. But God isn't like humans, who look for loopholes to break a contract. He is *the rememberer*. He remembers his covenants.

As God's beloved, you've entered into the new covenant; his law is written on your mind and heart (see Jeremiah 31:31–33). Others might have rejected you . . . he never will. Others will forget promises they've made . . . it's against his nature to forget. If you think he's forsaken you, think again . . . he is *the rememberer*.

For the next He Is, go to p. 169.

163

the value of a male at five shekels *a* of silver and that of a female at three shekels*b* of silver; [7] for a person sixty years old or more, set the value of a male at fifteen shekels*c* and of a female at ten shekels. [8] If anyone making the vow is too poor to pay the specified amount, the person being dedicated is to be presented to the priest, who will set the value according to what the one making the vow can afford.

[9] "'If what anyone vowed is an animal that is acceptable as an offering to the Lord, such an animal given to the Lord becomes holy. [10] They must not exchange it or substitute a good one for a bad one, or a bad one for a good one; if they should substitute one animal for another, both it and the substitute become holy. [11] If what they vowed is a ceremonially unclean animal—one that is not acceptable as an offering to the Lord—the animal must be presented to the priest, [12] who will judge its quality as good or bad. Whatever value the priest then sets, that is what it will be. [13] If the owner wishes to redeem the animal, a fifth must be added to its value.

[14] "'If anyone dedicates their house as something holy to the Lord, the priest will judge its quality as good or bad. Whatever value the priest then sets, so it will remain. [15] If the one who dedicates their house wishes to redeem it, they must add a fifth to its value, and the house will again become theirs.

[16] "'If anyone dedicates to the Lord part of their family land, its value is to be set according to the amount of seed required for it—fifty shekels of silver to a homer*d* of barley seed. [17] If they dedicate a field during the Year of Jubilee, the value that has been set remains. [18] But if they dedicate a field after the Jubilee, the priest will determine the value according to the number of years that remain until the next Year of Jubilee, and its set value will be reduced. [19] If the one who dedicates the field wishes to redeem it, they must add a fifth to its value, and the field will again become theirs. [20] If, however, they do not redeem the field, or if they have sold it to someone else, it can never be redeemed. [21] When the field is released in the Jubilee, it will become holy, like a field devoted to the Lord; it will become priestly property.

[22] "'If anyone dedicates to the Lord a field they have bought, which is not part of their family land, [23] the priest will determine its value up to the Year of Jubilee, and that person must pay its value on that day as something holy to the Lord. [24] In the Year of Jubilee the field will revert to the person from whom it was bought, the one whose land it was. [25] Every value is to be set according to the sanctuary shekel, twenty gerahs to the shekel.

[26] "'No one, however, may dedicate the firstborn of an animal, since the firstborn already belongs to the Lord; whether an ox*e* or a sheep, it is the Lord's. [27] If it is one of the unclean animals, it may be bought back at its set value, adding a fifth of the value to it. If it is not redeemed, it is to be sold at its set value.

[28] "'But nothing that a person owns and devotes*f* to the Lord—whether a human being or an animal or family land—may be sold or redeemed; everything so devoted is most holy to the Lord.

[29] "'No persons devoted to destruction*g* may be ransomed; they are to be put to death.

---

a 6 That is, about 2 ounces or about 55 grams *b 6* That is, about 1 1/4 ounces or about 35 grams *c 7* That is, about 6 ounces or about 170 grams *d 16* That is, probably about 300 pounds or about 135 kilograms *e 26* The Hebrew word can refer to either male or female. *f 28* The Hebrew term refers to the irrevocable giving over of things or persons to the Lord. *g 29* The Hebrew term refers to the irrevocable giving over of things or persons to the Lord, often by totally destroying them.

³⁰"'A tithe of everything from the land, whether grain from the soil or fruit from the trees, belongs to the Lord; it is holy to the Lord. ³¹Whoever would redeem any of their tithe must add a fifth of the value to it. ³²Every tithe of the herd and flock—every tenth animal that passes under the shepherd's rod—will be holy to the Lord. ³³No one may pick out the good from the bad or make any substitution. If anyone does make a substitution, both the animal and its substitute become holy and cannot be redeemed.'"

³⁴These are the commands the Lord gave Moses on Mount Sinai for the Israelites.

numbers

165

AUTHOR
Moses.

AUDIENCE
The people of Israel.

DATE
Between 1446 and 1406 B.C.

SETTING
After a year in the Sinai Desert, a census is
taken. Then onward to Canaan and 39 more
years of wandering in the desert.

VERSES TO REMEMBER
"They gave Moses this account: 'We went
into the land to which you sent us, and it
does flow with milk and honey! Here is its
fruit.'

"But the men who had gone up with him
said, 'We can't attack those people; they are
stronger than we are.'" (13:27,31)

THEME TO CONSIDER
Serving God means following his plan,
his way. If we refuse, we'll miss key opportunities.

The Census

1 The LORD spoke to Moses in the tent of meeting in the Desert of Sinai on the first day of the second month of the second year after the Israelites came out of Egypt. He said: ²"Take a census of the whole Israelite community by their clans and families, listing every man by name, one by one. ³You and Aaron are to count according to their divisions all the men in Israel who are twenty years old or more and able to serve in the army. ⁴One man from each tribe, each of them the head of his family, is to help you. ⁵These are the names of the men who are to assist you:

from Reuben, Elizur son of Shedeur;
⁶ from Simeon, Shelumiel son of Zurishaddai;
⁷ from Judah, Nahshon son of Amminadab;
⁸ from Issachar, Nethanel son of Zuar;
⁹ from Zebulun, Eliab son of Helon;
¹⁰ from the sons of Joseph:
from Ephraim, Elishama son of Ammihud;
from Manasseh, Gamaliel son of Pedahzur;
¹¹ from Benjamin, Abidan son of Gideoni;
¹² from Dan, Ahiezer son of Ammishaddai;
¹³ from Asher, Pagiel son of Okran;
¹⁴ from Gad, Eliasaph son of Deuel;
¹⁵ from Naphtali, Ahira son of Enan."

¹⁶These were the men appointed from the community, the leaders of their ancestral tribes. They were the heads of the clans of Israel.

¹⁷Moses and Aaron took these men whose names had been specified, ¹⁸and they called the whole community together on the first day of the second month. The people registered their ancestry by their clans and families, and the men twenty years old or more were listed by name, one by one, ¹⁹as the LORD commanded Moses. And so he counted them in the Desert of Sinai:

²⁰ From the descendants of Reuben the firstborn son of Israel:
All the men twenty years old or more who were able to serve in the army were listed by name, one by one, according to the records of their clans and families. ²¹The number from the tribe of Reuben was 46,500.

²² From the descendants of Simeon:
All the men twenty years old or more who were able to serve in the army were counted and listed by name, one by one, according to the records of their clans and families. ²³The number from the tribe of Simeon was 59,300.

²⁴ From the descendants of Gad:
All the men twenty years old or more who were able to serve in the army were listed by name, according to the records of their clans and families. ²⁵The number from the tribe of Gad was 45,650.

²⁶ From the descendants of Judah:
All the men twenty years old or more who were able to serve in the army were listed by name, according to the records of their clans and families. ²⁷The number from the tribe of Judah was 74,600.

²⁸ From the descendants of Issachar:
All the men twenty years old or more who were able to serve in the army were listed by name, according to the records of their clans and families. ²⁹The number from the tribe of Issachar was 54,400.

³⁰ From the descendants of Zebulun:
All the men twenty years old or more who were able to serve in the army were listed by name,

according to the records of their clans and families. [31]The number from the tribe of Zebulun was 57,400.

[32] From the sons of Joseph:

From the descendants of Ephraim:

All the men twenty years old or more who were able to serve in the army were listed by name, according to the records of their clans and families. [33]The number from the tribe of Ephraim was 40,500.

[34] From the descendants of Manasseh:

All the men twenty years old or more who were able to serve in the army were listed by name, according to the records of their clans and families. [35]The number from the tribe of Manasseh was 32,200.

[36] From the descendants of Benjamin:

All the men twenty years old or more who were able to serve in the army were listed by name, according to the records of their clans and families. [37]The number from the tribe of Benjamin was 35,400.

[38] From the descendants of Dan:

All the men twenty years old or more who were able to serve in the army were listed by name, according to the records of their clans and families. [39]The number from the tribe of Dan was 62,700.

[40] From the descendants of Asher:

All the men twenty years old or more who were able to serve in the army were listed by name, according to the records of their clans and families. [41]The number from the tribe of Asher was 41,500.

[42] From the descendants of Naphtali:

All the men twenty years old or more who were able to serve in the army were listed by name, according to the records of their clans and families. [43]The number from the tribe of Naphtali was 53,400.

[44]These were the men counted by Moses and Aaron and the twelve leaders of Israel, each one representing his family. [45]All the Israelites twenty years old or more who were able to serve in Israel's army were counted according to their families. [46]The total number was 603,550.

[47]The ancestral tribe of the Levites, however, was not counted along with the others. [48]The LORD had said to Moses: [49]"You must not count the tribe of Levi or include them in the census of the other Israelites. [50]Instead, appoint the Levites to be in charge of the tabernacle of the covenant law—over all its furnishings and everything belonging to it. They are to carry the tabernacle and all its furnishings; they are to take care of it and encamp around it. [51]Whenever the tabernacle is to move, the Levites are to take it down, and whenever the tabernacle is to be set up, the Levites shall do it. Anyone else who approaches it is to be put to death. [52]The Israelites are to set up their tents by divisions, each of them in their own camp under their standard. [53]The Levites, however, are to set up their tents around the tabernacle of the covenant law so that my wrath will not fall on the Israelite community. The Levites are to be responsible for the care of the tabernacle of the covenant law."

[54]The Israelites did all this just as the LORD commanded Moses.

The Arrangement of the Tribal Camps

2 The LORD said to Moses and Aaron: [2]"The Israelites are to camp around the tent of meeting some distance from it, each of them under their standard and holding the banners of their family."

[3]On the east, toward the sunrise, the divisions of the camp of Judah are to encamp under their standard. The leader of the people of Judah is Nahshon son of Amminadab. [4]His division numbers 74,600.

168

⁵The tribe of Issachar will camp next to them. The leader of the people of Issachar is Nethanel son of Zuar. ⁶His division numbers 54,400.

⁷The tribe of Zebulun will be next. The leader of the people of Zebulun is Eliab son of Helon. ⁸His division numbers 57,400.

⁹All the men assigned to the camp of Judah, according to their divisions, number 186,400. They will set out first.

¹⁰On the south will be the divisions of the camp of Reuben under their standard. The leader of the people of Reuben is Elizur son of Shedeur. ¹¹His division numbers 46,500.

¹²The tribe of Simeon will camp next to them. The leader of the people of Simeon is Shelumiel son of Zurishaddai. ¹³His division numbers 59,300.

¹⁴The tribe of Gad will be next. The leader of the people of Gad is Eliasaph son of Deuel.ᵃ ¹⁵His division numbers 45,650.

¹⁶All the men assigned to the camp of Reuben, according to their divisions, number 151,450. They will set out second.

¹⁷Then the tent of meeting and the camp of the Levites will set out in the middle of the camps. They will set out in the same order as they encamp, each in their own place under their standard.

¹⁸On the west will be the divisions of the camp of Ephraim under their standard. The leader of the people of Ephraim is Elishama son of Ammihud. ¹⁹His division numbers 40,500.

²⁰The tribe of Manasseh will be next to them. The leader of the people of Manasseh is Gamaliel son of Pedahzur. ²¹His division numbers 32,200.

²²The tribe of Benjamin will be next. The leader of the people of Benjamin is Abidan son of Gideoni. ²³His division numbers 35,400.

²⁴All the men assigned to the camp of Ephraim, according to their divisions, number 108,100. They will set out third.

²⁵On the north will be the divisions of the camp of Dan under their standard. The leader of the people of Dan is Ahiezer son of Ammishaddai. ²⁶His division numbers 62,700.

²⁷The tribe of Asher will camp next to them. The leader of the people of Asher is Pagiel son of Okran. ²⁸His division numbers 41,500.

²⁹The tribe of Naphtali will be next. The leader of the people of Naphtali is Ahira son of Enan. ³⁰His division numbers 53,400.

³¹All the men assigned to the camp of Dan number 157,600. They will set out last, under their standards.

³²These are the Israelites, counted according to their families. All the men in the camps, by their divisions, number 603,550. ³³The Levites, however, were not counted along with the other Israelites, as the LORD commanded Moses.

³⁴So the Israelites did everything the LORD commanded Moses; that is the way they encamped under their standards, and that is the way they set out, each of them with their clan and family.

The Levites

3 This is the account of the family of Aaron and Moses at the time the LORD spoke to Moses on Mount Sinai.

²The names of the sons of Aaron were Nadab the firstborn and Abihu, Eleazar and Ithamar. ³Those were the names of Aaron's sons, the anointed priests, who were ordained to serve as priests. ⁴Nadab and Abihu, however, died before the LORD when they made an offering with unauthorized fire before him in the Desert of Sinai. They had no sons, so Eleazar and Ithamar served as priests during the lifetime of their father Aaron.

⁵The LORD said to Moses, ⁶"Bring the tribe of Levi and present them to Aaron the priest to assist him.

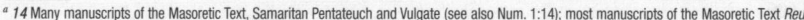

ᵃ 14 Many manuscripts of the Masoretic Text, Samaritan Pentateuch and Vulgate (see also Num. 1:14); most manuscripts of the Masoretic Text *Reuel*

HE IS: the appointer

3:5–10 God appointed Aaron to serve as high priest for the Israelites. But it was a big job, and he didn't expect Aaron to accomplish all the work alone. To ensure that Aaron's load was not too heavy, God told Moses, "Give the Levites to Aaron and his sons."

As *the appointer*, God has some kingdom work custom-made for you. Perhaps he has designated you to serve as a teacher, on a finance committee, in a children's ministry or in your neighborhood. You may see lots of needs, but don't despair. You're not alone in the work—God has more than enough people he can send to help carry the load.

For the next He Is, go to p. 176.

[7] They are to perform duties for him and for the whole community at the tent of meeting by doing the work of the tabernacle. [8] They are to take care of all the furnishings of the tent of meeting, fulfilling the obligations of the Israelites by doing the work of the tabernacle. [9] Give the Levites to Aaron and his sons; they are the Israelites who are to be given wholly to him.[a] [10] Appoint Aaron and his sons to serve as priests; anyone else who approaches the sanctuary is to be put to death."

[11] The LORD also said to Moses, [12] "I have taken the Levites from among the Israelites in place of the first male offspring of every Israelite woman. The Levites are mine, [13] for all the firstborn are mine. When I struck down all the firstborn in Egypt, I set apart for myself every firstborn in Israel, whether human or animal. They are to be mine. I am the LORD."

[14] The LORD said to Moses in the Desert of Sinai, [15] "Count the Levites by their families and clans. Count every male a month old or more." [16] So Moses counted them, as he was commanded by the word of the LORD.

[17] These were the names of the sons of Levi:

Gershon, Kohath and Merari.

[18] These were the names of the Gershonite clans:

Libni and Shimei.

[19] The Kohathite clans:

Amram, Izhar, Hebron and Uzziel.

[20] The Merarite clans:

Mahli and Mushi.

These were the Levite clans, according to their families.

[21] To Gershon belonged the clans of the Libnites and Shimeites; these were the Gershonite clans. [22] The number of all the males a month old or more who were counted was 7,500. [23] The Gershonite clans were to camp on the west, behind the tabernacle. [24] The leader of the families of the Gershonites was Eliasaph son of Lael. [25] At the tent of meeting the Gershonites were responsible for the care of the tabernacle and tent, its coverings, the curtain at the entrance to the tent of meeting, [26] the curtains of the courtyard, the curtain at the entrance to the courtyard surrounding the tabernacle and altar, and the ropes—and everything related to their use.

[27] To Kohath belonged the clans of the Amramites, Izharites, Hebronites and Uzzielites; these were the Kohathite clans. [28] The number of all the males a month old or more was 8,600.[b] The Kohathites were responsible for the care of the sanctuary. [29] The Kohathite clans were to camp on the south side of the tabernacle. [30] The leader of the families of the Kohathite clans was Elizaphan son of Uzziel. [31] They were responsible for the care of the ark, the table, the lampstand, the altars, the articles of the sanctuary used in ministering, the curtain, and everything related to their use. [32] The chief leader of the Levites was

169

[a] *9 Most manuscripts of the Masoretic Text; some manuscripts of the Masoretic Text, Samaritan Pentateuch and Septuagint (see also Num. 8:16) to me*
[b] *28 Hebrew; some Septuagint manuscripts 8,300*

Eleazar son of Aaron, the priest. He was appointed over those who were responsible for the care of the sanctuary.

³³To Merari belonged the clans of the Mahlites and the Mushites; these were the Merarite clans. ³⁴The number of all the males a month old or more who were counted was 6,200. ³⁵The leader of the families of the Merarite clans was Zuriel son of Abihail; they were to camp on the north side of the tabernacle. ³⁶The Merarites were appointed to take care of the frames of the tabernacle, its crossbars, posts, bases, all its equipment, and everything related to their use, ³⁷as well as the posts of the surrounding courtyard with their bases, tent pegs and ropes.

³⁸Moses and Aaron and his sons were to camp to the east of the tabernacle, toward the sunrise, in front of the tent of meeting. They were responsible for the care of the sanctuary on behalf of the Israelites. Anyone else who approached the sanctuary was to be put to death.

³⁹The total number of Levites counted at the LORD's command by Moses and Aaron according to their clans, including every male a month old or more, was 22,000.

⁴⁰The LORD said to Moses, "Count all the firstborn Israelite males who are a month old or more and make a list of their names. ⁴¹Take the Levites for me in place of all the firstborn of the Israelites, and the livestock of the Levites in place of all the firstborn of the livestock of the Israelites. I am the LORD."

⁴²So Moses counted all the firstborn of the Israelites, as the LORD commanded him. ⁴³The total number of firstborn males a month old or more, listed by name, was 22,273.

⁴⁴The LORD also said to Moses, ⁴⁵"Take the Levites in place of all the firstborn of Israel, and the livestock of the Levites in place of their livestock. The Levites are to be mine. I am the LORD. ⁴⁶To redeem the 273 firstborn Israelites who exceed the number of the Levites, ⁴⁷collect five shekels^a for each one, according to the sanctuary shekel, which weighs twenty gerahs. ⁴⁸Give the money for the redemption of the additional Israelites to Aaron and his sons."

⁴⁹So Moses collected the redemption money from those who exceeded the number redeemed by the Levites. ⁵⁰From the firstborn of the Israelites he collected silver weighing 1,365 shekels,^b according to the sanctuary shekel. ⁵¹Moses gave the redemption money to Aaron and his sons, as he was commanded by the word of the LORD.

The Kohathites

4 The LORD said to Moses and Aaron: ²"Take a census of the Kohathite branch of the Levites by their clans and families. ³Count all the men from thirty to fifty years of age who come to serve in the work at the tent of meeting.

⁴"This is the work of the Kohathites at the tent of meeting: the care of the most holy things. ⁵When the camp is to move, Aaron and his sons are to go in and take down the shielding curtain and put it over the ark of the covenant law. ⁶Then they are to cover the curtain with a durable leather,^c spread a cloth of solid blue over that and put the poles in place.

⁷"Over the table of the Presence they are to spread a blue cloth and put on it the plates, dishes and bowls, and the jars for drink offerings; the bread that is continually there is to remain on it. ⁸They are to spread a scarlet cloth over them, cover that with the durable leather and put the poles in place.

⁹"They are to take a blue cloth and cover the lampstand that is for light, together with its lamps, its wick trimmers and trays, and all its jars for the olive oil used to supply it. ¹⁰Then they are to wrap it and all its accessories in a covering of the durable leather and put it on a carrying frame.

¹¹"Over the gold altar they are to spread a blue cloth and cover that with the durable leather and put the poles in place.

¹²"They are to take all the articles used for ministering in the sanctuary, wrap them in a blue cloth, cover that with the durable leather and put them on a carrying frame.

---

^a *47* That is, about 2 ounces or about 55 grams   ^b *50* That is, about 35 pounds or about 16 kilograms   ^c *6* Possibly the hides of dugongs; also in verses 8, 10, 11, 12, 14 and 25

¹³"They are to remove the ashes from the bronze altar and spread a purple cloth over it. ¹⁴Then they are to place on it all the utensils used for ministering at the altar, including the firepans, meat forks, shovels and sprinkling bowls. Over it they are to spread a covering of the durable leather and put the poles in place.

¹⁵"After Aaron and his sons have finished covering the holy furnishings and all the holy articles, and when the camp is ready to move, only then are the Kohathites to come and do the carrying. But they must not touch the holy things or they will die. The Kohathites are to carry those things that are in the tent of meeting.

¹⁶"Eleazar son of Aaron, the priest, is to have charge of the oil for the light, the fragrant incense, the regular grain offering and the anointing oil. He is to be in charge of the entire tabernacle and everything in it, including its holy furnishings and articles."

¹⁷The LORD said to Moses and Aaron, ¹⁸"See that the Kohathite tribal clans are not destroyed from among the Levites. ¹⁹So that they may live and not die when they come near the most holy things, do this for them: Aaron and his sons are to go into the sanctuary and assign to each man his work and what he is to carry. ²⁰But the Kohathites must not go in to look at the holy things, even for a moment, or they will die."

The Gershonites

²¹The LORD said to Moses, ²²"Take a census also of the Gershonites by their families and clans. ²³Count all the men from thirty to fifty years of age who come to serve in the work at the tent of meeting.

²⁴"This is the service of the Gershonite clans in their carrying and their other work: ²⁵They are to carry the curtains of the tabernacle, that is, the tent of meeting, its covering and its outer covering of durable leather, the curtains for the entrance to the tent of meeting, ²⁶the curtains of the courtyard surrounding the tabernacle and altar, the curtain for the entrance to the courtyard, the ropes and all the equipment used in the service of the tent. The Gershonites are to do all that needs to be done with these things. ²⁷All their service, whether carrying or doing other work, is to be done under the direction of Aaron and his sons. You shall assign to them as their responsibility all they are to carry. ²⁸This is the service of the Gershonite clans at the tent of meeting. Their duties are to be under the direction of Ithamar son of Aaron, the priest.

The Merarites

²⁹"Count the Merarites by their clans and families. ³⁰Count all the men from thirty to fifty years of age who come to serve in the work at the tent of meeting. ³¹As part of all their service at the tent, they are to carry the frames of the tabernacle, its crossbars, posts and bases, ³²as well as the posts of the surrounding courtyard with their bases, tent pegs, ropes, all their equipment and everything related to their use. Assign to each man the specific things he is to carry. ³³This is the service of the Merarite clans as they work at the tent of meeting under the direction of Ithamar son of Aaron, the priest."

The Numbering of the Levite Clans

³⁴Moses, Aaron and the leaders of the community counted the Kohathites by their clans and families. ³⁵All the men from thirty to fifty years of age who came to serve in the work at the tent of meeting, ³⁶counted by clans, were 2,750. ³⁷This was the total of all those in the Kohathite clans who served at the tent of meeting. Moses and Aaron counted them according to the LORD's command through Moses.

³⁸The Gershonites were counted by their clans and families. ³⁹All the men from thirty to fifty years of age who came to serve in the work at the tent of meeting, ⁴⁰counted by their clans and families, were 2,630. ⁴¹This was the total of those in the Gershonite clans who served at the tent of meeting. Moses and Aaron counted them according to the LORD's command.

⁴²The Merarites were counted by their clans and families. ⁴³All the men from thirty to fifty years of age who came to serve in the work at the tent of meeting, ⁴⁴counted by their clans, were 3,200. ⁴⁵This was the total of those in the Merarite clans. Moses and Aaron counted them according to the LORD's command through Moses.

⁴⁶So Moses, Aaron and the leaders of Israel counted all the Levites by their clans and families. ⁴⁷All the men from thirty to fifty years of age who came to do the work of serving and carrying the tent of

meeting ⁴⁸numbered 8,580. ⁴⁹At the LORD's command through Moses, each was assigned his work and told what to carry.

Thus they were counted, as the LORD commanded Moses.

The Purity of the Camp

5 The LORD said to Moses, ²"Command the Israelites to send away from the camp anyone who has a defiling skin disease*ᵃ* or a discharge of any kind, or who is ceremonially unclean because of a dead body. ³Send away male and female alike; send them outside the camp so they will not defile their camp, where I dwell among them." ⁴The Israelites did so; they sent them outside the camp. They did just as the LORD had instructed Moses.

Restitution for Wrongs

⁵The LORD said to Moses, ⁶"Say to the Israelites: 'Any man or woman who wrongs another in any way*ᵇ* and so is unfaithful to the LORD is

conversations

making amends «» 5:5–10

1» What are some ways people wrong each other today?

2» How can we make full restitution after we wrong a person, company, government, etc.?

3» Who do you think is hurt more: the one committing the wrong or the one wronged? Why?

For more on **making amends**, check the index. For the next Conversations, go to p. 183.

172

guilty ⁷and must confess the sin they have committed. They must make full restitution for the wrong they have done, add a fifth of the value to it and give it all to the person they have wronged. ⁸But if that person has no close relative to whom restitution can be made for the wrong, the restitution belongs to the LORD and must be given to the priest, along with the ram with which atonement is made for the wrongdoer. ⁹All the sacred contributions the Israelites bring to a priest will belong to him. ¹⁰All sacred gifts belong to the donors, but what they give to the priest will belong to the priest.'"

The Test for an Unfaithful Wife

¹¹Then the LORD said to Moses, ¹²"Speak to the Israelites and say to them: 'If a man's wife goes astray and is unfaithful to him ¹³so that another man has sexual relations with her, and this is hidden from her husband and her impurity is undetected (since there is no witness against her and she has not been caught in the act), ¹⁴and if feelings of jealousy come over her husband and he suspects his wife and she is impure—or if he is jealous and suspects her even though she is not impure— ¹⁵then he is to take his wife to the priest. He must also take an offering of a tenth of an ephah*ᶜ* of barley flour on her behalf. He must not pour oil on it or put incense on it, because it is a grain offering for jealousy, a reminder-offering to draw attention to wrongdoing.

¹⁶"'The priest shall bring her and have her stand before the LORD. ¹⁷Then he shall take some holy water in a clay jar and put some dust from the tabernacle floor into the water. ¹⁸After the priest has had the woman stand before the LORD, he shall loosen her hair and place in her hands the reminder-offering, the grain offering for jealousy, while he himself holds the bitter water that brings a curse. ¹⁹Then the priest shall put the woman under oath and say to her, "If no other man has had sexual relations with you and you have not gone astray and become impure while married to your husband, may this bitter water that brings a curse not harm you. ²⁰But if you have gone astray while married to your husband and you have made yourself impure by having sexual relations with a man other than your husband"— ²¹here the priest is to put the woman under this curse—"may the LORD cause you to become a curse*ᵈ* among your people when he makes your womb miscarry and your abdomen swell. ²²May this water that brings a curse enter your body so that your abdomen swells or your womb miscarries."

"'Then the woman is to say, "Amen. So be it."

²³"'The priest is to write these curses on a scroll and then wash them off into the bitter water. ²⁴He shall make the woman drink the bitter water that brings a curse, and this water that brings a curse and

---

ᵃ 2 The Hebrew word for *defiling skin disease,* traditionally translated "leprosy," was used for various diseases affecting the skin. *ᵇ 6* Or *woman who commits any wrong common to humankind* *ᶜ 15* That is, probably about 3 1/2 pounds or about 1.6 kilograms *ᵈ 21* That is, may he cause your name to be used in cursing (see Jer. 29:22); or, may others see that you are cursed; similarly in verse 27.

causes bitter suffering will enter her. ²⁵The priest is to take from her hands the grain offering for jealousy, wave it before the LORD and bring it to the altar. ²⁶The priest is then to take a handful of the grain offering as a memorial*ᵃ* offering and burn it on the altar; after that, he is to have the woman drink the water. ²⁷If she has made herself impure and been unfaithful to her husband, this will be the result: When she is made to drink the water that brings a curse and causes bitter suffering, it will enter her, her abdomen will swell and her womb will miscarry, and she will become a curse. ²⁸If, however, the woman has not made herself impure, but is clean, she will be cleared of guilt and will be able to have children.

²⁹"'This, then, is the law of jealousy when a woman goes astray and makes herself impure while married to her husband, ³⁰or when feelings of jealousy come over a man because he suspects his wife. The priest is to have her stand before the LORD and is to apply this entire law to her. ³¹The husband will be innocent of any wrongdoing, but the woman will bear the consequences of her sin.'"

The Nazirite

6 The LORD said to Moses, ²"Speak to the Israelites and say to them: 'If a man or woman wants to make a special vow, a vow of dedication to the LORD as a Nazirite, ³they must abstain from wine and other fermented drink and must not drink vinegar made from wine or other fermented drink. They must not drink grape juice or eat grapes or raisins. ⁴As long as they remain under their Nazirite vow, they must not eat anything that comes from the grapevine, not even the seeds or skins.

⁵"'During the entire period of the Nazirite's vow, no razor may be used on their head. They must be holy until the period of their dedication to the LORD is over; they must let their hair grow long.

⁶"'Throughout the period of their dedication to the LORD, the Nazirite must not go near a dead body. ⁷Even if their own father or mother or brother or sister dies, they must not make themselves ceremonially unclean on account of them, because the symbol of their dedication to God is on their head. ⁸Throughout the period of their dedication, they are consecrated to the LORD.

⁹"'If someone dies suddenly in the Nazirite's presence, thus defiling the hair that symbolizes their dedication, they must shave their head on the seventh day—the day of their cleansing. ¹⁰Then on the eighth day they must bring two doves or two young pigeons to the priest at the entrance to the tent of meeting. ¹¹The priest is to offer one as a sin offering*ᵇ* and the other as a burnt offering to make atonement for the Nazirite because they sinned by being in the presence of the dead body. That same day they are to consecrate their head again. ¹²They must rededicate themselves to the LORD for the same period of dedication and must bring a year-old male lamb as a guilt offering. The previous days do not count, because they became defiled during their period of dedication.

¹³"'Now this is the law for the Nazirite when the period of their dedication is over. The Nazirite is to be brought to the entrance to the tent of meeting. ¹⁴There they are to present their offerings to the LORD: a year-old male lamb without defect for a burnt offering, a year-old ewe lamb without defect for a sin offering, a ram without defect for a fellowship offering, ¹⁵together with their grain offerings and drink offerings, and a basket of bread made with the finest flour and without yeast—thick loaves with olive oil mixed in, and thin loaves brushed with olive oil.

¹⁶"'The priest is to present the Nazirite before the LORD and make the sin offering and the burnt

---

a issue: infidelity

5:11–31 Cheating on your spouse wasn't invented by the guests on some sizzling daytime talk show. Nor was God ignorant of the possibility when he created the institution of marriage. He knew the temptation his people would face—men and women. That's why he gave the Israelites guidelines to deal with adultery. In our own marriages, God also gives us rules that protect us from the destruction of infidelity. However, he does not force us to obey them. That is what makes love love—it's a choice, a risk to trust another person, an active decision to protect a marriage.

173

ᵃ 26 Or *representative* *ᵇ 11* Or *purification offering;* also in verses 14 and 16

myth# 12 "SEXUAL FREEDOM IS GOOD FOR WOMEN."

My favorite movie? Pretty Woman, without a doubt! I watched it twice in one night when my friends and I sneaked back into the theater when we were in college. This is the ultimate chick flick. Julia Roberts had it made—a sexy, rich man wanted to take care of her and lavish attention on her with no strings attached. Of course, in 1990, the only way Hollywood could get away with portraying that ideal was to make the main character a prostitute—a likable one you'd want to be friends with—but a prostitute nonetheless. As if the picture of a woman who was in control of her sexuality and using it for her benefit was somehow unbecoming for the average woman.

Now we've grown into a more sophisticated sexual freedom. My girlfriends and I meet eligible single men at trendy clubs downtown. Most of the men there are stockbrokers or successful lawyers and doctors. We're adults with disposable incomes and time on our hands.

I was nervous the first time I had a guy I met at a club over to my flat. I poured some drinks, we talked about our families and work and then we messed around until he had to go home for work the next day. I recall looking in the mirror the next morning and strangely not recognizing my own face right away, but I also remember the rush of feeling empowered. Every time I hook up with a guy, I feel as if I break through some other barrier. It's as if I'm in control of my life in a way I couldn't have imagined before.

I'm not actually sleeping with these guys. Some of my girlfriends do, but I'm just out to have fun. It wasn't that long ago when only men were allowed to have fun like this, but this is an equal opportunity planet. More power to us!

—Nicole

THE SEXUAL REVOLUTION

drastically changed how women viewed their sexuality. In the past, women hid their sexuality under restrictive clothing and severe social codes. Now we flaunt it. Women used to be envious of men's supposed sexual freedom and the apparent power it gave them. Now we have that same "freedom," but where has it gotten us?

- Legalized abortion—A world in which even if a woman wants to keep her baby, her partner has no responsibility to stand beside her and support her. Too many women feel alone and pressured to abort their children. Is that freedom?

- Disappointment—Relationships in which men won't commit because they don't have to. Why buy the cow when you can get the milk for free?

- Emotional baggage—Past physical attachments, emotional scars and the weight of guilt so that women can't enter fully into their marriages or the relationships God intended for them.

- Disrespect—In a world of sexual freedom, women are often treated like (surprise, surprise) sex objects. When was the last time a man held the door for you?

- Expectations—Just because a man buys you dinner doesn't mean you owe him sex—not after one date, four dates, six months or two years.

We're no better off sexually than our mothers and grandmothers. We may feel a sense of control, but it comes at a very high price—the price of our clean consciences, of our whole relationships, of our sexual purity.

God wants women to experience the powerful, intoxicating pleasures of their sexuality. Yet he has specific parameters in which that experience should take place—in a monogamous, marital relationship, one man and one woman, for life. Satan exploits a woman's sexuality by enticing her to express herself sexually outside of God's ideal—through promiscuity, pre-marital sex or adultery.

Sexual freedom God's way

We think we feel empowered.	God says we are enslaved—either to sin or to righteousness (ROMANS 6:16).
We tell ourselves we're in control when we use sex in relationships (since we have what men want).	God calls that kind of control self-deception (1 CORINTHIANS 3:18).
The world assures us sexual freedom is life's highest reward.	God warns us that we will reap what we sow. (GALATIANS 6:7).

175

"'Free sex has proven to be quite costly—not only in terms of pregnancy but also with regard to sexually transmitted diseases (STDs). Since 1999, more than 12 million Americans contract an STD every year."

—Concerned Women for America

"YOU, MY BROTHERS AND SISTERS, WERE CALLED TO BE FREE. BUT DO NOT USE YOUR FREEDOM TO INDULGE THE SINFUL NATURE."

GALATIANS 5:13

SEE ALSO

Romans 1:24
1 Corinthians 6:12–20
Ephesians 5:3

For more on **Sex**, check the index.

HE IS: facing you

6:24-26 When God taught the priests how to bless the people, he mentioned his face twice. He turned his face toward his people to show them grace and to give them peace, even in the desert.

Because God is a personal God, he turns his face toward you, which shows that he is interested in you and cares for you. He is not a God who abandons you so that you're left to deal with life by yourself. If you're wandering in a desert of discontent, distress or disbelief, don't turn from God. Turn from your circumstances and look to him for comfort. His face is already turned toward you.

For the next He Is, go to p. 181.

offering. ¹⁷He is to present the basket of unleavened bread and is to sacrifice the ram as a fellowship offering to the LORD, together with its grain offering and drink offering.

¹⁸"Then at the entrance to the tent of meeting, the Nazirite must shave off the hair that symbolizes their dedication. They are to take the hair and put it in the fire that is under the sacrifice of the fellowship offering.

¹⁹"After the Nazirite has shaved off the hair that symbolizes their dedication, the priest is to place in their hands a boiled shoulder of the ram, and one thick loaf and one thin loaf from the basket, both made without yeast. ²⁰The priest shall then wave these before the LORD as a wave offering; they are holy and belong to the priest, together with the breast that was waved and the thigh that was presented. After that, the Nazirite may drink wine.

²¹"This is the law of the Nazirite who vows offerings to the LORD in accordance with their dedication, in addition to whatever else they can afford. They must fulfill the vows they have made, according to the law of the Nazirite.'"

The Priestly Blessing

²²The LORD said to Moses, ²³"Tell Aaron and his sons, 'This is how you are to bless the Israelites. Say to them:

²⁴"'"The LORD bless you
  and keep you;
²⁵the LORD make his face shine on you
  and be gracious to you;
²⁶the LORD turn his face toward you
  and give you peace."'

²⁷"So they will put my name on the Israelites, and I will bless them."

Offerings at the Dedication of the Tabernacle

7 When Moses finished setting up the tabernacle, he anointed and consecrated it and all its furnishings. He also anointed and consecrated the altar and all its utensils. ²Then the leaders of Israel, the heads of families who were the tribal leaders in charge of those who were counted, made offerings. ³They brought as their gifts before the LORD six covered carts and twelve oxen—an ox from each leader and a cart from every two. These they presented before the tabernacle.

⁴The LORD said to Moses, ⁵"Accept these from them, that they may be used in the work at the tent of meeting. Give them to the Levites as each man's work requires."

⁶So Moses took the carts and oxen and gave them to the Levites. ⁷He gave two carts and four oxen to the Gershonites, as their work required, ⁸and he gave four carts and eight oxen to the Merarites, as their work required. They were all under the direction of Ithamar son of Aaron, the priest. ⁹But Moses did not give any to the Kohathites, because they were to carry on their shoulders the holy things, for which they were responsible.

¹⁰When the altar was anointed, the leaders brought their offerings for its dedication and presented them before the altar. ¹¹For the Lord had said to Moses, "Each day one leader is to bring his offering for the dedication of the altar."

¹²The one who brought his offering on the first day was Nahshon son of Amminadab of the tribe of Judah.

¹³His offering was one silver plate weighing a hundred and thirty shekels *a* and one silver sprinkling bowl weighing seventy shekels, *b* both according to the sanctuary shekel, each filled with the finest flour mixed with olive oil as a grain offering; ¹⁴one gold dish weighing ten shekels, *c* filled with incense; ¹⁵one young bull, one ram and one male lamb a year old for a burnt offering; ¹⁶one male goat for a sin offering *d*; ¹⁷and two oxen, five rams, five male goats and five male lambs a year old to be sacrificed as a fellowship offering. This was the offering of Nahshon son of Amminadab.

¹⁸On the second day Nethanel son of Zuar, the leader of Issachar, brought his offering. ¹⁹The offering he brought was one silver plate weighing a hundred and thirty shekels and one silver sprinkling bowl weighing seventy shekels, both according to the sanctuary shekel, each filled with the finest flour mixed with olive oil as a grain offering; ²⁰one gold dish weighing ten shekels, filled with incense; ²¹one young bull, one ram and one male lamb a year old for a burnt offering; ²²one male goat for a sin offering; ²³and two oxen, five rams, five male goats and five male lambs a year old to be sacrificed as a fellowship offering. This was the offering of Nethanel son of Zuar.

²⁴On the third day, Eliab son of Helon, the leader of the people of Zebulun, brought his offering. ²⁵His offering was one silver plate weighing a hundred and thirty shekels and one silver sprinkling bowl weighing seventy shekels, both according to the sanctuary shekel, each filled with the finest flour mixed with olive oil as a grain offering; ²⁶one gold dish weighing ten shekels, filled with incense; ²⁷one young bull, one ram and one male lamb a year old for a burnt offering; ²⁸one male goat for a sin offering; ²⁹and two oxen, five rams, five male goats and five male lambs a year old to be sacrificed as a fellowship offering. This was the offering of Eliab son of Helon.

³⁰On the fourth day Elizur son of Shedeur, the leader of the people of Reuben, brought his offering. ³¹His offering was one silver plate weighing a hundred and thirty shekels and one silver sprinkling bowl weighing seventy shekels, both according to the sanctuary shekel, each filled with the finest flour mixed with olive oil as a grain offering; ³²one gold dish weighing ten shekels, filled with incense; ³³one young bull, one ram and one male lamb a year old for a burnt offering; ³⁴one male goat for a sin offering; ³⁵and two oxen, five rams, five male goats and five male lambs a year old to be sacrificed as a fellowship offering. This was the offering of Elizur son of Shedeur.

³⁶On the fifth day Shelumiel son of Zurishaddai, the leader of the people of Simeon, brought his offering. ³⁷His offering was one silver plate weighing a hundred and thirty shekels and one silver sprinkling bowl weighing seventy shekels, both according to the sanctuary shekel, each filled with the finest flour mixed with olive oil as a grain offering; ³⁸one gold dish weighing ten shekels, filled with incense; ³⁹one young bull, one ram and one male lamb a year old for a burnt offering; ⁴⁰one male goat for a sin offering; ⁴¹and two oxen, five rams, five male goats and five male lambs a year old to be sacrificed as a fellowship offering. This was the offering of Shelumiel son of Zurishaddai.

⁴²On the sixth day Eliasaph son of Deuel, the leader of the people of Gad, brought his offering. ⁴³His offering was one silver plate weighing a hundred and thirty shekels and one silver sprinkling bowl weighing seventy shekels, both according to the sanctuary shekel, each filled with the finest flour mixed with olive oil as a grain offering; ⁴⁴one gold dish weighing ten shekels, filled with incense; ⁴⁵one young bull, one ram and one male lamb a year old for a burnt offering; ⁴⁶one male goat for a sin offering; ⁴⁷and two oxen, five rams, five male goats and five male lambs a year old to be sacrificed as a fellowship offering. This was the offering of Eliasaph son of Deuel.

---

a 13 That is, about 3 1/4 pounds or about 1.5 kilograms; also elsewhere in this chapter   *b 13* That is, about 1 3/4 pounds or about 800 grams; also elsewhere in this chapter   *c 14* That is, about 4 ounces or about 115 grams; also elsewhere in this chapter   *d 16* Or *purification offering*; also elsewhere in this chapter

[48] On the seventh day Elishama son of Ammihud, the leader of the people of Ephraim, brought his offering.
[49] His offering was one silver plate weighing a hundred and thirty shekels and one silver sprinkling bowl weighing seventy shekels, both according to the sanctuary shekel, each filled with the finest flour mixed with olive oil as a grain offering; [50] one gold dish weighing ten shekels, filled with incense; [51] one young bull, one ram and one male lamb a year old for a burnt offering; [52] one male goat for a sin offering; [53] and two oxen, five rams, five male goats and five male lambs a year old to be sacrificed as a fellowship offering. This was the offering of Elishama son of Ammihud.

[54] On the eighth day Gamaliel son of Pedahzur, the leader of the people of Manasseh, brought his offering.
[55] His offering was one silver plate weighing a hundred and thirty shekels and one silver sprinkling bowl weighing seventy shekels, both according to the sanctuary shekel, each filled with the finest flour mixed with olive oil as a grain offering; [56] one gold dish weighing ten shekels, filled with incense; [57] one young bull, one ram and one male lamb a year old for a burnt offering; [58] one male goat for a sin offering; [59] and two oxen, five rams, five male goats and five male lambs a year old to be sacrificed as a fellowship offering. This was the offering of Gamaliel son of Pedahzur.

[60] On the ninth day Abidan son of Gideoni, the leader of the people of Benjamin, brought his offering.
[61] His offering was one silver plate weighing a hundred and thirty shekels and one silver sprinkling bowl weighing seventy shekels, both according to the sanctuary shekel, each filled with the finest flour mixed with olive oil as a grain offering; [62] one gold dish weighing ten shekels, filled with incense; [63] one young bull, one ram and one male lamb a year old for a burnt offering; [64] one male goat for a sin offering; [65] and two oxen, five rams, five male goats and five male lambs a year old to be sacrificed as a fellowship offering. This was the offering of Abidan son of Gideoni.

[66] On the tenth day Ahiezer son of Ammishaddai, the leader of the people of Dan, brought his offering.
[67] His offering was one silver plate weighing a hundred and thirty shekels and one silver sprinkling bowl weighing seventy shekels, both according to the sanctuary shekel, each filled with the finest flour mixed with olive oil as a grain offering; [68] one gold dish weighing ten shekels, filled with incense; [69] one young bull, one ram and one male lamb a year old for a burnt offering; [70] one male goat for a sin offering; [71] and two oxen, five rams, five male goats and five male lambs a year old to be sacrificed as a fellowship offering. This was the offering of Ahiezer son of Ammishaddai.

[72] On the eleventh day Pagiel son of Okran, the leader of the people of Asher, brought his offering.
[73] His offering was one silver plate weighing a hundred and thirty shekels and one silver sprinkling bowl weighing seventy shekels, both according to the sanctuary shekel, each filled with the finest flour mixed with olive oil as a grain offering; [74] one gold dish weighing ten shekels, filled with incense; [75] one young bull, one ram and one male lamb a year old for a burnt offering; [76] one male goat for a sin offering; [77] and two oxen, five rams, five male goats and five male lambs a year old to be sacrificed as a fellowship offering. This was the offering of Pagiel son of Okran.

[78] On the twelfth day Ahira son of Enan, the leader of the people of Naphtali, brought his offering.
[79] His offering was one silver plate weighing a hundred and thirty shekels and one silver sprinkling bowl weighing seventy shekels, both according to the sanctuary shekel, each filled with the finest flour mixed with olive oil as a grain offering; [80] one gold dish weighing ten shekels, filled with incense; [81] one young bull, one ram and one male lamb a year old for a burnt offering; [82] one male goat for a sin offering; [83] and two oxen, five rams, five male goats and five male lambs a year old to be sacrificed as a fellowship offering. This was the offering of Ahira son of Enan.

[84] These were the offerings of the Israelite leaders for the dedication of the altar when it was anointed: twelve silver plates, twelve silver sprinkling bowls and twelve gold dishes. [85] Each silver plate weighed a hundred and thirty shekels, and each sprinkling bowl seventy shekels. Altogether, the silver dishes weighed two thousand four hundred shekels,[a] according to the sanctuary shekel. [86] The twelve gold

---

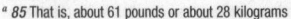

[a] 85 That is, about 61 pounds or about 28 kilograms

dishes filled with incense weighed ten shekels each, according to the sanctuary shekel. Altogether, the gold dishes weighed a hundred and twenty shekels.[a] [87] The total number of animals for the burnt offering came to twelve young bulls, twelve rams and twelve male lambs a year old, together with their grain offering. Twelve male goats were used for the sin offering. [88] The total number of animals for the sacrifice

---

[a] *86* That is, about 3 pounds or about 1.4 kilograms

ASKmeANYTHING

hagar
Genesis 16:1–16

You were in a terrible position—you were Sarah's servant and the mother of Abraham's son. What were some difficult aspects of your situation?

I was a slave girl, a foreigner, who was far from home and from any family. I had no one to turn to when the situation got ugly.

What happened?

When I got pregnant by Abraham—something my mistress had not been able to do—I lost all respect for Sarah. After all, *I* was the one who had conceived, not *her*. It was very important for a woman to have children—a woman's worth was tied to her ability to conceive. So in my eyes, I was the better woman. But my actions reaped terrible consequences. My relationship with Sarah deteriorated to the point where she began to abuse me. It was horrible. So I ran away. How much worse could my life get?

And did it get worse?

Actually, no. That's when the most amazing thing happened to me. I was out in the desert, on the road to Shur, but I had no idea of where I could go. It seemed I had very little chance for survival. And it was there, by the well, that God found me.

What do you mean by that?

God saw me at the well. He spoke to me. He knew every detail of my messy situation. He saw my shame, my loneliness, my rejection. And right then, when I needed it most, God gave me an incredible promise—that my son would have so many descendants that they would be too numerous to count. God accepted my child and me, even though others did not. That meant so much to me! And he assured me that he cared for me.

What can others learn from your experience?

When you reach the end of your road, when there is absolutely no place you can go or no one you can turn to, God is there. He is always there. He alone sees your situation. He alone knows your pain. And he alone will go with you whatever you face.

FOR MORE INSIGHT:
Read the rest of Hagar's story in Genesis 21:8–21 to see how God continued to provide and care for her. For other assurances of God's care in the midst of pain and loneliness, read Psalm 23:4; Isaiah 58:9; and Matthew 28:20.

179

of the fellowship offering came to twenty-four oxen, sixty rams, sixty male goats and sixty male lambs a year old. These were the offerings for the dedication of the altar after it was anointed.

⁸⁹When Moses entered the tent of meeting to speak with the LORD, he heard the voice speaking to him from between the two cherubim above the atonement cover on the ark of the covenant law. In this way the LORD spoke to him.

Setting Up the Lamps

8 The LORD said to Moses, ²"Speak to Aaron and say to him, 'When you set up the lamps, see that all seven light up the area in front of the lampstand.'"

³Aaron did so; he set up the lamps so that they faced forward on the lampstand, just as the LORD commanded Moses. ⁴This is how the lampstand was made: It was made of hammered gold—from its base to its blossoms. The lampstand was made exactly like the pattern the LORD had shown Moses.

The Setting Apart of the Levites

⁵The LORD said to Moses: ⁶"Take the Levites from among all the Israelites and make them ceremonially clean. ⁷To purify them, do this: Sprinkle the water of cleansing on them; then have them shave their whole bodies and wash their clothes. And so they will purify themselves. ⁸Have them take a young bull with its grain offering of the finest flour mixed with olive oil; then you are to take a second young bull for a sin offering.ᵃ ⁹Bring the Levites to the front of the tent of meeting and assemble the whole Israelite community. ¹⁰You are to bring the Levites before the LORD, and the Israelites are to lay their hands on them. ¹¹Aaron is to present the Levites before the LORD as a wave offering from the Israelites, so that they may be ready to do the work of the LORD.

¹²"Then the Levites are to lay their hands on the heads of the bulls, using one for a sin offering to the LORD and the other for a burnt offering, to make atonement for the Levites. ¹³Have the Levites stand in front of Aaron and his sons and then present them as a wave offering to the LORD. ¹⁴In this way you are to set the Levites apart from the other Israelites, and the Levites will be mine.

¹⁵"After you have purified the Levites and presented them as a wave offering, they are to come to do their work at the tent of meeting. ¹⁶They are the Israelites who are to be given wholly to me. I have taken them as my own in place of the firstborn, the first male offspring from every Israelite woman. ¹⁷Every firstborn male in Israel, whether human or animal, is mine. When I struck down all the firstborn in Egypt, I set them apart for myself. ¹⁸And I have taken the Levites in place of all the firstborn sons in Israel. ¹⁹From among all the Israelites, I have given the Levites as gifts to Aaron and his sons to do the work at the tent of meeting on behalf of the Israelites and to make atonement for them so that no plague will strike the Israelites when they go near the sanctuary."

²⁰Moses, Aaron and the whole Israelite community did with the Levites just as the LORD commanded Moses. ²¹The Levites purified themselves and washed their clothes. Then Aaron presented them as a wave offering before the LORD and made atonement for them to purify them. ²²After that, the Levites came to do their work at the tent of meeting under the supervision of Aaron and his sons. They did with the Levites just as the LORD commanded Moses.

²³The LORD said to Moses, ²⁴"This applies to the Levites: Men twenty-five years old or more shall come to take part in the work at the tent of meeting, ²⁵but at the age of fifty, they must retire from their regular service and work no longer. ²⁶They may assist their brothers in performing their duties at the tent of meeting, but they themselves must not do the work. This, then, is how you are to assign the responsibilities of the Levites."

The Passover

9 The LORD spoke to Moses in the Desert of Sinai in the first month of the second year after they came out of Egypt. He said, ²"Have the Israelites celebrate the Passover at the appointed time. ³Celebrate it at the appointed time, at twilight on the fourteenth day of this month, in accordance with all its rules and regulations."

⁴So Moses told the Israelites to celebrate the Passover, ⁵and they did so in the Desert of Sinai at twi-

---

ᵃ 8 Or purification offering; also in verse 12

light on the fourteenth day of the first month. The Israelites did everything just as the LORD commanded Moses.

[6]But some of them could not celebrate the Passover on that day because they were ceremonially unclean on account of a dead body. So they came to Moses and Aaron that same day [7]and said to Moses, "We have become unclean because of a dead body, but why should we be kept from presenting the LORD's offering with the other Israelites at the appointed time?"

[8]Moses answered them, "Wait until I find out what the LORD commands concerning you."

[9]Then the LORD said to Moses, [10]"Tell the Israelites: 'When any of you or your descendants are unclean because of a dead body or are away on a journey, they are still to celebrate the LORD's Passover, [11]but they are to do it on the fourteenth day of the second month at twilight. They are to eat the lamb, together with unleavened bread and bitter herbs. [12]They must not leave any of it till morning or break any of its bones. When they celebrate the Passover, they must follow all the regulations. [13]But if anyone who is ceremonially clean and not on a journey fails to celebrate the Passover, they must be cut off from their people for not presenting the LORD's offering at the appointed time. They will bear the consequences of their sin.

[14]"'A foreigner residing among you is also to celebrate the LORD's Passover in accordance with its rules and regulations. You must have the same regulations for both the foreigner and the native-born.'"

The Cloud Above the Tabernacle

[15]On the day the tabernacle, the tent of the covenant law, was set up, the cloud covered it. From evening till morning the cloud above the tabernacle looked like fire. [16]That is how it continued to be; the cloud covered it, and at night it looked like fire. [17]Whenever the cloud lifted from above the tent, the Israelites set out; wherever the cloud settled, the Israelites encamped. [18]At the LORD's command the Israelites set out, and at his command they encamped. As long as the cloud stayed over the tabernacle, they remained in camp. [19]When the cloud remained over the tabernacle a long time, the Israelites obeyed the LORD's order and did not set out. [20]Sometimes the cloud was over the tabernacle only a few days; at the LORD's command they would encamp, and then at his command they would set out. [21]Sometimes the cloud stayed only from evening till morning, and when it lifted in the morning, they set out. Whether by day or by night, whenever the cloud lifted, they set out. [22]Whether the cloud stayed over the tabernacle for two days or a month or a year, the Israelites would remain in camp and not set out; but when it lifted, they would set out. [23]At the LORD's command they encamped, and at the LORD's command they set out. They obeyed the LORD's order, in accordance with his command through Moses.

HE IS: the divine guide

9:15–23 The cloud covering the tabernacle was no ordinary cumulus. It was God himself guiding the nation of Israel through the desert. When the cloud moved, the people moved. When the cloud stopped, they stayed put. God acted as *the divine guide* for his people.

Today God doesn't lead us with a fiery light or a bright shining cloud, though we often wish he would. Instead, he guides us in other ways including his Word, his Spirit, people and our circumstances. If you sense God telling you to stop, stay put. If you see God telling you to move, go for it!

For the next He Is, go to p. 201.

The Silver Trumpets

10 The LORD said to Moses: [2]"Make two trumpets of hammered silver, and use them for calling the community together and for having the camps set out. [3]When both are sounded, the whole community is to assemble before you at the entrance to the tent of meeting. [4]If only one is sounded, the leaders—the heads of the clans of Israel—are to assemble before you. [5]When a trumpet blast is sounded, the tribes camping on the east are to set out. [6]At the sounding of a second blast, the camps on the south are

to set out. The blast will be the signal for setting out. ⁷To gather the assembly, blow the trumpets, but not with the signal for setting out.

⁸"The sons of Aaron, the priests, are to blow the trumpets. This is to be a lasting ordinance for you and the generations to come. ⁹When you go into battle in your own land against an enemy who is oppressing you, sound a blast on the trumpets. Then you will be remembered by the LORD your God and rescued from your enemies. ¹⁰Also at your times of rejoicing—your appointed festivals and New Moon feasts—you are to sound the trumpets over your burnt offerings and fellowship offerings, and they will be a memorial for you before your God. I am the LORD your God."

The Israelites Leave Sinai

¹¹On the twentieth day of the second month of the second year, the cloud lifted from above the tabernacle of the covenant law. ¹²Then the Israelites set out from the Desert of Sinai and traveled from place to place until the cloud came to rest in the Desert of Paran. ¹³They set out, this first time, at the LORD's command through Moses.

¹⁴The divisions of the camp of Judah went first, under their standard. Nahshon son of Amminadab was in command. ¹⁵Nethanel son of Zuar was over the division of the tribe of Issachar, ¹⁶and Eliab son of Helon was over the division of the tribe of Zebulun. ¹⁷Then the tabernacle was taken down, and the Gershonites and Merarites, who carried it, set out.

¹⁸The divisions of the camp of Reuben went next, under their standard. Elizur son of Shedeur was in command. ¹⁹Shelumiel son of Zurishaddai was over the division of the tribe of Simeon, ²⁰and Eliasaph son of Deuel was over the division of the tribe of Gad. ²¹Then the Kohathites set out, carrying the holy things. The tabernacle was to be set up before they arrived.

²²The divisions of the camp of Ephraim went next, under their standard. Elishama son of Ammihud was in command. ²³Gamaliel son of Pedahzur was over the division of the tribe of Manasseh, ²⁴and Abidan son of Gideoni was over the division of the tribe of Benjamin.

²⁵Finally, as the rear guard for all the units, the divisions of the camp of Dan set out under their standard. Ahiezer son of Ammishaddai was in command. ²⁶Pagiel son of Okran was over the division of the tribe of Asher, ²⁷and Ahira son of Enan was over the division of the tribe of Naphtali. ²⁸This was the order of march for the Israelite divisions as they set out.

²⁹Now Moses said to Hobab son of Reuel the Midianite, Moses' father-in-law, "We are setting out for the place about which the LORD said, 'I will give it to you.' Come with us and we will treat you well, for the LORD has promised good things to Israel."

³⁰He answered, "No, I will not go; I am going back to my own land and my own people."

³¹But Moses said, "Please do not leave us. You know where we should camp in the wilderness, and you can be our eyes. ³²If you come with us, we will share with you whatever good things the LORD gives us."

³³So they set out from the mountain of the LORD and traveled for three days. The ark of the covenant of the LORD went before them during those three days to find them a place to rest. ³⁴The cloud of the LORD was over them by day when they set out from the camp.

³⁵Whenever the ark set out, Moses said,

> "Rise up, LORD!
> May your enemies be scattered;
> may your foes flee before you."

182

atissue:giftedness

10:29–32 Within the body of Christ, certain roles have long been exalted over others. Who wouldn't want to preach like Billy Graham, write like Rick Warren or lead worship like Darlene Zschech? Yet Moses didn't need a theologian or a preacher out in the desert—he needed an outdoor guide, someone who knew the land. That might not sound spiritual, but it is. Don't attempt to take on gifts you don't have. Just be who God made you to be. Even if you can't see the value of your gifts, allow God to show you how your gifts can contribute to others.

³⁶Whenever it came to rest, he said,

"Return, LORD,
to the countless thousands of Israel."

Fire From the LORD

11 Now the people complained about their hardships in the hearing of the LORD, and when he heard them his anger was aroused. Then fire from the LORD burned among them and consumed some of the outskirts of the camp. ²When the people cried out to Moses, he prayed to the LORD and the fire died down. ³So that place was called Taberah,ᵃ because fire from the LORD had burned among them.

Quail From the LORD

⁴The rabble with them began to crave other food, and again the Israelites started wailing and said, "If only we had meat to eat! ⁵We remember the fish we ate in Egypt at no cost—also the cucumbers, melons, leeks, onions and garlic. ⁶But now we have lost our appetite; we never see anything but this manna!"

⁷The manna was like coriander seed and looked like resin. ⁸The people went around gathering it, and then ground it in a hand mill or crushed it in a mortar. They cooked it in a pot or made it into loaves. And it tasted like something made with olive oil. ⁹When the dew settled on the camp at night, the manna also came down.

¹⁰Moses heard the people of every family wailing at the entrance to their tents. The LORD became exceedingly angry, and Moses was troubled. ¹¹He asked the LORD, "Why have you brought this trouble on your servant? What have I done to displease you that you put the burden of all these people on me? ¹²Did I conceive all these people? Did I give them birth? Why do you tell me to carry them in my arms, as a nurse carries an infant, to the land you promised on oath to their ancestors? ¹³Where can I get meat for all these people? They keep wailing to me, 'Give us meat to eat!' ¹⁴I cannot carry all these people by myself; the burden is too heavy for me. ¹⁵If this is how you are going to treat me, please go ahead and kill me—if I have found favor in your eyes—and do not let me face my own ruin."

¹⁶The LORD said to Moses: "Bring me seventy of Israel's elders who are known to you as leaders and officials among the people. Have them come to the tent of meeting, that they may stand there with you. ¹⁷I will come down and speak with you there, and I will take some of the power of the Spirit that is on you and put it on them. They will share the burden of the people with you so that you will not have to carry it alone.

¹⁸"Tell the people: 'Consecrate yourselves in preparation for tomorrow, when you will eat meat. The LORD heard you when you wailed, "If only we had meat to eat! We were better off in Egypt!" Now the LORD will give you meat, and you will eat it. ¹⁹You will not eat it for just one day, or two days, or five, ten or twenty days, ²⁰but for a whole month—until it comes

conversations

complaining «» 11:1–3

1 » What do you tend to complain about in your life?

2 » What does a Christian's complaining communicate to a non-Christian?

3 » Why does God take our complaints so personally?

For more on **complaining,** check the index.
For the next Conversations, go to p. 189.

183

at issue : busyness

11:10–17 As women, we pride ourselves on our ability to multitask. If the job (or jobs) needs to get done, we're all over it. Unfortunately, our hunger for managing everything within our reach often leaves us stressed out and burned out at the end of the day. Like Moses, if you find yourself inching towards a total meltdown, stop and ask yourself the following questions. First, what do I achieve (or prove) by getting myself bogged down? And second, to whom could I delegate some of this work? God's not grading you on your personal GNP. Ask for help before you're forced to get help!

out of your nostrils and you loathe it—because you have rejected the LORD, who is among you, and have wailed before him, saying, "Why did we ever leave Egypt?"'"

²¹But Moses said, "Here I am among six hundred thousand men on foot, and you say, 'I will give them meat to eat for a whole month!' ²²Would they have enough if flocks and herds were slaughtered for them? Would they have enough if all the fish in the sea were caught for them?"

²³The LORD answered Moses, "Is the LORD's arm too short? Now you will see whether or not what I say will come true for you."

²⁴So Moses went out and told the people what the LORD had said. He brought together seventy of their elders and had them stand around the tent. ²⁵Then the LORD came down in the cloud and spoke with him, and he took some of the power of the Spirit that was on him and put it on the seventy elders. When the Spirit rested on them, they prophesied—but did not do so again.

²⁶However, two men, whose names were Eldad and Medad, had remained in the camp. They were listed among the elders, but did not go out to the tent. Yet the Spirit also rested on them, and they prophesied in the camp. ²⁷A young man ran and told Moses, "Eldad and Medad are prophesying in the camp."

²⁸Joshua son of Nun, who had been Moses' aide since youth, spoke up and said, "Moses, my lord, stop them!"

²⁹But Moses replied, "Are you jealous for my sake? I wish that all the LORD's people were prophets and that the LORD would put his Spirit on them!" ³⁰Then Moses and the elders of Israel returned to the camp.

³¹Now a wind went out from the LORD and drove quail in from the sea. It scattered them up to two cubits*a* deep all around the camp, as far as a day's walk in any direction. ³²All that day and night and all the next day the people went out and gathered quail. No one gathered less than ten homers.*b* Then they spread them out all around the camp. ³³But while the meat was still between their teeth and before it could be consumed, the anger of the LORD burned against the people, and he struck them with a severe plague. ³⁴Therefore the place was named Kibroth Hattaavah,*c* because there they buried the people who had craved other food.

³⁵From Kibroth Hattaavah the people traveled to Hazeroth and stayed there.

Miriam and Aaron Oppose Moses

12 Miriam and Aaron began to talk against Moses because of his Cushite wife, for he had married a Cushite. ²"Has the LORD spoken only through Moses?" they asked. "Hasn't he also spoken through us?" And the LORD heard this.

³(Now Moses was a very humble man, more humble than anyone else on the face of the earth.)

⁴At once the LORD said to Moses, Aaron and Miriam, "Come out to the tent of meeting, all three of you." So the three of them went out. ⁵Then the LORD came down in a pillar of cloud; he stood at the entrance to the tent and summoned Aaron and Miriam. When the two of them stepped forward, ⁶he said, "Listen to my words:

> "When there are prophets of the LORD
>   among you,
> I reveal myself to them in visions,
> I speak to them in dreams.
> ⁷But this is not true of my servant Moses;

184

atissue:racism

12:1–2 Our natural response to unfamiliar people or things is fear. This fear usually rises to the surface masked as some other emotion, such as anger or hate. Aaron and Miriam let their fear of Moses' foreign wife turn into suspicion. Then their suspicion quickly turned into feelings of jealousy and then superiority. If we don't proactively monitor our reactions to people who aren't like us, then we become carriers for racist, judgmental attitudes and actions. And this is pride in the face of God and his creation. You may not intentionally hold racist feelings, but how are you proactively fighting racism?

---

a 31 That is, about 3 feet or about 90 centimeters   *b 32* That is, possibly about 1 3/4 tons or about 1.6 metric tons   *c 34 Kibroth Hattaavah* means *graves of craving.*

he is faithful in all my house.
⁸With him I speak face to face,
   clearly and not in riddles;
   he sees the form of the LORD.
Why then were you not afraid
   to speak against my servant Moses?"

⁹The anger of the LORD burned against them, and he left them.

¹⁰When the cloud lifted from above the tent, Miriam's skin was leprous ᵃ—it became as white as snow. Aaron turned toward her and saw that she had a defiling skin disease, ¹¹and he said to Moses, "Please, my lord, I ask you not to hold against us the sin we have so foolishly committed. ¹²Do not let her be like a stillborn infant coming from its mother's womb with its flesh half eaten away."

¹³So Moses cried out to the LORD, "Please, God, heal her!"

¹⁴The LORD replied to Moses, "If her father had spit in her face, would she not have been in disgrace for seven days? Confine her outside the camp for seven days; after that she can be brought back." ¹⁵So Miriam was confined outside the camp for seven days, and the people did not move on till she was brought back.

¹⁶After that, the people left Hazeroth and encamped in the Desert of Paran.

Exploring Canaan

13 The LORD said to Moses, ²"Send some men to explore the land of Canaan, which I am giving to the Israelites. From each ancestral tribe send one of its leaders."

³So at the LORD's command Moses sent them out from the Desert of Paran. All of them were leaders of the Israelites. ⁴These are their names:

from the tribe of Reuben, Shammua son of Zakkur;
⁵ from the tribe of Simeon, Shaphat son of Hori;
⁶ from the tribe of Judah, Caleb son of Jephunneh;
⁷ from the tribe of Issachar, Igal son of Joseph;
⁸ from the tribe of Ephraim, Hoshea son of Nun;
⁹ from the tribe of Benjamin, Palti son of Raphu;
¹⁰ from the tribe of Zebulun, Gaddiel son of Sodi;
¹¹ from the tribe of Manasseh (a tribe of Joseph), Gaddi son of Susi;
¹² from the tribe of Dan, Ammiel son of Gemalli;
¹³ from the tribe of Asher, Sethur son of Michael;
¹⁴ from the tribe of Naphtali, Nahbi son of Vophsi;
¹⁵ from the tribe of Gad, Geuel son of Maki.

¹⁶These are the names of the men Moses sent to explore the land. (Moses gave Hoshea son of Nun the name Joshua.)

¹⁷When Moses sent them to explore Canaan, he said, "Go up through the Negev and on into the hill country. ¹⁸See what the land is like and whether the people who live there are strong or weak, few or many. ¹⁹What kind of land do they live in? Is it good or bad? What kind of towns do they live in? Are they unwalled or fortified? ²⁰How is the soil? Is it fertile or poor? Are there trees in it or not? Do your best to bring back some of the fruit of the land." (It was the season for the first ripe grapes.)

²¹So they went up and explored the land from the Desert of Zin as far as Rehob, toward Lebo Hamath. ²²They went up through the Negev and came to Hebron, where Ahiman, Sheshai and Talmai, the descendants of Anak, lived. (Hebron had been built seven years before Zoan in Egypt.) ²³When they reached the Valley of Eshkol,ᵇ they cut off a branch bearing a single cluster of grapes. Two of them carried it on a pole between them, along with some pomegranates and figs. ²⁴That place was called the Valley of Eshkol because of the cluster of grapes the Israelites cut off there. ²⁵At the end of forty days they returned from exploring the land.

ᵃ *10* The Hebrew for *leprous* was used for various diseases affecting the skin.   ᵇ *23* Eshkol means *cluster*; also in verse 24.

myth# 13 "I'LL ALWAYS HAVE CLOSE FRIENDS AROUND ME."

Maybe if I didn't know what I was missing, it wouldn't be so difficult.

When my husband followed God's call to move to Ohio after serving at a church in California for eight years, I was devastated. I'd assumed that we were going to be at our church and part of that community forever. We were settled in an established neighborhood with excellent schools, and we lived close to the beach in a house I simply adored. I was part of a circle of Christian women who had become my dearest friends. We met once a week for coffee and often talked to each other throughout the day. I thought I'd always have them in my life. However, God opened a unique door of ministry for my husband in Ohio, so I did my best to trust him as we packed our things and moved cross-country.

Even though my husband has been on staff at this church for three years now, I wouldn't say that I have any real friends here. Of course, I've met many women through Bible study groups and parties we host in our home. The people here are warm and hospitable. My husband and I love our new church, and my kids are crazy about their youth group. But I miss having a girlfriend I can confide in or call on a moment's notice to go shopping or out to lunch. I don't have any of those "just stop by" kind of friends. Some days I feel so lonely.

It's not as if I don't have any friends. My "California friends," as I call them, get together once a year for a girls' weekend. It's as if no time has passed at all, and we catch up on each other's lives. Then it's a long flight back home and back to life as usual. I keep a busy social calendar, as you'd imagine a minister's wife does, but is it too much to ask to have one close friend here?

—Jessica

WOMEN NEED CLOSE,

meaningful friendships with other women. It's the way God uniquely designed us! While men may be content to have one or two close friends in a lifetime, women are more likely to keep up with a range of friends—friends from grade school, college roommates, co-workers and neighbors from three neighborhoods ago. However, at times we may end up in places with no one on our side (like Moses in Numbers 12).

Relationships change. Life moves us on to different places—both physically and emotionally. A job change, a move, a time-consuming project at work, the birth of a child or the dissolution of a friend's marriage—all of these can drastically affect our friendships. Remember, friendships are not a given. We can't take them for granted and assume that we'll always have them.

If you feel relationally dry right now, consider the following:

- Start by examining your friendship with God. God is the only ever-present friend through all of life's circumstances (see Deuteronomy 31:8). Are you cultivating that friendship as you would a relationship with a best girl-friend?

- It's possible that you're in a place in life where God has not given you close girl-friends. What is God trying to teach you by forcing some alone-time?

- Consider changing your expectations for friendships. It's helpful to realize that some friendships never become very close, and they last for only a season. Don't close yourself off to these short-term opportunities just because someone may not become your *best* friend. You may be surprised how and where a friendship may develop if you give it a chance.

- Take the initiative to cultivate relationships that may have gone by the wayside.

"Science has proven that friendships with other women help decrease our stress levels—simply talking about our life issues with someone else who understands can do wonders for our emotional health."

187

"one who Has unreliaBle frienDs soon comes to ruin, BUT THere is a frienD WHO STICKS closer THan a BroTHer."

PROVERBS 18:24

SEE ALSO

1 Samuel 18:1–4
Psalm 88:8–9
John 15:13,15

For more on **Friendship**, check the index.

Report on the Exploration

²⁶They came back to Moses and Aaron and the whole Israelite community at Kadesh in the Desert of Paran. There they reported to them and to the whole assembly and showed them the fruit of the land. ²⁷They gave Moses this account: "We went into the land to which you sent us, and it does flow with milk and honey! Here is its fruit. ²⁸But the people who live there are powerful, and the cities are fortified and very large. We even saw descendants of Anak there. ²⁹The Amalekites live in the Negev; the Hittites, Jebusites and Amorites live in the hill country; and the Canaanites live near the sea and along the Jordan."

³⁰Then Caleb silenced the people before Moses and said, "We should go up and take possession of the land, for we can certainly do it."

³¹But the men who had gone up with him said, "We can't attack those people; they are stronger than we are." ³²And they spread among the Israelites a bad report about the land they had explored. They said, "The land we explored devours those living in it. All the people we saw there are of great size. ³³We saw the Nephilim there (the descendants of Anak come from the Nephilim). We seemed like grasshoppers in our own eyes, and we looked the same to them."

The People Rebel

14 That night all the members of the community raised their voices and wept aloud. ²All the Israelites grumbled against Moses and Aaron, and the whole assembly said to them, "If only we had died in Egypt! Or in this wilderness! ³Why is the LORD bringing us to this land only to let us fall by the sword? Our wives and children will be taken as plunder. Wouldn't it be better for us to go back to Egypt?" ⁴And they said to each other, "We should choose a leader and go back to Egypt."

⁵Then Moses and Aaron fell facedown in front of the whole Israelite assembly gathered there. ⁶Joshua son of Nun and Caleb son of Jephunneh, who were among those who had explored the land, tore their clothes ⁷and said to the entire Israelite assembly, "The land we passed through and explored is exceedingly good. ⁸If the LORD is pleased with us, he will lead us into that land, a land flowing with milk and honey, and will give it to us. ⁹Only do not rebel against the LORD. And do not be afraid of the people of the land, because we will devour them. Their protection is gone, but the LORD is with us. Do not be afraid of them."

¹⁰But the whole assembly talked about stoning them. Then the glory of the LORD appeared at the tent of meeting to all the Israelites. ¹¹The LORD said to Moses, "How long will these people treat me with contempt? How long will they refuse to believe in me, in spite of all the signs I have performed among them? ¹²I will strike them down with a plague and destroy them, but I will make you into a nation greater and stronger than they."

¹³Moses said to the LORD, "Then the Egyptians will hear about it! By your power you brought these people up from among them. ¹⁴And they will tell the inhabitants of this land about it. They have already heard that you, LORD, are with these people and that you, LORD, have been seen face to face, that your cloud stays over them, and that you go before them in a pillar of cloud by day and a pillar of fire by night. ¹⁵If you put these people to death all at one time, the nations who have heard this report about you will say, ¹⁶'The LORD was not able to bring these people into the land he promised them on oath, so he slaughtered them in the wilderness.'

¹⁷"Now may the Lord's strength be displayed, just as you have declared: ¹⁸'The LORD is slow to anger,

---

at issue: doubting God

14:1–4 We might not cry and grumble all night like the Israelites, but we still might harbor thoughts of faithlessness to God. We find subtle ways to doubt God each day—sometimes we're not even aware of what we're doing. Perhaps we find we're wishing for "the good old days." Or maybe we catch ourselves questioning God more often. It's normal to feel anxiety when we're faced with the unknown, but when we try to take matters into our own hands, we interfere with God's timing and his plan. When all you see is desert before you, don't let your doubts distract you from trusting God.

abounding in love and forgiving sin and rebellion. Yet he does not leave the guilty unpunished; he punishes the children for the sin of the parents to the third and fourth generation.' ¹⁹In accordance with your great love, forgive the sin of these people, just as you have pardoned them from the time they left Egypt until now."

²⁰The Lᴏʀᴅ replied, "I have forgiven them, as you asked. ²¹Nevertheless, as surely as I live and as surely as the glory of the Lᴏʀᴅ fills the whole earth, ²²not one of those who saw my glory and the signs I performed in Egypt and in the wilderness but who disobeyed me and tested me ten times— ²³not one of them will ever see the land I promised on oath to their ancestors. No one who has treated me with contempt will ever see it. ²⁴But because my servant Caleb has a different spirit and follows me wholeheartedly, I will bring him into the land he went to, and his descendants will inherit it. ²⁵Since the Amalekites and Canaanites are living in the valleys, turn back tomorrow and set out toward the desert along the route to the Red Sea.ᵃ"

²⁶The Lᴏʀᴅ said to Moses and Aaron: ²⁷"How long will this wicked community grumble against me? I have heard the complaints of these grumbling Israelites. ²⁸So tell them, 'As surely as I live, declares the Lᴏʀᴅ, I will do to you the very thing I heard you say: ²⁹In this wilderness your bodies will fall—every one of you twenty years old or more who was counted in the census and who has grumbled against me. ³⁰Not one of you will enter the land I swore with uplifted hand to make your home, except Caleb son of Jephunneh and Joshua son of Nun. ³¹As for your children that you said would be taken as plunder, I will bring them in to enjoy the land you have rejected. ³²But you—your bodies will fall in this wilderness. ³³Your children will be shepherds here for forty years, suffering for your unfaithfulness, until the last of your bodies lies in the wilderness. ³⁴For forty years—one year for each of the forty days you explored the land—you will suffer for your sins and know what it is like to have me against you.' ³⁵I, the Lᴏʀᴅ, have spoken, and I will surely do these things to this whole wicked community, which has banded together against me. They will meet their end in this wilderness; here they will die."

³⁶So the men Moses had sent to explore the land, who returned and made the whole community grumble against him by spreading a bad report about it— ³⁷these men who were responsible for spreading the bad report about the land were struck down and died of a plague before the Lᴏʀᴅ. ³⁸Of the men who went to explore the land, only Joshua son of Nun and Caleb son of Jephunneh survived.

³⁹When Moses reported this to all the Israelites, they mourned bitterly. ⁴⁰Early the next morning they set out for the highest point in the hill country, saying, "Now we are ready to go up to the land the Lᴏʀᴅ promised. Surely we have sinned!"

⁴¹But Moses said, "Why are you disobeying the Lᴏʀᴅ's command? This will not succeed! ⁴²Do not go up, because the Lᴏʀᴅ is not with you. You will be defeated by your enemies, ⁴³for the Amalekites and Canaanites will face you there. Because you have turned away from the Lᴏʀᴅ, he will not be with you and you will fall by the sword."

⁴⁴Nevertheless, in their presumption they went up toward the highest point in the hill country, though neither Moses nor the ark of the Lᴏʀᴅ's covenant moved from the camp. ⁴⁵Then the Amalekites and Canaanites who lived in that hill country came down and attacked them and beat them down all the way to Hormah.

conversations

attitude «» 14:20–35

1» Why do you still often reap the consequences of your complaining after God forgives you?

2» How do *others* suffer for *your* unfaithfulness (see v. 33)?

3» How can you develop an attitude of contentment about where you are in life now?

For more on **attitude**, check the index.
For the next Conversations, go to p. 194.

Supplementary Offerings

15 The Lᴏʀᴅ said to Moses, ²"Speak to the Israelites and say to them: 'After you enter the land I am giving you as a home ³and you present to the Lᴏʀᴅ food offerings from the herd or the flock, as an aroma pleasing to the Lᴏʀᴅ—whether burnt offerings or sacrifices, for special vows or freewill

---

ᵃ 25 Or *the Sea of Reeds*

offerings or festival offerings— ⁴then the person who brings an offering shall present to the LORD a grain offering of a tenth of an ephah*ᵃ* of the finest flour mixed with a quarter of a hin*ᵇ* of olive oil. ⁵With each lamb for the burnt offering or the sacrifice, prepare a quarter of a hin of wine as a drink offering.

⁶"With a ram prepare a grain offering of two-tenths of an ephah*ᶜ* of the finest flour mixed with a third of a hin*ᵈ* of olive oil, ⁷and a third of a hin of wine as a drink offering. Offer it as an aroma pleasing to the LORD.

⁸"When you prepare a young bull as a burnt offering or sacrifice, for a special vow or a fellowship offering to the LORD, ⁹bring with the bull a grain offering of three-tenths of an ephah*ᵉ* of the finest flour mixed with half a hin*ᶠ* of olive oil, ¹⁰and also bring half a hin of wine as a drink offering. This will be a food offering, an aroma pleasing to the LORD. ¹¹Each bull or ram, each lamb or young goat, is to be prepared in this manner. ¹²Do this for each one, for as many as you prepare.

¹³"Everyone who is native-born must do these things in this way when they present a food offering as an aroma pleasing to the LORD. ¹⁴For the generations to come, whenever a foreigner or anyone else living among you presents a food offering as an aroma pleasing to the LORD, they must do exactly as you do. ¹⁵The community is to have the same rules for you and for the foreigner residing among you; this is a lasting ordinance for the generations to come. You and the foreigner shall be the same before the LORD: ¹⁶The same laws and regulations will apply both to you and to the foreigner residing among you.'"

¹⁷The LORD said to Moses, ¹⁸"Speak to the Israelites and say to them: 'When you enter the land to which I am taking you ¹⁹and you eat the food of the land, present a portion as an offering to the LORD. ²⁰Present a loaf from the first of your ground meal and present it as an offering from the threshing floor. ²¹Throughout the generations to come you are to give this offering to the LORD from the first of your ground meal.

190

Offerings for Unintentional Sins

²²"Now if you as a community unintentionally fail to keep any of these commands the LORD gave Moses— ²³any of the LORD's commands to you through him, from the day the LORD gave them and continuing through the generations to come— ²⁴and if this is done unintentionally without the community being aware of it, then the whole community is to offer a young bull for a burnt offering as an aroma pleasing to the LORD, along with its prescribed grain offering and drink offering, and a male goat for a sin offering.*ᵍ* ²⁵The priest is to make atonement for the whole Israelite community, and they will be forgiven, for it was not intentional and they have presented to the LORD for their wrong a food offering and a sin offering. ²⁶The whole Israelite community and the foreigners residing among them will be forgiven, because all the people were involved in the unintentional wrong.

²⁷"But if just one person sins unintentionally, that person must bring a year-old female goat for a sin offering. ²⁸The priest is to make atonement before the LORD for the one who erred by sinning unintentionally, and when atonement has been made for them, they will be forgiven. ²⁹One and the same law applies to everyone who sins unintentionally, whether a native-born Israelite or a foreigner residing among you.

³⁰"But anyone who sins defiantly, whether native-born or foreigner, blasphemes the LORD and must be cut off from their people. ³¹Because they have despised the LORD's word and broken his commands, they must surely be cut off; their guilt remains on them.'"

The Sabbath-Breaker Put to Death

³²While the Israelites were in the wilderness, a man was found gathering wood on the Sabbath day. ³³Those who found him gathering wood brought him to Moses and Aaron and the whole assembly, ³⁴and they kept him in custody, because it was not clear what should be done to him. ³⁵Then the LORD said to Moses, "The man must die. The whole assembly must stone him outside the camp." ³⁶So the assembly took him outside the camp and stoned him to death, as the LORD commanded Moses.

Tassels on Garments

³⁷The LORD said to Moses, ³⁸"Speak to the Israelites and say to them: 'Throughout the generations to come you are to make tassels on the corners of your garments, with a blue cord on each tassel. ³⁹You will

---

ᵃ 4 That is, probably about 3 1/2 pounds or about 1.5 kilograms   ᵇ 4 That is, about 1 quart or about 0.9 liter; also in verse 5   ᶜ 6 That is, probably about 7 pounds or about 3 1/4 kilograms   ᵈ 6 That is, about 2 2/3 pints or about 1.2 liters; also in verse 7   ᵉ 9 That is, probably about 11 pounds or about 5 kilograms   ᶠ 9 That is, about 1/2 gallon or about 1.8 liters; also in verse 10   ᵍ 24 Or purification offering; also in verses 25 and 27 have these tassels to look at and so you will remember all the commands of the LORD, that you may obey them and not prostitute yourselves by chasing after the lusts of your own hearts and eyes. [40]Then you will remember to obey all my commands and will be consecrated to your God. [41]I am the LORD your God, who brought you out of Egypt to be your God. I am the LORD your God.'"

Korah, Dathan and Abiram

16 Korah son of Izhar, the son of Kohath, the son of Levi, and certain Reubenites—Dathan and Abiram, sons of Eliab, and On son of Peleth—became insolent[a] [2]and rose up against Moses. With them were 250 Israelite men, well-known community leaders who had been appointed members of the council. [3]They came as a group to oppose Moses and Aaron and said to them, "You have gone too far! The whole community is holy, every one of them, and the LORD is with them. Why then do you set yourselves above the LORD's assembly?"

[4]When Moses heard this, he fell facedown. [5]Then he said to Korah and all his followers: "In the morning the LORD will show who belongs to him and who is holy, and he will have that person come near him. The one he chooses he will cause to come near him. [6]You, Korah, and all your followers are to do this: Take censers [7]and tomorrow put burning coals and incense in them before the LORD. The man the LORD chooses will be the one who is holy. You Levites have gone too far!"

[8]Moses also said to Korah, "Now listen, you Levites! [9]Isn't it enough for you that the God of Israel has separated you from the rest of the Israelite community and brought you near himself to do the work at the LORD's tabernacle and to stand before the community and minister to them? [10]He has brought you and all your fellow Levites near himself, but now you are trying to get the priesthood too. [11]It is against the LORD that you and all your followers have banded together. Who is Aaron that you should grumble against him?"

[12]Then Moses summoned Dathan and Abiram, the sons of Eliab. But they said, "We will not come! [13]Isn't it enough that you have brought us up out of a land flowing with milk and honey to kill us in the wilderness? And now you also want to lord it over us! [14]Moreover, you haven't brought us into a land flowing with milk and honey or given us an inheritance of fields and vineyards. Do you want to treat these men like slaves[b]? No, we will not come!"

at issue: competition

16:1–35 Every day we're in competition for anything from a better position in the company to being first in the checkout lane. Competition isn't inherently wrong. However, when we compete with others in the body of Christ to gain a "better" position, we invite trouble. Korah had served the Lord faithfully with his skills, but his prideful desire for the priesthood cost him his life. If you feel the need to plant seeds of dissension in your church or to question the authority of your church leaders, remember Korah. Don't try to usurp someone else's God-given authority in order to get ahead.

[15]Then Moses became very angry and said to the LORD, "Do not accept their offering. I have not taken so much as a donkey from them, nor have I wronged any of them."

[16]Moses said to Korah, "You and all your followers are to appear before the LORD tomorrow—you and they and Aaron. [17]Each one is to take his censer and put incense in it—250 censers in all—and present it before the LORD. You and Aaron are to present your censers also." [18]So each one took his censer, put burning coals and incense in it, and stood with Moses and Aaron at the entrance to the tent of meeting. [19]When Korah had gathered all his followers in opposition to them at the entrance to the tent of meeting, the glory of the LORD appeared to the entire assembly. [20]The LORD said to Moses and Aaron, [21]"Separate yourselves from this assembly so I can put an end to them at once."

[22]But Moses and Aaron fell facedown and cried out, "O God, God of every human spirit, will you be angry with the entire assembly when only one man sins?"

[23]Then the LORD said to Moses, [24]"Say to the assembly, 'Move away from the tents of Korah, Dathan and Abiram.'"

---

[a] 1 Or Peleth—took men   [b] 14 Or to deceive these men; Hebrew Will you gouge out the eyes of these men

²⁵Moses got up and went to Dathan and Abiram, and the elders of Israel followed him. ²⁶He warned the assembly, "Move back from the tents of these wicked men! Do not touch anything belonging to them, or you will be swept away because of all their sins." ²⁷So they moved away from the tents of Korah, Dathan and Abiram. Dathan and Abiram had come out and were standing with their wives, children and little ones at the entrances to their tents.

²⁸Then Moses said, "This is how you will know that the LORD has sent me to do all these things and that it was not my idea: ²⁹If these men die a natural death and suffer the common fate of all human beings, then the LORD has not sent me. ³⁰But if the LORD brings about something totally new, and the earth opens its mouth and swallows them, with everything that belongs to them, and they go down alive into the realm of the dead, then you will know that these men have treated the LORD with contempt."

³¹As soon as he finished saying all this, the ground under them split apart ³²and the earth opened its mouth and swallowed them and their households, and all those associated with Korah, together with their possessions. ³³They went down alive into the realm of the dead, with everything they owned; the earth closed over them, and they perished and were gone from the community. ³⁴At their cries, all the Israelites around them fled, shouting, "The earth is going to swallow us too!"

³⁵And fire came out from the LORD and consumed the 250 men who were offering the incense.

*³⁶The LORD said to Moses, ³⁷"Tell Eleazar son of Aaron, the priest, to remove the censers from the charred remains and scatter the coals some distance away, for the censers are holy— ³⁸the censers of the men who sinned at the cost of their lives. Hammer the censers into sheets to overlay the altar, for they were presented before the LORD and have become holy. Let them be a sign to the Israelites."

³⁹So Eleazar the priest collected the bronze censers brought by those who had been burned to death, and he had them hammered out to overlay the altar, ⁴⁰as the LORD directed him through Moses. This was to remind the Israelites that no one except a descendant of Aaron should come to burn incense before the LORD, or he would become like Korah and his followers.

⁴¹The next day the whole Israelite community grumbled against Moses and Aaron. "You have killed the LORD's people," they said.

⁴²But when the assembly gathered in opposition to Moses and Aaron and turned toward the tent of meeting, suddenly the cloud covered it and the glory of the LORD appeared. ⁴³Then Moses and Aaron went to the front of the tent of meeting, ⁴⁴and the LORD said to Moses, ⁴⁵"Get away from this assembly so I can put an end to them at once." And they fell facedown.

⁴⁶Then Moses said to Aaron, "Take your censer and put incense in it, along with burning coals from the altar, and hurry to the assembly to make atonement for them. Wrath has come out from the LORD; the plague has started." ⁴⁷So Aaron did as Moses said, and ran into the midst of the assembly. The plague had already started among the people, but Aaron offered the incense and made atonement for them. ⁴⁸He stood between the living and the dead, and the plague stopped. ⁴⁹But 14,700 people died from the plague, in addition to those who had died because of Korah. ⁵⁰Then Aaron returned to Moses at the entrance to the tent of meeting, for the plague had stopped.

The Budding of Aaron's Staff

17 *The LORD said to Moses, ²"Speak to the Israelites and get twelve staffs from them, one from the leader of each of their ancestral tribes. Write the name of each man on his staff. ³On the staff of Levi write Aaron's name, for there must be one staff for the head of each ancestral tribe. ⁴Place them in the tent of meeting in front of the ark of the covenant law, where I meet with you. ⁵The staff belonging to the man I choose will sprout, and I will rid myself of this constant grumbling against you by the Israelites."

⁶So Moses spoke to the Israelites, and their leaders gave him twelve staffs, one for the leader of each of their ancestral tribes, and Aaron's staff was among them. ⁷Moses placed the staffs before the LORD in the tent of the covenant law.

⁸The next day Moses entered the tent and saw that Aaron's staff, which represented the house of Levi, had not only sprouted but had budded, blossomed and produced almonds. ⁹Then Moses brought out all

* 16:36-50 is numbered 17:1-15 in Hebrew texts.   * 17:1-13 is numbered 17:16-28 in Hebrew texts.

the staffs from the Lord's presence to all the Israelites. They looked at them, and each of the leaders took his own staff.

¹⁰The Lord said to Moses, "Put back Aaron's staff in front of the ark of the covenant law, to be kept as a sign to the rebellious. This will put an end to their grumbling against me, so that they will not die." ¹¹Moses did just as the Lord commanded him.

¹²The Israelites said to Moses, "We will die! We are lost, we are all lost! ¹³Anyone who even comes near the tabernacle of the Lord will die. Are we all going to die?"

Duties of Priests and Levites

18 The Lord said to Aaron, "You, your sons and your ancestral family are to bear the responsibility for offenses connected with the sanctuary, and you and your sons alone are to bear the responsibility for offenses connected with the priesthood. ²Bring your fellow Levites from your ancestral tribe to join you and assist you when you and your sons minister before the tent of the covenant law. ³They are to be responsible to you and are to perform all the duties of the tent, but they must not go near the furnishings of the sanctuary or the altar. Otherwise both they and you will die. ⁴They are to join you and be responsible for the care of the tent of meeting—all the work at the tent—and no one else may come near where you are.

⁵"You are to be responsible for the care of the sanctuary and the altar, so that my wrath will not fall on the Israelites again. ⁶I myself have selected your fellow Levites from among the Israelites as a gift to you, dedicated to the Lord to do the work at the tent of meeting. ⁷But only you and your sons may serve as priests in connection with everything at the altar and inside the curtain. I am giving you the service of the priesthood as a gift. Anyone else who comes near the sanctuary is to be put to death."

Offerings for Priests and Levites

⁸Then the Lord said to Aaron, "I myself have put you in charge of the offerings presented to me; all the holy offerings the Israelites give me I give to you and your sons as your portion, your perpetual share. ⁹You are to have the part of the most holy offerings that is kept from the fire. From all the gifts they bring me as most holy offerings, whether grain or sin*ᵃ* or guilt offerings, that part belongs to you and your sons. ¹⁰Eat it as something most holy; every male shall eat it. You must regard it as holy.

¹¹"This also is yours: whatever is set aside from the gifts of all the wave offerings of the Israelites. I give this to you and your sons and daughters as your perpetual share. Everyone in your household who is ceremonially clean may eat it.

¹²"I give you all the finest olive oil and all the finest new wine and grain they give the Lord as the firstfruits of their harvest. ¹³All the land's firstfruits that they bring to the Lord will be yours. Everyone in your household who is ceremonially clean may eat it.

¹⁴"Everything in Israel that is devoted*ᵇ* to the Lord is yours. ¹⁵The first offspring of every womb, both human and animal, that is offered to the Lord is yours. But you must redeem every firstborn son and every firstborn male of unclean animals. ¹⁶When they are a month old, you must redeem them at the redemption price set at five shekels*ᶜ* of silver, according to the sanctuary shekel, which weighs twenty gerahs.

¹⁷"But you must not redeem the firstborn of a cow, a sheep or a goat; they are holy. Splash their blood against the altar and burn their fat as a food offering, an aroma pleasing to the Lord. ¹⁸Their meat is to be yours, just as the breast of the wave offering and the right thigh are yours. ¹⁹Whatever is set aside from the holy offerings the Israelites present to the Lord I give to you and your sons and daughters as your perpetual share. It is an everlasting covenant of salt before the Lord for both you and your offspring."

²⁰The Lord said to Aaron, "You will have no inheritance in their land, nor will you have any share among them; I am your share and your inheritance among the Israelites.

²¹"I give to the Levites all the tithes in Israel as their inheritance in return for the work they do while serving at the tent of meeting. ²²From now on the Israelites must not go near the tent of meeting, or they will bear the consequences of their sin and will die. ²³It is the Levites who are to do the work at the tent

193

ᵃ 9 Or *purification*   *ᵇ 14* The Hebrew term refers to the irrevocable giving over of things or persons to the Lord.   *ᶜ 16* That is, about 2 ounces or about 55 grams of meeting and bear the responsibility for any offenses they commit against it. This is a lasting ordinance for the generations to come. They will receive no inheritance among the Israelites. ²⁴Instead, I give to the Levites as their inheritance the tithes that the Israelites present as an offering to the LORD. That is why I said concerning them: 'They will have no inheritance among the Israelites.'"

²⁵The LORD said to Moses, ²⁶"Speak to the Levites and say to them: 'When you receive from the Israelites the tithe I give you as your inheritance, you must present a tenth of that tithe as the LORD's offering. ²⁷Your offering will be reckoned to you as grain from the threshing floor or juice from the winepress. ²⁸In this way you also will present an offering to the LORD from all the tithes you receive from the Israelites. From these tithes you must give the LORD's portion to Aaron the priest. ²⁹You must present as the LORD's portion the best and holiest part of everything given to you.'

³⁰"Say to the Levites: 'When you present the best part, it will be reckoned to you as the product of the threshing floor or the winepress. ³¹You and your households may eat the rest of it anywhere, for it is your wages for your work at the tent of meeting. ³²By presenting the best part of it you will not be guilty in this matter; then you will not defile the holy offerings of the Israelites, and you will not die.'"

conversations

tithing «» 18

1» Why do you give?

2» Does God *need* your tithes and offerings? Why or why not?

3» Do you honestly give God the "best and holiest part" (v. 29) of everything you're given?

For more on tithing, check the index. For the next Conversations, go to p. 214.

The Water of Cleansing

19 The LORD said to Moses and Aaron: ²"This is a requirement of the law that the LORD has commanded: Tell the Israelites to bring you a red heifer without defect or blemish and that has never been under a yoke. ³Give it to Eleazar the priest; it is to be taken outside the camp and slaughtered in his presence. ⁴Then Eleazar the priest is to take some of its blood on his finger and sprinkle it seven times toward the front of the tent of meeting. ⁵While he watches, the heifer is to be burned—its hide, flesh, blood and intestines. ⁶The priest is to take some cedar wood, hyssop and scarlet wool and throw them onto the burning heifer. ⁷After that, the priest must wash his clothes and bathe himself with water. He may then come into the camp, but he will be ceremonially unclean till evening. ⁸The man who burns it must also wash his clothes and bathe with water, and he too will be unclean till evening.

⁹"A man who is clean shall gather up the ashes of the heifer and put them in a ceremonially clean place outside the camp. They are to be kept by the Israelite community for use in the water of cleansing; it is for purification from sin. ¹⁰The man who gathers up the ashes of the heifer must also wash his clothes, and he too will be unclean till evening. This will be a lasting ordinance both for the Israelites and for the foreigners residing among them.

¹¹"Whoever touches a human corpse will be unclean for seven days. ¹²They must purify themselves with the water on the third day and on the seventh day; then they will be clean. But if they do not purify themselves on the third and seventh days, they will not be clean. ¹³If they fail to purify themselves after touching a human corpse, they defile the LORD's tabernacle. They must be cut off from Israel. Because the water of cleansing has not been sprinkled on them, they are unclean; their uncleanness remains on them.

¹⁴"This is the law that applies when a person dies in a tent: Anyone who enters the tent and anyone who is in it will be unclean for seven days, ¹⁵and every open container without a lid fastened on it will be unclean.

¹⁶"Anyone out in the open who touches someone who has been killed with a sword or someone who has died a natural death, or anyone who touches a human bone or a grave, will be unclean for seven days.

¹⁷"For the unclean person, put some ashes from the burned purification offering into a jar and pour

fresh water over them. ¹⁸Then a man who is ceremonially clean is to take some hyssop, dip it in the water and sprinkle the tent and all the furnishings and the people who were there. He must also sprinkle anyone who has touched a human bone or a grave or anyone who has been killed or anyone who has died a natural death. ¹⁹The man who is clean is to sprinkle those who are unclean on the third and seventh days, and on the seventh day he is to purify them. Those who are being cleansed must wash their clothes and bathe with water, and that evening they will be clean. ²⁰But if those who are unclean do not purify themselves, they must be cut off from the community, because they have defiled the sanctuary of the LORD. The water of cleansing has not been sprinkled on them, and they are unclean. ²¹This is a lasting ordinance for them.

"The man who sprinkles the water of cleansing must also wash his clothes, and anyone who touches the water of cleansing will be unclean till evening. ²²Anything that an unclean person touches becomes unclean, and anyone who touches it becomes unclean till evening."

Water From the Rock

20 In the first month the whole Israelite community arrived at the Desert of Zin, and they stayed at Kadesh. There Miriam died and was buried.

²Now there was no water for the community, and the people gathered in opposition to Moses and Aaron. ³They quarreled with Moses and said, "If only we had died when our brothers fell dead before the LORD! ⁴Why did you bring the LORD's community into this wilderness, that we and our livestock should die here? ⁵Why did you bring us up out of Egypt to this terrible place? It has no grain or figs, grapevines or pomegranates. And there is no water to drink!"

⁶Moses and Aaron went from the assembly to the entrance to the tent of meeting and fell facedown, and the glory of the LORD appeared to them. ⁷The LORD said to Moses, ⁸"Take the staff, and you and your brother Aaron gather the assembly together. Speak to that rock before their eyes and it will pour out its water. You will bring water out of the rock for the community so they and their livestock can drink."

⁹So Moses took the staff from the LORD's presence, just as he commanded him. ¹⁰He and Aaron gathered the assembly together in front of the rock and Moses said to them, "Listen, you rebels, must we bring you water out of this rock?" ¹¹Then Moses raised his arm and struck the rock twice with his staff. Water gushed out, and the community and their livestock drank.

¹²But the LORD said to Moses and Aaron, "Because you did not trust in me enough to honor me as holy in the sight of the Israelites, you will not bring this community into the land I give them."

¹³These were the waters of Meribah,ᵃ where the Israelites quarreled with the LORD and where he was proved holy among them.

195

atissue:anger

20:1–13 Anger causes us to do crazy things. The news is full of headlines about people who got angry and completely lost control. Out in the middle of the desert, worn down by endless complaining, Moses vented his anger by beating a rock with a stick. God was displeased—not at Moses' anger but at the way he lost control and determined to do things his way, not God's. We all feel angry at times, and rightfully so. The key is to be angry yet still control our actions and honor God, even in the midst of our anger.

Edom Denies Israel Passage

¹⁴Moses sent messengers from Kadesh to the king of Edom, saying:

"This is what your brother Israel says: You know about all the hardships that have come on us. ¹⁵Our ancestors went down into Egypt, and we lived there many years. The Egyptians mistreated us and our ancestors, ¹⁶but when we cried out to the LORD, he heard our cry and sent an angel and brought us out of Egypt.

ᵃ 13 Meribah means quarreling.

myth# 14 "I'M IN CONTROL."

I have three kids under the age of four. There is no such thing as control in my house. In fact, the more I try to pull it together, the crazier life gets.

I can't remember the last time I arrived early to something. I plan to be somewhere at a certain time, but by the time Savannah has decided to change her clothes yet again, we're already 30 minutes late. I can get myself ready in nothing flat, but it takes forever to pack the car as if we're leaving for Singapore when we're only going to the church nursery.

Last month, the dishwasher broke. The timing belt on my Suburban needs to be replaced. Some days I slip into feeling sorry for myself, yet I realize that my circumstances are way beyond anyone's control at this point. What I worry about is feeling guilty because I should at least be in control of myself. I screamed at Jacob the other day when he stuck his ice cream sandwich into the DVD player. I mean, I got in his face and lost it. If people from church had seen me, they wouldn't believe it. I could hardly believe it myself. It was like an out-of-body experience where I was off to the side watching this insanely bitter woman scream at her child. I honestly didn't think I had a short fuse before I had children. I taught sixth grade (picture a roomful of electric Chihuahuas) for five years and loved it. Who knew my own children would be such a personal challenge?

I try to work through my anger and concentrate on being patient. Every night I ask God for the strength to keep my emotions in check. Yet by the end of each day I feel frazzled and frustrated. This is way beyond being hormonal. I'm just trying to survive each day and not emotionally scar my children for life.

—Tisha

WANTED: WOMAN IN

control of her emotions. Must be able to carry a screaming child out of grocery stores without committing an act of violence, kindly overlook a supervisor's ignorance without retort, complete at least nine LLPW (Laundry Loads Per Week) and have the patience to repeat everything at least twice without breaking a tender smile. Training in volume control a plus.

Who could qualify for that job? Not many of us. We like to tell ourselves, "I'm in control," but God isn't fooled. The Bible says it's impossible for us to keep a lid on what we say (see James 3:8). Look at Moses, God's chosen leader—even *he* lost it (see Numbers 20). None of us is in perfect control of his or her emotions, and it's OK to admit that we need help.

Feeling out of control? Remember . . .

- Self-control is not a result of our own efforts; it is a fruit of the Spirit (see Galatians 5:22–23).

- The Spirit provides the power we need to overcome the temptation to blast our kids, to let our unreasonable boss have it or to tell an obnoxious person exactly what we think. The same power that raised Christ from the dead is already living in us (see Romans 8:11).

- Accountability can go a long way in self-discipline. Ask a good friend to hold you accountable for your anger by asking you how you handled your stress each day. Give your friend permission to probe your heart so you can identify the underlying issues that are driving your anger. It's too easy to leave verbal casualties along the road of life.

- If you have directed verbal or physical abuse toward your child, you have crossed a line and need to seek counsel right away. The wise woman asks for help when she needs it—even if she has to humble herself and admit she's not perfect.

"American's don't like any area of life to be out of their control; in fact, 92 percent include 'self-sufficient' as one of their key self-descriptions."

—Barna Research Group (2000)

197

"BUT THE FRUIT OF THE SPIRIT IS . . . SELF-CONTROL."

GALATIANS 5:22–23

SEE ALSO

Proverbs 25:28
Ephesians 4:26–27
2 Timothy 1:7

For more on **Self-Control,** check the index.

"Now we are here at Kadesh, a town on the edge of your territory. [17] Please let us pass through your country. We will not go through any field or vineyard, or drink water from any well. We will travel along the King's Highway and not turn to the right or to the left until we have passed through your territory."

[18] But Edom answered:

"You may not pass through here; if you try, we will march out and attack you with the sword."

[19] The Israelites replied:

"We will go along the main road, and if we or our livestock drink any of your water, we will pay for it. We only want to pass through on foot—nothing else."

[20] Again they answered:

"You may not pass through."

Then Edom came out against them with a large and powerful army. [21] Since Edom refused to let them go through their territory, Israel turned away from them.

The Death of Aaron

[22] The whole Israelite community set out from Kadesh and came to Mount Hor. [23] At Mount Hor, near the border of Edom, the LORD said to Moses and Aaron, [24] "Aaron will be gathered to his people. He will not enter the land I give the Israelites, because both of you rebelled against my command at the waters of Meribah. [25] Get Aaron and his son Eleazar and take them up Mount Hor. [26] Remove Aaron's garments and put them on his son Eleazar, for Aaron will be gathered to his people; he will die there."

[27] Moses did as the LORD commanded: They went up Mount Hor in the sight of the whole community. [28] Moses removed Aaron's garments and put them on his son Eleazar. And Aaron died there on top of the mountain. Then Moses and Eleazar came down from the mountain, [29] and when the whole community learned that Aaron had died, the entire house of Israel mourned for him thirty days.

Arad Destroyed

21 When the Canaanite king of Arad, who lived in the Negev, heard that Israel was coming along the road to Atharim, he attacked the Israelites and captured some of them. [2] Then Israel made this vow to the LORD: "If you will deliver these people into our hands, we will totally destroy[a] their cities." [3] The LORD listened to Israel's plea and gave the Canaanites over to them. They completely destroyed them and their towns; so the place was named Hormah.[b]

The Bronze Snake

[4] They traveled from Mount Hor along the route to the Red Sea,[c] to go around Edom. But the people grew impatient on the way; [5] they spoke against God and against Moses, and said, "Why have you brought us up

---

atissue:complaining

21:4–9 "Quit complaining, or I'll give you something to complain about!" We've all heard (or used) these words before. Actually, there's some truth to this saying. When we whine, we lose sight of the big picture. Our problems become magnified and distort our view of our lives. In their complaining, the Israelites had completely forgotten just how bad life was in Egypt. So God *literally* gave them something to complain about. If you find yourself consistently feeling irritable or discontented, watch where you're headed. It's less painful to quit complaining now before you actually get something to complain about.

---

[a] 2 The Hebrew term refers to the irrevocable giving over of things or persons to the LORD, often by totally destroying them; also in verse 3.   [b] 3 Hormah means destruction.   [c] 4 Or the Sea of Reeds

out of Egypt to die in the wilderness? There is no bread! There is no water! And we detest this miserable food!"

[6]Then the Lord sent venomous snakes among them; they bit the people and many Israelites died. [7]The people came to Moses and said, "We sinned when we spoke against the Lord and against you. Pray that the Lord will take the snakes away from us." So Moses prayed for the people.

[8]The Lord said to Moses, "Make a snake and put it up on a pole; anyone who is bitten can look at it and live." [9]So Moses made a bronze snake and put it up on a pole. Then when anyone was bitten by a snake and looked at the bronze snake, they lived.

The Journey to Moab

[10]The Israelites moved on and camped at Oboth. [11]Then they set out from Oboth and camped in Iye Abarim, in the wilderness that faces Moab toward the sunrise. [12]From there they moved on and camped in the Zered Valley. [13]They set out from there and camped alongside the Arnon, which is in the wilderness extending into Amorite territory. The Arnon is the border of Moab, between Moab and the Amorites. [14]That is why the Book of the Wars of the Lord says:

> "... Zahab[a] in Suphah and the ravines,
>   the Arnon [15]and[b] the slopes of the ravines
> that lead to the settlement of Ar
> and lie along the border of Moab."

[16]From there they continued on to Beer, the well where the Lord said to Moses, "Gather the people together and I will give them water."

[17]Then Israel sang this song:

> "Spring up, O well!
>   Sing about it,
> [18]about the well that the princes dug,
>   that the nobles of the people sank—
>   the nobles with scepters and staffs."

Then they went from the wilderness to Mattanah, [19]from Mattanah to Nahaliel, from Nahaliel to Bamoth, [20]and from Bamoth to the valley in Moab where the top of Pisgah overlooks the wasteland.

Defeat of Sihon and Og

[21]Israel sent messengers to say to Sihon king of the Amorites:

[22]"Let us pass through your country. We will not turn aside into any field or vineyard, or drink water from any well. We will travel along the King's Highway until we have passed through your territory."

[23]But Sihon would not let Israel pass through his territory. He mustered his entire army and marched out into the wilderness against Israel. When he reached Jahaz, he fought with Israel. [24]Israel, however, put him to the sword and took over his land from the Arnon to the Jabbok, but only as far as the Ammonites, because their border was fortified. [25]Israel captured all the cities of the Amorites and occupied them, including Heshbon and all its surrounding settlements. [26]Heshbon was the city of Sihon king of the Amorites, who had fought against the former king of Moab and had taken from him all his land as far as the Arnon.

[27]That is why the poets say:

> "Come to Heshbon and let it be rebuilt;
>   let Sihon's city be restored.

> [28]"Fire went out from Heshbon,
>   a blaze from the city of Sihon.

---

[a] 14 Septuagint; Hebrew Waheb   [b] 14,15 Or "I have been given from Suphah and the ravines / of the Arnon [15]to

It consumed Ar of Moab,
the citizens of Arnon's heights.
²⁹Woe to you, Moab!
You are destroyed, people of Chemosh!
He has given up his sons as fugitives
and his daughters as captives
to Sihon king of the Amorites.

³⁰"But we have overthrown them;
Heshbon's dominion has been destroyed all the way to Dibon.
We have demolished them as far as Nophah,
which extends to Medeba."

³¹So Israel settled in the land of the Amorites.

³²After Moses had sent spies to Jazer, the Israelites captured its surrounding settlements and drove out the Amorites who were there. ³³Then they turned and went up along the road toward Bashan, and Og king of Bashan and his whole army marched out to meet them in battle at Edrei.

³⁴The LORD said to Moses, "Do not be afraid of him, for I have delivered him into your hands, along with his whole army and his land. Do to him what you did to Sihon king of the Amorites, who reigned in Heshbon."

³⁵So they struck him down, together with his sons and his whole army, leaving them no survivors. And they took possession of his land.

Balak Summons Balaam

22 Then the Israelites traveled to the plains of Moab and camped along the Jordan across from Jericho.

²Now Balak son of Zippor saw all that Israel had done to the Amorites, ³and Moab was terrified because there were so many people. Indeed, Moab was filled with dread because of the Israelites.

⁴The Moabites said to the elders of Midian, "This horde is going to lick up everything around us, as an ox licks up the grass of the field."

So Balak son of Zippor, who was king of Moab at that time, ⁵sent messengers to summon Balaam son of Beor, who was at Pethor, near the Euphrates River, in his native land. Balak said:

"A people has come out of Egypt; they cover the face of the land and have settled next to me. ⁶Now come and put a curse on these people, because they are too powerful for me. Perhaps then I will be able to defeat them and drive them out of the land. For I know that whoever you bless is blessed, and whoever you curse is cursed."

⁷The elders of Moab and Midian left, taking with them the fee for divination. When they came to Balaam, they told him what Balak had said.

⁸"Spend the night here," Balaam said to them, "and I will report back to you with the answer the LORD gives me." So the Moabite officials stayed with him.

⁹God came to Balaam and asked, "Who are these men with you?"

¹⁰Balaam said to God, "Balak son of Zippor, king of Moab, sent me this message: ¹¹'A people that has come out of Egypt covers the face of the land. Now come and put a curse on them for me. Perhaps then I will be able to fight them and drive them away.'"

¹²But God said to Balaam, "Do not go with them. You must not put a curse on those people, because they are blessed."

¹³The next morning Balaam got up and said to Balak's officials, "Go back to your own country, for the LORD has refused to let me go with you."

¹⁴So the Moabite officials returned to Balak and said, "Balaam refused to come with us."

¹⁵Then Balak sent other officials, more numerous and more distinguished than the first. ¹⁶They came to Balaam and said:

"This is what Balak son of Zippor says: Do not let anything keep you from coming to me, [17]because I will reward you handsomely and do whatever you say. Come and put a curse on these people for me."

[18]But Balaam answered them, "Even if Balak gave me all the silver and gold in his palace, I could not do anything great or small to go beyond the command of the LORD my God. [19]Now spend the night here so that I can find out what else the LORD will tell me."

[20]That night God came to Balaam and said, "Since these men have come to summon you, go with them, but do only what I tell you."

Balaam's Donkey

[21]Balaam got up in the morning, saddled his donkey and went with the Moabite officials. [22]But God was very angry when he went, and the angel of the LORD stood in the road to oppose him. Balaam was riding on his donkey, and his two servants were with him. [23]When the donkey saw the angel of the LORD standing in the road with a drawn sword in his hand, it turned off the road into a field. Balaam beat it to get it back on the road.

[24]Then the angel of the LORD stood in a narrow path through the vineyards, with walls on both sides. [25]When the donkey saw the angel of the LORD, it pressed close to the wall, crushing Balaam's foot against it. So he beat the donkey again.

[26]Then the angel of the LORD moved on ahead and stood in a narrow place where there was no room to turn, either to the right or to the left. [27]When the donkey saw the angel of the LORD, it lay down under Balaam, and he was angry and beat it with his staff. [28]Then the LORD opened the donkey's mouth, and it said to Balaam, "What have I done to you to make you beat me these three times?"

[29]Balaam answered the donkey, "You have made a fool of me! If only I had a sword in my hand, I would kill you right now."

[30]The donkey said to Balaam, "Am I not your own donkey, which you have always ridden, to this day? Have I been in the habit of doing this to you?"

"No," he said.

[31]Then the LORD opened Balaam's eyes, and he saw the angel of the LORD standing in the road with his sword drawn. So he bowed low and fell facedown.

[32]The angel of the LORD asked him, "Why have you beaten your donkey these three times? I have come here to oppose you because your path is a reckless one before me.[a] [33]The donkey saw me and turned away from me these three times. If it had not turned away, I would certainly have killed you by now, but I would have spared it."

[34]Balaam said to the angel of the LORD, "I have sinned. I did not realize you were standing in the road to oppose me. Now if you are displeased, I will go back."

---

[a] 32 The meaning of the Hebrew for this clause is uncertain.

HE IS: a creative communicator

22:21–35 Balaam was riding a donkey on a mission that displeased God. But God used the donkey to warn Balaam against his folly. In the natural world, donkeys are stubborn animals known for their loud bray. In the supernatural world, God can use even a donkey to speak to obstinate people.

If you are stubbornly set in your ways, don't be surprised when God shows you that he is *a creative communicator*. He may not speak through an animal, but he can get his message across using people, events—even pop culture. God has amazingly creative ways to get your attention.

For the next He Is, go to p. 211.

³⁵The angel of the LORD said to Balaam, "Go with the men, but speak only what I tell you." So Balaam went with Balak's officials.

³⁶When Balak heard that Balaam was coming, he went out to meet him at the Moabite town on the Arnon border, at the edge of his territory. ³⁷Balak said to Balaam, "Did I not send you an urgent summons? Why didn't you come to me? Am I really not able to reward you?"

³⁸"Well, I have come to you now," Balaam replied. "But I can't say whatever I please. I must speak only what God puts in my mouth."

³⁹Then Balaam went with Balak to Kiriath Huzoth. ⁴⁰Balak sacrificed cattle and sheep, and gave some to Balaam and the officials who were with him. ⁴¹The next morning Balak took Balaam up to Bamoth Baal, and from there he could see the outskirts of the Israelite camp.

Balaam's First Message

23 Balaam said, "Build me seven altars here, and prepare seven bulls and seven rams for me." ²Balak did as Balaam said, and the two of them offered a bull and a ram on each altar.

³Then Balaam said to Balak, "Stay here beside your offering while I go aside. Perhaps the LORD will come to meet with me. Whatever he reveals to me I will tell you." Then he went off to a barren height.

⁴God met with him, and Balaam said, "I have prepared seven altars, and on each altar I have offered a bull and a ram."

⁵The LORD put a word in Balaam's mouth and said, "Go back to Balak and give him this word."

⁶So he went back to him and found him standing beside his offering, with all the Moabite officials. ⁷Then Balaam spoke his message:

> "Balak brought me from Aram,
> the king of Moab from the eastern mountains.
> 'Come,' he said, 'curse Jacob for me;
> come, denounce Israel.'
> ⁸How can I curse
> those whom God has not cursed?
> How can I denounce
> those whom the LORD has not denounced?
> ⁹From the rocky peaks I see them,
> from the heights I view them.
> I see a people who live apart
> and do not consider themselves one of the nations.
> ¹⁰Who can count the dust of Jacob
> or number the fourth part of Israel?
> Let me die the death of the righteous,
> and may my final end be like theirs!"

¹¹Balak said to Balaam, "What have you done to me? I brought you to curse my enemies, but you have done nothing but bless them!"

¹²He answered, "Must I not speak what the LORD puts in my mouth?"

Balaam's Second Message

¹³Then Balak said to him, "Come with me to another place where you can see them; you will not see them all but only the outskirts of their camp. And from there, curse them for me." ¹⁴So he took him to the field of Zophim on the top of Pisgah, and there he built seven altars and offered a bull and a ram on each altar.

¹⁵Balaam said to Balak, "Stay here beside your offering while I meet with him over there."

¹⁶The LORD met with Balaam and put a word in his mouth and said, "Go back to Balak and give him this word."

¹⁷So he went to him and found him standing beside his offering, with the Moabite officials. Balak asked him, "What did the LORD say?"

¹⁸Then he spoke his message:

"Arise, Balak, and listen;
    hear me, son of Zippor.
¹⁹God is not a human, that he should lie,
    not a human being, that he should change his mind.
Does he speak and then not act?
    Does he promise and not fulfill?
²⁰I have received a command to bless;
    he has blessed, and I cannot change it.

²¹"No misfortune is seen in Jacob,
    no misery observed^a in Israel.
The Lord their God is with them;
    the shout of the King is among them.
²²God brought them out of Egypt;
    they have the strength of a wild ox.
²³There is no divination against^b Jacob,
    no evil omens against^b Israel.
It will now be said of Jacob
    and of Israel, 'See what God has done!'
²⁴The people rise like a lioness;
    they rouse themselves like a lion
that does not rest till it devours its prey
    and drinks the blood of its victims."

²⁵Then Balak said to Balaam, "Neither curse them at all nor bless them at all!"

²⁶Balaam answered, "Did I not tell you I must do whatever the Lord says?"

Balaam's Third Message

²⁷Then Balak said to Balaam, "Come, let me take you to another place. Perhaps it will please God to let you curse them for me from there." ²⁸And Balak took Balaam to the top of Peor, overlooking the wasteland.

²⁹Balaam said, "Build me seven altars here, and prepare seven bulls and seven rams for me." ³⁰Balak did as Balaam had said, and offered a bull and a ram on each altar.

24 Now when Balaam saw that it pleased the Lord to bless Israel, he did not resort to divination as at other times, but turned his face toward the wilderness. ²When Balaam looked out and saw Israel encamped tribe by tribe, the Spirit of God came on him ³and he spoke his message:

"The prophecy of Balaam son of Beor,
    the prophecy of one whose eye sees clearly,
⁴the prophecy of one who hears the words of God,
    who sees a vision from the Almighty,^c
    who falls prostrate, and whose eyes are opened:

⁵"How beautiful are your tents, Jacob,
    your dwelling places, Israel!

⁶"Like valleys they spread out,
    like gardens beside a river,
like aloes planted by the Lord,
    like cedars beside the waters.

---

^a 21 Or He has not looked on Jacob's offenses / or on the wrongs found   ^b 23 Or in   ^c 4 Hebrew Shaddai; also in verse 16

⁷Water will flow from their buckets;
    their seed will have abundant water.

"Their king will be greater than Agag;
    their kingdom will be exalted.

⁸"God brought them out of Egypt;
    they have the strength of a wild ox.
They devour hostile nations
    and break their bones in pieces;
    with their arrows they pierce them.
⁹Like a lion they crouch and lie down,
    like a lioness—who dares to rouse them?

"May those who bless you be blessed
    and those who curse you be cursed!"

¹⁰Then Balak's anger burned against Balaam. He struck his hands together and said to him, "I summoned you to curse my enemies, but you have blessed them these three times. ¹¹Now leave at once and go home! I said I would reward you handsomely, but the LORD has kept you from being rewarded."

¹²Balaam answered Balak, "Did I not tell the messengers you sent me, ¹³'Even if Balak gave me all the silver and gold in his palace, I could not do anything of my own accord, good or bad, to go beyond the command of the LORD—and I must say only what the LORD says'? ¹⁴Now I am going back to my people, but come, let me warn you of what this people will do to your people in days to come."

Balaam's Fourth Message

¹⁵Then he spoke his message:

"The prophecy of Balaam son of Beor,
    the prophecy of one whose eye sees clearly,
¹⁶the prophecy of one who hears the words of God,
    who has knowledge from the Most High,
who sees a vision from the Almighty,
    who falls prostrate, and whose eyes are opened:

¹⁷"I see him, but not now;
    I behold him, but not near.
A star will come out of Jacob;
    a scepter will rise out of Israel.
He will crush the foreheads of Moab,
    the skulls^a of^b all the people of Sheth.^c
¹⁸Edom will be conquered;
    Seir, his enemy, will be conquered,
    but Israel will grow strong.
¹⁹A ruler will come out of Jacob
    and destroy the survivors of the city."

Balaam's Fifth Message

²⁰Then Balaam saw Amalek and spoke his message:

"Amalek was first among the nations,
    but they will come to ruin at last."

---

^a 17 Samaritan Pentateuch (see also Jer. 48:45); the meaning of the word in the Masoretic Text is uncertain.   ^b 17 Or possibly Moab, / batter   ^c 17 Or all the noisy boasters

Balaam's Sixth Message

[21] Then he saw the Kenites and spoke his message:

"Your dwelling place is secure,
    your nest is set in a rock;
[22] yet you Kenites will be destroyed
    when Ashur takes you captive."

Balaam's Seventh Message

[23] Then he spoke his message:

"Ah, who can live when God does this?[a]
[24]   Ships will come from the shores of Cyprus;
    they will subdue Ashur and Eber,
        but they too will come to ruin."

[25] Then Balaam got up and returned home, and Balak went his own way.

Moab Seduces Israel

25 While Israel was staying in Shittim, the men began to indulge in sexual immorality with Moabite women, [2] who invited them to the sacrifices to their gods. The people ate the sacrificial meal and bowed down before these gods. [3] So Israel yoked themselves to the Baal of Peor. And the LORD's anger burned against them.

[4] The LORD said to Moses, "Take all the leaders of these people, kill them and expose them in broad daylight before the LORD, so that the LORD's fierce anger may turn away from Israel."

[5] So Moses said to Israel's judges, "Each of you must put to death those of your people who have yoked themselves to the Baal of Peor."

[6] Then an Israelite man brought into the camp a Midianite woman right before the eyes of Moses and the whole assembly of Israel while they were weeping at the entrance to the tent of meeting. [7] When Phinehas son of Eleazar, the son of Aaron, the priest, saw this, he left the assembly, took a spear in his hand [8] and followed the Israelite into the tent. He drove the spear into both of them, right through the Israelite man and into the woman's stomach. Then the plague against the Israelites was stopped; [9] but those who died in the plague numbered 24,000.

[10] The LORD said to Moses, [11] "Phinehas son of Eleazar, the son of Aaron, the priest, has turned my anger away from the Israelites. Since he was as zealous for my honor among them as I am, I did not put an end to them in my zeal. [12] Therefore tell him I am making my covenant of peace with him. [13] He and his descendants will have a covenant of a lasting priesthood, because he was zealous for the honor of his God and made atonement for the Israelites."

[14] The name of the Israelite who was killed with the Midianite woman was Zimri son of Salu, the leader of a Simeonite

205

atissue:non-christian friends

25:1–3 We all know people who aren't Christians. The only way to avoid non-Christians is to cut off all contact with the outside world—something God has specifically commanded us *not* to do.
Yet we need to be aware of the temptations we face when we make non-Christians our closest friends. The Israelites probably didn't foresee that they'd worship false gods with the Moabites, but that was the result of their close alignment. God wants you to love others and even to be friends with people who don't believe as you do. Yet watch closely the *degree* of your friendship. Your closest friends should be Christians too.

---

[a] 23 Masoretic Text; with a different word division of the Hebrew *The people from the islands will gather from the north.*

family. ¹⁵And the name of the Midianite woman who was put to death was Kozbi daughter of Zur, a tribal chief of a Midianite family.

¹⁶The LORD said to Moses, ¹⁷"Treat the Midianites as enemies and kill them. ¹⁸They treated you as enemies when they deceived you in the Peor incident involving their sister Kozbi, the daughter of a Midianite leader, the woman who was killed when the plague came as a result of that incident."

The Second Census

26 After the plague the LORD said to Moses and Eleazar son of Aaron, the priest, ²"Take a census of the whole Israelite community by families—all those twenty years old or more who are able to serve in the army of Israel." ³So on the plains of Moab by the Jordan across from Jericho, Moses and Eleazar the priest spoke with them and said, ⁴"Take a census of the men twenty years old or more, as the LORD commanded Moses."

These were the Israelites who came out of Egypt:

⁵The descendants of Reuben, the firstborn son of Israel, were:
through Hanok, the Hanokite clan;
through Pallu, the Palluite clan;
⁶ through Hezron, the Hezronite clan;
through Karmi, the Karmite clan.
⁷These were the clans of Reuben; those numbered were 43,730.

⁸The son of Pallu was Eliab, ⁹and the sons of Eliab were Nemuel, Dathan and Abiram. The same Dathan and Abiram were the community officials who rebelled against Moses and Aaron and were among Korah's followers when they rebelled against the LORD. ¹⁰The earth opened its mouth and swallowed them along with Korah, whose followers died when the fire devoured the 250 men. And they served as a warning sign. ¹¹The line of Korah, however, did not die out.

¹²The descendants of Simeon by their clans were:
through Nemuel, the Nemuelite clan;
through Jamin, the Jaminite clan;
through Jakin, the Jakinite clan;
¹³ through Zerah, the Zerahite clan;
through Shaul, the Shaulite clan.
¹⁴These were the clans of Simeon; those numbered were 22,200.

¹⁵The descendants of Gad by their clans were:
through Zephon, the Zephonite clan;
through Haggi, the Haggite clan;
through Shuni, the Shunite clan;
¹⁶ through Ozni, the Oznite clan;
through Eri, the Erite clan;
¹⁷ through Arodi,^a the Arodite clan;
through Areli, the Arelite clan.
¹⁸These were the clans of Gad; those numbered were 40,500.

¹⁹Er and Onan were sons of Judah, but they died in Canaan.
²⁰The descendants of Judah by their clans were:
through Shelah, the Shelanite clan;
through Perez, the Perezite clan;
through Zerah, the Zerahite clan.
²¹ The descendants of Perez were:
through Hezron, the Hezronite clan;
through Hamul, the Hamulite clan.

---

^a *17* Samaritan Pentateuch and Syriac (see also Gen. 46:16); Masoretic Text *Arod*

²²These were the clans of Judah; those numbered were 76,500.

²³The descendants of Issachar by their clans were:

through Tola, the Tolaite clan;

through Puah, the Puite*a* clan;

²⁴ through Jashub, the Jashubite clan;

through Shimron, the Shimronite clan.

²⁵These were the clans of Issachar; those numbered were 64,300.

²⁶The descendants of Zebulun by their clans were:

through Sered, the Seredite clan;

through Elon, the Elonite clan;

through Jahleel, the Jahleelite clan.

²⁷These were the clans of Zebulun; those numbered were 60,500.

²⁸The descendants of Joseph by their clans through Manasseh and Ephraim were:

²⁹The descendants of Manasseh:

through Makir, the Makirite clan (Makir was the father of Gilead);

through Gilead, the Gileadite clan.

³⁰ These were the descendants of Gilead:

through Iezer, the Iezerite clan;

through Helek, the Helekite clan;

³¹ through Asriel, the Asrielite clan;

through Shechem, the Shechemite clan;

³² through Shemida, the Shemidaite clan;

through Hepher, the Hepherite clan.

³³ (Zelophehad son of Hepher had no sons; he had only daughters, whose names were Mahlah, Noah, Hoglah, Milkah and Tirzah.)

³⁴These were the clans of Manasseh; those numbered were 52,700.

³⁵These were the descendants of Ephraim by their clans:

through Shuthelah, the Shuthelahite clan;

through Beker, the Bekerite clan;

through Tahan, the Tahanite clan.

³⁶ These were the descendants of Shuthelah:

through Eran, the Eranite clan.

³⁷These were the clans of Ephraim; those numbered were 32,500.

These were the descendants of Joseph by their clans.

³⁸The descendants of Benjamin by their clans were:

through Bela, the Belaite clan;

through Ashbel, the Ashbelite clan;

through Ahiram, the Ahiramite clan;

³⁹ through Shupham,*b* the Shuphamite clan;

through Hupham, the Huphamite clan.

⁴⁰ The descendants of Bela through Ard and Naaman were:

through Ard,*c* the Ardite clan;

through Naaman, the Naamite clan.

⁴¹These were the clans of Benjamin; those numbered were 45,600.

207

a 23 Samaritan Pentateuch, Septuagint, Vulgate and Syriac (see also 1 Chron. 7:1); Masoretic Text *through Puvah, the Punite*   *b 39* A few manuscripts of the Masoretic Text, Samaritan Pentateuch, Vulgate and Syriac (see also Septuagint); most manuscripts of the Masoretic Text *Shephupham*   *c 40* Samaritan Pentateuch and Vulgate (see also Septuagint); Masoretic Text does not have *through Ard.*

⁴²These were the descendants of Dan by their clans:

through Shuham, the Shuhamite clan.

These were the clans of Dan: ⁴³All of them were Shuhamite clans; and those numbered were 64,400.

⁴⁴The descendants of Asher by their clans were:

through Imnah, the Imnite clan;

through Ishvi, the Ishvite clan;

through Beriah, the Beriite clan;

⁴⁵ and through the descendants of Beriah:

through Heber, the Heberite clan;

through Malkiel, the Malkielite clan.

⁴⁶ (Asher had a daughter named Serah.)

⁴⁷These were the clans of Asher; those numbered were 53,400.

⁴⁸The descendants of Naphtali by their clans were:

through Jahzeel, the Jahzeelite clan;

through Guni, the Gunite clan;

⁴⁹ through Jezer, the Jezerite clan;

through Shillem, the Shillemite clan.

⁵⁰These were the clans of Naphtali; those numbered were 45,400.

⁵¹The total number of the men of Israel was 601,730.

⁵²The Lord said to Moses, ⁵³"The land is to be allotted to them as an inheritance based on the number of names. ⁵⁴To a larger group give a larger inheritance, and to a smaller group a smaller one; each is to receive its inheritance according to the number of those listed. ⁵⁵Be sure that the land is distributed by lot. What each group inherits will be according to the names for its ancestral tribe. ⁵⁶Each inheritance is to be distributed by lot among the larger and smaller groups."

⁵⁷These were the Levites who were counted by their clans:

through Gershon, the Gershonite clan;

through Kohath, the Kohathite clan;

through Merari, the Merarite clan.

⁵⁸ These also were Levite clans:

the Libnite clan,

the Hebronite clan,

the Mahlite clan,

the Mushite clan,

the Korahite clan.

(Kohath was the forefather of Amram; ⁵⁹the name of Amram's wife was Jochebed, a descendant of Levi, who was born to the Levites^a in Egypt. To Amram she bore Aaron, Moses and their sister Miriam. ⁶⁰Aaron was the father of Nadab and Abihu, Eleazar and Ithamar. ⁶¹But Nadab and Abihu died when they made an offering before the Lord with unauthorized fire.)

⁶²All the male Levites a month old or more numbered 23,000. They were not counted along with the other Israelites because they received no inheritance among them.

⁶³These are the men counted by Moses and Eleazar the priest when they counted the Israelites on the plains of Moab by the Jordan across from Jericho. ⁶⁴Not one of them was among those counted by Moses and Aaron the priest when they counted the Israelites in the Desert of Sinai. ⁶⁵For the Lord had told those Israelites they would surely die in the wilderness, and not one of them was left except Caleb son of Jephunneh and Joshua son of Nun.

---

^a 59 Or Jochebed, a daughter of Levi, who was born to Levi

Zelophehad's Daughters

27 The daughters of Zelophehad son of Hepher, the son of Gilead, the son of Makir, the son of Manasseh, belonged to the clans of Manasseh son of Joseph. The names of the daughters were Mahlah, Noah, Hoglah, Milkah and Tirzah. They came forward ²and stood before Moses, Eleazar the priest, the leaders and the whole assembly at the entrance to the tent of meeting and said, ³"Our father died in the wilderness. He was not among Korah's followers, who banded together against the LORD, but he died for his own sin and left no sons. ⁴Why should our father's name disappear from his clan because he had no son? Give us property among our father's relatives."

⁵So Moses brought their case before the LORD, ⁶and the LORD said to him, ⁷"What Zelophehad's daughters are saying is right. You must certainly give them property as an inheritance among their father's relatives and give their father's inheritance to them.

⁸"Say to the Israelites, 'If a man dies and leaves no son, give his inheritance to his daughter. ⁹If he has no daughter, give his inheritance to his brothers. ¹⁰If he has no brothers, give his inheritance to his father's brothers. ¹¹If his father had no brothers, give his inheritance to the nearest relative in his clan, that he may possess it. This is to have the force of law for the Israelites, as the LORD commanded Moses.'"

Joshua to Succeed Moses

¹²Then the LORD said to Moses, "Go up this mountain in the Abarim Range and see the land I have given the Israelites. ¹³After you have seen it, you too will be gathered to your people, as your brother Aaron was, ¹⁴for when the community rebelled at the waters in the Desert of Zin, both of you disobeyed my command to honor me as holy before their eyes." (These were the waters of Meribah Kadesh, in the Desert of Zin.)

¹⁵Moses said to the LORD, ¹⁶"May the LORD, the God of every human spirit, appoint someone over this community ¹⁷to go out and come in before them, one who will lead them out and bring them in, so the LORD's people will not be like sheep without a shepherd."

¹⁸So the LORD said to Moses, "Take Joshua son of Nun, a man in whom is the spirit of leadership,ᵃ and lay your hand on him. ¹⁹Have him stand before Eleazar the priest and the entire assembly and commission him in their presence. ²⁰Give him some of your authority so the whole Israelite community will obey him. ²¹He is to stand before Eleazar the priest, who will obtain decisions for him by inquiring of the Urim before the LORD. At his command he and the entire community of the Israelites will go out, and at his command they will come in."

²²Moses did as the LORD commanded him. He took Joshua and had him stand before Eleazar the priest and the whole assembly. ²³Then he laid his hands on him and commissioned him, as the LORD instructed through Moses.

Daily Offerings

28 The LORD said to Moses, ²"Give this command to the Israelites and say to them: 'Make sure that you present to me at the appointed time my food offerings, as an aroma pleasing to me.' ³Say to them: 'This is the food offering you are to present to the LORD: two lambs a year old without defect, as a regular burnt offering each day. ⁴Offer one lamb in the morning and the other at twilight, ⁵together with a grain offering of a tenth of an ephahᵇ of the finest flour mixed with a quarter of a hinᶜ of oil from pressed olives. ⁶This is the regular burnt offering instituted at Mount Sinai as a pleasing aroma, a food offering presented to the LORD. ⁷The accompanying drink offering is to be a quarter of a hin of fermented drink with each lamb. Pour out the drink offering to the LORD at the sanctuary. ⁸Offer the second lamb at twilight, along with the same kind of grain offering and drink offering that you offer in the morning. This is a food offering, an aroma pleasing to the LORD.

Sabbath Offerings

⁹"'On the Sabbath day, make an offering of two lambs a year old without defect, together with its drink offering and a grain offering of two-tenths of an ephahᵈ of the finest flour mixed with olive oil. ¹⁰This is the burnt offering for every Sabbath, in addition to the regular burnt offering and its drink offering.

209

ᵃ *18* Or *the Spirit*   ᵇ *5* That is, probably about 3 1/2 pounds or about 1.5 kilograms; also in verses 13, 21 and 29   ᶜ *5* That is, about 1 quart or about 0.9 liter; also in verses 7 and 14   ᵈ *9* That is, probably about 7 pounds or about 3 1/4 kilograms; also in verses 12, 20 and 28

Monthly Offerings

[11] "'On the first of every month, present to the Lord a burnt offering of two young bulls, one ram and seven male lambs a year old, all without defect. [12] With each bull there is to be a grain offering of three-tenths of an ephah[a] of the finest flour mixed with oil; with the ram, a grain offering of two-tenths of an ephah of the finest flour mixed with oil; [13] and with each lamb, a grain offering of a tenth of an ephah of the finest flour mixed with oil. This is for a burnt offering, a pleasing aroma, a food offering presented to the Lord. [14] With each bull there is to be a drink offering of half a hin[b] of wine; with the ram, a third of a hin[c]; and with each lamb, a quarter of a hin. This is the monthly burnt offering to be made at each new moon during the year. [15] Besides the regular burnt offering with its drink offering, one male goat is to be presented to the Lord as a sin offering.[d]

The Passover

[16] "'On the fourteenth day of the first month the Lord's Passover is to be held. [17] On the fifteenth day of this month there is to be a festival; for seven days eat bread made without yeast. [18] On the first day hold a sacred assembly and do no regular work. [19] Present to the Lord a food offering consisting of a burnt offering of two young bulls, one ram and seven male lambs a year old, all without defect. [20] With each bull offer a grain offering of three-tenths of an ephah of the finest flour mixed with oil; with the ram, two-tenths; [21] and with each of the seven lambs, one-tenth. [22] Include one male goat as a sin offering to make atonement for you. [23] Offer these in addition to the regular morning burnt offering. [24] In this way present the food offering every day for seven days as an aroma pleasing to the Lord; it is to be offered in addition to the regular burnt offering and its drink offering. [25] On the seventh day hold a sacred assembly and do no regular work.

The Festival of Weeks

[26] "'On the day of firstfruits, when you present to the Lord an offering of new grain during the Festival of Weeks, hold a sacred assembly and do no regular work. [27] Present a burnt offering of two young bulls, one ram and seven male lambs a year old as an aroma pleasing to the Lord. [28] With each bull there is to be a grain offering of three-tenths of an ephah of the finest flour mixed with oil; with the ram, two-tenths; [29] and with each of the seven lambs, one-tenth. [30] Include one male goat to make atonement for you. [31] Offer these together with their drink offerings, in addition to the regular burnt offering and its grain offering. Be sure the animals are without defect.

The Festival of Trumpets

29 "'On the first day of the seventh month hold a sacred assembly and do no regular work. It is a day for you to sound the trumpets. [2] As an aroma pleasing to the Lord, offer a burnt offering of one young bull, one ram and seven male lambs a year old, all without defect. [3] With the bull offer a grain offering of three-tenths of an ephah[e] of the finest flour mixed with olive oil; with the ram, two-tenths[f]; [4] and with each of the seven lambs, one-tenth.[g] [5] Include one male goat as a sin offering[h] to make atonement for you. [6] These are in addition to the monthly and daily burnt offerings with their grain offerings and drink offerings as specified. They are food offerings presented to the Lord, a pleasing aroma.

The Day of Atonement

[7] "'On the tenth day of this seventh month hold a sacred assembly. You must deny yourselves[i] and do no work. [8] Present as an aroma pleasing to the Lord a burnt offering of one young bull, one ram and seven male lambs a year old, all without defect. [9] With the bull offer a grain offering of three-tenths of an ephah of the finest flour mixed with olive oil; with the ram, two-tenths; [10] and with each of the seven lambs, one-tenth. [11] Include one male goat as a sin offering, in addition to the sin offering for atonement and the regular burnt offering with its grain offering, and their drink offerings.

---

[a] 12 That is, probably about 11 pounds or about 5 kilograms; also in verses 20 and 28   [b] 14 That is, about 1/2 gallon or about 1.8 liters   [c] 14 That is, about 2 2/3 pints or about 1.2 liters   [d] 15 Or purification offering; also in verse 22   [e] 3 That is, probably about 11 pounds or about 5 kilograms; also in verses 9 and 14   [f] 3 That is, probably about 7 pounds or about 3 1/4 kilograms; also in verses 9 and 14   [g] 4 That is, probably about 3 1/2 pounds or about 1 1/2 kilograms; also in verses 10 and 15   [h] 5 Or purification offering; also elsewhere in this chapter   [i] 7 Or must fast

The Festival of Tabernacles

¹²"On the fifteenth day of the seventh month, hold a sacred assembly and do no regular work. Celebrate a festival to the LORD for seven days. ¹³Present as an aroma pleasing to the LORD a food offering consisting of a burnt offering of thirteen young bulls, two rams and fourteen male lambs a year old, all without defect. ¹⁴With each of the thirteen bulls offer a grain offering of three-tenths of an ephah of the finest flour mixed with olive oil; with each of the two rams, two-tenths; ¹⁵and with each of the fourteen lambs, one-tenth. ¹⁶Include one male goat as a sin offering, in addition to the regular burnt offering with its grain offering and drink offering.

¹⁷"On the second day offer twelve young bulls, two rams and fourteen male lambs a year old, all without defect. ¹⁸With the bulls, rams and lambs, offer their grain offerings and drink offerings according to the number specified. ¹⁹Include one male goat as a sin offering, in addition to the regular burnt offering with its grain offering, and their drink offerings.

²⁰"On the third day offer eleven bulls, two rams and fourteen male lambs a year old, all without defect. ²¹With the bulls, rams and lambs, offer their grain offerings and drink offerings according to the number specified. ²²Include one male goat as a sin offering, in addition to the regular burnt offering with its grain offering and drink offering.

²³"On the fourth day offer ten bulls, two rams and fourteen male lambs a year old, all without defect. ²⁴With the bulls, rams and lambs, offer their grain offerings and drink offerings according to the number specified. ²⁵Include one male goat as a sin offering, in addition to the regular burnt offering with its grain offering and drink offering.

²⁶"On the fifth day offer nine bulls, two rams and fourteen male lambs a year old, all without defect. ²⁷With the bulls, rams and lambs, offer their grain offerings and drink offerings according to the number specified. ²⁸Include one male goat as a sin offering, in addition to the regular burnt offering with its grain offering and drink offering.

²⁹"On the sixth day offer eight bulls, two rams and fourteen male lambs a year old, all without defect. ³⁰With the bulls, rams and lambs, offer their grain offerings and drink offerings according to the number specified. ³¹Include one male goat as a sin offering, in addition to the regular burnt offering with its grain offering and drink offering.

211

HE IS: a party planner

29:1–39 Many people think of God as the big party pooper in the sky. That couldn't be further from the truth. In fact, God established a schedule of feasts for the Israelites to celebrate throughout the year. You see, he is *a party planner* and loves a gathering, especially in his honor.

The word *holiday* really means "holy day." Holidays are days we set aside to honor God. After all, he provides all that we have. He gives good and perfect gifts. So when the next holiday rolls around, be sure you celebrate it as a holy day to God. He's celebrating with you.

For the next He Is, go to p. 215.

³²"On the seventh day offer seven bulls, two rams and fourteen male lambs a year old, all without defect. ³³With the bulls, rams and lambs, offer their grain offerings and drink offerings according to the number specified. ³⁴Include one male goat as a sin offering, in addition to the regular burnt offering with its grain offering and drink offering.

³⁵"On the eighth day hold a closing special assembly and do no regular work. ³⁶Present as an aroma pleasing to the LORD a food offering consisting of a burnt offering of one bull, one ram and seven male lambs a year old, all without defect. ³⁷With the bull, the ram and the lambs, offer their grain offerings and drink offerings according to the number specified. ³⁸Include one male goat as a sin offering, in addition to the regular burnt offering with its grain offering and drink offering.

³⁹"'In addition to what you vow and your freewill offerings, offer these to the LORD at your appointed festivals: your burnt offerings, grain offerings, drink offerings and fellowship offerings.'"

*⁴⁰Moses told the Israelites all that the LORD commanded him.

Vows

30 *Moses said to the heads of the tribes of Israel: "This is what the LORD commands: ²When a man makes a vow to the LORD or takes an oath to obligate himself by a pledge, he must not break his word but must do everything he said.

³"When a young woman still living in her father's household makes a vow to the LORD or obligates herself by a pledge ⁴and her father hears about her vow or pledge but says nothing to her, then all her vows and every pledge by which she obligated herself will stand. ⁵But if her father forbids her when he hears about it, none of her vows or the pledges by which she obligated herself will stand; the LORD will release her because her father has forbidden her.

⁶"If she marries after she makes a vow or after her lips utter a rash promise by which she obligates herself ⁷and her husband hears about it but says nothing to her, then her vows or the pledges by which she obligated herself will stand. ⁸But if her husband forbids her when he hears about it, he nullifies the vow that obligates her or the rash promise by which she obligates herself, and the LORD will release her.

⁹"Any vow or obligation taken by a widow or divorced woman will be binding on her.

¹⁰"If a woman living with her husband makes a vow or obligates herself by a pledge under oath ¹¹and her husband hears about it but says nothing to her and does not forbid her, then all her vows or the pledges by which she obligated herself will stand. ¹²But if her husband nullifies them when he hears about them, then none of the vows or pledges that came from her lips will stand. Her husband has nullified them, and the LORD will release her. ¹³Her husband may confirm or nullify any vow she makes or any sworn pledge to deny herself.ᵃ ¹⁴But if her husband says nothing to her about it from day to day, then he confirms all her vows or the pledges binding on her. He confirms them by saying nothing to her when he hears about them. ¹⁵If, however, he nullifies them some time after he hears about them, then he must bear the consequences of her wrongdoing."

¹⁶These are the regulations the LORD gave Moses concerning relationships between a man and his wife, and between a father and his young daughter still living at home.

Vengeance on the Midianites

31 The LORD said to Moses, ²"Take vengeance on the Midianites for the Israelites. After that, you will be gathered to your people."

³So Moses said to the people, "Arm some of your men to go to war against the Midianites so that they may carry out the LORD's vengeance on them. ⁴Send into battle a thousand men from each of the tribes of Israel." ⁵So twelve thousand men armed for battle, a thousand from each tribe, were supplied from the clans of Israel. ⁶Moses sent them into battle, a thousand from each tribe, along with Phinehas son of Eleazar, the priest, who took with him articles from the sanctuary and the trumpets for signaling.

at issue: rash decisions

30:1–16 All of us are guilty at times of making rash decisions—speaking too quickly, making snap judgments, taking on more than we can handle, making promises we can't keep, buying items we can't afford. We think we know what we need, but only God knows what's truly best for us. If we'd learn to wait before speaking or acting and first ask for wisdom—from God and others—we'd save ourselves and those we love from a lot of pain. Before you commit yourself to something rash, first check with God.

ᵃ 13 Or to fast

* 29:40 is numbered 30:1 in Hebrew texts.   * 30:1-16 is numbered 30:2-17 in Hebrew texts.

[7] They fought against Midian, as the LORD commanded Moses, and killed every man. [8] Among their victims were Evi, Rekem, Zur, Hur and Reba—the five kings of Midian. They also killed Balaam son of Beor with the sword. [9] The Israelites captured the Midianite women and children and took all the Midianite herds, flocks and goods as plunder. [10] They burned all the towns where the Midianites had settled, as well as all their camps. [11] They took all the plunder and spoils, including the people and animals, [12] and brought the captives, spoils and plunder to Moses and Eleazar the priest and the Israelite assembly at their camp on the plains of Moab, by the Jordan across from Jericho.

[13] Moses, Eleazar the priest and all the leaders of the community went to meet them outside the camp. [14] Moses was angry with the officers of the army—the commanders of thousands and commanders of hundreds—who returned from the battle.

[15] "Have you allowed all the women to live?" he asked them. [16] "They were the ones who followed Balaam's advice and enticed the Israelites to be unfaithful to the LORD in the Peor incident, so that a plague struck the LORD's people. [17] Now kill all the boys. And kill every woman who has slept with a man, [18] but save for yourselves every girl who has never slept with a man.

[19] "Anyone who has killed someone or touched someone who was killed must stay outside the camp seven days. On the third and seventh days you must purify yourselves and your captives. [20] Purify every garment as well as everything made of leather, goat hair or wood."

[21] Then Eleazar the priest said to the soldiers who had gone into battle, "This is what is required by the law that the LORD gave Moses: [22] Gold, silver, bronze, iron, tin, lead [23] and anything else that can withstand fire must be put through the fire, and then it will be clean. But it must also be purified with the water of cleansing. And whatever cannot withstand fire must be put through that water. [24] On the seventh day wash your clothes and you will be clean. Then you may come into the camp."

Dividing the Spoils

[25] The LORD said to Moses, [26] "You and Eleazar the priest and the family heads of the community are to count all the women and animals that were captured. [27] Divide the spoils equally between the soldiers who took part in the battle and the rest of the community. [28] From the soldiers who fought in the battle, set apart as tribute for the LORD one out of every five hundred, whether women, cattle, donkeys or sheep. [29] Take this tribute from their half share and give it to Eleazar the priest as the LORD's part. [30] From the Israelites' half, select one out of every fifty, whether women, cattle, donkeys, sheep or other animals. Give them to the Levites, who are responsible for the care of the LORD's tabernacle." [31] So Moses and Eleazar the priest did as the LORD commanded Moses.

[32] The plunder remaining from the spoils that the soldiers took was 675,000 sheep, [33] 72,000 cattle, [34] 61,000 donkeys [35] and 32,000 women who had never slept with a man. [36] The half share of those who fought in the battle was:

337,500 sheep, [37] of which the tribute for the LORD was 675;

[38] 36,000 cattle, of which the tribute for the LORD was 72;

[39] 30,500 donkeys, of which the tribute for the LORD was 61;

[40] 16,000 women, of whom the tribute for the LORD was 32.

[41] Moses gave the tribute to Eleazar the priest as the LORD's part, as the LORD commanded Moses.

[42] The half belonging to the Israelites, which Moses set apart from that of the fighting men— [43] the community's half—was 337,500 sheep, [44] 36,000 cattle, [45] 30,500 donkeys [46] and 16,000 women. [47] From the Israelites' half, Moses selected one out of every fifty women and animals, as the LORD commanded him, and gave them to the Levites, who were responsible for the care of the LORD's tabernacle.

[48] Then the officers who were over the units of the army—the commanders of thousands and commanders of hundreds—went to Moses [49] and said to him, "Your servants have counted the soldiers under our command, and not one is missing. [50] So we have brought as an offering to the LORD the gold articles each of us acquired—armlets, bracelets, signet rings, earrings and necklaces—to make atonement for ourselves before the LORD."

[51] Moses and Eleazar the priest accepted from them the gold—all the crafted articles. [52] All the gold from the commanders of thousands and commanders of hundreds that Moses and Eleazar presented as

213

a gift to the Lord weighed 16,750 shekels.[a] [53]Each soldier had taken plunder for himself. [54]Moses and Eleazar the priest accepted the gold from the commanders of thousands and commanders of hundreds and brought it into the tent of meeting as a memorial for the Israelites before the Lord.

The Transjordan Tribes

32 The Reubenites and Gadites, who had very large herds and flocks, saw that the lands of Jazer and Gilead were suitable for livestock. [2]So they came to Moses and Eleazar the priest and to the leaders of the community, and said, [3]"Ataroth, Dibon, Jazer, Nimrah, Heshbon, Elealeh, Sebam, Nebo and Beon— [4]the land the Lord subdued before the people of Israel—are suitable for livestock, and your servants have livestock. [5]If we have found favor in your eyes," they said, "let this land be given to your servants as our possession. Do not make us cross the Jordan."

[6]Moses said to the Gadites and Reubenites, "Should your own people go to war while you sit here? [7]Why do you discourage the Israelites from crossing over into the land the Lord has given them? [8]This is what your fathers did when I sent them from Kadesh Barnea to look over the land. [9]After they went up to the Valley of Eshkol and viewed the land, they discouraged the Israelites from entering the land the Lord had given them. [10]The Lord's anger was aroused that day and he swore this oath: [11]'Because they have not followed me wholeheartedly, not one of those who were twenty years old or more when they came up out of Egypt will see the land I promised on oath to Abraham, Isaac and Jacob— [12]not one except Caleb son of Jephunneh the Kenizzite and Joshua son of Nun, for they followed the Lord wholeheartedly.' [13]The Lord's anger burned against Israel and he made them wander in the wilderness forty years, until the whole generation of those who had done evil in his sight was gone.

[14]"And here you are, a brood of sinners, standing in the place of your fathers and making the Lord even more angry with Israel. [15]If you turn away from following him, he will again leave all this people in the wilderness, and you will be the cause of their destruction."

[16]Then they came up to him and said, "We would like to build pens here for our livestock and cities for our women and children. [17]But we will arm ourselves for battle[b] and go ahead of the Israelites until we have brought them to their place. Meanwhile our women and children will live in fortified cities, for protection from the inhabitants of the land. [18]We will not return to our homes until all the Israelites have received their inheritance. [19]We will not receive any inheritance with them on the other side of the Jordan, because our inheritance has come to us on the east side of the Jordan."

[20]Then Moses said to them, "If you will do this—if you will arm yourselves before the Lord for battle [21]and if all of you who are armed cross over the Jordan before the Lord until he has driven his enemies out before him— [22]then when the land is subdued before the Lord, you may return and be free from your obligation to the Lord and to Israel. And this land will be your possession before the Lord.

[23]"But if you fail to do this, you will be sinning against the Lord; and you may be sure that your sin will find you out. [24]Build cities for your women and children, and pens for your flocks, but do what you have promised."

[25]The Gadites and Reubenites said to Moses, "We your servants will do as our lord commands. [26]Our children and wives, our flocks and herds will remain here in the cities of Gilead. [27]But your servants, every man who is armed for battle, will cross over to fight before the Lord, just as our lord says."

[28]Then Moses gave orders about them to Eleazar the priest and Joshua son of Nun and to the family heads of the Israelite tribes. [29]He said to them, "If the Gadites and Reubenites, all those armed for battle, cross over the Jordan with you before the Lord, then when the land is subdued before you, you must

conversations

negotiation «» 32:16–27

1 » Is it ever OK to negotiate with God (as the people did in vv. 16–19)? If so, when?

2 » How much input do Christians have into God's plans?

3 » What conditional agreements does God make with us? "If you will _____, then I will _____."

For more on negotiation, check the index.
For the next Conversations, go to p. 218.

214

---

[a] 52 That is, about 420 pounds or about 190 kilograms [b]17 Septuagint; Hebrew will be quick to arm ourselves

HE IS: unfailing

32:23 Failing God is a frightening prospect. The Israelites failed to believe that God would give them the promised land. As a result, they wandered in the desert for 40 years. God warned the Reubenites and Gadites not to fail in their commitment to conquer their part of the land lest their sin find them out and they suffer the consequences.

He is *unfailing* when it comes to sin. You may think you can hide sin, but it always comes to the surface. You may try to justify it, but there are no loopholes for disobedience. The only option when you sin is to confess it. Then God will unfailingly restore you.

For the next He Is, go to p. 219.

give them the land of Gilead as their possession. ³⁰But if they do not cross over with you armed, they must accept their possession with you in Canaan."

³¹The Gadites and Reubenites answered, "Your servants will do what the LORD has said. ³²We will cross over before the LORD into Canaan armed, but the property we inherit will be on this side of the Jordan."

³³Then Moses gave to the Gadites, the Reubenites and the half-tribe of Manasseh son of Joseph the kingdom of Sihon king of the Amorites and the kingdom of Og king of Bashan—the whole land with its cities and the territory around them.

³⁴The Gadites built up Dibon, Ataroth, Aroer, ³⁵Atroth Shophan, Jazer, Jogbehah, ³⁶Beth Nimrah and Beth Haran as fortified cities, and built pens for their flocks. ³⁷And the Reubenites rebuilt Heshbon, Elealeh and Kiriathaim, ³⁸as well as Nebo and Baal Meon (these names were changed) and Sibmah. They gave names to the cities they rebuilt.

³⁹The descendants of Makir son of Manasseh went to Gilead, captured it and drove out the Amorites who were there. ⁴⁰So Moses gave Gilead to the Makirites, the descendants of Manasseh, and they settled there. ⁴¹Jair, a descendant of Manasseh, captured their settlements and called them Havvoth Jair.ᵃ ⁴²And Nobah captured Kenath and its surrounding settlements and called it Nobah after himself.

Stages in Israel's Journey

33 Here are the stages in the journey of the Israelites when they came out of Egypt by divisions under the leadership of Moses and Aaron. ²At the LORD's command Moses recorded the stages in their journey. This is their journey by stages:

³The Israelites set out from Rameses on the fifteenth day of the first month, the day after the Passover. They marched out defiantly in full view of all the Egyptians, ⁴who were burying all their firstborn, whom the LORD had struck down among them; for the LORD had brought judgment on their gods.

⁵The Israelites left Rameses and camped at Sukkoth.

⁶They left Sukkoth and camped at Etham, on the edge of the desert.

⁷They left Etham, turned back to Pi Hahiroth, to the east of Baal Zephon, and camped near Migdol.

⁸They left Pi Hahirothᵇ and passed through the sea into the desert, and when they had traveled for three days in the Desert of Etham, they camped at Marah.

⁹They left Marah and went to Elim, where there were twelve springs and seventy palm trees, and they camped there.

¹⁰They left Elim and camped by the Red Sea.ᶜ

¹¹They left the Red Sea and camped in the Desert of Sin.

¹²They left the Desert of Sin and camped at Dophkah.

¹³They left Dophkah and camped at Alush.

215

ᵃ *41* Or *them the settlements of Jair*   ᵇ *8* Many manuscripts of the Masoretic Text, Samaritan Pentateuch and Vulgate; most manuscripts of the Masoretic Text *left from before Hahiroth*   ᶜ *10* Or *the Sea of Reeds*; also in verse 11

[14]They left Alush and camped at Rephidim, where there was no water for the people to drink.
[15]They left Rephidim and camped in the Desert of Sinai.
[16]They left the Desert of Sinai and camped at Kibroth Hattaavah.
[17]They left Kibroth Hattaavah and camped at Hazeroth.
[18]They left Hazeroth and camped at Rithmah.
[19]They left Rithmah and camped at Rimmon Perez.
[20]They left Rimmon Perez and camped at Libnah.
[21]They left Libnah and camped at Rissah.
[22]They left Rissah and camped at Kehelathah.
[23]They left Kehelathah and camped at Mount Shepher.
[24]They left Mount Shepher and camped at Haradah.
[25]They left Haradah and camped at Makheloth.
[26]They left Makheloth and camped at Tahath.
[27]They left Tahath and camped at Terah.
[28]They left Terah and camped at Mithkah.
[29]They left Mithkah and camped at Hashmonah.
[30]They left Hashmonah and camped at Moseroth.

216

[31]They left Moseroth and camped at Bene Jaakan.
[32]They left Bene Jaakan and camped at Hor Haggidgad.
[33]They left Hor Haggidgad and camped at Jotbathah.
[34]They left Jotbathah and camped at Abronah.
[35]They left Abronah and camped at Ezion Geber.
[36]They left Ezion Geber and camped at Kadesh, in the Desert of Zin.

[37]They left Kadesh and camped at Mount Hor, on the border of Edom. [38]At the Lord's command Aaron the priest went up Mount Hor, where he died on the first day of the fifth month of the fortieth year after the Israelites came out of Egypt. [39]Aaron was a hundred and twenty-three years old when he died on Mount Hor.

[40]The Canaanite king of Arad, who lived in the Negev of Canaan, heard that the Israelites were coming.

[41]They left Mount Hor and camped at Zalmonah.
[42]They left Zalmonah and camped at Punon.
[43]They left Punon and camped at Oboth.
[44]They left Oboth and camped at Iye Abarim, on the border of Moab.
[45]They left Iye Abarim and camped at Dibon Gad.
[46]They left Dibon Gad and camped at Almon Diblathaim.
[47]They left Almon Diblathaim and camped in the mountains of Abarim, near Nebo.
[48]They left the mountains of Abarim and camped on the plains of Moab by the Jordan across from Jericho. [49]There on the plains of Moab they camped along the Jordan from Beth Jeshimoth to Abel Shittim.

[50]On the plains of Moab by the Jordan across from Jericho the Lord said to Moses, [51]"Speak to the Israelites and say to them: 'When you cross the Jordan into Canaan, [52]drive out all the inhabitants of the land before you. Destroy all their carved images and their cast idols, and demolish all their high places. [53]Take possession of the land and settle in it, for I have given you the land to possess. [54]Distribute the land by lot, according to your clans. To a larger group give a larger inheritance, and to a smaller group a smaller one. Whatever falls to them by lot will be theirs. Distribute it according to your ancestral tribes.

[55]"'But if you do not drive out the inhabitants of the land, those you allow to remain will become barbs in your eyes and thorns in your sides. They will give you trouble in the land where you will live. [56]And then I will do to you what I plan to do to them.'"

Boundaries of Canaan

34 The Lord said to Moses, [2]"Command the Israelites and say to them: 'When you enter Canaan, the land that will be allotted to you as an inheritance is to have these boundaries:

³"'Your southern side will include some of the Desert of Zin along the border of Edom. Your southern boundary will start in the east from the southern end of the Dead Sea, ⁴cross south of Scorpion Pass, continue on to Zin and go south of Kadesh Barnea. Then it will go to Hazar Addar and over to Azmon, ⁵where it will turn, join the Wadi of Egypt and end at the Mediterranean Sea.

⁶"'Your western boundary will be the coast of the Mediterranean Sea. This will be your boundary on the west.

⁷"'For your northern boundary, run a line from the Mediterranean Sea to Mount Hor ⁸and from Mount Hor to Lebo Hamath. Then the boundary will go to Zedad, ⁹continue to Ziphron and end at Hazar Enan. This will be your boundary on the north.

¹⁰"'For your eastern boundary, run a line from Hazar Enan to Shepham. ¹¹The boundary will go down from Shepham to Riblah on the east side of Ain and continue along the slopes east of the Sea of Galilee.ᵃ ¹²Then the boundary will go down along the Jordan and end at the Dead Sea.

"'This will be your land, with its boundaries on every side.'"

¹³Moses commanded the Israelites: "Assign this land by lot as an inheritance. The LORD has ordered that it be given to the nine and a half tribes, ¹⁴because the families of the tribe of Reuben, the tribe of Gad and the half-tribe of Manasseh have received their inheritance. ¹⁵These two and a half tribes have received their inheritance east of the Jordan across from Jericho, toward the sunrise."

¹⁶The LORD said to Moses, ¹⁷"These are the names of the men who are to assign the land for you as an inheritance: Eleazar the priest and Joshua son of Nun. ¹⁸And appoint one leader from each tribe to help assign the land. ¹⁹These are their names:

217

Caleb son of Jephunneh,
    from the tribe of Judah;
²⁰ Shemuel son of Ammihud,
    from the tribe of Simeon;
²¹ Elidad son of Kislon,
    from the tribe of Benjamin;
²² Bukki son of Jogli,
    the leader from the tribe of Dan;
²³ Hanniel son of Ephod,
    the leader from the tribe of Manasseh son of Joseph;
²⁴ Kemuel son of Shiphtan,
    the leader from the tribe of Ephraim son of Joseph;
²⁵ Elizaphan son of Parnak,
    the leader from the tribe of Zebulun;
²⁶ Paltiel son of Azzan,
    the leader from the tribe of Issachar;
²⁷ Ahihud son of Shelomi,
    the leader from the tribe of Asher;
²⁸ Pedahel son of Ammihud,
    the leader from the tribe of Naphtali."

²⁹These are the men the LORD commanded to assign the inheritance to the Israelites in the land of Canaan.

Towns for the Levites

35 On the plains of Moab by the Jordan across from Jericho, the LORD said to Moses, ²"Command the Israelites to give the Levites towns to live in from the inheritance the Israelites will possess. And give them pasturelands around the towns. ³Then they will have towns to live in and pasturelands for the cattle they own and all their other animals.

⁴"The pasturelands around the towns that you give the Levites will extend a thousand cubitsᵇ from the town wall. ⁵Outside the town, measure two thousand cubitsᶜ on the east side, two thousand on the

---

ᵃ *11* Hebrew *Kinnereth* ᵇ *4* That is, about 1,500 feet or about 450 meters ᶜ *5* That is, about 3,000 feet or about 900 meters south side, two thousand on the west and two thousand on the north, with the town in the center. They will have this area as pastureland for the towns.

Cities of Refuge

⁶"Six of the towns you give the Levites will be cities of refuge, to which a person who has killed someone may flee. In addition, give them forty-two other towns. ⁷In all you must give the Levites forty-eight towns, together with their pasturelands. ⁸The towns you give the Levites from the land the Israelites possess are to be given in proportion to the inheritance of each tribe: Take many towns from a tribe that has many, but few from one that has few."

⁹Then the LORD said to Moses: ¹⁰"Speak to the Israelites and say to them: 'When you cross the Jordan into Canaan, ¹¹select some towns to be your cities of refuge, to which a person who has killed someone accidentally may flee. ¹²They will be places of refuge from the avenger, so that anyone accused of murder may not die before standing trial before the assembly. ¹³These six towns you give will be your cities of refuge. ¹⁴Give three on this side of the Jordan and three in Canaan as cities of refuge. ¹⁵These six towns will be a place of refuge for Israelites and for foreigners residing among them, so that anyone who has killed another accidentally can flee there.

¹⁶"'If anyone strikes someone a fatal blow with an iron object, that person is a murderer; the murderer is to be put to death. ¹⁷Or if anyone is holding a stone and strikes someone a fatal blow with it, that person is a murderer; the murderer is to be put to death. ¹⁸Or if anyone is holding a wooden object and strikes someone a fatal blow with it, that person is a murderer; the murderer is to be put to death. ¹⁹The avenger of blood shall put the murderer to death; when the avenger comes upon the murderer, the avenger shall put the murderer to death. ²⁰If anyone with malice aforethought shoves another or throws something at them intentionally so that they die ²¹or if out of enmity one person hits another with their fist so that the other dies, that person is to be put to death; that person is a murderer. The avenger of blood shall put the murderer to death when they meet.

²²"'But if without enmity someone suddenly pushes another or throws something at them unintentionally ²³or, without seeing them, drops on them a stone heavy enough to kill them, and they die, then since that other person was not an enemy and no harm was intended, ²⁴the assembly must judge between the accused and the avenger of blood according to these regulations. ²⁵The assembly must protect the one accused of murder from the avenger of blood and send the accused back to the city of refuge to which they fled. The accused must stay there until the death of the high priest, who was anointed with the holy oil.

²⁶"'But if the accused ever goes outside the limits of the city of refuge in which refuge was taken ²⁷and the avenger of blood finds that person outside the city, the avenger of blood may kill the accused without being guilty of murder. ²⁸The accused must stay in the city of refuge until the death of the high priest; only after the death of the high priest may an accused person return home.

²⁹"'This is to have the force of law for you throughout the generations to come, wherever you live.

³⁰"'Anyone who kills a person is to be put to death as a murderer only on the testimony of witnesses. But no one is to be put to death on the testimony of only one witness.

³¹"'Do not accept a ransom for the life of a murderer, who deserves to die. A murderer is to be put to death.

³²"'Do not accept a ransom for anyone who has fled to a city of refuge and so allow them to go back and live on their own land before the death of the high priest.

³³"'Do not pollute the land where you are. Bloodshed pollutes the land, and atonement cannot be made for the land on which blood has been shed, except by the blood of the one who shed it. ³⁴Do not defile the land where you live and where I dwell, for I, the LORD, dwell among the Israelites.'"

218

conversations

vulnerability «» 36:1–12

1» Do you trust God to be fair to you? Why or why not?

2» Does God always protect the vulnerable?

3» You know God is just. How does his justice influence what happens in your life?

For more on **vulnerability**, check the index.
For the next Conversations, go to p. 227.

Inheritance of Zelophehad's Daughters

36 The family heads of the clan of Gilead son of Makir, the son of Manasseh, who were from the clans of the descendants of Joseph, came and spoke before Moses and the leaders, the heads of the Israelite families. ²They said, "When the Lord commanded my lord to give the land as an inheritance to the Israelites by lot, he ordered you to give the inheritance of our brother Zelophehad to his daughters. ³Now suppose they marry men from other Israelite tribes; then their inheritance will be taken from our ancestral inheritance and added to that of the tribe they marry into. And so part of the inheritance allotted to us will be taken away. ⁴When the Year of Jubilee for the Israelites comes, their inheritance will be added to that of the tribe into which they marry, and their property will be taken from the tribal inheritance of our ancestors."

⁵Then at the Lord's command Moses gave this order to the Israelites: "What the tribe of the descendants of Joseph is saying is right. ⁶This is what the Lord commands for Zelophehad's daughters: They may marry anyone they please as long as they marry within their father's tribal clan. ⁷No inheritance in Israel is to pass from one tribe to another, for each of the Israelites shall keep the tribal inheritance of their ancestors. ⁸Every daughter who inherits land in any Israelite tribe must marry someone in her father's tribal clan, so that all Israelites will possess the inheritance of their ancestors. ⁹No inheritance may pass from one tribe to another, for each Israelite tribe is to keep the land it inherits."

219

HE IS: a match-maker

36:5–7 Moses decreed that a man's daughters could inherit his land. In many other nations, this would have been unheard of. However, God has different standards and treats people fairly. He gave one condition for this startling new law, to ensure that the inheritance stay within the family: Each daughter could marry anyone she pleased as long as he was in the tribal clan of her father.

So too God wants you to marry within the family of faith (see 2 Corinthians 6:14). To guard your spiritual inheritance, he desires for you to marry within the "clan" of your heavenly Father.

For the next He Is, go to p. 223.

¹⁰So Zelophehad's daughters did as the Lord commanded Moses. ¹¹Zelophehad's daughters—Mahlah, Tirzah, Hoglah, Milkah and Noah—married their cousins on their father's side. ¹²They married within the clans of the descendants of Manasseh son of Joseph, and their inheritance remained in their father's tribe and clan.

¹³These are the commands and regulations the Lord gave through Moses to the Israelites on the plains of Moab by the Jordan across from Jericho.

deuteronomy

AUTHOR
Moses.

AUDIENCE
The people of Israel.

DATE
About 1406 B.C.

SETTING
Moses delivers his farewell speeches to
the Israelites on the plains of Moab, east of
the Jordan River.

VERSES TO REMEMBER
"Hear, O Israel: The LORD our God, the LORD
is one. Love the LORD your God with all your
heart and with all your soul and with all
your strength." (6:4–5)

THEME TO CONSIDER
God is committed to his people—and he
longs for a similar commitment from us.

The Command to Leave Horeb

1 These are the words Moses spoke to all Israel in the wilderness east of the Jordan—that is, in the Arabah—opposite Suph, between Paran and Tophel, Laban, Hazeroth and Dizahab. ²(It takes eleven days to go from Horeb to Kadesh Barnea by the Mount Seir road.)

³In the fortieth year, on the first day of the eleventh month, Moses proclaimed to the Israelites all that the LORD had commanded him concerning them. ⁴This was after he had defeated Sihon king of the Amorites, who reigned in Heshbon, and at Edrei had defeated Og king of Bashan, who reigned in Ashtaroth.

⁵East of the Jordan in the territory of Moab, Moses began to expound this law, saying:

⁶The LORD our God said to us at Horeb, "You have stayed long enough at this mountain. ⁷Break camp and advance into the hill country of the Amorites; go to all the neighboring peoples in the Arabah, in the mountains, in the western foothills, in the Negev and along the coast, to the land of the Canaanites and to Lebanon, as far as the great river, the Euphrates. ⁸See, I have given you this land. Go in and take possession of the land that the LORD swore he would give to your fathers—to Abraham, Isaac and Jacob—and to their descendants after them."

The Appointment of Leaders

⁹At that time I said to you, "You are too heavy a burden for me to carry alone. ¹⁰The LORD your God has increased your numbers so that today you are as many as the stars in the sky. ¹¹May the LORD, the God of your ancestors, increase you a thousand times and bless you as he has promised! ¹²But how can I bear your problems and your burdens and your disputes all by myself? ¹³Choose some wise, understanding and respected men from each of your tribes, and I will set them over you."

¹⁴You answered me, "What you propose to do is good."

¹⁵So I took the leading men of your tribes, wise and respected men, and appointed them to have authority over you—as commanders of thousands, of hundreds, of fifties and of tens and as tribal officials. ¹⁶And I charged your judges at that time: Hear the disputes between your people and judge fairly, whether the case is between two Israelites or between an Israelite and a foreigner residing among you. ¹⁷Do not show partiality in judging; hear both small and great alike. Do not be afraid of anyone, for judgment belongs to God. Bring me any case too hard for you, and I will hear it. ¹⁸And at that time I told you everything you were to do.

Spies Sent Out

¹⁹Then, as the LORD our God commanded us, we set out from Horeb and went toward the hill country of the Amorites through all that vast and dreadful wilderness that you have seen, and so we reached Kadesh Barnea. ²⁰Then I said to you, "You have reached the hill country of the Amorites, which the LORD our God is giving us. ²¹See, the LORD your God has given you the land. Go up and take possession of it as the LORD, the God of your ancestors, told you. Do not be afraid; do not be discouraged."

²²Then all of you came to me and said, "Let us send men ahead to spy out the land for us and bring back a report about the route we are to take and the towns we will come to."

²³The idea seemed good to me; so I selected twelve of you, one man from each tribe. ²⁴They left and went up into the hill country, and came to the Valley of Eshkol and explored it. ²⁵Taking with them some of the fruit of the land, they brought it down to us and reported, "It is a good land that the LORD our God is giving us."

---

atissue:authority

1:9–18 We've been trained to think that a good leader is self-sufficient and independent. She must be able to get the job done on her own, without asking for help. Here's a secret: This framework leads to panic attacks and burn out. The truth is that a good leader knows when to delegate. Moses, God's mouthpiece and chosen leader, knew he couldn't handle the job alone. Did that make him a bad leader? Not at all! Don't believe the lie that taking on all the responsibility yourself makes you a strong leader. Have the courage to acknowledge your limitations and share the load.

221

Rebellion Against the Lord

²⁶But you were unwilling to go up; you rebelled against the command of the Lord your God. ²⁷You grumbled in your tents and said, "The Lord hates us; so he brought us out of Egypt to deliver us into the hands of the Amorites to destroy us. ²⁸Where can we go? Our brothers have made our hearts melt in fear. They say, 'The people are stronger and taller than we are; the cities are large, with walls up to the sky. We even saw the Anakites there.'"

²⁹Then I said to you, "Do not be terrified; do not be afraid of them. ³⁰The Lord your God, who is going before you, will fight for you, as he did for you in Egypt, before your very eyes, ³¹and in the wilderness. There you saw how the Lord your God carried you, as a father carries his son, all the way you went until you reached this place."

³²In spite of this, you did not trust in the Lord your God, ³³who went ahead of you on your journey, in fire by night and in a cloud by day, to search out places for you to camp and to show you the way you should go.

³⁴When the Lord heard what you said, he was angry and solemnly swore: ³⁵"No one from this evil generation shall see the good land I swore to give your ancestors, ³⁶except Caleb son of Jephunneh. He will see it, and I will give him and his descendants the land he set his feet on, because he followed the Lord wholeheartedly."

³⁷Because of you the Lord became angry with me also and said, "You shall not enter it, either. ³⁸But your assistant, Joshua son of Nun, will enter it. Encourage him, because he will lead Israel to inherit it. ³⁹And the little ones that you said would be taken captive, your children who do not yet know good from bad—they will enter the land. I will give it to them and they will take possession of it. ⁴⁰But as for you, turn around and set out toward the desert along the route to the Red Sea.ᵃ"

⁴¹Then you replied, "We have sinned against the Lord. We will go up and fight, as the Lord our God commanded us." So every one of you put on his weapons, thinking it easy to go up into the hill country.

⁴²But the Lord said to me, "Tell them, 'Do not go up and fight, because I will not be with you. You will be defeated by your enemies.'"

⁴³So I told you, but you would not listen. You rebelled against the Lord's command and in your arrogance you marched up into the hill country. ⁴⁴The Amorites who lived in those hills came out against you; they chased you like a swarm of bees and beat you down from Seir all the way to Hormah. ⁴⁵You came back and wept before the Lord, but he paid no attention to your weeping and turned a deaf ear to you. ⁴⁶And so you stayed in Kadesh many days—all the time you spent there.

Wanderings in the Wilderness

2 Then we turned back and set out toward the wilderness along the route to the Red Sea,ᵃ as the Lord had directed me. For a long time we made our way around the hill country of Seir.

²Then the Lord said to me, ³"You have made your way around this hill country long enough; now turn north. ⁴Give the people these orders: 'You are about to pass through the territory of your relatives the descendants of Esau, who live in Seir. They will be afraid of you, but be very careful. ⁵Do not provoke them to war, for I will not give you any of their land, not even enough to put your foot on. I have given Esau the hill country of Seir as his own. ⁶You are to pay them in silver for the food you eat and the water you drink.'"

⁷The Lord your God has blessed you in all the work of your hands. He has watched over your journey through this vast wilderness. These forty years the Lord your God has been with you, and you have not lacked anything.

⁸So we went on past our relatives the descendants of Esau, who live in Seir. We turned from the Arabah road, which comes up from Elath and Ezion Geber, and traveled along the desert road of Moab.

⁹Then the Lord said to me, "Do not harass the Moabites or provoke them to war, for I will not give you any part of their land. I have given Ar to the descendants of Lot as a possession."

¹⁰(The Emites used to live there—a people strong and numerous, and as tall as the Anakites. ¹¹Like the Anakites, they too were considered Rephaites, but the Moabites called them Emites. ¹²Horites used

---

to live in Seir, but the descendants of Esau drove them out. They destroyed the Horites from before them and settled in their place, just as Israel did in the land the LORD gave them as their possession.)

[13] And the LORD said, "Now get up and cross the Zered Valley." So we crossed the valley.

[14] Thirty-eight years passed from the time we left Kadesh Barnea until we crossed the Zered Valley. By then, that entire generation of fighting men had perished from the camp, as the LORD had sworn to them. [15] The LORD's hand was against them until he had completely eliminated them from the camp.

[16] Now when the last of these fighting men among the people had died, [17] the LORD said to me, [18] "Today you are to pass by the region of Moab at Ar. [19] When you come to the Ammonites, do not harass them or provoke them to war, for I will not give you possession of any land belonging to the Ammonites. I have given it as a possession to the descendants of Lot."

[20] (That too was considered a land of the Rephaites, who used to live there; but the Ammonites called them Zamzummites. [21] They were a people strong and numerous, and as tall as the Anakites. The LORD destroyed them from before the Ammonites, who drove them out and settled in their place. [22] The LORD had done the same for the descendants of Esau, who lived in Seir, when he destroyed the Horites from before them. They drove them out and have lived in their place to this day. [23] And as for the Avvites who lived in villages as far as Gaza, the Caphtorites coming out from Caphtor[a] destroyed them and settled in their place.)

HE IS: supportive

2:7 Before moving into the promised land, Moses reminded the people of God's love and support in the desert, carefully recounting their journey. They remembered that four decades in the desert had not left them desolate. For 40 years, God had been with them and had supported them.

Before you move forward toward a new challenge or goal, sometimes it's good to look back and recall how he has been *supportive* of you. Review the ways God has watched over your journey. Retell how God has been with you when you needed him most. And remember how you have not lacked anything.

For the next He Is, go to p. 231.

Defeat of Sihon King of Heshbon

[24] "Set out now and cross the Arnon Gorge. See, I have given into your hand Sihon the Amorite, king of Heshbon, and his country. Begin to take possession of it and engage him in battle. [25] This very day I will begin to put the terror and fear of you on all the nations under heaven. They will hear reports of you and will tremble and be in anguish because of you."

[26] From the Desert of Kedemoth I sent messengers to Sihon king of Heshbon offering peace and saying, [27] "Let us pass through your country. We will stay on the main road; we will not turn aside to the right or to the left. [28] Sell us food to eat and water to drink for their price in silver. Only let us pass through on foot— [29] as the descendants of Esau, who live in Seir, and the Moabites, who live in Ar, did for us—until we cross the Jordan into the land the LORD our God is giving us." [30] But Sihon king of Heshbon refused to let us pass through. For the LORD your God had made his spirit stubborn and his heart obstinate in order to give him into your hands, as he has now done.

[31] The LORD said to me, "See, I have begun to deliver Sihon and his country over to you. Now begin to conquer and possess his land."

[32] When Sihon and all his army came out to meet us in battle at Jahaz, [33] the LORD our God delivered him over to us and we struck him down, together with his sons and his whole army. [34] At that time we took all his towns and completely destroyed[b] them—men, women and children. We left no survivors.

---

[a] *23* That is, Crete [b] *34* The Hebrew term refers to the irrevocable giving over of things or persons to the LORD, often by totally destroying them.

224

³⁵But the livestock and the plunder from the towns we had captured we carried off for ourselves. ³⁶From Aroer on the rim of the Arnon Gorge, and from the town in the gorge, even as far as Gilead, not one town was too strong for us. The Lord our God gave us all of them. ³⁷But in accordance with the command of the Lord our God, you did not encroach on any of the land of the Ammonites, neither the land along the course of the Jabbok nor that around the towns in the hills.

Defeat of Og King of Bashan

3 Next we turned and went up along the road toward Bashan, and Og king of Bashan with his whole army marched out to meet us in battle at Edrei. ²The Lord said to me, "Do not be afraid of him, for I have delivered him into your hands, along with his whole army and his land. Do to him what you did to Sihon king of the Amorites, who reigned in Heshbon."

³So the Lord our God also gave into our hands Og king of Bashan and all his army. We struck them down, leaving no survivors. ⁴At that time we took all his cities. There was not one of the sixty cities that we did not take from them—the whole region of Argob, Og's kingdom in Bashan. ⁵All these cities were fortified with high walls and with gates and bars, and there were also a great many unwalled villages. ⁶We completely destroyed^a them, as we had done with Sihon king of Heshbon, destroying^a every city— men, women and children. ⁷But all the livestock and the plunder from their cities we carried off for ourselves.

⁸So at that time we took from these two kings of the Amorites the territory east of the Jordan, from the Arnon Gorge as far as Mount Hermon. ⁹(Hermon is called Sirion by the Sidonians; the Amorites call it Senir.) ¹⁰We took all the towns on the plateau, and all Gilead, and all Bashan as far as Salekah and Edrei, towns of Og's kingdom in Bashan. ¹¹(Og king of Bashan was the last of the Rephaites. His bed was decorated with iron and was more than nine cubits long and four cubits wide.^b It is still in Rabbah of the Ammonites.)

Division of the Land

¹²Of the land that we took over at that time, I gave the Reubenites and the Gadites the territory north of Aroer by the Arnon Gorge, including half the hill country of Gilead, together with its towns. ¹³The rest of Gilead and also all of Bashan, the kingdom of Og, I gave to the half-tribe of Manasseh. (The whole region of Argob in Bashan used to be known as a land of the Rephaites. ¹⁴Jair, a descendant of Manasseh, took the whole region of Argob as far as the border of the Geshurites and the Maakathites; it was named after him, so that to this day Bashan is called Havvoth Jair.^c) ¹⁵And I gave Gilead to Makir. ¹⁶But to the Reubenites and the Gadites I gave the territory extending from Gilead down to the Arnon Gorge (the middle of the gorge being the border) and out to the Jabbok River, which is the border of the Ammonites. ¹⁷Its western border was the Jordan in the Arabah, from Kinnereth to the Sea of the Arabah (that is, the Dead Sea), below the slopes of Pisgah.

¹⁸I commanded you at that time: "The Lord your God has given you this land to take possession of it. But all your able-bodied men, armed for battle, must cross over ahead of the other Israelites. ¹⁹However, your wives, your children and your livestock (I know you have much livestock) may stay in the towns I have given you, ²⁰until the Lord gives rest to all your people as he has to you, and they too have taken over the land that the Lord your God is giving them across the Jordan. After that, each of you may go back to the possession I have given you."

Moses Forbidden to Cross the Jordan

²¹At that time I commanded Joshua: "You have seen with your own eyes all that the Lord your God has done to these two kings. The Lord will do the same to all the kingdoms over there where you are going. ²²Do not be afraid of them; the Lord your God himself will fight for you."

²³At that time I pleaded with the Lord: ²⁴"Sovereign Lord, you have begun to show to your servant your greatness and your strong hand. For what god is there in heaven or on earth who can do the deeds

^a 6 The Hebrew term refers to the irrevocable giving over of things or persons to the Lord, often by totally destroying them.   ^b 11 That is, about 13 feet long and 6 feet wide or about 4 meters long and 1.8 meters wide   ^c 14 Or called the settlements of Jair

and mighty works you do? [25] Let me go over and see the good land beyond the Jordan—that fine hill country and Lebanon."

[26] But because of you the Lord was angry with me and would not listen to me. "That is enough," the Lord said. "Do not speak to me anymore about this matter. [27] Go up to the top of Pisgah and look west and north and south and east. Look at the land with your own eyes, since you are not going to cross this Jordan. [28] But commission Joshua, and encourage and strengthen him, for he will lead this people across and will cause them to inherit the land that you will see." [29] So we stayed in the valley near Beth Peor.

Obedience Commanded

4 Now, Israel, hear the decrees and laws I am about to teach you. Follow them so that you may live and may go in and take possession of the land that the Lord, the God of your ancestors, is giving you. [2] Do not add to what I command you and do not subtract from it, but keep the commands of the Lord your God that I give you.

[3] You saw with your own eyes what the Lord did at Baal Peor. The Lord your God destroyed from among you everyone who followed the Baal of Peor, [4] but all of you who held fast to the Lord your God are still alive today.

[5] See, I have taught you decrees and laws as the Lord my God commanded me, so that you may follow them in the land you are entering to take possession of it. [6] Observe them carefully, for this will show your wisdom and understanding to the nations, who will hear about all these decrees and say, "Surely this great nation is a wise and understanding people." [7] What other nation is so great as to have their gods near them the way the Lord our God is near us whenever we pray to him? [8] And what other nation is so great as to have such righteous decrees and laws as this body of laws I am setting before you today?

[9] Only be careful, and watch yourselves closely so that you do not forget the things your eyes have seen or let them slip from your heart as long as you live. Teach them to your children and to their children after them. [10] Remember the day you stood before the Lord your God at Horeb, when he said to me, "Assemble the people before me to hear my words so that they may learn to revere me as long as they live in the land and may teach them to their children." [11] You came near and stood at the foot of the mountain while it blazed with fire to the very heavens, with black clouds and deep darkness. [12] Then the Lord spoke to you out of the fire. You heard the sound of words but saw no form; there was only a voice. [13] He declared to you his covenant, the Ten Commandments, which he commanded you to follow and then wrote them on two stone tablets. [14] And the Lord directed me at that time to teach you the decrees and laws you are to follow in the land that you are crossing the Jordan to possess.

Idolatry Forbidden

[15] You saw no form of any kind the day the Lord spoke to you at Horeb out of the fire. Therefore watch yourselves very carefully, [16] so that you do not become corrupt and make for yourselves an idol, an image of any shape, whether formed like a man or a woman, [17] or like any animal on earth or any bird that flies in the air, [18] or like any creature that moves along the ground or any fish in the waters below. [19] And when you look up to the sky and see the sun, the moon and the stars—all the heavenly array—do not be enticed into bowing down to them and worshiping things the Lord your God has apportioned to all the

---

atissue:obedience

4:5–8 Obedience is an issue between you and God, right? Yes, but it's more than that. You never obey in a vacuum—your actions as a Christian woman are constantly on display for others to see. You make small choices to obey God throughout each day; non-Christians look on to see if you remain consistent. The tiny nation of Israel had a unique God with a unique plan for them. Other nations watched to see how God's plan worked. In the same way, your obedience communicates to others a vast amount about your relationship with God. What do your actions tell others?

225

nations under heaven. ²⁰But as for you, the LORD took you and brought you out of the iron-smelting furnace, out of Egypt, to be the people of his inheritance, as you now are.

²¹The LORD was angry with me because of you, and he solemnly swore that I would not cross the Jordan and enter the good land the LORD your God is giving you as your inheritance. ²²I will die in this land; I will not cross the Jordan; but you are about to cross over and take possession of that good land. ²³Be careful not to forget the covenant of the LORD your God that he made with you; do not make for yourselves an idol in the form of anything the LORD your God has forbidden. ²⁴For the LORD your God is a consuming fire, a jealous God.

²⁵After you have had children and grandchildren and have lived in the land a long time—if you then become corrupt and make any kind of idol, doing evil in the eyes of the LORD your God and arousing his anger, ²⁶I call the heavens and the earth as witnesses against you this day that you will quickly perish from the land that you are crossing the Jordan to possess. You will not live there long but will certainly be destroyed. ²⁷The LORD will scatter you among the peoples, and only a few of you will survive among the nations to which the LORD will drive you. ²⁸There you will worship gods of wood and stone made by human hands, which cannot see or hear or eat or smell. ²⁹But if from there you seek the LORD your God, you will find him if you seek him with all your heart and with all your soul. ³⁰When you are in distress and all these things have happened to you, then in later days you will return to the LORD your God and obey him. ³¹For the LORD your God is a merciful God; he will not abandon or destroy you or forget the covenant with your ancestors, which he confirmed to them by oath.

The LORD Is God

³²Ask now about the former days, long before your time, from the day God created human beings on the earth; ask from one end of the heavens to the other. Has anything so great as this ever happened, or has anything like it ever been heard of? ³³Has any other people heard the voice of God*a* speaking out of fire, as you have, and lived? ³⁴Has any god ever tried to take for himself one nation out of another nation, by testings, by signs and wonders, by war, by a mighty hand and an outstretched arm, or by great and awesome deeds, like all the things the LORD your God did for you in Egypt before your very eyes?

³⁵You were shown these things so that you might know that the LORD is God; besides him there is no other. ³⁶From heaven he made you hear his voice to discipline you. On earth he showed you his great fire, and you heard his words from out of the fire. ³⁷Because he loved your ancestors and chose their descendants after them, he brought you out of Egypt by his Presence and his great strength, ³⁸to drive out before you nations greater and stronger than you and to bring you into their land to give it to you for your inheritance, as it is today.

³⁹Acknowledge and take to heart this day that the LORD is God in heaven above and on the earth below. There is no other. ⁴⁰Keep his decrees and commands, which I am giving you today, so that it may go well with you and your children after you and that you may live long in the land the LORD your God gives you for all time.

Cities of Refuge

⁴¹Then Moses set aside three cities east of the Jordan, ⁴²to which anyone who had killed a person could flee if they had unintentionally killed a neighbor without malice aforethought. They could flee into one of these cities

---

atissue:parenting

4:39–40 If you're a mother, you have a unique position, both as a parent and as a child of God. Moms know what's best for their children. Our rules are for their good. We know that our children will be happier if they obey. In the same way, God, our heavenly Father, has rules meant for our good. Do we obey him the way we want our children to obey us? Do we trust that he knows best the way we want our children to trust us? Guess who's watching! Choose to openly obey God in front of your children. *Be* the model you want them to follow.

---

a 33 Or of a god

and save their life. ⁴³The cities were these: Bezer in the wilderness plateau, for the Reubenites; Ramoth in Gilead, for the Gadites; and Golan in Bashan, for the Manassites.

Introduction to the Law

⁴⁴This is the law Moses set before the Israelites. ⁴⁵These are the stipulations, decrees and laws Moses gave them when they came out of Egypt ⁴⁶and were in the valley near Beth Peor east of the Jordan, in the land of Sihon king of the Amorites, who reigned in Heshbon and was defeated by Moses and the Israelites as they came out of Egypt. ⁴⁷They took possession of his land and the land of Og king of Bashan, the two Amorite kings east of the Jordan. ⁴⁸This land extended from Aroer on the rim of the Arnon Gorge to Mount Sirion*a* (that is, Hermon), ⁴⁹and included all the Arabah east of the Jordan, as far as the Dead Sea,*b* below the slopes of Pisgah.

The Ten Commandments

5 Moses summoned all Israel and said:

Hear, Israel, the decrees and laws I declare in your hearing today. Learn them and be sure to follow them. ²The LORD our God made a covenant with us at Horeb. ³It was not with our ancestors*c* that the LORD made this covenant, but with us, with all of us who are alive here today. ⁴The LORD spoke to you face to face out of the fire on the mountain. ⁵(At that time I stood between the LORD and you to declare to you the word of the LORD, because you were afraid of the fire and did not go up the mountain.) And he said:

227

⁶ "I am the LORD your God, who brought you out of Egypt, out of the land of slavery.

⁷ "You shall have no other gods before*d* me.

⁸ "You shall not make for yourself an image in the form of anything in heaven above or on the earth beneath or in the waters below. ⁹You shall not bow down to them or worship them; for I, the LORD your God, am a jealous God, punishing the children for the sin of the parents to the third and fourth generation of those who hate me, ¹⁰but showing love to a thousand generations of those who love me and keep my commandments.

¹¹ "You shall not misuse the name of the LORD your God, for the LORD will not hold anyone guiltless who misuses his name.

¹² "Observe the Sabbath day by keeping it holy, as the LORD your God has commanded you. ¹³Six days you shall labor and do all your work, ¹⁴but the seventh day is a sabbath to the LORD your God. On it you shall not do any work, neither you, nor your son or daughter, nor your male or female servant, nor your ox, your donkey or any of your animals, nor any foreigner residing in your towns, so that your male and female servants may rest, as you do. ¹⁵Remember that you were slaves in Egypt and that the LORD your God brought you out of there with a mighty hand and an outstretched arm. Therefore the LORD your God has commanded you to observe the Sabbath day.

¹⁶ "Honor your father and your mother, as the LORD your God has commanded you, so that you may live long and that it may go well with you in the land the LORD your God is giving you.

¹⁷ "You shall not murder.

¹⁸ "You shall not commit adultery.

¹⁹ "You shall not steal.

²⁰ "You shall not give false testimony against your neighbor.

conversations

parents «»» 5:16

1 » What does it mean to "honor" your parents?

2 » What are some practical ways that you can show honor to your parents?

3 » How does honoring your parents change as you age?

For more on **parents**, check the index.
For the next Conversations, go to p. 234.

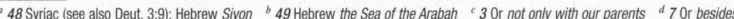

---

a 48 Syriac (see also Deut. 3:9); Hebrew *Siyon*   *b 49* Hebrew *the Sea of the Arabah*   *c 3* Or *not only with our parents*   *d 7* Or *besides*

myth# 15 "MY HUSBAND WOULD NEVER LOOK AT PORNOGRAPHY."

Is this cause for a divorce? I don't know. I am still so indescribably shocked that I'm not even sure if it really happened. Of course, I know it did. It's impossible to dream up something like this.

God, we're leaders in the student ministry—how could this happen to us? He's a coach for our daughter's softball team. A deacon at our church. How long has this been going on? Is he an addict like the perverts who fill the strip joints? My husband?

Before tonight, I had no reason to suspect my husband of doing anything as vulgar and repulsive as paying for smut. He is my best friend. We have a wonderful marriage. We talk to each other about everything. We spend time together. Our sex life isn't like it was when we were younger, but I thought it was healthy and normal. In fact, he just surprised me with a trip to Hawaii for our tenth wedding anniversary. I get nauseous whenever I think of him fantasizing about all these women whenever we made love.

Then, I get angry. All this time, and I had no idea.

What kind of a husband surprises his wife with a wedding anniversary trip to Hawaii and then downloads porn off the Internet in our own home? And what am I going to tell my parents? Your son-in-law is a pervert? He's not the person we thought he was all these years? It will absolutely break their hearts. I can't handle this, God. We had a good . . . we have a good marriage. I still want to believe we have a good marriage. That's why there must be some sort of mistake. It just can't be as bad as it seems. Please God, what did I do wrong?

—Haley

THE ALLURE OF pornography makes no distinction between Christian and non-Christian men. Unfortunately, as wives, mothers and sisters, women want to believe pornography could never be a problem for the men in their lives. However, we can't afford to be naïve when it comes to understanding the nature of sin and its addictive qualities.

- First, we have to admit that pornography addiction can happen in Christian homes, and it does. Frequently.

- Second, we must see that pornography is a true addiction—those who are involved in it may say they want to stop, even try desperately to stop, but they are often powerless to escape it without help. This is not to exonerate them from responsibility. Pornography is a deliberate choice that brings shame and pain to families.

- Third, women should recognize that their husbands need help, sometimes clinical aid, to break free from their addiction to pornography.

- Fourth, women cannot take the burden of accountability onto themselves. Men need other Christian men to hold them brutally accountable for their choices. Resources like Promise Keepers specialize in Internet accountability, even providing filters and software designed to monitor Internet use.

At the same time, women whose husbands look at pornography need to find someone to talk to about the grief associated with this violation against their marriage. The worst scenario is for a woman to feel so shamed and rejected by the discovery of her husband's addiction that she refuses to ask for help from the church or other family-centered crisis counseling. Pornography, like all sin, thrives in darkness. Bring it into the light by seeking help.

Create a climate of honesty in your home so that even if your husband fails, you can pray together for victory over this sin. It may feel very painful for you to talk and pray about this topic since you are the one who feels wronged, yet love is an endless act of dying to oneself.

Begin to pray for your sons or the young men in your life. Our culture is so sexually saturated, brimming with visual temptation for men, that men must fight proactively to guard their minds. Understand that the enemy wants to hook our sons early and hard. They need to hear from Christian men how they should start *now* to set up boundaries in their lives.

Finally, never give up. The Holy Spirit can bring freedom (see John 8:32); with God there is always hope for healing for your husband and your marriage.

229

> "47 percent of Christians admit that pornography is a major problem in their homes."
>
> —— Internet Filter Review, "Pornography Statistics 2003"

"HE WILL BRING TO LIGHT WHAT IS HIDDEN IN DARKNESS AND WILL EXPOSE THE MOTIVES OF PEOPLE'S HEARTS."

1 CORINTHIANS 4:5

SEE ALSO

John 3:19–21
Ephesians 5:3,11
Hebrews 13:4

For more on **Pornography**, check the index.

²¹ "You shall not covet your neighbor's wife. You shall not set your desire on your neighbor's house or land, his male or female servant, his ox or donkey, or anything that belongs to your neighbor."

²² These are the commandments the Lord proclaimed in a loud voice to your whole assembly there on the mountain from out of the fire, the cloud and the deep darkness; and he added nothing more. Then he wrote them on two stone tablets and gave them to me.

²³ When you heard the voice out of the darkness, while the mountain was ablaze with fire, all the leaders of your tribes and your elders came to me. ²⁴ And you said, "The Lord our God has shown us his glory and his majesty, and we have heard his voice from the fire. Today we have seen that people can live even if God speaks with them. ²⁵ But now, why should we die? This great fire will consume us, and we will die if we hear the voice of the Lord our God any longer. ²⁶ For what mortal has ever heard the voice of the living God speaking out of fire, as we have, and survived? ²⁷ Go near and listen to all that the Lord our God says. Then tell us whatever the Lord our God tells you. We will listen and obey."

²⁸ The Lord heard you when you spoke to me, and the Lord said to me, "I have heard what this people said to you. Everything they said was good. ²⁹ Oh, that their hearts would be inclined to fear me and keep all my commands always, so that it might go well with them and their children forever!

³⁰ "Go, tell them to return to their tents. ³¹ But you stay here with me so that I may give you all the commands, decrees and laws you are to teach them to follow in the land I am giving them to possess."

³² So be careful to do what the Lord your God has commanded you; do not turn aside to the right or to the left. ³³ Walk in obedience to all that the Lord your God has commanded you, so that you may live and prosper and prolong your days in the land that you will possess.

Love the Lord Your God

6 These are the commands, decrees and laws the Lord your God directed me to teach you to observe in the land that you are crossing the Jordan to possess, ² so that you, your children and their children after them may fear the Lord your God as long as you live by keeping all his decrees and commands that I give you, and so that you may enjoy long life. ³ Hear, Israel, and be careful to obey so that it may go well with you and that you may increase greatly in a land flowing with milk and honey, just as the Lord, the God of your ancestors, promised you.

⁴ Hear, O Israel: The Lord our God, the Lord is one.^a ⁵ Love the Lord your God with all your heart and with all your soul and with all your strength. ⁶ These commandments that I give you today are to be on your hearts. ⁷ Impress them on your children. Talk about them when you sit at home and when you walk along the road, when you lie down and when you get up. ⁸ Tie them as symbols on your hands and bind them on your foreheads. ⁹ Write them on the doorframes of your houses and on your gates.

¹⁰ When the Lord your God brings you into the land he swore to your fathers, to Abraham, Isaac and Jacob, to give you—a land with large, flourishing cities you did not build, ¹¹ houses filled with all kinds of good things you did not provide, wells you did not dig, and vineyards and olive groves you did not plant—then when you eat and are satisfied, ¹² be careful that you do not forget the Lord, who brought you out of Egypt, out of the land of slavery.

at issue: parenting

6:6–8 "If it were that important, I would have remembered it" is a big fat lie we tell ourselves. Our abundant use of Post-It notes, Palm Pilots and calendars on the fridge attests to the fact that we function best with constant reminders. When he first gave instructions to the Israelites, God knew that his people would need daily reminders. The most important information is not absorbed instantly— it is steeped into our hearts through repetition. Today, tell your children again about God's wisdom and love. They need to be reminded as much as you do.

---

^a 4 Or The Lord our God is one Lord; or The Lord is our God, the Lord is one; or The Lord is our God, the Lord alone

[13]Fear the LORD your God, serve him only and take your oaths in his name. [14]Do not follow other gods, the gods of the peoples around you; [15]for the LORD your God, who is among you, is a jealous God and his anger will burn against you, and he will destroy you from the face of the land. [16]Do not put the LORD your God to the test as you did at Massah. [17]Be sure to keep the commands of the LORD your God and the stipulations and decrees he has given you. [18]Do what is right and good in the LORD's sight, so that it may go well with you and you may go in and take over the good land that the LORD promised on oath to your ancestors, [19]thrusting out all your enemies before you, as the LORD said.

[20]In the future, when your children ask you, "What is the meaning of the stipulations, decrees and laws the LORD our God has commanded you?" [21]tell them: "We were slaves of Pharaoh in Egypt, but the LORD brought us out of Egypt with a mighty hand. [22]Before our eyes the LORD sent signs and wonders— great and terrible—on Egypt and Pharaoh and his whole household. [23]But he brought us out from there to bring us in and give us the land that he promised on oath to our ancestors. [24]The LORD commanded us to obey all these decrees and to fear the LORD our God, so that we might always prosper and be kept alive, as is the case today. [25]And if we are careful to obey all this law before the LORD our God, as he has commanded us, that will be our righteousness."

Driving Out the Nations

7 When the LORD your God brings you into the land you are entering to possess and drives out before you many nations—the Hittites, Girgashites, Amorites, Canaanites, Perizzites, Hivites and Jebusites, seven nations larger and stronger than you— [2]and when the LORD your God has delivered them over to you and you have defeated them, then you must destroy them totally.[a] Make no treaty with them, and show them no mercy. [3]Do not intermarry with them. Do not give your daughters to their sons or take their daughters for your sons, [4]for they will turn your children away from following me to serve other gods, and the LORD's anger will burn against you and will quickly destroy you. [5]This is what you are to do to them: Break down their altars, smash their sacred stones, cut down their Asherah poles[b] and burn their idols in the fire. [6]For you are a people holy to the LORD your God. The LORD your God has chosen you out of all the peoples on the face of the earth to be his people, his treasured possession.

[7]The LORD did not set his affection on you and choose you because you were more numerous than other peoples, for you were the fewest of all peoples. [8]But it was because the LORD loved you and kept the oath he swore to your ancestors that he brought you out with a mighty hand and redeemed you from the land of slavery, from the power of Pharaoh king of Egypt. [9]Know therefore that the LORD your God is God; he is the faithful God, keeping his covenant of love to a thousand generations of those who love him and keep his commandments. [10]But

> those who hate him he will repay to their face by destruction;
> he will not be slow to repay to their face those who hate him.

---

[a] *2* The Hebrew term refers to the irrevocable giving over of things or persons to the LORD, often by totally destroying them; also in verse 26.   [b] *5* That is, wooden symbols of the goddess Asherah; here and elsewhere in Deuteronomy

HE IS: unexplainable

7:7–9 There's no logical explanation for why God chose the chosen people. They weren't stronger, smarter or more special than others. He simply chose to love them because he loved them. Unexplainable? Perhaps. But an undeniable truth—God loves because he is love.

Your past could make you feel unworthy of God's affection. Join the club! No one deserves God's love. We've all sinned and fallen short of his standards. While you probably can't explain why God loves you, the *unexplainable* truth is unavoidable: the Lord loves you—not because of who you are, but because of who he is.

For the next He Is, go to p. 235.

myth# 16 "TODAY'S MEDIA CAN'T SIGNIFICANTLY INFLUENCE MY LIFE."

Although I personally don't have a problem with my entertainment choices, I'm selective about telling people in church about my media habits. Maybe it's because I'm afraid they'll think I'm too worldly because I like to listen to the morning show on the "new rock" station every morning or, even worse, that I'm peddling feminism to the youth I teach in Bible study just because I read Cosmo *in my spare time. If I happen to be listening to a secular CD when I pick up a friend from church for lunch, I subconsciously wonder if she expects me to tune into Dr. Dobson and Christian radio 24-7. Call me paranoid, but I don't think my suspicions are unfounded. That's not to say I don't have standards about my choices.*

For example, I've made a firm decision not to see R-rated movies in theaters. Although if they have some historical value (or have received that rating for something other than nudity or capricious violence), I may rent them to watch in the privacy of my home. I intentionally don't subscribe to premium movie channels whose convenience could tempt me to compromise my standards. However, when it comes to popular culture, I don't see the harm in keeping up with what's going on. So I occasionally buy US Weekly *or* People *magazine to catch up on the latest celebrity gossip. And I personally find reality TV shows ridiculous, but I think they're pretty harmless and overall mindless timewasters that keep me in the loop with everyone at work.*

However, I'm not naïve. I realize I'm walking a fine line between monitoring my own behavior, modeling what's appropriate for my Christian brothers and sisters and remaining sensitive to God's promptings in this area. But I think I'm doing an OK job. After all, I'm a strong Christian, and I don't think my choices are hurting anyone.

—Mary Ann

THE HUMAN HEART and

mind are delicate instruments. Sensitive to the least influence, our minds are constantly receiving input from our surroundings, shaping our hearts with an artist's precision. When our minds take their cues and impulses from the Word of God and wise counsel, our hearts follow suit. However, if we allow the culture to regulate our hearts and minds, we soon lose our perspective on our relationship with God.

While we may know better than to participate in outright sinful activities, we may not approach areas of subtle influence with such diligence. For example, did you know that the majority of women feel depressed after flipping through a fashion magazine? They're subconsciously reminded of how they don't look and what they can't afford. Harmless? Not quite.

The worldly influence of the media may appear as unobtrusive as fine grains of sand in the cogs of a machine. Some influences are so seemingly insignificant that we might not notice their effects right away. We assume our over-exposure to crime, domestic violence, profanity, crude humor, homosexuality, promiscuity and adultery as a mainstay of movies, television and radio is harmless. We hardly notice it anymore, so how could it be harming us?

However, over time, being out of rhythm with the Word of God and its principles can prove dangerous to our spiritual health. God instructed Israel to separate itself from the surrounding culture. Extended exposure to pagan cultures can influence even the strongest Christians—if not to break their moral commitments, then at least to bend them. How should you respond?

- Ask God to search your heart and your media habits (see Psalm 26:2–3).

- Examine your habits: Are they out of balance with your intake of God's Word and wise counsel?

- How does the media influence your attitudes, thought patterns, beliefs and actions?

- Discernment is key: How adept are you at viewing the world around you through the lens of Scripture?

- Remember, if you aren't looking out for your mental purity, who is?

"The average American watches 25 hours of television per week."

— Focus on the Family

"DO NOT CONFORM TO THE PATTERN OF THIS WORLD, BUT BE TRANSFORMED BY THE RENEWING OF YOUR MIND."

ROMANS 12:2

SEE ALSO

Proverbs 2:11; 4:23

Philippians 2:15; 4:8

1 Thessalonians 5:23

For more on **Discernment**, check the index.

234

¹¹Therefore, take care to follow the commands, decrees and laws I give you today.

¹²If you pay attention to these laws and are careful to follow them, then the LORD your God will keep his covenant of love with you, as he swore to your ancestors. ¹³He will love you and bless you and increase your numbers. He will bless the fruit of your womb, the crops of your land—your grain, new wine and olive oil—the calves of your herds and the lambs of your flocks in the land that he swore to your ancestors to give you. ¹⁴You will be blessed more than any other people; none of your men or women will be childless, nor any of your livestock without young. ¹⁵The LORD will keep you free from every disease. He will not inflict on you the horrible diseases you knew in Egypt, but he will inflict them on all who hate you. ¹⁶You must destroy all the peoples the LORD your God gives over to you. Do not look on them with pity and do not serve their gods, for that will be a snare to you.

¹⁷You may say to yourselves, "These nations are stronger than we are. How can we drive them out?" ¹⁸But do not be afraid of them; remember well what the LORD your God did to Pharaoh and to all Egypt. ¹⁹You saw with your own eyes the great trials, the signs and wonders, the mighty hand and outstretched arm, with which the LORD your God brought you out. The LORD your God will do the same to all the peoples you now fear. ²⁰Moreover, the LORD your God will send the hornet among them until even the survivors who hide from you have perished. ²¹Do not be terrified by them, for the LORD your God, who is among you, is a great and awesome God. ²²The LORD your God will drive out those nations before you, little by little. You will not be allowed to eliminate them all at once, or the wild animals will multiply around you. ²³But the LORD your God will deliver them over to you, throwing them into great confusion until they are destroyed. ²⁴He will give their kings into your hand, and you will wipe out their names from under heaven. No one will be able to stand up against you; you will destroy them. ²⁵The images of their gods you are to burn in the fire. Do not covet the silver and gold on them, and do not take it for yourselves, or you will be ensnared by it, for it is detestable to the LORD your God. ²⁶Do not bring a detestable thing into your house or you, like it, will be set apart for destruction. Regard it as vile and utterly detest it, for it is set apart for destruction.

Do Not Forget the LORD

8 Be careful to follow every command I am giving you today, so that you may live and increase and may enter and possess the land that the LORD promised on oath to your ancestors. ²Remember how the LORD your God led you all the way in the wilderness these forty years, to humble and test you in order to know what was in your heart, whether or not you would keep his commands. ³He humbled you, causing you to hunger and then feeding you with manna, which neither you nor your ancestors had known, to teach you that people do not live on bread alone but on every word that comes from the mouth of the LORD. ⁴Your clothes did not wear out and your feet did not swell during these forty years. ⁵Know then in your heart that as a man disciplines his son, so the LORD your God disciplines you.

⁶Observe the commands of the LORD your God, walking in obedience to him and revering him. ⁷For the LORD your God is bringing you into a good land—a land with streams and pools of water, with springs flowing in the valleys and hills; ⁸a land with wheat and barley, vines and fig trees, pomegranates, olive oil and honey; ⁹a land where bread will not be scarce and you will lack nothing; a land where the rocks are iron and you can dig copper out of the hills.

¹⁰When you have eaten and are satisfied, praise the LORD your God for the good land he has given you. ¹¹Be careful that you do not forget the LORD your God, failing to observe his commands, his laws and his decrees that I am giving you this day. ¹²Otherwise, when you eat and are satisfied, when you build fine houses and settle down, ¹³and when your herds and flocks grow large and your silver and gold increase and all you have is multiplied, ¹⁴then your heart will become proud and you will forget the LORD your God, who brought you out

conversations

pride «» 8:11–18

1 ⟫ What's the danger of being successful?

2 ⟫ Why is our society especially susceptible to pride?

3 ⟫ How can you avoid this type of pride?

For more on pride, check the index.
For the next Conversations, go to p. 241.

of Egypt, out of the land of slavery. ¹⁵He led you through the vast and dreadful wilderness, that thirsty and waterless land, with its venomous snakes and scorpions. He brought you water out of hard rock. ¹⁶He gave you manna to eat in the wilderness, something your ancestors had never known, to humble and test you so that in the end it might go well with you. ¹⁷You may say to yourself, "My power and the strength of my hands have produced this wealth for me." ¹⁸But remember the LORD your God, for it is he who gives you the ability to produce wealth, and so confirms his covenant, which he swore to your ancestors, as it is today.

¹⁹If you ever forget the LORD your God and follow other gods and worship and bow down to them, I testify against you today that you will surely be destroyed. ²⁰Like the nations the LORD destroyed before you, so you will be destroyed for not obeying the LORD your God.

Not Because of Israel's Righteousness

9 Hear, Israel: You are now about to cross the Jordan to go in and dispossess nations greater and stronger than you, with large cities that have walls up to the sky. ²The people are strong and tall—Anakites! You know about them and have heard it said: "Who can stand up against the Anakites?" ³But be assured today that the LORD your God is the one who goes across ahead of you like a devouring fire. He will destroy them; he will subdue them before you. And you will drive them out and annihilate them quickly, as the LORD has promised you.

235

HE IS: fire

9:3 Fire symbolizes God's presence and power. God spoke to Moses out of a burning bush and guided the Israelites with a pillar of fire. In this verse he promises to go before them like a devouring fire, judging the nations that defy him.

Fire can be either helpful or harmful. Contained, it provides light, warmth and fuel. Uncontained, it devours everything in its path. One way or another, God will be a *fire* in your life. If you defy him, he will burn with justice. If you serve him, he will illuminate the path before you

For the next He Is, go to p. 249.

⁴After the LORD your God has driven them out before you, do not say to yourself, "The LORD has brought me here to take possession of this land because of my righteousness." No, it is on account of the wickedness of these nations that the LORD is going to drive them out before you. ⁵It is not because of your righteousness or your integrity that you are going in to take possession of their land; but on account of the wickedness of these nations, the LORD your God will drive them out before you, to accomplish what he swore to your fathers, to Abraham, Isaac and Jacob. ⁶Understand, then, that it is not because of your righteousness that the LORD your God is giving you this good land to possess, for you are a stiff-necked people.

The Golden Calf

⁷Remember this and never forget how you aroused the anger of the LORD your God in the wilderness. From the day you left Egypt until you arrived here, you have been rebellious against the LORD. ⁸At Horeb you aroused the LORD's wrath so that he was angry enough to destroy you. ⁹When I went up on the mountain to receive the tablets of stone, the tablets of the covenant that the LORD had made with you, I stayed on the mountain forty days and forty nights; I ate no bread and drank no water. ¹⁰The LORD gave me two stone tablets inscribed by the finger of God. On them were all the commandments the LORD proclaimed to you on the mountain out of the fire, on the day of the assembly.

¹¹At the end of the forty days and forty nights, the LORD gave me the two stone tablets, the tablets of the covenant. ¹²Then the LORD told me, "Go down from here at once, because your people whom you

myth# 17 "I NEED TO MAINTAIN A CERTAIN LIFESTYLE."

"How do they do it?" asked my husband, Dan. He tossed his keys down and slumped into his old, forest green recliner, a relic from his bachelor days that he'd insisted we keep when we got married. "They must have inherited money. Honestly, do you think they make more than we do?"

I sighed. We'd just gotten home from a party at a friend's house. We had this conversation, or versions of it, all the time.

I guess it all started when we got involved in our church's young marrieds group. The people were very nice—and extremely successful. Although we were all in our early thirties, I couldn't believe my eyes when I saw one couple's lakeside home. They had all the toys—a boat and a jet ski in the boathouse (nearly as big as our house at the time) and a premium-packaged Tahoe in the three-car garage.

Once Dan and I started spending time with our new, affluent friends, our life didn't seem all that great anymore. Our modest, three-bedroom ranch felt cramped. Our used Honda looked cheap. I cringed when I looked at that old recliner and the rest of our hand-me-down furniture, which prior to visiting "Trump Tower Lakeside" had been tolerable (strictly functional, but tolerable). Our old TV with giant rabbit ears just couldn't compare with Tom and Kris's state-of-the-art entertainment system.

So every time the topic came up, we spent a good hour or so arguing. "Just because nearly everyone in our class shows off how rich they are doesn't mean we ought to run out and buy something we can't afford," I snapped at Dan.

"I make good money, Lauren," Dan shot back. "We could get financed for a fancy new home, you know, if that's what we wanted."

And so we did. Six months later, we moved from our affordable home to a new community near the lake with a gorgeous view from the front porch of our Georgian colonial. It wasn't more than our friends had; it was just more than we'd ever had. It was bigger than our parents' homes.

We agreed we wouldn't take a vacation that summer. But we can't take one next summer either because we're so behind on our payments. We do more than a little finagling to get the checkbook to balance most months. We're finally fitting in with our friends' lifestyles. I just hope we can keep the pace.

—Lauren

WOULD JESUS DRIVE
a BMW?

That question has floated around in the Christian community and even in an environmentalist ad campaign. Regardless of what you think about Jesus' supposed motor vehicle of choice, the root issue is this: "What should Christians do with their money?" No doubt, money—either the lack of it or its abundance—conditions our lifestyle choices. The temptation is to think that we're not successful until we have a large home, drive a nice car, put our kids in the best private schools and take exciting vacations to Aruba. Sadly, many of us are willing to risk our future well-being and financial freedom in order to be happy *today*, at any price.

The Bible says the world clamors and "runs" after all it can grab in this life (see Luke 12:29-30). Women who are committed to Jesus have to make counter-cultural choices in their lifestyles. Emulating Jesus' lifestyle does not necessarily mean pursuing poverty (as if by it one is inherently more spiritual). It means internally identifying with the overarching themes of his life. Consider the themes of Jesus' life:

- Contentment
- Outrageous generosity
- Impenetrable joy
- Unselfishness

These characteristics, not dollar signs, are the primary distinctions between Jesus' lifestyle versus the way the world lives.

Deciding you're not going to live like the rest of the world—even if you *can* afford it—is that much more difficult when you realize that Jesus is talking about a change of heart. Trading in a new BMW for a used Honda is much easier than taking a realistic look behind what is driving your lifestyle choices. Your *attitude* toward money, not what's in your garage, is one of the quickest external indicators of your inward commitment.

"[In our media-saturated culture,] people can see, in agonizing detail, all the expensive things they will never possess. This may make what a typical person possesses seem insufficient, even if the person is one of the tens of millions of Americans living, by the standards of history, in unprecedented comfort and freedom."

—Gregg Easterbrook

"KEEP YOUR LIVES FREE FROM THE LOVE OF MONEY AND BE CONTENT WITH WHAT YOU HAVE, BECAUSE GOD HAS SAID, 'NEVER WILL I LEAVE YOU; NEVER WILL I FORSAKE YOU.'"

HEBREWS 13:5

SEE ALSO

Deuteronomy 8:10–18
Matthew 19:23–29
1 Corinthians 3:12–13

For more on **Materialism**, check the index.

brought out of Egypt have become corrupt. They have turned away quickly from what I commanded them and have made an idol for themselves."

¹³And the LORD said to me, "I have seen this people, and they are a stiff-necked people indeed! ¹⁴Let me alone, so that I may destroy them and blot out their name from under heaven. And I will make you into a nation stronger and more numerous than they."

¹⁵So I turned and went down from the mountain while it was ablaze with fire. And the two tablets of the covenant were in my hands. ¹⁶When I looked, I saw that you had sinned against the LORD your God; you had made for yourselves an idol cast in the shape of a calf. You had turned aside quickly from the way that the LORD had commanded you. ¹⁷So I took the two tablets and threw them out of my hands, breaking them to pieces before your eyes.

¹⁸Then once again I fell prostrate before the LORD for forty days and forty nights; I ate no bread and drank no water, because of all the sin you had committed, doing what was evil in the LORD's sight and so arousing his anger. ¹⁹I feared the anger and wrath of the LORD, for he was angry enough with you to destroy you. But again the LORD listened to me. ²⁰And the LORD was angry enough with Aaron to destroy him, but at that time I prayed for Aaron too. ²¹Also I took that sinful thing of yours, the calf you had made, and burned it in the fire. Then I crushed it and ground it to powder as fine as dust and threw the dust into a stream that flowed down the mountain.

²²You also made the LORD angry at Taberah, at Massah and at Kibroth Hattaavah.

²³And when the LORD sent you out from Kadesh Barnea, he said, "Go up and take possession of the land I have given you." But you rebelled against the command of the LORD your God. You did not trust him or obey him. ²⁴You have been rebellious against the LORD ever since I have known you.

²⁵I lay prostrate before the LORD those forty days and forty nights because the LORD had said he would destroy you. ²⁶I prayed to the LORD and said, "Sovereign LORD, do not destroy your people, your own inheritance that you redeemed by your great power and brought out of Egypt with a mighty hand. ²⁷Remember your servants Abraham, Isaac and Jacob. Overlook the stubbornness of this people, their wickedness and their sin. ²⁸Otherwise, the country from which you brought us will say, 'Because the LORD was not able to take them into the land he had promised them, and because he hated them, he brought them out to put them to death in the wilderness.' ²⁹But they are your people, your inheritance that you brought out by your great power and your outstretched arm."

Tablets Like the First Ones

10 At that time the LORD said to me, "Chisel out two stone tablets like the first ones and come up to me on the mountain. Also make a wooden ark.^a ²I will write on the tablets the words that were on the first tablets, which you broke. Then you are to put them in the ark."

³So I made the ark out of acacia wood and chiseled out two stone tablets like the first ones, and I went up on the mountain with the two tablets in my hands. ⁴The LORD wrote on these tablets what he had written before, the Ten Commandments he had proclaimed to you on the mountain, out of the fire, on the day of the assembly. And the LORD gave them to me. ⁵Then I came back down the mountain and put the tablets in the ark I had made, as the LORD commanded me, and they are there now.

⁶(The Israelites traveled from the wells of Bene Jaakan to Moserah. There Aaron died and was buried, and Eleazar his son succeeded him as priest. ⁷From there they traveled to Gudgodah and on to Jotbathah, a land with streams of water. ⁸At that time the LORD set apart the tribe of Levi to carry the ark of the covenant of the LORD, to stand before the LORD to minister and to pronounce blessings in his name, as they still do today. ⁹That is why the Levites have no share or inheritance among their fellow Israelites; the LORD is their inheritance, as the LORD your God told them.)

¹⁰Now I had stayed on the mountain forty days and nights, as I did the first time, and the LORD listened to me at this time also. It was not his will to destroy you. ¹¹"Go," the LORD said to me, "and lead the people on their way, so that they may enter and possess the land that I swore to their ancestors to give them."

---

^a *1 That is, a chest*

Fear the LORD

¹²And now, Israel, what does the LORD your God ask of you but to fear the LORD your God, to walk in obedience to him, to love him, to serve the LORD your God with all your heart and with all your soul, ¹³and to observe the LORD's commands and decrees that I am giving you today for your own good?

¹⁴To the LORD your God belong the heavens, even the highest heavens, the earth and everything in it. ¹⁵Yet the LORD set his affection on your ancestors and loved them, and he chose you, their descendants, above all the nations—as it is today. ¹⁶Circumcise your hearts, therefore, and do not be stiff-necked any longer. ¹⁷For the LORD your God is God of gods and Lord of lords, the great God, mighty and awesome, who shows no partiality and accepts no bribes. ¹⁸He defends the cause of the fatherless and the widow, and loves the foreigners residing among you, giving them food and clothing. ¹⁹And you are to love those who are foreigners, for you yourselves were foreigners in Egypt. ²⁰Fear the LORD your God and serve him. Hold fast to him and take your oaths in his name. ²¹He is your praise; he is your God, who performed for you those great and awesome wonders you saw with your own eyes. ²²Your ancestors who went down into Egypt were seventy in all, and now the LORD your God has made you as numerous as the stars in the sky.

Love and Obey the LORD

11 Love the LORD your God and keep his requirements, his decrees, his laws and his commands always. ²Remember today that your children were not the ones who saw and experienced the discipline of the LORD your God: his majesty, his mighty hand, his outstretched arm; ³the signs he performed and the things he did in the heart of Egypt, both to Pharaoh king of Egypt and to his whole country; ⁴what he did to the Egyptian army, to its horses and chariots, how he overwhelmed them with the waters of the Red Sea*a* as they were pursuing you, and how the LORD brought lasting ruin on them. ⁵It was not your children who saw what he did for you in the wilderness until you arrived at this place, ⁶and what he did to Dathan and Abiram, sons of Eliab the Reubenite, when the earth opened its mouth right in the middle of all Israel and swallowed them up with their households, their tents and every living thing that belonged to them. ⁷But it was your own eyes that saw all these great things the LORD has done.

⁸Observe therefore all the commands I am giving you today, so that you may have the strength to go in and take over the land that you are crossing the Jordan to possess, ⁹and so that you may live long in the land that the LORD swore to your ancestors to give to them and their descendants, a land flowing with milk and honey. ¹⁰The land you are entering to take over is not like the land of Egypt, from which you have come, where you planted your seed and irrigated it by foot as in a vegetable garden. ¹¹But the land you are crossing the Jordan to take possession of is a land of mountains and valleys that drinks rain from heaven. ¹²It is a land the LORD your God cares for; the eyes of the LORD your God are continually on it from the beginning of the year to its end.

¹³So if you faithfully obey the commands I am giving you today—to love the LORD your God and to serve him with all your heart and with all your soul— ¹⁴then I will send rain on your land in its season, both autumn and spring rains, so that you may gather in your grain, new wine and olive oil. ¹⁵I will provide grass in the fields for your cattle, and you will eat and be satisfied.

¹⁶Be careful, or you will be enticed to turn away and worship other gods and bow down to them. ¹⁷Then the LORD's anger will burn against you, and he will shut the heavens so that it will not rain and the ground will yield no produce, and you will soon perish from the good land the LORD is giving you. ¹⁸Fix these words of mine in your hearts and minds; tie them as symbols on your hands and bind them on your foreheads. ¹⁹Teach them to your children, talking about them when you sit at home and when you walk along the road, when you lie down and when you get up. ²⁰Write them on the doorframes of your houses and on your gates, ²¹so that your days and the days of your children may be many in the land that the LORD swore to give your ancestors, as many as the days that the heavens are above the earth.

²²If you carefully observe all these commands I am giving you to follow—to love the LORD your God,

239

---

a 4 Or the Sea of Reeds

to walk in obedience to him and to hold fast to him— ²³then the LORD will drive out all these nations before you, and you will dispossess nations larger and stronger than you. ²⁴Every place where you set your foot will be yours: Your territory will extend from the desert to Lebanon, and from the Euphrates River to the Mediterranean Sea. ²⁵No one will be able to stand against you. The LORD your God, as he promised you, will put the terror and fear of you on the whole land, wherever you go.

²⁶See, I am setting before you today a blessing and a curse— ²⁷the blessing if you obey the commands of the LORD your God that I am giving you today; ²⁸the curse if you disobey the commands of the LORD your God and turn from the way that I command you today by following other gods, which you have not known. ²⁹When the LORD your God has brought you into the land you are entering to possess, you are to proclaim on Mount Gerizim the blessings, and on Mount Ebal the curses. ³⁰As you know, these mountains are across the Jordan, westward, toward the setting sun, near the great trees of Moreh, in the territory of those Canaanites living in the Arabah in the vicinity of Gilgal. ³¹You are about to cross the Jordan to enter and take possession of the land the LORD your God is giving you. When you have taken it over and are living there, ³²be sure that you obey all the decrees and laws I am setting before you today.

The One Place of Worship

12 These are the decrees and laws you must be careful to follow in the land that the LORD, the God of your ancestors, has given you to possess—as long as you live in the land. ²Destroy completely all the places on the high mountains, on the hills and under every spreading tree, where the nations you are dispossessing worship their gods. ³Break down their altars, smash their sacred stones and burn their Asherah poles in the fire; cut down the idols of their gods and wipe out their names from those places.

⁴You must not worship the LORD your God in their way. ⁵But you are to seek the place the LORD your God will choose from among all your tribes to put his Name there for his dwelling. To that place you must go; ⁶there bring your burnt offerings and sacrifices, your tithes and special gifts, what you have vowed to give and your freewill offerings, and the firstborn of your herds and flocks. ⁷There, in the presence of the LORD your God, you and your families shall eat and shall rejoice in everything you have put your hand to, because the LORD your God has blessed you.

⁸You are not to do as we do here today, everyone doing as they see fit, ⁹since you have not yet reached the resting place and the inheritance the LORD your God is giving you. ¹⁰But you will cross the Jordan and settle in the land the LORD your God is giving you as an inheritance, and he will give you rest from all your enemies around you so that you will live in safety. ¹¹Then to the place the LORD your God will choose as a dwelling for his Name—there you are to bring everything I command you: your burnt offerings and sacrifices, your tithes and special gifts, and all the choice possessions you have vowed to the LORD. ¹²And there rejoice before the LORD your God—you, your sons and daughters, your male and female servants, and the Levites from your towns who have no allotment or inheritance of their own. ¹³Be careful not to sacrifice your burnt offerings anywhere you please. ¹⁴Offer them only at the place the LORD will choose in one of your tribes, and there observe everything I command you.

¹⁵Nevertheless, you may slaughter your animals in any of your towns and eat as much of the meat as you want, as if it were gazelle or deer, according to the blessing the LORD your God gives you. Both the ceremonially unclean and the clean may eat it. ¹⁶But you must not eat the blood; pour it out on the

atissue: the body of Christ

12:1–32 Going to church doesn't buy you a free pass into heaven. Church attendance doesn't make you better in God's eyes or even guarantee you good behavior during the week. So why go? The Bible tells us about two kinds of relationships with God. The first one is personal—how you and God communicate. The second is communal—how you are a part of the body of Christ. Seeking the Lord with others is important, so important that God commanded it and gave abundant instructions for it. Don't let your focus on a personal relationship with God cause you to neglect your communal relationship.

240

ground like water. ¹⁷You must not eat in your own towns the tithe of your grain and new wine and olive oil, or the firstborn of your herds and flocks, or whatever you have vowed to give, or your freewill offerings or special gifts. ¹⁸Instead, you are to eat them in the presence of the Lord your God at the place the Lord your God will choose—you, your sons and daughters, your male and female servants, and the Levites from your towns—and you are to rejoice before the Lord your God in everything you put your hand to. ¹⁹Be careful not to neglect the Levites as long as you live in your land.

²⁰When the Lord your God has enlarged your territory as he promised you, and you crave meat and say, "I would like some meat," then you may eat as much of it as you want. ²¹If the place where the Lord your God chooses to put his Name is too far away from you, you may slaughter animals from the herds and flocks the Lord has given you, as I have commanded you, and in your own towns you may eat as much of them as you want. ²²Eat them as you would gazelle or deer. Both the ceremonially unclean and the clean may eat. ²³But be sure you do not eat the blood, because the blood is the life, and you must not eat the life with the meat. ²⁴You must not eat the blood; pour it out on the ground like water. ²⁵Do not eat it, so that it may go well with you and your children after you, because you will be doing what is right in the eyes of the Lord.

²⁶But take your consecrated things and whatever you have vowed to give, and go to the place the Lord will choose. ²⁷Present your burnt offerings on the altar of the Lord your God, both the meat and the blood. The blood of your sacrifices must be poured beside the altar of the Lord your God, but you may eat the meat. ²⁸Be careful to obey all these regulations I am giving you, so that it may always go well with you and your children after you, because you will be doing what is good and right in the eyes of the Lord your God.

²⁹The Lord your God will cut off before you the nations you are about to invade and dispossess. But when you have driven them out and settled in their land, ³⁰and after they have been destroyed before you, be careful not to be ensnared by inquiring about their gods, saying, "How do these nations serve their gods? We will do the same." ³¹You must not worship the Lord your God in their way, because in worshiping their gods, they do all kinds of detestable things the Lord hates. They even burn their sons and daughters in the fire as sacrifices to their gods.

*³²See that you do all I command you; do not add to it or take away from it.

Worshiping Other Gods

13 *If a prophet, or one who foretells by dreams, appears among you and announces to you a sign or wonder, ²and if the sign or wonder spoken of takes place, and the prophet says, "Let us follow other gods" (gods you have not known) "and let us worship them," ³you must not listen to the words of that prophet or dreamer. The Lord your God is testing you to find out whether you love him with all your heart and with all your soul. ⁴It is the Lord your God you must follow, and him you must revere. Keep his commands and obey him; serve him and hold fast to him. ⁵That prophet or dreamer must be put to death for inciting rebellion against the Lord your God, who brought you out of Egypt and redeemed you from the land of slavery. That prophet or dreamer tried to turn you from the way the Lord your God commanded you to follow. You must purge the evil from among you.

⁶If your very own brother, or your son or daughter, or the wife you love, or your closest friend secretly entices you, saying, "Let us go and worship other gods" (gods that neither you nor your ancestors have known, ⁷gods of the peoples around you, whether near or far, from one end of the land to the other), ⁸do not yield to them or listen to them. Show them no pity. Do not spare

"conversations"

manipulation «» 13:1–3

1» Describe a situation in which you had to determine if someone was speaking God's words.

2» How can you accurately judge who's speaking the truth?

3» How should you respond to those who manipulate God's message?

For more on **manipulation**, check the index.
For the next Conversations, go to p. 251.

241

myth# 18 "THE CHURCH
SHOULD MEET
MY NEEDS."

*Today's church service just didn't do anything for me. Sunday mornings
are my only day of the week to sleep late. It's incredibly frustrating to
drag myself out of bed to go to church and then not get anything out of it.*

*I went church shopping the first weekend I moved here and started my
new job. Over the next couple months, I tried out several different kinds of
churches, even though I come from a Methodist background. I did mega-
churches. Small churches. Funky retro churches that met in strip malls
and coffee bars. Stiff churches with ice-cold marble flooring that complemented the even cooler reception from their starched members.*

*The church I'm attending now is OK, but it's not really my style. I walked
into Sunday school and immediately knew these weren't "my people."
They invite me to their socials, but what's the point when I have nothing
in common with them? I occasionally glance over the bulletin, scanning
for ministries that might suit me, but I rarely find anything that garners
more than an occasional blip on my interest radar. It makes me wonder
where all my offering money is going. The most exciting thing I see happening is in the children's ministry—no way, thank you. I come to church
to relax, not to stress out over who's had their snack or to build a miniature church out of dried pinto beans and empty toilet paper rolls.*

*One would think a church this size would have something for everyone
(and some good-looking guys wouldn't hurt). Why is it so hard to find a
church that meets my needs, doesn't talk about money more than once a
year and has a decent music program?*

—Gabriela

WHEN IT COMES TO under-
standing the purpose of the church, we often
have it backwards. The church does not exist for
us, though we are central to its existence. The
capital-C Church—which is the big-picture,
universal Church that includes all believers—
exists for Jesus alone. The Church is his bride
(see Revelation 19:7; 21:2). The little-c church—
which is the local church in a neighborhood
near you—is how God reaches the masses with
his gospel and love. It is also an incubator for
baby Christians, a hospital for hurting people,
a gathering place for all to worship and an
opportunity for maturing believers to hone their
spiritual gifts through serving one another.
Although it is human nature to make life "all
about me," the church is all about serving Jesus
through serving his people.

That's why petty arguments about the music
being too loud, the music being too dull, the
pastor talking too long, the service starting too
early, the service starting too late and all the
other rationales for why we resent the church
for not catering to our preferences are just
that—petty preferences that do not matter. The
next time you try to make church all about you,
remember this:

- The church is Jesus' body (see 1 Corinthians
  12:27).
- Jesus promises to build his church—regardless of our personal tastes (see Matthew
  16:18).
- Jesus loved the church so much that he died
  for it. The church matters to him, so it should
  matter to us (see Ephesians 5:25–27).

When we begin to make church more about
Jesus and less about us, we look for ways to love
the body of Christ. Ironically, God rewards our
unselfish actions by meeting our needs in
return—if we will just put him and his church
first (see Matthew 6:33).

"The local church is the
classroom for learning how to
get along in God's family. It is a
lab for practicing unselfish,
sympathetic love."

—Rick Warren

243

"FROM HIM
THE WHOLE BODY,
JOINED AND HELD
TOGETHER BY
EVERY SUPPORTING
LIGAMENT, GROWS
AND BUILDS ITSELF
UP IN LOVE,
AS EACH PART
DOES ITS WORK."

SEE ALSO   EPHESIANS 4:16

For more on **Church**, check
the index.

them or shield them. ⁹You must certainly put them to death. Your hand must be the first in putting them to death, and then the hands of all the people. ¹⁰Stone them to death, because they tried to turn you away from the LORD your God, who brought you out of Egypt, out of the land of slavery. ¹¹Then all Israel will hear and be afraid, and no one among you will do such an evil thing again.

¹²If you hear it said about one of the towns the LORD your God is giving you to live in ¹³that wicked persons have arisen among you and have led the people of their town astray, saying, "Let us go and worship other gods" (gods you have not known), ¹⁴then you must inquire, probe and investigate it thoroughly. And if it is true and it has been proved that this detestable thing has been done among you, ¹⁵you must certainly put to the sword all who live in that town. Destroy it completely,ᵃ both its people and its livestock. ¹⁶Gather all the plunder of the town into the middle of the public square and completely burn the town and all its plunder as a whole burnt offering to the LORD your God. It is to remain a ruin forever, never to be rebuilt. ¹⁷None of those condemned thingsᵃ shall be found in your hands, so that the LORD will turn from his fierce anger; he will show you mercy, have compassion on you, and increase your numbers, as he promised on oath to your ancestors, ¹⁸because you obey the LORD your God, keeping all his commands that I am giving you today and doing what is right in his eyes.

Clean and Unclean Food

14 You are the children of the LORD your God. Do not cut yourselves or shave the front of your heads for the dead, ²for you are a people holy to the LORD your God. Out of all the peoples on the face of the earth, the LORD has chosen you to be his treasured possession.

³Do not eat any detestable thing. ⁴These are the animals you may eat: the ox, the sheep, the goat, ⁵the deer, the gazelle, the roe deer, the wild goat, the ibex, the antelope and the mountain sheep.ᵇ ⁶You may eat any animal that has a divided hoof and that chews the cud. ⁷However, of those that chew the cud or that have a divided hoof you may not eat the camel, the rabbit or the hyrax. Although they chew the cud, they do not have a divided hoof; they are ceremonially unclean for you. ⁸The pig is also unclean; although it has a divided hoof, it does not chew the cud. You are not to eat their meat or touch their carcasses.

⁹Of all the creatures living in the water, you may eat any that has fins and scales. ¹⁰But anything that does not have fins and scales you may not eat; for you it is unclean.

¹¹You may eat any clean bird. ¹²But these you may not eat: the eagle, the vulture, the black vulture, ¹³the red kite, the black kite, any kind of falcon, ¹⁴any kind of raven, ¹⁵the horned owl, the screech owl, the gull, any kind of hawk, ¹⁶the little owl, the great owl, the white owl, ¹⁷the desert owl, the osprey, the cormorant, ¹⁸the stork, any kind of heron, the hoopoe and the bat.

¹⁹All flying insects that swarm are unclean to you; do not eat them. ²⁰But any winged creature that is clean you may eat.

²¹Do not eat anything you find already dead. You may give it to the foreigners residing in any of your towns, and they may eat it, or you may sell it to any other foreigner. But you are a people holy to the LORD your God.

Do not cook a young goat in its mother's milk.

Tithes

²²Be sure to set aside a tenth of all that your fields produce each year. ²³Eat the tithe of your grain, new wine and olive oil, and the firstborn of your herds and flocks in the presence of the LORD your God at the place he will choose as a dwelling for his Name, so that you may learn to revere the LORD your God always. ²⁴But if that place is too distant and you have been blessed by the LORD your God and cannot carry your tithe (because the place where the LORD will choose to put his Name is so far away), ²⁵then exchange your tithe for silver, and take the silver with you and go to the place the LORD your God will choose. ²⁶Use the silver to buy whatever you like: cattle, sheep, wine or other fermented drink, or anything you wish. Then you and your household shall eat there in the presence of the LORD your God and

---

ᵃ 15,17 The Hebrew term refers to the irrevocable giving over of things or persons to the LORD, often by totally destroying them.   ᵇ 5 The precise identification of some of the birds and animals in this chapter is uncertain.

rejoice. ²⁷ And do not neglect the Levites living in your towns, for they have no allotment or inheritance of their own.

²⁸ At the end of every three years, bring all the tithes of that year's produce and store it in your towns, ²⁹ so that the Levites (who have no allotment or inheritance of their own) and the foreigners, the fatherless and the widows who live in your towns may come and eat and be satisfied, and so that the LORD your God may bless you in all the work of your hands.

The Year for Canceling Debts

15 At the end of every seven years you must cancel debts. ² This is how it is to be done: Every creditor shall cancel any loan they have made to another Israelite. They shall not require payment from anyone among their own people, because the LORD's time for canceling debts has been proclaimed. ³ You may require payment from a foreigner, but you must cancel any debt one of your people owes you. ⁴ However, there need be no poor people among you, for in the land the LORD your God is giving you to possess as your inheritance, he will richly bless you, ⁵ if only you fully obey the LORD your God and are careful to follow all these commands I am giving you today. ⁶ For the LORD your God will bless you as he has promised, and you will lend to many nations but will borrow from none. You will rule over many nations but none will rule over you.

⁷ If anyone is poor among your people in any of the towns of the land that the LORD your God is giving you, do not be hardhearted or tightfisted toward them. ⁸ Rather, be openhanded and freely lend them whatever they need. ⁹ Be careful not to harbor this wicked thought: "The seventh year, the year for canceling debts, is near," so that you do not show ill will toward the needy among your people and give them nothing. They may then appeal to the LORD against you, and you will be found guilty of sin. ¹⁰ Give generously to them and do so without a grudging heart; then because of this the LORD your God will bless you in all your work and in everything you put your hand to. ¹¹ There will always be poor people in the land. Therefore I command you to be openhanded toward those of your people who are poor and needy in your land.

Freeing Servants

¹² If any of your people, men or women, sell themselves to you and serve you six years, in the seventh year you must let them go free. ¹³ And when you release them, do not send them away empty-handed. ¹⁴ Supply them liberally from your flock, your threshing floor and your winepress. Give to them as the LORD your God has blessed you. ¹⁵ Remember that you were slaves in Egypt and the LORD your God redeemed you. That is why I give you this command today.

¹⁶ But if your servant says to you, "I do not want to leave you," because he loves you and your family and is well off with you, ¹⁷ then take an awl and push it through his ear lobe into the door, and he will become your servant for life. Do the same for your female servant.

¹⁸ Do not consider it a hardship to set your servants free, because their service to you these six years has been worth twice as much as that of a hired hand. And the LORD your God will bless you in everything you do.

The Firstborn Animals

¹⁹ Set apart for the LORD your God every firstborn male of your herds and flocks. Do not put the firstborn of your cows to work, and do not shear the firstborn of your sheep. ²⁰ Each year you and your

at issue: tithing

14:22–29 We often don't think about someone's power over us until we must yield to that power. We may not think about the government much during the year. Yet at tax time, we're reminded of the IRS's power. When we intentionally give God part of our income through tithing, we acknowledge his authority in our lives. Tithing teaches us to fear and honor God above all else. Tithing is more for our benefit than for God's—he certainly doesn't need our money! When you receive your next paycheck, tithe *first* as a reminder of the highest authority in your life.

245

family are to eat them in the presence of the Lord your God at the place he will choose. ²¹If an animal has a defect, is lame or blind, or has any serious flaw, you must not sacrifice it to the Lord your God. ²²You are to eat it in your own towns. Both the ceremonially unclean and the clean may eat it, as if it were gazelle or deer. ²³But you must not eat the blood; pour it out on the ground like water.

The Passover

16 Observe the month of Aviv and celebrate the Passover of the Lord your God, because in the month of Aviv he brought you out of Egypt by night. ²Sacrifice as the Passover to the Lord your God an animal from your flock or herd at the place the Lord will choose as a dwelling for his Name. ³Do not eat it with bread made with yeast, but for seven days eat unleavened bread, the bread of affliction, because you left Egypt in haste—so that all the days of your life you may remember the time of your departure from Egypt. ⁴Let no yeast be found in your possession in all your land for seven days. Do not let any of the meat you sacrifice on the evening of the first day remain until morning.

⁵You must not sacrifice the Passover in any town the Lord your God gives you ⁶except in the place he will choose as a dwelling for his Name. There you must sacrifice the Passover in the evening, when the sun goes down, on the anniversary*ᵃ* of your departure from Egypt. ⁷Roast it and eat it at the place the Lord your God will choose. Then in the morning return to your tents. ⁸For six days eat unleavened bread and on the seventh day hold an assembly to the Lord your God and do no work.

The Festival of Weeks

⁹Count off seven weeks from the time you begin to put the sickle to the standing grain. ¹⁰Then celebrate the Festival of Weeks to the Lord your God by giving a freewill offering in proportion to the blessings the Lord your God has given you. ¹¹And rejoice before the Lord your God at the place he will choose as a dwelling for his Name—you, your sons and daughters, your male and female servants, the Levites in your towns, and the foreigners, the fatherless and the widows living among you. ¹²Remember that you were slaves in Egypt, and follow carefully these decrees.

The Festival of Tabernacles

¹³Celebrate the Festival of Tabernacles for seven days after you have gathered the produce of your threshing floor and your winepress. ¹⁴Be joyful at your festival—you, your sons and daughters, your male and female servants, and the Levites, the foreigners, the fatherless and the widows who live in your towns. ¹⁵For seven days celebrate the festival to the Lord your God at the place the Lord will choose. For the Lord your God will bless you in all your harvest and in all the work of your hands, and your joy will be complete.

¹⁶Three times a year all your men must appear before the Lord your God at the place he will choose: at the Festival of Unleavened Bread, the Festival of Weeks and the Festival of Tabernacles. No one should appear before the Lord empty-handed: ¹⁷Each of you must bring a gift in proportion to the way the Lord your God has blessed you.

Judges

¹⁸Appoint judges and officials for each of your tribes in every town the Lord your God is giving you, and they shall judge the people fairly. ¹⁹Do not pervert justice or show partiality. Do not accept a bribe, for a bribe blinds the eyes of the wise and twists the words of the righteous. ²⁰Follow justice and justice alone, so that you may live and possess the land the Lord your God is giving you.

Worshiping Other Gods

²¹Do not set up any wooden Asherah pole beside the altar you build to the Lord your God, ²²and do not erect a sacred stone, for these the Lord your God hates.

17 Do not sacrifice to the Lord your God an ox or a sheep that has any defect or flaw in it, for that would be detestable to him.

²If a man or woman living among you in one of the towns the Lord gives you is found doing evil in the eyes of the Lord your God in violation of his covenant, ³and contrary to my command has worshiped

---

ᵃ 6 Or down, at the time of day

other gods, bowing down to them or to the sun or the moon or the stars in the sky, ⁴and this has been brought to your attention, then you must investigate it thoroughly. If it is true and it has been proved that this detestable thing has been done in Israel, ⁵take the man or woman who has done this evil deed to your city gate and stone that person to death. ⁶On the testimony of two or three witnesses a person is to be put to death, but no one is to be put to death on the testimony of only one witness. ⁷The hands of the witnesses must be the first in putting that person to death, and then the hands of all the people. You must purge the evil from among you.

Law Courts

⁸If cases come before your courts that are too difficult for you to judge—whether bloodshed, lawsuits or assaults—take them to the place the LORD your God will choose. ⁹Go to the Levitical priests and to the judge who is in office at that time. Inquire of them and they will give you the verdict. ¹⁰You must act according to the decisions they give you at the place the LORD will choose. Be careful to do everything they instruct you to do. ¹¹Act according to whatever they teach you and the decisions they give you. Do not turn aside from what they tell you, to the right or to the left. ¹²Anyone who shows contempt for the judge or for the priest who stands ministering there to the LORD your God is to be put to death. You must purge the evil from Israel. ¹³All the people will hear and be afraid, and will not be contemptuous again.

The King

¹⁴When you enter the land the LORD your God is giving you and have taken possession of it and settled in it, and you say, "Let us set a king over us like all the nations around us," ¹⁵be sure to appoint over you the king the LORD your God chooses. He must be from among your own people. Do not place a foreigner over you, one who is not an Israelite. ¹⁶The king, moreover, must not acquire great numbers of horses for himself or make the people return to Egypt to get more of them, for the LORD has told you, "You are not to go back that way again." ¹⁷He must not take many wives, or his heart will be led astray. He must not accumulate large amounts of silver and gold.

¹⁸When he takes the throne of his kingdom, he is to write for himself on a scroll a copy of this law, taken from that of the Levitical priests. ¹⁹It is to be with him, and he is to read it all the days of his life so that he may learn to revere the LORD his God and follow carefully all the words of this law and these decrees ²⁰and not consider himself better than his fellow Israelites and turn from the law to the right or to the left. Then he and his descendants will reign a long time over his kingdom in Israel.

Offerings for Priests and Levites

18 The Levitical priests—indeed, the whole tribe of Levi—are to have no allotment or inheritance with Israel. They shall live on the food offerings presented to the LORD, for that is their inheritance. ²They shall have no inheritance among their fellow Israelites; the LORD is their inheritance, as he promised them.

³This is the share due the priests from the people who sacrifice a bull or a sheep: the shoulder, the jowls and the internal organs. ⁴You are to give them the firstfruits of your grain, new wine and olive oil, and the first wool from the shearing of your sheep, ⁵for the LORD your God has chosen them and their descendants out of all your tribes to stand and minister in the LORD's name always.

⁶If a Levite moves from one of your towns anywhere in Israel where he is living, and comes in all earnestness to the place the LORD will choose, ⁷he may minister in the name of the LORD his God like all other Levites who serve there in the presence of the LORD. ⁸He is to share equally in their benefits, even though he has received money from the sale of family possessions.

247

atissue:leadership

17:14–20 Good leaders aren't born; they're made. In fact, the Bible describes certain habits and precautions that promote strong leadership. First, a good leader must not be focused on her own gain. Second, she must keep herself accountable to God's law and not let herself be influenced away from him. Third, she must not think she's better than others. Fourth, she must read, think about, focus on and follow God's rules. Want to become a good leader who can stand strong under pressure? Follow God's advice.

Occult Practices

⁹When you enter the land the Lᴏʀᴅ your God is giving you, do not learn to imitate the detestable ways of the nations there. ¹⁰Let no one be found among you who sacrifices their son or daughter in the fire, who practices divination or sorcery, interprets omens, engages in witchcraft, ¹¹or casts spells, or who is a medium or spiritist or who consults the dead. ¹²Anyone who does these things is detestable to the Lᴏʀᴅ, and because of these detestable practices the Lᴏʀᴅ your God will drive out those nations before you. ¹³You must be blameless before the Lᴏʀᴅ your God.

The Prophet

¹⁴The nations you will dispossess listen to those who practice sorcery or divination. But as for you, the Lᴏʀᴅ your God has not permitted you to do so. ¹⁵The Lᴏʀᴅ your God will raise up for you a prophet like me from among you, from your own people. You must listen to him. ¹⁶For this is what you asked of the Lᴏʀᴅ your God at Horeb on the day of the assembly when you said, "Let us not hear the voice of the Lᴏʀᴅ our God nor see this great fire anymore, or we will die."

¹⁷The Lᴏʀᴅ said to me: "What they say is good. ¹⁸I will raise up for them a prophet like you from among their people, and I will put my words in his mouth. He will tell them everything I command him. ¹⁹I myself will call to account anyone who does not listen to my words that the prophet speaks in my name. ²⁰But a prophet who presumes to speak in my name anything I have not commanded, or a prophet who speaks in the name of other gods, is to be put to death."

²¹You may say to yourselves, "How can we know when a message has not been spoken by the Lᴏʀᴅ?" ²²If what a prophet proclaims in the name of the Lᴏʀᴅ does not take place or come true, that is a message the Lᴏʀᴅ has not spoken. That prophet has spoken presumptuously. No one should be alarmed.

Cities of Refuge

19 When the Lᴏʀᴅ your God has destroyed the nations whose land he is giving you, and when you have driven them out and settled in their towns and houses, ²then set aside for yourselves three cities in the land the Lᴏʀᴅ your God is giving you to possess. ³Build roads to them and divide into three parts the land the Lᴏʀᴅ your God is giving you as an inheritance, so that anyone who kills someone else may flee there.

⁴This is the rule concerning anyone who kills a person and flees there for safety—anyone who kills a neighbor unintentionally, without malice aforethought. ⁵For instance, a man may go into the forest with his neighbor to cut wood, and as he swings his ax to fell a tree, the head may fly off and hit his neighbor and kill him. That man may flee to one of these cities and save his life. ⁶Otherwise, the avenger of blood might pursue him in a rage, overtake him if the distance is too great, and kill him even though he is not deserving of death, since he did it to his neighbor without malice aforethought. ⁷This is why I command you to set aside for yourselves three cities.

⁸If the Lᴏʀᴅ your God enlarges your territory, as he promised on oath to your ancestors, and gives you the whole land he promised them, ⁹because you carefully follow all these laws I command you today— to love the Lᴏʀᴅ your God and to walk always in obedience to him—then you are to set aside three more cities. ¹⁰Do this so that innocent blood will not be shed in your land, which the Lᴏʀᴅ your God is giving you as your inheritance, and so that you will not be guilty of bloodshed.

¹¹But if out of hate someone lies in wait, assaults and kills a neighbor, and then flees to one of these cities, ¹²the killer shall be sent for by the town elders, be brought back from the city, and be handed over to the avenger of blood to die. ¹³Show no pity. You must purge from Israel the guilt of shedding innocent blood, so that it may go well with you.

¹⁴Do not move your neighbor's boundary stone set up by your predecessors in the inheritance you receive in the land the Lᴏʀᴅ your God is giving you to possess.

Witnesses

¹⁵One witness is not enough to convict anyone accused of any crime or offense they may have committed. A matter must be established by the testimony of two or three witnesses.

¹⁶If a malicious witness takes the stand to accuse someone of a crime, ¹⁷the two involved in the dispute must stand in the presence of the Lᴏʀᴅ before the priests and the judges who are in office at the

time. ¹⁸The judges must make a thorough investigation, and if the witness proves to be a liar, giving false testimony, ¹⁹then do to the false witness as that witness intended to do to the other party. You must purge the evil from among you. ²⁰The rest of the people will hear of this and be afraid, and never again will such an evil thing be done among you. ²¹Show no pity: life for life, eye for eye, tooth for tooth, hand for hand, foot for foot.

Going to War

20 When you go to war against your enemies and see horses and chariots and an army greater than yours, do not be afraid of them, because the LORD your God, who brought you up out of Egypt, will be with you. ²When you are about to go into battle, the priest shall come forward and address the army. ³He shall say: "Hear, Israel: Today you are going into battle against your enemies. Do not be fainthearted or afraid; do not be terrified or give way to panic before them. ⁴For the LORD your God is the one who goes with you to fight for you against your enemies to give you victory."

HE IS: with you

20:1 After the exodus, the Israelites refused to enter the promised land because the inhabitants seemed so big and bad. As the next generation prepared to take a step of faith to enter the promised land, God encouraged them not to be afraid. The enemy was looming, but God promised he wouldn't leave them.

What step of faith is God asking you to take? Do the obstacles seem big? Might the outcome be bad? Do not be afraid! Jesus has already won the battle. Everything else you face is just a skirmish. Move forward with confidence, knowing that he is *with you.*

249

For the next He Is, go to p. 256.

⁵The officers shall say to the army: "Has anyone built a new house and not yet begun to live in it? Let him go home, or he may die in battle and someone else may begin to live in it. ⁶Has anyone planted a vineyard and not begun to enjoy it? Let him go home, or he may die in battle and someone else enjoy it. ⁷Has anyone become pledged to a woman and not married her? Let him go home, or he may die in battle and someone else marry her." ⁸Then the officers shall add, "Is anyone afraid or fainthearted? Let him go home so that the others will not become disheartened too." ⁹When the officers have finished speaking to the army, they shall appoint commanders over it.

¹⁰When you march up to attack a city, make its people an offer of peace. ¹¹If they accept and open their gates, all the people in it shall be subject to forced labor and shall work for you. ¹²If they refuse to make peace and they engage you in battle, lay siege to that city. ¹³When the LORD your God delivers it into your hand, put to the sword all the men in it. ¹⁴As for the women, the children, the livestock and everything else in the city, you may take these as plunder for yourselves. And you may use the plunder the LORD your God gives you from your enemies. ¹⁵This is how you are to treat all the cities that are at a distance from you and do not belong to the nations nearby.

¹⁶However, in the cities of the nations the LORD your God is giving you as an inheritance, do not leave alive anything that breathes. ¹⁷Completely destroy^a them—the Hittites, Amorites, Canaanites, Perizzites, Hivites and Jebusites—as the LORD your God has commanded you. ¹⁸Otherwise, they will teach you to follow all the detestable things they do in worshiping their gods, and you will sin against the LORD your God.

¹⁹When you lay siege to a city for a long time, fighting against it to capture it, do not destroy its trees by putting an ax to them, because you can eat their fruit. Do not cut them down. Are the trees people, that you should besiege them?^b ²⁰However, you may cut down trees that you know are not fruit trees and use them to build siege works until the city at war with you falls.

---

^a *17* The Hebrew term refers to the irrevocable giving over of things or persons to the LORD, often by totally destroying them. ^b *19* Or *down to use in the siege, for the fruit trees are for the benefit of people.*

Atonement for an Unsolved Murder

21 If someone is found slain, lying in a field in the land the Lord your God is giving you to possess, and it is not known who the killer was, [2] your elders and judges shall go out and measure the distance from the body to the neighboring towns. [3] Then the elders of the town nearest the body shall take a heifer that has never been worked and has never worn a yoke [4] and lead it down to a valley that has not been plowed or planted and where there is a flowing stream. There in the valley they are to break the heifer's neck. [5] The priests, the sons of Levi, shall step forward, for the Lord your God has chosen them to minister and to pronounce blessings in the name of the Lord and to decide all cases of dispute and assault. [6] Then all the elders of the town nearest the body shall wash their hands over the heifer whose neck was broken in the valley, [7] and they shall declare: "Our hands did not shed this blood, nor did our eyes see it done. [8] Accept this atonement for your people Israel, whom you have redeemed, Lord, and do not hold your people guilty of the blood of an innocent person." And the bloodshed will be atoned for. [9] So you will purge from yourselves the guilt of shedding innocent blood, since you have done what is right in the eyes of the Lord.

Marrying a Captive Woman

[10] When you go to war against your enemies and the Lord your God delivers them into your hands and you take captives, [11] if you notice among the captives a beautiful woman and are attracted to her, you may take her as your wife. [12] Bring her into your home and have her shave her head, trim her nails [13] and put aside the clothes she was wearing when captured. After she has lived in your house and mourned her father and mother for a full month, then you may go to her and be her husband and she shall be your wife. [14] If you are not pleased with her, let her go wherever she wishes. You must not sell her or treat her as a slave, since you have dishonored her.

The Right of the Firstborn

[15] If someone has two wives, and he loves one but not the other, and both bear him sons but the firstborn is the son of the wife he does not love, [16] when he wills his property to his sons, he must not give the rights of the firstborn to the son of the wife he loves in preference to his actual firstborn, the son of the wife he does not love. [17] He must acknowledge the son of his unloved wife as the firstborn by giving him a double share of all he has. That son is the first sign of his father's strength. The right of the firstborn belongs to him.

A Rebellious Son

[18] If someone has a stubborn and rebellious son who does not obey his father and mother and will not listen to them when they discipline him, [19] his father and mother shall take hold of him and bring him to the elders at the gate of his town. [20] They shall say to the elders, "This son of ours is stubborn and rebellious. He will not obey us. He is a profligate and a drunkard." [21] Then all the men of his town are to stone him to death. You must purge the evil from among you. All Israel will hear of it and be afraid.

Various Laws

[22] If anyone guilty of a capital offense is put to death and their body is exposed on a pole, [23] you must not leave the body hanging on the pole overnight. Be sure to bury it that same day, because anyone who is hung on a pole is under God's curse. You must not desecrate the land the Lord your God is giving you as an inheritance.

22 If you see someone else's ox or sheep straying, do not ignore it but be sure to take it back to its owner. [2] If the owner does not live near you or if you do not know who owns it, take it home with you and keep it until the owner comes looking for it. Then give it back. [3] Do the same if you find someone's donkey or cloak or anything else they have lost. Do not ignore it.

[4] If you see someone's donkey or ox fallen on the road, do not ignore it. Help the owner get it to its feet.

[5] A woman must not wear men's clothing, nor a man wear women's clothing, for the Lord your God detests anyone who does this.

[6] If you come across a bird's nest beside the road, either in a tree or on the ground, and the mother is sitting on the young or on the eggs, do not take the mother with the young. [7] You may take the young,

conversations

body image «» 22:5

1 » Why would God care about how his people dress?

2 » Should Christians follow clothing rules today?

3 » How does culture affect your body image and attitude toward what you wear?

For more on **body image**, check the index.
For the next Conversations, go to p. 253.

but be sure to let the mother go, so that it may go well with you and you may have a long life.

[8]When you build a new house, make a parapet around your roof so that you may not bring the guilt of bloodshed on your house if someone falls from the roof.

[9]Do not plant two kinds of seed in your vineyard; if you do, not only the crops you plant but also the fruit of the vineyard will be defiled.[a]

[10]Do not plow with an ox and a donkey yoked together.

[11]Do not wear clothes of wool and linen woven together.

[12]Make tassels on the four corners of the cloak you wear.

Marriage Violations

[13]If a man takes a wife and, after sleeping with her, dislikes her [14]and slanders her and gives her a bad name, saying, "I married this woman, but when I approached her, I did not find proof of her virginity," [15]then the young woman's father and mother shall bring to the town elders at the gate proof that she was a virgin. [16]Her father will say to the elders, "I gave my daughter in marriage to this man, but he dislikes her. [17]Now he has slandered her and said, 'I did not find your daughter to be a virgin.' But here is the proof of my daughter's virginity." Then her parents shall display the cloth before the elders of the town, [18]and the elders shall take the man and punish him. [19]They shall fine him a hundred shekels[b] of silver and give them to the young woman's father, because this man has given an Israelite virgin a bad name. She shall continue to be his wife; he must not divorce her as long as he lives.

[20]If, however, the charge is true and no proof of the young woman's virginity can be found, [21]she shall be brought to the door of her father's house and there the men of her town shall stone her to death. She has done an outrageous thing in Israel by being promiscuous while still in her father's house. You must purge the evil from among you.

[22]If a man is found sleeping with another man's wife, both the man who slept with her and the woman must die. You must purge the evil from Israel.

[23]If a man happens to meet in a town a virgin pledged to be married and he sleeps with her, [24]you shall take both of them to the gate of that town and stone them to death—the young woman because she was in a town and did not scream for help, and the man because he violated another man's wife. You must purge the evil from among you.

[25]But if out in the country a man happens to meet a young woman pledged to be married and rapes her, only the man who has done this shall die. [26]Do nothing to the woman; she has committed no sin deserving death. This case is like that of someone who attacks and murders a neighbor, [27]for the man found the young woman out in the country, and though the betrothed woman screamed, there was no one to rescue her.

at issue: virginity

22:13–21 Our society considers virginity an outdated idea, a strange and pointless precaution. These verses on marriage violations might seem strange and obsolete to many in our day. Yet deep down we know that the only emotionally, spiritually, physically and psychologically safe place to experience such a volatile, unifying act as sex is under the protection of a committed marriage. When we're faced with the temptation to have sex outside the security of marriage, we need to be willing to obey God totally instead of seeing how much we can get away with.

251

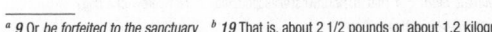

---

a 9 Or *be forfeited to the sanctuary*   *b 19* That is, about 2 1/2 pounds or about 1.2 kilograms

[28]If a man happens to meet a virgin who is not pledged to be married and rapes her and they are discovered, [29]he shall pay her father fifty shekels[a] of silver. He must marry the young woman, for he has violated her. He can never divorce her as long as he lives.

*[30]A man is not to marry his father's wife; he must not dishonor his father's bed.

Exclusion From the Assembly

23 *[1]No one who has been emasculated by crushing or cutting may enter the assembly of the LORD. [2]No one born of a forbidden marriage[b] nor any offspring from such a marriage may enter the assembly of the LORD, not even in the tenth generation.

[3]No Ammonite or Moabite or any of their descendants may enter the assembly of the LORD, not even in the tenth generation. [4]For they did not come to meet you with bread and water on your way when you came out of Egypt, and they hired Balaam son of Beor from Pethor in Aram Naharaim[c] to pronounce a curse on you. [5]However, the LORD your God would not listen to Balaam but turned the curse into a blessing for you, because the LORD your God loves you. [6]Do not seek a treaty of friendship with them as long as you live.

[7]Do not despise an Edomite, for the Edomites are related to you. Do not despise an Egyptian, because you resided as foreigners in their country. [8]The third generation of children born to them may enter the assembly of the LORD.

Uncleanness in the Camp

[9]When you are encamped against your enemies, keep away from everything impure. [10]If one of your men is unclean because of a nocturnal emission, he is to go outside the camp and stay there. [11]But as evening approaches he is to wash himself, and at sunset he may return to the camp.

[12]Designate a place outside the camp where you can go to relieve yourself. [13]As part of your equipment have something to dig with, and when you relieve yourself, dig a hole and cover up your excrement. [14]For the LORD your God moves about in your camp to protect you and to deliver your enemies to you. Your camp must be holy, so that he will not see among you anything indecent and turn away from you.

Miscellaneous Laws

[15]If a slave has taken refuge with you, do not hand them over to their master. [16]Let them live among you wherever they like and in whatever town they choose. Do not oppress them.

[17]No Israelite man or woman is to become a shrine prostitute. [18]You must not bring the earnings of a female prostitute or of a male prostitute[d] into the house of the LORD your God to pay any vow, because the LORD your God detests them both.

[19]Do not charge an Israelite interest, whether on money or food or anything else that may earn interest. [20]You may charge a foreigner interest, but not another Israelite, so that the LORD your God may bless you in everything you put your hand to in the land you are entering to possess.

[21]If you make a vow to the LORD your God, do not be slow to pay it, for the LORD your God will certainly demand it of you and you will be guilty of sin. [22]But if you refrain from making a vow, you will not be guilty. [23]Whatever your lips utter you must be sure to do, because you made your vow freely to the LORD your God with your own mouth.

[24]If you enter your neighbor's vineyard, you may eat all the grapes you want, but do not put any in your basket. [25]If you enter your neighbor's grainfield, you may pick kernels with your hands, but you must not put a sickle to the standing grain.

24 If a man marries a woman who becomes displeasing to him because he finds something indecent about her, and he writes her a certificate of divorce, gives it to her and sends her from his house, [2]and if after she leaves his house she becomes the wife of another man, [3]and her second husband dislikes her and writes her a certificate of divorce, gives it to her and sends her from his house, or if he dies, [4]then her first husband, who divorced her, is not allowed to marry her again after she has been

---

[a] 29 That is, about 1 1/4 pounds or about 575 grams   [b] 2 Or one of illegitimate birth   [c] 4 That is, Northwest Mesopotamia   [d] 18 Hebrew of a dog
* 22:30 is numbered 23:1 in Hebrew texts.   * 23:1-25 is numbered 23:2-26 in Hebrew texts.

defiled. That would be detestable in the eyes of the LORD. Do not bring sin upon the land the LORD your God is giving you as an inheritance.

⁵If a man has recently married, he must not be sent to war or have any other duty laid on him. For one year he is to be free to stay at home and bring happiness to the wife he has married.

⁶Do not take a pair of millstones—not even the upper one—as security for a debt, because that would be taking a person's livelihood as security.

⁷If someone is caught kidnapping another Israelite and treating or selling that Israelite as a slave, the kidnapper must die. You must purge the evil from among you.

⁸In cases of defiling skin diseases,ª be very careful to do exactly as the Levitical priests instruct you. You must follow carefully what I have commanded them. ⁹Remember what the LORD your God did to Miriam along the way after you came out of Egypt.

> ## "conversations
> marriage «» 24:5
>
> 1» Why is the first year so vital for a strong marriage?
>
> 2» What pressures do newlyweds face today?
>
> 3» If you're married, how can you place your marriage above all other responsibilities?
>
> For more on **marriage**, check the index.
> For the next Conversations, go to p. 263.

¹⁰When you make a loan of any kind to a neighbor, do not go into the neighbor's house to get what is offered to you as a pledge. ¹¹Stay outside and let the neighbor to whom you are making the loan bring the pledge out to you. ¹²If the neighbor is poor, do not go to sleep with that pledge in your possession. ¹³Return the cloak by sunset so that your neighbor may sleep in it. Then you will be thanked, and it will be regarded as a righteous act in the sight of the LORD your God.

¹⁴Do not take advantage of a hired worker who is poor and needy, whether that worker is an Israelite or is a foreigner residing in one of your towns. ¹⁵Pay them their wages each day before sunset, because they are poor and are counting on it. Otherwise they may cry to the LORD against you, and you will be guilty of sin.

¹⁶Parents are not to be put to death for their children, nor children put to death for their parents; each of you will die for your own sin.

¹⁷Do not deprive the foreigner or the fatherless of justice, or take the cloak of the widow as a pledge. ¹⁸Remember that you were slaves in Egypt and the LORD your God redeemed you from there. That is why I command you to do this.

¹⁹When you are harvesting in your field and you overlook a sheaf, do not go back to get it. Leave it for the foreigner, the fatherless and the widow, so that the LORD your God may bless you in all the work of your hands. ²⁰When you beat the olives from your trees, do not go over the branches a second time. Leave what remains for the foreigner, the fatherless and the widow. ²¹When you harvest the grapes in your vineyard, do not go over the vines again. Leave what remains for the foreigner, the fatherless and the widow. ²²Remember that you were slaves in Egypt. That is why I command you to do this.

25 When people have a dispute, they are to take it to court and the judges will decide the case, acquitting the innocent and condemning the guilty. ²If the one who is guilty deserves to be beaten, the judge shall make them lie down and have them flogged in his presence with the number of lashes the crime deserves, ³but the judge must not impose more than forty lashes. If the guilty party is flogged more than that, your Israelite neighbor will be degraded in your eyes.

⁴Do not muzzle an ox while it is treading out the grain.

⁵If brothers are living together and one of them dies without a son, his widow must not marry outside the family. Her husband's brother shall take her and marry her and fulfill the duty of a brother-in-law to her. ⁶The first son she bears shall carry on the name of the dead brother so that his name will not be blotted out from Israel.

⁷However, if a man does not want to marry his brother's wife, she shall go to the elders at the town gate and say, "My husband's brother refuses to carry on his brother's name in Israel. He will not fulfill the duty of a brother-in-law to me." ⁸Then the elders of his town shall summon him and talk to him. If he

---

ª 8 The Hebrew word for *defiling skin diseases*, traditionally translated "leprosy," was used for various diseases affecting the skin.

persists in saying, "I do not want to marry her," [9]his brother's widow shall go up to him in the presence of the elders, take off one of his sandals, spit in his face and say, "This is what is done to the man who will not build up his brother's family line." [10]That man's line shall be known in Israel as The Family of the Unsandaled.

[11]If two men are fighting and the wife of one of them comes to rescue her husband from his assailant, and she reaches out and seizes him by his private parts, [12]you shall cut off her hand. Show her no pity.

[13]Do not have two differing weights in your bag—one heavy, one light. [14]Do not have two differing measures in your house—one large, one small. [15]You must have accurate and honest weights and measures, so that you may live long in the land the Lord your God is giving you. [16]For the Lord your God detests anyone who does these things, anyone who deals dishonestly.

[17]Remember what the Amalekites did to you along the way when you came out of Egypt. [18]When you were weary and worn out, they met you on your journey and attacked all who were lagging behind; they had no fear of God. [19]When the Lord your God gives you rest from all the enemies around you in the land he is giving you to possess as an inheritance, you shall blot out the name of Amalek from under heaven. Do not forget!

Firstfruits and Tithes

26 When you have entered the land the Lord your God is giving you as an inheritance and have taken possession of it and settled in it, [2]take some of the firstfruits of all that you produce from the soil of the land the Lord your God is giving you and put them in a basket. Then go to the place the Lord your God will choose as a dwelling for his Name [3]and say to the priest in office at the time, "I declare today to the Lord your God that I have come to the land the Lord swore to our ancestors to give us." [4]The priest shall take the basket from your hands and set it down in front of the altar of the Lord your God. [5]Then you shall declare before the Lord your God: "My father was a wandering Aramean, and he went down into Egypt with a few people and lived there and became a great nation, powerful and numerous. [6]But the Egyptians mistreated us and made us suffer, subjecting us to harsh labor. [7]Then we cried out to the Lord, the God of our ancestors, and the Lord heard our voice and saw our misery, toil and oppression. [8]So the Lord brought us out of Egypt with a mighty hand and an outstretched arm, with great terror and with signs and wonders. [9]He brought us to this place and gave us this land, a land flowing with milk and honey; [10]and now I bring the firstfruits of the soil that you, Lord, have given me." Place the basket before the Lord your God and bow down before him. [11]Then you and the Levites and the foreigners residing among you shall rejoice in all the good things the Lord your God has given to you and your household.

[12]When you have finished setting aside a tenth of all your produce in the third year, the year of the tithe, you shall give it to the Levite, the foreigner, the fatherless and the widow, so that they may eat in your towns and be satisfied. [13]Then say to the Lord your God: "I have removed from my house the sacred portion and have given it to the Levite, the foreigner, the fatherless and the widow, according to all you commanded. I have not turned aside from your commands nor have I forgotten any of them. [14]I have not eaten any of the sacred portion while I was in mourning, nor have I removed any of it while I was unclean, nor have I offered any of it to the dead. I have obeyed the Lord my God; I have done everything you commanded me. [15]Look down from heaven, your holy dwelling place, and bless your people Israel and the land you have given us as you promised on oath to our ancestors, a land flowing with milk and honey."

Follow the Lord's Commands

[16]The Lord your God commands you this day to follow these decrees and laws; carefully observe them with all your heart and with all your soul. [17]You have declared this day that the Lord is your God and that you will walk in obedience to him, that you will keep his decrees, commands and laws—that you will listen to him. [18]And the Lord has declared this day that you are his people, his treasured possession as he promised, and that you are to keep all his commands. [19]He has declared that he will set you in praise, fame and honor high above all the nations he has made and that you will be a people holy to the Lord your God, as he promised.

The Altar on Mount Ebal

27 Moses and the elders of Israel commanded the people: "Keep all these commands that I give you today. ²When you have crossed the Jordan into the land the LORD your God is giving you, set up some large stones and coat them with plaster. ³Write on them all the words of this law when you have crossed over to enter the land the LORD your God is giving you, a land flowing with milk and honey, just as the LORD, the God of your ancestors, promised you. ⁴And when you have crossed the Jordan, set up these stones on Mount Ebal, as I command you today, and coat them with plaster. ⁵Build there an altar to the LORD your God, an altar of stones. Do not use any iron tool on them. ⁶Build the altar of the LORD your God with fieldstones and offer burnt offerings on it to the LORD your God. ⁷Sacrifice fellowship offerings there, eating them and rejoicing in the presence of the LORD your God. ⁸And you shall write very clearly all the words of this law on these stones you have set up."

Curses From Mount Ebal

⁹Then Moses and the Levitical priests said to all Israel, "Be silent, Israel, and listen! You have now become the people of the LORD your God. ¹⁰Obey the LORD your God and follow his commands and decrees that I give you today."

¹¹On the same day Moses commanded the people:

¹²When you have crossed the Jordan, these tribes shall stand on Mount Gerizim to bless the people: Simeon, Levi, Judah, Issachar, Joseph and Benjamin. ¹³And these tribes shall stand on Mount Ebal to pronounce curses: Reuben, Gad, Asher, Zebulun, Dan and Naphtali.

¹⁴The Levites shall recite to all the people of Israel in a loud voice:

255

¹⁵"Cursed is anyone who makes an idol—a thing detestable to the LORD, the work of skilled hands—and sets it up in secret."

Then all the people shall say, "Amen!"

¹⁶"Cursed is anyone who dishonors their father or mother."

Then all the people shall say, "Amen!"

¹⁷"Cursed is anyone who moves their neighbor's boundary stone."

Then all the people shall say, "Amen!"

¹⁸"Cursed is anyone who leads the blind astray on the road."

Then all the people shall say, "Amen!"

¹⁹"Cursed is anyone who withholds justice from the foreigner, the fatherless or the widow."

Then all the people shall say, "Amen!"

²⁰"Cursed is anyone who sleeps with his father's wife, for he dishonors his father's bed."

Then all the people shall say, "Amen!"

²¹"Cursed is anyone who has sexual relations with any animal."

Then all the people shall say, "Amen!"

²²"Cursed is anyone who sleeps with his sister, the daughter of his father or the daughter of his mother."

Then all the people shall say, "Amen!"

²³"Cursed is anyone who sleeps with his mother-in-law."

Then all the people shall say, "Amen!"

²⁴"Cursed is anyone who kills their neighbor secretly."

Then all the people shall say, "Amen!"

²⁵"Cursed is anyone who accepts a bribe to kill an innocent person."

Then all the people shall say, "Amen!"

²⁶"Cursed is anyone who does not uphold the words of this law by carrying them out."

Then all the people shall say, "Amen!"

Blessings for Obedience

28 If you fully obey the LORD your God and carefully follow all his commands I give you today, the LORD your God will set you high above all the nations on earth. ²All these blessings will come on you and accompany you if you obey the LORD your God:

HE IS: elevating

28:1–21 Elevating the Israelites above all the other nations on earth was God's intent. However, his promise was conditional: He would elevate them if they would elevate him. If the Israelites stooped to follow other gods or to follow the customs of their pagan neighbors, God would bring them down.

God intends to elevate you. If the world is dragging you down, trust that he is eager to help you rise above it all. He is *elevating;* all he asks is that you obey him. When you lift up his commands, he will lift you above your circumstances.

For the next He Is, go to p. 260.

³You will be blessed in the city and blessed in the country.

⁴The fruit of your womb will be blessed, and the crops of your land and the young of your livestock—the calves of your herds and the lambs of your flocks.

⁵Your basket and your kneading trough will be blessed.

⁶You will be blessed when you come in and blessed when you go out.

⁷The LORD will grant that the enemies who rise up against you will be defeated before you. They will come at you from one direction but flee from you in seven.

⁸The LORD will send a blessing on your barns and on everything you put your hand to. The LORD your God will bless you in the land he is giving you.

⁹The LORD will establish you as his holy people, as he promised you on oath, if you keep the commands of the LORD your God and walk in obedience to him. ¹⁰Then all the peoples on earth will see that you are called by the name of the LORD, and they will fear you. ¹¹The LORD will grant you abundant prosperity—in the fruit of your womb, the young of your livestock and the crops of your ground—in the land he swore to your ancestors to give you.

¹²The LORD will open the heavens, the storehouse of his bounty, to send rain on your land in season and to bless all the work of your hands. You will lend to many nations but will borrow from none. ¹³The LORD will make you the head, not the tail. If you pay attention to the commands of the LORD your God that I give you this day and carefully follow them, you will always be at the top, never at the bottom. ¹⁴Do not turn aside from any of the commands I give you today, to the right or to the left, following other gods and serving them.

Curses for Disobedience

¹⁵However, if you do not obey the LORD your God and do not carefully follow all his commands and decrees I am giving you today, all these curses will come on you and overtake you:

¹⁶You will be cursed in the city and cursed in the country.

¹⁷Your basket and your kneading trough will be cursed.

¹⁸The fruit of your womb will be cursed, and the crops of your land, and the calves of your herds and the lambs of your flocks.

¹⁹You will be cursed when you come in and cursed when you go out.

²⁰The LORD will send on you curses, confusion and rebuke in everything you put your hand to, until you are destroyed and come to sudden ruin because of the evil you have done in forsaking him.ᵃ ²¹The LORD will plague you with diseases until he has destroyed you from the land you are entering to possess. ²²The LORD will strike you with wasting disease, with fever and inflammation, with scorching heat and drought, with blight and mildew, which will plague you until you perish. ²³The sky over your head will

be bronze, the ground beneath you iron. [24]The LORD will turn the rain of your country into dust and powder; it will come down from the skies until you are destroyed.

[25]The LORD will cause you to be defeated before your enemies. You will come at them from one direction but flee from them in seven, and you will become a thing of horror to all the kingdoms on earth. [26]Your carcasses will be food for all the birds and the wild animals, and there will be no one to frighten them away. [27]The LORD will afflict you with the boils of Egypt and with tumors, festering sores and the itch, from which you cannot be cured. [28]The LORD will afflict you with madness, blindness and confusion of mind. [29]At midday you will grope about like a blind person in the dark. You will be unsuccessful in everything you do; day after day you will be oppressed and robbed, with no one to rescue you.

[30]You will be pledged to be married to a woman, but another will take her and ravish her. You will build a house, but you will not live in it. You will plant a vineyard, but you will not even begin to enjoy its fruit. [31]Your ox will be slaughtered before your eyes, but you will eat none of it. Your donkey will be forcibly taken from you and will not be returned. Your sheep will be given to your enemies, and no one will rescue them. [32]Your sons and daughters will be given to another nation, and you will wear out your eyes watching for them day after day, powerless to lift a hand. [33]A people that you do not know will eat what your land and labor produce, and you will have nothing but cruel oppression all your days. [34]The sights you see will drive you mad. [35]The LORD will afflict your knees and legs with painful boils that cannot be cured, spreading from the soles of your feet to the top of your head.

[36]The LORD will drive you and the king you set over you to a nation unknown to you or your ancestors. There you will worship other gods, gods of wood and stone. [37]You will become a thing of horror, a byword and an object of ridicule among all the peoples where the LORD will drive you.

257

[38]You will sow much seed in the field but you will harvest little, because locusts will devour it. [39]You will plant vineyards and cultivate them but you will not drink the wine or gather the grapes, because worms will eat them. [40]You will have olive trees throughout your country but you will not use the oil, because the olives will drop off. [41]You will have sons and daughters but you will not keep them, because they will go into captivity. [42]Swarms of locusts will take over all your trees and the crops of your land.

[43]The foreigners who reside among you will rise above you higher and higher, but you will sink lower and lower. [44]They will lend to you, but you will not lend to them. They will be the head, but you will be the tail.

[45]All these curses will come on you. They will pursue you and overtake you until you are destroyed, because you did not obey the LORD your God and observe the commands and decrees he gave you. [46]They will be a sign and a wonder to you and your descendants forever. [47]Because you did not serve the LORD your God joyfully and gladly in the time of prosperity, [48]therefore in hunger and thirst, in nakedness and dire poverty, you will serve the enemies the LORD sends against you. He will put an iron yoke on your neck until he has destroyed you.

[49]The LORD will bring a nation against you from far away, from the ends of the earth, like an eagle swooping down, a nation whose language you will not understand, [50]a fierce-looking nation without respect for the old or pity for the young. [51]They will devour the young of your livestock and the crops of your land until you are destroyed. They will leave you no grain, new wine or olive oil, nor any calves of your herds or lambs of your flocks until you are ruined. [52]They will lay siege to all the cities throughout your land until the high fortified walls in which you trust fall down. They will besiege all the cities throughout the land the LORD your God is giving you.

[53]Because of the suffering that your enemy will inflict on you during the siege, you will eat the fruit of the womb, the flesh of the sons and daughters the LORD your God has given you. [54]Even the most gentle and sensitive man among you will have no compassion on his own brother or the wife he loves or his surviving children, [55]and he will not give to one of them any of the flesh of his children that he is eating. It will be all he has left because of the suffering your enemy will inflict on you during the siege of all your cities. [56]The most gentle and sensitive woman among you—so sensitive and gentle that she would not venture to touch the ground with the sole of her foot—will begrudge the husband she loves and her own son or daughter [57]the afterbirth from her womb and the children she bears. For in her dire need she intends to eat them secretly because of the suffering your enemy will inflict on you during the siege of your cities.

⁵⁸If you do not carefully follow all the words of this law, which are written in this book, and do not revere this glorious and awesome name—the Lᴏʀᴅ your God— ⁵⁹the Lᴏʀᴅ will send fearful plagues on you and your descendants, harsh and prolonged disasters, and severe and lingering illnesses. ⁶⁰He will bring on you all the diseases of Egypt that you dreaded, and they will cling to you. ⁶¹The Lᴏʀᴅ will also bring on you every kind of sickness and disaster not recorded in this Book of the Law, until you are destroyed. ⁶²You who were as numerous as the stars in the sky will be left but few in number, because you did not obey the Lᴏʀᴅ your God. ⁶³Just as it pleased the Lᴏʀᴅ to make you prosper and increase in number, so it will please him to ruin and destroy you. You will be uprooted from the land you are entering to possess.

⁶⁴Then the Lᴏʀᴅ will scatter you among all nations, from one end of the earth to the other. There you will worship other gods—gods of wood and stone, which neither you nor your ancestors have known. ⁶⁵Among those nations you will find no repose, no resting place for the sole of your foot. There the Lᴏʀᴅ will give you an anxious mind, eyes weary with longing, and a despairing heart. ⁶⁶You will live in constant suspense, filled with dread both night and day, never sure of your life. ⁶⁷In the morning you will say, "If only it were evening!" and in the evening, "If only it were morning!"—because of the terror that will fill your hearts and the sights that your eyes will see. ⁶⁸The Lᴏʀᴅ will send you back in ships to Egypt on a journey I said you should never make again. There you will offer yourselves for sale to your enemies as male and female slaves, but no one will buy you.

Renewal of the Covenant

29 *These are the terms of the covenant the Lᴏʀᴅ commanded Moses to make with the Israelites in Moab, in addition to the covenant he had made with them at Horeb. *²Moses summoned all the Israelites and said to them:

Your eyes have seen all that the Lᴏʀᴅ did in Egypt to Pharaoh, to all his officials and to all his land. ³With your own eyes you saw those great trials, those signs and great wonders. ⁴But to this day the Lᴏʀᴅ has not given you a mind that understands or eyes that see or ears that hear. ⁵During the forty years that I led you through the wilderness, your clothes did not wear out, nor did the sandals on your feet. ⁶You ate no bread and drank no wine or other fermented drink. I did this so that you might know that I am the Lᴏʀᴅ your God.

⁷When you reached this place, Sihon king of Heshbon and Og king of Bashan came out to fight against us, but we defeated them. ⁸We took their land and gave it as an inheritance to the Reubenites, the Gadites and the half-tribe of Manasseh.

⁹Carefully follow the terms of this covenant, so that you may prosper in everything you do. ¹⁰All of you are standing today in the presence of the Lᴏʀᴅ your God—your leaders and chief men, your elders and officials, and all the other men of Israel, ¹¹together with your children and your wives, and the foreigners living in your camps who chop your wood and carry your water. ¹²You are standing here in order to enter into a covenant with the Lᴏʀᴅ your God, a covenant the Lᴏʀᴅ is making with you this day and sealing with an oath, ¹³to confirm you this day as his people, that he may be your God as he promised you and as he swore to your fathers, Abraham, Isaac and Jacob. ¹⁴I am making this covenant, with its oath, not only with you ¹⁵who are standing here with us today in the presence of the Lᴏʀᴅ our God but also with those who are not here today.

¹⁶You yourselves know how we lived in Egypt and how we passed through the countries on the way here. ¹⁷You saw among them their detestable images and idols of wood and stone, of silver and gold. ¹⁸Make sure there is no man or woman, clan or tribe among you today whose heart turns away from the Lᴏʀᴅ our God to go and worship the gods of those nations; make sure there is no root among you that produces such bitter poison.

¹⁹When such persons hear the words of this oath and invoke a blessing on themselves, thinking, "I will be safe, even though I persist in going my own way," they will bring disaster on the watered land as well as the dry. ²⁰The Lᴏʀᴅ will never be willing to forgive them; his wrath and zeal will burn against them. All the curses written in this book will fall on them, and the Lᴏʀᴅ will blot out their names from under

---

* 29:1 is numbered 28:69 in Hebrew texts.   * 29:2-29 is numbered 29:1-28 in Hebrew texts.

heaven. ²¹The LORD will single them out from all the tribes of Israel for disaster, according to all the curses of the covenant written in this Book of the Law.

²²Your children who follow you in later generations and foreigners who come from distant lands will see the calamities that have fallen on the land and the diseases with which the LORD has afflicted it. ²³The whole land will be a burning waste of salt and sulfur—nothing planted, nothing sprouting, no vegetation growing on it. It will be like the destruction of Sodom and Gomorrah, Admah and Zeboyim, which the LORD overthrew in fierce anger. ²⁴All the nations will ask: "Why has the LORD done this to this land? Why this fierce, burning anger?"

²⁵And the answer will be: "It is because this people abandoned the covenant of the LORD, the God of their ancestors, the covenant he made with them when he brought them out of Egypt. ²⁶They went off and worshiped other gods and bowed down to them, gods they did not know, gods he had not given them. ²⁷Therefore the LORD's anger burned against this land, so that he brought on it all the curses written in this book. ²⁸In furious anger and in great wrath the LORD uprooted them from their land and thrust them into another land, as it is now."

²⁹The secret things belong to the LORD our God, but the things revealed belong to us and to our children forever, that we may follow all the words of this law.

Prosperity After Turning to the LORD

30 When all these blessings and curses I have set before you come on you and you take them to heart wherever the LORD your God disperses you among the nations, ²and when you and your children return to the LORD your God and obey him with all your heart and with all your soul according to everything I command you today, ³then the LORD your God will restore your fortunes ^{a} and have compassion on you and gather you again from all the nations where he scattered you. ⁴Even if you have been banished to the most distant land under the heavens, from there the LORD your God will gather you and bring you back. ⁵He will bring you to the land that belonged to your ancestors, and you will take possession of it. He will make you more prosperous and numerous than your ancestors. ⁶The LORD your God will circumcise your hearts and the hearts of your descendants, so that you may love him with all your heart and with all your soul, and live. ⁷The LORD your God will put all these curses on your enemies who hate and persecute you. ⁸You will again obey the LORD and follow all his commands I am giving you today. ⁹Then the LORD your God will make you most prosperous in all the work of your hands and in the fruit of your womb, the young of your livestock and the crops of your land. The LORD will again delight in you and make you prosperous, just as he delighted in your ancestors, ¹⁰if you obey the LORD your God and keep his commands and decrees that are written in this Book of the Law and turn to the LORD your God with all your heart and with all your soul.

The Offer of Life or Death

¹¹Now what I am commanding you today is not too difficult for you or beyond your reach. ¹²It is not up in heaven, so that you have to ask, "Who will ascend into heaven to get it and proclaim it to us so we may obey it?" ¹³Nor is it beyond the sea, so that you have to ask, "Who will cross the sea to get it and proclaim it to us so we may obey it?" ¹⁴No, the word is very near you; it is in your mouth and in your heart so you may obey it.

¹⁵See, I set before you today life and prosperity, death and destruction. ¹⁶For I command you today to love the LORD your God, to walk in obedience to him, and to keep his commands, decrees and laws; then you will live and increase, and the LORD your God will bless you in the land you are entering to possess.

¹⁷But if your heart turns away and you are not obedient, and if you are drawn away to bow down to other gods and worship them, ¹⁸I declare to you this day that you will certainly be destroyed. You will not live long in the land you are crossing the Jordan to enter and possess.

¹⁹This day I call the heavens and the earth as witnesses against you that I have set before you life and death, blessings and curses. Now choose life, so that you and your children may live ²⁰and that you may love the LORD your God, listen to his voice, and hold fast to him. For the LORD is your life, and he will give you many years in the land he swore to give to your fathers, Abraham, Isaac and Jacob.

259

---

^{a} 3 Or will bring you back from captivity

Joshua to Succeed Moses

31 Then Moses went out and spoke these words to all Israel: ²"I am now a hundred and twenty years old and I am no longer able to lead you. The LORD has said to me, 'You shall not cross the Jordan.' ³The LORD your God himself will cross over ahead of you. He will destroy these nations before you, and you will take possession of their land. Joshua also will cross over ahead of you, as the LORD said. ⁴And the LORD will do to them what he did to Sihon and Og, the kings of the Amorites, whom he destroyed along with their land. ⁵The LORD will deliver them to you, and you must do to them all that I have command-ed you. ⁶Be strong and courageous. Do not be afraid or terrified because of them, for the LORD your God goes with you; he will never leave you nor forsake you."

HE IS: encouraging

31:6 Moses was not given the privilege of leading the Israelites into the promised land. But God had chosen his leader wisely. When it was time to pass the torch, rather than bemoan-ing his fate, Moses thought not of himself but of his people. He urged them to be strong and courageous. Through Moses, God encouraged the people to move ahead.

Encouragement is one of the best gifts we can offer one another. Think of someone who's going through a time of discouragement. Remind her that she's not alone, that God goes with her. Speak God's words to her. Just as he is *encouraging*, so you can be too.

For the next He Is, go to p. 273.

⁷Then Moses summoned Joshua and said to him in the presence of all Israel, "Be strong and coura-geous, for you must go with this people into the land that the LORD swore to their ancestors to give them, and you must divide it among them as their inheritance. ⁸The LORD himself goes before you and will be with you; he will never leave you nor forsake you. Do not be afraid; do not be discouraged."

Public Reading of the Law

⁹So Moses wrote down this law and gave it to the priests, the sons of Levi, who carried the ark of the covenant of the LORD, and to all the elders of Israel. ¹⁰Then Moses commanded them: "At the end of every seven years, in the year for canceling debts, during the Festival of Tabernacles, ¹¹when all Israel comes to appear before the LORD your God at the place he will choose, you shall read this law before them in their hearing. ¹²Assemble the people—men, women and children, and the foreigners residing in your towns—so they can listen and learn to fear the LORD your God and follow carefully all the words of this law. ¹³Their children, who do not know this law, must hear it and learn to fear the LORD your God as long as you live in the land you are crossing the Jordan to possess."

Israel's Rebellion Predicted

¹⁴The LORD said to Moses, "Now the day of your death is near. Call Joshua and present yourselves at the tent of meeting, where I will commission him." So Moses and Joshua came and presented themselves at the tent of meeting.

¹⁵Then the LORD appeared at the tent in a pillar of cloud, and the cloud stood over the entrance to the tent. ¹⁶And the LORD said to Moses: "You are going to rest with your ancestors, and these people will soon prostitute themselves to the foreign gods of the land they are entering. They will forsake me and break the covenant I made with them. ¹⁷And in that day I will become angry with them and forsake them; I will hide my face from them, and they will be destroyed. Many disasters and calamities will come on them, and in that day they will ask, 'Have not these disasters come on us because our God is not with us?' ¹⁸And I will certainly hide my face in that day because of all their wickedness in turning to other gods.

¹⁹"Now write down this song and teach it to the Israelites and have them sing it, so that it may be a witness for me against them. ²⁰When I have brought them into the land flowing with milk and honey,

the land I promised on oath to their ancestors, and when they eat their fill and thrive, they will turn to other gods and worship them, rejecting me and breaking my covenant. ²¹And when many disasters and calamities come on them, this song will testify against them, because it will not be forgotten by their descendants. I know what they are disposed to do, even before I bring them into the land I promised them on oath." ²²So Moses wrote down this song that day and taught it to the Israelites.

²³The LORD gave this command to Joshua son of Nun: "Be strong and courageous, for you will bring the Israelites into the land I promised them on oath, and I myself will be with you."

²⁴After Moses finished writing in a book the words of this law from beginning to end, ²⁵he gave this command to the Levites who carried the ark of the covenant of the LORD: ²⁶"Take this Book of the Law and place it beside the ark of the covenant of the LORD your God. There it will remain as a witness against you. ²⁷For I know how rebellious and stiff-necked you are. If you have been rebellious against the LORD while I am still alive and with you, how much more will you rebel after I die! ²⁸Assemble before me all the elders of your tribes and all your officials, so that I can speak these words in their hearing and call the heavens and the earth to testify against them. ²⁹For I know that after my death you are sure to become utterly corrupt and to turn from the way I have commanded you. In days to come, disaster will fall on you because you will do evil in the sight of the LORD and arouse his anger by what your hands have made."

The Song of Moses
³⁰And Moses recited the words of this song from beginning to end in the hearing of the whole assembly of Israel:

261

32
Listen, you heavens, and I will speak;
    hear, you earth, the words of my mouth.
²Let my teaching fall like rain
    and my words descend like dew,
like showers on new grass,
    like abundant rain on tender plants.

³I will proclaim the name of the LORD.
    Oh, praise the greatness of our God!
⁴He is the Rock, his works are perfect,
    and all his ways are just.
A faithful God who does no wrong,
    upright and just is he.

⁵They are corrupt and not his children;
    to their shame they are a warped and crooked generation.
⁶Is this the way you repay the LORD,
    you foolish and unwise people?
Is he not your Father, your Creator,ᵃ
    who made you and formed you?

⁷Remember the days of old;
    consider the generations long past.
Ask your father and he will tell you,
    your elders, and they will explain to you.
⁸When the Most High gave the nations their inheritance,
    when he divided all the human race,
he set up boundaries for the peoples
    according to the number of the sons of Israel.ᵇ

ᵃ *6* Or *Father, who bought you*   ᵇ *8* Masoretic Text; Dead Sea Scrolls (see also Septuagint) *sons of God*

⁹For the Lord's portion is his people,
    Jacob his allotted inheritance.

¹⁰In a desert land he found him,
    in a barren and howling waste.
He shielded him and cared for him;
    he guarded him as the apple of his eye,
¹¹like an eagle that stirs up its nest
    and hovers over its young,
that spreads its wings to catch them
    and carries them aloft.
¹²The Lord alone led him;
    no foreign god was with him.

¹³He made him ride on the heights of the land
    and fed him with the fruit of the fields.
He nourished him with honey from the rock,
    and with oil from the flinty crag,
¹⁴with curds and milk from herd and flock
    and with fattened lambs and goats,
with choice rams of Bashan
    and the finest kernels of wheat.
You drank the foaming blood of the grape.

¹⁵Jeshurun*ᵃ* grew fat and kicked;
    filled with food, he became heavy and sleek.
He abandoned the God who made him
    and rejected the Rock his Savior.
¹⁶They made him jealous with their foreign gods
    and angered him with their detestable idols.
¹⁷They sacrificed to demons, which are not God—
    gods they had not known,
    gods that recently appeared,
    gods your ancestors did not fear.
¹⁸You deserted the Rock, who bore you;
    you forgot the God who gave you birth.

¹⁹The Lord saw this and rejected them
    because he was angered by his sons and daughters.
²⁰"I will hide my face from them," he said,
    "and see what their end will be;
for they are a perverse generation,
    children who are unfaithful.
²¹They made me jealous by what is no god
    and angered me with their worthless idols.
I will make them envious by those who are not a people;
    I will make them angry by a nation that has no understanding.
²²For a fire will be kindled by my wrath,
    one that burns down to the realm of the dead below.
It will devour the earth and its harvests
    and set afire the foundations of the mountains.

ᵃ 15 *Jeshurun* means *the upright one,* that is, Israel.

²³"I will heap calamities on them
  and spend my arrows against them.
²⁴I will send wasting famine against them,
  consuming pestilence and deadly plague;
I will send against them the fangs of wild beasts,
  the venom of vipers that glide in the dust.
²⁵In the street the sword will make them childless;
  in their homes terror will reign.
The young men and young women will perish,
  the infants and those with gray hair.
²⁶I said I would scatter them
  and erase their name from human memory,
²⁷but I dreaded the taunt of the enemy,
  lest the adversary misunderstand
and say, 'Our hand has triumphed;
  the LORD has not done all this.'"

²⁸They are a nation without sense,
  there is no discernment in them.
²⁹If only they were wise and would understand this
  and discern what their end will be!
³⁰How could one man chase a thousand,
  or two put ten thousand to flight,
unless their Rock had sold them,
  unless the LORD had given them up?
³¹For their rock is not like our Rock,
  as even our enemies concede.
³²Their vine comes from the vine of Sodom
  and from the fields of Gomorrah.
Their grapes are filled with poison,
  and their clusters with bitterness.
³³Their wine is the venom of serpents,
  the deadly poison of cobras.

³⁴"Have I not kept this in reserve
  and sealed it in my vaults?
³⁵It is mine to avenge; I will repay.
  In due time their foot will slip;
their day of disaster is near
  and their doom rushes upon them."

³⁶The LORD will vindicate his people
  and relent concerning his servants
when he sees their strength is gone
  and no one is left, slave or free.ᵃ
³⁷He will say: "Now where are their gods,
  the rock they took refuge in,
³⁸the gods who ate the fat of their sacrifices
  and drank the wine of their drink offerings?
Let them rise up to help you!
  Let them give you shelter!

263

conversations

revenge «» 32:35

1» Describe a time when you wanted to take revenge on someone.

2» Why is it so hard to wait for God to avenge a wrong done to you?

3» How can God be both vengeful and merciful?

For more on **revenge**, check the index.
For the next Conversations, go to p. 275.

ᵃ 36 Or and they are without a ruler or leader

³⁹"See now that I myself am He!
    There is no god besides me.
I put to death and I bring to life,
    I have wounded and I will heal,
    and no one can deliver out of my hand.
⁴⁰I lift my hand to heaven and declare:
    As surely as I live forever,
⁴¹when I sharpen my flashing sword
    and my hand grasps it in judgment,
I will take vengeance on my adversaries
    and repay those who hate me.
⁴²I will make my arrows drunk with blood,
    while my sword devours flesh:
the blood of the slain and the captives,
    the heads of the enemy leaders."

⁴³Rejoice, you nations, with his people,[a,b]
    for he will avenge the blood of his servants;
he will take vengeance on his enemies
    and make atonement for his land and people.

⁴⁴Moses came with Joshua[c] son of Nun and spoke all the words of this song in the hearing of the people. ⁴⁵When Moses finished reciting all these words to all Israel, ⁴⁶he said to them, "Take to heart all the words I have solemnly declared to you this day, so that you may command your children to obey carefully all the words of this law. ⁴⁷They are not just idle words for you— they are your life. By them you will live long in the land you are crossing the Jordan to possess."

Moses to Die on Mount Nebo

⁴⁸On that same day the LORD told Moses, ⁴⁹"Go up into the Abarim Range to Mount Nebo in Moab, across from Jericho, and view Canaan, the land I am giving the Israelites as their own possession. ⁵⁰There on the mountain that you have climbed you will die and be gathered to your people, just as your brother Aaron died on Mount Hor and was gathered to his people. ⁵¹This is because both of you broke faith with me in the presence of the Israelites at the waters of Meribah Kadesh in the Desert of Zin and because you did not uphold my holiness among the Israelites. ⁵²Therefore, you will see the land only from a distance; you will not enter the land I am giving to the people of Israel."

Moses Blesses the Tribes

33 This is the blessing that Moses the man of God pronounced on the Israelites before his death. ²He said:

    "The LORD came from Sinai
      and dawned over them from Seir;
    he shone forth from Mount Paran.

atissue:regret

32:48–52 What do you do when you must live with the painful consequences of a past mistake? Moses must have felt deep regret as he looked across at the promised land he would never enter. For 40 years he had been leading the people to this place. While the consequences of past sins can be terribly disappointing, remember that God still loves you. Even Moses, the friend and servant of God, had to deal with regret. If you're struggling with regret, allow God's forgiveness to restore your hope and to help you deal with whatever consequences you may be facing.

---

^a *43* Or *Make his people rejoice, you nations*   ^b *43* Masoretic Text; Dead Sea Scrolls (see also Septuagint) *people, / and let all the angels worship him /*
^c *44* Hebrew *Hoshea,* a variant of *Joshua*

He came with*a* myriads of holy ones
    from the south, from his mountain slopes.*b*
³Surely it is you who love the people;
    all the holy ones are in your hand.
At your feet they all bow down,
    and from you receive instruction,
⁴the law that Moses gave us,
    the possession of the assembly of Jacob.
⁵He was king over Jeshurun*c*
    when the leaders of the people assembled,
    along with the tribes of Israel.

⁶"Let Reuben live and not die,
    nor*d* his people be few."

⁷And this he said about Judah:

"Hear, Lord, the cry of Judah;
    bring him to his people.
With his own hands he defends his cause.
    Oh, be his help against his foes!"

⁸About Levi he said:

"Your Thummim and Urim belong
    to your faithful servant.
You tested him at Massah;
    you contended with him at the waters of Meribah.
⁹He said of his father and mother,
    'I have no regard for them.'
He did not recognize his brothers
    or acknowledge his own children,
but he watched over your word
    and guarded your covenant.
¹⁰He teaches your precepts to Jacob
    and your law to Israel.
He offers incense before you
    and whole burnt offerings on your altar.
¹¹Bless all his skills, Lord,
    and be pleased with the work of his hands.
Strike down those who rise against him,
    his foes till they rise no more."

¹²About Benjamin he said:

"Let the beloved of the Lord rest secure in him,
    for he shields him all day long,
    and the one the Lord loves rests between his shoulders."

¹³About Joseph he said:

"May the Lord bless his land
    with the precious dew from heaven above
    and with the deep waters that lie below;

---

a 2 Or *from*   *b* 2 The meaning of the Hebrew for this phrase is uncertain.   *c* 5 *Jeshurun* means *the upright one,* that is, Israel; also in verse 26.   *d* 6 Or *but let*

¹⁴with the best the sun brings forth
and the finest the moon can yield;
¹⁵with the choicest gifts of the ancient mountains
and the fruitfulness of the everlasting hills;
¹⁶with the best gifts of the earth and its fullness
and the favor of him who dwelt in the burning bush.
Let all these rest on the head of Joseph,
on the brow of the prince among*ᵃ* his brothers.
¹⁷In majesty he is like a firstborn bull;
his horns are the horns of a wild ox.
With them he will gore the nations,
even those at the ends of the earth.
Such are the ten thousands of Ephraim;
such are the thousands of Manasseh."

¹⁸About Zebulun he said:

"Rejoice, Zebulun, in your going out,
and you, Issachar, in your tents.
¹⁹They will summon peoples to the mountain
and there offer the sacrifices of the righteous;
they will feast on the abundance of the seas,
on the treasures hidden in the sand."

²⁰About Gad he said:

"Blessed is he who enlarges Gad's domain!
Gad lives there like a lion,
tearing at arm or head.
²¹He chose the best land for himself;
the leader's portion was kept for him.
When the heads of the people assembled,
he carried out the LORD's righteous will,
and his judgments concerning Israel."

²²About Dan he said:

"Dan is a lion's cub,
springing out of Bashan."

²³About Naphtali he said:

"Naphtali is abounding with the favor of the LORD
and is full of his blessing;
he will inherit southward to the lake."

²⁴About Asher he said:

"Most blessed of sons is Asher;
let him be favored by his brothers,
and let him bathe his feet in oil.
²⁵The bolts of your gates will be iron and bronze,
and your strength will equal your days.

²⁶"There is no one like the God of Jeshurun,
who rides on the heavens to help you

ᵃ 16 Or *of the one separated from*

and on the clouds in his majesty.
²⁷The eternal God is your refuge,
    and underneath are the everlasting arms.
He will drive out your enemies before you,
    saying, 'Destroy them!'
²⁸So Israel will live in safety;
    Jacob will dwell*a* secure
in a land of grain and new wine,
    where the heavens drop dew.
²⁹Blessed are you, Israel!
    Who is like you,
a people saved by the LORD?
He is your shield and helper
    and your glorious sword.
Your enemies will cower before you,
    and you will tread on their heights."

The Death of Moses

34 Then Moses climbed Mount Nebo from the plains of Moab to the top of Pisgah, across from Jericho. There the LORD showed him the whole land—from Gilead to Dan, ²all of Naphtali, the territory of Ephraim and Manasseh, all the land of Judah as far as the Mediterranean Sea, ³the Negev and the whole region from the Valley of Jericho, the City of Palms, as far as Zoar. ⁴Then the LORD said to him, "This is the land I promised on oath to Abraham, Isaac and Jacob when I said, 'I will give it to your descendants.' I have let you see it with your eyes, but you will not cross over into it."

⁵And Moses the servant of the LORD died there in Moab, as the LORD had said. ⁶He buried him*b* in Moab, in the valley opposite Beth Peor, but to this day no one knows where his grave is. ⁷Moses was a hundred and twenty years old when he died, yet his eyes were not weak nor his strength gone. ⁸The Israelites grieved for Moses in the plains of Moab thirty days, until the time of weeping and mourning was over.

⁹Now Joshua son of Nun was filled with the spirit*c* of wisdom because Moses had laid his hands on him. So the Israelites listened to him and did what the LORD had commanded Moses.

¹⁰Since then, no prophet has risen in Israel like Moses, whom the LORD knew face to face, ¹¹who did all those signs and wonders the LORD sent him to do in Egypt—to Pharaoh and to all his officials and to his whole land. ¹²For no one has ever shown the mighty power or performed the awesome deeds that Moses did in the sight of all Israel.

270	302	334	342	381
JOSHUA	JUDGES	RUTH	1 SAMUEL	2 SAMUEL

419	459	498	546	591
1 KINGS	2 KINGS	1 CHRONICLES	2 CHRONICLES	EZRA

607	627
NEHEMIAH	ESTHER

the his
of isra

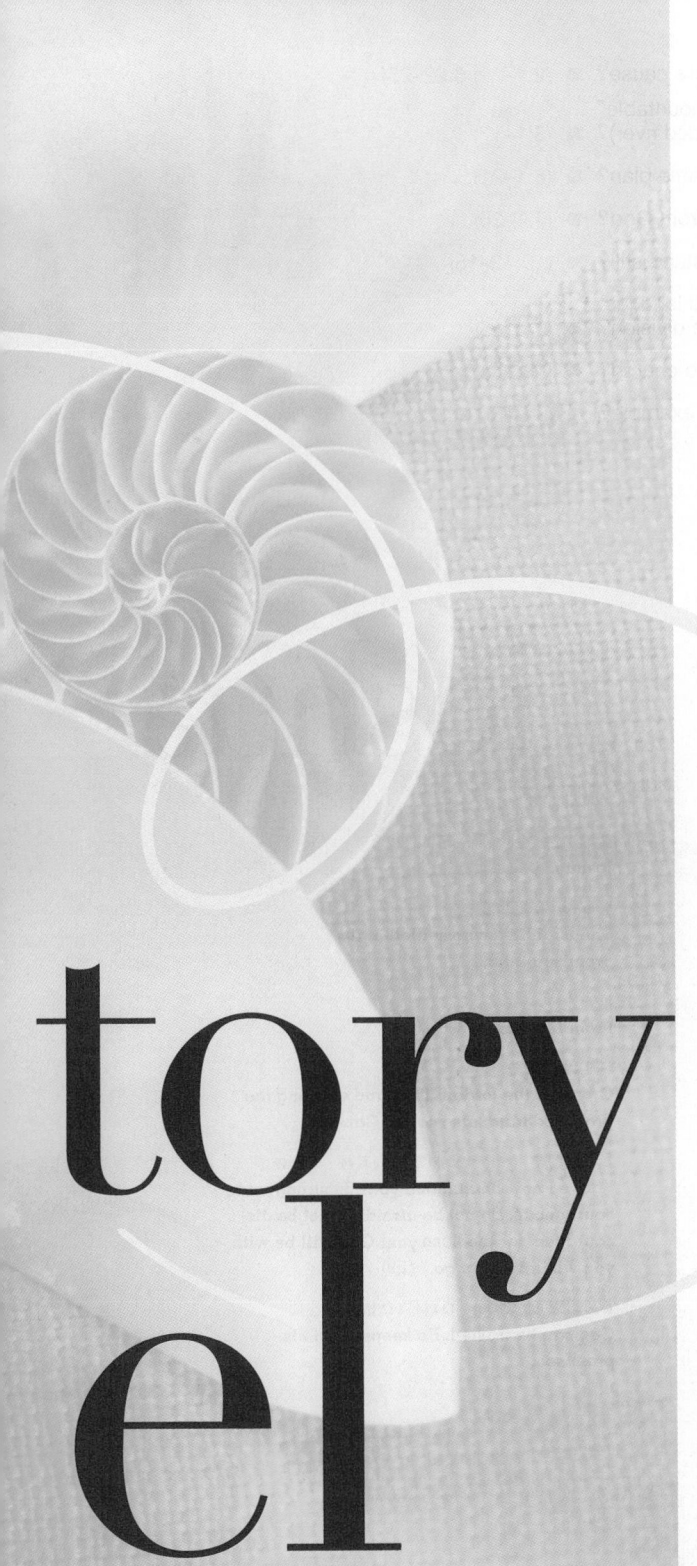

The History books of Israel are considered as two groups. The first group is comprised of Joshua through Kings. The pairs of 1 and 2 Samuel and 1 and 2 Kings were each originally a single book, so the five "books" of Joshua, Judges, Ruth, Samuel and Kings form a set that mirrors the five books of Moses. These texts, also known as the Former Prophets, relate the story of the Israelite journey from Egypt to take possession of the promised land and the events that followed.

The second group of books, Chronicles through Esther, is part of the Old Testament canon known as the Writings (the third and final major division of the Old Testament, along with the Law and the Prophets). These five books are prose texts and relate various narratives of the big events of the history of Israel.

tory
el

joshua

AUTHOR
Joshua.

AUDIENCE
The Israelites who settled in the promised land.

DATE
Probably about 1390 B.C.

SETTING
Crossing the Jordan River and entering the promised land, also called Canaan.

VERSE TO REMEMBER
"Have I not commanded you? Be strong and courageous. Do not be afraid; do not be discouraged, for the LORD your God will be with you wherever you go." (1:9)

THEME TO CONSIDER
God can be trusted. He keeps all of his promises.

The LORD Commands Joshua

1 After the death of Moses the servant of the LORD, the LORD said to Joshua son of Nun, Moses' aide: ²"Moses my servant is dead. Now then, you and all these people, get ready to cross the Jordan River into the land I am about to give to them—to the Israelites. ³I will give you every place where you set your foot, as I promised Moses. ⁴Your territory will extend from the desert to Lebanon, and from the great river, the Euphrates—all the Hittite country—to the Mediterranean Sea in the west. ⁵No one will be able to stand against you all the days of your life. As I was with Moses, so I will be with you; I will never leave you nor forsake you. ⁶Be strong and courageous, because you will lead these people to inherit the land I swore to their ancestors to give them.

⁷"Be strong and very courageous. Be careful to obey all the law my servant Moses gave you; do not turn from it to the right or to the left, that you may be successful wherever you go. ⁸Keep this Book of the Law always on your lips; meditate on it day and night, so that you may be careful to do everything written in it. Then you will be prosperous and successful. ⁹Have I not commanded you? Be strong and courageous. Do not be afraid; do not be discouraged, for the LORD your God will be with you wherever you go."

¹⁰So Joshua ordered the officers of the people: ¹¹"Go through the camp and tell the people, 'Get your provisions ready. Three days from now you will cross the Jordan here to go in and take possession of the land the LORD your God is giving you for your own.'"

¹²But to the Reubenites, the Gadites and the half-tribe of Manasseh, Joshua said, ¹³"Remember the command that Moses the servant of the LORD gave you after he said, 'The LORD your God will give you rest by giving you this land.' ¹⁴Your wives, your children and your livestock may stay in the land that Moses gave you east of the Jordan, but all your fighting men, ready for battle, must cross over ahead of the other Israelites. You are to help them ¹⁵until the LORD gives them rest, as he has done for you, and until they too have taken possession of the land that the LORD your God is giving them. After that, you may go back and occupy your own land, which Moses the servant of the LORD gave you east of the Jordan toward the sunrise."

¹⁶Then they answered Joshua, "Whatever you have commanded us we will do, and wherever you send us we will go. ¹⁷Just as we fully obeyed Moses, so we will obey you. Only may the LORD your God be with you as he was with Moses. ¹⁸Whoever rebels against your word and does not obey it, whatever you may command them, is to be put to death. Only be strong and courageous!"

Rahab and the Spies

2 Then Joshua son of Nun secretly sent two spies from Shittim. "Go, look over the land," he said, "especially Jericho." So they went and entered the house of a prostitute named Rahab and stayed there.

²The king of Jericho was told, "Look! Some of the Israelites have come here tonight to spy out the land." ³So the king of Jericho sent this message to Rahab: "Bring out the men who came to you and entered your house, because they have come to spy out the whole land."

⁴But the woman had taken the two men and hidden them. She said, "Yes, the men came to me, but I did not know where they had come from. ⁵At dusk, when it was time to close the city gate, they left. I don't know which way they went. Go after them quickly. You may catch up with them." ⁶(But she had taken them up to the roof and hidden them under the stalks of flax she had laid out on the roof.) ⁷So the men set out in pursuit of the spies on the road that leads to the fords of the Jordan, and as soon as the pursuers had gone out, the gate was shut.

---

atissue:success

1:7–8 To succeed at any task, you must have the proper tools. Success in changing a tire requires such things as a tire iron and a jack. Success in quilting requires needles and fabric. Without the right equipment, you're left empty-handed and guessing. These verses tell us that success in life requires one important tool—God's Word. It's not enough to *own* a copy of God's Word. You have to *use* it—read it, meditate on it, talk about it and obey it. God has given you all you need to succeed in life—if you'll use the tools he's given you.

271

⁸Before the spies lay down for the night, she went up on the roof ⁹and said to them, "I know that the LORD has given this land to you and that a great fear of you has fallen on us, so that all who live in this country are melting in fear because of you. ¹⁰We have heard how the LORD dried up the water of the Red Sea*ᵃ* for you when you came out of Egypt, and what you did to Sihon and Og, the two kings of the Amorites east of the Jordan, whom you completely destroyed.*ᵇ* ¹¹When we heard of it, our hearts melted in fear and everyone's courage failed because of you, for the LORD your God is God in heaven above and on the earth below.

¹²"Now then, please swear to me by the LORD that you will show kindness to my family, because I have shown kindness to you. Give me a sure sign ¹³that you will spare the lives of my father and mother, my brothers and sisters, and all who belong to them—and that you will save us from death."

¹⁴"Our lives for your lives!" the men assured her. "If you don't tell what we are doing, we will treat you kindly and faithfully when the LORD gives us the land."

¹⁵So she let them down by a rope through the window, for the house she lived in was part of the city wall. ¹⁶She said to them, "Go to the hills so the pursuers will not find you. Hide yourselves there three days until they return, and then go on your way."

¹⁷Now the men had said to her, "This oath you made us swear will not be binding on us ¹⁸unless, when we enter the land, you have tied this scarlet cord in the window through which you let us down, and unless you have brought your father and mother, your brothers and all your family into your house. ¹⁹If any of them go outside your house into the street, their blood will be on their own heads; we will not be responsible. As for those who are in the house with you, their blood will be on our head if a hand is laid on them. ²⁰But if you tell what we are doing, we will be released from the oath you made us swear."

²¹"Agreed," she replied. "Let it be as you say." So she sent them away, and they departed. And she tied the scarlet cord in the window.

²²When they left, they went into the hills and stayed there three days, until the pursuers had searched all along the road and returned without finding them. ²³Then the two men started back. They went down out of the hills, forded the river and came to Joshua son of Nun and told him everything that had happened to them. ²⁴They said to Joshua, "The LORD has surely given the whole land into our hands; all the people are melting in fear because of us."

atissue:risk

2:1–24 Great risks require great risk-takers. Rarely will we take risks unless we're certain that they're worth it. Rahab was willing to endanger her life because she knew the risk was worth it. She knew God was on Israel's side, and she wanted to align herself with him at any cost. In the end, her risky faith saved her life and the lives of her entire family (see 6:22–23). God doesn't fail to give us opportunities to take on challenges. Our problem is that we often fail to accept his terms. If there's something God wants you to do—do it! God will take you to the very edge of your faith if you'll let him.

Crossing the Jordan

3 Early in the morning Joshua and all the Israelites set out from Shittim and went to the Jordan, where they camped before crossing over. ²After three days the officers went throughout the camp, ³giving orders to the people: "When you see the ark of the covenant of the LORD your God, and the Levitical priests carrying it, you are to move out from your positions and follow it. ⁴Then you will know which way to go, since you have never been this way before. But keep a distance of about two thousand cubits*ᶜ* between you and the ark; do not go near it."

⁵Joshua told the people, "Consecrate yourselves, for tomorrow the LORD will do amazing things among you."

ᵃ 10 Or the Sea of Reeds   *ᵇ 10 The Hebrew term refers to the irrevocable giving over of things or persons to the LORD, often by totally destroying them.*
ᶜ 4 That is, about 3,000 feet or about 900 meters

⁶Joshua said to the priests, "Take up the ark of the covenant and pass on ahead of the people." So they took it up and went ahead of them.

⁷And the Lord said to Joshua, "Today I will begin to exalt you in the eyes of all Israel, so they may know that I am with you as I was with Moses. ⁸Tell the priests who carry the ark of the covenant: 'When you reach the edge of the Jordan's waters, go and stand in the river.'"

⁹Joshua said to the Israelites, "Come here and listen to the words of the Lord your God. ¹⁰This is how you will know that the living God is among you and that he will certainly drive out before you the Canaanites, Hittites, Hivites, Perizzites, Girgashites, Amorites and Jebusites. ¹¹See, the ark of the covenant of the Lord of all the earth will go into the Jordan ahead of you. ¹²Now then, choose twelve men from the tribes of Israel, one from each tribe. ¹³And as soon as the priests who carry the ark of the Lord—the Lord of all the earth—set foot in the Jordan, its waters flowing downstream will be cut off and stand up in a heap."

HE IS: ahead of you

3:11 Joshua told the people to follow the visible representation of God (the ark) into the promised land. "The ark of the covenant of the Lord of all the earth will go into the Jordan ahead of you." The Israelites realized that God was leading them when they saw the ark ahead of them.

Don't allow yourself to get ahead of God. He wants to lead you every step of the way. While you can't follow something tangible like the ark, you can let the living Word be your guide by reading the Bible. That way you'll know that God is *in* you and *ahead of you.*

For the next He Is, go to p. 282.

273

¹⁴So when the people broke camp to cross the Jordan, the priests carrying the ark of the covenant went ahead of them. ¹⁵Now the Jordan is at flood stage all during harvest. Yet as soon as the priests who carried the ark reached the Jordan and their feet touched the water's edge, ¹⁶the water from upstream stopped flowing. It piled up in a heap a great distance away, at a town called Adam in the vicinity of Zarethan, while the water flowing down to the Sea of the Arabah (that is, the Dead Sea) was completely cut off. So the people crossed over opposite Jericho. ¹⁷The priests who carried the ark of the covenant of the Lord stopped in the middle of the Jordan and stood on dry ground, while all Israel passed by until the whole nation had completed the crossing on dry ground.

4 When the whole nation had finished crossing the Jordan, the Lord said to Joshua, ²"Choose twelve men from among the people, one from each tribe, ³and tell them to take up twelve stones from the middle of the Jordan, from right where the priests are standing, and carry them over with you and put them down at the place where you stay tonight."

⁴So Joshua called together the twelve men he had appointed from the Israelites, one from each tribe, ⁵and said to them, "Go over before the ark of the Lord your God into the middle of the Jordan. Each of you is to take up a stone on his shoulder, according to the number of the tribes of the Israelites, ⁶to serve as a sign among you. In the future, when your children ask you, 'What do these stones mean?' ⁷tell them that the flow of the Jordan was cut off before the ark of the covenant of the Lord. When it crossed the Jordan, the waters of the Jordan were cut off. These stones are to be a memorial to the people of Israel forever."

⁸So the Israelites did as Joshua commanded them. They took twelve stones from the middle of the Jordan, according to the number of the tribes of the Israelites, as the Lord had told Joshua; and they carried them over with them to their camp, where they put them down. ⁹Joshua set up the twelve stones that had been*a* in the middle of the Jordan at the spot where the priests who carried the ark of the covenant had stood. And they are there to this day.

---

a 9 Or Joshua also set up twelve stones

¹⁰Now the priests who carried the ark remained standing in the middle of the Jordan until everything the LORD had commanded Joshua was done by the people, just as Moses had directed Joshua. The people hurried over, ¹¹and as soon as all of them had crossed, the ark of the LORD and the priests came to the other side while the people watched. ¹²The men of Reuben, Gad and the half-tribe of Manasseh crossed over, ready for battle, in front of the Israelites, as Moses had directed them. ¹³About forty thousand armed for battle crossed over before the LORD to the plains of Jericho for war.

¹⁴That day the LORD exalted Joshua in the sight of all Israel; and they stood in awe of him all the days of his life, just as they had stood in awe of Moses.

¹⁵Then the LORD said to Joshua, ¹⁶"Command the priests carrying the ark of the covenant law to come up out of the Jordan."

¹⁷So Joshua commanded the priests, "Come up out of the Jordan."

¹⁸And the priests came up out of the river carrying the ark of the covenant of the LORD. No sooner had they set their feet on the dry ground than the waters of the Jordan returned to their place and ran at flood stage as before.

¹⁹On the tenth day of the first month the people went up from the Jordan and camped at Gilgal on the eastern border of Jericho. ²⁰And Joshua set up at Gilgal the twelve stones they had taken out of the Jordan. ²¹He said to the Israelites, "In the future when your descendants ask their parents, 'What do these stones mean?' ²²tell them, 'Israel crossed the Jordan on dry ground.' ²³For the LORD your God dried up the Jordan before you until you had crossed over. The LORD your God did to the Jordan what he had done to the Red Sea^a when he dried it up before us until we had crossed over. ²⁴He did this so that all the peoples of the earth might know that the hand of the LORD is powerful and so that you might always fear the LORD your God."

5 Now when all the Amorite kings west of the Jordan and all the Canaanite kings along the coast heard how the LORD had dried up the Jordan before the Israelites until they^b had crossed over, their hearts melted in fear and they no longer had the courage to face the Israelites.

Circumcision and Passover at Gilgal

²At that time the LORD said to Joshua, "Make flint knives and circumcise the Israelites again." ³So Joshua made flint knives and circumcised the Israelites at Gibeath Haaraloth.^c

⁴Now this is why he did so: All those who came out of Egypt—all the men of military age—died in the wilderness on the way after leaving Egypt. ⁵All the people that came out had been circumcised, but all the people born in the wilderness during the journey from Egypt had not. ⁶The Israelites had moved about in the wilderness forty years until all the men who were of military age when they left Egypt had died, since they had not obeyed the LORD. For the LORD had sworn to them that they would not see the land that he had solemnly promised their ancestors to give us, a land flowing with milk and honey. ⁷So he raised up their sons in their place, and these were the ones Joshua circumcised. They were still uncircumcised because they had not been circumcised on the way. ⁸And after the whole nation had been circumcised, they remained where they were in camp until they were healed.

⁹Then the LORD said to Joshua, "Today I have rolled away the reproach of Egypt from you." So the place has been called Gilgal^d to this day.

¹⁰On the evening of the fourteenth day of the month, while camped at Gilgal on the plains of Jericho, the Israelites celebrated the Passover. ¹¹The day after the Passover, that very day, they ate some of the produce of the land: unleavened bread and roasted grain. ¹²The manna stopped the day after^e they ate this food from the land; there was no longer any manna for the Israelites, but that year they ate of the produce of Canaan.

The Fall of Jericho

¹³Now when Joshua was near Jericho, he looked up and saw a man standing in front of him with a drawn sword in his hand. Joshua went up to him and asked, "Are you for us or for our enemies?"

^a 23 Or the Sea of Reeds ^b 1 Another textual tradition we ^c 3 Gibeath Haaraloth means the hill of foreskins. ^d 9 Gilgal sounds like the Hebrew for roll.
^e 12 Or the day

¹⁴"Neither," he replied, "but as commander of the army of the Lord I have now come." Then Joshua fell facedown to the ground in reverence, and asked him, "What message does my Lord*ᵃ* have for his servant?"

¹⁵The commander of the Lord's army replied, "Take off your sandals, for the place where you are standing is holy." And Joshua did so.

6 Now the gates of Jericho were securely barred because of the Israelites. No one went out and no one came in.

²Then the Lord said to Joshua, "See, I have delivered Jericho into your hands, along with its king and its fighting men. ³March around the city once with all the armed men. Do this for six days. ⁴Have seven priests carry trumpets of rams' horns in front of the ark. On the seventh day, march around the city seven times, with the priests blowing the trumpets. ⁵When you hear them sound a long blast on the trumpets, have the whole army give a loud shout; then the wall of the city will collapse and the army will go up, everyone straight in."

⁶So Joshua son of Nun called the priests and said to them, "Take up the ark of the covenant of the Lord and have seven priests carry trumpets in front of it." ⁷And he ordered the army, "Advance! March around the city, with an armed guard going ahead of the ark of the Lord."

⁸When Joshua had spoken to the people, the seven priests carrying the seven trumpets before the Lord went forward, blowing their trumpets, and the ark of the Lord's covenant followed them. ⁹The armed guard marched ahead of the priests who blew the trumpets, and the rear guard followed the ark. All this time the trumpets were sounding. ¹⁰But Joshua had commanded the army, "Do not give a war cry, do not raise your voices, do not say a word until the day I tell you to shout. Then shout!" ¹¹So he had the ark of the Lord carried around the city, circling it once. Then the army returned to camp and spent the night there.

¹²Joshua got up early the next morning and the priests took up the ark of the Lord. ¹³The seven priests carrying the seven trumpets went forward, marching before the ark of the Lord and blowing the trumpets. The armed men went ahead of them and the rear guard followed the ark of the Lord, while the trumpets kept sounding. ¹⁴So on the second day they marched around the city once and returned to the camp. They did this for six days.

¹⁵On the seventh day, they got up at daybreak and marched around the city seven times in the same manner, except that on that day they circled the city seven times. ¹⁶The seventh time around, when the priests sounded the trumpet blast, Joshua commanded the army, "Shout! For the Lord has given you the city! ¹⁷The city and all that is in it

---

atissue: God's power

5:13–15 Whose side is God on? When you're in a conflict with someone—is God on your side? When you're competing for a promotion—is God on your side? When you're fighting wrongful charges on your cell phone bill—is God on your side? Actually, when Joshua asked the commander of the army of the Lord whose side he was on, he got a cryptic reply: "Neither." The question isn't whether God's on our side, but whether we're on *God's* side. God was ready to do something great through Joshua, but Joshua's first battle action was to bow and acknowledge that *God* was the one in authority. After he did, the walls of Jericho fell without a single blow.

275

"conversations"

winning «» 6:12–21

1 » Is it OK for Christians to love to win?

2 » What should be your attitude when you win?

3 » Why do Christians also lose?

For more on **winning**, check the index. For the next Conversations, go to p. 277.

---

are to be devoted[a] to the Lord. Only Rahab the prostitute and all who are with her in her house shall be spared, because she hid the spies we sent. [18]But keep away from the devoted things, so that you will not bring about your own destruction by taking any of them. Otherwise you will make the camp of Israel liable to destruction and bring trouble on it. [19]All the silver and gold and the articles of bronze and iron are sacred to the Lord and must go into his treasury."

[20]When the trumpets sounded, the army shouted, and at the sound of the trumpet, when the men gave a loud shout, the wall collapsed; so everyone charged straight in, and they took the city. [21]They devoted the city to the Lord and destroyed with the sword every living thing in it—men and women, young and old, cattle, sheep and donkeys.

[22]Joshua said to the two men who had spied out the land, "Go into the prostitute's house and bring her out and all who belong to her, in accordance with your oath to her." [23]So the young men who had done the spying went in and brought out Rahab, her father and mother, her brothers and sisters and all who belonged to her. They brought out her entire family and put them in a place outside the camp of Israel.

[24]Then they burned the whole city and everything in it, but they put the silver and gold and the articles of bronze and iron into the treasury of the Lord's house. [25]But Joshua spared Rahab the prostitute, with her family and all who belonged to her, because she hid the men Joshua had sent as spies to Jericho—and she lives among the Israelites to this day.

[26]At that time Joshua pronounced this solemn oath: "Cursed before the Lord is anyone who undertakes to rebuild this city, Jericho:

> "At the cost of his firstborn son
> he will lay its foundations;
> at the cost of his youngest
> he will set up its gates."

[27]So the Lord was with Joshua, and his fame spread throughout the land.

Achan's Sin

7 But the Israelites were unfaithful in regard to the devoted things[b]; Achan son of Karmi, the son of Zimri,[c] the son of Zerah, of the tribe of Judah, took some of them. So the Lord's anger burned against Israel.

[2]Now Joshua sent men from Jericho to Ai,[d] which is near Beth Aven to the east of Bethel, and told them, "Go up and spy out the region." So the men went up and spied out Ai.

[3]When they returned to Joshua, they said, "Not all the army will have to go up against Ai. Send two or three thousand men to take it and do not weary the whole army, for only a few people live there." [4]So about three thousand went up; but they were routed by the men of Ai, [5]who killed about thirty-six of them. They chased the Israelites from the city gate as far as the stone quarries and struck them down on the slopes. At this the hearts of the people melted in fear and became like water.

[6]Then Joshua tore his clothes and fell facedown to the ground before the ark of the Lord, remaining there till evening. The elders of Israel did the same, and sprinkled dust on their heads. [7]And Joshua said, "Ah, Sovereign Lord, why did you ever bring this people across the Jordan to deliver us into the hands of the Amorites to destroy us? If only we had been content to stay on the other side of the Jordan! [8]Pardon your servant, Lord. What can I say, now that Israel has been routed by its enemies? [9]The Canaanites and the other people of the country will hear about this and they will surround us and wipe out our name from the earth. What then will you do for your own great name?"

[10]The Lord said to Joshua, "Stand up! What are you doing down on your face? [11]Israel has sinned; they have violated my covenant, which I commanded them to keep. They have taken some of the devoted things; they have stolen, they have lied, they have put them with their own possessions. [12]That is why the Israelites cannot stand against their enemies; they turn their backs and run because they have been

---

[a] 17 The Hebrew term refers to the irrevocable giving over of things or persons to the Lord, often by totally destroying them; also in verses 18 and 21.
[b] 1 The Hebrew term refers to the irrevocable giving over of things or persons to the Lord, often by totally destroying them; also in verses 11, 12, 13 and 15.
[c] 1 See Septuagint and 1 Chron. 2:6; Hebrew Zabdi; also in verses 17 and 18.   [d] 2 Ai means the ruin.

made liable to destruction. I will not be with you anymore unless you destroy whatever among you is devoted to destruction.

¹³"Go, consecrate the people. Tell them, 'Consecrate yourselves in preparation for tomorrow; for this is what the LORD, the God of Israel, says: There are devoted things among you, Israel. You cannot stand against your enemies until you remove them.

¹⁴"'In the morning, present yourselves tribe by tribe. The tribe that the LORD chooses shall come forward clan by clan; the clan that the LORD chooses shall come forward family by family; and the family that the LORD chooses shall come forward man by man. ¹⁵Whoever is caught with the devoted things shall be destroyed by fire, along with all that belongs to him. He has violated the covenant of the LORD and has done an outrageous thing in Israel!'"

¹⁶Early the next morning Joshua had Israel come forward by tribes, and Judah was chosen. ¹⁷The clans of Judah came forward, and the Zerahites were chosen. He had the clan of the Zerahites come forward by families, and Zimri was chosen. ¹⁸Joshua had his family come forward man by man, and Achan son of Karmi, the son of Zimri, the son of Zerah, of the tribe of Judah, was chosen.

¹⁹Then Joshua said to Achan, "My son, give glory to the LORD, the God of Israel, and honor him. Tell me what you have done; do not hide it from me."

²⁰Achan replied, "It is true! I have sinned against the LORD, the God of Israel. This is what I have done: ²¹When I saw in the plunder a beautiful robe from Babylonia,ᵃ two hundred shekelsᵇ of silver and a bar of gold weighing fifty shekels,ᶜ I coveted them and took them. They are hidden in the ground inside my tent, with the silver underneath."

²²So Joshua sent messengers, and they ran to the tent, and there it was, hidden in his tent, with the silver underneath. ²³They took the things from the tent, brought them to Joshua and all the Israelites and spread them out before the LORD.

²⁴Then Joshua, together with all Israel, took Achan son of Zerah, the silver, the robe, the gold bar, his sons and daughters, his cattle, donkeys and sheep, his tent and all that he had, to the Valley of Achor. ²⁵Joshua said, "Why have you brought this trouble on us? The LORD will bring trouble on you today."

Then all Israel stoned him, and after they had stoned the rest, they burned them. ²⁶Over Achan they heaped up a large pile of rocks, which remains to this day. Then the LORD turned from his fierce anger. Therefore that place has been called the Valley of Achorᵈ ever since.

conversations

materialism «» 7:1–21

1 ›› How materialistic do you think you are?

2 ›› What feeds materialistic desires?

3 ›› What are the consequences of materialism?

For more on **materialism**, check the index.
For the next Conversations, go to p. 281.

Ai Destroyed

8 Then the LORD said to Joshua, "Do not be afraid; do not be discouraged. Take the whole army with you, and go up and attack Ai. For I have delivered into your hands the king of Ai, his people, his city and his land. ²You shall do to Ai and its king as you did to Jericho and its king, except that you may carry off their plunder and livestock for yourselves. Set an ambush behind the city."

³So Joshua and the whole army moved out to attack Ai. He chose thirty thousand of his best fighting men and sent them out at night ⁴with these orders: "Listen carefully. You are to set an ambush behind the city. Don't go very far from it. All of you be on the alert. ⁵I and all those with me will advance on the city, and when the men come out against us, as they did before, we will flee from them. ⁶They will pursue us until we have lured them away from the city, for they will say, 'They are running away from us as they did before.' So when we flee from them, ⁷you are to rise up from ambush and take the city. The LORD your God will give it into your hand. ⁸When you have taken the city, set it on fire. Do what the LORD has commanded. See to it; you have my orders."

277

ᵃ 21 Hebrew *Shinar*   ᵇ 21 That is, about 5 pounds or about 2.3 kilograms   ᶜ 21 That is, about 1 1/4 pounds or about 575 grams   ᵈ 26 Achor means *trouble.*

myth# 19 "I'VE GOT TO HAVE THOSE SHOES."

I shop, therefore I am.

Sling-backs. Strappy platforms. And my to-die-for Manolo Blahniks. If it's splashed across Elle or Cosmo in neon pink, 72-point headlines, I want it. Six Sizzling Party Looks. What's Hot Now. Flirty Florals. I've been through enough after-dark fashion emergencies to know how difficult it is to find the right outfit for a sudden invitation to a friend's holiday bash or the boss's last-minute cocktail party if a girl's caught unprepared. That's why impulse buying is not an entirely bad thing. Whether it's out with the girls or out on a date, women want to be ready and look good. (And you clearly can't wear the same category of outfit for a movie date, a dinner and dancing date and a meet-the-parents date.) If I had a dime for every party dress I picked up "just in case," well, I'd have enough money to put toward that cute little Prada tote I saw last week.

I've heard all the money-saving tips before. And I admit I may have too many things in my closet already, but I'm tired of those dated outfits. Waiting until the end-of-season sales to save money and taper my purchases sounds good, but wading through circular racks of last season's castoffs is just not appealing.

I'm not saying the meaning of life can be reduced to knowing how to wear a peasant blouse, the top ten places to wear a sarong or the finesse required to pull off knee-high boots on casual Friday. However, women who have harnessed the mood-altering power of purchasing a bit of boho cashmere as a little pick-me-up know what I'm talking about. When I've had a hard week, buying something in the guilty pleasures category is the only consolation that puts me in a good mood for the weekend. And buying something at a two-for-one sale is almost like making money, right?

—Patty

ELLE. COSMO. INSTYLE.

They're not to blame for our materialistic culture. They've just learned to capitalize on our vulnerabilities—those less closely guarded areas of our lives where, like Achan (see Joshua 7), we often succumb to peer pressure, impulse, desire and pride.

There's nothing wrong with scooping up some key pieces to make "endless ensembles" or nabbing a new handbag to "achieve a fabulous look." We're talking about balance. Control. Being good to yourself by avoiding the underside of greed—depression over debt, interpersonal conflicts, overspending, overindulgence, the inability to give generously to others, impatience and envy, just to name a few.

We all like to feel the rush of getting something new, but isn't it time for the material girl inside each of us to grow up? The one who goes shopping for retail therapy when she's depressed. The one who spontaneously makes purchases but feels the inevitable emotional crash soon afterward. The one who is never satisfied with what she has—only with what someone else has.

Materialism overrides our good intentions and laughs at our sworn promises to cut back. It only responds to practical measures that take the control over our desires out of our hands and put it in the hands of someone else—namely, Jesus. (Although accountability with friends and family can be a part of the maturing process.) Try these rules on for size:

- Before you buy, ask yourself: *What's driving this impulse?* Are you trying to find satisfaction in things, though deep down you know they will never satisfy you?

- Walk away from what appears to be a must-have purchase, and give yourself a mandatory 36-hour waiting period—even if it's on sale.

- Think through the ramifications of major purchases on your budget.

- If you don't have a budget, make one and stick to it.

- Think first. Detox from the euphoric feeling of what it would be like to wear that new outfit, work out on that at-home exercise machine or drive to work in that new car, and think through your decision.

No, following this advice is not as fun . . . in the short-term. Long-term, however, you'll be amazed at how much more content you are with yourself.

279

"Studies estimate that as many as 17 million Americans, better than 1 in 20 of us, can't control our urge to shop, even at the expense of our job, our marriage, our family and our finances."

"THEN HE SAID TO THEM, 'WATCH OUT! BE ON YOUR GUARD AGAINST ALL KINDS OF GREED; LIFE DOES NOT CONSIST IN AN ABUNDANCE OF POSSESSIONS.'"

LUKE 12:15

SEE ALSO

1 Corinthians 5:11
Philippians 4:10–12
1 Timothy 6:6–8,17

For more on **Materialism**, check the index.

⁹Then Joshua sent them off, and they went to the place of ambush and lay in wait between Bethel and Ai, to the west of Ai—but Joshua spent that night with the people.

¹⁰Early the next morning Joshua mustered his army, and he and the leaders of Israel marched before them to Ai. ¹¹The entire force that was with him marched up and approached the city and arrived in front of it. They set up camp north of Ai, with the valley between them and the city. ¹²Joshua had taken about five thousand men and set them in ambush between Bethel and Ai, to the west of the city. ¹³So the soldiers took up their positions—with the main camp to the north of the city and the ambush to the west of it. That night Joshua went into the valley.

¹⁴When the king of Ai saw this, he and all the men of the city hurried out early in the morning to meet Israel in battle at a certain place overlooking the Arabah. But he did not know that an ambush had been set against him behind the city. ¹⁵Joshua and all Israel let themselves be driven back before them, and they fled toward the wilderness. ¹⁶All the men of Ai were called to pursue them, and they pursued Joshua and were lured away from the city. ¹⁷Not a man remained in Ai or Bethel who did not go after Israel. They left the city open and went in pursuit of Israel.

¹⁸Then the Lord said to Joshua, "Hold out toward Ai the javelin that is in your hand, for into your hand I will deliver the city." So Joshua held out toward the city the javelin that was in his hand. ¹⁹As soon as he did this, the men in the ambush rose quickly from their position and rushed forward. They entered the city and captured it and quickly set it on fire.

²⁰The men of Ai looked back and saw the smoke of the city rising against the sky, but they had no chance to escape in any direction; the Israelites who had been fleeing toward the wilderness had turned back against their pursuers. ²¹For when Joshua and all Israel saw that the ambush had taken the city and that smoke was going up from the city, they turned around and attacked the men of Ai. ²²Those in the ambush also came out of the city against them, so that they were caught in the middle, with Israelites on both sides. Israel cut them down, leaving them neither survivors nor fugitives. ²³But they took the king of Ai alive and brought him to Joshua.

²⁴When Israel had finished killing all the men of Ai in the fields and in the wilderness where they had chased them, and when every one of them had been put to the sword, all the Israelites returned to Ai and killed those who were in it. ²⁵Twelve thousand men and women fell that day—all the people of Ai. ²⁶For Joshua did not draw back the hand that held out his javelin until he had destroyed[a] all who lived in Ai. ²⁷But Israel did carry off for themselves the livestock and plunder of this city, as the Lord had instructed Joshua.

²⁸So Joshua burned Ai[b] and made it a permanent heap of ruins, a desolate place to this day. ²⁹He impaled the body of the king of Ai on a pole and left it there until evening. At sunset, Joshua ordered them to take the body from the pole and throw it down at the entrance of the city gate. And they raised a large pile of rocks over it, which remains to this day.

The Covenant Renewed at Mount Ebal

³⁰Then Joshua built on Mount Ebal an altar to the Lord, the God of Israel, ³¹as Moses the servant of the Lord had commanded the Israelites. He built it according to what is written in the Book of the Law of Moses—an altar of uncut stones, on which no iron tool had been used. On it they offered to the Lord burnt offerings and sacrificed fellowship offerings. ³²There, in the presence of the Israelites, Joshua copied on stones the law of Moses, which he had written. ³³All the Israelites, with their elders, officials and judges, were standing on both sides of the ark of the covenant of the Lord, facing the Levitical priests who carried it. Both the foreigners living among them and the native-born were there. Half of the people stood in front of Mount Gerizim and half of them in front of Mount Ebal, as Moses the servant of the Lord had formerly commanded when he gave instructions to bless the people of Israel.

³⁴Afterward, Joshua read all the words of the law—the blessings and the curses—just as it is written in the Book of the Law. ³⁵There was not a word of all that Moses had commanded that Joshua did not read to the whole assembly of Israel, including the women and children, and the foreigners who lived among them.

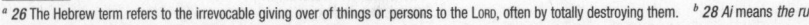

The Gibeonite Deception

9 Now when all the kings west of the Jordan heard about these things—those in the hill country, in the western foothills, and along the entire coast of the Mediterranean Sea as far as Lebanon (the kings of the Hittites, Amorites, Canaanites, Perizzites, Hivites and Jebusites)— ²they came together to make war against Joshua and Israel.

³However, when the people of Gibeon heard what Joshua had done to Jericho and Ai, ⁴they resorted to a ruse: They went as a delegation whose donkeys were loaded*a* with worn-out sacks and old wineskins, cracked and mended. ⁵They put worn and patched sandals on their feet and wore old clothes. All the bread of their food supply was dry and moldy. ⁶Then they went to Joshua in the camp at Gilgal and said to him and the Israelites, "We have come from a distant country; make a treaty with us."

⁷The Israelites said to the Hivites, "But perhaps you live near us, so how can we make a treaty with you?"

⁸"We are your servants," they said to Joshua.

But Joshua asked, "Who are you and where do you come from?"

⁹They answered: "Your servants have come from a very distant country because of the fame of the LORD your God. For we have heard reports of him: all that he did in Egypt, ¹⁰and all that he did to the two kings of the Amorites east of the Jordan—Sihon king of Heshbon, and Og king of Bashan, who reigned in Ashtaroth. ¹¹And our elders and all those living in our country said to us, 'Take provisions for your journey; go and meet them and say to them, "We are your servants; make a treaty with us."' ¹²This bread of ours was warm when we packed it at home on the day we left to come to you. But now see how dry and moldy it is. ¹³And these wineskins that we filled were new, but see how cracked they are. And our clothes and sandals are worn out by the very long journey."

¹⁴The Israelites sampled their provisions but did not inquire of the LORD. ¹⁵Then Joshua made a treaty of peace with them to let them live, and the leaders of the assembly ratified it by oath.

¹⁶Three days after they made the treaty with the Gibeonites, the Israelites heard that they were neighbors, living near them. ¹⁷So the Israelites set out and on the third day came to their cities: Gibeon, Kephirah, Beeroth and Kiriath Jearim. ¹⁸But the Israelites did not attack them, because the leaders of the assembly had sworn an oath to them by the LORD, the God of Israel.

The whole assembly grumbled against the leaders, ¹⁹but all the leaders answered, "We have given them our oath by the LORD, the God of Israel, and we cannot touch them now. ²⁰This is what we will do to them: We will let them live, so that God's wrath will not fall on us for breaking the oath we swore to them." ²¹They continued, "Let them live, but let them be woodcutters and water carriers for the entire community." So the leaders' promise to them was kept.

conversations

manipulation «» 9:1–14

1» Does the end ever justify the means? Is manipulation or stretching the truth always wrong?

2» How have you responded to being manipulated in the past?

3» Have you manipulated a situation for what you thought was a good outcome?

For more on **manipulation**, check the index.
For the next Conversations, go to p. 300.

²²Then Joshua summoned the Gibeonites and said, "Why did you deceive us by saying, 'We live a long way from you,' while actually you live near us? ²³You are now under a curse: You will never cease to serve as woodcutters and water carriers for the house of my God."

²⁴They answered Joshua, "Your servants were clearly told how the LORD your God had commanded his servant Moses to give you the whole land and to wipe out all its inhabitants from before you. So we feared for our lives because of you, and that is why we did this. ²⁵We are now in your hands. Do to us whatever seems good and right to you."

²⁶So Joshua saved them from the Israelites, and they did not kill them. ²⁷That day he made the Gibeonites woodcutters and water carriers for the community and for the altar of the LORD at the place the LORD would choose. And that is what they are to this day.

a 4 Most Hebrew manuscripts; some Hebrew manuscripts, Vulgate and Syriac (see also Septuagint) They prepared provisions and loaded their donkeys

joshua 10:1

The Sun Stands Still

10 Now Adoni-Zedek king of Jerusalem heard that Joshua had taken Ai and totally destroyed*a* it, doing to Ai and its king as he had done to Jericho and its king, and that the people of Gibeon had made a treaty of peace with Israel and had become their allies. ²He and his people were very much alarmed at this, because Gibeon was an important city, like one of the royal cities; it was larger than Ai, and all its men were good fighters. ³So Adoni-Zedek king of Jerusalem appealed to Hoham king of Hebron, Piram king of Jarmuth, Japhia king of Lachish and Debir king of Eglon. ⁴"Come up and help me attack Gibeon," he said, "because it has made peace with Joshua and the Israelites."

⁵Then the five kings of the Amorites—the kings of Jerusalem, Hebron, Jarmuth, Lachish and Eglon—joined forces. They moved up with all their troops and took up positions against Gibeon and attacked it.

⁶The Gibeonites then sent word to Joshua in the camp at Gilgal: "Do not abandon your servants. Come up to us quickly and save us! Help us, because all the Amorite kings from the hill country have joined forces against us."

⁷So Joshua marched up from Gilgal with his entire army, including all the best fighting men. ⁸The LORD said to Joshua, "Do not be afraid of them; I have given them into your hand. Not one of them will be able to withstand you."

⁹After an all-night march from Gilgal, Joshua took them by surprise. ¹⁰The LORD threw them into confusion before Israel, so Joshua and the Israelites defeated them completely at Gibeon. Israel pursued them along the road going up to Beth Horon and cut them down all the way to Azekah and Makkedah. ¹¹As they fled before Israel on the road down from Beth Horon to Azekah, the LORD hurled large hailstones down on them, and more of them died from the hail than were killed by the swords of the Israelites.

¹²On the day the LORD gave the Amorites over to Israel, Joshua said to the LORD in the presence of Israel:

> "Sun, stand still over Gibeon,
>   and you, moon, over the Valley of Aijalon."
> ¹³So the sun stood still,
>   and the moon stopped,
>   till the nation avenged itself on*b* its enemies,

as it is written in the Book of Jashar.

The sun stopped in the middle of the sky and delayed going down about a full day. ¹⁴There has never been a day like it before or since, a day when the LORD listened to a human being. Surely the LORD was fighting for Israel!

¹⁵Then Joshua returned with all Israel to the camp at Gilgal.

---

a 1 The Hebrew term refers to the irrevocable giving over of things or persons to the LORD, often by totally destroying them; also in verses 28, 35, 37, 39 and 40.
b 13 Or nation triumphed over

HE IS: over nature

10:12–14 The people of Israel were fiercely battling their enemies. The time was ripe for victory. All they needed was a few more hours of daylight. So Joshua asked God for the impossible, that the sun would stand still. Miraculously, it did! God proved without a doubt that he is *over nature*.

Life is so demanding that we could all use more hours in our day. When you're under a time crunch, use Joshua's tactics—pray. God may not make time stand still for you, but he can help you prioritize and spend your hours wisely. He can overcome your fatigue, your discouragement and your distractions.

For the next He Is, go to p. 294.

Five Amorite Kings Killed

[16]Now the five kings had fled and hidden in the cave at Makkedah. [17]When Joshua was told that the five kings had been found hiding in the cave at Makkedah, [18]he said, "Roll large rocks up to the mouth of the cave, and post some guards there. [19]But don't stop; pursue your enemies! Attack them from the rear and don't let them reach their cities, for the LORD your God has given them into your hand."

[20]So Joshua and the Israelites defeated them completely, but a few survivors managed to reach their fortified cities. [21]The whole army then returned safely to Joshua in the camp at Makkedah, and no one uttered a word against the Israelites.

[22]Joshua said, "Open the mouth of the cave and bring those five kings out to me." [23]So they brought the five kings out of the cave—the kings of Jerusalem, Hebron, Jarmuth, Lachish and Eglon. [24]When they had brought these kings to Joshua, he summoned all the men of Israel and said to the army commanders who had come with him, "Come here and put your feet on the necks of these kings." So they came forward and placed their feet on their necks.

[25]Joshua said to them, "Do not be afraid; do not be discouraged. Be strong and courageous. This is what the LORD will do to all the enemies you are going to fight." [26]Then Joshua put the kings to death and exposed their bodies on five poles, and they were left hanging on the poles until evening.

[27]At sunset Joshua gave the order and they took them down from the poles and threw them into the cave where they had been hiding. At the mouth of the cave they placed large rocks, which are there to this day.

283

Southern Cities Conquered

[28]That day Joshua took Makkedah. He put the city and its king to the sword and totally destroyed everyone in it. He left no survivors. And he did to the king of Makkedah as he had done to the king of Jericho.

[29]Then Joshua and all Israel with him moved on from Makkedah to Libnah and attacked it. [30]The LORD also gave that city and its king into Israel's hand. The city and everyone in it Joshua put to the sword. He left no survivors there. And he did to its king as he had done to the king of Jericho.

[31]Then Joshua and all Israel with him moved on from Libnah to Lachish; he took up positions against it and attacked it. [32]The LORD gave Lachish into Israel's hands, and Joshua took it on the second day. The city and everyone in it he put to the sword, just as he had done to Libnah. [33]Meanwhile, Horam king of Gezer had come up to help Lachish, but Joshua defeated him and his army—until no survivors were left.

[34]Then Joshua and all Israel with him moved on from Lachish to Eglon; they took up positions against it and attacked it. [35]They captured it that same day and put it to the sword and totally destroyed everyone in it, just as they had done to Lachish.

[36]Then Joshua and all Israel with him went up from Eglon to Hebron and attacked it. [37]They took the city and put it to the sword, together with its king, its villages and everyone in it. They left no survivors. Just as at Eglon, they totally destroyed it and everyone in it.

[38]Then Joshua and all Israel with him turned around and attacked Debir. [39]They took the city, its king and its villages, and put them to the sword. Everyone in it they totally destroyed. They left no survivors. They did to Debir and its king as they had done to Libnah and its king and to Hebron.

[40]So Joshua subdued the whole region, including the hill country, the Negev, the western foothills and the mountain slopes, together with all their kings. He left no survivors. He totally destroyed all who breathed, just as the LORD, the God of Israel, had commanded. [41]Joshua subdued them from Kadesh Barnea to Gaza and from the whole region of Goshen to Gibeon. [42]All these kings and their lands Joshua conquered in one campaign, because the LORD, the God of Israel, fought for Israel.

[43]Then Joshua returned with all Israel to the camp at Gilgal.

Northern Kings Defeated

11 When Jabin king of Hazor heard of this, he sent word to Jobab king of Madon, to the kings of Shimron and Akshaph, [2]and to the northern kings who were in the mountains, in the Arabah south of Kinnereth, in the western foothills and in Naphoth Dor on the west; [3]to the Canaanites in the east and west; to the Amorites, Hittites, Perizzites and Jebusites in the hill country; and to the Hivites

below Hermon in the region of Mizpah. [4]They came out with all their troops and a large number of horses and chariots—a huge army, as numerous as the sand on the seashore. [5]All these kings joined forces and made camp together at the Waters of Merom to fight against Israel.

[6]The LORD said to Joshua, "Do not be afraid of them, because by this time tomorrow I will hand all of them, slain, over to Israel. You are to hamstring their horses and burn their chariots."

[7]So Joshua and his whole army came against them suddenly at the Waters of Merom and attacked them, [8]and the LORD gave them into the hand of Israel. They defeated them and pursued them all the way to Greater Sidon, to Misrephoth Maim, and to the Valley of Mizpah on the east, until no survivors were left. [9]Joshua did to them as the LORD had directed: He hamstrung their horses and burned their chariots.

[10]At that time Joshua turned back and captured Hazor and put its king to the sword. (Hazor had been the head of all these kingdoms.) [11]Everyone in it they put to the sword. They totally destroyed[a] them, not sparing anyone that breathed, and he burned Hazor itself.

[12]Joshua took all these royal cities and their kings and put them to the sword. He totally destroyed them, as Moses the servant of the LORD had commanded. [13]Yet Israel did not burn any of the cities built on their mounds—except Hazor, which Joshua burned. [14]The Israelites carried off for themselves all the plunder and livestock of these cities, but all the people they put to the sword until they completely destroyed them, not sparing anyone that breathed. [15]As the LORD commanded his servant Moses, so Moses commanded Joshua, and Joshua did it; he left nothing undone of all that the LORD commanded Moses.

[16]So Joshua took this entire land: the hill country, all the Negev, the whole region of Goshen, the western foothills, the Arabah and the mountains of Israel with their foothills, [17]from Mount Halak, which rises toward Seir, to Baal Gad in the Valley of Lebanon below Mount Hermon. He captured all their kings and put them to death. [18]Joshua waged war against all these kings for a long time. [19]Except for the Hivites living in Gibeon, not one city made a treaty of peace with the Israelites, who took them all in battle. [20]For it was the LORD himself who hardened their hearts to wage war against Israel, so that he might destroy them totally, exterminating them without mercy, as the LORD had commanded Moses.

[21]At that time Joshua went and destroyed the Anakites from the hill country: from Hebron, Debir and Anab, from all the hill country of Judah, and from all the hill country of Israel. Joshua totally destroyed them and their towns. [22]No Anakites were left in Israelite territory; only in Gaza, Gath and Ashdod did any survive.

[23]So Joshua took the entire land, just as the LORD had directed Moses, and he gave it as an inheritance to Israel according to their tribal divisions. Then the land had rest from war.

List of Defeated Kings

12 These are the kings of the land whom the Israelites had defeated and whose territory they took over east of the Jordan, from the Arnon Gorge to Mount Hermon, including all the eastern side of the Arabah:

[2]Sihon king of the Amorites, who reigned in Heshbon.

He ruled from Aroer on the rim of the Arnon Gorge—from the middle of the gorge—to the Jabbok River, which is the border of the Ammonites. This included half of Gilead. [3]He also ruled over the eastern Arabah from the Sea of Galilee[b] to the Sea of the Arabah (that is, the Dead Sea), to Beth Jeshimoth, and then southward below the slopes of Pisgah.

[4]And the territory of Og king of Bashan, one of the last of the Rephaites, who reigned in Ashtaroth and Edrei.

[5]He ruled over Mount Hermon, Salekah, all of Bashan to the border of the people of Geshur and Maakah, and half of Gilead to the border of Sihon king of Heshbon.

[6]Moses, the servant of the LORD, and the Israelites conquered them. And Moses the servant of the LORD gave their land to the Reubenites, the Gadites and the half-tribe of Manasseh to be their possession.

---

[a] *11* The Hebrew term refers to the irrevocable giving over of things or persons to the LORD, often by totally destroying them; also in verses 12, 20 and 21.
[b] *3* Hebrew *Kinnereth*

[7]These are the kings of the land that Joshua and the Israelites conquered on the west side of the Jordan, from Baal Gad in the Valley of Lebanon to Mount Halak, which rises toward Seir (their lands Joshua gave as an inheritance to the tribes of Israel according to their tribal divisions— [8]the hill country, the western foothills, the Arabah, the mountain slopes, the wilderness and the Negev—the lands of the Hittites, Amorites, Canaanites, Perizzites, Hivites and Jebusites):

[9] the king of Jericho	one
the king of Ai (near Bethel)	one
[10] the king of Jerusalem	one
the king of Hebron	one
[11] the king of Jarmuth	one
the king of Lachish	one
[12] the king of Eglon	one
the king of Gezer	one
[13] the king of Debir	one
the king of Geder	one
[14] the king of Hormah	one
the king of Arad	one
[15] the king of Libnah	one
the king of Adullam	one
[16] the king of Makkedah	one
the king of Bethel	one
[17] the king of Tappuah	one
the king of Hepher	one
[18] the king of Aphek	one
the king of Lasharon	one
[19] the king of Madon	one
the king of Hazor	one
[20] the king of Shimron Meron	one
the king of Akshaph	one
[21] the king of Taanach	one
the king of Megiddo	one
[22] the king of Kedesh	one
the king of Jokneam in Carmel	one
[23] the king of Dor (in Naphoth Dor)	one
the king of Goyim in Gilgal	one
[24] the king of Tirzah	one
	thirty-one kings in all.

285

Land Still to Be Taken

13 When Joshua had grown old, the Lord said to him, "You are now very old, and there are still very large areas of land to be taken over.

[2]"This is the land that remains: all the regions of the Philistines and Geshurites, [3]from the Shihor River on the east of Egypt to the territory of Ekron on the north, all of it counted as Canaanite though held by the five Philistine rulers in Gaza, Ashdod, Ashkelon, Gath and Ekron; the territory of the Avvites [4]on the south; all the land of the Canaanites, from Arah of the Sidonians as far as Aphek and the border of the Amorites; [5]the area of Byblos; and all Lebanon to the east, from Baal Gad below Mount Hermon to Lebo Hamath.

[6]"As for all the inhabitants of the mountain regions from Lebanon to Misrephoth Maim, that is, all the Sidonians, I myself will drive them out before the Israelites. Be sure to allocate this land to Israel for an inheritance, as I have instructed you, [7]and divide it as an inheritance among the nine tribes and half of the tribe of Manasseh."

Division of the Land East of the Jordan

[8]The other half of Manasseh,[a] the Reubenites and the Gadites had received the inheritance that Moses had given them east of the Jordan, as he, the servant of the Lord, had assigned it to them.

[9]It extended from Aroer on the rim of the Arnon Gorge, and from the town in the middle of the gorge, and included the whole plateau of Medeba as far as Dibon, [10]and all the towns of Sihon king of the Amorites, who ruled in Heshbon, out to the border of the Ammonites. [11]It also included Gilead, the territory of the people of Geshur and Maakah, all of Mount Hermon and all Bashan as far as Salekah— [12]that is, the whole kingdom of Og in Bashan, who had reigned in Ashtaroth and Edrei. (He was the last of the Rephaites.) Moses had defeated them and taken over their land. [13]But the Israelites did not drive out the people of Geshur and Maakah, so they continue to live among the Israelites to this day.

[14]But to the tribe of Levi he gave no inheritance, since the food offerings presented to the Lord, the God of Israel, are their inheritance, as he promised them.

[15]This is what Moses had given to the tribe of Reuben, according to its clans:

[16]The territory from Aroer on the rim of the Arnon Gorge, and from the town in the middle of the gorge, and the whole plateau past Medeba [17]to Heshbon and all its towns on the plateau, including Dibon, Bamoth Baal, Beth Baal Meon, [18]Jahaz, Kedemoth, Mephaath, [19]Kiriathaim, Sibmah, Zereth Shahar on the hill in the valley, [20]Beth Peor, the slopes of Pisgah, and Beth Jeshimoth—[21]all the towns on the plateau and the entire realm of Sihon king of the Amorites, who ruled at Heshbon. Moses had defeated him and the Midianite chiefs, Evi, Rekem, Zur, Hur and Reba—princes allied with Sihon—who lived in that country. [22]In addition to those slain in battle, the Israelites had put to the sword Balaam son of Beor, who practiced divination. [23]The boundary of the Reubenites was the bank of the Jordan. These towns and their villages were the inheritance of the Reubenites, according to their clans.

[24]This is what Moses had given to the tribe of Gad, according to its clans:

[25]The territory of Jazer, all the towns of Gilead and half the Ammonite country as far as Aroer, near Rabbah; [26]and from Heshbon to Ramath Mizpah and Betonim, and from Mahanaim to the territory of Debir; [27]and in the valley, Beth Haram, Beth Nimrah, Sukkoth and Zaphon with the rest of the realm of Sihon king of Heshbon (the east side of the Jordan, the territory up to the end of the Sea of Galilee[b]). [28]These towns and their villages were the inheritance of the Gadites, according to their clans.

[29]This is what Moses had given to the half-tribe of Manasseh, that is, to half the family of the descendants of Manasseh, according to its clans:

[30]The territory extending from Mahanaim and including all of Bashan, the entire realm of Og king of Bashan—all the settlements of Jair in Bashan, sixty towns, [31]half of Gilead, and Ashtaroth and Edrei (the royal cities of Og in Bashan). This was for the descendants of Makir son of Manasseh— for half of the sons of Makir, according to their clans.

[32]This is the inheritance Moses had given when he was in the plains of Moab across the Jordan east of Jericho. [33]But to the tribe of Levi, Moses had given no inheritance; the Lord, the God of Israel, is their inheritance, as he promised them.

Division of the Land West of the Jordan

14 Now these are the areas the Israelites received as an inheritance in the land of Canaan, which Eleazar the priest, Joshua son of Nun and the heads of the tribal clans of Israel allotted to them. [2]Their inheritances were assigned by lot to the nine-and-a-half tribes, as the Lord had commanded

---

[a] 8 Hebrew *With it* (that is, with the other half of Manasseh)   [b] 27 Hebrew *Kinnereth*

through Moses. ³Moses had granted the two-and-a-half tribes their inheritance east of the Jordan but had not granted the Levites an inheritance among the rest, ⁴for the sons of Joseph had become two tribes—Manasseh and Ephraim. The Levites received no share of the land but only towns to live in, with pasturelands for their flocks and herds. ⁵So the Israelites divided the land, just as the Lord had commanded Moses.

Allotment for Caleb

⁶Now the people of Judah approached Joshua at Gilgal, and Caleb son of Jephunneh the Kenizzite said to him, "You know what the Lord said to Moses the man of God at Kadesh Barnea about you and me. ⁷I was forty years old when Moses the servant of the Lord sent me from Kadesh Barnea to explore the land. And I brought him back a report according to my convictions, ⁸but the others who went up with me made the hearts of the people melt in fear. I, however, followed the Lord my God wholeheartedly. ⁹So on that day Moses swore to me, 'The land on which your feet have walked will be your inheritance and that of your children forever, because you have followed the Lord my God wholeheartedly.'ᵃ

¹⁰"Now then, just as the Lord promised, he has kept me alive for forty-five years since the time he said this to Moses, while Israel moved about in the wilderness. So here I am today, eighty-five years old! ¹¹I am still as strong today as the day Moses sent me out; I'm just as vigorous to go out to battle now as I was then. ¹²Now give me this hill country that the Lord promised me that day. You yourself heard then that the Anakites were there and their cities were large and fortified, but, the Lord helping me, I will drive them out just as he said."

¹³Then Joshua blessed Caleb son of Jephunneh and gave him Hebron as his inheritance. ¹⁴So Hebron has belonged to Caleb son of Jephunneh the Kenizzite ever since, because he followed the Lord, the God of Israel, wholeheartedly. ¹⁵(Hebron used to be called Kiriath Arba after Arba, who was the greatest man among the Anakites.)

Then the land had rest from war.

aussie:impatience

14:6–15 How often we pass off our faults as socially acceptable character traits. We call our apathy "open-mindedness" and our impatience "enthusiasm" or "desire for productivity." These little lies we tell ourselves won't cut it when we're faced with a true challenge. Caleb had been given a promise that took *45 years* to fulfill. He could have forced something to happen sooner, claiming his rightful prize, but instead he waited on God. When you feel the twinge of impatience, don't lie to yourself. (You're not just "results-oriented.") Wait on God. Pray and release those impatient desires to him.

287

Allotment for Judah

15 The allotment for the tribe of Judah, according to its clans, extended down to the territory of Edom, to the Desert of Zin in the extreme south.

²Their southern boundary started from the bay at the southern end of the Dead Sea, ³crossed south of Scorpion Pass, continued on to Zin and went over to the south of Kadesh Barnea. Then it ran past Hezron up to Addar and curved around to Karka. ⁴It then passed along to Azmon and joined the Wadi of Egypt, ending at the Mediterranean Sea. This is theirᵇ southern boundary.

⁵The eastern boundary is the Dead Sea as far as the mouth of the Jordan.

The northern boundary started from the bay of the sea at the mouth of the Jordan, ⁶went up to Beth Hoglah and continued north of Beth Arabah to the Stone of Bohan son of Reuben. ⁷The boundary then went up to Debir from the Valley of Achor and turned north to Gilgal, which faces the Pass of Adummim south of the gorge. It continued along to the waters of En Shemesh and came out at En Rogel. ⁸Then it ran up the Valley of Ben Hinnom along the southern slope of the Jebusite city (that is, Jerusalem). From there it climbed to the top of the hill west of the Hinnom Valley at the northern end of the Valley of Rephaim. ⁹From the hilltop the boundary headed toward the spring of the waters of Nephtoah, came out at the towns of Mount Ephron and went down toward

ᵃ 9 Deut. 1:36   ᵇ 4 Septuagint; Hebrew your

Baalah (that is, Kiriath Jearim). ¹⁰Then it curved westward from Baalah to Mount Seir, ran along the northern slope of Mount Jearim (that is, Kesalon), continued down to Beth Shemesh and crossed to Timnah. ¹¹It went to the northern slope of Ekron, turned toward Shikkeron, passed along to Mount Baalah and reached Jabneel. The boundary ended at the sea.

¹²The western boundary is the coastline of the Mediterranean Sea.

These are the boundaries around the people of Judah by their clans.

¹³In accordance with the Lord's command to him, Joshua gave to Caleb son of Jephunneh a portion in Judah—Kiriath Arba, that is, Hebron. (Arba was the ancestor of Anak.) ¹⁴From Hebron Caleb drove out the three Anakites—Sheshai, Ahiman and Talmai, the sons of Anak. ¹⁵From there he marched against the people living in Debir (formerly called Kiriath Sepher). ¹⁶And Caleb said, "I will give my daughter Aksah in marriage to the man who attacks and captures Kiriath Sepher." ¹⁷Othniel son of Kenaz, Caleb's brother, took it; so Caleb gave his daughter Aksah to him in marriage.

¹⁸One day when she came to Othniel, she urged him^a to ask her father for a field. When she got off her donkey, Caleb asked her, "What can I do for you?"

¹⁹She replied, "Do me a special favor. Since you have given me land in the Negev, give me also springs of water." So Caleb gave her the upper and lower springs.

²⁰This is the inheritance of the tribe of Judah, according to its clans:

²¹The southernmost towns of the tribe of Judah in the Negev toward the boundary of Edom were:

Kabzeel, Eder, Jagur, ²²Kinah, Dimonah, Adadah, ²³Kedesh, Hazor, Ithnan, ²⁴Ziph, Telem, Bealoth, ²⁵Hazor Hadattah, Kerioth Hezron (that is, Hazor), ²⁶Amam, Shema, Moladah, ²⁷Hazar Gaddah, Heshmon, Beth Pelet, ²⁸Hazar Shual, Beersheba, Biziothiah, ²⁹Baalah, Iyim, Ezem, ³⁰Eltolad, Kesil, Hormah, ³¹Ziklag, Madmannah, Sansannah, ³²Lebaoth, Shilhim, Ain and Rimmon—a total of twenty-nine towns and their villages.

³³In the western foothills:

Eshtaol, Zorah, Ashnah, ³⁴Zanoah, En Gannim, Tappuah, Enam, ³⁵Jarmuth, Adullam, Sokoh, Azekah, ³⁶Shaaraim, Adithaim and Gederah (or Gederothaim)^b—fourteen towns and their villages.

³⁷Zenan, Hadashah, Migdal Gad, ³⁸Dilean, Mizpah, Joktheel, ³⁹Lachish, Bozkath, Eglon, ⁴⁰Kabbon, Lahmas, Kitlish, ⁴¹Gederoth, Beth Dagon, Naamah and Makkedah—sixteen towns and their villages.

⁴²Libnah, Ether, Ashan, ⁴³Iphtah, Ashnah, Nezib, ⁴⁴Keilah, Akzib and Mareshah—nine towns and their villages.

⁴⁵Ekron, with its surrounding settlements and villages; ⁴⁶west of Ekron, all that were in the vicinity of Ashdod, together with their villages; ⁴⁷Ashdod, its surrounding settlements and villages; and Gaza, its settlements and villages, as far as the Wadi of Egypt and the coastline of the Mediterranean Sea.

⁴⁸In the hill country:

Shamir, Jattir, Sokoh, ⁴⁹Dannah, Kiriath Sannah (that is, Debir), ⁵⁰Anab, Eshtemoh, Anim, ⁵¹Goshen, Holon and Giloh—eleven towns and their villages.

⁵²Arab, Dumah, Eshan, ⁵³Janim, Beth Tappuah, Aphekah, ⁵⁴Humtah, Kiriath Arba (that is, Hebron) and Zior—nine towns and their villages.

⁵⁵Maon, Carmel, Ziph, Juttah, ⁵⁶Jezreel, Jokdeam, Zanoah, ⁵⁷Kain, Gibeah and Timnah—ten towns and their villages.

⁵⁸Halhul, Beth Zur, Gedor, ⁵⁹Maarath, Beth Anoth and Eltekon—six towns and their villages.^c

⁶⁰Kiriath Baal (that is, Kiriath Jearim) and Rabbah—two towns and their villages.

⁶¹In the wilderness:

Beth Arabah, Middin, Sekakah, ⁶²Nibshan, the City of Salt and En Gedi—six towns and their villages.

^a 18 Hebrew and some Septuagint manuscripts; other Septuagint manuscripts (see also note at Judges 1:14) Othniel, he urged her   ^b 36 Or Gederah and Gederothaim   ^c 59 The Septuagint adds another district of eleven towns, including Tekoa and Ephrathah (Bethlehem).

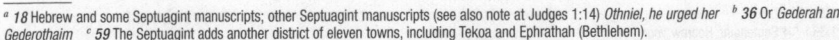

⁶³Judah could not dislodge the Jebusites, who were living in Jerusalem; to this day the Jebusites live there with the people of Judah.

Allotment for Ephraim and Manasseh

16 The allotment for Joseph began at the Jordan, east of the springs of Jericho, and went up from there through the desert into the hill country of Bethel. ²It went on from Bethel (that is, Luz),^a crossed over to the territory of the Arkites in Ataroth, ³descended westward to the territory of the Japhletites as far as the region of Lower Beth Horon and on to Gezer, ending at the Mediterranean Sea.

⁴So Manasseh and Ephraim, the descendants of Joseph, received their inheritance.

⁵This was the territory of Ephraim, according to its clans:

The boundary of their inheritance went from Ataroth Addar in the east to Upper Beth Horon ⁶and continued to the Mediterranean Sea. From Mikmethath on the north it curved eastward to Taanath Shiloh, passing by it to Janoah on the east. ⁷Then it went down from Janoah to Ataroth and Naarah, touched Jericho and came out at the Jordan. ⁸From Tappuah the border went west to the Kanah Ravine and ended at the Mediterranean Sea. This was the inheritance of the tribe of the Ephraimites, according to its clans. ⁹It also included all the towns and their villages that were set aside for the Ephraimites within the inheritance of the Manassites.

¹⁰They did not dislodge the Canaanites living in Gezer; to this day the Canaanites live among the people of Ephraim but are required to do forced labor.

17 This was the allotment for the tribe of Manasseh as Joseph's firstborn, that is, for Makir, Manasseh's firstborn. Makir was the ancestor of the Gileadites, who had received Gilead and Bashan because the Makirites were great soldiers. ²So this allotment was for the rest of the people of Manasseh—the clans of Abiezer, Helek, Asriel, Shechem, Hepher and Shemida. These are the other male descendants of Manasseh son of Joseph by their clans.

³Now Zelophehad son of Hepher, the son of Gilead, the son of Makir, the son of Manasseh, had no sons but only daughters, whose names were Mahlah, Noah, Hoglah, Milkah and Tirzah. ⁴They went to Eleazar the priest, Joshua son of Nun, and the leaders and said, "The LORD commanded Moses to give us an inheritance among our relatives." So Joshua gave them an inheritance along with the brothers of their father, according to the LORD's command. ⁵Manasseh's share consisted of ten tracts of land besides Gilead and Bashan east of the Jordan, ⁶because the daughters of the tribe of Manasseh received an inheritance among the sons. The land of Gilead belonged to the rest of the descendants of Manasseh.

⁷The territory of Manasseh extended from Asher to Mikmethath east of Shechem. The boundary ran southward from there to include the people living at En Tappuah. ⁸(Manasseh had the land of Tappuah, but Tappuah itself, on the boundary of Manasseh, belonged to the Ephraimites.) ⁹Then the boundary continued south to the Kanah Ravine. There were towns belonging to Ephraim lying among the towns of Manasseh, but the boundary of Manasseh was the northern side of the ravine and ended at the Mediterranean Sea. ¹⁰On the south the land belonged to Ephraim, on the north to Manasseh. The territory of Manasseh reached the Mediterranean Sea and bordered Asher on the north and Issachar on the east.

¹¹Within Issachar and Asher, Manasseh also had Beth Shan, Ibleam and the people of Dor, Endor, Taanach and Megiddo, together with their surrounding settlements (the third in the list is Naphoth^b).

¹²Yet the Manassites were not able to occupy these towns, for the Canaanites were determined to live in that region. ¹³However, when the Israelites grew stronger, they subjected the Canaanites to forced labor but did not drive them out completely.

¹⁴The people of Joseph said to Joshua, "Why have you given us only one allotment and one portion for an inheritance? We are a numerous people, and the LORD has blessed us abundantly."

¹⁵"If you are so numerous," Joshua answered, "and if the hill country of Ephraim is too small for you,

^a *2 Septuagint; Hebrew Bethel to Luz* ^b *11 That is, Naphoth Dor*

myth#20 "I AM WHAT I DO."

The home I grew up in resembles an Italian restaurant commercial. Whenever you entered my mom and dad's home, you were welcomed like you were family. Of course, you ate like you were family, too—cioppino, tortellini, passatelli. And that was before Mom served the main dish. Strict Catholics, my father raised me, my two sisters and three brothers with the fear of God and a phobia about skipping Mass. When I was old enough to go off to college, my parents' parting words to me were already so familiar, "You're the first Ciccione to go to college. Make us proud, Cici." No pressure. Just centuries of Ciccione history riding on my shoulders.

When I met Tony in graduate school, my parents were ecstatic. He was studying to be a lawyer. The first time I took him home to meet the family, my mother gushed about what "pretty grandbabies" Tony and I would make together. Cringing, I reminded her we'd only known each other three months. "No matter," Mom said. "The Cicciones always make good children."

Suddenly, it wasn't enough that I would graduate with honors or that I already had job offers from top companies in my field. Now, I had to make pretty babies with someone in order to have my parents' approval. They never tell me they love me. It's always about my latest achievement. That brings a smile to their faces. Sometimes I wonder if I weren't so successful or smart, how would their feelings about me change? I wonder if I'd still be the favored child if I (God forbid) failed. I'm starting to believe I am a human doing, not a human being. I need to know my family loves me for me, regardless of what I do in life.

—Ceclia

REGARDLESS OF WHAT

society or your family tells you (or even what you may secretly tell yourself), you are not the sum total of your pedigree, résumé and credentials. You have one identity in life upon which you should rest all your aspirations: You are a daughter of God. That's all. But how much that "all" entails!

- You are unconditionally accepted—not because you earned it, but because of grace (Ephesians 2:8–9).

- Your past is forgiven (2 Corinthians 5:17).

- You have a promising future (Jeremiah 29:11).

- He will never turn you away (John 6:37).

- You are loved as you are and not as you should be (Jeremiah 31:3).

- You are complete in Christ (Colossians 2:10).

Do you believe God wants an intimate relationship with you, not another impressive audition? The Bible's revelation to the over-achiever is this: There is nothing more for you to "do" to earn God's favor; Christ has already done it all. And because of the Cross (not by anything you've done), you are entitled to a promotion you didn't earn, favor you didn't seek, status beyond your wildest expectations and confidence in the court of the King. The world will try to point to what you do in order to define your worth—as if a salary, title or home address could ever encapsulate the wonder of a person's value. Remember, it's not *who* you are or *what* you do but *whose* you are. And you belong to the Almighty God.

"One indicator that Americans tend to identify themselves with their career is that most teens believe occupational or career success is necessary to lead a fulfilling adult life."

—Barna Research Group (1999)

291

"BUT NOW, THIS IS WHAT THE LORD SAYS— HE WHO created you, Jacob, he who formed you, Israel: 'DO NOT Fear, FOR I HAVE redeemed you; I Have summoned you by name; you are mine.'"

ISAIAH 43:1

SEE ALSO
Psalm 46:10
John 1:12
Ephesians 1:5

For more on **Identity**, check the index.

go up into the forest and clear land for yourselves there in the land of the Perizzites and Rephaites."

[16]The people of Joseph replied, "The hill country is not enough for us, and all the Canaanites who live in the plain have chariots fitted with iron, both those in Beth Shan and its settlements and those in the Valley of Jezreel."

[17]But Joshua said to the house of Joseph—to Ephraim and Manasseh—"You are numerous and very powerful. You will have not only one allotment [18]but the forested hill country as well. Clear it, and its farthest limits will be yours; though the Canaanites have chariots fitted with iron and though they are strong, you can drive them out."

Division of the Rest of the Land

18 The whole assembly of the Israelites gathered at Shiloh and set up the tent of meeting there. The country was brought under their control, [2]but there were still seven Israelite tribes who had not yet received their inheritance.

[3]So Joshua said to the Israelites: "How long will you wait before you begin to take possession of the land that the LORD, the God of your ancestors, has given you? [4]Appoint three men from each tribe. I will send them out to make a survey of the land and to write a description of it, according to the inheritance of each. Then they will return to me. [5]You are to divide the land into seven parts. Judah is to remain in its territory on the south and the house of Joseph in its territory on the north. [6]After you have written descriptions of the seven parts of the land, bring them here to me and I will cast lots for you in the presence of the LORD our God. [7]The Levites, however, do not get a portion among you, because the priestly service of the LORD is their inheritance. And Gad, Reuben and the half-tribe of Manasseh have already received their inheritance on the east side of the Jordan. Moses the servant of the LORD gave it to them."

[8]As the men started on their way to map out the land, Joshua instructed them, "Go and make a survey of the land and write a description of it. Then return to me, and I will cast lots for you here at Shiloh in the presence of the LORD." [9]So they left and went through the land. They wrote its description on a scroll, town by town, in seven parts, and returned to Joshua in the camp at Shiloh. [10]Joshua then cast lots for them in Shiloh in the presence of the LORD, and there he distributed the land to the Israelites according to their tribal divisions.

Allotment for Benjamin

[11]The first lot came up for the tribe of Benjamin according to its clans. Their allotted territory lay between the tribes of Judah and Joseph:

[12]On the north side their boundary began at the Jordan, passed the northern slope of Jericho and headed west into the hill country, coming out at the wilderness of Beth Aven. [13]From there it crossed to the south slope of Luz (that is, Bethel) and went down to Ataroth Addar on the hill south of Lower Beth Horon.

[14]From the hill facing Beth Horon on the south the boundary turned south along the western side and came out at Kiriath Baal (that is, Kiriath Jearim), a town of the people of Judah. This was the western side.

[15]The southern side began at the outskirts of Kiriath Jearim on the west, and the boundary came out at the spring of the waters of Nephtoah. [16]The boundary went down to the foot of the hill facing the Valley of Ben Hinnom, north of the Valley of Rephaim. It continued down the Hinnom Valley along the southern slope of the Jebusite city and so to En Rogel. [17]It then curved north, went to En Shemesh, continued to Geliloth, which faces the Pass of Adummim, and ran down to the Stone of Bohan son of Reuben. [18]It continued to the northern slope of Beth Arabah[a] and on down into the Arabah. [19]It then went to the northern slope of Beth Hoglah and came out at the northern bay of the Dead Sea, at the mouth of the Jordan in the south. This was the southern boundary.

[20]The Jordan formed the boundary on the eastern side.

These were the boundaries that marked out the inheritance of the clans of Benjamin on all sides.

[21]The tribe of Benjamin, according to its clans, had the following towns:

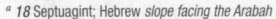

[a] 18 Septuagint; Hebrew slope facing the Arabah

Jericho, Beth Hoglah, Emek Keziz, ²²Beth Arabah, Zemaraim, Bethel, ²³Avvim, Parah, Ophrah, ²⁴Kephar Ammoni, Ophni and Geba—twelve towns and their villages.

²⁵Gibeon, Ramah, Beeroth, ²⁶Mizpah, Kephirah, Mozah, ²⁷Rekem, Irpeel, Taralah, ²⁸Zelah, Haeleph, the Jebusite city (that is, Jerusalem), Gibeah and Kiriath—fourteen towns and their villages.

This was the inheritance of Benjamin for its clans.

Allotment for Simeon

19 The second lot came out for the tribe of Simeon according to its clans. Their inheritance lay within the territory of Judah. ²It included:

Beersheba (or Sheba),^a Moladah, ³Hazar Shual, Balah, Ezem, ⁴Eltolad, Bethul, Hormah, ⁵Ziklag, Beth Markaboth, Hazar Susah, ⁶Beth Lebaoth and Sharuhen—thirteen towns and their villages;

⁷Ain, Rimmon, Ether and Ashan—four towns and their villages— ⁸and all the villages around these towns as far as Baalath Beer (Ramah in the Negev).

This was the inheritance of the tribe of the Simeonites, according to its clans. ⁹The inheritance of the Simeonites was taken from the share of Judah, because Judah's portion was more than they needed. So the Simeonites received their inheritance within the territory of Judah.

Allotment for Zebulun

¹⁰The third lot came up for Zebulun according to its clans:

The boundary of their inheritance went as far as Sarid. ¹¹Going west it ran to Maralah, touched Dabbesheth, and extended to the ravine near Jokneam. ¹²It turned east from Sarid toward the sunrise to the territory of Kisloth Tabor and went on to Daberath and up to Japhia. ¹³Then it continued eastward to Gath Hepher and Eth Kazin; it came out at Rimmon and turned toward Neah. ¹⁴There the boundary went around on the north to Hannathon and ended at the Valley of Iphtah El. ¹⁵Included were Kattath, Nahalal, Shimron, Idalah and Bethlehem. There were twelve towns and their villages.

¹⁶These towns and their villages were the inheritance of Zebulun, according to its clans.

Allotment for Issachar

¹⁷The fourth lot came out for Issachar according to its clans. ¹⁸Their territory included:

Jezreel, Kesulloth, Shunem, ¹⁹Hapharaim, Shion, Anaharath, ²⁰Rabbith, Kishion, Ebez, ²¹Remeth, En Gannim, En Haddah and Beth Pazzez. ²²The boundary touched Tabor, Shahazumah and Beth Shemesh, and ended at the Jordan. There were sixteen towns and their villages.

²³These towns and their villages were the inheritance of the tribe of Issachar, according to its clans.

Allotment for Asher

²⁴The fifth lot came out for the tribe of Asher according to its clans. ²⁵Their territory included:

Helkath, Hali, Beten, Akshaph, ²⁶Allammelek, Amad and Mishal. On the west the boundary touched Carmel and Shihor Libnath. ²⁷It then turned east toward Beth Dagon, touched Zebulun and the Valley of Iphtah El, and went north to Beth Emek and Neiel, passing Kabul on the left. ²⁸It went to Abdon,^b Rehob, Hammon and Kanah, as far as Greater Sidon. ²⁹The boundary then turned back toward Ramah and went to the fortified city of Tyre, turned toward Hosah and came out at the Mediterranean Sea in the region of Akzib, ³⁰Ummah, Aphek and Rehob. There were twenty-two towns and their villages.

³¹These towns and their villages were the inheritance of the tribe of Asher, according to its clans.

Allotment for Naphtali

³²The sixth lot came out for Naphtali according to its clans:

³³Their boundary went from Heleph and the large tree in Zaanannim, passing Adami Nekeb and Jabneel to Lakkum and ending at the Jordan. ³⁴The boundary ran west through Aznoth Tabor and

293

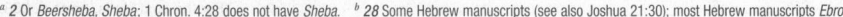

---

^a *2* Or *Beersheba, Sheba*; 1 Chron. 4:28 does not have *Sheba*.   ^b *28* Some Hebrew manuscripts (see also Joshua 21:30); most Hebrew manuscripts *Ebron*

came out at Hukkok. It touched Zebulun on the south, Asher on the west and the Jordan*[a]* on the east. [35] The fortified towns were Ziddim, Zer, Hammath, Rakkath, Kinnereth, [36] Adamah, Ramah, Hazor, [37] Kedesh, Edrei, En Hazor, [38] Iron, Migdal El, Horem, Beth Anath and Beth Shemesh. There were nineteen towns and their villages.

[39] These towns and their villages were the inheritance of the tribe of Naphtali, according to its clans.

Allotment for Dan

[40] The seventh lot came out for the tribe of Dan according to its clans. [41] The territory of their inheritance included:

Zorah, Eshtaol, Ir Shemesh, [42] Shaalabbin, Aijalon, Ithlah, [43] Elon, Timnah, Ekron, [44] Eltekeh, Gibbethon, Baalath, [45] Jehud, Bene Berak, Gath Rimmon, [46] Me Jarkon and Rakkon, with the area facing Joppa.

[47] (When the territory of the Danites was lost to them, they went up and attacked Leshem, took it, put it to the sword and occupied it. They settled in Leshem and named it Dan after their ancestor.) [48] These towns and their villages were the inheritance of the tribe of Dan, according to its clans.

Allotment for Joshua

[49] When they had finished dividing the land into its allotted portions, the Israelites gave Joshua son of Nun an inheritance among them, [50] as the LORD had commanded. They gave him the town he asked for— Timnath Serah*[b]* in the hill country of Ephraim. And he built up the town and settled there.

[51] These are the territories that Eleazar the priest, Joshua son of Nun and the heads of the tribal clans of Israel assigned by lot at Shiloh in the presence of the LORD at the entrance to the tent of meeting. And so they finished dividing the land.

Cities of Refuge

20 Then the LORD said to Joshua: [2] "Tell the Israelites to designate the cities of refuge, as I instructed you through Moses, [3] so that anyone who kills a person accidentally and unintentionally may flee there and find protection from the avenger of blood. [4] When they flee to one of these cities, they are to stand in the entrance of the city gate and state their case before the elders of that city. Then the elders are to admit them into their city and give them a place to live with them. [5] If the avenger of blood pursues them, the elders must not surrender the accused, because they killed their neighbor unintentionally and without malice aforethought. [6] They are to stay in that city until they have stood trial before the assembly and until the death of the high priest who is serving at that time. Then they may go back to their own home in the town from which they fled."

[7] So they set apart Kedesh in Galilee in the hill country of Naphtali, Shechem in the hill country of Ephraim, and Kiriath Arba (that is, Hebron) in the hill country of Judah. [8] East of the Jordan (on the other

---

[a] 34 Septuagint; Hebrew *west, and Judah, the Jordan,*   *[b]* 50 Also known as *Timnath Heres* (see Judges 2:9)

HE IS: a refuge

20:1–9 In ancient times people often sought personal revenge for a murder, even if the homicide was unintentional. So God provided a safe haven for those who killed someone accidentally—a city of refuge where the offender would be protected from the avenger until a trial could be held.

How often we need that place of refuge! Intentionally or not, we sin all the time. We harbor angry, murderous thoughts. We lash out with our words. We cut someone else down to build ourselves up. Thank God that he provides a safe haven for us— Jesus, our living city of *refuge.*

For the next He Is, go to p. 298.

side from Jericho) they designated Bezer in the wilderness on the plateau in the tribe of Reuben, Ramoth in Gilead in the tribe of Gad, and Golan in Bashan in the tribe of Manasseh. ⁹Any of the Israelites or any foreigner residing among them who killed someone accidentally could flee to these designated cities and not be killed by the avenger of blood prior to standing trial before the assembly.

Towns for the Levites

21 Now the family heads of the Levites approached Eleazar the priest, Joshua son of Nun, and the heads of the other tribal families of Israel ²at Shiloh in Canaan and said to them, "The Lord commanded through Moses that you give us towns to live in, with pasturelands for our livestock." ³So, as the Lord had commanded, the Israelites gave the Levites the following towns and pasturelands out of their own inheritance:

⁴The first lot came out for the Kohathites, according to their clans. The Levites who were descendants of Aaron the priest were allotted thirteen towns from the tribes of Judah, Simeon and Benjamin. ⁵The rest of Kohath's descendants were allotted ten towns from the clans of the tribes of Ephraim, Dan and half of Manasseh.

⁶The descendants of Gershon were allotted thirteen towns from the clans of the tribes of Issachar, Asher, Naphtali and the half-tribe of Manasseh in Bashan.

⁷The descendants of Merari, according to their clans, received twelve towns from the tribes of Reuben, Gad and Zebulun.

⁸So the Israelites allotted to the Levites these towns and their pasturelands, as the Lord had commanded through Moses.

⁹From the tribes of Judah and Simeon they allotted the following towns by name ¹⁰(these towns were assigned to the descendants of Aaron who were from the Kohathite clans of the Levites, because the first lot fell to them):

¹¹They gave them Kiriath Arba (that is, Hebron), with its surrounding pastureland, in the hill country of Judah. (Arba was the ancestor of Anak.) ¹²But the fields and villages around the city they had given to Caleb son of Jephunneh as his possession.

¹³So to the descendants of Aaron the priest they gave Hebron (a city of refuge for one accused of murder), Libnah, ¹⁴Jattir, Eshtemoa, ¹⁵Holon, Debir, ¹⁶Ain, Juttah and Beth Shemesh, together with their pasturelands—nine towns from these two tribes.

¹⁷And from the tribe of Benjamin they gave them Gibeon, Geba, ¹⁸Anathoth and Almon, together with their pasturelands—four towns.

¹⁹The total number of towns for the priests, the descendants of Aaron, came to thirteen, together with their pasturelands.

²⁰The rest of the Kohathite clans of the Levites were allotted towns from the tribe of Ephraim:

²¹In the hill country of Ephraim they were given Shechem (a city of refuge for one accused of murder) and Gezer, ²²Kibzaim and Beth Horon, together with their pasturelands—four towns.

²³Also from the tribe of Dan they received Eltekeh, Gibbethon, ²⁴Aijalon and Gath Rimmon, together with their pasturelands—four towns.

²⁵From half the tribe of Manasseh they received Taanach and Gath Rimmon, together with their pasturelands—two towns.

²⁶All these ten towns and their pasturelands were given to the rest of the Kohathite clans.

²⁷The Levite clans of the Gershonites were given:
from the half-tribe of Manasseh,
Golan in Bashan (a city of refuge for one accused of murder) and Be Eshterah, together with their pasturelands—two towns;
²⁸from the tribe of Issachar,
Kishion, Daberath, ²⁹Jarmuth and En Gannim, together with their pasturelands—four towns;
³⁰from the tribe of Asher,
Mishal, Abdon, ³¹Helkath and Rehob, together with their pasturelands—four towns;

295

³²from the tribe of Naphtali,

Kedesh in Galilee (a city of refuge for one accused of murder), Hammoth Dor and Kartan, together with their pasturelands—three towns.

³³The total number of towns of the Gershonite clans came to thirteen, together with their pasturelands.

³⁴The Merarite clans (the rest of the Levites) were given:

from the tribe of Zebulun,

Jokneam, Kartah, ³⁵Dimnah and Nahalal, together with their pasturelands—four towns;

³⁶from the tribe of Reuben,

Bezer, Jahaz, ³⁷Kedemoth and Mephaath, together with their pasturelands—four towns;

³⁸from the tribe of Gad,

Ramoth in Gilead (a city of refuge for one accused of murder), Mahanaim, ³⁹Heshbon and Jazer, together with their pasturelands—four towns in all.

⁴⁰The total number of towns allotted to the Merarite clans, who were the rest of the Levites, came to twelve.

⁴¹The towns of the Levites in the territory held by the Israelites were forty-eight in all, together with their pasturelands. ⁴²Each of these towns had pasturelands surrounding it; this was true for all these towns.

⁴³So the LORD gave Israel all the land he had sworn to give their ancestors, and they took possession of it and settled there. ⁴⁴The LORD gave them rest on every side, just as he had sworn to their ancestors. Not one of their enemies withstood them; the LORD gave all their enemies into their hands. ⁴⁵Not one of all the LORD's good promises to the house of Israel failed; every one was fulfilled.

Eastern Tribes Return Home

22 Then Joshua summoned the Reubenites, the Gadites and the half-tribe of Manasseh ²and said to them, "You have done all that Moses the servant of the LORD commanded, and you have obeyed me in everything I commanded. ³For a long time now—to this very day—you have not deserted the other Israelites but have carried out the mission the LORD your God gave you. ⁴Now that the LORD your God has given them rest as he promised, return to your homes in the land that Moses the servant of the LORD gave you on the other side of the Jordan. ⁵But be very careful to keep the commandment and the law that Moses the servant of the LORD gave you: to love the LORD your God, to walk in obedience to him, to keep his commands, to hold fast to him and to serve him with all your heart and with all your soul."

⁶Then Joshua blessed them and sent them away, and they went to their homes. ⁷(To the half-tribe of Manasseh Moses had given land in Bashan, and to the other half of the tribe Joshua gave land on the west side of the Jordan along with the other Israelites.) When Joshua sent them home, he blessed them, ⁸saying, "Return to your homes with your great wealth—with large herds of livestock, with silver, gold, bronze and iron, and a great quantity of clothing—and divide the plunder from your enemies with the other members of your tribes."

⁹So the Reubenites, the Gadites and the half-tribe of Manasseh left the Israelites at Shiloh in Canaan to return to Gilead, their own land, which they had acquired in accordance with the command of the LORD through Moses.

atissue:trustworthiness

22:1–5 Are you a woman of your word? If you say you'll do something, will you do it? Even if it gets hard? Even if it takes longer than you'd expected? Even if it interferes with your personal plans? Before Israel entered the promised land, 2½ of the 12 tribes staked out a perfect spot just east of the Jordan. God gave them permission to live there on one condition: that they first help the other 9½ tribes conquer the promised land. And they did—even though it was hard to leave home, to be apart from their families, to fight someone else's battles. Are you that true to your word?

¹⁰When they came to Geliloth near the Jordan in the land of Canaan, the Reubenites, the Gadites and the half-tribe of Manasseh built an imposing altar there by the Jordan. ¹¹And when the Israelites heard that they had built the altar on the border of Canaan at Geliloth near the Jordan on the Israelite side, ¹²the whole assembly of Israel gathered at Shiloh to go to war against them.

¹³So the Israelites sent Phinehas son of Eleazar, the priest, to the land of Gilead—to Reuben, Gad and the half-tribe of Manasseh. ¹⁴With him they sent ten of the chief men, one from each of the tribes of Israel, each the head of a family division among the Israelite clans.

¹⁵When they went to Gilead—to Reuben, Gad and the half-tribe of Manasseh—they said to them: ¹⁶"The whole assembly of the LORD says: 'How could you break faith with the God of Israel like this? How could you turn away from the LORD and build yourselves an altar in rebellion against him now? ¹⁷Was not the sin of Peor enough for us? Up to this very day we have not cleansed ourselves from that sin, even though a plague fell on the community of the LORD! ¹⁸And are you now turning away from the LORD?

"'If you rebel against the LORD today, tomorrow he will be angry with the whole community of Israel. ¹⁹If the land you possess is defiled, come over to the LORD's land, where the LORD's tabernacle stands, and share the land with us. But do not rebel against the LORD or against us by building an altar for yourselves, other than the altar of the LORD our God. ²⁰When Achan son of Zerah was unfaithful in regard to the devoted things,ᵃ did not wrath come on the whole community of Israel? He was not the only one who died for his sin.'"

297

²¹Then Reuben, Gad and the half-tribe of Manasseh replied to the heads of the clans of Israel: ²²"The Mighty One, God, the LORD! The Mighty One, God, the LORD! He knows! And let Israel know! If this has been in rebellion or disobedience to the LORD, do not spare us this day. ²³If we have built our own altar to turn away from the LORD and to offer burnt offerings and grain offerings, or to sacrifice fellowship offerings on it, may the LORD himself call us to account.

²⁴"No! We did it for fear that some day your descendants might say to ours, 'What do you have to do with the LORD, the God of Israel? ²⁵The LORD has made the Jordan a boundary between us and you—you Reubenites and Gadites! You have no share in the LORD.' So your descendants might cause ours to stop fearing the LORD.

²⁶"That is why we said, 'Let us get ready and build an altar—but not for burnt offerings or sacrifices.' ²⁷On the contrary, it is to be a witness between us and you and the generations that follow, that we will worship the LORD at his sanctuary with our burnt offerings, sacrifices and fellowship offerings. Then in the future your descendants will not be able to say to ours, 'You have no share in the LORD.'

²⁸"And we said, 'If they ever say this to us, or to our descendants, we will answer: Look at the replica of the LORD's altar, which our people built, not for burnt offerings and sacrifices, but as a witness between us and you.'

²⁹"Far be it from us to rebel against the LORD and turn away from him today by building an altar for burnt offerings, grain offerings and sacrifices, other than the altar of the LORD our God that stands before his tabernacle."

³⁰When Phinehas the priest and the leaders of the community—the heads of the clans of the Israelites—heard what Reuben, Gad and Manasseh had to say, they were pleased. ³¹And Phinehas son of Eleazar, the priest, said to Reuben, Gad and Manasseh, "Today we know that the LORD is with us, because you have not been unfaithful to the LORD in this matter. Now you have rescued the Israelites from the LORD's hand."

³²Then Phinehas son of Eleazar, the priest, and the leaders returned to Canaan from their meeting with the Reubenites and Gadites in Gilead and reported to the Israelites. ³³They were glad to hear the report and praised God. And they talked no more about going to war against them to devastate the country where the Reubenites and the Gadites lived.

³⁴And the Reubenites and the Gadites gave the altar this name: A Witness Between Us—that the LORD is God.

ᵃ 20 The Hebrew term refers to the irrevocable giving over of things or persons to the LORD, often by totally destroying them.

Joshua's Farewell to the Leaders

23 After a long time had passed and the LORD had given Israel rest from all their enemies around them, Joshua, by then a very old man, ²summoned all Israel—their elders, leaders, judges and officials—and said to them: "I am very old. ³You yourselves have seen everything the LORD your God has done to all these nations for your sake; it was the LORD your God who fought for you. ⁴Remember how I have allotted as an inheritance for your tribes all the land of the nations that remain—the nations I conquered—between the Jordan and the Mediterranean Sea in the west. ⁵The LORD your God himself will push them out for your sake. He will drive them out before you, and you will take possession of their land, as the LORD your God promised you.

⁶"Be very strong; be careful to obey all that is written in the Book of the Law of Moses, without turning aside to the right or to the left. ⁷Do not associate with these nations that remain among you; do not invoke the names of their gods or swear by them. You must not serve them or bow down to them. ⁸But you are to hold fast to the LORD your God, as you have until now.

⁹"The LORD has driven out before you great and powerful nations; to this day no one has been able to withstand you. ¹⁰One of you routs a thousand, because the LORD your God fights for you, just as he promised. ¹¹So be very careful to love the LORD your God.

HE IS: cautionary

23:10–11 Joshua offered a farewell speech to the leaders of the people, sharing advice that the Lord had taught him. God often speaks words of warning to us through our leaders in the hopes that we won't make mistakes that lead us into sin. He is *cautionary* and wants to protect us.

Think of the last piece of advice you received from a spiritual leader. Did you follow it? If not, did you find yourself in spiritual danger or sinful behavior? It's not too late to heed the warnings you've been given. "Be very careful to love the LORD your God."

For the next He Is, go to p. 305.

¹²"But if you turn away and ally yourselves with the survivors of these nations that remain among you and if you intermarry with them and associate with them, ¹³then you may be sure that the LORD your God will no longer drive out these nations before you. Instead, they will become snares and traps for you, whips on your backs and thorns in your eyes, until you perish from this good land, which the LORD your God has given you.

¹⁴"Now I am about to go the way of all the earth. You know with all your heart and soul that not one of all the good promises the LORD your God gave you has failed. Every promise has been fulfilled; not one has failed. ¹⁵But just as all the good things the LORD your God has promised you have come to you, so he will bring on you all the evil things he has threatened, until the LORD your God has destroyed you from this good land he has given you. ¹⁶If you violate the covenant of the LORD your God, which he commanded you, and go and serve other gods and bow down to them, the LORD's anger will burn against you, and you will quickly perish from the good land he has given you."

The Covenant Renewed at Shechem

24 Then Joshua assembled all the tribes of Israel at Shechem. He summoned the elders, leaders, judges and officials of Israel, and they presented themselves before God.

²Joshua said to all the people, "This is what the LORD, the God of Israel, says: 'Long ago your ancestors, including Terah the father of Abraham and Nahor, lived beyond the Euphrates River and worshiped other gods. ³But I took your father Abraham from the land beyond the Euphrates and led him throughout Canaan and gave him many descendants. I gave him Isaac, ⁴and to Isaac I gave Jacob and Esau. I assigned the hill country of Seir to Esau, but Jacob and his family went down to Egypt.

rebekah

Genesis 24–27

Tell us about your sons.

Isaac and I had been married 20 years before I finally got pregnant. And to have twins—what a blessing! It wasn't an easy pregnancy, though. The babies were constantly jostling and moving, so much so that I asked God what was going on. His answer was puzzling—he said two nations were struggling inside me. Then he said the older would serve the younger. How odd that seemed to me—the firstborn son always had more rights and blessings. But as I watched my sons grow, I realized that I had given birth to two completely different people.

How so?

Esau, my oldest, was a hunter. He lived for the outdoors and the hunt. Esau was bold, daring, adventurous. And Isaac, who enjoyed the luxury of fresh meat, loved Esau. Jacob was totally opposite of his brother. He was quiet, a thinker. He preferred staying near home. And I confess, I loved him more, not only because we were closer, but also because I knew that God favored Jacob over his brother.

How did your favoritism play itself out?

I did everything in my power to promote Jacob's cause and give him the advantage. Even though I knew God's plan for Jacob, I had such high hopes for my son and such strong ambitions that I felt compelled to move matters along myself. So I coached Jacob on how to trick his father so he could get the family blessing for himself. And it worked. Jacob got Isaac's blessing, and Esau was left with nothing. But in the end, so was I.

What do you mean?

Because of my singular desire to see my son succeed, I sacrificed the trust of my husband and permanently damaged my relationship with my older son. In bitterness and anger, he took even more pagan wives. And I eventually lost Jacob. Esau was so angry at what Jacob had done that he wanted to kill him. Jacob had to leave home immediately. I was left without either of my sons.

So what would you tell mothers about loving their children?

It was a difficult and bitter lesson for me, but favoritism has no place in a family. Absolutely none. Love that seeks success at the cost of truth and at the expense of other family members is not pleasing or honoring to God. And it leads only to conflict and heartache.

FOR MORE INSIGHT: For other instances of favoritism and its effect on families, read the stories of Joseph (Genesis 37:1–36) and of Hannah and Elkanah (1 Samuel 1:1–20).

⁵ "Then I sent Moses and Aaron, and I afflicted the Egyptians by what I did there, and I brought you out. ⁶When I brought your people out of Egypt, you came to the sea, and the Egyptians pursued them with chariots and horsemen*a* as far as the Red Sea.*b* ⁷But they cried to the LORD for help, and he put darkness between you and the Egyptians; he brought the sea over them and covered them. You saw with your own eyes what I did to the Egyptians. Then you lived in the wilderness for a long time.

⁸ "I brought you to the land of the Amorites who lived east of the Jordan. They fought against you, but I gave them into your hands. I destroyed them from before you, and you took possession of their land. ⁹When Balak son of Zippor, the king of Moab, prepared to fight against Israel, he sent for Balaam son of Beor to put a curse on you. ¹⁰But I would not listen to Balaam, so he blessed you again and again, and I delivered you out of his hand.

¹¹ "Then you crossed the Jordan and came to Jericho. The citizens of Jericho fought against you, as did also the Amorites, Perizzites, Canaanites, Hittites, Girgashites, Hivites and Jebusites, but I gave them into your hands. ¹²I sent the hornet ahead of you, which drove them out before you—also the two Amorite kings. You did not do it with your own sword and bow. ¹³So I gave you a land on which you did not toil and cities you did not build; and you live in them and eat from vineyards and olive groves that you did not plant.'

¹⁴ "Now fear the LORD and serve him with all faithfulness. Throw away the gods your ancestors worshiped beyond the Euphrates River and in Egypt, and serve the LORD. ¹⁵But if serving the LORD seems undesirable to you, then choose for yourselves this day whom you will serve, whether the gods your ancestors served beyond the Euphrates, or the gods of the Amorites, in whose land you are living. But as for me and my household, we will serve the LORD."

¹⁶Then the people answered, "Far be it from us to forsake the LORD to serve other gods! ¹⁷It was the LORD our God himself who brought us and our parents up out of Egypt, from that land of slavery, and performed those great signs before our eyes. He protected us on our entire journey and among all the nations through which we traveled. ¹⁸And the LORD drove out before us all the nations, including the Amorites, who lived in the land. We too will serve the LORD, because he is our God."

¹⁹Joshua said to the people, "You are not able to serve the LORD. He is a holy God; he is a jealous God. He will not forgive your rebellion and your sins. ²⁰If you forsake the LORD and serve foreign gods, he will turn and bring disaster on you and make an end of you, after he has been good to you."

conversations

parenting «» 24:15

1 ≫ Can a parent speak for the family, or does each family member have to choose to serve God?

2 ≫ How much influence do parents have over their children's beliefs?

3 ≫ What can you do to affect how your children believe?

For more on **parenting**, check the index.
For the next Conversations, go to p. 305.

²¹But the people said to Joshua, "No! We will serve the LORD."

²²Then Joshua said, "You are witnesses against yourselves that you have chosen to serve the LORD."

"Yes, we are witnesses," they replied.

²³ "Now then," said Joshua, "throw away the foreign gods that are among you and yield your hearts to the LORD, the God of Israel."

²⁴And the people said to Joshua, "We will serve the LORD our God and obey him."

²⁵On that day Joshua made a covenant for the people, and there at Shechem he reaffirmed for them decrees and laws. ²⁶And Joshua recorded these things in the Book of the Law of God. Then he took a large stone and set it up there under the oak near the holy place of the LORD.

²⁷ "See!" he said to all the people. "This stone will be a witness against us. It has heard all the words the LORD has said to us. It will be a witness against you if you are untrue to your God."

²⁸Then Joshua dismissed the people, each to their own inheritance.

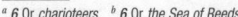

a 6 Or *charioteers*   *b* 6 Or *the Sea of Reeds*

Buried in the Promised Land

²⁹ After these things, Joshua son of Nun, the servant of the LORD, died at the age of a hundred and ten. ³⁰ And they buried him in the land of his inheritance, at Timnath Serah*ᵃ* in the hill country of Ephraim, north of Mount Gaash.

³¹ Israel served the LORD throughout the lifetime of Joshua and of the elders who outlived him and who had experienced everything the LORD had done for Israel.

³² And Joseph's bones, which the Israelites had brought up from Egypt, were buried at Shechem in the tract of land that Jacob bought for a hundred pieces of silver*ᵇ* from the sons of Hamor, the father of Shechem. This became the inheritance of Joseph's descendants.

³³ And Eleazar son of Aaron died and was buried at Gibeah, which had been allotted to his son Phinehas in the hill country of Ephraim.

atissue:leadership

24:31 Leaders are ultimately responsible for the actions of their subordinates. If the group succeeds, the leader is praised. If the group fails, the leader is blamed. No matter what difficult person may be in the group, a good leader is expected to make everyone work together. Joshua, throughout the time he led Israel, moved the nation closer to God. He achieved his goal. He led his people in three dynamic ways: by example, with authority and in the direction that God was leading him. When you're in a position of leadership, do you lead equally well in all three of those ways?

301

judges

302

AUTHOR
Likely Samuel.

AUDIENCE
The Israelites living in the promised land.

DATE
Around 1000 B.C.

SETTING
Israel's ups and (mostly) downs after the time of Joshua.

VERSE TO REMEMBER
"In those days Israel had no king; everyone did as they saw fit." (17:6)

THEME TO CONSIDER
It's easy to lose sight of our identity as God's people. God must deliver us from our own sinfulness.

Israel Fights the Remaining Canaanites

1 After the death of Joshua, the Israelites asked the Lord, "Who of us is to go up first to fight against the Canaanites?"

²The Lord answered, "Judah shall go up; I have given the land into their hands."

³The men of Judah then said to the Simeonites their fellow Israelites, "Come up with us into the territory allotted to us, to fight against the Canaanites. We in turn will go with you into yours." So the Simeonites went with them.

⁴When Judah attacked, the Lord gave the Canaanites and Perizzites into their hands, and they struck down ten thousand men at Bezek. ⁵It was there that they found Adoni-Bezek and fought against him, putting to rout the Canaanites and Perizzites. ⁶Adoni-Bezek fled, but they chased him and caught him, and cut off his thumbs and big toes.

⁷Then Adoni-Bezek said, "Seventy kings with their thumbs and big toes cut off have picked up scraps under my table. Now God has paid me back for what I did to them." They brought him to Jerusalem, and he died there.

⁸The men of Judah attacked Jerusalem also and took it. They put the city to the sword and set it on fire.

⁹After that, Judah went down to fight against the Canaanites living in the hill country, the Negev and the western foothills. ¹⁰They advanced against the Canaanites living in Hebron (formerly called Kiriath Arba) and defeated Sheshai, Ahiman and Talmai.

¹¹From there they advanced against the people living in Debir (formerly called Kiriath Sepher). ¹²And Caleb said, "I will give my daughter Aksah in marriage to the man who attacks and captures Kiriath Sepher." ¹³Othniel son of Kenaz, Caleb's younger brother, took it; so Caleb gave his daughter Aksah to him in marriage.

¹⁴One day when she came to Othniel, she urged him*a* to ask her father for a field. When she got off her donkey, Caleb asked her, "What can I do for you?"

¹⁵She replied, "Do me a special favor. Since you have given me land in the Negev, give me also springs of water." So Caleb gave her the upper and lower springs.

¹⁶The descendants of Moses' father-in-law, the Kenite, went up from the City of Palms*b* with the people of Judah to live among the inhabitants of the Desert of Judah in the Negev near Arad.

¹⁷Then the men of Judah went with the Simeonites their fellow Israelites and attacked the Canaanites living in Zephath, and they totally destroyed*c* the city. Therefore it was called Hormah.*d* ¹⁸Judah also took*e* Gaza, Ashkelon and Ekron—each city with its territory.

¹⁹The Lord was with the men of Judah. They took possession of the hill country, but they were unable to drive the people from the plains, because they had chariots fitted with iron. ²⁰As Moses had promised, Hebron was given to Caleb, who drove from it the three sons of Anak. ²¹The Benjamites, however, did not drive out the Jebusites, who were living in Jerusalem; to this day the Jebusites live there with the Benjamites.

²²Now the house of Joseph attacked Bethel, and the Lord was with them. ²³When they sent men to spy out Bethel (formerly called Luz), ²⁴the spies saw a man coming out of the city and they said to him, "Show us how to get into the city and we will see that you are treated well." ²⁵So he showed them, and they put the city to the sword but spared the man and his whole family. ²⁶He then went to the land of the Hittites, where he built a city and called it Luz, which is its name to this day.

²⁷But Manasseh did not drive out the people of Beth Shan or Taanach or Dor or Ibleam or Megiddo and their surrounding settlements, for the Canaanites were determined to live in that land. ²⁸When Israel became strong, they pressed the Canaanites into forced labor but never drove them out completely. ²⁹Nor did Ephraim drive out the Canaanites living in Gezer, but the Canaanites continued to live there among them. ³⁰Neither did Zebulun drive out the Canaanites living in Kitron or Nahalol, so these Canaanites lived among them, but Zebulun did subject them to forced labor. ³¹Nor did Asher drive out those living in Akko or Sidon or Ahlab or Akzib or Helbah or Aphek or Rehob. ³²The Asherites lived

303

---

a 14 Hebrew; Septuagint and Vulgate *Othniel, he urged her*   *b 16* That is, Jericho   *c 17* The Hebrew term refers to the irrevocable giving over of things or persons to the Lord, often by totally destroying them.   *d 17 Hormah* means *destruction.*   *e 18* Hebrew; Septuagint *Judah did not take* among the Canaanite inhabitants of the land because they did not drive them out. ³³ Neither did Naphtali drive out those living in Beth Shemesh or Beth Anath; but the Naphtalites too lived among the Canaanite inhabitants of the land, and those living in Beth Shemesh and Beth Anath became forced laborers for them. ³⁴ The Amorites confined the Danites to the hill country, not allowing them to come down into the plain. ³⁵ And the Amorites were determined also to hold out in Mount Heres, Aijalon and Shaalbim, but when the power of the house of Joseph increased, they too were pressed into forced labor. ³⁶ The boundary of the Amorites was from Scorpion Pass to Sela and beyond.

The Angel of the LORD at Bokim

2 The angel of the LORD went up from Gilgal to Bokim and said, "I brought you up out of Egypt and led you into the land that I swore to give to your ancestors. I said, 'I will never break my covenant with you, ² and you shall not make a covenant with the people of this land, but you shall break down their altars.' Yet you have disobeyed me. Why have you done this? ³ And I have also said, 'I will not drive them out before you; they will become traps for you, and their gods will become snares to you.'"

⁴ When the angel of the LORD had spoken these things to all the Israelites, the people wept aloud, ⁵ and they called that place Bokim.^a There they offered sacrifices to the LORD.

Disobedience and Defeat

⁶ After Joshua had dismissed the Israelites, they went to take possession of the land, each to their own inheritance. ⁷ The people served the LORD throughout the lifetime of Joshua and of the elders who outlived him and who had seen all the great things the LORD had done for Israel.

⁸ Joshua son of Nun, the servant of the LORD, died at the age of a hundred and ten. ⁹ And they buried him in the land of his inheritance, at Timnath Heres^b in the hill country of Ephraim, north of Mount Gaash.

¹⁰ After that whole generation had been gathered to their ancestors, another generation grew up who knew neither the LORD nor what he had done for Israel. ¹¹ Then the Israelites did evil in the eyes of the LORD and served the Baals. ¹² They forsook the LORD, the God of their ancestors, who had brought them out of Egypt. They followed and worshiped various gods of the peoples around them. They aroused the LORD's anger ¹³ because they forsook him and served Baal and the Ashtoreths. ¹⁴ In his anger against Israel the LORD gave them into the hands of raiders who plundered them. He sold them into the hands of their enemies all around, whom they were no longer able to resist. ¹⁵ Whenever Israel went out to fight, the hand of the LORD was against them to defeat them, just as he had sworn to them. They were in great distress.

¹⁶ Then the LORD raised up judges,^c who saved them out of the hands of these raiders. ¹⁷ Yet they would not listen to their judges but prostituted themselves to other gods and worshiped them. Unlike their ancestors, they quickly turned from following the way of their ancestors, the way of obedience to the LORD's commands. ¹⁸ Whenever the LORD raised up a judge for them, he was with the judge and saved them out of the hands of their enemies as long as the judge lived; for the LORD relented because of their groaning under those who oppressed and afflicted them. ¹⁹ But when the judge died, the people returned to ways even more corrupt than those of their ancestors, following

atissue:compromise

2:7–11 Sometimes in life you have to compromise. For example, in a marriage you have to compromise on lots of little decisions in order to live in harmony with another person. Sometimes you *shouldn't* compromise, though. When you compromise in your relationship with God, you're headed for danger. The Israelites thought they could worship pagan gods while keeping God as their official spokesman. Of course, that plan didn't work at all. God demands our total allegiance. When we try to serve him some of the time, we end up not serving him at all.

---

^a *5 Bokim* means *weepers.* ^b *9* Also known as *Timnath Serah* (see Joshua 19:50 and 24:30) ^c *16* Or *leaders*; similarly in verses 17-19

other gods and serving and worshiping them. They refused to give up their evil practices and stubborn ways.

²⁰Therefore the LORD was very angry with Israel and said, "Because this nation has violated the covenant I ordained for their ancestors and has not listened to me, ²¹I will no longer drive out before them any of the nations Joshua left when he died. ²²I will use them to test Israel and see whether they will keep the way of the LORD and walk in it as their ancestors did." ²³The LORD had allowed those nations to remain; he did not drive them out at once by giving them into the hands of Joshua.

HE IS: testing

2:20–22 During the time of the judges, the Israelites spun out of control into a cycle of sin and restoration. They disobeyed God, experienced his discipline, cried out in distress and were delivered. However, the cycle always started again. Throughout the years, God continually tested them to see whether they would keep his ways.

It's easy to fall into the sin cycle: disobedience, divine discipline, distress and deliverance by God. If God is *testing* you, then it's time to break the cycle. Start a new pattern by looking to him for the strength to obey his commands the first time. Then you'll have what you need to pass the test.

For the next He Is, go to p. 316.

3 These are the nations the LORD left to test all those Israelites who had not experienced any of the wars in Canaan ²(he did this only to teach warfare to the descendants of the Israelites who had not had previous battle experience): ³the five rulers of the Philistines, all the Canaanites, the Sidonians, and the Hivites living in the Lebanon mountains from Mount Baal Hermon to Lebo Hamath. ⁴They were left to test the Israelites to see whether they would obey the LORD's commands, which he had given their ancestors through Moses.

⁵The Israelites lived among the Canaanites, Hittites, Amorites, Perizzites, Hivites and Jebusites. ⁶They took their daughters in marriage and gave their own daughters to their sons, and served their gods.

Othniel

⁷The Israelites did evil in the eyes of the LORD; they forgot the LORD their God and served the Baals and the Asherahs. ⁸The anger of the LORD burned against Israel so that he sold them into the hands of Cushan-Rishathaim king of Aram Naharaim,ᵃ to whom the Israelites were subject for eight years. ⁹But when they cried out to the LORD, he raised up for them a deliverer, Othniel son of Kenaz, Caleb's younger brother, who saved them. ¹⁰The Spirit of the LORD came on him, so that he became Israel's judgeᵇ and went to war. The LORD gave Cushan-Rishathaim king of Aram into the hands of Othniel, who overpowered him. ¹¹So the land had peace for forty years, until Othniel son of Kenaz died.

Ehud

¹²Again the Israelites did evil in the eyes of the LORD, and because they did this evil the LORD gave Eglon king of Moab power over Israel. ¹³Getting the Ammonites and Amalekites to join him, Eglon came and attacked Israel, and they took possession of the City of Palms.ᶜ ¹⁴The Israelites were subject to Eglon king of Moab for eighteen years.

" conversations "

dating non-Christians ‹∞› 3:1–7

1 » How does dating a non-Christian differ from friendship with a non-Christian?

2 » How much influence does the person you're dating have on you?

3 » How will the non-Christian influence a Christian, even if she has a strong character?

For more on **dating non-Christians**, check the index.
For the next Conversations, go to p. 306.

ᵃ *8* That is, Northwest Mesopotamia   ᵇ *10* Or *leader*   ᶜ *13* That is, Jericho

¹⁵Again the Israelites cried out to the Lord, and he gave them a deliverer—Ehud, a left-handed man, the son of Gera the Benjamite. The Israelites sent him with tribute to Eglon king of Moab. ¹⁶Now Ehud had made a double-edged sword about a cubit^{*a*} long, which he strapped to his right thigh under his clothing. ¹⁷He presented the tribute to Eglon king of Moab, who was a very fat man. ¹⁸After Ehud had presented the tribute, he dismissed those who had carried it. ¹⁹But on reaching the stone images near Gilgal he himself went back to Eglon and said, "Your Majesty, I have a secret message for you."

The king said to his attendants, "Leave us!" And they all left.

²⁰Ehud then approached him while he was sitting alone in the upper room of his palace^{*b*} and said, "I have a message from God for you." As the king rose from his seat, ²¹Ehud reached with his left hand, drew the sword from his right thigh and plunged it into the king's belly. ²²Even the handle sank in after the blade, and his bowels discharged. Ehud did not pull the sword out, and the fat closed in over it. ²³Then Ehud went out to the porch^{*c*}; he shut the doors of the upper room behind him and locked them.

²⁴After he had gone, the servants came and found the doors of the upper room locked. They said, "He must be relieving himself in the inner room of the palace." ²⁵They waited to the point of embarrassment, but when he did not open the doors of the room, they took a key and unlocked them. There they saw their lord fallen to the floor, dead.

²⁶While they waited, Ehud got away. He passed by the stone images and escaped to Seirah. ²⁷When he arrived there, he blew a trumpet in the hill country of Ephraim, and the Israelites went down with him from the hills, with him leading them.

²⁸"Follow me," he ordered, "for the Lord has given Moab, your enemy, into your hands." So they followed him down and took possession of the fords of the Jordan that led to Moab; they allowed no one to cross over. ²⁹At that time they struck down about ten thousand Moabites, all vigorous and strong; not one escaped. ³⁰That day Moab was made subject to Israel, and the land had peace for eighty years.

Shamgar

³¹After Ehud came Shamgar son of Anath, who struck down six hundred Philistines with an oxgoad. He too saved Israel.

Deborah

4 Again the Israelites did evil in the eyes of the Lord, now that Ehud was dead. ²So the Lord sold them into the hands of Jabin king of Canaan, who reigned in Hazor. Sisera, the commander of his army, was based in Harosheth Haggoyim. ³Because he had nine hundred chariots fitted with iron and had cruelly oppressed the Israelites for twenty years, they cried to the Lord for help.

⁴Now Deborah, a prophet, the wife of Lappidoth, was leading^{*d*} Israel at that time. ⁵She held court under the Palm of Deborah between Ramah and Bethel in the hill country of Ephraim, and the Israelites went up to her to have their disputes decided. ⁶She sent for Barak son of Abinoam from Kedesh in Naphtali and said to him, "The Lord, the God of Israel, commands you: 'Go, take with you ten thousand men of Naphtali and Zebulun and lead them up to Mount Tabor. ⁷I will lead Sisera, the commander of Jabin's army, with his chariots and his troops to the Kishon River and give him into your hands.'"

⁸Barak said to her, "If you go with me, I will go; but if you don't go with me, I won't go."

⁹"Certainly I will go with you," said Deborah. "But because of the course you are taking, the honor will not be yours, for the Lord will deliver Sisera into the hands of a woman." So Deborah went with Barak to Kedesh. ¹⁰There Barak summoned Zebulun and

"conversations"

friendship with men «» 4:4–8

1» Is it OK for women and men to be friends? What if they're married to other people?

2» Is it possible for men and women to have purely platonic friendships?

3» What complicates male-female relationships at work? At church? Socially?

For more on friendship with men, check the index. For the next Conversations, go to p. 312.

---

^{*a*} *16* That is, about 18 inches or about 45 centimeters   ^{*b*} *20* The meaning of the Hebrew for this word is uncertain; also in verse 24.   ^{*c*} *23* The meaning of the Hebrew for this word is uncertain.   ^{*d*} *4* Traditionally *judging*

Naphtali, and ten thousand men went up under his command. Deborah also went up with him. ¹¹ Now Heber the Kenite had left the other Kenites, the descendants of Hobab, Moses' brother-in-law,ᵃ and pitched his tent by the great tree in Zaanannim near Kedesh.

¹² When they told Sisera that Barak son of Abinoam had gone up to Mount Tabor, ¹³ Sisera summoned from Harosheth Haggoyim to the Kishon River all his men and his nine hundred chariots fitted with iron.

¹⁴ Then Deborah said to Barak, "Go! This is the day the LORD has given Sisera into your hands. Has not the LORD gone ahead of you?" So Barak went down Mount Tabor, with ten thousand men following him. ¹⁵ At Barak's advance, the LORD routed Sisera and all his chariots and army by the sword, and Sisera got down from his chariot and fled on foot.

¹⁶ Barak pursued the chariots and army as far as Harosheth Haggoyim, and all Sisera's troops fell by the sword; not a man was left. ¹⁷ Sisera, meanwhile, fled on foot to the tent of Jael, the wife of Heber the Kenite, because there was an alliance between Jabin king of Hazor and the family of Heber the Kenite.

¹⁸ Jael went out to meet Sisera and said to him, "Come, my lord, come right in. Don't be afraid." So he entered her tent, and she covered him with a blanket.

¹⁹ "I'm thirsty," he said. "Please give me some water." She opened a skin of milk, gave him a drink, and covered him up.

²⁰ "Stand in the doorway of the tent," he told her. "If anyone comes by and asks you, 'Is there a man in here?' say 'No.'"

²¹ But Jael, Heber's wife, picked up a tent peg and a hammer and went quietly to him while he lay fast asleep, exhausted. She drove the peg through his temple into the ground, and he died.

²² Just then Barak came by in pursuit of Sisera, and Jael went out to meet him. "Come," she said, "I will show you the man you're looking for." So he went in with her, and there lay Sisera with the tent peg through his temple—dead.

²³ On that day God subdued Jabin king of Canaan before the Israelites. ²⁴ And the hand of the Israelites pressed harder and harder against Jabin king of Canaan until they destroyed him.

The Song of Deborah

5 On that day Deborah and Barak son of Abinoam sang this song:

²"When the princes in Israel take the lead,
    when the people willingly offer themselves—
    praise the LORD!

³"Hear this, you kings! Listen, you rulers!
    I, even I, will sing toᵇ the LORD;
    I will praise the LORD, the God of Israel, in song.

⁴"When you, LORD, went out from Seir,
    when you marched from the land of Edom,
the earth shook, the heavens poured,
    the clouds poured down water.
⁵The mountains quaked before the LORD, the One of Sinai,
    before the LORD, the God of Israel.

⁶"In the days of Shamgar son of Anath,
    in the days of Jael, the highways were abandoned;
    travelers took to winding paths.
⁷Villagers in Israel would not fight;
    they held back until I, Deborah, arose,
    until I arose, a mother in Israel.
⁸God chose new leaders

> when war came to the city gates,
> but not a shield or spear was seen
>   among forty thousand in Israel.
> ⁹My heart is with Israel's princes,
>   with the willing volunteers among the people.
>   Praise the LORD!
>
> ¹⁰"You who ride on white donkeys,
>   sitting on your saddle blankets,
>   and you who walk along the road,
> consider ¹¹the voice of the singers^a at the watering places.
>   They recite the victories of the LORD,
>   the victories of his villagers in Israel.
>
> "Then the people of the LORD
>   went down to the city gates.
> ¹²'Wake up, wake up, Deborah!
>   Wake up, wake up, break out in song!
> Arise, Barak!
>   Take captive your captives, son of Abinoam.'
>
> ¹³"The remnant of the nobles came down;
>   the people of the LORD came down to me against the mighty.
> ¹⁴Some came from Ephraim, whose roots were in Amalek;
>   Benjamin was with the people who followed you.
> From Makir captains came down,
>   from Zebulun those who bear a commander's^a staff.
> ¹⁵The princes of Issachar were with Deborah;
>   yes, Issachar was with Barak,
>   sent under his command into the valley.
> In the districts of Reuben
>   there was much searching of heart.
> ¹⁶Why did you stay among the sheep pens^b
>   to hear the whistling for the flocks?
> In the districts of Reuben
>   there was much searching of heart.
> ¹⁷Gilead stayed beyond the Jordan.
>   And Dan, why did he linger by the ships?
> Asher remained on the coast
>   and stayed in his coves.
> ¹⁸The people of Zebulun risked their very lives;
>   so did Naphtali on the terraced fields.
>
> ¹⁹"Kings came, they fought,
>   the kings of Canaan fought.
> At Taanach, by the waters of Megiddo,
>   they took no plunder of silver.
> ²⁰From the heavens the stars fought,
>   from their courses they fought against Sisera.
> ²¹The river Kishon swept them away,
>   the age-old river, the river Kishon.

308

---

^a *11,14* The meaning of the Hebrew for this word is uncertain.   ^b *16* Or *the campfires;* or *the saddlebags*

> March on, my soul; be strong!
> ²²Then thundered the horses' hooves—
>   galloping, galloping go his mighty steeds.
> ²³'Curse Meroz,' said the angel of the LORD.
>   'Curse its people bitterly,
> because they did not come to help the LORD,
>   to help the LORD against the mighty.'
>
> ²⁴"Most blessed of women be Jael,
>   the wife of Heber the Kenite,
>   most blessed of tent-dwelling women.
> ²⁵He asked for water, and she gave him milk;
>   in a bowl fit for nobles she brought him curdled milk.
> ²⁶Her hand reached for the tent peg,
>   her right hand for the laborer's hammer.
> She struck Sisera, she crushed his head,
>   she shattered and pierced his temple.
> ²⁷At her feet he sank,
>   he fell; there he lay.
> At her feet he sank, he fell;
>   where he sank, there he fell—dead.
>
> ²⁸"Through the window peered Sisera's mother;
>   behind the lattice she cried out,
>   'Why is his chariot so long in coming?
>   Why is the clatter of his chariots delayed?'
> ²⁹The wisest of her ladies answer her;
>   indeed, she keeps saying to herself,
> ³⁰'Are they not finding and dividing the spoils:
>   a woman or two for each man,
> colorful garments as plunder for Sisera,
>   colorful garments embroidered,
> highly embroidered garments for my neck—
>   all this as plunder?'
>
> ³¹"So may all your enemies perish, LORD!
>   But may all who love you be like the sun
>   when it rises in its strength."

Then the land had peace forty years.

Gideon

6 The Israelites did evil in the eyes of the LORD, and for seven years he gave them into the hands of the Midianites. ²Because the power of Midian was so oppressive, the Israelites prepared shelters for themselves in mountain clefts, caves and strongholds. ³Whenever the Israelites planted their crops, the Midianites, Amalekites and other eastern peoples invaded the country. ⁴They camped on the land and ruined the crops all the way to Gaza and did not spare a living thing for Israel, neither sheep nor cattle nor donkeys. ⁵They came up with their livestock and their tents like swarms of locusts. It was impossible to count them or their camels; they invaded the land to ravage it. ⁶Midian so impoverished the Israelites that they cried out to the LORD for help.

⁷When the Israelites cried out to the LORD because of Midian, ⁸he sent them a prophet, who said, "This is what the LORD, the God of Israel, says: I brought you up out of Egypt, out of the land of slavery.

⁹I rescued you from the hand of the Egyptians. And I delivered you from the hand of all your oppressors; I drove them out before you and gave you their land. ¹⁰I said to you, 'I am the LORD your God; do not worship the gods of the Amorites, in whose land you live.' But you have not listened to me."

¹¹The angel of the LORD came and sat down under the oak in Ophrah that belonged to Joash the Abiezrite, where his son Gideon was threshing wheat in a winepress to keep it from the Midianites. ¹²When the angel of the LORD appeared to Gideon, he said, "The LORD is with you, mighty warrior."

¹³"Pardon me, my lord," Gideon replied, "but if the LORD is with us, why has all this happened to us? Where are all his wonders that our ancestors told us about when they said, 'Did not the LORD bring us up out of Egypt?' But now the LORD has abandoned us and given us into the hand of Midian."

¹⁴The LORD turned to him and said, "Go in the strength you have and save Israel out of Midian's hand. Am I not sending you?"

¹⁵"Pardon me, my lord," Gideon replied, "but how can I save Israel? My clan is the weakest in Manasseh, and I am the least in my family."

¹⁶The LORD answered, "I will be with you, and you will strike down all the Midianites together."

¹⁷Gideon replied, "If now I have found favor in your eyes, give me a sign that it is really you talking to me. ¹⁸Please do not go away until I come back and bring my offering and set it before you."

And the LORD said, "I will wait until you return."

¹⁹Gideon went in, prepared a young goat, and from an ephah*a* of flour he made bread without yeast. Putting the meat in a basket and its broth in a pot, he brought them out and offered them to him under the oak.

²⁰The angel of God said to him, "Take the meat and the unleavened bread, place them on this rock, and pour out the broth." And Gideon did so. ²¹With the tip of the staff that was in his hand, the angel of the LORD touched the meat and the unleavened bread. Fire flared from the rock, consuming the meat and the bread. And the angel of the LORD disappeared. ²²When Gideon realized that it was the angel of the LORD, he exclaimed, "Ah, Sovereign LORD! I have seen the angel of the LORD face to face!"

²³But the LORD said to him, "Peace! Do not be afraid. You are not going to die."

²⁴So Gideon built an altar to the LORD there and called it The LORD Is Peace. To this day it stands in Ophrah of the Abiezrites.

²⁵That same night the LORD said to him, "Take the second bull from your father's herd, the one seven years old.*b* Tear down your father's altar to Baal and cut down the Asherah pole*c* beside it. ²⁶Then build a proper kind of*d* altar to the LORD your God on the top of this height. Using the wood of the Asherah pole that you cut down, offer the second*e* bull as a burnt offering."

²⁷So Gideon took ten of his servants and did as the LORD told him. But because he was afraid of his family and the townspeople, he did it at night rather than in the daytime.

²⁸In the morning when the people of the town got up, there was Baal's altar, demolished, with the Asherah pole beside it cut down and the second bull sacrificed on the newly built altar!

²⁹They asked each other, "Who did this?"

When they carefully investigated, they were told, "Gideon son of Joash did it."

³⁰The people of the town demanded of Joash, "Bring out your son. He must die, because he has broken down Baal's altar and cut down the Asherah pole beside it."

³¹But Joash replied to the hostile crowd around him, "Are you going to plead Baal's cause? Are you trying to save him? Whoever fights for him shall be put to death by morning! If Baal really is a god, he can defend himself when someone breaks down his altar." ³²So that day they gave Gideon the name Jerub-Baal,*f* saying, "Let Baal contend with him," because he broke down Baal's altar.

³³Now all the Midianites, Amalekites and other eastern peoples joined forces and crossed over the Jordan and camped in the Valley of Jezreel. ³⁴Then the Spirit of the LORD came on Gideon, and he blew a trumpet, summoning the Abiezrites to follow him. ³⁵He sent messengers throughout Manasseh, calling them to arms, and also into Asher, Zebulun and Naphtali, so that they too went up to meet them.

³⁶Gideon said to God, "If you will save Israel by my hand as you have promised— ³⁷look, I will place a

---

a 19 That is, probably about 36 pounds or about 16 kilograms   *b 25* Or *Take a full-grown, mature bull from your father's herd*   *c 25* That is, a wooden symbol of the goddess Asherah; also in verses 26, 28 and 30   *d 26* Or *build with layers of stone an*   *e 26* Or *full-grown*; also in verse 28   *f 32* Jerub-Baal probably means *let Baal contend.*

wool fleece on the threshing floor. If there is dew only on the fleece and all the ground is dry, then I will know that you will save Israel by my hand, as you said." [38] And that is what happened. Gideon rose early the next day; he squeezed the fleece and wrung out the dew—a bowlful of water.

[39] Then Gideon said to God, "Do not be angry with me. Let me make just one more request. Allow me one more test with the fleece, but this time make the fleece dry and let the ground be covered with dew." [40] That night God did so. Only the fleece was dry; all the ground was covered with dew.

Gideon Defeats the Midianites

7 Early in the morning, Jerub-Baal (that is, Gideon) and all his men camped at the spring of Harod. The camp of Midian was north of them in the valley near the hill of Moreh. [2] The LORD said to Gideon, "You have too many men. I cannot deliver Midian into their hands, or Israel would boast against me, 'My own strength has saved me.' [3] Now announce to the army, 'Anyone who trembles with fear may turn back and leave Mount Gilead.'" So twenty-two thousand men left, while ten thousand remained.

[4] But the LORD said to Gideon, "There are still too many men. Take them down to the water, and I will sift them for you there. If I say, 'This one shall go with you,' he shall go; but if I say, 'This one shall not go with you,' he shall not go."

[5] So Gideon took the men down to the water. There the LORD told him, "Separate those who lap the water with their tongues like a dog from those who kneel down to drink." [6] Three hundred of them lapped with their hands to their mouths. All the rest got down on their knees to drink.

[7] The LORD said to Gideon, "With the three hundred men that lapped I will save you and give the Midianites into your hands. Let all the others go, each to his own place." [8] So Gideon sent the rest of the Israelites to their tents but kept the three hundred, who took over the provisions and trumpets of the others.

Now the camp of Midian lay below him in the valley. [9] During that night the LORD said to Gideon, "Get up, go down against the camp, because I am going to give it into your hands. [10] If you are afraid to attack, go down to the camp with your servant Purah [11] and listen to what they are saying. Afterward, you will be encouraged to attack the camp." So he and Purah his servant went down to the outposts of the camp. [12] The Midianites, the Amalekites and all the other eastern peoples had settled in the valley, thick as locusts. Their camels could no more be counted than the sand on the seashore.

[13] Gideon arrived just as a man was telling a friend his dream. "I had a dream," he was saying. "A round loaf of barley bread came tumbling into the Midianite camp. It struck the tent with such force that the tent overturned and collapsed."

[14] His friend responded, "This can be nothing other than the sword of Gideon son of Joash, the Israelite. God has given the Midianites and the whole camp into his hands."

[15] When Gideon heard the dream and its interpretation, he bowed down and worshiped. He returned to the camp of Israel and called out, "Get up! The LORD has given the Midianite camp into your hands." [16] Dividing the three hundred men into three companies, he placed trumpets and empty jars in the hands of all of them, with torches inside.

[17] "Watch me," he told them. "Follow my lead. When I get to the edge of the camp, do exactly as I do. [18] When I and all who are with me blow our trumpets, then from all around the camp blow yours and shout, 'For the LORD and for Gideon.'"

[19] Gideon and the hundred men with him reached the edge of the camp at the beginning of the

atissue:decisions

6:36–40 "Prove it, God!" When you ask God to prove something to you, your request reveals more about you than it does about God. Your demand exposes your unspoken doubts and fears. *Why can't I take him at his word? Why am I so afraid?* When you face tough decisions, anxiety is a natural reaction. So, like Gideon, you may plead for assurance in a sign. Before you ask God for a sign, though, first recognize the fear or lack of faith that's motivating your request. Then ask God for the courage to overcome that fear so that you can take him at his word.

311

conversations

risk «» 7:1-25

1 » What does risk-taking for God teach you that safe decisions can never teach you?

2 » Name some positive and negative risks.

3 » What risks do you think God might want you to take?

For more on risk, check the index.
For the next Conversations, go to p. 315.

312

middle watch, just after they had changed the guard. They blew their trumpets and broke the jars that were in their hands. ²⁰The three companies blew the trumpets and smashed the jars. Grasping the torches in their left hands and holding in their right hands the trumpets they were to blow, they shouted, "A sword for the Lord and for Gideon!" ²¹While each man held his position around the camp, all the Midianites ran, crying out as they fled.

²²When the three hundred trumpets sounded, the Lord caused the men throughout the camp to turn on each other with their swords. The army fled to Beth Shittah toward Zererah as far as the border of Abel Meholah near Tabbath. ²³Israelites from Naphtali, Asher and all Manasseh were called out, and they pursued the Midianites. ²⁴Gideon sent messengers throughout the hill country of Ephraim, saying, "Come down against the Midianites and seize the waters of the Jordan ahead of them as far as Beth Barah."

So all the men of Ephraim were called out and they seized the waters of the Jordan as far as Beth Barah. ²⁵They also captured two of the Midianite leaders, Oreb and Zeeb. They killed Oreb at the rock of Oreb, and Zeeb at the winepress of Zeeb. They pursued the Midianites and brought the heads of Oreb and Zeeb to Gideon, who was by the Jordan.

Zebah and Zalmunna

8 Now the Ephraimites asked Gideon, "Why have you treated us like this? Why didn't you call us when you went to fight Midian?" And they challenged him vigorously.

²But he answered them, "What have I accomplished compared to you? Aren't the gleanings of Ephraim's grapes better than the full grape harvest of Abiezer? ³God gave Oreb and Zeeb, the Midianite leaders, into your hands. What was I able to do compared to you?" At this, their resentment against him subsided.

⁴Gideon and his three hundred men, exhausted yet keeping up the pursuit, came to the Jordan and crossed it. ⁵He said to the men of Sukkoth, "Give my troops some bread; they are worn out, and I am still pursuing Zebah and Zalmunna, the kings of Midian."

⁶But the officials of Sukkoth said, "Do you already have the hands of Zebah and Zalmunna in your possession? Why should we give bread to your troops?"

⁷Then Gideon replied, "Just for that, when the Lord has given Zebah and Zalmunna into my hand, I will tear your flesh with desert thorns and briers."

⁸From there he went up to Peniel[a] and made the same request of them, but they answered as the men of Sukkoth had. ⁹So he said to the men of Peniel, "When I return in triumph, I will tear down this tower."

¹⁰Now Zebah and Zalmunna were in Karkor with a force of about fifteen thousand men, all that were left of the armies of the eastern peoples; a hundred and twenty thousand swordsmen had fallen. ¹¹Gideon went up by the route of the nomads east of Nobah and Jogbehah and attacked the unsuspecting army. ¹²Zebah and Zalmunna, the two kings of Midian, fled, but he pursued them and captured them, routing their entire army.

¹³Gideon son of Joash then returned from the battle by the Pass of Heres. ¹⁴He caught a young man of Sukkoth and questioned him, and the young man wrote down for him the names of the seventy-seven officials of Sukkoth, the elders of the town. ¹⁵Then Gideon came and said to the men of Sukkoth, "Here are Zebah and Zalmunna, about whom you taunted me by saying, 'Do you already have the hands of Zebah and Zalmunna in your possession? Why should we give bread to your exhausted troops?'" ¹⁶He took the elders of the town and taught the men of Sukkoth a lesson by punishing them with desert thorns and briers. ¹⁷He also pulled down the tower of Peniel and killed the men of the town.

ᵃ 8 Hebrew Penuel, a variant of Peniel; also in verses 9 and 17

¹⁸ Then he asked Zebah and Zalmunna, "What kind of men did you kill at Tabor?"

"Men like you," they answered, "each one with the bearing of a prince."

¹⁹ Gideon replied, "Those were my brothers, the sons of my own mother. As surely as the LORD lives, if you had spared their lives, I would not kill you." ²⁰ Turning to Jether, his oldest son, he said, "Kill them!" But Jether did not draw his sword, because he was only a boy and was afraid.

²¹ Zebah and Zalmunna said, "Come, do it yourself. 'As is the man, so is his strength.'" So Gideon stepped forward and killed them, and took the ornaments off their camels' necks.

Gideon's Ephod

²² The Israelites said to Gideon, "Rule over us—you, your son and your grandson—because you have saved us from the hand of Midian."

²³ But Gideon told them, "I will not rule over you, nor will my son rule over you. The LORD will rule over you." ²⁴ And he said, "I do have one request, that each of you give me an earring from your share of the plunder." (It was the custom of the Ishmaelites to wear gold earrings.)

²⁵ They answered, "We'll be glad to give them." So they spread out a garment, and each of them threw a ring from his plunder onto it. ²⁶ The weight of the gold rings he asked for came to seventeen hundred shekels,^a not counting the ornaments, the pendants and the purple garments worn by the kings of Midian or the chains that were on their camels' necks. ²⁷ Gideon made the gold into an ephod, which he placed in Ophrah, his town. All Israel prostituted themselves by worshiping it there, and it became a snare to Gideon and his family.

Gideon's Death

²⁸ Thus Midian was subdued before the Israelites and did not raise its head again. During Gideon's lifetime, the land had peace forty years.

²⁹ Jerub-Baal son of Joash went back home to live. ³⁰ He had seventy sons of his own, for he had many wives. ³¹ His concubine, who lived in Shechem, also bore him a son, whom he named Abimelek. ³² Gideon son of Joash died at a good old age and was buried in the tomb of his father Joash in Ophrah of the Abiezrites.

³³ No sooner had Gideon died than the Israelites again prostituted themselves to the Baals. They set up Baal-Berith as their god ³⁴ and did not remember the LORD their God, who had rescued them from the hands of all their enemies on every side. ³⁵ They also failed to show any loyalty to the family of Jerub-Baal (that is, Gideon) in spite of all the good things he had done for them.

Abimelek

9 Abimelek son of Jerub-Baal went to his mother's brothers in Shechem and said to them and to all his mother's clan, ² "Ask all the citizens of Shechem, 'Which is better for you: to have all seventy of Jerub-Baal's sons rule over you, or just one man?' Remember, I am your flesh and blood."

³ When the brothers repeated all this to the citizens of Shechem, they were inclined to follow Abimelek, for they said, "He is related to us." ⁴ They gave him seventy shekels^b of silver from the temple of Baal-Berith, and Abimelek used it to hire reckless scoundrels, who became his followers. ⁵ He went to his father's home in Ophrah and on one stone murdered his seventy brothers, the sons of Jerub-Baal. But Jotham, the youngest son of Jerub-Baal, escaped by hiding. ⁶ Then all the citizens of Shechem and Beth Millo gathered beside the great tree at the pillar in Shechem to crown Abimelek king.

⁷ When Jotham was told about this, he climbed up on the top of Mount Gerizim and shouted to them, "Listen to me, citizens of Shechem, so that God may listen to you. ⁸ One day the trees went out to anoint a king for themselves. They said to the olive tree, 'Be our king.'

⁹ "But the olive tree answered, 'Should I give up my oil, by which both gods and human beings are honored, to hold sway over the trees?'

¹⁰ "Next, the trees said to the fig tree, 'Come and be our king.'

¹¹ "But the fig tree replied, 'Should I give up my fruit, so good and sweet, to hold sway over the trees?'

¹² "Then the trees said to the vine, 'Come and be our king.'

---

^a *26* That is, about 43 pounds or about 20 kilograms   ^b *4* That is, about 1 3/4 pounds or about 800 grams

¹³"But the vine answered, 'Should I give up my wine, which cheers both gods and human beings, to hold sway over the trees?'

¹⁴"Finally all the trees said to the thornbush, 'Come and be our king.'

¹⁵"The thornbush said to the trees, 'If you really want to anoint me king over you, come and take refuge in my shade; but if not, then let fire come out of the thornbush and consume the cedars of Lebanon!'

¹⁶"Have you acted honorably and in good faith by making Abimelek king? Have you been fair to Jerub-Baal and his family? Have you treated him as he deserves? ¹⁷Remember that my father fought for you and risked his life to rescue you from the hand of Midian. ¹⁸But today you have revolted against my father's family. You have murdered his seventy sons on a single stone and have made Abimelek, the son of his female slave, king over the citizens of Shechem because he is related to you. ¹⁹So have you acted honorably and in good faith toward Jerub-Baal and his family today? If you have, may Abimelek be your joy, and may you be his, too! ²⁰But if you have not, let fire come out from Abimelek and consume you, the citizens of Shechem and Beth Millo, and let fire come out from you, the citizens of Shechem and Beth Millo, and consume Abimelek!"

²¹Then Jotham fled, escaping to Beer, and he lived there because he was afraid of his brother Abimelek.

²²After Abimelek had governed Israel three years, ²³God stirred up animosity between Abimelek and the citizens of Shechem so that they acted treacherously against Abimelek. ²⁴God did this in order that the crime against Jerub-Baal's seventy sons, the shedding of their blood, might be avenged on their brother Abimelek and on the citizens of Shechem, who had helped him murder his brothers. ²⁵In opposition to him these citizens of Shechem set an ambush on the hilltops to rob everyone who passed by, and this was reported to Abimelek.

²⁶Now Gaal son of Ebed moved with his brothers into Shechem, and its citizens put their confidence in him. ²⁷After they had gone out into the fields and gathered the grapes and trodden them, they held a festival in the temple of their god. While they were eating and drinking, they cursed Abimelek. ²⁸Then Gaal son of Ebed said, "Who is Abimelek, and who is Shechem, that we should be subject to him? Isn't he Jerub-Baal's son, and isn't Zebul his deputy? Serve the people of Hamor, Shechem's father! Why should we serve Abimelek? ²⁹If only this people were under my command! Then I would get rid of him. I would say to Abimelek, 'Call out your whole army!'"^a

³⁰When Zebul the governor of the city heard what Gaal son of Ebed said, he was very angry. ³¹Under cover he sent messengers to Abimelek, saying, "Gaal son of Ebed and his relatives have come to Shechem and are stirring up the city against you. ³²Now then, during the night you and your men should come and lie in wait in the fields. ³³In the morning at sunrise, advance against the city. When Gaal and his men come out against you, do whatever your hand finds to do."

³⁴So Abimelek and all his troops set out by night and took up concealed positions near Shechem in four companies. ³⁵Now Gaal son of Ebed had gone out and was standing at the entrance of the city gate just as Abimelek and his troops came out from their hiding place.

³⁶When Gaal saw them, he said to Zebul, "Look, people are coming down from the tops of the mountains!"

Zebul replied, "You mistake the shadows of the mountains for men."

³⁷But Gaal spoke up again: "Look, people are coming down from the central hill,^b and a company is coming from the direction of the diviners' tree."

³⁸Then Zebul said to him, "Where is your big talk now, you who said, 'Who is Abimelek that we should be subject to him?' Aren't these the men you ridiculed? Go out and fight them!"

³⁹So Gaal led out^c the citizens of Shechem and fought Abimelek. ⁴⁰Abimelek chased him all the way to the entrance of the gate, and many fell slain as they fled. ⁴¹Abimelek stayed in Arumah, and Zebul drove Gaal and his relatives out of Shechem.

⁴²The next day the people of Shechem went out to the fields, and this was reported to Abimelek. ⁴³So

---

^a 29 Septuagint; Hebrew him." Then he said to Abimelek, "Call out your whole army!" ^b 37 The Hebrew for this phrase means the navel of the earth.
^c 39 Or Gaal went out in the sight of

he took his troops, divided them into three companies and set an ambush in the fields. When he saw the people coming out of the city, he rose to attack them. ⁴⁴Abimelek and the companies with him rushed forward to a position at the entrance of the city gate. Then two companies attacked those in the fields and struck them down. ⁴⁵All that day Abimelek pressed his attack against the city until he had captured it and killed its people. Then he destroyed the city and scattered salt over it.

⁴⁶On hearing this, the citizens in the tower of Shechem went into the stronghold of the temple of El-Berith. ⁴⁷When Abimelek heard that they had assembled there, ⁴⁸he and all his men went up Mount Zalmon. He took an ax and cut off some branches, which he lifted to his shoulders. He ordered the men with him, "Quick! Do what you have seen me do!" ⁴⁹So all the men cut branches and followed Abimelek. They piled them against the stronghold and set it on fire with the people still inside. So all the people in the tower of Shechem, about a thousand men and women, also died.

⁵⁰Next Abimelek went to Thebez and besieged it and captured it. ⁵¹Inside the city, however, was a strong tower, to which all the men and women—all the people of the city—had fled. They had locked themselves in and climbed up on the tower roof. ⁵²Abimelek went to the tower and attacked it. But as he approached the entrance to the tower to set it on fire, ⁵³a woman dropped an upper millstone on his head and cracked his skull.

⁵⁴Hurriedly he called to his armor-bearer, "Draw your sword and kill me, so that they can't say, 'A woman killed him.'" So his servant ran him through, and he died. ⁵⁵When the Israelites saw that Abimelek was dead, they went home.

⁵⁶Thus God repaid the wickedness that Abimelek had done to his father by murdering his seventy brothers. ⁵⁷God also made the people of Shechem pay for all their wickedness. The curse of Jotham son of Jerub-Baal came on them.

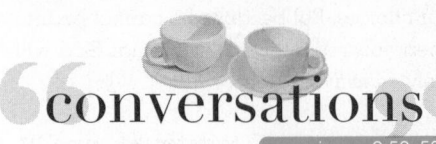

" conversations "

exercise «» 9:50–53

1 » What do this woman's impressive strength and aim tell us about her physical fitness?

2 » Does your level of fitness hold you back from anything God wants you to do?

3 » What is the relationship between physical and spiritual health?

For more on exercise, check the index.
For the next Conversations, go to p. 335.

315

Tola

10 After the time of Abimelek, a man of Issachar named Tola son of Puah, the son of Dodo, rose to save Israel. He lived in Shamir, in the hill country of Ephraim. ²He led*ᵃ* Israel twenty-three years; then he died, and was buried in Shamir.

Jair

³He was followed by Jair of Gilead, who led Israel twenty-two years. ⁴He had thirty sons, who rode thirty donkeys. They controlled thirty towns in Gilead, which to this day are called Havvoth Jair.*ᵇ* ⁵When Jair died, he was buried in Kamon.

Jephthah

⁶Again the Israelites did evil in the eyes of the LORD. They served the Baals and the Ashtoreths, and the gods of Aram, the gods of Sidon, the gods of Moab, the gods of the Ammonites and the gods of the Philistines. And because the Israelites forsook the LORD and no longer served him, ⁷he became angry with them. He sold them into the hands of the Philistines and the Ammonites, ⁸who that year shattered and crushed them. For eighteen years they oppressed all the Israelites on the east side of the Jordan in Gilead, the land of the Amorites. ⁹The Ammonites also crossed the Jordan to fight against Judah, Benjamin and the house of Ephraim; and Israel was in great distress. ¹⁰Then the Israelites cried out to the LORD, "We have sinned against you, forsaking our God and serving the Baals."

¹¹The LORD replied, "When the Egyptians, the Amorites, the Ammonites, the Philistines, ¹²the Sidonians, the Amalekites and the Maonites*ᶜ* oppressed you and you cried to me for help, did I not save

---

ᵃ 2 Traditionally judged; also in verse 3 ᵇ 4 Or called the settlements of Jair ᶜ 12 Hebrew; some Septuagint manuscripts Midianites you from their hands? ¹³But you have forsaken me and served other gods, so I will no longer save you. ¹⁴Go and cry out to the gods you have chosen. Let them save you when you are in trouble!"

¹⁵But the Israelites said to the LORD, "We have sinned. Do with us whatever you think best, but please rescue us now." ¹⁶Then they got rid of the foreign gods among them and served the LORD. And he could bear Israel's misery no longer.

HE IS: sensitive

10:16 God refused to put up with Israel's sin of serving false gods, so he allowed their enemies to take them captive. When the people showed proof of their repentance and got rid of their other gods, God graciously forgave them because he could not bear to see them suffer.

Because God cannot tolerate your serving other gods—things like money, power or pride—he will allow you to suffer the consequences of your choices. But because he cannot bear to see you suffer, he will forgive and restore you when you repent. Don't think that God will ignore either your sin or your suffering. He is divinely *sensitive* to you.

For the next He Is, go to p. 317.

¹⁷When the Ammonites were called to arms and camped in Gilead, the Israelites assembled and camped at Mizpah. ¹⁸The leaders of the people of Gilead said to each other, "Whoever will take the lead in attacking the Ammonites will be head over all who live in Gilead."

11 Jephthah the Gileadite was a mighty warrior. His father was Gilead; his mother was a prostitute. ²Gilead's wife also bore him sons, and when they were grown up, they drove Jephthah away. "You are not going to get any inheritance in our family," they said, "because you are the son of another woman." ³So Jephthah fled from his brothers and settled in the land of Tob, where a gang of scoundrels gathered around him and followed him.

⁴Some time later, when the Ammonites were fighting against Israel, ⁵the elders of Gilead went to get Jephthah from the land of Tob. ⁶"Come," they said, "be our commander, so we can fight the Ammonites."

⁷Jephthah said to them, "Didn't you hate me and drive me from my father's house? Why do you come to me now, when you're in trouble?"

⁸The elders of Gilead said to him, "Nevertheless, we are turning to you now; come with us to fight the Ammonites, and you will be head over all of us who live in Gilead."

⁹Jephthah answered, "Suppose you take me back to fight the Ammonites and the LORD gives them to me—will I really be your head?"

¹⁰The elders of Gilead replied, "The LORD is our witness; we will certainly do as you say." ¹¹So Jephthah went with the elders of Gilead, and the people made him head and commander over them. And he repeated all his words before the LORD in Mizpah.

¹²Then Jephthah sent messengers to the Ammonite king with the question: "What do you have against me that you have attacked my country?"

¹³The king of the Ammonites answered Jephthah's messengers, "When Israel came up out of Egypt, they took away my land from the Arnon to the Jabbok, all the way to the Jordan. Now give it back peaceably."

¹⁴Jephthah sent back messengers to the Ammonite king, ¹⁵saying:

"This is what Jephthah says: Israel did not take the land of Moab or the land of the Ammonites. ¹⁶But when they came up out of Egypt, Israel went through the wilderness to the Red Sea*ᵃ* and on to Kadesh. ¹⁷Then Israel sent messengers to the king of Edom, saying, 'Give us permission to go through your country,' but the king of Edom would not listen. They sent also to the king of Moab, and he refused. So Israel stayed at Kadesh.

[18] "Next they traveled through the wilderness, skirted the lands of Edom and Moab, passed along the eastern side of the country of Moab, and camped on the other side of the Arnon. They did not enter the territory of Moab, for the Arnon was its border.

[19] "Then Israel sent messengers to Sihon king of the Amorites, who ruled in Heshbon, and said to him, 'Let us pass through your country to our own place.' [20] Sihon, however, did not trust Israel[a] to pass through his territory. He mustered all his army and encamped at Jahaz and fought with Israel.

[21] "Then the LORD, the God of Israel, gave Sihon and his whole army into Israel's hands, and they defeated them. Israel took over all the land of the Amorites who lived in that country, [22] capturing all of it from the Arnon to the Jabbok and from the desert to the Jordan.

[23] "Now since the LORD, the God of Israel, has driven the Amorites out before his people Israel, what right have you to take it over? [24] Will you not take what your god Chemosh gives you? Likewise, whatever the LORD our God has given us, we will possess. [25] Are you any better than Balak son of Zippor, king of Moab? Did he ever quarrel with Israel or fight with them? [26] For three hundred years Israel occupied Heshbon, Aroer, the surrounding settlements and all the towns along the Arnon. Why didn't you retake them during that time? [27] I have not wronged you, but you are doing me wrong by waging war against me. Let the LORD, the Judge,[b] decide the dispute this day between the Israelites and the Ammonites."

[28] The king of Ammon, however, paid no attention to the message Jephthah sent him.

[29] Then the Spirit of the LORD came on Jephthah. He crossed Gilead and Manasseh, passed through Mizpah of Gilead, and from there he advanced against the Ammonites. [30] And Jephthah made a vow to the LORD: "If you give the Ammonites into my hands, [31] whatever comes out of the door of my house to meet me when I return in triumph from the Ammonites will be the LORD's, and I will sacrifice it as a burnt offering."

HE IS: unbiased

11:1–29 Jephthah was an unlikely judge. The child of a prostitute, he was cut out of his father's inheritance. He was driven away from his family and fell in with a rowdy group. However, God looked beyond the outward circumstances of Jephthah's life and saw a man who would serve him wholeheartedly. Graciously, God chose Jephthah.

He is *unbiased*. God does not judge you based on your pedigree or your network of friends. He sees beyond those things to the person you are inside and the person you could be. If you serve God with your whole heart, he will use you too.

For the next He Is, go to p. 324.

[32] Then Jephthah went over to fight the Ammonites, and the LORD gave them into his hands. [33] He devastated twenty towns from Aroer to the vicinity of Minnith, as far as Abel Keramim. Thus Israel subdued Ammon.

[34] When Jephthah returned to his home in Mizpah, who should come out to meet him but his daughter, dancing to the sound of timbrels! She was an only child. Except for her he had neither son nor daughter. [35] When he saw her, he tore his clothes and cried, "Oh! My daughter! You have brought me down and I am devastated. I have made a vow to the LORD that I cannot break."

[36] "My father," she replied, "you have given your word to the LORD. Do to me just as you promised, now that the LORD has avenged you of your enemies, the Ammonites. [37] But grant me this one request," she said. "Give me two months to roam the hills and weep with my friends, because I will never marry."

[38] "You may go," he said. And he let her go for two months. She and her friends went into the hills and

wept because she would never marry. ³⁹After the two months, she returned to her father, and he did to her as he had vowed. And she was a virgin.

From this comes the Israelite tradition ⁴⁰that each year the young women of Israel go out for four days to commemorate the daughter of Jephthah the Gileadite.

Jephthah and Ephraim

12 The Ephraimite forces were called out, and they crossed over to Zaphon and said to Jephthah, "Why did you go to fight the Ammonites without calling us to go with you? We're going to burn down your house over your head."

²Jephthah answered, "I and my people were engaged in a great struggle with the Ammonites, and although I called, you didn't save me out of their hands. ³When I saw that you wouldn't help, I took my life in my hands and crossed over to fight the Ammonites, and the LORD gave me the victory over them. Now why have you come up today to fight me?"

⁴Jephthah then called together the men of Gilead and fought against Ephraim. The Gileadites struck them down because the Ephraimites had said, "You Gileadites are renegades from Ephraim and Manasseh." ⁵The Gileadites captured the fords of the Jordan leading to Ephraim, and whenever a survivor of Ephraim said, "Let me cross over," the Gileadites asked him, "Are you an Ephraimite?" If he replied, "No," ⁶they said, "All right, say 'Shibboleth.'" If he said, "Sibboleth," because he could not pronounce the word correctly, they seized him and killed him at the fords of the Jordan. Forty-two thousand Ephraimites were killed at that time.

⁷Jephthah led*ᵃ* Israel six years. Then Jephthah the Gileadite died and was buried in a town in Gilead.

Ibzan, Elon and Abdon

⁸After him, Ibzan of Bethlehem led Israel. ⁹He had thirty sons and thirty daughters. He gave his daughters away in marriage to those outside his clan, and for his sons he brought in thirty young women as wives from outside his clan. Ibzan led Israel seven years. ¹⁰Then Ibzan died and was buried in Bethlehem.

¹¹After him, Elon the Zebulunite led Israel ten years. ¹²Then Elon died and was buried in Aijalon in the land of Zebulun.

¹³After him, Abdon son of Hillel, from Pirathon, led Israel. ¹⁴He had forty sons and thirty grandsons, who rode on seventy donkeys. He led Israel eight years. ¹⁵Then Abdon son of Hillel died and was buried at Pirathon in Ephraim, in the hill country of the Amalekites.

The Birth of Samson

13 Again the Israelites did evil in the eyes of the LORD, so the LORD delivered them into the hands of the Philistines for forty years.

²A certain man of Zorah, named Manoah, from the clan of the Danites, had a wife who was childless, unable to give birth. ³The angel of the LORD appeared to her and said, "You are barren and childless, but you are going to become pregnant and give birth to a son. ⁴Now see to it that you drink no wine or other fermented drink and that you do not eat anything unclean. ⁵You will become pregnant and have a son whose head

aussie:children

13:2–5 Even if you've never been pregnant, chances are that one or more of your friends has. And once you get talking about pregnancy, everyone has a story. Samson's mother certainly would've had a great story to share with her girlfriends. Her pregnancy was announced by an angel who gave her guidelines for Samson's special status before God. If you're a Christian, you have a desire for your children to be set apart to God, too. Thankfully, you don't have to follow the rules God gave to Samson's mother. But like her, it *is* important to raise your child with the knowledge of his or her special place as a child of God.

ᵃ 7 Traditionally judged; also in verses 8-14

is never to be touched by a razor because the boy is to be a Nazirite, dedicated to God from the womb. He will begin to deliver Israel from the hands of the Philistines."

⁶Then the woman went to her husband and told him, "A man of God came to me. He looked like an angel of God, very awesome. I didn't ask him where he came from, and he didn't tell me his name. ⁷But he said to me, 'You will become pregnant and have a son. Now then, drink no wine or other fermented drink and do not eat anything unclean, because the boy will be a Nazirite of God from the womb until the day of his death.'"

⁸Then Manoah prayed to the LORD: "Pardon your servant, Lord. I beg you to let the man of God you sent to us come again to teach us how to bring up the boy who is to be born."

⁹God heard Manoah, and the angel of God came again to the woman while she was out in the field; but her husband Manoah was not with her. ¹⁰The woman hurried to tell her husband, "He's here! The man who appeared to me the other day!"

¹¹Manoah got up and followed his wife. When he came to the man, he said, "Are you the man who talked to my wife?"

"I am," he said.

¹²So Manoah asked him, "When your words are fulfilled, what is to be the rule that governs the boy's life and work?"

¹³The angel of the LORD answered, "Your wife must do all that I have told her. ¹⁴She must not eat anything that comes from the grapevine, nor drink any wine or other fermented drink nor eat anything unclean. She must do everything I have commanded her."

¹⁵Manoah said to the angel of the LORD, "We would like you to stay until we prepare a young goat for you."

¹⁶The angel of the LORD replied, "Even though you detain me, I will not eat any of your food. But if you prepare a burnt offering, offer it to the LORD." (Manoah did not realize that it was the angel of the LORD.)

¹⁷Then Manoah inquired of the angel of the LORD, "What is your name, so that we may honor you when your word comes true?"

¹⁸He replied, "Why do you ask my name? It is beyond understanding.ᵃ" ¹⁹Then Manoah took a young goat, together with the grain offering, and sacrificed it on a rock to the LORD. And the LORD did an amazing thing while Manoah and his wife watched: ²⁰As the flame blazed up from the altar toward heaven, the angel of the LORD ascended in the flame. Seeing this, Manoah and his wife fell with their faces to the ground. ²¹When the angel of the LORD did not show himself again to Manoah and his wife, Manoah realized that it was the angel of the LORD.

²²"We are doomed to die!" he said to his wife. "We have seen God!"

²³But his wife answered, "If the LORD had meant to kill us, he would not have accepted a burnt offering and grain offering from our hands, nor shown us all these things or now told us this."

²⁴The woman gave birth to a boy and named him Samson. He grew and the LORD blessed him, ²⁵and the Spirit of the LORD began to stir him while he was in Mahaneh Dan, between Zorah and Eshtaol.

Samson's Marriage

14 Samson went down to Timnah and saw there a young Philistine woman. ²When he returned, he said to his father and mother, "I have seen a Philistine woman in Timnah; now get her for me as my wife."

³His father and mother replied, "Isn't there an acceptable woman among your relatives or among all our people? Must you go to the uncircumcised Philistines to get a wife?"

But Samson said to his father, "Get her for me. She's the right one for me." ⁴(His parents did not know that this was from the LORD, who was seeking an occasion to confront the Philistines; for at that time they were ruling over Israel.)

⁵Samson went down to Timnah together with his father and mother. As they approached the vineyards of Timnah, suddenly a young lion came roaring toward him. ⁶The Spirit of the LORD came on him in power so that he tore the lion apart with his bare hands as he might have torn a young goat. But he

319

ᵃ 18 Or is wonderful

told neither his father nor his mother what he had done. [7]Then he went down and talked with the woman, and he liked her.

[8]Some time later, when he went back to marry her, he turned aside to look at the lion's carcass, and in it he saw a swarm of bees and some honey. [9]He scooped out the honey with his hands and ate as he went along. When he rejoined his parents, he gave them some, and they too ate it. But he did not tell them that he had taken the honey from the lion's carcass.

[10]Now his father went down to see the woman. And there Samson held a feast, as was customary for young men. [11]When the people saw him, they chose thirty men to be his companions.

[12]"Let me tell you a riddle," Samson said to them. "If you can give me the answer within the seven days of the feast, I will give you thirty linen garments and thirty sets of clothes. [13]If you can't tell me the answer, you must give me thirty linen garments and thirty sets of clothes."

"Tell us your riddle," they said. "Let's hear it."

[14]He replied,

> "Out of the eater, something to eat;
> out of the strong, something sweet."

For three days they could not give the answer.

[15]On the fourth[a] day, they said to Samson's wife, "Coax your husband into explaining the riddle for us, or we will burn you and your father's household to death. Did you invite us here to steal our property?"

[16]Then Samson's wife threw herself on him, sobbing, "You hate me! You don't really love me. You've given my people a riddle, but you haven't told me the answer."

"I haven't even explained it to my father or mother," he replied, "so why should I explain it to you?" [17]She cried the whole seven days of the feast. So on the seventh day he finally told her, because she continued to press him. She in turn explained the riddle to her people.

[18]Before sunset on the seventh day the men of the town said to him,

> "What is sweeter than honey?
> What is stronger than a lion?"

Samson said to them,

> "If you had not plowed with my heifer,
> you would not have solved my riddle."

[19]Then the Spirit of the Lord came on him in power. He went down to Ashkelon, struck down thirty of their men, stripped them of everything and gave their clothes to those who had explained the riddle. Burning with anger, he returned to his father's home. [20]And Samson's wife was given to one of his companions who had attended him at the feast.

at issue: manipulation

14:12–20 "You don't really love me!" Have you ever heard someone say those words to a loved one? The speaker of these words rarely wants the listener to actually *prove* their love. These are words of control, meant to cause guilt so that the speaker can manipulate the listener. When we use words to force certain reactions, we trade true emotional intimacy for a tool of power. We may achieve our goal in getting our way, but at the same time, we sabotage the long-term relationship. By manipulating Samson, the Philistine woman who was to be his wife forfeited her marriage.

Samson's Vengeance on the Philistines

15 Later on, at the time of wheat harvest, Samson took a young goat and went to visit his wife. He said, "I'm going to my wife's room." But her father would not let him go in.

[2]"I was so sure you hated her," he said, "that I gave her to your companion. Isn't her younger sister more attractive? Take her instead."

---

[a] 15 Some Septuagint manuscripts and Syriac; Hebrew *seventh*

[3] Samson said to them, "This time I have a right to get even with the Philistines; I will really harm them." [4] So he went out and caught three hundred foxes and tied them tail to tail in pairs. He then fastened a torch to every pair of tails, [5] lit the torches and let the foxes loose in the standing grain of the Philistines. He burned up the shocks and standing grain, together with the vineyards and olive groves.

[6] When the Philistines asked, "Who did this?" they were told, "Samson, the Timnite's son-in-law, because his wife was given to his companion."

So the Philistines went up and burned her and her father to death. [7] Samson said to them, "Since you've acted like this, I swear that I won't stop until I get my revenge on you." [8] He attacked them viciously and slaughtered many of them. Then he went down and stayed in a cave in the rock of Etam.

[9] The Philistines went up and camped in Judah, spreading out near Lehi. [10] The people of Judah asked, "Why have you come to fight us?"

"We have come to take Samson prisoner," they answered, "to do to him as he did to us."

[11] Then three thousand men from Judah went down to the cave in the rock of Etam and said to Samson, "Don't you realize that the Philistines are rulers over us? What have you done to us?"

He answered, "I merely did to them what they did to me."

[12] They said to him, "We've come to tie you up and hand you over to the Philistines."

Samson said, "Swear to me that you won't kill me yourselves."

[13] "Agreed," they answered. "We will only tie you up and hand you over to them. We will not kill you." So they bound him with two new ropes and led him up from the rock. [14] As he approached Lehi, the Philistines came toward him shouting. The Spirit of the LORD came on him in power. The ropes on his arms became like charred flax, and the bindings dropped from his hands. [15] Finding a fresh jawbone of a donkey, he grabbed it and struck down a thousand men.

[16] Then Samson said,

> "With a donkey's jawbone
> I have made donkeys of them.[a]
> With a donkey's jawbone
> I have killed a thousand men."

[17] When he finished speaking, he threw away the jawbone; and the place was called Ramath Lehi.[b]

[18] Because he was very thirsty, he cried out to the LORD, "You have given your servant this great victory. Must I now die of thirst and fall into the hands of the uncircumcised?" [19] Then God opened up the hollow place in Lehi, and water came out of it. When Samson drank, his strength returned and he revived. So the spring was called En Hakkore,[c] and it is still there in Lehi.

[20] Samson led[d] Israel for twenty years in the days of the Philistines.

Samson and Delilah

16 One day Samson went to Gaza, where he saw a prostitute. He went in to spend the night with her. [2] The people of Gaza were told, "Samson is here!" So they surrounded the place and lay in wait for him all night at the city gate. They made no move during the night, saying, "At dawn we'll kill him."

[3] But Samson lay there only until the middle of the night. Then he got up and took hold of the doors of the city gate,

321

nonmanipulation·issue

16:1–31 Begging, prodding, pleading, imploring, entreating, demanding, pressuring—women are masters of manipulation. We may even pride ourselves on our ability to get our husbands or boyfriends to agree to anything. Delilah was an impressive manipulator. She knew how to use guilt as a weapon against the one she supposedly loved. As much as we would be horrified if a man used physical strength to control us, we should be careful not to use manipulation to control the men in our lives. You may have the skills to get what you want, but, like Delilah, you'll pay a high price for it.

---

[a] 16 Or made a heap or two; the Hebrew for donkey sounds like the Hebrew for heap.   [b] 17 Ramath Lehi means jawbone hill.   [c] 19 En Hakkore means caller's spring.   [d] 20 Traditionally judged

myth#21 "GOD WILL NEVER FORGIVE ME FOR . . ."

I would do things so differently—if only I could go back in time. Sometimes I dream that I am married to a wonderful man, and we're playing together in the park with our curly-haired little girl. When I first wake up, I feel so good and almost hopeful inside, but that feeling lasts only a few seconds as reality sets in and I begin remembering.

Remembering the traumatic fights my boyfriend and I used to have in our on-again, off-again relationship. Remembering how much I wanted him to love me . . . and realizing it would never be. Two years after we first met and six months after I moved in with him, he decided it wasn't worth it anymore and told me to leave. A few weeks later, I discovered I was pregnant. I had never slept with anyone before him. I think it will be a long time before I'll ever be able to let myself be close to a man again. It's foolish, I know, but part of me will always love him.

I didn't even tell him I was carrying his baby. I couldn't. It wouldn't matter anyway. It was as if I were walking around in a fog, not really thinking or feeling much of anything. In the meantime, I had no job and nowhere else to live. My mom let me move back home with her until I could figure something out. I was so plagued with guilt. I wanted it all to just go away. I felt like it was crushing the very life out of me. When I finally told my mom one night, crying hysterically, she held me tight and promised we'd get through this. The next day, she stayed home from work, and we went to two places. First, we went to her priest. Then, we went to her doctor. I remember talking about my options and just wanting it to be over. And now it's behind me—just like Mom promised me. But it will never really be over. I was so wrong, in so many ways. I wish I had died with that child. How can God ever forgive me?

—Courtney

ACCEPTING CHRIST'S FORGIVENESS

ACCEPTING CHRIST'S FORGIVENESS for our sins is a square-one issue. How can we grow in our faith if we can't get past square one and believe we're truly forgiven? For example, how can you share the Good News when you don't believe the news is all that good? And how would you counsel others about God's forgiveness if you're unsure it covers your sin? If you accept God's forgiveness intellectually yet fail to internalize it emotionally, you are practicing one of two options:

- You may be attempting to minimize your sin and convince yourself that it really isn't that bad.
- Or you're minimizing the work of the Cross by saying, in effect, that your sin is "so bad" that Christ's sacrificial death was not enough to pay for it.

Either option erroneously puts you in charge of your sin situation and sets aside the grace of God.

Why did Christ die? So he could forgive you for everything but _____? As he completed the payment for sin by spilling his precious blood, did he cry out a caveat from the cross, "It is finished . . . except for one thing" (John 19:30)? Moses was a murderer. David was an adulterer. Samson blew his potential. Saul murdered Christians. Zacchaeus was a thief. Peter denied Christ on the eve of his death—*three times*. Rahab was a prostitute. Their lives are a testimony to the outrageous, undeserved grace of God.

It's time to get practical and get past your own hang-ups.

- Do you need to talk with a Christian counselor to help you? Contact your church for recommendations.
- Write a "marker in time," sealed with today's date to keep in your Bible, to once and for all settle the issue of confessing, repenting and accepting God's forgiveness for that one sin you're still not sure his grace can cover.
- Meditate on the verses listed below as if reading them for the first time. Let their assurance spill over you like water on thirsty ground. Drink deeply, and determine to grow past square one in your faith today.

323

"Half of all adults (50 percent) believe that a person who does good can earn a place in heaven."

—Barna Research Group (2002)

> "I DO NOT SET ASIDE THE GRACE OF GOD, FOR IF RIGHTEOUSNESS COULD BE GAINED THROUGH THE LAW, CHRIST DIED FOR NOTHING!"
>
> GALATIANS 2:21

SEE ALSO

Psalm 51:17
Psalm 103:10–12
1 John 1:9

For more on **Forgiveness**, check the index.

together with the two posts, and tore them loose, bar and all. He lifted them to his shoulders and carried them to the top of the hill that faces Hebron.

⁴Some time later, he fell in love with a woman in the Valley of Sorek whose name was Delilah. ⁵The rulers of the Philistines went to her and said, "See if you can lure him into showing you the secret of his great strength and how we can overpower him so we may tie him up and subdue him. Each one of us will give you eleven hundred shekels*ᵃ* of silver."

⁶So Delilah said to Samson, "Tell me the secret of your great strength and how you can be tied up and subdued."

⁷Samson answered her, "If anyone ties me with seven fresh thongs*ᵇ* that have not been dried, I'll become as weak as any other man."

⁸Then the rulers of the Philistines brought her seven fresh thongs that had not been dried, and she tied him with them. ⁹With men hidden in the room, she called to him, "Samson, the Philistines are upon you!" But he snapped the thongs as easily as a piece of string snaps when it comes close to a flame. So the secret of his strength was not discovered.

¹⁰Then Delilah said to Samson, "You have made a fool of me; you lied to me. Come now, tell me how you can be tied."

¹¹He said, "If anyone ties me securely with new ropes that have never been used, I'll become as weak as any other man."

¹²So Delilah took new ropes and tied him with them. Then, with men hidden in the room, she called to him, "Samson, the Philistines are upon you!" But he snapped the ropes off his arms as if they were threads.

¹³Delilah then said to Samson, "Until now, you have been making a fool of me and lying to me. Tell me how you can be tied."

He replied, "If you weave the seven braids of my head into the fabric ⌊on the loom⌋ and tighten it with the pin, I'll become as weak as any other man." So while he was sleeping, Delilah took the seven braids of his head, wove them into the fabric ¹⁴and*ᶜ* tightened it with the pin.

Again she called to him, "Samson, the Philistines are upon you!" He awoke from his sleep and pulled up the pin and the loom, with the fabric.

¹⁵Then she said to him, "How can you say, 'I love you,' when you won't confide in me? This is the third time you have made a fool of me and haven't told me the secret of your great strength." ¹⁶With such nagging she prodded him day after day until he was tired to death.

¹⁷So he told her everything. "No razor has ever been used on my head," he said, "because I have been a Nazirite dedicated to God from my mother's womb. If my head were shaved, my strength would leave me, and I would become as weak as any other man."

¹⁸When Delilah saw that he had told her everything, she sent word to the rulers of the Philistines,

---

ᵃ 5 That is, about 28 pounds or about 13 kilograms   ᵇ 7 Or bowstrings; also in verses 8 and 9   ᶜ 13,14 Some Septuagint manuscripts; Hebrew ".I can⌋ if you weave the seven braids of my head into the fabric ⌊on the loom⌋." ¹⁴So she

HE IS: a restorer

16:1–31 Samson started on the right track, accomplishing great things with God's power. But he dabbled with danger, playing games with Delilah that led to his downfall. Finally, he repented, and God restored his strength—though it cost Samson his vision and his life.

There are many "Delilahs" out there looking for the secret that will topple you spiritually. Learn from Samson to fight the temptation of spiritual compromise. Otherwise, before you know it, you'll be blinded. He is *a restorer* and will help you when you fall, but it might cost you something precious.

For the next He Is, go to p. 338.

"Come back once more; he has told me everything." So the rulers of the Philistines returned with the silver in their hands. ¹⁹Having put him to sleep on her lap, she called for someone to shave off the seven braids of his hair, and so began to subdue him.ᵃ And his strength left him.

²⁰Then she called, "Samson, the Philistines are upon you!"

He awoke from his sleep and thought, "I'll go out as before and shake myself free." But he did not know that the Lᴏʀᴅ had left him.

²¹Then the Philistines seized him, gouged out his eyes and took him down to Gaza. Binding him with bronze shackles, they set him to grinding grain in the prison. ²²But the hair on his head began to grow again after it had been shaved.

The Death of Samson

²³Now the rulers of the Philistines assembled to offer a great sacrifice to Dagon their god and to celebrate, saying, "Our god has delivered Samson, our enemy, into our hands."

²⁴When the people saw him, they praised their god, saying,

> "Our god has delivered our enemy
>   into our hands,
>   the one who laid waste our land
>   and multiplied our slain."

²⁵While they were in high spirits, they shouted, "Bring out Samson to entertain us." So they called Samson out of the prison, and he performed for them.

When they stood him among the pillars, ²⁶Samson said to the servant who held his hand, "Put me where I can feel the pillars that support the temple, so that I may lean against them." ²⁷Now the temple was crowded with men and women; all the rulers of the Philistines were there, and on the roof were about three thousand men and women watching Samson perform. ²⁸Then Samson prayed to the Lᴏʀᴅ, "Sovereign Lᴏʀᴅ, remember me. Please, God, strengthen me just once more, and let me with one blow get revenge on the Philistines for my two eyes." ²⁹Then Samson reached toward the two central pillars on which the temple stood. Bracing himself against them, his right hand on the one and his left hand on the other, ³⁰Samson said, "Let me die with the Philistines!" Then he pushed with all his might, and down came the temple on the rulers and all the people in it. Thus he killed many more when he died than while he lived.

³¹Then his brothers and his father's whole family went down to get him. They brought him back and buried him between Zorah and Eshtaol in the tomb of Manoah his father. He had ledᵇ Israel twenty years.

Micah's Idols

17 Now a man named Micah from the hill country of Ephraim ²said to his mother, "The eleven hundred shekelsᶜ of silver that were taken from you and about which I heard you utter a curse—I have that silver with me; I took it."

Then his mother said, "The Lᴏʀᴅ bless you, my son!"

³When he returned the eleven hundred shekels of silver to his mother, she said, "I solemnly consecrate my silver to the Lᴏʀᴅ for my son to make an image overlaid with silver. I will give it back to you."

⁴So after he returned the silver to his mother, she took two hundred shekelsᵈ of silver and gave them to a silversmith, who used them to make the idol. And it was put in Micah's house.

⁵Now this man Micah had a shrine, and he made an ephod and some household gods and installed one of his sons as his priest. ⁶In those days Israel had no king; everyone did as they saw fit.

⁷A young Levite from Bethlehem in Judah, who had been living within the clan of Judah, ⁸left that town in search of some other place to stay. On his wayᵉ he came to Micah's house in the hill country of Ephraim.

⁹Micah asked him, "Where are you from?"

"I'm a Levite from Bethlehem in Judah," he said, "and I'm looking for a place to stay."

ᵃ 19 Hebrew; some Septuagint manuscripts *and he began to weaken* ᵇ31 Traditionally *judged* ᶜ 2 That is, about 28 pounds or about 13 kilograms
ᵈ 4 That is, about 5 pounds or about 2.3 kilograms ᵉ 8 Or *To carry on his profession*

myth#22

"I DON'T NEED TO GET INVOLVED— SOMEONE ELSE WILL DO IT."

I used to think I didn't need to get involved. "Someone else will do it," I told myself whenever I saw a situation and wondered if I should step in. "Who am I to tell someone else how to live his or her life?" I reassured myself, feeling justified simply to pray for the individual if I thought of it.

So, I looked the other way whenever we came up short closing the register at work. I knew who was stealing the money, but why should I say anything. After all, that was someone else's place—someone who earned the big bucks as the manager.

I turned a blind eye when I saw my neighbor's teenage daughter hanging out at the local park (often during school hours) with a man clearly much older than she was. They were kissing and causing quite a spectacle, so I was sure someone else would report it. After all, I don't know this neighbor that well. I wasn't sure how she'd take the news coming from me.

I also pretended not to see my old friend from high school, Brenda, at church on Sunday mornings. I looked right through her if I couldn't avoid her any other way. Not rudely, just as if I were focused on someone else. Somewhere else. Anywhere but looking into her eyes and seeing her raw pain up close. I'd heard the rumors—driving for hours by herself, drunk and lost. I'd even smelled the alcohol on her at our kids' soccer games. But what could I do to help her? After all, we're really not friends anymore. And I wouldn't know what to say anyway.

Then a crisis occurred in our family. It was a time when I really needed someone to enter into my daughter's life. She needed to hear the truth from someone other than her mom and dad. But no one else thought they needed to get involved. After all, everyone thought someone else would do it.

—Maya

WE HAVE A responsibility to our sisters and brothers in Christ. God instructs us to love each other above ourselves, even saying we ought to be willing to lay down our lives for others, yet we don't think we have a right to speak up when we see them in trouble? Too often we're content to stay uninvolved (other than carefully disguising gossip about them as "prayer requests"). We convince ourselves that we're being respectful of their privacy, waiting until we have more facts or depending on the paid professionals (church staff and counselors) to do something about it. Truthfully, as long as our own lives are comfortable, we tend to be more like the priest and Levite in Jesus' parable who ignored their neighbor's plight (see Luke 10:25–37). When we're slack in upholding our responsibility to look out for those within our church, then ignoring moral decay on the job, in our neighborhoods and in our nation is even easier.

The trickle-down effects of a "to each her own" philosophy we see in Judges 17:6 are obvious in our culture. We isolate ourselves in our own little worlds, living life as if it were a drive-up ATM that never required us to exit our cars.

Yes, getting involved in others' lives is messy. Yes, it demands your time. Yes, it makes you uncomfortable at times. Yes, it forces you to grow. But yes, it's the right thing to do. This is how God intends for you to live—to cry with those who cry, to celebrate with those who celebrate (see Romans 12:15). This is how Jesus lived his life—sharing people's messy lives, encouraging those who were faltering, picking the weak up off the ground and living out his love in action and in truth (see 1 John 3:18).

Get involved!

> "Although women are more active in church life than are men, their levels of participation in many aspects of church life—from worship attendance to volunteerism—are significantly declining."
>
> —Barna Research Group (2000)

327

"BROTHERS AND SISTERS, IF SOMEONE IS CAUGHT IN A SIN, YOU WHO LIVE BY THE SPIRIT SHOULD RESTORE THAT PERSON GENTLY."

GALATIANS 6:1

SEE ALSO

Deuteronomy 22:4

Ecclesiastes 4:9–12

Ephesians 4:15

For more on **Responsibility**, check the index.

¹⁰Then Micah said to him, "Live with me and be my father and priest, and I'll give you ten shekels*ᵃ* of silver a year, your clothes and your food." ¹¹So the Levite agreed to live with him, and the young man became like one of his sons to him. ¹²Then Micah installed the Levite, and the young man became his priest and lived in his house. ¹³And Micah said, "Now I know that the LORD will be good to me, since this Levite has become my priest."

The Danites Settle in Laish

18 In those days Israel had no king.

And in those days the tribe of the Danites was seeking a place of their own where they might settle, because they had not yet come into an inheritance among the tribes of Israel. ²So the Danites sent five of their leading men from Zorah and Eshtaol to spy out the land and explore it. These men represented all the Danites. They told them, "Go, explore the land."

So they entered the hill country of Ephraim and came to the house of Micah, where they spent the night. ³When they were near Micah's house, they recognized the voice of the young Levite; so they turned in there and asked him, "Who brought you here? What are you doing in this place? Why are you here?"

⁴He told them what Micah had done for him, and said, "He has hired me and I am his priest."

⁵Then they said to him, "Please inquire of God to learn whether our journey will be successful."

⁶The priest answered them, "Go in peace. Your journey has the LORD's approval."

⁷So the five men left and came to Laish, where they saw that the people were living in safety, like the Sidonians, unsuspecting and secure. And since their land lacked nothing, they were prosperous.ᵇ Also, they lived a long way from the Sidonians and had no relationship with anyone else.ᶜ

⁸When they returned to Zorah and Eshtaol, the Danites asked them, "How did you find things?"

⁹They answered, "Come on, let's attack them! We have seen the land, and it is very good. Aren't you going to do something? Don't hesitate to go there and take it over. ¹⁰When you get there, you will find an unsuspecting people and a spacious land that God has put into your hands, a land that lacks nothing whatever."

¹¹Then six hundred men of the Danites, armed for battle, set out from Zorah and Eshtaol. ¹²On their way they set up camp near Kiriath Jearim in Judah. This is why the place west of Kiriath Jearim is called Mahaneh Danᵈ to this day. ¹³From there they went on to the hill country of Ephraim and came to Micah's house.

¹⁴Then the five men who had spied out the land of Laish said to their fellow Danites, "Do you know that one of these houses has an ephod, some household gods and an image overlaid with silver? Now you know what to do." ¹⁵So they turned in there and went to the house of the young Levite at Micah's place and greeted him. ¹⁶The six hundred Danites, armed for battle, stood at the entrance of the gate. ¹⁷The five men who had spied out the land went inside and took the idol, the ephod and the household gods while the priest and the six hundred armed men stood at the entrance of the gate.

¹⁸When the five went into Micah's house and took the idol, the ephod and the household gods, the priest said to them, "What are you doing?"

¹⁹They answered him, "Be quiet! Don't say a word. Come with us, and be our father and priest. Isn't it better that you serve a tribe and clan in Israel as priest rather than just one man's household?" ²⁰The priest was very pleased. He took the ephod, the household gods and the idol and went along with the people. ²¹Putting their little children, their livestock and their possessions in front of them, they turned away and left.

²²When they had gone some distance from Micah's house, the men who lived near Micah were called together and overtook the Danites. ²³As they shouted after them, the Danites turned and said to Micah, "What's the matter with you that you called out your men to fight?"

²⁴He replied, "You took the gods I made, and my priest, and went away. What else do I have? How can you ask, 'What's the matter with you?'"

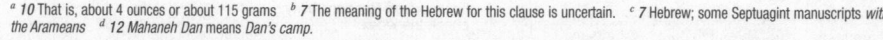

ᵃ *10* That is, about 4 ounces or about 115 grams   ᵇ *7* The meaning of the Hebrew for this clause is uncertain.   ᶜ *7* Hebrew; some Septuagint manuscripts *with the Arameans*   ᵈ *12 Mahaneh Dan* means *Dan's camp.*

²⁵The Danites answered, "Don't argue with us, or some of the men may get angry and attack you, and you and your family will lose your lives." ²⁶So the Danites went their way, and Micah, seeing that they were too strong for him, turned around and went back home.

²⁷Then they took what Micah had made, and his priest, and went on to Laish, against a peaceful and unsuspecting people. They attacked them with the sword and burned down their city. ²⁸There was no one to rescue them because they lived a long way from Sidon and had no relationship with anyone else. The city was in a valley near Beth Rehob.

The Danites rebuilt the city and settled there. ²⁹They named it Dan after their ancestor Dan, who was born to Israel—though the city used to be called Laish. ³⁰There the Danites set up for themselves the idol, and Jonathan son of Gershom, the son of Moses,[a] and his sons were priests for the tribe of Dan until the time of the captivity of the land. ³¹They continued to use the idol Micah had made, all the time the house of God was in Shiloh.

A Levite and His Concubine

19 In those days Israel had no king.

Now a Levite who lived in a remote area in the hill country of Ephraim took a concubine from Bethlehem in Judah. ²But she was unfaithful to him. She left him and went back to her parents' home in Bethlehem, Judah. After she had been there four months, ³her husband went to her to persuade her to return. He had with him his servant and two donkeys. She took him into her parents' home, and when her father saw him, he gladly welcomed him. ⁴His father-in-law, the woman's father, prevailed on him to stay; so he remained with him three days, eating and drinking, and sleeping there.

⁵On the fourth day they got up early and he prepared to leave, but the woman's father said to his son-in-law, "Refresh yourself with something to eat; then you can go." ⁶So the two of them sat down to eat and drink together. Afterward the woman's father said, "Please stay tonight and enjoy yourself." ⁷And when the man got up to go, his father-in-law persuaded him, so he stayed there that night. ⁸On the morning of the fifth day, when he rose to go, the woman's father said, "Refresh yourself. Wait till afternoon!" So the two of them ate together.

⁹Then when the man, with his concubine and his servant, got up to leave, his father-in-law, the woman's father, said, "Now look, it's almost evening. Spend the night here; the day is nearly over. Stay and enjoy yourself. Early tomorrow morning you can get up and be on your way home." ¹⁰But, unwilling to stay another night, the man left and went toward Jebus (that is, Jerusalem), with his two saddled donkeys and his concubine.

¹¹When they were near Jebus and the day was almost gone, the servant said to his master, "Come, let's stop at this city of the Jebusites and spend the night."

¹²His master replied, "No. We won't go into any city whose people are not Israelites. We will go on to Gibeah." ¹³He added, "Come, let's try to reach Gibeah or Ramah and spend the night in one of those places." ¹⁴So they went on, and the sun set as they neared Gibeah in Benjamin. ¹⁵There they stopped to spend the night. They went and sat in the city square, but no one took them in for the night.

¹⁶That evening an old man from the hill country of Ephraim, who was living in Gibeah (the inhabitants of the place were Benjamites), came in from his work in the fields. ¹⁷When he looked and saw the traveler in the city square, the old man asked, "Where are you going? Where did you come from?"

¹⁸He answered, "We are on our way from Bethlehem in Judah to a remote area in the hill country of Ephraim where I live. I have been to Bethlehem in Judah and now I am going to the house of the LORD.[b] No one has taken me in for the night. ¹⁹We have both straw and fodder for our donkeys and bread and wine for ourselves your servants—me, the woman and the young man with us. We don't need anything."

²⁰"You are welcome at my house," the old man said. "Let me supply whatever you need. Only don't spend the night in the square." ²¹So he took him into his house and fed his donkeys. After they had washed their feet, they had something to eat and drink.

---

^a *30* Many Hebrew manuscripts, some Septuagint manuscripts and Vulgate, other Hebrew and Septuagint manuscripts *Manasseh*   ^b *18* Hebrew, Vulgate, Syriac and Targum; Septuagint *going home*

²²While they were enjoying themselves, some of the wicked men of the city surrounded the house. Pounding on the door, they shouted to the old man who owned the house, "Bring out the man who came to your house so we can have sex with him."

²³The owner of the house went outside and said to them, "No, my friends, don't be so vile. Since this man is my guest, don't do this outrageous thing. ²⁴Look, here is my virgin daughter, and his concubine. I will bring them out to you now, and you can use them and do to them whatever you wish. But as for this man, don't do such an outrageous thing."

²⁵But the men would not listen to him. So the man took his concubine and sent her outside to them, and they raped her and abused her throughout the night, and at dawn they let her go. ²⁶At daybreak the woman went back to the house where her master was staying, fell down at the door and lay there until daylight.

²⁷When her master got up in the morning and opened the door of the house and stepped out to continue on his way, there lay his concubine, fallen in the doorway of the house, with her hands on the threshold. ²⁸He said to her, "Get up; let's go." But there was no answer. Then he put her on his donkey and set out for home.

²⁹When he reached home, he took a knife and cut up his concubine, limb by limb, into twelve parts and sent them into all the areas of Israel. ³⁰Everyone who saw it said, "Such a thing has never been seen or done, not since the day the Israelites came up out of Egypt. Think about it! Consider it! Tell us what to do!"

The Israelites Punish the Benjamites

20 Then all the Israelites from Dan to Beersheba and from the land of Gilead came out with one accord and assembled before the LORD in Mizpah. ²The leaders of all the people of the tribes of Israel took their places in the assembly of the people of God, four hundred thousand soldiers armed with swords. ³(The Benjamites heard that the Israelites had gone up to Mizpah.) Then the Israelites said, "Tell us how this awful thing happened."

⁴So the Levite, the husband of the murdered woman, said, "I and my concubine came to Gibeah in Benjamin to spend the night. ⁵During the night the men of Gibeah came after me and surrounded the house, intending to kill me. They raped my concubine, and she died. ⁶I took my concubine, cut her into pieces and sent one piece to each region of Israel's inheritance, because they committed this lewd and outrageous act in Israel. ⁷Now, all you Israelites, speak up and give your verdict."

⁸All the people rose with one accord, saying, "None of us will go home. No, not one of us will return to his house. ⁹But now this is what we'll do to Gibeah: We'll go up against it as the lot directs. ¹⁰We'll take ten men out of every hundred from all the tribes of Israel, and a hundred from a thousand, and a thousand from ten thousand, to get provisions for the army. Then, when the army arrives at Gibeah^a in Benjamin, it can give them what they deserve for this outrageous act done in Israel." ¹¹So all the Israelites got together and united against the city with one accord.

¹²The tribes of Israel sent messengers throughout the tribe of Benjamin, saying, "What about this awful crime that was committed among you? ¹³Now turn those wicked men of Gibeah over to us so that we may put them to death and purge the evil from Israel."

But the Benjamites would not listen to their fellow Israelites. ¹⁴From their towns they came together at Gibeah to fight against the Israelites. ¹⁵At once the Benjamites mobilized twenty-six thousand swordsmen from their towns, in addition to seven hundred able young men from those living in Gibeah. ¹⁶Among all these soldiers there were seven hundred who were left-handed, each of whom could sling a stone at a hair and not miss.

¹⁷Israel, apart from Benjamin, mustered four hundred thousand swordsmen, all of them fighting men.

¹⁸The Israelites went up to Bethel^b and inquired of God. They said, "Who of us is to go up first to fight against the Benjamites?"

The LORD replied, "Judah shall go first."

¹⁹The next morning the Israelites got up and pitched camp near Gibeah. ²⁰The Israelites went out to

---

^a 10 One Hebrew manuscript; most Hebrew manuscripts Geba, a variant of Gibeah   ^b 18 Or to the house of God; also in verse 26

ASKMEanYTHING

Leah

Genesis 29–30

Describe your marriage to Jacob.

Imagine starting out your married life being an absolute—and *unwelcome*—surprise to your husband. That was my wedding. Because my father was insistent that I, being the older daughter, had to marry first, I was brought to Jacob's wedding bed in darkness and deceit. And when he discovered that he had slept with me instead of Rachel . . . well, it was a horrible scene. So from day one of my marriage to Jacob, I knew he didn't love me. He loved my more beautiful sister, Rachel, and I had to live with that fact every day.

How were you able to do that?

331

What I lacked in love from my husband was given to me by God. God knew that I was unwanted. He knew how it hurt to be married to someone who didn't love me. And he chose to bless me with children—six sons and a daughter! The first son I named Reuben because I was certain God had seen my misery. The second I named Simeon because the Lord had heard that I was unloved. The third I named Levi because I thought that surely Jacob would be attached to me through our three sons.

But the fourth son I named Judah, which means *praise*. I finally quit focusing on Jacob and trying to win his affection and focused on God instead. I thanked God for how he had sustained me in this loveless marriage and how he had rewarded my faithfulness and loyalty to Jacob.

So what can we learn from your situation?

I wish I could tell you that Jacob finally loved me in the way that I so desperately wanted. He never did. But that didn't give me license to leave him and find satisfaction with someone else. I had to do the right thing, as painful as that was. I had to find my satisfaction in God, in his love, not my husband's, and in the children that he gave me. I'm grateful that God doesn't love us based on our outward appearances. Even though Jacob never did, God loved me for *me*.

FOR MORE INSIGHT: What Leah may have never known was that the savior of the world, Jesus Christ, came through her son Judah's lineage—not through Rachel's children. What a redeeming gift for an unloved wife!

This world often assigns value to us based on our physical appearance. This is what Leah experienced to a very painful degree. But what a contrast there is between the physical beauty that this world admires and the true, lasting beauty that God admires. Read more in Proverbs 31:30; Isaiah 3:16–24; and Ezekiel 16:14–19.

fight the Benjamites and took up battle positions against them at Gibeah. ²¹The Benjamites came out of Gibeah and cut down twenty-two thousand Israelites on the battlefield that day. ²²But the Israelites encouraged one another and again took up their positions where they had stationed themselves the first day. ²³The Israelites went up and wept before the Lord until evening, and they inquired of the Lord. They said, "Shall we go up again to fight against the Benjamites, our fellow Israelites?"

The Lord answered, "Go up against them."

²⁴Then the Israelites drew near to Benjamin the second day. ²⁵This time, when the Benjamites came out from Gibeah to oppose them, they cut down another eighteen thousand Israelites, all of them armed with swords.

²⁶Then all the Israelites, the whole army, went up to Bethel, and there they sat weeping before the Lord. They fasted that day until evening and presented burnt offerings and fellowship offerings to the Lord. ²⁷And the Israelites inquired of the Lord. (In those days the ark of the covenant of God was there, ²⁸with Phinehas son of Eleazar, the son of Aaron, ministering before it.) They asked, "Shall we go up again to fight against the Benjamites, our fellow Israelites, or not?"

The Lord responded, "Go, for tomorrow I will give them into your hands."

²⁹Then Israel set an ambush around Gibeah. ³⁰They went up against the Benjamites on the third day and took up positions against Gibeah as they had done before. ³¹The Benjamites came out to meet them and were drawn away from the city. They began to inflict casualties on the Israelites as before, so that about thirty of them fell in the open field and on the roads—the one leading to Bethel and the other to Gibeah.

³²While the Benjamites were saying, "We are defeating them as before," the Israelites were saying, "Let's retreat and draw them away from the city to the roads."

³³All the men of Israel moved from their places and took up positions at Baal Tamar, and the Israelite ambush charged out of its place on the west*a* of Gibeah.*b* ³⁴Then ten thousand of Israel's able young men made a frontal attack on Gibeah. The fighting was so heavy that the Benjamites did not realize how near disaster was. ³⁵The Lord defeated Benjamin before Israel, and on that day the Israelites struck down 25,100 Benjamites, all armed with swords. ³⁶Then the Benjamites saw that they were beaten.

Now the men of Israel had given way before Benjamin, because they relied on the ambush they had set near Gibeah. ³⁷Those who had been in ambush made a sudden dash into Gibeah, spread out and put the whole city to the sword. ³⁸The Israelites had arranged with the ambush that they should send up a great cloud of smoke from the city, ³⁹and then the Israelites would turn in the battle.

The Benjamites had begun to inflict casualties on the Israelites (about thirty), and they said, "We are defeating them as in the first battle." ⁴⁰But when the column of smoke began to rise from the city, the Benjamites turned and saw the smoke of the whole city going up into the sky. ⁴¹Then the Israelites turned on them, and the Benjamites were terrified, because they realized that disaster had come on them. ⁴²So they fled before the Israelites in the direction of the wilderness, but they could not escape the battle. And the Israelites who came out of the towns cut them down there. ⁴³They surrounded the Benjamites, chased them and easily*c* overran them in the vicinity of Gibeah on the east. ⁴⁴Eighteen thousand Benjamites fell, all of them valiant fighters. ⁴⁵As they turned and fled toward the wilderness to the rock of Rimmon, the Israelites cut down five thousand men along the roads. They kept pressing after the Benjamites as far as Gidom and struck down two thousand more.

⁴⁶On that day twenty-five thousand Benjamite swordsmen fell, all of them valiant fighters. ⁴⁷But six hundred men turned and fled into the wilderness to the rock of Rimmon, where they stayed four months. ⁴⁸The men of Israel went back to Benjamin and put all the towns to the sword, including the animals and everything else they found. All the towns they came across they set on fire.

Wives for the Benjamites

21 The men of Israel had taken an oath at Mizpah: "Not one of us will give his daughter in marriage to a Benjamite."

²The people went to Bethel,*d* where they sat before God until evening, raising their voices and weep-

---

a 33 Some Septuagint manuscripts and Vulgate; the meaning of the Hebrew for this word is uncertain. *b 33* Hebrew *Geba,* a variant of *Gibeah*
c 43 The meaning of the Hebrew for this word is uncertain. *d 2* Or *to the house of God*

332

ing bitterly. ³"LORD, God of Israel," they cried, "why has this happened to Israel? Why should one tribe be missing from Israel today?"

⁴Early the next day the people built an altar and presented burnt offerings and fellowship offerings.

⁵Then the Israelites asked, "Who from all the tribes of Israel has failed to assemble before the LORD?" For they had taken a solemn oath that anyone who failed to assemble before the LORD at Mizpah was to be put to death.

⁶Now the Israelites grieved for Benjamin, one of their tribes. "Today one tribe is cut off from Israel," they said. ⁷"How can we provide wives for those who are left, since we have taken an oath by the LORD not to give them any of our daughters in marriage?" ⁸Then they asked, "Which one of the tribes of Israel failed to assemble before the LORD at Mizpah?" They discovered that no one from Jabesh Gilead had come to the camp for the assembly. ⁹For when they counted the people, they found that none of the people of Jabesh Gilead were there.

¹⁰So the assembly sent twelve thousand fighting men with instructions to go to Jabesh Gilead and put to the sword those living there, including the women and children. ¹¹"This is what you are to do," they said. "Kill every male and every woman who is not a virgin." ¹²They found among the people living in Jabesh Gilead four hundred young women who had never slept with a man, and they took them to the camp at Shiloh in Canaan.

¹³Then the whole assembly sent an offer of peace to the Benjamites at the rock of Rimmon. ¹⁴So the Benjamites returned at that time and were given the women of Jabesh Gilead who had been spared. But there were not enough for all of them.

¹⁵The people grieved for Benjamin, because the LORD had made a gap in the tribes of Israel. ¹⁶And the elders of the assembly said, "With the women of Benjamin destroyed, how shall we provide wives for the men who are left? ¹⁷The Benjamite survivors must have heirs," they said, "so that a tribe of Israel will not be wiped out. ¹⁸We can't give them our daughters as wives, since we Israelites have taken this oath: 'Cursed be anyone who gives a wife to a Benjamite.' ¹⁹But look, there is the annual festival of the LORD in Shiloh, to the north of Bethel, and east of the road that goes from Bethel to Shechem, and to the south of Lebonah."

²⁰So they instructed the Benjamites, saying, "Go and hide in the vineyards ²¹and watch. When the young women of Shiloh come out to join in the dancing, then rush from the vineyards and each of you seize a wife from the young women of Shiloh and go to the land of Benjamin. ²²When their fathers or brothers complain to us, we will say to them, 'Do us a kindness by helping them, because we did not get wives for them during the war, and you are innocent, since you did not give your daughters to them.'"

²³So that is what the Benjamites did. While the young women were dancing, each man caught one and carried her off to be his wife. Then they returned to their inheritance and rebuilt the towns and settled in them.

²⁴At that time the Israelites left that place and went home to their tribes and clans, each to his own inheritance.

²⁵In those days Israel had no king; everyone did as they saw fit.

atissue:government

21:25 Why would it ever be wrong to do what you believe is right? What would happen if all drivers on the road drove as they saw fit? Or parked wherever was the most convenient for them? Or paid only the taxes they felt like paying? Without set standards or higher rules to govern our behavior, our society would quickly fall apart. Everything would be considered permissible, and the consequences would be grave. God has given us leaders to give our lives structure so that we can peaceably coexist.

333

What all did Ruth risk in order
to stick with Naomi? **»** (1:11–18)

Is there *really* such a thing as
love at first sight? **»** (2:1–23)

How did God use a love story to foreshadow
what Jesus would one day do for you? **»** (4:1–12)

AUTHOR
Unknown.

AUDIENCE
The people of Israel.

DATE
Around 1000 B.C.

SETTING
The story is set sometime during the time
of the judges when Israel and Moab were
at peace.

VERSES TO REMEMBER
"But Ruth replied, 'Don't urge me to leave
you or to turn back from you. Where you go I
will go, and where you stay I will stay. Your
people will be my people and your God my
God. Where you die I will die, and there I
will be buried. May the LORD deal with me,
be it ever so severely, if even death separates you and me.' " (1:16–17)

THEME TO CONSIDER
No matter how bleak and hopeless our
situation may seem, we can trust God for
our good and his glory.

Naomi Loses Her Husband and Sons

1 In the days when the judges ruled,ᵃ there was a famine in the land. So a man from Bethlehem in Judah, together with his wife and two sons, went to live for a while in the country of Moab. ²The man's name was Elimelek, his wife's name was Naomi, and the names of his two sons were Mahlon and Kilion. They were Ephrathites from Bethlehem, Judah. And they went to Moab and lived there.

³Now Elimelek, Naomi's husband, died, and she was left with her two sons. ⁴They married Moabite women, one named Orpah and the other Ruth. After they had lived there about ten years, ⁵both Mahlon and Kilion also died, and Naomi was left without her two sons and her husband.

Naomi and Ruth Return to Bethlehem

⁶When Naomi heard in Moab that the Lord had come to the aid of his people by providing food for them, she and her daughters-in-law prepared to return home from there. ⁷With her two daughters-in-law she left the place where she had been living and set out on the road that would take them back to the land of Judah.

⁸Then Naomi said to her two daughters-in-law, "Go back, each of you, to your mother's home. May the Lord show you kindness, as you have shown kindness to your dead and to me. ⁹May the Lord grant that each of you will find rest in the home of another husband."

Then she kissed them good-by and they wept aloud ¹⁰and said to her, "We will go back with you to your people."

¹¹But Naomi said, "Return home, my daughters. Why would you come with me? Am I going to have any more sons, who could become your husbands? ¹²Return home, my daughters; I am too old to have another husband. Even if I thought there was still hope for me—even if I had a husband tonight and then gave birth to sons— ¹³would you wait until they grew up? Would you remain unmarried for them? No, my daughters. It is more bitter for me than for you, because the Lord's hand has turned against me!"

¹⁴At this they wept aloud again. Then Orpah kissed her mother-in-law good-by, but Ruth clung to her.

¹⁵"Look," said Naomi, "your sister-in-law is going back to her people and her gods. Go back with her."

¹⁶But Ruth replied, "Don't urge me to leave you or to turn back from you. Where you go I will go, and where you stay I will stay. Your people will be my people and your God my God. ¹⁷Where you die I will die, and there I will be buried. May the Lord deal with me, be it ever so severely, if even death separates you and me." ¹⁸When Naomi realized that Ruth was determined to go with her, she stopped urging her.

¹⁹So the two women went on until they came to Bethlehem. When they arrived in Bethlehem, the whole town was stirred because of them, and the women exclaimed, "Can this be Naomi?"

²⁰"Don't call me Naomi,ᵇ" she told them. "Call me Mara,ᶜ because the Almightyᵈ has made my life very bitter. ²¹I went away full, but the Lord has brought me back empty. Why call me Naomi? The Lord has afflictedᵉ me; the Almighty has brought misfortune upon me."

²²So Naomi returned from Moab accompanied by Ruth the Moabite, her daughter-in-law, arriving in Bethlehem as the barley harvest was beginning.

"conversations"

mentors «» 1:16–17

1» What are the benefits of a mentoring relationship?

2» What would you look for in a mentor?

3» How can you grow so that you can mentor another woman?

For more on **mentors**, check the index. For the next Conversations, go to p. 343.

Ruth Meets Boaz in the Grain Field

2 Now Naomi had a relative on her husband's side, a man of standing from the clan of Elimelek, whose name was Boaz.

²And Ruth the Moabite said to Naomi, "Let me go to the fields and pick up the leftover grain behind anyone in whose eyes I find favor."

ᵃ 1 Traditionally *judged*   ᵇ 20 Naomi means *pleasant*; also in verse 21.   ᶜ 20 Mara means *bitter*.   ᵈ 20 Hebrew *Shaddai*; also in verse 21   ᵉ 21 Or *has testified against*

myth# 23 "WE SHOULD LIVE TOGETHER BEFORE WE GET MARRIED TO MAKE SURE WE'RE COMPATIBLE."

When I first met Doug at a church singles group, I practically knew from the start that he was the one. For one thing, he's totally hot. But that's not why I fell in love with him. We just had this connection. Doug said he knew practically from the first that he loved me too.

After three months of dating, I knew that someday I would marry Doug. But even the thought of marriage to someone as wonderful as Doug, someone who seemed so right for me, scared me—scared us both really. My parents divorced twenty years ago, when I was eleven. Mom never got over being bitter toward Dad. And even though Doug's parents are still married, they sometimes act like they hate each other.

So, when Doug and I really started getting serious, there was no question in my mind—in both our minds—that we would move in together. After all, we were going to get married someday. We already had the commitment. In my heart, we were already married. Besides, wouldn't it be better to know upfront whether or not we should get married? Even some of my friends told me, "You've got to test the waters, Shay. See if you're really right for each other."

My mom didn't like the idea of us moving in together. She kept saying, "Shannon, wait. Don't be hasty." But seeing what a mess her marriage was made me determined not to make the same mistake.

The first three months were great, coming home to someone I loved. But then there were little things that started to add up to bigger things. Like the guilt I feel. Like the fear I have that Doug might leave me someday. Like the fact that Doug suggested postponing the wedding until we work out some of our problems.

You know what? We fight a lot more than we used to, sometimes about stupid things. Maybe Mom was right. Maybe we should have waited.

—Shannon

YOU KNOW THERE are some

things you don't have to "road test"—drugs, pornography and prostitution, just to name a few. Some things are just givens—you know they're wrong or right, based on the Bible and on the consequences you see in people's lives. But before making long-term decisions where the stakes are high, many people want to stick a toe in the water to test the outcome. Marriage is one of those long-term decisions many people fear the most. Can you relate?

Statistically, more couples are living together before marriage than ever before. The high divorce rate has turned more people away from thoughts of "I do" to thoughts of "I want to, but I need to try it out first." They believe divorce is to be avoided at all costs, even at the cost of compromising what they may know to be the best way.

The problem with the living-together option is that it's commitment "lite"—a promise of commitment with a backdoor to it. All of the pleasures of intimacy without the messy aftermath—or so people think. But a commitment you can walk away from isn't really a commitment. And contrary to what the movies and TV programs show, it comes with a hidden emotional and spiritual cost.

So how can you really know that you'll stay together if you don't live together beforehand? What are some alternatives to living together?

- **Get Premarital Counseling.** Counseling can help you explore your fears or unrealistic fantasies about marriage. Many pastors offer counseling to help you explore whether or not you should marry and determine when you're ready.

- **Find "Marriage Mentors."** Get to know an older couple, one with whom you can feel comfortable discussing the hard realities of marriage.

- **Dump the Divorce Option.** The only guarantee that you'll stay together is to decide beforehand that divorce is not an option.

- **Know God's Word.** Don't just rely on the advice of your friends. Know what the Bible says. For example, Genesis 2:24 clearly states God's desire for marriage.

Living together before marriage isn't a guarantee that you'll avoid divorce later. On the contrary, people who live together before marriage have a higher chance of divorce, as well as sexual problems. Many couples wind up separating before they reach the altar.

Want God's absolute best for you? Wait for the wedding. You're worth waiting for.

337

> "Those who cohabitate or live together before marriage have a 50 percent higher possibility of divorce than those who do not."
>
> —M. D. Newcomb and P. M. Bentler

"FOR THIS reason a man WILL Leave HIS FaTHer and moTHer and Be UNITeD TO HIS WIFE, and THEY WILL Become one FLeSH."

GENESIS 2:24

SEE ALSO

Song of Songs 2:7

1 Corinthians 6:18–20

1 Thessalonians 4:3–8

For more on **Cohabitation,** check the index.

Naomi said to her, "Go ahead, my daughter." ³So she went out, entered a field and began to glean behind the harvesters. As it turned out, she found herself working in a field belonging to Boaz, who was from the clan of Elimelek.

⁴Just then Boaz arrived from Bethlehem and greeted the harvesters, "The LORD be with you!"

"The LORD bless you!" they answered.

⁵Boaz asked the overseer of his harvesters, "Who does that young woman belong to?"

⁶The overseer replied, "She is the Moabite who came back from Moab with Naomi. ⁷She said, 'Please let me glean and gather among the sheaves behind the harvesters.' She came into the field and has remained here from morning till now, except for a short rest in the shelter."

⁸So Boaz said to Ruth, "My daughter, listen to me. Don't go and glean in another field and don't go away from here. Stay here with the women who work for me. ⁹Watch the field where the harvesters are working, and follow along after the women. I have told the men not to lay a hand on you. And whenever you are thirsty, go and get a drink from the water jars the men have filled."

¹⁰At this, she bowed down with her face to the ground. She asked him, "Why have I found such favor in your eyes that you notice me—a foreigner?"

HE IS: unprejudiced

2:8–10 As a member of a despised people, Ruth was defenseless in the nation of Israel. But Boaz, a picture of Jesus Christ, had heard how the Moabitess showed kindness to Naomi, so he offered to protect her as a daughter. Later, he came to love her as a wife. Like God, Boaz was *unprejudiced* and gladly welcomed a foreigner into his family.

Because God is unprejudiced, he welcomes anyone of any race into his family (see Romans 2:11). He doesn't care where you're from, the color of your skin or what name you bear. And that same color-blind impartiality is what he expects his children to show others.

For the next He Is, go to p. 344.

¹¹Boaz replied, "I've been told all about what you have done for your mother-in-law since the death of your husband—how you left your father and mother and your homeland and came to live with a people you did not know before. ¹²May the LORD repay you for what you have done. May you be richly rewarded by the LORD, the God of Israel, under whose wings you have come to take refuge."

¹³"May I continue to find favor in your eyes, my lord," she said. "You have reassured me and have spoken kindly to your servant—though I do not have the standing of one of your servants."

¹⁴At mealtime Boaz said to her, "Come over here. Have some bread and dip it in the wine vinegar."

When she sat down with the harvesters, he offered her some roasted grain. She ate all she wanted and had some left over. ¹⁵As she got up to glean, Boaz gave orders to his men, "Let her gather among the sheaves and don't reprimand her. ¹⁶Even pull out some stalks for her from the bundles and leave them for her to pick up, and don't rebuke her."

¹⁷So Ruth gleaned in the field until evening. Then she threshed the barley she had gathered, and it amounted to about an ephah.ᵃ ¹⁸She carried it back to town, and her mother-in-law saw how much she had gathered. Ruth also brought out and gave her what she had left over after she had eaten enough.

¹⁹Her mother-in-law asked her, "Where did you glean today? Where did you work? Blessed be the man who took notice of you!"

Then Ruth told her mother-in-law about the one at whose place she had been working. "The name of the man I worked with today is Boaz," she said.

²⁰"The LORD bless him!" Naomi said to her daughter-in-law. "He has not stopped showing his kindness to the living and the dead." She added, "That man is our close relative; he is one of our family guardians.ᵇ"

ᵃ *17* That is, probably about 30 pounds or about 13 kilograms   ᵇ *20* The Hebrew word for *family guardian* is a legal term for one who has the obligation to redeem a relative in serious difficulty (see Lev. 25:25-55).

ruth

Ruth 1–4

ASKmeanYTHING

Describe your relationship with your mother-in-law.

I know that for many women the word *mother-in-law* brings to mind some negative connotations. *[laughs]* And that could have been true for Naomi and me. We are two very different people. I was raised in Moab; she was an Israelite. Our customs were very different. We worshiped different gods in different ways. But over the ten years that I was married to her son, Mahlon, I came to know Naomi and the God she worshiped—so very different than the gods of my people. I learned of a God who was loving, holy and kind. The stories Naomi and Mahlon told me of their God thrilled me.

Then after my husband, my brother-in-law and father-in-law died, the three of us—Naomi, Orpah and I—clung to each other. We cried together. We supported one another. We were bound together in our grief.

339

What made you decide to follow Naomi to Bethlehem?

As I mentioned, the bond between Naomi and me went beyond my marriage to her son. Naomi was more than a mother-in-law. She represented a link to a new life and to a God that gave me hope. So when she decided to return to Bethlehem, the decision was clear. I didn't want to lose her; I didn't want to lose that connection to her God. I wanted to be part of her life and to know her God. I was determined to stay with Naomi, no matter what.

What was the secret to your relationship with Naomi?

We were committed first to God and then to each other. There was nothing I would not do for Naomi, and I know that she felt as deeply for me. We loved the same God, and that spilled into every aspect of our relationship and how we treated each other.

What advice would you give to women whose relationships with their mothers-in-law are strained?

First, bring God into the relationship. Commit yourself to him, and commit that relationship to him. Second, support your mother-in-law in whatever ways you can. Look for the positive aspects of your relationship and build on that. You may be two very different people, but look for the good in her. And pray. Pray for her, pray for your relationship and pray that you'll give that relationship a second chance.

FOR MORE INSIGHT: For more stories of friendships where commitment to God is evident, read about David and Jonathan (see 1 Samuel 18:1–4; 23:16–18), David and Mephibosheth (see 2 Samuel 9:1–13), and Mary, Martha, Lazarus and Jesus (see John 11:1–44).

²¹Then Ruth the Moabite said, "He even said to me, 'Stay with my workers until they finish harvesting all my grain.'"

²²Naomi said to Ruth her daughter-in-law, "It will be good for you, my daughter, to go with the women who work for him, because in someone else's field you might be harmed."

²³So Ruth stayed close to the women of Boaz to glean until the barley and wheat harvests were finished. And she lived with her mother-in-law.

Ruth and Boaz at the Threshing Floor

3 One day Naomi her mother-in-law said to her, "My daughter, I must find a home[a] for you, where you will be well provided for. ²Now Boaz, with whose women you have worked, is a relative of ours. Tonight he will be winnowing barley on the threshing floor. ³Wash and perfume yourself, and put on your best clothes. Then go down to the threshing floor, but don't let him know you are there until he has finished eating and drinking. ⁴When he lies down, note the place where he is lying. Then go and uncover his feet and lie down. He will tell you what to do."

⁵"I will do whatever you say," Ruth answered. ⁶So she went down to the threshing floor and did everything her mother-in-law told her to do.

⁷When Boaz had finished eating and drinking and was in good spirits, he went over to lie down at the far end of the grain pile. Ruth approached quietly, uncovered his feet and lay down. ⁸In the middle of the night something startled the man; he turned—and there was a woman lying at his feet!

⁹"Who are you?" he asked.

"I am your servant Ruth," she said. "Spread the corner of your garment over me, since you are a family guardian."

¹⁰"The LORD bless you, my daughter," he replied. "This kindness is greater than that which you showed earlier: You have not run after the younger men, whether rich or poor. ¹¹And now, my daughter, don't be afraid. I will do for you all you ask. All the people of my town know that you are a woman of noble character. ¹²Although it is true that I am a family guardian, there is another who is more closely related than I. ¹³Stay here for the night, and in the morning if he wants to do his duty as your family guardian, good; let him redeem you. But if he is not willing, as surely as the LORD lives I will do it. Lie here until morning."

¹⁴So she lay at his feet until morning, but got up before anyone could be recognized; and he said, "No one must know that a woman came to the threshing floor."

¹⁵He also said, "Bring me the shawl you are wearing and hold it out." When she did so, he poured into it six measures of barley and put it on her. Then he[b] went back to town.

¹⁶When Ruth came to her mother-in-law, Naomi asked, "How did it go, my daughter?"

Then she told her everything Boaz had done for her ¹⁷and added, "He gave me these six measures of barley, saying, 'Don't go back to your mother-in-law empty-handed.'"

¹⁸Then Naomi said, "Wait, my daughter, until you find out what happens. For the man will not rest until the matter is settled today."

aussie:singleness

3:1–18 "How to Lure a Man in Five Easy Steps!" We groom, we primp, we suck it in and flair it out. All for one purpose—nabbing that man. When Ruth wanted to attract Boaz, Naomi was ready with strict grooming instructions. Obviously, putting our best foot forward in dating isn't a crime. However, when Ruth's date actually took place, Boaz couldn't get enough of her loyalty and honorable reputation. In the end, Ruth's character—not her appearance—landed her a husband. If you're SWTBM (Single Waiting To Be Married), let your good reputation, not your Gucci shoes, do the talking.

---

[a] 1 Hebrew *find rest* (see Ruth 1:9)   [b] 15 Most Hebrew manuscripts; many Hebrew manuscripts, Vulgate and Syriac *she*

Boaz Marries Ruth

4 Meanwhile Boaz went up to the town gate and sat down there just as the family guardian he had mentioned came along. Boaz said, "Come over here, my friend, and sit down." So he went over and sat down.

²Boaz took ten of the elders of the town and said, "Sit here," and they did so. ³Then he said to the family guardian, "Naomi, who has come back from Moab, is selling the piece of land that belonged to our relative Elimelek. ⁴I thought I should bring the matter to your attention and suggest that you buy it in the presence of these seated here and in the presence of the elders of my people. If you will redeem it, do so. But if you*ᵃ* will not, tell me, so I will know. For no one has the right to do it except you, and I am next in line."

"I will redeem it," he said.

⁵Then Boaz said, "On the day you buy the land from Naomi, you also acquire Ruth the Moabite, theᵇ dead man's widow, in order to maintain the name of the dead with his property."

⁶At this, the family guardian said, "Then I cannot redeem it because I might endanger my own estate. You redeem it yourself. I cannot do it."

⁷(Now in earlier times in Israel, for the redemption and transfer of property to become final, one party took off his sandal and gave it to the other. This was the method of legalizing transactions in Israel.)

⁸So the family guardian said to Boaz, "Buy it yourself." And he removed his sandal.

⁹Then Boaz announced to the elders and all the people, "Today you are witnesses that I have bought from Naomi all the property of Elimelek, Kilion and Mahlon. ¹⁰I have also acquired Ruth the Moabite, Mahlon's widow, as my wife, in order to maintain the name of the dead with his property, so that his name will not disappear from among his family or from his hometown. Today you are witnesses!"

¹¹Then the elders and all the people at the gate said, "We are witnesses. May the Lᴏʀᴅ make the woman who is coming into your home like Rachel and Leah, who together built up the house of Israel. May you have standing in Ephrathah and be famous in Bethlehem. ¹²Through the offspring the Lᴏʀᴅ gives you by this young woman, may your family be like that of Perez, whom Tamar bore to Judah."

Naomi Gains a Son

¹³So Boaz took Ruth and she became his wife. When he made love to her, the Lᴏʀᴅ enabled her to conceive, and she gave birth to a son. ¹⁴The women said to Naomi: "Praise be to the Lᴏʀᴅ, who this day has not left you without a family guardian. May he become famous throughout Israel! ¹⁵He will renew your life and sustain you in your old age. For your daughter-in-law, who loves you and who is better to you than seven sons, has given him birth."

¹⁶Then Naomi took the child in her arms and cared for him. ¹⁷The women living there said, "Naomi has a son!" And they named him Obed. He was the father of Jesse, the father of David.

The Genealogy of David

¹⁸This, then, is the family line of Perez:

Perez was the father of Hezron,
¹⁹Hezron the father of Ram,
 Ram the father of Amminadab,
²⁰Amminadab the father of Nahshon,
 Nahshon the father of Salmon,ᶜ
²¹Salmon the father of Boaz,
 Boaz the father of Obed,
²²Obed the father of Jesse,
 and Jesse the father of David.

341

---

1 samuel

AUTHOR
Unknown.

AUDIENCE
The people of Israel.

DATE
Sometime after the division of Israel into
the northern and southern kingdoms, around
930 B.C.

SETTING
The people of Israel want to shift from a
theocracy to a monarchy.

VERSE TO REMEMBER
"But the LORD said to Samuel, 'Do not
consider his appearance or his height, for I
have rejected him. The LORD does not look at
the things human beings look at. People look
at the outward appearance, but the LORD
looks at the heart.'" (16:7)

THEME TO CONSIDER
Leadership is a matter of the heart.

The Birth of Samuel

1 There was a certain man from Ramathaim, a Zuphite*a* from the hill country of Ephraim, whose name was Elkanah son of Jeroham, the son of Elihu, the son of Tohu, the son of Zuph, an Ephraimite. ²He had two wives; one was called Hannah and the other Peninnah. Peninnah had children, but Hannah had none.

³Year after year this man went up from his town to worship and sacrifice to the Lord Almighty at Shiloh, where Hophni and Phinehas, the two sons of Eli, were priests of the Lord. ⁴Whenever the day came for Elkanah to sacrifice, he would give portions of the meat to his wife Peninnah and to all her sons and daughters. ⁵But to Hannah he gave a double portion because he loved her, and the Lord had closed her womb. ⁶Because the Lord had closed Hannah's womb, her rival kept provoking her in order to irritate her. ⁷This went on year after year. Whenever Hannah went up to the house of the Lord, her rival provoked her till she wept and would not eat. ⁸Her husband Elkanah would say to her, "Hannah, why are you weeping? Why don't you eat? Why are you downhearted? Don't I mean more to you than ten sons?"

⁹Once when they had finished eating and drinking in Shiloh, Hannah stood up. Now Eli the priest was sitting on his chair by the doorpost of the Lord's house. ¹⁰In her deep anguish Hannah prayed to the Lord, weeping bitterly. ¹¹And she made a vow, saying, "Lord Almighty, if you will only look on your servant's misery and remember me, and not forget your servant but give her a son, then I will give him to the Lord for all the days of his life, and no razor will ever be used on his head."

¹²As she kept on praying to the Lord, Eli observed her mouth. ¹³Hannah was praying in her heart, and her lips were moving but her voice was not heard. Eli thought she was drunk ¹⁴and said to her, "How long are you going to stay drunk? Put away your wine."

¹⁵"Not so, my lord," Hannah replied, "I am a woman who is deeply troubled. I have not been drinking wine or beer; I was pouring out my soul to the Lord. ¹⁶Do not take your servant for a wicked woman; I have been praying here out of my great anguish and grief."

¹⁷Eli answered, "Go in peace, and may the God of Israel grant you what you have asked of him."

¹⁸She said, "May your servant find favor in your eyes." Then she went her way and ate something, and her face was no longer downcast.

¹⁹Early the next morning they arose and worshiped before the Lord and then went back to their home at Ramah. Elkanah made love to his wife Hannah, and the Lord remembered her. ²⁰So in the course of time Hannah

conversations
wanted pregnancy «» 1:5

1 » How does infertility affect a marriage?

2 » How far should a Christian go to overcome infertility?

3 » Does our society connect fertility and a woman's worth? How?

For more on **pregnancy**, check the index.
For the next Conversations, go to p. 357.

1:10–18 If someone called and said that you'd just won a million dollars, what would your first response be? "Wow, thanks! I'll expect it in my bank account today!" Not likely. Usually when we hear outrageous promises, our cynicism kicks into high gear. This is a natural response to most situations, except one—prayer. See, when God makes exorbitant promises (like answering our prayers of faith), he actually means what he says. He's a real "you've just won the jackpot!" kind of God. When you truly believe this, your response to prayer will be like Hannah's. You'll drop your suspicions because you expect God to answer for your good.

a 1 See Septuagint and 1 Chron. 6:26-27,33-35; or from Ramathaim Zuphim.

became pregnant and gave birth to a son. She named him Samuel,[a] saying, "Because I asked the LORD for him."

Hannah Dedicates Samuel

[21] When Elkanah went up with all his family to offer the annual sacrifice to the LORD and to fulfill his vow, [22] Hannah did not go. She said to her husband, "After the boy is weaned, I will take him and present him before the LORD, and he will live there always."[b]

[23] "Do what seems best to you," her husband Elkanah told her. "Stay here until you have weaned him; only may the LORD make good his[c] word." So the woman stayed at home and nursed her son until she had weaned him.

[24] After he was weaned, she took the boy with her, young as he was, along with a three-year-old bull,[d] an ephah[e] of flour and a skin of wine, and brought him to the house of the LORD at Shiloh. [25] When the bull had been sacrificed, they brought the boy to Eli, [26] and she said to him, "Pardon me, my lord. As surely as you live, I am the woman who stood here beside you praying to the LORD. [27] I prayed for this child, and the LORD has granted me what I asked of him. [28] So now I give him to the LORD. For his whole life he will be given over to the LORD." And he worshiped the LORD there.

Hannah's Prayer

2 Then Hannah prayed and said:

> "My heart rejoices in the LORD;
> in the LORD my horn[f] is lifted high.
> My mouth boasts over my enemies,
> for I delight in your deliverance.

[2] "There is no one holy like the LORD;
> there is no one besides you;
> there is no Rock like our God.

HE IS: delightful

2:1–2 Years earlier, God had given Hannah the delight of her heart by answering her prayer for a child. Now the time had come to release her son to the Lord's service. Amazingly, she could say, "My heart rejoices in the LORD." Rather than despairing, Hannah discovered that God is *delightful*.

Sometimes God asks us to turn our most precious things over to him. What would that be for you? A relationship? A responsibility? A personal right? If you release it with a heart of trusting devotion, you'll find that God fills your heart with delight.

For the next He Is, go to p. 352.

> [3] "Do not keep talking so proudly
> or let your mouth speak such arrogance,
> for the LORD is a God who knows,
> and by him deeds are weighed.

> [4] "The bows of the warriors are broken,
> but those who stumbled are armed with strength.
> [5] Those who were full hire themselves out for food,
> but those who were hungry are hungry no more.

---

[a] 20 *Samuel* sounds like the Hebrew for *heard by God.* [b] 22 Masoretic Text; Dead Sea Scrolls *always. I have dedicated him as a Nazirite—all the days of his life."* [c] 23 Masoretic Text; Dead Sea Scrolls, Septuagint and Syriac *your* [d] 24 Dead Sea Scrolls, Septuagint and Syriac; Masoretic Text *with three bulls*
[e] 24 That is, probably about 36 pounds or about 16 kilograms [f] 1 *Horn* here symbolizes strength; also in verse 10.

> She who was barren has borne seven children,
>   but she who has had many sons pines away.
>
> 6 "The LORD brings death and makes alive;
>   he brings down to the grave and raises up.
> 7 The LORD sends poverty and wealth;
>   he humbles and he exalts.
> 8 He raises the poor from the dust
>   and lifts the needy from the ash heap;
> he seats them with princes
>   and has them inherit a throne of honor.
>
> "For the foundations of the earth are the LORD's;
>   on them he has set the world.
> 9 He will guard the feet of his faithful servants,
>   but the wicked will be silenced in the place of darkness.
>
> "It is not by strength that one prevails;
> 10   those who oppose the LORD will be broken.
> The Most High will thunder from heaven;
>   the LORD will judge the ends of the earth.
>
> "He will give strength to his king
>   and exalt the horn of his anointed."

345

11 Then Elkanah went home to Ramah, but the boy ministered before the LORD under Eli the priest.

Eli's Wicked Sons

12 Eli's sons were scoundrels; they had no regard for the LORD. 13 Now it was the practice of the priests that, whenever any of the people offered a sacrifice, the priest's servant would come with a three-pronged fork in his hand while the meat was being boiled 14 and would plunge the fork into the pan or kettle or caldron or pot. Whatever the fork brought up the priest would take for himself. This is how they treated all the Israelites who came to Shiloh. 15 But even before the fat was burned, the priest's servant would come and say to the person who was sacrificing, "Give the priest some meat to roast; he won't accept boiled meat from you, but only raw."

16 If the person said to him, "Let the fat be burned first, and then take whatever you want," the servant would answer, "No, hand it over now; if you don't, I'll take it by force."

17 This sin of the young men was very great in the LORD's sight, for they*a* were treating the LORD's offering with contempt.

18 But Samuel was ministering before the LORD—a boy wearing a linen ephod. 19 Each year his mother made him a little robe and took it to him when she went up with her husband to offer the annual sacrifice. 20 Eli would bless Elkanah and his wife, saying, "May the LORD give you children by this woman to take the place of the one she prayed for and gave to*b* the LORD." Then they would go home. 21 And the LORD was gracious to Hannah; she gave birth to three sons and two daughters. Meanwhile, the boy Samuel grew up in the presence of the LORD.

22 Now Eli, who was very old, heard about everything his sons were doing to all Israel and how they slept with the women who served at the entrance to the tent of meeting. 23 So he said to them, "Why do you do such things? I hear from all the people about these wicked deeds of yours. 24 No, my sons; the report I hear spreading among the LORD's people is not good. 25 If anyone sins against another human being, God*c* may mediate for the offender; but if anyone sins against the LORD, who will intercede for them?" His sons, however, did not listen to their father's rebuke, for it was the LORD's will to put them to death.

26 And the boy Samuel continued to grow in stature and in favor with the LORD and with people.

---

a 17 Dead Sea Scrolls and Septuagint; Masoretic Text *people*   *b* 20 Dead Sea Scrolls; Masoretic Text *and asked from*   *c* 25 Or *the judges*

Prophecy Against the House of Eli

²⁷Now a man of God came to Eli and said to him, "This is what the Lord says: 'Did I not clearly reveal myself to the family of your ancestor when they were in Egypt under Pharaoh? ²⁸I chose your ancestor out of all the tribes of Israel to be my priest, to go up to my altar, to burn incense, and to wear an ephod in my presence. I also gave your ancestor's family all the food offerings presented by the Israelites. ²⁹Why do you*ᵃ* scorn my sacrifice and offering that I prescribed for my dwelling? Why do you honor your sons more than me by fattening yourselves on the choice parts of every offering made by my people Israel?'

³⁰"Therefore the Lord, the God of Israel, declares: 'I promised that the members of your family would minister before me forever.' But now the Lord declares: 'Far be it from me! Those who honor me I will honor, but those who despise me will be disdained. ³¹The time is coming when I will cut short your strength and the strength of the members of your family, so that no one in it will reach old age, ³²and you will see distress in my dwelling. Although good will be done to Israel, no one in your family line will ever reach old age. ³³Every one of you that I do not cut off from serving at my altar I will spare only to destroy your sight and sap your strength, and all your descendants will die in the prime of life.

³⁴"'And what happens to your two sons, Hophni and Phinehas, will be a sign to you—they will both die on the same day. ³⁵I will raise up for myself a faithful priest, who will do according to what is in my heart and mind. I will firmly establish his family line, and he will minister before my anointed one always. ³⁶Then everyone left in your family line will come and bow down before him for a piece of silver and a loaf of bread and plead, "Appoint me to some priestly office so I can have food to eat."'"

The Lord Calls Samuel

3 The boy Samuel ministered before the Lord under Eli. In those days the word of the Lord was rare; there were not many visions.

²One night Eli, whose eyes were becoming so weak that he could barely see, was lying down in his usual place. ³The lamp of God had not yet gone out, and Samuel was lying down in the house of the Lord, where the ark of God was. ⁴Then the Lord called Samuel.

Samuel answered, "Here I am." ⁵And he ran to Eli and said, "Here I am; you called me."

But Eli said, "I did not call; go back and lie down." So he went and lay down.

⁶Again the Lord called, "Samuel!" And Samuel got up and went to Eli and said, "Here I am; you called me."

"My son," Eli said, "I did not call; go back and lie down."

⁷Now Samuel did not yet know the Lord: The word of the Lord had not yet been revealed to him.

⁸A third time the Lord called, "Samuel!" And Samuel got up and went to Eli and said, "Here I am; you called me."

Then Eli realized that the Lord was calling the boy. ⁹So Eli told Samuel, "Go and lie down, and if he calls you, say, 'Speak, Lord, for your servant is listening.'" So Samuel went and lay down in his place.

¹⁰The Lord came and stood there, calling as at the other times, "Samuel! Samuel!"

Then Samuel said, "Speak, for your servant is listening."

¹¹And the Lord said to Samuel: "See, I am about to do something in Israel that will make the ears of everyone who hears about it tingle. ¹²At that time I will carry out against Eli everything I spoke against his family—from beginning to end. ¹³For I told him that I would judge his family forever because of the sin he knew about; his sons blasphemed God,*ᵇ* and he failed to restrain them. ¹⁴Therefore I swore to the house of Eli, 'The guilt of Eli's house will never be atoned for by sacrifice or offering.'"

¹⁵Samuel lay down until morning and then opened the doors of the house of the Lord. He was afraid to tell Eli the vision, ¹⁶but Eli called him and said, "Samuel, my son."

Samuel answered, "Here I am."

¹⁷"What was it he said to you?" Eli asked. "Do not hide it from me. May God deal with you, be it ever so severely, if you hide from me anything he told you." ¹⁸So Samuel told him everything, hiding nothing from him. Then Eli said, "He is the Lord; let him do what is good in his eyes."

¹⁹The Lord was with Samuel as he grew up, and he let none of Samuel's words fall to the ground. ²⁰And

---

ᵃ *29 The Hebrew is plural.*   ᵇ *13 An ancient Hebrew scribal tradition (see also Septuagint); Masoretic Text sons made themselves contemptible* all Israel from Dan to Beersheba recognized that Samuel was attested as a prophet of the LORD. ²¹The LORD continued to appear at Shiloh, and there he revealed himself to Samuel through his word.

4 And Samuel's word came to all Israel.

The Philistines Capture the Ark

Now the Israelites went out to fight against the Philistines. The Israelites camped at Ebenezer, and the Philistines at Aphek. ²The Philistines deployed their forces to meet Israel, and as the battle spread, Israel was defeated by the Philistines, who killed about four thousand of them on the battlefield. ³When the soldiers returned to camp, the elders of Israel asked, "Why did the LORD bring defeat on us today before the Philistines? Let us bring the ark of the LORD's covenant from Shiloh, so that he may go with us and save us from the hand of our enemies."

⁴So the people sent men to Shiloh, and they brought back the ark of the covenant of the LORD Almighty, who is enthroned between the cherubim. And Eli's two sons, Hophni and Phinehas, were there with the ark of the covenant of God.

⁵When the ark of the LORD's covenant came into the camp, all Israel raised such a great shout that the ground shook. ⁶Hearing the uproar, the Philistines asked, "What's all this shouting in the Hebrew camp?"

When they learned that the ark of the LORD had come into the camp, ⁷the Philistines were afraid. "A god has*a* come into the camp," they said. "We're in trouble! Nothing like this has happened before. ⁸Woe to us! Who will deliver us from the hand of these mighty gods? They are the gods who struck the Egyptians with all kinds of plagues in the wilderness. ⁹Be strong, Philistines! Be men, or you will be subject to the Hebrews, as they have been to you. Be men, and fight!"

¹⁰So the Philistines fought, and the Israelites were defeated and every man fled to his tent. The slaughter was very great; Israel lost thirty thousand foot soldiers. ¹¹The ark of God was captured, and Eli's two sons, Hophni and Phinehas, died.

Death of Eli

¹²That same day a Benjamite ran from the battle line and went to Shiloh with his clothes torn and dust on his head. ¹³When he arrived, there was Eli sitting on his chair by the side of the road, watching, because his heart feared for the ark of God. When the man entered the town and told what had happened, the whole town sent up a cry.

¹⁴Eli heard the outcry and asked, "What is the meaning of this uproar?"

The man hurried over to Eli, ¹⁵who was ninety-eight years old and whose eyes had failed so that he could not see. ¹⁶He told Eli, "I have just come from the battle line; I fled from it this very day."

Eli asked, "What happened, my son?"

¹⁷The one who brought the news replied, "Israel fled before the Philistines, and the army has suffered heavy losses. Also your two sons, Hophni and Phinehas, are dead, and the ark of God has been captured."

¹⁸When he mentioned the ark of God, Eli fell backward off his chair by the side of the gate. His neck was broken and he died, for he was an old man, and he was heavy. He had led*b* Israel forty years.

¹⁹His daughter-in-law, the wife of Phinehas, was pregnant and near the time of delivery. When she heard the news that the ark of God had been captured and that her father-in-law and her husband were dead, she went into labor and gave birth, but was overcome by her labor pains. ²⁰As she was dying, the

atissue:parenting

3:11–14 With all the ugly stories of child abuse that we hear, disciplining children has become a touchy subject. Yet we've all met people who grew up without discipline—and that neglect is another form of abuse. When Eli refused to discipline his children, God actually stepped in. God approves of discipline and expects us to lovingly discipline our children. Discipline provides a sense of structure for children, allowing them to feel safe. And giving children consequences for their actions while they're young spares them from greater consequences as adults.

347

---

a 7 Or "Gods have (see Septuagint) *b 18 Traditionally judged*

myth# 24 "I SHOULD KNOW GOD'S PLAN FOR MY LIFE."

Life is full of surprises. The most surprising place God called me was to unemployment. I was in a job that I didn't hate, but I didn't love it either. I could sense it was time for a change, but I thought the perfect job would come along at the right time, and then I would gracefully transition into it. After all, I was a college graduate with excellent work experience. I considered myself very marketable. I was sure I would have a new job offer in no time after I put some feelers out there.

So I sat back and waited for that perfect opportunity to come my way. I waited. And I waited. Hello, God. This would be a really good time for you to show up, I remember praying. However, all the time I was waiting on God to do something, God was actually waiting for me to make the first move. I didn't want to do it. I was really scared to do it. But after several months of job searching with no luck, I quit. I quit my job without having another one lined up.

Even the daredevil, Evel Knievel—the guy who jumped his motorcycle over 18-wheelers and walked out onto the wings of jet airplanes—knew the first principle of wing-walking: "Don't let go of something unless you have a firm grasp on something else." I don't recommend doing what I did. My mother doesn't recommend it. No one recommends it. However, that's what I sensed God wanted me to do. Within 30 days of leaving my former job, guess what happened? The perfect opportunity came my way. And I haven't looked back.

Ten years ago I don't think I would have been able to step out in faith like that. Two years ago I wouldn't have done it. I had always believed that following God's will meant having absolute certainty about his plan. I was never certain I understood the plan, so I rarely stepped out in faith.

I still didn't understand his plan when I left my job, but this time was different. I stepped out in faith anyway. And he rewarded me beyond my expectations.

—*Elizabeth*

SCRIPTURE HAS THIS to say about following God's plan, "Now faith is being sure of what we hope for and certain of what we do not see . . . By faith Abraham, when called to go to a place he would later receive as his inheritance, obeyed and went, *even though he did not know where he was going*" (Hebrews 11:1,8, emphasis added). Are you in the middle of one of life's surprises right now? Are you at a place you never expected to be? Are you unsure of what will happen next?

Welcome to reality.

While the myth that we should "know" God's plan for our lives still floats around Christian circles, the truth is quite different.

- We live by faith and not by sight (see 2 Corinthians 5:7). If you knew every aspect of God's plan for your life, clearly labeled in triplicate form, why would you need faith?

- The moment of absolute certainty rarely comes. Consider Abraham. He didn't have a clue where he was going. But he went anyway. Think of Samuel, whom God called as a child. Do you think a young boy understood the scope of God's plan for his life? Certainly not. But these people moved forward in faith, as did all the spiritual heroes.

- We must move forward. In preparation, we pray and seek godly counsel. We search the Scriptures and meditate on God's truths. And then it comes time to decide. To make a move. We may not feel ready or certain, but God lovingly gives us a chance to flex our faith and trust him for the outcome.

The Bible is about people in a fluid, dynamic relationship with God. It's not a treasure map. It's not a blueprint spelling out Steps A, B and C for God's plan for you. Instead of outlining methods to find God's plan, it teaches the principles of finding God's heart. The living God leads through *relationship*. When we understand this, we start to seek his face, not his hand. We stop wanting to find God's plan so that we might find God instead. No longer capriciously wanting the "answer," we want the one who knows the answer.

> "We do not seek a word from God to prove he is real so we can have a relationship with him. Rather, as we seek to develop an intimate relationship with him, we will hear him speak to us."
>
> —Henry Blackaby

349

"YOU WILL SEEK ME AND FIND ME WHEN YOU SEEK ME WITH ALL YOUR HEART."

JEREMIAH 29:13

SEE ALSO

Psalm 32:8
Psalm 73:24
1 Corinthians 1:9

For more on **Future** and **God's Will**, check the index.

women attending her said, "Don't despair; you have given birth to a son." But she did not respond or pay any attention.

²¹She named the boy Ichabod,*a* saying, "The Glory has departed from Israel"—because of the capture of the ark of God and the deaths of her father-in-law and her husband. ²²She said, "The Glory has departed from Israel, for the ark of God has been captured."

The Ark in Ashdod and Ekron

5 After the Philistines had captured the ark of God, they took it from Ebenezer to Ashdod. ²Then they carried the ark into Dagon's temple and set it beside Dagon. ³When the people of Ashdod rose early the next day, there was Dagon, fallen on his face on the ground before the ark of the LORD! They took Dagon and put him back in his place. ⁴But the following morning when they rose, there was Dagon, fallen on his face on the ground before the ark of the LORD! His head and hands had been broken off and were lying on the threshold; only his body remained. ⁵That is why to this day neither the priests of Dagon nor any others who enter Dagon's temple at Ashdod step on the threshold.

⁶The LORD's hand was heavy on the people of Ashdod and its vicinity; he brought devastation on them and afflicted them with tumors.*b* ⁷When the people of Ashdod saw what was happening, they said, "The ark of the god of Israel must not stay here with us, because his hand is heavy on us and on Dagon our god." ⁸So they called together all the rulers of the Philistines and asked them, "What shall we do with the ark of the god of Israel?"

They answered, "Have the ark of the god of Israel moved to Gath." So they moved the ark of the God of Israel.

⁹But after they had moved it, the LORD's hand was against that city, throwing it into a great panic. He afflicted the people of the city, both young and old, with an outbreak of tumors.*c* ¹⁰So they sent the ark of God to Ekron.

As the ark of God was entering Ekron, the people of Ekron cried out, "They have brought the ark of the god of Israel around to us to kill us and our people." ¹¹So they called together all the rulers of the Philistines and said, "Send the ark of the god of Israel away; let it go back to its own place, or it*d* will kill us and our people." For death had filled the city with panic; God's hand was very heavy on it. ¹²Those who did not die were afflicted with tumors, and the outcry of the city went up to heaven.

The Ark Returned to Israel

6 When the ark of the LORD had been in Philistine territory seven months, ²the Philistines called for the priests and the diviners and said, "What shall we do with the ark of the LORD? Tell us how we should send it back to its place."

³They answered, "If you return the ark of the god of Israel, do not send it back to him without a gift; by all means send a guilt offering to him. Then you will be healed, and you will know why his hand has not been lifted from you."

⁴The Philistines asked, "What guilt offering should we send to him?"

They replied, "Five gold tumors and five gold rats, according to the number of the Philistine rulers, because the same plague has struck both you and your rulers. ⁵Make models of the tumors and of the rats that are destroying the country, and give glory to Israel's god. Perhaps he will lift his hand from you

---

atissue:weight

4:18 Sure, we hate that our society tells us the "ideal" woman is 5'9" and weighs 110 pounds. We aren't all meant to look like supermodels! Plus, we know that God loves us just the way we are. Of course that's true . . . but hold on a second. Eli's life illustrates the fact that how we treat our bodies has serious consequences. So instead of thinking skinny—let's think *healthy*. Doesn't God want us to care for the bodies he gave us? Ask yourself what a healthy lifestyle looks like for you.

---

a 21 Ichabod means no glory. ᵇ 6 Hebrew; Septuagint and Vulgate tumors. And rats appeared in their land, and there was death and destruction throughout the city ᶜ 9 Or with tumors in the groin (see Septuagint) ᵈ 11 Or he

350

and your gods and your land. ⁶Why do you harden your hearts as the Egyptians and Pharaoh did? When Israel's god dealt harshly with them, did they not send the Israelites out so they could go on their way?

⁷"Now then, get a new cart ready, with two cows that have calved and have never been yoked. Hitch the cows to the cart, but take their calves away and pen them up. ⁸Take the ark of the LORD and put it on the cart, and in a chest beside it put the gold objects you are sending back to him as a guilt offering. Send it on its way, ⁹but keep watching it. If it goes up to its own territory, toward Beth Shemesh, then the LORD has brought this great disaster on us. But if it does not, then we will know that it was not his hand that struck us but that it happened to us by chance."

¹⁰So they did this. They took two such cows and hitched them to the cart and penned up their calves. ¹¹They placed the ark of the LORD on the cart and along with it the chest containing the gold rats and the models of the tumors. ¹²Then the cows went straight up toward Beth Shemesh, keeping on the road and lowing all the way; they did not turn to the right or to the left. The rulers of the Philistines followed them as far as the border of Beth Shemesh.

¹³Now the people of Beth Shemesh were harvesting their wheat in the valley, and when they looked up and saw the ark, they rejoiced at the sight. ¹⁴The cart came to the field of Joshua of Beth Shemesh, and there it stopped beside a large rock. The people chopped up the wood of the cart and sacrificed the cows as a burnt offering to the LORD. ¹⁵The Levites took down the ark of the LORD, together with the chest containing the gold objects, and placed them on the large rock. On that day the people of Beth Shemesh offered burnt offerings and made sacrifices to the LORD. ¹⁶The five rulers of the Philistines saw all this and then returned that same day to Ekron.

351

¹⁷These are the gold tumors the Philistines sent as a guilt offering to the LORD—one each for Ashdod, Gaza, Ashkelon, Gath and Ekron. ¹⁸And the number of the gold rats was according to the number of Philistine towns belonging to the five rulers—the fortified towns with their country villages. The large rock on which the Levites set the ark of the LORD is a witness to this day in the field of Joshua of Beth Shemesh.

¹⁹But God struck down some of the inhabitants of Beth Shemesh, putting seventy[a] of them to death because they looked into the ark of the LORD. The people mourned because of the heavy blow the LORD had dealt them. ²⁰And the people of Beth Shemesh asked, "Who can stand in the presence of the LORD, this holy God? To whom will the ark go up from here?"

²¹Then they sent messengers to the people of Kiriath Jearim, saying, "The Philistines 7 have returned the ark of the LORD. Come down and take it up to your town." ¹So the men of Kiriath Jearim came and took up the ark of the LORD. They brought it to Abinadab's house on the hill and consecrated Eleazar his son to guard the ark of the LORD. ²The ark remained at Kiriath Jearim a long time—twenty years in all.

Samuel Subdues the Philistines at Mizpah

Then all the people of Israel turned back to the LORD. ³So Samuel said to the whole house of Israel, "If you are returning to the LORD with all your hearts, then rid yourselves of the foreign gods and the Ashtoreths and commit yourselves to the LORD and serve him only, and he will deliver you out of the hand of the Philistines." ⁴So the Israelites put away their Baals and Ashtoreths, and served the LORD only.

⁵Then Samuel said, "Assemble all Israel at Mizpah, and I will intercede with the LORD for you." ⁶When they had assembled at Mizpah, they drew water and poured it out before the LORD. On that day they fasted and there they confessed, "We have sinned against the LORD." Now Samuel was serving as leader[b] of Israel at Mizpah.

⁷When the Philistines heard that Israel had assembled at Mizpah, the rulers of the Philistines came up to attack them. When the Israelites heard of it, they were afraid because of the Philistines. ⁸They said to Samuel, "Do not stop crying out to the LORD our God for us, that he may rescue us from the hand of the Philistines." ⁹Then Samuel took a suckling lamb and sacrificed it as a whole burnt offering to the LORD. He cried out to the LORD on Israel's behalf, and the LORD answered him.

¹⁰While Samuel was sacrificing the burnt offering, the Philistines drew near to engage Israel in battle.

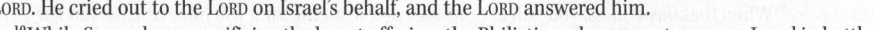

But that day the LORD thundered with loud thunder against the Philistines and threw them into such a panic that they were routed before the Israelites. [11]The men of Israel rushed out of Mizpah and pursued the Philistines, slaughtering them along the way to a point below Beth Kar.

[12]Then Samuel took a stone and set it up between Mizpah and Shen. He named it Ebenezer,[a] saying, "Thus far the LORD has helped us."

[13]So the Philistines were subdued and they stopped invading Israel's territory. Throughout Samuel's lifetime, the hand of the LORD was against the Philistines. [14]The towns from Ekron to Gath that the Philistines had captured from Israel were restored, and Israel delivered the neighboring territory from the hands of the Philistines. And there was peace between Israel and the Amorites.

[15]Samuel continued as Israel's leader all the days of his life. [16]From year to year he went on a circuit from Bethel to Gilgal to Mizpah, judging Israel in all those places. [17]But he always went back to Ramah, where his home was, and there he also held court for Israel. And he built an altar there to the LORD.

Israel Asks for a King

8 When Samuel grew old, he appointed his sons as Israel's leaders.[b] [2]The name of his firstborn was Joel and the name of his second was Abijah, and they served at Beersheba. [3]But his sons did not follow his ways. They turned aside after dishonest gain and accepted bribes and perverted justice.

[4]So all the elders of Israel gathered together and came to Samuel at Ramah. [5]They said to him, "You are old, and your sons do not follow your ways; now appoint a king to lead[c] us, such as all the other nations have."

[6]But when they said, "Give us a king to lead us," this displeased Samuel; so he prayed to the LORD. [7]And the LORD told him: "Listen to all that the people are saying to you; it is not you they have rejected, but they have rejected me as their king. [8]As they have done from the day I brought them up out of Egypt until this day, forsaking me and serving other gods, so they are doing to you. [9]Now listen to them; but warn them solemnly and let them know what the king who will reign over them will claim as his rights."

HE IS: on the throne

8:7–9 The Israelites demanded a human king so they could be like the surrounding countries. In his permissive will, God allowed the people to replace him with Saul, their new king. Though the Israelites didn't acknowledge it, God was still *on the throne*.

God doesn't preside over an earthly country, yet he is on the throne of this universe, and he also wants to rule in our hearts. However, he allows us to choose whether we'll make him our king. Be warned: He is *on the throne* and will one day reign over everyone. It's better to serve him willingly now (see Matthew 6:9–10).

For the next He Is, go to p. 364.

[10]Samuel told all the words of the LORD to the people who were asking him for a king. [11]He said, "This is what the king who will reign over you will claim as his rights: He will take your sons and make them serve with his chariots and horses, and they will run in front of his chariots. [12]Some he will assign to be commanders of thousands and commanders of fifties, and others to plow his ground and reap his harvest, and still others to make weapons of war and equipment for his chariots. [13]He will take your daughters to be perfumers and cooks and bakers. [14]He will take the best of your fields and vineyards and olive groves and give them to his attendants. [15]He will take a tenth of your grain and of your vintage and give it to his officials and attendants. [16]Your male and female servants and the best of your cattle[d] and donkeys he will take for his own use. [17]He will take a tenth of your flocks, and you yourselves will become his slaves. [18]When that day comes, you will cry out for relief from the king you have chosen, but the LORD will not answer you in that day."

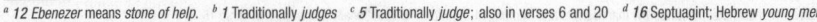

[a] 12 Ebenezer means *stone of help.*   [b] 1 Traditionally *judges*   [c] 5 Traditionally *judge*; also in verses 6 and 20   [d] 16 Septuagint; Hebrew *young men*

¹⁹But the people refused to listen to Samuel. "No!" they said. "We want a king over us. ²⁰Then we will be like all the other nations, with a king to lead us and to go out before us and fight our battles."

²¹When Samuel heard all that the people said, he repeated it before the LORD. ²²The LORD answered, "Listen to them and give them a king."

Then Samuel said to the Israelites, "Everyone go back to your own town."

Samuel Anoints Saul

9 There was a Benjamite, a man of standing, whose name was Kish son of Abiel, the son of Zeror, the son of Bekorath, the son of Aphiah of Benjamin. ²Kish had a son named Saul, as handsome a young man as could be found anywhere in Israel, and he was a head taller than anyone else.

³Now the donkeys belonging to Saul's father Kish were lost, and Kish said to his son Saul, "Take one of the servants with you and go and look for the donkeys." ⁴So he passed through the hill country of Ephraim and through the area around Shalisha, but they did not find them. They went on into the district of Shaalim, but the donkeys were not there. Then he passed through the territory of Benjamin, but they did not find them.

⁵When they reached the district of Zuph, Saul said to the servant who was with him, "Come, let's go back, or my father will stop thinking about the donkeys and start worrying about us."

⁶But the servant replied, "Look, in this town there is a man of God; he is highly respected, and everything he says comes true. Let's go there now. Perhaps he will tell us what way to take."

⁷Saul said to his servant, "If we go, what can we give the man? The food in our sacks is gone. We have no gift to take to the man of God. What do we have?"

⁸The servant answered him again. "Look," he said, "I have a quarter of a shekel*ᵃ* of silver. I will give it to the man of God so that he will tell us what way to take." ⁹(Formerly in Israel, if people went to inquire of God, they would say, "Come, let us go to the seer," because the prophet of today used to be called a seer.)

¹⁰"Good," Saul said to his servant. "Come, let's go." So they set out for the town where the man of God was.

¹¹As they were going up the hill to the town, they met some young women coming out to draw water, and they asked them, "Is the seer here?"

¹²"He is," they answered. "He's ahead of you. Hurry now; he has just come to our town today, for the people have a sacrifice at the high place. ¹³As soon as you enter the town, you will find him before he goes up to the high place to eat. The people will not begin eating until he comes, because he must bless the sacrifice; afterward, those who are invited will eat. Go up now; you should find him about this time."

¹⁴They went up to the town, and as they were entering it, there was Samuel, coming toward them on his way up to the high place.

¹⁵Now the day before Saul came, the LORD had revealed this to Samuel: ¹⁶"About this time tomorrow I will send you a man from the land of Benjamin. Anoint him ruler over my people Israel; he will deliver them from the hand of the Philistines. I have looked on my people, for their cry has reached me."

¹⁷When Samuel caught sight of Saul, the LORD said to him, "This is the man I spoke to you about; he will govern my people."

atissue:fitting in

8:1–22 Wouldn't it be great if the newest styles stuck around long enough so that you could actually wear out the clothes you spent so much money on? Fitting in can often feel like a full-time job, as the Israelites discovered. To blend in with the surrounding nations, Israel wanted a king. God warned them that a king wouldn't be all they'd hoped for. They'd have to give up things to fit in. Altering yourself or your faith to fit in is never worth it. In your hurry to blend in, don't sacrifice what's most important.

353

ᵃ 8 That is, about 1/10 ounce or about 3 grams

¹⁸Saul approached Samuel in the gateway and asked, "Would you please tell me where the seer's house is?"

¹⁹"I am the seer," Samuel replied. "Go up ahead of me to the high place, for today you are to eat with me, and in the morning I will send you on your way and will tell you all that is in your heart. ²⁰As for the donkeys you lost three days ago, do not worry about them; they have been found. And to whom is all the desire of Israel turned, if not to you and your whole family line?"

²¹Saul answered, "But am I not a Benjamite, from the smallest tribe of Israel, and is not my clan the least of all the clans of the tribe of Benjamin? Why do you say such a thing to me?"

²²Then Samuel brought Saul and his servant into the hall and seated them at the head of those who were invited—about thirty in number. ²³Samuel said to the cook, "Bring the piece of meat I gave you, the one I told you to lay aside."

²⁴So the cook took up the thigh with what was on it and set it in front of Saul. Samuel said, "Here is what has been kept for you. Eat, because it was set aside for you for this occasion from the time I said, 'I have invited guests.'" And Saul dined with Samuel that day.

²⁵After they came down from the high place to the town, Samuel talked with Saul on the roof of his house. ²⁶They rose about daybreak, and Samuel called to Saul on the roof, "Get ready, and I will send you on your way." When Saul got ready, he and Samuel went outside together. ²⁷As they were going down to the edge of the town, Samuel said to Saul, "Tell the servant to go on ahead of us"—and the servant did so—"but you stay here for a while, so that I may give you a message from God."

 Then Samuel took a bottle of olive oil and poured it on Saul's head and kissed him, saying, "Has not the LORD anointed you ruler over his inheritance?ᵃ ²When you leave me today, you will meet two men near Rachel's tomb, at Zelzah on the border of Benjamin. They will say to you, 'The donkeys you set out to look for have been found. And now your father has stopped thinking about them and is worried about you. He is asking, "What shall I do about my son?"'

³"Then you will go on from there until you reach the great tree of Tabor. Three men going up to God at Bethel will meet you there. One will be carrying three young goats, another three loaves of bread, and another a skin of wine. ⁴They will greet you and offer you two loaves of bread, which you will accept from them.

⁵"After that you will go to Gibeah of God, where there is a Philistine outpost. As you approach the town, you will meet a procession of prophets coming down from the high place with lyres, timbrels, pipes and harps being played before them, and they will be prophesying. ⁶The Spirit of the LORD will come on you in power, and you will prophesy with them; and you will be changed into a different person. ⁷Once these signs are fulfilled, do whatever your hand finds to do, for God is with you.

⁸"Go down ahead of me to Gilgal. I will surely come down to you to sacrifice burnt offerings and fellowship offerings, but you must wait seven days until I come to you and tell you what you are to do."

Saul Made King

⁹As Saul turned to leave Samuel, God changed Saul's heart, and all these signs were fulfilled that day. ¹⁰When he and his servant arrived at Gibeah, a procession of prophets met him; the Spirit of God came on him in power, and he joined in their prophesying. ¹¹When all those who had formerly known him saw him prophesying with the prophets, they asked each other, "What is this that has happened to the son of Kish? Is Saul also among the prophets?"

¹²A man who lived there answered, "And who is their father?" So it became a saying: "Is Saul also among the prophets?" ¹³After Saul stopped prophesying, he went to the high place.

¹⁴Now Saul's uncle asked him and his servant, "Where have you been?"

"Looking for the donkeys," he said. "But when we saw they were not to be found, we went to Samuel."

¹⁵Saul's uncle said, "Tell me what Samuel said to you."

¹⁶Saul replied, "He assured us that the donkeys had been found." But he did not tell his uncle what Samuel had said about the kingship.

¹⁷Samuel summoned the people of Israel to the LORD at Mizpah ¹⁸and said to them, "This is what

---

ᵃ 1 Hebrew; Septuagint and Vulgate *over his people Israel? You will reign over the LORD's people and save them from the power of their enemies round about. And this will be a sign to you that the LORD has anointed you ruler over his inheritance:*

the LORD, the God of Israel, says: 'I brought Israel up out of Egypt, and I delivered you from the power of Egypt and all the kingdoms that oppressed you.' ¹⁹But you have now rejected your God, who saves you out of all your disasters and calamities. And you have said, 'No, appoint a king over us.' So now present yourselves before the LORD by your tribes and clans."

²⁰When Samuel had all Israel come forward by tribes, the tribe of Benjamin was taken by lot. ²¹Then he brought forward the tribe of Benjamin, clan by clan, and Matri's clan was taken. Finally Saul son of Kish was taken. But when they looked for him, he was not to be found. ²²So they inquired further of the LORD, "Has the man come here yet?"

And the LORD said, "Yes, he has hidden himself among the supplies."

²³They ran and brought him out, and as he stood among the people he was a head taller than any of the others. ²⁴Samuel said to all the people, "Do you see the man the LORD has chosen? There is no one like him among all the people."

Then the people shouted, "Long live the king!"

²⁵Samuel explained to the people the rights and duties of kingship. He wrote them down on a scroll and deposited it before the LORD. Then Samuel dismissed the people to go to their own homes.

²⁶Saul also went to his home in Gibeah, accompanied by valiant men whose hearts God had touched. ²⁷But some scoundrels said, "How can this fellow save us?" They despised him and brought him no gifts. But Saul kept silent.

Saul Rescues the City of Jabesh

11 Nahash*ᵃ* the Ammonite went up and besieged Jabesh Gilead. And all the men of Jabesh said to him, "Make a treaty with us, and we will be subject to you."

²But Nahash the Ammonite replied, "I will make a treaty with you only on the condition that I gouge out the right eye of every one of you and so bring disgrace on all Israel."

³The elders of Jabesh said to him, "Give us seven days so we can send messengers throughout Israel; if no one comes to rescue us, we will surrender to you."

⁴When the messengers came to Gibeah of Saul and reported these terms to the people, they all wept aloud. ⁵Just then Saul was returning from the fields, behind his oxen, and he asked, "What is wrong with everyone? Why are they weeping?" Then they repeated to him what the men of Jabesh had said.

⁶When Saul heard their words, the Spirit of God came on him in power, and he burned with anger. ⁷He took a pair of oxen, cut them into pieces, and sent the pieces by messengers throughout Israel, proclaiming, "This is what will be done to the oxen of anyone who does not follow Saul and Samuel." Then the terror of the LORD fell on the people, and they turned out with one accord. ⁸When Saul mustered them at Bezek, the men of Israel numbered three hundred thousand and those of Judah thirty thousand.

⁹They told the messengers who had come, "Say to the men of Jabesh Gilead, 'By the time the sun is hot tomorrow, you will be rescued.'" When the messengers went and reported this to the men of Jabesh, they were elated. ¹⁰They said to the Ammonites, "Tomorrow we will surrender to you, and you can do to us whatever you like."

¹¹The next day Saul separated his men into three divisions; during the last watch of the night they

---

a:ssue:self-esteem

10:20–24 Why did Saul hide when his name was called? Was he afraid, knowing that God was displeased with the people's request for a king? Or did he have low self-esteem? Many of us can be found hiding in the baggage when God calls us to step forward. We doubt ourselves and doubt that God would use us. We even confuse low self-esteem with Christian humility. Trying not to appear arrogant, we may outright deny our talents. But this isn't humility—it's a denial of how God made us. The result? We miss God's will for us and a chance to serve others.

355

---

broke into the camp of the Ammonites and slaughtered them until the heat of the day. Those who survived were scattered, so that no two of them were left together.

Saul Confirmed as King

¹²The people then said to Samuel, "Who was it that asked, 'Shall Saul reign over us?' Turn these men over to us so that we may put them to death."

¹³But Saul said, "No one will be put to death today, for this day the Lord has rescued Israel."

¹⁴Then Samuel said to the people, "Come, let us go to Gilgal and there renew the kingship." ¹⁵So all the people went to Gilgal and made Saul king in the presence of the Lord. There they sacrificed fellowship offerings before the Lord, and Saul and all the Israelites held a great celebration.

Samuel's Farewell Speech

12 Samuel said to all Israel, "I have listened to everything you said to me and have set a king over you. ²Now you have a king as your leader. As for me, I am old and gray, and my sons are here with you. I have been your leader from my youth until this day. ³Here I stand. Testify against me in the presence of the Lord and his anointed. Whose ox have I taken? Whose donkey have I taken? Whom have I cheated? Whom have I oppressed? From whose hand have I accepted a bribe to make me shut my eyes? If I have done any of these things, I will make it right."

⁴"You have not cheated or oppressed us," they replied. "You have not taken anything from anyone's hand."

⁵Samuel said to them, "The Lord is witness against you, and also his anointed is witness this day, that you have not found anything in my hand."

"We agree," they said.

⁶Then Samuel said to the people, "It is the Lord who appointed Moses and Aaron and brought your ancestors up out of Egypt. ⁷Now then, stand here, because I am going to confront you with evidence before the Lord as to all the righteous acts performed by the Lord for you and your ancestors.

⁸"After Jacob entered Egypt, they cried to the Lord for help, and the Lord sent Moses and Aaron, who brought your ancestors out of Egypt and settled them in this place.

⁹"But they forgot the Lord their God; so he sold them into the hand of Sisera, the commander of the army of Hazor, and into the hands of the Philistines and the king of Moab, who fought against them. ¹⁰They cried out to the Lord and said, 'We have sinned; we have forsaken the Lord and served the Baals and the Ashtoreths. But now deliver us from the hands of our enemies, and we will serve you.' ¹¹Then the Lord sent Jerub-Baal,ᵃ Barak,ᵇ Jephthah and Samuel,ᶜ and he delivered you from the hands of your enemies all around you, so that you lived in safety.

¹²"But when you saw that Nahash king of the Ammonites was moving against you, you said to me, 'No, we want a king to rule over us'—even though the Lord your God was your king. ¹³Now here is the king you have chosen, the one you asked for; see, the Lord has set a king over you. ¹⁴If you fear the Lord and serve and obey him and do not rebel against his commands, and if both you and the king who reigns over you follow the Lord your God—good! ¹⁵But if you do not obey the Lord, and if you rebel against his commands, his hand will be against you, as it was against your ancestors.

¹⁶"Now then, stand still and see this great thing the Lord is about to do before your eyes! ¹⁷Is it not wheat harvest now? I will call on the Lord to send thunder and rain. And you will realize what an evil thing you did in the eyes of the Lord when you asked for a king."

¹⁸Then Samuel called on the Lord, and that same day the Lord sent thunder and rain. So all the people stood in awe of the Lord and of Samuel.

¹⁹The people all said to Samuel, "Pray to the Lord your God for your servants so that we will not die, for we have added to all our other sins the evil of asking for a king."

²⁰"Do not be afraid," Samuel replied. "You have done all this evil; yet do not turn away from the Lord, but serve the Lord with all your heart. ²¹Do not turn away after useless idols. They can do you no good, nor can they rescue you, because they are useless. ²²For the sake of his great name the Lord will not reject his people, because the Lord was pleased to make you his own. ²³As for me, far be it from me that

---

ᵃ 11 Also called *Gideon*   ᵇ 11 Some Septuagint manuscripts and Syriac; Hebrew *Bedan*   ᶜ 11 Hebrew; some Septuagint manuscripts and Syriac *Samson*

I should sin against the Lord by failing to pray for you. And I will teach you the way that is good and right. ²⁴But be sure to fear the Lord and serve him faithfully with all your heart; consider what great things he has done for you. ²⁵Yet if you persist in doing evil, both you and your king will perish."

Samuel Rebukes Saul

13 Saul was thirty[a] years old when he became king, and he reigned over Israel forty-[b] two years.

²Saul chose three thousand men from Israel; two thousand were with him at Mikmash and in the hill country of Bethel, and a thousand were with Jonathan at Gibeah in Benjamin. The rest he sent back to their homes.

³Jonathan attacked the Philistine outpost at Geba, and the Philistines heard about it. Then Saul had the trumpet blown throughout the land and said, "Let the Hebrews hear!" ⁴So all Israel heard the news: "Saul has attacked the Philistine outpost, and now Israel has become obnoxious to the Philistines." And the people were summoned to join Saul at Gilgal.

⁵The Philistines assembled to fight Israel, with three thousand[c] chariots, six thousand charioteers, and soldiers as numerous as the sand on the seashore. They went up and camped at Mikmash, east of Beth Aven. ⁶When the Israelites saw that their situation was critical and that their army was hard pressed, they hid in caves and thickets, among the rocks, and in pits and cisterns. ⁷Some Hebrews even crossed the Jordan to the land of Gad and Gilead.

Saul remained at Gilgal, and all the troops with him were quaking with fear. ⁸He waited seven days, the time set by Samuel; but Samuel did not come to Gilgal, and Saul's men began to scatter. ⁹So he said, "Bring me the burnt offering and the fellowship offerings." And Saul offered up the burnt offering. ¹⁰Just as he finished making the offering, Samuel arrived, and Saul went out to greet him.

¹¹"What have you done?" asked Samuel.

Saul replied, "When I saw that the men were scattering, and that you did not come at the set time, and that the Philistines were assembling at Mikmash, ¹²I thought, 'Now the Philistines will come down against me at Gilgal, and I have not sought the Lord's favor.' So I felt compelled to offer the burnt offering."

¹³"You have done a foolish thing," Samuel said. "You have not kept the command the Lord your God gave you; if you had, he would have established your kingdom over Israel for all time. ¹⁴But now your kingdom will not endure; the Lord has sought out a man after his own heart and appointed him ruler of his people, because you have not kept the Lord's command."

¹⁵Then Samuel left Gilgal[d] and went up to Gibeah in Benjamin, and Saul counted the men who were with him. They numbered about six hundred.

Israel Without Weapons

¹⁶Saul and his son Jonathan and the men with them were staying in Gibeah[e] in Benjamin, while the Philistines camped at Mikmash. ¹⁷Raiding parties went out from the Philistine camp in three detachments. One turned toward Ophrah in the vicinity of Shual, ¹⁸another toward Beth Horon, and the third toward the borderland overlooking the Valley of Zeboyim facing the wilderness.

¹⁹Not a blacksmith could be found in the whole land of Israel, because the Philistines had said, "Otherwise the Hebrews will make swords or spears!" ²⁰So all Israel went down to the Philistines to have their plowpoints, mattocks, axes and sickles[f] sharpened. ²¹The price was two-thirds of a shekel[g] for sharpening plowpoints and mattocks, and a third of a shekel[h] for sharpening forks and axes and for repointing goads.

conversations

prayer «» 12:23

1 » In what ways is prayerlessness a sin?

2 » How can you prioritize who to pray for?

3 » What is the purpose of intercessory prayer?

For more on **prayer**, check the index.
For the next Conversations, go to p. 360.

357

---

[a] 1 A few late manuscripts of the Septuagint; Hebrew does not have *thirty*.   [b] 1 Probable reading of the original Hebrew text (see Acts 13:21); Masoretic Text does not have *forty-*.   [c] 5 Some Septuagint manuscripts and Syriac; Hebrew *thirty thousand*   [d] 15 Hebrew; Septuagint *Gilgal and went his way; the rest of the people went after Saul to meet the army, and they went out of Gilgal*   [e] 16 Two Hebrew manuscripts; most Hebrew manuscripts *Geba*, a variant of *Gibeah*   [f] 20 Septuagint; Hebrew *plowpoints*   [g] 21 That is, about 1/4 ounce or about 8 grams   [h] 21 That is, about 1/8 ounce or about 4 grams

²²So on the day of the battle not a soldier with Saul and Jonathan had a sword or spear in his hand; only Saul and his son Jonathan had them.

Jonathan Attacks the Philistines

14 ²³Now a detachment of Philistines had gone out to the pass at Mikmash. ¹One day Jonathan son of Saul said to his young armor-bearer, "Come, let's go over to the Philistine outpost on the other side." But he did not tell his father.

²Saul was staying on the outskirts of Gibeah under a pomegranate tree in Migron. With him were about six hundred men, ³among whom was Ahijah, who was wearing an ephod. He was a son of Ichabod's brother Ahitub son of Phinehas, the son of Eli, the Lord's priest in Shiloh. No one was aware that Jonathan had left.

⁴On each side of the pass that Jonathan intended to cross to reach the Philistine outpost was a cliff; one was called Bozez and the other Seneh. ⁵One cliff stood to the north toward Mikmash, the other to the south toward Geba.

⁶Jonathan said to his young armor-bearer, "Come, let's go over to the outpost of those uncircumcised fellows. Perhaps the Lord will act in our behalf. Nothing can hinder the Lord from saving, whether by many or by few."

⁷"Do all that you have in mind," his armor-bearer said. "Go ahead; I am with you heart and soul."

⁸Jonathan said, "Come on, then; we will cross over toward them and let them see us. ⁹If they say to us, 'Wait there until we come to you,' we will stay where we are and not go up to them. ¹⁰But if they say, 'Come up to us,' we will climb up, because that will be our sign that the Lord has given them into our hands."

¹¹So both of them showed themselves to the Philistine outpost. "Look!" said the Philistines. "The Hebrews are crawling out of the holes they were hiding in." ¹²The men of the outpost shouted to Jonathan and his armor-bearer, "Come up to us and we'll teach you a lesson."

So Jonathan said to his armor-bearer, "Climb up after me; the Lord has given them into the hand of Israel."

¹³Jonathan climbed up, using his hands and feet, with his armor-bearer right behind him. The Philistines fell before Jonathan, and his armor-bearer followed and killed behind him. ¹⁴In that first attack Jonathan and his armor-bearer killed some twenty men in an area of about half an acre.

Israel Routs the Philistines

¹⁵Then panic struck the whole army—those in the camp and field, and those in the outposts and raiding parties—and the ground shook. It was a panic sent by God.*a*

¹⁶Saul's lookouts at Gibeah in Benjamin saw the army melting away in all directions. ¹⁷Then Saul said to the men who were with him, "Muster the forces and see who has left us." When they did, it was Jonathan and his armor-bearer who were not there.

¹⁸Saul said to Ahijah, "Bring the ark of God." (At that time it was with the Israelites.)*b* ¹⁹While Saul was talking to the priest, the tumult in the Philistine camp increased more and more. So Saul said to the priest, "Withdraw your hand."

²⁰Then Saul and all his men assembled and went to the battle. They found the Philistines in total confusion, striking each other with their swords. ²¹Those Hebrews who had previously been with the Philistines and had gone up with them to their camp went over to the Israelites who were with Saul and Jonathan. ²²When all the Israelites who had hidden in the hill country of Ephraim heard that the Philistines were on the run, they joined the battle in hot pursuit. ²³So on that day the Lord saved Israel, and the battle moved on beyond Beth Aven.

Jonathan Eats Honey

²⁴Now the Israelites were in distress that day, because Saul had bound the people under an oath, saying, "Cursed be anyone who eats food before evening comes, before I have avenged myself on my enemies!" So none of the troops tasted food.

---

a 15 Or *a terrible panic*   *b* 18 Hebrew; Septuagint *"Bring the ephod." (At that time he wore the ephod before the Israelites.)*

²⁵The entire army entered the woods, and there was honey on the ground. ²⁶When they went into the woods, they saw the honey oozing out; yet no one put his hand to his mouth, because they feared the oath. ²⁷But Jonathan had not heard that his father had bound the people with the oath, so he reached out the end of the staff that was in his hand and dipped it into the honeycomb. He raised his hand to his mouth, and his eyes brightened.^a ²⁸Then one of the soldiers told him, "Your father bound the army under a strict oath, saying, 'Cursed be anyone who eats food today!' That is why the men are faint."

²⁹Jonathan said, "My father has made trouble for the country. See how my eyes brightened^b when I tasted a little of this honey. ³⁰How much better it would have been if the men had eaten today some of the plunder they took from their enemies. Would not the slaughter of the Philistines have been even greater?"

³¹That day, after the Israelites had struck down the Philistines from Mikmash to Aijalon, they were exhausted. ³²They pounced on the plunder and, taking sheep, cattle and calves, they butchered them on the ground and ate them, together with the blood. ³³Then someone said to Saul, "Look, the men are sinning against the LORD by eating meat that has blood in it."

"You have broken faith," he said. "Roll a large stone over here at once." ³⁴Then he said, "Go out among the men and tell them, 'Each of you bring me your cattle and sheep, and slaughter them here and eat them. Do not sin against the LORD by eating meat with blood still in it.'"

So everyone brought his ox that night and slaughtered it there. ³⁵Then Saul built an altar to the LORD; it was the first time he had done this.

³⁶Saul said, "Let us go down and pursue the Philistines by night and plunder them till dawn, and let us not leave one of them alive."

"Do whatever seems best to you," they replied.

But the priest said, "Let us inquire of God here."

³⁷So Saul asked God, "Shall I go down and pursue the Philistines? Will you give them into Israel's hand?" But God did not answer him that day.

³⁸Saul therefore said, "Come here, all you who are leaders of the army, and let us find out what sin has been committed today. ³⁹As surely as the LORD who rescues Israel lives, even if it lies with my son Jonathan, he must die." But not one of them said a word.

⁴⁰Saul then said to all the Israelites, "You stand over there; I and Jonathan my son will stand over here."

"Do what seems best to you," they replied.

⁴¹Then Saul prayed to the LORD, the God of Israel, "Why have you not answered your servant today? If the fault is in me or my son Jonathan, respond with Urim, but if the men of Israel are at fault,^c respond with Thummim." Jonathan and Saul were taken by lot, and the men were cleared. ⁴²Saul said, "Cast the lot between me and Jonathan my son." And Jonathan was taken.

⁴³Then Saul said to Jonathan, "Tell me what you have done."

So Jonathan told him, "I tasted a little honey with the end of my staff. And now I must die!"

⁴⁴Saul said, "May God deal with me, be it ever so severely, if you do not die, Jonathan."

⁴⁵But the men said to Saul, "Should Jonathan die—he who has brought about this great deliverance in Israel? Never! As surely as the LORD lives, not a hair of his head will fall to the ground, for he did this today with God's help." So the men rescued Jonathan, and he was not put to death.

⁴⁶Then Saul stopped pursuing the Philistines, and they withdrew to their own land.

⁴⁷After Saul had assumed rule over Israel, he fought against their enemies on every side: Moab, the Ammonites, Edom, the kings^d of Zobah, and the Philistines. Wherever he turned, he inflicted punishment on them.^e ⁴⁸He fought valiantly and defeated the Amalekites, delivering Israel from the hands of those who had plundered them.

Saul's Family

⁴⁹Saul's sons were Jonathan, Ishvi and Malki-Shua. The name of his older daughter was Merab, and that of the younger was Michal. ⁵⁰His wife's name was Ahinoam daughter of Ahimaaz. The name of the

^a 27 Or his strength was renewed   ^b 29 Or my strength was renewed   ^c 41 Septuagint; Hebrew does not have "Why… at fault.   ^d 47 Masoretic Text; Dead Sea Scrolls and Septuagint king   ^e 47 Hebrew; Septuagint he was victorious

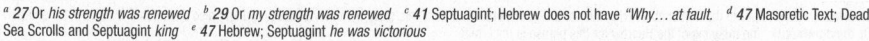

commander of Saul's army was Abner son of Ner, and Ner was Saul's uncle. [51] Saul's father Kish and Abner's father Ner were sons of Abiel.

[52] All the days of Saul there was bitter war with the Philistines, and whenever Saul saw a mighty or brave man, he took him into his service.

The LORD Rejects Saul as King

15 Samuel said to Saul, "I am the one the LORD sent to anoint you king over his people Israel; so listen now to the message from the LORD. [2] This is what the LORD Almighty says: 'I will punish the Amalekites for what they did to Israel when they waylaid them as they came up from Egypt. [3] Now go, attack the Amalekites and totally destroy[a] all that belongs to them. Do not spare them; put to death men and women, children and infants, cattle and sheep, camels and donkeys.'"

[4] So Saul summoned the men and mustered them at Telaim—two hundred thousand foot soldiers and ten thousand from Judah. [5] Saul went to the city of Amalek and set an ambush in the ravine. [6] Then he said to the Kenites, "Go away, leave the Amalekites so that I do not destroy you along with them; for you showed kindness to all the Israelites when they came up out of Egypt." So the Kenites moved away from the Amalekites.

[7] Then Saul attacked the Amalekites all the way from Havilah to Shur, near the eastern border of Egypt. [8] He took Agag king of the Amalekites alive, and all his people he totally destroyed with the sword. [9] But Saul and the army spared Agag and the best of the sheep and cattle, the fat calves[b] and lambs—everything that was good. These they were unwilling to destroy completely, but everything that was despised and weak they totally destroyed.

[10] Then the word of the LORD came to Samuel: [11] "I regret that I have made Saul king, because he has turned away from me and has not carried out my instructions." Samuel was angry, and he cried out to the LORD all that night.

[12] Early in the morning Samuel got up and went to meet Saul, but he was told, "Saul has gone to Carmel. There he has set up a monument in his own honor and has turned and gone on down to Gilgal."

[13] When Samuel reached him, Saul said, "The LORD bless you! I have carried out the LORD's instructions."

[14] But Samuel said, "What then is this bleating of sheep in my ears? What is this lowing of cattle that I hear?"

[15] Saul answered, "The soldiers brought them from the Amalekites; they spared the best of the sheep and cattle to sacrifice to the LORD your God, but we totally destroyed the rest."

[16] "Enough!" Samuel said to Saul. "Let me tell you what the LORD said to me last night."

"Tell me," Saul replied.

[17] Samuel said, "Although you were once small in your own eyes, did you not become the head of the tribes of Israel? The LORD anointed you king over Israel. [18] And he sent you on a mission, saying, 'Go and completely destroy those wicked people, the Amalekites; make war on them until you have wiped them out.' [19] Why did you not obey the LORD? Why did you pounce on the plunder and do evil in the eyes of the LORD?"

[20] "But I did obey the LORD," Saul said. "I went on the mission the LORD assigned me. I completely destroyed the Amalekites and brought back Agag their king. [21] The soldiers took sheep and cattle from the plunder, the best of what was devoted to God, in order to sacrifice them to the LORD your God at Gilgal."

[22] But Samuel replied:

conversations

obedience ‹› 15:20–23

1 Describe a time when you listened to God and obeyed him.

2 Describe a time when you did what you were supposed to, but your heart was far from God.

3 How can you listen to God if you can't literally hear him?

For more on **obedience**, check the index.
For the next Conversations, go to p. 365.

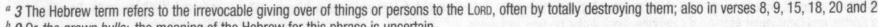

[a] 3 The Hebrew term refers to the irrevocable giving over of things or persons to the LORD, often by totally destroying them; also in verses 8, 9, 15, 18, 20 and 21.
[b] 9 Or the grown bulls; the meaning of the Hebrew for this phrase is uncertain.

"Does the Lord delight in burnt offerings and sacrifices
    as much as in obeying the Lord?
To obey is better than sacrifice,
    and to heed is better than the fat of rams.
²³For rebellion is like the sin of divination,
    and arrogance like the evil of idolatry.
Because you have rejected the word of the Lord,
    he has rejected you as king."

²⁴Then Saul said to Samuel, "I have sinned. I violated the Lord's command and your instructions. I was afraid of the men and so I gave in to them. ²⁵Now I beg you, forgive my sin and come back with me, so that I may worship the Lord."

²⁶But Samuel said to him, "I will not go back with you. You have rejected the word of the Lord, and the Lord has rejected you as king over Israel!"

²⁷As Samuel turned to leave, Saul caught hold of the hem of his robe, and it tore. ²⁸Samuel said to him, "The Lord has torn the kingdom of Israel from you today and has given it to one of your neighbors—to one better than you. ²⁹He who is the Glory of Israel does not lie or change his mind; for he is not a human being, that he should change his mind."

³⁰Saul replied, "I have sinned. But please honor me before the elders of my people and before Israel; come back with me, so that I may worship the Lord your God." ³¹So Samuel went back with Saul, and Saul worshiped the Lord.

³²Then Samuel said, "Bring me Agag king of the Amalekites."

Agag came to him in chains.ᵃ And he thought, "Surely the bitterness of death is past."
³³But Samuel said,

"As your sword has made women childless,
    so will your mother be childless among women."

And Samuel put Agag to death before the Lord at Gilgal.

³⁴Then Samuel left for Ramah, but Saul went up to his home in Gibeah of Saul. ³⁵Until the day Samuel died, he did not go to see Saul again, though Samuel mourned for him. And the Lord regretted that he had made Saul king over Israel.

Samuel Anoints David

16 The Lord said to Samuel, "How long will you mourn for Saul, since I have rejected him as king over Israel? Fill your horn with oil and be on your way; I am sending you to Jesse of Bethlehem. I have chosen one of his sons to be king."

²But Samuel said, "How can I go? If Saul hears about it, he will kill me."

The Lord said, "Take a heifer with you and say, 'I have come to sacrifice to the Lord.' ³Invite Jesse to the sacrifice, and I will show you what to do. You are to anoint for me the one I indicate."

⁴Samuel did what the Lord said. When he arrived at Bethlehem, the elders of the town trembled when they met him. They asked, "Do you come in peace?"

⁵Samuel replied, "Yes, in peace; I have come to sacrifice to the Lord. Consecrate yourselves and come to the sacrifice with me." Then he consecrated Jesse and his sons and invited them to the sacrifice.

⁶When they arrived, Samuel saw Eliab and thought, "Surely the Lord's anointed stands here before the Lord."

⁷But the Lord said to Samuel, "Do not consider his appearance or his height, for I have rejected him. The Lord does not look at the things human beings look at. People look at the outward appearance, but the Lord looks at the heart."

⁸Then Jesse called Abinadab and had him pass in front of Samuel. But Samuel said, "The Lord has not chosen this one either." ⁹Jesse then had Shammah pass by, but Samuel said, "Nor has the Lord chosen

---

ᵃ *32* The meaning of the Hebrew for this phrase is uncertain.

this one." ¹⁰Jesse had seven of his sons pass before Samuel, but Samuel said to him, "The LORD has not chosen these." ¹¹So he asked Jesse, "Are these all the sons you have?"

"There is still the youngest," Jesse answered. "He is tending the sheep."

Samuel said, "Send for him; we will not sit down until he arrives."

¹²So he sent and had him brought in. He was glowing with health and had a fine appearance and handsome features.

Then the LORD said, "Rise and anoint him; this is the one."

¹³So Samuel took the horn of oil and anointed him in the presence of his brothers, and from that day on the Spirit of the LORD came on David in power. Samuel then went to Ramah.

David in Saul's Service

¹⁴Now the Spirit of the LORD had departed from Saul, and an evil[a] spirit from the LORD tormented him.

¹⁵Saul's attendants said to him, "See, an evil spirit from God is tormenting you. ¹⁶Let our lord command his servants here to search for someone who can play the lyre. He will play when the evil spirit from God comes on you, and you will feel better."

¹⁷So Saul said to his attendants, "Find someone who plays well and bring him to me."

¹⁸One of the servants answered, "I have seen a son of Jesse of Bethlehem who knows how to play the lyre. He is a brave man and a warrior. He speaks well and is a fine-looking man. And the LORD is with him."

¹⁹Then Saul sent messengers to Jesse and said, "Send me your son David, who is with the sheep." ²⁰So Jesse took a donkey loaded with bread, a skin of wine and a young goat and sent them with his son David to Saul.

²¹David came to Saul and entered his service. Saul liked him very much, and David became one of his armor-bearers. ²²Then Saul sent word to Jesse, saying, "Allow David to remain in my service, for I am pleased with him."

²³Whenever the spirit from God came on Saul, David would take up his lyre and play. Then relief would come to Saul; he would feel better, and the evil spirit would leave him.

David and Goliath

17 Now the Philistines gathered their forces for war and assembled at Sokoh in Judah. They pitched camp at Ephes Dammim, between Sokoh and Azekah. ²Saul and the Israelites assembled and camped in the Valley of Elah and drew up their battle line to meet the Philistines. ³The Philistines occupied one hill and the Israelites another, with the valley between them.

⁴A champion named Goliath, who was from Gath, came out of the Philistine camp. His height was six cubits and a span.[b] ⁵He had a bronze helmet on his head and wore a coat of scale armor of bronze weighing five thousand shekels[c]; ⁶on his legs he wore bronze greaves, and a bronze javelin was slung on his back. ⁷His spear shaft was like a weaver's rod, and its iron point weighed six hundred shekels.[d] His shield bearer went ahead of him.

⁸Goliath stood and shouted to the ranks of Israel, "Why do you come out and line up for battle? Am I

atissue:appearance

16:7 How long does it take you to get ready in the morning? If you spend one hour each day, that's 30 hours a month (over a whole day!) just preparing your external features. How can we live in a world that judges us by our appearance while remaining true to the way God judges us? God doesn't require us to throw out our mirrors, melt our makeup and cancel our appointments at the salon. However, exterior grooming should always be balanced with internal development. What would be the result if you spent an equal amount of time each day with God?

---

[a] 14 Or *harmful*; also in verses 15, 16 and 23   [b] 4 That is, about 9 1/2 feet or about 2.9 meters   [c] 5 That is, about 125 pounds or about 57 kilograms
[d] 7 That is, about 15 pounds or about 6.9 kilograms

not a Philistine, and are you not the servants of Saul? Choose a man and have him come down to me. ⁹If he is able to fight and kill me, we will become your subjects; but if I overcome him and kill him, you will become our subjects and serve us." ¹⁰Then the Philistine said, "This day I defy the armies of Israel! Give me a man and let us fight each other." ¹¹On hearing the Philistine's words, Saul and all the Israelites were dismayed and terrified.

¹²Now David was the son of an Ephrathite named Jesse, who was from Bethlehem in Judah. Jesse had eight sons, and in Saul's time he was very old. ¹³Jesse's three oldest sons had followed Saul to the war: The firstborn was Eliab; the second, Abinadab; and the third, Shammah. ¹⁴David was the youngest. The three oldest followed Saul, ¹⁵but David went back and forth from Saul to tend his father's sheep at Bethlehem.

¹⁶For forty days the Philistine came forward every morning and evening and took his stand.

¹⁷Now Jesse said to his son David, "Take this ephah*ᵃ* of roasted grain and these ten loaves of bread for your brothers and hurry to their camp. ¹⁸Take along these ten cheeses to the commander of their unit. See how your brothers are and bring back some assurance*ᵇ* from them. ¹⁹They are with Saul and all the men of Israel in the Valley of Elah, fighting against the Philistines."

²⁰Early in the morning David left the flock in the care of a shepherd, loaded up and set out, as Jesse had directed. He reached the camp as the army was going out to its battle positions, shouting the war cry. ²¹Israel and the Philistines were drawing up their lines facing each other. ²²David left his things with the keeper of supplies, ran to the battle lines and asked his brothers how they were. ²³As he was talking with them, Goliath, the Philistine champion from Gath, stepped out from his lines and shouted his usual defiance, and David heard it. ²⁴Whenever the Israelites saw the man, they all fled from him in great fear.

²⁵Now the Israelites had been saying, "Do you see how this man keeps coming out? He comes out to defy Israel. The king will give great wealth to the man who kills him. He will also give him his daughter in marriage and will exempt his family line from taxes in Israel."

²⁶David asked those standing near him, "What will be done for the man who kills this Philistine and removes this disgrace from Israel? Who is this uncircumcised Philistine that he should defy the armies of the living God?"

²⁷They repeated to him what they had been saying and told him, "This is what will be done for the man who kills him."

²⁸When Eliab, David's oldest brother, heard him speaking with the men, he burned with anger at him and asked, "Why have you come down here? And with whom did you leave those few sheep in the wilderness? I know how conceited you are and how wicked your heart is; you came down only to watch the battle."

²⁹"Now what have I done?" said David. "Can't I even speak?" ³⁰He then turned away to someone else and brought up the same matter, and the men answered him as before. ³¹What David said was overheard and reported to Saul, and Saul sent for him.

³²David said to Saul, "Let no one lose heart on account of this Philistine; your servant will go and fight him."

³³Saul replied, "You are not able to go out against this Philistine and fight him; you are little more than a boy, and he has been a warrior from his youth."

³⁴But David said to Saul, "Your servant has been keeping his father's sheep. When a lion or a bear

363

aussue:risk

17:20–50 What if David's stone had missed? Goliath would have killed him, and the nation of Israel would have been conquered. In the world's eyes, David took a big (and frankly quite foolish) risk in picking up the slingshot. In David's eyes, he was just going for a sure bet on his God, and that made all the difference. Each of us must decide what risks in our lives are worth taking. Is it worth taking a stand for God in your workplace or with your friends? If the result depends on you—no way. If the result depends on God—sure bet.

ᵃ 17 That is, probably about 36 pounds or about 16 kilograms   *ᵇ 18* Or *some token;* or *some pledge of spoils* came and carried off a sheep from the flock, ³⁵I went after it, struck it and rescued the sheep from its mouth. When it turned on me, I seized it by its hair, struck it and killed it. ³⁶Your servant has killed both the lion and the bear; this uncircumcised Philistine will be like one of them, because he has defied the armies of the living God. ³⁷The LORD who rescued me from the paw of the lion and the paw of the bear will rescue me from the hand of this Philistine."

Saul said to David, "Go, and the LORD be with you."

³⁸Then Saul dressed David in his own tunic. He put a coat of armor on him and a bronze helmet on his head. ³⁹David fastened on his sword over the tunic and tried walking around, because he was not used to them.

"I cannot go in these," he said to Saul, "because I am not used to them." So he took them off. ⁴⁰Then he took his staff in his hand, chose five smooth stones from the stream, put them in the pouch of his shepherd's bag and, with his sling in his hand, approached the Philistine.

⁴¹Meanwhile, the Philistine, with his shield bearer in front of him, kept coming closer to David. ⁴²He looked David over and saw that he was little more than a boy, glowing with health and handsome, and he despised him. ⁴³He said to David, "Am I a dog, that you come at me with sticks?" And the Philistine cursed David by his gods. ⁴⁴"Come here," he said, "and I'll give your flesh to the birds and the wild animals!"

⁴⁵David said to the Philistine, "You come against me with sword and spear and javelin, but I come against you in the name of the LORD Almighty, the God of the armies of Israel, whom you have defied. ⁴⁶This day the LORD will deliver you into my hands, and I'll strike you down and cut off your head. This very day I will give the carcasses of the Philistine army to the birds and the wild animals, and the whole world will know that there is a God in Israel. ⁴⁷All those gathered here will know that it is not by sword or spear that the LORD saves; for the battle is the LORD's, and he will give all of you into our hands."

HE IS: the secret weapon

17:45–47 The giant Goliath had the Israelite army paralyzed with fear. Along came a shepherd boy named David who had a *secret weapon* in his arsenal: "I come against you in the name of the LORD Almighty." With God on his side, David couldn't lose.

Those who defy the living God can sometimes seem like Goliaths: They're often well-equipped, well-financed and stand tall in the world. But God uses small and faithful people to topple giants. Are there "Goliaths" standing in your path—situations or organizations, a law or our culture? Ask God to help you stand up to them in the power of his name. He is *the secret weapon*.

For the next He Is, go to p. 370.

⁴⁸As the Philistine moved closer to attack him, David ran quickly toward the battle line to meet him. ⁴⁹Reaching into his bag and taking out a stone, he slung it and struck the Philistine on the forehead. The stone sank into his forehead, and he fell facedown on the ground.

⁵⁰So David triumphed over the Philistine with a sling and a stone; without a sword in his hand he struck down the Philistine and killed him.

⁵¹David ran and stood over him. He took hold of the Philistine's sword and drew it from the sheath. After he killed him, he cut off his head with the sword.

When the Philistines saw that their hero was dead, they turned and ran. ⁵²Then the men of Israel and Judah surged forward with a shout and pursued the Philistines to the entrance of Gath ^a and to the gates of Ekron. Their dead were strewn along the Shaaraim road to Gath and Ekron. ⁵³When the Israelites returned from chasing the Philistines, they plundered their camp.

---

^a *52 Some Septuagint manuscripts; Hebrew of a valley*

⁵⁴David took the Philistine's head and brought it to Jerusalem; he put the Philistine's weapons in his own tent.

⁵⁵As Saul watched David going out to meet the Philistine, he said to Abner, commander of the army, "Abner, whose son is that young man?"

Abner replied, "As surely as you live, Your Majesty, I don't know."

⁵⁶The king said, "Find out whose son this young man is."

⁵⁷As soon as David returned from killing the Philistine, Abner took him and brought him before Saul, with David still holding the Philistine's head.

⁵⁸"Whose son are you, young man?" Saul asked him.

David said, "I am the son of your servant Jesse of Bethlehem."

Saul's Growing Fear of David

18 After David had finished talking with Saul, Jonathan became one in spirit with David, and he loved him as himself. ²From that day Saul kept David with him and did not let him return home to his family. ³And Jonathan made a covenant with David because he loved him as himself. ⁴Jonathan took off the robe he was wearing and gave it to David, along with his tunic, and even his sword, his bow and his belt.

⁵Whatever mission Saul sent him on, David was so successful that Saul gave him a high rank in the army. This pleased all the troops, and Saul's officers as well.

⁶When the men were returning home after David had killed the Philistine, the women came out from all the towns of Israel to meet King Saul with singing and dancing, with joyful songs and with timbrels and lyres. ⁷As they danced, they sang:

> "Saul has slain his thousands,
>   and David his tens of thousands."

⁸Saul was very angry; this refrain displeased him greatly. "They have credited David with tens of thousands," he thought, "but me with only thousands. What more can he get but the kingdom?" ⁹And from that time on Saul kept a close eye on David.

¹⁰The next day an evil*ᵃ* spirit from God came forcefully on Saul. He was prophesying in his house, while David was playing the lyre, as he usually did. Saul had a spear in his hand ¹¹and he hurled it, saying to himself, "I'll pin David to the wall." But David eluded him twice.

¹²Saul was afraid of David, because the LORD was with David but had departed from Saul. ¹³So he sent David away from him and gave him command over a thousand men, and David led the troops in their campaigns. ¹⁴In everything he did he had great success, because the LORD was with him. ¹⁵When Saul saw how successful he was, he was afraid of him. ¹⁶But all Israel and Judah loved David, because he led them in their campaigns.

¹⁷Saul said to David, "Here is my older daughter Merab. I will give her to you in marriage; only serve me bravely and

conversations
being a good friend «» 18:1–3

1» Describe the ideal friend.

2» What do all of your friends have in common?

3» How do you demonstrate love for your friends?

For more on **friendship**, check the index.
For the next Conversations, go to p. 365.

conversations
envy «» 18:7–9

1» Is it always wrong to want what another person has?

2» What is the root cause of envy?

3» Think of someone you envied in the past. Why did you envy her?

For more on **envy**, check the index.
For the next Conversations, go to p. 371.

365

ᵃ 10 Or *harmful*

fight the battles of the LORD." For Saul said to himself, "I will not raise a hand against him. Let the Philistines do that!"

¹⁸But David said to Saul, "Who am I, and what is my family or my clan in Israel, that I should become the king's son-in-law?" ¹⁹So*ᵃ* when the time came for Merab, Saul's daughter, to be given to David, she was given in marriage to Adriel of Meholah.

²⁰Now Saul's daughter Michal was in love with David, and when they told Saul about it, he was pleased. ²¹"I will give her to him," he thought, "so that she may be a snare to him and so that the hand of the Philistines may be against him." So Saul said to David, "Now you have a second opportunity to become my son-in-law."

²²Then Saul ordered his attendants: "Speak to David privately and say, 'Look, the king likes you, and his attendants all love you; now become his son-in-law.'"

²³They repeated these words to David. But David said, "Do you think it is a small matter to become the king's son-in-law? I'm only a poor man and little known."

²⁴When Saul's servants told him what David had said, ²⁵Saul replied, "Say to David, 'The king wants no other price for the bride than a hundred Philistine foreskins, to take revenge on his enemies.'" Saul's plan was to have David fall by the hands of the Philistines.

²⁶When the attendants told David these things, he was pleased to become the king's son-in-law. So before the allotted time elapsed, ²⁷David took his men with him and went out and killed two hundred Philistines and brought back their foreskins. They counted out the full number to the king so that David might become the king's son-in-law. Then Saul gave him his daughter Michal in marriage.

²⁸When Saul realized that the LORD was with David and that his daughter Michal loved David, ²⁹Saul became still more afraid of him, and he remained his enemy the rest of his days.

³⁰The Philistine commanders continued to go out to battle, and as often as they did, David met with more success than the rest of Saul's officers, and his name became well known.

Saul Tries to Kill David

19 Saul told his son Jonathan and all the attendants to kill David. But Jonathan had taken a great liking to David ²and warned him, "My father Saul is looking for a chance to kill you. Be on your guard tomorrow morning; go into hiding and stay there. ³I will go out and stand with my father in the field where you are. I'll speak to him about you and will tell you what I find out."

⁴Jonathan spoke well of David to Saul his father and said to him, "Let not the king do wrong to his servant David; he has not wronged you, and what he has done has benefited you greatly. ⁵He took his life in his hands when he killed the Philistine. The LORD won a great victory for all Israel, and you saw it and were glad. Why then would you do wrong to an innocent man like David by killing him for no reason?"

⁶Saul listened to Jonathan and took this oath: "As surely as the LORD lives, David will not be put to death."

⁷So Jonathan called David and told him the whole conversation. He brought him to Saul, and David was with Saul as before.

⁸Once more war broke out, and David went out and fought the Philistines. He struck them with such force that they fled before him.

⁹But an evil*ᵇ* spirit from the LORD came on Saul as he was sitting in his house with his spear in his hand. While David was playing the lyre, ¹⁰Saul tried to pin him to the wall with his spear, but David eluded him as Saul drove the spear into the wall. That night David made good his escape.

¹¹Saul sent men to David's house to watch it and to kill him in the morning. But Michal, David's wife, warned him, "If you don't run for your life tonight, tomorrow you'll be killed." ¹²So Michal let David down through a window, and he fled and escaped. ¹³Then Michal took an idol and laid it on the bed, covering it with a garment and putting some goats' hair at the head.

¹⁴When Saul sent the men to capture David, Michal said, "He is ill."

¹⁵Then Saul sent the men back to see David and told them, "Bring him up to me in his bed so that I

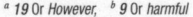

ᵃ 19 Or However, ᵇ 9 Or harmful

may kill him." ¹⁶But when the men entered, there was the idol in the bed, and at the head was some goats' hair.

¹⁷Saul said to Michal, "Why did you deceive me like this and send my enemy away so that he escaped?"

Michal told him, "He said to me, 'Let me get away. Why should I kill you?'"

¹⁸When David had fled and made his escape, he went to Samuel at Ramah and told him all that Saul had done to him. Then he and Samuel went to Naioth and stayed there. ¹⁹Word came to Saul: "David is in Naioth at Ramah"; ²⁰so he sent men to capture him. But when they saw a group of prophets prophesying, with Samuel standing there as their leader, the Spirit of God came on Saul's men, and they also prophesied. ²¹Saul was told about it, and he sent more men, and they prophesied too. Saul sent men a third time, and they also prophesied. ²²Finally, he himself left for Ramah and went to the great cistern at Seku. And he asked, "Where are Samuel and David?"

"Over in Naioth at Ramah," they said.

²³So Saul went to Naioth at Ramah. But the Spirit of God came even on him, and he walked along prophesying until he came to Naioth. ²⁴He stripped off his garments, and he too prophesied in Samuel's presence. He lay naked all that day and all that night. This is why people say, "Is Saul also among the prophets?"

David and Jonathan

20 Then David fled from Naioth at Ramah and went to Jonathan and asked, "What have I done? What is my crime? How have I wronged your father, that he is trying to take my life?"

²"Never!" Jonathan replied. "You are not going to die! Look, my father doesn't do anything, great or small, without letting me know. Why would he hide this from me? It isn't so!"

³But David took an oath and said, "Your father knows very well that I have found favor in your eyes, and he has said to himself, 'Jonathan must not know this or he will be grieved.' Yet as surely as the Lord lives and as you live, there is only a step between me and death."

⁴Jonathan said to David, "Whatever you want me to do, I'll do for you."

⁵So David said, "Look, tomorrow is the New Moon feast, and I am supposed to dine with the king; but let me go and hide in the field until the evening of the day after tomorrow. ⁶If your father misses me at all, tell him, 'David earnestly asked my permission to hurry to Bethlehem, his hometown, because an annual sacrifice is being made there for his whole clan.' ⁷If he says, 'Very well,' then your servant is safe. But if he loses his temper, you can be sure that he is determined to harm me. ⁸As for you, show kindness to your servant, for you have brought him into a covenant with you before the Lord. If I am guilty, then kill me yourself! Why hand me over to your father?"

⁹"Never!" Jonathan said. "If I had the least inkling that my father was determined to harm you, wouldn't I tell you?"

¹⁰David asked, "Who will tell me if your father answers you harshly?"

¹¹"Come," Jonathan said, "let's go out into the field." So they went there together.

¹²Then Jonathan said to David, "I swear by the Lord, the God of Israel, that I will surely sound out my father by this time the day after tomorrow! If he is favorably disposed toward you, will I not send you word and let you know? ¹³But if my father intends to harm you, may the Lord deal with Jonathan, be it ever so severely, if I do not let you know and send you away in peace. May the Lord be with you as he has been with my father. ¹⁴But show me unfailing kindness like the Lord's kindness as long as I live, so that I may not be killed, ¹⁵and do not ever cut off your kindness from my family—not even when the Lord has cut off every one of David's enemies from the face of the earth."

¹⁶So Jonathan made a covenant with the house of David, saying, "May the Lord call David's enemies to account." ¹⁷And Jonathan had David reaffirm his oath out of love for him, because he loved him as he loved himself.

¹⁸Then Jonathan said to David, "Tomorrow is the New Moon feast. You will be missed, because your seat will be empty. ¹⁹The day after tomorrow, toward evening, go to the place where you hid when this trouble began, and wait by the stone Ezel. ²⁰I will shoot three arrows to the side of it, as though I were

shooting at a target. ²¹Then I will send a boy and say, 'Go, find the arrows.' If I say to him, 'Look, the arrows are on this side of you; bring them here,' then come, because, as surely as the LORD lives, you are safe; there is no danger. ²²But if I say to the boy, 'Look, the arrows are beyond you,' then you must go, because the LORD has sent you away. ²³And about the matter you and I discussed—remember, the LORD is witness between you and me forever."

²⁴So David hid in the field, and when the New Moon feast came, the king sat down to eat. ²⁵He sat in his customary place by the wall, opposite Jonathan,ᵃ and Abner sat next to Saul, but David's place was empty. ²⁶Saul said nothing that day, for he thought, "Something must have happened to David to make him ceremonially unclean—surely he is unclean." ²⁷But the next day, the second day of the month, David's place was empty again. Then Saul said to his son Jonathan, "Why hasn't the son of Jesse come to the meal, either yesterday or today?"

²⁸Jonathan answered, "David earnestly asked me for permission to go to Bethlehem. ²⁹He said, 'Let me go, because our family is observing a sacrifice in the town and my brother has ordered me to be there. If I have found favor in your eyes, let me get away to see my brothers.' That is why he has not come to the king's table."

³⁰Saul's anger flared up at Jonathan and he said to him, "You son of a perverse and rebellious woman! Don't I know that you have sided with the son of Jesse to your own shame and to the shame of the mother who bore you? ³¹As long as the son of Jesse lives on this earth, neither you nor your kingdom will be established. Now send someone to bring him to me, for he must die!"

³²"Why should he be put to death? What has he done?" Jonathan asked his father. ³³But Saul hurled his spear at him to kill him. Then Jonathan knew that his father intended to kill David.

³⁴Jonathan got up from the table in fierce anger; on that second day of the feast he did not eat, because he was grieved at his father's shameful treatment of David.

³⁵In the morning Jonathan went out to the field for his meeting with David. He had a small boy with him, ³⁶and he said to the boy, "Run and find the arrows I shoot." As the boy ran, he shot an arrow beyond him. ³⁷When the boy came to the place where Jonathan's arrow had fallen, Jonathan called out after him, "Isn't the arrow beyond you?" ³⁸Then he shouted, "Hurry! Go quickly! Don't stop!" The boy picked up the arrow and returned to his master. ³⁹(The boy knew nothing about all this; only Jonathan and David knew.) ⁴⁰Then Jonathan gave his weapons to the boy and said, "Go, carry them back to town."

⁴¹After the boy had gone, David got up from the south side of the stone and bowed down before Jonathan three times, with his face to the ground. Then they kissed each other and wept together—but David wept the most.

⁴²Jonathan said to David, "Go in peace, for we have sworn friendship with each other in the name of the LORD, saying, 'The LORD is witness between you and me, and between your descendants and my descendants forever.'" *Then David left, and Jonathan went back to the town.

David at Nob

21 *David went to Nob, to Ahimelek the priest. Ahimelek trembled when he met him, and asked, "Why are you alone? Why is no one with you?"

²David answered Ahimelek the priest, "The king sent me on a mission and said to me, 'No one is to know anything about the mission I am sending you on.' As for my men, I have told them to meet me at a certain place. ³Now then, what do you have on hand? Give me five loaves of bread, or whatever you can find."

⁴But the priest answered David, "I don't have any ordinary bread on hand; however, there is some consecrated bread here—provided the men have kept themselves from women."

⁵David replied, "Indeed women have been kept from us, as usual wheneverᵇ I set out. The men's bodies are holy even on missions that are not holy. How much more so today!" ⁶So the priest gave him the consecrated bread, since there was no bread there except the bread of the Presence that had been removed from before the LORD and replaced by hot bread on the day it was taken away.

ᵃ 25 Septuagint; Hebrew *wall. Jonathan arose*   ᵇ 5 Or *from us in the past few days since*

* This sentence (20:42b) is numbered 21:1 in Hebrew texts.   * 21:1-15 is numbered 21:2-16 in Hebrew texts.

⁷Now one of Saul's servants was there that day, detained before the LORD; he was Doeg the Edomite, Saul's chief shepherd.

⁸David asked Ahimelek, "Don't you have a spear or a sword here? I haven't brought my sword or any other weapon, because the king's mission was urgent."

⁹The priest replied, "The sword of Goliath the Philistine, whom you killed in the Valley of Elah, is here; it is wrapped in a cloth behind the ephod. If you want it, take it; there is no sword here but that one."

David said, "There is none like it; give it to me."

David at Gath

¹⁰That day David fled from Saul and went to Achish king of Gath. ¹¹But the servants of Achish said to him, "Isn't this David, the king of the land? Isn't he the one they sing about in their dances:

> "'Saul has slain his thousands,
>   and David his tens of thousands'?"

¹²David took these words to heart and was very much afraid of Achish king of Gath. ¹³So he pretended to be insane in their presence; and while he was in their hands he acted like a madman, making marks on the doors of the gate and letting saliva run down his beard.

¹⁴Achish said to his servants, "Look at the man! He is insane! Why bring him to me? ¹⁵Am I so short of madmen that you have to bring this fellow here to carry on like this in front of me? Must this man come into my house?"

David at Adullam and Mizpah

22 David left Gath and escaped to the cave of Adullam. When his brothers and his father's household heard about it, they went down to him there. ²All those who were in distress or in debt or discontented gathered around him, and he became their commander. About four hundred men were with him.

³From there David went to Mizpah in Moab and said to the king of Moab, "Would you let my father and mother come and stay with you until I learn what God will do for me?" ⁴So he left them with the king of Moab, and they stayed with him as long as David was in the stronghold.

⁵But the prophet Gad said to David, "Do not stay in the stronghold. Go into the land of Judah." So David left and went to the forest of Hereth.

Saul Kills the Priests of Nob

⁶Now Saul heard that David and his men had been discovered. And Saul was seated, spear in hand, under the tamarisk tree on the hill at Gibeah, with all his officials standing at his side. ⁷He said to them, "Listen, men of Benjamin! Will the son of Jesse give all of you fields and vineyards? Will he make all of you commanders of thousands and commanders of hundreds? ⁸Is that why you have all conspired against me? No one tells me when my son makes a covenant with the son of Jesse. None of you is concerned about me or tells me that my son has incited my servant to lie in wait for me, as he does today."

⁹But Doeg the Edomite, who was standing with Saul's officials, said, "I saw the son of Jesse come to Ahimelek son of Ahitub at Nob. ¹⁰Ahimelek inquired of the LORD for him; he also gave him provisions and the sword of Goliath the Philistine."

¹¹Then the king sent for the priest Ahimelek son of Ahitub and all the men of his family, who were the priests at Nob, and they all came to the king. ¹²Saul said, "Listen now, son of Ahitub."

"Yes, my lord," he answered.

¹³Saul said to him, "Why have you conspired against me, you and the son of Jesse, giving him bread and a sword and inquiring of God for him, so that he has rebelled against me and lies in wait for me, as he does today?"

¹⁴Ahimelek answered the king, "Who of all your servants is as loyal as David, the king's son-in-law, captain of your bodyguard and highly respected in your household? ¹⁵Was that day the first time I inquired of God for him? Of course not! Let not the king accuse your servant or any of his father's family, for your servant knows nothing at all about this whole affair."

¹⁶But the king said, "You will surely die, Ahimelek, you and your whole family."

¹⁷Then the king ordered the guards at his side: "Turn and kill the priests of the LORD, because they too have sided with David. They knew he was fleeing, yet they did not tell me."

But the king's officials were unwilling to raise a hand to strike the priests of the LORD.

¹⁸The king then ordered Doeg, "You turn and strike down the priests." So Doeg the Edomite turned and struck them down. That day he killed eighty-five men who wore the linen ephod. ¹⁹He also put to the sword Nob, the town of the priests, with its men and women, its children and infants, and its cattle, donkeys and sheep.

²⁰But one son of Ahimelek son of Ahitub, named Abiathar, escaped and fled to join David. ²¹He told David that Saul had killed the priests of the LORD. ²²Then David said to Abiathar, "That day, when Doeg the Edomite was there, I knew he would be sure to tell Saul. I am responsible for the death of your whole family. ²³Stay with me; don't be afraid. The man who wants to take your life is trying to kill me too. You will be safe with me."

David Saves Keilah

23 When David was told, "Look, the Philistines are fighting against Keilah and are looting the threshing floors," ²he inquired of the LORD, saying, "Shall I go and attack these Philistines?"

The LORD answered him, "Go, attack the Philistines and save Keilah."

³But David's men said to him, "Here in Judah we are afraid. How much more, then, if we go to Keilah against the Philistine forces!"

⁴Once again David inquired of the LORD, and the LORD answered him, "Go down to Keilah, for I am going to give the Philistines into your hand." ⁵So David and his men went to Keilah, fought the Philistines and carried off their livestock. He inflicted heavy losses on the Philistines and saved the people of Keilah. ⁶(Now Abiathar son of Ahimelek had brought the ephod down with him when he fled to David at Keilah.)

370

HE IS: strategic

23:1–5 When David, a seasoned warrior, heard about the Philistines fighting against Keilah, he was deeply distressed. But he didn't rush into battle. Instead, he went to God for the right tactics and timing. God is *strategic* and gave David the go-ahead (twice) to fight his rivals and rescue the people.

You may be tempted to rush headlong into battle when you feel moved by an injustice at home, work or school. Why not follow David's example and ask the Lord when and how you should enter the fray? His timing is perfect.

For the next He Is, go to p. 379.

Saul Pursues David

⁷Saul was told that David had gone to Keilah, and he said, "God has delivered him into my hands, for David has imprisoned himself by entering a town with gates and bars." ⁸And Saul called up all his forces for battle, to go down to Keilah to besiege David and his men.

⁹When David learned that Saul was plotting against him, he said to Abiathar the priest, "Bring the ephod." ¹⁰David said, "LORD, God of Israel, your servant has heard definitely that Saul plans to come to Keilah and destroy the town on account of me. ¹¹Will the citizens of Keilah surrender me to him? Will Saul come down, as your servant has heard? LORD, God of Israel, tell your servant."

And the LORD said, "He will."

¹²Again David asked, "Will the citizens of Keilah surrender me and my men to Saul?"

And the LORD said, "They will."

¹³So David and his men, about six hundred in number, left Keilah and kept moving from place to place. When Saul was told that David had escaped from Keilah, he did not go there.

¹⁴David stayed in the wilderness strongholds and in the hills of the Desert of Ziph. Day after day Saul searched for him, but God did not give David into his hands.

¹⁵While David was at Horesh in the Desert of Ziph, he learned that Saul had come out to take his life.

conversations

friendship «» 23:15–18

1 » What is the greatest need your friends fill in your life?

2 » What needs do you fill in your friends' lives?

3 » Have you ever given up your rights so that a friend could succeed, as Jonathan did?

For more on friendship, check the index.
For the next Conversations, go to p. 378.

¹⁶And Saul's son Jonathan went to David at Horesh and helped him find strength in God. ¹⁷"Don't be afraid," he said. "My father Saul will not lay a hand on you. You will be king over Israel, and I will be second to you. Even my father Saul knows this." ¹⁸The two of them made a covenant before the LORD. Then Jonathan went home, but David remained at Horesh.

¹⁹The Ziphites went up to Saul at Gibeah and said, "Is not David hiding among us in the strongholds at Horesh, on the hill of Hakilah, south of Jeshimon? ²⁰Now, Your Majesty, come down whenever it pleases you to do so, and we will be responsible for giving him into your hands."

²¹Saul replied, "The LORD bless you for your concern for me. ²²Go and get more information. Find out where David usually goes and who has seen him there. They tell me he is very crafty. ²³Find out about all the hiding places he uses and come back to me with definite information. Then I will go with you; if he is in the area, I will track him down among all the clans of Judah."

²⁴So they set out and went to Ziph ahead of Saul. Now David and his men were in the Desert of Maon, in the Arabah south of Jeshimon. ²⁵Saul and his men began the search, and when David was told about it, he went down to the rock and stayed in the Desert of Maon. When Saul heard this, he went into the Desert of Maon in pursuit of David.

²⁶Saul was going along one side of the mountain, and David and his men were on the other side, hurrying to get away from Saul. As Saul and his forces were closing in on David and his men to capture them, ²⁷a messenger came to Saul, saying, "Come quickly! The Philistines are raiding the land." ²⁸Then Saul broke off his pursuit of David and went to meet the Philistines. That is why they call this place Sela Hammahlekoth.ᵃ * ²⁹And David went up from there and lived in the strongholds of En Gedi.

David Spares Saul's Life

24 *After Saul returned from pursuing the Philistines, he was told, "David is in the Desert of En Gedi." ²So Saul took three thousand able young men from all Israel and set out to look for David and his men near the Crags of the Wild Goats.

³He came to the sheep pens along the way; a cave was there, and Saul went in to relieve himself. David and his men were far back in the cave. ⁴The men said, "This is the day the LORD spoke of when he saidᵇ to you, 'I will give your enemy into your hands for you to deal with as you wish.'" Then David crept up unnoticed and cut off a corner of Saul's robe.

⁵Afterward, David was conscience-stricken for having cut off a corner of his robe. ⁶He said to his men, "The LORD forbid that I should do such a thing to my master, the LORD's anointed, or lay my hand on him; for he is the anointed of the LORD." ⁷With these words David sharply rebuked his men and did not allow them to attack Saul. And Saul left the cave and went his way.

⁸Then David went out of the cave and called out to Saul, "My lord the king!" When Saul looked behind him, David bowed down and prostrated himself with his face to the ground. ⁹He said to Saul, "Why do you listen when men say, 'David is bent on harming you'? ¹⁰This day you have seen with your own eyes how the LORD delivered you into my hands in the cave. Some urged me to kill you, but I spared you; I said, 'I will not lay my hand on my lord, because he is the LORD's anointed.' ¹¹See, my father, look at this piece

---

ᵃ 28 Sela Hammahlekoth means rock of parting.   ᵇ 4 Or "Today the LORD is saying

* 23:29 is numbered 24:1 in Hebrew texts.   * 24:1-22 is numbered 24:2-23 in Hebrew texts.

of your robe in my hand! I cut off the corner of your robe but did not kill you. See that there is nothing in my hand to indicate that I am guilty of wrongdoing or rebellion. I have not wronged you, but you are hunting me down to take my life. ¹²May the LORD judge between you and me. And may the LORD avenge the wrongs you have done to me, but my hand will not touch you. ¹³As the old saying goes, 'From evildoers come evil deeds,' so my hand will not touch you.

¹⁴"Against whom has the king of Israel come out? Whom are you pursuing? A dead dog? A flea? ¹⁵May the LORD be our judge and decide between us. May he consider my cause and uphold it; may he vindicate me by delivering me from your hand."

¹⁶When David finished saying this, Saul asked, "Is that your voice, David my son?" And he wept aloud. ¹⁷"You are more righteous than I," he said. "You have treated me well, but I have treated you badly. ¹⁸You have just now told me about the good you did to me; the LORD delivered me into your hands, but you did not kill me. ¹⁹When a man finds his enemy, does he let him get away unharmed? May the LORD reward you well for the way you treated me today. ²⁰I know that you will surely be king and that the kingdom of Israel will be established in your hands. ²¹Now swear to me by the LORD that you will not kill off my descendants or wipe out my name from my father's family."

²²So David gave his oath to Saul. Then Saul returned home, but David and his men went up to the stronghold.

David, Nabal and Abigail

25 Now Samuel died, and all Israel assembled and mourned for him; and they buried him at his home in Ramah. Then David moved down into the Desert of Paran.ᵃ

²A certain man in Maon, who had property there at Carmel, was very wealthy. He had a thousand goats and three thousand sheep, which he was shearing in Carmel. ³His name was Nabal and his wife's name was Abigail. She was an intelligent and beautiful woman, but her husband was surly and mean in his dealings—he was a Calebite.

⁴While David was in the wilderness, he heard that Nabal was shearing sheep. ⁵So he sent ten young men and said to them, "Go up to Nabal at Carmel and greet him in my name. ⁶Say to him: 'Long life to you! Good health to you and your household! And good health to all that is yours!

⁷"'Now I hear that it is sheep-shearing time. When your shepherds were with us, we did not mistreat them, and the whole time they were at Carmel nothing of theirs was missing. ⁸Ask your own servants and they will tell you. Therefore be favorable toward my men, since we come at a festive time. Please give your servants and your son David whatever you can find for them.'"

⁹When David's men arrived, they gave Nabal this message in David's name. Then they waited.

at issue: submitting

25:1–44 Newsflash! Submitting to our husbands doesn't mean we must always agree with their opinions or actions. *All* people act like fools sometimes. When her husband's poor choice put a price on his head, Abigail's quick thinking actually saved his life. Yet she did not nag him or argue with him. She just quietly did what was right, despite her husband's attitude. Her example teaches us that it's better to do something that's right and that's within our power than to waste time trying to convince our husbands that they're wrong. Trust in God, and let your actions do the talking.

¹⁰Nabal answered David's servants, "Who is this David? Who is this son of Jesse? Many servants are breaking away from their masters these days. ¹¹Why should I take my bread and water, and the meat I have slaughtered for my shearers, and give it to men coming from who knows where?"

¹²David's men turned around and went back. When they arrived, they reported every word. ¹³David said to his men, "Each of you strap on your sword!" So they did, and David strapped his on as well. About four hundred men went up with David, while two hundred stayed with the supplies.

ᵃ 1 Hebrew and some Septuagint manuscripts; other Septuagint manuscripts *Maon*

¹⁴One of the servants told Abigail, Nabal's wife, "David sent messengers from the wilderness to give our master his greetings, but he hurled insults at them. ¹⁵Yet these men were very good to us. They did not mistreat us, and the whole time we were out in the fields near them nothing was missing. ¹⁶Night and day they were a wall around us the whole time we were herding our sheep near them. ¹⁷Now think it over and see what you can do, because disaster is hanging over our master and his whole household. He is such a wicked man that no one can talk to him."

¹⁸Abigail acted quickly. She took two hundred loaves of bread, two skins of wine, five dressed sheep, five seahs^a of roasted grain, a hundred cakes of raisins and two hundred cakes of pressed figs, and loaded them on donkeys. ¹⁹Then she told her servants, "Go on ahead; I'll follow you." But she did not tell her husband Nabal.

²⁰As she came riding her donkey into a mountain ravine, there were David and his men descending toward her, and she met them. ²¹David had just said, "It's been useless—all my watching over this fellow's property in the wilderness so that nothing of his was missing. He has paid me back evil for good. ²²May God deal with David,^b be it ever so severely, if by morning I leave alive one male of all who belong to him!"

²³When Abigail saw David, she quickly got off her donkey and bowed down before David with her face to the ground. ²⁴She fell at his feet and said: "Pardon your servant, my lord, and let me speak to you; hear what your servant has to say. ²⁵Please pay no attention, my lord, to that wicked man Nabal. He is just like his name—his name means Fool, and folly goes with him. And as for me, your servant, I did not see the men my lord sent. ²⁶And now, my lord, as surely as the Lord your God lives and as you live, since the Lord has kept you from bloodshed and from avenging yourself with your own hands, may your enemies and all who are intent on harming my lord be like Nabal. ²⁷And let this gift, which your servant has brought to my lord, be given to the men who follow you.

²⁸"Please forgive your servant's presumption. The Lord your God will certainly make a lasting dynasty for my lord, because you fight the Lord's battles, and no wrongdoing will be found in you as long as you live. ²⁹Even though someone is pursuing you to take your life, the life of my lord will be bound securely in the bundle of the living by the Lord your God, but the lives of your enemies he will hurl away as from the pocket of a sling. ³⁰When the Lord has fulfilled for my lord every good thing he promised concerning him and has appointed him ruler over Israel, ³¹my lord will not have on his conscience the staggering burden of needless bloodshed or of having avenged himself. And when the Lord your God has brought my lord success, remember your servant."

³²David said to Abigail, "Praise be to the Lord, the God of Israel, who has sent you today to meet me. ³³May you be blessed for your good judgment and for keeping me from bloodshed this day and from avenging myself with my own hands. ³⁴Otherwise, as surely as the Lord, the God of Israel, lives, who has kept me from harming you, if you had not come quickly to meet me, not one male belonging to Nabal would have been left alive by daybreak."

³⁵Then David accepted from her hand what she had brought him and said, "Go home in peace. I have heard your words and granted your request."

³⁶When Abigail went to Nabal, he was in the house holding a banquet like that of a king. He was in high spirits and very drunk. So she told him nothing at all until daybreak. ³⁷Then in the morning, when Nabal was sober, his wife told him all these things, and his heart failed him and he became like a stone. ³⁸About ten days later, the Lord struck Nabal and he died.

³⁹When David heard that Nabal was dead, he said, "Praise be to the Lord, who has upheld my cause against Nabal for treating me with contempt. He has kept his servant from doing wrong and has brought Nabal's wrongdoing down on his own head."

Then David sent word to Abigail, asking her to become his wife. ⁴⁰His servants went to Carmel and said to Abigail, "David has sent us to you to take you to become his wife."

⁴¹She bowed down with her face to the ground and said, "I am your servant and am ready to serve you and wash the feet of my lord's servants." ⁴²Abigail quickly got on a donkey and, attended by her five female servants, went with David's messengers and became his wife. ⁴³David had also married Ahinoam

^a 18 That is, probably about 60 pounds or about 27 kilograms   ^b 22 Some Septuagint manuscripts; Hebrew *with David's enemies*

myth# 25 "I CAN NEVER PLAY A TRULY IMPORTANT ROLE IN CHURCH."

Honestly, sometimes I think my church is still about a hundred years in the past. For example, take the way women are treated. I attend a church of about three thousand members. Yet women aren't allowed to be ordained or to teach adults. Recently, I asked the teacher of my singles Sunday School class if I could teach a session on finances. I had just done an amazing in-depth study on my own, and I felt like I had a lot of insights to share, especially since I'm a CFA (certified financial analyst). He was very nice about it, but he basically told me that he had the whole year mapped out, and there just wasn't a place for me. Maybe I could teach fifth graders. He had heard there was a need.

I knew that my teacher was just putting me off. There was no way he would allow me to teach. The leaders of our church justify their position by quoting 1 Corinthians 14:34: "Women should remain silent in the churches." I believe that the whole Bible was inspired by God, but what exactly is Paul saying here? Obviously he didn't mean that literally or else we'd never have a woman sing a solo. Or have a woman missionary tell us about her work. Or have the woman who runs the vacation Bible school ask for volunteers. I'm so confused!

After my talk with my teacher, I felt very discouraged. I'm a natural teacher, and God made me a leader. Why would he make me that way if he didn't want me to use those gifts? And didn't Paul say in Galatians 3:28 that there is "neither male nor female, for you are all one in Christ Jesus"? I refuse to accept that God thinks more highly of men or that only men can have the important roles at church. But I can't see that my gifts can be used in my church. I guess it's either change churches or get used to being a "pew-flower."

—Amanda

THE ISSUE OF a woman's role in the church has been hotly debated for many years. Good, God-fearing churches vary widely on how they interpret various Scriptures that seem clear-cut to each party. If you disagree with your church's stance, should you just give up and not serve?

The Bible itself can be confusing in all the seemingly contradictory statements about men and women. For example, Paul reminds us that "There is neither Jew nor Greek, neither slave nor free, neither male nor female, for you are all one in Christ Jesus" (Galatians 3:28); yet later, he tells his readers that men and women have differing roles (see Ephesians 5:21–33). How can you make sense of the controversy?

- Remember that God wants men and women to celebrate and respect their differences—not use these differences as a license to judge others or to make assumptions about the "inferiority" or "superiority" of one sex.

- Different Christians interpret Scripture differently. You are not responsible for what others think, but you are responsible to think through the issues for yourself. Read some books on the issues of women's roles in the church. Do a Bible study on your own. Talk to wise people. Most of all, talk to God. Let him guide your thinking and your answers.

- Be inspired by the stories of great women of the Bible. In Abigail (see 1 Samuel 25), we see a woman of character who earned David's respect and admiration simply by being herself. In Judges 4, Deborah is viewed as a leader of integrity. In both cases, God worked through these women as they operated within the roles he gave them.

- Don't allow yourself to become disillusioned. If your church says you can't teach the class you want to, then find another way or another place to serve. Ask God to show you how he wants to use you. Be open to following his leading—even if that takes you somewhere

you hadn't expected or keeps you somewhere you might not want to be (see Colossians 1:9–14).

375

"Men are the senior pastors of more than 90 percent of Protestant churches. However, women shoulder most of the responsibility for the health and vitality of the Christian faith in the country. Women are 33 percent more likely to volunteer for a church than are men."

—Barna Research Group (2000)

"SO GOD created
HUMan BEInGS In
HIS own ImaGE,
In THE ImaGE
OF GOD HE
created THEM;
maLe anD FemaLe
HE created THEM."

GENESIS 1:27

SEE ALSO
1 Corinthians 11:3
Galatians 3:28
Ephesians 5:21–33

For more on **Female Roles**, check the index.

of Jezreel, and they both were his wives. [44]But Saul had given his daughter Michal, David's wife, to Paltiel[a] son of Laish, who was from Gallim.

David Again Spares Saul's Life

26 The Ziphites went to Saul at Gibeah and said, "Is not David hiding on the hill of Hakilah, which faces Jeshimon?"

[2]So Saul went down to the Desert of Ziph, with his three thousand able young Israelites, to search there for David. [3]Saul made his camp beside the road on the hill of Hakilah facing Jeshimon, but David stayed in the wilderness. When he saw that Saul had followed him there, [4]he sent out scouts and learned that Saul had definitely arrived.

[5]Then David set out and went to the place where Saul had camped. He saw where Saul and Abner son of Ner, the commander of the army, had lain down. Saul was lying inside the camp, with the army encamped around him.

[6]David then asked Ahimelek the Hittite and Abishai son of Zeruiah, Joab's brother, "Who will go down into the camp with me to Saul?"

"I'll go with you," said Abishai.

[7]So David and Abishai went to the army by night, and there was Saul, lying asleep inside the camp with his spear stuck in the ground near his head. Abner and the soldiers were lying around him.

[8]Abishai said to David, "Today God has delivered your enemy into your hands. Now let me pin him to the ground with one thrust of the spear; I won't strike him twice."

[9]But David said to Abishai, "Don't destroy him! Who can lay a hand on the LORD's anointed and be guiltless? [10]As surely as the LORD lives," he said, "the LORD himself will strike him, or his time will come and he will die, or he will go into battle and perish. [11]But the LORD forbid that I should lay a hand on the LORD's anointed. Now get the spear and water jug that are near his head, and let's go."

[12]So David took the spear and water jug near Saul's head, and they left. No one saw or knew about it, nor did anyone wake up. They were all sleeping, because the LORD had put them into a deep sleep.

[13]Then David crossed over to the other side and stood on top of the hill some distance away; there was a wide space between them. [14]He called out to the army and to Abner son of Ner, "Aren't you going to answer me, Abner?"

Abner replied, "Who are you who calls to the king?"

[15]David said, "You're a man, aren't you? And who is like you in Israel? Why didn't you guard your lord the king? Someone came to destroy your lord the king. [16]What you have done is not good. As surely as the LORD lives, you and your men must die, because you did not guard your master, the LORD's anointed. Look around you. Where are the king's spear and water jug that were near his head?"

[17]Saul recognized David's voice and said, "Is that your voice, David my son?"

David replied, "Yes it is, my lord the king." [18]And he added, "Why is my lord pursuing his servant? What have I done, and what wrong am I guilty of? [19]Now let my lord the king listen to his servant's words. If the LORD has incited you against me, then may he accept an offering. If, however, people have done it, may they be cursed before the LORD! They have driven me today from my share in the LORD's inheritance and have said, 'Go, serve other gods.' [20]Now do not let my blood fall to the ground far from

issue:integrity

26:1–25 Even though we might feel like it, we probably won't ever be in the position to decide the fate of an enemy. We do, however, get lots of chances each day to kill the people we dislike with words and actions. And each time we have an opportunity to subtly sabotage another person, God gives us a choice. We either uphold our honor as David did, or we strike out. Building integrity in God's eyes doesn't begin with life or death choices. It begins with the daily decision not to cut someone else down, no matter what she's done to you.

---
[a] 44 Hebrew *Palti*, a variant of *Paltiel*

the presence of the LORD. The king of Israel has come out to look for a flea—as one hunts a partridge in the mountains."

²¹Then Saul said, "I have sinned. Come back, David my son. Because you considered my life precious today, I will not try to harm you again. Surely I have acted like a fool and have been terribly wrong."

²²"Here is the king's spear," David answered. "Let one of your servants come over and get it. ²³The LORD rewards every man for his righteousness and faithfulness. The LORD delivered you into my hands today, but I would not lay a hand on the LORD's anointed. ²⁴As surely as I valued your life today, so may the LORD value my life and deliver me from all trouble."

²⁵Then Saul said to David, "May you be blessed, David my son; you will do great things and surely triumph."

So David went on his way, and Saul returned home.

David Among the Philistines

27 But David thought to himself, "One of these days I will be destroyed by the hand of Saul. The best thing I can do is to escape to the land of the Philistines. Then Saul will give up searching for me anywhere in Israel, and I will slip out of his hand."

²So David and the six hundred men with him left and went over to Achish son of Maok king of Gath. ³David and his men settled in Gath with Achish. Each man had his family with him, and David had his two wives: Ahinoam of Jezreel and Abigail of Carmel, the widow of Nabal. ⁴When Saul was told that David had fled to Gath, he no longer searched for him.

⁵Then David said to Achish, "If I have found favor in your eyes, let a place be assigned to me in one of the country towns, that I may live there. Why should your servant live in the royal city with you?"

⁶So on that day Achish gave him Ziklag, and it has belonged to the kings of Judah ever since. ⁷David lived in Philistine territory a year and four months.

⁸Now David and his men went up and raided the Geshurites, the Girzites and the Amalekites. (From ancient times these peoples had lived in the land extending to Shur and Egypt.) ⁹Whenever David attacked an area, he did not leave a man or woman alive, but took sheep and cattle, donkeys and camels, and clothes. Then he returned to Achish.

¹⁰When Achish asked, "Where did you go raiding today?" David would say, "Against the Negev of Judah" or "Against the Negev of Jerahmeel" or "Against the Negev of the Kenites." ¹¹He did not leave a man or woman alive to be brought to Gath, for he thought, "They might inform on us and say, 'This is what David did.'" And such was his practice as long as he lived in Philistine territory. ¹²Achish trusted David and said to himself, "He has become so obnoxious to his people, the Israelites, that he will be my servant for life."

28 In those days the Philistines gathered their forces to fight against Israel. Achish said to David, "You must understand that you and your men will accompany me in the army."

²David said, "Then you will see for yourself what your servant can do."

Achish replied, "Very well, I will make you my bodyguard for life."

Saul and the Medium at Endor

³Now Samuel was dead, and all Israel had mourned for him and buried him in his own town of Ramah. Saul had expelled the mediums and spiritists from the land.

⁴The Philistines assembled and came and set up camp at Shunem, while Saul gathered all Israel and set up camp at Gilboa. ⁵When Saul saw the Philistine army, he was afraid; terror filled his heart. ⁶He inquired of the LORD, but the LORD did not answer him by dreams or Urim or prophets. ⁷Saul then said to his attendants, "Find me a woman who is a medium, so I may go and inquire of her."

"There is one in Endor," they said.

⁸So Saul disguised himself, putting on other clothes, and at night he and two men went to the woman. "Consult a spirit for me," he said, "and bring up for me the one I name."

⁹But the woman said to him, "Surely you know what Saul has done. He has cut off the mediums and spiritists from the land. Why have you set a trap for my life to bring about my death?"

¹⁰Saul swore to her by the LORD, "As surely as the LORD lives, you will not be punished for this."

¹¹Then the woman asked, "Whom shall I bring up for you?"

"Bring up Samuel," he said.

¹²When the woman saw Samuel, she cried out at the top of her voice and said to Saul, "Why have you deceived me? You are Saul!"

¹³The king said to her, "Don't be afraid. What do you see?"

The woman said, "I see a ghostly figure*ᵃ* coming up out of the earth."

¹⁴"What does he look like?" he asked.

"An old man wearing a robe is coming up," she said.

Then Saul knew it was Samuel, and he bowed down and prostrated himself with his face to the ground.

¹⁵Samuel said to Saul, "Why have you disturbed me by bringing me up?"

"I am in great distress," Saul said. "The Philistines are fighting against me, and God has departed from me. He no longer answers me, either by prophets or by dreams. So I have called on you to tell me what to do."

¹⁶Samuel said, "Why do you consult me, now that the LORD has departed from you and become your enemy? ¹⁷The LORD has done what he predicted through me. The LORD has torn the kingdom out of your hands and given it to one of your neighbors—to David. ¹⁸Because you did not obey the LORD or carry out his fierce wrath against the Amalekites, the LORD has done this to you today. ¹⁹The LORD will deliver both Israel and you into the hands of the Philistines, and tomorrow you and your sons will be with me. The LORD will also give the army of Israel into the hands of the Philistines."

²⁰Immediately Saul fell full length on the ground, filled with fear because of Samuel's words. His strength was gone, for he had eaten nothing all that day and all that night.

²¹When the woman came to Saul and saw that he was greatly shaken, she said, "Look, your servant has obeyed you. I took my life in my hands and did what you told me to do. ²²Now please listen to your servant and let me give you some food so you may eat and have the strength to go on your way."

²³He refused and said, "I will not eat."

But his men joined the woman in urging him, and he listened to them. He got up from the ground and sat on the couch.

²⁴The woman had a fattened calf at the house, which she butchered at once. She took some flour, kneaded it and baked bread without yeast. ²⁵Then she set it before Saul and his men, and they ate. That same night they got up and left.

conversations

the future «» 28:1–25

1» How do fortunetellers, psychics and horoscopes give people a false sense of control?

2» Are such things inherently evil or harmlessly fun? What would God say?

3» If you knew the future, how might it help/hurt you?

For more on the future, check the index.
For the next Conversations, go to p. 382.

Achish Sends David Back to Ziklag

29 The Philistines gathered all their forces at Aphek, and Israel camped by the spring in Jezreel. ²As the Philistine rulers marched with their units of hundreds and thousands, David and his men were marching at the rear with Achish. ³The commanders of the Philistines asked, "What about these Hebrews?"

Achish replied, "Is this not David, who was an officer of Saul king of Israel? He has already been with me for over a year, and from the day he left Saul until now, I have found no fault in him."

⁴But the Philistine commanders were angry with Achish and said, "Send the man back, that he may return to the place you assigned him. He must not go with us into battle, or he will turn against us during the fighting. How better could he regain his master's favor than by taking the heads of our own men? ⁵Isn't this the David they sang about in their dances:

―――――
ᵃ 13 Or *see spirits;* or *see gods*

"'Saul has slain his thousands,
and David his tens of thousands'?"

⁶So Achish called David and said to him, "As surely as the LORD lives, you have been reliable, and I would be pleased to have you serve with me in the army. From the day you came to me until today, I have found no fault in you, but the rulers don't approve of you. ⁷Now turn back and go in peace; do nothing to displease the Philistine rulers."

⁸"But what have I done?" asked David. "What have you found against your servant from the day I came to you until now? Why can't I go and fight against the enemies of my lord the king?"

⁹Achish answered, "I know that you have been as pleasing in my eyes as an angel of God; nevertheless, the Philistine commanders have said, 'He must not go up with us into battle.' ¹⁰Now get up early, along with your master's servants who have come with you, and leave in the morning as soon as it is light."

¹¹So David and his men got up early in the morning to go back to the land of the Philistines, and the Philistines went up to Jezreel.

David Destroys the Amalekites

30 David and his men reached Ziklag on the third day. Now the Amalekites had raided the Negev and Ziklag. They had attacked Ziklag and burned it, ²and had taken captive the women who were in it, both young and old. They killed none of them, but carried them off as they went on their way.

³When David and his men reached Ziklag, they found it destroyed by fire and their wives and sons and daughters taken captive. ⁴So David and his men wept aloud until they had no strength left to weep. ⁵David's two wives had been captured—Ahinoam of Jezreel and Abigail, the widow of Nabal of Carmel. ⁶David was greatly distressed because the men were talking of stoning him; each one was bitter in spirit because of his sons and daughters. But David found strength in the LORD his God.

HE IS: strength within

30:6 Discharged from the Philistine army, David and his men returned to Ziklag to find tragedy—their camp destroyed and their loved ones taken captive. The men blame-shifted, wanting to punish David for their pain. David grieved and then wisely looked to God for guidance. He found strength in the Lord his God.

When something or someone you love gets taken away, or when you're unjustly blamed for a bad situation, you have two choices: You can grow bitter, or you can trust God to help you through the situation (see Psalm 31:1–5). Like David, you need time to grieve. Then turn to God and find *strength within*.

For the next He Is, go to p. 387.

⁷Then David said to Abiathar the priest, the son of Ahimelek, "Bring me the ephod." Abiathar brought it to him, ⁸and David inquired of the LORD, "Shall I pursue this raiding party? Will I overtake them?"

"Pursue them," he answered. "You will certainly overtake them and succeed in the rescue."

⁹David and the six hundred men with him came to the Besor Valley, where some stayed behind. ¹⁰Two hundred of them were too exhausted to cross the valley, but David and the other four hundred continued the pursuit.

¹¹They found an Egyptian in a field and brought him to David. They gave him water to drink and food to eat— ¹²part of a cake of pressed figs and two cakes of raisins. He ate and was revived, for he had not eaten any food or drunk any water for three days and three nights.

¹³David asked him, "Who do you belong to? Where do you come from?"

He said, "I am an Egyptian, the slave of an Amalekite. My master abandoned me when I became ill three days ago. ¹⁴We raided the Negev of the Kerethites, some territory belonging to Judah and the Negev of Caleb. And we burned Ziklag."

¹⁵David asked him, "Can you lead me down to this raiding party?"

He answered, "Swear to me before God that you will not kill me or hand me over to my master, and I will take you down to them."

¹⁶He led David down, and there they were, scattered over the countryside, eating, drinking and reveling because of the great amount of plunder they had taken from the land of the Philistines and from Judah. ¹⁷David fought them from dusk until the evening of the next day, and none of them got away, except four hundred young men who rode off on camels and fled. ¹⁸David recovered everything the Amalekites had taken, including his two wives. ¹⁹Nothing was missing: young or old, boy or girl, plunder or anything else they had taken. David brought everything back. ²⁰He took all the flocks and herds, and his men drove them ahead of the other livestock, saying, "This is David's plunder."

²¹Then David came to the two hundred men who had been too exhausted to follow him and who were left behind at the Besor Valley. They came out to meet David and the men with him. As David and his men approached, he asked them how they were. ²²But all the evil men and troublemakers among David's followers said, "Because they did not go out with us, we will not share with them the plunder we recovered. However, each man may take his wife and children and go."

²³David replied, "No, my brothers, you must not do that with what the Lord has given us. He has protected us and delivered into our hands the raiding party that came against us. ²⁴Who will listen to what you say? The share of the man who stayed with the supplies is to be the same as that of him who went down to the battle. All will share alike." ²⁵David made this a statute and ordinance for Israel from that day to this.

²⁶When David reached Ziklag, he sent some of the plunder to the elders of Judah, who were his friends, saying, "Here is a gift for you from the plunder of the Lord's enemies."

²⁷David sent it to those who were in Bethel, Ramoth Negev and Jattir; ²⁸to those in Aroer, Siphmoth, Eshtemoa ²⁹and Rakal; to those in the towns of the Jerahmeelites and the Kenites; ³⁰to those in Hormah, Bor Ashan, Athak ³¹and Hebron; and to those in all the other places where he and his men had roamed.

Saul Takes His Life

31 Now the Philistines fought against Israel; the Israelites fled before them, and many fell dead on Mount Gilboa. ²The Philistines were in hot pursuit of Saul and his sons, and they killed his sons Jonathan, Abinadab and Malki-Shua. ³The fighting grew fierce around Saul, and when the archers overtook him, they wounded him critically.

⁴Saul said to his armor-bearer, "Draw your sword and run me through, or these uncircumcised fellows will come and run me through and abuse me."

But his armor-bearer was terrified and would not do it; so Saul took his own sword and fell on it. ⁵When the armor-bearer saw that Saul was dead, he too fell on his sword and died with him. ⁶So Saul and his three sons and his armor-bearer and all his men died together that same day.

⁷When the Israelites along the valley and those across the Jordan saw that the Israelite army had fled and that Saul and his sons had died, they abandoned their towns and fled. And the Philistines came and occupied them.

⁸The next day, when the Philistines came to strip the dead, they found Saul and his three sons fallen on Mount Gilboa. ⁹They cut off his head and stripped off his armor, and they sent messengers throughout the land of the Philistines to proclaim the news in the temple of their idols and among their people. ¹⁰They put his armor in the temple of the Ashtoreths and fastened his body to the wall of Beth Shan.

¹¹When the people of Jabesh Gilead heard what the Philistines had done to Saul, ¹²all their valiant men marched through the night to Beth Shan. They took down the bodies of Saul and his sons from the wall of Beth Shan and went to Jabesh, where they burned them. ¹³Then they took their bones and buried them under a tamarisk tree at Jabesh, and they fasted seven days.

2samuel

AUTHOR
Unknown.

AUDIENCE
The people of Israel.

DATE
Sometime after the division of Israel into the
northern and southern kingdoms, around
930 B.C.

SETTING
Saul has proven to be a bad king, and David
is poised to begin his reign.

VERSES TO REMEMBER
"As for God, his way is perfect;
    the LORD's word is flawless.
    He shields all who take refuge in him.
For who is God besides the LORD?
    And who is the Rock except our God?
It is God who arms me with strength
    and keeps my way secure."   (22:31–33)

THEME TO CONSIDER
God's plan is unwavering. Obedience
advances it, but personal failure cannot
thwart it.

David Hears of Saul's Death

1 After the death of Saul, David returned from striking down the Amalekites and stayed in Ziklag two days. ²On the third day a man arrived from Saul's camp with his clothes torn and dust on his head. When he came to David, he fell to the ground to pay him honor.

³"Where have you come from?" David asked him.

He answered, "I have escaped from the Israelite camp."

⁴"What happened?" David asked. "Tell me."

"The men fled from the battle," he replied. "Many of them fell and died. And Saul and his son Jonathan are dead."

⁵Then David said to the young man who brought him the report, "How do you know that Saul and his son Jonathan are dead?"

⁶"I happened to be on Mount Gilboa," the young man said, "and there was Saul, leaning on his spear, with the chariots and their drivers in hot pursuit. ⁷When he turned around and saw me, he called out to me, and I said, 'What can I do?'

⁸"He asked me, 'Who are you?'

"'An Amalekite,' I answered.

⁹"Then he said to me, 'Stand here by me and kill me! I'm in the throes of death, but I'm still alive.'

¹⁰"So I stood beside him and killed him, because I knew that after he had fallen he could not survive. And I took the crown that was on his head and the band on his arm and have brought them here to my lord."

¹¹Then David and all the men with him took hold of their clothes and tore them. ¹²They mourned and wept and fasted till evening for Saul and his son Jonathan, and for the army of the LORD and the house of Israel, because they had fallen by the sword.

¹³David said to the young man who brought him the report, "Where are you from?"

"I am the son of a foreigner, an Amalekite," he answered.

¹⁴David asked him, "Why weren't you afraid to lift your hand to destroy the LORD's anointed?"

¹⁵Then David called one of his men and said, "Go, strike him down!" So he struck him down, and he died. ¹⁶For David had said to him, "Your blood be on your own head. Your own mouth testified against you when you said, 'I killed the LORD's anointed.'"

David's Lament for Saul and Jonathan

¹⁷David took up this lament concerning Saul and his son Jonathan, ¹⁸and he ordered that the people of Judah be taught this lament of the bow (it is written in the Book of Jashar):

> ¹⁹"A gazelle*a* lies slain on your
>   heights, Israel.
>   How the mighty have fallen!
>
> ²⁰"Tell it not in Gath,
>   proclaim it not in the
>   streets of Ashkelon,
>   lest the daughters of the
>   Philistines be glad,
>   lest the daughters of the
>   uncircumcised rejoice.
>
> ²¹"Mountains of Gilboa,
>   may you have neither dew nor rain,
>   may no showers fall on your terraced fields.*b*

conversations

grief «» 1:17–27

1» How should you react to an enemy's misfortune or death?

2» How have you reacted to the loss of someone close to you?

3» What are the benefits of grief?

For more on **grief**, check the index.
For the next Conversations, go to p. 396.

---

a 19 Gazelle here symbolizes a human dignitary.   *b 21* Or / nor fields that yield grain for offerings

> For there the shield of the mighty was despised,
>   the shield of Saul—no longer rubbed with oil.
>
> ²²"From the blood of the slain,
>   from the flesh of the mighty,
> the bow of Jonathan did not turn back,
>   the sword of Saul did not return unsatisfied.
> ²³Saul and Jonathan—
>   in life they were loved and admired,
>   and in death they were not parted.
> They were swifter than eagles,
>   they were stronger than lions.
>
> ²⁴"Daughters of Israel,
>   weep for Saul,
> who clothed you in scarlet and finery,
>   who adorned your garments with ornaments of gold.
>
> ²⁵"How the mighty have fallen in battle!
>   Jonathan lies slain on your heights.
> ²⁶I grieve for you, Jonathan my brother;
>   you were very dear to me.
> Your love for me was wonderful,
>   more wonderful than that of women.
>
> ²⁷"How the mighty have fallen!
>   The weapons of war have perished!"

David Anointed King Over Judah

2 In the course of time, David inquired of the LORD. "Shall I go up to one of the towns of Judah?" he asked.

The LORD said, "Go up."

David asked, "Where shall I go?"

"To Hebron," the LORD answered.

²So David went up there with his two wives, Ahinoam of Jezreel and Abigail, the widow of Nabal of Carmel. ³David also took the men who were with him, each with his family, and they settled in Hebron and its towns. ⁴Then the men of Judah came to Hebron, and there they anointed David king over the house of Judah.

When David was told that it was the men from Jabesh Gilead who had buried Saul, ⁵he sent messengers to them to say to them, "The LORD bless you for showing this kindness to Saul your master by burying him. ⁶May the LORD now show you kindness and faithfulness, and I too will show you the same favor because you have done this. ⁷Now then, be strong and brave, for Saul your master is dead, and the house of Judah has anointed me king over them."

War Between the Houses of David and Saul

⁸Meanwhile, Abner son of Ner, the commander of Saul's army, had taken Ish-Bosheth son of Saul and brought him over to Mahanaim. ⁹He made him king over Gilead, Ashuri and Jezreel, and also over Ephraim, Benjamin and all Israel.

¹⁰Ish-Bosheth son of Saul was forty years old when he became king over Israel, and he reigned two years. The house of Judah, however, remained loyal to David. ¹¹The length of time David was king in Hebron over the house of Judah was seven years and six months.

¹²Abner son of Ner, together with the men of Ish-Bosheth son of Saul, left Mahanaim and went to Gibeon. ¹³Joab son of Zeruiah and David's men went out and met them at the pool of Gibeon. One group sat down on one side of the pool and one group on the other side.

¹⁴Then Abner said to Joab, "Let's have some of the soldiers get up and fight hand to hand in front of us."

"All right, let them do it," Joab said.

¹⁵So they stood up and were counted off—twelve men for Benjamin and Ish-Bosheth son of Saul, and twelve for David. ¹⁶Then each man grabbed his opponent by the head and thrust his dagger into his opponent's side, and they fell down together. So that place in Gibeon was called Helkath Hazzurim.^a

¹⁷The battle that day was very fierce, and Abner and the Israelites were defeated by David's men.

¹⁸The three sons of Zeruiah were there: Joab, Abishai and Asahel. Now Asahel was as fleet-footed as a wild gazelle. ¹⁹He chased Abner, turning neither to the right nor to the left as he pursued him. ²⁰Abner looked behind him and asked, "Is that you, Asahel?"

"It is," he answered.

²¹Then Abner said to him, "Turn aside to the right or to the left; take on one of the soldiers and strip him of his weapons." But Asahel would not stop chasing him.

²²Again Abner warned Asahel, "Stop chasing me! Why should I strike you down? How could I look your brother Joab in the face?"

²³But Asahel refused to give up the pursuit; so Abner thrust the butt of his spear into Asahel's stomach, and the spear came out through his back. He fell there and died on the spot. And every man stopped when he came to the place where Asahel had fallen and died.

²⁴But Joab and Abishai pursued Abner, and as the sun was setting, they came to the hill of Ammah, near Giah on the way to the wasteland of Gibeon. ²⁵Then the men of Benjamin rallied behind Abner. They formed themselves into a group and took their stand on top of a hill.

²⁶Abner called out to Joab, "Must the sword devour forever? Don't you realize that this will end in bitterness? How long before you order your men to stop pursuing their fellow Israelites?"

²⁷Joab answered, "As surely as God lives, if you had not spoken, the men would have continued pursuing them until morning."

²⁸So Joab blew the trumpet, and everyone came to a halt; they no longer pursued Israel, nor did they fight anymore.

²⁹All that night Abner and his men marched through the Arabah. They crossed the Jordan, continued through the morning hours^b and came to Mahanaim.

³⁰Then Joab stopped pursuing Abner and assembled the whole army. Besides Asahel, nineteen of David's men were found missing. ³¹But David's men had killed three hundred and sixty Benjamites who were with Abner. ³²They took Asahel and buried him in his father's tomb at Bethlehem. Then Joab and his men marched all night and arrived at Hebron by daybreak.

3 The war between the house of Saul and the house of David lasted a long time. David grew stronger and stronger, while the house of Saul grew weaker and weaker.

²Sons were born to David in Hebron:

His firstborn was Amnon the son of Ahinoam of Jezreel;

³his second, Kileab the son of Abigail the widow of Nabal of Carmel;

the third, Absalom the son of Maakah daughter of Talmai king of Geshur;

⁴the fourth, Adonijah the son of Haggith;

the fifth, Shephatiah the son of Abital;

⁵and the sixth, Ithream the son of David's wife Eglah.

These were born to David in Hebron.

Abner Goes Over to David

⁶During the war between the house of Saul and the house of David, Abner had been strengthening his own position in the house of Saul. ⁷Now Saul had had a concubine named Rizpah daughter of Aiah. And Ish-Bosheth said to Abner, "Why did you sleep with my father's concubine?"

⁸Abner was very angry because of what Ish-Bosheth said. So he answered, "Am I a dog's head—on Judah's side? This very day I am loyal to the house of your father Saul and to his family and friends.

<hr />

^a *16 Helkath Hazzurim means field of daggers or field of hostilities.*   ^b *29 Or See Septuagint; the meaning of the Hebrew for this phrase is uncertain.*

I haven't handed you over to David. Yet now you accuse me of an offense involving this woman! ⁹May God deal with Abner, be it ever so severely, if I do not do for David what the LORD promised him on oath ¹⁰and transfer the kingdom from the house of Saul and establish David's throne over Israel and Judah from Dan to Beersheba." ¹¹Ish-Bosheth did not dare to say another word to Abner, because he was afraid of him.

¹²Then Abner sent messengers on his behalf to say to David, "Whose land is it? Make an agreement with me, and I will help you bring all Israel over to you."

¹³"Good," said David. "I will make an agreement with you. But I demand one thing of you: Do not come into my presence unless you bring Michal daughter of Saul when you come to see me." ¹⁴Then David sent messengers to Ish-Bosheth son of Saul, demanding, "Give me my wife Michal, whom I betrothed to myself for the price of a hundred Philistine foreskins."

¹⁵So Ish-Bosheth gave orders and had her taken away from her husband Paltiel son of Laish. ¹⁶Her husband, however, went with her, weeping behind her all the way to Bahurim. Then Abner said to him, "Go back home!" So he went back.

¹⁷Abner conferred with the elders of Israel and said, "For some time you have wanted to make David your king. ¹⁸Now do it! For the LORD promised David, 'By my servant David I will rescue my people Israel from the hand of the Philistines and from the hand of all their enemies.'"

¹⁹Abner also spoke to the Benjamites in person. Then he went to Hebron to tell David everything that Israel and the whole house of Benjamin wanted to do. ²⁰When Abner, who had twenty men with him, came to David at Hebron, David prepared a feast for him and his men. ²¹Then Abner said to David, "Let me go at once and assemble all Israel for my lord the king, so that they may make a covenant with you, and that you may rule over all that your heart desires." So David sent Abner away, and he went in peace.

Joab Murders Abner

²²Just then David's men and Joab returned from a raid and brought with them a great deal of plunder. But Abner was no longer with David in Hebron, because David had sent him away, and he had gone in peace. ²³When Joab and all the soldiers with him arrived, he was told that Abner son of Ner had come to the king and that the king had sent him away and that he had gone in peace.

²⁴So Joab went to the king and said, "What have you done? Look, Abner came to you. Why did you let him go? Now he is gone! ²⁵You know Abner son of Ner; he came to deceive you and observe your movements and find out everything you are doing."

²⁶Joab then left David and sent messengers after Abner, and they brought him back from the cistern at Sirah. But David did not know it. ²⁷Now when Abner returned to Hebron, Joab took him aside into an inner chamber, as if to speak with him privately. And there, to avenge the blood of his brother Asahel, Joab stabbed him in the stomach, and he died.

²⁸Later, when David heard about this, he said, "I and my kingdom are forever innocent before the LORD concerning the blood of Abner son of Ner. ²⁹May his blood fall on the head of Joab and on his whole family! May Joab's family never be without someone who has a running sore or leprosy*a* or who leans on a crutch or who falls by the sword or who lacks food."

385

atissue:revenge

3:22–30 Revenge is a funny thing. Even if we finally make things equal by leveling our opposition, we never feel satisfied. Joab's thirst for revenge for the death of his brother Asahel was met by a curse from King David (see v. 29). While we might not face such a severe consequence, the whole process of revenge inherently eats away at us. The next time someone offends you (and there *will* be a next time), ask God to help you control your anger and release the offender and the debt to God. God can give you the peace you will never find in revenge.

---

a 29 The Hebrew for *leprosy* was used for various diseases affecting the skin.

³⁰(Joab and his brother Abishai murdered Abner because he had killed their brother Asahel in the battle at Gibeon.)

³¹Then David said to Joab and all of Joab's men, "Tear your clothes and put on sackcloth and walk in mourning in front of Abner." King David himself walked behind the bier. ³²They buried Abner in Hebron, and the king wept aloud at Abner's tomb. All of Joab's men wept also.

³³The king sang this lament for Abner:

> "Should Abner have died as the lawless die?
> ³⁴   Your hands were not bound,
>   your feet were not fettered.
> You fell as one falls before the wicked."

And all of Joab's men wept over him again.

³⁵Then they all came and urged David to eat something while it was still day; but David took an oath, saying, "May God deal with me, be it ever so severely, if I taste bread or anything else before the sun sets!"

³⁶All of Joab's men took note and were pleased; indeed, everything the king did pleased them. ³⁷So on that day all of Joab's men and all Israel knew that the king had no part in the murder of Abner son of Ner.

³⁸Then the king said to his men, "Don't you realize that a great commander has fallen in Israel this day? ³⁹And today, though I am the anointed king, I am weak, and these sons of Zeruiah are too strong for me. May the LORD repay the evildoer according to his evil deeds!"

Ish-Bosheth Murdered

4 When Ish-Bosheth son of Saul heard that Abner had died in Hebron, he lost courage, and all Israel became alarmed. ²Now Saul's son had two leaders of raiding bands. One was named Baanah and the other Rekab; they were sons of Rimmon the Beerothite from the tribe of Benjamin—Beeroth is considered part of Benjamin, ³because the people of Beeroth fled to Gittaim and have resided there as foreigners to this day.

⁴(Jonathan son of Saul had a son who was lame in both feet. He was five years old when the news about Saul and Jonathan came from Jezreel. His nurse picked him up and fled, but as she hurried to leave, he fell and became disabled. His name was Mephibosheth.)

⁵Now Rekab and Baanah, the sons of Rimmon the Beerothite, set out for the house of Ish-Bosheth, and they arrived there in the heat of the day while he was taking his noonday rest. ⁶They went into the inner part of the house as if to get some wheat, and they stabbed him in the stomach. Then Rekab and his brother Baanah slipped away.

⁷They had gone into the house while he was lying on the bed in his bedroom. After they stabbed and killed him, they cut off his head. Taking it with them, they traveled all night by way of the Arabah. ⁸They brought the head of Ish-Bosheth to David at Hebron and said to the king, "Here is the head of Ish-Bosheth son of Saul, your enemy, who tried to take your life. This day the LORD has avenged my lord the king against Saul and his offspring."

⁹David answered Rekab and his brother Baanah, the sons of Rimmon the Beerothite, "As surely as the LORD lives, who has delivered me out of every trouble, ¹⁰when someone told me, 'Saul is dead,' and thought he was bringing good news, I seized him and put him to death in Ziklag. That was the reward I gave him for his news! ¹¹How much more—when wicked men have killed an innocent man in his own house and on his own bed—should I not now demand his blood from your hand and rid the earth of you!"

¹²So David gave an order to his men, and they killed them. They cut off their hands and feet and hung the bodies by the pool in Hebron. But they took the head of Ish-Bosheth and buried it in Abner's tomb at Hebron.

David Becomes King Over Israel

5 All the tribes of Israel came to David at Hebron and said, "We are your own flesh and blood. ²In the past, while Saul was king over us, you were the one who led Israel on their military campaigns. And the LORD said to you, 'You will shepherd my people Israel, and you will become their ruler.'"

HE IS: the power source

5:9–10 David's power didn't come from the sturdy walls of his fortress city or the strong arms of his mighty men. His strength didn't spring from the natural realm but from a supernatural reality: He became more and more powerful because the Lord God Almighty was with him. God was David's *power source* (see 1 Samuel 16:13).

Maybe you've sought power through positions, possessions or people. But you can be fired from a job, forfeit your property and lose the favor of people. Those sources of power are temporary, insecure and disloyal. God is the only sure *power source*.

For the next He Is, go to p. 391.

³When all the elders of Israel had come to King David at Hebron, the king made a covenant with them at Hebron before the Lord, and they anointed David king over Israel.

⁴David was thirty years old when he became king, and he reigned forty years. ⁵In Hebron he reigned over Judah seven years and six months, and in Jerusalem he reigned over all Israel and Judah thirty-three years.

David Conquers Jerusalem

⁶The king and his men marched to Jerusalem to attack the Jebusites, who lived there. The Jebusites said to David, "You will not get in here; even the blind and the lame can ward you off." They thought, "David cannot get in here." ⁷Nevertheless, David captured the fortress of Zion—which is the City of David.

⁸On that day David had said, "Anyone who conquers the Jebusites will have to use the water shaft to reach those 'lame and blind' who are David's enemies.ᵃ" That is why they say, "The 'blind and lame' will not enter the palace."

⁹David then took up residence in the fortress and called it the City of David. He built up the area around it, from the terracesᵇ inward. ¹⁰And he became more and more powerful, because the Lord God Almighty was with him.

¹¹Now Hiram king of Tyre sent messengers to David, along with cedar logs and carpenters and stonemasons, and they built a palace for David. ¹²And David knew that the Lord had established him as king over Israel and had exalted his kingdom for the sake of his people Israel.

¹³After he left Hebron, David took more concubines and wives in Jerusalem, and more sons and daughters were born to him. ¹⁴These are the names of the children born to him there: Shammua, Shobab, Nathan, Solomon, ¹⁵Ibhar, Elishua, Nepheg, Japhia, ¹⁶Elishama, Eliada and Eliphelet.

David Defeats the Philistines

¹⁷When the Philistines heard that David had been anointed king over Israel, they went up in full force to search for him, but David heard about it and went down to the stronghold. ¹⁸Now the Philistines had come and spread out in the Valley of Rephaim; ¹⁹so David inquired of the Lord, "Shall I go and attack the Philistines? Will you deliver them into my hands?"

The Lord answered him, "Go, for I will surely deliver the Philistines into your hands."

aussie:purpose

5:12 Say you just got a promotion at work, bought a new house or earned your Ph.D. God has blessed you. Now what are you going to do with it? God made David king so that he could bless God's people. God expects us to use what we've been given to help others too. Why did God bless you? Perhaps you got a raise so that you could give more generously to a ministry. Perhaps he gave you a new home so that you could welcome others into it. Only when you look beyond yourself will you be able to see God's greater purpose.

387

ᵃ *8 Or are hated by David* ᵇ *9 Or the Millo*

myth# 26 "GOD IS A REPUBLICAN."

I'm a black woman who happens to be a Republican. Unashamedly so. But here's what I'm not:

- *A rich property owner.*
- *Trying to "assimilate."*
- *A sellout.*

My family tries to make me believe there's something wrong with me for voting Republican. I've heard all the comments: "Some Republicans still have racist beliefs." "Republicans are too conservative." "Republicans are only in favor of the wealthy." Like I said, I'm not rich. And shouldn't Christians embrace conservative views? Take abortion, for instance. And what about the whole gay marriage issue? Hello? And shouldn't we all be concerned about quality health care? These are issues all Christians need to be aware of.

I was a Democrat when I voted for the first time ten years ago. My parents are Democrats, so I registered as a Democrat too. But later I noticed that many of the Republican candidates seemed to express conservative views that I believe in. Now, I'm not one to fall in with what everyone else is doing. I try to do my research. I try not to vote Republican just because a lot of the people in my church vote that way

Yet I can't help wondering why everyone's not Republican. I seriously wonder if people who claim to be believers but who aren't pro-life or aren't really interested in what's going on in the country are really Christians.

—Carrie

SOMETIMES WE CAN

believe in something so strongly that we feel everyone should believe the same way. While you might be allowed to disagree on the merits of Ford vs. Chevy (or vice versa), few subjects push the hot buttons like a discussion of one's political beliefs or affiliation.

Many Christians brand other Christians as traitors or "un-American" for choosing one political party over another. Because a group of people might feel one way, then it must be "the right way" to think. Sometimes these well-meaning Christians even go so far as labeling those who oppose them as un-Christian. But Jesus warns against this kind of judgmental attitude against other people. (See Matthew 7:1–5; see also Paul's follow-up argument in Romans 2:1–4.)

Some issues are black and white, while others—like political affiliation—are gray. When it comes to politics, God is neither for nor against any political party. After all, he's the King of the universe, not a closet Republican or Democrat. All true authority belongs to him. And he's not handing out wholesale endorsements to any one party.

Jesus said that his kingdom is not of this world (see John 18:36). Too often we blend the lines between faith and politics and confuse them as the same issue. However, we need to remember that Jesus never had a political agenda while he was on earth, and he declined opportunities to comment on political issues or become a political leader. When Jesus interacted with people, he cared about their heart issues, not their political affiliation—and so should we.

When it comes to political issues, we need to be wise. The Bible advises us to "be as shrewd as snakes and as innocent as doves" (Matthew 10:16). Instead of accepting at face value that one group or another has "the whole truth," the wise person investigates the facts for herself before she makes a decision.

While it's good to take our civic responsibilities seriously (and we could use more Christians in politics), it's unhealthy when we allow *politics* to become the defining issue in our lives. Political affiliation is only and always secondary to a personal relationship with Jesus Christ.

> "If God is a Republican, then most Christians in America are registered for the wrong party—40 percent of born again adults said they were Republicans, compared to 47 percent Democrats and Independents."
>
> —Barna Research Group (2001)

389

> "PETER BEGAN TO SPEAK: 'I NOW REALIZE HOW TRUE IT IS THAT GOD DOES NOT SHOW FAVORITISM BUT ACCEPTS THOSE FROM EVERY NATION WHO FEAR HIM AND DO WHAT IS RIGHT.'"
>
> ACTS 10:34–35

SEE ALSO

Deuteronomy 10:17

Acts 5:29

Romans 2:11

For more on **Politics,** check the index.

²⁰So David went to Baal Perazim, and there he defeated them. He said, "As waters break out, the LORD has broken out against my enemies before me." So that place was called Baal Perazim.ᵃ ²¹The Philistines abandoned their idols there, and David and his men carried them off.

²²Once more the Philistines came up and spread out in the Valley of Rephaim; ²³so David inquired of the LORD, and he answered, "Do not go straight up, but circle around behind them and attack them in front of the poplar trees. ²⁴As soon as you hear the sound of marching in the tops of the poplar trees, move quickly, because that will mean the LORD has gone out in front of you to strike the Philistine army." ²⁵So David did as the LORD commanded him, and he struck down the Philistines all the way from Gibeonᵇ to Gezer.

The Ark Brought to Jerusalem

6 David again brought together all the able young men of Israel—thirty thousand. ²He and all his men went to Baalahᶜ in Judah to bring up from there the ark of God, which is called by the Name,ᵈ the name of the LORD Almighty, who is enthroned between the cherubim on the ark. ³They set the ark of God on a new cart and brought it from the house of Abinadab, which was on the hill. Uzzah and Ahio, sons of Abinadab, were guiding the new cart ⁴with the ark of God on it,ᵉ and Ahio was walking in front of it. ⁵David and the whole house of Israel were celebrating with all their might before the LORD, with castanets,ᶠ harps, lyres, timbrels, sistrums and cymbals.

⁶When they came to the threshing floor of Nakon, Uzzah reached out and took hold of the ark of God, because the oxen stumbled. ⁷The LORD's anger burned against Uzzah because of his irreverent act; therefore God struck him down, and he died there beside the ark of God.

⁸Then David was angry because the LORD's wrath had broken out against Uzzah, and to this day that place is called Perez Uzzah.ᵍ

⁹David was afraid of the LORD that day and said, "How can the ark of the LORD ever come to me?" ¹⁰He was not willing to take the ark of the LORD to be with him in the City of David. Instead, he took it to the house of Obed-Edom the Gittite. ¹¹The ark of the LORD remained in the house of Obed-Edom the Gittite for three months, and the LORD blessed him and his entire household.

¹²Now King David was told, "The LORD has blessed the household of Obed-Edom and everything he has, because of the ark of God." So David went to bring up the ark of God from the house of Obed-Edom to the City of David with rejoicing. ¹³When those who were carrying the ark of the LORD had taken six steps, he sacrificed a bull and a fattened calf. ¹⁴Wearing a linen ephod, David was dancing before the LORD with all his might, ¹⁵while he and the entire house of Israel were bringing up the ark of the LORD with shouts and the sound of trumpets.

¹⁶As the ark of the LORD was entering the City of David, Michal daughter of Saul watched from a window. And when she saw King David leaping and dancing before the LORD, she despised him in her heart.

¹⁷They brought the ark of the LORD and set it in its place inside the tent that David had pitched for it, and David

---

atissue:relational sabotage

6:16 Like Michal, we don't always like what our husbands do. Michal reacted to David not only with anger but also with contempt and hatred. Why? Was she feeling left out? Insecure? Was she jealous or dissatisfied? Clearly, she wanted to cut her husband down for dancing before God. In this case, David's actions were justified. But even if our husbands do something foolish, does that give us the right to treat them with scorn? It is not our right as wives to humble our husbands. Instead, we are the ones who are supposed to extend the most grace to them.

ᵃ 20 Baal Perazim means the lord who breaks out.   ᵇ 25 Septuagint (see also 1 Chron. 14:16); Hebrew Geba   ᶜ 2 That is, Kiriath Jearim (see 1 Chron. 13:6)
ᵈ 2 Hebrew; Septuagint and Vulgate do not have the Name.   ᵉ 3,4 Dead Sea Scrolls and some Septuagint manuscripts; Masoretic Text cart ᵈand they brought it
with the ark of God from the house of Abinadab, which was on the hill   ᶠ 5 Masoretic Text; Dead Sea Scrolls and Septuagint (see also 1 Chron. 13:8) songs
ᵍ 8 Perez Uzzah means outbreak against Uzzah.

sacrificed burnt offerings and fellowship offerings before the LORD. ¹⁸After he had finished sacrificing the burnt offerings and fellowship offerings, he blessed the people in the name of the LORD Almighty. ¹⁹Then he gave a loaf of bread, a cake of dates and a cake of raisins to each person in the whole crowd of Israelites, both men and women. And all the people went to their homes.

²⁰When David returned home to bless his household, Michal daughter of Saul came out to meet him and said, "How the king of Israel has distinguished himself today, going around half-naked in full view of the slave girls of his servants as any vulgar fellow would!"

²¹David said to Michal, "It was before the LORD, who chose me rather than your father or anyone from his house when he appointed me ruler over the LORD's people Israel—I will celebrate before the LORD. ²²I will become even more undignified than this, and I will be humiliated in my own eyes. But by these slave girls you spoke of, I will be held in honor."

²³And Michal daughter of Saul had no children to the day of her death.

God's Promise to David

7 After the king was settled in his palace and the LORD had given him rest from all his enemies around him, ²he said to Nathan the prophet, "Here I am, living in a house of cedar, while the ark of God remains in a tent."

³Nathan replied to the king, "Whatever you have in mind, go ahead and do it, for the LORD is with you."

⁴But that night the word of the LORD came to Nathan, saying:

⁵"Go and tell my servant David, 'This is what the LORD says: Are you the one to build me a house to dwell in? ⁶I have not dwelt in a house from the day I brought the Israelites up out of Egypt to this day. I have been moving from place to place with a tent as my dwelling. ⁷Wherever I have moved with all the Israelites, did I ever say to any of their rulers whom I commanded to shepherd my people Israel, "Why have you not built me a house of cedar?"'

⁸"Now then, tell my servant David, 'This is what the LORD Almighty says: I took you from the pasture, from tending the flock, and appointed you ruler over my people Israel. ⁹I have been with you wherever you have gone, and I have cut off all your enemies from before you. Now I will make your name great, like the names of the greatest men on earth. ¹⁰And I will provide a place for my people Israel and will plant them so that they can have a home of their own and no longer be disturbed. Wicked people will not oppress them anymore, as they did at the beginning ¹¹and have done ever since the time I appointed leaders ᵃ over my people Israel. I will also give you rest from all your enemies.

"'The LORD declares to you that the LORD himself will establish a house for you: ¹²When your days are over and you rest with your ancestors, I will raise up your offspring to succeed you, who will come from your own body, and I will establish his kingdom. ¹³He is the one who will build a house for my Name, and I will establish the throne of his kingdom forever. ¹⁴I will be his father, and he

391

ᵃ 11 Traditionally judges

HE IS: a king-maker

7:8–16 God honored David beyond his wildest imagination, giving him and his descendants a kingdom that would endure forever. Reflecting on his life, David humbly realized he was unworthy of this honor. But God is a *king-maker*, elevating those who love and serve him.

God has prepared a crown of glory for you in heaven and gifts beyond your wildest dreams. You may feel like saying, "Who am I, that you have brought me this far?" Simply put, you are his. Demonstrate your royal position by striving to emulate your Father here on earth, knowing you'll wear a crown of glory in heaven (see 1 Peter 5:4).

For the next He Is, go to p. 409.

will be my son. When he does wrong, I will punish him with a rod wielded by human beings, with floggings inflicted by human hands. [15] But my love will never be taken away from him, as I took it away from Saul, whom I removed from before you. [16] Your house and your kingdom will endure forever before me[a]; your throne will be established forever.'"

[17] Nathan reported to David all the words of this entire revelation.

David's Prayer

[18] Then King David went in and sat before the LORD, and he said:

"Who am I, Sovereign LORD, and what is my family, that you have brought me this far? [19] And as if this were not enough in your sight, Sovereign LORD, you have also spoken about the future of the house of your servant—and this decree, Sovereign LORD, is for a human being![b]

[20] "What more can David say to you? For you know your servant, Sovereign LORD. [21] For the sake of your word and according to your will, you have done this great thing and made it known to your servant.

[22] "How great you are, Sovereign LORD! There is no one like you, and there is no God but you, as we have heard with our own ears. [23] And who is like your people Israel—the one nation on earth that God went out to redeem as a people for himself, and to make a name for himself, and to perform great and awesome wonders by driving out nations and their gods from before your people, whom you redeemed from Egypt?[c] [24] You have established your people Israel as your very own forever, and you, LORD, have become their God.

[25] "And now, LORD God, keep forever the promise you have made concerning your servant and his house. Do as you promised, [26] so that your name will be great forever. Then people will say, 'The LORD Almighty is God over Israel!' And the house of your servant David will be established in your sight.

[27] "LORD Almighty, God of Israel, you have revealed this to your servant, saying, 'I will build a house for you.' So your servant has found courage to pray this prayer to you. [28] Sovereign LORD, you are God! Your covenant is trustworthy, and you have promised these good things to your servant. [29] Now be pleased to bless the house of your servant, that it may continue forever in your sight; for you, Sovereign LORD, have spoken, and with your blessing the house of your servant will be blessed forever."

David's Victories

8 In the course of time, David defeated the Philistines and subdued them, and he took Metheg Ammah from the control of the Philistines.

[2] David also defeated the Moabites. He made them lie down on the ground and measured them off with a length of cord. Every two lengths of them were put to death, and the third length was allowed to live. So the Moabites became subject to David and brought him tribute.

[3] Moreover, David defeated Hadadezer son of Rehob, king of Zobah, when he went to restore his monument at[d] the Euphrates River. [4] David captured a thousand of his chariots, seven thousand charioteers[e] and twenty thousand foot soldiers. He hamstrung all but a hundred of the chariot horses.

[5] When the Arameans of Damascus came to help Hadadezer king of Zobah, David struck down twenty-two thousand of them. [6] He put garrisons in the Aramean kingdom of Damascus, and the Arameans became subject to him and brought tribute. The LORD gave David victory wherever he went.

[7] David took the gold shields that belonged to the officers of Hadadezer and brought them to Jerusalem. [8] From Tebah[f] and Berothai, towns that belonged to Hadadezer, King David took a great quantity of bronze.

[9] When Tou[g] king of Hamath heard that David had defeated the entire army of Hadadezer, [10] he sent his son Joram[h] to King David to greet him and congratulate him on his victory in battle over Hadad-

---

[a] 16 Some Hebrew manuscripts and Septuagint; most Hebrew manuscripts *you*   [b] 19 Or *for the human race*   [c] 23 See Septuagint and 1 Chron. 17:21; Hebrew *wonders for your land and before your people, whom you redeemed from Egypt, from the nations and their gods.*   [d] 3 Or *his control along*   [e] 4 Septuagint (see also Dead Sea Scrolls and 1 Chron. 18:4); Masoretic Text *captured seventeen hundred of his charioteers*   [f] 8 See some Septuagint manuscripts (see also 1 Chron. 18:8); Hebrew *Betah.*   [g] 9 Hebrew *Toi,* a variant of *Tou;* also in verse 10   [h] 10 A variant of *Hadoram*

ezer, who had been at war with Tou. Joram brought with him articles of silver, of gold and of bronze. ¹¹King David dedicated these articles to the LORD, as he had done with the silver and gold from all the nations he had subdued: ¹²Edom*a* and Moab, the Ammonites and the Philistines, and Amalek. He also dedicated the plunder taken from Hadadezer son of Rehob, king of Zobah.

¹³And David became famous after he returned from striking down eighteen thousand Edomites*b* in the Valley of Salt.

¹⁴He put garrisons throughout Edom, and all the Edomites became subject to David. The LORD gave David victory wherever he went.

David's Officials

¹⁵David reigned over all Israel, doing what was just and right for all his people. ¹⁶Joab son of Zeruiah was over the army; Jehoshaphat son of Ahilud was recorder; ¹⁷Zadok son of Ahitub and Ahimelek son of Abiathar were priests; Seraiah was secretary; ¹⁸Benaiah son of Jehoiada was over the Kerethites and Pelethites; and David's sons were priests.*c*

David and Mephibosheth

9 David asked, "Is there anyone still left of the house of Saul to whom I can show kindness for Jonathan's sake?"

²Now there was a servant of Saul's household named Ziba. They summoned him to appear before David, and the king said to him, "Are you Ziba?"

"At your service," he replied.

393

³The king asked, "Is there no one still left of the house of Saul to whom I can show God's kindness?"

Ziba answered the king, "There is still a son of Jonathan; he is lame in both feet."

⁴"Where is he?" the king asked.

Ziba answered, "He is at the house of Makir son of Ammiel in Lo Debar."

⁵So King David had him brought from Lo Debar, from the house of Makir son of Ammiel.

⁶When Mephibosheth son of Jonathan, the son of Saul, came to David, he bowed down to pay him honor.

David said, "Mephibosheth!"

"At your service," he replied.

⁷"Don't be afraid," David said to him, "for I will surely show you kindness for the sake of your father Jonathan. I will restore to you all the land that belonged to your grandfather Saul, and you will always eat at my table."

⁸Mephibosheth bowed down and said, "What is your servant, that you should notice a dead dog like me?"

⁹Then the king summoned Ziba, Saul's steward, and said to him, "I have given your master's grandson everything that belonged to Saul and his family. ¹⁰You and your sons and your servants are to farm the land for him and bring in the crops, so that your master's grandson may be provided for. And Mephibosheth, grandson of your master, will always eat at my table." (Now Ziba had fifteen sons and twenty servants.)

¹¹Then Ziba said to the king, "Your servant will do whatever my lord the king commands his servant to do." So Mephibosheth ate at David's*d* table like one of the king's sons.

¹²Mephibosheth had a young son named Mika, and all the members of Ziba's household were servants of Mephibosheth. ¹³And Mephibosheth lived in Jerusalem, because he always ate at the king's table; he was lame in both feet.

David Defeats the Ammonites

10 In the course of time, the king of the Ammonites died, and his son Hanun succeeded him as king. ²David thought, "I will show kindness to Hanun son of Nahash, just as his father showed kindness to me." So David sent a delegation to express his sympathy to Hanun concerning his father.

---

a 12 Some Hebrew manuscripts, Septuagint and Syriac (see also 1 Chron. 18:11); most Hebrew manuscripts *Aram*   *b 13* A few Hebrew manuscripts, Septuagint and Syriac (see also 1 Chron. 18:12); most Hebrew manuscripts *Aram* (that is, Arameans)   *c 18* Or *were chief officials* (see Septuagint and Targum; see also 1 Chron. 18:17)   *d 11* Septuagint; Hebrew *my*

When David's men came to the land of the Ammonites, [3]the Ammonite commanders said to Hanun their lord, "Do you think David is honoring your father by sending envoys to you to express sympathy? Hasn't David sent them to you only to explore the city and spy it out and overthrow it?" [4]So Hanun seized David's envoys, shaved off half of each man's beard, cut off their garments at the buttocks, and sent them away.

[5]When David was told about this, he sent messengers to meet the men, for they were greatly humiliated. The king said, "Stay at Jericho till your beards have grown, and then come back."

[6]When the Ammonites realized that they had become obnoxious to David, they hired twenty thousand Aramean foot soldiers from Beth Rehob and Zobah, as well as the king of Maakah with a thousand men, and also twelve thousand men from Tob.

[7]On hearing this, David sent Joab out with the entire army of fighting men. [8]The Ammonites came out and drew up in battle formation at the entrance of their city gate, while the Arameans of Zobah and Rehob and the men of Tob and Maakah were by themselves in the open country.

[9]Joab saw that there were battle lines in front of him and behind him; so he selected some of the best troops in Israel and deployed them against the Arameans. [10]He put the rest of the men under the command of Abishai his brother and deployed them against the Ammonites. [11]Joab said, "If the Arameans are too strong for me, then you are to come to my rescue; but if the Ammonites are too strong for you, then I will come to rescue you. [12]Be strong, and let us fight bravely for our people and the cities of our God. The LORD will do what is good in his sight."

[13]Then Joab and the troops with him advanced to fight the Arameans, and they fled before him. [14]When the Ammonites realized that the Arameans were fleeing, they fled before Abishai and went inside the city. So Joab returned from fighting the Ammonites and came to Jerusalem.

[15]After the Arameans saw that they had been routed by Israel, they regrouped. [16]Hadadezer had Arameans brought from beyond the Euphrates River; they went to Helam, with Shobak the commander of Hadadezer's army leading them.

[17]When David was told of this, he gathered all Israel, crossed the Jordan and went to Helam. The Arameans formed their battle lines to meet David and fought against him. [18]But they fled before Israel, and David killed seven hundred of their charioteers and forty thousand of their foot soldiers.[a] He also struck down Shobak the commander of their army, and he died there. [19]When all the kings who were vassals of Hadadezer saw that they had been routed by Israel, they made peace with the Israelites and became subject to them.

So the Arameans were afraid to help the Ammonites anymore.

David and Bathsheba

11 In the spring, at the time when kings go off to war, David sent Joab out with the king's men and the whole Israelite army. They destroyed the Ammonites and besieged Rabbah. But David remained in Jerusalem.

[2]One evening David got up from his bed and walked around on the roof of the palace. From the roof he saw a woman bathing. The woman was very beautiful, [3]and David sent someone to find out about her. The man said, "She is Bathsheba, the daughter of Eliam and the wife of Uriah the Hittite." [4]Then David sent messengers to get her. She came to him, and he slept with her. (Now she was purifying herself from her monthly uncleanness.) Then she went back home. [5]The woman conceived and sent word to David, saying, "I am pregnant."

[6]So David sent this word to Joab: "Send me Uriah the Hittite." And Joab sent him to David. [7]When Uriah came to him, David asked him how Joab was, how the soldiers were and how the war was going. [8]Then David said to Uriah, "Go down to your house and wash your feet." So Uriah left the palace, and a gift from the king was sent after him. [9]But Uriah slept at the entrance to the palace with all his master's servants and did not go down to his house.

[10]David was told, "Uriah did not go home." So he asked Uriah, "Haven't you just come from a military campaign? Why didn't you go home?"

---

[a] *18* Some Septuagint manuscripts (see also 1 Chron. 19:18); Hebrew *horsemen*

¹¹Uriah said to David, "The ark and Israel and Judah are staying in tents,^a and my commander Joab and my lord's men are camped in the open country. How could I go to my house to eat and drink and make love to my wife? As surely as you live, I will not do such a thing!"

¹²Then David said to him, "Stay here one more day, and tomorrow I will send you back." So Uriah remained in Jerusalem that day and the next. ¹³At David's invitation, he ate and drank with him, and David made him drunk. But in the evening Uriah went out to sleep on his mat among his master's servants; he did not go home.

¹⁴In the morning David wrote a letter to Joab and sent it with Uriah. ¹⁵In it he wrote, "Put Uriah out in front where the fighting is fiercest. Then withdraw from him so he will be struck down and die."

¹⁶So while Joab had the city under siege, he put Uriah at a place where he knew the strongest defenders were. ¹⁷When the men of the city came out and fought against Joab, some of the men in David's army fell; moreover, Uriah the Hittite died.

¹⁸Joab sent David a full account of the battle. ¹⁹He instructed the messenger: "When you have finished giving the king this account of the battle, ²⁰the king's anger may flare up, and he may ask you, 'Why did you get so close to the city to fight? Didn't you know they would shoot arrows from the wall? ²¹Who killed Abimelek son of Jerub-Besheth^b? Didn't a woman drop an upper millstone on him from the wall, so that he died in Thebez? Why did you get so close to the wall?' If he asks you this, then say to him, 'Moreover, your servant Uriah the Hittite is dead.'"

²²The messenger set out, and when he arrived he told David everything Joab had sent him to say. ²³The messenger said to David, "The men overpowered us and came out against us in the open, but we drove them back to the entrance of the city gate. ²⁴Then the archers shot arrows at your servants from the wall, and some of the king's men died. Moreover, your servant Uriah the Hittite is dead."

²⁵David told the messenger, "Say this to Joab: 'Don't let this upset you; the sword devours one as well as another. Press the attack against the city and destroy it.' Say this to encourage Joab."

²⁶When Uriah's wife heard that her husband was dead, she mourned for him. ²⁷After the time of mourning was over, David had her brought to his house, and she became his wife and bore him a son. But the thing David had done displeased the LORD.

Nathan Rebukes David

12 The LORD sent Nathan to David. When he came to him, he said, "There were two men in a certain town, one rich and the other poor. ²The rich man had a very large number of sheep and cattle, ³but the poor man had nothing except one little ewe lamb he had bought. He raised it, and it grew up with him and his children. It shared his food, drank from his cup and even slept in his arms. It was like a daughter to him.

⁴"Now a traveler came to the rich man, but the rich man refrained from taking one of his own sheep or cattle to prepare a meal for the traveler who had come to him. Instead, he took the ewe lamb that belonged to the poor man and prepared it for the one who had come to him."

⁵David burned with anger against the man and said to Nathan, "As surely as the LORD lives, the man who did this must die! ⁶He must pay for that lamb four times over, because he did such a thing and had no pity."

---

aussie:infidelity

11:1–27 It takes two to tango, and (if they're any good) no one else gets injured. It also takes two to commit adultery, but others will definitely get hurt. David and Bathsheba might have thought their affair was just between them. That might have been true—for a night. As a direct result of their adultery, Bathsheba's husband and son both died (and later many died during Absalom's revolt, a spin-off of David's punishment). Their choice to break the marriage covenant had serious consequences for them and others. Don't lie to yourself—infidelity will hurt those you love.

395

7Then Nathan said to David, "You are the man! This is what the LORD, the God of Israel, says: 'I anointed you king over Israel, and I delivered you from the hand of Saul. 8I gave your master's house to you, and your master's wives into your arms. I gave you the house of Israel and Judah. And if all this had been too little, I would have given you even more. 9Why did you despise the word of the LORD by doing what is evil in his eyes? You struck down Uriah the Hittite with the sword and took his wife to be your own. You killed him with the sword of the Ammonites. 10Now, therefore, the sword will never depart from your house, because you despised me and took the wife of Uriah the Hittite to be your own.'

11"This is what the LORD says: 'Out of your own household I am going to bring calamity on you. Before your very eyes I will take your wives and give them to one who is close to you, and he will sleep with your wives in broad daylight. 12You did it in secret, but I will do this thing in broad daylight before all Israel.'"

13Then David said to Nathan, "I have sinned against the LORD."

Nathan replied, "The LORD has taken away your sin. You are not going to die. 14But because by doing this you have shown utter contempt for^a the LORD, the son born to you will die."

15After Nathan had gone home, the LORD struck the child that Uriah's wife had borne to David, and he became ill. 16David pleaded with God for the child. He fasted and spent the nights lying in sackcloth^b on the ground. 17The elders of his household stood beside him to get him up from the ground, but he refused, and he would not eat any food with them.

18On the seventh day the child died. David's attendants were afraid to tell him that the child was dead, for they thought, "While the child was still living, he wouldn't listen to us when we spoke to him. How can we now tell him the child is dead? He may do something desperate."

19David noticed that his attendants were whispering among themselves, and he realized the child was dead. "Is the child dead?" he asked.

"Yes," they replied, "he is dead."

20Then David got up from the ground. After he had washed, put on lotions and changed his clothes, he went into the house of the LORD and worshiped. Then he went to his own house, and at his request they served him food, and he ate.

21His attendants asked him, "Why are you acting this way? While the child was alive, you fasted and wept, but now that the child is dead, you get up and eat!"

22He answered, "While the child was still alive, I fasted and wept. I thought, 'Who knows? The LORD may be gracious to me and let the child live.' 23But now that he is dead, why should I go on fasting? Can I bring him back again? I will go to him, but he will not return to me."

24Then David comforted his wife Bathsheba, and he went to her and made love to her. She gave birth to a son, and they named him Solomon. The LORD loved him; 25and because the LORD loved him, he sent word through Nathan the prophet to name him Jedidiah.^c

26Meanwhile Joab fought against Rabbah of the Ammonites and captured the royal citadel. 27Joab then sent messengers to David, saying, "I have fought against Rabbah and taken its water supply. 28Now muster the rest of the troops and besiege the city and capture it. Otherwise I will take the city, and it will be named after me."

29So David mustered the entire army and went to Rabbah, and attacked and captured it. 30David took the crown from their king's^d head, and it was placed on his own head. It weighed a talent^e of gold, and it was set with precious stones. David took a great quantity of plunder from the city 31and brought out

conversations

regret «» 12:1–31

1» What is the difference between regret and repentance?

2» What kind of deep regrets can haunt you all your life?

3» How can you bring good out of your regrets, rather than letting them bury you?

For more on regret, check the index.
For the next Conversations, go to p. 398.

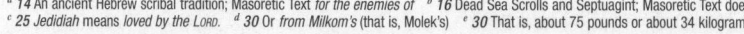

^a 14 An ancient Hebrew scribal tradition; Masoretic Text for the enemies of   ^b 16 Dead Sea Scrolls and Septuagint; Masoretic Text does not have in sackcloth.
^c 25 Jedidiah means loved by the LORD.   ^d 30 Or from Milkom's (that is, Molek's)   ^e 30 That is, about 75 pounds or about 34 kilograms

the people who were there, consigning them to labor with saws and with iron picks and axes, and he made them work at brickmaking.[a] David did this to all the Ammonite towns. Then he and his entire army returned to Jerusalem.

Amnon and Tamar

13 In the course of time, Amnon son of David fell in love with Tamar, the beautiful sister of Absalom son of David.

² Amnon became so obsessed with his sister Tamar that he made himself ill. She was a virgin, and it seemed impossible for him to do anything to her.

³ Now Amnon had an advisor named Jonadab son of Shimeah, David's brother. Jonadab was a very shrewd man. ⁴ He asked Amnon, "Why do you, the king's son, look so haggard morning after morning? Won't you tell me?"

Amnon said to him, "I'm in love with Tamar, my brother Absalom's sister."

⁵ "Go to bed and pretend to be ill," Jonadab said. "When your father comes to see you, say to him, 'I would like my sister Tamar to come and give me something to eat. Let her prepare the food in my sight so I may watch her and then eat it from her hand.'"

⁶ So Amnon lay down and pretended to be ill. When the king came to see him, Amnon said to him, "I would like my sister Tamar to come and make some special bread in my sight, so I may eat from her hand."

⁷ David sent word to Tamar at the palace: "Go to the house of your brother Amnon and prepare some food for him." ⁸ So Tamar went to the house of her brother Amnon, who was lying down. She took some dough, kneaded it, made the bread in his sight and baked it. ⁹ Then she took the pan and served him the bread, but he refused to eat.

"Send everyone out of here," Amnon said. So everyone left him. ¹⁰ Then Amnon said to Tamar, "Bring the food here into my bedroom so I may eat from your hand." And Tamar took the bread she had prepared and brought it to her brother Amnon in his bedroom. ¹¹ But when she took it to him to eat, he grabbed her and said, "Come to bed with me, my sister."

¹² "No, my brother!" she said to him. "Don't force me! Such a thing should not be done in Israel! Don't do this wicked thing. ¹³ What about me? Where could I get rid of my disgrace? And what about you? You would be like one of the wicked fools in Israel. Please speak to the king; he will not keep me from being married to you." ¹⁴ But he refused to listen to her, and since he was stronger than she, he raped her.

¹⁵ Then Amnon hated her with intense hatred. In fact, he hated her more than he had loved her. Amnon said to her, "Get up and get out!"

¹⁶ "No!" she said to him. "Sending me away would be a greater wrong than what you have already done to me."

But he refused to listen to her. ¹⁷ He called his personal servant and said, "Get this woman out of my sight and bolt the door after her." ¹⁸ So his servant put her out and bolted the door after her. She was wearing a richly ornamented[b] robe, for this was the kind of garment the virgin daughters of the king wore. ¹⁹ Tamar put ashes on her head and tore the ornamented[c] robe she was wearing. She put her hands on her head and went away, weeping aloud as she went.

---

atissue:flirting

13:1–3 True or False: If a man shows interest in you, it's because he genuinely likes you. And if a man wants to make love to you, then he really feels a deep connection with you. Did you answer *false* to both? Good! Many women receive the attention of men with blind naïveté. Men can have sex with women they don't even like. (And women can do the same.) If a man flirts with you, don't assume he's thinking about long-term commitment and family vacations. Like Amnon, he may be thinking only of sex. Don't let someone's flattery affect your good judgment.

397

---

[a] 31 The meaning of the Hebrew for this clause is uncertain.   [b] 18 The meaning of the Hebrew for this phrase is uncertain.   [c] 19 The meaning of the Hebrew for this word is uncertain.

²⁰Her brother Absalom said to her, "Has that Amnon, your brother, been with you? Be quiet for now, my sister; he is your brother. Don't take this thing to heart." And Tamar lived in her brother Absalom's house, a desolate woman.

²¹When King David heard all this, he was furious. ²²And Absalom never spoke to Amnon again; he hated Amnon because he had disgraced his sister Tamar.

Absalom Kills Amnon

²³Two years later, when Absalom's sheepshearers were at Baal Hazor near the border of Ephraim, he invited all the king's sons to come there. ²⁴Absalom went to the king and said, "Your servant has had shearers come. Will the king and his attendants please join me?"

²⁵"No, my son," the king replied. "All of us should not go; we would only be a burden to you." Although Absalom urged him, he still refused to go but gave him his blessing.

²⁶Then Absalom said, "If not, please let my brother Amnon come with us."

The king asked him, "Why should he go with you?" ²⁷But Absalom urged him, so he sent with him Amnon and the rest of the king's sons.

²⁸Absalom ordered his men, "Listen! When Amnon is in high spirits from drinking wine and I say to you, 'Strike Amnon down,' then kill him. Don't be afraid. Haven't I given you this order? Be strong and brave." ²⁹So Absalom's men did to Amnon what Absalom had ordered. Then all the king's sons got up, mounted their mules and fled.

³⁰While they were on their way, the report came to David: "Absalom has struck down all the king's sons; not one of them is left." ³¹The king stood up, tore his clothes and lay down on the ground; and all his attendants stood by with their clothes torn.

"conversations"

revenge «» 13:23–29

1» If you take revenge, what are the consequences?

2» How do you feel after you take revenge?

3» In what ways does taking revenge make you similar to the person who hurt you?

For more on revenge, check the index.
For the next Conversations, go to p. 411.

³²But Jonadab son of Shimeah, David's brother, said, "My lord should not think that they killed all the princes; only Amnon is dead. This has been Absalom's express intention ever since the day Amnon raped his sister Tamar. ³³My lord the king should not be concerned about the report that all the king's sons are dead. Only Amnon is dead."

³⁴Meanwhile, Absalom had fled.

Now the man standing watch looked up and saw many people on the road west of him, coming down the side of the hill. The watchman went and told the king, "I see men in the direction of Horonaim, on the side of the hill."ᵃ

³⁵Jonadab said to the king, "See, the king's sons have come; it has happened just as your servant said."

³⁶As he finished speaking, the king's sons came in, wailing loudly. The king, too, and all his attendants wept very bitterly.

³⁷Absalom fled and went to Talmai son of Ammihud, the king of Geshur. But King David mourned many days for his son.

³⁸After Absalom fled and went to Geshur, he stayed there three years. ³⁹And King David longed to go to Absalom, for he was consoled concerning Amnon's death.

Absalom Returns to Jerusalem

14 Joab son of Zeruiah knew that the king's heart longed for Absalom. ²So Joab sent someone to Tekoa and had a wise woman brought from there. He said to her, "Pretend you are in mourning. Dress in mourning clothes, and don't use any cosmetic lotions. Act like a woman who has spent many days grieving for the dead. ³Then go to the king and speak these words to him." And Joab put the words in her mouth.

ᵃ *34* Septuagint; Hebrew does not have this sentence.

[4]When the woman from Tekoa went[a] to the king, she fell with her face to the ground to pay him honor, and she said, "Help me, Your Majesty!"

[5]The king asked her, "What is troubling you?"

She said, "I am a widow; my husband is dead. [6]I your servant had two sons. They got into a fight with each other in the field, and no one was there to separate them. One struck the other and killed him. [7]Now the whole clan has risen up against your servant; they say, 'Hand over the one who struck his brother down, so that we may put him to death for the life of his brother whom he killed; then we will get rid of the heir as well.' They would put out the only burning coal I have left, leaving my husband neither name nor descendant on the face of the earth."

[8]The king said to the woman, "Go home, and I will issue an order in your behalf."

[9]But the woman from Tekoa said to him, "Let my lord the king pardon me and my family, and let the king and his throne be without guilt."

[10]The king replied, "If anyone says anything to you, bring them to me, and they will not bother you again."

[11]She said, "Then let the king invoke the LORD his God to prevent the avenger of blood from adding to the destruction, so that my son will not be destroyed."

"As surely as the LORD lives," he said, "not one hair of your son's head will fall to the ground."

[12]Then the woman said, "Let your servant speak a word to my lord the king."

"Speak," he replied.

[13]The woman said, "Why then have you devised a thing like this against the people of God? When the king says this, does he not convict himself, for the king has not brought back his banished son? [14]Like water spilled on the ground, which cannot be recovered, so we must die. But that is not what God desires; rather, he devises ways so that a banished person does not remain banished from him.

[15]"And now I have come to say this to my lord the king because the people have made me afraid. Your servant thought, 'I will speak to the king; perhaps he will grant his servant's request. [16]Perhaps the king will agree to deliver his servant from the hand of the man who is trying to cut off both me and my son from God's inheritance.'

[17]"And now your servant says, 'May the word of my lord the king secure my inheritance, for my lord the king is like an angel of God in discerning good and evil. May the LORD your God be with you.'"

[18]Then the king said to the woman, "Don't keep from me the answer to what I am going to ask you."

"Let my lord the king speak," the woman said.

[19]The king asked, "Isn't the hand of Joab with you in all this?"

The woman answered, "As surely as you live, my lord the king, no one can turn to the right or to the left from anything my lord the king says. Yes, it was your servant Joab who instructed me to do this and who put all these words into the mouth of your servant. [20]Your servant Joab did this to change the present situation. My lord has wisdom like that of an angel of God—he knows everything that happens in the land."

[21]The king said to Joab, "Very well, I will do it. Go, bring back the young man Absalom."

[22]Joab fell with his face to the ground to pay him honor, and he blessed the king. Joab said, "Today your servant knows that he has found favor in your eyes, my lord the king, because the king has granted his servant's request."

[23]Then Joab went to Geshur and brought Absalom back to Jerusalem. [24]But the king said, "He must go to his own house; he must not see my face." So Absalom went to his own house and did not see the face of the king.

[25]In all Israel there was not a man so highly praised for his handsome appearance as Absalom. From the top of his head to the sole of his foot there was no blemish in him. [26]Whenever he cut the hair of his head—he used to cut his hair once a year because it became too heavy for him—he would weigh it, and its weight was two hundred shekels[b] by the royal standard.

[27]Three sons and a daughter were born to Absalom. His daughter's name was Tamar, and she became a beautiful woman.

---

[a] 4 Many Hebrew manuscripts, Septuagint, Vulgate and Syriac; most Hebrew manuscripts *spoke*   [b] 26 That is, about 5 pounds or about 2.3 kilograms

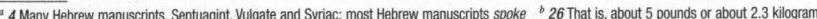

²⁸Absalom lived two years in Jerusalem without seeing the king's face. ²⁹Then Absalom sent for Joab in order to send him to the king, but Joab refused to come to him. So he sent a second time, but he refused to come. ³⁰Then he said to his servants, "Look, Joab's field is next to mine, and he has barley there. Go and set it on fire." So Absalom's servants set the field on fire.

³¹Then Joab did go to Absalom's house, and he said to him, "Why have your servants set my field on fire?"

³²Absalom said to Joab, "Look, I sent word to you and said, 'Come here so I can send you to the king to ask, "Why have I come from Geshur? It would be better for me if I were still there!"' Now then, I want to see the king's face, and if I am guilty of anything, let him put me to death."

³³So Joab went to the king and told him this. Then the king summoned Absalom, and he came in and bowed down with his face to the ground before the king. And the king kissed Absalom.

Absalom's Conspiracy

15 In the course of time, Absalom provided himself with a chariot and horses and with fifty men to run ahead of him. ²He would get up early and stand by the side of the road leading to the city gate. Whenever anyone came with a complaint to be placed before the king for a decision, Absalom would call out to him, "What town are you from?" He would answer, "Your servant is from one of the tribes of Israel." ³Then Absalom would say to him, "Look, your claims are valid and proper, but there is no representative of the king to hear you." ⁴And Absalom would add, "If only I were appointed judge in the land! Then everyone who has a complaint or case could come to me and I would see that they receive justice."

⁵Also, whenever anyone approached him to bow down before him, Absalom would reach out his hand, take hold of him and kiss him. ⁶Absalom behaved in this way toward all the Israelites who came to the king asking for justice, and so he stole the hearts of the people of Israel.

⁷At the end of four*a* years, Absalom said to the king, "Let me go to Hebron and fulfill a vow I made to the Lᴏʀᴅ. ⁸While your servant was living at Geshur in Aram, I made this vow: 'If the Lᴏʀᴅ takes me back to Jerusalem, I will worship the Lᴏʀᴅ in Hebron.*b*'"

⁹The king said to him, "Go in peace." So he went to Hebron.

¹⁰Then Absalom sent secret messengers throughout the tribes of Israel to say, "As soon as you hear the sound of the trumpets, then say, 'Absalom is king in Hebron.'" ¹¹Two hundred men from Jerusalem had accompanied Absalom. They had been invited as guests and went quite innocently, knowing nothing about the matter. ¹²While Absalom was offering sacrifices, he also sent for Ahithophel the Gilonite, David's counselor, to come from Giloh, his hometown. And so the conspiracy gained strength, and Absalom's following kept on increasing.

David Flees

¹³A messenger came and told David, "The hearts of the people of Israel are with Absalom."

¹⁴Then David said to all his officials who were with him in Jerusalem, "Come! We must flee, or none of us will escape from Absalom. We must leave immediately, or he will move quickly to overtake us and bring ruin on us and put the city to the sword."

atissue:vanity

14:25–26 Wise investors put their money in something they think will appreciate—hopefully even outlive them. Few of us consciously invest in something that's *guaranteed* to depreciate—except when it comes to our appearance. We devote exorbitant amounts of time and money to something we know can't last. Absalom was definitely proud of his hair. In the end, his remarkable hair actually contributed to his death (see 18:9–15). Of course, there's nothing wrong with caring for our bodies. But the fact remains that beauty fades, and we all grow older. Invest in something that won't depreciate.

---

a 7 Some Septuagint manuscripts, Syriac and Josephus; Hebrew forty   *b 8 Some Septuagint manuscripts; Hebrew does not have in Hebron.*

¹⁵The king's officials answered him, "Your servants are ready to do whatever our lord the king chooses."

¹⁶The king set out, with his entire household following him; but he left ten concubines to take care of the palace. ¹⁷So the king set out, with all the people following him, and they halted at the edge of the city. ¹⁸All his men marched past him, along with all the Kerethites and Pelethites; and all the six hundred Gittites who had accompanied him from Gath marched before the king.

¹⁹The king said to Ittai the Gittite, "Why should you come along with us? Go back and stay with King Absalom. You are a foreigner, an exile from your homeland. ²⁰You came only yesterday. And today shall I make you wander about with us, when I do not know where I am going? Go back, and take your people with you. May the LORD show you kindness and faithfulness."ᵃ

²¹But Ittai replied to the king, "As surely as the LORD lives, and as my lord the king lives, wherever my lord the king may be, whether it means life or death, there will your servant be."

²²David said to Ittai, "Go ahead, march on." So Ittai the Gittite marched on with all his men and the families that were with him.

²³The whole countryside wept aloud as all the people passed by. The king also crossed the Kidron Valley, and all the people moved on toward the wilderness.

²⁴Zadok was there, too, and all the Levites who were with him were carrying the ark of the covenant of God. They set down the ark of God, and Abiathar offered sacrifices until all the people had finished leaving the city.

²⁵Then the king said to Zadok, "Take the ark of God back into the city. If I find favor in the LORD's eyes, he will bring me back and let me see it and his dwelling place again. ²⁶But if he says, 'I am not pleased with you,' then I am ready; let him do to me whatever seems good to him."

²⁷The king also said to Zadok the priest, "Do you understand? Go back to the city with my blessing. Take your son Ahimaaz with you, and also Abiathar's son Jonathan. You and Abiathar return with your two sons. ²⁸I will wait at the fords in the wilderness until word comes from you to inform me." ²⁹So Zadok and Abiathar took the ark of God back to Jerusalem and stayed there.

³⁰But David continued up the Mount of Olives, weeping as he went; his head was covered and he was barefoot. All the people with him covered their heads too and were weeping as they went up. ³¹Now David had been told, "Ahithophel is among the conspirators with Absalom." So David prayed, "LORD, turn Ahithophel's counsel into foolishness."

³²When David arrived at the summit, where people used to worship God, Hushai the Arkite was there to meet him, his robe torn and dust on his head. ³³David said to him, "If you go with me, you will be a burden to me. ³⁴But if you return to the city and say to Absalom, 'Your Majesty, I will be your servant; I was your father's servant in the past, but now I will be your servant,' then you can help me by frustrating Ahithophel's advice. ³⁵Won't the priests Zadok and Abiathar be there with you? Tell them anything you hear in the king's palace. ³⁶Their two sons, Ahimaaz son of Zadok and Jonathan son of Abiathar, are there with them. Send them to me with anything you hear."

³⁷So Hushai, David's confidant, arrived at Jerusalem as Absalom was entering the city.

401

David and Ziba

16 When David had gone a short distance beyond the summit, there was Ziba, the steward of Mephibosheth, waiting to meet him. He had a string of donkeys saddled and loaded with two hundred loaves of bread, a hundred cakes of raisins, a hundred cakes of figs and a skin of wine.

²The king asked Ziba, "Why have you brought these?"

Ziba answered, "The donkeys are for the king's household to ride on, the bread and fruit are for the men to eat, and the wine is to refresh those who become exhausted in the wilderness."

³The king then asked, "Where is your master's grandson?"

Ziba said to him, "He is staying in Jerusalem, because he thinks, 'Today the house of Israel will restore to me my grandfather's kingdom.'"

⁴Then the king said to Ziba, "All that belonged to Mephibosheth is now yours."

"I humbly bow," Ziba said. "May I find favor in your eyes, my lord the king."

ᵃ 20 Septuagint; Hebrew *May kindness and faithfulness be with you*

Shimei Curses David

⁵As King David approached Bahurim, a man from the same clan as Saul's family came out from there. His name was Shimei son of Gera, and he cursed as he came out. ⁶He pelted David and all the king's officials with stones, though all the troops and the special guard were on David's right and left. ⁷As he cursed, Shimei said, "Get out, get out, you murderer, you scoundrel! ⁸The LORD has repaid you for all the blood you shed in the household of Saul, in whose place you have reigned. The LORD has given the kingdom into the hands of your son Absalom. You have come to ruin because you are a murderer!"

⁹Then Abishai son of Zeruiah said to the king, "Why should this dead dog curse my lord the king? Let me go over and cut off his head."

¹⁰But the king said, "What does this have to do with you, you sons of Zeruiah? If he is cursing because the LORD said to him, 'Curse David,' who can ask, 'Why do you do this?'"

¹¹David then said to Abishai and all his officials, "My son, who is of my own flesh, is trying to take my life. How much more, then, this Benjamite! Leave him alone; let him curse, for the LORD has told him to. ¹²It may be that the LORD will look upon my misery and restore to me his covenant blessing instead of his curse today."

¹³So David and his men continued along the road while Shimei was going along the hillside opposite him, cursing as he went and throwing stones at him and showering him with dirt. ¹⁴The king and all the people with him arrived at their destination exhausted. And there he refreshed himself.

The Advice of Ahithophel and Hushai

¹⁵Meanwhile, Absalom and all the men of Israel came to Jerusalem, and Ahithophel was with him. ¹⁶Then Hushai the Arkite, David's confidant, went to Absalom and said to him, "Long live the king! Long live the king!"

¹⁷Absalom said to Hushai, "So this is the love you show your friend? If he's your friend, why didn't you go with him?"

¹⁸Hushai said to Absalom, "No, the one chosen by the LORD, by these people, and by all the men of Israel—his I will be, and I will remain with him. ¹⁹Furthermore, whom should I serve? Should I not serve the son? Just as I served your father, so I will serve you."

²⁰Absalom said to Ahithophel, "Give us your advice. What should we do?"

²¹Ahithophel answered, "Sleep with your father's concubines whom he left to take care of the palace. Then all Israel will hear that you have made yourself obnoxious to your father, and the hands of everyone with you will be more resolute." ²²So they pitched a tent for Absalom on the roof, and he slept with his father's concubines in the sight of all Israel.

²³Now in those days the advice Ahithophel gave was like that of one who inquires of God. That was how both David and Absalom regarded all of Ahithophel's advice.

17 Ahithophel said to Absalom, "I would*ᵃ* choose twelve thousand men and set out tonight in pursuit of David. ²I would attack him while he is weary and weak. I would strike him with terror, and then all the people with him will flee. I would strike down only the king ³and bring all the people back to you. The death of the man you seek will mean the return of all; all the people will be unharmed." ⁴This plan seemed good to Absalom and to all the elders of Israel.

⁵But Absalom said, "Summon also Hushai the Arkite, so we can hear what he has to say as well." ⁶When Hushai came to him, Absalom said, "Ahithophel has given this advice. Should we do what he says? If not, give us your opinion."

⁷Hushai replied to Absalom, "The advice Ahithophel has given is not good this time. ⁸You know your father and his men; they are fighters, and as fierce as a wild bear robbed of her cubs. Besides, your father is an experienced fighter; he will not spend the night with the troops. ⁹Even now, he is hidden in a cave or some other place. If he should attack your troops first,*ᵇ* whoever hears about it will say, 'There has been a slaughter among the troops who follow Absalom.' ¹⁰Then even the bravest soldier, whose heart is like the heart of a lion, will melt with fear, for all Israel knows that your father is a fighter and that those with him are brave.

ᵃ 1 Or Let me *ᵇ 9 Or When some of the men fall at the first attack*

[11] "So I advise you: Let all Israel, from Dan to Beersheba—as numerous as the sand on the seashore—be gathered to you, with you yourself leading them into battle. [12]Then we will attack him wherever he may be found, and we will fall on him as dew settles on the ground. Neither he nor any of his men will be left alive. [13]If he withdraws into a city, then all Israel will bring ropes to that city, and we will drag it down to the valley until not so much as a pebble is left."

[14]Absalom and all the men of Israel said, "The advice of Hushai the Arkite is better than that of Ahithophel." For the LORD had determined to frustrate the good advice of Ahithophel in order to bring disaster on Absalom.

[15]Hushai told Zadok and Abiathar, the priests, "Ahithophel has advised Absalom and the elders of Israel to do such and such, but I have advised them to do so and so. [16]Now send a message at once and tell David, 'Do not spend the night at the fords in the wilderness; cross over without fail, or the king and all the people with him will be swallowed up.'"

[17]Jonathan and Ahimaaz were staying at En Rogel. A female servant was to go and inform them, and they were to go and tell King David, for they could not risk being seen entering the city. [18]But a young man saw them and told Absalom. So the two of them left at once and went to the house of a man in Bahurim. He had a well in his courtyard, and they climbed down into it. [19]His wife took a covering and spread it out over the opening of the well and scattered grain over it. No one knew anything about it.

[20]When Absalom's men came to the woman at the house, they asked, "Where are Ahimaaz and Jonathan?"

The woman answered them, "They crossed over the brook."[a] The men searched but found no one, so they returned to Jerusalem.

[21]After they had gone, the two climbed out of the well and went to inform King David. They said to him, "Set out and cross the river at once; Ahithophel has advised such and such against you." [22]So David and all the people with him set out and crossed the Jordan. By daybreak, no one was left who had not crossed the Jordan.

[23]When Ahithophel saw that his advice had not been followed, he saddled his donkey and set out for his house in his hometown. He put his house in order and then hanged himself. So he died and was buried in his father's tomb.

Absalom's Death

[24]David went to Mahanaim, and Absalom crossed the Jordan with all the men of Israel. [25]Absalom had appointed Amasa over the army in place of Joab. Amasa was the son of Jether,[b] an Ishmaelite[c] who had married Abigal, the daughter of Nahash and sister of Zeruiah the mother of Joab. [26]The Israelites and Absalom camped in the land of Gilead.

[27]When David came to Mahanaim, Shobi son of Nahash from Rabbah of the Ammonites, and Makir son of Ammiel from Lo Debar, and Barzillai the Gileadite from Rogelim [28]brought bedding and bowls and articles of pottery. They also brought wheat and barley, flour and roasted grain, beans and lentils,[d] [29]honey and curds, sheep, and cheese from cows' milk for David and his people to eat. For they said, "The people have become exhausted and hungry and thirsty in the wilderness."

18 David mustered the men who were with him and appointed over them commanders of thousands and commanders of hundreds. [2]David sent out his troops, a third under the command of Joab, a third under Joab's brother Abishai son of Zeruiah, and a third under Ittai the Gittite. The king told the troops, "I myself will surely march out with you."

[3]But the men said, "You must not go out; if we are forced to flee, they won't care about us. Even if half of us die, they won't care; but you are worth ten thousand of us.[e] It would be better now for you to give us support from the city."

[4]The king answered, "I will do whatever seems best to you."

So the king stood beside the gate while all his men marched out in units of hundreds and of

403

---

[a] 20 Or "They passed by the sheep pen toward the water."   [b] 25 Hebrew Ithra, a variant of Jether   [c] 25 Some Septuagint manuscripts (see also 1 Chron. 2:17); Hebrew and other Septuagint manuscripts Israelite   [d] 28 Most Septuagint manuscripts and Syriac; Hebrew lentils, and roasted grain   [e] 3 Two Hebrew manuscripts, some Septuagint manuscripts and Vulgate; most Hebrew manuscripts care; for now there are ten thousand like us

thousands. ⁵The king commanded Joab, Abishai and Ittai, "Be gentle with the young man Absalom for my sake." And all the troops heard the king giving orders concerning Absalom to each of the commanders.

⁶David's army marched out of the city to fight Israel, and the battle took place in the forest of Ephraim. ⁷There Israel's troops were routed by David's men, and the casualties that day were great—twenty thousand men. ⁸The battle spread out over the whole countryside, and the forest swallowed up more men that day than the sword.

⁹Now Absalom happened to meet David's men. He was riding his mule, and as the mule went under the thick branches of a large oak, Absalom's hair got caught in the tree. He was left hanging in midair, while the mule he was riding kept on going.

¹⁰When one of the men saw what had happened, he told Joab, "I just saw Absalom hanging in an oak tree."

¹¹Joab said to the man who had told him this, "What! You saw him? Why didn't you strike him to the ground right there? Then I would have had to give you ten shekels[a] of silver and a warrior's belt."

¹²But the man replied, "Even if a thousand shekels[b] were weighed out into my hands, I would not lay a hand on the king's son. In our hearing the king commanded you and Abishai and Ittai, 'Protect the young man Absalom for my sake.[c]' ¹³And if I had put my life in jeopardy[d]—and nothing is hidden from the king—you would have kept your distance from me."

¹⁴Joab said, "I'm not going to wait like this for you." So he took three javelins in his hand and plunged them into Absalom's heart while Absalom was still alive in the oak tree. ¹⁵And ten of Joab's armor-bearers surrounded Absalom, struck him and killed him.

¹⁶Then Joab sounded the trumpet, and the troops stopped pursuing Israel, for Joab halted them. ¹⁷They took Absalom, threw him into a big pit in the forest and piled up a large heap of rocks over him. Meanwhile, all the Israelites fled to their homes.

¹⁸During his lifetime Absalom had taken a pillar and erected it in the King's Valley as a monument to himself, for he thought, "I have no son to carry on the memory of my name." He named the pillar after himself, and it is called Absalom's Monument to this day.

David Mourns

¹⁹Now Ahimaaz son of Zadok said, "Let me run and take the news to the king that the LORD has vindicated him by delivering him from the hand of his enemies."

²⁰"You are not the one to take the news today," Joab told him. "You may take the news another time, but you must not do so today, because the king's son is dead."

²¹Then Joab said to a Cushite, "Go, tell the king what you have seen." The Cushite bowed down before Joab and ran off.

²²Ahimaaz son of Zadok again said to Joab, "Come what may, please let me run behind the Cushite."

But Joab replied, "My son, why do you want to go? You don't have any news that will bring you a reward."

²³He said, "Come what may, I want to run."

So Joab said, "Run!" Then Ahimaaz ran by way of the plain[e] and outran the Cushite.

²⁴While David was sitting between the inner and outer gates, the watchman went up to the roof of the gateway by the wall. As he looked out, he saw a man running alone. ²⁵The watchman called out to the king and reported it.

The king said, "If he is alone, he must have good news." And the runner came closer and closer.

²⁶Then the watchman saw another runner, and he called down to the gatekeeper, "Look, another man running alone!"

The king said, "He must be bringing good news, too."

²⁷The watchman said, "It seems to me that the first one runs like Ahimaaz son of Zadok."

"He's a good man," the king said. "He comes with good news."

²⁸Then Ahimaaz called out to the king, "All is well!" He bowed down before the king with his face to

404

ASKMEANYTHING

miriam
Exodus 2–15; Numbers 12:1-15

Tell us about your relationship with your brother Moses.

I was the typical older sister, protective of my little brother. Remember, *I* was the one who watched over Moses while he was in the basket. *I* was the one who approached Pharaoh's daughter and offered to "find" a Hebrew woman to nurse the baby. *I* was the one right beside Moses when he led the people out of Egypt and through the sea. *I* led the women in worship. All along *I* was with Moses, supporting him and helping him.

But you were mostly in the background, right? Was that hard?

Right. [*sighs*] Yes, it was hard. I watched Moses grow up in Pharaoh's palace. I was an onlooker as my kid brother led our people out of Egypt. I had to stay behind as Moses met with God—God himself!—on Mt. Sinai. Moses always got center stage. But me, well, I was there in the background, always there when Moses needed me. I guess it eventually got to me—and to Aaron, too. It's hard watching your younger brother get all the credit and attention. I admit it—I was more than a little jealous.

So how did you handle that?

I'm not proud of this, but both Aaron and I began criticizing Moses' wife. (He had married a Cushite woman, you know.) But that really wasn't the issue. The issue was that we both felt overlooked and unappreciated. I resented Moses' position and his influence. I resented how everyone looked up to him. I felt I had something to contribute, but no one seemed to notice.

So what changed your perspective?

Well, a touch of leprosy can really grab your attention! All of a sudden, what had seemed like a righteous cause looked petty. I had plenty of time to think about myself, my feelings and even my brother while I was exiled from camp for seven long days.

And what did you learn?

I realized that I needed to serve exactly where God put me, with the abilities that he had given me. I needed to keep my focus on myself and not on Moses or anyone else. Instead of worrying about what Moses did or how others responded to him, I needed to focus on my own faithfulness. It's a tough lesson to learn.

405

FOR MORE INSIGHT: Read these stories of jealousy and its harmful effects: Genesis 4:1–8; 1 Samuel 18:6–30; and Luke 15:25–32. To see what God has to say about jealousy, read Proverbs 14:30; Romans 13:11–14; and James 3:13–16.

the ground and said, "Praise be to the LORD your God! He has delivered up those who lifted their hands against my lord the king."

²⁹The king asked, "Is the young man Absalom safe?"

Ahimaaz answered, "I saw great confusion just as Joab was about to send the king's servant and me, your servant, but I don't know what it was."

³⁰The king said, "Stand aside and wait here." So he stepped aside and stood there.

³¹Then the Cushite arrived and said, "My lord the king, hear the good news! The LORD has vindicated you today by delivering you from the hand of all who rose up against you."

³²The king asked the Cushite, "Is the young man Absalom safe?"

The Cushite replied, "May the enemies of my lord the king and all who rise up to harm you be like that young man."

*³³The king was shaken. He went up to the room over the gateway and wept. As he went, he said: "O my son Absalom! My son, my son Absalom! If only I had died instead of you—O Absalom, my son, my son!"

19 *Joab was told, "The king is weeping and mourning for Absalom." ²And for the whole army the victory that day was turned into mourning, because on that day the troops heard it said, "The king is grieving for his son." ³The men stole into the city that day as men steal in who are ashamed when they flee from battle. ⁴The king covered his face and cried aloud, "O my son Absalom! O Absalom, my son, my son!"

⁵Then Joab went into the house to the king and said, "Today you have humiliated all your men, who have just saved your life and the lives of your sons and daughters and the lives of your wives and concubines. ⁶You love those who hate you and hate those who love you. You have made it clear today that the commanders and their men mean nothing to you. I see that you would be pleased if Absalom were alive today and all of us were dead. ⁷Now go out and encourage your men. I swear by the LORD that if you don't go out, not a man will be left with you by nightfall. This will be worse for you than all the calamities that have come on you from your youth till now."

⁸So the king got up and took his seat in the gateway. When the men were told, "The king is sitting in the gateway," they all came before him.

Meanwhile, the Israelites had fled to their homes.

David Returns to Jerusalem

⁹Throughout the tribes of Israel, all the people were arguing among themselves, saying, "The king delivered us from the hand of our enemies; he is the one who rescued us from the hand of the Philistines. But now he has fled the country to escape from Absalom; ¹⁰and Absalom, whom we anointed to rule over us, has died in battle. So why do you say nothing about bringing the king back?"

¹¹King David sent this message to Zadok and Abiathar, the priests: "Ask the elders of Judah, 'Why should you be the last to bring the king back to his palace, since what is being said throughout Israel has reached the king at his quarters? ¹²You are my relatives, my own flesh and blood. So why should you be the last to bring back the king?' ¹³And say to Amasa, 'Are you not my own flesh and blood? May God deal with me, be it ever so severely, if you are not the commander of my army for life in place of Joab.'"

¹⁴He won over the hearts of the men of Judah so that they were all of one accord. They sent word to the king, "Return, you and all your men." ¹⁵Then the king returned and went as far as the Jordan.

Now the men of Judah had come to Gilgal to go out and meet the king and bring him across the Jordan. ¹⁶Shimei son of Gera, the Benjamite from Bahurim, hurried down with the men of Judah to meet King David. ¹⁷With him were a thousand Benjamites, along with Ziba, the steward of Saul's household, and his fifteen sons and twenty servants. They rushed to the Jordan, where the king was. ¹⁸They crossed at the ford to take the king's household over and to do whatever he wished.

When Shimei son of Gera crossed the Jordan, he fell prostrate before the king ¹⁹and said to him, "May my lord not hold me guilty. Do not remember how your servant did wrong on the day my lord the king left Jerusalem. May the king put it out of his mind. ²⁰For I your servant know that I have sinned, but

* 18:33 is numbered 19:1 in Hebrew texts.   * 19:1-43 is numbered 19:2-44 in Hebrew texts.

today I have come here as the first of the whole house of Joseph to come down and meet my lord the king."

²¹Then Abishai son of Zeruiah said, "Shouldn't Shimei be put to death for this? He cursed the Lord's anointed."

²²David replied, "What does this have to do with you, you sons of Zeruiah? What right do you have to interfere? Should anyone be put to death in Israel today? Don't I know that today I am king over Israel?" ²³So the king said to Shimei, "You shall not die." And the king promised him on oath.

²⁴Mephibosheth, Saul's grandson, also went down to meet the king. He had not taken care of his feet or trimmed his mustache or washed his clothes from the day the king left until the day he returned safely. ²⁵When he came from Jerusalem to meet the king, the king asked him, "Why didn't you go with me, Mephibosheth?"

²⁶He said, "My lord the king, since I your servant am lame, I said, 'I will have my donkey saddled and will ride on it, so I can go with the king.' But Ziba my servant betrayed me. ²⁷And he has slandered your servant to my lord the king. My lord the king is like an angel of God; so do whatever you wish. ²⁸All my grandfather's descendants deserved nothing but death from my lord the king, but you gave your servant a place among those who eat at your table. So what right do I have to make any more appeals to the king?"

²⁹The king said to him, "Why say more? I order you and Ziba to divide the land."

³⁰Mephibosheth said to the king, "Let him take everything, now that my lord the king has returned home safely."

³¹Barzillai the Gileadite also came down from Rogelim to cross the Jordan with the king and to send him on his way from there. ³²Now Barzillai was very old, eighty years of age. He had provided for the king during his stay in Mahanaim, for he was a very wealthy man. ³³The king said to Barzillai, "Cross over with me and stay with me in Jerusalem, and I will provide for you."

³⁴But Barzillai answered the king, "How many more years will I live, that I should go up to Jerusalem with the king? ³⁵I am now eighty years old. Can I tell the difference between what is enjoyable and what is not? Can your servant taste what he eats and drinks? Can I still hear the voices of male and female singers? Why should your servant be an added burden to my lord the king? ³⁶Your servant will cross over the Jordan with the king for a short distance, but why should the king reward me in this way? ³⁷Let your servant return, that I may die in my own town near the tomb of my father and mother. But here is your servant Kimham. Let him cross over with my lord the king. Do for him whatever you wish."

³⁸The king said, "Kimham shall cross over with me, and I will do for him whatever you wish. And anything you desire from me I will do for you."

³⁹So all the people crossed the Jordan, and then the king crossed over. The king kissed Barzillai and bid him farewell, and Barzillai returned to his home.

⁴⁰When the king crossed over to Gilgal, Kimham crossed with him. All the troops of Judah and half the troops of Israel had taken the king over.

⁴¹Soon all the men of Israel were coming to the king and saying to him, "Why did our brothers, the men of Judah, steal the king away and bring him and his household across the Jordan, together with all his men?"

⁴²All the men of Judah answered the men of Israel, "We did this because the king is closely related to us. Why are you angry about it? Have we eaten any of the king's provisions? Have we taken anything for ourselves?"

⁴³Then the men of Israel answered the men of Judah, "We have ten shares in the king; so we have a greater claim on David than you have. Why then do you treat us with contempt? Weren't we the first to speak of bringing back our king?"

But the men of Judah responded even more harshly than the men of Israel.

Sheba Rebels Against David

20 Now a troublemaker named Sheba son of Bikri, a Benjamite, happened to be there. He sounded the trumpet and shouted,

> "We have no share in David,
>   no part in Jesse's son!
> Everyone to your tents, Israel!"

²So all the men of Israel deserted David to follow Sheba son of Bikri. But the men of Judah stayed by their king all the way from the Jordan to Jerusalem.

³When David returned to his palace in Jerusalem, he took the ten concubines he had left to take care of the palace and put them in a house under guard. He provided for them but had no sexual relations with them. They were kept in confinement till the day of their death, living as widows.

⁴Then the king said to Amasa, "Summon the men of Judah to come to me within three days, and be here yourself." ⁵But when Amasa went to summon Judah, he took longer than the time the king had set for him.

⁶David said to Abishai, "Now Sheba son of Bikri will do us more harm than Absalom did. Take your master's men and pursue him, or he will find fortified cities and escape from us." *ᵃ* ⁷So Joab's men and the Kerethites and Pelethites and all the mighty warriors went out under the command of Abishai. They marched out from Jerusalem to pursue Sheba son of Bikri.

⁸While they were at the great rock in Gibeon, Amasa came to meet them. Joab was wearing his military tunic, and strapped over it at his waist was a belt with a dagger in its sheath. As he stepped forward, it dropped out of its sheath.

⁹Joab said to Amasa, "How are you, my brother?" Then Joab took Amasa by the beard with his right hand to kiss him. ¹⁰Amasa was not on his guard against the dagger in Joab's hand, and Joab plunged it into his belly, and his intestines spilled out on the ground. Without being stabbed again, Amasa died. Then Joab and his brother Abishai pursued Sheba son of Bikri.

¹¹One of Joab's men stood beside Amasa and said, "Whoever favors Joab, and whoever is for David, let him follow Joab!" ¹²Amasa lay wallowing in his blood in the middle of the road, and the man saw that all the troops came to a halt there. When he realized that everyone who came up to Amasa stopped, he dragged him from the road into a field and threw a garment over him. ¹³After Amasa had been removed from the road, everyone went on with Joab to pursue Sheba son of Bikri.

¹⁴Sheba passed through all the tribes of Israel to Abel Beth Maakah and through the entire region of the Bikrites,*ᵇ* who gathered together and followed him. ¹⁵All the troops with Joab came and besieged Sheba in Abel Beth Maakah. They built a siege ramp up to the city, and it stood against the outer fortifications. While they were battering the wall to bring it down, ¹⁶a wise woman called from the city, "Listen! Listen! Tell Joab to come here so I can speak to him." ¹⁷He went toward her, and she asked, "Are you Joab?"

"I am," he answered.

She said, "Listen to what your servant has to say."

"I'm listening," he said.

¹⁸She continued, "Long ago they used to say, 'Get your answer at Abel,' and that settled it. ¹⁹We are the peaceful and faithful in Israel. You are trying to destroy a city that is a mother in Israel. Why do you want to swallow up the Lᴏʀᴅ's inheritance?"

²⁰"Far be it from me!" Joab replied, "Far be it from me to swallow up or destroy! ²¹That is not the case. A man named Sheba son of Bikri, from the hill country of Ephraim, has lifted up his hand against the king, against David. Hand over this one man, and I'll withdraw from the city."

The woman said to Joab, "His head will be thrown to you from the wall."

²²Then the woman went to all the people with her wise advice, and they cut off the head of Sheba son of Bikri and threw it to Joab. So he sounded the trumpet, and his men dispersed from the city, each returning to his home. And Joab went back to the king in Jerusalem.

David's Officials

²³Joab was over Israel's entire army; Benaiah son of Jehoiada was over the Kerethites and Pelethites; ²⁴Adoniram*ᶜ* was in charge of forced labor; Jehoshaphat son of Ahilud was recorder; ²⁵Sheva was secretary; Zadok and Abiathar were priests; ²⁶and Ira the Jairite*ᵈ* was David's priest.

ᵃ 6 Or *and do us serious injury*   *ᵇ 14* See Septuagint and Vulgate; Hebrew *Berites*.   *ᶜ 24* Some Septuagint manuscripts (see also 1 Kings 4:6 and 5:14); Hebrew *Adoram*   *ᵈ 26* Hebrew; some Septuagint manuscripts and Syriac (see also 2 Samuel 23:38) *Ithrite*

The Gibeonites Avenged

21 During the reign of David, there was a famine for three successive years; so David sought the face of the LORD. The LORD said, "It is on account of Saul and his blood-stained house; it is because he put the Gibeonites to death."

HE IS: approachable

21:1 Saul's past sins brought famine upon David's kingdom. In the Old Testament, famine was often a sign of God's judgment. Rather than planting crops more aggressively or rationing food, David sought the Lord's face. God revealed that the answer to the famine was to take action and right the prior wrongs.

Perhaps an old habit from your past is preventing you from growing in your faith. Or a wrong relationship is keeping you from becoming closer to God. If you're in a spiritual famine, seek the Lord's face. Ask him what you need to change. He is always *approachable*.

For the next He Is, go to p. 410.

For the next He Is, go to p. 410.

409

²The king summoned the Gibeonites and spoke to them. (Now the Gibeonites were not a part of Israel but were survivors of the Amorites; the Israelites had sworn to spare them, but Saul in his zeal for Israel and Judah had tried to annihilate them.) ³David asked the Gibeonites, "What shall I do for you? How shall I make atonement so that you will bless the LORD's inheritance?"

⁴The Gibeonites answered him, "We have no right to demand silver or gold from Saul or his family, nor do we have the right to put anyone in Israel to death."

"What do you want me to do for you?" David asked.

⁵They answered the king, "As for the man who destroyed us and plotted against us so that we have been decimated and have no place anywhere in Israel, ⁶let seven of his male descendants be given to us to be killed and their bodies exposed before the LORD at Gibeah of Saul—the LORD's chosen one."

So the king said, "I will give them to you."

⁷The king spared Mephibosheth son of Jonathan, the son of Saul, because of the oath before the LORD between David and Jonathan son of Saul. ⁸But the king took Armoni and Mephibosheth, the two sons of Aiah's daughter Rizpah, whom she had borne to Saul, together with the five sons of Saul's daughter Merab,ᵃ whom she had borne to Adriel son of Barzillai the Meholathite. ⁹He handed them over to the Gibeonites, who killed them and exposed their bodies on a hill before the LORD. All seven of them fell together; they were put to death during the first days of the harvest, just as the barley harvest was beginning.

¹⁰Rizpah daughter of Aiah took sackcloth and spread it out for herself on a rock. From the beginning of the harvest till the rain poured down from the heavens on the bodies, she did not let the birds touch them by day or the wild animals by night. ¹¹When David was told what Aiah's daughter Rizpah, Saul's concubine, had done, ¹²he went and took the bones of Saul and his son Jonathan from the citizens of Jabesh Gilead. (They had stolen their bodies from the public square at Beth Shan, where the Philistines had hung them after they struck Saul down on Gilboa.) ¹³David brought the bones of Saul and his son Jonathan from there, and the bones of those who had been killed and exposed were gathered up.

¹⁴They buried the bones of Saul and his son Jonathan in the tomb of Saul's father Kish, at Zela in Benjamin, and did everything the king commanded. After that, God answered prayer in behalf of the land.

Wars Against the Philistines

¹⁵Once again there was a battle between the Philistines and Israel. David went down with his men to fight against the Philistines, and he became exhausted. ¹⁶And Ishbi-Benob, one of the descendants of

---

ᵃ *8 Two Hebrew manuscripts, some Septuagint manuscripts and Syriac (see also 1 Samuel 18:19); most Hebrew and Septuagint manuscripts *Michal*

Rapha, whose bronze spearhead weighed three hundred shekels*ᵃ* and who was armed with a new ˌswordˌ, said he would kill David. ¹⁷But Abishai son of Zeruiah came to David's rescue; he struck the Philistine down and killed him. Then David's men swore to him, saying, "Never again will you go out with us to battle, so that the lamp of Israel will not be extinguished."

¹⁸In the course of time, there was another battle with the Philistines, at Gob. At that time Sibbekai the Hushathite killed Saph, one of the descendants of Rapha.

¹⁹In another battle with the Philistines at Gob, Elhanan son of Jair*ᵇ* the Bethlehemite killed the brother of*ᶜ* Goliath the Gittite, who had a spear with a shaft like a weaver's rod.

²⁰In still another battle, which took place at Gath, there was a huge man with six fingers on each hand and six toes on each foot—twenty-four in all. He also was descended from Rapha. ²¹When he taunted Israel, Jonathan son of Shimeah, David's brother, killed him.

²²These four were descendants of Rapha in Gath, and they fell at the hands of David and his men.

David's Song of Praise

22 David sang to the Lᴏʀᴅ the words of this song when the Lᴏʀᴅ delivered him from the hand of all his enemies and from the hand of Saul. ²He said:

> "The Lᴏʀᴅ is my rock, my fortress and my deliverer;
> ³   my God is my rock, in whom I take refuge,
>   my shield*ᵈ* and the horn*ᵉ* of my salvation.
> He is my stronghold, my refuge and my savior—
>   from violent people you save me.
>
> ⁴"I called to the Lᴏʀᴅ, who is worthy of praise,
>   and have been saved from my enemies.
> ⁵The waves of death swirled about me;
>   the torrents of destruction overwhelmed me.
> ⁶The cords of the grave coiled around me;
>   the snares of death confronted me.

HE IS: victorious

22:1–4 Winning the final battles and nearing the end of his life, David sang a song of thanks, proclaiming that the Lord had delivered him from all his enemies. God had proven time and again to David and the Israelites the he is *victorious*.

Though it sometimes seems like life is one battle after another, you can trust God to be your rock, fortress and deliverer. Whether you're nearing the end of this earthly life or you still have many battles ahead, you will find victory in your *victorious* God, your refuge and savior.

For the next He Is, go to p. 424.

> ⁷"In my distress I called to the Lᴏʀᴅ;
>   I called out to my God.
> From his temple he heard my voice;
>   my cry came to his ears.
> ⁸The earth trembled and quaked,
>   the foundations of the heavens*ᶠ* shook;
>   they trembled because he was angry.

ᵃ 16 That is, about 7 1/2 pounds or about 3.5 kilograms   ᵇ 19 See 1 Chron. 20:5; Hebrew Jaare-Oregim.   ᶜ 19 See 1 Chron. 20:5; Hebrew does not have the brother of.   ᵈ 3 Or sovereign   ᵉ 3 Horn here symbolizes strength.   ᶠ 8 Hebrew; Vulgate and Syriac (see also Psalm 18:7) mountains

⁹Smoke rose from his nostrils;
  consuming fire came from his
    mouth,
  burning coals blazed out of it.
¹⁰He parted the heavens and came down;
  dark clouds were under his feet.
¹¹He mounted the cherubim and flew;
  he soared*ᵃ* on the wings of the wind.
¹²He made darkness his canopy around
    him—
  the dark*ᵇ* rain clouds of the sky.
¹³Out of the brightness of his presence
  bolts of lightning blazed forth.
¹⁴The LORD thundered from heaven;
  the voice of the Most High resounded.
¹⁵He shot his arrows and scattered the
    enemy,
  with great bolts of lightning he routed them.
¹⁶The valleys of the sea were exposed
  and the foundations of the earth laid bare
at the rebuke of the LORD,
  at the blast of breath from his nostrils.

¹⁷"He reached down from on high and took hold of me;
  he drew me out of deep waters.
¹⁸He rescued me from my powerful enemy,
  from my foes, who were too strong for me.
¹⁹They confronted me in the day of my disaster,
  but the LORD was my support.
²⁰He brought me out into a spacious place;
  he rescued me because he delighted in me.

²¹"The LORD has dealt with me according to my righteousness;
  according to the cleanness of my hands he has rewarded me.
²²For I have kept the ways of the LORD;
  I am not guilty of turning from my God.
²³All his laws are before me;
  I have not turned away from his decrees.
²⁴I have been blameless before him
  and have kept myself from sin.
²⁵The LORD has rewarded me according to my righteousness,
  according to my cleanness*ᶜ* in his sight.

²⁶"To the faithful you show yourself faithful,
  to the blameless you show yourself blameless,
²⁷to the pure you show yourself pure,
  but to the devious you show yourself shrewd.
²⁸You save the humble,
  but your eyes are on the haughty to bring them low.
²⁹You, LORD, are my lamp;
  the LORD turns my darkness into light.

conversations

stress «» 22:7

1» What are several positive and negative ways you handle stress?

2» What are some long-term effects of stress in your life?

3» How does prayer help you cope with stress?

For more on **stress**, check the index.
For the next Conversations, go to p. 420.

411

ᵃ 11 Many Hebrew manuscripts (see also Psalm 18:10); most Hebrew manuscripts *appeared*   *ᵇ 12* Septuagint (see also Psalm 18:11); Hebrew *massed*
ᶜ 25 Hebrew; Septuagint and Vulgate (see also Psalm 18:24) *to the cleanness of my hands*

³⁰With your help I can advance against a troop*ᵃ*;
with my God I can scale a wall.

³¹"As for God, his way is perfect;
the Lord's word is flawless.
He shields all who take refuge in him.
³²For who is God besides the Lord?
And who is the Rock except our God?
³³It is God who arms me with strength*ᵇ*
and keeps my way secure.
³⁴He makes my feet like the feet of a deer
and causes me to stand on the heights.
³⁵He trains my hands for battle;
my arms can bend a bow of bronze.
³⁶You make your saving help my shield;
your help has made *ᶜ* me great.
³⁷You provide a broad path for my feet,
so that my ankles do not give way.

³⁸"I pursued my enemies and crushed them;
I did not turn back till they were destroyed.
³⁹I crushed them completely, and they could not rise;
they fell beneath my feet.
⁴⁰You armed me with strength for battle;
you humbled my adversaries before me.
⁴¹You made my enemies turn their backs in flight,
and I destroyed my foes.
⁴²They cried for help, but there was no one to save them—
to the Lord, but he did not answer.
⁴³I beat them as fine as the dust of the earth;
I pounded and trampled them like mud in the streets.

⁴⁴"You have delivered me from the attacks of the peoples;
you have preserved me as the head of nations.
People I did not know now serve me,
⁴⁵ foreigners cower before me;
as soon as they hear of me, they obey me.
⁴⁶They all lose heart;
they come trembling*ᵈ* from their strongholds.

⁴⁷"The Lord lives! Praise be to my Rock!
Exalted be my God, the Rock, my Savior!
⁴⁸He is the God who avenges me,
who puts the nations under me,
⁴⁹ who sets me free from my enemies.
You exalted me above my foes;
from violent people you rescued me.
⁵⁰Therefore I will praise you, Lord, among the nations;
I will sing the praises of your name.

ᵃ 30 Or *can run through a barricade* *ᵇ 33* Dead Sea Scrolls, some Septuagint manuscripts, Vulgate and Syriac (see also Psalm 18:32); Masoretic Text *who is my strong refuge* *ᶜ 36* Dead Sea Scrolls; Masoretic Text *shield; / you stoop down to make* *ᵈ 46* Some Septuagint manuscripts and Vulgate (see also Psalm 18:45); Masoretic Text *they arm themselves*

⁵¹"He gives his king great victories;
　he shows unfailing kindness to his anointed,
　to David and his descendants forever."

David's Last Words

23 These are the last words of David:

"The inspired utterance of David son of Jesse,
　the utterance of the man exalted by the Most High,
the man anointed by the God of Jacob,
　the hero of Israel's songs:

²"The Spirit of the LORD spoke through me;
　his word was on my tongue.
³The God of Israel spoke,
　the Rock of Israel said to me:
'When one rules over people in
　righteousness,
　when he rules in the fear of God,
⁴he is like the light of morning at sunrise
　on a cloudless morning,
like the brightness after rain
　that brings grass from the earth.'

⁵"If my house were not right with God,
　surely he would not have made with me
　an everlasting covenant,
　arranged and secured in every part;
surely he would not bring to fruition my
　salvation
　and grant me my every desire.
⁶But evil men are all to be cast aside like
　thorns,
　which are not gathered with the hand.
⁷Whoever touches thorns
　uses a tool of iron or the shaft of a spear;
　they are burned up where they lie."

aussue:security

413

23:5 There are few things completely secure in this world. Husbands die or leave us, property is destroyed, investments fail, jobs end. These facts of life shouldn't depress us but should instead wake us up. When we honestly face these possibilities, we are able to recognize true security. In David's last words, he spoke of God's promise to him as eternal and final. He knew God would never break his promise. God's promise to love you unconditionally and completely is the one secure thing that you can count on in life.

David's Mighty Warriors

⁸These are the names of David's mighty warriors:

Josheb-Basshebeth,ᵃ a Tahkemonite,ᵇ was chief of the Three; he raised his spear against eight hundred men, whom he killedᶜ in one encounter.

⁹Next to him was Eleazar son of Dodai the Ahohite. As one of the three mighty warriors, he was with David when they taunted the Philistines gathered ⌐at Pas Dammim.ᵈ for battle. Then the Israelites retreated, ¹⁰but Eleazar stood his ground and struck down the Philistines till his hand grew tired and froze to the sword. The LORD brought about a great victory that day. The troops returned to Eleazar, but only to strip the dead.

¹¹Next to him was Shammah son of Agee the Hararite. When the Philistines banded together at a place where there was a field full of lentils, Israel's troops fled from them. ¹²But Shammah took his stand in the middle of the field. He defended it and struck the Philistines down, and the LORD brought about a great victory.

ᵃ *8* Hebrew; some Septuagint manuscripts suggest *Ish-Bosheth,* that is, *Esh-Baal* (see also 1 Chron. 11:11 *Jashobeam*).　ᵇ *8* Probably a variant of *Hakmonite* (see 1 Chron. 11:11)　ᶜ *8* Some Septuagint manuscripts (see also 1 Chron. 11:11); Hebrew and other Septuagint manuscripts *Three; it was Adino the Eznite who killed eight hundred men*　ᵈ *9* See 1 Chron. 11:13; Hebrew *gathered there.*

¹³During harvest time, three of the thirty chief warriors came down to David at the cave of Adullam, while a band of Philistines was encamped in the Valley of Rephaim. ¹⁴At that time David was in the stronghold, and the Philistine garrison was at Bethlehem. ¹⁵David longed for water and said, "Oh, that someone would get me a drink of water from the well near the gate of Bethlehem!" ¹⁶So the three mighty warriors broke through the Philistine lines, drew water from the well near the gate of Bethlehem and carried it back to David. But he refused to drink it; instead, he poured it out before the LORD. ¹⁷"Far be it from me, LORD, to do this!" he said. "Is it not the blood of men who went at the risk of their lives?" And David would not drink it.

Such were the exploits of the three mighty warriors.

¹⁸Abishai the brother of Joab son of Zeruiah was chief of the Three.^{*a*} He raised his spear against three hundred men, whom he killed, and so he became as famous as the Three. ¹⁹Was he not held in greater honor than the Three? He became their commander, even though he was not included among them.

²⁰Benaiah son of Jehoiada, a valiant fighter from Kabzeel, performed great exploits. He struck down Moab's two mightiest warriors. He also went down into a pit on a snowy day and killed a lion. ²¹And he struck down a huge Egyptian. Although the Egyptian had a spear in his hand, Benaiah went against him with a club. He snatched the spear from the Egyptian's hand and killed him with his own spear. ²²Such were the exploits of Benaiah son of Jehoiada; he too was as famous as the three mighty warriors. ²³He was held in greater honor than any of the Thirty, but he was not included among the Three. And David put him in charge of his bodyguard.

²⁴Among the Thirty were:

    Asahel the brother of Joab,

    Elhanan son of Dodo from Bethlehem,

  ²⁵Shammah the Harodite,

    Elika the Harodite,

  ²⁶Helez the Paltite,

    Ira son of Ikkesh from Tekoa,

  ²⁷Abiezer from Anathoth,

    Sibbekai^{*b*} the Hushathite,

  ²⁸Zalmon the Ahohite,

    Maharai the Netophathite,

  ²⁹Heled^{*c*} son of Baanah the Netophathite,

    Ithai son of Ribai from Gibeah in Benjamin,

  ³⁰Benaiah the Pirathonite,

    Hiddai^{*d*} from the ravines of Gaash,

  ³¹Abi-Albon the Arbathite,

    Azmaveth the Barhumite,

  ³²Eliahba the Shaalbonite,

    the sons of Jashen,

    Jonathan ³³son of^{*e*} Shammah the Hararite,

    Ahiam son of Sharar^{*f*} the Hararite,

  ³⁴Eliphelet son of Ahasbai the Maakathite,

    Eliam son of Ahithophel the Gilonite,

  ³⁵Hezro the Carmelite,

    Paarai the Arbite,

  ³⁶Igal son of Nathan from Zobah,

    the son of Hagri,^{*g*}

  ³⁷Zelek the Ammonite,

    Naharai the Beerothite, the armor-bearer of Joab son of Zeruiah,

^{*a*} *18* Most Hebrew manuscripts (see also 1 Chron. 11:20); two Hebrew manuscripts and Syriac *Thirty*   ^{*b*} *27* Some Septuagint manuscripts (see also 21:18; 1 Chron. 11:29); Hebrew *Mebunnai*   ^{*c*} *29* Some Hebrew manuscripts and Vulgate (see also 1 Chron. 11:30); most Hebrew manuscripts *Heleb*   ^{*d*} *30* Hebrew; some Septuagint manuscripts (see also 1 Chron. 11:32) *Hurai*   ^{*e*} *33* Some Septuagint manuscripts (see also 1 Chron. 11:34); Hebrew does not have *son of.*   ^{*f*} *33* Hebrew; some Septuagint manuscripts (see also 1 Chron. 11:35) *Sakar*   ^{*g*} *36* Some Septuagint manuscripts (see also 1 Chron. 11:38); Hebrew *Haggadi*

³⁸ Ira the Ithrite,
Gareb the Ithrite
³⁹ and Uriah the Hittite.
There were thirty-seven in all.

David Enrolls the Fighting Men

24 Again the anger of the LORD burned against Israel, and he incited David against them, saying, "Go and take a census of Israel and Judah."

²So the king said to Joab and the army commanders^a with him, "Go throughout the tribes of Israel from Dan to Beersheba and enroll the fighting men, so that I may know how many there are."

³But Joab replied to the king, "May the LORD your God multiply the troops a hundred times over, and may the eyes of my lord the king see it. But why does my lord the king want to do such a thing?"

⁴The king's word, however, overruled Joab and the army commanders; so they left the presence of the king to enroll the fighting men of Israel.

⁵After crossing the Jordan, they camped near Aroer, south of the town in the gorge, and then went through Gad and on to Jazer. ⁶They went to Gilead and the region of Tahtim Hodshi, and on to Dan Jaan and around toward Sidon. ⁷Then they went toward the fortress of Tyre and all the towns of the Hivites and Canaanites. Finally, they went on to Beersheba in the Negev of Judah.

⁸After they had gone through the entire land, they came back to Jerusalem at the end of nine months and twenty days.

⁹Joab reported the number of the fighting men to the king: In Israel there were eight hundred thousand able-bodied men who could handle a sword, and in Judah five hundred thousand.

¹⁰David was conscience-stricken after he had counted the fighting men, and he said to the LORD, "I have sinned greatly in what I have done. Now, LORD, I beg you, take away the guilt of your servant. I have done a very foolish thing."

¹¹Before David got up the next morning, the word of the LORD had come to Gad the prophet, David's seer: ¹²"Go and tell David, 'This is what the LORD says: I am giving you three options. Choose one of them for me to carry out against you.'"

¹³So Gad went to David and said to him, "Shall there come on you three^b years of famine in your land? Or three months of fleeing from your enemies while they pursue you? Or three days of plague in your land? Now then, think it over and decide how I should answer the one who sent me."

¹⁴David said to Gad, "I am in deep distress. Let us fall into the hands of the LORD, for his mercy is great; but do not let me fall into human hands."

¹⁵So the LORD sent a plague on Israel from that morning until the end of the time designated, and seventy thousand of the people from Dan to Beersheba died. ¹⁶When the angel stretched out his hand to destroy Jerusalem, the LORD relented concerning the disaster and said to the angel who was afflicting the people, "Enough! Withdraw your hand." The angel of the LORD was then at the threshing floor of Araunah the Jebusite.

¹⁷When David saw the angel who was striking down the people, he said to the LORD, "I have sinned; I, the shepherd,^c have done wrong. These are but sheep. What have they done? Let your hand fall on me and my family."

David Builds an Altar

¹⁸On that day Gad went to David and said to him, "Go up and build an altar to the LORD on the threshing floor of Araunah the Jebusite." ¹⁹So David went up, as the LORD had commanded through Gad. ²⁰When Araunah looked and saw the king and his officials coming toward him, he went out and bowed down before the king with his face to the ground.

²¹Araunah said, "Why has my lord the king come to his servant?"

"To buy your threshing floor," David answered, "so I can build an altar to the LORD, that the plague on the people may be stopped."

415

---

^a *2* Septuagint (see also verse 4 and 1 Chron. 21:2); Hebrew *Joab the army commander*   ^b *13* Septuagint (see also 1 Chron. 21:12); Hebrew *seven*   ^c *17* Dead Sea Scrolls and Septuagint; Masoretic Text does not have *the shepherd.*

myth# 27 "IT MUST HAVE BEEN MY FAULT. I SHOULD HAVE DONE SOMETHING."

I get so angry with myself sometimes when something bad happens. I worry that I've blown it somehow or with someone or that I've failed in some way. Oh, I know I shouldn't say that. But that's the reality. I feel buried under a load of guilt sometimes.

Take my nine-year-old daughter Zoë's recent D in her science class. For weeks afterward I wondered if I could have helped her more or motivated her more (although I told her over and over, "Zoë, you've got to work harder").

Maybe if I had homeschooled my daughter instead of sending her to public school she'd be a better student. Maybe if her dad and I had stayed together instead of divorcing three years ago, she'd be a better student. As if I could've stopped Rick from going off with that woman he met in grad school. But . . . maybe I should've tried harder to save the marriage. Maybe if I hadn't nagged him so much . . .

My sister tells me, "Em, you worry too much. Didn't Jesus already die for everyone's sins?" That's her way of pointing out that I think I'm to blame for everything. I'm not neurotic. I just can't shake the feeling that I could do more—that all of this is my fault somehow.

—Emiko

A POPULAR PASTIME nowadays is the blame game. Many people who wish to avoid taking responsibility for an action choose to lay that blame on others: parents, friends, circumstance . . . the dog. After all, it must have been someone else's fault.

In contrast, others of us (especially us women) tend to go to the other extreme. Sometimes when we acknowledge personal responsibility, we might overdo it by accepting responsibility for things that we had no influence over or ability to change. We end up wallowing in guilt for our sins *and* everyone else's.

It's true that we all have blown it at some point or another. There are some actions that will result in difficult consequences that continue to haunt us. While our humanity isn't a license to commit every wrong under the sun, it is a reminder that no one is perfect. Only God is completely infallible.

However, some of us think that humility is expressed in thoughts of self-chastisement or guilt. But true humility involves a dependence on God's love and gratitude for his forgiveness. Once forgiven, we're no longer condemned.

The Bible has one story after another of Jesus' encounters with imperfect people. In one story in particular, the story of Zacchaeus (see Luke 19:1–10), Jesus chose to eat in the home of a man branded as a "sinner" by the rest of the community. Instead of condemning Zacchaeus, Jesus chose to befriend him. And instead of wallowing in the guilt of his past actions, Zacchaeus chose to accept Jesus' forgiveness, make amends and move on.

Jesus willingly died for us "while we were still sinners" (Romans 5:8) to allow all to be forgiven by God. Are you willing to forgive others? How about starting with yourself?

"80 percent of divorces are unilateral, rather than truly mutual, decisions. In other words, no amount of hard work can make your spouse remain committed to you."

—Frank F. Furstenberg, Jr. and Andrew J. Cherlin

417

"THere is now no condemnation For THOSe WHO are in CHRist Jesus."

ROMANS 8:1

SEE ALSO
Psalms 19:12
Luke 11:4
Colossians 1:13–14

For more on **Guilt,** check the index.

²²Araunah said to David, "Let my lord the king take whatever he wishes and offer it up. Here are oxen for the burnt offering, and here are threshing sledges and ox yokes for the wood. ²³Your Majesty, Araunah*ᵃ* gives all this to the king." Araunah also said to him, "May the LORD your God accept you."

²⁴But the king replied to Araunah, "No, I insist on paying you for it. I will not sacrifice to the LORD my God burnt offerings that cost me nothing."

So David bought the threshing floor and the oxen and paid fifty shekels*ᵇ* of silver for them. ²⁵David built an altar to the LORD there and sacrificed burnt offerings and fellowship offerings. Then the LORD answered his prayer in behalf of the land, and the plague on Israel was stopped.

ᵃ 23 Some Hebrew manuscripts and Septuagint; most Hebrew manuscripts *King Araunah*   *ᵇ 24* That is, about 1 1/4 pounds or about 575 grams

1 kings

419

AUTHOR
Unknown.

AUDIENCE
The people of Israel.

DATE
Originally, 1 and 2 Kings were one book,
probably written during the Israelites'
Babylonian exile, sometime between 560
and 550 B.C.

SETTING
David's faithful rule is the model for Israel's
future kings.

VERSE TO REMEMBER
"LORD, the God of Israel, there is no God like
you in heaven above or on earth below—
you who keep your covenant of love with
your servants who continue wholeheartedly
in your way." (8:23)

THEME TO CONSIDER
God's formula for success is simple: obedience yields blessing; disobedience yields
judgment.

Adonijah Sets Himself Up as King

1 When King David was very old, he could not keep warm even when they put covers over him. [2]So his attendants said to him, "Let us look for a young virgin to serve the king and take care of him. She can lie beside him so that our lord the king may keep warm."

[3]Then they searched throughout Israel for a beautiful girl and found Abishag, a Shunammite, and brought her to the king. [4]The girl was very beautiful; she took care of the king and waited on him, but the king had no sexual relations with her.

[5]Now Adonijah, whose mother was Haggith, put himself forward and said, "I will be king." So he got chariots and horses[a] ready, with fifty men to run ahead of him. [6](His father had never rebuked him by asking, "Why do you behave as you do?" He was also very handsome and was born next after Absalom.)

[7]Adonijah conferred with Joab son of Zeruiah and with Abiathar the priest, and they gave him their support. [8]But Zadok the priest, Benaiah son of Jehoiada, Nathan the prophet, Shimei and Rei and David's special guard did not join Adonijah.

[9]Adonijah then sacrificed sheep, cattle and fattened calves at the Stone of Zoheleth near En Rogel. He invited all his brothers, the king's sons, and all the royal officials of Judah, [10]but he did not invite Nathan the prophet or Benaiah or the special guard or his brother Solomon.

[11]Then Nathan asked Bathsheba, Solomon's mother, "Have you not heard that Adonijah, the son of Haggith, has become king, and our lord David knows nothing about it? [12]Now then, let me advise you how you can save your own life and the life of your son Solomon. [13]Go in to King David and say to him, 'My lord the king, did you not swear to me your servant: "Surely Solomon your son shall be king after me, and he will sit on my throne"? Why then has Adonijah become king?' [14]While you are still there talking to the king, I will come in and add my word to what you have said."

[15]So Bathsheba went to see the aged king in his room, where Abishag the Shunammite was attending him. [16]Bathsheba bowed down, prostrating herself before the king.

"What is it you want?" the king asked.

[17]She said to him, "My lord, you yourself swore to me your servant by the LORD your God: 'Solomon your son shall be king after me, and he will sit on my throne.' [18]But now Adonijah has become king, and you, my lord the king, do not know about it. [19]He has sacrificed great numbers of cattle, fattened calves, and sheep, and has invited all the king's sons, Abiathar the priest and Joab the commander of the army, but he has not invited Solomon your servant. [20]My lord the king, the eyes of all Israel are on you, to learn from you who will sit on the throne of my lord the king after him. [21]Otherwise, as soon as my lord the king is laid to rest with his ancestors, I and my son Solomon will be treated as criminals."

[22]While she was still speaking with the king, Nathan the prophet arrived. [23]And the king was told, "Nathan the prophet is here." So he went before the king and bowed with his face to the ground.

[24]Nathan said, "Have you, my lord the king, declared that Adonijah shall be king after you, and that he will sit on your throne? [25]Today he has gone down and sacrificed great numbers of cattle, fattened calves, and sheep. He has invited all the king's sons, the commanders of the army and Abiathar the priest. Right now they are eating and drinking with him and saying, 'Long live King Adonijah!' [26]But me your servant, and Zadok the priest, and Benaiah son of Jehoiada, and your servant Solomon he did not invite. [27]Is this something my lord the king has done without letting his servants know who should sit on the throne of my lord the king after him?"

"conversations"

parenting «» 1:6

1 » What is the goal of discipline?

2 » Do you know someone who grew up without any discipline? How has that affected her?

3 » What makes disciplining children so difficult?

For more on **parenting**, check the index. For the next Conversations, go to p. 423.

---

[a] 5 Or *charioteers*

David Makes Solomon King

²⁸Then King David said, "Call in Bathsheba." So she came into the king's presence and stood before him.

²⁹The king then took an oath: "As surely as the LORD lives, who has delivered me out of every trouble, ³⁰I will surely carry out this very day what I swore to you by the LORD, the God of Israel: Solomon your son shall be king after me, and he will sit on my throne in my place."

³¹Then Bathsheba bowed down with her face to the ground, prostrating herself before the king, and said, "May my lord King David live forever!"

³²King David said, "Call in Zadok the priest, Nathan the prophet and Benaiah son of Jehoiada." When they came before the king, ³³he said to them: "Take your lord's servants with you and have Solomon my son mount my own mule and take him down to Gihon. ³⁴There have Zadok the priest and Nathan the prophet anoint him king over Israel. Blow the trumpet and shout, 'Long live King Solomon!' ³⁵Then you are to go up with him, and he is to come and sit on my throne and reign in my place. I have appointed him ruler over Israel and Judah."

³⁶Benaiah son of Jehoiada answered the king, "Amen! May the LORD, the God of my lord the king, so declare it. ³⁷As the LORD was with my lord the king, so may he be with Solomon to make his throne even greater than the throne of my lord King David!"

³⁸So Zadok the priest, Nathan the prophet, Benaiah son of Jehoiada, the Kerethites and the Pelethites went down and had Solomon mount King David's mule, and they escorted him to Gihon. ³⁹Zadok the priest took the horn of oil from the sacred tent and anointed Solomon. Then they sounded the trumpet and all the people shouted, "Long live King Solomon!" ⁴⁰And all the people went up after him, playing pipes and rejoicing greatly, so that the ground shook with the sound.

⁴¹Adonijah and all the guests who were with him heard it as they were finishing their feast. On hearing the sound of the trumpet, Joab asked, "What's the meaning of all the noise in the city?"

⁴²Even as he was speaking, Jonathan son of Abiathar the priest arrived. Adonijah said, "Come in. A worthy man like you must be bringing good news."

⁴³"Not at all!" Jonathan answered. "Our lord King David has made Solomon king. ⁴⁴The king has sent with him Zadok the priest, Nathan the prophet, Benaiah son of Jehoiada, the Kerethites and the Pelethites, and they have put him on the king's mule, ⁴⁵and Zadok the priest and Nathan the prophet have anointed him king at Gihon. From there they have gone up cheering, and the city resounds with it. That's the noise you hear. ⁴⁶Moreover, Solomon has taken his seat on the royal throne. ⁴⁷Also, the royal officials have come to congratulate our lord King David, saying, 'May your God make Solomon's name more famous than yours and his throne greater than yours!' And the king bowed in worship on his bed ⁴⁸and said, 'Praise be to the LORD, the God of Israel, who has allowed my eyes to see a successor on my throne today.'"

⁴⁹At this, all Adonijah's guests rose in alarm and dispersed. ⁵⁰But Adonijah, in fear of Solomon, went and took hold of the horns of the altar. ⁵¹Then Solomon was told, "Adonijah is afraid of King Solomon and is clinging to the horns of the altar. He says, 'Let King Solomon swear to me today that he will not put his servant to death with the sword.'"

⁵²Solomon replied, "If he shows himself to be worthy, not a hair of his head will fall to the ground; but if evil is found in him, he will die." ⁵³Then King Solomon sent men, and they brought him down from the altar. And Adonijah came and bowed down to King Solomon, and Solomon said, "Go to your home."

David's Charge to Solomon

2 When the time drew near for David to die, he gave a charge to Solomon his son.

²"I am about to go the way of all the earth," he said. "So be strong, act like a man, ³and observe what the LORD your God requires: Walk in obedience to him, and keep his decrees and commands, his laws and regulations, as written in the Law of Moses. Do this so that you may prosper in all you do and wherever you go ⁴and that the LORD may keep his promise to me: 'If your descendants watch how they live, and if they walk faithfully before me with all their heart and soul, you will never fail to have a successor on the throne of Israel.'

⁵"Now you yourself know what Joab son of Zeruiah did to me—what he did to the two commanders of Israel's armies, Abner son of Ner and Amasa son of Jether. He killed them, shedding their blood in peacetime as if in battle, and with that blood he stained the belt around his waist and the sandals on his feet. ⁶Deal with him according to your wisdom, but do not let his gray head go down to the grave in peace.

⁷"But show kindness to the sons of Barzillai of Gilead and let them be among those who eat at your table. They stood by me when I fled from your brother Absalom.

⁸"And remember, you have with you Shimei son of Gera, the Benjamite from Bahurim, who called down bitter curses on me the day I went to Mahanaim. When he came down to meet me at the Jordan, I swore to him by the LORD: 'I will not put you to death by the sword.' ⁹But now, do not consider him innocent. You are a man of wisdom; you will know what to do to him. Bring his gray head down to the grave in blood."

¹⁰Then David rested with his ancestors and was buried in the City of David. ¹¹He had reigned forty years over Israel—seven years in Hebron and thirty-three in Jerusalem. ¹²So Solomon sat on the throne of his father David, and his rule was firmly established.

Solomon's Throne Established

¹³Now Adonijah, the son of Haggith, went to Bathsheba, Solomon's mother. Bathsheba asked him, "Do you come peacefully?"

He answered, "Yes, peacefully." ¹⁴Then he added, "I have something to say to you."

"You may say it," she replied.

¹⁵"As you know," he said, "the kingdom was mine. All Israel looked to me as their king. But things changed, and the kingdom has gone to my brother; for it has come to him from the LORD. ¹⁶Now I have one request to make of you. Do not refuse me."

"You may make it," she said.

¹⁷So he continued, "Please ask King Solomon—he will not refuse you—to give me Abishag the Shunammite as my wife."

¹⁸"Very well," Bathsheba replied, "I will speak to the king for you."

¹⁹When Bathsheba went to King Solomon to speak to him for Adonijah, the king stood up to meet her, bowed down to her and sat down on his throne. He had a throne brought for the king's mother, and she sat down at his right hand.

²⁰"I have one small request to make of you," she said. "Do not refuse me."

The king replied, "Make it, my mother; I will not refuse you."

²¹So she said, "Let Abishag the Shunammite be given in marriage to your brother Adonijah."

²²King Solomon answered his mother, "Why do you request Abishag the Shunammite for Adonijah? You might as well request the kingdom for him—after all, he is my older brother—yes, for him and for Abiathar the priest and Joab son of Zeruiah!"

²³Then King Solomon swore by the LORD: "May God deal with me, be it ever so severely, if Adonijah does not pay with his life for this request! ²⁴And now, as surely as the LORD lives—he who has established me securely on the throne of my father David and has founded a dynasty for me as he promised—Adonijah shall be put to death today!" ²⁵So King Solomon gave orders to Benaiah son of Jehoiada, and he struck down Adonijah and he died.

422

atissue:mentoring

2:1–12 Remember when you first considered yourself a grown woman? Who helped you understand what being a woman meant? Before he died, King David helped his son become a man by giving him royal advice. As women, we also must take over responsibilities, whether we like it or not. Few of us ever get clear instructions, as Solomon did, on how to do this. Now you may find yourself in a unique position to mentor younger women in their transition into womanhood. Is there someone in your life whom you could guide, as you would have wanted to be guided?

[26] To Abiathar the priest the king said, "Go back to your fields in Anathoth. You deserve to die, but I will not put you to death now, because you carried the ark of the Sovereign LORD before my father David and shared all my father's hardships." [27] So Solomon removed Abiathar from the priesthood of the LORD, fulfilling the word the LORD had spoken at Shiloh about the house of Eli.

[28] When the news reached Joab, who had conspired with Adonijah though not with Absalom, he fled to the tent of the LORD and took hold of the horns of the altar. [29] King Solomon was told that Joab had fled to the tent of the LORD and was beside the altar. Then Solomon ordered Benaiah son of Jehoiada, "Go, strike him down!"

[30] So Benaiah entered the tent of the LORD and said to Joab, "The king says, 'Come out!'"

But he answered, "No, I will die here."

Benaiah reported to the king, "This is how Joab answered me."

[31] Then the king commanded Benaiah, "Do as he says. Strike him down and bury him, and so clear me and my family line of the guilt of the innocent blood that Joab shed. [32] The LORD will repay him for the blood he shed, because without my father David knowing it he attacked two men and killed them with the sword. Both of them—Abner son of Ner, commander of Israel's army, and Amasa son of Jether, commander of Judah's army—were better men and more upright than he. [33] May the guilt of their blood rest on the head of Joab and his descendants forever. But on David and his descendants, his house and his throne, may there be the LORD's peace forever."

[34] So Benaiah son of Jehoiada went up and struck down Joab and killed him, and he was buried at his home out in the country. [35] The king put Benaiah son of Jehoiada over the army in Joab's position and replaced Abiathar with Zadok the priest.

[36] Then the king sent for Shimei and said to him, "Build yourself a house in Jerusalem and live there, but do not go anywhere else. [37] The day you leave and cross the Kidron Valley, you can be sure you will die; your blood will be on your own head."

[38] Shimei answered the king, "What you say is good. Your servant will do as my lord the king has said." And Shimei stayed in Jerusalem for a long time.

[39] But three years later, two of Shimei's slaves ran off to Achish son of Maakah, king of Gath, and Shimei was told, "Your slaves are in Gath." [40] At this, he saddled his donkey and went to Achish at Gath in search of his slaves. So Shimei went away and brought the slaves back from Gath.

[41] When Solomon was told that Shimei had gone from Jerusalem to Gath and had returned, [42] the king summoned Shimei and said to him, "Did I not make you swear by the LORD and warn you, 'On the day you leave to go anywhere else, you can be sure you will die'? At that time you said to me, 'What you say is good. I will obey.' [43] Why then did you not keep your oath to the LORD and obey the command I gave you?"

[44] The king also said to Shimei, "You know in your heart all the wrong you did to my father David. Now the LORD will repay you for your wrongdoing. [45] But King Solomon will be blessed, and David's throne will remain secure before the LORD forever."

[46] Then the king gave the order to Benaiah son of Jehoiada, and he went out and struck Shimei down and he died.

The kingdom was now established in Solomon's hands.

Solomon Asks for Wisdom

3 Solomon made an alliance with Pharaoh king of Egypt and married his daughter. He brought her to the City of David until he finished building his palace and the temple of the LORD, and the wall around Jerusalem. [2] The people, however, were still sacrificing at the high places, because a temple had not yet been built for the Name of the LORD. [3] Solomon showed his love for the LORD by walking according to the instructions given him by his father David, except that he offered sacrifices and burned incense on the high places.

conversations

leadership «» 3:3–9

1» What qualities must a good leader possess?

2» What is your personal leadership style?

3» Is a good leader born or made?

For more on **leadership**, check the index.
For the next Conversations, go to p. 434.

⁴The king went to Gibeon to offer sacrifices, for that was the most important high place, and Solomon offered a thousand burnt offerings on that altar. ⁵At Gibeon the LORD appeared to Solomon during the night in a dream, and God said, "Ask for whatever you want me to give you."

⁶Solomon answered, "You have shown great kindness to your servant, my father David, because he was faithful to you and righteous and upright in heart. You have continued this great kindness to him and have given him a son to sit on his throne this very day.

⁷"Now, LORD my God, you have made your servant king in place of my father David. But I am only a little child and do not know how to carry out my duties. ⁸Your servant is here among the people you have chosen, a great people, too numerous to count or number. ⁹So give your servant a discerning heart to govern your people and to distinguish between right and wrong. For who is able to govern this great people of yours?"

¹⁰The Lord was pleased that Solomon had asked for this. ¹¹So God said to him, "Since you have asked for this and not for long life or wealth for yourself, nor have asked for the death of your enemies but for discernment in administering justice, ¹²I will do what you have asked. I will give you a wise and discerning heart, so that there will never have been anyone like you, nor will there ever be. ¹³Moreover, I will give you what you have not asked for—both wealth and honor—so that in your lifetime you will have no equal among kings. ¹⁴And if you walk in obedience to me and keep my decrees and commands as David your father did, I will give you a long life." ¹⁵Then Solomon awoke—and he realized it had been a dream.

424

HE IS: giving

3:11–12 God made Solomon an incredible offer: "Ask for whatever you want me to give you." Imagine the possibilities! Solomon could have selfishly asked for a big kingdom and lots of money. Instead he selflessly asked God for discernment to distinguish between right and wrong. Gladly God granted his request and added wealth and honor.

Don't be afraid to tell God what you want—what you really, really want. He loves to be giving. And as you grow closer to him, you'll begin to pray for things that are what he wants for you (such as becoming more like him or asking for the wisdom to help others). Ask for his will; he'll gladly give it and more (see Matthew 6:33)!

For the next He Is, go to p. 433.

He returned to Jerusalem, stood before the ark of the Lord's covenant and sacrificed burnt offerings and fellowship offerings. Then he gave a feast for all his court.

A Wise Ruling

¹⁶Now two prostitutes came to the king and stood before him. ¹⁷One of them said, "Pardon me, my lord. This woman and I live in the same house. I had a baby while she was there with me. ¹⁸The third day after my child was born, this woman also had a baby. We were alone; there was no one in the house but the two of us.

¹⁹"During the night this woman's son died because she lay on him. ²⁰So she got up in the middle of the night and took my son from my side while I your servant was asleep. She put him by her breast and put her dead son by my breast. ²¹The next morning, I got up to nurse my son—and he was dead! But when I looked at him closely in the morning light, I saw that it wasn't the son I had borne."

²²The other woman said, "No! The living one is my son; the dead one is yours."

But the first one insisted, "No! The dead one is yours; the living one is mine." And so they argued before the king.

²³The king said, "This one says, 'My son is alive and your son is dead,' while that one says, 'No! Your son is dead and mine is alive.'"

²⁴Then the king said, "Bring me a sword." So they brought a sword for the king. ²⁵He then gave an order: "Cut the living child in two and give half to one and half to the other."

²⁶The woman whose son was alive was deeply moved out of love for her son and said to the king, "Please, my lord, give her the living baby! Don't kill him!"

But the other said, "Neither I nor you shall have him. Cut him in two!"

²⁷Then the king gave his ruling: "Give the living baby to the first woman. Do not kill him; she is his mother."

²⁸When all Israel heard the verdict the king had given, they held the king in awe, because they saw that he had wisdom from God to administer justice.

Solomon's Officials and Governors

4 So King Solomon ruled over all Israel. ²And these were his chief officials:

Azariah son of Zadok—the priest;
³ Elihoreph and Ahijah, sons of Shisha—secretaries;
Jehoshaphat son of Ahilud—recorder;
⁴ Benaiah son of Jehoiada—commander in chief;
Zadok and Abiathar—priests;
⁵ Azariah son of Nathan—in charge of the district governors;
Zabud son of Nathan—a priest and adviser to the king;
⁶ Ahishar—palace administrator;
Adoniram son of Abda—in charge of forced labor.

⁷Solomon had twelve district governors over all Israel, who supplied provisions for the king and the royal household. Each one had to provide supplies for one month in the year. ⁸These are their names:

Ben-Hur—in the hill country of Ephraim;
⁹ Ben-Deker—in Makaz, Shaalbim, Beth Shemesh and Elon Bethhanan;
¹⁰ Ben-Hesed—in Arubboth (Sokoh and all the land of Hepher were his);
¹¹ Ben-Abinadab—in Naphoth Dor (he was married to Taphath daughter of Solomon);
¹² Baana son of Ahilud—in Taanach and Megiddo, and in all of Beth Shan next to Zarethan below
    Jezreel, from Beth Shan to Abel Meholah across to Jokmeam;
¹³ Ben-Geber—in Ramoth Gilead (the settlements of Jair son of Manasseh in Gilead were his, as well
    as the region of Argob in Bashan and its sixty large walled cities with bronze gate bars);
¹⁴ Ahinadab son of Iddo—in Mahanaim;
¹⁵ Ahimaaz—in Naphtali (he had married Basemath daughter of Solomon);
¹⁶ Baana son of Hushai—in Asher and in Aloth;
¹⁷ Jehoshaphat son of Paruah—in Issachar;
¹⁸ Shimei son of Ela—in Benjamin;
¹⁹ Geber son of Uri—in Gilead (the country of Sihon king of the Amorites and the country of Og king
    of Bashan). He was the only governor over the district.

425

Solomon's Daily Provisions

²⁰The people of Judah and Israel were as numerous as the sand on the seashore; they ate, they drank and they were happy. * ²¹And Solomon ruled over all the kingdoms from the Euphrates River to the land of the Philistines, as far as the border of Egypt. These countries brought tribute and were Solomon's subjects all his life.

²²Solomon's daily provisions were thirty cors ᵃ of the finest flour and sixty cors ᵇ of meal, ²³ten head of stall-fed cattle, twenty of pasture-fed cattle and a hundred sheep and goats, as well as deer, gazelles,

myth# 28 "I SHOULD LISTEN TO MY HEART."

All my life everyone's told me what to do, when to do it and even how to do it. Until finally, at age 34, I realized that I didn't know what I really wanted.

I knew I wanted to follow God. Every Christian probably does. I knew God expected obedience, but I felt confused about what God expected of me (career-wise and marriage-wise). Sure I could read the Bible. But it's not as if the Bible only has two pages in it, both of which talk about what God's will is for my life.

One day I was watching a movie in which one of the characters struggled with a decision. Another character—the wise mentor—said, "Listen to your heart. What does it tell you?" That advice seemed to make sense to the first character. Suddenly it made sense to me. I needed to listen to my heart. And over the next few weeks I kept hearing that same message— "Listen to your heart"—everywhere.

I thought listening to your heart meant being in tune with your feelings. So I listened to my feelings and got involved with Greg—a guy I met through a friend. Gorgeous Greg. All-wrong-for-me Greg. Being involved with him was a mistake, a blind mistake. Something that felt so right turned out to be so wrong. And suddenly life felt unbearable to me. How did my heart lead me so far off?

If that wasn't bad enough—and it was bad—I passed up an opportunity to take a short-term missions trip to Guatemala. Again, I listened to my heart—listened to the fears I had, really—and decided not to go. Some of my friends went. Based on what they said about the trip, I probably would've loved the experience, despite how inadequate I felt.

So now at age 35, I'm back to feeling confused.

—Gretchen

OUR SOCIETY LOVES and
lives by the mantra, "Listen to your heart."
Undoubtedly you've heard that in a movie or TV
show. That seemingly sage advice is inescapable.
On the surface, it sounds good, especially if
you're a person of high self-reliance or you're
known for your common sense. After all, is
there anyone who knows what you want better
than *you*? Or so we're told. But this advice has a
flaw—it leaves God out of the equation.

God knows us better than we know ourselves.
Our hearts are sometimes undiscovered country—terrain he's traversed long before we
explore it. The prophet Jeremiah warns us not
to depend on what our hearts tell us because
our hearts can deceive us (see Jeremiah 17:9).
Sometimes that strong urge of the heart is nothing but a gut, emotional reaction or the onset of
PMS. We don't always know what's best, and
ignoring what our Counselor tells us sets us up
for trouble.

God promises to offer guidance and wisdom to
live the kind of life that's pleasing to him. Better
still, he offers us the Holy Spirit who takes up
residence within us and provides personalized
guidance. (See John 14:16–17,26; 16:7–11.) And
God's overall will for our lives can be summed
up by two commandments, "Love the Lord your
God with all your heart and with all your soul
and with all your mind," and "Love your neighbor as yourself" (Matthew 22:37,39).

Instead of depending on what we feel is best,
we're invited to listen to the Holy Spirit. He'll
never steer us wrong. A heart in tune with God
is a heart worth listening to.

"When asked the basis on
which they form their moral
choices, nearly half of all
adults (44 percent) cited their
desire to do whatever will
bring them the most pleasing
or satisfying results. About one
out of four adults (24 percent)
lean primarily upon religious
principles and teaching or
Bible content when making
moral decisions."

—Barna Research Group (2001)

427

"I PRAY THAT
THE EYES OF YOUR
HEART MAY BE
ENLIGHTENED IN
ORDER THAT YOU
MAY KNOW THE
HOPE TO WHICH HE
HAS CALLED YOU."

EPHESIANS 1:18

SEE ALSO
Psalm 32:8
Psalm 37:4
Proverbs 3:5–6

For more on **Future** and **God's
Will,** check the index.

roebucks and choice fowl. ²⁴For he ruled over all the kingdoms west of the Euphrates River, from Tiphsah to Gaza, and had peace on all sides. ²⁵During Solomon's lifetime Judah and Israel, from Dan to Beersheba, lived in safety, everyone under their own vine and fig tree.

²⁶Solomon had four*ª thousand stalls for chariot horses, and twelve thousand horses.*ᵇ

²⁷The district governors, each in his month, supplied provisions for King Solomon and all who came to the king's table. They saw to it that nothing was lacking. ²⁸They also brought to the proper place their quotas of barley and straw for the chariot horses and the other horses.

Solomon's Wisdom

²⁹God gave Solomon wisdom and very great insight, and a breadth of understanding as measureless as the sand on the seashore. ³⁰Solomon's wisdom was greater than the wisdom of all the people of the East, and greater than all the wisdom of Egypt. ³¹He was wiser than anyone else, including Ethan the Ezrahite—wiser than Heman, Kalkol and Darda, the sons of Mahol. And his fame spread to all the surrounding nations. ³²He spoke three thousand proverbs and his songs numbered a thousand and five. ³³He spoke about plant life, from the cedar of Lebanon to the hyssop that grows out of walls. He also spoke about animals and birds, reptiles and fish. ³⁴From all nations people came to listen to Solomon's wisdom, sent by all the kings of the world, who had heard of his wisdom.

Preparations for Building the Temple

428

5 *When Hiram king of Tyre heard that Solomon had been anointed king to succeed his father David, he sent his envoys to Solomon, because he had always been on friendly terms with David. ²Solomon sent back this message to Hiram:

³"You know that because of the wars waged against my father David from all sides, he could not build a temple for the Name of the LORD his God until the LORD put his enemies under his feet. ⁴But now the LORD my God has given me rest on every side, and there is no adversary or disaster. ⁵I intend, therefore, to build a temple for the Name of the LORD my God, as the LORD told my father David, when he said, 'Your son whom I will put on the throne in your place will build the temple for my Name.'

⁶"So give orders that cedars of Lebanon be cut for me. My men will work with yours, and I will pay you for your men whatever wages you set. You know that we have no one so skilled in felling timber as the Sidonians."

⁷When Hiram heard Solomon's message, he was greatly pleased and said, "Praise be to the LORD today, for he has given David a wise son to rule over this great nation."

⁸So Hiram sent word to Solomon:

"I have received the message you sent me and will do all you want in providing the cedar and juniper logs. ⁹My men will haul them down from Lebanon to the Mediterranean Sea, and I will float them as rafts by sea to the place you specify. There I will separate them and you can take them away. And you are to grant my wish by providing food for my royal household."

¹⁰In this way Hiram kept Solomon supplied with all the cedar and juniper logs he wanted, ¹¹and Solomon gave Hiram twenty thousand cors*ᶜ of wheat as food for his household, in addition to twenty thousand baths*ᵈ,ᵉ of pressed olive oil. Solomon continued to do this for Hiram year after year. ¹²The LORD gave Solomon wisdom, just as he had promised him. There were peaceful relations between Hiram and Solomon, and the two of them made a treaty.

¹³King Solomon conscripted laborers from all Israel—thirty thousand men. ¹⁴He sent them off to Lebanon in shifts of ten thousand a month, so that they spent one month in Lebanon and two months at home. Adoniram was in charge of the forced labor. ¹⁵Solomon had seventy thousand carriers and eighty thousand stonecutters in the hills, ¹⁶as well as thirty-three hundred*ᶠ overseers who supervised

---

ª 26 Some Septuagint manuscripts (see also 2 Chron. 9:25); Hebrew *forty*   *ᵇ 26* Or *charioteers*   *ᶜ 11* That is, probably about 3,600 tons or about 3,250 metric tons   *ᵈ 11* Septuagint (see also 2 Chron. 2:10); Hebrew *twenty cors*   *ᵉ 11* That is, about 120,000 gallons or about 440,000 liters   *ᶠ 16* Hebrew; some Septuagint manuscripts (see also 2 Chron. 2:2, 18) *thirty-six hundred*

* 5:1–18 is numbered 5:15–32 in Hebrew texts.

the project and directed the work. ¹⁷At the king's command they removed from the quarry large blocks of high-grade stone to provide a foundation of dressed stone for the temple. ¹⁸The skilled workers of Solomon and Hiram and those from Byblos cut and prepared the timber and stone for the building of the temple.

Solomon Builds the Temple

6 In the four hundred and eightieth*ᵃ* year after the Israelites came out of Egypt, in the fourth year of Solomon's reign over Israel, in the month of Ziv, the second month, he began to build the temple of the Lord.

²The temple that King Solomon built for the Lord was sixty cubits long, twenty wide and thirty high.*ᵇ* ³The portico at the front of the main hall of the temple extended the width of the temple, that is twenty cubits,*ᶜ* and projected ten cubits*ᵈ* from the front of the temple. ⁴He made narrow windows high up in the temple walls. ⁵Against the walls of the main hall and inner sanctuary he built a structure around the building, in which there were side rooms. ⁶The lowest floor was five cubits*ᵉ* wide, the middle floor six cubits*ᶠ* and the third floor seven.*ᵍ* He made offset ledges around the outside of the temple so that nothing would be inserted into the temple walls.

⁷In building the temple, only blocks dressed at the quarry were used, and no hammer, chisel or any other iron tool was heard at the temple site while it was being built.

⁸The entrance to the lowest*ʰ* floor was on the south side of the temple; a stairway led up to the middle level and from there to the third. ⁹So he built the temple and completed it, roofing it with beams and cedar planks. ¹⁰And he built the side rooms all along the temple. The height of each was five cubits, and they were attached to the temple by beams of cedar.

¹¹The word of the Lord came to Solomon: ¹²"As for this temple you are building, if you follow my decrees, observe my laws and keep all my commands and obey them, I will fulfill through you the promise I gave to David your father. ¹³And I will live among the Israelites and will not abandon my people Israel."

¹⁴So Solomon built the temple and completed it. ¹⁵He lined its interior walls with cedar boards, paneling them from the floor of the temple to the ceiling, and covered the floor of the temple with planks of juniper. ¹⁶He partitioned off twenty cubits at the rear of the temple with cedar boards from floor to ceiling to form within the temple an inner sanctuary, the Most Holy Place. ¹⁷The main hall in front of this room was forty cubits*ⁱ* long. ¹⁸The inside of the temple was cedar, carved with gourds and open flowers. Everything was cedar; no stone was to be seen.

¹⁹He prepared the inner sanctuary within the temple to set the ark of the covenant of the Lord there. ²⁰The inner sanctuary was twenty cubits long, twenty wide and twenty high. He overlaid the inside with pure gold, and he also overlaid the altar of cedar. ²¹Solomon covered the inside of the temple with pure gold, and he extended gold chains across the front of the inner sanctuary, which was overlaid with gold. ²²So he overlaid the whole interior with gold. He also overlaid with gold the altar that belonged to the inner sanctuary.

²³For the inner sanctuary he made a pair of cherubim out of olive wood, each ten cubits high. ²⁴One wing of the first cherub was five cubits long, and the other wing five cubits—ten cubits from wing tip to wing tip. ²⁵The second cherub also measured ten cubits, for the two cherubim were identical in size and shape. ²⁶The height of each cherub was ten cubits. ²⁷He placed the cherubim inside the innermost room of the temple, with their wings spread out. The wing of one cherub touched one wall, while the wing of the other touched the other wall, and their wings touched each other in the middle of the room. ²⁸He overlaid the cherubim with gold.

²⁹On the walls all around the temple, in both the inner and outer rooms, he carved cherubim, palm trees and open flowers. ³⁰He also covered the floors of both the inner and outer rooms of the temple with gold.

ᵃ 1 Hebrew; Septuagint *four hundred and fortieth*   *ᵇ 2* That is, about 90 feet long, 30 feet wide and 45 feet high or about 27 meters long, 9 meters wide and 13.5 meters high   *ᶜ 3* That is, about 30 feet or about 9 meters; also in verses 16 and 20   *ᵈ 3* That is, about 15 feet or about 4.5 meters; also in verse 23   *ᵉ 6* That is, about 7 1/2 feet or about 2.3 meters; also in verses 10 and 24   *ᶠ 6* That is, about 9 feet or about 2.7 meters   *ᵍ 6* That is, about 10 1/2 feet or about 3.2 meters   *ʰ 8* Septuagint; Hebrew *middle*   *ⁱ 17* That is, about 60 feet or about 18 meters

³¹For the entrance to the inner sanctuary he made doors out of olive wood that were one fifth of the width of the sanctuary. ³²And on the two olive-wood doors he carved cherubim, palm trees and open flowers, and overlaid the cherubim and palm trees with hammered gold. ³³In the same way, for the entrance to the main hall he made doorframes out of olive wood that were one fourth of the width of the hall. ³⁴He also made two doors out of juniper wood, each having two leaves that turned in sockets. ³⁵He carved cherubim, palm trees and open flowers on them and overlaid them with gold hammered evenly over the carvings.

³⁶And he built the inner courtyard of three courses of dressed stone and one course of trimmed cedar beams.

³⁷The foundation of the temple of the Lord was laid in the fourth year, in the month of Ziv. ³⁸In the eleventh year in the month of Bul, the eighth month, the temple was finished in all its details according to its specifications. He had spent seven years building it.

Solomon Builds His Palace

7 It took Solomon thirteen years, however, to complete the construction of his palace. ²He built the Palace of the Forest of Lebanon a hundred cubits long, fifty wide and thirty high,^a with four rows of cedar columns supporting trimmed cedar beams. ³It was roofed with cedar above the beams that rested on the columns—forty-five beams, fifteen to a row. ⁴Its windows were placed high in sets of three, facing each other. ⁵All the doorways had rectangular frames; they were in the front part in sets of three, facing each other.^b

⁶He made a colonnade fifty cubits long and thirty wide.^c In front of it was a portico, and in front of that were pillars and an overhanging roof.

⁷He built the throne hall, the Hall of Justice, where he was to judge, and he covered it with cedar from floor to ceiling.^d ⁸And the palace in which he was to live, set farther back, was similar in design. Solomon also made a palace like this hall for Pharaoh's daughter, whom he had married.

⁹All these structures, from the outside to the great courtyard and from foundation to eaves, were made of blocks of high-grade stone cut to size and trimmed with a saw on their inner and outer faces. ¹⁰The foundations were laid with large stones of good quality, some measuring ten cubits^e and some eight.^f ¹¹Above were high-grade stones, cut to size, and cedar beams. ¹²The great courtyard was surrounded by a wall of three courses of dressed stone and one course of trimmed cedar beams, as was the inner courtyard of the temple of the Lord with its portico.

The Temple's Furnishings

¹³King Solomon sent to Tyre and brought Huram,^g ¹⁴whose mother was a widow from the tribe of Naphtali and whose father was from Tyre and a skilled worker in bronze. Huram was filled with wisdom, with understanding and with knowledge to do all kinds of bronze work. He came to King Solomon and did all the work assigned to him.

¹⁵He cast two bronze pillars, each eighteen cubits high and twelve cubits in circumference.^h ¹⁶He also made two capitals of cast bronze to set on the tops of the pillars; each capital was five cubitsⁱ high. ¹⁷A network of interwoven chains adorned the capitals on top of the pillars, seven for each capital. ¹⁸He made pomegranates in two rows^j encircling each network to decorate the capitals on top of the pillars.^k He did the same for each capital. ¹⁹The capitals on top of the pillars in the portico were in the shape of lilies, four cubits^l high. ²⁰On the capitals of both pillars, above the bowl-shaped part next to the network, were the two hundred pomegranates in rows all around. ²¹He erected the pillars at the portico of the temple. The pillar to the south he named Jakin^m and the one to the north Boaz.ⁿ ²²The capitals on top were in the shape of lilies. And so the work on the pillars was completed.

²³He made the Sea of cast metal, circular in shape, measuring ten cubits from rim to rim and five

---

^a *2* That is, about 150 feet long, 75 feet wide and 45 feet high or about 45 meters long, 22.5 meters wide and 13.5 meters high   ^b *5* The meaning of the Hebrew for this verse is uncertain.   ^c *6* That is, about 75 feet long and 45 feet wide or about 22.5 meters long and 13.5 meters wide   ^d *7* Vulgate and Syriac; Hebrew *floor*   ^e *10* That is, about 15 feet or about 4.5 meters; also in verse 23   ^f *10* That is, about 12 feet or about 3.6 meters   ^g *13* Hebrew *Hiram*, a variant of *Huram*; also in verses 40 and 45   ^h *15* That is, about 27 feet high and 18 feet in circumference or about 8.2 meters high and 5.4 meters in circumference   ⁱ *16* That is, about 7 1/2 feet or about 2.3 meters; also in verse 23   ^j *18* Two Hebrew manuscripts and Septuagint; most Hebrew manuscripts *made the pillars, and there were two rows*   ^k *18* Many Hebrew manuscripts and Syriac; most Hebrew manuscripts *pomegranates*   ^l *19* That is, about 6 feet or about 1.8 meters; also in verse 38   ^m *21* Jakin probably means *he establishes*.   ⁿ *21* Boaz probably means *in him is strength*.

cubits high. It took a line of thirty cubits^{*a*} to measure around it. ²⁴Below the rim, gourds encircled it—ten to a cubit. The gourds were cast in two rows in one piece with the Sea.

²⁵The Sea stood on twelve bulls, three facing north, three facing west, three facing south and three facing east. The Sea rested on top of them, and their hindquarters were toward the center. ²⁶It was a handbreadth^{*b*} in thickness, and its rim was like the rim of a cup, like a lily blossom. It held two thousand baths.^{*c*}

²⁷He also made ten movable stands of bronze; each was four cubits long, four wide and three high.^{*d*} ²⁸This is how the stands were made: They had side panels attached to uprights. ²⁹On the panels between the uprights were lions, bulls and cherubim—and on the uprights as well. Above and below the lions and bulls were wreaths of hammered work. ³⁰Each stand had four bronze wheels with bronze axles, and each had a basin resting on four supports, cast with wreaths on each side. ³¹On the inside of the stand there was an opening that had a circular frame one cubit^{*e*} deep. This opening was round, and with its basework it measured a cubit and a half.^{*f*} Around its opening there was engraving. The panels of the stands were square, not round. ³²The four wheels were under the panels, and the axles of the wheels were attached to the stand. The diameter of each wheel was a cubit and a half. ³³The wheels were made like chariot wheels; the axles, rims, spokes and hubs were all of cast metal.

³⁴Each stand had four handles, one on each corner, projecting from the stand. ³⁵At the top of the stand there was a circular band half a cubit^{*g*} deep. The supports and panels were attached to the top of the stand. ³⁶He engraved cherubim, lions and palm trees on the surfaces of the supports and on the panels, in every available space, with wreaths all around. ³⁷This is the way he made the ten stands. They were all cast in the same molds and were identical in size and shape.

³⁸He then made ten bronze basins, each holding forty baths^{*h*} and measuring four cubits across, one basin to go on each of the ten stands. ³⁹He placed five of the stands on the south side of the temple and five on the north. He placed the Sea on the south side, at the southeast corner of the temple. ⁴⁰He also made the pots^{*i*} and shovels and sprinkling bowls.

So Huram finished all the work he had undertaken for King Solomon in the temple of the Lord:

⁴¹ the two pillars;
the two bowl-shaped capitals on top of the pillars;
the two sets of network decorating the two bowl-shaped capitals on top of the pillars;
⁴² the four hundred pomegranates for the two sets of network (two rows of pomegranates for each
  network decorating the bowl-shaped capitals on top of the pillars);
⁴³ the ten stands with their ten basins;
⁴⁴ the Sea and the twelve bulls under it;
⁴⁵ the pots, shovels and sprinkling bowls.

All these objects that Huram made for King Solomon for the temple of the Lord were of burnished bronze. ⁴⁶The king had them cast in clay molds in the plain of the Jordan between Sukkoth and Zarethan. ⁴⁷Solomon left all these things unweighed, because there were so many; the weight of the bronze was not determined.

⁴⁸Solomon also made all the furnishings that were in the Lord's temple:

the golden altar;
the golden table on which was the bread of the Presence;
⁴⁹ the lampstands of pure gold (five on the right and five on the left, in front of the inner sanctuary);
the gold floral work and lamps and tongs;
⁵⁰ the pure gold basins, wick trimmers, sprinkling bowls, dishes and censers;

^{*a*} *23* That is, about 45 feet or about 13.5 meters   ^{*b*} *26* That is, about 3 inches or about 7.5 centimeters   ^{*c*} *26* That is, about 12,000 gallons or about 44,000 liters; the Septuagint does not have this sentence.   ^{*d*} *27* That is, about 6 feet long and wide and about 4 1/2 feet high or about 1.8 meters long and wide and 1.4 meters high   ^{*e*} *31* That is, about 18 inches or about 45 centimeters   ^{*f*} *31* That is, about 2 1/4 feet or about 67 centimeters; also in verse 32   ^{*g*} *35* That is, about 9 inches or about 22.5 centimeters   ^{*h*} *38* That is, about 240 gallons or about 880 liters   ^{*i*} *40* Many Hebrew manuscripts, Septuagint, Syriac and Vulgate (see also verse 45 and 2 Chron. 4:11); many other Hebrew manuscripts *basins*

and the gold sockets for the doors of the innermost room, the Most Holy Place, and also for the doors of the main hall of the temple.

⁵¹When all the work King Solomon had done for the temple of the LORD was finished, he brought in the things his father David had dedicated—the silver and gold and the furnishings—and he placed them in the treasuries of the LORD's temple.

The Ark Brought to the Temple

8 Then King Solomon summoned into his presence at Jerusalem the elders of Israel, all the heads of the tribes and the chiefs of the Israelite families, to bring up the ark of the LORD's covenant from Zion, the City of David. ²All the Israelites came together to King Solomon at the time of the festival in the month of Ethanim, the seventh month.

³When all the elders of Israel had arrived, the priests took up the ark, ⁴and they brought up the ark of the LORD and the tent of meeting and all the sacred furnishings in it. The priests and Levites carried them up, ⁵and King Solomon and the entire assembly of Israel that had gathered about him were before the ark, sacrificing so many sheep and cattle that they could not be recorded or counted.

⁶The priests then brought the ark of the LORD's covenant to its place in the inner sanctuary of the temple, the Most Holy Place, and put it beneath the wings of the cherubim. ⁷The cherubim spread their wings over the place of the ark and overshadowed the ark and its carrying poles. ⁸These poles were so long that their ends could be seen from the Holy Place in front of the inner sanctuary, but not from outside the Holy Place; and they are still there today. ⁹There was nothing in the ark except the two stone tablets that Moses had placed in it at Horeb, where the LORD made a covenant with the Israelites after they came out of Egypt.

¹⁰When the priests withdrew from the Holy Place, the cloud filled the temple of the LORD. ¹¹And the priests could not perform their service because of the cloud, for the glory of the LORD filled his temple.

¹²Then Solomon said, "The LORD has said that he would dwell in a dark cloud; ¹³I have indeed built a magnificent temple for you, a place for you to dwell forever."

¹⁴While the whole assembly of Israel was standing there, the king turned around and blessed them. ¹⁵Then he said:

"Praise be to the LORD, the God of Israel, who with his own hand has fulfilled what he promised with his own mouth to my father David. For he said, ¹⁶'Since the day I brought my people Israel out of Egypt, I have not chosen a city in any tribe of Israel to have a temple built that my Name might be there, but I have chosen David to rule my people Israel.'

¹⁷"My father David had it in his heart to build a temple for the Name of the LORD, the God of Israel. ¹⁸But the LORD said to my father David, 'You did well to have it in your heart to build a temple for my Name. ¹⁹Nevertheless, you are not the one to build the temple, but your son, who is your own flesh and blood—he is the one who will build the temple for my Name.'

²⁰"The LORD has kept the promise he made: I have succeeded David my father and now I sit on the throne of Israel, just as the LORD promised, and I have built the temple for the Name of the LORD, the God of Israel. ²¹I have provided a place there for the ark, in which is the covenant of the LORD that he made with our ancestors when he brought them out of Egypt."

Solomon's Prayer of Dedication

²²Then Solomon stood before the altar of the LORD in front of the whole assembly of Israel, spread out his hands toward heaven ²³and said:

"LORD, the God of Israel, there is no God like you in heaven above or on earth below—you who keep your covenant of love with your servants who continue wholeheartedly in your way. ²⁴You have kept your promise to your servant David my father; with your mouth you have promised and with your hand you have fulfilled it—as it is today.

²⁵"Now LORD, the God of Israel, keep for your servant David my father the promises you made to him when you said, 'You shall never fail to have a successor to sit before me on the throne of Israel,

if only your descendants are careful in all they do to walk before me faithfully as you have done.' ²⁶ And now, God of Israel, let your word that you promised your servant David my father come true.

²⁷ "But will God really dwell on earth? The heavens, even the highest heaven, cannot contain you. How much less this temple I have built! ²⁸ Yet give attention to your servant's prayer and his plea for mercy, LORD my God. Hear the cry and the prayer that your servant is praying in your presence this day. ²⁹ May your eyes be open toward this temple night and day, this place of which you said, 'My Name shall be there,' so that you will hear the prayer your servant prays toward this place. ³⁰ Hear the supplication of your servant and of your people Israel when they pray toward this place. Hear from heaven, your dwelling place, and when you hear, forgive.

HE IS: uncontainable

8:27–30 Solomon's temple was a breath-taking structure, yet he realized that even this magnificent building could not hold the *uncontainable* God. In awe Solomon acknowledged that not even the highest heaven could contain God. Even though God can't be contained by a building, he is always accessible. Nothing can restrain him from hearing the prayers of his people.

You don't have to go to a church, a chapel or a prayer room to pray to God. He does not limit your prayers to certain places or particular times. He is *uncontainable*. Wherever you go, he's there. Whatever you say, he's listening. When you cry out, he'll answer.

For the next He Is, go to p. 435.

433

³¹ "When anyone wrongs their neighbor and is required to take an oath and they come and swear the oath before your altar in this temple, ³² then hear from heaven and act. Judge between your servants, condemning the guilty by bringing down on their heads what they have done, and vindicating the innocent by treating them in accordance with their innocence.

³³ "When your people Israel have been defeated by an enemy because they have sinned against you, and when they turn back to you and give praise to your name, praying and making supplication to you in this temple, ³⁴ then hear from heaven and forgive the sin of your people Israel and bring them back to the land you gave to their ancestors.

³⁵ "When the heavens are shut up and there is no rain because your people have sinned against you, and when they pray toward this place and give praise to your name and turn from their sin because you have afflicted them, ³⁶ then hear from heaven and forgive the sin of your servants, your people Israel. Teach them the right way to live, and send rain on the land you gave your people for an inheritance.

³⁷ "When famine or plague comes to the land, or blight or mildew, locusts or grasshoppers, or when an enemy besieges them in any of their cities, whatever disaster or disease may come, ³⁸ and when a prayer or plea is made by anyone among your people Israel—being aware of the afflictions of their own hearts, and spreading out their hands toward this temple— ³⁹ then hear from heaven, your dwelling place. Forgive and act; deal with everyone according to all they do, since you know their hearts (for you alone know every human heart), ⁴⁰ so that they will fear you all the time they live in the land you gave our ancestors.

⁴¹ "As for the foreigners who do not belong to your people Israel but have come from a distant land because of your name— ⁴² for they will hear of your great name and your mighty hand and your outstretched arm—when they come and pray toward this temple, ⁴³ then hear from heaven, your dwelling place. Do whatever the foreigners ask of you, so that all the peoples of the earth may know your name and fear you, as do your own people Israel, and may know that this house I have built bears your Name.

⁴⁴"When your people go to war against their enemies, wherever you send them, and when they pray to the LORD toward the city you have chosen and the temple I have built for your Name, ⁴⁵then hear from heaven their prayer and their plea, and uphold their cause.

⁴⁶"When they sin against you—for there is no one who does not sin—and you become angry with them and give them over to their enemies, who take them captive to their own lands, far away or near; ⁴⁷and if they have a change of heart in the land where they are held captive, and repent and plead with you in the land of their captors and say, 'We have sinned, we have done wrong, we have acted wickedly'; ⁴⁸and if they turn back to you with all their heart and soul in the land of their enemies who took them captive, and pray to you toward the land you gave their ancestors, toward the city you have chosen and the temple I have built for your Name; ⁴⁹then from heaven, your dwelling place, hear their prayer and their plea, and uphold their cause. ⁵⁰And forgive your people, who have sinned against you; forgive all the offenses they have committed against you, and cause their captors to show them mercy; ⁵¹for they are your people and your inheritance, whom you brought out of Egypt, out of that iron-smelting furnace.

⁵²"May your eyes be open to your servant's plea and to the plea of your people Israel, and may you listen to them whenever they cry out to you. ⁵³For you singled them out from all the nations of the world to be your own inheritance, just as you declared through your servant Moses when you, Sovereign LORD, brought our ancestors out of Egypt."

"conversations"

racism «» 8:41–43

1» Why did God choose Israel, and what does that mean for people who are not Jewish?

2» Who are the people of God?

3» How does your church or group accept people that are different from them?

For more on racism, check the index.
For the next Conversations, go to p. 442.

⁵⁴When Solomon had finished all these prayers and supplications to the LORD, he rose from before the altar of the LORD, where he had been kneeling with his hands spread out toward heaven. ⁵⁵He stood and blessed the whole assembly of Israel in a loud voice, saying:

⁵⁶"Praise be to the LORD, who has given rest to his people Israel just as he promised. Not one word has failed of all the good promises he gave through his servant Moses. ⁵⁷May the LORD our God be with us as he was with our ancestors; may he never leave us nor forsake us. ⁵⁸May he turn our hearts to him, to walk in obedience to him and keep the commands, decrees and laws he gave our ancestors. ⁵⁹And may these words of mine, which I have prayed before the LORD, be near to the LORD our God day and night, that he may uphold the cause of his servant and the cause of his people Israel according to each day's need, ⁶⁰so that all the peoples of the earth may know that the LORD is God and that there is no other. ⁶¹And may your hearts be fully committed to the LORD our God, to live by his decrees and obey his commands, as at this time."

The Dedication of the Temple

⁶²Then the king and all Israel with him offered sacrifices before the LORD. ⁶³Solomon offered a sacrifice of fellowship offerings to the LORD: twenty-two thousand cattle and a hundred and twenty thousand sheep and goats. So the king and all the Israelites dedicated the temple of the LORD.

⁶⁴On that same day the king consecrated the middle part of the courtyard in front of the temple of the LORD, and there he offered burnt offerings, grain offerings and the fat of the fellowship offerings, because the bronze altar that stood before the LORD was too small to hold the burnt offerings, the grain offerings and the fat of the fellowship offerings.

⁶⁵So Solomon observed the festival at that time, and all Israel with him—a vast assembly, people from Lebo Hamath to the Wadi of Egypt. They celebrated it before the LORD our God for seven days and seven days more, fourteen days in all. ⁶⁶On the following day he sent the people away. They blessed the king

and then went home, joyful and glad in heart for all the good things the LORD had done for his servant David and his people Israel.

The LORD Appears to Solomon

9 When Solomon had finished building the temple of the LORD and the royal palace, and had achieved all he had desired to do, ²the LORD appeared to him a second time, as he had appeared to him at Gibeon. ³The LORD said to him:

"I have heard the prayer and plea you have made before me; I have consecrated this temple, which you have built, by putting my Name there forever. My eyes and my heart will always be there.

⁴"As for you, if you walk before me faithfully with integrity of heart and uprightness, as David your father did, and do all I command and observe my decrees and laws, ⁵I will establish your royal throne over Israel forever, as I promised David your father when I said, 'You shall never fail to have a successor on the throne of Israel.'

⁶"But if you*ᵃ* or your descendants turn away from me and do not observe the commands and decrees I have given you*ᵃ* and go off to serve other gods and worship them, ⁷then I will cut off Israel from the land I have given them and will reject this temple I have consecrated for my Name. Israel will then become a byword and an object of ridicule among all peoples. ⁸This temple will become a heap of rubble. All*ᵇ* who pass by will be appalled and will scoff and say, 'Why has the LORD done such a thing to this land and to this temple?' ⁹People will answer, 'Because they have forsaken the LORD their God, who brought their ancestors out of Egypt, and have embraced other gods, worshiping and serving them—that is why the LORD brought all this disaster on them.'"

HE IS: forewarning

9:4–7 As a doting daddy, God *forewarns* his children against things that will harm them. And like a good father, he spells out the consequences for disobedience. Just as he had done with previous rulers, God cautioned King Solomon about the consequences for disobedience. God was upfront and fair about his expectations for Solomon.

The saying "forewarned is forearmed" is true. Your heavenly Father spells out his divine will in his Word to keep you from danger. It is his heart's desire to bless you when you follow the path of obedience and his heavenly duty to discipline you when you stray off course.

For the next He Is, go to p. 448.

Solomon's Other Activities

¹⁰At the end of twenty years, during which Solomon built these two buildings—the temple of the LORD and the royal palace— ¹¹King Solomon gave twenty towns in Galilee to Hiram king of Tyre, because Hiram had supplied him with all the cedar and juniper and gold he wanted. ¹²But when Hiram went from Tyre to see the towns that Solomon had given him, he was not pleased with them. ¹³"What kind of towns are these you have given me, my brother?" he asked. And he called them the Land of Kabul,*ᶜ* a name they have to this day. ¹⁴Now Hiram had sent to the king 120 talents*ᵈ* of gold.

¹⁵Here is the account of the forced labor King Solomon conscripted to build the LORD's temple, his own palace, the terraces,*ᵉ* the wall of Jerusalem, and Hazor, Megiddo and Gezer. ¹⁶(Pharaoh king of Egypt had attacked and captured Gezer. He had set it on fire. He killed its Canaanite inhabitants and then gave it as a wedding gift to his daughter, Solomon's wife. ¹⁷And Solomon rebuilt Gezer.) He built up Lower Beth Horon, ¹⁸Baalath, and Tadmor*ᶠ* in the desert, within his land, ¹⁹as well as all his store cities and the towns for his chariots and for his horses*ᵍ*—whatever he desired to build in Jerusalem, in Lebanon and throughout all the territory he ruled.

ᵃ 6 The Hebrew is plural.   *ᵇ 8* See some Septuagint manuscripts, Old Latin, Syriac, Arabic and Targum; Hebrew *And though this temple is now imposing, all*   *ᶜ 13* Kabul sounds like the Hebrew for *good-for-nothing.*   *ᵈ 14* That is, about 4 1/2 tons or about 4 metric tons   *ᵉ 15* Or *the Millo;* also in verse 24   *ᶠ 18* The Hebrew may also be read *Tamar.*   *ᵍ 19* Or *charioteers*

²⁰There were still people left from the Amorites, Hittites, Perizzites, Hivites and Jebusites (these peoples were not Israelites). ²¹Solomon conscripted the descendants of all these peoples remaining in the land—whom the Israelites could not exterminate*—to serve as slave labor, as it is to this day. ²²But Solomon did not make slaves of any of the Israelites; they were his fighting men, his government officials, his officers, his captains, and the commanders of his chariots and charioteers. ²³They were also the chief officials in charge of Solomon's projects—550 officials supervising those who did the work.

²⁴After Pharaoh's daughter had come up from the City of David to the palace Solomon had built for her, he constructed the terraces.

²⁵Three times a year Solomon sacrificed burnt offerings and fellowship offerings on the altar he had built for the LORD, burning incense before the LORD along with them, and so fulfilled the temple obligations.

²⁶King Solomon also built ships at Ezion Geber, which is near Elath in Edom, on the shore of the Red Sea.ᵇ ²⁷And Hiram sent his servants—sailors who knew the sea—to serve in the fleet with Solomon's servants. ²⁸They sailed to Ophir and brought back 420 talentsᶜ of gold, which they delivered to King Solomon.

The Queen of Sheba Visits Solomon

10 When the queen of Sheba heard about the fame of Solomon and his relationship to the LORD, she came to test Solomon with hard questions. ²Arriving at Jerusalem with a very great caravan—with camels carrying spices, large quantities of gold, and precious stones—she came to Solomon and talked with him about all that she had on her mind. ³Solomon answered all her questions; nothing was too hard for the king to explain to her. ⁴When the queen of Sheba saw all the wisdom of Solomon and the palace he had built, ⁵the food on his table, the seating of his officials, the attending servants in their robes, his cupbearers, and the burnt offerings he made atᵈ the temple of the LORD, she was overwhelmed.

⁶She said to the king, "The report I heard in my own country about your achievements and your wisdom is true. ⁷But I did not believe these things until I came and saw with my own eyes. Indeed, not even half was told me; in wisdom and wealth you have far exceeded the report I heard. ⁸How happy your people must be! How happy your officials, who continually stand before you and hear your wisdom! ⁹Praise be to the LORD your God, who has delighted in you and placed you on the throne of Israel. Because of the LORD's eternal love for Israel, he has made you king to maintain justice and righteousness."

¹⁰And she gave the king 120 talentsᵉ of gold, large quantities of spices, and precious stones. Never again were so many spices brought in as those the queen of Sheba gave to King Solomon.

¹¹(Hiram's ships brought gold from Ophir; and from there they brought great cargoes of almugwoodᶠ and precious stones. ¹²The king used the almugwood to make supportsᵍ for the temple of the LORD and for the royal palace, and to make harps and lyres for the musicians. So much almugwood has never been imported or seen since that day.)

¹³King Solomon gave the queen of Sheba all she desired and asked for, besides what he had given her out of his royal bounty. Then she left and returned with her retinue to her own country.

Solomon's Splendor

¹⁴The weight of the gold that Solomon received yearly was 666 talents,ʰ ¹⁵not including the revenues from merchants and traders and from all the Arabian kings and the governors of the territories.

¹⁶King Solomon made two hundred large shields of hammered gold; six hundred shekelsⁱ of gold went into each shield. ¹⁷He also made three hundred small shields of hammered gold, with three minasʲ of gold in each shield. The king put them in the Palace of the Forest of Lebanon.

¹⁸Then the king made a great throne inlaid with ivory and overlaid with fine gold. ¹⁹The throne had six steps, and its back had a rounded top. On both sides of the seat were armrests, with a lion standing beside each of them. ²⁰Twelve lions stood on the six steps, one at either end of each step. Nothing like it

---

ᵃ *21* The Hebrew term refers to the irrevocable giving over of things or persons to the LORD, often by totally destroying them.   ᵇ *26* Or *the Sea of Reeds*   ᶜ *28* That is, about 16 tons or about 14 metric tons   ᵈ *5* Or *the ascent by which he went up to*   ᵉ *10* That is, about 4 1/2 tons or about 4 metric tons   ᶠ *11* Probably a variant of *algumwood*; also in verse 12   ᵍ *12* The meaning of the Hebrew for this word is uncertain.   ʰ *14* That is, about 25 tons or about 23 metric tons   ⁱ *16* That is, about 15 pounds or about 6.9 kilograms; also in verse 29   ʲ *17* That is, about 3 3/4 pounds or about 1.7 kilograms; or perhaps reference is to double minas, that is, about 7 1/2 pounds or about 3.5 kilograms.

had ever been made for any other kingdom. ²¹All King Solomon's goblets were gold, and all the household articles in the Palace of the Forest of Lebanon were pure gold. Nothing was made of silver, because silver was considered of little value in Solomon's days. ²²The king had a fleet of trading ships*ᵃ* at sea along with the ships of Hiram. Once every three years it returned, carrying gold, silver and ivory, and apes and baboons.

²³King Solomon was greater in riches and wisdom than all the other kings of the earth. ²⁴The whole world sought audience with Solomon to hear the wisdom God had put in his heart. ²⁵Year after year, everyone who came brought a gift—articles of silver and gold, robes, weapons and spices, and horses and mules.

²⁶Solomon accumulated chariots and horses; he had fourteen hundred chariots and twelve thousand horses,*ᵇ* which he kept in the chariot cities and also with him in Jerusalem. ²⁷The king made silver as common in Jerusalem as stones, and cedar as plentiful as sycamore-fig trees in the foothills. ²⁸Solomon's horses were imported from Egypt and from Kue*ᶜ*—the royal merchants purchased them from Kue at the current price. ²⁹They imported a chariot from Egypt for six hundred shekels of silver, and a horse for a hundred and fifty.*ᵈ* They also exported them to all the kings of the Hittites and of the Arameans.

Solomon's Wives

11 King Solomon, however, loved many foreign women besides Pharaoh's daughter—Moabites, Ammonites, Edomites, Sidonians and Hittites. ²They were from nations about which the LORD had told the Israelites, "You must not intermarry with them, because they will surely turn your hearts after their gods." Nevertheless, Solomon held fast to them in love. ³He had seven hundred wives of royal birth and three hundred concubines, and his wives led him astray. ⁴As Solomon grew old, his wives turned his heart after other gods, and his heart was not fully devoted to the LORD his God, as the heart of David his father had been. ⁵He followed Ashtoreth the goddess of the Sidonians, and Molek the detestable god of the Ammonites. ⁶So Solomon did evil in the eyes of the LORD; he did not follow the LORD completely, as David his father had done.

⁷On a hill east of Jerusalem, Solomon built a high place for Chemosh the detestable god of Moab, and for Molek the detestable god of the Ammonites. ⁸He did the same for all his foreign wives, who burned incense and offered sacrifices to their gods.

⁹The LORD became angry with Solomon because his heart had turned away from the LORD, the God of Israel, who had appeared to him twice. ¹⁰Although he had forbidden Solomon to follow other gods, Solomon did not keep the LORD's command. ¹¹So the LORD said to Solomon, "Since this is your attitude and you have not kept my covenant and my decrees, which I commanded you, I will most certainly tear the kingdom away from you and give it to one of your subordinates. ¹²Nevertheless, for the sake of David your father, I will not do it during your lifetime. I will tear it out of the hand of your son. ¹³Yet I will not tear the whole kingdom from him, but will give him one tribe for the sake of David my servant and for the sake of Jerusalem, which I have chosen."

Solomon's Adversaries

¹⁴Then the LORD raised up against Solomon an adversary, Hadad the Edomite, from the royal line of Edom. ¹⁵Earlier when David was fighting with Edom, Joab the commander of

at issue: compromise

11:1–8 For all Solomon's wisdom, he sure made some terrible choices. He started his reign devoted to God and ended it bowing before his wives' pagan gods. Even this giant of the faith had his weak points. Perhaps Solomon wouldn't have compromised his faith so completely if he had identified the disobedience in his life sooner. Each of us has weak points and areas of disobedience we're inclined not to see, and *that's* where we're most likely to be tempted. Be honest with yourself and God (and find a friend who will be painfully honest with you too) so that you can avoid making poor choices.

ᵃ 22 Hebrew of ships of Tarshish   ᵇ 26 Or charioteers   ᶜ 28 Probably Cilicia   ᵈ 29 That is, about 3 3/4 pounds or about 1.7 kilograms

myth# 29 "THE WAY I DRESS IS NONE OF YOUR BUSINESS."

I overheard some women at work today talking about the way I dress. They said stuff like, "She dresses too sexy" and "Try a skirt next time instead of that handkerchief" and "She's too much of a distraction." (I've heard people say that one at church!) Sometimes I let comments like that just roll off my back. But sometimes they genuinely hurt.

One older friend at church had the nerve to come up to me after a service and try to advise me on my wardrobe! "Honey," she said, "you're showing just a little too much skin in that dress. You're causing some of the men to stumble." Why is everyone so concerned about what I wear? How I dress is my business and no one else's! If men are thinking thoughts they shouldn't be thinking, is that my problem?

Just because I like to look good . . . can I help that? I work out. I like how I look. Some women can be so jealous, so catty. They think I'm trying to steal their man or something. I try to love others and give to the poor—stuff God wants me to do. I try not to judge others. Yet why is it that people feel free to gossip about me and tell me what I'm doing wrong but don't deal with their own sin?

—Denitra

IN RESPONSE TO complaints by parents and others about her clothing choices and sex-symbol persona, one pop singer quickly responded that being a role model was not her responsibility. She brushed off complaints about the sexual explicitness of her photos and dismissed the complaints as "their opinion." In other words, "Your problem with what I wear is *your* problem."

As Christians, though, we're all accountable for our actions. The Bible warns against causing someone else to stumble (see 1 Corinthians 10:32). Maybe that's why the apostles Peter and Paul stressed the need for modesty. Let's face it: some clothing styles can be distracting or inappropriate for certain settings—particularly the worship setting.

Some may argue that we're not responsible for how other people think. After all, some men will lust after a woman no matter what she wears. That's true enough. But there's one thing that's within our control: our own motives. We can discern those by asking ourselves the following questions:

- Do I dress to get attention or to entice?
- Am I trying to maintain a certain image?
- Do I hope to boost my low self-esteem?
- Am I trying to push the envelope because of what I think is an unfair dress code?

Modesty doesn't have to mean wearing sackcloth or foregoing makeup and jewelry. As with all other decisions, wisdom is key.

"Modesty is a posture of the heart."

—Joshua Harris

439

"DO NOT cause anyone to stumble, whether jews, greeks or the church of god."

1 CORINTHIANS 10:32

SEE ALSO

Proverbs 31:25,30
Matthew 18:6–9
1 Timothy 2:9–10
1 Peter 3:3–6

For more on **Modesty,** check the index.

the army, who had gone up to bury the dead, had struck down all the men in Edom. [16]Joab and all the Israelites stayed there for six months, until they had destroyed all the men in Edom. [17]But Hadad, still only a boy, fled to Egypt with some Edomite officials who had served his father. [18]They set out from Midian and went to Paran. Then taking people from Paran with them, they went to Egypt, to Pharaoh king of Egypt, who gave Hadad a house and land and provided him with food.

[19]Pharaoh was so pleased with Hadad that he gave him a sister of his own wife, Queen Tahpenes, in marriage. [20]The sister of Tahpenes bore him a son named Genubath, whom Tahpenes brought up in the royal palace. There Genubath lived with Pharaoh's own children.

[21]While he was in Egypt, Hadad heard that David rested with his ancestors and that Joab the commander of the army was also dead. Then Hadad said to Pharaoh, "Let me go, that I may return to my own country."

[22]"What have you lacked here that you want to go back to your own country?" Pharaoh asked.

"Nothing," Hadad replied, "but do let me go!"

[23]And God raised up against Solomon another adversary, Rezon son of Eliada, who had fled from his master, Hadadezer king of Zobah. [24]When David destroyed Zobah's army, Rezon gathered a band of men around him and became their leader; they went to Damascus, where they settled and took control. [25]Rezon was Israel's adversary as long as Solomon lived, adding to the trouble caused by Hadad. So Rezon ruled in Aram and was hostile toward Israel.

Jeroboam Rebels Against Solomon

[26]Also, Jeroboam son of Nebat rebelled against the king. He was one of Solomon's officials, an Ephraimite from Zeredah, and his mother was a widow named Zeruah.

[27]Here is the account of how he rebelled against the king: Solomon had built the terraces*a* and had filled in the gap in the wall of the city of David his father. [28]Now Jeroboam was a man of standing, and when Solomon saw how well the young man did his work, he put him in charge of the whole labor force of the house of Joseph.

[29]About that time Jeroboam was going out of Jerusalem, and Ahijah the prophet of Shiloh met him on the way, wearing a new cloak. The two of them were alone out in the country, [30]and Ahijah took hold of the new cloak he was wearing and tore it into twelve pieces. [31]Then he said to Jeroboam, "Take ten pieces for yourself, for this is what the LORD, the God of Israel, says: 'See, I am going to tear the kingdom out of Solomon's hand and give you ten tribes. [32]But for the sake of my servant David and the city of Jerusalem, which I have chosen out of all the tribes of Israel, he will have one tribe. [33]I will do this because they have*b* forsaken me and worshiped Ashtoreth the goddess of the Sidonians, Chemosh the god of the Moabites, and Molek the god of the Ammonites, and have not walked in obedience to me, nor done what is right in my eyes, nor kept my decrees and laws as David, Solomon's father, did.

[34]"'But I will not take the whole kingdom out of Solomon's hand; I have made him ruler all the days of his life for the sake of David my servant, whom I chose and who obeyed my commands and decrees. [35]I will take the kingdom from his son's hands and give you ten tribes. [36]I will give one tribe to his son so that David my servant may always have a lamp before me in Jerusalem, the city where I chose to put my Name. [37]However, as for you, I will take you, and you will rule over all that your heart desires; you will be king over Israel. [38]If you do whatever I command you and walk in obedience to me and do what is right in my eyes by obeying my decrees and commands, as David my servant did, I will be with you. I will build you a dynasty as enduring as the one I built for David and will give Israel to you. [39]I will humble David's descendants because of this, but not forever.'"

[40]Solomon tried to kill Jeroboam, but Jeroboam fled to Egypt, to Shishak the king, and stayed there until Solomon's death.

Solomon's Death

[41]As for the other events of Solomon's reign—all he did and the wisdom he displayed—are they not written in the book of the annals of Solomon? [42]Solomon reigned in Jerusalem over all Israel forty years.

---

a 27 Or *the Millo*   *b 33* Hebrew; Septuagint, Vulgate and Syriac *because he has*

⁴³Then he rested with his ancestors and was buried in the city of David his father. And Rehoboam his son succeeded him as king.

Israel Rebels Against Rehoboam

12 Rehoboam went to Shechem, for all Israel had gone there to make him king. ²When Jeroboam son of Nebat heard this (he was still in Egypt, where he had fled from King Solomon), he returned from*ᵃ* Egypt. ³So they sent for Jeroboam, and he and the whole assembly of Israel went to Rehoboam and said to him: ⁴"Your father put a heavy yoke on us, but now lighten the harsh labor and the heavy yoke he put on us, and we will serve you."

⁵Rehoboam answered, "Go away for three days and then come back to me." So the people went away.

⁶Then King Rehoboam consulted the elders who had served his father Solomon during his lifetime. "How would you advise me to answer these people?" he asked.

⁷They replied, "If today you will be a servant to these people and serve them and give them a favorable answer, they will always be your servants."

⁸But Rehoboam rejected the advice the elders gave him and consulted the young men who had grown up with him and were serving him. ⁹He asked them, "What is your advice? How should we answer these people who say to me, 'Lighten the yoke your father put on us'?"

¹⁰The young men who had grown up with him replied, "These people have said to you, 'Your father put a heavy yoke on us, but make our yoke lighter.' Now tell them, 'My little finger is thicker than my father's waist. ¹¹My father laid on you a heavy yoke; I will make it even heavier. My father scourged you with whips; I will scourge you with scorpions.'"

¹²Three days later Jeroboam and all the people returned to Rehoboam, as the king had said, "Come back to me in three days." ¹³The king answered the people harshly. Rejecting the advice given him by the elders, ¹⁴he followed the advice of the young men and said, "My father made your yoke heavy; I will make it even heavier. My father scourged you with whips; I will scourge you with scorpions." ¹⁵So the king did not listen to the people, for this turn of events was from the LORD, to fulfill the word the LORD had spoken to Jeroboam son of Nebat through Ahijah the Shilonite.

¹⁶When all Israel saw that the king refused to listen to them, they answered the king:

> "What share do we have in David,
>   what part in Jesse's son?
> To your tents, Israel!
>   Look after your own house, David!"

So the Israelites went home. ¹⁷But as for the Israelites who were living in the towns of Judah, Rehoboam still ruled over them.

¹⁸King Rehoboam sent out Adoniram,*ᵇ* who was in charge of forced labor, but all Israel stoned him to death. King Rehoboam, however, managed to get into his chariot and escape to Jerusalem. ¹⁹So Israel has been in rebellion against the house of David to this day.

²⁰When all the Israelites heard that Jeroboam had returned, they sent and called him to the assembly and made him king over all Israel. Only the tribe of Judah remained loyal to the house of David.

²¹When Rehoboam arrived in Jerusalem, he mustered the whole house of Judah and the tribe of Benjamin—a hundred and eighty thousand able young men—to make war against the house of Israel and to regain the kingdom for Rehoboam son of Solomon.

²²But this word of God came to Shemaiah the man of God: ²³"Say to Rehoboam son of Solomon king of Judah, to the whole house of Judah and Benjamin, and to the rest of the people, ²⁴'This is what the LORD says: Do not go up to fight against your brothers, the Israelites. Go home, every one of you, for this is my doing.'" So they obeyed the word of the LORD and went home again, as the LORD had ordered.

Golden Calves at Bethel and Dan

²⁵Then Jeroboam fortified Shechem in the hill country of Ephraim and lived there. From there he went out and built up Peniel.*ᶜ*

441

---

[26]Jeroboam thought to himself, "The kingdom will now likely revert to the house of David. [27]If these people go up to offer sacrifices at the temple of the LORD in Jerusalem, they will again give their allegiance to their lord, Rehoboam king of Judah. They will kill me and return to King Rehoboam."

[28]After seeking advice, the king made two golden calves. He said to the people, "It is too much for you to go up to Jerusalem. Here are your gods, Israel, who brought you up out of Egypt." [29]One he set up in Bethel, and the other in Dan. [30]And this thing became a sin; the people came to worship the one at Bethel and went as far as Dan to worship the other.[a]

[31]Jeroboam built shrines on high places and appointed priests from all sorts of people, even though they were not Levites. [32]He instituted a festival on the fifteenth day of the eighth month, like the festival held in Judah, and offered sacrifices on the altar. This he did in Bethel, sacrificing to the calves he had made. And at Bethel he also installed priests at the high places he had made. [33]On the fifteenth day of the eighth month, a month of his own choosing, he offered sacrifices on the altar he had built at Bethel. So he instituted the festival for the Israelites and went up to the altar to make offerings.

conversations

compromise «» 12:25–33

1» What leads a person to compromise her faith?

2» What is the first warning sign that you're beginning to compromise?

3» In what ways are Christians tempted to compromise what they believe?

For more on compromise, check the index. For the next Conversations, go to p. 451.

The Man of God From Judah

13 By the word of the LORD a man of God came from Judah to Bethel, as Jeroboam was standing by the altar to make an offering. [2]He cried out against the altar by the word of the LORD: "Altar, altar! This is what the LORD says: 'A son named Josiah will be born to the house of David. On you he will sacrifice the priests of the high places who make offerings here, and human bones will be burned on you.'" [3]That same day the man of God gave a sign: "This is the sign the LORD has declared: The altar will be split apart and the ashes on it will be poured out."

[4]When King Jeroboam heard what the man of God cried out against the altar at Bethel, he stretched out his hand from the altar and said, "Seize him!" But the hand he stretched out toward the man shriveled up, so that he could not pull it back. [5]Also, the altar was split apart and its ashes poured out according to the sign given by the man of God by the word of the LORD.

[6]Then the king said to the man of God, "Intercede with the LORD your God and pray for me that my hand may be restored." So the man of God interceded with the LORD, and the king's hand was restored and became as it was before.

[7]The king said to the man of God, "Come home with me for a meal, and I will give you a gift."

[8]But the man of God answered the king, "Even if you were to give me half your possessions, I would not go with you, nor would I eat bread or drink water here. [9]For I was commanded by the word of the LORD: 'You must not eat bread or drink water or return by the way you came.'" [10]So he took another road and did not return by the way he had come to Bethel.

[11]Now there was a certain old prophet living in Bethel, whose sons came and told him all that the man of God had done there that day. They also told their father what he had said to the king. [12]Their father asked them, "Which way did he go?" And his sons showed him which road the man of God from Judah had taken. [13]So he said to his sons, "Saddle the donkey for me." And when they had saddled the donkey for him, he mounted it [14]and rode after the man of God. He found him sitting under an oak tree and asked, "Are you the man of God who came from Judah?"

"I am," he replied.

[15]So the prophet said to him, "Come home with me and eat."

[16]The man of God said, "I cannot turn back and go with you, nor can I eat bread or drink water with

---

[a] 30 Probable reading of the original Hebrew text; Masoretic Text *people went to the one as far as Dan*

you in this place. ¹⁷I have been told by the word of the LORD: 'You must not eat bread or drink water there or return by the way you came.'"

¹⁸The old prophet answered, "I too am a prophet, as you are. And an angel said to me by the word of the LORD: 'Bring him back with you to your house so that he may eat bread and drink water.'" (But he was lying to him.) ¹⁹So the man of God returned with him and ate and drank in his house.

²⁰While they were sitting at the table, the word of the LORD came to the old prophet who had brought him back. ²¹He cried out to the man of God who had come from Judah, "This is what the LORD says: 'You have defied the word of the LORD and have not kept the command the LORD your God gave you. ²²You came back and ate bread and drank water in the place where he told you not to eat or drink. Therefore your body will not be buried in the tomb of your ancestors.'"

²³When the man of God had finished eating and drinking, the prophet who had brought him back saddled his donkey for him. ²⁴As he went on his way, a lion met him on the road and killed him, and his body was left lying on the road, with both the donkey and the lion standing beside it. ²⁵Some people who passed by saw the body lying there, with the lion standing beside the body, and they went and reported it in the city where the old prophet lived.

²⁶When the prophet who had brought him back from his journey heard of it, he said, "It is the man of God who defied the word of the LORD. The LORD has given him over to the lion, which has mauled him and killed him, as the word of the LORD had warned him."

443

²⁷The prophet said to his sons, "Saddle the donkey for me," and they did so. ²⁸Then he went out and found the body lying on the road, with the donkey and the lion standing beside it. The lion had neither eaten the body nor mauled the donkey. ²⁹So the prophet picked up the body of the man of God, laid it on the donkey, and brought it back to his own city to mourn for him and bury him. ³⁰Then he laid the body in his own tomb, and they mourned over him and said, "Alas, my brother!"

³¹After burying him, he said to his sons, "When I die, bury me in the grave where the man of God is buried; lay my bones beside his bones. ³²For the message he declared by the word of the LORD against the altar in Bethel and against all the shrines on the high places in the towns of Samaria will certainly come true."

³³Even after this, Jeroboam did not change his evil ways, but once more appointed priests for the high places from all sorts of people. Anyone who wanted to become a priest he consecrated for the high places. ³⁴This was the sin of the house of Jeroboam that led to its downfall and to its destruction from the face of the earth.

Ahijah's Prophecy Against Jeroboam

14 At that time Abijah son of Jeroboam became ill, ²and Jeroboam said to his wife, "Go, disguise yourself, so you won't be recognized as the wife of Jeroboam. Then go to Shiloh. Ahijah the prophet is there—the one who told me I would be king over this people. ³Take ten loaves of bread with you, some cakes and a jar of honey, and go to him. He will tell you what will happen to the boy." ⁴So Jeroboam's wife did what he said and went to Ahijah's house in Shiloh.

Now Ahijah could not see; his sight was gone because of his age. ⁵But the LORD had told Ahijah, "Jeroboam's wife is coming to ask you about her son, for he is ill, and you are to give her such and such an answer. When she arrives, she will pretend to be someone else."

⁶So when Ahijah heard the sound of her footsteps at the door, he said, "Come in, wife of Jeroboam. Why this pretense? I have been sent to you with bad news. ⁷Go, tell Jeroboam that this is what the LORD, the God of Israel, says: 'I raised you up from among the people and appointed you ruler over my people Israel. ⁸I tore the kingdom away from the house of David and gave it to you, but you have not been like my servant David, who kept my commands and followed me with all his heart, doing only what was right in my eyes. ⁹You have done more evil than all who lived before you. You have made for yourself other gods, idols made of metal; you have aroused my anger and thrust me behind your back.

¹⁰"'Because of this, I am going to bring disaster on the house of Jeroboam. I will cut off from Jeroboam every last male in Israel—slave or free.ᵃ I will burn up the house of Jeroboam as one burns dung, until it

ᵃ 10 Or Israel—every ruler or leader

is all gone. [11]Dogs will eat those belonging to Jeroboam who die in the city, and the birds will feed on those who die in the country. The LORD has spoken!'

[12]"As for you, go back home. When you set foot in your city, the boy will die. [13]All Israel will mourn for him and bury him. He is the only one belonging to Jeroboam who will be buried, because he is the only one in the house of Jeroboam in whom the LORD, the God of Israel, has found anything good.

[14]"The LORD will raise up for himself a king over Israel who will cut off the family of Jeroboam. Even now this is beginning to happen.[a] [15]And the LORD will strike Israel, so that it will be like a reed swaying in the water. He will uproot Israel from this good land that he gave to their ancestors and scatter them beyond the Euphrates River, because they aroused the LORD's anger by making Asherah poles.[b] [16]And he will give Israel up because of the sins Jeroboam has committed and has caused Israel to commit."

[17]Then Jeroboam's wife got up and left and went to Tirzah. As soon as she stepped over the threshold of the house, the boy died. [18]They buried him, and all Israel mourned for him, as the LORD had said through his servant the prophet Ahijah.

[19]The other events of Jeroboam's reign, his wars and how he ruled, are written in the book of the annals of the kings of Israel. [20]He reigned for twenty-two years and then rested with his ancestors. And Nadab his son succeeded him as king.

Rehoboam King of Judah

[21]Rehoboam son of Solomon was king in Judah. He was forty-one years old when he became king, and he reigned seventeen years in Jerusalem, the city the LORD had chosen out of all the tribes of Israel in which to put his Name. His mother's name was Naamah; she was an Ammonite.

[22]Judah did evil in the eyes of the LORD. By the sins they committed they stirred up his jealous anger more than those who were before them had done. [23]They also set up for themselves high places, sacred stones and Asherah poles on every high hill and under every spreading tree. [24]There were even male shrine prostitutes in the land; the people engaged in all the detestable practices of the nations the LORD had driven out before the Israelites.

[25]In the fifth year of King Rehoboam, Shishak king of Egypt attacked Jerusalem. [26]He carried off the treasures of the temple of the LORD and the treasures of the royal palace. He took everything, including all the gold shields Solomon had made. [27]So King Rehoboam made bronze shields to replace them and assigned these to the commanders of the guard on duty at the entrance to the royal palace. [28]Whenever the king went to the LORD's temple, the guards bore the shields, and afterward they returned them to the guardroom.

[29]As for the other events of Rehoboam's reign, and all he did, are they not written in the book of the annals of the kings of Judah? [30]There was continual warfare between Rehoboam and Jeroboam. [31]And Rehoboam rested with his ancestors and was buried with them in the City of David. His mother's name was Naamah; she was an Ammonite. And Abijah[c] his son succeeded him as king.

Abijah King of Judah

15 In the eighteenth year of the reign of Jeroboam son of Nebat, Abijah[d] became king of Judah, [2]and he reigned in Jerusalem three years. His mother's name was Maakah daughter of Abishalom.[e]

[3]He committed all the sins his father had done before him; his heart was not fully devoted to the LORD his God, as the heart of David his forefather had been. [4]Nevertheless, for David's sake the LORD his God gave him a lamp in Jerusalem by raising up a son to succeed him and by making Jerusalem strong. [5]For David had done what was right in the eyes of the LORD and had not failed to keep any of the LORD's commands all the days of his life—except in the case of Uriah the Hittite.

[6]There was war between Abijah[f] and Jeroboam throughout Abijah's lifetime. [7]As for the other events of Abijah's reign, and all he did, are they not written in the book of the annals of the kings of Judah? There was war between Abijah and Jeroboam. [8]And Abijah rested with his ancestors and was buried in the City of David. And Asa his son succeeded him as king.

---

a 14 The meaning of the Hebrew for this sentence is uncertain.   *b 15* That is, wooden symbols of the goddess Asherah; here and elsewhere in 1 Kings
c 31 Some Hebrew manuscripts and Septuagint (see also 2 Chron. 12:16); most Hebrew manuscripts *Abijam*   *d 1* Some Hebrew manuscripts and Septuagint (see also 2 Chron. 12:16); most Hebrew manuscripts *Abijam*; also in verses 7 and 8   *e 2* A variant of *Absalom*; also in verse 10   *f 6* Some Hebrew manuscripts and Syriac *Abijam* (that is, Abijah); most Hebrew manuscripts *Rehoboam*

Asa King of Judah

⁹In the twentieth year of Jeroboam king of Israel, Asa became king of Judah, ¹⁰and he reigned in Jerusalem forty-one years. His grandmother's name was Maakah daughter of Abishalom.

¹¹Asa did what was right in the eyes of the LORD, as his father David had done. ¹²He expelled the male shrine prostitutes from the land and got rid of all the idols his ancestors had made. ¹³He even deposed his grandmother Maakah from her position as queen mother, because she had made a repulsive image for the worship of Asherah. Asa cut it down and burned it in the Kidron Valley. ¹⁴Although he did not remove the high places, Asa's heart was fully committed to the LORD all his life. ¹⁵He brought into the temple of the LORD the silver and gold and the articles that he and his father had dedicated.

¹⁶There was war between Asa and Baasha king of Israel throughout their reigns. ¹⁷Baasha king of Israel went up against Judah and fortified Ramah to prevent anyone from leaving or entering the territory of Asa king of Judah.

¹⁸Asa then took all the silver and gold that was left in the treasuries of the LORD's temple and of his own palace. He entrusted it to his officials and sent them to Ben-Hadad son of Tabrimmon, the son of Hezion, the king of Aram, who was ruling in Damascus. ¹⁹"Let there be a treaty between me and you," he said, "as there was between my father and your father. See, I am sending you a gift of silver and gold. Now break your treaty with Baasha king of Israel so he will withdraw from me."

²⁰Ben-Hadad agreed with King Asa and sent the commanders of his forces against the towns of Israel. He conquered Ijon, Dan, Abel Beth Maakah and all Kinnereth in addition to Naphtali. ²¹When Baasha heard this, he stopped building Ramah and withdrew to Tirzah. ²²Then King Asa issued an order to all Judah—no one was exempt—and they carried away from Ramah the stones and timber Baasha had been using there. With them King Asa built up Geba in Benjamin, and also Mizpah.

²³As for all the other events of Asa's reign, all his achievements, all he did and the cities he built, are they not written in the book of the annals of the kings of Judah? In his old age, however, his feet became diseased. ²⁴Then Asa rested with his ancestors and was buried with them in the city of his father David. And Jehoshaphat his son succeeded him as king.

Nadab King of Israel

²⁵Nadab son of Jeroboam became king of Israel in the second year of Asa king of Judah, and he reigned over Israel two years. ²⁶He did evil in the eyes of the LORD, following the ways of his father and committing the same sin his father had caused Israel to commit.

²⁷Baasha son of Ahijah of the house of Issachar plotted against him, and he struck him down at Gibbethon, a Philistine town, while Nadab and all Israel were besieging it. ²⁸Baasha killed Nadab in the third year of Asa king of Judah and succeeded him as king.

²⁹As soon as he began to reign, he killed Jeroboam's whole family. He did not leave Jeroboam anyone that breathed, but destroyed them all, according to the word of the LORD given through his servant Ahijah the Shilonite. ³⁰This happened because of the sins Jeroboam had committed and had caused Israel to commit, and because he aroused the anger of the LORD, the God of Israel.

³¹As for the other events of Nadab's reign, and all he did, are they not written in the book of the annals of the kings of Israel? ³²There was war between Asa and Baasha king of Israel throughout their reigns.

atissue:disappointment

15:1–15 All children face disappointment when they first realize their parents aren't perfect. Even more painful is discovering as adults that our parents may have left us with a legacy of lies, betrayal or unfaithfulness. Many of us fear that we're going to turn out just like them. God gives us hope for something completely different. King Asa chose to make a godly life out of the ashes of a bad heritage. You have a choice as well. Your background does not set your destiny. Choose, today, how you will spend your life—as a child of God or as a child of your heritage.

445

Baasha King of Israel

³³In the third year of Asa king of Judah, Baasha son of Ahijah became king of all Israel in Tirzah, and he reigned twenty-four years. ³⁴He did evil in the eyes of the LORD, following the ways of Jeroboam and committing the same sin Jeroboam had caused Israel to commit.

16 Then the word of the LORD came to Jehu son of Hanani concerning Baasha: ²"I lifted you up from the dust and appointed you ruler over my people Israel, but you followed the ways of Jeroboam and caused my people Israel to sin and to arouse my anger by their sins. ³So I am about to wipe out Baasha and his house, and I will make your house like that of Jeroboam son of Nebat. ⁴Dogs will eat those belonging to Baasha who die in the city, and birds will feed on those who die in the country."

⁵As for the other events of Baasha's reign, what he did and his achievements, are they not written in the book of the annals of the kings of Israel? ⁶Baasha rested with his ancestors and was buried in Tirzah. And Elah his son succeeded him as king.

⁷Moreover, the word of the LORD came through the prophet Jehu son of Hanani to Baasha and his house, because of all the evil he had done in the eyes of the LORD, arousing his anger by the things he did, becoming like the house of Jeroboam—and also because he destroyed it.

Elah King of Israel

⁸In the twenty-sixth year of Asa king of Judah, Elah son of Baasha became king of Israel, and he reigned in Tirzah two years.

⁹Zimri, one of his officials, who had command of half his chariots, plotted against him. Elah was in Tirzah at the time, getting drunk in the home of Arza, who was in charge of the palace at Tirzah. ¹⁰Zimri came in, struck him down and killed him in the twenty-seventh year of Asa king of Judah. Then he succeeded him as king.

¹¹As soon as he began to reign and was seated on the throne, he killed off Baasha's whole family. He did not spare a single male, whether relative or friend. ¹²So Zimri destroyed the whole family of Baasha, in accordance with the word of the LORD spoken against Baasha through the prophet Jehu— ¹³because of all the sins Baasha and his son Elah had committed and had caused Israel to commit, so that they aroused the anger of the LORD, the God of Israel, by their worthless idols.

¹⁴As for the other events of Elah's reign, and all he did, are they not written in the book of the annals of the kings of Israel?

Zimri King of Israel

¹⁵In the twenty-seventh year of Asa king of Judah, Zimri reigned in Tirzah seven days. The army was encamped near Gibbethon, a Philistine town. ¹⁶When the Israelites in the camp heard that Zimri had plotted against the king and murdered him, they proclaimed Omri, the commander of the army, king over Israel that very day there in the camp. ¹⁷Then Omri and all the Israelites with him withdrew from Gibbethon and laid siege to Tirzah. ¹⁸When Zimri saw that the city was taken, he went into the citadel of the royal palace and set the palace on fire around him. So he died, ¹⁹because of the sins he had committed, doing evil in the eyes of the LORD and following the ways of Jeroboam and committing the same sin Jeroboam had caused Israel to commit.

²⁰As for the other events of Zimri's reign, and the rebellion he carried out, are they not written in the book of the annals of the kings of Israel?

Omri King of Israel

²¹Then the people of Israel were split into two factions; half supported Tibni son of Ginath for king, and the other half supported Omri. ²²But Omri's followers proved stronger than those of Tibni son of Ginath. So Tibni died and Omri became king.

²³In the thirty-first year of Asa king of Judah, Omri became king of Israel, and he reigned twelve years, six of them in Tirzah. ²⁴He bought the hill of Samaria from Shemer for two talents*a* of silver and built a city on the hill, calling it Samaria, after Shemer, the name of the former owner of the hill.

²⁵But Omri did evil in the eyes of the LORD and sinned more than all those before him. ²⁶He followed

---

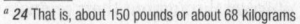

a 24 That is, about 150 pounds or about 68 kilograms

completely the ways of Jeroboam son of Nebat, committing the same sin Jeroboam had caused Israel to commit, so that they aroused the anger of the Lord, the God of Israel, by their worthless idols.

²⁷As for the other events of Omri's reign, what he did and the things he achieved, are they not written in the book of the annals of the kings of Israel? ²⁸Omri rested with his ancestors and was buried in Samaria. And Ahab his son succeeded him as king.

Ahab Becomes King of Israel

²⁹In the thirty-eighth year of Asa king of Judah, Ahab son of Omri became king of Israel, and he reigned in Samaria over Israel twenty-two years. ³⁰Ahab son of Omri did more evil in the eyes of the Lord than any of those before him. ³¹He not only considered it trivial to commit the sins of Jeroboam son of Nebat, but he also married Jezebel daughter of Ethbaal king of the Sidonians, and began to serve Baal and worship him. ³²He set up an altar for Baal in the temple of Baal that he built in Samaria. ³³Ahab also made an Asherah pole and did more to arouse the anger of the Lord, the God of Israel, than did all the kings of Israel before him.

³⁴In Ahab's time, Hiel of Bethel rebuilt Jericho. He laid its foundations at the cost of his firstborn son Abiram, and he set up its gates at the cost of his youngest son Segub, in accordance with the word of the Lord spoken by Joshua son of Nun.

Elijah Fed by Ravens

17 Now Elijah the Tishbite, from Tishbe*a* in Gilead, said to Ahab, "As the Lord, the God of Israel, lives, whom I serve, there will be neither dew nor rain in the next few years except at my word."

²Then the word of the Lord came to Elijah: ³"Leave here, turn eastward and hide in the Kerith Ravine, east of the Jordan. ⁴You will drink from the brook, and I have directed the ravens to supply you with food there."

⁵So he did what the Lord had told him. He went to the Kerith Ravine, east of the Jordan, and stayed there. ⁶The ravens brought him bread and meat in the morning and bread and meat in the evening, and he drank from the brook.

The Widow at Zarephath

⁷Some time later the brook dried up because there had been no rain in the land. ⁸Then the word of the Lord came to him: ⁹"Go at once to Zarephath in the region of Sidon and stay there. I have directed a widow there to supply you with food." ¹⁰So he went to Zarephath. When he came to the town gate, a widow was there gathering sticks. He called to her and asked, "Would you bring me a little water in a jar so I may have a drink?" ¹¹As she was going to get it, he called, "And bring me, please, a piece of bread."

¹²"As surely as the Lord your God lives," she replied, "I don't have any bread—only a handful of flour in a jar and a little olive oil in a jug. I am gathering a few sticks to take home and make a meal for myself and my son, that we may eat it—and die."

¹³Elijah said to her, "Don't be afraid. Go home and do as you have said. But first make a small loaf of bread for me from what you have and bring it to me, and then make something for yourself and your son. ¹⁴For this is what the Lord, the God of Israel, says: 'The jar of flour will not be used up and the jug of oil will not run dry until the day the Lord sends rain on the land.'"

¹⁵She went away and did as Elijah had told her. So there was food every day for Elijah and for the woman and her family. ¹⁶For the jar of flour was not used up and the jug of oil did not run dry, in keeping with the word of the Lord spoken by Elijah.

¹⁷Some time later the son of the woman who owned the house became ill. He grew worse and worse, and finally stopped breathing. ¹⁸She said to Elijah, "What do you have against me, man of God? Did you come to remind me of my sin and kill my son?"

¹⁹"Give me your son," Elijah replied. He took him from her arms, carried him to the upper room where he was staying, and laid him on his bed. ²⁰Then he cried out to the Lord, "Lord my God, have you brought tragedy even on this widow I am staying with, by causing her son to die?" ²¹Then he stretched himself out on the boy three times and cried out to the Lord, "Lord my God, let this boy's life return to him!"

a 1 Or *Tishbite, of the settlers*

²²The Lord heard Elijah's cry, and the boy's life returned to him, and he lived. ²³Elijah picked up the child and carried him down from the room into the house. He gave him to his mother and said, "Look, your son is alive!"

²⁴Then the woman said to Elijah, "Now I know that you are a man of God and that the word of the Lord from your mouth is the truth."

HE IS: life-giving

17:19–23 The widow of Zarephath shared her meager provisions with Elijah and was blessed with a miracle when God multiplied her flour and oil. But she felt as if she'd lost everything when her son died. In the midst of that tragedy, God proved that he is *life-giving*—supreme over death, giver of life.

One day all God's children who have died will rise again. Nothing is too hard for him! The God who resurrects the dead wields that same life-giving power in your life—giving you hope when you lose a loved one or when a dream or desire within you dies. What's dead will not always be so.

For the next He Is, go to p. 451.

Elijah and Obadiah

18 After a long time, in the third year, the word of the Lord came to Elijah: "Go and present yourself to Ahab, and I will send rain on the land." ²So Elijah went to present himself to Ahab.

Now the famine was severe in Samaria, ³and Ahab had summoned Obadiah, who was in charge of his palace. (Obadiah was a devout believer in the Lord. ⁴While Jezebel was killing off the Lord's prophets, Obadiah had taken a hundred prophets and hidden them in two caves, fifty in each, and had supplied them with food and water.) ⁵Ahab had said to Obadiah, "Go through the land to all the springs and valleys. Maybe we can find some grass to keep the horses and mules alive so we will not have to kill any of our animals." ⁶So they divided the land they were to cover, Ahab going in one direction and Obadiah in another.

⁷As Obadiah was walking along, Elijah met him. Obadiah recognized him, bowed down to the ground, and said, "Is it really you, my lord Elijah?"

⁸"Yes," he replied. "Go tell your master, 'Elijah is here.'"

⁹"What have I done wrong," asked Obadiah, "that you are handing your servant over to Ahab to be put to death? ¹⁰As surely as the Lord your God lives, there is not a nation or kingdom where my master has not sent someone to look for you. And whenever a nation or kingdom claimed you were not there, he made them swear they could not find you. ¹¹But now you tell me to go to my master and say, 'Elijah is here.' ¹²I don't know where the Spirit of the Lord may carry you when I leave you. If I go and tell Ahab and he doesn't find you, he will kill me. Yet I your servant have worshiped the Lord since my youth. ¹³Haven't you heard, my lord, what I did while Jezebel was killing the prophets of the Lord? I hid a hundred of the Lord's prophets in two caves, fifty in each, and supplied them with food and water. ¹⁴And now you tell me to go to my master and say, 'Elijah is here.' He will kill me!"

¹⁵Elijah said, "As the Lord Almighty lives, whom I serve, I will surely present myself to Ahab today."

Elijah on Mount Carmel

¹⁶So Obadiah went to meet Ahab and told him, and Ahab went to meet Elijah. ¹⁷When he saw Elijah, he said to him, "Is that you, you troubler of Israel?"

¹⁸"I have not made trouble for Israel," Elijah replied. "But you and your father's family have. You have abandoned the Lord's commands and have followed the Baals. ¹⁹Now summon the people from all over Israel to meet me on Mount Carmel. And bring the four hundred and fifty prophets of Baal and the four hundred prophets of Asherah, who eat at Jezebel's table."

²⁰So Ahab sent word throughout all Israel and assembled the prophets on Mount Carmel. ²¹Elijah went before the people and said, "How long will you waver between two opinions? If the LORD is God, follow him; but if Baal is God, follow him."

But the people said nothing.

²²Then Elijah said to them, "I am the only one of the LORD's prophets left, but Baal has four hundred and fifty prophets. ²³Get two bulls for us. Let Baal's prophets choose one for themselves, and let them cut it into pieces and put it on the wood but not set fire to it. I will prepare the other bull and put it on the wood but not set fire to it. ²⁴Then you call on the name of your god, and I will call on the name of the LORD. The god who answers by fire—he is God."

Then all the people said, "What you say is good."

²⁵Elijah said to the prophets of Baal, "Choose one of the bulls and prepare it first, since there are so many of you. Call on the name of your god, but do not light the fire." ²⁶So they took the bull given them and prepared it.

Then they called on the name of Baal from morning till noon. "Baal, answer us!" they shouted. But there was no response; no one answered. And they danced around the altar they had made.

²⁷At noon Elijah began to taunt them. "Shout louder!" he said. "Surely he is a god! Perhaps he is deep in thought, or busy, or traveling. Maybe he is sleeping and must be awakened." ²⁸So they shouted louder and slashed themselves with swords and spears, as was their custom, until their blood flowed. ²⁹Midday passed, and they continued their frantic prophesying until the time for the evening sacrifice. But there was no response, no one answered, no one paid attention.

³⁰Then Elijah said to all the people, "Come here to me." They came to him, and he repaired the altar of the LORD, which had been torn down. ³¹Elijah took twelve stones, one for each of the tribes descended from Jacob, to whom the word of the LORD had come, saying, "Your name shall be Israel." ³²With the stones he built an altar in the name of the LORD, and he dug a trench around it large enough to hold two seahs^a of seed. ³³He arranged the wood, cut the bull into pieces and laid it on the wood. Then he said to them, "Fill four large jars with water and pour it on the offering and on the wood."

³⁴"Do it again," he said, and they did it again.

"Do it a third time," he ordered, and they did it the third time. ³⁵The water ran down around the altar and even filled the trench.

³⁶At the time of sacrifice, the prophet Elijah stepped forward and prayed: "LORD, the God of Abraham, Isaac and Israel, let it be known today that you are God in Israel and that I am your servant and have done all these things at your command. ³⁷Answer me, LORD, answer me, so these people will know that you, LORD, are God, and that you are turning their hearts back again."

³⁸Then the fire of the LORD fell and burned up the sacrifice, the wood, the stones and the soil, and also licked up the water in the trench.

³⁹When all the people saw this, they fell prostrate and cried, "The LORD—he is God! The LORD—he is God!"

⁴⁰Then Elijah commanded them, "Seize the prophets of Baal. Don't let anyone get away!" They seized them, and Elijah had them brought down to the Kishon Valley and slaughtered there.

⁴¹And Elijah said to Ahab, "Go, eat and drink, for there is

449

a t issue: taking a stand

18:16–39 Elijah made a solo stand for God, and look at what God did with just that one man! Elijah's bold testimony humbled hundreds of his enemies before God. Few of us will ever be placed in a position like Elijah's face-off against the prophets of Baal. That doesn't mean, however, that our lives cannot make an impact. Begin with one person you talk to every day. How many other lives does that person's life touch? The impact of your bold stand for Christ is exponential. Like Elijah, you may never know what a difference you make in this world.

---

^a 32 That is, probably about 24 pounds or about 11 kilograms

the sound of a heavy rain." ⁴²So Ahab went off to eat and drink, but Elijah climbed to the top of Carmel, bent down to the ground and put his face between his knees.

⁴³"Go and look toward the sea," he told his servant. And he went up and looked.

"There is nothing there," he said.

Seven times Elijah said, "Go back."

⁴⁴The seventh time the servant reported, "A cloud as small as a man's hand is rising from the sea."

So Elijah said, "Go and tell Ahab, 'Hitch up your chariot and go down before the rain stops you.'"

⁴⁵Meanwhile, the sky grew black with clouds, the wind rose, a heavy rain came on and Ahab rode off to Jezreel. ⁴⁶The power of the LORD came on Elijah and, tucking his cloak into his belt, he ran ahead of Ahab all the way to Jezreel.

Elijah Flees to Horeb

19 Now Ahab told Jezebel everything Elijah had done and how he had killed all the prophets with the sword. ²So Jezebel sent a messenger to Elijah to say, "May the gods deal with me, be it ever so severely, if by this time tomorrow I do not make your life like that of one of them."

³Elijah was afraid*ᵃ* and ran for his life. When he came to Beersheba in Judah, he left his servant there, ⁴while he himself went a day's journey into the wilderness. He came to a broom bush, sat down under it and prayed that he might die. "I have had enough, LORD," he said. "Take my life; I am no better than my ancestors." ⁵Then he lay down under the tree and fell asleep.

All at once an angel touched him and said, "Get up and eat." ⁶He looked around, and there by his head was some bread baked over hot coals, and a jar of water. He ate and drank and then lay down again.

⁷The angel of the LORD came back a second time and touched him and said, "Get up and eat, for the journey is too much for you." ⁸So he got up and ate and drank. Strengthened by that food, he traveled forty days and forty nights until he reached Horeb, the mountain of God. ⁹There he went into a cave and spent the night.

The LORD Appears to Elijah

And the word of the LORD came to him: "What are you doing here, Elijah?"

¹⁰He replied, "I have been very zealous for the LORD God Almighty. The Israelites have rejected your covenant, torn down your altars, and put your prophets to death with the sword. I am the only one left, and now they are trying to kill me too."

¹¹The LORD said, "Go out and stand on the mountain in the presence of the LORD, for the LORD is about to pass by."

Then a great and powerful wind tore the mountains apart and shattered the rocks before the LORD, but the LORD was not in the wind. After the wind there was an earthquake, but the LORD was not in the earthquake. ¹²After the earthquake came a fire, but the LORD was not in the fire. And after the fire came a gentle whisper. ¹³When Elijah heard it, he pulled his cloak over his face and went out and stood at the mouth of the cave.

Then a voice said to him, "What are you doing here, Elijah?"

¹⁴He replied, "I have been very zealous for the LORD God Almighty. The Israelites have rejected your

atissue:depression

19:1–9 When we're depressed, our view of life gets distorted. We can no longer see our own lives with clarity. Elijah had just been a part of an amazing miracle by God, and now— later that very same day— he wanted to die. He believed what his feelings were telling him, and as a result, he lost connection with reality. He had forgotten that God loved him and would always protect him. If you feel hopeless and can't see past your own feelings, talk to someone. Get God's perspective and seek out a friend, pastor or a professional counselor to help balance out your view of life.

ᵃ 3 Or Elijah saw

covenant, torn down your altars, and put your prophets to death with the sword. I am the only one left, and now they are trying to kill me too."

¹⁵The LORD said to him, "Go back the way you came, and go to the Desert of Damascus. When you get there, anoint Hazael king over Aram. ¹⁶Also, anoint Jehu son of Nimshi king over Israel, and anoint Elisha son of Shaphat from Abel Meholah to succeed you as prophet. ¹⁷Jehu will put to death any who escape the sword of Hazael, and Elisha will put to death any who escape the sword of Jehu. ¹⁸Yet I reserve seven thousand in Israel—all whose knees have not bowed down to Baal and whose mouths have not kissed him."

The Call of Elisha

¹⁹So Elijah went from there and found Elisha son of Shaphat. He was plowing with twelve yoke of oxen, and he himself was driving the twelfth pair. Elijah went up to him and threw his cloak around him. ²⁰Elisha then left his oxen and ran after Elijah. "Let me kiss my father and mother good-by," he said, "and then I will come with you."

"Go back," Elijah replied. "What have I done to you?"

²¹So Elisha left him and went back. He took his yoke of oxen and slaughtered them. He burned the plowing equipment to cook the meat and gave it to the people, and they ate. Then he set out to follow Elijah and became his servant.

" conversations "

loneliness «» 19:14

1 » Do you ever feel lonely? Why?

2 » What's the difference between feeling lonely and being alone?

3 » How can loneliness lead to depression?

For more on **loneliness**, check the index.
For the next Conversations, go to p. 467.

451

HE IS: a gentle whisper

19:11–12 Just after Elijah had participated in miraculous displays of God's power, he became weary and spiritually despondent, thinking he was the only one to carry God's message. That's when God revealed that he doesn't communicate only through powerful presentations; he also speaks in *a gentle whisper*. God met Elijah's need by talking to him personally.

When you're feeling low, don't always look for God in dynamic displays outside your circumstances. Listen for his voice in the quiet places of your heart. Be still and listen—truly listen—for his *gentle whisper* that comes to soothe your soul.

For the next He Is, go to p. 466.

Ben-Hadad Attacks Samaria

20 Now Ben-Hadad king of Aram mustered his entire army. Accompanied by thirty-two kings with their horses and chariots, he went up and besieged Samaria and attacked it. ²He sent messengers into the city to Ahab king of Israel, saying, "This is what Ben-Hadad says: ³'Your silver and gold are mine, and the best of your wives and children are mine.'"

⁴The king of Israel answered, "Just as you say, my lord the king. I and all I have are yours."

⁵The messengers came again and said, "This is what Ben-Hadad says: 'I sent to demand your silver and gold, your wives and your children. ⁶But about this time tomorrow I am going to send my officials to search your palace and the houses of your officials. They will seize everything you value and carry it away.'"

⁷The king of Israel summoned all the elders of the land and said to them, "See how this man is looking for trouble! When he sent for my wives and my children, my silver and my gold, I did not refuse him."

⁸The elders and the people all answered, "Don't listen to him or agree to his demands."

⁹So he replied to Ben-Hadad's messengers, "Tell my lord the king, 'Your servant will do all you

demanded the first time, but this demand I cannot meet.'" They left and took the answer back to Ben-Hadad.

[10] Then Ben-Hadad sent another message to Ahab: "May the gods deal with me, be it ever so severely, if enough dust remains in Samaria to give each of my men a handful."

[11] The king of Israel answered, "Tell him: 'One who puts on his armor should not boast like one who takes it off.'"

[12] Ben-Hadad heard this message while he and the kings were drinking in their tents,[a] and he ordered his men: "Prepare to attack." So they prepared to attack the city.

Ahab Defeats Ben-Hadad

[13] Meanwhile a prophet came to Ahab king of Israel and announced, "This is what the LORD says: 'Do you see this vast army? I will give it into your hand today, and then you will know that I am the LORD.'"

[14] "But who will do this?" asked Ahab.

The prophet replied, "This is what the LORD says: 'The junior officers under the provincial commanders will do it.'"

"And who will start the battle?" he asked.

The prophet answered, "You will."

[15] So Ahab summoned the 232 junior officers under the provincial commanders. Then he assembled the rest of the Israelites, 7,000 in all. [16] They set out at noon while Ben-Hadad and the 32 kings allied with him were in their tents getting drunk. [17] The junior officers under the provincial commanders went out first.

Now Ben-Hadad had dispatched scouts, who reported, "Men are advancing from Samaria."

[18] He said, "If they have come out for peace, take them alive; if they have come out for war, take them alive."

[19] The junior officers under the provincial commanders marched out of the city with the army behind them [20] and each one struck down his opponent. At that, the Arameans fled, with the Israelites in pursuit. But Ben-Hadad king of Aram escaped on horseback with some of his horsemen. [21] The king of Israel advanced and overpowered the horses and chariots and inflicted heavy losses on the Arameans.

[22] Afterward, the prophet came to the king of Israel and said, "Strengthen your position and see what must be done, because next spring the king of Aram will attack you again."

[23] Meanwhile, the officials of the king of Aram advised him, "Their gods are gods of the hills. That is why they were too strong for us. But if we fight them on the plains, surely we will be stronger than they. [24] Do this: Remove all the kings from their commands and replace them with other officers. [25] You must also raise an army like the one you lost—horse for horse and chariot for chariot—so we can fight Israel on the plains. Then surely we will be stronger than they." He agreed with them and acted accordingly.

[26] The next spring Ben-Hadad mustered the Arameans and went up to Aphek to fight against Israel. [27] When the Israelites were also mustered and given provisions, they marched out to meet them. The Israelites camped opposite them like two small flocks of goats, while the Arameans covered the countryside.

[28] The man of God came up and told the king of Israel, "This is what the LORD says: 'Because the Arameans think the LORD is a god of the hills and not a god of the valleys, I will deliver this vast army into your hands, and you will know that I am the LORD.'"

[29] For seven days they camped opposite each other, and on the seventh day the battle was joined. The Israelites inflicted a hundred thousand casualties on the Aramean foot soldiers in one day. [30] The rest of them escaped to the city of Aphek, where the wall collapsed on twenty-seven thousand of them. And Ben-Hadad fled to the city and hid in an inner room.

[31] His officials said to him, "Look, we have heard that the kings of the house of Israel are merciful. Let us go to the king of Israel with sackcloth around our waists and ropes around our heads. Perhaps he will spare your life."

[32] Wearing sackcloth around their waists and ropes around their heads, they went to the king of Israel and said, "Your servant Ben-Hadad says: 'Please let me live.'"

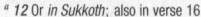

The king answered, "Is he still alive? He is an old ally."

³³The men took this as a good sign and were quick to pick up his word. "Yes, your old ally Ben-Hadad!" they said.

"Go and get him," the king said. When Ben-Hadad came out, Ahab had him come up into his chariot.

³⁴"I will return the cities my father took from your father," Ben-Hadad offered. "You may set up your own market areas in Damascus, as my father did in Samaria."

Ahab said, "On the basis of a treaty I will set you free." So he made a treaty with him, and let him go.

A Prophet Condemns Ahab

³⁵By the word of the LORD one of the company of the prophets said to his companion, "Strike me with your weapon," but he refused.

³⁶So the prophet said, "Because you have not obeyed the LORD, as soon as you leave me a lion will kill you." And after the man went away, a lion found him and killed him.

³⁷The prophet found another man and said, "Strike me, please." So the man struck him and wounded him. ³⁸Then the prophet went and stood by the road waiting for the king. He disguised himself with his headband down over his eyes. ³⁹As the king passed by, the prophet called out to him, "Your servant went into the thick of the battle, and someone came to me with a captive and said, 'Guard this man. If he is missing, it will be your life for his life, or you must pay a talent*a* of silver.' ⁴⁰While your servant was busy here and there, the man disappeared."

"That is your sentence," the king of Israel said. "You have pronounced it yourself."

⁴¹Then the prophet quickly removed the headband from his eyes, and the king of Israel recognized him as one of the prophets. ⁴²He said to the king, "This is what the LORD says: 'You have set free a man I had determined should die.*b* Therefore it is your life for his life, your people for his people.'" ⁴³Sullen and angry, the king of Israel went to his palace in Samaria.

Naboth's Vineyard

21 Some time later there was an incident involving a vineyard belonging to Naboth the Jezreelite. The vineyard was in Jezreel, close to the palace of Ahab king of Samaria. ²Ahab said to Naboth, "Let me have your vineyard to use for a vegetable garden, since it is close to my palace. In exchange I will give you a better vineyard or, if you prefer, I will pay you whatever it is worth."

³But Naboth replied, "The LORD forbid that I should give you the inheritance of my ancestors."

⁴So Ahab went home, sullen and angry because Naboth the Jezreelite had said, "I will not give you the inheritance of my ancestors." He lay on his bed sulking and refused to eat.

⁵His wife Jezebel came in and asked him, "Why are you so sullen? Why won't you eat?"

⁶He answered her, "Because I said to Naboth the Jezreelite, 'Sell me your vineyard; or if you prefer, I will give you another vineyard in its place.' But he said, 'I will not give you my vineyard.'"

⁷Jezebel his wife said, "Is this how you act as king over Israel? Get up and eat! Cheer up. I'll get you the vineyard of Naboth the Jezreelite."

atissue: selfishness

21:1–7 It's funny how quickly we adults turn into children when we don't get what we want. We pout, we beg, we turn on the charm or the guilt—whatever serves our purposes. King Ahab (a grown man, the ruler of a kingdom) decided not to eat. How childish! Too often when we want something, we want it *now*. However, God doesn't excuse our selfishness as childish immaturity. A selfish attitude opens us up for serious consequences when we don't relinquish our rights to God. Are you harboring selfishness? Don't sacrifice what is important trying to possess what you don't truly need.

---

a 39 That is, about 75 pounds or about 34 kilograms   b 42 The Hebrew term refers to the irrevocable giving over of things or persons to the LORD, often by totally destroying them.

[8]So she wrote letters in Ahab's name, placed his seal on them, and sent them to the elders and nobles who lived in Naboth's city with him. [9]In those letters she wrote:

"Proclaim a day of fasting and seat Naboth in a prominent place among the people. [10]But seat two scoundrels opposite him and have them bring charges that he has cursed both God and the king. Then take him out and stone him to death."

[11]So the elders and nobles who lived in Naboth's city did as Jezebel directed in the letters she had written to them. [12]They proclaimed a fast and seated Naboth in a prominent place among the people. [13]Then two scoundrels came and sat opposite him and brought charges against Naboth before the people, saying, "Naboth has cursed both God and the king." So they took him outside the city and stoned him to death. [14]Then they sent word to Jezebel: "Naboth has been stoned to death."

[15]As soon as Jezebel heard that Naboth had been stoned to death, she said to Ahab, "Get up and take possession of the vineyard of Naboth the Jezreelite that he refused to sell you. He is no longer alive, but dead." [16]When Ahab heard that Naboth was dead, he got up and went down to take possession of Naboth's vineyard.

[17]Then the word of the LORD came to Elijah the Tishbite: [18]"Go down to meet Ahab king of Israel, who rules in Samaria. He is now in Naboth's vineyard, where he has gone to take possession of it. [19]Say to him, 'This is what the LORD says: Have you not murdered a man and seized his property?' Then say to him, 'This is what the LORD says: In the place where dogs licked up Naboth's blood, dogs will lick up your blood—yes, yours!'"

[20]Ahab said to Elijah, "So you have found me, my enemy!"

"I have found you," he answered, "because you have sold yourself to do evil in the eyes of the LORD. [21]He says, 'I am going to bring disaster on you. I will wipe out your descendants and cut off from Ahab every last male in Israel—slave or free.[a] [22]I will make your house like that of Jeroboam son of Nebat and that of Baasha son of Ahijah, because you have aroused my anger and have caused Israel to sin.'

[23]"And also concerning Jezebel the LORD says: 'Dogs will devour Jezebel by the wall of[b] Jezreel.'

[24]"Dogs will eat those belonging to Ahab who die in the city, and the birds will feed on those who die in the country."

[25](There was never anyone like Ahab, who sold himself to do evil in the eyes of the LORD, urged on by Jezebel his wife. [26]He behaved in the vilest manner by going after idols, like the Amorites the LORD drove out before Israel.)

[27]When Ahab heard these words, he tore his clothes, put on sackcloth and fasted. He lay in sackcloth and went around meekly.

[28]Then the word of the LORD came to Elijah the Tishbite: [29]"Have you noticed how Ahab has humbled himself before me? Because he has humbled himself, I will not bring this disaster in his day, but I will bring it on his house in the days of his son."

Micaiah Prophesies Against Ahab

22 For three years there was no war between Aram and Israel. [2]But in the third year Jehoshaphat king of Judah went down to see the king of Israel. [3]The king of Israel had said to his officials, "Don't you know that Ramoth Gilead belongs to us and yet we are doing nothing to retake it from the king of Aram?"

[4]So he asked Jehoshaphat, "Will you go with me to fight against Ramoth Gilead?"

Jehoshaphat replied to the king of Israel, "I am as you are, my people as your people, my horses as your horses." [5]But Jehoshaphat also said to the king of Israel, "First seek the counsel of the LORD."

[6]So the king of Israel brought together the prophets—about four hundred men—and asked them, "Shall I go to war against Ramoth Gilead, or shall I refrain?"

"Go," they answered, "for the Lord will give it into the king's hand."

[7]But Jehoshaphat asked, "Is there no longer a prophet of the LORD here whom we can inquire of?"

[8]The king of Israel answered Jehoshaphat, "There is still one through whom we can inquire of the

---

[a] 21 Or Israel—every ruler or leader   [b] 23 Most Hebrew manuscripts; a few Hebrew manuscripts, Vulgate and Syriac (see also 2 Kings 9:26) the plot of ground at

LORD, but I hate him because he never prophesies anything good about me, but always bad. He is Micaiah son of Imlah."

"The king should not say such a thing," Jehoshaphat replied.

⁹So the king of Israel called one of his officials and said, "Bring Micaiah son of Imlah at once."

¹⁰Dressed in their royal robes, the king of Israel and Jehoshaphat king of Judah were sitting on their thrones at the threshing floor by the entrance of the gate of Samaria, with all the prophets prophesying before them. ¹¹Now Zedekiah son of Kenaanah had made iron horns and he declared, "This is what the LORD says: 'With these you will gore the Arameans until they are destroyed.'"

¹²All the other prophets were prophesying the same thing. "Attack Ramoth Gilead and be victorious," they said, "for the LORD will give it into the king's hand."

¹³The messenger who had gone to summon Micaiah said to him, "Look, the other prophets without exception are predicting success for the king. Let your word agree with theirs, and speak favorably."

¹⁴But Micaiah said, "As surely as the LORD lives, I can tell him only what the LORD tells me."

¹⁵When he arrived, the king asked him, "Micaiah, shall we go to war against Ramoth Gilead, or not?"

"Attack and be victorious," he answered, "for the LORD will give it into the king's hand."

¹⁶The king said to him, "How many times must I make you swear to tell me nothing but the truth in the name of the LORD?"

¹⁷Then Micaiah answered, "I saw all Israel scattered on the hills like sheep without a shepherd, and the LORD said, 'These people have no master. Let each one go home in peace.'"

¹⁸The king of Israel said to Jehoshaphat, "Didn't I tell you that he never prophesies anything good about me, but only bad?"

¹⁹Micaiah continued, "Therefore hear the word of the LORD: I saw the LORD sitting on his throne with all the host of heaven standing around him on his right and on his left. ²⁰And the LORD said, 'Who will entice Ahab into attacking Ramoth Gilead and going to his death there?'

"One suggested this, and another that. ²¹Finally, a spirit came forward, stood before the LORD and said, 'I will entice him.'

²²"'By what means?' the LORD asked.

"'I will go out and be a lying spirit in the mouths of all his prophets,' he said.

"'You will succeed in enticing him,' said the LORD. 'Go and do it.'

²³"So now the LORD has put a lying spirit in the mouths of all these prophets of yours. The LORD has decreed disaster for you."

²⁴Then Zedekiah son of Kenaanah went up and slapped Micaiah in the face. "Which way did the spirit from*a* the LORD go when he went from me to speak to you?" he asked.

²⁵Micaiah replied, "You will find out on the day you go to hide in an inner room."

²⁶The king of Israel then ordered, "Take Micaiah and send him back to Amon the ruler of the city and to Joash the king's son ²⁷and say, 'This is what the king says: Put this fellow in prison and give him nothing but bread and water until I return safely.'"

²⁸Micaiah declared, "If you ever return safely, the LORD has not spoken through me." Then he added, "Mark my words, all you people!"

Ahab Killed at Ramoth Gilead

²⁹So the king of Israel and Jehoshaphat king of Judah went up to Ramoth Gilead. ³⁰The king of Israel said to Jehoshaphat, "I will enter the battle in disguise, but you wear your royal robes." So the king of Israel disguised himself and went into battle.

³¹Now the king of Aram had ordered his thirty-two chariot commanders, "Do not fight with anyone, small or great, except the king of Israel." ³²When the chariot commanders saw Jehoshaphat, they thought, "Surely this is the king of Israel." So they turned to attack him, but when Jehoshaphat cried out, ³³the chariot commanders saw that he was not the king of Israel and stopped pursuing him.

³⁴But someone drew his bow at random and hit the king of Israel between the breastplate and the scale armor. The king told his chariot driver, "Wheel around and get me out of the fighting. I've been

---

a 24 Or *Spirit of*

myth# 30

"CHILDREN ARE RESILIENT; DIVORCE WON'T PERMANENTLY AFFECT THEM."

My brother Dominic is thirty-three. I'm thirty. He was older when our parents divorced, and he remembers a lot more about it than I do. So it's not that surprising for him to be reluctant about marriage and raising a family. Dominic says he's afraid of putting children through what he and I went through . . . what if his marriage ended in divorce? What if he has "issues" he can't get past and they affect his marriage?

These are his questions, not my own. I decided a long time ago that I couldn't control what happened with my parents in the past. But I was in charge of my future. I didn't have to carry baggage from my childhood into my marriage. So I decided I wouldn't.

When I was older, I went to counseling for a while, and it helped me ask the right questions about my feelings and experiences. Through the years, I talked with my parents about what happened and tried to understand it from their point of view. In hindsight, they both admitted their share in the problem. They probably should never have married each other in the first place.

That's why I took my time when I dated and eventually fell in love with my husband. I wanted to make sure he understood me, and even more, that I understood myself and my own expectations for marriage. We don't have a perfect marriage. (Who does?) And growing up in a divorced home has brought certain challenges into our relationship that wouldn't otherwise exist. However, in an odd way, I consider our marriage stronger because of the challenges. We don't take commitment for granted. We invest the time and energy it takes to work through our problems and get help when and if we need it.

I wish Dominic would give marriage a chance—he'd be such a good father. I don't understand his reasons. But I understand his pain. It's still there inside of me. It will never go away. But I'm somehow stronger for it.

—Lucia

DOMINIC'S AND LUCIA'S different takes on their parents' divorce is not uncommon. The temptation to make assumptions about a child's reaction is unwise in any scenario. Children are as unpredictable as they are resilient. One may internalize her emotions and become emotionally scarred as a result, while her sibling may express those same emotions in healthy ways and receive help and guidance. Predicting the long-term consequences in a child's life is an inexact science at best. However, we do know some truths about divorce are universal.

- To a certain degree, divorce *will* permanently affect anyone involved. This is one of the reasons God "hates" it (Malachi 2:16), as it is not what he intended.

- Studies have cited the increase in the likelihood that a child from a divorced home will . . .

    Experience poverty, out-of-wedlock pregnancy and behavioral problems.

    Attain less education.

    Experience a divorce in his or her own marriage.

In spite of the evidence, many couples contemplating divorce overestimate a child's resilience for the wrong reasons—to justify a decision loosely termed as "what's best for the children."

At the same time, underestimating God's redemptive power in a family is equally erroneous. Specifically, if you come from a divorced home, the writing is not on the wall regarding your future. There are, however, challenges unique to your situation. If you are wise, you will seek counseling, time for reflection, blame-free conversations with your parents if possible and many moments of solace with God to work through your experience. God can heal and restore you in ways you never thought possible.

> "We've seriously underestimated the long-term impact of divorce on children [and] . . . the numerous ways a child's experiences differ when growing up in a divorced family."
>
> —Judith Wallerstein,
> *The Unexpected Legacy of Divorce:*
> *A 25-Year Landmark Study*

457

> ## "I WILL repay you for THe years THe LOCUSTS Have eaten."
>
> JOEL 2:25

SEE ALSO

Psalm 68:5–6

Malachi 2:16

Romans 8:28

For more on **Divorce** and **Children**, check the index.

wounded." [35] All day long the battle raged, and the king was propped up in his chariot facing the Arameans. The blood from his wound ran onto the floor of the chariot, and that evening he died. [36] As the sun was setting, a cry spread through the army: "Everyone to your own town; everyone to your land!"

[37] So the king died and was brought to Samaria, and they buried him there. [38] They washed the chariot at a pool in Samaria (where the prostitutes bathed),[a] and the dogs licked up his blood, as the word of the LORD had declared.

[39] As for the other events of Ahab's reign, including all he did, the palace he built and inlaid with ivory, and the cities he fortified, are they not written in the book of the annals of the kings of Israel? [40] Ahab rested with his ancestors. And Ahaziah his son succeeded him as king.

Jehoshaphat King of Judah

[41] Jehoshaphat son of Asa became king of Judah in the fourth year of Ahab king of Israel. [42] Jehoshaphat was thirty-five years old when he became king, and he reigned in Jerusalem twenty-five years. His mother's name was Azubah daughter of Shilhi. [43] In everything he followed the ways of his father Asa and did not stray from them; he did what was right in the eyes of the LORD. *The high places, however, were not removed, and the people continued to offer sacrifices and burn incense there. * [44] Jehoshaphat was also at peace with the king of Israel.

[45] As for the other events of Jehoshaphat's reign, the things he achieved and his military exploits, are they not written in the book of the annals of the kings of Judah? [46] He rid the land of the rest of the male shrine prostitutes who remained there even after the reign of his father Asa. [47] There was then no king in Edom; a provincial governor ruled.

[48] Now Jehoshaphat built a fleet of trading ships[b] to go to Ophir for gold, but they never set sail—they were wrecked at Ezion Geber. [49] At that time Ahaziah son of Ahab said to Jehoshaphat, "Let my men sail with yours," but Jehoshaphat refused.

[50] Then Jehoshaphat rested with his ancestors and was buried with them in the city of David his father. And Jehoram his son succeeded him as king.

Ahaziah King of Israel

[51] Ahaziah son of Ahab became king of Israel in Samaria in the seventeenth year of Jehoshaphat king of Judah, and he reigned over Israel two years. [52] He did evil in the eyes of the LORD, because he followed the ways of his father and mother and of Jeroboam son of Nebat, who caused Israel to sin. [53] He served and worshiped Baal and aroused the anger of the LORD, the God of Israel, just as his father had done.

---

[a] *38* Or *Samaria and cleaned the weapons*   [b] *48* Hebrew *of ships of Tarshish*

* This sentence (22:43b) is numbered 22:44 in Hebrew texts.   * 22:44-53 is numbered 22:45-54 in Hebrew texts.

2kings

459

AUTHOR
Unknown.

AUDIENCE
The people of Israel.

DATE
Between 560 and 550 B.C.

SETTING
One kingdom has divided into two.

VERSE TO REMEMBER
"For out of Jerusalem will come a remnant,
and out of Mount Zion a band of survivors."
(19:31)

THEME TO CONSIDER
Where there is punishment for sin, there is
hope for redemption.

2 kings 1:1

The LORD's Judgment on Ahaziah

1 After Ahab's death, Moab rebelled against Israel. ²Now Ahaziah had fallen through the lattice of his upper room in Samaria and injured himself. So he sent messengers, saying to them, "Go and consult Baal-Zebub, the god of Ekron, to see if I will recover from this injury."

³But the angel of the LORD said to Elijah the Tishbite, "Go up and meet the messengers of the king of Samaria and ask them, 'Is it because there is no God in Israel that you are going off to consult Baal-Zebub, the god of Ekron?' ⁴Therefore this is what the LORD says: 'You will not leave the bed you are lying on. You will certainly die!'" So Elijah went.

⁵When the messengers returned to the king, he asked them, "Why have you come back?"

⁶"A man came to meet us," they replied. "And he said to us, 'Go back to the king who sent you and tell him, "This is what the LORD says: Is it because there is no God in Israel that you are sending messengers to consult Baal-Zebub, the god of Ekron? Therefore you will not leave the bed you are lying on. You will certainly die!"'"

⁷The king asked them, "What kind of man was it who came to meet you and told you this?"

⁸They replied, "He had a garment of hair*ᵃ* and had a leather belt around his waist."

The king said, "That was Elijah the Tishbite."

⁹Then he sent to Elijah a captain with his company of fifty men. The captain went up to Elijah, who was sitting on the top of a hill, and said to him, "Man of God, the king says, 'Come down!'"

¹⁰Elijah answered the captain, "If I am a man of God, may fire come down from heaven and consume you and your fifty men!" Then fire fell from heaven and consumed the captain and his men.

¹¹At this the king sent to Elijah another captain with his fifty men. The captain said to him, "Man of God, this is what the king says, 'Come down at once!'"

¹²"If I am a man of God," Elijah replied, "may fire come down from heaven and consume you and your fifty men!" Then the fire of God fell from heaven and consumed him and his fifty men.

¹³So the king sent a third captain with his fifty men. This third captain went up and fell on his knees before Elijah. "Man of God," he begged, "please have respect for my life and the lives of these fifty men, your servants! ¹⁴See, fire has fallen from heaven and consumed the first two captains and all their men. But now have respect for my life!"

¹⁵The angel of the LORD said to Elijah, "Go down with him; do not be afraid of him." So Elijah got up and went down with him to the king.

¹⁶He told the king, "This is what the LORD says: Is it because there is no God in Israel for you to consult that you have sent messengers to consult Baal-Zebub, the god of Ekron? Because you have done this, you will never leave the bed you are lying on. You will certainly die!" ¹⁷So he died, according to the word of the LORD that Elijah had spoken.

Because Ahaziah had no son, Joram*ᵇ* succeeded him as king in the second year of Jehoram son of Jehoshaphat king of Judah. ¹⁸As for all the other events of Ahaziah's reign, and what he did, are they not written in the book of the annals of the kings of Israel?

Elijah Taken Up to Heaven

2 When the LORD was about to take Elijah up to heaven in a whirlwind, Elijah and Elisha were on their way from Gilgal. ²Elijah said to Elisha, "Stay here; the LORD has sent me to Bethel."

But Elisha said, "As surely as the LORD lives and as you live, I will not leave you." So they went down to Bethel.

³The company of the prophets at Bethel came out to Elisha and asked, "Do you know that the LORD is going to take your master from you today?"

"Yes, I know," Elisha replied, "so be quiet."

⁴Then Elijah said to him, "Stay here, Elisha; the LORD has sent me to Jericho."

And he replied, "As surely as the LORD lives and as you live, I will not leave you." So they went to Jericho.

⁵The company of the prophets at Jericho went up to Elisha and asked him, "Do you know that the LORD is going to take your master from you today?"

ᵃ 8 Or He was a hairy man   *ᵇ 17 Hebrew Jehoram, a variant of Joram*

"Yes, I know," he replied, "so be quiet."

⁶Then Elijah said to him, "Stay here; the LORD has sent me to the Jordan."

And he replied, "As surely as the LORD lives and as you live, I will not leave you." So the two of them walked on.

⁷Fifty men from the company of the prophets went and stood at a distance, facing the place where Elijah and Elisha had stopped at the Jordan. ⁸Elijah took his cloak, rolled it up and struck the water with it. The water divided to the right and to the left, and the two of them crossed over on dry ground.

⁹When they had crossed, Elijah said to Elisha, "Tell me, what can I do for you before I am taken from you?"

"Let me inherit a double portion of your spirit," Elisha replied.

¹⁰"You have asked a difficult thing," Elijah said, "yet if you see me when I am taken from you, it will be yours—otherwise, it will not."

¹¹As they were walking along and talking together, suddenly a chariot of fire and horses of fire appeared and separated the two of them, and Elijah went up to heaven in a whirlwind. ¹²Elisha saw this and cried out, "My father! My father! The chariots and horsemen of Israel!" And Elisha saw him no more. Then he took hold of his garment and tore it in two.

¹³He picked up the cloak that had fallen from Elijah and went back and stood on the bank of the Jordan. ¹⁴Then he took the cloak that had fallen from him and struck the water with it. "Where now is the LORD, the God of Elijah?" he asked. When he struck the water, it divided to the right and to the left, and he crossed over.

¹⁵The company of the prophets from Jericho, who were watching, said, "The spirit of Elijah is resting on Elisha." And they went to meet him and bowed to the ground before him. ¹⁶"Look," they said, "we your servants have fifty able men. Let them go and look for your master. Perhaps the Spirit of the LORD has picked him up and set him down on some mountain or in some valley."

"No," Elisha replied, "do not send them."

¹⁷But they persisted until he was too embarrassed to refuse. So he said, "Send them." And they sent fifty men, who searched for three days but did not find him. ¹⁸When they returned to Elisha, who was staying in Jericho, he said to them, "Didn't I tell you not to go?"

Healing of the Water

¹⁹The people of the city said to Elisha, "Look, our lord, this town is well situated, as you can see, but the water is bad and the land is unproductive."

²⁰"Bring me a new bowl," he said, "and put salt in it." So they brought it to him.

²¹Then he went out to the spring and threw the salt into it, saying, "This is what the LORD says: 'I have healed this water. Never again will it cause death or make the land unproductive.'" ²²And the water has remained pure to this day, according to the word Elisha had spoken.

Elisha Is Jeered

²³From there Elisha went up to Bethel. As he was walking along the road, some boys came out of the town and jeered at him. "Get out of here, baldy!" they said. "Get out of here, baldy!" ²⁴He turned around, looked at them and called down a curse on them in the name of the LORD. Then two bears came out of

461

myth#31

"TO BE EFFECTIVE IN MINISTRY OR IN LIFE, I NEED TO EXPERIENCE ALL KINDS OF THINGS."

The other day at youth group (I'm one of the youth leaders), I heard the most amazing testimony from our guest speaker—a former drug addict who became a Christian. He talked about all of the wild things he'd done and how God had miraculously healed him and delivered him out of that lifestyle.

Sitting there, I couldn't help wondering how effective my life has been. I mean, what have I experienced? I grew up in church. I can't remember a time when I didn't know Jesus. I was a straight-A student all the way through high school, college and even grad school. I've never been drunk. Never smoked. I've never been rebellious, unless you call talking back to my dad a lot when I was 15 rebellious. I've never even shoplifted any-thing! And I don't have a good I've-been-dumped-by-the-worst-guy story like so many women seem to have. I met my husband in college and married him afterward. He's a great guy! (Not that there's anything wrong with that.)

See what I mean? No one would want to hear my story. It's boring! People want to hear about all of the wild stuff you've been into. That's why I don't feel like I'm as effective as the former drug addict. I mean, I love the kids I'm working with. But am I the best person to work with the youth?

Sometimes I wonder if I've missed out on things in life. Do I need to sow some wild oats? Should all of us do that?

—Elaine

YOU MAY HEAR that you've got to experience all kinds of things in order to be effective in ministry. After all, some may reason, how can you relate to people if you haven't experienced "all the meats of our cultural stew," as a well-known cartoon character once proclaimed?

There is a big difference between living a sheltered life—one that avoids all contact with non-Christians out of fear of "contamination"—and a life set apart by God. Jesus lived a sinless life. Yet even though he never got crazy at a party or committed a crime, he interacted with and related to all kinds of people. For example, Jesus never committed adultery, yet he had compassion on a woman who was caught in the act, and he stepped in to save her from being stoned to death (see John 8:1–11).

You don't have to experience everything to know that certain things are harmful and should be avoided. You don't have to read racy novels and watch R-rated movies so that you're "exposed to what's out there." You don't have to listen to profanity-laced rap with warning labels on the cover so that you know what kids-these-days are into. You don't have to fail miserably at a relationship so that you can relate to others who are hurting.

Yet living a "clean life" does not give one license to prejudge every experience or any person. Just think: Jesus was harshest with the Pharisees—the legalists of the day. They readily pointed out the "sinners" while excluding themselves from that group.

Want to be effective? Echo these words from David the psalmist: "Test me, LORD, and try me, examine my heart and my mind" (Psalm 26:2).

> "A person's response to the meaning and personal value of Jesus Christ's life, death and resurrection is usually determined before a person reaches eighteen. In fact, a majority of Americans make a lasting determination about the personal significance of Christ's death and resurrection by age twelve."
>
> —Barna Research Group (2003)

463

> "THE WORLD
> AND ITS DESIRES
> PASS AWAY,
> BUT WHOEVER DOES
> THE WILL OF GOD
> LIVES FOREVER."
>
> 1 JOHN 2:17

SEE ALSO

Matthew 7:1
Luke 15:11–32
2 Corinthians 10:12–18
Titus 2:11–14

For more on **Media** and **Testimony**, check the index.

the woods and mauled forty-two of the boys. ²⁵And he went on to Mount Carmel and from there returned to Samaria.

Moab Revolts

3 Joram[a] son of Ahab became king of Israel in Samaria in the eighteenth year of Jehoshaphat king of Judah, and he reigned twelve years. ²He did evil in the eyes of the LORD, but not as his father and mother had done. He got rid of the sacred stone of Baal that his father had made. ³Nevertheless he clung to the sins of Jeroboam son of Nebat, which he had caused Israel to commit; he did not turn away from them.

⁴Now Mesha king of Moab raised sheep, and he had to pay the king of Israel a tribute of a hundred thousand lambs and the wool of a hundred thousand rams. ⁵But after Ahab died, the king of Moab rebelled against the king of Israel. ⁶So at that time King Joram set out from Samaria and mobilized all Israel. ⁷He also sent this message to Jehoshaphat king of Judah: "The king of Moab has rebelled against me. Will you go with me to fight against Moab?"

"I will go with you," he replied. "I am as you are, my people as your people, my horses as your horses."

⁸"By what route shall we attack?" he asked.

"Through the Desert of Edom," he answered.

⁹So the king of Israel set out with the king of Judah and the king of Edom. After a roundabout march of seven days, the army had no more water for themselves or for the animals with them.

¹⁰"What!" exclaimed the king of Israel. "Has the LORD called us three kings together only to deliver us into the hands of Moab?"

¹¹But Jehoshaphat asked, "Is there no prophet of the LORD here, through whom we may inquire of the LORD?"

An officer of the king of Israel answered, "Elisha son of Shaphat is here. He used to pour water on the hands of Elijah.[b]"

¹²Jehoshaphat said, "The word of the LORD is with him." So the king of Israel and Jehoshaphat and the king of Edom went down to him.

¹³Elisha said to the king of Israel, "Why do you want to involve me? Go to the prophets of your father and the prophets of your mother."

"No," the king of Israel answered, "because it was the LORD who called us three kings together to deliver us into the hands of Moab."

¹⁴Elisha said, "As surely as the LORD Almighty lives, whom I serve, if I did not have respect for the presence of Jehoshaphat king of Judah, I would not pay any attention to you. ¹⁵But now bring me a harpist."

While the harpist was playing, the hand of the LORD came on Elisha ¹⁶and he said, "This is what the LORD says: I will fill this valley with pools of water. ¹⁷For this is what the LORD says: You will see neither wind nor rain, yet this valley will be filled with water, and you, your cattle and your other animals will drink. ¹⁸This is an easy thing in the eyes of the LORD; he will also deliver Moab into your hands. ¹⁹You will overthrow every fortified city and every major town. You will cut down every good tree, stop up all the springs, and ruin every good field with stones."

²⁰The next morning, about the time for offering the sacrifice, there it was—water flowing from the direction of Edom! And the land was filled with water.

²¹Now all the Moabites had heard that the kings had come to fight against them; so every man, young and old, who could bear arms was called up and stationed on the border. ²²When they got up early in the morning, the sun was shining on the water. To the Moabites across the way, the water looked red—like blood. ²³"That's blood!" they said. "Those kings must have fought and slaughtered each other. Now to the plunder, Moab!"

²⁴But when the Moabites came to the camp of Israel, the Israelites rose up and fought them until they fled. And the Israelites invaded the land and slaughtered the Moabites. ²⁵They destroyed the towns, and each man threw a stone on every good field until it was covered. They stopped up all the springs and cut

---

a 1 Hebrew *Jehoram*, a variant of *Joram*; also in verse 6   *b 11* That is, he was Elijah's personal servant.

down every good tree. Only Kir Hareseth was left with its stones in place, but men armed with slings surrounded it and attacked it.

²⁶When the king of Moab saw that the battle had gone against him, he took with him seven hundred swordsmen to break through to the king of Edom, but they failed. ²⁷Then he took his firstborn son, who was to succeed him as king, and offered him as a sacrifice on the city wall. The fury against Israel was great; they withdrew and returned to their own land.

The Widow's Oil

4 The wife of a man from the company of the prophets cried out to Elisha, "Your servant my husband is dead, and you know that he revered the LORD. But now his creditor is coming to take my two boys as his slaves."

²Elisha replied to her, "How can I help you? Tell me, what do you have in your house?"

"Your servant has nothing there at all," she said, "except a little olive oil."

³Elisha said, "Go around and ask all your neighbors for empty jars. Don't ask for just a few. ⁴Then go inside and shut the door behind you and your sons. Pour oil into all the jars, and as each is filled, put it to one side."

⁵She left him and shut the door behind her and her sons. They brought the jars to her and she kept pouring. ⁶When all the jars were full, she said to her son, "Bring me another one."

But he replied, "There is not a jar left." Then the oil stopped flowing.

⁷She went and told the man of God, and he said, "Go, sell the oil and pay your debts. You and your sons can live on what is left."

The Shunammite's Son Restored to Life

⁸One day Elisha went to Shunem. And a well-to-do woman was there, who urged him to stay for a meal. So whenever he came by, he stopped there to eat. ⁹She said to her husband, "I know that this man who often comes our way is a holy man of God. ¹⁰Let's make a small room on the roof and put in it a bed and a table, a chair and a lamp for him. Then he can stay there whenever he comes to us."

¹¹One day when Elisha came, he went up to his room and lay down there. ¹²He said to his servant Gehazi, "Call the Shunammite." So he called her, and she stood before him. ¹³Elisha said to him, "Tell her, 'You have gone to all this trouble for us. Now what can be done for you? Can we speak on your behalf to the king or the commander of the army?'"

She replied, "I have a home among my own people."

¹⁴"What can be done for her?" Elisha asked.

Gehazi said, "She has no son, and her husband is old."

¹⁵Then Elisha said, "Call her." So he called her, and she stood in the doorway. ¹⁶"About this time next year," Elisha said, "you will hold a son in your arms."

"No, my lord!" she objected. "Please, man of God, don't mislead your servant!"

¹⁷But the woman became pregnant, and the next year about that same time she gave birth to a son, just as Elisha had told her.

¹⁸The child grew, and one day he went out to his father, who was with the reapers. ¹⁹He said to his father, "My head! My head!"

His father told a servant, "Carry him to his mother." ²⁰After the servant had lifted him up and carried

---

at issue: financial stress

4:1–7 Money is frequently the last stronghold we relinquish to God's control. We give ourselves a false sense of security if we can balance our checkbooks and keep budgets. But if an unforeseen illness or accident happens, then suddenly we realize we're not in control anymore (as if we ever really were). The destitute widow came to Elisha when she had exhausted all other options for saving herself. And God was gracious. Include God in your finances from the beginning. He can help you with any financial situation you face; he wants you to depend solely on him.

465

him to his mother, the boy sat on her lap until noon, and then he died. ²¹She went up and laid him on the bed of the man of God, then shut the door and went out.

²²She called her husband and said, "Please send me one of the servants and a donkey so I can go to the man of God quickly and return."

²³"Why go to him today?" he asked. "It's not the New Moon or the Sabbath."

"That's all right," she said.

²⁴She saddled the donkey and said to her servant, "Lead on; don't slow down for me unless I tell you." ²⁵So she set out and came to the man of God at Mount Carmel.

When he saw her in the distance, the man of God said to his servant Gehazi, "Look! There's the Shunammite! ²⁶Run to meet her and ask her, 'Are you all right? Is your husband all right? Is your child all right?'"

"Everything is all right," she said.

²⁷When she reached the man of God at the mountain, she took hold of his feet. Gehazi came over to push her away, but the man of God said, "Leave her alone! She is in bitter distress, but the LORD has hidden it from me and has not told me why."

²⁸"Did I ask you for a son, my lord?" she said. "Didn't I tell you, 'Don't raise my hopes'?"

²⁹Elisha said to Gehazi, "Tuck your cloak into your belt, take my staff in your hand and run. Don't greet anyone you meet, and if anyone greets you, do not answer. Lay my staff on the boy's face."

³⁰But the child's mother said, "As surely as the LORD lives and as you live, I will not leave you." So he got up and followed her.

³¹Gehazi went on ahead and laid the staff on the boy's face, but there was no sound or response. So Gehazi went back to meet Elisha and told him, "The boy has not awakened."

³²When Elisha reached the house, there was the boy lying dead on his couch. ³³He went in, shut the door on the two of them and prayed to the LORD. ³⁴Then he got on the bed and lay on the boy, mouth to mouth, eyes to eyes, hands to hands. As he stretched himself out on him, the boy's body grew warm. ³⁵Elisha turned away and walked back and forth in the room and then got on the bed and stretched out on him once more. The boy sneezed seven times and opened his eyes.

³⁶Elisha summoned Gehazi and said, "Call the Shunammite." And he did. When she came, he said, "Take your son." ³⁷She came in, fell at his feet and bowed to the ground. Then she took her son and went out.

Death in the Pot

³⁸Elisha returned to Gilgal and there was a famine in that region. While the company of the prophets was meeting with him, he said to his servant, "Put on the large pot and cook some stew for this company."

³⁹One of them went out into the fields to gather herbs and found a wild vine. He gathered some of its gourds and filled the fold of his cloak. When he returned, he cut them up into the pot of stew, though no one knew what they were. ⁴⁰The stew was poured out for the men, but as they began to eat it, they cried out, "Man of God, there is death in the pot!" And they could not eat it.

HE IS: nourishing

4:38–44 God used Elisha to demonstrate that he is *nourishing*. During a famine, God used Elisha to remove the poison from the prophets' stew. Then, with only twenty loaves of bread, God's prophet fed one hundred men and had some left over!

God doesn't just care about our spiritual needs; he cares about our physical needs as well. God can use you to show people that he is *nourishing*. Give what you have from your pantry, your pocketbook or your possessions, and watch what happens. By meeting others' physical needs, you tangibly show God's love to those who hunger.

For the next He Is, go to p. 469.

[41] Elisha said, "Get some flour." He put it into the pot and said, "Serve it to the people to eat." And there was nothing harmful in the pot.

Feeding of a Hundred

[42] A man came from Baal Shalishah, bringing the man of God twenty loaves of barley bread baked from the first ripe grain, along with some heads of new grain. "Give it to the people to eat," Elisha said.

[43] "How can I set this before a hundred men?" his servant asked.

But Elisha answered, "Give it to the people to eat. For this is what the LORD says: 'They will eat and have some left over.'" [44] Then he set it before them, and they ate and had some left over, according to the word of the LORD.

Naaman Healed of Leprosy

5 Now Naaman was commander of the army of the king of Aram. He was a great man in the sight of his master and highly regarded, because through him the LORD had given victory to Aram. He was a valiant soldier, but he had leprosy.[a]

[2] Now bands of raiders from Aram had gone out and had taken captive a young girl from Israel, and she served Naaman's wife. [3] She said to her mistress, "If only my master would see the prophet who is in Samaria! He would cure him of his leprosy."

[4] Naaman went to his master and told him what the girl from Israel had said. [5] "By all means, go," the king of Aram replied. "I will send a letter to the king of Israel." So Naaman left, taking with him ten talents[b] of silver, six thousand shekels[c] of gold and ten sets of clothing. [6] The letter that he took to the king of Israel read: "With this letter I am sending my servant Naaman to you so that you may cure him of his leprosy."

[7] As soon as the king of Israel read the letter, he tore his robes and said, "Am I God? Can I kill and bring back to life? Why does this fellow send someone to me to be cured of his leprosy? See how he is trying to pick a quarrel with me!"

[8] When Elisha the man of God heard that the king of Israel had torn his robes, he sent him this message: "Why have you torn your robes? Have the man come to me and he will know that there is a prophet in Israel." [9] So Naaman went with his horses and chariots and stopped at the door of Elisha's house. [10] Elisha sent a messenger to say to him, "Go, wash yourself seven times in the Jordan, and your flesh will be restored and you will be cleansed."

[11] But Naaman went away angry and said, "I thought that he would surely come out to me and stand and call on the name of the LORD his God, wave his hand over the spot and cure me of my leprosy. [12] Are not Abana and Pharpar, the rivers of Damascus, better than all the waters of Israel? Couldn't I wash in them and be cleansed?" So he turned and went off in a rage.

[13] Naaman's servants went to him and said, "My father, if the prophet had told you to do some great thing, would you not have done it? How much more, then, when he tells you, 'Wash and be cleansed'!" [14] So he went down and dipped himself in the Jordan seven times, as the man of God had told him, and his flesh was restored and became clean like that of a young boy.

[15] Then Naaman and all his attendants went back to the man of God. He stood before him and said, "Now I know that there is no God in all the world except in Israel. So please accept a gift from your servant."

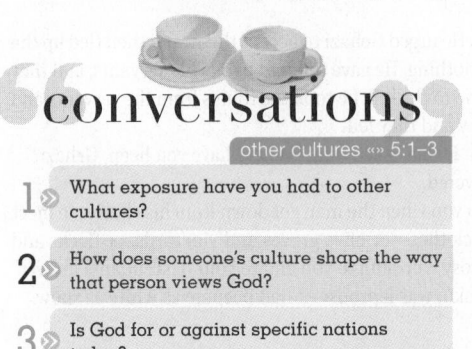

conversations

other cultures «» 5:1–3

1» What exposure have you had to other cultures?

2» How does someone's culture shape the way that person views God?

3» Is God for or against specific nations today?

For more on other **cultures**, check the index.
For the next Conversations, go to p. 479.

467

---

[a] *1* The Hebrew for *leprosy* was used for various diseases affecting the skin; also in verses 3, 6, 7, 11 and 27.   [b] *5* That is, about 750 pounds or about 340 kilograms   [c] *5* That is, about 150 pounds or about 68 kilograms

¹⁶The prophet answered, "As surely as the LORD lives, whom I serve, I will not accept a thing." And even though Naaman urged him, he refused.

¹⁷"If you will not," said Naaman, "please let me, your servant, be given as much earth as a pair of mules can carry, for your servant will never again make burnt offerings and sacrifices to any other god but the LORD. ¹⁸But may the LORD forgive your servant for this one thing: When my master enters the temple of Rimmon to bow down and he is leaning on my arm and I have to bow there also—when I bow down in the temple of Rimmon, may the LORD forgive your servant for this."

¹⁹"Go in peace," Elisha said.

After Naaman had traveled some distance, ²⁰Gehazi, the servant of Elisha the man of God, said to himself, "My master was too easy on Naaman, this Aramean, by not accepting from him what he brought. As surely as the LORD lives, I will run after him and get something from him."

²¹So Gehazi hurried after Naaman. When Naaman saw him running toward him, he got down from the chariot to meet him. "Is everything all right?" he asked.

²²"Everything is all right," Gehazi answered. "My master sent me to say, 'Two young men from the company of the prophets have just come to me from the hill country of Ephraim. Please give them a talent^a of silver and two sets of clothing.'"

²³"By all means, take two talents," said Naaman. He urged Gehazi to accept them, and then tied up the two talents of silver in two bags, with two sets of clothing. He gave them to two of his servants, and they carried them ahead of Gehazi. ²⁴When Gehazi came to the hill, he took the things from the servants and put them away in the house. He sent the men away and they left.

²⁵When he went in and stood before his master, Elisha asked him, "Where have you been, Gehazi?"

"Your servant didn't go anywhere," Gehazi answered.

²⁶But Elisha said to him, "Was not my spirit with you when the man got down from his chariot to meet you? Is this the time to take money or to accept clothes—or olive groves and vineyards, or flocks and herds, or male and female slaves? ²⁷Naaman's leprosy will cling to you and to your descendants forever." Then Gehazi went from Elisha's presence and his skin was leprous—it had become as white as snow.

An Axhead Floats

6 The company of the prophets said to Elisha, "Look, the place where we meet with you is too small for us. ²Let us go to the Jordan, where each of us can get a pole; and let us build a place there for us to meet."

And he said, "Go."

³Then one of them said, "Won't you please come with your servants?"

"I will," Elisha replied. ⁴And he went with them.

They went to the Jordan and began to cut down trees. ⁵As one of them was cutting down a tree, the iron axhead fell into the water. "Oh no, my lord!" he cried out. "It was borrowed!"

⁶The man of God asked, "Where did it fall?" When he showed him the place, Elisha cut a stick and threw it there, and made the iron float. ⁷"Lift it out," he said. Then the man reached out his hand and took it.

Elisha Traps Blinded Arameans

⁸Now the king of Aram was at war with Israel. After conferring with his officers, he said, "I will set up my camp in such and such a place."

⁹The man of God sent word to the king of Israel: "Beware of passing that place, because the Arameans are going down there." ¹⁰So the king of Israel checked on the place indicated by the man of God. Time and again Elisha warned the king, so that he was on his guard in such places.

¹¹This enraged the king of Aram. He summoned his officers and demanded of them, "Tell me! Which of us is on the side of the king of Israel?"

¹²"None of us, my lord the king," said one of his officers, "but Elisha, the prophet who is in Israel, tells the king of Israel the very words you speak in your bedroom."

^a 22 That is, about 75 pounds or about 34 kilograms

¹³"Go, find out where he is," the king ordered, "so I can send men and capture him." The report came back: "He is in Dothan." ¹⁴Then he sent horses and chariots and a strong force there. They went by night and surrounded the city.

¹⁵When the servant of the man of God got up and went out early the next morning, an army with horses and chariots had surrounded the city. "Oh no, my lord! What shall we do?" the servant asked.

¹⁶"Don't be afraid," the prophet answered. "Those who are with us are more than those who are with them."

¹⁷And Elisha prayed, "Open his eyes, LORD, so that he may see." Then the LORD opened the servant's eyes, and he looked and saw the hills full of horses and chariots of fire all around Elisha.

HE IS: eye-opening

6:16–17 Elisha didn't fear the enemy because he saw through eyes of faith. Wanting his servant to have confidence too, he prayed for the Lord to open the servant's eyes. As the man gazed into the spiritual realm, he understood that God had posted heavenly hosts to stand guard.

If only we could see as God sees, then we wouldn't be afraid! If the world's closing in on you, ask God to be *eye-opening* for you. Though you may not see chariots of fire as Elijah's servant did, you can have confidence that God has legions ready to surround and protect you.

469

For the next He Is, go to p. 471.

¹⁸As the enemy came down toward him, Elisha prayed to the LORD, "Strike this army with blindness." So he struck them with blindness, as Elisha had asked.

¹⁹Elisha told them, "This is not the road and this is not the city. Follow me, and I will lead you to the man you are looking for." And he led them to Samaria.

²⁰After they entered the city, Elisha said, "LORD, open the eyes of these men so they can see." Then the LORD opened their eyes and they looked, and there they were, inside Samaria.

²¹When the king of Israel saw them, he asked Elisha, "Shall I kill them, my father? Shall I kill them?"

²²"Do not kill them," he answered. "Would you kill those you have captured with your own sword or bow? Set food and water before them so that they may eat and drink and then go back to their master." ²³So he prepared a great feast for them, and after they had finished eating and drinking, he sent them away, and they returned to their master. So the bands from Aram stopped raiding Israel's territory.

Famine in Besieged Samaria

²⁴Some time later, Ben-Hadad king of Aram mobilized his entire army and marched up and laid siege to Samaria. ²⁵There was a great famine in the city; the siege lasted so long that a donkey's head sold for eighty shekels*ᵃ* of silver, and a quarter of a cab*ᵇ* of seed pods*ᶜ* for five shekels.*ᵈ*

²⁶As the king of Israel was passing by on the wall, a woman cried to him, "Help me, my lord the king!"

²⁷The king replied, "If the LORD does not help you, where can I get help for you? From the threshing floor? From the winepress?" ²⁸Then he asked her, "What's the matter?"

She answered, "This woman said to me, 'Give up your son so we may eat him today, and tomorrow we'll eat my son.' ²⁹So we cooked my son and ate him. The next day I said to her, 'Give up your son so we may eat him,' but she had hidden him."

³⁰When the king heard the woman's words, he tore his robes. As he went along the wall, the people looked, and they saw that, under his robes, he had sackcloth on his body. ³¹He said, "May God deal with me, be it ever so severely, if the head of Elisha son of Shaphat remains on his shoulders today!"

³²Now Elisha was sitting in his house, and the elders were sitting with him. The king sent a messenger

---

ᵃ 25 That is, about 2 pounds or about 920 grams   *ᵇ 25* That is, probably about 1/4 pound or about 100 grams   *ᶜ 25* Or *of doves' dung*   *ᵈ 25* That is, about 2 ounces or about 55 grams ahead, but before he arrived, Elisha said to the elders, "Don't you see how this murderer is sending some-one to cut off my head? Look, when the messenger comes, shut the door and hold it shut against him. Is not the sound of his master's footsteps behind him?" ³³While he was still talking to them, the messenger came down to him.

The king said, "This disaster is from the LORD. Why should I wait for the LORD any longer?"

7 Elisha replied, "Hear the word of the LORD. This is what the LORD says: About this time tomorrow, a seah^a of the finest flour will sell for a shekel^b and two seahs^c of barley for a shekel at the gate of Samaria."

²The officer on whose arm the king was leaning said to the man of God, "Look, even if the LORD should open the floodgates of the heavens, could this happen?"

"You will see it with your own eyes," answered Elisha, "but you will not eat any of it!"

The Siege Lifted

³Now there were four men with leprosy ^d at the entrance of the city gate. They said to each other, "Why stay here until we die? ⁴If we say, 'We'll go into the city'—the famine is there, and we will die. And if we stay here, we will die. So let's go over to the camp of the Arameans and surrender. If they spare us, we live; if they kill us, then we die."

⁵At dusk they got up and went to the camp of the Arameans. When they reached the edge of the camp, no one was there, ⁶for the Lord had caused the Arameans to hear the sound of chariots and horses and a great army, so that they said to one another, "Look, the king of Israel has hired the Hittite and Egyptian kings to attack us!" ⁷So they got up and fled in the dusk and abandoned their tents and their horses and donkeys. They left the camp as it was and ran for their lives.

⁸The men who had leprosy reached the edge of the camp, entered one of the tents and ate and drank. Then they took silver, gold and clothes, and went off and hid them. They returned and entered another tent and took some things from it and hid them also.

⁹Then they said to each other, "What we're doing is not right. This is a day of good news and we are keeping it to ourselves. If we wait until daylight, punishment will overtake us. Let's go at once and report this to the royal palace."

¹⁰So they went and called out to the city gatekeepers and told them, "We went into the Aramean camp and no one was there—not a sound of anyone—only tethered horses and donkeys, and the tents left just as they were." ¹¹The gatekeepers shouted the news, and it was reported within the palace.

¹²The king got up in the night and said to his officers, "I will tell you what the Arameans have done to us. They know we are starving; so they have left the camp to hide in the countryside, thinking, 'They will surely come out, and then we will take them alive and get into the city.'"

¹³One of his officers answered, "Have some men take five of the horses that are left in the city. Their plight will be like that of all the Israelites left here—yes, they will only be like all these Israelites who are doomed. So let us send them to find out what happened."

¹⁴So they selected two chariots with their horses, and the king sent them after the Aramean army. He commanded the drivers, "Go and find out what has happened." ¹⁵They followed them as far as the Jordan, and they found the whole road strewn with the clothing and equipment the Arameans had thrown away in their headlong flight. So the messengers returned and reported to the king. ¹⁶Then the people went out and plundered the camp of the Arameans. So a seah of the finest flour sold for a shekel, and two seahs of barley sold for a shekel, as the LORD had said.

¹⁷Now the king had put the officer on whose arm he leaned in charge of the gate, and the people trampled him in the gateway, and he died, just as the man of God had foretold when the king came down to his house. ¹⁸It happened as the man of God had said to the king: "About this time tomorrow, a seah of the finest flour will sell for a shekel and two seahs of barley for a shekel at the gate of Samaria."

¹⁹The officer had said to the man of God, "Look, even if the LORD should open the floodgates of the heavens, could this happen?" The man of God had replied, "You will see it with your own eyes, but you

---

^a *1* That is, probably about 12 pounds or about 5.5 kilograms; also in verses 16 and 18   ^b *1* That is, about 2/5 ounce or about 11.5 grams; also in verses 16 and 18   ^c *1* That is, probably about 20 pounds or about 9 kilograms; also in verses 16 and 18   ^d *3* The Hebrew for *leprosy* was used for various diseases affecting the skin; also in verse 8.

will not eat any of it!" [20] And that is exactly what happened to him, for the people trampled him in the gateway, and he died.

The Shunammite's Land Restored

8 Now Elisha had said to the woman whose son he had restored to life, "Go away with your family and stay for a while wherever you can, because the LORD has decreed a famine in the land that will last seven years." [2] The woman proceeded to do as the man of God said. She and her family went away and stayed in the land of the Philistines seven years.

[3] At the end of the seven years she came back from the land of the Philistines and went to appeal to the king for her house and land. [4] The king was talking to Gehazi, the servant of the man of God, and had said, "Tell me about all the great things Elisha has done." [5] Just as Gehazi was telling the king how Elisha had restored the dead to life, the woman whose son Elisha had brought back to life came to appeal to the king for her house and land.

Gehazi said, "This is the woman, my lord the king, and this is her son whom Elisha restored to life." [6] The king asked the woman about it, and she told him.

Then he assigned an official to her case and said to him, "Give back everything that belonged to her, including all the income from her land from the day she left the country until now."

Hazael Murders Ben-Hadad

[7] Elisha went to Damascus, and Ben-Hadad king of Aram was ill. When the king was told, "The man of God has come all the way up here," [8] he said to Hazael, "Take a gift with you and go to meet the man of God. Consult the LORD through him; ask him, 'Will I recover from this illness?'"

[9] Hazael went to meet Elisha, taking with him as a gift forty camel-loads of all the finest wares of Damascus. He went in and stood before him, and said, "Your son Ben-Hadad king of Aram has sent me to ask, 'Will I recover from this illness?'"

[10] Elisha answered, "Go and say to him, 'You will certainly recover.' Nevertheless,[a] the LORD has revealed to me that he will in fact die." [11] He stared at him with a fixed gaze until Hazael was embarrassed. Then the man of God began to weep.

[12] "Why is my lord weeping?" asked Hazael.

"Because I know the harm you will do to the Israelites," he answered. "You will set fire to their fortified places, kill their young men with the sword, dash their little children to the ground, and rip open their pregnant women."

[13] Hazael said, "How could your servant, a mere dog, accomplish such a feat?"

"The LORD has shown me that you will become king of Aram," answered Elisha.

[14] Then Hazael left Elisha and returned to his master. When Ben-Hadad asked, "What did Elisha say to you?" Hazael replied, "He told me that you would certainly recover." [15] But the next day he took a thick cloth, soaked it in water and spread it over the king's face, so that he died. Then Hazael succeeded him as king.

471

---

[a] 10 The Hebrew may also be read *Go and say, 'You will certainly not recover,' for.*

HE IS: heart-searching

8:11–13 God looked into Hazael's heart and saw a murderer who would kill his king, claim the throne and treat the Israelites with merciless brutality. This insight into Hazael's heart brought the prophet Elisha to tears. However, when Hazael was confronted with the evil in his soul, he questioned it.

God is *heart-searching*. He sees the evil we conceal. When God probes your heart and reveals the wickedness within, how do you respond? Like Hazael, do you deny the truth?

For the next He Is, go to p. 489.

2 kings 8:16

Jehoram King of Judah

¹⁶In the fifth year of Joram son of Ahab king of Israel, when Jehoshaphat was king of Judah, Jehoram son of Jehoshaphat began his reign as king of Judah. ¹⁷He was thirty-two years old when he became king, and he reigned in Jerusalem eight years. ¹⁸He followed the ways of the kings of Israel, as the house of Ahab had done, for he married a daughter of Ahab. He did evil in the eyes of the LORD. ¹⁹Nevertheless, for the sake of his servant David, the LORD was not willing to destroy Judah. He had promised to maintain a lamp for David and his descendants forever.

²⁰In the time of Jehoram, Edom rebelled against Judah and set up its own king. ²¹So Jehoram^{*a*} went to Zair with all his chariots. The Edomites surrounded him and his chariot commanders, but he rose up and broke through by night; his army, however, fled back home. ²²To this day Edom has been in rebellion against Judah. Libnah revolted at the same time.

²³As for the other events of Jehoram's reign, and all he did, are they not written in the book of the annals of the kings of Judah? ²⁴Jehoram rested with his ancestors and was buried with them in the City of David. And Ahaziah his son succeeded him as king.

Ahaziah King of Judah

²⁵In the twelfth year of Joram son of Ahab king of Israel, Ahaziah son of Jehoram king of Judah began to reign. ²⁶Ahaziah was twenty-two years old when he became king, and he reigned in Jerusalem one year. His mother's name was Athaliah, a granddaughter of Omri king of Israel. ²⁷He followed the ways of the house of Ahab and did evil in the eyes of the LORD, as the house of Ahab had done, for he was related by marriage to Ahab's family.

²⁸Ahaziah went with Joram son of Ahab to war against Hazael king of Aram at Ramoth Gilead. The Arameans wounded Joram; ²⁹so King Joram returned to Jezreel to recover from the wounds the Arameans had inflicted on him at Ramoth^{*b*} in his battle with Hazael king of Aram.

Then Ahaziah son of Jehoram king of Judah went down to Jezreel to see Joram son of Ahab, because he had been wounded.

Jehu Anointed King of Israel

9 The prophet Elisha summoned a man from the company of the prophets and said to him, "Tuck your cloak into your belt, take this flask of oil with you and go to Ramoth Gilead. ²When you get there, look for Jehu son of Jehoshaphat, the son of Nimshi. Go to him, get him away from his companions and take him into an inner room. ³Then take the flask and pour the oil on his head and declare, 'This is what the LORD says: I anoint you king over Israel.' Then open the door and run; don't delay!"

⁴So the young prophet went to Ramoth Gilead. ⁵When he arrived, he found the army officers sitting together. "I have a message for you, commander," he said.

"For which of us?" asked Jehu.

"For you, commander," he replied.

⁶Jehu got up and went into the house. Then the prophet poured the oil on Jehu's head and declared, "This is what the LORD, the God of Israel, says: 'I anoint you king over the LORD's people Israel. ⁷You are to destroy the house of Ahab your master, and I will avenge the blood of my servants the prophets and the blood of all the LORD's servants shed by Jezebel. ⁸The whole house of Ahab will perish. I will cut off from Ahab every last male in Israel—slave or free.^{*c*} ⁹I will make the house of Ahab like the house of Jeroboam son of Nebat and like the house of Baasha son of Ahijah. ¹⁰As for Jezebel, dogs will devour her on the plot of ground at Jezreel, and no one will bury her.'" Then he opened the door and ran.

¹¹When Jehu went out to his fellow officers, one of them asked him, "Is everything all right? Why did this maniac come to you?"

"You know the man and the sort of things he says," Jehu replied.

¹²"That's not true!" they said. "Tell us."

Jehu said, "Here is what he told me: 'This is what the LORD says: I anoint you king over Israel.'"

¹³They quickly took their cloaks and spread them under him on the bare steps. Then they blew the trumpet and shouted, "Jehu is king!"

---

^{*a*} *21* Hebrew *Joram*, a variant of *Jehoram*; also in verses 23 and 24   ^{*b*} *29* Hebrew *Ramah*, a variant of *Ramoth*   ^{*c*} *8* Or *Israel—every ruler or leader*

Jehu Kills Joram and Ahaziah

[14]So Jehu son of Jehoshaphat, the son of Nimshi, conspired against Joram. (Now Joram and all Israel had been defending Ramoth Gilead against Hazael king of Aram, [15]but King Joram[a] had returned to Jezreel to recover from the wounds the Arameans had inflicted on him in the battle with Hazael king of Aram.) Jehu said, "If you desire to make me king, don't let anyone slip out of the city to go and tell the news in Jezreel." [16]Then he got into his chariot and rode to Jezreel, because Joram was resting there and Ahaziah king of Judah had gone down to see him.

[17]When the lookout standing on the tower in Jezreel saw Jehu's troops approaching, he called out, "I see some troops coming."

"Get a horseman," Joram ordered. "Send him to meet them and ask, 'Do you come in peace?'"

[18]The horseman rode off to meet Jehu and said, "This is what the king says: 'Do you come in peace?'"

"What do you have to do with peace?" Jehu replied. "Fall in behind me."

The lookout reported, "The messenger has reached them, but he isn't coming back."

[19]So the king sent out a second horseman. When he came to them he said, "This is what the king says: 'Do you come in peace?'"

Jehu replied, "What do you have to do with peace? Fall in behind me."

[20]The lookout reported, "He has reached them, but he isn't coming back either. The driving is like that of Jehu son of Nimshi—he drives like a maniac."

[21]"Hitch up my chariot," Joram ordered. And when it was hitched up, Joram king of Israel and Ahaziah king of Judah rode out, each in his own chariot, to meet Jehu. They met him at the plot of ground that had belonged to Naboth the Jezreelite. [22]When Joram saw Jehu he asked, "Have you come in peace, Jehu?"

"How can there be peace," Jehu replied, "as long as all the idolatry and witchcraft of your mother Jezebel abound?"

[23]Joram turned about and fled, calling out to Ahaziah, "Treachery, Ahaziah!"

[24]Then Jehu drew his bow and shot Joram between the shoulders. The arrow pierced his heart and he slumped down in his chariot. [25]Jehu said to Bidkar, his chariot officer, "Pick him up and throw him on the field that belonged to Naboth the Jezreelite. Remember how you and I were riding together in chariots behind Ahab his father when the LORD spoke this prophecy against him: [26]'Yesterday I saw the blood of Naboth and the blood of his sons, declares the LORD, and I will surely make you pay for it on this plot of ground, declares the LORD.'[b] Now then, pick him up and throw him on that plot, in accordance with the word of the LORD."

[27]When Ahaziah king of Judah saw what had happened, he fled up the road to Beth Haggan.[c] Jehu chased him, shouting, "Kill him too!" They wounded him in his chariot on the way up to Gur near Ibleam, but he escaped to Megiddo and died there. [28]His servants took him by chariot to Jerusalem and buried him with his ancestors in his tomb in the City of David. [29](In the eleventh year of Joram son of Ahab, Ahaziah had become king of Judah.)

Jezebel Killed

[30]Then Jehu went to Jezreel. When Jezebel heard about it, she painted her eyes, arranged her hair and looked out of a window. [31]As Jehu entered the gate, she asked, "Have you come in peace, you Zimri, you murderer of your master?"[d]

473

atissue:appearance

9:30–37 Having expensive clothes and the best make-up might win you the first few minutes of a man's admiration, but your personality—what you have going on the inside—is the only thing that's going to keep the interest of a quality man after that. Jezebel might have been the diva of ancient Israel, but her looks couldn't hide her evil heart. Even her closest servants betrayed her in an instant. In the end, our appearance won't endear us to others.

[a] 15 Hebrew *Jehoram*, a variant of *Joram*; also in verses 17 and 21-24   [b] 26 See 1 Kings 21:19.   [c] 27 Or *fled by way of the garden house*   [d] 31 Or "Was there peace for Zimri, who murdered his master?"

³²He looked up at the window and called out, "Who is on my side? Who?" Two or three eunuchs looked down at him. ³³"Throw her down!" Jehu said. So they threw her down, and some of her blood spattered the wall and the horses as they trampled her underfoot.

³⁴Jehu went in and ate and drank. "Take care of that cursed woman," he said, "and bury her, for she was a king's daughter." ³⁵But when they went out to bury her, they found nothing except her skull, her feet and her hands. ³⁶They went back and told Jehu, who said, "This is the word of the LORD that he spoke through his servant Elijah the Tishbite: On the plot of ground at Jezreel dogs will devour Jezebel's flesh.ᵃ ³⁷Jezebel's body will be like dung on the ground in the plot at Jezreel, so that no one will be able to say, 'This is Jezebel.'"

Ahab's Family Killed

10 Now there were in Samaria seventy sons of the house of Ahab. So Jehu wrote letters and sent them to Samaria: to the officials of Jezreel,ᵇ to the elders and to the guardians of Ahab's children. He said, ²"You have your master's sons with you and you have chariots and horses, a fortified city and weapons. Now as soon as this letter reaches you, ³choose the best and most worthy of your master's sons and set him on his father's throne. Then fight for your master's house."

⁴But they were terrified and said, "If two kings could not resist him, how can we?"

⁵So the palace administrator, the city governor, the elders and the guardians sent this message to Jehu: "We are your servants and we will do anything you say. We will not appoint anyone as king; you do whatever you think best."

⁶Then Jehu wrote them a second letter, saying, "If you are on my side and will obey me, take the heads of your master's sons and come to me in Jezreel by this time tomorrow."

Now the royal princes, seventy of them, were with the leading men of the city, who were rearing them. ⁷When the letter arrived, they took the princes and slaughtered all seventy of them. They put their heads in baskets and sent them to Jehu in Jezreel. ⁸When the messenger arrived, he told Jehu, "They have brought the heads of the princes."

Then Jehu ordered, "Put them in two piles at the entrance of the city gate until morning."

⁹The next morning Jehu went out. He stood before all the people and said, "You are innocent. It was I who conspired against my master and killed him, but who killed all these? ¹⁰Know, then, that not a word the LORD has spoken against the house of Ahab will fail. The LORD has done what he announced through his servant Elijah." ¹¹So Jehu killed everyone in Jezreel who remained of the house of Ahab, as well as all his chief men, his close friends and his priests, leaving him no survivor.

¹²Jehu then set out and went toward Samaria. At Beth Eked of the Shepherds, ¹³he met some relatives of Ahaziah king of Judah and asked, "Who are you?"

They said, "We are relatives of Ahaziah, and we have come down to greet the families of the king and of the queen mother."

¹⁴"Take them alive!" he ordered. So they took them alive and slaughtered them by the well of Beth Eked—forty-two of them. He left no survivor.

¹⁵After he left there, he came upon Jehonadab son of Rekab, who was on his way to meet him. Jehu greeted him and said, "Are you in accord with me, as I am with you?"

"I am," Jehonadab answered.

"If so," said Jehu, "give me your hand." So he did, and Jehu helped him up into the chariot. ¹⁶Jehu said, "Come with me and see my zeal for the LORD." Then he had him ride along in his chariot.

¹⁷When Jehu came to Samaria, he killed all who were left there of Ahab's family; he destroyed them, according to the word of the LORD spoken to Elijah.

Servants of Baal Killed

¹⁸Then Jehu brought all the people together and said to them, "Ahab served Baal a little; Jehu will serve him much. ¹⁹Now summon all the prophets of Baal, all his servants and all his priests. See that no one is missing, because I am going to hold a great sacrifice for Baal. Anyone who fails to come will no longer live." But Jehu was acting deceptively in order to destroy the servants of Baal.

ᵃ *36* See 1 Kings 21:23.   ᵇ *1* Hebrew; some Septuagint manuscripts and Vulgate *of the city*

²⁰Jehu said, "Call an assembly in honor of Baal." So they proclaimed it. ²¹Then he sent word throughout Israel, and all the servants of Baal came; not one stayed away. They crowded into the temple of Baal until it was full from one end to the other. ²²And Jehu said to the keeper of the wardrobe, "Bring robes for all the servants of Baal." So he brought out robes for them.

²³Then Jehu and Jehonadab son of Rekab went into the temple of Baal. Jehu said to the servants of Baal, "Look around and see that no one who serves the LORD is here with you—only servants of Baal." ²⁴So they went in to make sacrifices and burnt offerings. Now Jehu had posted eighty men outside with this warning: "If one of you lets any of the men I am placing in your hands escape, it will be your life for his life."

²⁵As soon as Jehu had finished making the burnt offering, he ordered the guards and officers: "Go in and kill them; let no one escape." So they cut them down with the sword. The guards and officers threw the bodies out and then entered the inner shrine of the temple of Baal. ²⁶They brought the sacred stone out of the temple of Baal and burned it. ²⁷They demolished the sacred stone of Baal and tore down the temple of Baal, and people have used it for a latrine to this day.

²⁸So Jehu destroyed Baal worship in Israel. ²⁹However, he did not turn away from the sins of Jeroboam son of Nebat, which he had caused Israel to commit—the worship of the golden calves at Bethel and Dan.

³⁰The LORD said to Jehu, "Because you have done well in accomplishing what is right in my eyes and have done to the house of Ahab all I had in mind to do, your descendants will sit on the throne of Israel to the fourth generation." ³¹Yet Jehu was not careful to keep the law of the LORD, the God of Israel, with all his heart. He did not turn away from the sins of Jeroboam, which he had caused Israel to commit.

³²In those days the LORD began to reduce the size of Israel. Hazael overpowered the Israelites throughout their territory ³³east of the Jordan in all the land of Gilead (the region of Gad, Reuben and Manasseh), from Aroer by the Arnon Gorge through Gilead to Bashan.

³⁴As for the other events of Jehu's reign, all he did, and all his achievements, are they not written in the book of the annals of the kings of Israel?

³⁵Jehu rested with his ancestors and was buried in Samaria. And Jehoahaz his son succeeded him as king. ³⁶The time that Jehu reigned over Israel in Samaria was twenty-eight years.

Athaliah and Joash

11 When Athaliah the mother of Ahaziah saw that her son was dead, she proceeded to destroy the whole royal family. ²But Jehosheba, the daughter of King Jehoram^a and sister of Ahaziah, took Joash son of Ahaziah and stole him away from among the royal princes, who were about to be murdered. She put him and his nurse in a bedroom to hide him from Athaliah; so he was not killed. ³He remained hidden with his nurse at the temple of the LORD for six years while Athaliah ruled the land.

⁴In the seventh year Jehoiada sent for the commanders of units of a hundred, the Carites and the guards and had them brought to him at the temple of the LORD. He made a covenant with them and put them under oath at the temple of the LORD. Then he showed them the king's son. ⁵He commanded them, saying, "This is what you are to do: You who are in the three companies that are going on duty on the Sabbath—a third of you guarding the royal palace, ⁶a third at the Sur Gate, and a third at the gate behind the guard, who take turns guarding the temple— ⁷and you who are in the other two companies that normally go off Sabbath duty are all to guard the temple for the king. ⁸Station yourselves around the king, each of you with weapon in hand. Anyone who approaches your ranks^b is to be put to death. Stay close to the king wherever he goes."

⁹The commanders of units of a hundred did just as Jehoiada the priest ordered. Each one took his men—those who were going on duty on the Sabbath and those who were going off duty—and came to Jehoiada the priest. ¹⁰Then he gave the commanders the spears and shields that had belonged to King David and that were in the temple of the LORD. ¹¹The guards, each with weapon in hand, stationed themselves around the king—near the altar and the temple, from the south side to the north side of the temple.

---

^a 2 Hebrew Joram, a variant of Jehoram   ^b 8 Or approaches the precincts

myth# 32 "MY IN-LAWS WILL LOVE ME."

Things to do today:

Buy milk

Pick up clothes from cleaners

Continue planning in-laws' anniversary dinner (that they probably won't appreciate anyway)

When I married Jose, I had this hope that everything finally would be perfect. I've never had much of a family. My mother died when I was seven. My stepmother and I have never been close. Even my father is closer to my brother, Reynaldo. And I barely see any of my aunts and uncles, who live in Mexico. So I asked God to give me a family that I could feel close to.

He brought me Jose. Jose comes from this big, loving (so I thought) family, with seven sisters and two brothers. He kept telling me I'd fit right in. "They'll love you, just like I do," he assured me.

Everything seemed good at first, especially when we were dating. His mother always talked to me and complimented me. And his dad seemed to like me, as did Jose's siblings (the ones who lived nearby). But when Jose and I married, things changed—or maybe I finally noticed how things really were. For one thing, my mother-in-law seems so critical about the way I cook and clean and take care of our two daughters. It's like I can't do anything right. She says she's not being critical; I think otherwise.

Jose's father—Javier—sometimes acts like I'm not even there. When he calls, he'll say, "Put Jose on the phone." Like I'm his assistant or something. One brother and two sisters live in the same city. I get along great with his brother Joel and one of their sisters Magdala. But the other sister acts stuck-up, like she thinks she's better than me. We hardly ever talk.

For the first five years, I kept thinking that it would get better. We've been married seven years now. It hasn't yet. I still feel like I'm not really part of the family.

It's not as if my in-laws are evil. I just thought we'd be closer.

—Lola

EVERYONE HAS A desire to be loved and appreciated. Wouldn't it be great if all in-law relationships were as close and loving as that of Ruth and her mother-in-law, Naomi? Yet many aren't. Some situations are absolute nightmares. There's even a Web site devoted to stories of hideous relationships with mothers-in-law! Can you relate?

Some desires turn into expectations—expectations that may or may not be met. Our reaction to thwarted expectations is what's important. What are your expectations concerning your relationship with your in-laws? Can these expectations be met?

When it comes to relationships among imperfect people in a fallen world, there are no guarantees. Only God can love us in a way that exceeds our expectations. (See John 3:16; 14:23; Romans 5:8.) He's free of the human biases and imperfections that mar our relationships.

Love is a choice—an act of the will, rather than a feeling. During his time on earth Jesus chose to love and serve others every day. He came with an agenda—to show the full extent of his love (see John 13:1). Like Jesus, you can choose to love your in-laws regardless of how they treat you. By choosing to love with the love of God, you choose to focus on what you can give, rather than what you haven't received. You also choose to forgive.

But choosing to love doesn't mean you turn into a doormat. The choice to love can also mean you love yourself enough to establish boundaries, particularly in relationships where abuse is involved. Tough love is still love.

"Civility Tips for Relating to In-Laws:
Be proactive.
Do what you can to build the relationship.
Don't compete with other family members.
Refocus your perspective by looking for the positive.
Accept reality."

—David & Claudia Arp

477

"LOVE IS PATIENT. . . . IT DOES NOT DISHONOR OTHERS, IT IS NOT SELF-SEEKING, IT IS NOT EASILY ANGERED, IT KEEPS NO RECORD OF WRONGS."

1 CORINTHIANS 13:4-5

SEE ALSO
Ruth 1–2
Matthew 22:37–40
Mark 3:34–35
Ephesians 4:31–32

For more on **In-Laws**, check the index.

¹²Jehoiada brought out the king's son and put the crown on him; he presented him with a copy of the covenant and proclaimed him king. They anointed him, and the people clapped their hands and shouted, "Long live the king!"

¹³When Athaliah heard the noise made by the guards and the people, she went to the people at the temple of the LORD. ¹⁴She looked and there was the king, standing by the pillar, as the custom was. The officers and the trumpeters were beside the king, and all the people of the land were rejoicing and blowing trumpets. Then Athaliah tore her robes and called out, "Treason! Treason!"

¹⁵Jehoiada the priest ordered the commanders of units of a hundred, who were in charge of the troops: "Bring her out between the ranks^a and put to the sword anyone who follows her." For the priest had said, "She must not be put to death in the temple of the LORD." ¹⁶So they seized her as she reached the place where the horses enter the palace grounds, and there she was put to death.

¹⁷Jehoiada then made a covenant between the LORD and the king and people that they would be the LORD's people. He also made a covenant between the king and the people. ¹⁸All the people of the land went to the temple of Baal and tore it down. They smashed the altars and idols to pieces and killed Mattan the priest of Baal in front of the altars.

Then Jehoiada the priest posted guards at the temple of the LORD. ¹⁹He took with him the commanders of hundreds, the Carites, the guards and all the people of the land, and together they brought the king down from the temple of the LORD and went into the palace, entering by way of the gate of the guards. The king then took his place on the royal throne. ²⁰All the people of the land rejoiced, and the city was calm, because Athaliah had been slain with the sword at the palace.

478

* ²¹Joash^b was seven years old when he began to reign.

Joash Repairs the Temple

12 *In the seventh year of Jehu, Joash^c became king, and he reigned in Jerusalem forty years. His mother's name was Zibiah; she was from Beersheba. ²Joash did what was right in the eyes of the LORD all the years Jehoiada the priest instructed him. ³The high places, however, were not removed; the people continued to offer sacrifices and burn incense there.

⁴Joash said to the priests, "Collect all the money that is brought as sacred offerings to the temple of the LORD—the money collected in the census, the money received from personal vows and the money brought voluntarily to the temple. ⁵Let every priest receive the money from one of the treasurers, then use it to repair whatever damage is found in the temple."

⁶But by the twenty-third year of King Joash the priests still had not repaired the temple. ⁷Therefore King Joash summoned Jehoiada the priest and the other priests and asked them, "Why aren't you repairing the damage done to the temple? Take no more money from your treasurers, but hand it over for repairing the temple." ⁸The priests agreed that they would not collect any more money from the people and that they would not repair the temple themselves.

⁹Jehoiada the priest took a chest and bored a hole in its lid. He placed it beside the altar, on the right side as one enters the temple of the LORD. The priests who guarded the entrance put into the chest all the money that was brought to the temple of the LORD. ¹⁰Whenever they saw that there was a large amount of money in the chest, the royal secretary and the high priest came, counted the money that had been brought into the temple of the LORD and put it into bags. ¹¹When the amount had been determined, they gave the money to the men appointed to supervise the work on the temple. With it they paid those who worked on the temple of the LORD—the carpenters and builders, ¹²the masons and stonecutters. They purchased timber and blocks of dressed stone for the repair of the temple of the LORD, and met all the other expenses of restoring the temple.

¹³The money brought into the temple was not spent for making silver basins, wick trimmers, sprinkling bowls, trumpets or any other articles of gold or silver for the temple of the LORD; ¹⁴it was paid to the workers, who used it to repair the temple. ¹⁵They did not require an accounting from those to whom they gave the money to pay the workers, because they acted with complete honesty. ¹⁶The money from

^a 15 Or *out from the precincts*   ^b 21 Hebrew *Jehoash,* a variant of *Joash*   ^c 1 Hebrew *Jehoash,* a variant of *Joash;* also in verses 2, 4, 6, 7 and 18
* 11:21 is numbered 12:1 in Hebrew texts.   * 12:1–21 is numbered 12:2–22 in Hebrew texts.

the guilt offerings and sin offerings *a* was not brought into the temple of the Lord; it belonged to the priests.

[17] About this time Hazael king of Aram went up and attacked Gath and captured it. Then he turned to attack Jerusalem. [18] But Joash king of Judah took all the sacred objects dedicated by his predecessors—Jehoshaphat, Jehoram and Ahaziah, the kings of Judah—and the gifts he himself had dedicated and all the gold found in the treasuries of the temple of the Lord and of the royal palace, and he sent them to Hazael king of Aram, who then withdrew from Jerusalem.

[19] As for the other events of the reign of Joash, and all he did, are they not written in the book of the annals of the kings of Judah? [20] His officials conspired against him and assassinated him at Beth Millo, on the road down to Silla. [21] The officials who murdered him were Jozabad son of Shimeath and Jehozabad son of Shomer. He died and was buried with his ancestors in the City of David. And Amaziah his son succeeded him as king.

Jehoahaz King of Israel

13 In the twenty-third year of Joash son of Ahaziah king of Judah, Jehoahaz son of Jehu became king of Israel in Samaria, and he reigned seventeen years. [2] He did evil in the eyes of the Lord by following the sins of Jeroboam son of Nebat, which he had caused Israel to commit, and he did not turn away from them. [3] So the Lord's anger burned against Israel, and for a long time he kept them under the power of Hazael king of Aram and Ben-Hadad his son.

[4] Then Jehoahaz sought the Lord's favor, and the Lord listened to him, for he saw how severely the king of Aram was oppressing Israel. [5] The Lord provided a deliverer for Israel, and they escaped from the power of Aram. So the Israelites lived in their own homes as they had before. [6] But they did not turn away from the sins of the house of Jeroboam, which he had caused Israel to commit; they continued in them. Also, the Asherah pole *b* remained standing in Samaria.

[7] Nothing had been left of the army of Jehoahaz except fifty horsemen, ten chariots and ten thousand foot soldiers, for the king of Aram had destroyed the rest and made them like the dust at threshing time.

[8] As for the other events of the reign of Jehoahaz, all he did and his achievements, are they not written in the book of the annals of the kings of Israel? [9] Jehoahaz rested with his ancestors and was buried in Samaria. And Jehoash *c* his son succeeded him as king.

Jehoash King of Israel

[10] In the thirty-seventh year of Joash king of Judah, Jehoash son of Jehoahaz became king of Israel in Samaria, and he reigned sixteen years. [11] He did evil in the eyes of the Lord and did not turn away from any of the sins of Jeroboam son of Nebat, which he had caused Israel to commit; he continued in them.

[12] As for the other events of the reign of Jehoash, all he did and his achievements, including his war against Amaziah king of Judah, are they not written in the book of the annals of the kings of Israel? [13] Jehoash rested with his ancestors, and Jeroboam succeeded him on the throne. Jehoash was buried in Samaria with the kings of Israel.

[14] Now Elisha was suffering from the illness from which he died. Jehoash king of Israel went down to see him and wept over him. "My father! My father!" he cried. "The chariots and horsemen of Israel!"

[15] Elisha said, "Get a bow and some arrows," and he did so. [16] "Take the bow in your hands," he said to the king of Israel. When he had taken it, Elisha put his hands on the king's hands.

conversations

integrity «» 12:15

1 » What does it mean to act with complete honesty with your finances?

2 » What are some ways you might cut corners and compromise your financial integrity?

3 » How do you build a reputation of integrity?

For more on **integrity**, check the index. For the next Conversations, go to p. 488.

479

---

a 16 Or *purification offerings*   *b 6* That is, a wooden symbol of the goddess Asherah; here and elsewhere in 2 Kings   *c 9* Hebrew *Joash*, a variant of *Jehoash*; also in verses 12-14 and 25

¹⁷ "Open the east window," he said, and he opened it. "Shoot!" Elisha said, and he shot. "The LORD's arrow of victory, the arrow of victory over Aram!" Elisha declared. "You will completely destroy the Arameans at Aphek."

¹⁸ Then he said, "Take the arrows," and the king took them. Elisha told him, "Strike the ground." He struck it three times and stopped. ¹⁹ The man of God was angry with him and said, "You should have struck the ground five or six times; then you would have defeated Aram and completely destroyed it. But now you will defeat it only three times."

²⁰ Elisha died and was buried.

Now Moabite raiders used to enter the country every spring. ²¹ Once while some Israelites were burying a man, suddenly they saw a band of raiders; so they threw the man's body into Elisha's tomb. When the body touched Elisha's bones, the man came to life and stood up on his feet.

²² Hazael king of Aram oppressed Israel throughout the reign of Jehoahaz. ²³ But the LORD was gracious to them and had compassion and showed concern for them because of his covenant with Abraham, Isaac and Jacob. To this day he has been unwilling to destroy them or banish them from his presence.

²⁴ Hazael king of Aram died, and Ben-Hadad his son succeeded him as king. ²⁵ Then Jehoash son of Jehoahaz recaptured from Ben-Hadad son of Hazael the towns he had taken in battle from his father Jehoahaz. Three times Jehoash defeated him, and so he recovered the Israelite towns.

Amaziah King of Judah

14 In the second year of Jehoash^a son of Jehoahaz king of Israel, Amaziah son of Joash king of Judah began to reign. ² He was twenty-five years old when he became king, and he reigned in Jerusalem twenty-nine years. His mother's name was Jehoaddan; she was from Jerusalem. ³ He did what was right in the eyes of the LORD, but not as his father David had done. In everything he followed the example of his father Joash. ⁴ The high places, however, were not removed; the people continued to offer sacrifices and burn incense there.

⁵ After the kingdom was firmly in his grasp, he executed the officials who had murdered his father the king. ⁶ Yet he did not put the children of the assassins to death, in accordance with what is written in the Book of the Law of Moses where the LORD commanded: "Parents are not to be put to death for their children, nor children put to death for their parents; each of you will die for your own sin."^b

⁷ He was the one who defeated ten thousand Edomites in the Valley of Salt and captured Sela in battle, calling it Joktheel, the name it has to this day.

⁸ Then Amaziah sent messengers to Jehoash son of Jehoahaz, the son of Jehu, king of Israel, with the challenge: "Come, meet me face to face."

⁹ But Jehoash king of Israel replied to Amaziah king of Judah: "A thistle in Lebanon sent a message to a cedar in Lebanon, 'Give your daughter to my son in marriage.' Then a wild beast in Lebanon came along and trampled the thistle underfoot. ¹⁰ You have indeed defeated Edom and now you are arrogant. Glory in your victory, but stay at home! Why ask for trouble and cause your own downfall and that of Judah also?"

¹¹ Amaziah, however, would not listen, so Jehoash king of Israel attacked. He and Amaziah king of Judah faced each other at Beth Shemesh in Judah. ¹² Judah was routed by Israel, and every man fled to his home. ¹³ Jehoash king of Israel captured Amaziah king of Judah, the son of Joash, the son of Ahaziah, at Beth Shemesh. Then Jehoash went to Jerusalem and broke down the wall of Jerusalem from the Ephraim Gate to the Corner Gate—a section about four hundred cubits long.^c ¹⁴ He took all the gold and silver and all the articles found in the temple of the LORD and in the treasuries of the royal palace. He also took hostages and returned to Samaria.

¹⁵ As for the other events of the reign of Jehoash, what he did and his achievements, including his war against Amaziah king of Judah, are they not written in the book of the annals of the kings of Israel? ¹⁶ Jehoash rested with his ancestors and was buried in Samaria with the kings of Israel. And Jeroboam his son succeeded him as king.

¹⁷ Amaziah son of Joash king of Judah lived for fifteen years after the death of Jehoash son of Jehoahaz

^a 1 Hebrew *Joash*, a variant of *Jehoash*; also in verses 13, 23 and 27   ^b 6 Deut. 24:16   ^c 13 That is, about 600 feet or about 180 meters

king of Israel. ¹⁸As for the other events of Amaziah's reign, are they not written in the book of the annals of the kings of Judah?

¹⁹They conspired against him in Jerusalem, and he fled to Lachish, but they sent men after him to Lachish and killed him there. ²⁰He was brought back by horse and was buried in Jerusalem with his ancestors, in the City of David.

²¹Then all the people of Judah took Azariah,ᵃ who was sixteen years old, and made him king in place of his father Amaziah. ²²He was the one who rebuilt Elath and restored it to Judah after Amaziah rested with his ancestors.

Jeroboam II King of Israel

²³In the fifteenth year of Amaziah son of Joash king of Judah, Jeroboam son of Jehoash king of Israel became king in Samaria, and he reigned forty-one years. ²⁴He did evil in the eyes of the LORD and did not turn away from any of the sins of Jeroboam son of Nebat, which he had caused Israel to commit. ²⁵He was the one who restored the boundaries of Israel from Lebo Hamath to the Dead Sea,ᵇ in accordance with the word of the LORD, the God of Israel, spoken through his servant Jonah son of Amittai, the prophet from Gath Hepher.

²⁶The LORD had seen how bitterly everyone in Israel, whether slave or free, was suffering;ᶜ there was no one to help them. ²⁷And since the LORD had not said he would blot out the name of Israel from under heaven, he saved them by the hand of Jeroboam son of Jehoash.

²⁸As for the other events of Jeroboam's reign, all he did, and his military achievements, including how he recovered for Israel both Damascus and Hamath, which had belonged to Judah, are they not written in the book of the annals of the kings of Israel? ²⁹Jeroboam rested with his ancestors, the kings of Israel. And Zechariah his son succeeded him as king.

481

Azariah King of Judah

15 In the twenty-seventh year of Jeroboam king of Israel, Azariahᵈ son of Amaziah king of Judah began to reign. ²He was sixteen years old when he became king, and he reigned in Jerusalem fifty-two years. His mother's name was Jekoliah; she was from Jerusalem. ³He did what was right in the eyes of the LORD, just as his father Amaziah had done. ⁴The high places, however, were not removed; the people continued to offer sacrifices and burn incense there.

⁵The LORD afflicted the king with leprosyᵉ until the day he died, and he lived in a separate house.ᶠ Jotham the king's son had charge of the palace and governed the people of the land.

⁶As for the other events of Azariah's reign, and all he did, are they not written in the book of the annals of the kings of Judah? ⁷Azariah rested with his ancestors and was buried near them in the City of David. And Jotham his son succeeded him as king.

Zechariah King of Israel

⁸In the thirty-eighth year of Azariah king of Judah, Zechariah son of Jeroboam became king of Israel in Samaria, and he reigned six months. ⁹He did evil in the eyes of the LORD, as his predecessors had done. He did not turn away from the sins of Jeroboam son of Nebat, which he had caused Israel to commit.

¹⁰Shallum son of Jabesh conspired against Zechariah. He attacked him in front of the people,ᵍ assassinated him and succeeded him as king. ¹¹The other events of Zechariah's reign are written in the book of the annals of the kings of Israel. ¹²So the word of the LORD spoken to Jehu was fulfilled: "Your descendants will sit on the throne of Israel to the fourth generation."ʰ

Shallum King of Israel

¹³Shallum son of Jabesh became king in the thirty-ninth year of Uzziah king of Judah, and he reigned in Samaria one month. ¹⁴Then Menahem son of Gadi went from Tirzah up to Samaria. He attacked Shallum son of Jabesh in Samaria, assassinated him and succeeded him as king.

ᵃ 21 Also called Uzziah   ᵇ 25 Hebrew the Sea of the Arabah   ᶜ 26 Or Israel was suffering. They were without a ruler or leader, and   ᵈ 1 Also called Uzziah; also in verses 6, 7, 8, 17, 23 and 27   ᵉ 5 The Hebrew for leprosy was used for various diseases affecting the skin.   ᶠ 5 Or in a house where he was relieved of responsibilities   ᵍ 10 Hebrew; some Septuagint manuscripts in Ibleam   ʰ 12 2Kings 10:30

¹⁵The other events of Shallum's reign, and the conspiracy he led, are written in the book of the annals of the kings of Israel.

¹⁶At that time Menahem, starting out from Tirzah, attacked Tiphsah and everyone in the city and its vicinity, because they refused to open their gates. He sacked Tiphsah and ripped open all the pregnant women.

Menahem King of Israel

¹⁷In the thirty-ninth year of Azariah king of Judah, Menahem son of Gadi became king of Israel, and he reigned in Samaria ten years. ¹⁸He did evil in the eyes of the LORD. During his entire reign he did not turn away from the sins of Jeroboam son of Nebat, which he had caused Israel to commit.

¹⁹Then Pul*ᵃ* king of Assyria invaded the land, and Menahem gave him a thousand talents*ᵇ* of silver to gain his support and strengthen his own hold on the kingdom. ²⁰Menahem exacted this money from Israel. Every wealthy person had to contribute fifty shekels*ᶜ* of silver to be given to the king of Assyria. So the king of Assyria withdrew and stayed in the land no longer.

²¹As for the other events of Menahem's reign, and all he did, are they not written in the book of the annals of the kings of Israel? ²²Menahem rested with his ancestors. And Pekahiah his son succeeded him as king.

Pekahiah King of Israel

²³In the fiftieth year of Azariah king of Judah, Pekahiah son of Menahem became king of Israel in Samaria, and he reigned two years. ²⁴Pekahiah did evil in the eyes of the LORD. He did not turn away from the sins of Jeroboam son of Nebat, which he had caused Israel to commit. ²⁵One of his chief officers, Pekah son of Remaliah, conspired against him. Taking fifty Gileadites with him, he assassinated Pekahiah, along with Argob and Arieh, in the citadel of the royal palace at Samaria. So Pekah killed Pekahiah and succeeded him as king.

²⁶The other events of Pekahiah's reign, and all he did, are written in the book of the annals of the kings of Israel.

Pekah King of Israel

²⁷In the fifty-second year of Azariah king of Judah, Pekah son of Remaliah became king of Israel in Samaria, and he reigned twenty years. ²⁸He did evil in the eyes of the LORD. He did not turn away from the sins of Jeroboam son of Nebat, which he had caused Israel to commit.

²⁹In the time of Pekah king of Israel, Tiglath-Pileser king of Assyria came and took Ijon, Abel Beth Maakah, Janoah, Kedesh and Hazor. He took Gilead and Galilee, including all the land of Naphtali, and deported the people to Assyria. ³⁰Then Hoshea son of Elah conspired against Pekah son of Remaliah. He attacked and assassinated him, and then succeeded him as king in the twentieth year of Jotham son of Uzziah.

³¹As for the other events of Pekah's reign, and all he did, are they not written in the book of the annals of the kings of Israel?

Jotham King of Judah

³²In the second year of Pekah son of Remaliah king of Israel, Jotham son of Uzziah king of Judah began to reign. ³³He was twenty-five years old when he became king, and he reigned in Jerusalem sixteen years. His mother's name was Jerusha daughter of Zadok. ³⁴He did what was right in the eyes of the LORD, just as his father Uzziah had done. ³⁵The high places, however, were not removed; the people continued to offer sacrifices and burn incense there. Jotham rebuilt the Upper Gate of the temple of the LORD.

³⁶As for the other events of Jotham's reign, and what he did, are they not written in the book of the annals of the kings of Judah? ³⁷(In those days the LORD began to send Rezin king of Aram and Pekah son of Remaliah against Judah.) ³⁸Jotham rested with his ancestors and was buried with them in the City of David, the city of his father. And Ahaz his son succeeded him as king.

ᵃ 19 Also called *Tiglath-Pileser*   *ᵇ 19* That is, about 38 tons or about 34 metric tons   *ᶜ 20* That is, about 1 1/4 pounds or about 575 grams

ASKmeanyTHING

You don't exactly have a stellar past. Do you mind talking about it?

Stellar? Far from it! I was a prostitute; you know, one of the oldest professions in the world. I made a living selling my body to any interested male who could pay. It didn't get me much, though. I lived on the edge of society, you might say. My family and I lived in a house right in the walls of Jericho—not exactly where you want to be if an invading army is approaching. But that was my life.

How did the people react when they heard about Joshua's army coming toward Jericho?

Everyone feared for their lives. I mean, we'd all heard amazing stories about the Israelite army, especially about their God and how he'd fought for them and what he'd done for them. We knew that if Joshua and his God were going to attack Jericho, then it was all over for us. So when we got word that Joshua was camped right across the river, the entire city panicked.

483

So why did you decide to welcome the Israelite spies?

That's a good question. I feared Joshua's God, too, but not in the same way as the rest of the people. I knew in my heart that Joshua's God was *the* God of heaven and earth. Who else could have performed those miracles? If anyone was able to save us, it was the powerful, mighty God of Israel. So when those two spies knocked on my door, I saw it as an incredible gift, an opportunity for my family and me. It was a risk, but what did I have to lose?

Your courageous act of faith didn't go unnoticed, did it?

That is the best part of my story. You wouldn't believe what God did for me. Not only did God spare my family and me, but he also gave me a second chance. I got married—me, a married woman!—to Salmon and had children of my own. My life was totally changed!

So what do you think is the real lesson of your life?

Simply put, we have a God of second chances. No matter what is in your past—your failures, mistakes or sins—God can forgive you and offer you new life. If he can redeem someone like me, he can change *anyone*.

FOR MORE INSIGHT: Rahab became the great-great-grandmother of King David. And we all know who came from David's line—Jesus. What an incredible honor God bestowed upon someone with a sinful past! Rahab is also one of two women commended for her faith in Hebrews 11.

For stories of other women with sordid pasts who were given new life from God, read the story of Jesus' encounter with the Samaritan woman (see John 4:1–26,39–42) and the woman accused of adultery (see John 8:1–11).

Ahaz King of Judah

16 In the seventeenth year of Pekah son of Remaliah, Ahaz son of Jotham king of Judah began to reign. [2] Ahaz was twenty years old when he became king, and he reigned in Jerusalem sixteen years. Unlike David his father, he did not do what was right in the eyes of the LORD his God. [3] He followed the ways of the kings of Israel and even sacrificed his son in the fire, engaging in the detestable practices of the nations the LORD had driven out before the Israelites. [4] He offered sacrifices and burned incense at the high places, on the hilltops and under every spreading tree.

[5] Then Rezin king of Aram and Pekah son of Remaliah king of Israel marched up to fight against Jerusalem and besieged Ahaz, but they could not overpower him. [6] At that time, Rezin king of Aram recovered Elath for Aram by driving out the people of Judah. Edomites then moved into Elath and have lived there to this day.

[7] Ahaz sent messengers to say to Tiglath-Pileser king of Assyria, "I am your servant and vassal. Come up and save me out of the hand of the king of Aram and of the king of Israel, who are attacking me." [8] And Ahaz took the silver and gold found in the temple of the LORD and in the treasuries of the royal palace and sent it as a gift to the king of Assyria. [9] The king of Assyria complied by attacking Damascus and capturing it. He deported its inhabitants to Kir and put Rezin to death.

[10] Then King Ahaz went to Damascus to meet Tiglath-Pileser king of Assyria. He saw an altar in Damascus and sent to Uriah the priest a sketch of the altar, with detailed plans for its construction. [11] So Uriah the priest built an altar in accordance with all the plans that King Ahaz had sent from Damascus and finished it before King Ahaz returned. [12] When the king came back from Damascus and saw the altar, he approached it and presented offerings[a] on it. [13] He offered up his burnt offering and grain offering, poured out his drink offering, and splashed the blood of his fellowship offerings against the altar. [14] The bronze altar that stood before the LORD he brought from the front of the temple—from between the new altar and the temple of the LORD—and put it on the north side of the new altar.

[15] King Ahaz then gave these orders to Uriah the priest: "On the large new altar, offer the morning burnt offering and the evening grain offering, the king's burnt offering and his grain offering, and the burnt offering of all the people of the land, and their grain offering and their drink offering. Splash against this altar the blood of all the burnt offerings and sacrifices. But I will use the bronze altar for seeking guidance." [16] And Uriah the priest did just as King Ahaz had ordered.

[17] King Ahaz cut off the side panels and removed the basins from the movable stands. He removed the Sea from the bronze bulls that supported it and set it on a stone base. [18] He took away the Sabbath canopy[b] that had been built at the temple and removed the royal entryway outside the temple of the LORD, in deference to the king of Assyria.

[19] As for the other events of the reign of Ahaz, and what he did, are they not written in the book of the annals of the kings of Judah? [20] Ahaz rested with his ancestors and was buried with them in the City of David. And Hezekiah his son succeeded him as king.

Hoshea Last King of Israel

17 In the twelfth year of Ahaz king of Judah, Hoshea son of Elah became king of Israel in Samaria, and he reigned nine years. [2] He did evil in the eyes of the LORD, but not like the kings of Israel who preceded him.

[3] Shalmaneser king of Assyria came up to attack Hoshea, who had been Shalmaneser's vassal and had paid him tribute. [4] But the king of Assyria discovered that Hoshea was a traitor, for he had sent envoys to So[c] king of Egypt, and he no longer paid tribute to the king of Assyria, as he had done year by year. Therefore Shalmaneser seized him and put him in prison. [5] The king of Assyria invaded the entire land, marched against Samaria and laid siege to it for three years. [6] In the ninth year of Hoshea, the king of Assyria captured Samaria and deported the Israelites to Assyria. He settled them in Halah, in Gozan on the Habor River and in the towns of the Medes.

Israel Exiled Because of Sin

[7] All this took place because the Israelites had sinned against the LORD their God, who had brought them up out of Egypt from under the power of Pharaoh king of Egypt. They worshiped other gods [8] and

---

a 12 Or *and went up*   *b 18* Or *the dais of his throne* (see Septuagint)   *c 4 So* is probably an abbreviation for *Osorkon.*

followed the practices of the nations the LORD had driven out before them, as well as the practices that the kings of Israel had introduced. ⁹The Israelites secretly did things against the LORD their God that were not right. From watchtower to fortified city they built themselves high places in all their towns. ¹⁰They set up sacred stones and Asherah poles on every high hill and under every spreading tree. ¹¹At every high place they burned incense, as the nations whom the LORD had driven out before them had done. They did wicked things that aroused the LORD's anger. ¹²They worshiped idols, though the LORD had said, "You shall not do this."ᵃ ¹³The LORD warned Israel and Judah through all his prophets and seers: "Turn from your evil ways. Observe my commands and decrees, in accordance with the entire Law that I commanded your ancestors to obey and that I delivered to you through my servants the prophets."

¹⁴But they would not listen and were as stiff-necked as their ancestors, who did not trust in the LORD their God. ¹⁵They rejected his decrees and the covenant he had made with their ancestors and the statutes he had warned them to keep. They followed worthless idols and themselves became worthless. They imitated the nations around them although the LORD had ordered them, "Do not do as they do."

¹⁶They forsook all the commands of the LORD their God and made for themselves two idols cast in the shape of calves, and an Asherah pole. They bowed down to all the starry hosts, and they worshiped Baal. ¹⁷They sacrificed their sons and daughters in the fire. They practiced divination and sought omens and sold themselves to do evil in the eyes of the LORD, arousing his anger.

¹⁸So the LORD was very angry with Israel and removed them from his presence. Only the tribe of Judah was left, ¹⁹and even Judah did not keep the commands of the LORD their God. They followed the practices Israel had introduced. ²⁰Therefore the LORD rejected all the people of Israel; he afflicted them and gave them into the hands of plunderers, until he thrust them from his presence.

²¹When he tore Israel away from the house of David, they made Jeroboam son of Nebat their king. Jeroboam enticed Israel away from following the LORD and caused them to commit a great sin. ²²The Israelites persisted in all the sins of Jeroboam and did not turn away from them ²³until the LORD removed them from his presence, as he had warned through all his servants the prophets. So the people of Israel were taken from their homeland into exile in Assyria, and they are still there.

Samaria Resettled

²⁴The king of Assyria brought people from Babylon, Kuthah, Avva, Hamath and Sepharvaim and settled them in the towns of Samaria to replace the Israelites. They took over Samaria and lived in its towns. ²⁵When they first lived there, they did not worship the LORD; so he sent lions among them and they killed some of the people. ²⁶It was reported to the king of Assyria: "The people you deported and resettled in the towns of Samaria do not know what the god of that country requires. He has sent lions among them, which are killing them off, because the people do not know what he requires."

²⁷Then the king of Assyria gave this order: "Have one of the priests you took captive from Samaria go back to live there and teach the people what the god of the land requires." ²⁸So one of the priests who had been exiled from Samaria came to live in Bethel and taught them how to worship the LORD.

²⁹Nevertheless, each national group made its own gods in the several towns where they settled, and set them up in the shrines the people of Samaria had made at the high places. ³⁰The people from

17:1–20 When you begin to drift from God, you often hurry to fill the void with something else. You don't have to think about your deteriorating relationship with God if your closet is full or your house is clean or your company is doing well, right? This is the curse of worldly success— it can blind us to what miserable failures we might be in our relationships with God (or in our marriages or as parents). Your first steps away from God might be unconscious, unplanned and unannounced. Don't wait, as Israel did, to hit rock bottom before returning to God.

485

atissue:straying from God

ᵃ *12* Exodus 20:4,5

Babylon made Sukkoth Benoth, those from Kuthah made Nergal, and those from Hamath made Ashima; ³¹the Avvites made Nibhaz and Tartak, and the Sepharvites burned their children in the fire as sacrifices to Adrammelek and Anammelek, the gods of Sepharvaim. ³²They worshiped the LORD, but they also appointed all sorts of their own people to officiate for them as priests in the shrines at the high places. ³³They worshiped the LORD, but they also served their own gods in accordance with the customs of the nations from which they had been brought.

³⁴To this day they persist in their former practices. They neither worship the LORD nor adhere to the decrees and regulations, the laws and commands that the LORD gave the descendants of Jacob, whom he named Israel. ³⁵When the LORD made a covenant with the Israelites, he commanded them: "Do not worship any other gods or bow down to them, serve them or sacrifice to them. ³⁶But the LORD, who brought you up out of Egypt with mighty power and outstretched arm, is the one you must worship. To him you shall bow down and to him offer sacrifices. ³⁷You must always be careful to keep the decrees and regulations, the laws and commands he wrote for you. Do not worship other gods. ³⁸Do not forget the covenant I have made with you, and do not worship other gods. ³⁹Rather, worship the LORD your God; it is he who will deliver you from the hand of all your enemies."

⁴⁰They would not listen, however, but persisted in their former practices. ⁴¹Even while these people were worshiping the LORD, they were serving their idols. To this day their children and grandchildren continue to do as their ancestors did.

Hezekiah King of Judah

18 In the third year of Hoshea son of Elah king of Israel, Hezekiah son of Ahaz king of Judah began to reign. ²He was twenty-five years old when he became king, and he reigned in Jerusalem twenty-nine years. His mother's name was Abijah*ᵃ* daughter of Zechariah. ³He did what was right in the eyes of the LORD, just as his father David had done. ⁴He removed the high places, smashed the sacred stones and cut down the Asherah poles. He broke into pieces the bronze snake Moses had made, for up to that time the Israelites had been burning incense to it. (It was called Nehushtan.ᵇ)

⁵Hezekiah trusted in the LORD, the God of Israel. There was no one like him among all the kings of Judah, either before him or after him. ⁶He held fast to the LORD and did not cease to follow him; he kept the commands the LORD had given Moses. ⁷And the LORD was with him; he was successful in whatever he undertook. He rebelled against the king of Assyria and did not serve him. ⁸From watchtower to fortified city, he defeated the Philistines, as far as Gaza and its territory.

⁹In King Hezekiah's fourth year, which was the seventh year of Hoshea son of Elah king of Israel, Shalmaneser king of Assyria marched against Samaria and laid siege to it. ¹⁰At the end of three years the Assyrians took it. So Samaria was captured in Hezekiah's sixth year, which was the ninth year of Hoshea king of Israel. ¹¹The king of Assyria deported Israel to Assyria and settled them in Halah, in Gozan on the Habor River and in towns of the Medes. ¹²This happened because they had not obeyed the LORD their God, but had violated his covenant—all that Moses the servant of the LORD commanded. They neither listened to the commands nor carried them out.

¹³In the fourteenth year of King Hezekiah's reign, Sennacherib king of Assyria attacked all the fortified cities of Judah and captured them. ¹⁴So Hezekiah king of Judah sent this message to the king of Assyria at Lachish: "I have done wrong. Withdraw from me, and I will pay whatever you demand of me." The king of Assyria exacted from Hezekiah king of Judah three hundred talentsᶜ of silver and thirty talentsᵈ of gold. ¹⁵So Hezekiah gave him all the silver that was found in the temple of the LORD and in the treasuries of the royal palace.

¹⁶At this time Hezekiah king of Judah stripped off the gold with which he had covered the doors and doorposts of the temple of the LORD, and gave it to the king of Assyria.

Sennacherib Threatens Jerusalem

¹⁷The king of Assyria sent his supreme commander, his chief officer and his field commander with a large army, from Lachish to King Hezekiah at Jerusalem. They came up to Jerusalem and stopped at the

---

ᵃ *2* Hebrew *Abi,* a variant of *Abijah*   ᵇ *4 Nehushtan* sounds like the Hebrew for both *bronze* and *snake.*   ᶜ *14* That is, about 11 tons or about 10 metric tons
ᵈ *14* That is, about 1 ton or about 1 metric ton

aqueduct of the Upper Pool, on the road to the Washerman's Field. [18]They called for the king; and Eliakim son of Hilkiah the palace administrator, Shebna the secretary, and Joah son of Asaph the recorder went out to them.

[19]The field commander said to them, "Tell Hezekiah:

"'This is what the great king, the king of Assyria, says: On what are you basing this confidence of yours? [20]You say you have the counsel and the might for war—but you speak only empty words. On whom are you depending, that you rebel against me? [21]Look, I know you are depending on Egypt, that splintered reed of a staff, which pierces the hands of anyone who leans on it! Such is Pharaoh king of Egypt to all who depend on him. [22]But if you say to me, "We are depending on the LORD our God"—isn't he the one whose high places and altars Hezekiah removed, saying to Judah and Jerusalem, "You must worship before this altar in Jerusalem"?

[23]"'Come now, make a bargain with my master, the king of Assyria: I will give you two thousand horses—if you can put riders on them! [24]How can you repulse one officer of the least of my master's officials, even though you are depending on Egypt for chariots and horsemen[a]? [25]Furthermore, have I come to attack and destroy this place without word from the LORD? The LORD himself told me to march against this country and destroy it.'"

[26]Then Eliakim son of Hilkiah, and Shebna and Joah said to the field commander, "Please speak to your servants in Aramaic, since we understand it. Don't speak to us in Hebrew in the hearing of the people on the wall."

487

[27]But the commander replied, "Was it only to your master and you that my master sent me to say these things, and not to the people sitting on the wall—who, like you, will have to eat their own excrement and drink their own urine?"

[28]Then the commander stood and called out in Hebrew, "Hear the word of the great king, the king of Assyria! [29]This is what the king says: Do not let Hezekiah deceive you. He cannot deliver you from my hand. [30]Do not let Hezekiah persuade you to trust in the LORD when he says, 'The LORD will surely deliver us; this city will not be given into the hand of the king of Assyria.'

[31]"Do not listen to Hezekiah. This is what the king of Assyria says: Make peace with me and come out to me. Then every one of you will eat from your own vine and fig tree and drink water from your own cistern, [32]until I come and take you to a land like your own—a land of grain and new wine, a land of bread and vineyards, a land of olive trees and honey. Choose life and not death!

"Do not listen to Hezekiah, for he is misleading you when he says, 'The LORD will deliver us.' [33]Has the god of any nation ever delivered his land from the hand of the king of Assyria? [34]Where are the gods of Hamath and Arpad? Where are the gods of Sepharvaim, Hena and Ivvah? Have they rescued Samaria from my hand? [35]Who of all the gods of these countries has been able to save his land from me? How then can the LORD deliver Jerusalem from my hand?"

[36]But the people remained silent and said nothing in reply, because the king had commanded, "Do not answer him."

[37]Then Eliakim son of Hilkiah the palace administrator, Shebna the secretary, and Joah son of Asaph the recorder went to Hezekiah, with their clothes torn, and told him what the field commander had said.

---

[a] 24 Or charioteers

Jerusalem's Deliverance Foretold

19 When King Hezekiah heard this, he tore his clothes and put on sackcloth and went into the temple of the LORD. ²He sent Eliakim the palace administrator, Shebna the secretary and the leading priests, all wearing sackcloth, to the prophet Isaiah son of Amoz. ³They told him, "This is what Hezekiah says: This day is a day of distress and rebuke and disgrace, as when children come to the moment of birth and there is no strength to deliver them. ⁴It may be that the LORD your God will hear all the words of the field commander, whom his master, the king of Assyria, has sent to ridicule the living God, and that he will rebuke him for the words the LORD your God has heard. Therefore pray for the remnant that still survives."

⁵When King Hezekiah's officials came to Isaiah, ⁶Isaiah said to them, "Tell your master, 'This is what the LORD says: Do not be afraid of what you have heard—those words with which the underlings of the king of Assyria have blasphemed me. ⁷Listen! When he hears a certain report, I will make him want to return to his own country, and there I will have him cut down with the sword.'"

⁸When the field commander heard that the king of Assyria had left Lachish, he withdrew and found the king fighting against Libnah.

⁹Now Sennacherib received a report that Tirhakah, the king of Cush,[a] was marching out to fight against him. So he again sent messengers to Hezekiah with this word: ¹⁰"Say to Hezekiah king of Judah: Do not let the god you depend on deceive you when he says, 'Jerusalem will not be given into the hands of the king of Assyria.' ¹¹Surely you have heard what the kings of Assyria have done to all the countries, destroying them completely. And will you be delivered? ¹²Did the gods of the nations that were destroyed by my ancestors deliver them—the gods of Gozan, Harran, Rezeph and the people of Eden who were in Tel Assar? ¹³Where is the king of Hamath or the king of Arpad? Where are the kings of Lair, Sepharvaim, Hena and Ivvah?"

Hezekiah's Prayer

¹⁴Hezekiah received the letter from the messengers and read it. Then he went up to the temple of the LORD and spread it out before the LORD. ¹⁵And Hezekiah prayed to the LORD: "LORD, the God of Israel, enthroned between the cherubim, you alone are God over all the kingdoms of the earth. You have made heaven and earth. ¹⁶Give ear, LORD, and hear; open your eyes, LORD, and see; listen to the words Sennacherib has sent to ridicule the living God.

¹⁷"It is true, LORD, that the Assyrian kings have laid waste these nations and their lands. ¹⁸They have thrown their gods into the fire and destroyed them, for they were not gods but only wood and stone, fashioned by human hands. ¹⁹Now, LORD our God, deliver us from his hand, so that all the kingdoms of the earth may know that you alone, LORD, are God."

conversations
prayer «» 19:14–19

1 » What is usually the focus of your prayers?

2 » How do you address God when you pray?

3 » How does prayer change you?

For more on **prayer**, check the index.
For the next Conversations, go to p. 493.

Isaiah Prophesies Sennacherib's Fall

²⁰Then Isaiah son of Amoz sent a message to Hezekiah: "This is what the LORD, the God of Israel, says: I have heard your prayer concerning Sennacherib king of Assyria. ²¹This is the word that the LORD has spoken against him:

> "'Virgin Daughter Zion
>   despises you and mocks you.
> Daughter Jerusalem

---

a 9 That is, the upper Nile region

tosses her head as you flee.
²²Who is it you have ridiculed and blasphemed?
    Against whom have you raised your voice
and lifted your eyes in pride?
    Against the Holy One of Israel!
²³By your messengers
    you have ridiculed the Lord.
And you have said,
    "With my many chariots
I have ascended the heights of the mountains,
    the utmost heights of Lebanon.
I have cut down its tallest cedars,
    the choicest of its junipers.
I have reached its remotest parts,
    the finest of its forests.
²⁴I have dug wells in foreign lands
    and drunk the water there.
With the soles of my feet
    I have dried up all the streams of Egypt."

²⁵"'Have you not heard?
    Long ago I ordained it.
In days of old I planned it;
    now I have brought it to pass,
that you have turned fortified cities
    into piles of stone.
²⁶Their people, drained of power,
    are dismayed and put to shame.
They are like plants in the field,
    like tender green shoots,
like grass sprouting on the roof,
    scorched before it grows up.

²⁷"'But I know where you are
    and when you come and go
    and how you rage against me.
²⁸Because you rage against me
    and because your insolence has reached my ears,
I will put my hook in your nose

489

HE IS: my defender

19:20–37 Sennacherib, king of Assyria, had the audacity to heap insults on the Lord and to lay siege to the city of David. King Hezekiah knew that help could only come from heaven. He prayed that God would intervene to deliver them. The Lord miraculously went to battle to defend his city.

God takes insults against himself and his people personally. When you are besieged or belittled, rely on God to be *your defender*. Pray and ask him to defend your honor in his way. God can send your enemy packing or reconcile you to each other (see Matthew 5:43–44).

For the next He Is, go to p. 497.

and my bit in your mouth,
and I will make you return
by the way you came.'

29 "This will be the sign for you, Hezekiah:

"This year you will eat what grows by itself,
and the second year what springs from that.
But in the third year sow and reap,
plant vineyards and eat their fruit.
30 Once more a remnant of the house of Judah
will take root below and bear fruit above.
31 For out of Jerusalem will come a remnant,
and out of Mount Zion a band of survivors.

"The zeal of the Lord Almighty will accomplish this.

32 "Therefore this is what the Lord says concerning the king of Assyria:

"'He will not enter this city
or shoot an arrow here.
He will not come before it with shield
or build a siege ramp against it.
33 By the way that he came he will return;
he will not enter this city,

declares the Lord.

34 I will defend this city and save it,
for my sake and for the sake of David
my servant.'"

35 That night the angel of the Lord went out and put to death a hundred and eighty-five thousand in the Assyrian camp. When the people got up the next morning—there were all the dead bodies! 36 So Sennacherib king of Assyria broke camp and withdrew. He returned to Nineveh and stayed there.

37 One day, while he was worshiping in the temple of his god Nisrok, his sons Adrammelek and Sharezer killed him with the sword, and they escaped to the land of Ararat. And Esarhaddon his son succeeded him as king.

Hezekiah's Illness

20 In those days Hezekiah became ill and was at the point of death. The prophet Isaiah son of Amoz went to him and said, "This is what the Lord says: Put your house in order, because you are going to die; you will not recover."

2 Hezekiah turned his face to the wall and prayed to the Lord, 3 "Remember, Lord, how I have walked before you faithfully and with wholehearted devotion and have done what is good in your eyes." And Hezekiah wept bitterly.

4 Before Isaiah had left the middle court, the word of the Lord came to him: 5 "Go back and tell Hezekiah, the ruler of my people, 'This is what the Lord, the God of your father David, says: I have heard your prayer and seen your tears;

490

at issue: illness

20:1–7 It's amazing how much we take our bodies for granted when we're healthy. But one sharp pain—a migraine, cramps, even a stiff neck—can make everyday life difficult. All our attention is diverted toward that one nagging pain. Illness makes us acutely aware of our limitations. Whether God heals us or not, illness should remind us to turn to God and thank him for what he's given us. Physical pain can be a severe mercy, giving us a sharp focus on God that we wouldn't have apart from pain, so that we'll be less likely to forget him when we recover.

I will heal you. On the third day from now you will go up to the temple of the LORD. ⁶I will add fifteen years to your life. And I will deliver you and this city from the hand of the king of Assyria. I will defend this city for my sake and for the sake of my servant David.'"

⁷Then Isaiah said, "Prepare a poultice of figs." They did so and applied it to the boil, and he recovered.

⁸Hezekiah had asked Isaiah, "What will be the sign that the LORD will heal me and that I will go up to the temple of the LORD on the third day from now?"

⁹Isaiah answered, "This is the LORD's sign to you that the LORD will do what he has promised: Shall the shadow go forward ten steps, or shall it go back ten steps?"

¹⁰"It is a simple matter for the shadow to go forward ten steps," said Hezekiah. "Rather, have it go back ten steps."

¹¹Then the prophet Isaiah called on the LORD, and the LORD made the shadow go back the ten steps it had gone down on the stairway of Ahaz.

Envoys From Babylon

¹²At that time Marduk-Baladan son of Baladan king of Babylon sent Hezekiah letters and a gift, because he had heard of Hezekiah's illness. ¹³Hezekiah received the envoys and showed them all that was in his storehouses—the silver, the gold, the spices and the fine olive oil—his armory and everything found among his treasures. There was nothing in his palace or in all his kingdom that Hezekiah did not show them.

¹⁴Then Isaiah the prophet went to King Hezekiah and asked, "What did those men say, and where did they come from?"

"From a distant land," Hezekiah replied. "They came from Babylon."

¹⁵The prophet asked, "What did they see in your palace?"

"They saw everything in my palace," Hezekiah said. "There is nothing among my treasures that I did not show them."

¹⁶Then Isaiah said to Hezekiah, "Hear the word of the LORD: ¹⁷The time will surely come when everything in your palace, and all that your predecessors have stored up until this day, will be carried off to Babylon. Nothing will be left, says the LORD. ¹⁸And some of your descendants, your own flesh and blood who will be born to you, will be taken away, and they will become eunuchs in the palace of the king of Babylon."

¹⁹"The word of the LORD you have spoken is good," Hezekiah replied. For he thought, "Will there not be peace and security in my lifetime?"

²⁰As for the other events of Hezekiah's reign, all his achievements and how he made the pool and the tunnel by which he brought water into the city, are they not written in the book of the annals of the kings of Judah? ²¹Hezekiah rested with his ancestors. And Manasseh his son succeeded him as king.

Manasseh King of Judah

21 Manasseh was twelve years old when he became king, and he reigned in Jerusalem fifty-five years. His mother's name was Hephzibah. ²He did evil in the eyes of the LORD, following the detestable practices of the nations the LORD had driven out before the Israelites. ³He rebuilt the high places his father Hezekiah had destroyed; he also erected altars to Baal and made an Asherah pole, as Ahab king of Israel had done. He bowed down to all the starry hosts and worshiped them. ⁴He built altars in the temple of the LORD, of which the LORD had said, "In Jerusalem I will put my Name." ⁵In the two courts of the temple of the LORD, he built altars to all the starry hosts. ⁶He sacrificed his own son in the fire, practiced divination, sought omens, and consulted mediums and spiritists. He did much evil in the eyes of the LORD, arousing his anger.

⁷He took the carved Asherah pole he had made and put it in the temple, of which the LORD had said to David and to his son Solomon, "In this temple and in Jerusalem, which I have chosen out of all the tribes of Israel, I will put my Name forever. ⁸I will not again make the feet of the Israelites wander from the land I gave their ancestors, if only they will be careful to do everything I commanded them and will keep the whole Law that my servant Moses gave them." ⁹But the people did not listen. Manasseh led them astray, so that they did more evil than the nations the LORD had destroyed before the Israelites.

491

¹⁰The Lord said through his servants the prophets: ¹¹"Manasseh king of Judah has committed these detestable sins. He has done more evil than the Amorites who preceded him and has led Judah into sin with his idols. ¹²Therefore this is what the Lord, the God of Israel, says: I am going to bring such disaster on Jerusalem and Judah that the ears of everyone who hears of it will tingle. ¹³I will stretch out over Jerusalem the measuring line used against Samaria and the plumb line used against the house of Ahab. I will wipe out Jerusalem as one wipes a dish, wiping it and turning it upside down. ¹⁴I will forsake the remnant of my inheritance and give them into the hands of enemies. They will be looted and plundered by all their enemies; ¹⁵they have done evil in my eyes and have aroused my anger from the day their ancestors came out of Egypt until this day."

¹⁶Moreover, Manasseh also shed so much innocent blood that he filled Jerusalem from end to end—besides the sin that he had caused Judah to commit, so that they did evil in the eyes of the Lord.

¹⁷As for the other events of Manasseh's reign, and all he did, including the sin he committed, are they not written in the book of the annals of the kings of Judah? ¹⁸Manasseh rested with his ancestors and was buried in his palace garden, the garden of Uzza. And Amon his son succeeded him as king.

Amon King of Judah

¹⁹Amon was twenty-two years old when he became king, and he reigned in Jerusalem two years. His mother's name was Meshullemeth daughter of Haruz; she was from Jotbah. ²⁰He did evil in the eyes of the Lord, as his father Manasseh had done. ²¹He followed completely the ways of his father, worshiping the idols his father had worshiped, and bowing down to them. ²²He forsook the Lord, the God of his ancestors, and did not walk in obedience to him.

²³Amon's officials conspired against him and assassinated the king in his palace. ²⁴Then the people of the land killed all who had plotted against King Amon, and they made Josiah his son king in his place.

²⁵As for the other events of Amon's reign, and what he did, are they not written in the book of the annals of the kings of Judah? ²⁶He was buried in his tomb in the garden of Uzza. And Josiah his son succeeded him as king.

The Book of the Law Found

22 Josiah was eight years old when he became king, and he reigned in Jerusalem thirty-one years. His mother's name was Jedidah daughter of Adaiah; she was from Bozkath. ²He did what was right in the eyes of the Lord and followed completely the ways of his father David, not turning aside to the right or to the left.

³In the eighteenth year of his reign, King Josiah sent the secretary, Shaphan son of Azaliah, the son of Meshullam, to the temple of the Lord. He said: ⁴"Go up to Hilkiah the high priest and have him get ready the money that has been brought into the temple of the Lord, which the doorkeepers have collected from the people. ⁵Have them entrust it to the men appointed to supervise the work on the temple. And have these men pay the workers who repair the temple of the Lord— ⁶the carpenters, the builders and the masons. Also have them purchase timber and dressed stone to repair the temple. ⁷But they need not account for the money entrusted to them, because they are honest in their dealings."

⁸Hilkiah the high priest said to Shaphan the secretary, "I have found the Book of the Law in the temple of the Lord." He gave it to Shaphan, who read it. ⁹Then Shaphan the secretary went to the king and reported to him: "Your officials have paid out the money that was in the temple of the Lord and have entrusted it to the workers and supervisors at the temple." ¹⁰Then Shaphan the secretary informed the king, "Hilkiah the priest has given me a book." And Shaphan read from it in the presence of the king.

¹¹When the king heard the words of the Book of the Law, he tore his robes. ¹²He gave these orders to Hilkiah the priest, Ahikam son of Shaphan, Akbor son of Micaiah, Shaphan the secretary and Asaiah the king's attendant: ¹³"Go and inquire of the Lord for me and for the people and for all Judah about what is written in this book that has been found. Great is the Lord's anger that burns against us because those who have gone before us have not obeyed the words of this book; they have not acted in accordance with all that is written there concerning us."

¹⁴Hilkiah the priest, Ahikam, Akbor, Shaphan and Asaiah went to speak to the prophet Huldah, who

was the wife of Shallum son of Tikvah, the son of Harhas, keeper of the wardrobe. She lived in Jerusalem, in the New Quarter.

¹⁵She said to them, "This is what the Lord, the God of Israel, says: Tell the man who sent you to me, ¹⁶'This is what the Lord says: I am going to bring disaster on this place and its people, according to everything written in the book the king of Judah has read. ¹⁷Because they have forsaken me and burned incense to other gods and aroused my anger by all the idols their hands have made,[a] my anger will burn against this place and will not be quenched.' ¹⁸Tell the king of Judah, who sent you to inquire of the Lord, 'This is what the Lord, the God of Israel, says concerning the words you heard: ¹⁹Because your heart was responsive and you humbled yourself before the Lord when you heard what I have spoken against this place and its people—that they would become a curse[b] and be laid waste—and because you tore your robes and wept in my presence, I also have heard you, declares the Lord. ²⁰Therefore I will gather you to your ancestors, and you will be buried in peace. Your eyes will not see all the disaster I am going to bring on this place.'"

So they took her answer back to the king.

conversations

time with God «» 22:11–20

1 » What is the importance of reading the Bible every day?

2 » What happens when you cut off your regular intake of God's Word?

3 » Can a Christian grow without reading her Bible?

For more on **time with God**, check the index.
For the next Conversations, go to p. 493.

Josiah Renews the Covenant

23 Then the king called together all the elders of Judah and Jerusalem. ²He went up to the temple of the Lord with the people of Judah, the inhabitants of Jerusalem, the priests and the prophets—all the people from the least to the greatest. He read in their hearing all the words of the Book of the Covenant, which had been found in the temple of the Lord. ³The king stood by the pillar and renewed the covenant in the presence of the Lord—to follow the Lord and keep his commands, statutes and decrees with all his heart and all his soul, thus confirming the words of the covenant written in this book. Then all the people pledged themselves to the covenant.

conversations

authority «» 23:1–3

1 » How important is it for a leader to lead by example?

2 » How much influence do leaders have on their followers' commitment to God?

3 » Can you think of someone whose commitment to the Lord influences you?

For more on **authority**, check the index.
For the next Conversations, go to p. 507.

⁴The king ordered Hilkiah the high priest, the priests next in rank and the doorkeepers to remove from the temple of the Lord all the articles made for Baal and Asherah and all the starry hosts. He burned them outside Jerusalem in the fields of the Kidron Valley and took the ashes to Bethel. ⁵He did away with the idolatrous priests appointed by the kings of Judah to burn incense on the high places of the towns of Judah and on those around Jerusalem—those who burned incense to Baal, to the sun and moon, to the constellations and to all the starry hosts. ⁶He took the Asherah pole from the temple of the Lord to the Kidron Valley outside Jerusalem and burned it there. He ground it to powder and scattered the dust over the graves of the common people. ⁷He also tore down the quarters of the male shrine prostitutes that were in the temple of the Lord, the quarters where women did weaving for Asherah.

⁸Josiah brought all the priests from the towns of Judah and desecrated the high places, from Geba to Beersheba, where the priests had burned incense. He broke down the gateway at the entrance of the Gate of Joshua, the city governor, which was on the left of the city gate. ⁹Although the priests of the high

---

[a] 17 Or by everything they have done   [b] 19 That is, their names would be used in cursing (see Jer. 29:22); or, others would see that they are cursed.

places did not serve at the altar of the LORD in Jerusalem, they ate unleavened bread with their fellow priests.

¹⁰He desecrated Topheth, which was in the Valley of Ben Hinnom, so no one could use it to sacrifice their son or daughter in the fire to Molek. ¹¹He removed from the entrance to the temple of the LORD the horses that the kings of Judah had dedicated to the sun. They were in the court^a near the room of an official named Nathan-Melek. Josiah then burned the chariots dedicated to the sun.

¹²He pulled down the altars the kings of Judah had erected on the roof near the upper room of Ahaz, and the altars Manasseh had built in the two courts of the temple of the LORD. He removed them from there, smashed them to pieces and threw the rubble into the Kidron Valley. ¹³The king also desecrated the high places that were east of Jerusalem on the south of the Hill of Corruption—the ones Solomon king of Israel had built for Ashtoreth the vile goddess of the Sidonians, for Chemosh the vile god of Moab, and for Molek the detestable god of the people of Ammon. ¹⁴Josiah smashed the sacred stones and cut down the Asherah poles and covered the sites with human bones.

¹⁵Even the altar at Bethel, the high place made by Jeroboam son of Nebat, who had caused Israel to sin—even that altar and high place he demolished. He burned the high place and ground it to powder, and burned the Asherah pole also. ¹⁶Then Josiah looked around, and when he saw the tombs that were there on the hillside, he had the bones removed from them and burned on the altar to defile it, in accordance with the word of the LORD proclaimed by the man of God who foretold these things.

494

¹⁷The king asked, "What is that tombstone I see?"

The people of the city said, "It marks the tomb of the man of God who came from Judah and pronounced against the altar of Bethel the very things you have done to it."

¹⁸"Leave it alone," he said. "Don't let anyone disturb his bones." So they spared his bones and those of the prophet who had come from Samaria.

¹⁹Just as he had done at Bethel, Josiah removed all the shrines at the high places that the kings of Israel had built in the towns of Samaria and that had aroused the LORD's anger. ²⁰Josiah slaughtered all the priests of those high places on the altars and burned human bones on them. Then he went back to Jerusalem.

²¹The king gave this order to all the people: "Celebrate the Passover to the LORD your God, as it is written in this Book of the Covenant." ²²Neither in the days of the judges who led Israel nor in the days of the kings of Israel and the kings of Judah had any such Passover been observed. ²³But in the eighteenth year of King Josiah, this Passover was celebrated to the LORD in Jerusalem.

²⁴Furthermore, Josiah got rid of the mediums and spiritists, the household gods, the idols and all the other detestable things seen in Judah and Jerusalem. This he did to fulfill the requirements of the law written in the book that Hilkiah the priest had discovered in the temple of the LORD. ²⁵Neither before nor after Josiah was there a king like him who turned to the LORD as he did—with all his heart and with all his soul and with all his strength, in accordance with all the Law of Moses.

²⁶Nevertheless, the LORD did not turn away from the heat of his fierce anger, which burned against Judah because of all that Manasseh had done to arouse his anger. ²⁷So the LORD said, "I will remove Judah also from my presence as I removed Israel, and I will reject Jerusalem, the city I chose, and this temple, about which I said, 'There shall my Name be.'^b"

²⁸As for the other events of Josiah's reign, and all he did, are they not written in the book of the annals of the kings of Judah?

²⁹While Josiah was king, Pharaoh Necho king of Egypt went up to the Euphrates River to help the king of Assyria. King Josiah marched out to meet him in battle, but Necho faced him and killed him at Megiddo. ³⁰Josiah's servants brought his body in a chariot from Megiddo to Jerusalem and buried him in his own tomb. And the people of the land took Jehoahaz son of Josiah and anointed him and made him king in place of his father.

Jehoahaz King of Judah

³¹Jehoahaz was twenty-three years old when he became king, and he reigned in Jerusalem three months. His mother's name was Hamutal daughter of Jeremiah; she was from Libnah. ³²He did evil in

---

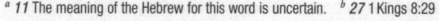

^a 11 The meaning of the Hebrew for this word is uncertain.   ^b 27 1 Kings 8:29

the eyes of the LORD, just as his predecessors had done. ³³Pharaoh Necho put him in chains at Riblah in the land of Hamath so that he might not reign in Jerusalem, and he imposed on Judah a levy of a hundred talents*ᵃ* of silver and a talent*ᵇ* of gold. ³⁴Pharaoh Necho made Eliakim son of Josiah king in place of his father Josiah and changed Eliakim's name to Jehoiakim. But he took Jehoahaz and carried him off to Egypt, and there he died. ³⁵Jehoiakim paid Pharaoh Necho the silver and gold he demanded. In order to do so, he taxed the land and exacted the silver and gold from the people of the land according to their assessments.

Jehoiakim King of Judah

³⁶Jehoiakim was twenty-five years old when he became king, and he reigned in Jerusalem eleven years. His mother's name was Zebidah daughter of Pedaiah; she was from Rumah. ³⁷And he did evil in the eyes of the LORD, just as his predecessors had done.

24 During Jehoiakim's reign, Nebuchadnezzar king of Babylon invaded the land, and Jehoiakim became his vassal for three years. But then he turned against Nebuchadnezzar and rebelled. ²The LORD sent Babylonian,*ᶜ* Aramean, Moabite and Ammonite raiders against him to destroy Judah, in accordance with the word of the LORD proclaimed by his servants the prophets. ³Surely these things happened to Judah according to the LORD's command, in order to remove them from his presence because of the sins of Manasseh and all he had done, ⁴including the shedding of innocent blood. For he had filled Jerusalem with innocent blood, and the LORD was not willing to forgive.

⁵As for the other events of Jehoiakim's reign, and all he did, are they not written in the book of the annals of the kings of Judah? ⁶Jehoiakim rested with his ancestors. And Jehoiachin his son succeeded him as king.

⁷The king of Egypt did not march out from his own country again, because the king of Babylon had taken all his territory, from the Wadi of Egypt to the Euphrates River.

495

Jehoiachin King of Judah

⁸Jehoiachin was eighteen years old when he became king, and he reigned in Jerusalem three months. His mother's name was Nehushta daughter of Elnathan; she was from Jerusalem. ⁹He did evil in the eyes of the LORD, just as his father had done.

¹⁰At that time the officers of Nebuchadnezzar king of Babylon advanced on Jerusalem and laid siege to it, ¹¹and Nebuchadnezzar himself came up to the city while his officers were besieging it. ¹²Jehoiachin king of Judah, his mother, his attendants, his nobles and his officials all surrendered to him.

In the eighth year of the reign of the king of Babylon, he took Jehoiachin prisoner. ¹³As the LORD had declared, Nebuchadnezzar removed the treasures from the temple of the LORD and from the royal palace, and cut up the gold articles that Solomon king of Israel had made for the temple of the LORD. ¹⁴He carried all Jerusalem into exile: all the officers and fighting men, and all the skilled workers and artisans—a total of ten thousand. Only the poorest people of the land were left.

¹⁵Nebuchadnezzar took Jehoiachin captive to Babylon. He also took from Jerusalem to Babylon the king's mother, his wives, his officials and the prominent people of the land. ¹⁶The king of Babylon also deported to Babylon the entire force of seven thousand fighting men, strong and fit for war, and a thousand skilled workers and artisans. ¹⁷He made Mattaniah, Jehoiachin's uncle, king in his place and changed his name to Zedekiah.

Zedekiah King of Judah

¹⁸Zedekiah was twenty-one years old when he became king, and he reigned in Jerusalem eleven years. His mother's name was Hamutal daughter of Jeremiah; she was from Libnah. ¹⁹He did evil in the eyes of the LORD, just as Jehoiakim had done. ²⁰It was because of the LORD's anger that all this happened to Jerusalem and Judah, and in the end he thrust them from his presence.

The Fall of Jerusalem

Now Zedekiah rebelled against the king of Babylon.

ᵃ 33 That is, about 3 3/4 tons or about 3.4 metric tons　*ᵇ 33* That is, about 75 pounds or about 34 kilograms　*ᶜ 2* Or *Chaldean*

25 So in the ninth year of Zedekiah's reign, on the tenth day of the tenth month, Nebuchadnezzar king of Babylon marched against Jerusalem with his whole army. He encamped outside the city and built siege works all around it. ²The city was kept under siege until the eleventh year of King Zedekiah.

³By the ninth day of the fourth*a* month the famine in the city had become so severe that there was no food for the people to eat. ⁴Then the city wall was broken through, and the whole army fled at night through the gate between the two walls near the king's garden, though the Babylonians*b* were surrounding the city. They fled toward the Arabah,*c* ⁵but the Babylonian*d* army pursued the king and overtook him in the plains of Jericho. All his soldiers were separated from him and scattered, ⁶and he was captured.

He was taken to the king of Babylon at Riblah, where sentence was pronounced on him. ⁷They killed the sons of Zedekiah before his eyes. Then they put out his eyes, bound him with bronze shackles and took him to Babylon.

⁸On the seventh day of the fifth month, in the nineteenth year of Nebuchadnezzar king of Babylon, Nebuzaradan commander of the imperial guard, an official of the king of Babylon, came to Jerusalem. ⁹He set fire to the temple of the LORD, the royal palace and all the houses of Jerusalem. Every important building he burned down. ¹⁰The whole Babylonian army under the commander of the imperial guard broke down the walls around Jerusalem. ¹¹Nebuzaradan the commander of the guard carried into exile the people who remained in the city, along with the rest of the populace and those who had deserted to the king of Babylon. ¹²But the commander left behind some of the poorest people of the land to work the vineyards and fields.

¹³The Babylonians broke up the bronze pillars, the movable stands and the bronze Sea that were at the temple of the LORD and they carried the bronze to Babylon. ¹⁴They also took away the pots, shovels, wick trimmers, dishes and all the bronze articles used in the temple service. ¹⁵The commander of the imperial guard took away the censers and sprinkling bowls—all that were made of pure gold or silver.

¹⁶The bronze from the two pillars, the Sea and the movable stands, which Solomon had made for the temple of the LORD, was more than could be weighed. ¹⁷Each pillar was eighteen cubits*e* high. The bronze capital on top of one pillar was three cubits*f* high and was decorated with a network and pomegranates of bronze all around. The other pillar, with its network, was similar.

¹⁸The commander of the guard took as prisoners Seraiah the chief priest, Zephaniah the priest next in rank and the three doorkeepers. ¹⁹Of those still in the city, he took the officer in charge of the fighting men, and five royal advisers. He also took the secretary who was chief officer in charge of conscripting the people of the land and sixty of the conscripts who were found in the city. ²⁰Nebuzaradan the commander took them all and brought them to the king of Babylon at Riblah. ²¹There at Riblah, in the land of Hamath, the king had them executed.

So Judah went into captivity, away from her land.

²²Nebuchadnezzar king of Babylon appointed Gedaliah son of Ahikam, the son of Shaphan, to be over the people he had left behind in Judah. ²³When all the army officers and their men heard that the king of Babylon had appointed Gedaliah as governor, they came to Gedaliah at Mizpah—Ishmael son of Nethaniah, Johanan son of Kareah, Seraiah son of Tanhumeth the Netophathite, Jaazaniah the son of the

496

at issue: failure

25:1–30 We don't like to think about failure as a teaching tool. We'd much rather have a lesson in prayer or even fasting . . . but not *failure*. Whether it's financial, emotional, physical or marital, there's nothing comfortable about a complete crash. The book of 2 Kings ends with the failure of the nation of Judah. The people refused to keep God's commands, so they were conquered and exiled. Their false stronghold, Jerusalem, was wiped away. We also set ourselves up for a difficult lesson in failure when we ignore God's repeated warnings. Is total failure the only way you'll return to God?

---

a 3 Probable reading of the original Hebrew text (see Jer. 52:6); Masoretic Text does not have *fourth.*   *b 4 Or Chaldeans*; also in verses 13, 25 and 26   *c 4 Or the Jordan Valley*   *d 5 Or Chaldean*; also in verses 10 and 24   *e 17* That is, about 27 feet or about 8.2 meters   *f 17* That is, about 4 1/2 feet or about 1.4 meters

HE IS: disciplining

25:1–30 Years of idolatry, ungodly rulers and ruinous alliances resulted in the Lord's *disciplining* Judah. Just as the prophets had predicted, God allowed his people to be taken into captivity by the Babylonians. The people had lived as idolaters; now they would live in the land of idolatry. God used this tragedy to show the people their sin.

If you are a child of God and have chosen to take a sinful path, don't be surprised when you experience God's divine discipline. He is *disciplining*. You may be going through chastisement now because the Lord wants to cleanse your life of sin (see Psalm 94:12).

For the next He Is, go to p. 518.

Maakathite, and their men. [24]Gedaliah took an oath to reassure them and their men. "Do not be afraid of the Babylonian officials," he said. "Settle down in the land and serve the king of Babylon, and it will go well with you."

[25]In the seventh month, however, Ishmael son of Nethaniah, the son of Elishama, who was of royal blood, came with ten men and assassinated Gedaliah and also the men of Judah and the Babylonians who were with him at Mizpah. [26]At this, all the people from the least to the greatest, together with the army officers, fled to Egypt for fear of the Babylonians.

Jehoiachin Released

[27]In the thirty-seventh year of the exile of Jehoiachin king of Judah, in the year Awel-Marduk became king of Babylon, he released Jehoiachin king of Judah from prison. He did this on the twenty-seventh day of the twelfth month. [28]He spoke kindly to him and gave him a seat of honor higher than those of the other kings who were with him in Babylon. [29]So Jehoiachin put aside his prison clothes and for the rest of his life ate regularly at the king's table. [30]Day by day the king gave Jehoiachin a regular allowance as long as he lived.

1 chronicles

AUTHOR
Unknown, but possibly Ezra.

AUDIENCE
All Israel.

DATE
About 430 B.C.

SETTING
The book begins with Israel's genealogical
records and then focuses on King David's
reign, paralleling many of the events
recorded in 2 Samuel.

VERSE TO REMEMBER
"And David knew that the LORD had established him as king over Israel and that his
kingdom had been highly exalted for the
sake of his people Israel." (14:2)

THEME TO CONSIDER
As the people of God, we can never forget
who we are and how far we've come, as told
in God's grand story.

Historical Records From Adam to Abraham

To Noah's Sons

1 Adam, Seth, Enosh, [2]Kenan, Mahalalel, Jared, [3]Enoch, Methuselah, Lamech, Noah.

[4]The sons of Noah:[a]
Shem, Ham and Japheth.

The Japhethites

[5] The sons[b] of Japheth:
Gomer, Magog, Madai, Javan, Tubal, Meshek and Tiras.
[6] The sons of Gomer:
Ashkenaz, Riphath[c] and Togarmah.
[7] The sons of Javan:
Elishah, Tarshish, the Kittites and the Rodanites.

The Hamites

[8] The sons of Ham:
Cush, Egypt, Put and Canaan.
[9] The sons of Cush:
Seba, Havilah, Sabta, Raamah and Sabteka.
The sons of Raamah:
Sheba and Dedan.
[10] Cush was the father[d] of
Nimrod, who became a mighty warrior on earth.
[11] Egypt was the father of
the Ludites, Anamites, Lehabites, Naphtuhites, [12]Pathrusites, Kasluhites (from whom the Philistines came) and Caphtorites.
[13] Canaan was the father of
Sidon his firstborn,[e] and of the Hittites, [14]Jebusites, Amorites, Girgashites, [15]Hivites, Arkites, Sinites, [16]Arvadites, Zemarites and Hamathites.

The Semites

[17] The sons of Shem:
Elam, Ashur, Arphaxad, Lud and Aram.
The sons of Aram:[f]
Uz, Hul, Gether and Meshek.
[18] Arphaxad was the father of Shelah,
and Shelah the father of Eber.
[19] Two sons were born to Eber:
One was named Peleg,[g] because in his time the earth was divided; his brother was named Joktan.
[20] Joktan was the father of
Almodad, Sheleph, Hazarmaveth, Jerah, [21]Hadoram, Uzal, Diklah, [22]Obal,[h] Abimael, Sheba, [23]Ophir, Havilah and Jobab. All these were sons of Joktan.

[24] Shem, Arphaxad,[i] Shelah,
[25] Eber, Peleg, Reu,
[26] Serug, Nahor, Terah
[27] and Abram (that is, Abraham).

499

---

[a] 4 Septuagint; Hebrew does not have this line. [b] 5 Sons may mean *descendants* or *successors* or *nations*; also in verses 6-10, 17 and 20. [c] 6 Many Hebrew manuscripts and Vulgate (see also Septuagint and Gen. 10:3); most Hebrew manuscripts *Diphath* [d] 10 Father may mean *ancestor* or *predecessor* or *founder*; also in verses 11, 13, 18 and 20. [e] 13 Or *of the Sidonians, the foremost* [f] 17 One Hebrew manuscript and some Septuagint manuscripts (see also Gen. 10:23); most Hebrew manuscripts do not have this line. [g] 19 Peleg means *division*. [h] 22 Some Hebrew manuscripts and Syriac (see also Gen. 10:28); most Hebrew manuscripts *Ebal* [i] 24 Hebrew; some Septuagint manuscripts *Arphaxad, Cainan* (see also note at Gen. 11:10)

The Family of Abraham

²⁸ The sons of Abraham:

Isaac and Ishmael.

Descendants of Hagar

²⁹ These were their descendants:

Nebaioth the firstborn of Ishmael, Kedar, Adbeel, Mibsam, ³⁰Mishma, Dumah, Massa, Hadad, Tema, ³¹Jetur, Naphish and Kedemah. These were the sons of Ishmael.

Descendants of Keturah

³² The sons born to Keturah, Abraham's concubine:

Zimran, Jokshan, Medan, Midian, Ishbak and Shuah.

The sons of Jokshan:

Sheba and Dedan.

³³ The sons of Midian:

Ephah, Epher, Hanok, Abida and Eldaah.

All these were descendants of Keturah.

Descendants of Sarah

³⁴ Abraham was the father of Isaac.

The sons of Isaac:

Esau and Israel.

Esau's Sons

³⁵ The sons of Esau:

Eliphaz, Reuel, Jeush, Jalam and Korah.

³⁶ The sons of Eliphaz:

Teman, Omar, Zepho,ᵃ Gatam and Kenaz;

by Timna: Amalek.ᵇ

³⁷ The sons of Reuel:

Nahath, Zerah, Shammah and Mizzah.

The People of Seir in Edom

³⁸ The sons of Seir:

Lotan, Shobal, Zibeon, Anah, Dishon, Ezer and Dishan.

³⁹ The sons of Lotan:

Hori and Homam. Timna was Lotan's sister.

⁴⁰ The sons of Shobal:

Alvan,ᶜ Manahath, Ebal, Shepho and Onam.

The sons of Zibeon:

Aiah and Anah.

⁴¹ The son of Anah:

Dishon.

The sons of Dishon:

Hemdan,ᵈ Eshban, Ithran and Keran.

⁴² The sons of Ezer:

Bilhan, Zaavan and Akan.ᵉ

The sons of Dishanᶠ:

Uz and Aran.

The Rulers of Edom

⁴³ These were the kings who reigned in Edom before any Israelite king reigned:

Bela son of Beor, whose city was named Dinhabah.

⁴⁴ When Bela died, Jobab son of Zerah from Bozrah succeeded him as king.

⁴⁵ When Jobab died, Husham from the land of the Temanites succeeded him as king.

⁴⁶ When Husham died, Hadad son of Bedad, who defeated Midian in the country of Moab, succeeded him as king. His city was named Avith.

⁴⁷ When Hadad died, Samlah from Masrekah succeeded him as king.

⁴⁸ When Samlah died, Shaul from Rehoboth on the river*ᵃ* succeeded him as king.

⁴⁹ When Shaul died, Baal-Hanan son of Akbor succeeded him as king.

⁵⁰ When Baal-Hanan died, Hadad succeeded him as king. His city was named Pau,*ᵇ* and his wife's name was Mehetabel daughter of Matred, the daughter of Me-Zahab. ⁵¹ Hadad also died.

The chiefs of Edom were:

Timna, Alvah, Jetheth, ⁵²Oholibamah, Elah, Pinon, ⁵³Kenaz, Teman, Mibzar, ⁵⁴Magdiel and Iram. These were the chiefs of Edom.

Israel's Sons

2 These were the sons of Israel:

Reuben, Simeon, Levi, Judah, Issachar, Zebulun, ²Dan, Joseph, Benjamin, Naphtali, Gad and Asher.

Judah

To Hezron's Sons

³ The sons of Judah:

Er, Onan and Shelah. These three were born to him by a Canaanite woman, the daughter of Shua. Er, Judah's firstborn, was wicked in the Lᴏʀᴅ's sight; so the Lᴏʀᴅ put him to death. ⁴Judah's daughter-in-law Tamar bore Perez and Zerah to Judah. He had five sons in all.

⁵ The sons of Perez:

Hezron and Hamul.

⁶ The sons of Zerah:

Zimri, Ethan, Heman, Kalkol and Darda*ᶜ*—five in all.

⁷ The son of Karmi:

Achar,*ᵈ* who brought trouble on Israel by violating the ban on taking devoted things.*ᵉ*

⁸ The son of Ethan:

Azariah.

⁹ The sons born to Hezron were:

Jerahmeel, Ram and Caleb.*ᶠ*

From Ram Son of Hezron

¹⁰ Ram was the father of

Amminadab, and Amminadab the father of Nahshon, the leader of the people of Judah. ¹¹Nahshon was the father of Salmon,*ᵍ* Salmon the father of Boaz, ¹²Boaz the father of Obed and Obed the father of Jesse.

¹³ Jesse was the father of

Eliab his firstborn; the second son was Abinadab, the third Shimea, ¹⁴the fourth Nethanel, the fifth Raddai, ¹⁵the sixth Ozem and the seventh David. ¹⁶Their sisters were Zeruiah and Abigail. Zeruiah's three sons were Abishai, Joab and Asahel. ¹⁷Abigail was the mother of Amasa, whose father was Jether the Ishmaelite.

501

ᵃ 48 Possibly the Euphrates   *ᵇ 50* Many Hebrew manuscripts, some Septuagint manuscripts, Vulgate and Syriac (see also Gen. 36:39); most Hebrew manuscripts *Pai*   *ᶜ 6* Many Hebrew manuscripts, some Septuagint manuscripts and Syriac (see also 1 Kings 4:31); most Hebrew manuscripts *Dara*   *ᵈ 7 Achar* means *trouble; Achar* is called *Achan* in Joshua.   *ᵉ 7* The Hebrew term refers to the irrevocable giving over of things or persons to the Lᴏʀᴅ, often by totally destroying them.   *ᶠ 9* Hebrew *Kelubai,* a variant of *Caleb*   *ᵍ 11* Septuagint (see also Ruth 4:21); Hebrew *Salma*

Caleb Son of Hezron

¹⁸ Caleb son of Hezron had children by his wife Azubah (and by Jerioth). These were her sons: Jesher, Shobab and Ardon. ¹⁹When Azubah died, Caleb married Ephrath, who bore him Hur. ²⁰Hur was the father of Uri, and Uri the father of Bezalel.

²¹ Later, Hezron, when he was sixty years old, married the daughter of Makir the father of Gilead. He made love to her, and she bore him Segub. ²²Segub was the father of Jair, who controlled twenty-three towns in Gilead. ²³(But Geshur and Aram captured Havvoth Jair,^a as well as Kenath with its surrounding settlements—sixty towns.) All these were descendants of Makir the father of Gilead.

²⁴ After Hezron died in Caleb Ephrathah, Abijah the wife of Hezron bore him Ashhur the father^b of Tekoa.

Jerahmeel Son of Hezron

²⁵ The sons of Jerahmeel the firstborn of Hezron:

Ram his firstborn, Bunah, Oren, Ozem and^c Ahijah. ²⁶Jerahmeel had another wife, whose name was Atarah; she was the mother of Onam.

²⁷ The sons of Ram the firstborn of Jerahmeel:

Maaz, Jamin and Eker.

²⁸ The sons of Onam:

Shammai and Jada.

The sons of Shammai:

Nadab and Abishur.

²⁹ Abishur's wife was named Abihail, who bore him Ahban and Molid.

³⁰ The sons of Nadab:

Seled and Appaim. Seled died without children.

³¹ The son of Appaim:

Ishi, who was the father of Sheshan.

Sheshan was the father of Ahlai.

³² The sons of Jada, Shammai's brother:

Jether and Jonathan. Jether died without children.

³³ The sons of Jonathan:

Peleth and Zaza.

These were the descendants of Jerahmeel.

³⁴ Sheshan had no sons—only daughters.

He had an Egyptian servant named Jarha. ³⁵Sheshan gave his daughter in marriage to his servant Jarha, and she bore him Attai.

³⁶ Attai was the father of Nathan,

Nathan the father of Zabad,

³⁷ Zabad the father of Ephlal,

Ephlal the father of Obed,

³⁸ Obed the father of Jehu,

Jehu the father of Azariah,

³⁹ Azariah the father of Helez,

Helez the father of Eleasah,

⁴⁰ Eleasah the father of Sismai,

Sismai the father of Shallum,

⁴¹ Shallum the father of Jekamiah,

and Jekamiah the father of Elishama.

---

^a *23* Or *captured the settlements of Jair*   ^b *24 Father* may mean *civic leader* or *military leader*; also in verses 42, 45, 49-52 and possibly elsewhere.
^c *25* Or *Oren and Ozem, by*

The Clans of Caleb

⁴² The sons of Caleb the brother of Jerahmeel:

Mesha his firstborn, who was the father of Ziph, and his son Mareshah,ᵃ who was the father of Hebron.

⁴³ The sons of Hebron:

Korah, Tappuah, Rekem and Shema. ⁴⁴Shema was the father of Raham, and Raham the father of Jorkeam. Rekem was the father of Shammai. ⁴⁵The son of Shammai was Maon, and Maon was the father of Beth Zur.

⁴⁶ Caleb's concubine Ephah was the mother of Haran, Moza and Gazez. Haran was the father of Gazez.

⁴⁷ The sons of Jahdai:

Regem, Jotham, Geshan, Pelet, Ephah and Shaaph.

⁴⁸ Caleb's concubine Maakah was the mother of Sheber and Tirhanah. ⁴⁹She also gave birth to Shaaph the father of Madmannah and to Sheva the father of Makbenah and Gibea. Caleb's daughter was Aksah. ⁵⁰These were the descendants of Caleb.

The sons of Hur the firstborn of Ephrathah:

Shobal the father of Kiriath Jearim, ⁵¹Salma the father of Bethlehem, and Hareph the father of Beth Gader.

⁵² The descendants of Shobal the father of Kiriath Jearim were:

Haroeh, half the Manahathites, ⁵³and the clans of Kiriath Jearim: the Ithrites, Puthites, Shumathites and Mishraites. From these descended the Zorathites and Eshtaolites.

⁵⁴ The descendants of Salma:

Bethlehem, the Netophathites, Atroth Beth Joab, half the Manahathites, the Zorites, ⁵⁵and the clans of scribesᵇ who lived at Jabez: the Tirathites, Shimeathites and Sucathites. These are the Kenites who came from Hammath, the father of the house of Rekab.ᶜ

The Sons of David

3 These were the sons of David born to him in Hebron:

The firstborn was Amnon the son of Ahinoam of Jezreel;

the second, Daniel the son of Abigail of Carmel;

² the third, Absalom the son of Maakah daughter of Talmai king of Geshur;

the fourth, Adonijah the son of Haggith;

³ the fifth, Shephatiah the son of Abital;

and the sixth, Ithream, by his wife Eglah.

⁴ These six were born to David in Hebron, where he reigned seven years and six months.

David reigned in Jerusalem thirty-three years, ⁵and these were the children born to him there:

Shammua,ᵈ Shobab, Nathan and Solomon. These four were by Bathshebaᵉ daughter of Ammiel. ⁶There were also Ibhar, Elishua,ᶠ Eliphelet, ⁷Nogah, Nepheg, Japhia, ⁸Elishama, Eliada and Eliphelet—nine in all. ⁹All these were the sons of David, besides his sons by his concubines. And Tamar was their sister.

503

atissue:sexual assault

3:9 Remember Tamar, David's daughter, who was raped by her half-brother, Amnon? Afterward, she lived a desolate life in her brother Absalom's house (see 2 Samuel 13). Amnon had said he loved Tamar, but what he felt wasn't love. Otherwise Amnon would have listened to her reasoning and her pleas. Rape is not an act of love. Maybe you know how Tamar felt after her brutal attack— alone and scared, used and ashamed, crushed and hopeless. You have someone you can turn to, just as Tamar turned to Absalom for care and solace. Jesus cares about your pain. He can comfort you and be with you as you heal.

ᵃ 42 The meaning of the Hebrew for this phrase is uncertain.   ᵇ 55 Or of the Sopherites   ᶜ 55 Or father of Beth Rekab   ᵈ 5 Hebrew Shimea, a variant of Shammua   ᵉ 5 One Hebrew manuscript and Vulgate (see also Septuagint and 2 Samuel 11:3); most Hebrew manuscripts Bathshua   ᶠ 6 Two Hebrew manuscripts (see also 2 Samuel 5:15 and 1 Chron. 14:5); most Hebrew manuscripts Elishama

myth# 33

"IT'S OK TO FLIRT— AS LONG AS EVERYONE'S JUST HAVING FUN."

When I landed a job as an advertising sales rep, I entered a completely different world from my inside sales position at a manufacturing firm. I was ready for more responsibility, and I was anxious to prove myself. I had a great first year, and I enjoyed making my mark in the company. When I was sent to the national convention within my second year, I felt like I had made the right career move.

I traveled to the convention with Paul, the VP of my division. He's in his mid-forties, married and very successful. He has this air of confidence about him. All the women in the office talk about how hot he is—tan, in great shape, with that sexy salt-and-pepper hair. We had worked together on some projects, and I could tell he really liked me. It's not every day you get to rub shoulders with a VP, so I was hoping to get to know him better at the convention and make a good impression.

The convention was a blast—lots of going out to great dinners on the company and late-night bar-hopping and parties. I'm a Christian, but I'm also a team player. So I made sure I was socializing and talking to everyone—especially Paul. At dinner on the last night, everyone was having a fabulous time, drinking and dancing and laughing. There were jokes and off-color innuendos flying back and forth, but no one meant anything by it. Paul was teasing me a lot, and also buying me drink after drink. I just played along, pretending not to notice that the jokes were getting more sexually-charged as the evening progressed. When Paul's hand grazed my thigh at the bar, I was taken aback. But I decided there was no harm done. The guy's married. A little flirting never hurts in the business world, as long as both parties understand what's going on.

When I got back to my room that night, a friend of mine (who is also a Christian) stopped by my room. She didn't mince words. "What are you doing, flirting with Paul?" she demanded.

Still a little giddy from that last martini, I laughed it off. "Who are you, my chaperone?"

"I'm serious," she said. "You're sending him an invitation. Don't think he won't act on it." Her look of disappointment sobered me for a moment. Was I going too far?

—Raisa

IT'S ONE THING to remain physically pure by not engaging in sex outside of marriage or having an extramarital affair. It's quite another thing to remain emotionally pure—not to flirt with another man, become emotionally attached to him, or talk with him about topics appropriate only between a husband and wife. Too often we ignore these "lesser" acts of impurity and justify them by saying "we haven't actually done anything." But Jesus said we are guilty all the same if we let impure thoughts infiltrate our minds (see Matthew 5:28).

What sets Christians apart from the rest of the world is not a list of "do's and don'ts." It's our hearts. Is it time for you to undergo a spiritual cardiogram so the Great Physician can diagnose any heart disorders? Consider taking these steps:

- *Ask God to monitor your motives and attitudes regarding your sexuality.* God gets to the heart of the matter—your motives, thoughts, attitudes. Take a realistic look at why you dress or act the way you do. What are you communicating about yourself and why?

- *Decide ahead of time to excuse yourself from questionable conversations at work.* Set some boundaries for yourself, lines you will not cross, and stick to them. Your first boundary shouldn't be physical touch (that's already too far)—it should be guarding your thoughts and your conversations. That will help protect you from acting on impure thoughts.

- *Refuse to demean your sexuality by using it to manipulate people and situations.* Let's face it—as women, our sexuality can be a powerful weapon. Will you abuse it, or will you use it for good? It's all too easy to spin your behavior in such a way that you can justify anything. *Flirting is OK as long as it gets you the job. Fantasizing is OK as long as you don't act on it.* False!

- *Get practical. Be accountable to a Christian girlfriend or mentor for your physical and emotional purity.* Be completely honest with each other.

> "59 percent of Americans surveyed considered having sexual fantasies 'morally acceptable,' and 42 percent considered having a sexual relationship with someone of the opposite sex other than their spouse 'morally acceptable.'"
>
> —Barna Research Group (2003)

> ## "FOR THE LORD searches every HEART and understands every DESIRE AND EVERY THOUGHT."
>
> 1 CHRONICLES 28:9

SEE ALSO

1 Corinthians 6:12–20

Ephesians 5:3–7

1 Thessalonians 4:3–8

For more on **Flirting**, check the index.

The Kings of Judah

¹⁰ Solomon's son was Rehoboam,
>   Abijah his son,
>   Asa his son,
>   Jehoshaphat his son,
¹¹ Jehoram^a his son,
>   Ahaziah his son,
>   Joash his son,
¹² Amaziah his son,
>   Azariah his son,
>   Jotham his son,
¹³ Ahaz his son,
>   Hezekiah his son,
>   Manasseh his son,
¹⁴ Amon his son,
>   Josiah his son.
¹⁵ The sons of Josiah:
>   Johanan the firstborn,
>   Jehoiakim the second son,
>   Zedekiah the third,
>   Shallum the fourth.
¹⁶ The successors of Jehoiakim:
>   Jehoiachin^b his son,
>   and Zedekiah.

The Royal Line After the Exile

¹⁷ The descendants of Jehoiachin the captive:
>   Shealtiel his son, ¹⁸Malkiram, Pedaiah, Shenazzar, Jekamiah, Hoshama and Nedabiah.
¹⁹ The sons of Pedaiah:
>   Zerubbabel and Shimei.
>   The sons of Zerubbabel:
>   Meshullam and Hananiah.
>   Shelomith was their sister.
²⁰ There were also five others:
>   Hashubah, Ohel, Berekiah, Hasadiah and Jushab-Hesed.
²¹ The descendants of Hananiah:
>   Pelatiah and Jeshaiah, and the sons of Rephaiah, of Arnan, of Obadiah and of Shekaniah.
²² The descendants of Shekaniah:
>   Shemaiah and his sons:
>   Hattush, Igal, Bariah, Neariah and Shaphat—six in all.
²³ The sons of Neariah:
>   Elioenai, Hizkiah and Azrikam—three in all.
²⁴ The sons of Elioenai:
>   Hodaviah, Eliashib, Pelaiah, Akkub, Johanan, Delaiah and Anani—seven in all.

Other Clans of Judah

4 The descendants of Judah:
>   Perez, Hezron, Karmi, Hur and Shobal.
² Reaiah son of Shobal was the father of Jahath, and Jahath the father of Ahumai and Lahad. These were the clans of the Zorathites.

---

^a *11* Hebrew *Joram,* a variant of *Jehoram*   ^b *16* Hebrew *Jeconiah,* a variant of *Jehoiachin;* also in verse 17

³ These were the sons*ᵃ* of Etam:

Jezreel, Ishma and Idbash. Their sister was named Hazzelelponi. ⁴Penuel was the father of Gedor, and Ezer the father of Hushah.

These were the descendants of Hur, the firstborn of Ephrathah and father*ᵇ* of Bethlehem.

⁵ Ashhur the father of Tekoa had two wives, Helah and Naarah.

⁶ Naarah bore him Ahuzzam, Hepher, Temeni and Haahashtari. These were the descendants of Naarah.

⁷ The sons of Helah:

Zereth, Zohar, Ethnan, ⁸and Koz, who was the father of Anub and Hazzobebah and of the clans of Aharhel son of Harum.

⁹ Jabez was more honorable than his brothers. His mother had named him Jabez,*ᶜ* saying, "I gave birth to him in pain." ¹⁰Jabez cried out to the God of Israel, "Oh, that you would bless me and enlarge my territory! Let your hand be with me, and keep me from harm so that I will be free from pain." And God granted his request.

¹¹ Kelub, Shuhah's brother, was the father of Mehir, who was the father of Eshton. ¹²Eshton was the father of Beth Rapha, Paseah and Tehinnah the father of Ir Nahash.*ᵈ* These were the men of Rekah.

¹³ The sons of Kenaz:

Othniel and Seraiah.

The sons of Othniel:

Hathath and Meonothai.*ᵉ* ¹⁴Meonothai was the father of Ophrah.

Seraiah was the father of Joab,

the father of GeHarashim.*ᶠ* It was called this because its people were skilled workers.

¹⁵ The sons of Caleb son of Jephunneh:

Iru, Elah and Naam.

The son of Elah:

Kenaz.

¹⁶ The sons of Jehallelel:

Ziph, Ziphah, Tiria and Asarel.

¹⁷ The sons of Ezrah:

Jether, Mered, Epher and Jalon. One of Mered's wives gave birth to Miriam, Shammai and Ishbah the father of Eshtemoa. ¹⁸(His wife from the tribe of Judah gave birth to Jered the father of Gedor, Heber the father of Soko, and Jekuthiel the father of Zanoah.) These were the children of Pharaoh's daughter Bithiah, whom Mered had married.

¹⁹ The sons of Hodiah's wife, the sister of Naham:

the father of Keilah the Garmite, and Eshtemoa the Maakathite.

²⁰ The sons of Shimon:

Amnon, Rinnah, Ben-Hanan and Tilon.

The descendants of Ishi:

Zoheth and Ben-Zoheth.

²¹ The sons of Shelah son of Judah:

Er the father of Lekah, Laadah the father of Mareshah and the clans of the linen workers at Beth Ashbea, ²²Jokim, the men of Kozeba, and Joash and Saraph, who ruled in Moab and Jashubi Lehem. (These records are from ancient times.) ²³They were the potters who lived at Netaim and Gederah; they stayed there and worked for the king.

507

conversations

prayer «» 4:9–10

1 » Is it always prideful to pray for personal blessing?

2 » Why are so many people today drawn to this prayer of Jabez?

3 » Does godliness lead to a less painful life?

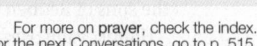

For more on **prayer**, check the index.
For the next Conversations, go to p. 515.

ᵃ 3 Some Septuagint manuscripts (see also Vulgate); Hebrew *father*   *ᵇ 4 Father* may mean *civic leader* or *military leader*; also in verses 12, 14, 17, 18 and possibly elsewhere.   *ᶜ 9 Jabez* sounds like the Hebrew for *pain*.   *ᵈ 12* Or *of the city of Nahash*   *ᵉ 13* Some Septuagint manuscripts and Vulgate; Hebrew does not have *and Meonothai*.   *ᶠ 14 GeHarashim* means *valley of skilled workers*.

Simeon

²⁴ The descendants of Simeon:

Nemuel, Jamin, Jarib, Zerah and Shaul;

²⁵ Shallum was Shaul's son, Mibsam his son and Mishma his son.

²⁶ The descendants of Mishma:

Hammuel his son, Zakkur his son and Shimei his son.

²⁷ Shimei had sixteen sons and six daughters, but his brothers did not have many children; so their entire clan did not become as numerous as the people of Judah. ²⁸ They lived in Beersheba, Moladah, Hazar Shual, ²⁹ Bilhah, Ezem, Tolad, ³⁰ Bethuel, Hormah, Ziklag, ³¹ Beth Markaboth, Hazar Susim, Beth Biri and Shaaraim. These were their towns until the reign of David. ³² Their surrounding villages were Etam, Ain, Rimmon, Token and Ashan—five towns— ³³ and all the villages around these towns as far as Baalath.ᵃ These were their settlements. And they kept a genealogical record.

³⁴ Meshobab, Jamlech, Joshah son of Amaziah, ³⁵ Joel, Jehu son of Joshibiah, the son of Seraiah, the son of Asiel, ³⁶ also Elioenai, Jaakobah, Jeshohaiah, Asaiah, Adiel, Jesimiel, Benaiah, ³⁷ and Ziza son of Shiphi, the son of Allon, the son of Jedaiah, the son of Shimri, the son of Shemaiah.

³⁸ The men listed above by name were leaders of their clans. Their families increased greatly, ³⁹ and they went to the outskirts of Gedor to the east of the valley in search of pasture for their flocks. ⁴⁰ They found rich, good pasture, and the land was spacious, peaceful and quiet. Some Hamites had lived there formerly.

⁴¹ The men whose names were listed came in the days of Hezekiah king of Judah. They attacked the Hamites in their dwellings and also the Meunites who were there and completely destroyedᵇ them, as is evident to this day. Then they settled in their place, because there was pasture for their flocks. ⁴² And five hundred of these Simeonites, led by Pelatiah, Neariah, Rephaiah and Uzziel, the sons of Ishi, invaded the hill country of Seir. ⁴³ They killed the remaining Amalekites who had escaped, and they have lived there to this day.

Reuben

5 The sons of Reuben the firstborn of Israel (he was the firstborn, but when he defiled his father's marriage bed, his rights as firstborn were given to the sons of Joseph son of Israel; so he could not be listed in the genealogical record in accordance with his birthright, ²and though Judah was the strongest of his brothers and a ruler came from him, the rights of the firstborn belonged to Joseph)— ³the sons of Reuben the firstborn of Israel:

Hanok, Pallu, Hezron and Karmi.

⁴ The descendants of Joel:

Shemaiah his son, Gog his son,

Shimei his son, ⁵ Micah his son,

Reaiah his son, Baal his son,

⁶ and Beerah his son, whom Tiglath-Pileserᶜ king of Assyria took into exile. Beerah was a leader of the Reubenites.

⁷ Their relatives by clans, listed according to their genealogical records:

Jeiel the chief, Zechariah, ⁸ and Bela son of Azaz, the son of Shema, the son of Joel. They settled in the area from Aroer to Nebo and Baal Meon. ⁹ To the east they occupied the land up to the edge of the desert that extends to the Euphrates River, because their livestock had increased in Gilead.

¹⁰ During Saul's reign they waged war against the Hagrites, who were defeated at their hands; they occupied the dwellings of the Hagrites throughout the entire region east of Gilead.

Gad

¹¹ The Gadites lived next to them in Bashan, as far as Salekah:

ᵃ 33 Some Septuagint manuscripts (see also Joshua 19:8); Hebrew *Baal*   ᵇ 41 The Hebrew term refers to the irrevocable giving over of things or persons to the Lᴏʀᴅ, often by totally destroying them.   ᶜ 6 Hebrew *Tilgath-Pilneser*, a variant of *Tiglath-Pileser*; also in verse 26

¹²Joel was the chief, Shapham the second, then Janai and Shaphat, in Bashan.
¹³Their relatives, by families, were:

Michael, Meshullam, Sheba, Jorai, Jakan, Zia and Eber—seven in all.

¹⁴These were the sons of Abihail son of Huri, the son of Jaroah, the son of Gilead, the son of Michael, the son of Jeshishai, the son of Jahdo, the son of Buz.

¹⁵Ahi son of Abdiel, the son of Guni, was head of their family.

¹⁶The Gadites lived in Gilead, in Bashan and its outlying villages, and on all the pasturelands of Sharon as far as they extended.

¹⁷All these were entered in the genealogical records during the reigns of Jotham king of Judah and Jeroboam king of Israel.

¹⁸The Reubenites, the Gadites and the half-tribe of Manasseh had 44,760 men ready for military service—able-bodied men who could handle shield and sword, who could use a bow, and who were trained for battle. ¹⁹They waged war against the Hagrites, Jetur, Naphish and Nodab. ²⁰They were helped in fighting them, and God delivered the Hagrites and all their allies into their hands, because they cried out to him during the battle. He answered their prayers, because they trusted in him. ²¹They seized the livestock of the Hagrites—fifty thousand camels, two hundred fifty thousand sheep and two thousand donkeys. They also took one hundred thousand people captive, ²²and many others fell slain, because the battle was God's. And they occupied the land until the exile.

The Half-Tribe of Manasseh

²³The people of the half-tribe of Manasseh were numerous; they settled in the land from Bashan to Baal Hermon, that is, to Senir (Mount Hermon).

²⁴These were the heads of their families: Epher, Ishi, Eliel, Azriel, Jeremiah, Hodaviah and Jahdiel. They were brave warriors, famous men, and heads of their families. ²⁵But they were unfaithful to the God of their ancestors and prostituted themselves to the gods of the peoples of the land, whom God had destroyed before them. ²⁶So the God of Israel stirred up the spirit of Pul king of Assyria (that is, Tiglath-Pileser king of Assyria), who took the Reubenites, the Gadites and the half-tribe of Manasseh into exile. He took them to Halah, Habor, Hara and the river of Gozan, where they are to this day.

Levi

6 *The sons of Levi:
Gershon, Kohath and Merari.
²The sons of Kohath:
Amram, Izhar, Hebron and Uzziel.
³The children of Amram:
Aaron, Moses and Miriam.
The sons of Aaron:
Nadab, Abihu, Eleazar and Ithamar.
⁴Eleazar was the father of Phinehas,
Phinehas the father of Abishua,

---

atissue:celebrities

5:24–25 Imagine you're chosen to be on a reality television show, and on the show you get to trade lives with another person for a month. Whose life would you want? Be honest! Would it be someone famous? Someone wealthy? Someone with a hunky husband? Let's get to the heart of it: What do you envy about someone else? What does your choice reveal about what's most important to you? The men from Manasseh were Israel's celebrities—famous, brave and powerful. But they weren't faithful to God. When it comes down to it, which do you admire more in a person—fame or faithfulness?

509

⁵ Abishua the father of Bukki,
  Bukki the father of Uzzi,
⁶ Uzzi the father of Zerahiah,
  Zerahiah the father of Meraioth,
⁷ Meraioth the father of Amariah,
  Amariah the father of Ahitub,
⁸ Ahitub the father of Zadok,
  Zadok the father of Ahimaaz,
⁹ Ahimaaz the father of Azariah,
  Azariah the father of Johanan,
¹⁰ Johanan the father of Azariah (it was he who served as priest in the temple Solomon built in Jerusalem),
¹¹ Azariah the father of Amariah,
  Amariah the father of Ahitub,
¹² Ahitub the father of Zadok,
  Zadok the father of Shallum,
¹³ Shallum the father of Hilkiah,
  Hilkiah the father of Azariah,
¹⁴ Azariah the father of Seraiah,
  and Seraiah the father of Jozadak.ᵃ

¹⁵ Jozadak was deported when the Lord sent Judah and Jerusalem into exile by the hand of Nebuchadnezzar.

*¹⁶ The sons of Levi:
  Gershon,ᵇ Kohath and Merari.
¹⁷ These are the names of the sons of Gershon:
  Libni and Shimei.
¹⁸ The sons of Kohath:
  Amram, Izhar, Hebron and Uzziel.
¹⁹ The sons of Merari:
  Mahli and Mushi.
These are the clans of the Levites listed according to their fathers:
²⁰ Of Gershon:
  Libni his son, Jahath his son,
  Zimmah his son, ²¹Joah his son,
  Iddo his son, Zerah his son
  and Jeatherai his son.
²² The descendants of Kohath:
  Amminadab his son, Korah his son,
  Assir his son, ²³Elkanah his son,
  Ebiasaph his son, Assir his son,
²⁴ Tahath his son, Uriel his son,
  Uzziah his son and Shaul his son.
²⁵ The descendants of Elkanah:
  Amasai, Ahimoth,
²⁶ Elkanah his son,ᶜ Zophai his son,
  Nahath his son, ²⁷Eliab his son,
  Jeroham his son, Elkanah his son
  and Samuel his son.ᵈ

ᵃ 14 Hebrew *Jehozadak*, a variant of *Jozadak*; also in verse 15   ᵇ 16 Hebrew *Gershom*, a variant of *Gershon*; also in verses 17, 20, 43, 62 and 71   ᶜ 26 Some Hebrew manuscripts, Septuagint and Syriac; most Hebrew manuscripts *Ahimoth* ²⁶*and Elkanah. The sons of Elkanah:*   ᵈ 27 Some Septuagint manuscripts (see also 1 Samuel 1:19,20 and 1 Chron. 6:33,34); Hebrew does not have *and Samuel his son.*
*6:16-81 is numbered 6:1-66 in Hebrew texts

510

²⁸ The sons of Samuel:

    Joel*a* the firstborn

    and Abijah the second son.

²⁹ The descendants of Merari:

    Mahli, Libni his son,

    Shimei his son, Uzzah his son,

    ³⁰ Shimea his son, Haggiah his son

    and Asaiah his son.

The Temple Musicians

³¹ These are the men David put in charge of the music in the house of the LORD after the ark came to rest there. ³² They ministered with music before the tabernacle, the tent of meeting, until Solomon built the temple of the LORD in Jerusalem. They performed their duties according to the regulations laid down for them.

³³ Here are the men who served, together with their sons:

From the Kohathites:

    Heman, the musician,

    the son of Joel, the son of Samuel,

    ³⁴ the son of Elkanah, the son of Jeroham,

    the son of Eliel, the son of Toah,

    ³⁵ the son of Zuph, the son of Elkanah,

    the son of Mahath, the son of Amasai,

    ³⁶ the son of Elkanah, the son of Joel,

    the son of Azariah, the son of Zephaniah,

    ³⁷ the son of Tahath, the son of Assir,

    the son of Ebiasaph, the son of Korah,

    ³⁸ the son of Izhar, the son of Kohath,

    the son of Levi, the son of Israel;

³⁹ and Heman's associate Asaph, who served at his right hand:

    Asaph son of Berekiah, the son of Shimea,

    ⁴⁰ the son of Michael, the son of Baaseiah,*b*

    the son of Malkijah, ⁴¹ the son of Ethni,

    the son of Zerah, the son of Adaiah,

    ⁴² the son of Ethan, the son of Zimmah,

    the son of Shimei, ⁴³ the son of Jahath,

    the son of Gershon, the son of Levi;

⁴⁴ and from their associates, the Merarites, at his left hand:

    Ethan son of Kishi, the son of Abdi,

    the son of Malluk, ⁴⁵ the son of Hashabiah,

    the son of Amaziah, the son of Hilkiah,

    ⁴⁶ the son of Amzi, the son of Bani,

    the son of Shemer, ⁴⁷ the son of Mahli,

    the son of Mushi, the son of Merari,

    the son of Levi.

⁴⁸ Their fellow Levites were assigned to all the other duties of the tabernacle, the house of God. ⁴⁹ But Aaron and his descendants were the ones who presented offerings on the altar of burnt offering and on the altar of incense in connection with all that was done in the Most Holy Place, making atonement for Israel, in accordance with all that Moses the servant of God had commanded.

511

---

a 28 Some Septuagint manuscripts and Syriac (see also 1 Samuel 8:2 and 1 Chron. 6:33); Hebrew does not have *Joel.* *b 40* Most Hebrew manuscripts; some Hebrew manuscripts, one Septuagint manuscript and Syriac *Maaseiah*

⁵⁰ These were the descendants of Aaron:
> Eleazar his son, Phinehas his son,
> Abishua his son, ⁵¹ Bukki his son,
> Uzzi his son, Zerahiah his son,
> ⁵² Meraioth his son, Amariah his son,
> Ahitub his son, ⁵³ Zadok his son
> and Ahimaaz his son.

⁵⁴ These were the locations of their settlements allotted as their territory (they were assigned to the descendants of Aaron who were from the Kohathite clan, because the first lot was for them): ⁵⁵ They were given Hebron in Judah with its surrounding pasturelands. ⁵⁶ But the fields and villages around the city were given to Caleb son of Jephunneh.

⁵⁷ So the descendants of Aaron were given Hebron (a city of refuge), and Libnah,ᵃ Jattir, Eshtemoa, ⁵⁸ Hilen, Debir, ⁵⁹ Ashan, Juttahᵇ and Beth Shemesh, together with their pasturelands. ⁶⁰ And from the tribe of Benjamin they were given Gibeon,ᶜ Geba, Alemeth and Anathoth, together with their pasturelands.

The total number of towns distributed among the Kohathite clans came to thirteen.

⁶¹ The rest of Kohath's descendants were allotted ten towns from the clans of half the tribe of Manasseh.

⁶² The descendants of Gershon, clan by clan, were allotted thirteen towns from the tribes of Issachar, Asher and Naphtali, and from the part of the tribe of Manasseh that is in Bashan.

⁶³ The descendants of Merari, clan by clan, were allotted twelve towns from the tribes of Reuben, Gad and Zebulun.

⁶⁴ So the Israelites gave the Levites these towns and their pasturelands. ⁶⁵ From the tribes of Judah, Simeon and Benjamin they allotted the previously named towns.

⁶⁶ Some of the Kohathite clans were given as their territory towns from the tribe of Ephraim.

⁶⁷ In the hill country of Ephraim they were given Shechem (a city of refuge), and Gezer,ᵈ ⁶⁸ Jokmeam, Beth Horon, ⁶⁹ Aijalon and Gath Rimmon, together with their pasturelands.

⁷⁰ And from half the tribe of Manasseh the Israelites gave Aner and Bileam, together with their pasturelands, to the rest of the Kohathite clans.

⁷¹ The Gershonites received the following:
> From the clan of the half-tribe of Manasseh
> > they received Golan in Bashan and also Ashtaroth, together with their pasturelands;
⁷² from the tribe of Issachar
> > they received Kedesh, Daberath, ⁷³ Ramoth and Anem, together with their pasturelands;
⁷⁴ from the tribe of Asher
> > they received Mashal, Abdon, ⁷⁵ Hukok and Rehob, together with their pasturelands;
⁷⁶ and from the tribe of Naphtali
> > they received Kedesh in Galilee, Hammon and Kiriathaim, together with their pasturelands.

⁷⁷ The Merarites (the rest of the Levites) received the following:
> From the tribe of Zebulun
> > they received Jokneam, Kartah,ᵉ Rimmono and Tabor, together with their pasturelands;
⁷⁸ from the tribe of Reuben across the Jordan east of Jericho
> > they received Bezer in the wilderness, Jahzah, ⁷⁹ Kedemoth and Mephaath, together with their pasturelands;
⁸⁰ and from the tribe of Gad
> > they received Ramoth in Gilead, Mahanaim, ⁸¹ Heshbon and Jazer, together with their pasturelands.

ᵃ 57 See Joshua 21:13; Hebrew given the cities of refuge: Hebron, Libnah. ᵇ 59 Syriac (see also Septuagint and Joshua 21:16); Hebrew does not have Juttah. ᶜ 60 See Joshua 21:17; Hebrew does not have Gibeon. ᵈ 67 See Joshua 21:21; Hebrew given the cities of refuge: Shechem, Gezer. ᵉ 77 See Septuagint and Joshua 21:34; Hebrew does not have Jokneam, Kartah.

Issachar

7 The sons of Issachar:

Tola, Puah, Jashub and Shimron—four in all.
² The sons of Tola:

Uzzi, Rephaiah, Jeriel, Jahmai, Ibsam and Samuel—heads of their families. During the reign of David, the descendants of Tola listed as fighting men in their genealogy numbered 22,600.
³ The son of Uzzi:

Izrahiah.

The sons of Izrahiah:

Michael, Obadiah, Joel and Ishiah. All five of them were chiefs. ⁴ According to their family genealogy, they had 36,000 men ready for battle, for they had many wives and children.
⁵ The relatives who were fighting men belonging to all the clans of Issachar, as listed in their genealogy, were 87,000 in all.

Benjamin

⁶ Three sons of Benjamin:

Bela, Beker and Jediael.
⁷ The sons of Bela:

Ezbon, Uzzi, Uzziel, Jerimoth and Iri, heads of families—five in all. Their genealogical record listed 22,034 fighting men.
⁸ The sons of Beker:

Zemirah, Joash, Eliezer, Elioenai, Omri, Jeremoth, Abijah, Anathoth and Alemeth. All these were the sons of Beker. ⁹ Their genealogical record listed the heads of families and 20,200 fighting men.
¹⁰ The son of Jediael:

Bilhan.

The sons of Bilhan:

Jeush, Benjamin, Ehud, Kenaanah, Zethan, Tarshish and Ahishahar. ¹¹ All these sons of Jediael were heads of families. There were 17,200 fighting men ready to go out to war.
¹² The Shuppites and Huppites were the descendants of Ir, and the Hushites[a] the descendants of Aher.

Naphtali

¹³ The sons of Naphtali:

Jahziel, Guni, Jezer and Shillem[b]—the descendants of Bilhah.

Manasseh

¹⁴ The descendants of Manasseh:

Asriel was his descendant through his Aramean concubine. She gave birth to Makir the father of Gilead. ¹⁵ Makir took a wife from among the Huppites and Shuppites. His sister's name was Maakah.

Another descendant was named Zelophehad, who had only daughters.

¹⁶ Makir's wife Maakah gave birth to a son and named him Peresh. His brother was named Sheresh, and his sons were Ulam and Rakem.
¹⁷ The son of Ulam:

Bedan.

These were the sons of Gilead son of Makir, the son of Manasseh. ¹⁸ His sister Hammoleketh gave birth to Ishhod, Abiezer and Mahlah.
¹⁹ The sons of Shemida were:

Ahian, Shechem, Likhi and Aniam.

ᵃ 12 Or Ir. The sons of Dan: Hushim, (see Gen. 46:23); Hebrew does not have The sons of Dan.   ᵇ 13 Some Hebrew and Septuagint manuscripts (see also Gen. 46:24 and Num. 26:49); most Hebrew manuscripts Shallum

Ephraim

²⁰ The descendants of Ephraim:

> Shuthelah, Bered his son,
> Tahath his son, Eleadah his son,
> Tahath his son, ²¹ Zabad his son
> and Shuthelah his son.

> Ezer and Elead were killed by the native-born men of Gath, when they went down to seize their livestock. ²² Their father Ephraim mourned for them many days, and his relatives came to comfort him. ²³ Then he made love to his wife again, and she became pregnant and gave birth to a son. He named him Beriah,^a because there had been misfortune in his family. ²⁴ His daughter was Sheerah, who built Lower and Upper Beth Horon as well as Uzzen Sheerah.

²⁵ Rephah was his son, Resheph his son,^b

> Telah his son, Tahan his son,
> ²⁶ Ladan his son, Ammihud his son,
> Elishama his son, ²⁷ Nun his son
> and Joshua his son.

²⁸ Their lands and settlements included Bethel and its surrounding villages, Naaran to the east, Gezer and its villages to the west, and Shechem and its villages all the way to Ayyah and its villages. ²⁹ Along the borders of Manasseh were Beth Shan, Taanach, Megiddo and Dor, together with their villages. The descendants of Joseph son of Israel lived in these towns.

Asher

³⁰ The sons of Asher:

> Imnah, Ishvah, Ishvi and Beriah. Their sister was Serah.

³¹ The sons of Beriah:

> Heber and Malkiel, who was the father of Birzaith.

³² Heber was the father of Japhlet, Shomer and Hotham and of their sister Shua.

³³ The sons of Japhlet:

> Pasak, Bimhal and Ashvath.
> These were Japhlet's sons.

³⁴ The sons of Shomer:

> Ahi, Rohgah,^c Hubbah and Aram.

³⁵ The sons of his brother Helem:

> Zophah, Imna, Shelesh and Amal.

³⁶ The sons of Zophah:

> Suah, Harnepher, Shual, Beri, Imrah, ³⁷ Bezer, Hod, Shamma, Shilshah, Ithran^d and Beera.

³⁸ The sons of Jether:

> Jephunneh, Pispah and Ara.

³⁹ The sons of Ulla:

> Arah, Hanniel and Rizia.

⁴⁰ All these were descendants of Asher—heads of families, choice men, brave warriors and outstanding leaders. The number of men ready for battle, as listed in their genealogy, was 26,000.

The Genealogy of Saul the Benjamite

8 Benjamin was the father of Bela his firstborn,
   Ashbel the second son, Aharah the third,
> ² Nohah the fourth and Rapha the fifth.

³ The sons of Bela were:

> Addar, Gera, Abihud,^e ⁴ Abishua, Naaman, Ahoah, ⁵ Gera, Shephuphan and Huram.

⁶ These were the descendants of Ehud, who were heads of families of those living in Geba and were deported to Manahath:

---

^a 23 Beriah sounds like the Hebrew for misfortune.   ^b 25 Some Septuagint manuscripts; Hebrew does not have his son.   ^c 34 Or of his brother Shomer: Rohgah
^d 37 Possibly a variant of Jether   ^e 3 Or Gera the father of Ehud

[7] Naaman, Ahijah, and Gera, who deported them and who was the father of Uzza and Ahihud.

[8] Sons were born to Shaharaim in Moab after he had divorced his wives Hushim and Baara. [9]By his wife Hodesh he had Jobab, Zibia, Mesha, Malkam, [10]Jeuz, Sakia and Mirmah. These were his sons, heads of families. [11]By Hushim he had Abitub and Elpaal.

[12] The sons of Elpaal:

Eber, Misham, Shemed (who built Ono and Lod with its surrounding villages), [13]and Beriah and Shema, who were heads of families of those living in Aijalon and who drove out the inhabitants of Gath.

[14] Ahio, Shashak, Jeremoth, [15]Zebadiah, Arad, Eder, [16]Michael, Ishpah and Joha were the sons of Beriah.

[17] Zebadiah, Meshullam, Hizki, Heber, [18]Ishmerai, Izliah and Jobab were the sons of Elpaal.

[19] Jakim, Zikri, Zabdi, [20]Elienai, Zillethai, Eliel, [21]Adaiah, Beraiah and Shimrath were the sons of Shimei.

[22] Ishpan, Eber, Eliel, [23]Abdon, Zikri, Hanan, [24]Hananiah, Elam, Anthothijah, [25]Iphdeiah and Penuel were the sons of Shashak.

[26] Shamsherai, Shehariah, Athaliah, [27]Jaareshiah, Elijah and Zikri were the sons of Jeroham.

[28] All these were heads of families, chiefs as listed in their genealogy, and they lived in Jerusalem.

[29] Jeiel[a] the father[b] of Gibeon lived in Gibeon.

His wife's name was Maakah, [30]and his firstborn son was Abdon, followed by Zur, Kish, Baal, Ner,[c] Nadab, [31]Gedor, Ahio, Zeker [32]and Mikloth, who was the father of Shimeah. They too lived near their relatives in Jerusalem.

[33] Ner was the father of Kish, Kish the father of Saul, and Saul the father of Jonathan, Malki-Shua, Abinadab and Esh-Baal.[d]

[34] The son of Jonathan:

Merib-Baal,[e] who was the father of Micah.

[35] The sons of Micah:

Pithon, Melek, Tarea and Ahaz.

[36] Ahaz was the father of Jehoaddah, Jehoaddah was the father of Alemeth, Azmaveth and Zimri, and Zimri was the father of Moza. [37]Moza was the father of Binea; Raphah was his son, Eleasah his son and Azel his son.

[38] Azel had six sons, and these were their names:

Azrikam, Bokeru, Ishmael, Sheariah, Obadiah and Hanan. All these were the sons of Azel.

[39] The sons of his brother Eshek:

Ulam his firstborn, Jeush the second son and Eliphelet the third. [40]The sons of Ulam were brave warriors who could handle the bow. They had many sons and grandsons—150 in all.

All these were the descendants of Benjamin.

9 All Israel was listed in the genealogies recorded in the book of the kings of Israel and Judah. They were taken captive to Babylon because of their unfaithfulness.

The People in Jerusalem

[2] Now the first to resettle on their own property in their own towns were some Israelites, priests, Levites and temple servants.

[3] Those from Judah, from Benjamin, and from Ephraim and Manasseh who lived in Jerusalem were:

[4] Uthai son of Ammihud, the son of Omri, the son of Imri, the son of Bani, a descendant of Perez son of Judah.

" conversations "

consequences «» 9:1

1 » What is considered "unfaithfulness" today?

2 » Are group consequences fair for all individuals—even those not sinning?

3 » What consequences are you reaping for bad choices you made in the past?

For more on consequences, check the index.
For the next Conversations, go to p. 517.

515

---

[a] 29 Some Septuagint manuscripts (see also 1 Chron. 9:35); Hebrew does not have *Jeiel*. [b] 29 *Father* may mean *civic leader* or *military leader*. [c] 30 Some Septuagint manuscripts (see also 1 Chron. 9:36); Hebrew does not have *Ner*. [d] 33 Also known as *Ish-Bosheth* [e] 34 Also known as *Mephibosheth*

⁵ Of the Shelanites[a]:

Asaiah the firstborn and his sons.

⁶ Of the Zerahites:

Jeuel.

The people from Judah numbered 690.

⁷ Of the Benjamites:

Sallu son of Meshullam, the son of Hodaviah, the son of Hassenuah;

⁸ Ibneiah son of Jeroham; Elah son of Uzzi, the son of Mikri; and Meshullam son of Shephatiah, the son of Reuel, the son of Ibnijah.

⁹The people from Benjamin, as listed in their genealogy, numbered 956. All these men were heads of their families.

¹⁰ Of the priests:

Jedaiah; Jehoiarib; Jakin;

¹¹ Azariah son of Hilkiah, the son of Meshullam, the son of Zadok, the son of Meraioth, the son of Ahitub, the official in charge of the house of God;

¹² Adaiah son of Jeroham, the son of Pashhur, the son of Malkijah; and Maasai son of Adiel, the son of Jahzerah, the son of Meshullam, the son of Meshillemith, the son of Immer.

¹³ The priests, who were heads of families, numbered 1,760. They were able men, responsible for ministering in the house of God.

¹⁴ Of the Levites:

Shemaiah son of Hasshub, the son of Azrikam, the son of Hashabiah, a Merarite; ¹⁵Bakbakkar, Heresh, Galal and Mattaniah son of Mika, the son of Zikri, the son of Asaph; ¹⁶Obadiah son of Shemaiah, the son of Galal, the son of Jeduthun; and Berekiah son of Asa, the son of Elkanah, who lived in the villages of the Netophathites.

¹⁷ The gatekeepers:

Shallum, Akkub, Talmon, Ahiman and their fellow Levites, Shallum their chief ¹⁸being stationed at the King's Gate on the east, up to the present time. These were the gatekeepers belonging to the camp of the Levites. ¹⁹Shallum son of Kore, the son of Ebiasaph, the son of Korah, and his fellow gatekeepers from his family (the Korahites) were responsible for guarding the thresholds of the tent just as their ancestors had been responsible for guarding the entrance to the dwelling of the LORD. ²⁰In earlier times Phinehas son of Eleazar was the official in charge of the gatekeepers, and the LORD was with him. ²¹Zechariah son of Meshelemiah was the gatekeeper at the entrance to the tent of meeting.

²²Altogether, those chosen to be gatekeepers at the thresholds numbered 212. They were registered by genealogy in their villages. The gatekeepers had been assigned to their positions of trust by David and Samuel the seer. ²³They and their descendants were in charge of guarding the gates of the house of the LORD—the house called the tent of meeting. ²⁴The gatekeepers were on the four sides: east, west, north and south. ²⁵Their fellow Levites in their villages had to come from time to time and share their duties for seven-day periods. ²⁶But the four principal gatekeepers, who were Levites, were entrusted with the responsibility for the rooms and treasuries in the house of God. ²⁷They would spend the night stationed around the house of God, because they had to guard it; and they had charge of the key for opening it each morning.

²⁸Some of them were in charge of the articles used in the temple service; they counted them when they were brought in and when they were taken out. ²⁹Others were assigned to take care of the furnishings and all the other articles of the sanctuary, as well as the special flour and wine, and the oil, incense and spices. ³⁰But some of the priests took care of mixing the spices. ³¹A Levite named Mattithiah, the firstborn son of Shallum the Korahite, was entrusted with the responsibility for baking the offering bread. ³²Some of the Kohathites, their fellow Levites, were in charge of preparing for every Sabbath the bread set out on the table.

---
a 5 See Num. 26:20; Hebrew *Shilonites.*

517

³³Those who were musicians, heads of Levite families, stayed in the rooms of the temple and were exempt from other duties because they were responsible for the work day and night.

³⁴All these were heads of Levite families, chiefs as listed in their genealogy, and they lived in Jerusalem.

The Genealogy of Saul

³⁵Jeiel the father*ᵃ* of Gibeon lived in Gibeon.

His wife's name was Maakah, ³⁶and his firstborn son was Abdon, followed by Zur, Kish, Baal, Ner, Nadab, ³⁷Gedor, Ahio, Zechariah and Mikloth. ³⁸Mikloth was the father of Shimeam. They too lived near their relatives in Jerusalem.

³⁹Ner was the father of Kish, Kish the father of Saul, and Saul the father of Jonathan, Malki-Shua, Abinadab and Esh-Baal.*ᵇ*

⁴⁰The son of Jonathan:

Merib-Baal,*ᶜ* who was the father of Micah.

⁴¹The sons of Micah:

Pithon, Melek, Tahrea and Ahaz.*ᵈ*

⁴²Ahaz was the father of Jadah, Jadah*ᵉ* was the father of Alemeth, Azmaveth and Zimri, and Zimri was the father of Moza. ⁴³Moza was the father of Binea; Rephaiah was his son, Eleasah his son and Azel his son.

⁴⁴Azel had six sons, and these were their names:

Azrikam, Bokeru, Ishmael, Sheariah, Obadiah and Hanan. These were the sons of Azel.

Saul Takes His Life

10 Now the Philistines fought against Israel; the Israelites fled before them, and many fell dead on Mount Gilboa. ²The Philistines were in hot pursuit of Saul and his sons, and they killed his sons Jonathan, Abinadab and Malki-Shua. ³The fighting grew fierce around Saul, and when the archers overtook him, they wounded him.

⁴Saul said to his armor-bearer, "Draw your sword and run me through, or these uncircumcised fellows will come and abuse me."

But his armor-bearer was terrified and would not do it; so Saul took his own sword and fell on it. ⁵When the armor-bearer saw that Saul was dead, he too fell on his sword and died. ⁶So Saul and his three sons died, and all his house died together.

⁷When all the Israelites in the valley saw that the army had fled and that Saul and his sons had died, they abandoned their towns and fled. And the Philistines came and occupied them.

⁸The next day, when the Philistines came to strip the dead, they found Saul and his sons fallen on Mount Gilboa. ⁹They stripped him and took his head and his armor, and sent messengers throughout the land of the Philistines to proclaim the news among their idols and their people. ¹⁰They put his armor in the temple of their gods and hung up his head in the temple of Dagon.

¹¹When all the inhabitants of Jabesh Gilead heard what the Philistines had done to Saul, ¹²all their valiant men went and took the bodies of Saul and his sons and brought them to Jabesh. Then they buried their bones under the great tree in Jabesh, and they fasted seven days.

¹³Saul died because he was unfaithful to the Lord; he did not keep the word of the Lord and even

conversations

suicide «» 10:1–6

1» How does God view suicide?

2» In what ways does suicide injure those left behind?

3» Why do some people resort to suicide?

For more on **suicide**, check the index.
For the next Conversations, go to p. 518.

ᵃ **35** *Father* may mean *civic leader* or *military leader.*   *ᵇ* **39** Also known as *Ish-Bosheth*   *ᶜ* **40** Also known as *Mephibosheth*   *ᵈ* **41** Vulgate and Syriac (see also Septuagint and 1 Chron. 8:35); Hebrew does not have *and Ahaz.*   *ᵉ* **42** Some Hebrew manuscripts and Septuagint (see also 1 Chron. 8:36); most Hebrew manuscripts *Jarah, Jarah* consulted a medium for guidance, [14]and did not inquire of the LORD. So the LORD put him to death and turned the kingdom over to David son of Jesse.

David Becomes King Over Israel

11 All Israel came together to David at Hebron and said, "We are your own flesh and blood. [2]In the past, even while Saul was king, you were the one who led Israel on their military campaigns. And the LORD your God said to you, 'You will shepherd my people Israel, and you will become their ruler.'"

[3]When all the elders of Israel had come to King David at Hebron, he made a covenant with them at Hebron before the LORD, and they anointed David king over Israel, as the LORD had promised through Samuel.

HE IS: the anointing one

11:3 Almost 20 years had passed since the prophet Samuel had first anointed David to be king of Israel. God had chosen David then, and the elders affirmed God's choice by anointing David again. God is the one who chooses and anoints people, setting them apart for special work in his kingdom. If you're a believer, then God has also anointed you, and he has a special purpose in mind for you. He is *the anointing one* who sets you apart with his Holy Spirit, pouring out his power to help you (see Acts 2:1–13).

For the next He Is, go to p. 525.

518

David Conquers Jerusalem

[4]David and all the Israelites marched to Jerusalem (that is, Jebus). The Jebusites who lived there [5]said to David, "You will not get in here." Nevertheless, David captured the fortress of Zion—which is the City of David.

[6]David had said, "Whoever leads the attack on the Jebusites will become commander-in-chief." Joab son of Zeruiah went up first, and so he received the command.

[7]David then took up residence in the fortress, and so it was called the City of David. [8]He built up the city around it, from the terraces[a] to the surrounding wall, while Joab restored the rest of the city. [9]And David became more and more powerful, because the LORD Almighty was with him.

David's Mighty Warriors

[10]These were the chiefs of David's mighty warriors— they, together with all Israel, gave his kingship strong support to extend it over the whole land, as the LORD had promised— [11]this is the list of David's mighty warriors:

Jashobeam,[b] a Hakmonite, was chief of the officers[c]; he raised his spear against three hundred men, whom he killed in one encounter.

[12]Next to him was Eleazar son of Dodai the Ahohite, one of the three mighty warriors. [13]He was with David at Pas Dammim when the Philistines gathered there for battle. At a place where there was a field full of barley, the troops fled from the Philistines. [14]But they took their stand in the middle of the field. They defended it and struck the Philistines down, and the LORD brought about a great victory.

[15]Three of the thirty chiefs came down to David to the rock at the cave of Adullam, while a band of Philistines was encamped in the Valley of Rephaim. [16]At that time David was in the stronghold, and the Philistine garrison was at Bethlehem. [17]David longed for

conversations

loyalty «» 11:10–19

1 Toward whom do you feel a strong sense of loyalty?

2 How much would you risk to prove your loyalty?

3 Should loyalty have limits?

For more on **loyalty**, check the index. For the next Conversations, go to p. 544.

---

[a] 8 Or *the Millo*   [b] 11 Possibly a variant of *Jashob-Baal*   [c] 11 Or *Thirty*; some Septuagint manuscripts *Three* (see also 2 Samuel 23:8)

water and said, "Oh, that someone would get me a drink of water from the well near the gate of Bethlehem!" ¹⁸So the Three broke through the Philistine lines, drew water from the well near the gate of Bethlehem and carried it back to David. But he refused to drink it; instead, he poured it out to the Lord. ¹⁹"God forbid that I should do this!" he said. "Should I drink the blood of these men who went at the risk of their lives?" Because they risked their lives to bring it back, David would not drink it.

Such were the exploits of the three mighty warriors.

²⁰Abishai the brother of Joab was chief of the Three. He raised his spear against three hundred men, whom he killed, and so he became as famous as the Three. ²¹He was doubly honored above the Three and became their commander, even though he was not included among them.

²²Benaiah son of Jehoiada, a valiant fighter from Kabzeel, performed great exploits. He struck down Moab's two mightiest warriors. He also went down into a pit on a snowy day and killed a lion. ²³And he struck down an Egyptian who was five cubits^a tall. Although the Egyptian had a spear like a weaver's rod in his hand, Benaiah went against him with a club. He snatched the spear from the Egyptian's hand and killed him with his own spear. ²⁴Such were the exploits of Benaiah son of Jehoiada; he too was as famous as the three mighty warriors. ²⁵He was held in greater honor than any of the Thirty, but he was not included among the Three. And David put him in charge of his bodyguard.

²⁶ The mighty warriors were:

Asahel the brother of Joab,
Elhanan son of Dodo from Bethlehem,
²⁷ Shammoth the Harorite,
Helez the Pelonite,
²⁸ Ira son of Ikkesh from Tekoa,
Abiezer from Anathoth,
²⁹ Sibbekai the Hushathite,
Ilai the Ahohite,
³⁰ Maharai the Netophathite,
Heled son of Baanah the Netophathite,
³¹ Ithai son of Ribai from Gibeah in Benjamin,
Benaiah the Pirathonite,
³² Hurai from the ravines of Gaash,
Abiel the Arbathite,
³³ Azmaveth the Baharumite,
Eliahba the Shaalbonite,
³⁴ the sons of Hashem the Gizonite,
Jonathan son of Shagee the Hararite,
³⁵ Ahiam son of Sakar the Hararite,
Eliphal son of Ur,
³⁶ Hepher the Mekerathite,
Ahijah the Pelonite,
³⁷ Hezro the Carmelite,
Naarai son of Ezbai,
³⁸ Joel the brother of Nathan,
Mibhar son of Hagri,
³⁹ Zelek the Ammonite,
Naharai the Berothite, the armor-bearer of Joab son of Zeruiah,
⁴⁰ Ira the Ithrite,
Gareb the Ithrite,
⁴¹ Uriah the Hittite,
Zabad son of Ahlai,

^a 23 That is, about 7 feet or about 2.3 meters

⁴²Adina son of Shiza the Reubenite, who was chief of the Reubenites, and the thirty with him,
⁴³Hanan son of Maakah,
  Joshaphat the Mithnite,
⁴⁴Uzzia the Ashterathite,
  Shama and Jeiel the sons of Hotham the Aroerite,
⁴⁵Jediael son of Shimri,
  his brother Joha the Tizite,
⁴⁶Eliel the Mahavite,
  Jeribai and Joshaviah the sons of Elnaam,
  Ithmah the Moabite,
⁴⁷Eliel, Obed and Jaasiel the Mezobaite.

Warriors Join David

12 These were the men who came to David at Ziklag, while he was banished from the presence of Saul son of Kish (they were among the warriors who helped him in battle; ²they were armed with bows and were able to shoot arrows or to sling stones right-handed or left-handed; they were relatives of Saul from the tribe of Benjamin):

³Ahiezer their chief and Joash the sons of Shemaah the Gibeathite; Jeziel and Pelet the sons of Azmaveth; Berakah, Jehu the Anathothite, ⁴and Ishmaiah the Gibeonite, a mighty warrior among the Thirty, who was a leader of the Thirty; *Jeremiah, Jahaziel, Johanan, Jozabad the Gederathite, * ⁵Eluzai, Jerimoth, Bealiah, Shemariah and Shephatiah the Haruphite; ⁶Elkanah, Ishiah, Azarel, Joezer and Jashobeam the Korahites; ⁷and Joelah and Zebadiah the sons of Jeroham from Gedor.

⁸Some Gadites defected to David at his stronghold in the wilderness. They were brave warriors, ready for battle and able to handle the shield and spear. Their faces were the faces of lions, and they were as swift as gazelles in the mountains.
⁹Ezer was the chief,
  Obadiah the second in command, Eliab the third,
¹⁰Mishmannah the fourth, Jeremiah the fifth,
¹¹Attai the sixth, Eliel the seventh,
¹²Johanan the eighth, Elzabad the ninth,
¹³Jeremiah the tenth and Makbannai the eleventh.

¹⁴These Gadites were army commanders; the least was a match for a hundred, and the greatest for a thousand. ¹⁵It was they who crossed the Jordan in the first month when it was overflowing all its banks, and they put to flight everyone living in the valleys, to the east and to the west.

¹⁶Other Benjamites and some men from Judah also came to David in his stronghold. ¹⁷David went out to meet them and said to them, "If you have come to me in peace to help me, I am ready for you to join me. But if you have come to betray me to my enemies when my hands are free from violence, may the God of our ancestors see it and judge you."

¹⁸Then the Spirit came on Amasai, chief of the Thirty, and he said:

  "We are yours, David!
    We are with you, son of Jesse!
  Success, success to you,
    and success to those who help you,
    for your God will help you."

So David received them and made them leaders of his raiding bands.

¹⁹Some of the tribe of Manasseh defected to David when he went with the Philistines to fight against Saul. (He and his men did not help the Philistines because, after consultation, their rulers sent him away. They said, "It will cost us our heads if he deserts to his master Saul.") ²⁰When David went to Ziklag, these

---

* The rest of this verse (12:4b) is numbered 12:5 in Hebrew texts.   * 12:5-40 is numbered 12:6-41 in Hebrew texts.

were the men of Manasseh who defected to him: Adnah, Jozabad, Jediael, Michael, Jozabad, Elihu and Zillethai, leaders of units of a thousand in Manasseh. ²¹They helped David against raiding bands, for all of them were brave warriors, and they were commanders in his army. ²²Day after day men came to help David, until he had a great army, like the army of God.ᵃ

Others Join David at Hebron

²³These are the numbers of the men armed for battle who came to David at Hebron to turn Saul's kingdom over to him, as the LORD had said:

²⁴ from Judah, carrying shield and spear—6,800 armed for battle;

²⁵ from Simeon, warriors ready for battle—7,100;

²⁶ from Levi—4,600, ²⁷including Jehoiada, leader of the family of Aaron, with 3,700 men, ²⁸and Zadok, a brave young warrior, with 22 officers from his family;

²⁹ from Benjamin, Saul's tribe—3,000, most of whom had remained loyal to Saul's house until then;

³⁰ from Ephraim, brave warriors, famous in their own clans—20,800;

³¹ from half the tribe of Manasseh, designated by name to come and make David king—18,000;

³² from Issachar, men who understood the times and knew what Israel should do—200 chiefs, with all their relatives under their command;

³³ from Zebulun, experienced soldiers prepared for battle with every type of weapon, to help David with undivided loyalty—50,000;

³⁴ from Naphtali—1,000 officers, together with 37,000 men carrying shields and spears;

³⁵ from Dan, ready for battle—28,600;

³⁶ from Asher, experienced soldiers prepared for battle—40,000;

³⁷ and from east of the Jordan, from Reuben, Gad and the half-tribe of Manasseh, armed with every type of weapon—120,000.

³⁸All these were fighting men who volunteered to serve in the ranks. They came to Hebron fully determined to make David king over all Israel. All the rest of the Israelites were also of one mind to make David king. ³⁹The men spent three days there with David, eating and drinking, for their families had supplied provisions for them. ⁴⁰Also, their neighbors from as far away as Issachar, Zebulun and Naphtali came bringing food on donkeys, camels, mules and oxen. There were plentiful supplies of flour, fig cakes, raisin cakes, wine, oil, cattle and sheep, for there was joy in Israel.

Bringing Back the Ark

13 David conferred with each of his officers, the commanders of thousands and commanders of hundreds. ²He then said to the whole assembly of Israel, "If it seems good to you and if it is the will of the LORD our God, let us send word far and wide to the rest of our people throughout the territories of Israel, and also to the priests and Levites who are with them in their towns and pasturelands, to come and join us. ³Let us bring the ark of our God back to us, for we did not inquire ofᵇ itᶜ during the reign of Saul." ⁴The whole assembly agreed to do this, because it seemed right to all the people.

⁵So David assembled all Israel, from the Shihor River in Egypt to Lebo Hamath, to bring the ark of God from Kiriath Jearim. ⁶David and all Israel went to Baalah of Judah (Kiriath Jearim) to bring up from there the ark of God the LORD, who is enthroned between the cherubim—the ark that is called by the Name.

⁷They moved the ark of God from Abinadab's house on a new cart, with Uzzah and Ahio guiding it. ⁸David and all the Israelites were celebrating with all their might before God, with songs and with harps, lyres, timbrels, cymbals and trumpets.

⁹When they came to the threshing floor of Kidon, Uzzah reached out his hand to steady the ark, because the oxen stumbled. ¹⁰The LORD's anger burned against Uzzah, and he struck him down because he had put his hand on the ark. So he died there before God.

¹¹Then David was angry because the LORD's wrath had broken out against Uzzah, and to this day that place is called Perez Uzzah.ᵈ

¹²David was afraid of God that day and asked, "How can I ever bring the ark of God to me?" ¹³He did

521

ᵃ 22 Or a great and mighty army ᵇ 3 Or we neglected ᶜ 3 Or him ᵈ 11 Perez Uzzah means outbreak against Uzzah.

not take the ark to be with him in the City of David. Instead, he took it to the house of Obed-Edom the Gittite. [14]The ark of God remained with the family of Obed-Edom in his house for three months, and the LORD blessed his household and everything he had.

David's House and Family

14 Now Hiram king of Tyre sent messengers to David, along with cedar logs, stonemasons and carpenters to build a palace for him. [2]And David knew that the LORD had established him as king over Israel and that his kingdom had been highly exalted for the sake of his people Israel.

[3]In Jerusalem David took more wives and became the father of more sons and daughters. [4]These are the names of the children born to him there: Shammua, Shobab, Nathan, Solomon, [5]Ibhar, Elishua, Elpelet, [6]Nogah, Nepheg, Japhia, [7]Elishama, Beeliada[a] and Eliphelet.

David Defeats the Philistines

[8]When the Philistines heard that David had been anointed king over all Israel, they went up in full force to search for him, but David heard about it and went out to meet them. [9]Now the Philistines had come and raided the Valley of Rephaim; [10]so David inquired of God: "Shall I go and attack the Philistines? Will you deliver them into my hands?"

The LORD answered him, "Go, I will deliver them into your hands."

[11]So David and his men went up to Baal Perazim, and there he defeated them. He said, "As waters break out, God has broken out against my enemies by my hand." So that place was called Baal Perazim.[b] [12]The Philistines had abandoned their gods there, and David gave orders to burn them in the fire.

[13]Once more the Philistines raided the valley; [14]so David inquired of God again, and God answered him, "Do not go directly after them, but circle around them and attack them in front of the poplar trees. [15]As soon as you hear the sound of marching in the tops of the poplar trees, move out to battle, because that will mean God has gone out in front of you to strike the Philistine army." [16]So David did as God commanded him, and they struck down the Philistine army, all the way from Gibeon to Gezer.

[17]So David's fame spread throughout every land, and the LORD made all the nations fear him.

The Ark Brought to Jerusalem

15 After David had constructed buildings for himself in the City of David, he prepared a place for the ark of God and pitched a tent for it. [2]Then David said, "No one but the Levites may carry the ark of God, because the LORD chose them to carry the ark of the LORD and to minister before him forever."

[3]David assembled all Israel in Jerusalem to bring up the ark of the LORD to the place he had prepared for it. [4]He called together the descendants of Aaron and the Levites:

[5]From the descendants of Kohath,

Uriel the leader and 120 relatives;

[6]from the descendants of Merari,

Asaiah the leader and 220 relatives;

[7]from the descendants of Gershon,[c]

---

a 7 A variant of *Eliada.*   *b* 11 Baal Perazim means *the lord who breaks out.*   *c* 7 Hebrew *Gershom,* a variant of *Gershon*

Joel the leader and 130 relatives;
[8] from the descendants of Elizaphan,
Shemaiah the leader and 200 relatives;
[9] from the descendants of Hebron,
Eliel the leader and 80 relatives;
[10] from the descendants of Uzziel,
Amminadab the leader and 112 relatives.

[11] Then David summoned Zadok and Abiathar the priests, and Uriel, Asaiah, Joel, Shemaiah, Eliel and Amminadab the Levites. [12] He said to them, "You are the heads of the Levitical families; you and your fellow Levites are to consecrate yourselves and bring up the ark of the LORD, the God of Israel, to the place I have prepared for it. [13] It was because you, the Levites, did not bring it up the first time that the LORD our God broke out in anger against us. We did not inquire of him about how to do it in the prescribed way." [14] So the priests and Levites consecrated themselves in order to bring up the ark of the LORD, the God of Israel. [15] And the Levites carried the ark of God with the poles on their shoulders, as Moses had commanded in accordance with the word of the LORD.

[16] David told the leaders of the Levites to appoint their fellow Levites as musicians to make a joyful sound with musical instruments: lyres, harps and cymbals.

[17] So the Levites appointed Heman son of Joel; from his relatives, Asaph son of Berekiah; and from their relatives the Merarites, Ethan son of Kushaiah; [18] and with them their relatives next in rank: Zechariah,[a] Jaaziel, Shemiramoth, Jehiel, Unni, Eliab, Benaiah, Maaseiah, Mattithiah, Eliphelehu, Mikneiah, Obed-Edom and Jeiel,[b] the gatekeepers.

[19] The musicians Heman, Asaph and Ethan were to sound the bronze cymbals; [20] Zechariah, Jaaziel,[c] Shemiramoth, Jehiel, Unni, Eliab, Maaseiah and Benaiah were to play the lyres according to *alamoth*,[d] [21] and Mattithiah, Eliphelehu, Mikneiah, Obed-Edom, Jeiel and Azaziah were to play the harps, directing according to *sheminith*.[e] [22] Kenaniah the head Levite was in charge of the singing; that was his responsibility because he was skillful at it.

[23] Berekiah and Elkanah were to be doorkeepers for the ark. [24] Shebaniah, Joshaphat, Nethanel, Amasai, Zechariah, Benaiah and Eliezer the priests were to blow trumpets before the ark of God. Obed-Edom and Jehiah were also to be doorkeepers for the ark.

[25] So David and the elders of Israel and the commanders of units of a thousand went to bring up the ark of the covenant of the LORD from the house of Obed-Edom, with rejoicing. [26] Because God had helped the Levites who were carrying the ark of the covenant of the LORD, seven bulls and seven rams were sacrificed. [27] Now David was clothed in a robe of fine linen, as were all the Levites who were carrying the ark, and as were the musicians, and Kenaniah, who was in charge of the singing of the choirs. David also wore a linen ephod. [28] So all Israel brought up the ark of the covenant of the LORD with shouts, with the sounding of rams' horns and trumpets, and of cymbals, and the playing of lyres and harps.

[29] As the ark of the covenant of the LORD was entering the City of David, Michal daughter of Saul watched from a window. And when she saw King David dancing and celebrating, she despised him in her heart.

523

atissue:control

15:29 What's Michal's problem?! Her husband was a godly man, a brave warrior and a respected king. Why despise him? Before you condemn her too quickly, take stock of the things you and Michal might have in common. Do you try to change your husband into someone he's not? Do you think *you* know best how he should act or what he should do—or maybe even how "spiritual" he should be? How concerned are you about "keeping up appearances"? Sure, Michal's attitude needed to change—but maybe yours does, too.

---

a 18 Three Hebrew manuscripts and most Septuagint manuscripts (see also verse 20 and 1 Chron. 16:5); most Hebrew manuscripts *Zechariah son and* or *Zechariah, Ben and*   *b 18* Hebrew; Septuagint (see also verse 21) *Jeiel and Azaziah*   *c 20* See verse 18; Hebrew *Aziel*, a variant of *Jaaziel*.   *d 20* Probably a musical term   *e 21* Probably a musical term

Ministering Before the Ark

16 They brought the ark of God and set it inside the tent that David had pitched for it, and they presented burnt offerings and fellowship offerings before God. [2]After David had finished sacrificing the burnt offerings and fellowship offerings, he blessed the people in the name of the LORD. [3]Then he gave a loaf of bread, a cake of dates and a cake of raisins to each Israelite man and woman.

[4]He appointed some of the Levites to minister before the ark of the LORD, to extol,[a] thank, and praise the LORD, the God of Israel: [5]Asaph was the chief, and next to him in rank were Zechariah, then Jaaziel,[b] Shemiramoth, Jehiel, Mattithiah, Eliab, Benaiah, Obed-Edom and Jeiel. They were to play the lyres and harps, Asaph was to sound the cymbals, [6]and Benaiah and Jahaziel the priests were to blow the trumpets regularly before the ark of the covenant of God.

[7]That day David first appointed Asaph and his associates to give praise to the LORD in this manner:

524

[8]Give praise to the LORD, call on his name;
    make known among the nations what he has done.
[9]Sing to him, sing praise to him;
    tell of all his wonderful acts.
[10]Glory in his holy name;
    let the hearts of those who seek the LORD rejoice.
[11]Look to the LORD and his strength;
    seek his face always.

[12]Remember the wonders he has done,
    his miracles, and the judgments he pronounced,
[13]you his servants, the descendants of Israel,
    his chosen ones, the children of Jacob.
[14]He is the LORD our God;
    his judgments are in all the earth.

[15]He remembers[c] his covenant forever,
    the promise he made, for a thousand generations,
[16]the covenant he made with Abraham,
    the oath he swore to Isaac.
[17]He confirmed it to Jacob as a decree,
    to Israel as an everlasting covenant:
[18]"To you I will give the land of Canaan
    as the portion you will inherit."

[19]When they were but few in number,
    few indeed, and strangers in it,
[20]they[d] wandered from nation to nation,
    from one kingdom to another.
[21]He allowed no one to oppress them;
    for their sake he rebuked kings:
[22]"Do not touch my anointed ones;
    do my prophets no harm."

[23]Sing to the LORD, all the earth;
    proclaim his salvation day after day.
[24]Declare his glory among the nations,
    his marvelous deeds among all peoples.

a 4 Or *petition;* or *invoke   b 5* See 15:18,20; Hebrew *Jeiel,* possibly another name for *Jaaziel.   c 15* Some Septuagint manuscripts (see also Psalm 105:8); Hebrew *Remember   d 18-20* One Hebrew manuscript, Septuagint and Vulgate (see also Psalm 105:12); most Hebrew manuscripts *inherit, / [19]though you are but few in number, / few indeed, and strangers in it." / [20]They*

²⁵For great is the LORD and most worthy of praise;
    he is to be feared above all gods.
²⁶For all the gods of the nations are idols,
    but the LORD made the heavens.
²⁷Splendor and majesty are before him;
    strength and joy are in his dwelling place.

²⁸Ascribe to the LORD, all you families of nations,
    ascribe to the LORD glory and strength.
²⁹Ascribe to the LORD the glory due his name;
    bring an offering and come before him.
  Worship the LORD in the splendor of his^a holiness.
³⁰ Tremble before him, all the earth!
    The world is firmly established; it cannot be moved.

³¹Let the heavens rejoice, let the earth be glad;
    let them say among the nations, "The LORD reigns!"
³²Let the sea resound, and all that is in it;
    let the fields be jubilant, and everything in them!
³³Let the trees of the forest sing,
    let them sing for joy before the LORD,
    for he comes to judge the earth.

³⁴Give thanks to the LORD, for he is good;
    his love endures forever.
³⁵Cry out, "Save us, God our Savior;
    gather us and deliver us from the nations,
  that we may give thanks to your holy name,
    and glory in your praise."
³⁶Praise be to the LORD, the God of Israel,
    from everlasting to everlasting.

Then all the people said "Amen" and "Praise the LORD."

HE IS: worthy of praise

16:34 As a righteous king, David wanted to instill praise in his people's hearts. What a good leader! First he taught the people *whom* to praise (the Lord) and then *why* they should praise him (because he is good, and his love lasts forever). And he gave them the words to say.

Remember that praise always begins with a heart of thankfulness—not just for what God has done but also for who he is. He is *worthy of praise* because he alone is good (see Mark 10:18), and he alone is capable of loving us forever.

For the next He Is, go to p. 528.

³⁷David left Asaph and his associates before the ark of the covenant of the LORD to minister there regularly, according to each day's requirements. ³⁸He also left Obed-Edom and his sixty-eight associates to minister with them. Obed-Edom son of Jeduthun, and also Hosah, were gatekeepers.
³⁹David left Zadok the priest and his fellow priests before the tabernacle of the LORD at the high place in Gibeon ⁴⁰to present burnt offerings to the LORD on the altar of burnt offering regularly, morning and

---

^a 29 Or LORD with the splendor of

myth# 34

"WHEN I TAKE CARE OF MY ISSUES, THEN I'LL GET SERIOUS ABOUT MY FAITH."

Wait a minute. That can't be right. I added up the numbers again in my head—and reached the same baffling conclusion. I've been a Christian for how many years now? Eighteen? That is just so wrong! That realization (how did the years go by so fast?) got me thinking . . .

When I became a Christian as a sophomore in high school, I had a picture in my head of where I'd be someday. I thought by the time I reached my thirties I would be so much further along than I am now. I remember thinking about the "older" leaders in my church. (Wow, forty doesn't seem so old anymore!) They were strong leaders, had great families and stable jobs and spent their free time serving the church. But here I am, mid-thirties and nowhere near the life I thought I'd have by now.

I'm still working on the "great family" thing. (But I am not optimistic that my boyfriend will pop the question anytime soon. And my biological clock is ticking.) My job is just that—a job. Temping is hardly a career move, but it pays the bills. And spiritually? Let's just say I've stopped making promises to God or myself anymore. Instead of being the mature Christian that I envisioned all those years ago, I seem to be a spiritual screw-up. I just have so many issues I need to deal with before I start living for God again. Like my relationship with my boyfriend. My career. My relationship with my father. My life in general. What kind of a God would want to use someone like me in ministry right now? I have nothing to offer anyone, least of all God.

If only I were married to a really solid Christian guy (not my boyfriend), and I had a respectable career in H.R., and my father and I were at least on speaking terms so I could move past all those issues from my childhood . . . if only I had a nice house and maybe a child someday . . . then I'd fit in with the other leaders at church.

I'm behind schedule, and the clock is ticking. But soon I'll get my life together, and then things will be different.

—Alexis

WE CAN'T GET our lives together apart from God's help. We can manage and cope, but we can't truly change apart from God's grace changing us from within. We have it all backwards when we strive to clean up our act single-handedly before we get serious about living for Christ. *Before* we loved him, he loved us. *Before* we chose him, he chose us. *Before* we even knew his name, he knew ours. What kind of a God loves, chooses and knows you as you are, not as you *should* be? The merciful God of the Bible, that's who. As long as we're alive, there will be emotional baggage and issues to deal with and problems to overcome. None of us is all we ought to be this side of heaven. None of us has it all together spiritually. King David didn't, but look how far God brought him (see 1 Chronicles 17).

Moreover, some of us need to call this "waiting till we've got it all together" what it really is—an excuse. We think we're doing God a favor by not bothering him, trying to take care of our problems on our own. In reality, we're just buying time so we don't have to face facts: something has to change.

Those who are willing to trade in their excuses for commitment will take action. This may mean . . .

- Finding a church home and plugging in.
- Signing up for a discipleship or Bible study class or joining a small group.
- Finding an area of service in the church.
- Meeting with a spiritual mentor.
- Seeking Christian counseling.

Whatever you need to do to jolt your slumbering spirituality, do it *today*. How much time do you think you'll have to get it together on your own? Time is short. You don't know how long you have on earth. A sudden illness, accident or the heavenly blast of a trumpet signaling the Lord's return to earth could blow your timeline. What are you waiting for?

"Possibly the most dangerous word in the English language is *tomorrow*. It implies that we have a choice to place would-be painful experiences into the uncontrollable abyss that we call the future."

—John Ortberg

527

"BUT encourage one another Daily, as long as it is called 'Today,' so that none of you may be Hardened by sin's Deceitfulness."

HEBREWS 3:13

SEE ALSO

Psalm 90:12
Galatians 3:3
Hebrews 4:7

For more on **Spiritual Growth**, check the index.

evening, in accordance with everything written in the Law of the LORD, which he had given Israel. [41]With them were Heman and Jeduthun and the rest of those chosen and designated by name to give thanks to the LORD, "for his love endures forever." [42]Heman and Jeduthun were responsible for the sounding of the trumpets and cymbals and for the playing of the other instruments for sacred song. The sons of Jeduthun were stationed at the gate.

[43]Then all the people left to go to their homes, and David returned home to bless his family.

God's Promise to David

17 After David was settled in his palace, he said to Nathan the prophet, "Here I am, living in a house of cedar, while the ark of the covenant of the LORD is under a tent."

[2]Nathan replied to David, "Whatever you have in mind, do it, for God is with you."

[3]But that night the word of God came to Nathan, saying:

[4]"Go and tell my servant David, 'This is what the LORD says: You are not the one to build me a house to dwell in. [5]I have not dwelt in a house from the day I brought Israel up out of Egypt to this day. I have moved from one tent site to another, from one dwelling place to another. [6]Wherever I have moved with all the Israelites, did I ever say to any of their leaders[a] whom I commanded to shepherd my people, "Why have you not built me a house of cedar?"'

[7]"Now then, tell my servant David, 'This is what the LORD Almighty says: I took you from the pasture, from tending the flock, and appointed you ruler over my people Israel. [8]I have been with you wherever you have gone, and I have cut off all your enemies from before you. Now I will make your name like the names of the greatest men on earth. [9]And I will provide a place for my people Israel and will plant them so that they can have a home of their own and no longer be disturbed. Wicked people will not oppress them anymore, as they did at the beginning [10]and have done ever since the time I appointed leaders over my people Israel. I will also subdue all your enemies.

"'I declare to you that the LORD will build a house for you: [11]When your days are over and you go to be with your ancestors, I will raise up your offspring to succeed you, one of your own sons, and I will establish his kingdom. [12]He is the one who will build a house for me, and I will establish his throne forever. [13]I will be his father, and he will be my son. I will never take my love away from him, as I took it away from your predecessor. [14]I will set him over my house and my kingdom forever; his throne will be established forever.'"

[15]Nathan reported to David all the words of this entire revelation.

David's Prayer

[16]Then King David went in and sat before the LORD, and he said:

"Who am I, LORD God, and what is my family, that you have brought me this far? [17]And as if this were not enough in your sight, my God, you have spoken about the future of the house of your servant. You, LORD God, have looked on me as though I were the most exalted of men.

---

[a] 6 Traditionally *judges*; also in verse 10

HE IS: matchless

17:16–22 When he received the promise of a kingly lineage, David realized that all of God's promises flow from how *matchless* he is. David acknowledged that there is no one like the Lord. No human compares to our great, almighty God or even falls into the same category.

God has made some amazing promises to you that only he, the *matchless* one, can keep. He has promised to be with you always, to provide for your needs, to give you an eternal inheritance. Acknowledge openly, as David did, that no one on earth or in heaven is like your God.

For the next He Is, go to p. 541.

¹⁸"What more can David say to you for honoring your servant? For you know your servant, ¹⁹Lord. For the sake of your servant and according to your will, you have done this great thing and made known all these great promises.

²⁰"There is no one like you, Lord, and there is no God but you, as we have heard with our own ears. ²¹And who is like your people Israel—the one nation on earth whose God went out to redeem a people for himself, and to make a name for yourself, and to perform great and awesome wonders by driving out nations from before your people, whom you redeemed from Egypt? ²²You made your people Israel your very own forever, and you, Lord, have become their God.

²³"And now, Lord, let the promise you have made concerning your servant and his house be established forever. Do as you promised, ²⁴so that it will be established and that your name will be great forever. Then people will say, 'The Lord Almighty, the God over Israel, is Israel's God!' And the house of your servant David will be established before you.

²⁵"You, my God, have revealed to your servant that you will build a house for him. So your servant has found courage to pray to you. ²⁶You, Lord, are God! You have promised these good things to your servant. ²⁷Now you have been pleased to bless the house of your servant, that it may continue forever in your sight; for you, Lord, have blessed it, and it will be blessed forever."

David's Victories

529

18 In the course of time, David defeated the Philistines and subdued them, and he took Gath and its surrounding villages from the control of the Philistines.

²David also defeated the Moabites, and they became subject to him and brought him tribute.

³Moreover, David defeated Hadadezer king of Zobah, in the vicinity of Hamath, when he went to set up his monument at*ᵃ* the Euphrates River. ⁴David captured a thousand of his chariots, seven thousand charioteers and twenty thousand foot soldiers. He hamstrung all but a hundred of the chariot horses.

⁵When the Arameans of Damascus came to help Hadadezer king of Zobah, David struck down twenty-two thousand of them. ⁶He put garrisons in the Aramean kingdom of Damascus, and the Arameans became subject to him and brought him tribute. The Lord gave David victory wherever he went.

⁷David took the gold shields carried by the officers of Hadadezer and brought them to Jerusalem. ⁸From Tebahᵇ and Kun, towns that belonged to Hadadezer, David took a great quantity of bronze, which Solomon used to make the bronze Sea, the pillars and various bronze articles.

⁹When Tou king of Hamath heard that David had defeated the entire army of Hadadezer king of Zobah, ¹⁰he sent his son Hadoram to King David to greet him and congratulate him on his victory in battle over Hadadezer, who had been at war with Tou. Hadoram brought all kinds of articles of gold, of silver and of bronze.

¹¹King David dedicated these articles to the Lord, as he had done with the silver and gold he had taken from all these nations: Edom and Moab, the Ammonites and the Philistines, and Amalek.

¹²Abishai son of Zeruiah struck down eighteen thousand Edomites in the Valley of Salt. ¹³He put garrisons in Edom, and all the Edomites became subject to David. The Lord gave David victory wherever he went.

David's Officials

¹⁴David reigned over all Israel, doing what was just and right for all his people. ¹⁵Joab son of Zeruiah was over the army; Jehoshaphat son of Ahilud was recorder; ¹⁶Zadok son of Ahitub and Ahimelekᶜ son of Abiathar were priests; Shavsha was secretary; ¹⁷Benaiah son of Jehoiada was over the Kerethites and Pelethites; and David's sons were chief officials at the king's side.

David Defeats the Ammonites

19 In the course of time, Nahash king of the Ammonites died, and his son succeeded him as king. ²David thought, "I will show kindness to Hanun son of Nahash, because his father showed kindness to me." So David sent a delegation to express his sympathy to Hanun concerning his father.

ᵃ *3* Or *to restore his control over* ᵇ *8* Hebrew *Tibhath,* a variant of *Tebah* ᶜ *16* Some Hebrew manuscripts, Vulgate and Syriac (see also 2 Samuel 8:17); most Hebrew manuscripts *Abimelek*

When David's envoys came to Hanun in the land of the Ammonites to express sympathy to him, ³the Ammonite commanders said to Hanun, "Do you think David is honoring your father by sending envoys to you to express sympathy? Haven't his envoys come to you only to explore and spy out the country and overthrow it?" ⁴So Hanun seized David's envoys, shaved them, cut off their garments at the buttocks, and sent them away.

⁵When someone came and told David about the men, he sent messengers to meet them, for they were greatly humiliated. The king said, "Stay at Jericho till your beards have grown, and then come back."

⁶When the Ammonites realized that they had become obnoxious to David, Hanun and the Ammonites sent a thousand talents*a* of silver to hire chariots and charioteers from Aram Naharaim,*b* Aram Maakah and Zobah. ⁷They hired thirty-two thousand chariots and charioteers, as well as the king of Maakah with his troops, who came and camped near Medeba, while the Ammonites were mustered from their towns and moved out for battle.

⁸On hearing this, David sent Joab out with the entire army of fighting men. ⁹The Ammonites came out and drew up in battle formation at the entrance to their city, while the kings who had come were by themselves in the open country.

¹⁰Joab saw that there were battle lines in front of him and behind him; so he selected some of the best troops in Israel and deployed them against the Arameans. ¹¹He put the rest of the men under the command of Abishai his brother, and they were deployed against the Ammonites. ¹²Joab said, "If the Arameans are too strong for me, then you are to rescue me; but if the Ammonites are too strong for you, then I will rescue you. ¹³Be strong, and let us fight bravely for our people and the cities of our God. The LORD will do what is good in his sight."

¹⁴Then Joab and the troops with him advanced to fight the Arameans, and they fled before him. ¹⁵When the Ammonites realized that the Arameans were fleeing, they too fled before his brother Abishai and went inside the city. So Joab went back to Jerusalem.

¹⁶After the Arameans saw that they had been routed by Israel, they sent messengers and had Arameans brought from beyond the Euphrates River, with Shophak the commander of Hadadezer's army leading them.

¹⁷When David was told of this, he gathered all Israel and crossed the Jordan; he advanced against them and formed his battle lines opposite them. David formed his lines to meet the Arameans in battle, and they fought against him. ¹⁸But they fled before Israel, and David killed seven thousand of their charioteers and forty thousand of their foot soldiers. He also killed Shophak the commander of their army.

¹⁹When the vassals of Hadadezer saw that they had been routed by Israel, they made peace with David and became subject to him.

So the Arameans were not willing to help the Ammonites anymore.

The Capture of Rabbah

20 In the spring, at the time when kings go off to war, Joab led out the armed forces. He laid waste the land of the Ammonites and went to Rabbah and besieged it, but David remained in Jerusalem. Joab attacked Rabbah and left it in ruins. ²David took the crown from the head of their king*c*—its weight was found to be a talent*d* of gold, and it was set with precious stones—and it was placed on David's head. He took a great quantity of plunder from the city ³and brought out the people who were there, consigning them to labor with saws and with iron picks and axes. David did this to all the Ammonite towns. Then David and his entire army returned to Jerusalem.

War With the Philistines

⁴In the course of time, war broke out with the Philistines, at Gezer. At that time Sibbekai the Hushathite killed Sippai, one of the descendants of the Rephaites, and the Philistines were subjugated.

⁵In another battle with the Philistines, Elhanan son of Jair killed Lahmi the brother of Goliath the Gittite, who had a spear with a shaft like a weaver's rod.

⁶In still another battle, which took place at Gath, there was a huge man with six fingers on each hand

---

a 6 That is, about 38 tons or about 34 metric tons *b 6* That is, Northwest Mesopotamia *c 2* Or *of Milkom,* that is, Molek *d 2* That is, about 75 pounds or about 34 kilograms and six toes on each foot—twenty-four in all. He also was descended from Rapha. [7] When he taunted Israel, Jonathan son of Shimea, David's brother, killed him.

[8] These were descendants of Rapha in Gath, and they fell at the hands of David and his men.

David Counts the Fighting Men

21 Satan rose up against Israel and incited David to take a census of Israel. [2] So David said to Joab and the commanders of the troops, "Go and count the Israelites from Beersheba to Dan. Then report back to me so that I may know how many there are."

[3] But Joab replied, "May the LORD multiply his troops a hundred times over. My lord the king, are they not all my lord's subjects? Why does my lord want to do this? Why should he bring guilt on Israel?"

[4] The king's word, however, overruled Joab; so Joab left and went throughout Israel and then came back to Jerusalem. [5] Joab reported the number of the fighting men to David: In all Israel there were one million one hundred thousand men who could handle a sword, including four hundred and seventy thousand in Judah.

[6] But Joab did not include Levi and Benjamin in the numbering, because the king's command was repulsive to him. [7] This command was also evil in the sight of God; so he punished Israel.

[8] Then David said to God, "I have sinned greatly by doing this. Now, I beg you, take away the guilt of your servant. I have done a very foolish thing."

[9] The LORD said to Gad, David's seer, [10] "Go and tell David, 'This is what the LORD says: I am giving you three options. Choose one of them for me to carry out against you.'"

[11] So Gad went to David and said to him, "This is what the LORD says: 'Take your choice: [12] three years of famine, three months of being swept away[a] before your enemies, with their swords overtaking you, or three days of the sword of the LORD—days of plague in the land, with the angel of the LORD ravaging every part of Israel.' Now then, decide how I should answer the one who sent me."

[13] David said to Gad, "I am in deep distress. Let me fall into the hands of the LORD, for his mercy is very great; but do not let me fall into human hands."

[14] So the LORD sent a plague on Israel, and seventy thousand men of Israel fell dead. [15] And God sent an angel to destroy Jerusalem. But as the angel was doing so, the LORD saw it and relented concerning the disaster and said to the angel who was destroying the people, "Enough! Withdraw your hand." The angel of the LORD was then standing at the threshing floor of Araunah[b] the Jebusite.

[16] David looked up and saw the angel of the LORD standing between heaven and earth, with a drawn sword in his hand extended over Jerusalem. Then David and the elders, clothed in sackcloth, fell facedown.

[17] David said to God, "Was it not I who ordered the fighting men to be counted? I, the shepherd,[c] have sinned and done wrong. These are but sheep. What have they done? LORD my God, let your hand fall on me and my family, but do not let this plague remain on your people."

531

a tissue: pride

21:1–8 You outmaneuver the competition and land the account. You get the man every girl wants. You sing the solo perfectly. Now, do you pat yourself on the back, saying, "I am *sooooooo* good"? Or do you humbly thank God for doing those things through you? David's counting of his troops wasn't really the problem—the pride in his heart was. Pride causes us to forget that we exist for God and his glory and makes us think life is about making ourselves look good. When we do that, we end up investing the life God gave us only in ourselves.

David Builds an Altar

[18] Then the angel of the LORD ordered Gad to tell David to go up and build an altar to the LORD on the threshing floor of Araunah the Jebusite. [19] So David went up in obedience to the word that Gad had spoken in the name of the LORD.

---

a 12 Hebrew; Septuagint and Vulgate (see also 2 Samuel 24:13) *of fleeing* *b 15* Hebrew *Ornan,* a variant of *Araunah*; also in verses 18-28 *c 17* Probable reading of the original Hebrew text (see 2 Samuel 24:17 and footnote); Masoretic Text does not have *the shepherd.*

[20] While Araunah was threshing wheat, he turned and saw the angel; his four sons who were with him hid themselves. [21] Then David approached, and when Araunah looked and saw him, he left the threshing floor and bowed down before David with his face to the ground.

[22] David said to him, "Let me have the site of your threshing floor so I can build an altar to the LORD, that the plague on the people may be stopped. Sell it to me at the full price."

[23] Araunah said to David, "Take it! Let my lord the king do whatever pleases him. Look, I will give the oxen for the burnt offerings, the threshing sledges for the wood, and the wheat for the grain offering. I will give all this."

[24] But King David replied to Araunah, "No, I insist on paying the full price. I will not take for the LORD what is yours, or sacrifice a burnt offering that costs me nothing."

[25] So David paid Araunah six hundred shekels[a] of gold for the site. [26] David built an altar to the LORD there and sacrificed burnt offerings and fellowship offerings. He called on the LORD, and the LORD answered him with fire from heaven on the altar of burnt offering.

[27] Then the LORD spoke to the angel, and he put his sword back into its sheath. [28] At that time, when David saw that the LORD had answered him on the threshing floor of Araunah the Jebusite, he offered sacrifices there. [29] The tabernacle of the LORD, which Moses had made in the wilderness, and the altar of burnt offering were at that time on the high place at Gibeon. [30] But David could not go before it to inquire of God, because he was afraid of the sword of the angel of the LORD.

22 Then David said, "The house of the LORD God is to be here, and also the altar of burnt offering for Israel."

Preparations for the Temple

[2] So David gave orders to assemble the foreigners residing in Israel, and from among them he appointed stonecutters to prepare dressed stone for building the house of God. [3] He provided a large amount of iron to make nails for the doors of the gateways and for the fittings, and more bronze than could be weighed. [4] He also provided more cedar logs than could be counted, for the Sidonians and Tyrians had brought large numbers of them to David.

[5] David said, "My son Solomon is young and inexperienced, and the house to be built for the LORD should be of great magnificence and fame and splendor in the sight of all the nations. Therefore I will make preparations for it." So David made extensive preparations before his death.

[6] Then he called for his son Solomon and charged him to build a house for the LORD, the God of Israel. [7] David said to Solomon: "My son, I had it in my heart to build a house for the Name of the LORD my God. [8] But this word of the LORD came to me: 'You have shed much blood and have fought many wars. You are not to build a house for my Name, because you have shed much blood on the earth in my sight. [9] But you will have a son who will be a man of peace and rest, and I will give him rest from all his enemies on every side. His name will be Solomon,[b] and I will grant Israel peace and quiet during his reign. [10] He is the one who will build a house for my Name. He will be my son, and I will be his father. And I will establish the throne of his kingdom over Israel forever.'

[11] "Now, my son, the LORD be with you, and may you have success and build the house of the LORD your God, as he said you would. [12] May the LORD give you discretion and understanding when he puts you in command over Israel, so that you may keep the law of the LORD your God. [13] Then you will have success

---

[a] *25* That is, about 15 pounds or about 6.9 kilograms   [b] *9 Solomon* sounds like and may be derived from the Hebrew for *peace.*

if you are careful to observe the decrees and laws that the LORD gave Moses for Israel. Be strong and courageous. Do not be afraid or discouraged.

¹⁴"I have taken great pains to provide for the temple of the LORD a hundred thousand talents*a* of gold, a million talents*b* of silver, quantities of bronze and iron too great to be weighed, and wood and stone. And you may add to them. ¹⁵You have many workers: stonecutters, masons and carpenters, as well as those skilled in every kind of work ¹⁶in gold and silver, bronze and iron—skilled workers beyond number. Now begin the work, and the LORD be with you."

¹⁷Then David ordered all the leaders of Israel to help his son Solomon. ¹⁸He said to them, "Is not the LORD your God with you? And has he not granted you rest on every side? For he has given the inhabitants of the land into my hands, and the land is subject to the LORD and to his people. ¹⁹Now devote your heart and soul to seeking the LORD your God. Begin to build the sanctuary of the LORD God, so that you may bring the ark of the covenant of the LORD and the sacred articles belonging to God into the temple that will be built for the Name of the LORD."

The Levites

23 When David was old and full of years, he made his son Solomon king over Israel.

²He also gathered together all the leaders of Israel, as well as the priests and Levites. ³The Levites thirty years old or more were counted, and the total number of men was thirty-eight thousand. ⁴David said, "Of these, twenty-four thousand are to be in charge of the work of the temple of the LORD and six thousand are to be officials and judges. ⁵Four thousand are to be gatekeepers and four thousand are to praise the LORD with the musical instruments I have provided for that purpose."

⁶David separated the Levites into divisions corresponding to the sons of Levi: Gershon, Kohath and Merari.

Gershonites

⁷Belonging to the Gershonites:
    Ladan and Shimei.
⁸ The sons of Ladan:
    Jehiel the first, Zetham and Joel—three in all.
⁹ The sons of Shimei:
    Shelomoth, Haziel and Haran—three in all.
    These were the heads of the families of Ladan.
¹⁰ And the sons of Shimei:
    Jahath, Ziza,*c* Jeush and Beriah.
    These were the sons of Shimei—four in all.
    ¹¹ Jahath was the first and Ziza the second, but Jeush and Beriah did not have many sons; so they were counted as one family with one assignment.

Kohathites

¹²The sons of Kohath:
    Amram, Izhar, Hebron and Uzziel—four in all.
¹³ The sons of Amram:
    Aaron and Moses.
    Aaron was set apart, he and his descendants forever, to consecrate the most holy things, to offer sacrifices before the LORD, to minister before him and to pronounce blessings in his name forever. ¹⁴The sons of Moses the man of God were counted as part of the tribe of Levi.
¹⁵ The sons of Moses:
    Gershom and Eliezer.
¹⁶ The descendants of Gershom:
    Shubael was the first.

---

a 14 That is, about 3,750 tons or about 3,400 metric tons   *b 14* That is, about 37,500 tons or about 34,000 metric tons   *c 10* One Hebrew manuscript, Septuagint and Vulgate (see also verse 11); most Hebrew manuscripts *Zina*

¹⁷ The descendants of Eliezer:

Rehabiah was the first.

Eliezer had no other sons, but the sons of Rehabiah were very numerous.

¹⁸ The sons of Izhar:

Shelomith was the first.

¹⁹ The sons of Hebron:

Jeriah the first, Amariah the second, Jahaziel the third and Jekameam the fourth.

²⁰ The sons of Uzziel:

Micah the first and Ishiah the second.

Merarites

²¹ The sons of Merari:

Mahli and Mushi.

The sons of Mahli:

Eleazar and Kish.

²² Eleazar died without having sons: he had only daughters. Their cousins, the sons of Kish, married them.

²³ The sons of Mushi:

Mahli, Eder and Jerimoth—three in all.

²⁴ These were the descendants of Levi by their families—the heads of families as they were registered under their names and counted individually, that is, the workers twenty years old or more who served in the temple of the LORD. ²⁵ For David had said, "Since the LORD, the God of Israel, has granted rest to his people and has come to dwell in Jerusalem forever, ²⁶ the Levites no longer need to carry the tabernacle or any of the articles used in its service." ²⁷ According to the last instructions of David, the Levites were counted from those twenty years old or more.

²⁸ The duty of the Levites was to help Aaron's descendants in the service of the temple of the LORD: to be in charge of the courtyards, the side rooms, the purification of all sacred things and the performance of other duties at the house of God. ²⁹ They were in charge of the bread set out on the table, the special flour for the grain offerings, the thin loaves made without yeast, the baking and the mixing, and all measurements of quantity and size. ³⁰ They were also to stand every morning to thank and praise the LORD. They were to do the same in the evening ³¹ and whenever burnt offerings were presented to the LORD on the Sabbaths, at the New Moon feasts and at the appointed festivals. They were to serve before the LORD regularly in the proper number and in the way prescribed for them.

³² And so the Levites carried out their responsibilities for the tent of meeting, for the Holy Place and, under their relatives the descendants of Aaron, for the service of the temple of the LORD.

The Divisions of Priests

24 These were the divisions of the descendants of Aaron:

The sons of Aaron were Nadab, Abihu, Eleazar and Ithamar. ² But Nadab and Abihu died before their father did, and they had no sons; so Eleazar and Ithamar served as the priests. ³ With the help of Zadok a descendant of Eleazar and Ahimelek a descendant of Ithamar, David separated them into divisions for their appointed order of ministering. ⁴ A larger number of leaders were found among Eleazar's descendants than among Ithamar's, and they were divided accordingly: sixteen heads of families from Eleazar's descendants and eight heads of families from Ithamar's descendants. ⁵ They divided them impartially by casting lots, for there were officials of the sanctuary and officials of God among the descendants of both Eleazar and Ithamar.

534

atissue:giftedness

23–27 Priests, musicians, gatekeepers, treasurers, commanders . . . the list goes on for chapters. What's the point of all these names? The point then— and now—is that each person has a role to play in the kingdom of God. *You* have a special place that only *you* can fill. You are a one-of-a-kind masterpiece created by God with a unique set of talents, gifts and experiences necessary to fulfill your role. Why waste your time wishing you could be like someone else? You've got a job to do—and you're the one God designed to do it!

⁶The scribe Shemaiah son of Nethanel, a Levite, recorded their names in the presence of the king and of the officials: Zadok the priest, Ahimelek son of Abiathar and the heads of families of the priests and of the Levites—one family being taken from Eleazar and then one from Ithamar.

⁷ The first lot fell to Jehoiarib,
　the second to Jedaiah,
⁸ the third to Harim,
　the fourth to Seorim,
⁹ the fifth to Malkijah,
　the sixth to Mijamin,
¹⁰ the seventh to Hakkoz,
　the eighth to Abijah,
¹¹ the ninth to Jeshua,
　the tenth to Shekaniah,
¹² the eleventh to Eliashib,
　the twelfth to Jakim,
¹³ the thirteenth to Huppah,
　the fourteenth to Jeshebeab,
¹⁴ the fifteenth to Bilgah,
　the sixteenth to Immer,
¹⁵ the seventeenth to Hezir,
　the eighteenth to Happizzez,
¹⁶ the nineteenth to Pethahiah,
　the twentieth to Jehezkel,
¹⁷ the twenty-first to Jakin,
　the twenty-second to Gamul,
¹⁸ the twenty-third to Delaiah
　and the twenty-fourth to Maaziah.

¹⁹This was their appointed order of ministering when they entered the temple of the LORD, according to the regulations prescribed for them by their ancestor Aaron, as the LORD, the God of Israel, had commanded him.

The Rest of the Levites

²⁰As for the rest of the descendants of Levi:
　from the sons of Amram: Shubael;
　　from the sons of Shubael: Jehdeiah.
　²¹ As for Rehabiah, from his sons:
　　Ishiah was the first.
²² From the Izharites: Shelomoth;
　from the sons of Shelomoth: Jahath.
²³ The sons of Hebron: Jeriah the first,ᵃ Amariah the second, Jahaziel the third and Jekameam the fourth.
²⁴ The son of Uzziel: Micah;
　from the sons of Micah: Shamir.
　²⁵ The brother of Micah: Ishiah;
　　from the sons of Ishiah: Zechariah.
²⁶ The sons of Merari: Mahli and Mushi.
　The son of Jaaziah: Beno.
²⁷ The sons of Merari:
　from Jaaziah: Beno, Shoham, Zakkur and Ibri.

ᵃ 23 Two Hebrew manuscripts and some Septuagint manuscripts (see also 1 Chron. 23:19); most Hebrew manuscripts *The sons of Jeriah:*

²⁸ From Mahli: Eleazar, who had no sons.
²⁹ From Kish: the son of Kish:
   Jerahmeel.
³⁰ And the sons of Mushi: Mahli, Eder and Jerimoth.

These were the Levites, according to their families. ³¹They also cast lots, just as their relatives the descendants of Aaron did, in the presence of King David and of Zadok, Ahimelek, and the heads of families of the priests and of the Levites. The families of the oldest brother were treated the same as those of the youngest.

The Musicians

25 David, together with the commanders of the army, set apart some of the sons of Asaph, Heman and Jeduthun for the ministry of prophesying, accompanied by harps, lyres and cymbals. Here is the list of the men who performed this service:

²From the sons of Asaph:
   Zakkur, Joseph, Nethaniah and Asarelah. The sons of Asaph were under the supervision of Asaph, who prophesied under the king's supervision.
³As for Jeduthun, from his sons:
   Gedaliah, Zeri, Jeshaiah, Shimei,ᵃ Hashabiah and Mattithiah, six in all, under the supervision of their father Jeduthun, who prophesied, using the harp in thanking and praising the LORD.
⁴As for Heman, from his sons:
   Bukkiah, Mattaniah, Uzziel, Shubael and Jerimoth; Hananiah, Hanani, Eliathah, Giddalti and Romamti-Ezer; Joshbekashah, Mallothi, Hothir and Mahazioth. ⁵(All these were sons of Heman the king's seer. They were given him through the promises of God to exalt him. God gave Heman fourteen sons and three daughters.)

⁶All these men were under the supervision of their father for the music of the temple of the LORD, with cymbals, lyres and harps, for the ministry at the house of God.
   Asaph, Jeduthun and Heman were under the supervision of the king. ⁷Along with their relatives—all of them trained and skilled in music for the LORD—they numbered 288. ⁸Young and old alike, teacher as well as student, cast lots for their duties.

⁹ The first lot, which was for Asaph, fell to Joseph,	
his sons and relativesᵇ	12ᶜ
the second to Gedaliah,	
him and his relatives and sons	12
¹⁰ the third to Zakkur,	
his sons and relatives	12
¹¹ the fourth to Izri,ᵈ	
his sons and relatives	12
¹² the fifth to Nethaniah,	
his sons and relatives	12
¹³ the sixth to Bukkiah,	
his sons and relatives	12
¹⁴ the seventh to Jesarelah,ᵉ	
his sons and relatives	12
¹⁵ the eighth to Jeshaiah,	
his sons and relatives	12
¹⁶ the ninth to Mattaniah,	
his sons and relatives	12
¹⁷ the tenth to Shimei,	

ᵃ *3 One Hebrew manuscript and some Septuagint manuscripts (see also verse 17); most Hebrew manuscripts do not have* Shimei.   ᵇ *9 See Septuagint; Hebrew does not have* his sons and relatives.   ᶜ *9 See the total in verse 7; Hebrew does not have* twelve.   ᵈ *11 A variant of Zerie*   ᵉ *14 A variant of Asarelah*

his sons and relatives	12
[18] the eleventh to Azarel,[a]	
his sons and relatives	12
[19] the twelfth to Hashabiah,	
his sons and relatives	12
[20] the thirteenth to Shubael,	
his sons and relatives	12
[21] the fourteenth to Mattithiah,	
his sons and relatives	12
[22] the fifteenth to Jerimoth,	
his sons and relatives	12
[23] the sixteenth to Hananiah,	
his sons and relatives	12
[24] the seventeenth to Joshbekashah,	
his sons and relatives	12
[25] the eighteenth to Hanani,	
his sons and relatives	12
[26] the nineteenth to Mallothi,	
his sons and relatives	12
[27] the twentieth to Eliathah,	
his sons and relatives	12
[28] the twenty-first to Hothir,	
his sons and relatives	12
[29] the twenty-second to Giddalti,	
his sons and relatives	12
[30] the twenty-third to Mahazioth,	
his sons and relatives	12
[31] the twenty-fourth to Romamti-Ezer,	
his sons and relatives	12.

The Gatekeepers

26

The divisions of the gatekeepers:

From the Korahites: Meshelemiah son of Kore, one of the sons of Asaph.
[2] Meshelemiah had sons:
Zechariah the firstborn,
Jediael the second,
Zebadiah the third,
Jathniel the fourth,
[3] Elam the fifth,
Jehohanan the sixth
and Eliehoenai the seventh.
[4] Obed-Edom also had sons:
Shemaiah the firstborn,
Jehozabad the second,
Joah the third,
Sakar the fourth,
Nethanel the fifth,
[5] Ammiel the sixth,
Issachar the seventh

---

[a] 18 A variant of Uzziel

and Peullethai the eighth.
(For God had blessed Obed-Edom.)

[6] Obed-Edom's son Shemaiah also had sons, who were leaders in their father's family because they were very capable men. [7] The sons of Shemaiah: Othni, Rephael, Obed and Elzabad; his relatives Elihu and Semakiah were also able men. [8] All these were descendants of Obed-Edom; they and their sons and their relatives were capable men with the strength to do the work—descendants of Obed-Edom, 62 in all.
[9] Meshelemiah had sons and relatives, who were able men—18 in all.

[10] Hosah the Merarite had sons: Shimri the first (although he was not the firstborn, his father had appointed him the first), [11] Hilkiah the second, Tabaliah the third and Zechariah the fourth. The sons and relatives of Hosah were 13 in all.
[12] These divisions of the gatekeepers, through their leaders, had duties for ministering in the temple of the Lord, just as their relatives had. [13] Lots were cast for each gate, according to their families, young and old alike.
[14] The lot for the East Gate fell to Shelemiah.[a] Then lots were cast for his son Zechariah, a wise counselor, and the lot for the North Gate fell to him. [15] The lot for the South Gate fell to Obed-Edom, and the lot for the storehouse fell to his sons. [16] The lots for the West Gate and the Shalleketh Gate on the upper road fell to Shuppim and Hosah.
Guard was alongside of guard: [17] There were six Levites a day on the east, four a day on the north, four a day on the south and two at a time at the storehouse. [18] As for the court[b] to the west, there were four at the road and two at the court[b] itself.
[19] These were the divisions of the gatekeepers who were descendants of Korah and Merari.

The Treasurers and Other Officials

[20] Their fellow Levites were[c] in charge of the treasuries of the house of God and the treasuries for the dedicated things.
[21] The descendants of Ladan, who were Gershonites through Ladan and who were heads of families belonging to Ladan the Gershonite, were Jehieli, [22] the sons of Jehieli, Zetham and his brother Joel. They were in charge of the treasuries of the temple of the Lord.
[23] From the Amramites, the Izharites, the Hebronites and the Uzzielites:

[24] Shubael, a descendant of Gershom son of Moses, was the official in charge of the treasuries. [25] His relatives through Eliezer: Rehabiah his son, Jeshaiah his son, Joram his son, Zikri his son and Shelomith his son. [26] Shelomith and his relatives were in charge of all the treasuries for the things dedicated by King David, by the heads of families who were the commanders of thousands and commanders of hundreds, and by the other army commanders. [27] Some of the plunder taken in battle they dedicated for the repair of the temple of the Lord. [28] And everything dedicated by Samuel the seer and by Saul son of Kish, Abner son of Ner and Joab son of Zeruiah, and all the other dedicated things were in the care of Shelomith and his relatives.
[29] From the Izharites: Kenaniah and his sons were assigned duties away from the temple, as officials and judges over Israel.
[30] From the Hebronites: Hashabiah and his relatives—seventeen hundred able men—were responsible in Israel west of the Jordan for all the work of the Lord and for the king's service. [31] As for the Hebronites, Jeriah was their chief according to the genealogical records of their families. In the fortieth year of David's reign a search was made in the records, and capable men among the Hebronites were found at Jazer in Gilead. [32] Jeriah had twenty-seven hundred relatives, who were able men and heads of families, and King David put them in charge of the Reubenites, the Gadites and the half-tribe of Manasseh for every matter pertaining to God and for the affairs of the king.

---

a 14 A variant of *Meshelemiah*   *b 18* The meaning of the Hebrew for this word is uncertain.   *c 20* Septuagint; Hebrew *As for the Levites, Ahijah was*

Army Divisions

27 This is the list of the Israelites—heads of families, commanders of thousands and commanders of hundreds, and their officers, who served the king in all that concerned the army divisions that were on duty month by month throughout the year. Each division consisted of 24,000 men.

²In charge of the first division, for the first month, was Jashobeam son of Zabdiel. There were 24,000 men in his division. ³He was a descendant of Perez and chief of all the army officers for the first month.

⁴In charge of the division for the second month was Dodai the Ahohite; Mikloth was the leader of his division. There were 24,000 men in his division.

⁵The third army commander, for the third month, was Benaiah son of Jehoiada the priest. He was chief and there were 24,000 men in his division. ⁶This was the Benaiah who was a mighty warrior among the Thirty and was over the Thirty. His son Ammizabad was in charge of his division.

⁷The fourth, for the fourth month, was Asahel the brother of Joab; his son Zebadiah was his successor. There were 24,000 men in his division.

⁸The fifth, for the fifth month, was the commander Shamhuth the Izrahite. There were 24,000 men in his division.

⁹The sixth, for the sixth month, was Ira the son of Ikkesh the Tekoite. There were 24,000 men in his division.

¹⁰The seventh, for the seventh month, was Helez the Pelonite, an Ephraimite. There were 24,000 men in his division.

¹¹The eighth, for the eighth month, was Sibbekai the Hushathite, a Zerahite. There were 24,000 men in his division.

¹²The ninth, for the ninth month, was Abiezer the Anathothite, a Benjamite. There were 24,000 men in his division.

¹³The tenth, for the tenth month, was Maharai the Netophathite, a Zerahite. There were 24,000 men in his division.

¹⁴The eleventh, for the eleventh month, was Benaiah the Pirathonite, an Ephraimite. There were 24,000 men in his division.

¹⁵The twelfth, for the twelfth month, was Heldai the Netophathite, from the family of Othniel. There were 24,000 men in his division.

Leaders of the Tribes

¹⁶The leaders of the tribes of Israel:

over the Reubenites: Eliezer son of Zikri;
over the Simeonites: Shephatiah son of Maakah;
¹⁷over Levi: Hashabiah son of Kemuel;
over Aaron: Zadok;
¹⁸over Judah: Elihu, a brother of David;
over Issachar: Omri son of Michael;
¹⁹over Zebulun: Ishmaiah son of Obadiah;
over Naphtali: Jerimoth son of Azriel;
²⁰over the Ephraimites: Hoshea son of Azaziah;
over half the tribe of Manasseh: Joel son of Pedaiah;
²¹over the half-tribe of Manasseh in Gilead: Iddo son of Zechariah;
over Benjamin: Jaasiel son of Abner;
²²over Dan: Azarel son of Jeroham.
These were the leaders of the tribes of Israel.

²³David did not take the number of the men twenty years old or less, because the Lᴏʀᴅ had promised to make Israel as numerous as the stars in the sky. ²⁴Joab son of Zeruiah began to count the men but did

not finish. God's wrath came on Israel on account of this numbering, and the number was not entered in the book[a] of the annals of King David.

The King's Overseers

[25] Azmaveth son of Adiel was in charge of the royal storehouses.

Jonathan son of Uzziah was in charge of the storehouses in the outlying districts, in the towns, the villages and the watchtowers.

[26] Ezri son of Kelub was in charge of the workers who farmed the land.

[27] Shimei the Ramathite was in charge of the vineyards.

Zabdi the Shiphmite was in charge of the produce of the vineyards for the wine vats.

[28] Baal-Hanan the Gederite was in charge of the olive and sycamore-fig trees in the western foothills.

Joash was in charge of the supplies of olive oil.

[29] Shitrai the Sharonite was in charge of the herds grazing in Sharon.

Shaphat son of Adlai was in charge of the herds in the valleys.

[30] Obil the Ishmaelite was in charge of the camels.

Jehdeiah the Meronothite was in charge of the donkeys.

[31] Jaziz the Hagrite was in charge of the flocks.

All these were the officials in charge of King David's property.

[32] Jonathan, David's uncle, was a counselor, a man of insight and a scribe. Jehiel son of Hakmoni took care of the king's sons.

[33] Ahithophel was the king's counselor.

Hushai the Arkite was the king's confidant. [34] Ahithophel was succeeded by Jehoiada son of Benaiah and by Abiathar.

Joab was the commander of the royal army.

David's Plans for the Temple

28 David summoned all the officials of Israel to assemble at Jerusalem: the officers over the tribes, the commanders of the divisions in the service of the king, the commanders of thousands and commanders of hundreds, and the officials in charge of all the property and livestock belonging to the king and his sons, together with the palace officials, the mighty warriors and all the brave fighting men.

[2] King David rose to his feet and said: "Listen to me, my fellow Israelites, my people. I had it in my heart to build a house as a place of rest for the ark of the covenant of the LORD, for the footstool of our God, and I made plans to build it. [3] But God said to me, 'You are not to build a house for my Name, because you are a warrior and have shed blood.'

[4] "Yet the LORD, the God of Israel, chose me from my whole family to be king over Israel forever. He chose Judah as leader, and from the house of Judah he chose my family, and from my father's sons he was pleased to make me king over all Israel. [5] Of all my sons—and the LORD has given me many—he has chosen my son Solomon to sit on the throne of the kingdom of the LORD over Israel. [6] He said to me: 'Solomon your son is the one who will build my house and my courts, for I have chosen him to be my son, and I will be his father. [7] I will establish his kingdom forever if he is unswerving in carrying out my commands and laws, as is being done at this time.'

[8] "So now I charge you in the sight of all Israel and of the assembly of the LORD, and in the hearing of our God: Be careful to follow all the commands of the LORD your God, that you may possess this good land and pass it on as an inheritance to your descendants forever.

[9] "And you, my son Solomon, acknowledge the God of your father, and serve him with wholehearted devotion and with a willing mind, for the LORD searches every heart and understands every desire and every thought. If you seek him, he will be found by you; but if you forsake him, he will reject you forever. [10] Consider now, for the LORD has chosen you to build a house as the sanctuary. Be strong and do the work."

[11] Then David gave his son Solomon the plans for the portico of the temple, its buildings, its store-

---

540

HE IS: all-knowing

28:9–10 Before he died, David warned his son that God searches our hearts and understands even the *motives* behind our thoughts. Nothing is hidden from the *all-knowing* God.

Does that fact scare you? It should . . . at least a little. When you do good things, is it for God or for yourself? He knows your motives. Are your words truly humble, or are you trying to draw attention to yourself? He knows. Do you appear to live a holy life yet hide a secret sin that you won't give up? He knows. Is your affection for him genuine and passionate or luke-warm? He knows.

For the next He Is, go to p. 544.

rooms, its upper parts, its inner rooms and the place of atonement. [12]He gave him the plans of all that the Spirit had put in his mind for the courts of the temple of the LORD and all the surrounding rooms, for the treasuries of the temple of God and for the treasuries for the dedicated things. [13]He gave him instructions for the divisions of the priests and Levites, and for all the work of serving in the temple of the LORD, as well as for all the articles to be used in its service. [14]He designated the weight of gold for all the gold articles to be used in various kinds of service, and the weight of silver for all the silver articles to be used in various kinds of service: [15]the weight of gold for the gold lampstands and their lamps, with the weight for each lampstand and its lamps; and the weight of silver for each silver lampstand and its lamps, according to the use of each lampstand; [16]the weight of gold for each table for consecrated bread; the weight of silver for the silver tables; [17]the weight of pure gold for the forks, sprinkling bowls and pitchers; the weight of gold for each gold dish; the weight of silver for each silver dish; [18]and the weight of the refined gold for the altar of incense. He also gave him the plan for the chariot, that is, the cherubim of gold that spread their wings and overshadow the ark of the covenant of the LORD.

[19]"All this," David said, "I have in writing as a result of the LORD's hand on me, and he enabled me to understand all the details of the plan."

[20]David also said to Solomon his son, "Be strong and courageous, and do the work. Do not be afraid or discouraged, for the LORD God, my God, is with you. He will not fail you or forsake you until all the work for the service of the temple of the LORD is finished. [21]The divisions of the priests and Levites are ready for all the work on the temple of God, and every willing person skilled in any craft will help you in all the work. The officials and all the people will obey your every command."

Gifts for Building the Temple

29 Then King David said to the whole assembly: "My son Solomon, the one whom God has chosen, is young and inexperienced. The task is great, because this palatial structure is not for human beings but for the LORD God. [2]With all my resources I have provided for the temple of my God—gold for the gold work, silver for the silver, bronze for the bronze, iron for the iron and wood for the wood, as well as onyx for the settings, turquoise,[a] stones of various colors, and all kinds of fine stone and marble—all of these in large quantities. [3]Besides, in my devotion to the temple of my God I now give my personal treasures of gold and silver for the temple of my God, over and above everything I have provided for this holy temple: [4]three thousand talents[b] of gold (gold of Ophir) and seven thousand talents[c] of refined silver, for the overlaying of the walls of the buildings, [5]for the gold work and the silver work, and for all the work to be done by the skilled workers. Now, who among you is willing to consecrate yourself to the LORD today?"

[6]Then the leaders of families, the officers of the tribes of Israel, the commanders of thousands and commanders of hundreds, and the officials in charge of the king's work gave willingly. [7]They gave toward the work on the temple of God five thousand talents[d] and ten thousand darics[e] of gold, ten thousand

541

---

[a] *2* The meaning of the Hebrew for this word is uncertain.   [b] *4* That is, about 110 tons or about 100 metric tons   [c] *4* That is, about 260 tons or about 235 metric tons   [d] *7* That is, about 190 tons or about 170 metric tons   [e] *7* That is, about 185 pounds or about 84 kilograms

myth# 35 "TITHING'S NOT FOR ME."

I'm sorry, but I think God loves me regardless of how much money I give or don't give to the church. It's not that I'm opposed to supporting God's work—I just don't share the same convictions about tithing as people my parents' age. I think tithing is a legalistic, outdated standard for determining how spiritual somebody is. My pastor talks as if we don't love God if we're not emptying our bank accounts every service. Meanwhile, I'm wondering where all the money is going. I don't want to help finance new pew cushions; I want my money going to real ministries.

Oh, I give. I give some money to the same inner-city ministry every Christmas. I just don't make a big deal about it, calculating some arbitrary percentage of my income. Between my car payment, rent, cell phone bill and insurance payments, I hardly have any money left to spend on the necessities, like food. If I have some extra cash left over at the end of the year, I don't mind giving it. If I don't have as much, I try to give extra the next year.

The whole emphasis on money in the church makes me uncomfortable. It sounds too much like those televangelists waving "anointed handkerchiefs" and asking people to send them their social security checks or grocery money. As long as tithing is referred to as voluntary, I'm fine with it. But don't try to make it one of the Ten Commandments.

—Chelsea

FAQs ON TITHING

Where's my money going? Remember, your offering is foremost and exclusively a gift to God, not to an organization, as a voluntary act of worship. The church is simply the vehicle for putting God's money into circulation. Find out where your money is going. Ask questions at your church. Join ministry teams. Experience the opportunities firsthand so you can see the difference your gift makes.

Who made up the magical "10-percent" rule? God did. The Bible gives examples of a *tithe*, which means "a tenth" (see Genesis 14:20). This amount is actually a Biblical minimum. A tithe represents the *first* 10 percent of our income (see Proverbs 3:9–10). That means before taxes (gross, not net) and before we pay our other bills and have "leftover" cash. Keep in mind that generosity is a Christian's *modus operandi*. As we grow, we may give beyond 10 percent—not because we have to, but because we want to.

What if I have too much debt to tithe? The Bible says that our money belongs first to God, not to creditors Honor your responsibility to pay back a debt, but don't neglect giving.

Tithing is more for us than it is for God. God doesn't *need* our money, as if he's going to go out of business without our donations. But tithing does something to our hearts. It's an act of submission, of putting God first, of getting to partner with God in what he's already doing on earth.

The only time God instructs us to test him is in the area of tithing (see Malachi 3:8–12). And he promises to bless us! If you haven't been tithing, try this six-month challenge to revamp your relationship with money and flex your faith.

- Give to God *before* you pay your bills. If you can't reasonably give 10 percent, start smaller and work your way up.

- Give regularly as part of your worship. Your attitude is what counts, not the size of your gift (see Mark 12:43–44).

- Refuse to incur more debt. Cut up your credit cards. Pay more than the monthly minimum to avoid more interest fees. God wants you to be financially free so that you don't live as a slave to your finances and so that you can have the joy of giving.

God himself is willing for you to put him to the test with tithing—and he has never failed anyone yet.

543

> "Tithing is down from 14 percent in 2001 to 6 percent in 2002 among born again Christians."
>
> —Barna Research Group (2003)

> "GIVE, AND IT WILL BE GIVEN TO YOU. A GOOD MEASURE, PRESSED DOWN, SHAKEN TOGETHER AND RUNNING OVER, WILL BE POURED INTO YOUR LAP."
>
> LUKE 6:38

SEE ALSO

2 Samuel 24:24

Proverbs 3:9–10

2 Corinthians 9:6–15

For more on **Tithing**, check the index.

talents *a* of silver, eighteen thousand talents *b* of bronze and a hundred thousand talents *c* of iron. ⁸Anyone who had precious stones gave them to the treasury of the temple of the Lord in the custody of Jehiel the Gershonite. ⁹The people rejoiced at the willing response of their leaders, for they had given freely and wholeheartedly to the Lord. David the king also rejoiced greatly.

 head over all

29:9–20 The Israelites gave freely to build God's house and enjoyed the act of giving. Rather than greedily clinging to their belongings, they recognized that everything belongs to God already, so they happily gave back to him, acknowledging that he is *head over all*.

You can tell a lot about your spiritual condition by how you use your resources. Do you *freely* give to God and his work? Or are you tight-fisted with your money and belongings? The easiest way to show that God is *head over all* of your life is to submit your time, talents and bank account to him.

For the next He Is, go to p. 550.

David's Prayer

¹⁰David praised the Lord in the presence of the whole assembly, saying,

> "Praise be to you, Lord,
> the God of our father Israel,
> from everlasting to everlasting.
> ¹¹Yours, Lord, is the greatness and the power
> and the glory and the majesty and the splendor,
> for everything in heaven and earth is yours.
> Yours, Lord, is the kingdom;
> you are exalted as head over all.
> ¹²Wealth and honor come from you;
> you are the ruler of all things.
> In your hands are strength and power
> to exalt and give strength to all.
> ¹³Now, our God, we give you thanks,
> and praise your glorious name.

¹⁴"But who am I, and who are my people, that we should be able to give as generously as this? Everything comes from you, and we have given you only what comes from your hand. ¹⁵We are foreigners and strangers in your sight, as were all our ancestors. Our days on earth are like a shadow, without hope. ¹⁶Lord our God, all this abundance that we have provided for building you a temple for your Holy Name comes from your hand, and all of it belongs to you. ¹⁷I know, my God, that you test the heart and are pleased with integrity. All these things have I given willingly and with honest intent. And now I have seen with joy how willingly your people who are here have given to you. ¹⁸Lord, the God of our

conversations

integrity «» 29:17

1 » What does it mean to have integrity?

2 » What's the opposite of integrity?

3 » In what areas is it hardest for you to maintain your integrity?

For more on integrity, check the index.
For the next Conversations, go to p. 565.

---

a *7 That is, about 375 tons or about 340 metric tons*   *b* *7 That is, about 675 tons or about 610 metric tons*   *c* *7 That is, about 3,750 tons or about 3,400 metric tons* fathers Abraham, Isaac and Israel, keep these desires and thoughts in the hearts of your people forever, and keep their hearts loyal to you. [19]And give my son Solomon the wholehearted devotion to keep your commands, statutes and decrees and to do everything to build the palatial structure for which I have provided."

[20]Then David said to the whole assembly, "Praise the LORD your God." So they all praised the LORD, the God of their fathers; they bowed down, prostrating themselves before the LORD and the king.

Solomon Acknowledged as King

[21]The next day they made sacrifices to the LORD and presented burnt offerings to him: a thousand bulls, a thousand rams and a thousand male lambs, together with their drink offerings, and other sacrifices in abundance for all Israel. [22]They ate and drank with great joy in the presence of the LORD that day.

Then they acknowledged Solomon son of David as king a second time, anointing him before the LORD to be ruler and Zadok to be priest. [23]So Solomon sat on the throne of the LORD as king in place of his father David. He prospered and all Israel obeyed him. [24]All the officers and mighty warriors, as well as all of King David's sons, pledged their submission to King Solomon.

[25]The LORD highly exalted Solomon in the sight of all Israel and bestowed on him royal splendor such as no king over Israel ever had before.

The Death of David

[26]David son of Jesse was king over all Israel. [27]He ruled over Israel forty years—seven in Hebron and thirty-three in Jerusalem. [28]He died at a good old age, having enjoyed long life, wealth and honor. His son Solomon succeeded him as king.

[29]As for the events of King David's reign, from beginning to end, they are written in the records of Samuel the seer, the records of Nathan the prophet and the records of Gad the seer, [30]together with the details of his reign and power, and the circumstances that surrounded him and Israel and the kingdoms of all the other lands.

545

2chronicles

546

AUTHOR
Unknown, but possibly Ezra.

AUDIENCE
All Israel.

DATE
About 430 B.C.

SETTING
The book covers the time from Solomon's
reign (970 B.C.) to the Babylonian exile
(586 B.C.), paralleling many of the events of
1 and 2 Kings.

VERSE TO REMEMBER
"If my people, who are called by my name,
will humble themselves and pray and seek
my face and turn from their wicked ways,
then I will hear from heaven, and I will forgive their sin and will heal their land." (7:14)

THEME TO CONSIDER
Learn life's lessons the hard way or
God's way.

Solomon Asks for Wisdom

1 Solomon son of David established himself firmly over his kingdom, for the LORD his God was with him and made him exceedingly great.

²Then Solomon spoke to all Israel—to the commanders of thousands and commanders of hundreds, to the judges and to all the leaders in Israel, the heads of families— ³and Solomon and the whole assembly went to the high place at Gibeon, for God's tent of meeting was there, which Moses the LORD's servant had made in the wilderness. ⁴Now David had brought up the ark of God from Kiriath Jearim to the place he had prepared for it, because he had pitched a tent for it in Jerusalem. ⁵But the bronze altar that Bezalel son of Uri, the son of Hur, had made was in Gibeon in front of the tabernacle of the LORD; so Solomon and the assembly inquired of him there. ⁶Solomon went up to the bronze altar before the LORD in the tent of meeting and offered a thousand burnt offerings on it.

⁷That night God appeared to Solomon and said to him, "Ask for whatever you want me to give you."

⁸Solomon answered God, "You have shown great kindness to David my father and have made me king in his place. ⁹Now, LORD God, let your promise to my father David be confirmed, for you have made me king over a people who are as numerous as the dust of the earth. ¹⁰Give me wisdom and knowledge, that I may lead this people, for who is able to govern this great people of yours?"

¹¹God said to Solomon, "Since this is your heart's desire and you have not asked for wealth, possessions or honor, nor for the death of your enemies, and since you have not asked for a long life but for wisdom and knowledge to govern my people over whom I have made you king, ¹²therefore wisdom and knowledge will be given you. And I will also give you wealth, possessions and honor, such as no king who was before you ever had and none after you will have."

¹³Then Solomon went to Jerusalem from the high place at Gibeon, from before the tent of meeting. And he reigned over Israel.

¹⁴Solomon accumulated chariots and horses; he had fourteen hundred chariots and twelve thousand horses,ᵃ which he kept in the chariot cities and also with him in Jerusalem. ¹⁵The king made silver and gold as common in Jerusalem as stones, and cedar as plentiful as sycamore-fig trees in the foothills. ¹⁶Solomon's horses were imported from Egypt and from Kueᵇ—the royal merchants purchased them from Kue at the current price. ¹⁷They imported a chariot from Egypt for six hundred shekelsᶜ of silver, and a horse for a hundred and fifty.ᵈ They also exported them to all the kings of the Hittites and of the Arameans.

547

atissue:selfishness

1:7–12 Rub the magic bottle, and the genie's willing to grant your one wish. Do you ask for fame and fortune? Beauty and health? If you're a new mom, maybe you'd simply be happy to get a full night's sleep, finish a meal and take a shower—all in the same day. When God made this wild offer to Solomon, the king could have asked for all kinds of favors for himself. But he didn't. He knew that life isn't about looking out for yourself; it's about loving God and serving others. If you focus on those two things, then you can trust that God will give you what you need.

Preparations for Building the Temple

2 *Solomon gave orders to build a temple for the Name of the LORD and a royal palace for himself. *²He conscripted 70,000 men as carriers and 80,000 as stonecutters in the hills and 3,600 as supervisors over them.

³Solomon sent this message to Hiramᵉ king of Tyre:

"Send me cedar logs as you did for my father David when you sent him cedar to build a palace to live in. ⁴Now I am about to build a temple for the Name of the LORD my God and to dedicate it

---

ᵃ *14* Or *charioteers*   ᵇ *16* Probably Cilicia   ᶜ *17* That is, about 15 pounds or about 6.9 kilograms   ᵈ *17* That is, about 3 3/4 pounds or about 1.7 kilograms
ᵉ *3* Hebrew *Huram*, a variant of *Hiram*; also in verses 11 and 12

* 2:1 is numbered 1:18 in Hebrew texts.   * 2:2-18 is numbered 2:1-17 in Hebrew texts.

to him for burning fragrant incense before him, for setting out the consecrated bread regularly, and for making burnt offerings every morning and evening and on the Sabbaths, at the New Moons and at the appointed festivals of the Lord our God. This is a lasting ordinance for Israel.

⁵"The temple I am going to build will be great, because our God is greater than all other gods. ⁶But who is able to build a temple for him, since the heavens, even the highest heavens, cannot contain him? Who then am I to build a temple for him, except as a place to burn sacrifices before him?

⁷"Send me, therefore, a man skilled to work in gold and silver, bronze and iron, and in purple, crimson and blue yarn, and experienced in the art of engraving, to work in Judah and Jerusalem with my skilled workers, whom my father David provided.

⁸"Send me also cedar, juniper and algum*ᵃ* logs from Lebanon, for I know that your servants are skilled in cutting timber there. My men will work with yours ⁹to provide me with plenty of lumber, because the temple I build must be large and magnificent. ¹⁰I will give your servants, those who cut the timber, twenty thousand cors*ᵇ* of ground wheat, twenty thousand cors*ᶜ* of barley, twenty thousand baths*ᵈ* of wine and twenty thousand baths of olive oil."

¹¹Hiram king of Tyre replied by letter to Solomon:

"Because the Lord loves his people, he has made you their king."

¹²And Hiram added:

"Praise be to the Lord, the God of Israel, who made heaven and earth! He has given King David a wise son, endowed with intelligence and discernment, who will build a temple for the Lord and a palace for himself.

¹³"I am sending you Huram-Abi, a man of great skill, ¹⁴whose mother was from Dan and whose father was from Tyre. He is trained to work in gold and silver, bronze and iron, stone and wood, and with purple and blue and crimson yarn and fine linen. He is experienced in all kinds of engraving and can execute any design given to him. He will work with your skilled workers and with those of my lord, David your father.

¹⁵"Now let my lord send his servants the wheat and barley and the olive oil and wine he promised, ¹⁶and we will cut all the logs from Lebanon that you need and will float them as rafts by sea down to Joppa. You can then take them up to Jerusalem."

¹⁷Solomon took a census of all the foreigners residing in Israel, after the census his father David had taken; and they were found to be 153,600. ¹⁸He assigned 70,000 of them to be carriers and 80,000 to be stonecutters in the hills, with 3,600 supervisors over them to keep the people working.

Solomon Builds the Temple

3 Then Solomon began to build the temple of the Lord in Jerusalem on Mount Moriah, where the Lord had appeared to his father David. It was on the threshing floor of Araunah*ᵉ* the Jebusite, the place provided by David. ²He began building on the second day of the second month in the fourth year of his reign.

³The foundation Solomon laid for building the temple of God was sixty cubits long and twenty cubits wide*ᶠ* (using the cubit of the old standard). ⁴The portico at the front of the temple was twenty cubits*ᵍ* long across the width of the building and twenty cubits*ʰ* high.

He overlaid the inside with pure gold. ⁵He paneled the main hall with juniper and covered it with fine gold and decorated it with palm tree and chain designs. ⁶He adorned the temple with precious stones. And the gold he used was gold of Parvaim. ⁷He overlaid the ceiling beams, doorframes, walls and doors of the temple with gold, and he carved cherubim on the walls.

⁸He built the Most Holy Place, its length corresponding to the width of the temple—twenty cubits

---

ᵃ *8* Probably a variant of *almug*   ᵇ *10* That is, probably about 3,600 tons or about 3,275 metric tons   ᶜ *10* That is, probably about 3,000 tons or about 2,700 metric tons   ᵈ *10* That is, about 120,000 gallons or about 440,000 liters   ᵉ *1* Hebrew *Ornan*, a variant of *Araunah*   ᶠ *3* That is, about 90 feet long and 30 feet wide or about 27 meters long and 9 meters wide   ᵍ *4* That is, about 30 feet or about 9 meters; also in verses 8, 11 and 13   ʰ *4* Some Septuagint and Syriac manuscripts; Hebrew *and a hundred and twenty* long and twenty cubits wide. He overlaid the inside with six hundred talents*a* of fine gold. [9]The gold nails weighed fifty shekels.*b* He also overlaid the upper parts with gold.

[10]For the Most Holy Place he made a pair of sculptured cherubim and overlaid them with gold. [11]The total wingspan of the cherubim was twenty cubits. One wing of the first cherub was five cubits*c* long and touched the temple wall, while its other wing, also five cubits long, touched the wing of the other cherub. [12]Similarly one wing of the second cherub was five cubits long and touched the other temple wall, and its other wing, also five cubits long, touched the wing of the first cherub. [13]The wings of these cherubim extended twenty cubits. They stood on their feet, facing the main hall.*d*

[14]He made the curtain of blue, purple and crimson yarn and fine linen, with cherubim worked into it.

[15]For the front of the temple he made two pillars, which totaled thirty-five cubits*e* in length, each with a capital five cubits high. [16]He made interwoven chains*f* and put them on top of the pillars. He also made a hundred pomegranates and attached them to the chains. [17]He erected the pillars in the front of the temple, one to the south and one to the north. The one to the south he named Jakin*g* and the one to the north Boaz.*h*

The Temple's Furnishings

4 He made a bronze altar twenty cubits long, twenty cubits wide and ten cubits high.*i* [2]He made the Sea of cast metal, circular in shape, measuring ten cubits from rim to rim and five cubits*j* high. It took a line of thirty cubits*k* to measure around it. [3]Below the rim, figures of bulls encircled it—ten to a cubit.*l* The bulls were cast in two rows in one piece with the Sea.

[4]The Sea stood on twelve bulls, three facing north, three facing west, three facing south and three facing east. The Sea rested on top of them, and their hindquarters were toward the center. [5]It was a handbreadth*m* in thickness, and its rim was like the rim of a cup, like a lily blossom. It held three thousand baths.*n*

[6]He then made ten basins for washing and placed five on the south side and five on the north. In them the things to be used for the burnt offerings were rinsed, but the Sea was to be used by the priests for washing.

[7]He made ten gold lampstands according to the specifications for them and placed them in the temple, five on the south side and five on the north.

[8]He made ten tables and placed them in the temple, five on the south side and five on the north. He also made a hundred gold sprinkling bowls.

[9]He made the courtyard of the priests, and the large court and the doors for the court, and overlaid the doors with bronze. [10]He placed the Sea on the south side, at the southeast corner.

[11]And Huram also made the pots and shovels and sprinkling bowls.

So Huram finished the work he had undertaken for King Solomon in the temple of God:

[12] the two pillars;

the two bowl-shaped capitals on top of the pillars;

the two sets of network decorating the two bowl-shaped capitals on top of the pillars;

[13] the four hundred pomegranates for the two sets of network (two rows of pomegranates for each network, decorating the bowl-shaped capitals on top of the pillars);

[14] the stands with their basins;

[15] the Sea and the twelve bulls under it;

[16] the pots, shovels, meat forks and all related articles.

All the objects that Huram-Abi made for King Solomon for the temple of the LORD were of polished bronze. [17]The king had them cast in clay molds in the plain of the Jordan between Sukkoth and Zarethan.*o* [18]All these things that Solomon made amounted to so much that the weight of the bronze could not be calculated.

549

---

a 8 That is, about 23 tons or about 20 metric tons   *b 9* That is, about 1 1/4 pounds or about 575 grams   *c 11* That is, about 7 1/2 feet or about 2.3 meters; also in verse 15   *d 13* Or *facing inward*   *e 15* That is, about 52 feet or about 16 meters   *f 16* Or possibly *made chains in the inner sanctuary*; the meaning of the Hebrew for this phrase is uncertain.   *g 17 Jakin* probably means *he establishes.*   *h 17 Boaz* probably means *in him is strength.*   *i 1* That is, about 30 feet long and wide and 15 feet high or about 9 meters long and wide and 4.5 meters high   *j 2* That is, about 7 1/2 feet or about 2.3 meters   *k 2* That is, about 45 feet or about 13.5 meters   *l 3* That is, about 18 inches or about 45 centimeters   *m 5* That is, about 3 inches or about 7.5 centimeters   *n 5* That is, about 18,000 gallons or about 66,000 liters   *o 17* Hebrew *Zeredatha,* a variant of *Zarethan*

¹⁹Solomon also made all the furnishings that were in God's temple:

the golden altar;
the tables on which was the bread of the Presence;
²⁰ the lampstands of pure gold with their lamps, to burn in front of the inner sanctuary as prescribed;
²¹ the gold floral work and lamps and tongs (they were solid gold);
²² the pure gold wick trimmers, sprinkling bowls, dishes and censers; and the gold doors of the temple: the inner doors to the Most Holy Place and the doors of the main hall.

5 When all the work Solomon had done for the temple of the LORD was finished, he brought in the things his father David had dedicated—the silver and gold and all the furnishings—and he placed them in the treasuries of God's temple.

The Ark Brought to the Temple

²Then Solomon summoned to Jerusalem the elders of Israel, all the heads of the tribes and the chiefs of the Israelite families, to bring up the ark of the LORD's covenant from Zion, the City of David. ³And all the Israelites came together to the king at the time of the festival in the seventh month.

⁴When all the elders of Israel had arrived, the Levites took up the ark, ⁵and they brought up the ark and the tent of meeting and all the sacred furnishings in it. The Levitical priests carried them up; ⁶and King Solomon and the entire assembly of Israel that had gathered about him were before the ark, sacrificing so many sheep and cattle that they could not be recorded or counted.

⁷The priests then brought the ark of the LORD's covenant to its place in the inner sanctuary of the temple, the Most Holy Place, and put it beneath the wings of the cherubim. ⁸The cherubim spread their wings over the place of the ark and covered the ark and its carrying poles. ⁹These poles were so long that their ends, extending from the ark, could be seen from in front of the inner sanctuary, but not from outside the Holy Place; and they are still there today. ¹⁰There was nothing in the ark except the two tablets that Moses had placed in it at Horeb, where the LORD made a covenant with the Israelites after they came out of Egypt.

¹¹The priests then withdrew from the Holy Place. All the priests who were there had consecrated themselves, regardless of their divisions. ¹²All the Levites who were musicians—Asaph, Heman, Jeduthun and their sons and relatives—stood on the east side of the altar, dressed in fine linen and playing cymbals, harps and lyres. They were accompanied by 120 priests sounding trumpets. ¹³The trumpeters and musicians joined in unison to give praise and thanks to the LORD. Accompanied by trumpets, cymbals and other instruments, the singers raised their voices in praise to the LORD and sang:

"He is good;
his love endures forever."

Then the temple of the LORD was filled with the cloud, ¹⁴and the priests could not perform their service because of the cloud, for the glory of the LORD filled the temple of God.

HE IS: unifying

5:13–14 Years of planning and work went into constructing the temple. But it wasn't until the people sang together in unison that the glory of the Lord filled the temple. God's glory is revealed when his people are unified.

He is *unifying*. Jesus said, "Where two or three come together in my name, there am I with them" (Matthew 18:20). When you join with other believers to praise, pray to or work for God, he creates unified reality among you. He brings together many people who would otherwise have nothing in common.

For the next He Is, go to p. 559.

6 Then Solomon said, "The LORD has said that he would dwell in a dark cloud; [2]I have built a magnificent temple for you, a place for you to dwell forever."

[3]While the whole assembly of Israel was standing there, the king turned around and blessed them. [4]Then he said:

"Praise be to the LORD, the God of Israel, who with his hands has fulfilled what he promised with his mouth to my father David. For he said, [5]'Since the day I brought my people out of Egypt, I have not chosen a city in any tribe of Israel to have a temple built so that my Name might be there, nor have I chosen anyone to be ruler over my people Israel. [6]But now I have chosen Jerusalem for my Name to be there, and I have chosen David to rule my people Israel.'

[7]"My father David had it in his heart to build a temple for the Name of the LORD, the God of Israel. [8]But the LORD said to my father David, 'You did well to have it in your heart to build a temple for my Name. [9]Nevertheless, you are not the one to build the temple, but your son, who is your own flesh and blood—he is the one who will build the temple for my Name.'

[10]"The LORD has kept the promise he made. I have succeeded David my father and now I sit on the throne of Israel, just as the LORD promised, and I have built the temple for the Name of the LORD, the God of Israel. [11]There I have placed the ark, in which is the covenant of the LORD that he made with the people of Israel."

Solomon's Prayer of Dedication

[12]Then Solomon stood before the altar of the LORD in front of the whole assembly of Israel and spread out his hands. [13]Now he had made a bronze platform, five cubits long, five cubits wide and three cubits high,[a] and had placed it in the center of the outer court. He stood on the platform and then knelt down before the whole assembly of Israel and spread out his hands toward heaven. [14]He said:

"LORD, the God of Israel, there is no God like you in heaven or on earth—you who keep your covenant of love with your servants who continue wholeheartedly in your way. [15]You have kept your promise to your servant David my father; with your mouth you have promised and with your hand you have fulfilled it—as it is today.

[16]"Now LORD, the God of Israel, keep for your servant David my father the promises you made to him when you said, 'You shall never fail to have a successor to sit before me on the throne of Israel, if only your descendants are careful in all they do to walk before me according to my law, as you have done.' [17]And now, LORD, the God of Israel, let your word that you promised your servant David come true.

[18]"But will God really dwell on earth with human beings? The heavens, even the highest heavens, cannot contain you. How much less this temple I have built! [19]Yet, LORD my God, give attention to your servant's prayer and his plea for mercy. Hear the cry and the prayer that your servant is praying in your presence. [20]May your eyes be open toward this temple day and night, this place of which you said you would put your Name there. May you hear the prayer your servant prays toward this place. [21]Hear the supplications of your servant and of your people Israel when they pray toward this place. Hear from heaven, your dwelling place; and when you hear, forgive.

[22]"When anyone wrongs their neighbor and is required to take an oath and they come and swear the oath before your altar in this temple, [23]then hear from heaven and act. Judge between your servants, condemning the guilty and bringing down on their heads what they have done, and vindicating the innocent by treating them in accordance with their innocence.

[24]"When your people Israel have been defeated by an enemy because they have sinned against you and when they turn back and give praise to your name, praying and making supplication before you in this temple, [25]then hear from heaven and forgive the sin of your people Israel and bring them back to the land you gave to them and their ancestors.

[26]"When the heavens are shut up and there is no rain because your people have sinned against you, and when they pray toward this place and give praise to your name and turn from their sin

---

[a] 13 That is, about 7 1/2 feet long and wide and 4 1/2 feet high or about 2.3 meters long and wide and 1.4 meters high

because you have afflicted them, ²⁷ then hear from heaven and forgive the sin of your servants, your people Israel. Teach them the right way to live, and send rain on the land you gave your people for an inheritance.

²⁸ "When famine or plague comes to the land, or blight or mildew, locusts or grasshoppers, or when enemies besiege them in any of their cities, whatever disaster or disease may come, ²⁹ and when a prayer or plea is made by anyone among your people Israel—being aware of their afflictions and pains, and spreading out their hands toward this temple— ³⁰ then hear from heaven, your dwelling place. Forgive, and deal with everyone according to all they do, since you know their hearts (for you alone know the human heart), ³¹ so that they will fear you and walk in obedience to you all the time they live in the land you gave our ancestors.

³² "As for foreigners who do not belong to your people Israel but have come from a distant land because of your great name and your mighty hand and your outstretched arm—when they come and pray toward this temple, ³³ then hear from heaven, your dwelling place. Do whatever the foreigner asks of you, so that all the peoples of the earth may know your name and fear you, as do your own people Israel, and may know that this house I have built bears your Name.

³⁴ "When your people go to war against their enemies, wherever you send them, and when they pray to you toward this city you have chosen and the temple I have built for your Name, ³⁵ then hear from heaven their prayer and their plea, and uphold their cause.

³⁶ "When they sin against you—for there is no one who does not sin—and you become angry with them and give them over to the enemy, who takes them captive to a land far away or near; ³⁷ and if they have a change of heart in the land where they are held captive, and repent and plead with you in the land of their captivity and say, 'We have sinned, we have done wrong and acted wickedly'; ³⁸ and if they turn back to you with all their heart and soul in the land of their captivity where they were taken, and pray toward the land you gave their ancestors, toward the city you have chosen and toward the temple I have built for your Name; ³⁹ then from heaven, your dwelling place, hear their prayer and their pleas, and uphold their cause. And forgive your people, who have sinned against you.

⁴⁰ "Now, my God, may your eyes be open and your ears attentive to the prayers offered in this place.

⁴¹ "Now arise, Lord God, and come to your resting place,
 you and the ark of your might.
May your priests, Lord God, be clothed with salvation,
 may your faithful people rejoice in your goodness.
⁴² Lord God, do not reject your anointed one.
 Remember the great love promised to David your servant."

The Dedication of the Temple

7 When Solomon finished praying, fire came down from heaven and consumed the burnt offering and the sacrifices, and the glory of the Lord filled the temple. ² The priests could not enter the temple of the Lord because the glory of the Lord filled it. ³ When all the Israelites saw the fire coming down and the glory of the Lord above the temple, they knelt on the pavement with their faces to the ground, and they worshiped and gave thanks to the Lord, saying,

"He is good;
 his love endures forever."

⁴ Then the king and all the people offered sacrifices before the Lord. ⁵ And King Solomon offered a sacrifice of twenty-two thousand head of cattle and a hundred and twenty thousand sheep and goats. So the king and all the people dedicated the temple of God. ⁶ The priests took their positions, as did the Levites with the Lord's musical instruments, which King David had made for praising the Lord and which were used when he gave thanks, saying, "His love endures forever." Opposite the Levites, the priests blew their trumpets, and all the Israelites were standing.

[7]Solomon consecrated the middle part of the courtyard in front of the temple of the LORD, and there he offered burnt offerings and the fat of the fellowship offerings, because the bronze altar he had made could not hold the burnt offerings, the grain offerings and the fat portions.

[8]So Solomon observed the festival at that time for seven days, and all Israel with him—a vast assembly, people from Lebo Hamath to the Wadi of Egypt. [9]On the eighth day they held an assembly, for they had celebrated the dedication of the altar for seven days and the festival for seven days more. [10]On the twenty-third day of the seventh month he sent the people to their homes, joyful and glad in heart for the good things the LORD had done for David and Solomon and for his people Israel.

The LORD Appears to Solomon

[11]When Solomon had finished the temple of the LORD and the royal palace, and had succeeded in carrying out all he had in mind to do in the temple of the LORD and in his own palace, [12]the LORD appeared to him at night and said:

"I have heard your prayer and have chosen this place for myself as a temple for sacrifices.

[13]"When I shut up the heavens so that there is no rain, or command locusts to devour the land or send a plague among my people, [14]if my people, who are called by my name, will humble themselves and pray and seek my face and turn from their wicked ways, then I will hear from heaven, and I will forgive their sin and will heal their land. [15]Now my eyes will be open and my ears attentive to the prayers offered in this place. [16]I have chosen and consecrated this temple so that my Name may be there forever. My eyes and my heart will always be there.

[17]"As for you, if you walk before me faithfully as David your father did, and do all I command, and observe my decrees and laws, [18]I will establish your royal throne, as I covenanted with David your father when I said, 'You shall never fail to have a successor to rule over Israel.'

[19]"But if you[a] turn away and forsake the decrees and commands I have given you[a] and go off to serve other gods and worship them, [20]then I will uproot Israel from my land, which I have given them, and will reject this temple I have consecrated for my Name. I will make it a byword and an object of ridicule among all peoples. [21]This temple will become a heap of rubble. All[b] who pass by will be appalled and say, 'Why has the LORD done such a thing to this land and to this temple?' [22]People will answer, 'Because they have forsaken the LORD, the God of their ancestors, who brought them out of Egypt, and have embraced other gods, worshiping and serving them—that is why he brought all this disaster on them.'"

553

atissue: guilt

7:13–14 What one sin from your past haunts you? Perhaps you fall into the more than 40 percent of women who've had an abortion. Perhaps you believed that it was your body, your choice. Perhaps you were told it would be hard, but you'd move on and forget. But you've never forgotten. For this sin or any other, do you feel like you crossed a line with God, a line past which he doesn't forgive? If you humble yourself, seek God and turn from your sin, you'll discover that he will do even more than forgive you—he'll heal you and make you whole.

Solomon's Other Activities

8 At the end of twenty years, during which Solomon built the temple of the LORD and his own palace, [2]Solomon rebuilt the villages that Hiram[c] had given him, and settled Israelites in them. [3]Solomon then went to Hamath Zobah and captured it. [4]He also built up Tadmor in the desert and all the store cities he had built in Hamath. [5]He rebuilt Upper Beth Horon and Lower Beth Horon as fortified cities, with walls and with gates and bars, [6]as well as Baalath and all his store cities, and all the cities for his chariots and for his horses[d]—whatever he desired to build in Jerusalem, in Lebanon and throughout all the territory he ruled.

---

[a] *19 The Hebrew is plural.*   [b] *21 See some Septuagint manuscripts, Old Latin, Syriac, Arabic and Targum; Hebrew And though this temple is now so imposing, all*   [c] *2 Hebrew Huram, a variant of Hiram; also in verse 18*   [d] *6 Or charioteers*

⁷There were still people left from the Hittites, Amorites, Perizzites, Hivites and Jebusites (these people were not Israelites). ⁸Solomon conscripted the descendants of all these people remaining in the land—whom the Israelites had not destroyed—to serve as slave labor, as it is to this day. ⁹But Solomon did not make slaves of the Israelites for his work; they were his fighting men, commanders of his captains, and commanders of his chariots and charioteers. ¹⁰They were also King Solomon's chief officials—two hundred and fifty officials supervising the men.

¹¹Solomon brought Pharaoh's daughter up from the City of David to the palace he had built for her, for he said, "My wife must not live in the palace of David king of Israel, because the places the ark of the Lord has entered are holy."

¹²On the altar of the Lord that he had built in front of the portico, Solomon sacrificed burnt offerings to the Lord, ¹³according to the daily requirement for offerings commanded by Moses for the Sabbaths, the New Moons and the three annual festivals—the Festival of Unleavened Bread, the Festival of Weeks and the Festival of Tabernacles. ¹⁴In keeping with the ordinance of his father David, he appointed the divisions of the priests for their duties, and the Levites to lead the praise and to assist the priests according to each day's requirement. He also appointed the gatekeepers by divisions for the various gates, because this was what David the man of God had ordered. ¹⁵They did not deviate from the king's commands to the priests or to the Levites in any matter, including that of the treasuries.

¹⁶All Solomon's work was carried out, from the day the foundation of the temple of the Lord was laid until its completion. So the temple of the Lord was finished.

¹⁷Then Solomon went to Ezion Geber and Elath on the coast of Edom. ¹⁸And Hiram sent him ships commanded by his own officers, sailors who knew the sea. These, with Solomon's servants, sailed to Ophir and brought back four hundred and fifty talents[a] of gold, which they delivered to King Solomon.

The Queen of Sheba Visits Solomon

9 When the queen of Sheba heard of Solomon's fame, she came to Jerusalem to test him with hard questions. Arriving with a very great caravan—with camels carrying spices, large quantities of gold, and precious stones—she came to Solomon and talked with him about all she had on her mind. ²Solomon answered all her questions; nothing was too hard for him to explain to her. ³When the queen of Sheba saw the wisdom of Solomon, as well as the palace he had built, ⁴the food on his table, the seating of his officials, the attending servants in their robes, the cupbearers in their robes and the burnt offerings he made at[b] the temple of the Lord, she was overwhelmed.

⁵She said to the king, "The report I heard in my own country about your achievements and your wisdom is true. ⁶But I did not believe what they said until I came and saw with my own eyes. Indeed, not even half the greatness of your wisdom was told me; you have far exceeded the report I heard. ⁷How happy your people must be! How happy your officials, who continually stand before you and hear your wisdom! ⁸Praise be to the Lord your God, who has delighted in you and placed you on his throne as king to rule for the Lord your God. Because of the love of your God for Israel and his desire to uphold them forever, he has made you king over them, to maintain justice and righteousness."

⁹Then she gave the king 120 talents[c] of gold, large quantities of spices, and precious stones. There had never been such spices as those the queen of Sheba gave to King Solomon.

¹⁰(The servants of Hiram and the servants of Solomon brought gold from Ophir; they also brought algumwood[d] and precious stones. ¹¹The king used the algumwood to make steps for the temple of the Lord and for the royal palace, and to make harps and lyres for the musicians. Nothing like them had ever been seen in Judah.)

¹²King Solomon gave the queen of Sheba all she desired and asked for; he gave her more than she had brought to him. Then she left and returned with her retinue to her own country.

Solomon's Splendor

¹³The weight of the gold that Solomon received yearly was 666 talents,[e] ¹⁴not including the revenues brought in by merchants and traders. Also all the kings of Arabia and the governors of the territories brought gold and silver to Solomon.

ᵃ *18* That is, about 17 tons or about 15 metric tons   ᵇ *4* Or *and the ascent by which he went up to*   ᶜ *9* That is, about 4 1/2 tons or about 4 metric tons
ᵈ *10* Probably a variant of *almugwood*   ᵉ *13* That is, about 25 tons or about 23 metric tons

¹⁵King Solomon made two hundred large shields of hammered gold; six hundred shekels*ᵃ* of hammered gold went into each shield. ¹⁶He also made three hundred small shields of hammered gold, with three hundred shekels*ᵇ* of gold in each shield. The king put them in the Palace of the Forest of Lebanon.

¹⁷Then the king made a great throne inlaid with ivory and overlaid with pure gold. ¹⁸The throne had six steps, and a footstool of gold was attached to it. On both sides of the seat were armrests, with a lion standing beside each of them. ¹⁹Twelve lions stood on the six steps, one at either end of each step. Nothing like it had ever been made for any other kingdom. ²⁰All King Solomon's goblets were gold, and all the household articles in the Palace of the Forest of Lebanon were pure gold. Nothing was made of silver, because silver was considered of little value in Solomon's day. ²¹The king had a fleet of trading ships*ᶜ* manned by Hiram's*ᵈ* servants. Once every three years it returned, carrying gold, silver and ivory, and apes and baboons.

²²King Solomon was greater in riches and wisdom than all the other kings of the earth. ²³All the kings of the earth sought audience with Solomon to hear the wisdom God had put in his heart. ²⁴Year after year, everyone who came brought a gift—articles of silver and gold, and robes, weapons and spices, and horses and mules.

²⁵Solomon had four thousand stalls for horses and chariots, and twelve thousand horses,*ᵉ* which he kept in the chariot cities and also with him in Jerusalem. ²⁶He ruled over all the kings from the Euphrates River to the land of the Philistines, as far as the border of Egypt. ²⁷The king made silver as common in Jerusalem as stones, and cedar as plentiful as sycamore-fig trees in the foothills. ²⁸Solomon's horses were imported from Egypt and from all other countries.

Solomon's Death

²⁹As for the other events of Solomon's reign, from beginning to end, are they not written in the records of Nathan the prophet, in the prophecy of Ahijah the Shilonite and in the visions of Iddo the seer concerning Jeroboam son of Nebat? ³⁰Solomon reigned in Jerusalem over all Israel forty years. ³¹Then he rested with his ancestors and was buried in the city of David his father. And Rehoboam his son succeeded him as king.

Israel Rebels Against Rehoboam

10 Rehoboam went to Shechem, for all Israel had gone there to make him king. ²When Jeroboam son of Nebat heard this (he was in Egypt, where he had fled from King Solomon), he returned from Egypt. ³So they sent for Jeroboam, and he and all Israel went to Rehoboam and said to him: ⁴"Your father put a heavy yoke on us, but now lighten the harsh labor and the heavy yoke he put on us, and we will serve you."

⁵Rehoboam answered, "Come back to me in three days." So the people went away.

⁶Then King Rehoboam consulted the elders who had served his father Solomon during his lifetime. "How would you advise me to answer these people?" he asked.

⁷They replied, "If you will be kind to these people and please them and give them a favorable answer, they will always be your servants."

⁸But Rehoboam rejected the advice the elders gave him and consulted the young men who had grown up with him and were serving him. ⁹He asked them, "What is your advice? How should we answer these people who say to me, 'Lighten the yoke your father put on us'?"

¹⁰The young men who had grown up with him replied, "The people have said to you, 'Your father put a heavy yoke on us, but make our yoke lighter.' Now tell them, 'My little finger is thicker than my father's waist. ¹¹My father laid on you a heavy yoke; I will make it even heavier. My father scourged you with whips; I will scourge you with scorpions.'"

¹²Three days later Jeroboam and all the people returned to Rehoboam, as the king had said, "Come back to me in three days." ¹³The king answered them harshly. Rejecting the advice of the elders, ¹⁴he followed the advice of the young men and said, "My father made your yoke heavy; I will make it even heavier. My father scourged you with whips; I will scourge you with scorpions." ¹⁵So the king did not listen to

555

ᵃ 15 That is, about 15 pounds or about 6.9 kilograms   *ᵇ 16* That is, about 7 1/2 pounds or about 3.5 kilograms   *ᶜ 21* Hebrew *of ships that could go to Tarshish*   *ᵈ 21* Hebrew *Huram,* a variant of *Hiram*   *ᵉ 25* Or *charioteers*

myth#30 "SEXUAL TEMPTATION WILL GO AWAY ONCE I'M MARRIED."

I am a happily married woman. Deep down I believe this, but I also keep trying to convince myself its true. I don't know what's wrong with me. I am married to an amazing man, Brian, who is so good to me. We have a healthy sex life. He's very attractive, quite sexy, and I work out to look my best for him too. I'd say I'm sexually fulfilled.

So how do I explain the fantasies I have about my co-worker? Why does my heart jump when he walks in the room? Why do I look my best every morning, not for Brian but for him? What's wrong with me?

I've always been something of a flirt, so I was relieved when I got married. I thought I'd find fulfillment in my marriage. I thought sexual temptation would go away once I got married. Brian and I were so young and in love when we got married—and so ready to be together physically. Fortunately, we were both Christians, and though we had both messed up sexually in our younger, rebellious years, we didn't have sex till we got married. (That felt like an accomplishment!) The first year we were married was sheer bliss.

Eighteen months into our marriage, I was astonished to find old feelings and emotions creeping into my heart and mind. I tried pushing them away, but they kept popping up.

It frightened me when I began to push Brian away for no reason, claiming I was tired or not in the mood. I began to entertain little fantasies in my mind and make unhealthy comparisons between Brian and other men. Silly ones about the Starbucks guy who was always ready with a smile and conversation during my morning java run. Or our Bible study leader who seemed so godly and successful. It devastated me to discover I still had needs that my husband wasn't meeting. And not just sexual needs—things like the need to feel like a woman, to be heard and understood, to feel excited—were all wrapped up in a jumbled mess.

No one really talks about a woman's sexual needs and temptations, but they're just as real as a man's—even if they express themselves in different ways.

—Jo

REALITIES ABOUT SEXUALITY

- While we live in these bodies, we will always face temptation—wedding ring or not. Don't be naïve about the power of the passions God gave you. Treat them as you would electricity—powerful and beneficial when under control, dangerous when left unchecked.

- Married women are less likely to indulge their sexual temptations physically. They tend to fantasize, compare or mentally play out their options—which is still sexual sin (see Matthew 5:28).

- Fantasizing, flirting, etc. Are these actions depriving your husband of the attention he rightfully deserves? First Corinthians 7:1–7 is clear that a married woman's first priority is her husband.

- Be accountable to others regarding your sexuality. Develop accountability with your husband. Are there fantasies, habits, movies, romance novels or other sexual compromises of which he is unaware? Also, confide in a trusted Christian (female!) friend or counselor about unruly passions. You'll be encouraged to know you're not alone—most Christian women struggle with this—and you'll be strengthened through their prayers. Don't try to master sexual temptation alone (see Ecclesiastes 4:9–12).

- As long as we live on this earth, we will never be 100 percent happy or fulfilled, especially by any earthly relationship. We will never be completely fulfilled until we are in heaven with Christ. Our wandering eyes and hearts are looking for something that doesn't exist this side of heaven.

> "It's true that women don't necessarily look lustfully at men. We engage in mental fantasies. We engage in emotional affairs. We engage in unhealthy comparisons of our husbands to other men and become disillusioned."
>
> —Shannon Etheridge

557

> "Be alert and of sober mind. Your enemy the devil prowls around like a roaring lion looking for someone to devour."
>
> 1 PETER 5:8

SEE ALSO

Proverbs 4:25–27
1 Corinthians 10:12–13
1 Peter 5:8–11

For more on **Sexual Temptation**, check the index.

the people, for this turn of events was from God, to fulfill the word the LORD had spoken to Jeroboam son of Nebat through Ahijah the Shilonite.

[16]When all Israel saw that the king refused to listen to them, they answered the king:

> "What share do we have in David,
>   what part in Jesse's son?
> To your tents, Israel!
>   Look after your own house, David!"

So all the Israelites went home. [17]But as for the Israelites who were living in the towns of Judah, Rehoboam still ruled over them.

[18]King Rehoboam sent out Adoniram,[a] who was in charge of forced labor, but the Israelites stoned him to death. King Rehoboam, however, managed to get into his chariot and escape to Jerusalem. [19]So Israel has been in rebellion against the house of David to this day.

11 When Rehoboam arrived in Jerusalem, he mustered the house of Judah and Benjamin—a hundred and eighty thousand able young men—to make war against Israel and to regain the kingdom for Rehoboam.

[2]But this word of the LORD came to Shemaiah the man of God: [3]"Say to Rehoboam son of Solomon king of Judah and to all Israel in Judah and Benjamin, [4]'This is what the LORD says: Do not go up to fight against your fellow Israelites. Go home, every one of you, for this is my doing.'" So they obeyed the words of the LORD and turned back from marching against Jeroboam.

Rehoboam Fortifies Judah

[5]Rehoboam lived in Jerusalem and built up towns for defense in Judah: [6]Bethlehem, Etam, Tekoa, [7]Beth Zur, Soko, Adullam, [8]Gath, Mareshah, Ziph, [9]Adoraim, Lachish, Azekah, [10]Zorah, Aijalon and Hebron. These were fortified cities in Judah and Benjamin. [11]He strengthened their defenses and put commanders in them, with supplies of food, olive oil and wine. [12]He put shields and spears in all the cities, and made them very strong. So Judah and Benjamin were his.

[13]The priests and Levites from all their districts throughout Israel sided with him. [14]The Levites even abandoned their pasturelands and property and came to Judah and Jerusalem, because Jeroboam and his sons had rejected them as priests of the LORD [15]when he appointed his own priests for the high places and for the goat and calf idols he had made. [16]Those from every tribe of Israel who set their hearts on seeking the LORD, the God of Israel, followed the Levites to Jerusalem to offer sacrifices to the LORD, the God of their ancestors. [17]They strengthened the kingdom of Judah and supported Rehoboam son of Solomon three years, following the ways of David and Solomon during this time.

Rehoboam's Family

[18]Rehoboam married Mahalath, who was the daughter of David's son Jerimoth and of Abihail, the daughter of Jesse's son Eliab. [19]She bore him sons: Jeush, Shemariah and Zaham. [20]Then he married Maakah daughter of

558

a tissue: rejection

11:13–17 Rejection hurts—when your boss hands you a pink slip, or your husband walks out on you, or a close friend deserts you. Rejection makes you doubt your abilities, your worth, your purpose in life. But not all rejection is bad. The Levites were rejected by Jeroboam, who wanted to choose his own priests to offer sacrifices to false gods. Painful as the rejection was, it motivated the Levites to move to Jerusalem to serve God there—a change they wouldn't have made otherwise. You may never welcome rejection, but you can trust that God will use even that to direct your life toward him.

---

[a] 18 Hebrew *Hadoram*, a variant of *Adoniram*

Absalom, who bore him Abijah, Attai, Ziza and Shelomith. ²¹Rehoboam loved Maakah daughter of Absalom more than any of his other wives and concubines. In all, he had eighteen wives and sixty concubines, twenty-eight sons and sixty daughters.

²²Rehoboam appointed Abijah son of Maakah as crown prince among his brothers, in order to make him king. ²³He acted wisely, dispersing some of his sons throughout the districts of Judah and Benjamin, and to all the fortified cities. He gave them abundant provisions and took many wives for them.

Shishak Attacks Jerusalem

12 After Rehoboam's position as king was established and he had become strong, he and all Israel[a] with him abandoned the law of the LORD. ²Because they had been unfaithful to the LORD, Shishak king of Egypt attacked Jerusalem in the fifth year of King Rehoboam. ³With twelve hundred chariots and sixty thousand horsemen and the innumerable troops of Libyans, Sukkites and Cushites[b] that came with him from Egypt, ⁴he captured the fortified cities of Judah and came as far as Jerusalem.

⁵Then the prophet Shemaiah came to Rehoboam and to the leaders of Judah who had assembled in Jerusalem for fear of Shishak, and he said to them, "This is what the LORD says, 'You have abandoned me; therefore, I now abandon you to Shishak.'"

⁶The leaders of Israel and the king humbled themselves and said, "The LORD is just."

⁷When the LORD saw that they humbled themselves, this word of the LORD came to Shemaiah: "Since they have humbled themselves, I will not destroy them but will soon give them deliverance. My wrath will not be poured out on Jerusalem through Shishak. ⁸They will, however, become subject to him, so that they may learn the difference between serving me and serving the kings of other lands."

HE IS: the perfect disciplinarian

12:7-8 God disciplined the people of Judah by allowing the Egyptians to invade their land. Realizing they were under divine justice, the Jewish rulers humbled themselves. God accepted their repentance and meted out chastisement but not destruction. God is *the perfect disciplinarian*, who wisely blends justice and mercy.

When you're called on to discipline those under your authority (your children, students or people who work for you), follow God's model. Sometimes love calls you to allow people to reap the consequences of their choices. Yet you must also be quick to show mercy, just as God is when you come running back to him (see James 2:12–13).

For the next He Is, go to p. 561.

⁹When Shishak king of Egypt attacked Jerusalem, he carried off the treasures of the temple of the LORD and the treasures of the royal palace. He took everything, including the gold shields Solomon had made. ¹⁰So King Rehoboam made bronze shields to replace them and assigned these to the commanders of the guard on duty at the entrance to the royal palace. ¹¹Whenever the king went to the LORD's temple, the guards went with him, bearing the shields, and afterward they returned them to the guardroom.

¹²Because Rehoboam humbled himself, the LORD's anger turned from him, and he was not totally destroyed. Indeed, there was some good in Judah.

¹³King Rehoboam established himself firmly in Jerusalem and continued as king. He was forty-one years old when he became king, and he reigned seventeen years in Jerusalem, the city the LORD had chosen out of all the tribes of Israel in which to put his Name. His mother's name was Naamah; she was an Ammonite. ¹⁴He did evil because he had not set his heart on seeking the LORD.

¹⁵As for the events of Rehoboam's reign, from beginning to end, are they not written in the records of Shemaiah the prophet and of Iddo the seer that deal with genealogies? There was continual warfare

---

[a] *1* That is, Judah, as frequently in 2 Chronicles   [b] *3* That is, people from the upper Nile region

between Rehoboam and Jeroboam. ¹⁶Rehoboam rested with his ancestors and was buried in the City of David. And Abijah his son succeeded him as king.

Abijah King of Judah

13 In the eighteenth year of the reign of Jeroboam, Abijah became king of Judah, ²and he reigned in Jerusalem three years. His mother's name was Maakah,ᵃ a daughterᵇ of Uriel of Gibeah.

There was war between Abijah and Jeroboam. ³Abijah went into battle with an army of four hundred thousand able fighting men, and Jeroboam drew up a battle line against him with eight hundred thousand able troops.

⁴Abijah stood on Mount Zemaraim, in the hill country of Ephraim, and said, "Jeroboam and all Israel, listen to me! ⁵Don't you know that the Lord, the God of Israel, has given the kingship of Israel to David and his descendants forever by a covenant of salt? ⁶Yet Jeroboam son of Nebat, an official of Solomon son of David, rebelled against his master. ⁷Some worthless scoundrels gathered around him and opposed Rehoboam son of Solomon when he was young and indecisive and not strong enough to resist them.

⁸"And now you plan to resist the kingdom of the Lord, which is in the hands of David's descendants. You are indeed a vast army and have with you the golden calves that Jeroboam made to be your gods. ⁹But didn't you drive out the priests of the Lord, the sons of Aaron, and the Levites, and make priests of your own as the peoples of other lands do? Whoever comes to consecrate himself with a young bull and seven rams may become a priest of what are not gods.

¹⁰"As for us, the Lord is our God, and we have not forsaken him. The priests who serve the Lord are sons of Aaron, and the Levites assist them. ¹¹Every morning and evening they present burnt offerings and fragrant incense to the Lord. They set out the bread on the ceremonially clean table and light the lamps on the gold lampstand every evening. We are observing the requirements of the Lord our God. But you have forsaken him. ¹²God is with us; he is our leader. His priests with their trumpets will sound the battle cry against you. People of Israel, do not fight against the Lord, the God of your ancestors, for you will not succeed."

¹³Now Jeroboam had sent troops around to the rear, so that while he was in front of Judah the ambush was behind them. ¹⁴Judah turned and saw that they were being attacked at both front and rear. Then they cried out to the Lord. The priests blew their trumpets ¹⁵and the men of Judah raised the battle cry. At the sound of their battle cry, God routed Jeroboam and all Israel before Abijah and Judah. ¹⁶The Israelites fled before Judah, and God delivered them into their hands. ¹⁷Abijah and his troops inflicted heavy losses on them, so that there were five hundred thousand casualties among Israel's able men. ¹⁸The Israelites were subdued on that occasion, and the men of Judah were victorious because they relied on the Lord, the God of their ancestors.

¹⁹Abijah pursued Jeroboam and took from him the towns of Bethel, Jeshanah and Ephron, with their surrounding villages. ²⁰Jeroboam did not regain power during the time of Abijah. And the Lord struck him down and he died.

²¹But Abijah grew in strength. He married fourteen wives and had twenty-two sons and sixteen daughters.

²²The other events of Abijah's reign, what he did and what he said, are written in the annotations of the prophet Iddo.

14 *And Abijah rested with his ancestors and was buried in the City of David. Asa his son succeeded him as king, and in his days the country was at peace for ten years.

Asa King of Judah

*²Asa did what was good and right in the eyes of the Lord his God. ³He removed the foreign altars and the high places, smashed the sacred stones and cut down the Asherah poles.ᶜ ⁴He commanded Judah to seek the Lord, the God of their ancestors, and to obey his laws and commands. ⁵He removed the high

---

ᵃ 2 Most Septuagint manuscripts and Syriac (see also 2 Chron. 11:20 and 1 Kings 15:2); Hebrew *Micaiah*   ᵇ 2 Or *granddaughter*   ᶜ 3 That is, wooden symbols of the goddess Asherah; here and elsewhere in 2 Chronicles

* 14:1 is numbered 13:23 in Hebrew texts.   * 14:2-15 is numbered 14:1-14 in Hebrew texts.

560

places and incense altars in every town in Judah, and the kingdom was at peace under him. ⁶He built up the fortified cities of Judah, since the land was at peace. No one was at war with him during those years, for the LORD gave him rest.

⁷"Let us build up these towns," he said to Judah, "and put walls around them, with towers, gates and bars. The land is still ours, because we have sought the LORD our God; we sought him and he has given us rest on every side." So they built and prospered.

⁸Asa had an army of three hundred thousand men from Judah, equipped with large shields and with spears, and two hundred and eighty thousand from Benjamin, armed with small shields and with bows. All these were brave fighting men.

⁹Zerah the Cushite marched out against them with an army of thousands upon thousands and three hundred chariots, and came as far as Mareshah. ¹⁰Asa went out to meet him, and they took up battle positions in the Valley of Zephathah near Mareshah.

¹¹Then Asa called to the LORD his God and said, "LORD, there is no one like you to help the powerless against the mighty. Help us, LORD our God, for we rely on you, and in your name we have come against this vast army. LORD, you are our God; do not let mere mortals prevail against you."

¹²The LORD struck down the Cushites before Asa and Judah. The Cushites fled, ¹³and Asa and his army pursued them as far as Gerar. Such a great number of Cushites fell that they could not recover; they were crushed before the LORD and his forces. The men of Judah carried off a large amount of plunder. ¹⁴They destroyed all the villages around Gerar, for the terror of the LORD had fallen on them. They plundered all these villages, since there was much booty there. ¹⁵They also attacked the camps of the herders and carried off droves of sheep and goats and camels. Then they returned to Jerusalem.

Asa's Reform

15 The Spirit of God came on Azariah son of Oded. ²He went out to meet Asa and said to him, "Listen to me, Asa and all Judah and Benjamin. The LORD is with you when you are with him. If you seek him, he will be found by you, but if you forsake him, he will forsake you. ³For a long time Israel was without the true God, without a priest to teach and without the law. ⁴But in their distress they turned to the LORD, the God of Israel, and sought him, and he was found by them. ⁵In those days it was not safe to travel about, for all the inhabitants of the lands were in great turmoil. ⁶One nation was being crushed by another and one city by another, because God was troubling them with every kind of distress. ⁷But as for you, be strong and do not give up, for your work will be rewarded."

561

HE IS: findable

15:1–7 Following a miraculous victory by King Asa's armies, God's prophet sought out the king to remind him of an important truth: If you seek God, he'll let you find him. The moral to Asa's story is simple: God is *findable*—he is with those who search for him and recognize their need for him.

If you're experiencing a time of triumph, learn a lesson from Asa. God is *findable*, but you must fight the temptation (which often follows success) of dropping your spiritual guard. You may *feel* strong now, but you'll never *be* spiritually strong until you seek—and find—the Lord.

For the next He Is, go to p. 568.

⁸When Asa heard these words and the prophecy of Azariah son of*ᵃ* Oded the prophet, he took courage. He removed the detestable idols from the whole land of Judah and Benjamin and from the towns he had captured in the hills of Ephraim. He repaired the altar of the LORD that was in front of the portico of the LORD's temple.

ᵃ 8 Vulgate and Syriac (see also Septuagint and verse 1); Hebrew does not have Azariah son of.

[9]Then he assembled all Judah and Benjamin and the people from Ephraim, Manasseh and Simeon who had settled among them, for large numbers had come over to him from Israel when they saw that the LORD his God was with him.

[10]They assembled at Jerusalem in the third month of the fifteenth year of Asa's reign. [11]At that time they sacrificed to the LORD seven hundred head of cattle and seven thousand sheep and goats from the plunder they had brought back. [12]They entered into a covenant to seek the LORD, the God of their ancestors, with all their heart and soul. [13]All who would not seek the LORD, the God of Israel, were to be put to death, whether small or great, man or woman. [14]They took an oath to the LORD with loud acclamation, with shouting and with trumpets and horns. [15]All Judah rejoiced about the oath because they had sworn it wholeheartedly. They sought God eagerly, and he was found by them. So the LORD gave them rest on every side.

[16]King Asa also deposed his grandmother Maakah from her position as queen mother, because she had made a repulsive image for the worship of Asherah. Asa cut it down, broke it up and burned it in the Kidron Valley. [17]Although he did not remove the high places from Israel, Asa's heart was fully committed ₜto the LORDﻻ all his life. [18]He brought into the temple of God the silver and gold and the articles that he and his father had dedicated.

[19]There was no more war until the thirty-fifth year of Asa's reign.

Asa's Last Years

16 In the thirty-sixth year of Asa's reign Baasha king of Israel went up against Judah and fortified Ramah to prevent anyone from leaving or entering the territory of Asa king of Judah.

[2]Asa then took the silver and gold out of the treasuries of the LORD's temple and of his own palace and sent it to Ben-Hadad king of Aram, who was ruling in Damascus. [3]"Let there be a treaty between me and you," he said, "as there was between my father and your father. See, I am sending you silver and gold. Now break your treaty with Baasha king of Israel so he will withdraw from me."

[4]Ben-Hadad agreed with King Asa and sent the commanders of his forces against the towns of Israel. They conquered Ijon, Dan, Abel Maim[a] and all the store cities of Naphtali. [5]When Baasha heard this, he stopped building Ramah and abandoned his work. [6]Then King Asa brought all the men of Judah, and they carried away from Ramah the stones and timber Baasha had been using. With them he built up Geba and Mizpah.

[7]At that time Hanani the seer came to Asa king of Judah and said to him: "Because you relied on the king of Aram and not on the LORD your God, the army of the king of Aram has escaped from your hand. [8]Were not the Cushites[b] and Libyans a mighty army with great numbers of chariots and horsemen[c]? Yet when you relied on the LORD, he delivered them into your hand. [9]For the eyes of the LORD range throughout the earth to strengthen those whose hearts are fully committed to him. You have done a foolish thing, and from now on you will be at war."

[10]Asa was angry with the seer because of this; he was so enraged that he put him in prison. At the same time Asa brutally oppressed some of the people.

[11]The events of Asa's reign, from beginning to end, are written in the book of the kings of Judah and Israel. [12]In the thirty-ninth year of his reign Asa was afflicted with a disease in his feet. Though his disease was severe, even in his illness he did not seek help from the LORD, but only from the physicians. [13]Then in the forty-first year of his reign Asa died and rested with his ancestors. [14]They buried him in the tomb that he had cut out for himself in the City of David. They laid him on a bier covered with spices and various blended perfumes, and they made a huge fire in his honor.

Jehoshaphat King of Judah

17 Jehoshaphat his son succeeded him as king and strengthened himself against Israel. [2]He stationed troops in all the fortified cities of Judah and put garrisons in Judah and in the towns of Ephraim that his father Asa had captured.

[3]The LORD was with Jehoshaphat because he followed the ways of his father David before him. He did not consult the Baals [4]but sought the God of his father and followed his commands rather than the prac-

---

[a] 4 Also known as *Abel Beth Maakah* [b] 8 That is, people from the upper Nile region [c] 8 Or *charioteers*

tices of Israel. ⁵The LORD established the kingdom under his control; and all Judah brought gifts to Jehoshaphat, so that he had great wealth and honor. ⁶His heart was devoted to the ways of the LORD; furthermore, he removed the high places and the Asherah poles from Judah.

⁷In the third year of his reign he sent his officials Ben-Hail, Obadiah, Zechariah, Nethanel and Micaiah to teach in the towns of Judah. ⁸With them were certain Levites—Shemaiah, Nethaniah, Zebadiah, Asahel, Shemiramoth, Jehonathan, Adonijah, Tobijah and Tob-Adonijah—and the priests Elishama and Jehoram. ⁹They taught throughout Judah, taking with them the Book of the Law of the LORD; they went around to all the towns of Judah and taught the people.

¹⁰The fear of the LORD fell on all the kingdoms of the lands surrounding Judah, so that they did not make war with Jehoshaphat. ¹¹Some Philistines brought Jehoshaphat gifts and silver as tribute, and the Arabs brought him flocks: seven thousand seven hundred rams and seven thousand seven hundred goats.

¹²Jehoshaphat became more and more powerful; he built forts and store cities in Judah ¹³and had large supplies in the towns of Judah. He also kept experienced fighting men in Jerusalem. ¹⁴Their enrollment by families was as follows:

From Judah, commanders of units of 1,000:
Adnah the commander, with 300,000 fighting men;
¹⁵next, Jehohanan the commander, with 280,000;
¹⁶next, Amasiah son of Zikri, who volunteered himself for the service of the LORD, with 200,000.
¹⁷From Benjamin:
Eliada, a valiant soldier, with 200,000 men armed with bows and shields;
¹⁸next, Jehozabad, with 180,000 men armed for battle.

¹⁹These were the men who served the king, besides those he stationed in the fortified cities throughout Judah.

Micaiah Prophesies Against Ahab

18 Now Jehoshaphat had great wealth and honor, and he allied himself with Ahab by marriage. ²Some years later he went down to see Ahab in Samaria. Ahab slaughtered many sheep and cattle for him and the people with him and urged him to attack Ramoth Gilead. ³Ahab king of Israel asked Jehoshaphat king of Judah, "Will you go with me against Ramoth Gilead?"

Jehoshaphat replied, "I am as you are, and my people as your people; we will join you in the war." ⁴But Jehoshaphat also said to the king of Israel, "First seek the counsel of the LORD."

⁵So the king of Israel brought together the prophets—four hundred men—and asked them, "Shall we go to war against Ramoth Gilead, or shall I not?"

"Go," they answered, "for God will give it into the king's hand."

⁶But Jehoshaphat asked, "Is there no longer a prophet of the LORD here whom we can inquire of?"

⁷The king of Israel answered Jehoshaphat, "There is still one through whom we can inquire of the LORD, but I hate him because he never prophesies anything good about me, but always bad. He is Micaiah son of Imlah."

"The king should not say such a thing," Jehoshaphat replied.

⁸So the king of Israel called one of his officials and said, "Bring Micaiah son of Imlah at once."

at issue: relationships

18:1 You may not realize how important it is to make good alliances. Think about it. A corrupt business partner could send you to jail. A close friend who likes to bar-hop could cause you to lower your standards. An unsaved husband could divide your family. Jehoshaphat made a poor choice in allying himself with Ahab—a well-known evil king. Who are your business partners, closest friends and mentors? Take care that your most important relationships draw you closer to God instead of pulling you away from him.

⁹Dressed in their royal robes, the king of Israel and Jehoshaphat king of Judah were sitting on their thrones at the threshing floor by the entrance of the gate of Samaria, with all the prophets prophesying before them. ¹⁰Now Zedekiah son of Kenaanah had made iron horns, and he declared, "This is what the LORD says: 'With these you will gore the Arameans until they are destroyed.'"

¹¹All the other prophets were prophesying the same thing. "Attack Ramoth Gilead and be victorious," they said, "for the LORD will give it into the king's hand."

¹²The messenger who had gone to summon Micaiah said to him, "Look, the other prophets without exception are predicting success for the king. Let your word agree with theirs, and speak favorably."

¹³But Micaiah said, "As surely as the LORD lives, I can tell him only what my God says."

¹⁴When he arrived, the king asked him, "Micaiah, shall we go to war against Ramoth Gilead, or shall I not?"

"Attack and be victorious," he answered, "for they will be given into your hand."

¹⁵The king said to him, "How many times must I make you swear to tell me nothing but the truth in the name of the LORD?"

¹⁶Then Micaiah answered, "I saw all Israel scattered on the hills like sheep without a shepherd, and the LORD said, 'These people have no master. Let each one go home in peace.'"

¹⁷The king of Israel said to Jehoshaphat, "Didn't I tell you that he never prophesies anything good about me, but only bad?"

¹⁸Micaiah continued, "Therefore hear the word of the LORD: I saw the LORD sitting on his throne with all the host of heaven standing on his right and on his left. ¹⁹And the LORD said, 'Who will entice Ahab king of Israel into attacking Ramoth Gilead and going to his death there?'

"One suggested this, and another that. ²⁰Finally, a spirit came forward, stood before the LORD and said, 'I will entice him.'

"'By what means?' the LORD asked.

²¹"'I will go and be a lying spirit in the mouths of all his prophets,' he said.

"'You will succeed in enticing him,' said the LORD. 'Go and do it.'

²²"So now the LORD has put a lying spirit in the mouths of these prophets of yours. The LORD has decreed disaster for you."

²³Then Zedekiah son of Kenaanah went up and slapped Micaiah in the face. "Which way did the spirit from*ᵃ* the LORD go when he went from me to speak to you?" he asked.

²⁴Micaiah replied, "You will find out on the day you go to hide in an inner room."

²⁵The king of Israel then ordered, "Take Micaiah and send him back to Amon the ruler of the city and to Joash the king's son, ²⁶and say, 'This is what the king says: Put this fellow in prison and give him nothing but bread and water until I return safely.'"

²⁷Micaiah declared, "If you ever return safely, the LORD has not spoken through me." Then he added, "Mark my words, all you people!"

Ahab Killed at Ramoth Gilead

²⁸So the king of Israel and Jehoshaphat king of Judah went up to Ramoth Gilead. ²⁹The king of Israel said to Jehoshaphat, "I will enter the battle in disguise, but you wear your royal robes." So the king of Israel disguised himself and went into battle.

³⁰Now the king of Aram had ordered his chariot commanders, "Do not fight with anyone, small or great, except the king of Israel." ³¹When the chariot commanders saw Jehoshaphat, they thought, "This is the king of Israel." So they turned to attack him, but Jehoshaphat cried out, and the LORD helped him. God drew them away from him, ³²for when the chariot commanders saw that he was not the king of Israel, they stopped pursuing him.

³³But someone drew his bow at random and hit the king of Israel between the breastplate and the scale armor. The king told the chariot driver, "Wheel around and get me out of the fighting. I've been wounded." ³⁴All day long the battle raged, and the king of Israel propped himself up in his chariot facing the Arameans until evening. Then at sunset he died.

ᵃ 23 Or *Spirit of*

19 When Jehoshaphat king of Judah returned safely to his palace in Jerusalem, ²Jehu the seer, the son of Hanani, went out to meet him and said to the king, "Should you help the wicked and love*ª* those who hate the LORD? Because of this, the wrath of the LORD is on you. ³There is, however, some good in you, for you have rid the land of the Asherah poles and have set your heart on seeking God."

Jehoshaphat Appoints Judges

⁴Jehoshaphat lived in Jerusalem, and he went out again among the people from Beersheba to the hill country of Ephraim and turned them back to the LORD, the God of their ancestors. ⁵He appointed judges in the land, in each of the fortified cities of Judah. ⁶He told them, "Consider carefully what you do, because you are not judging for mere mortals but for the LORD, who is with you whenever you give a verdict. ⁷Now let the fear of the LORD be on you. Judge carefully, for with the LORD our God there is no injustice or partiality or bribery."

⁸In Jerusalem also, Jehoshaphat appointed some of the Levites, priests and heads of Israelite families to administer the law of the LORD and to settle disputes. And they lived in Jerusalem. ⁹He gave them these orders: "You must serve faithfully and wholeheartedly in the fear of the LORD. ¹⁰In every case that comes before you from your people who live in the cities—whether bloodshed or other concerns of the law, commands, decrees or regulations—you are to warn them not to sin against the LORD; otherwise his wrath will come on you and your people. Do this, and you will not sin.

¹¹"Amariah the chief priest will be over you in any matter concerning the LORD, and Zebadiah son of Ishmael, the leader of the tribe of Judah, will be over you in any matter concerning the king, and the Levites will serve as officials before you. Act with courage, and may the LORD be with those who do well."

Jehoshaphat Defeats Moab and Ammon

20 After this, the Moabites and Ammonites with some of the Meunites*ᵇ* came to make war on Jehoshaphat.

²Some people came and told Jehoshaphat, "A vast army is coming against you from Edom,*ᶜ* from the other side of the Dead Sea. It is already in Hazezon Tamar" (that is, En Gedi). ³Alarmed, Jehoshaphat resolved to inquire of the LORD, and he proclaimed a fast for all Judah. ⁴The people of Judah came together to seek help from the LORD; indeed, they came from every town in Judah to seek him.

⁵Then Jehoshaphat stood up in the assembly of Judah and Jerusalem at the temple of the LORD in the front of the new courtyard ⁶and said:

"LORD, the God of our ancestors, are you not the God who is in heaven? You rule over all the kingdoms of the nations. Power and might are in your hand, and no one can withstand you. ⁷Our God, did you not drive out the inhabitants of this land before your people Israel and give it forever to the descendants of Abraham your friend? ⁸They have lived in it and have built in it a sanctuary for your Name, saying, ⁹'If calamity comes upon us, whether the sword of judgment, or plague or famine, we will stand in your presence before this temple that bears your Name and will cry out to you in our distress, and you will hear us and save us.'

¹⁰"But now here are men from Ammon, Moab and Mount Seir, whose territory you would not allow Israel to invade when they came from Egypt; so they turned away from them and did not destroy them. ¹¹See how they are repaying us by coming to drive us out of the possession you gave us as an inheritance. ¹²Our God, will you not judge them? For we have no power to face this vast army that is attacking us. We do not know what to do, but our eyes are on you."

"conversations"

favoritism «» 19:7

1» In what situations have you seen partiality for a certain group of people displayed?

2» Do you think our modern court decisions are just and impartial?

3» When have you made an unfair judgment about another person?

For more on favoritism, check the index. For the next Conversations, go to p. 569.

565

ª 2 Or and make alliances with   ᵇ 1 Some Septuagint manuscripts; Hebrew Ammonites   ᶜ 2 One Hebrew manuscript; most Hebrew manuscripts, Septuagint and Vulgate Aram

myth# 37 "I'M NOT HURTING ANYONE ELSE."

"How does the sanctity of my marriage affect the sanctity of yours?" the sign read. In the midst of all the media coverage on the issue of gay marriage, a photo of a lesbian and her partner holding up that sign gave me pause. Their question sounded very familiar. In fact, it sounded like the basis of a number of family discussions I've been a part of over the past seven years regarding my brother and his partner. How does one person's private choice possibly hurt anyone else?

Besides entirely discounting what the Bible says (or, according to him, does not say) about homosexuality, he contends that his relationship should not be construed as sin because it is not like other sexual sins, such as adultery or incest, which cause tremendous pain and deeply hurt other people. In contrast, how can we say his committed and loving relationship causes similar heartache and destruction? (I suppose my own personal grief doesn't count.)

The last time we talked about this issue, he challenged me to show him one fact that proved that legalizing his relationship with his partner would harm anyone in any way. "Christians can only say it's against their beliefs," he responded to my attempts to answer him. "That's fine. You don't have to be in favor of it to concede my relationship is not hurting anyone else."

Granted, he and his partner are some of the most giving individuals I know. They work with AIDS patients and the homeless. They give a lot of their money to ministries for orphans. They have been in a monogamous relationship for the past seven years, buying a house together and even talking about adopting a child. If he is happy, why can't we be happy for him?

I just can't. The hurt goes too deep.

—Amber

THE *ROOT* ISSUE in this myth is not whether gay marriage should be legalized but whether or not the nature of sin is as consequential as God's Word claims. We can live in naïveté about sin only so long. When King Josiah discovered that the people of Judah had been living outside God's law for years, he tore his clothes in anguish over their sin (see 2 Chronicles 34). Instead of reacting by saying, "Well, we've been doing fine all this time," he was swift to change his course.

God says sin is so serious that the result is spiritual death (see Romans 6:23). We tend to say some sins are not so bad. We use the same argument in a number of scenarios: Marijuana use is acceptable as long as it harms no one but the user. Addiction to prescription medicine is fine if it makes you sleep better. Cohabitation. Drunkenness. Pornography. Gambling addictions. We justify any number of seemingly isolated sins by saying, "But I'm not hurting anyone else."

The only problem with this argument is that sin is like second-hand smoke. It leaves a trail of destruction. Friends and family of someone dealing with sin know the power personal sin has to hurt other people. Families grieve. Reputations are ruined. Family names are tainted. Future hopes and dreams are tarnished. Instead of isolationism, the Bible teaches our inter-connectedness:

- We are examples to one another (1 Corinthians 11:1).
- We are to carry each other's burdens (Galatians 6:2) and honor one another more than ourselves (Romans 12:10).
- We ought to intervene with someone who's going astray (James 5:20).

There's no such thing as sin that doesn't harm anyone else. Sin, even a seemingly private choice, affects others—ask Adam and Eve. And it has far-reaching consequences—ask David. And it is deadly—ask Jesus. His precious blood was the only acceptable form of payment for the very sins we thought were inconsequential.

> "No man ever enters heaven until he is first convinced that he deserves hell."
>
> —John Everrett

567

"THE WRATH OF GOD IS BEING REVEALED FROM HEAVEN AGAINST ALL THE GODLESSNESS AND WICKEDNESS OF HUMAN BEINGS WHO SUPPRESS THE TRUTH BY THEIR WICKEDNESS."

ROMANS 1:18

SEE ALSO

Psalm 51:3–6
Romans 15:1–4
James 1:13–15

For more on **Consequences**, check the index.

¹³All the men of Judah, with their wives and children and little ones, stood there before the LORD.

¹⁴Then the Spirit of the LORD came on Jahaziel son of Zechariah, the son of Benaiah, the son of Jeiel, the son of Mattaniah, a Levite and descendant of Asaph, as he stood in the assembly.

¹⁵He said: "Listen, King Jehoshaphat and all who live in Judah and Jerusalem! This is what the LORD says to you: 'Do not be afraid or discouraged because of this vast army. For the battle is not yours, but God's. ¹⁶Tomorrow march down against them. They will be climbing up by the Pass of Ziz, and you will find them at the end of the gorge in the Desert of Jeruel. ¹⁷You will not have to fight this battle. Take up your positions; stand firm and see the deliverance the LORD will give you, Judah and Jerusalem. Do not be afraid; do not be discouraged. Go out to face them tomorrow, and the LORD will be with you.'"

HE IS: firm

20:15–17 A ruthless army was descending on Jerusalem. The people had every reason to be afraid and discouraged. Wouldn't you be? But Jehoshaphat trusted God to save the people of Judah. God sent word for them to stand firm. The people obeyed, and God dealt decisively with their enemies.

With God as your guide, you are never standing on shaky ground. He is *firm*. When you call out to him, he'll be the firm foundation on which to stand. If you see an enemy descending on you, set your feet and stand firm. The battle is not yours, but God's.

For the next He Is, go to p. 579.

¹⁸Jehoshaphat bowed down with his face to the ground, and all the people of Judah and Jerusalem fell down in worship before the LORD. ¹⁹Then some Levites from the Kohathites and Korahites stood up and praised the LORD, the God of Israel, with a very loud voice.

²⁰Early in the morning they left for the Desert of Tekoa. As they set out, Jehoshaphat stood and said, "Listen to me, Judah and people of Jerusalem! Have faith in the LORD your God and you will be upheld; have faith in his prophets and you will be successful." ²¹After consulting the people, Jehoshaphat appointed men to sing to the LORD and to praise him for the splendor of his*a* holiness as they went out at the head of the army, saying:

"Give thanks to the LORD,
for his love endures forever."

²²As they began to sing and praise, the LORD set ambushes against the men of Ammon and Moab and Mount Seir who were invading Judah, and they were defeated. ²³The Ammonites and Moabites rose up against the men from Mount Seir to destroy and annihilate them. After they finished slaughtering the men from Seir, they helped to destroy one another.

²⁴When the men of Judah came to the place that overlooks the desert and looked toward the vast army, they saw only dead bodies lying on the ground; no one had escaped. ²⁵So Jehoshaphat and his men went to carry off their plunder, and they found among them a great amount of equipment and clothing*b* and also articles of value—more than they could take away. There was so much plunder that it took three days to collect it. ²⁶On the fourth day they assembled in the Valley of Berakah, where they praised the LORD. This is why it is called the Valley of Berakah*c* to this day.

²⁷Then, led by Jehoshaphat, all the men of Judah and Jerusalem returned joyfully to Jerusalem, for the LORD had given them cause to rejoice over their enemies. ²⁸They entered Jerusalem and went to the temple of the LORD with harps and lyres and trumpets.

²⁹The fear of God came on all the surrounding kingdoms when they heard how the LORD had fought against the enemies of Israel. ³⁰And the kingdom of Jehoshaphat was at peace, for his God had given him rest on every side.

---

a 21 Or him with the splendor of *b 25 Some Hebrew manuscripts and Vulgate; most Hebrew manuscripts corpses* *c 26 Berakah means praise.*

The End of Jehoshaphat's Reign

³¹So Jehoshaphat reigned over Judah. He was thirty-five years old when he became king of Judah, and he reigned in Jerusalem twenty-five years. His mother's name was Azubah daughter of Shilhi. ³²He followed the ways of his father Asa and did not stray from them; he did what was right in the eyes of the LORD. ³³The high places, however, were not removed, and the people still had not set their hearts on the God of their ancestors.

³⁴The other events of Jehoshaphat's reign, from beginning to end, are written in the annals of Jehu son of Hanani, which are recorded in the book of the kings of Israel.

³⁵Later, Jehoshaphat king of Judah made an alliance with Ahaziah king of Israel, whose ways were wicked. ³⁶He agreed with him to construct a fleet of trading ships.*ᵃ* After these were built at Ezion Geber, ³⁷Eliezer son of Dodavahu of Mareshah prophesied against Jehoshaphat, saying, "Because you have made an alliance with Ahaziah, the LORD will destroy what you have made." The ships were wrecked and were not able to set sail to trade.*ᵇ*

21 Then Jehoshaphat rested with his ancestors and was buried with them in the City of David. And Jehoram his son succeeded him as king. ²Jehoram's brothers, the sons of Jehoshaphat, were Azariah, Jehiel, Zechariah, Azariahu, Michael and Shephatiah. All these were sons of Jehoshaphat king of Israel.*ᶜ* ³Their father had given them many gifts of silver and gold and articles of value, as well as fortified cities in Judah, but he had given the kingdom to Jehoram because he was his firstborn son.

569

Jehoram King of Judah

⁴When Jehoram established himself firmly over his father's kingdom, he put all his brothers to the sword along with some of the officials of Israel. ⁵Jehoram was thirty-two years old when he became king, and he reigned in Jerusalem eight years. ⁶He followed the ways of the kings of Israel, as the house of Ahab had done, for he married a daughter of Ahab. He did evil in the eyes of the LORD. ⁷Nevertheless, because of the covenant the LORD had made with David, the LORD was not willing to destroy the house of David. He had promised to maintain a lamp for him and his descendants forever.

⁸In the time of Jehoram, Edom rebelled against Judah and set up its own king. ⁹So Jehoram went there with his officers and all his chariots. The Edomites surrounded him and his chariot commanders, but he rose up and broke through by night. ¹⁰To this day Edom has been in rebellion against Judah.

Libnah revolted at the same time, because Jehoram had forsaken the LORD, the God of his ancestors. ¹¹He had also built high places on the hills of Judah and had caused the people of Jerusalem to prostitute themselves and had led Judah astray.

conversations

legacy «» 21:16–20

1» How should you react when others leave you with a bad legacy?

2» In what ways have your parents' choices affected your reputation?

3» Is it OK to express your disappointment with your parents?

For more on **legacy**, check the index.
For the next Conversations, go to p. 574.

¹²Jehoram received a letter from Elijah the prophet, which said:

"This is what the LORD, the God of your father David, says: 'You have not followed the ways of your father Jehoshaphat or of Asa king of Judah. ¹³But you have followed the ways of the kings of Israel, and you have led Judah and the people of Jerusalem to prostitute themselves, just as the house of Ahab did. You have also murdered your own brothers, members of your own family, men who were better than you. ¹⁴So now the LORD is about to strike your people, your sons, your wives and everything that is yours, with a heavy blow. ¹⁵You yourself will be very ill with a lingering disease of the bowels, until the disease causes your bowels to come out.'"

¹⁶The LORD aroused against Jehoram the hostility of the Philistines and of the Arabs who lived near the Cushites. ¹⁷They attacked Judah, invaded it and carried off all the goods found in the king's

---

ᵃ 36 Hebrew *of ships that could go to Tarshish*   *ᵇ 37* Hebrew *sail for Tarshish*   *ᶜ 2* That is, Judah, as frequently in 2 Chronicles palace, together with his sons and wives. Not a son was left to him except Ahaziah,[a] the youngest.

[18] After all this, the LORD afflicted Jehoram with an incurable disease of the bowels. [19] In the course of time, at the end of the second year, his bowels came out because of the disease, and he died in great pain. His people made no funeral fire in his honor, as they had for his predecessors.

[20] Jehoram was thirty-two years old when he became king, and he reigned in Jerusalem eight years. He passed away, to no one's regret, and was buried in the City of David, but not in the tombs of the kings.

Ahaziah King of Judah

22 The people of Jerusalem made Ahaziah, Jehoram's youngest son, king in his place, since the raiders, who came with the Arabs into the camp, had killed all the older sons. So Ahaziah son of Jehoram king of Judah began to reign.

[2] Ahaziah was twenty-two[b] years old when he became king, and he reigned in Jerusalem one year. His mother's name was Athaliah, a granddaughter of Omri.

[3] He too followed the ways of the house of Ahab, for his mother encouraged him to act wickedly. [4] He did evil in the eyes of the LORD, as the house of Ahab had done, for after his father's death they became his advisers, to his undoing. [5] He also followed their counsel when he went with Joram[c] son of Ahab king of Israel to war against Hazael king of Aram at Ramoth Gilead. The Arameans wounded Joram; [6] so he returned to Jezreel to recover from the wounds they had inflicted on him at Ramoth[d] in his battle with Hazael king of Aram.

Then Ahaziah[e] son of Jehoram king of Judah went down to Jezreel to see Joram son of Ahab because he had been wounded.

[7] Through Ahaziah's visit to Joram, God brought about Ahaziah's downfall. When Ahaziah arrived, he went out with Joram to meet Jehu son of Nimshi, whom the LORD had anointed to destroy the house of Ahab. [8] While Jehu was executing judgment on the house of Ahab, he found the officials of Judah and the sons of Ahaziah's relatives, who had been attending Ahaziah, and he killed them. [9] He then went in search of Ahaziah, and his men captured him while he was hiding in Samaria. He was brought to Jehu and put to death. They buried him, for they said, "He was a son of Jehoshaphat, who sought the LORD with all his heart." So there was no one in the house of Ahaziah powerful enough to retain the kingdom.

570

atissue:parenting

22:2–4 If you're a stay-at-home mom, it's tempting to feel like you're not doing "big things." Your circle of influence can feel small and therefore not as important as if you were out in the world. But small does *not* equal insignificant. You are the biggest influence in your children's lives—either for good or for bad. That's equally true if you work outside the home. Your time with your children is precious—no one can replace you in your kids' lives. How might Ahaziah have turned out if his mother hadn't affirmed his evil choices . . . or if he'd had *you* for a mom?

Athaliah and Joash

[10] When Athaliah the mother of Ahaziah saw that her son was dead, she proceeded to destroy the whole royal family of the house of Judah. [11] But Jehosheba,[f] the daughter of King Jehoram, took Joash son of Ahaziah and stole him away from among the royal princes who were about to be murdered and put him and his nurse in a bedroom. Because Jehosheba,[f] the daughter of King Jehoram and wife of the priest Jehoiada, was Ahaziah's sister, she hid the child from Athaliah so she could not kill him. [12] He remained hidden with them at the temple of God for six years while Athaliah ruled the land.

23 In the seventh year Jehoiada showed his strength. He made a covenant with the commanders of units of a hundred: Azariah son of Jeroham, Ishmael son of Jehohanan, Azariah son of Obed, Maaseiah son of Adaiah, and Elishaphat son of Zikri. [2] They went throughout Judah and gathered the

---

[a] 17 Hebrew *Jehoahaz*, a variant of *Ahaziah*   [b] 2 Some Septuagint manuscripts and Syriac (see also 2 Kings 8:26); Hebrew *forty-two*   [c] 5 Hebrew *Jehoram*, a variant of *Joram*; also in verses 6 and 7   [d] 6 Hebrew *Ramah*, a variant of *Ramoth*   [e] 6 Some Hebrew manuscripts, Septuagint, Vulgate and Syriac (see also 2 Kings 8:29); most Hebrew manuscripts *Azariah*   [f] 11 Hebrew *Jehoshabeath*, a variant of *Jehosheba*

Levites and the heads of Israelite families from all the towns. When they came to Jerusalem, ³the whole assembly made a covenant with the king at the temple of God.

Jehoiada said to them, "The king's son shall reign, as the LORD promised concerning the descendants of David. ⁴Now this is what you are to do: A third of you priests and Levites who are going on duty on the Sabbath are to keep watch at the doors, ⁵a third of you at the royal palace and a third at the Foundation Gate, and all the others are to be in the courtyards of the temple of the LORD. ⁶No one is to enter the temple of the LORD except the priests and Levites on duty; they may enter because they are consecrated, but all the others are to observe the LORD's command not to enter.ᵃ ⁷The Levites are to station themselves around the king, each with weapon in hand. Anyone who enters the temple is to be put to death. Stay close to the king wherever he goes."

⁸The Levites and all the men of Judah did just as Jehoiada the priest ordered. Each one took his men—those who were going on duty on the Sabbath and those who were going off duty—for Jehoiada the priest had not released any of the divisions. ⁹Then he gave the commanders of units of a hundred the spears and the large and small shields that had belonged to King David and that were in the temple of God. ¹⁰He stationed all the men, each with his weapon in his hand, around the king—near the altar and the temple, from the south side to the north side of the temple.

¹¹Jehoiada and his sons brought out the king's son and put the crown on him; they presented him with a copy of the covenant and proclaimed him king. They anointed him and shouted, "Long live the king!"

¹²When Athaliah heard the noise of the people running and cheering the king, she went to them at the temple of the LORD. ¹³She looked, and there was the king, standing by his pillar at the entrance. The officers and the trumpeters were beside the king, and all the people of the land were rejoicing and blowing trumpets, and musicians with their instruments were leading the praises. Then Athaliah tore her robes and shouted, "Treason! Treason!"

¹⁴Jehoiada the priest sent out the commanders of units of a hundred, who were in charge of the troops, and said to them: "Bring her out between the ranksᵇ and put to the sword anyone who follows her." For the priest had said, "Do not put her to death at the temple of the LORD." ¹⁵So they seized her as she reached the entrance of the Horse Gate on the palace grounds, and there they put her to death.

¹⁶Jehoiada then made a covenant that he, the people and the kingᶜ would be the LORD's people. ¹⁷All the people went to the temple of Baal and tore it down. They smashed the altars and idols and killed Mattan the priest of Baal in front of the altars.

¹⁸Then Jehoiada placed the oversight of the temple of the LORD in the hands of the Levitical priests, to whom David had made assignments in the temple, to present the burnt offerings of the LORD as written in the Law of Moses, with rejoicing and singing, as David had ordered. ¹⁹He also stationed gatekeepers at the gates of the LORD's temple so that no one who was in any way unclean might enter.

²⁰He took with him the commanders of hundreds, the nobles, the rulers of the people and all the people of the land and brought the king down from the temple of the LORD. They went into the palace through the Upper Gate and seated the king on the royal throne. ²¹All the people of the land rejoiced, and the city was calm, because Athaliah had been slain with the sword.

Joash Repairs the Temple

24 Joash was seven years old when he became king, and he reigned in Jerusalem forty years. His mother's name was Zibiah; she was from Beersheba. ²Joash did what was right in the eyes of the LORD all the years of Jehoiada the priest. ³Jehoiada chose two wives for him, and he had sons and daughters.

⁴Some time later Joash decided to restore the temple of the LORD. ⁵He called together the priests and Levites and said to them, "Go to the towns of Judah and collect the money due annually from all Israel, to repair the temple of your God. Do it now." But the Levites did not act at once.

⁶Therefore the king summoned Jehoiada the chief priest and said to him, "Why haven't you required the Levites to bring in from Judah and Jerusalem the tax imposed by Moses the servant of the LORD and by the assembly of Israel for the tent of the covenant law?"

ᵃ 6 Or are to stand guard where the LORD has assigned them   ᵇ 14 Or out from the precincts   ᶜ 16 Or covenant between ⌐the LORD⌐ and the people and the king that they (see 2 Kings 11:17)

[7]Now the sons of that wicked woman Athaliah had broken into the temple of God and had used even its sacred objects for the Baals.

[8]At the king's command, a chest was made and placed outside, at the gate of the temple of the LORD. [9]A proclamation was then issued in Judah and Jerusalem that they should bring to the LORD the tax that Moses the servant of God had required of Israel in the wilderness. [10]All the officials and all the people brought their contributions gladly, dropping them into the chest until it was full. [11]Whenever the chest was brought in by the Levites to the king's officials and they saw that there was a large amount of money, the royal secretary and the officer of the chief priest would come and empty the chest and carry it back to its place. They did this regularly and collected a great amount of money. [12]The king and Jehoiada gave it to those who carried out the work required for the temple of the LORD. They hired masons and carpenters to restore the LORD's temple, and also workers in iron and bronze to repair the temple.

[13]The men in charge of the work were diligent, and the repairs progressed under them. They rebuilt the temple of God according to its original design and reinforced it. [14]When they had finished, they brought the rest of the money to the king and Jehoiada, and with it were made articles for the LORD's temple: articles for the service and for the burnt offerings, and also dishes and other objects of gold and silver. As long as Jehoiada lived, burnt offerings were presented continually in the temple of the LORD.

[15]Now Jehoiada was old and full of years, and he died at the age of a hundred and thirty. [16]He was buried with the kings in the City of David, because of the good he had done in Israel for God and his temple.

The Wickedness of Joash

[17]After the death of Jehoiada, the officials of Judah came and paid homage to the king, and he listened to them. [18]They abandoned the temple of the LORD, the God of their ancestors, and worshiped Asherah poles and idols. Because of their guilt, God's anger came on Judah and Jerusalem. [19]Although the LORD sent prophets to the people to bring them back to him, and though they testified against them, they would not listen.

[20]Then the Spirit of God came on Zechariah son of Jehoiada the priest. He stood before the people and said, "This is what God says: 'Why do you disobey the LORD's commands? You will not prosper. Because you have forsaken the LORD, he has forsaken you.'"

[21]But they plotted against him, and by order of the king they stoned him to death in the courtyard of the LORD's temple. [22]King Joash did not remember the kindness Zechariah's father Jehoiada had shown him but killed his son, who said as he lay dying, "May the LORD see this and call you to account."

[23]At the turn of the year,[a] the army of Aram marched against Joash; it invaded Judah and Jerusalem and killed all the leaders of the people. They sent all the plunder to their king in Damascus. [24]Although the Aramean army had come with only a few men, the LORD delivered into their hands a much larger army. Because Judah had forsaken the LORD, the God of their ancestors, judgment was executed on Joash. [25]When the Arameans withdrew, they left Joash severely wounded. His officials conspired against him for murdering the son of Jehoiada the priest, and they killed him in his bed. So he died and was buried in the City of David, but not in the tombs of the kings.

[26]Those who conspired against him were Zabad,[b] son of Shimeath an Ammonite woman, and Jehozabad, son of Shimrith[c] a Moabite woman. [27]The account of his sons, the many prophecies about him, and the record of the restoration of the temple of God are written in the annotations on the book of the kings. And Amaziah his son succeeded him as king.

Amaziah King of Judah

25 Amaziah was twenty-five years old when he became king, and he reigned in Jerusalem twenty-nine years. His mother's name was Jehoaddan; she was from Jerusalem. [2]He did what was right in the eyes of the LORD, but not wholeheartedly. [3]After the kingdom was firmly in his control, he executed the officials who had murdered his father the king. [4]Yet he did not put their children to death, but acted in accordance with what is written in the Law, in the Book of Moses, where the LORD commanded: "Parents shall not be put to death for their children, nor children be put to death for their parents; each of you will die for your own sin."[d]

---

a 23 Probably in the spring   *b 26* A variant of *Jozabad*   *c 26* A variant of *Shomer*   *d 4* Deut. 24:16

⁵Amaziah called the people of Judah together and assigned them according to their families to commanders of thousands and commanders of hundreds for all Judah and Benjamin. He then mustered those twenty years old or more and found that there were three hundred thousand men fit for military service, able to handle the spear and shield. ⁶He also hired a hundred thousand fighting men from Israel for a hundred talents*ᵃ* of silver.

⁷But a man of God came to him and said, "Your Majesty, these troops from Israel must not march with you, for the LORD is not with Israel—not with any of the people of Ephraim. ⁸Even if you go and fight courageously in battle, God will overthrow you before the enemy, for God has the power to help or to overthrow."

⁹Amaziah asked the man of God, "But what about the hundred talents I paid for these Israelite troops?"

The man of God replied, "The LORD can give you much more than that."

¹⁰So Amaziah dismissed the troops who had come to him from Ephraim and sent them home. They were furious with Judah and left for home in a great rage.

¹¹Amaziah then marshaled his strength and led his army to the Valley of Salt, where he killed ten thousand men of Seir. ¹²The army of Judah also captured ten thousand men alive, took them to the top of a cliff and threw them down so that all were dashed to pieces.

¹³Meanwhile the troops that Amaziah had sent back and had not allowed to take part in the war raided towns belonging to Judah from Samaria to Beth Horon. They killed three thousand people and carried off great quantities of plunder.

¹⁴When Amaziah returned from slaughtering the Edomites, he brought back the gods of the people of Seir. He set them up as his own gods, bowed down to them and burned sacrifices to them. ¹⁵The anger of the LORD burned against Amaziah, and he sent a prophet to him, who said, "Why do you consult this people's gods, which could not save their own people from your hand?"

¹⁶While he was still speaking, the king said to him, "Have we appointed you an adviser to the king? Stop! Why be struck down?"

So the prophet stopped but said, "I know that God has determined to destroy you, because you have done this and have not listened to my counsel."

¹⁷After Amaziah king of Judah consulted his advisers, he sent this challenge to Jehoash*ᵇ* son of Jehoahaz, the son of Jehu, king of Israel: "Come, meet me face to face."

¹⁸But Jehoash king of Israel replied to Amaziah king of Judah: "A thistle in Lebanon sent a message to a cedar in Lebanon, 'Give your daughter to my son in marriage.' Then a wild beast in Lebanon came along and trampled the thistle underfoot. ¹⁹You say to yourself that you have defeated Edom, and now you are arrogant and proud. But stay at home! Why ask for trouble and cause your own downfall and that of Judah also?"

²⁰Amaziah, however, would not listen, for God so worked that he might deliver them into the hands of Jehoash, because they sought the gods of Edom. ²¹So Jehoash king of Israel attacked. He and Amaziah king of Judah faced each other at Beth Shemesh in Judah. ²²Judah was routed by Israel, and every man fled to his home. ²³Jehoash king of Israel captured Amaziah king of Judah, the son of Joash, the son of Ahaziah,*ᶜ* at Beth Shemesh. Then Jehoash brought him to Jerusalem and broke down the wall of Jerusalem from the Ephraim Gate to the Corner Gate—a section about four hundred cubits*ᵈ* long. ²⁴He took all the gold and silver and all the articles found in the temple of God that had been in the care of Obed-Edom, together with the palace treasures and the hostages, and returned to Samaria.

²⁵Amaziah son of Joash king of Judah lived for fifteen years after the death of Jehoash son of Jehoahaz king of Israel. ²⁶As for the other events of Amaziah's reign, from beginning to end, are they not written in the book of the kings of Judah and Israel? ²⁷From the time that Amaziah turned away from following the LORD, they conspired against him in Jerusalem and he fled to Lachish, but they sent men after him to Lachish and killed him there. ²⁸He was brought back by horse and was buried with his ancestors in the City of Judah.*ᵉ*

573

ᵃ 6 That is, about 3 3/4 tons or about 3.4 metric tons; also in verse 9   *ᵇ 17* Hebrew *Joash*, a variant of *Jehoash*; also in verses 18, 21, 23 and 25
ᶜ 23 Hebrew *Jehoahaz*, a variant of *Ahaziah*   *ᵈ 23* That is, about 600 feet or about 180 meters   *ᵉ 28* Most Hebrew manuscripts; some Hebrew manuscripts, Septuagint, Vulgate and Syriac (see also 2 Kings 14:20) *David*

Uzziah King of Judah

26 Then all the people of Judah took Uzziah,[a] who was sixteen years old, and made him king in place of his father Amaziah. [2]He was the one who rebuilt Elath and restored it to Judah after Amaziah rested with his ancestors.

[3]Uzziah was sixteen years old when he became king, and he reigned in Jerusalem fifty-two years. His mother's name was Jekoliah; she was from Jerusalem. [4]He did what was right in the eyes of the LORD, just as his father Amaziah had done. [5]He sought God during the days of Zechariah, who instructed him in the fear[b] of God. As long as he sought the LORD, God gave him success.

[6]He went to war against the Philistines and broke down the walls of Gath, Jabneh and Ashdod. He then rebuilt towns near Ashdod and elsewhere among the Philistines. [7]God helped him against the Philistines and against the Arabs who lived in Gur Baal and against the Meunites. [8]The Ammonites brought tribute to Uzziah, and his fame spread as far as the border of Egypt, because he had become very powerful.

[9]Uzziah built towers in Jerusalem at the Corner Gate, at the Valley Gate and at the angle of the wall, and he fortified them. [10]He also built towers in the wilderness and dug many cisterns, because he had much livestock in the foothills and in the plain. He had people working his fields and vineyards in the hills and in the fertile lands, for he loved the soil.

[11]Uzziah had a well-trained army, ready to go out by divisions according to their numbers as mustered by Jeiel the secretary and Maaseiah the officer under the direction of Hananiah, one of the royal officials. [12]The total number of family leaders over the fighting men was 2,600. [13]Under their command was an army of 307,500 men trained for war, a powerful force to support the king against his enemies. [14]Uzziah provided shields, spears, helmets, coats of armor, bows and slingstones for the entire army. [15]In Jerusalem he made devices designed by skilled workers for use on the towers and on the corner defenses so that soldiers could shoot arrows and hurl large stones from the walls. His fame spread far and wide, for he was greatly helped until he became powerful.

[16]But after Uzziah became powerful, his pride led to his downfall. He was unfaithful to the LORD his God, and entered the temple of the LORD to burn incense on the altar of incense. [17]Azariah the priest with eighty other courageous priests of the LORD followed him in. [18]They confronted King Uzziah and said, "It is not right for you, Uzziah, to burn incense to the LORD. That is for the priests, the descendants of Aaron, who have been consecrated to burn incense. Leave the sanctuary, for you have been unfaithful; and you will not be honored by the LORD God."

[19]Uzziah, who had a censer in his hand ready to burn incense, became angry. While he was raging at the priests in their presence before the incense altar in the LORD's temple, leprosy[c] broke out on his forehead. [20]When Azariah the chief priest and all the other priests looked at him, they saw that he had leprosy on his forehead, so they hurried him out. Indeed, he himself was eager to leave, because the LORD had afflicted him.

[21]King Uzziah had leprosy until the day he died. He lived in a separate house[d]—leprous, and excluded from the temple of the LORD. Jotham his son had charge of the palace and governed the people of the land.

[22]The other events of Uzziah's reign, from beginning to end, are recorded by the prophet Isaiah son of Amoz. [23]Uzziah rested with his ancestors and was buried near them in a cemetery that belonged to the kings, for people said, "He had leprosy." And Jotham his son succeeded him as king.

conversations

pride «» 26:16–21

1 Describe a recent decision you made that was motivated by pride.

2 What consequences resulted from your decision? How did you deal with them?

3 Does power always corrupt? Why or why not?

For more on **pride**, check the index.
For the next Conversations, go to p. 575.

574

---

[a] 1 Also called *Azariah* [b] 5 Many Hebrew manuscripts, Septuagint and Syriac; other Hebrew manuscripts *vision* [c] 19 The Hebrew for *leprosy* was used for various diseases affecting the skin; also in verses 20, 21 and 23. [d] 21 Or *in a house where he was relieved of responsibilities*

Jotham King of Judah

27 Jotham was twenty-five years old when he became king, and he reigned in Jerusalem sixteen years. His mother's name was Jerusha daughter of Zadok. ²He did what was right in the eyes of the LORD, just as his father Uzziah had done, but unlike him he did not enter the temple of the LORD. The people, however, continued their corrupt practices. ³Jotham rebuilt the Upper Gate of the temple of the LORD and did extensive work on the wall at the hill of Ophel. ⁴He built towns in the hill country of Judah and forts and towers in the wooded areas.

⁵Jotham made war on the king of the Ammonites and conquered them. That year the Ammonites paid him a hundred talents[a] of silver, ten thousand cors[b] of wheat and ten thousand cors[c] of barley. The Ammonites brought him the same amount also in the second and third years.

⁶Jotham grew powerful because he walked steadfastly before the LORD his God.

⁷The other events in Jotham's reign, including all his wars and the other things he did, are written in the book of the kings of Israel and Judah. ⁸He was twenty-five years old when he became king, and he reigned in Jerusalem sixteen years. ⁹Jotham rested with his ancestors and was buried in the City of David. And Ahaz his son succeeded him as king.

Ahaz King of Judah

28 Ahaz was twenty years old when he became king, and he reigned in Jerusalem sixteen years. Unlike David his father, he did not do what was right in the eyes of the LORD. ²He followed the ways of the kings of Israel and also made idols for worshiping the Baals. ³He burned sacrifices in the Valley of Ben Hinnom and sacrificed his children in the fire, engaging in the detestable practices of the nations the LORD had driven out before the Israelites. ⁴He offered sacrifices and burned incense at the high places, on the hilltops and under every spreading tree.

⁵Therefore the LORD his God delivered him into the hands of the king of Aram. The Arameans defeated him and took many of his people as prisoners and brought them to Damascus.

He was also given into the hands of the king of Israel, who inflicted heavy casualties on him. ⁶In one day Pekah son of Remaliah killed a hundred and twenty thousand soldiers in Judah—because Judah had forsaken the LORD, the God of their ancestors. ⁷Zikri, an Ephraimite warrior, killed Maaseiah the king's son, Azrikam the officer in charge of the palace, and Elkanah, second to the king. ⁸The men of Israel took captive from their fellow Israelites in Judah two hundred thousand wives, sons and daughters. They also took a great deal of plunder, which they carried back to Samaria.

⁹But a prophet of the LORD named Oded was there, and he went out to meet the army when it returned to Samaria. He said to them, "Because the LORD, the God of your ancestors, was angry with Judah, he gave them into your hand. But you have slaughtered them in a rage that reaches to heaven. ¹⁰And now you intend to make the men and women of Judah and Jerusalem your slaves. But aren't you also guilty of sins against the LORD your God? ¹¹Now listen to me! Send back your fellow Israelites you have taken as prisoners, for the LORD's fierce anger rests on you."

¹²Then some of the leaders in Ephraim—Azariah son of Jehohanan, Berekiah son of Meshillemoth, Jehizkiah son of Shallum, and Amasa son of Hadlai—confronted those who were arriving from the war. ¹³"You must not bring those prisoners here," they said, "or we will be guilty before the LORD. Do you intend to add to our sin and guilt? For our guilt is already great, and his fierce anger rests on Israel."

¹⁴So the soldiers gave up the prisoners and plunder in the presence of the officials and all the assembly. ¹⁵The men designated by name took the prisoners, and from the plunder they clothed all who were naked. They provided

575

conversations
poverty «» 28:14–15

1» Why is social aid important in the area where you live?

2» Could you help someone escape poverty? How?

3» What are other kinds of poverty (besides economic poverty)?

For more on **poverty**, check the index.
For the next Conversations, go to p. 579.

---

[a] 5 That is, about 3 3/4 tons or about 3.4 metric tons   [b] 5 That is, probably about 1,800 tons or about 1,600 metric tons   [c] 5 That is, probably about 1,500 tons or about 1,350 metric tons

them with clothes and sandals, food and drink, and healing balm. All those who were weak they put on donkeys. So they took them back to their fellow Israelites at Jericho, the City of Palms, and returned to Samaria.

[16] At that time King Ahaz sent to the kings[a] of Assyria for help. [17] The Edomites had again come and attacked Judah and carried away prisoners, [18] while the Philistines had raided towns in the foothills and in the Negev of Judah. They captured and occupied Beth Shemesh, Aijalon and Gederoth, as well as Soko, Timnah and Gimzo, with their surrounding villages. [19] The LORD had humbled Judah because of Ahaz king of Israel,[b] for he had promoted wickedness in Judah and had been most unfaithful to the LORD. [20] Tiglath-Pileser[c] king of Assyria came to him, but he gave him trouble instead of help. [21] Ahaz took some of the things from the temple of the LORD and from the royal palace and from the officials and presented them to the king of Assyria, but that did not help him.

[22] In his time of trouble King Ahaz became even more unfaithful to the LORD. [23] He offered sacrifices to the gods of Damascus, who had defeated him; for he thought, "Since the gods of the kings of Aram have helped them, I will sacrifice to them so they will help me." But they were his downfall and the downfall of all Israel.

[24] Ahaz gathered together the furnishings from the temple of God and cut them in pieces. He shut the doors of the LORD's temple and set up altars at every street corner in Jerusalem. [25] In every town in Judah he built high places to burn sacrifices to other gods and aroused the anger of the LORD, the God of his ancestors.

[26] The other events of his reign and all his ways, from beginning to end, are written in the book of the kings of Judah and Israel. [27] Ahaz rested with his ancestors and was buried in the city of Jerusalem, but he was not placed in the tombs of the kings of Israel. And Hezekiah his son succeeded him as king.

Hezekiah Purifies the Temple

29 Hezekiah was twenty-five years old when he became king, and he reigned in Jerusalem twenty-nine years. His mother's name was Abijah daughter of Zechariah. [2] He did what was right in the eyes of the LORD, just as his father David had done.

[3] In the first month of the first year of his reign, he opened the doors of the temple of the LORD and repaired them. [4] He brought in the priests and the Levites, assembled them in the square on the east side [5] and said: "Listen to me, Levites! Consecrate yourselves now and consecrate the temple of the LORD, the God of your ancestors. Remove all defilement from the sanctuary. [6] Our ancestors were unfaithful; they did evil in the eyes of the LORD our God and forsook him. They turned their faces away from the LORD's dwelling place and turned their backs on him. [7] They also shut the doors of the portico and put out the lamps. They did not burn incense or present any burnt offerings at the sanctuary to the God of Israel. [8] Therefore, the anger of the LORD has fallen on Judah and Jerusalem; he has made them an object of dread and horror and scorn, as you can see with your own eyes. [9] This is why our ancestors have fallen by the sword and why our sons and daughters and our wives are in captivity. [10] Now I intend to make a covenant with the LORD, the God of Israel, so that his fierce anger will turn away from us. [11] My sons, do not

aussie:dysfunctional family

29:1–2 Maybe growing up in your family was no picnic. Some would say you're doomed to repeat the failings you grew up with—you, too, will be an alcoholic, abuse your children or have an affair. While it takes some work and a lot of faith, it's not impossible to break the cycle of a dysfunctional family. Hezekiah's father, King Ahaz, sacrificed Hezekiah's brothers to false gods, closed up the temple and led the people in idol worship. In spite of this, Hezekiah "did what was right in the eyes of the LORD." There's hope! You don't have to be trapped by your past.

---

[a] 16 Most Hebrew manuscripts; one Hebrew manuscript, Septuagint and Vulgate (see also 2 Kings 16:7) king   [b] 19 That is, Judah, as frequently in 2 Chronicles
[c] 20 Hebrew Tilgath-Pilneser, a variant of Tiglath-Pileser

be negligent now, for the LORD has chosen you to stand before him and serve him, to minister before him and to burn incense."

¹²Then these Levites set to work:

from the Kohathites,

Mahath son of Amasai and Joel son of Azariah;

from the Merarites,

Kish son of Abdi and Azariah son of Jehallelel;

from the Gershonites,

Joah son of Zimmah and Eden son of Joah;

¹³from the descendants of Elizaphan,

Shimri and Jeiel;

from the descendants of Asaph,

Zechariah and Mattaniah;

¹⁴from the descendants of Heman,

Jehiel and Shimei;

from the descendants of Jeduthun,

Shemaiah and Uzziel.

¹⁵When they had assembled their fellow Levites and consecrated themselves, they went in to purify the temple of the LORD, as the king had ordered, following the word of the LORD. ¹⁶The priests went into the sanctuary of the LORD to purify it. They brought out to the courtyard of the LORD's temple everything unclean that they found in the temple of the LORD. The Levites took it and carried it out to the Kidron Valley. ¹⁷They began the consecration on the first day of the first month, and by the eighth day of the month they reached the portico of the LORD. For eight more days they consecrated the temple of the LORD itself, finishing on the sixteenth day of the first month.

¹⁸Then they went in to King Hezekiah and reported: "We have purified the entire temple of the LORD, the altar of burnt offering with all its utensils, and the table for setting out the consecrated bread, with all its articles. ¹⁹We have prepared and consecrated all the articles that King Ahaz removed in his unfaithfulness while he was king. They are now in front of the LORD's altar."

²⁰Early the next morning King Hezekiah gathered the city officials together and went up to the temple of the LORD. ²¹They brought seven bulls, seven rams, seven male lambs and seven male goats as a sin offering[a] for the kingdom, for the sanctuary and for Judah. The king commanded the priests, the descendants of Aaron, to offer these on the altar of the LORD. ²²So they slaughtered the bulls, and the priests took the blood and splashed it against the altar; next they slaughtered the rams and splashed their blood against the altar; then they slaughtered the lambs and splashed their blood against the altar. ²³The goats for the sin offering were brought before the king and the assembly, and they laid their hands on them. ²⁴The priests then slaughtered the goats and presented their blood on the altar for a sin offering to atone for all Israel, because the king had ordered the burnt offering and the sin offering for all Israel.

²⁵He stationed the Levites in the temple of the LORD with cymbals, harps and lyres in the way prescribed by David and Gad the king's seer and Nathan the prophet; this was commanded by the LORD through his prophets. ²⁶So the Levites stood ready with David's instruments, and the priests with their trumpets.

²⁷Hezekiah gave the order to sacrifice the burnt offering on the altar. As the offering began, singing to the LORD began also, accompanied by trumpets and the instruments of David king of Israel. ²⁸The whole assembly bowed in worship, while the musicians played and the trumpets sounded. All this continued until the sacrifice of the burnt offering was completed.

²⁹When the offerings were finished, the king and everyone present with him knelt down and worshiped. ³⁰King Hezekiah and his officials ordered the Levites to praise the LORD with the words of David and of Asaph the seer. So they sang praises with gladness and bowed down and worshiped.

³¹Then Hezekiah said, "You have now dedicated yourselves to the LORD. Come and bring sacrifices and

---

ᵃ 21 Or purification offering; also in verses 23 and 24

thank offerings to the temple of the Lord." So the assembly brought sacrifices and thank offerings, and all whose hearts were willing brought burnt offerings.

³²The number of burnt offerings the assembly brought was seventy bulls, a hundred rams and two hundred male lambs—all of them for burnt offerings to the Lord. ³³The animals consecrated as sacrifices amounted to six hundred bulls and three thousand sheep and goats. ³⁴The priests, however, were too few to skin all the burnt offerings; so their relatives the Levites helped them until the task was finished and until other priests had been consecrated, for the Levites had been more conscientious in consecrating themselves than the priests had been. ³⁵There were burnt offerings in abundance, together with the fat of the fellowship offerings and the drink offerings that accompanied the burnt offerings.

So the service of the temple of the Lord was reestablished. ³⁶Hezekiah and all the people rejoiced at what God had brought about for his people, because it was done so quickly.

Hezekiah Celebrates the Passover

30 Hezekiah sent word to all Israel and Judah and also wrote letters to Ephraim and Manasseh, inviting them to come to the temple of the Lord in Jerusalem and celebrate the Passover to the Lord, the God of Israel. ²The king and his officials and the whole assembly in Jerusalem decided to celebrate the Passover in the second month. ³They had not been able to celebrate it at the regular time because not enough priests had consecrated themselves and the people had not assembled in Jerusalem. ⁴The plan seemed right both to the king and to the whole assembly. ⁵They decided to send a proclamation throughout Israel, from Beersheba to Dan, calling the people to come to Jerusalem and celebrate the Passover to the Lord, the God of Israel. It had not been celebrated in large numbers according to what was written.

⁶At the king's command, couriers went throughout Israel and Judah with letters from the king and from his officials, which read:

"People of Israel, return to the Lord, the God of Abraham, Isaac and Israel, that he may return to you who are left, who have escaped from the hand of the kings of Assyria. ⁷Do not be like your parents and your fellow Israelites, who were unfaithful to the Lord, the God of their ancestors, so that he made them an object of horror, as you see. ⁸Do not be stiff-necked, as your parents were; submit to the Lord. Come to his sanctuary, which he has consecrated forever. Serve the Lord your God, so that his fierce anger will turn away from you. ⁹If you return to the Lord, then your fellow Israelites and your children will be shown compassion by their captors and will return to this land, for the Lord your God is gracious and compassionate. He will not turn his face from you if you return to him."

¹⁰The couriers went from town to town in Ephraim and Manasseh, as far as Zebulun, but people scorned and ridiculed them. ¹¹Nevertheless, some from Asher, Manasseh and Zebulun humbled themselves and went to Jerusalem. ¹²Also in Judah the hand of God was on the people to give them unity of mind to carry out what the king and his officials had ordered, following the word of the Lord.

¹³A very large crowd of people assembled in Jerusalem to celebrate the Festival of Unleavened Bread in the second month. ¹⁴They removed the altars in Jerusalem and cleared away the incense altars and threw them into the Kidron Valley.

¹⁵They slaughtered the Passover lamb on the fourteenth day of the second month. The priests and the Levites were ashamed and consecrated themselves and brought burnt offerings to the temple of the Lord. ¹⁶Then they took up their regular positions as prescribed in the Law of Moses the man of God. The priests splashed against the altar the blood handed to them by the Levites. ¹⁷Since many in the crowd had not consecrated themselves, the Levites had to kill the Passover lambs for all those who were not ceremonially clean and could not consecrate their lambs to the Lord. ¹⁸Although most of the many people who came from Ephraim, Manasseh, Issachar and Zebulun had not purified themselves, yet they ate the Passover, contrary to what was written. But Hezekiah prayed for them, saying, "May the Lord, who is good, pardon everyone ¹⁹who sets their heart on seeking God—the Lord, the God of their ancestors—even if they are not clean according to the rules of the sanctuary." ²⁰And the Lord heard Hezekiah and healed the people.

²¹The Israelites who were present in Jerusalem celebrated the Festival of Unleavened Bread for seven days with great rejoicing, while the Levites and priests praised the LORD every day with resounding instruments dedicated to the LORD.ᵃ

HE IS: pardoning

30:18–20 King Hezekiah invited those who escaped the Assyrian captivity to celebrate Passover. However, there was a problem—the people had not ceremonially purified themselves, as the law required. God graciously heard Hezekiah's intercessory prayer and pardoned all those who had set their hearts on seeking God.

Aren't you grateful that God pardons your sin? You can't possibly uphold every one of God's laws. You sin every day (every hour for some of us). But the good news is that God is *pardoning*. Even though your actions never merit God's acceptance, if you set your heart on seeking God, he pardons your sin (see 1 John 1:8–10).

For the next He Is, go to p. 581.

579

²²Hezekiah spoke encouragingly to all the Levites, who showed good understanding of the service of the LORD. For the seven days they ate their assigned portion and offered fellowship offerings and praisedᵇ the LORD, the God of their ancestors.

²³The whole assembly then agreed to celebrate the festival seven more days; so for another seven days they celebrated joyfully. ²⁴Hezekiah king of Judah provided a thousand bulls and seven thousand sheep and goats for the assembly, and the officials provided them with a thousand bulls and ten thousand sheep and goats. A great number of priests consecrated themselves. ²⁵The entire assembly of Judah rejoiced, along with the priests and Levites and all who had assembled from Israel, including the foreigners who had come from Israel and also those who resided in Judah. ²⁶There was great joy in Jerusalem, for since the days of Solomon son of David king of Israel there had been nothing like this in Jerusalem. ²⁷The priests and the Levites stood to bless the people, and God heard them, for their prayer reached heaven, his holy dwelling place.

31 When all this had ended, the Israelites who were there went out to the towns of Judah, smashed the sacred stones and cut down the Asherah poles. They destroyed the high places and the altars throughout Judah and Benjamin and in Ephraim and Manasseh. After they had destroyed all of them, the Israelites returned to their own towns and to their own property.

Contributions for Worship

²Hezekiah assigned the priests and Levites to divisions—each of them according to their duties as priests or Levites—to offer burnt offerings and fellowship offerings, to minister, to give thanks and to sing praises at the gates of the LORD's dwelling. ³The king contributed from his own possessions for the morning and evening burnt offerings and for the burnt offerings on the Sabbaths, at the New Moons and at the appointed festivals as written in the Law of the LORD. ⁴He ordered the people living in Jerusalem to give the portion due the priests and Levites so they could devote themselves to the Law of the LORD. ⁵As soon as the order went out, the Israelites generously gave the

conversations

tithing «» 31:5

1» What does it mean to give God your first-fruits? Do people need to do this today?

2» Why is having a generous attitude so important when you give to God?

3» Do you feel like your generosity is stifled when churches require you to tithe?

For more on **tithing**, check the index.
For the next Conversations, go to p. 589.

ᵃ 21 Or *priests sang to the LORD every day, accompanied by the LORD's instruments of praise*   ᵇ 22 Or *and confessed their sins to* firstfruits of their grain, new wine, oil and honey and all that the fields produced. They brought a great amount, a tithe of everything. ⁶The people of Israel and Judah who lived in the towns of Judah also brought a tithe of their herds and flocks and a tithe of the holy things dedicated to the LORD their God, and they piled them in heaps. ⁷They began doing this in the third month and finished in the seventh month. ⁸When Hezekiah and his officials came and saw the heaps, they praised the LORD and blessed his people Israel.

⁹Hezekiah asked the priests and Levites about the heaps; ¹⁰and Azariah the chief priest, from the family of Zadok, answered, "Since the people began to bring their contributions to the temple of the LORD, we have had enough to eat and plenty to spare, because the LORD has blessed his people, and this great amount is left over."

¹¹Hezekiah gave orders to prepare storerooms in the temple of the LORD, and this was done. ¹²Then they faithfully brought in the contributions, tithes and dedicated gifts. Konaniah, a Levite, was the overseer in charge of these things, and his brother Shimei was next in rank. ¹³Jehiel, Azaziah, Nahath, Asahel, Jerimoth, Jozabad, Eliel, Ismakiah, Mahath and Benaiah were assistants of Konaniah and Shimei his brother. All these served by appointment of King Hezekiah and Azariah the official in charge of the temple of God.

¹⁴Kore son of Imnah the Levite, keeper of the East Gate, was in charge of the freewill offerings given to God, distributing the contributions made to the LORD and also the consecrated gifts. ¹⁵Eden, Miniamin, Jeshua, Shemaiah, Amariah and Shekaniah assisted him faithfully in the towns of the priests, distributing to their fellow priests according to their divisions, old and young alike.

¹⁶In addition, they distributed to the males three years old or more whose names were in the genealogical records—all who would enter the temple of the LORD to perform the daily duties of their various tasks, according to their responsibilities and their divisions. ¹⁷And they distributed to the priests enrolled by their families in the genealogical records and likewise to the Levites twenty years old or more, according to their responsibilities and their divisions. ¹⁸They included all the little ones, the wives, and the sons and daughters of the whole community listed in these genealogical records. For they were faithful in consecrating themselves.

¹⁹As for the priests, the descendants of Aaron, who lived on the farm lands around their towns or in any other towns, men were designated by name to distribute portions to every male among them and to all who were recorded in the genealogies of the Levites.

²⁰This is what Hezekiah did throughout Judah, doing what was good and right and faithful before the LORD his God. ²¹In everything that he undertook in the service of God's temple and in obedience to the law and the commands, he sought his God and worked wholeheartedly. And so he prospered.

580

at issue: success

31:20–21 "success\suk-ses\n 1: the attainment of wealth and favor." The world generally defines success and prosperity in terms of money. Is God's definition different? You bet it is. According to God, Hezekiah prospered. It had nothing to do with money and everything to do with his heart. Hezekiah wanted to faithfully honor God in all things. He sought God and served him wholeheartedly. "And so he prospered." Do you define success by the clothes you wear, the car you drive and the balance in your bank account? Maybe it's time you start defining it by the state of your heart.

Sennacherib Threatens Jerusalem

32 After all that Hezekiah had so faithfully done, Sennacherib king of Assyria came and invaded Judah. He laid siege to the fortified cities, thinking to conquer them for himself. ²When Hezekiah saw that Sennacherib had come and that he intended to make war on Jerusalem, ³he consulted with his officials and military staff about blocking off the water from the springs outside the city, and they helped him. ⁴A large force assembled and blocked all the springs and the stream that flowed through the land. "Why should the kings*a* of Assyria come and find plenty of water?" they said. ⁵Then he worked hard repairing all the broken sections of the wall and building towers on it. He built another wall outside that one and reinforced the terraces*b* of the City of David. He also made large numbers of weapons and shields.

⁶He appointed military officers over the people and assembled them before him in the square at the city gate and encouraged them with these words: ⁷"Be strong and courageous. Do not be afraid or discouraged because of the king of Assyria and the vast army with him, for there is a greater power with us than with him. ⁸With him is only the arm of flesh, but with us is the LORD our God to help us and to fight our battles." And the people gained confidence from what Hezekiah the king of Judah said.

HE IS: the confidence builder

32:7–8 Hezekiah had led a great spiritual awakening, but it was followed by a time of testing when Sennacherib invaded Judah. The king reminded the people that their strength lay in the Lord, and God was the far stronger power. This reminder gave the people great confidence. God himself is *the confidence builder*.

Do you ever lack confidence when you face a difficult situation? Perhaps you doubt yourself or your worth, thinking, *I'm not good enough, smart enough, pretty enough* . . . Focus on the one who can fight your battles for you. He is the ultimate confidence builder (see 2 Corinthians 3:4–6).

For the next He Is, go to p. 583.

⁹Later, when Sennacherib king of Assyria and all his forces were laying siege to Lachish, he sent his officers to Jerusalem with this message for Hezekiah king of Judah and for all the people of Judah who were there:

¹⁰"This is what Sennacherib king of Assyria says: On what are you basing your confidence, that you remain in Jerusalem under siege? ¹¹When Hezekiah says, 'The LORD our God will save us from the hand of the king of Assyria,' he is misleading you, to let you die of hunger and thirst. ¹²Did not Hezekiah himself remove this god's high places and altars, saying to Judah and Jerusalem, 'You must worship before one altar and burn sacrifices on it'?

¹³"Do you not know what I and my predecessors have done to all the peoples of the other lands? Were the gods of those nations ever able to deliver their land from my hand? ¹⁴Who of all the gods of these nations that my predecessors destroyed has been able to save his people from me? How then can your god deliver you from my hand? ¹⁵Now do not let Hezekiah deceive you and mislead you like this. Do not believe him, for no god of any nation or kingdom has been able to deliver his people from my hand or the hand of my predecessors. How much less will your god deliver you from my hand!"

¹⁶Sennacherib's officers spoke further against the LORD God and against his servant Hezekiah. ¹⁷The king also wrote letters ridiculing the LORD, the God of Israel, and saying this against him: "Just as the gods of the peoples of the other lands did not rescue their people from my hand, so the god of Hezekiah will not rescue his people from my hand." ¹⁸Then they called out in Hebrew to the people of Jerusalem who were on the wall, to terrify them and make them afraid in order to capture the city. ¹⁹They spoke about the God of Jerusalem as they did about the gods of the other peoples of the world—the work of human hands.

²⁰King Hezekiah and the prophet Isaiah son of Amoz cried out in prayer to heaven about this. ²¹And the LORD sent an angel, who annihilated all the fighting men and the commanders and officers in the

a 4 Hebrew; Septuagint and Syriac king b 5 Or the Millo

camp of the Assyrian king. So he withdrew to his own land in disgrace. And when he went into the temple of his god, some of his sons cut him down with the sword.

²²So the LORD saved Hezekiah and the people of Jerusalem from the hand of Sennacherib king of Assyria and from the hand of all others. He took care of them*ᵃ* on every side. ²³Many brought offerings to Jerusalem for the LORD and valuable gifts for Hezekiah king of Judah. From then on he was highly regarded by all the nations.

Hezekiah's Pride, Success and Death

²⁴In those days Hezekiah became ill and was at the point of death. He prayed to the LORD, who answered him and gave him a miraculous sign. ²⁵But Hezekiah's heart was proud and he did not respond to the kindness shown him; therefore the LORD's wrath was on him and on Judah and Jerusalem. ²⁶Then Hezekiah repented of the pride of his heart, as did the people of Jerusalem; therefore the LORD's wrath did not come on them during the days of Hezekiah.

²⁷Hezekiah had very great wealth and honor, and he made treasuries for his silver and gold and for his precious stones, spices, shields and all kinds of valuables. ²⁸He also made buildings to store the harvest of grain, new wine and olive oil; and he made stalls for various kinds of cattle, and pens for the flocks. ²⁹He built villages and acquired great numbers of flocks and herds, for God had given him very great riches.

³⁰It was Hezekiah who blocked the upper outlet of the Gihon spring and channeled the water down to the west side of the City of David. He succeeded in everything he undertook. ³¹But when envoys were sent by the rulers of Babylon to ask him about the miraculous sign that had occurred in the land, God left him to test him and to know everything that was in his heart.

³²The other events of Hezekiah's reign and his acts of devotion are written in the vision of the prophet Isaiah son of Amoz in the book of the kings of Judah and Israel. ³³Hezekiah rested with his ancestors and was buried on the hill where the tombs of David's descendants are. All Judah and the people of Jerusalem honored him when he died. And Manasseh his son succeeded him as king.

Manasseh King of Judah

33 Manasseh was twelve years old when he became king, and he reigned in Jerusalem fifty-five years. ²He did evil in the eyes of the LORD, following the detestable practices of the nations the LORD had driven out before the Israelites. ³He rebuilt the high places his father Hezekiah had demolished; he also erected altars to the Baals and made Asherah poles. He bowed down to all the starry hosts and worshiped them. ⁴He built altars in the temple of the LORD, of which the LORD had said, "My Name will remain in Jerusalem forever." ⁵In both courts of the temple of the LORD, he built altars to all the starry hosts. ⁶He sacrificed his children in the fire in the Valley of Ben Hinnom, practiced divination and witchcraft, sought omens, and consulted mediums and spiritists. He did much evil in the eyes of the LORD, arousing his anger.

⁷He took the image he had made and put it in God's temple, of which God had said to David and to his son Solomon, "In this temple and in Jerusalem, which I have chosen out of all the tribes of Israel, I will put my Name forever. ⁸I will not again make the feet of the Israelites leave the land I assigned to your ancestors, if only they will be careful to do everything I commanded them concerning all the laws, decrees and regulations given through Moses." ⁹But Manasseh led Judah and the people of Jerusalem astray, so that they did more evil than the nations the LORD had destroyed before the Israelites.

¹⁰The LORD spoke to Manasseh and his people, but they paid no attention. ¹¹So the LORD brought against them the army commanders of the king of Assyria, who took Manasseh prisoner, put a hook in his nose, bound him with bronze shackles and took him to Babylon. ¹²In his distress he sought the favor of the LORD his God and humbled himself greatly before the God of his ancestors. ¹³And when he prayed to him, the LORD was moved by his entreaty and listened to his plea; so he brought him back to Jerusalem and to his kingdom. Then Manasseh knew that the LORD is God.

¹⁴Afterward he rebuilt the outer wall of the City of David, west of the Gihon spring in the valley, as far

---

ᵃ 22 Hebrew; Septuagint and Vulgate He gave them rest

HE IS: *moved*

33:10–13 Manasseh was an evil king. During his reign the people did more evil than the nations the Lord had destroyed before them. God punished Manasseh with humiliating captivity. However, when he truly repented, the Lord was *moved* by his plea and restored him.

When you worry that God might not forgive your sins, remember Manasseh, who sacrificed his sons, practiced sorcery and did much evil. And God forgave even him. God is *moved* by your plea for mercy. Nothing you've done—abortion, adultery, astrology, atheism, etc.—is unforgivable. Simply ask, and he'll move heaven and earth to forgive you.

For the next He Is, go to p. 592.

583

as the entrance of the Fish Gate and encircling the hill of Ophel; he also made it much higher. He stationed military commanders in all the fortified cities in Judah.

¹⁵He got rid of the foreign gods and removed the image from the temple of the Lord, as well as all the altars he had built on the temple hill and in Jerusalem; and he threw them out of the city. ¹⁶Then he restored the altar of the Lord and sacrificed fellowship offerings and thank offerings on it, and told Judah to serve the Lord, the God of Israel. ¹⁷The people, however, continued to sacrifice at the high places, but only to the Lord their God.

¹⁸The other events of Manasseh's reign, including his prayer to his God and the words the seers spoke to him in the name of the Lord, the God of Israel, are written in the annals of the kings of Israel.^a ¹⁹His prayer and how God was moved by his entreaty, as well as all his sins and unfaithfulness, and the sites where he built high places and set up Asherah poles and idols before he humbled himself—all these are written in the records of the seers.^b ²⁰Manasseh rested with his ancestors and was buried in his palace. And Amon his son succeeded him as king.

Amon King of Judah

²¹Amon was twenty-two years old when he became king, and he reigned in Jerusalem two years. ²²He did evil in the eyes of the Lord, as his father Manasseh had done. Amon worshiped and offered sacrifices to all the idols Manasseh had made. ²³But unlike his father Manasseh, he did not humble himself before the Lord; Amon increased his guilt.

²⁴Amon's officials conspired against him and assassinated him in his palace. ²⁵Then the people of the land killed all who had plotted against King Amon, and they made Josiah his son king in his place.

Josiah's Reforms

34 Josiah was eight years old when he became king, and he reigned in Jerusalem thirty-one years. ²He did what was right in the eyes of the Lord and followed the ways of his father David, not turning aside to the right or to the left.

³In the eighth year of his reign, while he was still young, he began to seek the God of his father David. In his twelfth year he began to purge Judah and Jerusalem of high places, Asherah poles and idols. ⁴Under his direction the altars of the Baals were torn down; he cut to pieces the incense altars that were above them, and smashed the Asherah poles and the idols. These he broke to pieces and scattered over the graves of those who had sacrificed to them. ⁵He burned the bones of the priests on their altars, and so he purged Judah and Jerusalem. ⁶In the towns of Manasseh, Ephraim and Simeon, as far as Naphtali, and in the ruins around them, ⁷he tore down the altars and the Asherah poles and crushed the idols to powder and cut to pieces all the incense altars throughout Israel. Then he went back to Jerusalem.

⁸In the eighteenth year of Josiah's reign, to purify the land and the temple, he sent Shaphan son of Azaliah and Maaseiah the ruler of the city, with Joah son of Joahaz, the recorder, to repair the temple of the Lord his God.

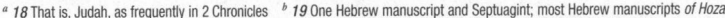

^a *18* That is, Judah, as frequently in 2 Chronicles   ^b *19* One Hebrew manuscript and Septuagint; most Hebrew manuscripts *of Hozai*

myth# 38 "I'LL ALWAYS HAVE MY HEALTH."

584

When I was in college, my metabolism was my best friend. I remember my roommate and I would order two large pizzas (delivery, of course) and eat them in one sitting. One for her and one for me. It was nothing to go through a whole pizza box each and still fit into our size 2 clothes the next day.

When I was in my late twenties, I had a job working with youth at a church in Colorado. Our youth trips always involved extreme sports—snowboarding, river rafting, trekking. I didn't order whole pizzas anymore, but I didn't really watch what I ate either. Whatever I consumed, I usually burned off that night playing broom hockey or an intense round of laser tag at a junior high all-nighter.

I eventually changed jobs and landed an office job I really enjoyed. But that's when it happened. My older sister, the self-proclaimed prophet, always warned me that my good fortune (and good figure) would change someday. "Yeah, whatever," I'd say as I stuffed my face with a burger. I figured she was just jealous. I honestly didn't believe her doomsday prediction. She got Mom's apple shape; I got Dad's athleticism.

It took three years into my thirties, giving birth to two children and trying on new swimsuits for the summer season before I finally conceded that aliens had absconded with my former body. I now live in one I don't recognize. Where'd I get that extra set of thighs, that spare tire and that growing double chin?

I talked to my doctor about my sedentary lifestyle and sluggish metabolism, expecting a $35-co-pay lecture on the benefits of exercise (which I would interpret as a free pass until my forties when I'd have to get serious). Instead, I received a shock. Turns out I also got Dad's predisposition to diabetes. Between my genetics, my obesity and my lack of exercise, I was headed for trouble. How could that be true?

—Rebecca

WHILE MANY OF us are blessed

with good health, we cannot take it for granted. It can be a shock when we get to the point when we realize that our bodies aren't what they used to be—or worse, that we have nagging or even debilitating health problems. Keep in mind . . .

- *Women take mental stress to heart (literally).* Stress is a common component in many women's daily lives. Between work, family, church and other responsibilities, taking time for ourselves to develop a healthy lifestyle and a regular exercise program often falls to the bottom of our lists. Studies suggest that stress can constrict blood flow and contribute to a number of heart-related ailments. See what Jesus has to say about worrying about earthly things in Matthew 6:25–34.

- *A healthy woman's lifestyle involves the whole person, body and soul.* Yoga isn't just for transcendentalists anymore! Nor is Pilates just for Hollywood. These types of exercise programs tone and lengthen the body's muscles while de-stressing the mind, building mental health and confidence.

- *It's not about losing weight; it's about developing a healthy lifestyle.* Yes, physical activity and lowering our caloric intake are the keys to weight loss, but they are much more than a means to an end. Exercise and healthy eating habits are choices we make for personal wellness.

- *Your health is a gift from the Lord.* Like any other gift we have received from God, we must be good stewards of our health. God encourages us to avoid laziness (see Proverbs 26:13–15). If we begin to take our bodies for granted, we risk losing something precious. Neglecting our health is a hard habit to break—many of us know too well that the spirit is willing, but the flesh is weak. Ask God to help you make the right choices to develop a healthy lifestyle—starting now.

"91 percent of adults rank good health as their number one priority in life."

—Barna Research Group (2000)

585

"YOU WERE BOUGHT AT A PRICE. THEREFORE HONOR GOD WITH YOUR BODIES."

1 CORINTHIANS 6:20

SEE ALSO

2 Corinthians 4:16–18

2 Corinthians 12:7–10

3 John 2

For more on **Health**, check the index.

⁹They went to Hilkiah the high priest and gave him the money that had been brought into the temple of God, which the Levites who were the gatekeepers had collected from the people of Manasseh, Ephraim and the entire remnant of Israel and from all the people of Judah and Benjamin and the inhabitants of Jerusalem. ¹⁰Then they entrusted it to the men appointed to supervise the work on the Lord's temple. These men paid the workers who repaired and restored the temple. ¹¹They also gave money to the carpenters and builders to purchase dressed stone, and timber for joists and beams for the buildings that the kings of Judah had allowed to fall into ruin.

¹²The workers did their work faithfully. Over them to direct them were Jahath and Obadiah, Levites descended from Merari, and Zechariah and Meshullam, descended from Kohath. The Levites—all who were skilled in playing musical instruments— ¹³had charge of the laborers and supervised all the workers from job to job. Some of the Levites were secretaries, scribes and gatekeepers.

The Book of the Law Found

¹⁴While they were bringing out the money that had been taken into the temple of the Lord, Hilkiah the priest found the Book of the Law of the Lord that had been given through Moses. ¹⁵Hilkiah said to Shaphan the secretary, "I have found the Book of the Law in the temple of the Lord." He gave it to Shaphan.

¹⁶Then Shaphan took the book to the king and reported to him: "Your officials are doing everything that has been committed to them. ¹⁷They have paid out the money that was in the temple of the Lord and have entrusted it to the supervisors and workers." ¹⁸Then Shaphan the secretary informed the king, "Hilkiah the priest has given me a book." And Shaphan read from it in the presence of the king.

¹⁹When the king heard the words of the Law, he tore his robes. ²⁰He gave these orders to Hilkiah, Ahikam son of Shaphan, Abdon son of Micah,ᵃ Shaphan the secretary and Asaiah the king's attendant: ²¹"Go and inquire of the Lord for me and for the remnant in Israel and Judah about what is written in this book that has been found. Great is the Lord's anger that is poured out on us because those who have gone before us have not kept the word of the Lord; they have not acted in accordance with all that is written in this book."

²²Hilkiah and those the king had sent with himᵇ went to speak to the prophet Huldah, who was the wife of Shallum son of Tokhath,ᶜ the son of Hasrah,ᵈ keeper of the wardrobe. She lived in Jerusalem, in the New Quarter.

²³She said to them, "This is what the Lord, the God of Israel, says: Tell the man who sent you to me, ²⁴'This is what the Lord says: I am going to bring disaster on this place and its people—all the curses written in the book that has been read in the presence of the king of Judah. ²⁵Because they have forsaken me and burned incense to other gods and aroused my anger by all that their hands have made,ᵉ my anger will be poured out on this place and will not be quenched.' ²⁶Tell the king of Judah, who sent you to inquire of the Lord, 'This is what the Lord, the God of Israel, says concerning the words you heard: ²⁷Because your heart was responsive and you humbled yourself before God when you heard what he spoke against this place and its people, and because you humbled yourself before me and tore your robes and wept in my presence, I have heard you, declares the Lord. ²⁸Now I will gather you to your ancestors, and you will be buried in peace. Your eyes will not see all the disaster I am going to bring on this place and on those who live here.'"

So they took her answer back to the king.

²⁹Then the king called together all the elders of Judah and Jerusalem. ³⁰He went up to the temple of the Lord with the people of Judah, the inhabitants of Jerusalem, the priests and the Levites—all the people from the least to the greatest. He read in their hearing all the words of the Book of the Covenant, which had been found in the temple of the Lord. ³¹The king stood by his pillar and renewed the covenant in the presence of the Lord—to follow the Lord and keep his commands, statutes and decrees with all his heart and all his soul, and to obey the words of the covenant written in this book.

³²Then he had everyone in Jerusalem and Benjamin pledge themselves to it; the people of Jerusalem did this in accordance with the covenant of God, the God of their ancestors.

ᵃ 20 Also called *Akbor son of Micaiah*   ᵇ 22 One Hebrew manuscript, Vulgate and Syriac; most Hebrew manuscripts do not have *had sent with him.*   ᶜ 22 Also called *Tikvah*   ᵈ 22 Also called *Harhas*   ᵉ 25 Or *by everything they have done*

ASKmeanything

deborah

Judges 4–5

You have some very impressive credentials. Tell us about yourself.

I was a prophetess, a wife, a warrior and a songwriter. But I suppose my main role was that of judge. Typically, I sat underneath the palm tree (which came to be known as my palm tree!) between the towns of Ramah and Bethel and heard the people's cases. Later, after Israel had defeated Sisera's army, I ruled Israel from that same palm tree for 40 years. But I suppose you most want to know about my role as a prophetess and warrior.

Yes, definitely. What can you tell us about that?

God had given me a message to pass on to one of our military leaders, Barak. It was during a very bleak period in our history. We had been harassed and oppressed by Sisera and his army for years. The people were dejected and basically had lost all hope. But God gave me the exact battle plan for defeating our enemies, and I summoned Barak and told him what to do. The odds were tremendously stacked against us, but God had assured us of victory. What more did we need?

Do you feel you were at a disadvantage, being a woman and giving military instructions?

Well, it always makes me wonder how Barak would have responded if, say, Joshua had given him those same instructions. Would he still have hesitated? Would he still have insisted that Joshua go along with him? I was definitely an oddity—a women in authority in a decidedly man's world. But I couldn't let that deter me from doing what I knew was right. God was my authority. That's all I needed.

In the end, Barak did obey, and we did defeat Sisera. But the Lord gave the final victory over Sisera to—you guessed it—another woman!

What advice would you give to women who are trying to find their place in male-dominated fields?

Remember who your ultimate authority is. God has given you unique talents and has equipped you for a specific role. He has placed you in that field. Trust God with the ultimate outcome of whatever you're attempting to achieve, and someday you may be able to sing your own victory song.

FOR MORE INSIGHT: For other instances of courageous women in the Bible, read about Jael and how she defeated Sisera (see Judges 4:18–22), Esther's courageous actions on behalf of the Jews in Persia (see Esther 4–5) and a young woman's amazing response to news of an unplanned pregnancy (see Luke 1:26–38).

587

³³Josiah removed all the detestable idols from all the territory belonging to the Israelites, and he had all who were present in Israel serve the Lord their God. As long as he lived, they did not fail to follow the Lord, the God of their ancestors.

Josiah Celebrates the Passover

35 Josiah celebrated the Passover to the Lord in Jerusalem, and the Passover lamb was slaughtered on the fourteenth day of the first month. ²He appointed the priests to their duties and encouraged them in the service of the Lord's temple. ³He said to the Levites, who instructed all Israel and who had been consecrated to the Lord: "Put the sacred ark in the temple that Solomon son of David king of Israel built. It is not to be carried about on your shoulders. Now serve the Lord your God and his people Israel. ⁴Prepare yourselves by families in your divisions, according to the instructions written by David king of Israel and by his son Solomon.

⁵"Stand in the holy place with a group of Levites for each subdivision of the families of your fellow Israelites, the lay people. ⁶Slaughter the Passover lambs, consecrate yourselves and prepare the lambs for your fellow Israelites, doing what the Lord commanded through Moses."

⁷Josiah provided for all the lay people who were there a total of thirty thousand lambs and goats for the Passover offerings, and also three thousand cattle—all from the king's own possessions.

⁸His officials also contributed voluntarily to the people and the priests and Levites. Hilkiah, Zechariah and Jehiel, the officials in charge of God's temple, gave the priests twenty-six hundred Passover offerings and three hundred cattle. ⁹Also Konaniah along with Shemaiah and Nethanel, his brothers, and Hashabiah, Jeiel and Jozabad, the leaders of the Levites, provided five thousand Passover offerings and five hundred head of cattle for the Levites.

¹⁰The service was arranged and the priests stood in their places with the Levites in their divisions as the king had ordered. ¹¹The Passover lambs were slaughtered, and the priests splashed against the altar the blood handed to them, while the Levites skinned the animals. ¹²They set aside the burnt offerings to give them to the subdivisions of the families of the people to offer to the Lord, as it is written in the Book of Moses. They did the same with the cattle. ¹³They roasted the Passover animals over the fire as prescribed, and boiled the holy offerings in pots, caldrons and pans and served them quickly to all the people. ¹⁴After this, they made preparations for themselves and for the priests, because the priests, the descendants of Aaron, were sacrificing the burnt offerings and the fat portions until nightfall. So the Levites made preparations for themselves and for the Aaronic priests.

¹⁵The musicians, the descendants of Asaph, were in the places prescribed by David, Asaph, Heman and Jeduthun the king's seer. The gatekeepers at each gate did not need to leave their posts, because their fellow Levites made the preparations for them.

¹⁶So at that time the entire service of the Lord was carried out for the celebration of the Passover and the offering of burnt offerings on the altar of the Lord, as King Josiah had ordered. ¹⁷The Israelites who were present celebrated the Passover at that time and observed the Festival of Unleavened Bread for seven days. ¹⁸The Passover had not been observed like this in Israel since the days of the prophet Samuel; and none of the kings of Israel had ever celebrated such a Passover as did Josiah, with the priests, the Levites and all Judah and Israel who were there with the people of Jerusalem. ¹⁹This Passover was celebrated in the eighteenth year of Josiah's reign.

The Death of Josiah

²⁰After all this, when Josiah had set the temple in order, Necho king of Egypt went up to fight at Carchemish on the Euphrates, and Josiah marched out to meet him in battle. ²¹But Necho sent messengers to him, saying, "What quarrel is there, king of Judah, between you and me? It is not you I am attacking at this time, but the house with which I am at war. God has told me to hurry; so stop opposing God, who is with me, or he will destroy you."

²²Josiah, however, would not turn away from him, but disguised himself to engage him in battle. He would not listen to what Necho had said at God's command but went to fight him on the plain of Megiddo.

²³Archers shot King Josiah, and he told his officers, "Take me away; I am badly wounded." ²⁴So they

took him out of his chariot, put him in his other chariot and brought him to Jerusalem, where he died. He was buried in the tombs of his ancestors, and all Judah and Jerusalem mourned for him.

²⁵Jeremiah composed laments for Josiah, and to this day all the male and female singers commemorate Josiah in the laments. These became a tradition in Israel and are written in the Laments.

²⁶The other events of Josiah's reign and his acts of devotion in accordance with what is written in the Law of the LORD— ²⁷all the events, from beginning to end, are written in the book of the kings of Israel and Judah. ¹And the people of the land took Jehoahaz son of Josiah and made him king in Jerusalem in place of his father.

36

Jehoahaz King of Judah

²Jehoahaz^a was twenty-three years old when he became king, and he reigned in Jerusalem three months. ³The king of Egypt dethroned him in Jerusalem and imposed on Judah a levy of a hundred talents^b of silver and a talent^c of gold. ⁴The king of Egypt made Eliakim, a brother of Jehoahaz, king over Judah and Jerusalem and changed Eliakim's name to Jehoiakim. But Necho took Eliakim's brother Jehoahaz and carried him off to Egypt.

Jehoiakim King of Judah

⁵Jehoiakim was twenty-five years old when he became king, and he reigned in Jerusalem eleven years. He did evil in the eyes of the LORD his God. ⁶Nebuchadnezzar king of Babylon attacked him and bound him with bronze shackles to take him to Babylon. ⁷Nebuchadnezzar also took to Babylon articles from the temple of the LORD and put them in his temple^d there.

⁸The other events of Jehoiakim's reign, the detestable things he did and all that was found against him, are written in the book of the kings of Israel and Judah. And Jehoiachin his son succeeded him as king.

Jehoiachin King of Judah

⁹Jehoiachin was eighteen^e years old when he became king, and he reigned in Jerusalem three months and ten days. He did evil in the eyes of the LORD. ¹⁰In the spring, King Nebuchadnezzar sent for him and brought him to Babylon, together with articles of value from the temple of the LORD, and he made Jehoiachin's uncle,^f Zedekiah, king over Judah and Jerusalem.

Zedekiah King of Judah

¹¹Zedekiah was twenty-one years old when he became king, and he reigned in Jerusalem eleven years. ¹²He did evil in the eyes of the LORD his God and did not humble himself before Jeremiah the prophet, who spoke the word of the LORD. ¹³He also rebelled against King Nebuchadnezzar, who had made him take an oath in God's name. He became stiff-necked and hardened his heart and would not turn to the LORD, the God of Israel. ¹⁴Furthermore, all the leaders of the priests and the people became more and more unfaithful, following all the detestable practices of the nations and defiling the temple of the LORD, which he had consecrated in Jerusalem.

The Fall of Jerusalem

¹⁵The LORD, the God of their ancestors, sent word to them through his messengers again and again, because he had pity on his people and on his dwelling place. ¹⁶But they mocked God's messengers, despised his words and scoffed at his prophets until the wrath of the LORD was aroused against his people and there was no remedy. ¹⁷He brought up against them the king of the Babylonians,^g who killed

589

conversations

consequences «» 36:15–16

1» What are the consequences of consistently disobeying God?

2» Is there a sinful area in your life that you refuse to change or feel you can't change?

3» Does a nation's sinfulness result in consequences? What kinds?

For more on **consequences**, check the index.
For the next Conversations, go to p. 594.

---

^a 2 Hebrew *Joahaz*, a variant of *Jehoahaz*; also in verse 4 ^b 3 That is, about 3 3/4 tons or about 3.4 metric tons ^c 3 That is, about 75 pounds or about 34 kilograms ^d 7 Or *palace* ^e 9 One Hebrew manuscript, some Septuagint manuscripts and Syriac (see also 2 Kings 24:8); most Hebrew manuscripts *eight* ^f 10 Hebrew *brother*, that is, relative (see 2 Kings 24:17) ^g 17 Or *Chaldeans*

their young men with the sword in the sanctuary, and spared neither young man nor young woman, the elderly or the aged. God gave them all into the hands of Nebuchadnezzar. ¹⁸He carried to Babylon all the articles from the temple of God, both large and small, and the treasures of the LORD's temple and the treasures of the king and his officials. ¹⁹They set fire to God's temple and broke down the wall of Jerusalem; they burned all the palaces and destroyed everything of value there.

²⁰He carried into exile to Babylon the remnant, who escaped from the sword, and they became servants to him and his successors until the kingdom of Persia came to power. ²¹The land enjoyed its sabbath rests; all the time of its desolation it rested, until the seventy years were completed in fulfillment of the word of the LORD spoken by Jeremiah.

²²In the first year of Cyrus king of Persia, in order to fulfill the word of the LORD spoken by Jeremiah, the LORD moved the heart of Cyrus king of Persia to make a proclamation throughout his realm and also to put it in writing:

²³"This is what Cyrus king of Persia says:

"'The LORD, the God of heaven, has given me all the kingdoms of the earth and he has appointed me to build a temple for him at Jerusalem in Judah. Any of his people among you—may the LORD their God be with them, and let them go up.'"

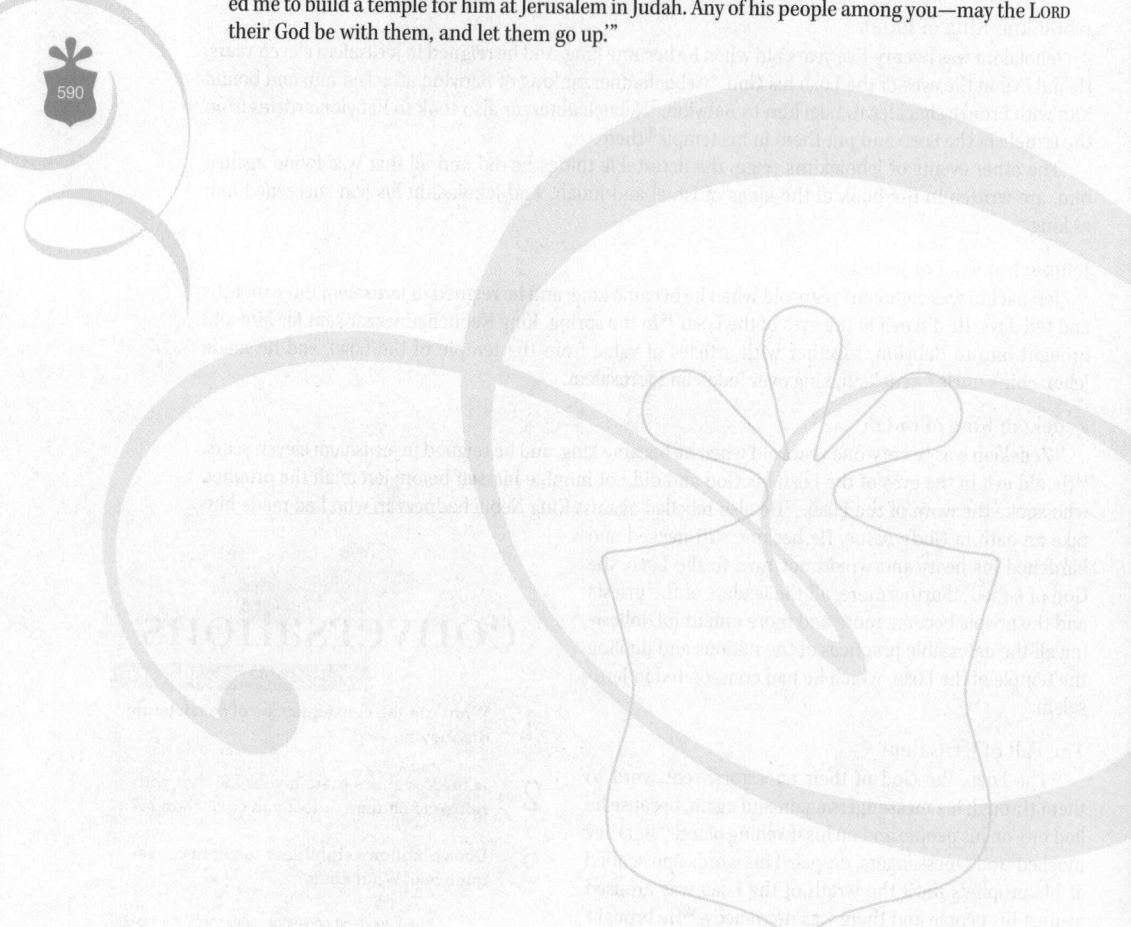

Can God use a pagan in his plans? » (1:1–4)

Is it possible to get a clean start, spiritually speaking? » (3:1–13)

If we're doing what God wants, then it shouldn't be this hard, right? » (4:1–24)

Was it worth the wait? » (8:15–36)

ezra

AUTHOR
Unknown, but possibly Ezra.

AUDIENCE
All Israel.

DATE
Around 440 B.C.

SETTING
The homecoming of the exiles from Babylon who will start rebuilding God's temple.

VERSE TO REMEMBER
"Any of his people among you—may their God be with them, and let them go up to Jerusalem in Judah and build the temple of the LORD, the God of Israel, the God who is in Jerusalem." (1:3)

THEME TO CONSIDER
Even when we we've strayed far away, God's grace lovingly calls us back to him.

Cyrus Helps the Exiles to Return

1 In the first year of Cyrus king of Persia, in order to fulfill the word of the LORD spoken by Jeremiah, the LORD moved the heart of Cyrus king of Persia to make a proclamation throughout his realm and also to put it in writing:

²"This is what Cyrus king of Persia says:

"'The LORD, the God of heaven, has given me all the kingdoms of the earth and he has appointed me to build a temple for him at Jerusalem in Judah. ³Any of his people among you—may their God be with them, and let them go up to Jerusalem in Judah and build the temple of the LORD, the God of Israel, the God who is in Jerusalem. ⁴And in any locality where survivors may now be living, the people are to provide them with silver and gold, with goods and livestock, and with freewill offerings for the temple of God in Jerusalem.'"

⁵Then the family heads of Judah and Benjamin, and the priests and Levites—everyone whose heart God had moved—prepared to go up and build the house of the LORD in Jerusalem. ⁶All their neighbors assisted them with articles of silver and gold, with goods and livestock, and with valuable gifts, in addition to all the freewill offerings.

⁷Moreover, King Cyrus brought out the articles belonging to the temple of the LORD, which Nebuchadnezzar had carried away from Jerusalem and had placed in the temple of his god.ᵃ ⁸Cyrus king of Persia had them brought by Mithredath the treasurer, who counted them out to Sheshbazzar the prince of Judah.

⁹This was the inventory:

gold dishes	30
silver dishes	1,000
silver pans ᵇ	29
¹⁰ gold bowls	30
matching silver bowls	410
other articles	1,000

¹¹In all, there were 5,400 articles of gold and of silver. Sheshbazzar brought all these along with the exiles when they came up from Babylon to Jerusalem.

The List of the Exiles Who Returned

2 Now these are the people of the province who came up from the captivity of the exiles, whom Nebuchadnezzar king of Babylon had taken captive to Babylon (they returned to Jerusalem and Judah, all to their own towns, ²in company with Zerubbabel, Joshua, Nehemiah, Seraiah, Reelaiah, Mordecai, Bilshan, Mispar, Bigvai, Rehum and Baanah):

The list of the men of the people of Israel:

ᵃ 7 Or gods   ᵇ 9 The meaning of the Hebrew for this word is uncertain.

HE IS: a builder

1:2–4 Though he had torn the Israelites away from their land, God kept his promise to restore them as a nation and rebuild their temple. Much to everyone's surprise, God compelled a pagan ruler to fulfill his divine design to build his temple.

It may seem that your life is in tatters—all you see is ruins where you once saw progress. You may feel discouraged, but don't give up. God is *a builder*, and a very creative one at that. Against all odds, he will use kings or commoners to restore your life to his intended design.

For the next He Is, go to p. 601.

³ the descendants of Parosh	2,172
⁴ of Shephatiah	372
⁵ of Arah	775
⁶ of Pahath-Moab (through the line of Jeshua and Joab)	2,812
⁷ of Elam	1,254
⁸ of Zattu	945
⁹ of Zakkai	760
¹⁰ of Bani	642
¹¹ of Bebai	623
¹² of Azgad	1,222
¹³ of Adonikam	666
¹⁴ of Bigvai	2,056
¹⁵ of Adin	454
¹⁶ of Ater (through Hezekiah)	98
¹⁷ of Bezai	323
¹⁸ of Jorah	112
¹⁹ of Hashum	223
²⁰ of Gibbar	95
²¹ the men of Bethlehem	123
²² of Netophah	56
²³ of Anathoth	128
²⁴ of Azmaveth	42
²⁵ of Kiriath Jearim,ᵃ Kephirah and Beeroth	743
²⁶ of Ramah and Geba	621
²⁷ of Mikmash	122
²⁸ of Bethel and Ai	223
²⁹ of Nebo	52
³⁰ of Magbish	156
³¹ of the other Elam	1,254
³² of Harim	320
³³ of Lod, Hadid and Ono	725
³⁴ of Jericho	345
³⁵ of Senaah	3,630

³⁶ The priests:

the descendants of Jedaiah (through the family of Jeshua)	973
³⁷ of Immer	1,052
³⁸ of Pashhur	1,247
³⁹ of Harim	1,017

⁴⁰ The Levites:

the descendants of Jeshua and Kadmiel (of the line of Hodaviah)	74

⁴¹ The musicians:

the descendants of Asaph	128

⁴² The gatekeepers of the temple:

the descendants of Shallum, Ater, Talmon, Akkub, Hatita and Shobai	139

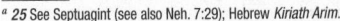

ᵃ 25 See Septuagint (see also Neh. 7:29); Hebrew *Kiriath Arim*.

⁴³The temple servants:

the descendants of
Ziha, Hasupha, Tabbaoth,
⁴⁴Keros, Siaha, Padon,
⁴⁵Lebanah, Hagabah, Akkub,
⁴⁶Hagab, Shalmai, Hanan,
⁴⁷Giddel, Gahar, Reaiah,
⁴⁸Rezin, Nekoda, Gazzam,
⁴⁹Uzza, Paseah, Besai,
⁵⁰Asnah, Meunim, Nephusim,
⁵¹Bakbuk, Hakupha, Harhur,
⁵²Bazluth, Mehida, Harsha,
⁵³Barkos, Sisera, Temah,
⁵⁴Neziah and Hatipha

⁵⁵The descendants of the servants of Solomon:

the descendants of
Sotai, Hassophereth, Peruda,
⁵⁶Jaala, Darkon, Giddel,
⁵⁷Shephatiah, Hattil,
Pokereth-Hazzebaim and Ami

⁵⁸The temple servants and the descendants
of the servants of Solomon   392

⁵⁹The following came up from the towns of Tel Melah, Tel Harsha, Kerub, Addon and Immer, but they could not show that their families were descended from Israel:

⁶⁰The descendants of
Delaiah, Tobiah and Nekoda   652

⁶¹And from among the priests:

The descendants of
Hobaiah, Hakkoz and Barzillai (a man who had married a daughter of Barzillai the Gileadite and was called by that name).

⁶²These searched for their family records, but they could not find them and so were excluded from the priesthood as unclean. ⁶³The governor ordered them not to eat any of the most sacred food until there was a priest ministering with the Urim and Thummim.

⁶⁴The whole company numbered 42,360, ⁶⁵besides their 7,337 male and female slaves; and they also had 200 male and female singers. ⁶⁶They had 736 horses, 245 mules, ⁶⁷435 camels and 6,720 donkeys.

⁶⁸When they arrived at the house of the LORD in Jerusalem, some of the heads of the families gave freewill offerings toward the rebuilding of the house of God on its site. ⁶⁹According to their ability they gave to the treasury for this work 61,000 darics*a* of gold, 5,000 minas*b* of silver and 100 priestly garments.

conversations

giving «» 2:68–69

1 » What financial responsibility (if any) do you feel you have towards your church?

2 » How important is it to support your church?

3 » What does it mean for you to give according to your ability?

For more on giving, check the index.
For the next Conversations, go to p. 595.

a 69 That is, about 1,100 pounds or about 500 kilograms   *b 69* That is, about 3 tons or about 2.8 metric tons

⁷⁰The priests, the Levites, the musicians, the gatekeepers and the temple servants settled in their own towns, along with some of the other people, and the rest of the Israelites settled in their towns.

Rebuilding the Altar

3 When the seventh month came and the Israelites had settled in their towns, the people assembled with one accord in Jerusalem. ²Then Joshua son of Jozadak and his fellow priests and Zerubbabel son of Shealtiel and his associates began to build the altar of the God of Israel to sacrifice burnt offerings on it, in accordance with what is written in the Law of Moses the man of God. ³Despite their fear of the peoples around them, they built the altar on its foundation and sacrificed burnt offerings on it to the LORD, both the morning and evening sacrifices. ⁴Then in accordance with what is written, they celebrated the Festival of Tabernacles with the required number of burnt offerings prescribed for each day. ⁵After that, they presented the regular burnt offerings, the New Moon sacrifices and the sacrifices for all the appointed sacred festivals of the LORD, as well as those brought as freewill offerings to the LORD. ⁶On the first day of the seventh month they began to offer burnt offerings to the LORD, though the foundation of the LORD's temple had not yet been laid.

Rebuilding the Temple

⁷Then they gave money to the masons and carpenters, and gave food and drink and olive oil to the people of Sidon and Tyre, so that they would bring cedar logs by sea from Lebanon to Joppa, as authorized by Cyrus king of Persia.

⁸In the second month of the second year after their arrival at the house of God in Jerusalem, Zerubbabel son of Shealtiel, Joshua son of Jozadak and the rest of the people (the priests and the Levites and all who had returned from the captivity to Jerusalem) began the work, appointing Levites twenty years old and older to supervise the building of the house of the LORD. ⁹Joshua and his sons and brothers and Kadmiel and his sons (descendants of Hodaviah[a]) and the sons of Henadad and their sons and brothers—all Levites—joined together in supervising those working on the house of God.

¹⁰When the builders laid the foundation of the temple of the LORD, the priests in their vestments and with trumpets, and the Levites (the sons of Asaph) with cymbals, took their places to praise the LORD, as prescribed by David king of Israel. ¹¹With praise and thanksgiving they sang to the LORD:

> "He is good;
> his love toward Israel endures forever."

And all the people gave a great shout of praise to the LORD, because the foundation of the house of the LORD was laid. ¹²But many of the older priests and Levites and family heads, who had seen the former temple, wept aloud when they saw the foundation of this temple being laid, while many others shouted for joy. ¹³No one could distinguish the sound of the shouts of joy from the sound of weeping, because the people made so much noise. And the sound was heard far away.

Opposition to the Rebuilding

4 When the enemies of Judah and Benjamin heard that the exiles were building a temple for the LORD, the God of Israel, ²they came to Zerubbabel and to the heads of the families and said, "Let us help you build because, like you, we seek your God and have been sacrificing to him since the time of Esarhaddon king of Assyria, who brought us here."

³But Zerubbabel, Joshua and the rest of the heads of the families of Israel answered, "You have no part with us in building a temple to our God. We alone will build it for the LORD, the God of Israel, as King Cyrus, the king of Persia, commanded us."

conversations

dissatisfaction «» 3:12–13

1» What dissatisfies you most about your life? Why?

2» Why do you compare your accomplishments with others' or with your past?

3» How can you find true contentment in your life?

For more on **dissatisfaction**, check the index. For the next Conversations, go to p. 613.

ᵃ 9 Hebrew *Yehudah*, a variant of *Hodaviah*

[4] Then the peoples around them set out to discourage the people of Judah and make them afraid to go on building.[a] [5] They bribed officials to work against them and frustrate their plans during the entire reign of Cyrus king of Persia and down to the reign of Darius king of Persia.

Later Opposition Under Xerxes and Artaxerxes

[6] At the beginning of the reign of Xerxes,[b] they lodged an accusation against the people of Judah and Jerusalem.

[7] And in the days of Artaxerxes king of Persia, Bishlam, Mithredath, Tabeel and the rest of his associates wrote a letter to Artaxerxes. The letter was written in Aramaic script and in the Aramaic language.[c][d]

[8] Rehum the commanding officer and Shimshai the secretary wrote a letter against Jerusalem to Artaxerxes the king as follows:

[9] Rehum the commanding officer and Shimshai the secretary, together with the rest of their associates—the judges, officials and administrators over the people from Persia, Uruk and Babylon, the Elamites of Susa, [10] and the other people whom the great and honorable Ashurbanipal deported and settled in the city of Samaria and elsewhere in Trans-Euphrates.

[11] (This is a copy of the letter they sent him.)

To King Artaxerxes,

From your servants in Trans-Euphrates:

[12] The king should know that the people who came up to us from you have gone to Jerusalem and are rebuilding that rebellious and wicked city. They are restoring the walls and repairing the foundations. [13] Furthermore, the king should know that if this city is built and its walls are restored, no more taxes, tribute or duty will be paid, and eventually the royal revenues will suffer.[e] [14] Now since we are under obligation to the palace and it is not proper for us to see the king dishonored, we are sending this message to inform the king, [15] so that a search may be made in the archives of your predecessors. In these records you will find that this city is a rebellious city, troublesome to kings and provinces, a place with a long history of sedition. That is why this city was destroyed. [16] We inform the king that if this city is built and its walls are restored, you will be left with nothing in Trans-Euphrates.

[17] The king sent this reply:

To Rehum the commanding officer, Shimshai the secretary and the rest of their associates living in Samaria and elsewhere in Trans-Euphrates:

Greetings.

[18] The letter you sent us has been read and translated in my presence. [19] I issued an order and a search was made, and it was found that this city has a long history of revolt against kings and has been a place of rebellion and sedition. [20] Jerusalem has had powerful kings ruling over the whole of Trans-Euphrates, and taxes, tribute and duty were paid to them. [21] Now issue an order to these peo-

596

at issue: conflict at work

4:4–6 Have you ever felt like someone at work was out to get you? She talks about you behind your back, makes you look bad in front of others and downplays your accomplishments. What should you do? First, make sure you're a woman of integrity so the accusations against you aren't believable. Next, like Ezra, pray and seek wisdom from God's Word. Pursue justice, when appropriate. Then, realizing what's beyond your control, do your best to be at peace. Forgive again and again, repaying evil with kindness—just as Christ has done with you. And trust God to work things out in his time.

ple to stop work, so that this city will not be rebuilt until I so order. ²²Be careful not to neglect this matter. Why let this threat grow, to the detriment of the royal interests?

²³As soon as the copy of the letter of King Artaxerxes was read to Rehum and Shimshai the secretary and their associates, they went immediately to the Jews in Jerusalem and compelled them by force to stop.

²⁴Thus the work on the house of God in Jerusalem came to a standstill until the second year of the reign of Darius king of Persia.

Tattenai's Letter to Darius

5 Now Haggai the prophet and Zechariah the prophet, a descendant of Iddo, prophesied to the Jews in Judah and Jerusalem in the name of the God of Israel, who was over them. ²Then Zerubbabel son of Shealtiel and Joshua son of Jozadak set to work to rebuild the house of God in Jerusalem. And the prophets of God were with them, supporting them.

³At that time Tattenai, governor of Trans-Euphrates, and Shethar-Bozenai and their associates went to them and asked, "Who authorized you to rebuild this temple and to finish it?" ⁴They[a] also asked, "What are the names of those who are constructing this building?" ⁵But the eye of their God was watching over the elders of the Jews, and they were not stopped until a report could go to Darius and his written reply be received.

⁶This is a copy of the letter that Tattenai, governor of Trans-Euphrates, and Shethar-Bozenai and their associates, the officials of Trans-Euphrates, sent to King Darius. ⁷The report they sent him read as follows:

To King Darius:

Cordial greetings.

⁸The king should know that we went to the district of Judah, to the temple of the great God. The people are building it with large stones and placing the timbers in the walls. The work is being carried on with diligence and is making rapid progress under their direction.

⁹We questioned the elders and asked them, "Who authorized you to rebuild this temple and to finish it?" ¹⁰We also asked them their names, so that we could write down the names of their leaders for your information.

¹¹This is the answer they gave us:

"We are the servants of the God of heaven and earth, and we are rebuilding the temple that was built many years ago, one that a great king of Israel built and finished. ¹²But because our ancestors angered the God of heaven, he gave them into the hands of Nebuchadnezzar the Chaldean, king of Babylon, who destroyed this temple and deported the people to Babylon.

¹³"However, in the first year of Cyrus king of Babylon, King Cyrus issued a decree to rebuild this house of God. ¹⁴He even removed from the temple[b] of Babylon the gold and silver articles of the house of God, which Nebuchadnezzar had taken from the temple in Jerusalem and brought to the temple[b] in Babylon. Then King Cyrus gave them to a man named Sheshbazzar, whom he had appointed governor, ¹⁵and he told him, 'Take these articles and go and deposit them in the temple in Jerusalem. And rebuild the house of God on its site.'

¹⁶"So this Sheshbazzar came and laid the foundations of the house of God in Jerusalem. From that day to the present it has been under construction but is not yet finished."

¹⁷Now if it pleases the king, let a search be made in the royal archives of Babylon to see if King Cyrus did in fact issue a decree to rebuild this house of God in Jerusalem. Then let the king send us his decision in this matter.

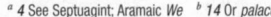

a 4 See Septuagint; Aramaic We   b 14 Or palace

myth# 39 "I SHOULDN'T LET ANYONE GET TOO CLOSE TO ME."

It could have gone either way.

I could have sworn off relationships forever. Or I could have learned to give love another chance. It's not as if I'd never had my heart broken before this happened. But this one was different. I felt like we could have been something special.

We met under the strangest circumstances—my moving halfway across the country for a new job. And his return to getting involved in church after a long absence. It had the makings of one of those great love stories you imagine telling your grandkids one day. I remember the first Sunday we met. We went out to lunch with a group after church, and he and I leaned across the table at the Italian restaurant and talked the entire time. I felt like I already knew him somehow. We ended up talking more in the parking lot that afternoon. And then he called that night to see if I wanted to go to dinner. We acted like old friends, and I told him things I had never told anyone else.

For the next three months, we spent nearly every day together—e-mailing each other back and forth from work, grabbing a bite at lunch or making dinner together. He was the first person I met in the city. And he'd found his way to me somehow. It'd been so long since I'd found anyone remotely interesting and with the same passions and viewpoints I had about life. We just clicked, and for the first time in a long time, I let a man into my heart.

I'm still not sure exactly how we broke up. I know my move back to California triggered it. We talked about him moving cross-country with me and getting a job there. He told me he could see himself married to me. Funny, at the time I didn't realize that I was in love with him, but how else can I explain the void I felt without him in my life? But he didn't come with me. And I couldn't go back to him. Days turned into weeks, into months, and I felt like my life had lost its dazzle. We'd been on the verge of a lifetime commitment, I think, and when that connection was broken, I was shattered.

I vowed I would never love anyone again the way I'd loved him. It hurt too much. In a way it feels like my loss, but I can't bear that kind of pain again.

—Misty

HEALING FROM PAST hurts

takes courage, tenacity and time. Women who deal with the temptation to keep others at arms' length are usually exercising a heightened response of self-preservation. Any number of situations, including parents' divorce in child-hood, sexual abuse, infidelity or a break-up in a relationship can cause this reflex. After some-one deeply wounds us, it's normal to feel like shutting down so that no one can hurt us again. However, if we indulge this natural response and develop a habit of putting up walls, we never move past our pain. Following Jesus Christ as our model for living means we must loosen the hold our pain has on us and truly engage with other people. And that involves risk—enormous risks for people from painful situations.

Are you willing to take that risk? Remember . . .

- Forgiving someone else doesn't make what he or she did to you OK. It helps to make you OK.

- Holding on to yesterday's hurts affects today's potential relationships. Will you allow those who hurt you in the past to continue influencing your future?

- Others need you. You may be withholding love and encouragement from friends who really need you to let them in—for their sake (see 1 Peter 4:8–10).

- Every relationship has the potential for both blessing and pain. Consider how Judas, part of the inner circle, betrayed Jesus. But the other 11 remained faithful friends to him.

> "A stronghold is a destructive pattern that has a strong hold on us; patterns that have become so deeply entrenched we live them out habitually, never recognizing that we are exhibiting un-Christlike behavior or that we even have a choice to resist."
>
> —Anabell Gillham

599

"two are Better Than one."

ECCLESIASTES 4:9

SEE ALSO

Genesis 2:18
Proverbs 17:17
Proverbs 27:6

For more on **Relationships**, check the index.

The Decree of Darius

6 King Darius then issued an order, and they searched in the archives stored in the treasury at Babylon. ²A scroll was found in the citadel of Ecbatana in the province of Media, and this was written on it:

Memorandum:

³In the first year of King Cyrus, the king issued a decree concerning the temple of God in Jerusalem:

Let the temple be rebuilt as a place to present sacrifices, and let its foundations be laid. It is to be sixty cubits*ᵃ* high and sixty cubits wide, ⁴with three courses of large stones and one of timbers. The costs are to be paid by the royal treasury. ⁵Also, the gold and silver articles of the house of God, which Nebuchadnezzar took from the temple in Jerusalem and brought to Babylon, are to be returned to their places in the temple in Jerusalem; they are to be deposited in the house of God.

⁶Now then, Tattenai, governor of Trans-Euphrates, and Shethar-Bozenai and you other officials of that province, stay away from there. ⁷Do not interfere with the work on this temple of God. Let the governor of the Jews and the Jewish elders rebuild this house of God on its site.

⁸Moreover, I hereby decree what you are to do for these elders of the Jews in the construction of this house of God:

Their expenses are to be fully paid out of the royal treasury, from the revenues of Trans-Euphrates, so that the work will not stop. ⁹Whatever is needed—young bulls, rams, male lambs for burnt offerings to the God of heaven, and wheat, salt, wine and olive oil, as requested by the priests in Jerusalem—must be given them daily without fail, ¹⁰so that they may offer sacrifices pleasing to the God of heaven and pray for the well-being of the king and his sons.

¹¹Furthermore, I decree that if anyone defies this edict, a beam is to be pulled from their house and they are to be impaled on it. And for this crime their house is to be made a pile of rubble. ¹²May God, who has caused his Name to dwell there, overthrow any king or people who lifts a hand to change this decree or to destroy this temple in Jerusalem.

I Darius have decreed it. Let it be carried out with diligence.

Completion and Dedication of the Temple

¹³Then, because of the decree King Darius had sent, Tattenai, governor of Trans-Euphrates, and Shethar-Bozenai and their associates carried it out with diligence. ¹⁴So the elders of the Jews continued to build and prosper under the preaching of Haggai the prophet and Zechariah, a descendant of Iddo. They finished building the temple according to the command of the God of Israel and the decrees of Cyrus, Darius and Artaxerxes, kings of Persia. ¹⁵The temple was completed on the third day of the month Adar, in the sixth year of the reign of King Darius.

¹⁶Then the people of Israel—the priests, the Levites and the rest of the exiles—celebrated the dedication of the house of God with joy. ¹⁷For the dedication of this house of God they offered a hundred bulls, two hundred rams, four hundred male lambs and, as a sin offering*ᵇ* for all Israel, twelve male goats, one for each of the tribes of Israel. ¹⁸And they installed the priests in their divisions and the Levites in their groups for the service of God at Jerusalem, according to what is written in the Book of Moses.

The Passover

¹⁹On the fourteenth day of the first month, the exiles celebrated the Passover. ²⁰The priests and Levites had purified themselves and were all ceremonially clean. The Levites slaughtered the Passover lamb for all the exiles, for their relatives the priests and for themselves. ²¹So the Israelites who had returned from the exile ate it, together with all who had separated themselves from the unclean practices of their Gentile neighbors in order to seek the LORD, the God of Israel. ²²For seven days they celebrated with joy the Festival of Unleavened Bread, because the LORD had filled them with joy by changing

---

ᵃ 3 That is, about 90 feet or about 27 meters   ᵇ 17 Or purification offering

601

HE IS: mind-changing

6:22 King Darius thought the Israelites and their temple posed a threat, so he ordered a halt to their building. However, God used the earlier decree by King Cyrus to change Darius's mind, so that the temple could be completed and worship restored. The people were filled with joy when they saw what God had done.

Perhaps you're surrounded by people who are threatened by your faith or who stubbornly refuse to hear God's Word. Remember that God is *mind-changing*. He can lovingly alter people's obstinate minds and hearts to turn toward him. When that happens, there's joy all around.

For the next He Is, go to p. 615.

the attitude of the king of Assyria so that he assisted them in the work on the house of God, the God of Israel.

Ezra Comes to Jerusalem

7 After these things, during the reign of Artaxerxes king of Persia, Ezra son of Seraiah, the son of Azariah, the son of Hilkiah, ²the son of Shallum, the son of Zadok, the son of Ahitub, ³the son of Amariah, the son of Azariah, the son of Meraioth, ⁴the son of Zerahiah, the son of Uzzi, the son of Bukki, ⁵the son of Abishua, the son of Phinehas, the son of Eleazar, the son of Aaron the chief priest— ⁶this Ezra came up from Babylon. He was a teacher well versed in the Law of Moses, which the Lord, the God of Israel, had given. The king had granted him everything he asked, for the hand of the Lord his God was on him. ⁷Some of the Israelites, including priests, Levites, musicians, gatekeepers and temple servants, also came up to Jerusalem in the seventh year of King Artaxerxes.

⁸Ezra arrived in Jerusalem in the fifth month of the seventh year of the king. ⁹He had begun his journey from Babylon on the first day of the first month, and he arrived in Jerusalem on the first day of the fifth month, for the gracious hand of his God was on him. ¹⁰For Ezra had devoted himself to the study and observance of the Law of the Lord, and to teaching its decrees and laws in Israel.

King Artaxerxes' Letter to Ezra

¹¹This is a copy of the letter King Artaxerxes had given to Ezra the priest, a teacher of the Law, a man learned in matters concerning the commands and decrees of the Lord for Israel:

¹²*ª* Artaxerxes, king of kings,

To Ezra the priest, teacher of the Law of the God of heaven:

Greetings.

¹³Now I decree that any of the Israelites in my kingdom, including priests and Levites, who volunteer to go to Jerusalem with you, may go. ¹⁴You are sent by the king and his seven advisers to inquire about Judah and Jerusalem with regard to the Law of your God, which is in your hand. ¹⁵Moreover, you are to take with you the silver and gold that the king and his advisers have freely given to the God of Israel, whose dwelling is in Jerusalem, ¹⁶together with all the silver and gold you may obtain from the province of Babylon, as well as the freewill offerings of the people and priests for the temple of their God in Jerusalem. ¹⁷With this money be sure to buy bulls, rams and male lambs, together with their grain offerings and drink offerings, and sacrifice them on the altar of the temple of your God in Jerusalem.

¹⁸You and your fellow Israelites may then do whatever seems best with the rest of the silver and

ª 12 The text of Ezra 7:12-26 is in Aramaic.

gold, in accordance with the will of your God. ¹⁹Deliver to the God of Jerusalem all the articles entrusted to you for worship in the temple of your God. ²⁰And anything else needed for the temple of your God that you are responsible to supply, you may provide from the royal treasury.

²¹Now I, King Artaxerxes, decree that all the treasurers of Trans-Euphrates are to provide with diligence whatever Ezra the priest, the teacher of the Law of the God of heaven, may ask of you—²²up to a hundred talents*a* of silver, a hundred cors*b* of wheat, a hundred baths*c* of wine, a hundred baths*c* of olive oil, and salt without limit. ²³Whatever the God of heaven has prescribed, let it be done with diligence for the temple of the God of heaven. Why should his wrath fall on the realm of the king and of his sons? ²⁴You are also to know that you have no authority to impose taxes, tribute or duty on any of the priests, Levites, musicians, gatekeepers, temple servants or other workers at this house of God.

²⁵And you, Ezra, in accordance with the wisdom of your God, which you possess, appoint magistrates and judges to administer justice to all the people of Trans-Euphrates—all who know the laws of your God. And you are to teach any who do not know them. ²⁶Whoever does not obey the law of your God and the law of the king must surely be punished by death, banishment, confiscation of property, or imprisonment.

²⁷Praise be to the LORD, the God of our ancestors, who has put it into the king's heart to bring honor to the house of the LORD in Jerusalem in this way ²⁸and who has extended his good favor to me before the king and his advisers and all the king's powerful officials. Because the hand of the LORD my God was on me, I took courage and gathered leaders from Israel to go up with me.

List of the Family Heads Returning With Ezra

8 These are the family heads and those registered with them who came up with me from Babylon during the reign of King Artaxerxes:

²of the descendants of Phinehas, Gershom;
of the descendants of Ithamar, Daniel;
of the descendants of David, Hattush ³of the descendants of Shekaniah;

of the descendants of Parosh, Zechariah, and with him were registered 150 men;
⁴of the descendants of Pahath-Moab, Eliehoenai son of Zerahiah, and with him 200 men;
⁵of the descendants of Zattu,*d* Shekaniah son of Jahaziel, and with him 300 men;
⁶of the descendants of Adin, Ebed son of Jonathan, and with him 50 men;
⁷of the descendants of Elam, Jeshaiah son of Athaliah, and with him 70 men;
⁸of the descendants of Shephatiah, Zebadiah son of Michael, and with him 80 men;
⁹of the descendants of Joab, Obadiah son of Jehiel, and with him 218 men;
¹⁰of the descendants of Bani,*e* Shelomith son of Josiphiah, and with him 160 men;
¹¹of the descendants of Bebai, Zechariah son of Bebai, and with him 28 men;
¹²of the descendants of Azgad, Johanan son of Hakkatan, and with him 110 men;
¹³of the descendants of Adonikam, the last ones, whose names were Eliphelet, Jeuel and Shemaiah, and with them 60 men;
¹⁴of the descendants of Bigvai, Uthai and Zakkur, and with them 70 men.

The Return to Jerusalem

¹⁵I assembled them at the canal that flows toward Ahava, and we camped there three days. When I checked among the people and the priests, I found no Levites there. ¹⁶So I summoned Eliezer, Ariel, Shemaiah, Elnathan, Jarib, Elnathan, Nathan, Zechariah and Meshullam, who were leaders, and Joiarib and Elnathan, who were men of learning, ¹⁷and I ordered them to go to Iddo, the leader in Kasiphia. I told them what to say to Iddo and his associates, the temple servants in Kasiphia, so that they might bring

---

a 22 That is, about 3 3/4 tons or about 3.4 metric tons   *b 22* That is, probably about 18 tons or about 16 metric tons   *c 22* That is, about 600 gallons or about 2,200 liters   *d 5* Some Septuagint manuscripts (also 1 Esdras 8:32); Hebrew does not have *Zattu*.   *e 10* Some Septuagint manuscripts (also 1 Esdras 8:36); Hebrew does not have *Bani*.

attendants to us for the house of our God. ¹⁸Because the gracious hand of our God was on us, they brought us Sherebiah, a capable man, from the descendants of Mahli son of Levi, the son of Israel, and Sherebiah's sons and brothers, 18 in all; ¹⁹and Hashabiah, together with Jeshaiah from the descendants of Merari, and his brothers and nephews, 20 in all. ²⁰They also brought 220 of the temple servants—a body that David and the officials had established to assist the Levites. All were registered by name.

²¹There, by the Ahava Canal, I proclaimed a fast, so that we might humble ourselves before our God and ask him for a safe journey for us and our children, with all our possessions. ²²I was ashamed to ask the king for soldiers and horsemen to protect us from enemies on the road, because we had told the king, "The gracious hand of our God is on everyone who looks to him, but his great anger is against all who forsake him." ²³So we fasted and petitioned our God about this, and he answered our prayer.

²⁴Then I set apart twelve of the leading priests, namely, Sherebiah, Hashabiah and ten of their brothers, ²⁵and I weighed out to them the offering of silver and gold and the articles that the king, his advisers, his officials and all Israel present there had donated for the house of our God. ²⁶I weighed out to them 650 talents*a* of silver, silver articles weighing 100 talents,*b* 100 talents*b* of gold, ²⁷20 bowls of gold valued at 1,000 darics,*c* and two fine articles of polished bronze, as precious as gold.

²⁸I said to them, "You as well as these articles are consecrated to the LORD. The silver and gold are a freewill offering to the LORD, the God of your ancestors. ²⁹Guard them carefully until you weigh them out in the chambers of the house of the LORD in Jerusalem before the leading priests and the Levites and the family heads of Israel." ³⁰Then the priests and Levites received the silver and gold and sacred articles that had been weighed out to be taken to the house of our God in Jerusalem.

³¹On the twelfth day of the first month we set out from the Ahava Canal to go to Jerusalem. The hand of our God was on us, and he protected us from enemies and bandits along the way. ³²So we arrived in Jerusalem, where we rested three days.

³³On the fourth day, in the house of our God, we weighed out the silver and gold and the sacred articles into the hands of Meremoth son of Uriah, the priest. Eleazar son of Phinehas was with him, and so were the Levites Jozabad son of Jeshua and Noadiah son of Binnui. ³⁴Everything was accounted for by number and weight, and the entire weight was recorded at that time.

³⁵Then the exiles who had returned from captivity sacrificed burnt offerings to the God of Israel: twelve bulls for all Israel, ninety-six rams, seventy-seven male lambs and, as a sin offering,*d* twelve male goats. All this was a burnt offering to the LORD. ³⁶They also delivered the king's orders to the royal satraps and to the governors of Trans-Euphrates, who then gave assistance to the people and to the house of God.

Ezra's Prayer About Intermarriage

9 After these things had been done, the leaders came to me and said, "The people of Israel, including the priests and the Levites, have not kept themselves separate from the neighboring peoples with their detestable practices, like those of the Canaanites, Hittites, Perizzites, Jebusites, Ammonites, Moabites, Egyptians and Amorites. ²They have taken some of their daughters as wives for themselves and their sons, and have mingled the holy race with the peoples around them. And the leaders and officials have led the way in this unfaithfulness."

603

atissue:risk

8:21-23 It's a lot easier to *say* you trust God than it is to live as if you really do. You may know that your neighbor needs to hear the Good News about Jesus— but what if she thinks you're being too pushy? Or you may feel God calling you to quit your job and go into a full-time position at your church—but what if you can't make enough to support yourself? You'd be amazed at how God can take a little bit of faith and make it grow. Follow Ezra's lead and see what happens when you humble yourself before God and take the risk of faith.

a 26 That is, about 24 tons or about 22 metric tons   *b 26* That is, about 3 3/4 tons or about 3.4 metric tons   *c 27* That is, about 19 pounds or about 8.5 kilograms   *d 35* Or *purification offering*

³When I heard this, I tore my tunic and cloak, pulled hair from my head and beard and sat down appalled. ⁴Then everyone who trembled at the words of the God of Israel gathered around me because of this unfaithfulness of the exiles. And I sat there appalled until the evening sacrifice.

⁵Then, at the evening sacrifice, I rose from my self-abasement, with my tunic and cloak torn, and fell on my knees with my hands spread out to the LORD my God ⁶and prayed:

"I am too ashamed and disgraced, my God, to lift up my face to you, because our sins are higher than our heads and our guilt has reached to the heavens. ⁷From the days of our ancestors until now, our guilt has been great. Because of our sins, we and our kings and our priests have been subjected to the sword and captivity, to pillage and humiliation at the hand of foreign kings, as it is today.

⁸"But now, for a brief moment, the LORD our God has been gracious in leaving us a remnant and giving us a firm place*a* in his sanctuary, and so our God gives light to our eyes and a little relief in our bondage. ⁹Though we are slaves, our God has not forsaken us in our bondage. He has shown us kindness in the sight of the kings of Persia: He has granted us new life to rebuild the house of our God and repair its ruins, and he has given us a wall of protection in Judah and Jerusalem.

¹⁰"But now, our God, what can we say after this? For we have forsaken the commands ¹¹you gave through your servants the prophets when you said: 'The land you are entering to possess is a land polluted by the corruption of its peoples. By their detestable practices they have filled it with their impurity from one end to the other. ¹²Therefore, do not give your daughters in marriage to their sons or take their daughters for your sons. Do not seek a treaty of friendship with them at any time, that you may be strong and eat the good things of the land and leave it to your children as an everlasting inheritance.'

¹³"What has happened to us is a result of our evil deeds and our great guilt, and yet, our God, you have punished us less than our sins deserved and have given us a remnant like this. ¹⁴Shall we then break your commands again and intermarry with the peoples who commit such detestable practices? Would you not be angry enough with us to destroy us, leaving us no remnant or survivor? ¹⁵LORD, the God of Israel, you are righteous! We are left this day as a remnant. Here we are before you in our guilt, though because of it not one of us can stand in your presence."

at issue: marriage

9:1–15 Ezra wasn't overreacting when he tore his robes, appalled at the intermarriage of the people. He knew how important it was to obey and love God wholeheartedly. If you marry someone who doesn't love God, your own heart naturally becomes divided. It's as if you're on the same team, but you're shooting on opposite goals. (It's tough to win that way!) If you're already married to a non-Christian, walk with God in faith, and know that he can do miracles. If you're not yet married, spare yourself the heartache—don't get involved with someone who doesn't truly share your faith.

The People's Confession of Sin

10 While Ezra was praying and confessing, weeping and throwing himself down before the house of God, a large crowd of Israelites—men, women and children—gathered around him. They too wept bitterly. ²Then Shekaniah son of Jehiel, one of the descendants of Elam, said to Ezra, "We have been unfaithful to our God by marrying foreign women from the peoples around us. But in spite of this, there is still hope for Israel. ³Now let us make a covenant before our God to send away all these women and their children, in accordance with the counsel of my lord and of those who fear the commands of our God. Let it be done according to the Law. ⁴Rise up; this matter is in your hands. We will support you, so take courage and do it."

a 8 Or a foothold

⁵So Ezra rose up and put the leading priests and Levites and all Israel under oath to do what had been suggested. And they took the oath. ⁶Then Ezra withdrew from before the house of God and went to the room of Jehohanan son of Eliashib. While he was there, he ate no food and drank no water, because he continued to mourn over the unfaithfulness of the exiles.

⁷A proclamation was then issued throughout Judah and Jerusalem for all the exiles to assemble in Jerusalem. ⁸Anyone who failed to appear within three days would forfeit all his property, in accordance with the decision of the officials and elders, and would himself be expelled from the assembly of the exiles.

⁹Within the three days, all the men of Judah and Benjamin had gathered in Jerusalem. And on the twentieth day of the ninth month, all the people were sitting in the square before the house of God, greatly distressed by the occasion and because of the rain. ¹⁰Then Ezra the priest stood up and said to them, "You have been unfaithful; you have married foreign women, adding to Israel's guilt. ¹¹Now honor*ᵃ the Lord, the God of your ancestors, and do his will. Separate yourselves from the peoples around you and from your foreign wives."

¹²The whole assembly responded with a loud voice: "You are right! We must do as you say. ¹³But there are many people here and it is the rainy season; so we cannot stand outside. Besides, this matter cannot be taken care of in a day or two, because we have sinned greatly in this thing. ¹⁴Let our officials act for the whole assembly. Then let everyone in our towns who has married a foreign woman come at a set time, along with the elders and judges of each town, until the fierce anger of our God in this matter is turned away from us." ¹⁵Only Jonathan son of Asahel and Jahzeiah son of Tikvah, supported by Meshullam and Shabbethai the Levite, opposed this.

¹⁶So the exiles did as was proposed. Ezra the priest selected men who were family heads, one from each family division, and all of them designated by name. On the first day of the tenth month they sat down to investigate the cases, ¹⁷and by the first day of the first month they finished dealing with all the men who had married foreign women.

Those Guilty of Intermarriage

¹⁸Among the descendants of the priests, the following had married foreign women:

From the descendants of Joshua son of Jozadak, and his brothers: Maaseiah, Eliezer, Jarib and Gedaliah. ¹⁹(They all gave their hands in pledge to put away their wives, and for their guilt they each presented a ram from the flock as a guilt offering.)

²⁰From the descendants of Immer:
Hanani and Zebadiah.
²¹From the descendants of Harim:
Maaseiah, Elijah, Shemaiah, Jehiel and Uzziah.
²²From the descendants of Pashhur:
Elioenai, Maaseiah, Ishmael, Nethanel, Jozabad and Elasah.

²³Among the Levites:

Jozabad, Shimei, Kelaiah (that is, Kelita), Pethahiah, Judah and Eliezer.
²⁴From the musicians:
Eliashib.
From the gatekeepers:
Shallum, Telem and Uri.

²⁵And among the other Israelites:

From the descendants of Parosh:
Ramiah, Izziah, Malkijah, Mijamin, Eleazar, Malkijah and Benaiah.

ᵃ 11 Or *Now make confession to*

[26] From the descendants of Elam:

Mattaniah, Zechariah, Jehiel, Abdi, Jeremoth and Elijah.

[27] From the descendants of Zattu:

Elioenai, Eliashib, Mattaniah, Jeremoth, Zabad and Aziza.

[28] From the descendants of Bebai:

Jehohanan, Hananiah, Zabbai and Athlai.

[29] From the descendants of Bani:

Meshullam, Malluk, Adaiah, Jashub, Sheal and Jeremoth.

[30] From the descendants of Pahath-Moab:

Adna, Kelal, Benaiah, Maaseiah, Mattaniah, Bezalel, Binnui and Manasseh.

[31] From the descendants of Harim:

Eliezer, Ishijah, Malkijah, Shemaiah, Shimeon, [32]Benjamin, Malluk and Shemariah.

[33] From the descendants of Hashum:

Mattenai, Mattattah, Zabad, Eliphelet, Jeremai, Manasseh and Shimei.

[34] From the descendants of Bani:

Maadai, Amram, Uel, [35]Benaiah, Bedeiah, Keluhi, [36]Vaniah, Meremoth, Eliashib, [37]Mattaniah, Mattenai and Jaasu.

[38] From the descendants of Binnui:[a]

Shimei, [39]Shelemiah, Nathan, Adaiah, [40]Maknadebai, Shashai, Sharai, [41]Azarel, Shelemiah, Shemariah, [42]Shallum, Amariah and Joseph.

[43] From the descendants of Nebo:

Jeiel, Mattithiah, Zabad, Zebina, Jaddai, Joel and Benaiah.

[44] All these had married foreign women, and some of them had children by these wives.[b]

---

[a] 37,38 See Septuagint (also 1 Esdras 9:34); Hebrew *Jaasu* [38]*and Bani and Binnui,*   [b] 44 Or *and they sent them away with their children*

Would you go to the boss with this request? ➤ (1:11—2:9)

Is following God a guarantee
that people will like you? ➤ (4:1–23)

How can discernment help you keep
your problems in perspective? ➤ (6:1–14)

How trustworthy are you when you don't have
someone looking over your shoulder? ➤ (13:1–30)

nehemiah

AUTHOR
Unknown, but possibly Ezra or Nehemiah.

AUDIENCE
All Israel.

DATE
Around 430 B.C.

SETTING
Battling harsh opposition, the exiles rebuild
the city wall in Jerusalem.

VERSES TO REMEMBER
"From that day on, half of my men did the
work, while the other half were equipped
with spears, shields, bows and armor. The
officers posted themselves behind all the
people of Judah who were building the wall.
Those who carried materials did their work
with one hand and held a weapon in the
other." (4:16–17)

THEME TO CONSIDER
Success is simply not giving up—even when
we most want to quit.

nehemiah 1:1

Nehemiah's Prayer

1 The words of Nehemiah son of Hakaliah:

In the month of Kislev in the twentieth year, while I was in the citadel of Susa, ²Hanani, one of my brothers, came from Judah with some other men, and I questioned them about the Jewish remnant that had survived the exile, and also about Jerusalem.

³They said to me, "Those who survived the exile and are back in the province are in great trouble and disgrace. The wall of Jerusalem is broken down, and its gates have been burned with fire."

⁴When I heard these things, I sat down and wept. For some days I mourned and fasted and prayed before the God of heaven. ⁵Then I said:

"Lᴏʀᴅ, the God of heaven, the great and awesome God, who keeps his covenant of love with those who love him and keep his commandments, ⁶let your ear be attentive and your eyes open to hear the prayer your servant is praying before you day and night for your servants, the people of Israel. I confess the sins we Israelites, including myself and my ancestral family, have committed against you. ⁷We have acted very wickedly toward you. We have not obeyed the commands, decrees and laws you gave your servant Moses.

⁸"Remember the instruction you gave your servant Moses, saying, 'If you are unfaithful, I will scatter you among the nations, ⁹but if you return to me and obey my commands, then even if your exiled people are at the farthest horizon, I will gather them from there and bring them to the place I have chosen as a dwelling for my Name.'

¹⁰"They are your servants and your people, whom you redeemed by your great strength and your mighty hand. ¹¹Lord, let your ear be attentive to the prayer of this your servant and to the prayer of your servants who delight in revering your name. Give your servant success today by granting him favor in the presence of this man."

I was cupbearer to the king.

Artaxerxes Sends Nehemiah to Jerusalem

2 In the month of Nisan in the twentieth year of King Artaxerxes, when wine was brought for him, I took the wine and gave it to the king. I had not been sad in his presence before, ²so the king asked me, "Why does your face look so sad when you are not ill? This can be nothing but sadness of heart."

I was very much afraid, ³but I said to the king, "May the king live forever! Why should my face not look sad when the city where my ancestors are buried lies in ruins, and its gates have been destroyed by fire?"

⁴The king said to me, "What is it you want?"

Then I prayed to the God of heaven, ⁵and I answered the king, "If it pleases the king and if your servant has found favor in his sight, let him send me to the city in Judah where my ancestors are buried so that I can rebuild it."

⁶Then the king, with the queen sitting beside him, asked me, "How long will your journey take, and when will you get back?" It pleased the king to send me; so I set a time.

⁷I also said to him, "If it pleases the king, may I have letters to the governors of Trans-Euphrates, so that they will provide me safe-conduct until I arrive in Judah? ⁸And may I have a letter to Asaph, keeper of the royal park, so he will

at issue: fear

2:1–9 What's your gut reaction when you feel afraid? Do you run to a friend? Act like nothing's wrong? Grit your teeth and get working on a plan? When Nehemiah was afraid in the face of the king, he prayed. Not a bad idea, is it? Prayer reminds us we're not alone. It reminds us we're not in charge. It reminds us we're loved and cared for by someone more powerful than anything we face. It reminds us that we don't have to—in fact, we shouldn't—depend on ourselves. And through those reminders, we find strength, hope and courage to face whatever comes our way.

give me timber to make beams for the gates of the citadel by the temple and for the city wall and for the residence I will occupy?" And because the gracious hand of my God was on me, the king granted my requests. ⁹So I went to the governors of Trans-Euphrates and gave them the king's letters. The king had also sent army officers and cavalry with me.

¹⁰When Sanballat the Horonite and Tobiah the Ammonite official heard about this, they were very much disturbed that someone had come to promote the welfare of the Israelites.

Nehemiah Inspects Jerusalem's Walls

¹¹I went to Jerusalem, and after staying there three days ¹²I set out during the night with a few others. I had not told anyone what my God had put in my heart to do for Jerusalem. There were no mounts with me except the one I was riding on.

¹³By night I went out through the Valley Gate toward the Jackal*ᵃ* Well and the Dung Gate, examining the walls of Jerusalem, which had been broken down, and its gates, which had been destroyed by fire. ¹⁴Then I moved on toward the Fountain Gate and the King's Pool, but there was not enough room for my mount to get through; ¹⁵so I went up the valley by night, examining the wall. Finally, I turned back and reentered through the Valley Gate. ¹⁶The officials did not know where I had gone or what I was doing, because as yet I had said nothing to the Jews or the priests or nobles or officials or any others who would be doing the work.

¹⁷Then I said to them, "You see the trouble we are in: Jerusalem lies in ruins, and its gates have been burned with fire. Come, let us rebuild the wall of Jerusalem, and we will no longer be in disgrace." ¹⁸I also told them about the gracious hand of my God on me and what the king had said to me.

They replied, "Let us start rebuilding." So they began this good work.

¹⁹But when Sanballat the Horonite, Tobiah the Ammonite official and Geshem the Arab heard about it, they mocked and ridiculed us. "What is this you are doing?" they asked. "Are you rebelling against the king?"

²⁰I answered them by saying, "The God of heaven will give us success. We his servants will start rebuilding, but as for you, you have no share in Jerusalem or any claim or historic right to it."

609

Builders of the Wall

3 Eliashib the high priest and his fellow priests went to work and rebuilt the Sheep Gate. They dedicated it and set its doors in place, building as far as the Tower of the Hundred, which they dedicated, and as far as the Tower of Hananel. ²The men of Jericho built the adjoining section, and Zakkur son of Imri built next to them.

³The Fish Gate was rebuilt by the sons of Hassenaah. They laid its beams and put its doors and bolts and bars in place. ⁴Meremoth son of Uriah, the son of Hakkoz, repaired the next section. Next to him Meshullam son of Berekiah, the son of Meshezabel, made repairs, and next to him Zadok son of Baana also made repairs. ⁵The next section was repaired by the men of Tekoa, but their nobles would not put their shoulders to the work under their supervisors.*ᵇ*

⁶The Jeshanah*ᶜ* Gate was repaired by Joiada son of Paseah and Meshullam son of Besodeiah. They laid its beams and put its doors with their bolts and bars in place. ⁷Next to them, repairs were made by men from Gibeon and Mizpah—Melatiah of Gibeon and Jadon of Meronoth—places under the authority of the governor of Trans-Euphrates. ⁸Uzziel son of Harhaiah, one of the goldsmiths, repaired the next section; and Hananiah, one of the perfume-makers, made repairs next to that. They restored Jerusalem as far as the Broad Wall. ⁹Rephaiah son of Hur, ruler of a half-district of Jerusalem, repaired the next section. ¹⁰Adjoining this, Jedaiah son of Harumaph made repairs opposite his house, and Hattush son of Hashabneiah made repairs next to him. ¹¹Malkijah son of Harim and Hasshub son of Pahath-Moab repaired another section and the Tower of the Ovens. ¹²Shallum son of Hallohesh, ruler of a half-district of Jerusalem, repaired the next section with the help of his daughters.

ᵃ *13* Or *Serpent* or *Fig*   ᵇ *5* Or *their Lord* or *the governor*   ᶜ *6* Or *Old* myth# 40 "I CAN DO IT ALL."

I'd never dreamed how hard being a mom would be. It's a 24/7 job. The biggest shocker for me was to realize there are no holidays, no personal days and no paid vacations in this job. How do other moms do it? I wondered as I tried to balance all the adjustments in my life with a baby and a freelance job. What about full-time working moms and those with several children? I can't imagine! . . . Oh, but I can, and it scares me!

Maybe I'm too selfish. I married at age 30 and had a baby at 33. I enjoyed a lot of time by myself when I was single. I had a corporate career, lived in a big city, traveled across the nation and even bought my own home. At the same time, I had always dreamed of being a wife, stay-at-home mom and a part-time freelancer.

When I quit my job to become a mom, I thought I'd have a spotless house, keep up with the laundry and cook nutritious meals from scratch. After all, isn't that what stay-at-home moms are supposed to do with all their extra time? Sure, I laugh now, too, but I honestly thought I could be June Cleaver! I have to admit, I used to look down on moms who looked frazzled or lost control of their kids or let their house fall apart or (worst of all) let their bodies go. I'd always thought I could do it all.

In my heart, I know raising my son is the most important job I have. But does that mean that I need to give up everything else? Sometimes I think so. After all, if I do everything I'm supposed to do, there's no extra time left. Yet I still have the desire to do my freelance work. So far, I've managed to keep my former employer as a client. I want to maintain that professional relationship and maybe even have some articles published in a national magazine. But sometimes I wonder how I'll stay afloat.

—Stacy

AH, THE NOTORIOUS

Proverbs 31 woman—the woman we sometimes love to hate! Super-mom activists point to her as a woman who "does it all" (and does it well). The more likely scenario is that this passage is a composite of many women, not one super-woman. The expectation of being perfect has to go. If you're a mom struggling to do it all, keep this in mind:

- *Put your children first.* That seems like a given, right? However, keeping your children first will look different for each woman. For some, this may mean home-schooling. For others, it may mean working to keep food on the table.

- *Ask yourself, "What regrets do I not want to have?"* Let this help guide your choices. For example, one argument against daycare is that your child spends more time during the day with someone else than he or she does with you. In contrast, some stay-at-home moms are so absorbed in their own lives and enroll their children in so many activities that they really aren't the biggest influence in their children's lives anyway.

- *Work as a team with your husband, and know what your marriage can afford.* Even if you stay home, you still desperately need your husband's help—marriage and parenting are joint efforts. Consider Nehemiah's strategy for his massive undertaking—he didn't do it by himself. He practiced a divide-and-con-quer philosophy (see Nehemiah 3). Utilize the support people in your life (if you're married, your husband; if you're a single mom, a family or church member, or friend) to enable you to do what you need to do (and occasionally what you want to do).

"Based on a 90-hour work week, a fair wage for the typical stay-at-home mom would be $88,276 for executing all of her daily tasks. Factor in overtime, and the appropriate salary leaps to $112,797."

—Salary.com

611

"Her CHILDreN arise aND caLL Her BLesseD."

PROVERBS 31:28

SEE ALSO

Psalm 127:3

Ecclesiastes 3:1

Philippians 4:6–7, 10–13

For more on **Parenting** and **Priorities**, check the index.

¹³The Valley Gate was repaired by Hanun and the residents of Zanoah. They rebuilt it and put its doors with their bolts and bars in place. They also repaired a thousand cubits^a of the wall as far as the Dung Gate.

¹⁴The Dung Gate was repaired by Malkijah son of Rekab, ruler of the district of Beth Hakkerem. He rebuilt it and put its doors with their bolts and bars in place.

¹⁵The Fountain Gate was repaired by Shallun son of Kol-Hozeh, ruler of the district of Mizpah. He rebuilt it, roofing it over and putting its doors and bolts and bars in place. He also repaired the wall of the Pool of Siloam,^b by the King's Garden, as far as the steps going down from the City of David. ¹⁶Beyond him, Nehemiah son of Azbuk, ruler of a half-district of Beth Zur, made repairs up to a point opposite the tombs^c of David, as far as the artificial pool and the House of the Heroes.

¹⁷Next to him, the repairs were made by the Levites under Rehum son of Bani. Beside him, Hashabiah, ruler of half the district of Keilah, carried out repairs for his district. ¹⁸Next to him, the repairs were made by their neighbors under Binnui^d son of Henadad, ruler of the other half-district of Keilah. ¹⁹Next to him, Ezer son of Jeshua, ruler of Mizpah, repaired another section, from a point facing the ascent to the armory as far as the angle of the wall. ²⁰Next to him, Baruch son of Zabbai zealously repaired another section, from the angle to the entrance of the house of Eliashib the high priest. ²¹Next to him, Meremoth son of Uriah, the son of Hakkoz, repaired another section, from the entrance of Eliashib's house to the end of it.

²²The repairs next to him were made by the priests from the surrounding region. ²³Beyond them, Benjamin and Hasshub made repairs in front of their house; and next to them, Azariah son of Maaseiah, the son of Ananiah, made repairs beside his house. ²⁴Next to him, Binnui son of Henadad repaired another section, from Azariah's house to the angle and the corner, ²⁵and Palal son of Uzai worked opposite the angle and the tower projecting from the upper palace near the court of the guard. Next to him, Pedaiah son of Parosh ²⁶and the temple servants living on the hill of Ophel made repairs up to a point opposite the Water Gate toward the east and the projecting tower. ²⁷Next to them, the men of Tekoa repaired another section, from the great projecting tower to the wall of Ophel.

²⁸Above the Horse Gate, the priests made repairs, each in front of his own house. ²⁹Next to them, Zadok son of Immer made repairs opposite his house. Next to him, Shemaiah son of Shekaniah, the guard at the East Gate, made repairs. ³⁰Next to him, Hananiah son of Shelemiah, and Hanun, the sixth son of Zalaph, repaired another section. Next to them, Meshullam son of Berekiah made repairs opposite his living quarters. ³¹Next to him, Malkijah, one of the goldsmiths, made repairs as far as the house of the temple servants and the merchants, opposite the Inspection Gate, and as far as the room above the corner; ³²and between the room above the corner and the Sheep Gate the goldsmiths and merchants made repairs.

Opposition to the Rebuilding

4 [*]When Sanballat heard that we were rebuilding the wall, he became angry and was greatly incensed. He ridiculed the Jews, ²and in the presence of his associates and the army of Samaria, he said, "What are those feeble Jews doing? Will they restore their wall? Will they offer sacrifices? Will they finish in a day? Can they bring the stones back to life from those heaps of rubble—burned as they are?"

³Tobiah the Ammonite, who was at his side, said, "What they are building—even a fox climbing up on it would break down their wall of stones!"

⁴Hear us, our God, for we are despised. Turn their insults back on their own heads. Give them over as plunder in a land of captivity. ⁵Do not cover up their guilt or blot out their sins from your sight, for they have thrown insults in the face of^e the builders.

⁶So we rebuilt the wall till all of it reached half its height, for the people worked with all their heart.

^{*7}But when Sanballat, Tobiah, the Arabs, the Ammonites and the people of Ashdod heard that the

---

^a 13 That is, about 1,500 feet or about 450 meters   ^b 15 Hebrew Shelah, a variant of Shiloah, that is, Siloam   ^c 16 Hebrew; Septuagint, some Vulgate manuscripts and Syriac tomb   ^d 18 Two Hebrew manuscripts and Syriac (see also Septuagint and verse 24); most Hebrew manuscripts Bavvai   ^e 5 Or have aroused your anger before

[*] 4:1-6 is numbered 3:33-38 in Hebrew texts.   [*] 4:7-23 is numbered 4:1-17 in Hebrew texts.

repairs to Jerusalem's walls had gone ahead and that the gaps were being closed, they were very angry. [8]They all plotted together to come and fight against Jerusalem and stir up trouble against it. [9]But we prayed to our God and posted a guard day and night to meet this threat.

conversations

prayer «» 4:9

1 » How do you balance prayer and taking action?

2 » Does making preparations show a lack of trust in God?

3 » Has prayer specifically guided your actions recently?

For more on **prayer**, check the index.
For the next Conversations, go to p. 613.

[10]Meanwhile, the people in Judah said, "The strength of the laborers is giving out, and there is so much rubble that we cannot rebuild the wall."

[11]Also our enemies said, "Before they know it or see us, we will be right there among them and will kill them and put an end to the work."

[12]Then the Jews who lived near them came and told us ten times over, "Wherever you turn, they will attack us."

[13]Therefore I stationed some of the people behind the lowest points of the wall at the exposed places, posting them by families, with their swords, spears and bows. [14]After I looked things over, I stood up and said to the nobles, the officials and the rest of the people, "Don't be afraid of them. Remember the Lord, who is great and awesome, and fight for your people, your sons and your daughters, your wives and your homes."

[15]When our enemies heard that we were aware of their plot and that God had frustrated it, we all returned to the wall, each to our own work.

[16]From that day on, half of my men did the work, while the other half were equipped with spears, shields, bows and armor. The officers posted themselves behind all the people of Judah [17]who were building the wall. Those who carried materials did their work with one hand and held a weapon in the other, [18]and each of the builders wore his sword at his side as he worked. But the man who sounded the trumpet stayed with me.

[19]Then I said to the nobles, the officials and the rest of the people, "The work is extensive and spread out, and we are widely separated from each other along the wall. [20]Wherever you hear the sound of the trumpet, join us there. Our God will fight for us!"

[21]So we continued the work with half the men holding spears, from the first light of dawn till the stars came out. [22]At that time I also said to the people, "Have every man and his helper stay inside Jerusalem at night, so they can serve us as guards by night and as workers by day." [23]Neither I nor my brothers nor my men nor the guards with me took off our clothes; each had his weapon, even when he went for water.[a]

Nehemiah Helps the Poor

5 Now the men and their wives raised a great outcry against their fellow Jews. [2]Some were saying, "We and our sons and daughters are numerous; in order for us to eat and stay alive, we must get grain."

[3]Others were saying, "We are mortgaging our fields, our vineyards and our homes to get grain during the famine."

[4]Still others were saying, "We have had to borrow money to pay the king's tax on our fields and vineyards. [5]Although we are of the same flesh and blood as the rest of our people and though our children are as good as theirs, yet we have to subject our sons and daughters to slavery. Some of our daughters have

conversations

compassion «» 5:1–13

1 » What's the difference between being business-savvy and taking advantage of people?

2 » Who are you in this story—outraged Nehemiah, a wealthy noble or a poor person?

3 » How could you demonstrate compassion toward someone less fortunate than you?

For more on **compassion**, check the index.
For the next Conversations, go to p. 621.

---
a 23 The meaning of the Hebrew for this clause is uncertain.

already been enslaved, but we are powerless, because our fields and our vineyards belong to others."

⁶When I heard their outcry and these charges, I was very angry. ⁷I pondered them in my mind and then accused the nobles and officials. I told them, "You are charging your own people interest!" So I called together a large meeting to deal with them ⁸and said: "As far as possible, we have bought back our fellow Jews who were sold to the Gentiles. Now you are selling your own people, only for them to be sold back to us!" They kept quiet, because they could find nothing to say.

⁹So I continued, "What you are doing is not right. Shouldn't you walk in the fear of our God to avoid the reproach of our Gentile enemies? ¹⁰I and my brothers and my men are also lending the people money and grain. But let us stop charging interest! ¹¹Give back to them immediately their fields, vineyards, olive groves and houses, and also the interest you are charging them—one percent of the money, grain, new wine and olive oil."

¹²"We will give it back," they said. "And we will not demand anything more from them. We will do as you say."

Then I summoned the priests and made the nobles and officials take an oath to do what they had promised. ¹³I also shook out the folds of my robe and said, "In this way may God shake out of their houses and possessions anyone who does not keep this promise. So may such a person be shaken out and emptied!"

At this the whole assembly said, "Amen," and praised the Lord. And the people did as they had promised.

¹⁴Moreover, from the twentieth year of King Artaxerxes, when I was appointed to be their governor in the land of Judah, until his thirty-second year—twelve years—neither I nor my brothers ate the food allotted to the governor. ¹⁵But the earlier governors—those preceding me—placed a heavy burden on the people and took forty shekels*ᵃ* of silver from them in addition to food and wine. Their assistants also lorded it over the people. But out of reverence for God I did not act like that. ¹⁶Instead, I devoted myself to the work on this wall. All my men were assembled there for the work; weᵇ did not acquire any land.

¹⁷Furthermore, a hundred and fifty Jews and officials ate at my table, as well as those who came to us from the surrounding nations. ¹⁸Each day one ox, six choice sheep and some poultry were prepared for me, and every ten days an abundant supply of wine of all kinds. In spite of all this, I never demanded the food allotted to the governor, because the demands were heavy on these people.

¹⁹Remember me with favor, my God, for all I have done for these people.

Further Opposition to the Rebuilding

6 When word came to Sanballat, Tobiah, Geshem the Arab and the rest of our enemies that I had rebuilt the wall and not a gap was left in it—though up to that time I had not set the doors in the gates— ²Sanballat and Geshem sent me this message: "Come, let us meet together in one of the villagesᶜ on the plain of Ono."

But they were scheming to harm me; ³so I sent messengers to them with this reply: "I am carrying on a great project and cannot go down. Why should the work stop while I leave it and go down to you?" ⁴Four times they sent me the same message, and each time I gave them the same answer.

⁵Then, the fifth time, Sanballat sent his aide to me with the same message, and in his hand was an unsealed letter ⁶in which was written:

"It is reported among the nations—and Geshemᵈ says it is true—that you and the Jews are plotting to revolt, and therefore you are building the wall. Moreover, according to these reports you are about to become their king ⁷and have even appointed prophets to make this proclamation about you in Jerusalem: 'There is a king in Judah!' Now this report will get back to the king; so come, let us meet together."

⁸I sent him this reply: "Nothing like what you are saying is happening; you are just making it up out of your head."

⁹They were all trying to frighten us, thinking, "Their hands will get too weak for the work, and it will not be completed."

HE IS: your helper

6:9–16 Nehemiah took on the task of rebuilding the wall around Jerusalem, facing opposition from without and intimidating foes within. Despite this resistance, the wall was completed. Nehemiah and even his *enemies* realized that the work had been done with God's help.

If God's enemies can't stop your spiritual work with outward opposition, such as mocking and stirring up logistical trouble, they'll resort to personal intimidation, even to the point of spreading lies. Don't give in to threats or subtle sabotage. Instead, pray as Nehemiah did, "Strengthen my hands." He is *your helper* who will enable you to complete your mission.

For the next He Is, go to p. 618.

But I prayed, "Now strengthen my hands."

¹⁰One day I went to the house of Shemaiah son of Delaiah, the son of Mehetabel, who was shut in at his home. He said, "Let us meet in the house of God, inside the temple, and let us close the temple doors, because some people are coming to kill you—by night they are coming to kill you."

¹¹But I said, "Should someone like me run away? Or should one like me go into the temple to save his life? I will not go!" ¹²I realized that God had not sent him, but that he had prophesied against me because Tobiah and Sanballat had hired him. ¹³He had been hired to intimidate me so that I would commit a sin by doing this, and then they would give me a bad name to discredit me.

¹⁴Remember Tobiah and Sanballat, my God, because of what they have done; remember also the prophet Noadiah and how she and the rest of the prophets have been trying to intimidate me. ¹⁵So the wall was completed on the twenty-fifth of Elul, in fifty-two days.

Opposition to the Completed Wall

¹⁶When all our enemies heard about this, all the surrounding nations were afraid and lost their self-confidence, because they realized that this work had been done with the help of our God.

¹⁷Also, in those days the nobles of Judah were sending many letters to Tobiah, and replies from Tobiah kept coming to them. ¹⁸For many in Judah were under oath to him, since he was son-in-law to Shekaniah son of Arah, and his son Jehohanan had married the daughter of Meshullam son of Berekiah. ¹⁹Moreover, they kept reporting to me his good deeds and then telling him what I said. And Tobiah sent letters to intimidate me.

7 After the wall had been rebuilt and I had set the doors in place, the gatekeepers, the musicians and the Levites were appointed. ²I put in charge of Jerusalem my brother Hanani, along with Hananiah the commander of the citadel, because he was trustworthy and feared God more than most people do. ³I said to them, "The gates of Jerusalem are not to be opened until the sun is hot. While the gatekeepers are still on duty, have them shut the doors and bar them. Also appoint residents of Jerusalem as guards, some at their posts and some near their own houses."

---

atissue:integrity

7:2 So you pad your expense report a little. No big deal, right? So you keep the extra five dollars the cashier mistakenly hands you. It's not worth making a fuss over, is it? God doesn't care about those harmless indiscretions, does he? Well, if you asked Hanani, he would disagree. He might say that character is a matter of who you are and what you do when no one but God is looking. He might say your life should reflect an understanding of how important honesty and integrity are to God. And you know what? He'd be right.

615

The List of the Exiles Who Returned

[4]Now the city was large and spacious, but there were few people in it, and the houses had not yet been rebuilt. [5]So my God put it into my heart to assemble the nobles, the officials and the common people for registration by families. I found the genealogical record of those who had been the first to return. This is what I found written there:

[6]These are the people of the province who came up from the captivity of the exiles whom Nebuchadnezzar king of Babylon had taken captive (they returned to Jerusalem and Judah, each to his own town, [7]in company with Zerubbabel, Joshua, Nehemiah, Azariah, Raamiah, Nahamani, Mordecai, Bilshan, Mispereth, Bigvai, Nehum and Baanah):

The list of the men of Israel:

616

[8]the descendants of Parosh	2,172
[9]of Shephatiah	372
[10]of Arah	652
[11]of Pahath-Moab (through the line of Jeshua and Joab)	2,818
[12]of Elam	1,254
[13]of Zattu	845
[14]of Zakkai	760
[15]of Binnui	648
[16]of Bebai	628
[17]of Azgad	2,322
[18]of Adonikam	667
[19]of Bigvai	2,067
[20]of Adin	655
[21]of Ater (through Hezekiah)	98
[22]of Hashum	328
[23]of Bezai	324
[24]of Hariph	112
[25]of Gibeon	95
[26]the men of Bethlehem and Netophah	188
[27]of Anathoth	128
[28]of Beth Azmaveth	42
[29]of Kiriath Jearim, Kephirah and Beeroth	743
[30]of Ramah and Geba	621
[31]of Mikmash	122
[32]of Bethel and Ai	123
[33]of the other Nebo	52
[34]of the other Elam	1,254
[35]of Harim	320
[36]of Jericho	345
[37]of Lod, Hadid and Ono	721
[38]of Senaah	3,930

[39]The priests:

the descendants of Jedaiah (through the family of Jeshua)	973
[40]of Immer	1,052
[41]of Pashhur	1,247
[42]of Harim	1,017

⁴³The Levites:

> the descendants of Jeshua (through Kadmiel
> through the line of Hodaviah)   74

⁴⁴The musicians:

> the descendants of Asaph   148

⁴⁵The gatekeepers:

> the descendants of
> Shallum, Ater, Talmon, Akkub, Hatita and Shobai   138

⁴⁶The temple servants:

> the descendants of
> Ziha, Hasupha, Tabbaoth,
> ⁴⁷Keros, Sia, Padon,
> ⁴⁸Lebana, Hagaba, Shalmai,
> ⁴⁹Hanan, Giddel, Gahar,
> ⁵⁰Reaiah, Rezin, Nekoda,
> ⁵¹Gazzam, Uzza, Paseah,
> ⁵²Besai, Meunim, Nephusim,
> ⁵³Bakbuk, Hakupha, Harhur,
> ⁵⁴Bazluth, Mehida, Harsha,
> ⁵⁵Barkos, Sisera, Temah,
> ⁵⁶Neziah and Hatipha

⁵⁷The descendants of the servants of Solomon:

> the descendants of
> Sotai, Sophereth, Perida,
> ⁵⁸Jaala, Darkon, Giddel,
> ⁵⁹Shephatiah, Hattil,
> Pokereth-Hazzebaim and Amon

> ⁶⁰The temple servants and the descendants of the servants of Solomon   392

⁶¹The following came up from the towns of Tel Melah, Tel Harsha, Kerub, Addon and Immer, but they could not show that their families were descended from Israel:

> ⁶²the descendants of
> Delaiah, Tobiah and Nekoda   642

⁶³And from among the priests:

> the descendants of
> Hobaiah, Hakkoz and Barzillai (a man who had married a daughter of
> Barzillai the Gileadite and was called by that name).

⁶⁴These searched for their family records, but they could not find them and so were excluded from the priesthood as unclean. ⁶⁵The governor, therefore, ordered them not to eat any of the most sacred food until there should be a priest ministering with the Urim and Thummim.

⁶⁶The whole company numbered 42,360, ⁶⁷besides their 7,337 male and female slaves; and they also had 245 male and female singers. ⁶⁸There were 736 horses, 245 mules,ᵃ ⁶⁹435 camels and 6,720 donkeys.

ᵃ 68 Some Hebrew manuscripts (see also Ezra 2:66); most Hebrew manuscripts do not have this verse.

⁷⁰Some of the heads of the families contributed to the work. The governor gave to the treasury 1,000 darics*a* of gold, 50 bowls and 530 garments for priests. ⁷¹Some of the heads of the families gave to the treasury for the work 20,000 darics*b* of gold and 2,200 minas*c* of silver. ⁷²The total given by the rest of the people was 20,000 darics of gold, 2,000 minas*d* of silver and 67 garments for priests.

⁷³The priests, the Levites, the gatekeepers, the musicians and the temple servants, along with certain of the people and the rest of the Israelites, settled in their own towns.

Ezra Reads the Law

8 When the seventh month came and the Israelites had settled in their towns, ¹all the people assembled with one accord in the square before the Water Gate. They told Ezra the teacher of the Law to bring out the Book of the Law of Moses, which the LORD had commanded for Israel.

²So on the first day of the seventh month Ezra the priest brought the Law before the assembly, which was made up of men and women and all who were able to understand. ³He read it aloud from daybreak till noon as he faced the square before the Water Gate in the presence of the men, women and others who could understand. And all the people listened attentively to the Book of the Law.

⁴Ezra the teacher of the Law stood on a high wooden platform built for the occasion. Beside him on his right stood Mattithiah, Shema, Anaiah, Uriah, Hilkiah and Maaseiah; and on his left were Pedaiah, Mishael, Malkijah, Hashum, Hashbaddanah, Zechariah and Meshullam.

⁵Ezra opened the book. All the people could see him because he was standing above them; and as he opened it, the people all stood up. ⁶Ezra praised the LORD, the great God; and all the people lifted their hands and responded, "Amen! Amen!" Then they bowed down and worshiped the LORD with their faces to the ground.

⁷The Levites—Jeshua, Bani, Sherebiah, Jamin, Akkub, Shabbethai, Hodiah, Maaseiah, Kelita, Azariah, Jozabad, Hanan and Pelaiah—instructed the people in the Law while the people were standing there. ⁸They read from the Book of the Law of God, making it clear*e* and giving the meaning so that the people understood what was being read.

⁹Then Nehemiah the governor, Ezra the priest and teacher of the Law, and the Levites who were instructing the people said to them all, "This day is holy to the LORD your God. Do not mourn or weep." For all the people had been weeping as they listened to the words of the Law.

¹⁰Nehemiah said, "Go and enjoy choice food and sweet drinks, and send some to those who have nothing prepared. This day is holy to our Lord. Do not grieve, for the joy of the LORD is your strength."

HE IS: the giver of joy

8:10 Ezra the priest read the words of the Law to the Israelites, and the people grieved over their disobedience. But Nehemiah realized that true repentance doesn't end in grief; it ultimately leads to change and then to joy. When the people returned to the Lord, they discovered God's joy, which was their strength.

When you hear God's Word and feel your conscience pricked, it's right to grieve. But don't be trapped indefinitely in your feelings of grief. Let your grief motivate you to change, and then move from your grief to *the giver of joy,* who is your strength.

For the next He Is, go to p. 634.

---

¹¹The Levites calmed all the people, saying, "Be still, for this is a holy day. Do not grieve." ¹²Then all the people went away to eat and drink, to send portions of food and to celebrate with great joy, because they now understood the words that had been made known to them.

¹³On the second day of the month, the heads of all the families, along with the priests and the Levites,

---

a 70 That is, about 19 pounds or about 8.5 kilograms   b 71 That is, about 375 pounds or about 170 kilograms; also in verse 72   c 71 That is, about 1 1/3 tons or about 1.2 metric tons   d 72 That is, about 1 1/4 tons or about 1.1 metric tons   e 8 Or God, translating it gathered around Ezra the teacher to give attention to the words of the Law. [14]They found written in the Law, which the Lord had commanded through Moses, that the Israelites were to live in temporary shelters during the festival of the seventh month [15]and that they should proclaim this word and spread it throughout their towns and in Jerusalem: "Go out into the hill country and bring back branches from olive and wild olive trees, and from myrtles, palms and shade trees, to make temporary shelters"—as it is written.[a]

[16]So the people went out and brought back branches and built themselves temporary shelters on their own roofs, in their courtyards, in the courts of the house of God and in the square by the Water Gate and the one by the Gate of Ephraim. [17]The whole company that had returned from exile built temporary shelters and lived in them. From the days of Joshua son of Nun until that day, the Israelites had not celebrated it like this. And their joy was very great.

[18]Day after day, from the first day to the last, Ezra read from the Book of the Law of God. They celebrated the festival for seven days, and on the eighth day, in accordance with the regulation, there was an assembly.

The Israelites Confess Their Sins

9 On the twenty-fourth day of the same month, the Israelites gathered together, fasting and wearing sackcloth and putting dust on their heads. [2]Those of Israelite descent had separated themselves from all foreigners. They stood in their places and confessed their sins and the sins of their ancestors. [3]They stood where they were and read from the Book of the Law of the Lord their God for a quarter of the day, and spent another quarter in confession and in worshiping the Lord their God. [4]Standing on the stairs of the Levites were Jeshua, Bani, Kadmiel, Shebaniah, Bunni, Sherebiah, Bani and Kenani. They cried out with loud voices to the Lord their God. [5]And the Levites—Jeshua, Kadmiel, Bani, Hashabneiah, Sherebiah, Hodiah, Shebaniah and Pethahiah—said: "Stand up and praise the Lord your God, who is from everlasting to everlasting.[b]"

"Blessed be your glorious name, and may it be exalted above all blessing and praise. [6]You alone are the Lord. You made the heavens, even the highest heavens, and all their starry host, the earth and all that is on it, the seas and all that is in them. You give life to everything, and the multitudes of heaven worship you.

[7]"You are the Lord God, who chose Abram and brought him out of Ur of the Chaldeans and named him Abraham. [8]You found his heart faithful to you, and you made a covenant with him to give to his descendants the land of the Canaanites, Hittites, Amorites, Perizzites, Jebusites and Girgashites. You have kept your promise because you are righteous.

[9]"You saw the suffering of our ancestors in Egypt; you heard their cry at the Red Sea.[c] [10]You sent signs and wonders against Pharaoh, against all his officials and all the people of his land, for you knew how arrogantly the Egyptians treated them. You made a name for yourself, which remains to this day. [11]You divided the sea before them, so that they passed through it on dry ground, but you hurled their pursuers into the depths, like a stone into mighty waters. [12]By day you led them with a pillar of cloud, and by night with a pillar of fire to give them light on the way they were to take.

[13]"You came down on Mount Sinai; you spoke to them from heaven. You gave them regulations and laws that are just and right, and decrees and commands that are good. [14]You made known to them your holy Sabbath and gave them commands, decrees and laws through your servant Moses. [15]In their hunger you gave them bread from heaven and in their thirst you brought them water from the rock; you told them to go in and take possession of the land you had sworn with uplifted hand to give them.

[16]"But they, our ancestors, became arrogant and stiff-necked, and did not obey your commands. [17]They refused to listen and failed to remember the miracles you performed among them. They became stiff-necked and in their rebellion appointed a leader in order to return to their slavery. But you are a forgiving God, gracious and compassionate, slow to anger and abounding in love.

---

[a] 15 See Lev. 23:37-40.   [b] 5 Or God for ever and ever   [c] 9 Or the Sea of Reeds

Therefore you did not desert them, [18]even when they cast for themselves an image of a calf and said, 'This is your god, who brought you up out of Egypt,' or when they committed awful blasphemies.

[19]"Because of your great compassion you did not abandon them in the wilderness. By day the pillar of cloud did not cease to guide them on their path, nor the pillar of fire by night to shine on the way they were to take. [20]You gave your good Spirit to instruct them. You did not withhold your manna from their mouths, and you gave them water for their thirst. [21]For forty years you sustained them in the wilderness; they lacked nothing, their clothes did not wear out nor did their feet become swollen.

[22]"You gave them kingdoms and nations, allotting to them even the remotest frontiers. They took over the country of Sihon[a] king of Heshbon and the country of Og king of Bashan. [23]You made their children as numerous as the stars in the sky, and you brought them into the land that you told their parents to enter and possess. [24]Their children went in and took possession of the land. You subdued before them the Canaanites, who lived in the land; you gave the Canaanites into their hands, along with their kings and the peoples of the land, to deal with them as they pleased. [25]They captured fortified cities and fertile land; they took possession of houses filled with all kinds of good things, wells already dug, vineyards, olive groves and fruit trees in abundance. They ate to the full and were well-nourished; they reveled in your great goodness.

620

[26]"But they were disobedient and rebelled against you; they put your law behind their backs. They killed your prophets, who had warned them in order to turn them back to you; they committed awful blasphemies. [27]So you delivered them into the hands of their enemies, who oppressed them. But when they were oppressed they cried out to you. From heaven you heard them, and in your great compassion you gave them deliverers, who rescued them from the hand of their enemies.

[28]"But as soon as they were at rest, they again did what was evil in your sight. Then you abandoned them to the hand of their enemies so that they ruled over them. And when they cried out to you again, you heard from heaven, and in your compassion you delivered them time after time.

[29]"You warned them in order to turn them back to your law, but they became arrogant and disobeyed your commands. They sinned against your ordinances, of which you said, 'Whoever obeys them will live by them.' Stubbornly they turned their backs on you, became stiff-necked and refused to listen. [30]For many years you were patient with them. By your Spirit you warned them through your prophets. Yet they paid no attention, so you gave them into the hands of the neighboring peoples. [31]But in your great mercy you did not put an end to them or abandon them, for you are a gracious and merciful God.

[32]"Now therefore, our God, the great God, mighty and awesome, who keeps his covenant of love, do not let all this hardship seem trifling in your eyes—the hardship that has come on us, on our kings and leaders, on our priests and prophets, on our ancestors and all your people, from the days of the kings of Assyria until today. [33]In all that has happened to us, you have remained righteous; you have acted faithfully, while we acted wickedly. [34]Our kings, our leaders, our priests and our ancestors did not follow your law; they did not pay attention to your commands or the statutes you warned them to keep. [35]Even while they were in their kingdom, enjoying your great goodness to them in the spacious and fertile land you gave them, they did not serve you or turn from their evil ways.

[36]"But see, we are slaves today, slaves in the land you gave our ancestors so they could eat its fruit and the other good things it produces. [37]Because of our sins, its abundant harvest goes to the kings you have placed over us. They rule over our bodies and our cattle as they please. We are in great distress.

The Agreement of the People

*[38]"In view of all this, we are making a binding agreement, putting it in writing, and our leaders, our Levites and our priests are affixing their seals to it."

---

[a] 22 One Hebrew manuscript and Septuagint; most Hebrew manuscripts *Sihon, that is, the country of the*

* 9:38 is numbered 10:1 in Hebrew texts.

10 *Those who sealed it were:

Nehemiah the governor, the son of Hakaliah.

Zedekiah, ²Seraiah, Azariah, Jeremiah,
³ Pashhur, Amariah, Malkijah,
⁴ Hattush, Shebaniah, Malluk,
⁵ Harim, Meremoth, Obadiah,
⁶ Daniel, Ginnethon, Baruch,
⁷ Meshullam, Abijah, Mijamin,
⁸ Maaziah, Bilgai and Shemaiah.
These were the priests.

⁹ The Levites:

Jeshua son of Azaniah, Binnui of the sons of Henadad, Kadmiel,
¹⁰ and their associates: Shebaniah,
Hodiah, Kelita, Pelaiah, Hanan,
¹¹ Mika, Rehob, Hashabiah,
¹² Zakkur, Sherebiah, Shebaniah,
¹³ Hodiah, Bani and Beninu.

¹⁴ The leaders of the people:

Parosh, Pahath-Moab, Elam, Zattu, Bani,
¹⁵ Bunni, Azgad, Bebai,
¹⁶ Adonijah, Bigvai, Adin,
¹⁷ Ater, Hezekiah, Azzur,
¹⁸ Hodiah, Hashum, Bezai,
¹⁹ Hariph, Anathoth, Nebai,
²⁰ Magpiash, Meshullam, Hezir,
²¹ Meshezabel, Zadok, Jaddua,
²² Pelatiah, Hanan, Anaiah,
²³ Hoshea, Hananiah, Hasshub,
²⁴ Hallohesh, Pilha, Shobek,
²⁵ Rehum, Hashabnah, Maaseiah,
²⁶ Ahiah, Hanan, Anan,
²⁷ Malluk, Harim and Baanah.

conversations

marriage «» 10:30

1» What are the risks in marrying a non-Christian?

2» Why is God so concerned about intermarriage between non-Christians and Christians?

3» How does a woman's faith affect her husband? And vice versa?

For more on **marriage**, check the index.
For the next Conversations, go to p. 631.

²⁸ "The rest of the people—priests, Levites, gatekeepers, musicians, temple servants and all who separated themselves from the neighboring peoples for the sake of the Law of God, together with their wives and all their sons and daughters who are able to understand— ²⁹ all these now join their fellow Israelites the nobles, and bind themselves with a curse and an oath to follow the Law of God given through Moses the servant of God and to obey carefully all the commands, regulations and decrees of the LORD our Lord.

³⁰ "We promise not to give our daughters in marriage to the peoples around us or take their daughters for our sons.

³¹ "When the neighboring peoples bring merchandise or grain to sell on the Sabbath, we will not buy from them on the Sabbath or on any holy day. Every seventh year we will forgo working the land and will cancel all debts.

³² "We assume the responsibility for carrying out the commands to give a third of a shekel*ᵃ* each year for the service of the house of our God: ³³ for the bread set out on the table; for the regular grain

---

ᵃ 32 That is, about 1/8 ounce or about 4 grams
* 10:1-39 is numbered 10:2-40 in Hebrew texts.

offerings and burnt offerings; for the offerings on the Sabbaths, at the New Moon feasts and at the appointed festivals; for the holy offerings; for sin offerings[a] to make atonement for Israel; and for all the duties of the house of our God.

[34]"We—the priests, the Levites and the people—have cast lots to determine when each of our families is to bring to the house of our God at set times each year a contribution of wood to burn on the altar of the Lord our God, as it is written in the Law.

[35]"We also assume responsibility for bringing to the house of the Lord each year the firstfruits of our crops and of every fruit tree.

[36]"As it is also written in the Law, we will bring the firstborn of our sons and of our cattle, of our herds and of our flocks to the house of our God, to the priests ministering there.

[37]"Moreover, we will bring to the storerooms of the house of our God, to the priests, the first of our ground meal, of our ⌞grain⌟ offerings, of the fruit of all our trees and of our new wine and olive oil. And we will bring a tithe of our crops to the Levites, for it is the Levites who collect the tithes in all the towns where we work. [38]A priest descended from Aaron is to accompany the Levites when they receive the tithes, and the Levites are to bring a tenth of the tithes up to the house of our God, to the storerooms of the treasury. [39]The people of Israel, including the Levites, are to bring their contributions of grain, new wine and olive oil to the storerooms, where the articles for the sanctuary and for the ministering priests, the gatekeepers and the musicians are also kept.

"We will not neglect the house of our God."

The New Residents of Jerusalem

11 Now the leaders of the people settled in Jerusalem. The rest of the people cast lots to bring one out of every ten of them to live in Jerusalem, the holy city, while the remaining nine were to stay in their own towns. [2]The people commended all who volunteered to live in Jerusalem.

[3]These are the provincial leaders who settled in Jerusalem (now some Israelites, priests, Levites, temple servants and descendants of Solomon's servants lived in the towns of Judah, each of them on their own property in the various towns, [4]while other people from both Judah and Benjamin lived in Jerusalem):

From the descendants of Judah:

Athaiah son of Uzziah, the son of Zechariah, the son of Amariah, the son of Shephatiah, the son of Mahalalel, a descendant of Perez; [5]and Maaseiah son of Baruch, the son of Kol-Hozeh, the son of Hazaiah, the son of Adaiah, the son of Joiarib, the son of Zechariah, a descendant of Shelah. [6]The descendants of Perez who lived in Jerusalem totaled 468 men of standing.

[7]From the descendants of Benjamin:

Sallu son of Meshullam, the son of Joed, the son of Pedaiah, the son of Kolaiah, the son of Maaseiah, the son of Ithiel, the son of Jeshaiah, [8]and his followers, Gabbai and Sallai—928 men. [9]Joel son of Zikri was their chief officer, and Judah son of Hassenuah was over the New Quarter of the city.

[10]From the priests:

Jedaiah; the son of Joiarib; Jakin; [11]Seraiah son of Hilkiah, the son of Meshullam, the son of Zadok, the son of Meraioth, the son of Ahitub, the official in charge of the house of God, [12]and their associates, who carried on work for the temple—822 men; Adaiah son of Jeroham, the son of Pelaliah, the son of Amzi, the son of Zechariah, the son of Pashhur, the son of Malkijah, [13]and his associates, who were heads of families—242 men; Amashsai son of Azarel, the son of Ahzai, the son of Meshillemoth, the son of Immer, [14]and his[b] associates, who were men of standing—128. Their chief officer was Zabdiel son of Haggedolim.

[15]From the Levites:

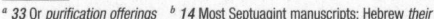

Shemaiah son of Hasshub, the son of Azrikam, the son of Hashabiah, the son of Bunni; ¹⁶Shabbethai and Jozabad, two of the heads of the Levites, who had charge of the outside work of the house of God; ¹⁷Mattaniah son of Mika, the son of Zabdi, the son of Asaph, the director who led in thanksgiving and prayer; Bakbukiah, second among his associates; and Abda son of Shammua, the son of Galal, the son of Jeduthun. ¹⁸The Levites in the holy city totaled 284.

¹⁹The gatekeepers:

Akkub, Talmon and their associates, who kept watch at the gates—172 men.

²⁰The rest of the Israelites, with the priests and Levites, were in all the towns of Judah, each of them on their ancestral property.

²¹The temple servants lived on the hill of Ophel, and Ziha and Gishpa were in charge of them.

²²The chief officer of the Levites in Jerusalem was Uzzi son of Bani, the son of Hashabiah, the son of Mattaniah, the son of Mika. Uzzi was one of Asaph's descendants, who were the musicians responsible for the service of the house of God. ²³The musicians were under the king's orders, which regulated their daily activity.

²⁴Pethahiah son of Meshezabel, one of the descendants of Zerah son of Judah, was the king's agent in all affairs relating to the people.

²⁵As for the villages with their fields, some of the people of Judah lived in Kiriath Arba and its surrounding settlements, in Dibon and its settlements, in Jekabzeel and its villages, ²⁶in Jeshua, in Moladah, in Beth Pelet, ²⁷in Hazar Shual, in Beersheba and its settlements, ²⁸in Ziklag, in Mekonah and its settlements, ²⁹in En Rimmon, in Zorah, in Jarmuth, ³⁰Zanoah, Adullam and their villages, in Lachish and its fields, and in Azekah and its settlements. So they were living all the way from Beersheba to the Valley of Hinnom.

³¹The descendants of the Benjamites from Geba lived in Mikmash, Aija, Bethel and its settlements, ³²in Anathoth, Nob and Ananiah, ³³in Hazor, Ramah and Gittaim, ³⁴in Hadid, Zeboim and Neballat, ³⁵in Lod and Ono, and in Ge Harashim.

³⁶Some of the divisions of the Levites of Judah settled in Benjamin.

Priests and Levites

12 These were the priests and Levites who returned with Zerubbabel son of Shealtiel and with Joshua:

Seraiah, Jeremiah, Ezra,

² Amariah, Malluk, Hattush,

³ Shekaniah, Rehum, Meremoth,

⁴ Iddo, Ginnethon,^a Abijah,

⁵ Mijamin,^b Moadiah, Bilgah,

⁶ Shemaiah, Joiarib, Jedaiah,

⁷ Sallu, Amok, Hilkiah and Jedaiah.

These were the leaders of the priests and their associates in the days of Joshua.

⁸The Levites were Jeshua, Binnui, Kadmiel, Sherebiah, Judah, and also Mattaniah, who, together with his associates, was in charge of the songs of thanksgiving. ⁹Bakbukiah and Unni, their associates, stood opposite them in the services.

¹⁰Joshua was the father of Joiakim, Joiakim the father of Eliashib, Eliashib the father of Joiada, ¹¹Joiada the father of Jonathan, and Jonathan the father of Jaddua.

¹²In the days of Joiakim, these were the heads of the priestly families:

of Seraiah's family, Meraiah;

of Jeremiah's, Hananiah;

¹³ of Ezra's, Meshullam;

of Amariah's, Jehohanan;

---

^a 4 Many Hebrew manuscripts and Vulgate (see also Neh. 12:16); most Hebrew manuscripts *Ginnethoi*   ^b 5 A variant of *Miniamin*

¹⁴ of Malluk's, Jonathan;
   of Shekaniah's,^a Joseph;
¹⁵ of Harim's, Adna;
   of Meremoth's,^b Helkai;
¹⁶ of Iddo's, Zechariah;
   of Ginnethon's, Meshullam;
¹⁷ of Abijah's, Zikri;
   of Miniamin's and of Moadiah's, Piltai;
¹⁸ of Bilgah's, Shammua;
   of Shemaiah's, Jehonathan;
¹⁹ of Joiarib's, Mattenai;
   of Jedaiah's, Uzzi;
²⁰ of Sallu's, Kallai;
   of Amok's, Eber;
²¹ of Hilkiah's, Hashabiah;
   of Jedaiah's, Nethanel.

²²The family heads of the Levites in the days of Eliashib, Joiada, Johanan and Jaddua, as well as those of the priests, were recorded in the reign of Darius the Persian. ²³The family heads among the descendants of Levi up to the time of Johanan son of Eliashib were recorded in the book of the annals. ²⁴And the leaders of the Levites were Hashabiah, Sherebiah, Jeshua son of Kadmiel, and their associates, who stood opposite them to give praise and thanksgiving, one section responding to the other, as prescribed by David the man of God.

²⁵Mattaniah, Bakbukiah, Obadiah, Meshullam, Talmon and Akkub were gatekeepers who guarded the storerooms at the gates. ²⁶They served in the days of Joiakim son of Joshua, the son of Jozadak, and in the days of Nehemiah the governor and of Ezra the priest, the teacher of the Law.

Dedication of the Wall of Jerusalem

²⁷At the dedication of the wall of Jerusalem, the Levites were sought out from where they lived and were brought to Jerusalem to celebrate joyfully the dedication with songs of thanksgiving and with the music of cymbals, harps and lyres. ²⁸The musicians also were brought together from the region around Jerusalem—from the villages of the Netophathites, ²⁹from Beth Gilgal, and from the area of Geba and Azmaveth, for the musicians had built villages for themselves around Jerusalem. ³⁰When the priests and Levites had purified themselves ceremonially, they purified the people, the gates and the wall.

³¹I had the leaders of Judah go up on top of ^c the wall. I also assigned two large choirs to give thanks. One was to proceed on top of ^d the wall to the right, toward the Dung Gate. ³²Hoshaiah and half the leaders of Judah followed them, ³³along with Azariah, Ezra, Meshullam, ³⁴Judah, Benjamin, Shemaiah, Jeremiah, ³⁵as well as some priests with trumpets, and also Zechariah son of Jonathan, the son of Shemaiah, the son of Mattaniah, the son of Micaiah, the son of Zakkur, the son of Asaph, ³⁶and his associates—Shemaiah, Azarel, Milalai, Gilalai, Maai, Nethanel, Judah and Hanani—with musical instruments prescribed by David the man of God. Ezra the teacher of the Law led the procession. ³⁷At the Fountain Gate they continued directly up the steps of the City of David on the ascent to the wall and passed above the site of David's palace to the Water Gate on the east.

³⁸The second choir proceeded in the opposite direction. I followed them on top of ^e the wall, together with half the people—past the Tower of the Ovens to the Broad Wall, ³⁹over the Gate of Ephraim, the Jeshanah ^f Gate, the Fish Gate, the Tower of Hananel and the Tower of the Hundred, as far as the Sheep Gate. At the Gate of the Guard they stopped.

⁴⁰The two choirs that gave thanks then took their places in the house of God; so did I, together with half the officials, ⁴¹as well as the priests—Eliakim, Maaseiah, Miniamin, Micaiah, Elioenai, Zechariah and Hananiah with their trumpets— ⁴²and also Maaseiah, Shemaiah, Eleazar, Uzzi, Jehohanan, Malkijah, Elam and Ezer. The choirs sang under the direction of Jezrahiah. ⁴³And on that day they offered great

sacrifices, rejoicing because God had given them great joy. The women and children also rejoiced. The sound of rejoicing in Jerusalem could be heard far away.

⁴⁴At that time men were appointed to be in charge of the storerooms for the contributions, firstfruits and tithes. From the fields around the towns they were to bring into the storerooms the portions required by the Law for the priests and the Levites, for Judah was pleased with the ministering priests and Levites. ⁴⁵They performed the service of their God and the service of purification, as did also the musicians and gatekeepers, according to the commands of David and his son Solomon. ⁴⁶For long ago, in the days of David and Asaph, there had been directors for the musicians and for the songs of praise and thanksgiving to God. ⁴⁷So in the days of Zerubbabel and of Nehemiah, all Israel contributed the daily portions for the musicians and the gatekeepers. They also set aside the portion for the other Levites, and the Levites set aside the portion for the descendants of Aaron.

Nehemiah's Final Reforms

13 On that day the Book of Moses was read aloud in the hearing of the people and there it was found written that no Ammonite or Moabite should ever be admitted into the assembly of God, ²because they had not met the Israelites with food and water but had hired Balaam to call a curse down on them. (Our God, however, turned the curse into a blessing.) ³When the people heard this law, they excluded from Israel all who were of foreign descent.

⁴Before this, Eliashib the priest had been put in charge of the storerooms of the house of our God. He was closely associated with Tobiah, ⁵and he had provided him with a large room formerly used to store the grain offerings and incense and temple articles, and also the tithes of grain, new wine and olive oil prescribed for the Levites, musicians and gatekeepers, as well as the contributions for the priests.

⁶But while all this was going on, I was not in Jerusalem, for in the thirty-second year of Artaxerxes king of Babylon I had returned to the king. Some time later I asked his permission ⁷and came back to Jerusalem. Here I learned about the evil thing Eliashib had done in providing Tobiah a room in the courts of the house of God. ⁸I was greatly displeased and threw all Tobiah's household goods out of the room. ⁹I gave orders to purify the rooms, and then I put back into them the equipment of the house of God, with the grain offerings and the incense.

¹⁰I also learned that the portions assigned to the Levites had not been given to them, and that all the Levites and musicians responsible for the service had gone back to their own fields. ¹¹So I rebuked the officials and asked them, "Why is the house of God neglected?" Then I called them together and stationed them at their posts.

¹²All Judah brought the tithes of grain, new wine and olive oil into the storerooms. ¹³I put Shelemiah the priest, Zadok the scribe, and a Levite named Pedaiah in charge of the storerooms and made Hanan son of Zakkur, the son of Mattaniah, their assistant, because they were considered trustworthy. They were made responsible for distributing the supplies to their fellow Levites.

¹⁴Remember me for this, my God, and do not blot out what I have so faithfully done for the house of my God and its services.

¹⁵In those days I saw people in Judah treading winepresses on the Sabbath and bringing in grain and loading it on donkeys, together with wine, grapes, figs and all other kinds of loads. And they were bringing all this into Jerusalem on the Sabbath. Therefore I warned them against selling food on that day. ¹⁶People from Tyre who lived in Jerusalem were bringing in fish and all kinds of merchandise and selling them in Jerusalem on the Sabbath to the people of Judah. ¹⁷I rebuked the nobles of Judah and said to

a tissue of joy

12:43 Deadlines, laundry, bills, voice mail, husband, kids, parents, errands . . . It's enough just to make it through the day alive. Forget about actually enjoying it. It's true that life is difficult, and you can't depend on your circumstances to bring true joy. But you can always find joy in all that Jesus did for you on the cross, in all that is yours on earth through him and in all that awaits you in heaven. When life seems to suck the joy right out of you, look to God to give you great joy.

625

them, "What is this wicked thing you are doing—desecrating the Sabbath day? [18]Didn't your ancestors do the same things, so that our God brought all this calamity on us and on this city? Now you are stirring up more wrath against Israel by desecrating the Sabbath."

[19]When evening shadows fell on the gates of Jerusalem before the Sabbath, I ordered the doors to be shut and not opened until the Sabbath was over. I stationed some of my own men at the gates so that no load could be brought in on the Sabbath day. [20]Once or twice the merchants and sellers of all kinds of goods spent the night outside Jerusalem. [21]But I warned them and said, "Why do you spend the night by the wall? If you do this again, I will lay hands on you." From that time on they no longer came on the Sabbath. [22]Then I commanded the Levites to purify themselves and go and guard the gates in order to keep the Sabbath day holy.

Remember me for this also, my God, and show mercy to me according to your great love.

[23]Moreover, in those days I saw men of Judah who had married women from Ashdod, Ammon and Moab. [24]Half of their children spoke the language of Ashdod or the language of one of the other peoples, and did not know how to speak the language of Judah. [25]I rebuked them and called curses down on them. I beat some of them and pulled out their hair. I made them take an oath in God's name and said: "You are not to give your daughters in marriage to their sons, nor are you to take their daughters in marriage for your sons or for yourselves. [26]Was it not because of marriages like these that Solomon king of Israel sinned? Among the many nations there was no king like him. He was loved by his God, and God made him king over all Israel, but even he was led into sin by foreign women. [27]Must we hear now that you too are doing all this terrible wickedness and are being unfaithful to our God by marrying foreign women?"

[28]One of the sons of Joiada son of Eliashib the high priest was son-in-law to Sanballat the Horonite. And I drove him away from me.

[29]Remember them, my God, because they defiled the priestly office and the covenant of the priesthood and of the Levites.

[30]So I purified the priests and the Levites of everything foreign, and assigned them duties, each to his own task. [31]I also made provision for contributions of wood at designated times, and for the firstfruits.

Remember me with favor, my God.

a tissue: marriage

13:23–27 Say a friend of yours signed up for a risky new eye surgery to give her perfect vision. How cool! But what if your friend's surgery had complications, and she lost her sight? You probably wouldn't say, "Sign me up. I want to try it for myself. Maybe I'll be different." Just like the eye surgery, marrying a non-Christian is something that can seem like a good decision at the time, but in this case, there are far worse risks. What are the odds your husband will decide to follow Christ? There's no guarantee. If he doesn't, then you'll suffer the hard consequences of your choice.

esther

AUTHOR
Unknown.

AUDIENCE
All Israel.

DATE
Written in hindsight, after the events
described in the book. About 460 B.C.

SETTING
Susa, the capital of the Persian Empire,
during a turbulent time for the Jews.

VERSE TO REMEMBER
"For if you remain silent at this time, relief
and deliverance for the Jews will arise from
another place, but you and your father's
family will perish. And who knows but that
you have come to royal position for such a
time as this?" (4:14)

THEME TO CONSIDER
God providentially places us in the
right place, at the right time, for all the
right reasons.

Queen Vashti Deposed

1 This is what happened during the time of Xerxes,[a] the Xerxes who ruled over 127 provinces stretching from India to Cush[b]: [2]At that time King Xerxes reigned from his royal throne in the citadel of Susa, [3]and in the third year of his reign he gave a banquet for all his nobles and officials. The military leaders of Persia and Media, the princes, and the nobles of the provinces were present.

[4]For a full 180 days he displayed the vast wealth of his kingdom and the splendor and glory of his majesty. [5]When these days were over, the king gave a banquet, lasting seven days, in the enclosed garden of the king's palace, for all the people from the least to the greatest who were in the citadel of Susa. [6]The garden had hangings of white and blue linen, fastened with cords of white linen and purple material to silver rings on marble pillars. There were couches of gold and silver on a mosaic pavement of porphyry, marble, mother-of-pearl and other costly stones. [7]Wine was served in goblets of gold, each one different from the other, and the royal wine was abundant, in keeping with the king's liberality. [8]By the king's command each guest was allowed to drink with no restrictions, for the king instructed all the wine stewards to serve each man what he wished.

[9]Queen Vashti also gave a banquet for the women in the royal palace of King Xerxes.

[10]On the seventh day, when King Xerxes was in high spirits from wine, he commanded the seven eunuchs who served him—Mehuman, Biztha, Harbona, Bigtha, Abagtha, Zethar and Karkas— [11]to bring before him Queen Vashti, wearing her royal crown, in order to display her beauty to the people and nobles, for she was lovely to look at. [12]But when the attendants delivered the king's command, Queen Vashti refused to come. Then the king became furious and burned with anger.

[13]Since it was customary for the king to consult experts in matters of law and justice, he spoke with the wise men who understood the times [14]and were closest to the king—Karshena, Shethar, Admatha, Tarshish, Meres, Marsena and Memukan, the seven nobles of Persia and Media who had special access to the king and were highest in the kingdom.

[15]"According to law, what must be done to Queen Vashti?" he asked. "She has not obeyed the command of King Xerxes that the eunuchs have taken to her."

[16]Then Memukan replied in the presence of the king and the nobles, "Queen Vashti has done wrong, not only against the king but also against all the nobles and the peoples of all the provinces of King Xerxes. [17]For the queen's conduct will become known to all the women, and so they will despise their husbands and say, 'King Xerxes commanded Queen Vashti to be brought before him, but she would not come.' [18]This very day the Persian and Median women of the nobility who have heard about the queen's conduct will respond to all the king's nobles in the same way. There will be no end of disrespect and discord.

[19]"Therefore, if it pleases the king, let him issue a royal decree and let it be written in the laws of Persia and Media, which cannot be repealed, that Vashti is never again to enter the presence of King Xerxes. Also let the king give her royal position to someone else who is better than she. [20]Then when the king's edict is proclaimed throughout all his vast realm, all the women will respect their husbands, from the least to the greatest."

[21]The king and his nobles were pleased with this advice, so the king did as Memukan proposed. [22]He sent dispatches to all parts of the kingdom, to each province in its own script and to each people in their own language, proclaiming that every man should be ruler over his own household, using his native tongue.

Esther Made Queen

2 Later when King Xerxes' fury had subsided, he remembered Vashti and what she had done and what he had decreed about her. [2]Then the king's personal attendants proposed, "Let a search be made for beautiful young virgins for the king. [3]Let the king appoint commissioners in every province of his realm to bring all these beautiful young women into the harem at the citadel of Susa. Let them be placed under the care of Hegai, the king's eunuch, who is in charge of the women; and let beauty treatments be given to them. [4]Then let the young woman who pleases the king be queen instead of Vashti." This advice appealed to the king, and he followed it.

---

[a] 1 Hebrew *Ahasuerus*; here and throughout Esther [b] 1 That is, the upper Nile region

[5]Now there was in the citadel of Susa a Jew of the tribe of Benjamin, named Mordecai son of Jair, the son of Shimei, the son of Kish, [6]who had been carried into exile from Jerusalem by Nebuchadnezzar king of Babylon, among those taken captive with Jehoiachin[a] king of Judah. [7]Mordecai had a cousin named Hadassah, whom he had brought up because she had neither father nor mother. This young woman, who was also known as Esther, had a lovely figure and was beautiful. Mordecai had taken her as his own daughter when her father and mother died.

[8]When the king's order and edict had been proclaimed, many young women were brought to the citadel of Susa and put under the care of Hegai. Esther also was taken to the king's palace and entrusted to Hegai, who had charge of the harem. [9]She pleased him and won his favor. Immediately he provided her with her beauty treatments and special food. He assigned to her seven female attendants selected from the king's palace and moved her and her attendants into the best place in the harem.

[10]Esther had not revealed her nationality and family background, because Mordecai had forbidden her to do so. [11]Every day he walked back and forth near the courtyard of the harem to find out how Esther was and what was happening to her.

[12]Before a young woman's turn came to go in to King Xerxes, she had to complete twelve months of beauty treatments prescribed for the women, six months with oil of myrrh and six with perfumes and cosmetics. [13]And this is how she would go to the king: Anything she wanted was given her to take with her from the harem to the king's palace. [14]In the evening she would go there and in the morning return to another part of the harem to the care of Shaashgaz, the king's eunuch who was in charge of the concubines. She would not return to the king unless he was pleased with her and summoned her by name.

[15]When the turn came for Esther (the young woman Mordecai had adopted, the daughter of his uncle Abihail) to go to the king, she asked for nothing other than what Hegai, the king's eunuch who was in charge of the harem, suggested. And Esther won the favor of everyone who saw her. [16]She was taken to King Xerxes in the royal residence in the tenth month, the month of Tebeth, in the seventh year of his reign.

[17]Now the king was attracted to Esther more than to any of the other women, and she won his favor and approval more than any of the other virgins. So he set a royal crown on her head and made her queen instead of Vashti. [18]And the king gave a great banquet, Esther's banquet, for all his nobles and officials. He proclaimed a holiday throughout the provinces and distributed gifts with royal liberality.

Mordecai Uncovers a Conspiracy

[19]When the virgins were assembled a second time, Mordecai was sitting at the king's gate. [20]But Esther had kept secret her family background and nationality just as Mordecai had told her to do, for she continued to follow Mordecai's instructions as she had done when he was bringing her up.

[21]During the time Mordecai was sitting at the king's gate, Bigthana[b] and Teresh, two of the king's officers who guarded the doorway, became angry and conspired to assassinate King Xerxes. [22]But Mordecai found out about the plot and told Queen Esther, who in turn reported it to the king, giving credit to Mordecai. [23]And when the report was investigated and found to be true, the two officials were impaled on poles. All this was recorded in the book of the annals in the presence of the king.

Haman's Plot to Destroy the Jews

3 After these events, King Xerxes honored Haman son of Hammedatha, the Agagite, elevating him and giving him a seat of honor higher than that of all the other nobles. [2]All the royal officials at the king's gate knelt down and paid honor to Haman, for the king had commanded this concerning him. But Mordecai would not kneel down or pay him honor.

[3]Then the royal officials at the king's gate asked Mordecai, "Why do you disobey the king's command?" [4]Day after day they spoke to him but he refused to comply. Therefore they told Haman about it to see whether Mordecai's behavior would be tolerated, for he had told them he was a Jew.

[5]When Haman saw that Mordecai would not kneel down or pay him honor, he was enraged. [6]Yet having learned who Mordecai's people were, he scorned the idea of killing only Mordecai. Instead Haman looked for a way to destroy all Mordecai's people, the Jews, throughout the whole kingdom of Xerxes.

629

---

a 6 Hebrew *Jeconiah*, a variant of *Jehoiachin*   *b 21* Hebrew *Bigthan*, a variant of *Bigthana*

630

[7]In the twelfth year of King Xerxes, in the first month, the month of Nisan, the *pur* (that is, the lot) was cast in the presence of Haman to select a day and month. And the lot fell on[a] the twelfth month, the month of Adar.

[8]Then Haman said to King Xerxes, "There is a certain people dispersed among the peoples in all the provinces of your kingdom who keep themselves separate. Their customs are different from those of all other people, and they do not obey the king's laws; it is not in the king's best interest to tolerate them. [9]If it pleases the king, let a decree be issued to destroy them, and I will give ten thousand talents[b] of silver to the king's administrators for the royal treasury."

[10]So the king took his signet ring from his finger and gave it to Haman son of Hammedatha, the Agagite, the enemy of the Jews. [11]"Keep the money," the king said to Haman, "and do with the people as you please."

[12]Then on the thirteenth day of the first month the royal secretaries were summoned. They wrote out in the script of each province and in the language of each people all Haman's orders to the king's satraps, the governors of the various provinces and the nobles of the various peoples. These were written in the name of King Xerxes himself and sealed with his own ring. [13]Dispatches were sent by couriers to all the king's provinces with the order to destroy, kill and annihilate all the Jews—young and old, women and children—on a single day, the thirteenth day of the twelfth month, the month of Adar, and to plunder their goods. [14]A copy of the text of the edict was to be issued as law in every province and made known to the people of every nationality so they would be ready for that day.

[15]The couriers went out, spurred on by the king's command, and the edict was issued in the citadel of Susa. The king and Haman sat down to drink, but the city of Susa was bewildered.

atissue:racism

3:8–9 Haman was neither the first nor the last person to hate and fear an ethnic group. After the September 11, 2001, terrorist attacks on the U.S. by Muslim extremists, a wave of prejudice resulted in the dramatic rise of hate crimes and suspicion directed at Arabs—Muslim or not. While it's true that a few Arab Muslim extremists proved dangerous, they didn't represent the majority. What makes a person dangerous or subversive isn't her race—it's her heart. Good and evil exist in all races; God judges us by our hearts. Shouldn't we do the same?

Mordecai Persuades Esther to Help

4 When Mordecai learned of all that had been done, he tore his clothes, put on sackcloth and ashes, and went out into the city, wailing loudly and bitterly. [2]But he went only as far as the king's gate, because no one clothed in sackcloth was allowed to enter it. [3]In every province to which the edict and order of the king came, there was great mourning among the Jews, with fasting, weeping and wailing. Many lay in sackcloth and ashes.

[4]When Esther's eunuchs and female attendants came and told her about Mordecai, she was in great distress. She sent clothes for him to put on instead of his sackcloth, but he would not accept them. [5]Then Esther summoned Hathak, one of the king's eunuchs assigned to attend her, and ordered him to find out what was troubling Mordecai and why.

[6]So Hathak went out to Mordecai in the open square of the city in front of the king's gate. [7]Mordecai told him everything that had happened to him, including the exact amount of money Haman had promised to pay into the royal treasury for the destruction of the Jews. [8]He also gave him a copy of the text of the edict for their annihilation, which had been published in Susa, to show to Esther and explain it to her, and he told him to instruct her to go into the king's presence to beg for mercy and plead with him for her people.

[9]Hathak went back and reported to Esther what Mordecai had said. [10]Then she instructed him to say

---

[a] 7 Septuagint; Hebrew does not have *And the lot fell on.*   [b] 9 That is, about 375 tons or about 335 metric tons

to Mordecai, [11]"All the king's officials and the people of the royal provinces know that for any man or woman who approaches the king in the inner court without being summoned the king has but one law: that they be put to death unless the king extends the gold scepter to them and spares their lives. But thirty days have passed since I was called to go to the king."

[12]When Esther's words were reported to Mordecai, [13]he sent back this answer: "Do not think that because you are in the king's house you alone of all the Jews will escape. [14]For if you remain silent at this time, relief and deliverance for the Jews will arise from another place, but you and your father's family will perish. And who knows but that you have come to royal position for such a time as this?"

[15]Then Esther sent this reply to Mordecai: [16]"Go, gather together all the Jews who are in Susa, and fast for me. Do not eat or drink for three days, night or day. I and my attendants will fast as you do. When this is done, I will go to the king, even though it is against the law. And if I perish, I perish."

[17]So Mordecai went away and carried out all of Esther's instructions.

conversations

making a difference «» 4:12–17

1» Who is one person who made a dramatic difference in your life?

2» How do you think God might use your life to make a difference for others?

3» What are the consequences for keeping quiet when you could take a stand for God?

For more on **making a difference**, check the index. For the next Conversations, go to p. 662.

631

Esther's Request to the King

5 On the third day Esther put on her royal robes and stood in the inner court of the palace, in front of the king's hall. The king was sitting on his royal throne in the hall, facing the entrance. [2]When he saw Queen Esther standing in the court, he was pleased with her and held out to her the gold scepter that was in his hand. So Esther approached and touched the tip of the scepter.

[3]Then the king asked, "What is it, Queen Esther? What is your request? Even up to half the kingdom, it will be given you."

[4]"If it pleases the king," replied Esther, "let the king, together with Haman, come today to a banquet I have prepared for him."

[5]"Bring Haman at once," the king said, "so that we may do what Esther asks."

So the king and Haman went to the banquet Esther had prepared. [6]As they were drinking wine, the king again asked Esther, "Now what is your petition? It will be given you. And what is your request? Even up to half the kingdom, it will be granted."

[7]Esther replied, "My petition and my request is this: [8]If the king regards me with favor and if it pleases the king to grant my petition and fulfill my request, let the king and Haman come tomorrow to the banquet I will prepare for them. Then I will answer the king's question."

Haman's Rage Against Mordecai

[9]Haman went out that day happy and in high spirits. But when he saw Mordecai at the king's gate and observed that he neither rose nor showed fear in his presence, he was filled with rage against Mordecai. [10]Nevertheless, Haman restrained himself and went home.

Calling together his friends and Zeresh, his wife, [11]Haman boasted to them about his vast wealth, his many sons, and all the ways the king had honored him and how he had elevated him above the other nobles and officials. [12]"And that's not all," Haman added. "I'm the only person Queen Esther invited to accompany the king to the banquet she gave. And she has invited me along with the king tomorrow. [13]But all this gives me no satisfaction as long as I see that Jew Mordecai sitting at the king's gate."

[14]His wife Zeresh and all his friends said to him, "Have a pole set up, reaching to a height of fifty cubits,[a] and ask the king in the morning to have Mordecai impaled on it. Then go with the king to the banquet and enjoy yourself." This suggestion delighted Haman, and he had the pole set up.

---

[a] *14* That is, about 75 feet or about 22.5 meters

myth# 41 "MEN WILL BE MEN— I CAN'T EXPECT THEM TO BE FAITHFUL."

I formed my own opinions about men by watching my parents' relationship. My dad got drunk when he wanted to, staying out late at the bars downtown with women he'd meet. My mom just carried on as if nothing was wrong. When I was in my teens, I remember asking her one day why she stayed with him. She said in a matter-of-fact voice, "Men will be men, honey. You just can't expect them to be faithful." We talked that first and only time about it. But I remembered her words.

I've been dating a man for three years this December. I've seen him look at waitresses when we go out. He flirts with them right in front of me—as if I'm not even there. If I call him on it, he just gets upset and turns it on me. "Why are you overreacting? You're so insecure. You know I love you." And somehow I end up apologizing.

Whenever he is late for our dates, he always has some excuse. Sometimes he doesn't call till the next day to explain where he's been. The problem is, I'm not just paranoid. I caught him cheating on me once. He told me it was because I was on a business trip, and he just missed me so much.

I never feel comfortable when he goes out with his guy friends, whether it's just a guy's night out or a bachelor party. I know they have strippers there. How degrading! But he tells me that all men are the same. "It's just our sexual nature—it's not that I don't love you." I'm afraid if I push him too hard I'll lose him.

Why do I stay with him? I don't know. Maybe my mom was right. Maybe this really is as good as it gets. Men are driven sexually, and as long as he says he loves me, I should just learn to deal with his indiscretions the best I can.

—Sarah

"MEN WILL BE MEN" is a lame excuse, so don't buy it or enable it. If your boyfriend treats you with disrespect, don't expect him to change on his own. As hard as it may feel to break off the relationship, it's better to be alone and waiting for a good man than to be with a man who doesn't respect you. You have immense worth in God's eyes, so be courageous, like Esther. Consider talking to someone about why you chose to be with such a man in the first place.

If you're married to a man who treats women inappropriately, talk to a pastor or Christian counselor to begin to address this issue. Don't excuse it; bring it into the light to begin the process of healing and change. Whenever you are tempted to believe that you don't deserve love and faithfulness in your relationships, stop and remember your WORTH.

W—Women and men have the same Biblical standard: faithfulness. Expecting a man to be faithful in a love relationship is a reasonable request.

O—Only God can change your man and your relationship. Your nagging or wishful thinking isn't going to work. Pray, live respectfully and let God deal with your husband (see 1 Peter 3:1–2).

R—Raise the bar. Sometimes we confuse our self-worth with how others treat us. Instead of lowering the bar of expectations, taking what you can get in the love department, know that you are worthy of extravagant love—the kind of love that motivated Jesus to die for you.

T—Tell yourself that your identity in Christ makes you his precious, prized possession. Because you are created in his image and you belong to him, you deserve love, respect and honor.

H—He is faithful. God sees. Do what's right, regardless of what your husband does, and entrust yourself to God to make things right in the end (see 1 Peter 2:23).

"My dream for every married man is that his wife, regardless of her age, is the most beautiful woman in his eyes, because she is the only woman in his eyes; . . . that the flicker in his eyes caused by the candles on his fiftieth anniversary cake reflect a man who has remained pure throughout his marriage, and that someday (whether married or not) that man will face Christ unashamed and hear the words, 'Well done, thou good and faithful servant.' "

—Joe White,
Promise Keepers

633

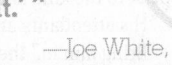

"THE LORD rewards every man FOR HIS rIGHTEOUSNESS and FAITHFULNESS."

1 SAMUEL 26:23

SEE ALSO

Proverbs 5:18–23
Song of Songs 8:6–7.
Luke 1:37

For more on **Relationships**, check the index.

Mordecai Honored

6 That night the king could not sleep; so he ordered the book of the chronicles, the record of his reign, to be brought in and read to him. [2] It was found recorded there that Mordecai had exposed Bigthana and Teresh, two of the king's officers who guarded the doorway, who had conspired to assassinate King Xerxes.

HE IS: ## providential

6:1–2 God isn't mentioned in the book of Esther, but his fingerprints are everywhere. Who but God could give a king insomnia, ensure that the section of the chronicles recording Mordecai's intercession for the king was read and bring to light the evil that Haman had planned? God is *providential*, coordinating events ahead of time and intervening for his people.

You may not realize God's at work, but he's busy behind the scenes, working in your life. Look for him in the people you meet and the places you go. Your *providential* God will make things happen for your good and his glory (see Romans 8:28–30).

For the next He Is, go to p. 640.

[3] "What honor and recognition has Mordecai received for this?" the king asked.

"Nothing has been done for him," his attendants answered.

[4] The king said, "Who is in the court?" Now Haman had just entered the outer court of the palace to speak to the king about impaling Mordecai on the pole he had set up for him.

[5] His attendants answered, "Haman is standing in the court."

"Bring him in," the king ordered.

[6] When Haman entered, the king asked him, "What should be done for the man the king delights to honor?"

Now Haman thought to himself, "Who is there that the king would rather honor than me?" [7] So he answered the king, "For the man the king delights to honor, [8] have them bring a royal robe the king has worn and a horse the king has ridden, one with a royal crest placed on its head. [9] Then let the robe and horse be entrusted to one of the king's most noble princes. Let them robe the man the king delights to honor, and lead him on the horse through the city streets, proclaiming before him, 'This is what is done for the man the king delights to honor!'"

[10] "Go at once," the king commanded Haman. "Get the robe and the horse and do just as you have suggested for Mordecai the Jew, who sits at the king's gate. Do not neglect anything you have recommended."

[11] So Haman got the robe and the horse. He robed Mordecai, and led him on horseback through the city streets, proclaiming before him, "This is what is done for the man the king delights to honor!"

[12] Afterward Mordecai returned to the king's gate. But Haman rushed home, with his head covered in grief, [13] and told Zeresh his wife and all his friends everything that had happened to him.

His advisers and his wife Zeresh said to him, "Since Mordecai, before whom your downfall has started, is of Jewish origin, you cannot stand against him—you will surely come to ruin!" [14] While they were still talking with him, the king's eunuchs arrived and hurried Haman away to the banquet Esther had prepared.

Haman Impaled

7 So the king and Haman went to Queen Esther's banquet, [2] and as they were drinking wine on the second day, the king again asked, "Queen Esther, what is your petition? It will be given you. What is your request? Even up to half the kingdom, it will be granted."

[3] Then Queen Esther answered, "If I have found favor with you, Your Majesty, and if it pleases you,

grant me my life—this is my petition. And spare my people—this is my request. ⁴For I and my people have been sold to be destroyed, killed and annihilated. If we had merely been sold as male and female slaves, I would have kept quiet, because no such distress would justify disturbing the king.ᵃ"

⁵King Xerxes asked Queen Esther, "Who is he? Where is he—the man who has dared to do such a thing?"

⁶Esther said, "An adversary and enemy! This vile Haman!"

Then Haman was terrified before the king and queen. ⁷The king got up in a rage, left his wine and went out into the palace garden. But Haman, realizing that the king had already decided his fate, stayed behind to beg Queen Esther for his life.

⁸Just as the king returned from the palace garden to the banquet hall, Haman was falling on the couch where Esther was reclining.

The king exclaimed, "Will he even molest the queen while she is with me in the house?"

As soon as the word left the king's mouth, they covered Haman's face. ⁹Then Harbona, one of the eunuchs attending the king, said, "A pole reaching to a height of fifty cubitsᵇ stands by Haman's house. He had it set up for Mordecai, who spoke up to help the king."

The king said, "Impale him on it!" ¹⁰So they impaled Haman on the pole he had set up for Mordecai. Then the king's fury subsided.

> **atissue:risk**
>
> **7:3–7** When it comes to risk, most of us are "trunk-huggers." Rather than go out on a limb and risk having it break beneath us, we choose to safely hug the tree trunk. Because Esther trusted God, she went out on a limb to save God's people. What limb does God want *you* to step out on? Perhaps it's time to reach out to someone new, to open up your heart, to expose evil. Challenge the status quo, and watch God do amazing things when you let go of that trunk.

The King's Edict in Behalf of the Jews

8 That same day King Xerxes gave Queen Esther the estate of Haman, the enemy of the Jews. And Mordecai came into the presence of the king, for Esther had told how he was related to her. ²The king took off his signet ring, which he had reclaimed from Haman, and presented it to Mordecai. And Esther appointed him over Haman's estate.

³Esther again pleaded with the king, falling at his feet and weeping. She begged him to put an end to the evil plan of Haman the Agagite, which he had devised against the Jews. ⁴Then the king extended the gold scepter to Esther and she arose and stood before him.

⁵"If it pleases the king," she said, "and if he regards me with favor and thinks it the right thing to do, and if he is pleased with me, let an order be written overruling the dispatches that Haman son of Hammedatha, the Agagite, devised and wrote to destroy the Jews in all the king's provinces. ⁶For how can I bear to see disaster fall on my people? How can I bear to see the destruction of my family?"

⁷King Xerxes replied to Queen Esther and to Mordecai the Jew, "Because Haman attacked the Jews, I have given his estate to Esther, and they have impaled him on the pole he set up. ⁸Now write another decree in the king's name in behalf of the Jews as seems best to you, and seal it with the king's signet ring—for no document written in the king's name and sealed with his ring can be revoked."

⁹At once the royal secretaries were summoned—on the twenty-third day of the third month, the month of Sivan. They wrote out all Mordecai's orders to the Jews, and to the satraps, governors and nobles of the 127 provinces stretching from India to Cush.ᶜ These orders were written in the script of each province and the language of each people and also to the Jews in their own script and language. ¹⁰Mordecai wrote in the name of King Xerxes, sealed the dispatches with the king's signet ring, and sent them by mounted couriers, who rode fast horses especially bred for the king.

¹¹The king's edict granted the Jews in every city the right to assemble and protect themselves; to destroy, kill and annihilate the armed men of any nationality or province who might attack them and their women and children,ᵈ and to plunder the property of their enemies. ¹²The day appointed for the

---

ᵃ *4 Or quiet, but the compensation our adversary offers cannot be compared with the loss the king would suffer*   ᵇ *9 That is, about 75 feet or about 22.5 meters*
ᶜ *9 That is, the upper Nile region*   ᵈ *11 Or province, together with their women and children, who might attack them;*

Jews to do this in all the provinces of King Xerxes was the thirteenth day of the twelfth month, the month of Adar. ¹³A copy of the text of the edict was to be issued as law in every province and made known to the people of every nationality so that the Jews would be ready on that day to avenge themselves on their enemies.

¹⁴The couriers, riding the royal horses, went out, spurred on by the king's command, and the edict was issued in the citadel of Susa.

The Triumph of the Jews

¹⁵When Mordecai left the king's presence, he was wearing royal garments of blue and white, a large crown of gold and a purple robe of fine linen. And the city of Susa held a joyous celebration. ¹⁶For the Jews it was a time of happiness and joy, gladness and honor. ¹⁷In every province and in every city to which the edict of the king came, there was joy and gladness among the Jews, with feasting and celebrating. And many people of other nationalities became Jews because fear of the Jews had seized them.

9 On the thirteenth day of the twelfth month, the month of Adar, the edict commanded by the king was to be carried out. On this day the enemies of the Jews had hoped to overpower them, but now the tables were turned and the Jews got the upper hand over those who hated them. ²The Jews assembled in their cities in all the provinces of King Xerxes to attack those seeking their destruction. No one could stand against them, because the people of all the other nationalities were afraid of them. ³And all the nobles of the provinces, the satraps, the governors and the king's administrators helped the Jews, because fear of Mordecai had seized them. ⁴Mordecai was prominent in the palace; his reputation spread throughout the provinces, and he became more and more powerful.

⁵The Jews struck down all their enemies with the sword, killing and destroying them, and they did what they pleased to those who hated them. ⁶In the citadel of Susa, the Jews killed and destroyed five hundred men. ⁷They also killed Parshandatha, Dalphon, Aspatha, ⁸Poratha, Adalia, Aridatha, ⁹Parmashta, Arisai, Aridai and Vaizatha, ¹⁰the ten sons of Haman son of Hammedatha, the enemy of the Jews. But they did not lay their hands on the plunder.

¹¹The number of those killed in the citadel of Susa was reported to the king that same day. ¹²The king said to Queen Esther, "The Jews have killed and destroyed five hundred men and the ten sons of Haman in the citadel of Susa. What have they done in the rest of the king's provinces? Now what is your petition? It will be given you. What is your request? It will also be granted."

¹³"If it pleases the king," Esther answered, "give the Jews in Susa permission to carry out this day's edict tomorrow also, and let Haman's ten sons be impaled on poles."

¹⁴So the king commanded that this be done. An edict was issued in Susa, and they impaled the ten sons of Haman. ¹⁵The Jews in Susa came together on the fourteenth day of the month of Adar, and they put to death in Susa three hundred men, but they did not lay their hands on the plunder.

¹⁶Meanwhile, the remainder of the Jews who were in the king's provinces also assembled to protect themselves and get relief from their enemies. They killed seventy-five thousand of them but did not lay their hands on the plunder. ¹⁷This happened on the thirteenth day of the month of Adar, and on the fourteenth they rested and made it a day of feasting and joy.

¹⁸The Jews in Susa, however, had assembled on the thirteenth and fourteenth, and then on the fifteenth they rested and made it a day of feasting and joy.

¹⁹That is why rural Jews—those living in villages—observe the fourteenth of the month of Adar as a day of joy and feasting, a day for giving presents to each other.

Purim Established

²⁰Mordecai recorded these events, and he sent letters to all the Jews throughout the provinces of King Xerxes, near and far, ²¹to have them celebrate annually the fourteenth and fifteenth days of the month of Adar ²²as the time when the Jews got relief from their enemies, and as the month when their sorrow was turned into joy and their mourning into a day of celebration. He wrote them to observe the days as days of feasting and joy and giving presents of food to one another and gifts to the poor.

²³So the Jews agreed to continue the celebration they had begun, doing what Mordecai had written to them. ²⁴For Haman son of Hammedatha, the Agagite, the enemy of all the Jews, had plotted against the

Jews to destroy them and had cast the *pur* (that is, the lot) for their ruin and destruction. [25] But when the plot came to the king's attention,[a] he issued written orders that the evil scheme Haman had devised against the Jews should come back onto his own head, and that he and his sons should be impaled on poles. [26] (Therefore these days were called Purim, from the word *pur*.) Because of everything written in this letter and because of what they had seen and what had happened to them, [27] the Jews took it on themselves to establish the custom that they and their descendants and all who join them should without fail observe these two days every year, in the way prescribed and at the time appointed. [28] These days should be remembered and observed in every generation by every family, and in every province and in every city. And these days of Purim should never cease to be celebrated by the Jews, nor should the memory of them die out among their descendants.

[29] So Queen Esther, daughter of Abihail, along with Mordecai the Jew, wrote with full authority to confirm this second letter concerning Purim. [30] And Mordecai sent letters to all the Jews in the 127 provinces of Xerxes' kingdom—words of goodwill and assurance— [31] to establish these days of Purim at their designated times, as Mordecai the Jew and Queen Esther had decreed for them, and as they had established for themselves and their descendants in regard to their times of fasting and lamentation. [32] Esther's decree confirmed these regulations about Purim, and it was written down in the records.

The Greatness of Mordecai

10 King Xerxes imposed tribute throughout the empire, to its distant shores. [2] And all his acts of power and might, together with a full account of the greatness of Mordecai to which the king had raised him, are they not written in the book of the annals of the kings of Media and Persia? [3] Mordecai the Jew was second in rank to King Xerxes, preeminent among the Jews, and held in high esteem by his many fellow Jews, because he worked for the good of his people and spoke up for the welfare of all the Jews.

640 700 862
JOB PSALMS PROVERBS

919 937
ECCLESIASTES SONG OF SONGS

the bo
of poe

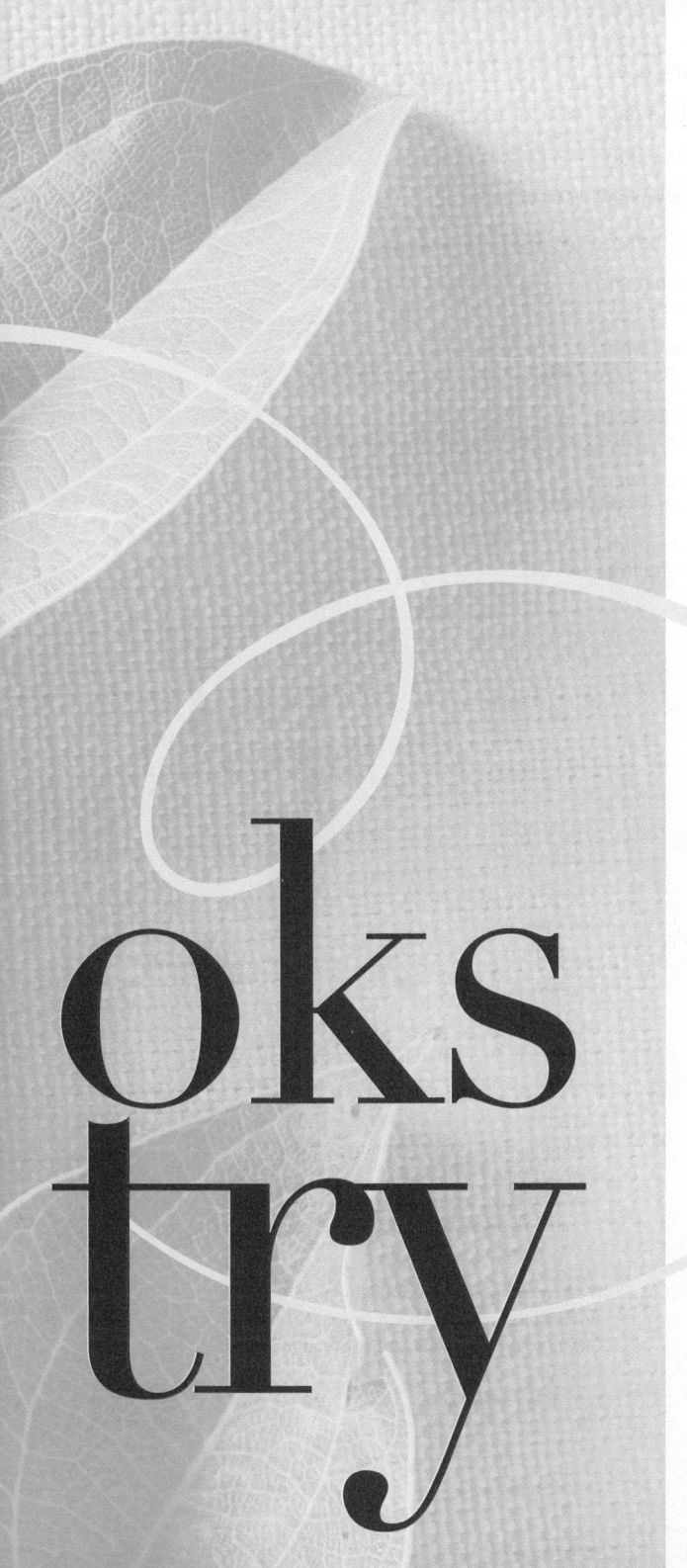

The books of Poetry form the latter half of the Writings (along with Chronicles through Esther). These texts vary in form and content but in general represent some of the most enduring literary achievements in the history of the written word. The books of Poetry cover a variety of functions, from wisdom literature to the liturgical and personal prayers and worship of the people of Israel.

Other than some narrative elements present at the beginning and end of the book of Job, these books are almost entirely composed of poetry. Ancient Hebrew poetry employed a number of formulas and unique structures that require different interpretive insights than those of Hebrew narrative. These beautiful, passionate, and often deeply personal writings are a reflection of the hearts of the writers and the heart of God.

640

job

AUTHOR
Unknown.

AUDIENCE
God's people.

DATE
Unknown B.C.

SETTING
Job lived in Uz, east of Canaan. His story is one of personal tragedy.

VERSE TO REMEMBER
"Naked I came from my mother's womb, and naked I will depart.
The LORD gave and the LORD has taken away; may the name of the LORD be praised." (1:21)

THEME TO CONSIDER
We may never understand why good people suffer in this world. All we can do is trust that God is sovereign. This is the lesson of life.

Prologue

1 In the land of Uz there lived a man whose name was Job. This man was blameless and upright; he feared God and shunned evil. ²He had seven sons and three daughters, ³and he owned seven thousand sheep, three thousand camels, five hundred yoke of oxen and five hundred donkeys, and had a large number of servants. He was the greatest man among all the people of the East.

⁴His sons used to hold feasts in their homes on their birthdays, and they would invite their three sisters to eat and drink with them. ⁵When a period of feasting had run its course, Job would make arrangements for them to be purified. Early in the morning he would sacrifice a burnt offering for each of them, thinking, "Perhaps my children have sinned and cursed God in their hearts." This was Job's regular custom.

⁶One day the angels*ᵃ* came to present themselves before the LORD, and Satan*ᵇ* also came with them. ⁷The LORD said to Satan, "Where have you come from?"

Satan answered the LORD, "From roaming through the earth and going back and forth in it."

⁸Then the LORD said to Satan, "Have you considered my servant Job? There is no one on earth like him; he is blameless and upright, a man who fears God and shuns evil."

⁹"Does Job fear God for nothing?" Satan replied. ¹⁰"Have you not put a hedge around him and his household and everything he has? You have blessed the work of his hands, so that his flocks and herds are spread throughout the land. ¹¹But now stretch out your hand and strike everything he has, and he will surely curse you to your face."

¹²The LORD said to Satan, "Very well, then, everything he has is in your power, but on the man himself do not lay a finger."

Then Satan went out from the presence of the LORD.

641

HE IS: in charge

1:6–12 When the angels came to present themselves before the LORD, Satan appeared with them. His purpose was to question Job's loyalty to God and ask if he could test Job's faith. However, God proved he is truly *in charge* by limiting the trials Job would endure.

You may be in the middle of a test of faith and find yourself wondering, "Where's God in this? Who's in control?" Rest assured that he is *in charge* of the situation. Though it may seem that evil is dictating your current circumstances, every trial comes with God's permission for the purpose of building your faith.

For the next He Is, go to p. 664.

¹³One day when Job's sons and daughters were feasting and drinking wine at the oldest brother's house, ¹⁴a messenger came to Job and said, "The oxen were plowing and the donkeys were grazing nearby, ¹⁵and the Sabeans attacked and made off with them. They put the servants to the sword, and I am the only one who has escaped to tell you!"

¹⁶While he was still speaking, another messenger came and said, "The fire of God fell from the sky and burned up the sheep and the servants, and I am the only one who has escaped to tell you!"

¹⁷While he was still speaking, another messenger came and said, "The Chaldeans formed three raiding parties and swept down on your camels and made off with them. They put the servants to the sword, and I am the only one who has escaped to tell you!"

¹⁸While he was still speaking, yet another messenger came and said, "Your sons and daughters were feasting and drinking wine at the oldest brother's house, ¹⁹when suddenly a mighty wind swept in from the desert and struck the four corners of the house. It collapsed on them and they are dead, and I am the only one who has escaped to tell you!"

²⁰At this, Job got up and tore his robe and shaved his head. Then he fell to the ground in worship ²¹and said:

ᵃ 6 Hebrew *the sons of God* *ᵇ 6* Hebrew *satan* means *adversary.*

> "Naked I came from my mother's womb,
>   and naked I will depart.*a*
> The L<small>ORD</small> gave and the L<small>ORD</small> has taken away;
>   may the name of the L<small>ORD</small> be praised."

²²In all this, Job did not sin by charging God with wrongdoing.

2 On another day the angels*b* came to present them- selves before the L<small>ORD</small>, and Satan also came with them to present himself before him. ²And the L<small>ORD</small> said to Satan, "Where have you come from?"

Satan answered the L<small>ORD</small>, "From roaming through the earth and going back and forth in it."

³Then the L<small>ORD</small> said to Satan, "Have you considered my servant Job? There is no one on earth like him; he is blame- less and upright, a man who fears God and shuns evil. And he still maintains his integrity, though you incited me against him to ruin him without any reason."

⁴"Skin for skin!" Satan replied. "A man will give all he has for his own life. ⁵But now stretch out your hand and strike his flesh and bones, and he will surely curse you to your face."

⁶The L<small>ORD</small> said to Satan, "Very well, then, he is in your hands; but you must spare his life."

⁷So Satan went out from the presence of the L<small>ORD</small> and afflicted Job with painful sores from the soles of his feet to the crown of his head. ⁸Then Job took a piece of broken pot- tery and scraped himself with it as he sat among the ashes.

⁹His wife said to him, "Are you still maintaining your integrity? Curse God and die!"

¹⁰He replied, "You are talking like a foolish*c* woman. Shall we accept good from God, and not trouble?"

In all this, Job did not sin in what he said.

2:7–10 Hearing "I have ter- minal cancer" from some- one you love can turn your world upside down and inside out. Nothing's ever the same again. Sharing the suffering, you wonder why God would allow this to happen. Job's wife thought God was being unfair and believed her husband no longer owed God his loyalty. Her faith wasn't strong enough to see her through the hard times—but Job's was. He could accept any- thing from God because he trusted that God is good and wise, always. Will you ask God to strengthen your faith so you can trust him too?

a tissue:illness

¹¹When Job's three friends, Eliphaz the Temanite, Bildad the Shuhite and Zophar the Naamathite, heard about all the troubles that had come upon him, they set out from their homes and met together by agreement to go and sympathize with him and comfort him. ¹²When they saw him from a distance, they could hardly recognize him; they began to weep aloud, and they tore their robes and sprinkled dust on their heads. ¹³Then they sat on the ground with him for seven days and seven nights. No one said a word to him, because they saw how great his suffering was.

Job Speaks

3 After this, Job opened his mouth and cursed the day of his birth. ²He said:

> ³"May the day of my birth perish,
>   and the night that said, 'A boy is conceived!'
> ⁴That day—may it turn to darkness;
>   may God above not care about it;
>   may no light shine on it.
> ⁵May gloom and utter darkness claim it once more;
>   may a cloud settle over it;
>   may blackness overwhelm it.
> ⁶That night—may thick darkness seize it;

---

a 21 Or *will return there*   *b 1* Hebrew *the sons of God*   *c 10* The Hebrew word rendered *foolish* denotes moral deficiency.

Job's wife

Job 1:1 – 2:10

This is painful for you, but can you tell us about your loss?

Loss? How about loss*es*, plural? In one terrible, horrible day, I lost everything. *Everything.* Job and I lost our children, our livestock, our home, our servants. Everything that I had built my life on was gone—except for my husband.

Why did you tell him to give up?

Why? Isn't it obvious to you? First, we get the news about our livestock being stolen, then the news that all our servants were killed. Then we find out that all our sheep and shepherds were burned to a crisp. Next came the news that our sons and daughters were killed in a freak accident. Later, Job suddenly breaks out in horrible, festering sores. And what does he do? He goes out and *worships* God. Surrenders to what God wants. Tells him that he's wonderful. What is *that*? Does that sound normal to you?

643

So how did you react?

I was beside myself with grief; I didn't know what to do. I couldn't make sense of anything. Then I got angry. I was angry with Job because he refused to blame God. But most of all I was angry with God. Why did he let this happen? What was he doing? Was he really in control? And Job just sat there—literally sitting in ashes, covered with wounds—and told me that *I* was the fool. Can you believe that?

Why do you think he said that?

It was difficult for me to understand at the time, but Job saw it all as a test from God. He said to me, "Shall we accept good from God, and not trouble?" Whereas I allowed my emotions to rule my response, Job chose to learn and grow from the pain. It's not that he didn't question God. He did; oh, but he did. But Job came out at a much different point than I did. I was bogged down in bitterness and anger. Job emerged with a closer, deeper relationship with God. So I guess in the end, it was *I* who was the fool.

So what can we learn from your experiences?

When suffering and troubles come—and they will come—you have a choice. You can curse God like I did and end up living in bitterness and anger. Or you can see your situation as a test of faith and an opportunity, albeit a painful one, to grow closer to God. From experience, I suggest the latter.

FOR MORE INSIGHT: To find out how God uses suffering in our lives, read Proverbs 17:3; Isaiah 48:10; James 1:2–4; and 1 Peter 1:6–7; 4:12–19.

myth#42 "MY SOUL MATE IS OUT THERE SOMEWHERE."

I didn't really believe in soul mates. Until I met John. He is, in a word, amazing. There is no limit to what he's willing to do for me. If I need to talk, he listens. And no matter what's going on in my life, he just seems to understand. Sometimes I don't have to say anything at all—he just reads my mind and knows exactly what I'm thinking.

He came into my life in such a fast, unexpected way. After our first few conversations at work, I knew there was something special about him. It was as if I were somehow speaking with the other half of myself. He seemed to reflect my feelings and emotions—even about the tiniest, most insignificant things. There's nothing I can't talk about with him.

No one has ever made me feel the way he makes me feel inside—complete, whole, safe. This must be the kind of Great Love people throughout time have written about in poems and songs—it's something so rare that it's hard to believe you've somehow found it. I've been wrong before, but this time I've finally found the one person who completes me, and I do the same for him. Every time we're together, I'm convinced even more that our relationship was just meant to be. He is undeniably my soul mate.

Sometimes when I can't sleep, I want to call him in the middle of the night to hear his voice on the other end of the line. I can't wait until the next time we will be together again. There's only one problem . . .

I'm already married.

—Tyne

ONE DANGER OF the "soul-mate philosophy" is that it's possible to believe you married the wrong person and to think that someone else must be your soul mate. Many affairs and divorces have resulted from recklessly pursuing this line of thinking as people go from relationship to relationship.

Do soul mates exist? Some people believe that God has one person for them; others believe there are a number of people they could be compatible with. No matter which perspective you hold to, one truth stands clear: once you make the choice to marry, stop looking for your soul mate. After you marry, your husband *becomes* "the one" as the two of you become one (see Genesis 2:24).

How do two people become one? The Bible gives us clear, unwavering guidance on making love last:

Beware of idealizing your mate. It's true—those "little things" you found so attractive in your mate initially often become the source of irritation later in marriage. In marriage, guards are down and the masks removed. There is no perfect man—or woman! (See Romans 3:23.)

Relationships are hard work. All relationships require attention. If your idea of a perfect relationship is one that exists to meet your needs and requires low maintenance, consider getting a pet, not a husband! (See Proverbs 31:10–31.)

Don't idolize happiness. Many of us have a skewed idea that we deserve happiness and that the pursuit of happiness should guide our choices about relationships. So we give up on a struggling relationship, and we forfeit what amazing things God would do in our marriages if we worked through our difficulties.

Choose to love. Sometimes you won't *feel* like you love him or you'll feel confused by your emotions for another man. That's when you have to *choose* to love your husband—not because he deserves it or because you want to, but because you know that's pleasing to God.

Act out love toward him (see 1 Corinthians 13), and your feelings will eventually follow.

Focus on becoming the kind of person you'd like to marry. Remember listing all those traits about your dream guy in high school? Do you want a kind-hearted, generous man? How would your friends describe you? Take the top five character items on your list of the "perfect guy," and measure your own progress in those areas.

645

"Soul mates are made, not born. You start with the ingredients for a highly compatible, successful relationship, and then you work to develop closeness and intimacy."

—Neil Clark Warren,
founder, Eharmony.com

"FOR THIS reason a man WILL Leave HIS FATHER anD MOTHER anD Be UNITED TO HIS WIFE, anD THEY WILL BECOME one FLESH."

GENESIS 2:24

SEE ALSO
Proverbs 19:22
1 Corinthians 13
1 John 4:16–21

For more on **Relationships**, check the index.

may it not be included among the days of the year
nor be entered in any of the months.
⁷May that night be barren;
may no shout of joy be heard in it.
⁸May those who curse days *a* curse that day,
those who are ready to rouse Leviathan.
⁹May its morning stars become dark;
may it wait for daylight in vain
and not see the first rays of dawn,
¹⁰for it did not shut the doors of the womb on me
to hide trouble from my eyes.

¹¹"Why did I not perish at birth,
and die as I came from the womb?
¹²Why were there knees to receive me
and breasts that I might be nursed?
¹³For now I would be lying down in peace;
I would be asleep and at rest
¹⁴with kings and rulers of the earth,
who built for themselves places now lying in ruins,
¹⁵with princes who had gold,
who filled their houses with silver.
¹⁶Or why was I not hidden away in the ground like a stillborn child,
like an infant who never saw the light of day?
¹⁷There the wicked cease from turmoil,
and there the weary are at rest.
¹⁸Captives also enjoy their ease;
they no longer hear the slave driver's shout.
¹⁹The small and the great are there,
and the slaves are freed from their owners.

²⁰"Why is light given to those in misery,
and life to the bitter of soul,
²¹to those who long for death that does not come,
who search for it more than for hidden treasure,
²²who are filled with gladness
and rejoice when they reach the grave?
²³Why is life given to a man
whose way is hidden,
whom God has hedged in?
²⁴For sighing has become my daily food;
my groans pour out like water.
²⁵What I feared has come upon me;
what I dreaded has happened to me.
²⁶I have no peace, no quietness;
I have no rest, but only turmoil."

Eliphaz

4 Then Eliphaz the Temanite replied:

²"If someone ventures a word with you, will you be impatient?
But who can keep from speaking?

---

a 8 Or *the sea*

job 5:2

³Think how you have instructed many,
     how you have strengthened feeble
          hands.
⁴Your words have supported those who
          stumbled;
     you have strengthened faltering knees.
⁵But now trouble comes to you, and you are
          discouraged;
     it strikes you, and you are dismayed.
⁶Should not your piety be your confidence
     and your blameless ways your hope?

⁷"Consider now: Who, being innocent, has
          ever perished?
     Where were the upright ever destroyed?
⁸As I have observed, those who plow evil
     and those who sow trouble reap it.
⁹At the breath of God they perish;
     at the blast of his anger they are no
          more.
¹⁰The lions may roar and growl,
     yet the teeth of the great lions are
          broken.
¹¹The lion perishes for lack of prey,
     and the cubs of the lioness are scattered.

¹²"A word was secretly brought to me,
     my ears caught a whisper of it.
¹³Amid disquieting dreams in the night,
     when deep sleep falls on people,
¹⁴fear and trembling seized me
     and made all my bones shake.
¹⁵A spirit glided past my face,
     and the hair on my body stood on end.
¹⁶It stopped,
     but I could not tell what it was.
  A form stood before my eyes,
     and I heard a hushed voice:
¹⁷'Can a mortal be more righteous than God?
     Can human beings be more pure than their Maker?
¹⁸If God places no trust in his servants,
     if he charges his angels with error,
¹⁹how much more those who live in houses of clay,
     whose foundations are in the dust,
     who are crushed more readily than a moth!
²⁰Between dawn and dusk they are broken to pieces;
     unnoticed, they perish forever.
²¹Are not the cords of their tent pulled up,
     so that they die without wisdom?'

  "Call if you will, but who will answer you?
     To which of the holy ones will you turn?
²Resentment kills a fool,

at issue: counsel

4:1–2 When someone's hurting, we often want to say something to help stop the pain or fix the problem. But many times our words reflect a poor understanding either of the situation or of God who is at work in it. And like the counsel of Job's friends, our words may only make things worse. Most of the time, the best thing we can do is shut up and wrap our arms around our friend. We can also shower her with love and tenderness, pray for her often and listen again and again. And if we do say something, we need to make sure our words are God's, not trite platitudes.

647

5

and envy slays the simple.
³I myself have seen a fool taking root,
  but suddenly his house was cursed.
⁴His children are far from safety,
  crushed in court without a defender.
⁵The hungry consume his harvest,
  taking it even from among thorns,
  and the thirsty pant after his wealth.
⁶For hardship does not spring from the soil,
  nor does trouble sprout from the ground.
⁷Yet human beings are born to trouble
  as surely as sparks fly upward.

⁸"But if I were you, I would appeal to God;
  I would lay my cause before him.
⁹He performs wonders that cannot be fathomed,
  miracles that cannot be counted.
¹⁰He bestows rain on the earth;
  he sends water on the countryside.
¹¹The lowly he sets on high,
  and those who mourn are lifted to safety.
¹²He thwarts the plans of the crafty,
  so that their hands achieve no success.
¹³He catches the wise in their craftiness,
  and the schemes of the wily are swept away.
¹⁴Darkness comes upon them in the daytime;
  at noon they grope as in the night.
¹⁵He saves the needy from the sword in their mouth;
  he saves them from the clutches of the powerful.
¹⁶So the poor have hope,
  and injustice shuts its mouth.

¹⁷"Blessed are those whom God corrects;
  so do not despise the discipline of the Almighty.ᵃ
¹⁸For he wounds, but he also binds up;
  he injures, but his hands also heal.
¹⁹From six calamities he will rescue you;
  in seven no harm will touch you.
²⁰In famine he will deliver you from death,
  and in battle from the stroke of the sword.
²¹You will be protected from the lash of the tongue,
  and need not fear when destruction comes.
²²You will laugh at destruction and famine,
  and need not fear the wild animals.
²³For you will have a covenant with the stones of the field,
  and the wild animals will be at peace with you.
²⁴You will know that your tent is secure;
  you will take stock of your property and find nothing missing.
²⁵You will know that your children will be many,
  and your descendants like the grass of the earth.

ᵃ 17 Hebrew *Shaddai*; here and throughout Job

²⁶You will come to the grave in full vigor,
  like sheaves gathered in season.

²⁷"We have examined this, and it is true.
  So hear it and apply it to yourself."

Job

6

Then Job replied:

²"If only my anguish could be weighed
  and all my misery be placed on the
    scales!
³It would surely outweigh the sand of the
    seas—
  no wonder my words have been
    impetuous.
⁴The arrows of the Almighty are in me,
  my spirit drinks in their poison;
  God's terrors are marshaled against me.
⁵Does a wild donkey bray when it has grass,
  or an ox bellow when it has fodder?
⁶Is tasteless food eaten without salt,
  or is there flavor in the sap of the
    mallow*ᵃ*?
⁷I refuse to touch it;
  such food makes me ill.

⁸"Oh, that I might have my request,
  that God would grant what I hope for,
⁹that God would be willing to crush me,
  to let loose his hand and cut off my life!
¹⁰Then I would still have this consolation—
  my joy in unrelenting pain—
  that I had not denied the words of the
    Holy One.

¹¹"What strength do I have, that I should still hope?
  What prospects, that I should be patient?
¹²Do I have the strength of stone?
  Is my flesh bronze?
¹³Do I have any power to help myself,
  now that success has been driven from me?

¹⁴"Anyone who withholds kindness from a friend
  forsakes the fear of the Almighty.
¹⁵But my brothers are as undependable as intermittent streams,
  as the streams that overflow
¹⁶when darkened by thawing ice
  and swollen with melting snow,
¹⁷but that cease to flow in the dry season,
  and in the heat vanish from their channels.
¹⁸Caravans turn aside from their routes;

at issue: suffering

6:1–10 When Job's life fell apart, he asked the same questions human beings have asked for millennia: Why me? What did I do to deserve this? How could God allow this to happen to me? Maybe you're in Job's shoes—feeling abandoned, rejected and hopeless. Maybe you are demanding answers from God. But as Job discovered, knowing the God who created you is better than knowing the answers to all your questions. Because when you know and trust his love, you'll find the freedom and hope that will enable you to trust in God's control over all things, even your suffering.

649

ᵃ 6 The meaning of the Hebrew for this phrase is uncertain.

they go off into the wasteland and perish.
¹⁹The caravans of Tema look for water,
    the traveling merchants of Sheba look in hope.
²⁰They are distressed, because they had been confident;
    they arrive there, only to be disappointed.
²¹Now you too have proved to be of no help;
    you see something dreadful and are afraid.
²²Have I ever said, 'Give something on my behalf,
    pay a ransom for me from your wealth,
²³deliver me from the hand of the enemy,
    rescue me from the clutches of the ruthless'?

²⁴"Teach me, and I will be quiet;
    show me where I have been wrong.
²⁵How painful are honest words!
    But what do your arguments prove?
²⁶Do you mean to correct what I say,
    and treat my desperate words as wind?
²⁷You would even cast lots for the fatherless
    and barter away your friend.

²⁸"But now be so kind as to look at me.
    Would I lie to your face?
²⁹Relent, do not be unjust;
    reconsider, for my integrity is at stake.ᵃ
³⁰Is there any wickedness on my lips?
    Can my mouth not discern malice?

7 "Do not mortals have hard service on earth?
    Are not their days like those of hired laborers?
²Like a slave longing for the evening shadows,
    or a hired laborer waiting to be paid,
³so I have been allotted months of futility,
    and nights of misery have been assigned to me.
⁴When I lie down I think, 'How long before I get up?'
    The night drags on, and I toss and turn until dawn.
⁵My body is clothed with worms and scabs,
    my skin is broken and festering.

⁶"My days are swifter than a weaver's shuttle,
    and they come to an end without hope.
⁷Remember, O God, that my life is but a breath;
    my eyes will never see happiness again.
⁸The eye that now sees me will see me no longer;
    you will look for me, but I will be no more.
⁹As a cloud vanishes and is gone,
    so those who go down to the grave do not return.
¹⁰They will never come to their homes again;
    their places will know them no more.

¹¹"Therefore I will not keep silent;
    I will speak out in the anguish of my spirit,

ᵃ 29 Or my righteousness still stands

I will complain in the bitterness of my soul.
¹²Am I the sea, or the monster of the deep,
    that you put me under guard?
¹³When I think my bed will comfort me
    and my couch will ease my complaint,
¹⁴even then you frighten me with dreams
    and terrify me with visions,
¹⁵so that I prefer strangling and death,
    rather than this body of mine.
¹⁶I despise my life; I would not live forever.
    Let me alone; my days have no meaning.

¹⁷"What are human beings that you make so much of them,
    that you give them so much attention,
¹⁸that you examine them every morning
    and test them every moment?
¹⁹Will you never look away from me,
    or let me alone even for an instant?
²⁰If I have sinned, what have I done to you,
    you who watch over us all?
Why have you made me your target?
Have I become a burden to you?^a
²¹Why do you not pardon my offenses
    and forgive my sins?
For I will soon lie down in the dust;
    you will search for me, but I will be no more."

Bildad

8 Then Bildad the Shuhite replied:

²"How long will you say such things?
    Your words are a blustering wind.
³Does God pervert justice?
    Does the Almighty pervert what is right?
⁴When your children sinned against him,
    he gave them over to the penalty of their sin.
⁵But if you will seek God earnestly
    and plead with the Almighty,
⁶if you are pure and upright,
    even now he will rouse himself on your behalf
    and restore you to your prosperous state.
⁷Your beginnings will seem humble,
    so prosperous will your future be.

⁸"Ask the former generation
    and find out what their ancestors learned,
⁹for we were born only yesterday and know nothing,
    and our days on earth are but a shadow.
¹⁰Will they not instruct you and tell you?
    Will they not bring forth words from their understanding?
¹¹Can papyrus grow tall where there is no marsh?

651

---

^a *20* A few manuscripts of the Masoretic Text, an ancient Hebrew scribal tradition and Septuagint; most manuscripts of the Masoretic Text *I have become a burden to myself.*

Can reeds thrive without water?
¹²While still growing and uncut,
they wither more quickly than grass.
¹³Such is the destiny of all who forget
God;
so perishes the hope of the godless.
¹⁴What they trust in is fragile[a];
what they rely on is a spider's web.
¹⁵They lean on the web, but it gives way;
they cling to it, but it does not hold.
¹⁶They are like a well-watered plant in the
sunshine,
spreading its shoots over the garden;
¹⁷it entwines its roots around a pile of
rocks
and looks for a place among the
stones.
¹⁸But when it is torn from its spot,
that place disowns it and says, 'I
never saw you.'
¹⁹Surely its life withers away,
and[b] from the soil other plants grow.

²⁰"Surely God does not reject the
blameless
or strengthen the hands of evildoers.
²¹He will yet fill your mouth with laughter
and your lips with shouts of joy.
²²Your enemies will be clothed in shame,
and the tents of the wicked will be no
more."

Job

9 Then Job replied:

²"Indeed, I know that this is true.
But how can mere mortals prove their innocence before God?
³Though they wished to dispute with him,
they could not answer him one time out of a thousand.
⁴His wisdom is profound, his power is vast.
Who has resisted him and come out unscathed?
⁵He moves mountains without their knowing it
and overturns them in his anger.
⁶He shakes the earth from its place
and makes its pillars tremble.
⁷He speaks to the sun and it does not shine;
he seals off the light of the stars.
⁸He alone stretches out the heavens
and treads on the waves of the sea.
⁹He is the Maker of the Bear[c] and Orion,
the Pleiades and the constellations of the south.

atissue:education

8:8–13 Getting a degree (or multiple degrees) is a wonderful, satisfying accomplishment that we should look on with pride. However, our society tends to value formal education more than the wisdom of age. Reflecting on Job's suffering, Bildad urged him to learn from the instruction of former generations. While there's great value in both education and in learning from our elders, there's also a difference between a formal education and wisdom—applying that knowledge. No matter how many degrees you have, education doesn't make you always right or better than others. Work at having a teachable heart that learns from others, not one that hides behind a degree.

652

---

[a] *14* The meaning of the Hebrew for this word is uncertain.   [b] *19* Or *Surely all the joy it has / is that*   [c] *9* Or *of Leo*

¹⁰He performs wonders that cannot be fathomed,
    miracles that cannot be counted.
¹¹When he passes me, I cannot see him;
    when he goes by, I cannot perceive him.
¹²If he snatches away, who can stop him?
    Who can say to him, 'What are you doing?'
¹³God does not restrain his anger;
    even the cohorts of Rahab cowered at his feet.

¹⁴"How then can I dispute with him?
    How can I find words to argue with him?
¹⁵Though I were innocent, I could not answer him;
    I could only plead with my Judge for mercy.
¹⁶Even if I summoned him and he responded,
    I do not believe he would give me a hearing.
¹⁷He would crush me with a storm
    and multiply my wounds for no reason.
¹⁸He would not let me catch my breath
    but would overwhelm me with misery.
¹⁹If it is a matter of strength, he is mighty!
    And if it is a matter of justice, who can challenge him^a?
²⁰Even if I were innocent, my mouth would condemn me;
    if I were blameless, it would pronounce me guilty.

²¹"Although I am blameless,
    I have no concern for myself;
    I despise my own life.
²²It is all the same; that is why I say,
    'He destroys both the blameless and the wicked.'
²³When a scourge brings sudden death,
    he mocks the despair of the innocent.
²⁴When a land falls into the hands of the wicked,
    he blindfolds its judges.
    If it is not he, then who is it?

²⁵"My days are swifter than a runner;
    they fly away without a glimpse of joy.
²⁶They skim past like boats of papyrus,
    like eagles swooping down on their prey.
²⁷If I say, 'I will forget my complaint,
    I will change my expression, and smile,'
²⁸I still dread all my sufferings,
    for I know you will not hold me innocent.
²⁹Since I am already found guilty,
    why should I struggle in vain?
³⁰Even if I washed myself with soap
    and my hands with cleansing powder,
³¹you would plunge me into a slime pit
    so that even my clothes would detest me.

³²"He is not a mere mortal like me that I might answer him,
    that we might confront each other in court.

^a 19 See Septuagint; Hebrew *me*.

33 If only there were someone to arbitrate between us,
  to lay a hand on us both,
34 someone to remove God's rod from me,
  so that his terror would frighten me no more.
35 Then I would speak up without fear of him,
  but as it now stands with me, I cannot.

10

"I loathe my very life;
  therefore I will give free rein to my
    complaint
  and speak out in the bitterness of my
    soul.
2 I say to God: Do not declare me guilty,
  but tell me what charges you have
    against me.
3 Does it please you to oppress me,
  to spurn the work of your hands,
  while you smile on the plans of the
    wicked?
4 Do you have eyes of flesh?
  Do you see as a mortal sees?
5 Are your days like those of a mortal
  or your years like those of a human
    being,
6 that you must search out my faults
  and probe after my sin—
7 though you know that I am not guilty
  and that no one can rescue me from
    your hand?

8 "Your hands shaped me and made me.
  Will you now turn and destroy me?
9 Remember that you molded me like
    clay.
  Will you now turn me to dust again?
10 Did you not pour me out like milk
  and curdle me like cheese,
11 clothe me with skin and flesh
  and knit me together with bones and sinews?
12 You gave me life and showed me kindness,
  and in your providence watched over my spirit.

13 "But this is what you concealed in your heart,
  and I know that this was in your mind:
14 If I sinned, you would be watching me
  and would not let my offense go unpunished.
15 If I am guilty—woe to me!
  Even if I am innocent, I cannot lift my head,
for I am full of shame
  and drowned in *a* my affliction.
16 If I hold my head high, you stalk me like a lion
  and again display your awesome power against me.

at issue: anger at God

10:1–22 Your husband abandons you. Cancer claims a loved one. Your baby doesn't make it. You've been sexually assaulted. And you want to know: Is it OK to be angry with God? First answer this: Does being angry with God mean that you think God is wrong or has made a mistake? When Job directed his anger at God, God reminded Job (for four chapters!) of his incomparable wisdom and power. He reminded Job that he's *never* wrong. If you're angry with God, talk to him about it. In your anger, don't sin by turning from God, blaming God or believing he's wrong (see Psalm 4:4; Ephesians 4:26). Ask him to help you accept his wisdom and work through your feelings.

a 15 Or and aware of

654

¹⁷You bring new witnesses against me
    and increase your anger toward me;
    your forces come against me wave upon wave.

¹⁸"Why then did you bring me out of the womb?
    I wish I had died before any eye saw me.
¹⁹If only I had never come into being,
    or had been carried straight from the womb to the grave!
²⁰Are not my few days almost over?
    Turn away from me so I can have a moment's joy
²¹before I go to the place of no return,
    to the land of gloom and utter darkness,
²²to the land of deepest night,
    of utter darkness and disorder,
    where even the light is like darkness."

Zophar

11

Then Zophar the Naamathite replied:

²"Are all these words to go unanswered?
    Is this talker to be vindicated?
³Will your idle talk reduce others to silence?
    Will no one rebuke you when you mock?
⁴You say to God, 'My beliefs are flawless
    and I am pure in your sight.'
⁵Oh, how I wish that God would speak,
    that he would open his lips against you
⁶and disclose to you the secrets of wisdom,
    for true wisdom has two sides.
    Know this: God has even forgotten some of your sin.

⁷"Can you fathom the mysteries of God?
    Can you probe the limits of the Almighty?
⁸They are higher than the heavens above—what can you do?
    They are deeper than the depths below—what can you know?
⁹Their measure is longer than the earth
    and wider than the sea.

¹⁰"If he comes along and confines you in prison
    and convenes a court, who can oppose him?
¹¹Surely he recognizes deceivers;
    and when he sees evil, does he not take note?
¹²But the witless can no more become wise
    than a wild donkey's colt can be born a human being.^a

¹³"Yet if you devote your heart to him
    and stretch out your hands to him,
¹⁴if you put away the sin that is in your hand
    and allow no evil to dwell in your tent,
¹⁵then, free of fault, you will lift up your face;
    you will stand firm and without fear.
¹⁶You will surely forget your trouble,

---
^a 12 Or wild donkey can be born tame

recalling it only as waters gone by.
17 Life will be brighter than noonday,
   and darkness will become like morning.
18 You will be secure, because there is hope;
   you will look about you and take your rest in safety.
19 You will lie down, with no one to make you afraid,
   and many will court your favor.
20 But the eyes of the wicked will fail,
   and escape will elude them;
   their hope will become a dying gasp."

Job 12

Then Job replied:

2 "Doubtless you are the people,
   and wisdom will die with you!
3 But I have a mind as well as you;
   I am not inferior to you.
   Who does not know all these things?

4 "I have become a laughingstock to my friends,
   though I called on God and he answered—
   a mere laughingstock, though righteous and blameless!
5 Those who are at ease have contempt for misfortune
   as the fate of those whose feet are slipping.
6 The tents of marauders are
      undisturbed,
   and those who provoke God are
      secure—
   those God has in his hand.[a]

7 "But ask the animals, and they will
      teach you,
   or the birds in the sky, and they will
      tell you;
8 or speak to the earth, and it will teach
      you,
   or let the fish in the sea inform you.
9 Which of all these does not know
   that the hand of the LORD has done
      this?
10 In his hand is the life of every creature
   and the breath of every human being.
11 Does not the ear test words
   as the tongue tastes food?
12 Is not wisdom found among the aged?
   Does not long life bring
      understanding?

13 "To God belong wisdom and power;
   counsel and understanding are his.
14 What he tears down cannot be rebuilt;

12:7–10 *I can't be pregnant. We're already struggling, and a baby's only going to make it worse. We were so careful. How could this happen?* God tends to shake up your life and remind you that no matter how much you think you're in control, you're not. When that happens, you can try harder to control everything (which will only frustrate you more). Or you can find comfort in knowing that God holds in his hand the life of every creature. You are secure, and you can trust him even with the unexpected things he allows to enter your life.

atissue:pregnancy

---

[a] 6 Or those whose god is in their own hand

those he imprisons cannot be released.
¹⁵If he holds back the waters, there is drought;
   if he lets them loose, they devastate the land.
¹⁶To him belong strength and insight;
   both deceived and deceiver are his.
¹⁷He leads rulers away stripped
   and makes fools of judges.
¹⁸He takes off the shackles put on by kings
   and ties a loincloth^a around their waist.
¹⁹He leads priests away stripped
   and overthrows officials long established.
²⁰He silences the lips of trusted advisers
   and takes away the discernment of elders.
²¹He pours contempt on nobles
   and disarms the mighty.
²²He reveals the deep things of darkness
   and brings utter darkness into the light.
²³He makes nations great, and destroys them;
   he enlarges nations, and disperses them.
²⁴He deprives the leaders of the earth of their reason;
   he makes them wander in a trackless waste.
²⁵They grope in darkness with no light;
   he makes them stagger like drunkards.

13

  "My eyes have seen all this,
   my ears have heard and understood it.
²What you know, I also know;
   I am not inferior to you.
³But I desire to speak to the Almighty
   and to argue my case with God.
⁴You, however, smear me with lies;
   you are worthless physicians, all of you!
⁵If only you would be altogether silent!
   For you, that would be wisdom.
⁶Hear now my argument;
   listen to the pleas of my lips.
⁷Will you speak wickedly on God's behalf?
   Will you speak deceitfully for him?
⁸Will you show him partiality?
   Will you argue the case for God?
⁹Would it turn out well if he examined you?
   Could you deceive him as you might deceive mortals?
¹⁰He would surely call you to account
   if you secretly showed partiality.
¹¹Would not his splendor terrify you?
   Would not the dread of him fall on you?
¹²Your maxims are proverbs of ashes;
   your defenses are defenses of clay.

¹³"Keep silent and let me speak;
   then let come to me what may.

657

---

¹⁴Why do I put myself in jeopardy
    and take my life in my hands?
¹⁵Though he slay me, yet will I hope in him;
    I will surely^{*a*} defend my ways to his face.
¹⁶Indeed, this will turn out for my deliverance,
    for no godless person would dare come before him!
¹⁷Listen carefully to what I say;
    let my words ring in your ears.
¹⁸Now that I have prepared my case,
    I know I will be vindicated.
¹⁹Can anyone bring charges against me?
    If so, I will be silent and die.

²⁰"Only grant me these two things, God,
    and then I will not hide from you:
²¹Withdraw your hand far from me,
    and stop frightening me with your terrors.
²²Then summon me and I will answer,
    or let me speak, and you reply to me.
²³How many wrongs and sins have I committed?
    Show me my offense and my sin.
²⁴Why do you hide your face
    and consider me your enemy?
²⁵Will you torment a windblown leaf?
    Will you chase after dry chaff?
²⁶For you write down bitter things against me
    and make me reap the sins of my youth.
²⁷You fasten my feet in shackles;
    you keep close watch on all my paths
    by putting marks on the soles of my feet.

²⁸"So humans waste away like something rotten,
    like a garment eaten by moths.

14

    "Mortals, born of woman,
    are of few days and full of trouble.
²They spring up like flowers and wither away;
    like fleeting shadows, they do not endure.
³Do you fix your eye on such as these?
    Will you bring them^{*b*} before you for judgment?
⁴Who can bring what is pure from the impure?
    No one!
⁵The days of mortals are determined;
    you have decreed the number of their months
    and have set limits they cannot exceed.
⁶So look away from us and leave us alone,
    till we have put in our time like hired laborers.

⁷"At least there is hope for a tree:
    If it is cut down, it will sprout again,
    and its new shoots will not fail.
⁸Its roots may grow old in the ground

^{*a*} *15 Or He will surely slay me; I have no hope — / yet I will*   ^{*b*} *3 Septuagint, Vulgate and Syriac; Hebrew me*

and its stump die in the soil,
⁹yet at the scent of water it will bud
    and put forth shoots like a plant.
¹⁰But human beings die and are laid low;
    they breathe their last and are no more.
¹¹As the water of a lake dries up
    or a riverbed becomes parched and dry,
¹²so they lie down and do not rise;
    till the heavens are no more, they will not awake
    or be roused from their sleep.

¹³"If only you would hide me in the grave
    and conceal me till your anger has passed!
 If only you would set me a time
    and then remember me!
¹⁴If someone dies, will they live again?
    All the days of my hard service
    I will wait for my renewal*a* to come.
¹⁵You will call and I will answer you;
    you will long for the creature your hands have made.
¹⁶Surely then you will count my steps
    but not keep track of my sin.
¹⁷My offenses will be sealed up in a bag;
    you will cover over my sin.

¹⁸"But as a mountain erodes and crumbles
    and as a rock is moved from its place,
¹⁹as water wears away stones
    and torrents wash away the soil,
    so you destroy everyone's hope.
²⁰You overpower them once for all, and they are gone;
    you change their countenance and send them away.
²¹If their children are honored, they do not know it;
    if their offspring are brought low, they do not see it.
²²They feel but the pain of their own bodies
    and mourn only for themselves."

Eliphaz

15 Then Eliphaz the Temanite replied:

²"Would the wise answer with empty notions
    or fill their bellies with the hot east wind?
³Would they argue with useless words,
    with speeches that have no value?
⁴But you even undermine piety
    and hinder devotion to God.
⁵Your sin prompts your mouth;
    you adopt the tongue of the crafty.
⁶Your own mouth condemns you, not mine;
    your own lips testify against you.

a 14 Or *release*

⁷"Are you the first man ever born?
  Were you brought forth before the hills?
⁸Do you listen in on God's council?
  Do you have a monopoly on wisdom?
⁹What do you know that we do not know?
  What insights do you have that we do not have?
¹⁰The gray-haired and the aged are on our side,
  men even older than your father.
¹¹Are God's consolations not enough for you,
  words spoken gently to you?
¹²Why has your heart carried you away,
  and why do your eyes flash,
¹³so that you vent your rage against God
  and pour out such words from your mouth?

¹⁴"What are mortals, that they could be pure,
  or those born of woman, that they could be righteous?
¹⁵If God places no trust in his holy ones,
  if even the heavens are not pure in his eyes,
¹⁶how much less mortals, who are vile and corrupt,
  who drink up evil like water!

¹⁷"Listen to me and I will explain to you;
  let me tell you what I have seen,
¹⁸what the wise have declared,
  hiding nothing received from their ancestors
¹⁹(to whom alone the land was given
  when no foreigners moved among them):
²⁰All their days the wicked suffer torment,
  the ruthless through all the years stored up for them.
²¹Terrifying sounds fill their ears;
  when all seems well, marauders attack them.
²²They despair of escaping the realm of darkness;
  they are marked for the sword.
²³They wander about for food like vultures;
  they know the day of darkness is at hand.
²⁴Distress and anguish fill them with terror;
  troubles overwhelm them, like a king poised to attack,
²⁵because they shake their fists at God
  and vaunt themselves against the Almighty,
²⁶defiantly charging against him
  with thick, strong shields.

²⁷"Though their faces are covered with fat
  and their waists bulge with flesh,
²⁸they will inhabit ruined towns
  and houses where no one lives,
  houses crumbling to rubble.
²⁹They will no longer be rich and their wealth will not endure,
  nor will their possessions spread over the land.
³⁰They will not escape the darkness;
  a flame will wither their shoots,
  and the breath of God's mouth will carry them away.

³¹Let them not deceive themselves by trusting what is worthless,
  for they will get nothing in return.
³²Before their time they will wither,
  and their branches will not flourish.
³³They will be like a vine stripped of its unripe grapes,
  like an olive tree shedding its blossoms.
³⁴For the company of the godless will be barren,
  and fire will consume the tents of those who love bribes.
³⁵They conceive trouble and give birth to evil;
  their womb fashions deceit."

Job

16

Then Job replied:

²"I have heard many things like these;
  you are miserable comforters, all of you!
³Will your long-winded speeches never end?
  What ails you that you keep on arguing?
⁴I also could speak like you,
  if you were in my place;
 I could make fine speeches against you
  and shake my head at you.
⁵But my mouth would encourage you;
  comfort from my lips would bring you relief.

⁶"Yet if I speak, my pain is not relieved;
  and if I refrain, it does not go away.
⁷Surely, God, you have worn me out;
  you have devastated my entire household.
⁸You have shriveled me up—and it has become a witness;
  my gauntness rises up and testifies against me.
⁹God assails me and tears me in his anger
  and gnashes his teeth at me;
  my opponent fastens on me his piercing eyes.
¹⁰People open their mouths to jeer at me;
  they strike my cheek in scorn
  and unite together against me.
¹¹God has turned me over to the ungodly
  and thrown me into the clutches of the wicked.
¹²All was well with me, but he shattered me;
  he seized me by the neck and crushed me.
 He has made me his target;
¹³ his archers surround me.
 Without pity, he pierces my kidneys
  and spills my gall on the ground.
¹⁴Again and again he bursts upon me;
  he rushes at me like a warrior.

¹⁵"I have sewed sackcloth over my skin
  and buried my brow in the dust.
¹⁶My face is red with weeping,
  dark shadows ring my eyes;
¹⁷yet my hands have been free of violence
  and my prayer is pure.

661

myth# 43 "IF I PRAY ABOUT MY PROBLEM, IT WILL GO AWAY."

On our honeymoon, I found out that my husband was addicted to drugs. I knew he had a history of drug use, but that was years ago. When we met, he was a committed Christian who claimed he'd completely cleaned up his act. We fell in love quickly, but I wanted to wait to get married to make sure he had really changed. I guess I didn't wait long enough.

Our married life became a living nightmare. We came home from our honeymoon to a ransacked apartment, with most of our new wedding gifts missing. Turns out, my husband owed some drug money to some unforgiving people. Quinn was no longer the man I thought I knew. He would take my car and be gone for hours. I never knew where he was. I feared for my life and for his. I prayed earnestly, tears streaming down my face, for God to heal him of this addiction. I knew it was God's will that he be healed, and I believed God had the power to heal him.

The next couple years were agonizing as I continued to pray for Quinn to change. Only the situation wasn't getting better; it was getting worse. Quinn was in and out of some of the best rehab clinics in the country. He would come clean for a while, and I thought God had answered my prayers. Then he would be back to using again. As a Christian, I knew divorce was wrong. Besides, I loved him. I was afraid he'd completely self-destruct if I left him.

After I became pregnant, I thought Quinn might change for the sake of our child. I think he tried but just couldn't pull it together. He was still using drugs off and on, and though I knew he couldn't be a husband or father, I still believed in a miracle. He barely made it to the hospital the day our daughter was born. I thought God answered prayer. What happened?

—Dawn

IF GOD HAS the power to change a bad situation, then why doesn't he? If he's all-powerful and loving, then why won't he answer our prayers? *Why, God, why?*

These are the timeless questions that humans have been asking for thousands of years. These are the very questions that Job cried out to God. God never directly answered Job's questions. Instead he answered Job by explaining who he is. He is powerful. He is beyond our reason. He is above our reproaches. *He is good.*

What we forget is that God sees good from his eternal perspective (see Romans 8:28). All we can see is the immediate—what's right before our eyes—and it sure doesn't look good from our limited view. Have you found yourself thinking any of the following statements?

God doesn't listen to me. "No" and "wait" are both valid answers to prayer. Don't allow yourself to believe that God is uncaring, aloof and distant. Cling to the fact that he cares deeply for you; he's near and he's good.

God didn't answer because I didn't have enough faith. This logic implies that the outcome depends on a human being. We don't have a magic formula to fix a situation; we have to trust God.

If God loved me, he would make this problem go away. Our problems are often tied to other people, who also have choices. God doesn't override a Christian's free will and force him or her to choose the right way. God often uses a range of people and situations to bring something good out of our pain, even though we can't always see it right away or ever . . . this side of eternity.

"I'd started believing that if I just met certain standards of performance such as Bible reading and prayer (both good things in themselves), then God would essentially become my fairy godparent and do my bidding."

—Ruth Van Reken

663

"GOING A LITTLE FARTHER, HE FELL WITH HIS FACE TO THE GROUND AND PRAYED, 'MY FATHER, IF IT IS POSSIBLE, MAY THIS CUP BE TAKEN FROM ME. YET NOT AS I WILL, BUT AS YOU WILL.'"

MATTHEW 26:39

SEE ALSO
Job 23:9–10
Psalm 4:3
Psalm 145:9

For more on **Prayer**, check the index.

¹⁸"Earth, do not cover my blood;
    may my cry never be laid to rest!
¹⁹Even now my witness is in heaven;
    my advocate is on high.
²⁰My intercessor is my friend*ᵃ*
    as my eyes pour out tears to God;
²¹on behalf of a human being he pleads with God
    as one pleads for a friend.

²²"Only a few years will pass
    before I take the path of no return.

HE IS: my friend

16:18–22 Job's earthly friends were miserable comforters throughout his many trials (see 16:2). Rather than wallowing in self-pity, Job turned to his true friend and advocate, one who would plead his case as a persuasive lawyer pleads for a friend. Clearly, Job had pinned all his hopes on God.

Human friends may disappoint you, disappear on you or disapprove of you. How much better to rely on your *friend* who is in heaven! Jesus will stand beside you and stand up for you, no matter what circumstances you face. Like Job, you can say through your tears, "My redeemer lives" (19:25–27)!

For the next He Is, go to p. 673.

17

¹My spirit is broken,
    my days are cut short,
    the grave awaits me.
²Surely mockers surround me;
    my eyes must dwell on their hostility.

³"Give me, O God, the pledge you demand.
    Who else will put up security for me?
⁴You have closed their minds to understanding;
    therefore you will not let
        them triumph.
⁵If people denounce their
        friends for reward,
    the eyes of their children
        will fail.

⁶"God has made me a byword
        to everyone,
    a man in whose face people
        spit.
⁷My eyes have grown dim with
        grief;
    my whole frame is but a
        shadow.
⁸The upright are appalled at
        this;

conversations

grief «» 17:7

1» What has been the hardest (most Job-like) season in your life so far?

2» Does grief make you stronger or weaker? How?

3» When you are grieving, what do you do to hold on to hope?

For more on **grief**, check the index.
For the next Conversations, go to p. 667.

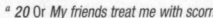

ᵃ 20 Or *My friends treat me with scorn*

the innocent are aroused against the ungodly.
⁹Nevertheless, the righteous will hold to their ways,
  and those with clean hands will grow stronger.

¹⁰"But come on, all of you, try again!
  I will not find a wise man among you.
¹¹My days have passed, my plans are shattered.
  Yet the desires of my heart
¹²turn night into day;
  in the face of the darkness light is near.
¹³If the only home I hope for is the grave,
  if I spread out my bed in the realm of darkness,
¹⁴if I say to corruption, 'You are my father,'
  and to the worm, 'My mother' or 'My sister,'
¹⁵where then is my hope—
  who can see any hope for me?
¹⁶Will it go down to the gates of death?
  Will we descend together into the dust?"

Bildad

18 Then Bildad the Shuhite replied:

²"When will you end these speeches?
  Be sensible, and then we can talk.
³Why are we regarded as cattle
  and considered stupid in your sight?
⁴You who tear yourself to pieces in your anger,
  is the earth to be abandoned for your sake?
  Or must the rocks be moved from their place?

⁵"The lamp of a wicked man is snuffed out;
  the flame of his fire stops burning.
⁶The light in his tent becomes dark;
  the lamp beside him goes out.
⁷The vigor of his step is weakened;
  his own schemes throw him down.
⁸His feet thrust him into a net;
  he wanders into its mesh.
⁹A trap seizes him by the heel;
  a snare holds him fast.
¹⁰A noose is hidden for him on the ground;
  a trap lies in his path.
¹¹Terrors startle him on every side
  and dog his every step.
¹²Calamity is hungry for him;
  disaster is ready for him when he falls.
¹³It eats away parts of his skin;
  death's firstborn devours his limbs.
¹⁴He is torn from the security of his tent
  and marched off to the king of terrors.
¹⁵Fire resides *a* in his tent;

665

---

a 15 Or Nothing he had remains

burning sulfur is scattered over his dwelling.
¹⁶His roots dry up below
    and his branches wither above.
¹⁷The memory of him perishes from the earth;
    he has no name in the land.
¹⁸He is driven from light into the realm of darkness
    and is banished from the world.
¹⁹He has no offspring or descendants among his people,
    no survivor where once he lived.
²⁰People of the west are appalled at his fate;
    those of the east are seized with horror.
²¹Surely such is the dwelling of an evil man;
    such is the place of one who knows not God."

Job

19

666

Then Job replied:

²"How long will you torment me
    and crush me with words?
³Ten times now you have reproached me;
    shamelessly you attack me.
⁴If it is true that I have gone astray,
    my error remains my concern alone.
⁵If indeed you would exalt yourselves above me
    and use my humiliation against me,
⁶then know that God has wronged me
    and drawn his net around me.

⁷"Though I cry, 'Violence!' I get no response;
    though I call for help, there is no justice.
⁸He has blocked my way so I cannot pass;
    he has shrouded my paths in darkness.
⁹He has stripped me of my honor
    and removed the crown from my head.
¹⁰He tears me down on every side till I am gone;
    he uproots my hope like a tree.
¹¹His anger burns against me;
    he counts me among his enemies.
¹²His troops advance in force;
    they build a siege ramp against me
    and encamp around my tent.

¹³"He has alienated my family from me;
    my acquaintances are completely estranged from me.
¹⁴My relatives have gone away;
    my friends have forgotten me.
¹⁵My guests and my female servants count me a foreigner;
    they look on me as on a stranger.
¹⁶I summon my servant, but he does not answer,
    though I beg him with my own mouth.
¹⁷My breath is offensive to my wife;
    I am loathsome to my own family.
¹⁸Even the little boys scorn me;

when I appear, they ridicule me.
¹⁹All my intimate friends detest me;
  those I love have turned against me.
²⁰I am nothing but skin and bones;
  I have escaped only by the skin of my teeth.ᵃ

²¹"Have pity on me, my friends, have pity,
  for the hand of God has struck me.
²²Why do you pursue me as God does?
  Will you never get enough of my
    flesh?

²³"Oh, that my words were recorded,
  that they were written on a scroll,
²⁴that they were inscribed with an iron
    tool onᵇ lead,
  or engraved in rock forever!
²⁵I know that my redeemerᶜ lives,
  and that in the end he will stand on
    the earth.ᵈ
²⁶And after my skin has been destroyed,
  yetᵉ inᶠ my flesh I will see God;
²⁷I myself will see him
  with my own eyes—I, and not another.
  How my heart yearns within me!

²⁸"If you say, 'How we will hound him,
  since the root of the trouble lies in him,ᵍ'
²⁹you should fear the sword yourselves;
  for wrath will bring punishment by the sword,
  and then you will know that there is judgment.ʰ"

conversations

security «» 19:25

1» What does it mean to have a redeemer?

2» How is *security* different from *safety*?

3» Which does God promise you?

667

For more on security, check the index.
For the next Conversations, go to p. 672.

Zophar

20 Then Zophar the Naamathite replied:

²"My troubled thoughts prompt me to answer
  because I am greatly disturbed.
³I hear a rebuke that dishonors me,
  and my understanding inspires me to reply.

⁴"Surely you know how it has been from of old,
  ever since people wereⁱ placed on the earth,
⁵that the mirth of the wicked is brief,
  the joy of the godless lasts but a moment.
⁶Though his pride reaches to the heavens
  and his head touches the clouds,
⁷he will perish forever, like his own dung;
  those who have seen him will say, 'Where is he?'
⁸Like a dream he flies away, no more to be found,
  banished like a vision of the night.
⁹The eye that saw him will not see him again;

ᵃ 20 Or only by my gums   ᵇ 24 Or and   ᶜ 25 Or vindicator   ᵈ 25 Or on my grave   ᵉ 26 Or And after I awake, / though this ⌊body⌋ has been destroyed, / then
ᶠ 26 Or destroyed, / apart from   ᵍ 28 Many Hebrew manuscripts, Septuagint and Vulgate; most Hebrew manuscripts me   ʰ 29 Or sword, / that you may come to
know the Almighty   ⁱ 4 Or since Adam was

his place will look on him no more.
¹⁰His children must make amends to the poor;
his own hands must give back his wealth.
¹¹The youthful vigor that fills his bones
will lie with him in the dust.

¹²"Though evil is sweet in his mouth
and he hides it under his tongue,
¹³though he cannot bear to let it go
and lets it linger in his mouth,
¹⁴yet his food will turn sour in his stomach;
it will become the venom of serpents within him.
¹⁵He will spit out the riches he swallowed;
God will make his stomach vomit them up.
¹⁶He will suck the poison of serpents;
the fangs of an adder will kill him.
¹⁷He will not enjoy the streams,
the rivers flowing with honey and cream.
¹⁸What he toiled for he must give back uneaten;
he will not enjoy the profit from his trading.
¹⁹For he has oppressed the poor and left them destitute;
he has seized houses he did not build.

²⁰"Surely he will have no respite from his craving;
he cannot save himself by his treasure.
²¹Nothing is left for him to devour;
his prosperity will not endure.
²²In the midst of his plenty, distress will overtake him;
the full force of misery will come upon him.
²³When he has filled his belly,
God will vent his burning anger against him
and rain down his blows on him.
²⁴Though he flees from an iron weapon,
a bronze-tipped arrow pierces him.
²⁵He pulls it out of his back,
the gleaming point out of his liver.
Terrors will come over him;
²⁶ total darkness lies in wait for his treasures.
A fire unfanned will consume him
and devour what is left in his tent.
²⁷The heavens will expose his guilt;
the earth will rise up against him.
²⁸A flood will carry off his house,
rushing waters^a on the day of God's wrath.
²⁹Such is the fate God allots the wicked,
the heritage appointed for them by God."

Job
21 Then Job replied:

²"Listen carefully to my words;
let this be the consolation you give me.

^a 28 Or The possessions in his house will be carried off, / washed away

³Bear with me while I speak,
  and after I have spoken, mock on.

⁴"Is my complaint directed to a human being?
  Why should I not be impatient?
⁵Look at me and be appalled;
  clap your hand over your mouth.
⁶When I think about this, I am terrified;
  trembling seizes my body.
⁷Why do the wicked live on,
  growing old and increasing in power?
⁸They see their children established around them,
  their offspring before their eyes.
⁹Their homes are safe and free from fear;
  the rod of God is not on them.
¹⁰Their bulls never fail to breed;
  their cows calve and do not miscarry.
¹¹They send forth their children as a flock;
  their little ones dance about.
¹²They sing to the music of timbrel and lyre;
  they make merry to the sound of the pipe.
¹³They spend their years in prosperity
  and go down to the grave in peace.ᵃ
¹⁴Yet they say to God, 'Leave us alone!
  We have no desire to know your ways.
¹⁵Who is the Almighty, that we should serve him?
  What would we gain by praying to him?'
¹⁶But their prosperity is not in their own hands,
  so I stand aloof from the counsel of the wicked.

¹⁷"Yet how often is the lamp of the wicked snuffed out?
  How often does calamity come upon them,
  the fate God allots in his anger?
¹⁸How often are they like straw before the wind,
  like chaff swept away by a gale?
¹⁹It is said, 'God stores up the punishment of the wicked for their children.'
  Let him repay the wicked, so that they themselves will experience it!
²⁰Let their own eyes see their destruction;
  let them drink of the wrath of the Almighty.
²¹For what do they care about the families they leave behind
  when their allotted months come to an end?

²²"Can anyone teach knowledge to God,
  since he judges even the highest?
²³One person dies in full vigor,
  completely secure and at ease,
²⁴well nourished in body,ᵇ
  bones rich with marrow.
²⁵Another dies in bitterness of soul,
  never having enjoyed anything good.
²⁶Side by side they lie in the dust,
  and worms cover them both.

ᵃ 13 Or *in an instant*   ᵇ 24 The meaning of the Hebrew for this word is uncertain.

²⁷"I know full well what you are thinking,
the schemes by which you would wrong me.
²⁸You say, 'Where now is the house of the great,
the tents where the wicked lived?'
²⁹Have you never questioned those who travel?
Have you paid no regard to their accounts—
³⁰that the wicked are spared from the day of calamity,
that they are delivered from ᵃ the day of wrath?
³¹Who denounces their conduct to their face?
Who repays them for what they have done?
³²They are carried to the grave,
and watch is kept over their tombs.
³³The soil in the valley is sweet to them;
everyone follows after them,
and a countless throng goes ᵇ before them.

³⁴"So how can you console me with your nonsense?
Nothing is left of your answers but falsehood!"

670

Eliphaz

22 Then Eliphaz the Temanite replied:

²"Can a human being be of benefit to God?
Can even the wise benefit him?
³What pleasure would it give the
Almighty if you were righteous?
What would he gain if your ways were
blameless?

⁴"Is it for your piety that he rebukes you
and brings charges against you?
⁵Is not your wickedness great?
Are not your sins endless?
⁶You demanded security from your
relatives for no reason;
you stripped people of their clothing,
leaving them naked.
⁷You gave no water to the weary
and you withheld food from the
hungry,
⁸though you were a powerful man,
owning land—
an honored man, living on it.
⁹And you sent widows away empty-
handed
and broke the strength of the
fatherless.
¹⁰That is why snares are all around you,
why sudden peril terrifies you,
¹¹why it is so dark you cannot see,
and why a flood of water covers you.

at issue: suffering

22:1–11 Many people view
God as the "principal" in the
"school of life." When bad
things happen to them, they
think God is punishing them
for breaking some rule. Do
you view God that way?
Job's friends did. They were
convinced Job's suffering
resulted from some secret
sin in his life. While it's true
that affliction may often
result from our sin, Job's
pure life demonstrates that
personal sin is not the only
reason for suffering. While
we may never know all the
reasons for our hardships,
we can trust that God
knows and will always use
trials for our good and his
glory.

ᵃ 30 Or are reserved for the day of calamity, / that they are brought forth to ᵇ 33 Or them, / as a countless throng went

¹² "Is not God in the heights of heaven?
  And see how lofty are the highest stars!
¹³ Yet you say, 'What does God know?
  Does he judge through such darkness?
¹⁴ Thick clouds veil him, so he does not see us
  as he goes about in the vaulted heavens.'
¹⁵ Will you keep to the old path
  that the wicked have trod?
¹⁶ They were carried off before their time,
  their foundations washed away by a flood.
¹⁷ They said to God, 'Leave us alone!
  What can the Almighty do to us?'
¹⁸ Yet it was he who filled their houses with good things,
  so I stand aloof from the counsel of the wicked.
¹⁹ The righteous see their ruin and rejoice;
  the innocent mock them, saying,
²⁰ 'Surely our foes are destroyed,
  and fire devours their wealth.'

²¹ "Submit to God and be at peace with him;
  in this way prosperity will come to you.
²² Accept instruction from his mouth
  and lay up his words in your heart.
²³ If you return to the Almighty, you will be restored:
  If you remove wickedness far from your tent
²⁴ and assign your nuggets to the dust,
  your gold of Ophir to the rocks in the ravines,
²⁵ then the Almighty will be your gold,
  the choicest silver for you.
²⁶ Surely then you will find delight in the Almighty
  and will lift up your face to God.
²⁷ You will pray to him, and he will hear you,
  and you will fulfill your vows.
²⁸ What you decide on will be done,
  and light will shine on your ways.
²⁹ When people are brought low and you say, 'Lift them up!'
  then he will save the downcast.
³⁰ He will deliver even one who is not innocent,
  who will be delivered through the cleanness of your hands."

671

Job
23

Then Job replied:

² "Even today my complaint is bitter;
  his hand^a is heavy in spite of^b my groaning.
³ If only I knew where to find him;
  if only I could go to his dwelling!
⁴ I would state my case before him
  and fill my mouth with arguments.
⁵ I would find out what he would answer me,
  and consider what he would say to me.

^a 2 Septuagint and Syriac; Hebrew / the hand on me   ^b 2 Or heavy on me in

⁶Would he vigorously oppose me?
No, he would not press charges against me.
⁷There the upright can establish their innocence before him,
and there I would be delivered forever from my judge.

⁸"But if I go to the east, he is not there;
if I go to the west, I do not find him.
⁹When he is at work in the north, I do not see him;
when he turns to the south, I catch no glimpse of him.
¹⁰But he knows the way that I take;
when he has tested me, I will come forth as gold.
¹¹My feet have closely followed his steps;
I have kept to his way without turning aside.
¹²I have not departed from the commands of his lips;
I have treasured the words of his mouth more than my daily bread.

¹³"But he stands alone, and who can oppose him?
He does whatever he pleases.
¹⁴He carries out his decree
against me,
and many such plans he
still has in store.
¹⁵That is why I am terrified
before him;
when I think of all this, I
fear him.
¹⁶God has made my heart faint;
the Almighty has terrified
me.
¹⁷Yet I am not silenced by the
darkness,
by the thick darkness that
covers my face.

" conversations "

complaining «» 23–24

1» What are we trying to control when we complain?

2» What does complaining do to an already-bad situation?

3» How is complaining related to fear?

For more on **complaining**, check the index.
For the next Conversations, go to p. 682.

24 "Why does the Almighty not
set times for judgment?
Why must those who know him look in vain for such days?
²There are those who move boundary stones;
they pasture flocks they have stolen.
³They drive away the orphan's donkey
and take the widow's ox in pledge.
⁴They thrust the needy from the path
and force all the poor of the land into hiding.
⁵Like wild donkeys in the desert,
the poor go about their labor of foraging food;
the wasteland provides food for their children.
⁶They gather fodder in the fields
and glean in the vineyards of the wicked.
⁷Lacking clothes, they spend the night naked;
they have nothing to cover themselves in the cold.
⁸They are drenched by mountain rains
and hug the rocks for lack of shelter.
⁹The fatherless child is snatched from the breast;

the infant of the poor is seized for a debt.
[10]Lacking clothes, they go about naked;
    they carry the sheaves, but still go hungry.
[11]They crush olives among the terraces[a];
    they tread the winepresses, yet suffer thirst.
[12]The groans of the dying rise from the city,
    and the souls of the wounded cry out for help.
    But God charges no one with wrongdoing.

[13]"There are those who rebel against the light,
    who do not know its ways
    or stay in its paths.
[14]When daylight is gone, the murderer rises up,
    kills the poor and needy,
    and in the night steals forth like a thief.
[15]The eye of the adulterer watches for dusk;
    he thinks, 'No eye will see me,'
    and he keeps his face concealed.
[16]In the dark, thieves break into houses,
    but by day they shut themselves in;
    they want nothing to do with the light.
[17]For all of them, midnight is their morning;
    they make friends with the terrors of darkness.

[18]"Yet they are foam on the surface of the water;
    their portion of the land is cursed,
    so that no one goes to the vineyards.
[19]As heat and drought snatch away the melted snow,
    so the grave snatches away those who have sinned.
[20]The womb forgets them,
    the worm feasts on them;
  the wicked are no longer remembered
    but are broken like a tree.
[21]They prey on the barren and childless woman,
    and to the widow show no kindness.
[22]But God drags away the mighty by his power;

---

[a] 11 The meaning of the Hebrew for this word is uncertain.

HE IS: overseeing

24:22–24 In every generation we ask the same question: Why do the wicked prosper? Job gives us insight into God's character by reminding his friends that God sees all people. Though the wicked may prosper for a season, God is *overseeing*. He will ensure that the wicked are repaid.

  Do you wonder why some people prosper and get away with sin while you endure pain or difficult times (see Matthew 5:45)? Remember that God is *overseeing*. He views things—all things—from an eternal perspective. In his perfect time, he'll bring the wicked down and raise the righteous up.

For the next He Is, go to p. 687.

though they become established, they have no assurance of life.
²³He may let them rest in a feeling of security,
　　but his eyes are on their ways.
²⁴For a little while they are exalted, and then they are gone;
　　they are brought low and gathered up like all others;
　　they are cut off like heads of grain.

²⁵"If this is not so, who can prove me false
　　and reduce my words to nothing?"

Bildad

25

Then Bildad the Shuhite replied:

²"Dominion and awe belong to God;
　　he establishes order in the heights of heaven.
³Can his forces be numbered?
　　On whom does his light not rise?
⁴How then can a mortal be righteous before God?
　　How can one born of woman be pure?
⁵If even the moon is not bright
　　and the stars are not pure in his eyes,
⁶how much less a mortal, who is but a maggot—
　　a human being, who is only a worm!"

Job

26

Then Job replied:

²"How you have helped the powerless!
　　How you have saved the arm that is feeble!
³What advice you have offered to one without wisdom!
　　And what great insight you have displayed!
⁴Who has helped you utter these words?
　　And whose spirit spoke from your mouth?

⁵"The dead are in deep anguish,
　　those beneath the waters and all that live in them.
⁶Death is naked before God;
　　Destruction*a* lies uncovered.
⁷He spreads out the northern ˻skies˼ over empty space;
　　he suspends the earth over nothing.
⁸He wraps up the waters in his clouds,
　　yet the clouds do not burst under their weight.
⁹He covers the face of the full moon,
　　spreading his clouds over it.
¹⁰He marks out the horizon on the face of the waters
　　for a boundary between light and darkness.
¹¹The pillars of the heavens quake,
　　aghast at his rebuke.
¹²By his power he churned up the sea;
　　by his wisdom he cut Rahab to pieces.
¹³By his breath the skies became fair;

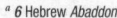

his hand pierced the gliding serpent.
¹⁴And these are but the outer fringe of his works;
how faint the whisper we hear of him!
Who then can understand the thunder of his power?"

Job's Final Word to His Friends

27 And Job continued his discourse:

²"As surely as God lives, who has denied me justice,
the Almighty, who has made my life bitter,
³as long as I have life within me,
the breath of God in my nostrils,
⁴my lips will not say anything wicked,
and my tongue will not utter lies.
⁵I will never admit you are in the right;
till I die, I will not deny my integrity.
⁶I will maintain my innocence and never let go of it;
my conscience will not reproach me as long as I live.

⁷"May my enemies be like the wicked,
my adversaries like the unjust!
⁸For what hope have the godless when they are cut off,
when God takes away their life?
⁹Does God listen to their cry
when distress comes upon them?
¹⁰Will they find delight in the Almighty?
Will they call on God at all times?

¹¹"I will teach you about the power of God;
the ways of the Almighty I will not conceal.
¹²You have all seen this yourselves.
Why then this meaningless talk?

¹³"Here is the fate God allots to the wicked,
the heritage a ruthless man receives from the Almighty:
¹⁴However many his children, their fate is the sword;
his offspring will never have enough to eat.
¹⁵The plague will bury those who survive him,
and their widows will not weep for them.
¹⁶Though he heaps up silver like dust
and clothes like piles of clay,
¹⁷what he lays up the righteous will wear,
and the innocent will divide his silver.
¹⁸The house he builds is like a moth's cocoon,
like a hut made by a watchman.
¹⁹He lies down wealthy, but will do so no more;
when he opens his eyes, all is gone.
²⁰Terrors overtake him like a flood;
a tempest snatches him away in the night.
²¹The east wind carries him off, and he is gone;
it sweeps him out of his place.
²²It hurls itself against him without mercy
as he flees headlong from its power.

675

²³It claps its hands in derision
    and hisses them out of their place."

Interlude: Where Wisdom Is Found

28 There is a mine for silver
    and a place where gold is refined.
²Iron is taken from the earth,
    and copper is smelted from ore.
³Miners put an end to the darkness;
    they search out the farthest recesses
    for ore in the blackest darkness.
⁴Far from human dwellings they cut a shaft,
    in places untouched by human feet;
    far from other people they dangle and sway.
⁵The earth, from which food comes,
    is transformed below as by fire;
⁶lapis lazuli comes from its rocks,
    and its dust contains nuggets of gold.
⁷No bird of prey knows that hidden path,
    no falcon's eye has seen it.
⁸Proud beasts do not set foot on it,
    and no lion prowls there.
⁹The miners' hands assault the flinty rock
    and lay bare the roots of the mountains.
¹⁰They tunnel through the rock;
    their eyes see all its treasures.
¹¹They search*a* the sources of the rivers
    and bring hidden things to light.

¹²But where can wisdom be found?
    Where does understanding dwell?
¹³No mortal comprehends its worth;
    it cannot be found in the land of the living.
¹⁴The deep says, "It is not in me";
    the sea says, "It is not with me."
¹⁵It cannot be bought with the finest gold,
    nor can its price be weighed out in silver.
¹⁶It cannot be bought with the gold of Ophir,
    with precious onyx or lapis lazuli.
¹⁷Neither gold nor crystal can compare with it,
    nor can it be had for jewels of gold.
¹⁸Coral and jasper are not worthy of mention;
    the price of wisdom is beyond rubies.
¹⁹The topaz of Cush cannot compare with it;
    it cannot be bought with pure gold.

²⁰Where then does wisdom come from?
    Where does understanding dwell?
²¹It is hidden from the eyes of every living thing,
    concealed even from the birds in the sky.
²²Destruction*b* and Death say,

---
a 11 Septuagint, Aquila and Vulgate; Hebrew They dam up   b 22 Hebrew Abaddon

"Only a rumor of it has reached our ears."
²³God understands the way to it
   and he alone knows where it dwells,
²⁴for he views the ends of the earth
   and sees everything under the heavens.
²⁵When he established the force of the wind
   and measured out the waters,
²⁶when he made a decree for the rain
   and a path for the thunderstorm,
²⁷then he looked at wisdom and appraised it;
   he confirmed it and tested it.
²⁸And he said to the human race,
   "The fear of the Lord—that is wisdom,
   and to shun evil is understanding."

Job's Final Defense

29
Job continued his discourse:

²"How I long for the months gone by,
   for the days when God watched over me,
³when his lamp shone on my head
   and by his light I walked through darkness!
⁴Oh, for the days when I was in my prime,
   when God's intimate friendship blessed my house,
⁵when the Almighty was still with me
   and my children were around me,
⁶when my path was drenched with cream
   and the rock poured out for me streams of olive oil.

⁷"When I went to the gate of the city
   and took my seat in the public square,
⁸the young men saw me and stepped aside
   and the old men rose to their feet;
⁹the chief men refrained from speaking
   and covered their mouths with their hands;
¹⁰the voices of the nobles were hushed,
   and their tongues stuck to the roof of their mouths.
¹¹Whoever heard me spoke well of me,
   and those who saw me commended me,
¹²because I rescued the poor who cried for help,
   and the fatherless who had none to assist them.
¹³Those who were dying blessed me;
   I made the widow's heart sing.
¹⁴I put on righteousness as my clothing;
   justice was my robe and my turban.
¹⁵I was eyes to the blind
   and feet to the lame.
¹⁶I was a father to the needy;
   I took up the case of the stranger.
¹⁷I broke the fangs of the wicked
   and snatched the victims from their teeth.

myth# 44 "IF I FEEL THIS WAY, IT MUST BE TRUE."

I was afraid my husband was cheating on me. Although he had always been a loving husband, I felt it in the depths of my bones. I had just had a baby, and I was feeling fat and very un-sexy in my post-maternity wear. Even though I couldn't pinpoint exactly why, I started feeling neglected. Ben assured me all the time that he loved me and found me sexually attractive. But I didn't believe him.

Not long after I started feeling this way, some friends told me they saw my husband having lunch with a woman who works for him. According to my friends, the two of them were laughing and having too good of a time for a "working lunch." When I asked Ben not to have lunch with women from the office alone, he agreed, though he felt I was overreacting. When he saw I was still unconvinced, he suggested we go to counseling to help us in our marriage. But I still didn't trust him.

I talked to a few friends about the problems we were having, and everyone counseled me to separate or file for divorce. Why stay married if I felt the love between us was gone? I should follow my instincts. A woman just knows these things about her husband—how could I live with those suspicions? Even my counselor—not a Christian, but all I could afford through our insurance—told me to leave my husband if I felt I didn't want to try working it out. I didn't want to talk to my Christian friends. I knew they would remind me that my hormones were all out of whack and tell me to process my emotions through prayer. Frankly, I didn't feel like praying. I felt overwhelmed by my failing marriage.

Even though I felt very strongly about leaving, I didn't know if it was the right choice. If I left Ben, it would devastate our families. I would have to get a full-time job to support my three children and me. A divorce could stretch on for years. I didn't know what to do. I couldn't see past what I felt.

—Taylor

WHAT SHOULD WE do when
we are on emotional overload?

- Remember, *feelings aren't facts.* Too often we base life-changing decisions on over-powering feelings. Our hearts can deceive us (see Jeremiah 17:9) and blind us with a half-truth. That's why we need God to help us sort through our thoughts and emotions.

- Before making any life-changing decisions, seek the counsel of several Christians. If you only get non-Christian opinions on what you should do, you'll always miss important pieces of the equation. In the same way, any one Christian can miss something, so seek counsel from your pastor, godly friends and family.

- Don't do anything rash. Instead, whenever your emotions are all over the place, wait. Talk to other people—especially your spouse.

- If needed, consult a doctor. Sometimes you may experience a hormonal imbalance due to pregnancy, stress or other conditions. You may also have a chemical imbalance, which may produce paranoia, depression, obsessiveness and other traits. God can use medical care to help give you a clearer perspective on reality.

- Pray. Ask God to help you sort through your feelings. What you see from a skewed perspective, he sees clearly. And he invites you to ask him for widom (see James 1:5–8).

"By a 3-to-1 margin (64 percent vs. 22 percent), adults said truth is always relative to the person and his or her situation. Nearly 31 percent described doing whatever feels right or comfortable in a situation as their primary consideration for moral decision-making."

——Barna Research Group (2002)

679

"WALK WITH THE WISE AND BECOME WISE, FOR a companion OF FOOLS suffers Harm."

PROVERBS 13:20

SEE ALSO
Isaiah 30:19–21
Philippians 4:6–8
1 John 3:18–20

For more on **Emotions,** check the index.

¹⁸"I thought, 'I will die in my own house,
  my days as numerous as the grains of sand.
¹⁹My roots will reach to the water,
  and the dew will lie all night on my branches.
²⁰My glory will remain fresh in me,
  the bow ever new in my hand.'

²¹"People listened to me expectantly,
  waiting in silence for my counsel.
²²After I had spoken, they spoke no more;
  my words fell gently on their ears.
²³They waited for me as for showers
  and drank in my words as the spring rain.
²⁴When I smiled at them, they scarcely believed it;
  the light of my face was precious to them.[a]
²⁵I chose the way for them and sat as their chief;
  I dwelt as a king among his troops;
  I was like one who comforts mourners.

30 "But now they mock me,
  men younger than I,
  whose fathers I would have disdained
  to put with my sheep dogs.
²Of what use was the strength of their hands to me,
  since their vigor had gone from them?
³Haggard from want and hunger,
  they roamed[b] the parched land
  in desolate wastelands at night.
⁴In the brush they gathered salt herbs,
  and their food[c] was the root of the broom bush.
⁵They were banished from human society,
  shouted at as if they were thieves.
⁶They were forced to live in the dry stream beds,
  among the rocks and in holes in the ground.
⁷They brayed among the bushes
  and huddled in the undergrowth.
⁸A base and nameless brood,
  they were driven out of the land.

⁹"And now those young men mock me in song;
  I have become a byword among them.
¹⁰They detest me and keep their distance;
  they do not hesitate to spit in my face.
¹¹Now that God has unstrung my bow and afflicted me,
  they throw off restraint in my presence.
¹²On my right the tribe[d] attacks;
  they lay snares for my feet,
  they build their siege ramps against me.
¹³They break up my road;
  they succeed in destroying me.
  'No one can help him,' they say.

---

[a] 24 The meaning of the Hebrew for this clause is uncertain. [b] 3 Or gnawed [c] 4 Or fuel [d] 12 The meaning of the Hebrew for this word is uncertain.

¹⁴They advance as through a gaping breach;
  amid the ruins they come rolling in.
¹⁵Terrors overwhelm me;
  my dignity is driven away as by the wind,
  my safety vanishes like a cloud.

¹⁶"And now my life ebbs away;
  days of suffering grip me.
¹⁷Night pierces my bones;
  my gnawing pains never rest.
¹⁸In his great power ⌞God⌟ becomes like
    clothing to me ᵃ;
  he binds me like the neck of my
    garment.
¹⁹He throws me into the mud,
  and I am reduced to dust and ashes.

²⁰"I cry out to you, God, but you do not
    answer;
  I stand up, but you merely look at me.
²¹You turn on me ruthlessly;
  with the might of your hand you attack
    me.
²²You snatch me up and drive me before the
    wind;
  you toss me about in the storm.
²³I know you will bring me down to death,
  to the place appointed for all the living.

²⁴"Surely no one lays a hand on those who
    are crushed
  when they cry for help in their distress.
²⁵Have I not wept for those in trouble?
  Has not my soul grieved for the poor?
²⁶Yet when I hoped for good, evil came;
  when I looked for light, then came
    darkness.
²⁷The churning inside me never stops;
  days of suffering confront me.
²⁸I go about blackened, but not by the sun;
  I stand up in the assembly and cry for help.
²⁹I have become a brother of jackals,
  a companion of owls.
³⁰My skin grows black and peels;
  my body burns with fever.
³¹My lyre is tuned to mourning,
  and my pipe to the sound of wailing.

31

  "I made a covenant with my eyes
    not to look lustfully at a virgin.
²For what is our lot from God above,
  our heritage from the Almighty on high?

atissue:despair

30:16–31 Job felt life slipping away from him. He cried out to God but didn't hear any answer. He experienced a heavy feeling of sadness and despair. Does it surprise you that Job experienced what you may feel at times? When you're suffering from deep sadness or depression, it's easy to think you're all alone or that a "good Christian" wouldn't feel this way. But if all the "good" women were completely honest, you'd discover that many of them struggle with the same feelings you do. Don't be paralyzed by your feelings. Reach out to God and to others for help. There is hope!

681

ᵃ *18 Hebrew; Septuagint ⌞God⌟ grasps my clothing*

³Is it not ruin for the wicked,
    disaster for those who do wrong?
⁴Does he not see my ways
    and count my every step?

⁵"If I have walked with falsehood
    or my foot has hurried after deceit—
⁶let God weigh me in honest scales
    and he will know that I am blameless—
⁷if my steps have turned from the path,
    if my heart has been led by my eyes,
    or if my hands have been defiled,
⁸then may others eat what I have sown,
    and may my crops be uprooted.

⁹"If my heart has been enticed by a woman,
    or if I have lurked at my neighbor's door,
¹⁰then may my wife grind another man's grain,
    and may other men sleep with her.
¹¹For that would have been wicked,
    a sin to be judged.
¹²It is a fire that burns to Destruction*;
    it would have uprooted my harvest.

¹³"If I have denied justice to any of my servants,
    whether male or female,
    when they had a grievance against me,
¹⁴what will I do when God
        confronts me?
    What will I answer when
        called to account?
¹⁵Did not he who made me in
        the womb make them?
    Did not the same one form
        us both within our
        mothers?

¹⁶"If I have denied the desires of
        the poor
    or let the eyes of the widow
        grow weary,
¹⁷if I have kept my bread to
        myself,
    not sharing it with the
        fatherless—
¹⁸but from my youth I reared them as a father would,
    and from my birth I guided the widow—
¹⁹if I have seen anyone perishing for lack of clothing,
    or the needy without garments,
²⁰and their hearts did not bless me
    for warming them with the fleece from my sheep,
²¹if I have raised my hand against the fatherless,

"conversations"

pregnancy · «» 31:15

1» Based on this verse, is any person less important than another in God's eyes?

2» How can you show you value all people?

3» In what ways does God plan and shape our lives from conception?

For more on **pregnancy**, check the index.
For the next Conversations, go to p. 699.

ᵃ 12 Hebrew Abaddon

knowing that I had influence in court,
²²then let my arm fall from the shoulder,
   let it be broken off at the joint.
²³For I dreaded destruction from God,
   and for fear of his splendor I could not do such things.

²⁴"If I have put my trust in gold
   or said to pure gold, 'You are my security,'
²⁵if I have rejoiced over my great wealth,
   the fortune my hands had gained,
²⁶if I have regarded the sun in its radiance
   or the moon moving in splendor,
²⁷so that my heart was secretly enticed
   and my hand offered them a kiss of homage,
²⁸then these also would be sins to be judged,
   for I would have been unfaithful to God on high.

²⁹"If I have rejoiced at my enemies' misfortune
   or gloated over the trouble that came to them—
³⁰I have not allowed my mouth to sin
   by invoking a curse against their life—
³¹if those of my household have never said,
   'Who has not been filled with Job's meat?'—
³²but no stranger had to spend the night in the street,
   for my door was always open to the traveler—
³³if I have concealed my sin as people do,ᵃ
   by hiding my guilt in my heart
³⁴because I so feared the crowd
   and so dreaded the contempt of the clans
   that I kept silent and would not go outside—

³⁵("Oh, that I had someone to hear me!
   I sign now my defense—let the Almighty answer me;
   let my accuser put his indictment in writing.
³⁶Surely I would wear it on my shoulder,
   I would put it on like a crown.
³⁷I would give him an account of my every step;
   I would present it to him as to a ruler.)—

³⁸"if my land cries out against me
   and all its furrows are wet with tears,
³⁹if I have devoured its yield without payment
   or broken the spirit of its tenants,
⁴⁰then let briers come up instead of wheat
   and stinkweed instead of barley."

The words of Job are ended.

Elihu

32 So these three men stopped answering Job, because he was righteous in his own eyes. ²But Elihu son of Barakel the Buzite, of the family of Ram, became very angry with Job for justifying himself rather than God. ³He was also angry with the three friends, because they had found no way to

---

ᵃ *33 Or as Adam did*

refute Job, and yet had condemned him.[a] [4]Now Elihu had waited before speaking to Job because they were older than he. [5]But when he saw that the three men had nothing more to say, his anger was aroused.

[6]So Elihu son of Barakel the Buzite said:

> "I am young in years,
>   and you are old;
> that is why I was fearful,
>   not daring to tell you what I know.
> [7]I thought, 'Age should speak;
>   advanced years should teach wisdom.'
> [8]But it is the spirit[b] in mortals,
>   the breath of the Almighty, that gives them understanding.
> [9]It is not only the old[c] who are wise,
>   not only the aged who understand what is right.
>
> [10]"Therefore I say: Listen to me;
>   I too will tell you what I know.
> [11]I waited while you spoke,
>   I listened to your reasoning;
> while you were searching for words,
> [12]   I gave you my full attention.
> But not one of you has proved Job wrong;
>   none of you has answered his arguments.
> [13]Do not say, 'We have found wisdom;
>   let God refute him, not a mere mortal.'
> [14]But Job has not marshaled his words against me,
>   and I will not answer him with your arguments.
>
> [15]"They are dismayed and have no more to say;
>   words have failed them.
> [16]Must I wait, now that they are silent,
>   now that they stand there with no reply?
> [17]I too will have my say;
>   I too will tell what I know.
> [18]For I am full of words,
>   and the spirit within me compels me;
> [19]inside I am like bottled-up wine,
>   like new wineskins ready to burst.
> [20]I must speak and find relief;
>   I must open my lips and reply.
> [21]I will show no partiality,
>   nor will I flatter anyone;
> [22]for if I were skilled in flattery,
>   my Maker would soon take me away.

33

> "But now, Job, listen to my words;
>   pay attention to everything I say.
> [2]I am about to open my mouth;
>   my words are on the tip of my tongue.
> [3]My words come from an upright heart;

---

[a] 3 Masoretic Text; an ancient Hebrew scribal tradition *Job, and so had condemned God*   [b] 8 Or *Spirit*; also in verse 18   [c] 9 Or *many; or great*

my lips sincerely speak what I know.
⁴The Spirit of God has made me;
  the breath of the Almighty gives me life.
⁵Answer me then, if you can;
  stand up and argue your case before me.
⁶I am the same as you in God's sight;
  I too am a piece of clay.
⁷No fear of me should alarm you,
  nor should my hand be heavy on you.

⁸"But you have said in my hearing—
  I heard the very words—
⁹'I am pure, I have done no wrong;
  I am clean and free from sin.
¹⁰Yet God has found fault with me;
  he considers me his enemy.
¹¹He fastens my feet in shackles;
  he keeps close watch on all my paths.'

¹²"But I tell you, in this you are not right,
  for God is greater than any mortal.
¹³Why do you complain to him
  that he responds to no one's words*ᵃ*?
¹⁴For God does speak—now one way, now another—
  though no one perceives it.
¹⁵In a dream, in a vision of the night,
  when deep sleep falls on people
  as they slumber in their beds,
¹⁶he may speak in their ears
  and terrify them with warnings,
¹⁷to turn them from wrongdoing
  and keep them from pride,
¹⁸to preserve them from the pit,
  their lives from perishing by the sword.*ᵇ*

¹⁹"Or they may be chastened on a bed of pain
  with constant distress in their bones,
²⁰so that their bodies find food repulsive
  and their souls loathe the choicest meal.
²¹Their flesh wastes away to nothing,
  and their bones, once hidden, now stick out.
²²They draw near to the pit,
  and their lives to the messengers of death.*ᶜ*
²³Yet if there is an angel at their side,
  a messenger, one out of a thousand,
  sent to tell them how to be upright,
²⁴and he is gracious to them and says to God,
  'Spare them from going down to the pit;
  I have found a ransom for them—
²⁵let their flesh be renewed like a child's;
  let them be restored as in the days of their youth'—

685

ᵃ 13 Or *that he does not answer for any of his actions*   *ᵇ 18* Or *from crossing the river*   *ᶜ 22* Or *to the place of the dead*

²⁶then they can pray to God and find favor with him,
    they will see God's face and shout for joy;
    he will restore them to full well-being.
²⁷And they will go to others and say,
    'We have sinned, we have perverted what is right,
    but we did not get what we deserved.
²⁸God has delivered us from going down to the pit,
    and we shall live to enjoy the light of life.'

²⁹"God does all these things to people—
    twice, even three times—
³⁰to turn them back from the pit,
    that the light of life may shine on them.

³¹"Pay attention, Job, and listen to me;
    be silent, and I will speak.
³²If you have anything to say, answer me;
    speak up, for I want to vindicate you.
³³But if not, then listen to me;
    be silent, and I will teach you wisdom."

686

34 Then Elihu said:

²"Hear my words, you wise men;
    listen to me, you men of learning.
³For the ear tests words
    as the tongue tastes food.
⁴Let us discern for ourselves what is right;
    let us learn together what is good.

⁵"Job says, 'I am innocent,
    but God denies me justice.
⁶Although I am right,
    I am considered a liar;
although I am guiltless,
    his arrow inflicts an incurable wound.'
⁷Is there anyone like Job,
    who drinks scorn like water?
⁸He keeps company with evildoers;
    he associates with the wicked.
⁹For he says, 'There is no profit
    in trying to please God.'

¹⁰"So listen to me, you men of understanding.
    Far be it from God to do evil,
    from the Almighty to do wrong.
¹¹He repays everyone for what they have done;
    he brings on them what their conduct deserves.
¹²It is unthinkable that God would do wrong,
    that the Almighty would pervert justice.
¹³Who appointed him over the earth?
    Who put him in charge of the whole world?
¹⁴If it were his intention

HE IS: never wrong

34:10–12 Elihu was the last of the friends to speak, and he, too, attempted to explain what God was doing in Job's life through his trials and tribulations. Though God's dealings with people are sometimes incomprehensible, Elihu sure got one thing right: It is unthinkable that God would do wrong. God cannot do evil; he brings good to his children.

You may not understand what God is doing in your life right now. You may even feel that he is doing everything wrong. But faith realizes that God is *never wrong*. He can't be. You can trust that God's plan is perfect, even if its details are not revealed to you in this life.

For the next He Is, go to p. 691.

and he withdrew his spirit*ᵃ* and breath,
¹⁵all people would perish together
and would return to the dust.

687

¹⁶"If you have understanding, hear this;
listen to what I say.
¹⁷Can one who hates justice govern?
Will you condemn the just and mighty One?
¹⁸Is he not the One who says to kings, 'You are worthless,'
and to nobles, 'You are wicked,'
¹⁹who shows no partiality to princes
and does not favor the rich over the poor,
for they are all the work of his hands?
²⁰They die in an instant, in the middle of the night;
the people are shaken and they pass away;
the mighty are removed without human hand.

²¹"His eyes are on the ways of mortals;
he sees their every step.
²²There is no deep shadow, no utter darkness,
where evildoers can hide.
²³God has no need to examine people further,
that they should come before him for judgment.
²⁴Without inquiry he shatters the mighty
and sets up others in their place.
²⁵Because he takes note of their deeds,
he overthrows them in the night and they are crushed.
²⁶He punishes them for their wickedness
where everyone can see them,
²⁷because they turned from following him
and had no regard for any of his ways.
²⁸They caused the cry of the poor to come before him,
so that he heard the cry of the needy.
²⁹But if he remains silent, who can condemn him?
If he hides his face, who can see him?
Yet he is over individual and nation alike,
³⁰   to keep the godless from ruling,
from laying snares for the people.

ᵃ 14 Or Spirit

³¹"Suppose someone says to God,
    'I am guilty but will offend no more.
³²Teach me what I cannot see;
    if I have done wrong, I will not do so again.'
³³Should God then reward you on your terms,
    when you refuse to repent?
  You must decide, not I;
    so tell me what you know.

³⁴"Men of understanding declare,
    wise men who hear me say to me,
³⁵'Job speaks without knowledge;
    his words lack insight.'
³⁶Oh, that Job might be tested to the utmost
    for answering like a wicked man!
³⁷To his sin he adds rebellion;
    scornfully he claps his hands among us
    and multiplies his words against God."

35 Then Elihu said:

²"Do you think this is just?
    You say, 'I am in the right, not God.'
³Yet you ask him, 'What profit is it to me,ᵃ
    and what do I gain by not sinning?'

⁴"I would like to reply to you
    and to your friends with you.
⁵Look up at the heavens and see;
    gaze at the clouds so high above you.
⁶If you sin, how does that affect him?
    If your sins are many, what does that do to him?
⁷If you are righteous, what do you give to him,
    or what does he receive from your hand?
⁸Your wickedness only affects human beings like yourself,
    and your righteousness only members of the human race.

⁹"People cry out under a load of oppression;
    they plead for relief from the arm of the powerful.
¹⁰But no one says, 'Where is God my Maker,
    who gives songs in the night,
¹¹who teaches us more than he teachesᵇ the beasts of the earth
    and makes us wiser thanᶜ the birds in the sky?'
¹²He does not answer when people cry out
    because of the arrogance of the wicked.
¹³Indeed, God does not listen to their empty plea;
    the Almighty pays no attention to it.
¹⁴How much less, then, will he listen
    when you say that you do not see him,
  that your case is before him
    and you must wait for him,

ᵃ 3 Or you   ᵇ 10,11 Or night, / ¹¹who teaches us by   ᶜ 11 Or us wise by

¹⁵and further, that his anger never punishes
    and he does not take the least notice of wickedness.^a
¹⁶So Job opens his mouth with empty talk;
    without knowledge he multiplies words."

36

Elihu continued:

²"Bear with me a little longer and I will show you
    that there is more to be said in God's behalf.
³I get my knowledge from afar;
    I will ascribe justice to my Maker.
⁴Be assured that my words are not false;
    one who has perfect knowledge is with you.

⁵"God is mighty, but despises no one;
    he is mighty, and firm in his purpose.
⁶He does not keep the wicked alive
    but gives the afflicted their rights.
⁷He does not take his eyes off the righteous;
    he enthrones them with kings
    and exalts them forever.
⁸But if people are bound in chains,
    held fast by cords of affliction,
⁹he tells them what they have done—
    that they have sinned arrogantly.
¹⁰He makes them listen to correction
    and commands them to repent of their evil.
¹¹If they obey and serve him,
    they will spend the rest of their days in prosperity
    and their years in contentment.
¹²But if they do not listen,
    they will perish by the sword^b
    and die without knowledge.

¹³"The godless in heart harbor resentment;
    even when he fetters them, they do not cry for help.
¹⁴They die in their youth,
    among male prostitutes of the shrines.
¹⁵But those who suffer he delivers in their suffering;
    he speaks to them in their affliction.

¹⁶"He is wooing you from the jaws of distress
    to a spacious place free from restriction,
    to the comfort of your table laden with choice food.
¹⁷But now you are laden with the judgment due the wicked;
    judgment and justice have taken hold of you.
¹⁸Be careful that no one entices you by riches;
    do not let a large bribe turn you aside.
¹⁹Would your wealth or even all your mighty efforts
    sustain you so you would not be in distress?
²⁰Do not long for the night,

---

^a *15* Symmachus, Theodotion and Vulgate; the meaning of the Hebrew for this word is uncertain. ^b *12* Or *will cross the river*

to drag people away from their homes.^a
²¹Beware of turning to evil,
    which you seem to prefer to affliction.

²²"God is exalted in his power.
    Who is a teacher like him?
²³Who has prescribed his ways for him,
    or said to him, 'You have done wrong'?
²⁴Remember to extol his work,
    which people have praised in song.
²⁵All human beings have seen it;
    mortals gaze on it from afar.
²⁶How great is God—beyond our understanding!
    The number of his years is past finding out.

²⁷"He draws up the drops of water,
    which distill as rain to the streams^b;
²⁸the clouds pour down their moisture
    and abundant showers fall on the human race.
²⁹Who can understand how he spreads out the clouds,
    how he thunders from his pavilion?
³⁰See how he scatters his lightning about him,
    bathing the depths of the sea.
³¹This is the way he governs^c the nations
    and provides food in abundance.
³²He fills his hands with lightning
    and commands it to strike its mark.
³³His thunder announces the coming storm;
    even the cattle make known its approach.^d

37 "At this my heart pounds
    and leaps from its place.
²Listen! Listen to the roar of his voice,
    to the rumbling that comes from his mouth.
³He unleashes his lightning beneath the whole heaven
    and sends it to the ends of the earth.
⁴After that comes the sound of his roar;
    he thunders with his majestic voice.
When his voice resounds,
    he holds nothing back.
⁵God's voice thunders in marvelous ways;
    he does great things beyond our understanding.
⁶He says to the snow, 'Fall on the earth,'
    and to the rain shower, 'Be a mighty downpour.'
⁷So that everyone he has made may know his work,
    he stops all mortals from their labor.^e
⁸The animals take cover;
    they remain in their dens.
⁹The tempest comes out from its chamber,
    the cold from the driving winds.

---

^a 20 The meaning of the Hebrew for verses 18-20 is uncertain. ^b 27 Or *distill from the mist as rain* ^c 31 Or *nourishes* ^d 33 Or *announces his coming— / the One zealous against evil* ^e 7 Or *work, / he fills all mortals with fear by his power*

¹⁰The breath of God produces ice,
    and the broad waters become frozen.
¹¹He loads the clouds with moisture;
    he scatters his lightning through them.
¹²At his direction they swirl around
    over the face of the whole earth
    to do whatever he commands them.
¹³He brings the clouds to punish people,
    or to water his earth and show his love.

¹⁴"Listen to this, Job;
    stop and consider God's wonders.
¹⁵Do you know how God controls the clouds
    and makes his lightning flash?
¹⁶Do you know how the clouds hang poised,
    those wonders of him who has perfect knowledge?
¹⁷You who swelter in your clothes
    when the land lies hushed under the south wind,
¹⁸can you join him in spreading out the skies,
    hard as a mirror of cast bronze?

¹⁹"Tell us what we should say to him;
    we cannot draw up our case because of our darkness.
²⁰Should he be told that I want to speak?
    Would anyone ask to be swallowed up?
²¹Now no one can look at the sun,
    bright as it is in the skies
    after the wind has swept them clean.
²²Out of the north he comes in golden splendor;
    God comes in awesome majesty.
²³The Almighty is beyond our reach and exalted in power;
    in his justice and great righteousness, he does not oppress.
²⁴Therefore, people revere him,
    for does he not have regard for all the wise in heart?^a"

691

---

^a 24 Or for he does not have regard for any who think they are wise.

 HE IS: awesome

37:22–23 When Elihu described God as one who comes in golden splendor, he drew Job's attention away from his dismal circumstances and toward the *awesome* majesty of God. Sometimes we need a change in perspective—to take our eyes off ourselves and put them on our awesome God and his creation.

If you're going through a dark time or you've lost your joy in living, look for God's golden splendor. You can see evidence in the sun, the sky, the intricacy of creation. God's glory is even more awesome than what you are able to see! Experiencing God's creation can change your perspective on the *awesome* Creator (see Romans 1:20).

For the next He Is, go to p. 696.

The Lord Speaks

38 Then the Lord spoke to Job out of the storm. He said:

> ²"Who is this that obscures my plans
>   with words without knowledge?
> ³Prepare to defend yourself;
>   I will question you,
>   and you shall answer me.

> ⁴"Where were you when I laid the earth's foundation?
>   Tell me, if you understand.
> ⁵Who marked off its dimensions? Surely you know!
>   Who stretched a measuring line across it?
> ⁶On what were its footings set,
>   or who laid its cornerstone—
> ⁷while the morning stars sang together
>   and all the angels*a* shouted for joy?

> ⁸"Who shut up the sea behind doors
>   when it burst forth from the womb,
> ⁹when I made the clouds its garment
>   and wrapped it in thick darkness,
> ¹⁰when I fixed limits for it
>   and set its doors and bars in place,
> ¹¹when I said, 'This far you may come and no farther;
>   here is where your proud waves halt'?

> ¹²"Have you ever given orders to the morning,
>   or shown the dawn its place,
> ¹³that it might take the earth by the edges
>   and shake the wicked out of it?
> ¹⁴The earth takes shape like clay under a seal;
>   its features stand out like those of a garment.
> ¹⁵The wicked are denied their light,
>   and their upraised arm is broken.

> ¹⁶"Have you journeyed to the springs of the sea
>   or walked in the recesses of the deep?
> ¹⁷Have the gates of death been shown to you?
>   Have you seen the gates of the deepest darkness?
> ¹⁸Have you comprehended the vast expanses of the earth?
>   Tell me, if you know all this.

> ¹⁹"What is the way to the abode of light?
>   And where does darkness reside?
> ²⁰Can you take them to their places?
>   Do you know the paths to their dwellings?
> ²¹Surely you know, for you were already born!
>   You have lived so many years!

> ²²"Have you entered the storehouses of the snow
>   or seen the storehouses of the hail,
> ²³which I reserve for times of trouble,

---

a 7 Hebrew *the sons of God*

for days of war and battle?
²⁴What is the way to the place where the lightning is dispersed,
  or the place where the east winds are scattered over the earth?
²⁵Who cuts a channel for the torrents of rain,
  and a path for the thunderstorm,
²⁶to water a land where no one lives,
  an uninhabited desert,
²⁷to satisfy a desolate wasteland
  and make it sprout with grass?
²⁸Does the rain have a father?
  Who fathers the drops of dew?
²⁹From whose womb comes the ice?
  Who gives birth to the frost from the heavens
³⁰when the waters become hard as stone,
  when the surface of the deep is frozen?

³¹"Can you bind the chains^a of the Pleiades?
  Can you loosen Orion's belt?
³²Can you bring forth the constellations in their seasons^b
  or lead out the Bear^c with its cubs?
³³Do you know the laws of the heavens?
  Can you set up ⌞God's^d⌟ dominion over the earth?

³⁴"Can you raise your voice to the clouds
  and cover yourself with a flood of water?
³⁵Do you send the lightning bolts on their way?
  Do they report to you, 'Here we are'?
³⁶Who gives the ibis wisdom ⌞about the flooding of the Nile⌟,
  or gives the rooster understanding ⌞of when to crow⌟?^e
³⁷Who has the wisdom to count the clouds?
  Who can tip over the water jars of the heavens
³⁸when the dust becomes hard
  and the clods of earth stick together?

³⁹"Do you hunt the prey for the lioness
  and satisfy the hunger of the lions
⁴⁰when they crouch in their dens
  or lie in wait in a thicket?
⁴¹Who provides food for the raven
  when its young cry out to God
  and wander about for lack of food?

39

"Do you know when the mountain goats give birth?
  Do you watch when the doe bears her fawn?
²Do you count the months till they bear?
  Do you know the time they give birth?
³They crouch down and bring forth their young;
  their labor pains are ended.
⁴Their young thrive and grow strong in the wilds;
  they leave and do not return.

⁵"Who let the wild donkey go free?
  Who untied its ropes?

---

^a 31 Septuagint; Hebrew beauty   ^b 32 Or the morning star in its season   ^c 32 Or out Leo   ^d 33 Or his; or their   ^e 36 The meaning of the Hebrew for this verse is uncertain.

⁶I gave it the wasteland as its home,
  the salt flats as its habitat.
⁷It laughs at the commotion in the town;
  it does not hear a driver's shout.
⁸It ranges the hills for its pasture
  and searches for any green thing.

⁹"Will the wild ox consent to serve you?
  Will it stay by your manger at night?
¹⁰Can you hold it to the furrow with a harness?
  Will it till the valleys behind you?
¹¹Will you rely on it for its great strength?
  Will you leave your heavy work to it?
¹²Can you trust it to haul in your grain
  and bring it to your threshing floor?

¹³"The wings of the ostrich flap joyfully,
  though they cannot compare
  with the wings and feathers of the stork.
¹⁴She lays her eggs on the ground
  and lets them warm in the sand,
¹⁵unmindful that a foot may crush them,
  that some wild animal may trample them.
¹⁶She treats her young harshly, as if they were not hers;
  she cares not that her labor was in vain,
¹⁷for God did not endow her with wisdom
  or give her a share of good sense.
¹⁸Yet when she spreads her feathers to run,
  she laughs at horse and rider.

¹⁹"Do you give the horse its strength
  or clothe its neck with a flowing mane?
²⁰Do you make it leap like a locust,
  striking terror with its proud snorting?
²¹It paws fiercely, rejoicing in its strength,
  and charges into the fray.
²²It laughs at fear, afraid of nothing;
  it does not shy away from the sword.
²³The quiver rattles against its side,
  along with the flashing spear and lance.
²⁴In frenzied excitement it eats up the ground;
  it cannot stand still when the trumpet sounds.
²⁵At the blast of the trumpet it snorts, 'Aha!'
  It catches the scent of battle from afar,
  the shout of commanders and the battle cry.

²⁶"Does the hawk take flight by your wisdom
  and spread its wings toward the south?
²⁷Does the eagle soar at your command
  and build its nest on high?
²⁸It dwells on a cliff and stays there at night;
  a rocky crag is its stronghold.
²⁹From there it looks for food;

its eyes detect it from afar.
³⁰Its young ones feast on blood,
  and where the slain are, there it is."

40 The LORD said to Job:

²"Will the one who contends with the Almighty correct him?
  Let him who accuses God answer him!"

³Then Job answered the LORD:

⁴"I am unworthy—how can I reply to you?
  I put my hand over my mouth.
⁵I spoke once, but I have no answer—
  twice, but I will say no more."

⁶Then the LORD spoke to Job out of the storm:

⁷"Prepare to defend yourself;
  I will question you,
  and you shall answer me.

⁸"Would you discredit my justice?
  Would you condemn me to justify
    yourself?
⁹Do you have an arm like God's,
  and can your voice thunder like his?
¹⁰Then adorn yourself with glory and
    splendor,
  and clothe yourself in honor and
    majesty.
¹¹Unleash the fury of your wrath,
  look at all who are proud and bring
    them low,
¹²look at all who are proud and humble
    them,
  crush the wicked where they stand.
¹³Bury them all in the dust together;
  shroud their faces in the grave.
¹⁴Then I myself will admit to you
  that your own right hand can save you.

¹⁵"Look at the behemoth,ᵃ
  which I made along with you
  and which feeds on grass like an ox.
¹⁶What strength it has in its loins,
  what power in the muscles of its belly!
¹⁷Its tail sways like a cedar;
  the sinews of its thighs are close-knit.
¹⁸Its bones are tubes of bronze,
  its limbs like rods of iron.
¹⁹It ranks first among the works of God,
  yet its Maker can approach it with his sword.

atissue:dealing with sin

40:3–5 When confronted with your sin, what do you do? Do you make excuses, try to shift blame or attempt to justify your actions? *I couldn't help myself. I had PMS, my boss threatened to fire me for no reason and my mother called and nagged me for a full hour. It's no wonder I lost it, and anyway, it's really not that big a deal.* Right? Wrong. Job demonstrated the only right response to sin: "Lord, you're right. I was wrong. I'm so sorry." The only way to know the freedom of forgiveness is to first be willing to confess your sin.

695

ᵃ *15* Possibly the hippopotamus or the elephant

²⁰The hills bring it their produce,
 and all the wild animals play nearby.
²¹Under the lotus plants it lies,
 hidden among the reeds in the marsh.
²²The lotuses conceal it in their shadow;
 the poplars by the stream surround it.
²³A raging river does not alarm it;
 it is secure, though the Jordan should surge against its mouth.
²⁴Can anyone capture it by the eyes,
 or trap it and pierce its nose?

41

* "Can you pull in the leviathan*ᵃ* with a fishhook
 or tie down its tongue with a rope?
²Can you put a cord through its nose
 or pierce its jaw with a hook?
³Will it keep begging you for mercy?
 Will it speak to you with gentle words?
⁴Will it make an agreement with you
 for you to take it as your slave for life?
⁵Can you make a pet of it like a bird
 or put it on a leash for the young women in your house?
⁶Will traders barter for it?
 Will they divide it up among the merchants?
⁷Can you fill its hide with harpoons
 or its head with fishing spears?
⁸If you lay a hand on it,
 you will remember the struggle and never do it again!
*⁹Any hope of subduing it is false;
 the mere sight of it is overpowering.
¹⁰No one is fierce enough to rouse it.
 Who then is able to stand against me?
¹¹Who has a claim against me that I must pay?
 Everything under heaven belongs to me.

¹²"I will not fail to speak of Leviathan's limbs,
 its strength and its graceful form.

ᵃ 1 Possibly the crocodile
* 41:1-8 is numbered 40:25-32 in Hebrew texts.   * 41:9-34 is numbered 41:1-26 in Hebrew texts.

HE IS: owner

41:11 God reminded Job of an important truth: Everything belongs to him. Humans talk about God, question God and even try to act like God, but at the end of the day, there is only one God. He made everything, holds everything together and owns everything.

Have you been guilty of thinking that you are the ruler of your domain? Maybe it's time to acknowledge that everything belongs to God. When you realize that he is *owner*, it can take a great burden off your shoulders—you can stop acting like God and, instead, live like you belong to God.

For the next He Is, go to p. 723.

ASKmeanyTHING

Ruth 1–4

Tell us about your situation.

As you know, I lost my husband, Elimelek, while we were living in Moab. At that time, being a widow was one of the lowest circumstances a woman could find herself in. I had to rely on my relatives and the generosity of others. And being a widow in a *foreign* country, where the people didn't believe in God or follow his laws, was even worse.

Later, both my sons died. Now I had no means of support other than my two daughters-in-law—and they were widows too!

What did you do?

My only option was to make the long journey home to Judah. I heard that the famine was over, and if I had any hope at all, it was among my own people. At first, my daughters-in-law set out with me. But I couldn't make them leave their home. I didn't have any hope, so what hope could I offer them—foreigners, Moabites!—among Israelites? Their best chance of survival was with their own people, so I urged them to go back to their own families.

697

Where was God in all of this?

I'm afraid I was so angry about my circumstances that all I could see was how much God was against me. In fact, when we first arrived back in Bethlehem, no one even recognized me because my bitterness had altered me so much. I told people to call me "Mara" because the Lord had made my life bitter. I left Bethlehem with a husband and two sons and returned with nothing. Why shouldn't I be bitter?

What changed your attitude?

Ruth. My daughter-in-law was so kind, so loving. Even when I couldn't think for myself, she was looking for ways to support us, even if it meant picking up the leftover grain in the field. She was completely devoted to me and to God. Somehow she was able to overcome every obstacle—the fact that she was poor, a widow, and a foreigner in a strange country with people she did not know. God blessed her faithfulness, and in turn, he blessed me. Through Ruth, I realized that God had not forgotten me and had not stopped loving me.

Any words of advice?

When life looks bleakest, God is there. When you can't see him, and you feel he must have deserted you, he's still there. God is faithful to his promises. He will never leave you. He knows what you are going through and will get you to the other side. Believe it. Cling to it, and don't let bitterness drive you from the one who can help.

FOR MORE INSIGHT

For more on God's faithfulness, read Psalm 146; Lamentations 3:22–23; and Hebrews 10:23.

¹³Who can strip off its outer coat?
  Who can penetrate its double coat of armor?^a
¹⁴Who dares open the doors of its mouth,
  ringed about with fearsome teeth?
¹⁵Its back has^b rows of shields
  tightly sealed together;
¹⁶each is so close to the next
  that no air can pass between.
¹⁷They are joined fast to one another;
  they cling together and cannot be parted.
¹⁸Its snorting throws out flashes of light;
  its eyes are like the rays of dawn.
¹⁹Flames stream from its mouth;
  sparks of fire shoot out.
²⁰Smoke pours from its nostrils
  as from a boiling pot over burning reeds.
²¹Its breath sets coals ablaze,
  and flames dart from its mouth.
²²Strength resides in its neck;
  dismay goes before it.
²³The folds of its flesh are tightly joined;
  they are firm and immovable.
²⁴Its chest is hard as rock,
  hard as a lower millstone.
²⁵When it rises up, the mighty are terrified;
  they retreat before its thrashing.
²⁶The sword that reaches it has no effect,
  nor does the spear or the dart or the javelin.
²⁷Iron it treats like straw
  and bronze like rotten wood.
²⁸Arrows do not make it flee;
  slingstones are like chaff to it.
²⁹A club seems to it but a piece of straw;
  it laughs at the rattling of the lance.
³⁰Its undersides are jagged potsherds,
  leaving a trail in the mud like a threshing sledge.
³¹It makes the depths churn like a boiling caldron
  and stirs up the sea like a pot of ointment.
³²It leaves a glistening wake behind it;
  one would think the deep had white hair.
³³Nothing on earth is its equal—
  a creature without fear.
³⁴It looks down on all that are haughty;
  it is king over all that are proud."

Job
42 Then Job replied to the LORD:

²"I know that you can do all things;
  no purpose of yours can be thwarted.

---
^a *13 Septuagint; Hebrew double bridle* ^b *15 Or Its pride is its*

³You asked, 'Who is this that obscures my plans without knowledge?'
Surely I spoke of things I did not understand,
things too wonderful for me to know.

⁴"You said, 'Listen now, and I will speak;
I will question you,
and you shall answer me.'
⁵My ears had heard of you
but now my eyes have seen you.
⁶Therefore I despise myself
and repent in dust and ashes."

Epilogue

⁷After the LORD had said these things to Job, he said to Eliphaz the Temanite, "I am angry with you and your two friends, because you have not spoken of me what is right, as my servant Job has. ⁸So now take seven bulls and seven rams and go to my servant Job and sacrifice a burnt offering for yourselves. My servant Job will pray for you, and I will accept his prayer and not deal with you according to your folly. You have not spoken of me what is right, as my servant Job has." ⁹So Eliphaz the Temanite, Bildad the Shuhite and Zophar the Naamathite did what the LORD told them; and the LORD accepted Job's prayer.

¹⁰After Job had prayed for his friends, the LORD restored his fortunes and gave him twice as much as he had before. ¹¹All his brothers and sisters and everyone who had known him before came and ate with him in his house. They comforted and consoled him over all the trouble the LORD had brought on him, and each one gave him a piece of silver^a and a gold ring.

¹²The LORD blessed the latter part of Job's life more than the former part. He had fourteen thousand sheep, six thousand camels, a thousand yoke of oxen and a thousand donkeys. ¹³And he also had seven sons and three daughters. ¹⁴The first daughter he named Jemimah, the second Keziah and the third Keren-Happuch. ¹⁵Nowhere in all the land were there found women as beautiful as Job's daughters, and their father granted them an inheritance along with their brothers.

¹⁶After this, Job lived a hundred and forty years; he saw his children and their children to the fourth generation. ¹⁷And so he died, old and full of years.

conversations

friendship «» 42:7–9

1 » How should you react when a friend hurts you?

2 » In what ways can friends lead you toward God? Away from God?

3 » Which of your friends desperately needs your prayers today?

For more on **friendship**, check the index.
For the next Conversations, go to p. 706.

699

---

^a 11 Hebrew *him a kesitah*; a kesitah was a unit of money of unknown weight and value.

psalms

700

AUTHOR
David, Asaph, the sons of Korah, Solomon,
Heman, Ethan and Moses.

AUDIENCE
All Israel.

DATE
Written between the time of Moses (about
1440 B.C.) and the time following the
Babylonian captivity (after 538 B.C.).

SETTING
Picture a passionate worship service in
God's temple with God's people.

VERSE TO REMEMBER
"Let me live that I may praise you,
 and may your laws sustain me." (119:175)

THEME TO CONSIDER
Sharing our hearts with God leads us to a
deeper relationship with him.

BOOK I

Psalms 1–41

Psalm 1

¹Blessed are those
    who do not walk in step with the wicked
or stand in the way that sinners take
    or sit in the company of mockers,
²but who delight in the law of the Lord
    and meditate on his law day and night.
³They are like a tree planted by streams of
       water,
    which yields its fruit in season
and whose leaf does not wither—
    whatever they do prospers.

⁴Not so the wicked!
    They are like chaff
    that the wind blows away.
⁵Therefore the wicked will not stand in the
       judgment,
    nor sinners in the assembly of the
       righteous.

⁶For the Lord watches over the way of the
       righteous,
    but the way of the wicked will be
       destroyed.

Psalm 2

¹Why do the nations conspire[a]
    and the peoples plot in vain?
²The kings of the earth rise up
    and the rulers band together
    against the Lord and against his anointed, saying,
³"Let us break their chains
    and throw off their shackles."

⁴The One enthroned in heaven laughs;
    the Lord scoffs at them.
⁵He rebukes them in his anger
    and terrifies them in his wrath, saying,
⁶"I have installed my king
    on Zion, my holy mountain."

⁷I will proclaim the Lord's decree:

    He said to me, "You are my son;
       today I have become your father.
⁸Ask me,
    and I will make the nations your inheritance,
    the ends of the earth your possession.

---

atissue: God's Word

1:1–3 Without strong roots, a tree won't grow and produce fruit. Deep roots are a source of sustenance and an anchor in storms. You need to be strongly rooted in God for the same reasons. So, how do you develop roots? Absorb God's Word daily. As life gets busier, this may require creativity. During your child's soccer practice, memorize Bible verses you keep on cards in your purse. Use your lunch hour to read your Bible. Listen to the Bible on CD while you drive. Look for every opportunity to soak up God's truth and send down those roots.

701

ᵃ *1* Hebrew; Septuagint *rage*

myth# 45 "I HAVE TO DO WHATEVER MY COMPANY ASKS."

Call me compliant. I have always been one of those people who does what I'm told. My parents taught me not to question authority. Teacher's pet. A/B honor roll. Perfect attendance in church. That was me.

For most of my adult life, especially in my career, a follower's strategy has served me well. My supervisors have shown their appreciation through regular raises and promotions. I am happy to say that others know me as someone who does her job well and does it without rocking the boat. That is, until yesterday.

Yesterday my manager came into my office and quietly shut the door behind her. It was Friday afternoon and I panicked. I was terrified that I was getting fired. "What is it?" I stammered.

Her voice was stern. "I have something very important to ask you. This could potentially affect your career."

As I listened to her carefully worded speech, I realized that she was asking me to lie about some information regarding one of our accounts. I got the idea she wanted me to cover for her and some of the other "higher-ups" in accounting by overlooking some slightly inflated figures on the next quarterly report. If I complied, she made it clear that they would reward me for my loyalty.

At first I was shocked. I didn't know how to respond. Luckily, someone knocked on the door, cutting short our conversation so that I didn't have to answer her right away.

What am I going to do? Do I lie for my boss and have that indiscretion on my conscience? I mean, it's not really lying. All I have to do is not notice a few numbers that are off. Or do I correct the numbers and risk losing my job and seriously damaging my career? There is no way I can take a middle ground on this issue. I am going to have to make a choice.

—Melia

MANY OF THE ethical dilemmas we face seem complex at first glance. We don't know what to do! However, the issues often come down to some basic questions we must answer.

- *Is what you're being asked to do contradictory to Scripture or godly principles?* While God's Word tells us that we are to obey authority and submit to our earthly masters (1 Peter 2:13–14), that principle doesn't apply when we are asked to do anything that contradicts God's Word and ways.

- *Will you honor and obey God, your ultimate authority, or someone else?* There may be times when we must go against an earthly authority in order to obey God and risk losing our job, status, reputation or friends.

- *Would you rather suffer now for what's right or suffer later for doing wrong?* The Bible teaches us that we may have to suffer for what is right. At times, God may call you to take a stand for truth, even though others are asking you to compromise.

- *Will you find favor with God for whatever you're being asked to do?* God emphasizes that we will find favor with *him* if we obey him. Wouldn't you rather have God's blessings than the favor of others, who may turn on you at any moment?

Jesus' disciples were ordered to stop preaching about him, but they decided to obey God rather than other people (Acts 5:29–32,40–42). You may be asked to make hard decisions as well. You have to decide if any job or working relationship is worth sacrificing your integrity and obedience to God.

Deep down you know what's right . . . but are you willing to pay that price?

"Our lives begin to end the day we become silent about things that matter."

—Martin Luther King, Jr.

 703

"BUT HOW IS IT TO YOUR CREDIT IF YOU RECEIVE A BEATING FOR DOING WRONG AND ENDURE IT? BUT IF YOU SUFFER FOR DOING GOOD AND YOU ENDURE IT, THIS IS COMMENDABLE BEFORE GOD."

1 PETER 2:20

SEE ALSO
Psalm 1:1–3
John 15:18—6:4
Acts 5:27–32,40–42
1 Peter 4:12–19

For more on **Lying**, check the index.

704

⁹You will break them with a rod of iron*ᵃ*;
  you will dash them to pieces like pottery."

¹⁰Therefore, you kings, be wise;
  be warned, you rulers of the earth.
¹¹Serve the LORD with fear
  and celebrate his rule with trembling.
¹²Kiss his son, or he will be angry
  and you and your ways will be destroyed,
for his wrath can flare up in a moment.
  Blessed are all who take refuge in him.

Psalm 3

A psalm of David. When he fled from his son Absalom.

* ¹LORD, how many are my foes!
  How many rise up against me!
²Many are saying of me,
  "God will not deliver him."*ᵇ*

³But you, LORD, are a shield around me,
  my glory, the one who lifts my head
    high.
⁴I call out to the LORD,
  and he answers me from his holy
    mountain.

⁵I lie down and sleep;
  I wake again, because the LORD
    sustains me.
⁶I will not fear though tens of thousands
  assail me on every side.

⁷Arise, LORD!
  Deliver me, my God!
Strike all my enemies on the jaw;
  break the teeth of the wicked.

⁸From the LORD comes deliverance.
  May your blessing be on your people.

Psalm 4

For the director of music. With stringed instruments. A psalm of David.

* ¹Answer me when I call to you,
  my righteous God.
Give me relief from my distress;
  have mercy on me and hear my prayer.

²How long will you men turn my glory into shame?
  How long will you love delusions and seek false gods*ᶜ*?*ᵈ*
³Know that the LORD has set apart his faithful servant for himself;
  the LORD hears when I call to him.

---

atissue:abuse

3:3–4 He said you were worthless. He said you deserved everything he dished out. He said no one would believe you or take your side. Maybe he's still saying it. Whether he's your father, husband, boyfriend or boss—whoever he is—he's wrong. Listen to what God says. He knows the truth. He's on your side. He gives you his glory and says that makes you precious and valuable. He lifts up your head and tells you to look down to no one because of who you are in him. Won't you start listening to God instead?

ᵃ 9 Or will rule them with an iron scepter (see Septuagint and Syriac)   *ᵇ 2 The Hebrew has Selah (a word of uncertain meaning) here and at the end of verses 4 and 8.*   *ᶜ 2 Or seek lies*   *ᵈ 2 The Hebrew has Selah (a word of uncertain meaning) here and at the end of verse 4.*
* 3:1-8 is numbered 3:2-9 in Hebrew texts.   * 4:1-8 is numbered 4:2-9 in Hebrew texts.

⁴Tremble and^a do not sin;
    when you are on your beds,
    search your hearts and be silent.
⁵Offer the sacrifices of the righteous
    and trust in the Lord.

⁶Many, Lord, are asking, "Who will bring us prosperity?"
    Let the light of your face shine on us.
⁷Fill my heart with joy
    when their grain and new wine abound.

⁸In peace I will lie down and sleep,
    for you alone, Lord,
    make me dwell in safety.

Psalm 5

For the director of music. For pipes. A psalm of David.

* ¹Listen to my words, Lord,
    consider my lament.
²Hear my cry for help,
    my King and my God,
    for to you I pray.

³In the morning, Lord, you hear my voice;
    in the morning I lay my requests before you
    and wait expectantly.
⁴For you are not a God who is pleased with wickedness;
    with you, evil people are not welcome.
⁵The arrogant cannot stand
    in your presence.
You hate all who do wrong;
⁶   you destroy those who tell lies.
The bloodthirsty and deceitful
    you, Lord, detest.
⁷But I, by your great love,
    can come into your house;
in reverence I bow down
    toward your holy temple.

⁸Lead me, Lord, in your righteousness
    because of my enemies—
    make your way straight before me.
⁹Not a word from their mouth can be trusted;
    their heart is filled with malice.
Their throat is an open grave;
    with their tongues they tell lies.
¹⁰Declare them guilty, O God!
    Let their intrigues be their downfall.
Banish them for their many sins,
    for they have rebelled against you.
¹¹But let all who take refuge in you be glad;

705

let them ever sing for joy.
Spread your protection over them,
that those who love your name may rejoice in you.

[12] Surely, LORD, you bless the righteous;
you surround them with your favor as with a shield.

Psalm 6

For the director of music. With stringed instruments.
According to sheminith.[a] A psalm of David.

* [1] LORD, do not rebuke me in your anger
or discipline me in your wrath.
[2] Have mercy on me, LORD, for I am faint;
heal me, LORD, for my bones are in agony.
[3] My soul is in deep anguish.
How long, LORD, how long?

[4] Turn, LORD, and deliver me;
save me because of your
unfailing love.
[5] Among the dead no one
proclaims your name.
Who praises you from the
grave?

[6] I am worn out from my
groaning.

All night long I flood my bed
with weeping
and drench my couch with
tears.
[7] My eyes grow weak with sorrow;
they fail because of all my foes.

[8] Away from me, all you who do evil,
for the LORD has heard my weeping.
[9] The LORD has heard my cry for mercy;
the LORD accepts my prayer.
[10] All my enemies will be overwhelmed with shame and anguish;
they will turn back and suddenly be put to shame.

conversations

despair «» 6:1–10

1 Have you ever gotten to a point where you felt despair? What was going on in your life?

2 When you feel like you're drowning in problems, what can you do?

3 What can keep you from getting to the point of despair?

For more on **despair**, check the index.
For the next Conversations, go to p. 712.

Psalm 7

A shiggaion[b] of David, which he sang to the LORD concerning Cush, a Benjamite.

* [1] LORD my God, I take refuge in you;
save and deliver me from all who pursue me,
[2] or they will tear me apart like a lion
and rip me to pieces with no one to rescue me.

[3] LORD my God, if I have done this
and there is guilt on my hands—
[4] if I have repaid my ally with evil

[a] Title: Probably a musical term   [b] Title: Probably a literary or musical term
* 6:1-10 is numbered 6:2-11 in Hebrew texts.   * 7:1-17 is numbered 7:2-18 in Hebrew texts.
706

or without cause have robbed my foe—
⁵then let my enemy pursue and overtake me;
    let him trample my life to the ground
    and make me sleep in the dust.ᵃ

⁶Arise, LORD, in your anger;
    rise up against the rage of my enemies.
    Awake, my God; decree justice.
⁷Let the assembled peoples gather around you,
    while you sit enthroned over them on high.
⁸   Let the LORD judge the peoples.
 Vindicate me, LORD, according to my righteousness,
    according to my integrity, O Most High.
⁹Bring to an end the violence of the wicked
    and make the righteous secure—
 you, the righteous God
    who probes minds and hearts.

¹⁰My shieldᵇ is God Most High,
    who saves the upright in heart.
¹¹God is a righteous judge,
    a God who displays his wrath every day.
¹²If he does not relent,
    heᶜ will sharpen his sword;
    he will bend and string his bow.
¹³He has prepared his deadly weapons;
    he makes ready his flaming arrows.

¹⁴Those who are pregnant with evil
    conceive trouble and give birth to disillusionment.
¹⁵Those who dig a hole and scoop it out
    fall into the pit they have made.
¹⁶The trouble they cause recoils on them;
    their violence comes down on their own heads.

¹⁷I will give thanks to the LORD because of his righteousness;
    I will sing the praises of the name of the LORD Most High.

Psalm 8

For the director of music. According to gittith.ᵈ *A psalm of David.*
* ¹LORD, our Lord,
    how majestic is your name in all the earth!

 You have set your glory
    above the heavens.
²Through the praise of children and infants
    you have established a stronghold against your enemies,
    to silence the foe and the avenger.
³When I consider your heavens,
    the work of your fingers,
    the moon and the stars,

which you have set in place,
[4] what are mere mortals that you are mindful of them,
human beings that you care for them?[a]

[5] You have made them[b] a little lower than the heavenly beings[c]
and crowned them[b] with glory and honor.
[6] You made them rulers over the works of your hands;
you put everything under their[d] feet:
[7] all flocks and herds,
and the animals of the wild,
[8] the birds in the sky,
and the fish in the sea,
all that swim the paths of the seas.

[9] Lord, our Lord,
how majestic is your name in all the earth!

Psalm 9[e]

For the director of music. To the tune of "The Death of the Son." A psalm of David.

* [1] I will praise you, Lord, with all my heart;
I will tell of all your wonderful deeds.
[2] I will be glad and rejoice in you;
I will sing the praises of your name, O Most High.

[3] My enemies turn back;
they stumble and perish before you.
[4] For you have upheld my right and my cause,
sitting enthroned as the righteous judge.
[5] You have rebuked the nations and destroyed the wicked;
you have blotted out their name for ever and ever.
[6] Endless ruin has overtaken my enemies,
you have uprooted their cities;
even the memory of them has perished.

[7] The Lord reigns forever;
he has established his throne for judgment.
[8] He rules the world in righteousness
and judges the peoples with equity.
[9] The Lord is a refuge for the oppressed,
a stronghold in times of trouble.
[10] Those who know your name trust in you,
for you, Lord, have never forsaken those who seek you.

[11] Sing the praises of the Lord, enthroned in Zion;
proclaim among the nations what he has done.
[12] For he who avenges blood remembers;
he does not ignore the cries of the afflicted.

[13] Lord, see how my enemies persecute me!
Have mercy and lift me up from the gates of death,
[14] that I may declare your praises

---

[a] *4* Or *what is a human being that you are mindful of him, / a son of man that you care for him?*   [b] *5* Or *him*   [c] *5* Or *than God*   [d] *6* Or *made him ruler . . . ; / . . . his*   [e] Psalms *9* and *10* may originally have been a single acrostic poem in which alternating lines began with the successive letters of the Hebrew alphabet. In the Septuagint they constitute one psalm.

* 9:1-20 is numbered 9:2-21 in Hebrew texts.

in the gates of Daughter Zion,
    and there rejoice in your salvation.

¹⁵The nations have fallen into the pit they have dug;
    their feet are caught in the net they have hidden.
¹⁶The Lord is known by his acts of justice;
    the wicked are ensnared by the work of their hands.ᵃ
¹⁷The wicked go down to the realm of the dead,
    all the nations that forget God.
¹⁸But God will never forget the needy;
    the hope of the afflicted will never perish.

¹⁹Arise, Lord, do not let mortals triumph;
    let the nations be judged in your presence.
²⁰Strike them with terror, Lord;
    let the nations know they are only mortals.

Psalm 10ᵇ

¹Why, Lord, do you stand far off?
    Why do you hide yourself in times of trouble?

²In their arrogance the wicked hunt down the weak,
    catching them in the schemes they devise.
³They boast about the cravings of their hearts;
    they bless the greedy and revile the Lord.
⁴In their pride the wicked do not seek him;
    in all their thoughts there is no room for God.
⁵Their ways are always prosperous;
    your laws are rejected byᶜ them;
    they sneer at all their enemies.
⁶They say to themselves, "Nothing will ever shake us."
    They swear, "No one will ever do us harm."

⁷Their mouths are full of lies and threats;
    trouble and evil are under their tongues.
⁸They lie in wait near the villages;
    from ambush they murder the innocent.
    Their eyes watch in secret for their victims;
⁹   like a lion in cover they lie in wait.
    They lie in wait to catch the helpless;
    they catch the helpless and drag them off in their nets.
¹⁰The innocent are crushed, they collapse;
    they fall victim to superior strength.
¹¹The wicked say to themselves, "God will never notice;
    he covers his face and never sees."

¹²Arise, Lord! Lift up your hand, O God.
    Do not forget the helpless.
¹³Why do the wicked revile God?
    Why do they say to themselves,
    "He won't call us to account"?
¹⁴But you, God, see the trouble of the afflicted;

709

ᵃ *16* The Hebrew has *Higgaion* and *Selah* (words of uncertain meaning) here; *Selah* occurs also at the end of verse 20.   ᵇ Psalms *9* and *10* may originally have been a single acrostic poem in which alternating lines began with the successive letters of the Hebrew alphabet. In the Septuagint they constitute one psalm.
ᶜ *5* See Septuagint; Hebrew / they are haughty, and your laws are far from

you consider their grief and take it in hand.
The victims commit themselves to you;
 you are the helper of the fatherless.
[15]Break the arms of the wicked and the evildoers;
 call them to account for their wickedness
 that would not otherwise be found out.

[16]The Lord is King for ever and ever;
 the nations will perish from his land.
[17]You, Lord, hear the desire of the afflicted;
 you encourage them, and you listen to their cry,
[18]defending the fatherless and the oppressed,
 so that mere earthly mortals
 will never again strike terror.

Psalm 11

For the director of music. Of David.

[1]In the Lord I take refuge.
 How then can you say to me:
 "Flee like a bird to your mountain.
[2]For look, the wicked bend their bows;
 they set their arrows against the strings
to shoot from the shadows
 at the upright in heart.
[3]When the foundations are being destroyed,
 what can the righteous do?"

[4]The Lord is in his holy temple;
 the Lord is on his heavenly throne.
He observes everyone on earth;
 his eyes examine them.
[5]The Lord examines the righteous,
 but the wicked, those who love violence,
 he hates with a passion.
[6]On the wicked he will rain
 fiery coals and burning sulfur;
 a scorching wind will be their lot.

[7]For the Lord is righteous,
 he loves justice;
 the upright will see his face.

Psalm 12

For the director of music. According to sheminith.*[a] A psalm of David.*

* [1]Help, Lord, for no one is faithful anymore;
 those who are loyal have vanished from the human race.
[2]Everyone lies to their neighbor;
 they flatter with their lips
 but harbor deception in their hearts.

---

a Title: Probably a musical term

* 12:1-8 is numbered 12:2-9 in Hebrew texts.

³May the LORD silence all flattering lips
  and every boastful tongue—
⁴those who say,
  "By our tongues we will prevail;
  our own lips will defend us—who is lord over us?"

⁵"Because the poor are plundered and the needy groan,
  I will now arise," says the LORD.
  "I will protect them from those who malign them."
⁶And the words of the LORD are flawless,
  like silver purified in a crucible,
  like gold*ᵃ* refined seven times.

⁷You, LORD, will keep the needy safe
  and will protect us forever from the wicked,
⁸who freely strut about
  while depravity is honored by the human race.

Psalm 13

For the director of music. A psalm of David.

* ¹How long, LORD? Will you forget me
      forever?
  How long will you hide your face from
      me?
²How long must I wrestle with my thoughts
  and day after day have sorrow in my
      heart?
  How long will my enemy triumph over me?

³Look on me and answer, LORD my God.
  Give light to my eyes, or I will sleep in
      death,
⁴and my enemy will say, "I have overcome
      him,"
  and my foes will rejoice when I fall.

⁵But I trust in your unfailing love;
  my heart rejoices in your salvation.
⁶I will sing the LORD's praise,
  for he has been good to me.

Psalm 14

For the director of music. Of David.

¹Fools*ᵇ* say in their hearts,
  "There is no God."
They are corrupt, their deeds are vile;
  there is no one who does good.

²The LORD looks down from heaven
  on the human race
to see if there are any who understand,
  any who seek God.

711

at issue: depression

13:1–6 Don't you just love David's honesty? He didn't act like he had it all together. He knew God already saw his heart, so he held nothing back. *Then* he chose to cling to the truth. Despite his pain, he trusted in God's unfailing love. Even when life looked bleak, he still praised God. How was he able to maintain that perspective? We're given a clue: David focused on God's *goodness* to him. When you're struggling, share your feelings with God. Then let him remind you of his goodness to you to give you comfort in the midst of your pain.

ᵃ *6* Probable reading of the original Hebrew text; Masoretic Text *earth*   ᵇ *1* The Hebrew words rendered *fool* in Psalms denote one who is morally deficient.

* 13:1-6 is numbered 13:2-6 in Hebrew texts.

³ All have turned away, all have become corrupt;
   there is no one who does good,
   not even one.

⁴ Do all these evildoers know
      nothing?

They devour my people as
      though eating bread;
   they never call on the LORD.
⁵ But there they are,
      overwhelmed with
      dread,
   for God is present in the
      company of the
      righteous.
⁶ You evildoers frustrate the
      plans of the poor,
   but the LORD is their refuge.

"conversations"

atheism «» 14:1

1» What attitudes about life does atheism
   promote?

2» Is God threatened by atheism? Should
   you be? Why?

3» How should you respond to a person who
   holds views such as atheism?

For more on **atheism**, check the index.
For the next Conversations, go to p. 726.

⁷ Oh, that salvation for Israel would come out of Zion!
   When the LORD restores his people,
   let Jacob rejoice and Israel be glad!

Psalm 15

A psalm of David.

¹ LORD, who may dwell in your sanctuary?
   Who may live on your holy mountain?

² Those whose walk is blameless,
   who do what is righteous,
   who speak the truth from their hearts;
³ who have no slander on their tongues,
   who do their neighbors no wrong,
   who cast no slur on others;
⁴ who despise those whose ways are vile
   but honor whoever fears the LORD;
   who keep their oaths even when it hurts;
⁵ who lend money to the poor without interest
   and do not accept bribes against the innocent.

Whoever does these things
   will never be shaken.

Psalm 16

A miktam^a of David.

¹ Keep me safe, my God,
   for in you I take refuge.

² I say to the LORD, "You are my Lord;
   apart from you I have no good thing."
³ I say of the godly who are in the land,
   "They are the noble people

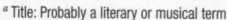

^a Title: Probably a literary or musical term

in whom is all my delight."
⁴Those who run after other gods
    will suffer more and more.
 I will not pour out their libations of blood
    or take up their names on my lips.

⁵Lᴏʀᴅ, you have assigned me my portion and my cup;
    you have made my lot secure.
⁶The boundary lines have fallen for me in pleasant places;
    surely I have a delightful inheritance.

⁷I will praise the Lᴏʀᴅ, who counsels me;
    even at night my heart instructs me.
⁸I keep my eyes always on the Lᴏʀᴅ.
    With him at my right hand, I will not be shaken.

⁹Therefore my heart is glad and my tongue rejoices;
    my body also will rest secure,
¹⁰because you will not abandon me to the realm of the dead,
    nor will you let your faithful*ᵃ* one see decay.
¹¹You make known to me the path of life;
    you will fill me with joy in your presence,
    with eternal pleasures at your right hand.

713

Psalm 17

A prayer of David.

¹Hear me, Lᴏʀᴅ, my plea is just;
    listen to my cry.
Hear my prayer—
    it does not rise from deceitful lips.
²Let my vindication come from you;
    may your eyes see what is right.

³Though you probe my heart,
    though you examine me at night and test me,
you will find that I have planned no evil;
    my mouth has not transgressed.
⁴Though people tried to bribe me,
    I have kept myself from the ways of the violent
    through what your lips have commanded.
⁵My steps have held to your paths;
    my feet have not stumbled.

⁶I call on you, my God, for you will answer me;
    turn your ear to me and hear my prayer.
⁷Show me the wonders of your great love,
    you who save by your right hand
    those who take refuge in you from their foes.
⁸Keep me as the apple of your eye;
    hide me in the shadow of your wings
⁹from the wicked who are out to destroy me,
    from my mortal enemies who surround me.

ᵃ *10* Or *holy*

myth# 46

"SINCE I WASN'T BORN WITH GOOD LOOKS OR A PERFECT BODY, I SHOULD JUST CHANGE THEM."

I love to watch medical fairy tales—the before-and-after TV shows where the miracles of surgery, dentistry and a little cosmetology transform ugly ducklings into beautiful swans. Despite a few unfortunate laps in the wrong gene pool, the man with buckteeth and a bald head becomes the most handsome man in his family. In just a few months, his whole life is radically changed. His wife adores him. His parents are bursting with pride. His teenagers may actually allow him to pick them up in front of the school instead of down the block—they're suddenly proud of old Dad, ready to show off his new looks.

I guess I love those shows so much because I wish that were my story. I certainly wasn't born perfect-looking, and I haven't exactly aged well. A couple of kids, a busy life with no time to exercise and some pretty lousy genetics have left me unhappy with my body (to say the least). Oh, if only I could take a couple of months out of my life in order to reappear with a fabulous new look. I know I would feel so much better about myself.

I realize it sounds shallow, but isn't that how the rest of the world works? If first impressions are everything, then I don't impress anyone. I know my family and friends love me just the way I am. I'm relatively successful at work, and I'm a good mom. But I know I would be so much happier if I could just change my appearance. What would be the harm in that?

—Samantha

ACCORDING TO OUR

culture, anything that's sagging, bulging, gaping or waning needs to be nipped, tucked or sucked to be acceptable. In a society that worships perfection, physical appearance seems to be the most important aspect of our humanity. We just have to turn on the television or leaf through a magazine to see glorified images of perfect-looking people. Beauty and science have joined forces by selling us surgery and serums to change how we look.

Is that so wrong? Well, yes and no.

It's wrong if we become so focused on our externals that we forget that we are created in God's image, that he blessed us and called us "good." God calls us the "apple of [his] eye" (Psalm 17:8). Perhaps for some of us the issue is less physical than it is spiritual. If you're dissatisfied with your appearance, think through the following questions:

- *What are your motives for wanting a change?* Are you trying to earn someone else's acceptance, perhaps even your own? Is your identity wrapped up in how you look? Are you trying to get more attention from men? Have you made beauty a god?

- *Why do those who are closest to you love you?* Is it more important to them that you are a good friend, faithful wife, loving mother and committed worker or that you look beautiful? Could it be that you are the only one who labels yourself "imperfect"?

- *What do your choices about your appearance communicate about your values?* Are you investing your time, energy and money into your physical appearance or into your heart and into God's kingdom?

- *Which is worse: being harshly critical of your appearance or being vain?* What's at the root of both?

If you stumbled through those questions, then perhaps it's your heart that needs an extreme makeover, not your body.

There's nothing wrong with wanting to look your best and taking care of your body *within reason.* On the makeover spectrum that ranges from putting on a little mascara and lip gloss to getting full-body cosmetic surgery, there's no clear-cut line for how much is too much. Examine your own heart to decide whether your beauty comes from "outward adornment, such as elaborate hairstyles and the wearing of gold jewelry and fine clothes" or from "your inner self, the unfading beauty of a gentle and quiet spirit, which is of great worth in God's sight" (1 Peter 3:3–4).

715

"8.7 million Americans received some form of plastic surgery in 2003—a 32 percent increase from 2002."

—American Society of Plastic Surgeons

"CHARM IS DECEPTIVE, AND BEAUTY IS FLEETING; BUT A WOMAN WHO FEARS THE LORD IS TO BE PRAISED."

PROVERBS 31:30

SEE ALSO
1 Samuel 16:7
Matthew 19:21
1 Timothy 2:9–10

For more on **Appearance,**
check the index.

¹⁰They close up their callous hearts,
   and their mouths speak with arrogance.
¹¹They have tracked me down, they now surround me,
   with eyes alert, to throw me to the ground.
¹²They are like a lion hungry for prey,
   like a fierce lion crouching in cover.

¹³Rise up, Lᴏʀᴅ, confront them, bring them down;
   with your sword rescue me from the wicked.
¹⁴By your hand save me from such people, Lᴏʀᴅ,
   from those of this world whose reward is in this life.
May what you have stored up for the wicked fill their bellies;
   may their children gorge themselves on it,
   may there be leftovers for their little ones.

¹⁵As for me, I will be vindicated and will see your face;
   when I awake, I will be satisfied with seeing your likeness.

Psalm 18

For the director of music. Of David the servant of the Lᴏʀᴅ. He sang to the Lᴏʀᴅ
   the words of this song when the Lᴏʀᴅ delivered him from the hand
   of all his enemies and from the hand of Saul. He said:

* ¹I love you, Lᴏʀᴅ, my strength.

²The Lᴏʀᴅ is my rock, my fortress and my deliverer;
   my God is my rock, in whom I take refuge,
   my shield*ᵃ* and the horn*ᵇ* of my salvation, my stronghold.

³I called to the Lᴏʀᴅ, who is worthy of praise,
   and I have been saved from my enemies.
⁴The cords of death entangled me;
   the torrents of destruction overwhelmed me.
⁵The cords of the grave coiled around me;
   the snares of death confronted me.

⁶In my distress I called to the Lᴏʀᴅ;
   I cried to my God for help.
From his temple he heard my voice;
   my cry came before him, into his ears.
⁷The earth trembled and quaked,
   and the foundations of the mountains shook;
   they trembled because he was angry.
⁸Smoke rose from his nostrils;
   consuming fire came from his mouth,
   burning coals blazed out of it.
⁹He parted the heavens and came down;
   dark clouds were under his feet.
¹⁰He mounted the cherubim and flew;
   he soared on the wings of the wind.
¹¹He made darkness his covering, his canopy around him—
   the dark rain clouds of the sky.

ᵃ 2 Or sovereign   *ᵇ 2 Horn here symbolizes strength.*
* 18:1-50 is numbered 18:2-51 in Hebrew texts.

¹²Out of the brightness of his presence clouds advanced,
  with hailstones and bolts of lightning.
¹³The LORD thundered from heaven;
  the voice of the Most High resounded.ᵃ
¹⁴He shot his arrows and scattered the enemy,
  with great bolts of lightning he routed them.
¹⁵The valleys of the sea were exposed
  and the foundations of the earth laid bare
at your rebuke, LORD,
  at the blast of breath from your nostrils.

¹⁶He reached down from on high and took hold of me;
  he drew me out of deep waters.
¹⁷He rescued me from my powerful enemy,
  from my foes, who were too strong for me.
¹⁸They confronted me in the day of my disaster,
  but the LORD was my support.
¹⁹He brought me out into a spacious place;
  he rescued me because he delighted in me.

²⁰The LORD has dealt with me according to my righteousness;
  according to the cleanness of my hands he has rewarded me.
²¹For I have kept the ways of the LORD;
  I am not guilty of turning from my God.
²²All his laws are before me;
  I have not turned away from his decrees.
²³I have been blameless before him
  and have kept myself from sin.
²⁴The LORD has rewarded me according to
    my righteousness,
  according to the cleanness of my hands
    in his sight.

²⁵To the faithful you show yourself faithful,
  to the blameless you show yourself
    blameless,
²⁶to the pure you show yourself pure,
  but to the devious you show yourself
    shrewd.
²⁷You save the humble
  but bring low those whose eyes are
    haughty.
²⁸You, LORD, keep my lamp burning;
  my God turns my darkness into light.
²⁹With your help I can advance against a
    troopᵇ;
  with my God I can scale a wall.

³⁰As for God, his way is perfect:
  The LORD's word is flawless;
  he shields all who take refuge in him.
³¹For who is God besides the LORD?

atissue:exhaustion

18:30–36 Life in general can wear you out. Life with children can be especially tiring—nurse the baby, change diapers, do laundry, go grocery shopping, make meals, wash dishes, drive to practices, discipline and train, play make-believe, read a favorite book, answer a thousand questions . . . how can you fit it all in one day? Do you sometimes dread waking up, knowing you're already behind? Try taking a few minutes each morning to ask God to arm you with strength. He will support you, guide you and encourage you. If you start your day with God, you may find you have more energy to actually enjoy the tasks you have before you.

ᵃ 13 Some Hebrew manuscripts and Septuagint (see also 2 Samuel 22:14); most Hebrew manuscripts resounded, / amid hailstones and bolts of lightning
ᵇ 29 Or can run through a barricade

And who is the Rock except our God?
³²It is God who arms me with strength
    and keeps my way secure.
³³He makes my feet like the feet of a deer;
    he causes me to stand on the heights.
³⁴He trains my hands for battle;
    my arms can bend a bow of bronze.
³⁵You make your saving help my shield,
    and your right hand sustains me;
    your help has made me great.
³⁶You provide a broad path for my feet,
    so that my ankles do not give way.

³⁷I pursued my enemies and overtook them;
    I did not turn back till they were destroyed.
³⁸I crushed them so that they could not rise;
    they fell beneath my feet.
³⁹You armed me with strength for battle;
    you humbled my adversaries before me.
⁴⁰You made my enemies turn their backs in flight,
    and I destroyed my foes.
⁴¹They cried for help, but there was no one to save them—
    to the Lord, but he did not answer.
⁴²I beat them as fine as windblown dust;
    I trampled them^a like mud in the streets.
⁴³You have delivered me from the attacks of the people;
    you have made me the head of nations.
People I did not know now serve me,
⁴⁴   foreigners cower before me;
    as soon as they hear of me, they obey me.
⁴⁵They all lose heart;
    they come trembling from their strongholds.

⁴⁶The Lord lives! Praise be to my Rock!
    Exalted be God my Savior!
⁴⁷He is the God who avenges me,
    who subdues nations under me,
⁴⁸   who saves me from my enemies.
You exalted me above my foes;
    from violent people you rescued me.
⁴⁹Therefore I will praise you, Lord, among the nations;
    I will sing the praises of your name.

⁵⁰He gives his king great victories;
    he shows unfailing love to his anointed,
    to David and to his descendants forever.

Psalm 19

For the director of music. A psalm of David.

[*] ¹The heavens declare the glory of God;
    the skies proclaim the work of his hands.

718

---

^a *42* Many Hebrew manuscripts, Septuagint, Syriac and Targum (see also 2 Samuel 22:43); Masoretic Text *I poured them out*
[*] 19:1-14 is numbered 19:2-15 in Hebrew texts.

²Day after day they pour forth speech;
   night after night they display knowledge.
³They have no speech, they use no words;
   no sound is heard from them.
⁴Yet their voice*ᵃ* goes out into all the earth,
   their words to the ends of the world.
 In the heavens he has pitched a tent for the sun,
⁵   which is like a bridegroom coming out of his chamber,
   like a champion rejoicing to run his course.
⁶It rises at one end of the heavens
   and makes its circuit to the other;
   nothing is deprived of its warmth.

⁷The law of the Lᴏʀᴅ is perfect,
   refreshing the soul.
 The statutes of the Lᴏʀᴅ are trustworthy,
   making wise the simple.
⁸The precepts of the Lᴏʀᴅ are right,
   giving joy to the heart.
 The commands of the Lᴏʀᴅ are radiant,
   giving light to the eyes.
⁹The fear of the Lᴏʀᴅ is pure,
   enduring forever.
 The ordinances of the Lᴏʀᴅ are sure,
   and all of them are righteous.

¹⁰They are more precious than gold,
   than much pure gold;
 they are sweeter than honey,
   than honey from the honeycomb.
¹¹By them your servant is warned;
   in keeping them there is great reward.
¹²But who can discern their own errors?
   Forgive my hidden faults.
¹³Keep your servant also from willful sins;
   may they not rule over me.
 Then I will be blameless,
   innocent of great transgression.

¹⁴May these words of my mouth and this meditation of my heart
   be pleasing in your sight,
 Lᴏʀᴅ, my Rock and my Redeemer.

Psalm 20

For the director of music. A psalm of David.

* ¹May the Lᴏʀᴅ answer you when you are in distress;
   may the name of the God of Jacob protect you.
²May he send you help from the sanctuary
   and grant you support from Zion.
³May he remember all your sacrifices
   and accept your burnt offerings.*ᵇ*

ᵃ 4 Septuagint, Jerome and Syriac; Hebrew *line*   *ᵇ 3* The Hebrew has *Selah* (a word of uncertain meaning) here.

* 20:1-9 is numbered 20:2-10 in Hebrew texts.

⁴May he give you the desire of your heart
  and make all your plans succeed.
⁵May we shout for joy over your victory
  and lift up our banners in the name of our God.

May the LORD grant all your requests.

⁶Now this I know:
  The LORD gives victory to his anointed.
He answers him from his heavenly sanctuary
  with the victorious power of his right hand.
⁷Some trust in chariots and some in horses,
  but we trust in the name of the LORD our God.
⁸They are brought to their knees and fall,
  but we rise up and stand firm.
⁹LORD, give victory to the king!
  Answer us when we call!

Psalm 21

For the director of music. A psalm of David.

* ¹The king rejoices in your strength, LORD.
  How great is his joy in the victories you give!

²You have granted him his heart's desire
  and have not withheld the request of his lips.*ᵃ*
³You came to greet him with rich blessings
  and placed a crown of pure gold on his head.
⁴He asked you for life, and you gave it to him—
  length of days, for ever and ever.
⁵Through the victories you gave, his glory is great;
  you have bestowed on him splendor and majesty.
⁶Surely you have granted him unending blessings
  and made him glad with the joy of your presence.
⁷For the king trusts in the LORD;
  through the unfailing love of the Most High
  he will not be shaken.

⁸Your hand will lay hold on all your enemies;
  your right hand will seize your foes.
⁹When you appear for battle,
  you will burn them up as in a blazing furnace.
The LORD will swallow them up in his wrath,
  and his fire will consume them.
¹⁰You will destroy their descendants from the earth,
  their posterity from the human race.
¹¹Though they plot evil against you
  and devise wicked schemes, they cannot succeed.
¹²You will make them turn their backs
  when you aim at them with drawn bow.

¹³Be exalted in your strength, LORD;
  we will sing and praise your might.

ᵃ 2 The Hebrew has *Selah* (a word of uncertain meaning) here.
* 21:1-13 is numbered 21:2-14 in Hebrew texts.

Psalm 22

For the director of music. To the tune of "The Doe of the Morning." A psalm of David.

*[1] My God, my God, why have you forsaken me?
    Why are you so far from saving me,
    so far from the words of my groaning?
[2] My God, I cry out by day, but you do not answer,
    by night, but I find no rest.[a]

[3] Yet you are enthroned as the Holy One;
    you are the praise[b] of Israel.
[4] In you our ancestors put their trust;
    they trusted and you delivered them.
[5] They cried to you and were saved;
    in you they trusted and were not disappointed.

[6] But I am a worm, not a human being;
    I am scorned by everyone, despised by the people.
[7] All who see me mock me;
    they hurl insults, shaking their heads.
[8] "He trusts in the Lord," they say,
    "let the Lord rescue him.
  Let him deliver him,
    since he delights in him."

[9] Yet you brought me out of the womb;
    you made me feel secure on my mother's breast.
[10] From birth I was cast on you;
    from my mother's womb you have been my God.
[11] Do not be far from me,
    for trouble is near
    and there is no one to help.

[12] Many bulls surround me;
    strong bulls of Bashan encircle me.
[13] Roaring lions that tear their prey
    open their mouths wide against me.
[14] I am poured out like water,
    and all my bones are out of joint.
  My heart has turned to wax;
    it has melted within me.
[15] My mouth[c] is dried up like a potsherd,
    and my tongue sticks to the roof of my mouth;
    you lay me[d] in the dust of death.
[16] Dogs surround me,
    a pack of villains encircles me;
    they pierce[e] my hands and my feet.
[17] All my bones are on display;
    people stare and gloat over me.
[18] They divide my clothes among them
    and cast lots for my garment.

---

[a] *2 Or night, and am not silent*   [b] *3 Or Yet you are holy, / enthroned on the praises*   [c] *15 Probable reading of the original Hebrew text; Masoretic Text* strength
[d] *15 Or mouth; / I am laid*   [e] *16 Some Hebrew manuscripts, Septuagint and Syriac; most Hebrew manuscripts* me, / like a lion

* 22:1-31 is numbered 22:2-32 in Hebrew texts.

¹⁹But you, Lord, do not be far from me.
  You are my strength; come quickly to help me.
²⁰Deliver me from the sword,
  my precious life from the power of the dogs.
²¹Rescue me from the mouth of the lions;
  save me from the horns of the wild oxen.

²²I will declare your name to my people;
  in the assembly I will praise you.
²³You who fear the Lord, praise him!
  All you descendants of Jacob, honor him!
Revere him,
  all you descendants of Israel!
²⁴For he has not despised or scorned
  the suffering of the afflicted one;
he has not hidden his face from him
  but has listened to his cry for help.

²⁵From you comes the theme of my praise in the great assembly;
  before those who fear you^a I will fulfill my vows.
²⁶The poor will eat and be satisfied;
  those who seek the Lord will praise him—
  may your hearts live forever!
²⁷All the ends of the earth
  will remember and turn to the Lord,
and all the families of the nations
  will bow down before him,
²⁸for dominion belongs to the Lord
  and he rules over the nations.

²⁹All the rich of the earth will feast and worship;
  all who go down to the dust will kneel before him—
  those who cannot keep themselves alive.
³⁰Posterity will serve him;
  future generations will be told about the Lord.
³¹They will proclaim his righteousness,
  declaring to a people yet unborn:
  He has done it!

Psalm 23

A psalm of David.

¹The Lord is my shepherd, I lack nothing.
² He makes me lie down in green pastures,
he leads me beside quiet waters,
³ he refreshes my soul.
He guides me along the right paths
  for his name's sake.
⁴Even though I walk
  through the darkest valley,^b
I will fear no evil,
  for you are with me;

---
^a 25 Hebrew *him*   ^b 4 Or *the valley of the shadow of death*

HE IS: my shepherd

23:1–6 The Bible often compares humans to sheep: skittish, scattered and silly—not exactly a compliment. Scripture reveals that, like sheep, we need a shepherd. And here is the great comfort: God is not *a* shepherd or *the* shepherd but *my shepherd*.

If you're hiding from your shepherd, or if you've wandered from the flock, remember that the Lord is your shepherd (see John 10:14). He will make sure you lack nothing. He'll restore your soul, and he will personally guide you and provide for you all the days of your life. What freedom you'll find when you acknowledge that you're a helpless sheep and you need him.

For the next He Is, go to p. 727.

your rod and your staff,
>   they comfort me.

⁵You prepare a table before me
>   in the presence of my enemies.
You anoint my head with oil;
>   my cup overflows.
⁶Surely your goodness and love will follow me
>   all the days of my life,
and I will dwell in the house of the Lᴏʀᴅ
>   forever.

Psalm 24

Of David. A psalm.

¹The earth is the Lᴏʀᴅ's, and everything in it,
>   the world, and all who live in it;
²for he founded it on the seas
>   and established it on the waters.

³Who may ascend the mountain of the Lᴏʀᴅ?
>   Who may stand in his holy place?
⁴Those who have clean hands and a pure heart,
>   who do not put their trust in an idol
>   or swear by a false god.ᵃ

⁵They will receive blessing from the Lᴏʀᴅ
>   and vindication from God their Savior.
⁶Such is the generation of those who seek him,
>   who seek your face, God of Jacob.ᵇ, ᶜ

⁷Lift up your heads, you gates;
>   be lifted up, you ancient doors,
>   that the King of glory may come in.
⁸Who is this King of glory?
>   The Lᴏʀᴅ strong and mighty,
>   the Lᴏʀᴅ mighty in battle.
⁹Lift up your heads, you gates;
>   lift them up, you ancient doors,

ᵃ *4* Or *swear falsely*   ᵇ *6* Two Hebrew manuscripts and Syriac (see also Septuagint); most Hebrew manuscripts *face, Jacob*   ᶜ *6* The Hebrew has *Selah* (a word of uncertain meaning) here and at the end of verse 10.

that the King of glory may come in.
¹⁰Who is he, this King of glory?
The Lord Almighty—
he is the King of glory.

Psalm 25ᵃ

Of David.

¹In you, Lord my God,
    I put my trust.

²I trust in you;
        do not let me be put to shame,
        nor let my enemies triumph over me.
³No one who hopes in you
        will ever be put to shame,
    but shame will come on those
        who are treacherous without cause.

⁴Show me your ways, Lord,
        teach me your paths.
⁵Guide me in your truth and teach me,
        for you are God my Savior,
        and my hope is in you all day long.
⁶Remember, Lord, your great mercy and love,
        for they are from of old.
⁷Do not remember the sins of my youth
        and my rebellious ways;
    according to your love remember me,
        for you, Lord, are good.

⁸Good and upright is the Lord;
        therefore he instructs sinners in his ways.
⁹He guides the humble in what is right
        and teaches them his way.
¹⁰All the ways of the Lord are loving and faithful
        toward those who keep the demands of his covenant.
¹¹For the sake of your name, Lord,
        forgive my iniquity, though it is great.

¹²Who, then, are those who fear the Lord?
        He will instruct them in the ways they should choose.
¹³They will spend their days in prosperity,
        and their descendants will inherit the land.
¹⁴The Lord confides in those who fear him;
        he makes his covenant known to them.
¹⁵My eyes are ever on the Lord,
        for only he will release my feet from the snare.

¹⁶Turn to me and be gracious to me,
        for I am lonely and afflicted.
¹⁷Relieve the troubles of my heart
        and free me from my anguish.

724

ᵃ This psalm is an acrostic poem, the verses of which begin with the successive letters of the Hebrew alphabet.

¹⁸Look on my affliction and my distress
and take away all my sins.
¹⁹See how numerous are my enemies
and how fiercely they hate me!

²⁰Guard my life and rescue me;
do not let me be put to shame,
for I take refuge in you.
²¹May integrity and uprightness protect me,
because my hope, LORD,ᵃ is in you.

²²Redeem Israel, O God,
from all their troubles!

Psalm 26

Of David.

¹Vindicate me, LORD,
for I have led a blameless life;
I have trusted in the LORD
and have not faltered.
²Test me, LORD, and try me,
examine my heart and my mind;
³for I have always been mindful of your
unfailing love
and have lived in reliance on your
faithfulness.

⁴I do not sit with the deceitful,
nor do I associate with hypocrites.
⁵I abhor the assembly of evildoers
and refuse to sit with the wicked.
⁶I wash my hands in innocence,
and go about your altar, LORD,
⁷proclaiming aloud your praise
and telling of all your wonderful deeds.

⁸LORD, I love the house where you live,
the place where your glory dwells.
⁹Do not take away my soul along with sinners,
my life with those who are bloodthirsty,
¹⁰in whose hands are wicked schemes,
whose right hands are full of bribes.
¹¹I lead a blameless life;
redeem me and be merciful to me.

¹²My feet stand on level ground;
in the great congregation I will praise the LORD.

Psalm 27

Of David.

¹The LORD is my light and my salvation—
whom shall I fear?

atissue:loneliness

25:16 In the beloved book *Anne of Green Gables,* Anne longs for a "bosom friend." Can you relate? Unfortunately, most of us have known the pain at times of not having a close friend. Yet loneliness is not entirely bad. Painful as it is, loneliness is good when it pushes us to grow closer to the best friend we'll ever have—God. No other friendship can compare to his. He knows and accepts us completely. He is right there with us, always. In the good times we take our friend for granted. In the bad times we realize we need him—and he's right there.

725

ᵃ *21* Septuagint; Hebrew does not have LORD.

The LORD is the stronghold of my life—
of whom shall I be afraid?

²When the wicked advance against me
to devour*a* me,
it is my enemies and my foes
who will stumble and fall.
³Though an army besiege me,
my heart will not fear;
though war break out against me,
even then I will be confident.

⁴One thing I ask from the LORD,
this only do I seek:
that I may dwell in the house
of the LORD
all the days of my life,
to gaze on the beauty of the
LORD
and to seek him in his
temple.
⁵For in the day of trouble
he will keep me safe in his
dwelling;
he will hide me in the shelter
of his tabernacle
and set me high upon a
rock.

⁶Then my head will be exalted
above the enemies who
surround me;
at his tabernacle I will sacrifice with shouts of joy;
I will sing and make music to the LORD.

⁷Hear my voice when I call, LORD;
be merciful to me and answer me.
⁸My heart says of you, "Seek his face!"
Your face, LORD, I will seek.
⁹Do not hide your face from me,
do not turn your servant away in anger;
you have been my helper.
Do not reject me or forsake me,
God my Savior.
¹⁰Though my father and mother forsake me,
the LORD will receive me.
¹¹Teach me your way, LORD;
lead me in a straight path
because of my oppressors.
¹²Do not turn me over to the desire of my foes,
for false witnesses rise up against me,
spouting malicious accusations.

conversations

fear «» 27:1–14

1 » Is it wrong or unspiritual to feel afraid?

2 » What are you most afraid of?

3 » What aspect of God's nature comforts you
most when you feel afraid?

For more on **fear**, check the index.
For the next Conversations, go to p. 731.

---

a 2 Or slander

¹³I remain confident of this:
  I will see the goodness of the Lᴏʀᴅ
  in the land of the living.
¹⁴Wait for the Lᴏʀᴅ;
  be strong and take heart
  and wait for the Lᴏʀᴅ.

Psalm 28

Of David.

¹To you, Lᴏʀᴅ, I call;
  you are my Rock,
  do not turn a deaf ear to me.
For if you remain silent,
  I will be like those who go down to the pit.
²Hear my cry for mercy
  as I call to you for help,
  as I lift up my hands
  toward your Most Holy Place.

HE IS: my rock

28:1 In a time when he felt crushed by opposition within his kingdom, David turned to the Lord, begging God to save him. David called God *my rock*. This powerful image suggests that God is both strong and immovable.

Because God is your rock, you will not be shaken. His stability becomes your stability. His strength, your strength. His steadiness, your steadiness. When you feel overwhelmed by problems or people in your life, follow David's lead and cry out to God, your rock. He will not turn a deaf ear to you but will hear your prayer and be your strength.

For the next He Is, go to p. 732.

³Do not drag me away with the wicked,
  with those who do evil,
who speak cordially with their neighbors
  but harbor malice in their hearts.
⁴Repay them for their deeds
  and for their evil work;
repay them for what their hands have done
  and bring back on them what they deserve.

⁵Because they have no regard for the deeds of the Lᴏʀᴅ
  and what his hands have done,
he will tear them down
  and never build them up again.

⁶Praise be to the Lᴏʀᴅ,
  for he has heard my cry for mercy.
⁷The Lᴏʀᴅ is my strength and my shield;
  my heart trusts in him, and he helps me.
My heart leaps for joy,
  and with my song I praise him.

⁸The Lord is the strength of his people,
a fortress of salvation for his anointed one.
⁹Save your people and bless your inheritance;
be their shepherd and carry them forever.

Psalm 29

A psalm of David.

¹Ascribe to the Lord, you heavenly beings,
ascribe to the Lord glory and strength.
²Ascribe to the Lord the glory due his name;
worship the Lord in the splendor of his^{*a*} holiness.

³The voice of the Lord is over the waters;
the God of glory thunders,
the Lord thunders over the mighty waters.
⁴The voice of the Lord is powerful;
the voice of the Lord is majestic.
⁵The voice of the Lord breaks the cedars;
the Lord breaks in pieces the cedars of Lebanon.
⁶He makes Lebanon leap like a calf,
Sirion^{*b*} like a young wild ox.
⁷The voice of the Lord strikes
with flashes of lightning.
⁸The voice of the Lord shakes the desert;
the Lord shakes the Desert of Kadesh.
⁹The voice of the Lord twists the oaks^{*c*}
and strips the forests bare.
And in his temple all cry, "Glory!"

¹⁰The Lord sits enthroned over the flood;
the Lord is enthroned as King forever.
¹¹The Lord gives strength to his people;
the Lord blesses his people with peace.

Psalm 30

A psalm. A song. For the dedication of the temple.^d Of David.

* ¹I will exalt you, Lord,
for you lifted me out of the depths
and did not let my enemies gloat over me.
²Lord my God, I called to you for help,
and you healed me.
³You, Lord, brought me up from the realm of the dead;
you spared me from going down to the pit.

⁴Sing the praises of the Lord, you his faithful people;
praise his holy name.
⁵For his anger lasts only a moment,
but his favor lasts a lifetime;

---

^{*a*} *2* Or Lord *with the splendor of*   ^{*b*} *6* That is, Mount Hermon   ^{*c*} *9* Or Lord *makes the deer give birth*   ^{*d*} Title: Or *palace*
* 30:1-12 is numbered 30:2-13 in Hebrew texts.

weeping may remain for a night,
  but rejoicing comes in the morning.

⁶When I felt secure, I said,
  "I will never be shaken."
⁷LORD, when you favored me,
  you made my royal mountain*ᵃ* stand firm;
but when you hid your face,
  I was dismayed.

⁸To you, LORD, I called;
  to the Lord I cried for mercy:
⁹"What is gained if I am silenced,
  if I go down to the pit?
Will the dust praise you?
  Will it proclaim your faithfulness?
¹⁰Hear, LORD, and be merciful to me;
  LORD, be my help."

¹¹You turned my wailing into dancing;
  you removed my sackcloth and clothed me with joy,
¹²that my heart may sing your praises and not be silent.
  LORD my God, I will praise you forever.

Psalm 31

For the director of music. A psalm of David.

*¹In you, LORD, I have taken refuge;
  let me never be put to shame;
  deliver me in your righteousness.
²Turn your ear to me,
  come quickly to my rescue;
be my rock of refuge,
  a strong fortress to save me.
³Since you are my rock and my fortress,
  for the sake of your name lead and guide me.
⁴Keep me free from the trap that is set for me,
  for you are my refuge.
⁵Into your hands I commit my spirit;
  redeem me, LORD, my faithful God.

⁶I hate those who cling to worthless idols;
  as for me, I trust in the LORD.
⁷I will be glad and rejoice in your love,
  for you saw my affliction
  and knew the anguish of my soul.
⁸You have not given me into the hands of the enemy
  but have set my feet in a spacious place.

⁹Be merciful to me, LORD, for I am in distress;
  my eyes grow weak with sorrow,
  my soul and body with grief.

ᵃ 7 That is, Mount Zion
* 31:1-24 is numbered 31:2-25 in Hebrew texts.

[10] My life is consumed by anguish
   and my years by groaning;
my strength fails because of my affliction,[a]
   and my bones grow weak.
[11] Because of all my enemies,
   I am the utter contempt of my neighbors;
I am a dread to my friends—
   those who see me on the street flee from me.
[12] I am forgotten as though I were dead;
   I have become like broken pottery.
[13] For I hear many whispering,
   "Terror on every side!"
They conspire against me
   and plot to take my life.

[14] But I trust in you, LORD;
   I say, "You are my God."
[15] My times are in your hands;
   deliver me from the hands of my enemies,
   from those who pursue me.
[16] Let your face shine on your servant;
   save me in your unfailing love.
[17] Let me not be put to shame, LORD,
   for I have cried out to you;
but let the wicked be put to shame
   and be silent in the realm of the dead.
[18] Let their lying lips be silenced,
   for with pride and contempt
   they speak arrogantly against the righteous.

[19] How great is your goodness,
   which you have stored up for those who fear you,
which you bestow in the sight of all
   on those who take refuge in you.
[20] In the shelter of your presence you hide them
   from all human intrigues;
you keep them safe in your dwelling
   from accusing tongues.

[21] Praise be to the LORD,
   for he showed me the wonders of his love
   when I was in a city under siege.
[22] In my alarm I said,
   "I am cut off from your sight!"
Yet you heard my cry for mercy
   when I called to you for help.

[23] Love the LORD, all his faithful people!
   The LORD preserves those who are true to him,
   but the proud he pays back in full.
[24] Be strong and take heart,
   all you who hope in the LORD.

_____
a 10 Or guilt

Psalm 32

Of David. A maskil.[a]

¹Blessed are those
    whose transgressions are forgiven,
    whose sins are covered.
²Blessed are those
    whose sin the LORD does not count against them
    and in whose spirit is no deceit.

³When I kept silent,
    my bones wasted away
    through my groaning all day long.
⁴For day and night
    your hand was heavy on me;
my strength was sapped
    as in the heat of summer.[b]

⁵Then I acknowledged my sin to you
    and did not cover up my iniquity.
I said, "I will confess
    my transgressions to the LORD."
And you forgave
    the guilt of my sin.

⁶Therefore let all the faithful pray to you
    while you may be found;
surely the rising of the mighty waters
    will not reach them.
⁷You are my hiding place;
    you will protect me from trouble
    and surround me with songs of deliverance.

⁸I will instruct you and teach you in the
        way you should go;
    I will counsel you with my loving eye
        on you.
⁹Do not be like the horse or the mule,
    which have no understanding
but must be controlled by bit and bridle
    or they will not come to you.
¹⁰Many are the woes of the wicked,
    but the LORD's unfailing love
    surrounds those who trust in him.

¹¹Rejoice in the LORD and be glad, you
        righteous;
    sing, all you who are upright in heart!

conversations

decisions «» 32:8–10

1 Describe a time when you stubbornly went your own way. What happened?

2 How does your relationship with God change the way you make decisions?

3 How much control do you really have in your decisions?

For more on **decisions**, check the index.
For the next Conversations, go to p. 738.

Psalm 33

¹Sing joyfully to the LORD, you righteous;
    it is fitting for the upright to praise him.
²Praise the LORD with the harp;

---

[a] Title: Probably a literary or musical term   [b] **4** The Hebrew has *Selah* (a word of uncertain meaning) here and at the end of verses 5 and 7.

make music to him on the ten-stringed lyre.
³Sing to him a new song;
    play skillfully, and shout for joy.

⁴For the word of the LORD is right and true;
    he is faithful in all he does.
⁵The LORD loves righteousness and justice;
    the earth is full of his unfailing love.

⁶By the word of the LORD the heavens were made,
    their starry host by the breath of his mouth.
⁷He gathers the waters of the sea into jars*;
    he puts the deep into storehouses.
⁸Let all the earth fear the LORD;
    let all the people of the world revere him.
⁹For he spoke, and it came to be;
    he commanded, and it stood firm.

¹⁰The LORD foils the plans of the nations;
    he thwarts the purposes of the peoples.
¹¹But the plans of the LORD stand firm forever,
    the purposes of his heart through all generations.

¹²Blessed is the nation whose God is the LORD,
    the people he chose for his inheritance.
¹³From heaven the LORD looks down
    and sees all humankind;
¹⁴from his dwelling place he watches
    all who live on earth—
¹⁵he who forms the hearts of all,
    who considers everything they do.

¹⁶No king is saved by the size of his army;
    no warrior escapes by his great strength.
¹⁷A horse is a vain hope for deliverance;
    despite all its great strength it cannot save.
¹⁸But the eyes of the LORD are on those who fear him,

ᵃ 7 Or sea as into a heap

HE IS: my shield

33:18–20 In Psalm 33, the psalmist praises God for his Word, his creation and his sovereignty. This time of praise helped the psalmist put life in perspective and reminded him to wait for the Lord, his shield.

Sometimes we lack the strength or courage to face difficult situations in our lives, as the psalmist did. In times like these, the best way to remind ourselves that God is our protection today is to remember what he did for us in the past. This gives us a whole new perspective on what we're facing and reminds us that God is *our shield* to protect us and give us hope. See also Ephesians 6:10–18.

For the next He Is, go to p. 743.

on those whose hope is in his unfailing love,
¹⁹to deliver them from death
    and keep them alive in famine.

²⁰We wait in hope for the LORD;
    he is our help and our shield.
²¹In him our hearts rejoice,
    for we trust in his holy name.
²²May your unfailing love be with us, LORD,
    even as we put our hope in you.

Psalm 34[a]

*Of David. When he pretended to be insane before Abimelek,
who drove him away, and he left.*

* ¹I will extol the LORD at all times;
    his praise will always be on my lips.
²I will glory in the LORD;
    let the afflicted hear and rejoice.
³Glorify the LORD with me;
    let us exalt his name together.

⁴I sought the LORD, and he answered me;
    he delivered me from all my fears.
⁵Those who look to him are radiant;
    their faces are never covered with shame.
⁶This poor man called, and the LORD heard him;
    he saved him out of all his troubles.
⁷The angel of the LORD encamps around those who fear him,
    and he delivers them.

⁸Taste and see that the LORD is good;
    blessed are those who take refuge in him.
⁹Fear the LORD, you his holy people,
    for those who fear him lack nothing.
¹⁰The lions may grow weak and hungry,
    but those who seek the LORD lack no good thing.
¹¹Come, my children, listen to me;
    I will teach you the fear of the LORD.
¹²Whoever of you loves life
    and desires to see many good days,
¹³keep your tongue from evil
    and your lips from telling lies.
¹⁴Turn from evil and do good;
    seek peace and pursue it.

¹⁵The eyes of the LORD are on the righteous
    and his ears are attentive to their cry.
¹⁶The face of the LORD is against those who do evil,
    to blot out their name from the earth.

¹⁷The righteous cry out, and the LORD hears them;
    he delivers them from all their troubles.

---

^a This psalm is an acrostic poem, the verses of which begin with the successive letters of the Hebrew alphabet.

* 34:1-22 is numbered 34:2-23 in Hebrew texts.

¹⁸The Lord is close to the brokenhearted
   and saves those who are crushed in spirit.

¹⁹The righteous may have many troubles,
   but the Lord delivers them from them all;
²⁰he protects all their bones,
   not one of them will be broken.

²¹Evil will slay the wicked;
   the foes of the righteous will be condemned.
²²The Lord redeems his servants;
   no one who takes refuge in him will be condemned.

Psalm 35

Of David.

¹Contend, Lord, with those who contend with me;
   fight against those who fight against me.
²Take up shield and armor;
   arise and come to my aid.
³Brandish spear and javelin^a
   against those who pursue me.
 Say to me,
   "I am your salvation."

⁴May those who seek my life
   be disgraced and put to shame;
 may those who plot my ruin
   be turned back in dismay.
⁵May they be like chaff before the wind,
   with the angel of the Lord driving them away;
⁶may their path be dark and slippery,
   with the angel of the Lord pursuing them.

⁷Since they hid their net for me without cause
   and without cause dug a pit for me,
⁸may ruin overtake them by surprise—
   may the net they hid entangle them,
   may they fall into the pit, to their ruin.
⁹Then my soul will rejoice in the Lord
   and delight in his salvation.
¹⁰My whole being will exclaim,
   "Who is like you, Lord?
 You rescue the poor from those too strong for them,
   the poor and needy from those who rob them."

¹¹Ruthless witnesses come forward;
   they question me on things I know nothing about.
¹²They repay me evil for good
   and leave me like one bereaved.
¹³Yet when they were ill, I put on sackcloth
   and humbled myself with fasting.
 When my prayers returned to me unanswered,

^a *3 Or and block the way*

¹⁴ I went about mourning
   as though for my friend or brother.
 I bowed my head in grief
   as though weeping for my mother.
¹⁵ But when I stumbled, they gathered in glee;
   assailants gathered against me without my knowledge.
   They slandered me without ceasing.
¹⁶ Like the ungodly they maliciously mocked^a;
   they gnashed their teeth at me.

¹⁷ How long, Lord, will you look on?
   Rescue me from their ravages,
   my precious life from these lions.
¹⁸ I will give you thanks in the great assembly;
   among the throngs I will praise you.
¹⁹ Do not let those gloat over me
   who are my enemies without cause;
 do not let those who hate me without reason
   maliciously wink the eye.
²⁰ They do not speak peaceably,
   but devise false accusations
   against those who live quietly in the land.
²¹ They sneer at me and say, "Aha! Aha!
   With our own eyes we have seen it."

²² Lord, you have seen this; do not be silent.
   Do not be far from me, Lord.
²³ Awake, and rise to my defense!
   Contend for me, my God and Lord.
²⁴ Vindicate me in your righteousness, Lord my God;
   do not let them gloat over me.
²⁵ Do not let them think, "Aha, just what we wanted!"
   or say, "We have swallowed him up."

²⁶ May all who gloat over my distress
   be put to shame and confusion;
 may all who exalt themselves over me
   be clothed with shame and disgrace.
²⁷ May those who delight in my vindication
   shout for joy and gladness;
 may they always say, "The Lord be exalted,
   who delights in the well-being of his servant."

²⁸ My tongue will proclaim your righteousness,
   your praises all day long.

Psalm 36

For the director of music. Of David the servant of the Lord.

[*] ¹ I have a message from God in my heart
   concerning the sinfulness of the wicked:^b

---

^a *16* Septuagint; Hebrew may mean *ungodly circle of mockers.*   ^b *1* Or *A message from God: The transgression of the wicked / resides in their hearts.*
[*] *36:1-12 is numbered 36:2-13 in Hebrew texts.*

There is no fear of God
 before their eyes.

2 In their own eyes they flatter themselves
 too much to detect or hate their sin.
3 The words of their mouths are wicked and deceitful;
 they have ceased to be wise and to do good.
4 Even on their beds they plot evil;
 they commit themselves to a sinful course
 and do not reject what is wrong.

5 Your love, LORD, reaches to the heavens,
 your faithfulness to the skies.
6 Your righteousness is like the highest mountains,
 your justice like the great deep.
 You, LORD, preserve both people and animals.
7 How priceless is your unfailing love, O God!
 People take refuge in the shadow of your wings.
8 They feast on the abundance of your house;
 you give them drink from your river of delights.
9 For with you is the fountain of life;
 in your light we see light.

10 Continue your love to those who know you,
 your righteousness to the upright in heart.
11 May the foot of the proud not come against me,
 nor the hand of the wicked drive me away.
12 See how the evildoers lie fallen—
 thrown down, not able to rise!

Psalm 37[a]

Of David.

1 Do not fret because of those who are evil
 or be envious of those who do wrong;
2 for like the grass they will soon wither,
 like green plants they will soon die away.

3 Trust in the LORD and do good;
 dwell in the land and enjoy safe pasture.
4 Take delight in the LORD
 and he will give you the desires of your heart.

5 Commit your way to the LORD;
 trust in him and he will do this:
6 He will make your righteous reward shine like the dawn,
 your vindication like the noonday sun.

7 Be still before the LORD
 and wait patiently for him;
do not fret when people succeed in their ways,
 when they carry out their wicked schemes.

---

[a] This psalm is an acrostic poem, the stanzas of which begin with the successive letters of the Hebrew alphabet.

⁸Refrain from anger and turn from wrath;
   do not fret—it leads only to evil.
⁹For those who are evil will be destroyed,
   but those who hope in the LORD will inherit the land.

¹⁰A little while, and the wicked will be no more;
   though you look for them, they will not be found.
¹¹But the meek will inherit the land
   and enjoy peace and prosperity.

¹²The wicked plot against the righteous
   and gnash their teeth at them;
¹³but the Lord laughs at the wicked,
   for he knows their day is coming.

¹⁴The wicked draw the sword
   and bend the bow
 to bring down the poor and needy,
   to slay those whose ways are upright.
¹⁵But their swords will pierce their own hearts,
   and their bows will be broken.

¹⁶Better the little that the righteous have
   than the wealth of many wicked;
¹⁷for the power of the wicked will be broken,
   but the LORD upholds the righteous.

¹⁸The blameless spend their days under the
      LORD's care,
   and their inheritance will endure forever.
¹⁹In times of disaster they will not wither;
   in days of famine they will enjoy plenty.

²⁰But the wicked will perish:
   Though the LORD's enemies are like the
      flowers of the field,
   they will be consumed, they will go up in
      smoke.

²¹The wicked borrow and do not repay,
   but the righteous give generously;
²²those the LORD blesses will inherit the land,
   but those he curses will be destroyed.

²³The LORD makes firm the steps
   of those who delight in him;
²⁴though they stumble, they will not fall,
   for the LORD upholds them with his hand.

²⁵I was young and now I am old,
   yet I have never seen the righteous
      forsaken
   or their children begging bread.
²⁶They are always generous and lend freely;
   their children will be a blessing.ᵃ

atissue:generosity

37:21–26 What if God were stingy and gave us just enough to get by? What if he hoarded his blessings to make sure he didn't run out? What if he hovered over us whenever he let us use anything of his to make sure we didn't take too much? Aren't you glad God doesn't act stingy toward us, the way we often act toward others? And he wants you to be just as openhanded with others as he's been with you. What you'll discover is that as you give of your time, possessions and love, you'll always have more to give. As you pour generously onto others, God keeps pouring generously onto you.

737

ᵃ 26 Or freely; / the names of their children will be used in blessings (see Gen. 48:20); or freely; / others will see that their children are blessed

738

²⁷Turn from evil and do good;
  then you will dwell in the land forever.
²⁸For the LORD loves the just
  and will not forsake his faithful ones.

  Wrongdoers will be completely destroyed ᵃ;
  the offspring of the wicked will perish.
²⁹The righteous will inherit the land
  and dwell in it forever.

³⁰The mouths of the righteous utter wisdom,
  and their tongues speak what is just.
³¹The law of their God is in their hearts;
  their feet do not slip.

³²The wicked lie in wait for the righteous,
  seeking their very lives;
³³but the LORD will not leave them in their power
  or let them be condemned when brought to trial.

³⁴Hope in the LORD
  and keep his way.
He will exalt you to inherit the land;
  when the wicked are destroyed, you will see it.

³⁵I have seen the wicked and ruthless
  flourishing like a luxuriant native tree,
³⁶but they soon passed away and were no more;
  though I looked for them, they could not be found.

³⁷Consider the blameless, observe the upright;
  a future awaits those who seek peace. ᵇ
³⁸But all sinners will be destroyed;
  there will be no future ᶜ for the wicked.

³⁹The salvation of the righteous comes from the LORD;
  he is their stronghold in
    time of trouble.
⁴⁰The LORD helps them and
    delivers them;
  he delivers them from the
    wicked and saves them,
  because they take refuge in
    him.

Psalm 38

A psalm of David. A petition.
* ¹LORD, do not rebuke me in
    your anger
  or discipline me in your
    wrath.
²Your arrows have pierced me,
  and your hand has come down on me.

conversations

guilt «» 38:1–4

1 » Is guilt a good thing? Why or why not?

2 » Besides confession, what actions will lessen feelings of guilt?

3 » Why do some Christians still feel guilty even after they've confessed a sin?

For more on **guilt**, check the index.
For the next Conversations, go to p. 760.

ᵃ *28* See Septuagint; Hebrew *They will be protected forever*   ᵇ *37* Or */ those who seek peace will have posterity*   ᶜ *38* Or *posterity*
* 38:1-22 is numbered 38:2-23 in Hebrew texts.

³Because of your wrath there is no health in my body;
   there is no soundness in my bones because of my sin.
⁴My guilt has overwhelmed me
   like a burden too heavy to bear.

⁵My wounds fester and are loathsome
   because of my sinful folly.
⁶I am bowed down and brought very low;
   all day long I go about mourning.
⁷My back is filled with searing pain;
   there is no health in my body.
⁸I am feeble and utterly crushed;
   I groan in anguish of heart.

⁹All my longings lie open before you, Lord;
   my sighing is not hidden from you.
¹⁰My heart pounds, my strength fails me;
   even the light has gone from my eyes.
¹¹My friends and companions avoid me because of my wounds;
   my neighbors stay far away.
¹²Those who seek my life set their traps,
   those who would harm me talk of my ruin;
   all day long they scheme and lie.

¹³I am like the deaf, who cannot hear,
   like the mute, who cannot speak;
¹⁴I have become like one who does not hear,
   whose mouth can offer no reply.
¹⁵Lord, I wait for you;
   you will answer, Lord my God.
¹⁶For I said, "Do not let them gloat
   or exalt themselves over me when my feet slip."

¹⁷For I am about to fall,
   and my pain is ever with me.
¹⁸I confess my iniquity;
   I am troubled by my sin.
¹⁹Many have become my enemies without cause[a];
   those who hate me without reason are numerous.
²⁰Those who repay my good with evil
   lodge accusations against me,
   though I seek only to do what is good.

²¹Lord, do not forsake me;
   do not be far from me, my God.
²²Come quickly to help me,
   my Lord and my Savior.

Psalm 39

For the director of music. For Jeduthun. A psalm of David.

* ¹I said, "I will watch my ways
   and keep my tongue from sin;

---

[a] *19* One Dead Sea Scrolls manuscript; Masoretic Text *my vigorous enemies*
* 39:1-13 is numbered 39:2-14 in Hebrew texts.

I will put a muzzle on my mouth
　　while in the presence of the wicked."
[2] So I remained utterly silent,
　　not even saying anything good.
But my anguish increased;
[3]　my heart grew hot within me.
While I meditated, the fire burned;
　　then I spoke with my tongue:

[4] "Show me, LORD, my life's end
　　and the number of my days;
　　let me know how fleeting my life is.
[5] You have made my days a mere
　　handbreadth;
　　the span of my years is as nothing
　　before you.
Everyone is but a breath,
　　even those who seem secure.[a]

[6] "Surely everyone goes around like a
　　mere phantom;
　　in vain they rush about, heaping up
　　wealth
　　without knowing whose it will finally be.

[7] "But now, Lord, what do I look for?
　　My hope is in you.
[8] Save me from all my transgressions;
　　do not make me the scorn of fools.
[9] I was silent; I would not open my mouth,
　　for you are the one who has done this.
[10] Remove your scourge from me;
　　I am overcome by the blow of your hand.
[11] When you rebuke and discipline people for their sins,
　　you consume their wealth like a moth—
　　surely everyone is but a breath.

[12] "Hear my prayer, LORD,
　　listen to my cry for help;
　　do not be deaf to my weeping.
I dwell with you as a foreigner,
　　a stranger, as all my ancestors were.
[13] Look away from me, that I may enjoy life again
　　before I depart and am no more."

Psalm 40

For the director of music. Of David. A psalm.

[*][1] I waited patiently for the LORD;
　　he turned to me and heard my cry.
[2] He lifted me out of the slimy pit,
　　out of the mud and mire;

---

atissue:mortality

39:1–13 Remember being 16 and thinking that the big 3-0 sounded ancient, and that 40 was near death? Maybe you're discouraged that life feels like it's rushing past in a blur. When David concluded that life is short and death comes sooner than we wish, he put his hope in the one who lasts forever. He looked to God for joy and meaning in light of the brevity of his life. Don't waste your time here wishing for more. Make the most of every moment you have, and find your hope in God and what he has in store for you—now and in eternity.

740

---

[a] *5* The Hebrew has *Selah* (a word of uncertain meaning) here and at the end of verse 11.
[*] 40:1-17 is numbered 40:2-18 in Hebrew texts.

he set my feet on a rock
    and gave me a firm place to stand.
³He put a new song in my mouth,
    a hymn of praise to our God.
Many will see and fear the Lᴏʀᴅ
    and put their trust in him.

⁴Blessed are those
    who make the Lᴏʀᴅ their trust,
who do not look to the proud,
    to those who turn aside to false gods.ᵃ
⁵Many, Lᴏʀᴅ my God,
    are the wonders you have done,
    the things you planned for us.
None can compare with you;
    were I to speak and tell of your deeds,
    they would be too many to declare.

⁶Sacrifice and offering you did not desire—
    but my ears you have openedᵇ—
    burnt offerings and sin offeringsᶜ you did not require.
⁷Then I said, "Here I am, I have come—
    it is written about me in the scroll.ᵈ
⁸I desire to do your will, my God;
    your law is within my heart."

⁹I proclaim your saving acts in the great assembly;
    I do not seal my lips, Lᴏʀᴅ,
    as you know.
¹⁰I do not hide your righteousness in my heart;
    I speak of your faithfulness and your saving help.
I do not conceal your love and your faithfulness
    from the great assembly.

¹¹Do not withhold your mercy from me, Lᴏʀᴅ;
    may your love and faithfulness always protect me.
¹²For troubles without number surround me;
    my sins have overtaken me, and I cannot see.
They are more than the hairs of my head,
    and my heart fails within me.
¹³Be pleased to save me, Lᴏʀᴅ;
    come quickly, Lᴏʀᴅ, to help me.

¹⁴May all who seek to take my life
    be put to shame and confusion;
may all who desire my ruin
    be turned back in disgrace.
¹⁵May those who say to me, "Aha! Aha!"
    be appalled at their own shame.
¹⁶But may all who seek you
    rejoice and be glad in you;

741

ᵃ 4 Or to lies   ᵇ 6 Hebrew; some Septuagint manuscripts but a body you have prepared for me   ᶜ 6 Or purification offerings   ᵈ 7 Or come / with the scroll written for me

may those who long for your saving help always say,
  "The LORD is great!"

[17] But as for me, I am poor and needy;
  may the Lord think of me.
You are my help and my deliverer;
  you are my God, do not delay.

Psalm 41

For the director of music. A psalm of David.

* [1] Blessed are those who have regard for the weak;
  the LORD delivers them in times of trouble.
[2] The LORD protects and preserves them—
  they are counted among the blessed in the land—
  he does not give them over to the desire of their foes.
[3] The LORD sustains them on their sickbed
  and restores them from their bed of illness.

[4] I said, "Have mercy on me, LORD;
  heal me, for I have sinned against
    you."
[5] My enemies say of me in malice,
  "When will he die and his name
    perish?"
[6] Whenever they come to see me,
  they speak falsely, while their hearts
    gather slander;
  then they go out and spread it
    abroad.

[7] All my enemies whisper together
    against me;
  they imagine the worst for me,
    saying,
[8] "A vile disease has beset him;
  he will never get up from the place
    where he lies."
[9] Even my close friend,
  someone I trusted,
one who shared my bread,
  has lifted up his heel against me.

[10] But may you have mercy on me, LORD;
  raise me up, that I may repay them.
[11] I know that you are pleased with me,
  for my enemy does not triumph
    over me.
[12] In my integrity you uphold me
  and set me in your presence forever.
[13] Praise be to the LORD, the God of Israel,
  from everlasting to everlasting.
        Amen and Amen.

---

atissue: distrust of men

41:7–9 Have you been betrayed by a man? Perhaps you thought he was your best friend, your soul mate, your Prince Charming. But he turned out to be a slimy frog—a cheater, liar and pretender. Perhaps he took your trust and violated it. And having dealt with more than one frog, perhaps you swore you'd never trust a man again. Maybe the solution isn't trusting men less; it's trusting God more. Trust God to heal your heart, to sustain you through your hurt and to help you be ready to someday trust again.

---

* 41:1-13 is numbered 41:2-14 in Hebrew texts.

BOOK II

Psalms 42–72

Psalm 42 *ᵃ*

For the director of music. A maskil *ᵇ of the Sons of Korah.*

** ¹*As the deer pants for streams of water,
    so my soul pants for you, my God.
²My soul thirsts for God, for the living God.
    When can I go and meet with God?
³My tears have been my food
    day and night,
while people say to me all day long,
    "Where is your God?"
⁴These things I remember
    as I pour out my soul:
how I used to go to the house of God
    under the protection of the Mighty One*ᶜ*
with shouts of joy and praise
    among the festive throng.

⁵Why, my soul, are you downcast?
    Why so disturbed within me?
Put your hope in God,
    for I will yet praise him,
    my Savior and my God.

⁶My soul is downcast within me;
    therefore I will remember you
from the land of the Jordan,
    the heights of Hermon—from Mount Mizar.
⁷Deep calls to deep
    in the roar of your waterfalls;
all your waves and breakers
    have swept over me.

ᵃ In many Hebrew manuscripts Psalms 42 and 43 constitute one psalm.   *ᵇ* Title: Probably a literary or musical term   *ᶜ 4* See Septuagint and Syriac; the meaning of the Hebrew for this line is uncertain.

*42:1-11 is numbered 42:2-12 in Hebrew texts.

HE IS: deep

42:5–11 The psalmist was in deep despair as his enemies mocked, "Where is your God?" Though in a time of depression, he wisely reminded himself that God isn't only in the heights; he is also in the depths. *"Deep* calls to deep . . ."

Perhaps you, like the psalmist, have felt waves of despair sweeping over you, threatening to take you under. Perhaps you feel so down you can't look up. Learn from the psalmist to remember God and share your feelings with him. When your thoughts take you to deep, dark places, let God take you deep into himself.

For the next He Is, go to p. 763.

myth# 47 "I SHOULD JUST GET OVER IT."

It's been three months since my mom died. I can't stop thinking about her and how much I miss her. We used to talk every day. It's as if a cloud has settled over my mind and heart, and I can't seem to see past it. I try to laugh with my boys at home, but nothing is funny. Even my eating habits have changed. I wanted to lose weight—but not in this way, and not this much.

My friends don't know what to say to me. They've said they're sorry about a thousand times. But I'm sure they're tired of being with me when I'm this quiet and listless. I hate being so sad and wish the pain would ease so I could move on. But it's impossible when the hurt is so fresh. How do I keep on living after I've lost my biggest fan and my best friend?

The other day after church, my friend Michelle was so comforting. She asked me about my mom and listened to me reminisce about our relationship. She didn't try to interject any advice; she just hugged me and told me to call her if I wanted to talk more. But then as I was getting into my car, another friend came over and commented on how sad I've been looking lately. She confided that her mother had died when she was my age. I thought she was going to say something helpful, but then her voice got cold and she said, "The fact is, everyone dies at some point. You need to accept that. It's time to move past it and go on again, at least for your boys' sake." As if I were somehow damaging my children by grieving for my mother.

I couldn't believe her bluntness. Does she think I like being sad all the time? I just stared at her, not knowing what to say. She gave my arm a little pat and walked away. I just stood there, trying to blink away hot tears. Finally I got in my car and just cried. Maybe she's right. Maybe I should just get over it.

—Grace

OUR CULTURE FEEDS the desire for a quick fix for everything. In movies, characters' complex life issues work themselves out in two hours or less. If we're hungry, we pop something in the microwave or dash off to the nearest restaurant to satisfy our hunger within minutes. Any info we need is instantly available online. However, this isn't how our emotions work. It isn't how our brains work. Processing a deep loss takes time. It may take many months or years. If you're on this journey after a significant loss or painful experience, keep this in mind:

- **You are not alone.** God promises to comfort you and guide you. He often uses others in your life to comfort you as well—friends, family and counselors. Find a grief support group or a Christian counselor to help you process your emotions. Asking for help when you need it isn't a sign of weakness; it's a sign of wisdom.

- **You need time.** Taking time to honor the loss, the sorrow, the anger or whatever other overwhelming emotions you feel can be difficult and painful, but that's how you work through those feelings. Just because you don't immediately bounce back from a loss doesn't mean you're less spiritual—it means you're fully human.

- **You are normal.** The Bible is clear that we will all experience times of sorrow and suffering. Psalm 42 reveals the heartfelt concerns and sadness David experienced. In fact, many Bible characters grieved and went through severe losses and painful experiences—including Jesus himself (see John 11:1–44).

745

"Recent research has shown that intense grieving lasts from three months to a year and many people continue experiencing profound grief for two years or more. Others' response to this extended grieving process may sometimes cause people to feel there is something wrong with them or they are behaving abnormally. This is not the case ... Prolonged bereavement is not unusual."

—Family Caregiver Alliance

"BLESSED are THOSE WHO mourn, FOR THEY WILL BE comforted."

MATTHEW 5:4

SEE ALSO

Psalm 23
Ecclesiastes 3:1–8
Isaiah 57:1–2
1 Thessalonians 4:13–18

For more on **Grief**, check the index.

⁸By day the LORD directs his love,
    at night his song is with me—
    a prayer to the God of my life.

⁹I say to God my Rock,
    "Why have you forgotten me?
Why must I go about mourning,
    oppressed by the enemy?"
¹⁰My bones suffer mortal agony
    as my foes taunt me,
saying to me all day long,
    "Where is your God?"

¹¹Why, my soul, are you downcast?
    Why so disturbed within me?
Put your hope in God,
    for I will yet praise him,
    my Savior and my God.

Psalm 43 ᵃ

¹Vindicate me, my God,
    and plead my cause
    against an unfaithful nation.
Rescue me from those who are
    deceitful and wicked.
²You are God my stronghold.
    Why have you rejected me?
Why must I go about mourning,
    oppressed by the enemy?
³Send me your light and your faithful care,
    let them lead me;
let them bring me to your holy mountain,
    to the place where you dwell.
⁴Then I will go to the altar of God,
    to God, my joy and my delight.
I will praise you with the lyre,
    O God, my God.

⁵Why, my soul, are you downcast?
    Why so disturbed within me?
Put your hope in God,
    for I will yet praise him,
    my Savior and my God.

Psalm 44

For the director of music. Of the Sons of Korah. A maskil. ᵇ

* ¹We have heard it with our ears, O God;
    our ancestors have told us
what you did in their days,
    in days long ago.

ᵃ In many Hebrew manuscripts Psalms 42 and 43 constitute one psalm.   ᵇ Title: Probably a literary or musical term
* 44:1-26 is numbered 44:2-27 in Hebrew texts.

²With your hand you drove out the nations
    and planted our ancestors;
you crushed the peoples
    and made our ancestors flourish.
³It was not by their sword that they won the land,
    nor did their arm bring them victory;
it was your right hand, your arm,
    and the light of your face, for you loved them.

⁴You are my King and my God,
    who decrees *ᵃ* victories for Jacob.
⁵Through you we push back our enemies;
    through your name we trample our foes.
⁶I put no trust in my bow,
    my sword does not bring me victory;
⁷but you give us victory over our enemies,
    you put our adversaries to shame.
⁸In God we make our boast all day long,
    and we will praise your name forever. *ᵇ*

⁹But now you have rejected and humbled us;
    you no longer go out with our armies.
¹⁰You made us retreat before the enemy,
    and our adversaries have plundered us.
¹¹You gave us up to be devoured like sheep
    and have scattered us among the nations.
¹²You sold your people for a pittance,
    gaining nothing from their sale.

¹³You have made us a reproach to our neighbors,
    the scorn and derision of those around us.
¹⁴You have made us a byword among the nations;
    the peoples shake their heads at us.
¹⁵I live in disgrace all day long,
    and my face is covered with shame
¹⁶at the taunts of those who reproach and revile me,
    because of the enemy, who is bent on revenge.

¹⁷All this came upon us,
    though we had not forgotten you;
    we had not been false to your covenant.
¹⁸Our hearts had not turned back;
    our feet had not strayed from your path.
¹⁹But you crushed us and made us a haunt for jackals;
    you covered us over with deep darkness.

²⁰If we had forgotten the name of our God
    or spread out our hands to a foreign god,
²¹would not God have discovered it,
    since he knows the secrets of the heart?
²²Yet for your sake we face death all day long;
    we are considered as sheep to be slaughtered.

ᵃ 4 Septuagint, Aquila and Syriac; Hebrew King, O God; / command   *ᵇ 8 The Hebrew has Selah (a word of uncertain meaning) here.*

²³Awake, Lord! Why do you sleep?
    Rouse yourself! Do not reject us forever.
²⁴Why do you hide your face
    and forget our misery and oppression?

²⁵We are brought down to the dust;
    our bodies cling to the ground.
²⁶Rise up and help us;
    redeem us because of your unfailing love.

Psalm 45

For the director of music. To the tune of "Lilies." Of the Sons of Korah. A maskil.^a *A wedding song.*

* ¹My heart is stirred by a noble theme
    as I recite my verses for the king;
    my tongue is the pen of a skillful writer.

²You are the most excellent of men
    and your lips have been anointed with grace,
    since God has blessed you forever.

³Gird your sword on your side, you mighty one;
    clothe yourself with splendor and majesty.
⁴In your majesty ride forth victoriously
    in the cause of truth, humility and justice;
    let your right hand achieve awesome deeds.
⁵Let your sharp arrows pierce the hearts of the king's enemies;
    let the nations fall beneath your feet.
⁶Your throne, O God,^b will last for ever and ever;
    a scepter of justice will be the scepter of your kingdom.
⁷You love righteousness and hate wickedness;
    therefore God, your God, has set you above your companions
    by anointing you with the oil of joy.
⁸All your robes are fragrant with myrrh and aloes and cassia;
    from palaces adorned with ivory
    the music of the strings makes you glad.
⁹Daughters of kings are among your honored women;
    at your right hand is the royal bride in gold of Ophir.

¹⁰Listen, daughter, and pay careful attention:
    Forget your people and your father's house.
¹¹Let the king be enthralled by your beauty;
    honor him, for he is your lord.
¹²The city of Tyre will come with a gift,^c
    people of wealth will seek your favor.
¹³All glorious is the princess within her chamber;
    her gown is interwoven with gold.
¹⁴In embroidered garments she is led to the king;
    her virgin companions follow her—
    those brought to be with her.
¹⁵Led in with joy and gladness,
    they enter the palace of the king.

748

---

^a Title: Probably a literary or musical term   ^b *6* Here the king is addressed as God's representative.   ^c *12* Or *A Tyrian robe is among the gifts*
* 45:1-17 is numbered 45:2-18 in Hebrew texts.

¹⁶Your sons will take the place of your fathers;
    you will make them princes throughout the land.

¹⁷I will perpetuate your memory through all generations;
    therefore the nations will praise you for ever and ever.

Psalm 46

For the director of music. Of the Sons of Korah. According to alamoth.ᵃ *A song.*

* ¹God is our refuge and strength,
    an ever-present help in trouble.
²Therefore we will not fear, though the
        earth give way
    and the mountains fall into the heart of
        the sea,
³though its waters roar and foam
    and the mountains quake with their
        surging.ᵇ

⁴There is a river whose streams make glad
        the city of God,
    the holy place where the Most High
        dwells.
⁵God is within her, she will not fall;
    God will help her at break of day.
⁶Nations are in uproar, kingdoms fall;
    he lifts his voice, the earth melts.

⁷The Lᴏʀᴅ Almighty is with us;
    the God of Jacob is our fortress.

⁸Come and see what the Lᴏʀᴅ has done,
    the desolations he has brought on the
        earth.
⁹He makes wars cease
    to the ends of the earth.
  He breaks the bow and shatters the spear;
    he burns the shieldsᶜ with fire.
¹⁰"Be still, and know that I am God;
    I will be exalted among the nations,
    I will be exalted in the earth."

¹¹The Lᴏʀᴅ Almighty is with us;
    the God of Jacob is our fortress.

Psalm 47

For the director of music. Of the Sons of Korah. A psalm.

* ¹Clap your hands, all you nations;
    shout to God with cries of joy.

²For the Lᴏʀᴅ Most High is awesome,
    the great King over all the earth.
³He subdued nations under us,

---

atissue:stress

46:1–3,10 Things in life often fall apart all at once. Name your *crisis du jour.* You have a bitter fight with your husband or boyfriend—and it seems as if a piece of your secure life falls at your feet. Layoffs threaten your job—another chunk drops. Your single mom breaks her hip—yet another piece falls. When life is crashing down around you, do you work even harder to hold it together? Try a different approach: Be still. Find comfort and strength in God, and stop trying so hard to fix everything. No matter how many pieces fall, you will have God's inner peace.

749

ᵃ Title: Probably a musical term   ᵇ *3* The Hebrew has *Selah* (a word of uncertain meaning) here and at the end of verses 7 and 11.   ᶜ *9* Or *chariots*
* 46:1-11 is numbered 46:2-12 in Hebrew texts.   * 47:1-9 is numbered 47:2-10 in Hebrew texts.

peoples under our feet.
⁴He chose our inheritance for us,
   the pride of Jacob, whom he loved.ᵃ

⁵God has ascended amid shouts of joy,
   the Lᴏʀᴅ amid the sounding of trumpets.
⁶Sing praises to God, sing praises;
   sing praises to our King, sing praises.
⁷For God is the King of all the earth;
   sing to him a psalm of praise.

⁸God reigns over the nations;
   God is seated on his holy throne.
⁹The nobles of the nations assemble
   as the people of the God of Abraham,
for the kingsᵇ of the earth belong to God;
   he is greatly exalted.

Psalm 48

A song. A psalm of the Sons of Korah.

*¹Great is the Lᴏʀᴅ, and most worthy of praise,
   in the city of our God, his holy mountain.

²Beautiful in its loftiness,
   the joy of the whole earth,
like the heights of Zaphonᶜ is Mount Zion,
   the city of the Great King.
³God is in her citadels;
   he has shown himself to be her fortress.

⁴When the kings joined forces,
   when they advanced together,
⁵they saw her and were astounded;
   they fled in terror.
⁶Trembling seized them there,
   pain like that of a woman in labor.
⁷You destroyed them like ships of Tarshish
   shattered by an east wind.

⁸As we have heard,
   so we have seen
in the city of the Lᴏʀᴅ Almighty,
   in the city of our God:
God makes her secure
   forever.ᵈ

⁹Within your temple, O God,
   we meditate on your unfailing love.
¹⁰Like your name, O God,
   your praise reaches to the ends of the earth;
   your right hand is filled with righteousness.

ᵃ *4* The Hebrew has *Selah* (a word of uncertain meaning) here. ᵇ *9* Or *shields* ᶜ *2 Zaphon* was the most sacred mountain of the Canaanites. ᵈ *8* The Hebrew
has *Selah* (a word of uncertain meaning) here.

* 48:1-14 is numbered 48:2-15 in Hebrew texts.

¹¹Mount Zion rejoices,
      the villages of Judah are glad
      because of your judgments.

¹²Walk about Zion, go around her,
      count her towers,
¹³consider well her ramparts,
      view her citadels,
   that you may tell of them
      to the next generation.

¹⁴For this God is our God for ever and ever;
      he will be our guide even to the end.

Psalm 49

For the director of music. Of the Sons of Korah. A psalm.

*¹Hear this, all you peoples;
      listen, all who live in this world,
²both low and high,
      rich and poor alike:
³My mouth will speak words of wisdom;
      the meditation of my heart will give you understanding.
⁴I will turn my ear to a proverb;
      with the harp I will expound my riddle:

⁵Why should I fear when evil days come,
      when wicked deceivers surround me—
⁶those who trust in their wealth
      and boast of their great riches?
⁷No one can redeem the life of another
      or give to God a sufficient ransom—
⁸the ransom for a life is costly,
      no payment is ever enough—
⁹so that someone should live on forever
      and not see decay.
¹⁰For all can see that the wise die,
      that the foolish and the senseless also perish,
      leaving their wealth to others.
¹¹Their tombs will remain their houses*ᵃ* forever,
      their dwellings for endless generations,
      though they had*ᵇ* named lands after themselves.

¹²Human beings, despite their wealth, do not endure;
      they are like the beasts that perish.

¹³This is the fate of those who trust in themselves,
      and of their followers, who approve their sayings.*ᶜ*
¹⁴They are like sheep and are destined to die;
      death will be their shepherd
      (but the upright will prevail over them in the morning).
   Their forms will decay in the grave,

751

ᵃ 11 Septuagint and Syriac; Hebrew *In their thoughts their houses will remain*   *ᵇ 11* Or *generations, / for they have*   *ᶜ13* The Hebrew has *Selah* (a word of uncertain meaning) here and at the end of verse 15.

* 49:1-20 is numbered 49:2-21 in Hebrew texts.

far from their princely mansions.

15But God will redeem me from the realm
      of the dead;
   he will surely take me to
      himself.
16Do not be overawed when others grow
      rich,
   when the splendor of their houses
      increases;
17for they will take nothing with them
      when they die,
   their splendor will not descend with
      them.
18Though while they live they count
      themselves blessed—
   and people praise you when you
      prosper—
19they will join those who have gone
      before them,
   who will never again see the light of
      life.

20Human beings who have wealth but
      lack understanding
   are like the beasts that perish.

atissue:materialism

49:16–20 Have you ever imagined what you would do if you won the lottery? All your worries would be over, right? Actually, money is not all it's cracked up to be. Certainly, people look at you in awe when you're wealthy, and they praise you when you prosper. And you likely count yourself blessed. It's not a lasting blessing, though, because no matter how much money you have, you can't take it with you when you die. If you are wealthy but don't understand who you really are—and who God really is—then you're no better off than road-kill on the highway.

Psalm 50

A psalm of Asaph.

1The Mighty One, God, the LORD,
   speaks and summons the earth
   from the rising of the sun to where it sets.
2From Zion, perfect in beauty,
   God shines forth.
3Our God comes
   and will not be silent;
 a fire devours before him,
   and around him a tempest rages.
4He summons the heavens above,
   and the earth, that he may judge his people:
5"Gather to me this consecrated people,
   who made a covenant with me by sacrifice."
6And the heavens proclaim his righteousness,
   for he is a God of justice.*a,b*

7"Listen, my people, and I will speak;
   I will testify against you, Israel:
   I am God, your God.
8I bring no charges against you concerning your sacrifices
   or concerning your burnt offerings, which are ever before me.
9I have no need of a bull from your stall

752

a 6 With a different word division of the Hebrew; Masoretic Text *for God himself is judge*   *b 6* The Hebrew has *Selah* (a word of uncertain meaning) here.

or of goats from your pens,
¹⁰for every animal of the forest is mine,
and the cattle on a thousand hills.
¹¹I know every bird in the mountains,
and the creatures of the field are mine.
¹²If I were hungry I would not tell you,
for the world is mine, and all that is in it.
¹³Do I eat the flesh of bulls
or drink the blood of goats?

¹⁴"Sacrifice thank offerings to God,
fulfill your vows to the Most High,
¹⁵and call on me in the day of trouble;
I will deliver you, and you will honor me."

¹⁶But to the wicked, God says:

"What right have you to recite my laws
or take my covenant on your lips?
¹⁷You hate my instruction
and cast my words behind you.
¹⁸When you see thieves, you join with them;
you throw in your lot with adulterers.
¹⁹You use your mouth for evil
and harness your tongue to deceit.
²⁰You sit and testify against your brother
and slander your own mother's son.
²¹When you did these things and I kept silent,
you thought I was exactly^a like you.
But I now arraign you
and set my accusations before you.

²²"Consider this, you who forget God,
or I will tear you to pieces, with no one to rescue:
²³Those who sacrifice thank offerings honor me,
and to the blameless^b I will show my salvation."

Psalm 51

*For the director of music. A psalm of David. When the prophet Nathan
came to him after David had committed adultery with Bathsheba.*

^{* 1}Have mercy on me, O God,
according to your unfailing love;
according to your great compassion
blot out my transgressions.
²Wash away all my iniquity
and cleanse me from my sin.

³For I know my transgressions,
and my sin is always before me.
⁴Against you, you only, have I sinned
and done what is evil in your sight;

753

myth# 48 "AT LEAST I'M NOT AS BAD AS *SHE* IS."

I know I shouldn't do it, but I can't help it. Work gets so boring at times, doing the same things over and over again. Talking about other people's lives in the office keeps things lively. And working the graveyard shift, conversation and caffeine keep me awake. It's always interesting to hear who's dating, who's not, what they did last weekend, etc. It's not as if this mindless talk is hurting anyone; we're just keeping up on everyone's social lives. Whenever I start to feel guilty about why I want to be in the know, I remind myself that at least I'm not as bad as Cindy is.

She knows the dirt on everyone. I don't know how she does it, but Cindy always has the daily dish. (I wonder sometimes how much of what she tells is the truth and how much she makes up.) Even so, whenever she's on vacation or out sick, we all mourn the loss—it's so boring without her juicy details.

I'm not a gossip. I just listen in on the conversations. I don't say any-thing—usually. Oh, a couple of times I've made a meager contribution. Once, I saw two people from the office out together on the weekend. Hardly news. I was merely making conversation, something to pass the time. Still, Cindy has a way of turning an insignificant detail into a full-fledged rumor. I'd hate to run into her somewhere I shouldn't be and have her report it back to the whole gang. At least I'm not like her.

—Isabel

COMPARING YOURSELF

to someone else is a common way to alleviate your own guilty feelings. That act of comparison may ease your conscience, but, as David reminds us in Psalm 51:4, it does nothing to repair the damage that sin does in your relationship with God. Sometimes you may feel so sure you've pinpointed someone else's sin, but you are oblivious to your own wrongdoing. The next time you are tempted to compare yourself with someone else, remember to **think**—twice, small and smart.

- **Think twice.** In Isabel's story, we might be tempted to deny what gossip really is. Gossip is talking about others, usually with the intent to hurt them. It can also be idle chatter about others. We may try to convince ourselves that we aren't gossiping because we're just "listening." However, the Bible warns against even associating with those who gossip. Whatever the sin in your life that you're trying to rationalize, let's call it what it is: *sin.*

- **Think small.** Even a little gossip is still gossip. Even a little lie is still a lie. Even a little cheating is still cheating. Even a little . . . you fill in the blank. The size of the sin is irrelevant. *So what if I slip up a little, only on occasion? Compared to someone else who is completely caught up in sin, it's not that bad, right?* Wrong. We may feel less guilty. But are we? There is no such thing as a tiny, insignificant sin.

- **Think smart.** Learn from your mistakes. A better way to lessen guilt is to avoid the sin in the first place. Instead of looking for a quick fix in the comparison game, trying to make yourself feel better about your sin, figure out how to proactively address your own area of weakness (or avoid it altogether) next time.

"The habit of judging and condemning others can be a more serious blemish than the things we so glibly point out as others' faults."

—J. Hudson Taylor

755

"THOSE WHO HAVE NO SENSE DERIDE THEIR NEIGHBORS, BUT THOSE WHO HAVE UNDERSTANDING HOLD THEIR TONGUES."

PROVERBS 11:12

SEE ALSO

Psalm 51:1–4

Matthew 7:1–5

Romans 6:11–14

1 Timothy 1:15–17

For more on **Gossip**, check the index.

so you are right in your verdict
  and justified when you judge.
⁵Surely I was sinful at birth,
  sinful from the time my mother
    conceived me.
⁶Yet you desired faithfulness even in the
    womb;
  you taught me wisdom in that secret
    place.

⁷Cleanse me with hyssop, and I will be
    clean;
  wash me, and I will be whiter than
    snow.
⁸Let me hear joy and gladness;
  let the bones you have crushed
    rejoice.
⁹Hide your face from my sins
  and blot out all my iniquity.

¹⁰Create in me a pure heart, O God,
  and renew a steadfast spirit within me.
¹¹Do not cast me from your presence
  or take your Holy Spirit from me.
¹²Restore to me the joy of your salvation
  and grant me a willing spirit, to
    sustain me.

¹³Then I will teach transgressors your ways,
  and sinners will turn back to you.
¹⁴Deliver me from bloodguilt, O God,
  you who are God my Savior,
  and my tongue will sing of your righteousness.
¹⁵Open my lips, Lord,
  and my mouth will declare your praise.
¹⁶You do not delight in sacrifice, or I would bring it;
  you do not take pleasure in burnt offerings.
¹⁷My sacrifice, O God, is ᵃ a broken spirit;
  a broken and contrite heart
  you, God, will not despise.

¹⁸May it please you to prosper Zion,
  to build up the walls of Jerusalem.
¹⁹Then you will delight in the sacrifices of the righteous,
  in burnt offerings offered whole;
  then bulls will be offered on your altar.

Psalm 52

*For the director of music. A maskil ᵇ of David. When Doeg the Edomite had gone
to Saul and told him: "David has gone to the house of Ahimelek."*

* ¹Why do you boast of evil, you mighty hero?

a tissue: forgiveness

51:1–19 David had reached the end of himself. His sins—adultery, murder, lying—had caught up with him. He knew the depth of his sin, but he also knew the depth of God's love and compassion. That's what gave him hope. As much as David was a sinner, God was a forgiver, so David threw himself on God's mercy. And that's what God gave him—not begrudging forgiveness, but lavish cleansing. If you think you're beyond forgiveness, or if you're trying to earn your way back to God, take a lesson from David. Throw yourself on God's grace. He will forgive.

756

ᵃ 17 Or *The sacrifices of God are*   ᵇ Title: Probably a literary or musical term
* 52:1-9 is numbered 52:3-11 in Hebrew texts.

Why do you boast all day long,
 you who are a disgrace in the eyes of God?
²You who practice deceit,
  your tongue plots destruction;
  it is like a sharpened razor.
³You love evil rather than good,
  falsehood rather than speaking the truth.ᵃ
⁴You love every harmful word,
  you deceitful tongue!

⁵Surely God will bring you down to everlasting ruin:
  He will snatch you up and pluck you from your tent;
  he will uproot you from the land of the living.
⁶The righteous will see and fear;
  they will laugh at you, saying,
⁷"Here now is the one
   who did not make God his stronghold
 but trusted in his great wealth
   and grew strong by destroying others!"

⁸But I am like an olive tree
  flourishing in the house of God;
I trust in God's unfailing love
  for ever and ever.
⁹For what you have done I will always praise you
  in the presence of your faithful people.
And I will hope in your name,
  for your name is good.

Psalm 53

For the director of music. According to mahalath.ᵇ *A maskilᶜ of David.*

* ¹Fools say in their hearts,
   "There is no God."
 They are corrupt, and their ways are vile;
   there is no one who does good.

²God looks down from heaven
  on the human race
to see if there are any who understand,
  any who seek God.
³Everyone has turned away, all have become corrupt;
   there is no one who does good,
   not even one.

⁴Do all these evildoers know nothing?

 They devour my people as though eating bread;
   they never call on God.
⁵But there they are, overwhelmed with dread,
   where there was nothing to dread.

ᵃ *3* The Hebrew has *Selah* (a word of uncertain meaning) here and at the end of verse 5.   ᵇ Title: Probably a musical term   ᶜ Title: Probably a literary or musical term

* 53:1-6 is numbered 53:2-7 in Hebrew texts.

God scattered the bones of those who attacked you;
  you put them to shame, for God despised them.

[6] Oh, that salvation for Israel would come out of Zion!
  When God restores his people,
  let Jacob rejoice and Israel be glad!

Psalm 54

*For the director of music. With stringed instruments. A maskil[a] of David.
When the Ziphites had gone to Saul and said, "Is not David hiding among us?"*

* [1] Save me, O God, by your name;
  vindicate me by your might.
[2] Hear my prayer, O God;
  listen to the words of my mouth.

[3] Arrogant foes are attacking me;
  ruthless people seek my life—
  people without regard for God.[b]

[4] Surely God is my help;
  the Lord is the one who sustains me.

[5] Let evil recoil on those who slander me;
  in your faithfulness destroy them.

[6] I will sacrifice a freewill offering to you;
  I will praise your name, Lord, for it is good.
[7] You have delivered me from all my troubles,
  and my eyes have looked in triumph on my foes.

Psalm 55

For the director of music. With stringed instruments. A maskil[a] of David.

* [1] Listen to my prayer, O God,
  do not ignore my plea;
[2] hear me and answer me.
  My thoughts trouble me and I am distraught
[3] because of what my enemy is saying,
  because of the threats of the wicked;
  for they bring down suffering on me
  and assail me in their anger.

[4] My heart is in anguish within me;
  the terrors of death have fallen on me.
[5] Fear and trembling have beset me;
  horror has overwhelmed me.
[6] I said, "Oh, that I had the wings of a dove!
  I would fly away and be at rest.
[7] I would flee far away
  and stay in the desert;[c]

---

[a] Title: Probably a literary or musical term   [b] The Hebrew has *Selah* (a word of uncertain meaning) here.   [c] 7 The Hebrew has *Selah* (a word of uncertain meaning) here and in the middle of verse 19.

* 54:1-7 is numbered 54:3-9 in Hebrew texts.   * 55:1-23 is numbered 55:2-24 in Hebrew texts.

⁸ I would hurry to my place of shelter,
  far from the tempest and storm."

⁹ Lord, confuse the wicked, confound their words,
  for I see violence and strife in the city.
¹⁰ Day and night they prowl about on its walls;
  malice and abuse are within it.
¹¹ Destructive forces are at work in the city;
  threats and lies never leave its streets.

¹² If an enemy were insulting me,
  I could endure it;
 if a foe were rising against me,
  I could hide.
¹³ But it is you, one like myself,
  my companion, my close friend,
¹⁴ with whom I once enjoyed sweet fellowship
  at the house of God,
 as we walked about
  among the worshipers.

¹⁵ Let death take my enemies by surprise;
  let them go down alive to the realm of the dead,
  for evil finds lodging among them.

¹⁶ As for me, I call to God,
  and the Lord saves me.
¹⁷ Evening, morning and noon
  I cry out in distress,
  and he hears my voice.
¹⁸ He rescues me unharmed
  from the battle waged against me,
  even though many oppose me.
¹⁹ God, who is enthroned from of old,
  who does not change—
 he will hear them and humble them,
  because they have no fear of God.

²⁰ My companion attacks his friends;
  he violates his covenant.
²¹ His talk is smooth as butter,
  yet war is in his heart;
 his words are more soothing than oil,
  yet they are drawn swords.

²² Cast your cares on the Lord
  and he will sustain you;
 he will never let
  the righteous be shaken.
²³ But you, God, will bring down the wicked
  into the pit of decay;
 the bloodthirsty and deceitful
  will not live out half their days.

 But as for me, I trust in you.

759

Psalm 56

For the director of music. To the tune of "A Dove on Distant Oaks." Of David.
A miktam.ᵃ When the Philistines had seized him in Gath.

* ¹Be merciful to me, my God,
for my enemies are in hot pursuit;
all day long they press their attack.
²My adversaries pursue me all day long;
in their pride many are attacking me.

³When I am afraid, I put my
trust in you.
⁴   In God, whose word I
praise—
in God I trust and am not
afraid.
What can mere mortals do
to me?

⁵All day long they twist my
words;
all their schemes are for my
ruin.
⁶They conspire, they lurk,
they watch my steps,
hoping to take my life.
⁷Because of their wickedness do notᵇ let them escape;
in your anger, God, bring the nations down.

⁸Record my misery;
list my tears on your scrollᶜ—
are they not in your record?
⁹Then my enemies will turn back
when I call for help.
By this I will know that God is for me.

¹⁰In God, whose word I praise,
in the LORD, whose word I praise—
¹¹in God I trust and am not afraid.
What can mere human beings do to me?

¹²I am under vows to you, my God;
I will present my thank offerings to you.
¹³For you have delivered me from death
and my feet from stumbling,
that I may walk before God
in the light of life.

"conversations"

fear «» 56:1–13

1 » How can praising God lessen your fear?

2 » Why can you still trust God, even though he'll
sometimes allow bad things to happen to you?

3 » How can the fear of something actually be
more disabling than the bad thing itself?

For more on **fear**, check the index.
For the next Conversations, go to p. 771.

Psalm 57

For the director of music. To the tune of "Do Not Destroy." Of David.
A miktam.ᵃ When he had fled from Saul into the cave.

* ¹Have mercy on me, my God, have mercy on me,

760

ᵃ Title: Probably a literary or musical term   ᵇ 7 Probable reading of the original Hebrew text; Masoretic Text does not have *do not*.   ᶜ 8 Or *misery; / put my tears in your wineskin*

* 56:1-13 is numbered 56:2-14 in Hebrew texts.   * 57:1-11 is numbered 57:2-12 in Hebrew texts.

for in you I take refuge.
I will take refuge in the shadow of your wings
    until the disaster has passed.

²I cry out to God Most High,
    to God, who vindicates me.
³He sends from heaven and saves me,
    rebuking those who hotly pursue me—ᵃ
God sends forth his love and his faithfulness.

⁴I am in the midst of lions;
    I am forced to dwell among man-eating beasts,
whose teeth are spears and arrows,
    whose tongues are sharp swords.

⁵Be exalted, O God, above the heavens;
    let your glory be over all the earth.

⁶They spread a net for my feet—
    I was bowed down in distress.
They dug a pit in my path—
    but they have fallen into it themselves.

⁷My heart, O God, is steadfast,
    my heart is steadfast;
    I will sing and make music.
⁸Awake, my soul!
    Awake, harp and lyre!
    I will awaken the dawn.

⁹I will praise you, Lord, among the nations;
    I will sing of you among the peoples.
¹⁰For great is your love, reaching to the heavens;
    your faithfulness reaches to the skies.

¹¹Be exalted, O God, above the heavens;
    let your glory be over all the earth.

Psalm 58

*For the director of music. To the tune of "Do Not Destroy." Of David. A miktam.*ᵇ

* ¹Do you rulers indeed speak justly?
    Do you judge people with equity?
²No, in your heart you devise injustice,
    and your hands mete out violence on the earth.

³Even from birth the wicked go astray;
    from the womb they are wayward, spreading lies.
⁴Their venom is like the venom of a snake,
    like that of a cobra that has stopped its ears,
⁵that will not heed the tune of the charmer,
    however skillful the enchanter may be.

⁶Break the teeth in their mouths, O God;
    LORD, tear out the fangs of those lions!

ᵃ 3 The Hebrew has *Selah* (a word of uncertain meaning) here and at the end of verse 6.   ᵇ Title: Probably a literary or musical term
* 58:1-11 is numbered 58:2-12 in Hebrew texts.

⁷Let them vanish like water that flows away;
  when they draw the bow, let their arrows fall short.
⁸May they be like a slug that melts away as it moves along,
  like a stillborn child that never sees the sun.

⁹Before your pots can feel the heat of the thorns—
  whether they are green or dry—the wicked will be swept away.ᵃ
¹⁰The righteous will be glad when they are avenged,
  when they dip their feet in the blood of the wicked.
¹¹Then people will say,
  "Surely the righteous still are rewarded;
  surely there is a God who judges the earth."

Psalm 59

For the director of music. To the tune of "Do Not Destroy." Of David. A miktam.ᵇ
When Saul had sent men to watch David's house in order to kill him.

* ¹Deliver me from my enemies, O God;
  be my fortress against those who are attacking me.
²Deliver me from evildoers
  and save me from those who are after my blood.

³See how they lie in wait for me!
  Powerful people conspire against me
  for no offense or sin of mine, LORD.
⁴I have done no wrong, yet they are ready to attack me.
  Arise to help me; look on my plight!
⁵You, LORD God Almighty,
  you who are the God of Israel,
rouse yourself to punish all the nations;
  show no mercy to wicked traitors.ᶜ

⁶They return at evening,
  snarling like dogs,
  and prowl about the city.
⁷See what they spew from their mouths—
  the words from their lips are sharp as swords,
  and they think, "Who can hear us?"
⁸But you laugh at them, LORD;
  you scoff at all those nations.

⁹You are my strength, I watch for you;
  you, God, are my fortress,
¹⁰ my God on whom I can rely.

God will go before me
  and will let me gloat over those who slander me.
¹¹But do not kill them, Lord our shield,ᵈ
  or my people will forget.
In your might uproot them
  and bring them down.
¹²For the sins of their mouths,

ᵃ *9* The meaning of the Hebrew for this verse is uncertain.   ᵇ Title: Probably a literary or musical term   ᶜ *5* The Hebrew has *Selah* (a word of uncertain meaning) here and at the end of verse 13.   ᵈ *11* Or *sovereign*

* 59:1-17 is numbered 59:2-18 in Hebrew texts.

for the words of their lips,
    let them be caught in their pride.
For the curses and lies they utter,
¹³   consume them in wrath,
    consume them till they are no more.
Then it will be known to the ends of the earth
    that God rules over Jacob.

¹⁴They return at evening,
    snarling like dogs,
    and prowl about the city.
¹⁵They wander about for food
    and howl if not satisfied.
¹⁶But I will sing of your strength,
    in the morning I will sing of your love;
for you are my fortress,
    my refuge in times of trouble.

¹⁷You are my strength, I sing praise to you;
    you, God, are my fortress,
    my God on whom I can rely.

763

HE IS: my strength

59:14–17 Saul (David's own father-in-law) sent men to lie in wait at David's house to assassinate him. Like a pack of wild dogs, these men were willing to prey on an innocent man. But God proved stronger than the king's evil plot, and thus David praised God, his strength.

It may be that people at work are threatened by your value system or that your unbelieving family doesn't relate to the whole "God thing." That's when the snarling and sniping begins. Take heart! God can protect you in a hostile environment. You, too, can say, "He is *my strength.*"

For the next He Is, go to p. 778.

Psalm 60

For the director of music. To the tune of "The Lily of the Covenant." A miktam ᵃ of David. For teaching. When he fought Aram Naharaim ᵇ and Aram Zobah, ᶜ and when Joab returned and struck down twelve thousand Edomites in the Valley of Salt.

* ¹You have rejected us, God, and burst upon us;
    you have been angry—now restore us!
²You have shaken the land and torn it open;
    mend its fractures, for it is quaking.
³You have shown your people desperate times;
    you have given us wine that makes us stagger.
⁴But for those who fear you, you have raised a banner
    to be unfurled against the bow.ᵈ

ᵃ Title: Probably a literary or musical term   ᵇ Title: That is, Arameans of Northwest Mesopotamia   ᶜ Title: That is, Arameans of central Syria   ᵈ 4 The Hebrew has *Selah* (a word of uncertain meaning) here.

* 60:1-12 is numbered 60:3-14 in Hebrew texts.

⁵Save us and help us with your right hand,
that those you love may be delivered.
⁶God has spoken from his sanctuary:
"In triumph I will parcel out Shechem
and measure off the Valley of Sukkoth.
⁷Gilead is mine, and Manasseh is mine;
Ephraim is my helmet,
Judah is my scepter.
⁸Moab is my washbasin,
on Edom I toss my sandal;
over Philistia I shout in triumph."

⁹Who will bring me to the fortified city?
Who will lead me to Edom?
¹⁰Is it not you, God, you who have now rejected us
and no longer go out with our armies?
¹¹Give us aid against the enemy,
for human help is worthless.
¹²With God we will gain the victory,
and he will trample down our enemies.

Psalm 61

For the director of music. With stringed instruments. Of David.

¹Hear my cry, O God;
listen to my prayer.

²From the ends of the earth I call to you,
I call as my heart grows faint;
lead me to the rock that is higher than I.
³For you have been my refuge,
a strong tower against the foe.

⁴I long to dwell in your tent forever
and take refuge in the shelter of your wings.^a
⁵For you, God, have heard my vows;
you have given me the heritage of those who fear your name.

⁶Increase the days of the king's life,
his years for many generations.
⁷May he be enthroned in God's presence forever;
appoint your love and faithfulness to protect him.

⁸Then I will ever sing in praise of your name
and fulfill my vows day after day.

Psalm 62

For the director of music. For Jeduthun. A psalm of David.

¹Truly my soul finds rest in God;
my salvation comes from him.
²Truly he is my rock and my salvation;
he is my fortress, I will never be shaken.

---

^a *4* The Hebrew has *Selah* (a word of uncertain meaning) here.
* 61:1-8 is numbered 61:2-9 in Hebrew texts.   * 62:1-12 is numbered 62:2-13 in Hebrew texts.

³How long will you assault me?
   Would all of you throw me down—
   this leaning wall, this tottering fence?
⁴Surely they intend to topple me
   from my lofty place;
   they take delight in lies.
With their mouths they bless,
   but in their hearts they curse.^a

⁵Yes, my soul, find rest in God;
   my hope comes from him.
⁶Truly he is my rock and my salvation;
   he is my fortress, I will not be shaken.
⁷My salvation and my honor depend on
      God^b;
   he is my mighty rock, my refuge.
⁸Trust in him at all times, you people;
   pour out your hearts to him,
   for God is our refuge.

⁹Surely the lowborn are but a breath,
   the highborn are but a lie.
If weighed on a balance, they are nothing;
   together they are only a breath.
¹⁰Do not trust in extortion
   or put vain hope in stolen goods;
though your riches increase,
   do not set your heart on them.

¹¹One thing God has spoken,
   two things I have heard:
"Power belongs to you, God,
¹²   and with you, Lord, is unfailing love";
and, "You reward everyone
   according to what they have done."

at issue: aging parents

62:5–8 Growing up, most of us found security in our parents. It didn't matter what happened as long as they hugged us and told us everything would be fine. As we got older, we realized our parents couldn't fix every problem, but we still felt more secure knowing they were there. It hurts to think about living without them, let alone actually doing it. It's one hard reality of these decades of life. Whenever you experience that loss, let it remind you to find security in God alone. He's the only refuge you can count on in an ever-changing world.

765

Psalm 63

A psalm of David. When he was in the Desert of Judah.

* ¹You, God, are my God,
   earnestly I seek you;
I thirst for you,
   my whole being longs for you,
in a dry and parched land
   where there is no water.

²I have seen you in the sanctuary
   and beheld your power and your glory.
³Because your love is better than life,
   my lips will glorify you.
⁴I will praise you as long as I live,
   and in your name I will lift up my hands.

---

^a *4* The Hebrew has *Selah* (a word of uncertain meaning) here and at the end of verse 8.   ^b *7* Or / *God Most High is my salvation and my honor*
* 63:1-11 is numbered 63:2-12 in Hebrew texts.

⁵I will be fully satisfied as with the
    richest of foods;
  with singing lips my mouth will praise
    you.

⁶On my bed I remember you;
  I think of you through the watches of
    the night.
⁷Because you are my help,
  I sing in the shadow of your wings.
⁸I cling to you;
  your right hand upholds me.

⁹Those who seek my life will be
    destroyed;
  they will go down to the depths of the
    earth.
¹⁰They will be given over to the sword
  and become food for jackals.

¹¹But the king will rejoice in God;
  all who swear by God will glory in
    him,
  while the mouths of liars will be
    silenced.

766

at issue: loving God

63:1–11 Do you truly love God? It's hard to feel an emotion toward an invisible deity. Then again, cultivating your love for God is like cultivating love in any relationship. It takes time. It involves actions, not just feelings. God wants you to look for every opportunity to spend time with him. He wants you to value him more than life itself. He wants you to find satisfaction in him. He wants you to think and talk of him often, look to him for protection, cling to him for comfort and strength. Do you have that kind of intimacy with God yet?

Psalm 64

For the director of music. A psalm of David.

*¹Hear me, my God, as I voice my complaint;
  protect my life from the threat of the enemy.

²Hide me from the conspiracy of the wicked,
  from the plots of evildoers.
³They sharpen their tongues like swords
  and aim cruel words like deadly arrows.
⁴They shoot from ambush at the innocent;
  they shoot suddenly, without fear.

⁵They encourage each other in evil plans,
  they talk about hiding their snares;
  they say, "Who will see it*ᵃ*?"
⁶They plot injustice and say,
  "We have devised a perfect plan!"
  Surely the human mind and heart are cunning.

⁷But God will shoot them with his arrows;
  they will suddenly be struck down.
⁸He will turn their own tongues against them
  and bring them to ruin;
  all who see them will shake their heads in scorn.
⁹All people will fear;
  they will proclaim the works of God
  and ponder what he has done.

ᵃ *5* Or *us*

* 64:1-10 is numbered 64:2-11 in Hebrew texts.

¹⁰The righteous will rejoice in the LORD
    and take refuge in him;
    all the upright in heart will glory in him!

Psalm 65

For the director of music. A psalm of David. A song.

* ¹Praise awaits^{*a*} you, our God, in Zion;
    to you our vows will be fulfilled.
²You who answer prayer,
    to you all people will come.
³When we were overwhelmed by sins,
    you forgave^{*b*} our transgressions.
⁴Blessed are those you choose
    and bring near to live in your courts!
We are filled with the good things of your house,
    of your holy temple.

⁵You answer us with awesome and righteous deeds,
    God our Savior,
the hope of all the ends of the earth
    and of the farthest seas,
⁶who formed the mountains by your power,
    having armed yourself with strength,
⁷who stilled the roaring of the seas,
    the roaring of their waves,
    and the turmoil of the nations.
⁸The whole earth is filled with awe at your wonders;
    where morning dawns, where evening fades,
    you call forth songs of joy.

⁹You care for the land and water it;
    you enrich it abundantly.
The streams of God are filled with water
    to provide the people with grain,
    for so you have ordained it.^{*c*}
¹⁰You drench its furrows and level its ridges;
    you soften it with showers and bless its crops.
¹¹You crown the year with your bounty,
    and your carts overflow with abundance.
¹²The grasslands of the wilderness overflow;
    the hills are clothed with gladness.
¹³The meadows are covered with flocks
    and the valleys are mantled with grain;
    they shout for joy and sing.

Psalm 66

For the director of music. A song. A psalm.

¹Shout for joy to God, all the earth!
²   Sing the glory of his name;
    make his praise glorious.

---

^{*a*} *1* Or *befits*; the meaning of the Hebrew for this word is uncertain.   ^{*b*} *3* Or *made atonement for*   ^{*c*} *9* Or *for that is how you prepare the land*
* 65:1-13 is numbered 65:2-14 in Hebrew texts.

768

³Say to God, "How awesome are your deeds!
    So great is your power
    that your enemies cringe before you.
⁴All the earth bows down to you;
    they sing praise to you,
    they sing the praises of your name." ᵃ

⁵Come and see what God has done,
    his awesome deeds for humankind!
⁶He turned the sea into dry land,
    they passed through the waters on foot—
    come, let us rejoice in him.
⁷He rules forever by his power,
    his eyes watch the nations—
    let not the rebellious rise up against him.

⁸Praise our God, all peoples,
    let the sound of his praise be heard;
⁹he has preserved our lives
    and kept our feet from slipping.
¹⁰For you, God, tested us;
    you refined us like silver.
¹¹You brought us into prison
    and laid burdens on our backs.
¹²You let people ride over our heads;
    we went through fire and water,
    but you brought us to a place of abundance.

¹³I will come to your temple with burnt offerings
    and fulfill my vows to you—
¹⁴vows my lips promised and my mouth spoke
    when I was in trouble.
¹⁵I will sacrifice fat animals to you
    and an offering of rams;
    I will offer bulls and goats.

¹⁶Come and hear, all you who fear God;
    let me tell you what he has done for me.
¹⁷I cried out to him with my mouth;
    his praise was on my tongue.
¹⁸If I had cherished sin in my heart,
    the Lord would not have listened;
¹⁹but God has surely listened
    and has heard my prayer.
²⁰Praise be to God,
    who has not rejected my prayer
    or withheld his love from me!

Psalm 67

For the director of music. With stringed instruments. A psalm. A song.

* ¹May God be gracious to us and bless us

ᵃ *4* The Hebrew has *Selah* (a word of uncertain meaning) here and at the end of verses 7 and 15.

* 67:1-7 is numbered 67:2-8 in Hebrew texts.

and make his face shine on us—[a]
²so that your ways may be known on earth,
      your salvation among all nations.

³May the peoples praise you, God;
      may all the peoples praise you.
⁴May the nations be glad and sing for joy,
      for you rule the peoples with equity
      and guide the nations of the earth.
⁵May the peoples praise you, God;
      may all the peoples praise you.

⁶The land yields its harvest;
      God, our God, blesses us.
⁷May God bless us still,
      so that all the ends of the earth will fear him.

Psalm 68

For the director of music. Of David. A psalm. A song.

* ¹May God arise, may his enemies be scattered;
      may his foes flee before him.
²May you blow them away like smoke—
      as wax melts before the fire,
      may the wicked perish before God.
³But may the righteous be glad
      and rejoice before God;
      may they be happy and joyful.

⁴Sing to God, sing in praise of his name,
      extol him who rides on the clouds[b];
      rejoice before him—his name is the
            LORD.
⁵A father to the fatherless, a defender of
            widows,
      is God in his holy dwelling.
⁶God sets the lonely in families,[c]
      he leads out the prisoners with singing;
      but the rebellious live in a sun-scorched
            land.

⁷When you, God, went out before your
            people,
      when you marched through the
            wilderness,[d]
⁸the earth shook, the heavens poured down
            rain,
      before God, the One of Sinai,
      before God, the God of Israel.
⁹You gave abundant showers, O God;
      you refreshed your weary inheritance.

atissue:single-parenting

68:4–6 "Wanted: Woman to fill the role of both father and mother. Applicant should be prepared to feel totally inadequate to meet the requirements of at least half of this job. She must be willing to work on her own without a back-up. No break time allowed." Whether you applied for it or not, you may find yourself filling this position. Being a single parent is tough! But remember that you and your children are not alone. God promises to be a father to the fatherless and to defend those without husbands. Trust yourself and your children to his care. He will be with you.

---

[a] *1* Hebrew has *Selah* (a word of uncertain meaning) here and at the end of verse 4.   [b] *4* Or *name, / prepare the way for him who rides through the deserts*
[c] *6* Or *the desolate in a homeland*   [d] *7* The Hebrew has *Selah* (a word of uncertain meaning) here and at the end of verses 19 and 32.

* *68:1-35 is numbered 68:2-36 in Hebrew texts.*

770

¹⁰Your people settled in it,
 and from your bounty, God, you provided for the poor.

¹¹The Lord announced the word,
 and great was the company of those who proclaimed it:
¹²"Kings and armies flee in haste;
 every household shares in the plunder.
¹³Even while you sleep among the sheep pens,^{*a*}
 the wings of my dove are sheathed with silver,
 its feathers with shining gold."
¹⁴When the Almighty^{*b*} scattered the kings in the land,
 it was like snow fallen on Mount Zalmon.

¹⁵Mount Bashan, majestic mountain,
 Mount Bashan, rugged mountain,
¹⁶why gaze in envy, you rugged mountain,
 at the mountain where God chooses to reign,
 where the Lord himself will dwell forever?
¹⁷The chariots of God are tens of thousands
 and thousands of thousands;
 the Lord has come from Sinai into his sanctuary.^{*c*}
¹⁸When you ascended on high,
 you took many captives;
 you received gifts from people,
even from^{*d*} the rebellious—
 that you,^{*e*} Lord God, might dwell there.

¹⁹Praise be to the Lord, to God our Savior,
 who daily bears our burdens.
²⁰Our God is a God who saves;
 from the Sovereign Lord comes escape from death.
²¹Surely God will crush the heads of his enemies,
 the hairy crowns of those who go on in their sins.
²²The Lord says, "I will bring them from Bashan;
 I will bring them from the depths of the sea,
²³that your feet may wade in the blood of your foes,
 while the tongues of your dogs have their share."

²⁴Your procession, God, has come into view,
 the procession of my God and King into the sanctuary.
²⁵In front are the singers, after them the musicians;
 with them are the young women playing the timbrels.
²⁶Praise God in the great congregation;
 praise the Lord in the assembly of Israel.
²⁷There is the little tribe of Benjamin, leading them,
 there the great throng of Judah's princes,
 and there the princes of Zebulun and of Naphtali.

²⁸Summon your power, God^{*f*};
 show us your strength, our God, as you have done before.
²⁹Because of your temple at Jerusalem

---

^{*a*} *13* Or *the campfires; or the saddlebags*   ^{*b*} *14* Hebrew *Shaddai*   ^{*c*} *17* Probable reading of the original Hebrew text; Masoretic Text *Lord is among them at Sinai in holiness*   ^{*d*} *18* Or *gifts for people, / even*   ^{*e*} *18* Or *they*   ^{*f*} *28* Many Hebrew manuscripts, Septuagint and Syriac; most Hebrew manuscripts *Your God has summoned power for you*

kings will bring you gifts.
³⁰Rebuke the beast among the reeds,
the herd of bulls among the calves of the nations.
Humbled, may it bring bars of silver.
Scatter the nations who delight in war.
³¹Envoys will come from Egypt;
Cush^a will submit herself to God.

³²Sing to God, you kingdoms of the earth,
sing praise to the Lord,
³³to him who rides the ancient skies above,
who thunders with mighty voice.
³⁴Proclaim the power of God,
whose majesty is over Israel,
whose power is in the skies.
³⁵You, God, are awesome in your sanctuary;
the God of Israel gives power and strength to his people.

Praise be to God!

Psalm 69

For the director of music. To the tune of "Lilies." Of David.

* ¹Save me, O God,
for the waters have come up to my neck.
²I sink in the miry depths,
where there is no foothold.
I have come into the deep waters;
the floods engulf me.
³I am worn out calling for help;
my throat is parched.
My eyes fail,
looking for my God.
⁴Those who hate me without reason
outnumber the hairs of my head;
many are my enemies without cause,
those who seek to destroy me.
I am forced to restore
what I did not steal.

⁵You, God, know my folly;
my guilt is not hidden from you.

⁶Lord, the LORD Almighty,
may those who hope in you
not be disgraced because of me;
God of Israel,
may those who seek you
not be put to shame because of me.
⁷For I endure scorn for your sake,
and shame covers my face.
⁸I am a foreigner to my own family,

conversations

overcommitment ⟨⟩ 69:1–3

1 » Why is it that trying to please everyone can actually result in letting everyone down?

2 » When you find yourself drowning in commitments, why is it still so difficult to say no?

3 » When you feel overwhelmed, as David did by his circumstances, what should you do?

For more on **overcommitment**, check the index.
For the next Conversations, go to p. 799.

For the next Conversations, go to p. 799.

---

^a *31* That is, the upper Nile region
* 69:1-36 is numbered 69:2-37 in Hebrew texts.

a stranger to my own mother's children;
⁹for zeal for your house consumes me,
  and the insults of those who insult you fall on me.
¹⁰When I weep and fast,
  I must endure scorn;
¹¹when I put on sackcloth,
  people make sport of me.
¹²Those who sit at the gate mock me,
  and I am the song of the drunkards.

¹³But I pray to you, LORD,
  in the time of your favor;
 in your great love, O God,
  answer me with your sure salvation.
¹⁴Rescue me from the mire,
  do not let me sink;
 deliver me from those who hate me,
  from the deep waters.
¹⁵Do not let the floodwaters engulf me
  or the depths swallow me up
  or the pit close its mouth over me.

¹⁶Answer me, LORD, out of the goodness of your love;
  in your great mercy turn to me.
¹⁷Do not hide your face from your servant;
  answer me quickly, for I am in trouble.
¹⁸Come near and rescue me;
  redeem me because of my foes.

¹⁹You know how I am scorned, disgraced and shamed;
  all my enemies are before you.
²⁰Scorn has broken my heart
  and has left me helpless;
 I looked for sympathy, but there was none,
  for comforters, but I found none.
²¹They put gall in my food
  and gave me vinegar for my thirst.

²²May the table set before them become a snare;
  may it become retribution and ᵃ a trap.
²³May their eyes be darkened so they cannot see,
  and their backs be bent forever.
²⁴Pour out your wrath on them;
  let your fierce anger overtake them.
²⁵May their place be deserted;
  let there be no one to dwell in their tents.
²⁶For they persecute those you wound
  and talk about the pain of those you hurt.
²⁷Charge them with crime upon crime;
  do not let them share in your salvation.
²⁸May they be blotted out of the book of life
  and not be listed with the righteous.

ᵃ 22 Or snare / and their fellowship become

ASKmeanYTHING

Tell us about yourself.

I was the youngest daughter of King Saul, the first king of Israel. I grew up in the royal palace. It seemed only appropriate that I would one day marry someone befitting my status. Then David came along.

Tell us about David.

[smiles, looks off into the distance] When I first saw David, I couldn't take my eyes off him. He was young, strong, courageous, handsome—every girl's dream. I fell in love with him instantly.

Your marriage had a rocky start, didn't it?

That's an understatement. From day one, my father did everything he could to disrupt our relationship. Even after our marriage, my father would not leave David alone. One night, my dad sent his men to kill David. I risked my father's wrath to help David escape. I couldn't sit by and allow him to be killed! But as punishment, my father gave me away to become the wife of another man. And I lost David.

773

What happened?

Years went by with my father chasing David and David running from him. I never saw or heard from my first husband. It was a nightmare. Then one day, after it was clear my father and his kingly line had been defeated, David asked that I be brought to him. If only life were that simple . . . by this time, I'd made a new life with my new husband, and David now had several other wives in addition to me. Imagine the kind of painful adjustment I was forced to make.

How did things turn out for you?

Well, I got what I had once hoped for—the title of queen, a royal position, respect. But just when it was all within my grasp, it was gone. At the moment of his greatest triumph, there was my husband out in the streets, dancing and carrying on like a commoner. I couldn't believe it! It was humiliating, absolutely humiliating. What would people think? How was I supposed to feel? But David didn't care how I felt. What was important to him was worshiping God.

What happened then?

I spent the rest of my life childless, alone, filled with regrets. It was far too great a price to pay. I had the opportunity to use my position for good. But I was too concerned with what others would think. It was a foolish choice.

FOR MORE INSIGHT: Michal's story is a hard one. Though we are often quick to blame her for her scorn of David, she likely went through great heartache of her own. For a fuller understanding of her situation, read more of her story, which appears in snippets throughout 1 Samuel 14—2 Samuel 6. Also, check out Psalm 18:27; and Proverbs 11:2; 31:30 to see how God regards vanity and pride, and their consequences.

²⁹But as for me, afflicted and in pain—
 may your salvation, God, protect me.

³⁰I will praise God's name in song
 and glorify him with thanksgiving.
³¹This will please the LORD more than an ox,
 more than a bull with its horns and hooves.
³²The poor will see and be glad—
 you who seek God, may your hearts live!
³³The LORD hears the needy
 and does not despise his captive people.

³⁴Let heaven and earth praise him,
 the seas and all that move in them,
³⁵for God will save Zion
 and rebuild the cities of Judah.
 Then people will settle there and possess it;
³⁶ the children of his servants will inherit it,
 and those who love his name will dwell there.

Psalm 70

For the director of music. Of David. A petition.

* ¹Hasten, O God, to save me;
 come quickly, LORD, to help me.

²May those who seek my life
 be put to shame and confusion;
 may all who desire my ruin
 be turned back in disgrace.
³May those who say to me, "Aha! Aha!"
 turn back because of their shame.
⁴But may all who seek you
 rejoice and be glad in you;
 may those who long for your saving help always say,
 "The LORD is great!"

⁵But as for me, I am poor and needy;
 come quickly to me, O God.
 You are my help and my deliverer;
 LORD, do not delay.

Psalm 71

¹In you, LORD, I have taken refuge;
 let me never be put to shame.
²In your righteousness, rescue me and deliver me;
 turn your ear to me and save me.
³Be my rock of refuge,
 to which I can always go;
 give the command to save me,
 for you are my rock and my fortress.
⁴Deliver me, my God, from the hand of the wicked,
 from the grasp of those who are evil and cruel.

* 70:1-5 is numbered 70:2-6 in Hebrew texts.

⁵For you have been my hope, Sovereign LORD,
  my confidence since my youth.
⁶From birth I have relied on you;
  you brought me forth from my mother's womb.
  I will ever praise you.
⁷I have become like a portent to many,
  but you are my strong refuge.
⁸My mouth is filled with your praise,
  declaring your splendor all day long.

⁹Do not cast me away when I am old;
  do not forsake me when my strength is gone.
¹⁰For my enemies speak against me;
  those who wait to kill me conspire together.
¹¹They say, "God has forsaken him;
  pursue him and seize him,
  for no one will rescue him."
¹²Do not be far from me, my God;
  come quickly, God, to help me.
¹³May my accusers perish in shame;
  may those who want to harm me
  be covered with scorn and disgrace.

¹⁴As for me, I will always have hope;
  I will praise you more and more.

¹⁵My mouth will tell of your righteous deeds,
  of your saving acts all day long—
  though I know not how to relate them all.
¹⁶I will come and proclaim your mighty acts, Sovereign LORD;
  I will proclaim your righteous deeds, yours alone.
¹⁷Since my youth, God, you have taught me,
  and to this day I declare your marvelous deeds.
¹⁸Even when I am old and gray,
  do not forsake me, my God,
 till I declare your power to the next generation,
  your mighty acts to all who are to come.

¹⁹Your righteousness, God, reaches to the skies,
  you who have done great things.
  Who is like you, God?
²⁰Though you have made me see troubles,
  many and bitter,
  you will restore my life again;
 from the depths of the earth
  you will again bring me up.
²¹You will increase my honor
  and comfort me once more.

²²I will praise you with the harp
  for your faithfulness, my God;
 I will sing praise to you with the lyre,
  Holy One of Israel.
²³My lips will shout for joy

775

when I sing praise to you—
I, whom you have redeemed.
²⁴My tongue will tell of your righteous acts
all day long,
for those who wanted to harm me
have been put to shame and confusion.

Psalm 72

Of Solomon.

¹Endow the king with your justice, O God,
the royal son with your righteousness.
²May he judge your people in righteousness,
your afflicted ones with justice.

³May the mountains bring prosperity to the people,
the hills the fruit of righteousness.
⁴May he defend the afflicted among the people
and save the children of the needy;
may he crush the oppressor.
⁵May he endure*ᵃ* as long as the sun,
as long as the moon, through all generations.
⁶May he be like rain falling on a mown field,
like showers watering the earth.
⁷In his days may the righteous flourish
and prosperity abound till the moon is no more.

⁸May he rule from sea to sea
and from the River*ᵇ* to the ends of the earth.
⁹May the desert tribes bow before him
and his enemies lick the dust.
¹⁰May the kings of Tarshish and of distant shores
bring tribute to him.
May the kings of Sheba and Seba
present him gifts.
¹¹May all kings bow down to him
and all nations serve him.

¹²For he will deliver the needy who cry out,
the afflicted who have no one to help.
¹³He will take pity on the weak and the needy
and save the needy from death.
¹⁴He will rescue them from oppression and violence,
for precious is their blood in his sight.

¹⁵Long may he live!
May gold from Sheba be given him.
May people ever pray for him
and bless him all day long.
¹⁶May grain abound throughout the land;
on the tops of the hills may it sway.
May the crops flourish like Lebanon
and thrive*ᶜ* like the grass of the field.

ᵃ 5 Septuagint; Hebrew *You will be feared*   *ᵇ 8* That is, the Euphrates   *ᶜ 16* Probable reading of the original Hebrew text; Masoretic Text *Lebanon, / from the city*

¹⁷May his name endure forever;
  may it continue as long as the sun.

Then all nations will be blessed through him,^a
  and they will call him blessed.

¹⁸Praise be to the L<small>ORD</small> God, the God of Israel,
  who alone does marvelous deeds.
¹⁹Praise be to his glorious name forever;
  may the whole earth be filled with his glory.
            Amen and Amen.

²⁰This concludes the prayers of David son of Jesse.

BOOK III

Psalms 73–89

Psalm 73

A psalm of Asaph.

¹Surely God is good to Israel,
  to those who are pure in heart.

²But as for me, my feet had almost slipped;
  I had nearly lost my foothold.
³For I envied the arrogant
  when I saw the prosperity of the wicked.

⁴They have no struggles;
  their bodies are healthy and strong.^b
⁵They are free from common human burdens;
  they are not plagued by human ills.
⁶Therefore pride is their necklace;
  they clothe themselves with violence.
⁷From their callous hearts comes iniquity^c;
  the evil conceits of their minds know no limits.
⁸They scoff, and speak with malice;
  with arrogance they threaten oppression.
⁹Their mouths lay claim to heaven,
  and their tongues take possession of the earth.
¹⁰Therefore their people turn to them
  and drink up waters in abundance.^d
¹¹They say, "How would God know?
  Does the Most High know anything?"

¹²This is what the wicked are like—
  always free of care, they go on amassing wealth.

¹³Surely in vain I have kept my heart pure
  and have washed my hands in innocence.

---

^a *17* Or *will use his name in blessings* (see Gen. 48:20)   ^b *4* With a different word division of the Hebrew; Masoretic Text *struggles at their death; / their bodies are healthy*   ^c *7* Syriac (see also Septuagint); Hebrew *Their eyes bulge with fat*   ^d *10* The meaning of the Hebrew for this verse is uncertain.

¹⁴All day long I have been afflicted,
and every morning brings new punishments.

¹⁵If I had spoken out like that,
I would have betrayed your children.
¹⁶When I tried to understand all this,
it troubled me deeply
¹⁷till I entered the sanctuary of God;
then I understood their final destiny.

¹⁸Surely you place them on slippery ground;
you cast them down to ruin.
¹⁹How suddenly are they destroyed,
completely swept away by terrors!
²⁰They are like a dream when one awakes;
when you arise, Lord,
you will despise them as fantasies.

²¹When my heart was grieved
and my spirit embittered,
²²I was senseless and ignorant;
I was a brute beast before you.

²³Yet I am always with you;
you hold me by my right hand.
²⁴You guide me with your counsel,
and afterward you will take me into glory.
²⁵Whom have I in heaven but you?
And earth has nothing I desire besides you.
²⁶My flesh and my heart may fail,
but God is the strength of my heart
and my portion forever.

HE IS: my portion

73:1–26 The psalmist was jealous that the wicked seemed to prosper. But he didn't hold his feelings in; he poured them out to God and let God change his viewpoint. He came to realize that though some people may have earthly treasures for a time, God was his forever.

Because God himself is your portion, you can let go of the world's definition of success, the praise you feel you're due and the injustices you feel subjected to. You can be satisfied without the perfect husband, the respectable career, 2.4 children and whatever else is on your wish list because you have something better: God himself is *your portion*.

For the next He Is, go to p. 782.

²⁷Those who are far from you will perish;
you destroy all who are unfaithful to you.
²⁸But as for me, it is good to be near God.
I have made the Sovereign Lord my refuge;
I will tell of all your deeds.

Psalm 74

A maskil [a] of Asaph.

¹O God, why have you rejected us forever?
    Why does your anger smolder against the sheep of your pasture?
²Remember the people you purchased long ago,
    the tribe of your inheritance, whom you redeemed—
    Mount Zion, where you dwell.
³Turn your steps toward these everlasting ruins,
    all this destruction the enemy has brought on the sanctuary.

⁴Your foes roared in the place where you met with us;
    they set up their standards as signs.
⁵They behaved like men wielding axes
    to cut through a thicket of trees.
⁶They smashed all the carved paneling
    with their axes and hatchets.
⁷They burned your sanctuary to the ground;
    they defiled the dwelling place of your Name.
⁸They said in their hearts, "We will crush them completely!"
    They burned every place where God was worshiped in the land.

⁹We are given no signs from God;
    no prophets are left,
    and none of us knows how long this will be.
¹⁰How long will the enemy mock you, God?
    Will the foe revile your name forever?
¹¹Why do you hold back your hand, your right hand?
    Take it from the folds of your garment and destroy them!

¹²But God is my King from long ago;
    he brings salvation on the earth.

¹³It was you who split open the sea by your power;
    you broke the heads of the monster in the waters.
¹⁴It was you who crushed the heads of Leviathan
    and gave it as food to the creatures of the desert.
¹⁵It was you who opened up springs and streams;
    you dried up the ever-flowing rivers.
¹⁶The day is yours, and yours also the night;
    you established the sun and moon.
¹⁷It was you who set all the boundaries of the earth;
    you made both summer and winter.

¹⁸Remember how the enemy has mocked you, Lord,
    how foolish people have reviled your name.
¹⁹Do not hand over the life of your dove to wild beasts;
    do not forget the lives of your afflicted people forever.
²⁰Have regard for your covenant,
    because haunts of violence fill the dark places of the land.
²¹Do not let the oppressed retreat in disgrace;
    may the poor and needy praise your name.
²²Rise up, O God, and defend your cause;

779

---
a Title: Probably a literary or musical term

remember how fools mock you all day long.
[23]Do not ignore the clamor of your adversaries,
the uproar of your enemies, which rises continually.

Psalm 75

For the director of music. To the tune of "Do Not Destroy." A psalm of Asaph. A song.

*[1]We praise you, God,
we praise you, for your Name is near;
people tell of your wonderful deeds.

[2]You say, "I choose the appointed time;
it is I who judge with equity.
[3]When the earth and all its people quake,
it is I who hold its pillars firm.[a]
[4]To the arrogant I say, 'Boast no more,'
and to the wicked, 'Do not lift up your horns.[b]
[5]Do not lift your horns against heaven;
do not speak with outstretched neck.'"

[6]No one from the east or the west
or from the desert can exalt themselves.
[7]It is God who judges:
He brings one down, he exalts another.
[8]In the hand of the Lord is a cup
full of foaming wine mixed with spices;
he pours it out, and all the wicked of the earth
drink it down to its very dregs.

[9]As for me, I will declare this forever;
I will sing praise to the God of Jacob,
[10]who says, "I will cut off the horns of all the wicked,
but the horns of the righteous will be lifted up."

Psalm 76

For the director of music. With stringed instruments. A psalm of Asaph. A song.

*[1]God is renowned in Judah;
in Israel his name is great.
[2]His tent is in Salem,
his dwelling place in Zion.
[3]There he broke the flashing arrows,
the shields and the swords, the weapons of war.[c]

[4]You are resplendent with light,
more majestic than mountains rich with game.
[5]The valiant lie plundered,
they sleep their last sleep;
not one of the warriors
can lift his hands.
[6]At your rebuke, God of Jacob,
both horse and chariot lie still.

780

---

^a *3* The Hebrew has *Selah* (a word of uncertain meaning) here.   ^b *4 Horns* here symbolize strength; also in verses 5 and 10.   ^c *3* The Hebrew has *Selah* (a word of uncertain meaning) here and at the end of verse 9.

* 75:1-10 is numbered 75:2-11 in Hebrew texts.   * 76:1-12 is numbered 76:2-13 in Hebrew texts.

781

⁷It is you alone who are to be feared.
　Who can stand before you when you are angry?
⁸From heaven you pronounced judgment,
　and the land feared and was quiet—
⁹when you, God, rose up to judge,
　to save all the afflicted of the land.
¹⁰Surely your wrath against human beings brings you praise,
　and the survivors of your wrath are restrained.ᵃ

¹¹Make vows to the LORD your God and fulfill them;
　let all the neighboring lands
　bring gifts to the One to be feared.
¹²He breaks the spirit of rulers;
　he is feared by the kings of the earth.

Psalm 77

For the director of music. For Jeduthun. Of Asaph. A psalm.

* ¹I cried out to God for help;
　I cried out to God to hear me.
²When I was in distress, I sought the Lord;
　at night I stretched out untiring hands,
　and I would not be comforted.

³I remembered you, God, and I groaned;
　I meditated, and my spirit grew faint.ᵇ
⁴You kept my eyes from closing;
　I was too troubled to speak.
⁵I thought about the former days,
　the years of long ago;
⁶I remembered my songs in the night.
　My heart meditated and my spirit asked:

⁷"Will the Lord reject forever?
　Will he never show his favor again?
⁸Has his unfailing love vanished forever?
　Has his promise failed for all time?
⁹Has God forgotten to be merciful?
　Has he in anger withheld his compassion?"

¹⁰Then I thought, "To this I will appeal:
　the years when the Most High stretched out his right hand.
¹¹I will remember the deeds of the LORD;
　yes, I will remember your miracles of long ago.
¹²I will consider all your works
　and meditate on all your mighty deeds."

¹³Your ways, God, are holy.
　What god is as great as our God?
¹⁴You are the God who performs miracles;
　you display your power among the peoples.

ᵃ *10* Or *Surely human wrath brings you praise, / and with the remainder of wrath you arm yourself*　　ᵇ *3* The Hebrew has *Selah* (a word of uncertain meaning)
here and at the end of verses 9 and 15.

* 77:1-20 is numbered 77:2-21 in Hebrew texts.

HE IS: worth considering

77:12–13 The psalmist made a conscious decision to think about God. He didn't say, "I might reflect on God." He said, "I will consider all your works and meditate on all your mighty deeds." God is *worth considering* because no one is his equal.

When do you stop and consider God? Before you start your day? Before you eat? Before you sleep? He is *worth considering* before, during and after your day. You may think your schedule is too hectic to take time to think about God. If so, then what god in your life are you making as great as our God?

For the next He Is, go to p. 792.

782

¹⁵With your mighty arm you redeemed your people,
   the descendants of Jacob and Joseph.

¹⁶The waters saw you, God,
   the waters saw you and writhed;
   the very depths were convulsed.
¹⁷The clouds poured down water,
   the heavens resounded with thunder;
   your arrows flashed back and forth.
¹⁸Your thunder was heard in the whirlwind,
   your lightning lit up the world;
   the earth trembled and quaked.
¹⁹Your path led through the sea,
   your way through the mighty waters,
   though your footprints were not seen.

²⁰You led your people like a flock
   by the hand of Moses and Aaron.

Psalm 78

A maskil ᵃ of Asaph.

¹My people, hear my teaching;
   listen to the words of my mouth.
²I will open my mouth with a parable;
   I will teach you lessons from the past—
³things we have heard and known,
   things our ancestors have told us.
⁴We will not hide them from their descendants;
   we will tell the next generation
the praiseworthy deeds of the LORD,
   his power, and the wonders he has done.
⁵He decreed statutes for Jacob
   and established the law in Israel,
which he commanded our ancestors
   to teach their children,
⁶so the next generation would know them,
   even the children yet to be born,

ᵃ Title: Probably a literary or musical term

and they in turn would tell their children.
⁷Then they would put their trust in God
 and would not forget his deeds
 but would keep his commands.
⁸They would not be like their ancestors—
 a stubborn and rebellious generation,
whose hearts were not loyal to God,
 whose spirits were not faithful to him.

⁹The men of Ephraim, though armed with bows,
 turned back on the day of battle;
¹⁰they did not keep God's covenant
 and refused to live by his law.
¹¹They forgot what he had done,
 the wonders he had shown them.
¹²He did miracles in the sight of their ancestors
 in the land of Egypt, in the region of Zoan.
¹³He divided the sea and led them through;
 he made the water stand up like a wall.
¹⁴He guided them with the cloud by day
 and with light from the fire all night.
¹⁵He split the rocks in the wilderness
 and gave them water as abundant as the seas;
¹⁶he brought streams out of a rocky crag
 and made water flow down like rivers.

¹⁷But they continued to sin against him,
 rebelling in the wilderness against the Most High.
¹⁸They willfully put God to the test
 by demanding the food they craved.
¹⁹They spoke against God;
 they said, "Can God really
 spread a table in the wilderness?
²⁰True, he struck the rock,
 and water gushed out,
 streams flowed abundantly,
but can he also give us bread?
 Can he supply meat for his people?"
²¹When the Lᴏʀᴅ heard them, he was furious;
 his fire broke out against Jacob,
 and his wrath rose against Israel,
²²for they did not believe in God
 or trust in his deliverance.
²³Yet he gave a command to the skies above
 and opened the doors of the heavens;
²⁴he rained down manna for the people to eat,
 he gave them the grain of heaven.
²⁵Human beings ate the bread of angels;
 he sent them all the food they could eat.
²⁶He let loose the east wind from the heavens
 and by his power made the south wind blow.
²⁷He rained meat down on them like dust,

783

birds like sand on the seashore.
²⁸He made them come down inside their camp,
all around their tents.
²⁹They ate till they were gorged—
he had given them what they craved.
³⁰But before they turned from what they craved,
even while the food was still in their mouths,
³¹God's anger rose against them;
he put to death the sturdiest among them,
cutting down the young men of Israel.

³²In spite of all this, they kept on sinning;
in spite of his wonders, they did not believe.
³³So he ended their days in futility
and their years in terror.
³⁴Whenever God slew them, they would seek him;
they eagerly turned to him again.
³⁵They remembered that God was their Rock,
that God Most High was their Redeemer.
³⁶But then they would flatter him with their mouths,
lying to him with their tongues;
³⁷their hearts were not loyal to him,
they were not faithful to his covenant.
³⁸Yet he was merciful;
he forgave their iniquities
and did not destroy them.
Time after time he restrained his anger
and did not stir up his full wrath.
³⁹He remembered that they were but flesh,
a passing breeze that does not return.

⁴⁰How often they rebelled against him in the wilderness
and grieved him in the wasteland!
⁴¹Again and again they put God to the test;
they vexed the Holy One of Israel.
⁴²They did not remember his power—
the day he redeemed them from the oppressor,
⁴³the day he displayed his signs in Egypt,
his wonders in the region of Zoan.
⁴⁴He turned their river into blood;
they could not drink from their streams.
⁴⁵He sent swarms of flies that devoured them,
and frogs that devastated them.
⁴⁶He gave their crops to the grasshopper,
their produce to the locust.
⁴⁷He destroyed their vines with hail
and their sycamore-figs with sleet.
⁴⁸He gave over their cattle to the hail,
their livestock to bolts of lightning.
⁴⁹He unleashed against them his hot anger,
his wrath, indignation and hostility—
a band of destroying angels.

784

⁵⁰He prepared a path for his anger;
    he did not spare them from death
    but gave them over to the plague.
⁵¹He struck down all the firstborn of Egypt,
    the firstfruits of manhood in the tents of Ham.
⁵²But he brought his people out like a flock;
    he led them like sheep through the wilderness.
⁵³He guided them safely, so they were unafraid;
    but the sea engulfed their enemies.
⁵⁴And so he brought them to the border of his holy land,
    to the hill country his right hand had taken.
⁵⁵He drove out nations before them
    and allotted their lands to them as an inheritance;
    he settled the tribes of Israel in their homes.

⁵⁶But they put God to the test
    and rebelled against the Most High;
    they did not keep his statutes.
⁵⁷Like their ancestors they were disloyal and faithless,
    as unreliable as a faulty bow.
⁵⁸They angered him with their high places;
    they aroused his jealousy with their idols.
⁵⁹When God heard them, he was furious;
    he rejected Israel completely.
⁶⁰He abandoned the tabernacle of Shiloh,
    the tent he had set up among mortals.
⁶¹He sent the ark of his might into captivity,
    his splendor into the hands of the enemy.
⁶²He gave his people over to the sword;
    he was furious with his inheritance.
⁶³Fire consumed their young men,
    and their young women had no wedding songs;
⁶⁴their priests were put to the sword,
    and their widows could not weep.

⁶⁵Then the Lord awoke as from sleep,
    as a warrior wakes from the stupor of wine.
⁶⁶He beat back his enemies;
    he put them to everlasting shame.
⁶⁷Then he rejected the tents of Joseph,
    he did not choose the tribe of Ephraim;
⁶⁸but he chose the tribe of Judah,
    Mount Zion, which he loved.
⁶⁹He built his sanctuary like the heights,
    like the earth that he established forever.
⁷⁰He chose David his servant
    and took him from the sheep pens;
⁷¹from tending the sheep he brought him
    to be the shepherd of his people Jacob,
    of Israel his inheritance.
⁷²And David shepherded them with integrity of heart;
    with skillful hands he led them.

785

myth# 49 "I DON'T NEED TO RELAX."

786

I live by my tasks list. I scroll through it at least ten times a day to see what I need to do next. I have my to-do items arranged by due date so I won't forget anything urgent.

I'm the kind of person who never runs out of things to do. My roommate gets home from work and collapses on the couch to watch TV. She drags herself into the kitchen to make dinner and a few phone calls, and then it's back to the couch till she's ready for bed. That's not me at all.

I go straight from work to the gym. As soon as I get home I sort through my mail, itemize any bills, recycle the junk mail, shred anything confidential, ask my roommate how her day was, start making dinner and then dive into a project. It could be a house project (cleaning, laundry, reorganizing) or a personal project (phone calls, e-mail, scrap-booking, coffee with a friend). I try to use my evenings well. There's never enough time in the day.

My friends and family tell me I need to slow down and relax. But I can always relax when I'm retired someday. For now, I want to make the most of the time I have. I did try to relax one day last month and cleared my calendar of all obligations. I went to a park with just my Bible and a sack lunch, but I grew restless in about thirty minutes. After I prayed for everyone I could think of and read a few psalms, I realized that relaxing just wasn't for me. It just doesn't fit my "go-go" personality. I am at my best when there is a lot going on in my life. I'm a very productive person. Besides, I don't want to miss anything. What if someone needs me? What if I miss something exciting while I'm resting?

Sure, sometimes I get tired. I can go on turbo speed for about a month, and then one morning I'll just crash and feel as if I can't get out of bed. It's annoying because my mind doesn't want to slow down, but my body makes me.

—Natalie

MANY WOMEN FEEL guilty if
they relax. They think they must be *doing* something at all times. The root of this issue for some
women is that they base their identities on what
they achieve. A day is only valuable or productive if they accomplish something or many
things. This is an exhausting way to live.

In contrast, God sees us as valuable because we
are his. What a radical shift in our thinking!
Seeing ourselves the way God sees us brings us
true freedom, security and best of all, *rest*.
Think about the following suggestions:

- God rested on the seventh day after creation
  (see Genesis 2:2–3). Try taking a literal day of
  Sabbath rest each week to relax and remind
  yourself that God is in control. If you build
  this day of rest into your week, you will protect yourself from burnout. The other six
  days of your week will be more rewarding and
  productive.

- If you never relax, your body will eventually
  wear down from the long-term effects of
  stress. Life is a marathon, not a sprint, so
  pace yourself.

- Resting and trusting in God means you won't
  try to accomplish things in your own
  strength. God can empower you to accomplish what is essential in any given day (see
  Psalm 46:10).

- If you learn to balance work and rest, you will
  be more effective in your Christian life.
  When you don't understand this balance,
  you'll end up tired and ineffective.

- Jesus regularly went away by himself to
  recharge and pray. He wasn't "on" 24 hours a
  day. Instead, he rested and recharged in
  times alone. If Jesus needed time to relax,
  how much more do you? Will you follow his
  example and set aside a regular time each
  week to relax?

"A spiritual discipline of regular rest from the constant drive
to check items off a to-do list
can be a powerful symbol of
our trust in God's sufficiency."
—ChristianityToday.com

787

"come to me,
all you who
are weary and
burdened,
and I will give
you rest."

MATTHEW 11:28

SEE ALSO
Exodus 16:23
Psalm 37:7
Hebrews 4:9–10

For more on **Rest**, check
the index.

Psalm 79

A psalm of Asaph.

¹O God, the nations have invaded your inheritance;
  they have defiled your holy temple,
  they have reduced Jerusalem to rubble.
²They have left the dead bodies of your servants
  as food for the birds of the sky,
  the flesh of your own people for the animals of the wild.
³They have poured out blood like water
  all around Jerusalem,
  and there is no one to bury the dead.
⁴We are objects of contempt to our neighbors,
  of scorn and derision to those around us.

⁵How long, LORD? Will you be angry forever?
  How long will your jealousy burn like fire?
⁶Pour out your wrath on the nations
  that do not acknowledge you,
on the kingdoms
  that do not call on your name;
⁷for they have devoured Jacob
  and devastated his homeland.

⁸Do not hold against us the sins of past generations;
  may your mercy come quickly to meet us,
  for we are in desperate need.
⁹Help us, God our Savior,
  for the glory of your name;
deliver us and forgive our sins
  for your name's sake.
¹⁰Why should the nations say,
  "Where is their God?"

Before our eyes, make known among the nations
  that you avenge the outpoured blood of your servants.
¹¹May the groans of the prisoners come before you;
  with your strong arm preserve those condemned to die.
¹²Pay back into the laps of our neighbors seven times
  the contempt they have hurled at you, Lord.
¹³Then we your people, the sheep of your pasture,
  will praise you forever;
from generation to generation
  we will proclaim your praise.

Psalm 80

*For the director of music. To the tune of "The Lilies of the Covenant."
Of Asaph. A psalm.*

* ¹Hear us, Shepherd of Israel,
  you who lead Joseph like a flock.
You who sit enthroned between the cherubim,
  shine forth ²before Ephraim, Benjamin and Manasseh.

---

* 80:1-19 is numbered 80:2-20 in Hebrew texts.

Awaken your might;
come and save us.

³Restore us, O God;
make your face shine on us,
that we may be saved.

⁴How long, Lᴏʀᴅ God Almighty,
will your anger smolder
against the prayers of your people?
⁵You have fed them with the bread of tears;
you have made them drink tears by the bowlful.
⁶You have made us an object of derision*a* to our neighbors,
and our enemies mock us.

⁷Restore us, God Almighty;
make your face shine on us,
that we may be saved.

⁸You transplanted a vine from Egypt;
you drove out the nations and planted it.
⁹You cleared the ground for it,
and it took root and filled the land.
¹⁰The mountains were covered with its shade,
the mighty cedars with its branches.
¹¹Its branches reached as far as the Sea,*b*
its shoots as far as the River.*c*

¹²Why have you broken down its walls
so that all who pass by pick its grapes?
¹³Boars from the forest ravage it
and wild animals feed on it.
¹⁴Return to us, God Almighty!
Look down from heaven and see!
Watch over this vine,
¹⁵ the root your right hand has planted,
the son*d* you have raised up for yourself.

¹⁶Your vine is cut down, it is burned with fire;
at your rebuke your people perish.
¹⁷Let your hand rest on the man at your right hand,
the son of man you have raised up for yourself.
¹⁸Then we will not turn away from you;
revive us, and we will call on your name.

¹⁹Restore us, Lᴏʀᴅ God Almighty;
make your face shine on us,
that we may be saved.

789

Psalm 81

For the director of music. According to gittith.*e* *Of Asaph.*

* ¹Sing for joy to God our strength;
shout aloud to the God of Jacob!

---

a 6 Probable reading of the original Hebrew text; Masoretic Text *contention*   *b* 11 Probably the Mediterranean   *c* 11 That is, the Euphrates   *d* 15 Or *branch*
e Title: Probably a musical term

* 81:1-16 is numbered 81:2-17 in Hebrew texts.

²Begin the music, strike the timbrel,
    play the melodious harp and lyre.

³Sound the ram's horn at the New Moon,
    and when the moon is full, on the day of our festival;
⁴this is a decree for Israel,
    an ordinance of the God of Jacob.
⁵When God went out against Egypt,
    he established it as a statute for Joseph.

I heard an unknown voice say:

⁶"I removed the burden from their shoulders;
    their hands were set free from the basket.
⁷In your distress you called and I rescued you,
    I answered you out of a thundercloud;
    I tested you at the waters of Meribah.ᵃ
⁸Hear me, my people, and I will warn you—
    if you would only listen to me, Israel!
⁹You shall have no foreign god among you;
    you shall not worship any god other than me.
¹⁰I am the LORD your God,
    who brought you up out of Egypt.
Open wide your mouth and I will fill it.

¹¹"But my people would not listen to me;
    Israel would not submit to me.
¹²So I gave them over to their stubborn hearts
    to follow their own devices.

¹³"If my people would only listen to me,
    if Israel would only follow my ways,
¹⁴how quickly I would subdue their enemies
    and turn my hand against their foes!
¹⁵Those who hate the LORD would cringe before him,
    and their punishment would last forever.
¹⁶But you would be fed with the finest of wheat;
    with honey from the rock I would satisfy you."

Psalm 82

A psalm of Asaph.

¹God presides in the great assembly;
    he gives judgment among the "gods":

²"How long will youᵇ defend the unjust
    and show partiality to the wicked?ᵃ
³Defend the weak and the fatherless;
    uphold the cause of the poor and the oppressed.
⁴Rescue the weak and the needy;
    deliver them from the hand of the wicked.

⁵"The 'gods' know nothing, they understand nothing.
    They walk about in darkness;
    all the foundations of the earth are shaken.

ᵃ *7* The Hebrew has *Selah* (a word of uncertain meaning) here.   ᵇ *2* The Hebrew is plural.

⁶"I said, 'You are "gods";
 you are all sons of the Most High.'
⁷But you will die like mere mortals;
 you will fall like every other ruler."

⁸Rise up, O God, judge the earth,
 for all the nations are your inheritance.

Psalm 83

A song. A psalm of Asaph.

* ¹O God, do not remain silent;
 do not turn a deaf ear,
 do not stand aloof, O God.
²See how your enemies growl,
 how your foes rear their heads.
³With cunning they conspire against your people;
 they plot against those you cherish.
⁴"Come," they say, "let us destroy them as a nation,
 so that Israel's name is remembered no more."

⁵With one mind they plot together;
 they form an alliance against you—
⁶the tents of Edom and the Ishmaelites,
 of Moab and the Hagrites,
⁷Byblos, Ammon and Amalek,
 Philistia, with the people of Tyre.
⁸Even Assyria has joined them
 to reinforce Lot's descendants.^a

⁹Do to them as you did to Midian,
 as you did to Sisera and Jabin at the river Kishon,
¹⁰who perished at Endor
 and became like dung on the ground.
¹¹Make their nobles like Oreb and Zeeb,
 all their princes like Zebah and Zalmunna,
¹²who said, "Let us take possession
 of the pasturelands of God."

¹³Make them like tumbleweed, my God,
 like chaff before the wind.
¹⁴As fire consumes the forest
 or a flame sets the mountains ablaze,
¹⁵so pursue them with your tempest
 and terrify them with your storm.
¹⁶Cover their faces with shame, LORD,
 so that they will seek your name.

¹⁷May they ever be ashamed and dismayed;
 may they perish in disgrace.
¹⁸Let them know that you, whose name is the LORD—
 that you alone are the Most High over all the earth.

---

^a *8* The Hebrew has *Selah* (a word of uncertain meaning) here.
* 83:1-18 is numbered 83:2-19 in Hebrew texts.

Psalm 84

For the director of music. According to gittith.[a] *Of the Sons of Korah. A psalm.*

* [1] How lovely is your dwelling place,
  LORD Almighty!
[2] My soul yearns, even faints,
  for the courts of the LORD;
my heart and my flesh cry out
  for the living God.
[3] Even the sparrow has found a home,
  and the swallow a nest for herself,
  where she may have her young—
a place near your altar,
  LORD Almighty, my King and my God.
[4] Blessed are those who dwell in your house;
  they are ever praising you.[b]

HE IS: the living God

84:1–4 This beautiful psalm echoes with the deep longing of a spiritual pilgrim whose soul craved to be in God's courts. The psalmist's journey was not to reach a place but to meet a person. His whole body and heart longed for *the living God.*

On your pilgrimage through life, don't settle for anything less than the living God himself. You will be tempted to turn aside to lesser things, distractions, false panaceas or even diluted theologies of God. But what your body, heart and soul long for is one thing, which cannot be substituted or replaced, *the living God* himself (see Luke 20:37–38).

For the next He Is, go to p. 802.

[5] Blessed are those whose strength is in you,
  whose hearts are set on pilgrimage.
[6] As they pass through the Valley of Baka,
  they make it a place of springs;
  the autumn rains also cover it with pools.[c]
[7] They go from strength to strength,
  till each appears before God in Zion.

[8] Hear my prayer, LORD God Almighty;
  listen to me, God of Jacob.
[9] Look on our shield,[d] O God;
  look with favor on your anointed one.

[10] Better is one day in your courts
  than a thousand elsewhere;
I would rather be a doorkeeper in the house of my God
  than dwell in the tents of the wicked.
[11] For the LORD God is a sun and shield;
  the LORD bestows favor and honor;
no good thing does he withhold
  from those whose walk is blameless.

---

[a] Title: Probably a musical term   [b] 4 The Hebrew has *Selah* (a word of uncertain meaning) here and at the end of verse 8.   [c] 6 Or *blessings*   [d] 9 Or *sovereign*
* 84:1-12 is numbered 84:2-13 in Hebrew texts.

¹²Lord Almighty,
    blessed are those who trust in you.

Psalm 85

For the director of music. Of the Sons of Korah. A psalm.

* ¹You, Lord, showed favor to your land;
    you restored the fortunes of Jacob.
²You forgave the iniquity of your people
    and covered all their sins.^a
³You set aside all your wrath
    and turned from your fierce anger.

⁴Restore us again, God our Savior,
    and put away your displeasure toward us.
⁵Will you be angry with us forever?
    Will you prolong your anger through all generations?
⁶Will you not revive us again,
    that your people may rejoice in you?
⁷Show us your unfailing love, Lord,
    and grant us your salvation.

⁸I will listen to what God the Lord says;
    he promises peace to his people, his faithful servants—
    but let them not turn to folly.
⁹Surely his salvation is near those who fear him,
    that his glory may dwell in our land.

¹⁰Love and faithfulness meet together;
    righteousness and peace kiss each other.
¹¹Faithfulness springs forth from the earth,
    and righteousness looks down from heaven.
¹²The Lord will indeed give what is good,
    and our land will yield its harvest.
¹³Righteousness goes before him
    and prepares the way for his steps.

Psalm 86

A prayer of David.

¹Hear me, Lord, and answer me,
    for I am poor and needy.
²Guard my life, for I am faithful to you;
    save your servant who trusts in you.
 You are my God; ³have mercy on me, Lord,
    for I call to you all day long.
⁴Bring joy to your servant, Lord,
    for I put my trust in you.

⁵You, Lord, are forgiving and good,
    abounding in love to all who call to you.
⁶Hear my prayer, Lord;
    listen to my cry for mercy.

793

---

^a 2 The Hebrew has *Selah* (a word of uncertain meaning) here.

* 85:1-13 is numbered 85:2-14 in Hebrew texts.

⁷When I am in distress, I call to you,
  because you answer me.

⁸Among the gods there is none like you, Lord;
  no deeds can compare with yours.
⁹All the nations you have made
  will come and worship before you, Lord;
  they will bring glory to your name.
¹⁰For you are great and do marvelous deeds;
  you alone are God.

¹¹Teach me your way, LORD,
  that I may rely on your faithfulness;
  give me an undivided heart,
  that I may fear your name.
¹²I will praise you, Lord my God, with all
    my heart;
  I will glorify your name forever.
¹³For great is your love toward me;
  you have delivered me from the
    depths,
  from the realm of the dead.

¹⁴Arrogant foes are attacking me, O God;
  a band of ruthless people seeks my
    life—
  they have no regard for you.
¹⁵But you, Lord, are a compassionate and
    gracious God,
  slow to anger, abounding in love and
    faithfulness.
¹⁶Turn to me and have mercy on me;
  show your strength in behalf of your
    servant
  and save the son of a woman
  who served you before me.
¹⁷Give me a sign of your goodness,
  that my enemies may see it and be
    put to shame,
  for you, LORD, have helped me and comforted me.

at issue: identity

86:11–13 Can you spot the woman with the divided heart? She has a split personality—she acts one way at church and another at work, one way around her family and another around her friends. Depending on her situation, she shifts her speech, clothes and standards. Why does she live this way? Why would anyone live like this? We want to fit in. We want to be accepted and liked. We want a relationship with God, but we want to live like the rest of the world. But God tells us we can't have it both ways. He wants us to find our identity in him alone.

Psalm 87

Of the Sons of Korah. A psalm. A song.

¹He has founded his city on the holy mountain.
²The LORD loves the gates of Zion
  more than all the other dwellings of Jacob.

³Glorious things are said of you,
  city of God:*ᵃ*
⁴"I will record Rahab*ᵇ* and Babylon
  among those who acknowledge me—
  Philistia too, and Tyre, along with Cush*ᶜ*—

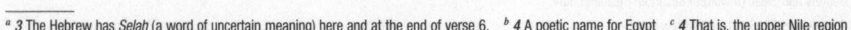

ᵃ 3 The Hebrew has *Selah* (a word of uncertain meaning) here and at the end of verse 6.   *ᵇ 4* A poetic name for Egypt   *ᶜ 4* That is, the upper Nile region

and will say, 'This one was born in Zion.'"*ᵃ
⁵Indeed, of Zion it will be said,
 "This one and that one were born in her,
 and the Most High himself will establish her."
⁶The Lᴏʀᴅ will write in the register of the peoples:
 "This one was born in Zion."

⁷As they make music they will sing,
 "All my fountains are in you."

Psalm 88

*A song. A psalm of the Sons of Korah. For the director of music.
According to mahalath leannoth.ᵇ A maskil ᶜ of Heman the Ezrahite.*

*ᵃ ¹Lᴏʀᴅ, you are the God who saves me;
 day and night I cry out to you.
²May my prayer come before you;
 turn your ear to my cry.

³I am overwhelmed with troubles
 and my life draws near to death.
⁴I am counted among those who go down to the pit;
 I am like one without strength.
⁵I am set apart with the dead,
 like the slain who lie in the grave,
whom you remember no more,
 who are cut off from your care.

⁶You have put me in the lowest pit,
 in the darkest depths.
⁷Your wrath lies heavily on me;
 you have overwhelmed me with all your waves.ᵈ
⁸You have taken from me my closest friends
 and have made me repulsive to them.
 I am confined and cannot escape;
⁹ my eyes are dim with grief.

 I call to you, Lᴏʀᴅ, every day;
 I spread out my hands to you.
¹⁰Do you show your wonders to the dead?
 Do their spirits rise up and praise you?
¹¹Is your love declared in the grave,
 your faithfulness in Destructionᵉ?
¹²Are your wonders known in the place of darkness,
 or your righteous deeds in the land of oblivion?

¹³But I cry to you for help, Lᴏʀᴅ;
 in the morning my prayer comes before you.
¹⁴Why, Lᴏʀᴅ, do you reject me
 and hide your face from me?

¹⁵From my youth I have suffered and been close to death;
   I have borne your terrors and am in despair.
¹⁶Your wrath has swept over me;
   your terrors have destroyed me.
¹⁷All day long they surround me like a flood;
   they have completely engulfed me.
¹⁸You have taken from me friend and neighbor—
   darkness is my closest friend.

Psalm 89

A maskil^a of Ethan the Ezrahite.

* ¹I will sing of the Lord's great love forever;
   with my mouth I will make your faithfulness known
   through all generations.
²I will declare that your love stands firm forever,
   that you have established your faithfulness in heaven itself.
³You said, "I have made a covenant with my chosen one,
   I have sworn to David my servant,
⁴'I will establish your line forever
   and make your throne firm through all generations.'"^b

⁵The heavens praise your wonders, Lord,
   your faithfulness too, in the assembly of the holy ones.
⁶For who in the skies above can compare with the Lord?
   Who is like the Lord among the heavenly beings?
⁷In the council of the holy ones God is greatly feared;
   he is more awesome than all who surround him.
⁸Who is like you, Lord God Almighty?
   You, Lord, are mighty, and your faithfulness surrounds you.

⁹You rule over the surging sea;
   when its waves mount up, you still them.
¹⁰You crushed Rahab like one of the slain;
   with your strong arm you scattered your enemies.
¹¹The heavens are yours, and yours also the earth;
   you founded the world and all that is in it.
¹²You created the north and the south;
   Tabor and Hermon sing for joy at your name.
¹³Your arm is endued with power;
   your hand is strong, your right hand exalted.

¹⁴Righteousness and justice are the foundation of your throne;
   love and faithfulness go before you.
¹⁵Blessed are those who have learned to acclaim you,
   who walk in the light of your presence, Lord.
¹⁶They rejoice in your name all day long;
   they exult in your righteousness.
¹⁷For you are their glory and strength,
   and by your favor you exalt our horn.^c

---

^a Title: Probably a literary or musical term   ^b *4* The Hebrew has *Selah* (a word of uncertain meaning) here and at the end of verses 37, 45 and 48.   ^c *17 Horn* here symbolizes strong one.

* 89:1-52 is numbered 89:2-53 in Hebrew texts.

¹⁸Indeed, our shield^{*a*} belongs to the LORD,
    our king to the Holy One of Israel.

¹⁹Once you spoke in a vision,
    to your faithful people you said:
 "I have bestowed strength on a warrior;
    I have raised up a young man from among the people.
²⁰I have found David my servant;
    with my sacred oil I have anointed him.
²¹My hand will sustain him;
    surely my arm will strengthen him.
²²No enemy will get the better of him;
    no wicked person will oppress him.
²³I will crush his foes before him
    and strike down his adversaries.
²⁴My faithful love will be with him,
    and through my name his horn^{*b*} will be exalted.
²⁵I will set his hand over the sea,
    his right hand over the rivers.
²⁶He will call out to me, 'You are my Father,
    my God, the Rock my Savior.'
²⁷And I will appoint him to be my firstborn,
    the most exalted of the kings of the earth.
²⁸I will maintain my love to him forever,
    and my covenant with him will never fail.
²⁹I will establish his line forever,
    his throne as long as the heavens endure.

³⁰"If his sons forsake my law
    and do not follow my statutes,
³¹if they violate my decrees
    and fail to keep my commands,
³²I will punish their sin with the rod,
    their iniquity with flogging;
³³but I will not take my love from him,
    nor will I ever betray my faithfulness.
³⁴I will not violate my covenant
    or alter what my lips have uttered.
³⁵Once for all, I have sworn by my holiness—
    and I will not lie to David—
³⁶that his line will continue forever
    and his throne endure before me like the sun;
³⁷it will be established forever like the moon,
    the faithful witness in the sky."

³⁸But you have rejected, you have spurned,
    you have been very angry with your anointed one.
³⁹You have renounced the covenant with your servant
    and have defiled his crown in the dust.
⁴⁰You have broken through all his walls
    and reduced his strongholds to ruins.

---

a *18* Or *sovereign* *b* *24* *Horn* here symbolizes strength.

⁴¹All who pass by have plundered him;
   he has become the scorn of his neighbors.
⁴²You have exalted the right hand of his foes;
   you have made all his enemies rejoice.
⁴³Indeed, you have turned back the edge of his sword
   and have not supported him in battle.
⁴⁴You have put an end to his splendor
   and cast his throne to the ground.
⁴⁵You have cut short the days of his youth;
   you have covered him with a mantle of shame.

⁴⁶How long, Lord? Will you hide yourself forever?
   How long will your wrath burn like fire?
⁴⁷Remember how fleeting is my life.
   For what futility you have created all humanity!
⁴⁸Who can live and not see death,
   or who can escape the power of the grave?
⁴⁹Lord, where is your former great love,
   which in your faithfulness you swore to David?
⁵⁰Remember, Lord, how your servant has*ᵃ* been mocked,
   how I bear in my heart the taunts of all the nations,
⁵¹the taunts with which your enemies, Lord, have mocked,
   with which they have mocked every step of your anointed one.

⁵²Praise be to the Lord forever!
                  Amen and Amen.

BOOK IV
Psalms 90–106

Psalm 90

A prayer of Moses the man of God.

¹Lord, you have been our dwelling place
   throughout all generations.
²Before the mountains were born
   or you brought forth the whole world,
   from everlasting to everlasting you are God.

³You turn people back to dust,
   saying, "Return to dust, you mortals."
⁴A thousand years in your sight
   are like a day that has just gone by,
   or like a watch in the night.
⁵Yet you sweep people away in the sleep of death—
   they are like the new grass of the morning:
⁶In the morning it springs up new,
   but by evening it is dry and withered.

⁷We are consumed by your anger
   and terrified by your indignation.

ᵃ 50 Or your servants have

⁸You have set our iniquities before you,
  our secret sins in the light of your presence.
⁹All our days pass away under your wrath;
  we finish our years with a moan.
¹⁰Our days may come to seventy years,
  or eighty, if our strength endures;
 yet the best of them are but trouble and sorrow,
  for they quickly pass, and we fly away.
¹¹If only we knew the power of your anger!
  Your wrath is as great as the fear that is your due.
¹²Teach us to number our days,
  that we may gain a heart of wisdom.

¹³Relent, LORD! How long will it be?
  Have compassion on your servants.
¹⁴Satisfy us in the morning with your unfailing love,
  that we may sing for joy and be glad all our days.
¹⁵Make us glad for as many days as you have afflicted us,
  for as many years as we have seen trouble.
¹⁶May your deeds be shown to your servants,
  your splendor to their children.

¹⁷May the favor*ᵃ* of the Lord our God rest
    on us;
  establish the work of our hands
    for us—
  yes, establish the work of our hands.

Psalm 91

¹Whoever dwells in the shelter of the
    Most High
  will rest in the shadow of the
    Almighty.*ᵇ*
²They say of the LORD, "He is my refuge
    and my fortress,
  my God, in whom I trust."

³Surely he will save you
  from the fowler's snare
  and from the deadly pestilence.
⁴He will cover you with his feathers,
  and under his wings you will find refuge;
  his faithfulness will be your shield and rampart.
⁵You will not fear the terror of night,
  nor the arrow that flies by day,
⁶nor the pestilence that stalks in the darkness,
  nor the plague that destroys at midday.
⁷A thousand may fall at your side,
  ten thousand at your right hand,
  but it will not come near you.
⁸You will only observe with your eyes
  and see the punishment of the wicked.

799

" conversations "

dissatisfaction ❮❯ 90:13–16

1 ❯❯ With what kind of attitude do you begin your day? How does that affect the rest of your day?

2 ❯❯ Why is it important to reflect on God specifically in the morning?

3 ❯❯ Who is responsible for keeping you satisfied in life?

For more on **dissatisfaction**, check the index. For the next Conversations, go to p. 806.

ᵃ 17 Or *beauty* *ᵇ 1* Hebrew *Shaddai*

⁹If you say, "The Lᴏʀᴅ is my refuge,"
and you make the Most High your dwelling,
¹⁰no harm will overtake you,
no disaster will come near your tent.
¹¹For he will command his angels concerning you
to guard you in all your ways;
¹²they will lift you up in their hands,
so that you will not strike your foot against a stone.
¹³You will tread on the lion and the cobra;
you will trample the great lion and the serpent.

¹⁴"Because they love me," says the Lᴏʀᴅ, "I will rescue them;
I will protect them, for they acknowledge my name.
¹⁵They will call on me, and I will answer them;
I will be with them in trouble,
I will deliver them and honor them.
¹⁶With long life I will satisfy them
and show them my salvation."

Psalm 92

A psalm. A song. For the Sabbath day.

* ¹It is good to praise the Lᴏʀᴅ
and make music to your name, O Most High,
²proclaiming your love in the morning
and your faithfulness at night,
³to the music of the ten-stringed lyre
and the melody of the harp.

⁴For you make me glad by your deeds, Lᴏʀᴅ;
I sing for joy at what your hands have done.
⁵How great are your works, Lᴏʀᴅ,
how profound your thoughts!
⁶Senseless people do not know,
fools do not understand,
⁷that though the wicked spring up like grass
and all evildoers flourish,
they will be destroyed forever.

⁸But you, Lᴏʀᴅ, are forever exalted.

⁹For surely your enemies, Lᴏʀᴅ,
surely your enemies will perish;
all evildoers will be scattered.
¹⁰You have exalted my horn*a* like that of a wild ox;
fine oils have been poured on me.
¹¹My eyes have seen the defeat of my adversaries;
my ears have heard the rout of my wicked foes.

¹²The righteous will flourish like a palm tree,
they will grow like a cedar of Lebanon;
¹³planted in the house of the Lᴏʀᴅ,

---

a 10 *Horn* here symbolizes strength.

* 92:1-15 is numbered 92:2-16 in Hebrew texts.

they will flourish in the courts of our God.
¹⁴They will still bear fruit in old age,
they will stay fresh and green,
¹⁵proclaiming, "The Lord is upright;
he is my Rock, and there is no wickedness in him."

Psalm 93

¹The Lord reigns, he is robed in majesty;
the Lord is robed in majesty and armed with strength;
indeed, the world is established, firm and secure.
²Your throne was established long ago;
you are from all eternity.

³The seas have lifted up, Lord,
the seas have lifted up their voice;
the seas have lifted up their pounding waves.
⁴Mightier than the thunder of the great waters,
mightier than the breakers of the sea—
the Lord on high is mighty.

⁵Your statutes, Lord, stand firm;
holiness adorns your house
for endless days.

Psalm 94

¹The Lord is a God who avenges.
O God who avenges, shine forth.
²Rise up, Judge of the earth;
pay back to the proud what they deserve.
³How long, Lord, will the wicked,
how long will the wicked be jubilant?

⁴They pour out arrogant words;
all the evildoers are full of boasting.
⁵They crush your people, Lord;
they oppress your inheritance.
⁶They slay the widow and the foreigner;
they murder the fatherless.
⁷They say, "The Lord does not see;
the God of Jacob takes no notice."

⁸Take notice, you senseless ones among the people;
you fools, when will you become wise?
⁹Does he who fashioned the ear not hear?
Does he who formed the eye not see?
¹⁰Does he who disciplines nations not punish?
Does he who teaches human beings lack knowledge?
¹¹The Lord knows all human plans;
he knows that they are futile.

¹²Blessed are those you discipline, Lord,
those you teach from your law;
¹³you grant them relief from days of trouble,
till a pit is dug for the wicked.
¹⁴For the Lord will not reject his people;

801

he will never forsake his inheritance.
¹⁵Judgment will again be founded on righteousness,
and all the upright in heart will follow it.

¹⁶Who will rise up for me against the wicked?
Who will take a stand for me against evildoers?
¹⁷Unless the Lord had given me help,
I would soon have dwelt in the silence of death.
¹⁸When I said, "My foot is slipping,"
your unfailing love, Lord, supported me.
¹⁹When anxiety was great within me,
your consolation brought me joy.

HE IS: consoling

94:17–19 Psalm 94 begins by asking God to right the wrongs done to the nation of Israel. Then the psalmist gets personal and asks, "Who will rise up for me against the wicked?" When he admits his private anxiety, notice how God responds—with consolation. God gives tender comfort and solace to his children.

Should you pray for your nation and the world around you? Absolutely. And when you feel yourself overwhelmed by the evil you see, when you feel anxious or afraid, discover for yourself that your *consoling* God will bring you joy (see 2 Corinthians 1:3–7).

For the next He Is, go to p. 812.

²⁰Can a corrupt throne be allied with you—
a throne that brings on misery by its decrees?
²¹The wicked band together against the righteous
and condemn the innocent to death.
²²But the Lord has become my fortress,
and my God the rock in whom I take refuge.
²³He will repay them for their sins
and destroy them for their wickedness;
the Lord our God will destroy them.

Psalm 95

¹Come, let us sing for joy to the Lord;
let us shout aloud to the Rock of our salvation.
²Let us come before him with thanksgiving
and extol him with music and song.

³For the Lord is the great God,
the great King above all gods.
⁴In his hand are the depths of the earth,
and the mountain peaks belong to him.
⁵The sea is his, for he made it,
and his hands formed the dry land.

⁶Come, let us bow down in worship,
let us kneel before the Lord our Maker;
⁷for he is our God

and we are the people of his pasture,
    the flock under his care.

  Today, if only you would hear his voice,
[8]"Do not harden your hearts as you did at Meribah,[a]
    as you did that day at Massah[b] in the wilderness,
[9]where your ancestors tested me;
    they tried me, though they had seen what I did.
[10]For forty years I was angry with that generation;
    I said, 'They are a people whose hearts go astray,
    and they have not known my ways.'
[11]So I declared on oath in my anger,
    'They shall never enter my rest.'"

Psalm 96

[1]Sing to the LORD a new song;
    sing to the LORD, all the earth.
[2]Sing to the LORD, praise his name;
    proclaim his salvation day after day.
[3]Declare his glory among the nations,
    his marvelous deeds among all peoples.

[4]For great is the LORD and most worthy of praise;
    he is to be feared above all gods.
[5]For all the gods of the nations are idols,
    but the LORD made the heavens.
[6]Splendor and majesty are before him;
    strength and glory are in his sanctuary.

[7]Ascribe to the LORD, all you families of nations,
    ascribe to the LORD glory and strength.
[8]Ascribe to the LORD the glory due his name;
    bring an offering and come into his courts.
[9]Worship the LORD in the splendor of his[c] holiness;
    tremble before him, all the earth.
[10]Say among the nations, "The LORD reigns."
    The world is firmly established, it cannot be moved;
    he will judge the peoples with equity.

[11]Let the heavens rejoice, let the earth be glad;
    let the sea resound, and all that is in it.
[12]Let the fields be jubilant, and everything in them;
    let all the trees of the forest sing for joy.
[13]Let all creation rejoice before the LORD, for he comes,
    he comes to judge the earth.
  He will judge the world in righteousness
    and the peoples in his faithfulness.

Psalm 97

[1]The LORD reigns, let the earth be glad;
    let the distant shores rejoice.
[2]Clouds and thick darkness surround him;
    righteousness and justice are the foundation of his throne.

---

[a] 8 Meribah means quarreling. [b] 8 Massah means testing. [c] 9 Or LORD with the splendor of

³Fire goes before him
  and consumes his foes on every side.
⁴His lightning lights up the world;
  the earth sees and trembles.
⁵The mountains melt like wax before the Lᴏʀᴅ,
  before the Lord of all the earth.
⁶The heavens proclaim his righteousness,
  and all peoples see his glory.

⁷All who worship images are put to shame,
  those who boast in idols—
  worship him, all you gods!

⁸Zion hears and rejoices
  and the villages of Judah are glad
  because of your judgments, Lᴏʀᴅ.
⁹For you, Lᴏʀᴅ, are the Most High over all the earth;
  you are exalted far above all gods.
¹⁰Let those who love the Lᴏʀᴅ hate evil,
  for he guards the lives of his faithful ones
  and delivers them from the hand of the wicked.
¹¹Light shines*ᵃ* on the righteous
  and joy on the upright in heart.
¹²Rejoice in the Lᴏʀᴅ, you who are righteous,
  and praise his holy name.

Psalm 98

A psalm.

¹Sing to the Lᴏʀᴅ a new song,
  for he has done marvelous things;
his right hand and his holy arm
  have worked salvation for him.
²The Lᴏʀᴅ has made his salvation known
  and revealed his righteousness to the nations.
³He has remembered his love
  and his faithfulness to the house of Israel;
all the ends of the earth have seen
  the salvation of our God.

⁴Shout for joy to the Lᴏʀᴅ, all the earth,
  burst into jubilant song with music;
⁵make music to the Lᴏʀᴅ with the harp,
  with the harp and the sound of singing,
⁶with trumpets and the blast of the ram's horn—
  shout for joy before the Lᴏʀᴅ, the King.

⁷Let the sea resound, and everything in it,
  the world, and all who live in it.
⁸Let the rivers clap their hands,
  let the mountains sing together for joy;
⁹let them sing before the Lᴏʀᴅ,
  for he comes to judge the earth.

ᵃ 11 One Hebrew manuscript and ancient versions (see also 112:4); most Hebrew manuscripts *Light is sown*

ASKmeanyTHING

Tell us about your husband, Nabal.

His name means *fool,* and that pretty much sums it up. Nabal was arrogant, stubborn and hot-tempered. Rude, harsh, selfish . . . need I go on?

What happened between Nabal and David?

As usual, my husband couldn't see the benefit of helping someone else. Nabal completely overlooked the fact that David's men had protected his herds and shepherds while they were out in the fields. So instead of welcoming and thanking David's men when they came asking for food and supplies, my husband rudely insulted them and turned them away. That, of course, made David very angry.

And you were stuck in the middle?

Right between a fool and an ill-tempered warrior with 400 armed men looking for revenge. Not a good place to be.

805

What did you do?

I knew that if I didn't do something, a lot of innocent blood would be lost. I couldn't stand by and let that happen—not to David, who had so much at stake, and not to the innocent men who had the misfortune of working for my husband. So I quickly gathered up some supplies and literally threw myself at David's feet. I took the blame for my husband's actions and begged David to reconsider. Wouldn't *God* take revenge on Nabal?

What happened?

David realized that he was making a terrible decision. So he accepted my gifts and went away. And as for Nabal—that fool was home getting drunk at a party. When I told him what had happened, he realized the danger he had been in and his heart, literally, gave out. He died ten days later. And I ended up marrying David!

What can we learn from your experience?

No matter what your circumstances, God wants you to be faithful to him. Just take the right steps and leave the consequences up to God. I didn't know if God would ever rescue me from Nabal and our loveless marriage. I didn't know how David would respond to my pleas. I didn't know what Nabal would do when he heard what I had done. But I knew someone needed to intervene before the situation got out of hand. Thankfully, God was able to use me in that situation. And he will use you, too.

FOR MORE INSIGHT: Read these stories of courageous conviction to take the right action: Genesis 22:1–18; Daniel 3:12–30; and Acts 4:19–20; 5:29–32.

He will judge the world in righteousness
    and the peoples with equity.

Psalm 99

[1]The LORD reigns,
    let the nations tremble;
he sits enthroned between the cherubim,
    let the earth shake.
[2]Great is the LORD in Zion;
    he is exalted over all the nations.
[3]Let them praise your great and awesome name—
    he is holy.

[4]The King is mighty, he loves justice—
    you have established equity;
in Jacob you have done
    what is just and right.
[5]Exalt the LORD our God
    and worship at his footstool;
    he is holy.

[6]Moses and Aaron were among his priests,
    Samuel was among those who called on his name;
they called on the LORD
    and he answered them.
[7]He spoke to them from the pillar of cloud;
    they kept his statutes and the decrees he gave them.

[8]LORD our God,
    you answered them;
you were to Israel a forgiving God,
    though you punished their misdeeds.[a]
[9]Exalt the LORD our God
    and worship at his holy mountain,
    for the LORD our God is holy.

Psalm 100

A psalm. For giving grateful praise.
[1]Shout for joy to the LORD, all
    the earth.
[2] Worship the LORD with
    gladness;
    come before him with
    joyful songs.
[3]Know that the LORD is God.
    It is he who made us, and
    we are his[b];
    we are his people, the sheep
    of his pasture.

[4]Enter his gates with
    thanksgiving

"conversations"

self-esteem «» 100:1–5

1» How does knowing who God is teach you
about who you are?

2» Do you think God wants you to feel good
about yourself? Why?

3» How would you describe who you are (your
identity) to someone in one minute or less?

For more on **self-esteem**, check the index.
For the next Conversations, go to p. 828.

---

[a] 8 Or God, / an avenger of the wrongs done to them   [b] 3 Or and not we ourselves

and his courts with praise;
    give thanks to him and praise his name.
⁵For the Lᴏʀᴅ is good and his love endures forever;
    his faithfulness continues through all generations.

Psalm 101

Of David. A psalm.

¹I will sing of your love and justice;
    to you, Lᴏʀᴅ, I will sing praise.
²I will be careful to lead a blameless life—
    when will you come to me?

I will conduct the affairs of my house
    with a blameless heart.
³I will not look with approval
    on anything that is vile.

I hate what faithless people do;
    I will have no part in it.
⁴The perverse of heart shall be far from me;
    I will have nothing to do with what is evil.

⁵Whoever slanders their neighbor in secret,
    I will put to silence;
whoever has haughty eyes and a proud
        heart,
    I will not endure.

⁶My eyes will be on the faithful in the land,
    that they may dwell with me;
those whose walk is blameless
    will minister to me.

⁷No one who practices deceit
    will dwell in my house;
no one who speaks falsely
    will stand in my presence.

⁸Every morning I will put to silence
    all the wicked in the land;
I will cut off every evildoer
    from the city of the Lᴏʀᴅ.

aussie:entertainment

101:1–4 Eyes don't have many choices. They basically see what's in front of them. So David made a promise to his eyes to set nothing vile before them. Have you made the same deal with your eyes? Do you make sure that nothing that God hates is set in front of them? When you open a magazine or book or watch a movie or TV show, ask yourself: What message is being communicated? How does that message compare with what God says is good and true? If what you're looking at fails the test, have nothing to do with it.

807

Psalm 102

A prayer of an afflicted person who has grown weak and pours out a lament before the Lᴏʀᴅ.

* ¹Hear my prayer, Lᴏʀᴅ;
    let my cry for help come to you.
²Do not hide your face from me
    when I am in distress.
Turn your ear to me;
    when I call, answer me quickly.

³For my days vanish like smoke;
    my bones burn like glowing embers.

---

* 102:1-28 is numbered 102:2-29 in Hebrew texts.

myth# 50 "I CAN CHANGE MY MAN."

We used to call it "missionary dating" in college. You know, a Christian girl falls for a non-Christian guy and tries to convert him. Every youth pastor told us not to do it—but we were young and naïve. We believed that our love was strong enough to change whatever was wrong.

Now that I'm married to someone I was trying to save, I realize how foolish that line of thinking is. I don't mean save him—he was already a Christian when we met. But he had so many issues from his childhood that I thought I could help him overcome. It's hard for him to communicate how he feels. He's very possessive of me. He struggles with anger and controlling his temper. He closes himself off from the kids and me. They want his love and affection so desperately, and, sadly, I know just how they feel. I thought that once we got married, I could make a difference in his life. Like the girl in the movie Jerry McGuire, I fell in love with "the man he almost was." If only I could draw out that better person inside of him, then he would be the husband and father I'd dreamed all along he could be.

Truthfully, I've spent so much time trying to change him that I think I've lost myself in the process. My friends tell me to stop trying to fix him and to worry about myself. I'm dying in this marriage, yet all I focus on is how I could make things better, what I could do to make him happier, what it would take to get through to him. I never realized how hard this would be . . . that he might not want to or be able to change.

—Chloe

WE WOMEN OFTEN spend more energy on helping and fixing others than on helping ourselves. Foolishly, we believe that we are capable of helping everyone who crosses our paths. The truth is that our not-so-subtle tactics (nagging, hinting, scheming) don't work. We will never change another person; only God can do that. If Chloe's experience sounds familiar to you, then you may be attempting the impossible—changing another person. Sometimes we have to let go of how others need to change and focus on how God would change us (see 1 Peter 3:1–2).

Where this thinking becomes particularly dangerous is in abusive relationships. Some women in abusive relationships believe that if they could just change their man or fix something about themselves, then he'd stop hurting them. That's not true. Abuse has nothing to do with what a woman is doing or not doing. The best thing a woman can do is to change her thinking and get some help for herself or her children. After all, a man may never decide to change, and staying in that abusive relationship only enables his patterns. If you are in an abusive situation, remember:

- One in three women will be abused in her own home by someone she loves at some point in her life. God did not intend for there to be abuse in relationships. He loves you and wants to keep you from harm (see Psalm 121:7–8). He has great plans for you to live your life to the fullest—and those plans *don't* include abuse.

- Emotional abuse—name calling, yelling, manipulation, threats—is often worse than physical abuse since it doesn't leave visible bruises, and family and friends may not believe you. You do not have to put up with this behavior.

- It's OK to seek help at a domestic violence agency or with a counselor. Many people are trained to help you make the changes you need to make.

"Yes, we need a changed partner, but the partner that needs to change is not our spouse, it's us!"

—Gary L. Thomas

809

"WHY DO YOU LOOK AT THE SPECK OF SAWDUST IN SOMEONE ELSE'S EYE AND PAY NO ATTENTION TO THE PLANK IN YOUR OWN EYE?"

MATTHEW 7:3

SEE ALSO
Jeremiah 29:11
1 Corinthians 13:4–7
Ephesians 5:21–33

For more on **Abuse** and **Relationships**, check the index.

⁴My heart is blighted and withered like grass;
   I forget to eat my food.
⁵In my distress I groan aloud
   and am reduced to skin and bones.
⁶I am like a desert owl,
   like an owl among the ruins.
⁷I lie awake; I have become
   like a bird alone on a roof.
⁸All day long my enemies taunt me;
   those who rail against me use my name as a curse.
⁹For I eat ashes as my food
   and mingle my drink with tears
¹⁰because of your great wrath,
   for you have taken me up and thrown me aside.
¹¹My days are like the evening shadow;
   I wither away like grass.

¹²But you, Lord, sit enthroned forever;
   your renown endures through all generations.
¹³You will arise and have compassion on Zion,
   for it is time to show favor to her;
   the appointed time has come.
¹⁴For her stones are dear to your servants;
   her very dust moves them to pity.
¹⁵The nations will fear the name of the Lord,
   all the kings of the earth will revere your glory.
¹⁶For the Lord will rebuild Zion
   and appear in his glory.
¹⁷He will respond to the prayer of the destitute;
   he will not despise their plea.

¹⁸Let this be written for a future generation,
   that a people not yet created may praise the Lord:
¹⁹"The Lord looked down from his sanctuary on high,
   from heaven he viewed the earth,
²⁰to hear the groans of the prisoners
   and release those condemned to death."
²¹So the name of the Lord will be declared in Zion
   and his praise in Jerusalem
²²when the peoples and the kingdoms
   assemble to worship the Lord.

²³In the course of my life^a he broke my strength;
   he cut short my days.
²⁴So I said:
"Do not take me away, my God, in the midst of my days;
   your years go on through all generations.
²⁵In the beginning you laid the foundations of the earth,
   and the heavens are the work of your hands.
²⁶They will perish, but you remain;
   they will all wear out like a garment.

---
^a 23 Or By his power

Like clothing you will change them
and they will be discarded.
²⁷But you remain the same,
and your years will never end.
²⁸The children of your servants will live in your presence;
their descendants will be established before you."

Psalm 103

Of David.

¹Praise the Lord, my soul;
all my inmost being, praise his holy name.
²Praise the Lord, my soul,
and forget not all his benefits—
³who forgives all your sins
and heals all your diseases,
⁴who redeems your life from the pit
and crowns you with love and compassion,
⁵who satisfies your desires with good things
so that your youth is renewed like the eagle's.

⁶The Lord works righteousness
and justice for all the oppressed.

⁷He made known his ways to Moses,
his deeds to the people of Israel:
⁸The Lord is compassionate and gracious,
slow to anger, abounding in love.
⁹He will not always accuse,
nor will he harbor his anger forever;
¹⁰he does not treat us as our sins deserve
or repay us according to our iniquities.
¹¹For as high as the heavens are above the
earth,
so great is his love for those who fear
him;
¹²as far as the east is from the west,
so far has he removed our transgressions
from us.

¹³As a father has compassion on his children,
so the Lord has compassion on those
who fear him;
¹⁴for he knows how we are formed,
he remembers that we are dust.
¹⁵As for mortals, their days are like grass,
they flourish like a flower of the field;
¹⁶the wind blows over it and it is gone,
and its place remembers it no more.
¹⁷But from everlasting to everlasting
the Lord's love is with those who fear
him,
and his righteousness with their
children's children—

811

at issue : guilt

103:7–14 Do you ever find yourself mentally reviewing the list of your failures? If you've never confessed those sins and asked God to forgive you, then the Spirit's telling you that you need to deal with those past mistakes. But if you've already asked God to forgive those sins and have been reconciled with those you sinned against, then it's not the Spirit talking. Because he loves us so much, God has completely removed our sin from us and covered us with his grace. Instead of listing your failures, think about all that God's done for you. If God has let go of your sin, why won't you?

¹⁸ with those who keep his covenant
　　and remember to obey his precepts.

¹⁹ The Lᴏʀᴅ has established his throne in heaven,
　　and his kingdom rules over all.

²⁰ Praise the Lᴏʀᴅ, you his angels,
　　you mighty ones who do his bidding,
　　who obey his word.
²¹ Praise the Lᴏʀᴅ, all his heavenly hosts,
　　you his servants who do his will.
²² Praise the Lᴏʀᴅ, all his works
　　everywhere in his dominion.

　　Praise the Lᴏʀᴅ, my soul.

Psalm 104

¹ Praise the Lᴏʀᴅ, my soul.

　Lᴏʀᴅ my God, you are very great;
　　you are clothed with splendor and majesty.

² The Lᴏʀᴅ wraps himself in light as with a garment;
　　he stretches out the heavens like a tent
³ 　and lays the beams of his upper chambers on their waters.
　He makes the clouds his chariot
　　and rides on the wings of the wind.
⁴ He makes winds his messengers,ᵃ
　　flames of fire his servants.

HE IS: clothed with splendor

104:1–4 Trying to describe the indescribable, the psalmist offers a beautiful word picture of what God wears: "[He] wraps himself in light as with a garment." Wrapped in light, God is bright, blinding and mesmerizing. Nothing can compare with our God, who is *clothed with splendor*.

If you're a child of God, then you are like a moon, reflecting the light of the sun, God himself, in your life. You do not create your own light; you merely reflect his. Put off any darkness or sin in your life (see Romans 13:12) so that you can reflect his splendor to others.

For the next He Is, go to p. 823.

⁵ He set the earth on its foundations;
　　it can never be moved.
⁶ You covered it with the deep as with a garment;
　　the waters stood above the mountains.
⁷ But at your rebuke the waters fled,
　　at the sound of your thunder they took to flight;
⁸ they flowed over the mountains,
　　they went down into the valleys,
　　to the place you assigned for them.

ᵃ 4 Or *angels*

⁹You set a boundary they cannot cross;
    never again will they cover the earth.

¹⁰He makes springs pour water into the ravines;
    it flows between the mountains.
¹¹They give water to all the beasts of the field;
    the wild donkeys quench their thirst.
¹²The birds of the sky nest by the waters;
    they sing among the branches.
¹³He waters the mountains from his upper chambers;
    the land is satisfied by the fruit of his work.
¹⁴He makes grass grow for the cattle,
    and plants for people to cultivate—
    bringing forth food from the earth:
¹⁵wine that gladdens human hearts,
    oil to make their faces shine,
    and bread that sustains their hearts.
¹⁶The trees of the Lord are well watered,
    the cedars of Lebanon that he planted.
¹⁷There the birds make their nests;
    the stork has its home in the junipers.
¹⁸The high mountains belong to the wild goats;
    the crags are a refuge for the hyrax.

¹⁹He made the moon to mark the seasons,
    and the sun knows when to go down.
²⁰You bring darkness, it becomes night,
    and all the beasts of the forest prowl.
²¹The lions roar for their prey
    and seek their food from God.
²²The sun rises, and they steal away;
    they return and lie down in their dens.
²³Then people go out to their work,
    to their labor until evening.

²⁴How many are your works, Lord!
    In wisdom you made them all;
    the earth is full of your creatures.
²⁵There is the sea, vast and spacious,
    teeming with creatures beyond number—
    living things both large and small.
²⁶There the ships go to and fro,
    and the leviathan, which you formed to frolic there.

²⁷All creatures look to you
    to give them their food at the proper time.
²⁸When you give it to them,
    they gather it up;
when you open your hand,
    they are satisfied with good things.
²⁹When you hide your face,
    they are terrified;
when you take away their breath,

813

they die and return to the dust.
³⁰When you send your Spirit,
      they are created,
      and you renew the face of the ground.

³¹May the glory of the LORD endure forever;
      may the LORD rejoice in his works—
³²he who looks at the earth, and it trembles,
      who touches the mountains, and they smoke.

³³I will sing to the LORD all my life;
      I will sing praise to my God as long as I live.
³⁴May my meditation be pleasing to him,
      as I rejoice in the LORD.
³⁵But may sinners vanish from the earth
      and the wicked be no more.

Praise the LORD, my soul.

Praise the LORD.ᵃ

814

Psalm 105

¹Give praise to the LORD, call on his name;
      make known among the nations what he has done.
²Sing of him, sing his praises;
      tell of all his wonderful acts.
³Glory in his holy name;
      let the hearts of those who seek the LORD rejoice.
⁴Look to the LORD and his strength;
      seek his face always.

⁵Remember the wonders he has done,
      his miracles, and the judgments he pronounced,
⁶you his servants, the descendants of Abraham,
      his chosen ones, the children of Jacob.
⁷He is the LORD our God;
      his judgments are in all the earth.

⁸He remembers his covenant forever,
      the promise he made, for a thousand generations,
⁹the covenant he made with Abraham,
      the oath he swore to Isaac.
¹⁰He confirmed it to Jacob as a decree,
      to Israel as an everlasting covenant:
¹¹"To you I will give the land of Canaan
      as the portion you will inherit."

¹²When they were but few in number,
      few indeed, and strangers in it,
¹³they wandered from nation to nation,
      from one kingdom to another.
¹⁴He allowed no one to oppress them;
      for their sake he rebuked kings:

ᵃ 35 Hebrew Hallelu Yah; in the Septuagint this line stands at the beginning of Psalm 105.

¹⁵"Do not touch my anointed ones;
  do my prophets no harm."

¹⁶He called down famine on the land
  and destroyed all their supplies of food;
¹⁷and he sent a man before them—
  Joseph, sold as a slave.
¹⁸They bruised his feet with shackles,
  his neck was put in irons,
¹⁹till what he foretold came to pass,
  till the word of the Lord proved him true.
²⁰The king sent and released him,
  the ruler of peoples set him free.
²¹He made him master of his household,
  ruler over all he possessed,
²²to instruct his princes as he pleased
  and teach his elders wisdom.

²³Then Israel entered Egypt;
  Jacob resided as a foreigner in the land of Ham.
²⁴The Lord made his people very fruitful;
  he made them too numerous for their foes,
²⁵whose hearts he turned to hate his people,
  to conspire against his servants.
²⁶He sent Moses his servant,
  and Aaron, whom he had chosen.
²⁷They performed his signs among them,
  his wonders in the land of Ham.
²⁸He sent darkness and made the land dark—
  for had they not rebelled against his words?
²⁹He turned their waters into blood,
  causing their fish to die.
³⁰Their land teemed with frogs,
  which went up into the bedrooms of their rulers.
³¹He spoke, and there came swarms of flies,
  and gnats throughout their country.
³²He turned their rain into hail,
  with lightning throughout their land;
³³he struck down their vines and fig trees
  and shattered the trees of their country.
³⁴He spoke, and the locusts came,
  grasshoppers without number;
³⁵they ate up every green thing in their land,
  ate up the produce of their soil.
³⁶Then he struck down all the firstborn in their land,
  the firstfruits of all their manhood.
³⁷He brought out Israel, laden with silver and gold,
  and from among their tribes no one faltered.
³⁸Egypt was glad when they left,
  because dread of Israel had fallen on them.

³⁹He spread out a cloud as a covering,
  and a fire to give light at night.

⁴⁰They asked, and he brought them quail;
  he fed them well with the bread of heaven.
⁴¹He opened the rock, and water gushed out;
  it flowed like a river in the desert.

⁴²For he remembered his holy promise
  given to his servant Abraham.
⁴³He brought out his people with rejoicing,
  his chosen ones with shouts of joy;
⁴⁴he gave them the lands of the nations,
  and they fell heir to what others had toiled for—
⁴⁵that they might keep his precepts
  and observe his laws.

Praise the LORD.^a

Psalm 106

¹Praise the LORD.^b

Give thanks to the LORD, for he is good;
  his love endures forever.

²Who can proclaim the mighty acts of the LORD
  or fully declare his praise?
³Blessed are those who act justly,
  who always do what is right.

⁴Remember me, LORD, when you show favor to your people,
  come to my aid when you save them,
⁵that I may enjoy the prosperity of your chosen ones,
  that I may share in the joy of your nation
  and join your inheritance in giving praise.

⁶We have sinned, even as our ancestors did;
  we have done wrong and acted wickedly.
⁷When our ancestors were in Egypt,
  they gave no thought to your miracles;
they did not remember your many kindnesses,
  and they rebelled by the sea, the Red Sea.^c
⁸Yet he saved them for his name's sake,
  to make his mighty power known.
⁹He rebuked the Red Sea, and it dried up;
  he led them through the depths as through a desert.
¹⁰He saved them from the hand of the foe;
  from the hand of the enemy he redeemed them.
¹¹The waters covered their adversaries;
  not one of them survived.
¹²Then they believed his promises
  and sang his praise.

¹³But they soon forgot what he had done
  and did not wait for his plan to unfold.
¹⁴In the desert they gave in to their craving;
  in the wilderness they put God to the test.

---

^a 45 Hebrew *Hallelu Yah*   ^b 1 Hebrew *Hallelu Yah*; also in verse 48   ^c 7 Or *the Sea of Reeds*; also in verses 9 and 22

¹⁵So he gave them what they asked for,
   but sent a wasting disease among them.

¹⁶In the camp they grew envious of Moses
   and of Aaron, who was consecrated to the LORD.
¹⁷The earth opened up and swallowed Dathan;
   it buried the company of Abiram.
¹⁸Fire blazed among their followers;
   a flame consumed the wicked.
¹⁹At Horeb they made a calf
   and worshiped an idol cast from metal.
²⁰They exchanged their glorious God
   for an image of a bull, which eats grass.
²¹They forgot the God who saved them,
   who had done great things in Egypt,
²²miracles in the land of Ham
   and awesome deeds by the Red Sea.
²³So he said he would destroy them—
   had not Moses, his chosen one,
stood in the breach before him
   to keep his wrath from destroying them.

²⁴Then they despised the pleasant land;
   they did not believe his promise.
²⁵They grumbled in their tents
   and did not obey the LORD.
²⁶So he swore to them with uplifted hand
   that he would make them fall in the wilderness,
²⁷make their descendants fall among the nations
   and scatter them throughout the lands.

²⁸They yoked themselves to the Baal of Peor
   and ate sacrifices offered to lifeless gods;
²⁹they aroused the LORD's anger by their wicked deeds,
   and a plague broke out among them.
³⁰But Phinehas stood up and intervened,
   and the plague was checked.
³¹This was credited to him as righteousness
   for endless generations to come.
³²By the waters of Meribah they angered the LORD,
   and trouble came to Moses because of them;
³³for they rebelled against the Spirit of God,
   and rash words came from Moses' lips.^a

³⁴They did not destroy the peoples
   as the LORD had commanded them,
³⁵but they mingled with the nations
   and adopted their customs.
³⁶They worshiped their idols,
   which became a snare to them.
³⁷They sacrificed their sons
   and their daughters to demons.

---

^a *33 Or against his spirit, / and rash words came from his lips*

³⁸They shed innocent blood,
  the blood of their sons and daughters,
whom they sacrificed to the idols of Canaan,
  and the land was desecrated by their blood.
³⁹They defiled themselves by what they did;
  by their deeds they prostituted themselves.

⁴⁰Therefore the Lord was angry with his people
  and abhorred his inheritance.
⁴¹He gave them into the hands of the nations,
  and their foes ruled over them.
⁴²Their enemies oppressed them
  and subjected them to their power.
⁴³Many times he delivered them,
  but they were bent on rebellion
  and they wasted away in their sin.
⁴⁴Yet he took note of their distress
  when he heard their cry;
⁴⁵for their sake he remembered his covenant
  and out of his great love he relented.
⁴⁶He caused all who held them captive
  to show them mercy.

⁴⁷Save us, Lord our God,
  and gather us from the nations,
that we may give thanks to your holy name
  and glory in your praise.

⁴⁸Praise be to the Lord, the God of Israel,
  from everlasting to everlasting.

Let all the people say, "Amen!"

Praise the Lord.

BOOK V

Psalms 107–150

Psalm 107

¹Give thanks to the Lord, for he is good;
  his love endures forever.

²Let the redeemed of the Lord tell their story—
  those he redeemed from the hand of the foe,
³those he gathered from the lands,
  from east and west, from north and south.ᵃ

⁴Some wandered in desert wastelands,
  finding no way to a city where they could settle.
⁵They were hungry and thirsty,
  and their lives ebbed away.
⁶Then they cried out to the Lord in their trouble,
  and he delivered them from their distress.

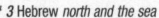

ᵃ *3 Hebrew north and the sea*

⁷He led them by a straight way
    to a city where they could settle.
⁸Let them give thanks to the LORD for his unfailing love
    and his wonderful deeds for humankind,
⁹for he satisfies the thirsty
    and fills the hungry with good things.

¹⁰Some sat in darkness, in utter darkness,
    prisoners suffering in iron chains,
¹¹because they rebelled against God's commands
    and despised the plans of the Most High.
¹²So he subjected them to bitter labor;
    they stumbled, and there was no one to help.
¹³Then they cried to the LORD in their trouble,
    and he saved them from their distress.
¹⁴He brought them out of darkness, the utter darkness,
    and broke away their chains.
¹⁵Let them give thanks to the LORD for his unfailing love
    and his wonderful deeds for humankind,
¹⁶for he breaks down gates of bronze
    and cuts through bars of iron.

¹⁷Some became fools through their rebellious ways
    and suffered affliction because of their iniquities.
¹⁸They loathed all food
    and drew near the gates of death.
¹⁹Then they cried to the LORD in their trouble,
    and he saved them from their distress.
²⁰He sent out his word and healed them;
    he rescued them from the grave.
²¹Let them give thanks to the LORD for his unfailing love
    and his wonderful deeds for humankind.
²²Let them sacrifice thank offerings
    and tell of his works with songs of joy.

²³Some went out on the sea in ships;
    they were merchants on the mighty waters.
²⁴They saw the works of the LORD,
    his wonderful deeds in the deep.
²⁵For he spoke and stirred up a tempest
    that lifted high the waves.
²⁶They mounted up to the heavens and went down to the depths;
    in their peril their courage melted away.
²⁷They reeled and staggered like drunkards;
    they were at their wits' end.
²⁸Then they cried out to the LORD in their trouble,
    and he brought them out of their distress.
²⁹He stilled the storm to a whisper;
    the waves of the sea^a were hushed.
³⁰They were glad when it grew calm,
    and he guided them to their desired haven.

---

^a 29 Dead Sea Scrolls; Masoretic Text / *their waves*

³¹Let them give thanks to the LORD for his unfailing love
      and his wonderful deeds for humankind.
³²Let them exalt him in the assembly of the people
      and praise him in the council of the elders.

³³He turned rivers into a desert,
      flowing springs into thirsty ground,
³⁴and fruitful land into a salt waste,
      because of the wickedness of those who lived there.
³⁵He turned the desert into pools of water
      and the parched ground into flowing springs;
³⁶there he brought the hungry to live,
      and they founded a city where they could settle.
³⁷They sowed fields and planted vineyards
      that yielded a fruitful harvest;
³⁸he blessed them, and their numbers greatly increased,
      and he did not let their herds diminish.

³⁹Then their numbers decreased, and they were humbled
      by oppression, calamity and sorrow;
⁴⁰he who pours contempt on nobles
      made them wander in a trackless waste.
⁴¹But he lifted the needy out of their affliction
      and increased their families like flocks.
⁴²The upright see and rejoice,
      but all the wicked shut their mouths.

⁴³Let all who are wise heed these things
      and ponder the loving deeds of the LORD.

Psalm 108

A song. A psalm of David.

* ¹My heart, O God, is steadfast;
      I will sing and make music with all my soul.
²Awake, harp and lyre!
      I will awaken the dawn.
³I will praise you, LORD, among the nations;
      I will sing of you among the peoples.
⁴For great is your love, higher than the heavens;
      your faithfulness reaches to the skies.
⁵Be exalted, O God, above the heavens;
      let your glory be over all the earth.

⁶Save us and help us with your right hand,
      that those you love may be delivered.
⁷God has spoken from his sanctuary:
      "In triumph I will parcel out Shechem
      and measure off the Valley of Sukkoth.
⁸Gilead is mine, Manasseh is mine;
      Ephraim is my helmet,
      Judah is my scepter.
⁹Moab is my washbasin,

---

* 108:1-13 is numbered 108:2-14 in Hebrew texts.

on Edom I toss my sandal;
    over Philistia I shout in triumph."

¹⁰Who will bring me to the fortified city?
    Who will lead me to Edom?
¹¹Is it not you, God, you who have rejected us
    and no longer go out with our armies?
¹²Give us aid against the enemy,
    for human help is worthless.
¹³With God we will gain the victory,
    and he will trample down our enemies.

Psalm 109

For the director of music. Of David. A psalm.

¹My God, whom I praise,
    do not remain silent,
²for people who are wicked and deceitful
    have opened their mouths against me;
    they have spoken against me with lying tongues.
³With words of hatred they surround me;
    they attack me without cause.
⁴In return for my friendship they accuse me,
    but I am a man of prayer.
⁵They repay me evil for good,
    and hatred for my friendship.

⁶Appoint someone evil to oppose my enemy;
    let an accuser stand at his right hand.
⁷When he is tried, let him be found guilty,
    and may his prayers condemn him.
⁸May his days be few;
    may another take his place of leadership.
⁹May his children be fatherless
    and his wife a widow.
¹⁰May his children be wandering beggars;
    may they be driven*ᵃ* from their ruined homes.
¹¹May a creditor seize all he has;
    may strangers plunder the fruits of his labor.
¹²May no one extend kindness to him
    or take pity on his fatherless children.
¹³May his descendants be cut off,
    their names blotted out from the next generation.
¹⁴May the iniquity of his fathers be remembered before the LORD;
    may the sin of his mother never be blotted out.
¹⁵May their sins always remain before the LORD,
    that he may blot out their name from the earth.

¹⁶For he never thought of doing a kindness,
    but hounded to death the poor
    and the needy and the brokenhearted.
¹⁷He loved to pronounce a curse—

821

ᵃ 10 Septuagint; Hebrew *sought*

may it come on him.
He found no pleasure in blessing—
    may it be far from him.
¹⁸He wore cursing as his garment;
    it entered into his body like water,
    into his bones like oil.
¹⁹May it be like a cloak wrapped about him,
    like a belt tied forever around him.
²⁰May this be the LORD's payment to my accusers,
    to those who speak evil of me.

²¹But you, Sovereign LORD,
    help me for your name's sake;
    out of the goodness of your love,
        deliver me.
²²For I am poor and needy,
    and my heart is wounded within me.
²³I fade away like an evening shadow;
    I am shaken off like a locust.
²⁴My knees give way from fasting;
    my body is thin and gaunt.
²⁵I am an object of scorn to my
        accusers;
    when they see me, they shake their
        heads.

²⁶Help me, LORD my God;
    save me according to your unfailing
        love.
²⁷Let them know that it is your hand,
    that you, LORD, have done it.
²⁸While they curse, may you bless;
    may those who attack me be put to
        shame,
    but may your servant rejoice.
²⁹May my accusers be clothed with
        disgrace
    and wrapped in shame as in a cloak.

³⁰With my mouth I will greatly extol the
        LORD;
    in the great throng of worshipers I will praise him.
³¹For he stands at the right hand of the needy,
    to save their lives from those who would condemn them.

Psalm 110

Of David. A psalm.

¹The LORD says to my lord:^a
    "Sit at my right hand
until I make your enemies
    a footstool for your feet."

---

an issue: eating disorders

109:21–26 David describes the negative physical effects of his mental stress—his gaunt body giving way, his physical strength worn thin. Sadly, we see people today suffering similar physical effects—not only for lack of food, but for mental reasons as well. Some women who are tormented by mental stress try to find a semblance of control through what they eat—or don't eat. Others take a good physical activity (like exercise) and distort it. An eating disorder of any kind, left unchecked, can consume you. Get help. Talk to a trusted pastor, Christian friend or counselor. Call out, "Help me, LORD my God!"

---

²The L ORD will extend your mighty scepter from Zion, saying,
> "Rule in the midst of your enemies."

³Your troops will be willing
> on your day of battle.
Arrayed in holy splendor,
> your young men will come to you
> like dew from the morning's womb.*ᵃ*

⁴The L ORD has sworn
> and will not change his mind:
"You are a priest forever,
> in the order of Melchizedek."

⁵The Lord is at your right hand*ᵇ*;
> he will crush kings on the day of his wrath.
⁶He will judge the nations, heaping up the dead
> and crushing the rulers of the whole earth.
⁷He will drink from a brook along the way,*ᶜ*
> and so he will lift up his head.

Psalm 111*ᵈ*

¹Praise the L ORD.*ᵉ*

I will extol the L ORD with all my heart
> in the council of the upright and in the assembly.

²Great are the works of the L ORD;
> they are pondered by all who delight in them.
³Glorious and majestic are his deeds,
> and his righteousness endures forever.
⁴He has caused his wonders to be remembered;
> the L ORD is gracious and compassionate.
⁵He provides food for those who fear him;
> he remembers his covenant forever.

⁶He has shown his people the power of his works,
> giving them the lands of other nations.

ᵃ 3 The meaning of the Hebrew for this sentence is uncertain.   *ᵇ 5* Or *My lord is at your right hand, L ORD*   *ᶜ 7* The meaning of the Hebrew for this clause is uncertain.   *ᵈ* This psalm is an acrostic poem, the lines of which begin with the successive letters of the Hebrew alphabet.   *ᵉ 1* Hebrew *Hallelu Yah*

HE IS: enduring

111:2–9 Psalm 111 commemorates the first Passover, when God saved the firstborn of Israel from death. Lamb's blood on the doorposts of the Israelite houses indicated to the destroyer to bypass that house (see Exodus 11–12). God's salvation is to be remembered forever. His acts are *enduring,* and this psalm ensures that the story of his redeeming love reaches all who listen.

God sent Jesus, the Lamb of God, as a blood sacrifice to spare you the penalty of death. Praise him for being gracious and compassionate! Thank him that he is *enduring.* Your righteousness depends on him alone; his righteousness endures forever.

For the next He Is, go to p. 837.

⁷The works of his hands are faithful and just;
　　all his precepts are trustworthy.
⁸They are established for ever and ever,
　　enacted in faithfulness and uprightness.
⁹He provided redemption for his people;
　　he ordained his covenant forever—
　　holy and awesome is his name.

¹⁰The fear of the LORD is the beginning of wisdom;
　　all who follow his precepts have good understanding.
　　To him belongs eternal praise.

Psalm 112^a

¹Praise the LORD.^b

Blessed are those who fear the LORD,
　　who find great delight in his commands.

²Their children will be mighty in the land;
　　the generation of the upright will be blessed.
³Wealth and riches are in their houses,
　　and their righteousness endures forever.
⁴Even in darkness light dawns for the upright,
　　for those who are gracious and compassionate and righteous.
⁵Good will come to those who are generous and lend freely,
　　who conduct their affairs with justice.

⁶Surely the righteous will never be shaken;
　　they will be remembered forever.
⁷They will have no fear of bad news;
　　their hearts are steadfast, trusting in the LORD.
⁸Their hearts are secure, they will have no fear;
　　in the end they will look in triumph on their foes.
⁹They have scattered abroad their gifts to the poor,
　　their righteousness endures forever;
　　their horn^c will be lifted high in honor.

¹⁰The wicked will see and be vexed,
　　they will gnash their teeth and waste away;
　　the longings of the wicked will come to nothing.

Psalm 113

¹Praise the LORD.^d

Praise the LORD, you his servants;
　　praise the name of the LORD.
²Let the name of the LORD be praised,
　　both now and forevermore.
³From the rising of the sun to the place where it sets,
　　the name of the LORD is to be praised.

⁴The LORD is exalted over all the nations,
　　his glory above the heavens.

824

---

^a This psalm is an acrostic poem, the lines of which begin with the successive letters of the Hebrew alphabet.　^b 1 Hebrew Hallelu Yah　^c 9 Horn here
symbolizes dignity.　^{<i>d</i>} 1 Hebrew <i>Hallelu Yah;</i> also in verse 9

⁵Who is like the LORD our God,
  the One who sits enthroned on high,
⁶who stoops down to look
  on the heavens and the earth?

⁷He raises the poor from the dust
  and lifts the needy from the ash heap;
⁸he seats them with princes,
  with the princes of his people.
⁹He settles the childless woman in her home
  as a happy mother of children.

  Praise the LORD.

Psalm 114

¹When Israel came out of Egypt,
  the house of Jacob from a people of foreign tongue,
²Judah became God's sanctuary,
  Israel his dominion.

³The sea looked and fled,
  the Jordan turned back;
⁴the mountains leaped like rams,
  the hills like lambs.

⁵Why was it, sea, that you fled?
  Why, Jordan, did you turn back?
⁶Why, mountains, did you leap like rams,
  you hills, like lambs?

⁷Tremble, earth, at the presence of the Lord,
  at the presence of the God of Jacob,
⁸who turned the rock into a pool,
  the hard rock into springs of water.

Psalm 115

¹Not to us, LORD, not to us
  but to your name be the glory,
  because of your love and faithfulness.

²Why do the nations say,
  "Where is their God?"
³Our God is in heaven;
  he does whatever pleases him.
⁴But their idols are silver and gold,
  made by human hands.
⁵They have mouths, but cannot speak,
  eyes, but cannot see.
⁶They have ears, but cannot hear,
  noses, but cannot smell.
⁷They have hands, but cannot feel,
  feet, but cannot walk,
  nor can they utter a sound with their
    throats.

at issue: pride

115:1 Let's face it—we really do want the glory. We may not *want* to want it, but we do. We like people to think we're incredible and amazing. We like how it feels when people notice us and praise us. And we find it's easy to forget that God created us for his glory—not our own—and that he's the only one who deserves it. What do you do with these mixed motives? Ask God to work in your heart so that you can genuinely pray, "Not to me, Lord, not to me but to *your* name be the glory."

825

⁸Those who make them will be like them,
and so will all who trust in them.

⁹House of Israel, trust in the L<small>ORD</small>—
he is their help and shield.
¹⁰House of Aaron, trust in the L<small>ORD</small>—
he is their help and shield.
¹¹You who fear him, trust in the L<small>ORD</small>—
he is their help and shield.

¹²The L<small>ORD</small> remembers us and will bless us:
He will bless the house of Israel,
he will bless the house of Aaron,
¹³he will bless those who fear the L<small>ORD</small>—
small and great alike.

¹⁴May the L<small>ORD</small> cause you to increase,
both you and your children.
¹⁵May you be blessed by the L<small>ORD</small>,
the Maker of heaven and earth.

¹⁶The highest heavens belong to the L<small>ORD</small>,
but the earth he has given to humankind.
¹⁷It is not the dead who praise the L<small>ORD</small>,
those who go down to the place of silence;
¹⁸it is we who extol the L<small>ORD</small>,
both now and forevermore.

Praise the L<small>ORD</small>.^a

Psalm 116

¹I love the L<small>ORD</small>, for he heard my voice;
he heard my cry for mercy.
²Because he turned his ear to me,
I will call on him as long as I live.

³The cords of death entangled me,
the anguish of the grave came over me;
I was overcome by distress and sorrow.
⁴Then I called on the name of the L<small>ORD</small>:
"L<small>ORD</small>, save me!"

⁵The L<small>ORD</small> is gracious and righteous;
our God is full of compassion.
⁶The L<small>ORD</small> protects the unwary;
when I was brought low, he saved me.

⁷Return to your rest, my soul,
for the L<small>ORD</small> has been good to you.

⁸For you, L<small>ORD</small>, have delivered me from death,
my eyes from tears,
my feet from stumbling,
⁹that I may walk before the L<small>ORD</small>
in the land of the living.

---

^a 18 Hebrew *Hallelu Yah*

¹⁰I trusted in the LORD when I said,
   "I am greatly afflicted";
¹¹in my alarm I said,
   "Everyone is a liar."

¹²What shall I return to the LORD
   for all his goodness to me?

¹³I will lift up the cup of salvation
   and call on the name of the LORD.
¹⁴I will fulfill my vows to the LORD
   in the presence of all his people.

¹⁵Precious in the sight of the LORD
   is the death of those faithful to him.
¹⁶Truly I am your servant, LORD;
   I am your servant, as was my mother before me;
   you have loosed my bonds of affliction.

¹⁷I will sacrifice a thank offering to you
   and call on the name of the LORD.
¹⁸I will fulfill my vows to the LORD
   in the presence of all his people,
¹⁹in the courts of the house of the LORD—
   in your midst, Jerusalem.

Praise the LORD.^a

Psalm 117

¹Praise the LORD, all you nations;
   extol him, all you peoples.
²For great is his love toward us,
   and the faithfulness of the LORD endures forever.

Praise the LORD.^b

Psalm 118

¹Give thanks to the LORD, for he is good;
   his love endures forever.

²Let Israel say:
   "His love endures forever."
³Let the house of Aaron say:
   "His love endures forever."
⁴Let those who fear the LORD say:
   "His love endures forever."

⁵When hard pressed, I cried to the LORD;
   he brought me into a spacious place.
⁶The LORD is with me; I will not be afraid.
   What can human beings do to me?
⁷The LORD is with me; he is my helper.
   I look in triumph on my enemies.

^a 19 Hebrew *Hallelu Yah*   ^b 2 Hebrew *Hallelu Yah*

⁸It is better to take refuge in
  the LORD
  than to trust in human
  beings.
⁹It is better to take refuge in
  the LORD
  than to trust in princes.
¹⁰All the nations surrounded
  me,
  but in the name of the LORD
  I cut them down.
¹¹They surrounded me on every
  side,
  but in the name of the LORD
  I cut them down.
¹²They swarmed around me
  like bees,
  but they were consumed as quickly as burning thorns;
  in the name of the LORD I cut them down.
¹³I was pushed back and about to fall,
  but the LORD helped me.
¹⁴The LORD is my strength and my defense*a*;
  he has become my salvation.

¹⁵Shouts of joy and victory
  resound in the tents of the righteous:
  "The LORD's right hand has done mighty things!
¹⁶   The LORD's right hand is lifted high;
  the LORD's right hand has done mighty things!"
¹⁷I will not die but live,
  and will proclaim what the LORD has done.
¹⁸The LORD has chastened me severely,
  but he has not given me over to death.
¹⁹Open for me the gates of the righteous;
  I will enter and give thanks to the LORD.
²⁰This is the gate of the LORD
  through which the righteous may enter.
²¹I will give you thanks, for you answered me;
  you have become my salvation.

²²The stone the builders rejected
  has become the cornerstone;
²³the LORD has done this,
  and it is marvelous in our eyes.
²⁴The LORD has done it this very day;
  let us rejoice today and be glad.

²⁵LORD, save us!
  LORD, grant us success!

²⁶Blessed is he who comes in the name of the LORD.
  From the house of the LORD we bless you.*b*

conversations

trust «» 118:8–9

1» Is it ever safe to completely trust another person?

2» Would you describe yourself as a trusting person or not? What's made you this way?

3» Does your level of trust in others affect your trust in God?

For more on trust, check the index.
For the next Conversations, go to p. 829.

---

a 14 Or *song*   *b* 26 The Hebrew is plural.

²⁷The Lᴏʀᴅ is God,
  and he has made his light shine on us.
  With boughs in hand, join in the festal procession
    up*ᵃ* to the horns of the altar.

²⁸You are my God, and I will praise you;
  you are my God, and I will exalt you.

²⁹Give thanks to the Lᴏʀᴅ, for he is good;
  his love endures forever.

Psalm 119 *ᵇ*

א Aleph

¹Blessed are those whose ways are blameless,
  who walk according to the law of the Lᴏʀᴅ.
²Blessed are those who keep his statutes
  and seek him with all their heart—
³they do no wrong
  but follow his ways.
⁴You have laid down precepts
  that are to be fully obeyed.
⁵Oh, that my ways were steadfast
  in obeying your decrees!
⁶Then I would not be put to shame
  when I consider all your commands.
⁷I will praise you with an upright heart
  as I learn your righteous laws.
⁸I will obey your decrees;
  do not utterly forsake me.

ב Beth

⁹How can those who are young keep their way pure?
  By living according to your word.
¹⁰I seek you with all my heart;
  do not let me stray from your
    commands.
¹¹I have hidden your word in my heart
  that I might not sin against you.
¹²Praise be to you, Lᴏʀᴅ;
  teach me your decrees.
¹³With my lips I recount
  all the laws that come from your
    mouth.
¹⁴I rejoice in following your statutes
  as one rejoices in great riches.
¹⁵I meditate on your precepts
  and consider your ways.
¹⁶I delight in your decrees;
  I will not neglect your word.

"conversations"

purity «» 119:9–16

1» What does it mean to be *pure* in our world today?

2» In what areas of your life do you have the most difficulty with purity?

3» How does God's Word help you remain pure?

For more on **purity**, check the index.
For the next Conversations, go to p. 841.

ᵃ 27 Or *Bind the festal sacrifice with ropes / and take it*   *ᵇ* This psalm is an acrostic poem; the verses of each stanza begin with the same letter of the Hebrew alphabet.

ג Gimel

¹⁷Be good to your servant while I live,
  that I may obey your word.
¹⁸Open my eyes that I may see
  wonderful things in your law.
¹⁹I am a stranger on earth;
  do not hide your commands from me.
²⁰My soul is consumed with longing
  for your laws at all times.
²¹You rebuke the arrogant, who are accursed,
  those who stray from your commands.
²²Remove from me scorn and contempt,
  for I keep your statutes.
²³Though rulers sit together and slander me,
  your servant will meditate on your decrees.
²⁴Your statutes are my delight;
  they are my counselors.

ד Daleth

²⁵I am laid low in the dust;
  preserve my life according to your word.
²⁶I gave an account of my ways and you answered me;
  teach me your decrees.
²⁷Cause me to understand the way of your precepts,
  that I may meditate on your wonderful deeds.
²⁸My soul is weary with sorrow;
  strengthen me according to your word.
²⁹Keep me from deceitful ways;
  be gracious to me and teach me your law.
³⁰I have chosen the way of faithfulness;
  I have set my heart on your laws.
³¹I hold fast to your statutes, LORD;
  do not let me be put to shame.
³²I run in the path of your commands,
  for you have set my heart free.

ה He

³³Teach me, LORD, the way of your decrees,
  that I may follow it to the end.^a
³⁴Give me understanding, so that I may keep your law
  and obey it with all my heart.
³⁵Direct me in the path of your commands,
  for there I find delight.
³⁶Turn my heart toward your statutes
  and not toward selfish gain.
³⁷Turn my eyes away from worthless things;
  preserve my life according to your word.^b
³⁸Fulfill your promise to your servant,
  so that you may be feared.

---

^a *33* Or *follow it for its reward*   ^b *37* Two manuscripts of the Masoretic Text and Dead Sea Scrolls; most manuscripts of the Masoretic Text *life in your way*

³⁹ Take away the disgrace I dread,
for your laws are good.
⁴⁰ How I long for your precepts!
In your righteousness preserve my life.

ו Waw

⁴¹ May your unfailing love come to me, LORD,
your salvation, according to your promise;
⁴² then I can answer anyone who taunts me,
for I trust in your word.
⁴³ Never take your word of truth from my mouth,
for I have put my hope in your laws.
⁴⁴ I will always obey your law,
for ever and ever.
⁴⁵ I will walk about in freedom,
for I have sought out your precepts.
⁴⁶ I will speak of your statutes before kings
and will not be put to shame,
⁴⁷ for I delight in your commands
because I love them.
⁴⁸ I reach out for your commands, which I love,
that I may meditate on your decrees.

ז Zayin

⁴⁹ Remember your word to your servant,
for you have given me hope.
⁵⁰ My comfort in my suffering is this:
Your promise preserves my life.
⁵¹ The arrogant mock me unmercifully,
but I do not turn from your law.
⁵² I remember, LORD, your ancient laws,
and I find comfort in them.
⁵³ Indignation grips me because of the wicked,
who have forsaken your law.
⁵⁴ Your decrees are the theme of my song
wherever I lodge.
⁵⁵ In the night, LORD, I remember your name,
that I may keep your law.
⁵⁶ This has been my practice:
I obey your precepts.

ח Heth

⁵⁷ You are my portion, LORD;
I have promised to obey your words.
⁵⁸ I have sought your face with all my heart;
be gracious to me according to your promise.
⁵⁹ I have considered my ways
and have turned my steps to your statutes.
⁶⁰ I will hasten and not delay
to obey your commands.
⁶¹ Though the wicked bind me with ropes,

831

I will not forget your law.
⁶²At midnight I rise to give you thanks
    for your righteous laws.
⁶³I am a friend to all who fear you,
    to all who follow your precepts.
⁶⁴The earth is filled with your love, LORD;
    teach me your decrees.

ט Teth

⁶⁵Do good to your servant
    according to your word, LORD.
⁶⁶Teach me knowledge and good judgment,
    for I trust your commands.
⁶⁷Before I was afflicted I went astray,
    but now I obey your word.
⁶⁸You are good, and what you do is good;
    teach me your decrees.
⁶⁹Though the arrogant have smeared me with lies,
    I keep your precepts with all my heart.
⁷⁰Their hearts are callous and unfeeling,
    but I delight in your law.
⁷¹It was good for me to be afflicted
    so that I might learn your decrees.
⁷²The law from your mouth is more precious to me
    than thousands of pieces of silver and gold.

י Yodh

⁷³Your hands made me and formed me;
    give me understanding to learn your commands.
⁷⁴May those who fear you rejoice when they see me,
    for I have put my hope in your word.
⁷⁵I know, LORD, that your laws are righteous,
    and that in faithfulness you have afflicted me.
⁷⁶May your unfailing love be my comfort,
    according to your promise to your servant.
⁷⁷Let your compassion come to me that I may live,
    for your law is my delight.
⁷⁸May the arrogant be put to shame for wronging me without cause;
    but I will meditate on your precepts.
⁷⁹May those who fear you turn to me,
    those who understand your statutes.
⁸⁰May my heart be blameless toward your decrees,
    that I may not be put to shame.

כ Kaph

⁸¹My soul faints with longing for your salvation,
    but I have put my hope in your word.
⁸²My eyes fail, looking for your promise;
    I say, "When will you comfort me?"
⁸³Though I am like a wineskin in the smoke,
    I do not forget your decrees.

832

⁸⁴How long must your servant wait?
   When will you punish my persecutors?
⁸⁵The arrogant dig pits to trap me,
   contrary to your law.
⁸⁶All your commands are trustworthy;
   help me, for I am being persecuted without cause.
⁸⁷They almost wiped me from the earth,
   but I have not forsaken your precepts.
⁸⁸In your unfailing love preserve my life,
   that I may obey the statutes of your mouth.

ל **Lamedh**

⁸⁹Your word, Lord, is eternal;
   it stands firm in the heavens.
⁹⁰Your faithfulness continues through all generations;
   you established the earth, and it endures.
⁹¹Your laws endure to this day,
   for all things serve you.
⁹²If your law had not been my delight,
   I would have perished in my affliction.
⁹³I will never forget your precepts,
   for by them you have preserved my life.
⁹⁴Save me, for I am yours;
   I have sought out your precepts.
⁹⁵The wicked are waiting to destroy me,
   but I will ponder your statutes.
⁹⁶To all perfection I see a limit,
   but your commands are boundless.

מ **Mem**

⁹⁷Oh, how I love your law!
   I meditate on it all day long.
⁹⁸Your commands are always with me
   and make me wiser than my enemies.
⁹⁹I have more insight than all my teachers,
   for I meditate on your statutes.
¹⁰⁰I have more understanding than the elders,
   for I obey your precepts.
¹⁰¹I have kept my feet from every evil path
   so that I might obey your word.
¹⁰²I have not departed from your laws,
   for you yourself have taught me.
¹⁰³How sweet are your words to my taste,
   sweeter than honey to my mouth!
¹⁰⁴I gain understanding from your precepts;
   therefore I hate every wrong path.

נ **Nun**

¹⁰⁵Your word is a lamp to my feet
   and a light for my path.
¹⁰⁶I have taken an oath and confirmed it,

833

that I will follow your righteous laws.
¹⁰⁷ I have suffered much;
     preserve my life, Lord, according to your word.
¹⁰⁸ Accept, Lord, the willing praise of my mouth,
     and teach me your laws.
¹⁰⁹ Though I constantly take my life in my hands,
     I will not forget your law.
¹¹⁰ The wicked have set a snare for me,
     but I have not strayed from your precepts.
¹¹¹ Your statutes are my heritage forever;
     they are the joy of my heart.
¹¹² My heart is set on keeping your decrees
     to the very end.ᵃ

ס Samekh

¹¹³ I hate double-minded people,
     but I love your law.
¹¹⁴ You are my refuge and my shield;
     I have put my hope in your word.
¹¹⁵ Away from me, you evildoers,
     that I may keep the commands of my God!
¹¹⁶ Sustain me according to your promise, and I will live;
     do not let my hopes be dashed.
¹¹⁷ Uphold me, and I will be delivered;
     I will always have regard for your decrees.
¹¹⁸ You reject all who stray from your decrees,
     for their delusions come to nothing.
¹¹⁹ All the wicked of the earth you discard like dross;
     therefore I love your statutes.
¹²⁰ My flesh trembles in fear of you;
     I stand in awe of your laws.

ע Ayin

¹²¹ I have done what is righteous and just;
     do not leave me to my oppressors.
¹²² Ensure your servant's well-being;
     do not let the arrogant oppress me.
¹²³ My eyes fail, looking for your salvation,
     looking for your righteous promise.
¹²⁴ Deal with your servant according to your love
     and teach me your decrees.
¹²⁵ I am your servant; give me discernment
     that I may understand your statutes.
¹²⁶ It is time for you to act, Lord;
     your law is being broken.
¹²⁷ Because I love your commands
     more than gold, more than pure gold,
¹²⁸ and because I consider all your precepts right,
     I hate every wrong path.

ᵃ 112 Or / for their enduring reward

פ Pe

¹²⁹ Your statutes are wonderful;
  therefore I obey them.
¹³⁰ The unfolding of your words gives light;
  it gives understanding to the simple.
¹³¹ I open my mouth and pant,
  longing for your commands.
¹³² Turn to me and have mercy on me,
  as you always do to those who love your name.
¹³³ Direct my footsteps according to your word;
  let no sin rule over me.
¹³⁴ Redeem me from human oppression,
  that I may obey your precepts.
¹³⁵ Make your face shine on your servant
  and teach me your decrees.
¹³⁶ Streams of tears flow from my eyes,
  for your law is not obeyed.

צ Tsadhe

¹³⁷ You are righteous, Lord,
  and your laws are right.
¹³⁸ The statutes you have laid down are righteous;
  they are fully trustworthy.
¹³⁹ My zeal wears me out,
  for my enemies ignore your words.
¹⁴⁰ Your promises have been thoroughly tested,
  and your servant loves them.
¹⁴¹ Though I am lowly and despised,
  I do not forget your precepts.
¹⁴² Your righteousness is everlasting
  and your law is true.
¹⁴³ Trouble and distress have come upon me,
  but your commands give me delight.
¹⁴⁴ Your statutes are always righteous;
  give me understanding that I may live.

ק Qoph

¹⁴⁵ I call with all my heart; answer me, Lord,
  and I will obey your decrees.
¹⁴⁶ I call out to you; save me
  and I will keep your statutes.
¹⁴⁷ I rise before dawn and cry for help;
  I have put my hope in your word.
¹⁴⁸ My eyes stay open through the watches of the night,
  that I may meditate on your promises.
¹⁴⁹ Hear my voice in accordance with your love;
  preserve my life, Lord, according to your laws.
¹⁵⁰ Those who devise wicked schemes are near,
  but they are far from your law.
¹⁵¹ Yet you are near, Lord,

and all your commands are true.
¹⁵²Long ago I learned from your statutes
that you established them to last forever.

ר **Resh**

¹⁵³Look on my suffering and deliver me,
for I have not forgotten your law.
¹⁵⁴Defend my cause and redeem me;
preserve my life according to your promise.
¹⁵⁵Salvation is far from the wicked,
for they do not seek out your decrees.
¹⁵⁶Your compassion, Lord, is great;
preserve my life according to your laws.
¹⁵⁷Many are the foes who persecute me,
but I have not turned from your statutes.
¹⁵⁸I look on the faithless with loathing,
for they do not obey your word.
¹⁵⁹See how I love your precepts;
preserve my life, Lord, in accordance with your love.
¹⁶⁰All your words are true;
all your righteous laws are eternal.

ש **Sin and Shin**

¹⁶¹Rulers persecute me without cause,
but my heart trembles at your word.
¹⁶²I rejoice in your promise
like one who finds great spoil.
¹⁶³I hate and detest falsehood
but I love your law.
¹⁶⁴Seven times a day I praise you
for your righteous laws.
¹⁶⁵Great peace have those who love your law,
and nothing can make them stumble.
¹⁶⁶I wait for your salvation, Lord,
and I follow your commands.
¹⁶⁷I obey your statutes,
for I love them greatly.
¹⁶⁸I obey your precepts and your statutes,
for all my ways are known to you.

ת **Taw**

¹⁶⁹May my cry come before you, Lord;
give me understanding according to your word.
¹⁷⁰May my supplication come before you;
deliver me according to your promise.
¹⁷¹May my lips overflow with praise,
for you teach me your decrees.
¹⁷²May my tongue sing of your word,
for all your commands are righteous.
¹⁷³May your hand be ready to help me,
for I have chosen your precepts.

¹⁷⁴I long for your salvation, Lord,
  and your law gives me delight.
¹⁷⁵Let me live that I may praise you,
  and may your laws sustain me.
¹⁷⁶I have strayed like a lost sheep.
  Seek your servant,
  for I have not forgotten your commands.

Psalm 120

A song of ascents.

¹I call on the Lord in my distress,
  and he answers me.
²Save me, Lord,
  from lying lips
  and from deceitful tongues.

³What will he do to you,
  and what more besides,
  you deceitful tongue?
⁴He will punish you with a warrior's sharp arrows,
  with burning coals of the broom bush.

⁵Woe to me that I dwell in Meshek,
  that I live among the tents of Kedar!
⁶Too long have I lived
  among those who hate peace.
⁷I am for peace;
  but when I speak, they are for war.

Psalm 121

A song of ascents.

¹I lift up my eyes to the mountains—
  where does my help come from?
²My help comes from the Lord,
  the Maker of heaven and earth.

³He will not let your foot slip—
  he who watches over you will not slumber;
⁴indeed, he who watches over Israel
  will neither slumber nor sleep.

837

HE IS: my shade

121:1–8 Desert wanderers long for relief from the glaring heat of the hot sun. The psalmist likens God's followers to people wandering in the dry desert and promises that God will provide relief from the harsh elements. God is *our shade.*

If you've been wandering in a difficult desert, lift up your eyes. Your help comes from the Lord. Though the world often leaves you feeling helpless and exposed in a sea of dry, hot sand, God promises to be *your shade.* He is beckoning like an oasis in the middle of a wasteland.

For the next He Is, go to p. 839.

⁵The Lord watches over you—
  the Lord is your shade at your right hand;
⁶the sun will not harm you by day,
  nor the moon by night.

⁷The Lord will keep you from all harm—
  he will watch over your life;
⁸the Lord will watch over your coming and going
  both now and forevermore.

Psalm 122

A song of ascents. Of David.

¹I rejoiced with those who said to me,
  "Let us go to the house of the Lord."
²Our feet are standing
  in your gates, Jerusalem.

³Jerusalem is built like a city
  that is closely compacted together.
⁴That is where the tribes go up—
  the tribes of the Lord—
to praise the name of the Lord
  according to the statute given to Israel.
⁵There stand the thrones for judgment,
  the thrones of the house of David.

⁶Pray for the peace of Jerusalem:
  "May those who love you be secure.
⁷May there be peace within your walls
  and security within your citadels."
⁸For the sake of my friends and of all the people,
  I will say, "Peace be within you."
⁹For the sake of the house of the Lord our God,
  I will seek your prosperity.

Psalm 123

A song of ascents.

¹I lift up my eyes to you,
  to you who sit enthroned in heaven.
²As the eyes of slaves look to the hand of their master,
  as the eyes of a female slave look to the hand of her mistress,
so our eyes look to the Lord our God,
  till he shows us his mercy.

³Have mercy on us, Lord, have mercy on us,
  for we have endured no end of contempt.
⁴We have endured no end
  of ridicule from the arrogant,
  of contempt from the proud.

Psalm 124

A song of ascents. Of David.

¹If the Lord had not been on our side—
  let Israel say—

838

²if the LORD had not been on our side
    when people attacked us,
³they would have swallowed us alive
    when their anger flared against us;
⁴the flood would have engulfed us,
    the torrent would have swept over us,
⁵the raging waters
    would have swept us away.

⁶Praise be to the LORD,
    who has not let us be torn by their teeth.
⁷We have escaped like a bird
    from the fowler's snare;
the snare has been broken,
    and we have escaped.
⁸Our help is in the name of the LORD,
    the Maker of heaven and earth.

Psalm 125

A song of ascents.

¹Those who trust in the LORD are like Mount Zion,
    which cannot be shaken but endures forever.
²As the mountains surround Jerusalem,
    so the LORD surrounds his people
    both now and forevermore.

HE IS: encompassing

125:1–5 Jerusalem was a haven, built on Mount Zion and surrounded by mountains. Pilgrims who reached the city felt an immense feeling of safety and security. The psalmist assures the spiritual pilgrim that God is *encompassing.* Just as the mountains surround Jerusalem, so the Lord surrounds his people, including you.

In a world filled with uncertainty and danger, isn't it comforting to know that he is *encompassing*? Your loving Lord surrounds you with his power, his presence and his people (see Acts 17:24). Though evildoers may seek to invade your territory, God promises to surround you with his incomprehensible peace.

For the next He Is, go to p. 846.

³The scepter of the wicked will not remain
    over the land allotted to the righteous,
for then the righteous might use
    their hands to do evil.

⁴LORD, do good to those who are good,
    to those who are upright in heart.
⁵But those who turn to crooked ways
    the LORD will banish with the evildoers.

Peace be on Israel.

Psalm 126

A song of ascents.

¹When the LORD restored the fortunes of *ᵃ* Zion,
    we were like those who dreamed.*ᵇ*
²Our mouths were filled with laughter,
    our tongues with songs of joy.
Then it was said among the nations,
    "The LORD has done great things for them."
³The LORD has done great things for us,
    and we are filled with joy.

⁴Restore our fortunes,*ᶜ* LORD,
    like streams in the Negev.
⁵Those who sow with tears
    will reap with songs of joy.
⁶Those who go out weeping,
    carrying seed to sow,
will return with songs of joy,
    carrying sheaves with them.

840

Psalm 127

A song of ascents. Of Solomon.

¹Unless the LORD builds the house,
    the builders labor in vain.
Unless the LORD watches over the city,
    the guards stand watch in vain.
²In vain you rise early
    and stay up late,
toiling for food to eat—
    for he grants sleep to*ᵈ* those he loves.

³Children are a heritage from the LORD,
    offspring a reward from him.
⁴Like arrows in the hands of a warrior
    are children born in one's youth.
⁵Blessed is the man
    whose quiver is full of them.
They will not be put to shame
    when they contend with their
        opponents in court.

Psalm 128

A song of ascents.

¹Blessed are all who fear the LORD,
    who walk in obedience to him.
²You will eat the fruit of your labor;
    blessings and prosperity will be yours.
³Your wife will be like a fruitful vine
    within your house;
your children will be like olive shoots
    around your table.

atissue:marriage

127:1–5 Imagine that for years you've been planning your dream home. When you're about to begin construction, the most famous builder in the world approaches you and offers to build the house for you. Wouldn't it be utterly foolish to reject his offer and instead try doing it on your own? In the same way, God is the Master Builder of the family. Let him show you how to build a marriage and family that will exceed your most cherished expectations and dreams. Follow his recommended guidelines. Trust him to show you how to build something that will last.

ᵃ 1 Or LORD brought back the captives to   ᵇ 1 Or those restored to health   ᶜ 4 Or Bring back our captives   ᵈ 2 Or eat— / for while they sleep he provides for

⁴Yes, this will be the blessing
　　for the man who fears the LORD.

⁵May the LORD bless you from Zion;
　　may you see the prosperity of
　　　Jerusalem
　　all the days of your life.
⁶May you live to see your children's
　　children—
　　peace be on Israel.

Psalm 129

A song of ascents.

¹"They have greatly oppressed me from
　　my youth,"
　　let Israel say;
²"they have greatly oppressed me from my youth,
　　but they have not gained the victory over me.
³Plowmen have plowed my back
　　and made their furrows long.
⁴But the LORD is righteous;
　　he has cut me free from the cords of the wicked."

⁵May all who hate Zion
　　be turned back in shame.
⁶May they be like grass on the roof,
　　which withers before it can grow;
⁷reapers cannot fill their hands with it,
　　nor those who gather fill their arms.
⁸May those who pass by not say to them,
　　"The blessing of the LORD be on you;
　　we bless you in the name of the LORD."

Psalm 130

A song of ascents.

¹Out of the depths I cry to you, LORD;
²　Lord, hear my voice.
Let your ears be attentive
　　to my cry for mercy.

³If you, LORD, kept a record of sins,
　　Lord, who could stand?
⁴But with you there is forgiveness,
　　so that we can, with reverence, serve
　　　you.

⁵I wait for the LORD, my whole being waits,
　　and in his word I put my hope.
⁶I wait for the Lord
　　more than watchmen wait for the morning,
　　more than watchmen wait for the morning.

⁷Israel, put your hope in the LORD,
　　for with the LORD is unfailing love

conversations

success «» 128:1–6

1» Does fearing the Lord guarantee success?
What kind of success?

2» How has God blessed you because of
your faith?

3» What happens when you are not successful? Do you doubt God?

For more on **success**, check the index.
For the next Conversations, go to p. 841.

841

conversations

depression «» 130:1–2

1» Does God ever get tired of hearing about
your pain? How do you know?

2» Is it wrong to be depressed? Why or
why not?

3» What is unique about how a Christian can
deal with depression?

For more on **depression**, check the index.
For the next Conversations, go to p. 849.

myth# 51 "MY DEGREE
IS MY TICKET
TO SUCCESS."

We were always just scraping by in my family. My mom cleaned houses, and my dad worked for a Christian mission. He'd given up a career in sales (and a good salary) to take this job. I knew things were tight, but it wasn't until I got older that I realized just how bad things were. I'd watch my dad trying to pay the bills, and I'd see the stress in his face. I'd hear my mom pray over and over again that God would provide.

We did things that other families didn't do. We had a wood stove to heat our house, and my dad and brother used to spend every Saturday chopping and hauling free wood for the coming week. In the worst months, we used to get free cans from the supermarket—the cans that were dented or the labels had fallen off—and that would be dinner. My mom made it a game—"What do you think is inside this can, Megan?" For family vacations, we went either to my grandma's house or to my aunt and uncle's shore house.

When I got older, I determined that I would never be "without." I always dreamed (and still do) about one day having enough money to help pay my mom and dad back for all their sacrifices. I worked hard in high school and made good grades so that I could get into the best college. With my bachelor's and master's degrees behind me, I'm now wrapping up my doctorate. I'm on track at my institution to get a big raise once I complete my dissertation.

The American dream of being a self-made woman is almost within my reach. It gives me a good feeling to know my children will never know what it means to struggle financially as I did as a child. Once I am financially comfortable, I will never have to worry about the future again.

—Megan

WHILE GOD WANTS us to work hard to provide for our families, he doesn't want us to put our hope or our trust in our own abilities. He is our source, our provider. He gives us the energy to do our work (see Colossians 1:28–29). This is a fine line to walk. While we want to do our best and work as if we were working for God (see Colossians 3:23–24), we also want to make sure that our security and our dependence are in him and not in our jobs, our emergency savings accounts or our 401(k)s.

You'll know that you are relying on him and not on yourself if you are . . .

- *Humbly relying on his promise to take care of you and provide for your needs (Matthew 6:33).* Anytime you start to put confidence in yourself, you risk becoming proud and arrogant. Your best efforts are in vain unless God is directing you (see Psalm 127:1).

- *Seeking God's definition of success over the world's definition.* To you, is success financial wealth and comfort? Or is it being rich in God's eyes? One leads to an empty life, and one leads to full and abundant living.

- *Not focusing too much on amassing earthly wealth.* If you're busy wishing you had more money, then you're missing opportunities to grow and trust God. The Bible says that financial success will never satisfy you anyway. In fact, while there is nothing wrong with money, the love of money can lead to all kinds of trouble. Wealth can be a curse.

- *Using the energy and resources God gave you for him and his kingdom, not for your own interests.* The money you earn and the education and training you receive is not for you alone. Put it in circulation, and share with those in need (see Ephesians 4:28).

- *Admitting that you do not control your own destiny (James 4:13–17).* You have no idea what the future holds. Only God does.

> "Between 1990 and 2000 the number of men enrolled in college rose 7 percent, while the number of women increased by twice that amount (14 percent)."
>
> —U.S. Department of Education, National Center for Education Statistics (2003)

843

"BUT SEEK FIRST HIS KINGDOM AND HIS RIGHTEOUSNESS, AND ALL THESE THINGS WILL BE GIVEN TO YOU AS WELL."

MATTHEW 6:33

SEE ALSO

Psalm 127:1
Ecclesiastes 5:10
1 Timothy 6:10

For more on **Money** and **Success**, check the index.

and with him is full redemption.
⁸He himself will redeem Israel
    from all their sins.

Psalm 131

A song of ascents. Of David.

¹My heart is not proud, Lord,
    my eyes are not haughty;
I do not concern myself with great matters
    or things too wonderful for me.
²But I have calmed myself
    and quieted my ambitions.
I am like a weaned child with its mother;
    like a weaned child I am content.

³Israel, put your hope in the Lord
    both now and forevermore.

Psalm 132

A song of ascents.

¹Lord, remember David
    and all his self-denial.

²He swore an oath to the Lord
    and made a vow to the Mighty One of Jacob:
³"I will not enter my house
    or go to my bed,
⁴I will allow no sleep to my eyes
    or slumber to my eyelids,
⁵till I find a place for the Lord,
    a dwelling for the Mighty One of Jacob."

⁶We heard it in Ephrathah,
    we came upon it in the fields of Jaar:ᵃ
⁷"Let us go to his dwelling place,
    let us worship at his footstool, saying,
⁸'Arise, Lord, and come to your resting place,
    you and the ark of your might.
⁹May your priests be clothed with your righteousness;
    may your faithful people sing for joy.'"

¹⁰For the sake of your servant David,
    do not reject your anointed one.

¹¹The Lord swore an oath to David,
    a sure oath that he will not revoke:
"One of your own descendants
    I will place on your throne.
¹²If your sons keep my covenant
    and the statutes I teach them,
then their sons will sit
    on your throne for ever and ever."

ᵃ *6 Or heard of it in Ephrathah, / we found it in the fields of Jearim.* (See 1 Chron. 13:5,6) (And no quotation marks around verses 7-9)

¹³For the LORD has chosen Zion,
   he has desired it for his dwelling, saying,
¹⁴"This is my resting place for ever and ever;
   here I will sit enthroned, for I have desired it.
¹⁵I will bless her with abundant provisions;
   her poor I will satisfy with food.
¹⁶I will clothe her priests with salvation,
   and her faithful people will ever sing for joy.

¹⁷"Here I will make a horn*ᵃ* grow for David
   and set up a lamp for my anointed one.
¹⁸I will clothe his enemies with shame,
   but his head will be adorned with a resplendent crown."

Psalm 133

A song of ascents. Of David.

¹How good and pleasant it is
   when God's people live together in unity!

²It is like precious oil poured on the head,
   running down on the beard,
running down on Aaron's beard,
   down on the collar of his robe.
³It is as if the dew of Hermon
   were falling on Mount Zion.
For there the LORD bestows his blessing,
   even life forevermore.

Psalm 134

A song of ascents.

¹Praise the LORD, all you servants of the LORD
   who minister by night in the house of the LORD.
²Lift up your hands in the sanctuary
   and praise the LORD.

³May the LORD bless you from Zion,
   he who is the Maker of heaven and earth.

Psalm 135

¹Praise the LORD.*ᵇ*

Praise the name of the LORD;
   praise him, you servants of the LORD,
²you who minister in the house of the LORD,
   in the courts of the house of our God.

³Praise the LORD, for the LORD is good;
   sing praise to his name, for that is pleasant.
⁴For the LORD has chosen Jacob to be his own,
   Israel to be his treasured possession.

⁵I know that the LORD is great,
   that our Lord is greater than all gods.

ᵃ 17 Horn here symbolizes strong one, that is, king.   *ᵇ 1* Hebrew Hallelu Yah; also in verses 3 and 21

⁶The LORD does whatever pleases him,
    in the heavens and on the earth,
    in the seas and all their depths.
⁷He makes clouds rise from the ends of the earth;
    he sends lightning with the rain
    and brings out the wind from his storehouses.

⁸He struck down the firstborn of Egypt,
    the firstborn of people and animals.
⁹He sent his signs and wonders into your midst, Egypt,
    against Pharaoh and all his servants.
¹⁰He struck down many nations
    and killed mighty kings—
¹¹Sihon king of the Amorites,
    Og king of Bashan,
    and all the kings of Canaan—
¹²and he gave their land as an inheritance,
    an inheritance to his people Israel.

¹³Your name, LORD, endures forever,
    your renown, LORD, through all generations.
¹⁴For the LORD will vindicate his people
    and relent concerning his servants.

HE IS: renowned

135:13–14 This is a psalm of praise, reminding the worshiper of God's special relationship with Israel and his mighty works on their behalf. Pointing to God's renown through all generations, the psalmist celebrates God's compassion on his servants.

He is *renowned* throughout the world. To their shame, many people use God's name as a curse (see Exodus 20:7). Do you use God's name disrespectfully, casually or flippantly? Or do you speak his name with respect and praise, elevating him above the gods of the world and telling others about his compassion to you? God's fame *will* spread—will you be a messenger for spreading it?

For the next He Is, go to p. 855.

¹⁵The idols of the nations are silver and gold,
    made by human hands.
¹⁶They have mouths, but cannot speak,
    eyes, but cannot see.
¹⁷They have ears, but cannot hear,
    nor is there breath in their mouths.
¹⁸Those who make them will be like them,
    and so will all who trust in them.

¹⁹House of Israel, praise the LORD;
    house of Aaron, praise the LORD;
²⁰house of Levi, praise the LORD;
    you who fear him, praise the LORD.

²¹Praise be to the LORD from Zion,
  to him who dwells in Jerusalem.

  Praise the LORD.

Psalm 136

¹Give thanks to the LORD, for he is good.

His love endures forever.

²Give thanks to the God of gods.

His love endures forever.

³Give thanks to the Lord of lords:

His love endures forever.

⁴to him who alone does great wonders,

His love endures forever.

⁵who by his understanding made the heavens,

His love endures forever.

⁶who spread out the earth upon the waters,

His love endures forever.

⁷who made the great lights—

His love endures forever.

⁸the sun to govern the day,

His love endures forever.

⁹the moon and stars to govern the night;

His love endures forever.

¹⁰to him who struck down the firstborn of Egypt

His love endures forever.

¹¹and brought Israel out from among them

His love endures forever.

¹²with a mighty hand and outstretched arm;

His love endures forever.

¹³to him who divided the Red Sea^a asunder

His love endures forever.

¹⁴and brought Israel through the midst of it,

His love endures forever.

¹⁵but swept Pharaoh and his army into the Red Sea;

His love endures forever.

¹⁶to him who led his people through the wilderness;

His love endures forever.

¹⁷to him who struck down great kings,

His love endures forever.

¹⁸and killed mighty kings—

His love endures forever.

¹⁹Sihon king of the Amorites

His love endures forever.

²⁰and Og king of Bashan—

His love endures forever.

²¹and gave their land as an inheritance,

His love endures forever.

847

---

^a *13* Or *the Sea of Reeds*; also in verse 15

²² an inheritance to his servant Israel.

His love endures forever.

²³ He remembered us in our low estate

His love endures forever.

²⁴ and freed us from our enemies.

His love endures forever.

²⁵ He gives food to every creature.

His love endures forever.

²⁶ Give thanks to the God of heaven.

His love endures forever.

Psalm 137

¹ By the rivers of Babylon we sat and wept
    when we remembered Zion.
² There on the poplars
    we hung our harps,
³ for there our captors asked us for songs,
    our tormentors demanded songs of joy;
    they said, "Sing us one of the songs of Zion!"

⁴ How can we sing the songs of the LORD
    while in a foreign land?
⁵ If I forget you, Jerusalem,
    may my right hand forget its skill.
⁶ May my tongue cling to the roof of my mouth
    if I do not remember you,
  if I do not consider Jerusalem
    my highest joy.

⁷ Remember, LORD, what the Edomites did
    on the day Jerusalem fell.
"Tear it down," they cried,
    "tear it down to its foundations!"
⁸ Daughter Babylon, doomed to destruction,
    happy are those who repay you
    according to what you have done to us.
⁹ Happy are those who seize your infants
    and dash them against the rocks.

Psalm 138

Of David.

¹ I will praise you, LORD, with all my heart;
    before the "gods" I will sing your praise.
² I will bow down toward your holy temple
    and will praise your name
    for your unfailing love and your faithfulness,
for you have so exalted your solemn decree
    that it surpasses your fame.
³ When I called, you answered me;
    you greatly emboldened me.

⁴ May all the kings of the earth praise you, LORD,
    when they hear what you have decreed.

848

⁵May they sing of the ways of the LORD,
    for the glory of the LORD is great.

⁶Though the LORD is exalted, he looks kindly
      on the lowly,
  but he takes notice of the proud from
      afar.
⁷Though I walk in the midst of trouble,
    you preserve my life.
You stretch out your hand against the
      anger of my foes;
  with your right hand you save me.
⁸The LORD will vindicate me;
    your love, LORD, endures forever—
  do not abandon the works of your
      hands.

Psalm 139

For the director of music. Of David. A psalm.

¹You have searched me, LORD,
    and you know me.
²You know when I sit and when I rise;
    you perceive my thoughts from afar.
³You discern my going out and my lying
      down;
  you are familiar with all my ways.
⁴Before a word is on my tongue
  you, LORD, know it completely.
⁵You hem me in behind and before,
    and you lay your hand upon me.
⁶Such knowledge is too wonderful for me,
    too lofty for me to attain.

⁷Where can I go from your Spirit?
    Where can I flee from your presence?
⁸If I go up to the heavens, you are there;
  if I make my bed in the depths, you
      are there.
⁹If I rise on the wings of the dawn,
    if I settle on the far side of the sea,
¹⁰even there your hand will guide me,
    your right hand will hold me fast.
¹¹If I say, "Surely the darkness will
      hide me
  and the light become night
      around me,"
¹²even the darkness will not be dark
      to you;
  the night will shine like the day,
    for darkness is as light to you.

¹³For you created my inmost being;
    you knit me together in my mother's womb.

atissue: singleness

138:6–8 Perhaps by now you thought you'd be married and have two children, a beautiful home and a job you love. Instead, you feel hopelessly single, hate your tiny apartment and dread each day at your job. So you just bide your time, waiting for your life to really start. This is a common story of discontentment for many women, no matter what the particulars are. If it's your story, then you're missing out on God's purpose for you right now. He's chosen you to bring him glory today. And you can fulfill that purpose no matter what your life is like now.

849

conversations

change «» 139:7–12

1» What's hard for you about changing your environment (work, home, city, etc.)?

2» How can a change of environment teach you new things about God?

3» What are the never-changing constants in your life?

For more on **change**, check the index.
For the next Conversations, go to p. 857.

myth# 52 "ABORTION IS MY ONLY OPTION."

I never, never intended for this to happen. I ran into an old boyfriend at a particularly vulnerable time in my life, and we talked late into the night. One thing led to another, and soon we were back into our old habits. It was such a brief period of time—a week, maybe two?—but I got pregnant.

I feel trapped. God, I can't have a baby at this point in my life. I can't quit working, and I am nowhere near being emotionally or physically prepared to be a mother.

The irony is, I am in ministry at my church and am a role model in my circles of friends. If people find out that I messed up this badly, it will for-ever damage my reputation and destroy my Christian witness. Surely God doesn't want me to bring this out in the open and make Christians look bad. If I tell my ex-boyfriend, he will certainly not want to have anything to do with the baby or me. If I tell my family, they will disown me. If my Christian friends find out, they will never look at me the same.

I've weighed all my options. It seems that I only have a few—no easy ones either. I went to a clinic in another town, and they suggested that I have a procedure to terminate the pregnancy. They were so understanding. The woman said that it would be relatively quick and painless. According to her, the doctor would eliminate the fetus from my body. Tomorrow my life would be back to normal, and no one would ever know.

I feel so alone and confused. I don't have anyone to talk to about this. The people at the clinic seem to be the most comforting and nonjudgmen-tal people that I can talk to right now. That seems like my only choice.

—Deborah

WHY DO SOME Christian women abort their unborn children? Is it because deep down they don't believe it's a child? No. Is it because they don't think abortion is a sin (murder) and displeasing to God? No. Is it because they really believe in abortion and a woman's right to choose? No.

It's because they feel alone.

Facing an unplanned pregnancy feels over-whelming and scary. It feels like life has come to an end. It feels like you're in a trap and there's no way out.

But you are not alone.

No, your heavenly Father knows and sees, and he loves you just as much as he did before you got pregnant. No matter what your circumstance or how you came to this point in your life, he still embraces you and holds you in his hand.

If you're facing an unplanned pregnancy, the last things you need to hear are preaching and trite advice. Let's be realistic—you are in a very difficult situation. Sometimes abortion feels like the best option because it's the quickest fix, and no one ever knows. But don't believe the lie that your life will go on as usual. If you have an abortion, you will never be the same. You will be haunted by guilt for years. You will miss that child that could have been yours. You will won-der what God had in mind for that little life (see Jeremiah 1:5). You will carry debilitating emo-tional scars into every relationship in your future, and you may carry physical scars too.

Granted, your other options are also difficult—raising the child on your own, under the scruti-ny and judgment of so-called Christians and your friends and family. Or giving your child up for adoption, which involves all of the shame of the pregnancy and then the feeling of loss of giving up your child.

But abortion will not fix your problem. Hard as it is, adoption may give a couple who desper-ately wants a child the baby they'd always hoped

for. And a true Christian friend will love you and stand beside you—in the maternity store and the delivery room. God can provide those types of friends.

Our God is a God of second chances, a God of untold grace and unending love. If you choose to do things God's way, rather than compounding one sin with another (a sin that will change you for life), then God will bring beauty out of ashes (see Isaiah 61:1–3), hope out of despair, new life out of the death of self you feel.

Exercise your freedom to choose, and choose what's right. If you need to talk to someone, call toll-free, (800) 848-LOVE, the National Life Center, 24 hours a day, 365 days a year.

God is with you.

851

"Approximately 93 percent of all induced abortions are done for elective, non-medical reasons."

—National Right to Life Web site

"FOR YOU CREATED MY INMOST BEING; YOU KNIT ME TOGETHER IN MY MOTHER'S WOMB."

PSALM 139:13

SEE ALSO
Deuteronomy 30:11–14,19–20
Psalm 22:9–11
Psalm 139:13–16

For more on **Abortion**, check the index.

¹⁴I praise you because I am fearfully and
　　wonderfully made;
　　your works are wonderful,
　　I know that full well.
¹⁵My frame was not hidden from you
　　when I was made in the secret place.
　When I was woven together in the
　　depths of the earth,
¹⁶ 　your eyes saw my unformed body.
　All the days ordained for me
　　were written in your book
　　before one of them came to be.
¹⁷How precious to me are your thoughts,ᵃ
　　God!
　　How vast is the sum of them!
¹⁸Were I to count them,
　　they would outnumber the grains of
　　　sand—
　　when I awake, I am still with you.

¹⁹If only you, God, would slay the wicked!
　Away from me, you who are
　　bloodthirsty!
²⁰They speak of you with evil intent;
　　your adversaries misuse your name.
²¹Do I not hate those who hate you, LORD,
　　and abhor those who are in rebellion against you?
²²I have nothing but hatred for them;
　　I count them my enemies.
²³Search me, God, and know my heart;
　　test me and know my anxious thoughts.
²⁴See if there is any offensive way in me,
　　and lead me in the way everlasting.

Psalm 140

For the director of music. A psalm of David.

* ¹Rescue me, LORD, from evildoers;
　　protect me from the violent,
²who devise evil plans in their hearts
　　and stir up war every day.
³They make their tongues as sharp as a serpent's;
　　the poison of vipers is on their lips.ᵇ

⁴Keep me safe, LORD, from the hands of the wicked;
　　protect me from the violent,
　　who devise ways to trip my feet.
⁵The arrogant have hidden a snare for me;
　　they have spread out the cords of their net
　　and have set traps for me along my path.

⁶I say to the LORD, "You are my God."
　　Hear, LORD, my cry for mercy.

at issue: body image

139:13–18 You are a masterpiece. Yes, you. You are the pinnacle of the creation of the Master Artist. You—with your too-big hips and your out-of-control hair and your pointy chin. You—with your tendency to repeat yourself and your inability to carry a tune and your goofy laugh. You are exactly who God designed you to be. And you are infinitely precious to him, just the way you are. Quit worrying about what other people see when they look at you. Start seeing yourself as God sees you: his beloved, priceless work of art.

ᵃ *17 Or precious are your thoughts concerning me*　ᵇ *3 The Hebrew has* Selah *(a word of uncertain meaning) here and at the end of verses 5 and 8.*
* *140:1-13 is numbered 140:2-14 in Hebrew texts.*

⁷Sovereign Lᴏʀᴅ, my strong deliverer,
  you shield my head in the day of battle.
⁸Do not grant the wicked their desires, Lᴏʀᴅ;
  do not let their plans succeed.

⁹Those who surround me proudly rear their heads;
  may the mischief of their lips engulf them.
¹⁰May burning coals fall on them;
  may they be thrown into the fire,
  into miry pits, never to rise.
¹¹May slanderers not be established in the land;
  may disaster hunt down the violent.

¹²I know that the Lᴏʀᴅ secures justice for the poor
  and upholds the cause of the needy.
¹³Surely the righteous will praise your name,
  and the upright will live in your presence.

Psalm 141

A psalm of David.

¹I call to you, Lᴏʀᴅ, come quickly to me;
  hear me when I call to you.
²May my prayer be set before you like incense;
  may the lifting up of my hands be like the evening sacrifice.

³Set a guard over my mouth, Lᴏʀᴅ;
  keep watch over the door of my lips.
⁴Do not let my heart be drawn to what is evil
  so that I take part in wicked deeds
along with those who are evildoers;
  do not let me eat of their delicacies.

⁵Let a righteous man strike me—that is a kindness;
  let him rebuke me—that is oil on my head.
My head will not refuse it,
  for my prayer will still be against the deeds of evildoers.

⁶Their rulers will be thrown down from the cliffs,
  and the wicked will learn that my words were well spoken.
⁷They will say, "As one plows and breaks up the earth,
  so our bones have been scattered at the mouth of the grave."

⁸But my eyes are fixed on you, Sovereign Lᴏʀᴅ;
  in you I take refuge—do not give me over to death.
⁹Keep me safe from the traps set by evildoers,
  from the snares they have laid for me.
¹⁰Let the wicked fall into their own nets,
  while I pass by in safety.

Psalm 142

A maskil ᵃ of David. When he was in the cave. A prayer.

* ¹I cry aloud to the Lᴏʀᴅ;
  I lift up my voice to the Lᴏʀᴅ for mercy.

853

ᵃ Title: Probably a literary or musical term

* 142:1-7 is numbered 142:2-8 in Hebrew texts.

²I pour out before him my complaint;
  before him I tell my trouble.

³When my spirit grows faint within me,
  it is you who watch over my way.
 In the path where I walk
  people have hidden a snare for me.
⁴Look and see, there is no one at my right hand;
  no one is concerned for me.
 I have no refuge;
  no one cares for my life.

⁵I cry to you, Lord;
 I say, "You are my refuge,
  my portion in the land of the living."

⁶Listen to my cry,
  for I am in desperate need;
 rescue me from those who pursue me,
  for they are too strong for me.
⁷Set me free from my prison,
  that I may praise your name.
 Then the righteous will gather about me
  because of your goodness to me.

854

Psalm 143

A psalm of David.

¹Lord, hear my prayer,
  listen to my cry for mercy;
 in your faithfulness and righteousness
  come to my relief.
²Do not bring your servant into judgment,
  for no one living is righteous before you.
³The enemy pursues me,
  he crushes me to the ground;
 he makes me dwell in the darkness
  like those long dead.
⁴So my spirit grows faint within me;
  my heart within me is dismayed.
⁵I remember the days of long ago;
  I meditate on all your works
  and consider what your hands have done.
⁶I spread out my hands to you;
  I thirst for you like a parched land.^a

⁷Answer me quickly, Lord;
  my spirit fails.
 Do not hide your face from me
  or I will be like those who go down to the pit.
⁸Let the morning bring me word of your unfailing love,
  for I have put my trust in you.
 Show me the way I should go,

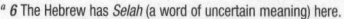

^a *6* The Hebrew has *Selah* (a word of uncertain meaning) here.

HE IS: Spirit

143:7–12 In this, a soldier's prayer, David cried to God when the enemy was in hot pursuit. He asked God to remind him of God's unfailing love, to show him the way and to rescue him from harm. David realized that God, who is *Spirit*, knew his plight and could lead him to safety.

Life is more boot camp than summer camp. It seems that we all fight battles every day. When the enemy is hot on your heels, ask God to show you his unfailing love. Make David's psalm your personal prayer: "May your good *Spirit* lead me on level ground."

For the next He Is, go to p. 861.

855

for to you I entrust my life.
⁹Rescue me from my enemies, LORD,
  for I hide myself in you.
¹⁰Teach me to do your will,
  for you are my God;
may your good Spirit
  lead me on level ground.

¹¹For your name's sake, LORD, preserve my life;
  in your righteousness, bring me out of trouble.
¹²In your unfailing love, silence my enemies;
  destroy all my foes,
  for I am your servant.

Psalm 144

Of David.

¹Praise be to the LORD my Rock,
  who trains my hands for war,
  my fingers for battle.
²He is my loving God and my fortress,
  my stronghold and my deliverer,
my shield, in whom I take refuge,
  who subdues peoples*ᵃ* under me.

³LORD, what are human beings that you care for them,
  mere mortals that you think of them?
⁴They are like a breath;
  their days are like a fleeting shadow.

⁵Part your heavens, LORD, and come down;
  touch the mountains, so that they smoke.
⁶Send forth lightning and scatter the enemy;
  shoot your arrows and rout them.
⁷Reach down your hand from on high;
  deliver me and rescue me
from the mighty waters,
  from the hands of foreigners
⁸whose mouths are full of lies,
  whose right hands are deceitful.

ᵃ *2* Many manuscripts of the Masoretic Text, Dead Sea Scrolls, Aquila, Jerome and Syriac; most manuscripts of the Masoretic Text *subdues my people*

⁹I will sing a new song to you, my God;
 on the ten-stringed lyre I will make music to you,
¹⁰to the One who gives victory to kings,
 who delivers his servant David.

From the deadly sword ¹¹deliver me;
 rescue me from the hands of foreigners
whose mouths are full of lies,
 whose right hands are deceitful.

¹²Then our sons in their youth
 will be like well-nurtured plants,
and our daughters will be like pillars
 carved to adorn a palace.
¹³Our barns will be filled
 with every kind of provision.
Our sheep will increase by thousands,
 by tens of thousands in our fields;
¹⁴ our oxen will draw heavy loads.*
There will be no breaching of walls,
 no going into captivity,
 no cry of distress in our streets.
¹⁵Blessed is the people of whom this is true;
 blessed is the people whose God is the LORD.

Psalm 145 *ᵇ*

A psalm of praise. Of David.

¹I will exalt you, my God the King;
 I will praise your name for ever and ever.
²Every day I will praise you
 and extol your name for ever and ever.

³Great is the LORD and most worthy of praise;
 his greatness no one can fathom.
⁴One generation commends your works to another;
 they tell of your mighty acts.
⁵They speak of the glorious splendor of your majesty—
 and I will meditate on your wonderful works.*ᶜ*
⁶They tell of the power of your awesome works—
 and I will proclaim your great deeds.
⁷They celebrate your abundant goodness
 and joyfully sing of your righteousness.

⁸The LORD is gracious and compassionate,
 slow to anger and rich in love.

⁹The LORD is good to all;
 he has compassion on all he has made.
¹⁰All your works praise you, LORD;
 your faithful people extol you.
¹¹They tell of the glory of your kingdom

ᵃ 14 Or our chieftains will be firmly established   ᵇ This psalm is an acrostic poem, the verses of which (including verse 13b) begin with the successive letters of the Hebrew alphabet.   ᶜ 5 Dead Sea Scrolls and Syriac (see also Septuagint); Masoretic Text On the glorious splendor of your majesty / and on your wonderful works I will meditate

and speak of your might,
¹²so that all people may know of your mighty acts
and the glorious splendor of your kingdom.
¹³Your kingdom is an everlasting kingdom,
and your dominion endures through all generations.

The Lord is trustworthy in all he
promises
and faithful in all he does.ᵃ
¹⁴The Lord upholds all who fall
and lifts up all who are bowed down.
¹⁵The eyes of all look to you,
and you give them their food at the
proper time.
¹⁶You open your hand
and satisfy the desires of every living
thing.

¹⁷The Lord is righteous in all his ways
and faithful in all he does.
¹⁸The Lord is near to all who call on him,
to all who call on him in truth.
¹⁹He fulfills the desires of those who fear him;
he hears their cry and saves them.
²⁰The Lord watches over all who love him,
but all the wicked he will destroy.

²¹My mouth will speak in praise of the Lord.
Let every creature praise his holy name
for ever and ever.

Psalm 146

¹Praise the Lord.ᵇ

Praise the Lord, my soul.

²I will praise the Lord all my life;
I will sing praise to my God as long as I live.
³Do not put your trust in princes,
in human beings, who cannot save.
⁴When their spirit departs, they return to the ground;
on that very day their plans come to nothing.
⁵Blessed are those whose help is the God of Jacob,
whose hope is in the Lord their God.

⁶He is the Maker of heaven and earth,
the sea, and everything in them—
he remains faithful forever.
⁷He upholds the cause of the oppressed
and gives food to the hungry.
The Lord sets prisoners free,
⁸ the Lord gives sight to the blind,
the Lord lifts up those who are bowed down,

conversations

fulfillment «» 145:13b–16

1 » Is it OK to ask God to fulfill your personal desires?

2 » What gives you true fulfillment in life?

3 » Do you think God cares about whether you feel fulfilled?

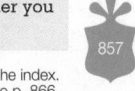

For more on fulfillment, check the index.
For the next Conversations, go to p. 866.

857

ᵃ 13 One manuscript of the Masoretic Text, Dead Sea Scrolls and Syriac (see also Septuagint); most manuscripts of the Masoretic Text do not have the last two lines of verse 13.   ᵇ 1 Hebrew *Hallelu Yah*; also in verse 10

the LORD loves the righteous.
⁹The LORD watches over the foreigner
and sustains the fatherless and the widow,
but he frustrates the ways of the wicked.

¹⁰The LORD reigns forever,
your God, O Zion, for all generations.

Praise the LORD.

Psalm 147

¹Praise the LORD.ᵃ

How good it is to sing praises to our God,
how pleasant and fitting to praise him!

²The LORD builds up Jerusalem;
he gathers the exiles of Israel.
³He heals the brokenhearted
and binds up their wounds.
⁴He determines the number of the stars
and calls them each by name.
⁵Great is our Lord and mighty in power;
his understanding has no limit.
⁶The LORD sustains the humble
but casts the wicked to the ground.

⁷Sing to the LORD with grateful praise;
make music to our God on the harp.

⁸He covers the sky with clouds;
he supplies the earth with rain
and makes grass grow on the hills.
⁹He provides food for the cattle
and for the young ravens when they
call.

¹⁰His pleasure is not in the strength of the
horse,
nor his delight in the power of human
legs;
¹¹the LORD delights in those who fear him,
who put their hope in his unfailing love.

¹²Extol the LORD, Jerusalem;
praise your God, Zion.

¹³He strengthens the bars of your gates
and blesses your people within you.
¹⁴He grants peace to your borders
and satisfies you with the finest of wheat.

¹⁵He sends his command to the earth;
his word runs swiftly.
¹⁶He spreads the snow like wool
and scatters the frost like ashes.

at issue : divorce

147:2–3 We are the walking wounded. All women have deep hurts. Some of us carry small wounds inflicted by a stinging remark or an unjust situation or an unappreciative boss. But if you've experienced a divorce, you know what it feels like to carry a large, gaping wound. You might not want others to see the pain you live with, so you may be good at hiding your pain. But God still sees it. Trust yourself to his tender, loving, healing touch. Let him mend your broken heart and bind up your wounds. He's the only one who can.

ᵃ 1 Hebrew *Hallelu Yah*; also in verse 20

ASKmeanyTHING

2 Samuel 13:1–33

859

You have a difficult story to tell.

Yes. Even now the pain and guilt of what happened so long ago is difficult to talk about. Not in my wildest dreams could I have imagined something like that happening to me—me, David's own daughter, a princess.

Tell us what happened as best you can.

As I said, I was David's daughter by Maacah. I was a sister of Absalom and half-sister to Amnon. I didn't realize it at the time, but Amnon was in love with me [laughs bitterly]. Love is probably not the right word here. He was in lust with me. Sex was all Amnon wanted. And when he tried to get me in his bed, I resisted as best I could. I told him that it was wrong, and that if he waited our father wouldn't prevent us from getting married. But he refused to listen or wait. He was much stronger and . . . he raped me.

Can you tell us what happened then?

It was a nightmare, a living hell. Amnon immediately realized that what he had done was horrible, and he hated me. He threw me out. I was humiliated, filled with self-loathing and guilt. What had I done to deserve this? What could I do to get rid of the horrible shame that I felt? Where could I go? My brother and my father were no help. Although they both were angry and disgusted with Amnon, they did nothing to help me. I can still hear the words: "Oh, you'll get over it. Everything will be fine. Don't worry about it, Tamar."

What did you do?

Absalom took me in, but I was a shell of a person. I lived in despair, loneliness, hopelessness.

How can others learn from your situation?

What happened to me was beyond my control. I lived for so many years with the haunting "what ifs"—*What if I had not gone to Amnon's room? What if I had seen what was coming? How naïve I was not to be suspicious!* Yet I know that what happened was not my choice or my fault. What *was* my choice, though, was how I dealt with my pain. Instead of focusing inwardly, I could have looked outside myself and sought help from God and others. To those living with the shame of rape or incest or whatever it might be, I would say this—don't isolate yourself. Get help. Ask God for healing. Don't let your past choke out the hope for your future. God can help. He really can. Go to him.

FOR MORE INSIGHT: For words on the hope that we have in God, look up Psalm 42:11; Psalm 130; and Lamentations 3:21–26.

¹⁷He hurls down his hail like pebbles.
    Who can withstand his icy blast?
¹⁸He sends his word and melts them;
    he stirs up his breezes, and the waters flow.

¹⁹He has revealed his word to Jacob,
    his laws and decrees to Israel.
²⁰He has done this for no other nation;
    they do not know his laws.^a

Praise the LORD.

Psalm 148

¹Praise the LORD.^b

Praise the LORD from the heavens;
    praise him in the heights above.
²Praise him, all his angels;
    praise him, all his heavenly hosts.
³Praise him, sun and moon;
    praise him, all you shining stars.
⁴Praise him, you highest heavens
    and you waters above the skies.

⁵Let them praise the name of the LORD,
    for at his command they were created,
⁶and he established them for ever and ever—
    he issued a decree that will never pass away.

⁷Praise the LORD from the earth,
    you great sea creatures and all ocean depths,
⁸lightning and hail, snow and clouds,
    stormy winds that do his bidding,
⁹you mountains and all hills,
    fruit trees and all cedars,
¹⁰wild animals and all cattle,
    small creatures and flying birds,
¹¹kings of the earth and all nations,
    you princes and all rulers on earth,
¹²young men and women,
    old men and children.

¹³Let them praise the name of the LORD,
    for his name alone is exalted;
    his splendor is above the earth and the heavens.
¹⁴And he has raised up for his people a horn,^c
    the praise of all his faithful servants,
    of Israel, the people close to his heart.

Praise the LORD.

Psalm 149

¹Praise the LORD.^d

Sing to the LORD a new song,
    his praise in the assembly of his faithful people.

---

^a 20 Masoretic Text; Dead Sea Scrolls and Septuagint / *he has not made his laws known to them* ^b 1 Hebrew *Hallelu Yah*; also in verse 14 ^c 14 *Horn* here symbolizes strength. ^d 1 Hebrew *Hallelu Yah*; also in verse 9

²Let Israel rejoice in their Maker;
    let the people of Zion be glad in their King.
³Let them praise his name with dancing
    and make music to him with timbrel and harp.
⁴For the LORD takes delight in his people;
    he crowns the humble with victory.
⁵Let his faithful people rejoice in this honor
    and sing for joy on their beds.

HE IS: praiseworthy

149:1–5 The psalmist tells us to sing to the Lord a new song. Songs of praise can be sung in a church assembly or in the privacy of our homes. The songs' themes are always the same: praising God.

Whether you have the voice of an angel or sing like a frog, God is *praiseworthy* and loves your songs. When you're in the shower, praise him for washing you clean from sin. When at work, praise him for providing for your needs. When at church, praise him for your spiritual family. Before you go to sleep, praise him for giving you rest. Whatever the circumstances, praise the Lord!

For the next He Is, go to p. 875.

861

⁶May the praise of God be in their mouths
    and a double-edged sword in their hands,
⁷to inflict vengeance on the nations
    and punishment on the peoples,
⁸to bind their kings with fetters,
    their nobles with shackles of iron,
⁹to carry out the sentence written against them—
    this is the glory of all his faithful people.

Praise the LORD.

Psalm 150

¹Praise the LORD.*

Praise God in his sanctuary;
    praise him in his mighty heavens.
²Praise him for his acts of power;
    praise him for his surpassing greatness.
³Praise him with the sounding of the trumpet,
    praise him with the harp and lyre,
⁴praise him with timbrel and dancing,
    praise him with the strings and pipe,
⁵praise him with the clash of cymbals,
    praise him with resounding cymbals.

⁶Let everything that has breath praise the LORD.

Praise the LORD.

ᵃ 1 Hebrew *Hallelu Yah*; also in verse 6

proverbs

AUTHOR
Primarily King Solomon.

AUDIENCE
All Israel.

DATE
Solomon wrote most of the proverbs during
his reign (970 to 930 B.C.), but the book wasn't
fully compiled until around 700 B.C.

SETTING
Written during Solomon's wiser days.
Solomon had great wisdom, but he gave in to
temptation later on in his life.

VERSES TO REMEMBER
"Trust in the LORD with all your heart
   and lean not on your own
      understanding;
in all your ways submit to him,
   and he will make your paths straight." (3:5–6)

THEME TO CONSIDER
True wisdom comes from God.

Purpose and Theme

1 The proverbs of Solomon son of David, king of Israel:

> ²for gaining wisdom and instruction;
> for understanding words of insight;
> ³for receiving instruction in prudent behavior,
> doing what is right and just and fair;
> ⁴for giving prudence to those who are simple,*^a*
> knowledge and discretion to the young—
> ⁵let the wise listen and add to their learning,
> and let the discerning get guidance—
> ⁶for understanding proverbs and parables,
> the sayings and riddles of the wise.*^b*

> ⁷The fear of the Lord is the beginning of knowledge,
> but fools*^c* despise wisdom and instruction.

Prologue: Exhortations to Embrace Wisdom

Warning Against the Invitation of Sinful Men

> ⁸Listen, my son, to your father's instruction
> and do not forsake your mother's teaching.
> ⁹They are a garland to grace your head
> and a chain to adorn your neck.

> ¹⁰My son, if sinful men entice you,
> do not give in to them.
> ¹¹If they say, "Come along with us;
> let's lie in wait for innocent blood,
> let's ambush some harmless soul;
> ¹²let's swallow them alive, like the grave,
> and whole, like those who go down to the pit;
> ¹³we will get all sorts of valuable things
> and fill our houses with plunder;
> ¹⁴cast lots with us;
> we will all share the loot"—
> ¹⁵my son, do not go along with them,
> do not set foot on their paths;
> ¹⁶for their feet rush into evil,
> they are swift to shed blood.
> ¹⁷How useless to spread a net
> where every bird can see it!
> ¹⁸These men lie in wait for their own blood;
> they ambush only themselves!
> ¹⁹Such are the paths of all who go after ill-gotten gain;
> it takes away the life of those who get it.

Wisdom's Rebuke

> ²⁰Out in the open wisdom calls aloud,
> she raises her voice in the public square;

---

^a 4 The Hebrew word rendered *simple* in Proverbs denotes a person who is gullible, without moral direction and inclined to evil.   *^b 6* Or *understanding a proverb, namely, a parable, / and the sayings of the wise, their riddles*   *^c 7* The Hebrew words rendered *fool* in Proverbs, and often elsewhere in the Old Testament, denote a person who is morally deficient.

²¹on top of the wall*ᵃ* she cries out,
   at the city gate she makes her speech:

²²"How long will you who are simple love your simple ways?
   How long will mockers delight in mockery
   and fools hate knowledge?
²³Repent at my rebuke!
   Then I will pour out my thoughts to you,
   I will make known to you my teachings.
²⁴But since you refuse to listen when I call
   and no one pays attention when I stretch out my hand,
²⁵since you disregard all my advice
   and do not accept my rebuke,
²⁶I in turn will laugh when disaster strikes you;
   I will mock when calamity overtakes you—
²⁷when calamity overtakes you like a storm,
   when disaster sweeps over you like a whirlwind,
   when distress and trouble overwhelm you.

²⁸"Then they will call to me but I will not answer;
   they will look for me but will not find me,
²⁹since they hated knowledge
   and did not choose to fear the Lᴏʀᴅ.
³⁰Since they would not accept my advice
   and spurned my rebuke,
³¹they will eat the fruit of their ways
   and be filled with the fruit of their schemes.
³²For the waywardness of the simple will kill them,
   and the complacency of fools will destroy them;
³³but whoever listens to me will live in safety
   and be at ease, without fear of harm."

Moral Benefits of Wisdom

2 My son, if you accept my words
   and store up my commands within you,
²turning your ear to wisdom
   and applying your heart to understanding—
³indeed, if you call out for insight
   and cry aloud for understanding,
⁴and if you look for it as for silver
   and search for it as for hidden treasure,
⁵then you will understand the fear of the Lᴏʀᴅ
   and find the knowledge of God.
⁶For the Lᴏʀᴅ gives wisdom;
   from his mouth come knowledge and understanding.
⁷He holds success in store for the upright,
   he is a shield to those whose walk is blameless,
⁸for he guards the course of the just
   and protects the way of his faithful ones.

⁹Then you will understand what is right and just
   and fair—every good path.

ᵃ 21 Septuagint; Hebrew / at noisy street corners

¹⁰For wisdom will enter your heart,
  and knowledge will be pleasant to your soul.
¹¹Discretion will protect you,
  and understanding will guard you.

¹²Wisdom will save you from the ways of wicked men,
  from men whose words are perverse,
¹³who have left the straight paths
  to walk in dark ways,
¹⁴who delight in doing wrong
  and rejoice in the perverseness of evil,
¹⁵whose paths are crooked
  and who are devious in their ways.

¹⁶Wisdom will save you also from the
  adulterous woman,
  from the wayward woman with her
  seductive words,
¹⁷who has left the partner of her youth
  and ignored the covenant she made
  before God.^a
¹⁸Surely her house leads down to death
  and her paths to the spirits of the dead.
¹⁹None who go to her return
  or attain the paths of life.

²⁰Thus you will walk in the ways of the just
  and keep to the paths of the righteous.
²¹For the upright will live in the land,
  and the blameless will remain in it;
²²but the wicked will be cut off from the
  land,
  and the unfaithful will be torn from it.

Wisdom Bestows Well-Being

3 My son, do not forget my teaching,
  but keep my commands in your heart,
²for they will prolong your life many years
  and bring you peace and prosperity.

³Let love and faithfulness never leave you;
  bind them around your neck,
  write them on the tablet of your heart.
⁴Then you will win favor and a good name
  in the sight of God and humankind.

⁵Trust in the LORD with all your heart
  and lean not on your own understanding;
⁶in all your ways submit to him,
  and he will make your paths straight.^b

⁷Do not be wise in your own eyes;
  fear the LORD and shun evil.

---

at issue: infidelity

2:16–19 How does a woman get to the point of having an affair? It starts with little things. Feeling indignant that her husband isn't meeting her needs. Discontentment. A desire to be appreciated and understood. A sense of entitlement—she deserves to be happy. A growing friendship with or admiration for another man. Too much time alone. Seductive words. The first touch. Justification of her choice. Avoiding God. Each little step leads her further down a path to destruction. So how can a righteous woman keep from taking those first steps that are all too easy to take? By finding protection in God's *wisdom.*

865

---

^a 17 Or *covenant of her God*   ^b 6 Or *will direct your paths*

⁸This will bring health to your body
and nourishment to your bones.

⁹Honor the LORD with your wealth,
with the firstfruits of all your crops;
¹⁰then your barns will be filled to overflowing,
and your vats will brim over with new wine.

¹¹My son, do not despise the LORD's discipline,
and do not resent his rebuke,
¹²because the LORD disciplines those he loves,
as a father the son he delights in.ᵃ

¹³Blessed are those who find wisdom,
those who gain understanding,
¹⁴for she is more profitable than silver
and yields better returns than gold.
¹⁵She is more precious than rubies;
nothing you desire can compare with her.
¹⁶Long life is in her right hand;
in her left hand are riches and honor.
¹⁷Her ways are pleasant ways,
and all her paths are peace.
¹⁸She is a tree of life to those who take hold of her;
those who hold her fast will be blessed.

¹⁹By wisdom the LORD laid the earth's foundations,
by understanding he set the heavens in place;
²⁰by his knowledge the deeps were divided,
and the clouds let drop the dew.

²¹My son, do not let wisdom and understanding out of your sight,
preserve sound judgment and discretion;
²²they will be life for you,
an ornament to grace your neck.
²³Then you will go on your way in safety,
and your foot will not stumble.
²⁴When you lie down, you will not be afraid;
when you lie down, your sleep will be sweet.
²⁵Have no fear of sudden disaster
or of the ruin that overtakes the wicked,
²⁶for the LORD will be at your side
and will keep your foot from being snared.

²⁷Do not withhold good from those to whom it is due,
when it is in your power to act.

"conversations"

health «» 3:7–8

1» How are your physical, emotional and spiritual health related (or are they)?

2» How can trusting God be good for your health?

3» How may sin affect you physically?

For more on health, check the index.
For the next Conversations, go to p. 867.

ᵃ 12 Hebrew; Septuagint / and he chastens everyone he accepts as his child

²⁸ Do not say to your neighbor,
  "Come back tomorrow and I'll give it to you"—
    when you already have it with you.
²⁹ Do not plot harm against your neighbor,
  who lives trustfully near you.
³⁰ Do not accuse anyone for no reason—
  when they have done you no harm.

³¹ Do not envy the violent
  or choose any of their ways.

³² For the LORD detests the perverse
  but takes the upright into his confidence.
³³ The LORD's curse is on the house of the wicked,
  but he blesses the home of the righteous.
³⁴ He mocks proud mockers
  but shows favor to the humble and oppressed.
³⁵ The wise inherit honor,
  but fools get only shame.

Get Wisdom At Any Cost

4 Listen, my sons, to a father's instruction;
    pay attention and gain understanding.
² I give you sound learning,
  so do not forsake my teaching.
³ For I too was a son to my father,
  still tender, and cherished by my mother.
⁴ Then he taught me, and he said to me,
  "Take hold of my words with all your heart;
    keep my commands, and you will live.
⁵ Get wisdom, get understanding;
  do not forget my words or turn away from them.
⁶ Do not forsake wisdom, and she will protect you;
  love her, and she will watch over you.
⁷ The beginning of wisdom is this: Get^a wisdom.
  Though it cost all you have,^b get
    understanding.
⁸ Cherish her, and she will exalt you;
  embrace her, and she will honor you.
⁹ She will give you a garland to grace your
    head
  and present you with a glorious
    crown."

¹⁰ Listen, my son, accept what I say,
  and the years of your life will be many.
¹¹ I instruct you in the way of wisdom
  and lead you along straight paths.
¹² When you walk, your steps will not be
    hampered;
  when you run, you will not stumble.

867

conversations

unhealthy relationships «» 4:10–17

1» What standards do you hold about the company you keep?

2» Do you have any unhealthy relationships in your life? How can you change or end them?

3» How can you reach out to unbelievers while maintaining spiritual integrity?

For more on unhealthy relationships, check the index.
For the next Conversations, go to p. 891.

---

^a 7 Or *Wisdom is supreme; therefore get*   ^b 7 Or *Whatever else you get*

¹³Hold on to instruction, do not let it go;
  guard it well, for it is your life.
¹⁴Do not set foot on the path of the wicked
  or walk in the way of evildoers.
¹⁵Avoid it, do not travel on it;
  turn from it and go on your way.
¹⁶For they cannot rest until they do evil;
  they are robbed of sleep till they make someone stumble.
¹⁷They eat the bread of wickedness
  and drink the wine of violence.

¹⁸The path of the righteous is like the morning sun,
  shining ever brighter till the full light of day.
¹⁹But the way of the wicked is like deep darkness;
  they do not know what makes them stumble.

²⁰My son, pay attention to what I say;
  turn your ear to my words.
²¹Do not let them out of your sight,
  keep them within your heart;
²²for they are life to those who find them
  and health to one's whole body.
²³Above all else, guard your heart,
  for everything you do flows from it.
²⁴Keep your mouth free of perversity;
  keep corrupt talk far from your lips.
²⁵Let your eyes look straight ahead;
  fix your gaze directly before you.
²⁶Give careful thought to the*a* paths for your feet
  and be steadfast in all your ways.
²⁷Do not turn to the right or the left;
  keep your foot from evil.

4:23 We closely watch over our possessions, health, appearance and loved ones. While safeguarding those things is important, God says—above all else—to guard your heart. Why? Because it affects everything else in your life. One of the most important ways you do this is by guarding the growth of your emotions for the opposite sex. If you're married, your husband should be the man your heart looks to for intimacy, encouragement, advice and protection. If you're single, don't give your heart away to just anyone; reserve it for the one man you'll marry. And keep your guard up!

atissue:emotional purity

Warning Against Adultery

5 My son, pay attention to my wisdom,
    turn your ear to my words of insight,
²that you may maintain discretion
  and your lips may preserve knowledge.
³For the lips of the adulterous woman drip honey,
  and her speech is smoother than oil;
⁴but in the end she is bitter as gall,
  sharp as a double-edged sword.
⁵Her feet go down to death;
  her steps lead straight to the grave.
⁶She gives no thought to the way of life;
  her paths wander aimlessly, but she does not know it.

a 26 Or Make level

⁷Now then, my sons, listen to me;
    do not turn aside from what I say.
⁸Keep to a path far from her,
    do not go near the door of her house,
⁹lest you lose your honor to others
    and your dignity ^a to one who is cruel,
¹⁰lest strangers feast on your wealth
    and your toil enrich the house of another.
¹¹At the end of your life you will groan,
    when your flesh and body are spent.
¹²You will say, "How I hated discipline!
    How my heart spurned correction!
¹³I would not obey my teachers
    or turn my ear to my instructors.
¹⁴And I was soon in serious trouble
    in the assembly of God's people."

¹⁵Drink water from your own cistern,
    running water from your own well.
¹⁶Should your springs overflow in the streets,
    your streams of water in the public squares?
¹⁷Let them be yours alone,
    never to be shared with strangers.
¹⁸May your fountain be blessed,
    and may you rejoice in the wife of your youth.
¹⁹A loving doe, a graceful deer—
    may her breasts satisfy you always,
    may you ever be intoxicated with her love.
²⁰Why, my son, be intoxicated with another man's wife?
    Why embrace the bosom of a wayward woman?

²¹For your ways are in full view of the Lord,
    and he examines all your paths.
²²The evil deeds of the wicked ensnare them;
    the cords of their sins hold them fast.
²³For lack of discipline they will die,
    led astray by their own great folly.

869

Warnings Against Folly

6 My son, if you have put up security for your neighbor,
    if you have shaken hands in pledge for a stranger,
²you have been trapped by what you said,
    ensnared by the words of your mouth.
³So do this, my son, to free yourself,
    since you have fallen into your neighbor's hands:
Go—to the point of exhaustion—^b
    and give your neighbor no rest!
⁴Allow no sleep to your eyes,
    no slumber to your eyelids.
⁵Free yourself, like a gazelle from the hand of the hunter,
    like a bird from the snare of the fowler.

---

^a *9* Or *years* ^b *3* Or *Go and humble yourself,*

myth# 53 "MY TIME IS MY OWN. I DESERVE TO INDULGE MYSELF."

I settled into our cozy chair-and-a-half and turned up the volume on the TV while my children slept. One of my favorite talk shows was recognizing women for unusual "acts of courage." I expected to see a dramatic portrayal of a woman lifting a burning car to free her trapped children. I was surprised to see an altogether different kind of hero.

The young wife and mother on this segment was no Purple Heart recipient. Her story was that she had left her family for several months because she was tired of their constant demands. So she skipped out. Hasta la vista! She camped out in a beach condo until her family got their act together and stopped leeching off her. After a full month of reading and relaxing on the beach, she returned home to national recognition for standing up for herself.

I was shocked, enraged . . . and then a little envious.

A whole month with time for myself? That would be amazing! Of course, I don't plan to leave my family under any circumstances—no matter how demanding they can be. I love them with all my heart. However, I do sometimes long for my single days when I could sleep late, travel impulsively and stay in my pajamas all day. When my time was my own. As a working mother of three, my time now belongs to my children, my son's baseball coach (who also happens to be my husband), my daughter's dance teacher, my boss and the local PTA. And the women's ministry director at church is trying to guilt-trip me into leading a Bible study.

I admit, those magazine headlines at the grocery store still tempt me with their siren appeal. "Indulge Yourself." "You Deserve It." I realize that I didn't indulge myself enough when I was young and single. Now, I'm looking forward to the time when I can do whatever I want with my time again.

—Julie

T—Time is short. Time is passing so quickly. You think you have all kinds of time to do what's important—spending time with your kids, building your marriage, serving in ministry or witnessing to non-Christian friends. But you don't know when Christ will return (see Matthew 24:36–44) or if you'll ever get another chance to do ____. Don't miss your opportunities!

I—It's a gift. While there's nothing wrong with relishing some time to yourself to recharge and recuperate from life's demands, each 24-hour period is a gift from God. How do you really want to spend that time you've been given? Make sure you're not misusing that gift, taking it for granted or just trying to get through it.

M—Make time for what's important. If you're not deliberate about how you spend your time, then your days will be filled up with the tyranny of the urgent or your favorite time-wasters, such as watching television. Prioritize what matters to you, and then build your schedule around those things. Don't feel bad saying no to something that's less important—you can't do everything.

E—Everyone has the same 24 hours. Mathematically, that's correct. Practically, however, it seems that some women have been endowed with greater time management skills than others. Don't resent or envy these people—seek them as time management mentors! Ask for their secrets. The writer of Proverbs observed the ways of an ant (see Proverbs 6:6–11); you have the chance to learn from a wise woman.

"30 percent of Americans believe the main purpose of life is personal fulfillment and enjoyment."

—Barna Research Group (1994)

871

"TEACH US TO NUMBER OUR DAYS, THAT WE MAY GAIN A HEART OF WISDOM."

PSALM 90:12

SEE ALSO

Proverbs 6:6–11

John 4:34–38

Ephesians 5:15–16

For more on **Time Management**, check the index.

⁶Go to the ant, you sluggard;
   consider its ways and be wise!
⁷It has no commander,
   no overseer or ruler,
⁸yet it stores its provisions in summer
   and gathers its food at harvest.

⁹How long will you lie there, you sluggard?
   When will you get up from your sleep?
¹⁰A little sleep, a little slumber,
   a little folding of the hands to rest—
¹¹and poverty will come on you like a thief
   and scarcity like an armed man.

¹²Troublemakers and villains,
   who go about with corrupt mouths,
¹³   who wink maliciously with their eyes,
   signal with their feet
   and motion with their fingers,
¹⁴   who plot evil with deceit in their hearts—
   they always stir up dissension.
¹⁵Therefore disaster will overtake them in an instant;
   they will suddenly be destroyed—without remedy.

¹⁶There are six things the LORD hates,
   seven that are detestable to him:
¹⁷   haughty eyes,
   a lying tongue,
   hands that shed innocent blood,
¹⁸   a heart that devises wicked schemes,
   feet that are quick to rush into evil,
¹⁹   a false witness who pours out lies
   and a person who stirs up dissension in the community.

Warning Against Adultery

²⁰My son, keep your father's command
   and do not forsake your mother's teaching.
²¹Bind them always on your heart;
   fasten them around your neck.
²²When you walk, they will guide you;
   when you sleep, they will watch over you;
   when you awake, they will speak to you.
²³For this command is a lamp,
   this teaching is a light,
   and correction and instruction
   are the way to life,
²⁴keeping you from your neighbor's wife,
   from the smooth talk of a wayward woman.

²⁵Do not lust in your heart after her beauty
   or let her captivate you with her eyes.

²⁶For a prostitute can be had for a loaf of bread,
   but another man's wife preys on your very life.

²⁷Can a man scoop fire into his lap
  without his clothes being burned?
²⁸Can a man walk on hot coals
  without his feet being scorched?
²⁹So is he who sleeps with another man's wife;
  no one who touches her will go unpunished.

³⁰People do not despise a thief if he steals
  to satisfy his hunger when he is starving.
³¹Yet if he is caught, he must pay sevenfold,
  though it costs him all the wealth of his house.
³²But a man who commits adultery has no sense;
  whoever does so destroys himself.
³³Blows and disgrace are his lot,
  and his shame will never be wiped away.

³⁴For jealousy arouses a husband's fury,
  and he will show no mercy when he takes revenge.
³⁵He will not accept any compensation;
  he will refuse a bribe, however great it is.

Warning Against the Adulterous Woman

7 My son, keep my words
  and store up my commands within you.
²Keep my commands and you will live;
  guard my teachings as the apple of your eye.
³Bind them on your fingers;
  write them on the tablet of your heart.
⁴Say to wisdom, "You are my sister,"
  and to insight, "You are my relative."
⁵They will keep you from the adulterous woman,
  from the wayward woman with her seductive words.

⁶At the window of my house
  I looked down through the lattice.
⁷I saw among the simple,
  I noticed among the young men,
  a youth who had no sense.
⁸He was going down the street near her corner,
  walking along in the direction of her house
⁹at twilight, as the day was fading,
  as the dark of night set in.

¹⁰Then out came a woman to meet him,
  dressed like a prostitute and with crafty intent.
¹¹(She is unruly and defiant,
  her feet never stay at home;
¹²now in the street, now in the squares,
  at every corner she lurks.)
¹³She took hold of him and kissed him
  and with a brazen face she said:

¹⁴"Today I fulfilled my vows,
  and I have food from my fellowship offering at home.

¹⁵So I came out to meet you;
   I looked for you and have found you!
¹⁶I have covered my bed
   with colored linens from Egypt.
¹⁷I have perfumed my bed
   with myrrh, aloes and cinnamon.
¹⁸Come, let's drink deep of love till morning;
   let's enjoy ourselves with love!
¹⁹My husband is not at home;
   he has gone on a long journey.
²⁰He took his purse filled with money
   and will not be home till full moon."

²¹With persuasive words she led him astray;
   she seduced him with her smooth talk.
²²All at once he followed her
   like an ox going to the slaughter,
   like a deer^a stepping into a noose^b
²³   till an arrow pierces his liver,
   like a bird darting into a snare,
      little knowing it will cost him his life.

²⁴Now then, my sons, listen to me;
   pay attention to what I say.
²⁵Do not let your heart turn to her ways
   or stray into her paths.
²⁶Many are the victims she has brought down;
   her slain are a mighty throng.
²⁷Her house is a highway to the grave,
   leading down to the chambers of death.

Wisdom's Call

8 Does not wisdom call out?
   Does not understanding raise her voice?
²At the highest point along the way,
   where the paths meet, she takes her stand;
³beside the gate leading into the city,
   at the entrance, she cries aloud:
⁴"To you, O people, I call out;
   I raise my voice to all humankind.
⁵You who are simple, gain prudence;
   you who are foolish, set your hearts on it.^c
⁶Listen, for I have trustworthy things to say;
   I open my lips to speak what is right.
⁷My mouth speaks what is true,
   for my lips detest wickedness.
⁸All the words of my mouth are just;
   none of them is crooked or perverse.
⁹To the discerning all of them are right;
   they are upright to those who have found knowledge.
¹⁰Choose my instruction instead of silver,

---

^a 22 Syriac (see also Septuagint); Hebrew *fool*   ^b 22 The meaning of the Hebrew for this line is uncertain.   ^c 5 Septuagint; Hebrew *foolish, instruct your minds*

knowledge rather than choice gold,
[11] for wisdom is more precious than rubies,
    and nothing you desire can compare with her.

[12] "I, wisdom, dwell together with prudence;
    I possess knowledge and discretion.
[13] To fear the LORD is to hate evil;
    I hate pride and arrogance,
    evil behavior and perverse speech.
[14] Counsel and sound judgment are mine;
    I have insight, I have power.
[15] By me kings reign
    and rulers issue decrees that are just;
[16] by me princes govern,
    and nobles—all who rule on earth.[a]
[17] I love those who love me,
    and those who seek me find me.
[18] With me are riches and honor,
    enduring wealth and prosperity.
[19] My fruit is better than fine gold;
    what I yield surpasses choice silver.
[20] I walk in the way of righteousness,
    along the paths of justice,
[21] bestowing a rich inheritance on those who love me
    and making their treasuries full.

[22] "The LORD brought me forth as the first of his works,[b, c]
    before his deeds of old;
[23] I was formed long ages ago,
    at the very beginning, when the world came to be.
[24] When there were no oceans, I was given birth,
    when there were no springs abounding with water;
[25] before the mountains were settled in place,
    before the hills, I was given birth,
[26] before he made the world or its fields

---

[a] 16 Some Hebrew manuscripts and Septuagint; other Hebrew manuscripts *all righteous rulers*   [b] 22 Or *way;* or *dominion*   [c] 22 Or *The LORD possessed me at the beginning of his work;* or *The LORD brought me forth at the beginning of his work*

HE IS: the master craftsman

8:22–31 Everything God created was designed with wisdom. In this passage, wisdom is personified as being at God's side throughout the creative process. God made sure that the whole world, including humanity, was fashioned to be a delight to him. As *the master craftsman,* God rejoices in what he created.

With great wisdom, God created you exactly the way you are. And he made you for a purpose—to bring him delight day after day. God rejoices when you obey his Word and accept his Son. He's disappointed when you don't fulfill your purpose or when you resent how he made you. Who are you to question *the master craftsman?*

For the next He Is, go to p. 887.

or any of the dust of the earth.
²⁷ I was there when he set the heavens in place,
   when he marked out the horizon on the face of the deep,
²⁸ when he established the clouds above
   and fixed securely the fountains of the deep,
²⁹ when he gave the sea its boundary
   so the waters would not overstep his command,
and when he marked out the foundations of the earth.
³⁰   Then I was constantly[a] at his side.
I was filled with delight day after day,
   rejoicing always in his presence,
³¹ rejoicing in his whole world
   and delighting in humankind.

³² "Now then, my children, listen to me;
   blessed are those who keep my ways.
³³ Listen to my instruction and be wise;
   do not disregard it.
³⁴ Blessed are those who listen to me,
   watching daily at my doors,
   waiting at my doorway.
³⁵ For those who find me find life
   and receive favor from the Lord.
³⁶ But those who fail to find me harm themselves;
   all who hate me love death."

Invitations of Wisdom and Folly

9   Wisdom has built her house;
   she has set up[b] its seven pillars.
² She has prepared her meat and mixed her wine;
   she has also set her table.
³ She has sent out her servants, and she calls
   from the highest point of the city,
⁴   "Let all who are simple come to my house!"
To those who have no sense she says,
⁵   "Come, eat my food
   and drink the wine I have mixed.
⁶ Leave your simple ways and you will live;
   walk in the way of insight."

⁷ Whoever corrects a mocker invites insults;
   whoever rebukes the wicked incurs abuse.
⁸ Do not rebuke mockers or they will hate you;
   rebuke the wise and they will love you.
⁹ Instruct the wise and they will be wiser still;
   teach the righteous and they will add to their learning.

¹⁰ The fear of the Lord is the beginning of wisdom,
   and knowledge of the Holy One is understanding.
¹¹ For through wisdom[c] your days will be many,
   and years will be added to your life.

---

^a 30 Or *was the artisan*; or *was a little child*   ^b 1 Septuagint, Syriac and Targum; Hebrew *has hewn out*   ^c 11 Septuagint, Syriac and Targum; Hebrew *me*

¹²If you are wise, your wisdom will reward you;
     if you are a mocker, you alone will suffer.

¹³Folly is an unruly woman;
     she is simple and knows nothing.
¹⁴She sits at the door of her house,
     on a seat at the highest point of the city,
¹⁵calling out to those who pass by,
     who go straight on their way,
¹⁶ "Let all who are simple come to my house!"
   To those who have no sense she says,
¹⁷ "Stolen water is sweet;
     food eaten in secret is delicious!"
¹⁸But little do they know that the dead are there,
     that her guests are deep in the realm of the dead.

Proverbs of Solomon

10 The proverbs of Solomon:

     Wise children bring joy to their father,
         but foolish children bring grief to their mother.

²Ill-gotten treasures have no lasting value,
     but righteousness delivers from death.

³The Lord does not let the righteous go hungry,
     but he thwarts the craving of the wicked.

⁴Lazy hands make for poverty,
     but diligent hands bring wealth.

⁵He who gathers crops in summer is a prudent son,
     but he who sleeps during harvest is a disgraceful son.

⁶Blessings crown the head of the righteous,
     but violence overwhelms the mouth of the wicked.ᵃ

⁷The name of the righteous is used in blessings,ᵇ
     but the name of the wicked will rot.

⁸The wise in heart accept commands,
     but a chattering fool comes to ruin.

⁹Whoever walks in integrity walks securely,
     but whoever takes crooked paths will be found out.

¹⁰Whoever winks maliciously causes grief,
     and a chattering fool comes to ruin.

¹¹The mouth of the righteous is a fountain of life,
     but the mouth of the wicked conceals violence.

¹²Hatred stirs up dissension,
     but love covers over all wrongs.

¹³Wisdom is found on the lips of the discerning,
     but a rod is for the back of one who has no sense.

ᵃ 6 Or but the mouth of the wicked conceals violence   ᵇ 7 See Gen. 48:20.

¹⁴The wise store up knowledge,
    but the mouth of a fool invites ruin.

¹⁵The wealth of the rich is their fortified
        city,
    but poverty is the ruin of the poor.

¹⁶The wages of the righteous is life,
    but the earnings of the wicked are sin
        and death.

¹⁷Whoever heeds discipline shows the
        way to life,
    but whoever ignores correction leads
        others astray.

¹⁸Whoever conceals hatred with lying
        lips
    and spreads slander is a fool.

¹⁹Sin is not ended by multiplying words,
    but the prudent hold their tongues.

²⁰The tongue of the righteous is choice
        silver,
    but the heart of the wicked is of little
        value.

²¹The lips of the righteous nourish many,
    but fools die for lack of sense.

²²The blessing of the LORD brings wealth,
    without painful toil for it.

²³Fools find pleasure in wicked schemes,
    but those who have understanding delight in wisdom.

²⁴What the wicked dread will overtake them;
    what the righteous desire will be granted.

²⁵When the storm has swept by, the wicked are gone,
    but the righteous stand firm forever.

²⁶As vinegar to the teeth and smoke to the eyes,
    so are sluggards to those who send them.

²⁷The fear of the LORD adds length to life,
    but the years of the wicked are cut short.

²⁸The prospect of the righteous is joy,
    but the hopes of the wicked come to nothing.

²⁹The way of the LORD is a refuge for the blameless,
    but it is the ruin of those who do evil.

³⁰The righteous will never be uprooted,
    but the wicked will not remain in the land.

³¹From the mouth of the righteous comes the fruit of wisdom,
    but a perverse tongue will be silenced.

at issue: in-laws

10:12 No matter how great your in-laws are, you'll likely have conflicts at some point. You may disagree about where you spend holidays, how you discipline your children or even denominational or doctrinal matters. You may sometimes feel like the daughter your in-laws wish they never had. How you respond will either bring you closer together as a family or drive you further apart. When conflicts arise, choose to cover over wrongs done to you with love. This takes humility, but let it go. Refuse to dwell on it. Choose to not even see it anymore because you know that God's love covers over your own wrongs.

³²The lips of the righteous know what finds
favor,
but the mouth of the wicked only what
is perverse.

11 The LORD detests dishonest scales,
but accurate weights find favor
with him.

²When pride comes, then comes disgrace,
but with humility comes wisdom.

³The integrity of the upright guides them,
but the unfaithful are destroyed by their
duplicity.

⁴Wealth is worthless in the day of wrath,
but righteousness delivers from death.

⁵The righteousness of the blameless makes
their paths straight,
but the wicked are brought down by
their own wickedness.

⁶The righteousness of the upright delivers
them,
but the unfaithful are trapped by evil
desires.

⁷Hopes placed in mortals die with them;
all the promise of^a their power comes to nothing.

⁸The righteous are rescued from trouble,
and it falls on the wicked instead.

⁹With their mouths the godless destroy their neighbors,
but through knowledge the righteous escape.

¹⁰When the righteous prosper, the city rejoices;
when the wicked perish, there are shouts of joy.

¹¹Through the blessing of the upright a city is exalted,
but by the mouth of the wicked it is destroyed.

¹²Those who have no sense deride their neighbors,
but those who have understanding hold their tongues.

¹³Gossips betray a confidence,
but the trustworthy keep a secret.

¹⁴For lack of guidance a nation falls,
but victory is won through many advisers.

¹⁵Whoever puts up security for a stranger will surely suffer,
but whoever refuses to shake hands in pledge is safe.

¹⁶A kindhearted woman gains honor,
but ruthless men gain only wealth.

atissue:shoplifting

10:23 Some women view shoplifting as a harmless prank, an exhilarating dare. They love the rush of getting away with something. If they do feel a twinge of conscience, they justify it by saying that the store will never notice and that it doesn't hurt anyone. But shoplifting does hurt others, and it is a big deal. No matter how you look at it, it's stealing. That adrenaline high may fool you into thinking it's OK when it's not. In God's eyes, the only person who's fooled by your excuses is you, which makes you either a thief or a fool—or both.

879

---

^a 7 Two Hebrew manuscripts; most Hebrew manuscripts, Vulgate, Syriac and Targum *When the wicked die, their hope perishes; / all they expected from*

880

¹⁷Those who are kind benefit themselves,
    but the cruel bring ruin on
      themselves.

¹⁸The wicked earn deceptive wages,
    but those who sow righteousness
      reap a sure reward.

¹⁹Truly the righteous attain life,
    but those who pursue evil go to their
      death.

²⁰The LORD detests those whose hearts are
      perverse,
    but he delights in those whose ways
      are blameless.

²¹Be sure of this: The wicked will not go
      unpunished,
    but those who are righteous will go
      free.

²²Like a gold ring in a pig's snout
    is a beautiful woman who shows no
      discretion.

²³The desire of the righteous ends only in
      good,
    but the hope of the wicked only in
      wrath.

²⁴One person gives freely, yet gains even more;
    another withholds unduly, but comes to poverty.

²⁵A generous person will prosper;
    whoever refreshes others will be refreshed.

²⁶People curse those who hoard grain,
    but they pray God's blessing on those who are willing to sell.

²⁷Whoever seeks good finds favor,
    but evil comes to those who search for it.

²⁸Those who trust in their riches will fall,
    but the righteous will thrive like a green leaf.

²⁹Those who bring ruin on their families will inherit only wind,
    and the fool will be servant to the wise.

³⁰The fruit of the righteous is a tree of life,
    and those who win souls are wise.

³¹If the righteous receive their due on earth,
    how much more the ungodly and the sinner!

12
    Whoever loves discipline loves knowledge,
      but whoever hates correction is stupid.

²Good people obtain favor from the LORD,
    but he condemns those who devise wicked schemes.

³No one can be established through wickedness,
  but the righteous cannot be uprooted.

⁴A wife of noble character is her husband's crown,
  but a disgraceful wife is like decay in his bones.

⁵The plans of the righteous are just,
  but the advice of the wicked is deceitful.

⁶The words of the wicked lie in wait for blood,
  but the speech of the upright rescues them.

⁷The wicked are overthrown and are no more,
  but the house of the righteous stands firm.

⁸People are praised according to their prudence,
  and those with warped minds are despised.

⁹Better to be a nobody and yet have a servant
  than pretend to be somebody and have no food.

¹⁰The righteous care for the needs of their animals,
  but the kindest acts of the wicked are cruel.

¹¹Those who work their land will have abundant food,
  but those who chase fantasies have no sense.

¹²The wicked desire the plunder^a of evildoers,
  but the root of the righteous flourishes.

¹³Evildoers are trapped by their sinful talk,
  and so the innocent escape trouble.

¹⁴From the fruit of their lips people are filled with good things,
  and the work of their hands brings them reward.

¹⁵The way of fools seems right to them,
  but the wise listen to advice.

¹⁶Fools show their annoyance at once,
  but the prudent overlook an insult.

¹⁷An honest witness tells the truth,
  but a false witness tells lies.

¹⁸The words of the reckless pierce like swords,
  but the tongue of the wise brings healing.

¹⁹Truthful lips endure forever,
  but a lying tongue lasts only a moment.

²⁰Deceit is in the hearts of those who plot evil,
  but those who promote peace have joy.

²¹No harm overtakes the righteous,
  but the wicked have their fill of trouble.

²²The LORD detests lying lips,
  but he delights in people who are trustworthy.

---

^a 12 Or stronghold

²³The prudent keep their knowledge to themselves,
  but a fool's heart blurts out folly.

²⁴Diligent hands will rule,
  but laziness ends in forced labor.

²⁵Anxiety weighs down the heart,
  but a kind word cheers it up.

²⁶The righteous choose their friends carefully,
  but the way of the wicked leads them astray.

²⁷The lazy do not roast*ᵃ* any game,
  but the diligent feed on the riches of the hunt.

²⁸In the way of righteousness there is life;
  along that path is immortality.

13

A wise child heeds a parent's instruction,
  but a mocker does not respond to rebukes.

²From the fruit of their lips people enjoy good things,
  but the unfaithful have an appetite for violence.

³Those who guard their lips preserve their lives,
  but those who speak rashly will come to ruin.

⁴A sluggard's appetite is never filled,
  but the desires of the diligent are fully satisfied.

⁵The righteous hate what is false,
  but the wicked make themselves a stench
  and are filled with shame.

⁶Righteousness guards the person of integrity,
  but wickedness overthrows the sinner.

⁷One person pretends to be rich, yet has nothing;
  another pretends to be poor, yet has great wealth.

⁸The rich may be able to ransom their lives,
  but the poor cannot respond to threatening rebukes.

⁹The light of the righteous shines brightly,
  but the lamp of the wicked is snuffed out.

¹⁰Where there is strife, there is pride,
  but wisdom is found in those who take advice.

¹¹Dishonest money dwindles away,
  but whoever gathers money little by little makes it grow.

¹²Hope deferred makes the heart sick,
  but a longing fulfilled is a tree of life.

¹³Whoever scorns instruction will pay for it,
  but whoever respects a command is rewarded.

¹⁴The teaching of the wise is a fountain of life,
  turning a person from the snares of death.

882

ᵃ 27 The meaning of the Hebrew for this word is uncertain.

¹⁵Good judgment wins favor,
   but the way of the unfaithful leads to their destruction.^a

¹⁶All who are prudent act with^b knowledge,
   but fools expose their folly.

¹⁷A wicked messenger falls into trouble,
   but a trustworthy envoy brings healing.

¹⁸Whoever disregards discipline comes to poverty and shame,
   but whoever heeds correction is honored.

¹⁹A longing fulfilled is sweet to the soul,
   but fools detest turning from evil.

²⁰Walk with the wise and become wise,
   for a companion of fools suffers harm.

²¹Trouble pursues the sinner,
   but the righteous are rewarded with good things.

²²Good people leave an inheritance for their children's children,
   but a sinner's wealth is stored up for the righteous.

²³An unplowed field produces food for the poor,
   but injustice sweeps it away.

²⁴Those who spare the rod hate their children,
   but those who love them are careful to discipline them.

²⁵The righteous eat to their hearts' content,
   but the stomach of the wicked goes hungry.

14 The wise woman builds her house,
   but with her own hands the foolish one tears hers down.

²Whoever fears the Lord walks uprightly,
   but those who despise him are devious in their ways.

³A fool's mouth lashes out with pride,
   but the lips of the wise protect them.

⁴Where there are no oxen, the manger is empty,
   but from the strength of an ox come abundant harvests.

⁵An honest witness does not deceive,
   but a false witness pours out lies.

⁶The mocker seeks wisdom and finds none,
   but knowledge comes easily to the discerning.

⁷Stay away from the foolish,
   for you will not find knowledge on their lips.

⁸The wisdom of the prudent is to give thought to their ways,
   but the folly of fools is deception.

⁹Fools mock at making amends for sin,
   but goodwill is found among the upright.

---

^a *15* Septuagint and Syriac; the meaning of the Hebrew for this phrase is uncertain.   ^b *16* Or *prudent protect themselves through*

myth# 54 "I SHOULD ALWAYS BE MY CHILD'S FRIEND."

We waited so long to have children. After a few frustrating years of trying to get pregnant, we started fertility treatments and finally conceived. Now Abbie is four years old, and Austin is nearly a year old.

As much as we enjoy being parents, we're struggling with Abbie. She's at a stage when she has fits every day. I think it must be the stress of having a new baby brother. For example, a few weeks ago at the mall, she asked me to buy her ice cream. When I told her no, she punched my leg with her little fist and then screamed in frustration. And that wasn't an isolated incident. It's tough taking her in public anymore. I've learned it's easier just to give her what she wants than to be embarrassed by her behavior.

Even though she's so good with Austin most of the time, she gets frustrated with him and pushes him away or screams at him, which of course makes him cry. It's just sibling rivalry, and I tell myself they'll work it out eventually; I don't want to get involved. Besides, if I reprimand her, she'll resent me. I've put her to bed angry with me many times. She turns her head to the side and won't even hug me good night. If only she knew how much it hurt me to see her upset!

I want to have a good relationship with my kids, the kind I wish I'd had with my parents. We waited so long to have kids and went through so much with the fertility treatments. I can't bring myself to hurt my children by disciplining them.

—Latasha

THE IDEA OF being friends with our small children is a relatively new phenomenon in our society. Have you ever thought about why we are tempted to do so today?

- Is it because our generation has so little time to spend with our kids, and we feel guilty and want to make up for it by being their friends?

- Is it because those of us coming from broken homes or bad relationships see our kids as easy ways to fill that lonely void?

- Do we believe that discipline is too hard or too outdated?

- Do we care too much about looking like inept parents in front of others if we have to discipline our children?

Regardless of why we confuse our roles, maintaining them in the family is important for everyone's sake. A child's role is to learn and grow. A parent's role is to teach and train. Asking children to take on the role of a friend is too big of a burden, and it will affect how they feel about themselves and how they interact with others throughout life.

Consider the following tips for maintaining balance in your family life:

- You must be your child's parent first, not his or her friend. Friendship comes later down the road, *after* you've been a good parent.

- Let your children be children. Asking them to be your friend is asking more than they should have to handle, and they may act out to protect themselves.

- The Bible says that discipline is providing clear boundaries for your children and helping them understand the consequences of their actions in a loving, supportive way (see Proverbs 13:24).

- Many women in a turbulent home situation—such as dealing with domestic violence or

going through a divorce—are especially vulnerable to this trap of trying to be their children's friends. They may feel so guilty about having to put their children through a painful situation that they overcompensate.

885

"Plenty of toddlers control their entire family, especially mom. If you as a parent find yourself in this situation, you need to take steps to stop the children from dominating you, or you'll really pay the price when your child is a teenager."

—Dennis Rainey

"NO DISCIPLINE SEEMS PLEASANT AT THE TIME, BUT PAINFUL. LATER ON, HOWEVER, IT PRODUCES A HARVEST OF RIGHTEOUSNESS AND PEACE FOR THOSE WHO HAVE BEEN TRAINED BY IT."

HEBREWS 12:11

SEE ALSO

Deuteronomy 6:1–9
Proverbs 22:6
Ephesians 6:4

For more on **Parenting**, check the index.

[10] Each heart knows its own bitterness,
and no one else can share its joy.

[11] The house of the wicked will be destroyed,
but the tent of the upright will flourish.

[12] There is a way that appears to be right,
but in the end it leads to death.

[13] Even in laughter the heart may ache,
and rejoicing may end in grief.

[14] The faithless will be fully repaid for their ways,
and the good rewarded for theirs.

[15] The simple believe anything,
but the prudent give thought to their steps.

[16] The wise fear the LORD and shun evil,
but a fool is hotheaded and yet feels secure.

[17] The quick-tempered do foolish things,
and those who devise evil schemes are hated.

[18] The simple inherit folly,
but the prudent are crowned with knowledge.

[19] Evildoers will bow down in the presence of the good,
and the wicked at the gates of the righteous.

[20] The poor are shunned even by their
neighbors,
but the rich have many friends.

[21] It is a sin to despise one's neighbor,
but blessed are those who are kind to
the needy.

[22] Do not those who plot evil go astray?
But those who plan what is good
find[a] love and faithfulness.

[23] All hard work brings a profit,
but mere talk leads only to poverty.

[24] The wealth of the wise is their crown,
but the folly of fools yields folly.

[25] A truthful witness saves lives,
but a false witness is deceitful.

[26] Those who fear the LORD have a secure
fortress,
and for their children it will be a
refuge.

[27] The fear of the LORD is a fountain of life,
turning a person from the snares of
death.

[a] 22 Or show

atissue:procrastination

14:23 Are you a "big talker"? Maybe you talk a lot about doing things. You make checklists and plan to complete them but find it hard to follow through. Phone calls get postponed. Tasks at work or home get put off. Good intentions to reach out at church or to a hurting friend don't result in actions. And that new leaf you keep meaning to turn over just keeps getting older. If that's you, then you're wasting precious time. If you want to reap the rewards of your labor, then you've got to get to work. Talk is cheap—so get moving!

For the next He Is, go to p. 896.

HE IS: a fountain of life

14:26–27 Fearing God doesn't mean being afraid of him; it means standing in awe of him. Fear connotes a healthy respect and honor. God's goodness cascades like a fountain over those who respect him, protecting them from the things that could bring them harm.

He is *a fountain of life* on earth and in eternity. On earth, when you show you fear God by obeying his commands, you will avoid the people and places that are physically and spiritually dangerous to you. Your fear for God will carry you into eternal life, where his love will pour over you forever.

887

²⁸A large population is a king's glory,
    but without subjects a prince is ruined.

²⁹Those who are patient have great understanding,
    but the quick-tempered display folly.

³⁰A heart at peace gives life to the body,
    but envy rots the bones.

³¹Whoever oppresses the poor shows contempt for their Maker,
    but whoever is kind to the needy honors God.

³²When calamity comes, the wicked are brought down,
    but even in death the righteous seek refuge in God.

³³Wisdom reposes in the heart of the discerning
    and even among fools she lets herself be known.*

³⁴Righteousness exalts a nation,
    but sin condemns any people.

³⁵A king delights in a wise servant,
    but a shameful servant arouses his fury.

15   A gentle answer turns away wrath,
    but a harsh word stirs up anger.

²The tongue of the wise adorns knowledge,
    but the mouth of the fool gushes folly.

³The eyes of the LORD are everywhere,
    keeping watch on the wicked and the good.

⁴The soothing tongue is a tree of life,
    but a perverse tongue crushes the spirit.

⁵A fool spurns a parent's discipline,
    but whoever heeds correction shows prudence.

⁶The house of the righteous contains great treasure,
    but the income of the wicked brings ruin.

ª 33 Hebrew; Septuagint and Syriac / *but in the heart of fools she is not known*

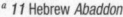
888

⁷The lips of the wise spread knowledge,
   but the hearts of fools are not upright.

⁸The Lord detests the sacrifice of the wicked,
   but the prayer of the upright pleases him.

⁹The Lord detests the way of the wicked,
   but he loves those who pursue righteousness.

¹⁰Stern discipline awaits those who leave the path;
   those who hate correction will die.

¹¹Death and Destruction*ᵃ* lie open before the Lord—
   how much more do human hearts!

¹²Mockers resent correction,
   so they avoid the wise.

¹³A happy heart makes the face cheerful,
   but heartache crushes the spirit.

¹⁴The discerning heart seeks knowledge,
   but the mouth of a fool feeds on folly.

¹⁵All the days of the oppressed are wretched,
   but the cheerful heart has a continual feast.

¹⁶Better a little with the fear of the Lord
   than great wealth with turmoil.

¹⁷Better a small serving of vegetables with love
   than a fattened calf with hatred.

¹⁸The hot-tempered stir up dissension,
   but those who are patient calm a quarrel.

¹⁹The way of the sluggard is blocked with thorns,
   but the path of the upright is a highway.

²⁰Wise children bring joy to their father,
   but foolish children despise their mother.

²¹Folly brings joy to those who have no sense,
   but those who have understanding keep a straight course.

²²Plans fail for lack of counsel,
   but with many advisers they succeed.

²³A person finds joy in giving an apt reply—
   and how good is a timely word!

²⁴The path of life leads upward for the prudent
   to keep them from going down to the realm of the dead.

²⁵The Lord tears down the house of the proud,
   but he sets the widow's boundary stones in place.

²⁶The Lord detests the thoughts of the wicked,
   but gracious words are pure in his sight.

_____

ᵃ 11 Hebrew Abaddon

²⁷The greedy bring ruin to their households,
    but those who hate bribes will live.

²⁸The heart of the righteous weighs its answers,
    but the mouth of the wicked gushes evil.

²⁹The Lord is far from the wicked,
    but he hears the prayer of the righteous.

³⁰Light in a messenger's eyes brings joy to the heart,
    and good news gives health to the bones.

³¹Whoever heeds life-giving correction
    will be at home among the wise.

³²Those who disregard discipline despise themselves,
    but those who heed correction gain understanding.

³³Wisdom's instruction is to fear the Lord,
    and humility comes before honor.

16 To human beings belong the plans of the heart,
    but from the Lord comes the proper answer of the tongue.

²People may think all their ways are pure,
    but motives are weighed by the Lord.

³Commit to the Lord whatever you do,
    and he will establish your plans.

⁴The Lord works out everything to its proper end—
    even the wicked for a day of disaster.

⁵The Lord detests all the proud of heart.
    Be sure of this: They will not go unpunished.

⁶Through love and faithfulness sin is atoned for;
    through the fear of the Lord evil is avoided.

⁷When the Lord takes pleasure in anyone's way,
    he causes their enemies to make peace with them.

⁸Better a little with righteousness
    than much gain with injustice.

⁹In their hearts human beings plan their course,
    but the Lord establishes their steps.

¹⁰The lips of a king speak as an oracle,
    and his mouth does not betray justice.

¹¹Honest scales and balances belong to the Lord;
    all the weights in the bag are of his making.

¹²Kings detest wrongdoing,
    for a throne is established through righteousness.

¹³Kings take pleasure in honest lips;
    they value persons who speak what is right.

¹⁴A king's wrath is a messenger of death,
    but the wise will appease it.

889

¹⁵When a king's face brightens, it means life;
his favor is like a rain cloud in spring.

¹⁶How much better to get wisdom than
gold,
to get insight rather than silver!

¹⁷The highway of the upright avoids evil;
those who guard their ways preserve
their lives.

¹⁸Pride goes before destruction,
a haughty spirit before a fall.

¹⁹Better to be lowly in spirit along with
the oppressed
than to share plunder with the proud.

²⁰Those who give heed to instruction
prosper,ᵃ
and blessed are those who trust in the
LORD.

²¹The wise in heart are called discerning,
and gracious words promote
instruction.ᵇ

²²Prudence is a fountain of life to the
prudent,
but folly brings punishment to fools.

²³The hearts of the wise make their
mouths prudent,
and their lips promote instruction.ᶜ

²⁴Gracious words are a honeycomb,
sweet to the soul and healing to the bones.

²⁵There is a way that appears to be right,
but in the end it leads to death.

²⁶The appetite of laborers works for them;
their hunger drives them on.

²⁷Scoundrels plot evil,
and on their lips it is like a scorching fire.

²⁸The perverse stir up dissension,
and gossips separate close friends.

²⁹The violent entice their neighbors
and lead them down a path that is not good.

³⁰Those who wink with their eyes are plotting perversity;
those who purse their lips are bent on evil.

³¹Gray hair is a crown of splendor;
it is attained in the way of righteousness.

at issue: gambling

16:16 Some Christians think there's nothing wrong with a little gambling—dropping a quarter in a slot machine or buying a lottery ticket for fun. They may be right—the Bible does not expressly forbid gambling. But the Bible does forbid several behaviors often associated with gambling—wasting money, needless debt, not providing for your family's needs and addiction to any substance or habit. The Bible is also very clear that our hope is to be found only in God. If you gamble because you hope that winning will solve your problems, then you're placing your trust in something besides God. And *that's* a real problem.

ᵃ 20 Or who speak prudently find what is good   ᵇ 21 Or words make a person persuasive   ᶜ 23 Or prudent / and make their lips persuasive

conversations

aging «» 16:31

32Better a patient person than a warrior,
those with self-control than those
who take a city.

33The lot is cast into the lap,
but its every decision is from the LORD.

17

Better a dry crust with peace and quiet
than a house full of feasting, with
strife.

2A prudent servant will rule over a
disgraceful son,
and will share the inheritance as one
of the family.

1 » How do you feel about aging? Is it a welcome friend or a dreaded enemy (or neither)?

2 » How can righteousness prolong your life?

3 » What specific ways have your grown spiritually as you've aged?

For more on aging, check the index.
For the next Conversations, go to p. 894.

3The crucible for silver and the furnace
for gold,
but the LORD tests the heart.

4A wicked person listens to deceitful lips;
a liar pays attention to a destructive tongue.

5Whoever mocks the poor shows contempt for their Maker;
whoever gloats over disaster will not go unpunished.

6Children's children are a crown to the aged,
and parents are the pride of their children.

7Eloquent lips are unsuited to a godless fool—
how much worse lying lips to a ruler!

8A bribe is seen as a charm by those who give it;
they think success will come at every turn.

9Whoever would foster love covers over an offense,
but whoever repeats the matter separates close friends.

10A rebuke impresses a discerning person
more than a hundred lashes a fool.

11Evildoers foster rebellion against God;
the messenger of death will be sent against them.

12Better to meet a bear robbed of her cubs
than a fool bent on folly.

13Evil will never leave the house
of one who pays back evil for good.

14Starting a quarrel is like breaching a dam;
so drop the matter before a dispute breaks out.

15Acquitting the guilty and condemning the innocent—
the LORD detests them both.

16Why should fools have money in hand to buy wisdom,
when they are not able to understand it?

17A friend loves at all times,
and a brother is born for a time of adversity.

¹⁸One who has no sense shakes hands in pledge
and puts up security for a neighbor.

¹⁹Whoever loves a quarrel loves sin;
whoever builds a high gate invites destruction.

²⁰One whose heart is corrupt does not prosper;
one whose tongue is perverse falls into trouble.

²¹To have a fool for a child brings grief;
there is no joy for the parent of a godless fool.

²²A cheerful heart is good medicine,
but a crushed spirit dries up the bones.

²³The wicked accept bribes in secret
to pervert the course of justice.

²⁴A discerning person keeps wisdom in view,
but a fool's eyes wander to the ends of the earth.

²⁵Foolish children bring grief to their father
and bitterness to the mother who bore them.

²⁶If imposing a fine on the innocent is not good,
surely to flog honest officials is not right.

²⁷Those who have knowledge use words with restraint,
and those who have understanding are even-tempered.

²⁸Even fools are thought wise if they keep silent,
and discerning if they hold their tongues.

18 An unfriendly person pursues selfish ends
and against all sound judgment starts quarrels.

²Fools find no pleasure in understanding
but delight in airing their own opinions.

³When wickedness comes, so does contempt,
and with shame comes reproach.

⁴The words of the mouth are deep waters,
but the fountain of wisdom is a rushing stream.

⁵It is not good to be partial to the wicked
and so deprive the innocent of justice.

⁶The lips of fools bring them strife,
and their mouths invite a beating.

⁷The mouths of fools are their undoing,
and their lips are a snare to their very lives.

⁸The words of a gossip are like choice morsels;
they go down to the inmost parts.

⁹One who is slack in his work
is a close relative of one who destroys.

¹⁰The name of the LORD is a fortified tower;
the righteous run to it and are safe.

¹¹The wealth of the rich is their fortified city;
     they imagine it a wall too high to scale.

¹²Before a downfall the heart is haughty,
     but humility comes before honor.

¹³To answer before listening—
     that is folly and shame.

¹⁴The human spirit can endure in sickness,
     but a crushed spirit who can bear?

¹⁵The heart of the discerning acquires knowledge,
     for the ears of the wise seek it out.

¹⁶A gift opens the way
     and ushers the giver into the presence of the great.

¹⁷In a lawsuit the first to speak seems right,
     until someone comes forward and cross-examines.

¹⁸Casting the lot settles disputes
     and keeps strong opponents apart.

¹⁹A brother wronged is more unyielding than a fortified city;
     disputes are like the barred gates of a citadel.

²⁰From the fruit of their mouths people's stomachs are filled;
     with the harvest of their lips they are satisfied.

²¹The tongue has the power of life and death,
     and those who love it will eat its fruit.

²²He who finds a wife finds what is good
     and receives favor from the LORD.

²³The poor plead for mercy,
     but the rich answer harshly.

²⁴One who has unreliable friends soon comes to ruin,
     but there is a friend who sticks closer than a brother.

19
     Better the poor whose walk is blameless
     than a fool whose lips are perverse.

²Desire without knowledge is not good—
     how much more will hasty feet miss the way!

³One's own folly leads to ruin,
     yet the heart rages against the LORD.

⁴Wealth attracts many friends,
     but even the closest friends of the poor desert them.

⁵A false witness will not go unpunished,
     and whoever pours out lies will not go free.

⁶Many curry favor with a ruler,
     and everyone is the friend of one who gives gifts.

⁷The poor are shunned by all their relatives—
     how much more do their friends avoid them!

Though they pursue them with pleading,
they are nowhere to be found.[a]

⁸Those who get wisdom love their own lives;
those who cherish understanding will soon prosper.

⁹A false witness will not go unpunished,
and whoever pours out lies will perish.

¹⁰It is not fitting for a fool to live in luxury—
how much worse for a slave to rule over princes!

¹¹A person's wisdom yields patience;
it is to one's glory to overlook an offense.

¹²A king's rage is like the roar of a lion,
but his favor is like dew on the grass.

¹³A foolish child is a father's ruin,
and a quarrelsome wife is like
the constant dripping of a leaky roof.

¹⁴Houses and wealth are inherited from parents,
but a prudent wife is from the LORD.

¹⁵Laziness brings on deep sleep,
and the shiftless go hungry.

¹⁶Those who obey instructions
preserve their lives,
but those who are
contemptuous of their
ways will die.

¹⁷Those who are kind to the
poor lend to the LORD,
and he will reward them for
what they have done.

¹⁸Discipline your children, for
in that there is hope;
do not be a willing party to
their death.

¹⁹The hot-tempered must pay the penalty;
rescue them, and you will have to do it again.

²⁰Listen to advice and accept discipline,
and at the end you will be counted among the wise.

²¹Many are the plans in a human heart,
but it is the LORD's purpose that prevails.

²²What a person desires is unfailing love[b];
better to be poor than a liar.

²³The fear of the LORD leads to life;
then one rests content, untouched by trouble.

"conversations"

laziness 19:15

1 What are some immediate consequences
of laziness?

2 In what areas of your life are you tempted
to be lazy?

3 Why is laziness such an alluring trap?

For more on **laziness**, check the index.
For the next Conversations, go to p. 901.

---

[a] 7 The meaning of the Hebrew for this sentence is uncertain.   [b] 22 Or *Greed is a person's shame*

²⁴Sluggards bury their hands in the dish
    and will not even bring them back to their mouths!

²⁵Flog a mocker, and the simple will learn prudence;
    rebuke the discerning, and they will gain knowledge.

²⁶Whoever robs their father and drives out their mother
    is a child who brings shame and disgrace.

²⁷Stop listening to instruction, my child,
    and you will stray from the words of knowledge.

²⁸A corrupt witness mocks at justice,
    and the mouth of the wicked gulps down evil.

²⁹Penalties are prepared for mockers,
    and beatings for the backs of fools.

20

Wine is a mocker and beer a brawler;
    whoever is led astray by them is not wise.

²A king's wrath strikes terror like the roar of a lion;
    those who anger him forfeit their lives.

³It is to one's honor to avoid strife,
    but every fool is quick to quarrel.

⁴Sluggards do not plow in season;
    so at harvest time they look but find nothing.

⁵The purposes of the human heart are deep waters,
    but those who have insight draw them out.

⁶Many claim to have unfailing love,
    but a faithful person who can find?

⁷The righteous lead blameless lives;
    blessed are their children after them.

⁸When a king sits on his throne to judge,
    he winnows out all evil with his eyes.

⁹Who can say, "I have kept my heart pure;
    I am clean and without sin"?

¹⁰Differing weights and differing measures—
    the Lord detests them both.

¹¹Even small children are known by their actions,
    so is their conduct really pure and upright?

¹²Ears that hear and eyes that see—
    the Lord has made them both.

¹³Do not love sleep or you will grow poor;
    stay awake and you will have food to spare.

¹⁴"It's no good, it's no good!" says the buyer—
    then goes off and boasts about the purchase.

¹⁵Gold there is, and rubies in abundance,
    but lips that speak knowledge are a rare jewel.

¹⁶Take the garment of one who puts up security for a stranger;
  hold it in pledge if it is done for an outsider.

¹⁷Food gained by fraud tastes sweet,
  but one ends up with a mouth full of gravel.

¹⁸Plans are established by seeking advice;
  so if you wage war, obtain guidance.

¹⁹A gossip betrays a confidence;
  so avoid anyone who talks too much.

²⁰If you curse your father or mother,
  your lamp will be snuffed out in pitch darkness.

²¹An inheritance claimed too soon
  will not be blessed at the end.

²²Do not say, "I'll pay you back for this wrong!"
  Wait for the LORD, and he will avenge you.

²³The LORD detests differing weights,
  and dishonest scales do not please him.

²⁴A person's steps are directed by the LORD.
  How then can anyone understand their own way?

²⁵It is a trap to dedicate something rashly
  and only later to consider one's vows.

²⁶A wise king winnows out the wicked;
  he drives the threshing wheel over them.

²⁷The human spirit is*a* the lamp of the LORD
  that sheds light on one's inmost being.

HE IS: searching

20:27 Is God ever lost? Does he ever wonder what's hidden that he cannot see? No, of course not. God's vision is better than perfect. He sees inside us, past us and ahead of us. Our God is *searching*; his vision penetrates us.

Unlike God, we are mistresses of self-deception. Often our true motives mystify us. The good news is that God is *searching* out our inner beings. He is not distracted by our layers of meaning, motives or excuses. His eyes penetrate us—he knows us far better than we do. If you're searching for answers, stop trying to figure things out on your own; ask God to search your heart.

For the next He Is, go to p. 907.

²⁸Love and faithfulness keep a king safe;
  through love his throne is made secure.

²⁹The glory of young men is their strength,
  gray hair the splendor of the old.

---

a 27 Or *A person's words are*

³⁰Blows and wounds cleanse away evil,
    and beatings purge the inmost being.

21 In the Lord's hand the king's heart is a stream of water
    that he channels toward all who please him.

²People may think all their ways are right,
    but the Lord weighs the heart.

³To do what is right and just
    is more acceptable to the Lord than sacrifice.

⁴Haughty eyes and a proud heart—
    the unplowed field of the wicked—produce sin.

⁵The plans of the diligent lead to profit
    as surely as haste leads to poverty.

⁶A fortune made by a lying tongue
    is a fleeting vapor and a deadly snare.^a

⁷The violence of the wicked will drag them away,
    for they refuse to do what is right.

⁸The way of the guilty is devious,
    but the conduct of the innocent is upright.

⁹Better to live on a corner of the roof
    than share a house with a quarrelsome wife.

¹⁰The wicked crave evil;
    their neighbors get no mercy from them.

¹¹When a mocker is punished, the simple gain wisdom;
    by paying attention to the wise they get knowledge.

¹²The Righteous One^b takes note of the house of the wicked
    and brings the wicked to ruin.

¹³Those who shut their ears to the cry of the poor
    will also cry out and not be answered.

¹⁴A gift given in secret soothes anger,
    and a bribe concealed in the cloak pacifies great wrath.

¹⁵When justice is done, it brings joy to the righteous
    but terror to evildoers.

¹⁶Whoever strays from the path of prudence
    comes to rest in the company of the dead.

¹⁷Whoever loves pleasure will become poor;
    whoever loves wine and olive oil will never be rich.

¹⁸The wicked become a ransom for the righteous,
    and the unfaithful for the upright.

¹⁹Better to live in a desert
    than with a quarrelsome and nagging wife.

---

myth# 55 "I SHOULD NEVER SAY NO TO A MINISTRY OPPORTUNITY."

When someone asks me if I can help serve at the church, I feel guilty if I say no. As a result, everyone seems to come to me for help, all the time! People see me as always willing, the go-to person. I like the way people perceive me. I have the reputation for being a servant. The pastors know that if there is a need, they can expect to see me there, just as Jesus would be.

I teach a weekly women's Bible study, serve on the student ministry leadership team and the building committee, volunteer in the nursery and do anything else anyone asks me to do. I know I'm qualified in many areas of service, and I can make a difference. In fact, in some areas I have so much experience that it's just easier to do the ministry myself rather than train someone else to do it. I want to use the talents God gave me for him.

My husband thinks I overdo it with the hectic volunteer schedule I keep. "No wonder you've been getting sick," he says. I simply don't have time to eat healthy or rest when I am making an investment in eternity by serving others. I like being needed.

What bothers me is that sometimes when I am rushing from one ministry opportunity to the next, I secretly resent the people I'm serving. It's also frustrating that my work for Christ takes me away from time with my husband and children. I hardly see them because of the frantic pace I keep. However, I know that I shouldn't say no to a chance to serve because God and others need me—and I want to please God by working for him.

—Lisa

TOO OFTEN WE equate busyness for Christ with devotion to Christ. But the two are not the same. Like Martha, we may be working so hard for Jesus that we miss what's most important (see Luke 10:38–42).

Nowhere does the Bible tell us to accept every ministry opportunity that comes our way. Our model for ministry is Jesus. With only three short years of public ministry, he could have frantically rushed from one need to the next; instead, he asked the Father what *he* wanted him to do. He didn't heal every sick person or talk with every seeker. In fact, Jesus often went away by himself or with his disciples to rest (see Mark 6:32).

If you feel overwhelmed by your ministry commitments, then you need to evaluate with God whether you're trying to establish your identity in your ministry work. Your identity should come from who you are in Christ rather than what you do for him. Ask yourself:

- **What is my motivation for doing ministry (see Proverbs 21:2)?** Do you feel guilty or obligated? Deep down, are you trying to *earn* God's favor or the approval of others? These feelings shouldn't motivate you to do ministry—instead, you should minister out of the overflow of the work God is doing in you.

- **Am I trying to please God or other people?** People-pleasers often have a hard time saying no. If you are more concerned with pleasing God, then you won't worry so much about what others think of you.

- **Am I being faithful to what God has called me to do?** God's calling on your life is first to love him and then to love those he's placed in your immediate circle of care (your husband, children, parents, siblings, grandparents, etc.). You should not serve outside that circle if you are neglecting time with God or those closest to you.

- **Am I taking away from someone else's gift?** If you agree to every task, you potentially rob others of the ministry opportunities God prepared for them. If you think you're the only woman for the job, check yourself and see if pride is creeping in where you least expect it.

"Too much ministry involvement can be harmful. 49 percent of pastors, for instance, reveal that their family life has suffered significantly as a result of the pressure and demands of ministry."

—Barna Research Group (1998)

"FOR WE ARE GOD'S HANDIWORK, CREATED IN CHRIST JESUS TO DO GOOD WORKS, WHICH GOD PREPARED IN ADVANCE FOR US TO DO."

EPHESIANS 2:10

SEE ALSO
Psalm 127:1–2
Mark 6:30–32
1 Corinthians 3:5–9

For more on **Service** and **Time Management**, check the index.

²⁰The wise store up choice food and olive oil,
  but fools gulp theirs down.

²¹Whoever pursues righteousness and love
  finds life, prosperity^a and honor.

²²One who is wise can go up against the city of the mighty
  and pull down the stronghold in which they trust.

²³Those who guard their mouths and their tongues
  keep themselves from calamity.

²⁴The proud and arrogant—"Mocker" is their name;
  they behave with insolent fury.

²⁵The craving of sluggards will be the death of them,
  because their hands refuse to work.
²⁶All day long they crave for more,
  but the righteous give without sparing.

²⁷The sacrifice of the wicked is detestable—
  how much more so when brought with evil intent!

²⁸Those who give false witness will perish,
  but a careful listener will testify successfully.

²⁹The wicked put up a bold front,
  but the upright give thought to their ways.

³⁰There is no wisdom, no insight, no plan
  that can succeed against the Lord.

³¹The horse is made ready for the day of battle,
  but victory rests with the Lord.

22

A good name is more desirable than great riches;
  to be esteemed is better than silver or gold.

²Rich and poor have this in common:
  The Lord is the Maker of them all.

³The prudent see danger and take refuge,
  but the simple keep going and pay the penalty.

⁴Humility is the fear of the Lord;
  its wages are riches and honor and life.

⁵In the paths of the wicked are snares and pitfalls,
  but those who would preserve their life stay far from them.

⁶Start children off on the way they should go,
  and even when they are old they will not turn from it.

⁷The rich rule over the poor,
  and the borrower is slave to the lender.

⁸Those who sow injustice reap calamity,
  and the rod they wield in fury will be broken.

---

^a 21 Or righteousness

⁹The generous will themselves be
    blessed,
  for they share their food with the
    poor.

¹⁰Drive out the mocker, and out goes
    strife;
  quarrels and insults are ended.

¹¹One who loves a pure heart and who
    speaks with grace
  will have the king for a friend.

¹²The eyes of the LORD keep watch over
    knowledge,
  but he frustrates the words of the
    unfaithful.

¹³The sluggard says, "There's a lion
    outside!
  I'll be killed in the public square!"

¹⁴The mouth of an adulterous woman is a deep pit;
  a man who is under the LORD's wrath falls into it.

¹⁵Folly is bound up in the heart of a child,
  but the rod of discipline will drive it far away.

¹⁶Those who oppress the poor to increase their wealth
  and those who give gifts to the rich—both come to poverty.

conversations

parenting «» 22:6

1» What do you think it means to "start children off on the way they should go"?

2» How much responsibility do parents have for their children's success or failure?

3» As a parent, how long will your direct influence last in your child's life?

For more on **parenting**, check the index.
For the next Conversations, go to p. 913.

901

Thirty Sayings of the Wise

Saying 1

¹⁷Pay attention and turn your ear to the sayings of the wise;
  apply your heart to what I teach,
¹⁸for it is pleasing when you keep them in your heart
  and have all of them ready on your lips.
¹⁹So that your trust may be in the LORD,
  I teach you today, even you.
²⁰Have I not written thirty sayings for you,
  sayings of counsel and knowledge,
²¹teaching you to be honest and to speak the truth,
  so that you bring back truthful reports
  to those you serve?

Saying 2

²²Do not exploit the poor because they are poor
  and do not crush the needy in court,
²³for the LORD will take up their case
  and will exact life for life.

Saying 3

²⁴Do not make friends with the hot-tempered,
  do not associate with those who are easily angered,

²⁵or you may learn their ways
and get yourself ensnared.

Saying 4

²⁶Do not be one who shakes hands in pledge
or puts up security for debts;
²⁷if you lack the means to pay,
your very bed will be snatched from under you.

Saying 5

²⁸Do not move an ancient boundary stone
set up by your ancestors.

Saying 6

²⁹Do you see those who are skilled in their work?
They will serve before kings;
they will not serve before officials of low rank.

Saying 7

23 When you sit to dine with a ruler,
note well what ᵃ is before you,
²and put a knife to your throat
if you are given to gluttony.
³Do not crave his delicacies,
for that food is deceptive.

Saying 8

⁴Do not wear yourself out to get rich;
do not trust your own cleverness.
⁵Cast but a glance at riches, and they are gone,
for they will surely sprout wings
and fly off to the sky like an eagle.

Saying 9

⁶Do not eat the food of a begrudging host,
do not crave his delicacies;
⁷for he is the kind of person
who is always thinking about the cost.ᵇ
"Eat and drink," he says to you,
but his heart is not with you.
⁸You will vomit up the little you have eaten
and will have wasted your compliments.

Saying 10

⁹Do not speak to fools,
for they will scorn your prudent words.

Saying 11

¹⁰Do not move an ancient boundary stone
or encroach on the fields of the fatherless,
¹¹for their Defender is strong;
he will take up their case against you.

ᵃ *1* Or *who*   ᵇ *7* Or *for as he thinks within himself, / so he is; or for as he puts on a feast, / so he is*

Saying 12

¹²Apply your heart to instruction
and your ears to words of knowledge.

Saying 13

¹³Do not withhold discipline from children;
if you punish them with the rod, they will not die.
¹⁴Punish them with the rod
and save them from death.

Saying 14

¹⁵My son, if your heart is wise,
then my heart will be glad indeed;
¹⁶my inmost being will rejoice
when your lips speak what is right.

Saying 15

¹⁷Do not let your heart envy sinners,
but always be zealous for the fear of the LORD.
¹⁸There is surely a future hope for you,
and your hope will not be cut off.

Saying 16

¹⁹Listen, my son, and be wise,
and set your heart on the right path:
²⁰Do not join those who drink too much wine
or gorge themselves on meat,
²¹for drunkards and gluttons become poor,
and drowsiness clothes them in rags.

Saying 17

²²Listen to your father, who gave you life,
and do not despise your mother when she is old.
²³Buy the truth and do not sell it—
wisdom, instruction and insight as well.
²⁴The father of a righteous child has great joy;
a man who fathers a wise son rejoices in him.
²⁵May your father and mother rejoice;
may she who gave you birth be joyful!

Saying 18

²⁶My son, give me your heart
and let your eyes delight in my ways,
²⁷for an adulterous woman is a deep pit
and a wayward wife is a narrow well.
²⁸Like a bandit she lies in wait,
and multiplies the unfaithful among men.

Saying 19

²⁹Who has woe? Who has sorrow?
Who has strife? Who has complaints?
Who has needless bruises? Who has bloodshot eyes?
³⁰Those who linger over wine,
who go to sample bowls of mixed wine.

903

³¹Do not gaze at wine when it is red,
  when it sparkles in the cup,
  when it goes down smoothly!
³²In the end it bites like a snake
  and poisons like a viper.
³³Your eyes will see strange sights
  and your mind imagine confusing things.
³⁴You will be like one sleeping on the high
    seas,
  lying on top of the rigging.
³⁵"They hit me," you will say, "but I'm not
    hurt!
  They beat me, but I don't feel it!
  When will I wake up
  so I can find another drink?"

Saying 20

24

Do not envy the wicked,
  do not desire their company;
²for their hearts plot violence,
  and their lips talk about making trouble.

Saying 21

³By wisdom a house is built,
  and through understanding it is
    established;
⁴through knowledge its rooms are filled
  with rare and beautiful treasures.

Saying 22

⁵The wise prevail through great power,
  and those who have knowledge muster their strength.
⁶Surely you need guidance to wage war,
  and victory is won through many advisers.

Saying 23

⁷Wisdom is too high for fools;
  in the assembly at the gate they must not open their mouths.

Saying 24

⁸Whoever plots evil
  will be known as a schemer.
⁹The schemes of folly are sin,
  and people detest a mocker.

Saying 25

¹⁰If you falter in a time of trouble,
  how small is your strength!
¹¹Rescue those being led away to death;
  hold back those staggering toward slaughter.
¹²If you say, "But we knew nothing about this,"
  does not he who weighs the heart perceive it?
  Does not he who guards your life know it?
  Will he not repay everyone according to what they have done?

a t i s s u e : a l c o h o l i s m

23:29–35 She has blood-shot eyes and bruises she can't remember receiving. Her drinking hurts the people she loves. She finds her hope and her help in alcohol. But in the end it doesn't make anything better; it makes things worse. It clouds her thinking and blinds her to the danger she's in. Her main concern is when she can get that next drink. Do you recognize yourself in her? If you do, it's time to talk to a friend, a pastor or a counselor. It's time to take back your life and start really living again.

904

Saying 26

¹³Eat honey, my son, for it is good;
    honey from the comb is sweet to your taste.
¹⁴Know also that wisdom is like honey for you:
    If you find it, there is a future hope for you,
    and your hope will not be cut off.

Saying 27

¹⁵Do not lurk like a thief near the house of the righteous,
    do not plunder their dwelling place;
¹⁶for though the righteous fall seven times, they rise again,
    but the wicked stumble when calamity strikes.

Saying 28

¹⁷Do not gloat when your enemies fall;
    when they stumble, do not let your heart rejoice,
¹⁸or the LORD will see and disapprove
    and turn his wrath away from them.

Saying 29

¹⁹Do not fret because of evildoers
    or be envious of the wicked,
²⁰for the evildoer has no future hope,
    and the lamp of the wicked will be snuffed out.

905

Saying 30

²¹Fear the LORD and the king, my son,
    and do not join with rebellious officials,
²²for those two will send sudden destruction on them,
    and who knows what calamities they can bring?

Further Sayings of the Wise

²³These also are sayings of the wise:

    To show partiality in judging is not good:
²⁴Whoever says to the guilty, "You are innocent,"
    will be cursed by peoples and denounced by nations.
²⁵But it will go well with those who convict the guilty,
    and rich blessing will come on them.

²⁶An honest answer
    is like a kiss on the lips.

²⁷Put your outdoor work in order
    and get your fields ready;
    after that, build your house.

²⁸Do not testify against your neighbor without cause—
    would you use your lips to mislead?
²⁹Do not say, "I'll do to them as they have done to me;
    I'll pay them back for what they did."

³⁰I went past the field of a sluggard,
    past the vineyard of someone who has no sense;
³¹thorns had come up everywhere,
    the ground was covered with weeds,

and the stone wall was in ruins.
³²I applied my heart to what I observed
  and learned a lesson from what I saw:
³³A little sleep, a little slumber,
  a little folding of the hands to rest—
³⁴and poverty will come on you like a thief
  and scarcity like an armed man.

More Proverbs of Solomon

25 These are more proverbs of Solomon, compiled by the men of Hezekiah king of Judah:

²It is the glory of God to conceal a matter;
  to search out a matter is the glory of kings.
³As the heavens are high and the earth is deep,
  so the hearts of kings are unsearchable.

⁴Remove the dross from the silver,
  and a silversmith can produce a vessel;
⁵remove wicked officials from the king's presence,
  and his throne will be established through righteousness.

⁶Do not exalt yourself in the king's presence,
  and do not claim a place among his great men;
⁷it is better for him to say to you, "Come up here,"
  than for him to humiliate you before his nobles.

What you have seen with your eyes
⁸ do not bring^a hastily to court,
for what will you do in the end
  if your neighbor puts you to shame?

⁹If you take your neighbor to court,
  do not betray another's confidence,
¹⁰or the one who hears it may shame you
  and the charge against you will stand.

¹¹Like apples^b of gold in settings of silver
  is a ruling rightly given.
¹²Like an earring of gold or an ornament of fine gold
  is the rebuke of a wise judge to a listening ear.

¹³Like a snow-cooled drink at harvest time
  is a trustworthy messenger to the one who sends him;
  he refreshes the spirit of his master.
¹⁴Like clouds and wind without rain
  is one who boasts of gifts never given.

¹⁵Through patience a ruler can be persuaded,
  and a gentle tongue can break a bone.

¹⁶If you find honey, eat just enough—
  too much of it, and you will vomit.
¹⁷Seldom set foot in your neighbor's house—
  too much of you, and you will be hated.

---

^a 7,8 Or nobles / on whom you had set your eyes. / ⁸Do not go ^b 11 Or possibly apricots

906

¹⁸Like a club or a sword or a sharp arrow
    is one who gives false testimony against a neighbor.
¹⁹Like a broken tooth or a lame foot
    is reliance on the unfaithful in a time of trouble.
²⁰Like one who takes away a garment on a cold day,
    or like vinegar poured on a wound,
    is one who sings songs to a heavy heart.

²¹If your enemy is hungry, give him food to eat;
    if he is thirsty, give him water to drink.
²²In doing this, you will heap burning coals on his head,
    and the LORD will reward you.

HE IS: rewarding

25:21–22 God is a giving God who encourages his people to be generous. He doesn't ask his people to give only to those who deserve it but to their enemies as well. When we give to our enemies, he is *rewarding*.

What does your enemy need? Some encouragement or affirmation? Help on a project at work? A personal invitation to church? When you show kindness to someone who does not deserve it, you're exhibiting a characteristic of God. Though the person you are kind to may not appreciate it, God will, and he will reward you, as a father does his children. See also Luke 6:32–36.

For the next He Is, go to p. 914.

907

²³Like a north wind that brings unexpected rain
    is a sly tongue—which provokes a horrified look.

²⁴Better to live on a corner of the roof
    than share a house with a quarrelsome wife.

²⁵Like cold water to a weary soul
    is good news from a distant land.
²⁶Like a muddied spring or a polluted well
    are the righteous who give way to the wicked.

²⁷It is not good to eat too much honey,
    nor is it honorable to search out matters that are too deep.

²⁸Like a city whose walls are broken through
    is a person who lacks self-control.

26 Like snow in summer or rain in harvest,
    honor is not fitting for a fool.
²Like a fluttering sparrow or a darting swallow,
    an undeserved curse does not come to rest.
³A whip for the horse, a bridle for the donkey,
    and a rod for the backs of fools!
⁴Do not answer fools according to their folly,
    or you yourself will be just like them.
⁵Answer fools according to their folly,
    or they will be wise in their own eyes.

⁶To send a message by the hands of a fool
   is like cutting off one's feet or drinking poison.
⁷Like the useless legs of one who is lame
   is a proverb in the mouth of a fool.
⁸Like tying a stone in a sling
   is the giving of honor to a fool.
⁹Like a thornbush in a drunkard's hand
   is a proverb in the mouth of a fool.
¹⁰Like an archer who wounds at random
   is one who hires a fool or any passer-by.
¹¹As a dog returns to its vomit,
   so fools repeat their folly.
¹²Do you see people who are wise in their own eyes?
   There is more hope for fools than for them.

¹³A sluggard says, "There's a lion in the
      road,
   a fierce lion roaming the streets!"
¹⁴As a door turns on its hinges,
   so a sluggard turns on the bed.
¹⁵Sluggards bury their hands in the dish
   and are too lazy to bring them back
      to their mouths.
¹⁶Sluggards are wiser in their own eyes
   than seven people who answer
      discreetly.

¹⁷Like one who grabs a stray dog by the
      ears
   is someone who rushes into a quarrel
      not their own.

¹⁸Like a maniac shooting
   flaming arrows of death
¹⁹is one who deceives a neighbor
   and says, "I was only joking!"

²⁰Without wood a fire goes out;
   without a gossip a quarrel dies down.
²¹As charcoal to embers and as wood to
      fire,
   so is a quarrelsome person for
      kindling strife.
²²The words of a gossip are like choice morsels;
   they go down to the inmost parts.

²³Like a coating of silver dross on earthenware
   are fervent *a* lips with an evil heart.
²⁴Enemies disguise themselves with their lips,
   but in their hearts they harbor deceit.
²⁵Though their speech is charming, do not believe them,
   for seven abominations fill their hearts.
²⁶Their malice may be concealed by deception,

at issue: lazy husband

26:13–16 Do you have a lazy or irresponsible husband? He's full of excuses for his laziness: His back hurts . . . Recent studies show work's bad for your health . . . It's his dad's fault. He doesn't notice that you're carrying more than your share of the load. What can you do? First, pray for him and for your own heart. Then tell him how you feel—without accusing, condemning or assigning motives to him. See how he responds. If he ignores or belittles your concerns, go talk to someone you both trust and respect. And through it all, make sure you don't grow lazy in loving him.

---
a 23 Hebrew; Septuagint *smooth*

but their wickedness will be exposed in the assembly.
²⁷If anyone digs a pit, they themselves will fall into it;
    if anyone rolls a stone, it will roll back on them.
²⁸A lying tongue hates those it hurts,
    and a flattering mouth works ruin.

27

Do not boast about tomorrow,
    for you do not know what a day may bring.

²Let someone else praise you, and not your own mouth;
    an outsider, and not your own lips.

³Stone is heavy and sand a burden,
    but a fool's provocation is heavier than both.

⁴Anger is cruel and fury overwhelming,
    but who can stand before jealousy?

⁵Better is open rebuke
    than hidden love.

⁶Wounds from a friend can be trusted,
    but an enemy multiplies kisses.

⁷One who is full loathes honey from the comb,
    but to the hungry even what is bitter tastes sweet.

⁸Like a bird that flees its nest
    is anyone who flees from home.

⁹Perfume and incense bring joy to the heart,
    and the pleasantness of a friend
    springs from their heartfelt advice.

¹⁰Do not forsake your friend or a friend of
    your family,
    and do not go to your relative's house
      when disaster strikes you—
    better a neighbor nearby than a relative
      far away.

¹¹Be wise, my child, and bring joy to my
    heart;
    then I can answer anyone who treats me
      with contempt.

¹²The prudent see danger and take refuge,
    but the simple keep going and pay the
      penalty.

¹³Take the garment of one who puts up
    security for a stranger;
    hold it in pledge if it is done for an
      outsider.

¹⁴If anyone loudly blesses a neighbor early in
    the morning,
    it will be taken as a curse.

909

atissue:friendship

27:9 The success of stores like Bath & Body Works® proves that women love to smell good. There's something about a pretty fragrance that just cheers us up. Did you know that in the same way you can be a pleasant aroma to your friends? Your friendship can lift the spirits of others and bring them joy, just like the smell of a beautiful fragrance. When you express heartfelt concern over them and the issues they're facing, you refresh them. When you care enough to get involved in their lives on a deeper level and offer encouragement and love, you are being a true friend.

¹⁵A quarrelsome wife is like the dripping
  of a leaky roof in a rainstorm;
¹⁶restraining her is like restraining the wind
  or grasping oil with the hand.

¹⁷As iron sharpens iron,
  so one person sharpens another.

¹⁸Those who guard a fig tree will eat its fruit,
  and those who protect their masters will be honored.

¹⁹As water reflects the face,
  so one's life reflects the heart.^a

²⁰Death and Destruction^b are never satisfied,
  and neither are human eyes.

²¹The crucible for silver and the furnace for gold,
  but people are tested by their praise.

²²Though you grind fools in a mortar,
  grinding them like grain with a pestle,
  you will not remove their folly from them.

²³Be sure you know the condition of your flocks,
  give careful attention to your herds;
²⁴for riches do not endure forever,
  and a crown is not secure for all generations.
²⁵When the hay is removed and new growth appears
  and the grass from the hills is gathered in,
²⁶the lambs will provide you with clothing,
  and the goats with the price of a field.
²⁷You will have plenty of goats' milk to feed your family
  and to nourish your women servants.

28

The wicked flee though no one pursues,
  but the righteous are as bold as a lion.

²When a country is rebellious, it has many rulers,
  but a ruler with discernment and knowledge maintains order.

³A ruler^c who oppresses the poor
  is like a driving rain that leaves no crops.

⁴Those who forsake instruction praise the wicked,
  but those who heed it resist them.

⁵Evildoers do not understand what is right,
  but those who seek the LORD understand it fully.

⁶Better the poor whose walk is blameless
  than the rich whose ways are perverse.

⁷Those who heed instruction are discerning children,
  but companions of gluttons disgrace their parents.

---

^a 19 Or so others reflect your heart back to you   ^b 20 Hebrew Abaddon   ^c 3 Or A poor person

[8]Whoever increases wealth by taking interest or profit from the poor
  amasses it for another, who will be kind to the poor.

[9]If anyone turns a deaf ear to my instruction,
  even their prayers are detestable.

[10]Those who lead the upright along an evil path
  will fall into their own trap,
  but the blameless will receive a good inheritance.

[11]The rich are wise in their own eyes;
  one who is poor and discerning sees how deluded they are.

[12]When the righteous triumph, there is great elation;
  but when the wicked rise to power, people go into hiding.

[13]Those who conceal their sins do not
    prosper,
  but those who confess and renounce
    them find mercy.

[14]Blessed are those who always tremble
    before God,
  but those who harden their hearts fall
    into trouble.

[15]Like a roaring lion or a charging bear
  is a wicked ruler over a helpless people.

[16]A tyrannical ruler practices extortion,
  but one who hates ill-gotten gain will
    enjoy a long reign.

[17]Anyone tormented by the guilt of murder
  will seek refuge in the grave;
  let no one hold them back.

[18]Those whose walk is blameless are kept
    safe,
  but those whose ways are perverse will
    fall into the pit.[a]

[19]Those who work their land will have
    abundant food,
  but those who chase fantasies will have
    their fill of poverty.

[20]A faithful person will be richly blessed,
  but one eager to get rich will not go unpunished.

[21]To show partiality is not good—
  yet a person will do wrong for a piece of bread.

[22]The stingy are eager to get rich
  and are unaware that poverty awaits them.

[23]Whoever rebukes a person will in the end gain favor
  rather than one who has a flattering tongue.

atissue:hidden sin

28:13 When you sin, it's natural to try to hide your wrong. But hidden sin festers. It makes things worse, not better. It begins to infect every area of your life—your relationship with God, your self-image, your relationships with others, your peace of mind, your ability to focus, and on and on. As long as that sin is hidden, you don't prosper. Eventually, your sin must be dealt with. When you confess your sin and renounce it, you'll experience the incredible forgiveness of your heavenly Father. He draws you close and whispers, "Yes, your sin is great. But my mercy is greater."

911

[a] *18* Syriac (see Septuagint); Hebrew *into one*

²⁴Whoever robs their father or mother
 and says, "It's not wrong,"
 is partner to one who destroys.

²⁵The greedy stir up dissension,
 but those who trust in the Lord will prosper.

²⁶Those who trust in themselves are fools,
 but those who walk in wisdom are kept safe.

²⁷Those who give to the poor will lack nothing,
 but those who close their eyes to them receive many curses.

²⁸When the wicked rise to power, people go into hiding;
 but when the wicked perish, the righteous thrive.

29

 Whoever remains stiff-necked after many rebukes
 will suddenly be destroyed—without remedy.

²When the righteous thrive, the people rejoice;
 when the wicked rule, the people groan.

³A man who loves wisdom brings joy to his father,
 but a companion of prostitutes squanders his wealth.

⁴By justice a king gives a country stability,
 but those who are greedy for^a bribes tear it down.

⁵Those who flatter their neighbors
 are spreading nets for their feet.

⁶Evildoers are snared by their own sin,
 but the righteous shout for joy and are glad.

⁷The righteous care about justice for the poor,
 but the wicked have no such concern.

⁸Mockers stir up a city,
 but the wise turn away anger.

⁹If a wise person goes to court with a fool,
 the fool rages and scoffs, and there is no peace.

¹⁰The bloodthirsty hate people of integrity
 and seek to kill the upright.

¹¹Fools give full vent to their rage,
 but the wise bring calm in the end.

¹²If a ruler listens to lies,
 all his officials become wicked.

¹³The poor and the oppressor have this in common:
 The Lord gives sight to the eyes of both.

¹⁴If a king judges the poor with fairness,
 his throne will be established forever.

¹⁵A rod and a reprimand impart wisdom,
 but children left to themselves disgrace their mother.

^a 4 Or who give

¹⁶When the wicked thrive, so does sin,
    but the righteous will see their downfall.

¹⁷Discipline your children, and they will give you peace;
    they will bring you the delights you desire.

¹⁸Where there is no revelation, people
        cast off restraint;
    but blessed are those who heed
        wisdom's instruction.

¹⁹Servants cannot be corrected by mere
        words;
    though they understand, they will not
        respond.

²⁰Do you see someone who speaks in
        haste?
    There is more hope for a fool than for
        them.

²¹A servant pampered from youth
    will turn out to be insolent.

²²An angry person stirs up dissension,
    and a hot-tempered person commits many sins.

²³Pride brings a person low,
    but the lowly in spirit gain honor.

²⁴The accomplices of thieves are their own enemies;
    they are put under oath and dare not testify.

²⁵To fear anyone will prove to be a snare,
    but whoever trusts in the LORD is kept safe.

²⁶Many seek an audience with a ruler,
    but it is from the LORD that one gets justice.

²⁷The righteous detest the dishonest;
    the wicked detest the upright.

conversations

parenting «» 29:15,17

1 » In what way are many children "left to themselves" today?

2 » If you're a parent, how can you ensure that your activities don't distract you from having a positive influence in your child's life?

3 » What are the benefits of discipline to a child? To a parent?

For more on **parenting**, check the index.
For the next Conversations, go to p. 921.

913

Sayings of Agur

30 The sayings of Agur son of Jakeh—an inspired utterance.

This man's utterance to Ithiel:

"I am weary, God,
    but I can prevail.ᵃ
²Surely I am only a brute, not a man;
    I do not have human understanding.
³I have not learned wisdom,
    nor have I attained to the knowledge of the Holy One.
⁴Who has gone up to heaven and come down?
    Whose hands have gathered up the wind?
    Who has wrapped up the waters in a cloak?

<hr>

ᵃ *1* With a different word division of the Hebrew; Masoretic Text *utterance to Ithiel, / to Ithiel and Ukal:*

Who has established all the ends of the earth?
What is his name, and what is the name of his son?
Surely you know!

⁵"Every word of God is flawless;
he is a shield to those who take refuge in him.
⁶Do not add to his words,
or he will rebuke you and prove you a liar.

HE IS: flawless

30:5–6 God reveals who he is in his Word, the holy Bible. Since every word of God is flawless, this means that God himself is *flawless*. Every word spoken by him, every decision made by him, every outcome allowed by him is perfect.

When skeptics question God's Word, calling it mere opinion or human interpretation, don't believe it! The Bible is a divinely inspired message from God to humanity. Do not doubt the truth or the God of the Bible—he is *flawless*. Time and again he'll prove to you that he knows what he's doing and that he does all things perfectly.

For the next He Is, go to p. 925.

914

⁷"Two things I ask of you, LORD;
do not refuse me before I die:
⁸Keep falsehood and lies far from me;
give me neither poverty nor riches,
but give me only my daily bread.
⁹Otherwise, I may have too much and disown you
and say, 'Who is the LORD?'
Or I may become poor and steal,
and so dishonor the name of my God.

¹⁰"Do not slander servants to their master,
or they will curse you, and you will pay for it.

¹¹"There are those who curse their fathers
and do not bless their mothers;
¹²those who are pure in their own eyes
and yet are not cleansed of their filth;
¹³those whose eyes are ever so haughty,
whose glances are so disdainful;
¹⁴those whose teeth are swords
and whose jaws are set with knives
to devour the poor from the earth
and the needy from among humankind.

¹⁵"The leech has two daughters.
'Give! Give!' they cry.

"There are three things that are never satisfied,
four that never say, 'Enough!':
¹⁶the grave, the barren womb,
land, which is never satisfied with water,
and fire, which never says, 'Enough!'

¹⁷"The eye that mocks a father,
   that scorns an aged mother,
will be pecked out by the ravens of the valley,
   will be eaten by the vultures.

¹⁸"There are three things that are too amazing for me,
   four that I do not understand:
¹⁹the way of an eagle in the sky,
   the way of a snake on a rock,
the way of a ship on the high seas,
   and the way of a man with a young woman.

²⁰"This is the way of an adulterous woman:
   She eats and wipes her mouth
   and says, 'I've done nothing wrong.'

²¹"Under three things the earth trembles,
   under four it cannot bear up:
²²a servant who becomes king,
   a godless fool who gets plenty to eat,
²³a contemptible woman who gets married,
   and a servant who displaces her mistress.

²⁴"Four things on earth are small,
   yet they are extremely wise:
²⁵Ants are creatures of little strength,
   yet they store up their food in the summer;
²⁶hyraxes are creatures of little power,
   yet they make their home in the crags;
²⁷locusts have no king,
   yet they advance together in ranks;
²⁸a lizard can be caught with the hand,
   yet it is found in kings' palaces.

²⁹"There are three things that are stately in their stride,
   four that move with stately bearing:
³⁰a lion, mighty among beasts,
   who retreats before nothing;
³¹a strutting rooster, a he-goat,
   and a king secure against revolt.^a

³²"If you play the fool and exalt yourself,
   or if you plan evil,
   clap your hand over your mouth!
³³For as churning cream produces butter,
   and as twisting the nose produces blood,
   so stirring up anger produces strife."

Sayings of King Lemuel

31 The sayings of King Lemuel—an inspired utterance his mother taught him.

²Listen, my son! Listen, son of my womb!
   Listen, my son, the answer to my prayers!

915

---

^a *31* The meaning of the Hebrew for this phrase is uncertain.

³Do not spend your strength^a on women,
   your vigor on those who ruin kings.

⁴It is not for kings, Lemuel—
   it is not for kings to drink wine,
   not for rulers to crave beer,
⁵lest they drink and forget what has been decreed,
   and deprive all the oppressed of their rights.
⁶Let beer be for those who are perishing,
   wine for those who are in anguish!
⁷Let them drink and forget their poverty
   and remember their misery no more.

⁸Speak up for those who cannot speak for themselves,
   for the rights of all who are destitute.
⁹Speak up and judge fairly;
   defend the rights of the poor and needy.

Epilogue: The Wife of Noble Character

¹⁰ᵇ A wife of noble character who can find?
   She is worth far more than rubies.
¹¹Her husband has full confidence in her
   and lacks nothing of value.
¹²She brings him good, not harm,
   all the days of her life.
¹³She selects wool and flax
   and works with eager hands.
¹⁴She is like the merchant ships,
   bringing her food from afar.
¹⁵She gets up while it is still night;
   she provides food for her family
   and portions for her women servants.
¹⁶She considers a field and buys it;
   out of her earnings she plants a vineyard.
¹⁷She sets about her work vigorously;
   her arms are strong for her tasks.
¹⁸She sees that her trading is profitable,
   and her lamp does not go out at night.
¹⁹In her hand she holds the distaff
   and grasps the spindle with her fingers.
²⁰She opens her arms to the poor
   and extends her hands to the needy.
²¹When it snows, she has no fear for her household;
   for all of them are clothed in scarlet.
²²She makes coverings for her bed;
   she is clothed in fine linen and purple.
²³Her husband is respected at the city gate,
   where he takes his seat among the elders of the land.
²⁴She makes linen garments and sells them,
   and supplies the merchants with sashes.
²⁵She is clothed with strength and dignity;

---

^a 3 Or wealth   ^b 10 Verses 10–31 are an acrostic poem, the verses of which begin with the successive letters of the Hebrew alphabet.

rachel

Genesis 29:1—35:20

Tell us about your relationship with your sister, Leah.

Have you ever heard of sibling rivalry? Well, we defined the term. Leah was older, and it was my father's desire that she marry first. Unfortunately for her, I was the one with all the looks in the family. Poor Leah, she was painfully plain. Not even an extreme makeover could have helped her. No boyfriends, no prospects of a husband.

What happened between you?

I was the first to meet Jacob at the well as I was tending the sheep. It was love at first sight—especially for Jacob. He fell hard for me. Jacob agreed to work for seven years in exchange for marrying me. Seven years! If that isn't diehard true love, what is? Neither of us knew that my father had other plans in mind. And when the time came for the wedding—my wedding!—my father tricked Jacob and gave him Leah as his bride. My father knew that was the only way anyone would marry my sister. Jacob was livid! He couldn't believe what my dad had done. So he demanded that I be his wife also. My father agreed, but only after Jacob agreed to work for another *seven* years.

917

How did both of you being married to Jacob affect your relationship as sisters?

My relationship with Leah became very competitive. It quickly became apparent that Leah was a baby-making machine. While I could not get pregnant, Leah was producing son after son. It seemed that God was blessing her and not me. I felt crazy with jealousy and shame. I had to have a child! Talk about a tense household. Jacob loved me, but I was angry and frustrated because I couldn't get pregnant. Meanwhile, Leah was having all these kids, but she still desperately wanted Jacob's love. Neither Leah nor I was happy.

Did you ever reconcile with your sister?

I can't say that we ever did. Even after I had Joseph, I still asked God for more, for another son. I was not satisfied with the love of Jacob and child of my own. I had to outdo my sister.

What can we learn from your situation?

When I look back, I realize how much God had given me. I was blessed with beauty. I had a man who loved me so much that he willingly endured 14 years of hard labor and a marriage to a woman he did not love, just so he could be with me. Not many women receive that kind of undying devotion. Yet all I focused on was how God had blessed my sister, not me. I never got past those bitter feelings. Leah and I could have supported each other instead of tearing each other down. We could have been friends instead of rivals. But that never happened.

FOR MORE INSIGHT: Check out Proverbs 15:13; Ecclesiastes 7:14; and 1 Thessalonians 5:16–18 on maintaining an attitude of thankfulness, no matter what your situation may be.

she can laugh at the days to come.
²⁶ She speaks with wisdom,
and faithful instruction is on her
tongue.
²⁷ She watches over the affairs of her
household
and does not eat the bread of
idleness.
²⁸ Her children arise and call her blessed;
her husband also, and he praises her:
²⁹ "Many women do noble things,
but you surpass them all."
³⁰ Charm is deceptive, and beauty is
fleeting;
but a woman who fears the LORD is to
be praised.
³¹ Honor her for all that her hands have
done,
and let her works bring her praise at
the city gate.

at issue:appearance

31:30 Admit it. It feels good when someone notices your appearance, appreciates your latest hairstyle or comments on how much weight you've lost. But don't get sucked into believing that's what is most important about you. No matter how much anti-aging cream you use, outward beauty is fleeting. It's fading fast. And ultimately, so many other things are more valuable. If you're going to be praised for something, let it be for your godly life. Let people notice your love for God and see your concern for others. Those are qualities that will only grow more beautiful with time and age.

ecclesiastes

AUTHOR
The Teacher, who was probably King
Solomon.

AUDIENCE
All Israel.

DATE
Most likely near the end of Solomon's life,
930 B.C.

SETTING
In the twilight of his life, the wise Teacher
reflects on human existence.

VERSE TO REMEMBER
"There is a time for everything, and a season
for every activity under the heavens." (3:1)

THEME TO CONSIDER
Even the best the world has to offer will
never truly satisfy us. Life apart from God is
meaningless.

ecclesiastes 1:1

Everything Is Meaningless

1 The words of the Teacher,[a] son of David, king in Jerusalem:

> [2] "Meaningless! Meaningless!"
>   says the Teacher.
> "Utterly meaningless!
>   Everything is meaningless."

> [3] What does anyone gain from all their labors
>   at which they toil under the sun?
> [4] Generations come and generations go,
>   but the earth remains forever.
> [5] The sun rises and the sun sets,
>   and hurries back to where it rises.
> [6] The wind blows to the south
>   and turns to the north;
> round and round it goes,
>   ever returning on its course.
> [7] All streams flow into the sea,
>   yet the sea is never full.
> To the place the streams come from,
>   there they return again.
> [8] All things are wearisome,
>   more than one can say.
> The eye never has enough of seeing,
>   nor the ear its fill of hearing.
> [9] What has been will be again,
>   what has been done will be done again;
>   there is nothing new under the sun.
> [10] Is there anything of which one can say,
>   "Look! This is something new"?
> It was here already, long ago;
>   it was here before our time.
> [11] There is no remembrance of people of old,
>   and even those who are yet to come
> will not be remembered
>   by those who follow them.

Wisdom Is Meaningless

[12] I, the Teacher, was king over Israel in Jerusalem. [13] I applied my mind to study and to explore by wisdom all that is done under the heavens. What a heavy burden God has laid on the human race! [14] I have seen all the things that are done under the sun; all of them are meaningless, a chasing after the wind.

> [15] What is crooked cannot be straightened;
>   what is lacking cannot be counted.

[16] I said to myself, "Look, I have grown and increased in wisdom more than anyone who has ruled over Jerusalem before me; I have experienced much of wisdom and knowledge." [17] Then I applied myself to the understanding of wisdom, and also of madness and folly, but I learned that this, too, is a chasing after the wind.

> [18] For with much wisdom comes much sorrow;
>   the more knowledge, the more grief.

---

[a] *1 Or* the leader of the assembly; *also in verses 2 and 12*

Pleasures Are Meaningless

2 I said to myself, "Come now, I will test you with pleasure to find out what is good." But that also proved to be meaningless. [2]"Laughter," I said, "is madness. And what does pleasure accomplish?" [3]I tried cheering myself with wine, and embracing folly—my mind still guiding me with wisdom. I wanted to see what was good for people to do under the heavens during the few days of their lives.

[4]I undertook great projects: I built houses for myself and planted vineyards. [5]I made gardens and parks and planted all kinds of fruit trees in them. [6]I made reservoirs to water groves of flourishing trees. [7]I bought male and female slaves and had other slaves who were born in my house. I also owned more herds and flocks than anyone in Jerusalem before me. [8]I amassed silver and gold for myself, and the treasure of kings and provinces. I acquired male and female singers, and a harem[a] as well—the delights of a man's heart. [9]I became greater by far than anyone in Jerusalem before me. In all this my wisdom stayed with me.

> [10]I denied myself nothing my eyes desired;
> I refused my heart no pleasure.
> My heart took delight in all my labor,
> and this was the reward for all my toil.
> [11]Yet when I surveyed all that my hands had done
> and what I had toiled to achieve,
> everything was meaningless, a chasing after the wind;
> nothing was gained under the sun.

Wisdom and Folly Are Meaningless

> [12]Then I turned my thoughts to consider wisdom,
> and also madness and folly.
> What more can the king's successor do
> than what has already been done?
> [13]I saw that wisdom is better than folly,
> just as light is better than darkness.
> [14]The wise have eyes in their heads,
> while fools walk in the darkness;
> but I came to realize
> that the same fate overtakes them both.

> [15]Then I said to myself,

> "The fate of the fool will overtake me also.
> What then do I gain by being wise?"
> I said to myself,
> "This too is meaningless."
> [16]For the wise, like the fool, will not be long remembered;
> the days have already come when both have been forgotten.
> Like the fool, the wise too must die!

conversations

dissatisfaction «» 2:1–2

1» Why does chasing after pleasure leave you feeling dissatisfied?

2» How would you picture a truly satisfied life?

3» What in your life causes you to feel dissatisfied?

For more on **dissatisfaction**, check the index.
For the next Conversations, go to p. 922.

921

---

a 8 The meaning of the Hebrew for this phrase is uncertain.

Toil Is Meaningless

[17] So I hated life, because the work that is done under the sun was grievous to me. All of it is meaningless, a chasing after the wind. [18] I hated all the things I had toiled for under the sun, because I must leave them to the one who comes after me. [19] And who knows whether that person will be wise or foolish? Yet they will have control over all the toil into which I have poured my effort and skill under the sun. This too is meaningless. [20] So my heart began to despair over all my toilsome labor under the sun. [21] For people may labor with wisdom, knowledge and skill, and then they must leave all they own to others who have not toiled for it. This too is meaningless and a great misfortune. [22] What do people get for all the toil and anxious striving with which they labor under the sun? [23] All their days their work is grief and pain; even at night their minds do not rest. This too is meaningless.

[24] People can do nothing better than to eat and drink and find satisfaction in their toil. This too, I see, is from the hand of God, [25] for without him, who can eat or find enjoyment? [26] To the person who pleases him, God gives wisdom, knowledge and happiness, but to the sinner he gives the task of gathering and storing up wealth to hand it over to the one who pleases God. This too is meaningless, a chasing after the wind.

A Time for Everything

3 There is a time for everything,
and a season for every activity under the heavens:

[2]   a time to be born and a time to die,
    a time to plant and a time to uproot,
[3]   a time to kill and a time to heal,
    a time to tear down and a time to build,
[4]   a time to weep and a time to laugh,
    a time to mourn and a time to dance,
[5]   a time to scatter stones and a time to gather them,
    a time to embrace and a time to refrain,
[6]   a time to search and a time to give up,
    a time to keep and a time to throw away,
[7]   a time to tear and a time to mend,
    a time to be silent and a time to speak,
[8]   a time to love and a time to hate,
    a time for war and a time for peace.

[9] What do workers gain from their toil? [10] I have seen the burden God has laid on the human race. [11] He has made everything beautiful in its time. He has also set eternity in the human heart; yet no one can fathom what God has done from beginning to end. [12] I know that there is nothing better for people than to be happy and to do good while they live. [13] That each of them may eat and drink, and find satisfaction in all their toil—this is the gift of God. [14] I know that everything God does will endure forever; nothing can be added to it and nothing taken from it. God does it so that people will fear him.

[15] Whatever is has already been,
  and what will be has been before;
  and God will call the past to account.[a]

conversations

infertility «» 3:10–14

1» How does our timing often differ from God's timing?

2» What makes dealing with infertility so difficult?

3» Could God make even infertility beautiful in his timing? How?

For more on infertility, check the index.
For the next Conversations, go to p. 944.

---

[a] 15 Or God calls back the past

¹⁶ And I saw something else under the sun:

> In the place of judgment—wickedness was there,
>> in the place of justice—wickedness was there.

¹⁷ I said to myself,

> "God will bring into judgment
>> both the righteous and the wicked,
> for there will be a time for every activity,
>> a time to judge every deed."

¹⁸ I also said to myself, "As for human beings, God tests them so that they may see that they are like the animals. ¹⁹ Surely the fate of human beings is like that of the animals; the same fate awaits them both: As one dies, so dies the other. All have the same breath^a; humans have no advantage over animals. Everything is meaningless. ²⁰ All go to the same place; all come from dust, and to dust all return. ²¹ Who knows if the human spirit rises upward and if the spirit of the animal goes down into the earth?"

²² So I saw that there is nothing better for people than to enjoy their work, because that is their lot. For who can bring them to see what will happen after them?

Oppression, Toil, Friendlessness

4 Again I looked and saw all the oppression that was taking place under the sun:

923

> I saw the tears of the oppressed—
>> and they have no comforter;
> power was on the side of their oppressors—
>> and they have no comforter.
> ² And I declared that the dead,
>> who had already died,
> are happier than the living,
>> who are still alive.
> ³ But better than both
>> is the one who has not yet been,
> who has not seen the evil
>> that is done under the sun.

⁴ And I saw that all toil and all achievement spring from one person's envy of another. This too is meaningless, a chasing after the wind.

> ⁵ Fools fold their hands
>> and ruin themselves.
> ⁶ Better one handful with tranquillity
>> than two handfuls with toil
>> and chasing after the wind.

⁷ Again I saw something meaningless under the sun:

> ⁸ There was a man all alone;
>> he had neither son nor brother.
> There was no end to his toil,
>> yet his eyes were not content with his wealth.
> "For whom am I toiling," he asked,
>> "and why am I depriving myself of enjoyment?"

---

^a 19 Or *spirit*

This too is meaningless—
a miserable business!

[9]Two are better than one,
because they have a good return for
their labor:
[10]If they fall down,
they can help each other up.
But pity those who fall
and have no one to help them up!
[11]Also, if two lie down together, they will
keep warm.
But how can one keep warm alone?
[12]Though one may be overpowered,
two can defend themselves.
A cord of three strands is not quickly
broken.

Advancement Is Meaningless

[13]Better a poor but wise youth than an old but foolish king who no longer knows how to heed a warning. [14]The youth may have come from prison to the kingship, or he may have been born in poverty within his kingdom. [15]I saw that all who lived and walked under the sun followed the youth, the king's successor. [16]There was no end to all the people who were before them. But those who came later were not pleased with the successor. This too is meaningless, a chasing after the wind.

924

atissue:husband's friends

4:9–12 We all need friends to encourage and support us in life. Yet many a husband feels his wife is the only friend he needs. How can you encourage your husband to build deep friendships with other guys? Make time in your schedule for him to spend time with his male friends. Notice which friends he connects with, and support his efforts to spend time with those men. Encourage him to join a men's small group. Pray for him to find true friendship and accountability with other men. And remind him that while two are better than one, a cord of *three* strands is even better.

Fulfill Your Vow to God

5 *Guard your steps when you go to the house of God. Go near to listen rather than to offer the sacrifice of fools, who do not know that they do wrong.

*[2]Do not be quick with your mouth,
do not be hasty in your heart
to utter anything before God.
God is in heaven
and you are on earth,
so let your words be few.
[3]A dream comes when there are many cares,
and many words mark the speech of a fool.

[4]When you make a vow to God, do not delay to fulfill it. He has no pleasure in fools; fulfill your vow. [5]It is better not to make a vow than to make one and not fulfill it. [6]Do not let your mouth lead you into sin. And do not protest to the temple messenger, "My vow was a mistake." Why should God be angry at what you say and destroy the work of your hands? [7]Much dreaming and many words are meaningless. Therefore fear God.

Riches Are Meaningless

[8]If you see the poor oppressed in a district, and justice and rights denied, do not be surprised at such things; for one official is eyed by a higher one, and over them both are others higher still. [9]The increase from the land is taken by all; the king himself profits from the fields.

---

* 5:1 is numbered 4:17 in Hebrew texts.   * 5:2-20 is numbered 5:1-19 in Hebrew texts.

HE IS: listening

5:4–7 The Teacher cautions against making a vow to God without quickly following through. Those who don't fulfill their promises to him are considered fools in his eyes. God would rather his people keep silent than make promises they can't keep.

Do you foolishly make promises? *God, if you give me this, I promise to ____. God, if you get me out of this mess, I'll never do ____ again.* Remember, he is *listening* and holds you accountable for every word you utter. If you can't do what you say, don't say anything at all (see Matthew 5:33–36).

For the next He Is, go to p. 930.

¹⁰Those who love money never have enough;
    those who love wealth are never satisfied with their income.
    This too is meaningless.

¹¹As goods increase,
    so do those who consume them.
And what benefit are they to the owners
    except to feast their eyes on them?

¹²The sleep of laborers is sweet,
    whether they eat little or much,
but the abundance of the rich
    permits them no sleep.

¹³I have seen a grievous evil under the sun:

    wealth hoarded to the harm of its owners,
¹⁴ or wealth lost through some misfortune,
so that when they have children
    there is nothing left for them to inherit.
¹⁵Everyone comes naked from their mother's womb,
    and as everyone comes, so they depart.
They take nothing from their toil
    that they can carry in their hands.

¹⁶This too is a grievous evil:

    As everyone comes, so they depart,
    and what do they gain,
    since they toil for the wind?
¹⁷All their days they eat in darkness,
    with great frustration, affliction and anger.

¹⁸This is what I have observed to be good: that it is appropriate for people to eat, to drink and to find satisfaction in their toilsome labor under the sun during the few days of life God has given them—for this is their lot. ¹⁹Moreover, when God gives people wealth and possessions, and the ability to enjoy them, to accept their lot and be happy in their toil—this is a gift of God. ²⁰They seldom reflect on the days of their lives, because God keeps them occupied with gladness of heart.

6 I have seen another evil under the sun, and it weighs heavily on the human race: ²God gives some people wealth, possessions and honor, so that they lack nothing their hearts desire, but God does not grant the ability to enjoy them, and strangers enjoy them instead. This is meaningless, a grievous evil.

925

³A man may have a hundred children and live many years; yet no matter how long he lives, if he cannot enjoy his prosperity and does not receive proper burial, I say that a stillborn child is better off than he. ⁴It comes without meaning, it departs in darkness, and in darkness its name is shrouded. ⁵Though it never saw the sun or knew anything, it has more rest than does that man— ⁶even if he lives a thousand years twice over but fails to enjoy his prosperity. Do not all go to the same place?

⁷Everyone's toil is for the mouth,
    yet the appetite is never satisfied.
⁸What advantage have the wise over
        fools?
What do the poor gain
    by knowing how to conduct
        themselves before others?
⁹Better what the eye sees
    than the roving of the appetite.
This too is meaningless,
    a chasing after the wind.

¹⁰Whatever exists has already been
        named,
    and what humanity is has been
        known;
no one can contend
    with someone who is stronger.
¹¹The more the words,
    the less the meaning,
    and how does that profit anyone?

¹²For who knows what is good for people in life, during the few and meaningless days they pass through like a shadow? Who can tell them what will happen under the sun after they are gone?

Wisdom

7

A good name is better than fine perfume,
    and the day of death better than the day of birth.
²It is better to go to a house of mourning
    than to go to a house of feasting,
for death is the destiny of everyone;
    the living should take this to heart.
³Frustration is better than laughter,
    because a sad face is good for the heart.
⁴The heart of the wise is in the house of mourning,
    but the heart of fools is in the house of pleasure.
⁵It is better to heed the rebuke of a wise person
    than to listen to the song of fools.
⁶Like the crackling of thorns under the pot,
    so is the laughter of fools.
    This too is meaningless.

⁷Extortion turns the wise into fools,
    and a bribe corrupts the heart.

atissue:credit card debt

6:1–9 *CHARGE IT!* is the battle cry of our generation. *If you buy it, you'll be happy.* Our culture tells us we need more—in fact, we *deserve* more—and we won't be truly happy until we get it. We've somehow missed the fine print: *Money cannot buy happiness. No matter how much stuff you acquire, it never feels like enough. When you die, you can't take it with you.* Credit card debt enslaves us and feeds our unhappiness; true financial freedom comes when we learn to be content with what we have and pin our hopes on God, not possessions.

⁸The end of a matter is better than its
   beginning,
   and patience is better than pride.
⁹Do not be quickly provoked in your spirit,
   for anger resides in the lap of fools.

¹⁰Do not say, "Why were the old days better
   than these?"
   For it is not wise to ask such questions.

¹¹Wisdom, like an inheritance, is a good
   thing
   and benefits those who see the sun.
¹²Wisdom is a shelter
   as money is a shelter,
but the advantage of knowledge is this:
   Wisdom preserves the life of its
   possessor.

¹³Consider what God has done:

   Who can straighten
   what he has made crooked?
¹⁴When times are good, be happy;
   but when times are bad, consider:
God has made the one
   as well as the other.
Therefore, you cannot discover
   anything about your future.

¹⁵In this meaningless life of mine I have seen both of these:

   the righteous perishing in their righteousness,
   and the wicked living long in their wickedness.
¹⁶Do not be overrighteous,
   neither be overwise—
   why destroy yourself?
¹⁷Do not be overwicked,
   and do not be a fool—
   why die before your time?
¹⁸It is good to grasp the one
   and not let go of the other.
   Whoever fears God will avoid all extremes.ᵃ

¹⁹Wisdom makes one wise person more powerful
   than ten rulers in a city.

²⁰Indeed, there is no one on earth who is righteous,
   no one who does what is right and never sins.

²¹Do not pay attention to every word people say,
   or you may hear your servant cursing you—
²²for you know in your heart
   that many times you yourself have cursed others.

---

a tissue: impatience

7:8–9 Do your children push buttons you didn't even know you had? Does your fuse seem to be getting shorter as the demands on you become greater? Do you grow quickly frustrated over even small things? As the volume and intensity of your voice go up, do you wonder, *Who is this angry person I've become?* If so, then it's time to slow down. Carve out some quiet time each day to focus on God's grace and mercy and his infinite patience towards you. Confess your quick, unfounded anger. And ask God to help you be patient with others, as he's been with you.

927

ᵃ *18 Or will follow them both*

²³ All this I tested by wisdom and I said,

> "I am determined to be wise"—
> but this was beyond me.
> ²⁴ Whatever exists is far off and most profound—
> who can discover it?
> ²⁵ So I turned my mind to understand,
> to investigate and to search out wisdom and the scheme of things
> and to understand the stupidity of wickedness
> and the madness of folly.

> ²⁶ I find more bitter than death
> the woman who is a snare,
> whose heart is a trap
> and whose hands are chains.
> The man who pleases God will escape her,
> but the sinner she will ensnare.

²⁷ "Look," says the Teacher,ᵃ "this is what I have discovered:

> "Adding one thing to another to discover the scheme of things—
> ²⁸   while I was still searching
> but not finding—
> I found one ⌊upright⌋ man among a thousand,
> but not one ⌊upright⌋ woman among them all.
> ²⁹ This only have I found:
> God created humankind upright,
> but they have gone in search of many schemes."

8
> Who is like the wise?
> Who knows the explanation of things?
> Wisdom brightens the face
> and changes its hard appearance.

Obey the King

² Obey the king's command, I say, because you took an oath before God. ³ Do not be in a hurry to leave the king's presence. Do not stand up for a bad cause, for he will do whatever he pleases. ⁴ Since a king's word is supreme, who can say to him, "What are you doing?"

> ⁵ Whoever obeys his command will come to no harm,
> and the wise heart will know the proper time and procedure.
> ⁶ For there is a proper time and procedure for every matter,
> though a person may be weighed down by misery.

> ⁷ Since no one knows the future,
> who can say what is to come?
> ⁸ As no one has power over the wind to contain it,
> soᵇ no one has power over the time of their death.
> As no one is discharged in time of war,
> so wickedness will not release those who practice it.

⁹ All this I saw, as I applied my mind to everything done under the sun. There is a time when a man lords it over others to his ownᶜ hurt. ¹⁰ Then too, I saw the wicked buried—those who used to come and go from the holy place and receive praiseᵈ in the city where they did this. This too is meaningless.

ᵃ *27 Or the leader of the assembly*   ᵇ *8 Or over the human spirit to retain it, / and so*   ᶜ *9 Or to their*   ᵈ *10 Some Hebrew manuscripts and Septuagint (Aquila); most Hebrew manuscripts and are forgotten*

[11]When the sentence for a crime is not quickly carried out, people's hearts are filled with schemes to do wrong. [12]Although a wicked person who commits a hundred crimes may live a long time, I know that it will go better with those who fear God, who are reverent before him. [13]Yet because the wicked do not fear God, it will not go well with them, and their days will not lengthen like a shadow.

[14]There is something else meaningless that occurs on earth: the righteous who get what the wicked deserve, and the wicked who get what the righteous deserve. This too, I say, is meaningless. [15]So I commend the enjoyment of life, because there is nothing better for people under the sun than to eat and drink and be glad. Then joy will accompany them in their toil all the days of the life God has given them under the sun.

[16]When I applied my mind to know wisdom and to observe the labor that is done on earth—people getting no sleep day or night— [17]then I saw all that God has done. No one can comprehend what goes on under the sun. People toil to search it out, but no one can discover its meaning. Even if the wise claim they know, they cannot really comprehend it.

A Common Destiny for All

9 So I reflected on all this and concluded that the righteous and the wise and what they do are in God's hands, but no one knows whether love or hate awaits them. [2]All share a common destiny—the righteous and the wicked, the good and the bad,[a] the clean and the unclean, those who offer sacrifices and those who do not.

> As it is with the good,
>   so with the sinful;
> as it is with those who take oaths,
>   so with those who are afraid to take them.

[3]This is the evil in everything that happens under the sun: The same destiny overtakes all. The hearts of people, moreover, are full of evil and there is madness in their hearts while they live, and afterward they join the dead. [4]Anyone who is among the living has hope[b]—even a live dog is better off than a dead lion!

> [5]For the living know that they will die,
>   but the dead know nothing;
> they have no further reward,
>   and even their name is forgotten.
> [6]Their love, their hate
>   and their jealousy have long since vanished;
> never again will they have a part
>   in anything that happens under the sun.

[7]Go, eat your food with gladness, and drink your wine with a joyful heart, for God has already approved what you do. [8]Always be clothed in white, and always anoint your head with oil. [9]Enjoy life with your wife, whom you love, all the days of this meaningless life that God has given you under the sun—all your meaningless days. For this is your lot in life and in your toilsome labor under the sun.

---

atissue:cynicism

8:11–15 At some point as a child, you probably got punished for a "crime" another kid committed. That may have been your first experience with injustice— but certainly not your last. Wrongdoers often get away with their crimes and prosper. And those who follow the rules often have nothing to show for it. It's easy to grow cynical and wonder if doing the right thing is worth it. *Since life isn't fair, you might think, I'd better stand up for myself and grab whatever I can get.* While God's justice may appear slow, it's sure. Don't grow cynical while you're waiting for God's justice.

929

---

[a] 2 Septuagint (Aquila), Vulgate and Syriac; Hebrew does not have *and the bad*.   [b] 4 Or *What then is to be chosen? With all who live, there is hope*

HE IS: monogamous

9:9–10 Though Solomon had many wives, he realized that true fulfillment in marriage comes from a *monogamous* relationship. God established marriage as a relationship between one man and one woman for life. When this divine pattern is followed, you can enjoy life with your husband, whom you love.

Marriage is a picture of God's relationship with his bride, the church. God is *monogamous* in his affections toward his church and his people—he will never be unfaithful; he will never divorce you; he will always love you. He is the husband who will never disappoint you (see also Hosea 2:19–20).

For the next He Is, go to p. 940.

[930]

[10]Whatever your hand finds to do, do it with all your might, for in the realm of the dead, where you are going, there is neither working nor planning nor knowledge nor wisdom.

[11]I have seen something else under the sun:

> The race is not to the swift
>   or the battle to the strong,
> nor does food come to the wise
>   or wealth to the brilliant
>   or favor to the learned;
> but time and chance happen to them all.

[12]Moreover, no one knows when their hour will come:

> As fish are caught in a cruel net,
>   or birds are taken in a snare,
> so people are trapped by evil times
>   that fall unexpectedly upon them.

Wisdom Better Than Folly

[13]I also saw under the sun this example of wisdom that greatly impressed me: [14]There was once a small city with only a few people in it. And a powerful king came against it, surrounded it and built huge siege works against it. [15]Now there lived in that city a man poor but wise, and he saved the city by his wisdom. But nobody remembered that poor man. [16]So I said, "Wisdom is better than strength." But the poor man's wisdom is despised, and his words are no longer heeded.

> [17]The quiet words of the wise are more to be heeded
>   than the shouts of a ruler of fools.
> [18]Wisdom is better than weapons of war,
>   but one sinner destroys much good.

10

> As dead flies give perfume a bad smell,
>   so a little folly outweighs wisdom and honor.
> [2]The heart of the wise inclines to the right,
>   but the heart of the fool to the left.
> [3]Even as fools walk along the road,
>   they lack sense
>   and show everyone how stupid they are.
> [4]If a ruler's anger rises against you,
>   do not leave your post;
>   calmness can lay great offenses to rest.

ASKmeanYTHING

You certainly experienced an incredible rise to power, didn't you?

One moment I was an anonymous Jewish girl without a country and without parents. All I had going for me was my appearance. The next thing I knew I was taken into the king's harem along with many other girls. We were all to receive beauty treatments and pampering for 12 months before being brought to the king. When the time came to choose a new queen, the king chose me.

But then you were asked to risk it all, weren't you?

931

Yes, I was. Let me explain. Throughout this entire crazy chain of events, my cousin Mordecai was my sounding board, my mentor. He helped me keep my head on straight and grounded me in our faith—even though he told me to keep my Jewish heritage a secret. But when the situation became life-threatening for the Jews, Mordecai told me it was time to speak up for our people. He wanted me to go and ask the king to spare our people. But no one—not even I, the queen—was allowed to approach the king unless he initiated it. The penalty was death.

What made you decide to go ahead and speak to the king?

It was something Mordecai said to me. "And who knows but that you have come to royal position for such a time as this?" *For such a time as this.* It made me stop and think. I mean, have you ever wondered why your life is a certain way, why you're working with a certain person, or living next to a difficult neighbor, or going through a particular trial? *For such a time as this.* I certainly had wondered, but now it seemed clear to me. Everything that God had given to me—my looks, my position, my relatives, my nationality, my influence—all led up to this one event, this one moment. I couldn't let it go by. I had to speak up.

Not many of us will be called to step up and save an entire group of people. Or become queen. So what can we learn from your life?

Don't look at your life as just a series of random events. God has a plan for everyone and for every situation in your life. Understand that the resources you have, the people in your life, the experiences you have had, everything is for a reason. Consider how all these elements in your life can be used to serve God's purpose.

FOR MORE INSIGHT: Read more about God's incredible plans for you in Psalm 40:5; Jeremiah 29:11; Ephesians 2:10; and Philippians 2:13.

myth# 56 "CHRISTIANS SHOULDN'T TOUCH ALCOHOL."

I feel guilty if I don't feel guilty. And then sometimes I wonder, Why do I feel so guilty?

It's not as if I actually get drunk. In fact, I can't even say what it's like to have a hard buzz. Every month or so, my friends at work talk me into going out with them to their favorite jazz club. I love listening to the live music, and it's a great time to talk and just relax.

I can never seem to resist the frozen drinks. If everyone is having one, I give in and have one too. The names alone are enough to tempt me— Paradise Slush, Mocha Mudslide, Mango Margarita. And the little straws, colorful tiki umbrellas and cool glasses they come in are so cute.

It's not as if I'm guzzling hard liquor out of a paper sack. Even though my work friends think nothing of ordering two, three, six drinks, I'm content to nurse one or two all night. But I still end up feeling sinful when I'm in a cab on the way home.

I know that if my friends at church knew I drink, even a little, they'd be shocked. I know none of them would dare touch a drop of alcohol. I'm almost losing sleep over this issue, partly because I'm not convinced that what I'm doing is wrong and partly because I fear other people will think it is wrong. Maybe I should confess to the pastor . . . no, he would probably bring it up in a sermon.

I've been taught that real Christians shouldn't touch alcohol . . . right?

—Erica

IN CHRISTIAN CIRCLES

you won't find a definitive answer on the hot topic of social drinking. Many good, thoughtful Christians have conflicting views on alcohol.

What we do know is that the Bible clearly forbids drunkenness (see Ephesians 5:18). God also warns us against becoming a slave to anything (see 2 Peter 2:19). If you use alcohol to lower your inhibitions so you feel better about yourself, or if you're dependent on it to dull the pain of your problems or if you feel like you *need* alcohol, then you're a slave to it. And God warns against such actions.

But what about drinking alcohol in moderation? Some Christians' personal views and interpretation of Scripture lead them to completely abstain from alcohol. Other Christians believe responsible social drinking is acceptable. As you think through the issue for yourself, keep these principles in mind:

- Jesus turned water into wine (see John 2:1–11), and Paul advised Timothy to drink a little wine for health benefits (see 1 Timothy 5:23). *You may want to avoid a legalistic stance on this issue.*

- Paul cautioned Christians not to pass judgment on "disputable matters" for the sake of the greater good of the community (see Romans 14:1–15:3). If it distressed members of the community for Christians to eat the sacrificed meat, then they should be willing to do without it. And neither group should pass judgment on the other. *If your drinking unduly upsets your Christian friends, forego it.*

- If you drink in moderation, does that convey to your non-Christian friends that you're no different than they are? Or does it show them that Christ cares about heart issues, not legalistic issues? *Think through the message you're sending to non-Christians.*

- If you feel guilty about drinking, then pray that the Holy Spirit would clearly speak to

you. *If he is prompting you not to drink, then don't drink.*

- A position of leadership in the church or a sensitive family situation (like a history of alcoholism) may lead you to take a strict personal stand on this issue. *Ask God what standards he wants you to set regarding social drinking.*

The conclusion? Read the Scriptures and let the Holy Spirit guide you as you make decisions on this sensitive issue.

933

"32 percent of Christians say they drank an alcoholic beverage within the last month."
——Barna Research Group (1997)

"IT IS BETTER NOT TO EAT MEAT OR DRINK WINE OR TO DO ANYTHING ELSE THAT WILL CAUSE YOUR BROTHER OR SISTER TO FALL."

ROMANS 14:21

SEE ALSO

Psalm 73:24
Proverbs 20:1
Proverbs 23:31–35

For more on **Alcohol**, check the index.

934

⁵There is an evil I have seen under the sun,
   the sort of error that arises from a ruler:
⁶Fools are put in many high positions,
   while the rich occupy the low ones.
⁷I have seen slaves on horseback,
   while princes go on foot like slaves.

⁸Whoever digs a pit may fall into it;
   whoever breaks through a wall may be bitten by a snake.
⁹Whoever quarries stones may be injured by them;
   whoever splits logs may be endangered by them.

¹⁰If the ax is dull
   and its edge unsharpened,
more strength is needed,
   but skill will bring success.

¹¹If a snake bites before it is charmed,
   the charmer receives no fee.

¹²Words from the mouth of the wise are gracious,
   but fools are consumed by their own lips.
¹³At the beginning their words are folly;
   at the end they are wicked madness—
¹⁴   and fools multiply words.

No one knows what is coming—
   who can tell them what will happen after them?

¹⁵The toil of fools wearies them;
   they do not know the way to town.

¹⁶Woe to the land whose king was a servant^a
   and whose princes feast in the morning.
¹⁷Blessed is the land whose king is of noble birth
   and whose princes eat at a proper time—
   for strength and not for drunkenness.

¹⁸Through laziness, the rafters sag;
   because of idle hands, the house leaks.

¹⁹A feast is made for laughter,
   wine makes life merry,
   and money is the answer for everything.

²⁰Do not revile the king even in your thoughts,
   or curse the rich in your bedroom,
because a bird in the sky may carry your words,
   and a bird on the wing may report what you say.

Invest in Many Ventures

11 Ship your grain across the sea;
   after many days you may receive a return.
²Invest in seven ventures, yes, in eight;
   you do not know what disaster may come upon the land.

---

^a 16 Or *king is a child*

³If clouds are full of water,
    they pour rain on the earth.
Whether a tree falls to the south or to the north,
    in the place where it falls, there it will lie.
⁴Whoever watches the wind will not plant;
    whoever looks at the clouds will not reap.

⁵As you do not know the path of the wind,
    or how the body is formed*ᵃ* in a mother's womb,
so you cannot understand the work of God,
    the Maker of all things.

⁶Sow your seed in the morning,
    and at evening let your hands not be idle,
for you do not know which will succeed,
    whether this or that,
    or whether both will do equally well.

Remember Your Creator While Young

⁷Light is sweet,
    and it pleases the eyes to see the sun.
⁸However many years anyone may live,
    let them enjoy them all.
But let them remember the days of darkness,
    for there will be many.
    Everything to come is meaningless.

⁹You who are young, be happy while you are young,
    and let your hearts give you joy in the days of your youth.
Follow the ways of your heart
    and whatever your eyes see,
but know that for all these things
    God will bring you into judgment.
¹⁰So then, banish anxiety from your heart
    and cast off the troubles of your body,
    for youth and vigor are meaningless.

12   Remember your Creator
    in the days of your youth,
before the days of trouble come
    and the years approach when you will say,
    "I find no pleasure in them"—
²before the sun and the light
    and the moon and the stars grow dark,
    and the clouds return after the rain;
³when the keepers of the house tremble,
    and the strong men stoop,
when the grinders cease because they are few,
    and those looking through the windows grow dim;
⁴when the doors to the street are closed
    and the sound of grinding fades;
when people rise up at the sound of birds,
    but all their songs grow faint;

935

ᵃ 5 Or know how life (or the spirit) / enters the body being formed

⁵when people are afraid of heights
  and of dangers in the streets;
when the almond tree blossoms
  and the grasshopper drags itself along
  and desire no longer is stirred.
Then people go to their eternal home
  and mourners go about the streets.

⁶Remember him—before the silver cord is severed,
  and the golden bowl is broken;
before the pitcher is shattered at the spring,
  and the wheel broken at the well,
⁷and the dust returns to the ground it came from,
  and the spirit returns to God who
    gave it.

⁸"Meaningless! Meaningless!" says the
    Teacher.ᵃ
  "Everything is meaningless!"

The Conclusion of the Matter

⁹Not only was the Teacher wise, but also he imparted knowledge to the people. He pondered and searched out and set in order many proverbs. ¹⁰The Teacher searched to find just the right words, and what he wrote was upright and true.

¹¹The words of the wise are like goads, their collected sayings like firmly embedded nails—given by one shepherd.ᵇ ¹²Be warned, my son, of anything in addition to them.

Of making many books there is no end, and much study wearies the body.

¹³Now all has been heard;
    here is the conclusion of the matter:
Fear God and keep his commandments,
    for this is the ᵗduty of every human
      being.
¹⁴For God will bring every deed into
      judgment,
    including every hidden thing,
    whether it is good or evil.

12:13–14 Solomon looked for meaning in life through riches, success, power, pleasure, knowledge and relationships, but he found that everything is meaningless—*when it's enjoyed apart from God.* Life without God is like buying a gorgeous new dress that you're excited to wear, but then you realize it's three sizes too small. As beautiful as the dress is, there's no point in owning it. Do you want your life to have lasting meaning and true purpose? Then fear God and keep his commands—love him and love others with all that you are. Only then can you truly enjoy everything in life.

aussie: the meaning of life

ᵃ *8 Or the leader of the assembly; also in verses 9 and 10*   ᵇ *11 Or Shepherd*

song of songs

AUTHOR
Probably King Solomon.

AUDIENCE
All Israel.

DATE
Most likely early in Solomon's reign, around 965 B.C.

SETTING
Storybook romance and steamy dialogue between two God-fearing, passionate lovers.

VERSE TO REMEMBER
"Place me like a seal over your heart, like a seal on your arm; for love is as strong as death, its jealousy as unyielding as the grave. It burns like blazing fire, like a mighty flame." (8:6)

THEME TO CONSIDER
God created the sexual relationship as a good and beautiful thing. Within the bounds of a committed marriage there's great freedom to enjoy your husband in a passionate, sensual way.

1 Solomon's Song of Songs.

She[a]

²Let him kiss me with the kisses of his mouth—
　　for your love is more delightful than wine.
³Pleasing is the fragrance of your perfumes;
　　your name is like perfume poured
　　　　out.
　　No wonder the young women love
　　　　you!
⁴Take me away with you—let us hurry!
　　Let the king bring me into his
　　　　chambers.

Friends

We rejoice and delight in you[b];
　　we will praise your love more than
　　　　wine.

She

How right they are to adore you!

⁵Dark am I, yet lovely,
　　daughters of Jerusalem,
　　dark like the tents of Kedar,
　　　　like the tent curtains of Solomon.[c]
⁶Do not stare at me because I am dark,
　　because I am darkened by the sun.
　　My mother's sons were angry with me
　　　　and made me take care of the
　　　　　　vineyards;
　　my own vineyard I had to neglect.
⁷Tell me, you whom I love,
　　where you graze your flock
　　and where you rest your sheep at
　　　　midday.
　　Why should I be like a veiled woman
　　　　beside the flocks of your friends?

Friends

⁸If you do not know, most beautiful of women,
　　follow the tracks of the sheep
　　and graze your young goats
　　　　by the tents of the shepherds.

He

⁹I liken you, my darling, to a mare
　　among Pharaoh's chariot horses.
¹⁰Your cheeks are beautiful with earrings,
　　your neck with strings of jewels.
¹¹We will make you earrings of gold,
　　studded with silver.

at issue: sex

1:1—2:6 God designed your sexuality to be like a plant that only flourishes in the right greenhouse. That greenhouse is marriage. God wants you to enjoy your husband's caresses, to long for his arms around you and to find comfort, joy and strength in your sexual relationship. If you're just enduring sex rather than enjoying it, then you need to talk to your husband. Is there an underlying problem in your marriage that's interfering? Are unresolved issues from your past choking out your pleasure? Are there things your husband could do differently? When you talk openly about your sex life, it will flourish.

---

[a] The main male and female speakers (identified primarily on the basis of the gender of the relevant Hebrew forms) are indicated by the captions *He* and *She* respectively. The words of others are marked *Friends*. In some instances the divisions and their captions are debatable.　　[b] 4 The Hebrew is masculine singular.
[c] 5 Or *Salma*

938

She

¹²While the king was at his table,
    my perfume spread its fragrance.
¹³My beloved is to me a sachet of myrrh
    resting between my breasts.
¹⁴My beloved is to me a cluster of henna blossoms
    from the vineyards of En Gedi.

He

¹⁵How beautiful you are, my darling!
    Oh, how beautiful!
    Your eyes are doves.

She

¹⁶How handsome you are, my beloved!
    Oh, how charming!
    And our bed is verdant.

He

¹⁷The beams of our house are cedars;
    our rafters are firs.

939

Sheᵃ

2 I am a roseᵇ of Sharon,
    a lily of the valleys.

He

²Like a lily among thorns
    is my darling among the young women.

She

³Like an appleᶜ tree among the trees of the forest
    is my beloved among the young men.
 I delight to sit in his shade,
    and his fruit is sweet to my taste.
⁴Let him lead me to the banquet hall,
    and let his banner over me be love.
⁵Strengthen me with raisins,
    refresh me with apples,
    for I am faint with love.
⁶His left arm is under my head,
    and his right arm embraces me.
⁷Daughters of Jerusalem, I charge you
    by the gazelles and by the does of the field:
 Do not arouse or awaken love
    until it so desires.

⁸Listen! My beloved!
    Look! Here he comes,
 leaping across the mountains,
    bounding over the hills.
⁹My beloved is like a gazelle or a young stag.
    Look! There he stands behind our wall,

ᵃ Or *He* ᵇ *1* Probably a member of the crocus family ᶜ *3* Or possibly *apricot*; here and elsewhere in Song of Songs

gazing through the windows,
    peering through the lattice.
¹⁰My beloved spoke and said to me,
    "Arise, my darling,
    my beautiful one, come with me.
¹¹See! The winter is past;
    the rains are over and gone.
¹²Flowers appear on the earth;
    the season of singing has come,
the cooing of doves
    is heard in our land.
¹³The fig tree forms its early fruit;
    the blossoming vines spread their fragrance.
Arise, come, my darling;
    my beautiful one, come with me."

HE IS: my beloved

2:8–13 Solomon's song tells of the passionate love between a man and a woman, which also symbolizes Christ's intense love for his church. In beautiful, poetic dialogue, the lovers express their feelings. Those in a personal relationship with Christ can also call him *my beloved*. In turn, he calls you *my darling, my beautiful one*.

Perhaps you've never thought of Jesus as your *lover*. You know that he's your Savior and your friend. But you should also understand that he loves you personally and passionately. If you've let your feelings grow cold, he cries: "Arise, my darling, my beautiful one, come with me."

For the next He Is, go to p. 969.

He

¹⁴My dove in the clefts of the rock,
    in the hiding places on the mountainside,
show me your face,
    let me hear your voice;
for your voice is sweet,
    and your face is lovely.
¹⁵Catch for us the foxes,
    the little foxes
that ruin the vineyards,
    our vineyards that are in bloom.

She

¹⁶My beloved is mine and I am his;
    he browses among the lilies.
¹⁷Until the day breaks
    and the shadows flee,
turn, my beloved,
    and be like a gazelle
or like a young stag
    on the rugged hills.ᵃ

ᵃ 17 Or *the hills of Bether*

3 All night long on my bed
    I looked for the one my heart loves;
    I looked for him but did not find him.
²I will get up now and go about the city,
    through its streets and squares;
I will search for the one my heart loves.
    So I looked for him but did not find him.
³The watchmen found me
    as they made their rounds in the city.
    "Have you seen the one my heart loves?"
⁴Scarcely had I passed them
    when I found the one my heart loves.
I held him and would not let him go
    till I had brought him to my mother's house,
    to the room of the one who conceived me.
⁵Daughters of Jerusalem, I charge you
    by the gazelles and by the does of the
        field:
Do not arouse or awaken love
    until it so desires.

⁶Who is this coming up from the wilderness
    like a column of smoke,
perfumed with myrrh and incense
    made from all the spices of the
        merchant?
⁷Look! It is Solomon's carriage,
    escorted by sixty warriors,
    the noblest of Israel,
⁸all of them wearing the sword,
    all experienced in battle,
each with his sword at his side,
    prepared for the terrors of the night.
⁹King Solomon made for himself the
        carriage;
    he made it of wood from Lebanon.
¹⁰Its posts he made of silver,
    its base of gold.
Its seat was upholstered with purple,
    its interior inlaid with love.
Daughters of Jerusalem, ¹¹come out,
    and look, you daughters of Zion.
Look*ᵃ* on King Solomon wearing a crown,
    the crown with which his mother crowned him
on the day of his wedding,
    the day his heart rejoiced.

He
4 How beautiful you are, my darling!
    Oh, how beautiful!
    Your eyes behind your veil are doves.

atissue:dating

3:5 Women spend a lot of time, energy and money trying to make a relationship happen. We agonize over the perfect outfit that will get *his* attention. We spend hours talking with our girlfriends, analyzing his every word and action and spinning ideas for how to keep the relationship going. We flirt, tease and manipulate in order to catch his interest. We're afraid we might miss him if we're not paying attention. Are we going about this all wrong? God tells us to quit trying so hard and wait for *God* to stir the waters of love at the right time and in the right place.

941

ᵃ 10,11 Or *interior lovingly inlaid / by the daughters of Jerusalem. / ¹¹Come out, you daughters of Zion, / and look*

myth# 57 "HAVING A MAN WILL SOLVE MY PROBLEMS."

I cried the whole way home from work last night. It's not unusual. I'm doing it more and more recently. I don't want to go home again to my empty apartment. The loneliness overwhelms me—another dinner-for-one, another evening alone. Sometimes I don't think I can take it one more day. By now, most of my friends have been married for several years. While I'm flipping through channels on the couch, eating supper from a sack, I imagine them with their husbands and children eating a home-cooked meal and catching up on each other's days.

They seem to have everything I don't.

They've had the weddings; I have more bridesmaid dresses in my closet than I care to count.

They've had the babies; I baby-sit when they go out with their husbands for date nights.

They have the beautiful houses. I house-sit while they're on vacation.

Every time I get my car serviced, I curse the fact that I don't have a man in my life. Each time I drive to church alone, I wonder what it would be like to have a man to sit with in worship. When I pay my bills, I wish for a husband to help support me financially. If I could just meet someone, I know I would be happy. He doesn't have to be perfect. He doesn't even have to be tall, dark or handsome. At this point, I'm not that picky.

These are all normal, healthy desires, right? I just can't understand why God is holding out on me. I have prayed and asked him to bring me someone, and he hasn't. It feels like he isn't listening or doesn't care about the fact that I feel so alone. As the birthdays come and go, I feel panic setting in, and I think, What if I never meet anyone?

—Emma

TOO OFTEN WOMEN convince themselves that if they could just have the one thing they don't have, *then* they would be happy. Consider meeting a man, for example. You may think that loneliness would disappear. Financial strain would melt. Your love and intimacy needs would be consistently met. But the reality is that having a man in your life will not solve all of your problems. Life will still have its challenges and difficulties. Being in a relationship means trading in one set of concerns for another.

When you are careful to base your joy on God and not on the circumstances of life, you receive at least four gifts:

- **Freedom.** It comes not when you get everything you want, but when you are content with what God has given you. If you learn to accept whatever circumstances you're in, you'll be free from misleading ideals that drain your energy without any return for your investment.

- **Blessings.** When you look for the good in every situation, you stumble onto blessings you didn't realize you had. Choosing to see blessings that God has given you (even though they might not be the ones you would have chosen for yourself) is a sign of spiritual and emotional maturity.

- **Satisfaction.** Psalm 106:13–15 tells about a time when the Israelites got what they selfishly wanted but missed out on being satisfied with God. Learn a lesson from them. Don't focus so much on what you don't have that you miss the chance to be fully satisfied in God. It's your relationship with God, not with a man, that will bring you true fulfillment.

- **Purpose.** If you are single, do you use your status to glorify and honor God? Or have you put your life on hold, thinking that you'll only be happy when a man comes along? The answer to this question reveals the focus of your heart. Colossians 3:2 tells us to set our hearts on things above instead of earthly things. Are you constantly focusing on your personal life or on God's will?

God can use your struggles to deepen your relationship with him and to teach you lessons about trust and faith that someone who is married could never learn. Will you let this legitimate desire in your life drive you to seek God wholeheartedly?

"More than four out of every ten adults in the United States is not married, producing a singles population that is larger than the total national population of all but eleven of the world's 192 nations."

——Barna Research Group (2002)

"set your mind on things above, not on earthly things."

COLOSSIANS 3:2

SEE ALSO

Psalm 73:25–26

Isaiah 54:5

1 Corinthians 7:32–35

For more on **Dating** and **Loneliness**, check the index.

Your hair is like a flock of goats
  descending from the hills of Gilead.
²Your teeth are like a flock of sheep just shorn,
  coming up from the
    washing.
Each has its twin;
  not one of them is alone.
³Your lips are like a scarlet
    ribbon;
  your mouth is lovely.
Your temples behind your veil
  are like the halves of a
    pomegranate.
⁴Your neck is like the tower of
    David,
  built with courses of stone*ᵃ*;
on it hang a thousand shields,
  all of them shields of
    warriors.
⁵Your breasts are like two
    fawns,
  like twin fawns of a gazelle
  that browse among the lilies.
⁶Until the day breaks
  and the shadows flee,
I will go to the mountain of myrrh
  and to the hill of incense.
⁷All beautiful you are, my darling;
  there is no flaw in you.

⁸Come with me from Lebanon, my bride,
  come with me from Lebanon.
Descend from the crest of Amana,
  from the top of Senir, the summit of Hermon,
from the lions' dens
  and the mountain haunts of leopards.
⁹You have stolen my heart, my sister, my bride;
  you have stolen my heart
with one glance of your eyes,
  with one jewel of your necklace.
¹⁰How delightful is your love, my sister, my bride!
  How much more pleasing is your love than wine,
and the fragrance of your perfume
    more than any spice!
¹¹Your lips drop sweetness as the honeycomb, my bride;
  milk and honey are under your tongue.
The fragrance of your garments
  is like the fragrance of Lebanon.
¹²You are a garden locked up, my sister, my bride;
  you are a spring enclosed, a sealed fountain.

"conversations"

marriage «» 4:1–16

1» Do you think intense sexual passion in a marriage naturally fades over time? Should it?

2» Why is enjoying and taking delight in your spouse so important?

3» If marriage is already a strong bond, then why invest time and energy to protect it?

For more on **marriage**, check the index.
For the next Conversations, go to p. 948.

ᵃ 4 The meaning of the Hebrew for this phrase is uncertain.

¹³Your plants are an orchard of pomegranates
    with choice fruits,
    with henna and nard,
¹⁴ nard and saffron,
    calamus and cinnamon,
    with every kind of incense tree,
    with myrrh and aloes
    and all the finest spices.
¹⁵You are^{*a*} a garden fountain,
    a well of flowing water
    streaming down from Lebanon.

She

¹⁶Awake, north wind,
    and come, south wind!
Blow on my garden,
    that its fragrance may spread abroad.
Let my beloved come into his garden
    and taste its choice fruits.

He

5

I have come into my garden, my sister, my bride;
    I have gathered my myrrh with my spice.
I have eaten my honeycomb and my honey;
    I have drunk my wine and my milk.

Friends

Eat, friends, and drink;
    drink your fill of love.

She

²I slept but my heart was awake.
    Listen! My beloved is knocking:
"Open to me, my sister, my darling,
    my dove, my flawless one.
My head is drenched with dew,
    my hair with the dampness of the night."
³I have taken off my robe—
    must I put it on again?
I have washed my feet—
    must I soil them again?
⁴My beloved thrust his hand through the
       latch-opening;
    my heart began to pound for him.
⁵I arose to open for my beloved,
    and my hands dripped with myrrh,
my fingers with flowing myrrh,
    on the handles of the bolt.
⁶I opened for my beloved,
    but my beloved had left; he was gone.
My heart sank at his departure.^{*b*}
I looked for him but did not find him.

atissue: falling out of love

5:2–8 As a newlywed, you adored your husband and eagerly expressed your love to him. Then the honeymoon ended, and you probably started to take each other for granted. The responsibilities of life weighed you down so that you didn't have the physical or emotional energy you once had to invest in your relationship. Like the woman in this poem, you have come to a crossroads and have a choice: Live with the loss of love or work to find that love again. The woman here passionately pursues her lover as if her life depended on it. Will you?

945

---

^{*a*} *15* Or *I am* (spoken by *She*) ^{*b*} *6* Or *heart had gone out to him when he spoke*

I called him but he did not answer.
⁷The watchmen found me
　　as they made their rounds in the city.
They beat me, they bruised me;
　　they took away my cloak,
　　those watchmen of the walls!
⁸Daughters of Jerusalem, I charge you—
　　if you find my beloved,
what will you tell him?
　　Tell him I am faint with love.

Friends

⁹How is your beloved better than others,
　　most beautiful of women?
How is your beloved better than others,
　　that you so charge us?

She

¹⁰My beloved is radiant and ruddy,
　　outstanding among ten thousand.
¹¹His head is purest gold;
　　his hair is wavy
　　and black as a raven.
¹²His eyes are like doves
　　by the water streams,
washed in milk,
　　mounted like jewels.
¹³His cheeks are like beds of spice
　　yielding perfume.
His lips are like lilies
　　dripping with myrrh.
¹⁴His arms are rods of gold
　　set with topaz.
His body is like polished ivory
　　decorated with lapis lazuli.
¹⁵His legs are pillars of marble
　　set on bases of pure gold.
His appearance is like Lebanon,
　　choice as its cedars.
¹⁶His mouth is sweetness itself;
　　he is altogether lovely.
This is my beloved, this is my friend,
　　daughters of Jerusalem.

Friends

6

Where has your beloved gone,
　　most beautiful of women?
Which way did your beloved turn,
　　that we may look for him with you?

She

²My beloved has gone down to his garden,
　　to the beds of spices,

ASKmeanything

bathsheba

2 Samuel 11:1 – 12:24

947

Tell us about that fateful night.

It was a beautiful spring night, really the first warm night of the season. The rains were over, the harvest was in and the men were off to war—including my husband, Uriah. I was enjoying the ritual bath that marked the end of my monthly period.

What happened next?

The events that followed changed my life forever. After my bath there was a knock on my door. To my complete amazement, there stood messengers from King David saying the king wanted to see me. To reject the summons of the king would be unthinkable, so I went to him.

And afterwards?

My one night with the king led to a series of tragic events. I became pregnant with David's child. When I told him about the pregnancy, he tried to cover up his sin—first by sending Uriah home to sleep with me, and when that didn't work, by having my husband killed. Then he took me into the palace and treated me as one of his wives.

What happened to your child?

After our baby was born—a son—the prophet Nathan went to David and confronted him. David was humbled and repentant, but the consequences remained. Our son died. And I was devastated.

What can others learn from your experience?

There is nothing that can happen to us, no matter how awful, that is beyond God's healing. God can take the worst parts of our lives and find a way to shape them into something good. That doesn't mean the consequences of what happened will be removed. Think of all I lost—Uriah, my way of life and my son. Still, something good came of all this. God gave me another son, Solomon. He was destined for great things, and I got to see him rise to power and become a wise and successful king.

FOR MORE INSIGHT: We may never know all the details of Bathsheba's story. Was she forced to go to David or did she choose to go? Was David's summons an invitation or a command? Was she aware David wanted sex or was she blinded by the king's flattering attention? Even though we may not know exactly what happened, we know that Bathsheba shared in the consequences of David's sin. Her life was forever changed by that one fateful night.

Take note of some other Biblical words on adultery: Numbers 15:39; Job 24:15; Proverbs 6:32; Matthew 5:27–30; Mark 7:20–23; and 1 Corinthians 6:18–20.

to browse in the gardens
and to gather lilies.
³I am my beloved's and my
beloved is mine;
he browses among the lilies.

He

⁴You are as beautiful as Tirzah,
my darling,
as lovely as Jerusalem,
as majestic as troops with
banners.
⁵Turn your eyes from me;
they overwhelm me.
Your hair is like a flock of
goats
descending from Gilead.
⁶Your teeth are like a flock of sheep
coming up from the washing.
Each has its twin,
not one of them is missing.
⁷Your temples behind your veil
are like the halves of a pomegranate.
⁸Sixty queens there may be,
and eighty concubines,
and virgins beyond number;
⁹but my dove, my perfect one, is unique,
the only daughter of her mother,
the favorite of the one who bore her.
The young women saw her and called her blessed;
the queens and concubines praised her.

Friends

¹⁰Who is this that appears like the dawn,
fair as the moon, bright as the sun,
majestic as the stars in procession?

He

¹¹I went down to the grove of nut trees
to look at the new growth in the valley,
to see if the vines had budded
or the pomegranates were in bloom.
¹²Before I realized it,
my desire set me among the royal chariots of my people.ᵃ

Friends

* ¹³Come back, come back, O Shulammite;
come back, come back, that we may gaze on you!

He

Why would you gaze on the Shulammite
as on the dance of Mahanaim?

conversations

sex «» 6:2–3

1» Do some Christians feel that sex is a bad or dirty act? What does this say about their view of God?

2» How important is sex in a marriage?

3» What issues block you from being completely receptive to your husband?

For more on **sex**, check the index.
For the next Conversations, go to p. 960.

948

ᵃ *12* Or *among the chariots of Amminadab*; or *among the chariots of the people of the prince*
* 6:13 is numbered 7:1 in Hebrew texts.

7

* [1] How beautiful your sandaled feet,
O prince's daughter!
Your graceful legs are like jewels,
the work of an artist's hands.
[2] Your navel is a rounded goblet
that never lacks blended wine.
Your waist is a mound of wheat
encircled by lilies.
[3] Your breasts are like two fawns,
like twin fawns of a gazelle.
[4] Your neck is like an ivory tower.
Your eyes are the pools of Heshbon
by the gate of Bath Rabbim.
Your nose is like the tower of Lebanon
looking toward Damascus.
[5] Your head crowns you like Mount Carmel.
Your hair is like royal tapestry;
the king is held captive by its tresses.
[6] How beautiful you are and how pleasing,
my love, with your delights!
[7] Your stature is like that of the palm,
and your breasts like clusters of fruit.
[8] I said, "I will climb the palm tree;
I will take hold of its fruit."
May your breasts be like clusters of grapes
on the vine,
the fragrance of your breath like apples,
[9] and your mouth like the best wine.

She

May the wine go straight to my beloved,
flowing gently over lips and teeth.[a]
[10] I belong to my beloved,
and his desire is for me.
[11] Come, my beloved, let us go to the countryside,
let us spend the night in the villages.[b]
[12] Let us go early to the vineyards
to see if the vines have budded,
if their blossoms have opened,
and if the pomegranates are in bloom—
there I will give you my love.
[13] The mandrakes send out their fragrance,
and at our door is every delicacy,
both new and old,
that I have stored up for you, my beloved.

8

If only you were to me like a brother,
who was nursed at my mother's breasts!
Then, if I found you outside,
I would kiss you,

---

aussie.loss of sexual interest

7:1–9 For an Israelite, this was fan-your-face, make-you-blush sensual poetry. Telling her very clearly just how attractive and sexy she was to him, the man praises his beloved's appearance from her feet up to her hair. Do you wish your husband would do the same? Maybe it seems he's no longer attracted to you. He's not interested in sex. And this rejection wounds you deeply. Talk to someone who can help you both. And remember that your value isn't based on your husband's sexual interest in you. *God* cherishes you as a beloved bride. *He* thinks you're beautiful. And his love for you will never change.

949

---

a 9 Septuagint, Aquila, Vulgate and Syriac; Hebrew *lips of sleepers*   *b 11* Or *the henna bushes*

* 7:1-13 is numbered 7:2-14 in Hebrew texts.

and no one would despise me.
² I would lead you
　and bring you to my mother's house—
　she who has taught me.
I would give you spiced wine to drink,
　the nectar of my pomegranates.
³ His left arm is under my head
　and his right arm embraces me.
⁴ Daughters of Jerusalem, I charge you:
　Do not arouse or awaken love
　until it so desires.

Friends

⁵ Who is this coming up from the wilderness
　leaning on her beloved?

She

Under the apple tree I roused you;
　there your mother conceived you,
　there she who was in labor gave you birth.
⁶ Place me like a seal over your heart,
　like a seal on your arm;
for love is as strong as death,
　its jealousy *a* unyielding as the grave.
It burns like blazing fire,
　like a mighty flame. *b*
⁷ Many waters cannot quench love;
　rivers cannot sweep it away.
If one were to give
　all the wealth of one's house for love,
　it *c* would be utterly scorned.

Friends

⁸ We have a little sister,
　and her breasts are not yet grown.
What shall we do for our sister
　on the day she is spoken for?
⁹ If she is a wall,
　we will build towers of silver on her.
If she is a door,
　we will enclose her with panels of cedar.

She

¹⁰ I am a wall,
　and my breasts are like towers.
Thus I have become in his eyes
　like one bringing contentment.
¹¹ Solomon had a vineyard in Baal Hamon;
　he let out his vineyard to tenants.
Each was to bring for its fruit
　a thousand shekels *d* of silver.
¹² But my own vineyard is mine to give;

---

a 6 Or *ardor*　*b 6* Or *fire, / like the very flame of the* LORD　*c 7* Or *he*　*d 11* That is, about 25 pounds or about 11.5 kilograms; also in verse 12

the thousand shekels are for you, Solomon,
and two hundred[a] are for those who tend its fruit.

He

¹³You who dwell in the gardens
with friends in attendance,
let me hear your voice!

She

¹⁴Come away, my beloved,
and be like a gazelle
or like a young stag
on the spice-laden mountains.

951

---

954 **ISAIAH**

1073 **JEREMIAH**

1174 **LAMENTATIONS**

1190 **EZEKIEL**

1256 **DANIEL**

1276 **HOSEA**

1297 **JOEL**

1305 **AMOS**

1319 **OBADIAH**

1322 **JONAH**

1326 **MICAH**

1339 **NAHUM**

1345 **HABAKKUK**

1351 **ZEPHANIAH**

1358 **HAGGAI**

1363 **ZECHARIAH**

1378 **MALACHI**

the
prop

Along with the books of Joshua through Kings, the books in this section form the second major division of the Old Testament, the Prophets. These 17 texts are together known as the Latter Prophets and are often further divided into two groups.

The Major Prophets are the books of Isaiah through Daniel, and are named this because of their relative length and the variety of topics addressed. The remaining texts are called the Minor Prophets. These are relatively shorter, usually addressing a particular context or dealing with a more singular theme. While a measure of prophetic activity included visions and dreams of the future, the primary task of all the prophets was to call the people of Israel back to faithfulness to their covenant with God.

hets

isaiah

AUTHOR
Isaiah.

AUDIENCE
Judah, Israel, surrounding pagan nations.

DATE
Between 701 and 681 B.C.

SETTING
Judgment is on the horizon for Judah as the
Assyrians threaten to overtake them.

VERSE TO REMEMBER
"Come now, let us reason together," says
the LORD. "Though your sins are like scarlet,
they shall be as white as snow; though they
are red as crimson, they shall be like wool."
(1:18)

THEME TO CONSIDER
Because of God's justice and holiness, sin
must be punished. Because of God's mercy,
Jesus paid the price for us.

1 The vision concerning Judah and Jerusalem that Isaiah son of Amoz saw during the reigns of Uzziah, Jotham, Ahaz and Hezekiah, kings of Judah.

A Rebellious Nation

²Hear me, you heavens! Listen, earth!
　　For the Lord has spoken:
"I reared children and brought them up,
　　but they have rebelled against me.
³The ox knows its master,
　　the donkey its owner's manger,
but Israel does not know,
　　my people do not understand."

⁴Ah, sinful nation,
　　a people whose guilt is great,
a brood of evildoers,
　　children given to corruption!
They have forsaken the Lord;
　　they have spurned the Holy One of Israel
　　and turned their backs on him.

955

⁵Why should you be beaten anymore?
　　Why do you persist in rebellion?
Your whole head is injured,
　　your whole heart afflicted.
⁶From the sole of your foot to the top of your head
　　there is no soundness—
only wounds and welts
　　and open sores,
not cleansed or bandaged
　　or soothed with olive oil.

⁷Your country is desolate,
　　your cities burned with fire;
your fields are being stripped by foreigners
　　right before you,
　　laid waste as when overthrown by strangers.
⁸Daughter Zion is left
　　like a shelter in a vineyard,
like a hut in a field of melons,
　　like a city under siege.
⁹Unless the Lord Almighty
　　had left us some survivors,
we would have become like Sodom,
　　we would have been like Gomorrah.

¹⁰Hear the word of the Lord,
　　you rulers of Sodom;
listen to the instruction of our God,
　　you people of Gomorrah!
¹¹"The multitude of your sacrifices—
　　what are they to me?" says the Lord.
"I have more than enough of burnt offerings,
　　of rams and the fat of fattened animals;

I have no pleasure
    in the blood of bulls and lambs and
      goats.
¹²When you come to appear before me,
    who has asked this of you,
    this trampling of my courts?
¹³Stop bringing meaningless offerings!
    Your incense is detestable to me.
New Moons, Sabbaths and
      convocations—
    I cannot bear your evil assemblies.
¹⁴Your New Moon feasts and your
      appointed festivals
    I hate with all my being.
They have become a burden to me;
    I am weary of bearing them.
¹⁵When you spread out your hands in
      prayer,
    I will hide my eyes from you;
even if you offer many prayers,
    I will not listen.
Your hands are full of blood;
¹⁶   wash and make yourselves clean.
Take your evil deeds
    out of my sight!
Stop doing wrong,
¹⁷   learn to do right!
Seek justice,
    encourage the oppressed.ᵃ
Defend the cause of the fatherless,
    plead the case of the widow.

¹⁸"Come now, let us reason together,"
    says the LORD.
"Though your sins are like scarlet,
    they shall be as white as snow;
though they are red as crimson,
    they shall be like wool.
¹⁹If you are willing and obedient,
    you will eat the best from the land;
²⁰but if you resist and rebel,
    you will be devoured by the sword."

        For the mouth of the LORD has spoken.

²¹See how the faithful city
    has become a prostitute!
She once was full of justice;
    righteousness used to dwell in her—
    but now murderers!
²²Your silver has become dross,
    your choice wine is diluted with water.

1:10–20 Consider the two types of actions Isaiah describes in these verses: the "religious" activities of sacrifice and worship and the "right" activities of defending the cause of those in need. Both are actions, but the former is not acceptable to God without the latter. Those who act "religious" but ignore their obligation to love their neighbor are hypocrites in God's eyes. God's acceptance is tied to whether you really *do* the right thing—not just in church or when people are looking, but in all areas of your life. How could you truly love, serve or worship God without also loving others?

atissue:God's acceptance

956

ᵃ *17 Or justice, / rebuke the oppressor*

²³Your rulers are rebels,
    companions of thieves;
they all love bribes
    and chase after gifts.
They do not defend the cause of the fatherless;
    the widow's case does not come before them.
²⁴Therefore the Lord, the LORD Almighty,
    the Mighty One of Israel, declares:
"Ah, I will vent my wrath on my foes
    and avenge myself on my enemies.
²⁵I will turn my hand against you;
    I will thoroughly purge away your dross
    and remove all your impurities.
²⁶I will restore your judges as in days of old,
    your rulers as at the beginning.
Afterward you will be called
    the City of Righteousness,
    the Faithful City."

²⁷Zion will be delivered with justice,
    her penitent ones with righteousness.
²⁸But rebels and sinners will both be broken,
    and those who forsake the LORD will perish.

²⁹"You will be ashamed because of the sacred oaks
    in which you have delighted;
you will be disgraced because of the gardens
    that you have chosen.
³⁰You will be like an oak with fading leaves,
    like a garden without water.
³¹The mighty man will become tinder
    and his work a spark;
both will burn together,
    with no one to quench the fire."

The Mountain of the LORD

2 This is what Isaiah son of Amoz saw concerning Judah and Jerusalem:

²In the last days

the mountain of the LORD's temple will be established
    as the highest of the mountains;
it will be exalted above the hills,
    and all nations will stream to it.

³Many peoples will come and say,

"Come, let us go up to the mountain of the LORD,
    to the house of the God of Jacob.
He will teach us his ways,
    so that we may walk in his paths."
The law will go out from Zion,
    the word of the LORD from Jerusalem.
⁴He will judge between the nations

and will settle disputes for many peoples.
They will beat their swords into plowshares
    and their spears into pruning hooks.
Nation will not take up sword against nation,
    nor will they train for war anymore.

⁵Come, house of Jacob,
    let us walk in the light of the Lord.

The Day of the Lord

⁶You have abandoned your people,
    the house of Jacob.
They are full of superstitions from the East;
    they practice divination like the Philistines
    and clasp hands with pagans.
⁷Their land is full of silver and gold;
    there is no end to their treasures.
Their land is full of horses;
    there is no end to their chariots.
⁸Their land is full of idols;
    they bow down to the work of their hands,
    to what their fingers have made.
⁹So people will be brought low
    and everyone humbled—
    do not forgive them.ᵃ

¹⁰Go into the rocks, hide in the ground
    from the fearful presence of the Lord
    and the splendor of his majesty!
¹¹The eyes of the arrogant will be humbled
    and human pride brought low;
    the Lord alone will be exalted in that day.

¹²The Lord Almighty has a day in store
    for all the proud and lofty,
    for all that is exalted
        (and they will be humbled),
¹³for all the cedars of Lebanon, tall and lofty,
    and all the oaks of Bashan,
¹⁴for all the towering mountains
    and all the high hills,
¹⁵for every lofty tower
    and every fortified wall,
¹⁶for every trading shipᵇ
    and every stately vessel.
¹⁷The arrogance of all people will be brought low
    and human pride humbled;
    the Lord alone will be exalted in that day,
¹⁸   and the idols will totally disappear.

¹⁹People will flee to caves in the rocks
    and to holes in the ground

ᵃ 9 Or not raise them up   ᵇ 16 Hebrew every ship of Tarshish

from the fearful presence of the Lord
 and the splendor of his majesty,
 when he rises to shake the earth.
²⁰In that day people will throw away
 to the moles and bats
their idols of silver and idols of gold,
 which they made to worship.
²¹They will flee to caverns in the rocks
 and to the overhanging crags
from the fearful presence of the Lord
 and the splendor of his majesty,
 when he rises to shake the earth.

²²Stop trusting in human beings,
 who have but a breath in their nostrils.
 Why hold them in esteem?

Judgment on Jerusalem and Judah

3 See now, the Lord,
 the Lord Almighty,
is about to take from Jerusalem and Judah
 both supply and support:
all supplies of food and all supplies of water,
² the hero and the warrior,
the judge and the prophet,
 the diviner and the elder,
³the captain of fifty and the person of rank,
 the counselor, skilled worker and clever enchanter.

⁴I will make mere youths their officials;
 children will govern them.
⁵People will oppress each other—
 one against another, neighbor against neighbor.
The young will rise up against the old,
 the nobody against the honored.

⁶A man will seize one of his brothers
 in his father's house, and say,
"You have a cloak, you be our leader;
 take charge of this heap of ruins!"
⁷But in that day he will cry out,
 "I have no remedy.
I have no food or clothing in my house;
 do not make me the leader of the people."

⁸Jerusalem staggers,
 Judah is falling;
their words and deeds are against the Lord,
 defying his glorious presence.
⁹The look on their faces testifies against them;
 they parade their sin like Sodom;
 they do not hide it.
Woe to them!
 They have brought disaster upon themselves.

959

960

¹⁰Tell the righteous it will be well with them,
　　for they will enjoy the fruit of their deeds.
¹¹Woe to the wicked!
　　Disaster is upon them!
　They will be paid back
　　for what their hands have done.

¹²Youths oppress my people,
　　women rule over them.
　My people, your guides lead you astray;
　　they turn you from the path.

¹³The Lᴏʀᴅ takes his place in court;
　　he rises to judge the people.
¹⁴The Lᴏʀᴅ enters into judgment
　　against the elders and leaders of his people:
　"It is you who have ruined my vineyard;
　　the plunder from the poor is in your houses.
¹⁵What do you mean by crushing my people
　　and grinding the faces of the poor?"

　　　　declares the Lord, the Lᴏʀᴅ Almighty.

¹⁶The Lᴏʀᴅ says,
　　"The women of Zion are haughty,
　walking along with outstretched necks,
　　flirting with their eyes,
　tripping along with mincing
　　　steps,
　　with ornaments jingling on
　　　their ankles.
¹⁷Therefore the Lord will bring
　　sores on the heads of
　　the women of Zion;
　　the Lᴏʀᴅ will make their
　　scalps bald."

¹⁸In that day the Lord will snatch away their finery: the bangles and headbands and crescent necklaces, ¹⁹the earrings and bracelets and veils, ²⁰the headdresses and ankle chains and sashes, the perfume bottles and charms, ²¹the signet rings and nose rings, ²²the fine robes and the capes and cloaks, the purses ²³and mirrors, and the linen garments and tiaras and shawls.

²⁴Instead of fragrance there will be a stench;
　　instead of a sash, a rope;
　instead of well-dressed hair, baldness;
　　instead of fine clothing, sackcloth;
　　instead of beauty, branding.
²⁵Your men will fall by the sword,
　　your warriors in battle.
²⁶The gates of Zion will lament and mourn;
　　destitute, she will sit on the ground.

conversations

flirting «» 3:16–17

1 » Is flirting harmless or dangerous? Why?

2 » What unmet needs might cause you to flirt?

3 » What in your behavior toward men could be construed as flirting?

For more on flirting, check the index.
For the next Conversations, go to p. 966.

4 In that day seven women
　　will take hold of one man
　and say, "We will eat our own food
　　and provide our own clothes;
　only let us be called by your name.
　　Take away our disgrace!"

The Branch of the Lord

²In that day the Branch of the Lord will be beautiful and glorious, and the fruit of the land will be the pride and glory of the survivors in Israel. ³Those who are left in Zion, who remain in Jerusalem, will be called holy, all who are recorded among the living in Jerusalem. ⁴The Lord will wash away the filth of the women of Zion; he will cleanse the bloodstains from Jerusalem by a spirit[a] of judgment and a spirit[a] of fire. ⁵Then the Lord will create over all of Mount Zion and over those who assemble there a cloud of smoke by day and a glow of flaming fire by night; over everything the glory[b] will be a canopy. ⁶It will be a shelter and shade from the heat of the day, and a refuge and hiding place from the storm and rain.

The Song of the Vineyard

5 I will sing for the one I love
　　a song about his vineyard:
　My loved one had a vineyard
　　on a fertile hillside.
²He dug it up and cleared it of stones
　　and planted it with the choicest vines.
　He built a watchtower in it
　　and cut out a winepress as well.
　Then he looked for a crop of good grapes,
　　but it yielded only bad fruit.

³"Now you dwellers in Jerusalem and people of Judah,
　　judge between me and my vineyard.
⁴What more could have been done for my vineyard
　　than I have done for it?
　When I looked for good grapes,
　　why did it yield only bad?
⁵Now I will tell you
　　what I am going to do to my vineyard:
　I will take away its hedge,
　　and it will be destroyed;
　I will break down its wall,
　　and it will be trampled.
⁶I will make it a wasteland,
　　neither pruned nor cultivated,
　　and briers and thorns will grow there.
　I will command the clouds
　　not to rain on it."

⁷The vineyard of the Lord Almighty
　　is the house of Israel,
　and the people of Judah
　　are the vines he delighted in.
　And he looked for justice, but saw bloodshed;
　　for righteousness, but heard cries of distress.

---

a 4 Or *the Spirit* *b 5* Or *over all the glory there*

myth# 58 "IT'S OK IF MY HUSBAND IS MY ONLY FRIEND."

When my husband and I started dating, I wanted to know everything about him, and I wanted him to know everything about me. We spent almost every waking hour together. I guess it was during that time that I lost touch with many of my girlfriends, which so often happens. I was so wrapped up in Luke that I just grew apart from everyone else.

Fast forward to today, and my life is much the same. If someone asked me to list my three best friends, I would put my husband as #1, #2 and #3. He's my soul mate. I tell him everything. I save all of my emotional energy for him, and when he is gone or traveling, I sometimes feel lost, as if I'm half of a whole.

My mother is always pestering me to "get out there and make friends." She says that I'll drain my husband dry if I don't find some women friends. She doesn't understand how close Luke and I are. Besides, our relationship is so easy. Making new friends takes a lot of time and energy, neither of which I have. I work a lot of hours, and I just don't have the extra time in my schedule to go out and meet up with women for lunch. Also, women friends are much more complicated than just being with my husband. He doesn't judge me, talk about me behind my back or hold a grudge. Girlfriends can be so petty and high maintenance—most of the women I work with are prime examples of this. The way I see it, I have all the friends I need wrapped up in one wonderful man.

—Jenny

WHILE IT IS important that you have a close friendship with your husband, it is also vital that he is not the only friend you have. It takes work to meet and sustain deep and meaningful friendships, but the benefits of friendships far outweigh the costs or risks. Keep this in mind:

- **We need friendships with other women to reciprocate encouragement and wisdom (see Ephesians 4:29).** Will you courageously seek out friendships in which you can *give* as well as *receive?* As much as you need the friendship of another woman, another woman needs your friendship too. She's waiting for you to come alongside her.

- **Girlfriends can understand us in ways that men never can.** Can a man truly understand PMS, what it's like to be a sister, the "biological clock" or shopping? Even the most well-rounded man can't fully relate. Girlfriends can understand us, empathize with us and pray for our unique struggles (see Proverbs 18:1; 27:9).

- **Your marriage will be healthier and more balanced if you and your husband both have strong, same-sex friendships.** Men need other men; women need other women. You and your husband will both benefit from godly friendships and accountability.

- **It is not fair to ask your husband to be your only friend.** While your husband should be your closest friend and your primary emotional partner, expecting him to be your *only* friend puts undue pressure on your marriage. It's impossible for one person to meet all your needs. God is the only one who can meet all of your needs in one relationship (see Psalm 18:1–2). If you expect anyone else to do what only God can do, you are setting yourself up for continual disappointment (see Isaiah 55:2).

"Somewhere in the meaning of the word 'trust' is the assumption that a friend has your best interest at heart. Friends can be the collaborators, the instigators who make change possible. They are often the ones who urge us to take a leap, who jump with us or help us scramble back up the other side."

—Ellen Goodman and Patricia O'Brien

963

"PERFUME AND INCENSE BRING JOY TO THE HEART, AND THE PLEASANTNESS OF A FRIEND SPRINGS FROM THEIR HEARTFELT ADVICE."

PROVERBS 27:9

SEE ALSO
Proverbs 17:17
Proverbs 18:1
Proverbs 27:17

For more on **Friendship** and **Marriage**, check the index.

Woes and Judgments

[8]Woe to you who add house to house
    and join field to field
till no space is left
    and you live alone in the land.

[9]The LORD Almighty has declared in my hearing:

"Surely the great houses will become desolate,
    the fine mansions left without occupants.
[10]A ten-acre vineyard will produce only a bath[a] of wine,
    a homer[b] of seed only an ephah[c] of grain."

[11]Woe to those who rise early in the morning
    to run after their drinks,
who stay up late at night
    till they are inflamed with wine.
[12]They have harps and lyres at their banquets,
    pipes and timbrels and wine,
but they have no regard for the deeds of the LORD,
    no respect for the work of his hands.
[13]Therefore my people will go into exile
    for lack of understanding;
those of high rank will die of hunger
    and the common people will be parched with thirst.
[14]Therefore the grave enlarges its appetite
    and opens wide its mouth;
into it will descend their nobles and masses
    with all their brawlers and revelers.
[15]So people will be brought low
    and everyone humbled,
    the eyes of the arrogant humbled.
[16]But the LORD Almighty will be exalted by his justice,
    and the holy God will be proved holy by his righteous acts.
[17]Then sheep will graze as in their own pasture;
    lambs will feed[d] among the ruins of the rich.

[18]Woe to those who draw sin along with cords of deceit,
    and wickedness as with cart ropes,
[19]to those who say, "Let God hurry;
    let him hasten his work
    so we may see it.
The plan of the Holy One of Israel—
    let it approach, let it come into view,
    so we may know it."

[20]Woe to those who call evil good
    and good evil,
who put darkness for light
    and light for darkness,
who put bitter for sweet
    and sweet for bitter.

964

---

[a] *10* That is, about 6 gallons or about 22 liters   [b] *10* That is, probably about 360 pounds or about 160 kilograms   [c] *10* That is, probably about 36 pounds or about 16 kilograms   [d] *17* Septuagint; Hebrew / *strangers will eat*

²¹Woe to those who are wise in their own eyes
  and clever in their own sight.

²²Woe to those who are heroes at drinking wine
  and champions at mixing drinks,
²³who acquit the guilty for a bribe,
  but deny justice to the innocent.
²⁴Therefore, as tongues of fire lick up straw
  and as dry grass sinks down in the flames,
so their roots will decay
  and their flowers blow away like dust;
for they have rejected the law of the LORD Almighty
  and spurned the word of the Holy One of
    Israel.
²⁵Therefore the LORD's anger burns against
    his people;
  his hand is raised and he strikes them
    down.
The mountains shake,
  and the dead bodies are like refuse in the
    streets.

Yet for all this, his anger is not turned away,
  his hand is still upraised.

²⁶He lifts up a banner for the distant nations,
  he whistles for those at the ends of the
    earth.
Here they come,
  swiftly and speedily!
²⁷Not one of them grows tired or stumbles,
  not one slumbers or sleeps;
not a belt is loosened at the waist,
  not a sandal thong is broken.
²⁸Their arrows are sharp,
  all their bows are strung;
their horses' hooves seem like flint,
  their chariot wheels like a whirlwind.
²⁹Their roar is like that of the lion,
  they roar like young lions;
they growl as they seize their prey
  and carry it off with no one to rescue.
³⁰In that day they will roar over it
  like the roaring of the sea.
And if one looks at the land,
  there is only darkness and distress;
  even the sun will be darkened by clouds.

at issue: sexual sin

5:20 Our society tries to blend the lines that God has drawn on sexuality. Society says it's fine to sleep with someone—of any sex—as long as you're careful, or you care about each other or it makes you happy. But God issues a harsh indictment on those who try to call good what he calls evil. He created us, and he's drawn the lines for our good. He designed sex to be enjoyed only between a husband and wife. Any creative variation on that (bisexuality, homosexuality, premarital sex) isn't "personal preference"; it's sin.

965

Isaiah's Commission

6 In the year that King Uzziah died, I saw the Lord seated on a throne, high and exalted, and the train of his robe filled the temple. ²Above him were seraphs, each with six wings: With two wings they covered their faces, with two they covered their feet, and with two they were flying. ³And they were calling to one another:

"Holy, holy, holy is the Lord
Almighty;
    the whole earth is full of his
        glory."

[4]At the sound of their voices the doorposts and thresholds shook and the temple was filled with smoke.

[5]"Woe to me!" I cried. "I am ruined! For I am a man of unclean lips, and I live among a people of unclean lips, and my eyes have seen the King, the Lord Almighty."

[6]Then one of the seraphs flew to me with a live coal in his hand, which he had taken with tongs from the altar. [7]With it he touched my mouth and said, "See, this has touched your lips; your guilt is taken away and your sin atoned for."

[8]Then I heard the voice of the Lord saying, "Whom shall I send? And who will go for us?"
And I said, "Here am I. Send me!"
[9]He said, "Go and tell this people:

    "'Be ever hearing, but never understanding;
        be ever seeing, but never perceiving.'
[10]Make the heart of this people calloused;
        make their ears dull
        and close their eyes.[a]
Otherwise they might see with their eyes,
        hear with their ears,
        understand with their hearts,
        and turn and be healed."

[11]Then I said, "For how long, Lord?"
And he answered:

    "Until the cities lie ruined
        and without inhabitant,
    until the houses are left deserted
        and the fields ruined and ravaged,
[12]until the Lord has sent everyone far away
        and the land is utterly forsaken.
[13]And though a tenth remains in the land,
        it will again be laid waste.
    But as the terebinth and oak
        leave stumps when they are cut down,
        so the holy seed will be the stump in the land."

The Sign of Immanuel

7 When Ahaz son of Jotham, the son of Uzziah, was king of Judah, King Rezin of Aram and Pekah son of Remaliah king of Israel marched up to fight against Jerusalem, but they could not overpower it.

[2]Now the house of David was told, "Aram has allied itself with[b] Ephraim"; so the hearts of Ahaz and his people were shaken, as the trees of the forest are shaken by the wind.

"conversations"

purpose «» 6:1–8

1» Does your life have a God-given purpose? If so, what is it?

2» Is your purpose in life tied more to who God is or to who you are? Explain your answer.

3» Why would God include unstable, unreliable people (like us) in his purposes?

For more on **purpose**, check the index.
For the next Conversations, go to p. 968.

966

---

[a] 9,10 Hebrew; Septuagint 'You will be ever hearing, but never understanding; / you will be ever seeing, but never perceiving.' / [10]This people's heart has become calloused; / they hardly hear with their ears, / and they have closed their eyes   [b] 2 Or has set up camp in

³Then the LORD said to Isaiah, "Go out, you and your son Shear-Jashub,ᵃ to meet Ahaz at the end of the aqueduct of the Upper Pool, on the road to the Launderer's Field. ⁴Say to him, 'Be careful, keep calm and don't be afraid. Do not lose heart because of these two smoldering stubs of firewood—because of the fierce anger of Rezin and Aram and of the son of Remaliah. ⁵Aram, Ephraim and Remaliah's son have plotted your ruin, saying, ⁶"Let us invade Judah; let us tear it apart and divide it among ourselves, and make the son of Tabeel king over it." ⁷Yet this is what the Sovereign LORD says:

> "'It will not take place,
>   it will not happen,
> ⁸for the head of Aram is Damascus,
>   and the head of Damascus is only Rezin.
> Within sixty-five years
>   Ephraim will be too shattered to be a people.
> ⁹The head of Ephraim is Samaria,
>   and the head of Samaria is only Remaliah's son.
> If you do not stand firm in your faith,
>   you will not stand at all.'"

¹⁰Again the LORD spoke to Ahaz, ¹¹"Ask the LORD your God for a sign, whether in the deepest depths or in the highest heights."

¹²But Ahaz said, "I will not ask; I will not put the LORD to the test."

¹³Then Isaiah said, "Hear now, you house of David! Is it not enough to try the patience of human beings? Will you try the patience of my God also? ¹⁴Therefore the Lord himself will give youᵇ a sign: The virginᶜ will conceive and give birth to a son, andᵈ will call him Immanuel.ᵉ ¹⁵He will be eating curds and honey when he knows enough to reject the wrong and choose the right, ¹⁶for before the boy knows enough to reject the wrong and choose the right, the land of the two kings you dread will be laid waste. ¹⁷The LORD will bring on you and on your people and on the house of your father a time unlike any since Ephraim broke away from Judah—he will bring the king of Assyria."

Assyria, the LORD's Instrument

¹⁸In that day the LORD will whistle for flies from the Nile delta in Egypt and for bees from the land of Assyria. ¹⁹They will all come and settle in the steep ravines and in the crevices in the rocks, on all the thornbushes and at all the water holes. ²⁰In that day the Lord will use a razor hired from beyond the Euphrates River—the king of Assyria—to shave your head and the hair of your legs, and to take off your beards also. ²¹In that day, a person will keep alive a young cow and two goats. ²²And because of the abundance of the milk they give, there will be curds to eat. All who remain in the land will eat curds and honey. ²³In that day, in every place where there were a thousand vines worth a thousand silver shekels,ᶠ there will be only briers and thorns. ²⁴Hunters will go there with bow and arrow, for the land will be covered with briers and thorns. ²⁵As for all the hills once cultivated by the hoe, you will no longer go there for fear of the briers and thorns; they will become places where cattle are turned loose and where sheep run.

Isaiah and His Children as Signs

8 The LORD said to me, "Take a large scroll and write on it with an ordinary pen: Maher-Shalal-Hash-Baz."ᵍ ²So I called in Uriah the priest and Zechariah son of Jeberekiah as reliable witnesses for me. ³Then I made love to the prophetess, and she conceived and gave birth to a son. And the LORD said to me, "Name him Maher-Shalal-Hash-Baz. ⁴Before the boy knows how to say 'My father' or 'My mother,' the wealth of Damascus and the plunder of Samaria will be carried off by the king of Assyria."

⁵The LORD spoke to me again:

> ⁶"Because this people has rejected
>   the gently flowing waters of Shiloah

ᵃ *3 Shear-Jashub means a remnant will return.* ᵇ *14 The Hebrew is plural.* ᶜ *14 Or young woman* ᵈ *14 Masoretic Text; Dead Sea Scrolls and he or and they* ᵉ *14 Immanuel means God with us.* ᶠ *23 That is, about 25 pounds or about 11.5 kilograms* ᵍ *1 Maher-Shalal-Baz means quick to the plunder, swift to the spoil; also in verse 3.*

and rejoices over Rezin
and the son of Remaliah,
⁷therefore the Lord is about to bring against them
the mighty floodwaters of the Euphrates—
the king of Assyria with all his pomp.
It will overflow all its channels,
run over all its banks
⁸and sweep on into Judah, swirling over it,
passing through it and reaching up to the neck.
Its outspread wings will cover the breadth of your land,
Immanuel^a!"

⁹Raise the war cry,^b you nations, and be shattered!
Listen, all you distant lands.
Prepare for battle, and be shattered!
Prepare for battle, and be shattered!
¹⁰Devise your strategy, but it will be thwarted;
propose your plan, but it will not stand,
for God is with us.^c

¹¹This is what the LORD says to me with his strong hand upon me, warning me not to follow the way of this people:

¹²"Do not call conspiracy
everything this people calls a conspiracy;
do not fear what they fear,
and do not dread it.
¹³The LORD Almighty is the one you are to regard as holy,
he is the one you are to fear,
he is the one you are to dread.
¹⁴He will be a holy place;
for both houses of Israel he will be
a stone that causes people to stumble
and a rock that makes them fall.
And for the people of
Jerusalem he will be
a trap and a snare.
¹⁵Many of them will stumble;
they will fall and be broken,
they will be snared and
captured."

¹⁶Bind up this testimony of
warning
and seal up God's
instruction among my
disciples.
¹⁷I will wait for the LORD,
who is hiding his face from
the house of Jacob.
I will put my trust in him.

968

"conversations"

patience «» 8:17

1» How much is your trust in God dependent on his actions?

2» What gives you hope while you wait for God's answers?

3» How does practicing patience increase your trust in God?

For more on patience, check the index.
For the next Conversations, go to p. 996.

^a 8 Immanuel means God with us.   ^b 9 Or Do your worst   ^c 10 Hebrew Immanuel

¹⁸Here am I, and the children the LORD has given me. We are signs and symbols in Israel from the LORD Almighty, who dwells on Mount Zion.

The Darkness Turns to Light

¹⁹When someone tells you to consult mediums and spiritists, who whisper and mutter, should not a people inquire of their God? Why consult the dead on behalf of the living? ²⁰Consult God's instruction and the testimony of warning. If anyone does not speak according to this word, they have no light of dawn. ²¹Distressed and hungry, they will roam through the land; when they are famished, they will become enraged and, looking upward, will curse their king and their God. ²²Then they will look toward the earth and see only distress and darkness and fearful gloom, and they will be thrust into utter darkness.

9 *Nevertheless, there will be no more gloom for those who were in distress. In the past he humbled the land of Zebulun and the land of Naphtali, but in the future he will honor Galilee of the nations, by the Way of the Sea, beyond the Jordan—

969

> * ²The people walking in darkness
>   have seen a great light;
>   on those living in the land of deep darkness
>   a light has dawned.
> ³You have enlarged the nation
>   and increased their joy;
>   they rejoice before you
>   as people rejoice at the harvest,
>   as soldiers rejoice
>   when dividing the plunder.
> ⁴For as in the day of Midian's defeat,
>   you have shattered
>   the yoke that burdens them,
>   the bar across their shoulders,
>   the rod of their oppressor.
> ⁵Every warrior's boot used in battle
>   and every garment rolled in blood
>   will be destined for burning,
>   will be fuel for the fire.
> ⁶For to us a child is born,

* 9:1 is numbered 8:23 in Hebrew texts.   * 9:2-21 is numbered 9:1-20 in Hebrew texts.

HE IS: my everything

9:6–7 Isaiah predicted that a child would be born who would be *our everything*. The variety of names reveals his character qualities: Wonderful Counselor, Mighty God, Everlasting Father, Prince of Peace.

Until Christ comes to govern the world, he wants to govern your heart and be *your everything*. When you're perplexed, let him be your *Wonderful Counselor*. When you're weak and fragile, trust him to be your *Mighty God*. When you feel that everything around you is changing, remember he is your *Everlasting Father*. When anxiety knocks, lean on the *Prince of Peace*. When you're searching for what completes you, look to *your everything*.

For the next He Is, go to p. 974.

to us a son is given,
  and the government will be on his shoulders.
And he will be called
  Wonderful Counselor, Mighty God,
  Everlasting Father, Prince of Peace.
⁷Of the increase of his government and peace
  there will be no end.
He will reign on David's throne
  and over his kingdom,
establishing and upholding it
  with justice and righteousness
  from that time on and forever.
The zeal of the LORD Almighty
  will accomplish this.

The LORD's Anger Against Israel

⁸The Lord has sent a message against Jacob;
  it will fall on Israel.
⁹All the people will know it—
  Ephraim and the inhabitants of Samaria—
who say with pride
  and arrogance of heart,
¹⁰"The bricks have fallen down,
  but we will rebuild with dressed stone;
the fig trees have been felled,
  but we will replace them with cedars."
¹¹But the LORD has strengthened Rezin's foes against them
  and has spurred their enemies on.
¹²Arameans from the east and Philistines from the west
  have devoured Israel with open mouth.

  Yet for all this, his anger is not turned away,
    his hand is still upraised.

¹³But the people have not returned to him who struck them,
  nor have they sought the LORD Almighty.
¹⁴So the LORD will cut off from Israel both head and tail,
  both palm branch and reed in a single day;
¹⁵the elders and dignitaries are the head,
  the prophets who teach lies are the tail.
¹⁶Those who guide this people mislead them,
  and those who are guided are led astray.
¹⁷Therefore the Lord will take no pleasure in the young men,
  nor will he pity the fatherless and widows,
for everyone is ungodly and wicked,
  every mouth speaks folly.

  Yet for all this, his anger is not turned away,
    his hand is still upraised.

¹⁸Surely wickedness burns like a fire;
  it consumes briers and thorns,
it sets the forest thickets ablaze,
  so that it rolls upward in a column of smoke.

¹⁹By the wrath of the Lord Almighty
    the land will be scorched
and the people will be fuel for the fire;
    they will not spare each other.
²⁰On the right they will devour,
    but still be hungry;
on the left they will eat,
    but not be satisfied.
They will all feed on the flesh of their own offspring^a:
²¹ Manasseh will feed on Ephraim, and Ephraim on Manasseh;
    together they will turn against Judah.

Yet for all this, his anger is not turned away,
    his hand is still upraised.

10

Woe to those who make unjust laws,
    to those who issue oppressive decrees,
²to deprive the poor of their rights
    and withhold justice from the oppressed of my people,
making widows their prey
    and robbing the fatherless.
³What will you do on the day of reckoning,
    when disaster comes from afar?
To whom will you run for help?
    Where will you leave your riches?
⁴Nothing will remain but to cringe among the captives
    or fall among the slain.

Yet for all this, his anger is not turned away,
    his hand is still upraised.

God's Judgment on Assyria

⁵"Woe to the Assyrian, the rod of my anger,
    in whose hand is the club of my wrath!
⁶I send him against a godless nation,
    I dispatch him against a people who anger me,
to seize loot and snatch plunder,
    and to trample them down like mud in the streets.
⁷But this is not what he intends,
    this is not what he has in mind;
his purpose is to destroy,
    to put an end to many nations.
⁸'Are not my commanders all kings?' he says.
⁹ 'Has not Kalno fared like Carchemish?
Is not Hamath like Arpad,
    and Samaria like Damascus?
¹⁰As my hand seized the kingdoms of the idols,
    kingdoms whose images excelled those of Jerusalem and Samaria—
¹¹shall I not deal with Jerusalem and her images
    as I dealt with Samaria and her idols?'"

---

^a *20* Or *arm*

972

¹²When the Lord has finished all his work against Mount Zion and Jerusalem, he will say, "I will punish the king of Assyria for the willful pride of his heart and the haughty look in his eyes. ¹³For he says:

"'By the strength of my hand I have done this,
 and by my wisdom, because I have understanding.
I removed the boundaries of nations,
 I plundered their treasures;
 like a mighty one I subdued*ᵃ* their kings.
¹⁴As one reaches into a nest,
 so my hand reached for the wealth of the nations;
as people gather abandoned eggs,
 so I gathered all the countries;
not one flapped a wing,
 or opened its mouth to chirp.'"

¹⁵Does the ax raise itself above the one who swings it,
 or the saw boast against the one who uses it?
As if a rod were to wield the person who lifts it up,
 or a club brandish one who is not wood!
¹⁶Therefore, the Lord, the Lᴏʀᴅ Almighty,
 will send a wasting disease upon his sturdy warriors;
under his pomp a fire will be kindled
 like a blazing flame.
¹⁷The Light of Israel will become a fire,
 their Holy One a flame;
in a single day it will burn and consume
 his thorns and his briers.
¹⁸The splendor of his forests and fertile fields
 it will completely destroy,
 as when sick people waste away.
¹⁹And the remaining trees of his forests will be so few
 that a child could write them down.

The Remnant of Israel

²⁰In that day the remnant of Israel,
 the survivors of the house of Jacob,
will no longer rely on him
 who struck them down
but will truly rely on the Lᴏʀᴅ,
 the Holy One of Israel.
²¹A remnant will return,*ᵇ* a remnant of Jacob
 will return to the Mighty God.
²²Though your people be like the sand by the sea, Israel,
 only a remnant will return.
Destruction has been decreed,
 overwhelming and righteous.
²³The Lord, the Lᴏʀᴅ Almighty, will carry out
 the destruction decreed upon the whole land.

²⁴Therefore, this is what the Lord, the Lᴏʀᴅ Almighty, says:

"My people who live in Zion,

ᵃ 13 Or *treasures; / I subdued the mighty,*   *ᵇ 21* Hebrew *shear-jashub; also in verse 22*

do not be afraid of the Assyrians,
who beat you with a rod
and lift up a club against you, as Egypt did.
25 Very soon my anger against you will end
and my wrath will be directed to their destruction."

26 The Lord Almighty will lash them with a whip,
as when he struck down Midian at the rock of Oreb;
and he will raise his staff over the waters,
as he did in Egypt.
27 In that day their burden will be lifted from your shoulders,
their yoke from your neck;
the yoke will be broken
because you have grown so fat.*a*

28 They enter Aiath;
they pass through Migron;
they store supplies at Mikmash.
29 They go over the pass, and say,
"We will camp overnight at Geba."
Ramah trembles;
Gibeah of Saul flees.
30 Cry out, Daughter Gallim!
Listen, Laishah!
Poor Anathoth!
31 Madmenah is in flight;
the people of Gebim take cover.
32 This day they will halt at Nob;
they will shake their fist
at the mount of Daughter Zion,
at the hill of Jerusalem.

33 See, the Lord, the Lord Almighty,
will lop off the boughs with great power.
The lofty trees will be felled,
the tall ones will be brought low.
34 He will cut down the forest thickets with an ax;
Lebanon will fall before the Mighty One.

The Branch From Jesse

11 A shoot will come up from the stump of Jesse;
from his roots a Branch will bear fruit.
2 The Spirit of the Lord will rest on him—
the Spirit of wisdom and of understanding,
the Spirit of counsel and of might,
the Spirit of the knowledge and fear of the Lord—
3 and he will delight in the fear of the Lord.

He will not judge by what he sees with his eyes,
or decide by what he hears with his ears;
4 but with righteousness he will judge the needy,

973

---

a 27 Hebrew; Septuagint *broken / from your shoulders*

with justice he will give decisions for the poor of the earth.
He will strike the earth with the rod of his mouth;
   with the breath of his lips he will slay the wicked.
[5]Righteousness will be his belt
   and faithfulness the sash around his waist.

[6]The wolf will live with the lamb,
   the leopard will lie down with the goat,
the calf and the lion and the yearling[a] together;
   and a little child will lead them.
[7]The cow will feed with the bear,
   their young will lie down together,
   and the lion will eat straw like the ox.
[8]Infants will play near the hole of the cobra;
   young children will put their hands into the viper's nest.
[9]They will neither harm nor destroy
   on all my holy mountain,
for the earth will be filled with the knowledge of the LORD
   as the waters cover the sea.

974

HE IS: the Branch

11:1–9 The faithless kings of Judah were called "the stump of Jesse"—worthless and fruitless. Yet from the spiritually dead root of Jesse's line, God promised that a shoot would grow and a Branch would bear fruit. In fulfillment, Jesus, *the Branch*, emerged from the barren stump, bearing the fruit of righteousness.

Would your spiritual life be described as a dead and fruitless stump or a living vine? Are you more like the faithless kings or the Faithful King? The answer should be obvious through the fruit of your life. If you're truly connected to *the Branch*, then you will bear fruit (see John 15:1–17).

For the next He Is, go to p. 975.

[10]In that day the Root of Jesse will stand as a banner for the peoples; the nations will rally to him, and his resting place will be glorious. [11]In that day the Lord will reach out his hand a second time to reclaim the surviving remnant of his people from Assyria, from Lower Egypt, from Upper Egypt, from Cush,[b] from Elam, from Babylonia,[c] from Hamath and from the islands of the Mediterranean.

[12]He will raise a banner for the nations
   and gather the exiles of Israel;
he will assemble the scattered people of Judah
   from the four quarters of the earth.
[13]Ephraim's jealousy will vanish,
   and Judah's enemies[d] will be destroyed;
Ephraim will not be jealous of Judah,
   nor Judah hostile toward Ephraim.
[14]They will swoop down on the slopes of Philistia to the west;
   together they will plunder the people to the east.
They will lay hands on Edom and Moab,

---

a 6 Hebrew; Septuagint *lion will feed*   *b 11* That is, the upper Nile region   *c 11* Hebrew *Shinar*   *d 13* Or *hostility*

and the Ammonites will be subject to them.
¹⁵The LORD will dry up
    the gulf of the Egyptian sea;
with a scorching wind he will sweep his hand
    over the Euphrates River.
He will break it up into seven streams
    so that anyone can cross over in sandals.
¹⁶There will be a highway for the remnant of his people
    that is left from Assyria,
as there was for Israel
    when they came up from Egypt.

Songs of Praise

12 In that day you will say:

    "I will praise you, LORD.
        Although you were angry with me,
    your anger has turned away
        and you have comforted me.
  ²Surely God is my salvation;
    I will trust and not be afraid.
The LORD, the LORD, is my strength and my defense^a;
    he has become my salvation."
³With joy you will draw water
    from the wells of salvation.

HE IS: not angry

12:1–3 The prophet predicted the time when the Messiah would come to save his people. When the people turned to the Messiah, God would in turn strengthen and comfort his children, and Israel would praise the Lord because his anger had turned away.

He is *not angry*. While God is angry at your sin, he does not hold on to his anger with you. When you turn to the Messiah for salvation, he turns from his anger over your sin. He has an amazing capacity to hate the sin and love the sinner. As his child, you are the recipient of his comfort, not his anger (see also Hosea 14:4–8).

For the next He Is, go to p. 983.

⁴In that day you will say:

    "Give praise to the LORD, call on his name;
        make known among the nations what he has done,
        and proclaim that his name is exalted.
  ⁵Sing to the LORD, for he has done glorious things;
    let this be known to all the world.
  ⁶Shout aloud and sing for joy, people of Zion,
    for great is the Holy One of Israel among you."

---

^a *2* Or *song*

A Prophecy Against Babylon

13 A prophecy concerning Babylon that Isaiah son of Amoz saw:

²Raise a banner on a bare hilltop,
  shout to them;
beckon to them
  to enter the gates of the nobles.
³I have commanded my holy ones;
  I have summoned my warriors to carry out my wrath—
  those who rejoice in my triumph.

⁴Listen, a noise on the mountains,
  like that of a great multitude!
Listen, an uproar among the kingdoms,
  like nations massing together!
The LORD Almighty is mustering
  an army for war.
⁵They come from faraway lands,
  from the ends of the heavens—
the LORD and the weapons of his wrath—
  to destroy the whole country.

⁶Wail, for the day of the LORD is near;
  it will come like destruction from the Almighty.ᵃ
⁷Because of this, all hands will go limp,
  every man's heart will melt.
⁸Terror will seize them,
  pain and anguish will grip them;
  they will writhe like a woman in labor.
They will look aghast at each other,
  their faces aflame.

⁹See, the day of the LORD is coming
  —a cruel day, with wrath and fierce anger—
to make the land desolate
  and destroy the sinners within it.
¹⁰The stars of heaven and their constellations
  will not show their light.
The rising sun will be darkened
  and the moon will not give its light.
¹¹I will punish the world for its evil,
  the wicked for their sins.
I will put an end to the arrogance of the haughty
  and will humble the pride of the ruthless.
¹²I will make people scarcer than pure gold,
  more rare than the gold of Ophir.
¹³Therefore I will make the heavens tremble;
  and the earth will shake from its place
at the wrath of the LORD Almighty,
  in the day of his burning anger.

¹⁴Like a hunted gazelle,
  like sheep without a shepherd,

ᵃ *6 Hebrew Shaddai*

    they will all return to their own people,
      they will flee to their native land.
¹⁵Whoever is captured will be thrust through;
      all who are caught will fall by the sword.
¹⁶Their infants will be dashed to pieces before their eyes;
      their houses will be looted and their wives ravished.

¹⁷See, I will stir up against them the Medes,
    who do not care for silver
      and have no delight in gold.
¹⁸Their bows will strike down the young men;
    they will have no mercy on infants
      nor will they look with compassion on children.
¹⁹Babylon, the jewel of kingdoms,
    the pride and glory of the Babylonians,^a
will be overthrown by God
    like Sodom and Gomorrah.
²⁰She will never be inhabited
    or lived in through all generations;
there no nomads will pitch their tents,
    there no shepherds will rest their flocks.
²¹But desert creatures will lie there,
    jackals will fill her houses;
there the owls will dwell,
    and there the wild goats will leap about.
²²Hyenas will inhabit her strongholds,
    jackals her luxurious palaces.
Her time is at hand,
    and her days will not be prolonged.

14

    The Lord will have compassion on Jacob;
      once again he will choose Israel
      and will settle them in their own land.
    Foreigners will join them
      and unite with the house of Jacob.
²Nations will take them
    and bring them to their own place.
And the house of Israel will take possession of the nations
    and make them male and female servants in the Lord's land.
They will make captives of their captors
    and rule over their oppressors.

³On the day the Lord gives you relief from your suffering and turmoil and from the harsh labor forced on you, ⁴you will take up this taunt against the king of Babylon:

    How the oppressor has come to an end!
      How his fury^b has ended!
⁵The Lord has broken the rod of the wicked,
    the scepter of the rulers,
⁶which in anger struck down peoples
    with unceasing blows,

---

^a 19 Or Chaldeans   ^b 4 Dead Sea Scrolls, Septuagint and Syriac; the meaning of the word in the Masoretic Text is uncertain.

and in fury subdued nations
with relentless aggression.
⁷All the lands are at rest and at peace;
they break into singing.
⁸Even the junipers and the cedars of Lebanon
exult over you and say,
"Now that you have been laid low,
no one comes to cut us down."

⁹The realm of the dead below is all astir
to meet you at your coming;
it rouses the spirits of the departed to greet you—
all those who were leaders in the world;
it makes them rise from their thrones—
all those who were kings over the nations.
¹⁰They will all respond,
they will say to you,
"You also have become weak, as we are;
you have become like us."
¹¹All your pomp has been brought down to the grave,
along with the noise of your harps;
maggots are spread out beneath you
and worms cover you.

978

¹²How you have fallen from heaven,
morning star, son of the dawn!
You have been cast down to the earth,
you who once laid low the nations!
¹³You said in your heart,
"I will ascend to heaven;
I will raise my throne
above the stars of God;
I will sit enthroned on the mount of assembly,
on the utmost heights of Mount Zaphon.^a
¹⁴I will ascend above the tops of the clouds;
I will make myself like the Most High."
¹⁵But you are brought down to the realm of the dead,
to the depths of the pit.

¹⁶Those who see you stare at you,
they ponder your fate:
"Is this the man who shook the earth
and made kingdoms tremble,
¹⁷the man who made the world a wilderness,
who overthrew its cities
and would not let his captives go home?"

¹⁸All the kings of the nations lie in state,
each in his own tomb.
¹⁹But you are cast out of your tomb
like a rejected branch;
you are covered with the slain,

---

^a 13 Or of the north; Zaphon was the most sacred mountain of the Canaanites.

with those pierced by the sword,
    those who descend to the stones of the pit.
Like a corpse trampled underfoot,
²⁰ you will not join them in burial,
for you have destroyed your land
    and killed your people.

Let the offspring of the wicked
    never be mentioned again.
²¹Prepare a place to slaughter his children
    for the sins of their ancestors;
they are not to rise to inherit the land
    and cover the earth with their cities.

²²"I will rise up against them,"
    declares the Lord Almighty.
"I will wipe out Babylon's name and survivors,
    her offspring and descendants,"

                                      declares the Lord.

979

²³"I will turn her into a place for owls
    and into swampland;
I will sweep her with the broom of destruction,"
    declares the Lord Almighty.

²⁴The Lord Almighty has sworn,

"Surely, as I have planned, so it will be,
    and as I have purposed, so it will happen.
²⁵I will crush the Assyrian in my land;
    on my mountains I will trample him down.
His yoke will be taken from my people,
    and his burden removed from their shoulders."

²⁶This is the plan determined for the whole world;
    this is the hand stretched out over all nations.
²⁷For the Lord Almighty has purposed, and who can thwart him?
    His hand is stretched out, and who can turn it back?

A Prophecy Against the Philistines

²⁸This prophecy came in the year King Ahaz died:

²⁹Do not rejoice, all you Philistines,
    that the rod that struck you is broken;
from the root of that snake will spring up a viper,
    its fruit will be a darting, venomous serpent.
³⁰The poorest of the poor will find pasture,
    and the needy will lie down in safety.
But your root I will destroy by famine;
    it will slay your survivors.

³¹Wail, you gate! Howl, you city!
    Melt away, all you Philistines!
A cloud of smoke comes from the north,
    and there is not a straggler in its ranks.
³²What answer shall be given

to the envoys of that nation?
"The Lord has established Zion,
and in her his afflicted people will find refuge."

A Prophecy Against Moab

15 A prophecy concerning Moab:

Ar in Moab is ruined,
   destroyed in a night!
Kir in Moab is ruined,
   destroyed in a night!
²Dibon goes up to its temple,
   to its high places to weep;
Moab wails over Nebo and Medeba.
Every head is shaved
   and every beard cut off.
³In the streets they wear sackcloth;
   on the roofs and in the public squares
they all wail,
   prostrate with weeping.
⁴Heshbon and Elealeh cry out,
   their voices are heard all the way to Jahaz.
Therefore the armed men of Moab cry out,
   and their hearts are faint.

⁵My heart cries out over Moab;
   her fugitives flee as far as Zoar,
   as far as Eglath Shelishiyah.
They go up the hill to Luhith,
   weeping as they go;
on the road to Horonaim
   they lament their destruction.
⁶The waters of Nimrim are dried up
   and the grass is withered;
the vegetation is gone
   and nothing green is left.
⁷So the wealth they have acquired and stored up
   they carry away over the Ravine of the Poplars.
⁸Their outcry echoes along the border of Moab;
   their wailing reaches as far as Eglaim,
   their lamentation as far as Beer Elim.
⁹The waters of Dimon*ᵃ* are full of blood,
   but I will bring still more upon Dimon*ᵃ*—
a lion upon the fugitives of Moab
   and upon those who remain in the land.

16 Send lambs as tribute
   to the ruler of the land,
from Sela, across the desert,
   to the mount of Daughter Zion.
²Like fluttering birds

ᵃ 9 Dimon, a wordplay on Dibon (see verse 2), sounds like the Hebrew for *blood.*

ASKmeanYTHING

What made you leave your country and travel all that way to Jerusalem?

Word had come from afar about King Solomon—his riches, his achievements, his palace and temple, his God and of course, his wisdom. Others considered him the wisest man in the world, and I needed to see him for myself.

What was it you wanted to know?

Well, Solomon was supposed to be very great and rich and wise. I had heard the rumors from travelers. People talked about it in my country, and I was intrigued. Were all the reports true? They seemed too good to be true, actually. And I wanted to see for myself.

What did you find out?

Well, I went with the toughest questions I could think of, and being a queen myself I knew some of the difficulties that leaders often face. And as I pressed Solomon with everything that was on my mind, he astounded me. No question was too hard for him. He explained everything that I wanted to know—and then some! Clearly, the reports I had heard were not exaggerations or the flattering attempts to glorify a king. Solomon's wisdom, wealth and achievements far exceeded what I had heard.

So what conclusions did you draw?

The only conclusion possible: Solomon clearly had been blessed by his God. The super-human wisdom that Solomon possessed could only come from one source—the Lord God, the God of Israel. I came to believe that Solomon's God was delighted with him and had handpicked him to rule his nation. What other explanation could there be? Israel's God loved his people and blessed them with a king to rule with justice and righteousness.

Based on what you discovered, what advice would you give to others?

I would refer them to one of Solomon's proverbs: "The fear of the LORD is the beginning of knowledge." If you want true wisdom, you have to start with God and end with God. He is the source of the kind of wisdom that I was searching for, the only source for all people who seek wisdom throughout time.

FOR MORE INSIGHT: Look at what others writers have discovered about wisdom: Job 28:28; Isaiah 11:2; Hosea 14:9; 1 Corinthians 1:30; 2:6–16; and James 3:13–18.

981

pushed from the nest,
so are the women of Moab
at the fords of the Arnon.

³"Make up your mind," Moab says.
"Render a decision.
Make your shadow like night—
at high noon.
Hide the fugitives,
do not betray the refugees.
⁴Let the Moabite fugitives stay with you;
be their shelter from the destroyer."

The oppressor will come to an end,
and destruction will cease;
the aggressor will vanish from the land.
⁵In love a throne will be established;
in faithfulness a man will sit on it—
one from the house^a of David—
one who in judging seeks justice
and speeds the cause of righteousness.

⁶We have heard of Moab's pride—
her overweening pride and conceit,
her pride and her insolence—
but her boasts are empty.
⁷Therefore the Moabites wail,
they wail together for Moab.
Lament and grieve
for the raisin cakes of Kir Hareseth.
⁸The fields of Heshbon wither,
the vines of Sibmah also.
The rulers of the nations
have trampled down the choicest vines,
which once reached Jazer
and spread toward the desert.
Their shoots spread out
and went as far as the sea.^b
⁹So I weep, as Jazer weeps,
for the vines of Sibmah.
Heshbon and Elealeh,
I drench you with tears!
The shouts of joy over your ripened fruit
and over your harvests have been stilled.
¹⁰Joy and gladness are taken away from the orchards;
no one sings or shouts in the vineyards;
no one treads out wine at the presses,
for I have put an end to the shouting.
¹¹My heart laments for Moab like a harp,
my inmost being for Kir Hareseth.
¹²When Moab appears at her high place,

---

^a 5 Hebrew *tent*   ^b 8 Probably the Dead Sea

she only wears herself out;
    when she goes to her shrine to pray,
        it is to no avail.

¹³This is the word the LORD has already spoken concerning Moab. ¹⁴But now the LORD says: "Within three years, as a servant bound by contract would count them, Moab's splendor and all her many people will be despised, and her survivors will be very few and feeble."

A Prophecy Against Damascus

17 A prophecy concerning Damascus:

"See, Damascus will no longer be a city
    but will become a heap of ruins.
²The cities of Aroer will be deserted
    and left to flocks, which will lie down,
        with no one to make them afraid.
³The fortified city will disappear from Ephraim,
    and royal power from Damascus;
the remnant of Aram will be
    like the glory of the Israelites,"

                    declares the LORD Almighty.

⁴"In that day the glory of Jacob will fade;
    the fat of his body will waste away.
⁵It will be as when reapers harvest the standing grain,
    gathering the grain in their arms—
as when someone gleans heads of grain
    in the Valley of Rephaim.
⁶Yet some gleanings will remain,
    as when an olive tree is beaten,
leaving two or three olives on the topmost branches,
    four or five on the fruitful boughs,"

                    declares the LORD, the God of Israel.

⁷In that day people will look to their Maker
    and turn their eyes to the Holy One of Israel.
⁸They will not look to the altars,
    the work of their hands,

983

HE IS: the maker and breaker

17:7–11 God is *the maker and breaker.* Isaiah prophetically saw the day when people would look to their Maker during a time of desolation. He recorded the paradoxical power of the Holy One of Israel to make and break empires and individuals.

If you feel broken, understand that God often breaks us in order to make us. Like a doctor who fractures a bone to properly reform it, God uses brokenness to reform our hearts (see 2 Corinthians 7:10). Allow the Great Physician to break you of sin and self-sufficiency so he can make you into the woman he created you to be.

For the next He Is, go to p. 991.

and they will have no regard for the Asherah poles*a*
and the incense altars their fingers have made.

⁹In that day their strong cities, which they left because of the Israelites, will be like places abandoned to thickets and undergrowth. And all will be desolation.

¹⁰You have forgotten God your Savior;
you have not remembered the Rock, your fortress.
Therefore, though you set out the finest plants
and plant imported vines,
¹¹though on the day you set them out, you make them grow,
and on the morning when you plant them, you bring them to bud,
yet the harvest will be as nothing
in the day of disease and incurable pain.

¹²Woe to the many nations that rage—
they rage like the raging sea!
Woe to the peoples who roar—
they roar like the roaring of great waters!
¹³Although the peoples roar like the roar of surging waters,
when he rebukes them they flee far away,
driven before the wind like chaff on the hills,
like tumbleweed before a gale.
¹⁴In the evening, sudden terror!
Before the morning, they are gone!
This is the portion of those who loot us,
the lot of those who plunder us.

A Prophecy Against Cush

18 Woe to the land of whirring wings*b*
along the rivers of Cush,*c*
²which sends envoys by sea
in papyrus boats over the water.

Go, swift messengers,
to a people tall and smooth-skinned,
to a people feared far and wide,
an aggressive nation of strange speech,
whose land is divided by rivers.

³All you people of the world,
you who live on the earth,
when a banner is raised on the mountains,
you will see it,
and when a trumpet sounds,
you will hear it.
⁴This is what the LORD says to me:
"I will remain quiet and will look on from my dwelling place,
like shimmering heat in the sunshine,
like a cloud of dew in the heat of harvest."
⁵For, before the harvest, when the blossom is gone
and the flower becomes a ripening grape,

---

a 8 That is, wooden symbols of the goddess Asherah   *b 1* Or *of locusts*   *c 1* That is, the upper Nile region

he will cut off the shoots with pruning knives,
   and cut down and take away the spreading branches.
⁶They will all be left to the mountain birds of prey
   and to the wild animals;
the birds will feed on them all summer,
   the wild animals all winter.

⁷At that time gifts will be brought to the Lᴏʀᴅ Almighty

   from a people tall and smooth-skinned,
      from a people feared far and wide,
   an aggressive nation of strange speech,
      whose land is divided by rivers—

the gifts will be brought to Mount Zion, the place of the Name of the Lᴏʀᴅ Almighty.

A Prophecy Against Egypt

19 A prophecy concerning Egypt:

   See, the Lᴏʀᴅ rides on a swift cloud
      and is coming to Egypt.
   The idols of Egypt tremble before him,
      and the hearts of the Egyptians melt within them.

²"I will stir up Egyptian against Egyptian—
      brother will fight against brother,
      neighbor against neighbor,
      city against city,
      kingdom against kingdom.
³The Egyptians will lose heart,
      and I will bring their plans to nothing;
   they will consult the idols and the spirits of the dead,
      the mediums and the spiritists.
⁴I will hand the Egyptians over
      to the power of a cruel master,
   and a fierce king will rule over them,"
      declares the Lord, the Lᴏʀᴅ Almighty.

⁵The waters of the river will dry up,
      and the riverbed will be parched and dry.
⁶The canals will stink;
      the streams of Egypt will dwindle and dry up.
   The reeds and rushes will wither,
⁷   also the plants along the Nile,
      at the mouth of the river.
   Every sown field along the Nile
      will become parched, will blow away and be no more.
⁸Those who fish will groan and lament,
      all who cast hooks into the Nile;
   those who throw nets on the water
      will pine away.
⁹Those who work with combed flax will despair,
      the weavers of fine linen will lose hope.

985

¹⁰The workers in cloth will be dejected,
   and all the wage earners will be sick at heart.

¹¹The officials of Zoan are nothing but fools;
   the wise counselors of Pharaoh give senseless advice.
How can you say to Pharaoh,
   "I am one of the wise men,
   a disciple of the ancient kings"?

¹²Where are your wise men now?
   Let them show you and make known
what the Lᴏʀᴅ Almighty
   has planned against Egypt.
¹³The officials of Zoan have become fools,
   the leaders of Memphis are deceived;
the cornerstones of her peoples
   have led Egypt astray.
¹⁴The Lᴏʀᴅ has poured into them
   a spirit of dizziness;
they make Egypt stagger in all that she does,
   as drunkards stagger around in their vomit.
¹⁵There is nothing Egypt can do—
   head or tail, palm branch or reed.

¹⁶In that day the Egyptians will become weaklings. They will shudder with fear at the uplifted hand that the Lᴏʀᴅ Almighty raises against them. ¹⁷And the land of Judah will bring terror to the Egyptians; everyone to whom Judah is mentioned will be terrified, because of what the Lᴏʀᴅ Almighty is planning against them.

¹⁸In that day five cities in Egypt will speak the language of Canaan and swear allegiance to the Lᴏʀᴅ Almighty. One of them will be called the City of the Sun.ᵃ

¹⁹In that day there will be an altar to the Lᴏʀᴅ in the heart of Egypt, and a monument to the Lᴏʀᴅ at its border. ²⁰It will be a sign and witness to the Lᴏʀᴅ Almighty in the land of Egypt. When they cry out to the Lᴏʀᴅ because of their oppressors, he will send them a savior and defender, and he will rescue them. ²¹So the Lᴏʀᴅ will make himself known to the Egyptians, and in that day they will acknowledge the Lᴏʀᴅ. They will worship with sacrifices and grain offerings; they will make vows to the Lᴏʀᴅ and keep them. ²²The Lᴏʀᴅ will strike Egypt with a plague; he will strike them and heal them. They will turn to the Lᴏʀᴅ, and he will respond to their pleas and heal them.

²³In that day there will be a highway from Egypt to Assyria. The Assyrians will go to Egypt and the Egyptians to Assyria. The Egyptians and Assyrians will worship together. ²⁴In that day Israel will be the third, along with Egypt and Assyria, a blessingᵇ on the earth. ²⁵The Lᴏʀᴅ Almighty will bless them, saying, "Blessed be Egypt my people, Assyria my handiwork, and Israel my inheritance."

A Prophecy Against Egypt and Cush

20 In the year that the supreme commander, sent by Sargon king of Assyria, came to Ashdod and attacked and captured it— ²at that time the Lᴏʀᴅ spoke through Isaiah son of Amoz. He said to him, "Take off the sackcloth from your body and the sandals from your feet." And he did so, going around stripped and barefoot.

³Then the Lᴏʀᴅ said, "Just as my servant Isaiah has gone stripped and barefoot for three years, as a sign and portent against Egypt and Cush,ᶜ ⁴so the king of Assyria will lead away stripped and barefoot the Egyptian captives and Cushite exiles, young and old, with buttocks bared—to Egypt's shame. ⁵Those

ᵃ 18 Some manuscripts of the Masoretic Text, Dead Sea Scrolls, Symmachus and Vulgate; most manuscripts of the Masoretic Text *the City of Destruction*
ᵇ 24 Or *Assyria, whose names will be used in blessings* (see Gen. 48:20); or *Assyria, who will be seen by others as blessed*   ᶜ 3 That is, the upper Nile region; also in verse 5

who trusted in Cush and boasted in Egypt will be dismayed and put to shame. ⁶In that day the people who live on this coast will say, 'See what has happened to those we relied on, those we fled to for help and deliverance from the king of Assyria! How then can we escape?'"

A Prophecy Against Babylon

21 A prophecy concerning the Desert by the Sea:

> Like whirlwinds sweeping through the
>   southland,
>   an invader comes from the desert,
>   from a land of terror.

> ²A dire vision has been shown to me:
>   The traitor betrays, the looter takes
>   loot.
>   Elam, attack! Media, lay siege!
>   I will bring to an end all the groaning
>   she caused.

> ³At this my body is racked with pain,
>   pangs seize me, like those of a woman
>   in labor;
>   I am staggered by what I hear,
>   I am bewildered by what I see.
> ⁴My heart falters,
>   fear makes me tremble;
>   the twilight I longed for
>   has become a horror to me.

> ⁵They set the tables,
>   they spread the rugs,
>   they eat, they drink!
>   Get up, you officers,
>   oil the shields!

⁶This is what the Lord says to me:

> "Go, post a lookout
>   and have him report what he sees.
> ⁷When he sees chariots
>   with teams of horses,
>   riders on donkeys
>   or riders on camels,
>   let him be alert,
>   fully alert."

⁸And the lookout*ᵃ* shouted,

> "Day after day, my lord, I stand on the watchtower;
>   every night I stay at my post.
> ⁹Look, here comes a man in a chariot
>   with a team of horses.

987

ᵃ 8 Dead Sea Scrolls and Syriac; Masoretic Text A lion

> And he gives back the answer:
>> 'Babylon has fallen, has fallen!
> All the images of its gods
>> lie shattered on the ground!'"

[10] My people who are crushed on the threshing floor,
> I tell you what I have heard
from the LORD Almighty,
> from the God of Israel.

A Prophecy Against Edom

[11] A prophecy concerning Dumah[a]:

> Someone calls to me from Seir,
>> "Watchman, what is left of the night?
>> Watchman, what is left of the night?"
> [12] The watchman replies,
>> "Morning is coming, but also the night.
> If you would ask, then ask;
>> and come back yet again."

A Prophecy Against Arabia

[13] A prophecy concerning Arabia:

> You caravans of Dedanites,
>> who camp in the thickets of Arabia,
> [14]   bring water for the thirsty;
> you who live in Tema,
>> bring food for the fugitives.
> [15] They flee from the sword,
>> from the drawn sword,
> from the bent bow
>> and from the heat of battle.

[16] This is what the Lord says to me: "Within one year, as a servant bound by contract would count it, all the splendor of Kedar will come to an end. [17] The survivors of the archers, the warriors of Kedar, will be few." The LORD, the God of Israel, has spoken.

A Prophecy About Jerusalem

22 A prophecy concerning the Valley of Vision:

> What troubles you now,
>> that you have all gone up on the roofs,
> [2] you town so full of commotion,
>> you city of tumult and revelry?
> Your slain were not killed by the sword,
>> nor did they die in battle.
> [3] All your leaders have fled together;
>> they have been captured without using the bow.
> All you who were caught were taken prisoner together,
>> having fled while the enemy was still far away.
> [4] Therefore I said, "Turn away from me;
>> let me weep bitterly.

---

[a] 11 Dumah, a wordplay on Edom, means silence or stillness.

Do not try to console me
over the destruction of my people."

⁵The Lord, the LORD Almighty, has a day
of tumult and trampling and terror
in the Valley of Vision,
a day of battering down walls
and of crying out to the mountains.
⁶Elam takes up the quiver,
with her charioteers and horses;
Kir uncovers the shield.
⁷Your choicest valleys are full of chariots,
and horsemen are posted at the city gates.

⁸The Lord stripped away the defenses of
Judah,
and you looked in that day
to the weapons in the Palace of the
Forest.
⁹You saw that the City of David
had many breaches in its defenses;
you stored up water
in the Lower Pool.
¹⁰You counted the buildings in Jerusalem
and tore down houses to strengthen the
wall.
¹¹You built a reservoir between the two walls
for the water of the Old Pool,
but you did not look to the One who
made it,
or have regard for the One who planned
it long ago.

¹²The Lord, the LORD Almighty,
called you on that day
to weep and to wail,
to tear out your hair and put on
sackcloth.
¹³But see, there is joy and revelry,
slaughtering of cattle and killing of
sheep,
eating of meat and drinking of wine!
"Let us eat and drink," you say,
"for tomorrow we die!"

¹⁴The LORD Almighty has revealed this in my hearing: "Till your dying day this sin will not be atoned for," says the Lord, the LORD Almighty.

¹⁵This is what the Lord, the LORD Almighty, says:

"Go, say to this steward,
to Shebna, who is in charge of the palace:
¹⁶What are you doing here and who gave you permission
to cut out a grave for yourself here,

at issue: self-reliance

22:8–11 At first glance, the Israelites looked like hard-working, industrious go-getters. They had a problem, and they set out to fix it. What's wrong with that? Plenty. They did not look to the one who created their defenses and held them in his hands. Sadly, we are so much like the Israelites! When problems arise, we start making our plans and gathering our resources. In doing so, we often bypass our greatest resource and the best plan of all. The next time disaster strikes, don't rely on your own strengths and talents—rely on the one who created them.

989

hewing your grave on the height
and chiseling your resting place in the rock?

[17] "Beware, the LORD is about to take firm hold of you
and hurl you away, you mighty man.
[18] He will roll you up tightly like a ball
and throw you into a large country.
There you will die
and there the chariots you were so proud of
will become a disgrace to your master's house.
[19] I will depose you from your office,
and you will be ousted from your position.

[20] "In that day I will summon my servant, Eliakim son of Hilkiah. [21] I will clothe him with your robe and fasten your sash around him and hand your authority over to him. He will be a father to those who live in Jerusalem and to the house of Judah. [22] I will place on his shoulder the key to the house of David; what he opens no one can shut, and what he shuts no one can open. [23] I will drive him like a peg into a firm place; he will become a seat[a] of honor for the house of his father. [24] All the glory of his family will hang on him: its offspring and offshoots—all its lesser vessels, from the bowls to all the jars.

[25] "In that day," declares the LORD Almighty, "the peg driven into the firm place will give way; it will be sheared off and will fall, and the load hanging on it will be cut down." The LORD has spoken.

A Prophecy Against Tyre

23 A prophecy concerning Tyre:

Wail, you ships of Tarshish!
For Tyre is destroyed
and left without house or harbor.
From the land of Cyprus
word has come to them.

[2] Be silent, you people of the island
and you merchants of Sidon,
whom the seafarers have enriched.
[3] On the great waters
came the grain of the Shihor;
the harvest of the Nile[b] was the revenue of Tyre,
and she became the marketplace of the nations.

[4] Be ashamed, Sidon, and you fortress of the sea,
for the sea has spoken:
"I have neither been in labor nor given birth;
I have neither reared sons nor brought up daughters."
[5] When word comes to Egypt,
they will be in anguish at the report from Tyre.

[6] Cross over to Tarshish;
wail, you people of the island.
[7] Is this your city of revelry,
the old, old city,
whose feet have taken her
to settle in far-off lands?

---

[a] 23 Or throne   [b] 2,3 Masoretic Text; Dead Sea Scrolls Sidon, / who cross over the sea; / your envoys [3] are on the great waters. / The grain of the Shihor, / the harvest of the Nile,

⁸Who planned this against Tyre,
　the bestower of crowns,
　whose merchants are princes,
　　whose traders are renowned in the earth?
⁹The Lord Almighty planned it,
　to bring down her pride in all her splendor
　and to humble all who are renowned on the earth.

¹⁰Till*ᵃ* your land as they do along the Nile,
　Daughter Tarshish,
　for you no longer have a harbor.
¹¹The Lord has stretched out his hand over the sea
　and made its kingdoms tremble.
He has given an order concerning Phoenicia
　that her fortresses be destroyed.
¹²He said, "No more of your reveling,
　Virgin Daughter Sidon, now crushed!

HE IS: a destroyer

23:6–12 Isaiah predicted that God would destroy the sea trade of Phoenicia's two mighty cities, Tyre and Sidon. God methodically destroyed the sinful empires that proudly stood against him. The Lord himself planned it to humble the proud and self-reliant Phoenicians.

You may be sailing on smooth seas now, but if you are constructing a business, family or reputation without building upon God, then remember that he is *a destroyer*, able to humble you and remind you of his power (see Matthew 7:24–27). Choose to stretch out your hand to the Lord before he stretches out his hand against you.

For the next He Is, go to p. 1001.

"Up, cross over to Cyprus;
　even there you will find no rest."
¹³Look at the land of the Babylonians,*ᵇ*
　this people that is now of no account!
The Assyrians have made it
　a place for desert creatures;
they raised up their siege towers,
　they stripped its fortresses bare
　and turned it into a ruin.

¹⁴Wail, you ships of Tarshish;
　your fortress is destroyed!

¹⁵At that time Tyre will be forgotten for seventy years, the span of a king's life. But at the end of these seventy years, it will happen to Tyre as in the song of the prostitute:

¹⁶"Take up a harp, walk through the city,
　you forgotten prostitute;
play the harp well, sing many a song,
　so that you will be remembered."

ᵃ 10 Dead Sea Scrolls and some Septuagint manuscripts; Masoretic Text *Go through*　*ᵇ 13* Or *Chaldeans* myth# 59 "HER MARRIAGE IS PERFECT."

992

Everyone thinks we have a perfect marriage. We're both strong Christians and active in our church. My husband is very attentive and compliments me in public. He has a great job that provides us with a comfortable lifestyle. We have a beautiful home in a gated neighborhood. I drive a new Lexus. And we have a beautiful baby boy, Caleb.

Our friends are blind to the fact that there's a dark side to our marriage. When my husband is stressed, he gets angry and takes it out on me. He keeps a mental list of all the things I do wrong in his eyes. Behind closed doors, he calls me stupid, incompetent and much worse. He accuses me of cheating on him. He questions whether I'm a good mother. He's punched holes in the walls (which I dutifully cover with framed prints).

I'm terrified of his rages. But I have to own some of the responsibility myself. I get angry too. There have been times when I've thrown things across the room. I've tried to blame him for all the problems in our marriage. We've gone to counseling off and on together, but he can't see that it helps, so we stopped.

My husband has never turned his anger toward Caleb, and I don't think he ever would. But I know that Caleb can sense the hostility in our home. I thought my husband's outbursts would go away once Caleb was born. This is my second marriage, and I told myself I would never go through another divorce. I wish I were as naïve about our problems as everyone else seems to be. They think our marriage is perfect. Who would guess I secretly envy theirs?

—Linda

SINCE THE Garden of Eden, women have been tempted to fantasize about a "perfect" world. Eve thought that one piece of fruit would make her life perfect; instead, it cost her everything (see Genesis 3).

Today women believe similar lies. We fantasize that someone else's marriage is perfect and if only ours were like hers, our lives would be perfect, too. However, there are more than a few problems with comparisons.

- Fantasies are selective. Envy usually focuses on only part of a person's life: the good part (or the part we think is good). Her marriage. Her car. Her career. Her clothes. Her child.

- Fantasies thrive on misinformation. When we think someone's life is perfect, we usually don't know her as well as we think we do. Like the woman in this story, the object of our fantasy may have serious hidden issues, which we know nothing about.

- Fantasies of perfection prevent us from realistically working on our own problems. We have to deal with our problems head-on in order to make spiritual and emotional progress.

- As women, we do each other a terrible disservice by believing, feeding, envying and perpetuating the lie of a perfect life. The woman who seems to have it all together may be dying inside. If you have a friend who is trying hard to appear perfect, chances are she may need you more than all the rest of your friends combined. Don't encourage the lie. Be honest and available so that she knows that she can be honest with you and that you won't be disappointed in her.

- Fantasies stunt the growth of our friendships. Until we're willing to be honest with our Christian girlfriends, we never fully know each other.

There are no perfect marriages or lives because there are no perfect people. Many of the people we envy or put up on pedestals have endured or are enduring serious heartache— broken homes, financial crises, abuse, illness and countless other personal anguishes. Let's commit to being real and honest with our Christian sisters (see James 5:13–16).

"A successful marriage requires a vision that is larger than itself, a vision that transcends its earthly limitations, confusion and setbacks."
—Barry R. Leventhal, Ph.D.

993

"EACH OF YOU SHOULD TEST YOUR OWN ACTIONS. THEN YOU CAN TAKE PRIDE IN YOURSELF, WITHOUT COMPARING YOURSELF TO SOMEBODY ELSE."

GALATIANS 6:4

SEE ALSO

Exodus 20:17
Proverbs 14:10,30
James 3:13–18

For more on **Envy** and **Marriage** , check the index.

¹⁷At the end of seventy years, the L<small>ORD</small> will deal with Tyre. She will return to her lucrative prostitution and will ply her trade with all the kingdoms on the face of the earth. ¹⁸Yet her profit and her earnings will be set apart for the L<small>ORD</small>; they will not be stored up or hoarded. Her profits will go to those who live before the L<small>ORD</small>, for abundant food and fine clothes.

The L<small>ORD</small>'s Devastation of the Earth

24 See, the L<small>ORD</small> is going to lay waste the earth
　　and devastate it;
he will ruin its face
　　and scatter its inhabitants—
²it will be the same
　　for priest as for people,
　　for master as for his servant,
　　for mistress as for her servant,
　　for seller as for buyer,
　　for borrower as for lender,
　　for debtor as for creditor.
³The earth will be completely laid waste
　　and totally plundered.

　　　　　　　　　　The L<small>ORD</small> has spoken this word.

⁴The earth dries up and withers,
　　the world languishes and withers,
　　the heavens languish with the earth.
⁵The earth is defiled by its people;
　　they have disobeyed the laws,
violated the statutes
　　and broken the everlasting covenant.
⁶Therefore a curse consumes the earth;
　　its people must bear their guilt.
Therefore earth's inhabitants are burned up,
　　and very few are left.
⁷The new wine dries up and the vine withers;
　　all the merrymakers groan.
⁸The gaiety of the timbrels is stilled,
　　the noise of the revelers has stopped,
　　the joyful harp is silent.
⁹No longer do they drink wine with a song;
　　the beer is bitter to its drinkers.
¹⁰The ruined city lies desolate;
　　the entrance to every house is barred.
¹¹In the streets they cry out for wine;
　　all joy turns to gloom,
　　all gaiety is banished from the earth.
¹²The city is left in ruins,
　　its gate is battered to pieces.
¹³So will it be on the earth
　　and among the nations,
as when an olive tree is beaten,
　　or as when gleanings are left after the grape harvest.

¹⁴They raise their voices, they shout for joy;
　　from the west they acclaim the L<small>ORD</small>'s majesty.

994

¹⁵Therefore in the east give glory to the Lord;
>   exalt the name of the Lord, the God of Israel,
>   in the islands of the sea.
¹⁶From the ends of the earth we hear singing:
>   "Glory to the Righteous One."

>   But I said, "I waste away, I waste away!
>   Woe to me!
>   The treacherous betray!
>   With treachery the treacherous betray!"
¹⁷Terror and pit and snare await you,
>   people of the earth.
¹⁸Whoever flees at the sound of terror
>   will fall into a pit;
>   whoever climbs out of the pit
>   will be caught in a snare.

>   The floodgates of the heavens are opened,
>   the foundations of the earth shake.
¹⁹The earth is broken up,
>   the earth is split asunder,
>   the earth is violently shaken.
²⁰The earth reels like a drunkard,
>   it sways like a hut in the wind;
>   so heavy upon it is the guilt of its rebellion
>   that it falls—never to rise again.

²¹In that day the Lord will punish
>   the powers in the heavens above
>   and the kings on the earth below.
²²They will be herded together
>   like prisoners bound in a dungeon;
>   they will be shut up in prison
>   and be punished^a after many days.
²³The moon will be dismayed,
>   the sun ashamed;
>   for the Lord Almighty will reign
>   on Mount Zion and in Jerusalem,
>   and before its elders—with great glory.

Praise to the Lord

25 Lord, you are my God;
>   I will exalt you and praise your name,
>   for in perfect faithfulness
>   you have done wonderful things,
>   things planned long ago.
²You have made the city a heap of rubble,
>   the fortified town a ruin,
>   the foreigners' stronghold a city no more;
>   it will never be rebuilt.
³Therefore strong peoples will honor you;

995

---
^a 22 Or *released*

cities of ruthless nations will revere you.
⁴You have been a refuge for the poor,
    a refuge for the needy in their distress,
a shelter from the storm
    and a shade from the heat.
For the breath of the ruthless
    is like a storm driving against a wall
⁵   and like the heat of the desert.
You silence the uproar of foreigners;
    as heat is reduced by the shadow of a cloud,
    so the song of the ruthless is stilled.

⁶On this mountain the Lord
    Almighty will prepare
a feast of rich food for all
    peoples,
a banquet of aged wine—
    the best of meats and the
    finest of wines.
⁷On this mountain he will
    destroy
the shroud that enfolds all
    peoples,
the sheet that covers all
    nations;
⁸   he will swallow up death
    forever.
The Sovereign Lord will wipe
    away the tears
from all faces;
he will remove his people's disgrace
    from all the earth.

conversations

death «» 25:6–8

1» What distinguishes a Christian's view of death from a non-Christian's?

2» Describe the times in your life when you've had to grapple with the issue of death.

3» How do God's promises to wipe away your tears in the future comfort you *now*?

For more on **death**, check the index.
For the next Conversations, go to p. 1003.

⁹In that day they will say,

"Surely this is our God;
    we trusted in him, and he saved us.
This is the Lord, we trusted in him;
    let us rejoice and be glad in his salvation."

¹⁰The hand of the Lord will rest on this mountain;
    but Moab will be trampled in their land
    as straw is trampled down in the manure.
¹¹They will stretch out their hands in it,
    as swimmers stretch out their hands to swim.
God will bring down their pride
    despite the cleverness^a of their hands.
¹²He will bring down your high fortified walls
    and lay them low;
he will bring them down to the ground,
    to the very dust.

The Lord has spoken.

^a *11 The meaning of the Hebrew for this word is uncertain.*

A Song of Praise

26 In that day this song will be sung in the land of Judah:

We have a strong city;
    God makes salvation
    its walls and ramparts.
²Open the gates
    that the righteous nation may enter,
    the nation that keeps faith.
³You will keep in perfect peace
    those whose minds are steadfast,
    because they trust in you.
⁴Trust in the Lᴏʀᴅ forever,
    for the Lᴏʀᴅ, the Lᴏʀᴅ, is the Rock
    eternal.
⁵He humbles those who dwell on high,
    he lays the lofty city low;
he levels it to the ground
    and casts it down to the dust.
⁶Feet trample it down—
    the feet of the oppressed,
    the footsteps of the poor.

⁷The path of the righteous is level;
    you, the Upright One, make the way of
        the righteous smooth.
⁸Yes, Lᴏʀᴅ, walking in the way of your laws,ᵃ
    we wait for you;
your name and renown
    are the desire of our hearts.
⁹My soul yearns for you in the night;
    in the morning my spirit longs for you.
When your judgments come upon the earth,
    the people of the world learn righteousness.
¹⁰But when grace is shown to the wicked,
    they do not learn righteousness;
even in a land of uprightness they go on doing evil
    and do not regard the majesty of the Lᴏʀᴅ.
¹¹Lᴏʀᴅ, your hand is lifted high,
    but they do not see it.
Let them see your zeal for your people and be put to shame;
    let the fire reserved for your enemies consume them.

¹²Lᴏʀᴅ, you establish peace for us;
    all that we have accomplished you have done for us.
¹³Lᴏʀᴅ our God, other lords besides you have ruled over us,
    but your name alone do we honor.
¹⁴They are now dead, they live no more;
    their spirits do not rise.
You punished them and brought them to ruin;
    you wiped out all memory of them.

---

atissue:worry

26:3–4 *What if I can't get everything done today? What if I say something stupid? What if I never find a true friend? What if I can't lose weight? What if I get cancer? What if my mom dies? What if my husband loses his job? What if we fall out of love? What if . . . what if . . . what if . . .* It's amazing how many things we find to worry about. But we have a choice—we can worry or we can pray. Only when we rely on the Rock eternal will we find the perfect peace we long for.

997

¹⁵You have enlarged the nation, L<small>ORD</small>;
    you have enlarged the nation.
You have gained glory for yourself;
    you have extended all the borders of the land.

¹⁶L<small>ORD</small>, they came to you in their distress;
    when you disciplined them,
    they could barely whisper a prayer.^{*a*}
¹⁷As a pregnant woman about to give birth
    writhes and cries out in her pain,
    so were we in your presence, L<small>ORD</small>.
¹⁸We were with child, we writhed in pain,
    but we gave birth to wind.
We have not brought salvation to the earth,
    and the people of the world have not been reborn.^{*b*}

¹⁹But your dead will live, L<small>ORD</small>;
    their bodies will rise—
let those who dwell in the dust
    wake up and shout for joy—
your dew is like the dew of the morning;
    you will make it fall on the spirits of the dead.

²⁰Go, my people, enter your rooms
    and shut the doors behind you;
hide yourselves for a little while
    until his wrath has passed by.
²¹See, the L<small>ORD</small> is coming out of his dwelling
    to punish the people of the earth for their sins.
The earth will disclose the blood shed on it;
    the earth will conceal its slain no longer.

Deliverance of Israel

27 In that day,

    the L<small>ORD</small> will punish with his sword—
    his fierce, great and powerful sword—
Leviathan the gliding serpent,
    Leviathan the coiling serpent;
he will slay the monster of the sea.

²In that day—

    "Sing about a fruitful vineyard:
³ I, the L<small>ORD</small>, watch over it;
    I water it continually.
I guard it day and night
    so that no one may harm it.
⁴ I am not angry.
If only there were briers and thorns confronting me!
    I would march against them in battle;
    I would set them all on fire.

---

^{*a*} *16* The meaning of the Hebrew for this clause is uncertain. ^{*b*} *18* Or *have not fallen*

⁵Or else let them come to me for refuge;
  let them make peace with me,
  yes, let them make peace with me."

⁶In days to come Jacob will take root,
  Israel will bud and blossom
  and fill all the world with fruit.

⁷Has ⸤the LORD⸥ struck her
  as he struck down those who struck her?
  Has she been killed
  as those were killed who killed her?
⁸By warfare*a* and exile you contend with her—
  with his fierce blast he drives her out,
  as on a day the east wind blows.
⁹By this, then, will Jacob's guilt be atoned for,
  and this will be the full fruit of the removal of his sin:
  When he makes all the altar stones
  to be like limestone crushed to pieces,
  no Asherah poles*b* or incense altars
  will be left standing.
¹⁰The fortified city stands desolate,
  an abandoned settlement, forsaken like the wilderness;
  there the calves graze,
  there they lie down;
  they strip its branches bare.
¹¹When its twigs are dry, they are broken off
  and women come and make fires with them.
  For this is a people without understanding;
  so their Maker has no compassion on them,
  and their Creator shows them no favor.

¹²In that day the LORD will thresh from the flowing Euphrates to the Wadi of Egypt, and you, Israel, will be gathered up one by one. ¹³And in that day a great trumpet will sound. Those who were perishing in Assyria and those who were exiled in Egypt will come and worship the LORD on the holy mountain in Jerusalem.

Woe to the Leaders of Ephraim and Judah

28 Woe to that wreath, the pride of Ephraim's drunkards,
  to the fading flower, his glorious beauty,
  set on the head of a fertile valley—
  to that city, the pride of those laid low by wine!
²See, the Lord has one who is powerful and strong.
  Like a hailstorm and a destructive wind,
  like a driving rain and a flooding downpour,
  he will throw it forcefully to the ground.
³That wreath, the pride of Ephraim's drunkards,
  will be trampled underfoot.
⁴That fading flower, his glorious beauty,
  set on the head of a fertile valley,
  will be like figs ripe before harvest—

---

a **8** See Septuagint; the meaning of the Hebrew for this word is uncertain.   *b* **9** That is, wooden symbols of the goddess Asherah

as soon as people see them and take them in hand,
   they swallow them.

⁵In that day the Lord Almighty
   will be a glorious crown,
a beautiful wreath
   for the remnant of his people.
⁶He will be a spirit of justice
   to those who sit in judgment,
a source of strength
   to those who turn back the battle at the gate.

⁷And these also stagger from wine
   and reel from beer:
Priests and prophets stagger from beer
   and are befuddled with wine;
they reel from beer,
   they stagger when seeing visions,
   they stumble when rendering decisions.
⁸All the tables are covered with vomit
   and there is not a spot without filth.

⁹"Who is it he is trying to teach?
   To whom is he explaining his message?
To children weaned from their milk,
   to those just taken from the breast?
¹⁰For it is:
   Do this, do that,
   a rule for this, a rule for that^a;
   a little here, a little there."

¹¹Very well then, with foreign lips and strange tongues
   God will speak to this people,
¹²to whom he said,
   "This is the resting place, let the weary rest";
and, "This is the place of repose"—
   but they would not listen.
¹³So then, the word of the Lord to them will become:
   Do this, do that,
   a rule for this, a rule for that;
   a little here, a little there—
so that as they go they will fall backward;
   they will be injured and snared and captured.

¹⁴Therefore hear the word of the Lord, you scoffers
   who rule this people in Jerusalem.
¹⁵You boast, "We have entered into a covenant with death,
   with the realm of the dead we have made an agreement.
When an overwhelming scourge sweeps by,
   it cannot touch us,
for we have made a lie our refuge
   and falsehood^b our hiding place."

---

^a *10* Hebrew / *sav lasav sav lasav / kav lakav kav lakav* (probably meaningless sounds mimicking the prophet's words); also in verse 13   ^b *15* Or *false gods*

HE IS: the precious cornerstone

28:16 In ancient times, the cornerstone of a building gave it stability. This critical point united two walls and bore the weight of the structure so that it would stand firm. The prophet portrays the Messiah as *the precious cornerstone* on which God will build a strong church.

Jesus is the only cornerstone, the only sure foundation for life (see Psalm 118:22–23). If you're building your life on anything else—yourself, your accomplishments, your status, wealth, appearance or relationships—then your life may crumble at any time. However, if you're building your life on him, the tested stone, then your foundation is sure.

For the next He Is, go to p. 1012.

¹⁶So this is what the Sovereign LORD says:

"See, I lay a stone in Zion, a tested stone,
　a precious cornerstone for a sure foundation;
the one who relies on it
　will never be stricken with panic.
¹⁷I will make justice the measuring line
　and righteousness the plumb line;
hail will sweep away your refuge, the lie,
　and water will overflow your hiding place.
¹⁸Your covenant with death will be annulled;
　your agreement with the realm of the dead will not stand.
When the overwhelming scourge sweeps by,
　you will be beaten down by it.
¹⁹As often as it comes it will carry you away;
　morning after morning, by day and by night,
　it will sweep through."

The understanding of this message
　will bring sheer terror.
²⁰The bed is too short to stretch out on,
　the blanket too narrow to wrap around you.
²¹The LORD will rise up as he did at Mount Perazim,
　he will rouse himself as in the Valley of Gibeon—
to do his work, his strange work,
　and perform his task, his alien task.
²²Now stop your mocking,
　or your chains will become heavier;
the Lord, the LORD Almighty, has told me
　of the destruction decreed against the whole land.

²³Listen and hear my voice;
　pay attention and hear what I say.
²⁴When farmers plow for planting, do they plow continually?
　Do they keep on breaking up and working the soil?
²⁵When they have leveled the surface,
　do they not sow caraway and scatter cumin?
Do they not plant wheat in its place,ᵃ

ᵃ *25* The meaning of the Hebrew for this word is uncertain.

barley in its plot,[a]
and spelt in its field?
[26]Their God instructs them
and teaches them the right way.

[27]Caraway is not threshed with a sledge,
nor is a cartwheel rolled over cumin;
caraway is beaten out with a rod,
and cumin with a stick.
[28]Grain must be ground to make bread;
so one does not go on threshing it forever.
The wheels of a threshing cart may be rolled over it,
but one does not use horses to grind grain.
[29]All this also comes from the Lord Almighty,
whose plan is wonderful,
whose wisdom is magnificent.

Woe to David's City

29 Woe to you, Ariel, Ariel,
the city where David settled!
Add year to year
and let your cycle of festivals go on.
[2]Yet I will besiege Ariel;
she will mourn and lament,
she will be to me like an altar hearth.[b]
[3]I will encamp against you on all sides;
I will encircle you with towers
and set up my siege works against you.
[4]Brought low, you will speak from the ground;
your speech will mumble out of the dust.
Your voice will come ghostlike from the earth;
out of the dust your speech will whisper.

[5]But your many enemies will become like fine dust,
the ruthless hordes like blown chaff.
Suddenly, in an instant,
[6]   the Lord Almighty will come
with thunder and earthquake and great noise,
with windstorm and tempest and flames of a devouring fire.
[7]Then the hordes of all the nations that fight against Ariel,
that attack her and her fortress and besiege her,
will be as it is with a dream,
with a vision in the night—
[8]as when hungry people dream they are eating,
but they awaken, and their hunger remains;
as when thirsty people dream they are drinking,
but they awaken faint, with their thirst unquenched.
So will it be with the hordes of all the nations
that fight against Mount Zion.

[9]Be stunned and amazed,
blind yourselves and be sightless;

---

[a] 25 The meaning of the Hebrew for this word is uncertain.   [b] 2 The Hebrew for *altar hearth* sounds like the Hebrew for *Ariel.*

be drunk, but not from wine,
>   stagger, but not from beer.
[10] The LORD has brought over you a deep sleep:
>   He has sealed your eyes (the prophets);
>   he has covered your heads (the seers).

[11] For you this whole vision is nothing but words sealed in a scroll. And if you give the scroll to someone who can read, and say, "Read this, please," they will answer, "I can't; it is sealed." [12] Or if you give the scroll to someone who cannot read, and say, "Read this, please," they will answer, "I don't know how to read."

[13] The Lord says:

> "These people come near to me with
>   their mouth
> and honor me with their lips,
>   but their hearts are far from me.
> Their worship of me
>   is based on merely human rules they
>   have been taught.[a]
[14] Therefore once more I will astound
>   these people
> with wonder upon wonder;
> the wisdom of the wise will perish,
>   the intelligence of the intelligent will
>   vanish."
[15] Woe to those who go to great depths
>   to hide their plans from the LORD,
> who do their work in darkness and think,
>   "Who sees us? Who will know?"
[16] You turn things upside down,
>   as if the potter were thought to be like the clay!
> Shall what is formed say to the one who formed it,
>   "You did not make me"?
> Can the pot say to the potter,
>   "You know nothing"?

[17] In a very short time, will not Lebanon be turned into a fertile field
>   and the fertile field seem like a forest?
[18] In that day the deaf will hear the words of the scroll,
>   and out of gloom and darkness
>   the eyes of the blind will see.
[19] Once more the humble will rejoice in the LORD;
>   the needy will rejoice in the Holy One of Israel.
[20] The ruthless will vanish,
>   the mockers will disappear,
>   and all who have an eye for evil will be cut down—
[21] those who with a word make someone out to be guilty,
>   who ensnare the defender in court
>   and with false testimony deprive the innocent of justice.

[22] Therefore this is what the LORD, who redeemed Abraham, says to the house of Jacob:

conversations

hypocrisy «» 29:13

1» Why is it so easy to slip from true worship into a spiritual façade?

2» How do hypocritical Christians damage the church's reputation and affect non-Christians?

3» In what ways can *religion* interfere with true *worship*?

For more on **hypocrisy**, check the index.
For the next Conversations, go to p. 1011.

1003

---

[a] *13 Hebrew; Septuagint They worship me in vain; / their teachings are merely human rules*

"No longer will Jacob be ashamed;
    no longer will their faces grow pale.
²³When they see among them their children,
    the work of my hands,
they will keep my name holy;
    they will acknowledge the holiness of the Holy One of Jacob,
    and will stand in awe of the God of Israel.
²⁴Those who are wayward in spirit will gain understanding;
    those who complain will accept instruction."

Woe to the Obstinate Nation

30 "Woe to the obstinate children,"
        declares the LORD,

"to those who carry out plans that are not mine,
    forming an alliance, but not by my Spirit,
    heaping sin upon sin;
²who go down to Egypt
    without consulting me;
who look for help to Pharaoh's protection,
    to Egypt's shade for refuge.
³But Pharaoh's protection will be to your shame,
    Egypt's shade will bring you disgrace.
⁴Though they have officials in Zoan
    and their envoys have arrived in Hanes,
⁵everyone will be put to shame
    because of a people useless to them,
who bring neither help nor advantage,
    but only shame and disgrace."

⁶A prophecy concerning the animals of the Negev:

Through a land of hardship and distress,
    of lions and lionesses,
    of adders and darting snakes,
the envoys carry their riches on donkeys' backs,
    their treasures on the humps of camels,
to that unprofitable nation,
⁷   to Egypt, whose help is utterly useless.
Therefore I call her
    Rahab the Do-Nothing.

⁸Go now, write it on a tablet for them,
    inscribe it on a scroll,
that for the days to come
    it may be an everlasting witness.
⁹For these are rebellious people, deceitful children,
    children unwilling to listen to the LORD's instruction.
¹⁰They say to the seers,
    "See no more visions!"
and to the prophets,
    "Give us no more visions of what is right!
Tell us pleasant things,
    prophesy illusions.

1004

¹¹Leave this way,
   get off this path,
and stop confronting us
   with the Holy One of Israel!"

¹²Therefore, this is what the Holy One of Israel says:

"Because you have rejected this message,
   relied on oppression
   and depended on deceit,
¹³this sin will become for you
   like a high wall, cracked and bulging,
   that collapses suddenly, in an instant.
¹⁴It will break in pieces like pottery,
   shattered so mercilessly
that among its pieces not a fragment will
      be found
   for taking coals from a hearth
   or scooping water out of a cistern."

¹⁵This is what the Sovereign Lord, the Holy One of Is-
rael, says:

"In repentance and rest is your salvation,
   in quietness and trust is your strength,
   but you would have none of it.
¹⁶You said, 'No, we will flee on horses.'
   Therefore you will flee!
You said, 'We will ride off on swift horses.'
   Therefore your pursuers will be swift!
¹⁷A thousand will flee
   at the threat of one;
at the threat of five
   you will all flee away,
till you are left
   like a flagstaff on a mountaintop,
   like a banner on a hill."

¹⁸Yet the Lord longs to be gracious to you;
   therefore he will rise up to show you
      compassion.
For the Lord is a God of justice.
   Blessed are all who wait for him!

atissue:sin

30:12–18 Have you noticed how we often try to fix or deal with sin on our own? We attempt to clean things up, sort them out and make them right—*then* bring them to God. Perhaps we fear that God will respond to our sin as people would: with anger, disgust or rejection. But that's not God. He longs to be gracious to us. He is eager to show compassion. Skip the frenzied activity; instead, come to him in repentance and rest, in quietness and trust. You will be amazed at the blessings he heaps on those who wait for him.

1005

¹⁹People of Zion, who live in Jerusalem, you will weep no more. How gracious he will be when you cry for help! As soon as he hears, he will answer you. ²⁰Although the Lord gives you the bread of adversity and the water of affliction, your teachers will be hidden no more; with your own eyes you will see them. ²¹Whether you turn to the right or to the left, your ears will hear a voice behind you, saying, "This is the way; walk in it." ²²Then you will desecrate your idols overlaid with silver and your images covered with gold; you will throw them away like a menstrual cloth and say to them, "Away with you!"

²³He will also send you rain for the seed you sow in the ground, and the food that comes from the land will be rich and plentiful. In that day your cattle will graze in broad meadows. ²⁴The oxen and donkeys that work the soil will eat fodder and mash, spread out with fork and shovel. ²⁵In the day of great slaughter, when the towers fall, streams of water will flow on every high mountain and every lofty hill. ²⁶The

myth# 60

"IT'S NOT MY PLACE TO CONFRONT MY FRIEND."

It started out innocently enough. My friend Trina simply wanted to fit in with the people at her new job. She has always struggled with self-esteem, and I was happy that she finally found a group of friends to accept her—even if they aren't the best influences. At first, she would just go out for drinks with them after work. Then she started staying out late with them, not getting home till 10 or 11 every night, and then she started hanging out with them on weekends—partying, the club scene, getting drunk and only God knows what else. (Literally, only he would know—she often couldn't remember.) Over time it seems to me she has basically forgotten how she used to walk with God. It's as if she's become a completely different person.

I haven't known what to do about the situation. Truthfully, at first I thought it was just a phase, and I wouldn't have to say anything. Lately, I've realized that Trina's actions are becoming her lifestyle. So I've thought about saying something to her. I've even rehearsed what I would say to her in my head. The only problem is that I just can't make myself say it. We've been out to lunch or shopping a few times, and I've felt as if I should bring it up. But I don't want to stick my nose in her business if she doesn't want me there, and I don't want to ruin our friendship. After all, I'm her last connection to God.

If I push her too hard, I'm afraid she'll accuse me of being "holier than thou" and write me off as her friend. It's not as if I haven't made mistakes—ones she could easily name off the top of her head. I guess what I'm trying to say is that every time I think I'll confront her about her compromising actions, I remember the saying "Live and let live." Isn't that somewhere in the Bible? I don't want to ruin our friendship. After all, it's her life to live as she chooses.

—Nadirah

IS IT YOUR place to confront your friend who's going astray? Yes . . .

If she's a Christian. Christians are not the guardians of all social morality. If your friend does not follow Jesus and believe in the authority of God's Word, then she won't feel bound by the same standards you do. It's much easier to rebuke someone in love when there is a common standard of morality to appeal to (see 2 Timothy 4:2). Your method of confronting a non-Christian should be much different than that of confronting a Christian (see Ephesians 4:25). However, if your non-Christian friend is making self-destructive choices, she may need some advice and encouragement from you, though you may have to appeal to common sense or shared values rather than God's Word as your authority.

If she has invited you into her life. If you two are close enough friends that she has invited your opinion on her choices in the past, then you have a responsibility to speak up. But don't assert yourself if you two don't have the level of friendship that invites intimacy.

If after praying about it, you firmly believe the Lord wants you to speak up. Pray that the Lord would give you pure motives and the right words.

If you can do so lovingly. If you tend to come across as judgmental, condescending or harsh, then confrontation may not be the role for you.

Assuming you passed the test above, then how should you go about Biblically confronting a friend?

- **Choose the right time.** Oftentimes the last thing guilt-ridden Christians want to hear is rebuke—consider the prophet Isaiah's hostile reception (see Isaiah 30:10–11). However, James 5:19–20 says that it's possible to turn a sinner from the error of her way. God may lead you to speak to a friend at a particularly receptive moment.

- **Use your influence.** Christians are called to encourage each other and speak truth in a loving way when others need to hear it.

- **Keep your tone gentle and humble.** Don't feel that you can't confront your friend unless your life is perfect. Make sure you approach the situation with gentleness, humility and a pure heart.

- **Keep it private.** Matthew 18:15–20 instructs that you should first go to your sister *in private.* How tempting it is to want to tell others about the situation first! Don't gossip; instead, talk directly and only to her.

A true friend will speak the truth when someone needs to hear it. Are you the kind of friend who will risk rejection in order to do what is right, even when it is uncomfortable or difficult?

1007

"We will never win the battle and convince people we are right if we don't have love. We must have hearts filled with the restorative love of Christ and plenty of grace and forgiveness for people who have failed."

—Dennis Rainey

"IF A BROTHER OR SISTER SINS, GO AND POINT OUT THE FAULT, JUST BETWEEN THE TWO OF YOU. IF THEY LISTEN TO YOU, YOU HAVE WON THEM OVER."

MATTHEW 18:15

SEE ALSO

Proverbs 27:5–6
Galatians 6:1
Hebrews 10:24

For more on **Friendship** and **Confrontation**, check the index.

moon will shine like the sun, and the sunlight will be seven times brighter, like the light of seven full days, when the LORD binds up the bruises of his people and heals the wounds he inflicted.

²⁷See, the Name of the LORD comes from afar,
    with burning anger and dense clouds of smoke;
his lips are full of wrath,
    and his tongue is a consuming fire.
²⁸His breath is like a rushing torrent,
    rising up to the neck.
He shakes the nations in the sieve of destruction;
    he places in the jaws of the peoples
    a bit that leads them astray.
²⁹And you will sing
    as on the night you celebrate a holy festival;
your hearts will rejoice
    as when people playing pipes go up
to the mountain of the LORD,
    to the Rock of Israel.
³⁰The LORD will cause people to hear his majestic voice
    and will make them see his arm coming down
with raging anger and consuming fire,
    with cloudburst, thunderstorm and hail.
³¹The voice of the LORD will shatter Assyria;
    with his rod he will strike them down.
³²Every stroke the LORD lays on them
    with his punishing club
will be to the music of timbrels and
    harps,
as he fights them in battle with the
    blows of his arm.
³³Topheth has long been prepared;
    it has been made ready for the king.
Its fire pit has been made deep and
    wide,
    with an abundance of fire and wood;
the breath of the LORD,
    like a stream of burning sulfur,
    sets it ablaze.

Woe to Those Who Rely on Egypt

31 Woe to those who go down to Egypt for
    help,
who rely on horses,
who trust in the multitude of their
    chariots
    and in the great strength of their
    horsemen,
but do not look to the Holy One of Israel,
    or seek help from the LORD.
²Yet he too is wise and can bring
    disaster;
he does not take back his words.

1008

atissue:security

31:1–3 What do you find security in? Your job? Your husband? Your investments and savings? Your family? Your own talents and beauty? God says that woe—which means *anguish*, *affliction* and *misery*—will come to those who put their trust in anything but the Holy One of Israel. Everything else will ultimately fail. When it does, both you and what you were relying on will come crashing to the ground. Only if your security is grounded in God will you avoid being smashed to pieces. He alone provides true security. Better to learn that lesson the easy way than from experience.

He will rise up against the house of the wicked,
    against those who help evildoers.
³But the Egyptians are mortals and not God;
    their horses are flesh and not spirit.
When the LORD stretches out his hand,
    those who help will stumble,
    those who are helped will fall;
    all will perish together.

⁴This is what the LORD says to me:

    "As a lion growls,
      a great lion over its prey—
    and though a whole band of shepherds
      is called together against it,
    it is not frightened by their shouts
      or disturbed by their clamor—
    so the LORD Almighty will come down
      to do battle on Mount Zion and on its heights.
⁵Like birds hovering overhead,
    the LORD Almighty will shield Jerusalem;
he will shield it and deliver it,
    he will 'pass over' it and will rescue it."

⁶Return, you Israelites, to the One you have so greatly revolted against. ⁷For in that day every one of you will reject the idols of silver and gold your sinful hands have made.

⁸"Assyria will fall by no human sword;
    a sword, not of mortals, will devour them.
They will flee before the sword
    and their young men will be put to forced labor.
⁹Their stronghold will fall because of terror;
    at the sight of the battle standard their commanders will panic,"
declares the LORD,
    whose fire is in Zion,
    whose furnace is in Jerusalem.

The Kingdom of Righteousness

32   See, a king will reign in righteousness
      and rulers will rule with justice.
²Each one will be like a shelter from the wind
    and a refuge from the storm,
like streams of water in the desert
    and the shadow of a great rock in a thirsty land.

³Then the eyes of those who see will no longer be closed,
    and the ears of those who hear will listen.
⁴The fearful heart will know and understand,
    and the stammering tongue will be fluent and clear.
⁵No longer will the fool be called noble
    nor the scoundrel be highly respected.
⁶For fools speak folly,
    their hearts are bent on evil:
They practice ungodliness

1009

and spread error concerning the LORD;
    the hungry they leave empty
        and from the thirsty they withhold water.
⁷Scoundrels use wicked methods,
    they make up evil schemes
to destroy the poor with lies,
    even when the plea of the needy is just.
⁸But the noble make noble plans,
    and by noble deeds they stand.

The Women of Jerusalem

⁹You women who are so complacent,
    rise up and listen to me;
you daughters who feel secure,
    hear what I have to say!
¹⁰In little more than a year
    you who feel secure will tremble;
the grape harvest will fail,
    and the harvest of fruit will not come.
¹¹Tremble, you complacent women;
    shudder, you daughters who feel secure!
Strip off your clothes,
    put sackcloth around your waists.
¹²Beat your breasts for the pleasant fields,
    for the fruitful vines
¹³and for the land of my people,
    a land overgrown with thorns and briers—
yes, mourn for all houses of merriment
    and for this city of revelry.
¹⁴The fortress will be abandoned,
    the noisy city deserted;
citadel and watchtower will become a wasteland forever,
    the delight of donkeys, a pasture for flocks,
¹⁵till the Spirit is poured on us from on high,
    and the desert becomes a fertile field,
    and the fertile field seems like a forest.
¹⁶The LORD's justice will dwell in the desert,
    his righteousness live in the fertile field.
¹⁷The fruit of that righteousness will be peace;
    its effect will be quietness and confidence forever.
¹⁸My people will live in peaceful dwelling places,
    in secure homes,
    in undisturbed places of rest.
¹⁹Though hail flattens the forest
    and the city is leveled completely,
²⁰how blessed you will be,
    sowing your seed by every stream,
    and letting your cattle and donkeys range free.

Distress and Help

33 Woe to you, destroyer,
    you who have not been destroyed!
Woe to you, betrayer,

1010

you who have not been betrayed!
When you stop destroying,
   you will be destroyed;
when you stop betraying,
   you will be betrayed.

²LORD, be gracious to us;
   we long for you.
Be our strength every morning,
   our salvation in time of distress.
³At the uproar of your army, the peoples
      flee;
   when you rise up, the nations scatter.
⁴Their plunder is harvested as by young
      locusts;
   like a swarm of locusts people pounce
      on it.

⁵The LORD is exalted, for he dwells on high;
   he will fill Zion with his justice and righteousness.
⁶He will be the sure foundation for your times,
   a rich store of salvation and wisdom and knowledge;
   the fear of the LORD is the key to this treasure.^a

⁷Look, their brave men cry aloud in the streets;
   the envoys of peace weep bitterly.
⁸The highways are deserted,
   no travelers are on the roads.
The treaty is broken,
   its witnesses^b are despised,
   no one is respected.
⁹The land dries up and wastes away,
   Lebanon is ashamed and withers;
Sharon is like the Arabah,
   and Bashan and Carmel drop their leaves.

¹⁰"Now will I arise," says the LORD.
   "Now will I be exalted;
   now will I be lifted up.
¹¹You conceive chaff,
   you give birth to straw;
   your breath is a fire that consumes you.
¹²The peoples will be burned as if to lime;
   like cut thornbushes they will be set ablaze."

¹³You who are far away, hear what I have done;
   you who are near, acknowledge my power!
¹⁴The sinners in Zion are terrified;
   trembling grips the godless:
"Who of us can dwell with the consuming fire?
   Who of us can dwell with everlasting burning?"
¹⁵Those who walk righteously

conversations

worry «» 33:2–6

1 Why is worry such a natural response when you feel stressed?

2 Are you a worrier? What kinds of things do you worry about?

3 What promises from God help you deal with worry?

For more on **worry**, check the index.
For the next Conversations, go to p. 1014.

1011

---

^a 6 Or *is a treasure from him*   ^b 8 Dead Sea Scrolls; Masoretic Text / *the cities*

and speak what is right,
who reject gain from extortion
and keep their hands from accepting bribes,
who stop their ears against plots of murder
and shut their eyes against contemplating evil—
¹⁶they are the ones who will dwell on the heights,
whose refuge will be the mountain fortress.
Their bread will be supplied,
and water will not fail them.

¹⁷Your eyes will see the king in his beauty
and view a land that stretches afar.
¹⁸In your thoughts you will ponder the former terror:
"Where is that chief officer?
Where is the one who took the revenue?
Where is the officer in charge of the towers?"
¹⁹You will see those arrogant people no more,
people whose speech is obscure,
whose language is strange and incomprehensible.

²⁰Look on Zion, the city of our festivals;
your eyes will see Jerusalem,
a peaceful abode, a tent that will not be moved;
its stakes will never be pulled up,
nor any of its ropes broken.
²¹There the LORD will be our Mighty One.
It will be like a place of broad rivers and streams.
No galley with oars will ride them,
no mighty ship will sail them.
²²For the LORD is our judge,
the LORD is our lawgiver,
the LORD is our king;
it is he who will save us.

²³Your rigging hangs loose:
The mast is not held secure,
the sail is not spread.
Then an abundance of spoils will be divided
and even the lame will carry off plunder.

HE IS: our Mighty One

33:20–22 Throughout history, Jerusalem has been one of the most fought-over pieces of real estate in the world. The prophet looked forward to the time when *our Mighty One*, the Messiah, will return, and Jerusalem will be a peaceful abode.

But God's first priority is not a piece of real estate; it's a person—you. *Our Mighty One* first came to win the war for your soul. It's being fought between the flesh and the Spirit, between sin and freedom. Just as he'll do with Jerusalem, let the *Mighty One* win the battle for your heart and make your life a peaceful abode.

For the next He Is, go to p. 1029.

²⁴No one living in Zion will say, "I am ill";
　　and the sins of those who dwell there will be forgiven.

Judgment Against the Nations

34 Come near, you nations, and listen;
　　pay attention, you peoples!
Let the earth hear, and all that is in it,
　　the world, and all that comes out of it!
²The Lord is angry with all nations;
　　his wrath is on all their armies.
He will totally destroy^a them,
　　he will give them over to slaughter.
³Their slain will be thrown out,
　　their dead bodies will send up a stench;
　　the mountains will be soaked with their blood.
⁴All the stars in the sky will be dissolved
　　and the heavens rolled up like a scroll;
all the starry host will fall
　　like withered leaves from the vine,
　　like shriveled figs from the fig tree.

⁵My sword has drunk its fill in the heavens;
　　see, it descends in judgment on Edom,
　　the people I have totally destroyed.
⁶The sword of the Lord is bathed in blood,
　　it is covered with fat—
the blood of lambs and goats,
　　fat from the kidneys of rams.
For the Lord has a sacrifice in Bozrah
　　and a great slaughter in Edom.
⁷And the wild oxen will fall with them,
　　the bull calves and the great bulls.
Their land will be drenched with blood,
　　and the dust will be soaked with fat.

⁸For the Lord has a day of vengeance,
　　a year of retribution, to uphold Zion's cause.
⁹Edom's streams will be turned into pitch,
　　her dust into burning sulfur;
　　her land will become blazing pitch!
¹⁰It will not be quenched night or day;
　　its smoke will rise forever.
From generation to generation it will lie desolate;
　　no one will ever pass through it again.
¹¹The desert owl^b and screech owl^b will possess it;
　　the great owl^b and the raven will nest there.
God will stretch out over Edom
　　the measuring line of chaos
　　and the plumb line of desolation.
¹²Her nobles will have nothing there to be called a kingdom,
　　all her princes will vanish away.

^a 2 The Hebrew term refers to the irrevocable giving over of things or persons to the Lord, often by totally destroying them; also in verse 5.　^b 11 The precise identification of these birds is uncertain.

¹³Thorns will overrun her citadels,
    nettles and brambles her strongholds.
She will become a haunt for jackals,
    a home for owls.
¹⁴Desert creatures will meet with hyenas,
    and wild goats will bleat to each other;
there the night creatures will also lie down
    and find for themselves places of rest.
¹⁵The owl will nest there and lay eggs,
    she will hatch them, and care for her young
    under the shadow of her wings;
there also the falcons will gather,
    each with its mate.

¹⁶Look in the scroll of the LORD and read:

None of these will be missing,
    not one will lack her mate.
For it is his mouth that has given the order,
    and his Spirit will gather them together.
¹⁷He allots their portions;
    his hand distributes them by measure.
They will possess it forever
    and dwell there from generation to generation.

1014

Joy of the Redeemed

35

The desert and the parched land will be glad;
    the wilderness will rejoice and blossom.
Like the crocus, ²it will burst into bloom;
    it will rejoice greatly and
        shout for joy.
The glory of Lebanon will be
        given to it,
    the splendor of Carmel and
        Sharon;
they will see the glory of the
        LORD,
    the splendor of our God.

³Strengthen the feeble hands,
    steady the knees that give
        way;
⁴say to those with fearful
        hearts,
    "Be strong, do not fear;
your God will come,
    he will come with
        vengeance;
with divine retribution
    he will come to save you."

⁵Then will the eyes of the blind be opened
    and the ears of the deaf unstopped.

"conversations"

assurance «» 35:1–4

1 » What's the difference between encouragement and assurance of salvation?

2 » What causes you to doubt your salvation?

3 » What gives you assurance?

For more on **assurance**, check the index.
For the next Conversations, go to p. 1028.

⁶Then will the lame leap like a deer,
  and the mute tongue shout for joy.
Water will gush forth in the wilderness
  and streams in the desert.
⁷The burning sand will become a pool,
  the thirsty ground bubbling springs.
In the haunts where jackals once lay,
  grass and reeds and papyrus will grow.

⁸And a highway will be there;
  it will be called the Way of Holiness;
  it will be for those who walk on that Way.
The unclean will not journey on it;
  wicked fools will not go about on it.
⁹No lion will be there,
  nor any ravenous beast;
  they will not be found there.
But only the redeemed will walk there,
¹⁰ and those the LORD has rescued will return.
They will enter Zion with singing;
  everlasting joy will crown their heads.
Gladness and joy will overtake them,
  and sorrow and sighing will flee away.

Sennacherib Threatens Jerusalem

36 In the fourteenth year of King Hezekiah's reign, Sennacherib king of Assyria attacked all the fortified cities of Judah and captured them. ²Then the king of Assyria sent his field commander with a large army from Lachish to King Hezekiah at Jerusalem. When the commander stopped at the aqueduct of the Upper Pool, on the road to the Launderer's Field, ³Eliakim son of Hilkiah the palace administrator, Shebna the secretary, and Joah son of Asaph the recorder went out to him.

⁴The field commander said to them, "Tell Hezekiah:

"'This is what the great king, the king of Assyria, says: On what are you basing this confidence of yours? ⁵You say you have counsel and might for war—but you speak only empty words. On whom are you depending, that you rebel against me? ⁶Look, I know you are depending on Egypt, that splintered reed of a staff, which pierces the hand of anyone who leans on it! Such is Pharaoh king of Egypt to all who depend on him. ⁷But if you say to me, "We are depending on the LORD our God"—isn't he the one whose high places and altars Hezekiah removed, saying to Judah and Jerusalem, "You must worship before this altar"?

⁸"'Come now, make a bargain with my master, the king of Assyria: I will give you two thousand horses—if you can put riders on them! ⁹How then can you repulse one officer of the least of my master's officials, even though you are depending on Egypt for chariots and horsemen*ᵃ*? ¹⁰Furthermore, have I come to attack and destroy this land without the LORD? The LORD himself told me to march against this country and destroy it.'"

¹¹Then Eliakim, Shebna and Joah said to the field commander, "Please speak to your servants in Aramaic, since we understand it. Don't speak to us in Hebrew in the hearing of the people on the wall."

¹²But the commander replied, "Was it only to your master and you that my master sent me to say these things, and not to the people sitting on the wall—who, like you, will have to eat their own excrement and drink their own urine?"

¹³Then the commander stood and called out in Hebrew, "Hear the words of the great king, the king of Assyria! ¹⁴This is what the king says: Do not let Hezekiah deceive you. He cannot deliver you! ¹⁵Do not

ᵃ 9 Or charioteers

let Hezekiah persuade you to trust in the LORD when he says, 'The LORD will surely deliver us; this city will not be given into the hand of the king of Assyria.'

¹⁶"Do not listen to Hezekiah. This is what the king of Assyria says: Make peace with me and come out to me. Then every one of you will eat from your own vine and fig tree and drink water from your own cistern, ¹⁷until I come and take you to a land like your own—a land of grain and new wine, a land of bread and vineyards.

¹⁸"Do not let Hezekiah mislead you when he says, 'The LORD will deliver us.' Have the gods of any nations ever delivered their lands from the hand of the king of Assyria? ¹⁹Where are the gods of Hamath and Arpad? Where are the gods of Sepharvaim? Have they rescued Samaria from my hand? ²⁰Who of all the gods of these countries have been able to save their lands from me? How then can the LORD deliver Jerusalem from my hand?"

²¹But the people remained silent and said nothing in reply, because the king had commanded, "Do not answer him."

²²Then Eliakim son of Hilkiah the palace administrator, Shebna the secretary and Joah son of Asaph the recorder went to Hezekiah, with their clothes torn, and told him what the field commander had said.

Jerusalem's Deliverance Foretold

37 When King Hezekiah heard this, he tore his clothes and put on sackcloth and went into the temple of the LORD. ²He sent Eliakim the palace administrator, Shebna the secretary, and the leading priests, all wearing sackcloth, to the prophet Isaiah son of Amoz. ³They told him, "This is what Hezekiah says: This day is a day of distress and rebuke and disgrace, as when children come to the moment of birth and there is no strength to deliver them. ⁴It may be that the LORD your God will hear the words of the field commander, whom his master, the king of Assyria, has sent to ridicule the living God, and that he will rebuke him for the words the LORD your God has heard. Therefore pray for the remnant that still survives."

⁵When King Hezekiah's officials came to Isaiah, ⁶Isaiah said to them, "Tell your master, 'This is what the LORD says: Do not be afraid of what you have heard—those words with which the underlings of the king of Assyria have blasphemed me. ⁷Listen! When he hears a certain report, I will make him want to return to his own country, and there I will have him cut down with the sword.'"

⁸When the field commander heard that the king of Assyria had left Lachish, he withdrew and found the king fighting against Libnah.

⁹Now Sennacherib received a report that Tirhakah, the king of Cush,ᵃ was marching out to fight against him. When he heard it, he sent messengers to Hezekiah with this word: ¹⁰"Say to Hezekiah king of Judah: Do not let the god you depend on deceive you when he says, 'Jerusalem will not be given into the hands of the king of Assyria.' ¹¹Surely you have heard what the kings of Assyria have done to all the countries, destroying them completely. And will you be delivered? ¹²Did the gods of the nations that were destroyed by my ancestors deliver them—the gods of Gozan, Harran, Rezeph and the people of Eden who were in Tel Assar? ¹³Where is the king of Hamath or the king of Arpad? Where are the kings of Lair, Sepharvaim, Hena and Ivvah?"

Hezekiah's Prayer

¹⁴Hezekiah received the letter from the messengers and read it. Then he went up to the temple of the LORD and spread it out before the LORD. ¹⁵And Hezekiah prayed to the LORD: ¹⁶"LORD Almighty, the God of Israel, enthroned between the cherubim, you alone are God over all the kingdoms of the earth. You have made heaven and earth. ¹⁷Give ear, LORD, and hear; open your eyes, LORD, and see; listen to all the words Sennacherib has sent to ridicule the living God.

¹⁸"It is true, LORD, that the Assyrian kings have laid waste all these peoples and their lands. ¹⁹They have thrown their gods into the fire and destroyed them, for they were not gods but only wood and stone, fashioned by human hands. ²⁰Now, LORD our God, deliver us from his hand, so that all the kingdoms of the earth may know that you, LORD, are the only God.ᵇ"

ᵃ *9* That is, the upper Nile region   ᵇ *20* Dead Sea Scrolls (see also 2 Kings 19:19); Masoretic Text *you alone are the* LORD

Sennacherib's Fall

²¹Then Isaiah son of Amoz sent a message to Hezekiah: "This is what the Lord, the God of Israel, says: Because you have prayed to me concerning Sennacherib king of Assyria, ²²this is the word the Lord has spoken against him:

> "Virgin Daughter Zion
>   despises and mocks you.
> Daughter Jerusalem
>   tosses her head as you flee.
> ²³Who is it you have ridiculed and blasphemed?
>   Against whom have you raised your voice
> and lifted your eyes in pride?
>   Against the Holy One of Israel!
> ²⁴By your messengers
>   you have ridiculed the Lord.
> And you have said,
>   'With my many chariots
> I have ascended the heights of the mountains,
>   the utmost heights of Lebanon.
> I have cut down its tallest cedars,
>   the choicest of its junipers.
> I have reached its remotest heights,
>   the finest of its forests.
> ²⁵I have dug wells in foreign lands*ᵃ*
>   and drunk the water there.
> With the soles of my feet
>   I have dried up all the streams of Egypt.'
>
> ²⁶"Have you not heard?
>   Long ago I ordained it.
> In days of old I planned it;
>   now I have brought it to pass,
> that you have turned fortified cities
>   into piles of stone.
> ²⁷Their people, drained of power,
>   are dismayed and put to shame.
> They are like plants in the field,
>   like tender green shoots,
> like grass sprouting on the roof,
>   scorched*ᵇ* before it grows up.
>
> ²⁸"But I know where you are
>   and when you come and go
>   and how you rage against me.
> ²⁹Because you rage against me
>   and because your insolence has reached my ears,
> I will put my hook in your nose
>   and my bit in your mouth,
> and I will make you return
>   by the way you came.

1017

---

³⁰"This will be the sign for you, Hezekiah:

"This year you will eat what grows by itself,
    and the second year what springs from that.
But in the third year sow and reap,
    plant vineyards and eat their fruit.
³¹Once more a remnant of the house of Judah
    will take root below and bear fruit above.
³²For out of Jerusalem will come a remnant,
    and out of Mount Zion a band of survivors.
The zeal of the Lord Almighty
    will accomplish this.

³³"Therefore this is what the Lord says concerning the king of Assyria:

"He will not enter this city
    or shoot an arrow here.
He will not come before it with shield
    or build a siege ramp against it.
³⁴By the way that he came he will return;
    he will not enter this city,"

                                   declares the Lord.

³⁵"I will defend this city and save it,
    for my sake and for the sake of David my servant!"

³⁶Then the angel of the Lord went out and put to death a hundred and eighty-five thousand in the Assyrian camp. When the people got up the next morning—there were all the dead bodies! ³⁷So Sennacherib king of Assyria broke camp and withdrew. He returned to Nineveh and stayed there.

³⁸One day, while he was worshiping in the temple of his god Nisrok, his sons Adrammelek and Sharezer killed him with the sword, and they escaped to the land of Ararat. And Esarhaddon his son succeeded him as king.

Hezekiah's Illness

38 In those days Hezekiah became ill and was at the point of death. The prophet Isaiah son of Amoz went to him and said, "This is what the Lord says: Put your house in order, because you are going to die; you will not recover."

²Hezekiah turned his face to the wall and prayed to the Lord, ³"Remember, Lord, how I have walked before you faithfully and with wholehearted devotion and have done what is good in your eyes." And Hezekiah wept bitterly.

⁴Then the word of the Lord came to Isaiah: ⁵"Go and tell Hezekiah, 'This is what the Lord, the God of your father David, says: I have heard your prayer and seen your tears; I will add fifteen years to your life. ⁶And I will deliver you and this city from the hand of the king of Assyria. I will defend this city.

⁷"This is the Lord's sign to you that the Lord will do what he has promised: ⁸I will make the shadow cast by the sun go back the ten steps it has gone down on the stairway of Ahaz.'" So the sunlight went back the ten steps it had gone down.

⁹A writing of Hezekiah king of Judah after his illness and recovery:

¹⁰I said, "In the prime of my life
    must I go through the gates of death
    and be robbed of the rest of my years?"
¹¹I said, "I will not again see the Lord,
    the Lord, in the land of the living;
no longer will I look on my fellow mortals,
    or be with those who now dwell in this world.

¹²Like a shepherd's tent my house
    has been pulled down and taken from me.
Like a weaver I have rolled up my life,
    and he has cut me off from the loom;
    day and night you made an end of me.
¹³I waited patiently till dawn,
    but like a lion he broke all my bones;
    day and night you made an end of me.
¹⁴I cried like a swift or thrush,
    I moaned like a mourning dove.
My eyes grew weak as I looked to the
        heavens.
    I am being threatened; Lord, come to
        my aid!"

¹⁵But what can I say?
    He has spoken to me, and he himself has
        done this.
I will walk humbly all my years
    because of this anguish of my soul.
¹⁶Lord, by such things people live;
    and my spirit finds life in them too.
You restored me to health
    and let me live.
¹⁷Surely it was for my benefit
    that I suffered such anguish.
In your love you kept me
    from the pit of destruction;
you have put all my sins
    behind your back.
¹⁸For the grave cannot praise you,
    death cannot sing your praise;
those who go down to the pit
    cannot hope for your faithfulness.
¹⁹The living, the living—they praise you,
    as I am doing today;
parents tell their children
    about your faithfulness.

²⁰The LORD will save me,
    and we will sing with stringed instruments
all the days of our lives
    in the temple of the LORD.

²¹Isaiah had said, "Prepare a poultice of figs and apply it to the boil, and he will recover."
²²Hezekiah had asked, "What will be the sign that I will go up to the temple of the LORD?"

Envoys From Babylon

39 At that time Marduk-Baladan son of Baladan king of Babylon sent Hezekiah letters and a gift, because he had heard of his illness and recovery. ²Hezekiah received the envoys gladly and showed them what was in his storehouses—the silver, the gold, the spices, the fine olive oil—his entire armory and everything found among his treasures. There was nothing in his palace or in all his kingdom that Hezekiah did not show them.

1019

³Then Isaiah the prophet went to King Hezekiah and asked, "What did those men say, and where did they come from?"

"From a distant land," Hezekiah replied. "They came to me from Babylon."

⁴The prophet asked, "What did they see in your palace?"

"They saw everything in my palace," Hezekiah said. "There is nothing among my treasures that I did not show them."

⁵Then Isaiah said to Hezekiah, "Hear the word of the Lord Almighty: ⁶The time will surely come when everything in your palace, and all that your predecessors have stored up until this day, will be carried off to Babylon. Nothing will be left, says the Lord. ⁷And some of your descendants, your own flesh and blood who will be born to you, will be taken away, and they will become eunuchs in the palace of the king of Babylon."

⁸"The word of the Lord you have spoken is good," Hezekiah replied. For he thought, "There will be peace and security in my lifetime."

Comfort for God's People

40 Comfort, comfort my people,
   says your God.
²Speak tenderly to Jerusalem,
   and proclaim to her
that her hard service has been completed,
   that her sin has been paid for,
that she has received from the Lord's hand
   double for all her sins.

³A voice of one calling:
"In the wilderness prepare
   the way for the Lord*ᵃ*;
make straight in the desert
   a highway for our God.*ᵇ*
⁴Every valley shall be raised up,
   every mountain and hill made low;
the rough ground shall become level,
   the rugged places a plain.
⁵And the glory of the Lord will be revealed,
   and all people will see it together.
                    For the mouth of the Lord has spoken."

⁶A voice says, "Cry out."
   And I said, "What shall I cry?"

"All people are like grass,
   and all human faithfulness is like the flowers of the field.
⁷The grass withers and the flowers fall,
   because the breath of the Lord blows on them.
   Surely the people are grass.
⁸The grass withers and the flowers fall,
   but the word of our God endures forever."

⁹You who bring good news to Zion,
   go up on a high mountain.
You who bring good news to Jerusalem,*ᶜ*
   lift up your voice with a shout,

ᵃ 3 Or A voice of one calling in the wilderness: / "Prepare the way for the Lord   ᵇ 3 Hebrew; Septuagint make straight the paths of our God   ᶜ 9 Or Zion, bringer of good news, / go up on a high mountain. / Jerusalem, bringer of good news

lift it up, do not be afraid;
    say to the towns of Judah,
    "Here is your God!"
¹⁰See, the Sovereign Lord comes with power,
    and his arm rules for him.
  See, his reward is with him,
    and his recompense accompanies him.
¹¹He tends his flock like a shepherd:
    He gathers the lambs in his arms
  and carries them close to his heart;
    he gently leads those that have young.

¹²Who has measured the waters in the hollow of his hand,
    or with the breadth of his hand marked off the heavens?
  Who has held the dust of the earth in a basket,
    or weighed the mountains on the scales
    and the hills in a balance?
¹³Who can fathom the Spirit*a* of the Lord,
    or instruct the Lord as his counselor?
¹⁴Whom did the Lord consult to enlighten him,
    and who taught him the right way?
  Who was it that taught him knowledge,
    or showed him the path of understanding?

¹⁵Surely the nations are like a drop in a bucket;
    they are regarded as dust on the scales;
  he weighs the islands as though they were fine dust.
¹⁶Lebanon is not sufficient for altar fires,
    nor its animals enough for burnt offerings.
¹⁷Before him all the nations are as nothing;
    they are regarded by him as worthless
    and less than nothing.

¹⁸With whom, then, will you compare God?
    To what image will you liken him?
¹⁹As for an idol, a metal worker casts it,
    and a goldsmith overlays it with gold
    and fashions silver chains for it.
²⁰People too poor to present such an offering
    select wood that will not rot.
  They look for a skilled worker
    to set up an idol that will not topple.

²¹Do you not know?
    Have you not heard?
  Has it not been told you from the beginning?
    Have you not understood since the earth was founded?
²²He sits enthroned above the circle of the earth,
    and its people are like grasshoppers.
  He stretches out the heavens like a canopy,
    and spreads them out like a tent to live in.
²³He brings princes to naught

1021

---

a 13 Or *mind*

and reduces the rulers of this world to nothing.
²⁴No sooner are they planted,
    no sooner are they sown,
    no sooner do they take root in the ground,
than he blows on them and they wither,
    and a whirlwind sweeps them away like chaff.

²⁵"To whom will you compare me?
    Or who is my equal?" says the Holy One.
²⁶Lift up your eyes and look to the heavens:
    Who created all these?
He who brings out the starry host one
        by one,
    and calls them each by name.
Because of his great power and mighty
        strength,
    not one of them is missing.

²⁷Why do you complain, Jacob?
    Why do you say, Israel,
"My way is hidden from the LORD;
    my cause is disregarded by my God"?
²⁸Do you not know?
    Have you not heard?
The LORD is the everlasting God,
    the Creator of the ends of the earth.
He will not grow tired or weary,
    and his understanding no one can
        fathom.
²⁹He gives strength to the weary
    and increases the power of the weak.
³⁰Even youths grow tired and weary,
    and young men stumble and fall;
³¹but those who hope in the LORD
    will renew their strength.
They will soar on wings like eagles;
    they will run and not grow weary,
    they will walk and not be faint.

The Helper of Israel

41 "Be silent before me, you islands!
        Let the nations renew their strength!
    Let them come forward and speak;
        let us meet together at the place of judgment.

²"Who has stirred up one from the east,
    calling him in righteousness to his service*a*?
He hands nations over to him
    and subdues kings before him.
He turns them to dust with his sword,
    to windblown chaff with his bow.
³He pursues them and moves on unscathed,

40:26–31 Does your marriage seem hopeless? Perhaps you've tried and tried, yet nothing has changed. You've pleaded with God to fix the problems, but he doesn't seem to be listening. So you've decided to solve it on your own. You feel you have no choice but to get out of the marriage. Don't give up! God is bigger than your problems. In very few cases does God condone divorce. In the majority of struggling marriages, God will make a way if you will wait for him. You may feel as if he doesn't see your struggle, but he does. He will give you strength to fight for your marriage.

aissue:considering divorce

1022

a 2 Or east, / whom victory meets at every step

by a path his feet have not traveled before.
⁴Who has done this and carried it through,
    calling forth the generations from the beginning?
I, the LORD—with the first of them
    and with the last—I am he."

⁵The islands have seen it and fear;
    the ends of the earth tremble.
They approach and come forward;
⁶   they help each other
    and say to their companions, "Be strong!"
⁷The metal worker encourages the goldsmith,
    and the one who smooths with the hammer
    spurs on the one who strikes the anvil.
One says of the welding, "It is good."
    The other nails down the idol so it will not topple.

⁸"But you, Israel, my servant,
    Jacob, whom I have chosen,
    you descendants of Abraham my friend,
⁹I took you from the ends of the earth,
    from its farthest corners I called you.
I said, 'You are my servant';
    I have chosen you and have not rejected you.
¹⁰So do not fear, for I am with you;
    do not be dismayed, for I am your God.
I will strengthen you and help you;
    I will uphold you with my righteous right
      hand.

¹¹"All who rage against you
    will surely be ashamed and disgraced;
those who oppose you
    will be as nothing and perish.
¹²Though you search for your enemies,
    you will not find them.
Those who wage war against you
    will be as nothing at all.
¹³For I am the LORD your God
    who takes hold of your right hand
and says to you, Do not fear;
    I will help you.
¹⁴Do not be afraid, you worm Jacob,
    little Israel, do not fear,
for I myself will help you," declares the
      LORD,
    your Redeemer, the Holy One of Israel.
¹⁵"See, I will make you into a threshing
      sledge,
new and sharp, with many teeth.
You will thresh the mountains and crush them,
    and reduce the hills to chaff.
¹⁶You will winnow them, the wind will pick them up,

at issue: fear

41:10 We all harbor secret fears. They hide in the dark corners of our hearts—until our life circumstances bring them charging out from the corners to terrify us. Only God can banish your fears from your heart altogether. The more you know the God who upholds you, the more you see that his power is greater than anything you face. His strength has no limit; his love for you has no end. May you come to know, deep in your heart, that even if the worst befalls you, you will be OK with God on your side. He is enough.

and a gale will blow them away.
But you will rejoice in the LORD
and glory in the Holy One of Israel.

¹⁷"The poor and needy search for water,
but there is none;
their tongues are parched with thirst.
But I the LORD will answer them;
I, the God of Israel, will not forsake them.
¹⁸I will make rivers flow on barren heights,
and springs within the valleys.
I will turn the desert into pools of water,
and the parched ground into springs.
¹⁹I will put in the desert
the cedar and the acacia, the myrtle and the olive.
I will set junipers in the wasteland,
the fir and the cypress together,
²⁰so that people may see and know,
may consider and understand,
that the hand of the LORD has done this,
that the Holy One of Israel has created it.

²¹"Present your case," says the LORD.
"Set forth your arguments," says Jacob's King.
²²"Tell us, you idols,
what is going to happen.
Tell us what the former things were,
so that we may consider them
and know their final outcome.
Or declare to us the things to come,
²³   tell us what the future holds,
so we may know that you are gods.
Do something, whether good or bad,
so that we will be dismayed and filled with fear.
²⁴But you are less than nothing
and you can do nothing;
those who choose you are detestable.

²⁵"I have stirred up one from the north, and he comes—
one from the rising sun who calls on my name.
He treads on rulers as if they were mortar,
as if he were a potter treading the clay.
²⁶Who told of this from the beginning, so we could know,
or beforehand, so we could say, 'He was right'?
No one told of this,
no one foretold it,
no one heard any words from you.
²⁷I was the first to tell Zion, 'Look, here they are!'
I gave to Jerusalem a messenger of good news.
²⁸I look but there is no one—
no one among the gods to give counsel,
no one to give answer when I ask them.
²⁹See, they are all false!

Their deeds amount to nothing;
    their images are but wind and confusion.

The Servant of the LORD

42 "Here is my servant, whom I uphold,
        my chosen one in whom I delight;
    I will put my Spirit on him,
        and he will bring justice to the nations.
²He will not shout or cry out,
        or raise his voice in the streets.
³A bruised reed he will not break,
        and a smoldering wick he will not snuff out.
    In faithfulness he will bring forth justice;
⁴   he will not falter or be discouraged
    till he establishes justice on earth.
        In his teaching the islands will put their hope."

⁵This is what God the LORD says—
he who created the heavens and stretched them out,
    who spread out the earth with all that springs from it,
who gives breath to its people,
    and life to those who walk on it:
⁶"I, the LORD, have called you in righteousness;
    I will take hold of your hand.
I will keep you and will make you
    to be a covenant for the people
    and a light for the Gentiles,
⁷to open eyes that are blind,
    to free captives from prison
    and to release from the dungeon those who sit in darkness.

⁸"I am the LORD; that is my name!
    I will not yield my glory to another
    or my praise to idols.
⁹See, the former things have taken place,
    and new things I declare;
before they spring into being
    I announce them to you."

Song of Praise to the LORD

¹⁰Sing to the LORD a new song,
    his praise from the ends of the earth,
you who go down to the sea, and all that is in it,
    you islands, and all who live in them.
¹¹Let the wilderness and its towns raise their voices;
    let the settlements where Kedar lives rejoice.
Let the people of Sela sing for joy;
    let them shout from the mountaintops.
¹²Let them give glory to the LORD
    and proclaim his praise in the islands.
¹³The LORD will march out like a champion,
    like a warrior he will stir up his zeal;

1025

with a shout he will raise the battle cry
and will triumph over his enemies.

¹⁴"For a long time I have kept silent,
I have been quiet and held myself back.
But now, like a woman in childbirth,
I cry out, I gasp and pant.
¹⁵I will lay waste the mountains and hills
and dry up all their vegetation;
I will turn rivers into islands
and dry up the pools.
¹⁶I will lead the blind by ways they have not known,
along unfamiliar paths I will guide them;
I will turn the darkness into light before them
and make the rough places smooth.
These are the things I will do;
I will not forsake them.
¹⁷But those who trust in idols,
who say to images, 'You are our gods,'
will be turned back in utter shame.

Israel Blind and Deaf

¹⁸"Hear, you deaf;
look, you blind, and see!
¹⁹Who is blind but my servant,
and deaf like the messenger I send?
Who is blind like the one in covenant with me,
blind like the servant of the LORD?
²⁰You have seen many things, but have paid no attention;
your ears are open, but you hear nothing."
²¹It pleased the LORD
for the sake of his righteousness
to make his law great and glorious.
²²But this is a people plundered and looted,
all of them trapped in pits
or hidden away in prisons.
They have become plunder,
with no one to rescue them;
they have been made loot,
with no one to say, "Send them back."

²³Which of you will listen to this
or pay close attention in time to come?
²⁴Who handed Jacob over to become loot,
and Israel to the plunderers?
Was it not the LORD,
against whom we have sinned?
For they would not follow his ways;
they did not obey his law.
²⁵So he poured out on them his burning anger,
the violence of war.
It enveloped them in flames, yet they did not understand;
it consumed them, but they did not take it to heart.

Israel's Only Savior

43 But now, this is what the LORD says—
he who created you, Jacob,
he who formed you, Israel:
"Do not fear, for I have redeemed you;
I have summoned you by name; you are mine.
²When you pass through the waters,
I will be with you;
and when you pass through the rivers,
they will not sweep over you.
When you walk through the fire,
you will not be burned;
the flames will not set you ablaze.
³For I am the LORD your God,
the Holy One of Israel, your Savior;
I give Egypt for your ransom,
Cushᵃ and Seba in your stead.
⁴Since you are precious and honored in my sight,
and because I love you,
I will give nations in exchange for you,
and peoples in exchange for your life.
⁵Do not be afraid, for I am with you;
I will bring your children from the east
and gather you from the west.
⁶I will say to the north, 'Give them up!'
and to the south, 'Do not hold them back.'
Bring my sons from afar
and my daughters from the ends of the earth—
⁷everyone who is called by my name,
whom I created for my glory,
whom I formed and made."

⁸Lead out those who have eyes but are blind,
who have ears but are deaf.
⁹All the nations gather together
and the peoples assemble.
Which of their gods foretold this
and proclaimed to us the former things?
Let them bring in their witnesses to prove they were right,
so that others may hear and say, "It is true."
¹⁰"You are my witnesses," declares the LORD,
"and my servant whom I have chosen,
so that you may know and believe me
and understand that I am he.
Before me no god was formed,
nor will there be one after me.
¹¹I, even I, am the LORD,
and apart from me there is no savior.
¹²I have revealed and saved and proclaimed—
I, and not some foreign god among you.

ᵃ *3* That is, the upper Nile region

You are my witnesses," declares the Lord, "that I am God.
  ¹³ Yes, and from ancient days I am he.
  No one can deliver out of my hand.
  When I act, who can reverse it?"

God's Mercy and Israel's Unfaithfulness

¹⁴This is what the Lord says—
  your Redeemer, the Holy One of Israel:
  "For your sake I will send to Babylon
    and bring down as fugitives all the Babylonians,ᵃ
    in the ships in which they took pride.
¹⁵I am the Lord, your Holy One,
  Israel's Creator, your King."

¹⁶This is what the Lord says—
  he who made a way
    through the sea,
  a path through the mighty
    waters,
¹⁷who drew out the chariots
    and horses,
  the army and
    reinforcements
    together,
  and they lay there, never to
    rise again,
  extinguished, snuffed out
    like a wick:
¹⁸"Forget the former things;
  do not dwell on the past.
¹⁹See, I am doing a new thing!
  Now it springs up; do you
    not perceive it?
  I am making a way in the wilderness
    and streams in the wasteland.
²⁰The wild animals honor me,
  the jackals and the owls,
  because I provide water in the wilderness
    and streams in the wasteland,
  to give drink to my people, my chosen,
²¹   the people I formed for myself
  that they may proclaim my praise.

²²"Yet you have not called on me, Jacob,
  you have not wearied yourselves for ᵇ me, Israel.
²³You have not brought me sheep for burnt offerings,
  nor honored me with your sacrifices.
  I have not burdened you with grain offerings
    nor wearied you with demands for incense.
²⁴You have not bought any fragrant calamus for me,
  or lavished on me the fat of your sacrifices.

1028

conversations

guilt over past sin «» 43:16–21

1 What are some consequences of dwelling on the past?

2 Could you ever reach a point where God would not help you start again?

3 How can guilt from your past blind you to the new things God is doing?

For more on **guilt**, check the index.
For the next Conversations, go to p. 1042.

ᵃ 14 Or Chaldeans   ᵇ 22 Or Jacob; / surely you have grown weary of

But you have burdened me with your sins
    and wearied me with your offenses.

25 "I, even I, am he who blots out
    your transgressions, for my own sake,
    and remembers your sins no more.
26 Review the past for me,
    let us argue the matter together;
    state the case for your innocence.
27 Your first father sinned;
    those I sent to teach you rebelled against me.
28 So I disgraced the dignitaries of your temple;
    I consigned Jacob to destruction[a]
    and Israel to scorn.

Israel the Chosen

44   "But now listen, Jacob, my servant,
    Israel, whom I have chosen.
2 This is what the LORD says—
    he who made you, who formed you in the womb,
    and who will help you:
Do not be afraid, Jacob, my servant,
    Jeshurun,[b] whom I have chosen.
3 For I will pour water on the thirsty land,
    and streams on the dry ground;
I will pour out my Spirit on your offspring,
    and my blessing on your descendants.
4 They will spring up like grass in a meadow,
    like poplar trees by flowing streams.
5 Some will say, 'I belong to the LORD';
    others will call themselves by the name of Jacob;
still others will write on their hand, 'The LORD's,'
    and will take the name Israel.

The LORD, Not Idols

6 "This is what the LORD says—
    Israel's King and Redeemer, the LORD Almighty:

1029

---

[a] 28 The Hebrew term refers to the irrevocable giving over of things or persons to the LORD, often by totally destroying them.   [b] 2 Jeshurun means the upright one, that is, Israel.

HE IS: first and last

44:6 The covenant people were going to be taken captive by a nation enmeshed in idolatry. Therefore, God warned them against worshiping idols by reminding them that he alone is God. He proclaimed that he is the *first and the last,* the only God.

    We too live in a land where people bow to false gods. Beware! Anything you value above God is an idol. Is he the *first* thing you consider in the morning and the *last* on your mind at night? If he's not *first and last* in your life, then maybe he's not Lord at all.

For the next He Is, go to p. 1035.

I am the first and I am the last;
　　apart from me there is no God.
⁷Who then is like me? Let them proclaim it.
　　Let them declare and lay out before me
what has happened since I established my ancient people,
　　and what is yet to come—
　　yes, let them foretell what will come.
⁸Do not tremble, do not be afraid.
　　Did I not proclaim this and foretell it long ago?
You are my witnesses. Is there any God besides me?
　　No, there is no other Rock; I know not one."

⁹All who make idols are nothing,
　　and the things they treasure are worthless.
Those who would speak up for them are blind;
　　they are ignorant, to their own shame.
¹⁰Who shapes a god and casts an idol,
　　which can profit nothing?
¹¹People like that will be put to shame;
　　skilled workers are only human beings.
Let them all come together and take their stand;
　　they will be brought down to terror and shame.

¹²The blacksmith takes a tool
　　and works with it in the coals;
he shapes an idol with hammers,
　　he forges it with the might of his arm.
He gets hungry and loses his strength;
　　he drinks no water and grows faint.
¹³The carpenter measures with a line
　　and makes an outline with a marker;
he roughs it out with chisels
　　and marks it with compasses.
He shapes it in human form,
　　human form in all its glory,
　　that it may dwell in a shrine.
¹⁴He cut down cedars,
　　or perhaps took a cypress or oak.
He let it grow among the trees of the forest,
　　or planted a pine, and the rain made it grow.
¹⁵It is used as fuel for burning;
　　some of it he takes and warms himself,
　　he kindles a fire and bakes bread.
But he also fashions a god and worships it;
　　he makes an idol and bows down to it.
¹⁶Half of the wood he burns in the fire;
　　over it he prepares his meal,
　　he roasts his meat and eats his fill.
He also warms himself and says,
　　"Ah! I am warm; I see the fire."
¹⁷From the rest he makes a god, his idol;
　　he bows down to it and worships.

He prays to it and says,
    "Save me! You are my god!"
¹⁸They know nothing, they understand nothing;
    their eyes are plastered over so they cannot see,
    and their minds closed so they cannot understand.
¹⁹No one stops to think,
    no one has the knowledge or understanding to say,
"Half of it I used for fuel;
    I even baked bread over its coals,
    I roasted meat and I ate.
Shall I make a detestable thing from what is left?
    Shall I bow down to a block of wood?"
²⁰Such people feed on ashes, a deluded heart misleads them;
    they cannot save themselves, or say,
    "Is not this thing in my right hand a lie?"

²¹"Remember these things, Jacob,
    for you, Israel, are my servant.
I have made you, you are my servant;
    Israel, I will not forget you.
²²I have swept away your offenses like a cloud,
    your sins like the morning mist.
Return to me,
    for I have redeemed you."

²³Sing for joy, you heavens, for the LORD has done this;
    shout aloud, you earth beneath.
Burst into song, you mountains,
    you forests and all your trees,
for the LORD has redeemed Jacob,
    he displays his glory in Israel.

Jerusalem to Be Inhabited

²⁴"This is what the LORD says—
    your Redeemer, who formed you in the womb:

I am the LORD,
    who has made all things,
    who alone stretched out the heavens,
    who spread out the earth by myself,

²⁵who foils the signs of false prophets
    and makes fools of diviners,
who overthrows the learning of the wise
    and turns it into nonsense,
²⁶who carries out the words of his servants
    and fulfills the predictions of his messengers,

who says of Jerusalem, 'It shall be inhabited,'
    of the towns of Judah, 'They shall be rebuilt,'
    and of their ruins, 'I will restore them,'
²⁷who says to the watery deep, 'Be dry,
    and I will dry up your streams,'
²⁸who says of Cyrus, 'He is my shepherd

and will accomplish all that I please;
he will say of Jerusalem, "Let it be rebuilt,"
and of the temple, "Let its foundations be laid."'

45 "This is what the Lord says to his anointed,
to Cyrus, whose right hand I take hold of
to subdue nations before him
and to strip kings of their armor,
to open doors before him
so that gates will not be shut:
²I will go before you
and will level the mountains^a;
I will break down gates of bronze
and cut through bars of iron.
³I will give you the treasures of darkness,
riches stored in secret places,
so that you may know that I am the Lord,
the God of Israel, who summons you by name.
⁴For the sake of Jacob my servant,
of Israel my chosen,
I summon you by name
and bestow on you a title of honor,
though you do not acknowledge me.
⁵I am the Lord, and there is no other;
apart from me there is no God.
I will strengthen you,
though you have not acknowledged
me,
⁶so that from the rising of the sun
to the place of its setting
people may know there is none besides
me.
I am the Lord, and there is no other.
⁷I form the light and create darkness,
I bring prosperity and create disaster;
I, the Lord, do all these things.

⁸"You heavens above, rain down my
righteousness;
let the clouds shower it down.
Let the earth open wide,
let salvation spring up,
let righteousness flourish with it;
I, the Lord, have created it.

⁹"Woe to those who quarrel with their
Maker,
those who are nothing but potsherds
among the potsherds on the ground.
Does the clay say to the potter,
'What are you making?'

at·issue:plurality

45:5–7 *You've got your God. I have mine. Some people think there is no God. It's all good.* That attitude reflects the dominant tenet of postmodern thinking: There's no absolute truth. Many people who think this way believe that right and wrong can be defined on an individual basis—"whatever's right for you." Fewer and fewer people believe there's only one true God. However, we as Christians know that God's Word contains the absolute truth, and there *is* a right way and a wrong way to view God. No matter what anyone else says, there's only one Lord—apart from him there is no God.

---

^a 2 Dead Sea Scrolls and Septuagint; the meaning of the word in the Masoretic Text is uncertain.

Does your work say,
　'The potter has no hands'?
[10] Woe to those who say to their father,
　'What have you begotten?'
or to their mother,
　'What have you brought to birth?'

[11] "This is what the LORD says—
　the Holy One of Israel, and its Maker:
Concerning things to come,
　do you question me about my children,
　or give me orders about the work of my hands?
[12] It is I who made the earth
　and created human beings on it.
My own hands stretched out the heavens;
　I marshaled their starry hosts.
[13] I will raise up Cyrus[a] in my righteousness:
　I will make all his ways straight.
He will rebuild my city
　and set my exiles free,
but not for a price or reward,
　says the LORD Almighty."

[14] This is what the LORD says:
　"The products of Egypt and the merchandise of Cush,[b]
　and those tall Sabeans—
they will come over to you
　and will be yours;
they will trudge behind you,
　coming over to you in chains.
They will bow down before you
　and plead with you, saying,
'Surely God is with you, and there is no other;
　there is no other god.'"

[15] Truly you are a God who has been hiding himself,
　the God and Savior of Israel.
[16] All the makers of idols will be put to shame and disgraced;
　they will go off into disgrace together.
[17] But Israel will be saved by the LORD
　with an everlasting salvation;
you will never be put to shame or disgraced,
　to ages everlasting.

[18] For this is what the LORD says—
he who created the heavens,
　he is God;
he who fashioned and made the earth,
　he founded it;
he did not create it to be empty,
　but formed it to be inhabited—
he says:

1033

"I am the LORD,
   and there is no other.
¹⁹I have not spoken in secret,
   from somewhere in a land of darkness;
I have not said to Jacob's descendants,
   'Seek me in vain.'
I, the LORD, speak the truth;
   I declare what is right.

²⁰"Gather together and come;
   assemble, you fugitives from the nations.
Ignorant are those who carry about idols of wood,
   who pray to gods that cannot save.
²¹Declare what is to be, present it—
   let them take counsel together.
Who foretold this long ago,
   who declared it from the distant past?
Was it not I, the LORD?
   And there is no God apart from me,
a righteous God and a Savior;
   there is none but me.

²²"Turn to me and be saved,
   all you ends of the earth;
for I am God, and there is no other.
²³By myself I have sworn,
   my mouth has uttered in all integrity
   a word that will not be revoked:
Before me every knee will bow;
   by me every tongue will swear.
²⁴They will say of me, 'In the LORD alone
   are deliverance and strength.'"
All who have raged against him
   will come to him and be put to shame.
²⁵But all the descendants of Israel
   will find deliverance in the LORD
   and will make their boast in him.

Gods of Babylon

46

Bel bows down, Nebo stoops low;
   their idols are borne by beasts of burden.[a]
The images that are carried about are burdensome,
   a burden for the weary.
²They stoop and bow down together;
   unable to rescue the burden,
   they themselves go off into captivity.

³"Listen to me, house of Jacob,
   all the remnant of the house of Israel,
you whom I have upheld since your birth,
   and have carried since you were born.
⁴Even to your old age and gray hairs

ᵃ 1 Or are but beasts and cattle

HE IS: the sustainer

46:3–4 Even though the people had wandered from God and were destined for punishment, God offered them hope. He promised to sustain them. He didn't promise a life of ease, but he did promise to be their *sustainer*. The same God who had carried them thus far would carry them through their trials.

Though you may be experiencing hardship and heartache, don't doubt that God has loved you from the moment you were conceived. Throughout your life, he is *the sustainer* who will carry you from the cradle to the grave (see Psalms 37:23–24; 55:22).

For the next He Is, go to p. 1049.

1035

I am he, I am he who will sustain you.
I have made you and I will carry you;
    I will sustain you and I will rescue you.

⁵"With whom will you compare me or count me equal?
    To whom will you liken me that we may be compared?
⁶Some pour out gold from their bags
    and weigh out silver on the scales;
they hire a goldsmith to make it into a god,
    and they bow down and worship it.
⁷They lift it to their shoulders and carry it;
    they set it up in its place, and there it stands.
    From that spot it cannot move.
Though people cry out to it, it does not answer;
    it cannot save them from their troubles.

⁸"Remember this, keep it in mind,
    take it to heart, you rebels.
⁹Remember the former things, those of long ago;
    I am God, and there is no other;
    I am God, and there is none like me.
¹⁰I make known the end from the beginning,
    from ancient times, what is still to come.
I say, 'My purpose will stand,
    and I will do all that I please.'
¹¹From the east I summon a bird of prey;
    from a far-off land, a man to fulfill my purpose.
What I have said, that I will bring about;
    what I have planned, that I will do.
¹²Listen to me, you stubborn-hearted,
    you who are now far from my righteousness.
¹³I am bringing my righteousness near,
    it is not far away;
    and my salvation will not be delayed.
I will grant salvation to Zion,
    my splendor to Israel.

The Fall of Babylon

47 "Go down, sit in the dust,
    Virgin Daughter Babylon;
sit on the ground without a throne,
    queen city of the Babylonians.*a*
No more will you be called
    tender or delicate.
² Take millstones and grind flour;
    take off your veil.
Lift up your skirts, bare your legs,
    and wade through the streams.
³ Your nakedness will be exposed
    and your shame uncovered.
I will take vengeance;
    I will spare no one."

⁴ Our Redeemer—the LORD Almighty is his name—
    is the Holy One of Israel.

⁵ "Sit in silence, go into darkness,
    queen city of the Babylonians;
no more will you be called
    queen of kingdoms.
⁶ I was angry with my people
    and desecrated my inheritance;
I gave them into your hand,
    and you showed them no mercy.
Even on the aged
    you laid a very heavy yoke.
⁷ You said, 'I am forever—
    the eternal queen!'
But you did not consider these things
    or reflect on what might happen.

⁸ "Now then, listen, you lover of pleasure,
    lounging in your security
and saying to yourself,
    'I am, and there is none besides me.
I will never be a widow
    or suffer the loss of children.'
⁹ Both of these will overtake you
    in a moment, on a single day:
loss of children and widowhood.
They will come upon you in full measure,
    in spite of your many sorceries
    and all your potent spells.
¹⁰ You have trusted in your wickedness
    and have said, 'No one sees me.'
Your wisdom and knowledge mislead you
    when you say to yourself,
    'I am, and there is none besides me.'

---

a 1 Or Chaldeans; also in verse 5

¹¹Disaster will come upon you,
    and you will not know how to conjure it away.
A calamity will fall upon you
    that you cannot ward off with a ransom;
a catastrophe you cannot foresee
    will suddenly come upon you.

¹²"Keep on, then, with your magic spells
    and with your many sorceries,
    which you have labored at since childhood.
Perhaps you will succeed,
    perhaps you will cause terror.
¹³All the counsel you have received has only worn you out!
    Let your astrologers come forward,
those stargazers who make predictions month by month,
    let them save you from what is coming upon you.
¹⁴Surely they are like stubble;
    the fire will burn them up.
They cannot even save themselves
    from the power of the flame.
Here are no coals to warm anyone;
    here is no fire to sit by.
¹⁵That is all they can do for you—
    these you have dealt with
    and labored with since childhood.
All of them go on in their error;
    there is not one that can save you.

Stubborn Israel

48   "Listen to this, house of Jacob,
    you who are called by the name of Israel
    and come from the line of Judah,
you who take oaths in the name of the Lord
    and invoke the God of Israel—
    but not in truth or righteousness—
²you who call yourselves citizens of the holy city
    and claim to rely on the God of Israel—
    the Lord Almighty is his name:
³I foretold the former things long ago,
    my mouth announced them and I made them known;
    then suddenly I acted, and they came to pass.
⁴For I knew how stubborn you were;
    the sinews of your neck were iron,
    your forehead was bronze.
⁵Therefore I told you these things long ago;
    before they happened I announced them to you
so that you could not say,
    'My images brought them about;
    my wooden image and metal god ordained them.'
⁶You have heard these things; look at them all.
    Will you not admit them?

"From now on I will tell you of new things,
of hidden things unknown to you.
[7] They are created now, and not long ago;
you have not heard of them before today.
So you cannot say,
'Yes, I knew of them.'
[8] You have neither heard nor understood;
from of old your ears have not been open.
Well do I know how treacherous you are;
you were called a rebel from birth.
[9] For my own name's sake I delay my wrath;
for the sake of my praise I hold it back from you,
so as not to destroy you completely.
[10] See, I have refined you, though not as silver;
I have tested you in the furnace of affliction.
[11] For my own sake, for my own sake, I do this.
How can I let myself be defamed?
I will not yield my glory to another.

Israel Freed

[12] "Listen to me, Jacob,
Israel, whom I have called:
I am he;
I am the first and I am the last.
[13] My own hand laid the foundations of the earth,
and my right hand spread out the heavens;
when I summon them,
they all stand up together.

[14] "Come together, all of you, and listen:
Which of the idols has foretold these things?
The LORD's chosen ally
will carry out his purpose against Babylon;
his arm will be against the Babylonians.[a]
[15] I, even I, have spoken;
yes, I have called him.
I will bring him,
and he will succeed in his mission.

[16] "Come near me and listen to this:

"From the first announcement I have not spoken in secret;
at the time it happens, I am there."

And now the Sovereign LORD has sent me,
endowed with his Spirit.

[17] This is what the LORD says—
your Redeemer, the Holy One of Israel:
"I am the LORD your God,
who teaches you what is best for you,
who directs you in the way you should go.

---
[a] 14 Or *Chaldeans*; also in verse 20

¹⁸ If only you had paid attention to my commands,
    your peace would have been like a river,
    your well-being like the waves of the sea.
¹⁹ Your descendants would have been like the sand,
    your children like its numberless grains;
their name would never be blotted out
    nor destroyed from before me."

²⁰ Leave Babylon,
    flee from the Babylonians!
Announce this with shouts of joy
    and proclaim it.
Send it out to the ends of the earth;
    say, "The LORD has redeemed his servant Jacob."
²¹ They did not thirst when he led them through the deserts;
    he made water flow for them from the rock;
he split the rock
    and water gushed out.

²² "There is no peace," says the LORD, "for the wicked."

The Servant of the LORD

49 Listen to me, you islands;
    hear this, you distant nations:
Before I was born the LORD called me;
    from my birth he has made mention of my name.
² He made my mouth like a sharpened sword,
    in the shadow of his hand he hid me;
he made me into a polished arrow
    and concealed me in his quiver.
³ He said to me, "You are my servant,
    Israel, in whom I will display my splendor."
⁴ But I said, "I have labored in vain;
    I have spent my strength for nothing at all.
Yet what is due me is in the LORD's hand,
    and my reward is with my God."

⁵ And now the LORD says—
    he who formed me in the womb to be his servant
to bring Jacob back to him
    and gather Israel to himself,
for I am^a honored in the eyes of the LORD
    and my God has been my strength—
⁶ he says:
"It is too small a thing for you to be my servant
    to restore the tribes of Jacob
    and bring back those of Israel I have kept.
I will also make you a light for the Gentiles,
    that my salvation may reach to the ends of the earth."

⁷ This is what the LORD says—
    the Redeemer and Holy One of Israel—

---

^a 5 Or him, / but Israel would not be gathered; / yet I will be

myth#61

"MY PARENTS WILL ALWAYS BE THERE FOR ME."

I remember as a little girl my dad would count to three and I would jump off a brick wall on our patio and into his arms. It was my favorite game. Even though it was a long way to the ground, I was never afraid. I knew that he would always catch me. And he did—I never once fell. As soon as I landed, I'd climb back up on the wall and beg, "Again, Daddy!"

I always knew that no matter what happened in life my dad would be there for me. So would my mom. While they weren't perfect parents, they were pretty amazing. They sacrificed to send me to a private school. They came to every concert, awards night or play I was ever in. It never occurred to me that my dad had to take time off work to come to my mid-day concerts. I took it for granted that my parents would be there. They knew all my friends, and ours was the house that was always open. My dad swore to me that if I was ever in trouble, he would move heaven and earth to come get me. Even when I went off to college, I knew that all I had to do was call, and he'd be there. I have always counted on my parents in a way I've never counted on anyone else in my life. Sometimes I feel like I trust them more than I trust God.

Some of my friends' parents now have serious health problems, and my friend's dad just died of a heart attack. I've started to think about my own mom and dad getting older. They're visibly slowing down, not quite as confident or as agile as they used to be. I feel like our roles are starting to reverse, and it scares me. I don't know what I would do without them.

—Kyoko

REGARDLESS OF HOW

old we are, losing our parents is a life-changing event. At any age, a person who loses a parent feels orphaned, as if she's completely alone in the world for the first time. She steps into full adulthood where she's now her own authority figure. She grapples with complicated emotions and a heightened sense of vulnerability, whether she's 10 years old or 60 years old. For most of us, having our parents alive gives us a sense of security, identity and acceptance, and a source of friendship, advice and approval. When we lose our parents, we feel as if a piece of us is missing. Remember . . .

- **Parents are human.** They can't always be there for us because they can't predict the future. As they age, they will slow down. Chances are high that at some point they will become sick. While we shouldn't live with a sense of dread, we can't put all of our hopes into the stability of parental relationships. God wants us to look to him as our primary source of love and security.

- **Parents are imperfect.** They may get divorced. They may make unwise choices. They may fail in their careers or investments. While God commands us to honor them, we must not idolize them. Parents may let us down or abandon us, but God promises he will never do so. He is the perfect father (see Psalm 2:7). He won't lose his memory or his health. He promises to always be there for us and never forget us (see Isaiah 49:15–16).

- **We often outlive our parents.** The sad truth is that you will probably bury your parents someday. Let this fact remind you to savor the time you have with them. Let it also remind you to put your hope and trust in the Eternal One. Even though your parents will die someday, you can rest in the fact that if they know Christ, they are with him. Of course you will grieve, but you will also have the hope and assurance of seeing them again one day in heaven (see 1 Thessalonians 4:13–14).

> "Every year 5 percent of the population loses a parent to death."
>
> —Shari Butler

> ## "A FATHER TO THE FATHERLESS, A DEFENDER OF WIDOWS, IS GOD IN HIS HOLY DWELLING."
>
> PSALM 68:5

SEE ALSO

Isaiah 26:3–4
Isaiah 57:1–2
Jeremiah 3:19

For more on **Family**, check the index.

to him who was despised and abhorred by the nation,
    to the servant of rulers:
"Kings will see you and stand up,
    princes will see and bow down,
because of the LORD, who is faithful,
    the Holy One of Israel, who has chosen you."

Restoration of Israel

⁸This is what the LORD says:

"In the time of my favor I will answer you,
    and in the day of salvation I will help you;
I will keep you and will make you
    to be a covenant for the people,
to restore the land
    and to reassign its desolate inheritances,
⁹to say to the captives, 'Come out,'
    and to those in darkness, 'Be free!'

"They will feed beside the roads
    and find pasture on every barren hill.
¹⁰They will neither hunger nor thirst,
    nor will the desert heat or the sun beat down on them.
He who has compassion on them will guide them
    and lead them beside springs of water.
¹¹I will turn all my mountains into roads,
    and my highways will be raised up.
¹²See, they will come from afar—
    some from the north, some from the west,
    some from the region of Aswan.ᵃ"

¹³Shout for joy, you heavens;
    rejoice, you earth;
    burst into song, you mountains!
For the LORD comforts his
    people
    and will have compassion
    on his afflicted ones.

¹⁴But Zion said, "The LORD has
    forsaken me,
    the Lord has forgotten me."

¹⁵"Can a mother forget the baby
    at her breast
    and have no compassion on
    the child she has
    borne?
Though she may forget,
    I will not forget you!
¹⁶See, I have engraved you on
    the palms of my
    hands;

1042

conversations

abandonment «» 49:15–16

1» Have you ever felt abandoned? Who or what caused you to feel that way?

2» Could God ever abandon you? Would he? How do you know?

3» How does finding your security in God give you confidence?

For more on **abandonment**, check the index.
For the next Conversations, go to p. 1054.

ᵃ 12 Dead Sea Scrolls; Masoretic Text *Sinim*

your walls are ever before me.
¹⁷Your children hasten back,
and those who laid you waste depart from you.
¹⁸Lift up your eyes and look around;
all your children gather and come to you.
As surely as I live," declares the Lord,
"you will wear them all as ornaments;
you will put them on, like a bride.

¹⁹"Though you were ruined and made desolate
and your land laid waste,
now you will be too small for your people,
and those who devoured you will be far away.
²⁰The children born during your bereavement
will yet say in your hearing,
'This place is too small for us;
give us more space to live in.'
²¹Then you will say in your heart,
'Who bore me these?
I was bereaved and barren;
I was exiled and rejected.
Who brought these up?
I was left all alone,
but these—where have they come from?'"

²²This is what the Sovereign Lord says:

"See, I will beckon to the nations,
I will lift up my banner to the peoples;
they will bring your sons in their arms
and carry your daughters on their hips.
²³Kings will be your foster fathers,
and their queens your nursing mothers.
They will bow down before you with their faces to the ground;
they will lick the dust at your feet.
Then you will know that I am the Lord;
those who hope in me will not be disappointed."

²⁴Can plunder be taken from warriors,
or captives be rescued from the fierce^a?

²⁵But this is what the Lord says:

"Yes, captives will be taken from warriors,
and plunder retrieved from the fierce;
I will contend with those who contend with you,
and your children I will save.
²⁶I will make your oppressors eat their own flesh;
they will be drunk on their own blood, as with wine.
Then the whole human race will know
that I, the Lord, am your Savior,
your Redeemer, the Mighty One of Jacob."

1043

---

^a 24 Dead Sea Scrolls, Vulgate and Syriac (see also Septuagint and verse 25); Masoretic Text *righteous*

Israel's Sin and the Servant's Obedience

50 This is what the LORD says:

"Where is your mother's certificate of divorce
    with which I sent her away?
Or to which of my creditors
    did I sell you?
Because of your sins you were sold;
    because of your transgressions your mother was sent away.
²When I came, why was there no one?
    When I called, why was there no one to answer?
Was my arm too short to deliver you?
    Do I lack the strength to rescue you?
By a mere rebuke I dry up the sea,
    I turn rivers into a desert;
their fish rot for lack of water
    and die of thirst.
³I clothe the heavens with darkness
    and make sackcloth its covering."

⁴The Sovereign LORD has given me an instructed tongue,
    to know the word that sustains the weary.
He wakens me morning by morning,
    wakens my ear to listen like one being taught.
⁵The Sovereign LORD has opened my ears;
    I have not been rebellious,
    I have not turned away.
⁶I offered my back to those who beat me,
    my cheeks to those who pulled out my beard;
I did not hide my face
    from mocking and spitting.
⁷Because the Sovereign LORD helps me,
    I will not be disgraced.
Therefore have I set my face like flint,
    and I know I will not be put to shame.
⁸He who vindicates me is near.
    Who then will bring charges against me?
    Let us face each other!
Who are my accusers?
    Let them confront me!
⁹It is the Sovereign LORD who helps me.
    Who will condemn me?
They will all wear out like a garment;
    the moths will eat them up.

¹⁰Who among you fears the LORD
    and obeys the word of his servant?
Let those who walk in the dark,
    who have no light,
trust in the name of the LORD
    and rely on their God.
¹¹But now, all you who light fires

and provide yourselves with flaming torches,
go, walk in the light of your fires
  and of the torches you have set ablaze.
This is what you shall receive from my hand:
  You will lie down in torment.

Everlasting Salvation for Zion

51 "Listen to me, you who pursue righteousness
  and who seek the Lord:
Look to the rock from which you were cut
  and to the quarry from which you were hewn;
²look to Abraham, your father,
  and to Sarah, who gave you birth.
When I called him he was only one man,
  and I blessed him and made him many.
³The Lord will surely comfort Zion
  and will look with compassion on all her ruins;
he will make her deserts like Eden,
  her wastelands like the garden of the Lord.
Joy and gladness will be found in her,
  thanksgiving and the sound of singing.

⁴"Listen to me, my people;
  hear me, my nation:
Instruction will go out from me;
  my justice will become a light to the nations.
⁵My righteousness draws near speedily,
  my salvation is on the way,
  and my arm will bring justice to the nations.
The islands will look to me
  and wait in hope for my arm.
⁶Lift up your eyes to the heavens,
  look at the earth beneath;
the heavens will vanish like smoke,
  the earth will wear out like a garment
  and its inhabitants die like flies.
But my salvation will last forever,
  my righteousness will never fail.

⁷"Hear me, you who know what is right,
  you people who have taken my instruction to heart:
Do not fear the reproach of mere mortals
  or be terrified by their insults.
⁸For the moth will eat them up like a garment;
  the worm will devour them like wool.
But my righteousness will last forever,
  my salvation through all generations."

⁹Awake, awake, arm of the Lord,
  clothe yourself with strength!
Awake, as in days gone by,
  as in generations of old.
Was it not you who cut Rahab to pieces,

1046

who pierced that monster through?
¹⁰Was it not you who dried up the sea,
    the waters of the great deep,
who made a road in the depths of the sea
    so that the redeemed might cross over?
¹¹Those the LORD has rescued will return.
    They will enter Zion with singing;
    everlasting joy will crown their heads.
Gladness and joy will overtake them,
    and sorrow and sighing will flee away.

¹²"I, even I, am he who comforts you.
    Who are you that you fear mere
        mortals,
    human beings, who are but grass,
¹³that you forget the LORD your Maker,
    who stretched out the heavens
    and laid the foundations of the earth,
that you live in constant terror every
        day
    because of the wrath of the oppressor,
    who is bent on destruction?
For where is the wrath of the oppressor?
¹⁴   The cowering prisoners will soon be
        set free;
they will not die in their dungeon,
    nor will they lack bread.
¹⁵For I am the LORD your God,
    who stirs up the sea so that its waves
        roar—
    the LORD Almighty is his name.
¹⁶I have put my words in your mouth
    and covered you with the shadow of
        my hand—
I who set the heavens in place,
    who laid the foundations of the earth,
    and who say to Zion, 'You are my people.'"

The Cup of the LORD's Wrath

¹⁷Awake, awake!
    Rise up, Jerusalem,
you who have drunk from the hand of the LORD
    the cup of his wrath,
you who have drained to its dregs
    the goblet that makes people stagger.
¹⁸Among all the children she bore
    there was none to guide her;
among all the children she reared
    there was none to take her by the hand.
¹⁹These double calamities have come upon you—
    who can comfort you?—
ruin and destruction, famine and sword—

---

at issue: fear of people

51:12–16 Each of us has an "oppressor" in our lives. Oppressors are the people who seem to go out of their way to make our lives miserable. It might be a co-worker, an abusive or critical family member, an ex-husband, a so-called friend, even someone at church. They come in all shapes and sizes, but the effect they have on us is the same: fear. We see them coming and want to run and hide. We start shrinking inside ourselves. But God reminds us that he is so much more powerful than mere people. Find comfort and courage knowing his hand is on your life.

who can*a* console you?
20 Your children have fainted;
　they lie at every street corner,
　like antelope caught in a net.
They are filled with the wrath of the LORD,
　with the rebuke of your God.

21 Therefore hear this, you afflicted one,
　made drunk, but not with wine.
22 This is what your Sovereign LORD says,
　your God, who defends his people:
"See, I have taken out of your hand
　the cup that made you stagger;
from that cup, the goblet of my wrath,
　you will never drink again.
23 I will put it into the hands of your tormentors,
　who said to you,
　'Fall prostrate that we may walk on you.'
And you made your back like the ground,
　like a street to be walked on."

52 Awake, awake, Zion,
　clothe yourself with strength!
Put on your garments of splendor,
　Jerusalem, the holy city.
The uncircumcised and defiled
　will not enter you again.
2 Shake off your dust;
　rise up, sit enthroned, Jerusalem.
Free yourself from the chains on your neck,
　Daughter Zion, now a captive.

3 For this is what the LORD says:

"You were sold for nothing,
　and without money you will be redeemed."

4 For this is what the Sovereign LORD says:

"At first my people went down to Egypt to live;
　lately, Assyria has oppressed them.

5 "And now what do I have here?" declares the LORD.

"For my people have been taken away for nothing,
　and those who rule them mock,*b*"

declares the LORD.

"And all day long
　my name is constantly blasphemed.
6 Therefore my people will know my name;
　therefore in that day they will know
that it is I who foretold it.
　Yes, it is I."

1047

---

a 19 Dead Sea Scrolls, Septuagint, Vulgate and Syriac; Masoretic Text / *how can I*　*b* 5 Dead Sea Scrolls and Vulgate; Masoretic Text *wail*

⁷How beautiful on the mountains
  are the feet of those who bring good
      news,
who proclaim peace,
  who bring good tidings,
  who proclaim salvation,
who say to Zion,
  "Your God reigns!"
⁸Listen! Your watchmen lift up their
      voices;
  together they shout for joy.
When the LORD returns to Zion,
  they will see it with their own eyes.
⁹Burst into songs of joy together,
  you ruins of Jerusalem,
for the LORD has comforted his people,
  he has redeemed Jerusalem.
¹⁰The LORD will lay bare his holy arm
  in the sight of all the nations,
and all the ends of the earth will see
  the salvation of our God.

¹¹Depart, depart, go out from there!
  Touch no unclean thing!
Come out from it and be pure,
  you who carry the articles of the
      LORD's house.
¹²But you will not leave in haste
  or go in flight;
for the LORD will go before you,
  the God of Israel will be your rear guard.

The Suffering and Glory of the Servant
¹³See, my servant will act wisely*a*;
  he will be raised and lifted up and highly exalted.
¹⁴Just as there were many who were appalled at him*b*—
  his appearance was so disfigured beyond that of any human being
  and his form marred beyond human likeness—
¹⁵so he will sprinkle many nations,*c*
  and kings will shut their mouths because of him.
For what they were not told, they will see,
  and what they have not heard, they will understand.

53 Who has believed our message
  and to whom has the arm of the LORD been revealed?
²He grew up before him like a tender shoot,
  and like a root out of dry ground.
He had no beauty or majesty to attract us to him,
  nothing in his appearance that we should desire him.
³He was despised and rejected by others,
  a man of suffering, and familiar with pain.

52:7–10 What is it about a pedicure that makes you feel so good? Did you know that you can get eternally beautiful feet without ever stepping into a salon? God says the way to have truly beautiful feet is to let them take you where you can share the Good News of Jesus Christ. The beauty of the message makes the messenger herself beautiful. What God has done for you should cause you to want to share him with others—that is the purist motive for evangelism. Sharing the Good News with others makes all of you, from your feet up, beautiful.

atissue:evangelism

1048

a 13 Or will prosper b 14 Hebrew you c 15 Or so will many nations be amazed at him (see also Septuagint)

Like one from whom people hide their faces
    he was despised, and we held him in low esteem.

⁴Surely he took up our pain
    and bore our suffering,
yet we considered him punished by God,
    stricken by him, and afflicted.
⁵But he was pierced for our transgressions,
    he was crushed for our iniquities;
the punishment that brought us peace was on him,
    and by his wounds we are healed.
⁶We all, like sheep, have gone astray,
    each of us has turned to our own way;
and the Lord has laid on him
    the iniquity of us all.

HE IS: a man of suffering

53:1–6 The prophet foresaw that the Messiah would be *a man of suffering*. During his life Jesus experienced loss, unfair treatment, rejection, physical pain and spiritual sorrow. On the cross, he took the sin and misery of the world onto his own shoulders.

Aren't you glad that Jesus understands pain? Isn't it comforting to know that the God-man did not choose an easy, sheltered life? He knows what it feels like to hurt. What sorrows are you carrying? Let him bear them for you (see Matthew 11:28–30). Place your pain on his strong shoulders. He's familiar with suffering and will carry your pain for you.

For the next He Is, go to p. 1067.

⁷He was oppressed and afflicted,
    yet he did not open his mouth;
he was led like a lamb to the slaughter,
    and as a sheep before its shearers is silent,
    so he did not open his mouth.
⁸By oppression ᵃ and judgment he was taken away.
    Yet who of his generation protested?
For he was cut off from the land of the living;
    for the transgression of my people he was punished. ᵇ
⁹He was assigned a grave with the wicked,
    and with the rich in his death,
though he had done no violence,
    nor was any deceit in his mouth.

¹⁰Yet it was the Lord's will to crush him and cause him to suffer,
    and though the Lord makes ᶜ his life an offering for sin,
he will see his offspring and prolong his days,
    and the will of the Lord will prosper in his hand.
¹¹After he has suffered,
    he will see the light of life ᵈ and be satisfied ᵉ;

ᵃ 8 Or *From arrest*　ᵇ 8 Or *generation considered / that he was cut off from the land of the living, / that he was punished for the transgression of my people?*　ᶜ 10 Hebrew *though you make*　ᵈ 11 Dead Sea Scrolls (see also Septuagint); Masoretic Text does not have *the light of life.*　ᵉ 11 Or (with Masoretic Text) ¹¹He will see the fruit of his suffering / and will be satisfied

myth# 62 "IF I'M GOOD, GOD WILL LOVE ME."

I wonder if my parents ever really loved me. They worked hard to support all of us; I'm not sure they had time to love us. I always tried to do well in school so my parents would notice me. I did anything I could to get their attention. When I turned 18, I left home in search of love and ended up marrying the first man who told me what I longed to hear. He was so thoughtful, buying me little gifts and bringing home flowers every Friday.

Several years into our marriage, I received a phone call from a hotel in a town 40 miles away. They'd found my husband's day timer. He'd left it there yesterday—did I want them to mail it to the house? I knew something was wrong, but I didn't want to lose the only love I'd ever known. Besides, we had two children, and I couldn't raise them alone.

My plan was to try my best to get him to love me again. I let my hair grow long (though a shorter cut was much easier with kids). I dressed up more around the house and wore makeup every day. I tried improving our sex life and never let on that I knew.

I was good at playing this game—I'd been playing it since I was a child. If you want love, work harder to earn it. The problem is that I always seem to lose. When I tried to be the best child, it didn't work. When I worked to be an irresistible wife and mother so my husband wouldn't leave me, it didn't work either.

But I know that God is different. God knows how hard I try to follow his commandments and be the best Christian I can be. I could never earn anyone's love, but I know I can win his. After all, he is God. If I keep trying hard enough, I will get what I've wanted all my life.

—Janie

WITHOUT EVEN realizing it, many of us are trying to win God's favor. This world has reinforced for us time and time again that we have to do something in order to be loved. So we try to "be a good girl" and do things that will make God happier with us—working tirelessly to try to prove that we're worthy of him.

But the fact is that we're not worthy of him and will never be. The gospel turns this world's logic on its head. The Good News of Jesus Christ is that he offers free, undeserved, unconditional, eternal love and grace to any sin-stained, hopeless, ragamuffin person who turns to him. Because of that, you can . . .

Revel in his grace. This is the greatest gift in the universe; enjoy it. Live like you're free because you are (see Ephesians 2:4–5).

Relax and rest in the only unconditional love available. Human love always has limits. God's love has no limits. Stop trying to earn or win his love. Discard that performance-based faith. Let go and fall back into his safe and loving arms. You are accepted and deeply loved.

Remember that God's love for you has nothing, absolutely nothing, to do with you. It's not because of your good behavior that he saved you (see Romans 5:6–8). He saved you because of him, because he loved you, not because of you or something you did to earn it. His very personal love for you depends on him, not you—and he never changes.

> "The hunger for love is much more difficult to remove than the hunger for bread."
>
> —Mother Teresa

1051

"FOR GOD SO LOVED THE WORLD THAT HE GAVE HIS ONE AND ONLY SON, THAT WHOEVER BELIEVES IN HIM SHALL NOT PERISH BUT HAVE ETERNAL LIFE."

JOHN 3:16

SEE ALSO
Psalm 36:7
Ephesians 3:16–19
1 John 3:1

For more on **Grace** and **Love**, check the index.

by his knowledge[a] my righteous servant will justify many,
    and he will bear their iniquities.
[12]Therefore I will give him a portion among the great,[b]
    and he will divide the spoils with the strong,[c]
because he poured out his life unto death,
    and was numbered with the transgressors.
For he bore the sin of many,
    and made intercession for the transgressors.

The Future Glory of Zion

54 "Sing, barren woman,
    you who never bore a child;
burst into song, shout for joy,
    you who were never in labor;
because more are the children of the desolate woman
    than of her who has a husband,"
                        says the LORD.

[2]"Enlarge the place of your tent,
    stretch your tent curtains wide,
    do not hold back;
lengthen your cords,
    strengthen your stakes.
[3]For you will spread out to the right and to the left;
    your descendants will dispossess
        nations
    and settle in their desolate cities.

[4]"Do not be afraid; you will not be put to
    shame.
Do not fear disgrace; you will not be
    humiliated.
You will forget the shame of your youth
    and remember no more the reproach
    of your widowhood.
[5]For your Maker is your husband—
    the LORD Almighty is his name—
the Holy One of Israel is your Redeemer;
    he is called the God of all the earth.
[6]The LORD will call you back
    as if you were a wife deserted and
        distressed in spirit—
a wife who married young,
    only to be rejected," says your God.
[7]"For a brief moment I abandoned you,
    but with deep compassion I will bring
    you back.
[8]In a surge of anger
    I hid my face from you for a moment,
but with everlasting kindness
    I will have compassion on you,"
    says the LORD your Redeemer.

a issue:divorce

54:4–10 God compared the nation of Israel to a wife who had been painfully separated from her husband. Perhaps you've been there—rejected by your husband, feeling cast off and abandoned. You've longed to remove that stigma, to be called back and loved, to have your husband want you back again. But now he's getting remarried, crushing your hopes of regaining what you once had together. In your hurt, look to your Maker, who is your husband, to comfort you, to give you value, security and peace. Know that his unfailing love for you will *never* be shaken.

---

a 11 Or *by knowledge of him*   b 12 Or *many*   c 12 Or *numerous*

⁹"To me this is like the days of Noah,
    when I swore that the waters of Noah would never again cover the earth.
  So now I have sworn not to be angry with you,
    never to rebuke you again.
¹⁰Though the mountains be shaken
    and the hills be removed,
  yet my unfailing love for you will not be shaken
    nor my covenant of peace be removed,"
    says the LORD, who has compassion on you.

¹¹"Afflicted city, lashed by storms and not comforted,
    I will rebuild you with stones of turquoise,ᵃ
    your foundations with lapis lazuli.
¹²I will make your battlements of rubies,
    your gates of sparkling jewels,
    and all your walls of precious stones.
¹³All your children will be taught by the LORD,
    and great will be their peace.
¹⁴In righteousness you will be established:
  Tyranny will be far from you;
    you will have nothing to fear.
  Terror will be far removed;
    it will not come near you.
¹⁵If anyone does attack you, it will not be my doing;
    whoever attacks you will surrender to you.

¹⁶"See, it is I who created the blacksmith
    who fans the coals into flame
    and forges a weapon fit for its work.
  And it is I who have created the destroyer to work havoc;
¹⁷   no weapon forged against you will prevail,
    and you will refute every tongue that accuses you.
  This is the heritage of the servants of the LORD,
    and this is their vindication from me,"
                                        declares the LORD.

Invitation to the Thirsty

55 "Come, all you who are thirsty,
    come to the waters;
  and you who have no money,
    come, buy and eat!
  Come, buy wine and milk
    without money and without cost.
²Why spend money on what is not bread,
    and your labor on what does not satisfy?
  Listen, listen to me, and eat what is good,
    and you will delight in the richest of fare.
³Give ear and come to me;
    listen, that you may live.
  I will make an everlasting covenant with you,
    my faithful love promised to David.

ᵃ 11 The meaning of the Hebrew for this word is uncertain.

⁴See, I have made him a witness to the peoples,
　　a ruler and commander of the peoples.
⁵Surely you will summon nations you know not,
　　and nations you do not know will come running to you,
　because of the LORD your God,
　　the Holy One of Israel,
　　for he has endowed you with splendor."

⁶Seek the LORD while he may be found;
　　call on him while he is near.
⁷Let the wicked forsake their ways
　　and the unrighteous their thoughts.
　Let them turn to the LORD, and he will have mercy on them,
　　and to our God, for he will freely pardon.

⁸"For my thoughts are not your
　　　thoughts,
　neither are your ways my
　　　ways,"
　　　　declares the LORD.
⁹"As the heavens are higher
　　　than the earth,
　so are my ways higher than
　　　your ways
　and my thoughts than your
　　　thoughts.
¹⁰As the rain and the snow
　　　come down from heaven,
　and do not return to it
　　　without watering the earth
　and making it bud and
　　　flourish,
　so that it yields seed for the sower and bread for the eater,
¹¹so is my word that goes out from my mouth:
　It will not return to me empty,
　but will accomplish what I desire
　　and achieve the purpose for which I sent it.
¹²You will go out in joy
　　　and be led forth in peace;
　the mountains and hills
　　　will burst into song before you,
　and all the trees of the field
　　　will clap their hands.
¹³Instead of the thornbush will grow the juniper,
　　and instead of briers the myrtle will grow.
　This will be for the LORD's renown,
　　for an everlasting sign,
　　that will endure forever."

conversations

trusting God «» 55:6–13

1» Is it easier to doubt God than to trust him? Why?

2» Is it necessary that you understand God in order to trust him? Why or why not?

3» Give an example of how God's ways and thoughts are superior to yours.

For more on **trusting God**, check the index.
For the next Conversations, go to p. 1057.

Salvation for Others

56 This is what the LORD says:

　"Maintain justice
　　and do what is right,

for my salvation is close at hand
    and my righteousness will soon be revealed.
²Blessed are those who do this—
    who hold it fast,
those who keep the Sabbath without desecrating it,
    and keep their hands from doing any evil."

³Let no foreigners who have bound themselves to the LORD say,
    "The LORD will surely exclude me from his people."
And let no eunuch complain,
    "I am only a dry tree."

⁴For this is what the LORD says:

"To the eunuchs who keep my Sabbaths,
    who choose what pleases me
    and hold fast to my covenant—
⁵to them I will give within my temple and its walls
    a memorial and a name
    better than sons and daughters;
I will give them an everlasting name
    that will endure forever.
⁶And foreigners who bind themselves to the LORD
    to minister to him,
to love the name of the LORD,
    and to be his servants,
all who keep the Sabbath without desecrating it
    and who hold fast to my covenant—
⁷these I will bring to my holy mountain
    and give them joy in my house of prayer.
Their burnt offerings and sacrifices
    will be accepted on my altar;
for my house will be called
    a house of prayer for all nations."
⁸The Sovereign LORD declares—
    he who gathers the exiles of Israel:
"I will gather still others to them
    besides those already gathered."

God's Accusation Against the Wicked

⁹Come, all you beasts of the field,
    come and devour, all you beasts of the forest!
¹⁰Israel's watchmen are blind,
    they all lack knowledge;
they are all mute dogs,
    they cannot bark;
they lie around and dream,
    they love to sleep.
¹¹They are dogs with mighty appetites;
    they never have enough.
They are shepherds who lack understanding;
    they all turn to their own way,
    they seek their own gain.

¹²"Come," each one cries, "let me get wine!
Let us drink our fill of beer!
And tomorrow will be like today,
or even far better."

57

The righteous perish,
and no one takes it to heart;
the devout are taken away,
and no one understands
that the righteous are taken away
to be spared from evil.
²Those who walk uprightly
enter into peace;
they find rest as they lie in death.

³"But you—come here, you children of a sorceress,
you offspring of adulterers and prostitutes!
⁴Whom are you mocking?
At whom do you sneer
and stick out your tongue?
Are you not a brood of rebels,
the offspring of liars?
⁵You burn with lust among the oaks
and under every spreading tree;
you sacrifice your children in the ravines
and under the overhanging crags.
⁶The idols among the smooth stones of the ravines are your portion;
they, they are your lot.
Yes, to them you have poured out drink offerings
and offered grain offerings.
In view of all this, should I relent?
⁷You have made your bed on a high and lofty hill;
there you went up to offer your sacrifices.
⁸Behind your doors and your doorposts
you have put your pagan symbols.
Forsaking me, you uncovered your bed,
you climbed into it and opened it wide;
you made a pact with those whose beds you love,
and you looked on their nakedness.
⁹You went to Molek^a with olive oil
and increased your perfumes.
You sent your ambassadors^b far away;
you descended to the very realm of the dead!
¹⁰You wearied yourself by such going about,
but you would not say, 'It is hopeless.'
You found renewal of your strength,
and so you did not faint.

¹¹"Whom have you so dreaded and feared
that you have not been true to me,
and have neither remembered me

---

^a 9 Or to the king   ^b 9 Or idols

nor taken this to heart?
Is it not because I have long been silent
    that you do not fear me?
[12] I will expose your righteousness and your works,
    and they will not benefit you.
[13] When you cry out for help,
    let your collection of idols save you!
The wind will carry all of them off,
    a mere breath will blow them away.
But whoever takes refuge in me
    will inherit the land
    and possess my holy mountain."

Comfort for the Contrite

[14] And it will be said:

"Build up, build up, prepare the road!
    Remove the obstacles out of the way of my people."
[15] For this is what the high and exalted
    One says—
he who lives forever, whose name is
    holy:
"I live in a high and holy place,
    but also with those who are contrite
      and lowly in spirit,
to revive the spirit of the lowly
    and to revive the heart of the contrite.
[16] I will not accuse them forever,
    nor will I always be angry,
for then they would faint away because
    of me—
    the very people I have created.
[17] I was enraged by their sinful greed;
    I punished them, and hid my face in
      anger,
    yet they kept on in their willful ways.
[18] I have seen their ways, but I will heal them;
    I will guide them and restore comfort to them,
[19]   creating praise on the lips of the mourners in Israel.
Peace, peace, to those far and near,"
    says the LORD. "And I will heal them."
[20] But the wicked are like the tossing sea,
    which cannot rest,
    whose waves cast up mire and mud.
[21] "There is no peace," says my God, "for the wicked."

True Fasting

58

"Shout it aloud, do not hold back.
    Raise your voice like a trumpet.
Declare to my people their rebellion
    and to the house of Jacob their sins.
[2] For day after day they seek me out;
    they seem eager to know my ways,

1057

conversations

failure «» 57:15–19

1 » Does God have any conditions for you to be healed from your failures?

2 » Why does God choose to heal you even though you continue to sin?

3 » What does it mean to have a truly contrite heart? Could that be said of you?

For more on **failure**, check the index.
For the next Conversations, go to p. 1069.

as if they were a nation that does what is right
and has not forsaken the commands of its God.
They ask me for just decisions
and seem eager for God to come near them.
³'Why have we fasted,' they say,
'and you have not seen it?
Why have we humbled ourselves,
and you have not noticed?'

"Yet on the day of your fasting, you do as you please
and exploit all your workers.
⁴Your fasting ends in quarreling and strife,
and in striking each other with wicked fists.
You cannot fast as you do today
and expect your voice to be heard on high.
⁵Is this the kind of fast I have chosen,
only a day for people to humble themselves?
Is it only for bowing one's head like a reed
and for lying in sackcloth and ashes?
Is that what you call a fast,
a day acceptable to the LORD?

⁶"Is not this the kind of fasting I have chosen:
to loose the chains of injustice
and untie the cords of the yoke,
to set the oppressed free
and break every yoke?
⁷Is it not to share your food with the hungry
and to provide the poor wanderer with shelter—
when you see the naked, to clothe them,
and not to turn away from your own flesh and blood?
⁸Then your light will break forth like the dawn,
and your healing will quickly appear;
then your righteousness^a will go before you,
and the glory of the LORD will be your rear guard.
⁹Then you will call, and the LORD will answer;
you will cry for help, and he will say: Here am I.

"If you do away with the yoke of oppression,
with the pointing finger and malicious talk,
¹⁰and if you spend yourselves in behalf of the hungry
and satisfy the needs of the oppressed,
then your light will rise in the darkness,
and your night will become like the noonday.
¹¹The LORD will guide you always;
he will satisfy your needs in a sun-scorched land
and will strengthen your frame.
You will be like a well-watered garden,
like a spring whose waters never fail.
¹²Your people will rebuild the ancient ruins
and will raise up the age-old foundations;

ᵃ 8 Or your righteous One

you will be called Repairer of Broken Walls,
    Restorer of Streets with Dwellings.

13 "If you keep your feet from breaking the Sabbath
    and from doing as you please on my holy day,
if you call the Sabbath a delight
    and the LORD's holy day honorable,
and if you honor it by not going your own way
    and not doing as you please or speaking idle words,
14 then you will find your joy in the LORD,
    and I will cause you to ride in triumph on the heights of the land
    and to feast on the inheritance of your father Jacob."
                For the mouth of the LORD has spoken.

Sin, Confession and Redemption

59

Surely the arm of the LORD is not too short
    to save,
  nor his ear too dull to hear.
2 But your iniquities have separated
    you from your God;
your sins have hidden his face from you,
    so that he will not hear.
3 For your hands are stained with blood,
    your fingers with guilt.
Your lips have spoken falsely,
    and your tongue mutters wicked things.
4 No one calls for justice;
    no one pleads their case with integrity.
They rely on empty arguments, they utter
    lies;
    they conceive trouble and give birth to
    evil.
5 They hatch the eggs of vipers
    and spin a spider's web.
Whoever eats their eggs will die,
    and when one is broken, an adder is
    hatched.
6 Their cobwebs are useless for clothing;
    they cannot cover themselves with what they make.
Their deeds are evil deeds,
    and acts of violence are in their hands.
7 Their feet rush into sin;
    they are swift to shed innocent blood.
They pursue evil schemes;
    acts of violence mark their ways.
8 The way of peace they do not know;
    there is no justice in their paths.
They have turned them into crooked roads;
    no one who walks along them will know peace.

9 So justice is far from us,
    and righteousness does not reach us.

at issue: unconfessed sin

59:1–2 There are many reasons to hate your sin. Let's consider one: Sin separates you from your holy God. Sin prevents you from knowing him. Through the Cross, God provided a way for your sin to be forgiven so that you could enter into a relationship with him. Once you belong to God, even your sin cannot sever that relationship—but it does get in the way. You will never know true intimacy with God if you harbor unconfessed sin in your heart. If you stubbornly cling to your sin, he will not hear you.

1059

We look for light, but all is darkness;
for brightness, but we walk in deep shadows.
¹⁰Like the blind we grope along the wall,
feeling our way like people without eyes.
At midday we stumble as if it were twilight;
among the strong, we are like the dead.
¹¹We all growl like bears;
we moan mournfully like doves.
We look for justice, but find none;
for deliverance, but it is far away.

¹²For our offenses are many in your sight,
and our sins testify against us.
Our offenses are ever with us,
and we acknowledge our iniquities:
¹³rebellion and treachery against the LORD,
turning our backs on our God,
inciting revolt and oppression,
uttering lies our hearts have conceived.
¹⁴So justice is driven back,
and righteousness stands at a distance;
truth has stumbled in the streets,
honesty cannot enter.
¹⁵Truth is nowhere to be found,
and whoever shuns evil becomes a prey.

The LORD looked and was displeased
that there was no justice.
¹⁶He saw that there was no one,
he was appalled that there was no one to intervene;
so his own arm achieved salvation for him,
and his own righteousness sustained him.
¹⁷He put on righteousness as his breastplate,
and the helmet of salvation on his head;
he put on the garments of vengeance
and wrapped himself in zeal as in a cloak.
¹⁸According to what they have done,
so will he repay
wrath to his enemies
and retribution to his foes;
he will repay the islands their due.
¹⁹From the west, people will fear the name of the LORD,
and from the rising of the sun, they will revere his glory.
For he will come like a pent-up flood
that the breath of the LORD drives along.ᵃ

²⁰"The Redeemer will come to Zion,
to those in Jacob who repent of their sins,"

declares the LORD.

²¹"As for me, this is my covenant with them," says the LORD. "My Spirit, who is on you, and my words that I have put in your mouth will not depart from your mouth, or from the mouths of your children, or from the mouths of their descendants from this time on and forever," says the LORD.

ᵃ *19* Or *When enemies come in like a flood, / the Spirit of the LORD will put them to flight*

The Glory of Zion

60 "Arise, shine, for your light has come,
and the glory of the Lord rises upon you.
[2]See, darkness covers the earth
and thick darkness is over the peoples,
but the Lord rises upon you
and his glory appears over you.
[3]Nations will come to your light,
and kings to the brightness of your dawn.

[4]"Lift up your eyes and look about you:
All assemble and come to you;
your sons come from afar,
and your daughters are carried on the hip.
[5]Then you will look and be radiant,
your heart will throb and swell with joy;
the wealth on the seas will be brought to you,
to you the riches of the nations will come.
[6]Herds of camels will cover your land,
young camels of Midian and Ephah.
And all from Sheba will come,
bearing gold and incense
and proclaiming the praise of the Lord.
[7]All Kedar's flocks will be gathered to you,
the rams of Nebaioth will serve you;
they will be accepted as offerings on my altar,
and I will adorn my glorious temple.

[8]"Who are these that fly along like clouds,
like doves to their nests?
[9]Surely the islands look to me;
in the lead are the ships of Tarshish,[a]
bringing your children from afar,
with their silver and gold,
to the honor of the Lord your God,
the Holy One of Israel,
for he has endowed you with splendor.

[10]"Foreigners will rebuild your walls,
and their kings will serve you.
Though in anger I struck you,
in favor I will show you compassion.
[11]Your gates will always stand open,
they will never be shut, day or night,
so that people may bring you the wealth of the nations—
their kings led in triumphal procession.
[12]For the nation or kingdom that will not serve you will perish;
it will be utterly ruined.

[13]"The glory of Lebanon will come to you,
the juniper, the fir and the cypress together,

1061

to adorn my sanctuary;
    and I will glorify the place for my feet.
¹⁴ The children of your oppressors will come bowing before you;
    all who despise you will bow down at your feet
and will call you the City of the LORD,
    Zion of the Holy One of Israel.

¹⁵ "Although you have been forsaken and hated,
    with no one traveling through,
I will make you the everlasting pride
    and the joy of all generations.
¹⁶ You will drink the milk of nations
    and be nursed at royal breasts.
Then you will know that I, the LORD, am your Savior,
    your Redeemer, the Mighty One of Jacob.
¹⁷ Instead of bronze I will bring you gold,
    and silver in place of iron.
Instead of wood I will bring you bronze,
    and iron in place of stones.
I will make peace your governor
    and well-being your ruler.
¹⁸ No longer will violence be heard in your land,
    nor ruin or destruction within your borders,
but you will call your walls Salvation
    and your gates Praise.
¹⁹ The sun will no more be your light by day,
    nor will the brightness of the moon shine on you,
for the LORD will be your everlasting light,
    and your God will be your glory.
²⁰ Your sun will never set again,
    and your moon will wane no more;
the LORD will be your everlasting light,
    and your days of sorrow will end.
²¹ Then will all your people be righteous
    and they will possess the land forever.
They are the shoot I have planted,
    the work of my hands,
    for the display of my splendor.
²² The least of you will become a thousand,
    the smallest a mighty nation.
I am the LORD;
    in its time I will do this swiftly."

The Year of the LORD's Favor

61 The Spirit of the Sovereign LORD is on me,
    because the LORD has anointed me
    to proclaim good news to the poor.
He has sent me to bind up the brokenhearted,
    to proclaim freedom for the captives
    and release from darkness for the prisoners,ᵃ

ᵃ *1* Hebrew; Septuagint *the blind*

²to proclaim the year of the L<small>ORD</small>'s favor
  and the day of vengeance of our God,
to comfort all who mourn,
³ and provide for those who grieve in Zion—
to bestow on them a crown of beauty
    instead of ashes,
the oil of joy
    instead of mourning,
and a garment of praise
    instead of a spirit of despair.
They will be called mighty oaks,
    a planting of the L<small>ORD</small>
  for the display of his splendor.

⁴They will rebuild the ancient ruins
  and restore the places long devastated;
they will renew the ruined cities
  that have been devastated for
      generations.
⁵Strangers will shepherd your flocks;
  foreigners will work your fields and
      vineyards.
⁶And you will be called priests of the L<small>ORD</small>,
  you will be named ministers of our God.
You will feed on the wealth of nations,
  and in their riches you will boast.

⁷Instead of your shame
  you will receive a double portion,
and instead of disgrace
  you will rejoice in your inheritance.
And so you will inherit a double portion in
      your land,
  and everlasting joy will be yours.

⁸"For I, the L<small>ORD</small>, love justice;
  I hate robbery and wrongdoing.
In my faithfulness I will reward my people
  and make an everlasting covenant with
      them.
⁹Their descendants will be known among the nations
  and their offspring among the peoples.
All who see them will acknowledge
  that they are a people the L<small>ORD</small> has blessed."

¹⁰I delight greatly in the L<small>ORD</small>;
  my soul rejoices in my God.
For he has clothed me with garments of salvation
  and arrayed me in a robe of his righteousness,
as a bridegroom adorns his head like a priest,
  and as a bride adorns herself with her jewels.
¹¹For as the soil makes the sprout come up
  and a garden causes seeds to grow,

tissue:joy

61:10 When we were little girls, most of us dreamed about our wedding day. (If you're still dreaming, keep it up!) We imagined the flowers and the music, and of course, we fantasized about the dress. There's something memorable and extraordinary about a wedding dress. Just as no outfit can compare to a wedding ensemble, so God's garments of salvation and righteousness are unparalleled. The pleasure a bride feels as she dresses for her wedding is a picture of the joy our salvation brings. No matter how bad your life may get, you always have one reason for joy: the unchanging gift of your salvation.

1063

so the Sovereign Lord will make righteousness
and praise spring up before all nations.

Zion's New Name

62 For Zion's sake I will not keep silent,
for Jerusalem's sake I will not remain quiet,
till her vindication shines out like the dawn,
her salvation like a blazing torch.
²The nations will see your vindication,
and all kings your glory;
you will be called by a new name
that the mouth of the Lord will bestow.
³You will be a crown of splendor in the Lord's hand,
a royal diadem in the hand of your God.
⁴No longer will they call you Deserted,
or name your land Desolate.
But you will be called Hephzibah,ᵃ
and your land Beulahᵇ;
for the Lord will take delight in you,
and your land will be married.
⁵As a young man marries a young woman,
so will your Builder marry you;
as a bridegroom rejoices over his bride,
so will your God rejoice over you.

⁶I have posted watchmen on your walls, Jerusalem;
they will never be silent day or night.
You who call on the Lord,
give yourselves no rest,
⁷and give him no rest till he establishes Jerusalem
and makes her the praise of the earth.

⁸The Lord has sworn by his right hand
and by his mighty arm:
"Never again will I give your grain
as food for your enemies,
and never again will foreigners drink the new wine
for which you have toiled;
⁹but those who harvest it will eat it
and praise the Lord,
and those who gather the grapes will drink it
in the courts of my sanctuary."

¹⁰Pass through, pass through the gates!
Prepare the way for the people.
Build up, build up the highway!
Remove the stones.
Raise a banner for the nations.

¹¹The Lord has made proclamation
to the ends of the earth:
"Say to Daughter Zion,

ᵃ 4 Hephzibah means my delight is in her. ᵇ 4 Beulah means married.

'See, your Savior comes!
See, his reward is with him,
    and his recompense accompanies him.'"
¹²They will be called the Holy People,
    the Redeemed of the LORD;
and you will be called Sought After,
    the City No Longer Deserted.

God's Day of Vengeance and Redemption

63 Who is this coming from Edom,
        from Bozrah, with his garments stained crimson?
Who is this, robed in splendor,
    striding forward in the greatness of his strength?

"It is I, speaking in righteousness,
    mighty to save."

²Why are your garments red,
    like those of one treading the winepress?

³"I have trodden the winepress alone;
    from the nations no one was with me.
I trampled them in my anger
    and trod them down in my wrath;
their blood spattered my garments,
    and I stained all my clothing.
⁴It was for me the day of vengeance;
    the year for me to redeem had come.
⁵I looked, but there was no one to help,
    I was appalled that no one gave support;
so my own arm achieved salvation for me,
    and my own wrath sustained me.
⁶I trampled the nations in my anger;
    in my wrath I made them drunk
    and poured their blood on the ground."

Praise and Prayer

⁷I will tell of the kindnesses of the LORD,
    the deeds for which he is to be praised,
    according to all the LORD has done for us—
yes, the many good things he has done
    for the house of Israel,
    according to his compassion and many kindnesses.
⁸He said, "Surely they are my people,
    children who will be true to me";
    and so he became their Savior.
⁹In all their distress he too was distressed,
    and the angel of his presence saved them.ᵃ
In his love and mercy he redeemed them;
    he lifted them up and carried them
    all the days of old.
¹⁰Yet they rebelled

1065

ᵃ 9 Or Savior ⁹in their distress. / It was no envoy or angel / but his own presence that saved them

and grieved his Holy Spirit.
So he turned and became their enemy
and he himself fought against them.

[11] Then his people recalled[a] the days of old,
the days of Moses and his people—
where is he who brought them through the sea,
with the shepherd of his flock?
Where is he who set
his Holy Spirit among them,
[12] who sent his glorious arm of power
to be at Moses' right hand,
who divided the waters before them,
to gain for himself everlasting renown,
[13] who led them through the depths?
Like a horse in open country,
they did not stumble;
[14] like cattle that go down to the plain,
they were given rest by the Spirit of the LORD.
This is how you guided your people
to make for yourself a glorious name.

[15] Look down from heaven and see,
from your lofty throne, holy and glorious.
Where are your zeal and your might?
Your tenderness and compassion are withheld from us.
[16] But you are our Father,
though Abraham does not know us
or Israel acknowledge us;
you, LORD, are our Father,
our Redeemer from of old is your name.
[17] Why, LORD, do you make us wander from your ways
and harden our hearts so we do not revere you?
Return for the sake of your servants,
the tribes that are your inheritance.
[18] For a little while your people possessed your holy place,
but now our enemies have trampled down your sanctuary.
[19] We are yours from of old;
but you have not ruled over them,
they have not been called[b] by your name.

64 *Oh, that you would rend the heavens and come down,
that the mountains would tremble before you!
* [2] As when fire sets twigs ablaze
and causes water to boil,
come down to make your name known to your enemies
and cause the nations to quake before you!
[3] For when you did awesome things that we did not expect,
you came down, and the mountains trembled before you.
[4] Since ancient times no one has heard,

---

no ear has perceived,
   no eye has seen any God besides you,
      who acts on behalf of those who wait for him.
⁵You come to the help of those who gladly do right,
   who remember your ways.
But when we continued to sin against them,
   you were angry.
   How then can we be saved?
⁶All of us have become like one who is unclean,
   and all our righteous acts are like filthy rags;
we all shrivel up like a leaf,
   and like the wind our sins sweep us away.
⁷No one calls on your name
   or strives to lay hold of you;
for you have hidden your face from us
   and have given us over to^a our sins.

⁸Yet you, LORD, are our Father.
   We are the clay, you are the potter;
   we are all the work of your hand.
⁹Do not be angry beyond measure, LORD;
   do not remember our sins forever.
Oh, look on us, we pray,
   for we are all your people.
¹⁰Your sacred cities have become a wasteland;
   even Zion is a wasteland, Jerusalem a desolation.
¹¹Our holy and glorious temple, where our ancestors praised you,
   has been burned with fire,
   and all that we treasured lies in ruins.
¹²After all this, LORD, will you hold yourself back?
   Will you keep silent and punish us beyond measure?

HE IS: the potter

64:8 The prophet Isaiah understood that human beings, like clay, can be shaped and molded for service by surrendering to God *the potter*. At our best, we are the work of God's hand.

   The potter created you for a purpose—to serve him. If you allow it, he will make you into a vessel that pours out his love to others. You must be supple clay in God's hands, not resistant to his sometimes-painful process of molding your character. Repentance of sin softens your spirit so you can be formed into his divine design.

For the next He Is, go to p. 1071.

Judgment and Salvation

65

"I revealed myself to those who did not ask for me;
   I was found by those who did not seek me.
To a nation that did not call on my name,
   I said, 'Here am I, here am I.'

---
^a 7 Septuagint, Syriac and Targum; Hebrew *have made us melt because of*

²All day long I have held out my hands
    to an obstinate people,
who walk in ways not good,
    pursuing their own imaginations—
³a people who continually provoke me
    to my very face,
offering sacrifices in gardens
    and burning incense on altars of brick;
⁴who sit among the graves
    and spend their nights keeping secret vigil;
who eat the flesh of pigs,
    and whose pots hold broth of impure meat;
⁵who say, 'Keep away; don't come near me,
    for I am too sacred for you!'
Such people are smoke in my nostrils,
    a fire that keeps burning all day.

⁶"See, it stands written before me:
    I will not keep silent but will pay back in full;
    I will pay it back into their laps—
⁷both your sins and the sins of your ancestors,"
    says the LORD.
"Because they burned sacrifices on the mountains
    and defied me on the hills,
I will measure into their laps
    the full payment for their former deeds."

⁸This is what the LORD says:

"As when juice is still found in a cluster of grapes
    and people say, 'Don't destroy it,
    there is still a blessing in it,'
so will I do in behalf of my servants;
    I will not destroy them all.
⁹I will bring forth descendants from Jacob,
    and from Judah those who will possess my mountains;
my chosen people will inherit them,
    and there will my servants live.
¹⁰Sharon will become a pasture for flocks,
    and the Valley of Achor a resting place for herds,
    for my people who seek me.

¹¹"But as for you who forsake the LORD
    and forget my holy mountain,
who spread a table for Fortune
    and fill bowls of mixed wine for Destiny,
¹²I will destine you for the sword,
    and all of you will fall in the slaughter;
for I called but you did not answer,
    I spoke but you did not listen.
You did evil in my sight
    and chose what displeases me."

¹³Therefore this is what the Sovereign LORD says:

"My servants will eat,
    but you will go hungry;
my servants will drink,
    but you will go thirsty;
my servants will rejoice,
    but you will be put to shame.
¹⁴My servants will sing
    out of the joy of their hearts,
but you will cry out
        from anguish of heart
        and wail in brokenness of spirit.
¹⁵You will leave your name
    for my chosen ones to use in their curses;
the Sovereign LORD will put you to death,
    but to his servants he will give another name.
¹⁶Whoever invokes a blessing in the land
    will do so by the one true God;
whoever takes an oath in the land
    will swear by the one true God.
For the past troubles will be forgotten
    and hidden from my eyes.

New Heavens and a New Earth

¹⁷"See, I will create
    new heavens and a new earth.
The former things will not be
        remembered,
    nor will they come to mind.
¹⁸But be glad and rejoice forever
    in what I will create,
for I will create Jerusalem to be a delight
    and its people a joy.
¹⁹I will rejoice over Jerusalem
    and take delight in my people;
the sound of weeping and of crying
    will be heard in it no more.

²⁰"Never again will there be in it
    infants who live but a few days,
    or older people who do not live out their years;
those who die at a hundred
    will be thought mere youths;
those who fail to reach*ᵃ* a hundred
    will be considered accursed.
²¹They will build houses and dwell in them;
    they will plant vineyards and eat their fruit.
²²No longer will they build houses and others live in them,
    or plant and others eat.
For as the days of a tree,

conversations

security «» 65:17–25

1» Is it foolish to strive for the earthly security of having a family and home? Why or why not?

2» How do God's promises of security differ from the security we create for ourselves?

3» Which aspects of your life feel insecure? Which feel secure?

For more on security, check the index.
For the next Conversations, go to p. 1074.

ᵃ 20 Or youths; / sinners who reach

so will be the days of my people;
my chosen ones will long enjoy
the work of their hands.
²³They will not labor in vain,
nor will they bear children doomed to misfortune;
for they will be a people blessed by the LORD,
they and their descendants with them.
²⁴Before they call I will answer;
while they are still speaking I will hear.
²⁵The wolf and the lamb will feed together,
and the lion will eat straw like the ox,
but dust will be the serpent's food.
They will neither harm nor destroy
on all my holy mountain,"

says the LORD.

Judgment and Hope

66 This is what the LORD says:

"Heaven is my throne,
and the earth is my footstool.
Where is the house you will build for me?
Where will my resting place be?
²Has not my hand made all these things,
and so they came into being?"

declares the LORD.

"These are the ones I look on with favor:
those who are humble and contrite in spirit,
and who tremble at my word.
³But whoever sacrifices a bull
is like one who kills a human being,
and whoever offers a lamb
is like one who breaks a dog's neck;
whoever makes a grain offering
is like one who presents pig's blood,
and whoever burns memorial incense
is like one who worships an idol.
They have chosen their own ways,
and they delight in their abominations;
⁴so I also will choose harsh treatment for them
and will bring on them what they dread.
For when I called, no one answered,
when I spoke, no one listened.
They did evil in my sight
and chose what displeases me."

⁵Hear the word of the LORD,
you who tremble at his word:
"Your own people who hate you,
and exclude you because of my name, have said,
'Let the LORD be glorified,

that we may see your joy!'
    Yet they will be put to shame.
⁶Hear that uproar from the city,
    hear that noise from the temple!
It is the sound of the LORD
    repaying his enemies all they deserve.

⁷"Before she goes into labor,
    she gives birth;
before the pains come upon her,
    she delivers a child.
⁸Who has ever heard of such things?
    Who has ever seen things like this?
Can a country be born in a day
    or a nation be brought forth in a moment?
Yet no sooner is Zion in labor
    than she gives birth to her children.
⁹Do I bring to the moment of birth
    and not give delivery?" says the LORD.
"Do I close up the womb
    when I bring to delivery?" says your God.
¹⁰"Rejoice with Jerusalem and be glad for her,
    all you who love her;
rejoice greatly with her,
    all you who mourn over her.
¹¹For you will nurse and be satisfied
    at her comforting breasts;
you will drink deeply
    and delight in her overflowing abundance."

¹²For this is what the LORD says:

"I will extend peace to her like a river,
    and the wealth of nations like a flooding stream;
you will nurse and be carried on her arm
    and dandled on her knees.
¹³As a mother comforts her child,
    so will I comfort you;
and you will be comforted over Jerusalem."

HE IS: the comforter

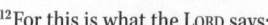

66:12–13 Isaiah foresaw that Israel would be restored. God promised to comfort his people as a mother comforts her child. What a tender picture of God's care!

Like a mother who nurses her baby and carries her little one in her arms, so God holds you close, pressed up against him. His comfort is available to you *today*. The indwelling Holy Spirit says, "I will extend peace to her like a river." Though outwardly you may be experiencing conflict and chaos, inwardly you can trust *the comforter* to hold you close (see John 14:25–27).

For the next He Is, go to p. 1096.

¹⁴When you see this, your heart will rejoice
　　and you will flourish like grass;
　the hand of the LORD will be made known to his servants,
　　but his fury will be shown to his foes.
¹⁵See, the LORD is coming with fire,
　　and his chariots are like a whirlwind;
　he will bring down his anger with fury,
　　and his rebuke with flames of fire.
¹⁶For with fire and with his sword
　　the LORD will execute judgment on all people,
　　and many will be those slain by the LORD.

¹⁷"Those who consecrate and purify themselves to go into the gardens, following one who is among those who eat the flesh of pigs, rats and other unclean things—they will meet their end together with the one they follow," declares the LORD.

¹⁸"And I, because of what they have planned and done, am about to come^a and gather the people of all nations and languages, and they will come and see my glory.

¹⁹"I will set a sign among them, and I will send some of those who survive to the nations—to Tarshish, to the Libyans^b and Lydians (famous as archers), to Tubal and Greece, and to the distant islands that have not heard of my fame or seen my glory. They will proclaim my glory among the nations. ²⁰And they will bring all your people, from all the nations, to my holy mountain in Jerusalem as an offering to the LORD—on horses, in chariots and wagons, and on mules and camels," says the LORD. "They will bring them, as the Israelites bring their grain offerings, to the temple of the LORD in ceremonially clean vessels. ²¹And I will select some of them also to be priests and Levites," says the LORD.

²²"As the new heavens and the new earth that I make will endure before me," declares the LORD, "so will your name and descendants endure. ²³From one New Moon to another and from one Sabbath to another, all people will come and bow down before me," says the LORD. ²⁴"And they will go out and look on the dead bodies of those who rebelled against me; their worm will not die, nor will their fire be quenched, and they will be loathsome to the whole human race."

---

^a *18* The meaning of the Hebrew for this clause is uncertain.　^b *19* Some Septuagint manuscripts *Put* (Libyans); Hebrew *Pul*

jeremiah

1073

AUTHOR
Jeremiah.

AUDIENCE
Jerusalem—Judah's capital city.

DATE
Jeremiah wrote from 626 B.C. through sometime after the fall of Jerusalem in 586 B.C.

SETTING
Jeremiah's message is Judah's last hope before God allows Babylon to sweep the country away.

VERSE TO REMEMBER
" 'For I know the plans I have for you,' declares the LORD, 'plans to prosper you and not to harm you, plans to give you hope and a future.' " (29:11)

THEME TO CONSIDER
The nation of Judah was dying spiritually, and Jeremiah was sent to beg the people to return to God. Because they wouldn't listen, they were taken captive.

1 The words of Jeremiah son of Hilkiah, one of the priests at Anathoth in the territory of Benjamin. ²The word of the LORD came to him in the thirteenth year of the reign of Josiah son of Amon king of Judah, ³and through the reign of Jehoiakim son of Josiah king of Judah, down to the fifth month of the eleventh year of Zedekiah son of Josiah king of Judah, when the people of Jerusalem went into exile.

The Call of Jeremiah

⁴The word of the LORD came to me, saying,

> ⁵"Before I formed you in the
>   womb I knew *a* you,
> before you were born I set
>   you apart;
> I appointed you as a
>   prophet to the
>   nations."

1074

⁶"Ah, Sovereign LORD," I said, "I do not know how to speak; I am too young." ⁷But the LORD said to me, "Do not say, 'I am too young.' You must go to everyone I send you to and say whatever I command you. ⁸Do not be afraid of them, for I am with you and will rescue you," declares the LORD.

⁹Then the LORD reached out his hand and touched my mouth and said to me, "I have put my words in your mouth. ¹⁰See, today I appoint you over nations and kingdoms to uproot and tear down, to destroy and overthrow, to build and to plant."

¹¹The word of the LORD came to me: "What do you see, Jeremiah?"

"I see the branch of an almond tree," I replied.

¹²The LORD said to me, "You have seen correctly, for I am watching *b* to see that my word is fulfilled."

¹³The word of the LORD came to me again: "What do you see?"

"I see a pot that is boiling," I answered. "It is tilting toward us from the north."

¹⁴The LORD said to me, "From the north disaster will be poured out on all who live in the land. ¹⁵I am about to summon all the peoples of the northern kingdoms," declares the LORD.

> "Their kings will come and set up their thrones
>   in the entrance of the gates of Jerusalem;
> they will come against all her surrounding walls
>   and against all the towns of Judah.
> ¹⁶I will pronounce my judgments on my people
>   because of their wickedness in forsaking me,
> in burning incense to other gods
>   and in worshiping what their hands have made.

¹⁷"Get yourself ready! Stand up and say to them whatever I command you. Do not be terrified by them, or I will terrify you before them. ¹⁸Today I have made you a fortified city, an iron pillar and a bronze wall to stand against the whole land—against the kings of Judah, its officials, its priests and the people of the land. ¹⁹They will fight against you but will not overcome you, for I am with you and will rescue you," declares the LORD.

Israel Forsakes God

2 The word of the LORD came to me: ²"Go and proclaim in the hearing of Jerusalem:

"This is what the LORD says:

"conversations"

self-esteem «» 1:5

1» How should the fact that God handmade you affect your self-esteem?

2» What would it be like to really live as if you were specially formed and set apart by God?

3» What unique ministry and purpose do you think God might have for you?

For more on **self-esteem**, check the index. For the next Conversations, go to p. 1093.

---

a 5 Or chose *b 12 The Hebrew for watching sounds like the Hebrew for almond tree.*

"'I remember the devotion of your youth,
how as a bride you loved me
and followed me through the wilderness,
through a land not sown.
³Israel was holy to the LORD,
the firstfruits of his harvest;
all who devoured her were held guilty,
and disaster overtook them,'"

declares the LORD.

⁴Hear the word of the LORD, house of Jacob,
all you clans of the house of Israel.

⁵This is what the LORD says:

"What fault did your ancestors find in me,
that they strayed so far from me?
They followed worthless idols
and became worthless themselves.
⁶They did not ask, 'Where is the LORD,
who brought us up out of Egypt
and led us through the barren wilderness,
through a land of deserts and ravines,
a land of drought and utter darkness,
a land where no one travels and no one lives?'
⁷I brought you into a fertile land
to eat its fruit and rich produce.
But you came and defiled my land
and made my inheritance detestable.
⁸The priests did not ask,
'Where is the LORD?'
Those who deal with the law did not know me;
the leaders rebelled against me.
The prophets prophesied by Baal,
following worthless idols.

⁹"Therefore I bring charges against you again,"

declares the LORD.

"And I will bring charges against your children's children.
¹⁰Cross over to the coasts of Cyprus and look,
send to Kedar*ᵃ* and observe closely;
see if there has ever been anything like this:
¹¹Has a nation ever changed its gods?
(Yet they are not gods at all.)
But my people have exchanged their glorious God
for worthless idols.
¹²Be appalled at this, you heavens,
and shudder with great horror,"

declares the LORD.

¹³"My people have committed two sins:
They have forsaken me,

ᵃ 10 In the Syro-Arabian desert

myth# 63 "USE CREDIT NOW AND PAY FOR IT LATER."

Look out, good life—here I come! After living on Ramen noodles all the way through college and graduate school and scraping by just to pay my tuition and rent, I'm ready to start living a real life. And it seems ready for me! Ever since I found a great job and moved to an upscale neighborhood, the credit card applications just keep coming. They overflow my mailbox every day. I feel so important. I pick and choose which ones I want and then fill them out and send them back. I got a Starbucks card, a Visa with a cute kitten on the front and a shiny Platinum Discover card (gotta love that cash back). Clearly I must have good credit—otherwise, why would credit card companies keep pursuing me?

Every time I whip out my card to pay for a purchase, I feel rich. I love having the power to buy something when I want it without having to wait till I get my next paycheck. And I appreciate being able to pay the minimum balance and then choose when to pay the rest. It's living life on my own terms, finally. I must be doing something right because the companies keep raising my credit limit.

Now that I have a good job, I know that I'll never have to worry about money again. I've taken trips and charged all of the expenses to my card. (Isn't it nice not to have to carry cash when you're overseas?) I've bought nice gifts for family members (and some for myself). I have a completely new wardrobe—something I'd always hoped for. For me, credit is the way to go.

—Helene

7 REASONS NOT to Abuse Credit

7. Credit card debt leads to bondage, not freedom.

6. Racking up a lot of credit card debt now reduces the chances of getting a loan for a legitimate need (like a house) later.

5. "Buy now, pay later" means you *will* pay for the fun you have on your credit card—and you'll pay with interest.

4. If you spend more than you earn, you're not being a wise steward of the money that God has entrusted to you.

3. Paying high interest charges is simply throwing money away. A simple expense, such as a dinner out, multiplies in price.

2. Having a high level of debt limits your choices in life. You won't be able to give or live as you'd like—you'll be a slave to your debt.

1. Feeding the urge to have whatever you want *now* is dangerous thinking and puts your dependence on your possessions rather than on God.

While there are some forms of debt that are necessary, such as a house mortgage or school loan, credit that guarantees high interest rate payments is a trap to avoid.

So, what should you do if you are facing a mountain of credit card debt? **STOP.**

S—Set aside your credit cards in a drawer. Better yet, cancel them and cut them in half. Save one with a reasonable credit limit for emergencies. Don't wait until you're in critical danger to quit charging (see Jeremiah 2:25 for God's warning to people who were so taken with other gods that they wore themselves out).

T—Talk to someone to start a repayment plan. Contact consumer-counseling services or join a faith-based financial study (such as Crown Ministries) in a local church.

O—Only use cash. The next time you are tempted to charge something you can't pay cash for, evaluate whether the item is a legitimate need or simply a want.

P—Practice self-control. It doesn't matter how much you make. What matters is the state of your heart. Are you living in a Spirit-controlled and self-controlled manner (see Galatians 5:22–26)? Do you respect yourself enough to say "no" or "maybe later"?

"Americans' average credit card debt is $8400 per household. Americans pay, on average, an 18.9 percent interest rate on credit cards. On average, the typical credit card purchase is 112 percent higher than if using cash. More than 40 percent of American families spend more than they earn."
—Consumer Credit Counseling Service

"THE BORROWER IS SLAVE TO THE LENDER."

PROVERBS 22:7

SEE ALSO

Proverbs 21:5
Proverbs 23:4–5
Galatians 5:22–24

For more on **Finances**, check the index.

the spring of living water,
and have dug their own cisterns,
  broken cisterns that cannot hold
    water.
¹⁴Is Israel a servant, a slave by birth?
  Why then has he become plunder?
¹⁵Lions have roared;
  they have growled at him.
They have laid waste his land;
  his towns are burned and deserted.
¹⁶Also, the men of Memphis and
    Tahpanhes
  have cracked your skull.
¹⁷Have you not brought this on yourselves
  by forsaking the LORD your God
  when he led you in the way?
¹⁸Now why go to Egypt
  to drink water from the Nile*?
And why go to Assyria
  to drink water from the Euphrates?
¹⁹Your wickedness will punish you;
  your backsliding will rebuke you.
Consider then and realize
  how evil and bitter it is for you
when you forsake the LORD your God
  and have no awe of me,"

declares the Lord, the LORD Almighty.

²⁰"Long ago you broke off your yoke
  and tore off your bonds;
  you said, 'I will not serve you!'
Indeed, on every high hill
  and under every spreading tree
  you lay down as a prostitute.
²¹I had planted you like a choice vine
  of sound and reliable stock.
How then did you turn against me
  into a corrupt, wild vine?
²²Although you wash yourself with soap
  and use an abundance of cleansing powder,
  the stain of your guilt is still before me,"
    declares the Sovereign LORD.
²³"How can you say, 'I am not defiled;
  I have not run after the Baals'?
See how you behaved in the valley;
  consider what you have done.
You are a swift she-camel
  running here and there,
²⁴a wild donkey accustomed to the desert,
  sniffing the wind in her craving—
  in her heat who can restrain her?

*at*issue:*fulfillment*

2:13 Every soul has a thirst only God can satisfy. Yet we often turn from God and try to quench our soul thirst in other ways. We pursue money, power and success, thinking they'll satisfy us. We search for fulfillment in our appearance, reputation, possessions and relationships. When all else fails, we may even turn to drugs and alcohol to slake our thirst. But those things are all like broken jars that can never hold water, so they still leave us thirsty. Only God is a spring of living water. He alone can quench the thirst of our souls.

1078

---

^a *18* Hebrew *Shihor*; that is, a branch of the Nile

Any males that pursue her need not tire themselves;
  at mating time they will find her.
²⁵Do not run until your feet are bare
  and your throat is dry.
But you said, 'It's no use!
  I love foreign gods,
  and I must go after them.'

²⁶"As a thief is disgraced when he is caught,
  so the house of Israel is disgraced—
they, their kings and their officials,
  their priests and their prophets.
²⁷They say to wood, 'You are my father,'
  and to stone, 'You gave me birth.'
They have turned their backs to me
  and not their faces;
yet when they are in trouble, they say,
  'Come and save us!'
²⁸Where then are the gods you made for yourselves?
  Let them come if they can save you
  when you are in trouble!
For you, Judah, have as many gods
  as you have towns.

²⁹"Why do you bring charges against me?
  You have all rebelled against me,"

declares the LORD.

³⁰"In vain I punished your people;
  they did not respond to correction.
Your sword has devoured your prophets
  like a ravenous lion.

³¹"You of this generation, consider the word of the LORD:

"Have I been a desert to Israel
  or a land of great darkness?
Why do my people say, 'We are free to roam;
  we will come to you no more'?
³²Does a young woman forget her jewelry,
  a bride her wedding ornaments?
Yet my people have forgotten me,
  days without number.
³³How skilled you are at pursuing love!
  Even the worst of women can learn from your ways.
³⁴On your clothes is found
  the lifeblood of the innocent poor,
  though you did not catch them breaking in.
Yet in spite of all this
³⁵ you say, 'I am innocent;
  he is not angry with me.'
But I will pass judgment on you
  because you say, 'I have not sinned.'
³⁶Why do you go about so much,

1079

changing your ways?
You will be disappointed by Egypt
    as you were by Assyria.
³⁷You will also leave that place
    with your hands on your head,
for the LORD has rejected those you trust;
    you will not be helped by them.

3 "If a man divorces his wife
    and she leaves him and marries another man,
should he return to her again?
    Would not the land be completely defiled?
But you have lived as a prostitute with many lovers—
    would you now return to me?"

declares the LORD.

²"Look up to the barren heights and see.
    Is there any place where you have not been ravished?
By the roadside you sat waiting for lovers,
    sat like a nomad in the desert.
You have defiled the land
    with your prostitution and wickedness.
³Therefore the showers have been withheld,
    and no spring rains have fallen.
Yet you have the brazen look of a prostitute;
    you refuse to blush with shame.
⁴Have you not just called to me:
    'My Father, my friend from my youth,
⁵will you always be angry?
    Will your wrath continue forever?'
This is how you talk,
    but you do all the evil you can."

Unfaithful Israel

⁶During the reign of King Josiah, the LORD said to me, "Have you seen what faithless Israel has done? She has gone up on every high hill and under every spreading tree and has committed adultery there. ⁷I thought that after she had done all this she would return to me but she did not, and her unfaithful sister Judah saw it. ⁸I gave faithless Israel her certificate of divorce and sent her away because of all her adulteries. Yet I saw that her unfaithful sister Judah had no fear; she also went out and committed adultery. ⁹Because Israel's immorality mattered so little to her, she defiled the land and committed adultery with stone and wood. ¹⁰In spite of all this, her unfaithful sister Judah did not return to me with all her heart, but only in pretense," declares the LORD.

¹¹The LORD said to me, "Faithless Israel is more righteous than unfaithful Judah. ¹²Go, proclaim this message toward the north:

"'Return, faithless Israel,' declares the LORD,
    'I will frown on you no longer,
for I am faithful,' declares the LORD,
    'I will not be angry forever.
¹³Only acknowledge your guilt—
    you have rebelled against the LORD your God,
you have scattered your favors to foreign gods
    under every spreading tree,

and have not obeyed me,'"

declares the LORD.

[14]"Return, faithless people," declares the LORD, "for I am your husband. I will choose you—one from a town and two from a clan—and bring you to Zion. [15]Then I will give you shepherds after my own heart, who will lead you with knowledge and understanding. [16]In those days, when your numbers have increased greatly in the land," declares the LORD, "people will no longer say, 'The ark of the covenant of the LORD.' It will never enter their minds or be remembered; it will not be missed, nor will another one be made. [17]At that time they will call Jerusalem The Throne of the LORD, and all nations will gather in Jerusalem to honor the name of the LORD. No longer will they follow the stubbornness of their evil hearts. [18]In those days the house of Judah will join the house of Israel, and together they will come from a northern land to the land I gave your ancestors as an inheritance.

[19]"I myself said,

"'How gladly would I treat you like my
        children
    and give you a pleasant land,
    the most beautiful inheritance of any
        nation.'
    I thought you would call me 'Father'
        and not turn away from following me.
[20]But like a woman unfaithful to her
        husband,
    so you, house of Israel, have been unfaithful to me,"

declares the LORD.

[21]A cry is heard on the barren heights,
    the weeping and pleading of the people of Israel,
because they have perverted their ways
    and have forgotten the LORD their God.

[22]"Return, faithless people;
    I will cure you of backsliding."

"Yes, we will come to you,
    for you are the LORD our God.
[23]Surely the idolatrous commotion on the hills
    and mountains is a deception;
surely in the LORD our God
    is the salvation of Israel.
[24]From our youth shameful gods have consumed
    the fruits of our ancestors' labor—
their flocks and herds,
    their sons and daughters.
[25]Let us lie down in our shame,
    and let our disgrace cover us.
We have sinned against the LORD our God,
    both we and our ancestors;

atissue:confessing sin

3:12–13 It's well known that Alcoholics Anonymous requires its members to admit out loud that they are alcoholics. The reason is simple: The first step to recovery is admitting you have a problem. Maybe we should form a new organization—Sinners Anonymous—that would require us to openly admit that we're sinners. The first step to being set free from your sin is coming clean with it. You have to acknowledge your guilt and confess your sin in order to experience God's forgiveness and mercy. So go on, say it: "My name is _____. I am a sinner."

1081

from our youth till this day
we have not obeyed the Lord our God."

4 "If you, Israel, will return,
then return to me,"

declares the Lord.

"If you put your detestable idols out of my sight
and no longer go astray,
[2] and if in a truthful, just and righteous way
you swear, 'As surely as the Lord lives,'
then the nations will invoke blessings by him
and in him they will boast."

[3] This is what the Lord says to the people of Judah and to Jerusalem:

"Break up your unplowed ground
and do not sow among thorns.
[4] Circumcise yourselves to the Lord,
circumcise your hearts,
you people of Judah and inhabitants of Jerusalem,
or my wrath will flare up and burn like fire
because of the evil you have done—
burn with no one to quench it.

Disaster From the North

[5] "Announce in Judah and proclaim in Jerusalem and say:
'Sound the trumpet throughout the land!'
Cry aloud and say:
'Gather together!
Let us flee to the fortified cities!'
[6] Raise the signal to go to Zion!
Flee for safety without delay!
For I am bringing disaster from the north,
even terrible destruction."

[7] A lion has come out of his lair;
a destroyer of nations has set out.
He has left his place
to lay waste your land.
Your towns will lie in ruins
without inhabitant.
[8] So put on sackcloth,
lament and wail,
for the fierce anger of the Lord
has not turned away from us.

[9] "In that day," declares the Lord,
"the king and the officials will lose heart,
the priests will be horrified,
and the prophets will be appalled."

[10] Then I said, "Ah, Sovereign Lord, how completely you have deceived this people and Jerusalem by saying, 'You will have peace,' when the sword is at our throats."

[11] At that time this people and Jerusalem will be told, "A scorching wind from the barren heights in the

desert blows toward my people, but not to winnow or cleanse; ¹²a wind too strong for that comes from me.^a Now I pronounce my judgments against them."

¹³Look! He advances like the clouds,
    his chariots come like a whirlwind,
his horses are swifter than eagles.
    Woe to us! We are ruined!
¹⁴Jerusalem, wash the evil from your heart and be saved.
    How long will you harbor wicked thoughts?
¹⁵A voice is announcing from Dan,
    proclaiming disaster from the hills of Ephraim.
¹⁶"Tell this to the nations,
    proclaim concerning Jerusalem:
'A besieging army is coming from a distant land,
    raising a war cry against the cities of Judah.
¹⁷They surround her like people guarding a field,
    because she has rebelled against me,'"

                                  declares the LORD.

¹⁸"Your own conduct and actions
    have brought this on you.
This is your punishment.
    How bitter it is!
    How it pierces to the heart!"

¹⁹Oh, my anguish, my anguish!
    I writhe in pain.
Oh, the agony of my heart!
    My heart pounds within me,
    I cannot keep silent.
For I have heard the sound of the trumpet;
    I have heard the battle cry.
²⁰Disaster follows disaster;
    the whole land lies in ruins.
In an instant my tents are destroyed,
    my shelter in a moment.
²¹How long must I see the battle standard
    and hear the sound of the trumpet?

²²"My people are fools;
    they do not know me.
They are senseless children;
    they have no understanding.
They are skilled in doing evil;
    they know not how to do good."

²³I looked at the earth,
    and it was formless and empty;
and at the heavens,
    and their light was gone.
²⁴I looked at the mountains,
    and they were quaking;
all the hills were swaying.

^a *12 Or comes at my command*

²⁵I looked, and there were no people;
   every bird in the sky had flown away.
²⁶I looked, and the fruitful land was a desert;
   all its towns lay in ruins
   before the LORD, before his fierce anger.

²⁷This is what the LORD says:

   "The whole land will be ruined,
      though I will not destroy it completely.
²⁸Therefore the earth will mourn
      and the heavens above grow dark,
   because I have spoken and will not relent,
      I have decided and will not turn back."

²⁹At the sound of horsemen and archers
      every town takes to flight.
   Some go into the thickets;
      some climb up among the rocks.
   All the towns are deserted;
      no one lives in them.

³⁰What are you doing, you devastated one?
   Why dress yourself in scarlet
      and put on jewels of gold?
   Why color your eyes with paint?
      You adorn yourself in vain.
   Your lovers despise you;
      they seek your life.

³¹I hear a cry as of a woman in labor,
   a groan as of one bearing her first
      child—
   the cry of Daughter Zion gasping for
      breath,
   stretching out her hands and saying,
   "Alas! I am fainting;
      my life is given over to murderers."

Not One Is Upright

5   "Go up and down the streets of
         Jerusalem,
      look around and consider,
         search through her squares.
      If you can find but one person
         who deals honestly and seeks the
            truth,
      I will forgive this city.
   ²Although they say, 'As surely as the LORD
         lives,'
      still they are swearing falsely."

³LORD, do not your eyes look for truth?
   You struck them, but they felt no
      pain;

1084

you crushed them, but they refused correction.
They made their faces harder than stone
and refused to repent.
⁴I thought, "These are only the poor;
they are foolish,
for they do not know the way of the LORD,
the requirements of their God.
⁵So I will go to the leaders
and speak to them;
surely they know the way of the LORD,
the requirements of their God."
But with one accord they too had broken off the yoke
and torn off the bonds.
⁶Therefore a lion from the forest will attack them,
a wolf from the desert will ravage them,
a leopard will lie in wait near their towns
to tear to pieces any who venture out,
for their rebellion is great
and their backslidings many.

⁷"Why should I forgive you?
Your children have forsaken me
and sworn by gods that are not gods.
I supplied all their needs,
yet they committed adultery
and thronged to the houses of prostitutes.
⁸They are well-fed, lusty stallions,
each neighing for another man's wife.
⁹Should I not punish them for this?"
declares the LORD.
"Should I not avenge myself
on such a nation as this?

¹⁰"Go through her vineyards and ravage them,
but do not destroy them completely.
Strip off her branches,
for these people do not belong to the LORD.
¹¹The house of Israel and the house of Judah
have been utterly unfaithful to me,"

declares the LORD.

¹²They have lied about the LORD;
they said, "He will do nothing!
No harm will come to us;
we will never see sword or famine.
¹³The prophets are but wind
and the word is not in them;
so let what they say be done to them."

¹⁴Therefore this is what the LORD God Almighty says:

"Because the people have spoken these words,
I will make my words in your mouth a fire
and these people the wood it consumes.

1085

¹⁵House of Israel," declares the LORD,
"I am bringing a distant nation against you—
an ancient and enduring nation,
    a people whose language you do not know,
    whose speech you do not understand.
¹⁶Their quivers are like an open grave;
    all of them are mighty warriors.
¹⁷They will devour your harvests and food,
    devour your sons and daughters;
they will devour your flocks and herds,
    devour your vines and fig trees.
With the sword they will destroy
    the fortified cities in which you trust.

¹⁸"Yet even in those days," declares the LORD, "I will not destroy you completely. ¹⁹And when the people ask, 'Why has the LORD our God done all this to us?' you will tell them, 'As you have forsaken me and served foreign gods in your own land, so now you will serve foreigners in a land not your own.'

1086

²⁰"Announce this to the house of Jacob
    and proclaim it in Judah:
²¹Hear this, you foolish and senseless people,
    who have eyes but do not see,
    who have ears but do not hear:
²²Should you not fear me?" declares the LORD.
    "Should you not tremble in my presence?
I made the sand a boundary for the sea,
    an everlasting barrier it cannot cross.
The waves may roll, but they cannot prevail;
    they may roar, but they cannot cross it.
²³But these people have stubborn and rebellious hearts;
    they have turned aside and gone away.
²⁴They do not say to themselves,
    'Let us fear the LORD our God,
who gives autumn and spring rains in season,
    who assures us of the regular weeks of harvest.'
²⁵Your wrongdoings have kept these away;
    your sins have deprived you of good.

²⁶"Among my people are the wicked
    who lie in wait like those who snare birds
    and like those who set traps to catch people.
²⁷Like cages full of birds,
    their houses are full of deceit;
they have become rich and powerful
²⁸   and have grown fat and sleek.
Their evil deeds have no limit;
    they do not seek justice.
They do not promote the case of the fatherless;
    they do not defend the just cause of the poor.
²⁹Should I not punish them for this?"
    declares the LORD.
"Should I not avenge myself
    on such a nation as this?

³⁰"A horrible and shocking thing
    has happened in the land:
³¹The prophets prophesy lies,
    the priests rule by their own authority,
and my people love it this way.
    But what will you do in the end?

Jerusalem Under Siege

6 "Flee for safety, people of Benjamin!
    Flee from Jerusalem!
Sound the trumpet in Tekoa!
    Raise the signal over Beth Hakkerem!
For disaster looms out of the north,
    even terrible destruction.
²I will destroy Daughter Zion,
    so beautiful and delicate.
³Shepherds with their flocks will come against her;
    they will pitch their tents around her,
    each of them tending their own portion."

⁴"Prepare for battle against her!
    Arise, let us attack at noon!
But, alas, the daylight is fading,
    and the shadows of evening grow long.
⁵So arise, let us attack at night
    and destroy her fortresses!"

⁶This is what the LORD Almighty says:

"Cut down the trees
    and build siege ramps against Jerusalem.
This city must be punished;
    it is filled with oppression.
⁷As a well pours out its water,
    so she pours out her wickedness.
Violence and destruction resound in her;
    her sickness and wounds are ever before me.
⁸Take warning, Jerusalem,
    or I will turn away from you
and make your land desolate
    so no one can live in it."

⁹This is what the LORD Almighty says:

"Let them glean the remnant of Israel
    as thoroughly as a vine;
pass your hand over the branches again,
    like one gathering grapes."

¹⁰To whom can I speak and give warning?
    Who will listen to me?
Their ears are closed^a
    so they cannot hear.

---

^a *10* Hebrew *uncircumcised*

The word of the LORD is offensive to them;
  they find no pleasure in it.
[11]But I am full of the wrath of the LORD,
  and I cannot hold it in.

"Pour it out on the children in the street
  and on the youths gathered together;
both husband and wife will be caught in it,
  and the old, those weighed down with years.
[12]Their houses will be turned over to others,
  together with their fields and their wives,
when I stretch out my hand
  against those who live in the land,"

declares the LORD.

[13]"From the least to the greatest,
  all are greedy for gain;
prophets and priests alike,
  all practice deceit.
[14]They dress the wound of my people
  as though it were not serious.
'Peace, peace,' they say,
  when there is no peace.
[15]Are they ashamed of their detestable conduct?
  No, they have no shame at all;
  they do not even know how to blush.
So they will fall among the fallen;
  they will be brought down when I punish them,"

says the LORD.

[16]This is what the LORD says:

"Stand at the crossroads and look;
  ask for the ancient paths,
ask where the good way is, and walk in it,
  and you will find rest for your souls.
  But you said, 'We will not walk in it.'
[17]I appointed watchmen over you and said,
  'Listen to the sound of the trumpet!'
  But you said, 'We will not listen.'
[18]Therefore hear, you nations;
  you who are witnesses,
  observe what will happen to them.
[19]Hear, you earth:
  I am bringing disaster on this people,
    the fruit of their schemes,
because they have not listened to my words
  and have rejected my law.
[20]What do I care about incense from Sheba
  or sweet calamus from a distant land?
Your burnt offerings are not acceptable;
  your sacrifices do not please me."

[21]Therefore this is what the LORD says:

> "I will put obstacles before this people.
>> Parents and children alike will stumble over them;
>> neighbors and friends will perish.""

22 This is what the LORD says:

> "Look, an army is coming
>> from the land of the north;
>> a great nation is being stirred up
>> from the ends of the earth.
> 23 They are armed with bow and spear;
>> they are cruel and show no mercy.
> They sound like the roaring sea
>> as they ride on their horses;
> they come like men in battle formation
>> to attack you, Daughter Zion."

> 24 We have heard reports about them,
>> and our hands hang limp.
> Anguish has gripped us,
>> pain like that of a woman in labor.
> 25 Do not go out to the fields
>> or walk on the roads,
> for the enemy has a sword,
>> and there is terror on every side.
> 26 Put on sackcloth, my people,
>> and roll in ashes;
> mourn with bitter wailing
>> as for an only son,
> for suddenly the destroyer
>> will come upon us.

> 27 "I have made you a tester of metals
>> and my people the ore,
> that you may observe
>> and test their ways.
> 28 They are all hardened rebels,
>> going about to slander.
> They are bronze and iron;
>> they all act corruptly.
> 29 The bellows blow fiercely
>> to burn away the lead with fire,
> but the refining goes on in vain;
>> the wicked are not purged out.
> 30 They are called rejected silver,
>> because the LORD has rejected them."

False Religion Worthless

7 This is the word that came to Jeremiah from the LORD: 2 "Stand at the gate of the LORD's house and there proclaim this message:

"'Hear the word of the LORD, all you people of Judah who come through these gates to worship the LORD. 3 This is what the LORD Almighty, the God of Israel, says: Reform your ways and your actions, and I will let you live in this place. 4 Do not trust in deceptive words and say, "This is the temple of the LORD, the temple of the LORD, the temple of the LORD!" 5 If you really change your ways and your actions and deal with each other justly, [6]if you do not oppress the foreigner, the fatherless or the widow and do not shed innocent blood in this place, and if you do not follow other gods to your own harm, [7]then I will let you live in this place, in the land I gave your ancestors for ever and ever. [8]But look, you are trusting in deceptive words that are worthless.

[9]"Will you steal and murder, commit adultery and perjury,[a] burn incense to Baal and follow other gods you have not known, [10]and then come and stand before me in this house, which bears my Name, and say, "We are safe"—safe to do all these detestable things? [11]Has this house, which bears my Name, become a den of robbers to you? But I have been watching! declares the LORD.

[12]"Go now to the place in Shiloh where I first made a dwelling for my Name, and see what I did to it because of the wickedness of my people Israel. [13]While you were doing all these things, declares the LORD, I spoke to you again and again, but you did not listen; I called you, but you did not answer. [14]Therefore, what I did to Shiloh I will now do to the house that bears my Name, the temple you trust in, the place I gave to you and your ancestors. [15]I will thrust you from my presence, just as I did all your fellow Israelites, the people of Ephraim.'

[16]"So do not pray for this people nor offer any plea or petition for them; do not plead with me, for I will not listen to you. [17]Do you not see what they are doing in the towns of Judah and in the streets of Jerusalem? [18]The children gather wood, the fathers light the fire, and the women knead the dough and make cakes to offer to the Queen of Heaven. They pour out drink offerings to other gods to arouse my anger. [19]But am I the one they are provoking? declares the LORD. Are they not rather harming themselves, to their own shame?

[20]"Therefore this is what the Sovereign LORD says: My anger and my wrath will be poured out on this place—on people and animals, on the trees of the field and on the crops of your land—and it will burn and not be quenched.

[21]"This is what the LORD Almighty, the God of Israel, says: Go ahead, add your burnt offerings to your other sacrifices and eat the meat yourselves! [22]For when I brought your ancestors out of Egypt and spoke to them, I did not just give them commands about burnt offerings and sacrifices, [23]but I gave them this command: Obey me, and I will be your God and you will be my people. Walk in obedience to all I command you, that it may go well with you. [24]But they did not listen or pay attention; instead, they followed the stubborn inclinations of their evil hearts. They went backward and not forward. [25]From the time your ancestors left Egypt until now, day after day, again and again I sent you my servants the prophets. [26]But they did not listen to me or pay attention. They were stiff-necked and did more evil than their ancestors.'

[27]"When you tell them all this, they will not listen to you; when you call to them, they will not answer. [28]Therefore say to them, 'This is the nation that has not obeyed the LORD its God or responded to correction. Truth has perished; it has vanished from their lips.

[29]"Cut off your hair and throw it away; take up a lament on the barren heights, for the LORD has rejected and abandoned this generation that is under his wrath.

The Valley of Slaughter

[30]"The people of Judah have done evil in my eyes, declares the LORD. They have set up their detestable idols in the house that bears my Name and have defiled it. [31]They have built the high places of Topheth

atissue:hypocrisy

7:21–26 Although the Israelites offered sacrifices, they did not choose to obey God's other commands— to let him be their God and to be his people. Put in modern-day terms, they did the "church thing" on Sundays and then did whatever they wanted the rest of the time. They didn't have a full-time relationship with God. *That* was the problem. God doesn't want you to put on an act of knowing him; he wants you to truly know him. He doesn't want a little of your time; he wants all of you, all the time. He will not settle for anything less.

1090

---

in the Valley of Ben Hinnom to burn their sons and daughters in the fire—something I did not command, nor did it enter my mind. ³²So beware, the days are coming, declares the LORD, when people will no longer call it Topheth or the Valley of Ben Hinnom, but the Valley of Slaughter, for they will bury the dead in Topheth until there is no more room. ³³Then the carcasses of this people will become food for the birds and the wild animals, and there will be no one to frighten them away. ³⁴I will bring an end to the sounds of joy and gladness and to the voices of bride and bridegroom in the towns of Judah and the streets of Jerusalem, for the land will become desolate.

8 "At that time, declares the LORD, the bones of the kings and officials of Judah, the bones of the priests and prophets, and the bones of the people of Jerusalem will be removed from their graves. ²They will be exposed to the sun and the moon and all the stars of the heavens, which they have loved and served and which they have followed and consulted and worshiped. They will not be gathered up or buried, but will be like dung lying on the ground. ³Wherever I banish them, all the survivors of this evil nation will prefer death to life, declares the LORD Almighty.'

Sin and Punishment

⁴"Say to them, 'This is what the LORD says:

"'When people fall down, do they not get up?
    When people turn away, do they not return?
⁵Why then have these people turned away?
    Why does Jerusalem always turn away?
They cling to deceit;
    they refuse to return.
⁶I have listened attentively,
    but they do not say what is right.
None of them repent of their wickedness,
    saying, "What have I done?"
They each pursue their own course
    like a horse charging into battle.
⁷Even the stork in the sky
    knows her appointed seasons,
and the dove, the swift and the thrush
    observe the time of their migration.
But my people do not know
    the requirements of the LORD.

⁸"'How can you say, "We are wise,
    for we have the law of the LORD,"
when actually the lying pen of the scribes
    has handled it falsely?
⁹The wise will be put to shame;
    they will be dismayed and trapped.
Since they have rejected the word of the LORD,
    what kind of wisdom do they have?
¹⁰Therefore I will give their wives to other men
    and their fields to new owners.
From the least to the greatest,
    all are greedy for gain;
prophets and priests alike,
    all practice deceit.
¹¹They dress the wound of my people
    as though it were not serious.
"Peace, peace," they say,

1091

when there is no peace.
¹²Are they ashamed of their detestable conduct?
No, they have no shame at all;
they do not even know how to blush.
So they will fall among the fallen;
they will be brought down when they are punished,

says the LORD.

¹³"'I will take away their harvest,

declares the LORD.

There will be no grapes on the vine.
There will be no figs on the tree,
and their leaves will wither.
What I have given them
will be taken from them.ᵃ'"

¹⁴Why are we sitting here?
Gather together!
Let us flee to the fortified cities
and perish there!
For the LORD our God has doomed us to perish
and given us poisoned water to drink,
because we have sinned against him.
¹⁵We hoped for peace
but no good has come,
for a time of healing
but there is only terror.
¹⁶The snorting of the enemy's horses
is heard from Dan;
at the neighing of their stallions
the whole land trembles.
They have come to devour
the land and everything in it,
the city and all who live there.

¹⁷"See, I will send venomous snakes among you,
vipers that cannot be charmed,
and they will bite you,"

declares the LORD.

¹⁸You who are my Comforterᵇ in sorrow,
my heart is faint within me.
¹⁹Listen to the cry of my people
from a land far away:
"Is the LORD not in Zion?
Is her King no longer there?"

"Why have they aroused my anger with their images,
with their worthless foreign idols?"

²⁰"The harvest is past,
the summer has ended,
and we are not saved."

ᵃ *13* The meaning of the Hebrew for this sentence is uncertain.   ᵇ *18* The meaning of the Hebrew for this word is uncertain.

²¹ Since my people are crushed, I am
    crushed;
  I mourn, and horror grips me.
²² Is there no balm in Gilead?
  Is there no physician there?
  Why then is there no healing
    for the wound of my people?

9

*¹ Oh, that my head were a spring of
    water
  and my eyes a fountain of tears!
  I would weep day and night
    for the slain of my people.
*² Oh, that I had in the desert
    a lodging place for travelers,
  so that I might leave my people
    and go away from them;
  for they are all adulterers,
    a crowd of unfaithful people.

³ "They make ready their tongue
    like a bow, to shoot lies;
  it is not by truth
    that they triumph*a* in the land.
  They go from one sin to another;
    they do not acknowledge me,"

                                    declares the LORD.

⁴ "Beware of your friends;
    do not trust any of your people.
  For every one of them is a deceiver,*b*
    and every friend a slanderer.
⁵ Friend deceives friend,
    and no one speaks the truth.
  They have taught their tongues to lie;
    they weary themselves with sinning.
⁶ You*c* live in the midst of deception;
    in their deceit they refuse to acknowledge me,"

                                    declares the LORD.

⁷ Therefore this is what the LORD Almighty says:

  "See, I will refine and test them,
    for what else can I do
    because of the sin of my people?
⁸ Their tongue is a deadly arrow;
    it speaks deceitfully.
  With their mouths they all speak cordially to their neighbors,
    but in their hearts they set traps for them.
⁹ Should I not punish them for this?"
    declares the LORD.
  "Should I not avenge myself
    on such a nation as this?"

conversations

suffering «» 8:21–22

1» Describe a time when you felt moved by the suffering of others.

2» Why does suffering continue in this world?

3» Is it possible to avoid suffering in this life by the way you live?

For more on **suffering**, check the index.
For the next Conversations, go to p. 1110.

1093

---

a 3 Or *lies; / they are not valiant for truth*   *b 4* Or *a deceiving Jacob*   *c 6* That is, Jeremiah (the Hebrew is singular)
* 9:1 is numbered 8:23 in Hebrew texts.   * 9:2-26 is numbered 9:1-25 in Hebrew texts.

¹⁰I will weep and wail for the mountains
   and take up a lament concerning the wilderness grasslands.
They are desolate and untraveled,
   and the lowing of cattle is not heard.
The birds have all fled
   and the animals are gone.

¹¹"I will make Jerusalem a heap of ruins,
   a haunt of jackals;
and I will lay waste the towns of Judah
   so no one can live there."

¹²Who is wise enough to understand this? Who has been instructed by the Lord and can explain it? Why has the land been ruined and laid waste like a desert that no one can cross?

¹³The Lord said, "It is because they have forsaken my law, which I set before them; they have not obeyed me or followed my law. ¹⁴Instead, they have followed the stubbornness of their hearts; they have followed the Baals, as their ancestors taught them." ¹⁵Therefore, this is what the Lord Almighty, the God of Israel, says: "See, I will make this people eat bitter food and drink poisoned water. ¹⁶I will scatter them among nations that neither they nor their ancestors have known, and I will pursue them with the sword until I have made an end of them."

¹⁷This is what the Lord Almighty says:

"Consider now! Call for the wailing women to come;
   send for the most skillful of them.
¹⁸Let them come quickly
   and wail over us
till our eyes overflow with tears
   and water streams from our eyelids.
¹⁹The sound of wailing is heard from Zion:
   'How ruined we are!
   How great is our shame!
We must leave our land
   because our houses are in ruins.'"

²⁰Now, you women, hear the word of the Lord;
   open your ears to the words of his mouth.
Teach your daughters how to wail;
   teach one another a lament.
²¹Death has climbed in through our windows
   and has entered our fortresses;
it has removed the children from the streets
   and the youths from the public squares.

²²Say, "This is what the Lord declares:

"'Dead bodies will lie
   like dung on the open field,
like cut grain behind the reaper,
   with no one to gather them.'"

²³This is what the Lord says:

"Let not the wise boast of their wisdom
   or the strong boast of their strength
   or the rich boast of their riches,

²⁴but let those who boast boast about this:
    that they understand and know me,
that I am the LORD, who exercises kindness,
    justice and righteousness on earth,
    for in these I delight,"
                  declares the LORD.

²⁵"The days are coming," declares the LORD, "when I will punish all who are circumcised only in the flesh— ²⁶Egypt, Judah, Edom, Ammon, Moab and all who live in the wilderness in distant places.ᵃ For all these nations are really uncircumcised, and even the whole house of Israel is uncircumcised in heart."

God and Idols

10 Hear what the LORD says to you, house of Israel. ²This is what the LORD says:

"Do not learn the ways of the nations
    or be terrified by signs in the sky,
    though the nations are terrified by them.
³For the practices of the peoples are
      worthless;
they cut a tree out of the forest,
    and a skilled worker shapes it with a chisel.
⁴They adorn it with silver and gold;
    they fasten it with hammer and nails
    so it will not totter.
⁵Like a scarecrow in a melon patch,
    their idols cannot speak;
they must be carried
    because they cannot walk.
Do not fear them;
    they can do no harm
    nor can they do any good."

⁶No one is like you, LORD;
    you are great,
    and your name is mighty in power.
⁷Who should not fear you,
    King of the nations?
    This is your due.
Among all the wise rulers of the nations
    and in all their kingdoms,
    there is no one like you.

⁸They are all senseless and foolish;
    they are taught by worthless wooden idols.
⁹Hammered silver is brought from Tarshish
    and gold from Uphaz.
What the goldsmith and engraver have made
    is then dressed in blue and purple—

at issue: identity

9:23–24 Stop and think for a minute about how you define yourself. Is it by your knowledge or wisdom? By your talents, abilities or strengths? By your possessions or relationships? The sense of pride and accomplishment you find in those things only gives you a false sense of self-worth. God reminds us that our lives are not meant to be about promoting ourselves. Instead, they ought to be about glorifying him. Let go of everything else and find your identity—your value, your purpose and your sense of *who you are*—in knowing God and being the woman *he* wants you to be.

1095

ᵃ *26* Or *wilderness and who clip the hair by their foreheads*

all made by skilled workers.
¹⁰But the Lᴏʀᴅ is the true God;
he is the living God, the eternal King.
When he is angry, the earth trembles;
the nations cannot endure his wrath.

HE IS: the true God

10:5–10 Idols are as false as a scarecrow dangling from a pole in a melon patch. Idols cannot speak or walk; they can do no harm, nor can they do any good. While idols are worthless, worshiping *the true God* is completely worthwhile.

Don't hang your heart on the gods of this world: strength, sexuality or status. There is only one *true God*. Listen to him when he speaks to you through his Word. Feel his presence when you gather among his people. Pin all your hopes and dreams on him, the one *true God*.

For the next He Is, go to p. 1102.

1096

¹¹"Tell them this: 'These gods, who did not make the heavens and the earth, will perish from the earth and from under the heavens.'"*ᵃ*

¹²But God made the earth by his power;
he founded the world by his wisdom
and stretched out the heavens by his understanding.
¹³When he thunders, the waters in the heavens roar;
he makes clouds rise from the ends of the earth.
He sends lightning with the rain
and brings out the wind from his storehouses.

¹⁴Everyone is senseless and without knowledge;
all goldsmiths are shamed by their idols.
Their images are a fraud;
they have no breath in them.
¹⁵They are worthless, the objects of mockery;
when their judgment comes, they will perish.
¹⁶He who is the Portion of Jacob is not like these,
for he is the Maker of all things,
including Israel, the tribe of his inheritance—
the Lᴏʀᴅ Almighty is his name.

Coming Destruction

¹⁷Gather up your belongings to leave the land,
you who live under siege.
¹⁸For this is what the Lᴏʀᴅ says:
"At this time I will hurl out
those who live in this land;
I will bring distress on them
so that they may be captured."

¹⁹Woe to me because of my injury!
My wound is incurable!

ᵃ 11 The text of this verse is in Aramaic.

Yet I said to myself,
    "This is my sickness, and I must endure it."
²⁰My tent is destroyed;
    all its ropes are snapped.
My children are gone from me and are no more;
    no one is left now to pitch my tent
    or to set up my shelter.
²¹The shepherds are senseless
    and do not inquire of the LORD;
so they do not prosper
    and all their flock is scattered.
²²Listen! The report is coming—
    a great commotion from the land of the north!
It will make the towns of Judah desolate,
    a haunt of jackals.

Jeremiah's Prayer

²³LORD, I know that people's lives are not their own;
    it is not for them to direct their steps.
²⁴Discipline me, LORD, but only in due measure—
    not in your anger,
    or you will reduce me to nothing.
²⁵Pour out your wrath on the nations
    that do not acknowledge you,
    on the peoples who do not call on your name.
For they have devoured Jacob;
    they have devoured him completely
    and destroyed his homeland.

The Covenant Is Broken

11 This is the word that came to Jeremiah from the LORD: ²"Listen to the terms of this covenant and tell them to the people of Judah and to those who live in Jerusalem. ³Tell them that this is what the LORD, the God of Israel, says: 'Cursed is everyone who does not obey the terms of this covenant— ⁴the terms I commanded your ancestors when I brought them out of Egypt, out of the iron-smelting furnace.' I said, 'Obey me and do everything I command you, and you will be my people, and I will be your God. ⁵Then I will fulfill the oath I swore to your ancestors, to give them a land flowing with milk and honey'— the land you possess today."

I answered, "Amen, LORD."

⁶The LORD said to me, "Proclaim all these words in the towns of Judah and in the streets of Jerusalem: 'Listen to the terms of this covenant and follow them. ⁷From the time I brought your ancestors up from Egypt until today, I warned them again and again, saying, "Obey me." ⁸But they did not listen or pay attention; instead, they followed the stubbornness of their evil hearts. So I brought on them all the curses of the covenant I had commanded them to follow but that they did not keep.'"

⁹Then the LORD said to me, "There is a conspiracy among the people of Judah and those who live in Jerusalem. ¹⁰They have returned to the sins of their ancestors, who refused to listen to my words. They have followed other gods to serve them. Both the house of Israel and the house of Judah have broken the covenant I made with their ancestors. ¹¹Therefore this is what the LORD says: 'I will bring on them a disaster they cannot escape. Although they cry out to me, I will not listen to them. ¹²The towns of Judah and the people of Jerusalem will go and cry out to the gods to whom they burn incense, but they will not help them at all when disaster strikes. ¹³You, Judah, have as many gods as you have towns; and the altars you have set up to burn incense to that shameful god Baal are as many as the streets of Jerusalem.'

14"Do not pray for this people or offer any plea or petition for them, because I will not listen when they call to me in the time of their distress.

> 15"What is my beloved doing in my
>   temple
>   as she, with many others, works out
>   her evil schemes?
>   Can consecrated meat avert your
>   punishment?
>   When you engage in your wickedness,
>   then you rejoice.ᵃ"

> 16The LORD called you a thriving olive tree
>   with fruit beautiful in form.
>   But with the roar of a mighty storm
>   he will set it on fire,
>   and its branches will be broken.

17The LORD Almighty, who planted you, has decreed disaster for you, because the house of Israel and the house of Judah have done evil and aroused my anger by burning incense to Baal.

Plot Against Jeremiah

18Because the LORD revealed their plot to me, I knew it, for at that time he showed me what they were doing. 19I had been like a gentle lamb led to the slaughter; I did not realize that they had plotted against me, saying,

> "Let us destroy the tree and its fruit;
>   let us cut him off from the land of the
>   living,
>   that his name be remembered no
>   more."
> 20But you, LORD Almighty, who judge righteously
>   and test the heart and mind,
>   let me see your vengeance on them,
>   for to you I have committed my cause.

21"Therefore this is what the LORD says about the people of Anathoth who are seeking your life and saying, 'Do not prophesy in the name of the LORD or you will die by our hands'— 22therefore this is what the LORD Almighty says: 'I will punish them. Their young men will die by the sword, their sons and daughters by famine. 23Not even a remnant will be left to them, because I will bring disaster on the people of Anathoth in the year of their punishment.'"

Jeremiah's Complaint

12 You are always righteous, LORD,
>   when I bring a case before you.
>   Yet I would speak with you about your justice:
>   Why does the way of the wicked prosper?
>   Why do all the faithless live at ease?
> 2You have planted them, and they have taken root;

1098

ᵃ 15 Or Could consecrated meat avert your punishment? / Then you would rejoice

they grow and bear fruit.
You are always on their lips
   but far from their hearts.
³Yet you know me, LORD;
   you see me and test my thoughts about you.
Drag them off like sheep to be butchered!
   Set them apart for the day of slaughter!
⁴How long will the land lie parched
   and the grass in every field be withered?
Because those who live in it are wicked,
   the animals and birds have perished.
Moreover, the people are saying,
   "He will not see what happens to us."

God's Answer

⁵"If you have raced with people on foot
   and they have worn you out,
   how can you compete with horses?
If you stumble*ᵃ* in safe country,
   how will you manage in the thickets by*ᵇ* the Jordan?
⁶Your relatives, members of your own family—
   even they have betrayed you;
   they have raised a loud cry against you.
Do not trust them,
   though they speak well of you.

⁷"I will forsake my house,
   abandon my inheritance;
I will give the one I love
   into the hands of her enemies.
⁸My inheritance has become to me
   like a lion in the forest.
She roars at me;
   therefore I hate her.
⁹Has not my inheritance become to me
   like a speckled bird of prey
   that other birds of prey surround and attack?
Go and gather all the wild beasts;
   bring them to devour.
¹⁰Many shepherds will ruin my vineyard
   and trample down my field;
they will turn my pleasant field
   into a desolate wasteland.
¹¹It will be made a wasteland,
   parched and desolate before me;
the whole land will be laid waste
   because there is no one who cares.
¹²Over all the barren heights in the desert
   destroyers will swarm,
for the sword of the LORD will devour
   from one end of the land to the other;

1099

ᵃ 5 Or *you feel secure only*   *ᵇ 5* Or *the flooding of*

no one will be safe.
¹³They will sow wheat but reap thorns;
they will wear themselves out but gain nothing.
They will bear the shame of their harvest
because of the LORD's fierce anger."

¹⁴This is what the LORD says: "As for all my wicked neighbors who seize the inheritance I gave my people Israel, I will uproot them from their lands and I will uproot the house of Judah from among them. ¹⁵But after I uproot them, I will again have compassion and will bring each of them back to their own inheritance and their own country. ¹⁶And if they learn well the ways of my people and swear by my name, saying, 'As surely as the LORD lives'—even as they once taught my people to swear by Baal—then they will be established among my people. ¹⁷But if any nation does not listen, I will completely uproot and destroy it," declares the LORD.

A Linen Belt

13 This is what the LORD said to me: "Go and buy a linen belt and put it around your waist, but do not let it touch water." ²So I bought a belt, as the LORD directed, and put it around my waist.

³Then the word of the LORD came to me a second time: ⁴"Take the belt you bought and are wearing around your waist, and go now to Perath^a and hide it there in a crevice in the rocks." ⁵So I went and hid it at Perath, as the LORD told me.

⁶Many days later the LORD said to me, "Go now to Perath and get the belt I told you to hide there." ⁷So I went to Perath and dug up the belt and took it from the place where I had hidden it, but now it was ruined and completely useless.

⁸Then the word of the LORD came to me: ⁹"This is what the LORD says: 'In the same way I will ruin the pride of Judah and the great pride of Jerusalem. ¹⁰These wicked people, who refuse to listen to my words, who follow the stubbornness of their hearts and go after other gods to serve and worship them, will be like this belt—completely useless! ¹¹For as a belt is bound around the waist, so I bound the whole house of Israel and the whole house of Judah to me,' declares the LORD, 'to be my people for my renown and praise and honor. But they have not listened.'

Wineskins

¹²"Say to them: 'This is what the LORD, the God of Israel, says: Every wineskin should be filled with wine.' And if they say to you, 'Don't we know that every wineskin should be filled with wine?' ¹³then tell them, 'This is what the LORD says: I am going to fill with drunkenness all who live in this land, including the kings who sit on David's throne, the priests, the prophets and all those living in Jerusalem. ¹⁴I will smash them one against the other, parents and children alike, declares the LORD. I will allow no pity or mercy or compassion to keep me from destroying them.'"

Threat of Captivity

¹⁵Hear and pay attention,
do not be arrogant,
for the LORD has spoken.
¹⁶Give glory to the LORD your God
before he brings the darkness,
before your feet stumble
on the darkening hills.
You hope for light,
but he will turn it to utter darkness
and change it to deep gloom.
¹⁷If you do not listen,
I will weep in secret
because of your pride;

^a 4 Or possibly to the Euphrates; also similarly in verses 5-7

my eyes will weep bitterly,
    overflowing with tears,
because the Lord's flock will be taken captive.

¹⁸Say to the king and to the queen mother,
    "Come down from your thrones,
for your glorious crowns
    will fall from your heads."
¹⁹The cities in the Negev will be shut up,
    and there will be no one to open them.
All Judah will be carried into exile,
    carried completely away.

²⁰Look up and see
    those who are coming from the north.
Where is the flock that was entrusted to you,
    the sheep of which you boasted?
²¹What will you say when the Lord sets over you
    those you cultivated as your special allies?
Will not pain grip you
    like that of a woman in labor?
²²And if you ask yourself,
    "Why has this happened to me?"—
it is because of your many sins
    that your skirts have been torn off
    and your body mistreated.
²³Can an Ethiopian^a change his skin
    or a leopard its spots?
Neither can you do good
    who are accustomed to doing evil.

²⁴"I will scatter you like chaff
    driven by the desert wind.
²⁵This is your lot,
    the portion I have decreed for you,"

declares the Lord,

"because you have forgotten me
    and trusted in false gods.
²⁶I will pull up your skirts over your face
    that your shame may be seen—
²⁷your adulteries and lustful neighings,
    your shameless prostitution!
I have seen your detestable acts
    on the hills and in the fields.
Woe to you, Jerusalem!
    How long will you be unclean?"

Drought, Famine, Sword

14 This is the word of the Lord that came to Jeremiah concerning the drought:

²"Judah mourns,
    her cities languish;

^a 23 Hebrew *Cushite* (probably a person from the upper Nile region)

they wail for the land,
 and a cry goes up from Jerusalem.
³The nobles send their servants for water;
 they go to the cisterns
 but find no water.
They return with their jars unfilled;
 dismayed and despairing,
 they cover their heads.
⁴The ground is cracked
 because there is no rain in the land;
the farmers are dismayed
 and cover their heads.
⁵Even the doe in the field
 deserts her newborn fawn
 because there is no grass.
⁶Wild donkeys stand on the barren heights
 and pant like jackals;
their eyes fail
 for lack of food."

1102

⁷Although our sins testify against us,
 do something, Lord, for the sake of your name.
For our backsliding is great;
 we have sinned against you.
⁸You who are the hope of Israel,
 its Savior in times of distress,
why are you like a stranger in the land,
 like a traveler who stays only a night?
⁹Why are you like someone taken by surprise,
 like a warrior powerless to save?
You are among us, Lord,
 and we bear your name;
 do not forsake us!

HE IS: the only hope

14:7–9 Judah's drought was a sign of God's displeasure with his people's sinfulness. So Jeremiah talked with God, acknowledging the people's backsliding and sin. God was Judah's *only hope*, but the people failed to repent.

Are you experiencing a spiritual drought? Has drinking at the wells of pleasure left you thirsting for true fulfillment? If your backsliding is great, know that he is *the only hope*. Return to God and talk with him. Confess your tendency to wander. He will quench your thirst, save you in times of distress and be your true and lasting hope (see Romans 15:13).

For the next He Is, go to p. 1106.

¹⁰This is what the Lord says about this people:

"They greatly love to wander;
 they do not restrain their feet.
So the Lord does not accept them;

he will now remember their wickedness
and punish them for their sins."

[11]Then the LORD said to me, "Do not pray for the well-being of this people. [12]Although they fast, I will not listen to their cry; though they offer burnt offerings and grain offerings, I will not accept them. Instead, I will destroy them with the sword, famine and plague."

[13]But I said, "Ah, Sovereign LORD, the prophets keep telling them, 'You will not see the sword or suffer famine. Indeed, I will give you lasting peace in this place.'"

[14]Then the LORD said to me, "The prophets are prophesying lies in my name. I have not sent them or appointed them or spoken to them. They are prophesying to you false visions, divinations, idolatries[a] and the delusions of their own minds. [15]Therefore, this is what the LORD says about the prophets who are prophesying in my name: I did not send them, yet they are saying, 'No sword or famine will touch this land.' Those same prophets will perish by sword and famine. [16]And the people they are prophesying to will be thrown out into the streets of Jerusalem because of the famine and sword. There will be no one to bury them, their wives, their sons and their daughters. I will pour out on them the calamity they deserve.

[17]"Speak this word to them:

> "'Let my eyes overflow with tears
>   night and day without ceasing;
> for the Virgin Daughter, my people,
>   has suffered a grievous wound,
>   a crushing blow.
> [18]If I go into the country,
>   I see those slain by the sword;
> if I go into the city,
>   I see the ravages of famine.
> Both prophet and priest
>   have gone to a land they know not.'"

> [19]Have you rejected Judah completely?
>   Do you despise Zion?
> Why have you afflicted us
>   so that we cannot be healed?
> We hoped for peace
>   but no good has come,
> for a time of healing
>   but there is only terror.
> [20]We acknowledge our wickedness, LORD,
>   and the guilt of our ancestors;
>   we have indeed sinned against you.
> [21]For the sake of your name do not despise us;
>   do not dishonor your glorious throne.
> Remember your covenant with us
>   and do not break it.
> [22]Do any of the worthless idols of the nations bring rain?
>   Do the skies themselves send down showers?
> No, it is you, LORD our God.
>   Therefore our hope is in you,
>   for you are the one who does all this.

----

15 Then the LORD said to me: "Even if Moses and Samuel were to stand before me, my heart would not go out to this people. Send them away from my presence! Let them go! ² And if they ask you, 'Where shall we go?' tell them, 'This is what the LORD says:

> "'Those destined for death, to death;
>   those for the sword, to the sword;
>   those for starvation, to starvation;
>   those for captivity, to captivity.'

³ "I will send four kinds of destroyers against them," declares the LORD, "the sword to kill and the dogs to drag away and the birds and the wild animals to devour and destroy. ⁴ I will make them abhorrent to all the kingdoms of the earth because of what Manasseh son of Hezekiah king of Judah did in Jerusalem.

> ⁵ "Who will have pity on you, Jerusalem?
>   Who will mourn for you?
>   Who will stop to ask how you are?
> ⁶ You have rejected me," declares the LORD.
>   "You keep on backsliding.
> So I will lay hands on you and destroy you;
>   I am tired of holding back.
> ⁷ I will winnow them with a winnowing fork
>   at the city gates of the land.
> I will bring bereavement and destruction on my people,
>   for they have not changed their ways.
> ⁸ I will make their widows more numerous
>   than the sand of the sea.
> At midday I will bring a destroyer
>   against the mothers of their young men;
> suddenly I will bring down on them
>   anguish and terror.
> ⁹ The mother of seven will grow faint
>   and breathe her last.
> Her sun will set while it is still day;
>   she will be disgraced and humiliated.
> I will put the survivors to the sword
>   before their enemies,"

declares the LORD.

> ¹⁰ Alas, my mother, that you gave me birth,
>   a man with whom the whole land strives and contends!
> I have neither lent nor borrowed,
>   yet everyone curses me.

¹¹ The LORD said,

> "Surely I will deliver you for a good purpose;
>   surely I will make your enemies plead with you
>   in times of disaster and times of distress.

> ¹² "Can anyone break iron—
>   iron from the north—or bronze?

> ¹³ "Your wealth and your treasures
>   I will give as plunder, without charge,
>   because of all your sins

1104

throughout your country.
¹⁴I will enslave you to your enemies
    in*ᵃ* a land you do not know,
for my anger will kindle a fire
    that will burn against you."

¹⁵Lᴏʀᴅ, you understand;
    remember me and care for me.
    Avenge me on my persecutors.
You are long-suffering—do not take me away;
    think of how I suffer reproach for your sake.
¹⁶When your words came, I ate them;
    they were my joy and my heart's delight,
for I bear your name,
    Lᴏʀᴅ God Almighty.
¹⁷I never sat in the company of revelers,
    never made merry with them;
I sat alone because your hand was on me
    and you had filled me with indignation.
¹⁸Why is my pain unending
    and my wound grievous and incurable?
You are to me like a deceptive brook,
    like a spring that fails.

¹⁹Therefore this is what the Lᴏʀᴅ says:

"If you repent, I will restore you
    that you may serve me;
if you utter worthy, not worthless, words,
    you will be my spokesman.
Let this people turn to you,
    but you must not turn to them.
²⁰I will make you a wall to this people,
    a fortified wall of bronze;
they will fight against you
    but will not overcome you,
for I am with you
    to rescue and save you,"

declares the Lᴏʀᴅ.

²¹"I will save you from the hands of the wicked
    and deliver you from the grasp of the cruel."

Day of Disaster

16 Then the word of the Lᴏʀᴅ came to me: ²"You must not marry and have sons or daughters in this place." ³For this is what the Lᴏʀᴅ says about the sons and daughters born in this land and about the women who are their mothers and the men who are their fathers: ⁴"They will die of deadly diseases. They will not be mourned or buried but will be like dung lying on the ground. They will perish by sword and famine, and their dead bodies will become food for the birds and the wild animals."

⁵For this is what the Lᴏʀᴅ says: "Do not enter a house where there is a funeral meal; do not go to mourn or show sympathy, because I have withdrawn my blessing, my love and my pity from this people," declares the Lᴏʀᴅ. ⁶"Both high and low will die in this land. They will not be buried or mourned, nor will people cut themselves or shave their heads for them. ⁷No one will offer food to comfort those who

---

ᵃ 14 Some Hebrew manuscripts, Septuagint and Syriac (see also Jer. 17:4); most Hebrew manuscripts I will cause your enemies to bring you / into mourn for the dead—not even for a father or a mother—nor will anyone give them a drink to console them.

⁸"And do not enter a house where there is feasting and sit down to eat and drink. ⁹For this is what the LORD Almighty, the God of Israel, says: Before your eyes and in your days I will bring an end to the sounds of joy and gladness and to the voices of bride and bridegroom in this place.

¹⁰"When you tell these people all this and they ask you, 'Why has the LORD decreed such a great disaster against us? What wrong have we done? What sin have we committed against the LORD our God?' ¹¹then say to them, 'It is because your ancestors forsook me,' declares the LORD, 'and followed other gods and served and worshiped them. They forsook me and did not keep my law. ¹²But you have behaved more wickedly than your ancestors. See how all of you are following the stubbornness of your evil hearts instead of obeying me. ¹³So I will throw you out of this land into a land neither you nor your ancestors have known, and there you will serve other gods day and night, for I will show you no favor.'

¹⁴"However, the days are coming," declares the LORD, "when people will no longer say, 'As surely as the LORD lives, who brought the Israelites up out of Egypt,' ¹⁵but they will say, 'As surely as the LORD lives, who brought the Israelites up out of the land of the north and out of all the countries where he had banished them.' For I will restore them to the land I gave their ancestors.

¹⁶"But now I will send for many fishermen," declares the LORD, "and they will catch them. After that I will send for many hunters, and they will hunt them down on every mountain and hill and from the crevices of the rocks. ¹⁷My eyes are on all their ways; they are not hidden from me, nor is their sin concealed from my eyes. ¹⁸I will repay them double for their wickedness and their sin, because they have defiled my land with the lifeless forms of their vile images and have filled my inheritance with their detestable idols."

¹⁹LORD, my strength and my fortress,
　　my refuge in time of distress,
　to you the nations will come
　　from the ends of the earth and say,
"Our ancestors possessed nothing but false gods,
　　worthless idols that did them no good.
²⁰Do people make their own gods?
　　Yes, but they are not gods!"

HE IS: my refuge

16:16–20 Like fish caught by fishermen and animals tracked down by hunters, so the people of Judah would be taken captive by the Babylonians. Yet despite his personal distress and his nation's impending doom, Jeremiah could say with confidence that God was his *refuge*.

Perhaps you feel like a fish caught in a net of circumstances beyond your control. Maybe you are being preyed upon by people who don't have your best interests at heart. Know that, like Jeremiah, you can turn to the Lord, *your refuge* in times of distress, your strength and your safe fortress.

For the next He Is, go to p. 1111.

²¹"Therefore I will teach them—
　　this time I will teach them
　　my power and might.
　Then they will know
　　that my name is the LORD.

17

"Judah's sin is engraved with an iron tool,
  inscribed with a flint point,
on the tablets of their hearts
  and on the horns of their altars.
[2]Even their children remember
  their altars and Asherah poles[a]
beside the spreading trees
  and on the high hills.
[3]My mountain in the land
  and your[b] wealth and all your treasures
I will give away as plunder,
  together with your high places,
  because of sin throughout your country.
[4]Through your own fault you will lose
  the inheritance I gave you.
I will enslave you to your enemies
  in a land you do not know,
for you have kindled my anger,
  and it will burn forever."

[5]This is what the LORD says:

"Cursed are those who trust in mortals,
  who depend on flesh for their strength
  and whose hearts turn away from the
    LORD.
[6]They will be like a bush in the wastelands;
  they will not see prosperity when it
    comes.
They will dwell in the parched places of the
    desert,
  in a salt land where no one lives.

[7]"But blessed are those who trust in the
    LORD,
  whose confidence is in him.
[8]They will be like a tree planted by the water
  that sends out its roots by the stream.
It does not fear when heat comes;
  its leaves are always green.
It has no worries in a year of drought
  and never fails to bear fruit."

[9]The heart is deceitful above all things
  and beyond cure.
  Who can understand it?

[10]"I the LORD search the heart
  and examine the mind,
to reward everyone according to their
    conduct,
  according to what their deeds deserve."

1107

atissue:emotions

17:9 *Follow your heart.* You've probably heard this advice a thousand times— from books, movies, mentors, friends or family. However, this counsel has one major flaw that you can't afford to ignore: Your heart is deceitful and cannot be trusted. Following your heart can lead you to dangerous places, such as an unhealthy dating relationship or an affair. Your heart can cause you to justify credit card debt, abuse, divorce, anger, bitterness, gossip, slander . . . The list is endless. Don't let your emotions cloud your reason. Instead, follow God's truth, a sure and unchanging guide.

---

[a] *2* That is, wooden symbols of the goddess Asherah   [b] *2,3* Or *hills* / [3]*and the mountains of the land. / Your*

myth# 64 "I DESERVE THIS. IT'S MY RIGHT TO BE HAPPY."

"I'm sorry. I thought I was your wife, not your maid," I felt like saying. I came in from work this evening to see my husband sitting on the couch, feet propped up on my coffee table, asking me when dinner would be ready. Meanwhile, I had just picked up his offspring from school, shuttled them to their after-school activities and dropped off his dry-cleaning. Next I ran to the grocery store and then made an appointment with the plumber to repair the sink my husband "fixed" last week. And he wonders why dinner isn't on the table on time. I wish he would occasionally acknowledge all the hard work I do to keep our house running smoothly.

Needless to say, I feel unappreciated—by my husband. The story is completely opposite at work.

I have the best boss in the world. He sees all of the work I do and compliments me every day. He not only thinks I'm smart and capable; he also thinks that I'm beautiful. At first, it alarmed me when he tossed out a compliment about a certain outfit I was wearing. But I secretly craved his attention. The more he flatters me, the more I want to linger in our conversations or find excuses to meet with him.

I never thought I would be the kind of person who would want to have an affair, but the thought keeps entering my mind. Honestly, I feel like I deserve the attention. I know I have to be careful, but these harmless compliments keep me going from one exhausting day to the next. He constantly says things that make me feel valued and appreciated. He pays attention to how I look and what I think. He couldn't be any more opposite than my husband.

—Denise

ANYTIME WE USE language that asserts our rights or emphasizes the strength of our emotions over God's unchanging standard of truth, we are living dangerously. Anything can be justifiable, it seems, if we feel it strongly enough. Take an affair, for example. No woman expects that it will happen to her, but many fall prey. While outside circumstances like stress or an unappreciative spouse may fuel a misstep, the match that lights the flame is our self-talk. "I deserve to be happy." "I need this." "I have a right to it."

Strange how we never need to justify doing the right thing, not in our minds or to anyone else. Righteousness stands on its own, unaided, while sin usually involves complicated attempts to justify something that deep down we know is wrong. Apply the theory to almost any situation, and you'll see what Jeremiah described as the deceitfulness of one's own heart (see 17:9). Women who are addicted to gambling tell themselves that one big win will justify all the cash advances on their credit cards and the grocery money they've gambled away. Women who embezzle money from their companies justify themselves by saying, "I'm supporting my family" or "The company owes me." Yet the more we talk ourselves into sin, the further away from God's truth we slide. In the end, we may believe our own lies.

Proverbs 6:32 says that those who commit adultery destroy themselves. That's true of sin in general. Often, the things that we tell ourselves will fulfill us instead will destroy us and bury us in regret.

"The fastest growing rate of infidelity is among young married women. Many of them have been molested or are the adult children of divorce. They are looking for marriage to make up a deficit that comes from their childhood. 'Intimacy deficits' stem from your family of origin. They may be from a lack of touching or hugging, from a need for a lot of admiration, affirmation, and adoration, or from another vacuum that a spouse wants satisfied. Everybody has deficits."

—Cindy Crosby

1109

"THERE IS A WAY THAT APPEARS TO BE RIGHT, BUT IN THE END IT LEADS TO DEATH."

PROVERBS 16:25

SEE ALSO

Proverbs 2:12–19
Proverbs 6:27–29,32
2 Peter 2:18–19

For more on **Purity**, check the index.

[1110]

¹¹Like a partridge that hatches eggs it did not lay
    are those who gain riches by unjust means.
When their lives are half gone, their riches will desert them,
    and in the end they will prove to be fools.

¹²A glorious throne, exalted from the beginning,
    is the place of our sanctuary.
¹³LORD, you are the hope of Israel;
    all who forsake you will be put to shame.
Those who turn away from you will be written in the dust
    because they have forsaken the LORD,
    the spring of living water.

¹⁴Heal me, LORD, and I will be healed;
    save me and I will be saved,
    for you are the one I praise.
¹⁵They keep saying to me,
    "Where is the word of the LORD?
    Let it now be fulfilled!"
¹⁶I have not run away from being your shepherd;
    you know I have not desired the day of despair.
What passes my lips is open before you.
¹⁷Do not be a terror to me;
    you are my refuge in the day of disaster.
¹⁸Let my persecutors be put to shame,
    but keep me from shame;
let them be terrified,
    but keep me from terror.
Bring on them the day of disaster;
    destroy them with double destruction.

Keeping the Sabbath Holy

¹⁹This is what the LORD said to me: "Go and stand at the gate of the people, through which the kings of Judah go in and out; stand also at all the other gates of Jerusalem. ²⁰Say to them, 'Hear the word of the LORD, you kings of Judah and all people of Judah and everyone living in Jerusalem who come through these gates. ²¹This is what the LORD says: Be careful not to carry a load on the Sabbath day or bring it through the gates of Jerusalem. ²²Do not bring a load out of your houses or do any work on the Sabbath, but keep the Sabbath day holy, as I commanded your ancestors. ²³Yet they did not listen or pay attention; they were stiff-necked and would not listen or respond to discipline. ²⁴But if you are careful to obey me, declares the LORD, and bring no load through the gates of this city on the Sabbath, but keep the Sabbath day holy by not doing any work on it, ²⁵then kings who sit on David's throne will come through the gates of this city with their officials. They and their officials will come riding in chariots and on horses, accompanied by the men of Judah and those living in Jerusalem, and this city will be inhabited forever. ²⁶People will come from the towns of Judah and the villages around Jerusalem, from the territory of Benjamin and the western foothills, from the hill country and the Negev, bringing burnt offerings and sacrifices, grain offerings and incense, and bringing thank offerings to the house of the LORD. ²⁷But if you

conversations

rest «» 17:19–27

1 » Why do you think God placed such great importance on a Sabbath day of rest?

2 » How does our culture promote workaholism rather than rest?

3 » What can you do to avoid working to the point of exhaustion?

For more on rest, check the index.
For the next Conversations, go to p. 1114.

do not obey me to keep the Sabbath day holy by not carrying any load as you come through the gates of Jerusalem on the Sabbath day, then I will kindle an unquenchable fire in the gates of Jerusalem that will consume her fortresses.'"

At the Potter's House

18 This is the word that came to Jeremiah from the LORD: [2]"Go down to the potter's house, and there I will give you my message." [3]So I went down to the potter's house, and I saw him working at the wheel. [4]But the pot he was shaping from the clay was marred in his hands; so the potter formed it into another pot, shaping it as seemed best to him.

[5]Then the word of the LORD came to me. [6]He said, "Can I not do with you, house of Israel, as this potter does?" declares the LORD. "Like clay in the hand of the potter, so are you in my hand, house of Israel. [7]If at any time I announce that a nation or kingdom is to be uprooted, torn down and destroyed, [8]and if that nation I warned repents of its evil, then I will relent and not inflict on it the disaster I had planned. [9]And if at another time I announce that a nation or kingdom is to be built up and planted, [10]and if it does evil in my sight and does not obey me, then I will reconsider the good I had intended to do for it.

[11]"Now therefore say to the people of Judah and those living in Jerusalem, 'This is what the LORD says: Look! I am preparing a disaster for you and devising a plan against you. So turn from your evil ways, each one of you, and reform your ways and your actions.' [12]But they will reply, 'It's no use. We will continue with our own plans; we will all follow the stubbornness of our evil hearts.'"

HE IS: a reformer

18:1–11 Jeremiah saw that the potter could form marred clay into a whole new pot, shaping it as seemed best to him. This illustration showed Jeremiah that God can reform sinful people who turn from their evil ways. Sadly, however, the people resisted both the message and the messenger.

Are you a marred pot? (The only honest answer is yes.) Take heart! The potter can take the flawed clay of your life and create something brand new. But he shapes it as seems best to him, so you must be willing, moldable, teachable and responsive so the *reformer* can re-form your life (see 2 Timothy 2:20–21).

For the next He Is, go to p. 1118.

[13]Therefore this is what the LORD says:

> "Inquire among the nations:
>   Who has ever heard anything like this?
> A most horrible thing has been done
>   by Virgin Israel.
> [14]Does the snow of Lebanon
>   ever vanish from its rocky slopes?
> Do its cool waters from distant sources
>   ever cease to flow?[a]
> [15]Yet my people have forgotten me;
>   they burn incense to worthless idols,
> which made them stumble in their ways,
>   in the ancient paths.
> They made them walk in byways,
>   on roads not built up.

---

[a] *14* The meaning of the Hebrew for this sentence is uncertain.

¹⁶Their land will be an object of horror
　　and of lasting scorn;
　all who pass by will be appalled
　　and will shake their heads.
¹⁷Like a wind from the east,
　　I will scatter them before their enemies;
　I will show them my back and not my face
　　in the day of their disaster."

¹⁸They said, "Come, let's make plans against Jeremiah; for the teaching of the law by the priest will not cease, nor will counsel from the wise, nor the word from the prophets. So come, let's attack him with our tongues and pay no attention to anything he says."

¹⁹Listen to me, LORD;
　　hear what my accusers are saying!
²⁰Should good be repaid with evil?
　　Yet they have dug a pit for me.
　Remember that I stood before you
　　and spoke in their behalf
　　to turn your wrath away from them.
²¹So give their children over to famine;
　　hand them over to the power of the sword.
　Let their wives be made childless and widows;
　　let their men be put to death,
　　their young men slain by the sword in battle.
²²Let a cry be heard from their houses
　　when you suddenly bring invaders against them,
　for they have dug a pit to capture me
　　and have hidden snares for my feet.
²³But you, LORD, know
　　all their plots to kill me.
　Do not forgive their crimes
　　or blot out their sins from your sight.
　Let them be overthrown before you;
　　deal with them in the time of your anger.

19 This is what the LORD says: "Go and buy a clay jar from a potter. Take along some of the elders of the people and of the priests ²and go out to the Valley of Ben Hinnom, near the entrance of the Potsherd Gate. There proclaim the words I tell you, ³and say, 'Hear the word of the LORD, you kings of Judah and people of Jerusalem. This is what the LORD Almighty, the God of Israel, says: Listen! I am going to bring a disaster on this place that will make the ears of everyone who hears of it tingle. ⁴For they have forsaken me and made this a place of foreign gods; they have burned incense in it to gods that neither they nor their ancestors nor the kings of Judah ever knew, and they have filled this place with the blood of the innocent. ⁵They have built the high places of Baal to burn their children in the fire as offerings to Baal—something I did not command or mention, nor did it enter my mind. ⁶So beware, the days are coming, declares the LORD, when people will no longer call this place Topheth or the Valley of Ben Hinnom, but the Valley of Slaughter.

⁷"'In this place I will ruinᵃ the plans of Judah and Jerusalem. I will make them fall by the sword before their enemies, at the hands of those who seek their lives, and I will give their carcasses as food to the birds and the wild animals. ⁸I will devastate this city and make it an object of horror and scorn; all who pass by will be appalled and will scoff because of all its wounds. ⁹I will make them eat the flesh of their

---

ᵃ 7 The Hebrew for *ruin* sounds like the Hebrew for *jar* (see verses 1 and 10).

sons and daughters, and they will eat one another's flesh because their enemies will press the siege so hard against them to destroy them.'

¹⁰"Then break the jar while those who go with you are watching, ¹¹and say to them, 'This is what the LORD Almighty says: I will smash this nation and this city just as this potter's jar is smashed and cannot be repaired. They will bury the dead in Topheth until there is no more room. ¹²This is what I will do to this place and to those who live here, declares the LORD. I will make this city like Topheth. ¹³The houses in Jerusalem and those of the kings of Judah will be defiled like this place, Topheth—all the houses where they burned incense on the roofs to all the starry hosts and poured out drink offerings to other gods.'"

¹⁴Jeremiah then returned from Topheth, where the LORD had sent him to prophesy, and stood in the court of the LORD's temple and said to all the people, ¹⁵"This is what the LORD Almighty, the God of Israel, says: 'Listen! I am going to bring on this city and all the villages around it every disaster I pronounced against them, because they were stiff-necked and would not listen to my words.'"

Jeremiah and Pashhur

20 When the priest Pashhur son of Immer, the official in charge of the temple of the LORD, heard Jeremiah prophesying these things, ²he had Jeremiah the prophet beaten and put in the stocks at the Upper Gate of Benjamin at the LORD's temple. ³The next day, when Pashhur released him from the stocks, Jeremiah said to him, "The LORD's name for you is not Pashhur, but Terror on Every Side. ⁴For this is what the LORD says: 'I will make you a terror to yourself and to all your friends; with your own eyes you will see them fall by the sword of their enemies. I will give all Judah into the hands of the king of Babylon, who will carry them away to Babylon or put them to the sword. ⁵I will deliver all the wealth of this city into the hands of their enemies—all its products, all its valuables and all the treasures of the kings of Judah. They will take it away as plunder and carry it off to Babylon. ⁶And you, Pashhur, and all who live in your house will go into exile to Babylon. There you will die and be buried, you and all your friends to whom you have prophesied lies.'"

Jeremiah's Complaint

⁷You deceived*ᵃ* me, LORD, and I was deceived*ᵇ*;
  you overpowered me and prevailed.
I am ridiculed all day long;
  everyone mocks me.
⁸Whenever I speak, I cry out
  proclaiming violence and destruction.
So the word of the LORD has brought me
  insult and reproach all day long.
⁹But if I say, "I will not mention his word
  or speak anymore in his name,"
his word is in my heart like a fire,
  a fire shut up in my bones.
I am weary of holding it in;
  indeed, I cannot.
¹⁰I hear many whispering,

atissue:pride

19:15 Although the people of Judah tried to shift the blame, the disaster they experienced was a direct result of their own pride and refusal to listen to God. Though we hate to admit it, we also try to do things our own way instead of God's way. This stubborn pride shows up in our dating relationships, in our marriages, in how we raise our kids, in how we use our time, in setting our priorities, in the things we pursue and in what we value in life. If left unchecked, pride leads us to disaster. Is doing it your own way really worth it?

1113

"Terror on every side!
Denounce him! Let's
denounce him!"
All my friends
are waiting for me to slip,
saying,
"Perhaps he will be deceived;
then we will prevail over
him
and take our revenge on
him."

¹¹But the LORD is with me like a
mighty warrior;
so my persecutors will
stumble and not
prevail.
They will fail and be thoroughly disgraced;
their dishonor will never be forgotten.
¹²LORD Almighty, you who examine the righteous
and probe the heart and mind,
let me see your vengeance on them,
for to you I have committed my cause.

¹³Sing to the LORD!
Give praise to the LORD!
He rescues the life of the needy
from the hands of the wicked.

¹⁴Cursed be the day I was born!
May the day my mother bore me not be blessed!
¹⁵Cursed be the man who brought my father the news,
who made him very glad, saying,
"A child is born to you—a son!"
¹⁶May that man be like the towns
the LORD overthrew without pity.
May he hear wailing in the morning,
a battle cry at noon.
¹⁷For he did not kill me in the womb,
with my mother as my grave,
her womb enlarged forever.
¹⁸Why did I ever come out of the womb
to see trouble and sorrow
and to end my days in shame?

conversations

complaining «» 20:7–12

1» Is it OK to complain about your difficulties to God? Why or why not?

2» What's the difference between sharing your struggles and complaining about them?

3» When problems arise, what can you do to keep your eyes on God and not on your problems?

For more on **complaining**, check the index.
For the next Conversations, go to p. 1115.

God Rejects Zedekiah's Request

21 The word came to Jeremiah from the LORD when King Zedekiah sent to him Pashhur son of Malkijah and the priest Zephaniah son of Maaseiah. They said: ²"Inquire now of the LORD for us because Nebuchadnezzar^a king of Babylon is attacking us. Perhaps the LORD will perform wonders for us as in times past so that he will withdraw from us."

³But Jeremiah answered them, "Tell Zedekiah, ⁴'This is what the LORD, the God of Israel, says: I am about to turn against you the weapons of war that are in your hands, which you are using to fight the

^a 2 Hebrew Nebuchadrezzar, of which Nebuchadnezzar is a variant; here and often in Jeremiah and Ezekiel

king of Babylon and the Babylonians*a* who are outside the wall besieging you. And I will gather them inside this city. [5] I myself will fight against you with an outstretched hand and a mighty arm in furious anger and in great wrath. [6] I will strike down those who live in this city—both people and animals—and they will die of a terrible plague. [7] After that, declares the LORD, I will give Zedekiah king of Judah, his officials and the people in this city who survive the plague, sword and famine, into the hands of Nebuchadnezzar king of Babylon and to their enemies who seek their lives. He will put them to the sword; he will show them no mercy or pity or compassion.'

[8] "Furthermore, tell the people, 'This is what the LORD says: See, I am setting before you the way of life and the way of death. [9] Whoever stays in this city will die by the sword, famine or plague. But whoever goes out and surrenders to the Babylonians who are besieging you will live; they will escape with their lives. [10] I have determined to do this city harm and not good, declares the LORD. It will be given into the hands of the king of Babylon, and he will destroy it with fire.'

[11] "Moreover, say to the royal house of Judah, 'Hear the word of the LORD. [12] This is what the LORD says to you, house of David:

> "'Administer justice every morning;
>   rescue from the hands of their oppressors
>   those who have been robbed,
> or my wrath will break out and burn like fire
>   because of the evil you have done—
>   burn with no one to quench it.
> [13] I am against you, Jerusalem,
>   you who live above this valley
>   on the rocky plateau, declares the LORD—
> you who say, "Who can come against us?
>   Who can enter our refuge?"
> [14] I will punish you as your deeds deserve,
>   declares the LORD.
> I will kindle a fire in your forests
>   that will consume everything around you."'

Judgment Against Wicked Kings

22 This is what the LORD says: "Go down to the palace of the king of Judah and proclaim this message there: [2] 'Hear the word of the LORD to you, king of Judah, you who sit on David's throne—you, your officials and your people who come through these gates. [3] This is what the LORD says: Do what is just and right. Rescue from the hands of their oppressors those who have been robbed. Do no wrong or violence to the foreigner, the fatherless or the widow, and do not shed innocent blood in this place. [4] For if you are careful to carry out these commands, then kings who sit on David's throne will come through the gates of this palace, riding in chariots and on horses, accompanied by their officials and their people. [5] But if you do not obey these commands, declares the LORD, I swear by myself that this palace will become a ruin.'"

[6] For this is what the LORD says about the palace of the king of Judah:

> "Though you are like Gilead to me,
>   like the summit of Lebanon,
> I will surely make you like a wasteland,

conversations

compassion «» 22:1–5,15–16

1» In what specific ways have you practiced compassion recently?

2» Who in your life could most benefit from your compassion?

3» What are the consequences of remaining idle or calloused toward those in need?

For more on **compassion**, check the index.
For the next Conversations, go to p. 1131.

a 4 Or *Chaldeans*; also in verse 9

like towns not inhabited.
⁷I will send destroyers against you,
    each man with his weapons,
and they will cut up your fine cedar beams
    and throw them into the fire.

⁸"People from many nations will pass by this city and will ask one another, 'Why has the LORD done such a thing to this great city?' ⁹And the answer will be: 'Because they have forsaken the covenant of the LORD their God and have worshiped and served other gods.'"

¹⁰Do not weep for the dead king, or mourn his loss;
    rather, weep bitterly for him who is exiled,
because he will never return
    nor see his native land again.

¹¹For this is what the LORD says about Shallum^a son of Josiah, who succeeded his father as king of Judah but has gone from this place: "He will never return. ¹²He will die in the place where they have led him captive; he will not see this land again."

¹³"Woe to him who builds his palace by unrighteousness,
    his upper rooms by injustice,
making his subjects work for nothing,
    not paying them for their labor.
¹⁴He says, 'I will build myself a great palace
    with spacious upper rooms.'
So he makes large windows in it,
    panels it with cedar
    and decorates it in red.

¹⁵"Does it make you a king
    to have more and more cedar?
Did not your father have food and drink?
    He did what was right and just,
    so all went well with him.
¹⁶He defended the cause of the poor and needy,
    and so all went well.
Is that not what it means to know me?"
    declares the LORD.
¹⁷"But your eyes and your heart
    are set only on dishonest gain,
on shedding innocent blood
    and on oppression and extortion."

¹⁸Therefore this is what the LORD says about Jehoiakim son of Josiah king of Judah:

"They will not mourn for him:
    'Alas, my brother! Alas, my sister!'
They will not mourn for him:
    'Alas, my master! Alas, his splendor!'
¹⁹He will have the burial of a donkey—
    dragged away and thrown
    outside the gates of Jerusalem."

20"Go up to Lebanon and cry out,
    let your voice be heard in Bashan,
cry out from Abarim,
    for all your allies are crushed.
21 I warned you when you felt secure,
    but you said, 'I will not listen!'
This has been your way from your youth;
    you have not obeyed me.
22 The wind will drive all your shepherds away,
    and your allies will go into exile.
Then you will be ashamed and disgraced
    because of all your wickedness.
23 You who live in 'Lebanon,'ᵃ'
    who are nestled in cedar buildings,
how you will groan when pangs come upon you,
    pain like that of a woman in labor!

24"As surely as I live," declares the Lord, "even if you, Jehoiachinᵇ son of Jehoiakim king of Judah, were a signet ring on my right hand, I would still pull you off. 25 I will deliver you into the hands of those who seek your life, those you fear—Nebuchadnezzar king of Babylon and the Babylonians.ᶜ 26 I will hurl you and the mother who gave you birth into another country, where neither of you was born, and there you both will die. 27 You will never come back to the land you long to return to."

28 Is this man Jehoiachin a despised, broken pot,
    an object no one wants?
Why will he and his children be hurled out,
    cast into a land they do not know?
29 O land, land, land,
    hear the word of the Lord!
30 This is what the Lord says:
    "Record this man as if childless,
    a man who will not prosper in his lifetime,
for none of his offspring will prosper,
    none will sit on the throne of David
    or rule anymore in Judah."

The Righteous Branch

23 "Woe to the shepherds who are destroying and scattering the sheep of my pasture!" declares the Lord. 2 Therefore this is what the Lord, the God of Israel, says to the shepherds who tend my people: "Because you have scattered my flock and driven them away and have not bestowed care on them, I will bestow punishment on you for the evil you have done," declares the Lord. 3 "I myself will gather the remnant of my flock out of all the countries where I have driven them and will bring them back to their pasture, where they will be fruitful and increase in number. 4 I will place shepherds over them who will tend them, and they will no longer be afraid or terrified, nor will any be missing," declares the Lord.

5"The days are coming," declares the Lord,
    "when I will raise up for Davidᵈ a righteous Branch,
a King who will reign wisely
    and do what is just and right in the land.
6 In his days Judah will be saved

ᵃ 23 That is, the palace in Jerusalem (see 1 Kings 7:2)   ᵇ 24 Hebrew Koniah, a variant of Jehoiachin; also in verse 28   ᶜ 25 Or Chaldeans   ᵈ 5 Or up from David's line

and Israel will live in safety.
This is the name by which he will be called:
The LORD Our Righteous Savior.

HE IS: the Lord Our Righteous Savior

23:1–6 Jeremiah denounced Judah's faithless kings as destructive shepherds who scattered the sheep of God's pasture. He saw a future day when a King would reign wisely and do what is just and right. Jeremiah spoke of the Messiah, *the Lord Our Righteous Savior*.

Earthly rulers come and go, but one day Jesus Christ will come to reign forever, dispensing righteousness to everyone. If you've been the victim of injustice, look toward the day when *the Lord Our Righteous Savior* will govern justly. The Shepherd King will do all the right things for all the right reasons.

For the next He Is, go to p. 1128.

1118

⁷"So then, the days are coming," declares the LORD, "when people will no longer say, 'As surely as the LORD lives, who brought the Israelites up out of Egypt,' ⁸but they will say, 'As surely as the LORD lives, who brought the descendants of Israel up out of the land of the north and out of all the countries where he had banished them.' Then they will live in their own land."

Lying Prophets

⁹Concerning the prophets:

My heart is broken within me;
all my bones tremble.
I am like a drunken man,
like one overcome by wine,
because of the LORD
and his holy words.
¹⁰The land is full of adulterers;
because of the curse*ᵃ* the land lies parched
and the pastures in the wilderness are withered.
The ⌞prophets⌟ follow an evil course
and use their power unjustly.

¹¹"Both prophet and priest are godless;
even in my temple I find their wickedness,"
declares the LORD.
¹²"Therefore their path will become slippery;
they will be banished to darkness
and there they will fall.
I will bring disaster on them
in the year they are punished,"
declares the LORD.

¹³"Among the prophets of Samaria
I saw this repulsive thing:
They prophesied by Baal
and led my people Israel astray.

ᵃ 10 Or because of these things

¹⁴And among the prophets of Jerusalem
 I have seen something horrible:
 They commit adultery and live a lie.
 They strengthen the hands of evildoers,
  so that none of them turn from their wickedness.
 They are all like Sodom to me;
  the people of Jerusalem are like Gomorrah."

¹⁵Therefore, this is what the LORD Almighty says concerning the prophets:

 "I will make them eat bitter food
  and drink poisoned water,
 because from the prophets of Jerusalem
  ungodliness has spread throughout the land."

¹⁶This is what the LORD Almighty says:

 "Do not listen to what the prophets are
   prophesying to you;
  they fill you with false hopes.
 They speak visions from their own minds,
  not from the mouth of the LORD.
 ¹⁷They keep saying to those who despise
   me,
  'The LORD says: You will have peace.'
 And to all who follow the stubbornness of
   their hearts
  they say, 'No harm will come to you.'
 ¹⁸But which of them has stood in the council
   of the LORD
  to see or to hear his word?
  Who has listened and heard his word?
 ¹⁹See, the storm of the LORD
  will burst out in wrath,
 a whirlwind swirling down
  on the heads of the wicked.
 ²⁰The anger of the LORD will not turn back
  until he fully accomplishes
  the purposes of his heart.
 In days to come
  you will understand it clearly.
 ²¹I did not send these prophets,
  yet they have run with their message;
 I did not speak to them,
  yet they have prophesied.
 ²²But if they had stood in my council,
  they would have proclaimed my words to my people
 and would have turned them from their evil ways
  and from their evil deeds.

 ²³"Am I only a God nearby,"

declares the LORD,

 "and not a God far away?
 ²⁴Who can hide in secret places

1119

---

atissue:friendship

23:16–18 Do you have a friend who tells you that it's OK to do something God says not to? Maybe she's the one encouraging you to wear tight, low-cut shirts and saying a wife's allowed to flirt a little. Or telling you there's nothing wrong with dating a non-Christian or leaving your husband if another man will make you happy. Or telling you it's OK to skim a little personal "bonus" from your company's profits. Listen closely: Ignore any friend whose message contradicts God's Word. God is always right—so she must be wrong.

so that I cannot see them?"

declares the LORD.

"Do not I fill heaven and earth?"

declares the LORD.

²⁵"I have heard what the prophets say who prophesy lies in my name. They say, 'I had a dream! I had a dream!' ²⁶How long will this continue in the hearts of these lying prophets, who prophesy the delusions of their own minds? ²⁷They think the dreams they tell one another will make my people forget my name, just as their ancestors forgot my name through Baal worship. ²⁸Let the prophets who have dreams tell their dreams, but let the one who has my word speak it faithfully. For what has straw to do with grain?" declares the LORD. ²⁹"Is not my word like fire," declares the LORD, "and like a hammer that breaks a rock in pieces?

³⁰"Therefore," declares the LORD, "I am against the prophets who steal from one another words supposedly from me. ³¹Yes," declares the LORD, "I am against the prophets who wag their own tongues and yet declare, 'The LORD declares.' ³²Indeed, I am against those who prophesy false dreams," declares the LORD. "They tell them and lead my people astray with their reckless lies, yet I did not send or appoint them. They do not benefit these people in the least," declares the LORD.

False Prophecy

³³"When these people, or a prophet or a priest, ask you, 'What is the message from the LORD?' say to them, 'What message? I will forsake you, declares the LORD.' ³⁴If a prophet or a priest or anyone else claims, 'This is a message from the LORD,' I will punish them and their households. ³⁵This is what each of you keeps saying to your friends and other Israelites: 'What is the LORD's answer?' or 'What has the LORD spoken?' ³⁶But you must not mention 'a message from the LORD' again, because everyone's own word becomes a message from God. So you distort the words of the living God, the LORD Almighty, our God. ³⁷This is what you keep saying to a prophet: 'What is the LORD's answer to you?' or 'What has the LORD spoken?' ³⁸Although you claim, 'This is a message from the LORD,' this is what the LORD says: You used the words, 'This is a message from the LORD,' even though I told you that you must not claim, 'This is a message from the LORD.' ³⁹Therefore, I will surely forget you and cast you out of my presence along with the city I gave to you and your ancestors. ⁴⁰I will bring on you everlasting disgrace—everlasting shame that will not be forgotten."

Two Baskets of Figs

24 After Jehoiachin^a son of Jehoiakim king of Judah and the officials, the artisans and the other skilled workers of Judah were carried into exile from Jerusalem to Babylon by Nebuchadnezzar king of Babylon, the LORD showed me two baskets of figs placed in front of the temple of the LORD. ²One basket had very good figs, like those that ripen early; the other basket had very bad figs, so bad they could not be eaten.

³Then the LORD asked me, "What do you see, Jeremiah?"

"Figs," I answered. "The good ones are very good, but the bad ones are so bad they cannot be eaten."

⁴Then the word of the LORD came to me: ⁵"This is what the LORD, the God of Israel, says: 'Like these good figs, I regard as good the exiles from Judah, whom I sent away from this place to the land of the Babylonians.^b ⁶My eyes will watch over them for their good, and I will bring them back to this land. I will build them up and not tear them down; I will plant them and not uproot them. ⁷I will give them a heart to know me, that I am the LORD. They will be my people, and I will be their God, for they will return to me with all their heart.

⁸"But like the bad figs, which are so bad they cannot be eaten,' says the LORD, 'so will I deal with Zedekiah king of Judah, his officials and the survivors from Jerusalem, whether they remain in this land or live in Egypt. ⁹I will make them abhorrent and an offense to all the kingdoms of the earth, a reproach and a byword, a curse^c and an object of ridicule, wherever I banish them. ¹⁰I will send the sword, famine and plague against them until they are destroyed from the land I gave to them and their ancestors.'"

---

^a *1* Hebrew *Jeconiah,* a variant of *Jehoiachin* ^b *5* Or *Chaldeans* ^c *9* That is, their names will be used in cursing (see Jer. 29:22); or, others will see that they are cursed.

Seventy Years of Captivity

25 The word came to Jeremiah concerning all the people of Judah in the fourth year of Jehoiakim son of Josiah king of Judah, which was the first year of Nebuchadnezzar king of Babylon. ²So Jeremiah the prophet said to all the people of Judah and to all those living in Jerusalem: ³For twenty-three years—from the thirteenth year of Josiah son of Amon king of Judah until this very day—the word of the LORD has come to me and I have spoken to you again and again, but you have not listened.

⁴And though the LORD has sent all his servants the prophets to you again and again, you have not listened or paid any attention. ⁵They said, "Turn now, each of you, from your evil ways and your evil practices, and you can stay in the land the LORD gave to you and your ancestors for ever and ever. ⁶Do not follow other gods to serve and worship them; do not arouse my anger with what your hands have made. Then I will not harm you."

⁷"But you did not listen to me," declares the LORD, "and you have aroused my anger with what your hands have made, and you have brought harm to yourselves."

⁸Therefore the LORD Almighty says this: "Because you have not listened to my words, ⁹I will summon all the peoples of the north and my servant Nebuchadnezzar king of Babylon," declares the LORD, "and I will bring them against this land and its inhabitants and against all the surrounding nations. I will completely destroy*ᵃ* them and make them an object of horror and scorn, and an everlasting ruin. ¹⁰I will banish from them the sounds of joy and gladness, the voices of bride and bridegroom, the sound of millstones and the light of the lamp. ¹¹This whole country will become a desolate wasteland, and these nations will serve the king of Babylon seventy years.

1121

¹²"But when the seventy years are fulfilled, I will punish the king of Babylon and his nation, the land of the Babylonians,*ᵇ* for their guilt," declares the LORD, "and will make it desolate forever. ¹³I will bring on that land all the things I have spoken against it, all that are written in this book and prophesied by Jeremiah against all the nations. ¹⁴They themselves will be enslaved by many nations and great kings; I will repay them according to their deeds and the work of their hands."

The Cup of God's Wrath

¹⁵This is what the LORD, the God of Israel, said to me: "Take from my hand this cup filled with the wine of my wrath and make all the nations to whom I send you drink it. ¹⁶When they drink it, they will stagger and go mad because of the sword I will send among them."

¹⁷So I took the cup from the LORD's hand and made all the nations to whom he sent me drink it: ¹⁸Jerusalem and the towns of Judah, its kings and officials, to make them a ruin and an object of horror and scorn, a curse*ᶜ*—as they are today; ¹⁹Pharaoh king of Egypt, his attendants, his officials and all his people, ²⁰and all the foreign people there; all the kings of Uz; all the kings of the Philistines (those of Ashkelon, Gaza, Ekron, and the people left at Ashdod); ²¹Edom, Moab and Ammon; ²²all the kings of Tyre and Sidon; the kings of the coastlands across the sea; ²³Dedan, Tema, Buz and all who are in distant places*ᵈ*; ²⁴all the kings of Arabia and all the kings of the foreign people who live in the wilderness; ²⁵all the kings of Zimri, Elam and Media; ²⁶and all the kings of the north, near and far, one after the other—all the kingdoms on the face of the earth. And after all of them, the king of Sheshak*ᵉ* will drink it too.

²⁷"Then tell them, 'This is what the LORD Almighty, the God of Israel, says: Drink, get drunk and vomit, and fall to rise no more because of the sword I will send among you.' ²⁸But if they refuse to take the cup from your hand and drink, tell them, 'This is what the LORD Almighty says: You must drink it! ²⁹See, I am beginning to bring disaster on the city that bears my Name, and will you indeed go unpunished? You will not go unpunished, for I am calling down a sword on all who live on the earth, declares the LORD Almighty.'

³⁰"Now prophesy all these words against them and say to them:

> "'The LORD will roar from on high;
> he will thunder from his holy dwelling
> and roar mightily against his land.

ᵃ 9 The Hebrew term refers to the irrevocable giving over of things or persons to the LORD, often by totally destroying them.   *ᵇ 12* Or *Chaldeans*   *ᶜ 18* That is, their names to be used in cursing (see Jer. 29:22); or, to be seen by others as cursed   *ᵈ 23* Or *who clip the hair by their foreheads*   *ᵉ 26* *Sheshak* is a cryptogram for Babylon.

He will shout like those who tread the grapes,
    shout against all who live on the earth.
³¹The tumult will resound to the ends of the earth,
    for the LORD will bring charges against the nations;
he will bring judgment on all humankind
    and put the wicked to the sword,'"

                                                    declares the LORD.

³²This is what the LORD Almighty says:

"Look! Disaster is spreading
    from nation to nation;
a mighty storm is rising
    from the ends of the earth."

³³At that time those slain by the LORD will be everywhere—from one end of the earth to the other. They will not be mourned or gathered up or buried, but will be like dung lying on the ground.

³⁴Weep and wail, you shepherds;
    roll in the dust, you leaders of the flock.
For your time to be slaughtered has come;
    you will fall like the best of the rams.^a
³⁵The shepherds will have nowhere to flee,
    the leaders of the flock no place to escape.
³⁶Hear the cry of the shepherds,
    the wailing of the leaders of the flock,
    for the LORD is destroying their pasture.
³⁷The peaceful meadows will be laid waste
    because of the fierce anger of the LORD.
³⁸Like a lion he will leave his lair,
    and their land will become desolate
because of the sword^b of the oppressor
    and because of the LORD's fierce anger.

Jeremiah Threatened With Death

26 Early in the reign of Jehoiakim son of Josiah king of Judah, this word came from the LORD: ²"This is what the LORD says: Stand in the courtyard of the LORD's house and speak to all the people of the towns of Judah who come to worship in the house of the LORD. Tell them everything I command you; do not omit a word. ³Perhaps they will listen and each will turn from their evil ways. Then I will relent and not inflict on them the disaster I was planning because of the evil they have done. ⁴Say to them, 'This is what the LORD says: If you do not listen to me and follow my law, which I have set before you, ⁵and if you do not listen to the words of my servants the prophets, whom I have sent to you again and again (though you have not listened), ⁶then I will make this house like Shiloh and this city a curse^c among all the nations of the earth.'"

⁷The priests, the prophets and all the people heard Jeremiah speak these words in the house of the LORD. ⁸But as soon as Jeremiah finished telling all the people everything the LORD had commanded him to say, the priests, the prophets and all the people seized him and said, "You must die! ⁹Why do you prophesy in the LORD's name that this house will be like Shiloh and this city will be desolate and deserted?" And all the people crowded around Jeremiah in the house of the LORD.

¹⁰When the officials of Judah heard about these things, they went up from the royal palace to the house of the LORD and took their places at the entrance of the New Gate of the LORD's house. ¹¹Then the priests and the prophets said to the officials and all the people, "This man should be sentenced to death

---

^a *34* Septuagint; Hebrew *fall and be shattered like fine pottery*   ^b *38* Some Hebrew manuscripts and Septuagint (see also Jer. 46:16 and 50:16); most Hebrew manuscripts *anger*   ^c *6* That is, their names will be used in cursing (see Jer. 29:22); or, others will see that they are cursed.

because he has prophesied against this city. You have heard it with your own ears!"

[12] Then Jeremiah said to all the officials and all the people: "The LORD sent me to prophesy against this house and this city all the things you have heard. [13] Now reform your ways and your actions and obey the LORD your God. Then the LORD will relent and not bring the disaster he has pronounced against you. [14] As for me, I am in your hands; do with me whatever you think is good and right. [15] Be assured, however, that if you put me to death, you will bring the guilt of innocent blood on yourselves and on this city and on those who live in it, for in truth the LORD has sent me to you to speak all these words in your hearing."

[16] Then the officials and all the people said to the priests and the prophets, "This man should not be sentenced to death! He has spoken to us in the name of the LORD our God."

[17] Some of the elders of the land stepped forward and said to the entire assembly of people, [18] "Micah of Moresheth prophesied in the days of Hezekiah king of Judah. He told all the people of Judah, 'This is what the LORD Almighty says:

> "'Zion will be plowed like a field,
>   Jerusalem will become a heap of rubble,
>   the temple hill a mound overgrown with
>   thickets.'[a]

[19] "Did Hezekiah king of Judah or anyone else in Judah put him to death? Did not Hezekiah fear the LORD and seek his favor? And did not the LORD relent, so that he did not bring the disaster he pronounced against them? We are about to bring a terrible disaster on ourselves!"

[20] (Now Uriah son of Shemaiah from Kiriath Jearim was another man who prophesied in the name of the LORD; he prophesied the same things against this city and this land as Jeremiah did. [21] When King Jehoiakim and all his officers and officials heard his words, the king sought to put him to death. But Uriah heard of it and fled in fear to Egypt. [22] King Jehoiakim, however, sent Elnathan son of Akbor to Egypt, along with some other men. [23] They brought Uriah out of Egypt and took him to King Jehoiakim, who had him struck down with a sword and his body thrown into the burial place of the common people.)

[24] Furthermore, Ahikam son of Shaphan supported Jeremiah, and so he was not handed over to the people to be put to death.

Judah to Serve Nebuchadnezzar

27 Early in the reign of Zedekiah[b] son of Josiah king of Judah, this word came to Jeremiah from the LORD: [2] This is what the LORD said to me: "Make a yoke out of straps and crossbars and put it on your neck. [3] Then send word to the kings of Edom, Moab, Ammon, Tyre and Sidon through the envoys who have come to Jerusalem to Zedekiah king of Judah. [4] Give them a message for their masters and say, 'This is what the LORD Almighty, the God of Israel, says: "Tell this to your masters: [5] With my great power and outstretched arm I made the earth and its people and the animals that are on it, and I give it to anyone I please. [6] Now I will give all your countries into the hands of my servant Nebuchadnezzar king of Babylon; I will make even the wild animals subject to him. [7] All nations will serve him and his son and his grandson until the time for his land comes; then many nations and great kings will subjugate him.

[8] "'"If, however, any nation or kingdom will not serve Nebuchadnezzar king of Babylon or bow its neck

---

a issue:sacrifice

26:7–9 Telling people the truth may come at a cost. Although you need to do your best not to be offensive in how you share the gospel with others, it's inevitable that the message itself will offend some people. Speaking for God is not likely to get you promoted at work, or make your neighbors like you more, or cause the other parents at school to look up to you. In fact, you may find yourself misunderstood, ostracized and maligned. Remember, though, that the price you pay now is tiny compared to the reward you'll receive later. Keep sharing the truth.

1123

---

under his yoke, I will punish that nation with the sword, famine and plague, declares the Lord, until I destroy it by his hand. [9]So do not listen to your prophets, your diviners, your interpreters of dreams, your mediums or your sorcerers who tell you, 'You will not serve the king of Babylon.' [10]They prophesy lies to you that will only serve to remove you far from your lands; I will banish you and you will perish. [11]But if any nation will bow its neck under the yoke of the king of Babylon and serve him, I will let that nation remain in its own land to till it and to live there, declares the Lord."'"

[12]I gave the same message to Zedekiah king of Judah. I said, "Bow your neck under the yoke of the king of Babylon; serve him and his people, and you will live. [13]Why will you and your people die by the sword, famine and plague with which the Lord has threatened any nation that will not serve the king of Babylon? [14]Do not listen to the words of the prophets who say to you, 'You will not serve the king of Babylon,' for they are prophesying lies to you. [15]'I have not sent them,' declares the Lord. 'They are prophesying lies in my name. Therefore, I will banish you and you will perish, both you and the prophets who prophesy to you.'"

[16]Then I said to the priests and all these people, "This is what the Lord says: Do not listen to the prophets who say, 'Very soon now the articles from the Lord's house will be brought back from Babylon.' They are prophesying lies to you. [17]Do not listen to them. Serve the king of Babylon, and you will live. Why should this city become a ruin? [18]If they are prophets and have the word of the Lord, let them plead with the Lord Almighty that the articles remaining in the house of the Lord and in the palace of the king of Judah and in Jerusalem not be taken to Babylon. [19]For this is what the Lord Almighty says about the pillars, the Sea, the movable stands and the other articles that are left in this city, [20]which Nebuchadnezzar king of Babylon did not take away when he carried Jehoiachin[a] son of Jehoiakim king of Judah into exile from Jerusalem to Babylon, along with all the nobles of Judah and Jerusalem— [21]yes, this is what the Lord Almighty, the God of Israel, says about the things that are left in the house of the Lord and in the palace of the king of Judah and in Jerusalem: [22]'They will be taken to Babylon and there they will remain until the day I come for them,' declares the Lord. 'Then I will bring them back and restore them to this place.'"

The False Prophet Hananiah

28 In the fifth month of that same year, the fourth year, early in the reign of Zedekiah king of Judah, the prophet Hananiah son of Azzur, who was from Gibeon, said to me in the house of the Lord in the presence of the priests and all the people: [2]"This is what the Lord Almighty, the God of Israel, says: 'I will break the yoke of the king of Babylon. [3]Within two years I will bring back to this place all the articles of the Lord's house that Nebuchadnezzar king of Babylon removed from here and took to Babylon. [4]I will also bring back to this place Jehoiachin[a] son of Jehoiakim king of Judah and all the other exiles from Judah who went to Babylon,' declares the Lord, 'for I will break the yoke of the king of Babylon.'"

[5]Then the prophet Jeremiah replied to the prophet Hananiah before the priests and all the people who were standing in the house of the Lord. [6]He said, "Amen! May the Lord do so! May the Lord fulfill the words you have prophesied by bringing the articles of the Lord's house and all the exiles back to this place from Babylon. [7]Nevertheless, listen to what I have to say in your hearing and in the hearing of all the people: [8]From early times the prophets who preceded you and me have prophesied war, disaster and plague against many countries and great kingdoms. [9]But the prophet who prophesies peace will be recognized as one truly sent by the Lord only if his prediction comes true."

[10]Then the prophet Hananiah took the yoke off the neck of the prophet Jeremiah and broke it, [11]and he said before all the people, "This is what the Lord says: 'In the same way I will break the yoke of Nebuchadnezzar king of Babylon off the neck of all the nations within two years.'" At this, the prophet Jeremiah went on his way.

[12]After the prophet Hananiah had broken the yoke off the neck of the prophet Jeremiah, the word of the Lord came to Jeremiah: [13]"Go and tell Hananiah, 'This is what the Lord says: You have broken a wooden yoke, but in its place you will get a yoke of iron. [14]This is what the Lord Almighty, the God of

---

[a] 20,4 Hebrew *Jeconiah*, a variant of *Jehoiachin*

Israel, says: I will put an iron yoke on the necks of all these nations to make them serve Nebuchadnezzar king of Babylon, and they will serve him. I will even give him control over the wild animals.'"

¹⁵Then the prophet Jeremiah said to Hananiah the prophet, "Listen, Hananiah! The LORD has not sent you, yet you have persuaded this nation to trust in lies. ¹⁶Therefore, this is what the LORD says: 'I am about to remove you from the face of the earth. This very year you are going to die, because you have preached rebellion against the LORD.'"

¹⁷In the seventh month of that same year, Hananiah the prophet died.

A Letter to the Exiles

29 This is the text of the letter that the prophet Jeremiah sent from Jerusalem to the surviving elders among the exiles and to the priests, the prophets and all the other people Nebuchadnezzar had carried into exile from Jerusalem to Babylon. ²(This was after King Jehoiachin[a] and the queen mother, the court officials and the leaders of Judah and Jerusalem, the artisans and the other skilled workers had gone into exile from Jerusalem.) ³He entrusted the letter to Elasah son of Shaphan and to Gemariah son of Hilkiah, whom Zedekiah king of Judah sent to King Nebuchadnezzar in Babylon. It said:

⁴This is what the LORD Almighty, the God of Israel, says to all those I carried into exile from Jerusalem to Babylon: ⁵"Build houses and settle down; plant gardens and eat what they produce. ⁶Marry and have sons and daughters; find wives for your sons and give your daughters in marriage, so that they too may have sons and daughters. Increase in number there; do not decrease. ⁷Also, seek the peace and prosperity of the city to which I have carried you into exile. Pray to the LORD for it, because if it prospers, you too will prosper." ⁸Yes, this is what the LORD Almighty, the God of Israel, says: "Do not let the prophets and diviners among you deceive you. Do not listen to the dreams you encourage them to have. ⁹They are prophesying lies to you in my name. I have not sent them," declares the LORD.

¹⁰This is what the LORD says: "When seventy years are completed for Babylon, I will come to you and fulfill my good promise to bring you back to this place. ¹¹For I know the plans I have for you," declares the LORD, "plans to prosper you and not to harm you, plans to give you hope and a future. ¹²Then you will call on me and come and pray to me, and I will listen to you. ¹³You will seek me and find me when you seek me with all your heart. ¹⁴I will be found by you," declares the LORD, "and will bring you back from captivity.[b] I will gather you from all the nations and places where I have banished you," declares the LORD, "and will bring you back to the place from which I carried you into exile."

¹⁵You may say, "The LORD has raised up prophets for us in Babylon," ¹⁶but this is what the LORD says about the king who sits on David's throne and all the people who remain in this city, your fellow citizens who did not go with you into exile— ¹⁷yes, this is what the LORD Almighty says: "I will send the sword, famine and plague against them and I will make them like figs that are so bad they cannot be eaten. ¹⁸I will pursue them with the sword, famine and plague and will make them abhorrent to all the kingdoms of the earth, a curse[c] and an

atissue:suffering

29:10–14 Have you ever felt that God had it in for you? When everything in your life feels like it's crashing down around you, you may conclude that either a) God doesn't exist, or b) he's out to get you. Neither is true. Whenever a difficult circumstance occurs in your life—whether it's a trial to enrich your character, suffering to display your commitment to God or discipline as a consequence for your sin—God's goal is not to crush you but to restore you. You can trust that God will bring about good for you. You have a hope and a future with him.

---

a 4 Hebrew Jeconiah, a variant of Jehoiachin b 14 Or will restore your fortunes c 18 That is, their names will be used in cursing (see Jer. 29:22); or, others will see that they are cursed.

object of horror, of scorn and reproach, among all the nations where I drive them. ¹⁹For they have not listened to my words," declares the LORD, "words that I sent to them again and again by my servants the prophets. And you exiles have not listened either," declares the LORD.

²⁰Therefore, hear the word of the LORD, all you exiles whom I have sent away from Jerusalem to Babylon. ²¹This is what the LORD Almighty, the God of Israel, says about Ahab son of Kolaiah and Zedekiah son of Maaseiah, who are prophesying lies to you in my name: "I will deliver them into the hands of Nebuchadnezzar king of Babylon, and he will put them to death before your very eyes. ²²Because of them, all the exiles from Judah who are in Babylon will use this curse: 'May the LORD treat you like Zedekiah and Ahab, whom the king of Babylon burned in the fire.' ²³For they have done outrageous things in Israel; they have committed adultery with their neighbors' wives, and in my name they have uttered lies—which I did not authorize. I know it and am a witness to it," declares the LORD.

Message to Shemaiah

²⁴Tell Shemaiah the Nehelamite, ²⁵"This is what the LORD Almighty, the God of Israel, says: You sent letters in your own name to all the people in Jerusalem, to the priest Zephaniah son of Maaseiah, and to all the other priests. You said to Zephaniah, ²⁶'The LORD has appointed you priest in place of Jehoiada to be in charge of the house of the LORD; you should put any crazy person who acts like a prophet into the stocks and neck-irons. ²⁷So why have you not reprimanded Jeremiah from Anathoth, who poses as a prophet among you? ²⁸He has sent this message to us in Babylon: It will be a long time. Therefore build houses and settle down; plant gardens and eat what they produce.'"

²⁹Zephaniah the priest, however, read the letter to Jeremiah the prophet. ³⁰Then the word of the LORD came to Jeremiah: ³¹"Send this message to all the exiles: 'This is what the LORD says about Shemaiah the Nehelamite: Because Shemaiah has prophesied to you, even though I did not send him, and has persuaded you to trust in lies, ³²this is what the LORD says: I will surely punish Shemaiah the Nehelamite and his descendants. He will have no one left among this people, nor will he see the good things I will do for my people, declares the LORD, because he has preached rebellion against me.'"

Restoration of Israel

30 This is the word that came to Jeremiah from the LORD: ²"This is what the LORD, the God of Israel, says: 'Write in a book all the words I have spoken to you. ³The days are coming,' declares the LORD, 'when I will bring my people Israel and Judah back from captivity*ᵃ* and restore them to the land I gave their ancestors to possess,' says the LORD."

⁴These are the words the LORD spoke concerning Israel and Judah: ⁵"This is what the LORD says:

"'Cries of fear are heard—
    terror, not peace.
⁶Ask and see:
    Can a man bear children?
Then why do I see every strong man
    with his hands on his stomach like a woman in labor,
    every face turned deathly pale?
⁷How awful that day will be!
    None will be like it.
It will be a time of trouble for Jacob,
    but he will be saved out of it.

⁸"'In that day,' declares the LORD Almighty,
    'I will break the yoke off their necks
and will tear off their bonds;
    no longer will foreigners enslave them.
⁹Instead, they will serve the LORD their God

ᵃ 3 Or *will restore the fortunes of my people Israel and Judah*

and David their king,
  whom I will raise up for them.

10 "'So do not be afraid, Jacob my servant;
  do not be dismayed, Israel,'

declares the LORD.

'I will surely save you out of a distant place,
  your descendants from the land of their exile.
Jacob will again have peace and security,
  and no one will make him afraid.
11 I am with you and will save you,'
  declares the LORD.
'Though I completely destroy all the nations
  among which I scatter you,
  I will not completely destroy you.
I will discipline you but only in due measure;
  I will not let you go entirely unpunished.'

12 "This is what the LORD says:

  "'Your wound is incurable,
    your injury beyond healing.
13 There is no one to plead your cause,
    no remedy for your sore,
    no healing for you.
14 All your allies have forgotten you;
    they care nothing for you.
I have struck you as an enemy would
    and punished you as would the cruel,
  because your guilt is so great
    and your sins so many.
15 Why do you cry out over your wound,
    your pain that has no cure?
Because of your great guilt and many sins
    I have done these things to you.

16 "'But all who devour you will be devoured;
    all your enemies will go into exile.
Those who plunder you will be plundered;
    all who make spoil of you I will despoil.
17 But I will restore you to health
    and heal your wounds,'

declares the LORD,

'because you are called an outcast,
    Zion for whom no one cares.'

18 "This is what the LORD says:

  "'I will restore the fortunes of Jacob's tents
    and have compassion on his dwellings;
  the city will be rebuilt on her ruins,
    and the palace will stand in its proper place.
19 From them will come songs of thanksgiving
    and the sound of rejoicing.

I will add to their numbers,
and they will not be decreased;
I will bring them honor,
and they will not be disdained.
²⁰Their children will be as in days of old,
and their community will be established before me;
I will punish all who oppress them.
²¹Their leader will be one of their own;
their ruler will arise from among them.
I will bring him near and he will come close to me—
for who is he who will devote himself
to be close to me?'

declares the LORD.

²²"'So you will be my people,
and I will be your God.'"

²³See, the storm of the LORD
will burst out in wrath,
a driving wind swirling down
on the heads of the wicked.
²⁴The fierce anger of the LORD will not turn back
until he fully accomplishes
the purposes of his heart.
In days to come
you will understand this.

1128

31 "At that time," declares the LORD, "I will be the God of all the families of Israel, and they will be my people."
²This is what the LORD says:

"The people who survive the sword
will find favor in the wilderness;
I will come to give rest to Israel."

³The LORD appeared to us in the past,ᵃ saying:

_____
ᵃ 3 Or LORD has appeared to us from afar

HE IS: coming

31:2–6 In a dream God told Jeremiah that he would come to give rest to Israel. He promised to rebuild and restore the people he had never stopped loving. Though God's people had been dispersed and persecuted, the time was coming when they would be fully re-established.

Remember that despite the upheaval on the earth and the persecution of Christians around the world today, he is coming again. When you begin to despair, or you see evil people succeed or God's plans seem to languish, set your heart on the certainty that he is *coming* (see 1 Thessalonians 4:16–18; Revelation 22:12–13).

For the next He Is, go to p. 1133.

"I have loved you with an everlasting love;
    I have drawn you with unfailing kindness.
⁴I will build you up again,
    and you, Virgin Israel, will be rebuilt.
Again you will take up your timbrels
    and go out to dance with the joyful.
⁵Again you will plant vineyards
    on the hills of Samaria;
the farmers will plant them
    and enjoy their fruit.
⁶There will be a day when watchmen cry out
    on the hills of Ephraim,
'Come, let us go up to Zion,
    to the Lord our God.'"

⁷This is what the Lord says:

"Sing with joy for Jacob;
    shout for the foremost of the nations.
Make your praises heard, and say,
    'Lord, save your people,
    the remnant of Israel.'
⁸See, I will bring them from the land of the north
    and gather them from the ends of the earth.
Among them will be the blind and the lame,
    expectant mothers and women in labor;
    a great throng will return.
⁹They will come with weeping;
    they will pray as I bring them back.
I will lead them beside streams of water
    on a level path where they will not stumble,
because I am Israel's father,
    and Ephraim is my firstborn son.

¹⁰"Hear the word of the Lord, you nations;
    proclaim it in distant coastlands:
'He who scattered Israel will gather them
    and will watch over his flock like a shepherd.'
¹¹For the Lord will deliver Jacob
    and redeem them from the hand of those stronger than they.
¹²They will come and shout for joy on the heights of Zion;
    they will rejoice in the bounty of the Lord—
the grain, the new wine and the olive oil,
    the young of the flocks and herds.
They will be like a well-watered garden,
    and they will sorrow no more.
¹³Then young women will dance and be glad,
    young men and old as well.
I will turn their mourning into gladness;
    I will give them comfort and joy instead of sorrow.
¹⁴I will satisfy the priests with abundance,
    and my people will be filled with my bounty,"

declares the Lord.

1129

¹⁵This is what the LORD says:

> "A voice is heard in Ramah,
>> mourning and great weeping,
> Rachel weeping for her children
>> and refusing to be comforted,
>> because they are no more."

¹⁶This is what the LORD says:

> "Restrain your voice from weeping
>> and your eyes from tears,
> for your work will be rewarded,"

declares the LORD.

> "They will return from the land of the enemy.
> ¹⁷So there is hope for your descendants,"

declares the LORD.

> "Your children will return to their own land.

> ¹⁸"I have surely heard Ephraim's moaning:
>> 'You disciplined me like an unruly calf,
>> and I have been disciplined.
> Restore me, and I will return,
>> because you are the LORD my God.
> ¹⁹After I strayed,
>> I repented;
> after I came to understand,
>> I beat my breast.
> I was ashamed and humiliated
>> because I bore the disgrace of my youth.'
> ²⁰Is not Ephraim my dear son,
>> the child in whom I delight?
> Though I often speak against him,
>> I still remember him.
> Therefore my heart yearns for him;
>> I have great compassion for him,"

declares the LORD.

> ²¹"Set up road signs;
>> put up guideposts.
> Take note of the highway,
>> the road that you take.
> Return, Virgin Israel,
>> return to your towns.
> ²²How long will you wander,
>> unfaithful Daughter Israel?
> The LORD will create a new thing on earth—
>> the woman will return to*ᵃ* the man."

²³This is what the LORD Almighty, the God of Israel, says: "When I bring them back from captivity,*ᵇ* the people in the land of Judah and in its towns will once again use these words: 'The LORD bless you, you prosperous city, you sacred mountain.' ²⁴People will live together in Judah and all its towns—farmers and those who move about with their flocks. ²⁵I will refresh the weary and satisfy the faint."

ᵃ 22 Or will protect ᵇ 23 Or I restore their fortunes

26 At this I awoke and looked around. My sleep had been pleasant to me.

27 "The days are coming," declares the Lord, "when I will plant the house of Israel and the house of Judah with the offspring of people and of animals. 28 Just as I watched over them to uproot and tear down, and to overthrow, destroy and bring disaster, so I will watch over them to build and to plant," declares the Lord. 29 "In those days people will no longer say,

> 'The parents have eaten sour grapes,
>   and the children's teeth are set on edge.'

30 Instead, everyone will die for their own sin; whoever eats sour grapes—their own teeth will be set on edge.

> 31 "The days are coming," declares the Lord,
>   "when I will make a new covenant
> with the house of Israel
>   and with the house of Judah.
> 32 It will not be like the covenant
>   I made with their ancestors
> when I took them by the hand
>   to lead them out of Egypt,
> because they broke my covenant,
>   though I was a husband to *a* them, *b*"
>   declares the Lord.
> 33 "This is the covenant I will make with
>   the house of Israel
>   after that time," declares the Lord.
> "I will put my law in their minds
>   and write it on their hearts.
> I will be their God,
>   and they will be my people.
> 34 No longer will they teach their
>   neighbors,
>   or say to one another, 'Know the
>   Lord,'
> because they will all know me,
>   from the least of them to the greatest,"

> "For I will forgive their wickedness
>   and will remember their sins no more."

35 This is what the Lord says,

> he who appoints the sun
>   to shine by day,
> who decrees the moon and stars
>   to shine by night,
> who stirs up the sea
>   so that its waves roar—
> the Lord Almighty is his name:
> 36 "Only if these decrees vanish from my sight,"
>   declares the Lord,
> "will the descendants of Israel ever cease
>   to be a nation before me."

conversations

forgiveness «» 31:31–34

1» What have you learned about God through his forgiveness in your life?

2» How can you teach others about the unconditional nature of God's forgiveness?

3» Are you a good forgiver? How do you convey forgiveness to someone who's wronged you?

For more on **forgiveness**, check the index.
For the next Conversations, go to p. 1138.

declares the Lord.

---

a 32 Hebrew; Septuagint and Syriac / *and I turned away from*   *b 32* Or *was their master*

³⁷This is what the Lord says:

> "Only if the heavens above can be measured
>> and the foundations of the earth below be searched out
> will I reject all the descendants of Israel
>> because of all they have done,"

declares the Lord.

³⁸"The days are coming," declares the Lord, "when this city will be rebuilt for me from the Tower of Hananel to the Corner Gate. ³⁹The measuring line will stretch from there straight to the hill of Gareb and then turn to Goah. ⁴⁰The whole valley where dead bodies and ashes are thrown, and all the terraces out to the Kidron Valley on the east as far as the corner of the Horse Gate, will be holy to the Lord. The city will never again be uprooted or demolished."

Jeremiah Buys a Field

32 This is the word that came to Jeremiah from the Lord in the tenth year of Zedekiah king of Judah, which was the eighteenth year of Nebuchadnezzar. ²The army of the king of Babylon was then besieging Jerusalem, and Jeremiah the prophet was confined in the courtyard of the guard in the royal palace of Judah.

³Now Zedekiah king of Judah had imprisoned him there, saying, "Why do you prophesy as you do? You say, 'This is what the Lord says: I am about to give this city into the hands of the king of Babylon, and he will capture it. ⁴Zedekiah king of Judah will not escape the Babylonians^a but will certainly be given into the hands of the king of Babylon, and will speak with him face to face and see him with his own eyes. ⁵He will take Zedekiah to Babylon, where he will remain until I deal with him, declares the Lord. If you fight against the Babylonians, you will not succeed.'"

⁶Jeremiah said, "The word of the Lord came to me: ⁷Hanamel son of Shallum your uncle is going to come to you and say, 'Buy my field at Anathoth, because as nearest relative it is your right and duty to buy it.'

⁸"Then, just as the Lord had said, my cousin Hanamel came to me in the courtyard of the guard and said, 'Buy my field at Anathoth in the territory of Benjamin. Since it is your right to redeem it and possess it, buy it for yourself.'

"I knew that this was the word of the Lord; ⁹so I bought the field at Anathoth from my cousin Hanamel and weighed out for him seventeen shekels^b of silver. ¹⁰I signed and sealed the deed, had it witnessed, and weighed out the silver on the scales. ¹¹I took the deed of purchase—the sealed copy containing the terms and conditions, as well as the unsealed copy— ¹²and I gave this deed to Baruch son of Neriah, the son of Mahseiah, in the presence of my cousin Hanamel and of the witnesses who had signed the deed and of all the Jews sitting in the courtyard of the guard.

¹³"In their presence I gave Baruch these instructions: ¹⁴'This is what the Lord Almighty, the God of Israel, says: Take these documents, both the sealed and unsealed copies of the deed of purchase, and put them in a clay jar so they will last a long time. ¹⁵For this is what the Lord Almighty, the God of Israel, says: Houses, fields and vineyards will again be bought in this land.'

¹⁶"After I had given the deed of purchase to Baruch son of Neriah, I prayed to the Lord:

¹⁷"Ah, Sovereign Lord, you have made the heavens and the earth by your great power and outstretched arm. Nothing is too hard for you. ¹⁸You show love to thousands but bring the punishment for the parents' sins into the laps of their children after them. Great and mighty God, whose name is the Lord Almighty, ¹⁹great are your purposes and mighty are your deeds. Your eyes are open to the ways of all; you reward everyone according to their conduct and as their deeds deserve. ²⁰You performed signs and wonders in Egypt and have continued them to this day, both in Israel and among all nations, and have gained the renown that is still yours. ²¹You brought your people Israel out of Egypt with signs and wonders, by a mighty hand and an outstretched arm and with great terror. ²²You gave them this land you had sworn to give their ancestors, a land flowing

---

^a 4 Or *Chaldeans*; also in verses 5, 24, 25, 28, 29 and 43   ^b 9 That is, about 7 ounces or about 200 grams

with milk and honey. [23] They came in and took possession of it, but they did not obey you or follow your law; they did not do what you commanded them to do. So you brought all this disaster on them.

[24] "See how the siege ramps are built up to take the city. Because of the sword, famine and plague, the city will be given into the hands of the Babylonians who are attacking it. What you said has happened, as you now see. [25] And though the city will be given into the hands of the Babylonians, you, Sovereign LORD, say to me, 'Buy the field with silver and have the transaction witnessed.'"

[26] Then the word of the LORD came to Jeremiah: [27] "I am the LORD, the God of the whole human race. Is anything too hard for me? [28] Therefore, this is what the LORD says: I am about to give this city into the hands of the Babylonians and to Nebuchadnezzar king of Babylon, who will capture it. [29] The Babylonians who are attacking this city will come in and set it on fire; they will burn it down, along with the houses where the people aroused my anger by burning incense on the roofs to Baal and by pouring out drink offerings to other gods.

[30] "The people of Israel and Judah have done nothing but evil in my sight from their youth; indeed, the people of Israel have done nothing but arouse my anger with what their hands have made, declares the LORD. [31] From the day it was built until now, this city has so aroused my anger and wrath that I must remove it from my sight. [32] The people of Israel and Judah have provoked me by all the evil they have done—they, their kings and officials, their priests and prophets, the people of Judah and those living in Jerusalem. [33] They turned their backs to me and not their faces; though I taught them again and again, they would not listen or respond to discipline. [34] They set up their vile images in the house that bears my Name and defiled it. [35] They built high places for Baal in the Valley of Ben Hinnom to sacrifice their sons and daughters to Molek, though I never commanded—nor did it enter my mind—that they should do such a detestable thing and so make Judah sin.

[36] "You are saying about this city, 'By the sword, famine and plague it will be given into the hands of the king of Babylon'; but this is what the LORD, the God of Israel, says: [37] I will surely gather them from all the lands where I banish them in my furious anger and great wrath; I will bring them back to this place and let them live in safety. [38] They will be my people, and I will be their God. [39] I will give them singleness of heart and action, so that they will always fear me and that all will then go well for them and for their children after them. [40] I will make an everlasting covenant with them: I will never stop doing good to them, and I will inspire them to fear me, so that they will never turn away from me. [41] I will rejoice in doing them good and will assuredly plant them in this land with all my heart and soul.

HE IS: foreseeing

32:1–25 God instructed Jeremiah to buy his uncle's field, knowing full well the Babylonians would soon conquer the land. This signified to the people of Israel that God was planning to bring them back to their home. Because God *foresees* the future, Jeremiah could trust God's seemingly ill-timed instructions. (Who invests in land right before captivity?!)

Nothing is too hard for God—not your housing situation, your health or your happiness. He *foresees* what will happen before it happens and has a plan to redeem whatever you're facing. You can trust God to bring his promises to pass in his perfect way and time.

For the next He Is, go to p. 1142.

[42] "This is what the LORD says: As I have brought all this great calamity on this people, so I will give them all the prosperity I have promised them. [43] Once more fields will be bought in this land of which you say, 'It is a desolate waste, without people or animals, for it has been given into the hands of the Babylonians.' [44] Fields will be bought for silver, and deeds will be signed, sealed and witnessed in the territory of Benjamin, in the villages around Jerusalem, in the towns of Judah and in the towns of the hill

country, of the western foothills and of the Negev, because I will restore their fortunes,*a* declares the LORD."

Promise of Restoration

33 While Jeremiah was still confined in the courtyard of the guard, the word of the LORD came to him a second time: [2]"This is what the LORD says, he who made the earth, the LORD who formed it and established it—the LORD is his name: [3]'Call to me and I will answer you and tell you great and unsearchable things you do not know.' [4]For this is what the LORD, the God of Israel, says about the houses in this city and the royal palaces of Judah that have been torn down to be used against the siege ramps and the sword [5]in the fight with the Babylonians*b*: 'They will be filled with the dead bodies of the people I will slay in my anger and wrath. I will hide my face from this city because of all its wickedness.

[6]"'Nevertheless, I will bring health and healing to it; I will heal my people and will let them enjoy abundant peace and security. [7]I will bring Judah and Israel back from captivity*c* and will rebuild them as they were before. [8]I will cleanse them from all the sin they have committed against me and will forgive all their sins of rebellion against me. [9]Then this city will bring me renown, joy, praise and honor before all nations on earth that hear of all the good things I do for it; and they will be in awe and will tremble at the abundant prosperity and peace I provide for it.'

[10]"This is what the LORD says: 'You say about this place, "It is a desolate waste, without people or animals." Yet in the towns of Judah and the streets of Jerusalem that are deserted, inhabited by neither people nor animals, there will be heard once more [11]the sounds of joy and gladness, the voices of bride and bridegroom, and the voices of those who bring thank offerings to the house of the LORD, saying,

> "Give thanks to the LORD Almighty,
>   for the LORD is good;
>   his love endures forever."

For I will restore the fortunes of the land as they were before,' says the LORD.

[12]"This is what the LORD Almighty says: 'In this place, desolate and without people or animals—in all its towns there will again be pastures for shepherds to rest their flocks. [13]In the towns of the hill country, of the western foothills and of the Negev, in the territory of Benjamin, in the villages around Jerusalem and in the towns of Judah, flocks will again pass under the hand of the one who counts them,' says the LORD.

[14]"'The days are coming,' declares the LORD, 'when I will fulfill the good promise I made to the house of Israel and to the house of Judah.

> [15]"'In those days and at that time
>   I will make a righteous Branch sprout from David's line;
>   he will do what is just and right in the land.
> [16]In those days Judah will be saved
>   and Jerusalem will live in safety.
> This is the name by which it*d* will be called:
>   The LORD Our Righteous Savior.'

1134

atissue:prayer

33:3 *Great and unsearchable things*—that's what God promised to tell Jeremiah. When we call to God, he also tells us great and unsearchable things. *Like what?* you may wonder. Like the depth of love that would motivate him to send his Son to die in your place. Like the unending supply of his mercy and grace available to you today. Like what he's doing in this world and how he wants to use *you* in his plan. For many of us, the problem is that we think prayer is an exercise in talking. But to hear great and unsearchable things, we must also be listening.

a 44 Or will bring them back from captivity   b 5 Or Chaldeans   c 7 Or will restore the fortunes of Judah and Israel   d 16 Or he

[17]For this is what the LORD says: 'David will never fail to have a man to sit on the throne of the house of Israel, [18]nor will the Levitical priests ever fail to have a man to stand before me continually to offer burnt offerings, to burn grain offerings and to present sacrifices.'"

[19]The word of the LORD came to Jeremiah: [20]"This is what the LORD says: 'If you can break my covenant with the day and my covenant with the night, so that day and night no longer come at their appointed time, [21]then my covenant with David my servant—and my covenant with the Levites who are priests ministering before me—can be broken and David will no longer have a descendant to reign on his throne. [22]I will make the descendants of David my servant and the Levites who minister before me as countless as the stars in the sky and as measureless as the sand on the seashore.'"

[23]The word of the LORD came to Jeremiah: [24]"Have you not noticed that these people are saying, 'The LORD has rejected the two kingdoms[a] he chose'? So they despise my people and no longer regard them as a nation. [25]This is what the LORD says: 'If I have not made my covenant with day and night and established the laws of heaven and earth, [26]then I will reject the descendants of Jacob and David my servant and will not choose one of his sons to rule over the descendants of Abraham, Isaac and Jacob. For I will restore their fortunes[b] and have compassion on them.'"

Warning to Zedekiah

34 While Nebuchadnezzar king of Babylon and all his army and all the kingdoms and peoples in the empire he ruled were fighting against Jerusalem and all its surrounding towns, this word came to Jeremiah from the LORD: [2]"This is what the LORD, the God of Israel, says: Go to Zedekiah king of Judah and tell him, 'This is what the LORD says: I am about to give this city into the hands of the king of Babylon, and he will burn it down. [3]You will not escape from his grasp but will surely be captured and given into his hands. You will see the king of Babylon with your own eyes, and he will speak with you face to face. And you will go to Babylon.

[4]"'Yet hear the LORD's promise to you, Zedekiah king of Judah. This is what the LORD says concerning you: You will not die by the sword; [5]you will die peacefully. As people made a funeral fire in honor of your ancestors, the former kings who preceded you, so they will make a fire in your honor and lament, "Alas, master!" I myself make this promise, declares the LORD.'"

[6]Then Jeremiah the prophet told all this to Zedekiah king of Judah, in Jerusalem, [7]while the army of the king of Babylon was fighting against Jerusalem and the other cities of Judah that were still holding out—Lachish and Azekah. These were the only fortified cities left in Judah.

Freedom for Slaves

[8]The word came to Jeremiah from the LORD after King Zedekiah had made a covenant with all the people in Jerusalem to proclaim freedom for the slaves. [9]Everyone was to free their Hebrew slaves, both male and female; no one was to hold another Jew in bondage. [10]So all the officials and people who entered into this covenant agreed that they would free their male and female slaves and no longer hold them in bondage. They agreed, and set them free. [11]But afterward they changed their minds and took back the slaves they had freed and enslaved them again.

[12]Then the word of the LORD came to Jeremiah: [13]"This is what the LORD, the God of Israel, says: I made a covenant with your ancestors when I brought them out of Egypt, out of the land of slavery. I said, [14]'Every seventh year each of you must free any other Hebrews who have sold themselves to you. After they have served you six years, you must let them go free.'[c] Your ancestors, however, did not listen to me or pay attention to me. [15]Recently you repented and did what is right in my sight: Each of you proclaimed freedom to your own people. You even made a covenant before me in the house that bears my Name. [16]But now you have turned around and profaned my name; each of you has taken back the male and female slaves you had set free to go where they wished. You have forced them to become your slaves again.

[17]"Therefore, this is what the LORD says: You have not obeyed me; you have not proclaimed freedom to your own people. So I now proclaim 'freedom' for you, declares the LORD—'freedom' to fall by the sword, plague and famine. I will make you abhorrent to all the kingdoms of the earth. [18]Those who have

1135

---

violated my covenant and have not fulfilled the terms of the covenant they made before me, I will treat like the calf they cut in two and then walked between its pieces. ¹⁹The leaders of Judah and Jerusalem, the court officials, the priests and all the people of the land who walked between the pieces of the calf, ²⁰I will deliver into the hands of their enemies who seek their lives. Their dead bodies will become food for the birds and the wild animals.

²¹"I will deliver Zedekiah king of Judah and his officials into the hands of their enemies who seek their lives, to the army of the king of Babylon, which has withdrawn from you. ²²I am going to give the order, declares the Lord, and I will bring them back to this city. They will fight against it, take it and burn it down. And I will lay waste the towns of Judah so no one can live there."

The Rekabites

35 This is the word that came to Jeremiah from the Lord during the reign of Jehoiakim son of Josiah king of Judah: ²"Go to the Rekabite family and invite them to come to one of the side rooms of the house of the Lord and give them wine to drink."

³So I went to get Jaazaniah son of Jeremiah, the son of Habazziniah, and his brothers and all his sons—the whole family of the Rekabites. ⁴I brought them into the house of the Lord, into the room of the sons of Hanan son of Igdaliah the man of God. It was next to the room of the officials, which was over that of Maaseiah son of Shallum the doorkeeper. ⁵Then I set bowls full of wine and some cups before the members of the Rekabite family and said to them, "Drink some wine."

⁶But they replied, "We do not drink wine, because our ancestor Jehonadab[a] son of Rekab gave us this command: 'Neither you nor your descendants must ever drink wine. ⁷Also you must never build houses, sow seed or plant vineyards; you must never have any of these things, but must always live in tents. Then you will live a long time in the land where you are nomads.' ⁸We have obeyed everything our ancestor Jehonadab son of Rekab commanded us. Neither we nor our wives nor our sons and daughters have ever drunk wine ⁹or built houses to live in or had vineyards, fields or crops. ¹⁰We have lived in tents and have fully obeyed everything our ancestor Jehonadab commanded us. ¹¹But when Nebuchadnezzar king of Babylon invaded this land, we said, 'Come, we must go to Jerusalem to escape the Babylonian[b] and Aramean armies.' So we have remained in Jerusalem."

¹²Then the word of the Lord came to Jeremiah, saying: ¹³"This is what the Lord Almighty, the God of Israel, says: Go and tell the people of Judah and those living in Jerusalem, 'Will you not learn a lesson and obey my words?' declares the Lord. ¹⁴'Jehonadab son of Rekab ordered his descendants not to drink wine and this command has been kept. To this day they do not drink wine, because they obey their ancestor's command. But I have spoken to you again and again, yet you have not obeyed me. ¹⁵Again and again I sent all my servants the prophets to you. They said, "Each of you must turn from your wicked ways and reform your actions; do not follow other gods to serve them. Then you will live in the land I have given to you and your ancestors." But you have not paid attention or listened to me. ¹⁶The descendants of Jehonadab son of Rekab have carried out the command their ancestor gave them, but these people have not obeyed me.'

¹⁷"Therefore, this is what the Lord God Almighty, the God of Israel, says: 'Listen! I am going to bring on Judah and on everyone living in Jerusalem every disaster I pronounced against them. I spoke to them, but they did not listen; I called to them, but they did not answer.'"

¹⁸Then Jeremiah said to the family of the Rekabites, "This is what the Lord Almighty, the God of Israel, says: 'You have obeyed the command of your ancestor Jehonadab and have followed all his instructions and have done everything he ordered.' ¹⁹Therefore, this is what the Lord Almighty, the God of Israel, says: 'Jehonadab son of Rekab will never fail to have a descendant to serve me.'"

Jehoiakim Burns Jeremiah's Scroll

36 In the fourth year of Jehoiakim son of Josiah king of Judah, this word came to Jeremiah from the Lord: ²"Take a scroll and write on it all the words I have spoken to you concerning Israel, Judah and all the other nations from the time I began speaking to you in the reign of Josiah till now. ³Perhaps

---

ᵃ 6 Hebrew Jonadab, a variant of Jehonadab; here and often in this chapter   ᵇ 11 Or Chaldean when the people of Judah hear about every disaster I plan to inflict on them, they will each turn from their wicked ways; then I will forgive their wickedness and their sin."

⁴So Jeremiah called Baruch son of Neriah, and while Jeremiah dictated all the words the LORD had spoken to him, Baruch wrote them on the scroll. ⁵Then Jeremiah told Baruch, "I am restricted; I am not allowed to go to the LORD's temple. ⁶So you go to the house of the LORD on a day of fasting and read to the people from the scroll the words of the LORD that you wrote as I dictated. Read them to all the people of Judah who come in from their towns. ⁷Perhaps they will bring their petition before the LORD, and will all turn from their wicked ways, for the anger and wrath pronounced against this people by the LORD are great."

⁸Baruch son of Neriah did everything Jeremiah the prophet told him to do; at the LORD's temple he read the words of the LORD from the scroll. ⁹In the ninth month of the fifth year of Jehoiakim son of Josiah king of Judah, a time of fasting before the LORD was proclaimed for all the people in Jerusalem and those who had come from the towns of Judah. ¹⁰From the room of Gemariah son of Shaphan the secretary, which was in the upper courtyard at the entrance of the New Gate of the temple, Baruch read to all the people at the LORD's temple the words of Jeremiah from the scroll.

¹¹When Micaiah son of Gemariah, the son of Shaphan, heard all the words of the LORD from the scroll, ¹²he went down to the secretary's room in the royal palace, where all the officials were sitting: Elishama the secretary, Delaiah son of Shemaiah, Elnathan son of Akbor, Gemariah son of Shaphan, Zedekiah son of Hananiah, and all the other officials. ¹³After Micaiah told them everything he had heard Baruch read to the people from the scroll, ¹⁴all the officials sent Jehudi son of Nethaniah, the son of Shelemiah, the son of Cushi, to say to Baruch, "Bring the scroll from which you have read to the people and come." So Baruch son of Neriah went to them with the scroll in his hand. ¹⁵They said to him, "Sit down, please, and read it to us."

So Baruch read it to them. ¹⁶When they heard all these words, they looked at each other in fear and said to Baruch, "We must report all these words to the king." ¹⁷Then they asked Baruch, "Tell us, how did you come to write all this? Did Jeremiah dictate it?"

¹⁸"Yes," Baruch replied, "he dictated all these words to me, and I wrote them in ink on the scroll."

¹⁹Then the officials said to Baruch, "You and Jeremiah, go and hide. Don't let anyone know where you are."

²⁰After they put the scroll in the room of Elishama the secretary, they went to the king in the courtyard and reported everything to him. ²¹The king sent Jehudi to get the scroll, and Jehudi brought it from the room of Elishama the secretary and read it to the king and all the officials standing beside him. ²²It was the ninth month and the king was sitting in the winter apartment, with a fire burning in the firepot in front of him. ²³Whenever Jehudi had read three or four columns of the scroll, the king cut them off with a scribe's knife and threw them into the firepot, until the entire scroll was burned in the fire. ²⁴The king and all his attendants who heard all these words showed no fear, nor did they tear their clothes. ²⁵Even though Elnathan, Delaiah and Gemariah urged the king not to burn the scroll, he would not listen to them. ²⁶Instead, the king commanded Jerahmeel, a son of the king, Seraiah son of Azriel and Shelemiah son of Abdeel to arrest Baruch the scribe and Jeremiah the prophet. But the LORD had hidden them.

²⁷After the king burned the scroll containing the words that Baruch had written at Jeremiah's dictation, the word of the LORD came to Jeremiah: ²⁸"Take another scroll and write on it all the words that were on the first scroll, which Jehoiakim king of Judah burned up. ²⁹Also tell Jehoiakim king of Judah, 'This is what the LORD says: You burned that scroll and said, "Why did you write on it that the king of Babylon would certainly come and destroy this land and wipe from it both people and animals?" ³⁰Therefore, this is what the LORD says about Jehoiakim king of Judah: He will have no one to sit on the throne of David; his body will be thrown out and exposed to the heat by day and the frost by night. ³¹I will punish him and his children and his attendants for their wickedness; I will bring on them and those living in Jerusalem and the people of Judah every disaster I pronounced against them, because they have not listened.'"

³²So Jeremiah took another scroll and gave it to the scribe Baruch son of Neriah, and as Jeremiah dictated, Baruch wrote on it all the words of the scroll that Jehoiakim king of Judah had burned in the fire. And many similar words were added to them.

1137

Jeremiah in Prison

37 Zedekiah son of Josiah was made king of Judah by Nebuchadnezzar king of Babylon; he reigned in place of Jehoiachin[a] son of Jehoiakim. ²Neither he nor his attendants nor the people of the land paid any attention to the words the LORD had spoken through Jeremiah the prophet.

³King Zedekiah, however, sent Jehukal son of Shelemiah with the priest Zephaniah son of Maaseiah to Jeremiah the prophet with this message: "Please pray to the LORD our God for us."

⁴Now Jeremiah was free to come and go among the people, for he had not yet been put in prison. ⁵Pharaoh's army had marched out of Egypt, and when the Babylonians[b] who were besieging Jerusalem heard the report about them, they withdrew from Jerusalem.

⁶Then the word of the LORD came to Jeremiah the prophet: ⁷"This is what the LORD, the God of Israel, says: Tell the king of Judah, who sent you to inquire of me, 'Pharaoh's army, which has marched out to support you, will go back to its own land, to Egypt. ⁸Then the Babylonians will return and attack this city; they will capture it and burn it down.'

⁹"This is what the LORD says: Do not deceive yourselves, thinking, 'The Babylonians will surely leave us.' They will not! ¹⁰Even if you were to defeat the entire Babylonian[c] army that is attacking you and only wounded men were left in their tents, they would come out and burn this city down."

¹¹After the Babylonian army had withdrawn from Jerusalem because of Pharaoh's army, ¹²Jeremiah started to leave the city to go to the territory of Benjamin to get his share of the property among the people there. ¹³But when he reached the Benjamin Gate, the captain of the guard, whose name was Irijah son of Shelemiah, the son of Hananiah, arrested him and said, "You are deserting to the Babylonians!"

¹⁴"That's not true!" Jeremiah said. "I am not deserting to the Babylonians." But Irijah would not listen to him; instead, he arrested Jeremiah and brought him to the officials. ¹⁵They were angry with Jeremiah and had him beaten and imprisoned in the house of Jonathan the secretary, which they had made into a prison.

¹⁶Jeremiah was put into a vaulted cell in a dungeon, where he remained a long time. ¹⁷Then King Zedekiah sent for him and had him brought to the palace, where he asked him privately, "Is there any word from the LORD?"

"Yes," Jeremiah replied, "you will be delivered into the hands of the king of Babylon."

¹⁸Then Jeremiah said to King Zedekiah, "What crime have I committed against you or your attendants or this people, that you have put me in prison? ¹⁹Where are your prophets who prophesied to you, 'The king of Babylon will not attack you or this land'? ²⁰But now, my lord the king, please listen. Let me bring my petition before you: Do not send me back to the house of Jonathan the secretary, or I will die there."

²¹King Zedekiah then gave orders for Jeremiah to be placed in the courtyard of the guard and given a loaf of bread from the street of the bakers each day until all the bread in the city was gone. So Jeremiah remained in the courtyard of the guard.

Jeremiah Thrown Into a Cistern

38 Shephatiah son of Mattan, Gedaliah son of Pashhur, Jehukal[d] son of Shelemiah, and Pashhur son of Malkijah heard what Jeremiah was telling all the people when he said, ²"This is what the LORD says: 'Whoever stays in this city will die by the sword, famine or plague, but whoever goes over to the Babylonians[e] will live. They will escape with their lives; they will live.' ³And this is what the LORD

conversations

compassion «» 38:1–13

1 » Think of a time when you saw someone treated unjustly. How did you feel, watching that person suffer?

2 » What power does your social position give you to respond to those treated unjustly?

3 » Christian leaders are often targets of unjust criticism. What leader could you encourage?

For more on **compassion**, check the index. For the next Conversations, go to p. 1148.

---

[a] *1* Hebrew *Koniah*, a variant of *Jehoiachin* [b] *5* Or *Chaldeans*; also in verses 8, 9, 13 and 14 [c] *10* Or *Chaldean*; also in verse 11 [d] *1* Hebrew *Jukal*, a variant of *Jehukal* [e] *2* Or *Chaldeans*; also in verses 18, 19 and 23

says: 'This city will certainly be given into the hands of the army of the king of Babylon, who will capture it.'"

⁴Then the officials said to the king, "This man should be put to death. He is discouraging the soldiers who are left in this city, as well as all the people, by the things he is saying to them. This man is not seeking the good of these people but their ruin."

⁵"He is in your hands," King Zedekiah answered. "The king can do nothing to oppose you."

⁶So they took Jeremiah and put him into the cistern of Malkijah, the king's son, which was in the courtyard of the guard. They lowered Jeremiah by ropes into the cistern; it had no water in it, only mud, and Jeremiah sank down into the mud.

⁷But Ebed-Melek, a Cushite,ᵃ an officialᵇ in the royal palace, heard that they had put Jeremiah into the cistern. While the king was sitting in the Benjamin Gate, ⁸Ebed-Melek went out of the palace and said to him, ⁹"My lord the king, these men have acted wickedly in all they have done to Jeremiah the prophet. They have thrown him into a cistern, where he will starve to death when there is no longer any bread in the city."

¹⁰Then the king commanded Ebed-Melek the Cushite, "Take thirty men from here with you and lift Jeremiah the prophet out of the cistern before he dies."

¹¹So Ebed-Melek took the men with him and went to a room under the treasury in the palace. He took some old rags and worn-out clothes from there and let them down with ropes to Jeremiah in the cistern. ¹²Ebed-Melek the Cushite said to Jeremiah, "Put these old rags and worn-out clothes under your arms to pad the ropes." Jeremiah did so, ¹³and they pulled him up with the ropes and lifted him out of the cistern. And Jeremiah remained in the courtyard of the guard.

Zedekiah Questions Jeremiah Again

¹⁴Then King Zedekiah sent for Jeremiah the prophet and had him brought to the third entrance to the temple of the Lord. "I am going to ask you something," the king said to Jeremiah. "Do not hide anything from me."

¹⁵Jeremiah said to Zedekiah, "If I give you an answer, will you not kill me? Even if I did give you counsel, you would not listen to me."

¹⁶But King Zedekiah swore this oath secretly to Jeremiah: "As surely as the Lord lives, who has given us breath, I will neither kill you nor hand you over to those who are seeking your life."

¹⁷Then Jeremiah said to Zedekiah, "This is what the Lord God Almighty, the God of Israel, says: 'If you surrender to the officers of the king of Babylon, your life will be spared and this city will not be burned down; you and your family will live. ¹⁸But if you will not surrender to the officers of the king of Babylon, this city will be given into the hands of the Babylonians and they will burn it down; you yourself will not escape from them.'"

¹⁹King Zedekiah said to Jeremiah, "I am afraid of the Jews who have gone over to the Babylonians, for the Babylonians may hand me over to them and they will mistreat me."

²⁰"They will not hand you over," Jeremiah replied. "Obey the Lord by doing what I tell you. Then it will go well with you, and your life will be spared. ²¹But if you refuse to surrender, this is what the Lord has revealed to me: ²²All the women left in the palace of the king of Judah will be brought out to the officials of the king of Babylon. Those women will say to you:

> "'They misled you and overcame you—
> those trusted friends of yours.
> Your feet are sunk in the mud;
> your friends have deserted you.'

²³"All your wives and children will be brought out to the Babylonians. You yourself will not escape from their hands but will be captured by the king of Babylon; and this city willᶜ be burned down."

²⁴Then Zedekiah said to Jeremiah, "Do not let anyone know about this conversation, or you may die. ²⁵If the officials hear that I talked with you, and they come to you and say, 'Tell us what you said to the

---

ᵃ 7 Probably from the upper Nile region   ᵇ 7 Or a eunuch   ᶜ 23 Or and you will cause this city to

myth #65 "GOD LOVES EVERONE. I HAVE NO RIGHT TO SAY SOMEONE ELSE'S LIFESTYLE IS WRONG."

I wish I knew how to talk to my brother. He's not a Christian, and I'm afraid I might say the wrong thing and set him off or offend him permanently. Let me tell you from experience—that kid knows how to hold a grudge! It will be hard enough for him to hear what I want to say . . . one wrong word on my part, and I'll lose him completely. Last year he started dating someone from his work. I was glad he was finally settling down enough to consider dating. However, one thing led to another, and within a few months they were living together.

She's very nice and has done a lot for him—he's much more organized, he actually remembers my birthday and he's decided to go back to school. I'm not saying the changes are all because of her, but she's clearly been a positive influence in his life. I'm glad they're together, but it makes me uncomfortable that they're living together. I know it's wrong, and I've read that living together before you get married makes your relationship less likely to succeed. They've talked about marriage, but my brother seems hesitant about it. He doesn't seem excited about the idea of marrying her. She's a fun person, but she can also be controlling and moody. They seem to argue a lot, and he doesn't sound as happy as he was at first.

So here I am, the perpetual big sister, watching my brother struggle through this relationship. I feel like I should say something to him about the direction his life is taking. But then I think that it's not right for me to judge his lifestyle—especially since he's not even a Christian. I don't have the right to do that. So should I just sit back and watch?

—Brooke

IT IS HARD to watch someone you love struggle in life—especially when you feel like you know the answers she needs. We know we have a responsibility to lovingly confront other Christians about certain sins they might be blind to in their lives (see Matthew 18:15–20). But what about non-Christians—what right do we have to comment on their lifestyles?

- *If someone doesn't know Christ, then that person is spiritually blinded.* We shouldn't chide unbelievers for making decisions that go against God's Word. They don't know any better. We can't expect unbelievers to live up to our standards when the Bible isn't their guide for living.

- *When you're tempted to judge another person, think about where you would be without Christ.* You'd probably be in exactly the same spot your unsaved friend is in—or worse. Judging someone shows justice without mercy—something Jesus never did. God's Word gives us the authority to judge right from wrong but not the permission to go around judging others.

- *Get at the root, heart issue.* In Brooke's case, her brother's root issue is that he needs Jesus in his life. Don't be distracted by the moral issue on the surface—whether that's cohabitation, homosexuality or abuse of alcohol. Jesus always saw past a person's external issues to her spiritual need. In John 4, Jesus acknowledged the Samaritan woman's external sin (five marriages and cohabitation), yet he didn't dwell on that; he went straight to her true need: living water. Once a person gets Jesus in her life, her other issues will get worked out over time. We can be confident that the Samaritan woman made some lifestyle changes after she met Jesus—but only after she met Jesus.

- *Make your life attractive and irresistible to non-Christians.* Show your non-Christian friends that God has a better way. They are watching closely to see if your life is going any better than their lives.

- *Leave the results to God.* Jeremiah talked to the Israelites about repentance for years—and never saw any results. It was his job to speak up, and he fulfilled God's expectation of him. The rest was up to God.

If you have some people on your heart as you read these words, write their names down today, and ask God to give you an opportunity to speak to them. And if he does, approach them with love, confident that God's ways are best, but humble as you share with them to meet their true needs—just like your Savior did.

"60 percent of people ages 36 and older and 75 percent of adults 18 to 35 embraced moral relativism and rejected unchanging moral absolutes."
—Barna Research Group (2002)

"THE WAY OF FOOLS SEEMS RIGHT TO THEM, BUT THE WISE LISTEN TO ADVICE."

PROVERBS 12:15

SEE ALSO

For more on **Confrontation** and **Witnessing**, check the index.

king and what the king said to you; do not hide it from us or we will kill you,' ²⁶then tell them, 'I was pleading with the king not to send me back to Jonathan's house to die there.'"

²⁷All the officials did come to Jeremiah and question him, and he told them everything the king had ordered him to say. So they said no more to him, for no one had heard his conversation with the king.

²⁸And Jeremiah remained in the courtyard of the guard until the day Jerusalem was captured.

The Fall of Jerusalem

39 This is how Jerusalem was taken: ¹In the ninth year of Zedekiah king of Judah, in the tenth month, Nebuchadnezzar king of Babylon marched against Jerusalem with his whole army and laid siege to it. ²And on the ninth day of the fourth month of Zedekiah's eleventh year, the city wall was broken through. ³Then all the officials of the king of Babylon came and took seats in the Middle Gate: Nergal-Sharezer of Samgar, Nebo-Sarsekim*ᵃ* a chief officer, Nergal-Sharezer a high official and all the other officials of the king of Babylon. ⁴When Zedekiah king of Judah and all the soldiers saw them, they fled; they left the city at night by way of the king's garden, through the gate between the two walls, and headed toward the Arabah.*ᵇ*

⁵But the Babylonian*ᶜ* army pursued them and overtook Zedekiah in the plains of Jericho. They captured him and took him to Nebuchadnezzar king of Babylon at Riblah in the land of Hamath, where he pronounced sentence on him. ⁶There at Riblah the king of Babylon slaughtered the sons of Zedekiah before his eyes and also killed all the nobles of Judah. ⁷Then he put out Zedekiah's eyes and bound him with bronze shackles to take him to Babylon.

⁸The Babylonians*ᵈ* set fire to the royal palace and the houses of the people and broke down the walls of Jerusalem. ⁹Nebuzaradan commander of the imperial guard carried into exile to Babylon the people who remained in the city, along with those who had gone over to him, and the rest of the people. ¹⁰But Nebuzaradan the commander of the guard left behind in the land of Judah some of the poor people, who owned nothing; and at that time he gave them vineyards and fields.

¹¹Now Nebuchadnezzar king of Babylon had given these orders about Jeremiah through Nebuzaradan commander of the imperial guard: ¹²"Take him and look after him; don't harm him but do for him whatever he asks." ¹³So Nebuzaradan the commander of the guard, Nebushazban a chief officer, Nergal-Sharezer a high official and all the other officers of the king of Babylon ¹⁴sent and had Jeremiah taken out of the courtyard of the guard. They turned him over to Gedaliah son of Ahikam, the son of Shaphan, to take him back to his home. So he remained among his own people.

¹⁵While Jeremiah had been confined in the courtyard of the guard, the word of the Lord came to him: ¹⁶"Go and tell Ebed-Melek the Cushite, 'This is what the Lord Almighty, the God of Israel, says: I am about to fulfill my words against this city—words concerning disaster, not prosperity. At that time they will be fulfilled before your eyes. ¹⁷But I will rescue you on that day, declares the Lord; you will not be given into the hands of those you fear. ¹⁸I will save you; you will not fall by the sword but will escape with your life, because you trust in me, declares the Lord.'"

ᵃ 3 Or Nergal-Sharezer, Samgar-Nebo, Sarsekim   ᵇ 4 Or the Jordan Valley   ᶜ 5 Or Chaldean   ᵈ 8 Or Chaldeans

HE IS: the rescuer

39:17–18 The long-prophesied time of destruction and captivity had arrived, and the Babylonians marched against Jerusalem. Yet God showed mercy to Ebed-Melek, who had interceded on Jeremiah's behalf. And God promised Ebed-Melek, "I will rescue you on that day . . . because you trust in me."

A time of judgment is coming upon the earth, but you have nothing to fear if you have put your trust in the Lord Jesus. He is *the rescuer*. If you have chosen Jesus, you will be saved. However, if you have not repented, he will not rescue you—and you cannot rescue yourself.

For the next He Is, go to p. 1150.

Jeremiah Freed

40 The word came to Jeremiah from the LORD after Nebuzaradan commander of the imperial guard had released him at Ramah. He had found Jeremiah bound in chains among all the captives from Jerusalem and Judah who were being carried into exile to Babylon. [2] When the commander of the guard found Jeremiah, he said to him, "The LORD your God decreed this disaster for this place. [3] And now the LORD has brought it about; he has done just as he said he would. All this happened because you people sinned against the LORD and did not obey him. [4] But today I am freeing you from the chains on your wrists. Come with me to Babylon, if you like, and I will look after you; but if you do not want to, then don't come. Look, the whole country lies before you; go wherever you please." [5] However, before Jeremiah turned to go,[a] Nebuzaradan added, "Go back to Gedaliah son of Ahikam, the son of Shaphan, whom the king of Babylon has appointed over the towns of Judah, and live with him among the people, or go anywhere else you please."

Then the commander gave him provisions and a present and let him go. [6] So Jeremiah went to Gedaliah son of Ahikam at Mizpah and stayed with him among the people who were left behind in the land.

Gedaliah Assassinated

[7] When all the army officers and their men who were still in the open country heard that the king of Babylon had appointed Gedaliah son of Ahikam as governor over the land and had put him in charge of the men, women and children who were the poorest in the land and who had not been carried into exile to Babylon, [8] they came to Gedaliah at Mizpah—Ishmael son of Nethaniah, Johanan and Jonathan the sons of Kareah, Seraiah son of Tanhumeth, the sons of Ephai the Netophathite, and Jaazaniah[b] the son of the Maakathite, and their men. [9] Gedaliah son of Ahikam, the son of Shaphan, took an oath to reassure them and their men. "Do not be afraid to serve the Babylonians,[c]" he said. "Settle down in the land and serve the king of Babylon, and it will go well with you. [10] I myself will stay at Mizpah to represent you before the Babylonians who come to us, but you are to harvest the wine, summer fruit and olive oil, and put them in your storage jars, and live in the towns you have taken over."

[11] When all the Jews in Moab, Ammon, Edom and all the other countries heard that the king of Babylon had left a remnant in Judah and had appointed Gedaliah son of Ahikam, the son of Shaphan, as governor over them, [12] they all came back to the land of Judah, to Gedaliah at Mizpah, from all the countries where they had been scattered. And they harvested an abundance of wine and summer fruit.

[13] Johanan son of Kareah and all the army officers still in the open country came to Gedaliah at Mizpah [14] and said to him, "Don't you know that Baalis king of the Ammonites has sent Ishmael son of Nethaniah to take your life?" But Gedaliah son of Ahikam did not believe them.

[15] Then Johanan son of Kareah said privately to Gedaliah in Mizpah, "Let me go and kill Ishmael son of Nethaniah, and no one will know it. Why should he take your life and cause all the Jews who are gathered around you to be scattered and the remnant of Judah to perish?"

[16] But Gedaliah son of Ahikam said to Johanan son of Kareah, "Don't do such a thing! What you are saying about Ishmael is not true."

41 In the seventh month Ishmael son of Nethaniah, the son of Elishama, who was of royal blood and had been one of the king's officers, came with ten men to Gedaliah son of Ahikam at Mizpah. While they were eating together there, [2] Ishmael son of Nethaniah and the ten men who were with him got up and struck down Gedaliah son of Ahikam, the son of Shaphan, with the sword, killing the one whom the king of Babylon had appointed as governor over the land. [3] Ishmael also killed all the men of Judah who were with Gedaliah at Mizpah, as well as the Babylonian[d] soldiers who were there.

[4] The day after Gedaliah's assassination, before anyone knew about it, [5] eighty men who had shaved off their beards, torn their clothes and cut themselves came from Shechem, Shiloh and Samaria, bringing grain offerings and incense with them to the house of the LORD. [6] Ishmael son of Nethaniah went out from Mizpah to meet them, weeping as he went. When he met them, he said, "Come to Gedaliah son of Ahikam." [7] When they went into the city, Ishmael son of Nethaniah and the men who were with him

slaughtered them and threw them into a cistern. [8]But ten of them said to Ishmael, "Don't kill us! We have wheat and barley, olive oil and honey, hidden in a field." So he let them alone and did not kill them with the others. [9]Now the cistern where he threw all the bodies of the men he had killed along with Gedaliah was the one King Asa had made as part of his defense against Baasha king of Israel. Ishmael son of Nethaniah filled it with the dead.

[10]Ishmael made captives of all the rest of the people who were in Mizpah—the king's daughters along with all the others who were left there, over whom Nebuzaradan commander of the imperial guard had appointed Gedaliah son of Ahikam. Ishmael son of Nethaniah took them captive and set out to cross over to the Ammonites.

[11]When Johanan son of Kareah and all the army officers who were with him heard about all the crimes Ishmael son of Nethaniah had committed, [12]they took all their men and went to fight Ishmael son of Nethaniah. They caught up with him near the great pool in Gibeon. [13]When all the people Ishmael had with him saw Johanan son of Kareah and the army officers who were with him, they were glad. [14]All the people Ishmael had taken captive at Mizpah turned and went over to Johanan son of Kareah. [15]But Ishmael son of Nethaniah and eight of his men escaped from Johanan and fled to the Ammonites.

Flight to Egypt

[16]Then Johanan son of Kareah and all the army officers who were with him led away all the people of Mizpah who had survived, whom Johanan had recovered from Ishmael son of Nethaniah after Ishmael had assassinated Gedaliah son of Ahikam—the soldiers, women, children and court officials he had recovered from Gibeon. [17]And they went on, stopping at Geruth Kimham near Bethlehem on their way to Egypt [18]to escape the Babylonians.[a] They were afraid of them because Ishmael son of Nethaniah had killed Gedaliah son of Ahikam, whom the king of Babylon had appointed as governor over the land.

42 Then all the army officers, including Johanan son of Kareah and Jezaniah[b] son of Hoshaiah, and all the people from the least to the greatest approached [2]Jeremiah the prophet and said to him, "Please hear our petition and pray to the LORD your God for this entire remnant. For as you now see, though we were once many, now only a few are left. [3]Pray that the LORD your God will tell us where we should go and what we should do."

[4]"I have heard you," replied Jeremiah the prophet. "I will certainly pray to the LORD your God as you have requested; I will tell you everything the LORD says and will keep nothing back from you."

[5]Then they said to Jeremiah, "May the LORD be a true and faithful witness against us if we do not act in accordance with everything the LORD your God sends you to tell us. [6]Whether it is favorable or unfavorable, we will obey the LORD our God, to whom we are sending you, so that it will go well with us, for we will obey the LORD our God."

[7]Ten days later the word of the LORD came to Jeremiah. [8]So he called together Johanan son of Kareah and all the army officers who were with him and all the people from the least to the greatest. [9]He said to them, "This is what the LORD, the God of Israel, to whom you sent me to present your petition, says: [10]'If you stay in this land, I will build you up and not tear you down; I will plant you and not uproot you, for I have relented concerning the disaster I have inflicted on you. [11]Do not be afraid of the king of Babylon, whom you now fear. Do not be afraid of him, declares the LORD, for I am with you and will save you and deliver you from his hands. [12]I will show you compassion so that he will have compassion on you and restore you to your land.'

[13]"However, if you say, 'We will not stay in this land,' and so disobey the LORD your God, [14]and if you say, 'No, we will go and live in Egypt, where we will not see war or hear the trumpet or be hungry for bread,' [15]then hear the word of the LORD, you remnant of Judah. This is what the LORD Almighty, the God of Israel, says: 'If you are determined to go to Egypt and you do go to settle there, [16]then the sword you fear will overtake you there, and the famine you dread will follow you into Egypt, and there you will die. [17]Indeed, all who are determined to go to Egypt to settle there will die by the sword, famine and plague; not one of them will survive or escape the disaster I will bring on them.' [18]This is what the LORD Almighty, the God of Israel, says: 'As my anger and wrath have been poured out on those who lived in Jerusalem,

---

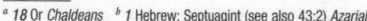

[a] 18 Or *Chaldeans*   [b] 1 Hebrew; Septuagint (see also 43:2) *Azariah*

so will my wrath be poured out on you when you go to Egypt. You will be a curse^{*a*} and an object of horror, a curse^{*a*} and an object of reproach; you will never see this place again.'

¹⁹"Remnant of Judah, the LORD has told you, 'Do not go to Egypt.' Be sure of this: I warn you today ²⁰that you made a fatal mistake when you sent me to the LORD your God and said, 'Pray to the LORD our God for us; tell us everything he says and we will do it.' ²¹I have told you today, but you still have not obeyed the LORD your God in all he sent me to tell you. ²²So now, be sure of this: You will die by the sword, famine and plague in the place where you want to go to settle."

43 When Jeremiah had finished telling the people all the words of the LORD their God—everything the LORD had sent him to tell them— ²Azariah son of Hoshaiah and Johanan son of Kareah and all the arrogant men said to Jeremiah, "You are lying! The LORD our God has not sent you to say, 'You must not go to Egypt to settle there.' ³But Baruch son of Neriah is inciting you against us to hand us over to the Babylonians,^{*b*} so they may kill us or carry us into exile to Babylon."

⁴So Johanan son of Kareah and all the army officers and all the people disobeyed the LORD's command to stay in the land of Judah. ⁵Instead, Johanan son of Kareah and all the army officers led away all the remnant of Judah who had come back to live in the land of Judah from all the nations where they had been scattered. ⁶They also led away all those whom Nebuzaradan commander of the imperial guard had left with Gedaliah son of Ahikam, the son of Shaphan—the men, the women, the children and the king's daughters. And they took Jeremiah the prophet and Baruch son of Neriah along with them. ⁷So they entered Egypt in disobedience to the LORD and went as far as Tahpanhes.

1145

⁸In Tahpanhes the word of the LORD came to Jeremiah: ⁹"While the Jews are watching, take some large stones with you and bury them in clay in the brick pavement at the entrance to Pharaoh's palace in Tahpanhes. ¹⁰Then say to them, 'This is what the LORD Almighty, the God of Israel, says: I will send for my servant Nebuchadnezzar king of Babylon, and I will set his throne over these stones I have buried here; he will spread his royal canopy above them. ¹¹He will come and attack Egypt, bringing death to those destined for death, captivity to those destined for captivity, and the sword to those destined for the sword. ¹²He will set fire to the temples of the gods of Egypt; he will burn their temples and take their gods captive. As a shepherd picks his garment clean of lice, so he will pick Egypt clean and depart. ¹³There in the temple of the sun^{*c*} in Egypt he will demolish the sacred pillars and will burn down the temples of the gods of Egypt.'"

Disaster Because of Idolatry

44 This word came to Jeremiah concerning all the Jews living in Lower Egypt—in Migdol, Tahpanhes and Memphis—and in Upper Egypt: ²"This is what the LORD Almighty, the God of Israel, says: You saw the great disaster I brought on Jerusalem and on all the towns of Judah. Today they lie deserted and in ruins ³because of the evil they have done. They aroused my anger by burning incense to and worshiping other gods that neither they nor you nor your ancestors ever knew. ⁴Again and again I sent my servants the prophets, who said, 'Do not do this detestable thing that I hate!' ⁵But they did not listen or pay attention; they did not turn from their wickedness or stop burning incense to other gods. ⁶Therefore, my fierce anger was poured out; it raged against the towns of Judah and the streets of Jerusalem and made them the desolate ruins they are today.

⁷"Now this is what the LORD God Almighty, the God of Israel, says: Why bring such great disaster on yourselves by cutting off from Judah the men and women, the children and infants, and so leave yourselves without a remnant? ⁸Why arouse my anger with what your hands have made, burning incense to other gods in Egypt, where you have come to live? You will destroy yourselves and make yourselves a curse^{*d*} and an object of reproach among all the nations on earth. ⁹Have you forgotten the wickedness committed by your ancestors and by the kings and queens of Judah and the wickedness committed by you and your wives in the land of Judah and the streets of Jerusalem? ¹⁰To this day they have not humbled themselves or shown reverence, nor have they followed my law and the decrees I set before you and your ancestors.

---

^{*a*} *18* That is, your name will be used in cursing (see Jer. 29:22); or, others will see that you are cursed.   ^{*b*} *3* Or *Chaldeans*   ^{*c*} *13* Or *in Heliopolis*   ^{*d*} *8* That is, your name will be used in cursing (see Jer. 29:22); or, others will see that you are cursed; also in verse 12; similarly in verse 22.

myth# 66

"I CAN STILL HAVE CLOSE MALE FRIENDS AFTER I'M MARRIED."

I've always felt closer to men than women. It's probably because I have five older brothers who have always treated me like a princess. I've just never felt as comfortable around women.

When I decided to get married, my family was so excited for me. I think my brothers were relieved I wouldn't be dating any more. They found that more stressful than I did. Last week, however, something came up in a conversation with my family, and I'm not sure what to think about it.

I still have three close male friends from college and one from work, and I don't know how Steve, my fiancé, will handle that when we're married. My mom asked me how Steve felt about my spending time with my guy friends. I told her that he hasn't said anything about it. He seems fine with the situation, and I think he likes those guys. When I mentioned that I still have lunch alone with my friend from work every week, my brothers looked skeptical. "Steve is very secure," I retorted. They argued that every guy is jealous of a woman's male friends—and if he isn't, he should be.

My friends have been important to me through the years. They were there for me during some tough times before I even knew Steve—when my father died and I struggled with depression. I'm not sure how things will change once we're married. I know they'll still be my friends, but I'm not sure how close I can be to them. I'd hate to lose their friendship when they've been so faithful to me.

—Heidi

THIS MYTH IS a popular one today. Many people, Christians and non-Christians, flirt with danger by maintaining close friendships with the opposite sex after they get married. Even secular experts agree that intimate friendships with the opposite sex can be a breeding ground for emotional infidelity. Yet many people don't see the potential for harm. If you or a friend is struggling with this issue, consider the following guidelines:

- **Think about how you would feel if the roles were reversed.** How comfortable would you feel if your husband had a close, intimate, female friend? Would you mind if he's sharing personal information with another woman? Spending time alone with her? Building dependence on her and meeting her needs?

- **Be realistic about your emotional needs.** Some women unwittingly allow someone else to meet their emotional needs—even under the guise of friendship. Do you need someone to listen to you and understand you? If you're married, that *someone* needs to be your husband.

- **Invest in your marriage.** If your marriage isn't all it should be and if your husband isn't meeting your needs, work on your marriage rather than looking outside your marriage to get your needs met. Find a couple whose marriage you admire, and ask them to mentor you. Or find a Christian marriage counselor with whom you both feel comfortable.

- **Build moral fences to protect yourself and your marriage.** The dissolution of a marriage usually begins with small choices, mini-betrayals that multiply over time. And Satan is just waiting for you to show weakness (see 1 Peter 5:8). Many good Christians have had moral lapses that cost them their marriage. How can you protect yourself? Establish clear, strict boundaries that you and your husband will both abide by. For example, limit the amount of time you spend with someone of the opposite sex, and develop guidelines you both follow regarding being alone with someone of the opposite sex.

At the end of the day, close male-female friendships after marriage do not work. That doesn't mean you can't have male friends. It does mean that your male friends shouldn't be your closest friends.

"Even if you never touch this other person, you have still used another person to relate to, and in doing so, you relate away from your spouse."

—M. Gary Neuman,
Emotional Infidelity

"BUT AMONG YOU THERE MUST NOT EVEN BE A HINT OF SEXUAL IMMORALITY, OR OF ANY KIND OF IMPURITY, OR OF GREED, BECAUSE THESE ARE IMPROPER FOR THE LORD'S PEOPLE."

EPHESIANS 5:3

SEE ALSO
Matthew 18:7–9
Mark 10:7–9
1 Corinthians 7:2–5

For more on **Marriage** and **Relationships**, check the index.

¹¹ "Therefore, this is what the LORD Almighty, the God of Israel, says: I am determined to bring disaster on you and to destroy all Judah. ¹²I will take away the remnant of Judah who were determined to go to Egypt to settle there. They will all perish in Egypt; they will fall by the sword or die from famine. From the least to the greatest, they will die by sword or famine. They will become a curse and an object of horror, a curse and an object of reproach. ¹³I will punish those who live in Egypt with the sword, famine and plague, as I punished Jerusalem. ¹⁴None of the remnant of Judah who have gone to live in Egypt will escape or survive to return to the land of Judah, to which they long to return and live; none will return except a few fugitives."

¹⁵Then all the men who knew that their wives were burning incense to other gods, along with all the women who were present—a large assembly—and all the people living in Lower and Upper Egypt, said to Jeremiah, ¹⁶ "We will not listen to the message you have spoken to us in the name of the LORD! ¹⁷We will certainly do everything we said we would: We will burn incense to the Queen of Heaven and will pour out drink offerings to her just as we and our ancestors, our kings and our officials did in the towns of Judah and in the streets of Jerusalem. At that time we had plenty of food and were well off and suffered no harm. ¹⁸But ever since we stopped burning incense to the Queen of Heaven and pouring out drink offerings to her, we have had nothing and have been perishing by sword and famine."

conversations

communication «» 44:15–30

1 ›› Have you had to deliver a hard message from God to someone who didn't want to hear it?

2 ›› Have you had to hear a hard message from God? How responsive were you to it?

3 ›› How can you best communicate your message to someone who's opposed to the truth?

For more on **communication**, check the index. For the next Conversations, go to p. 1149.

¹⁹The women added, "When we burned incense to the Queen of Heaven and poured out drink offerings to her, did not our husbands know that we were making cakes impressed with her image and pouring out drink offerings to her?"

²⁰Then Jeremiah said to all the people, both men and women, who were answering him, ²¹ "Did not the LORD remember and call to mind the incense burned in the towns of Judah and the streets of Jerusalem by you and your ancestors, your kings and your officials and the people of the land? ²²When the LORD could no longer endure your wicked actions and the detestable things you did, your land became a curse and a desolate waste without inhabitants, as it is today. ²³Because you have burned incense and have sinned against the LORD and have not obeyed him or followed his law or his decrees or his stipulations, this disaster has come upon you, as you now see."

²⁴Then Jeremiah said to all the people, including the women, "Hear the word of the LORD, all you people of Judah in Egypt. ²⁵This is what the LORD Almighty, the God of Israel, says: You and your wives have done what you said you would do when you promised, 'We will certainly carry out the vows we made to burn incense and pour out drink offerings to the Queen of Heaven.'

"Go ahead then, do what you promised! Keep your vows! ²⁶But hear the word of the LORD, all you Jews living in Egypt: 'I swear by my great name,' says the LORD, 'that no one from Judah living anywhere in Egypt will ever again invoke my name or swear, "As surely as the Sovereign LORD lives." ²⁷For I am watching over them for harm, not for good; the Jews in Egypt will perish by sword and famine until they are all destroyed. ²⁸Those who escape the sword and return to the land of Judah from Egypt will be very few. Then the whole remnant of Judah who came to live in Egypt will know whose word will stand—mine or theirs.

²⁹ "This will be the sign to you that I will punish you in this place,' declares the LORD, 'so that you will know that my threats of harm against you will surely stand.' ³⁰This is what the LORD says: 'I am going to deliver Pharaoh Hophra king of Egypt into the hands of his enemies who seek his life, just as I gave Zedekiah king of Judah into the hands of Nebuchadnezzar king of Babylon, the enemy who was seeking his life.'"

A Message to Baruch

45 When Baruch son of Neriah wrote on a scroll the words Jeremiah the prophet dictated in the fourth year of Jehoiakim son of Josiah king of Judah, Jeremiah said this to Baruch: ²"This is what the LORD, the God of Israel, says to you, Baruch: ³You said, 'Woe to me! The LORD has added sorrow to my pain; I am worn out with groaning and find no rest.' ⁴But the LORD has told me to say to you, 'This is what the LORD says: I will overthrow what I have built and uproot what I have planted, throughout the earth. ⁵Should you then seek great things for yourself? Do not seek them. For I will bring disaster on all people, declares the LORD, but wherever you go I will let you escape with your life.'"

A Message About Egypt

46 This is the word of the LORD that came to Jeremiah the prophet concerning the nations:

²Concerning Egypt:

This is the message against the army of Pharaoh Necho king of Egypt, which was defeated at Carchemish on the Euphrates River by Nebuchadnezzar king of Babylon in the fourth year of Jehoiakim son of Josiah king of Judah:

³"Prepare your shields, both large and small,
   and march out for battle!
⁴Harness the horses,
   mount the steeds!
Take your positions
   with helmets on!
Polish your spears,
   put on your armor!
⁵What do I see?
   They are terrified,
they are retreating,
   their warriors are defeated.
They flee in haste
   without looking back,
   and there is terror on every side,"
      declares the LORD.
⁶"The swift cannot flee
   nor the strong escape.
In the north by the River Euphrates
   they stumble and fall.

⁷"Who is this that rises like the Nile,
   like rivers of surging waters?
⁸Egypt rises like the Nile,
   like rivers of surging waters.
She says, 'I will rise and cover the earth;
   I will destroy cities and their people.'
⁹Charge, you horses!
   Drive furiously, you charioteers!

conversations

selfishness «» 45:4–5

1 » When have you experienced pain or sorrow because of your selfish choices?

2 » When have you allowed God to alter your plans?

3 » What does it mean to have a selfless attitude in response to God's plans?

For more on **selfishness**, check the index.
For the next Conversations, go to p. 1154.

March on, you warriors—men of Cush[a] and Put who carry shields,
men of Lydia who draw the bow.
[10] But that day belongs to the Lord, the LORD Almighty—
a day of vengeance, for vengeance on his foes.
The sword will devour till it is satisfied,
till it has quenched its thirst with blood.
For the Lord, the LORD Almighty, will offer sacrifice
in the land of the north by the River Euphrates.

[11] "Go up to Gilead and get balm,
Virgin Daughter Egypt.
But you multiply remedies in vain;
there is no healing for you.
[12] The nations will hear of your shame;
your cries will fill the earth.
One warrior will stumble over another;
both will fall down together."

[13] This is the message the LORD spoke to Jeremiah the prophet about the coming of Nebuchadnezzar king of Babylon to attack Egypt:

[14] "Announce this in Egypt, and proclaim it in Migdol;
proclaim it also in Memphis and Tahpanhes:
'Take your positions and get ready,
for the sword devours those around you.'
[15] Why will your warriors be laid low?
They cannot stand, for the LORD will push them down.
[16] They will stumble repeatedly;
they will fall over each other.
They will say, 'Get up, let us go back
to our own people and our native lands,
away from the sword of the oppressor.'
[17] There they will exclaim,
'Pharaoh king of Egypt is only a loud noise;
he has missed his opportunity.'

[18] "As surely as I live," declares the King,
whose name is the LORD Almighty,
"one will come who is like Tabor among the mountains,

---

[a] *9* That is, the upper Nile region

HE IS: the true king

46:18–28 After scolding his own people, God turned his prophetic attention to the Gentile nations. Through Jeremiah he predicted that he would bring punishment on Pharaoh, king of Egypt; on Egypt itself; the gods of Egypt; and on those who relied on Pharaoh. Thus, God would prove that he is *the true king*, who controls the fate of nations.

While God does intervene in the world's kingdoms, he is also busy establishing his kingdom of heaven (see John 18:36–37). He wants to be *the true king* of your soul. Don't be like Pharaoh, who missed his opportunity; instead place God on your heart's throne today.

For the next He Is, go to p. 1166.

      like Carmel by the sea.
¹⁹ Pack your belongings for exile,
    you who live in Egypt,
  for Memphis will be laid waste
    and lie in ruins without inhabitant.

²⁰ "Egypt is a beautiful heifer,
    but a gadfly is coming
    against her from the north.
²¹ The mercenaries in her ranks
    are like fattened calves.
  They too will turn and flee together,
    they will not stand their ground,
  for the day of disaster is coming upon them,
    the time for them to be punished.
²² Egypt will hiss like a fleeing serpent
    as the enemy advances in force;
  they will come against her with axes,
    like those who cut down trees.
²³ They will chop down her forest,"

                                 declares the LORD,

    "dense though it be.
  They are more numerous than locusts,
    they cannot be counted.
²⁴ Daughter Egypt will be put to shame,
    given into the hands of the people of the north."

²⁵ The LORD Almighty, the God of Israel, says: "I am about to bring punishment on Amon god of Thebes, on Pharaoh, on Egypt and her gods and her kings, and on those who rely on Pharaoh. ²⁶ I will give them into the hands of those who seek their lives—Nebuchadnezzar king of Babylon and his officers. Later, however, Egypt will be inhabited as in times past," declares the LORD.

²⁷ "Do not be afraid, Jacob my servant;
    do not be dismayed, Israel.
  I will surely save you out of a distant place,
    your descendants from the land of their exile.
  Jacob will again have peace and security,
    and no one will make him afraid.
²⁸ Do not be afraid, Jacob my servant,
    for I am with you," declares the LORD.
  "Though I completely destroy all the nations
    among which I scatter you,
  I will not completely destroy you.
  I will discipline you but only in due measure;
    I will not let you go entirely unpunished."

A Message About the Philistines

47 This is the word of the LORD that came to Jeremiah the prophet concerning the Philistines before Pharaoh attacked Gaza:

² This is what the LORD says:

    "See how the waters are rising in the north;
    they will become an overflowing torrent.

1151

They will overflow the land and everything in it,
the towns and those who live in them.
The people will cry out;
all who dwell in the land will wail
[3]at the sound of the hooves of galloping steeds,
at the noise of enemy chariots
and the rumble of their wheels.
Parents will not turn to help their children;
their hands will hang limp.
[4]For the day has come
to destroy all the Philistines
and to remove all survivors
who could help Tyre and Sidon.
The LORD is about to destroy the Philistines,
the remnant from the coasts of Caphtor.[a]
[5]Gaza will shave her head in mourning;
Ashkelon will be silenced.
You remnant on the plain,
how long will you cut yourselves?

[6]"'Ah, sword of the LORD,' you cry,
'how long till you rest?
Return to your sheath;
cease and be still.'
[7]But how can it rest
when the LORD has commanded it,
when he has ordered it
to attack Ashkelon and the coast?"

A Message About Moab

48

Concerning Moab:

This is what the LORD Almighty, the God of Israel, says:

"Woe to Nebo, for it will be ruined.
Kiriathaim will be disgraced and captured;
the stronghold[b] will be disgraced and shattered.
[2]Moab will be praised no more;
in Heshbon[c] people will plot her downfall:
'Come, let us put an end to that nation.'
You, the people of Madmen,[d] will also be silenced;
the sword will pursue you.
[3]Cries of anguish arise from Horonaim,
cries of great havoc and destruction.
[4]Moab will be broken;
her little ones will cry out.[e]
[5]They go up the hill to Luhith,
weeping bitterly as they go;
on the road down to Horonaim
anguished cries over the destruction are heard.

---

a 4 That is, Crete   *b 1* Or *captured; / Misgab*   *c 2* The Hebrew for *Heshbon* sounds like the Hebrew for *plot.*   *d 2* The name of the Moabite town Madmen sounds like the Hebrew for *be silenced.*   *e 4* Hebrew; Septuagint / *proclaim it to Zoar*

⁶Flee! Run for your lives;
    become like a bush*ᵃ* in the desert.
⁷Since you trust in your deeds and riches,
    you too will be taken captive,
and Chemosh will go into exile,
    together with his priests and officials.
⁸The destroyer will come against every town,
    and not a town will escape.
The valley will be ruined
    and the plateau destroyed,
    because the LORD has spoken.
⁹Put salt on Moab,
    for she will be laid waste*ᵇ*;
her towns will become desolate,
    with no one to live in them.

¹⁰"A curse on those who are lax in doing the LORD's work!
    A curse on those who keep their swords from bloodshed!

¹¹"Moab has been at rest from youth,
    like wine left on its dregs,
not poured from one jar to another—
    she has not gone into exile.
So she tastes as she did,
    and her aroma is unchanged.
¹²But days are coming,"
    declares the LORD,
"when I will send people who pour from jars,
    and they will pour her out;
they will empty her jars
    and smash her jugs.
¹³Then Moab will be ashamed of Chemosh,
    as the house of Israel was ashamed
    when they trusted in Bethel.

¹⁴"How can you say, 'We are warriors,
    men valiant in battle'?
¹⁵Moab will be destroyed and her towns invaded;
    her finest young men will go down in the slaughter,"
    declares the King, whose name is the LORD Almighty.
¹⁶"The fall of Moab is at hand;
    her calamity will come quickly.
¹⁷Mourn for her, all who live around her,
    all who know her fame;
say, 'How broken is the mighty scepter,
    how broken the glorious staff!'

¹⁸"Come down from your glory
    and sit on the parched ground,
    you inhabitants of Daughter Dibon,
for Moab's destroyer
    will come up against you

ᵃ 6 Or like Aroer   ᵇ 9 Or Give wings to Moab, / for she will fly away

and ruin your fortified cities.
¹⁹Stand by the road and watch,
    you who live in Aroer.
Ask the man fleeing and the woman escaping,
    ask them, 'What has happened?'
²⁰Moab is disgraced, for she is shattered.
    Wail and cry out!
Announce by the Arnon
    that Moab is destroyed.
²¹Judgment has come to the plateau—
    to Holon, Jahzah and Mephaath,
²²   to Dibon, Nebo and Beth Diblathaim,
²³   to Kiriathaim, Beth Gamul and Beth Meon,
²⁴   to Kerioth and Bozrah—
    to all the towns of Moab, far and near.
²⁵Moab's horn*ᵃ* is cut off;
    her arm is broken,"
        declares the LORD.

²⁶"Make her drunk,
    for she has defied the LORD.
Let Moab wallow in her vomit;
    let her be an object of ridicule.
²⁷Was not Israel the object of your ridicule?
    Was she caught among thieves,
that you shake your head in scorn
    whenever you speak of her?
²⁸Abandon your towns and dwell among the rocks,
    you who live in Moab.
Be like a dove that makes its nest
    at the mouth of a cave.

²⁹"We have heard of Moab's
        pride—
    her overweening pride and
        conceit,
her pride and arrogance
    and the haughtiness of her
        heart.
³⁰I know her insolence but it is
        futile,"
        declares the LORD,
    "and her boasts accomplish
        nothing.
³¹Therefore I wail over Moab,
    for all Moab I cry out,
    I moan for the people of Kir
        Hareseth.
³²I weep for you, as Jazer weeps,
    you vines of Sibmah.

conversations

pride «» 48:29–30

1 » Why is pride such a dangerous sin?

2 » Is it easy to conceal your pride? How?

3 » How can you recognize pride in your own life?

For more on **pride**, check the index.
For the next Conversations, go to p. 1157.

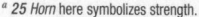

ᵃ 25 Horn here symbolizes strength.

Your branches spread as far as the sea*a*;
    they reached as far as*b* Jazer.
The destroyer has fallen
    on your ripened fruit and grapes.
³³Joy and gladness are gone
    from the orchards and fields of Moab.
I have stopped the flow of wine from the presses;
    no one treads them with shouts of joy.
Although there are shouts,
    they are not shouts of joy.

³⁴"The sound of their cry rises
    from Heshbon to Elealeh and Jahaz,
from Zoar as far as Horonaim and Eglath Shelishiyah,
    for even the waters of Nimrim are dried up.
³⁵In Moab I will put an end
    to those who make offerings on the high places
    and burn incense to their gods,"

                            declares the LORD.

1155

³⁶"So my heart laments for Moab like the music of a pipe;
    it laments like a pipe for the people of Kir Hareseth.
    The wealth they acquired is gone.
³⁷Every head is shaved
    and every beard cut off;
every hand is slashed
    and every waist is covered with sackcloth.
³⁸On all the roofs in Moab
    and in the public squares
there is nothing but mourning,
    for I have broken Moab
    like a jar that no one wants,"

                            declares the LORD.

³⁹"How shattered she is! How they wail!
    How Moab turns her back in shame!
Moab has become an object of ridicule,
    an object of horror to all those around her."

⁴⁰This is what the LORD says:

    "Look! An eagle is swooping down,
        spreading its wings over Moab.
⁴¹Kerioth*c* will be captured
    and the strongholds taken.
In that day the hearts of Moab's warriors
    will be like the heart of a woman in labor.
⁴²Moab will be destroyed as a nation
    because she defied the LORD.
⁴³Terror and pit and snare await you,
    you people of Moab,"

                            declares the LORD.

⁴⁴"Whoever flees from the terror

---

a 32 Probably the Dead Sea   *b 32* Two Hebrew manuscripts and Septuagint; most Hebrew manuscripts *as far as the Sea of*   *c 41* Or *The cities*

will fall into a pit,
    whoever climbs out of the pit
        will be caught in a snare;
    for I will bring on Moab
        the year of her punishment,"

declares the LORD.

⁴⁵"In the shadow of Heshbon
    the fugitives stand helpless,
for a fire has gone out from Heshbon,
    a blaze from the midst of Sihon;
it burns the foreheads of Moab,
    the skulls of the noisy boasters.
⁴⁶Woe to you, Moab!
    The people of Chemosh are destroyed;
your sons are taken into exile
    and your daughters into captivity.

⁴⁷"Yet I will restore the fortunes of Moab
    in days to come,"

declares the LORD.

Here ends the judgment on Moab.

A Message About Ammon

49 Concerning the Ammonites:

This is what the LORD says:

"Has Israel no children?
    Has she no heirs?
Why then has Molek*ᵃ* taken possession of Gad?
    Why do his people live in its towns?
²But the days are coming,"
    declares the LORD,
"when I will sound the battle cry
    against Rabbah of the Ammonites;
it will become a mound of ruins,
    and its surrounding villages will be set on fire.
Then Israel will drive out
    those who drove her out,"

says the LORD.

³"Wail, Heshbon, for Ai is destroyed!
    Cry out, you inhabitants of Rabbah!
Put on sackcloth and mourn;
    rush here and there inside the walls,
for Molek will go into exile,
    together with his priests and officials.
⁴Why do you boast of your valleys,
    boast of your valleys so fruitful?
Unfaithful Daughter Ammon,
    you trust in your riches and say,

ᵃ *1 Or* their king; *also in verse 3*

'Who will attack me?'
⁵I will bring terror on you
  from all those around you,"

                    declares the Lord, the LORD Almighty.

"Every one of you will be driven away,
  and no one will gather the fugitives.

⁶"Yet afterward, I will restore the fortunes of the Ammonites,"

                    declares the LORD.

A Message About Edom

⁷Concerning Edom:

This is what the LORD Almighty says:

"Is there no longer wisdom in Teman?
  Has counsel perished from the prudent?
  Has their wisdom decayed?
⁸Turn and flee, hide in deep caves,
  you who live in Dedan,
for I will bring disaster on Esau
  at the time when I punish him.
⁹If grape pickers came to you,
  would they not leave a few grapes?
If thieves came during the night,
  would they not steal only as much as
    they wanted?
¹⁰But I will strip Esau bare;
  I will uncover his hiding places,
  so that he cannot conceal himself.
His armed men are destroyed,
  also his allies and neighbors,
  so there is no one to say,
¹¹'Leave your fatherless children; I will
    keep them alive.
Your widows too can depend on me.'"

conversations

protection «» 49:11

1» Why does God promise special care for orphans and widows?

2» Describe a time when God clearly protected you.

3» What kinds of protection do you need in your life?

For more on **protection**, check the index.
For the next Conversations, go to p. 1183.

¹²This is what the LORD says: "If those who do not deserve to drink the cup must drink it, why should you go unpunished? You will not go unpunished, but must drink it. ¹³I swear by myself," declares the LORD, "that Bozrah will become a ruin and a curse,ᵃ an object of horror and reproach; and all its towns will be in ruins forever."

¹⁴I have heard a message from the LORD;
  an envoy was sent to the nations to say,
"Assemble yourselves to attack it!
  Rise up for battle!"

¹⁵"Now I will make you small among the nations,
  despised among the peoples.
¹⁶The terror you inspire
  and the pride of your heart have deceived you,
you who live in the clefts of the rocks,
  who occupy the heights of the hill.

ᵃ 13 That is, its name will be used in cursing (see Jer. 29:22); or, others will see that it is cursed.

Though you build your nest as high as the eagle's,
　　from there I will bring you down,"

declares the LORD.

¹⁷"Edom will become an object of horror;
　　all who pass by will be appalled and will scoff
　　because of all its wounds.
¹⁸As Sodom and Gomorrah were overthrown,
　　along with their neighboring towns,"

says the LORD,

"so no one will live there;
　　no one will dwell in it.

¹⁹"Like a lion coming up from Jordan's thickets
　　to a rich pastureland,
I will chase Edom from its land in an instant.
　　Who is the chosen one I will appoint for this?
Who is like me and who can challenge me?
　　And what shepherd can stand against me?"

²⁰Therefore, hear what the LORD has planned against Edom,
　　what he has purposed against those who live in Teman:
The young of the flock will be dragged away;
　　their pasture will be appalled at their fate.
²¹At the sound of their fall the earth will tremble;
　　their cry will resound to the Red Sea.^a
²²Look! An eagle will soar and swoop down,
　　spreading its wings over Bozrah.
In that day the hearts of Edom's warriors
　　will be like the heart of a woman in labor.

A Message About Damascus

²³Concerning Damascus:

"Hamath and Arpad are dismayed,
　　for they have heard bad news.
They are disheartened,
　　troubled like^b the restless sea.
²⁴Damascus has become feeble,
　　she has turned to flee
　　and panic has gripped her;
anguish and pain have seized her,
　　pain like that of a woman in labor.
²⁵Why has the city of renown not been abandoned,
　　the town in which I delight?
²⁶Surely, her young men will fall in the streets;
　　all her soldiers will be silenced in that day,"

declares the LORD Almighty.

²⁷"I will set fire to the walls of Damascus;
　　it will consume the fortresses of Ben-Hadad."

A Message About Kedar and Hazor

²⁸Concerning Kedar and the kingdoms of Hazor, which Nebuchadnezzar king of Babylon attacked:

^a 21 Or the Sea of Reeds ^b 23 Hebrew on or by

This is what the LORD says:

> "Arise, and attack Kedar
>> and destroy the people of the East.
> ²⁹Their tents and their flocks will be taken;
>> their shelters will be carried off
>> with all their goods and camels.
> People will shout to them,
>> 'Terror on every side!'

> ³⁰"Flee quickly away!
>> Stay in deep caves, you who live in Hazor,"

>> declares the LORD.

> "Nebuchadnezzar king of Babylon has plotted against you;
>> he has devised a plan against you.

> ³¹"Arise and attack a nation at ease,
>> which lives in confidence,"

>> declares the LORD,

> "a nation that has neither gates nor bars;
>> its people live far from danger.
> ³²Their camels will become plunder,
>> and their large herds will be booty.
> I will scatter to the winds those who are in distant places^a
>> and will bring disaster on them from every side,"

>> declares the LORD.

> ³³"Hazor will become a haunt of jackals,
>> a desolate place forever.
> No one will live there;
>> no one will dwell in it."

A Message About Elam

³⁴This is the word of the LORD that came to Jeremiah the prophet concerning Elam, early in the reign of Zedekiah king of Judah:

³⁵This is what the LORD Almighty says:

> "See, I will break the bow of Elam,
>> the mainstay of their might.
> ³⁶I will bring against Elam the four winds
>> from the four quarters of the heavens;
> I will scatter them to the four winds,
>> and there will not be a nation
>> where Elam's exiles do not go.
> ³⁷I will shatter Elam before their foes,
>> before those who seek their lives;
> I will bring disaster on them,
>> even my fierce anger,"

>> declares the LORD.

> "I will pursue them with the sword
>> until I have made an end of them.
> ³⁸I will set my throne in Elam

---

^a *32 Or who clip the hair by their foreheads*

and destroy her king and officials,"

> declares the LORD.

³⁹"Yet I will restore the fortunes of Elam
   in days to come,"

> declares the LORD.

A Message About Babylon

50 This is the word the LORD spoke through Jeremiah the prophet concerning Babylon and the land of the Babylonians^a:

²"Announce and proclaim among the nations,
   lift up a banner and proclaim it;
   keep nothing back, but say,
'Babylon will be captured;
   Bel will be put to shame,
   Marduk filled with terror.
Her images will be put to shame
   and her idols filled with terror.'
³A nation from the north will attack her
   and lay waste her land.
No one will live in it;
   both people and animals will flee away.

⁴"In those days, at that time,"
   declares the LORD,
"the people of Israel and the people of Judah together
   will go in tears to seek the LORD their God.
⁵They will ask the way to Zion
   and turn their faces toward it.
They will come and bind themselves to the LORD
   in an everlasting covenant
   that will not be forgotten.

⁶"My people have been lost sheep;
   their shepherds have led them astray
   and caused them to roam on the mountains.
They wandered over mountain and hill
   and forgot their own resting place.
⁷Whoever found them devoured them;
   their enemies said, 'We are not guilty,
for they sinned against the LORD, their verdant pasture,
   the LORD, the hope of their ancestors.'

⁸"Flee out of Babylon;
   leave the land of the Babylonians,
   and be like the goats that lead the flock.
⁹For I will stir up and bring against Babylon
   an alliance of great nations from the land of the north.
They will take up their positions against her,
   and from the north she will be captured.
Their arrows will be like skilled warriors

---

^a *1 Or Chaldeans*; also in verses 8, 25, 35 and 45

who do not return empty-handed.
¹⁰So Babylonia*a* will be plundered;
    all who plunder her will have their fill,"

                        declares the Lord.

¹¹"Because you rejoice and are glad,
    you who pillage my inheritance,
because you frolic like a heifer threshing grain
    and neigh like stallions,
¹²your mother will be greatly ashamed;
    she who gave you birth will be disgraced.
She will be the least of the nations—
    a wilderness, a dry land, a desert.
¹³Because of the Lord's anger she will not be inhabited
    but will be completely desolate.
All who pass Babylon will be appalled;
    they will scoff because of all her wounds.

¹⁴"Take up your positions around Babylon,
    all you who draw the bow.
Shoot at her! Spare no arrows,
    for she has sinned against the Lord.
¹⁵Shout against her on every side!
    She surrenders, her towers fall,
    her walls are torn down.
Since this is the vengeance of the Lord,
    take vengeance on her;
    do to her as she has done to others.
¹⁶Cut off from Babylon the sowers,
    and the reapers with their sickles at harvest.
Because of the sword of the oppressor
    let everyone return to their own people,
    let everyone flee to their own land.

¹⁷"Israel is a scattered flock
    that lions have chased away.
The first to devour them
    was the king of Assyria;
the last to crush their bones
    was Nebuchadnezzar king of Babylon."
¹⁸Therefore this is what the Lord Almighty, the God of Israel, says:

    "I will punish the king of Babylon and his land
        as I punished the king of Assyria.
¹⁹But I will bring Israel back to their own pasture,
    and they will graze on Carmel and Bashan;
their appetite will be satisfied
    on the hills of Ephraim and Gilead.
²⁰In those days, at that time,"
    declares the Lord,
"search will be made for Israel's guilt,
    but there will be none,

---

myth# 67 "TIME THAT COUNTS WITH MY KIDS IS *QUALITY, NOT QUANTITY.*"

As a VP of a telecomm company, I know I'm busier than most moms. My husband has his own successful dental practice. Our daughter, Emily, is very intelligent and driven to succeed, much like her parents. I'm glad we can afford extra tutoring twice a week for her to ensure her science and math scores are where they should be. She wants to go to our alma mater, and we couldn't be more thrilled. She does Tae Kwon Do, plays soccer and piano and just made swim team for her sophomore year. I know Emily appreciates her father's sacrifices and my hard work to be able to provide her with all these opportunities.

Her nanny has been in our family since Emily was six months old. She's done a fantastic job with her. I'm so glad there are other people in her life who are able to be with her and support her. I get to most of her soccer games, at least the ones on the weekends, unless I'm traveling for work. I pick her up from piano lessons when I can, and the two of us have the car ride home together every Tuesday.

Sometimes I feel guilty about how little time I actually spend with her one-on-one. But then again, I don't remember how to play the piano, and I've never played soccer. How could I help her with her interests? Besides, she's very close to her nanny, whom I trust completely.

I like to think of the time that we spend together as quality time. We try to pack as much as we can into the few hours a week her father and I can spare away from the office. We've had some unforgettable vacations to Fiji, the Virgin Islands and Monaco. Focusing on the quality of our time together helps me to feel like a good mom.

—Jill

CHILDREN CRAVE THE

time and attention of their parents. God gives parents the ultimate responsibility of taking care of children. His teachings imply that spending time with children, even time that might not seem important, can have a positive effect on them (see Deuteronomy 11:19). Some moms hide behind a "quality time" excuse to assuage a guilty conscience because they aren't spending enough time with their kids. So why is *quantity* just as important as *quality* time?

- Spending time with your children is vital to their well-being and self-esteem. Providing for your children includes meeting their emotional needs, not just their physical needs.

- When you're an active part of your children's lives, you get to shape them. Spending just a few hours a week with your children may not be enough time to teach them everything you want them to know.

- They are only young once, and the time goes quickly.

- At the end of your life, you won't wish you'd spent more time at the office, chasing your career dreams or volunteering on another committee at church. You'll wish you'd spent more time with the people you love—especially your children.

This advice isn't meant to bash working moms or make stretched-thin mothers feel guilty. It's meant to help *all* busy moms (a redundant phrase) evaluate the time they're spending with their children. Ask yourself:

- Does my children's behavior suggest that they could use more "mommy time"?

- Do I spend time with them doing both special activities (playing, talking, going places together) and mundane tasks (cleaning, errands, reading)? Do they feel that I'm

there for the special events and plain old everyday living?

- Do I know who my child's best friend is? What my child likes on her hamburger? How she behaves at school?

- Who is the *primary* influence in my child's life? Is it me . . . or a daycare worker or nanny?

- Is the time I spend with my child enough *for my child* (not just my own preferences)?

"Only 57 percent of U. S. teens indicate they are emotionally close to their mothers, and only 39 percent indicate they are emotionally close to their fathers."

—Barna Research Group (1997)

"TEACH THEM TO YOUR CHILDREN, TALKING ABOUT THEM WHEN YOU SIT AT HOME AND WHEN YOU WALK ALONG THE ROAD, WHEN YOU LIE DOWN AND WHEN YOU GET UP."

DEUTERONOMY 11:19

SEE ALSO

Psalm 90:12
Proverbs 20:7
Proverbs 22:15

For more on **Children**, check the index.

and for the sins of Judah,
  but none will be found,
  for I will forgive the remnant I
    spare.

²¹"Attack the land of Merathaim
  and those who live in Pekod.
Pursue, kill and completely destroy^a
    them,"
                    declares the LORD.
  "Do everything I have commanded
    you.
²²The noise of battle is in the land,
  the noise of great destruction!
²³How broken and shattered
  is the hammer of the whole earth!
  How desolate is Babylon
    among the nations!
²⁴I set a trap for you, Babylon,
  and you were caught before you
    knew it;
  you were found and captured
    because you opposed the LORD.
²⁵The LORD has opened his arsenal
  and brought out the weapons of his
    wrath,
  for the Sovereign LORD Almighty has work to do
  in the land of the Babylonians.
²⁶Come against her from afar.
  Break open her granaries;
  pile her up like heaps of grain.
  Completely destroy her
    and leave her no remnant.
²⁷Kill all her young bulls;
  let them go down to the slaughter!
Woe to them! For their day has come,
  the time for them to be punished.
²⁸Listen to the fugitives and refugees from Babylon
    declaring in Zion
how the LORD our God has taken vengeance,
  vengeance for his temple.

²⁹"Summon archers against Babylon,
  all those who draw the bow.
Encamp all around her;
  let no one escape.
Repay her for her deeds;
  do to her as she has done.
For she has defied the LORD,
  the Holy One of Israel.
³⁰Therefore, her young men will fall in the streets;

50:20 Do you ever feel as if you're walking around with a scarlet "A" sewed to your clothes? Even if your sin was something other than adultery, you may still feel branded for life, as if you can't escape your sin no matter how hard you try. Did you know that when you confess your sin to God with genuine sorrow, God forgives you completely? Not just part of the sin, but *all* of it is wiped out. Even if someone looked for your guilt and your sin, it couldn't be found. You don't have to wear that scarlet letter anymore.

atissue:forgiveness

1164

---

^a *21* The Hebrew term refers to the irrevocable giving over of things or persons to the LORD, often by totally destroying them; also in verse 26.

all her soldiers will be silenced in that day,"

declares the Lord.

³¹"See, I am against you, you arrogant one,"
    declares the Lord, the Lord Almighty,
"for your day has come,
    the time for you to be punished.
³²The arrogant one will stumble and fall
    and no one will help her up;
I will kindle a fire in her towns
    that will consume all who are around her."

³³This is what the Lord Almighty says:

"The people of Israel are oppressed,
    and the people of Judah as well.
All their captors hold them fast,
    refusing to let them go.
³⁴Yet their Redeemer is strong;
    the Lord Almighty is his name.
He will vigorously defend their cause
    so that he may bring rest to their land,
    but unrest to those who live in Babylon.

³⁵"A sword against the Babylonians!"
    declares the Lord—
"against those who live in Babylon
    and against her officials and wise counselors!
³⁶A sword against her false prophets!
    They will become fools.
A sword against her warriors!
    They will be filled with terror.
³⁷A sword against her horses and chariots
    and all the foreigners in her ranks!
    They will become weaklings.
A sword against her treasures!
    They will be plundered.
³⁸A drought on*ᵃ* her waters!
    They will dry up.
For it is a land of idols,
    idols that will go mad with terror.

³⁹"So desert creatures and hyenas will live there,
    and there the owl will dwell.
It will never again be inhabited
    or lived in from generation to generation.
⁴⁰As I overthrew Sodom and Gomorrah
    along with their neighboring towns,"

declares the Lord,

"so no one will live there;
    no one will dwell in it.

⁴¹"Look! An army is coming from the north;
    a great nation and many kings

ᵃ **38** Or *A sword against*

are being stirred up from the ends of the earth.
⁴²They are armed with bows and spears;
    they are cruel and without mercy.
They sound like the roaring sea
    as they ride on their horses;
they come like men in battle formation
    to attack you, Daughter Babylon.
⁴³The king of Babylon has heard reports about them,
    and his hands hang limp.
Anguish has gripped him,
    pain like that of a woman in labor.
⁴⁴Like a lion coming up from Jordan's thickets
    to a rich pastureland,
I will chase Babylon from its land in an instant.
    Who is the chosen one I will appoint for this?
Who is like me and who can challenge me?
    And what shepherd can stand against me?"

⁴⁵Therefore, hear what the LORD has planned against Babylon,
    what he has purposed against the land of the Babylonians:
The young of the flock will be dragged away;
    their pasture will be appalled at their fate.
⁴⁶At the sound of Babylon's capture the earth will tremble;
    its cry will resound among the nations.

51 This is what the LORD says:

"See, I will stir up the spirit of a destroyer
    against Babylon and the people of Leb Kamai.ᵃ
²I will send foreigners to Babylon
    to winnow her and to devastate her land;
they will oppose her on every side
    in the day of her disaster.
³Let not the archer string his bow,
    nor let him put on his armor.
Do not spare her young men;
    completely destroyᵇ her army.

ᵃ 1 Leb Kamai is a cryptogram for Chaldea, that is, Babylonia. ᵇ 3 The Hebrew term refers to the irrevocable giving over of things or persons to the LORD, often by totally destroying them.

HE IS: vindicating

51:1–10 God didn't forsake his people. He never does. Instead, Jeremiah predicted that Babylon would fall because of its sins against God and the mistreatment of his people. The people of God would be set free and would proclaim how God had vindicated them.

God calls our evil world system today *Babylon*. He sees how some governments allow his people to be mocked, mistreated and even murdered. But he is *vindicating*. If you've been persecuted because of your faith, the day is coming when Babylon will suddenly fall, and you will be able to tell what the Lord our God has done.

For the next He Is, go to p. 1185.

⁴They will fall down slain in Babylon,ᵃ
　fatally wounded in her streets.
⁵For Israel and Judah have not been forsaken
　by their God, the Lord Almighty,
though their landᵇ is full of guilt
　before the Holy One of Israel.

⁶"Flee from Babylon!
　Run for your lives!
　Do not be destroyed because of her sins.
It is time for the Lord's vengeance;
　he will repay her what she deserves.
⁷Babylon was a gold cup in the Lord's hand;
　she made the whole earth drunk.
The nations drank her wine;
　therefore they have now gone mad.
⁸Babylon will suddenly fall and be broken.
　Wail over her!
Get balm for her pain;
　perhaps she can be healed.

⁹"We would have healed Babylon,
　but she cannot be healed;
let us leave her and each go to our own land,
　for her judgment reaches to the skies,
　it rises as high as the heavens.'

¹⁰"The Lord has vindicated us;
　come, let us tell in Zion
　what the Lord our God has done.'

¹¹"Sharpen the arrows,
　take up the shields!
The Lord has stirred up the kings of the Medes,
　because his purpose is to destroy Babylon.
The Lord will take vengeance,
　vengeance for his temple.
¹²Lift up a banner against the walls of Babylon!
　Reinforce the guard,
station the watchmen,
　prepare an ambush!
The Lord will carry out his purpose,
　his decree against the people of Babylon.
¹³You who live by many waters
　and are rich in treasures,
your end has come,
　the time for you to be destroyed.
¹⁴The Lord Almighty has sworn by himself:
　I will surely fill you with troops, as with a swarm of locusts,
　and they will shout in triumph over you.

¹⁵"He made the earth by his power;
　he founded the world by his wisdom

1167

and stretched out the heavens by his understanding.
¹⁶When he thunders, the waters in the heavens roar;
  he makes clouds rise from the ends of the earth.
He sends lightning with the rain
  and brings out the wind from his storehouses.

¹⁷"Everyone is senseless and without knowledge;
  all goldsmiths are shamed by their idols.
Their images are a fraud;
  they have no breath in them.
¹⁸They are worthless, the objects of mockery;
  when their judgment comes, they will perish.
¹⁹He who is the Portion of Jacob is not like these,
  for he is the Maker of all things,
including the tribe of his inheritance—
  the LORD Almighty is his name.

²⁰"You are my war club,
  my weapon for battle—
with you I shatter nations,
  with you I destroy kingdoms,
²¹with you I shatter horse and rider,
  with you I shatter chariot and driver,
²²with you I shatter man and woman,
  with you I shatter old man and youth,
  with you I shatter young man and young woman,
²³with you I shatter shepherd and flock,
  with you I shatter farmer and oxen,
  with you I shatter governors and officials.

²⁴"Before your eyes I will repay Babylon and all who live in Babylonia^a for all the wrong they have done in Zion," declares the LORD.

²⁵"I am against you, you destroying mountain,
  you who destroy the whole earth,"

declares the LORD.

"I will stretch out my hand against you,
  roll you off the cliffs,
  and make you a burned-out mountain.
²⁶No rock will be taken from you for a cornerstone,
  nor any stone for a foundation,
  for you will be desolate forever,"

declares the LORD.

²⁷"Lift up a banner in the land!
  Blow the trumpet among the nations!
Prepare the nations for battle against her;
  summon against her these kingdoms:
  Ararat, Minni and Ashkenaz.
Appoint a commander against her;
  send up horses like a swarm of locusts.
²⁸Prepare the nations for battle against her—

_____
^a 24 Or Chaldea; also in verse 35

the kings of the Medes,
their governors and all their officials,
and all the countries they rule.
²⁹ The land trembles and writhes,
for the LORD's purposes against Babylon stand—
to lay waste the land of Babylon
so that no one will live there.
³⁰ Babylon's warriors have stopped fighting;
they remain in their strongholds.
Their strength is exhausted;
they have become weaklings.
Her dwellings are set on fire;
the bars of her gates are broken.
³¹ One courier follows another
and messenger follows messenger
to announce to the king of Babylon
that his entire city is captured,
³² the river crossings seized,
the marshes set on fire,
and the soldiers terrified."

³³ This is what the LORD Almighty, the God of Israel, says:

"Daughter Babylon is like a threshing floor
at the time it is trampled;
the time to harvest her will soon come."

³⁴ "Nebuchadnezzar king of Babylon has devoured us,
he has thrown us into confusion,
he has made us an empty jar.
Like a serpent he has swallowed us
and filled his stomach with our delicacies,
and then has spewed us out.
³⁵ May the violence done to our flesh *a* be on Babylon,"
say the inhabitants of Zion.
"May our blood be on those who live in Babylonia,"
says Jerusalem.

³⁶ Therefore, this is what the LORD says:

"See, I will defend your cause
and avenge you;
I will dry up her sea
and make her springs dry.
³⁷ Babylon will be a heap of ruins,
a haunt of jackals,
an object of horror and scorn,
a place where no one lives.
³⁸ Her people all roar like young lions,
they growl like lion cubs.
³⁹ But while they are aroused,
I will set out a feast for them

1169

---

a 35 Or done to us and to our children

and make them drunk,
so that they shout with laughter—
then sleep forever and not awake,"

declares the LORD.

40 "I will bring them down
like lambs to the slaughter,
like rams and goats.

41 "How Sheshak^a will be captured,
the boast of the whole earth seized!
How desolate Babylon will be
among the nations!
42 The sea will rise over Babylon;
its roaring waves will cover her.
43 Her towns will be desolate,
a dry and desert land,
a land where no one lives,
through which no one travels.
44 I will punish Bel in Babylon
and make him spew out what he has swallowed.
The nations will no longer stream to him.
And the wall of Babylon will fall.

45 "Come out of her, my people!
Run for your lives!
Run from the fierce anger of the LORD.
46 Do not lose heart or be afraid
when rumors are heard in the land;
one rumor comes this year, another the next,
rumors of violence in the land
and of ruler against ruler.
47 For the time will surely come
when I will punish the idols of Babylon;
her whole land will be disgraced
and her slain will all lie fallen within her.
48 Then heaven and earth and all that is in them
will shout for joy over Babylon,
for out of the north
destroyers will attack her,"

declares the LORD.

49 "Babylon must fall because of Israel's slain,
just as the slain in all the earth
have fallen because of Babylon.
50 You who have escaped the sword,
leave and do not linger!
Remember the LORD in a distant land,
and call to mind Jerusalem."

51 "We are disgraced,
for we have been insulted
and shame covers our faces,

---

^a 41 *Sheshak* is a cryptogram for Babylon.

because foreigners have entered
 the holy places of the Lord's house."

52 "But days are coming," declares the Lord,
 "when I will punish her idols,
and throughout her land
 the wounded will groan.
53 Even if Babylon reaches the sky
 and fortifies her lofty stronghold,
 I will send destroyers against her,"

declares the Lord.

54 "The sound of a cry comes from Babylon,
 the sound of great destruction
 from the land of the Babylonians.[a]
55 The Lord will destroy Babylon;
 he will silence her noisy din.
Waves of enemies will rage like great waters;
 the roar of their voices will resound.
56 A destroyer will come against Babylon;
 her warriors will be captured,
 and their bows will be broken.
For the Lord is a God of retribution;
 he will repay in full.
57 I will make her officials and wise counselors drunk,
 her governors, officers and warriors as well;
they will sleep forever and not awake,"
 declares the King, whose name is the Lord Almighty.

58 This is what the Lord Almighty says:

 "Babylon's thick wall will be leveled
 and her high gates set on fire;
 the peoples exhaust themselves for nothing,
 the nations' labor is only fuel for the flames."

59 This is the message Jeremiah the prophet gave to the staff officer Seraiah son of Neriah, the son of Mahseiah, when he went to Babylon with Zedekiah king of Judah in the fourth year of his reign. 60 Jeremiah had written on a scroll about all the disasters that would come upon Babylon—all that had been recorded concerning Babylon. 61 He said to Seraiah, "When you get to Babylon, see that you read all these words aloud. 62 Then say, 'Lord, you have said you will destroy this place, so that neither people nor animals will live in it; it will be desolate forever.' 63 When you finish reading this scroll, tie a stone to it and throw it into the Euphrates. 64 Then say, 'So will Babylon sink to rise no more because of the disaster I will bring on her. And her people will fall.'"

The words of Jeremiah end here.

The Fall of Jerusalem

52 Zedekiah was twenty-one years old when he became king, and he reigned in Jerusalem eleven years. His mother's name was Hamutal daughter of Jeremiah; she was from Libnah. 2 He did evil in the eyes of the Lord, just as Jehoiakim had done. 3 It was because of the Lord's anger that all this happened to Jerusalem and Judah, and in the end he thrust them from his presence.

Now Zedekiah rebelled against the king of Babylon.

⁴So in the ninth year of Zedekiah's reign, on the tenth day of the tenth month, Nebuchadnezzar king of Babylon marched against Jerusalem with his whole army. They encamped outside the city and built siege works all around it. ⁵The city was kept under siege until the eleventh year of King Zedekiah.

⁶By the ninth day of the fourth month the famine in the city had become so severe that there was no food for the people to eat. ⁷Then the city wall was broken through, and the whole army fled. They left the city at night through the gate between the two walls near the king's garden, though the Babylonians^a were surrounding the city. They fled toward the Arabah,^b ⁸but the Babylonian^c army pursued King Zedekiah and overtook him in the plains of Jericho. All his soldiers were separated from him and scattered, ⁹and he was captured.

He was taken to the king of Babylon at Riblah in the land of Hamath, where he pronounced sentence on him. ¹⁰There at Riblah the king of Babylon killed the sons of Zedekiah before his eyes; he also killed all the officials of Judah. ¹¹Then he put out Zedekiah's eyes, bound him with bronze shackles and took him to Babylon, where he put him in prison till the day of his death.

¹²On the tenth day of the fifth month, in the nineteenth year of Nebuchadnezzar king of Babylon, Nebuzaradan commander of the imperial guard, who served the king of Babylon, came to Jerusalem. ¹³He set fire to the temple of the Lord, the royal palace and all the houses of Jerusalem. Every important building he burned down. ¹⁴The whole Babylonian army, under the commander of the imperial guard, broke down all the walls around Jerusalem. ¹⁵Nebuzaradan the commander of the guard carried into exile some of the poorest people and those who remained in the city, along with the rest of the skilled workers^d and those who had deserted to the king of Babylon. ¹⁶But Nebuzaradan left behind the rest of the poorest people of the land to work the vineyards and fields.

¹⁷The Babylonians broke up the bronze pillars, the movable stands and the bronze Sea that were at the temple of the Lord and they carried all the bronze to Babylon. ¹⁸They also took away the pots, shovels, wick trimmers, sprinkling bowls, dishes and all the bronze articles used in the temple service. ¹⁹The commander of the imperial guard took away the basins, censers, sprinkling bowls, pots, lampstands, dishes and bowls used for drink offerings—all that were made of pure gold or silver.

²⁰The bronze from the two pillars, the Sea and the twelve bronze bulls under it, and the movable stands, which King Solomon had made for the temple of the Lord, was more than could be weighed. ²¹Each pillar was eighteen cubits high and twelve cubits in circumference^e; each was four fingers thick, and hollow. ²²The bronze capital on top of one pillar was five cubits^f high and was decorated with a network and pomegranates of bronze all around. The other pillar, with its pomegranates, was similar. ²³There were ninety-six pomegranates on the sides; the total number of pomegranates above the surrounding network was a hundred.

²⁴The commander of the guard took as prisoners Seraiah the chief priest, Zephaniah the priest next in rank and the three doorkeepers. ²⁵Of those still in the city, he took the officer in charge of the fighting men, and seven royal advisers. He also took the secretary who was chief officer in charge of conscripting the people of the land, sixty of whom were found in the city. ²⁶Nebuzaradan the commander took them all and brought them to the king of Babylon at Riblah. ²⁷There at Riblah, in the land of Hamath, the king had them executed.

So Judah went into captivity, away from her land. ²⁸This is the number of the people Nebuchadnezzar carried into exile:

in the seventh year, 3,023 Jews;
²⁹in Nebuchadnezzar's eighteenth year,
832 people from Jerusalem;
³⁰in his twenty-third year,
745 Jews taken into exile by Nebuzaradan the commander of the imperial guard.
There were 4,600 people in all.

---

^a 7 Or Chaldeans; also in verse 17 ^b 7 Or the Jordan Valley ^c 8 Or Chaldean; also in verse 14 ^d 15 Or the populace ^e 21 That is, about 27 feet high and 18 feet in circumference or about 8.2 meters high and 5.4 meters in circumference ^f 22 That is, about 7 1/2 feet or about 2.3 meters

Jehoiachin Released

³¹In the thirty-seventh year of the exile of Jehoiachin king of Judah, in the year Awel-Marduk became king of Babylon, on the twenty-fifth day of the twelfth month, he released Jehoiachin king of Judah and freed him from prison. ³²He spoke kindly to him and gave him a seat of honor higher than those of the other kings who were with him in Babylon. ³³So Jehoiachin put aside his prison clothes and for the rest of his life ate regularly at the king's table. ³⁴Day by day the king of Babylon gave Jehoiachin a regular allowance as long as he lived, till the day of his death.

1173

God, is it going to get any better? ⟫ (1:1—3:20)

God, do you still love me? ⟫ (3:21–66)

God, have you forgotten about me? ⟫ (5:19–22)

lamentations

AUTHOR
Anonymous (possibly Jeremiah).

AUDIENCE
All who mourned Jerusalem's destruction.

DATE
Shortly after the fall of Jerusalem in 586 B.C.

SETTING
The Babylonians had destroyed God's holy city of Jerusalem. Those who weren't killed or tortured were taken as prisoners.

VERSES TO REMEMBER
"Because of the LORD's great love we are not consumed, for his compassions never fail. They are new every morning; great is your faithfulness." (3:22–23)

THEME TO CONSIDER
What causes God to grieve should also cause us to grieve. But we do not grieve as those who have no hope. Because of God's great love we have hope for tomorrow.

1 *a*

How deserted lies the city,
    once so full of people!
How like a widow is she,
    who once was great among the nations!
She who was queen among the provinces
    has now become a slave.

²Bitterly she weeps at night,
    tears are on her cheeks.
Among all her lovers
    there is none to comfort her.
All her friends have betrayed her;
    they have become her enemies.

³After affliction and harsh labor,
    Judah has gone into exile.
She dwells among the nations;
    she finds no resting place.
All who pursue her have overtaken her
    in the midst of her distress.

⁴The roads to Zion mourn,
    for no one comes to her appointed festivals.
All her gateways are desolate,
    her priests groan,
her young women grieve,
    and she is in bitter anguish.

⁵Her foes have become her masters;
    her enemies are at ease.
The LORD has brought her grief
    because of her many sins.
Her children have gone into exile,
    captive before the foe.

⁶All the splendor has departed
    from Daughter Zion.
Her princes are like deer
    that find no pasture;
in weakness they have fled
    before the pursuer.

⁷In the days of her affliction and wandering
    Jerusalem remembers all the treasures
    that were hers in days of old.
When her people fell into enemy hands,
    there was no one to help her.
Her enemies looked at her
    and laughed at her destruction.

⁸Jerusalem has sinned greatly
    and so has become unclean.
All who honored her despise her,

1175

for they have seen her nakedness;
she herself groans
and turns away.

⁹Her filthiness clung to her skirts;
she did not consider her future.
Her fall was astounding;
there was none to comfort her.
"Look, Lord, on my affliction,
for the enemy has triumphed."

¹⁰The enemy laid hands
on all her treasures;
she saw pagan nations
enter her sanctuary—
those you had forbidden
to enter your assembly.

¹¹All her people groan
as they search for bread;
they barter their treasures for food
to keep themselves alive.
"Look, Lord, and consider,
for I am despised."

¹²"Is it nothing to you, all you who pass by?
Look around and see.
Is any suffering like my suffering
that was inflicted on me,
that the Lord brought on me
in the day of his fierce anger?

¹³"From on high he sent fire,
sent it down into my bones.
He spread a net for my feet
and turned me back.
He made me desolate,
faint all the day long.

¹⁴"My sins have been bound into a yoke*ᵃ*;
by his hands they were woven together.
They have been hung on my neck,
and the Lord has sapped my strength.
He has given me into the hands
of those I cannot withstand.

¹⁵"The Lord has rejected
all the warriors in my midst;
he has summoned an army against me
to*ᵇ* crush my young men.
In his winepress the Lord has trampled
Virgin Daughter Judah.

¹⁶"This is why I weep
and my eyes overflow with tears.

ᵃ 14 Most Hebrew manuscripts; many Hebrew manuscripts and Septuagint *He kept watch over my sins*   *ᵇ 15* Or *has set a time for me / when he will*
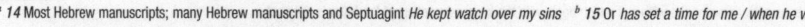

No one is near to comfort me,
    no one to restore my spirit.
My children are destitute
    because the enemy has prevailed."

¹⁷Zion stretches out her hands,
    but there is no one to comfort her.
The Lord has decreed for Jacob
    that his neighbors become his foes;
Jerusalem has become
    an unclean thing among them.

¹⁸"The Lord is righteous,
    yet I rebelled against his command.
Listen, all you peoples;
    look on my suffering.
My young men and young women
    have gone into exile.

¹⁹"I called to my allies
    but they betrayed me.
My priests and my elders
    perished in the city
while they searched for food
    to keep themselves alive.

²⁰"See, Lord, how distressed I am!
    I am in torment within,
and in my heart I am disturbed,
    for I have been most rebellious.
Outside, the sword bereaves;
    inside, there is only death.

²¹"People have heard my groaning,
    but there is no one to comfort me.
All my enemies have heard of my distress;
    they rejoice at what you have done.
May you bring the day you have announced
    so they may become like me.

²²"Let all their wickedness come before you;
    deal with them
as you have dealt with me
    because of all my sins.
My groans are many
    and my heart is faint."

2 ^a

How the Lord has covered Daughter Zion
    with the cloud of his anger^b!
He has hurled down the splendor of Israel
    from heaven to earth;
he has not remembered his footstool
    in the day of his anger.

---

^a This chapter is an acrostic poem, the verses of which begin with the successive letters of the Hebrew alphabet.   ^b 1 Or *How the Lord in his anger / has treated Daughter Zion with contempt*

²Without pity the Lord has swallowed up
 all the dwellings of Jacob;
in his wrath he has torn down
 the strongholds of Daughter Judah.
He has brought her kingdom and its princes
 down to the ground in dishonor.

³In fierce anger he has cut off
 every horn*ᵃ* of Israel.
He has withdrawn his right hand
 at the approach of the enemy.
He has burned in Jacob like a flaming fire
 that consumes everything around it.

⁴Like an enemy he has strung his bow;
 his right hand is ready.
Like a foe he has slain
 all who were pleasing to the eye;
he has poured out his wrath like fire
 on the tent of Daughter Zion.

⁵The Lord is like an enemy;
 he has swallowed up Israel.
He has swallowed up all her palaces
 and destroyed her strongholds.
He has multiplied mourning and lamentation
 for Daughter Judah.

⁶He has laid waste his dwelling like a garden;
 he has destroyed his place of meeting.
The Lᴏʀᴅ has made Zion forget
 her appointed festivals and her Sabbaths;
in his fierce anger he has spurned
 both king and priest.

⁷The Lord has rejected his altar
 and abandoned his sanctuary.
He has given the walls of her palaces
 into the hands of the enemy;
they have raised a shout in the house of the Lᴏʀᴅ
 as on the day of an appointed festival.

⁸The Lᴏʀᴅ determined to tear down
 the wall around Daughter Zion.
He stretched out a measuring line
 and did not withhold his hand from destroying.
He made ramparts and walls lament;
 together they wasted away.

⁹Her gates have sunk into the ground;
 their bars he has broken and destroyed.
Her king and her princes are exiled among the nations,
 the law is no more,

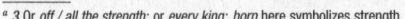

ASKmeanyTHING

It's no secret that you struggled with infertility. How did you handle it?

It was very difficult for me. My husband, Elkanah, was also married to another woman, Peninnah. Peninnah had given Elkanah several children, and she flaunted it and tormented me for having no children. I knew that Elkanah loved me, but it wasn't enough to overcome Peninnah's constant harassment.

So what did you do?

I was miserable and at a loss for what to do. So I poured out my bitterness, my anguish and my soul to God. I prayed as if my life depended upon it, with tears streaming down my cheeks. And then and there, I made a promise, that if God would remember me and give me a son, then I would give that child back to God for life.

1179

And that's what you did, isn't it?

Yes. God did hear my prayer, and he answered it by giving me a son, Samuel. What a gift! Three years later, after he had been weaned, I took Samuel back to the temple and gave him to Eli, the priest, to serve the Lord.

That couldn't have been easy to do.

[laughs softly] There were many women in our village who thought I had completely lost my mind. But I knew in my heart that Samuel was not mine. God had given me the gift of this child, but Samuel truly belonged to the Lord. All we have and receive is on loan from God. We need to hold it loosely. I discovered that the greatest joy in having a child is giving that child freely and completely to God.

What advice do you have for mothers today?

Love the children that God has placed in your care, but do so understanding that one day you will need to release them back to God. Remember that children are a gift from God, on loan to you. Your role is to nurture, train and guide them into becoming independent people that God can use for his purposes.

FOR MORE INSIGHT: Read Genesis 33:5; Psalm 127; Proverbs 22:15; and 29:17 on God's gift of children and on training them to serve the Lord.

myth# 68

"HER CHILD IS PERFECT."

I can't admit this to my friend Gwen, but sometimes I can't stand to be around her son Tyrell. It's not that he's a bad kid. I simply can't stand the fact that he seems to do everything so much better than my son, Imaran. They're both on the middle school soccer team. While my son sits on the bench, her son's out there starting. He's the team's highest scorer.

Not only that, but he's also very polite to adults—not like some of these other surly 13-year-olds. I don't think I've ever heard him talk back to Gwen or his dad. Even Imaran isn't always polite, although I'm always on him about that.

And of course, Tyrell is a straight-A student, and Gwen makes sure to tell me about that. I'm starting to resent those announcements, especially since my baby tries so hard and winds up with only Bs and Cs.

Every time I look at Tyrell I think, Is this kid perfect or what? Then I feel resentful that he is or seems to be, and I have to pray to God to help me say something nice to the boy. Imaran doesn't seem bothered by Tyrell's successes at all—or so he says. Tyrell's his best friend. He's happy when Tyrell does well. I'm not! I want my baby to excel too.

I wonder what Gwen's secret is. She doesn't seem to work with Tyrell any more than I do with Imaran. Whatever her secret, it's causing me to question my abilities as a parent. Am I doing something wrong with Imaran? Is there more I could be doing?

—Tamyra

EVER KNOW A family that seemed too good to be true? They always look put together, and the children seem to embody perfection itself. But, as the old saying goes, looks can be deceiving. Many times perfection is simply an illusion.

When we envy the "unattainable" level of success in parenting that someone else seems to have achieved, it's time to evaluate what we believe.

- What's really behind the thought that someone else is perfect? Do we seek perfection in our children? In ourselves? Is perfection a realistic goal for imperfect people?

- What do we believe about God and his plans for us and our children (see Jeremiah 29:11)? Do we believe that he has our best interests at heart?

Seeing someone else as perfect sets up a barrier between that person and us. Comparing ourselves or our children to others also leads to discouragement. It takes our focus off God. And over time, our children will pick up on the dissatisfaction and discouragement we feel, and they may take that personally, concluding that we're dissatisfied with them.

God, the giver of life, is also the one who gives each person his or her unique abilities. It grieves him when we envy the abilities of others, even if we do so on behalf of someone else. He gives us the power to avoid the trap of discouragement or depression when we compare ourselves to others. But the best way to avoid that trap is to avoid the comparison altogether.

"Remember that a friend's victories are your victories. So when she receives a promotion, a new car, or diamond earrings, learn to say, 'I'm so happy for you' without gritting your teeth. Don't let the stab of envy rob you of the joy of shared celebration."

—Nancy Beach

1181

"IF YOU HARBOR BITTER ENVY AND SELFISH AMBITION IN YOUR HEARTS, DO NOT BOAST ABOUT IT OR DENY THE TRUTH."

JAMES 3:14

SEE ALSO

Isaiah 26:3
2 Corinthians 10:12
James 1:17

For more on **Parenting**, check the index.

and her prophets no longer find
    visions from the L ord.

¹⁰The elders of Daughter Zion
    sit on the ground in silence;
they have sprinkled dust on their heads
    and put on sackcloth.
The young women of Jerusalem
    have bowed their heads to the ground.

¹¹My eyes fail from weeping,
    I am in torment within;
my heart is poured out on the ground
    because my people are destroyed,
because children and infants faint
    in the streets of the city.

1182

¹²They say to their mothers,
    "Where is bread and wine?"
as they faint like the wounded
    in the streets of the city,
as their lives ebb away
    in their mothers' arms.

¹³What can I say for you?
    With what can I compare you,
    Daughter Jerusalem?
To what can I liken you,
    that I may comfort you,
    Virgin Daughter Zion?
Your wound is as deep as the sea.
    Who can heal you?

¹⁴The visions of your prophets
    were false and worthless;
they did not expose your sin
    to ward off your captivity.
The prophecies they gave you
    were false and misleading.

¹⁵All who pass your way
    clap their hands at you;
they scoff and shake their heads
    at Daughter Jerusalem:
"Is this the city that was called
    the perfection of beauty,
    the joy of the whole earth?"

¹⁶All your enemies open their mouths
    wide against you;
they scoff and gnash their teeth
    and say, "We have swallowed her up.
This is the day we have waited for;
    we have lived to see it."

¹⁷ The Lord has done what he planned;
    he has fulfilled his word,
    which he decreed long ago.
He has overthrown you without pity,
    he has let the enemy gloat over you,
    he has exalted the horn*ᵃ* of your foes.

¹⁸ The hearts of the people
    cry out to the Lord.
You walls of Daughter Zion,
    let your tears flow like a river
    day and night;
give yourself no relief,
    your eyes no rest.

¹⁹ Arise, cry out in the night,
    as the watches of the night begin;
pour out your heart like water
    in the presence of the Lord.
Lift up your hands to him
    for the lives of your children,
who faint from hunger
    at every street corner.

²⁰ "Look, Lord, and consider:
    Whom have you ever treated like
        this?
Should women eat their offspring,
    the children they have cared for?
Should priest and prophet be killed
    in the sanctuary of the Lord?

²¹ "Young and old lie together
    in the dust of the streets;
my young men and young women
    have fallen by the sword.
You have slain them in the day of your anger;
    you have slaughtered them without pity.

²² "As you summon to a feast day,
    so you summoned against me terrors on every side.
In the day of the Lord's anger
    no one escaped or survived;
those I cared for and reared
    my enemy has destroyed."

3 *ᵇ*   I am one who has seen affliction
        by the rod of the Lord's wrath.
² He has driven me away and made me walk
        in darkness rather than light;
³ indeed, he has turned his hand against me
        again and again, all day long.

conversations

dealing with past sin «» 2:18–19

1 » What do these verses teach you about the meaning of repentance?

2 » How does unconfessed sin affect your life?

1183

3 » What does it mean to truly repent?

For more on **dealing with past sin**, check the index.
For the next Conversations, go to p. 1196.

ᵃ 17 *Horn* here symbolizes strength.   *ᵇ* This chapter is an acrostic poem; the verses of each stanza begin with the successive letters of the Hebrew alphabet, and the verses within each stanza begin with the same letter.

⁴He has made my skin and my flesh grow old
 and has broken my bones.
⁵He has besieged me and surrounded me
 with bitterness and hardship.
⁶He has made me dwell in darkness
 like those long dead.

⁷He has walled me in so I cannot escape;
 he has weighed me down with chains.
⁸Even when I call out or cry for help,
 he shuts out my prayer.
⁹He has barred my way with blocks of stone;
 he has made my paths crooked.

¹⁰Like a bear lying in wait,
 like a lion in hiding,
¹¹he dragged me from the path and mangled me
 and left me without help.
¹²He drew his bow
 and made me the target for his arrows.

¹³He pierced my heart
 with arrows from his quiver.
¹⁴I became the laughingstock of all my people;
 they mock me in song all day long.
¹⁵He has filled me with bitter herbs
 and sated me with gall.

¹⁶He has broken my teeth with gravel;
 he has trampled me in the dust.
¹⁷I have been deprived of peace;
 I have forgotten what prosperity is.
¹⁸So I say, "My splendor is gone
 and all that I had hoped from the Lord."

¹⁹I remember my affliction and my wandering,
 the bitterness and the gall.
²⁰I well remember them,
 and my soul is downcast within me.
²¹Yet this I call to mind
 and therefore I have hope:

²²Because of the Lord's great love we are not consumed,
 for his compassions never fail.
²³They are new every morning;
 great is your faithfulness.
²⁴I say to myself, "The Lord is my portion;
 therefore I will wait for him."

²⁵The Lord is good to those whose hope is in him,
 to the one who seeks him;
²⁶it is good to wait quietly
 for the salvation of the Lord.
²⁷It is good for people to bear the yoke
 while they are young.

HE IS: good

3:22–26 The weeping prophet, Jeremiah, grieved over the fall of Jerusalem. Yet he found consolation in the fact that God's compassions are new every morning. Although the people had sinned and the city was destroyed, Jeremiah knew that God is *good* to those who hope in him.

If you're grieving over the destruction in your life and you're longing for a fresh start, seek the Lord. He is *good* and is able and willing to give you a new beginning. Because he offers a fresh batch of compassion every morning, he'll help you put the past behind you when you hope in him.

For the next He Is, go to p. 1191.

²⁸ Let them sit alone in silence,
    for the LORD has laid it on them.
²⁹ Let them bury their faces in the dust—
    there may yet be hope.
³⁰ Let them offer their cheeks to one who would strike them,
    and let them be filled with disgrace.

³¹ For people are not cast off
    by the Lord forever.
³² Though he brings grief, he will show compassion,
    so great is his unfailing love.
³³ For he does not willingly bring affliction
    or grief to any human being.

³⁴ To crush underfoot
    all prisoners in the land,
³⁵ to deny people their rights
    before the Most High,
³⁶ to deprive them of justice—
    would not the Lord see such things?

³⁷ Who can speak and have it happen
    if the Lord has not decreed it?
³⁸ Is it not from the mouth of the Most High
    that both calamities and good things come?
³⁹ Why should the living complain
    when punished for their sins?

⁴⁰ Let us examine our ways and test them,
    and let us return to the LORD.
⁴¹ Let us lift up our hearts and our hands
    to God in heaven, and say:
⁴² "We have sinned and rebelled
    and you have not forgiven.

⁴³ "You have covered yourself with anger and pursued us;
    you have slain without pity.
⁴⁴ You have covered yourself with a cloud
    so that no prayer can get through.

⁴⁵You have made us scum and refuse
  among the nations.

⁴⁶"All our enemies have opened their mouths
  wide against us.
⁴⁷We have suffered terror and pitfalls,
  ruin and destruction."
⁴⁸Streams of tears flow from my eyes
  because my people are destroyed.

⁴⁹My eyes will flow unceasingly,
  without relief,
⁵⁰until the Lord looks down
  from heaven and sees.
⁵¹What I see brings grief to my soul
  because of all the women of my city.

⁵²Those who were my enemies without cause
  hunted me like a bird.
⁵³They tried to end my life in a pit
  and threw stones at me;
⁵⁴the waters closed over my head,
  and I thought I was about to perish.

⁵⁵I called on your name, Lord,
  from the depths of the pit.
⁵⁶You heard my plea: "Do not close your ears
  to my cry for relief."
⁵⁷You came near when I called you,
  and you said, "Do not fear."

⁵⁸You, Lord, took up my case;
  you redeemed my life.
⁵⁹Lord, you have seen the wrong done to me.
  Uphold my cause!
⁶⁰You have seen the depth of their vengeance,
  all their plots against me.

⁶¹Lord, you have heard their insults,
  all their plots against me—
⁶²what my enemies whisper and mutter
  against me all day long.
⁶³Look at them! Sitting or standing,
  they mock me in their songs.

⁶⁴Pay them back what they deserve, Lord,
  for what their hands have done.
⁶⁵Put a veil over their hearts,
  and may your curse be on them!
⁶⁶Pursue them in anger and destroy them
  from under the heavens of the Lord.

4 ^a How the gold has lost its luster,
  the fine gold become dull!

^a This chapter is an acrostic poem, the verses of which begin with the successive letters of the Hebrew alphabet.

The sacred gems are scattered
    at every street corner.

²How the precious children of Zion,
    once worth their weight in gold,
are now considered as pots of clay,
    the work of a potter's hands!

³Even jackals offer their breasts
    to nurse their young,
but my people have become heartless
    like ostriches in the desert.

⁴Because of thirst the infant's tongue
    sticks to the roof of its mouth;
the children beg for bread,
    but no one gives it to them.

⁵Those who once ate delicacies
    are destitute in the streets.
Those nurtured in purple
    now lie on ash heaps.

⁶The punishment of my people
    is greater than that of Sodom,
which was overthrown in a moment
    without a hand turned to help her.

⁷Their princes were brighter than snow
    and whiter than milk,
their bodies more ruddy than rubies,
    their appearance like lapis lazuli.

⁸But now they are blacker than soot;
    they are not recognized in the streets.
Their skin has shriveled on their bones;
    it has become as dry as a stick.

⁹Those killed by the sword are better off
    than those who die of famine;
racked with hunger, they waste away
    for lack of food from the field.

¹⁰With their own hands compassionate
      women
    have cooked their own children,
who became their food
    when my people were destroyed.

¹¹The LORD has given full vent to his wrath;
    he has poured out his fierce anger.
He kindled a fire in Zion
    that consumed her foundations.

¹²The kings of the earth did not believe,
    nor did any of the peoples of the world,

1187

at issue: poverty

4:1–10 Have you ever visited a third-world country or an overpopulated city and witnessed poverty firsthand? When Jeremiah saw the people of Jerusalem desperate and dying from lack of food and water, his heart broke for them. Though their own sin had ushered in their suffering, Jeremiah grieved when he saw their hopeless state. Human suffering in any form should break our hearts too. Does it distress you to see someone in need? Thank God for giving you a tender heart, then ask him to show you how you can help. Though you can't solve the whole problem, you *can* make a difference.

that enemies and foes could enter
    the gates of Jerusalem.

¹³But it happened because of the sins of her prophets
    and the iniquities of her priests,
who shed within her
    the blood of the righteous.

¹⁴Now they grope through the streets
    as if they were blind.
They are so defiled with blood
    that no one dares to touch their garments.

¹⁵"Go away! You are unclean!" people cry to them.
    "Away! Away! Don't touch us!"
When they flee and wander about,
    people among the nations say,
    "They can stay here no longer."

¹⁶The Lord himself has scattered them;
    he no longer watches over them.
The priests are shown no honor,
    the elders no favor.

¹⁷Moreover, our eyes failed,
    looking in vain for help;
from our towers we watched
    for a nation that could not save us.

¹⁸People stalked us at every step,
    so we could not walk in our streets.
Our end was near, our days were numbered,
    for our end had come.

¹⁹Our pursuers were swifter
    than eagles in the sky;
they chased us over the mountains
    and lay in wait for us in the desert.

²⁰The Lord's anointed, our very life breath,
    was caught in their traps.
We thought that under his shadow
    we would live among the nations.

²¹Rejoice and be glad, Daughter Edom,
    you who live in the land of Uz.
But to you also the cup will be passed;
    you will be drunk and stripped naked.

²²Your punishment will end, Daughter Zion;
    he will not prolong your exile.
But he will punish your sin, Daughter Edom,
    and expose your wickedness.

Remember, Lord, what has happened to us;
    look, and see our disgrace.

²Our inheritance has been turned over to strangers,
  our homes to foreigners.
³We have become fatherless,
  our mothers are widows.
⁴We must buy the water we drink;
  our wood can be had only at a price.
⁵Those who pursue us are at our heels;
  we are weary and find no rest.
⁶We submitted to Egypt and Assyria
  to get enough bread.
⁷Our parents sinned and are no more,
  and we bear their punishment.
⁸Slaves rule over us,
  and there is none to free us from their hands.
⁹We get our bread at the risk of our lives
  because of the sword in the desert.
¹⁰Our skin is hot as an oven,
  feverish from hunger.
¹¹Women have been ravished in Zion,
  and virgins in the towns of Judah.
¹²Princes have been hung up by their hands;
  elders are shown no respect.
¹³Young men toil at the millstones;
  boys stagger under loads of wood.
¹⁴The elders are gone from the city gate;
  the young men have stopped their music.
¹⁵Joy is gone from our hearts;
  our dancing has turned to mourning.
¹⁶The crown has fallen from our head.
  Woe to us, for we have sinned!
¹⁷Because of this our hearts are faint,
  because of these things our eyes grow dim
¹⁸for Mount Zion, which lies desolate,
  with jackals prowling over it.

¹⁹You, LORD, reign forever;
  your throne endures from generation to generation.
²⁰Why do you always forget us?
  Why do you forsake us so long?
²¹Restore us to yourself, LORD, that we may return;
  renew our days as of old
²²unless you have utterly rejected us
  and are angry with us beyond measure.

ezekiel

AUTHOR
Ezekiel.

AUDIENCE
Ezekiel's fellow Jewish exiles in Babylon.

DATE
Between 593 and 571 B.C.

SETTING
The priest Ezekiel prophesied to his fellow
Jews, who were taken as prisoners to
Babylon in 597 B.C.

VERSE TO REMEMBER
"I will give you a new heart and put a new
spirit in you; I will remove from you your
heart of stone and give you a heart of flesh."
(36:26)

THEME TO CONSIDER
No matter what happened in the past or
what lies ahead of us, God is still and
always in control.

Ezekiel's Inaugural Vision

1 In my thirtieth year, in the fourth month on the fifth day, while I was among the exiles by the Kebar River, the heavens were opened and I saw visions of God.

² On the fifth of the month—it was the fifth year of the exile of King Jehoiachin— ³ the word of the LORD came to Ezekiel the priest, the son of Buzi, by the Kebar River in the land of the Babylonians.*ª* There the hand of the LORD was on him.

⁴ I looked, and I saw a windstorm coming out of the north—an immense cloud with flashing lightning and surrounded by brilliant light. The center of the fire looked like glowing metal, ⁵ and in the fire was what looked like four living creatures. In appearance their form was human, ⁶ but each of them had four faces and four wings. ⁷ Their legs were straight; their feet were like those of a calf and gleamed like burnished bronze. ⁸ Under their wings on their four sides they had human hands. All four of them had faces and wings, ⁹ and the wings of one touched the wings of another. Each one went straight ahead; they did not turn as they moved.

¹⁰ Their faces looked like this: Each of the four had the face of a human being, and on the right side each had the face of a lion, and on the left the face of an ox; each also had the face of an eagle. ¹¹ Such were their faces. They each had two wings spreading out upward, each wing touching that of the creature on either side; and each had two other wings covering its body. ¹² Each one went straight ahead. Wherever the spirit would go, they would go, without turning as they went. ¹³ The appearance of the living creatures was like burning coals of fire or like torches. Fire moved back and forth among the creatures; it was bright, and lightning flashed out of it. ¹⁴ The creatures sped back and forth like flashes of lightning.

¹⁵ As I looked at the living creatures, I saw a wheel on the ground beside each creature with its four faces. ¹⁶ This was the appearance and structure of the wheels: They sparkled like topaz, and all four looked alike. Each appeared to be made like a wheel intersecting a wheel. ¹⁷ As they moved, they would go in any one of the four directions the creatures faced; the wheels did not change direction as the creatures went. ¹⁸ Their rims were high and awesome, and all four rims were full of eyes all around.

¹⁹ When the living creatures moved, the wheels beside them moved; and when the living creatures rose from the ground, the wheels also rose. ²⁰ Wherever the spirit would go, they would go, and the wheels would rise along with them, because the spirit of the living creatures was in the wheels. ²¹ When the creatures moved, they also moved; when the creatures stood still, they also stood still; and when the creatures rose from the ground, the wheels rose along with them, because the spirit of the living creatures was in the wheels.

²² Spread out above the heads of the living creatures was what looked something like a vault, sparkling like crystal, and awesome. ²³ Under the vault their wings were stretched out one toward the other, and each had two wings covering its body. ²⁴ When the creatures moved, I heard the sound of their wings, like the roar of rushing waters, like the voice of the Almighty,*ᵇ* like the tumult of an army. When they stood still, they lowered their wings.

ª 3 Or *Chaldeans*   *ᵇ 24* Hebrew *Shaddai*

1191

high above

1:22–28 Ezekiel saw a mind-blowing vision: A storm came, the heavens opened and the prophet was privy to a glimpse into the supernatural realm. Of all the wondrous things he saw, the most magnificent was God, *high above* on the throne.

When the storms of life hit you, you may fear being swept away. But your God who is *high above* is unaffected by the hurricane force of that storm. Pray that God will allow you to see beyond the tempest to him, reigning *high above* the clouds. He is on his throne and can change your situation—or how you view it.

For the next He Is, go to p. 1212.

²⁵Then there came a voice from above the vault over their heads as they stood with lowered wings. ²⁶Above the vault over their heads was what looked like a throne of lapis lazuli, and high above on the throne was a figure like that of a man. ²⁷I saw that from what appeared to be his waist up he looked like glowing metal, as if full of fire, and that from there down he looked like fire; and brilliant light surrounded him. ²⁸Like the appearance of a rainbow in the clouds on a rainy day, so was the radiance around him.

This was the appearance of the likeness of the glory of the LORD. When I saw it, I fell facedown, and I heard the voice of one speaking.

Ezekiel's Call to Be a Prophet

2 He said to me, "Son of man,ᵃ stand up on your feet and I will speak to you." ²As he spoke, the Spirit came into me and raised me to my feet, and I heard him speaking to me.

³He said: "Son of man, I am sending you to the Israelites, to a rebellious nation that has rebelled against me; they and their ancestors have been in revolt against me to this very day. ⁴The people to whom I am sending you are obstinate and stubborn. Say to them, 'This is what the Sovereign LORD says.' ⁵And whether they listen or fail to listen—for they are a rebellious house—they will know that a prophet has been among them. ⁶And you, son of man, do not be afraid of them or their words. Do not be afraid, though briers and thorns are all around you and you live among scorpions. Do not be afraid of what they say or be terrified by them, though they are a rebellious house. ⁷You must speak my words to them, whether they listen or fail to listen, for they are rebellious. ⁸But you, son of man, listen to what I say to you. Do not rebel like that rebellious house; open your mouth and eat what I give you."

⁹Then I looked, and I saw a hand stretched out to me. In it was a scroll, ¹⁰which he unrolled before me. On both sides of it were written words of lament and mourning and woe.

3 And he said to me, "Son of man, eat what is before you, eat this scroll; then go and speak to the house of Israel." ²So I opened my mouth, and he gave me the scroll to eat.

³Then he said to me, "Son of man, eat this scroll I am giving you and fill your stomach with it." So I ate it, and it tasted as sweet as honey in my mouth.

⁴He then said to me: "Son of man, go now to the house of Israel and speak my words to them. ⁵You are not being sent to a people of obscure speech and strange language, but to the house of Israel— ⁶not to many peoples of obscure speech and strange language, whose words you cannot understand. Surely if I had sent you to them, they would have listened to you. ⁷But the house of Israel is not willing to listen to you because they are not willing to listen to me, for the whole house of Israel is hardened and obstinate. ⁸But I will make you as unyielding and hardened as they are. ⁹I will make your forehead like the hardest stone, harder than flint. Do not be afraid of them or terrified by them, though they are a rebellious house."

¹⁰And he said to me, "Son of man, listen carefully and take to heart all the words I speak to you. ¹¹Go now to your people in exile and speak to them. Say to them, 'This is what the Sovereign LORD says,' whether they listen or fail to listen."

at issue: witnessing

2:3–8 It's natural to want to "pick and choose" the people with whom you share the gospel. Certain people may seem more likely to listen to and respect what you have to say, so it's easier to want to share with them. If someone seems openly hostile towards God, you may hesitate to witness at all. But God doesn't hold you accountable for the other person's response; he holds you accountable for speaking the truth. Like Ezekiel, God may send you to speak to a stubborn, rebellious, intimidating or unresponsive person. If so, be faithful to speak God's words, and then trust him with the outcome.

ᵃ *1* The Hebrew phrase *ben adam* means *human being*. The phrase *son of man* is retained as a form of address here and throughout Ezekiel because of its traditional associations.

¹²Then the Spirit lifted me up, and I heard behind me a loud rumbling sound as the glory of the LORD rose from the place where it was standing.ᵃ ¹³It was the sound of the wings of the living creatures brushing against each other and the sound of the wheels beside them, a loud rumbling sound. ¹⁴The Spirit then lifted me up and took me away, and I went in bitterness and in the anger of my spirit, with the strong hand of the LORD on me. ¹⁵I came to the exiles who lived at Tel Aviv near the Kebar River. And there, where they were living, I sat among them for seven days—deeply distressed.

Ezekiel's Task as Watchman

¹⁶At the end of seven days the word of the LORD came to me: ¹⁷"Son of man, I have made you a watchman for the house of Israel; so hear the word I speak and give them warning from me. ¹⁸When I say to the wicked, 'You will surely die,' and you do not warn them or speak out to dissuade them from their evil ways in order to save their lives, those wicked people will die forᵇ their sins, and I will hold you accountable for their blood. ¹⁹But if you do warn the wicked and they do not turn from their wickedness or from their evil ways, they will die for their sins; but you will have saved yourself.

²⁰"Again, when the righteous turn from their righteousness and do evil, and I put a stumbling block before them, they will die. Since you did not warn them, they will die for their sins. The righteous things they did will not be remembered, and I will hold you accountable for their blood. ²¹But if you do warn the righteous not to sin and they do not sin, they will surely live because they took warning, and you will have saved yourself."

²²The hand of the LORD was on me there, and he said to me, "Get up and go out to the plain, and there I will speak to you." ²³So I got up and went out to the plain. And the glory of the LORD was standing there, like the glory I had seen by the Kebar River, and I fell facedown. ²⁴Then the Spirit came into me and raised me to my feet. He spoke to me and said: "Go, shut yourself inside your house. ²⁵And you, son of man, they will tie with ropes; you will be bound so that you cannot go out among the people. ²⁶I will make your tongue stick to the roof of your mouth so that you will be silent and unable to rebuke them, for they are a rebellious house. ²⁷But when I speak to you, I will open your mouth and you shall say to them, 'This is what the Sovereign LORD says.' Whoever will listen let them listen, and whoever will refuse let them refuse; for they are a rebellious house.

Siege of Jerusalem Symbolized

4 "Now, son of man, take a block of clay, put it in front of you and draw the city of Jerusalem on it. ²Then lay siege to it: Erect siege works against it, build a ramp up to it, set up camps against it and put battering rams around it. ³Then take an iron pan, place it as an iron wall between you and the city and turn your face toward it. It will be under siege, and you shall besiege it. This will be a sign to the house of Israel.

⁴"Then lie on your left side and put the sin of the house of Israel upon yourself.ᶜ You are to bear their sin for the number of days you lie on your side. ⁵I have assigned you the same number of days as the years of their sin. So for 390 days you will bear the sin of the house of Israel.

⁶"After you have finished this, lie down again, this time on your right side, and bear the sin of the

at issue: responsibility

3:18–21 Imagine that your friend is blindfolded, walking toward a 300-foot drop-off. Would you tell yourself, *It's none of my business. Surely someone else already warned her. I should keep my mouth shut*? No way! You'd yell, "Stop!" You'd run to take off her blindfold and show her the danger ahead. You'd try to steer her in a different direction. While she might still choose to walk off that cliff, you would have done all you could to stop her. This is the kind of responsibility you have for your friends who are blinded by their sin. Wouldn't you want someone to do the same for you?

1193

---

myth# 69 "MY HUSBAND IS THE ONLY ONE WHO NEEDS TO CHANGE."

1194

Scott and I recently had an argument—a bad one. I can't take anymore of his stubbornness and moodiness. Something's got to change!

It all started when I decided to go back to school for a Master's degree as an art therapist. At first Scott said he was all for it. "Sure, honey, you've always wanted to do this. It will be good for you to go back to school."

He knew that I had put my goals on hold to stay home with our two sons. After my relationship with God, they're our first priority. But when they turned 12 and 10 and were in school all day, plus involved in extra-curricular activities, I decided to enroll.

Scott even helped me with my application, and I was accepted into the program of my choice! But ever since my first semester (I'm in the second semester now), Scott started complaining. "I never seem to have any clean shirts." (Why can't he do the laundry now? I did it all for 12 years!) "You don't have as much time for me." (I have to study!)

He's even accused me of "shortchanging" (his word) our kids. Like his 60-hour a week job doesn't? He barely sees the kids!

Lately, he's questioned whether or not it's "God's will" for me to be in this program. That's what prompted our last argument. When he said that, I hit the roof. Why is it that I always have to sacrifice my goals and dreams? Scott never has to do that.

Even though he apologized for saying what he did, I'm finding it hard to be civil to him lately. I love my husband, but sometimes I don't like him very much. I wish he were more understanding. Some days I feel as if he doesn't even try.

—Nora

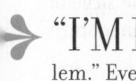

"I'M NOT THE one with the problem." Ever hear that (or think it)? It's far more satisfying to place the blame 100 percent on someone else, especially if that person has wronged you. But God has a better way. Consider this:

- Jesus tells you to love your enemies—even when your enemy takes the form of your husband, your mother or your best friend—and to pray for them. Your loving example might convict your husband of his selfishness.

- Settling heated disagreements requires humility, along with love, a willingness to forgive and faith in God's ability to change a person—even if that person is you. It takes humility to admit that though the other person is at fault, you may be partly at fault too. Often a resolution takes the form of a compromise, in which both of you admit some fault and work together to find ways to avoid more conflict in the future. In Nora and Scott's case, the compromise might be that Scott has to do a larger share of housework now while Nora works on her career.

- The need to place blame and demand that someone else change could be a signal of bitterness in your heart. Paul warned against allowing bitterness to take root (see Ephesians 4:31–32). Bitterness can strangle the life of a believer. Refusing to be bitter doesn't mean that the person who wronged you is without fault. It's a way to acknowledge that God has the right to decide if, how and when to change a life, and it shows your dependence on his ability to make those changes.

- One word you might not want to consider is *submission*. For many years this concept has been misunderstood and misused. However, God clearly tells women to submit to their husbands (see Ephesians 5:22), just as he tells a husband to sacrifice himself for his wife (see Ephesians 5:25). Remember that this passage about love and submission starts with the command for all people to submit to one another—but that doesn't mean that if your husband isn't submitting that you don't have to! Both you and your husband share a responsibility to each other. If you want your husband to change, the first step is to remember that Christ gave up his life for others—for you! This is what should motivate you to sacrifice, love and submit to those closest to you, including and especially your husband. Though submission is hard, and it grates against our willful spirits, it works wonders in relationships.

"We have this inborn habit of pouncing on the negative and not noticing the positive. Most people don't realize how negative they are toward their partners. When they examine their own words and actions, they're shocked to find how critical they are."

—Michele Weiner-Davis,
marriage therapist

"BE KIND AND COMPASSIONATE TO ONE ANOTHER, FORGIVING EACH OTHER, JUST AS IN CHRIST GOD FORGAVE YOU."

EPHESIANS 4:32

SEE ALSO

Proverbs 25:21–22

Matthew 7:5

John 8:7

For more on **Marriage**, check the index.

house of Judah. I have assigned you 40 days, a day for each year. ⁷Turn your face toward the siege of Jerusalem and with bared arm prophesy against her. ⁸I will tie you up with ropes so that you cannot turn from one side to the other until you have finished the days of your siege.

⁹"Take wheat and barley, beans and lentils, millet and spelt; put them in a storage jar and use them to make bread for yourself. You are to eat it during the 390 days you lie on your side. ¹⁰Weigh out twenty shekels*ᵃ* of food to eat each day and eat it at set times. ¹¹Also measure out a sixth of a hin*ᵇ* of water and drink it at set times. ¹²Eat the food as you would a loaf of barley bread; bake it in the sight of the people, using human excrement for fuel." ¹³The LORD said, "In this way the people of Israel will eat defiled food among the nations where I will drive them."

¹⁴Then I said, "Not so, Sovereign LORD! I have never defiled myself. From my youth until now I have never eaten anything found dead or torn by wild animals. No impure meat has ever entered my mouth."

conversations

obedience «» 4:1–17

1» What does it mean for you to obey God in life's *details*, as Ezekiel did?

2» What does your obedience convey to others about God?

3» Are there some areas in your life where you've not fully obeyed God?

For more on **obedience**, check the index.
For the next Conversations, go to p. 1202.

¹⁵"Very well," he said, "I will let you bake your bread over cow dung instead of human excrement."

¹⁶He then said to me: "Son of man, I am about to cut off the food supply in Jerusalem. The people will eat rationed food in anxiety and drink rationed water in despair, ¹⁷for food and water will be scarce. They will be appalled at the sight of each other and will waste away because of*ᶜ* their sin.

God's Razor of Judgment

5 "Now, son of man, take a sharp sword and use it as a barber's razor to shave your head and your beard. Then take a set of scales and divide up the hair. ²When the days of your siege come to an end, burn a third of the hair inside the city. Take a third and strike it with the sword all around the city. And scatter a third to the wind. For I will pursue them with drawn sword. ³But take a few hairs and tuck them away in the folds of your garment. ⁴Again, take a few of these and throw them into the fire and burn them up. A fire will spread from there to the whole house of Israel.

⁵"This is what the Sovereign LORD says: This is Jerusalem, which I have set in the center of the nations, with countries all around her. ⁶Yet in her wickedness she has rebelled against my laws and decrees more than the nations and countries around her. She has rejected my laws and has not followed my decrees.

⁷"Therefore this is what the Sovereign LORD says: You have been more unruly than the nations around you and have not followed my decrees or kept my laws. You have not even*ᵈ* conformed to the standards of the nations around you.

⁸"Therefore this is what the Sovereign LORD says: I myself am against you, Jerusalem, and I will inflict punishment on you in the sight of the nations. ⁹Because of all your detestable idols, I will do to you what I have never done before and will never do again. ¹⁰Therefore in your midst parents will eat their children, and children will eat their parents. I will inflict punishment on you and will scatter all your survivors to the winds. ¹¹Therefore as surely as I live, declares the Sovereign LORD, because you have defiled my sanctuary with all your vile images and detestable practices, I myself will shave you; I will not look on you with pity or spare you. ¹²A third of your people will die of the plague or perish by famine inside you; a third will fall by the sword outside your walls; and a third I will scatter to the winds and pursue with drawn sword.

¹³"Then my anger will cease and my wrath against them will subside, and I will be avenged. And when I have spent my wrath on them, they will know that I the LORD have spoken in my zeal.

¹⁴"I will make you a ruin and a reproach among the nations around you, in the sight of all who pass

---

ᵃ 10 That is, about 8 ounces or about 230 grams   *ᵇ 11* That is, about 1 1/3 pints or about 0.6 liter   *ᶜ 17* Or *away in*   *ᵈ 7* Most Hebrew manuscripts; some Hebrew manuscripts and Syriac *You have* by. [15]You will be a reproach and a taunt, a warning and an object of horror to the nations around you when I inflict punishment on you in anger and in wrath and with stinging rebuke. I the LORD have spoken. [16]When I shoot at you with my deadly and destructive arrows of famine, I will shoot to destroy you. I will bring more and more famine upon you and cut off your supply of food. [17]I will send famine and wild beasts against you, and they will leave you childless. Plague and bloodshed will sweep through you, and I will bring the sword against you. I the LORD have spoken."

Doom for the Mountains of Israel

6 The word of the LORD came to me: [2]"Son of man, set your face against the mountains of Israel; prophesy against them [3]and say: 'You mountains of Israel, hear the word of the Sovereign LORD. This is what the Sovereign LORD says to the mountains and hills, to the ravines and valleys: I am about to bring a sword against you, and I will destroy your high places. [4]Your altars will be demolished and your incense altars will be smashed; and I will slay your people in front of your idols. [5]I will lay the dead bodies of the Israelites in front of their idols, and I will scatter your bones around your altars. [6]Wherever you live, the towns will be laid waste and the high places demolished, so that your altars will be laid waste and devastated, your idols smashed and ruined, your incense altars broken down, and what you have made wiped out. [7]Your people will fall slain among you, and you will know that I am the LORD.

[8]"But I will spare some, for some of you will escape the sword when you are scattered among the lands and nations. [9]Then in the nations where they have been carried captive, those who escape will remember me—how I have been grieved by their adulterous hearts, which have turned away from me, and by their eyes, which have lusted after their idols. They will loathe themselves for the evil they have done and for all their detestable practices. [10]And they will know that I am the LORD; I did not threaten in vain to bring this calamity on them.

[11]"This is what the Sovereign LORD says: Strike your hands together and stamp your feet and cry out "Alas!" because of all the wicked and detestable practices of the house of Israel, for they will fall by the sword, famine and plague. [12]Those who are far away will die of the plague, and those who are near will fall by the sword, and those who survive and are spared will die of famine. So will I spend my wrath on them. [13]And they will know that I am the LORD, when their people lie slain among their idols around their altars, on every high hill and on all the mountaintops, under every spreading tree and every leafy oak—places where they offered fragrant incense to all their idols. [14]And I will stretch out my hand against them and make the land a desolate waste from the desert to Diblah[a]—wherever they live. Then they will know that I am the LORD.'"

The End Has Come

7 The word of the LORD came to me: [2]"Son of man, this is what the Sovereign LORD says to the land of Israel:

> "'The end! The end has come
>   upon the four corners of the land!
> [3]The end is now upon you,
>   and I will unleash my anger against you.
> I will judge you according to your conduct
>   and repay you for all your detestable practices.
> [4]I will not look on you with pity;
>   I will not spare you.
> I will surely repay you for your conduct
>   and for the detestable practices among you.

"'Then you will know that I am the LORD.'

[5]"This is what the Sovereign LORD says:

---

[a] 14 Most Hebrew manuscripts; a few Hebrew manuscripts *Riblah*

"'Disaster! Unheard-of[a] disaster!
 See, it comes!
[6]The end has come!
 The end has come!
It has roused itself against you.
 See, it comes!
[7]Doom has come upon you,
 upon you who dwell in the land.
The time has come! The day is near!
 There is panic, not joy, on the mountains.
[8]I am about to pour out my wrath on you
 and spend my anger against you.
I will judge you according to your conduct
 and repay you for all your detestable practices.
[9]I will not look on you with pity;
 I will not spare you.
I will repay you for your conduct
 and for the detestable practices among you.

"'Then you will know that it is I the Lord who strikes you.

[10]"'See, the day!
 See, it comes!
Doom has burst forth,
 the rod has budded,
 arrogance has blossomed!
[11]Violence has arisen,[b]
 a rod to punish the wicked.
None of the people will be left,
 none of that crowd—
 none of their wealth,
 nothing of value.
[12]The time has come!
 The day has arrived!
Let not the buyer rejoice
 nor the seller grieve,
 for my wrath is on the whole crowd.
[13]The sellers will not recover
 the property they have sold—
 as long as both buyers and sellers live.
For the vision concerning the whole crowd
 will not be reversed.
Because of their sins, not one of them
 will preserve their life.

[14]"'They have blown the trumpet,
 they have made all things ready,
but no one will go into battle,
 for my wrath is on the whole crowd.
[15]Outside is the sword;
 inside are plague and famine.

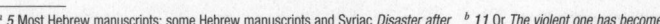

[a] 5 Most Hebrew manuscripts; some Hebrew manuscripts and Syriac *Disaster after* [b] 11 Or *The violent one has become*

Those in the country
    will die by the sword;
those in the city
    will be devoured by famine and plague.
¹⁶The fugitives who escape
    will flee to the mountains.
Like doves of the valleys,
    they will all moan,
    each for their own sins.
¹⁷Every hand will go limp;
    every knee will be wet with urine.
¹⁸They will put on sackcloth
    and be clothed with terror.
Every face will be covered with shame,
    and every head will be shaved.

¹⁹"They will throw their silver into the
    streets,
    and their gold will be treated as a thing
    unclean.
Their silver and gold
    will not be able to deliver them
    in the day of the Lord's wrath.
It will not satisfy their hunger
    or fill their stomachs,
    for it has caused them to stumble into
    sin.
²⁰They took pride in their beautiful jewelry
    and used it to make their detestable
    idols.
They made it into vile images;
    therefore I will make it a thing unclean
    for them.
²¹I will give their wealth as plunder to
    foreigners
    and as loot to the wicked of the earth,
    who will defile it.
²²I will turn my face away from the people,
    and robbers will desecrate the place I treasure.
They will enter it
    and will defile it.

²³"Prepare chains!
    For the land is full of bloodshed,
    and the city is full of violence.
²⁴I will bring the most wicked of nations
    to take possession of their houses.
I will put an end to the pride of the mighty,
    and their sanctuaries will be desecrated.
²⁵When terror comes,
    they will seek peace in vain.
²⁶Calamity upon calamity will come,
    and rumor upon rumor.

---

atissue:money stress

7:19 Money—we spend so much time pursuing it, managing it and thinking about it. How much should you save, invest and tithe? If you're married, how much should go toward your shopping versus your husband's golf game? Who should pay the bills? Stress over money can make a person feel torn or drive a couple apart. But the Israelites discovered that money has no real, eternal value. In the end, it's basically worthless. It cannot save you or satisfy you, and it can distract from what's really important. The next time a conflict over money erupts in your heart or house, ask yourself: Is it really worth this worry?

1199

> They will go searching for a vision from the prophet,
>> priestly instruction in the law will cease,
>> the counsel of the elders will come to an end.
> ²⁷The king will mourn,
>> the prince will be clothed with despair,
>> and the hands of the people of the land will tremble.
> I will deal with them according to their conduct,
>> and by their own standards I will judge them.

"'Then they will know that I am the Lord.'"

Idolatry in the Temple

8 In the sixth year, in the sixth month on the fifth day, while I was sitting in my house and the elders of Judah were sitting before me, the hand of the Sovereign Lord came on me there. ²I looked, and I saw a figure like that of a man.ᵃ From what appeared to be his waist down he was like fire, and from there up his appearance was as bright as glowing metal. ³He stretched out what looked like a hand and took me by the hair of my head. The Spirit lifted me up between earth and heaven and in visions of God he took me to Jerusalem, to the entrance of the north gate of the inner court, where the idol that provokes to jealousy stood. ⁴And there before me was the glory of the God of Israel, as in the vision I had seen in the plain.

⁵Then he said to me, "Son of man, look toward the north." So I looked, and in the entrance north of the gate of the altar I saw this idol of jealousy.

⁶And he said to me, "Son of man, do you see what they are doing—the utterly detestable things the house of Israel is doing here, things that will drive me far from my sanctuary? But you will see things that are even more detestable."

⁷Then he brought me to the entrance to the court. I looked, and I saw a hole in the wall. ⁸He said to me, "Son of man, now dig into the wall." So I dug into the wall and saw a doorway there.

⁹And he said to me, "Go in and see the wicked and detestable things they are doing here." ¹⁰So I went in and looked, and I saw portrayed all over the walls all kinds of crawling things and unclean animals and all the idols of the house of Israel. ¹¹In front of them stood seventy elders of the house of Israel, and Jaazaniah son of Shaphan was standing among them. Each had a censer in his hand, and a fragrant cloud of incense was rising.

¹²He said to me, "Son of man, have you seen what the elders of the house of Israel are doing in the darkness, each at the shrine of his own idol? They say, 'The Lord does not see us; the Lord has forsaken the land.'" ¹³Again, he said, "You will see them doing things that are even more detestable."

¹⁴Then he brought me to the entrance of the north gate of the house of the Lord, and I saw women sitting there, mourning the god Tammuz. ¹⁵He said to me, "Do you see this, son of man? You will see things that are even more detestable than this."

¹⁶He then brought me into the inner court of the house of the Lord, and there at the entrance to the temple, between the portico and the altar, were about twenty-five men. With their backs toward the temple of the Lord and their faces toward the east, they were bowing down to the sun in the east.

¹⁷He said to me, "Have you seen this, son of man? Is it a trivial matter for the house of Judah to do the detestable things they are doing here? Must they also fill the land with violence and continually arouse my anger? Look at them putting the branch to their nose! ¹⁸Therefore I will deal with them in anger; I will not look on them with pity or spare them. Although they shout in my ears, I will not listen to them."

Judgment on the Idolaters

9 Then I heard him call out in a loud voice, "Bring near those who are appointed to execute judgment on the city, each with weapon in hand." ²And I saw six men coming from the direction of the upper gate, which faces north, each with a deadly weapon in his hand. With them was a man clothed in linen who had a writing kit at his side. They came in and stood beside the bronze altar.

ᵃ 2 Or *saw a fiery figure*

³Now the glory of the God of Israel went up from above the cherubim, where it had been, and moved to the threshold of the temple. Then the LORD called to the man clothed in linen who had the writing kit at his side ⁴and said to him, "Go throughout the city of Jerusalem and put a mark on the foreheads of those who grieve and lament over all the detestable things that are done in it."

⁵As I listened, he said to the others, "Follow him through the city and kill, without showing pity or compassion. ⁶Slaughter the old men, the young men and women, the mothers and children, but do not touch anyone who has the mark. Begin at my sanctuary." So they began with the old men who were in front of the temple.

⁷Then he said to them, "Defile the temple and fill the courts with the slain. Go!" So they went out and began killing throughout the city. ⁸While they were killing and I was left alone, I fell facedown, crying out, "Ah, Sovereign LORD! Are you going to destroy the entire remnant of Israel in this outpouring of your wrath on Jerusalem?"

⁹He answered me, "The sin of the house of Israel and Judah is exceedingly great; the land is full of bloodshed and the city is full of injustice. They say, 'The LORD has forsaken the land; the LORD does not see.' ¹⁰So I will not look on them with pity or spare them, but I will bring down on their own heads what they have done."

¹¹Then the man in linen with the writing kit at his side brought back word, saying, "I have done as you commanded."

God's Glory Departs From the Temple

10 I looked, and I saw the likeness of a throne of lapis lazuli above the vault that was over the heads of the cherubim. ²The LORD said to the man clothed in linen, "Go in among the wheels beneath the cherubim. Fill your hands with burning coals from among the cherubim and scatter them over the city." And as I watched, he went in.

³Now the cherubim were standing on the south side of the temple when the man went in, and a cloud filled the inner court. ⁴Then the glory of the LORD rose from above the cherubim and moved to the threshold of the temple. The cloud filled the temple, and the court was full of the radiance of the glory of the LORD. ⁵The sound of the wings of the cherubim could be heard as far away as the outer court, like the voice of God Almighty*a* when he speaks.

⁶When the LORD commanded the man in linen, "Take fire from among the wheels, from among the cherubim," the man went in and stood beside a wheel. ⁷Then one of the cherubim reached out his hand to the fire that was among them. He took up some of it and put it into the hands of the man in linen, who took it and went out. ⁸(Under the wings of the cherubim could be seen what looked like human hands.)

⁹I looked, and I saw beside the cherubim four wheels, one beside each of the cherubim; the wheels sparkled like topaz. ¹⁰As for their appearance, the four of them looked alike; each was like a wheel intersecting a wheel. ¹¹As they moved, they would go in any one of the four directions the cherubim faced; the wheels did not turn about*b* as the cherubim went. The cherubim went in whatever direction the head faced, without turning as they went. ¹²Their entire bodies, including their backs, their hands and their wings, were completely full of eyes, as were their four wheels. ¹³I heard the wheels being called "the whirling wheels." ¹⁴Each of the cherubim had four faces: One face was that of a cherub, the second the face of a human being, the third the face of a lion, and the fourth the face of an eagle.

¹⁵Then the cherubim rose upward. These were the living creatures I had seen by the Kebar River. ¹⁶When the cherubim moved, the wheels beside them moved; and when the cherubim spread their wings to rise from the ground, the wheels did not leave their side. ¹⁷When the cherubim stood still, they also stood still; and when the cherubim rose, they rose with them, because the spirit of the living creatures was in them.

¹⁸Then the glory of the LORD departed from over the threshold of the temple and stopped above the cherubim. ¹⁹While I watched, the cherubim spread their wings and rose from the ground, and as they went, the wheels went with them. They stopped at the entrance of the east gate of the LORD's house, and the glory of the God of Israel was above them.

---

a 5 Hebrew *El-Shaddai* *b* 11 Or *aside*

²⁰These were the living creatures I had seen beneath the God of Israel by the Kebar River, and I realized that they were cherubim. ²¹Each had four faces and four wings, and under their wings was what looked like human hands. ²²Their faces had the same appearance as those I had seen by the Kebar River. Each one went straight ahead.

God's Sure Judgment on Jerusalem

11 Then the Spirit lifted me up and brought me to the gate of the house of the Lord that faces east. There at the entrance of the gate were twenty-five men, and I saw among them Jaazaniah son of Azzur and Pelatiah son of Benaiah, leaders of the people. ²The Lord said to me, "Son of man, these are the men who are plotting evil and giving wicked advice in this city. ³They say, 'Haven't our houses been recently rebuilt? This city is a pot, and we are the meat in it.' ⁴Therefore prophesy against them; prophesy, son of man."

⁵Then the Spirit of the Lord came on me, and he told me to say: "This is what the Lord says: That is what you are saying, house of Israel, but I know what is going through your mind. ⁶You have killed many people in this city and filled its streets with the dead.

⁷"Therefore this is what the Sovereign Lord says: The bodies you have thrown there are the meat and this city is the pot, but I will drive you out of it. ⁸You fear the sword, and the sword is what I will bring against you, declares the Sovereign Lord. ⁹I will drive you out of the city and deliver you into the hands of foreigners and inflict punishment on you. ¹⁰You will fall by the sword, and I will execute judgment on you at the borders of Israel. Then you will know that I am the Lord. ¹¹This city will not be a pot for you, nor will you be the meat in it; I will execute judgment on you at the borders of Israel. ¹²And you will know that I am the Lord, for you have not followed my decrees or kept my laws but have conformed to the standards of the nations around you."

¹³Now as I was prophesying, Pelatiah son of Benaiah died. Then I fell facedown and cried out in a loud voice, "Ah, Sovereign Lord! Will you completely destroy the remnant of Israel?"

The Promise of Israel's Return

¹⁴The word of the Lord came to me: ¹⁵"Son of man, the people of Jerusalem have said of your fellow exiles and the whole house of Israel,ᵃ 'They are far away from the Lord; this land was given to us as our possession.'

¹⁶"Therefore say: 'This is what the Sovereign Lord says: Although I sent them far away among the nations and scattered them among the countries, yet for a little while I have been a sanctuary for them in the countries where they have gone.'

¹⁷"Therefore say: 'This is what the Sovereign Lord says: I will gather you from the nations and bring you back from the countries where you have been scattered, and I will give you back the land of Israel again.'

¹⁸"They will return to it and remove all its vile images and detestable idols. ¹⁹I will give them an undivided heart and put a new spirit in them; I will remove from them their heart of stone and give them a heart of flesh. ²⁰Then they will follow my decrees and be careful to keep my laws. They will be my people, and I will be their God. ²¹But as for those whose hearts are devoted to their vile images and detestable idols, I will bring down on their own heads what they have done, declares the Sovereign Lord."

²²Then the cherubim, with the wheels beside them, spread their wings, and the glory of the

conversations
acceptance «» 11:17-21

1» What did the Israelites have to do to be once again accepted by God?

2» What do you have to do in order for God to accept you?

3» In your heart, do you feel fully accepted by God? Why do you think that is?

For more on **acceptance**, check the index.
For the next Conversations, go to p. 1221.

ᵃ 15 Or said of your brothers—your brothers who are your blood relatives and the whole house of Israel—

God of Israel was above them. ²³The glory of the Lord went up from within the city and stopped above the mountain east of it. ²⁴The Spirit lifted me up and brought me to the exiles in Babylonia*ᵃ* in the vision given by the Spirit of God.

Then the vision I had seen went up from me, ²⁵and I told the exiles everything the Lord had shown me.

The Exile Symbolized

12 The word of the Lord came to me: ²"Son of man, you are living among a rebellious people. They have eyes to see but do not see and ears to hear but do not hear, for they are a rebellious people.

³"Therefore, son of man, pack your belongings for exile and in the daytime, as they watch, set out and go from where you are to another place. Perhaps they will understand, though they are a rebellious house. ⁴During the daytime, while they watch, bring out your belongings packed for exile. Then in the evening, while they are watching, go out like those who go into exile. ⁵While they watch, dig through the wall and take your belongings out through it. ⁶Put them on your shoulder as they are watching and carry them out at dusk. Cover your face so that you cannot see the land, for I have made you a sign to the house of Israel."

⁷So I did as I was commanded. During the day I brought out my things packed for exile. Then in the evening I dug through the wall with my hands. I took my belongings out at dusk, carrying them on my shoulders while they watched.

⁸In the morning the word of the Lord came to me: ⁹"Son of man, did not that rebellious house of Israel ask you, 'What are you doing?'

¹⁰"Say to them, 'This is what the Sovereign Lord says: This prophecy concerns the prince in Jerusalem and the whole house of Israel who are there.' ¹¹Say to them, 'I am a sign to you.'

"As I have done, so it will be done to them. They will go into exile as captives.

¹²"The prince among them will put his things on his shoulder at dusk and leave, and a hole will be dug in the wall for him to go through. He will cover his face so that he cannot see the land. ¹³I will spread my net for him, and he will be caught in my snare; I will bring him to Babylonia, the land of the Chaldeans, but he will not see it, and there he will die. ¹⁴I will scatter to the winds all those around him—his staff and all his troops—and I will pursue them with drawn sword.

¹⁵"They will know that I am the Lord, when I disperse them among the nations and scatter them through the countries. ¹⁶But I will spare a few of them from the sword, famine and plague, so that in the nations where they go they may acknowledge all their detestable practices. Then they will know that I am the Lord."

¹⁷The word of the Lord came to me: ¹⁸"Son of man, tremble as you eat your food, and shudder in fear as you drink your water. ¹⁹Say to the people of the land: 'This is what the Sovereign Lord says about those living in Jerusalem and in the land of Israel: They will eat their food in anxiety and drink their water in despair, for their land will be stripped of everything in it because of the violence of all who live there. ²⁰The inhabited towns will be laid waste and the land will be desolate. Then you will know that I am the Lord.'"

There Will Be No Delay

²¹The word of the Lord came to me: ²²"Son of man, what is this proverb you have in the land of Israel: 'The days go by and every vision comes to nothing'? ²³Say to them, 'This is what the Sovereign Lord says: I am going to put an end to this proverb, and they will no longer quote it in Israel.' Say to them, 'The days are near when every vision will be fulfilled. ²⁴For there will be no more false visions or flattering divinations among the people of Israel. ²⁵But I the Lord will speak what I will, and it shall be fulfilled without delay. For in your days, you rebellious house, I will fulfill whatever I say, declares the Sovereign Lord.'"

²⁶The word of the Lord came to me: ²⁷"Son of man, the house of Israel is saying, 'The vision he sees is for many years from now, and he prophesies about the distant future.'

²⁸"Therefore say to them, 'This is what the Sovereign Lord says: None of my words will be delayed any longer; whatever I say will be fulfilled, declares the Sovereign Lord.'"

1203

ᵃ 24 Or *Chaldea*

False Prophets Condemned

13 The word of the LORD came to me: [2] "Son of man, prophesy against the prophets of Israel who are now prophesying. Say to those who prophesy out of their own imagination: 'Hear the word of the LORD! [3] This is what the Sovereign LORD says: Woe to the foolish[a] prophets who follow their own spirit and have seen nothing! [4] Your prophets, Israel, are like jackals among ruins. [5] You have not gone up to the breaches in the wall to repair it for the house of Israel so that it will stand firm in the battle on the day of the LORD. [6] Their visions are false and their divinations a lie. Even though the LORD has not sent them, they say, "The LORD declares," and expect him to fulfill their words. [7] Have you not seen false visions and uttered lying divinations when you say, "The LORD declares," though I have not spoken?

[8] "Therefore this is what the Sovereign LORD says: Because of your false words and lying visions, I am against you, declares the Sovereign LORD. [9] My hand will be against the prophets who see false visions and utter lying divinations. They will not belong to the council of my people or be listed in the records of the house of Israel, nor will they enter the land of Israel. Then you will know that I am the Sovereign LORD.

[10] "Because they lead my people astray, saying, "Peace," when there is no peace, and because, when a flimsy wall is built, they cover it with whitewash, [11] therefore tell those who cover it with whitewash that it is going to fall. Rain will come in torrents, and I will send hailstones hurtling down, and violent winds will burst forth. [12] When the wall collapses, will people not ask you, "Where is the whitewash you covered it with?"

[13] "Therefore this is what the Sovereign LORD says: In my wrath I will unleash a violent wind, and in my anger hailstones and torrents of rain will fall with destructive fury. [14] I will tear down the wall you have covered with whitewash and will level it to the ground so that its foundation will be laid bare. When it[b] falls, you will be destroyed in it; and you will know that I am the LORD. [15] So I will spend my wrath against the wall and against those who covered it with whitewash. I will say to you, "The wall is gone and so are those who whitewashed it, [16] those prophets of Israel who prophesied to Jerusalem and saw visions of peace for her when there was no peace, declares the Sovereign LORD."'

[17] "Now, son of man, set your face against the daughters of your people who prophesy out of their own imagination. Prophesy against them [18] and say, 'This is what the Sovereign LORD says: Woe to the women who sew magic charms on all their wrists and make veils of various lengths for their heads in order to ensnare people. Will you ensnare the lives of my people but preserve your own? [19] You have profaned me among my people for a few handfuls of barley and scraps of bread. By lying to my people, who listen to lies, you have killed those who should not have died and have spared those who should not live.

[20] "Therefore this is what the Sovereign LORD says: I am against your magic charms with which you ensnare people like birds and I will tear them from your arms; I will set free the people that you ensnare like birds. [21] I will tear off your veils and save my people from your hands, and they will no longer fall prey to your power. Then you will know that I am the LORD. [22] Because you disheartened the righteous with your lies, when I had brought them no grief, and because you encouraged the wicked not to turn from their evil ways and so save their lives, [23] therefore you will no longer see false visions or practice divination. I will save my people from your hands. And then you will know that I am the LORD.'"

atissue:lying

13:19 What's the big deal about a little lie? It's not as if I killed anybody . . . But any lie is a very big deal to God because God *is* truth. Truth is an integral part of his nature. Even a small, seemingly inconsequential lie is an infringement on the truth—and thereby a violation against God himself. Because of who he is, it's no wonder that truth is so important to him. Loving God means caring about what he cares about, which means you'll also care about truth—full truth, only truth, always truth.

---

[a] 3 Or *wicked*   [b] 14 Or *the city*

Idolaters Condemned

14 Some of the elders of Israel came to me and sat down in front of me. ²Then the word of the Lord came to me: ³"Son of man, these men have set up idols in their hearts and put wicked stumbling blocks before their faces. Should I let them inquire of me at all? ⁴Therefore speak to them and tell them, 'This is what the Sovereign Lord says: When any of the Israelites set up idols in their hearts and put a wicked stumbling block before their faces and then go to a prophet, I the Lord will answer them myself in keeping with their great idolatry. ⁵I will do this to recapture the hearts of the people of Israel, who have all deserted me for their idols.'

⁶"Therefore say to the house of Israel, 'This is what the Sovereign Lord says: Repent! Turn from your idols and renounce all your detestable practices!

⁷"'When any of the Israelites or any foreigner residing in Israel separate themselves from me and set up idols in their hearts and put a wicked stumbling block before their faces and then go to a prophet to inquire of me, I the Lord will answer them myself. ⁸I will set my face against them and make them an example and a byword. I will remove them from my people. Then you will know that I am the Lord.

⁹"'And if the prophet is enticed to utter a prophecy, I the Lord have enticed that prophet, and I will stretch out my hand against him and destroy him from among my people Israel. ¹⁰They will bear their guilt—the prophet will be as guilty as the one who consults him. ¹¹Then the people of Israel will no longer stray from me, nor will they defile themselves anymore with all their sins. They will be my people, and I will be their God, declares the Sovereign Lord.'"

1205

Jerusalem's Judgment Inescapable

¹²The word of the Lord came to me: ¹³"Son of man, if a country sins against me by being unfaithful and I stretch out my hand against it to cut off its food supply and send famine upon it and kill its people and their animals, ¹⁴even if these three men—Noah, Daniel[a] and Job—were in it, they could save only themselves by their righteousness, declares the Sovereign Lord.

¹⁵"Or if I send wild beasts through that country and they leave it childless and it becomes desolate so that no one can pass through it because of the beasts, ¹⁶as surely as I live, declares the Sovereign Lord, even if these three men were in it, they could not save their own sons or daughters. They alone would be saved, but the land would be desolate.

¹⁷"Or if I bring a sword against that country and say, 'Let the sword pass throughout the land,' and I kill its people and their animals, ¹⁸as surely as I live, declares the Sovereign Lord, even if these three men were in it, they could not save their own sons or daughters. They alone would be saved.

¹⁹"Or if I send a plague into that land and pour out my wrath on it through bloodshed, killing its people and their animals, ²⁰as surely as I live, declares the Sovereign Lord, even if Noah, Daniel and Job were in it, they could save neither son nor daughter. They would save only themselves by their righteousness.

²¹"For this is what the Sovereign Lord says: How much worse will it be when I send against Jerusalem my four dreadful judgments—sword and famine and wild beasts and plague—to kill its men and their animals! ²²Yet there will be some survivors—sons and daughters who will be brought out of it. They will come to you, and when you see their conduct and their actions, you will be consoled regarding the disaster I have brought on Jerusalem—every disaster I have brought on it. ²³You will be consoled when you see their conduct and their actions, for you will know that I have done nothing in it without cause, declares the Sovereign Lord."

Jerusalem as a Useless Vine

15 The word of the Lord came to me: ²"Son of man, how is the wood of a vine different from that of a branch from any of the trees in the forest? ³Is wood ever taken from it to make anything useful? Do they make pegs from it to hang things on? ⁴And after it is thrown on the fire as fuel and the fire burns both ends and chars the middle, is it then useful for anything? ⁵If it was not useful for anything when it was whole, how much less can it be made into something useful when the fire has burned it and it is charred?

⁶"Therefore this is what the Sovereign Lord says: As I have given the wood of the vine among the trees

---

a 14 Or *Danel*, a man of renown in ancient literature; also in verse 20 of the forest as fuel for the fire, so will I treat the people living in Jerusalem. [7]I will set my face against them. Although they have come out of the fire, the fire will yet consume them. And when I set my face against them, you will know that I am the Lord. [8]I will make the land desolate because they have been unfaithful, declares the Sovereign Lord."

Jerusalem as an Adulterous Wife

16 The word of the Lord came to me: [2]"Son of man, confront Jerusalem with her detestable practices [3]and say, 'This is what the Sovereign Lord says to Jerusalem: Your ancestry and birth were in the land of the Canaanites; your father was an Amorite and your mother a Hittite. [4]On the day you were born your cord was not cut, nor were you washed with water to make you clean, nor were you rubbed with salt or wrapped in cloths. [5]No one looked on you with pity or had compassion enough to do any of these things for you. Rather, you were thrown out into the open field, for on the day you were born you were despised.

[6]"'Then I passed by and saw you kicking about in your blood, and as you lay there in your blood I said to you, "Live!"[a] [7]I made you grow like a plant of the field. You grew and developed and entered puberty. Your breasts had formed and your hair had grown, yet you were stark naked.

[8]"'Later I passed by, and when I looked at you and saw that you were old enough for love, I spread the corner of my garment over you and covered your nakedness. I gave you my solemn oath and entered into a covenant with you, declares the Sovereign Lord, and you became mine.

[9]"'I bathed you with water and washed the blood from you and put ointments on you. [10]I clothed you with an embroidered dress and put sandals of fine leather on you. I dressed you in fine linen and covered you with costly garments. [11]I adorned you with jewelry: I put bracelets on your arms and a necklace around your neck, [12]and I put a ring on your nose, earrings on your ears and a beautiful crown on your head. [13]So you were adorned with gold and silver; your clothes were of fine linen and costly fabric and embroidered cloth. Your food was honey, olive oil and the finest flour. You became very beautiful and rose to be a queen. [14]And your fame spread among the nations on account of your beauty, because the splendor I had given you made your beauty perfect, declares the Sovereign Lord.

[15]"'But you trusted in your beauty and used your fame to become a prostitute. You lavished your favors on anyone who passed by and your beauty became his. [16]You took some of your garments to make gaudy high places, where you carried on your prostitution. You went to him, and he possessed your beauty.[b] [17]You also took the fine jewelry I gave you, the jewelry made of my gold and silver, and you made for yourself male idols and engaged in prostitution with them. [18]And you took your embroidered clothes to put on them, and you offered my oil and incense before them. [19]Also the food I provided for you—the flour, olive oil and honey I gave you to eat—you offered as fragrant incense before them. That is what happened, declares the Sovereign Lord.

[20]"'And you took your sons and daughters whom you bore to me and sacrificed them as food to the idols. Was your prostitution not enough? [21]You slaughtered my children and sacrificed them to the idols. [22]In all your detestable practices and your prostitution you did not remember the days of your youth, when you were naked and bare, kicking about in your blood.

[23]"'Woe! Woe to you, declares the Sovereign Lord. In addition to all your other wickedness, [24]you built a mound for yourself and made a lofty shrine in every public square. [25]At every street corner you built your lofty shrines and degraded your beauty, spreading your legs with increasing promiscuity to anyone who passed by. [26]You engaged in prostitution with the Egyptians, your neighbors with large genitals, and aroused my anger with your increasing promiscuity. [27]So I stretched out my hand against you and reduced your territory; I gave you over to the greed of your enemies, the daughters of the Philistines, who were shocked by your lewd conduct. [28]You engaged in prostitution with the Assyrians too, because you were insatiable; and even after that, you still were not satisfied. [29]Then you increased your promiscuity to include Babylonia,[c] a land of merchants, but even with this you were not satisfied.

[30]"'I am filled with fury against you,[d] declares the Sovereign Lord, when you do all these things, act-

[a] 6 A few Hebrew manuscripts, Septuagint and Syriac; most Hebrew manuscripts repeat the last clause.   [b] 16 The meaning of the Hebrew for this sentence is uncertain.   [c] 29 Or Chaldea   [d] 30 Or How feverish is your heart,

ing like a brazen prostitute! ³¹When you built your mounds at every street corner and made your lofty shrines in every public square, you were unlike a prostitute, because you scorned payment.

³²"You adulterous wife! You prefer strangers to your own husband! ³³All prostitutes receive gifts, but you give gifts to all your lovers, bribing them to come to you from everywhere for your illicit favors. ³⁴So in your prostitution you are the opposite of others; no one runs after you for your favors. You are the very opposite, for you give payment and none is given to you.

³⁵"Therefore, you prostitute, hear the word of the LORD! ³⁶This is what the Sovereign LORD says: Because you poured out your lust and exposed your nakedness in your promiscuity with your lovers, and because of all your detestable idols, and because you gave them your children's blood, ³⁷therefore I am going to gather all your lovers, with whom you found pleasure, those you loved as well as those you hated. I will gather them against you from all around and will strip you in front of them, and they will see all your nakedness. ³⁸I will sentence you to the punishment of women who commit adultery and who shed blood; I will bring on you the blood vengeance of my wrath and jealous anger. ³⁹Then I will deliver you into the hands of your lovers, and they will tear down your mounds and destroy your lofty shrines. They will strip you of your clothes and take your fine jewelry and leave you naked and bare. ⁴⁰They will bring a mob against you, who will stone you and hack you to pieces with their swords. ⁴¹They will burn down your houses and inflict punishment on you in the sight of many women. I will put a stop to your prostitution, and you will no longer pay your lovers. ⁴²Then my wrath against you will subside and my jealous anger will turn away from you; I will be calm and no longer angry.

⁴³"Because you did not remember the days of your youth but enraged me with all these things, I will surely bring down on your head what you have done, declares the Sovereign LORD. Did you not add lewdness to all your other detestable practices?

⁴⁴"Everyone who quotes proverbs will quote this proverb about you: "Like mother, like daughter." ⁴⁵You are a true daughter of your mother, who despised her husband and her children; and you are a true sister of your sisters, who despised their husbands and their children. Your mother was a Hittite and your father an Amorite. ⁴⁶Your older sister was Samaria, who lived to the north of you with her daughters; and your younger sister, who lived to the south of you with her daughters, was Sodom. ⁴⁷You not only followed their ways and copied their detestable practices, but in all your ways you soon became more depraved than they. ⁴⁸As surely as I live, declares the Sovereign LORD, your sister Sodom and her daughters never did what you and your daughters have done.

⁴⁹"Now this was the sin of your sister Sodom: She and her daughters were arrogant, overfed and unconcerned; they did not help the poor and needy. ⁵⁰They were haughty and did detestable things before me. Therefore I did away with them as you have seen. ⁵¹Samaria did not commit half the sins you did. You have done more detestable things than they, and have made your sisters seem righteous by all these things you have done. ⁵²Bear your disgrace, for you have furnished some justification for your sisters. Because your sins were more vile than theirs, they appear more righteous than you. So then, be ashamed and bear your disgrace, for you have made your sisters appear righteous.

⁵³"However, I will restore the fortunes of Sodom and her daughters and of Samaria and her daughters, and your fortunes along with them, ⁵⁴so that you may bear your disgrace and be ashamed of all you have done in giving them comfort. ⁵⁵And your sisters, Sodom with her daughters and Samaria with her daughters, will return to what they were before; and you and your daughters will return to what you were before. ⁵⁶You would not even mention your sister Sodom in the day of your pride, ⁵⁷before your wickedness was uncovered. Even

1207

atissue:compassion

16:49–50 *Arrogant. Overfed. Unconcerned.* Those words could easily describe our society in general. Do they describe you, even a little? Don't answer too quickly. It's easy to get so consumed by your own life that you don't look beyond yourself to see the needs of others. This was Sodom's sin. Is it your sin, too? Ask God to help you take your eyes off yourself and to start seeing the needs of others. Ask him to show you ways you can help the poor and needy who are all around you.

so, you are now scorned by the daughters of Edom*a* and all her neighbors and the daughters of the Philistines—all those around you who despise you. ⁵⁸You will bear the consequences of your lewdness and your detestable practices, declares the LORD.

⁵⁹"'This is what the Sovereign LORD says: I will deal with you as you deserve, because you have despised my oath by breaking the covenant. ⁶⁰Yet I will remember the covenant I made with you in the days of your youth, and I will establish an everlasting covenant with you. ⁶¹Then you will remember your ways and be ashamed when you receive your sisters, both those who are older than you and those who are younger. I will give them to you as daughters, but not on the basis of my covenant with you. ⁶²So I will establish my covenant with you, and you will know that I am the LORD. ⁶³Then, when I make atonement for you for all you have done, you will remember and be ashamed and never again open your mouth because of your humiliation, declares the Sovereign LORD.'"

Two Eagles and a Vine

17 The word of the LORD came to me: ²"Son of man, set forth an allegory and tell it to the house of Israel as a parable. ³Say to them, 'This is what the Sovereign LORD says: A great eagle with powerful wings, long feathers and full plumage of varied colors came to Lebanon. Taking hold of the top of a cedar, ⁴he broke off its topmost shoot and carried it away to a land of merchants, where he planted it in a city of traders.

⁵"'He took one of the seedlings of the land and put it in fertile soil. He planted it like a willow by abundant water, ⁶and it sprouted and became a low, spreading vine. Its branches turned toward him, but its roots remained under it. So it became a vine and produced branches and put out leafy boughs.

⁷"'But there was another great eagle with powerful wings and full plumage. The vine now sent out its roots toward him from the plot where it was planted and stretched out its branches to him for water. ⁸It had been planted in good soil by abundant water so that it would produce branches, bear fruit and become a splendid vine.'

⁹"Say to them, 'This is what the Sovereign LORD says: Will it thrive? Will it not be uprooted and stripped of its fruit so that it withers? All its new growth will wither. It will not take a strong arm or many people to pull it up by the roots. ¹⁰It has been planted, but will it thrive? Will it not wither completely when the east wind strikes it—wither away in the plot where it grew?'"

¹¹Then the word of the LORD came to me: ¹²"Say to this rebellious house, 'Do you not know what these things mean?' Say to them: 'The king of Babylon went to Jerusalem and carried off her king and her nobles, bringing them back with him to Babylon. ¹³Then he took a member of the royal family and made a treaty with him, putting him under oath. He also carried away the leading men of the land, ¹⁴so that the kingdom would be brought low, unable to rise again, surviving only by keeping his treaty. ¹⁵But the king rebelled against him by sending his envoys to Egypt to get horses and a large army. Will he succeed? Will he who does such things escape? Will he break the treaty and yet escape?

¹⁶"'As surely as I live, declares the Sovereign LORD, he shall die in Babylon, in the land of the king who put him on the throne, whose oath he despised and whose treaty he broke. ¹⁷Pharaoh with his mighty army and great horde will be of no help to him in war, when ramps are built and siege works erected to destroy many lives. ¹⁸He despised the oath by breaking the covenant. Because he had given his hand in pledge and yet did all these things, he shall not escape.

¹⁹"'Therefore this is what the Sovereign LORD says: As surely as I live, I will bring down on his head my oath that he despised and my covenant that he broke. ²⁰I will spread my net for him, and he will be caught in my snare. I will bring him to Babylon and execute judgment on him there because he was unfaithful to me. ²¹All his choice troops will fall by the sword, and the survivors will be scattered to the winds. Then you will know that I the LORD have spoken.

²²"'This is what the Sovereign LORD says: I myself will take a shoot from the very top of a cedar and plant it; I will break off a tender sprig from its topmost shoots and plant it on a high and lofty mountain. ²³On the mountain heights of Israel I will plant it; it will produce branches and bear fruit and become a splendid cedar. Birds of every kind will nest in it; they will find shelter in the shade of its branches. ²⁴All

---

a 57 Many Hebrew manuscripts and Syriac; most Hebrew manuscripts, Septuagint and Vulgate Aram the trees of the forest will know that I the LORD bring down the tall tree and make the low tree grow tall. I dry up the green tree and make the dry tree flourish.

"'I the LORD have spoken, and I will do it.'"

The One Who Sins Will Die

18 The word of the LORD came to me: [2]"What do you people mean by quoting this proverb about the land of Israel:

> "'The parents eat sour grapes,
>   and the children's teeth are set on edge'?

[3]"As surely as I live, declares the Sovereign LORD, you will no longer quote this proverb in Israel. [4]For everyone belongs to me, the parent as well as the child—both alike belong to me. The one who sins is the one who will die.

> [5]"Suppose there is a righteous man
>   who does what is just and right.
> [6]He does not eat at the mountain shrines
>   or look to the idols of the house of Israel.
> He does not defile his neighbor's wife
>   or have sexual relations with a woman during her period.
> [7]He does not oppress anyone,
>   but returns what he took in pledge for a loan.
> He does not commit robbery
>   but gives his food to the hungry
>   and provides clothing for the naked.
> [8]He does not lend to them at interest
>   or take a profit from them.
> He withholds his hand from doing wrong
>   and judges fairly between two parties.
> [9]He follows my decrees
>   and faithfully keeps my laws.
> That man is righteous;
>   he will surely live,

declares the Sovereign LORD.

[10]"Suppose he has a violent son, who sheds blood or does any of these other things[a] [11](though the father has done none of them):

> "He eats at the mountain shrines.
> He defiles his neighbor's wife.
> [12]He oppresses the poor and needy.
> He commits robbery.
> He does not return what he took in pledge.
> He looks to the idols.
> He does detestable things.
> [13]He lends at interest and takes a profit.

Will such a man live? He will not! Because he has done all these detestable things, he is to be put to death; his blood will be on his own head.

[14]"But suppose this son has a son who sees all the sins his father commits, and though he sees them, he does not do such things:

---

[a] 10 Or things to a brother

myth#70

"IT'S NOT MY FAULT. IT'S THE WAY I WAS RAISED."

I'm so tired of hearing about what someone thinks I've done wrong now. Lately, it's been, "Makayla, you really let us down," just because I forgot to show up for set-up at church a few times. Or I hear, "Makayla, you're just playing with Eric. Don't hurt him." Yada yada yada. You'd think I was a terrible person or something.

I can't help the fact that I struggle with commitment. Issues in my past and the way I grew up make it almost impossible for me to stick with something. No one stayed committed to anything in my family. We didn't stay in the same place long enough to be committed.

I was an Air Force brat. We lived all over the States and even overseas. I always knew that I'd have to say good-bye to new friends within six months to a year. I got so tired of saying good-bye. But that's what my family always did—we said good-bye. And that's what my parents did to each other after they divorced.

I quickly learned to leave my options open. I never knew where life would take me. That's why I haven't become a member of the church I've been attending. After all, I don't know how long I'll be here. I don't know why I keep volunteering at church. Just to connect with people, I guess. But then after I sign up, it seems like things just come up. You'd think that people would be understanding—we're all busy, you know—but they're so uptight. So if I don't show, everyone gets mad. But isn't it better that I don't do something than feel coerced to do it?

I feel the same way with relationships. I tell guys up front, "I'm not looking for a commitment. I just want to hang out and have fun." Is it my fault if they try to get serious and end up hurt? Honestly, I usually try to leave them before they leave me. It's inevitable, so I might as well keep the upper hand.

I'll say this one last time, so everyone, please pay attention: I can't help it. It's just the way I am.

—Makayla

EVER MEET SOMEONE who seemed to wear her faults like a badge of honor? She might say, "I can't help it. I'm high-maintenance." Or she might even use a more "spiritual" excuse: "I know I've got issues, but I'm just a sinner saved by grace." She might hide behind her past or blame her parents or others for her actions. But blaming someone else or refusing to take responsibility for our actions isn't fair to us or others.

We might feel trapped in the patterns that ruined relationships in our families in the past (for example, a predisposition to alcoholism or drug addiction, the failures of parents, etc.). Or, because of wounds due to past trauma (rape or some other violent crime), we might feel pulled into self-destructive behaviors. But the Bible promises freedom from even the most invincible of prisons. That's why God tells us to confess our sins and receive his forgiveness and freedom. No need to deny our mistakes, hide behind excuses or let the past control us.

Through the Holy Spirit, he also gives us the power to change and to resist temptation. (See Romans 8:1–17; 1 Corinthians 10:13; Galatians 5:13–26.) God can do the impossible. The Spirit transforms us into new creatures (see 2 Corinthians 5:17) so that we no longer have to hold on to our belief that we're helpless to overcome our pasts.

God makes readily available to us the power to resist temptation. He also places the responsibility for our choices squarely on our shoulders.

"Maybe you have been struggling to change and tempted by the notion that a change of environment will change the way you're feeling. A new job or a new city or a new spouse. 'Out with the old and in with the new and then I will be happy.' It's a lie! Our problem is inside us, not around us. We are the ones who need to change, not our environment."

—James MacDonald, pastor

1211

"IF WE CLAIM TO BE WITHOUT SIN, WE DECEIVE OURSELVES AND THE TRUTH IS NOT IN US."

1 JOHN 1:8

SEE ALSO
Deuteronomy 30:11–20
Ezekiel 18:20
Galatians 5:1

For more on **Responsibility**, check the index.

1212

¹⁵"He does not eat at the mountain shrines
    or look to the idols of the house of Israel.
He does not defile his neighbor's wife.
¹⁶He does not oppress anyone
    or require a pledge for a loan.
He does not commit robbery
    but gives his food to the hungry
    and provides clothing for the naked.
¹⁷He withholds his hand from mistreating the poor
    and takes no interest or profit from them.
He keeps my laws and follows my decrees.

He will not die for his father's sin; he will surely live. ¹⁸But his father will die for his own sin, because he practiced extortion, robbed his brother and did what was wrong among his people.

¹⁹"Yet you ask, 'Why does the son not share the guilt of his father?' Since the son has done what is just and right and has been careful to keep all my decrees, he will surely live. ²⁰The one who sins is the one who will die. The child will not share the guilt of the parent, nor will the parent share the guilt of the child. The righteousness of the righteous will be credited to them, and the wickedness of the wicked will be charged against them.

²¹"But if the wicked turn away from all the sins they have committed and keep all my decrees and do what is just and right, they will surely live; they will not die. ²²None of the offenses they have committed will be remembered against them. Because of the righteous things they have done, they will live. ²³Do I take any pleasure in the death of the wicked? declares the Sovereign LORD. Rather, am I not pleased when they turn from their ways and live?

²⁴"But if the righteous turn from their righteousness and commit sin and do the same detestable things the wicked do, will they live? None of the righteous things they have done will be remembered. Because of the unfaithfulness they are guilty of and because of the sins they have committed, they will die.

²⁵"Yet you say, 'The way of the Lord is not just.' Hear, house of Israel: Is my way unjust? Is it not your ways that are unjust? ²⁶If the righteous turn from their righteousness and commit sin, they will die for it; because of the sin they have committed they will die. ²⁷But if the wicked turn away from the wickedness they have committed and do what is just and right, they will save their lives. ²⁸Because they consider all the offenses they have committed and turn away from them, they will surely live; they will not die. ²⁹Yet the house of Israel says, 'The way of the Lord is not just.' Are my ways unjust, house of Israel? Is it not your ways that are unjust?

³⁰"Therefore, house of Israel, I will judge each of you according to your own ways, declares the Sovereign LORD. Repent! Turn away from all your offenses; then sin will not be your downfall. ³¹Rid your-

HE IS: pleased

18:23–32 Some people portray God as a cruel deity who wants to zap unsuspecting sinners. In Ezekiel's day, the Israelites accused God of unfairly punishing the people for the sins of their parents. But through Ezekiel, God revealed that people are responsible for their own sin and that he is *pleased* when people turn to him.

God is not begrudging. He doesn't overcomplicate salvation in the hopes of disqualifying some. He doesn't enjoy anyone's death. Rather, he is *pleased*—thrilled, delighted and satisfied—when you come to him and live (see Luke 15:7). Imagine—the God of the universe, pleased with *you*!

For the next He Is, go to p. 1241.

selves of all the offenses you have committed, and get a new heart and a new spirit. Why will you die, house of Israel? ³²For I take no pleasure in the death of anyone, declares the Sovereign Lᴏʀᴅ. Repent and live!

A Lament Over Israel's Princes

19 "Take up a lament concerning the princes of Israel ²and say:

> "'What a lioness was your mother
>   among the lions!
> She lay down among them
>   and reared her cubs.
> ³She brought up one of her cubs,
>   and he became a strong lion.
> He learned to tear the prey
>   and he devoured people.
> ⁴The nations heard about him,
>   and he was trapped in their pit.
> They led him with hooks
>   to the land of Egypt.
>
> ⁵"'When she saw her hope unfulfilled,
>   her expectation gone,
> she took another of her cubs
>   and made him a strong lion.
> ⁶He prowled among the lions,
>   for he was now a strong lion.
> He learned to tear the prey
>   and he devoured people.
> ⁷He broke down*ᵃ* their strongholds
>   and devastated their towns.
> The land and all who were in it
>   were terrified by his roaring.
> ⁸Then the nations came against him,
>   those from regions round about.
> They spread their net for him,
>   and he was trapped in their pit.
> ⁹With hooks they pulled him into a cage
>   and brought him to the king of Babylon.
> They put him in prison,
>   so his roar was heard no longer
>   on the mountains of Israel.
>
> ¹⁰"'Your mother was like a vine in your vineyard*ᵇ*
>   planted by the water;
> it was fruitful and full of branches
>   because of abundant water.
> ¹¹Its branches were strong,
>   fit for a ruler's scepter.
> It towered high
>   above the thick foliage,
> conspicuous for its height

ᵃ 7 Targum (see Septuagint); Hebrew *He knew*   *ᵇ 10* Two Hebrew manuscripts; most Hebrew manuscripts *your blood*

and for its many branches.
¹²But it was uprooted in fury
and thrown to the ground.
The east wind made it shrivel,
it was stripped of its fruit;
its strong branches withered
and fire consumed them.
¹³Now it is planted in the desert,
in a dry and thirsty land.
¹⁴Fire spread from one of its main^a branches
and consumed its fruit.
No strong branch is left on it
fit for a ruler's scepter.'

"This is a lament and is to be used as a lament."

Rebellious Israel Purged

20 In the seventh year, in the fifth month on the tenth day, some of the elders of Israel came to inquire of the LORD, and they sat down in front of me.

²Then the word of the LORD came to me: ³"Son of man, speak to the elders of Israel and say to them, 'This is what the Sovereign LORD says: Have you come to inquire of me? As surely as I live, I will not let you inquire of me, declares the Sovereign LORD.'

⁴"Will you judge them? Will you judge them, son of man? Then confront them with the detestable practices of their ancestors ⁵and say to them: 'This is what the Sovereign LORD says: On the day I chose Israel, I swore with uplifted hand to the descendants of the house of Jacob and revealed myself to them in Egypt. With uplifted hand I said to them, "I am the LORD your God." ⁶On that day I swore to them that I would bring them out of Egypt into a land I had searched out for them, a land flowing with milk and honey, the most beautiful of all lands. ⁷And I said to them, "Each of you, get rid of the vile images you have set your eyes on, and do not defile yourselves with the idols of Egypt. I am the LORD your God."

⁸"But they rebelled against me and would not listen to me; they did not get rid of the vile images they had set their eyes on, nor did they forsake the idols of Egypt. So I said I would pour out my wrath on them and spend my anger against them in Egypt. ⁹But for the sake of my name, I brought them out of Egypt. I did it to keep my name from being profaned in the eyes of the nations among whom they lived and in whose sight I had revealed myself to the Israelites. ¹⁰Therefore I led them out of Egypt and brought them into the wilderness. ¹¹I gave them my decrees and made known to them my laws, through which people will live if they obey them. ¹²Also I gave them my Sabbaths as a sign between us, so they would know that I the LORD made them holy.

¹³"Yet the people of Israel rebelled against me in the wilderness. They did not follow my decrees but rejected my laws—through which people will live if they obey them—and they utterly desecrated my Sabbaths. So I said I would pour out my wrath on them and destroy them in the wilderness. ¹⁴But for the sake of my name I did what would keep it from being profaned in the eyes of the nations in whose sight I had brought them out. ¹⁵Also with uplifted hand I swore to them in the wilderness that I would not bring them into the land I had given them—a land flowing with milk and honey, the most beautiful of all lands— ¹⁶because they rejected my laws and did not follow my decrees and desecrated my Sabbaths. For their hearts were devoted to their idols. ¹⁷Yet I looked on them with pity and did not destroy them or put an end to them in the wilderness. ¹⁸I said to their children in the wilderness, "Do not follow the statutes of your parents or keep their laws or defile yourselves with their idols. ¹⁹I am the LORD your God; follow my decrees and be careful to keep my laws. ²⁰Keep my Sabbaths holy, that they may be a sign between us. Then you will know that I am the LORD your God."

²¹"But the children rebelled against me: They did not follow my decrees, they were not careful to keep my laws, of which I said, "Whoever obeys them will live by them," and they desecrated my Sabbaths. So

---

^a *14 Or from under its*

I said I would pour out my wrath on them and spend my anger against them in the wilderness. ²²But I withheld my hand, and for the sake of my name I did what would keep it from being profaned in the eyes of the nations in whose sight I had brought them out. ²³Also with uplifted hand I swore to them in the wilderness that I would disperse them among the nations and scatter them through the countries, ²⁴because they had not obeyed my laws but had rejected my decrees and desecrated my Sabbaths, and their eyes ⸢lusted⸥ after their parents' idols. ²⁵So I gave them other statutes that were not good and laws through which they could not live; ²⁶I defiled them through their gifts—the sacrifice of every firstborn— that I might fill them with horror so they would know that I am the Lord.'

²⁷"Therefore, son of man, speak to the people of Israel and say to them, 'This is what the Sovereign Lord says: In this also your ancestors blasphemed me by being unfaithful to me: ²⁸When I brought them into the land I had sworn to give them and they saw any high hill or any leafy tree, there they offered their sacrifices, made offerings that aroused my anger, presented their fragrant incense and poured out their drink offerings. ²⁹Then I said to them: What is this high place you go to?'" (It is called Bamah*ᵃ* to this day.)

Rebellious Israel Renewed

³⁰"Therefore say to the house of Israel: 'This is what the Sovereign Lord says: Will you defile yourselves the way your ancestors did and lust after their vile images? ³¹When you offer your gifts—the sacrifice of your children in the fire—you continue to defile yourselves with all your idols to this day. Am I to let you inquire of me, house of Israel? As surely as I live, declares the Sovereign Lord, I will not let you inquire of me.

³²"'You say, "We want to be like the nations, like the peoples of the world, who serve wood and stone." But what you have in mind will never happen. ³³As surely as I live, declares the Sovereign Lord, I will reign over you with a mighty hand and an outstretched arm and with outpoured wrath. ³⁴I will bring you from the nations and gather you from the countries where you have been scattered—with a mighty hand and an outstretched arm and with outpoured wrath. ³⁵I will bring you into the wilderness of the nations and there, face to face, I will execute judgment upon you. ³⁶As I judged your ancestors in the wilderness of the land of Egypt, so I will judge you, declares the Sovereign Lord. ³⁷I will take note of you as you pass under my rod, and I will bring you into the bond of the covenant. ³⁸I will purge you of those who revolt and rebel against me. Although I will bring them out of the land where they are living, yet they will not enter the land of Israel. Then you will know that I am the Lord.

³⁹"'As for you, house of Israel, this is what the Sovereign Lord says: Go and serve your idols, every one of you! But afterward you will surely listen to me and no longer profane my holy name with your gifts and idols. ⁴⁰For on my holy mountain, the high mountain of Israel, declares the Sovereign Lord, there in the land the entire house of Israel will serve me, and there I will accept them. There I will require your offerings and your choice gifts,*ᵇ* along with all your holy sacrifices. ⁴¹I will accept you as fragrant incense when I bring you out from the nations and gather you from the countries where you have been scattered, and I will be proved holy through you in the sight of the nations. ⁴²Then you will know that I am the Lord, when I bring you into the land of Israel, the land I had sworn with uplifted hand to give to your ancestors. ⁴³There you will remember your conduct and all the actions by which you have defiled yourselves, and you will loathe yourselves for all the evil you have done. ⁴⁴You will know that I am the Lord, when I deal with you for my name's sake and not according to your evil ways and your corrupt practices, house of Israel, declares the Sovereign Lord.'"

Prophecy Against the South

* ⁴⁵The word of the Lord came to me: ⁴⁶"Son of man, set your face toward the south; preach against the south and prophesy against the forest of the southland. ⁴⁷Say to the southern forest: 'Hear the word of the Lord. This is what the Sovereign Lord says: I am about to set fire to you, and it will consume all your trees, both green and dry. The blazing flame will not be quenched, and every face from south to north will be scorched by it. ⁴⁸Everyone will see that I the Lord have kindled it; it will not be quenched.'"

⁴⁹Then I said, "Ah, Sovereign Lord! They are saying of me, 'Isn't he just telling parables?'"

ᵃ 29 Bamah means *high place.*   *ᵇ 40* Or *and the gifts of your firstfruits*

* 20:45-49 is numbered 21:1-5 in Hebrew texts.

Babylon as God's Sword of Judgment

21 [1]The word of the Lord came to me: [2]"Son of man, set your face against Jerusalem and preach against the sanctuary. Prophesy against the land of Israel [3]and say to her: 'This is what the Lord says: I am against you. I will draw my sword from its sheath and cut off from you both the righteous and the wicked. [4]Because I am going to cut off the righteous and the wicked, my sword will be unsheathed against everyone from south to north. [5]Then all people will know that I the Lord have drawn my sword from its sheath; it will not return again.'

[6]"Therefore groan, son of man! Groan before them with broken heart and bitter grief. [7]And when they ask you, 'Why are you groaning?' you shall say, 'Because of the news that is coming. Every heart will melt and every hand go limp; every spirit will become faint and every knee be wet with urine.' It is coming! It will surely take place, declares the Sovereign Lord."

[8]The word of the Lord came to me: [9]"Son of man, prophesy and say, 'This is what the Lord says:

> "'A sword, a sword,
>   sharpened and polished—
> [10]sharpened for the slaughter,
>   polished to flash like lightning!

"'Shall we rejoice in the scepter of my royal son? The sword despises every such stick.

> [11]"'The sword is appointed to be polished,
>   to be grasped with the hand;
> it is sharpened and polished,
>   made ready for the hand of the slayer.
> [12]Cry out and wail, son of man,
>   for it is against my people;
>   it is against all the princes of Israel.
> They are thrown to the sword
>   along with my people.
> Therefore beat your breast.

[13]"'Testing will surely come. And what if even the scepter, which the sword despises, does not continue? declares the Sovereign Lord.'

> [14]"So then, son of man, prophesy
>   and strike your hands together.
> Let the sword strike twice,
>   even three times.
> It is a sword for slaughter—
>   a sword for great slaughter,
>   closing in on them from every side.
> [15]So that hearts may melt
>   and the fallen be many,
> I have stationed the sword for slaughter[a]
>   at all their gates.
> Oh! It is made to flash like lightning,
>   it is grasped for slaughter.
> [16]Slash to the right, you sword,
>   then to the left,
>   wherever your blade is turned.
> [17]I too will strike my hands together,

---

[a] *15* Septuagint; the meaning of the Hebrew for this word is uncertain.

* 21:1-32 is numbered 21:6-37 in Hebrew texts.

and my wrath will subside.
    I the LORD have spoken."

¹⁸The word of the LORD came to me: ¹⁹"Son of man, mark out two roads for the sword of the king of Babylon to take, both starting from the same country. Make a signpost where the road branches off to the city. ²⁰Mark out one road for the sword to come against Rabbah of the Ammonites and another against Judah and fortified Jerusalem. ²¹For the king of Babylon will stop at the fork in the road, at the junction of the two roads, to seek an omen: He will cast lots with arrows, he will consult his idols, he will examine the liver. ²²Into his right hand will come the lot for Jerusalem, where he is to set up battering rams, to give the command to slaughter, to sound the battle cry, to set battering rams against the gates, to build a ramp and to erect siege works. ²³It will seem like a false omen to those who have sworn allegiance to him, but he will remind them of their guilt and take them captive.

²⁴"Therefore this is what the Sovereign LORD says: 'Because you people have brought to mind your guilt by your open rebellion, revealing your sins in all that you do—because you have done this, you will be taken captive.

²⁵"You profane and wicked prince of Israel, whose day has come, whose time of punishment has reached its climax, ²⁶this is what the Sovereign LORD says: Take off the turban, remove the crown. It will not be as it was: The lowly will be exalted and the exalted will be brought low. ²⁷A ruin! A ruin! I will make it a ruin! The crown will not be restored until he to whom it rightfully belongs shall come; to him I will give it.'

²⁸"And you, son of man, prophesy and say, 'This is what the Sovereign LORD says about the Ammonites and their insults:

> "'A sword, a sword,
>> drawn for the slaughter,
> polished to consume
>> and to flash like lightning!
> ²⁹Despite false visions concerning you
>> and lying divinations about you,
> it will be laid on the necks
>> of the wicked who are to be slain,
> whose day has come,
>> whose time of punishment has reached its climax.

> ³⁰"'Let the sword return to its sheath.
>> In the place where you were created,
> in the land of your ancestry,
>> I will judge you.
> ³¹I will pour out my wrath on you
>> and breathe out my fiery anger against you;
> I will deliver you into the hands of brutal men,
>> men skilled in destruction.
> ³²You will be fuel for the fire,
>> your blood will be shed in your land,
> you will be remembered no more;
>> for I the LORD have spoken.'"

Judgment on Jerusalem's Sins

22 The word of the LORD came to me:

²"Son of man, will you judge her? Will you judge this city of bloodshed? Then confront her with all her detestable practices ³and say: 'This is what the Sovereign LORD says: You city that brings on herself doom by shedding blood in her midst and defiles herself by making idols, ⁴you have become guilty because of

the blood you have shed and have become defiled by the idols you have made. You have brought your days to a close, and the end of your years has come. Therefore I will make you an object of scorn to the nations and a laughingstock to all the countries. ⁵Those who are near and those who are far away will mock you, you infamous city, full of turmoil.

⁶"'See how each of the princes of Israel who are in you uses his power to shed blood. ⁷In you they have treated father and mother with contempt; in you they have oppressed the foreigner and mistreated the fatherless and the widow. ⁸You have despised my holy things and desecrated my Sabbaths. ⁹In you are slanderers who are bent on shedding blood; in you are those who eat at the mountain shrines and commit lewd acts. ¹⁰In you are those who dishonor their father's bed; in you are those who violate women during their period, when they are ceremonially unclean. ¹¹In you one man commits a detestable offense with his neighbor's wife, another shamefully defiles his daughter-in-law, and another violates his sister, his own father's daughter. ¹²In you are people who accept bribes to shed blood; you take interest and make a profit from the poor. You extort unjust gain from your neighbors. And you have forgotten me, declares the Sovereign LORD.

¹³"'I will surely strike my hands together at the unjust gain you have made and at the blood you have shed in your midst. ¹⁴Will your courage endure or your hands be strong in the day I deal with you? I the LORD have spoken, and I will do it. ¹⁵I will disperse you among the nations and scatter you through the countries; and I will put an end to your uncleanness. ¹⁶When you have been defiled*a* in the eyes of the nations, you will know that I am the LORD.'"

¹⁷Then the word of the LORD came to me: ¹⁸"Son of man, the house of Israel has become dross to me; all of them are the copper, tin, iron and lead left inside a furnace. They are but the dross of silver. ¹⁹Therefore this is what the Sovereign LORD says: 'Because you have all become dross, I will gather you into Jerusalem. ²⁰As silver, copper, iron, lead and tin are gathered into a furnace to be melted with a fiery blast, so will I gather you in my anger and my wrath and put you inside the city and melt you. ²¹I will gather you and I will blow on you with my fiery wrath, and you will be melted inside her. ²²As silver is melted in a furnace, so you will be melted inside her, and you will know that I the LORD have poured out my wrath on you.'"

²³Again the word of the LORD came to me: ²⁴"Son of man, say to the land, 'You are a land that has not been cleansed or rained on in the day of wrath.' ²⁵There is a conspiracy of her princes*b* within her like a roaring lion tearing its prey; they devour people, take treasures and precious things and make many widows within her. ²⁶Her priests do violence to my law and profane my holy things; they do not distinguish between the holy and the common; they teach that there is no difference between the unclean and the clean; and they shut their eyes to the keeping of my Sabbaths, so that I am profaned among them. ²⁷Her officials within her are like wolves tearing their prey; they shed blood and kill people to make unjust gain. ²⁸Her prophets whitewash these deeds for them by false visions and lying divinations. They say, 'This is what the Sovereign LORD says'—when the LORD has not spoken. ²⁹The people of the land practice extortion and commit robbery; they oppress the poor and needy and mistreat the foreigner, denying them justice.

³⁰"I looked for someone among them who would build up the wall and stand before me in the gap on behalf of the land so I would not have to destroy it, but I found no one. ³¹So I will pour out my wrath on them and consume them with my fiery anger, bringing down on their own heads all they have done, declares the Sovereign LORD."

Two Adulterous Sisters

23 The word of the LORD came to me: ²"Son of man, there were two women, daughters of the same mother. ³They became prostitutes in Egypt, engaging in prostitution from their youth. In that land their breasts were fondled and their virgin bosoms caressed. ⁴The older was named Oholah, and her sister was Oholibah. They were mine and gave birth to sons and daughters. Oholah is Samaria, and Oholibah is Jerusalem.

⁵"Oholah engaged in prostitution while she was still mine; and she lusted after her lovers, the

Assyrians—warriors [6]clothed in blue, governors and commanders, all of them handsome young men, and mounted horsemen. [7]She gave herself as a prostitute to all the elite of the Assyrians and defiled herself with all the idols of everyone she lusted after. [8]She did not give up the prostitution she began in Egypt, when during her youth men slept with her, caressed her virgin bosom and poured out their lust on her.

[9]"Therefore I delivered her into the hands of her lovers, the Assyrians, for whom she lusted. [10]They stripped her naked, took away her sons and daughters and killed her with the sword. She became a byword among women, and punishment was inflicted on her.

[11]"Her sister Oholibah saw this, yet in her lust and prostitution she was more depraved than her sister. [12]She too lusted after the Assyrians—governors and commanders, warriors in full dress, mounted horsemen, all handsome young men. [13]I saw that she too defiled herself; both of them went the same way.

[14]"But she carried her prostitution still further. She saw men portrayed on a wall, figures of Chaldeans[a] portrayed in red, [15]with belts around their waists and flowing turbans on their heads; all of them looked like Babylonian chariot officers, natives of Chaldea.[b] [16]As soon as she saw them, she lusted after them and sent messengers to them in Chaldea. [17]Then the Babylonians came to her, to the bed of love, and in their lust they defiled her. After she had been defiled by them, she turned away from them in disgust. [18]When she carried on her prostitution openly and exposed her nakedness, I turned away from her in disgust, just as I had turned away from her sister. [19]Yet she became more and more promiscuous as she recalled the days of her youth, when she was a prostitute in Egypt. [20]There she lusted after her lovers, whose genitals were like those of donkeys and whose emission was like that of horses. [21]So you longed for the lewdness of your youth, when in Egypt your bosom was caressed and your young breasts fondled.[c]

[22]"Therefore, Oholibah, this is what the Sovereign LORD says: I will stir up your lovers against you, those you turned away from in disgust, and I will bring them against you from every side— [23]the Babylonians and all the Chaldeans, the men of Pekod and Shoa and Koa, and all the Assyrians with them, handsome young men, all of them governors and commanders, chariot officers and men of high rank, all mounted on horses. [24]They will come against you with weapons,[d] chariots and wagons and with a throng of people; they will take up positions against you on every side with large and small shields and with helmets. I will turn you over to them for punishment, and they will punish you according to their standards. [25]I will direct my jealous anger against you, and they will deal with you in fury. They will cut off your noses and your ears, and those of you who are left will fall by the sword. They will take away your sons and daughters, and those of you who are left will be consumed by fire. [26]They will also strip you of your clothes and take your fine jewelry. [27]So I will put a stop to the lewdness and prostitution you began in Egypt. You will not look on these things with longing or remember Egypt anymore.

[28]"For this is what the Sovereign LORD says: I am about to deliver you into the hands of those you hate, to those you turned away from in disgust. [29]They will deal with you in hatred and take away everything you have worked for. They will leave you stark naked, and the shame of your prostitution will be exposed. Your lewdness and promiscuity [30]have brought this on you, because you lusted after the nations and defiled yourself with their idols. [31]You have gone the way of your sister; so I will put her cup into your hand.

[32]"This is what the Sovereign LORD says:

> "You will drink your sister's cup,
>   a cup large and deep;
> it will bring scorn and derision,
>   for it holds so much.
> [33]You will be filled with drunkenness and sorrow,
>   the cup of ruin and desolation,
>   the cup of your sister Samaria.

---

[a] *14* Or *Babylonians*   [b] *15* Or *Babylonia*; also in verse 16   [c] *21* Syriac (see also verse 3); Hebrew *caressed because of your young breasts*   [d] *24* The meaning of the Hebrew for this word is uncertain.

³⁴You will drink it and drain it dry
    and chew on its pieces—
    and you will tear your breasts.

I have spoken, declares the Sovereign Lord.

³⁵"Therefore this is what the Sovereign Lord says: Since you have forgotten me and thrust me behind your back, you must bear the consequences of your lewdness and prostitution."

³⁶The Lord said to me: "Son of man, will you judge Oholah and Oholibah? Then confront them with their detestable practices, ³⁷for they have committed adultery and blood is on their hands. They committed adultery with their idols; they even sacrificed their children, whom they bore to me, as food for them. ³⁸They have also done this to me: At that same time they defiled my sanctuary and desecrated my Sabbaths. ³⁹On the very day they sacrificed their children to their idols, they entered my sanctuary and desecrated it. That is what they did in my house.

⁴⁰"They even sent messengers for men who came from far away, and when they arrived you bathed yourself for them, painted your eyes and put on your jewelry. ⁴¹You sat on an elegant couch, with a table spread before it on which you had placed the incense and olive oil that belonged to me.

⁴²"The noise of a carefree crowd was around her; drunkards were brought from the desert along with men from the rabble, and they put bracelets on the arms of the woman and her sister and beautiful crowns on their heads. ⁴³Then I said about the one worn out by adultery, 'Now let them use her as a prostitute, for that is all she is.' ⁴⁴And they slept with her. As men sleep with a prostitute, so they slept with those lewd women, Oholah and Oholibah. ⁴⁵But righteous judges will sentence them to the punishment of women who commit adultery and shed blood, because they are adulterous and blood is on their hands.

⁴⁶"This is what the Sovereign Lord says: Bring a mob against them and give them over to terror and plunder. ⁴⁷The mob will stone them and cut them down with their swords; they will kill their sons and daughters and burn down their houses.

⁴⁸"So I will put an end to lewdness in the land, that all women may take warning and not imitate you. ⁴⁹You will suffer the penalty for your lewdness and bear the consequences of your sins of idolatry. Then you will know that I am the Sovereign Lord."

Jerusalem as a Cooking Pot

24 In the ninth year, in the tenth month on the tenth day, the word of the Lord came to me: ²"Son of man, record this date, this very date, because the king of Babylon has laid siege to Jerusalem this very day. ³Tell this rebellious house a parable and say to them: 'This is what the Sovereign Lord says:

    "'Put on the cooking pot; put it on
        and pour water into it.
⁴Put into it the pieces of meat,
        all the choice pieces—the leg and the shoulder.
Fill it with the best of these bones;
⁵   take the pick of the flock.
Pile wood beneath it for the bones;
        bring it to a boil
        and cook the bones in it.

⁶"'For this is what the Sovereign Lord says:

    "'Woe to the city of bloodshed,
        to the pot now encrusted,
        whose deposit will not go away!
Take the meat out piece by piece
        in whatever order it comes.

7 "'For the blood she shed is in her midst:
  She poured it on the bare rock;
 she did not pour it on the ground,
  where the dust would cover it.
8 To stir up wrath and take revenge
 I put her blood on the bare rock,
  so that it would not be covered.

9 "'Therefore this is what the Sovereign Lord says:

"'Woe to the city of bloodshed!
  I, too, will pile the wood high.
10 So heap on the wood
  and kindle the fire.
 Cook the meat well,
  mixing in the spices;
  and let the bones be charred.
11 Then set the empty pot on the coals
  till it becomes hot and its copper glows,
 so that its impurities may be melted
  and its deposit burned away.
12 It has frustrated all efforts;
  its heavy deposit has not been removed,
  not even by fire.

13 "'Now your impurity is lewdness. Because I tried to cleanse you but you would not be cleansed from your impurity, you will not be clean again until my wrath against you has subsided.

14 "'I the Lord have spoken. The time has come for me to act. I will not hold back; I will not have pity, nor will I relent. You will be judged according to your conduct and your actions, declares the Sovereign Lord.'"

Ezekiel's Wife Dies

15 The word of the Lord came to me: 16 "Son of man, with one blow I am about to take away from you the delight of your eyes. Yet do not lament or weep or shed any tears. 17 Groan quietly; do not mourn for the dead. Keep your turban fastened and your sandals on your feet; do not cover your mustache and beard or eat the customary food ˌof mournersˌ."

18 So I spoke to the people in the morning, and in the evening my wife died. The next morning I did as I had been commanded.

19 Then the people asked me, "Won't you tell us what these things have to do with us? Why are you acting like this?"

20 So I said to them, "The word of the Lord came to me: 21 Say to the house of Israel, 'This is what the Sovereign Lord says: I am about to desecrate my sanctuary—the stronghold in which you take pride, the delight of your eyes, the object of your affection. The sons and daughters you left behind will fall by the sword. 22 And you will do as I have done. You will not cover your mustache and beard or eat the customary food ˌof mournersˌ. 23 You will keep your turbans on your heads and your sandals on your feet. You will not mourn or weep but will waste away because of[a] your sins and groan among yourselves. 24 Ezekiel will be

" conversations "

grief «» 24:15–27

1 » Why does God allow us to experience personal pain and loss?

2 » How does grieving help us cope with the pain of our loss?

3 » Have you ever had to withhold grieving, as Ezekiel did? If so, how did that affect you?

For more on grief, check the index.
For the next Conversations, go to p. 1234.

---
a 23 Or away in

a sign to you; you will do just as he has done. When this happens, you will know that I am the Sovereign Lord.'

²⁵"And you, son of man, on the day I take away their stronghold, their joy and glory, the delight of their eyes, their heart's desire, and their sons and daughters as well— ²⁶on that day a fugitive will come to tell you the news. ²⁷At that time your mouth will be opened; you will speak with him and will no longer be silent. So you will be a sign to them, and they will know that I am the Lord."

A Prophecy Against Ammon

25 The word of the Lord came to me: ²"Son of man, set your face against the Ammonites and prophesy against them. ³Say to them, 'Hear the word of the Sovereign Lord. This is what the Sovereign Lord says: Because you said "Aha!" over my sanctuary when it was desecrated and over the land of Israel when it was laid waste and over the people of Judah when they went into exile, ⁴therefore I am going to give you to the people of the East as a possession. They will set up their camps and pitch their tents among you; they will eat your fruit and drink your milk. ⁵I will turn Rabbah into a pasture for camels and Ammon into a resting place for sheep. Then you will know that I am the Lord. ⁶For this is what the Sovereign Lord says: Because you have clapped your hands and stamped your feet, rejoicing with all the malice of your heart against the land of Israel, ⁷therefore I will stretch out my hand against you and give you as plunder to the nations. I will wipe you out from among the nations and exterminate you from the countries. I will destroy you, and you will know that I am the Lord.'"

A Prophecy Against Moab

⁸"This is what the Sovereign Lord says: 'Because Moab and Seir said, "Look, the house of Judah has become like all the other nations," ⁹therefore I will expose the flank of Moab, beginning at its frontier towns—Beth Jeshimoth, Baal Meon and Kiriathaim—the glory of that land. ¹⁰I will give Moab along with the Ammonites to the people of the East as a possession, so that the Ammonites will not be remembered among the nations; ¹¹and I will inflict punishment on Moab. Then they will know that I am the Lord.'"

A Prophecy Against Edom

¹²"This is what the Sovereign Lord says: 'Because Edom took revenge on the house of Judah and became very guilty by doing so, ¹³therefore this is what the Sovereign Lord says: I will stretch out my hand against Edom and kill its people and their animals. I will lay it waste, and from Teman to Dedan they will fall by the sword. ¹⁴I will take vengeance on Edom by the hand of my people Israel, and they will deal with Edom in accordance with my anger and my wrath; they will know my vengeance, declares the Sovereign Lord.'"

A Prophecy Against Philistia

¹⁵"This is what the Sovereign Lord says: 'Because the Philistines acted in vengeance and took revenge with malice in their hearts, and with ancient hostility sought to destroy Judah, ¹⁶therefore this is what the Sovereign Lord says: I am about to stretch out my hand against the Philistines, and I will wipe out the Kerethites and destroy those remaining along the coast. ¹⁷I will carry out great vengeance on them and punish them in my wrath. Then they will know that I am the Lord, when I take vengeance on them.'"

atissue:gloating

25:1–7 The Ammonites were absolutely delighted to see God's people conquered. How shallow and wicked of them! But do we do the same? Do we secretly enjoy watching someone else fail? Does it make us feel better to hear of someone else who lost her job or her husband or her beauty? Do we wish that those we envy would fail, at least once? When we rejoice in another's downfall, we bring judgment upon ourselves. Instead of rejoicing when someone falls, do all you can to reach out and lift her up. Next time you may be the one in need of help.

A Prophecy Against Tyre

26 In the eleventh month of the twelfth[a] year, on the first day of the month, the word of the LORD came to me: [2]"Son of man, because Tyre has said of Jerusalem, 'Aha! The gate to the nations is broken, and its doors have swung open to me; now that she lies in ruins I will prosper,' [3]therefore this is what the Sovereign LORD says: I am against you, Tyre, and I will bring many nations against you, like the sea casting up its waves. [4]They will destroy the walls of Tyre and pull down her towers; I will scrape away her rubble and make her a bare rock. [5]Out in the sea she will become a place to spread fishnets, for I have spoken, declares the Sovereign LORD. She will become plunder for the nations, [6]and her settlements on the mainland will be ravaged by the sword. Then they will know that I am the LORD.

[7]"For this is what the Sovereign LORD says: From the north I am going to bring against Tyre Nebuchadnezzar[b] king of Babylon, king of kings, with horses and chariots, with horsemen and a great army. [8]He will ravage your settlements on the mainland with the sword; he will set up siege works against you, build a ramp up to your walls and raise his shields against you. [9]He will direct the blows of his battering rams against your walls and demolish your towers with his weapons. [10]His horses will be so many that they will cover you with dust. Your walls will tremble at the noise of the warhorses, wagons and chariots when he enters your gates as men enter a city whose walls have been broken through. [11]The hooves of his horses will trample all your streets; he will kill your people with the sword, and your strong pillars will fall to the ground. [12]They will plunder your wealth and loot your merchandise; they will break down your walls and demolish your fine houses and throw your stones, timber and rubble into the sea. [13]I will put an end to your noisy songs, and the music of your harps will be heard no more. [14]I will make you a bare rock, and you will become a place to spread fishnets. You will never be rebuilt, for I the LORD have spoken, declares the Sovereign LORD.

[15]"This is what the Sovereign LORD says to Tyre: Will not the coastlands tremble at the sound of your fall, when the wounded groan and the slaughter takes place in you? [16]Then all the princes of the coast will step down from their thrones and lay aside their robes and take off their embroidered garments. Clothed with terror, they will sit on the ground, trembling every moment, appalled at you. [17]Then they will take up a lament concerning you and say to you:

> "'How you are destroyed, city of renown,
>   peopled by men of the sea!
> You were a power on the seas,
>   you and your citizens;
> you put your terror
>   on all who lived there.
> [18]Now the coastlands tremble
>   on the day of your fall;
> the islands in the sea
>   are terrified at your collapse.'

[19]"This is what the Sovereign LORD says: When I make you a desolate city, like cities no longer inhabited, and when I bring the ocean depths over you and its vast waters cover you, [20]then I will bring you down with those who go down to the pit, to the people of long ago. I will make you dwell in the earth below, as in ancient ruins, with those who go down to the pit, and you will not return or take your place[c] in the land of the living. [21]I will bring you to a horrible end and you will be no more. You will be sought, but you will never again be found, declares the Sovereign LORD."

A Lament Over Tyre

27 The word of the LORD came to me: [2]"Son of man, take up a lament concerning Tyre. [3]Say to Tyre, situated at the gateway to the sea, merchant of peoples on many coasts, 'This is what the Sovereign LORD says:

---

[a] *1 Probable reading of the original Hebrew text; Masoretic Text does not have* month of the twelfth.   [b] *7 Hebrew* Nebuchadrezzar, *of which* Nebuchadnezzar *is a variant; here and often in Ezekiel and Jeremiah*   [c] *20 Septuagint; Hebrew* return, and I will give glory

"'You say, Tyre,
    "I am perfect in beauty."
⁴Your domain was on the high seas;
    your builders brought your beauty to perfection.
⁵They made all your timbers
    of juniper from Senir*ᵃ*;
they took a cedar from Lebanon
    to make a mast for you.
⁶Of oaks from Bashan
    they made your oars;
of cypress wood*ᵇ* from the coasts of Cyprus
    they made your deck, inlaid with ivory.
⁷Fine embroidered linen from Egypt was your sail
    and served as your banner;
your awnings were of blue and purple
    from the coasts of Elishah.
⁸Men of Sidon and Arvad were your oarsmen;
    your skilled men, Tyre, were aboard as your sailors.
⁹Veteran craftsmen of Byblos were on board
    as shipwrights to caulk your seams.
All the ships of the sea and their sailors
    came alongside to trade for your wares.

¹⁰"'Men of Persia, Lydia and Put
    served as soldiers in your army.
They hung their shields and helmets on your walls,
    bringing you splendor.
¹¹Men of Arvad and Helek
    guarded your walls on every side;
men of Gammad
    were in your towers.
They hung their shields around your walls;
    they brought your beauty to perfection.

¹²"'Tarshish did business with you because of your great wealth of goods; they exchanged silver, iron, tin and lead for your merchandise.
¹³"'Greece, Tubal and Meshek did business with you; they traded human beings and articles of bronze for your wares.
¹⁴"'Men of Beth Togarmah exchanged chariot horses, cavalry horses and mules for your merchandise.
¹⁵"'The men of Rhodes*ᶜ* traded with you, and many coastlands were your customers; they paid you with ivory tusks and ebony.
¹⁶"'Aram*ᵈ* did business with you because of your many products; they exchanged turquoise, purple fabric, embroidered work, fine linen, coral and rubies for your merchandise.
¹⁷"'Judah and Israel traded with you; they exchanged wheat from Minnith and confections,*ᵉ* honey, olive oil and balm for your wares.
¹⁸"'Damascus did business with you because of your many products and great wealth of goods. They offered wine from Helbon, wool from Zahar ¹⁹and casks of wine from Izal in exchange for your wares: wrought iron, cassia and calamus.
²⁰"'Dedan traded in saddle blankets with you.
²¹"'Arabia and all the princes of Kedar were your customers; they did business with you in lambs, rams and goats.

ᵃ 5 That is, Mount Hermon   *ᵇ 6* Targum; the Masoretic Text has a different division of the consonants.   *ᶜ 15* Septuagint; Hebrew *Dedan*   *ᵈ 16* Most Hebrew manuscripts; some Hebrew manuscripts and Syriac *Edom*   *ᵉ 17* The meaning of the Hebrew for this word is uncertain.

²²"'The merchants of Sheba and Raamah traded with you; for your merchandise they exchanged the finest of all kinds of spices and precious stones, and gold.

²³"'Harran, Kanneh and Eden and merchants of Sheba, Ashur and Kilmad traded with you. ²⁴In your marketplace they traded with you beautiful garments, blue fabric, embroidered work and multicolored rugs with cords twisted and tightly knotted.

²⁵"'The ships of Tarshish serve
    as carriers for your wares.
You are filled with heavy cargo
    as you sail the sea.
²⁶Your oarsmen take you
    out to the high seas.
But the east wind will break you to pieces
    far out at sea.
²⁷Your wealth, merchandise and wares,
    your mariners, sailors and shipwrights,
your merchants and all your soldiers,
    and everyone else on board
will sink into the heart of the sea
    on the day of your shipwreck.
²⁸The shorelands will quake
    when your sailors cry out.
²⁹All who handle the oars
    will abandon their ships;
the mariners and all the sailors
    will stand on the shore.
³⁰They will raise their voice
    and cry bitterly over you;
they will sprinkle dust on their heads
    and roll in ashes.
³¹They will shave their heads because of you
    and will put on sackcloth.
They will weep over you with anguish of soul
    and with bitter mourning.
³²As they wail and mourn over you,
    they will take up a lament concerning you:
"Who was ever silenced like Tyre,
    surrounded by the sea?"
³³When your merchandise went out on the seas,
    you satisfied many nations;
with your great wealth and your wares
    you enriched the kings of the earth.
³⁴Now you are shattered by the sea
    in the depths of the waters;
your wares and all your company
    have gone down with you.
³⁵All who live in the coastlands
    are appalled at you;
their kings shudder with horror
    and their faces are distorted with fear.
³⁶The merchants among the nations scoff at you;

1225

you have come to a horrible end
and will be no more.'"

A Prophecy Against the King of Tyre

28 The word of the LORD came to me: [2]"Son of man, say to the ruler of Tyre, 'This is what the Sovereign LORD says:

"'In the pride of your heart
you say, "I am a god;
I sit on the throne of a god
in the heart of the seas."
But you are a mortal and not a god,
though you think you are as wise as a
god.
[3]Are you wiser than Daniel[a]?
Is no secret hidden from you?
[4]By your wisdom and understanding
you have gained wealth for yourself
and amassed gold and silver
in your treasuries.
[5]By your great skill in trading
you have increased your wealth,
and because of your wealth
your heart has grown proud.

[6]"'Therefore this is what the Sovereign LORD says:

"'Because you think you are wise,
as wise as a god,
[7]I am going to bring foreigners against
you,
the most ruthless of nations;
they will draw their swords against your
beauty and wisdom
and pierce your shining splendor.
[8]They will bring you down to the pit,
and you will die a violent death
in the heart of the seas.
[9]Will you then say, "I am a god,"
in the presence of those who kill you?
You will be but a mortal, not a god,
in the hands of those who slay you.
[10]You will die the death of the uncircumcised
at the hands of foreigners.

I have spoken, declares the Sovereign LORD.'"

[11]The word of the LORD came to me: [12]"Son of man, take up a lament concerning the king of Tyre and say to him: 'This is what the Sovereign LORD says:

"'You were the seal of perfection,
full of wisdom and perfect in beauty.
[13]You were in Eden,

---

atissue:pride

28:2–10 Pride is a sneaky thing. It can masquerade as something more acceptable-sounding, such as self-reliance, independence or self-confidence. Pride infiltrates your heart, and before you even realize it, you may be making decisions without asking God for guidance first. Pride causes you to be self-sufficient rather than God-dependent, and it persuades you to justify your sins. Pride implies that God doesn't know best, but you do. Pride tells you that all your accomplishments were your doing. When your pride tries to assert itself, remind yourself that there's only one God—and you are not he. The price of pride is self-destruction.

---

a 3 Or Daniel, a man of renown in ancient literature

1226

the garden of God;
    every precious stone adorned you:
      carnelian, chrysolite and emerald,
      topaz, onyx and jasper,
      lapis lazuli, turquoise and beryl.*a*
    Your settings and mountings*b* were made of gold;
      on the day you were created they were prepared.
¹⁴You were anointed as a guardian cherub,
    for so I ordained you.
You were on the holy mount of God;
    you walked among the fiery stones.
¹⁵You were blameless in your ways
    from the day you were created
    till wickedness was found in you.
¹⁶Through your widespread trade
    you were filled with violence,
    and you sinned.
So I drove you in disgrace from the mount of God,
    and I expelled you, guardian cherub,
    from among the fiery stones.
¹⁷Your heart became proud
    on account of your beauty,
and you corrupted your wisdom
    because of your splendor.
So I threw you to the earth;
    I made a spectacle of you before kings.
¹⁸By your many sins and dishonest trade
    you have desecrated your sanctuaries.
So I made a fire come out from you,
    and it consumed you,
and I reduced you to ashes on the ground
    in the sight of all who were watching.
¹⁹All the nations who knew you
    are appalled at you;
you have come to a horrible end
    and will be no more.'"

A Prophecy Against Sidon

²⁰The word of the Lord came to me: ²¹"Son of man, set your face against Sidon; prophesy against her ²²and say: 'This is what the Sovereign Lord says:

"'I am against you, Sidon,
    and among you I will display my glory.
You will know that I am the Lord,
    when I inflict punishment on you
    and within you am proved to be holy.
²³I will send a plague upon you
    and make blood flow in your streets.
The slain will fall within you,
    with the sword against you on every side.
Then you will know that I am the Lord.

---

a 13 The precise identification of some of these precious stones is uncertain.   *b 13* The meaning of the Hebrew for this phrase is uncertain.

²⁴"'No longer will the people of Israel have malicious neighbors who are painful briers and sharp thorns. Then they will know that I am the Sovereign Lord.

²⁵"'This is what the Sovereign Lord says: When I gather the people of Israel from the nations where they have been scattered, I will be proved holy through them in the sight of the nations. Then they will live in their own land, which I gave to my servant Jacob. ²⁶They will live there in safety and will build houses and plant vineyards; they will live in safety when I inflict punishment on all their neighbors who maligned them. Then they will know that I am the Lord their God.'"

A Prophecy Against Egypt

Judgment on Pharaoh

29 In the tenth year, in the tenth month on the twelfth day, the word of the Lord came to me: ²"Son of man, set your face against Pharaoh king of Egypt and prophesy against him and against all Egypt. ³Speak to him and say: 'This is what the Sovereign Lord says:

> "'I am against you, Pharaoh king of Egypt,
>   you great monster lying among your streams.
> You say, "The Nile belongs to me;
>   I made it for myself."
> ⁴But I will put hooks in your jaws
>   and make the fish of your streams stick to your scales.
> I will pull you out from among your streams,
>   with all the fish sticking to your scales.
> ⁵I will leave you in the desert,
>   you and all the fish of your streams.
> You will fall on the open field
>   and not be gathered or picked up.
> I will give you as food
>   to the beasts of the earth and the birds of the sky.

⁶Then all who live in Egypt will know that I am the Lord.

"'You have been a staff of reed for the house of Israel. ⁷When they grasped you with their hands, you splintered and you tore open their shoulders; when they leaned on you, you broke and their backs were wrenched.^a

⁸"'Therefore this is what the Sovereign Lord says: I will bring a sword against you and kill your people and their animals. ⁹Egypt will become a desolate wasteland. Then they will know that I am the Lord.

"'Because you said, "The Nile is mine; I made it," ¹⁰therefore I am against you and against your streams, and I will make the land of Egypt a ruin and a desolate waste from Migdol to Aswan, as far as the border of Cush.^b ¹¹No foot will pass through it, neither people nor animals; no one will live there for forty years. ¹²I will make the land of Egypt desolate among devastated lands, and her cities will lie desolate forty years among ruined cities. And I will disperse the Egyptians among the nations and scatter them through the countries.

¹³"'Yet this is what the Sovereign Lord says: At the end of forty years I will gather the Egyptians from the nations where they were scattered. ¹⁴I will bring them back from captivity and return them to Upper Egypt, the land of their ancestry. There they will be a lowly kingdom. ¹⁵It will be the lowliest of kingdoms and will never again exalt itself above the other nations. I will make it so weak that it will never again rule over the nations. ¹⁶Egypt will no longer be a source of confidence for the people of Israel but will be a reminder of their sin in turning to her for help. Then they will know that I am the Sovereign Lord.'"

Nebuchadnezzar's Reward

¹⁷In the twenty-seventh year, in the first month on the first day, the word of the Lord came to me: ¹⁸"Son of man, Nebuchadnezzar king of Babylon drove his army in a hard campaign against Tyre; every

---

^a 7 Syriac (see also Septuagint and Vulgate); Hebrew *and you caused their backs to stand* ^b 10 That is, the upper Nile region

head was rubbed bare and every shoulder made raw. Yet he and his army got no reward from the campaign he led against Tyre. ¹⁹Therefore this is what the Sovereign Lord says: I am going to give Egypt to Nebuchadnezzar king of Babylon, and he will carry off its wealth. He will loot and plunder the land as pay for his army. ²⁰I have given him Egypt as a reward for his efforts because he and his army did it for me, declares the Sovereign Lord.

²¹"On that day I will make a horn*ᵃ* grow for the house of Israel, and I will open your mouth among them. Then they will know that I am the Lord."

A Lament Over Egypt

30 The word of the Lord came to me: ²"Son of man, prophesy and say: 'This is what the Sovereign Lord says:

> "'Wail and say,
>   "Alas for that day!"
> ³For the day is near,
>   the day of the Lord is near—
> a day of clouds,
>   a time of doom for the nations.
> ⁴A sword will come against Egypt,
>   and anguish will come upon Cush.*ᵇ*
> When the slain fall in Egypt,
>   her wealth will be carried away
>   and her foundations torn down.

⁵Cush and Libya, Lydia and all Arabia, Kub and the people of the covenant land will fall by the sword along with Egypt.

⁶"This is what the Lord says:

> "'The allies of Egypt will fall
>   and her proud strength will fail.
> From Migdol to Aswan
>   they will fall by the sword within her,

> declares the Sovereign Lord.

> ⁷"'They will be desolate
>   among desolate lands,
> and their cities will lie
>   among ruined cities.
> ⁸Then they will know that I am the Lord,
>   when I set fire to Egypt
>   and all her helpers are crushed.

⁹"'On that day messengers will go out from me in ships to frighten Cush out of her complacency. Anguish will take hold of them on the day of Egypt's doom, for it is sure to come.

¹⁰"This is what the Sovereign Lord says:

> "'I will put an end to the hordes of Egypt
>   by the hand of Nebuchadnezzar king of Babylon.
> ¹¹He and his army—the most ruthless of nations—
>   will be brought in to destroy the land.
> They will draw their swords against Egypt
>   and fill the land with the slain.
> ¹²I will dry up the waters of the Nile

1229

ᵃ 21 *Horn* here symbolizes strength.   *ᵇ* 4 That is, the upper Nile region; also in verses 5 and 9

and sell the land to an evil nation;
   by the hand of foreigners
     I will lay waste the land and everything in it.

I the LORD have spoken.

¹³"This is what the Sovereign LORD says:

"'I will destroy the idols
   and put an end to the images in Memphis.
No longer will there be a prince in Egypt,
   and I will spread fear throughout the land.
¹⁴I will lay waste Upper Egypt,
   set fire to Zoan
   and inflict punishment on Thebes.
¹⁵I will pour out my wrath on Pelusium,
   the stronghold of Egypt,
   and wipe out the hordes of Thebes.
¹⁶I will set fire to Egypt;
   Pelusium will writhe in agony.
Thebes will be taken by storm;
   Memphis will be in constant distress.
¹⁷The young men of Heliopolis and Bubastis
   will fall by the sword,
   and the cities themselves will go into captivity.
¹⁸Dark will be the day at Tahpanhes
   when I break the yoke of Egypt;
   there her proud strength will come to an end.
She will be covered with clouds,
   and her villages will go into captivity.
¹⁹So I will inflict punishment on Egypt,
   and they will know that I am the LORD.'"

Pharaoh's Arms Are Broken

²⁰In the eleventh year, in the first month on the seventh day, the word of the LORD came to me: ²¹"Son of man, I have broken the arm of Pharaoh king of Egypt. It has not been bound up to be healed or put in a splint so that it may become strong enough to hold a sword. ²²Therefore this is what the Sovereign LORD says: I am against Pharaoh king of Egypt. I will break both his arms, the good arm as well as the broken one, and make the sword fall from his hand. ²³I will disperse the Egyptians among the nations and scatter them through the countries. ²⁴I will strengthen the arms of the king of Babylon and put my sword in his hand, but I will break the arms of Pharaoh, and he will groan before him like someone mortally wounded. ²⁵I will strengthen the arms of the king of Babylon, but the arms of Pharaoh will fall limp. Then they will know that I am the LORD, when I put my sword into the hand of the king of Babylon and he brandishes it against Egypt. ²⁶I will disperse the Egyptians among the nations and scatter them through the countries. Then they will know that I am the LORD."

Pharaoh as a Felled Cedar of Lebanon

31 In the eleventh year, in the third month on the first day, the word of the LORD came to me: ²"Son of man, say to Pharaoh king of Egypt and to his hordes:

"'Who can be compared with you in majesty?
³Consider Assyria, once a cedar in Lebanon,
   with beautiful branches overshadowing the forest;
it towered on high,
   its top above the thick foliage.

⁴The waters nourished it,
  deep springs made it grow tall;
their streams flowed
  all around its base
and sent their channels
  to all the trees of the field.
⁵So it towered higher
  than all the trees of the field;
its boughs increased
  and its branches grew long,
  spreading because of abundant waters.
⁶All the birds of the sky
  nested in its boughs,
all the animals of the wild
  gave birth under its branches;
all the great nations
  lived in its shade.
⁷It was majestic in beauty,
  with its spreading boughs,
for its roots went down
  to abundant waters.
⁸The cedars in the garden of God
  could not rival it,
nor could the junipers
  equal its boughs,
nor could the plane trees
  compare with its branches—
no tree in the garden of God
  could match its beauty.
⁹I made it beautiful
  with abundant branches,
the envy of all the trees of Eden
  in the garden of God.

¹⁰"'Therefore this is what the Sovereign Lord says: Because the great cedar towered over the thick foliage, and because it was proud of its height, ¹¹I gave it into the hands of the ruler of the nations, for him to deal with according to its wickedness. I cast it aside, ¹²and the most ruthless of foreign nations cut it down and left it. Its boughs fell on the mountains and in all the valleys; its branches lay broken in all the ravines of the land. All the nations of the earth came out from under its shade and left it. ¹³All the birds settled on the fallen tree, and all the wild animals lived among its branches. ¹⁴Therefore no other trees by the waters are ever to tower proudly on high, lifting their tops above the thick foliage. No other trees so well-watered are ever to reach such a height; they are all destined for death, for the earth below, among mortals who go down to the realm of the dead.

¹⁵"'This is what the Sovereign Lord says: On the day it was brought down to the realm of the dead I covered the deep springs with mourning for it; I held back its streams, and its abundant waters were restrained. Because of it I clothed Lebanon with gloom, and all the trees of the field withered away. ¹⁶I made the nations tremble at the sound of its fall when I brought it down to the realm of the dead to be with those who go down to the pit. Then all the trees of Eden, the choicest and best of Lebanon, the well-watered trees, were consoled in the earth below. ¹⁷They too, like the great cedar, had gone down to the realm of the dead, to those killed by the sword, along with the armed men who lived in its shade among the nations.

¹⁸"'Which of the trees of Eden can be compared with you in splendor and majesty? Yet you, too, will

be brought down with the trees of Eden to the earth below; you will lie among the uncircumcised, with those killed by the sword.

"'This is Pharaoh and all his hordes, declares the Sovereign LORD.'"

A Lament Over Pharaoh

32 In the twelfth year, in the twelfth month on the first day, the word of the LORD came to me: ² "Son of man, take up a lament concerning Pharaoh king of Egypt and say to him:

> "'You are like a lion among the nations;
>   you are like a monster in the seas
> thrashing about in your streams,
>   churning the water with your feet
>   and muddying the streams.

³ "'This is what the Sovereign LORD says:

> "'With a great throng of people
>   I will cast my net over you,
>   and they will haul you up in my net.
> ⁴ I will throw you on the land
>   and hurl you on the open field.
> I will let all the birds of the sky settle on you
>   and all the animals of the wild gorge themselves on you.
> ⁵ I will spread your flesh on the mountains
>   and fill the valleys with your remains.
> ⁶ I will drench the land with your flowing blood
>   all the way to the mountains,
>   and the ravines will be filled with your flesh.
> ⁷ When I snuff you out, I will cover the heavens
>   and darken their stars;
> I will cover the sun with a cloud,
>   and the moon will not give its light.
> ⁸ All the shining lights in the heavens
>   I will darken over you;
>   I will bring darkness over your land,
>
>   declares the Sovereign LORD.
> ⁹ I will trouble the hearts of many peoples
>   when I bring about your destruction among the nations,
>   among *a* lands you have not known.
> ¹⁰ I will cause many peoples to be appalled at you,
>   and their kings will shudder with horror because of you
>   when I brandish my sword before them.
> On the day of your downfall
>   each of them will tremble
>   every moment for his life.

¹¹ "'For this is what the Sovereign LORD says:

> "'The sword of the king of Babylon
>   will come against you.
> ¹² I will cause your hordes to fall
>   by the swords of mighty men—
>   the most ruthless of all nations.

---

a 9 Hebrew; Septuagint *bring you into captivity among the nations, / to*

> They will shatter the pride of Egypt,
>   and all her hordes will be overthrown.
> [13]I will destroy all her cattle
>   from beside abundant waters
> no longer to be stirred by human feet
>   or muddied by the hooves of cattle.
> [14]Then I will let her waters settle
>   and make her streams flow like oil,
>
>   declares the Sovereign LORD.
>
> [15]When I make Egypt desolate
>   and strip the land of everything in it,
> when I strike down all who live there,
>   then they will know that I am the LORD.'

[16]"This is the lament they will chant for her. The daughters of the nations will chant it; for Egypt and all her hordes they will chant it, declares the Sovereign LORD."

Egypt's Descent Into the Realm of the Dead

[17]In the twelfth year, on the fifteenth day of the month, the word of the LORD came to me: [18]"Son of man, wail for the hordes of Egypt and consign to the earth below both her and the daughters of mighty nations, along with those who go down to the pit. [19]Say to them, 'Are you more favored than others? Go down and be laid among the uncircumcised.' [20]They will fall among those killed by the sword. The sword is drawn; let her be dragged off with all her hordes. [21]From within the realm of the dead the mighty leaders will say of Egypt and her allies, 'They have come down and they lie with the uncircumcised, with those killed by the sword.'

[22]"Assyria is there with her whole army; she is surrounded by the graves of all her slain, all who have fallen by the sword. [23]Their graves are in the depths of the pit and her army lies around her grave. All who had spread terror in the land of the living are slain, fallen by the sword.

[24]"Elam is there, with all her hordes around her grave. All of them are slain, fallen by the sword. All who had spread terror in the land of the living went down uncircumcised to the earth below. They bear their shame with those who go down to the pit. [25]A bed is made for her among the slain, with all her hordes around her grave. All of them are uncircumcised, killed by the sword. Because their terror had spread in the land of the living, they bear their shame with those who go down to the pit; they are laid among the slain.

[26]"Meshek and Tubal are there, with all their hordes around their graves. All of them are uncircumcised, killed by the sword because they spread their terror in the land of the living. [27]But they do not lie with the fallen warriors of old,[a] who went down to the realm of the dead with their weapons of war—their swords placed under their heads and their shields[b] resting on their bones—though these warriors also had terrorized the land of the living.

[28]"You too, Pharaoh, will be broken and will lie among the uncircumcised, with those killed by the sword.

[29]"Edom is there, her kings and all her princes; despite their power, they are laid with those killed by the sword. They lie with the uncircumcised, with those who go down to the pit.

[30]"All the princes of the north and all the Sidonians are there; they went down with the slain in disgrace despite the terror caused by their power. They lie uncircumcised with those killed by the sword and bear their shame with those who go down to the pit.

[31]"Pharaoh—he and all his army—will see them and he will be consoled for all his hordes that were killed by the sword, declares the Sovereign LORD. [32]Although I had him spread terror in the land of the living, Pharaoh and all his hordes will be laid among the uncircumcised, with those killed by the sword, declares the Sovereign LORD."

[a] 27 Septuagint; Hebrew *warriors who were uncircumcised*   [b] 27 Probable reading of the original Hebrew text; Masoretic Text *punishment*

Renewal of Ezekiel's Call as Watchman

33 The word of the Lord came to me: [2]"Son of man, speak to your people and say to them: 'When I bring the sword against a land, and the people of the land choose one of their men and make him their watchman, [3]and he sees the sword coming against the land and blows the trumpet to warn the people, [4]then if anyone hears the trumpet but does not heed the warning and the sword comes and takes their life, their blood will be on their own head. [5]Since they heard the sound of the trumpet but did not heed the warning, their blood will be on their own head. If they had heeded the warning, they would have saved themselves. [6]But if the watchman sees the sword coming and does not blow the trumpet to warn the people and the sword comes and takes someone's life, that person's life will be taken because of their sin, but I will hold the watchman accountable for their blood.'

[7]"Son of man, I have made you a watchman for the house of Israel; so hear the word I speak and give them warning from me. [8]When I say to the wicked, 'You wicked people, you will surely die,' and you do not speak out to dissuade them from their ways, those wicked people will die for[a] their sins, and I will hold you accountable for their blood. [9]But if you do warn the wicked to turn from their ways and they do not do so, they will die for their sins, though you yourself will be saved.

conversations

accountability «» 33:1–9

1» For what did God hold the prophet Ezekiel accountable?

2» How are you acting as a watchman for the people you know?

3» To what extent do you feel a sense of responsibility for those around you?

For more on **accountability**, check the index.
For the next Conversations, go to p. 1260.

[10]"Son of man, say to the house of Israel, 'This is what you are saying: "Our offenses and sins weigh us down, and we are wasting away because of[b] them. How then can we live?"' [11]Say to them, 'As surely as I live, declares the Sovereign Lord, I take no pleasure in the death of the wicked, but rather that they turn from their ways and live. Turn! Turn from your evil ways! Why will you die, house of Israel?'

[12]"Therefore, son of man, say to your people, 'If someone who is righteous disobeys, that person's former righteousness will count for nothing. And if someone who is wicked repents, that person's former wickedness will not bring condemnation. The righteous, if they sin, will not be allowed to live because of their former righteousness.' [13]If I tell the righteous that they will surely live, but then they trust in their righteousness and do evil, none of the righteous things they have done will be remembered; they will die for the evil they have done. [14]And if I say to the wicked, 'You will surely die,' but they then turn away from their sins and do what is just and right— [15]if they give back what they took in pledge for a loan, return what they have stolen, follow the decrees that give life, and do no evil, they will surely live; they will not die. [16]None of the sins they have committed will be remembered against them. They have done what is just and right; they will surely live.

[17]"Yet your people say, 'The way of the Lord is not just.' But it is their way that is not just. [18]If the righteous turn from their righteousness and do evil, they will die for it. [19]And if the wicked turn away from their wickedness and do what is just and right, they will live by doing so. [20]Yet you say, house of Israel, 'The way of the Lord is not just.' But I will judge each of you according to your own ways."

Jerusalem's Fall Explained

[21]In the twelfth year of our exile, in the tenth month on the fifth day, a man who had escaped from Jerusalem came to me and said, "The city has fallen!" [22]Now the evening before the man arrived, the hand of the Lord was on me, and he opened my mouth before the man came to me in the morning. So my mouth was opened and I was no longer silent.

[23]Then the word of the Lord came to me: [24]"Son of man, the people living in those ruins in the land of Israel are saying, 'Abraham was only one man, yet he possessed the land. But we are many; surely the

---

[a] *8 Or in; also in verse 9*   [b] *10 Or away in*

land has been given to us as our possession.' ²⁵Therefore say to them, 'This is what the Sovereign LORD says: Since you eat meat with the blood still in it and look to your idols and shed blood, should you then possess the land? ²⁶You rely on your sword, you do detestable things, and each of you defiles his neighbor's wife. Should you then possess the land?'

²⁷"Say this to them: 'This is what the Sovereign LORD says: As surely as I live, those who are left in the ruins will fall by the sword, those out in the country I will give to the wild animals to be devoured, and those in strongholds and caves will die of a plague. ²⁸I will make the land a desolate waste, and her proud strength will come to an end, and the mountains of Israel will become desolate so that no one will cross them. ²⁹Then they will know that I am the LORD, when I have made the land a desolate waste because of all the detestable things they have done.'

³⁰"As for you, son of man, your people are talking together about you by the walls and at the doors of the houses, saying to each other, 'Come and hear the message that has come from the LORD.' ³¹My people come to you, as they usually do, and sit before you to hear your words, but they do not put them into practice. Their mouths speak of love, but their hearts are greedy for unjust gain. ³²Indeed, to them you are nothing more than one who sings love songs with a beautiful voice and plays an instrument well, for they hear your words but do not put them into practice.

³³"When all this comes true—and it surely will—then they will know that a prophet has been among them."

1235

The LORD Will Be Israel's Shepherd

34 The word of the LORD came to me: ²"Son of man, prophesy against the shepherds of Israel; prophesy and say to them: 'This is what the Sovereign LORD says: Woe to you shepherds of Israel who only take care of yourselves! Should not shepherds take care of the flock? ³You eat the curds, clothe yourselves with the wool and slaughter the choice animals, but you do not take care of the flock. ⁴You have not strengthened the weak or healed the sick or bound up the injured. You have not brought back the strays or searched for the lost. You have ruled them harshly and brutally. ⁵So they were scattered because there was no shepherd, and when they were scattered they became food for all the wild animals. ⁶My sheep wandered over all the mountains and on every high hill. They were scattered over the whole earth, and no one searched or looked for them.

⁷"'Therefore, you shepherds, hear the word of the LORD: ⁸As surely as I live, declares the Sovereign LORD, because my flock lacks a shepherd and so has been plundered and has become food for all the wild animals, and because my shepherds did not search for my flock but cared for themselves rather than for my flock, ⁹therefore, you shepherds, hear the word of the LORD: ¹⁰This is what the Sovereign LORD says: I am against the shepherds and will hold them accountable for my flock. I will remove them from tending the flock so that the shepherds can no longer feed themselves. I will rescue my flock from their mouths, and it will no longer be food for them.

¹¹"'For this is what the Sovereign LORD says: I myself will search for my sheep and look after them. ¹²As shepherds look after their scattered flocks when they are with them, so will I look after my sheep. I will rescue them from all the places where they were scattered on a day of clouds and darkness. ¹³I will bring them out from the nations and gather them from the countries, and I will bring them into their own land. I will pasture them on the mountains of Israel, in the ravines and in all the settlements in the land. ¹⁴I will tend them in a good pasture, and the mountain heights of Israel will be their grazing land. There

myth# 71

"A SUCCESSFUL CAREER IS MORE IMPORTANT THAN BEING AT HOME WITH MY CHILDREN."

I finally feel like I'm successful, although some people may criticize the choices I've made to get where I am. I worked hard in college and graduate school and had to make a lot of sacrifices to advance in my career. But it's what I've always wanted, and it's certainly what my parents sacrificed for so that I could have the best education possible.

Some people I know are critical of my drive to succeed—especially those who elected to stay at home with their kids. They think I'm depriving my children of the attention they need because I'm so focused on my job.

My sister Gail is often the most hurtful. She keeps asking me what I'm building into my children's lives if I stay at work late every night. Just because she decided to be a stay-at-home mom, she thinks every woman should make the same choice. She never had any career aspirations. Her higher ambition in life was to get married and have babies.

I haven't failed my kids. I think my kids are happier and better adjusted with a mom who's fulfilled in her career than with a mom who sits at home simply because everyone tells her she should. Plus, my daughters are in school all day and are involved in so many activities—music, sports, drama, etc. If I stayed home, I'd be at home alone, twiddling my thumbs, bored and unfulfilled. Then what kind of mother would I be?

—Naomi

LIFE IS ALL about choices. Some of the choices you make affect your life for years to come. One of those choices is the decision to have children. Once you have children, you face a whole new series of choices on how to raise them.

Society tells us that a woman who forgoes a career to stay at home with her kids isn't contributing to the world. She's sometimes viewed as unfulfilled or unproductive, as the following conversation implies.

New acquaintance: "What do you do?"

Woman: "I'm a stay-at-home mom."

New acquaintance: "Oh . . . But what do you *do?*"

If you've ever been pegged that way, then you know how much it hurts. That condescending attitude is unfair to women who are making a sacrifice to do what they believe is best for their kids.

At the same time, some stay-at-home moms harshly judge any mother who chooses to work. Judging another woman's choice isn't loving, and it's not your job—it's God's.

The Bible clearly tells us the importance of a mother's influence in her child's life—for good (like Eunice in 2 Timothy 1:5) or for evil (like Athaliah in 2 Chronicles 22:2–4). A parent can only influence a child if she spends time with that child.

Some women, particularly single moms, can't afford to stay at home. Maybe that's your experience. If so, you know the time-juggling you have to do to make sure your child has time with you. But time together is of immeasurable worth.

Regardless of your station in life, ask yourself:

- What message am I sending my children?

- Do my children know that they are the most important thing in my life?

- Do my kids know that I'm willing to make sacrifices in order to be with them?

- If you choose to pursue a career, what is your motive—personal fulfillment, genuine need to earn money, a desire to maintain a certain lifestyle, a conviction that this is what God wants for you, or . . . ?

- If you choose to stay home, what is your motive—guilt, genuine desire, pressure from others, a conviction that this is what God wants for you, or . . . ?

1237

"Census data reveal that more women with graduate or professional degrees—the very women who seemed destined to blast through the glass ceiling—are now choosing to stay at home. Now 22 percent of them are home with their kids."

—TIME magazine, "The Case for Staying Home," March 22, 2004

"CHILDren are a Heritage From THE LORD, OFFSPRING a rewarD From HIM."

PSALM 127:3

SEE ALSO

Deuteronomy 6:4–9
Deuteronomy 11:18–21
Proverbs 31:10–28

For more on **Parenting** and **Work**, check the index.

they will lie down in good grazing land, and there they will feed in a rich pasture on the mountains of Israel. [15]I myself will tend my sheep and have them lie down, declares the Sovereign Lord. [16]I will search for the lost and bring back the strays. I will bind up the injured and strengthen the weak, but the sleek and the strong I will destroy. I will shepherd the flock with justice.

[17]"'As for you, my flock, this is what the Sovereign Lord says: I will judge between one sheep and another, and between rams and goats. [18]Is it not enough for you to feed on the good pasture? Must you also trample the rest of your pasture with your feet? Is it not enough for you to drink clear water? Must you also muddy the rest with your feet? [19]Must my flock feed on what you have trampled and drink what you have muddied with your feet?

[20]"'Therefore this is what the Sovereign Lord says to them: See, I myself will judge between the fat sheep and the lean sheep. [21]Because you shove with flank and shoulder, butting all the weak sheep with your horns until you have driven them away, [22]I will save my flock, and they will no longer be plundered. I will judge between one sheep and another. [23]I will place over them one shepherd, my servant David, and he will tend them; he will tend them and be their shepherd. [24]I the Lord will be their God, and my servant David will be prince among them. I the Lord have spoken.

[25]"'I will make a covenant of peace with them and rid the land of savage beasts so that they may live in the wilderness and sleep in the forests in safety. [26]I will make them and the places surrounding my hill a blessing.[a] I will send down showers in season; there will be showers of blessing. [27]The trees will yield their fruit and the ground will yield its crops; the people will be secure in their land. They will know that I am the Lord, when I break the bars of their yoke and rescue them from the hands of those who enslaved them. [28]They will no longer be plundered by the nations, nor will wild animals devour them. They will live in safety, and no one will make them afraid. [29]I will provide for them a land renowned for its crops, and they will no longer be victims of famine in the land or bear the scorn of the nations. [30]Then they will know that I, the Lord their God, am with them and that they, the house of Israel, are my people, declares the Sovereign Lord. [31]You are my sheep, the sheep of my pasture, and I am your God, declares the Sovereign Lord.'"

A Prophecy Against Edom

35 The word of the Lord came to me: [2]"Son of man, set your face against Mount Seir; prophesy against it [3]and say: 'This is what the Sovereign Lord says: I am against you, Mount Seir, and I will stretch out my hand against you and make you a desolate waste. [4]I will turn your towns into ruins and you will be desolate. Then you will know that I am the Lord.

[5]"'Because you harbored an ancient hostility and delivered the Israelites over to the sword at the time of their calamity, the time their punishment reached its climax, [6]therefore as surely as I live, declares the Sovereign Lord, I will give you over to bloodshed and it will pursue you. Since you did not hate bloodshed, bloodshed will pursue you. [7]I will make Mount Seir a desolate waste and cut off from it all who come and go. [8]I will fill your mountains with the slain; those killed by the sword will fall on your hills and in your valleys and in all your ravines. [9]I will make you desolate forever; your towns will not be inhabited. Then you will know that I am the Lord.

[10]"'Because you have said, "These two nations and countries will be ours and we will take possession of them," even though I the Lord was there, [11]therefore as surely as I live, declares the Sovereign Lord, I will treat you in accordance with the anger and jealousy you showed in your hatred of them and I will make myself known among them when I judge you. [12]Then you will know that I the Lord have heard all the contemptible things you have said against the mountains of Israel. You said, "They have been laid waste and have been given over to us to devour." [13]You boasted against me and spoke against me without restraint, and I heard it. [14]This is what the Sovereign Lord says: While the whole earth rejoices, I will make you desolate. [15]Because you rejoiced when the inheritance of the house of Israel became desolate, that is how I will treat you. You will be desolate, Mount Seir, you and all of Edom. Then they will know that I am the Lord.'"

---

[a] 26 Or I will cause them and the places surrounding my hill to be named in blessings (see Gen. 48:20); or I will cause them and the places surrounding my hill to be seen as blessed

Hope for the Mountains of Israel

36 "Son of man, prophesy to the mountains of Israel and say, 'Mountains of Israel, hear the word of the LORD. ²This is what the Sovereign LORD says: The enemy said of you, "Aha! The ancient heights have become our possession."' ³Therefore prophesy and say, 'This is what the Sovereign LORD says: Because they ravaged and crushed you from every side so that you became the possession of the rest of the nations and the object of people's malicious talk and slander, ⁴therefore, mountains of Israel, hear the word of the Sovereign LORD: This is what the Sovereign LORD says to the mountains and hills, to the ravines and valleys, to the desolate ruins and the deserted towns that have been plundered and ridiculed by the rest of the nations around you— ⁵this is what the Sovereign LORD says: In my burning zeal I have spoken against the rest of the nations, and against all Edom, for with glee and with malice in their hearts they made my land their own possession so that they might plunder its pastureland.' ⁶Therefore prophesy concerning the land of Israel and say to the mountains and hills, to the ravines and valleys: 'This is what the Sovereign LORD says: I speak in my jealous wrath because you have suffered the scorn of the nations. ⁷Therefore this is what the Sovereign LORD says: I swear with uplifted hand that the nations around you will also suffer scorn.

⁸"'But you, mountains of Israel, will produce branches and fruit for my people Israel, for they will soon come home. ⁹I am concerned for you and will look on you with favor; you will be plowed and sown, ¹⁰and I will multiply the number of people living on you, even the whole house of Israel. The towns will be inhabited and the ruins rebuilt. ¹¹I will increase the number of people and animals living on you, and they will be fruitful and become numerous. I will settle people on you as in the past and will make you prosper more than before. Then you will know that I am the LORD. ¹²I will cause people, my people Israel, to live on you. They will possess you, and you will be their inheritance; you will never again deprive them of their children.

¹³"'This is what the Sovereign LORD says: Because some say to you, "You devour your people and deprive your nation of its children," ¹⁴therefore you will no longer devour people or make your nation childless, declares the Sovereign LORD. ¹⁵No longer will I make you hear the taunts of the nations, and no longer will you suffer the scorn of the peoples or cause your nation to fall, declares the Sovereign LORD.'"

Israel's Restoration Assured

¹⁶Again the word of the LORD came to me: ¹⁷"Son of man, when the people of Israel were living in their own land, they defiled it by their conduct and their actions. Their conduct was like a woman's monthly uncleanness in my sight. ¹⁸So I poured out my wrath on them because they had shed blood in the land and because they had defiled it with their idols. ¹⁹I dispersed them among the nations, and they were scattered through the countries; I judged them according to their conduct and their actions. ²⁰And wherever they went among the nations they profaned my holy name, for it was said of them, 'These are the LORD's people, and yet they had to leave his land.' ²¹I had concern for my holy name, which the house of Israel profaned among the nations where they had gone.

²²"Therefore say to the house of Israel, 'This is what the Sovereign LORD says: It is not for your sake, house of Israel, that I am going to do these things, but for the sake of my holy name, which you have profaned among the nations where you have gone. ²³I will show the holiness of my great name, which has been profaned among the nations, the name you have profaned among them. Then the nations will know that I am the LORD, declares the Sovereign LORD, when I am proved holy through you before their eyes.

²⁴"'For I will take you out of the nations; I will gather you

1239

atissue:purity

36:24–30 When you think of "all your impurities," what comes to mind? Blatant sin? Ignoring God? Living for yourself? Hurting others? Perhaps you feel like the filth of your past clings to you so that you can never feel clean. The good news is that you can be. When you come to God, he cleanses you from all your grimy sin and makes you 100 percent pure—brand new, undamaged goods in his eyes. He gives you a new heart and makes you a new person, and this should give you a new desire to follow him.

from all the countries and bring you back into your own land. [25] I will sprinkle clean water on you, and you will be clean; I will cleanse you from all your impurities and from all your idols. [26] I will give you a new heart and put a new spirit in you; I will remove from you your heart of stone and give you a heart of flesh. [27] And I will put my Spirit in you and move you to follow my decrees and be careful to keep my laws. [28] Then you will live in the land I gave your ancestors; you will be my people, and I will be your God. [29] I will save you from all your uncleanness. I will call for the grain and make it plentiful and will not bring famine upon you. [30] I will increase the fruit of the trees and the crops of the field, so that you will no longer suffer disgrace among the nations because of famine. [31] Then you will remember your evil ways and wicked deeds, and you will loathe yourselves for your sins and detestable practices. [32] I want you to know that I am not doing this for your sake, declares the Sovereign LORD. Be ashamed and disgraced for your conduct, house of Israel!

[33] "This is what the Sovereign LORD says: On the day I cleanse you from all your sins, I will resettle your towns, and the ruins will be rebuilt. [34] The desolate land will be cultivated instead of lying desolate in the sight of all who pass through it. [35] They will say, "This land that was laid waste has become like the garden of Eden; the cities that were lying in ruins, desolate and destroyed, are now fortified and inhabited." [36] Then the nations around you that remain will know that I the LORD have rebuilt what was destroyed and have replanted what was desolate. I the LORD have spoken, and I will do it.'

[37] "This is what the Sovereign LORD says: Once again I will yield to the plea of the house of Israel and do this for them: I will make their people as numerous as sheep, [38] as numerous as the flocks for offerings at Jerusalem during her appointed festivals. So will the ruined cities be filled with flocks of people. Then they will know that I am the LORD."

The Valley of Dry Bones

37 The hand of the LORD was on me, and he brought me out by the Spirit of the LORD and set me in the middle of a valley; it was full of bones. [2] He led me back and forth among them, and I saw a great many bones on the floor of the valley, bones that were very dry. [3] He asked me, "Son of man, can these bones live?"

I said, "Sovereign LORD, you alone know."

[4] Then he said to me, "Prophesy to these bones and say to them, 'Dry bones, hear the word of the LORD! [5] This is what the Sovereign LORD says to these bones: I will make breath[a] enter you, and you will come to life. [6] I will attach tendons to you and make flesh come upon you and cover you with skin; I will put breath in you, and you will come to life. Then you will know that I am the LORD.'"

[7] So I prophesied as I was commanded. And as I was prophesying, there was a noise, a rattling sound, and the bones came together, bone to bone. [8] I looked, and tendons and flesh appeared on them and skin covered them, but there was no breath in them.

[9] Then he said to me, "Prophesy to the breath; prophesy, son of man, and say to it, 'This is what the Sovereign LORD says: Come, breath, from the four winds and breathe into these slain, that they may live.'" [10] So I prophesied as he commanded me, and breath entered them; they came to life and stood up on their feet—a vast army.

[11] Then he said to me: "Son of man, these bones are the whole house of Israel. They say, 'Our bones are dried up and our hope is gone; we are cut off.' [12] Therefore prophesy and say to them: 'This is what the Sovereign LORD says: My people, I am going to open your graves and bring you up from them; I will bring you back to the land of Israel. [13] Then you, my people, will know that I am the LORD, when I open your graves and bring you up from them. [14] I will put my Spirit in you and you will live, and I will settle you in your own land. Then you will know that I the LORD have spoken, and I have done it, declares the LORD.'"

One Nation Under One King

[15] The word of the LORD came to me: [16] "Son of man, take a stick of wood and write on it, 'Belonging to Judah and the Israelites associated with him.' Then take another stick of wood, and write on it, 'Belonging to Joseph (that is, to Ephraim) and all the house of Israel associated with him.' [17] Join them together into one stick so that they will become one in your hand.

---

a 5 The Hebrew for this word can also mean *wind* or *spirit* (see verses 6-14).

[18]"When your people ask you, 'Won't you tell us what you mean by this?' [19]say to them, 'This is what the Sovereign Lord says: I am going to take the stick of Joseph—which is in Ephraim's hand—and of the Israelite tribes associated with him, and join it to Judah's stick. I will make them into a single stick of wood, and they will become one in my hand.' [20]Hold before their eyes the sticks you have written on [21]and say to them, 'This is what the Sovereign Lord says: I will take the Israelites out of the nations where they have gone. I will gather them from all around and bring them back into their own land. [22]I will make them one nation in the land, on the mountains of Israel. There will be one king over all of them and they will never again be two nations or be divided into two kingdoms. [23]They will no longer defile themselves with their idols and vile images or with any of their offenses, for I will save them from all their sinful backsliding,[a] and I will cleanse them. They will be my people, and I will be their God.

[24]"'My servant David will be king over them, and they will all have one shepherd. They will follow my laws and be careful to keep my decrees. [25]They will live in the land I gave to my servant Jacob, the land where your ancestors lived. They and their children and their children's children will live there forever, and David my servant will be their prince forever. [26]I will make a covenant of peace with them; it will be an everlasting covenant. I will establish them and increase their numbers, and I will put my sanctuary among them forever. [27]My dwelling place will be with them; I will be their God, and they will be my people. [28]Then the nations will know that I the Lord make Israel holy, when my sanctuary is among them forever.'"

HE IS: among you

37:25–28 God promised to one day put his sanctuary among his people and make Israel his dwelling place. He promised to be their God and make them his people.

When you wonder about God's mailing address, don't envision him in far-off heaven or on vacation in some distant galaxy. He is right here, with you! When you go to work, he is with you. When you're in your car, at home, with your friends—he is there. What an intimate sign of love that of all places your God could choose to dwell, he chose to make his home *among you.*

For the next He Is, go to p. 1249.

The Lord's Great Victory Over the Nations

38 The word of the Lord came to me: [2]"Son of man, set your face against Gog, of the land of Magog, the chief prince of[b] Meshek and Tubal; prophesy against him [3]and say: 'This is what the Sovereign Lord says: I am against you, Gog, chief prince of[c] Meshek and Tubal. [4]I will turn you around, put hooks in your jaws and bring you out with your whole army—your horses, your horsemen fully armed, and a great horde with large and small shields, all of them brandishing their swords. [5]Persia, Cush[d] and Put will be with them, all with shields and helmets, [6]also Gomer with all its troops, and Beth Togarmah from the far north with all its troops—the many nations with you.

[7]"'Get ready; be prepared, you and all the hordes gathered about you, and take command of them. [8]After many days you will be called to arms. In future years you will invade a land that has recovered from war, whose people were gathered from many nations to the mountains of Israel, which had long been desolate. They had been brought out from the nations, and now all of them live in safety. [9]You and all your troops and the many nations with you will go up, advancing like a storm; you will be like a cloud covering the land.

[10]"'This is what the Sovereign Lord says: On that day thoughts will come into your mind and you will devise an evil scheme. [11]You will say, "I will invade a land of unwalled villages; I will attack a peaceful and unsuspecting people—all of them living without walls and without gates and bars. [12]I will plunder

---

[a] 23 Many Hebrew manuscripts (see also Septuagint); most Hebrew manuscripts *all their dwelling places where they sinned*   [b] 2 Or *the prince of Rosh,*
[c] 3 Or *Gog, prince of Rosh,*   [d] 5 That is, the upper Nile region

myth#72 "GOD IS DISTANT."

I can't admit this to many people, but I feel very far away from God these days. I've noticed this for the past few months. It's almost like I'm in a wilderness of some kind, alone. I've had a lot of setbacks lately, which have caused me to feel a little depressed. When I pray (and I've had a hard time praying recently), it feels as if God isn't listening. I can't sense his presence in my life at all anymore.

At church, I feel as if I'm just going through the motions. When I was asked to pray at the missions council meeting, I wanted to say no. But I prayed anyway. I felt as if I was just mouthing the words—not really feeling or believing them.

I feel abandoned by God. I thought he promised never to leave or forsake me. But that's how I feel now—forsaken.

One of our pastors said that if you're not hearing from God, then maybe you have unconfessed sin in your life. I was so angry when I heard that. Why is God's silence all my fault? I'm not used to this. It's not like I'm a new Christian. I've been a believer for over 25 years.

Just a few months ago, I was on top of the world. Many of my prayers were answered with a resounding yes. I felt so close to the Lord. Now I wonder what went wrong.

—Charity

CAN YOU RELATE to Charity's

story? Elijah could. He went through a time when God seemed distant.

What's ironic is that Elijah's time of struggle came right after his (literal) mountaintop experience, a tremendous show of God's power that enabled Elijah to single-handedly defeat the 450 prophets of Baal on Mount Carmel (see 1 Kings 18). After that awesome display, the wicked Queen Jezebel threatened to kill Elijah by the next day (see 1 Kings 19:1–2). In the wake of Elijah's unshakable confidence on Mount Carmel, the fear and depression he felt right after that seem shocking. But Elijah knew all too well that Jezebel wasn't one to make idle threats. So the exhausted prophet ran for his life.

A lull after a spiritual high is often the time when the enemy moves in for an attack. In a dark night of the soul, like depression, the believer's focus can turn from praise to thoughts of *Where is God?*

Does God seem distant to you? Every relationship experiences an ebb and flow of feelings. A relationship with God is no exception. What can you do during those times?

- *Keep spending time with God, even when you don't feel like it.* In a marriage, the partners may not always feel close, but they keep making time for each other for the sake of their marriage. Your relationship with God is like a marriage. Spending time with him is necessary for the health of your relationship and your spiritual health. Jesus used the illustration of staying attached to the vine. "Remain in me, as I also remain in you" (John 15:4). Eventually the feelings will return.

- *When God seems silent, you have to trust him.* Sometimes God seems silent in order to stretch your faith in him. Are you willing to trust and wait on his answers, even when his time frame may be much different than yours?

- *Examine your heart.* Sometimes (not always) it's a hidden sin that has come between you and God (see Isaiah 59:1–2). If God seems far away, examine your heart. Do you have any hidden or unconfessed sin that might be blocking your relationship with God?

- *Believe that God has not moved.* God is where he said he'd be—with you. Meditate on verses that assure you of this truth (see Hebrews 13:5–6).

- *Talk with other believers.* You aren't the only one who has been in a wilderness. Talk with other believers. Let their experiences encourage you during this time.

1243

"**Nearly half of regular church attenders (48 percent) say they have not experienced God's presence in the past year.**"
—Barna Research Group (1997)

"**THE LORD YOUR GOD GOES WITH YOU; HE WILL never Leave YOU nor Forsake YOU.**"
DEUTERONOMY 31:6

SEE ALSO

Psalms 43:5; 145:13–20
Jeremiah 23:23–24
Romans 8:38–39

For more on **Doubting God**, check the index.

and loot and turn my hand against the resettled ruins and the people gathered from the nations, rich in livestock and goods, living at the center of the land.ᵃ" ¹³Sheba and Dedan and the merchants of Tarshish and all her villagesᵇ will say to you, "Have you come to plunder? Have you gathered your hordes to loot, to carry off silver and gold, to take away livestock and goods and to seize much plunder?"'

¹⁴"Therefore, son of man, prophesy and say to Gog: 'This is what the Sovereign Lord says: In that day, when my people Israel are living in safety, will you not take notice of it? ¹⁵You will come from your place in the far north, you and many nations with you, all of them riding on horses, a great horde, a mighty army. ¹⁶You will advance against my people Israel like a cloud that covers the land. In days to come, Gog, I will bring you against my land, so that the nations may know me when I am proved holy through you before their eyes.

¹⁷"This is what the Sovereign Lord says: You are the one I spoke of in former days by my servants the prophets of Israel. At that time they prophesied for years that I would bring you against them. ¹⁸This is what will happen in that day: When Gog attacks the land of Israel, my hot anger will be aroused, declares the Sovereign Lord. ¹⁹In my zeal and fiery wrath I declare that at that time there shall be a great earthquake in the land of Israel. ²⁰The fish in the sea, the birds in the sky, the beasts of the field, every creature that moves along the ground, and all the people on the face of the earth will tremble at my presence. The mountains will be overturned, the cliffs will crumble and every wall will fall to the ground. ²¹I will summon a sword against Gog on all my mountains, declares the Sovereign Lord. Every man's sword will be against his fellow. ²²I will execute judgment on him with plague and bloodshed; I will pour down torrents of rain, hailstones and burning sulfur on him and on his troops and on the many nations with him. ²³And so I will show my greatness and my holiness, and I will make myself known in the sight of many nations. Then they will know that I am the Lord.'

39 "Son of man, prophesy against Gog and say: 'This is what the Sovereign Lord says: I am against you, Gog, chief prince ofᶜ Meshek and Tubal. ²I will turn you around and drag you along. I will bring you from the far north and send you against the mountains of Israel. ³Then I will strike your bow from your left hand and make your arrows drop from your right hand. ⁴On the mountains of Israel you will fall, you and all your troops and the nations with you. I will give you as food to all kinds of carrion birds and to the wild animals. ⁵You will fall in the open field, for I have spoken, declares the Sovereign Lord. ⁶I will send fire on Magog and on those who live in safety in the coastlands, and they will know that I am the Lord.

⁷"I will make known my holy name among my people Israel. I will no longer let my holy name be profaned, and the nations will know that I the Lord am the Holy One in Israel. ⁸It is coming! It will surely take place, declares the Sovereign Lord. This is the day I have spoken of.

⁹"Then those who live in the towns of Israel will go out and use the weapons for fuel and burn them up—the small and large shields, the bows and arrows, the war clubs and spears. For seven years they will use them for fuel. ¹⁰They will not need to gather wood from the fields or cut it from the forests, because they will use the weapons for fuel. And they will plunder those who plundered them and loot those who looted them, declares the Sovereign Lord.

¹¹"On that day I will give Gog a burial place in Israel, in the valley of those who travel east of the Sea. It will block the way of travelers, because Gog and all his hordes will be buried there. So it will be called the Valley of Hamon Gog.ᵈ

> **atissue:atheism**
>
> **39:7–8** One day there won't be any room left for argument, denial or doubt. From the most cynical atheist to the most gentle, compassionate Christian, all the nations will know God is the Holy One and Sovereign Lord. His reign and his rule will be declared. He will cause every person to bow before him, and no one will question his authority or power. When you find yourself frustrated at a world that refuses to acknowledge God, be patient. Their day is coming. And be thankful now that by his grace you already know him.

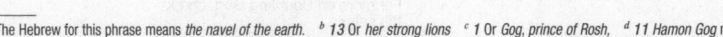

ᵃ *12 The Hebrew for this phrase means the navel of the earth.*   ᵇ *13 Or her strong lions*   ᶜ *1 Or Gog, prince of Rosh,*   ᵈ *11 Hamon Gog means hordes of Gog.*

¹²"'For seven months the house of Israel will be burying them in order to cleanse the land. ¹³All the people of the land will bury them, and the day I display my glory will be a memorable day for them, declares the Sovereign Lᴏʀᴅ. ¹⁴People will be continually employed in cleansing the land. They will spread out across the land and, along with others, they will bury any bodies that are lying on the ground.

"'After the seven months they will carry out a more detailed search. ¹⁵As they go through the land, anyone who sees a human bone will leave a marker beside it until the gravediggers bury it in the Valley of Hamon Gog, ¹⁶near a town called Hamonah.ᵃ And so they will cleanse the land.'

¹⁷"Son of man, this is what the Sovereign Lᴏʀᴅ says: Call out to every kind of bird and all the wild animals: 'Assemble and come together from all around to the sacrifice I am preparing for you, the great sacrifice on the mountains of Israel. There you will eat flesh and drink blood. ¹⁸You will eat the flesh of mighty men and drink the blood of the princes of the earth as if they were rams and lambs, goats and bulls—all of them fattened animals from Bashan. ¹⁹At the sacrifice I am preparing for you, you will eat fat till you are glutted and drink blood till you are drunk. ²⁰At my table you will eat your fill of horses and riders, mighty men and soldiers of every kind,' declares the Sovereign Lᴏʀᴅ.

²¹"I will display my glory among the nations, and all the nations will see the punishment I inflict and the hand I lay on them. ²²From that day forward the house of Israel will know that I am the Lᴏʀᴅ their God. ²³And the nations will know that the people of Israel went into exile for their sin, because they were unfaithful to me. So I hid my face from them and handed them over to their enemies, and they all fell by the sword. ²⁴I dealt with them according to their uncleanness and their offenses, and I hid my face from them.

²⁵"Therefore this is what the Sovereign Lᴏʀᴅ says: I will now restore the fortunes of Jacobᵇ and will have compassion on all the people of Israel, and I will be zealous for my holy name. ²⁶They will forget their shame and all the unfaithfulness they showed toward me when they lived in safety in their land with no one to make them afraid. ²⁷When I have brought them back from the nations and have gathered them from the countries of their enemies, I will be proved holy through them in the sight of many nations. ²⁸Then they will know that I am the Lᴏʀᴅ their God, for though I sent them into exile among the nations, I will gather them to their own land, not leaving any behind. ²⁹I will no longer hide my face from them, for I will pour out my Spirit on the house of Israel, declares the Sovereign Lᴏʀᴅ."

The Temple Area Restored

40 In the twenty-fifth year of our exile, at the beginning of the year, on the tenth of the month, in the fourteenth year after the fall of the city—on that very day the hand of the Lᴏʀᴅ was on me and he took me there. ²In visions of God he took me to the land of Israel and set me on a very high mountain, on whose south side were some buildings that looked like a city. ³He took me there, and I saw a man whose appearance was like bronze; he was standing in the gateway with a linen cord and a measuring rod in his hand. ⁴The man said to me, "Son of man, look carefully and listen closely and pay attention to everything I am going to show you, for that is why you have been brought here. Tell the house of Israel everything you see."

The East Gate to the Outer Court

⁵I saw a wall completely surrounding the temple area. The length of the measuring rod in the man's hand was six long cubits,ᶜ each of which was a cubit and a handbreadth. He measured the wall; it was one measuring rod thick and one rod high.

⁶Then he went to the east gate. He climbed its steps and measured the threshold of the gate; it was one rod deep. ⁷The alcoves for the guards were one rod long and one rod wide, and the projecting walls between the alcoves were five cubitsᵈ thick. And the threshold of the gate next to the portico facing the temple was one rod deep.

⁸Then he measured the portico of the gateway; ⁹itᵉ was eight cubitsᶠ deep and its jambs were two cubitsᵍ thick. The portico of the gateway faced the temple.

ᵃ 16 Hamonah means horde.   ᵇ 25 Or now bring Jacob back from captivity   ᶜ 5 That is, about 10 feet or about 3.1 meters; also in verse 12. The long cubit of about 21 inches or about 52 centimeters is the basic unit of measurement of length throughout Ezekiel 40–48.   ᵈ 7 That is, about 8 1/2 feet or about 2.6 meters; also in verse 48   ᵉ 8,9 Many Hebrew manuscripts, Septuagint, Vulgate and Syriac; most Hebrew manuscripts gateway facing the temple; it was one rod deep.
⁹Then he measured the portico of the gateway; it   ᶠ 9 That is, about 14 feet or about 4.2 meters.   ᵍ 9 That is, about 3 1/2 feet or about 1 meter

¹⁰Inside the east gate were three alcoves on each side; the three had the same measurements, and the faces of the projecting walls on each side had the same measurements. ¹¹Then he measured the width of the entrance of the gateway; it was ten cubits and its length was thirteen cubits.ᵃ ¹²In front of each alcove was a wall one cubit high, and the alcoves were six cubits square. ¹³Then he measured the gateway from the top of the rear wall of one alcove to the top of the opposite one; the distance was twenty-five cubitsᵇ from one parapet opening to the opposite one. ¹⁴He measured along the faces of the projecting walls all around the inside of the gateway—sixty cubits.ᶜ The measurement was up to the porticoᵈ facing the courtyard.ᵉ ¹⁵The distance from the entrance of the gateway to the far end of its portico was fifty cubits.ᶠ ¹⁶The alcoves and the projecting walls inside the gateway were surmounted by narrow parapet openings all around, as was the portico; the openings all around faced inward. The faces of the projecting walls were decorated with palm trees.

The Outer Court

¹⁷Then he brought me into the outer court. There I saw some rooms and a pavement that had been constructed all around the court; there were thirty rooms along the pavement. ¹⁸It abutted the sides of the gateways and was as wide as they were long; this was the lower pavement. ¹⁹Then he measured the distance from the inside of the lower gateway to the outside of the inner court; it was a hundred cubitsᵍ on the east side as well as on the north.

The North Gate

²⁰Then he measured the length and width of the north gate, leading into the outer court. ²¹Its alcoves—three on each side—its projecting walls and its portico had the same measurements as those of the first gateway. It was fifty cubits long and twenty-five cubits wide. ²²Its openings, its portico and its palm tree decorations had the same measurements as those of the gate facing east. Seven steps led up to it, with its portico opposite them. ²³There was a gate to the inner court facing the north gate, just as there was on the east. He measured from one gate to the opposite one; it was a hundred cubits.

The South Gate

²⁴Then he led me to the south side and I saw the south gate. He measured its jambs and its portico, and they had the same measurements as the others. ²⁵The gateway and its portico had narrow openings all around, like the openings of the others. It was fifty cubits long and twenty-five cubits wide. ²⁶Seven steps led up to it, with its portico opposite them; it had palm tree decorations on the faces of the projecting walls on each side. ²⁷The inner court also had a gate facing south, and he measured from this gate to the outer gate on the south side; it was a hundred cubits.

The Gates to the Inner Court

²⁸Then he brought me into the inner court through the south gate, and he measured the south gate; it had the same measurements as the others. ²⁹Its alcoves, its projecting walls and its portico had the same measurements as the others. The gateway and its portico had openings all around. It was fifty cubits long and twenty-five cubits wide. ³⁰(The porticoes of the gateways around the inner court were twenty-five cubits wide and five cubits deep.) ³¹Its portico faced the outer court; palm trees decorated its jambs, and eight steps led up to it.

³²Then he brought me to the inner court on the east side, and he measured the gateway; it had the same measurements as the others. ³³Its alcoves, its projecting walls and its portico had the same measurements as the others. The gateway and its portico had openings all around. It was fifty cubits long and twenty-five cubits wide. ³⁴Its portico faced the outer court; palm trees decorated the jambs on either side, and eight steps led up to it.

³⁵Then he brought me to the north gate and measured it. It had the same measurements as the others, ³⁶as did its alcoves, its projecting walls and its portico, and it had openings all around. It was fifty cubits long and twenty-five cubits wide. ³⁷Its porticoʰ faced the outer court; palm trees decorated the jambs on either side, and eight steps led up to it.

ᵃ *11* That is, about 17 feet wide and 22 feet long or about 5.2 meters wide and 6.8 meters long   ᵇ *13* That is, about 43 feet or about 13 meters; also in verses 21, 25, 29, 30, 33 and 36   ᶜ *14* That is, about 103 feet or about 31 meters   ᵈ *14* Septuagint; Hebrew *projecting wall*   ᵉ *14* The meaning of the Hebrew for this verse is uncertain.   ᶠ *15* That is, about 85 feet or about 26 meters; also in verses 21, 25, 29, 33 and 36   ᵍ *19* That is, about 170 feet or about 52 meters; also in verses 23, 27 and 47   ʰ *37* Septuagint (see also verses 31 and 34); Hebrew *jambs*

The Rooms for Preparing Sacrifices

[38] A room with a doorway was by the portico in each of the inner gateways, where the burnt offerings were washed. [39] In the portico of the gateway were two tables on each side, on which the burnt offerings, sin offerings[a] and guilt offerings were slaughtered. [40] By the outside wall of the portico of the gateway, near the steps at the entrance of the north gateway were two tables, and on the other side of the steps were two tables. [41] So there were four tables on one side of the gateway and four on the other—eight tables in all—on which the sacrifices were slaughtered. [42] There were also four tables of dressed stone for the burnt offerings, each a cubit and a half long, a cubit and a half wide and a cubit high.[b] On them were placed the utensils for slaughtering the burnt offerings and the other sacrifices. [43] And double-pronged hooks, each a handbreadth[c] long, were attached to the wall all around. The tables were for the flesh of the offerings.

The Rooms for the Priests

[44] Outside the inner gate, within the inner court, were two rooms, one[d] at the side of the north gate and facing south, and another at the side of the south[e] gate and facing north. [45] He said to me, "The room facing south is for the priests who guard the temple, [46] and the room facing north is for the priests who guard the altar. These are the sons of Zadok, who are the only Levites who may draw near to the LORD to minister before him."

[47] Then he measured the court: It was square—a hundred cubits long and a hundred cubits wide. And the altar was in front of the temple.

The New Temple

[48] He brought me to the portico of the temple and measured the jambs of the portico; they were five cubits wide on either side. The width of the entrance was fourteen cubits[f] and its projecting walls were[g] three cubits[h] wide on either side. [49] The portico was twenty cubits[i] wide, and twelve[j] cubits[k] from front to back. It was reached by a flight of stairs,[l] and there were pillars on each side of the jambs.

41 Then the man brought me to the main hall and measured the jambs; the width of the jambs was six cubits[m] on each side.[n] [2] The entrance was ten cubits[o] wide, and the projecting walls on each side of it were five cubits[p] wide. He also measured the main hall; it was forty cubits long and twenty cubits[q] wide.

[3] Then he went into the inner sanctuary and measured the jambs of the entrance; each was two cubits[r] wide. The entrance was six cubits wide, and the projecting walls on each side of it were seven cubits[s] wide. [4] And he measured the length of the inner sanctuary; it was twenty cubits, and its width was twenty cubits across the end of the main hall. He said to me, "This is the Most Holy Place."

[5] Then he measured the wall of the temple; it was six cubits thick, and each side room around the temple was four cubits[t] wide. [6] The side rooms were on three levels, one above another, thirty on each level. There were ledges all around the wall of the temple to serve as supports for the side rooms, so that the supports were not inserted into the wall of the temple. [7] The side rooms all around the temple were wider at each successive level. The structure surrounding the temple was built in ascending stages, so that the rooms widened as one went upward. A stairway went up from the lowest floor to the top floor through the middle floor.

[8] I saw that the temple had a raised base all around it, forming the foundation of the side rooms. It was the length of the rod, six long cubits. [9] The outer wall of the side rooms was five cubits thick. The open area between the side rooms of the temple [10] and the ⌊priests'⌋ rooms was twenty cubits wide all around the temple. [11] There were entrances to the side rooms from the open area, one on the north and another on the south; and the base adjoining the open area was five cubits wide all around.

1247

¹²The building facing the temple courtyard on the west side was seventy cubits*ᵃ* wide. The wall of the building was five cubits thick all around, and its length was ninety cubits.*ᵇ*

¹³Then he measured the temple; it was a hundred cubits*ᶜ* long, and the temple courtyard and the building with its walls were also a hundred cubits long. ¹⁴The width of the temple courtyard on the east, including the front of the temple, was a hundred cubits.

¹⁵Then he measured the length of the building facing the courtyard at the rear of the temple, including its galleries on each side; it was a hundred cubits.

The main hall, the inner sanctuary and the portico facing the court, ¹⁶as well as the thresholds and the narrow windows and galleries around the three of them—everything beyond and including the threshold was covered with wood. The floor, the wall up to the windows, and the windows were covered. ¹⁷In the space above the outside of the entrance to the inner sanctuary and on the walls at regular intervals all around the inner and outer sanctuary ¹⁸were carved cherubim and palm trees. Palm trees alternated with cherubim. Each cherub had two faces: ¹⁹the face of a human being toward the palm tree on one side and the face of a lion toward the palm tree on the other. They were carved all around the whole temple. ²⁰From the floor to the area above the entrance, cherubim and palm trees were carved on the wall of the main hall.

²¹The main hall had a rectangular doorframe, and the one at the front of the Most Holy Place was similar. ²²There was a wooden altar three cubits*ᵈ* high and two cubits square*ᵉ*; its corners, its base*ᶠ* and its sides were of wood. The man said to me, "This is the table that is before the LORD." ²³Both the main hall and the Most Holy Place had double doors. ²⁴Each door had two leaves—two hinged leaves for each door. ²⁵And on the doors of the main hall were carved cherubim and palm trees like those carved on the walls, and there was a wooden overhang on the front of the portico. ²⁶On the sidewalls of the portico were narrow windows with palm trees carved on each side. The side rooms of the temple also had overhangs.

The Rooms for the Priests

42 Then the man led me northward into the outer court and brought me to the rooms opposite the temple courtyard and opposite the outer wall on the north side. ²The building whose door faced north was a hundred cubits long and fifty cubits wide.*ᵍ* ³Both in the section twenty cubits*ʰ* from the inner court and in the section opposite the pavement of the outer court, gallery faced gallery at the three levels. ⁴In front of the rooms was an inner passageway ten cubits wide and a hundred cubits*ⁱ* long.*ʲ* Their doors were on the north. ⁵Now the upper rooms were narrower, for the galleries took more space from them than from the rooms on the lower and middle floors of the building. ⁶The rooms on the top floor had no pillars, as the courts had; so they were smaller in floor space than those on the lower and middle floors. ⁷There was an outer wall parallel to the rooms and the outer court; it extended in front of the rooms for fifty cubits. ⁸While the row of rooms on the side next to the outer court was fifty cubits long, the row on the side nearest the sanctuary was a hundred cubits long. ⁹The lower rooms had an entrance on the east side as one enters them from the outer court.

¹⁰On the south side*ᵏ* along the length of the wall of the outer court, adjoining the temple courtyard and opposite the outer wall, were rooms ¹¹with a passageway in front of them. These were like the rooms on the north; they had the same length and width, with similar exits and dimensions. Similar to the doorways on the north ¹²were the doorways of the rooms on the south. There was a doorway at the beginning of the passageway that was parallel to the corresponding wall extending eastward, by which one enters the rooms.

¹³Then he said to me, "The north and south rooms facing the temple courtyard are the priests' rooms, where the priests who approach the LORD will eat the most holy offerings. There they will put the most holy offerings—the grain offerings, the sin offerings*ˡ* and the guilt offerings—for the place is holy. ¹⁴Once the priests enter the holy precincts, they are not to go into the outer court until they leave behind the

---

ᵃ 12 That is, about 120 feet or about 36 meters   *ᵇ 12* That is, about 154 feet or about 47 meters   *ᶜ 13* That is, about 170 feet or about 52 meters; also in verses 14 and 15   *ᵈ 22* That is, about 5 1/4 feet or about 1.5 meters   *ᵉ 22* Septuagint; Hebrew *long*   *ᶠ 22* Septuagint; Hebrew *length*   *ᵍ 2* That is, about 170 feet long and 85 feet wide or about 52 meters long and 26 meters wide   *ʰ 3* That is, about 34 feet or about 10.4 meters   *ⁱ 4* Septuagint and Syriac; Hebrew *and one cubit*   *ʲ 4* That is, about 17 feet wide and 170 feet long or about 5.2 meters wide and 52 meters long   *ᵏ 10* Septuagint; Hebrew *Eastward*   *ˡ 13* Or *purification offerings* garments in which they minister, for these are holy. They are to put on other clothes before they go near the places that are for the people."

¹⁵When he had finished measuring what was inside the temple area, he led me out by the east gate and measured the area all around: ¹⁶He measured the east side with the measuring rod; it was five hundred cubits.*ᵃ, ᵇ* ¹⁷He measured the north side; it was five hundred cubits*ᶜ* by the measuring rod. ¹⁸He measured the south side; it was five hundred cubits by the measuring rod. ¹⁹Then he turned to the west side and measured; it was five hundred cubits by the measuring rod. ²⁰So he measured the area on all four sides. It had a wall around it, five hundred cubits long and five hundred cubits wide, to separate the holy from the common.

God's Glory Returns to the Temple

43 Then the man brought me to the gate facing east, ²and I saw the glory of the God of Israel coming from the east. His voice was like the roar of rushing waters, and the land was radiant with his glory. ³The vision I saw was like the vision I had seen when he*ᵈ* came to destroy the city and like the visions I had seen by the Kebar River, and I fell facedown. ⁴The glory of the LORD entered the temple through the gate facing east. ⁵Then the Spirit lifted me up and brought me into the inner court, and the glory of the LORD filled the temple.

HE IS: radiant

43:1–5 Ezekiel was shown a vision of the glory of the Lord filling the temple. God's glory had departed from the temple because the people had turned from him, but one day the indescribable brilliance of God will return, making the land *radiant* with his glory.

Scripture teaches that, as a believer, you "are God's temple" (1 Corinthians 3:16). With the *radiant* God within you, you too become radiant—shining with the life he gives you, glowing from within, bright and shimmering in a dark world.

For the next He Is, go to p. 1261.

⁶While the man was standing beside me, I heard someone speaking to me from inside the temple. ⁷He said: "Son of man, this is the place of my throne and the place for the soles of my feet. This is where I will live among the Israelites forever. The house of Israel will never again defile my holy name—neither they nor their kings—by their prostitution and the funeral offerings*ᵉ* for their kings at their death.*ᶠ* ⁸When they placed their threshold next to my threshold and their doorposts beside my doorposts, with only a wall between me and them, they defiled my holy name by their detestable practices. So I destroyed them in my anger. ⁹Now let them put away from me their prostitution and the funeral offerings for their kings, and I will live among them forever.

¹⁰"Son of man, describe the temple to the people of Israel, that they may be ashamed of their sins. Let them consider its perfection, ¹¹and if they are ashamed of all they have done, make known to them the design of the temple—its arrangement, its exits and entrances—its whole design and all its regulations*ᵍ* and laws. Write these down before them so that they may be faithful to its design and follow all its regulations.

¹²"This is the law of the temple: All the surrounding area on top of the mountain will be most holy. Such is the law of the temple.

The Great Altar Restored

¹³"These are the measurements of the altar in long cubits,*ʰ* that cubit being a cubit and a handbreadth: Its gutter is a cubit deep and a cubit wide, with a rim of one span*ⁱ* around the edge. And this is

---

ᵃ 16 See Septuagint of verse 17; Hebrew *rods*; also in verses 18 and 19.   *ᵇ 16* Five hundred cubits equal about 850 feet or about 260 meters; also in verses 17, 18 and 19.   *ᶜ 17* Septuagint; Hebrew *rods*   *ᵈ 3* Some Hebrew manuscripts and Vulgate; most Hebrew manuscripts *I*   *ᵉ 7* Or *the memorial monuments*; also in verse 9   *ᶠ 7* Or *their high places*   *ᵍ 11* Some Hebrew manuscripts and Septuagint; most Hebrew manuscripts *regulations and its whole design*   *ʰ 13* That is, about 21 inches or about 52 centimeters; also in verses 14 and 17. The long cubit is the basic unit for linear measurement throughout Ezekiel 40–48.   *ⁱ 13* That is, about 10 inches or about 26 centimeters the height of the altar: ¹⁴From the gutter on the ground up to the lower ledge that goes around the altar it is two cubits high, and the ledge is a cubit wide.ᵃ From this lower ledge to the upper ledge that goes around the altar it is four cubits high, and that ledge is also a cubit wide.ᵇ ¹⁵Above that, the altar hearth is four cubits high, and four horns project upward from the hearth. ¹⁶The altar hearth is square, twelve cubitsᶜ long and twelve cubits wide. ¹⁷The upper ledge also is square, fourteen cubitsᵈ long and fourteen cubits wide. All around the altar is a gutter of one cubit with a rim of half a cubit.ᵉ The steps of the altar face east."

¹⁸Then he said to me, "Son of man, this is what the Sovereign Lord says: These will be the regulations for sacrificing burnt offerings and splashing blood against the altar when it is built: ¹⁹You are to give a young bull as a sin offeringᶠ to the Levitical priests of the family of Zadok, who come near to minister before me, declares the Sovereign Lord. ²⁰You are to take some of its blood and put it on the four horns of the altar and on the four corners of the upper ledge and all around the rim, and so purify the altar and make atonement for it. ²¹You are to take the bull for the sin offering and burn it in the designated part of the temple area outside the sanctuary.

²²"On the second day you are to offer a male goat without defect for a sin offering, and the altar is to be purified as it was purified with the bull. ²³When you have finished purifying it, you are to offer a young bull and a ram from the flock, both without defect. ²⁴You are to offer them before the Lord, and the priests are to sprinkle salt on them and sacrifice them as a burnt offering to the Lord.

²⁵"For seven days you are to provide a male goat daily for a sin offering; you are also to provide a young bull and a ram from the flock, both without defect. ²⁶For seven days they are to make atonement for the altar and cleanse it; thus they will dedicate it. ²⁷At the end of these days, from the eighth day on, the priests are to present your burnt offerings and fellowship offerings on the altar. Then I will accept you, declares the Sovereign Lord."

The Priesthood Restored

44 Then the man brought me back to the outer gate of the sanctuary, the one facing east, and it was shut. ²The Lord said to me, "This gate is to remain shut. It must not be opened; no one may enter through it. It is to remain shut because the Lord, the God of Israel, has entered through it. ³The prince himself is the only one who may sit inside the gateway to eat in the presence of the Lord. He is to enter by way of the portico of the gateway and go out the same way."

⁴Then the man brought me by way of the north gate to the front of the temple. I looked and saw the glory of the Lord filling the temple of the Lord, and I fell facedown.

⁵The Lord said to me, "Son of man, look carefully, listen closely and give attention to everything I tell you concerning all the regulations and instructions regarding the temple of the Lord. Give attention to the entrance to the temple and all the exits of the sanctuary. ⁶Say to the rebellious house of Israel, 'This is what the Sovereign Lord says: Enough of your detestable practices, house of Israel! ⁷In addition to all your other detestable practices, you brought foreigners uncircumcised in heart and flesh into my sanctuary, desecrating my temple while you offered me food, fat and blood, and you broke my covenant. ⁸Instead of carrying out your duty in regard to my holy things, you put others in charge of my sanctuary. ⁹This is what the Sovereign Lord says: No foreigner uncircumcised in heart and flesh is to enter my sanctuary, not even the foreigners who live among the Israelites.

¹⁰"'The Levites who went far from me when Israel went astray and who wandered from me after their idols must bear the consequences of their sin. ¹¹They may serve in my sanctuary, having charge of the gates of the temple and serving in it; they may slaughter the burnt offerings and sacrifices for the people and stand before the people and serve them. ¹²But because they served them in the presence of their idols and made the house of Israel fall into sin, therefore I have sworn with uplifted hand that they must bear the consequences of their sin, declares the Sovereign Lord. ¹³They are not to come near to serve me as priests or come near any of my holy things or my most holy offerings; they must bear the shame of

---

ᵃ *14* That is, about 3 1/2 feet high and 1 3/4 feet wide or about 104 centimeters high and 52 centimeters wide   ᵇ *14* That is, about 7 feet high and 1 3/4 feet wide or about 2.1 meters high and 52 centimeters wide   ᶜ *16* That is, about 21 feet or about 6.2 meters   ᵈ *17* That is, about 24 feet or about 7.3 meters   ᵉ *17* That is, about 10 inches or about 26 centimeters   ᶠ *19* Or *purification offering*; also in verses 21, 22 and 25 their detestable practices. ¹⁴And I will appoint them to guard the temple for all the work that is to be done in it.

¹⁵"But the Levitical priests, who are descendants of Zadok and who guarded my sanctuary when the Israelites went astray from me, are to come near to minister before me; they are to stand before me to offer sacrifices of fat and blood, declares the Sovereign Lord. ¹⁶They alone are to enter my sanctuary; they alone are to come near my table to minister before me and serve me as guards.

¹⁷"When they enter the gates of the inner court, they are to wear linen clothes; they must not wear any woolen garment while ministering at the gates of the inner court or inside the temple. ¹⁸They are to wear linen turbans on their heads and linen undergarments around their waists. They must not wear anything that makes them perspire. ¹⁹When they go out into the outer court where the people are, they are to take off the clothes they have been ministering in and are to leave them in the sacred rooms, and put on other clothes, so that the people are not consecrated through contact with their garments.

²⁰"They must not shave their heads or let their hair grow long, but they are to keep the hair of their heads trimmed. ²¹No priest is to drink wine when he enters the inner court. ²²They must not marry widows or divorced women; they may marry only virgins of Israelite descent or widows of priests. ²³They are to teach my people the difference between the holy and the common and show them how to distinguish between the unclean and the clean.

²⁴"In any dispute, the priests are to serve as judges and decide it according to my ordinances. They are to keep my laws and my decrees for all my appointed festivals, and they are to keep my Sabbaths holy.

²⁵"A priest must not defile himself by going near a dead person; however, if the dead person was his father or mother, son or daughter, brother or unmarried sister, then he may defile himself. ²⁶After he is cleansed, he must wait seven days. ²⁷On the day he goes into the inner court of the sanctuary to minister in the sanctuary, he is to offer a sin offering*a* for himself, declares the Sovereign Lord.

²⁸"I am to be the only inheritance the priests have. You are to give them no possession in Israel; I will be their possession. ²⁹They will eat the grain offerings, the sin offerings and the guilt offerings; and everything in Israel devoted*b* to the Lord will belong to them. ³⁰The best of all the firstfruits and of all your special gifts will belong to the priests. You are to give them the first portion of your ground meal so that a blessing may rest on your household. ³¹The priests must not eat anything, whether bird or animal, found dead or torn by wild animals.

Israel Fully Restored

45 "'When you allot the land as an inheritance, you are to present to the Lord a portion of the land as a sacred district, 25,000 cubits*c* long and 20,000*d* cubits*e* wide; the entire area will be holy. ²Of this, a section 500 cubits*f* square is to be for the sanctuary, with 50 cubits*g* around it for open land. ³In the sacred district, measure off a section 25,000 cubits long and 10,000 cubits*h* wide. In it will be the sanctuary, the Most Holy Place. ⁴It will be the sacred portion of the land for the priests, who minister in the sanctuary and who draw near to minister before the Lord. It will be a place for their houses as well as a holy place for the sanctuary. ⁵An area 25,000 cubits long and 10,000 cubits wide will belong to the Levites, who serve in the temple, as their possession for towns to live in.*i*

⁶"You are to give the city as its property an area 5,000 cubits*j* wide and 25,000 cubits long, adjoining the sacred portion; it will belong to the whole house of Israel.

⁷"The prince will have the land bordering each side of the area formed by the sacred district and the property of the city. It will extend westward from the west side and eastward from the east side, running lengthwise from the western to the eastern border parallel to one of the tribal portions. ⁸This land will be his possession in Israel. And my princes will no longer oppress my people but will allow the house of Israel to possess the land according to their tribes.

⁹"This is what the Sovereign Lord says: You have gone far enough, princes of Israel! Give up your violence and oppression and do what is just and right. Stop dispossessing my people, declares the Sovereign

Lord. ¹⁰You are to use accurate scales, an accurate ephah ᵃ and an accurate bath.ᵇ ¹¹The ephah and the bath are to be the same size, the bath containing a tenth of a homer and the ephah a tenth of a homer; the homer is to be the standard measure for both. ¹²The shekelᶜ is to consist of twenty gerahs. Twenty shekels plus twenty-five shekels plus fifteen shekels equal one mina.ᵈ

¹³"'This is the special gift you are to offer: a sixth of an ephahᵉ from each homer of wheat and a sixth of an ephahᶠ from each homer of barley. ¹⁴The prescribed portion of olive oil, measured by the bath,ᵍ is a tenth of a bath from each cor (which consists of ten baths or one homer, for ten baths are equivalent to a homer). ¹⁵Also one sheep is to be taken from every flock of two hundred from the well-watered pastures of Israel. These will be used for the grain offerings, burnt offerings and fellowship offerings to make atonement for the people, declares the Sovereign Lord. ¹⁶All the people of the land will be required to give this special offering to the prince in Israel. ¹⁷It will be the duty of the prince to provide the burnt offerings, grain offerings and drink offerings at the festivals, the New Moons and the Sabbaths—at all the appointed festivals of the house of Israel. He will provide the sin offerings,ʰ grain offerings, burnt offerings and fellowship offerings to make atonement for the house of Israel.

¹⁸"'This is what the Sovereign Lord says: In the first month on the first day you are to take a young bull without defect and purify the sanctuary. ¹⁹The priest is to take some of the blood of the sin offering and put it on the doorposts of the temple, on the four corners of the upper ledge of the altar and on the gateposts of the inner court. ²⁰You are to do the same on the seventh day of the month for anyone who sins unintentionally or through ignorance; so you are to make atonement for the temple.

²¹"'In the first month on the fourteenth day you are to observe the Passover, a festival lasting seven days, during which you shall eat bread made without yeast. ²²On that day the prince is to provide a bull as a sin offering for himself and for all the people of the land. ²³Every day during the seven days of the festival he is to provide seven bulls and seven rams without defect as a burnt offering to the Lord, and a male goat for a sin offering. ²⁴He is to provide as a grain offering an ephah for each bull and an ephah for each ram, along with a hinⁱ of olive oil for each ephah.

²⁵"'During the seven days of the festival, which begins in the seventh month on the fifteenth day, he is to make the same provision for sin offerings, burnt offerings, grain offerings and oil.

46 "'This is what the Sovereign Lord says: The gate of the inner court facing east is to be shut on the six working days, but on the Sabbath day and on the day of the New Moon it is to be opened. ²The prince is to enter from the outside through the portico of the gateway and stand by the gatepost. The priests are to sacrifice his burnt offering and his fellowship offerings. He is to bow down in worship at the threshold of the gateway and then go out, but the gate will not be shut until evening. ³On the Sabbaths and New Moons the people of the land are to worship in the presence of the Lord at the entrance of that gateway. ⁴The burnt offering the prince brings to the Lord on the Sabbath day is to be six male lambs and a ram, all without defect. ⁵The grain offering given with the ram is to be an ephah,ʲ and the grain offering with the lambs is to be as much as he pleases, along with a hinᵏ of olive oil for each ephah. ⁶On the day of the New Moon he is to offer a young bull, six lambs and a ram, all without defect. ⁷He is to provide as a grain offering one ephah with the bull, one ephah with the ram, and with the lambs as much as he wants to give, along with a hin of oil for each ephah. ⁸When the prince enters, he is to go in through the portico of the gateway, and he is to come out the same way.

⁹"'When the people of the land come before the Lord at the appointed festivals, whoever enters by the north gate to worship is to go out the south gate; and whoever enters by the south gate is to go out the north gate. No one is to return through the gate by which he entered, but each is to go out the opposite gate. ¹⁰The prince is to be among them, going in when they go in and going out when they go out. ¹¹At the feasts and the appointed festivals, the grain offering is to be an ephah with a bull, an ephah with a ram, and with the lambs as much as he pleases, along with a hin of oil for each ephah.

¹²"'When the prince provides a freewill offering to the Lord—whether a burnt offering or fellowship

ᵃ 10 An ephah was a dry measure equaling about 3/5 bushel or about 22 liters.   ᵇ 10 A bath was a liquid measure equaling about 6 gallons or about 22 liters.
ᶜ 12 A shekel weighed about 2/5 ounce or about 11.5 grams.   ᵈ 12 That is, 60 shekels; the common mina was 50 shekels. Sixty shekels were about 1 1/2 pounds or about 680 grams.   ᵉ 13 That is, probably about 6 pounds or about 23/4 kilograms   ᶠ 13 That is, probably about 5 pounds or about 2 1/4 kilograms
ᵍ 14 That is, about 5 pints or about 2.2 liters   ʰ 17 Or purification offerings; also in verses 19, 22, 23 and 25   ⁱ 24 That is, about 1 gallon or about 3.6 liters
ʲ 5 That is, probably about 36 pounds or about 16 kilograms; also in verses 7 and 11   ᵏ 5 That is, about 1 gallon or about 3.6 liters; also in verses 7 and 11

offerings—the gate facing east is to be opened for him. He shall offer his burnt offering or his fellowship offerings as he does on the Sabbath day. Then he shall go out, and after he has gone out, the gate will be shut.

¹³"'Every day you are to provide a year-old lamb without defect for a burnt offering to the LORD; morning by morning you shall provide it. ¹⁴You are also to provide with it morning by morning a grain offering, consisting of a sixth of an ephah*a* with a third of a hin*b* of oil to moisten the flour. The presenting of this grain offering to the LORD is a lasting ordinance. ¹⁵So the lamb and the grain offering and the oil shall be provided morning by morning for a regular burnt offering.

¹⁶"'This is what the Sovereign LORD says: If the prince makes a gift from his inheritance to one of his sons, it will also belong to his descendants; it is to be their property by inheritance. ¹⁷If, however, he makes a gift from his inheritance to one of his servants, the servant may keep it until the year of freedom; then it will revert to the prince. His inheritance belongs to his sons only; it is theirs. ¹⁸The prince must not take any of the inheritance of the people, driving them off their property. He is to give his sons their inheritance out of his own property, so that not one of my people will be separated from their property.'"

¹⁹Then the man brought me through the entrance at the side of the gate to the sacred rooms facing north, which belonged to the priests, and showed me a place at the western end. ²⁰He said to me, "This is the place where the priests are to cook the guilt offering and the sin offering*c* and bake the grain offering, to avoid bringing them into the outer court and consecrating the people."

²¹He then brought me to the outer court and led me around to its four corners, and I saw in each corner another court. ²²In the four corners of the outer court were enclosed*d* courts, forty cubits long and thirty cubits wide;*e* each of the courts in the four corners was the same size. ²³Around the inside of each of the four courts was a ledge of stone, with places for fire built all around under the ledge. ²⁴He said to me, "These are the kitchens where those who minister at the temple are to cook the sacrifices of the people."

The River From the Temple

47 The man brought me back to the entrance to the temple, and I saw water coming out from under the threshold of the temple toward the east (for the temple faced east). The water was coming down from under the south side of the temple, south of the altar. ²He then brought me out through the north gate and led me around the outside to the outer gate facing east, and the water was trickling from the south side.

³As the man went eastward with a measuring line in his hand, he measured off a thousand cubits*f* and then led me through water that was ankle-deep. ⁴He measured off another thousand cubits and led me through water that was knee-deep. He measured off another thousand and led me through water that was up to the waist. ⁵He measured off another thousand, but now it was a river that I could not cross, because the water had risen and was deep enough to swim in—a river that no one could cross. ⁶He asked me, "Son of man, do you see this?"

Then he led me back to the bank of the river. ⁷When I arrived there, I saw a great number of trees on each side of the river. ⁸He said to me, "This water flows toward the eastern region and goes down into the Arabah,*g* where it enters the Dead Sea. When it empties into the sea, the salty water there becomes fresh. ⁹Swarms of living creatures will live wherever the river flows. There will be large numbers of fish, because this water flows there and makes the salt water fresh; so where the river flows everything will live. ¹⁰People will fish along the shore; from En Gedi to En Eglaim there will be places for spreading nets. The fish will be of many kinds—like the fish of the Mediterranean Sea. ¹¹But the swamps and marshes will not become fresh; they will be left for salt. ¹²Fruit trees of all kinds will grow on both banks of the river. Their leaves will not wither, nor will their fruit fail. Every month they will bear fruit, because the water from the sanctuary flows to them. Their fruit will serve for food and their leaves for healing."

---

a 14 That is, probably about 6 pounds or about 2 3/4 kilograms   *b 14* That is, about 2 2/3 pints or about 1.2 liters   *c 20* Or *purification offering*
d 22 The meaning of the Hebrew for this word is uncertain.   *e 22* That is, about 68 feet long and 51 feet wide or about 21 meters long and 16 meters wide
f 3 That is, about 1,700 feet or about 520 meters   *g 8* Or *the Jordan Valley*

The Boundaries of the Land

¹³This is what the Sovereign Lord says: "These are the boundaries of the land that you will divide among the twelve tribes of Israel as their inheritance, with two portions for Joseph. ¹⁴You are to divide it equally among them. Because I swore with uplifted hand to give it to your ancestors, this land will become your inheritance.

¹⁵"This is to be the boundary of the land:

"On the north side it will run from the Mediterranean Sea by the Hethlon road past Lebo Hamath to Zedad, ¹⁶Berothah*ᵃ* and Sibraim (which lies on the border between Damascus and Hamath), as far as Hazer Hattikon, which is on the border of Hauran. ¹⁷The boundary will extend from the sea to Hazar Enan,*ᵇ* along the northern border of Damascus, with the border of Hamath to the north. This will be the northern boundary.

¹⁸"On the east side the boundary will run between Hauran and Damascus, along the Jordan between Gilead and the land of Israel, to the Dead Sea and as far as Tamar.*ᶜ* This will be the eastern boundary.

¹⁹"On the south side it will run from Tamar as far as the waters of Meribah Kadesh, then along the Wadi of Egypt to the Mediterranean Sea. This will be the southern boundary.

²⁰"On the west side, the Mediterranean Sea will be the boundary to a point opposite Lebo Hamath. This will be the western boundary.

²¹"You are to distribute this land among yourselves according to the tribes of Israel. ²²You are to allot it as an inheritance for yourselves and for the foreigners residing among you and who have children. You are to consider them as native-born Israelites; along with you they are to be allotted an inheritance among the tribes of Israel. ²³In whatever tribe foreigners reside, there you are to give them their inheritance," declares the Sovereign Lord.

The Division of the Land

48 "These are the tribes, listed by name: At the northern frontier, Dan will have one portion; it will follow the Hethlon road to Lebo Hamath; Hazar Enan and the northern border of Damascus next to Hamath will be part of its border from the east side to the west side.

²"Asher will have one portion; it will border the territory of Dan from east to west.

³"Naphtali will have one portion; it will border the territory of Asher from east to west.

⁴"Manasseh will have one portion; it will border the territory of Naphtali from east to west.

⁵"Ephraim will have one portion; it will border the territory of Manasseh from east to west.

⁶"Reuben will have one portion; it will border the territory of Ephraim from east to west.

⁷"Judah will have one portion; it will border the territory of Reuben from east to west.

⁸"Bordering the territory of Judah from east to west will be the portion you are to present as a special gift. It will be 25,000 cubits*ᵈ* wide, and its length from east to west will equal one of the tribal portions; the sanctuary will be in the center of it.

⁹"The special portion you are to offer to the Lord will be 25,000 cubits long and 10,000 cubits*ᵉ* wide. ¹⁰This will be the sacred portion for the priests. It will be 25,000 cubits long on the north side, 10,000 cubits wide on the west side, 10,000 cubits wide on the east side and 25,000 cubits long on the south side. In the center of it will be the sanctuary of the Lord. ¹¹This will be for the consecrated priests, the Zadokites, who were faithful in serving me and did not go astray as the Levites did when the Israelites went astray. ¹²It will be a special gift to them from the sacred portion of the land, a most holy portion, bordering the territory of the Levites.

¹³"Alongside the territory of the priests, the Levites will have an allotment 25,000 cubits long and 10,000 cubits wide. Its total length will be 25,000 cubits and its width 10,000 cubits. ¹⁴They must not sell or exchange any of it. This is the best of the land and must not pass into other hands, because it is holy to the Lord.

¹⁵"The remaining area, 5,000 cubits*^a* wide and 25,000 cubits long, will be for the common use of the city, for houses and for pastureland. The city will be in the center of it ¹⁶and will have these measurements: the north side 4,500 cubits,*^b* the south side 4,500 cubits, the east side 4,500 cubits, and the west side 4,500 cubits. ¹⁷The pastureland for the city will be 250 cubits*^c* on the north, 250 cubits on the south, 250 cubits on the east, and 250 cubits on the west. ¹⁸What remains of the area, bordering on the sacred portion and running the length of it, will be 10,000 cubits on the east side and 10,000 cubits on the west side. Its produce will supply food for the workers of the city. ¹⁹The workers from the city who farm it will come from all the tribes of Israel. ²⁰The entire portion will be a square, 25,000 cubits on each side. As a special gift you will set aside the sacred portion, along with the property of the city.

²¹"What remains on both sides of the area formed by the sacred portion and the property of the city will belong to the prince. It will extend eastward from the 25,000 cubits of the sacred portion to the eastern border, and westward from the 25,000 cubits to the western border. Both these areas running the length of the tribal portions will belong to the prince, and the sacred portion with the temple sanctuary will be in the center of them. ²²So the property of the Levites and the property of the city will lie in the center of the area that belongs to the prince. The area belonging to the prince will lie between the border of Judah and the border of Benjamin.

²³"As for the rest of the tribes: Benjamin will have one portion; it will extend from the east side to the west side.

²⁴"Simeon will have one portion; it will border the territory of Benjamin from east to west.

²⁵"Issachar will have one portion; it will border the territory of Simeon from east to west.

²⁶"Zebulun will have one portion; it will border the territory of Issachar from east to west.

²⁷"Gad will have one portion; it will border the territory of Zebulun from east to west.

²⁸"The southern boundary of Gad will run south from Tamar to the waters of Meribah Kadesh, then along the Wadi of Egypt to the Mediterranean Sea.

²⁹"This is the land you are to allot as an inheritance to the tribes of Israel, and these will be their portions," declares the Sovereign Lord.

The Gates of the New City

³⁰"These will be the exits of the city: Beginning on the north side, which is 4,500 cubits long, ³¹the gates of the city will be named after the tribes of Israel. The three gates on the north side will be the gate of Reuben, the gate of Judah and the gate of Levi.

³²"On the east side, which is 4,500 cubits long, will be three gates: the gate of Joseph, the gate of Benjamin and the gate of Dan.

³³"On the south side, which measures 4,500 cubits, will be three gates: the gate of Simeon, the gate of Issachar and the gate of Zebulun.

³⁴"On the west side, which is 4,500 cubits long, will be three gates: the gate of Gad, the gate of Asher and the gate of Naphtali.

³⁵"The distance all around will be 18,000 cubits.*^d*

"And the name of the city from that time on will be:

THE Lord IS THERE."

1255

daniel

AUTHOR
Daniel.

AUDIENCE
Exiles in Babylon and all of God's people.

DATE
About 530 B.C.

SETTING
The Jews are taken into captivity by the
Babylonians.

VERSES TO REMEMBER
"If the God we serve is able to deliver us,
then he will deliver us from the blazing
furnace and from Your Majesty's hand.
But even if he does not, we want you to
know, Your Majesty, that we will not serve
your gods or worship the image of gold you
have set up." (3:17–18)

THEME TO CONSIDER
Our God is an awesome God—worthy of our
devotion in this lifetime and the next.

1256

Daniel's Training in Babylon

1 In the third year of the reign of Jehoiakim king of Judah, Nebuchadnezzar king of Babylon came to Jerusalem and besieged it. [2]And the Lord delivered Jehoiakim king of Judah into his hand, along with some of the articles from the temple of God. These he carried off to the temple of his god in Babylonia[a] and put in the treasure house of his god.

[3]Then the king ordered Ashpenaz, chief of his court officials, to bring into the king's service some of the Israelites from the royal family and the nobility— [4]young men without any physical defect, handsome, showing aptitude for every kind of learning, well informed, quick to understand, and qualified to serve in the king's palace. He was to teach them the language and literature of the Babylonians.[b] [5]The king assigned them a daily amount of food and wine from the king's table. They were to be trained for three years, and after that they were to enter the king's service.

[6]Among those who were chosen were some from Judah: Daniel, Hananiah, Mishael and Azariah. [7]The chief official gave them new names: to Daniel, the name Belteshazzar; to Hananiah, Shadrach; to Mishael, Meshach; and to Azariah, Abednego.

[8]But Daniel resolved not to defile himself with the royal food and wine, and he asked the chief official for permission not to defile himself this way. [9]Now God had caused the official to show favor and compassion to Daniel, [10]but the official told Daniel, "I am afraid of my lord the king, who has assigned your[c] food and drink. Why should he see you looking worse than the other young men your age? The king would then have my head because of you."

[11]Daniel then said to the guard whom the chief official had appointed over Daniel, Hananiah, Mishael and Azariah, [12]"Please test your servants for ten days: Give us nothing but vegetables to eat and water to drink. [13]Then compare our appearance with that of the young men who eat the royal food, and treat your servants in accordance with what you see." [14]So he agreed to this and tested them for ten days.

[15]At the end of the ten days they looked healthier and better nourished than any of the young men who ate the royal food. [16]So the guard took away their choice food and the wine they were to drink and gave them vegetables instead.

[17]To these four young men God gave knowledge and understanding of all kinds of literature and learning. And Daniel could understand visions and dreams of all kinds.

[18]At the end of the time set by the king to bring them into his service, the chief official presented them to Nebuchadnezzar. [19]The king talked with them, and he found none equal to Daniel, Hananiah, Mishael and Azariah; so they entered the king's service. [20]In every matter of wisdom and understanding about which the king questioned them, he found them ten times better than all the magicians and enchanters in his whole kingdom.

[21]And Daniel remained there until the first year of King Cyrus.

atissue:health

1:8–16 Daniel could have tried to justify eating the defiled food—after all, what else would he eat, and was this issue really worth taking a stand on? Yet Daniel knew that honoring God above all else should permeate every area of his life, including his diet. For Daniel, it was likely that the foods in question didn't correspond with Jewish dietary laws and parts of the food had been sacrificed to idols. While our issues are different, the principle is still the same: God wants us to honor him in every area of our lives. Even what we do with our bodies should reflect his authority.

Nebuchadnezzar's Dream

2 In the second year of his reign, Nebuchadnezzar had dreams; his mind was troubled and he could not sleep. [2]So the king summoned the magicians, enchanters, sorcerers and astrologers[d] to tell him what he had dreamed. When they came in and stood before the king, [3]he said to them, "I have had a dream that troubles me and I want to know what it means.[e]"

---

a 2 Hebrew *Shinar*   *b 4* Or *Chaldeans*   *c 10* The Hebrew for *your* and *you* in this verse is plural.   *d 2* Or *Chaldeans;* also in verses 4, 5 and 10
e 3 Or *was*

myth#73 "I'M SMARTER THAN SHE IS."

I don't understand it. I've got two Master's degrees from one of the best colleges in the country. I've been working at this company for ten years. So, why did Simone get the promotion, not me?

God? Hello? I don't understand something here. (OK. Deep breath, Kara.) I don't mean to complain. But let's face it, God. You know I could do this job. And—I didn't want to go here, but I can't help but think it: I'm smarter than Simone. I'm not trying to brag. I'm just stating a fact.

Is this some kind of lesson in humility, Lord? I hope not.

God, I earned that promotion. I've given this company everything—nights, weekends, new clients, killer presentations. I don't think Simone works nearly as many hours as I do. And although Simone is nice and all, could she really be a better manager than I'd be? Honestly?

I'm the one who always has to help her with her computer problems and remind her of meetings. (She can't remember when a meeting is sched-uled, yet she remembers the janitor's birthday. He doesn't even work in our department!) Yet no one seems to notice how little she knows. Or maybe they do, but they're too polite to say anything. Instead, every-one says she's so nice.

Lord, you know how hard I worked for those degrees so that I could advance in my career. Maybe it's time for me to go where I'm more appreciated.

—Kara

"IF YOU'VE GOT IT, flaunt it," or so the saying goes. We're encouraged to crow about our "stuff" (a Prada handbag at a Prada-knockoff price, our latest jewelry acquisition, our professionally decorated home) and advertise our pedigrees or academic accomplishments, especially if these raise our status above someone else's.

Some of us, if we're honest, will admit that we compare ourselves to others. Maybe we don't exactly say, "God, I thank you that I am not like other people," as the self-righteous Pharisee boasted (Luke 18:11). But we secretly think that we have more going for us. Consequently, we might think we deserve more perks than someone with fewer accomplishments.

Paul could have boasted about his pedigree. He was highly educated, a religious purebred and a citizen of Rome on top of that (see Philippians 3:4–6 and Acts 16:37). But he willingly gave up his envied status as a Pharisee to boast about Christ (see 2 Corinthians 10:12–18). He used his abundant intellect and other abilities to further God's kingdom. His motto: "For to me, to live is Christ" (Philippians 1:21)

In the Bible, we read of Daniel, Joseph and Deborah, who used their abilities to advise kings and judge the affairs of the people under their jurisdiction. Humility was the key that unlocked the door to their success. They knew the source of their abilities and used their gifts to serve God.

Humility isn't sitting in a corner or having a self-deprecating attitude. Rather, it is an acknowledgment of how God has gifted you (musically, intellectually, financially—whatever) and a willingness to use your abilities for God's kingdom.

Are you smarter than she is? Perhaps God made you smarter to give you more responsibility to further his kingdom in serving others. "From the one who has been entrusted with much, much more will be asked" (Luke 12:48).

> "Yet every day, everywhere, from every age bracket, and even despite our faith in Jesus Christ, we size each other up, comparing supposed weaknesses and trying to make ourselves feel better by ignoring or brushing off one another. The sad truth is, we're doing what comes naturally—in the flesh."
>
> —Julie Ann Barnhill

1259

"EACH OF YOU SHOULD USE WHATEVER GIFT YOU HAVE RECEIVED TO SERVE OTHERS, AS FAITHFUL STEWARDS OF GOD'S GRACE IN ITS VARIOUS FORMS."

1 PETER 4:10

SEE ALSO

1 Corinthians 1:28–31
2 Corinthians 12:9
Titus 3:1–2

For more on **Humility** and **Pride**, check the index.

[4]Then the astrologers answered the king,[a] "May the king live forever! Tell your servants the dream, and we will interpret it."

[5]The king replied to the astrologers, "This is what I have firmly decided: If you do not tell me what my dream was and interpret it, I will have you cut into pieces and your houses turned into piles of rubble. [6]But if you tell me the dream and explain it, you will receive from me gifts and rewards and great honor. So tell me the dream and interpret it for me."

[7]Once more they replied, "Let the king tell his servants the dream, and we will interpret it."

[8]Then the king answered, "I am certain that you are trying to gain time, because you realize that this is what I have firmly decided: [9]If you do not tell me the dream, there is only one penalty for you. You have conspired to tell me misleading and wicked things, hoping the situation will change. So then, tell me the dream, and I will know that you can interpret it for me."

[10]The astrologers answered the king, "There is not a person on earth who can do what the king asks! No king, however great and mighty, has ever asked such a thing of any magician or enchanter or astrologer. [11]What the king asks is too difficult. No one can reveal it to the king except the gods, and they do not live among human beings."

[12]This made the king so angry and furious that he ordered the execution of all the wise men of Babylon. [13]So the decree was issued to put the wise men to death, and men were sent to look for Daniel and his friends to put them to death.

[14]When Arioch, the commander of the king's guard, had gone out to put to death the wise men of Babylon, Daniel spoke to him with wisdom and tact. [15]He asked the king's officer, "Why did the king issue such a harsh decree?" Arioch then explained the matter to Daniel. [16]At this, Daniel went in to the king and asked for time, so that he might interpret the dream for him.

[17]Then Daniel returned to his house and explained the matter to his friends Hananiah, Mishael and Azariah. [18]He urged them to plead for mercy from the God of heaven concerning this mystery, so that he and his friends might not be executed with the rest of the wise men of Babylon. [19]During the night the mystery was revealed to Daniel in a vision. Then Daniel praised the God of heaven [20]and said:

> "Praise be to the name of God for ever and ever;
>   wisdom and power are his.
> [21]He changes times and seasons;
>   he deposes kings and raises
>   up others.
> He gives wisdom to the wise
>   and knowledge to the
>   discerning.
> [22]He reveals deep and hidden
>   things;
>   he knows what lies in
>   darkness,
>   and light dwells with him.
> [23]I thank and praise you, God of
>   my ancestors:
>   You have given me wisdom
>   and power,
> you have made known to me what we asked of you,
>   you have made known to us the dream of the king."

conversations

hidden sin «» 2:22

1» Even though God knows everything about us, why do we still try to hide things from him?

2» What are the "deep and hidden things" in your life that you try to conceal?

3» What sins in your life has God revealed to you recently?

For more on **hidden sin**, check the index. For the next Conversations, go to p. 1262.

Daniel Interprets the Dream

[24]Then Daniel went to Arioch, whom the king had appointed to execute the wise men of Babylon, and said to him, "Do not execute the wise men of Babylon. Take me to the king, and I will interpret his dream for him."

---

[a] 4 At this point the Hebrew text has *in Aramaic*, indicating that the text from here through the end of chapter 7 is in Aramaic.

²⁵Arioch took Daniel to the king at once and said, "I have found a man among the exiles from Judah who can tell the king what his dream means."

²⁶The king asked Daniel (also called Belteshazzar), "Are you able to tell me what I saw in my dream and interpret it?"

²⁷Daniel replied, "No wise man, enchanter, magician or diviner can explain to the king the mystery he has asked about, ²⁸but there is a God in heaven who reveals mysteries. He has shown King Nebuchadnezzar what will happen in days to come. Your dream and the visions that passed through your mind as you were lying in bed are these:

²⁹"As Your Majesty was lying there, your mind turned to things to come, and the revealer of mysteries showed you what is going to happen. ³⁰As for me, this mystery has been revealed to me, not because I have greater wisdom than anyone else alive, but so that Your Majesty may know the interpretation and that you may understand what went through your mind.

³¹"Your Majesty looked, and there before you stood a large statue—an enormous, dazzling statue, awesome in appearance. ³²The head of the statue was made of pure gold, its chest and arms of silver, its belly and thighs of bronze, ³³its legs of iron, its feet partly of iron and partly of baked clay. ³⁴While you were watching, a rock was cut out, but not by human hands. It struck the statue on its feet of iron and clay and smashed them. ³⁵Then the iron, the clay, the bronze, the silver and the gold were all broken to pieces and became like chaff on a threshing floor in the summer. The wind swept them away without leaving a trace. But the rock that struck the statue became a huge mountain and filled the whole earth.

³⁶"This was the dream, and now we will interpret it to the king. ³⁷Your Majesty, you are the king of kings. The God of heaven has given you dominion and power and might and glory; ³⁸in your hands he has placed all people everywhere and the beasts of the field and the birds in the sky. Wherever they live, he has made you ruler over them all. You are that head of gold.

³⁹"After you, another kingdom will arise, inferior to yours. Next, a third kingdom, one of bronze, will rule over the whole earth. ⁴⁰Finally, there will be a fourth kingdom, strong as iron—for iron breaks and smashes everything—and as iron breaks things to pieces, so it will crush and break all the others. ⁴¹Just as you saw that the feet and toes were partly of baked clay and partly of iron, so this will be a divided kingdom; yet it will have some of the strength of iron in it, even as you saw iron mixed with clay. ⁴²As the toes were partly iron and partly clay, so this kingdom will be partly strong and partly brittle. ⁴³And just as you saw the iron mixed with baked clay, so the people will be a mixture and will not remain united, any more than iron mixes with clay.

⁴⁴"In the time of those kings, the God of heaven will set up a kingdom that will never be destroyed, nor will it be left to another people. It will crush all those kingdoms and bring them to an end, but it will itself endure forever. ⁴⁵This is the meaning of the vision of the rock cut out of a mountain, but not by human hands—a rock that broke the iron, the bronze, the clay, the silver and the gold to pieces.

"The great God has shown the king what will take place in the future. The dream is true and its interpretation is trustworthy."

HE IS: a revealer of mysteries

2:27–47 King Nebuchadnezzar demanded that his "wise men" reveal his disturbing dream and its interpretation—or risk death. Flustered, they explained that the task was too difficult. But nothing is too hard for God. As *a revealer of mysteries*, God gave his servant, Daniel, the wisdom to help the king understand his dream.

If you are seeking spiritual guidance from psychics, advice from an astrologer or help from a horoscope, you should know that the task is too difficult for them. Only God can truthfully communicate the complexities of the spiritual world. He alone is *a revealer of mysteries* (see also Ephesians 3:2–6).

For the next He Is, go to p. 1269.

[46]Then King Nebuchadnezzar fell prostrate before Daniel and paid him honor and ordered that an offering and incense be presented to him. [47]The king said to Daniel, "Surely your God is the God of gods and the Lord of kings and a revealer of mysteries, for you were able to reveal this mystery."

[48]Then the king placed Daniel in a high position and lavished many gifts on him. He made him ruler over the entire province of Babylon and placed him in charge of all its wise men. [49]Moreover, at Daniel's request the king appointed Shadrach, Meshach and Abednego administrators over the province of Babylon, while Daniel himself remained at the royal court.

The Image of Gold and the Blazing Furnace

3 King Nebuchadnezzar made an image of gold, sixty cubits high and six cubits wide,[a] and set it up on the plain of Dura in the province of Babylon. [2]He then summoned the satraps, prefects, governors, advisers, treasurers, judges, magistrates and all the other provincial officials to come to the dedication of the image he had set up. [3]So the satraps, prefects, governors, advisers, treasurers, judges, magistrates and all the other provincial officials assembled for the dedication of the image that King Nebuchadnezzar had set up, and they stood before it.

conversations

pride «» 3:1–7

1» How did Nebuchadnezzar's gold image reveal an attitude of pride on his part?

2» What "images of pride" have you erected in your own life?

3» How does pride actually reveal weakness?

For more on pride, check the index.
For the next Conversations, go to p. 1274.

[4]Then the herald loudly proclaimed, "Nations and peoples of every language, this is what you are commanded to do: [5]As soon as you hear the sound of the horn, flute, zither, lyre, harp, pipe and all kinds of music, you must fall down and worship the image of gold that King Nebuchadnezzar has set up. [6]Whoever does not fall down and worship will immediately be thrown into a blazing furnace."

[7]Therefore, as soon as they heard the sound of the horn, flute, zither, lyre, harp and all kinds of music, all the nations and peoples of every language fell down and worshiped the image of gold that King Nebuchadnezzar had set up.

[8]At this time some astrologers[b] came forward and denounced the Jews. [9]They said to King Nebuchadnezzar, "May the king live forever! [10]Your Majesty has issued a decree that everyone who hears the sound of the horn, flute, zither, lyre, harp, pipe and all kinds of music must fall down and worship the image of gold, [11]and that whoever does not fall down and worship will be thrown into a blazing furnace. [12]But there are some Jews whom you have set over the affairs of the province of Babylon—Shadrach, Meshach and Abednego—who pay no attention to you, Your Majesty. They neither serve your gods nor worship the image of gold you have set up."

[13]Furious with rage, Nebuchadnezzar summoned Shadrach, Meshach and Abednego. So these men were brought before the king, [14]and Nebuchadnezzar said to them, "Is it true, Shadrach, Meshach and Abednego, that you do not serve my gods or worship the image of gold I have set up? [15]Now when you hear the sound of the horn, flute, zither, lyre, harp, pipe and all kinds of music, if you are ready to fall down and worship the image I made, very good. But if you do not worship it, you will be thrown immediately into a blazing furnace. Then what god will be able to rescue you from my hand?"

[16]Shadrach, Meshach and Abednego replied to him, "King Nebuchadnezzar, we do not need to defend ourselves before you in this matter. [17]If the God we serve is able to deliver us, then he will deliver us from the blazing furnace and from Your Majesty's hand. [18]But even if he does not, we want you to know, Your Majesty, that we will not serve your gods or worship the image of gold you have set up."

[19]Then Nebuchadnezzar was furious with Shadrach, Meshach and Abednego, and his attitude toward them changed. He ordered the furnace heated seven times hotter than usual [20]and commanded some of

---

[a] 1 That is, about 90 feet high and 9 feet wide or about 27 meters high and 2.7 meters wide   [b] 8 Or Chaldeans

the strongest soldiers in his army to tie up Shadrach, Meshach and Abednego and throw them into the blazing furnace. ²¹So these men, wearing their robes, trousers, turbans and other clothes, were bound and thrown into the blazing furnace. ²²The king's command was so urgent and the furnace so hot that the flames of the fire killed the soldiers who took up Shadrach, Meshach and Abednego, ²³and these three men, firmly tied, fell into the blazing furnace.

²⁴Then King Nebuchadnezzar leaped to his feet in amazement and asked his advisers, "Weren't there three men that we tied up and threw into the fire?"

They replied, "Certainly, Your Majesty."

²⁵He said, "Look! I see four men walking around in the fire, unbound and unharmed, and the fourth looks like a son of the gods."

²⁶Nebuchadnezzar then approached the opening of the blazing furnace and shouted, "Shadrach, Meshach and Abednego, servants of the Most High God, come out! Come here!"

So Shadrach, Meshach and Abednego came out of the fire, ²⁷and the satraps, prefects, governors and royal advisers crowded around them. They saw that the fire had not harmed their bodies, nor was a hair of their heads singed; their robes were not scorched, and there was no smell of fire on them.

²⁸Then Nebuchadnezzar said, "Praise be to the God of Shadrach, Meshach and Abednego, who has sent his angel and rescued his servants! They trusted in him and defied the king's command and were willing to give up their lives rather than serve or worship any god except their own God. ²⁹Therefore I decree that the people of any nation or language who say anything against the God of Shadrach, Meshach and Abednego be cut into pieces and their houses be turned into piles of rubble, for no other god can save in this way."

³⁰Then the king promoted Shadrach, Meshach and Abednego in the province of Babylon.

Nebuchadnezzar's Dream of a Tree

4 *King Nebuchadnezzar,

To the nations and peoples of every language, who live in all the earth:

May you prosper greatly!

²It is my pleasure to tell you about the miraculous signs and wonders that the Most High God has performed for me.

³How great are his signs,
    how mighty his wonders!
His kingdom is an eternal kingdom;
    his dominion endures from generation to generation.

* ⁴I, Nebuchadnezzar, was at home in my palace, contented and prosperous. ⁵I had a dream that made me afraid. As I was lying in bed, the images and visions that passed through my mind terrified me. ⁶So I commanded that all the wise men of Babylon be brought before me to interpret the dream for me. ⁷When the magicians, enchanters, astrologersᵃ and diviners came, I told them the dream, but they could not interpret it for me. ⁸Finally, Daniel came into my presence and I told him

1263

atissue:trusting God

3:17–18 Perhaps you asked God to protect your baby, but you lost him. Or you pleaded with God to heal your mother's cancer, but she died. Or you begged God to save your marriage, but your husband left you. If God is so powerful, then why does he allow these things to happen? Shadrach, Meshach and Abednego knew that God *could* save them, but they also trusted him *even if* he chose not to do so. When life doesn't go the way you'd hoped, and you're stuck in the furnace, will you choose to trust that God is still good?

ᵃ 7 Or *Chaldeans*
* 4:1-3 is numbered 3:31-33 in Aramaic texts.   * 4:4-37 is numbered 4:1-34 in Aramaic texts.

the dream. (He is called Belteshazzar, after the name of my god, and the spirit of the holy gods is in him.)

⁹I said, "Belteshazzar, chief of the magicians, I know that the spirit of the holy gods is in you, and no mystery is too difficult for you. Here is my dream; interpret it for me. ¹⁰These are the visions I saw while lying in bed: I looked, and there before me stood a tree in the middle of the land. Its height was enormous. ¹¹The tree grew large and strong and its top touched the sky; it was visible to the ends of the earth. ¹²Its leaves were beautiful, its fruit abundant, and on it was food for all. Under it the wild animals found shelter, and the birds lived in its branches; from it every creature was fed.

¹³"In the visions I saw while lying in bed, I looked, and there before me was a holy one, a messenger,ᵃ coming down from heaven. ¹⁴He called in a loud voice: 'Cut down the tree and trim off its branches; strip off its leaves and scatter its fruit. Let the animals flee from under it and the birds from its branches. ¹⁵But let the stump and its roots, bound with iron and bronze, remain in the ground, in the grass of the field.

"'Let him be drenched with the dew of heaven, and let him live with the animals among the plants of the earth. ¹⁶Let his mind be changed from that of a human being and let him be given the mind of an animal, till seven timesᵇ pass by for him.

¹⁷"'The decision is announced by messengers, the holy ones declare the verdict, so that the living may know that the Most High is sovereign over the kingdoms on earth and gives them to anyone he wishes and sets over them the lowliest of people.'

¹⁸"This is the dream that I, King Nebuchadnezzar, had. Now, Belteshazzar, tell me what it means, for none of the wise men in my kingdom can interpret it for me. But you can, because the spirit of the holy gods is in you."

Daniel Interprets the Dream

¹⁹Then Daniel (also called Belteshazzar) was greatly perplexed for a time, and his thoughts terrified him. So the king said, "Belteshazzar, do not let the dream or its meaning alarm you."

Belteshazzar answered, "My lord, if only the dream applied to your enemies and its meaning to your adversaries! ²⁰The tree you saw, which grew large and strong, with its top touching the sky, visible to the whole earth, ²¹with beautiful leaves and abundant fruit, providing food for all, giving shelter to the wild animals, and having nesting places in its branches for the birds— ²²Your Majesty, you are that tree! You have become great and strong; your greatness has grown until it reaches the sky, and your dominion extends to distant parts of the earth.

²³"Your Majesty saw a holy one, a messenger, coming down from heaven and saying, 'Cut down the tree and destroy it, but leave the stump, bound with iron and bronze, in the grass of the field, while its roots remain in the ground. Let him be drenched with the dew of heaven; let him live with the wild animals, until seven times pass by for him.'

²⁴"This is the interpretation, Your Majesty, and this is the decree the Most High has issued against my lord the king: ²⁵You will be driven away from people and will live with the wild animals; you will eat grass like the ox and be drenched with the dew of heaven. Seven times will pass by for you until you acknowledge that the Most High is sovereign over the kingdoms on earth and gives them to anyone he wishes. ²⁶The command to leave the stump of the tree with its roots means that your kingdom will be restored to you when you acknowledge that Heaven rules. ²⁷Therefore, Your Majesty, be pleased to accept my advice: Renounce your sins by doing what is right, and your wickedness by being kind to the oppressed. It may be that then your prosperity will continue."

The Dream Is Fulfilled

²⁸All this happened to King Nebuchadnezzar. ²⁹Twelve months later, as the king was walking on the roof of the royal palace of Babylon, ³⁰he said, "Is not this the great Babylon I have built as the royal residence, by my mighty power and for the glory of my majesty?"

ᵃ *13* Or *watchman*; also in verses 17 and 23   ᵇ *16* Or *years*; also in verses 23, 25 and 32

³¹Even as the words were on his lips, a voice came from heaven, "This is what is decreed for you, King Nebuchadnezzar: Your royal authority has been taken from you. ³²You will be driven away from people and will live with the wild animals; you will eat grass like the ox. Seven times will pass by for you until you acknowledge that the Most High is sovereign over the kingdoms on earth and gives them to anyone he wishes."

³³Immediately what had been said about Nebuchadnezzar was fulfilled. He was driven away from people and ate grass like the ox. His body was drenched with the dew of heaven until his hair grew like the feathers of an eagle and his nails like the claws of a bird.

³⁴At the end of that time, I, Nebuchadnezzar, raised my eyes toward heaven, and my sanity was restored. Then I praised the Most High; I honored and glorified him who lives forever.

His dominion is an eternal dominion;
    his kingdom endures from generation to
        generation.
³⁵All the peoples of the earth
    are regarded as nothing.
He does as he pleases
    with the powers of heaven
    and the peoples of the earth.
No one can hold back his hand
    or say to him: "What have you done?"

³⁶At the same time that my sanity was restored, my honor and splendor were returned to me for the glory of my kingdom. My advisers and nobles sought me out, and I was restored to my throne and became even greater than before. ³⁷Now I, Nebuchadnezzar, praise and exalt and glorify the King of heaven, because everything he does is right and all his ways are just. And those who walk in pride he is able to humble.

The Writing on the Wall

5 King Belshazzar gave a great banquet for a thousand of his nobles and drank wine with them. ²While Belshazzar was drinking his wine, he gave orders to bring in the gold and silver goblets that Nebuchadnezzar his father ᵃ had taken from the temple in Jerusalem, so that the king and his nobles, his wives and his concubines might drink from them. ³So they brought in the gold goblets that had been taken from the temple of God in Jerusalem, and the king and his nobles, his wives and his concubines drank from them. ⁴As they drank the wine, they praised the gods of gold and silver, of bronze, iron, wood and stone.

⁵Suddenly the fingers of a human hand appeared and wrote on the plaster of the wall, near the lampstand in the royal palace. The king watched the hand as it wrote. ⁶His face turned pale and he was so frightened that his legs became weak and his knees were knocking.

⁷The king summoned the enchanters, astrologers ᵇ and diviners. Then he said to these wise men of Babylon, "Whoever reads this writing and tells me what it means will be clothed in purple and have a gold chain placed around his neck, and he will be made the third highest ruler in the kingdom."

⁸Then all the king's wise men came in, but they could not read the writing or tell the king what it meant. ⁹So King Belshazzar became even more terrified and his face grew more pale. His nobles were baffled.

ᵃ 2 Or ancestor; or predecessor; also in verses 11, 13 and 18   ᵇ 7 Or Chaldeans; also in verse 11

1266

¹⁰The queen,ᵃ hearing the voices of the king and his nobles, came into the banquet hall. "May the king live forever!" she said. "Don't be alarmed! Don't look so pale! ¹¹There is a man in your kingdom who has the spirit of the holy gods in him. In the time of your father he was found to have insight and intelligence and wisdom like that of the gods. Your father, King Nebuchadnezzar, appointed him chief of the magicians, enchanters, astrologers and diviners. ¹²He did this because Daniel, whom the king called Belteshazzar, was found to have a keen mind and knowledge and understanding, and also the ability to interpret dreams, explain riddles and solve difficult problems. Call for Daniel, and he will tell you what the writing means."

¹³So Daniel was brought before the king, and the king said to him, "Are you Daniel, one of the exiles my father the king brought from Judah? ¹⁴I have heard that the spirit of the gods is in you and that you have insight, intelligence and outstanding wisdom. ¹⁵The wise men and enchanters were brought before me to read this writing and tell me what it means, but they could not explain it. ¹⁶Now I have heard that you are able to give interpretations and to solve difficult problems. If you can read this writing and tell me what it means, you will be clothed in purple and have a gold chain placed around your neck, and you will be made the third highest ruler in the kingdom."

¹⁷Then Daniel answered the king, "You may keep your gifts for yourself and give your rewards to someone else. Nevertheless, I will read the writing for the king and tell him what it means.

¹⁸"Your Majesty, the Most High God gave your father Nebuchadnezzar sovereignty and greatness and glory and splendor. ¹⁹Because of the high position he gave him, all the nations and peoples of every language dreaded and feared him. Those the king wanted to put to death, he put to death; those he wanted to spare, he spared; those he wanted to promote, he promoted; and those he wanted to humble, he humbled. ²⁰But when his heart became arrogant and hardened with pride, he was deposed from his royal throne and stripped of his glory. ²¹He was driven away from people and given the mind of an animal; he lived with the wild donkeys and ate grass like the ox; and his body was drenched with the dew of heaven, until he acknowledged that the Most High God is sovereign over the kingdoms on earth and sets over them anyone he wishes.

²²"But you, Belshazzar, his son,ᵇ have not humbled yourself, though you knew all this. ²³Instead, you have set yourself up against the Lord of heaven. You had the goblets from his temple brought to you, and you and your nobles, your wives and your concubines drank wine from them. You praised the gods of silver and gold, of bronze, iron, wood and stone, which cannot see or hear or understand. But you did not honor the God who holds in his hand your life and all your ways. ²⁴Therefore he sent the hand that wrote the inscription.

²⁵"This is the inscription that was written:

MENE, MENE, TEKEL, PARSIN

²⁶"This is what these words mean:

> *Mene*ᶜ: God has numbered the days of your reign and brought it to an end.
> ²⁷ *Tekel*ᵈ: You have been weighed on the scales and found wanting.
> ²⁸ *Peres*ᵉ: Your kingdom is divided and given to the Medes and Persians."

²⁹Then at Belshazzar's command, Daniel was clothed in purple, a gold chain was placed around his neck, and he was proclaimed the third highest ruler in the kingdom.

³⁰That very night Belshazzar, king of the Babylonians,ᶠ was slain, * ³¹and Darius the Mede took over the kingdom, at the age of sixty-two.

Daniel in the Den of Lions

6 *It pleased Darius to appoint 120 satraps to rule throughout the kingdom, ²with three administrators over them, one of whom was Daniel. The satraps were made accountable to them so that the king might not suffer loss. ³Now Daniel so distinguished himself among the administrators and the

---

ᵃ *10* Or *queen mother*   ᵇ *22* Or *descendant*; or *successor*   ᶜ *26 Mene* can mean *numbered* or *mina* (a unit of money).   ᵈ *27 Tekel* can mean *weighed* or *shekel*.   ᵉ *28 Peres* (the singular of *Parsin*) can mean *divided* or *Persia* or *a half mina* or *a half shekel*.   ᶠ *30* Or *Chaldeans*

* *5:31* is numbered 6:1 in Aramaic texts.   * *6:1-28* is numbered 6:2-29 in Aramaic texts.

satraps by his exceptional qualities that the king planned to set him over the whole kingdom. ⁴At this, the administrators and the satraps tried to find grounds for charges against Daniel in his conduct of government affairs, but they were unable to do so. They could find no corruption in him, because he was trustworthy and neither corrupt nor negligent. ⁵Finally these men said, "We will never find any basis for charges against this man Daniel unless it has something to do with the law of his God."

⁶So these administrators and satraps went as a group to the king and said: "May King Darius live forever! ⁷The royal administrators, prefects, satraps, advisers and governors have all agreed that the king should issue an edict and enforce the decree that anyone who prays to any god or human being during the next thirty days, except to you, Your Majesty, shall be thrown into the lions' den. ⁸Now, Your Majesty, issue the decree and put it in writing so that it cannot be altered—in accordance with the law of the Medes and Persians, which cannot be repealed." ⁹So King Darius put the decree in writing.

¹⁰Now when Daniel learned that the decree had been published, he went home to his upstairs room where the windows opened toward Jerusalem. Three times a day he got down on his knees and prayed, giving thanks to his God, just as he had done before. ¹¹Then these men went as a group and found Daniel praying and asking God for help. ¹²So they went to the king and spoke to him about his royal decree: "Did you not publish a decree that during the next thirty days anyone who prays to any god or human being except to you, Your Majesty, would be thrown into the lions' den?"

The king answered, "The decree stands—in accordance with the law of the Medes and Persians, which cannot be repealed."

¹³Then they said to the king, "Daniel, who is one of the exiles from Judah, pays no attention to you, Your Majesty, or to the decree you put in writing. He still prays three times a day." ¹⁴When the king heard this, he was greatly distressed; he was determined to rescue Daniel and made every effort until sundown to save him.

¹⁵Then the men went as a group to King Darius and said to him, "Remember, Your Majesty, that according to the law of the Medes and Persians no decree or edict that the king issues can be changed."

¹⁶So the king gave the order, and they brought Daniel and threw him into the lions' den. The king said to Daniel, "May your God, whom you serve continually, rescue you!"

¹⁷A stone was brought and placed over the mouth of the den, and the king sealed it with his own signet ring and with the rings of his nobles, so that Daniel's situation might not be changed. ¹⁸Then the king returned to his palace and spent the night without eating and without any entertainment being brought to him. And he could not sleep.

¹⁹At the first light of dawn, the king got up and hurried to the lions' den. ²⁰When he came near the den, he called to Daniel in an anguished voice, "Daniel, servant of the living God, has your God, whom you serve continually, been able to rescue you from the lions?"

²¹Daniel answered, "May the king live forever! ²²My God sent his angel, and he shut the mouths of the lions. They have not hurt me, because I was found innocent in his sight. Nor have I ever done any wrong before you, Your Majesty."

²³The king was overjoyed and gave orders to lift Daniel out of the den. And when Daniel was lifted from the den, no wound was found on him, because he had trusted in his God.

²⁴At the king's command, the men who had falsely accused Daniel were brought in and thrown into the lions' den, along with their wives and children. And before they reached the floor of the den, the lions overpowered them and crushed all their bones.

atissue:identity

6:1–22 Every day you face pressure to compromise your Christianity. It might be subtle pressure, but it's still pressure. So you might smile when your co-workers badmouth the boss. Or you might get drunk with your friends so you won't stand out. And you might choose to never, ever bring up God with the other moms at Little League. Daniel also knew the pressure to conform. Though his very life was on the line, he chose to remain true to himself and true to God. Now it's your turn to stand up to the pressure and live to please God alone.

1267

²⁵Then King Darius wrote to all the nations and peoples of every language in all the earth:

"May you prosper greatly!

²⁶"I issue a decree that in every part of my kingdom people must fear and reverence the God of Daniel.

> "For he is the living God
>> and he endures forever;
> his kingdom will not be destroyed,
>> his dominion will never end.
> ²⁷He rescues and he saves;
>> he performs signs and wonders
>> in the heavens and on the earth.
> He has rescued Daniel
>> from the power of the lions."

²⁸So Daniel prospered during the reign of Darius and the reign of Cyrus^a the Persian.

Daniel's Dream of Four Beasts

7 In the first year of Belshazzar king of Babylon, Daniel had a dream, and visions passed through his mind as he was lying in bed. He wrote down the substance of his dream.
²Daniel said: "In my vision at night I looked, and there before me were the four winds of heaven churning up the great sea. ³Four great beasts, each different from the others, came up out of the sea.

⁴"The first was like a lion, and it had the wings of an eagle. I watched until its wings were torn off and it was lifted from the ground so that it stood on two feet like a human being, and a human mind was given to it.

⁵"And there before me was a second beast, which looked like a bear. It was raised up on one of its sides, and it had three ribs in its mouth between its teeth. It was told, 'Get up and eat your fill of flesh!'

⁶"After that, I looked, and there before me was another beast, one that looked like a leopard. And on its back it had four wings like those of a bird. This beast had four heads, and it was given authority to rule.

⁷"After that, in my vision at night I looked, and there before me was a fourth beast—terrifying and frightening and very powerful. It had large iron teeth; it crushed and devoured its victims and trampled underfoot whatever was left. It was different from all the former beasts, and it had ten horns.

⁸"While I was thinking about the horns, there before me was another horn, a little one, which came up among them; and three of the first horns were uprooted before it. This horn had eyes like the eyes of a human being and a mouth that spoke boastfully.

⁹"As I looked,

> "thrones were set in place,
>> and the Ancient of Days took his seat.
> His clothing was as white as snow;
>> the hair of his head was white like wool.
> His throne was flaming with fire,
>> and its wheels were all ablaze.
> ¹⁰A river of fire was flowing,
>> coming out from before him.
> Thousands upon thousands attended him;
>> ten thousand times ten thousand stood before him.
> The court was seated,
>> and the books were opened.

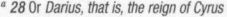

^a 28 Or Darius, that is, the reign of Cyrus

the Ancient of Days

7:9–10 Daniel saw a vision of world history where each successive empire was depicted as a fierce beast, culminating in the rule of the antichrist. In the midst of the vision, Daniel saw *the Ancient of Days,* God himself, regally seated on his throne to judge the nations.

He is *the Ancient of Days*—timeless, enduring, unchanging. How unlike us. While our lives are quick blips on the screen of time, he was, is and is to come. And *the Ancient of Days* freely offers us eternal life with him—a permanence, security and future we could never earn for ourselves.

For the next He Is, go to p. 1284.

¹¹"Then I continued to watch because of the boastful words the horn was speaking. I kept looking until the beast was slain and its body destroyed and thrown into the blazing fire. ¹²(The other beasts had been stripped of their authority, but were allowed to live for a period of time.)

¹³"In my vision at night I looked, and there before me was one like a son of man,ᵃ coming with the clouds of heaven. He approached the Ancient of Days and was led into his presence. ¹⁴He was given authority, glory and sovereign power; all nations and peoples of every language worshiped him. His dominion is an everlasting dominion that will not pass away, and his kingdom is one that will never be destroyed.

The Interpretation of the Dream

¹⁵"I, Daniel, was troubled in spirit, and the visions that passed through my mind disturbed me. ¹⁶I approached one of those standing there and asked him the meaning of all this.

"So he told me and gave me the interpretation of these things: ¹⁷'The four great beasts are four kings that will rise from the earth. ¹⁸But the holy people of the Most High will receive the kingdom and will possess it forever—yes, for ever and ever.'

¹⁹"Then I wanted to know the meaning of the fourth beast, which was different from all the others and most terrifying, with its iron teeth and bronze claws—the beast that crushed and devoured its victims and trampled underfoot whatever was left. ²⁰I also wanted to know about the ten horns on its head and about the other horn that came up, before which three of them fell—the horn that looked more imposing than the others and that had eyes and a mouth that spoke boastfully. ²¹As I watched, this horn was waging war against the holy people and defeating them, ²²until the Ancient of Days came and pronounced judgment in favor of the holy people of the Most High, and the time came when they possessed the kingdom.

²³"He gave me this explanation: 'The fourth beast is a fourth kingdom that will appear on earth. It will be different from all the other kingdoms and will devour the whole earth, trampling it down and crushing it. ²⁴The ten horns are ten kings who will come from this kingdom. After them another king will arise, different from the earlier ones; he will subdue three kings. ²⁵He will speak against the Most High and oppress his holy people and try to change the set times and the laws. The holy people will be delivered into his hands for a time, times and half a time.ᵇ

²⁶"'But the court will sit, and his power will be taken away and completely destroyed forever. ²⁷Then the sovereignty, power and greatness of all the kingdoms under heaven will be handed over to the holy people of the Most High. His kingdom will be an everlasting kingdom, and all rulers will worship and obey him.'

²⁸"This is the end of the matter. I, Daniel, was deeply troubled by my thoughts, and my face turned pale, but I kept the matter to myself."

ᵃ *13* The Aramaic phrase *bar enash* means *human being.* The phrase *son of man* is retained as a form of address here because of its traditional associations.
ᵇ *25* Or *for a year, two years and half a year*

Daniel's Vision of a Ram and a Goat

8 In the third year of King Belshazzar's reign, I, Daniel, had a vision, after the one that had already appeared to me. ²In my vision I saw myself in the citadel of Susa in the province of Elam; in the vision I was beside the Ulai Canal. ³I looked up, and there before me was a ram with two horns, standing beside the canal, and the horns were long. One of the horns was longer than the other but grew up later. ⁴I watched the ram as it charged toward the west and the north and the south. No animal could stand against it, and none could rescue from its power. It did as it pleased and became great.

⁵As I was thinking about this, suddenly a goat with a prominent horn between its eyes came from the west, crossing the whole earth without touching the ground. ⁶It came toward the two-horned ram I had seen standing beside the canal and charged at it in great rage. ⁷I saw it attack the ram furiously, striking the ram and shattering its two horns. The ram was powerless to stand against it; the goat knocked it to the ground and trampled on it, and none could rescue the ram from its power. ⁸The goat became very great, but at the height of its power the large horn was broken off, and in its place four prominent horns grew up toward the four winds of heaven.

⁹Out of one of them came another horn, which started small but grew in power to the south and to the east and toward the Beautiful Land. ¹⁰It grew until it reached the host of the heavens, and it threw some of the starry host down to the earth and trampled on them. ¹¹It set itself up to be as great as the commander of the army of the Lord; it took away the daily sacrifice from the Lord, and his sanctuary was thrown down. ¹²Because of rebellion, the Lord's people[a] and the daily sacrifice were given over to it. It prospered in everything it did, and truth was thrown to the ground.

¹³Then I heard a holy one speaking, and another holy one said to him, "How long will it take for the vision to be fulfilled—the vision concerning the daily sacrifice, the rebellion that causes desolation, the surrender of the sanctuary and the trampling underfoot of the Lord's people?"

¹⁴He said to me, "It will take 2,300 evenings and mornings; then the sanctuary will be reconsecrated."

The Interpretation of the Vision

¹⁵While I, Daniel, was watching the vision and trying to understand it, there before me stood one who looked like a man. ¹⁶And I heard a man's voice from the Ulai calling, "Gabriel, tell this man the meaning of the vision."

¹⁷As he came near the place where I was standing, I was terrified and fell prostrate. "Son of man,"[b] he said to me, "understand that the vision concerns the time of the end."

¹⁸While he was speaking to me, I was in a deep sleep, with my face to the ground. Then he touched me and raised me to my feet.

¹⁹He said: "I am going to tell you what will happen later in the time of wrath, because the vision concerns the appointed time of the end.[c] ²⁰The two-horned ram that you saw represents the kings of Media and Persia. ²¹The shaggy goat is the king of Greece, and the large horn between its eyes is the first king. ²²The four horns that replaced the one that was broken off represent four kingdoms that will emerge from his nation but will not have the same power.

²³"In the latter part of their reign, when rebels have become completely wicked, a fierce-looking king, a master of intrigue, will arise. ²⁴He will become very strong, but not by his own power. He will cause astounding devastation and will succeed in whatever he does. He will destroy the mighty warriors, the holy people. ²⁵He will cause deceit to prosper, and he will consider himself superior. When they feel secure, he will destroy many and take his stand against the Prince of princes. Yet he will be destroyed, but not by human power.

²⁶"The vision of the evenings and mornings that has been given you is true, but seal up the vision, for it concerns the distant future."

²⁷I, Daniel, was worn out. I lay exhausted for several days. Then I got up and went about the king's business. I was appalled by the vision; it was beyond understanding.

---

a 12 Or *rebellion, the armies*   *b 17* The Hebrew phrase *ben adam* means *human being.* The phrase *son of man* is retained as a form of address here because of its traditional associations.   *c 19* Or *because the end will be at the appointed time*

Daniel's Prayer

9 In the first year of Darius son of Xerxes[a] (a Mede by descent), who was made ruler over the Babylonian[b] kingdom— ²in the first year of his reign, I, Daniel, understood from the Scriptures, according to the word of the LORD given to Jeremiah the prophet, that the desolation of Jerusalem would last seventy years. ³So I turned to the Lord God and pleaded with him in prayer and petition, in fasting, and in sackcloth and ashes.

⁴I prayed to the LORD my God and confessed:

"Lord, the great and awesome God, who keeps his covenant of love with those who love him and keep his commandments, ⁵we have sinned and done wrong. We have been wicked and have rebelled; we have turned away from your commands and laws. ⁶We have not listened to your servants the prophets, who spoke in your name to our kings, our princes and our ancestors, and to all the people of the land.

⁷"Lord, you are righteous, but this day we are covered with shame—the people of Judah and Jerusalem and all Israel, both near and far, in all the countries where you have scattered us because of our unfaithfulness to you. ⁸We and our kings, our princes and our ancestors are covered with shame, LORD, because we have sinned against you. ⁹The Lord our God is merciful and forgiving, even though we have rebelled against him; ¹⁰we have not obeyed the LORD our God or kept the laws he gave us through his servants the prophets. ¹¹All Israel has transgressed your law and turned away, refusing to obey you.

"Therefore the curses and sworn judgments written in the Law of Moses, the servant of God, have been poured out on us, because we have sinned against you. ¹²You have fulfilled the words spoken against us and against our rulers by bringing on us great disaster. Under the whole heaven nothing has ever been done like what has been done to Jerusalem. ¹³Just as it is written in the Law of Moses, all this disaster has come on us, yet we have not sought the favor of the LORD our God by turning from our sins and giving attention to your truth. ¹⁴The LORD did not hesitate to bring the disaster on us, for the LORD our God is righteous in everything he does; yet we have not obeyed him.

¹⁵"Now, Lord our God, who brought your people out of Egypt with a mighty hand and who made for yourself a name that endures to this day, we have sinned, we have done wrong. ¹⁶Lord, in keeping with all your righteous acts, turn away your anger and your wrath from Jerusalem, your city, your holy hill. Our sins and the iniquities of our ancestors have made Jerusalem and your people an object of scorn to all those around us.

¹⁷"Now, our God, hear the prayers and petitions of your servant. For your sake, Lord, look with favor on your desolate sanctuary. ¹⁸Give ear, our God, and hear; open your eyes and see the desolation of the city that bears your Name. We do not make requests of you because we are righteous, but because of your great mercy. ¹⁹Lord, listen! Lord, forgive! Lord, hear and act! For your sake, my God, do not delay, because your city and your people bear your Name."

The Seventy "Sevens"

²⁰While I was speaking and praying, confessing my sin and the sin of my people Israel and making my request to the LORD my God for his holy hill— ²¹while I was still in prayer, Gabriel, the man I had seen in the earlier vision, came to me in swift flight about the time of the evening sacrifice. ²²He instructed me and said to me, "Daniel, I have now come to give you insight and understanding. ²³As soon as you began to pray, a word went out, which I have come to tell you, for you are highly esteemed. Therefore, consider the word and understand the vision:

²⁴"Seventy 'sevens'[c] are decreed for your people and your holy city to finish[d] transgression, to put an end to sin, to atone for wickedness, to bring in everlasting righteousness, to seal up vision and prophecy and to anoint the Most Holy Place.[e]

²⁵"Know and understand this: From the time the word goes out to restore and rebuild Jerusalem until the Anointed One,[f] the ruler, comes, there will be seven 'sevens,' and sixty-two 'sevens.' It will be rebuilt

1271

---

[a] *1* Hebrew *Ahasuerus*   [b] *1* Or *Chaldean*   [c] *24* Or *'weeks'*; also in verses 25 and 26   [d] *24* Or *restrain*   [e] *24* Or *the most holy One*   [f] *25* Or *an anointed one*; also in verse 26

with streets and a trench, but in times of trouble. ²⁶After the sixty-two 'sevens,' the Anointed One will be put to death and will have nothing.ᵃ The people of the ruler who will come will destroy the city and the sanctuary. The end will come like a flood: War will continue until the end, and desolations have been decreed. ²⁷He will confirm a covenant with many for one 'seven.'ᵇ In the middle of the 'seven'ᵇ he will put an end to sacrifice and offering. And at the templeᶜ he will set up an abomination that causes desolation, until the end that is decreed is poured out on him.ᵈ"ᵉ

Daniel's Vision of a Man

10 In the third year of Cyrus king of Persia, a revelation was given to Daniel (who was called Belteshazzar). Its message was true and it concerned a great war.ᶠ The understanding of the message came to him in a vision.

²At that time I, Daniel, mourned for three weeks. ³I ate no choice food; no meat or wine touched my lips; and I used no lotions at all until the three weeks were over.

⁴On the twenty-fourth day of the first month, as I was standing on the bank of the great river, the Tigris, ⁵I looked up and there before me was a man dressed in linen, with a belt of fine gold from Uphaz around his waist. ⁶His body was like topaz, his face like lightning, his eyes like flaming torches, his arms and legs like the gleam of burnished bronze, and his voice like the sound of a multitude.

⁷I, Daniel, was the only one who saw the vision; those who were with me did not see it, but such terror overwhelmed them that they fled and hid themselves. ⁸So I was left alone, gazing at this great vision; I had no strength left, my face turned deathly pale and I was helpless. ⁹Then I heard him speaking, and as I listened to him, I fell into a deep sleep, my face to the ground.

¹⁰A hand touched me and set me trembling on my hands and knees. ¹¹He said, "Daniel, you who are highly esteemed, consider carefully the words I am about to speak to you, and stand up, for I have now been sent to you." And when he said this to me, I stood up trembling.

¹²Then he continued, "Do not be afraid, Daniel. Since the first day that you set your mind to gain understanding and to humble yourself before your God, your words were heard, and I have come in response to them. ¹³But the prince of the Persian kingdom resisted me twenty-one days. Then Michael, one of the chief princes, came to help me, because I was detained there with the king of Persia. ¹⁴Now I have come to explain to you what will happen to your people in the future, for the vision concerns a time yet to come."

¹⁵While he was saying this to me, I bowed with my face toward the ground and was speechless. ¹⁶Then one who looked like a manᵍ touched my lips, and I opened my mouth and began to speak. I said to the one standing before me, "I am overcome with anguish because of the vision, my lord, and I feel very weak. ¹⁷How can I, your servant, talk with you, my lord? My strength is gone and I can hardly breathe."

¹⁸Again the one who looked like a man touched me and gave me strength. ¹⁹"Do not be afraid, you who are highly esteemed," he said. "Peace! Be strong now; be strong."

When he spoke to me, I was strengthened and said, "Speak, my lord, since you have given me strength."

atissue:prayer

10:12–13 If you've ever felt like God didn't hear your prayer, then you're not alone. We all like to receive an immediate response to our requests. When we don't get one, we may begin to think that God doesn't hear or doesn't care. But neither is true. God always hears—and he always answers—every single prayer. However, sometimes his answer is delayed, for reasons that are out of your control or have nothing to do with you. Wait patiently on God, knowing that he'll answer in his way and in his time.

ᵃ 26 Or death and will have no one; or death, but not for himself   ᵇ 27 Or 'week'   ᶜ 27 Septuagint and Theodotion; Hebrew wing   ᵈ 27 Or it   ᵉ 27 Or And one who causes desolation will come upon the wing of the abominable ⌊temple⌋, until the end that is decreed is poured out on the desolated ⌊city⌋   ᶠ 1 Or true and burdensome   ᵍ 16 Most manuscripts of the Masoretic Text; one manuscript of the Masoretic Text, Dead Sea Scrolls and Septuagint Then something that looked like a human hand

²⁰So he said, "Do you know why I have come to you? Soon I will return to fight against the prince of Persia, and when I go, the prince of Greece will come; ²¹but first I will tell you what is written in the Book of Truth. (No one supports me against them except Michael, your prince. ¹And in the first year of Darius the Mede, I took my stand to support and protect him.)

The Kings of the South and the North

²"Now then, I tell you the truth: Three more kings will arise in Persia, and then a fourth, who will be far richer than all the others. When he has gained power by his wealth, he will stir up everyone against the kingdom of Greece. ³Then a mighty king will arise, who will rule with great power and do as he pleases. ⁴After he has arisen, his empire will be broken up and parceled out toward the four winds of heaven. It will not go to his descendants, nor will it have the power he exercised, because his empire will be uprooted and given to others.

⁵"The king of the South will become strong, but one of his commanders will become even stronger than he and will rule his own kingdom with great power. ⁶After some years, they will become allies. The daughter of the king of the South will go to the king of the North to make an alliance, but she will not retain her power, and he and his power*ᵃ* will not last. In those days she will be betrayed, together with her royal escort and her father*ᵇ* and the one who supported her.

⁷"One from her family line will arise to take her place. He will attack the forces of the king of the North and enter his fortress; he will fight against them and be victorious. ⁸He will also seize their gods, their metal images and their valuable articles of silver and gold and carry them off to Egypt. For some years he will leave the king of the North alone. ⁹Then the king of the North will invade the realm of the king of the South but will retreat to his own country. ¹⁰His sons will prepare for war and assemble a great army, which will sweep on like an irresistible flood and carry the battle as far as his fortress.

¹¹"Then the king of the South will march out in a rage and fight against the king of the North, who will raise a large army, but it will be defeated. ¹²When the army is carried off, the king of the South will be filled with pride and will slaughter many thousands, yet he will not remain triumphant. ¹³For the king of the North will muster another army, larger than the first; and after several years, he will advance with a huge army fully equipped.

¹⁴"In those times many will rise against the king of the South. Those who are violent among your own people will rebel in fulfillment of the vision, but without success. ¹⁵Then the king of the North will come and build up siege ramps and will capture a fortified city. The forces of the South will be powerless to resist; even their best troops will not have the strength to stand. ¹⁶The invader will do as he pleases; no one will be able to stand against him. He will establish himself in the Beautiful Land and will have the power to destroy it. ¹⁷He will determine to come with the might of his entire kingdom and will make an alliance with the king of the South. And he will give him a daughter in marriage in order to overthrow the kingdom, but his plans*ᶜ* will not succeed or help him. ¹⁸Then he will turn his attention to the coastlands and will take many of them, but a commander will put an end to his insolence and will turn his insolence back on him. ¹⁹After this, he will turn back toward the fortresses of his own country but will stumble and fall, to be seen no more.

²⁰"His successor will send out a tax collector to maintain the royal splendor. In a few years, however, he will be destroyed, yet not in anger or in battle.

²¹"He will be succeeded by a contemptible person who has not been given the honor of royalty. He will invade the kingdom when its people feel secure, and he will seize it through intrigue. ²²Then an overwhelming army will be swept away before him; both it and a prince of the covenant will be destroyed. ²³After coming to an agreement with him, he will act deceitfully, and with only a few people he will rise to power. ²⁴When the richest provinces feel secure, he will invade them and will achieve what neither his fathers nor his forefathers did. He will distribute plunder, loot and wealth among his followers. He will plot the overthrow of fortresses—but only for a time.

²⁵"With a large army he will stir up his strength and courage against the king of the South. The king of the South will wage war with a large and very powerful army, but he will not be able to stand because

---

of the plots devised against him. [26]Those who eat from the king's provisions will try to destroy him; his army will be swept away, and many will fall in battle. [27]The two kings, with their hearts bent on evil, will sit at the same table and lie to each other, but to no avail, because an end will still come at the appointed time. [28]The king of the North will return to his own country with great wealth, but his heart will be set against the holy covenant. He will take action against it and then return to his own country.

[29]"At the appointed time he will invade the South again, but this time the outcome will be different from what it was before. [30]Ships of the western coastlands will oppose him, and he will lose heart. Then he will turn back and vent his fury against the holy covenant. He will return and show favor to those who forsake the holy covenant.

[31]"His armed forces will rise up to desecrate the temple fortress and will abolish the daily sacrifice. Then they will set up the abomination that causes desolation. [32]With flattery he will corrupt those who have violated the covenant, but the people who know their God will firmly resist him.

[33]"Those who are wise will instruct many, though for a time they will fall by the sword or be burned or captured or plundered. [34]When they fall, they will receive a little help, and many who are not sincere will join them. [35]Some of the wise will stumble, so that they may be refined, purified and made spotless until the time of the end, for it will still come at the appointed time.

The King Who Exalts Himself

[36]"The king will do as he pleases. He will exalt and magnify himself above every god and will say unheard-of things against the God of gods. He will be successful until the time of wrath is completed, for what has been determined must take place. [37]He will show no regard for the gods of his ancestors or for the one desired by women, nor will he regard any god, but will exalt himself above them all. [38]Instead of them, he will honor a god of fortresses; a god unknown to his ancestors he will honor with gold and silver, with precious stones and costly gifts. [39]He will attack the mightiest fortresses with the help of a foreign god and will greatly honor those who acknowledge him. He will make them rulers over many people and will distribute the land at a price.[a]

[40]"At the time of the end the king of the South will engage him in battle, and the king of the North will storm out against him with chariots and cavalry and a great fleet of ships. He will invade many countries and sweep through them like a flood. [41]He will also invade the Beautiful Land. Many countries will fall, but Edom, Moab and the leaders of Ammon will be delivered from his hand. [42]He will extend his power over many countries; Egypt will not escape. [43]He will gain control of the treasures of gold and silver and all the riches of Egypt, with the Libyans and Cushites[b] in submission. [44]But reports from the east and the north will alarm him, and he will set out in a great rage to destroy and annihilate many. [45]He will pitch his royal tents between the seas at[c] the beautiful holy mountain. Yet he will come to his end, and no one will help him.

The End Times

12 "At that time Michael, the great prince who protects your people, will arise. There will be a time of distress such as has not happened from the beginning of nations until then. But at that time your people—everyone whose name is found written in the book—will be delivered. [2]Multitudes who sleep in the dust of the earth will awake: some to everlasting life, others to shame and everlasting contempt. [3]Those who are wise[d] will shine like the brightness of the heavens, and those who lead many to righteousness, like the stars for ever and ever.

conversations

witnessing «» 12:3

1» What does it mean to "shine like the brightness of the heavens"? Do you do that?

2» What does it mean to "lead many to righteousness"? Do you do that?

3» Why are both wisdom and witnessing likened to light?

For more on **witnessing**, check the index. For the next Conversations, go to p. 1280.

---

[a] 39 Or land for a reward   [b] 43 That is, people from the upper Nile region   [c] 45 Or the sea and   [d] 3 Or who impart wisdom

⁴But you, Daniel, close up and seal the words of the scroll until the time of the end. Many will go here and there to increase knowledge."

⁵Then I, Daniel, looked, and there before me stood two others, one on this bank of the river and one on the opposite bank. ⁶One of them said to the man clothed in linen, who was above the waters of the river, "How long will it be before these astonishing things are fulfilled?"

⁷The man clothed in linen, who was above the waters of the river, lifted his right hand and his left hand toward heaven, and I heard him swear by him who lives forever, saying, "It will be for a time, times and half a time.ᵃ When the power of the holy people has been finally broken, all these things will be completed."

⁸I heard, but I did not understand. So I asked, "My lord, what will the outcome of all this be?"

⁹He replied, "Go your way, Daniel, because the words are closed up and sealed until the time of the end. ¹⁰Many will be purified, made spotless and refined, but the wicked will continue to be wicked. None of the wicked will understand, but those who are wise will understand.

¹¹"From the time that the daily sacrifice is abolished and the abomination that causes desolation is set up, there will be 1,290 days. ¹²Blessed is the one who waits for and reaches the end of the 1,335 days.

¹³"As for you, go your way till the end. You will rest, and then at the end of the days you will rise to receive your allotted inheritance."

ᵃ 7 Or a year, two years and half a year

hosea

AUTHOR
Hosea.

AUDIENCE
The northern kingdom of Israel and all of
God's people.

DATE
Written about 715 B.C.

SETTING
Hosea lived during the time of the end of the
northern kingdom, which fell to the
Assyrians in 722 B.C.

VERSE TO REMEMBER
"For I desire mercy, not sacrifice, and
acknowledgment of God rather than burnt
offerings." (6:6)

THEME TO CONSIDER
Our love relationship with God is based on
his faithfulness, not our unfaithfulness.

1 The word of the Lord that came to Hosea son of Beeri during the reigns of Uzziah, Jotham, Ahaz and Hezekiah, kings of Judah, and during the reign of Jeroboam son of Jehoash[a] king of Israel:

Hosea's Wife and Children

²When the Lord began to speak through Hosea, the Lord said to him, "Go, marry a promiscuous woman and have children with her, for like an adulterous wife this land is guilty of unfaithfulness to the Lord." ³So he married Gomer daughter of Diblaim, and she conceived and bore him a son.

⁴Then the Lord said to Hosea, "Call him Jezreel, because I will soon punish the house of Jehu for the massacre at Jezreel, and I will put an end to the kingdom of Israel. ⁵In that day I will break Israel's bow in the Valley of Jezreel."

⁶Gomer conceived again and gave birth to a daughter. Then the Lord said to Hosea, "Call her Lo-Ruhamah (which means "not loved"), for I will no longer show love to the house of Israel, that I should at all forgive them. ⁷Yet I will show love to the house of Judah; and I will save them—not by bow, sword or battle, or by horses and horsemen, but by the Lord their God."

⁸After she had weaned Lo-Ruhamah, Gomer had another son. ⁹Then the Lord said, "Call him Lo-Ammi (which means "not my people"), for you are not my people, and I am not your God.[b]

*¹⁰"Yet the Israelites will be like the sand on the seashore, which cannot be measured or counted. In the place where it was said to them, 'You are not my people,' they will be called 'children of the living God.' ¹¹The people of Judah and the people of Israel will come together; they will appoint one leader and will come up out of the land, for great will be the day of Jezreel.

2 *"Say of your brothers, 'My people,' and of your sisters, 'My loved one.'

1277

Israel Punished and Restored

²"Rebuke your mother, rebuke her,
    for she is not my wife,
    and I am not her husband.
Let her remove the adulterous look from her face
    and the unfaithfulness from between her breasts.
³Otherwise I will strip her naked
    and make her as bare as on the day she was born;
I will make her like a desert,
    turn her into a parched land,
    and slay her with thirst.
⁴I will not show my love to her children,
    because they are the children of adultery.
⁵Their mother has been unfaithful
    and has conceived them in disgrace.
She said, 'I will go after my lovers,
    who give me my food and my water,
    my wool and my linen, my olive oil and my drink.'
⁶Therefore I will block her path with thornbushes;
    I will wall her in so that she cannot find her way.
⁷She will chase after her lovers but not catch them;
    she will look for them but not find them.
Then she will say,
    'I will go back to my husband as at first,
    for then I was better off than now.'
⁸She has not acknowledged that I was the one

a 1 Hebrew *Joash*, a variant of *Jehoash* *b* 9 Or *your I AM*

* 1:10-11 is numbered 2:1-2 in Hebrew texts. * 2:1-23 is numbered 2:3-25 in Hebrew texts.

myth# 74 "THERE MUST BE SOMETHING WRONG WITH ME IF I DON'T HAVE A MAN."

I'm almost 35 years old. I thought I'd be married by now. I feel like—dare I say it?—a freak.

For the third week in a row I don't have a date for Friday or Saturday. And even worse, I was invited to a friend's wedding coming up next weekend. I shouldn't go since I have no one to bring. Besides, weddings depress me these days.

When my co-workers asked me about my plans for this weekend, I was so tempted to lie. Of course, all of them have plans. And having to say, "I'm not sure what I'll do" for the third week in a row was humiliating.

I hate not being in a relationship. And it's not as if I haven't been proactive about this—I've been hanging out at the health club more, joining online dating services and singles groups, asking friends to hook me up with their friends. I've even prayed about it. So far, nothing lasting has come my way.

It doesn't help that all of my friends are either married or dating someone, so I can't count on girls' nights every weekend, and I also can't expect them to understand what it feels like to be alone. I don't know what to do with myself without a man in my life. Somehow I like myself better when I'm in a relationship.

My mom thinks I should get out more. I certainly wouldn't eat in a restaurant or go to the movies alone. I would feel like I have the word LOSER tattooed on my forehead. I know I shouldn't think that way, but I do.

I wonder all the time whether I should've stayed with Phil. Sure, it wasn't the best relationship for my spiritual growth. (I'm a Christian; he's . . . well, atheist seems like a strong word; maybe non-religious.) But he loved me and took me to nice places and treated me well. At least with Phil I wouldn't be alone.

—Tracy

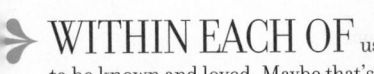

WITHIN EACH OF us is a desire to be known and loved. Maybe that's why we take to heart the words of Genesis 2:18, "It is not good . . . to be alone." Being alone can be very hard, and it's natural to want a relationship so we have companionship. The danger comes when our desire to escape being alone turns into an expectation or agenda. You can be easily disappointed if God doesn't seem to follow your plans.

The world may tell you that you're somehow incomplete if you're single, especially if you're not in a romantic relationship at all. God tells you you're complete if you have him. You may know that intellectually, but how do you truly accept that and live as if you're whole, regardless of whether or not you're in a relationship?

- Remember that not all relationships are blissful—and some are downright painful. Singleness isn't just an escape route from a bad relationship or a waiting period between relationships. As many women would attest, it's better to be single than to be in a bad relationship.

- Consider some of the benefits of being single. Read 1 Corinthians 7:32–35 and ask God to show you what's good about your station in life.

- As the old saying goes, "The grass is always greener on the other side of the fence." Explore what's good about your side of the fence. Contentment is the way to start exploring your territory. As Paul says, "I have learned the secret of being content in any and every situation, whether well fed or hungry, whether living in plenty or in want" (Philippians 4:12). He might have added "whether single or married"!

- Remind yourself of the truth about God's love for you. As Psalm 84:11 says, "No good thing does he withhold from those whose

walk is blameless." In other words, if you're his child, he won't withhold anything from you that you need.

> "Those who have never been married make up the lion's share of America's 82 million single adults, representing nearly six out of every ten singles. Adults who are currently divorced are one-quarter of the singles population."
>
> —Barna Research Group (2002)

"THE LORD IS MY SHEPHERD, I LACK NOTHING."

PSALM 23:1

SEE ALSO

For more on **Loneliness** and **Dating**, check the index.

who gave her the grain, the new wine and oil,
who lavished on her the silver and gold—
which they used for Baal.

⁹"Therefore I will take away my grain when it ripens,
and my new wine when it is ready.
I will take back my wool and my linen,
intended to cover her nakedness.
¹⁰So now I will expose her lewdness
before the eyes of her lovers;
no one will take her out of my hands.
¹¹I will stop all her celebrations:
her yearly festivals, her New Moons,
her Sabbath days—all her appointed festivals.
¹²I will ruin her vines and her fig trees,
which she said were her pay from her lovers;
I will make them a thicket,
and wild animals will devour them.
¹³I will punish her for the days
she burned incense to the Baals;
she decked herself with rings and jewelry,
and went after her lovers,
but me she forgot,"

declares the LORD.

¹⁴"Therefore I am now going to allure her;
I will lead her into the wilderness
and speak tenderly to her.
¹⁵There I will give her back her vineyards,
and will make the Valley of Achor ᵃ a door of hope.
There she will respond ᵇ as in the days of her youth,
as in the day she came up out of Egypt.

¹⁶"In that day," declares the
LORD,
"you will call me 'my
husband';
you will no longer call me
'my master.' ᶜ
¹⁷I will remove the names of the
Baals from her lips;
no longer will their names
be invoked.
¹⁸In that day I will make a
covenant for them
with the beasts of the field,
the birds in the sky
and the creatures that
move along the
ground.
Bow and sword and battle
I will abolish from the land,

conversations

security «» 2:16–23

1 Should a relationship with God make you feel more secure in life? Does it for you?

2 Is it wrong to enjoy the security of human relationships? Why or why not?

3 Deep down, do you trust God to be faithful to you for life?

For more on security, check the index.
For the next Conversations, go to p. 1288.

ᵃ 15 Achor means trouble.   ᵇ 15 Or sing   ᶜ 16 Hebrew baal

so that all may lie down in safety.
¹⁹I will betroth you to me forever;
    I will betroth you in*ᵃ* righteousness and justice,
    in*ᵇ* love and compassion.
²⁰I will betroth you in faithfulness,
    and you will acknowledge the LORD.

²¹"In that day I will respond,"
    declares the LORD—
"I will respond to the skies,
    and they will respond to the earth;
²²and the earth will respond to the grain,
    the new wine and the olive oil,
    and they will respond to Jezreel.*ᶜ*
²³I will plant her for myself in the land;
    I will show my love to the one I called 'Not my loved one.'*ᵈ*
I will say to those called 'Not my people,'*ᵉ* 'You are my people';
    and they will say, 'You are my God.'"

Hosea's Reconciliation With His Wife

3 The LORD said to me, "Go, show your love to your wife again, though she is loved by another and is an adulteress. Love her as the LORD loves the Israelites, though they turn to other gods and love the sacred raisin cakes."

²So I bought her for fifteen shekels*ᶠ* of silver and about a homer and a lethek*ᵍ* of barley. ³Then I told her, "You are to live with me many days; you must not be a prostitute or be intimate with any man, and I will behave the same way toward you."

⁴For the Israelites will live many days without king or prince, without sacrifice or sacred stones, without ephod or household gods. ⁵Afterward the Israelites will return and seek the LORD their God and David their king. They will come trembling to the LORD and to his blessings in the last days.

The Charge Against Israel

4   Hear the word of the LORD, you Israelites,
        because the LORD has a charge to bring
        against you who live in the land:
    "There is no faithfulness, no love,
        no acknowledgment of God in the
            land.
²There is only cursing,*ʰ* lying and murder,
        stealing and adultery;
    they break all bounds,
        and bloodshed follows bloodshed.
³Because of this the land dries up,
        and all who live in it waste away;
    the beasts of the field, the birds in the sky
        and the fish in the sea are swept away.

atissue:infidelity

1281

3:1–3 If your husband has cheated on you, then you understand the deepest level of pain and betrayal. You may wonder if you will ever get past this—or if you even want your marriage to survive. After you have taken the first steps—confrontation (the affair must end) and the beginning of forgiveness (whether you reconcile or not, for your sake, you must forgive him)—then you can ask God for restoration. Hosea experienced this miracle of God's healing. God can heal you and make your marriage better than it ever was. Only God can do such miracles.

ᵃ 19 Or *with;* also in verse 20   *ᵇ 19* Or *with*   *ᶜ 22 Jezreel* means *God plants.*   *ᵈ 23* Hebrew *Lo-Ruhamah* (see 1:6)   *ᵉ 23* Hebrew *Lo-Ammi* (see 1:9)   *ᶠ 2* That is, about 6 ounces or about 170 grams   *ᵍ 2* A homer and a lethek possibly weighed about 430 pounds or about 195 kilograms.   *ʰ 2* That is, to pronounce a curse on

⁴"But let no one bring a charge,
    let no one accuse another,
for your people are like those
    who bring charges against a priest.
⁵You stumble day and night,
    and the prophets stumble with you.
So I will destroy your mother—
⁶ my people are destroyed from lack of knowledge.

"Because you have rejected knowledge,
    I also reject you as my priests;
because you have ignored the law of your God,
    I also will ignore your children.
⁷The more the priests increased,
    the more they sinned against me;
    they exchanged their glorious God*ᵃ* for something disgraceful.
⁸They feed on the sins of my people
    and relish their wickedness.
⁹And it will be: Like people, like priests.
    I will punish both of them for their ways
    and repay them for their deeds.

¹⁰"They will eat but not have enough;
    they will engage in prostitution but not increase,
because they have deserted the Lord
    to give themselves ¹¹to prostitution;
old wine and new wine
    take away their understanding.
¹²My people consult a wooden idol
    and are answered by a stick of wood.
A spirit of prostitution leads them astray;
    they are unfaithful to their God.
¹³They sacrifice on the mountaintops
    and burn offerings on the hills,
under oak, poplar and terebinth,
    where the shade is pleasant.
Therefore your daughters turn to prostitution
    and your daughters-in-law to adultery.

¹⁴"I will not punish your daughters
    when they turn to prostitution,
nor your daughters-in-law
    when they commit adultery,
because the men themselves consort with harlots
    and sacrifice with shrine prostitutes—
a people without understanding will come to ruin!

¹⁵"Though you, Israel, commit adultery,
    do not let Judah become guilty.

"Do not go to Gilgal;
    do not go up to Beth Aven.*ᵇ*

ᵃ 7 Syriac (see also an ancient Hebrew scribal tradition); Masoretic Text *I will exchange their glory*   *ᵇ* 15 Beth Aven means *house of wickedness* (a derogatory name for Bethel, which means *house of God*).

And do not swear, 'As surely as the LORD lives!'
¹⁶The Israelites are stubborn,
    like a stubborn heifer.
How then can the LORD pasture them
    like lambs in a meadow?
¹⁷Ephraim is joined to idols;
    leave him alone!
¹⁸Even when their drinks are gone,
    they continue their prostitution;
    their rulers dearly love shameful ways.
¹⁹A whirlwind will sweep them away,
    and their sacrifices will bring them shame.

Judgment Against Israel

5   "Hear this, you priests!
    Pay attention, you Israelites!
Listen, royal house!
    This judgment is against you:
You have been a snare at Mizpah,
    a net spread out on Tabor.
²The rebels are deep in slaughter.
    I will discipline all of them.
³I know all about Ephraim;
    Israel is not hidden from me.
Ephraim, you have now turned to prostitution;
    Israel is corrupt.

⁴"Their deeds do not permit them
    to return to their God.
A spirit of prostitution is in their heart;
    they do not acknowledge the LORD.
⁵Israel's arrogance testifies against them;
    the Israelites, even Ephraim, stumble in their sin;
    Judah also stumbles with them.
⁶When they go with their flocks and herds
    to seek the LORD,
they will not find him;
    he has withdrawn himself from them.
⁷They are unfaithful to the LORD;
    they give birth to illegitimate children.
When they celebrate their New Moon feasts,
    he will devour ᵃ their fields.

⁸"Sound the trumpet in Gibeah,
    the horn in Ramah.
Raise the battle cry in Beth Aven ᵇ;
    lead on, Benjamin.
⁹Ephraim will be laid waste
    on the day of reckoning.
Among the tribes of Israel
    I proclaim what is certain.

ᵃ *7 Or Now their New Moon feasts / will devour them and* ᵇ *8 Beth Aven* means *house of wickedness* (a derogatory name for Bethel, which means *house of God*).

¹⁰Judah's leaders are like those
  who move boundary stones.
  I will pour out my wrath on them
  like a flood of water.
¹¹Ephraim is oppressed,
  trampled in judgment,
  intent on pursuing idols.^a
¹²I am like a moth to Ephraim,
  like rot to the people of Judah.

¹³"When Ephraim saw his sickness,
  and Judah his sores,
then Ephraim turned to Assyria,
  and sent to the great king for help.
But he is not able to cure you,
  not able to heal your sores.
¹⁴For I will be like a lion to Ephraim,
  like a great lion to Judah.
I will tear them to pieces and go away;
  I will carry them off, with no one to
    rescue them.
¹⁵Then I will return to my lair
  until they have borne their guilt
  and seek my face—
in their misery
  they will earnestly seek me."

Israel Unrepentant

6 "Come, let us return to the LORD.
  He has torn us to pieces
  but he will heal us;
he has injured us
  but he will bind up our wounds.
²After two days he will revive us;
  on the third day he will restore us,
  that we may live in his presence.
³Let us acknowledge the LORD;

---

^a 11 The meaning of the Hebrew for this word is uncertain.

at issue : conviction

5:15 There are two kinds of conviction: one is a tool of God, the other a tool of Satan. Satan uses conviction to paralyze you, convincing you that you have no hope of change. He uses it to remind you of your failures long after God has both forgiven and forgotten them. Satan wrongly convicts you to rob you of your joy. In contrast, God uses conviction to cause you to turn to him for forgiveness and cleansing. He uses conviction to show you your need for a Savior and to draw you to him. So who's wielding this tool in your life now?

HE IS: healing

6:1–3 Hosea recognized that the God who, in justice, chastises his children for turning away from him will also, in mercy, *heal* them. The Lord rains his refreshing, *healing* forgiveness on those who acknowledge him.

God may allow pain in your life. He may allow you to be torn to pieces and injured by life. Why? So that you will return to him. These afflictions are a severe mercy—though painful, they are the catalyst for you to press on to acknowledge God. He will heal you, bind up your wounds, restore you and invite you to live in his presence.

For the next He Is, go to p. 1287.

let us press on to acknowledge him.
As surely as the sun rises,
    he will appear;
he will come to us like the winter rains,
    like the spring rains that water the earth."

4"What can I do with you, Ephraim?
    What can I do with you, Judah?
Your love is like the morning mist,
    like the early dew that disappears.
5Therefore I cut you in pieces with my prophets,
    I killed you with the words of my mouth—
then my judgments go forth like the sun.*a*
6For I desire mercy, not sacrifice,
    and acknowledgment of God rather than burnt offerings.
7As at Adam,*b* they have broken the covenant;
    they were unfaithful to me there.
8Gilead is a city of wicked people,
    stained with footprints of blood.
9As marauders lie in ambush for a victim,
    so do bands of priests;
they murder on the road to Shechem,
    carrying out their wicked schemes.
10I have seen a horrible thing
    in the house of Israel.
There Ephraim is given to prostitution
    and Israel is defiled.

11"Also for you, Judah,
    a harvest is appointed.

7

"Whenever I would restore the fortunes of my people,
1   whenever I would heal Israel,
the sins of Ephraim are exposed
    and the crimes of Samaria revealed.
They practice deceit,
    thieves break into houses,
    bandits rob in the streets;
2but they do not realize
    that I remember all their evil deeds.
Their sins engulf them;
    they are always before me.

3"They delight the king with their wickedness,
    the princes with their lies.
4They are all adulterers,
    burning like an oven
whose fire the baker need not stir
    from the kneading of the dough till it rises.
5On the day of the festival of our king
    the princes become inflamed with wine,
    and he joins hands with the mockers.

---

a 5 The meaning of the Hebrew for this line is uncertain.   *b* 7 Or *Like Adam; or Like human beings*

⁶Their hearts are like an oven;
    they approach him with intrigue.
Their passion smolders all night;
    in the morning it blazes like a flaming fire.
⁷All of them are hot as an oven;
    they devour their rulers.
All their kings fall,
    and none of them calls on me.

⁸"Ephraim mixes with the nations;
    Ephraim is a flat loaf not turned over.
⁹Foreigners sap his strength,
    but he does not realize it.
His hair is sprinkled with gray,
    but he does not notice.
¹⁰Israel's arrogance testifies against him,
    but despite all this
he does not return to the LORD his God
    or search for him.

¹¹"Ephraim is like a dove,
    easily deceived and senseless—
now calling to Egypt,
    now turning to Assyria.
¹²When they go, I will throw my net over them;
    I will pull them down like the birds in the sky.
When I hear them flocking together,
    I will catch them.
¹³Woe to them,
    because they have strayed from me!
Destruction to them,
    because they have rebelled against me!
I long to redeem them
    but they speak about me falsely.
¹⁴They do not cry out to me from their hearts
    but wail on their beds.
They slash themselves,ᵃ appealing to their gods
    for grain and new wine,
    but they turn away from me.
¹⁵I trained them and strengthened their arms,
    but they plot evil against me.
¹⁶They do not turn to the Most High;
    they are like a faulty bow.
Their leaders will fall by the sword
    because of their insolent words.
For this they will be ridiculed
    in the land of Egypt.

Israel to Reap the Whirlwind

8 "Put the trumpet to your lips!
    An eagle is over the house of the LORD
    because the people have broken my covenant

ᵃ *14* Some Hebrew manuscripts and Septuagint; most Hebrew manuscripts *They gather together*

and rebelled against my law.
² Israel cries out to me,
　'Our God, we acknowledge you!'
³ But Israel has rejected what is good;
　an enemy will pursue him.
⁴ They set up kings without my consent;
　they choose princes without my approval.
With their silver and gold
　they make idols for themselves
　to their own destruction.
⁵ Throw out your calf-idol, Samaria!
　My anger burns against them.
How long will they be incapable of purity?
⁶　They are from Israel!
This calf—a metalworker has made it;
　it is not God.
It will be broken in pieces,
　that calf of Samaria.

⁷ "They sow the wind
　and reap the whirlwind.
The stalk has no head;
　it will produce no flour.
Were it to yield grain,
　foreigners would swallow it up.
⁸ Israel is swallowed up;
　now she is among the nations
　like something no one wants.
⁹ For they have gone up to Assyria
　like a wild donkey wandering alone.
Ephraim has sold herself to lovers.
¹⁰ Although they have sold themselves among the nations,
　I will now gather them together.
They will begin to waste away
　under the oppression of the mighty king.

¹¹ "Though Ephraim built many altars for sin offerings,
　these have become altars for sinning.

1287

HE IS: not pleased

8:11–14 The people of Ephraim were doing the right things for the wrong reasons. They built altars to God—in addition to their idol worship. They offered sacrifices to God—but didn't truly feel sorry. God was *not pleased* that his people followed the letter of the law but forgot the Lord of the law.

If your religion looks good from the outside but hasn't changed you from the inside out, something's wrong (see Matthew 23:25–28). God is *not pleased* when you observe the proper rituals without cultivating a personal relationship with him. He is pleased when you do the right things out of heartfelt love, not from habit or routine.

For the next He Is, go to p. 1302.

¹²I wrote for them the many things of my law,
 but they regarded them as something foreign.
¹³Though they offer sacrifices as gifts to me,
 and though they eat the meat,
 the LORD is not pleased with them.
Now he will remember their wickedness
 and punish their sins:
 They will return to Egypt.
¹⁴Israel has forgotten his Maker
 and built palaces;
 Judah has fortified many towns.
But I will send fire on their cities
 that will consume their fortresses."

Punishment for Israel

9 Do not rejoice, Israel;
 do not be jubilant like the other nations.
For you have been unfaithful to your God;
 you love the wages of a prostitute
 at every threshing floor.
²Threshing floors and winepresses will not feed the people;
 the new wine will fail them.
³They will not remain in the LORD's land;
 Ephraim will return to Egypt
 and eat unclean food in Assyria.
⁴They will not pour out wine offerings to the LORD,
 nor will their sacrifices please him.
Such sacrifices will be to them like the bread of mourners;
 all who eat them will be unclean.
This food will be for themselves;
 it will not come into the temple of the LORD.

⁵What will you do on the day of your appointed festivals,
 on the festal days of the LORD?
⁶Even if they escape from
 destruction,
 Egypt will gather them,
 and Memphis will bury
 them.
Their treasures of silver will
 be taken over by
 briers,
 and thorns will overrun
 their tents.
⁷The days of punishment are
 coming,
 the days of reckoning are at
 hand.
Let Israel know this.
Because your sins are so
 many
 and your hostility so great,
the prophet is considered a fool,

conversations

consequences «» 9:7

1» How does sin affect your conscience?

2» How can sin skew your perception of God's messages (as it did for Israel in v. 7)?

3» What have been the consequences of willful sin in your life?

For more on **consequences**, check the index.
For the next Conversations, go to p. 1298.

ASKmeanything

gomer

Your story is pretty painful to tell, isn't it?

[Laughs bitterly] Definitely. If you're looking for an uplifting story of moral fortitude, you're not going to find it in my life-story. I suppose most people would sympathize with my husband, Hosea, and wonder why he would ever marry a woman like me. To most people who know my story, my very name is synonymous with adultery and prostitution. What a way to be remembered.

Tell us about your life with Hosea.

Hosea was a good man and insisted that he was marrying me because God had commanded it. I didn't know about that. I tried to be a good wife to him at first, but I don't think I was ready for marriage. I just couldn't remain faithful to my husband. Eventually, my cheating cost me my freedom, as my husband cast me out and I became a slave . . . until Hosea bought me and brought me back to his house to live.

1289

And you had children?

Three. Other than the first, I'm not sure who the fathers of the other two were. It was actually God who named them all. The first was named *Jezreel* because God was going to punish King Jehu's dynasty for the murders committed at Jezreel. Then *Lo-Ruhamah,* which means "not loved." And my youngest was *Lo-Ammi,* which means "not my people." Those names don't exactly inspire confidence, do they? But God was using my children to say something to the people of Israel about their unfaithfulness to him.

How did you feel when Hosea wanted you back after you had become a slave?

Stunned. Confused. Amazed. I mean, I certainly wasn't expecting anyone to rescue me. After what I had done? So to me, it just didn't make any sense that Hosea would want me back. But I went back with him, and, according to his demands, I stopped sleeping around. I stayed with Hosea from that day on.

What can we learn from your experiences?

Two things, I suppose. One is how serious God considers unfaithfulness. Just look at the names of my children! The same way my marital unfaithfulness was an insult to Hosea, so spiritual unfaithfulness is a serious affront to God. Then there's the second lesson that I still don't fully understand. In spite of my legendary unfaithfulness, God was still willing to take me back, to love me and to remain faithful to me. I'm not sure how much of that I really understood while I lived with Hosea. But everything Hosea said and how he acted toward me demonstrated this unconditional love. So the good news for others is that if God can love and accept someone like *me,* he can do the same for *all* sinners.

FOR MORE INSIGHT: For more on how seriously God views our sin, read Jeremiah 23:13–14; and Amos 5:12. For more on God's unconditional love and acceptance of us, read Hosea 2:19—3:1; 14:1–4.

anyone who is inspired a maniac.
⁸The prophet, along with my God,
    is the watchman over Ephraim,^{*a*}
yet snares await him on all his paths,
    and hostility in the house of his God.
⁹They have sunk deep into corruption,
    as in the days of Gibeah.
God will remember their wickedness
    and punish them for their sins.

¹⁰"When I found Israel,
    it was like finding grapes in the desert;
when I saw your ancestors,
    it was like seeing the early fruit on the fig tree.
But when they came to Baal Peor,
    they consecrated themselves to that shameful idol
    and became as vile as the thing they loved.
¹¹Ephraim's glory will fly away like a bird—
    no birth, no pregnancy, no conception.
¹²Even if they rear children,
    I will bereave them of every one.
Woe to them
    when I turn away from them!
¹³I have seen Ephraim, like Tyre,
    planted in a pleasant place.
But Ephraim will bring out
    their children to the slayer."

¹⁴Give them, LORD—
    what will you give them?
Give them wombs that miscarry
    and breasts that are dry.

¹⁵"Because of all their wickedness in Gilgal,
    I hated them there.
Because of their sinful deeds,
    I will drive them out of my house.
I will no longer love them;
    all their leaders are rebellious.
¹⁶Ephraim is blighted,
    their root is withered,
    they yield no fruit.
Even if they bear children,
    I will slay their cherished offspring."

¹⁷My God will reject them
    because they have not obeyed him;
    they will be wanderers among the nations.

10

Israel was a spreading vine;
    he brought forth fruit for himself.
As his fruit increased,

---

a 8 Or The prophet is the watchman over Ephraim, / the people of my God

he built more altars;
as his land prospered,
he adorned his sacred stones.
²Their heart is deceitful,
and now they must bear their guilt.
The Lord will demolish their altars
and destroy their sacred stones.

³Then they will say, "We have no king
because we did not revere the Lord.
But even if we had a king,
what could he do for us?"
⁴They make many promises,
take false oaths
and make agreements;
therefore lawsuits spring up
like poisonous weeds in a plowed field.
⁵The people who live in Samaria fear
for the calf-idol of Beth Aven.ᵃ
Its people will mourn over it,
and so will its idolatrous priests,
those who had rejoiced over its splendor,
because it is taken from them into exile.
⁶It will be carried to Assyria
as tribute for the great king.
Ephraim will be disgraced;
Israel will be ashamed of its foreign alliances.
⁷Samaria's king will be destroyed,
swept away like a twig on the surface of the waters.
⁸The high places of wickednessᵇ will be destroyed—
it is the sin of Israel.
Thorns and thistles will grow up
and cover their altars.
Then they will say to the mountains, "Cover us!"
and to the hills, "Fall on us!"

⁹"Since the days of Gibeah, you have sinned, Israel,
and there you have remained.ᶜ
Will not war again overtake
the evildoers in Gibeah?
¹⁰When I please, I will punish them;
nations will be gathered against them
to put them in bonds for their double sin.
¹¹Ephraim is a trained heifer
that loves to thresh;
so I will put a yoke
on her fair neck.
I will drive Ephraim,
Judah must plow,
and Jacob must break up the ground.

ᵃ 5 Beth Aven means house of wickedness (a derogatory name for Bethel, which means house of God).   ᵇ 8 Hebrew aven, a reference to Beth Aven (a derogatory name for Bethel); see verse 5.   ᶜ 9 Or there a stand was taken

¹²Sow for yourselves righteousness,
　　reap the fruit of unfailing love,
and break up your unplowed ground;
　　for it is time to seek the Lord,
until he comes
　　and showers his righteousness on you.
¹³But you have planted wickedness,
　　you have reaped evil,
　　you have eaten the fruit of deception.
Because you have depended on your
　　　own strength
　　and on your many warriors,
¹⁴the roar of battle will rise against your
　　　people,
so that all your fortresses will be
　　　devastated—
as Shalman devastated Beth Arbel on
　　the day of battle,
when mothers were dashed to the
　　ground with their children.
¹⁵So will it happen to you, Bethel,
　　because your wickedness is great.
When that day dawns,
　　the king of Israel will be completely destroyed.

God's Love for Israel

11 "When Israel was a child, I loved him,
　　and out of Egypt I called my son.
²But the more they were called,
　　the more they went away from me.^a
They sacrificed to the Baals
　　and they burned incense to images.
³It was I who taught Ephraim to walk,
　　taking them by the arms;
but they did not realize
　　it was I who healed them.
⁴I led them with cords of human kindness,
　　with ties of love.
To them I was like one who lifts
　　a little child to the cheek,
　　and I bent down to feed them.

⁵"Will they not return to Egypt
　　and will not Assyria rule over them
　　because they refuse to repent?
⁶Swords will flash in their cities,
　　will destroy the bars of their gates
　　and put an end to their plans.
⁷My people are determined to turn from me.
　　Even though they call me God Most High,
　　I will by no means exalt them.

1292

^a 2 Septuagint; Hebrew them

8 "How can I give you up, Ephraim?
    How can I hand you over, Israel?
How can I treat you like Admah?
    How can I make you like Zeboyim?
My heart is changed within me;
    all my compassion is aroused.
9 I will not carry out my fierce anger,
    nor will I devastate Ephraim again.
For I am God, and not a human being—
    the Holy One among you.
I will not come against their cities.
10 They will follow the LORD;
    he will roar like a lion.
When he roars,
    his children will come trembling from
        the west.
11 They will come trembling
    like birds from Egypt,
    like doves from Assyria.
I will settle them in their homes,"
    declares the LORD.

Israel's Sin

* 12 Ephraim has surrounded me with lies,
    the house of Israel with deceit.
And Judah is unruly against God,
    even against the faithful Holy One.

12 * 1 Ephraim feeds on the wind;
    he pursues the east wind all day
    and multiplies lies and violence.
He makes a treaty with Assyria
    and sends olive oil to Egypt.
2 The LORD has a charge to bring against Judah;
    he will punish Jacob[a] according to his ways
    and repay him according to his deeds.
3 In the womb he grasped his brother's heel;
    as a man he struggled with God.
4 He struggled with the angel and overcame him;
    he wept and begged for his favor.
He found him at Bethel
    and talked with him there—
5 the LORD God Almighty,
    the LORD is his name!
6 But you must return to your God;
    maintain love and justice,
    and wait for your God always.

7 The merchants use dishonest scales;
    they love to defraud.
8 Ephraim boasts,

---

at issue: forgiveness

11:8–11 God does not give up on his children. He is not human and doesn't act like we do. He is full of compassion. He calls his children, who hear his familiar, commanding voice and run back to him. No matter how heinous your sin, he invites you to return to him in repentance. Murder, adultery, stealing, drugs, premarital sex, pornography, abortion, _____ (fill in your "unforgivable" sin)—no sin can take you beyond the reach of God's compassion. He longs to redeem you. Turn from your sin and to him, and find complete forgiveness.

1293

---

a 2 *Jacob* means *he grasps the heel,* a Hebrew idiom for *he takes advantage of* or *he deceives.*

* 11:12 is numbered 12:1 in Hebrew texts.   * 12:1-14 is numbered 12:2-15 in Hebrew texts.

"I am very rich; I have become wealthy.
　With all my wealth they will not find in me
　　any iniquity or sin."

⁹"I have been the LORD your God
　　ever since you came out of Egypt;
I will make you live in tents again,
　　as in the days of your appointed festivals.
¹⁰I spoke to the prophets,
　　gave them many visions
　　and told parables through them."

¹¹Is Gilead wicked?
　　Its people are worthless!
Do they sacrifice bulls in Gilgal?
　　Their altars will be like piles of stones
　　on a plowed field.
¹²Jacob fled to the country of Aram ᵃ;
　　Israel served to get a wife,
　　and to pay for her he tended sheep.
¹³The LORD used a prophet to bring Israel up from Egypt,
　　by a prophet he cared for him.
¹⁴But Ephraim has aroused his bitter anger;
　　his Lord will leave on him the guilt of his bloodshed
　　and will repay him for his contempt.

The LORD's Anger Against Israel

13 When Ephraim spoke, people trembled;
　　he was exalted in Israel.
But he became guilty of Baal worship
　　and died.
²Now they sin more and more;
　　they make idols for themselves from
　　　their silver,
cleverly fashioned images,
　　all of them the work of skilled hands.
It is said of them,
　　"They offer human sacrifices!
　　They kiss ᵇ calf-idols!"
³Therefore they will be like the morning
　　mist,
like the early dew that disappears,
　　like chaff swirling from a threshing
　　　floor,
like smoke escaping through a
　　window.

⁴"But I have been the LORD your God
　　ever since you came out of Egypt.
You shall acknowledge no God but me,
　　no Savior except me.
⁵I cared for you in the wilderness,

atissue:forgetting God

13:5–6 When life is difficult, we naturally cling to God. We realize that we can't make it through a single day without him, so we hold on tightly. But as the weight of the trial lightens, we loosen our grip. It's a sad human pattern: When God blesses us, we become satisfied, then proud and then we forget God. We start thinking we can make it through life on our own; we become self-sufficient. Ask God to help you cling to him in the good times and the bad so that it won't take a bad time to remind you of him.

ᵃ *12* That is, Northwest Mesopotamia　　ᵇ *2* Or *"Men who sacrifice / kiss*

in the land of burning heat.
⁶When I fed them, they were satisfied;
  when they were satisfied, they became proud;
  then they forgot me.
⁷So I will come upon them like a lion,
  like a leopard I will lurk by the path.
⁸Like a bear robbed of her cubs,
  I will attack them and rip them open;
like a lion I will devour them—
  a wild animal will tear them apart.

⁹"You are destroyed, Israel,
  because you are against me, against your helper.
¹⁰Where is your king, that he may save you?
  Where are your rulers in all your towns,
of whom you said,
  'Give me a king and princes'?
¹¹So in my anger I gave you a king,
  and in my wrath I took him away.
¹²The guilt of Ephraim is stored up,
  his sins are kept on record.
¹³Pains as of a woman in childbirth come to him,
  but he is a child without wisdom;
when the time arrives,
  he does not come to the opening of the womb.

¹⁴"I will deliver them from the power of the grave;
  I will redeem them from death.
Where, O death, are your plagues?
  Where, O grave, is your destruction?

"I will have no compassion,
¹⁵ even though he thrives among his brothers.
An east wind from the LORD will come,
  blowing in from the desert;
his spring will fail
  and his well dry up.
His storehouse will be plundered
  of all its treasures.
*¹⁶The people of Samaria must bear their guilt,
  because they have rebelled against their God.
They will fall by the sword;
  their little ones will be dashed to the ground,
  their pregnant women ripped open."

Repentance to Bring Blessing

14 *¹Return, Israel, to the LORD your God.
  Your sins have been your downfall!
²Take words with you
  and return to the LORD.
Say to him:
  "Forgive all our sins

and receive us graciously,
    that we may offer the fruit of our lips."[a]
[3]Assyria cannot save us;
    we will not mount warhorses.
We will never again say 'Our gods'
    to what our own hands have made,
    for in you the fatherless find compassion."

[4]"I will heal their waywardness
    and love them freely,
    for my anger has turned away from
        them.
[5]I will be like the dew to Israel;
    he will blossom like a lily.
Like a cedar of Lebanon
    he will send down his roots;
[6] his young shoots will grow.
His splendor will be like an olive tree,
    his fragrance like a cedar of Lebanon.
[7]People will dwell again in his shade;
    they will flourish like the grain,
they will blossom like the vine—
    Israel's fame will be like the wine of
        Lebanon.
[8]Ephraim, what more have I[b] to do with
        idols?
I will answer him and care for him.
I am like a flourishing juniper;
    your fruitfulness comes from me."

[9]Who is wise? Let them realize these
        things.
    Who is discerning? Let them
        understand.
The ways of the LORD are right;
    the righteous walk in them,
    but the rebellious stumble in them.

aussie:total obedience

14:9 The ways of your best friend might seem right. The ways of your husband might seem right. The ways of your parents might seem right. The ways of your therapist might seem right. But if their ways—their habits, motives, goals, beliefs, lifestyles, choices—conflict with God's ways, then their ways are wrong. Walk only in God's ways. Be your own woman, willing to obey God, no matter what anyone else does. If you rebel against God's ways, you'll find yourself stumbling instead of walking victoriously through life.

---

[a] 2 Or *offer our lips as sacrifices of bulls*   [b] 8 Or Hebrew; Septuagint *What more has Ephraim*

What tiny but mighty force nearly
destroyed Judah? »» (1:2–12)

If you've been biding your time, when is
the *best* time to return to God? »» (2:12)

What happens on the day of the Lord? »» (2:28–32)

joel

1297

AUTHOR
Joel.

AUDIENCE
The southern kingdom (Judah) and all of
God's people.

DATE
About 835 B.C.

SETTING
The people of Judah trusted in their great
wealth, not in God.

VERSE TO REMEMBER
"I will repay you for the years the locusts
have eaten—the great locust and the
young locust, the other locusts and the
locust swarm—my great army that I sent
among you." (2:25)

THEME TO CONSIDER
When we sincerely repent, God wholeheartedly redeems us.

1 The word of the LORD that came to Joel son of Pethuel.

An Invasion of Locusts

²Hear this, you elders;
　　listen, all who live in the
　　　　land.
Has anything like this ever
　　　happened in your days
　　or in the days of your
　　　　ancestors?
³Tell it to your children,
　　and let your children tell it
　　　to their children,
　　and their children to the
　　　next generation.
⁴What the locust swarm has
　　left
　　the great locusts have eaten;
what the great locusts have left
　　the young locusts have eaten;
what the young locusts have left
　　other locusts*ᵃ* have eaten.

⁵Wake up, you drunkards, and weep!
　　Wail, all you drinkers of wine;
wail because of the new wine,
　　for it has been snatched from your lips.
⁶A nation has invaded my land,
　　a mighty army without number;
it has the teeth of a lion,
　　the fangs of a lioness.
⁷It has laid waste my vines
　　and ruined my fig trees.
It has stripped off their bark
　　and thrown it away,
　　leaving their branches white.

⁸Mourn like a virgin in sackcloth
　　grieving for the betrothed of her youth.
⁹Grain offerings and drink offerings
　　are cut off from the house of the LORD.
The priests are in mourning,
　　those who minister before the LORD.
¹⁰The fields are ruined,
　　the ground is dried up;
the grain is destroyed,
　　the new wine is dried up,
　　the olive oil fails.

¹¹Despair, you farmers,
　　wail, you vine growers;

"conversations"

children «» 1:1–3

1» What is your responsibility to the children in your life?

2» Why is it important to pass on stories to the next generation?

3» How could your life story help a child close to you?

For more on **children**, check the index.
For the next Conversations, go to p. 1310.

ᵃ 4 The precise meaning of the four Hebrew words used here for locusts is uncertain.

grieve for the wheat and the barley,
  because the harvest of the field is destroyed.
¹²The vine is dried up
  and the fig tree is withered;
the pomegranate, the palm and the apple[a] tree—
  all the trees of the field—are dried up.
Surely the people's joy
  is withered away.

A Call to Lamentation

¹³Put on sackcloth, you priests, and mourn;
  wail, you who minister before the altar.
Come, spend the night in sackcloth,
  you who minister before my God;
for the grain offerings and drink offerings
  are withheld from the house of your God.
¹⁴Declare a holy fast;
  call a sacred assembly.
Summon the elders
  and all who live in the land
to the house of the LORD your God,
  and cry out to the LORD.

¹⁵Alas for that day!
  For the day of the LORD is near;
  it will come like destruction from the Almighty.[b]

¹⁶Has not the food been cut off
  before our very eyes—
joy and gladness
  from the house of our God?
¹⁷The seeds are shriveled
  beneath the clods.[c]
The storehouses are in ruins,
  the granaries have been broken down,
  for the grain has dried up.
¹⁸How the cattle moan!
  The herds mill about
because they have no pasture;
  even the flocks of sheep are suffering.

¹⁹To you, LORD, I call,
  for fire has devoured the pastures in the wilderness
  and flames have burned up all the trees of the field.
²⁰Even the wild animals pant for you;
  the streams of water have dried up
  and fire has devoured the pastures in the wilderness.

An Army of Locusts

2 Blow the trumpet in Zion;
  sound the alarm on my holy hill.

Let all who live in the land tremble,
  for the day of the LORD is coming.

1299

---

a 12 Or possibly *apricot*   *b 15* Hebrew *Shaddai*   *c 17* The meaning of the Hebrew for this word is uncertain.

It is close at hand—
² a day of darkness and gloom,
a day of clouds and blackness.
Like dawn spreading across the mountains
a large and mighty army comes,
such as never was of old
nor ever will be in ages to come.

³Before them fire devours,
behind them a flame blazes.
Before them the land is like the garden of Eden,
behind them, a desert waste—
nothing escapes them.
⁴They have the appearance of horses;
they gallop along like cavalry.
⁵With a noise like that of chariots
they leap over the mountaintops,
like a crackling fire consuming stubble,
like a mighty army drawn up for battle.

1300

⁶At the sight of them, nations are in anguish;
every face turns pale.
⁷They charge like warriors;
they scale walls like soldiers.
They all march in line,
not swerving from their course.
⁸They do not jostle each other;
each marches straight ahead.
They plunge through defenses
without breaking ranks.
⁹They rush upon the city;
they run along the wall.
They climb into the houses;
like thieves they enter through the
windows.

¹⁰Before them the earth shakes,
the heavens tremble,
the sun and moon are darkened,
and the stars no longer shine.
¹¹The LORD thunders
at the head of his army;
his forces are beyond number,
and mighty is the army that obeys his
command.
The day of the LORD is great;
it is dreadful.
Who can endure it?

Rend Your Heart

¹²"Even now," declares the LORD,
"return to me with all your heart,
with fasting and weeping and
mourning."

at·issue:repentance

2:12–13 Have you ever received an insincere apology? Although the words were spoken, you could tell that they weren't meant. It would have been better for the person to have said nothing at all. An insincere apology adds insult to injury, doesn't it? God hates it when we offer him insincere repentance, when we go through the motions out of obligation, but our hearts aren't in it. Instead, he wants us to return to him with our whole hearts—to not just say we're sorry, but to show it in our actions. When we do, we discover the depth of his mercy.

1301

¹³Rend your heart
    and not your garments.
Return to the LORD your God,
    for he is gracious and compassionate,
slow to anger and abounding in love,
    and he relents from sending calamity.
¹⁴Who knows? He may turn and relent
    and leave behind a blessing—
grain offerings and drink offerings
    for the LORD your God.

¹⁵Blow the trumpet in Zion,
    declare a holy fast,
    call a sacred assembly.
¹⁶Gather the people,
    consecrate the assembly;
bring together the elders,
    gather the children,
    those nursing at the breast.
Let the bridegroom leave his room
    and the bride her chamber.
¹⁷Let the priests, who minister before the LORD,
    weep between the portico and the altar.
Let them say, "Spare your people, LORD.
    Do not make your inheritance an object of scorn,
    a byword among the nations.
Why should they say among the peoples,
    'Where is their God?'"

The LORD's Answer

¹⁸Then the LORD was jealous for his land
    and took pity on his people.
¹⁹The LORD replied*ᵃ* to them:
    "I am sending you grain, new wine and olive oil,
    enough to satisfy you fully;
never again will I make you
    an object of scorn to the nations.

²⁰"I will drive the northern horde far from you,
    pushing it into a parched and barren land;
its eastern ranks will drown in the Dead Sea
    and its western ranks in the Mediterranean Sea.
And its stench will go up;
    its smell will rise."

Surely he has done great things!
²¹ Do not be afraid, land of Judah;
    be glad and rejoice.
Surely the LORD has done great things!
²² Do not be afraid, you wild animals,
    for the pastures in the wilderness are becoming green.

ᵃ 18,19 Or *LORD will be jealous… / and take pity… / ¹⁹The LORD will reply*

The trees are bearing their fruit;
    the fig tree and the vine yield their riches.
²³ Be glad, people of Zion,
    rejoice in the Lord your God,
for he has given you
    the autumn rains in righteousness.
He sends you abundant showers,
    both autumn and spring rains, as before.
²⁴ The threshing floors will be filled with grain;
    the vats will overflow with new wine and oil.

²⁵ "I will repay you for the years the locusts have eaten—
    the great locust and the young locust,
    the other locusts and the locust swarm*—
my great army that I sent among you.
²⁶ You will have plenty to eat, until you are full,
    and you will praise the name of the Lord your God,
    who has worked wonders for you;
never again will my people be shamed.
²⁷ Then you will know that I am in Israel,
    that I am the Lord your God,
    and that there is no other;
never again will my people be shamed.

The Day of the Lord

*²⁸ "And afterward,
    I will pour out my Spirit on all people.
Your sons and daughters will prophesy,
    your old men will dream dreams,
    your young men will see visions.
²⁹ Even on my servants, both men and women,
    I will pour out my Spirit in those days.
³⁰ I will show wonders in the heavens
    and on the earth,
    blood and fire and billows of smoke.
³¹ The sun will be turned to darkness

---

a 25 The precise meaning of the four Hebrew words used here for locusts is uncertain.
* 2:28-32 is numbered 3:1-5 in Hebrew texts.

HE IS: pouring out

2:28–32 Joel spoke of a time to come when God promised to pour out his Spirit on all people. He predicted that in those days, the Spirit would not be sent just to prophets, priests and kings, but to everyone—young and old, men and women, slave and free.

This was a shocking announcement—God's Holy Spirit, available to many! God fulfilled this promise at Pentecost, sending his Spirit to indwell all who believed in Jesus (see Acts 2:1–4). Today, God continues *pouring out* his Spirit on all who believe. When you receive Christ as Lord, he'll pour his Spirit into your heart (see 1 Corinthians 12:4–11).

For the next He Is, go to p. 1318.

and the moon to blood
before the coming of the great and dreadful day of the LORD.
³²And everyone who calls
on the name of the LORD will be saved;
for on Mount Zion and in Jerusalem
there will be deliverance,
as the LORD has said,
even among the survivors
whom the LORD calls.

The Nations Judged

3 *"In those days and at that time,
when I restore the fortunes of Judah and Jerusalem,
²I will gather all nations
and bring them down to the Valley of Jehoshaphat.ᵃ
There I will enter into judgment against them
concerning my inheritance, my people Israel,
for they scattered my people among the nations
and divided up my land.
³They cast lots for my people
and traded boys for prostitutes;
they sold girls for wine
that they might drink.

⁴"Now what have you against me, Tyre and Sidon and all you regions of Philistia? Are you repaying me for something I have done? If you are paying me back, I will swiftly and speedily return on your own heads what you have done. ⁵For you took my silver and my gold and carried off my finest treasures to your temples.ᵇ ⁶You sold the people of Judah and Jerusalem to the Greeks, that you might send them far from their homeland.

⁷"See, I am going to rouse them out of the places to which you sold them, and I will return on your own heads what you have done. ⁸I will sell your sons and daughters to the people of Judah, and they will sell them to the Sabeans, a nation far away." The LORD has spoken.

⁹Proclaim this among the nations:
Prepare for war!
Rouse the warriors!
Let all the fighting men draw near and attack.
¹⁰Beat your plowshares into swords
and your pruning hooks into spears.
Let the weakling say,
"I am strong!"
¹¹Come quickly, all you nations from every side,
and assemble there.

Bring down your warriors, LORD!

¹²"Let the nations be roused;
let them advance into the Valley of Jehoshaphat,
for there I will sit
to judge all the nations on every side.
¹³Swing the sickle,

ᵃ 2 *Jehoshaphat* means *the LORD judges*; also in verse 12. ᵇ 5 Or *palaces*
* 3:1-21 is numbered 4:1-21 in Hebrew texts.

for the harvest is ripe.
Come, trample the grapes,
    for the winepress is full
    and the vats overflow—
so great is their wickedness!"

¹⁴Multitudes, multitudes
    in the valley of decision!
For the day of the LORD is near
    in the valley of decision.
¹⁵The sun and moon will be darkened,
    and the stars no longer shine.
¹⁶The LORD will roar from Zion
    and thunder from Jerusalem;
    the earth and the heavens will tremble.
But the LORD will be a refuge for his people,
    a stronghold for the people of Israel.

Blessings for God's People

¹⁷"Then you will know that I, the LORD your God,
    dwell in Zion, my holy hill.
Jerusalem will be holy;
    never again will foreigners invade her.

¹⁸"In that day the mountains will drip new wine,
    and the hills will flow with milk;
    all the ravines of Judah will run with water.
A fountain will flow out of the LORD's house
    and will water the valley of acacias.ᵃ
¹⁹But Egypt will be desolate,
    Edom a desert waste,
because of violence done to the people of Judah,
    in whose land they shed innocent blood.
²⁰Judah will be inhabited forever
    and Jerusalem through all generations.
²¹Shall I leave their innocent blood unpunished?
    No, I will not."

The LORD dwells in Zion!

1304

What was Amos's pre-prophet occupation? »» (1:1; 7:14–15)

How had Israel treated its poor? »» (2:6–8)

In your opinion, which is Amos's most
striking use of imagery? »» (2:13; 3:8,12; 4:1; 8:1–2)

Does God feel laid-back about our complacency? »» (6:1,3–7)

amos

1305

AUTHOR
Amos.

AUDIENCE
The northern kingdom (Israel) and all of
God's people.

DATE
About 760–750 B.C.

SETTING
Wealthy people were oppressing the poor in
Israel.

VERSE TO REMEMBER
"But let justice roll on like a river, righteousness like a never-failing stream!" (5:24)

THEME TO CONSIDER
God's love for the overlooked cannot be
overstated.

1 The words of Amos, one of the shepherds of Tekoa—the vision he saw concerning Israel two years
before the earthquake, when Uzziah was king of Judah and Jeroboam son of Jehoash[a] was king
of Israel.

²He said:

> "The Lord roars from Zion
>   and thunders from Jerusalem;
> the pastures of the shepherds dry up,
>   and the top of Carmel withers."

Judgment on Israel's Neighbors

³This is what the Lord says:

> "For three sins of Damascus,
>   even for four, I will not turn back ⌞my wrath⌟.
> Because she threshed Gilead
>   with sledges having iron teeth,
> ⁴I will send fire on the house of Hazael
>   that will consume the fortresses of Ben-Hadad.
> ⁵I will break down the gate of Damascus;
>   I will destroy the king who is in[b] the Valley of Aven[c]
> and the one who holds the scepter in Beth Eden.
>   The people of Aram will go into exile to Kir,"

says the Lord.

⁶This is what the Lord says:

> "For three sins of Gaza,
>   even for four, I will not turn back ⌞my wrath⌟.
> Because she took captive whole communities
>   and sold them to Edom,
> ⁷I will send fire on the walls of Gaza
>   that will consume her fortresses.
> ⁸I will destroy the king[d] of Ashdod
>   and the one who holds the scepter in Ashkelon.
> I will turn my hand against Ekron,
>   till the last of the Philistines are dead,"

says the Sovereign Lord.

⁹This is what the Lord says:

> "For three sins of Tyre,
>   even for four, I will not turn back ⌞my wrath⌟.
> Because she sold whole communities of captives to Edom,
>   disregarding a treaty of brotherhood,
> ¹⁰I will send fire on the walls of Tyre
>   that will consume her fortresses."

¹¹This is what the Lord says:

> "For three sins of Edom,
>   even for four, I will not turn back ⌞my wrath⌟.
> Because he pursued his brother with a sword
>   and slaughtered the women of the land,

ᵃ 1 Hebrew Joash, a variant of Jehoash   ᵇ 5 Or the inhabitants of   ᶜ 5 Aven means wickedness.   ᵈ 8 Or inhabitants

because his anger raged continually
  and his fury flamed unchecked,
[12]I will send fire on Teman
  that will consume the fortresses of Bozrah."

[13]This is what the LORD says:

"For three sins of Ammon,
  even for four, I will not turn back ⌐my wrath⌐.
Because he ripped open the pregnant women of Gilead
  in order to extend his borders,
[14]I will set fire to the walls of Rabbah
  that will consume her fortresses
amid war cries on the day of battle,
  amid violent winds on a stormy day.
[15]Their king[a] will go into exile,
  he and his officials together,"

says the LORD.

2 This is what the LORD says:

"For three sins of Moab,
  even for four, I will not turn back ⌐my wrath⌐.
Because he burned to lime
  the bones of Edom's king,
[2]I will send fire on Moab
  that will consume the fortresses of Kerioth.[b]
Moab will go down in great tumult
  amid war cries and the blast of the trumpet.
[3]I will destroy her ruler
  and kill all her officials with him,"

says the LORD.

[4]This is what the LORD says:

"For three sins of Judah,
  even for four, I will not turn back ⌐my wrath⌐.
Because they have rejected the law of the LORD
  and have not kept his decrees,
because they have been led astray by false gods,[c]
  the gods[d] their ancestors followed,
[5]I will send fire on Judah
  that will consume the fortresses of Jerusalem."

Judgment on Israel

[6]This is what the LORD says:

"For three sins of Israel,
  even for four, I will not turn back ⌐my wrath⌐.
They sell the innocent for silver,
  and the needy for a pair of sandals.
[7]They trample on the heads of the poor
  as on the dust of the ground

1307

---

[a] 15 Or / Molek   [b] 2 Or of her cities   [c] 4 Or by lies   [d] 4 Or lies

and deny justice to the oppressed.
Father and son use the same girl
and so profane my holy name.
[8]They lie down beside every altar
on garments taken in pledge.
In the house of their god
they drink wine taken as fines.

[9]"Yet I destroyed the Amorites before them,
though they were tall as the cedars
and strong as the oaks.
I destroyed their fruit above
and their roots below.
[10]I brought you up out of Egypt
and led you forty years in the wilderness
to give you the land of the Amorites.

[11]"I also raised up prophets from among your children
and Nazirites from among your youths.
Is this not true, people of Israel?"

declares the LORD.

[12]"But you made the Nazirites drink wine
and commanded the prophets not to prophesy.

[13]"Now then, I will crush you
as a cart crushes when loaded with grain.
[14]The swift will not escape,
the strong will not muster their strength,
and the warrior will not save his life.
[15]The archer will not stand his ground,
the fleet-footed soldier will not get away,
and the horseman will not save his life.
[16]Even the bravest warriors
will flee naked on that day,"

declares the LORD.

Witnesses Summoned Against Israel

3 Hear this word, people of Israel, the word the LORD has spoken against you—against the whole family I brought up out of Egypt:

[2]"You only have I chosen
of all the families of the earth;
therefore I will punish you
for all your sins."

[3]Do two walk together
unless they have agreed to do so?
[4]Does a lion roar in the thicket
when it has no prey?
Does it growl in its den
when it has caught nothing?
[5]Does a bird swoop down to a trap on the ground
when no bait is there?
Does a trap spring up from the ground

if it has not caught anything?
⁶When a trumpet sounds in a city,
    do not the people tremble?
When disaster comes to a city,
    has not the Lord caused it?

⁷Surely the Sovereign Lord does nothing
    without revealing his plan
    to his servants the prophets.

⁸The lion has roared—
    who will not fear?
The Sovereign Lord has spoken—
    who can but prophesy?

⁹Proclaim to the fortresses of Ashdod
    and to the fortresses of Egypt:
"Assemble yourselves on the mountains of Samaria;
    see the great unrest within her
    and the oppression among her people."

¹⁰"They do not know how to do right," declares the Lord,
    "who store up in their fortresses
    what they have plundered and looted."

¹¹Therefore this is what the Sovereign Lord says:

"An enemy will overrun your land,
    pull down your strongholds
    and plunder your fortresses."

¹²This is what the Lord says:

"As a shepherd saves from the lion's mouth
    only two leg bones or a piece of an ear,
    so will the Israelites be saved,
those who sit in Samaria
    on the edge of their beds
    and in Damascus on their couches.ᵃ"

¹³"Hear this and testify against the house of Jacob," declares the Lord, the Lord God Almighty.

¹⁴"On the day I punish Israel for her sins,
    I will destroy the altars of Bethel;
the horns of the altar will be cut off
    and fall to the ground.
¹⁵I will tear down the winter house
    along with the summer house;
the houses adorned with ivory will be destroyed
    and the mansions will be demolished,"

declares the Lord.

Israel Has Not Returned to God

4 Hear this word, you cows of Bashan on Mount Samaria,
    you women who oppress the poor and crush the needy
    and say to your husbands, "Bring us some drinks!"

ᵃ 12 Or Israelites living in Samaria be saved, / with only the head of a bed / and a piece of fabric from a couch

²The Sovereign Lord has sworn
    by his holiness:
    "The time will surely come
when you will be taken away
    with hooks,
    the last of you with
      fishhooks.ᵃ
³You will each go straight out
    through breaches in the
      wall,
    and you will be cast out
      toward Harmon,ᵇ"
        declares the Lord.
⁴"Go to Bethel and sin;
    go to Gilgal and sin yet
      more.
Bring your sacrifices every morning,
    your tithes every three years.ᶜ
⁵Burn leavened bread as a thank offering
    and brag about your freewill offerings—
boast about them, you Israelites,
    for this is what you love to do,"

          declares the Sovereign Lord.

⁶"I gave you empty stomachs in every city
    and lack of bread in every town,
    yet you have not returned to me,"

          declares the Lord.

⁷"I also withheld rain from you
    when the harvest was still three months away.
I sent rain on one town,
    but withheld it from another.
One field had rain;
    another had none and dried up.
⁸People staggered from town to town for water
    but did not get enough to drink,
    yet you have not returned to me,"

          declares the Lord.

⁹"Many times I struck your gardens and vineyards,
    destroying them with blight and mildew.
Locusts devoured your fig and olive trees,
    yet you have not returned to me,"

          declares the Lord.

¹⁰"I sent plagues among you
    as I did to Egypt.
I killed your young men with the sword,
    along with your captured horses.
I filled your nostrils with the stench of your camps,

conversations

selfishness «» 4:1–3

1 » How can you relate to these women's selfish and indulgent behaviors?

2 » How does selfishness contradict the gospel?

3 » How does selfishness strangle your relationships and stunt your spiritual growth?

For more on **selfishness**, check the index. For the next Conversations, go to p. 1321.

ᵃ *2 Or away in baskets, / the last of you in fish baskets*   ᵇ *3 Masoretic Text; with a different word division of the Hebrew (see Septuagint)* out, you mountain of oppression   ᶜ *4 Or days* yet you have not returned to me,"

declares the Lord.

¹¹"I overthrew some of you
    as I overthrew Sodom and Gomorrah.
  You were like a burning stick snatched from the fire,
    yet you have not returned to me,"

declares the Lord.

¹²"Therefore this is what I will do to you, Israel,
    and because I will do this to you, Israel,
    prepare to meet your God."

¹³He who forms the mountains,
    who creates the wind,
    and who reveals his thoughts to mortals,
  who turns dawn to darkness,
    and treads on the heights of the earth—
    the Lord God Almighty is his name.

A Lament and Call to Repentance

5 Hear this word, house of Israel, this lament I take up concerning you:

²"Fallen is Virgin Israel,
    never to rise again,
  deserted in her own land,
    with no one to lift her up."

³This is what the Sovereign Lord says to the house of Israel:

"Your city that marches out a thousand strong
    will have only a hundred left;
your town that marches out a hundred strong
    will have only ten left."

⁴This is what the Lord says to the house of Israel:

"Seek me and live;
⁵ do not seek Bethel,
do not go to Gilgal,
    do not journey to Beersheba.
For Gilgal will surely go into exile,
    and Bethel will be reduced to nothing.^a"
⁶Seek the Lord and live,
    or he will sweep through the house of Joseph like a fire;
it will devour them,
    and Bethel will have no one to quench it.

⁷There are those who turn justice into bitterness
    and cast righteousness to the ground.

⁸He who made the Pleiades and Orion,
    who turns midnight into dawn
    and darkens day into night,
  who calls for the waters of the sea

^a 5 Hebrew *aven*, a reference to Beth Aven (a derogatory name for Bethel); see Hosea 4:15.

and pours them out over the face of the land—
the Lord is his name.
⁹He flashes destruction on the stronghold
and brings the fortified city to ruin.

¹⁰There are those who hate the one who reproves in court
and detest the one who tells the truth.

¹¹You levy a straw tax on the poor
and impose a tax on their grain.
Therefore, though you have built stone mansions,
you will not live in them;
though you have planted lush vineyards,
you will not drink their wine.
¹²For I know how many are your offenses
and how great your sins.

There are those who oppress the innocent and take bribes
and deprive the poor of justice in the courts.
¹³Therefore the prudent keep quiet in such times,
for the times are evil.

¹⁴Seek good, not evil,
that you may live.
Then the Lord God Almighty will be with you,
just as you say he is.
¹⁵Hate evil, love good;
maintain justice in the courts.
Perhaps the Lord God Almighty will have mercy
on the remnant of Joseph.

¹⁶Therefore this is what the Lord, the Lord God Almighty, says:

"There will be wailing in all the streets
and cries of anguish in every public square.
The farmers will be summoned to weep
and the mourners to wail.
¹⁷There will be wailing in all the vineyards,
for I will pass through your midst,"

says the Lord.

The Day of the Lord

¹⁸Woe to you who long
for the day of the Lord!
Why do you long for the day of the Lord?
That day will be darkness, not light.
¹⁹It will be as though a man fled from a lion
only to meet a bear,
as though he entered his house
and rested his hand on the wall
only to have a snake bite him.
²⁰Will not the day of the Lord be darkness, not light—
pitch-dark, without a ray of brightness?

²¹"I hate, I despise your religious festivals;
I cannot stand your assemblies.

22 Even though you bring me burnt offerings
  and grain offerings,
 I will not accept them.
Though you bring choice fellowship offerings,
 I will have no regard for them.
23 Away with the noise of your songs!
 I will not listen to the music of your harps.
24 But let justice roll on like a river,
 righteousness like a never-failing stream!

25 "Did you bring me sacrifices and offerings
 forty years in the wilderness, house of Israel?
26 You have lifted up the shrine of your king,
 the pedestal of your idols,
 the star of your god[a]—
 which you made for yourselves.
27 Therefore I will send you into exile beyond Damascus,"
 says the LORD, whose name is God Almighty.

at issue: hypocrisy

5:21–24 Since God himself instituted Israel's feasts and offerings, why would he despise them? Why would he not want to hear the people sing praises? The answer is simple: God wants *genuine* worship. This means living righteously every day, not just when you show up to church. If being a Christian is a sometimes-identity that you put on and take off each Sunday, then you're missing the point. Not only is God not impressed by that, but he will not even listen to or accept that kind of hypocritical worship.

1313

Woe to the Complacent

6 Woe to you who are complacent in Zion,
 and to you who feel secure on Mount Samaria,
 you notable men of the foremost nation,
 to whom the people of Israel come!
2 Go to Kalneh and look at it;
 go from there to great Hamath,
 and then go down to Gath in Philistia.
 Are they better off than your two kingdoms?
 Is their land larger than yours?
3 You put off the evil day
 and bring near a reign of terror.
4 You lie on beds inlaid with ivory
 and lounge on your couches.
 You dine on choice lambs
 and fattened calves.
5 You strum away on your harps like David
 and improvise on musical instruments.
6 You drink wine by the bowlful
 and use the finest lotions,
 but you do not grieve over the ruin of Joseph.
7 Therefore you will be among the first to go into exile;
 your feasting and lounging will end.

The LORD Abhors the Pride of Israel

8 The Sovereign LORD has sworn by himself—the LORD God Almighty declares:

---

[a] 26 Or lifted up Sakkuth your king / and Kaiwan your idols, / your star-gods; Septuagint lifted up the shrine of Molek / and the star of your god Rephan, / their idols

> "I abhor the pride of Jacob
>   and detest his fortresses;
> I will deliver up the city
>   and everything in it."

⁹If ten people are left in one house, they too will die. ¹⁰And if the relative who comes to carry the bodies out of the house to burn them*ᵃ* asks anyone who might be hiding there, "Is anyone else with you?" and he says, "No," then he will go on to say, "Hush! We must not mention the name of the LORD."

> ¹¹For the LORD has given the command,
>   and he will smash the great house into pieces
>   and the small house into bits.

> ¹²Do horses run on the rocky crags?
>   Does one plow the sea*ᵇ* with oxen?
> But you have turned justice into poison
>   and the fruit of righteousness into bitterness—
> ¹³you who rejoice in the conquest of Lo Debar*ᶜ*
>   and say, "Did we not take Karnaim*ᵈ* by our own strength?"

> ¹⁴For the LORD God Almighty declares,
>   "I will stir up a nation against you, house of Israel,
> that will oppress you all the way
>   from Lebo Hamath to the valley of the Arabah."

Locusts, Fire and a Plumb Line

7 This is what the Sovereign LORD showed me: He was preparing swarms of locusts after the king's share had been harvested and just as the late crops were coming up. ²When they had stripped the land clean, I cried out, "Sovereign LORD, forgive! How can Jacob survive? He is so small!"

³So the LORD relented.

"This will not happen," the LORD said.

⁴This is what the Sovereign LORD showed me: The Sovereign LORD was calling for judgment by fire; it dried up the great deep and devoured the land. ⁵Then I cried out, "Sovereign LORD, I beg you, stop! How can Jacob survive? He is so small!"

⁶So the LORD relented.

"This will not happen either," the Sovereign LORD said.

⁷This is what he showed me: The Lord was standing by a wall that had been built true to plumb,*ᵉ* with a plumb line*ᵉ* in his hand. ⁸And the LORD asked me, "What do you see, Amos?"

"A plumb line," I replied.

Then the Lord said, "Look, I am setting a plumb line among my people Israel; I will spare them no longer.

> ⁹"The high places of Isaac will be destroyed
>   and the sanctuaries of Israel will be ruined;
>   with my sword I will rise against the house of Jeroboam."

Amos and Amaziah

¹⁰Then Amaziah the priest of Bethel sent a message to Jeroboam king of Israel: "Amos is raising a conspiracy against you in the very heart of Israel. The land cannot bear all his words. ¹¹For this is what Amos is saying:

ᵃ 10 Or to make a funeral fire in honor of the dead   *ᵇ 12 With a different word division of the Hebrew; Masoretic Text plow there*   *ᶜ 13 Lo Debar means nothing.*
ᵈ 13 Karnaim means horns; horn here symbolizes strength.   *ᵉ 7 The meaning of the Hebrew for this phrase is uncertain.*

> "'Jeroboam will die by the sword,
>   and Israel will surely go into exile,
>   away from their native land.'"

¹²Then Amaziah said to Amos, "Get out, you seer! Go back to the land of Judah. Earn your bread there and do your prophesying there. ¹³Don't prophesy anymore at Bethel, because this is the king's sanctuary and the temple of the kingdom."

¹⁴Amos answered Amaziah, "I was neither a prophet nor the disciple of a prophet, but I was a shepherd, and I also took care of sycamore-fig trees. ¹⁵But the Lord took me from tending the flock and said to me, 'Go, prophesy to my people Israel.' ¹⁶Now then, hear the word of the Lord. You say,

> "'Do not prophesy against Israel,
>   and stop preaching against the house of Isaac.'

¹⁷"Therefore this is what the Lord says:

> "'Your wife will become a prostitute in the city,
>   and your sons and daughters will fall by the sword.
> Your land will be measured and divided up,
>   and you yourself will die in a pagan^a country.
> And Israel will surely go into exile,
>   away from their native land.'"

A Basket of Ripe Fruit

8 This is what the Sovereign Lord showed me: a basket of ripe fruit. ²"What do you see, Amos?" he asked.

"A basket of ripe fruit," I answered.

Then the Lord said to me, "The time is ripe for my people Israel; I will spare them no longer.

³"In that day," declares the Sovereign Lord, "the songs in the temple will turn to wailing.^b Many, many bodies—flung everywhere! Silence!"

> ⁴Hear this, you who trample the needy
>   and do away with the poor of the land,

⁵saying,

> "When will the New Moon be over
>   that we may sell grain,
> and the Sabbath be ended
>   that we may market wheat?"—
> skimping on the measure,
>   boosting the price
>   and cheating with dishonest scales,
> ⁶buying the poor with silver
>   and the needy for a pair of sandals,
>   selling even the sweepings with the wheat.

⁷The Lord has sworn by himself, the Pride of Jacob: "I will never forget anything they have done.

> ⁸"Will not the land tremble for this,
>   and all who live in it mourn?
> The whole land will rise like the Nile;
>   it will be stirred up and then sink
>   like the river of Egypt.

1315

---

^a 17 Hebrew *an unclean*   ^b 3 Or *"the temple singers will wail"*

⁹"In that day," declares the Sovereign LORD,

> "I will make the sun go down at noon
>   and darken the earth in broad
>   daylight.
> ¹⁰I will turn your religious festivals into
>   mourning
>   and all your singing into weeping.
> I will make all of you wear sackcloth
>   and shave your heads.
> I will make that time like mourning for
>   an only son
>   and the end of it like a bitter day.
>
> ¹¹"The days are coming," declares the
>   Sovereign LORD,
>   "when I will send a famine through
>   the land—
> not a famine of food or a thirst for
>   water,
>   but a famine of hearing the words of
>   the LORD.
> ¹²People will stagger from sea to sea
>   and wander from north to east,
> searching for the word of the LORD,
>   but they will not find it.

¹³"In that day

> "the lovely young women and strong
>   young men
>   will faint because of thirst.
> ¹⁴Those who swear by the sin of Samaria—
> who say, 'As surely as your god lives, Dan,'
> or, 'As surely as the god*a* of Beersheba lives'—
>   they will fall, never to rise again."

Israel to Be Destroyed

9 I saw the Lord standing by the altar, and he said:

> "Strike the tops of the pillars
>   so that the thresholds shake.
> Bring them down on the heads of all the people;
>   those who are left I will kill with the sword.
> Not one will get away,
>   none will escape.
> ²Though they dig down to the depths below,
>   from there my hand will take them.
> Though they climb up to the heavens above,
>   from there I will bring them down.
> ³Though they hide themselves on the top of Carmel,
>   there I will hunt them down and seize them.

1316

8:11–12 There are many things we take for granted— until we no longer have them. Things necessary to survival, such as food, water and air. Important things, such as friendships, meaningful work and good neighbors. The people of Israel took God's words for granted. Do you? Do you appreciate that God has communicated to you in a tangible way that you can hold in your hands? Do you value the freedom you have to hear God's Word taught? Don't forget that your freedom is a gift to be appreciated, not a universal right that you'll always have. How much do you really appreciate this gift?

---

a 14 Hebrew *the way*

Though they hide from my eyes at the bottom of the sea,
  there I will command the serpent to bite them.
⁴Though they are driven into exile by their enemies,
  there I will command the sword to slay them.

  "I will fix my eyes on them
  for evil and not for good."

⁵The Lord, the LORD Almighty—
he touches the earth and it melts,
  and all who live in it mourn;
the whole land rises like the Nile,
  then sinks like the river of Egypt;
⁶he builds his lofty palace*a* in the heavens
  and sets its foundation*b* on the earth;
he calls for the waters of the sea
  and pours them out over the face of the land—
  the LORD is his name.

⁷"Are not you Israelites
  the same to me as the Cushites*c*?"

declares the LORD.

  "Did I not bring Israel up from Egypt,
  the Philistines from Caphtor*d*
  and the Arameans from Kir?

⁸"Surely the eyes of the Sovereign LORD
  are on the sinful kingdom.
I will destroy it
  from the face of the earth.
Yet I will not totally destroy
  the house of Jacob,"

declares the LORD.

⁹"For I will give the command,
  and I will shake the house of Israel
  among all the nations
as grain is shaken in a sieve,
  and not a pebble will reach the ground.
¹⁰All the sinners among my people
  will die by the sword,
all those who say,
  'Disaster will not overtake or meet us.'

Israel's Restoration

¹¹"In that day

  I will restore David's fallen shelter—
  I will repair its broken walls
  and restore its ruins—
  and will rebuild it as it used to be,
¹²so that they may possess the remnant of Edom
  and all the nations that bear my name,*e*"

declares the LORD, who will do these things.

1317

---

a 6 The meaning of the Hebrew for this phrase is uncertain. *b* 6 The meaning of the Hebrew for this word is uncertain. *c* 7 That is, people from the upper Nile region *d* 7 That is, Crete *e* 12 Hebrew; Septuagint *so that the remnant of people / and all the nations that bear my name may seek* the Lord

obadiah

1319

AUTHOR
Obadiah.

AUDIENCE
The Edomites, Judah and all of God's
people.

DATE
Probably during the Babylonian attacks on
Jerusalem (605–586 B.C.)

SETTING
The Edomites, who were descendants of
Esau and related to the Israelites, were
harassing the people of Israel.

VERSE TO REMEMBER
"The pride of your heart has deceived you,
you who live in the clefts of the rocks and
make your home on the heights, you who
say to yourself, 'Who can bring me down to
the ground?' " (3)

THEME TO CONSIDER
Watch out—picking on God's people gets
his attention!

¹The vision of Obadiah.

This is what the Sovereign Lord says about Edom—

> We have heard a message from the Lord:
> > An envoy was sent to the nations to say,
> > "Rise, let us go against her for battle"—

²"See, I will make you small among the
> > nations;
> > you will be utterly despised.
³The pride of your heart has deceived
> > you,
> > you who live in the clefts of the rocks[a]
> > and make your home on the heights,
> you who say to yourself,
> > 'Who can bring me down to the
> > ground?'
⁴Though you soar like the eagle
> > and make your nest among the stars,
> > from there I will bring you down,"
> > > declares the Lord.
⁵"If thieves came to you,
> > if robbers in the night—
> oh, what a disaster awaits you—
> > would they not steal only as much as
> > they wanted?
> If grape pickers came to you,
> > would they not leave a few grapes?
⁶But how Esau will be ransacked,
> > his hidden treasures pillaged!
⁷All your allies will force you to the
> > border;
> > your friends will deceive and
> > overpower you;
> those who eat your bread will set a trap for you,[b]
> > but you will not detect it.

⁸"In that day," declares the Lord,
> > "will I not destroy the wise in Edom,
> > people of understanding in the mountains of Esau?
⁹Your warriors, Teman, will be terrified,
> > and everyone in Esau's mountains
> > will be cut down in the slaughter.
¹⁰Because of the violence against your brother Jacob,
> > you will be covered with shame;
> > you will be destroyed forever.
¹¹On the day you stood aloof
> > while strangers carried off his wealth
> and foreigners entered his gates
> > and cast lots for Jerusalem,
> > you were like one of them.

1320

atissue:pride

3–4 We can be deceived by many things in life—the media, advertisements, other people. But the worst kind of deceit is self-deceit. Our pride tells us lies—delectable, addictive lies: *My life is secure. I've earned all these good things. I deserve this. I will always have this good of a life.* Like the Edomites who had a seemingly impenetrable rock fortress, you may believe that your good life and good fortune are invincible. But at any moment, you could lose everything. However, when you put your security in God alone, then you cannot lose the good life you have; no one can take it from you.

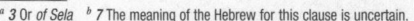

ᵃ 3 Or of Sela *ᵇ 7 The meaning of the Hebrew for this clause is uncertain.*

¹²You should not gloat over your brother
in the day of his misfortune,
nor rejoice over the people of Judah
in the day of their destruction,
nor boast so much
in the day of their trouble.
¹³You should not march through the gates
of my people
in the day of their disaster,
nor gloat over them in their calamity
in the day of their disaster,
nor seize their wealth
in the day of their disaster.
¹⁴You should not wait at the crossroads
to cut down their fugitives,
nor hand over their survivors
in the day of their trouble.

¹⁵"The day of the LORD is near
for all nations.
As you have done, it will be done to you;
your deeds will return upon your own head.
¹⁶Just as you drank on my holy hill,
so all the nations will drink continually;
they will drink and drink
and be as if they had never been.
¹⁷But on Mount Zion will be deliverance;
it will be holy,
and the house of Jacob
will possess its inheritance.
¹⁸The house of Jacob will be a fire
and the house of Joseph a flame;
the house of Esau will be stubble,
and they will set it on fire and consume it.
There will be no survivors
from the house of Esau."

The LORD has spoken.

¹⁹People from the Negev will occupy
the mountains of Esau,
and people from the foothills will possess
the land of the Philistines.
They will occupy the fields of Ephraim and Samaria,
and Benjamin will possess Gilead.
²⁰This company of Israelite exiles who are in Canaan
will possess ⌊the land⌋ as far as Zarephath;
the exiles from Jerusalem who are in Sepharad
will possess the towns of the Negev.
²¹Deliverers will go up on^a Mount Zion
to govern the mountains of Esau.
And the kingdom will be the LORD's.

conversations

revenge «» 12–14

1» Why do you think God forbids gloating over others when they get what they deserve?

2» What are several ways you can short-circuit feelings of revenge?

3» How can you deliberately do good to someone who's hurt you?

For more on **revenge**, check the index.
For the next Conversations, go to p. 1325.

1321

---

^a 21 Or from

jonah

AUTHOR
Jonah.

AUDIENCE
Israel and all of God's people.

DATE
Probably about 785–750 B.C.

SETTING
God sends a reluctant Jonah to Nineveh, the
capital city of the dreaded nation of Assyria,
to preach repentance.

VERSE TO REMEMBER
"And should I not have concern for the great
city Nineveh, in which there are more than a
hundred and twenty thousand people who
cannot tell their right hand from their left—
and also many animals?" (4:11)

THEME TO CONSIDER
Too easily we grow indignant and calloused
toward the wicked. In contrast, God has
great compassion for them.

Jonah Flees From the Lord

1 The word of the Lord came to Jonah son of Amittai: ²"Go to the great city Nineveh and preach against it, because its wickedness has come up before me."

³But Jonah ran away from the Lord and headed for Tarshish. He went down to Joppa, where he found a ship bound for that port. After paying the fare, he went aboard and sailed for Tarshish to flee from the Lord.

⁴Then the Lord sent a great wind on the sea, and such a violent storm arose that the ship threatened to break up. ⁵All the sailors were afraid and each cried out to his own god. And they threw the cargo into the sea to lighten the ship.

But Jonah had gone below deck, where he lay down and fell into a deep sleep. ⁶The captain went to him and said, "How can you sleep? Get up and call on your god! Maybe he will take notice of us so that we will not perish."

⁷Then the sailors said to each other, "Come, let us cast lots to find out who is responsible for this calamity." They cast lots and the lot fell on Jonah. ⁸So they asked him, "Tell us, who is responsible for making all this trouble for us? What kind of work do you do? Where do you come from? What is your country? From what people are you?"

⁹He answered, "I am a Hebrew and I worship the Lord, the God of heaven, who made the sea and the dry land."

¹⁰This terrified them and they asked, "What have you done?" (They knew he was running away from the Lord, because he had already told them so.)

1323

HE IS: inescapable

1:3–10 Defying God's orders to preach against Nineveh, Jonah ran the opposite direction. But with a fierce storm and a huge fish, God prevented Jonah from getting away from him. Jonah found he could try to run, but he couldn't escape the call of God.

He is *inescapable*. You may think you've outrun God, heading in the opposite direction from the path he's mapped out for you. But there is nowhere you can hide from the presence of God. You cannot ignore him forever. He will search the highest mountains and the deepest oceans to bring you back.

For the next He Is, go to p. 1338.

¹¹The sea was getting rougher and rougher. So they asked him, "What should we do to you to make the sea calm down for us?"

¹²"Pick me up and throw me into the sea," he replied, "and it will become calm. I know that it is my fault that this great storm has come upon you."

¹³Instead, the men did their best to row back to land. But they could not, for the sea grew even wilder than before. ¹⁴Then they cried out to the Lord, "Please, Lord, do not let us die for taking this man's life. Do not hold us accountable for killing an innocent man, for you, Lord, have done as you pleased." ¹⁵Then they took Jonah and threw him overboard, and the raging sea grew calm. ¹⁶At this the men greatly feared the Lord, and they offered a sacrifice to the Lord and made vows to him.

*¹⁷Now the Lord provided a huge fish to swallow Jonah, and Jonah was in the belly of the fish three days and three nights.

Jonah's Prayer

2 *From inside the fish Jonah prayed to the Lord his God. ²He said:

"In my distress I called to the Lord,
    and he answered me.

---

* 1:17 is numbered 2:1 in Hebrew texts.   * 2:1-10 is numbered 2:2-11 in Hebrew texts.

From deep in the realm of the dead I called for help,
  and you listened to my cry.
³You hurled me into the deep,
  into the very heart of the seas,
  and the currents swirled about me;
all your waves and breakers
  swept over me.
⁴I said, 'I have been banished
  from your sight;
yet I will look again
  toward your holy temple.'
⁵The engulfing waters threatened me,ᵃ
  the deep surrounded me;
  seaweed was wrapped around my
    head.
⁶To the roots of the mountains I sank
    down;
  the earth beneath barred me in
    forever.
But you, Lᴏʀᴅ my God,
  brought my life up from the pit.

⁷"When my life was ebbing away,
  I remembered you, Lᴏʀᴅ,
and my prayer rose to you,
  to your holy temple.

⁸"Those who cling to worthless idols
  forfeit God's love for them.
⁹But I, with shouts of grateful praise,
  will sacrifice to you.
What I have vowed I will make good.
  I will say, 'Salvation comes from the
    Lᴏʀᴅ.'"

atissue:idols

2:8 In what do you invest your time and money? What item holds the most cherished place in your life? To whom do you cling for security? Maybe it's your appearance, your beautiful home or your great job. Perhaps it's your relationship with your husband or boyfriend. It might be your friends, family or children. Those are all good things to invest in, but when they start taking God's place in your life, they become worthless idols. Clinging to them will only cause you to forfeit God's grace and all that could be yours if you held tight to God alone.

¹⁰And the Lᴏʀᴅ commanded the fish, and it vomited Jonah onto dry land.

Jonah Goes to Nineveh

3 Then the word of the Lᴏʀᴅ came to Jonah a second time: ²"Go to the great city of Nineveh and proclaim to it the message I give you."

³Jonah obeyed the word of the Lᴏʀᴅ and went to Nineveh. Now Nineveh was a very large city; it took three days to go through it. ⁴Jonah began by going a day's journey into the city, proclaiming, "Forty more days and Nineveh will be overthrown." ⁵The Ninevites believed God. They declared a fast, and all of them, from the greatest to the least, put on sackcloth.

⁶When the news reached the king of Nineveh, he rose from his throne, took off his royal robes, covered himself with sackcloth and sat down in the dust. ⁷Then he issued a proclamation in Nineveh:

"By the decree of the king and his nobles:

Do not let people or animals, herds or flocks, taste anything; do not let them eat or drink. ⁸But let people and animals be covered with sackcloth. Let everyone call urgently on God. Let them give up their evil ways and their violence. ⁹Who knows? God may yet relent and with compassion turn from his fierce anger so that we will not perish."

ᵃ 5 Or waters were at my throat

¹⁰When God saw what they did and how they turned from their evil ways, he relented and did not bring on them the destruction he had threatened.

Jonah's Anger at the LORD's Compassion

4 But to Jonah this seemed very wrong, and he became angry. ²He prayed to the LORD, "Isn't this what I said, LORD, when I was still at home? That is what I tried to forestall by fleeing to Tarshish. I knew that you are a gracious and compassionate God, slow to anger and abounding in love, a God who relents from sending calamity. ³Now, LORD, take away my life, for it is better for me to die than to live."

⁴But the LORD replied, "Is it right for you to be angry?"

⁵Jonah went out and sat down at a place east of the city. There he made himself a shelter, sat in its shade and waited to see what would happen to the city. ⁶Then the LORD God provided a gourdᵃ and made it grow up over Jonah to give shade for his head to ease his discomfort, and Jonah was very happy about the gourd. ⁷But at dawn the next day God provided a worm, which chewed the gourd so that it withered. ⁸When the sun rose, God provided a scorching east wind, and the sun blazed on Jonah's head so that he grew faint. He wanted to die, and said, "It would be better for me to die than to live."

⁹But God said to Jonah, "Is it right for you to be angry about the gourd?"

"It is," he said. "And I'm so angry I wish I were dead."

¹⁰But the LORD said, "You have been concerned about this gourd, though you did not tend it or make it grow. It sprang up overnight and died overnight. ¹¹And should I not have concern for the great city Nineveh, in which there are more than a hundred and twenty thousand people who cannot tell their right hand from their left—and also many animals?"

---

atissue:compassion

3:10—4:2 Let's count a few of the many ways God has shown you compassion. He's given you life and breath each day. If you belong to him, he's adopted you into his family and given you an eternal inheritance. He's forgiven your sin and made you righteous. He's been with you in both your joys and your sorrows. Now, with that in mind, ask God to open your eyes to see who he would have *you* show compassion to. Jonah failed to extend to the Ninevites the same compassion that God had shown to him. Don't repeat Jonah's mistake.

1325

"conversations"

anger at God «» 4:5–11

1» Is it ever OK to be angry with God? If so, when?

2» When have you felt angry with God? Why did you feel that way?

3» How can anger make you shortsighted?

For more on **anger at God**, check the index.
For the next Conversations, go to p. 1336.

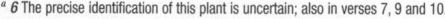

ᵃ *6* The precise identification of this plant is uncertain; also in verses 7, 9 and 10.

Why did Israel and Judah get into so much trouble? ➤ (1:5–7; 2:1–2; 3:1–4)

Who makes a surprise appearance in Micah's book of prophecy? ➤ (5:2–5)

After we repent, what does God do with our sins? ➤ (7:18–20)

micah

1326

AUTHOR
Micah.

AUDIENCE
The southern kingdom (Judah) and northern kingdom (Israel).

DATE
Likely between 742 and 687 B.C., during the time of Isaiah and Hosea.

SETTING
Political mayhem has the kingdoms reeling from one bad king to another. Micah steps in to prophesy judgment.

VERSE TO REMEMBER
"Who is a God like you, who pardons sin and forgives the transgression of the remnant of his inheritance? You do not stay angry forever but delight to show mercy." (7:18)

THEME TO CONSIDER
What God wants is simple: justice, mercy and humility.

1 The word of the LORD that came to Micah of Moresheth during the reigns of Jotham, Ahaz and
Hezekiah, kings of Judah—the vision he saw concerning Samaria and Jerusalem.

²Hear, you peoples, all of you,
    listen, earth and all who live in it,
that the Sovereign LORD may witness against you,
    the Lord from his holy temple.

Judgment Against Samaria and Jerusalem

³Look! The LORD is coming from his dwelling place;
    he comes down and treads on the heights of the earth.
⁴The mountains melt beneath him
    and the valleys split apart,
like wax before the fire,
    like water rushing down a slope.
⁵All this is because of Jacob's transgression,
    because of the sins of the house of Israel.
What is Jacob's transgression?
    Is it not Samaria?
What is Judah's high place?
    Is it not Jerusalem?

⁶"Therefore I will make Samaria a heap of rubble,
    a place for planting vineyards.
I will pour her stones into the valley
    and lay bare her foundations.
⁷All her idols will be broken to pieces;
    all her temple gifts will be burned with fire;
    I will destroy all her images.
Since she gathered her gifts from the wages of prostitutes,
    as the wages of prostitutes they will again be used."

Weeping and Mourning

⁸Because of this I will weep and wail;
    I will go about barefoot and naked.
I will howl like a jackal
    and moan like an owl.
⁹For Samaria's wound is incurable;
    it has come to Judah.
It has reached the very gate of my people,
    even to Jerusalem itself.
¹⁰Tell it not in Gath[a];
    weep not at all.
In Beth Ophrah[b]
    roll in the dust.
¹¹Pass on in nakedness and shame,
    you who live in Shaphir.[c]
Those who live in Zaanan[d]
    will not come out.
Beth Ezel is in mourning;
    its protection is taken from you.

---

[a] 10 Gath sounds like the Hebrew for tell. [b] 10 Beth Ophrah means house of dust. [c] 11 Shaphir means pleasant. [d] 11 Zaanan sounds like the Hebrew for come out.

¹²Those who live in Maroth *ᵃ* writhe in pain,
    waiting for relief,
because disaster has come from the LORD,
    even to the gate of Jerusalem.
¹³You who live in Lachish, *ᵇ*
    harness the team to the chariot.
You were the beginning of sin
    to Daughter Zion,
for the transgressions of Israel
    were found in you.
¹⁴Therefore you will give parting gifts
    to Moresheth Gath.
The town of Akzib *ᶜ* will prove deceptive
    to the kings of Israel.
¹⁵I will bring a conqueror against you
    who live in Mareshah. *ᵈ*
The nobles of Israel
    will flee to Adullam.
¹⁶Shave your head in mourning
    for the children in whom you delight;
make yourself as bald as the vulture,
    for they will go from you into exile.

Human Plans and God's Plans

2 Woe to those who plan iniquity,
    to those who plot evil on their beds!
At morning's light they carry it out
    because it is in their power to do it.
²They covet fields and seize them,
    and houses, and take them.
They defraud people of their homes,
    they rob them of their inheritance.

³Therefore, the LORD says:

"I am planning disaster against this
        people,
    from which you cannot save
        yourselves.
You will no longer walk proudly,
    for it will be a time of calamity.
⁴In that day people will ridicule you;
    they will taunt you with this
        mournful song:
'We are utterly ruined;
    my people's possession is divided up.
He takes it from me!
    He assigns our fields to traitors.'"

⁵Therefore you will have no one in the
        assembly of the LORD
    to divide the land by lot.

2:1–5 The old saying "might makes right" too often holds true. When people have the power to do something, they think that gives them the right to do it. If powerful people want something, they get it, one way or another. We see this abuse of power everywhere—from government to the medical community to Hollywood to big business. But that's not God's way. His is the way of selflessness and denial, of compassion and generosity. His way means using your power to stand up to injustice and show kindness even to those who don't deserve it. Will you make *his* way *your* way?

ᵃ 12 Maroth sounds like the Hebrew for *bitter.* *ᵇ 13 Lachish* sounds like the Hebrew for *team.* *ᶜ 14 Akzib* means *deception.* *ᵈ 15 Mareshah* sounds like the Hebrew for *conqueror.*

False Prophets

⁶"Do not prophesy," their prophets say.
  "Do not prophesy about these things;
    disgrace will not overtake us."
⁷House of Jacob, should it be said,
  "Does the Lord become^a impatient?
  Does he do such things?"

  "Do not my words do good
    to those whose ways are upright?
⁸Lately my people have risen up
    like an enemy.
  You strip off the rich robe
    from those who pass by without a care,
    like men returning from battle.
⁹You drive the women of my people
    from their pleasant homes.
  You take away my blessing
    from their children forever.
¹⁰Get up, go away!
    For this is not your resting place,
  because it is defiled,
    it is ruined, beyond all remedy.
¹¹If liars and deceivers come and say,
    'We will prophesy for you plenty of wine and beer,'
    they would be just the prophets for this people!

Deliverance Promised

¹²"I will surely gather all of you, Jacob;
    I will surely bring together the remnant of Israel.
  I will bring them together like sheep in a pen,
    like a flock in its pasture;
    the place will throng with people.
¹³One who breaks open the way will go up before them;
    they will break through the gate and go out.
  Their King will pass through before them,
    the Lord at their head."

Leaders and Prophets Rebuked

3 Then I said,

  "Listen, you leaders of Jacob,
    you rulers of the house of Israel.
  Should you not know justice,
²   you who hate good and love evil;
  who tear the skin from my people
    and the flesh from their bones;
³who eat my people's flesh,
    strip off their skin
    and break their bones in pieces;
  who chop them up like meat for the pan,
    like flesh for the pot?"

^a 7 Or Is the Spirit of the Lord

⁴Then they will cry out to the Lord,
   but he will not answer them.
At that time he will hide his face from them
   because of the evil they have done.

⁵This is what the Lord says:

   "As for the prophets
      who lead my people astray,
   if you feed them,
      they proclaim 'peace';
   if you do not,
      they prepare to wage war against you.
⁶Therefore night will come over you, without visions,
      and darkness, without divination.
   The sun will set for the prophets,
      and the day will go dark for them.
⁷The seers will be ashamed
      and the diviners disgraced.
   They will all cover their faces
      because there is no answer from God."
⁸But as for me, I am filled with power,
      with the Spirit of the Lord,
   and with justice and might,
   to declare to Jacob his transgression,
      to Israel his sin.

⁹Hear this, you leaders of the house of Jacob,
      you rulers of the house of Israel,
   who despise justice
      and distort all that is right;
¹⁰who build Zion with bloodshed,
      and Jerusalem with wickedness.
¹¹Her leaders judge for a bribe,
      her priests teach for a price,
      and her prophets tell fortunes for money.
   Yet they lean upon the Lord and say,
      "Is not the Lord among us?
      No disaster will come upon us."
¹²Therefore because of you,
      Zion will be plowed like a field,
   Jerusalem will become a heap of rubble,
      the temple hill a mound overgrown with thickets.

The Mountain of the Lord

4 In the last days

      the mountain of the Lord's temple will be established
         as chief among the mountains;
      it will be raised above the hills,
         and peoples will stream to it.

²Many nations will come and say,

1330

"Come, let us go up to the mountain of the LORD,
    to the house of the God of Jacob.
He will teach us his ways,
    so that we may walk in his paths."
The law will go out from Zion,
    the word of the LORD from Jerusalem.
³He will judge between many peoples
    and will settle disputes for strong nations far and wide.
They will beat their swords into plowshares
    and their spears into pruning hooks.
Nation will not take up sword against nation,
    nor will they train for war anymore.
⁴Everyone will sit under their own vine
    and under their own fig tree,
and no one will make them afraid,
    for the LORD Almighty has spoken.
⁵All the nations may walk
    in the name of their gods;
we will walk in the name of the LORD
    our God for ever and ever.

The LORD's Plan

⁶"In that day," declares the LORD,

"I will gather the lame;
    I will assemble the exiles
    and those I have brought to grief.
⁷I will make the lame a remnant,
    those driven away a strong nation.
The LORD will rule over them in Mount
    Zion
    from that day and forever.
⁸As for you, watchtower of the flock,
    stronghold*ᵃ* of Daughter Zion,
the former dominion will be restored to
    you;
    kingship will come to Daughter
    Jerusalem."

⁹Why do you now cry aloud—
    have you no king*ᵇ*?
Has your ruler*ᶜ* perished,
    that pain seizes you like that of a woman
    in labor?
¹⁰Writhe in agony, Daughter Zion,
    like a woman in labor,
for now you must leave the city
    to camp in the open field.
You will go to Babylon;
    there you will be rescued.
There the LORD will redeem you
    out of the hand of your enemies.

atissue:brokenness

4:6–8 We are broken people—lame, exiled and grieving—some of us physically, others of us emotionally, all of us spiritually. Over time the trials of life beat us down and force us to choose: Is following God worth it, despite the pain, or will we abandon God and turn away from him? Though your past may be depressing and your present bleak, your future is hopeful if you are God's. As you look forward to what God has for you, you'll find encouragement to persevere. When trials bring you to that fork in the road, what will you choose?

ᵃ 8 Or hill   *ᵇ* 9 Or King   *ᶜ* 9 Or Ruler

¹¹But now many nations
    are gathered against you.
They say, "Let her be defiled,
    let our eyes gloat over Zion!"
¹²But they do not know
    the thoughts of the Lord;
they do not understand his plan,
    he who gathers them like sheaves to the threshing floor.
¹³"Rise and thresh, Daughter Zion,
    for I will give you horns of iron;
I will give you hooves of bronze,
    and you will break to pieces many nations."
You will devote their ill-gotten gains to the Lord,
    their wealth to the Lord of all the earth.

A Promised Ruler From Bethlehem

5 *Marshal your troops now, city of troops,
    for a siege is laid against us.
They will strike Israel's ruler
    on the cheek with a rod.

*²"But you, Bethlehem Ephrathah,
    though you are small among the clans^a of Judah,
out of you will come for me
    one who will be ruler over Israel,
whose origins are from of old,
    from ancient times."

³Therefore Israel will be abandoned
    until the time when she who is in labor gives birth
and the rest of his brothers return
    to join the Israelites.

⁴He will stand and shepherd his flock
    in the strength of the Lord,
    in the majesty of the name of the Lord his God.
And they will live securely, for then his greatness
    will reach to the ends of the earth.

⁵And he will be our peace
    when the Assyrians invade our land
    and march through our fortresses.
We will raise against them seven shepherds,
    even eight commanders,
⁶who will rule^b the land of Assyria with the sword,
    the land of Nimrod with drawn sword.^c
He will deliver us from the Assyrians
    when they invade our land
    and march into our borders.

⁷The remnant of Jacob will be
    in the midst of many peoples

---

^a 2 Or rulers   ^b 6 Or crush   ^c 6 Or Nimrod in its gates

* 5:1 is numbered 4:14 in Hebrew texts.   * 5:2-15 is numbered 5:1-14 in Hebrew texts.

like dew from the LORD,
    like showers on the grass,
which do not wait for mortals
    or depend on any human being.
⁸The remnant of Jacob will be among the nations,
    in the midst of many peoples,
like a lion among the beasts of the forest,
    like a young lion among flocks of sheep,
which mauls and mangles as it goes,
    and no one can rescue.
⁹Your hand will be lifted up in triumph over your enemies,
    and all your foes will be destroyed.

¹⁰"In that day," declares the LORD,

"I will destroy your horses from among you
    and demolish your chariots.
¹¹I will destroy the cities of your land
    and tear down all your strongholds.
¹²I will destroy your witchcraft
    and you will no longer cast spells.
¹³I will destroy your idols
    and your sacred stones from among you;
you will no longer bow down
    to the work of your hands.
¹⁴I will uproot from among you your Asherah poles[a]
    when I demolish your cities.
¹⁵I will take vengeance in anger and wrath
    on the nations that have not obeyed me."

The LORD's Case Against Israel

6 Listen to what the LORD says:

"Stand up, plead my case before the mountains;
    let the hills hear what you have to say.

²"Hear, you mountains, the LORD's accusation;
    listen, you everlasting foundations of the earth.
For the LORD has a case against his people;
    he is lodging a charge against Israel.

³"My people, what have I done to you?
    How have I burdened you? Answer me.
⁴I brought you up out of Egypt
    and redeemed you from the land of slavery.
I sent Moses to lead you,
    also Aaron and Miriam.
⁵My people, remember
    what Balak king of Moab plotted
    and what Balaam son of Beor answered.
Remember your journey from Shittim to Gilgal,
    that you may know the righteous acts of the LORD."

---

a 14 That is, wooden symbols of the goddess Asherah

myth# 75 "LEAVE THE EVANGELISM TO PASTORS AND MISSIONARIES."

My pastor always asks us who we've shared the gospel with this week. I'm tired of being asked that. I mean, isn't that his job? Isn't that why we have full-time missionaries? Isn't that what I give my money to support? Those people are professionals, and they're trained in how to share their faith. Me? I come across as awkward and nervous. I can't just start a conversation with someone and ask if she believes in Jesus. That's so not me. I'm not outgoing at all, and I don't like to intrude into people's personal lives.

The leader of my Bible study said, "If you're not sharing your faith, then do you really have faith?" I resented that remark. Didn't Jesus say the greatest commandment was to love God and others? We all do that in different ways. My spiritual gift is hospitality, so I open my home to others. In fact, I recently hosted a missionary family while they were on furlough. If that's not showing love, I don't know what is (they had three small children!).

I've been a Christian for as long as I can remember. I know I'm not bold or outspoken. Quite frankly, I don't believe God demands that we walk up to strangers and force them to listen to the gospel or take a tract. I could never do that anyway! Isn't that what people in those other religions (Jehovah's Witnesses, maybe) do? Isn't that trying to earn your salvation? Doesn't the Bible warn against that?

—Donna

HOW WOULD YOU complete the following statement?

When Jesus said, "Go and make disciples" (Matthew 28:19), he was talking to . . .

A. The 11 remaining disciples.

B. Pastors, missionaries and those in full-time ministry.

C. Anyone who believes in him.

If you polled a group of believers, most Christians would answer C. We *say* that evangelism is something we all *should* do (with an emphasis on the word *should*), but do we really believe that? Sadly many Christians rarely or never tell others about Jesus. Why are many of us so hesitant to share the Good News with others?

Some people are content to believe that pastors and missionaries are better at evangelism because "that's their job."

Some Christians avoid sharing their faith out of fear of rejection or persecution. Jesus never promised that believers *wouldn't* experience persecution. In fact, he guaranteed we would: "In this world you will have trouble" (John 16:33).

Others look askance at evangelism because they think of it as an invasive, uncomfortable experience. They cringe at the thought of handing out tracts or explaining with color illustrations "The Four Spiritual Laws."

But evangelism in its purest form is simply sharing Good News with someone, anyone—the Good News of what Jesus has done in your life. No theological arguments or polished talks necessary. Evangelism is a *partnership* between you and the Holy Spirit. Before Jesus left the earth, he promised to send the Holy Spirit, who would "teach you all things and will remind you of everything [Jesus said]" (John 14:26). You're not on your own. The Holy Spirit helps you know what to say and how to say it when an evangelism opportunity arises and you take it.

Evangelism is also more than just words. It's about how you live your life, consistently and with love. And what you will discover (if you haven't yet) is that sharing the Good News of Jesus Christ will be one of the most exhilarating, rewarding experiences of your life. For more information, read the article, "Your Most Powerful Possession; Using Your Personal Testimony to Touch Others" on page 1796.

1335

"76 percent of born again Christians believe they 'personally have a responsibility to tell other people their religious beliefs.' "

—Barna Research Group (2001)

"GO AND MAKE DISCIPLES OF ALL NATIONS."

MATTHEW 28:19

SEE ALSO

Matthew 10:17–20
Romans 1:16
1 Peter 3:15

For more on **Evangelism**, check the index.

⁶With what shall I come before the LORD
and bow down before the exalted God?
Shall I come before him with burnt offerings,
with calves a year old?
⁷Will the LORD be pleased with
thousands of rams,
with ten thousand rivers of
olive oil?
Shall I offer my firstborn for
my transgression,
the fruit of my body for the
sin of my soul?
⁸He has shown all you people
what is good.
And what does the LORD
require of you?
To act justly and to love mercy
and to walk humbly^a with
your God.

conversations
attitudes «» 6:8

1» Throughout your life, how have you tried to please God?

2» Which is more important—your attitude or your actions? Why?

3» What does it mean to act justly, love mercy and walk humbly with your God?

For more on **attitudes**, check the index.
For the next Conversations, go to p. 1341.

Israel's Guilt and Punishment

⁹Listen! The LORD is calling to the city—
and to fear your name is wisdom—
"Heed the rod and the One who appointed it.^b
¹⁰Am I still to forget your ill-gotten treasures, you wicked house,
and the short ephah,^c which is accursed?
¹¹Shall I acquit a person with dishonest scales,
with a bag of false weights?
¹²Her rich people are violent;
her inhabitants are liars
and their tongues speak deceitfully.
¹³Therefore, I have begun to destroy you,
to ruin^d you because of your sins.
¹⁴You will eat but not be satisfied;
your stomach will still be empty.^e
You will store up but save nothing,
because what you save^f I will give to the sword.
¹⁵You will plant but not harvest;
you will press olives but not use the oil on yourselves,
you will crush grapes but not drink the wine.
¹⁶You have observed the statutes of Omri
and all the practices of Ahab's house;
you have followed their traditions.
Therefore I will give you over to ruin
and your people to derision;
you will bear the scorn of the nations.^g"

Israel's Misery

7 What misery is mine!
I am like one who gathers summer fruit

---

^a **8** Or *prudently* ^b **9** The meaning of the Hebrew for this line is uncertain. ^c **10** An ephah was a dry measure. ^d **13** Or *Therefore, I will make you ill and destroy you; / I will ruin* ^e **14** The meaning of the Hebrew for this word is uncertain. ^f **14** Or *You will press toward birth but not give birth, / and what you bring to birth* ^g **16** Septuagint; Hebrew *scorn due my people*

at the gleaning of the vineyard;
  there is no cluster of grapes to eat,
    none of the early figs that I crave.
[2] The faithful have been swept from the land;
  not one upright person remains.
Everyone lies in wait to shed blood;
  they hunt each other with nets.
[3] Both hands are skilled in doing evil;
  the ruler demands gifts,
the judge accepts bribes,
  the powerful dictate what they desire—
  they all conspire together.
[4] The best of them is like a brier,
  the most upright worse than a thorn hedge.
The day of your watchmen has come,
  the day God visits you.
  Now is the time of their confusion.
[5] Do not trust a neighbor;
  put no confidence in a friend.
Even with the woman who lies in your embrace
  be careful of your words.
[6] For a son dishonors his father,
  a daughter rises up against her mother,
a daughter-in-law against her mother-in-law—
  your enemies are the members of your own household.

[7] But as for me, I watch in hope for the Lord,
  I wait for God my Savior;
  my God will hear me.

Israel Will Rise

[8] Do not gloat over me, my enemy!
  Though I have fallen, I will rise.
Though I sit in darkness,
  the Lord will be my light.
[9] Because I have sinned against him,
  I will bear the Lord's wrath,
until he pleads my case
  and establishes my right.
He will bring me out into the light;
  I will see his righteousness.
[10] Then my enemy will see it
  and will be covered with shame,
she who said to me,
  "Where is the Lord your God?"
My eyes will see her downfall;
  even now she will be trampled underfoot
  like mire in the streets.

[11] The day for building your walls will come,
  the day for extending your boundaries.
[12] In that day people will come to you
  from Assyria and the cities of Egypt,

1337

even from Egypt to the Euphrates
and from sea to sea
and from mountain to mountain.
¹³The earth will become desolate because of its inhabitants,
as the result of their deeds.

Prayer and Praise

¹⁴Shepherd your people with your staff,
the flock of your inheritance,
which lives by itself in a forest,
in fertile pasturelands.*
Let them feed in Bashan and Gilead
as in days long ago.

¹⁵"As in the days when you came out of Egypt,
I will show them my wonders."

¹⁶Nations will see and be ashamed,
deprived of all their power.
They will put their hands over their mouths
and their ears will become deaf.
¹⁷They will lick dust like a snake,
like creatures that crawl on the ground.
They will come trembling out of their dens;
they will turn in fear to the Lord our God
and will be afraid of you.
¹⁸Who is a God like you,
who pardons sin and forgives the transgression
of the remnant of his inheritance?
You do not stay angry forever
but delight to show mercy.
¹⁹You will again have compassion on us;
you will tread our sins underfoot
and hurl all our iniquities into the depths of the sea.
²⁰You will be faithful to Jacob,
and show love to Abraham,
as you pledged on oath to our ancestors
in days long ago.

---

a 14 Or in the middle of Carmel

HE IS: unique

7:18–19 Micah's rhetorical question, "Who is a God like you?" begs the answer, "No one!" God is *unique*. Only God pardons sin. Only God hurls our sins far from us, into the deepest part of the ocean. All other gods are counterfeits, making false claims and promises.

What counterfeit gods have you sought to fulfill your needs? Have you looked to the almighty dollar to find status? To pleasing people to gain acceptance? To intellectual enterprises to appear wise? These false gods are hard taskmasters, never satisfied, always demanding more. Only God has compassion. He is *unique* and always willing to show mercy.

For the next He Is, go to p. 1340.

What does God reveal about himself
in the book of Nahum? ≫ (1:2–8)

What event would headline Judah's
morning papers? ≫ (1:15—2:2)

How would surrounding nations
react to the news? ≫ (3:19)

nahum

AUTHOR
Nahum.

AUDIENCE
The residents of Nineveh and Judah.

DATE
Likely written shortly before the fall of
Nineveh in 612 B.C.

SETTING
Assyria had just conquered the Egyptian
city of Thebes in 663 B.C. (see 3:8–10), and
Judah seemed to be next. However, Assyria
would fall in 612 B.C.

VERSE TO REMEMBER
"The LORD is good, a refuge in times of
trouble. He cares for those who trust in
him." (1:7)

THEME TO CONSIDER
Read this book and take heart. Injustice,
rebellion, cruelty and disobedience will not
go unpunished.

nahum 1:1

1 A prophecy concerning Nineveh. The book of the vision of Nahum the Elkoshite.

The Lord's Anger Against Nineveh

²The Lord is a jealous and avenging God;
    the Lord takes vengeance and is filled with wrath.
The Lord takes vengeance on his foes
    and vents his wrath against his enemies.
³The Lord is slow to anger but great in power;
    the Lord will not leave the guilty unpunished.
His way is in the whirlwind and the storm,
    and clouds are the dust of his feet.

HE IS: slow to anger

1:2–3 Pronouncing impending judgment on Nineveh, Nahum reminded the people that the Lord is *slow to anger*. God had shown mercy to Nineveh 150 years earlier when the people repented in response to Jonah's warnings. But the Lord won't leave the guilty unpunished. Though he waits, his judgment is sure.

Aren't you glad he is *slow to anger*? If he weren't, he might have judged you before you became a Christian. Fortunately, God doesn't want anyone to die (see Jonah 4:2–3). He wants everyone to have a chance to come to him. How willing are you to exhibit this kind of patience with those who mistreat you?

For the next He Is, go to p. 1350.

⁴He rebukes the sea and dries it up;
    he makes all the rivers run dry.
Bashan and Carmel wither
    and the blossoms of Lebanon fade.
⁵The mountains quake before him
    and the hills melt away.
The earth trembles at his presence,
    the world and all who live in it.
⁶Who can withstand his indignation?
    Who can endure his fierce anger?
His wrath is poured out like fire;
    the rocks are shattered before him.

⁷The Lord is good,
    a refuge in times of trouble.
He cares for those who trust in him,
⁸   but with an overwhelming flood
he will make an end of Nineveh;
    he will pursue his foes into darkness.

⁹Whatever they plot against the Lord
    he*a* will bring to an end;
    trouble will not come a second time.
¹⁰They will be entangled among thorns

---

a 9 Or What do you foes plot against the Lord? / He

⁵Nineveh summons her picked troops,
   yet they stumble on their way.
They dash to the city wall;
   the protective shield is put in place.
⁶The river gates are thrown open
   and the palace collapses.
⁷It is decreed*a* that Nineveh
   be exiled and carried away.
Her female slaves moan like doves
   and beat on their breasts.
⁸Nineveh is like a pool
   whose water is draining away.
"Stop! Stop!" they cry,
   but no one turns back.
⁹Plunder the silver!
   Plunder the gold!
The supply is endless,
   the wealth from all its treasures!
¹⁰She is pillaged, plundered, stripped!
   Hearts melt, knees give way,
   bodies tremble, every face grows pale.

¹¹Where now is the lions' den,
   the place where they fed their young,
where the lion and lioness went,
   and the cubs, with nothing to fear?
¹²The lion killed enough for his cubs
   and strangled the prey for his mate,
filling his lairs with the kill
   and his dens with the prey.

¹³"I am against you,"
   declares the Lord Almighty.
"I will burn up your chariots in smoke,
   and the sword will devour your young lions.
I will leave you no prey on the earth.
The voices of your messengers
   will no longer be heard."

Woe to Nineveh

3 Woe to the city of blood,
   full of lies,
full of plunder,
   never without victims!
²The crack of whips,
   the clatter of wheels,
galloping horses
   and jolting chariots!
³Charging cavalry,
   flashing swords
   and glittering spears!

---

a 7 The meaning of the Hebrew for this word is uncertain.

Many casualties,
    piles of dead,
bodies without number,
    people stumbling over the corpses—
⁴all because of the wanton lust of a prostitute,
    alluring, the mistress of sorceries,
who enslaved nations by her prostitution
    and peoples by her witchcraft.

⁵"I am against you," declares the Lord Almighty.
    "I will lift your skirts over your face.
I will show the nations your nakedness
    and the kingdoms your shame.
⁶I will pelt you with filth,
    I will treat you with contempt
    and make you a spectacle.
⁷All who see you will flee from you and say,
    'Nineveh is in ruins—who will mourn for her?'
    Where can I find anyone to comfort you?"

⁸Are you better than Thebes,
    situated on the Nile,
    with water around her?
The river was her defense,
    the waters her wall.
⁹Cush^a and Egypt were her boundless strength;
    Put and Libya were among her allies.
¹⁰Yet she was taken captive
    and went into exile.
Her infants were dashed to pieces
    at every street corner.
Lots were cast for her nobles,
    and all her great men were put in chains.
¹¹You too will become drunk;
    you will go into hiding
    and seek refuge from the enemy.

¹²All your fortresses are like fig trees
    with their first ripe fruit;
when they are shaken,
    the figs fall into the mouth of the eater.
¹³Look at your troops—
    they are all weaklings.
The gates of your land
    are wide open to your enemies;
    fire has consumed the bars of your gates.

¹⁴Draw water for the siege,
    strengthen your defenses!
Work the clay,
    tread the mortar,
    repair the brickwork!

^a *9* That is, the upper Nile region

¹⁵There the fire will consume you;
    the sword will cut you down—
    and it will devour you like a swarm of locusts.
Multiply like grasshoppers,
    multiply like locusts!
¹⁶You have increased the number of your merchants
    till they are more than the stars in the sky,
but like locusts they strip the land
    and then fly away.
¹⁷Your guards are like locusts,
    your officials like swarms of locusts
    that settle in the walls on a cold day—
but when the sun appears they fly away,
    and no one knows where.

¹⁸King of Assyria, your shepherds*a* slumber;
    your nobles lie down to rest.
Your people are scattered on the mountains
    with no one to gather them.
¹⁹Nothing can heal you;
    your wound is fatal.
All who hear the news about you
    clap their hands at your fall,
for who has not felt
    your endless cruelty?

---

a 18 That is, rulers

How long should you wait on God for an answer to your prayers? » (2:1–3)

How would this verse read if you rewrote the phrases in the terms of your life? » (3:17)

Could you then echo Habakkuk's resolution in this verse? » (3:18)

habakkuk

AUTHOR
Habakkuk.

AUDIENCE
The southern kingdom of Judah and all of God's people.

DATE
About 605 B.C.

SETTING
Babylon was about to destroy Judah.

VERSE TO REMEMBER
"LORD, I have heard of your fame; I stand in awe of your deeds, LORD. Renew them in our day, in our time make them known; in wrath remember mercy." (3:2)

THEME TO CONSIDER
Is God still trustworthy, even when all that we see points to the contrary? Habakkuk answers with a resounding yes!

1 The prophecy that Habakkuk the prophet received.

Habakkuk's Complaint

² How long, LORD, must I call for help,
 but you do not listen?
Or cry out to you, "Violence!"
 but you do not save?
³ Why do you make me look at
 injustice?
Why do you tolerate
 wrongdoing?
Destruction and violence are
 before me;
there is strife, and conflict
 abounds.
⁴ Therefore the law is
 paralyzed,
and justice never prevails.
The wicked hem in the
 righteous,
so that justice is perverted.

The LORD's Answer

⁵ "Look at the nations and watch—
 and be utterly amazed.
For I am going to do something in your days
 that you would not believe,
 even if you were told.
⁶ I am raising up the Babylonians,ᵃ
 that ruthless and impetuous people,
who sweep across the whole earth
 to seize dwellings not their own.
⁷ They are a feared and dreaded people;
 they are a law to themselves
 and promote their own honor.
⁸ Their horses are swifter than leopards,
 fiercer than wolves at dusk.
Their cavalry gallops headlong;
 their horsemen come from afar.
They fly like a vulture swooping to devour;
⁹ they all come bent on violence.
Their hordesᵇ advance like a desert wind
 and gather prisoners like sand.
¹⁰ They mock kings
 and scoff at rulers.
They laugh at all fortified cities;
 by building earthen ramps they capture them.
¹¹ Then they sweep past like the wind and go on—
 guilty people, whose own strength is their god."

conversations
prayer «» 1:1–11

1» When you pray, do you share with God your feelings or do you try to hide them? Why?

2» Why might God let a prayer for peace go unanswered?

3» In the midst of injustice, how can prayer preserve your hope?

For more on **prayer**, check the index.
For the next Conversations, go to p. 1356.

1346

ᵃ 6 Or *Chaldeans*   ᵇ 9 The meaning of the Hebrew for this word is uncertain.

Habakkuk's Second Complaint

¹²Lord, are you not from everlasting?
    My God, my Holy One, you^{*a*} will never die.
  You, Lord, have appointed them to execute judgment;
    you, my Rock, have ordained them to punish.
¹³Your eyes are too pure to look on evil;
    you cannot tolerate wrongdoing.
  Why then do you tolerate the treacherous?
    Why are you silent while the wicked
    swallow up those more righteous than themselves?
¹⁴You have made people like the fish in the sea,
    like the sea creatures that have no ruler.
¹⁵The wicked foe pulls all of them up with hooks,
    he catches them in his net,
  he gathers them up in his dragnet;
    and so he rejoices and is glad.
¹⁶Therefore he sacrifices to his net
    and burns incense to his dragnet,
  for by his net he lives in luxury
    and enjoys the choicest food.
¹⁷Is he to keep on emptying his net,
    destroying nations without mercy?

2

I will stand at my watch
    and station myself on the ramparts;
I will look to see what he will say to me,
    and what answer I am to give to this
        complaint.^{*b*}

The Lord's Answer

²Then the Lord replied:

"Write down the revelation
  and make it plain on tablets
  so that a herald^{*c*} may run with it.
³For the revelation awaits an appointed
    time;
  it speaks of the end
  and will not prove false.
Though it linger, wait for it;
  it^{*d*} will certainly come
  and will not delay.

⁴"See, he is puffed up;
  his desires are not upright—
  but the righteous will live by their
    faithfulness^{*e*}—
⁵indeed, wine betrays him;
  he is arrogant and never at rest.
Because he is as greedy as the grave
  and like death is never satisfied,

atissue:dissatisfaction

2:4 When I meet someone, then I'll be happy. When I'm engaged, then I'll be happy. When I'm married, then I'll be happy. When I have children, then I'll be happy. When I get the promotion, then I'll be happy. When I . . . When you live your life always looking for your happiness in "the next thing," you miss out on enjoying all the good things that are part of "right now." Instead, be one of the righteous who lives by faith. Walk faithfully with God every day of your life, and enjoy each gift he gives you now.

---

^{*a*} *12* An ancient Hebrew scribal tradition; Masoretic Text *we* ^{*b*} *1* Or *and what to answer when I am rebuked* ^{*c*} *2* Or *so that whoever reads it* ^{*d*} *3* Or *Though he linger, wait for him; / he* ^{*e*} *4* Or *faith*

he gathers to himself all the nations
and takes captive all the peoples.

[6] "Will not all of them taunt him with ridicule and scorn, saying,

"'Woe to him who piles up stolen goods
and makes himself wealthy by extortion!
How long must this go on?'
[7] Will not your creditors suddenly arise?
Will they not wake up and make you tremble?
Then you will become their prey.
[8] Because you have plundered many nations,
the peoples who are left will plunder you.
For you have shed human blood;
you have destroyed lands and cities and everyone in them.

[9] "Woe to him who builds his house by unjust gain,
setting his nest on high
to escape the clutches of ruin!
[10] You have plotted the ruin of many peoples,
shaming your own house and forfeiting your life.
[11] The stones of the wall will cry out,
and the beams of the woodwork will echo it.

[12] "Woe to him who builds a city with bloodshed
and establishes a town by injustice!
[13] Has not the LORD Almighty determined
that the people's labor is only fuel for the fire,
that the nations exhaust themselves for nothing?
[14] For the earth will be filled with the knowledge of the glory of the LORD
as the waters cover the sea.

[15] "Woe to him who gives drink to his neighbors,
pouring it from the wineskin till they are drunk,
so that he can gaze on their naked bodies!
[16] You will be filled with shame instead of glory.
Now it is your turn! Drink and let your nakedness be exposed[a]!
The cup from the LORD's right hand is coming around to you,
and disgrace will cover your glory.
[17] The violence you have done to Lebanon will overwhelm you,
and your destruction of animals will terrify you.
For you have shed human blood;
you have destroyed lands and cities and everyone in them.

[18] "Of what value is an idol that someone has carved?
Or an image that teaches lies?
For those who make them trust in their own creations;
they make idols that cannot speak.
[19] Woe to him who says to wood, 'Come to life!'
Or to lifeless stone, 'Wake up!'
Can it give guidance?
It is covered with gold and silver;
there is no breath in it."

---

a *16* Masoretic Text; Dead Sea Scrolls, Aquila, Vulgate and Syriac (see also Septuagint) *and stagger*

²⁰The L<small>ORD</small> is in his holy temple;
    let all the earth be silent before him.

Habakkuk's Prayer

3 A prayer of Habakkuk the prophet. On *shigionoth.*^a

²L<small>ORD</small>, I have heard of your fame;
    I stand in awe of your deeds, L<small>ORD</small>.
Renew them in our day,
    in our time make them known;
    in wrath remember mercy.

³God came from Teman,
    the Holy One from Mount Paran.^b
His glory covered the heavens
    and his praise filled the earth.
⁴His splendor was like the sunrise;
    rays flashed from his hand,
    where his power was hidden.
⁵Plague went before him;
    pestilence followed his steps.
⁶He stood, and shook the earth;
    he looked, and made the nations tremble.
The ancient mountains crumbled
    and the age-old hills collapsed—
    but he marches on forever.
⁷I saw the tents of Cushan in distress,
    the dwellings of Midian in anguish.

⁸Were you angry with the rivers, L<small>ORD</small>?
    Was your wrath against the streams?
Did you rage against the sea
    when you rode your horses
    and your chariots to victory?
⁹You uncovered your bow,
    you called for many arrows.
You split the earth with rivers;
¹⁰   the mountains saw you and writhed.
Torrents of water swept by;
    the deep roared
    and lifted its waves on high.

¹¹Sun and moon stood still in the heavens
    at the glint of your flying arrows,
    at the lightning of your flashing spear.
¹²In wrath you strode through the earth
    and in anger you threshed the nations.
¹³You came out to deliver your people,
    to save your anointed one.
You crushed the leader of the land of wickedness,
    you stripped him from head to foot.
¹⁴With his own spear you pierced his head

---

^a *1* Probably a literary or musical term   ^b *3* The Hebrew has *Selah* (a word of uncertain meaning) here and at the middle of verse 9 and at the end of verse 13.

when his warriors stormed out to scatter us,
gloating as though about to devour
the wretched who were in hiding.
¹⁵You trampled the sea with your horses,
churning the great waters.

¹⁶I heard and my heart pounded,
my lips quivered at the sound;
decay crept into my bones,
and my legs trembled.
Yet I will wait patiently for the day of calamity
to come on the nation invading us.
¹⁷Though the fig tree does not bud
and there are no grapes on the vines,
though the olive crop fails
and the fields produce no food,
though there are no sheep in the pen
and no cattle in the stalls,
¹⁸yet I will rejoice in the LORD,
I will be joyful in God my Savior.

¹⁹The Sovereign LORD is my strength;
he makes my feet like the feet of a deer,
he enables me to tread on the heights.

For the director of music. On my stringed instruments.

1350

HE IS: my strength

3:16–19 Knowing that the land faced devastation, Habakkuk set his mind on God rather than circumstances. He told himself, *I choose to be patient; I choose to rejoice—even when* (*not if*) *disaster comes.* With this perspective on life, he could confidently say that God was his *strength.*

Sometimes faith requires that we make a hard choice that contradicts what we can see. When the circumstances of your life look bad, remind yourself that God is in control. Like Habakkuk, you can *choose* to trust God. By making the choice to trust, you too can discover that God is *your strength.*

For the next He Is, go to p. 1357.

How useful will our hard-earned money be
on the great and terrible day of the Lord? ⟫ (1:17–18)

What was and is the only means of escape
from the coming judgment? ⟫ (2:1–3)

After that depressing prophecy of doom and gloom,
what hope is there for God's people? ⟫ (3:18–20)

zephaniah

AUTHOR
Zephaniah.

AUDIENCE
Judah and all nations.

DATE
Likely during the early years of the reign of
King Josiah (640–609 B.C.)

SETTING
Zephaniah's prophecy encouraged King
Josiah to bring spiritual reform to Judah.

VERSE TO REMEMBER
"The LORD your God is with you, the Mighty
Warrior who saves. He will take great
delight in you; in his love he will no longer
rebuke you, but will rejoice over you with
singing." (3:17)

THEME TO CONSIDER
Painful as it sometimes is, discipline is part
of God's greater plan for our lives.

zephaniah 1:1

1 The word of the Lord that came to Zephaniah son of Cushi, the son of Gedaliah, the son of Amariah, the son of Hezekiah, during the reign of Josiah son of Amon king of Judah:

Judgment on the Whole Earth in the Day of the Lord

2 "I will sweep away everything
    from the face of the earth,"

                                        declares the Lord.

3 "I will sweep away both people and animals;
    I will sweep away the birds in the sky
    and the fish in the sea—
    and the idols that cause the wicked to stumble."[a]

"When I destroy all people
    on the face of the earth,"

                                        declares the Lord,

4 "I will stretch out my hand against Judah
    and against all who live in Jerusalem.
I will destroy every remnant of Baal worship in this place,
    every remembrance of the idolatrous priests—
5 those who bow down on the roofs
    to worship the starry host,
those who bow down and swear by the Lord
    and who also swear by Molek,[b]
6 those who turn back from following the Lord
    and neither seek the Lord nor inquire of him."

7 Be silent before the Sovereign Lord,
    for the day of the Lord is near.
The Lord has prepared a sacrifice;
    he has consecrated those he has invited.

8 "On the day of the Lord's sacrifice
    I will punish the officials
    and the king's sons
and all those clad
    in foreign clothes.
9 On that day I will punish
    all who avoid stepping on the threshold,[c]
who fill the temple of their gods
    with violence and deceit.

10 "On that day,"
    declares the Lord,
"a cry will go up from the Fish Gate,
    wailing from the New Quarter,
    and a loud crash from the hills.
11 Wail, you who live in the market district[d];
    all your merchants will be wiped out,
    all who trade with[e] silver will be destroyed.
12 At that time I will search Jerusalem with lamps
    and punish those who are complacent,
    who are like wine left on its dregs,

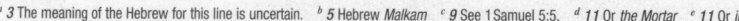

---

a 3 The meaning of the Hebrew for this line is uncertain. *b 5* Hebrew *Malkam* *c 9* See 1 Samuel 5:5. *d 11* Or *the Mortar* *e 11* Or *in*

who think, 'The Lord will do nothing,
    either good or bad.'
¹³Their wealth will be plundered,
    their houses demolished.
Though they build houses,
    they will not live in them;
though they plant vineyards,
    they will not drink the wine."

¹⁴The great day of the Lord is near—
    near and coming quickly.
The cry on the day of the Lord is bitter;
    the Mighty Warrior shouts his battle cry.
¹⁵That day will be a day of wrath—
    a day of distress and anguish,
      a day of trouble and ruin,
      a day of darkness and gloom,
      a day of clouds and blackness—
¹⁶   a day of trumpet and battle cry
against the fortified cities
    and against the corner towers.

¹⁷"I will bring such distress on all people
    that they will grope about like those who are blind,
    because they have sinned against the Lord.
Their blood will be poured out like dust
    and their entrails like dung.
¹⁸Neither their silver nor their gold
    will be able to save them
    on the day of the Lord's wrath."

In the fire of his jealousy
    the whole earth will be consumed,
for he will make a sudden end
    of all who live on the earth.

Judah and Jerusalem Judged Along With the Nations

Judah Summoned to Repent

2 Gather together, gather yourselves
      together,
    you shameful nation,
²before the decree takes effect
    and that day passes like windblown
      chaff,
before the Lord's fierce anger
    comes upon you,
before the day of the Lord's wrath
    comes upon you.
³Seek the Lord, all you humble of the land,
    you who do what he commands.
Seek righteousness, seek humility;
    perhaps you will be sheltered
    on the day of the Lord's anger.

1353

at issue: sin

2:1–3 Blowing off our sin is a full-time occupation for some of us. *I was wrong—oh well. I made a mistake—everyone does. I know I'm not perfect—but I'm not as bad as some other people I know.* In our attempts to assuage our guilty consciences, we lose sight of the fact that one "tiny" sin is enough for us to earn God's full, terrifying wrath. That's the bad news of what we've earned. The good news is what we've been given: full pardon, at the price of Jesus' death. Jesus gives us the only option for shelter on the day when God repays people for what they've done.

Philistia

⁴Gaza will be abandoned
    and Ashkelon left in ruins.
At midday Ashdod will be emptied
    and Ekron uprooted.
⁵Woe to you who live by the sea,
    you Kerethite people;
the word of the LORD is against you,
    Canaan, land of the Philistines.
He says, "I will destroy you,
    and none will be left."
⁶The land by the sea will become pastures
    having wells for shepherds
    and pens for flocks.
⁷That land will belong
    to the remnant of the house of Judah;
    there they will find pasture.
In the evening they will lie down
    in the houses of Ashkelon.
The LORD their God will care for them;
    he will restore their fortunes.ᵃ

Moab and Ammon

⁸"I have heard the insults of Moab
    and the taunts of the Ammonites,
who insulted my people
    and made threats against their land.
⁹Therefore, as surely as I live,"
    declares the LORD Almighty,
    the God of Israel,
"surely Moab will become like Sodom,
    the Ammonites like Gomorrah—
a place of weeds and salt pits,
    a wasteland forever.
The remnant of my people will plunder them;
    the survivors of my nation will inherit their land."

¹⁰This is what they will get in return for their pride,
    for insulting and mocking
    the people of the LORD Almighty.
¹¹The LORD will be awesome to them
    when he destroys all the gods of the earth.
Distant nations will bow down to him,
    all of them in their own lands.

Cush

¹²"You Cushites,ᵇ too,
    will be slain by my sword."

Assyria

¹³He will stretch out his hand against the north
    and destroy Assyria,

ᵃ 7 Or will bring back their captives   ᵇ 12 That is, people from the upper Nile region

leaving Nineveh utterly desolate
and dry as the desert.
[14]Flocks and herds will lie down there,
creatures of every kind.
The desert owl and the screech owl
will roost on her columns.
Their hooting will echo through the windows,
rubble will fill the doorways,
the beams of cedar will be exposed.
[15]This is the city of revelry
that lived in safety.
She said to herself,
"I am the one! And there is none besides me."
What a ruin she has become,
a lair for wild beasts!
All who pass by her scoff
and shake their fists.

Jerusalem

3

Woe to the city of oppressors,
rebellious and defiled!
[2]She obeys no one,
she accepts no correction.
She does not trust in the LORD,
she does not draw near to her God.
[3]Her officials within her
are roaring lions;
her rulers are evening wolves,
who leave nothing for the morning.
[4]Her prophets are unprincipled;
they cannot be trusted.
Her priests profane the sanctuary
and do violence to the law.
[5]The LORD within her is righteous;
he does no wrong.
Morning by morning he dispenses his justice,
and every new day he does not fail,
yet the unrighteous know no shame.

Jerusalem Remains Unrepentant

[6]"I have destroyed nations;
their strongholds are demolished.
I have left their streets deserted,
with no one passing through.
Their cities are laid waste;
they are deserted and empty.
[7]Of Jerusalem I thought,
'Surely you will fear me
and accept correction!'
Then her place of refuge[a] would not be destroyed,
nor all my punishments come upon[b] her.

1355

But they were still eager
   to act corruptly in all they did.
⁸"Therefore wait for me,"
   declares the Lord,
   "for the day I will stand up to testify.ᵃ
I have decided to assemble the nations,
   to gather the kingdoms
and to pour out my wrath on them—
   all my fierce anger.
The whole world will be consumed
   by the fire of my jealous anger.

Restoration of Israel's Remnant

⁹"Then I will purify the lips of the peoples,
   that all of them may call on the name of the Lord
   and serve him shoulder to shoulder.
¹⁰From beyond the rivers of Cushᵇ
   my worshipers, my scattered people,
   will bring me offerings.
¹¹On that day you, Jerusalem, will not be put to shame
   for all the wrongs you have done to me,
because I will remove from you
   those who revel in your glory.
Never again will you be haughty
   on my holy hill.
¹²But I will leave within you
   the meek and humble.
The remnant of Israel
   will trust in the name of the Lord.
¹³They will do no wrong;
   they will tell no lies.
A deceitful tongue
   will not be found in their
     mouths.
They will eat and lie down
   and no one will make them
     afraid."

¹⁴Sing, Daughter Zion;
   shout aloud, Israel!
Be glad and rejoice with all
     your heart,
   Daughter Jerusalem!
¹⁵The Lord has taken away your
     punishment,
   he has turned back your
     enemy.
The Lord, the King of Israel, is with you;
   never again will you fear any harm.
¹⁶On that day
   they will say to Jerusalem,

conversations

lying «» 3:13

1» Why does God hate lying?

2» Is there a type of lie that you most commonly fall into (exaggeration, denial, etc.)? If so, why?

3» Is it possible to avoid suffering in this life by the way you live?

For more on **lying**, check the index.
For the next Conversations, go to p. 1359.

ᵃ 8 Septuagint and Syriac; Hebrew *will rise up to plunder* ᵇ 10 That is, the upper Nile region

"Do not fear, Zion;
    do not let your hands hang limp.
¹⁷ The LORD your God is with you,
    the Mighty Warrior who saves.
He will take great delight in you;
    in his love he will no longer rebuke you,
    but will rejoice over you with singing."

HE IS: the Mighty Warrior who saves

3:17 Zephaniah's prophesies concerning God's judgment of Israel and the nations are gloomy, yet his final words ignite hope. In the end, he reveals that God's mercy will triumph over judgment. When God is with his people, he is the saving, *Mighty Warrior*.

When Jesus conquered sin and death, God proved that he is able to save souls. In the future at Armageddon, God will prove himself *the Mighty Warrior who saves* his people. Today, when you believe in him, he will take pleasure in you, lovingly calm you and rejoice over you.

For the next He Is, go to p. 1359.

1357

¹⁸ "I will remove from you
    all who mourn over the loss of your appointed festivals,
    which is a burden and reproach for you.
¹⁹ At that time I will deal
    with all who oppressed you.
I will rescue the lame;
    I will gather the exiles.
I will give them praise and honor
    in every land where they have suffered shame.
²⁰ At that time I will gather you;
    at that time I will bring you home.
I will give you honor and praise
    among all the peoples of the earth
when I restore your fortunes*ᵃ*
    before your very eyes,"

says the LORD.

ᵃ 20 Or *I bring back your captives*

"Nice house. Now, what are you going
to do about mine?"—God »» (1:2–11)

The new temple was far inferior to the original
in all ways except what? »» (2:1–9)

What happens when we finally "get it right"? »» (2:18–19)

haggai

AUTHOR
Haggai.

AUDIENCE
The exiles who returned to Jerusalem.

DATE
520 B.C.

SETTING
The Persian King Cyrus allowed the Jews to
return to Jerusalem to rebuild the temple.
However, misplaced priorities and local opposition brought work to a halt.

VERSES TO REMEMBER
"Now this is what the LORD Almighty says:
'Give careful thought to your ways. You have
planted much, but have harvested little. You
eat, but never have enough. You drink, but
never have your fill. You put on clothes, but
are not warm. You earn wages, only to put
them in a purse with holes in it.'" (1:5–6)

THEME TO CONSIDER
Give careful consideration to your priorities—
they will guide your steps or lead you astray.

A Call to Build the House of the LORD

1 In the second year of King Darius, on the first day of the sixth month, the word of the LORD came through the prophet Haggai to Zerubbabel son of Shealtiel, governor of Judah, and to Joshua[a] son of Jozadak,[b] the high priest:

2 This is what the LORD Almighty says: "These people say, 'The time has not yet come to rebuild the LORD's house.'"

3 Then the word of the LORD came through the prophet Haggai: 4 "Is it a time for you yourselves to be living in your paneled houses, while this house remains a ruin?"

5 Now this is what the LORD Almighty says: "Give careful thought to your ways. 6 You have planted much, but have harvested little. You eat, but never have enough. You drink, but never have your fill. You put on clothes, but are not warm. You earn wages, only to put them in a purse with holes in it."

7 This is what the LORD Almighty says: "Give careful thought to your ways. 8 Go up into the mountains and bring down timber and build the house, so that I may take pleasure in it and be honored," says the LORD. 9 "You expected much, but see, it turned out to be little. What you brought home, I blew away. Why?" declares the LORD Almighty. "Because of my house, which remains a ruin, while each of you is busy with his own house. 10 Therefore, because of you the heavens have withheld their dew and the earth its crops. 11 I called for a drought on the fields and the mountains, on the grain, the new wine, the olive oil and everything else the ground produces, on people and livestock, and on all the labor of your hands."

12 Then Zerubbabel son of Shealtiel, Joshua son of Jozadak, the high priest, and the whole remnant of the people obeyed the voice of the LORD their God and the message of the prophet Haggai, because the LORD their God had sent him. And the people feared the LORD.

13 Then Haggai, the LORD's messenger, gave this message of the LORD to the people: "I am with you," declares the LORD. 14 So the LORD stirred up the spirit of Zerubbabel son of Shealtiel, governor of Judah, and the spirit of Joshua son of Jozadak, the high priest, and the spirit of the whole remnant of the people. They came and began to work on the house of the LORD Almighty, their God, 15 on the twenty-fourth day of the sixth month.

"conversations"

priorities «» 1:3–11

1 » Based on how you spend your time and money, what would an outside observer conclude are your priorities in life?

2 » What are some realistic, practical ways to make God your highest priority?

3 » Have you ever experienced a "drought" in your life when God did not bless you (v. 6)? What did you learn?

For more on **priorities**, check the index.
For the next Conversations, go to p. 1375.

1359

---

[a] 1 A variant of *Jeshua*; here and elsewhere in Haggai   [b] 1 Hebrew *Jehozadak*, a variant of *Jozadak*; also in verses 12 and 14

HE IS: stirring

1:13–14 As the Lord's messenger, Haggai reminded the people that they had put much energy into building their own homes, yet God's house remained a ruin. God himself stirred up the people to work on his house, the building project he was passionate about.

God is also *stirring* in the hearts of his people today. What is he stirring you to do? Build his house? Reach out to a hurting friend? Witness to your unsaved neighbor? Give? When you are attuned to his stirring in your heart, and open to doing whatever project he is passionate about, he will use you.

For the next He Is, go to p. 1367.

myth# 76 "I'LL HAVE PLENTY OF TIME TO SAVE MONEY LATER."

My parents went ballistic the other day when I announced that I've decided to spend my tax return on a trip to Spain.

"What's so wrong with seeing the world?" I asked them.

But Mom went, "You've been spending a lot of money, Dar. Are you saving anything? Maybe you should invest that money." While she was on the phone, I could hear Dad in the background, "Yeah, Darci, invest."

Invest? How often do I get a chance to go to Spain? Besides, I'm 30 years old; I can invest money later. I figure I've got at least 30 more years to work and sock my money away. Plenty of time to save. Right now is my time to enjoy myself.

Which is why I bought a new car this year. I was so tired of driving that piece of junk I'd had since college. So that's why my parents are freaking out about the trip to Spain. They think I'm spending way too much money, and they want me to stick to a budget.

The thing is, I'm not in major amounts of debt like some of my friends. I have some debt, but it's not unmanageable. Plus, I have good job, and I know that soon I'll have to get serious and stop spending so much. In the meantime, I'm young; I have no ties; I feel like I really want to enjoy myself now while I can.

I don't want to be like my grandfather. All he did was save money. I don't think he ever went to Europe, bought a brand new car or did anything extra or fun. Instead he lived, saved and died. Now someone else gets his money. That's not the kind of life I want.

—Darci

WE CAN MAKE elaborate plans for our lives, but really we have no idea what the future holds. That's why David wrote, "My times are in your hands" (Psalm 31:15). Only God knows what will happen in the future.

But aren't many of our plans made with the assumption that we have plenty of time? The credit card commercials promise us a world of fun if we spend now and pay later. Many bright (but misled) people buy into the belief that there's always time to save later, just like many bright (but deceived) people believe there's always time to give their lives to God later. But God sometimes has a way of surprising us and upending our well-laid plans, just as he did in Jesus' parable about the rich fool (see Luke 12:16–21). Having hoarded his money, the rich fool thought he had time to sit back and enjoy it. But God had a surprise for him.

Think back to a time as a child when you were handed a sum of money to spend. Was your first thought to save it or to spend it? Most kids think about spending money as fast as they can. A parent might force a child to save some of the money he or she is given, in the hopes of instilling the discipline of saving money. Saving truly does take discipline.

The way we handle money reveals a lot about the state of our emotions and spiritual growth. The extremes—hoarding money on the one end and spending every cent of it on the other—show our fears and our focus (on self, rather than on God). That's why the Bible warns against the love of money and encourages wisdom in all matters. A balanced view of money is healthy. Perhaps that's why Proverbs 30:8 says, "Give me neither poverty nor riches."

God wants his people to be responsible with the resources he gives them, including money. As a steward of God's money, how will you use it?

> "On average, Americans save only 1.9 percent of their disposable income."
> —U.S. Bureau of Economic Analysis (2004)

1361

"DISHONEST MONEY DWINDLES AWAY, BUT WHOEVER GATHERS MONEY LITTLE BY LITTLE MAKES IT GROW."

PROVERBS 13:11

SEE ALSO
Proverbs 30:8–9

Ecclesiastes 5:13–15

2 Corinthians 9:6–11

For more on **Money**, check the index.

The Promised Glory of the New House

2 In the second year of King Darius, ¹on the twenty-first day of the seventh month, the word of the Lord came through the prophet Haggai: ²"Speak to Zerubbabel son of Shealtiel, governor of Judah, to Joshua son of Jozadak,ᵃ the high priest, and to the remnant of the people. Ask them, ³'Who of you is left who saw this house in its former glory? How does it look to you now? Does it not seem to you like nothing? ⁴But now be strong, Zerubbabel,' declares the Lord. 'Be strong, Joshua son of Jozadak, the high priest. Be strong, all you people of the land,' declares the Lord, 'and work. For I am with you,' declares the Lord Almighty. ⁵'This is what I covenanted with you when you came out of Egypt. And my Spirit remains among you. Do not fear.'

⁶"This is what the Lord Almighty says: 'In a little while I will once more shake the heavens and the earth, the sea and the dry land. ⁷I will shake all nations, and what is desired by all nations will come, and I will fill this house with glory,' says the Lord Almighty. ⁸'The silver is mine and the gold is mine,' declares the Lord Almighty. ⁹'The glory of this present house will be greater than the glory of the former house,' says the Lord Almighty. 'And in this place I will grant peace,' declares the Lord Almighty."

Blessings for a Defiled People

¹⁰On the twenty-fourth day of the ninth month, in the second year of Darius, the word of the Lord came to the prophet Haggai: ¹¹"This is what the Lord Almighty says: 'Ask the priests what the law says: ¹²If a person carries consecrated meat in the fold of his garment, and that fold touches some bread or stew, some wine, olive oil or other food, does it become consecrated?'"

The priests answered, "No."

¹³Then Haggai said, "If a person defiled by contact with a dead body touches one of these things, does it become defiled?"

"Yes," the priests replied, "it becomes defiled."

¹⁴Then Haggai said, "'So it is with this people and this nation in my sight,' declares the Lord. 'Whatever they do and whatever they offer there is defiled.

¹⁵"'Now give careful thought to this from this day on ᵇ— consider how things were before one stone was laid on another in the Lord's temple. ¹⁶When anyone came to a heap of twenty measures, there were only ten. When anyone went to a wine vat to draw fifty measures, there were only twenty. ¹⁷I struck all the work of your hands with blight, mildew and hail, yet you did not return to me,' declares the Lord. ¹⁸'From this day on, from this twenty-fourth day of the ninth month, give careful thought to the day when the foundation of the Lord's temple was laid. Give careful thought: ¹⁹Is there yet any seed left in the barn? Until now, the vine and the fig tree, the pomegranate and the olive tree have not borne fruit.

"'From this day on I will bless you.'"

Zerubbabel the Lord's Signet Ring

²⁰The word of the Lord came to Haggai a second time on the twenty-fourth day of the month: ²¹"Tell Zerubbabel governor of Judah that I am going to shake the heavens and the earth. ²²I will overturn royal thrones and shatter the power of the foreign kingdoms. I will overthrow chariots and their drivers; horses and their riders will fall, each by the sword of his comrade.

²³"'On that day,' declares the Lord Almighty, 'I will take you, my servant Zerubbabel son of Shealtiel,' declares the Lord, 'and I will make you like my signet ring, for I have chosen you,' declares the Lord Almighty."

atissue:fear

2:5 When you feel afraid, telling yourself there's nothing to be afraid of doesn't often work. Trying to control or manipulate the situation doesn't often work. Worrying through every possible scenario doesn't work either. So, how can you combat fear? When God tells us not to be afraid, he reminds us that he's with us. We have nothing to fear *because* God is with us. He's more powerful than our circumstances or enemies. During the most stressful situation, he's still on his throne. And his love and comfort are more abundant than our pain or anxiety. So don't be afraid— God is near.

ᵃ 2 Hebrew *Jehozadak*, a variant of *Jozadak*; also in verse 4   ᵇ 15 Or *to the days past*

zechariah

AUTHOR
Zechariah.

AUDIENCE
The exiles who returned to Jerusalem.

DATE
Between about 520 and 480 B.C.

SETTING
Zechariah, like Haggai, encouraged the
exiles who had returned to Jerusalem from
Babylon to complete the rebuilding of the
temple.

VERSE TO REMEMBER
"Therefore tell the people: This is what the
LORD Almighty says: 'Return to me,' declares
the LORD Almighty, 'and I will return to you,'
says the LORD Almighty." (1:3)

THEME TO CONSIDER
Return to the Lord, and he will return to you.

A Call to Return to the Lord

1 In the eighth month of the second year of Darius, the word of the Lord came to the prophet Zechariah son of Berekiah, the son of Iddo:

²"The Lord was very angry with your ancestors. ³Therefore tell the people: This is what the Lord Almighty says: 'Return to me,' declares the Lord Almighty, 'and I will return to you,' says the Lord Almighty. ⁴Do not be like your ancestors, to whom the earlier prophets proclaimed: This is what the Lord Almighty says: 'Turn from your evil ways and your evil practices.' But they would not listen or pay attention to me, declares the Lord. ⁵Where are your ancestors now? And the prophets, do they live forever? ⁶But did not my words and my decrees, which I commanded my servants the prophets, overtake your ancestors?

"Then they repented and said, 'The Lord Almighty has done to us what our ways and practices deserve, just as he determined to do.'"

The Man Among the Myrtle Trees

⁷On the twenty-fourth day of the eleventh month, the month of Shebat, in the second year of Darius, the word of the Lord came to the prophet Zechariah son of Berekiah, the son of Iddo.

⁸During the night I had a vision, and there before me was a man mounted on a red horse. He was standing among the myrtle trees in a ravine. Behind him were red, brown and white horses.

⁹I asked, "What are these, my lord?"

The angel who was talking with me answered, "I will show you what they are."

¹⁰Then the man standing among the myrtle trees explained, "They are the ones the Lord has sent to go throughout the earth."

¹¹And they reported to the angel of the Lord who was standing among the myrtle trees, "We have gone throughout the earth and found the whole world at rest and in peace."

¹²Then the angel of the Lord said, "Lord Almighty, how long will you withhold mercy from Jerusalem and from the towns of Judah, which you have been angry with these seventy years?" ¹³So the Lord spoke kind and comforting words to the angel who talked with me.

¹⁴Then the angel who was speaking to me said, "Proclaim this word: This is what the Lord Almighty says: 'I am very jealous for Jerusalem and Zion, ¹⁵and I am very angry with the nations that feel secure. I was only a little angry, but they added to the calamity.'

¹⁶"Therefore, this is what the Lord says: 'I will return to Jerusalem with mercy, and there my house will be rebuilt. And the measuring line will be stretched out over Jerusalem,' declares the Lord Almighty.

¹⁷"Proclaim further: This is what the Lord Almighty says: 'My towns will again overflow with prosperity, and the Lord will again comfort Zion and choose Jerusalem.'"

Four Horns and Four Craftsmen

*¹⁸Then I looked up, and there before me were four horns. ¹⁹I asked the angel who was speaking to me, "What are these?"

He answered me, "These are the horns that scattered Judah, Israel and Jerusalem."

²⁰Then the Lord showed me four craftsmen. ²¹I asked, "What are these coming to do?"

He answered, "These are the horns that scattered Judah so its people could not raise their heads, but the craftsmen have come to terrify them and throw down these horns of the nations who lifted up their horns against the land of Judah to scatter its people."

A Man With a Measuring Line

2 *Then I looked up, and there before me was a man with a measuring line in his hand. ²I asked, "Where are you going?"

He answered me, "To measure Jerusalem, to find out how wide and how long it is."

³While the angel who was speaking to me was leaving, another angel came to meet him ⁴and said to him: "Run, tell that young man, 'Jerusalem will be a city without walls because of the great number of

---

* 1:18-21 is numbered 2:1-4 in Hebrew texts.   * 2:1-13 is numbered 2:5-17 in Hebrew texts.

people and animals in it. ⁵And I myself will be a wall of fire around it,' declares the Lord, 'and I will be its glory within.'

⁶"Come! Come! Flee from the land of the north," declares the Lord, "for I have scattered you to the four winds of heaven," declares the Lord.

⁷"Come, Zion! Escape, you who live in Daughter Babylon!" ⁸For this is what the Lord Almighty says: "After the Glorious One has sent me against the nations that have plundered you—for whoever touches you touches the apple of his eye— ⁹I will surely raise my hand against them so that their slaves will plunder them.ᵃ Then you will know that the Lord Almighty has sent me.

¹⁰"Shout and be glad, Daughter Zion. For I am coming, and I will live among you," declares the Lord. ¹¹"Many nations will be joined with the Lord in that day and will become my people. I will live among you and you will know that the Lord Almighty has sent me to you. ¹²The Lord will inherit Judah as his portion in the holy land and will again choose Jerusalem. ¹³Be still before the Lord, all people, because he has roused himself from his holy dwelling."

Clean Garments for the High Priest

3 Then he showed me Joshuaᵇ the high priest standing before the angel of the Lord, and Satanᶜ standing at his right side to accuse him. ²The Lord said to Satan, "The Lord rebuke you, Satan! The Lord, who has chosen Jerusalem, rebuke you! Is not this man a burning stick snatched from the fire?"

³Now Joshua was dressed in filthy clothes as he stood before the angel. ⁴The angel said to those who were standing before him, "Take off his filthy clothes."

Then he said to Joshua, "See, I have taken away your sin, and I will put fine garments on you."

⁵Then I said, "Put a clean turban on his head." So they put a clean turban on his head and clothed him, while the angel of the Lord stood by.

⁶The angel of the Lord gave this charge to Joshua: ⁷"This is what the Lord Almighty says: 'If you will walk in obedience to me and keep my requirements, then you will govern my house and have charge of my courts, and I will give you a place among these standing here.

⁸"'Listen, High Priest Joshua, you and your associates seated before you, you who are symbolic of things to come: I am going to bring my servant, the Branch. ⁹See, the stone I have set in front of Joshua! There are seven eyesᵈ on that one stone, and I will engrave an inscription on it,' says the Lord Almighty, 'and I will remove the sin of this land in a single day.

¹⁰"'In that day each of you will invite your neighbor to sit under your vine and fig tree,' declares the Lord Almighty."

The Gold Lampstand and the Two Olive Trees

4 Then the angel who talked with me returned and wakened me, as one is wakened from sleep. ²He asked me, "What do you see?"

I answered, "I see a solid gold lampstand with a bowl at the top and seven lamps on it, with seven channels to the lamps. ³Also there are two olive trees by it, one on the right of the bowl and the other on its left."

⁴I asked the angel who talked with me, "What are these, my lord?"

⁵He answered, "Do you not know what these are?"

"No, my lord," I replied.

1365

ᵃ 8,9 Or says after… eye: ⁹"I… plunder them."   ᵇ 1 A variant of Jesus; here and elsewhere in Zechariah   ᶜ 1 Hebrew satan means adversary.   ᵈ 9 Or facets

⁶So he said to me, "This is the word of the Lord to Zerubbabel: 'Not by might nor by power, but by my Spirit,' says the Lord Almighty.

⁷"What are you, mighty mountain? Before Zerubbabel you will become level ground. Then he will bring out the capstone to shouts of 'God bless it! God bless it!'"

⁸Then the word of the Lord came to me: ⁹"The hands of Zerubbabel have laid the foundation of this temple; his hands will also complete it. Then you will know that the Lord Almighty has sent me to you.

¹⁰"Who dares despise the day of small things, since the seven eyes of the Lord that range throughout the earth will rejoice when they see the chosen capstone*a* in the hand of Zerubbabel?"

¹¹Then I asked the angel, "What are these two olive trees on the right and the left of the lampstand?"

¹²Again I asked him, "What are these two olive branches beside the two gold pipes that pour out golden oil?"

¹³He replied, "Do you not know what these are?"

"No, my lord," I said.

¹⁴So he said, "These are the two who are anointed to*b* serve the Lord of all the earth."

The Flying Scroll

5 I looked again, and there before me was a flying scroll.

²He asked me, "What do you see?"

I answered, "I see a flying scroll, twenty cubits long and ten cubits wide.*c*"

³And he said to me, "This is the curse that is going out over the whole land; for according to what it says on one side, every thief will be banished, and according to what it says on the other, everyone who swears falsely will be banished. ⁴The Lord Almighty declares, 'I will send it out, and it will enter the house of the thief and the house of anyone who swears falsely by my name. It will remain in that house and destroy it completely, both its timbers and its stones.'"

The Woman in a Basket

⁵Then the angel who was speaking to me came forward and said to me, "Look up and see what this is that is appearing."

⁶I asked, "What is it?"

He replied, "It is a basket." And he added, "This is the iniquity*d* of the people throughout the land."

⁷Then the cover of lead was raised, and there in the basket sat a woman! ⁸He said, "This is wickedness," and he pushed her back into the basket and pushed the lead cover down over its mouth.

⁹Then I looked up—and there before me were two women, with the wind in their wings! They had wings like those of a stork, and they lifted up the basket between heaven and earth.

¹⁰"Where are they taking the basket?" I asked the angel who was speaking to me.

¹¹He replied, "To the country of Babylonia*e* to build a house for it. When it is ready, the basket will be set there in its place."

Four Chariots

6 I looked up again, and there before me were four chariots coming out from between two mountains—mountains of bronze. ²The first chariot had red horses, the second black, ³the third white,

> **at issue: self-reliance**
>
> **4:6** God brings us to the end of ourselves to show us how much, how desperately, we need him. We need the power of his Spirit to help us walk in obedience, no matter the cost. We need his help to forgive as we've been forgiven, to love as we've been loved, to be patient with others as he's been patient with us. Only through the Spirit can we break the power of sin in our lives—whether it's addiction or bitterness or gossip. So remember, it's not by *your* might or power, but by God's. Admit your dependence on him.

1366

---

a 10 Or *the plumb line*   *b* 14 Or *two who bring oil and*   *c* 2 That is, about 30 feet long and 15 feet wide or about 9 meters long and 4.5 meters wide
d 6 Or *appearance*   *e* 11 Hebrew *Shinar*

and the fourth dappled—all of them powerful. ⁴I asked the angel who was speaking to me, "What are these, my lord?"

⁵The angel answered me, "These are the four spirits*ᵃ* of heaven, going out from standing in the presence of the Lord of the whole world. ⁶The one with the black horses is going toward the north country, the one with the white horses toward the west,*ᵇ* and the one with the dappled horses toward the south."

⁷When the powerful horses went out, they were straining to go throughout the earth. And he said, "Go throughout the earth!" So they went throughout the earth.

⁸Then he called to me, "Look, those going toward the north country have given my Spirit*ᶜ* rest in the land of the north."

A Crown for Joshua

⁹The word of the LORD came to me: ¹⁰"Take ⌐silver and gold⌐ from the exiles Heldai, Tobijah and Jedaiah, who have arrived from Babylon. Go the same day to the house of Josiah son of Zephaniah. ¹¹Take the silver and gold and make a crown, and set it on the head of the high priest, Joshua son of Jozadak.*ᵈ* ¹²Tell him this is what the LORD Almighty says: 'Here is the man whose name is the Branch, and he will branch out from his place and build the temple of the LORD. ¹³It is he who will build the temple of the LORD, and he will be clothed with majesty and will sit and rule on his throne. And he*ᵉ* will be a priest on his throne. And there will be harmony between the two.' ¹⁴The crown will be given to Heldai,*ᶠ* Tobijah, Jedaiah and Hen*ᵍ* son of Zephaniah as a memorial in the temple of the LORD. ¹⁵Those who are far away will come and help to build the temple of the LORD, and you will know that the LORD Almighty has sent me to you. This will happen if you diligently obey the LORD your God."

HE IS: the Branch

6:12–13 In ancient Israel, priests didn't sit on the throne, and kings didn't perform priestly duties. The two were distinct offices. But Zechariah saw a day when the two would be united. The Messiah, *the Branch*, would be the priest-king who would finally bring harmony to earth.

Because Jesus fills both offices of priest and king, he brings harmony to wherever he rules—including your life. As king of your heart, he'll govern your decisions and royally bless you. As high priest, he personally made the ultimate sin offering on your behalf and intercedes for you in prayer to the Father (see Hebrews 6:19—7:3). What divine harmony!

For the next He Is, go to p. 1371.

Justice and Mercy, Not Fasting

7 In the fourth year of King Darius, the word of the LORD came to Zechariah on the fourth day of the ninth month, the month of Kislev. ²The people of Bethel had sent Sharezer and Regem-Melek, together with their men, to entreat the LORD ³by asking the priests of the house of the LORD Almighty and the prophets, "Should I mourn and fast in the fifth month, as I have done for so many years?"

⁴Then the word of the LORD Almighty came to me: ⁵"Ask all the people of the land and the priests, 'When you fasted and mourned in the fifth and seventh months for the past seventy years, was it really for me that you fasted? ⁶And when you were eating and drinking, were you not just feasting for yourselves? ⁷Are these not the words the LORD proclaimed through the earlier prophets when Jerusalem and its surrounding towns were at rest and prosperous, and the Negev and the western foothills were settled?'"

⁸And the word of the LORD came again to Zechariah: ⁹"This is what the LORD Almighty said:

ᵃ 5 Or winds ᵇ 6 Or horses after them ᶜ 8 Or spirit ᵈ 11 Hebrew Jehozadak, a variant of Jozadak ᵉ 13 Or there ᶠ 14 Syriac; Hebrew Helem ᵍ 14 Or and the gracious one, the

myth# 77 "IF THE POOR REALLY WANTED TO IMPROVE THEMSELVES, THEY COULD."

I see them everywhere. The homeless people, I mean. I commute into the city every day and have a six-block walk from the train to my office. I used to feel guilty when I didn't give them money, but now I've gotten to the point where I ignore them. You can tell the true city people by how they can tune them out. Honestly, if I gave money to some, I'd feel like I have to give to them all. Is it my responsibility to give to people who are probably on the street because of something that's their own fault? Like maybe they got into drugs like my cousin Leon, or maybe they're alcoholics. Or maybe they dropped out of school like some of the people at my high school. That's always a big mistake.

My family didn't have a heap of money when I was growing up. But my parents still made sure my sisters and I went to college. The fact is, we went and graduated. We didn't drop out. We wanted to make something of ourselves because our parents sacrificed to get us to college. Now my little sister is in law school. I graduated from med school nine years ago. I'm thankful to God that I made it through.

I really think that if people wanted to improve themselves, they could. I mean, why be content to just live on welfare? Why not work hard, earn a GED and try to get a decent job?

I can't help thinking of my ex-roommate from college, Molly. A perfect example of what I mean. Haven't seen her since she dropped out during our freshman year after spending most of the year partying. She got into some drugs, too. But I hear about her from time to time through some of our friends. They hear from her whenever she needs money. She's gone from dead-end job to dead-end job and equally dead-end boyfriends. The fact is she's broke now because of her poor choices.

To think that she arrived at school with a 3.75 GPA. She wasted it.

—Veneta

IT'S EASY TO judge someone without knowing her whole story. Take someone who may be poor, for instance. It seems logical to assume that if only she could improve herself, everything would work out for her. But sometimes things aren't that simple.

During his days on earth, Jesus showed compassion for all kinds of people. He never told anyone, "If only you would try to improve yourself, your life would be better." Instead, he often challenged people to move out of their comfort zones. Take the rich young man, for example, to whom Jesus said, "Go, sell everything you have and give to the poor" (Mark 10:21).

Give to the poor. God has always shown compassion for the poor. In fact, you could say he's obsessed with showing compassion for the poor. Throughout the Law of Moses, the Israelites were commanded to show mercy to the poor, widowed and orphaned. (See Exodus 22:22; Leviticus 19:10; 23:22; Deuteronomy 10:18; 24:14–15,17–22; 26:12.) God had harsh words for those who exploited or ignored the poor. He understood their painful and sometimes unfair circumstances.

In the parable of the Good Samaritan (see Luke 10:25–37), Jesus gives us a clear model of compassion for those in need. According to Jesus' teaching, showing compassion means . . .

- Going out of your way for someone in need— even if it's inconvenient for you and costs you time and money.

- Treating that person with dignity, as a human being and a real person with real needs.

- Helping to solve that person's problems—not by coldly ignoring her; not by throwing money at her to get her to leave you alone; but by providing for her physical and spiritual needs.

Could that mean buying a homeless man a sandwich and talking with him while he eats it?

Could that mean housing a pregnant girl who has nowhere else to go? Could that mean giving of your time and money to a mission or shelter? How can *you* translate Jesus' teaching into action in your life?

"Only 47 percent of Americans believe they have a personal responsibility to share what they have with those who are in need or struggling."
—Barna Research Group (1994)

 1369

"THERE WILL ALWAYS BE POOR PEOPLE IN THE LAND. THEREFORE I COMMAND YOU TO BE OPEN-HANDED TOWARD THOSE OF YOUR PEOPLE WHO ARE POOR AND NEEDY IN YOUR LAND."

SEE ALSO

DEUTERONOMY 15:11

Proverbs 22:16
Micah 6:8
Zechariah 7:9–10

For more on **Compassion,** check the index.

'Administer true justice; show mercy and compassion to one another. [10]Do not oppress the widow or the fatherless, the foreigner or the poor. Do not plot evil against each other.'

[11]"But they refused to pay attention; stubbornly they turned their backs and covered their ears. [12]They made their hearts as hard as flint and would not listen to the law or to the words that the LORD Almighty had sent by his Spirit through the earlier prophets. So the LORD Almighty was very angry.

[13]"When I called, they did not listen; so when they called, I would not listen,' says the LORD Almighty. [14]'I scattered them with a whirlwind among all the nations, where they were strangers. The land they left behind them was so desolate that no one traveled through it. This is how they made the pleasant land desolate.'"

The LORD Promises to Bless Jerusalem

8 The word of the LORD Almighty came to me.

[2]This is what the LORD Almighty says: "I am very jealous for Zion; I am burning with jealousy for her."

[3]This is what the LORD says: "I will return to Zion and dwell in Jerusalem. Then Jerusalem will be called the City of Truth, and the mountain of the LORD Almighty will be called the Holy Mountain."

[4]This is what the LORD Almighty says: "Once again men and women of ripe old age will sit in the streets of Jerusalem, each of them with cane in hand because of their age. [5]The city streets will be filled with boys and girls playing there."

[6]This is what the LORD Almighty says: "It may seem marvelous to the remnant of this people at that time, but will it seem marvelous to me?" declares the LORD Almighty.

[7]This is what the LORD Almighty says: "I will save my people from the countries of the east and the west. [8]I will bring them back to live in Jerusalem; they will be my people, and I will be faithful and righteous to them as their God."

[9]This is what the LORD Almighty says: "Now hear these words, 'Let your hands be strong so that the temple may be built.' This is also what the prophets said who were present when the foundation was laid for the house of the LORD Almighty. [10]Before that time there were no wages for people or animals. People could not go about their business safely because of conflicts, since I had turned them all against each other. [11]But now I will not deal with the remnant of this people as I did in the past," declares the LORD Almighty.

[12]"The seed will grow well, the vine will yield its fruit, the ground will produce its crops, and the heavens will drop their dew. I will give all these things as an inheritance to the remnant of this people. [13]Just as you, Judah and Israel, have been a curse[a] among the nations, so I will save you, and you will be a blessing.[b] Do not be afraid, but let your hands be strong."

[14]This is what the LORD Almighty says: "Just as I had determined to bring disaster on you and showed no pity when your ancestors angered me," says the LORD Almighty, [15]"so now I have determined to do good again to Jerusalem and Judah. Do not be afraid. [16]These are the things you are to do: Speak the truth to each other, and render true and sound judgment in your courts; [17]do not plot evil against each other, and do not love to swear falsely. I hate all this," declares the LORD.

[18]The word of the LORD Almighty came to me. [19]This is what the LORD Almighty says: "The fasts of the fourth, fifth, seventh and tenth months will become joyful and glad occasions and happy festivals for Judah. Therefore love truth and peace."

[20]This is what the LORD Almighty says: "Many peoples and the inhabitants of many cities will yet come, [21]and the inhabitants of one city will go to another and say, 'Let us go at once to entreat the LORD and seek the LORD Almighty. I myself am going.' [22]And many peoples and powerful nations will come to Jerusalem to seek the LORD Almighty and to entreat him."

[23]This is what the LORD Almighty says: "In those days ten people from all languages and nations will take firm hold of one Jew by the hem of his robe and say, 'Let us go with you, because we have heard that God is with you.'"

---

[a] 13 That is, your name has been used in cursing (see Jer. 29:23); or, you have been regarded as under a curse. [b] 13 Or and your name will be used in blessings (see Gen. 48:20); or and you will be seen as blessed

Judgment on Israel's Enemies

9 A prophecy:

> The word of the Lord is against the land of Hadrak
>   and will come to rest on Damascus—
> for the eyes of all people and all the tribes of Israel
>   are on the Lord—[a]
> [2] and on Hamath too, which borders on it,
>   and on Tyre and Sidon, though they are very skillful.
> [3] Tyre has built herself a stronghold;
>   she has heaped up silver like dust,
>   and gold like the dirt of the streets.
> [4] But the Lord will take away her possessions
>   and destroy her power on the sea,
>   and she will be consumed by fire.
> [5] Ashkelon will see it and fear;
>   Gaza will writhe in agony,
>   and Ekron too, for her hope will wither.
> Gaza will lose her king
>   and Ashkelon will be deserted.
> [6] A mongrel people will occupy Ashdod,
>   and I will put an end to the pride of the Philistines.
> [7] I will take the blood from their mouths,
>   the forbidden food from between their teeth.
> Those who are left will belong to our God
>   and become a clan in Judah,
>   and Ekron will be like the Jebusites.
> [8] But I will encamp at my temple
>   to guard it against marauding forces.
> Never again will an oppressor overrun my people,
>   for now I am keeping watch.

The Coming of Zion's King

> [9] Rejoice greatly, Daughter Zion!
>   Shout, Daughter Jerusalem!
> See, your king comes to you,

---

[a] 1 Or Damascus. / For the eye of the Lord is on all people, / as well as on the tribes of Israel,

---

HE IS: lowly

9:9–10 Zechariah predicted that the Messiah would arrive in a lowly state, riding on a donkey. Jesus fulfilled this prophecy when he triumphantly rode into Jerusalem (see Matthew 21:7–11). Zechariah also predicted that at Jesus' second coming, he will come as a powerful judge and disarm his foes (see Matthew 25:31–33).

Jesus is *lowly*, or *humble*, and came first as a suffering servant. He will not force you to choose him. However, if you choose not to receive his mercy, one day he will come forcefully. The choice is yours: Would you rather meet Jesus as servant or judge?

For the next He Is, go to p. 1383.

>   righteous and having salvation,
>   lowly and riding on a donkey,
>   on a colt, the foal of a donkey.
> ¹⁰I will take away the chariots from Ephraim
>   and the warhorses from Jerusalem,
>   and the battle bow will be broken.
> He will proclaim peace to the nations.
>   His rule will extend from sea to sea
>   and from the River[a] to the ends of the earth.
> ¹¹As for you, because of the blood of my covenant with you,
>   I will free your prisoners from the waterless pit.
> ¹²Return to your fortress, you prisoners of hope;
>   even now I announce that I will restore twice as much to you.
> ¹³I will bend Judah as I bend my bow
>   and fill it with Ephraim.
> I will rouse your sons, Zion,
>   against your sons, Greece,
>   and make you like a warrior's sword.

The Lord Will Appear

> ¹⁴Then the Lord will appear over them;
>   his arrow will flash like lightning.
> The Sovereign Lord will sound the trumpet;
>   he will march in the storms of the
>   south,
> ¹⁵ and the Lord Almighty will shield
>   them.
> They will destroy
>   and overcome with slingstones.
> They will drink and roar as with wine;
>   they will be full like a bowl
>   used for sprinkling[b] the corners of the
>   altar.
> ¹⁶The Lord their God will save his people
>   on that day
>   as a shepherd saves his flock.
> They will sparkle in his land
>   like jewels in a crown.
> ¹⁷How attractive and beautiful they
>   will be!
> Grain will make the young men
>   thrive,
>   and new wine the young women.

The Lord Will Care for Judah

10 Ask the Lord for rain in the springtime;
>   it is the Lord who sends the
>   thunderstorms.
> He gives showers of rain to all people,
>   and plants of the field to everyone.

atissue:prayer

10:1 If you needed help with computer software, you'd get the best assistance from the software designer. If you needed to make sense of a confusing recipe, the original chef would know best. If your new dishwasher started malfunctioning, you'd call the manufacturer. It pays to go to the source. The same is true for the bigger things in life. When you need something that only God can give you, go to God. Why look to anyone else for wisdom and strength, healing in relationships, rain in the droughts of your life? Go straight to the source to find all that you need.

---

[a] 10 That is, the Euphrates   [b] 15 Or bowl, / like

²The idols speak deceitfully,
   diviners see visions that lie;
they tell dreams that are false,
   they give comfort in vain.
Therefore the people wander like sheep
   oppressed for lack of a shepherd.

³"My anger burns against the shepherds,
   and I will punish the leaders;
for the LORD Almighty will care
   for his flock, the house of Judah,
   and make them like a proud horse in battle.
⁴From Judah will come the cornerstone,
   from him the tent peg,
from him the battle bow,
   from him every ruler.
⁵Together they^a will be like mighty warriors in battle
   trampling their enemy into the mud of the streets.
They will fight because the LORD is with them,
   and they will put the enemy horsemen to shame.

⁶"I will strengthen the house of Judah
   and save the house of Joseph.
I will restore them
   because I have compassion on them.
They will be as though
   I had not rejected them,
for I am the LORD their God
   and I will answer them.
⁷The Ephraimites will become like mighty warriors,
   and their hearts will be glad as with wine.
Their children will see it and be joyful;
   their hearts will rejoice in the LORD.
⁸I will signal for them
   and gather them in.
Surely I will redeem them;
   they will be as numerous as before.
⁹Though I scatter them among the
      peoples,
   yet in distant lands they will remember me.
They and their children will survive,
   and they will return.
¹⁰I will bring them back from Egypt
   and gather them from Assyria.
I will bring them to Gilead and Lebanon,
   and there will not be room enough for them.
¹¹They will pass through the sea of trouble;
   the surging sea will be subdued
   and all the depths of the Nile will dry up.
Assyria's pride will be brought down
   and Egypt's scepter will pass away.

---

^a *4,5* Or *ruler, all of them together.* / ⁵*They*

¹²I will strengthen them in the Lord
and in his name they will live securely,"
declares the Lord.

11

Open your doors, Lebanon,
so that fire may devour your cedars!
²Wail, you juniper, for the cedar has fallen;
the stately trees are ruined!
Wail, oaks of Bashan;
the dense forest has been cut down!
³Listen to the wail of the shepherds;
their rich pastures are destroyed!
Listen to the roar of the lions;
the lush thicket of the Jordan is ruined!

Two Shepherds

⁴This is what the Lord my God says: "Shepherd the flock marked for slaughter. ⁵Their buyers slaughter them and go unpunished. Those who sell them say, 'Praise the Lord, I am rich!' Their own shepherds do not spare them. ⁶For I will no longer have pity on the people of the land," declares the Lord. "I will give everyone into the hands of their neighbors and their king. They will devastate the land, and I will not rescue them from their hands."

⁷So I shepherded the flock marked for slaughter, particularly the oppressed of the flock. Then I took two staffs and called one Favor and the other Union, and I shepherded the flock. ⁸In one month I got rid of the three shepherds.

The flock detested me, and I grew weary of them ⁹and said, "I will not be your shepherd. Let the dying die, and the perishing perish. Let those who are left eat one another's flesh."

¹⁰Then I took my staff called Favor and broke it, revoking the covenant I had made with all the nations. ¹¹It was revoked on that day, and so the oppressed of the flock who were watching me knew it was the word of the Lord.

¹²I told them, "If you think it best, give me my pay; but if not, keep it." So they paid me thirty pieces of silver.

¹³And the Lord said to me, "Throw it to the potter"—the handsome price at which they valued me! So I took the thirty pieces of silver and threw them to the potter at the house of the Lord.

¹⁴Then I broke my second staff called Union, breaking the family bond between Judah and Israel.

¹⁵Then the Lord said to me, "Take again the equipment of a foolish shepherd. ¹⁶For I am going to raise up a shepherd over the land who will not care for the lost, or seek the young, or heal the injured, or feed the healthy, but will eat the meat of the choice sheep, tearing off their hooves.

¹⁷"Woe to the worthless shepherd,
who deserts the flock!
May the sword strike his arm and his right eye!
May his arm be completely withered,
his right eye totally blinded!"

Jerusalem's Enemies to Be Destroyed

12

A prophecy: The word of the Lord concerning Israel.

The Lord, who stretches out the heavens, who lays the foundation of the earth, and who forms the spirit in human beings, declares: ²"I am going to make Jerusalem a cup that sends all the surrounding peoples reeling. Judah will be besieged as well as Jerusalem. ³On that day, when all the nations of the earth are gathered against her, I will make Jerusalem an immovable rock for all the nations. All who try to move it will injure themselves. ⁴On that day I will strike every horse with panic and its rider with madness," declares the Lord. "I will keep a watchful eye over the house of Judah, but I will blind all the horses of the nations. ⁵Then the clans of Judah will say in their hearts, 'The people of Jerusalem are strong, because the Lᴏʀᴅ Almighty is their God.'

⁶"On that day I will make the clans of Judah like a firepot in a woodpile, like a flaming torch among sheaves. They will consume right and left all the surrounding peoples, but Jerusalem will remain intact in her place.

⁷"The Lᴏʀᴅ will save the dwellings of Judah first, so that the honor of the house of David and of Jerusalem's inhabitants may not be greater than that of Judah. ⁸On that day the Lᴏʀᴅ will shield those who live in Jerusalem, so that the feeblest among them will be like David, and the house of David will be like God, like the angel of the Lᴏʀᴅ going before them. ⁹On that day I will set out to destroy all the nations that attack Jerusalem.

Mourning for the One They Pierced

¹⁰"And I will pour out on the house of David and the inhabitants of Jerusalem a spirit*a* of grace and supplication. They will look on*b* me, the one they have pierced, and they will mourn for him as one mourns for an only child, and grieve bitterly for him as one grieves for a firstborn son. ¹¹On that day the weeping in Jerusalem will be great, like the weeping of Hadad Rimmon in the plain of Megiddo. ¹²The land will mourn, each clan by itself, with their wives by themselves: the clan of the house of David and their wives, the clan of the house of Nathan and their wives, ¹³the clan of the house of Levi and their wives, the clan of Shimei and their wives, ¹⁴and all the rest of the clans and their wives.

Cleansing From Sin

13 "On that day a fountain will be opened to the house of David and the inhabitants of Jerusalem, to cleanse them from sin and impurity.

²"On that day, I will banish the names of the idols from the land, and they will be remembered no more," declares the Lᴏʀᴅ Almighty. "I will remove both the prophets and the spirit of impurity from the land. ³And if some still prophesy, their fathers and mothers, to whom they were born, will say to them, 'You must die, because you have told lies in the Lᴏʀᴅ's name.' When they prophesy, their own parents will stab them.

⁴"On that day the prophets will all be ashamed of their prophetic visions. They will not put on a prophet's garment of hair in order to deceive. ⁵Every one of them will say, 'I am not a prophet. I am a farmer; the land has been my livelihood since my youth.*c*' ⁶If someone asks, 'What are these wounds on your body*d*?' they will answer, 'The wounds I was given at the house of my friends.'

The Shepherd Struck, the Sheep Scattered

⁷"Awake, sword, against my shepherd,
against the man who is close to me!"
declares the Lᴏʀᴅ Almighty.
"Strike the shepherd,
and the sheep will be scattered,
and I will turn my hand against the little ones.
⁸In the whole land," declares the Lᴏʀᴅ,
"two-thirds will be struck down and perish;
yet one-third will be left in it.
⁹This third I will bring into the fire;
I will refine them like silver

conversations

purity «» 13:1

1» Is cleansing from sin a one-time episode or an ongoing experience? Explain your answer.

2» Are there impurities in your life you still need to be cleansed from? If so, what are they?

3» What does living a pure life look like?

For more on **purity**, check the index.
For the next Conversations, go to p. 1383.

1375

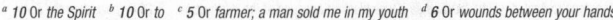

a 10 Or the Spirit b 10 Or to c 5 Or farmer; a man sold me in my youth d 6 Or wounds between your hands

and test them like gold.
> They will call on my name
> and I will answer them;
> I will say, 'They are my people,'
> and they will say, 'The LORD is our God.'"

The LORD Comes and Reigns

14 A day of the LORD is coming, Jerusalem, when your possessions will be plundered and divided up within your very walls.

[2] I will gather all the nations to Jerusalem to fight against it; the city will be captured, the houses ransacked, and the women ravished. Half of the city will go into exile, but the rest of the people will not be taken from the city. [3] Then the LORD will go out and fight against those nations, as he fights on a day of battle. [4] On that day his feet will stand on the Mount of Olives, east of Jerusalem, and the Mount of Olives will be split in two from east to west, forming a great valley, with half of the mountain moving north and half moving south. [5] You will flee by my mountain valley, for it will extend to Azel. You will flee as you fled from the earthquake[a] in the days of Uzziah king of Judah. Then the LORD my God will come, and all the holy ones with him.

[6] On that day there will be no sunlight, no cold, frosty darkness. [7] It will be a unique day—a day known only to the LORD—with no distinction between day and night. When evening comes, there will be light.

[8] On that day living water will flow out from Jerusalem, half of it east to the Dead Sea and half of it west to the Mediterranean Sea, in summer and in winter.

[9] The LORD will be king over the whole earth. On that day there will be one LORD, and his name the only name.

[10] The whole land, from Geba to Rimmon, south of Jerusalem, will become like the Arabah. But Jerusalem will be raised up high from the Benjamin Gate to the site of the First Gate, to the Corner Gate, and from the Tower of Hananel to the royal winepresses, and will remain in its place. [11] It will be inhabited; never again will it be destroyed. Jerusalem will be secure.

[12] This is the plague with which the LORD will strike all the nations that fought against Jerusalem: Their flesh will rot while they are still standing on their feet, their eyes will rot in their sockets, and their tongues will rot in their mouths. [13] On that day people will be stricken by the LORD with great panic. They will seize each other by the hand and attack one another. [14] Judah too will fight at Jerusalem. The wealth of all the surrounding nations will be collected—great quantities of gold and silver and clothing. [15] A similar plague will strike the horses and mules, the camels and donkeys, and all the animals in those camps.

[16] Then the survivors from all the nations that have attacked Jerusalem will go up year after year to worship the King, the LORD Almighty, and to celebrate the Festival of Tabernacles. [17] If any of the peoples of the earth do not go up to Jerusalem to worship the King, the LORD Almighty, they will have no rain. [18] If the Egyptian people do not go up and take part, they will have no rain. The LORD[b] will bring on them the plague he inflicts on the nations that do not go up to celebrate the Festival of Tabernacles. [19] This

1376

issue:unknown future

14:8–9,20–21 Why do people read horoscopes or consult psychics? It's primarily because they don't like living with the uncertainty of the future. They think they could live better today if they knew what tomorrow held. God doesn't give us the exact details of the future because he wants us to trust him. However, he *does* tell us the end of the story so that we can have hope, even as we live in uncertainty, wondering how the story will unfold. No matter what happens today or tomorrow, you can rest securely knowing that your future in heaven with God is secure.

---

[a] 5 Or [5] *My mountain valley will be blocked and will extend to Azel. It will be blocked as it was blocked because of the earthquake*   [b] 18 Or *part, then the LORD*

will be the punishment of Egypt and the punishment of all the nations that do not go up to celebrate the Festival of Tabernacles.

²⁰On that day HOLY TO THE LORD will be inscribed on the bells of the horses, and the cooking pots in the LORD's house will be like the sacred bowls in front of the altar. ²¹Every pot in Jerusalem and Judah will be holy to the LORD Almighty, and all who come to sacrifice will take some of the pots and cook in them. And on that day there will no longer be a Canaanite*a* in the house of the LORD Almighty.

a 21 Or merchant

1378

malachi

AUTHOR
Malachi.

AUDIENCE
Jews in Jerusalem and all of God's people.

DATE
About 430 B.C.

SETTING
Although the temple in Jerusalem and the city walls had been rebuilt, the Jews languished in their worship.

VERSE TO REMEMBER
"I the LORD do not change. So you, the descendants of Jacob, are not destroyed." (3:6)

THEME TO CONSIDER
Meaningless rituals are no substitute for wholehearted worship.

1 A prophecy: The word of the LORD to Israel through Malachi.*

Israel Doubts God's Love

²"I have loved you," says the LORD.

"But you ask, 'How have you loved us?'

"Was not Esau Jacob's brother?" declares the LORD. "Yet I have loved Jacob, ³but Esau I have hated, and I have turned his hill country into a wasteland and left his inheritance to the desert jackals."

⁴Edom may say, "Though we have been crushed, we will rebuild the ruins."

But this is what the LORD Almighty says: "They may build, but I will demolish. They will be called the Wicked Land, a people always under the wrath of the LORD. ⁵You will see it with your own eyes and say, 'Great is the LORD—even beyond the borders of Israel!'

Breaking Covenant Through Blemished Sacrifices

⁶"A son honors his father, and slaves honor their master. If I am a father, where is the honor due me? If I am a master, where is the respect due me?" says the LORD Almighty.

"It is you priests who show contempt for my name.

"But you ask, 'How have we shown contempt for your name?'

⁷"By offering defiled food on my altar.

"But you ask, 'How have we defiled you?'

"By saying that the LORD's table is contemptible. ⁸When you offer blind animals for sacrifice, is that not wrong? When you sacrifice lame or diseased animals, is that not wrong? Try offering them to your governor! Would he be pleased with you? Would he accept you?" says the LORD Almighty.

⁹"Now implore God to be gracious to us. With such offerings from your hands, will he accept you?"—says the LORD Almighty.

¹⁰"Oh, that one of you would shut the temple doors, so that you would not light useless fires on my altar! I am not pleased with you," says the LORD Almighty, "and I will accept no offering from your hands. ¹¹My name will be great among the nations, from where the sun rises to where it sets. In every place incense and pure offerings will be brought to me, because my name will be great among the nations," says the LORD Almighty.

¹²"But you profane it by saying, 'The Lord's table is defiled,' and, 'Its food is contemptible.' ¹³And you say, 'What a burden!' and you sniff at it contemptuously," says the LORD Almighty.

"When you bring injured, lame or diseased animals and offer them as sacrifices, should I accept them from your hands?" says the LORD. ¹⁴"Cursed is the cheat who has an acceptable male in his flock and vows to give it, but then sacrifices a blemished animal to the Lord. For I am a great king," says the LORD Almighty, "and my name is to be feared among the nations.

Additional Warning to the Priests

2 "And now, you priests, this warning is for you. ²If you do not listen, and if you do not resolve to honor my name," says the LORD Almighty, "I will send a curse on you, and I will curse your blessings. Yes, I have already cursed them, because you have not resolved to honor me.

³"Because of you I will rebuke your descendants*; I will smear on your faces the dung from your festival sacrifices, and you will be carried off with it. ⁴And you will know that I have sent you this warning so that my covenant with Levi may continue," says the LORD Almighty. ⁵"My covenant was with him, a covenant of life and peace, and I gave them to him; this called for reverence and he revered me and stood in awe of my name. ⁶True instruction was in his mouth and nothing false was found on his lips. He walked with me in peace and uprightness, and turned many from sin.

⁷"For the lips of a priest ought to preserve knowledge, because he is the messenger of the LORD Almighty and people seek instruction from his mouth. ⁸But you have turned from the way and by your teaching have caused many to stumble; you have violated the covenant with Levi," says the LORD

a 1 Malachi means my messenger.   b 3 Or will blight your grain myth# 78 "DIVORCE DOESN'T HAPPEN TO CHRISTIANS."

Craig wants out of our marriage. That's obvious now.

The last thing he told me before moving out a month ago was that he never really loved me and doesn't plan to come back. I felt like I cried for two weeks straight.

We were separated once, a year ago, but got back together. This time is different. I know him well enough to know when he really means something. He's not coming back.

I feel so ashamed. I was raised to believe that Christians don't get divorced. You try to work things out, even if it seems impossible. But even after I pleaded with Craig to at least try to work at it and maybe go back to counseling, he said he doesn't want to reconcile. He doesn't think God meant for us to be together. He wants a new life with Ginny, one of his co-workers. He says he's tired of sneaking around with her.

He's tired? He doesn't know what it's like to wait for someone to make up his mind about whether or not he wants to stay married. For the last two years of our marriage, we've drifted apart, ever since his last promotion. Now that he has the job of his dreams, it's as if our life together doesn't fit the "new and improved" Craig.

I don't know what to do. I can't make him stay. My pastor and my parents keep giving me advice about reconciliation. Aside from begging Craig to stay (yes, I've done that), I don't know what else to do.

—Rachael

JUDGING BY THE percentage of divorce among Christians, divorce can and does happen to Christians. Based on verses such as, " 'I hate divorce,' says the LORD God of Israel" (Malachi 2:16), some Christians presume that a person ceases to be a believer if his or her marriage ends. Consequently, many Christians feel a tremendous amount of stress and guilt in addition to the grief caused by marital trauma.

The best-case scenario for a marriage, and what we should do everything in our power to fight for, is for a man and woman to be joined for life, à la Genesis 2:24. But in a fallen world, many heartbreaking choices are made—some that are out of our control, like Rachael's helplessness over Craig's choice to leave her.

Because of sin, God allowed a clause about divorce to be included in the Law of Moses (see Deuteronomy 24:1–4). He wanted to prevent men from dumping their wives for frivolous reasons. Yet this allowance is not a license to maintain a cavalier attitude about marriage, such as, "Oh well. If this doesn't work out, we can always get divorced." Nor does it preclude a couple's responsibility to work hard at a marriage. After all, God still hates divorce. His mercy, however, is shown in the grace he extends to his people.

Unfortunately, we believers aren't always so gracious to each other. We load guilt on people who are already wounded. Maybe you've experienced this firsthand.

In a perfect world, divorce wouldn't happen. Unfortunately, in our world, it does.

> "Christians have the same incidence of divorce as non-Christians. Among married born again Christians, 35 percent have experienced a divorce. That figure is identical to the outcome among married adults who are not born again: 35 percent."
>
> —Barna Research Group (2004)

1381

> "JESUS REPLIED, 'MOSES PERMITTED YOU TO DIVORCE YOUR WIVES BECAUSE YOUR HEARTS WERE HARD. BUT IT WAS NOT THIS WAY FROM THE BEGINNING.' "
>
> MATTHEW 19:8

SEE ALSO
Matthew 5:31–32
Matthew 19:1–11
1 Corinthians 7:10–16

For more on **Divorce**, check the index.

Almighty. ⁹"So I have caused you to be despised and humiliated before all the people, because you have not followed my ways but have shown partiality in matters of the law."

Breaking Covenant Through Divorce

¹⁰Do we not all have one Father*? Did not one God create us? Why do we profane the covenant of our ancestors by being unfaithful to one another?

¹¹Judah has been unfaithful. A detestable thing has been committed in Israel and in Jerusalem: Judah has desecrated the sanctuary the LORD loves by marrying women who worship a foreign god. ¹²If anyone does this, whoever he may be, may the LORD remove him from the tents of Jacob*—even though he brings an offering to the LORD Almighty.

¹³Another thing you do: You flood the LORD's altar with tears. You weep and wail because he no longer looks with favor on your offerings or accepts them with pleasure from your hands. ¹⁴You ask, "Why?" It is because the LORD is the witness between you and the wife of your youth. You have been unfaithful to her, though she is your partner, the wife of your marriage covenant.

¹⁵Has not the LORD made the two of you one? You belong to him in body and spirit. And why has he made you one? Because he was seeking godly offspring.* So be on your guard, and do not be unfaithful to the wife of your youth.

¹⁶"I hate divorce," says the LORD God of Israel, "and I hate it when people clothe themselves with injustice," says the LORD Almighty.

So be on your guard, and do not be unfaithful.

Breaking Covenant Through Injustice

¹⁷You have wearied the LORD with your words.

"How have we wearied him?" you ask.

By saying, "All who do evil are good in the eyes of the LORD, and he is pleased with them" or "Where is the God of justice?"

3 "I will send my messenger, who will prepare the way before me. Then suddenly the Lord you are seeking will come to his temple; the messenger of the covenant, whom you desire, will come," says the LORD Almighty.

²But who can endure the day of his coming? Who can stand when he appears? For he will be like a refiner's fire or a launderer's soap. ³He will sit as a refiner and purifier of silver; he will purify the Levites and refine them like gold and silver. Then the LORD will have men who will bring offerings in righteousness, ⁴and the offerings of Judah and Jerusalem will be acceptable to the LORD, as in days gone by, as in former years.

⁵"So I will come to put you on trial. I will be quick to testify against sorcerers, adulterers and perjurers, against those who defraud laborers of their wages, who oppress the widows and the fatherless, and deprive the foreigners among you of justice, but do not fear me," says the LORD Almighty.

Breaking Covenant by Withholding Tithes

⁶"I the LORD do not change. So you, the descendants of Jacob, are not destroyed. ⁷Ever since the time of your ancestors you have turned away from my decrees and have not kept them. Return to me, and I will return to you," says the LORD Almighty.

"But you ask, 'How are we to return?'

aussie:considering divorce

2:13–16 On the topic of divorce, God doesn't say he's comfortable with whatever's best for us, or he'd *prefer* we stay together or he *dislikes* divorce so please try to avoid it. He uses a strong word: "I hate divorce." *Hate*, as in abhor, detest, loathe. When you're experiencing marital problems, exhaust every possible resource God gives you—wise counsel, encouraging friends, prayer. With only a few exceptions, if you will close the door to divorce, God will open another door for you. You and your husband are one in God's eyes, and God will help you fight to preserve that unity.

ª 10 Or *father*   *ᵇ 12* Or *¹²May the LORD remove from the tents of Jacob anyone who gives testimony in behalf of the man who does this*

HE IS: a refiner

3:3 The people had grown indifferent to the Lord, but Malachi saw that because of their backsliding, God would turn up the heat to bring them back to righteousness. He predicted that God would sit as a *refiner*.

If the heat has been turned up in your life, perhaps God is refining you. He monitors the temperature of your trials so the dross of sin will rise to the surface. He wants to sweep away your iniquities as the silversmith sweeps away the impurities tainting precious metals. Though the heat might feel painful, it's purifying, making you shine and reflect his glory.

For the next He Is, go to p. 1390.

8"Will a mere mortal rob God? Yet you rob me.

"But you ask, 'How are we robbing you?'

"In tithes and offerings. 9You are under a curse—your whole nation—because you are robbing me. 10Bring the whole tithe into the storehouse, that there may be food in my house. Test me in this," says the LORD Almighty, "and see if I will not throw open the floodgates of heaven and pour out so much blessing that there will not be room enough to store it. 11I will prevent pests from devouring your crops, and the vines in your fields will not drop their fruit before it is ripe," says the LORD Almighty. 12"Then all the nations will call you blessed, for yours will be a delightful land," says the LORD Almighty.

Israel Speaks Arrogantly Against God

13"You have spoken arrogantly against me," says the LORD.

"Yet you ask, 'What have we said against you?'

14"You have said, 'It is futile to serve God. What do we gain by carrying out his requirements and going about like mourners before the LORD Almighty? 15But now we call the arrogant blessed. Certainly evildoers prosper, and even when they put God to the test, they get away with it.'"

conversations

tithing «» 3:10

1» Why does God allow us to test him on the issue of tithing?

2» What do you consider to be your "whole tithe"?

3» What makes tithing so hard to do? What's at the heart of those issues?

For more on tithing, check the index.
For the next Conversations, go to p. 1400.

The Faithful Remnant

16Then those who feared the LORD talked with each other, and the LORD listened and heard. A scroll of remembrance was written in his presence concerning those who feared the LORD and honored his name.

17"On the day when I act," says the LORD Almighty, "they will be my treasured possession. I will spare them, just as a father has compassion and spares his son who serves him. 18And you will again see the distinction between the righteous and the wicked, between those who serve God and those who do not.

Judgment and Covenant Renewal

4 *"Surely the day is coming; it will burn like a furnace. All the arrogant and every evildoer will be stubble, and that day that is coming will set them on fire," says the LORD Almighty. "Not a root or a branch will be left to them. 2But for you who revere my name, the sun of righteousness will rise with healing in its rays. And you will go out and frolic like well-fed calves. 3Then you will trample on the wicked; they will be ashes under the soles of your feet on the day when I act," says the LORD Almighty.

---

* 4:1-6 is numbered 3:19-24 in Hebrew texts.

4 "Remember the law of my servant Moses, the decrees and laws I gave him at Horeb for all Israel.

5 "See, I will send the prophet Elijah to you before that great and dreadful day of the LORD comes. 6 He will turn the hearts of the parents to their children, and the hearts of the children to their parents; or else I will come and strike the land with total destruction."

The New Testament

1388 1436 1466
MATTHEW MARK LUKE

1514 1550
JOHN ACTS

the gos
& the
early

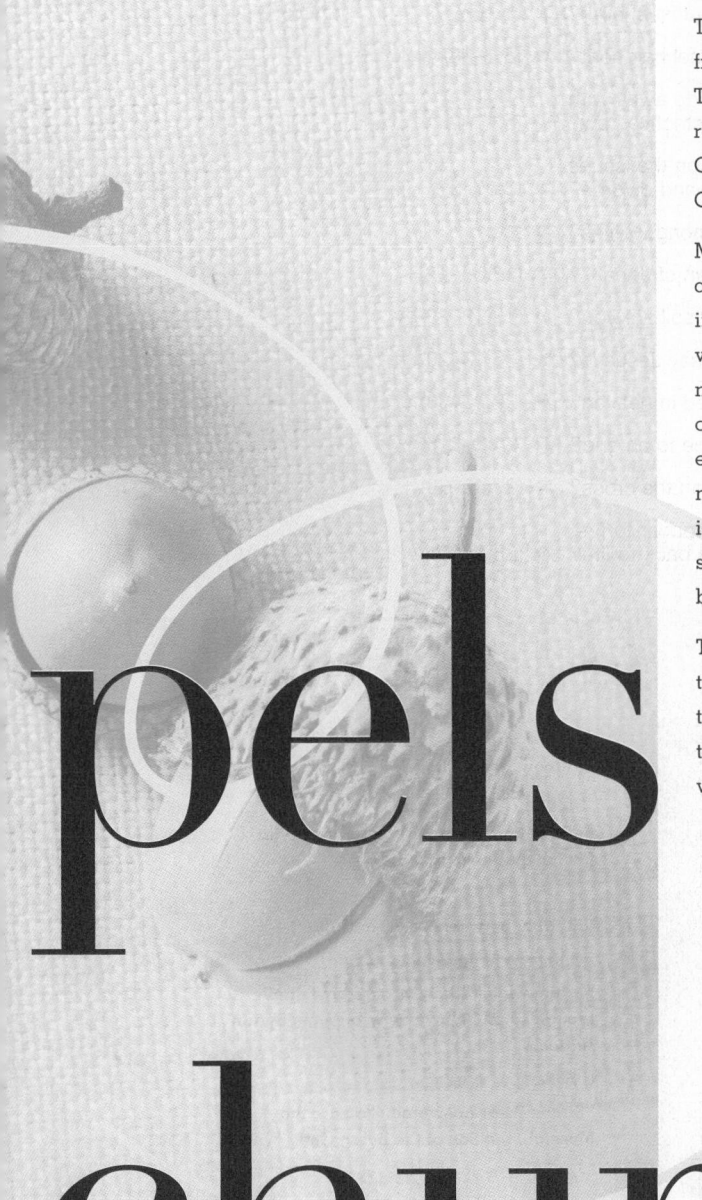

The first four books of the New Testament are known as the *Gospels*, from the Greek word for "good news." The "Good News" is that of the redemptive life and work of Jesus Christ, the Messiah foretold in the Old Testament.

Matthew, Mark and Luke are often called the "synoptic" Gospels, meaning that they are written from a similar viewpoint. These texts are historical narratives, relating the story of the life of Christ. The Gospel of John differs in emphasis from the synoptics. With a more theological tone, the book of John is concerned more with examining the special significance and meaning behind Jesus' life, work and identity.

The book of Acts is a companion piece to the book of Luke, picking up where the Gospel narrative ends and telling the story of the early church and the work of the apostle Paul.

pels

church

matthew

AUTHOR
Matthew, also called Levi.

AUDIENCE
Followers of Jesus. Matthew wrote with a Jewish audience in mind.

DATE
Probably between A.D. 60 and 70.

SETTING
Matthew most likely wrote from Israel, though some believe he wrote from Syrian Antioch.

VERSE TO REMEMBER
"Simon Peter answered, 'You are the Messiah, the Son of the living God.'" (16:16)

THEME TO CONSIDER
Jesus claimed to be the Messiah, the Son of God. Who do you say Jesus is?

The Genealogy of Jesus the Messiah

1 This is the genealogy*a* of Jesus the Messiah*b* the son of David, the son of Abraham:

² Abraham was the father of Isaac,
    Isaac the father of Jacob,
    Jacob the father of Judah and his brothers,
    ³ Judah the father of Perez and Zerah, whose mother was Tamar,
    Perez the father of Hezron,
    Hezron the father of Ram,
    ⁴ Ram the father of Amminadab,
    Amminadab the father of Nahshon,
    Nahshon the father of Salmon,
    ⁵ Salmon the father of Boaz, whose mother was Rahab,
    Boaz the father of Obed, whose mother was Ruth,
    Obed the father of Jesse,
    ⁶ and Jesse the father of King David.

    David was the father of Solomon, whose mother had been Uriah's wife,
    ⁷ Solomon the father of Rehoboam,
    Rehoboam the father of Abijah,
    Abijah the father of Asa,
    ⁸ Asa the father of Jehoshaphat,
    Jehoshaphat the father of Jehoram,
    Jehoram the father of Uzziah,
    ⁹ Uzziah the father of Jotham,
    Jotham the father of Ahaz,
    Ahaz the father of Hezekiah,
    ¹⁰ Hezekiah the father of Manasseh,
    Manasseh the father of Amon,
    Amon the father of Josiah,
    ¹¹ and Josiah the father of Jeconiah*c* and his brothers at the time of the exile to Babylon.

¹² After the exile to Babylon:
    Jeconiah was the father of Shealtiel,
    Shealtiel the father of Zerubbabel,
    ¹³ Zerubbabel the father of Abiud,
    Abiud the father of Eliakim,
    Eliakim the father of Azor,
    ¹⁴ Azor the father of Zadok,
    Zadok the father of Akim,
    Akim the father of Eliud,
    ¹⁵ Eliud the father of Eleazar,
    Eleazar the father of Matthan,
    Matthan the father of Jacob,
    ¹⁶ and Jacob the father of Joseph, the husband of Mary, and Mary was the mother of Jesus who is called the Messiah.

¹⁷ Thus there were fourteen generations in all from Abraham to David, fourteen from David to the exile to Babylon, and fourteen from the exile to the Messiah.

---

a 1 Or *is an account of the origin*   *b* 1 Or *Jesus Christ. Messiah* (Hebrew) and *Christ* (Greek) both mean *Anointed One*; also in verse 18.   *c* 11 That is, Jehoiachin; also in verse 12

Joseph Accepts Jesus as His Son

¹⁸This is how the birth of Jesus the Messiah came about*a*: His mother Mary was pledged to be married to Joseph, but before they came together, she was found to be pregnant through the Holy Spirit. ¹⁹Because Joseph her husband was a righteous man and did not want to expose her to public disgrace, he had in mind to divorce her quietly.

²⁰But after he had considered this, an angel of the Lord appeared to him in a dream and said, "Joseph son of David, do not be afraid to take Mary home as your wife, because what is conceived in her is from the Holy Spirit. ²¹She will give birth to a son, and you are to give him the name Jesus,*b* because he will save his people from their sins."

²²All this took place to fulfill what the Lord had said through the prophet: ²³"The virgin will conceive and give birth to a son, and they will call him Immanuel"*c* (which means "God with us").

²⁴When Joseph woke up, he did what the angel of the Lord had commanded him and took Mary home as his wife. ²⁵But he had no union with her until she gave birth to a son. And he gave him the name Jesus.

HE IS: God with us

1:22–23 Jesus Christ's birth, prophesied by Isaiah, was divinely mortal. Conceived by the Holy Spirit, he was a child of the heavenly Father and a human mother, and nurtured in Mary's womb. Through this miracle, the reality of Immanuel, *God with us*, was fulfilled (see Isaiah 7:14).

If you believe Jesus was only a man, you're mistaken. If you think of him as only God, you're off-track. Jesus is God who became human so that you can know him personally. He is *God with us*, and his constant, divine presence is forever, always with you, no matter how alone you may feel.

For the next He Is, go to p. 1394.

The Magi Visit the Messiah

2 After Jesus was born in Bethlehem in Judea, during the time of King Herod, Magi*d* from the east came to Jerusalem ²and asked, "Where is the one who has been born king of the Jews? We saw his star when it rose and have come to worship him."

³When King Herod heard this he was disturbed, and all Jerusalem with him. ⁴When he had called together all the people's chief priests and teachers of the law, he asked them where the Messiah was to be born. ⁵"In Bethlehem in Judea," they replied, "for this is what the prophet has written:

⁶"'But you, Bethlehem, in the land of Judah,
    are by no means least among the rulers of Judah;
for out of you will come a ruler
    who will shepherd my people Israel.'*e*"

⁷Then Herod called the Magi secretly and found out from them the exact time the star had appeared. ⁸He sent them to Bethlehem and said, "Go and make a careful search for the child. As soon as you find him, report to me, so that I too may go and worship him."

⁹After they had heard the king, they went on their way, and the star they had seen when it rose went ahead of them until it stopped over the place where the child was. ¹⁰When they saw the star, they were overjoyed. ¹¹On coming to the house, they saw the child with his mother Mary, and they bowed down and worshiped him. Then they opened their treasures and presented him with gifts of gold, frankincense and myrrh. ¹²And having been warned in a dream not to go back to Herod, they returned to their country by another route.

---

a 18 Or *The origin of Jesus the Messiah was like this* *b 21* Jesus is the Greek form of *Joshua*, which means *the Lᴏʀᴅ saves.* *c 23* Isaiah 7:14 *d 1* Traditionally *wise men* *e 6* Micah 5:2,4

Matthew 1:18-25; Luke 1:26-56

ASKmeanyTHING

How did you handle the news of your pregnancy?

[laughs softly] Not quite the news I ever expected to hear—and from an *angel*. I'm not sure I can even put into words all the thoughts that were racing through my mind when Gabriel appeared. How do you even begin to understand that God has singled you out to be the mother of the "Son of the Most High"? What did that mean? How could that happen, especially since I was a virgin? It made no sense.

So what did you do?

I guess I reacted in the only way I knew how—to accept what my God had planned for me. You see, I had grown up knowing the power of the God we served and worshiped. I knew of his love and his provision. If this is what God wanted for me, then how could I do anything but accept his plan?

It couldn't have been easy being an unwed mother.

No, it was extremely difficult. You know, many women who had sex outside of marriage were stoned. I was so thankful that Joseph stayed by my side and married me. But the fact remained: I was the town scandal. My pregnancy was the subject of gossip everywhere. It didn't matter what I said—people were going to think what they wanted. Both Joseph and I knew that we had not done anything wrong. But who would believe two young people who were already engaged? At times I felt so isolated. My cousin Elizabeth understood, and I spent quite a bit of time with her. But outside of Elizabeth and Joseph, there was no one who really understood.

So how did you cope?

I coped the only way I knew how—I had to trust God completely. Daily, hour by hour, minute by minute, I had to remind myself that God was in complete control and that he knew what he was doing.

How can others benefit from your story?

Well, I know that my situation is unique. But I think we all face unexpected events or shocking news. For some that may mean a pregnancy outside of marriage. Or maybe it's an illness or job loss. It's tempting to let those situations overwhelm you, isolate you or make you doubt God. My hope is that others can learn from my story and see that God will come through for them. Your life may not turn out how you expected, but it will turn out better than it ever could apart from God.

1391

FOR MORE INSIGHT: For more on the benefits of trusting God in your circumstances, read Proverbs 16:20; Isaiah 28:16; Nahum 1:7; and Romans 15:13.

The Escape to Egypt

¹³When they had gone, an angel of the Lord appeared to Joseph in a dream. "Get up," he said, "take the child and his mother and escape to Egypt. Stay there until I tell you, for Herod is going to search for the child to kill him."

¹⁴So he got up, took the child and his mother during the night and left for Egypt, ¹⁵where he stayed until the death of Herod. And so was fulfilled what the Lord had said through the prophet: "Out of Egypt I called my son."*ᵃ*

¹⁶When Herod realized that he had been outwitted by the Magi, he was furious, and he gave orders to kill all the boys in Bethlehem and its vicinity who were two years old and under, in accordance with the time he had learned from the Magi. ¹⁷Then what was said through the prophet Jeremiah was fulfilled:

¹⁸"A voice is heard in Ramah,
  weeping and great mourning,
  Rachel weeping for her children
    and refusing to be comforted,
  because they are no more."*ᵇ*

The Return to Nazareth

¹⁹After Herod died, an angel of the Lord appeared in a dream to Joseph in Egypt ²⁰and said, "Get up, take the child and his mother and go to the land of Israel, for those who were trying to take the child's life are dead."

²¹So he got up, took the child and his mother and went to the land of Israel. ²²But when he heard that Archelaus was reigning in Judea in place of his father Herod, he was afraid to go there. Having been warned in a dream, he withdrew to the district of Galilee, ²³and he went and lived in a town called Nazareth. So was fulfilled what was said through the prophets: "He will be called a Nazarene."

John the Baptist Prepares the Way

3 In those days John the Baptist came, preaching in the wilderness of Judea ²and saying, "Repent, for the kingdom of heaven has come near." ³This is he who was spoken of through the prophet Isaiah:

"A voice of one calling in the wilderness,
  'Prepare the way for the Lord,
    make straight paths for him.'"*ᶜ*

⁴John's clothes were made of camel's hair, and he had a leather belt around his waist. His food was locusts and wild honey. ⁵People went out to him from Jerusalem and all Judea and the whole region of the Jordan. ⁶Confessing their sins, they were baptized by him in the Jordan River.

⁷But when he saw many of the Pharisees and Sadducees coming to where he was baptizing, he said to them: "You brood of vipers! Who warned you to flee from the coming wrath? ⁸Produce fruit in keeping with repentance. ⁹And do not think you can say to yourselves, 'We have Abraham as our father.' I tell you that out of these stones God can raise up children for Abraham. ¹⁰The ax is already at the root of the trees, and every tree that does not produce good fruit will be cut down and thrown into the fire.

¹¹"I baptize you with*ᵈ* water for repentance. But after me comes one who is more powerful than I, whose sandals I am not worthy to carry. He will baptize you with*ᵉ* the Holy Spirit and fire. ¹²His winnowing fork is in his hand, and he will clear his threshing floor, gathering his wheat into the barn and burning up the chaff with unquenchable fire."

The Baptism of Jesus

¹³Then Jesus came from Galilee to the Jordan to be baptized by John. ¹⁴But John tried to deter him, saying, "I need to be baptized by you, and do you come to me?"

¹⁵Jesus replied, "Let it be so now; it is proper for us to do this to fulfill all righteousness." Then John consented.

elizabeth

Luke 1:5–80

You waited your entire life to have a child, didn't you?

Oh yes. Zechariah and I prayed for a child for years—since the day we were married. Even as we got older, we never stopped praying, although our age became more of a factor. I mean, who would believe a woman my age having a child? I guess we had both come to a point in life where we just didn't believe it would happen.

What was it like to be the wife of a priest and not have any children?

It was humiliating, completely humiliating for both Zechariah and me. To see my friends get pregnant and have baby after baby, and then to watch their children playing and growing up while I couldn't even conceive. I felt like I was less of a woman. I felt devalued. My barrenness was a constant reminder of my deficiency as a wife. For years I clung to the story of Sarah and the miracle baby she had in her old age. If anyone was capable of giving us a child, it was our magnificent, wonderful God.

1393

So it wasn't a total surprise when Zechariah came and told, oh wait, **wrote** you the news that Gabriel had given him?

Oh, it was a surprise, a complete surprise. I had never doubted that God *could* do it, but I doubted that he *would* do it. At least I didn't become mute like my husband! Imagine a priest, of all people, questioning one of God's angels! Me? I was just so overjoyed. A child! A *son*. After years of waiting, God had done this for us. In an instant, my disgrace was removed. But that's not all. Our son would be the one to prepare people for the coming of our Messiah! Can you believe that? Our God does so much more for us than we could ever possibly dream about or think to ask for.

What can other women learn from your experience?

I think the main thing is to remember while you're waiting on God for whatever it is—a child, a job, a husband, a dream, a direction—that God is at work. He is in control of everything. It may not seem that God is even listening to your prayers, but he is. And he will act on your behalf in his timing and his plan. Trust, even when you don't see. Especially when you don't see. And always believe.

FOR MORE INSIGHT: Read the following verses for more insight on trusting God and waiting for his timing: Psalm 27:13–14; Isaiah 26:3–4; and Galatians 6:9.

HE IS: God's Son

3:17 At Jesus' baptism, the heavenly Father proudly testified from heaven about his relationship with his Son. With his bold announcement he expelled any doubts about who Jesus is. Jesus' baptism symbolized his sinless life, atoning death and miraculous resurrection.

Because Jesus came to earth as *God's Son* and pleased the Father through his life and death, he created a way for you to become God's daughter. When you put your faith in Jesus, God will baptize you into his family and proudly proclaim, "This is my daughter, whom I love; with her I am well pleased."

For the next He Is, go to p. 1407.

¹⁶As soon as Jesus was baptized, he went up out of the water. At that moment heaven was opened, and he saw the Spirit of God descending like a dove and alighting on him. ¹⁷And a voice from heaven said, "This is my Son, whom I love; with him I am well pleased."

Jesus Is Tested in the Wilderness

4 Then Jesus was led by the Spirit into the wilderness to be tempted^a by the devil. ²After fasting forty days and forty nights, he was hungry. ³The tempter came to him and said, "If you are the Son of God, tell these stones to become bread."

⁴Jesus answered, "It is written: 'People do not live on bread alone, but on every word that comes from the mouth of God.'^b"

⁵Then the devil took him to the holy city and had him stand on the highest point of the temple. ⁶"If you are the Son of God," he said, "throw yourself down. For it is written:

"'He will command his angels
concerning you,
and they will lift you up in their hands,
so that you will not strike your foot
against a stone.'^c"

⁷Jesus answered him, "It is also written: 'Do not put the Lord your God to the test.'^d"

⁸Again, the devil took him to a very high mountain and showed him all the kingdoms of the world and their splendor. ⁹"All this I will give you," he said, "if you will bow down and worship me."

¹⁰Jesus said to him, "Away from me, Satan! For it is written: 'Worship the Lord your God, and serve him only.'^e"

¹¹Then the devil left him, and angels came and attended him.

Jesus Begins to Preach

¹²When Jesus heard that John had been put in prison, he withdrew to Galilee. ¹³Leaving Nazareth, he went and lived in Capernaum, which was by the lake in the area of Zebulun and Naphtali— ¹⁴to fulfill what was said through the prophet Isaiah:

at issue: temptation

4:1–11 Temptation comes to us in so many forms: juicy gossip practically begging to be passed on, your co-workers or children pushing you to the end of your patience, images in movies that you should never allow yourself to see in the first place. You probably know your own personal weaknesses, but do you know how to battle them? When Satan tempted Jesus, Jesus responded with God's Word. He combated temptation by naming Satan's lies and then holding on to God's truth. You can only use that strategy if you know God's Word—and that's the only sure weapon against temptation.

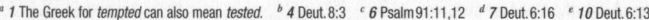

---

^a *1* The Greek for *tempted* can also mean *tested.*   ^b *4* Deut. 8:3   ^c *6* Psalm 91:11,12   ^d *7* Deut. 6:16   ^e *10* Deut. 6:13

¹⁵"Land of Zebulun and land of Naphtali,
　　the Way of the Sea, beyond the Jordan,
　　Galilee of the Gentiles—
¹⁶the people living in darkness
　　have seen a great light;
　　on those living in the land of the shadow of death
　　a light has dawned."*ᵃ*

¹⁷From that time on Jesus began to preach, "Repent, for the kingdom of heaven has come near."

Jesus Calls His First Disciples

¹⁸As Jesus was walking beside the Sea of Galilee, he saw two brothers, Simon called Peter and his brother Andrew. They were casting a net into the lake, for they were fishermen. ¹⁹"Come, follow me," Jesus said, "and I will send you out to fish for people." ²⁰At once they left their nets and followed him.

²¹Going on from there, he saw two other brothers, James son of Zebedee and his brother John. They were in a boat with their father Zebedee, preparing their nets. Jesus called them, ²²and immediately they left the boat and their father and followed him.

Jesus Heals the Sick

²³Jesus went throughout Galilee, teaching in their synagogues, proclaiming the good news of the kingdom, and healing every disease and sickness among the people. ²⁴News about him spread all over Syria, and people brought to him all who were ill with various diseases, those suffering severe pain, the demon-possessed, those having seizures, and the paralyzed; and he healed them. ²⁵Large crowds from Galilee, the Decapolis,*ᵇ* Jerusalem, Judea and the region across the Jordan followed him.

Introduction to the Sermon on the Mount

5 Now when Jesus saw the crowds, he went up on a mountainside and sat down. His disciples came to him, ²and he began to teach them.

The Beatitudes

He said:

³"Blessed are the poor in spirit,
　　for theirs is the kingdom of heaven.
⁴Blessed are those who mourn,
　　for they will be comforted.
⁵Blessed are the meek,
　　for they will inherit the earth.
⁶Blessed are those who hunger and thirst for righteousness,
　　for they will be filled.
⁷Blessed are the merciful,
　　for they will be shown mercy.
⁸Blessed are the pure in heart,
　　for they will see God.
⁹Blessed are the peacemakers,
　　for they will be called children of God.
¹⁰Blessed are those who are persecuted because of righteousness,
　　for theirs is the kingdom of heaven.

¹¹"Blessed are you when people insult you, persecute you and falsely say all kinds of evil against you because of me. ¹²Rejoice and be glad, because great is your reward in heaven, for in the same way they persecuted the prophets who were before you.

ᵃ 16 Isaiah 9:1,2　　*ᵇ 25* That is, the Ten Cities

Salt and Light

¹³"You are the salt of the earth. But if the salt loses its saltiness, how can it be made salty again? It is no longer good for anything, except to be thrown out and trampled underfoot.

¹⁴"You are the light of the world. A city on a hill cannot be hidden. ¹⁵Neither do people light a lamp and put it under a bowl. Instead they put it on its stand, and it gives light to everyone in the house. ¹⁶In the same way, let your light shine before others, that they may see your good deeds and glorify your Father in heaven.

The Fulfillment of the Law

¹⁷"Do not think that I have come to abolish the Law or the Prophets; I have not come to abolish them but to fulfill them. ¹⁸Truly I tell you, until heaven and earth disappear, not the smallest letter, not the least stroke of a pen, will by any means disappear from the Law until everything is accomplished. ¹⁹Anyone who sets aside one of the least of these commands and teaches others accordingly will be called least in the kingdom of heaven, but whoever practices and teaches these commands will be called great in the kingdom of heaven. ²⁰For I tell you that unless your righteousness surpasses that of the Pharisees and the teachers of the law, you will certainly not enter the kingdom of heaven.

Murder

²¹"You have heard that it was said to the people long ago, 'You shall not murder,'ᵃ and anyone who murders will be subject to judgment.' ²²But I tell you that anyone who is angry with a brother or sisterᵇ will be subject to judgment. Again, anyone who says to a brother or sister, 'Raca,'ᶜ is answerable to the Sanhedrin. And anyone who says, 'You fool!' will be in danger of the fire of hell.

²³"Therefore, if you are offering your gift at the altar and there remember that your brother or sister has something against you, ²⁴leave your gift there in front of the altar. First go and be reconciled to that person; then come and offer your gift.

²⁵"Settle matters quickly with your adversary who is taking you to court. Do it while you are still together on the way, or your adversary may hand you over to the judge, and the judge may hand you over to the officer, and you may be thrown into prison. ²⁶Truly I tell you, you will not get out until you have paid the last penny.

Adultery

²⁷"You have heard that it was said, 'You shall not commit adultery.'ᵈ ²⁸But I tell you that anyone who looks at a woman lustfully has already committed adultery with her in his heart. ²⁹If your right eye causes you to stumble, gouge it out and throw it away. It is better for you to lose one part of your body than for your whole body to be thrown into hell. ³⁰And if your right hand causes you to stumble, cut it off and throw it away. It is better for you to lose one part of your body than for your whole body to go into hell.

Divorce

³¹"It has been said, 'Anyone who divorces his wife must give her a certificate of divorce.'ᵉ ³²But I tell you that any-

1396

atissue:lust

5:27–30 Our society loves the little loopholes—on our taxes, on our timesheets, in the courtroom, in our obligations. But in God's eyes, violating the spirit of his law is the same as actually breaking the letter of it. Having a sexual fantasy about your handsome neighbor is as sinful as if you had actually engaged in a physical affair. Investing your emotions into a male friend or man you met online and becoming dependent on him at the expense of your husband is an affair, even if you never gave him your body. Lustful thoughts are a breach of the purity God desires for you. God doesn't honor our "technicalities."

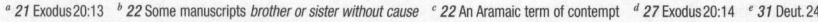

ᵃ 21 Exodus 20:13 ᵇ 22 Some manuscripts *brother or sister without cause* ᶜ 22 An Aramaic term of contempt ᵈ 27 Exodus 20:14 ᵉ 31 Deut. 24:1

one who divorces his wife, except for sexual immorality, causes her to become an adulteress, and anyone who marries the divorced woman commits adultery.

Oaths

³³ "Again, you have heard that it was said to the people long ago, 'Do not break your oath, but fulfill to the Lord the vows you have made.' ³⁴ But I tell you, do not swear an oath at all: either by heaven, for it is God's throne; ³⁵ or by the earth, for it is his footstool; or by Jerusalem, for it is the city of the Great King. ³⁶ And do not swear by your head, for you cannot make even one hair white or black. ³⁷ All you need to say is simply 'Yes,' or 'No'; anything beyond this comes from the evil one.ᵃ

Eye for Eye

³⁸ "You have heard that it was said, 'Eye for eye, and tooth for tooth.'ᵇ ³⁹ But I tell you, do not resist an evil person. If anyone slaps you on the right cheek, turn to them the other cheek also. ⁴⁰ And if anyone wants to sue you and take your shirt, hand over your coat as well. ⁴¹ If anyone forces you to go one mile, go with them two miles. ⁴² Give to the one who asks you, and do not turn away from the one who wants to borrow from you.

Love for Enemies

⁴³ "You have heard that it was said, 'Love your neighborᶜ and hate your enemy.' ⁴⁴ But I tell you, love your enemies and pray for those who persecute you, ⁴⁵ that you may be children of your Father in heaven. He causes his sun to rise on the evil and the good, and sends rain on the righteous and the unrighteous. ⁴⁶ If you love those who love you, what reward will you get? Are not even the tax collectors doing that? ⁴⁷ And if you greet only your own people, what are you doing more than others? Do not even pagans do that? ⁴⁸ Be perfect, therefore, as your heavenly Father is perfect.

Giving to the Needy

6 "Be careful not to do your 'acts of righteousness' in front of others, to be seen by them. If you do, you will have no reward from your Father in heaven.

² "So when you give to the needy, do not announce it with trumpets, as the hypocrites do in the synagogues and on the streets, to be honored by others. Truly I tell you, they have received their reward in full. ³ But when you give to the needy, do not let your left hand know what your right hand is doing, ⁴ so that your giving may be in secret. Then your Father, who sees what is done in secret, will reward you.

Prayer

⁵ "And when you pray, do not be like the hypocrites, for they love to pray standing in the synagogues and on the street corners to be seen by others. Truly I tell you, they have received their reward in full. ⁶ But when you pray, go into your room, close the door and pray to your Father, who is unseen. Then your Father, who sees what is done in secret, will reward you. ⁷ And when you pray, do not keep on babbling like pagans, for they think they will be heard because of their many words. ⁸ Do not be like them, for your Father knows what you need before you ask him.

⁹ "This, then, is how you should pray:

> " 'Our Father in heaven,
> hallowed be your name,
> ¹⁰ your kingdom come,
> your will be done,
> on earth as it is in heaven.
> ¹¹ Give us today our daily bread.
> ¹² And forgive us our debts,
> as we also have forgiven our debtors.
> ¹³ And lead us not into temptation,ᵈ
> but deliver us from the evil one.ᵉ'

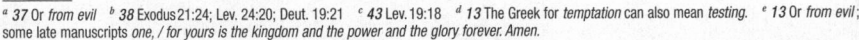

ᵃ *37* Or *from evil*   ᵇ *38* Exodus 21:24; Lev. 24:20; Deut. 19:21   ᶜ *43* Lev. 19:18   ᵈ *13* The Greek for *temptation* can also mean *testing.*   ᵉ *13* Or *from evil*; some late manuscripts *one, / for yours is the kingdom and the power and the glory forever. Amen.*

myth#

"MY COMPANY OWES ME."

My co-worker told me how to do it. She said everyone does it, and no one ever gets caught. Besides, my company owes me.

How many of my son's soccer games had I missed that month? I'd lost track. And how many nights had I eaten take-out dinners at my desk while finishing some work for my boss? It seems as if my life consists of driving to work, working, driving home and dropping into bed exhausted, only to wake up and do it all over again. Other people at normal jobs can take off for an appointment or leave early if they need to. Not me! I work for an abnormally demanding boss and an impersonal company that's only concerned about the bottom line: performance.

True, I chose to work here. And the long hours didn't bother me at first. But having to explain my schedule to my son has been getting to me. I resent the time away from him. My boss sees me as an employee—not a real person. And that's exactly how I felt the day I crossed the line. It wasn't really me manipulating the numbers in my June expense account. When I turned in the padded report to Accounting, I had suddenly become someone I didn't recognize.

"This company owes me," I remember repeating to myself as I drove home that night, nervous about what I'd just done. I didn't think of it as outright lying—more like just inflating the truth so that I could get what was due me. I justified it to myself all night and the next morning. I do so much for this company, practically sacrificing all of my time and energy. The executives make so much money; they won't miss this little bit. It doesn't hurt anyone. I won't let myself feel guilty for taking what I deserve.

Oh, if only I'd known the truth about the lies I was telling myself.

—Erin

WHILE MANY PEOPLE

separate their lives into compartments, such as "sacred" and "secular," God is concerned with our lives as a whole. He expects us to honor him in all areas, including our work, recreation, relationships—everything. What does our integrity at work tell us about our spirituality?

- Our decisions at work reveal what's really in our hearts. Under pressure, does our faith hold up? Do we let God's principles guide our decisions in and out of the office?

- Our integrity in the little decisions shows who we are really serving. Do we work for our company as if we're working for God himself and not a human boss (see Colossians 3:22–25)? That sets a high standard for us, regardless of how unreasonable our human bosses may be.

- God is "supervising" our work even when we think no one sees us stretch the truth or cheat in little ways. Our real Boss knows our hearts and actions. He sees everything (see Matthew 6:18). Do you do the right thing when no one else is looking?

- If we claim to be Christians, then we are often under intense scrutiny in the workplace. Others are watching us to see if we are really living what we claim to believe. When someone else finds out about our dishonest decisions, how does that damage our testimony?

- It's easy to justify our actions or convince ourselves that we deserve certain liberties. Are we listening to our deceptive hearts (see Jeremiah 17:9) or to God's unchanging Word (see Psalm 119:11)?

- Being right before God is more satisfying than any amount of dishonest gain. Which would you choose: To do your best, be honest and honor God *or* to have more money but forfeit God's blessing on your work? God will

reward you with far more than you can grab for yourself—sometimes financially but also with peace of mind and a sense of his favor and presence.

"Four out of five adults stated that living with a high degree of integrity is a very desirable goal for their future."

—Barna Research Group (2000)

"Better a little with the fear of the Lord than great wealth with turmoil."

PROVERBS 15:16

SEE ALSO

Psalm 15:2

Daniel 6:1–5

Colossians 3:22–25

For more on **Career** and **Honesty,** check the index.

[1400]

¹⁴For if you forgive others when they sin against you, your heavenly Father will also forgive you. ¹⁵But if you do not forgive others their sins, your Father will not forgive your sins.

Fasting

¹⁶"When you fast, do not look somber as the hypocrites do, for they disfigure their faces to show others they are fasting. Truly I tell you, they have received their reward in full. ¹⁷But when you fast, put oil on your head and wash your face, ¹⁸so that it will not be obvious to others that you are fasting, but only to your Father, who is unseen; and your Father, who sees what is done in secret, will reward you.

Treasures in Heaven

¹⁹"Do not store up for yourselves treasures on earth, where moth and rust destroy, and where thieves break in and steal. ²⁰But store up for yourselves treasures in heaven, where moth and rust do not destroy, and where thieves do not break in and steal. ²¹For where your treasure is, there your heart will be also.

²²"The eye is the lamp of the body. If your eyes are healthy,ᵃ your whole body will be full of light. ²³But if your eyes are unhealthy,ᵇ your whole body will be full of darkness. If then the light within you is darkness, how great is that darkness!

²⁴"No one can serve two masters. Either you will hate the one and love the other, or you will be devoted to the one and despise the other. You cannot serve both God and Money.

Do Not Worry

²⁵"Therefore I tell you, do not worry about your life, what you will eat or drink; or about your body, what you will wear. Is not life more important than food, and the body more important than clothes? ²⁶Look at the birds of the air; they do not sow or reap or store away in barns, and yet your heavenly Father feeds them. Are you not much more valuable than they? ²⁷Can any one of you by worrying add a single hour to your lifeᶜ?

²⁸"And why do you worry about clothes? See how the flowers of the field grow. They do not labor or spin. ²⁹Yet I tell you that not even Solomon in all his splendor was dressed like one of these. ³⁰If that is how God clothes the grass of the field, which is here today and tomorrow is thrown into the fire, will he not much more clothe you—you of little faith? ³¹So do not worry, saying, 'What shall we eat?' or 'What shall we drink?' or 'What shall we wear?' ³²For the pagans run after all these things, and your heavenly Father knows that you need them. ³³But seek first his kingdom and his righteousness, and all these things will be given to you as well. ³⁴Therefore do not worry about tomorrow, for tomorrow will worry about itself. Each day has enough trouble of its own.

"conversations"

fashion ⟨⟩ 6:28–34

1» Is it OK for Christian women to be concerned about being in style?

2» How much time do you spend worrying about your clothing?

3» What does it mean to seek God's kingdom first, even when it comes to fashion?

For more on fashion, check the index.
For the next Conversations, go to p. 1406.

Judging Others

7 "Do not judge, or you too will be judged. ²For in the same way you judge others, you will be judged, and with the measure you use, it will be measured to you.

³"Why do you look at the speck of sawdust in someone else's eye and pay no attention to the plank in your own eye? ⁴How can you say, 'Let me take the speck out of your eye,' when all the time there is a plank in your own eye? ⁵You hypocrite, first take the plank out of your own eye, and then you will see clearly to remove the speck from the other person's eye.

⁶"Do not give dogs what is sacred; do not throw your pearls to pigs. If you do, they may trample them under their feet, and then turn and tear you to pieces.

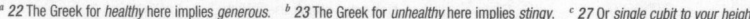

ᵃ 22 The Greek for *healthy* here implies *generous.*   ᵇ 23 The Greek for *unhealthy* here implies *stingy.*   ᶜ 27 Or *single cubit to your height*

Ask, Seek, Knock

[7]"Ask and it will be given to you; seek and you will find; knock and the door will be opened to you. [8]For everyone who asks receives; those who seek find; and to those who knock, the door will be opened.

[9]"Which of you, if your son asks for bread, will give him a stone? [10]Or if he asks for a fish, will give him a snake? [11]If you, then, though you are evil, know how to give good gifts to your children, how much more will your Father in heaven give good gifts to those who ask him! [12]So in everything, do to others what you would have them do to you, for this sums up the Law and the Prophets.

The Narrow and Wide Gates

[13]"Enter through the narrow gate. For wide is the gate and broad is the road that leads to destruction, and many enter through it. [14]But small is the gate and narrow the road that leads to life, and only a few find it.

True and False Prophets

[15]"Watch out for false prophets. They come to you in sheep's clothing, but inwardly they are ferocious wolves. [16]By their fruit you will recognize them. Do people pick grapes from thornbushes, or figs from thistles? [17]Likewise, every good tree bears good fruit, but a bad tree bears bad fruit. [18]A good tree cannot bear bad fruit, and a bad tree cannot bear good fruit. [19]Every tree that does not bear good fruit is cut down and thrown into the fire. [20]Thus, by their fruit you will recognize them.

True and False Disciples

[21]"Not everyone who says to me, 'Lord, Lord,' will enter the kingdom of heaven, but only those who do the will of my Father who is in heaven. [22]Many will say to me on that day, 'Lord, Lord, did we not prophesy in your name and in your name drive out demons and in your name perform many miracles?' [23]Then I will tell them plainly, 'I never knew you. Away from me, you evildoers!'

The Wise and Foolish Builders

[24]"Therefore everyone who hears these words of mine and puts them into practice is like a wise man who built his house on the rock. [25]The rain came down, the streams rose, and the winds blew and beat against that house; yet it did not fall, because it had its foundation on the rock. [26]But everyone who hears these words of mine and does not put them into practice is like a foolish man who built his house on sand. [27]The rain came down, the streams rose, and the winds blew and beat against that house, and it fell with a great crash."

[28]When Jesus had finished saying these things, the crowds were amazed at his teaching, [29]because he taught as one who had authority, and not as their teachers of the law.

Jesus Heals a Man With Leprosy

8 When Jesus came down from the mountainside, large crowds followed him. [2]A man with leprosy[a] came and knelt before him and said, "Lord, if you are willing, you can make me clean."

[3]Jesus reached out his hand and touched the man. "I am willing," he said. "Be clean!" Immediately he was cleansed of his leprosy. [4]Then Jesus said to him, "See that you don't tell anyone. But go, show yourself to the priest and offer the gift Moses commanded, as a testimony to them."

The Faith of the Centurion

[5]When Jesus had entered Capernaum, a centurion came to him, asking for help. [6]"Lord," he said, "my servant lies at home paralyzed, suffering terribly."

[7]Jesus said to him, "Shall I come and heal him?"

[8]The centurion replied, "Lord, I do not deserve to have you come under my roof. But just say the word, and my servant will be healed. [9]For I myself am a man under authority, with soldiers under me. I tell this one, 'Go,' and he goes; and that one, 'Come,' and he comes. I say to my servant, 'Do this,' and he does it."

[10]When Jesus heard this, he was amazed and said to those following him, "Truly I tell you, I have not found anyone in Israel with such great faith. [11]I say to you that many will come from the east and the

---

a 2 The Greek word traditionally translated leprosy was used for various diseases affecting the skin.

west, and will take their places at the feast with Abraham, Isaac and Jacob in the kingdom of heaven. [12]But the subjects of the kingdom will be thrown outside, into the darkness, where there will be weeping and gnashing of teeth."

[13]Then Jesus said to the centurion, "Go! Let it be done just as you believed it would." And his servant was healed at that very hour.

Jesus Heals Many

[14]When Jesus came into Peter's house, he saw Peter's mother-in-law lying in bed with a fever. [15]He touched her hand and the fever left her, and she got up and began to wait on him.

[16]When evening came, many who were demon-possessed were brought to him, and he drove out the spirits with a word and healed all the sick. [17]This was to fulfill what was spoken through the prophet Isaiah:

> "He took up our infirmities
> and bore our diseases."[a]

The Cost of Following Jesus

[18]When Jesus saw the crowd around him, he gave orders to cross to the other side of the lake. [19]Then a teacher of the law came to him and said, "Teacher, I will follow you wherever you go."

[20]Jesus replied, "Foxes have holes and birds have nests, but the Son of Man has no place to lay his head."

[21]Another disciple said to him, "Lord, first let me go and bury my father."

[22]But Jesus told him, "Follow me, and let the dead bury their own dead."

Jesus Calms the Storm

[23]Then he got into the boat and his disciples followed him. [24]Suddenly a furious storm came up on the lake, so that the waves swept over the boat. But Jesus was sleeping. [25]The disciples went and woke him, saying, "Lord, save us! We're going to drown!"

[26]He replied, "You of little faith, why are you so afraid?" Then he got up and rebuked the winds and the waves, and it was completely calm.

[27]The men were amazed and asked, "What kind of man is this? Even the winds and the waves obey him!"

Jesus Restores Two Demon-Possessed Men

[28]When he arrived at the other side in the region of the Gadarenes,[b] two demon-possessed men coming from the tombs met him. They were so violent that no one could pass that way. [29]"What do you want with us, Son of God?" they shouted. "Have you come here to torture us before the appointed time?"

[30]Some distance from them a large herd of pigs was feeding. [31]The demons begged Jesus, "If you drive us out, send us into the herd of pigs."

[32]He said to them, "Go!" So they came out and went into the pigs, and the whole herd rushed down the steep bank into the lake and died in the water. [33]Those tending the pigs ran off, went into the town and reported all this, including what had happened to the demon-possessed men. [34]Then the whole town went out to meet Jesus. And when they saw him, they pleaded with him to leave their region.

atissue:fear

8:23–27 When you feel afraid, does it ever seem like Jesus is sleeping, oblivious to your desperation? You of little faith, is he not stronger than the storm you face? Is he not more powerful than your fears? He gives you faith to overcome your fears. That faith comes from a deep relationship with the one who controls not only the wind and the waves but also all the circumstances of your life. When the storms of life threaten to overwhelm you, replace your fear with faith, prayer and God's Word. He is holding onto you, and *that* keeps your fears from taking over.

1402

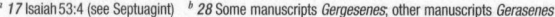

---

[a] *17* Isaiah 53:4 (see Septuagint)   [b] *28* Some manuscripts *Gergesenes;* other manuscripts *Gerasenes*

Jesus Forgives and Heals a Paralyzed Man

9 Jesus stepped into a boat, crossed over and came to his own town. [2]Some men brought to him a paralyzed man, lying on a mat. When Jesus saw their faith, he said to the man, "Take heart, son; your sins are forgiven."

[3]At this, some of the teachers of the law said to themselves, "This fellow is blaspheming!"

[4]Knowing their thoughts, Jesus said, "Why do you entertain evil thoughts in your hearts? [5]Which is easier: to say, 'Your sins are forgiven,' or to say, 'Get up and walk'? [6]But I want you to know that the Son of Man has authority on earth to forgive sins." So he said to the paralyzed man, "Get up, take your mat and go home." [7]Then the man got up and went home. [8]When the crowd saw this, they were filled with awe; and they praised God, who had given such authority to human beings.

The Calling of Matthew

[9]As Jesus went on from there, he saw a man named Matthew sitting at the tax collector's booth. "Follow me," he told him, and Matthew got up and followed him.

[10]While Jesus was having dinner at Matthew's house, many tax collectors and sinners came and ate with him and his disciples. [11]When the Pharisees saw this, they asked his disciples, "Why does your teacher eat with tax collectors and sinners?"

[12]On hearing this, Jesus said, "It is not the healthy who need a doctor, but the sick. [13]But go and learn what this means: 'I desire mercy, not sacrifice.'[a] For I have not come to call the righteous, but sinners."

Jesus Questioned About Fasting

[14]Then John's disciples came and asked him, "How is it that we and the Pharisees fast often, but your disciples do not fast?"

[15]Jesus answered, "How can the guests of the bridegroom mourn while he is with them? The time will come when the bridegroom will be taken from them; then they will fast.

[16]"No one sews a patch of unshrunk cloth on an old garment, for the patch will pull away from the garment, making the tear worse. [17]Neither do people pour new wine into old wineskins. If they do, the skins will burst; the wine will run out and the wineskins will be ruined. No, they pour new wine into new wineskins, and both are preserved."

a tissue: non-believers

9:9–13 The Pharisees had it all wrong. They thought they could earn God's favor by cutting themselves off from those who didn't know him (though the Pharisees didn't realize that many of their own did not even know him). God has mercy and compassion on those who are lost in sin. He reaches out to non-believers and desires a relationship with them. Like Jesus, we need to be purposeful about cultivating relationships with those who don't know God. Jesus was on a mission to point the lost to their need for the one, true God. Is that your mission, too?

1403

Jesus Raises a Dead Girl and Heals a Sick Woman

[18]While he was saying this, a synagogue leader came and knelt before him and said, "My daughter has just died. But come and put your hand on her, and she will live." [19]Jesus got up and went with him, and so did his disciples.

[20]Just then a woman who had been subject to bleeding for twelve years came up behind him and touched the edge of his cloak. [21]She said to herself, "If I only touch his cloak, I will be healed." [22]Jesus turned and saw her. "Take heart, daughter," he said, "your faith has healed you." And the woman was healed from that moment.

[23]When Jesus entered the synagogue leader's house and saw the noisy crowd and people playing pipes, [24]he said, "Go away. The girl is not dead but asleep." But they laughed at him. [25]After the crowd had been put outside, he went in and took the girl by the hand, and she got up. [26]News of this spread through all that region.

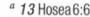
a 13 Hosea 6:6

Jesus Heals the Blind and the Mute

²⁷As Jesus went on from there, two blind men followed him, calling out, "Have mercy on us, Son of David!"

²⁸When he had gone indoors, the blind men came to him, and he asked them, "Do you believe that I am able to do this?"

"Yes, Lord," they replied.

²⁹Then he touched their eyes and said, "According to your faith let it be done to you"; ³⁰and their sight was restored. Jesus warned them sternly, "See that no one knows about this." ³¹But they went out and spread the news about him all over that region.

³²While they were going out, a man who was demon-possessed and could not talk was brought to Jesus. ³³And when the demon was driven out, the man who had been mute spoke. The crowd was amazed and said, "Nothing like this has ever been seen in Israel."

³⁴But the Pharisees said, "It is by the prince of demons that he drives out demons."

The Workers Are Few

³⁵Jesus went through all the towns and villages, teaching in their synagogues, proclaiming the good news of the kingdom and healing every disease and sickness. ³⁶When he saw the crowds, he had compassion on them, because they were harassed and helpless, like sheep without a shepherd. ³⁷Then he said to his disciples, "The harvest is plentiful but the workers are few. ³⁸Ask the Lord of the harvest, therefore, to send out workers into his harvest field."

Jesus Sends Out the Twelve

10 Jesus called his twelve disciples to him and gave them authority to drive out evil*ᵃ* spirits and to heal every disease and sickness.

²These are the names of the twelve apostles: first, Simon (who is called Peter) and his brother Andrew; James son of Zebedee, and his brother John; ³Philip and Bartholomew; Thomas and Matthew the tax collector; James son of Alphaeus, and Thaddaeus; ⁴Simon the Zealot and Judas Iscariot, who betrayed him.

⁵These twelve Jesus sent out with the following instructions: "Do not go among the Gentiles or enter any town of the Samaritans. ⁶Go rather to the lost sheep of Israel. ⁷As you go, proclaim this message: 'The kingdom of heaven has come near.' ⁸Heal the sick, raise the dead, cleanse those who have leprosy,*ᵇ* drive out demons. Freely you have received, freely give.

⁹"Do not get any gold or silver or copper to take with you in your belts— ¹⁰no bag for the journey or extra shirt or sandals or a staff, for workers are worth their keep. ¹¹Whatever town or village you enter, search for some worthy person there and stay at that person's house until you leave. ¹²As you enter the home, give it your greeting. ¹³If the home is deserving, let your peace rest on it; if it is not, let your peace return to you. ¹⁴If anyone will not welcome you or listen to your words, shake the dust off your feet when you leave that home or town. ¹⁵Truly I tell you, it will be more bearable for Sodom and Gomorrah on the day of judgment than for that town.

¹⁶"I am sending you out like sheep among wolves. Therefore be as shrewd as snakes and as innocent as doves. ¹⁷Be on your guard; you will be handed over to the local councils and be flogged in the synagogues. ¹⁸On my account you will be brought before governors and kings as witnesses to them and to the Gentiles. ¹⁹But when they arrest you, do not worry about what to say or how to say it. At that time you will be given what to say, ²⁰for it will not be you speaking, but the Spirit of your Father speaking through you.

²¹"Brother will betray brother to death, and a father his child; children will rebel against their parents and have them put to death. ²²Everyone will hate you because of me, but those who stand firm to the end will be saved. ²³When you are persecuted in one place, flee to another. Truly I tell you, you will not finish going through the towns of Israel before the Son of Man comes.

²⁴"Students are not above their teacher, nor servants above their master. ²⁵It is enough for students to be like their teacher, and servants like their master. If the head of the house has been called Beelzebul, how much more the members of his household!

ᵃ 1 Greek *unclean* *ᵇ 8* The Greek word traditionally translated *leprosy* was used for various diseases affecting the skin.

²⁶"So do not be afraid of them. There is nothing concealed that will not be disclosed, or hidden that will not be made known. ²⁷What I tell you in the dark, speak in the daylight; what is whispered in your ear, proclaim from the roofs. ²⁸Do not be afraid of those who kill the body but cannot kill the soul. Rather, be afraid of the One who can destroy both soul and body in hell. ²⁹Are not two sparrows sold for a penny? Yet not one of them will fall to the ground outside your Father's care.^a ³⁰And even the very hairs of your head are all numbered. ³¹So don't be afraid; you are worth more than many sparrows.

³²"Whoever publicly acknowledges me I will also acknowledge before my Father in heaven. ³³But whoever publicly disowns me I will disown before my Father in heaven.

³⁴"Do not suppose that I have come to bring peace to the earth. I did not come to bring peace, but a sword. ³⁵For I have come to turn

> "'a man against his father,
> a daughter against her mother,
> a daughter-in-law against her mother-in-law—
> ³⁶ your enemies will be the members of your own household.'^b

³⁷"Anyone who loves their father or mother more than me is not worthy of me; anyone who loves a son or daughter more than me is not worthy of me. ³⁸Whoever does not take up their cross and follow me is not worthy of me. ³⁹Whoever finds their life will lose it, and whoever loses their life for my sake will find it.

1405

⁴⁰"Anyone who welcomes you welcomes me, and anyone who welcomes me welcomes the one who sent me. ⁴¹Whoever welcomes someone known to be a prophet will receive a prophet's reward, and whoever welcomes someone known to be righteous will receive a righteous person's reward. ⁴²And if anyone gives even a cup of cold water to one of these little ones who is known to be my disciple, truly I tell you, that person will certainly be rewarded."

Jesus and John the Baptist

11 After Jesus had finished instructing his twelve disciples, he went on from there to teach and preach in the towns of Galilee.^c

²When John heard in prison what the Messiah was doing, he sent his disciples ³to ask him, "Are you the one who was to come, or should we expect someone else?"

⁴Jesus replied, "Go back and report to John what you hear and see: ⁵The blind receive sight, the lame walk, those who have leprosy^d are cleansed, the deaf hear, the dead are raised, and the good news is proclaimed to the poor. ⁶Blessed is anyone who does not stumble on account of me."

⁷As John's disciples were leaving, Jesus began to speak to the crowd about John: "What did you go out into the wilderness to see? A reed swayed by the wind? ⁸If not, what did you go out to see? A man dressed in fine clothes? No, those who wear fine clothes are in kings' palaces. ⁹Then what did you go out to see? A prophet? Yes, I tell you, and more than a prophet. ¹⁰This is the one about whom it is written:

> "'I will send my messenger ahead of you,
> who will prepare your way before you.'^e

¹¹Truly I tell you, among those born of women there has not risen anyone greater than John the Baptist; yet whoever is least in the kingdom of heaven is greater than he. ¹²From the days of John the Baptist until now, the kingdom of heaven has been subjected to violence,^f and violent people have been raiding it. ¹³For all the Prophets and the Law prophesied until John. ¹⁴And if you are willing to accept it, he is the Elijah who was to come. ¹⁵Whoever has ears, let them hear.

¹⁶"To what can I compare this generation? They are like children sitting in the marketplaces and calling out to others:

> ¹⁷"'We played the pipe for you,
> and you did not dance;

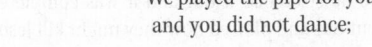

^a *29* Or *will,* or *knowledge*   ^b *36* Micah 7:6   ^c *1* Greek *in their towns*   ^d *5* The Greek word traditionally translated *leprosy* was used for various diseases affecting the skin.   ^e *10* Mal. 3:1   ^f *12* Or *been forcefully advancing*

> we sang a dirge,
> and you did not mourn.'

¹⁸For John came neither eating nor drinking, and they say, 'He has a demon.' ¹⁹The Son of Man came eating and drinking, and they say, 'Here is a glutton and a drunkard, a friend of tax collectors and sinners.' But wisdom is proved right by her actions."

Woe on Unrepentant Towns

²⁰Then Jesus began to denounce the towns in which most of his miracles had been performed, because they did not repent. ²¹"Woe to you, Chorazin! Woe to you, Bethsaida! If the miracles that were performed in you had been performed in Tyre and Sidon, they would have repented long ago in sackcloth and ashes. ²²But I tell you, it will be more bearable for Tyre and Sidon on the day of judgment than for you. ²³And you, Capernaum, will you be lifted up to the skies? No, you will go down to the depths.ᵃ If the miracles that were performed in you had been performed in Sodom, it would have remained to this day. ²⁴But I tell you that it will be more bearable for Sodom on the day of judgment than for you."

The Father Revealed in the Son

²⁵At that time Jesus said, "I praise you, Father, Lord of heaven and earth, because you have hidden these things from the wise and learned, and revealed them to little children. ²⁶Yes, Father, for this was your good pleasure.

²⁷"All things have been committed to me by my Father. No one knows the Son except the Father, and no one knows the Father except the Son and those to whom the Son chooses to reveal him.

²⁸"Come to me, all you who are weary and burdened, and I will give you rest. ²⁹Take my yoke upon you and learn from me, for I am gentle and humble in heart, and you will find rest for your souls. ³⁰For my yoke is easy and my burden is light."

1406

conversations

stress «» 11:28-30

1 » What are the major stressors in your life?

2 » How can taking Jesus' advice in these verses help you handle these stress points?

3 » What burdens do you have a hard time relinquishing to God?

For more on **stress**, check the index.
For the next Conversations, go to p. 1410.

Jesus Is Lord of the Sabbath

12 At that time Jesus went through the grainfields on the Sabbath. His disciples were hungry and began to pick some heads of grain and eat them. ²When the Pharisees saw this, they said to him, "Look! Your disciples are doing what is unlawful on the Sabbath."

³He answered, "Haven't you read what David did when he and his companions were hungry? ⁴He entered the house of God, and he and his companions ate the consecrated bread—which was not lawful for them to do, but only for the priests. ⁵Or haven't you read in the Law that the priests on Sabbath duty in the temple desecrate the Sabbath and yet are innocent? ⁶I tell you that oneᵇ greater than the temple is here. ⁷If you had known what these words mean, 'I desire mercy, not sacrifice,'ᶜ you would not have condemned the innocent. ⁸For the Son of Man is Lord of the Sabbath."

⁹Going on from that place, he went into their synagogue, ¹⁰and a man with a shriveled hand was there. Looking for a reason to accuse Jesus, they asked him, "Is it lawful to heal on the Sabbath?"

¹¹He said to them, "If any of you has a sheep and it falls into a pit on the Sabbath, will you not take hold of it and lift it out? ¹²How much more valuable is a human being than a sheep! Therefore it is lawful to do good on the Sabbath."

¹³Then he said to the man, "Stretch out your hand." So he stretched it out and it was completely restored, just as sound as the other. ¹⁴But the Pharisees went out and plotted how they might kill Jesus.

ᵃ 23 Greek to Hades   ᵇ 6 Or something   ᶜ 7 Hosea 6:6

God's Chosen Servant

¹⁵Aware of this, Jesus withdrew from that place. A large crowd followed him, and he healed all who were ill. ¹⁶He warned them not to tell others about him. ¹⁷This was to fulfill what was spoken through the prophet Isaiah:

> ¹⁸"Here is my servant whom I have chosen,
>   the one I love, in whom I delight;
> I will put my Spirit on him,
>   and he will proclaim justice to the nations.
> ¹⁹He will not quarrel or cry out;
>   no one will hear his voice in the streets.
> ²⁰A bruised reed he will not break,
>   and a smoldering wick he will not snuff out,
> till he leads justice to victory.
> ²¹   In his name the nations will put their hope."ᵃ

Jesus and Beelzebul

²²Then they brought him a demon-possessed man who was blind and mute, and Jesus healed him, so that he could both talk and see. ²³All the people were astonished and said, "Could this be the Son of David?"

²⁴But when the Pharisees heard this, they said, "It is only by Beelzebul, the prince of demons, that this fellow drives out demons."

²⁵Jesus knew their thoughts and said to them, "Every kingdom divided against itself will be ruined, and every city or household divided against itself will not stand. ²⁶If Satan drives out Satan, he is divided against himself. How then can his kingdom stand? ²⁷And if I drive out demons by Beelzebul, by whom do your people drive them out? So then, they will be your judges. ²⁸But if it is by the Spirit of God that I drive out demons, then the kingdom of God has come upon you.

1407

HE IS: a mind reader

12:22–28 When Jesus healed a demon-possessed man, the Pharisees began murmuring, quietly accusing him of driving out demons with the power of the prince of demons. But Jesus knew their thoughts and exposed their false accusations. He is *a mind reader* who reveals people's dark ideas and brings the truth to light.

Maybe you've questioned God's methods or motives because things haven't turned out as you expected. If you've murmured against God, remember that he is *a mind reader*. Rather than hiding your fears and criticism, bring Jesus your honest questions, and allow him to enlighten you about his will and his ways.

For the next He Is, go to p. 1417.

---

²⁹"Or again, how can anyone enter a strong man's house and carry off his possessions without first tying up the strong man? Then his house can be plundered.

³⁰"Whoever is not with me is against me, and whoever does not gather with me scatters. ³¹And so I tell you, people will be forgiven every sin and blasphemy. But blasphemy against the Spirit will not be forgiven. ³²Anyone who speaks a word against the Son of Man will be forgiven, but anyone who speaks against the Holy Spirit will not be forgiven, either in this age or in the age to come.

³³"Make a tree good and its fruit will be good, or make a tree bad and its fruit will be bad, for a tree is recognized by its fruit. ³⁴You brood of vipers, how can you who are evil say anything good? For out of the

---

ᵃ *21* Isaiah 42:1-4

overflow of the heart the mouth speaks. ³⁵Good people bring good things out of the good stored up in them, and evil people bring evil things out of the evil stored up in them. ³⁶But I tell you that people will have to give account on the day of judgment for every empty word they have spoken. ³⁷For by your words you will be acquitted, and by your words you will be condemned."

The Sign of Jonah

³⁸Then some of the Pharisees and teachers of the law said to him, "Teacher, we want to see a sign from you."

³⁹He answered, "A wicked and adulterous generation asks for a sign! But none will be given it except the sign of the prophet Jonah. ⁴⁰For as Jonah was three days and three nights in the belly of a huge fish, so the Son of Man will be three days and three nights in the heart of the earth. ⁴¹The people of Nineveh will stand up at the judgment with this generation and condemn it; for they repented at the preaching of Jonah, and now one*ᵃ* greater than Jonah is here. ⁴²The Queen of the South will rise at the judgment with this generation and condemn it; for she came from the ends of the earth to listen to Solomon's wisdom, and now one greater than Solomon is here.

⁴³"When an evil*ᵇ* spirit comes out of anyone, it goes through arid places seeking rest and does not find it. ⁴⁴Then it says, 'I will return to the house I left.' When it arrives, it finds the house unoccupied, swept clean and put in order. ⁴⁵Then it goes and takes with it seven other spirits more wicked than itself, and they go in and live there. And the final condition of that person is worse than the first. That is how it will be with this wicked generation."

Jesus' Mother and Brothers

⁴⁶While Jesus was still talking to the crowd, his mother and brothers stood outside, wanting to speak to him. ⁴⁷Someone told him, "Your mother and brothers are standing outside, wanting to speak to you."

⁴⁸He replied to him, "Who is my mother, and who are my brothers?" ⁴⁹Pointing to his disciples, he said, "Here are my mother and my brothers. ⁵⁰For whoever does the will of my Father in heaven is my brother and sister and mother."

The Parable of the Sower

13 That same day Jesus went out of the house and sat by the lake. ²Such large crowds gathered around him that he got into a boat and sat in it, while all the people stood on the shore. ³Then he told them many things in parables, saying: "A farmer went out to sow his seed. ⁴As he was scattering the seed, some fell along the path, and the birds came and ate it up. ⁵Some fell on rocky places, where it did not have much soil. It sprang up quickly, because the soil was shallow. ⁶But when the sun came up, the plants were scorched, and they withered because they had no root. ⁷Other seed fell among thorns, which grew up and choked the plants. ⁸Still other seed fell on good soil, where it produced a crop—a hundred, sixty or thirty times what was sown. ⁹Whoever has ears, let them hear."

¹⁰The disciples came to him and asked, "Why do you speak to the people in parables?"

¹¹He replied, "The knowledge of the secrets of the kingdom of heaven has been given to you, but not to them. ¹²Those who have will be given more, and they will have an abundance. As for those who do not have, even what they have will be taken from them. ¹³This is why I speak to them in parables:

"Though seeing, they do not see;
        though hearing, they do not hear or understand.

¹⁴In them is fulfilled the prophecy of Isaiah:

"'You will be ever hearing but never understanding;
        you will be ever seeing but never perceiving.
¹⁵For this people's heart has become calloused;
        they hardly hear with their ears,
        and they have closed their eyes.
Otherwise they might see with their eyes,

ᵃ 41 Or *something*; also in verse 42   *ᵇ 43* Greek *unclean*

> hear with their ears,
> understand with their hearts
> and turn, and I would heal them.'*

¹⁶But blessed are your eyes because they see, and your ears because they hear. ¹⁷Truly I tell you, many prophets and righteous people longed to see what you see but did not see it, and to hear what you hear but did not hear it.

¹⁸"Listen then to what the parable of the sower means: ¹⁹When people hear the message about the kingdom and do not understand it, the evil one comes and snatches away what was sown in their hearts. This is the seed sown along the path. ²⁰The seed falling on rocky ground refers to people who hear the word and at once receive it with joy. ²¹But since they have no root, they last only a short time. When trouble or persecution comes because of the word, they quickly fall away. ²²The seed falling among the thorns refers to people who hear the word, but the worries of this life and the deceitfulness of wealth choke the word, making it unfruitful. ²³But the seed falling on good soil refers to people who hear the word and understand it. They produce a crop, yielding a hundred, sixty or thirty times what was sown."

The Parable of the Weeds

²⁴Jesus told them another parable: "The kingdom of heaven is like a man who sowed good seed in his field. ²⁵But while everyone was sleeping, his enemy came and sowed weeds among the wheat, and went away. ²⁶When the wheat sprouted and formed heads, then the weeds also appeared.

²⁷"The owner's servants came to him and said, 'Sir, didn't you sow good seed in your field? Where then did the weeds come from?'

²⁸"'An enemy did this,' he replied.

"The servants asked him, 'Do you want us to go and pull them up?'

²⁹"'No,' he answered, 'because while you are pulling the weeds, you may uproot the wheat with them. ³⁰Let both grow together until the harvest. At that time I will tell the harvesters: First collect the weeds and tie them in bundles to be burned; then gather the wheat and bring it into my barn.'"

The Parables of the Mustard Seed and the Yeast

³¹He told them another parable: "The kingdom of heaven is like a mustard seed, which a man took and planted in his field. ³²Though it is the smallest of all seeds, yet when it grows, it is the largest of garden plants and becomes a tree, so that the birds come and perch in its branches."

³³He told them still another parable: "The kingdom of heaven is like yeast that a woman took and mixed into about sixty pounds*ᵇ* of flour until it worked all through the dough."

³⁴Jesus spoke all these things to the crowd in parables; he did not say anything to them without using a parable. ³⁵So was fulfilled what was spoken through the prophet:

> "I will open my mouth in parables,
> I will utter things hidden since the creation of the world."*ᶜ*

The Parable of the Weeds Explained

³⁶Then he left the crowd and went into the house. His disciples came to him and said, "Explain to us the parable of the weeds in the field."

³⁷He answered, "The one who sowed the good seed is the Son of Man. ³⁸The field is the world, and the good seed stands for the people of the kingdom. The weeds are the people of the evil one, ³⁹and the enemy who sows them is the devil. The harvest is the end of the age, and the harvesters are angels.

⁴⁰"As the weeds are pulled up and burned in the fire, so it will be at the end of the age. ⁴¹The Son of Man will send out his angels, and they will weed out of his kingdom everything that causes sin and all who do evil. ⁴²They will throw them into the blazing furnace, where there will be weeping and gnashing of teeth. ⁴³Then the righteous will shine like the sun in the kingdom of their Father. Whoever has ears, let them hear.

ᵃ 15 Isaiah 6:9,10 (see Septuagint)   *ᵇ 33* Or about 27 kilograms   *ᶜ 35* Psalm 78:2

The Parables of the Hidden Treasure and the Pearl

⁴⁴ "The kingdom of heaven is like treasure hidden in a field. When a man found it, he hid it again, and then in his joy went and sold all he had and bought that field.

⁴⁵ "Again, the kingdom of heaven is like a merchant looking for fine pearls. ⁴⁶ When he found one of great value, he went away and sold everything he had and bought it.

The Parable of the Net

⁴⁷ "Once again, the kingdom of heaven is like a net that was let down into the lake and caught all kinds of fish. ⁴⁸ When it was full, the fishermen pulled it up on the shore. Then they sat down and collected the good fish in baskets, but threw the bad away. ⁴⁹ This is how it will be at the end of the age. The angels will come and separate the wicked from the righteous ⁵⁰ and throw them into the blazing furnace, where there will be weeping and gnashing of teeth.

⁵¹ "Have you understood all these things?" Jesus asked.

"Yes," they replied.

⁵² He said to them, "Therefore every teacher of the law who has been instructed about the kingdom of heaven is like the owner of a house who brings out of his storeroom new treasures as well as old."

A Prophet Without Honor

⁵³ When Jesus had finished these parables, he moved on from there. ⁵⁴ Coming to his hometown, he began teaching the people in their synagogue, and they were amazed. "Where did this man get this wisdom and these miraculous powers?" they asked. ⁵⁵ "Isn't this the carpenter's son? Isn't his mother's name Mary, and aren't his brothers James, Joseph, Simon and Judas? ⁵⁶ Aren't all his sisters with us? Where then did this man get all these things?" ⁵⁷ And they took offense at him.

But Jesus said to them, "Only in their own towns and in their own homes are prophets without honor."

⁵⁸ And he did not do many miracles there because of their lack of faith.

1410

John the Baptist Beheaded

14 At that time Herod the tetrarch heard the reports about Jesus, ²and he said to his attendants, "This is John the Baptist; he has risen from the dead! That is why miraculous powers are at work in him."

³ Now Herod had arrested John and bound him and put him in prison because of Herodias, his brother Philip's wife, ⁴ for John had been saying to him: "It is not lawful for you to have her." ⁵ Herod wanted to kill John, but he was afraid of the people, because they considered him a prophet.

⁶ On Herod's birthday the daughter of Herodias danced for them and pleased Herod so much ⁷ that he promised with an oath to give her whatever she asked. ⁸ Prompted by her mother, she said, "Give me here on a platter the head of John the Baptist." ⁹ The king was distressed, but because of his oaths and his dinner guests, he ordered that her request be granted ¹⁰ and had John beheaded in the prison. ¹¹ His head was brought in on a platter and given to the girl, who carried it to her mother. ¹² John's disciples came and took his body and buried it. Then they went and told Jesus.

Jesus Feeds the Five Thousand

¹³ When Jesus heard what had happened, he withdrew by boat privately to a solitary place. Hearing of this, the crowds followed him on foot from the towns. ¹⁴ When Jesus landed and saw a large crowd, he had compassion on them and healed their sick.

¹⁵ As evening approached, the disciples came to him and said, "This is a remote place, and it's already getting late. Send the crowds away, so they can go to the villages and buy themselves some food."

conversations

poverty «» 14:15–21

1» What physically or spiritually impoverished people is Jesus asking you to help?

2» Today, how can you specifically respond to one of these needs?

3» Instead of the hopelessness the disciples felt, how should Christians counter poverty?

For more on **poverty**, check the index.
For the next Conversations, go to p. 1421.

¹⁶Jesus replied, "They do not need to go away. You give them something to eat."

¹⁷"We have here only five loaves of bread and two fish," they answered.

¹⁸"Bring them here to me," he said. ¹⁹And he directed the people to sit down on the grass. Taking the five loaves and the two fish and looking up to heaven, he gave thanks and broke the loaves. Then he gave them to the disciples, and the disciples gave them to the people. ²⁰They all ate and were satisfied, and the disciples picked up twelve basketfuls of broken pieces that were left over. ²¹The number of those who ate was about five thousand men, besides women and children.

Jesus Walks on the Water

²²Immediately Jesus made the disciples get into the boat and go on ahead of him to the other side, while he dismissed the crowd. ²³After he had dismissed them, he went up on a mountainside by himself to pray. When evening came, he was there alone, ²⁴but the boat was already a considerable distance from land, buffeted by the waves because the wind was against it.

²⁵Shortly before dawn Jesus went out to them, walking on the lake. ²⁶When the disciples saw him walking on the lake, they were terrified. "It's a ghost," they said, and cried out in fear.

²⁷But Jesus immediately said to them: "Take courage! It is I. Don't be afraid."

²⁸"Lord, if it's you," Peter replied, "tell me to come to you on the water."

²⁹"Come," he said.

Then Peter got down out of the boat, walked on the water and came toward Jesus. ³⁰But when he saw the wind, he was afraid and, beginning to sink, cried out, "Lord, save me!"

³¹Immediately Jesus reached out his hand and caught him. "You of little faith," he said, "why did you doubt?"

³²And when they climbed into the boat, the wind died down. ³³Then those who were in the boat worshiped him, saying, "Truly you are the Son of God."

aussie:doubting God

14:22–33 Let's say you start a business, or go back to school, or reach out to mend a broken relationship or take on a new ministry. Stepping out in faith feels scary! When things start to get a little rough, keep your eyes focused on Jesus. Don't start looking at the troubles that surround you. Don't doubt him and his ability to carry you through because that will only cause you to sink. The one who brought you out on the water can keep you from drowning. So keep walking in faith!

1411

³⁴When they had crossed over, they landed at Gennesaret. ³⁵And when the men of that place recognized Jesus, they sent word to all the surrounding country. People brought all their sick to him ³⁶and begged him to let the sick just touch the edge of his cloak, and all who touched him were healed.

That Which Defiles

15 Then some Pharisees and teachers of the law came to Jesus from Jerusalem and asked, ²"Why do your disciples break the tradition of the elders? They don't wash their hands before they eat!"

³Jesus replied, "And why do you break the command of God for the sake of your tradition? ⁴For God said, 'Honor your father and mother'ᵃ and 'Anyone who curses their father or mother is to be put to death.'ᵇ ⁵But you say that if anyone declares that what might have been used to help their father or mother is 'devoted to God,' ⁶they are not to 'honor their father or mother' with it. Thus you nullify the word of God for the sake of your tradition. ⁷You hypocrites! Isaiah was right when he prophesied about you:

⁸"'These people honor me with their lips,
  but their hearts are far from me.
⁹They worship me in vain;
  their teachings are merely human rules.'ᶜ"

ᵃ 4 Exodus 20:12; Deut. 5:16 ᵇ 4 Exodus 21:17; Lev. 20:9 ᶜ 9 Isaiah 29:13

¹⁰Jesus called the crowd to him and said, "Listen and understand. ¹¹What goes into your mouth does not defile you, but what comes out of your mouth, that is what defiles you."

¹²Then the disciples came to him and asked, "Do you know that the Pharisees were offended when they heard this?"

¹³He replied, "Every plant that my heavenly Father has not planted will be pulled up by the roots. ¹⁴Leave them; they are blind guides.^a If the blind lead the blind, both will fall into a pit."

¹⁵Peter said, "Explain the parable to us."

¹⁶"Are you still so dull?" Jesus asked them. ¹⁷"Don't you see that whatever enters the mouth goes into the stomach and then out of the body? ¹⁸But the things that come out of the mouth come from the heart, and these defile you. ¹⁹For out of the heart come evil thoughts, murder, adultery, sexual immorality, theft, false testimony, slander. ²⁰These are what defile you; but eating with unwashed hands does not defile you."

The Faith of a Canaanite Woman

²¹Leaving that place, Jesus withdrew to the region of Tyre and Sidon. ²²A Canaanite woman from that vicinity came to him, crying out, "Lord, Son of David, have mercy on me! My daughter is demon-possessed and suffering terribly."

²³Jesus did not answer a word. So his disciples came to him and urged him, "Send her away, for she keeps crying out after us."

²⁴He answered, "I was sent only to the lost sheep of Israel."

²⁵The woman came and knelt before him. "Lord, help me!" she said.

²⁶He replied, "It is not right to take the children's bread and toss it to the dogs."

²⁷"Yes it is, Lord," she said. "Even the dogs eat the crumbs that fall from their master's table."

²⁸Then Jesus said to her, "Woman,^b you have great faith! Your request is granted." And her daughter was healed from that very hour.

Jesus Feeds the Four Thousand

²⁹Jesus left there and went along the Sea of Galilee. Then he went up on a mountainside and sat down. ³⁰Great crowds came to him, bringing the lame, the blind, the crippled, the mute and many others, and laid them at his feet; and he healed them. ³¹The people were amazed when they saw the mute speaking, the crippled made well, the lame walking and the blind seeing. And they praised the God of Israel.

³²Jesus called his disciples to him and said, "I have compassion for these people; they have already been with me three days and have nothing to eat. I do not want to send them away hungry, or they may collapse on the way."

³³His disciples answered, "Where could we get enough bread in this remote place to feed such a crowd?"

³⁴"How many loaves do you have?" Jesus asked.

"Seven," they replied, "and a few small fish."

³⁵He told the crowd to sit down on the ground. ³⁶Then he took the seven loaves and the fish, and when he had given thanks, he broke them and gave them to the disciples, and they in turn to the people. ³⁷They all ate and were satisfied. Afterward the disciples picked up seven basketfuls of broken pieces that were

atissue:parents

15:1–9 It's never a good idea to use a "spiritual" excuse to get out of obeying God. Just ask the Pharisees. When they tried to get out of caring for their aging parents by saying that all their resources were already "devoted to God," Jesus took them to task. He called them hypocrites who only made a show of honoring God, while not really doing so in their hearts. Caring for your parents as they get older may require sacrifices of time, money, energy and love. Apparently Jesus considers those sacrifices more pleasing to God than any "religious" act.

1412

---

^a 14 Some manuscripts *blind guides of the blind*   ^b 28 The Greek for *Woman* does not denote any disrespect.

left over. [38]The number of those who ate was four thousand men, besides women and children. [39]After Jesus had sent the crowd away, he got into the boat and went to the vicinity of Magadan.

The Demand for a Sign

16 The Pharisees and Sadducees came to Jesus and tested him by asking him to show them a sign from heaven.

[2]He replied,[a] "When evening comes, you say, 'It will be fair weather, for the sky is red,' [3]and in the morning, 'Today it will be stormy, for the sky is red and overcast.' You know how to interpret the appearance of the sky, but you cannot interpret the signs of the times. [4]A wicked and adulterous generation looks for a sign, but none will be given it except the sign of Jonah." Jesus then left them and went away.

The Yeast of the Pharisees and Sadducees

[5]When they went across the lake, the disciples forgot to take bread. [6]"Be careful," Jesus said to them. "Be on your guard against the yeast of the Pharisees and Sadducees."

[7]They discussed this among themselves and said, "It is because we didn't bring any bread."

[8]Aware of their discussion, Jesus asked, "You of little faith, why are you talking among yourselves about having no bread? [9]Do you still not understand? Don't you remember the five loaves for the five thousand, and how many basketfuls you gathered? [10]Or the seven loaves for the four thousand, and how many basketfuls you gathered? [11]How is it you don't understand that I was not talking to you about bread? But be on your guard against the yeast of the Pharisees and Sadducees." [12]Then they understood that he was not telling them to guard against the yeast used in bread, but against the teaching of the Pharisees and Sadducees.

Peter Declares That Jesus Is the Messiah

[13]When Jesus came to the region of Caesarea Philippi, he asked his disciples, "Who do people say the Son of Man is?"

[14]They replied, "Some say John the Baptist; others say Elijah; and still others, Jeremiah or one of the prophets."

[15]"But what about you?" he asked. "Who do you say I am?"

[16]Simon Peter answered, "You are the Messiah, the Son of the living God."

[17]Jesus replied, "Blessed are you, Simon son of Jonah, for this was not revealed to you by flesh and blood, but by my Father in heaven. [18]And I tell you that you are Peter,[b] and on this rock I will build my church, and the gates of death[c] will not overcome it. [19]I will give you the keys of the kingdom of heaven; whatever you bind on earth will be[d] bound in heaven, and whatever you loose on earth will be[e] loosed in heaven." [20]Then he ordered his disciples not to tell anyone that he was the Messiah.

Jesus Predicts His Death

[21]From that time on Jesus began to explain to his disciples that he must go to Jerusalem and suffer many things at the hands of the elders, the chief priests and the teachers of the law, and that he must be killed and on the third day be raised to life.

[22]Peter took him aside and began to rebuke him. "Never, Lord!" he said. "This shall never happen to you!"

[23]Jesus turned and said to Peter, "Get behind me, Satan! You are a stumbling block to me; you do not have in mind the concerns of God, but merely human concerns."

[24]Then Jesus said to his disciples, "Whoever wants to be my disciple must deny themselves and take up their cross and follow me. [25]For whoever wants to save their life[f] will lose it, but whoever loses their life for me will find it. [26]What good will it be for you to gain the whole world, yet forfeit your soul? Or what can you give in exchange for your soul? [27]For the Son of Man is going to come in his Father's glory with his angels, and then he will reward everyone according to what they have done.

[28]"Truly I tell you, some who are standing here will not taste death before they see the Son of Man coming in his kingdom."

---

[a] *2* Some early manuscripts do not have the rest of verse 2 and all of verse 3.   [b] *18* The Greek for *Peter* means *rock*.   [c] *18* Greek *Hades*   [d] *19* Or *will have been*   [e] *19* Or *will have been*   [f] *25* The Greek word means either *life* or *soul*; also in verse 26.

The Transfiguration

17 After six days Jesus took with him Peter, James and John the brother of James, and led them up a high mountain by themselves. ²There he was transfigured before them. His face shone like the sun, and his clothes became as white as the light. ³Just then there appeared before them Moses and Elijah, talking with Jesus.

⁴Peter said to Jesus, "Lord, it is good for us to be here. If you wish, I will put up three shelters—one for you, one for Moses and one for Elijah."

⁵While he was still speaking, a bright cloud covered them, and a voice from the cloud said, "This is my Son, whom I love; with him I am well pleased. Listen to him!"

⁶When the disciples heard this, they fell facedown to the ground, terrified. ⁷But Jesus came and touched them. "Get up," he said. "Don't be afraid." ⁸When they looked up, they saw no one except Jesus.

⁹As they were coming down the mountain, Jesus instructed them, "Don't tell anyone what you have seen, until the Son of Man has been raised from the dead."

¹⁰The disciples asked him, "Why then do the teachers of the law say that Elijah must come first?"

¹¹Jesus replied, "To be sure, Elijah comes and will restore all things. ¹²But I tell you, Elijah has already come, and they did not recognize him, but have done to him everything they wished. In the same way the Son of Man is going to suffer at their hands." ¹³Then the disciples understood that he was talking to them about John the Baptist.

Jesus Heals a Demon-Possessed Boy

¹⁴When they came to the crowd, a man approached Jesus and knelt before him. ¹⁵"Lord, have mercy on my son," he said. "He has seizures and is suffering greatly. He often falls into the fire or into the water. ¹⁶I brought him to your disciples, but they could not heal him."

¹⁷"You unbelieving and perverse generation," Jesus replied, "how long shall I stay with you? How long shall I put up with you? Bring the boy here to me." ¹⁸Jesus rebuked the demon, and it came out of the boy, and he was healed from that moment.

¹⁹Then the disciples came to Jesus in private and asked, "Why couldn't we drive it out?"

²⁰[²¹]He replied, "Because you have so little faith. Truly I tell you, if you have faith as small as a mustard seed, you can say to this mountain, 'Move from here to there,' and it will move. Nothing will be impossible for you."

Jesus Predicts His Death a Second Time

²²When they came together in Galilee, he said to them, "The Son of Man is going to be delivered over to human hands. ²³He will be killed, and on the third day he will be raised to life." And the disciples were filled with grief.

The Temple Tax

²⁴After Jesus and his disciples arrived in Capernaum, the collectors of the two-drachma temple tax came to Peter and asked, "Doesn't your teacher pay the temple tax?"

²⁵"Yes, he does," he replied.

When Peter came into the house, Jesus was the first to speak. "What do you think, Simon?" he asked. "From whom do the kings of the earth collect duty and taxes—from their own children or from others?"

²⁶"From others," Peter answered.

"Then the children are exempt," Jesus said to him. ²⁷"But so that we may not cause offense, go to the lake and throw out your line. Take the first fish you catch; open its mouth and you will find a four-drachma coin. Take it and give it to them for my tax and yours."

The Greatest in the Kingdom of Heaven

18 At that time the disciples came to Jesus and asked, "Who, then, is the greatest in the kingdom of heaven?"

²He called a little child, whom he placed among them. ³And he said: "Truly I tell you, unless you change and become like little children, you will never enter the kingdom of heaven. ⁴Therefore, who-

ever takes a humble place—becoming like this child—is the greatest in the kingdom of heaven. [5]And whoever welcomes one such child in my name welcomes me.

Causing to Stumble

[6]"If anyone causes one of these little ones—those who believe in me—to stumble, it would be better for them if a large millstone were hung around their neck and they were drowned in the depths of the sea. [7]Woe to the world because of the things that cause people to stumble! Such things must come, but woe to the person through whom they come! [8]If your hand or your foot causes you to stumble, cut it off and throw it away. It is better for you to enter life maimed or crippled than to have two hands or two feet and be thrown into eternal fire. [9]And if your eye causes you to stumble, gouge it out and throw it away. It is better for you to enter life with one eye than to have two eyes and be thrown into the fire of hell.

The Parable of the Wandering Sheep

[10][11]"See that you do not despise one of these little ones. For I tell you that their angels in heaven always see the face of my Father in heaven.

[12]"What do you think? If a man owns a hundred sheep, and one of them wanders away, will he not leave the ninety-nine on the hills and go to look for the one that wandered off? [13]And if he finds it, truly I tell you, he is happier about that one sheep than about the ninety-nine that did not wander off. [14]In the same way your Father in heaven is not willing that any of these little ones should perish.

1415

Dealing With Sin in the Church

[15]"If a brother or sister sins,[a] go and point out the fault, just between the two of you. If they listen to you, you have won them over. [16]But if they will not listen, take one or two others along, so that 'every matter may be established by the testimony of two or three witnesses.'[b] [17]If they still refuse to listen, tell it to the church; and if they refuse to listen even to the church, treat them as you would a pagan or a tax collector.

[18]"Truly I tell you, whatever you bind on earth will be[c] bound in heaven, and whatever you loose on earth will be[d] loosed in heaven.

[19]"Again, truly I tell you that if two of you on earth agree about anything you ask for, it will be done for you by my Father in heaven. [20]For where two or three come together in my name, there am I with them."

The Parable of the Unmerciful Servant

[21]Then Peter came to Jesus and asked, "Lord, how many times shall I forgive someone who sins against me? Up to seven times?"

[22]Jesus answered, "I tell you, not seven times, but seventy-seven times.[e]

[23]"Therefore, the kingdom of heaven is like a king who wanted to settle accounts with his servants. [24]As he began the settlement, a man who owed him ten thousand bags of gold[f] was brought to him. [25]Since he was not able to pay, the master ordered that he and his wife and his children and all that he had be sold to repay the debt.

---

a 15 Some manuscripts *sins against you*   *b 16* Deut. 19:15   *c 18* Or *will have been*   *d 18* Or *will have been*   *e 22* Or *seventy times seven*   *f 24* Greek *ten thousand talents*; a talent was worth about 20 years of a day laborer's wages.

²⁶"The servant fell on his knees before him. 'Be patient with me,' he begged, 'and I will pay back every-thing.' ²⁷The servant's master took pity on him, canceled the debt and let him go.

²⁸"But when that servant went out, he found one of his fellow servants who owed him a hundred sil-ver coins.ᵃ He grabbed him and began to choke him. 'Pay back what you owe me!' he demanded.

²⁹"His fellow servant fell to his knees and begged him, 'Be patient with me, and I will pay you back.'

³⁰"But he refused. Instead, he went off and had the man thrown into prison until he could pay the debt. ³¹When the other servants saw what had happened, they were greatly distressed and went and told their master everything that had happened.

³²"Then the master called the servant in. 'You wicked servant,' he said, 'I canceled all that debt of yours because you begged me to. ³³Shouldn't you have had mercy on your fellow servant just as I had on you?' ³⁴In anger his master handed him over to the jailers to be tortured, until he should pay back all he owed.

³⁵"This is how my heavenly Father will treat each of you unless you forgive a brother or sister from your heart."

Divorce

19 When Jesus had finished saying these things, he left Galilee and went into the region of Judea to the other side of the Jordan. ²Large crowds followed him, and he healed them there.

³Some Pharisees came to him to test him. They asked, "Is it lawful for a man to divorce his wife for any and every reason?"

⁴"Haven't you read," he replied, "that at the beginning the Creator 'made them male and female,'ᵇ ⁵and said, 'For this reason a man will leave his father and mother and be united to his wife, and the two will become one flesh'ᶜ? ⁶So they are no longer two, but one. Therefore what God has joined together, let no one separate."

⁷"Why then," they asked, "did Moses command that a man give his wife a certificate of divorce and send her away?"

⁸Jesus replied, "Moses permitted you to divorce your wives because your hearts were hard. But it was not this way from the beginning. ⁹I tell you that anyone who divorces his wife, except for sexual immorality, and marries another woman commits adultery."

¹⁰The disciples said to him, "If this is the situation between a husband and wife, it is better not to marry."

¹¹Jesus replied, "Not everyone can accept this word, but only those to whom it has been given. ¹²For some are eunuchs because they were born that way; others have been made eunuchs; and others have renounced marriageᵈ because of the kingdom of heaven. The one who can accept this should accept it."

The Little Children and Jesus

¹³Then people brought little children to Jesus for him to place his hands on them and pray for them. But the disciples rebuked them.

¹⁴Jesus said, "Let the little children come to me, and do not hinder them, for the kingdom of heaven belongs to such as these." ¹⁵When he had placed his hands on them, he went on from there.

The Rich and the Kingdom of God

¹⁶Just then a man came up to Jesus and asked, "Teacher, what good thing must I do to get eternal life?"

¹⁷"Why do you ask me about what is good?" Jesus replied. "There is only One who is good. If you want to enter life, keep the commandments."

¹⁸"Which ones?" he inquired.

Jesus replied, "'You shall not murder, you shall not commit adultery, you shall not steal, you shall not give false testimony, ¹⁹honor your father and mother,'ᵉ and 'love your neighbor as yourself.'ᶠ"

²⁰"All these I have kept," the young man said. "What do I still lack?"

²¹Jesus answered, "If you want to be perfect, go, sell your possessions and give to the poor, and you will have treasure in heaven. Then come, follow me."

ᵃ 28 Greek *a hundred denarii*; a denarius was the daily wage of a day laborer (see Matt. 20:2).   ᵇ 4 Gen. 1:27   ᶜ 5 Gen. 2:24   ᵈ 12 Or *have made themselves eunuchs*   ᵉ 19 Exodus 20:12-16; Deut. 5:16-20   ᶠ 19 Lev. 19:18

HE IS: the God of the impossible

19:23–26 Jesus pointed out the difficulties that the rich have in entering God's kingdom because of their divided loyalties. The disciples then wondered who could ever be saved. Jesus underscored the impossibility of people saving themselves but explained that with God, all things are possible.

You'll never appreciate the price of your salvation until you understand how impossible it was for you, the rich woman with divided loyalties, to get to God on your own. You cannot buy or earn a spot in God's eternity (see Hebrews 11:6). What you could not do for yourself *the God of the impossible* did for you.

For the next He Is, go to p. 1421.

²²When the young man heard this, he went away sad, because he had great wealth.

²³Then Jesus said to his disciples, "Truly I tell you, it is hard for the rich to enter the kingdom of heaven. ²⁴Again I tell you, it is easier for a camel to go through the eye of a needle than for the rich to enter the kingdom of God."

²⁵When the disciples heard this, they were greatly astonished and asked, "Who then can be saved?"

²⁶Jesus looked at them and said, "With human beings this is impossible, but with God all things are possible."

²⁷Peter answered him, "We have left everything to follow you! What then will there be for us?"

²⁸Jesus said to them, "Truly I tell you, at the renewal of all things, when the Son of Man sits on his glorious throne, you who have followed me will also sit on twelve thrones, judging the twelve tribes of Israel. ²⁹And everyone who has left houses or brothers or sisters or father or mother or wife*ᵃ* or children or fields for my sake will receive a hundred times as much and will inherit eternal life. ³⁰But many who are first will be last, and many who are last will be first.

The Parable of the Workers in the Vineyard

20 "For the kingdom of heaven is like a landowner who went out early in the morning to hire workers for his vineyard. ²He agreed to pay them a denarius for the day and sent them into his vineyard.

³"About nine in the morning he went out and saw others standing in the marketplace doing nothing. ⁴He told them, 'You also go and work in my vineyard, and I will pay you whatever is right.' ⁵So they went.

"He went out again about noon and about three in the afternoon and did the same thing. ⁶About five in the afternoon he went out and found still others standing around. He asked them, 'Why have you been standing here all day long doing nothing?'

⁷"'Because no one has hired us,' they answered.

"He said to them, 'You also go and work in my vineyard.'

⁸"When evening came, the owner of the vineyard said to his supervisor, 'Call the workers and pay them their wages, beginning with the last ones hired and going on to the first.'

⁹"The workers who were hired about five in the afternoon came and each received a denarius. ¹⁰So when those came who were hired first, they expected to receive more. But each one of them also received a denarius. ¹¹When they received it, they began to grumble against the landowner. ¹²'These men who were hired last worked only one hour,' they said, 'and you have made them equal to us who have borne the burden of the work and the heat of the day.'

¹³"But he answered one of them, 'Friend, I am not being unfair to you. Didn't you agree to work for a denarius? ¹⁴Take your pay and go. I want to give the one who was hired last the same as I gave you. ¹⁵Don't I have the right to do what I want with my own money? Or are you envious because I am generous?'

¹⁶"So the last will be first, and the first will be last."

ᵃ 29 Some manuscripts do not have *or wife.*

1417

myth# 80

"MARRIAGE IS EASY. I WON'T HAVE TO WORK AT IT."

I thought it would be so much easier than this.

When we were dating, our relationship seemed natural. We got along so well—which, believe me, is a minor miracle for two people in their late thirties who are single and set in their ways. Somehow we just kind of slipped into a comfortable way of being together. Nothing forced or contrived. Just an easy friendship that had its share of passion too. Not a bad combination, I remember thinking to myself early on. I could see myself married to this guy for the rest of my life.

Now that we are married, all that's changed. Instead of aging naturally together like a pair of comfortable shoes, everything is such an effort. I mean everything. Deciding how to divide household chores, where we'll go on vacation, who will pay the bills or even the best way to sort laundry. These are weekly sources of debate in our home. Because we married later in life, we each had our own way of doing things for years. Which means we have to discuss every single thing that happens or we end up fighting about what didn't turn out the way we wanted.

I look at my parents' marriage, and I don't understand why mine is so tough. They seem to be able to read each other's minds. My dad can sense when my mom is getting upset about something, and my mom knows exactly how to make him smile again. They can finish each other's sentences. And not to be understated in importance, they have the same decorating taste.

Maybe Arthur and I made a mistake. Maybe we're really not that good together. Marriage is supposed to be way easier than all this work. Why was dating such a breeze?

—Audra

CONTRARY TO POPULAR

belief, romantic love does not conquer all. Marriage is much more than two people who are attracted to each other. If a marriage is built to last, it also needs a love that encompasses commitment, faithfulness, communication, understanding, forgiveness, honesty, patience, time, common experiences and humor, to name just a few essentials (see 1 Corinthians 13). And a loving marriage especially needs W-O-R-K:

W—Work in progress. Although you may look at a married couple you admire and expect the same for your marriage, you have to remember that you only see a small piece of a work in progress. It takes time to get to know someone, and you *will* find some surprises along the way. This discovery doesn't have to be bad, but you'll have to work through it together. That takes effort.

O—Other couples. Instead of comparing your marriage to another couple you admire, use them as a resource. Can they give you any advice for your marriage? Can they share any stories about the work they've put into their relationship? How do other couples work through issues? Find out for yourself.

R—Reality check. Sometimes the strain on a young marriage comes from unrealistic expectations—of who your husband is and of how your marriage will work out. Use the challenges in your marriage and the war stories of other couples to help you adjust your expectations. Your marriage is not unusual—*all* marriages require a lot of work. Having realistic expectations will help you pick your battles and let go of the things that don't matter.

K—Keep praying. Prayer transforms struggling marriages. Nothing is impossible when you turn to God in faith (see Matthew 17:20). Invite God into your marriage. Make him first in your life. If your husband is open

to it, pray together for your marriage. Then allow God to use both of you to buff each other's rough edges and to glorify him through your marriage.

"Couples that learn how to persevere through the tough times are the ones that emerge with even stronger relationships."

—Focus on the Family

1419

"BEAR WITH EACH OTHER AND FORGIVE ONE ANOTHER IF ANY OF YOU HAS A GRIEVANCE AGAINST SOMEONE."

COLOSSIANS 3:13

SEE ALSO

Proverbs 27:17

Romans 15:5–6

Colossians 3:13–17

For more on **Marriage**, check the index.

Jesus Predicts His Death a Third Time

¹⁷Now Jesus was going up to Jerusalem. On the way, he took the Twelve aside and said to them, ¹⁸"We are going up to Jerusalem, and the Son of Man will be delivered over to the chief priests and the teachers of the law. They will condemn him to death ¹⁹and will hand him over to the Gentiles to be mocked and flogged and crucified. On the third day he will be raised to life!"

A Mother's Request

²⁰Then the mother of Zebedee's sons came to Jesus with her sons and, kneeling down, asked a favor of him.

²¹"What is it you want?" he asked.

She said, "Grant that one of these two sons of mine may sit at your right and the other at your left in your kingdom."

²²"You don't know what you are asking," Jesus said to them. "Can you drink the cup I am going to drink?"

"We can," they answered.

²³Jesus said to them, "You will indeed drink from my cup, but to sit at my right or left is not for me to grant. These places belong to those for whom they have been prepared by my Father."

²⁴When the ten heard about this, they were indignant with the two brothers. ²⁵Jesus called them together and said, "You know that the rulers of the Gentiles lord it over them, and their high officials exercise authority over them. ²⁶Not so with you. Instead, whoever wants to become great among you must be your servant, ²⁷and whoever wants to be first must be your slave— ²⁸just as the Son of Man did not come to be served, but to serve, and to give his life as a ransom for many."

Two Blind Men Receive Sight

²⁹As Jesus and his disciples were leaving Jericho, a large crowd followed him. ³⁰Two blind men were sitting by the roadside, and when they heard that Jesus was going by, they shouted, "Lord, Son of David, have mercy on us!"

³¹The crowd rebuked them and told them to be quiet, but they shouted all the louder, "Lord, Son of David, have mercy on us!"

³²Jesus stopped and called them. "What do you want me to do for you?" he asked.

³³"Lord," they answered, "we want our sight."

³⁴Jesus had compassion on them and touched their eyes. Immediately they received their sight and followed him.

Jesus Comes to Jerusalem as King

21 As they approached Jerusalem and came to Bethphage on the Mount of Olives, Jesus sent two disciples, ²saying to them, "Go to the village ahead of you, and at once you will find a donkey tied there, with her colt by her. Untie them and bring them to me. ³If anyone says anything to you, say that the Lord needs them, and he will send them right away."

⁴This took place to fulfill what was spoken through the prophet:

> ⁵"Say to Daughter Zion,
>   'See, your king comes to you,
> gentle and riding on a donkey,
>   and on a colt, the foal of a donkey.'"ᵃ

⁶The disciples went and did as Jesus had instructed them. ⁷They brought the donkey and the colt and placed their cloaks on them for Jesus to sit on. ⁸A very large crowd spread their cloaks on the road, while others cut branches from the trees and spread them on the road. ⁹The crowds that went ahead of him and those that followed shouted,

> "Hosannaᵇ to the Son of David!"

1420

HE IS: the Son of David

21:8–9 It was Passover in Jerusalem when Jesus entered the city riding on a donkey. The crowds shouted that he was *the Son of David*, signifying that he had the pedigree to be rightful heir to King David's throne. Their cries of *Hosanna* literally meant, "Save us, please!"

The Israelites were controlled by the Romans and longed for salvation. What controls you? Your personal relationships? Your petty thoughts? Your private habits? Isn't it time you recognized *the Son of David* as King of kings and asked him to triumphantly enter your life? Shout "*Hosanna!* Save me, please!" and he will come to your rescue.

For the next He Is, go to p. 1426.

"Blessed is he who comes in the name of the Lord!"*ᵃ*

"Hosanna*ᵇ* in the highest heaven!"

¹⁰When Jesus entered Jerusalem, the whole city was stirred and asked, "Who is this?"
¹¹The crowds answered, "This is Jesus, the prophet from Nazareth in Galilee."

Jesus at the Temple

¹²Jesus entered the temple courts and drove out all who were buying and selling there. He overturned the tables of the money changers and the benches of those selling doves. ¹³"It is written," he said to them, "'My house will be called a house of prayer,'*ᶜ* but you are making it 'a den of robbers.'*ᵈ*"

¹⁴The blind and the lame came to him at the temple, and he healed them. ¹⁵But when the chief priests and the teachers of the law saw the wonderful things he did and the children shouting in the temple courts, "Hosanna to the Son of David," they were indignant.

¹⁶"Do you hear what these children are saying?" they asked him.

"Yes," replied Jesus, "have you never read,

"'From the lips of children and infants
    you have ordained praise'*ᵉ*?"

¹⁷And he left them and went out of the city to Bethany, where he spent the night.

Jesus Curses a Fig Tree

¹⁸Early in the morning, as he was on his way back to the city, he was hungry. ¹⁹Seeing a fig tree by the road, he went up to it but found nothing on it except leaves. Then he said to it, "May you never bear fruit again!" Immediately the tree withered.

²⁰When the disciples saw this, they were amazed. "How did the fig tree wither so quickly?" they asked.

²¹Jesus replied, "Truly I tell you, if you have faith and do not doubt, not only can you do what was done to the fig tree, but also you can say to this mountain, 'Go, throw yourself into the sea,' and it will be done. ²²If you believe, you will receive whatever you ask for in prayer."

conversations

prayer «» 21:21–22

1» Is Jesus saying here that, with faith, we will actually receive whatever we ask for in prayer?

2» With what attitude do you usually approach prayer? Why?

3» Why is lack of faith so damaging to your prayer life?

For more on **prayer**, check the index.
For the next Conversations, go to p. 1431.

The Authority of Jesus Questioned

²³Jesus entered the temple courts, and, while he was teaching, the chief priests and the elders of the people came to him. "By what authority are you doing these things?" they asked. "And who gave you this authority?"

ᵃ 9 Psalm 118:25,26 *ᵇ 9* A Hebrew expression meaning "Save!" which became an exclamation of praise; also in verse 15 *ᶜ 13* Isaiah 56:7 *ᵈ 13* Jer. 7:11
ᵉ 16 Psalm 8:2 (see Septuagint)

²⁴Jesus replied, "I will also ask you one question. If you answer me, I will tell you by what authority I am doing these things. ²⁵John's baptism—where did it come from? Was it from heaven, or of human origin?"

They discussed it among themselves and said, "If we say, 'From heaven,' he will ask, 'Then why didn't you believe him?' ²⁶But if we say, 'Of human origin'—we are afraid of the people, for they all hold that John was a prophet."

²⁷So they answered Jesus, "We don't know."

Then he said, "Neither will I tell you by what authority I am doing these things.

The Parable of the Two Sons

²⁸"What do you think? There was a man who had two sons. He went to the first and said, 'Son, go and work today in the vineyard.'

²⁹"'I will not,' he answered, but later he changed his mind and went.

³⁰"Then the father went to the other son and said the same thing. He answered, 'I will, sir,' but he did not go.

³¹"Which of the two did what his father wanted?"

"The first," they answered.

Jesus said to them, "Truly I tell you, the tax collectors and the prostitutes are entering the kingdom of God ahead of you. ³²For John came to you to show you the way of righteousness, and you did not believe him, but the tax collectors and the prostitutes did. And even after you saw this, you did not repent and believe him.

The Parable of the Tenants

³³"Listen to another parable: There was a landowner who planted a vineyard. He put a wall around it, dug a winepress in it and built a watchtower. Then he rented the vineyard to some farmers and moved to another place. ³⁴When the harvest time approached, he sent his servants to the tenants to collect his fruit.

³⁵"The tenants seized his servants; they beat one, killed another, and stoned a third. ³⁶Then he sent other servants to them, more than the first time, and the tenants treated them the same way. ³⁷Last of all, he sent his son to them. 'They will respect my son,' he said.

³⁸"But when the tenants saw the son, they said to each other, 'This is the heir. Come, let's kill him and take his inheritance.' ³⁹So they took him and threw him out of the vineyard and killed him.

⁴⁰"Therefore, when the owner of the vineyard comes, what will he do to those tenants?"

⁴¹"He will bring those wretches to a wretched end," they replied, "and he will rent the vineyard to other tenants, who will give him his share of the crop at harvest time."

⁴²Jesus said to them, "Have you never read in the Scriptures:

> "'The stone the builders rejected
>   has become the cornerstone;
> the Lord has done this,
>   and it is marvelous in our eyes'ᵃ?

⁴³"Therefore I tell you that the kingdom of God will be taken away from you and given to a people who will produce its fruit. ⁴⁴Anyone who falls on this stone will be broken to pieces, but anyone on whom it falls will be crushed."ᵇ

⁴⁵When the chief priests and the Pharisees heard Jesus' parables, they knew he was talking about them. ⁴⁶They looked for a way to arrest him, but they were afraid of the crowd because the people held that he was a prophet.

The Parable of the Wedding Banquet

22 Jesus spoke to them again in parables, saying: ²"The kingdom of heaven is like a king who prepared a wedding banquet for his son. ³He sent his servants to those who had been invited to the banquet to tell them to come, but they refused to come.

ᵃ 42 Psalm 118:22,23   ᵇ 44 Some manuscripts do not have verse 44.

⁴"Then he sent some more servants and said, 'Tell those who have been invited that I have prepared my dinner: My oxen and fattened cattle have been butchered, and everything is ready. Come to the wedding banquet.'

⁵"But they paid no attention and went off—one to his field, another to his business. ⁶The rest seized his servants, mistreated them and killed them. ⁷The king was enraged. He sent his army and destroyed those murderers and burned their city.

⁸"Then he said to his servants, 'The wedding banquet is ready, but those I invited did not deserve to come. ⁹Go to the street corners and invite to the banquet anyone you find.' ¹⁰So the servants went out into the streets and gathered all the people they could find, the bad as well as the good, and the wedding hall was filled with guests.

¹¹"But when the king came in to see the guests, he noticed a man there who was not wearing wedding clothes. ¹²'Friend,' he asked, 'how did you get in here without wedding clothes?' The man was speechless.

¹³"Then the king told the attendants, 'Tie him hand and foot, and throw him outside, into the darkness, where there will be weeping and gnashing of teeth.'

¹⁴"For many are invited, but few are chosen."

Paying the Imperial Tax to Caesar

¹⁵Then the Pharisees went out and laid plans to trap him in his words. ¹⁶They sent their disciples to him along with the Herodians. "Teacher," they said, "we know that you are a man of integrity and that you teach the way of God in accordance with the truth. You aren't swayed by others, because you pay no attention to who they are. ¹⁷Tell us then, what is your opinion? Is it right to pay the imperial tax[a] to Caesar or not?"

¹⁸But Jesus, knowing their evil intent, said, "You hypocrites, why are you trying to trap me? ¹⁹Show me the coin used for paying the tax." They brought him a denarius, ²⁰and he asked them, "Whose image is this? And whose inscription?"

²¹"Caesar's," they replied.

Then he said to them, "Give back to Caesar what is Caesar's, and to God what is God's."

²²When they heard this, they were amazed. So they left him and went away.

Marriage at the Resurrection

²³That same day the Sadducees, who say there is no resurrection, came to him with a question. ²⁴"Teacher," they said, "Moses told us that if a man dies without having children, his brother must marry the widow and raise up offspring for him. ²⁵Now there were seven brothers among us. The first one married and died, and since he had no children, he left his wife to his brother. ²⁶The same thing happened to the second and third brother, right on down to the seventh. ²⁷Finally, the woman died. ²⁸Now then, at the resurrection, whose wife will she be of the seven, since all of them were married to her?"

²⁹Jesus replied, "You are in error because you do not know the Scriptures or the power of God. ³⁰At the resurrection people will neither marry nor be given in marriage; they will be like the angels in heaven. ³¹But about the resurrection of the dead—have you not read what God said to you, ³²'I am the God of Abraham, the God of Isaac, and the God of Jacob'[b]? He is not the God of the dead but of the living."

³³When the crowds heard this, they were astonished at his teaching.

The Greatest Commandment

³⁴Hearing that Jesus had silenced the Sadducees, the Pharisees got together. ³⁵One of them, an expert in the law, tested him with this question: ³⁶"Teacher, which is the greatest commandment in the Law?"

³⁷Jesus replied: "'Love the Lord your God with all your heart and with all your soul and with all your mind.'[c] ³⁸This is the first and greatest commandment. ³⁹And the second is like it: 'Love your neighbor as yourself.'[d] ⁴⁰All the Law and the Prophets hang on these two commandments."

Whose Son Is the Messiah?

⁴¹While the Pharisees were gathered together, Jesus asked them, ⁴²"What do you think about the Messiah? Whose son is he?"

---

[a] 17 A special tax levied on subject peoples, not on Roman citizens   [b] 32 Exodus 3:6   [c] 37 Deut. 6:5   [d] 39 Lev. 19:18

"The son of David," they replied.

[43] He said to them, "How is it then that David, speaking by the Spirit, calls him 'Lord'? For he says,

[44] "'The Lord said to my Lord:
"Sit at my right hand
until I put your enemies
under your feet."'[a]

[45] "If then David calls him 'Lord,' how can he be his son?" [46] No one could say a word in reply, and from that day on no one dared to ask him any more questions.

A Warning Against Hypocrisy

23 Then Jesus said to the crowds and to his disciples: [2] "The teachers of the law and the Pharisees sit in Moses' seat. [3] So you must be careful to do everything they tell you. But do not do what they do, for they do not practice what they preach. [4] They tie up heavy, cumbersome loads and put them on other people's shoulders, but they themselves are not willing to lift a finger to move them.

[5] "Everything they do is done for people to see: They make their phylacteries[b] wide and the tassels on their garments long; [6] they love the place of honor at banquets and the most important seats in the synagogues; [7] they love to be greeted with respect in the marketplaces and to have people call them 'Rabbi.'

[8] "But you are not to be called 'Rabbi,' for you have only one Master and you are all brothers. [9] And do not call anyone on earth 'father,' for you have one Father, and he is in heaven. [10] Nor are you to be called 'teacher,' for you have one Teacher, the Messiah. [11] The greatest among you will be your servant. [12] For those who exalt themselves will be humbled, and those who humble themselves will be exalted.

Seven Woes on the Teachers of the Law and the Pharisees

[13] [14] "Woe to you, teachers of the law and Pharisees, you hypocrites! You shut the door of the kingdom of heaven in people's faces. You yourselves do not enter, nor will you let those enter who are trying to.

[15] "Woe to you, teachers of the law and Pharisees, you hypocrites! You travel over land and sea to win a single convert, and then you make that convert twice as much a child of hell as you are.

[16] "Woe to you, blind guides! You say, 'If anyone swears by the temple, it means nothing; but whoever swears by the gold of the temple is bound by the oath.' [17] You blind fools! Which is greater: the gold, or the temple that makes the gold sacred? [18] You also say, 'If anyone swears by the altar, it means nothing; but whoever swears by the gift on the altar is bound by the oath.' [19] You blind men! Which is greater: the gift, or the altar that makes the gift sacred? [20] Therefore, anyone who swears by the altar swears by it and by everything on it. [21] And anyone who swears by the temple swears by it and by the one who dwells in it. [22] And anyone who swears by heaven swears by God's throne and by the one who sits on it.

[23] "Woe to you, teachers of the law and Pharisees, you hypocrites! You give a tenth of your spices—mint, dill and cumin. But you have neglected the more important matters of the law—justice, mercy and faithfulness. You should have practiced the latter, without neglecting the former. [24] You blind guides! You strain out a gnat but swallow a camel.

[25] "Woe to you, teachers of the law and Pharisees, you hypocrites! You clean the outside of the cup and dish, but inside they are full of greed and self-indulgence. [26] Blind Pharisee! First clean the inside of the cup and dish, and then the outside also will be clean.

at issue: priorities

22:34–40 As you get older, life gets more complicated. Demands on your time and attention continue to mount, and there's never enough time or energy in a day to get to everything. Do you find yourself longing for a simpler life? When all is said and done, the focus of your life should be to love God and love others. Do the things that fill your heart, life and schedule reflect those priorities? By discovering and focusing your energy on what God considers most important, you begin to find clarity and purpose for each day of your life.

---

[a] 44 Psalm 110:1   [b] 5 That is, boxes containing Scripture verses, worn on forehead and arm

²⁷"Woe to you, teachers of the law and Pharisees, you hypocrites! You are like whitewashed tombs, which look beautiful on the outside but on the inside are full of the bones of the dead and everything unclean. ²⁸In the same way, on the outside you appear to people as righteous but on the inside you are full of hypocrisy and wickedness.

²⁹"Woe to you, teachers of the law and Pharisees, you hypocrites! You build tombs for the prophets and decorate the graves of the righteous. ³⁰And you say, 'If we had lived in the days of our ancestors, we would not have taken part with them in shedding the blood of the prophets.' ³¹So you testify against yourselves that you are the descendants of those who murdered the prophets. ³²Fill up, then, the measure of the sin of your ancestors!

³³"You snakes! You brood of vipers! How will you escape being condemned to hell? ³⁴Therefore I am sending you prophets and sages and teachers. Some of them you will kill and crucify; others you will flog in your synagogues and pursue from town to town. ³⁵And so upon you will come all the righteous blood that has been shed on earth, from the blood of righteous Abel to the blood of Zechariah son of Berekiah, whom you murdered between the temple and the altar. ³⁶Truly I tell you, all this will come on this generation.

³⁷"Jerusalem, Jerusalem, you who kill the prophets and stone those sent to you, how often I have longed to gather your children together, as a hen gathers her chicks under her wings, and you were not willing. ³⁸Look, your house is left to you desolate. ³⁹For I tell you, you will not see me again until you say, 'Blessed is he who comes in the name of the Lord.'^a"

The Destruction of the Temple and Signs of the End Times

24 Jesus left the temple and was walking away when his disciples came up to him to call his attention to its buildings. ²"Do you see all these things?" he asked. "Truly I tell you, not one stone here will be left on another; every one will be thrown down."

³As Jesus was sitting on the Mount of Olives, the disciples came to him privately. "Tell us," they said, "when will this happen, and what will be the sign of your coming and of the end of the age?"

⁴Jesus answered: "Watch out that no one deceives you. ⁵For many will come in my name, claiming, 'I am the Messiah,' and will deceive many. ⁶You will hear of wars and rumors of wars, but see to it that you are not alarmed. Such things must happen, but the end is still to come. ⁷Nation will rise against nation, and kingdom against kingdom. There will be famines and earthquakes in various places. ⁸All these are the beginning of birth pains.

⁹"Then you will be handed over to be persecuted and put to death, and you will be hated by all nations because of me. ¹⁰At that time many will turn away from the faith and will betray and hate each other, ¹¹and many false prophets will appear and deceive many people. ¹²Because of the increase of wickedness, the love of most will grow cold, ¹³but whoever stands firm to the end will be saved. ¹⁴And this gospel of the kingdom will be preached in the whole world as a testimony to all nations, and then the end will come.

¹⁵"So when you see standing in the holy place 'the abomination that causes desolation,'^b spoken of through the prophet Daniel—let the reader understand— ¹⁶then let those who are in Judea flee to the mountains. ¹⁷Let no one on the housetop go down to take anything out of the house. ¹⁸Let no one in the field go back to get their cloak. ¹⁹How dreadful it will be in those days for pregnant women and nursing mothers! ²⁰Pray that your flight will not take place in winter or on the Sabbath. ²¹For then there will be great distress, unequaled from the beginning of the world until now—and never to be equaled again.

²²"If those days had not been cut short, no one would survive, but for the sake of the elect those days will be shortened. ²³At that time if anyone says to you, 'Look, here is the Messiah!' or, 'There he is!' do not believe it. ²⁴For false messiahs and false prophets will appear and perform great signs and wonders to deceive, if possible, even the elect. ²⁵See, I have told you ahead of time.

²⁶"So if anyone tells you, 'There he is, out in the wilderness,' do not go out; or, 'Here he is, in the inner rooms,' do not believe it. ²⁷For as lightning that comes from the east is visible even in the west, so will be the coming of the Son of Man. ²⁸Wherever there is a carcass, there the vultures will gather.

---

^a *39* Psalm 118:26   ^b *15* Daniel 9:27; 11:31; 12:11

²⁹"Immediately after the distress of those days

"'the sun will be darkened,
and the moon will not give its light;
the stars will fall from the sky,
and the heavenly bodies will be shaken.'ᵃ

³⁰"At that time the sign of the Son of Man will appear in the sky, and all the peoples of the earthᵇ will mourn. They will see the Son of Man coming on the clouds of heaven, with power and great glory. ³¹And he will send his angels with a loud trumpet call, and they will gather his elect from the four winds, from one end of the heavens to the other.

³²"Now learn this lesson from the fig tree: As soon as its twigs get tender and its leaves come out, you know that summer is near. ³³Even so, when you see all these things, you know that itᶜ is near, right at the door. ³⁴Truly I tell you, this generation will certainly not pass away until all these things have happened. ³⁵Heaven and earth will pass away, but my words will never pass away.

The Day and Hour Unknown

³⁶"But about that day or hour no one knows, not even the angels in heaven, nor the Son,ᵈ but only the Father. ³⁷As it was in the days of Noah, so it will be at the coming of the Son of Man. ³⁸For in the days before the flood, people were eating and drinking, marrying and giving in marriage, up to the day Noah entered the ark; ³⁹and they knew nothing about what would happen until the flood came and took them all away. That is how it will be at the coming of the Son of Man. ⁴⁰Two men will be in the field; one will be taken and the other left. ⁴¹Two women will be grinding with a hand mill; one will be taken and the other left.

HE IS: the Son of Man

24:26–31 Jesus spoke of a future full of distress that will be visible to the whole world. The faithful will be persecuted for their faith in the Messiah, but then all will see *the Son of Man* coming on heaven's clouds with power and great glory (see 1 Thessalonians 4:16–18).

Is someone or something in your life causing you such distress that you despair for the future? *The Son of Man* comes with power to free your heart and mind from the forces that would destroy you. Pray that his Word, his people and his providential care for you will give you victory.

For the next He Is, go to p. 1438.

⁴²"Therefore keep watch, because you do not know on what day your Lord will come. ⁴³But understand this: If the owner of the house had known at what time of night the thief was coming, he would have kept watch and would not have let his house be broken into. ⁴⁴So you also must be ready, because the Son of Man will come at an hour when you do not expect him.

⁴⁵"Who then is the faithful and wise servant, whom the master has put in charge of the servants in his household to give them their food at the proper time? ⁴⁶It will be good for that servant whose master finds him doing so when he returns. ⁴⁷Truly I tell you, he will put him in charge of all his possessions. ⁴⁸But suppose that servant is wicked and says to himself, 'My master is staying away a long time,' ⁴⁹and he then begins to beat his fellow servants and to eat and drink with drunkards. ⁵⁰The master of that servant will come on a day when he does not expect him and at an hour he is not aware of. ⁵¹He will cut him to pieces and assign him a place with the hypocrites, where there will be weeping and gnashing of teeth.

ᵃ *29* Isaiah 13:10; 34:4   ᵇ *30* Or *the tribes of the land*   ᶜ *33* Or *he*   ᵈ *36* Some manuscripts do not have *nor the Son.*

The Parable of the Ten Virgins

25 "At that time the kingdom of heaven will be like ten virgins who took their lamps and went out to meet the bridegroom. [2]Five of them were foolish and five were wise. [3]The foolish ones took their lamps but did not take any oil with them. [4]The wise, however, took oil in jars along with their lamps. [5]The bridegroom was a long time in coming, and they all became drowsy and fell asleep.

[6]"At midnight the cry rang out: 'Here's the bridegroom! Come out to meet him!'

[7]"Then all the virgins woke up and trimmed their lamps. [8]The foolish ones said to the wise, 'Give us some of your oil; our lamps are going out.'

[9]"'No,' they replied, 'there may not be enough for both us and you. Instead, go to those who sell oil and buy some for yourselves.'

[10]"But while they were on their way to buy the oil, the bridegroom arrived. The virgins who were ready went in with him to the wedding banquet. And the door was shut.

[11]"Later the others also came. 'Sir! Sir!' they said. 'Open the door for us!'

[12]"But he replied, 'Truly I tell you, I don't know you.'

[13]"Therefore keep watch, because you do not know the day or the hour.

The Parable of the Bags of Gold

[14]"Again, it will be like a man going on a journey, who called his servants and entrusted his wealth to them. [15]To one he gave five bags of gold, to another two bags, and to another one bag,[a] each according to his ability. Then he went on his journey. [16]The man who had received five bags of gold went at once and put his money to work and gained five bags more. [17]So also, the one with two bags of gold gained two more. [18]But the man who had received one bag went off, dug a hole in the ground and hid his master's money.

[19]"After a long time the master of those servants returned and settled accounts with them. [20]The man who had received five bags of gold brought the other five. 'Master,' he said, 'you entrusted me with five bags of gold. See, I have gained five more.'

[21]"His master replied, 'Well done, good and faithful servant! You have been faithful with a few things; I will put you in charge of many things. Come and share your master's happiness!'

[22]"The man with two bags of gold also came. 'Master,' he said, 'you entrusted me with two bags of gold; see, I have gained two more.'

[23]"His master replied, 'Well done, good and faithful servant! You have been faithful with a few things; I will put you in charge of many things. Come and share your master's happiness!'

[24]"Then the man who had received one bag of gold came. 'Master,' he said, 'I knew that you are a hard man, harvesting where you have not sown and gathering where you have not scattered seed. [25]So I was afraid and went out and hid your gold in the ground. See, here is what belongs to you.'

[26]"His master replied, 'You wicked, lazy servant! So you knew that I harvest where I have not sown and gather where I have not scattered seed? [27]Well then, you should have put my money on deposit with the bankers, so that when I returned I would have received it back with interest.

[28]"'Take the bag of gold from him and give it to the one who has ten bags. [29]For those who have will be given more, and they will have an abundance. As for those who do not have, even what they have will be taken from them. [30]And throw that worthless servant outside, into the darkness, where there will be weeping and gnashing of teeth.'

The Sheep and the Goats

[31]"When the Son of Man comes in his glory, and all the angels with him, he will sit on his glorious throne. [32]All the nations will be gathered before him, and he will separate the people one from another as a shepherd separates the sheep from the goats. [33]He will put the sheep on his right and the goats on his left.

[34]"Then the King will say to those on his right, 'Come, you who are blessed by my Father; take your inheritance, the kingdom prepared for you since the creation of the world. [35]For I was hungry and you gave me something to eat, I was thirsty and you gave me something to drink, I was a stranger and you

---

[a] 15 Greek *five talents… two talents… one talent*; also throughout this parable; a talent was worth about 20 years of a day laborer's wage.

myth# 81 "WHAT HE EARNS IS HIS; WHAT I EARN IS MINE."

"What's wrong with letting him take care of you, Jacinta? That's what your husband is supposed to do."

My friend meant well. After all, she was just trying to encourage me to buy a little something for myself. We were shopping at a boutique where a few cute things in the window caught my eye. "No, I just don't feel right about it," I said and kept walking.

My husband, Corey, and I have always had a good arrangement. We both worked and shared the bills and expenses. I could spend the extra money I made on shopping, decorating, whatever I wanted, and he spent his on golf, his car, electronics, whatever he wanted. We always had plenty of money to eat at expensive restaurants or take nice trips. After all, it was just the two of us, and we denied ourselves nothing. Then we decided to start a family.

Now I'm home on extended maternity leave, and life is so different. Ethan was born prematurely and is still struggling with some lingering health issues. We decided it would be best for me to take at least six months off to care for him. I'm glad for the time to be with him, but for the first time in our lives, our money situation is tight. Our income is cut in half, and Corey's earning all the money. Even though neither of us misses the extravagant lifestyle we had, we still have to be careful. The hardest part for me is that now I feel guilty about spending my husband's money since I'm not making any money of my own. Sure, I buy groceries and things for the baby, but it would be nice to have some new clothes— some that fit my "mommy body." I still feel that what Corey earns is his, and I shouldn't spend any on me.

—Jacinta

JESUS SAID THAT marriage is

all about two people coming together and becoming one (see Matthew 19:4–6). While that doesn't necessarily mean a couple has to have one joint bank account (in fact, some marriages may operate better with separate accounts), the key principle is *sharing*. There may be times in a marriage when one spouse, not necessarily the husband, is making more money than the other. To put it in business terms, a marriage is a partnership when it comes to finances. This partnership has a set of shared expectations that lead to mutual benefits. How can you improve the effectiveness of your marriage partnership?

- You will face conflicts; the key is how you handle those conflicts. Rather than ignoring the issues or exploding over them, deal with them. This requires good communication. Before you got married, did you and your husband talk about how you would handle finances? Does the current arrangement work for you? If not, it's not too late to devise a "financial agreement" instead of just hoping things will work out.

- Relationships must be able to navigate change. When your financial situation changes, from something such as a job loss, major purchase or the birth of a child, is your financial agreement able to change to accommodate your new situation?

- Talking with other couples about how they handle their money can be helpful. What's worked for someone else can give you and your spouse new ideas. Also consider meeting with a professional financial planner who can give you some ideas on how to handle your money as a couple.

- Finances are a volatile issue and a leading cause of divorce. Unsettled conflicts over money can cost you what's truly valuable—your marriage. Take preventative measures to protect your marriage; don't allow money to divide you.

"Learning to listen to and respect your mate's money perspective is one way to invest in a valuable commodity—your marriage."

—Beverly L. Burch

1429

"FOR THIS reason a man WILL LeAVE HIS FATHER AND MOTHER AND BE UNITED TO HIS WIFE, AND THEY WILL BECOME ONE FLESH."

GENESIS 2:24

SEE ALSO

Acts 4:32

1 Timothy 6:10

Hebrews 13:5,16

For more on **Money** and **Marriage**, check the index.

invited me in, [36]I needed clothes and you clothed me, I was sick and you looked after me, I was in prison and you came to visit me.'

[37]"Then the righteous will answer him, 'Lord, when did we see you hungry and feed you, or thirsty and give you something to drink? [38]When did we see you a stranger and invite you in, or needing clothes and clothe you? [39]When did we see you sick or in prison and go to visit you?'

[40]"The King will reply, 'Truly I tell you, whatever you did for one of the least of these brothers and sisters of mine, you did for me.'

[41]"Then he will say to those on his left, 'Depart from me, you who are cursed, into the eternal fire prepared for the devil and his angels. [42]For I was hungry and you gave me nothing to eat, I was thirsty and you gave me nothing to drink, [43]I was a stranger and you did not invite me in, I needed clothes and you did not clothe me, I was sick and in prison and you did not look after me.'

[44]"They also will answer, 'Lord, when did we see you hungry or thirsty or a stranger or needing clothes or sick or in prison, and did not help you?'

[45]"He will reply, 'Truly I tell you, whatever you did not do for one of the least of these, you did not do for me.'

[46]"Then they will go away to eternal punishment, but the righteous to eternal life."

25:31–46 Many people consider themselves good people—but they're not. They think they have God's approval—but they don't. When you have a genuine relationship with God, the love you have for him spills out onto others. Your actions toward the poor and downtrodden of this world won't save you, but they do reflect whether or not God's love fills your heart. Don't fool yourself into thinking you know God if you really don't. Take this moment to reflect on whether you have genuine faith. True faith reveals itself when you show other people the same love and mercy God has shown you.

1430

The Plot Against Jesus

26 When Jesus had finished saying all these things, he said to his disciples, [2]"As you know, the Passover is two days away—and the Son of Man will be handed over to be crucified."

[3]Then the chief priests and the elders of the people assembled in the palace of the high priest, whose name was Caiaphas, [4]and they plotted to arrest Jesus in some sly way and kill him. [5]"But not during the festival," they said, "or there may be a riot among the people."

Jesus Anointed at Bethany

[6]While Jesus was in Bethany in the home of Simon the Leper, [7]a woman came to him with an alabaster jar of very expensive perfume, which she poured on his head as he was reclining at the table.

[8]When the disciples saw this, they were indignant. "Why this waste?" they asked. [9]"This perfume could have been sold at a high price and the money given to the poor."

[10]Aware of this, Jesus said to them, "Why are you bothering this woman? She has done a beautiful thing to me. [11]The poor you will always have with you,[a] but you will not always have me. [12]When she poured this perfume on my body, she did it to prepare me for burial. [13]Truly I tell you, wherever this gospel is preached throughout the world, what she has done will also be told, in memory of her."

Judas Agrees to Betray Jesus

[14]Then one of the Twelve—the one called Judas Iscariot—went to the chief priests [15]and asked, "What are you willing to give me if I deliver him over to you?" So they counted out for him thirty pieces of silver. [16]From then on Judas watched for an opportunity to hand him over.

The Last Supper

[17]On the first day of the Festival of Unleavened Bread, the disciples came to Jesus and asked, "Where do you want us to make preparations for you to eat the Passover?"

[a] 11 See Deut. 15:11.

¹⁸He replied, "Go into the city to a certain man and tell him, 'The Teacher says: My appointed time is near. I am going to celebrate the Passover with my disciples at your house.'" ¹⁹So the disciples did as Jesus had directed them and prepared the Passover.

²⁰When evening came, Jesus was reclining at the table with the Twelve. ²¹And while they were eating, he said, "Truly I tell you, one of you will betray me."

²²They were very sad and began to say to him one after the other, "Surely not I, Lord?"

²³Jesus replied, "The one who has dipped his hand into the bowl with me will betray me. ²⁴The Son of Man will go just as it is written about him. But woe to that man who betrays the Son of Man! It would be better for him if he had not been born."

²⁵Then Judas, the one who would betray him, said, "Surely not I, Rabbi?"

Jesus answered, "You have said so."

²⁶While they were eating, Jesus took bread, and when he had given thanks, he broke it and gave it to his disciples, saying, "Take and eat; this is my body."

²⁷Then he took the cup, and when he had given thanks, he gave it to them, saying, "Drink from it, all of you. ²⁸This is my blood of the*ᵃ* covenant, which is poured out for many for the forgiveness of sins. ²⁹I tell you, I will not drink of this fruit of the vine from now on until that day when I drink it new with you in my Father's kingdom."

³⁰When they had sung a hymn, they went out to the Mount of Olives.

Jesus Predicts Peter's Denial

³¹Then Jesus told them, "This very night you will all fall away on account of me, for it is written:

> "'I will strike the shepherd,
>   and the sheep of the flock will be scattered.'ᵇ

³²But after I have risen, I will go ahead of you into Galilee."

³³Peter replied, "Even if all fall away on account of you, I never will."

³⁴"Truly I tell you," Jesus answered, "this very night, before the rooster crows, you will disown me three times."

³⁵But Peter declared, "Even if I have to die with you, I will never disown you." And all the other disciples said the same.

Gethsemane

³⁶Then Jesus went with his disciples to a place called Gethsemane, and he said to them, "Sit here while I go over there and pray." ³⁷He took Peter and the two sons of Zebedee along with him, and he began to be sorrowful and troubled. ³⁸Then he said to them, "My soul is overwhelmed with sorrow to the point of death. Stay here and keep watch with me."

³⁹Going a little farther, he fell with his face to the ground and prayed, "My Father, if it is possible, may this cup be taken from me. Yet not as I will, but as you will."

⁴⁰Then he returned to his disciples and found them sleeping. "Couldn't you men keep watch with me for one hour?" he asked Peter. ⁴¹"Watch and pray so that you will not fall into temptation. The spirit is willing, but the flesh is weak."

conversations

prayer «» 26:41

1» What temptations tend to arise when you aren't praying consistently?

2» How can "watching and praying" help you resist those temptations?

3» When do you feel the weakest spiritually and physically?

For more on **prayer**, check the index.
For the next Conversations, go to p. 1433.

⁴²He went away a second time and prayed, "My Father, if it is not possible for this cup to be taken away unless I drink it, may your will be done."

⁴³When he came back, he again found them sleeping, because their eyes were heavy. ⁴⁴So he left them and went away once more and prayed the third time, saying the same thing.

ᵃ *28* Some manuscripts *the new* ᵇ *31* Zech. 13:7

⁴⁵Then he returned to the disciples and said to them, "Are you still sleeping and resting? Look, the hour is near, and the Son of Man is delivered into the hands of sinners. ⁴⁶Rise! Let us go! Here comes my betrayer!"

Jesus Arrested

⁴⁷While he was still speaking, Judas, one of the Twelve, arrived. With him was a large crowd armed with swords and clubs, sent from the chief priests and the elders of the people. ⁴⁸Now the betrayer had arranged a signal with them: "The one I kiss is the man; arrest him." ⁴⁹Going at once to Jesus, Judas said, "Greetings, Rabbi!" and kissed him.

⁵⁰Jesus replied, "Friend, do what you came for."ᵃ

Then the men stepped forward, seized Jesus and arrested him. ⁵¹With that, one of Jesus' companions reached for his sword, drew it out and struck the servant of the high priest, cutting off his ear.

⁵²"Put your sword back in its place," Jesus said to him, "for all who draw the sword will die by the sword. ⁵³Do you think I cannot call on my Father, and he will at once put at my disposal more than twelve legions of angels? ⁵⁴But how then would the Scriptures be fulfilled that say it must happen in this way?"

⁵⁵In that hour Jesus said to the crowd, "Am I leading a rebellion, that you have come out with swords and clubs to capture me? Every day I sat in the temple courts teaching, and you did not arrest me. ⁵⁶But this has all taken place that the writings of the prophets might be fulfilled." Then all the disciples deserted him and fled.

Jesus Before the Sanhedrin

⁵⁷Those who had arrested Jesus took him to Caiaphas the high priest, where the teachers of the law and the elders had assembled. ⁵⁸But Peter followed him at a distance, right up to the courtyard of the high priest. He entered and sat down with the guards to see the outcome.

⁵⁹The chief priests and the whole Sanhedrin were looking for false evidence against Jesus so that they could put him to death. ⁶⁰But they did not find any, though many false witnesses came forward.

Finally two came forward ⁶¹and declared, "This fellow said, 'I am able to destroy the temple of God and rebuild it in three days.'"

⁶²Then the high priest stood up and said to Jesus, "Are you not going to answer? What is this testimony that these men are bringing against you?" ⁶³But Jesus remained silent.

The high priest said to him, "I charge you under oath by the living God: Tell us if you are the Messiah, the Son of God."

⁶⁴"You have said so," Jesus replied. "But I say to all of you: From now on you will see the Son of Man sitting at the right hand of the Mighty One and coming on the clouds of heaven."ᵇ

⁶⁵Then the high priest tore his clothes and said, "He has spoken blasphemy! Why do we need any more witnesses? Look, now you have heard the blasphemy. ⁶⁶What do you think?"

"He is worthy of death," they answered.

⁶⁷Then they spit in his face and struck him with their fists. Others slapped him ⁶⁸and said, "Prophesy to us, Messiah. Who hit you?"

Peter Disowns Jesus

⁶⁹Now Peter was sitting out in the courtyard, and a servant girl came to him. "You also were with Jesus of Galilee," she said.

⁷⁰But he denied it before them all. "I don't know what you're talking about," he said.

⁷¹Then he went out to the gateway, where another servant girl saw him and said to the people there, "This fellow was with Jesus of Nazareth."

⁷²He denied it again, with an oath: "I don't know the man!"

⁷³After a little while, those standing there went up to Peter and said, "Surely you are one of them; your accent gives you away."

⁷⁴Then he began to call down curses, and he swore to them, "I don't know the man!"

Immediately a rooster crowed. ⁷⁵Then Peter remembered the word Jesus had spoken: "Before the rooster crows, you will disown me three times." And he went outside and wept bitterly.

ᵃ *50* Or *"Friend, why have you come?"*   ᵇ *64* See Psalm 110:1; Daniel 7:13.

Judas Hangs Himself

27 Early in the morning, all the chief priests and the elders of the people came to the decision to put Jesus to death. [2]They bound him, led him away and handed him over to Pilate the governor.

[3]When Judas, who had betrayed him, saw that Jesus was condemned, he was seized with remorse and returned the thirty pieces of silver to the chief priests and the elders. [4]"I have sinned," he said, "for I have betrayed innocent blood."

"What is that to us?" they replied. "That's your responsibility."

[5]So Judas threw the money into the temple and left. Then he went away and hanged himself.

[6]The chief priests picked up the coins and said, "It is against the law to put this into the treasury, since it is blood money." [7]So they decided to use the money to buy the potter's field as a burial place for foreigners. [8]That is why it has been called the Field of Blood to this day. [9]Then what was spoken by Jeremiah the prophet was fulfilled: "They took the thirty pieces of silver, the price set on him by the people of Israel, [10]and they used them to buy the potter's field, as the Lord commanded me."[a]

Jesus Before Pilate

[11]Meanwhile Jesus stood before the governor, and the governor asked him, "Are you the king of the Jews?"

"You have said so," Jesus replied.

[12]When he was accused by the chief priests and the elders, he gave no answer. [13]Then Pilate asked him, "Don't you hear the testimony they are bringing against you?" [14]But Jesus made no reply, not even to a single charge—to the great amazement of the governor.

[15]Now it was the governor's custom at the festival to release a prisoner chosen by the crowd. [16]At that time they had a well-known prisoner whose name was Jesus[b] Barabbas. [17]So when the crowd had gathered, Pilate asked them, "Which one do you want me to release to you: Jesus Barabbas, or Jesus who is called the Messiah?" [18]For he knew it was out of envy that they had handed Jesus over to him.

[19]While Pilate was sitting on the judge's seat, his wife sent him this message: "Don't have anything to do with that innocent man, for I have suffered a great deal today in a dream because of him."

[20]But the chief priests and the elders persuaded the crowd to ask for Barabbas and to have Jesus executed.

[21]"Which of the two do you want me to release to you?" asked the governor.

"Barabbas," they answered.

[22]"What shall I do, then, with Jesus who is called the Messiah?" Pilate asked.

They all answered, "Crucify him!"

[23]"Why? What crime has he committed?" asked Pilate.

But they shouted all the louder, "Crucify him!"

[24]When Pilate saw that he was getting nowhere, but that instead an uproar was starting, he took water and washed his hands in front of the crowd. "I am innocent of this man's blood," he said. "It is your responsibility!"

[25]All the people answered, "His blood is on us and on our children!"

[26]Then he released Barabbas to them. But he had Jesus flogged, and handed him over to be crucified.

The Soldiers Mock Jesus

[27]Then the governor's soldiers took Jesus into the Praetorium and gathered the whole company of soldiers around him. [28]They stripped him and put a scarlet robe on him, [29]and then twisted together a

1433

conversations

envy «» 27:18

1» Can you identify a time you acted out of envy? What was the result?

2» How have you, like the Jewish leaders, envied another's position?

3» What will protect you from developing an envious attitude?

For more on **envy**, check the index.
For the next Conversations, go to p. 1442.

---

[a] *10* See Zech. 11:12,13; Jer. 19:1-13; 32:6-9. [b] *16* Many manuscripts do not have *Jesus*; also in verse 17.

crown of thorns and set it on his head. They put a staff in his right hand as a scepter. Then they knelt in front of him and mocked him. "Hail, king of the Jews!" they said. [30]They spit on him, and took the staff and struck him on the head again and again. [31]After they had mocked him, they took off the robe and put his own clothes on him. Then they led him away to crucify him.

The Crucifixion of Jesus

[32]As they were going out, they met a man from Cyrene, named Simon, and they forced him to carry the cross. [33]They came to a place called Golgotha (which means "the place of the skull"). [34]There they offered Jesus wine to drink, mixed with gall; but after tasting it, he refused to drink it. [35]When they had crucified him, they divided up his clothes by casting lots. [36]And sitting down, they kept watch over him there. [37]Above his head they placed the written charge against him: THIS IS JESUS, THE KING OF THE JEWS.

[38]Two rebels were crucified with him, one on his right and one on his left. [39]Those who passed by hurled insults at him, shaking their heads [40]and saying, "You who are going to destroy the temple and build it in three days, save yourself! Come down from the cross, if you are the Son of God!"

[41]In the same way the chief priests, the teachers of the law and the elders mocked him. [42]"He saved others," they said, "but he can't save himself! He's the king of Israel! Let him come down now from the cross, and we will believe in him. [43]He trusts in God. Let God rescue him now if he wants him, for he said, 'I am the Son of God.'" [44]In the same way the rebels who were crucified with him also heaped insults on him.

The Death of Jesus

[45]From noon until three in the afternoon darkness came over all the land. [46]About three in the afternoon Jesus cried out in a loud voice, *"Eli, Eli,[a] lema sabachthani?"* (which means "My God, my God, why have you forsaken me?").[b]

[47]When some of those standing there heard this, they said, "He's calling Elijah."

[48]Immediately one of them ran and got a sponge. He filled it with wine vinegar, put it on a staff, and offered it to Jesus to drink. [49]The rest said, "Now leave him alone. Let's see if Elijah comes to save him."

[50]And when Jesus had cried out again in a loud voice, he gave up his spirit.

[51]At that moment the curtain of the temple was torn in two from top to bottom. The earth shook, the rocks split [52]and the tombs broke open. The bodies of many holy people who had died were raised to life. [53]They came out of the tombs after Jesus' resurrection and[c] went into the holy city and appeared to many people.

[54]When the centurion and those with him who were guarding Jesus saw the earthquake and all that had happened, they were terrified, and exclaimed, "Surely he was the Son of God!"

[55]Many women were there, watching from a distance. They had followed Jesus from Galilee to care for his needs. [56]Among them were Mary Magdalene, Mary the mother of James and Joseph,[d] and the mother of Zebedee's sons.

The Burial of Jesus

[57]As evening approached, there came a rich man from Arimathea, named Joseph, who had himself become a disciple of Jesus. [58]Going to Pilate, he asked for Jesus' body, and Pilate ordered that it be given to him. [59]Joseph took the body, wrapped it in a clean linen cloth, [60]and placed it in his own new tomb that he had cut out of the rock. He rolled a big stone in front of the entrance to the tomb and went away. [61]Mary Magdalene and the other Mary were sitting there opposite the tomb.

The Guard at the Tomb

[62]The next day, the one after Preparation Day, the chief priests and the Pharisees went to Pilate. [63]"Sir," they said, "we remember that while he was still alive that deceiver said, 'After three days I will rise again.' [64]So give the order for the tomb to be made secure until the third day. Otherwise, his disciples may come and steal the body and tell the people that he has been raised from the dead. This last deception will be worse than the first."

---

[a] 46 Some manuscripts *Eloi, Eloi*   [b] 46 Psalm 22:1   [c] 53 Or *tombs, and after Jesus' resurrection they*   [d] 56 Greek *Joses*, a variant of *Joseph*

[65] "Take a guard," Pilate answered. "Go, make the tomb as secure as you know how." [66] So they went and made the tomb secure by putting a seal on the stone and posting the guard.

Jesus Has Risen

28 After the Sabbath, at dawn on the first day of the week, Mary Magdalene and the other Mary went to look at the tomb.

[2] There was a violent earthquake, for an angel of the Lord came down from heaven and, going to the tomb, rolled back the stone and sat on it. [3] His appearance was like lightning, and his clothes were white as snow. [4] The guards were so afraid of him that they shook and became like dead men.

[5] The angel said to the women, "Do not be afraid, for I know that you are looking for Jesus, who was crucified. [6] He is not here; he has risen, just as he said. Come and see the place where he lay. [7] Then go quickly and tell his disciples: 'He has risen from the dead and is going ahead of you into Galilee. There you will see him.' Now I have told you."

[8] So the women hurried away from the tomb, afraid yet filled with joy, and ran to tell his disciples. [9] Suddenly Jesus met them. "Greetings," he said. They came to him, clasped his feet and worshiped him. [10] Then Jesus said to them, "Do not be afraid. Go and tell my brothers to go to Galilee; there they will see me."

The Guards' Report

[11] While the women were on their way, some of the guards went into the city and reported to the chief priests everything that had happened. [12] When the chief priests had met with the elders and devised a plan, they gave the soldiers a large sum of money, [13] telling them, "You are to say, 'His disciples came during the night and stole him away while we were asleep.' [14] If this report gets to the governor, we will satisfy him and keep you out of trouble." [15] So the soldiers took the money and did as they were instructed. And this story has been widely circulated among the Jews to this very day.

The Great Commission

[16] Then the eleven disciples went to Galilee, to the mountain where Jesus had told them to go. [17] When they saw him, they worshiped him; but some doubted. [18] Then Jesus came to them and said, "All authority in heaven and on earth has been given to me. [19] Therefore go and make disciples of all nations, baptizing them in[a] the name of the Father and of the Son and of the Holy Spirit, [20] and teaching them to obey everything I have commanded you. And surely I am with you always, to the very end of the age."

1435

atissue:purpose in life

28:19–20 Jesus' "Great Commission" has four simple points: 1) Go and make disciples. 2) Baptize them to show they belong to God's family. 3) Teach them to obey God's commands. 4) Know that Christ is with you as you do this. This was Jesus' final charge to his followers—including us. Is this your mission in life? This is God's purpose for you with your children. It's your purpose in your workplace. It's your purpose in your neighborhood, with your friends, in your world. Ask God to show you what part you can have in fulfilling his call.

---

[a] 19 Or into; see Acts 8:16; 19:5; Romans 6:3; 1 Cor. 1:13; 10:2; Gal. 3:27.

mark

1436

AUTHOR
John Mark.

AUDIENCE
Followers of Jesus. Mark wrote with a Roman audience in mind.

DATE
Probably between A.D. 55 and 65.

SETTING
Mark most likely wrote from Rome. Early church sources tell us the apostle Peter relayed information to Mark for his Gospel.

VERSE TO REMEMBER
"Jesus said to them, 'It is not the healthy who need a doctor, but the sick. I have not come to call the righteous, but sinners.'" (2:17)

THEME TO CONSIDER
In Jesus' short, three-year public ministry, he sought out, helped, saved and loved sinners.

John the Baptist Prepares the Way

1 The beginning of the good news about Jesus the Messiah,[a, b] [2]as it is written in Isaiah the prophet:

> "I will send my messenger ahead of you,
>   who will prepare your way"[c]—
> [3]"a voice of one calling in the wilderness,
> 'Prepare the way for the Lord,
>   make straight paths for him.'"[d]

[4]And so John the Baptist appeared in the wilderness, preaching a baptism of repentance for the forgiveness of sins. [5]The whole Judean countryside and all the people of Jerusalem went out to him. Confessing their sins, they were baptized by him in the Jordan River. [6]John wore clothing made of camel's hair, with a leather belt around his waist, and he ate locusts and wild honey. [7]And this was his message: "After me comes the one more powerful than I, the thongs of whose sandals I am not worthy to stoop down and untie. [8]I baptize you with[e] water, but he will baptize you with[f] the Holy Spirit."

The Baptism and Testing of Jesus

[9]At that time Jesus came from Nazareth in Galilee and was baptized by John in the Jordan. [10]Just as Jesus was coming up out of the water, he saw heaven being torn open and the Spirit descending on him like a dove. [11]And a voice came from heaven: "You are my Son, whom I love; with you I am well pleased."

[12]At once the Spirit sent him out into the wilderness, [13]and he was in the wilderness forty days, being tempted[g] by Satan. He was with the wild animals, and angels attended him.

Jesus Announces the Good News

[14]After John was put in prison, Jesus went into Galilee, proclaiming the good news of God. [15]"The time has come," he said. "The kingdom of God has come near. Repent and believe the good news!"

Jesus Calls His First Disciples

[16]As Jesus walked beside the Sea of Galilee, he saw Simon and his brother Andrew casting a net into the lake, for they were fishermen. [17]"Come, follow me," Jesus said, "and I will send you out to fish for people." [18]At once they left their nets and followed him.

[19]When he had gone a little farther, he saw James son of Zebedee and his brother John in a boat, preparing their nets. [20]Without delay he called them, and they left their father Zebedee in the boat with the hired men and followed him.

Jesus Drives Out an Evil Spirit

[21]They went to Capernaum, and when the Sabbath came, Jesus went into the synagogue and began to teach. [22]The people were amazed at his teaching, because he taught them as one who had authority, not as the teachers of the law. [23]Just then a man in their synagogue who was possessed by an evil[h] spirit cried out, [24]"What do you want with us, Jesus of Nazareth? Have you come to destroy us? I know who you are—the Holy One of God!"

[25]"Be quiet!" said Jesus sternly. "Come out of him!" [26]The evil spirit shook the man violently and came out of him with a shriek.

[27]The people were all so amazed that they asked each other, "What is this? A new teaching—and with authority! He even gives orders to evil spirits and they obey him." [28]News about him spread quickly over the whole region of Galilee.

Jesus Heals Many

[29]As soon as they left the synagogue, they went with James and John to the home of Simon and Andrew. [30]Simon's mother-in-law was in bed with a fever, and they immediately told Jesus about her. [31]So he went to her, took her hand and helped her up. The fever left her and she began to wait on them.

---

[a] *1* Or *Jesus Christ. Messiah* (Hebrew) and *Christ* (Greek) both mean *Anointed One.*   [b] *1* Many manuscripts *Messiah, the Son of God*   [c] *2* Mal. 3:1
[d] *3* Isaiah 40:3   [e] *8* Or *in*   [f] *8* Or *in*   [g] *13* The Greek for *tempted* can also mean *tested.*   [h] *23* Greek *unclean*; also in verses 26 and 27

³²That evening after sunset the people brought to Jesus all the sick and demon-possessed. ³³The whole town gathered at the door, ³⁴and Jesus healed many who had various diseases. He also drove out many demons, but he would not let the demons speak because they knew who he was.

Jesus Prays in a Solitary Place

³⁵Very early in the morning, while it was still dark, Jesus got up, left the house and went off to a solitary place, where he prayed. ³⁶Simon and his companions went to look for him, ³⁷and when they found him, they exclaimed: "Everyone is looking for you!"

³⁸Jesus replied, "Let us go somewhere else—to the nearby villages—so I can preach there also. That is why I have come." ³⁹So he traveled throughout Galilee, preaching in their synagogues and driving out demons.

Jesus Heals a Man With Leprosy

⁴⁰A man with leprosy^{*a*} came to him and begged him on his knees, "If you are willing, you can make me clean."

⁴¹Jesus was indignant.^{*b*} He reached out his hand and touched the man. "I am willing," he said. "Be clean!" ⁴²Immediately the leprosy left him and he was cleansed.

⁴³Jesus sent him away at once with a strong warning: ⁴⁴"See that you don't tell this to anyone. But go, show yourself to the priest and offer the sacrifices that Moses commanded for your cleansing, as a testimony to them." ⁴⁵Instead he went out and began to talk freely, spreading the news. As a result, Jesus could no longer enter a town openly but stayed outside in lonely places. Yet the people still came to him from everywhere.

Jesus Forgives and Heals a Paralyzed Man

2 A few days later, when Jesus again entered Capernaum, the people heard that he had come home. ²They gathered in such large numbers that there was no room left, not even outside the door, and he preached the word to them. ³Some men came, bringing to him a paralyzed man, carried by four of them. ⁴Since they could not get him to Jesus because of the crowd, they made an opening in the roof above Jesus by digging through it and then lowered the mat the man was lying on. ⁵When Jesus saw their faith, he said to the paralyzed man, "Son, your sins are forgiven."

---

^{*a*} *40* The Greek word traditionally translated *leprosy* was used for various diseases affecting the skin.   ^{*b*} *41* Many manuscripts *Jesus was filled with compassion*

a tissue : prayer

1:35 If we're honest, many of us will admit that our lives are not characterized by deep, intimate times of prayer. Do we think we don't need time with God? Jesus needed to be with him. Do we have too many other things to do? Check out Jesus' packed schedule. Is it hard to find time alone? Jesus had demanding crowds following him. Do we believe prayer doesn't work? Jesus knew it does. It's time for us to start choosing to make time alone with God. You may need to be creative or make some difficult choices. But prayer is our renouncement of self-sufficiency and our admission of God-dependency.

1438

HE IS: God alone

2:1–7 When a paralyzed man was brought by his four friends to Jesus, the Lord first healed the man's soul, not his body. The criticism by the teachers of the law actually revealed Jesus' true identity, for no one but *God alone* can forgive sins.

Because Jesus is God, he alone can heal you or any friend of yours who's hurting. He first heals the soul—of the fatality of sin, of sadness, fear, failure or despair. If you have a friend who's hurting, bring her to Jesus. He is *God alone* and is able to liberate body and soul from sin.

For the next He Is, go to p. 1449.

⁶Now some teachers of the law were sitting there, thinking to themselves, ⁷"Why does this fellow talk like that? He's blaspheming! Who can forgive sins but God alone?"

⁸Immediately Jesus knew in his spirit that this was what they were thinking in their hearts, and he said to them, "Why are you thinking these things? ⁹Which is easier: to say to this paralyzed man, 'Your sins are forgiven,' or to say, 'Get up, take your mat and walk'? ¹⁰But I want you to know that the Son of Man has authority on earth to forgive sins." So he said to the man, ¹¹"I tell you, get up, take your mat and go home." ¹²He got up, took his mat and walked out in full view of them all. This amazed everyone and they praised God, saying, "We have never seen anything like this!"

Jesus Calls Levi and Eats With Sinners

¹³Once again Jesus went out beside the lake. A large crowd came to him, and he began to teach them. ¹⁴As he walked along, he saw Levi son of Alphaeus sitting at the tax collector's booth. "Follow me," Jesus told him, and Levi got up and followed him.

¹⁵While Jesus was having dinner at Levi's house, many tax collectors and sinners were eating with him and his disciples, for there were many who followed him. ¹⁶When the teachers of the law who were Pharisees saw him eating with the sinners and tax collectors, they asked his disciples: "Why does he eat with tax collectors and sinners?"

¹⁷On hearing this, Jesus said to them, "It is not the healthy who need a doctor, but the sick. I have not come to call the righteous, but sinners."

Jesus Questioned About Fasting

1439

¹⁸Now John's disciples and the Pharisees were fasting. Some people came and asked Jesus, "How is it that John's disciples and the disciples of the Pharisees are fasting, but yours are not?"

¹⁹Jesus answered, "How can the guests of the bridegroom fast while he is with them? They cannot, so long as they have him with them. ²⁰But the time will come when the bridegroom will be taken from them, and on that day they will fast.

²¹"No one sews a patch of unshrunk cloth on an old garment. If they do, the new piece will pull away from the old, making the tear worse. ²²And people do not pour new wine into old wineskins. If they do, the wine will burst the skins, and both the wine and the wineskins will be ruined. No, they pour new wine into new wineskins."

Jesus Is Lord of the Sabbath

²³One Sabbath Jesus was going through the grainfields, and as his disciples walked along, they began to pick some heads of grain. ²⁴The Pharisees said to him, "Look, why are they doing what is unlawful on the Sabbath?"

²⁵He answered, "Have you never read what David did when he and his companions were hungry and in need? ²⁶In the days of Abiathar the high priest, he entered the house of God and ate the consecrated bread, which is lawful only for priests to eat. And he also gave some to his companions."

²⁷Then he said to them, "The Sabbath was made for people, not people for the Sabbath. ²⁸So the Son of Man is Lord even of the Sabbath."

Jesus Heals on the Sabbath

3 Another time Jesus went into the synagogue, and a man with a shriveled hand was there. ²Some of them were looking for a reason to accuse Jesus, so they watched him closely to see if he would heal him on the Sabbath. ³Jesus said to the man with the shriveled hand, "Stand up in front of everyone."

⁴Then Jesus asked them, "Which is lawful on the Sabbath: to do good or to do evil, to save life or to kill?" But they remained silent.

⁵He looked around at them in anger and, deeply distressed at their stubborn hearts, said to the man, "Stretch out your hand." He stretched it out, and his hand was completely restored. ⁶Then the Pharisees went out and began to plot with the Herodians how they might kill Jesus.

Crowds Follow Jesus

⁷Jesus withdrew with his disciples to the lake, and a large crowd from Galilee followed. ⁸When they heard all he was doing, many people came to him from Judea, Jerusalem, Idumea, and the regions across

myth# 82 "IF I WERE A GOOD CHRISTIAN, I WOULDN'T STRUGGLE WITH THIS SIN."

I can't get the thought out of my head. Katrina, if you were a good Christian, you would forgive Fran and move on with your life. I envision my mom, my eighth-grade Sunday school teacher and my college religious education prof all nodding their heads in agreement. I am not the mature Christian everyone thinks I am.

But I feel stuck. I tell myself that I'm over it; then the memories, as fresh as if it happened yesterday, flood my mind. What Fran did to me was inexcusable, unforgivable. But shouldn't I be able to forgive her and move past this?

I opened myself up to her. I was the one who told her about the job opening at work. Even though she would be my supervisor, I encouraged her to pursue it. "You'd be a great boss," I told her. I even helped her write her résumé! After all, we were friends (or so I thought). When she had a personal crisis last year, I invited her and her children to come stay with me, which they did for a few weeks.

After that, she turned on me. When the company began to struggle, I was one of the first people Fran laid off! I feel so betrayed—because I was. I know that I don't have to trust her again, but I can't even begin to forgive her. My friends compliment me on how well I'm handling everything—unemployment, the job hunt, keeping a good attitude. They don't know what I'm hiding—anger, bitterness and unforgiveness in my heart. If I were half the Christian people think I am, I wouldn't be struggling with this.

—Katrina

BEING A CHRISTIAN does

not mean being perfect. In fact, Jesus didn't come to seek people who thought they were perfect; he came for those who *knew* they needed help (see Mark 2:17). How quickly we forget that! How slow we are to admit our hidden sins, our secret struggles, our personal addictions. Yet the sad truth is that trying to maintain that flawless façade just isolates us and makes our sins even more difficult to overcome. Consider this strategy:

- *Know your weaknesses.* Your spiritual adversary, the devil, knows your weaknesses well. Although your issue may seem like a trifle temptation to someone else, it can trip you up spiritually every time. Know your own weaknesses so that you can better prepare yourself when you know where the battle lines will likely be drawn.

- *All Christians struggle, even the "good" ones.* Consider the heroes and heroines of our faith—Moses struggled with anger, David struggled with lust and Martha struggled with worry. It's quite possible for Christians to become addicts—enslaved to habitual sins.

- *You are not helpless.* Instead of wallowing in a sin pattern, learn from your struggle. Ask other Christian women to hold you accountable for your actions. Look at why you continue to sin, and figure out what's beneath that tendency. If you are dealing with an addiction, these steps are essential to your recovery. And don't let pride keep you from getting professional and pastoral help.

- *Share your struggle with others.* As a member of the body of Christ, you can encourage and help others by sharing your story and asking others to pray for you (see James 5:16).

- *Be focused.* Accept God's love and forgiveness rather than focusing on your sin. Be tough on sin, but gentle with yourself, know-

ing that the Spirit is working in you every day to bring you closer to God.

God loves us no matter what. Even after we've committed the same sin for the one hundredth time, God still loves us and takes us back.

> "Whether we've been the villain or the victim—our dark secrets can be potent sources of shame, pain, and bondage."
>
> —Karen Linamen

1441

> "THEN I ACKNOWLEDGED MY SIN TO YOU AND DID NOT COVER UP MY INIQUITY. I SAID, 'I WILL CONFESS MY TRANSGRESSIONS TO THE LORD.' AND YOU FORGAVE THE GUILT OF MY SIN."
>
> PSALM 32:5

SEE ALSO

For more on **Sin**, check the index.

the Jordan and around Tyre and Sidon. [9]Because of the crowd he told his disciples to have a small boat ready for him, to keep the people from crowding him. [10]For he had healed many, so that those with diseases were pushing forward to touch him. [11]Whenever the evil[a] spirits saw him, they fell down before him and cried out, "You are the Son of God." [12]But he gave them strict orders not to tell others about him.

Jesus Appoints the Twelve

[13]Jesus went up on a mountainside and called to him those he wanted, and they came to him. [14]He appointed twelve[b] that they might be with him and that he might send them out to preach [15]and to have authority to drive out demons. [16]These are the twelve he appointed: Simon (to whom he gave the name Peter), [17]James son of Zebedee and his brother John (to them he gave the name Boanerges, which means "sons of thunder"), [18]Andrew, Philip, Bartholomew, Matthew, Thomas, James son of Alphaeus, Thaddaeus, Simon the Zealot [19]and Judas Iscariot, who betrayed him.

Jesus Accused by His Family and by Teachers of the Law

[20]Then Jesus entered a house, and again a crowd gathered, so that he and his disciples were not even able to eat. [21]When his family[c] heard about this, they went to take charge of him, for they said, "He is out of his mind."

[22]And the teachers of the law who came down from Jerusalem said, "He is possessed by Beelzebul! By the prince of demons he is driving out demons."

[23]So Jesus called them over to him and began to speak to them in parables: "How can Satan drive out Satan? [24]If a kingdom is divided against itself, that kingdom cannot stand. [25]If a house is divided against itself, that house cannot stand. [26]And if Satan opposes himself and is divided, he cannot stand; his end has come. [27]In fact, no one can enter a strong man's house without first tying him up. Then he can plunder the strong man's house. [28]Truly I tell you, people will be forgiven all their sins and all the blasphemies they utter. [29]But whoever blasphemes against the Holy Spirit will never be forgiven, but is guilty of an eternal sin."

[30]He said this because they were saying, "He has an evil spirit."

[31]Then Jesus' mother and brothers arrived. Standing outside, they sent someone in to call him. [32]A crowd was sitting around him, and they told him, "Your mother and brothers are outside looking for you."

[33]"Who are my mother and my brothers?" he asked.

[34]Then he looked at those seated in a circle around him and said, "Here are my mother and my brothers! [35]Whoever does God's will is my brother and sister and mother."

" conversations "

acceptance «» 3:31–34

1» How does Jesus' description of his family differ from how you would define a family?

2» What do Jesus' words teach us about God's acceptance?

3» What does it mean to do God's will?

For more on **acceptance**, check the index.
For the next Conversations, go to p. 1444.

The Parable of the Sower

4 Again Jesus began to teach by the lake. The crowd that gathered around him was so large that he got into a boat and sat in it out on the lake, while all the people were along the shore at the water's edge. [2]He taught them many things by parables, and in his teaching said: [3]"Listen! A farmer went out to sow his seed. [4]As he was scattering the seed, some fell along the path, and the birds came and ate it up. [5]Some fell on rocky places, where it did not have much soil. It sprang up quickly, because the soil was shallow. [6]But when the sun came up, the plants were scorched, and they withered because they had no root. [7]Other seed fell among thorns, which grew up and choked the plants, so that they did not bear grain. [8]Still other seed fell on good soil. It came up, grew and produced a crop, some multiplying thirty, some sixty, some a hundred times."

---

[a] 11 Greek unclean; also in verse 30   [b] 14 Some manuscripts twelve—designating them apostles—   [c] 21 Or his associates

⁹Then Jesus said, "Whoever has ears to hear, let them hear."

¹⁰When he was alone, the Twelve and the others around him asked him about the parables. ¹¹He told them, "The secret of the kingdom of God has been given to you. But to those on the outside everything is said in parables ¹²so that,

> "'they may be ever seeing but never perceiving,
> and ever hearing but never understanding;
> otherwise they might turn and be forgiven!'ᵃ"

¹³Then Jesus said to them, "Don't you understand this parable? How then will you understand any parable? ¹⁴The farmer sows the word. ¹⁵Some people are like seed along the path, where the word is sown. As soon as they hear it, Satan comes and takes away the word that was sown in them. ¹⁶Others, like seed sown on rocky places, hear the word and at once receive it with joy. ¹⁷But since they have no root, they last only a short time. When trouble or persecution comes because of the word, they quickly fall away. ¹⁸Still others, like seed sown among thorns, hear the word; ¹⁹but the worries of this life, the deceitfulness of wealth and the desires for other things come in and choke the word, making it unfruitful. ²⁰Others, like seed sown on good soil, hear the word, accept it, and produce a crop—some thirty, some sixty, some a hundred times what was sown."

A Lamp on a Stand

²¹He said to them, "Do you bring in a lamp to put it under a bowl or a bed? Instead, don't you put it on its stand? ²²For whatever is hidden is meant to be disclosed, and whatever is concealed is meant to be brought out into the open. ²³If anyone has ears to hear, let them hear."

²⁴"Consider carefully what you hear," he continued. "With the measure you use, it will be measured to you—and even more. ²⁵Those who have will be given more; as for those who do not have, even what they have will be taken from them."

The Parable of the Growing Seed

²⁶He also said, "This is what the kingdom of God is like. A man scatters seed on the ground. ²⁷Night and day, whether he sleeps or gets up, the seed sprouts and grows, though he does not know how. ²⁸All by itself the soil produces grain—first the stalk, then the head, then the full kernel in the head. ²⁹As soon as the grain is ripe, he puts the sickle to it, because the harvest has come."

The Parable of the Mustard Seed

³⁰Again he said, "What shall we say the kingdom of God is like, or what parable shall we use to describe it? ³¹It is like a mustard seed, which is the smallest of all seeds on earth. ³²Yet when planted, it grows and becomes the largest of all garden plants, with such big branches that the birds can perch in its shade."

³³With many similar parables Jesus spoke the word to them, as much as they could understand. ³⁴He did not say anything to them without using a parable. But when he was alone with his own disciples, he explained everything.

Jesus Calms the Storm

³⁵That day when evening came, he said to his disciples, "Let us go over to the other side." ³⁶Leaving the crowd behind, they took him along, just as he was, in the boat. There were also other boats with him. ³⁷A furious squall came up, and the waves broke over the boat, so that it was nearly swamped. ³⁸Jesus was in the stern, sleeping on a cushion. The disciples woke him and said to him, "Teacher, don't you care if we drown?"

³⁹He got up, rebuked the wind and said to the waves, "Quiet! Be still!" Then the wind died down and it was completely calm.

⁴⁰He said to his disciples, "Why are you so afraid? Do you still have no faith?"

⁴¹They were terrified and asked each other, "Who is this? Even the wind and the waves obey him!"

 ᵃ 12 Isaiah 6:9,10

Jesus Restores a Demon-Possessed Man

5 They went across the lake to the region of the Gerasenes.[a] [2]When Jesus got out of the boat, a man with an evil[b] spirit came from the tombs to meet him. [3]This man lived in the tombs, and no one could bind him anymore, not even with a chain. [4]For he had often been chained hand and foot, but he tore the chains apart and broke the irons on his feet. No one was strong enough to subdue him. [5]Night and day among the tombs and in the hills he would cry out and cut himself with stones.

[6]When he saw Jesus from a distance, he ran and fell on his knees in front of him. [7]He shouted at the top of his voice, "What do you want with me, Jesus, Son of the Most High God? In God's name don't torture me!" [8]For Jesus had said to him, "Come out of this man, you evil spirit!"

[9]Then Jesus asked him, "What is your name?"

"My name is Legion," he replied, "for we are many." [10]And he begged Jesus again and again not to send them out of the area.

[11]A large herd of pigs was feeding on the nearby hillside. [12]The demons begged Jesus, "Send us among the pigs; allow us to go into them." [13]He gave them permission, and the evil spirits came out and went into the pigs. The herd, about two thousand in number, rushed down the steep bank into the lake and were drowned.

[14]Those tending the pigs ran off and reported this in the town and countryside, and the people went out to see what had happened. [15]When they came to Jesus, they saw the man who had been possessed by the legion of demons, sitting there, dressed and in his right mind; and they were afraid. [16]Those who had seen it told the people what had happened to the demon-possessed man— and told about the pigs as well. [17]Then the people began to plead with Jesus to leave their region.

[18]As Jesus was getting into the boat, the man who had been demon-possessed begged to go with him. [19]Jesus did not let him, but said, "Go home to your own people and tell them how much the Lord has done for you, and how he has had mercy on you." [20]So the man went away and began to tell in the Decapolis[c] how much Jesus had done for him. And all the people were amazed.

conversations

witnessing «» 5:19–20

1» What true works of God have you seen in your own life or in others' lives?

2» Who are "your own people" to whom you can be a witness?

3» How do you overcomplicate the simple act of sharing what God has done for you?

For more on **witnessing**, check the index.
For the next Conversations, go to p. 1446.

Jesus Raises a Dead Girl and Heals a Sick Woman

[21]When Jesus had again crossed over by boat to the other side of the lake, a large crowd gathered around him while he was by the lake. [22]Then one of the synagogue leaders, named Jairus, came, and when he saw Jesus, he fell at his feet. [23]He pleaded earnestly with him, "My little daughter is dying. Please come and put your hands on her so that she will be healed and live." [24]So Jesus went with him.

A large crowd followed and pressed around him. [25]And a woman was there who had been subject to bleeding for twelve years. [26]She had suffered a great deal under the care of many doctors and had spent all she had, yet instead of getting better she grew worse. [27]When she heard about Jesus, she came up behind him in the crowd and touched his cloak, [28]because she thought, "If I just touch his clothes, I will be healed." [29]Immediately her bleeding stopped and she felt in her body that she was freed from her suffering.

[30]At once Jesus realized that power had gone out from him. He turned around in the crowd and asked, "Who touched my clothes?"

[31]"You see the people crowding against you," his disciples answered, "and yet you can ask, 'Who touched me?'"

---

[a] *1* Some manuscripts *Gadarenes*; other manuscripts *Gergesenes*   [b] *2* Greek *unclean*; also in verses 8 and 13   [c] *20* That is, the Ten Cities

³²But Jesus kept looking around to see who had done it. ³³Then the woman, knowing what had happened to her, came and fell at his feet and, trembling with fear, told him the whole truth. ³⁴He said to her, "Daughter, your faith has healed you. Go in peace and be freed from your suffering."

³⁵While Jesus was still speaking, some people came from the house of Jairus, the synagogue leader. "Your daughter is dead," they said. "Why bother the teacher anymore?"

³⁶Overhearing*a* what they said, Jesus told him, "Don't be afraid; just believe."

³⁷He did not let anyone follow him except Peter, James and John the brother of James. ³⁸When they came to the home of the synagogue leader, Jesus saw a commotion, with people crying and wailing loudly. ³⁹He went in and said to them, "Why all this commotion and wailing? The child is not dead but asleep." ⁴⁰But they laughed at him.

After he put them all out, he took the child's father and mother and the disciples who were with him, and went in where the child was. ⁴¹He took her by the hand and said to her, *"Talitha koum!"* (which means "Little girl, I say to you, get up!"). ⁴²Immediately the girl stood up and began to walk around (she was twelve years old). At this they were completely astonished. ⁴³He gave strict orders not to let anyone know about this, and told them to give her something to eat.

A Prophet Without Honor

6 Jesus left there and went to his hometown, accompanied by his disciples. ²When the Sabbath came, he began to teach in the synagogue, and many who heard him were amazed.

"Where did this man get these things?" they asked. "What's this wisdom that has been given him? What are these remarkable miracles he is performing? ³Isn't this the carpenter? Isn't this Mary's son and the brother of James, Joseph,*b* Judas and Simon? Aren't his sisters here with us?" And they took offense at him.

⁴Jesus said to them, "Only in their own towns, among their relatives and in their own homes are prophets without honor." ⁵He could not do any miracles there, except lay his hands on a few sick people and heal them. ⁶He was amazed at their lack of faith.

1445

Jesus Sends Out the Twelve

Then Jesus went around teaching from village to village. ⁷Calling the Twelve to him, he began to send them out two by two and gave them authority over evil*c* spirits.

⁸These were his instructions: "Take nothing for the journey except a staff—no bread, no bag, no money in your belts. ⁹Wear sandals but not an extra shirt. ¹⁰Whenever you enter a house, stay there until you leave that town. ¹¹And if any place will not welcome you or listen to you, shake the dust off your feet when you leave, as a testimony against them."

¹²They went out and preached that people should repent. ¹³They drove out many demons and anointed many sick people with oil and healed them.

John the Baptist Beheaded

¹⁴King Herod heard about this, for Jesus' name had become well known. Some were saying,*d* "John the Baptist has been raised from the dead, and that is why miraculous powers are at work in him."

¹⁵Others said, "He is Elijah."

And still others claimed, "He is a prophet, like one of the prophets of long ago."

¹⁶But when Herod heard this, he said, "John, whom I beheaded, has been raised from the dead!"

¹⁷For Herod himself had given orders to have John arrested, and he had him bound and put in prison. He did this because of Herodias, his brother Philip's wife, whom he had married. ¹⁸For John had been saying to Herod, "It is not lawful for you to have your brother's wife." ¹⁹So Herodias nursed a grudge against John and wanted to kill him. But she was not able to, ²⁰because Herod feared John and protected him, knowing him to be a righteous and holy man. When Herod heard John, he was greatly puzzled*e*; yet he liked to listen to him.

²¹Finally the opportune time came. On his birthday Herod gave a banquet for his high officials and

---

a 36 Or *Ignoring*   *b* 3 Greek *Joses*, a variant of *Joseph*   *c* 7 Greek *unclean*   *d* 14 Some early manuscripts *He was saying*   *e* 20 Some early manuscripts *he did many things* military commanders and the leading men of Galilee. ²²When the daughter of ᵃ Herodias came in and danced, she pleased Herod and his dinner guests.

The king said to the girl, "Ask me for anything you want, and I'll give it to you." ²³And he promised her with an oath, "Whatever you ask I will give you, up to half my kingdom."

²⁴She went out and said to her mother, "What shall I ask for?"

"The head of John the Baptist," she answered.

²⁵At once the girl hurried in to the king with the request: "I want you to give me right now the head of John the Baptist on a platter."

²⁶The king was greatly distressed, but because of his oaths and his dinner guests, he did not want to refuse her. ²⁷So he immediately sent an executioner with orders to bring John's head. The man went, beheaded John in the prison, ²⁸and brought back his head on a platter. He presented it to the girl, and she gave it to her mother. ²⁹On hearing of this, John's disciples came and took his body and laid it in a tomb.

conversations

sexual sin «» 6:17–20

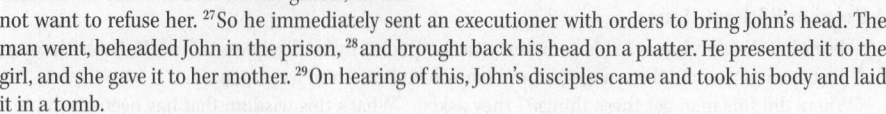

1» What are the repercussions of sexual sin of any kind?

2» If you were harboring sexual sin, how would you feel toward someone who confronted you?

3» Is it your business to address sexual sin when you see it in others' lives? If so, how?

For more on **sexual sin**, check the index.
For the next Conversations, go to p. 1457.

1446

Jesus Feeds the Five Thousand

³⁰The apostles gathered around Jesus and reported to him all they had done and taught. ³¹Then, because so many people were coming and going that they did not even have a chance to eat, he said to them, "Come with me by yourselves to a quiet place and get some rest."

³²So they went away by themselves in a boat to a solitary place. ³³But many who saw them leaving recognized them and ran on foot from all the towns and got there ahead of them. ³⁴When Jesus landed and saw a large crowd, he had compassion on them, because they were like sheep without a shepherd. So he began teaching them many things.

³⁵By this time it was late in the day, so his disciples came to him. "This is a remote place," they said, "and it's already very late. ³⁶Send the people away so that they can go to the surrounding countryside and villages and buy themselves something to eat."

³⁷But he answered, "You give them something to eat."

They said to him, "That would take almost a year's wages ᵇ! Are we to go and spend that much on bread and give it to them to eat?"

³⁸"How many loaves do you have?" he asked. "Go and see."

When they found out, they said, "Five—and two fish."

³⁹Then Jesus directed them to have all the people sit down in groups on the green grass. ⁴⁰So they sat down in groups of hundreds and fifties. ⁴¹Taking the five loaves and the two fish and looking up to heaven, he gave thanks and broke the loaves. Then he gave them to his disciples to set before the people. He also divided the two fish among them all. ⁴²They all ate and were satisfied, ⁴³and the disciples picked up twelve basketfuls of broken pieces of bread and fish. ⁴⁴The number of the men who had eaten was five thousand.

Jesus Walks on the Water

⁴⁵Immediately Jesus made his disciples get into the boat and go on ahead of him to Bethsaida, while he dismissed the crowd. ⁴⁶After leaving them, he went up on a mountainside to pray.

⁴⁷When evening came, the boat was in the middle of the lake, and he was alone on land. ⁴⁸He saw the disciples straining at the oars, because the wind was against them. Shortly before dawn he went out to them, walking on the lake. He was about to pass by them, ⁴⁹but when they saw him walking on the lake, they thought he was a ghost. They cried out, ⁵⁰because they all saw him and were terrified.

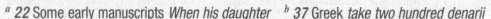

ᵃ 22 Some early manuscripts *When his daughter*   ᵇ 37 Greek *take two hundred denarii*

Immediately he spoke to them and said, "Take courage! It is I. Don't be afraid." ⁵¹Then he climbed into the boat with them, and the wind died down. They were completely amazed, ⁵²for they had not understood about the loaves; their hearts were hardened.

⁵³When they had crossed over, they landed at Gennesaret and anchored there. ⁵⁴As soon as they got out of the boat, people recognized Jesus. ⁵⁵They ran throughout that whole region and carried the sick on mats to wherever they heard he was. ⁵⁶And wherever he went—into villages, towns or countryside—they placed the sick in the marketplaces. They begged him to let them touch even the edge of his cloak, and all who touched him were healed.

That Which Defiles

7 The Pharisees and some of the teachers of the law who had come from Jerusalem gathered around Jesus ²and saw some of his disciples eating food with hands that were defiled, that is, unwashed. ³(The Pharisees and all the Jews do not eat unless they give their hands a ceremonial washing, holding to the tradition of the elders. ⁴When they come from the marketplace they do not eat unless they wash. And they observe many other traditions, such as the washing of cups, pitchers and kettles.ᵃ)

⁵So the Pharisees and teachers of the law asked Jesus, "Why don't your disciples live according to the tradition of the elders instead of eating their food with defiled hands?"

⁶He replied, "Isaiah was right when he prophesied about you hypocrites; as it is written:

> "'These people honor me with their lips,
>   but their hearts are far from me.
> ⁷They worship me in vain;
>   their teachings are merely human rules.'ᵇ

⁸You have let go of the commands of God and are holding on to human traditions."

⁹And he continued, "You have a fine way of setting aside the commands of God in order to observeᶜ your own traditions! ¹⁰For Moses said, 'Honor your father and mother,'ᵈ and, 'Anyone who curses their father or mother is to be put to death.'ᵉ ¹¹But you say that if anyone declares that what might have been used to help their father or mother is Corban (that is, devoted to God)— ¹²then you no longer let them do anything for their father or mother. ¹³Thus you nullify the word of God by your tradition that you have handed down. And you do many things like that."

¹⁴Again Jesus called the crowd to him and said, "Listen to me, everyone, and understand this. ¹⁵ [¹⁶]Nothing outside you can defile you by going into you. Rather, it is what comes out of you that defiles you."

¹⁷After he had left the crowd and entered the house, his disciples asked him about this parable. ¹⁸"Are you so dull?" he asked. "Don't you see that nothing that enters you from the outside can defile you? ¹⁹For it doesn't go into your heart but into your stomach, and then out of your body." (In saying this, Jesus declared all foods clean.)

²⁰He went on: "What comes out of you is what defiles you. ²¹For from within, out of your hearts, come evil thoughts, sexual immorality, theft, murder, ²²adultery, greed, malice, deceit, lewdness, envy, slander, arrogance and folly. ²³All these evils come from inside and defile you."

at issue: sexual sin

7:21–23 Human beings naturally focus on the external. We fashion our words, our actions and our appearances to gain others' approval. We tend to measure our spirituality by the things others can see on the outside instead of what's truly in our hearts. This makes it easier to justify the sin that no one else sees, the private sins and obsessions we keep so well hidden—sexual fantasies, adultery, sexual immorality, vulgarity. But God sees our hearts and every action no one else sees. Don't believe your own façade; repent of any sexual sin today, and be pure within.

ᵃ *4 Some early manuscripts pitchers, kettles and dining couches*   ᵇ *6,7 Isaiah 29:13*   ᶜ *9 Some manuscripts set up*   ᵈ *10 Exodus 20:12; Deut. 5:16*
ᵉ *10 Exodus 21:17; Lev. 20:9*

Jesus Honors a Syrophoenician Woman's Faith

²⁴Jesus left that place and went to the vicinity of Tyre.ᵃ He entered a house and did not want anyone to know it; yet he could not keep his presence secret. ²⁵In fact, as soon as she heard about him, a woman whose little daughter was possessed by an evilᵇ spirit came and fell at his feet. ²⁶The woman was a Greek, born in Syrian Phoenicia. She begged Jesus to drive the demon out of her daughter.

²⁷"First let the children eat all they want," he told her, "for it is not right to take the children's bread and toss it to the dogs."

²⁸"Lord," she replied, "even the dogs under the table eat the children's crumbs."

²⁹Then he told her, "For such a reply, you may go; the demon has left your daughter."

³⁰She went home and found her child lying on the bed, and the demon gone.

Jesus Heals a Deaf and Mute Man

³¹Then Jesus left the vicinity of Tyre and went through Sidon, down to the Sea of Galilee and into the region of the Decapolis.ᶜ ³²There some people brought to him a man who was deaf and could hardly talk, and they begged Jesus to place his hand on him.

³³After he took him aside, away from the crowd, Jesus put his fingers into the man's ears. Then he spit and touched the man's tongue. ³⁴He looked up to heaven and with a deep sigh said to him, *"Ephphatha!"* (which means "Be opened!"). ³⁵At this, the man's ears were opened, his tongue was loosened and he began to speak plainly.

³⁶Jesus commanded them not to tell anyone. But the more he did so, the more they kept talking about it. ³⁷People were overwhelmed with amazement. "He has done everything well," they said. "He even makes the deaf hear and the mute speak."

Jesus Feeds the Four Thousand

8 During those days another large crowd gathered. Since they had nothing to eat, Jesus called his disciples to him and said, ²"I have compassion for these people; they have already been with me three days and have nothing to eat. ³If I send them home hungry, they will collapse on the way, because some of them have come a long distance."

⁴His disciples answered, "But where in this remote place can anyone get enough bread to feed them?"

⁵"How many loaves do you have?" Jesus asked.

"Seven," they replied.

⁶He told the crowd to sit down on the ground. When he had taken the seven loaves and given thanks, he broke them and gave them to his disciples to set before the people, and they did so. ⁷They had a few small fish as well; he gave thanks for them also and told the disciples to distribute them. ⁸The people ate and were satisfied. Afterward the disciples picked up seven basketfuls of broken pieces that were left over. ⁹About four thousand were present. And having sent them away, ¹⁰he got into the boat with his disciples and went to the region of Dalmanutha.

¹¹The Pharisees came and began to question Jesus. To test him, they asked him for a sign from heaven. ¹²He sighed deeply and said, "Why does this generation ask for a sign? Truly I tell you, no sign will be given to it." ¹³Then he left them, got back into the boat and crossed to the other side.

The Yeast of the Pharisees and Herod

¹⁴The disciples had forgotten to bring bread, except for one loaf they had with them in the boat. ¹⁵"Be careful," Jesus warned them. "Watch out for the yeast of the Pharisees and that of Herod."

¹⁶They discussed this with one another and said, "It is because we have no bread."

¹⁷Aware of their discussion, Jesus asked them: "Why are you talking about having no bread? Do you still not see or understand? Are your hearts hardened? ¹⁸Do you have eyes but fail to see, and ears but fail to hear? And don't you remember? ¹⁹When I broke the five loaves for the five thousand, how many basketfuls of pieces did you pick up?"

"Twelve," they replied.

²⁰"And when I broke the seven loaves for the four thousand, how many basketfuls of pieces did you pick up?"

ᵃ *24* Many early manuscripts *Tyre and Sidon*   ᵇ *25* Greek *unclean*   ᶜ *31* That is, the Ten Cities

They answered, "Seven."

[21] He said to them, "Do you still not understand?"

Jesus Heals a Blind Man at Bethsaida

[22] They came to Bethsaida, and some people brought a blind man and begged Jesus to touch him. [23] He took the blind man by the hand and led him outside the village. When he had spit on the man's eyes and put his hands on him, Jesus asked, "Do you see anything?"

[24] He looked up and said, "I see people; they look like trees walking around."

[25] Once more Jesus put his hands on the man's eyes. Then his eyes were opened, his sight was restored, and he saw everything clearly. [26] Jesus sent him home, saying, "Don't even go into[a] the village."

Peter Declares That Jesus Is the Messiah

[27] Jesus and his disciples went on to the villages around Caesarea Philippi. On the way he asked them, "Who do people say I am?"

[28] They replied, "Some say John the Baptist; others say Elijah; and still others, one of the prophets."

[29] "But what about you?" he asked. "Who do you say I am?"

Peter answered, "You are the Messiah."

[30] Jesus warned them not to tell anyone about him.

HE IS: the Messiah

1449

8:27–29 The people didn't understand who Jesus really was, so he asked his disciples what they thought. Peter passed the test of faith by rightly calling Jesus the Christ, *the Messiah*, acknowledging that Jesus was the anointed one sent from God to deliver his people.

The most important question you'll ever answer is the same one posed by Jesus: *Who do you say I am?* If you say he was just a good man, or a powerful prophet, then he couldn't be the God-man—and he wouldn't have the power to save you. The only correct answer is Peter's, though you must answer for yourself.

For the next He Is, go to p. 1461.

Jesus Predicts His Death

[31] He then began to teach them that the Son of Man must suffer many things and be rejected by the elders, the chief priests and the teachers of the law, and that he must be killed and after three days rise again. [32] He spoke plainly about this, and Peter took him aside and began to rebuke him.

[33] But when Jesus turned and looked at his disciples, he rebuked Peter. "Get behind me, Satan!" he said. "You do not have in mind the concerns of God, but merely human concerns."

The Way of the Cross

[34] Then he called the crowd to him along with his disciples and said: "Whoever wants to be my disciple must deny themselves and take up their cross and follow me. [35] For whoever wants to save their life[b] will lose it, but whoever loses their life for me and for the gospel will save it. [36] What good is it for you to gain the whole world, yet forfeit your soul? [37] Or what can you give in exchange for your soul? [38] If any of you are ashamed of me and my words in this adulterous and sinful generation, the Son of Man will be ashamed of you when he comes in his Father's glory with the holy angels."

9 And he said to them, "Truly I tell you, some who are standing here will not taste death before they see that the kingdom of God has come with power."

The Transfiguration

[2] After six days Jesus took Peter, James and John with him and led them up a high mountain, where they were all alone. There he was transfigured before them. [3] His clothes became dazzling white, whiter

---

[a] 26 Some manuscripts *go and tell anyone in*   [b] 35 The Greek word means either *life* or *soul*; also in verses 36 and 37.

than anyone in the world could bleach them. ⁴And there appeared before them Elijah and Moses, who were talking with Jesus.

⁵Peter said to Jesus, "Rabbi, it is good for us to be here. Let us put up three shelters—one for you, one for Moses and one for Elijah." ⁶(He did not know what to say, they were so frightened.)

⁷Then a cloud appeared and covered them, and a voice came from the cloud: "This is my Son, whom I love. Listen to him!"

⁸Suddenly, when they looked around, they no longer saw anyone with them except Jesus.

⁹As they were coming down the mountain, Jesus gave them orders not to tell anyone what they had seen until the Son of Man had risen from the dead. ¹⁰They kept the matter to themselves, discussing what "rising from the dead" meant.

¹¹And they asked him, "Why do the teachers of the law say that Elijah must come first?"

¹²Jesus replied, "To be sure, Elijah does come first, and restores all things. Why then is it written that the Son of Man must suffer much and be rejected? ¹³But I tell you, Elijah has come, and they have done to him everything they wished, just as it is written about him."

Jesus Heals a Boy Possessed by an Evil Spirit

¹⁴When they came to the other disciples, they saw a large crowd around them and the teachers of the law arguing with them. ¹⁵As soon as all the people saw Jesus, they were overwhelmed with wonder and ran to greet him.

¹⁶"What are you arguing with them about?" he asked.

¹⁷A man in the crowd answered, "Teacher, I brought you my son, who is possessed by a spirit that has robbed him of speech. ¹⁸Whenever it seizes him, it throws him to the ground. He foams at the mouth, gnashes his teeth and becomes rigid. I asked your disciples to drive out the spirit, but they could not."

¹⁹"You unbelieving generation," Jesus replied, "how long shall I stay with you? How long shall I put up with you? Bring the boy to me."

²⁰So they brought him. When the spirit saw Jesus, it immediately threw the boy into a convulsion. He fell to the ground and rolled around, foaming at the mouth.

²¹Jesus asked the boy's father, "How long has he been like this?"

"From childhood," he answered. ²²"It has often thrown him into fire or water to kill him. But if you can do anything, take pity on us and help us."

²³"'If you can'?" said Jesus. "Everything is possible for one who believes."

²⁴Immediately the boy's father exclaimed, "I do believe; help me overcome my unbelief!"

²⁵When Jesus saw that a crowd was running to the scene, he rebuked the evil^{*a*} spirit. "You deaf and mute spirit," he said, "I command you, come out of him and never enter him again."

²⁶The spirit shrieked, convulsed him violently and came out. The boy looked so much like a corpse that many said, "He's dead." ²⁷But Jesus took him by the hand and lifted him to his feet, and he stood up.

²⁸After Jesus had gone indoors, his disciples asked him privately, "Why couldn't we drive it out?"

²⁹He replied, "This kind can come out only by prayer.^{*b*}"

Jesus Predicts His Death a Second Time

³⁰They left that place and passed through Galilee. Jesus did not want anyone to know where they were, ³¹because he was teaching his disciples. He said to them, "The Son of Man is going to be delivered over to human hands. He will be killed, and after three days he will rise." ³²But they did not understand what he meant and were afraid to ask him about it.

³³They came to Capernaum. When he was in the house, he asked them, "What were you arguing about on the road?" ³⁴But they kept quiet because on the way they had argued about who was the greatest.

³⁵Sitting down, Jesus called the Twelve and said, "Anyone who wants to be first must be the very last, and the servant of all."

³⁶He took a little child whom he placed among them. Taking the child in his arms, he said to them, ³⁷"Whoever welcomes one of these little children in my name welcomes me; and whoever welcomes me does not welcome me but the one who sent me."

Whoever Is Not Against Us Is for Us

[38]"Teacher," said John, "we saw someone driving out demons in your name and we told him to stop, because he was not one of us."

[39]"Do not stop him," Jesus said. "No one who does a miracle in my name can in the next moment say anything bad about me, [40]for whoever is not against us is for us. [41]Truly I tell you, anyone who gives you a cup of water in my name because you belong to the Messiah will certainly be rewarded.

Causing to Stumble

[42]"If anyone causes one of these little ones—those who believe in me—to stumble, it would be better for them if a large millstone were hung around their neck and they were thrown into the sea. [43] [44]If your hand causes you to stumble, cut it off. It is better for you to enter life maimed than with two hands to go into hell, where the fire never goes out. [45] [46]And if your foot causes you to stumble, cut it off. It is better for you to enter life crippled than to have two feet and be thrown into hell. [47]And if your eye causes you to stumble, pluck it out. It is better for you to enter the kingdom of God with one eye than to have two eyes and be thrown into hell, [48]where

> "'their worm does not die,
>   and the fire is not quenched.'[a]

[49]Everyone will be salted with fire.

[50]"Salt is good, but if it loses its saltiness, how can you make it salty again? Have salt in yourselves, and be at peace with each other."

Divorce

10 Jesus then left that place and went into the region of Judea and across the Jordan. Again crowds of people came to him, and as was his custom, he taught them.

[2]Some Pharisees came and tested him by asking, "Is it lawful for a man to divorce his wife?"

[3]"What did Moses command you?" he replied.

[4]They said, "Moses permitted a man to write a certificate of divorce and send her away."

[5]"It was because your hearts were hard that Moses wrote you this law," Jesus replied. [6]"But at the beginning of creation God 'made them male and female.'[b] [7]'For this reason a man will leave his father and mother and be united to his wife,[c] [8]and the two will become one flesh.'[d] So they are no longer two, but one. [9]Therefore what God has joined together, let no one separate."

[10]When they were in the house again, the disciples asked Jesus about this. [11]He answered, "Anyone who divorces his wife and marries another woman commits adultery against her. [12]And if she divorces her husband and marries another man, she commits adultery."

The Little Children and Jesus

[13]People were bringing little children to Jesus for him to place his hands on them, but the disciples rebuked them. [14]When Jesus saw this, he was indignant. He said to them, "Let the little children come to me, and do not hinder them, for the kingdom of God belongs to such as these. [15]Truly I tell you, anyone who will not receive the kingdom of God like a

1451

at issue: marriage

10:1–12 It used to be that when couples pledged themselves in marriage "till death do us part," they meant it. Sadly, many Christian couples today enter into marriage thinking they can always get out and try again if this marriage doesn't work. Yet God designed marriage as a permanent union of two people into one for his glory—not a temporary alliance until something goes awry or one of the two parties finds a better option. When you enter into marriage, understand that you are making a covenant. You should take this as seriously as God does.

---

[a] 48 Isaiah 66:24   [b] 6 Gen. 1:27   [c] 7 Some early manuscripts do not have *and be united to his wife*.   [d] 8 Gen. 2:24

myth# 83

"IF I COULD LOSE TEN POUNDS, THEN I'D BE SATISFIED."

The invitation came in the mail today—my fifteen-year high school reunion. The ten-year reunion I could handle—at least I resembled my high school photos. This time I'm not so sure. When I look at pictures of me in high school, it makes me want to cry. I was so much thinner then— my face, my arms. Every time I look in the mirror now, all I see is fat and disgusting cellulite.

Yes, I have tried every diet out there. Low-fat, low-carb, detox. You name it, I've been on it. And I have the pills, the books and the videos to prove it. I work out faithfully too. My parents constantly tell me that I'm not fat. (Thankfully) they don't see me naked in front of an unforgiving mirror every day! But I do. When I'm getting ready in the morning, a glance in certain areas will ruin my entire day. I see my hips in my pants or the skin that hangs over my belt, and I feel sick. But instead of eating less, I can't help but eat more to numb the pain.

I just wish I could lose the ten pounds I've put on since high school. If I were thin enough to fit into my old prom dress—and zip it—then I would be completely satisfied with my looks. I would finally feel comfortable in my clothes. And I wouldn't have to worry about what people thought of me when I walk into that ballroom next month at the reunion.

—Liz

OUR CULTURE PLACES

tremendous importance on women's outward appearances—as if our own personal obsessions aren't enough. Movies and magazines constantly define for us how a beautiful woman should look—bone-thin, sexy, impeccably dressed, with flawless skin and gleaming white teeth. With that unrealistic standard before us, it's easy to become critical of ourselves and, like Liz, allow that to grow into self-hatred.

God's Word defines a beautiful woman altogether differently. Her beauty radiates from within. In fact, while God creates physically "beautiful people," he doesn't linger on the outward appearance; he focuses on the heart (see 1 Samuel 16:7). We should care for our bodies because God lives inside us (see 2 Corinthians 6:16), but focusing on our bodies breeds discontentment, which can grow into self-hatred and unhealthy self-esteem.

Where is your focus? Ask yourself the following questions:

- *How do I spend my time?* If you put all your emphasis on developing your external beauty, what will happen when you grow old (which will happen), or if an accident or sickness steals your beauty?

- *Am I satisfied?* Jesus said it is possible to gain the whole world and still be completely empty inside (see Mark 8:34–37). Outer beauty may promise satisfaction, but it can't deliver. Once you get to the perfect weight, you'll want even more. Your heart will still have the same longings for meaning and purpose that only God can fill.

- *How am I feeding these unhealthy desires?* The majority of women feel mildly depressed after looking through a fashion magazine— they're reminded of how they don't look and what they can't afford. Filling your mind with unrealistic images feeds those feelings of dissatisfaction with your body. You may

need to limit your intake of magazines, movies and even shopping to protect yourself.

- *What is the point of my life?* Joy comes not from being the perfect weight but from living a life of purpose. Think of Mother Teresa's lasting legacy. She's remembered not for her external beauty but for her life of love and service. What will others remember about you?

1453

"89 percent of women want to lose weight. The average woman weighs 140 pounds; the preferred weight is 125 pounds."

—David M. Garner

"THE Lord DOES NOT LOOK AT THE THINGS HUMAN BEINGS LOOK AT. PEOPLE LOOK AT THE OUTWARD APPEARANCE, BUT THE Lord LOOKS AT THE HEART."

1 SAMUEL 16:7

SEE ALSO

For more on **Appearance**, check the index.

little child will never enter it." [16] And he took the children in his arms, placed his hands on them and blessed them.

The Rich and the Kingdom of God

[17] As Jesus started on his way, a man ran up to him and fell on his knees before him. "Good teacher," he asked, "what must I do to inherit eternal life?"

[18] "Why do you call me good?" Jesus answered. "No one is good—except God alone. [19] You know the commandments: 'You shall not murder, you shall not commit adultery, you shall not steal, you shall not give false testimony, you shall not defraud, honor your father and mother.'[a]"

[20] "Teacher," he declared, "all these I have kept since I was a boy."

[21] Jesus looked at him and loved him. "One thing you lack," he said. "Go, sell everything you have and give to the poor, and you will have treasure in heaven. Then come, follow me."

[22] At this the man's face fell. He went away sad, because he had great wealth.

[23] Jesus looked around and said to his disciples, "How hard it is for the rich to enter the kingdom of God!"

[24] The disciples were amazed at his words. But Jesus said again, "Children, how hard it is[b] to enter the kingdom of God! [25] It is easier for a camel to go through the eye of a needle than for the rich to enter the kingdom of God."

[26] The disciples were even more amazed, and said to each other, "Who then can be saved?"

[27] Jesus looked at them and said, "With human beings this is impossible, but not with God; all things are possible with God."

[28] Then Peter spoke up, "We have left everything to follow you!"

[29] "Truly I tell you," Jesus replied, "no one who has left home or brothers or sisters or mother or father or children or fields for me and the gospel [30] will fail to receive a hundred times as much in this present age: homes, brothers, sisters, mothers, children and fields—along with persecutions—and in the age to come eternal life. [31] But many who are first will be last, and the last first."

Jesus Predicts His Death a Third Time

[32] They were on their way up to Jerusalem, with Jesus leading the way, and the disciples were astonished, while those who followed were afraid. Again he took the Twelve aside and told them what was going to happen to him. [33] "We are going up to Jerusalem," he said, "and the Son of Man will be delivered over to the chief priests and the teachers of the law. They will condemn him to death and will hand him over to the Gentiles, [34] who will mock him and spit on him, flog him and kill him. Three days later he will rise."

The Request of James and John

[35] Then James and John, the sons of Zebedee, came to him. "Teacher," they said, "we want you to do for us whatever we ask."

[36] "What do you want me to do for you?" he asked.

[37] They replied, "Let one of us sit at your right and the other at your left in your glory."

[38] "You don't know what you are asking," Jesus said. "Can you drink the cup I drink or be baptized with the baptism I am baptized with?"

[39] "We can," they answered.

Jesus said to them, "You will drink the cup I drink and be baptized with the baptism I am baptized with, [40] but to sit at my right or left is not for me to grant. These places belong to those for whom they have been prepared."

[41] When the ten heard about this, they became indignant with James and John. [42] Jesus called them together and said, "You know that those who are regarded as rulers of the Gentiles lord it over them, and their high officials exercise authority over them. [43] Not so with you. Instead, whoever wants to become great among you must be your servant, [44] and whoever wants to be first must be slave of all. [45] For even the Son of Man did not come to be served, but to serve, and to give his life as a ransom for many."

---

[a] 19 Exodus 20:12-16; Deut. 5:16-20   [b] 24 Some manuscripts *is for those who trust in riches*

Blind Bartimaeus Receives His Sight

[46]Then they came to Jericho. As Jesus and his disciples, together with a large crowd, were leaving the city, a blind man, Bartimaeus (which means "son of Timaeus"), was sitting by the roadside begging. [47]When he heard that it was Jesus of Nazareth, he began to shout, "Jesus, Son of David, have mercy on me!"

[48]Many rebuked him and told him to be quiet, but he shouted all the more, "Son of David, have mercy on me!"

[49]Jesus stopped and said, "Call him."

So they called to the blind man, "Cheer up! On your feet! He's calling you." [50]Throwing his cloak aside, he jumped to his feet and came to Jesus.

[51]"What do you want me to do for you?" Jesus asked him.

The blind man said, "Rabbi, I want to see."

[52]"Go," said Jesus, "your faith has healed you." Immediately he received his sight and followed Jesus along the road.

Jesus Comes to Jerusalem as King

11 As they approached Jerusalem and came to Bethphage and Bethany at the Mount of Olives, Jesus sent two of his disciples, [2]saying to them, "Go to the village ahead of you, and just as you enter it, you will find a colt tied there, which no one has ever ridden. Untie it and bring it here. [3]If anyone asks you, 'Why are you doing this?' say, 'The Lord needs it and will send it back here shortly.'"

[4]They went and found a colt outside in the street, tied at a doorway. As they untied it, [5]some people standing there asked, "What are you doing, untying that colt?" [6]They answered as Jesus had told them to, and the people let them go. [7]When they brought the colt to Jesus and threw their cloaks over it, he sat on it. [8]Many people spread their cloaks on the road, while others spread branches they had cut in the fields. [9]Those who went ahead and those who followed shouted,

> "Hosanna![a]"
>
> "Blessed is he who comes in the name of the Lord!"[b]
>
> [10]"Blessed is the coming kingdom of our father David!"
>
> "Hosanna in the highest heaven!"

[11]Jesus entered Jerusalem and went into the temple courts. He looked around at everything, but since it was already late, he went out to Bethany with the Twelve.

Jesus Curses a Fig Tree and Clears the Temple Courts

[12]The next day as they were leaving Bethany, Jesus was hungry. [13]Seeing in the distance a fig tree in leaf, he went to find out if it had any fruit. When he reached it, he found nothing but leaves, because it was not the season for figs. [14]Then he said to the tree, "May no one ever eat fruit from you again." And his disciples heard him say it.

[15]On reaching Jerusalem, Jesus entered the temple courts and began driving out those who were buying and selling there. He overturned the tables of the money changers and the benches of those selling doves, [16]and would not allow anyone to carry merchandise through the temple courts. [17]And as he taught them, he said, "Is it not written: 'My house will be called a house of prayer for all nations'[c]? But you have made it 'a den of robbers.'[d]"

[18]The chief priests and the teachers of the law heard this and began looking for a way to kill him, for they feared him, because the whole crowd was amazed at his teaching.

[19]When evening came, Jesus and his disciples[e] went out of the city.

[20]In the morning, as they went along, they saw the fig tree withered from the roots. [21]Peter remembered and said to Jesus, "Rabbi, look! The fig tree you cursed has withered!"

[22]"Have faith in God," Jesus answered. [23]"Truly[f] I tell you, if you say to this mountain, 'Go, throw

---

[a] 9 A Hebrew expression meaning "Save!" which became an exclamation of praise; also in verse 10   [b] 9 Psalm 118:25,26   [c] 17 Isaiah 56:7   [d] 17 Jer. 7:11
[e] 19 Some early manuscripts came, Jesus   [f] 22,23 Some early manuscripts "If you have faith in God," Jesus answered, [23]"truly

yourself into the sea,' and do not doubt in your heart but believe that what you say will happen, it will be done for you. [24]Therefore I tell you, whatever you ask for in prayer, believe that you have received it, and it will be yours. [25][26]And when you stand praying, if you hold anything against anyone, forgive them, so that your Father in heaven may forgive you your sins."

The Authority of Jesus Questioned

[27]They arrived again in Jerusalem, and while Jesus was walking in the temple courts, the chief priests, the teachers of the law and the elders came to him. [28]"By what authority are you doing these things?" they asked. "And who gave you authority to do this?"

[29]Jesus replied, "I will ask you one question. Answer me, and I will tell you by what authority I am doing these things. [30]John's baptism—was it from heaven, or of human origin? Tell me!"

[31]They discussed it among themselves and said, "If we say, 'From heaven,' he will ask, 'Then why didn't you believe him?' [32]But if we say, 'Of human origin'...." (They feared the people, for everyone held that John really was a prophet.)

[33]So they answered Jesus, "We don't know."

Jesus said, "Neither will I tell you by what authority I am doing these things."

The Parable of the Tenants

12 Jesus then began to speak to them in parables: "A man planted a vineyard. He put a wall around it, dug a pit for the winepress and built a watchtower. Then he rented the vineyard to some farmers and moved to another place. [2]At harvest time he sent a servant to the tenants to collect from them some of the fruit of the vineyard. [3]But they seized him, beat him and sent him away empty-handed. [4]Then he sent another servant to them; they struck this man on the head and treated him shamefully. [5]He sent still another, and that one they killed. He sent many others; some of them they beat, others they killed.

[6]"He had one left to send, a son, whom he loved. He sent him last of all, saying, 'They will respect my son.'

[7]"But the tenants said to one another, 'This is the heir. Come, let's kill him, and the inheritance will be ours.' [8]So they took him and killed him, and threw him out of the vineyard.

[9]"What then will the owner of the vineyard do? He will come and kill those tenants and give the vineyard to others. [10]Haven't you read this passage of Scripture:

> "'The stone the builders rejected
>   has become the cornerstone;
> [11]the Lord has done this,
>   and it is marvelous in our eyes'[a]?"

[12]Then the chief priests, the teachers of the law and the elders looked for a way to arrest him because they knew he had spoken the parable against them. But they were afraid of the crowd; so they left him and went away.

Paying the Imperial Tax to Caesar

[13]Later they sent some of the Pharisees and Herodians to Jesus to catch him in his words. [14]They came to him and said, "Teacher, we know that you are a man of integrity. You aren't swayed by others, because you pay no attention to who they are; but you teach the way of God in accordance with the truth. Is it right to pay the imperial tax[b] to Caesar or not? [15]Should we pay or shouldn't we?"

But Jesus knew their hypocrisy. "Why are you trying to trap me?" he asked. "Bring me a denarius and let me look at it." [16]They brought the coin, and he asked them, "Whose image is this? And whose inscription?"

"Caesar's," they replied.

[17]Then Jesus said to them, "Give back to Caesar what is Caesar's and to God what is God's."

And they were amazed at him.

---

[a] 11 Psalm 118:22,23   [b] 14 A special tax levied on subject peoples, not on Roman citizens

Marriage at the Resurrection

[18] Then the Sadducees, who say there is no resurrection, came to him with a question. [19] "Teacher," they said, "Moses wrote for us that if a man's brother dies and leaves a wife but no children, the man must marry the widow and raise up offspring for his brother. [20] Now there were seven brothers. The first one married and died without leaving any children. [21] The second one married the widow, but he also died, leaving no child. It was the same with the third. [22] In fact, none of the seven left any children. Last of all, the woman died too. [23] At the resurrection[a] whose wife will she be, since the seven were married to her?"

[24] Jesus replied, "Are you not in error because you do not know the Scriptures or the power of God? [25] When the dead rise, they will neither marry nor be given in marriage; they will be like the angels in heaven. [26] Now about the dead rising—have you not read in the Book of Moses, in the account of the burning bush, how God said to him, 'I am the God of Abraham, the God of Isaac, and the God of Jacob'[b]? [27] He is not the God of the dead, but of the living. You are badly mistaken!"

conversations

loving God «» 12:28–34

1. Identify some examples of how you've loved God with your heart, soul, mind and strength.

2. How does loving God cause you to develop a love for others?

3. What steps can you take to increase your love for God and your neighbor?

For more on **loving God**, check the index. For the next Conversations, go to p. 1467.

1457

The Greatest Commandment

[28] One of the teachers of the law came and heard them debating. Noticing that Jesus had given them a good answer, he asked him, "Of all the commandments, which is the most important?"

[29] "The most important one," answered Jesus, "is this: 'Hear, O Israel: The Lord our God, the Lord is one.[c] [30] Love the Lord your God with all your heart and with all your soul and with all your mind and with all your strength.'[d] [31] The second is this: 'Love your neighbor as yourself.'[e] There is no commandment greater than these."

[32] "Well said, teacher," the man replied. "You are right in saying that God is one and there is no other but him. [33] To love him with all your heart, with all your understanding and with all your strength, and to love your neighbor as yourself is more important than all burnt offerings and sacrifices."

[34] When Jesus saw that he had answered wisely, he said to him, "You are not far from the kingdom of God." And from then on no one dared ask him any more questions.

Whose Son Is the Messiah?

[35] While Jesus was teaching in the temple courts, he asked, "Why do the teachers of the law say that the Messiah is the son of David? [36] David himself, speaking by the Holy Spirit, declared:

> "'The Lord said to my Lord:
> "Sit at my right hand
> until I put your enemies
> under your feet."'[f]

[37] David himself calls him 'Lord.' How then can he be his son?"

The large crowd listened to him with delight.

Warning Against the Teachers of the Law

[38] As he taught, Jesus said, "Watch out for the teachers of the law. They like to walk around in flowing robes and be greeted with respect in the marketplaces, [39] and have the most important seats in the

---

[a] *23 Some manuscripts resurrection, when people rise from the dead,*   [b] *26 Exodus 3:6*   [c] *29 Or The Lord our God is one Lord*   [d] *30 Deut. 6:4,5*
[e] *31 Lev. 19:18*   [f] *36 Psalm 110:1*

synagogues and the places of honor at banquets. ⁴⁰They devour widows' houses and for a show make lengthy prayers. These men will be punished most severely."

The Widow's Offering

⁴¹Jesus sat down opposite the place where the offerings were put and watched the crowd putting their money into the temple treasury. Many rich people threw in large amounts. ⁴²But a poor widow came and put in two very small copper coins, worth only a fraction of a penny.

⁴³Calling his disciples to him, Jesus said, "Truly I tell you, this poor widow has put more into the treasury than all the others. ⁴⁴They all gave out of their wealth; but she, out of her poverty, put in everything— all she had to live on."

The Destruction of the Temple and Signs of the End Times

13 As Jesus was leaving the temple, one of his disciples said to him, "Look, Teacher! What massive stones! What magnificent buildings!"

²"Do you see all these great buildings?" replied Jesus. "Not one stone here will be left on another; every one will be thrown down."

³As Jesus was sitting on the Mount of Olives opposite the temple, Peter, James, John and Andrew asked him privately, ⁴"Tell us, when will these things happen? And what will be the sign that they are all about to be fulfilled?"

⁵Jesus said to them: "Watch out that no one deceives you. ⁶Many will come in my name, claiming, 'I am he,' and will deceive many. ⁷When you hear of wars and rumors of wars, do not be alarmed. Such things must happen, but the end is still to come. ⁸Nation will rise against nation, and kingdom against kingdom. There will be earthquakes in various places, and famines. These are the beginning of birth pains.

⁹"You must be on your guard. You will be handed over to the local councils and flogged in the synagogues. On account of me you will stand before governors and kings as witnesses to them. ¹⁰And the gospel must first be preached to all nations. ¹¹Whenever you are arrested and brought to trial, do not worry beforehand about what to say. Just say whatever is given you at the time, for it is not you speaking, but the Holy Spirit.

¹²"Brother will betray brother to death, and a father his child. Children will rebel against their parents and have them put to death. ¹³Everyone will hate you because of me, but those who stand firm to the end will be saved.

¹⁴"When you see 'the abomination that causes desolation'ᵃ standing where itᵇ does not belong—let the reader understand—then let those who are in Judea flee to the mountains. ¹⁵Let no one on the housetop go down or enter the house to take anything out. ¹⁶Let no one in the field go back to get their cloak. ¹⁷How dreadful it will be in those days for pregnant women and nursing mothers! ¹⁸Pray that this will not take place in winter, ¹⁹because those will be days of distress unequaled from the beginning, when God created the world, until now—and never to be equaled again.

²⁰"If the Lord had not cut short those days, no one would survive. But for the sake of the elect, whom he has chosen, he has shortened them. ²¹At that time if anyone says to you, 'Look, here is the Messiah!' or, 'Look, there he is!' do not believe it. ²²For false messiahs and false prophets will appear and perform signs and wonders to deceive, if possible, even the elect. ²³So be on your guard; I have told you everything ahead of time.

²⁴"But in those days, following that distress,

> "'the sun will be darkened,
>   and the moon will not give its light;
> ²⁵the stars will fall from the sky,
>   and the heavenly bodies will be shaken.'ᶜ

ᵃ *14* Daniel 9:27; 11:31; 12:11   ᵇ *14* Or *he*   ᶜ *25* Isaiah 13:10; 34:4

²⁶"At that time people will see the Son of Man coming in clouds with great power and glory. ²⁷And he will send his angels and gather his elect from the four winds, from the ends of the earth to the ends of the heavens.

²⁸"Now learn this lesson from the fig tree: As soon as its twigs get tender and its leaves come out, you know that summer is near. ²⁹Even so, when you see these things happening, you know that it^a is near, right at the door. ³⁰Truly I tell you, this generation will certainly not pass away until all these things have happened. ³¹Heaven and earth will pass away, but my words will never pass away.

The Day and Hour Unknown

³²"But about that day or hour no one knows, not even the angels in heaven, nor the Son, but only the Father. ³³Be on guard! Be alert^b! You do not know when that time will come. ³⁴It's like a man going away: He leaves his house and puts his servants in charge, each with an assigned task, and tells the one at the door to keep watch.

³⁵"Therefore keep watch because you do not know when the owner of the house will come back— whether in the evening, or at midnight, or when the rooster crows, or at dawn. ³⁶If he comes suddenly, do not let him find you sleeping. ³⁷What I say to you, I say to everyone: 'Watch!'"

Jesus Anointed at Bethany

14 Now the Passover and the Festival of Unleavened Bread were only two days away, and the chief priests and the teachers of the law were looking for some sly way to arrest Jesus and kill him. ²"But not during the festival," they said, "or the people may riot."

1459

³While he was in Bethany, reclining at the table in the home of Simon the Leper, a woman came with an alabaster jar of very expensive perfume, made of pure nard. She broke the jar and poured the perfume on his head.

⁴Some of those present were saying indignantly to one another, "Why this waste of perfume? ⁵It could have been sold for more than a year's wages^c and the money given to the poor." And they rebuked her harshly.

⁶"Leave her alone," said Jesus. "Why are you bothering her? She has done a beautiful thing to me. ⁷The poor you will always have with you,^d and you can help them any time you want. But you will not always have me. ⁸She did what she could. She poured perfume on my body beforehand to prepare for my burial. ⁹Truly I tell you, wherever the gospel is preached throughout the world, what she has done will also be told, in memory of her."

¹⁰Then Judas Iscariot, one of the Twelve, went to the chief priests to betray Jesus to them. ¹¹They were delighted to hear this and promised to give him money. So he watched for an opportunity to hand him over.

The Last Supper

¹²On the first day of the Festival of Unleavened Bread, when it was customary to sacrifice the Passover lamb, Jesus' disciples asked him, "Where do you want us to go and make preparations for you to eat the Passover?"

¹³So he sent two of his disciples, telling them, "Go into the city, and a man carrying a jar of water will meet you. Follow him. ¹⁴Say to the owner of the house he enters, 'The Teacher asks: Where is my guest room, where I may eat the Passover with my disciples?' ¹⁵He will show you a large room upstairs, furnished and ready. Make preparations for us there."

¹⁶The disciples left, went into the city and found things just as Jesus had told them. So they prepared the Passover.

¹⁷When evening came, Jesus arrived with the Twelve. ¹⁸While they were reclining at the table eating, he said, "Truly I tell you, one of you will betray me—one who is eating with me."

¹⁹They were saddened, and one by one they said to him, "Surely not I?"

²⁰"It is one of the Twelve," he replied, "one who dips bread into the bowl with me. ²¹The Son of Man will go just as it is written about him. But woe to that man who betrays the Son of Man! It would be better for him if he had not been born."

---

^a 29 Or he   ^b 33 Some manuscripts alert and pray   ^c 5 Greek than three hundred denarii   ^d 7 See Deut. 15:11.

²²While they were eating, Jesus took bread, and when he had given thanks, he broke it and gave it to his disciples, saying, "Take it; this is my body."

²³Then he took the cup, and when he had given thanks, he gave it to them, and they all drank from it.

²⁴"This is my blood of the *ᵃ* covenant, which is poured out for many," he said to them. ²⁵"Truly I tell you, I will not drink again of the fruit of the vine until that day when I drink it new in the kingdom of God."

²⁶When they had sung a hymn, they went out to the Mount of Olives.

Jesus Predicts Peter's Denial

²⁷"You will all fall away," Jesus told them, "for it is written:

> "'I will strike the shepherd,
> and the sheep will be scattered.'ᵇ

²⁸But after I have risen, I will go ahead of you into Galilee."

²⁹Peter declared, "Even if all fall away, I will not."

³⁰"Truly I tell you," Jesus answered, "today—yes, tonight—before the rooster crows twiceᶜ you yourself will disown me three times."

³¹But Peter insisted emphatically, "Even if I have to die with you, I will never disown you." And all the others said the same.

Gethsemane

³²They went to a place called Gethsemane, and Jesus said to his disciples, "Sit here while I pray." ³³He took Peter, James and John along with him, and he began to be deeply distressed and troubled. ³⁴"My soul is overwhelmed with sorrow to the point of death," he said to them. "Stay here and keep watch."

³⁵Going a little farther, he fell to the ground and prayed that if possible the hour might pass from him. ³⁶ "Abba,ᵈ Father," he said, "everything is possible for you. Take this cup from me. Yet not what I will, but what you will."

³⁷Then he returned to his disciples and found them sleeping. "Simon," he said to Peter, "are you asleep? Could you not keep watch for one hour? ³⁸Watch and pray so that you will not fall into temptation. The spirit is willing, but the flesh is weak."

³⁹Once more he went away and prayed the same thing. ⁴⁰When he came back, he again found them sleeping, because their eyes were heavy. They did not know what to say to him.

⁴¹Returning the third time, he said to them, "Are you still sleeping and resting? Enough! The hour has come. Look, the Son of Man is delivered into the hands of sinners. ⁴²Rise! Let us go! Here comes my betrayer!"

Jesus Arrested

⁴³Just as he was speaking, Judas, one of the Twelve, appeared. With him was a crowd armed with swords and clubs, sent from the chief priests, the teachers of the law, and the elders.

⁴⁴Now the betrayer had arranged a signal with them: "The one I kiss is the man; arrest him and lead him away under guard." ⁴⁵Going at once to Jesus, Judas said, "Rabbi!" and kissed him. ⁴⁶The men seized Jesus and arrested him. ⁴⁷Then one of those standing near drew his sword and struck the servant of the high priest, cutting off his ear.

⁴⁸"Am I leading a rebellion," said Jesus, "that you have come out with swords and clubs to capture me? ⁴⁹Every day I was with you, teaching in the temple courts, and you did not arrest me. But the Scriptures must be fulfilled." ⁵⁰Then everyone deserted him and fled.

⁵¹A young man, wearing nothing but a linen garment, was following Jesus. When they seized him, ⁵²he fled naked, leaving his garment behind.

Jesus Before the Sanhedrin

⁵³They took Jesus to the high priest, and all the chief priests, the elders and the teachers of the law came together. ⁵⁴Peter followed him at a distance, right into the courtyard of the high priest. There he sat with the guards and warmed himself at the fire.

ᵃ 24 Some manuscripts *the new*   *ᵇ 27* Zech. 13:7   *ᶜ 30* Some early manuscripts do not have *twice.*   *ᵈ 36* Aramaic for *Father*

⁵⁵The chief priests and the whole Sanhedrin were looking for evidence against Jesus so that they could put him to death, but they did not find any. ⁵⁶Many testified falsely against him, but their statements did not agree.

⁵⁷Then some stood up and gave this false testimony against him: ⁵⁸"We heard him say, 'I will destroy this temple made with human hands and in three days will build another, not made with hands.'" ⁵⁹Yet even then their testimony did not agree.

⁶⁰Then the high priest stood up before them and asked Jesus, "Are you not going to answer? What is this testimony that these men are bringing against you?" ⁶¹But Jesus remained silent and gave no answer.

Again the high priest asked him, "Are you the Messiah, the Son of the Blessed One?"

⁶²"I am," said Jesus. "And you will see the Son of Man sitting at the right hand of the Mighty One and coming on the clouds of heaven."

HE IS: I am

14:60–62 When Jesus stood trial before the hypocritical religious leaders who had plotted to put him to death, he showed silent restraint when false accusations were brought against him. But there was one question he answered. When asked, *Are you the Messiah?* Jesus responded, *I am.*

I AM—the very name God revealed to Moses at the burning bush (see Exodus 3:14). Is Jesus the *I AM* to you? If you asked who he is, he would answer, *I am* your provider, *I am* your peace, *I am* your friend, *I am* always with you . . . *I am* your everything.

For the next He Is, go to p. 1470.

1461

⁶³The high priest tore his clothes. "Why do we need any more witnesses?" he asked. ⁶⁴"You have heard the blasphemy. What do you think?"

They all condemned him as worthy of death. ⁶⁵Then some began to spit at him; they blindfolded him, struck him with their fists, and said, "Prophesy!" And the guards took him and beat him.

Peter Disowns Jesus

⁶⁶While Peter was below in the courtyard, one of the servant girls of the high priest came by. ⁶⁷When she saw Peter warming himself, she looked closely at him.

"You also were with that Nazarene, Jesus," she said.

⁶⁸But he denied it. "I don't know or understand what you're talking about," he said, and went out into the entryway.*ᵃ*

⁶⁹When the servant girl saw him there, she said again to those standing around, "This fellow is one of them." ⁷⁰Again he denied it.

After a little while, those standing near said to Peter, "Surely you are one of them, for you are a Galilean."

⁷¹He began to call down curses, and he swore to them, "I don't know this man you're talking about."

⁷²Immediately the rooster crowed the second time.*ᵇ* Then Peter remembered the word Jesus had spoken to him: "Before the rooster crows twice*ᶜ* you will disown me three times." And he broke down and wept.

Jesus Before Pilate

15 Very early in the morning, the chief priests, with the elders, the teachers of the law and the whole Sanhedrin, reached a decision. They bound Jesus, led him away and handed him over to Pilate.
²"Are you the king of the Jews?" asked Pilate.

ᵃ 68 Some early manuscripts *entryway and the rooster crowed*   *ᵇ 72* Some early manuscripts do not have *the second time.*   *ᶜ 72* Some early manuscripts do not have *twice.*

"You have said so," Jesus replied.

[3]The chief priests accused him of many things. [4]So again Pilate asked him, "Aren't you going to answer? See how many things they are accusing you of."

[5]But Jesus still made no reply, and Pilate was amazed.

[6]Now it was the custom at the festival to release a prisoner whom the people requested. [7]A man called Barabbas was in prison with the insurrectionists who had committed murder in the uprising. [8]The crowd came up and asked Pilate to do for them what he usually did.

[9]"Do you want me to release to you the king of the Jews?" asked Pilate, [10]knowing it was out of envy that the chief priests had handed Jesus over to him. [11]But the chief priests stirred up the crowd to have Pilate release Barabbas instead.

[12]"What shall I do, then, with the one you call the king of the Jews?" Pilate asked them.

[13]"Crucify him!" they shouted.

[14]"Why? What crime has he committed?" asked Pilate.

But they shouted all the louder, "Crucify him!"

[15]Wanting to satisfy the crowd, Pilate released Barabbas to them. He had Jesus flogged, and handed him over to be crucified.

The Soldiers Mock Jesus

[16]The soldiers led Jesus away into the palace (that is, the Praetorium) and called together the whole company of soldiers. [17]They put a purple robe on him, then twisted together a crown of thorns and set it on him. [18]And they began to call out to him, "Hail, king of the Jews!" [19]Again and again they struck him on the head with a staff and spit on him. Falling on their knees, they paid homage to him. [20]And when they had mocked him, they took off the purple robe and put his own clothes on him. Then they led him out to crucify him.

The Crucifixion of Jesus

[21]A certain man from Cyrene, Simon, the father of Alexander and Rufus, was passing by on his way in from the country, and they forced him to carry the cross. [22]They brought Jesus to the place called Golgotha (which means "the place of the skull"). [23]Then they offered him wine mixed with myrrh, but he did not take it. [24]And they crucified him. Dividing up his clothes, they cast lots to see what each would get.

[25]It was nine in the morning when they crucified him. [26]The written notice of the charge against him read: THE KING OF THE JEWS. [27][28]They crucified two rebels with him, one on his right and one on his left. [29]Those who passed by hurled insults at him, shaking their heads and saying, "So! You who are going to destroy the temple and build it in three days, [30]come down from the cross and save yourself!"

[31]In the same way the chief priests and the teachers of the law mocked him among themselves. "He saved others," they said, "but he can't save himself! [32]Let this Messiah, this king of Israel, come down now from the cross, that we may see and believe." Those crucified with him also heaped insults on him.

The Death of Jesus

[33]At noon, darkness came over the whole land until three in the afternoon. [34]And at three in the afternoon Jesus cried out in a loud voice, *"Eloi, Eloi, lema sabachthani?"* (which means "My God, my God, why have you forsaken me?"). [a]

[35]When some of those standing near heard this, they said, "Listen, he's calling Elijah."

[36]Someone ran, filled a sponge with wine vinegar, put it on a staff, and offered it to Jesus to drink. "Now leave him alone. Let's see if Elijah comes to take him down," he said.

[37]With a loud cry, Jesus breathed his last.

[38]The curtain of the temple was torn in two from top to bottom. [39]And when the centurion, who stood there in front of Jesus, saw how he died, [b] he said, "Surely this man was the Son of God!"

[40]Some women were watching from a distance. Among them were Mary Magdalene, Mary the

---

[a] 34 Psalm 22:1   [b] 39 Some manuscripts *saw that he died with such a cry*

ASKMEANYTHING

Tell us about your sons, James and John.

My husband and I raised our two sons near Capernaum, by the Sea of Galilee. The boys were fishermen like their father. We fully expected them to go into the family business. In fact, the boys were fishing when *he* arrived on the shore and called them.

That would be Jesus, right?

Correct. Of course, we had heard about this Teacher. I think the boys had heard him teach on several occasions. But to be his disciples! Well, what could Zebedee and I say? We had raised our sons to serve God. Even though we didn't fully understand what it meant for Jesus to be the Messiah, we recognized that this man was from God.

You became a follower of Jesus yourself, didn't you?

1463

Yes. In fact, I was with Jesus' mother and some of the other women when he was crucified. It was horrible. Afterwards a few of us went to the tomb to anoint his body and heard the incredible news that Jesus was alive! I will never forget that day!

But you also asked Jesus a particular favor. What was that?

Well, as you can imagine, I was extremely proud of my sons. They were two of Jesus' closest companions. And I thought Jesus' kingdom was going to be established here on earth during his lifetime. Naturally, I wanted to make sure that my sons were going to play an important role in that kingdom. So I asked Jesus if he would place my two sons on seats of power next to him. Looking back, I think I overstepped my boundaries, but as a mother, I was only thinking of my boys.

How did Jesus respond?

Jesus didn't condemn me, nor did he take it out on my sons. That really wasn't his nature at all. But he did make it clear that my request was based on ignorance—I really didn't know what I was asking for. Jesus wanted to know only one thing—were my sons willing to *suffer* for his kingdom? It was only after witnessing Jesus' gruesome death and later the persecution of his followers that I realized what he meant by that comment. And my sons did suffer for Jesus' kingdom: James was the first apostle to be killed for following Jesus, and John was the last apostle to suffer for Christ.

What did you learn from your experience?

I learned that it wasn't by serving in any high position in an earthly kingdom that my sons would earn honor. No, they were willing to sacrifice everything for Jesus—including their very lives—and through that they gained the greatest honor. I think the same is true for every one of us as well. It's only in losing ourselves, in giving up everything, that we gain the most.

FOR MORE INSIGHT For other verses on the cost of discipleship, read Matthew 10:32–39; Luke 14:26–35; and John 21:15–19.

mother of James the younger and of Joseph,^a and Salome. ⁴¹ In Galilee these women had followed him and cared for his needs. Many other women who had come up with him to Jerusalem were also there.

The Burial of Jesus

⁴² It was Preparation Day (that is, the day before the Sabbath). So as evening approached, ⁴³ Joseph of Arimathea, a prominent member of the Council, who was himself waiting for the kingdom of God, went boldly to Pilate and asked for Jesus' body. ⁴⁴ Pilate was surprised to hear that he was already dead. Summoning the centurion, he asked him if Jesus had already died. ⁴⁵ When he learned from the centurion that it was so, he gave the body to Joseph. ⁴⁶ So Joseph bought some linen cloth, took down the body, wrapped it in the linen, and placed it in a tomb cut out of rock. Then he rolled a stone against the entrance of the tomb. ⁴⁷ Mary Magdalene and Mary the mother of Joseph saw where he was laid.

Jesus Has Risen

16 When the Sabbath was over, Mary Magdalene, Mary the mother of James, and Salome bought spices so that they might go to anoint Jesus' body. ² Very early on the first day of the week, just after sunrise, they were on their way to the tomb ³ and they asked each other, "Who will roll the stone away from the entrance of the tomb?"

⁴ But when they looked up, they saw that the stone, which was very large, had been rolled away. ⁵ As they entered the tomb, they saw a young man dressed in a white robe sitting on the right side, and they were alarmed.

⁶ "Don't be alarmed," he said. "You are looking for Jesus the Nazarene, who was crucified. He has risen! He is not here. See the place where they laid him. ⁷ But go, tell his disciples and Peter, 'He is going ahead of you into Galilee. There you will see him, just as he told you.'"

⁸ Trembling and bewildered, the women went out and fled from the tomb. They said nothing to anyone, because they were afraid.

[The earliest manuscripts and some other ancient witnesses do not have Mark 16:9–20.]

⁹ *When Jesus rose early on the first day of the week, he appeared first to Mary Magdalene, out of whom he had driven seven demons.* ¹⁰ *She went and told those who had been with him and who were mourning and weeping.* ¹¹ *When they heard that Jesus was alive and that she had seen him, they did not believe it.*

¹² *Afterward Jesus appeared in a different form to two of them while they were walking in the country.* ¹³ *These returned and reported it to the rest; but they did not believe them either.*

¹⁴ *Later Jesus appeared to the Eleven as they were eating; he rebuked them for their lack of faith and their stubborn refusal to believe those who had seen him after he had risen.*

¹⁵ *He said to them, "Go into all the world and preach the gospel to all creation.* ¹⁶ *Whoever believes and is baptized will*

1464

be saved, but whoever does not believe will be condemned. [17] *And these signs will accompany those who believe: In my name they will drive out demons; they will speak in new tongues;* [18] *they will pick up snakes with their hands; and when they drink deadly poison, it will not hurt them at all; they will place their hands on sick people, and they will get well."*

[19] *After the Lord Jesus had spoken to them, he was taken up into heaven and he sat at the right hand of God.* [20] *Then the disciples went out and preached everywhere, and the Lord worked with them and confirmed his word by the signs that accompanied it.*

luke

1466

AUTHOR
Luke, a doctor and Gentile Christian.

AUDIENCE
Followers of Jesus. Luke wanted the Gentiles to hear the true details about the life of Jesus.

DATE
Probably about A.D. 60.

SETTING
Luke wrote to the Gentiles from Rome or perhaps Caesarea, Achaia or Ephesus.

VERSE TO REMEMBER
"Jesus replied, 'What is impossible with human beings is possible with God.'" (18:27)

THEME TO CONSIDER
Jesus communicates the love of God through his relationships with people. Notice Luke's emphasis on women and how Jesus included them in his ministry.

Introduction

1 Many have undertaken to draw up an account of the things that have been fulfilled[a] among us, [2]just as they were handed down to us by those who from the first were eyewitnesses and servants of the word. [3]With this in mind, since I myself have carefully investigated everything from the beginning, I too decided to write an orderly account for you, most excellent Theophilus, [4]so that you may know the certainty of the things you have been taught.

The Birth of John the Baptist Foretold

[5]In the time of Herod king of Judea there was a priest named Zechariah, who belonged to the priestly division of Abijah; his wife Elizabeth was also a descendant of Aaron. [6]Both of them were righteous in the sight of God, observing all the Lord's commands and decrees blamelessly. [7]But they were childless because Elizabeth was not able to conceive, and they were both well advanced in years.

[8]Once when Zechariah's division was on duty and he was serving as priest before God, [9]he was chosen by lot, according to the custom of the priesthood, to go into the temple of the Lord and burn incense. [10]And when the time for the burning of incense came, all the assembled worshipers were praying outside.

[11]Then an angel of the Lord appeared to him, standing at the right side of the altar of incense. [12]When Zechariah saw him, he was startled and was gripped with fear. [13]But the angel said to him: "Do not be afraid, Zechariah; your prayer has been heard. Your wife Elizabeth will bear you a son, and you are to call him John. [14]He will be a joy and delight to you, and many will rejoice because of his birth, [15]for he will be great in the sight of the Lord. He is never to take wine or other fermented drink, and he will be filled with the Holy Spirit even before he is born. [16]Many of the people of Israel will he bring back to the Lord their God. [17]And he will go on before the Lord, in the spirit and power of Elijah, to turn the hearts of the parents to their children and the disobedient to the wisdom of the righteous—to make ready a people prepared for the Lord."

[18]Zechariah asked the angel, "How can I be sure of this? I am an old man and my wife is well along in years."

[19]The angel said to him, "I am Gabriel. I stand in the presence of God, and I have been sent to speak to you and to tell you this good news. [20]And now you will be silent and not able to speak until the day this happens, because you did not believe my words, which will come true at their appointed time."

[21]Meanwhile, the people were waiting for Zechariah and wondering why he stayed so long in the temple. [22]When he came out, he could not speak to them. They realized he had seen a vision in the temple, for he kept making signs to them but remained unable to speak.

[23]When his time of service was completed, he returned home. [24]After this his wife Elizabeth became pregnant and for five months remained in seclusion. [25]"The Lord has done this for me," she said. "In these days he has shown his favor and taken away my disgrace among the people."

The Birth of Jesus Foretold

[26]In the sixth month of Elizabeth's pregnancy, God sent the angel Gabriel to Nazareth, a town in Galilee, [27]to a virgin pledged to be married to a man named Joseph, a descendant of David. The virgin's name was Mary. [28]The angel went to her and said, "Greetings, you who are highly favored! The Lord is with you."

[29]Mary was greatly troubled at his words and wondered what kind of greeting this might be. [30]But the angel said to her, "Do not be afraid, Mary, you have found favor with God. [31]You will conceive and give birth to a son, and you are to call him Jesus. [32]He will be great and will be called the Son of the Most High.

conversations

pregnancy «» 1:5–7

1» Do you think that infertility or pregnancy is connected to your obedience to God?

2» How does the ability to conceive affect how you view yourself as a woman?

3» How can you know if it's God's will that you get pregnant?

For more on **pregnancy**, check the index. For the next Conversations, go to p. 1472.

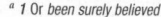

[a] 1 Or *been surely believed*

The Lord God will give him the throne of his father David, ³³and he will reign over the house of Jacob forever; his kingdom will never end."

³⁴"How will this be," Mary asked the angel, "since I am a virgin?"

³⁵The angel answered, "The Holy Spirit will come on you, and the power of the Most High will overshadow you. So the holy one to be born will be called*a* the Son of God. ³⁶Even Elizabeth your relative is going to have a child in her old age, and she who was said to be unable to conceive is in her sixth month. ³⁷For no word from God will ever fail."

³⁸"I am the Lord's servant," Mary answered. "May it be to me according to your word." Then the angel left her.

Mary Visits Elizabeth

³⁹At that time Mary got ready and hurried to a town in the hill country of Judea, ⁴⁰where she entered Zechariah's home and greeted Elizabeth. ⁴¹When Elizabeth heard Mary's greeting, the baby leaped in her womb, and Elizabeth was filled with the Holy Spirit. ⁴²In a loud voice she exclaimed: "Blessed are you among women, and blessed is the child you will bear! ⁴³But why am I so favored, that the mother of my Lord should come to me? ⁴⁴As soon as the sound of your greeting reached my ears, the baby in my womb leaped for joy. ⁴⁵Blessed is she who has believed that the Lord would fulfill his promises to her!"

Mary's Song

⁴⁶And Mary said:

> "My soul glorifies the Lord
> ⁴⁷   and my spirit rejoices in God my Savior,
> ⁴⁸for he has been mindful
>   of the humble state of his servant.
>   From now on all generations will call me blessed,
> ⁴⁹   for the Mighty One has done great things for me—
>   holy is his name.
> ⁵⁰His mercy extends to those who fear him,
>   from generation to generation.
> ⁵¹He has performed mighty deeds with his arm;
>   he has scattered those who are proud in their inmost thoughts.
> ⁵²He has brought down rulers from their thrones
>   but has lifted up the humble.
> ⁵³He has filled the hungry with good things
>   but has sent the rich away empty.
> ⁵⁴He has helped his servant Israel,
>   remembering to be merciful
> ⁵⁵to Abraham and his descendants forever,
>   just as he promised our ancestors."

⁵⁶Mary stayed with Elizabeth for about three months and then returned home.

---

a 35 Or So the child to be born will be called holy,

1:38 Most likely, Mary planned to marry and raise a family—every Jewish girl's dream, nothing unusual. Then God revealed *his* plans for her, and the future Mary envisioned suddenly vanished before her eyes. She had no way of knowing what this change would mean in her life. Did she argue with God? Try to cling to her own plans? Ignore what God was doing? No. Mary humbly accepted what God had for her because she knew her life belonged to him. She saw herself as God's servant. How do you respond to the changes God brings into your life?

1468

The Birth of John the Baptist

⁵⁷When it was time for Elizabeth to have her baby, she gave birth to a son. ⁵⁸Her neighbors and relatives heard that the Lord had shown her great mercy, and they shared her joy.

⁵⁹On the eighth day they came to circumcise the child, and they were going to name him after his father Zechariah, ⁶⁰but his mother spoke up and said, "No! He is to be called John."

⁶¹They said to her, "There is no one among your relatives who has that name."

⁶²Then they made signs to his father, to find out what he would like to name the child. ⁶³He asked for a writing tablet, and to everyone's astonishment he wrote, "His name is John." ⁶⁴Immediately his mouth was opened and his tongue was loosed, and he began to speak, praising God. ⁶⁵The neighbors were all filled with awe, and throughout the hill country of Judea people were talking about all these things. ⁶⁶Everyone who heard this wondered about it, asking, "What then is this child going to be?" For the Lord's hand was with him.

Zechariah's Song

⁶⁷His father Zechariah was filled with the Holy Spirit and prophesied:

> ⁶⁸"Praise be to the Lord, the God of Israel,
>   because he has come to his people and redeemed them.
> ⁶⁹He has raised up a horn^a of salvation for us
>   in the house of his servant David
> ⁷⁰(as he said through his holy prophets of long ago),
> ⁷¹salvation from our enemies
>   and from the hand of all who hate us—
> ⁷²to show mercy to our ancestors
>   and to remember his holy covenant,
> ⁷³   the oath he swore to our father Abraham:
> ⁷⁴to rescue us from the hand of our enemies,
>   and to enable us to serve him without fear
> ⁷⁵   in holiness and righteousness before him all our days.
>
> ⁷⁶And you, my child, will be called a prophet of the Most High;
>   for you will go on before the Lord to prepare the way for him,
> ⁷⁷to give his people the knowledge of salvation
>   through the forgiveness of their sins,
> ⁷⁸because of the tender mercy of our God,
>   by which the rising sun will come to us from heaven
> ⁷⁹to shine on those living in darkness
>   and in the shadow of death,
>   to guide our feet into the path of peace."

⁸⁰And the child grew and became strong in spirit^b; and he lived in the wilderness until he appeared publicly to Israel.

The Birth of Jesus

2 In those days Caesar Augustus issued a decree that a census should be taken of the entire Roman world. ²(This was the first census that took place while Quirinius was governor of Syria.) ³And everyone went to their own town to register.

⁴So Joseph also went up from the town of Nazareth in Galilee to Judea, to Bethlehem the town of David, because he belonged to the house and line of David. ⁵He went there to register with Mary, who was pledged to be married to him and was expecting a child. ⁶While they were there, the time came for the baby to be born, ⁷and she gave birth to her firstborn, a son. She wrapped him in cloths and placed him in a manger, because there was no guest room available for them.

1469

---

^a 69 Horn here symbolizes a strong king.   ^b 80 Or in the Spirit

HE IS: on time

2:1–7 The people of Israel had eagerly waited for centuries for the Messiah to arrive, but it wasn't until the perfect moment in history, during the census of the entire Roman world, when the baby was born. Jesus was born right on *time* and in the right place, fulfilling many Old Testament prophecies.

He's consistently, perfectly, always on *time*. You may be waiting for God to fulfill a promise to you. Don't lose hope; he's on *time* and always keeps his promises. However, sometimes God's waiting room can be God's training room. Waiting helps you grow into the woman he intends you to be.

For the next He Is, go to p. 1497.

The Shepherds and the Angels

⁸And there were shepherds living out in the fields nearby, keeping watch over their flocks at night. ⁹An angel of the Lord appeared to them, and the glory of the Lord shone around them, and they were terrified. ¹⁰But the angel said to them, "Do not be afraid. I bring you good news of great joy that will be for all the people. ¹¹Today in the town of David a Savior has been born to you; he is the Messiah, the Lord. ¹²This will be a sign to you: You will find a baby wrapped in cloths and lying in a manger."

¹³Suddenly a great company of the heavenly host appeared with the angel, praising God and saying,

¹⁴"Glory to God in the highest heaven,
    and on earth peace to those on whom his favor rests."

¹⁵When the angels had left them and gone into heaven, the shepherds said to one another, "Let's go to Bethlehem and see this thing that has happened, which the Lord has told us about."

¹⁶So they hurried off and found Mary and Joseph, and the baby, who was lying in the manger. ¹⁷When they had seen him, they spread the word concerning what had been told them about this child, ¹⁸and all who heard it were amazed at what the shepherds said to them. ¹⁹But Mary treasured up all these things and pondered them in her heart. ²⁰The shepherds returned, glorifying and praising God for all the things they had heard and seen, which were just as they had been told.

Jesus Presented in the Temple

²¹On the eighth day, when it was time to circumcise the child, he was named Jesus, the name the angel had given him before he was conceived.

²²When the time came for the purification rites required by the Law of Moses, Joseph and Mary took him to Jerusalem to present him to the Lord ²³(as it is written in the Law of the Lord, "Every firstborn male is to be consecrated to the Lord"ᵃ), ²⁴and to offer a sacrifice in keeping with what is said in the Law of the Lord: "a pair of doves or two young pigeons."ᵇ

²⁵Now there was a man in Jerusalem called Simeon, who was righteous and devout. He was waiting for the consolation of Israel, and the Holy Spirit was on him. ²⁶It had been revealed to him by the Holy Spirit that he would not die before he had seen the Lord's Messiah. ²⁷Moved by the Spirit, he went into the temple courts. When the parents brought in the child Jesus to do for him what the custom of the Law required, ²⁸Simeon took him in his arms and praised God, saying:

²⁹"Sovereign Lord, as you have promised,
    you may now dismissᶜ your servant in peace.
³⁰For my eyes have seen your salvation,
³¹   which you have prepared in the sight of all nations:
³²a light for revelation to the Gentiles,
    and the glory of your people Israel."

ASKmeanYTHING

anna

Luke 2:36–38

Tell us about your background.

I had been married only seven years when my husband died. I had no children, so I was basically alone. I never remarried and remained a widow for the rest of my life.

Was that a lonely time for you?

You know, it could have been. But my days and nights were filled. The temple became my home, and I spent my time serving and worshiping the Lord. You might think that's not much of a life, but when God fills your life with his presence, you are never alone, never without hope or purpose.

1471

What did it mean to you to get to see the Messiah?

Can you even imagine what that was like for me? As a prophet, I had spent years waiting for the Messiah. I knew the promises that God had given to his people throughout the centuries, and I had spent my life praying and fasting, longing for the Messiah to appear. So that morning when I overheard Simeon giving thanks to God because he had seen the Lord's Messiah, I knew I had to see this child. When I saw that young couple proudly carrying their newborn son, I could hardly believe my old eyes. Here in that tiny body was the hope of Jerusalem, the redemption of our people. Praise God! I had seen the promised Messiah—me, a lowly widow. What a privilege!

What can others learn from your life?

There is worth and value in whatever passage of life you may find yourself. Many people might consider an elderly woman worthless or those lonely years of widowhood unbearable. But our God can make any time in our lives worthwhile and useful. You may be washing floors and wiping up after young children right now. Or maybe you are in-between jobs and uncertain about what step to take next. Maybe you're waiting for a husband or for financial security. Wherever you are in life, look for ways to serve God in and through your life situation. And I know this: If you are faithful, God will honor you.

FOR MORE INSIGHT: Take a look at the following verses for more on waiting on the Lord: Psalm 25:5; Psalm 130:5; Isaiah 40:30–31; Lamentations 3:25–26; Hosea 12:6; and 1 Corinthians 4:4–5.

33 The child's father and mother marveled at what was said about him. 34 Then Simeon blessed them and said to Mary, his mother: "This child is destined to cause the falling and rising of many in Israel, and to be a sign that will be spoken against, 35 so that the thoughts of many hearts will be revealed. And a sword will pierce your own soul too."

36 There was also a prophet, Anna, the daughter of Phanuel, of the tribe of Asher. She was very old; she had lived with her husband seven years after her marriage, 37 and then had been a widow for eighty-four years.^a She never left the temple but worshiped night and day, fasting and praying. 38 Coming up to them at that very moment, she gave thanks to God and spoke about the child to all who were looking forward to the redemption of Jerusalem.

39 When Joseph and Mary had done everything required by the Law of the Lord, they returned to Galilee to their own town of Nazareth. 40 And the child grew and became strong; he was filled with wisdom, and the grace of God was on him.

conversations

aging «» 2:36–38

1» What unique roles do older women have within God's family?

2» As you age, do you feel your value increases or decreases in your job? At home or church?

3» How can you be involved in the life of a younger Christian woman?

For more on aging, check the index.
For the next Conversations, go to p. 1486.

The Boy Jesus at the Temple

41 Every year Jesus' parents went to Jerusalem for the Festival of the Passover. 42 When he was twelve years old, they went up to the festival, according to the custom. 43 After the festival was over, while his parents were returning home, the boy Jesus stayed behind in Jerusalem, but they were unaware of it. 44 Thinking he was in their company, they traveled on for a day. Then they began looking for him among their relatives and friends. 45 When they did not find him, they went back to Jerusalem to look for him. 46 After three days they found him in the temple courts, sitting among the teachers, listening to them and asking them questions. 47 Everyone who heard him was amazed at his understanding and his answers. 48 When his parents saw him, they were astonished. His mother said to him, "Son, why have you treated us like this? Your father and I have been anxiously searching for you."

49 "Why were you searching for me?" he asked. "Didn't you know I had to be in my Father's house?"^b 50 But they did not understand what he was saying to them.

51 Then he went down to Nazareth with them and was obedient to them. But his mother treasured all these things in her heart. 52 And as Jesus grew up, he increased in wisdom and in favor with God and people.

John the Baptist Prepares the Way

3 In the fifteenth year of the reign of Tiberius Caesar—when Pontius Pilate was governor of Judea, Herod tetrarch of Galilee, his brother Philip tetrarch of Iturea and Traconitis, and Lysanias tetrarch of Abilene— 2 during the high-priesthood of Annas and Caiaphas, the word of God came to John son of Zechariah in the wilderness. 3 He went into all the country around the Jordan, preaching a baptism of repentance for the forgiveness of sins. 4 As it is written in the book of the words of Isaiah the prophet:

"A voice of one calling in the wilderness,
'Prepare the way for the Lord,
make straight paths for him.
5 Every valley shall be filled in,
every mountain and hill made low.
The crooked roads shall become straight,
the rough ways smooth.
6 And all people will see God's salvation.'"^c

⁷John said to the crowds coming out to be baptized by him, "You brood of vipers! Who warned you to flee from the coming wrath? ⁸Produce fruit in keeping with repentance. And do not begin to say to yourselves, 'We have Abraham as our father.' For I tell you that out of these stones God can raise up children for Abraham. ⁹The ax is already at the root of the trees, and every tree that does not produce good fruit will be cut down and thrown into the fire."

¹⁰"What should we do then?" the crowd asked.

¹¹John answered, "Anyone who has two shirts should share with the one who has none, and anyone who has food should do the same."

¹²Even tax collectors came to be baptized. "Teacher," they asked, "what should we do?"

¹³"Don't collect any more than you are required to," he told them.

¹⁴Then some soldiers asked him, "And what should we do?"

He replied, "Don't extort money and don't accuse people falsely—be content with your pay."

¹⁵The people were waiting expectantly and were all wondering in their hearts if John might possibly be the Messiah. ¹⁶John answered them all, "I baptize you with ᵃ water. But one who is more powerful than I will come, the thongs of whose sandals I am not worthy to untie. He will baptize you with ᵃ the Holy Spirit and fire. ¹⁷His winnowing fork is in his hand to clear his threshing floor and to gather the wheat into his barn, but he will burn up the chaff with unquenchable fire." ¹⁸And with many other words John exhorted the people and proclaimed the good news to them.

¹⁹But when John rebuked Herod the tetrarch because of his marriage to Herodias, his brother's wife, and all the other evil things he had done, ²⁰Herod added this to them all: He locked John up in prison.

The Baptism and Genealogy of Jesus

²¹When all the people were being baptized, Jesus was baptized too. And as he was praying, heaven was opened ²²and the Holy Spirit descended on him in bodily form like a dove. And a voice came from heaven: "You are my Son, whom I love; with you I am well pleased."

²³Now Jesus himself was about thirty years old when he began his ministry. He was the son, so it was thought, of Joseph,

the son of Heli, ²⁴the son of Matthat,
the son of Levi, the son of Melki,
the son of Jannai, the son of Joseph,
²⁵ the son of Mattathias, the son of Amos,
the son of Nahum, the son of Esli,
the son of Naggai, ²⁶the son of Maath,
the son of Mattathias, the son of Semein,
the son of Josek, the son of Joda,
²⁷ the son of Joanan, the son of Rhesa,
the son of Zerubbabel, the son of Shealtiel,
the son of Neri, ²⁸the son of Melki,
the son of Addi, the son of Cosam,
the son of Elmadam, the son of Er,
²⁹ the son of Joshua, the son of Eliezer,
the son of Jorim, the son of Matthat,
the son of Levi, ³⁰the son of Simeon,
the son of Judah, the son of Joseph,
the son of Jonam, the son of Eliakim,
³¹ the son of Melea, the son of Menna,
the son of Mattatha, the son of Nathan,
the son of David, ³²the son of Jesse,
the son of Obed, the son of Boaz,

ᵃ 16 Or in

the son of Salmon,^a the son of Nahshon,
³³ the son of Amminadab, the son of Ram,^b
the son of Hezron, the son of Perez,
the son of Judah, ³⁴ the son of Jacob,
the son of Isaac, the son of Abraham,
the son of Terah, the son of Nahor,
³⁵ the son of Serug, the son of Reu,
the son of Peleg, the son of Eber,
the son of Shelah, ³⁶ the son of Cainan,
the son of Arphaxad, the son of Shem,
the son of Noah, the son of Lamech,
³⁷ the son of Methuselah, the son of Enoch,
the son of Jared, the son of Mahalalel,
the son of Kenan, ³⁸ the son of Enosh,
the son of Seth, the son of Adam,
the son of God.

Jesus Is Tested in the Wilderness

4 Jesus, full of the Holy Spirit, left the Jordan and was led by the Spirit into the wilderness, ² where for forty days he was tempted^c by the devil. He ate nothing during those days, and at the end of them he was hungry.

³ The devil said to him, "If you are the Son of God, tell this stone to become bread."

⁴ Jesus answered, "It is written: 'People do not live on bread alone.'^d"

⁵ The devil led him up to a high place and showed him in an instant all the kingdoms of the world. ⁶ And he said to him, "I will give you all their authority and splendor; it has been given to me, and I can give it to anyone I want to. ⁷ If you worship me, it will all be yours."

⁸ Jesus answered, "It is written: 'Worship the Lord your God and serve him only.'^e"

⁹ The devil led him to Jerusalem and had him stand on the highest point of the temple. "If you are the Son of God," he said, "throw yourself down from here. ¹⁰ For it is written:

> "'He will command his angels concerning you
>   to guard you carefully;
> ¹¹ they will lift you up in their hands,
>   so that you will not strike your foot against a stone.'^f"

¹² Jesus answered, "It is said: 'Do not put the Lord your God to the test.'^g"

¹³ When the devil had finished all this tempting, he left him until an opportune time.

Jesus Rejected at Nazareth

¹⁴ Jesus returned to Galilee in the power of the Spirit, and news about him spread through the whole countryside. ¹⁵ He was teaching in their synagogues, and everyone praised him.

¹⁶ He went to Nazareth, where he had been brought up, and on the Sabbath day he went into the synagogue, as was his custom. He stood up to read, ¹⁷ and the scroll of the prophet Isaiah was handed to him. Unrolling it, he found the place where it is written:

> ¹⁸ "The Spirit of the Lord is on me,
>   because he has anointed me
>   to proclaim good news to the poor.
> He has sent me to proclaim freedom for the prisoners
>   and recovery of sight for the blind,
>   to set the oppressed free,
> ¹⁹   to proclaim the year of the Lord's favor."^h

²⁰Then he rolled up the scroll, gave it back to the attendant and sat down. The eyes of everyone in the synagogue were fastened on him. ²¹He began by saying to them, "Today this scripture is fulfilled in your hearing."

²²All spoke well of him and were amazed at the gracious words that came from his lips. "Isn't this Joseph's son?" they asked.

²³Jesus said to them, "Surely you will quote this proverb to me: 'Physician, heal yourself!' And you will tell me, 'Do here in your hometown what we have heard that you did in Capernaum.'"

²⁴"Truly I tell you," he continued, "prophets are not accepted in their hometowns. ²⁵I assure you that there were many widows in Israel in Elijah's time, when the sky was shut for three and a half years and there was a severe famine throughout the land. ²⁶Yet Elijah was not sent to any of them, but to a widow in Zarephath in the region of Sidon. ²⁷And there were many in Israel with leprosy ᵃ in the time of Elisha the prophet, yet not one of them was cleansed—only Naaman the Syrian."

²⁸All the people in the synagogue were furious when they heard this. ²⁹They got up, drove him out of the town, and took him to the brow of the hill on which the town was built, in order to throw him off the cliff. ³⁰But he walked right through the crowd and went on his way.

Jesus Drives Out an Evil Spirit

³¹Then he went down to Capernaum, a town in Galilee, and on the Sabbath he taught the people. ³²They were amazed at his teaching, because his words had authority.

³³In the synagogue there was a man possessed by a demon, an evil ᵇ spirit. He cried out at the top of his voice, ³⁴"Go away! What do you want with us, Jesus of Nazareth? Have you come to destroy us? I know who you are—the Holy One of God!"

³⁵"Be quiet!" Jesus said sternly. "Come out of him!" Then the demon threw the man down before them all and came out without injuring him.

³⁶All the people were amazed and said to each other, "What words these are! With authority and power he gives orders to evil spirits and they come out!" ³⁷And the news about him spread throughout the surrounding area.

Jesus Heals Many

³⁸Jesus left the synagogue and went to the home of Simon. Now Simon's mother-in-law was suffering from a high fever, and they asked Jesus to help her. ³⁹So he bent over her and rebuked the fever, and it left her. She got up at once and began to wait on them.

⁴⁰At sunset, the people brought to Jesus all who had various kinds of sickness, and laying his hands on each one, he healed them. ⁴¹Moreover, demons came out of many people, shouting, "You are the Son of God!" But he rebuked them and would not allow them to speak, because they knew he was the Messiah.

⁴²At daybreak, Jesus went out to a solitary place. The people were looking for him and when they came to where he was, they tried to keep him from leaving them. ⁴³But he said, "I must proclaim the good news of the kingdom of God to the other towns also, because that is why I was sent." ⁴⁴And he kept on preaching in the synagogues of Judea.

Jesus Calls His First Disciples

5 One day as Jesus was standing by the Lake of Gennesaret,ᶜ the people were crowding around him and listening to the word of God. ²He saw at the water's edge two boats, left there by the fishermen, who were washing their nets. ³He got into one of the boats, the one belonging to Simon, and asked him to put out a little from shore. Then he sat down and taught the people from the boat.

⁴When he had finished speaking, he said to Simon, "Put out into deep water, and let down the nets for a catch."

⁵Simon answered, "Master, we've worked hard all night and haven't caught anything. But because you say so, I will let down the nets."

⁶When they had done so, they caught such a large number of fish that their nets began to break. ⁷So

---

ᵃ *27* The Greek word traditionally translated *leprosy* was used for various diseases affecting the skin.   ᵇ *33* Greek *unclean*; also in verse 36   ᶜ *1* That is, Sea of Galilee they signaled their partners in the other boat to come and help them, and they came and filled both boats so full that they began to sink.

[8] When Simon Peter saw this, he fell at Jesus' knees and said, "Go away from me, Lord; I am a sinful man!" [9] For he and all his companions were astonished at the catch of fish they had taken, [10] and so were James and John, the sons of Zebedee, Simon's partners.

Then Jesus said to Simon, "Don't be afraid; from now on you will fish for people." [11] So they pulled their boats up on shore, left everything and followed him.

Jesus Heals a Man With Leprosy

[12] While Jesus was in one of the towns, a man came along who was covered with leprosy.[a] When he saw Jesus, he fell with his face to the ground and begged him, "Lord, if you are willing, you can make me clean."

[13] Jesus reached out his hand and touched the man. "I am willing," he said. "Be clean!" And immediately the leprosy left him.

[14] Then Jesus ordered him, "Don't tell anyone, but go, show yourself to the priest and offer the sacrifices that Moses commanded for your cleansing, as a testimony to them."

[15] Yet the news about him spread all the more, so that crowds of people came to hear him and to be healed of their sicknesses. [16] But Jesus often withdrew to lonely places and prayed.

Jesus Forgives and Heals a Paralyzed Man

[17] One day Jesus was teaching, and Pharisees and teachers of the law were sitting there. They had come from every village of Galilee and from Judea and Jerusalem. And the power of the Lord was with Jesus to heal the sick. [18] Some men came carrying a paralyzed man on a mat and tried to take him into the house to lay him before Jesus. [19] When they could not find a way to do this because of the crowd, they went up on the roof and lowered him on his mat through the tiles into the middle of the crowd, right in front of Jesus.

[20] When Jesus saw their faith, he said, "Friend, your sins are forgiven."

[21] The Pharisees and the teachers of the law began thinking to themselves, "Who is this fellow who speaks blasphemy? Who can forgive sins but God alone?"

[22] Jesus knew what they were thinking and asked, "Why are you thinking these things in your hearts? [23] Which is easier: to say, 'Your sins are forgiven,' or to say, 'Get up and walk'? [24] But I want you to know that the Son of Man has authority on earth to forgive sins." So he said to the paralyzed man, "I tell you, get up, take your mat and go home." [25] Immediately he stood up in front of them, took what he had been lying on and went home praising God. [26] Everyone was amazed and gave praise to God. They were filled with awe and said, "We have seen remarkable things today."

Jesus Calls Levi and Eats With Sinners

[27] After this, Jesus went out and saw a tax collector by the name of Levi sitting at his tax booth. "Follow me," Jesus said to him, [28] and Levi got up, left everything and followed him.

[29] Then Levi held a great banquet for Jesus at his house, and a large crowd of tax collectors and others were eating with them. [30] But the Pharisees and the teachers of the law who belonged to their sect complained to his disciples, "Why do you eat and drink with tax collectors and sinners?"

atissue:busyness

5:15–16 Jesus knew the pressure of a packed schedule. Crowds of people clamored for his attention. The Pharisees continually attacked him. Teaching his followers required a huge investment of his time. Yet he never let his schedule rule over him. He knew the mission God had given him, and he didn't allow others' demands dictate how he spent his time. He was never too busy to focus on what was most important— including time alone with his Father. If you're too busy to spend time with God, then perhaps you're too busy.

---

a 12 The Greek word traditionally translated leprosy was used for various diseases affecting the skin.

³¹Jesus answered them, "It is not the healthy who need a doctor, but the sick. ³²I have not come to call the righteous, but sinners to repentance."

Jesus Questioned About Fasting

³³They said to him, "John's disciples often fast and pray, and so do the disciples of the Pharisees, but yours go on eating and drinking."

³⁴Jesus answered, "Can you make the friends of the bridegroom fast while he is with them? ³⁵But the time will come when the bridegroom will be taken from them; in those days they will fast."

³⁶He told them this parable: "No one tears a piece out of a new garment to patch an old one. If they do, they will have torn the new garment, and the patch from the new will not match the old. ³⁷And people do not pour new wine into old wineskins. If they do, the new wine will burst the skins; the wine will run out and the wineskins will be ruined. ³⁸No, new wine must be poured into new wineskins. ³⁹And none of you, after drinking old wine, wants the new, for you say, 'The old is better.'"

Jesus Is Lord of the Sabbath

6 One Sabbath Jesus was going through the grainfields, and his disciples began to pick some heads of grain, rub them in their hands and eat the kernels. ²Some of the Pharisees asked, "Why are you doing what is unlawful on the Sabbath?"

³Jesus answered them, "Have you never read what David did when he and his companions were hungry? ⁴He entered the house of God, and taking the consecrated bread, he ate what is lawful only for priests to eat. And he also gave some to his companions." ⁵Then Jesus said to them, "The Son of Man is Lord of the Sabbath."

⁶On another Sabbath he went into the synagogue and was teaching, and a man was there whose right hand was shriveled. ⁷The Pharisees and the teachers of the law were looking for a reason to accuse Jesus, so they watched him closely to see if he would heal on the Sabbath. ⁸But Jesus knew what they were thinking and said to the man with the shriveled hand, "Get up and stand in front of everyone." So he got up and stood there.

⁹Then Jesus said to them, "I ask you, which is lawful on the Sabbath: to do good or to do evil, to save life or to destroy it?"

¹⁰He looked around at them all, and then said to the man, "Stretch out your hand." He did so, and his hand was completely restored. ¹¹But the Pharisees and the teachers of the law were furious and began to discuss with one another what they might do to Jesus.

The Twelve Apostles

¹²One of those days Jesus went out to a mountainside to pray, and spent the night praying to God. ¹³When morning came, he called his disciples to him and chose twelve of them, whom he also designated apostles: ¹⁴Simon (whom he named Peter), his brother Andrew, James, John, Philip, Bartholomew, ¹⁵Matthew, Thomas, James son of Alphaeus, Simon who was called the Zealot, ¹⁶Judas son of James, and Judas Iscariot, who became a traitor.

Blessings and Woes

¹⁷He went down with them and stood on a level place. A large crowd of his disciples was there and a great number of people from all over Judea, from Jerusalem, and from the coastal region around Tyre and Sidon, ¹⁸who had come to hear him and to be healed of their diseases. Those troubled by evil*a* spirits were cured, ¹⁹and the people all tried to touch him, because power was coming from him and healing them all.

²⁰Looking at his disciples, he said:

"Blessed are you who are poor,
for yours is the kingdom of God.
²¹Blessed are you who hunger now,
for you will be satisfied.

a 18 Greek *unclean*

"IT'S NOT A BIG DEAL."

I've always wanted to be the director of this division, and I've finally gotten my chance. I've been biding my time and waiting six years for this, so I can't mess it up. I know I can do a better job than the previous director, and now is my golden opportunity to prove it during this three-month trial period.

Here's what bothers me, though: I know why I got this chance. It wasn't because my VP (Sam) saw such potential in me. It wasn't because he's been impressed with my numbers or my leadership ability or even my MBA. It's because he is clearly attracted to me, and he also thinks that he can mold me into someone as ruthless as he is. Everyone knows what he's looking for: 1) A pretty blonde who will travel with him. 2) Someone he can clone.

I've seen the pattern before. The other director who reports to Sam is Dana. Dana is fairly nice but openly ambitious. Sam saw that Dana was willing to step on other people to get what she wants, so Sam took her under his wing and coached her on how to lead by intimidation and threat, just like he does. She's the female version of Sam.

So it's very clear what he wants of me. But I also know what else he wants. He makes that very clear with his eyes. This is part of corporate America, though. Every woman in big business faces this. I've seen so many of the top-level women in our company who I know didn't get there because they're brilliant. They're all using their charm to get to the top, and it's clearly working for them. If I can get through the next three months, then the job will be permanently mine.

—Rae

ASIDE FROM THE other moral issues Rae is facing—how to stay sexually and emotionally pure and how to lead a business in a God-honoring way—she is dealing with that age-old lie that Satan tells us (and we tell ourselves) a thousand times in this life: "Everyone else is doing it. You should too."

But people do many things in life even though they know such things are wrong. It's tempting to follow the crowd and join in. We don't feel so bad when we look around and see how many other people are participating.

But God calls us to be holy, set apart. Holiness is not making big headlines these days. But it is as relevant to Christians today as it was when God first called his people "holy" (see Exodus 19:5–6; Leviticus 20:7–8). It means that we should not buy into this world. It means we live for eternity, not for the moment. It means there is a choice we must make, and it will cost us something in order to give Jesus everything.

Does that mean we're going to lose out on the "good life"? That depends on what kind of life we want. The Bible elaborates on the choices some of God's people made:

- When Ruth followed her godly mother-in-law instead of returning to her pagan country, she was blessed.

- When King David lived a holy life, he prospered. When he turned away from God's ways in pursuit of what he thought would bring him happiness, he suffered.

- When Mary agreed to be the mother of Jesus, instead of insisting on following the natural pursuits of a teenager, she was blessed.

We all want to succeed and be happy. We can choose the way of the world to try and achieve that happiness. Or we can choose what Jesus described as the "narrow door" (Luke 13:24). If we do, we never have to worry about our choices working out in the end. God already promises they will.

> "35 percent of Christians said that to get by in life these days, sometimes you have to bend the rules for your own benefit."
> —Barna Research Group (1997)

1479

> ## "KEEP MY DECREES AND FOLLOW THEM. I AM THE LORD, WHO MAKES YOU HOLY."
> LEVITICUS 20:8

SEE ALSO

Ephesians 1:3–4
1 Peter 1:14–16
1 Peter 2:9–10

For more on **Temptation**, check the index.

Blessed are you who weep now,
for you will laugh.
²²Blessed are you when people hate you,
when they exclude you and insult you
and reject your name as evil,
because of the Son of Man.

²³"Rejoice in that day and leap for joy, because great is your reward in heaven. For that is how their ancestors treated the prophets.

²⁴"But woe to you who are rich,
for you have already received your comfort.
²⁵Woe to you who are well fed now,
for you will go hungry.
Woe to you who laugh now,
for you will mourn and weep.
²⁶Woe to you when everyone speaks well of you,
for that is how their ancestors treated the false prophets.

Love for Enemies

²⁷"But to you who are listening I say: Love your enemies, do good to those who hate you, ²⁸bless those who curse you, pray for those who mistreat you. ²⁹If someone slaps you on one cheek, turn the other also. If someone takes your coat, do not withhold your shirt. ³⁰Give to everyone who asks you, and if anyone takes what belongs to you, do not demand it back. ³¹Do to others as you would have them do to you.

³²"If you love those who love you, what credit is that to you? Even sinners love those who love them. ³³And if you do good to those who are good to you, what credit is that to you? Even sinners do that. ³⁴And if you lend to those from whom you expect repayment, what credit is that to you? Even sinners lend to sinners, expecting to be repaid in full. ³⁵But love your enemies, do good to them, and lend to them without expecting to get anything back. Then your reward will be great, and you will be children of the Most High, because he is kind to the ungrateful and wicked. ³⁶Be merciful, just as your Father is merciful.

Judging Others

³⁷"Do not judge, and you will not be judged. Do not condemn, and you will not be condemned. Forgive, and you will be forgiven. ³⁸Give, and it will be given to you. A good measure, pressed down, shaken together and running over, will be poured into your lap. For with the measure you use, it will be measured to you."

³⁹He also told them this parable: "Can the blind lead the blind? Will they not both fall into a pit? ⁴⁰Students are not above their teacher, but all who are fully trained will be like their teacher.

⁴¹"Why do you look at the speck of sawdust in someone else's eye and pay no attention to the plank in your own eye? ⁴²How can you say, 'Friend, let me take the speck out of your eye,' when you yourself fail to see the plank in your own eye? You hypocrite, first take the plank out of your eye, and then you will see clearly to remove the speck from the other person's eye.

1480

at issue: judgmentalism

6:37–42 With a hunk of wood in your own eye, why would you concern yourself with the speck in someone else's eye? Yet we spend an embarrassing amount of time doing just that. In our insecurity, we subconsciously think that if we can find faults in others, then we'll feel better about ourselves. This judgmentalism is the very quality that turns many non-Christians away from the church. We are *all* weak and need a huge dose of grace—which God freely gives us. Be generous in extending that grace to others, and others will be more likely to extend that same generosity to you.

A Tree and Its Fruit

⁴³"No good tree bears bad fruit, nor does a bad tree bear good fruit. ⁴⁴Each tree is recognized by its own fruit. People do not pick figs from thornbushes, or grapes from briers. ⁴⁵Good people bring good things out of the good stored up in their heart, and evil people bring evil things out of the evil stored up in their heart. For out of the overflow of the heart the mouth speaks.

The Wise and Foolish Builders

⁴⁶"Why do you call me, 'Lord, Lord,' and do not do what I say? ⁴⁷As for those who come to me and hear my words and put them into practice, I will show you what they are like. ⁴⁸They are like a man building a house, who dug down deep and laid the foundation on rock. When a flood came, the torrent struck that house but could not shake it, because it was well built. ⁴⁹But those who hear my words and do not put them into practice are like a man who built a house on the ground without a foundation. The moment the torrent struck that house, it collapsed and its destruction was complete."

The Faith of the Centurion

7 When Jesus had finished saying all this to the people who were listening, he entered Capernaum. ²There a centurion's servant, whom his master valued highly, was sick and about to die. ³The centurion heard of Jesus and sent some elders of the Jews to him, asking him to come and heal his servant. ⁴When they came to Jesus, they pleaded earnestly with him, "This man deserves to have you do this, ⁵because he loves our nation and has built our synagogue." ⁶So Jesus went with them.

He was not far from the house when the centurion sent friends to say to him: "Lord, don't trouble yourself, for I do not deserve to have you come under my roof. ⁷That is why I did not even consider myself worthy to come to you. But say the word, and my servant will be healed. ⁸For I myself am a man under authority, with soldiers under me. I tell this one, 'Go,' and he goes; and that one, 'Come,' and he comes. I say to my servant, 'Do this,' and he does it."

⁹When Jesus heard this, he was amazed at him, and turning to the crowd following him, he said, "I tell you, I have not found such great faith even in Israel." ¹⁰Then the men who had been sent returned to the house and found the servant well.

Jesus Raises a Widow's Son

¹¹Soon afterward, Jesus went to a town called Nain, and his disciples and a large crowd went along with him. ¹²As he approached the town gate, a dead person was being carried out—the only son of his mother, and she was a widow. And a large crowd from the town was with her. ¹³When the Lord saw her, his heart went out to her and he said, "Don't cry."

¹⁴Then he went up and touched the bier they were carrying him on, and the bearers stood still. He said, "Young man, I say to you, get up!" ¹⁵The dead man sat up and began to talk, and Jesus gave him back to his mother.

¹⁶They were all filled with awe and praised God. "A great prophet has appeared among us," they said. "God has come to help his people." ¹⁷This news about Jesus spread throughout Judea and the surrounding country.

Jesus and John the Baptist

¹⁸John's disciples told him about all these things. Calling two of them, ¹⁹he sent them to the Lord to ask, "Are you the one who was to come, or should we expect someone else?"

²⁰When the men came to Jesus, they said, "John the Baptist sent us to you to ask, 'Are you the one who was to come, or should we expect someone else?'"

²¹At that very time Jesus cured many who had diseases, sicknesses and evil spirits, and gave sight to many who were blind. ²²So he replied to the messengers, "Go back and report to John what you have seen and heard: The blind receive sight, the lame walk, those who have leprosy ᵃ are cleansed, the deaf hear, the dead are raised, and the good news is proclaimed to the poor. ²³Blessed is anyone who does not stumble on account of me."

ᵃ 22 The Greek word traditionally translated *leprosy* was used for various diseases affecting the skin.

²⁴ After John's messengers left, Jesus began to speak to the crowd about John: "What did you go out into the wilderness to see? A reed swayed by the wind? ²⁵ If not, what did you go out to see? A man dressed in fine clothes? No, those who wear expensive clothes and indulge in luxury are in palaces. ²⁶ But what did you go out to see? A prophet? Yes, I tell you, and more than a prophet. ²⁷ This is the one about whom it is written:

> "'I will send my messenger ahead of you,
>   who will prepare your way before you.'^a

²⁸ I tell you, among those born of women there is no one greater than John; yet the one who is least in the kingdom of God is greater than he."

²⁹ (All the people, even the tax collectors, when they heard Jesus' words, acknowledged that God's way was right, because they had been baptized by John. ³⁰ But the Pharisees and the experts in the law rejected God's purpose for themselves, because they had not been baptized by John.)

³¹ Jesus went on to say, "To what, then, can I compare the people of this generation? What are they like? ³² They are like children sitting in the marketplace and calling out to each other:

> "'We played the pipe for you,
>   and you did not dance;
> we sang a dirge,
>   and you did not cry.'

³³ For John the Baptist came neither eating bread nor drinking wine, and you say, 'He has a demon.' ³⁴ The Son of Man came eating and drinking, and you say, 'Here is a glutton and a drunkard, a friend of tax collectors and sinners.' ³⁵ But wisdom is proved right by all her children."

Jesus Anointed by a Sinful Woman

³⁶ When one of the Pharisees invited Jesus to have dinner with him, he went to the Pharisee's house and reclined at the table. ³⁷ A woman in that town who lived a sinful life learned that Jesus was eating at the Pharisee's house, so she came there with an alabaster jar of perfume. ³⁸ As she stood behind him at his feet weeping, she began to wet his feet with her tears. Then she wiped them with her hair, kissed them and poured perfume on them.

³⁹ When the Pharisee who had invited him saw this, he said to himself, "If this man were a prophet, he would know who is touching him and what kind of woman she is—that she is a sinner."

⁴⁰ Jesus answered him, "Simon, I have something to tell you."

"Tell me, teacher," he said.

⁴¹ "Two people owed money to a certain moneylender. One owed him five hundred denarii,^b and the other fifty. ⁴² Neither of them had the money to pay him back, so he forgave the debts of both. Now which of them will love him more?"

⁴³ Simon replied, "I suppose the one who had the bigger debt forgiven."

"You have judged correctly," Jesus said.

⁴⁴ Then he turned toward the woman and said to Simon,

at issue: forgiveness by God

7:36–50 Don't miss the profoundness of Jesus' teaching in this passage. Those of us who consider ourselves "minor sinners" will never appreciate God's forgiveness. Our love for God will be shallow and choked, like that of the Pharisees. In contrast, those of us who understand how absurd and undeserved God's forgiveness is will love him deeply and passionately and gratefully, like the woman in this story. Our love for God is in direct proportion to our gratitude for his forgiveness and our understanding of how much we need it. Who are you in this story—the Pharisee or the woman?

---

^a 27 Mal. 3:1   ^b 41 A denarius was the daily wage of a day laborer (see Matt. 20:2).

"Do you see this woman? I came into your house. You did not give me any water for my feet, but she wet my feet with her tears and wiped them with her hair. ⁴⁵You did not give me a kiss, but this woman, from the time I entered, has not stopped kissing my feet. ⁴⁶You did not put oil on my head, but she has poured perfume on my feet. ⁴⁷Therefore, I tell you, her many sins have been forgiven—as her great love has shown. But whoever has been forgiven little loves little."

⁴⁸Then Jesus said to her, "Your sins are forgiven."

⁴⁹The other guests began to say among themselves, "Who is this who even forgives sins?"

⁵⁰Jesus said to the woman, "Your faith has saved you; go in peace."

The Parable of the Sower

8 After this, Jesus traveled about from one town and village to another, proclaiming the good news of the kingdom of God. The Twelve were with him, ²and also some women who had been cured of evil spirits and diseases: Mary (called Magdalene) from whom seven demons had come out; ³Joanna the wife of Chuza, the manager of Herod's household; Susanna; and many others. These women were helping to support them out of their own means.

⁴While a large crowd was gathering and people were coming to Jesus from town after town, he told this parable: ⁵"A farmer went out to sow his seed. As he was scattering the seed, some fell along the path; it was trampled on, and the birds ate it up. ⁶Some fell on rock, and when it came up, the plants withered because they had no moisture. ⁷Other seed fell among thorns, which grew up with it and choked the plants. ⁸Still other seed fell on good soil. It came up and yielded a crop, a hundred times more than was sown."

When he said this, he called out, "Whoever has ears to hear, let them hear."

⁹His disciples asked him what this parable meant. ¹⁰He said, "The knowledge of the secrets of the kingdom of God has been given to you, but to others I speak in parables, so that,

> "'though seeing, they may not see;
> though hearing, they may not
> understand.'ᵃ

¹¹"This is the meaning of the parable: The seed is the word of God. ¹²Those along the path are the ones who hear, and then the devil comes and takes away the word from their hearts, so that they may not believe and be saved. ¹³Those on the rock are the ones who receive the word with joy when they hear it, but they have no root. They believe for a while, but in the time of testing they fall away. ¹⁴The seed that fell among thorns stands for those who hear, but as they go on their way they are choked by life's worries, riches and pleasures, and they do not mature. ¹⁵But the seed on good soil stands for those with a noble and good heart, who hear the word, retain it, and by persevering produce a crop.

A Lamp on a Stand

¹⁶"No one lights a lamp and hides it in a clay jar or puts it under a bed. Instead, they put it on a stand, so that those who come in can see the light. ¹⁷For there is nothing hidden that will not be disclosed, and nothing concealed that will not be known or brought out into the open. ¹⁸Therefore consider carefully how you listen. Those who have will be given more; as for those who do not have, even what they think they have will be taken from them."

at issue: responsibility

8:4–15 As women we often feel responsible for those around us—our friends, co-workers, parents and especially our children. Yet Jesus reminds us that our job is to plant the seeds in other's lives; we cannot take responsibility for how others respond to the gospel message. It's hard to release that sense of control, especially with our children. However, it's not your job to control your children's (or friends', or co-workers') choices. However, it *is* your job to be a farmer in their lives—to sow and nurture the seed of God's truth in their hearts. Then trust God as you wait to see what kind of crop he grows.

ᵃ *10* Isaiah 6:9

Jesus' Mother and Brothers

[19]Now Jesus' mother and brothers came to see him, but they were not able to get near him because of the crowd. [20]Someone told him, "Your mother and brothers are standing outside, wanting to see you."

[21]He replied, "My mother and brothers are those who hear God's word and put it into practice."

Jesus Calms the Storm

[22]One day Jesus said to his disciples, "Let us go over to the other side of the lake." So they got into a boat and set out. [23]As they sailed, he fell asleep. A squall came down on the lake, so that the boat was being swamped, and they were in great danger.

[24]The disciples went and woke him, saying, "Master, Master, we're going to drown!"

He got up and rebuked the wind and the raging waters; the storm subsided, and all was calm. [25]"Where is your faith?" he asked his disciples.

In fear and amazement they asked one another, "Who is this? He commands even the winds and the water, and they obey him."

Jesus Restores a Demon-Possessed Man

[26]They sailed to the region of the Gerasenes,[a] which is across the lake from Galilee. [27]When Jesus stepped ashore, he was met by a demon-possessed man from the town. For a long time this man had not worn clothes or lived in a house, but had lived in the tombs. [28]When he saw Jesus, he cried out and fell at his feet, shouting at the top of his voice, "What do you want with me, Jesus, Son of the Most High God? I beg you, don't torture me!" [29]For Jesus had commanded the evil[b] spirit to come out of the man. Many times it had seized him, and though he was chained hand and foot and kept under guard, he had broken his chains and had been driven by the demon into solitary places.

[30]Jesus asked him, "What is your name?"

"Legion," he replied, because many demons had gone into him. [31]And they begged Jesus repeatedly not to order them to go into the Abyss.

[32]A large herd of pigs was feeding there on the hillside. The demons begged Jesus to let them go into the pigs, and he gave them permission. [33]When the demons came out of the man, they went into pigs, and the herd rushed down the steep bank into the lake and was drowned.

[34]When those tending the pigs saw what had happened, they ran off and reported this in the town and countryside, [35]and the people went out to see what had happened. When they came to Jesus, they found the man from whom the demons had gone out, sitting at Jesus' feet, dressed and in his right mind; and they were afraid. [36]Those who had seen it told the people how the demon-possessed man had been cured. [37]Then all the people of the region of the Gerasenes asked Jesus to leave them, because they were overcome with fear. So he got into the boat and left.

[38]The man from whom the demons had gone out begged to go with him, but Jesus sent him away, saying, [39]"Return home and tell how much God has done for you." So the man went away and told all over town how much Jesus had done for him.

Jesus Raises a Dead Girl and Heals a Sick Woman

[40]Now when Jesus returned, a crowd welcomed him, for they were all expecting him. [41]Then a man named Jairus, a synagogue leader, came and fell at Jesus' feet, pleading with him to come to his house [42]because his only daughter, a girl of about twelve, was dying.

As Jesus was on his way, the crowds almost crushed him. [43]And a woman was there who had been subject to bleeding for twelve years,[c] but no one could heal her. [44]She came up behind him and touched the edge of his cloak, and immediately her bleeding stopped.

[45]"Who touched me?" Jesus asked.

When they all denied it, Peter said, "Master, the people are crowding and pressing against you."

[46]But Jesus said, "Someone touched me; I know that power has gone out from me."

[47]Then the woman, seeing that she could not go unnoticed, came trembling and fell at his feet. In the

---

a 26 Some manuscripts *Gadarenes*; other manuscripts *Gergesenes*; also in verse 37   *b 29* Greek *unclean*   *c 43* Many manuscripts *years, and she had spent all she had on doctors* presence of all the people, she told why she had touched him and how she had been instantly healed. [48]Then he said to her, "Daughter, your faith has healed you. Go in peace."

[49]While Jesus was still speaking, someone came from the house of Jairus, the synagogue leader. "Your daughter is dead," he said. "Don't bother the teacher anymore."

[50]Hearing this, Jesus said to Jairus, "Don't be afraid; just believe, and she will be healed."

[51]When he arrived at the house of Jairus, he did not let anyone go in with him except Peter, John and James, and the child's father and mother. [52]Meanwhile, all the people were wailing and mourning for her. "Stop wailing," Jesus said. "She is not dead but asleep."

[53]They laughed at him, knowing that she was dead. [54]But he took her by the hand and said, "My child, get up!" [55]Her spirit returned, and at once she stood up. Then Jesus told them to give her something to eat. [56]Her parents were astonished, but he ordered them not to tell anyone what had happened.

Jesus Sends Out the Twelve

9 When Jesus had called the Twelve together, he gave them power and authority to drive out all demons and to cure diseases, [2]and he sent them out to proclaim the kingdom of God and to heal the sick. [3]He told them: "Take nothing for the journey—no staff, no bag, no bread, no money, no extra shirt. [4]Whatever house you enter, stay there until you leave that town. [5]If people do not welcome you, shake the dust off your feet when you leave their town, as a testimony against them." [6]So they set out and went from village to village, proclaiming the good news and healing people everywhere.

[7]Now Herod the tetrarch heard about all that was going on. And he was perplexed because some were saying that John had been raised from the dead, [8]others that Elijah had appeared, and still others that one of the prophets of long ago had come back to life. [9]But Herod said, "I beheaded John. Who, then, is this I hear such things about?" And he tried to see him.

1485

Jesus Feeds the Five Thousand

[10]When the apostles returned, they reported to Jesus what they had done. Then he took them with him and they withdrew by themselves to a town called Bethsaida, [11]but the crowds learned about it and followed him. He welcomed them and spoke to them about the kingdom of God, and healed those who needed healing.

[12]Late in the afternoon the Twelve came to him and said, "Send the crowd away so they can go to the surrounding villages and countryside and find food and lodging, because we are in a remote place here."

[13]He replied, "You give them something to eat."

They answered, "We have only five loaves of bread and two fish—unless we go and buy food for all this crowd." [14](About five thousand men were there.)

But he said to his disciples, "Have them sit down in groups of about fifty each." [15]The disciples did so, and everyone sat down. [16]Taking the five loaves and the two fish and looking up to heaven, he gave thanks and broke them. Then he gave them to the disciples to set before the people. [17]They all ate and were satisfied, and the disciples picked up twelve basketfuls of broken pieces that were left over.

Peter Declares That Jesus Is the Messiah

[18]Once when Jesus was praying in private and his disciples were with him, he asked them, "Who do the crowds say I am?"

[19]They replied, "Some say John the Baptist; others say Elijah; and still others, that one of the prophets of long ago has come back to life."

[20]"But what about you?" he asked. "Who do you say I am?"

Peter answered, "God's Messiah."

Jesus Predicts His Death

[21]Jesus strictly warned them not to tell this to anyone. [22]And he said, "The Son of Man must suffer many things and be rejected by the elders, the chief priests and the teachers of the law, and he must be killed and on the third day be raised to life."

[23]Then he said to them all: "Whoever wants to be my disciple must deny themselves and take up their cross daily and follow me. [24]For whoever wants to save their life will lose it, but whoever loses their life

for me will save it. ²⁵What good is it for you to gain the whole world, and yet lose or forfeit your very self? ²⁶If any of you are ashamed of me and my words, the Son of Man will be ashamed of you when he comes in his glory and in the glory of the Father and of the holy angels.

²⁷"Truly I tell you, some who are standing here will not taste death before they see the kingdom of God."

The Transfiguration

²⁸About eight days after Jesus said this, he took Peter, John and James with him and went up onto a mountain to pray. ²⁹As he was praying, the appearance of his face changed, and his clothes became as bright as a flash of lightning. ³⁰Two men, Moses and Elijah, ³¹appeared in glorious splendor, talking with Jesus. They spoke about his departure,ᵃ which he was about to bring to fulfillment at Jerusalem. ³²Peter and his companions were very sleepy, but when they became fully awake, they saw his glory and the two men standing with him. ³³As the men were leaving Jesus, Peter said to him, "Master, it is good for us to be here. Let us put up three shelters—one for you, one for Moses and one for Elijah." (He did not know what he was saying.)

³⁴While he was speaking, a cloud appeared and covered them, and they were afraid as they entered the cloud. ³⁵A voice came from the cloud, saying, "This is my Son, whom I have chosen; listen to him." ³⁶When the voice had spoken, they found that Jesus was alone. The disciples kept this to themselves and did not tell anyone at that time what they had seen.

Jesus Heals a Demon-Possessed Boy

³⁷The next day, when they came down from the mountain, a large crowd met him. ³⁸A man in the crowd called out, "Teacher, I beg you to look at my son, for he is my only child. ³⁹A spirit seizes him and he suddenly screams; it throws him into convulsions so that he foams at the mouth. It scarcely ever leaves him and is destroying him. ⁴⁰I begged your disciples to drive it out, but they could not."

⁴¹"You unbelieving and perverse generation," Jesus replied, "how long shall I stay with you and put up with you? Bring your son here."

⁴²Even while the boy was coming, the demon threw him to the ground in a convulsion. But Jesus rebuked the evilᵇ spirit, healed the boy and gave him back to his father. ⁴³And they were all amazed at the greatness of God.

Jesus Predicts His Death a Second Time

While everyone was marveling at all that Jesus did, he said to his disciples, ⁴⁴"Listen carefully to what I am about to tell you: The Son of Man is going to be delivered over to human hands." ⁴⁵But they did not understand what this meant. It was hidden from them, so that they did not grasp it, and they were afraid to ask him about it.

⁴⁶An argument started among the disciples as to which of them would be the greatest. ⁴⁷Jesus, knowing their thoughts, took a little child and had him stand beside him. ⁴⁸Then he said to them, "Whoever welcomes this little child in my name welcomes me; and whoever welcomes me welcomes the one who sent me. For whoever is least among you all is the greatest."

⁴⁹"Master," said John, "we saw someone driving out demons in your name and we tried to stop him, because he is not one of us."

⁵⁰"Do not stop him," Jesus said, "for whoever is not against you is for you."

conversations

greed «» 9:23–27

1» How does our society promote greedy attitudes?

2» What things do you find the most difficult to deny yourself?

3» Today, what must you do to "take up your cross"?

For more on **greed**, check the index.
For the next Conversations, go to p. 1488.

1486

ᵃ 31 Greek *exodus*   ᵇ 42 Greek *unclean*

Samaritan Opposition

⁵¹As the time approached for him to be taken up to heaven, Jesus resolutely set out for Jerusalem. ⁵²And he sent messengers on ahead, who went into a Samaritan village to get things ready for him; ⁵³but the people there did not welcome him, because he was heading for Jerusalem. ⁵⁴When the disciples James and John saw this, they asked, "Lord, do you want us to call fire down from heaven to destroy them*ᵃ*?" ⁵⁵But Jesus turned and rebuked them. ⁵⁶Then he and his disciples went to another village.

The Cost of Following Jesus

⁵⁷As they were walking along the road, a man said to him, "I will follow you wherever you go."

⁵⁸Jesus replied, "Foxes have holes and birds have nests, but the Son of Man has no place to lay his head."

⁵⁹He said to another man, "Follow me."

But he replied, "Lord, first let me go and bury my father."

⁶⁰Jesus said to him, "Let the dead bury their own dead, but you go and proclaim the kingdom of God."

⁶¹Still another said, "I will follow you, Lord; but first let me go back and say good-by to my family."

⁶²Jesus replied, "No one who puts a hand to the plow and looks back is fit for service in the kingdom of God."

Jesus Sends Out the Seventy-Two

10 After this the Lord appointed seventy-two*ᵇ* others and sent them two by two ahead of him to every town and place where he was about to go. ²He told them, "The harvest is plentiful, but the workers are few. Ask the Lord of the harvest, therefore, to send out workers into his harvest field. ³Go! I am sending you out like lambs among wolves. ⁴Do not take a purse or bag or sandals; and do not greet anyone on the road.

⁵"When you enter a house, first say, 'Peace to this house.' ⁶If the head of the house loves peace, your peace will rest on that house; if not, it will return to you. ⁷Stay there, eating and drinking whatever they give you, for workers deserve their wages. Do not move around from house to house.

⁸"When you enter a town and are welcomed, eat what is set before you. ⁹Heal the sick who are there and tell them, 'The kingdom of God has come near to you.' ¹⁰But when you enter a town and are not welcomed, go into its streets and say, ¹¹'Even the dust of your town we wipe from our feet as a warning to you. Yet be sure of this: The kingdom of God has come near.' ¹²I tell you, it will be more bearable on that day for Sodom than for that town.

¹³"Woe to you, Chorazin! Woe to you, Bethsaida! For if the miracles that were performed in you had been performed in Tyre and Sidon, they would have repented long ago, sitting in sackcloth and ashes. ¹⁴But it will be more bearable for Tyre and Sidon at the judgment than for you. ¹⁵And you, Capernaum, will you be lifted up to the skies? No, you will go down to the depths.*ᶜ*

¹⁶"Whoever listens to you listens to me; whoever rejects you rejects me; but whoever rejects me rejects him who sent me."

¹⁷The seventy-two returned with joy and said, "Lord, even the demons submit to us in your name."

¹⁸He replied, "I saw Satan fall like lightning from heaven. ¹⁹I have given you authority to trample on snakes and scorpions and to overcome all the power of the enemy; nothing will harm you. ²⁰However, do not rejoice that the spirits submit to you, but rejoice that your names are written in heaven."

²¹At that time Jesus, full of joy through the Holy Spirit, said, "I praise you, Father, Lord of heaven and earth, because you have hidden these things from the wise and learned, and revealed them to little children. Yes, Father, for this was your good pleasure.

²²"All things have been committed to me by my Father. No one knows who the Son is except the Father, and no one knows who the Father is except the Son and those to whom the Son chooses to reveal him."

²³Then he turned to his disciples and said privately, "Blessed are the eyes that see what you see. ²⁴For I tell you that many prophets and kings wanted to see what you see but did not see it, and to hear what you hear but did not hear it."

ᵃ 54 Some manuscripts *them, just as Elijah did*   *ᵇ 1* Some manuscripts *seventy; also in verse 17*   *ᶜ 15* Greek *to Hades*

The Parable of the Good Samaritan

²⁵On one occasion an expert in the law stood up to test Jesus. "Teacher," he asked, "what must I do to inherit eternal life?"

²⁶"What is written in the Law?" he replied. "How do you read it?"

²⁷He answered, "'Love the Lord your God with all your heart and with all your soul and with all your strength and with all your mind'ᵃ; and, 'Love your neighbor as yourself.'ᵇ"

²⁸"You have answered correctly," Jesus replied. "Do this and you will live."

²⁹But he wanted to justify himself, so he asked Jesus, "And who is my neighbor?"

³⁰In reply Jesus said: "A man was going down from Jerusalem to Jericho, when he fell into the hands of robbers. They stripped him of his clothes, beat him and went away, leaving him half dead. ³¹A priest happened to be going down the same road, and when he saw the man, he passed by on the other side. ³²So too, a Levite, when he came to the place and saw him, passed by on the other side. ³³But a Samaritan, as he traveled, came where the man was; and when he saw him, he took pity on him. ³⁴He went to him and bandaged his wounds, pouring on oil and wine. Then he put the man on his own donkey, brought him to an inn and took care of him. ³⁵The next day he took out two denariiᶜ and gave them to the innkeeper. 'Look after him,' he said, 'and when I return, I will reimburse you for any extra expense you may have.'

³⁶"Which of these three do you think was a neighbor to the man who fell into the hands of robbers?"

³⁷The expert in the law replied, "The one who had mercy on him."

Jesus told him, "Go and do likewise."

conversations

racism «» 10:29–37

1» How would you answer the expert's question, "Who is my neighbor?"

2» Do you have any "neighbors" of a different race whom you look down on or feel reluctant to serve? Why?

3» Like the Samaritan, how can you take an active position against racism?

For more on racism, check the index.
For the next Conversations, go to p. 1496.

At the Home of Martha and Mary

³⁸As Jesus and his disciples were on their way, he came to a village where a woman named Martha opened her home to him. ³⁹She had a sister called Mary, who sat at the Lord's feet listening to what he said. ⁴⁰But Martha was distracted by all the preparations that had to be made. She came to him and asked, "Lord, don't you care that my sister has left me to do the work by myself? Tell her to help me!"

⁴¹"Martha, Martha," the Lord answered, "you are worried and upset about many things, ⁴²but few things are needed—or indeed only one.ᵈ Mary has chosen what is better, and it will not be taken away from her."

Jesus' Teaching on Prayer

11 One day Jesus was praying in a certain place. When he finished, one of his disciples said to him, "Lord, teach us to pray, just as John taught his disciples."

²He said to them, "When you pray, say:

"'Father,ᵉ
hallowed be your name,
    your kingdom come.ᶠ
³Give us each day our daily bread.
⁴Forgive us our sins,
    for we also forgive everyone who sins against us.ᵍ
    And lead us not into temptation.ʰ'"

ᵃ 27 Deut. 6:5   ᵇ 27 Lev. 19:18   ᶜ 35 A denarius was the daily wage of a day laborer (see Matt. 20:2).   ᵈ 42 Some manuscripts but only one thing is needed
ᵉ 2 Some manuscripts Our Father in heaven   ᶠ 2 Some manuscripts come. May your will be done on earth as it is in heaven.   ᵍ 4 Greek everyone who is indebted to us   ʰ 4 Some manuscripts temptation, but deliver us from the evil one

⁵Then Jesus said to them, "Suppose you have a friend, and you go to him at midnight and say, 'Friend, lend me three loaves of bread; ⁶a friend of mine on a journey has come to me, and I have nothing to set before him.' ⁷And suppose the one inside answers, 'Don't bother me. The door is already locked, and my children and I are in bed. I can't get up and give you anything.' ⁸I tell you, even though he will not get up and give you the bread because of friendship, yet because of your shameless audacity*ᵃ* he will surely get up and give you as much as you need.

⁹"So I say to you: Ask and it will be given to you; seek and you will find; knock and the door will be opened to you. ¹⁰For everyone who asks receives; those who seek find; and to those who knock, the door will be opened.

¹¹"Which of you fathers, if your son asks for*ᵇ* a fish, will give him a snake instead? ¹²Or if he asks for an egg, will give him a scorpion? ¹³If you then, though you are evil, know how to give good gifts to your children, how much more will your Father in heaven give the Holy Spirit to those who ask him!"

Jesus and Beelzebul

¹⁴Jesus was driving out a demon that was mute. When the demon left, the man who had been mute spoke, and the crowd was amazed. ¹⁵But some of them said, "By Beelzebul, the prince of demons, he is driving out demons." ¹⁶Others tested him by asking for a sign from heaven.

¹⁷Jesus knew their thoughts and said to them: "Any kingdom divided against itself will be ruined, and a house divided against itself will fall. ¹⁸If Satan is divided against himself, how can his kingdom stand? I say this because you claim that I drive out demons by Beelzebul. ¹⁹Now if I drive out demons by Beelzebul, by whom do your followers drive them out? So then, they will be your judges. ²⁰But if I drive out demons by the finger of God, then the kingdom of God has come upon you.

²¹"When a strong man, fully armed, guards his own house, his possessions are safe. ²²But when someone stronger attacks and overpowers him, he takes away the armor in which the man trusted and divides up his plunder.

²³"Whoever is not with me is against me, and whoever does not gather with me scatters.

²⁴"When an evil*ᶜ* spirit comes out of anyone, it goes through arid places seeking rest and does not find it. Then it says, 'I will return to the house I left.' ²⁵When it arrives, it finds the house swept clean and put in order. ²⁶Then it goes and takes seven other spirits more wicked than itself, and they go in and live there. And the final condition of that person is worse than the first."

²⁷As Jesus was saying these things, a woman in the crowd called out, "Blessed is the mother who gave you birth and nursed you."

²⁸He replied, "Blessed rather are those who hear the word of God and obey it."

The Sign of Jonah

²⁹As the crowds increased, Jesus said, "This is a wicked generation. It asks for a sign, but none will be given it except the sign of Jonah. ³⁰For as Jonah was a sign to the Ninevites, so also will the Son of Man be to this generation. ³¹The Queen of the South will rise at the judgment with the people of this generation and condemn them, for she came from the ends of the earth to listen to Solomon's wisdom; and now one*ᵈ* greater than Solomon is here. ³²The people of Nineveh will stand up at the judgment with this generation and condemn it, for they repented at the preaching of Jonah; and now one greater than Jonah is here.

---

atissue:prayer

11:1–13 Prayer isn't like giving "the Santa Claus in the sky" a list of what you want because you've been good. And it's not rubbing the bottle, forcing the genie to grant you three wishes because he's obligated. Instead, prayer is the humble recognition of your own lack and God's great ability to supply. It's the respectful, persistent pouring out of your heart's desires to the only one who can change or fulfill them. It's your expression of your longing to commune with God. Perhaps your first prayer request needs to be, "Lord, teach me to pray."

1489

The Lamp of the Body

[33] "None of you lights a lamp and puts it in a place where it will be hidden, or under a bowl. Instead you put it on its stand, so that those who come in may see the light. [34] Your eye is the lamp of your body. When your eyes are healthy,[a] your whole body also is full of light. But when they are unhealthy,[b] your body also is full of darkness. [35] See to it, then, that the light within you is not darkness. [36] Therefore, if your whole body is full of light, and no part of it dark, it will be just as full of light as when a lamp shines its light on you."

Woes on the Pharisees and the Experts in the Law

[37] When Jesus had finished speaking, a Pharisee invited him to eat with him; so he went in and reclined at the table. [38] But the Pharisee was surprised when he noticed that Jesus did not first wash before the meal.

[39] Then the Lord said to him, "Now then, you Pharisees clean the outside of the cup and dish, but inside you are full of greed and wickedness. [40] You foolish people! Did not the one who made the outside make the inside also? [41] But now as for what is inside you—be generous to the poor, and everything will be clean for you.

[42] "Woe to you Pharisees, because you give God a tenth of your mint, rue and all other kinds of garden herbs, but you neglect justice and the love of God. You should have practiced the latter without leaving the former undone.

[43] "Woe to you Pharisees, because you love the most important seats in the synagogues and respectful greetings in the marketplaces.

[44] "Woe to you, because you are like unmarked graves, which people walk over without knowing it."

[45] One of the experts in the law answered him, "Teacher, when you say these things, you insult us also."

[46] Jesus replied, "And you experts in the law, woe to you, because you load people down with burdens they can hardly carry, and you yourselves will not lift one finger to help them.

[47] "Woe to you, because you build tombs for the prophets, and it was your ancestors who killed them. [48] So you testify that you approve of what your ancestors did; they killed the prophets, and you build their tombs. [49] Because of this, God in his wisdom said, 'I will send them prophets and apostles, some of whom they will kill and others they will persecute.' [50] Therefore this generation will be held responsible for the blood of all the prophets that has been shed since the beginning of the world, [51] from the blood of Abel to the blood of Zechariah, who was killed between the altar and the sanctuary. Yes, I tell you, this generation will be held responsible for it all.

[52] "Woe to you experts in the law, because you have taken away the key to knowledge. You yourselves have not entered, and you have hindered those who were entering."

[53] When Jesus went outside, the Pharisees and the teachers of the law began to oppose him fiercely and to besiege him with questions, [54] waiting to catch him in something he might say.

Warnings and Encouragements

12 Meanwhile, when a crowd of many thousands had gathered, so that they were trampling on one another, Jesus began to speak first to his disciples, saying: "Be[c] on your guard against the yeast of the Pharisees, which is hypocrisy. [2] There is nothing concealed that will not be disclosed, or hidden that will not be made known. [3] What you have said in the dark will be heard in the daylight, and what you have whispered in the ear in the inner rooms will be proclaimed from the roofs.

[4] "I tell you, my friends, do not be afraid of those who kill the body and after that can do no more. [5] But I will show you whom you should fear: Fear him who, after your body has been killed, has authority to throw you into hell. Yes, I tell you, fear him. [6] Are not five sparrows sold for two pennies? Yet not one of them is forgotten by God. [7] Indeed, the very hairs of your head are all numbered. Don't be afraid; you are worth more than many sparrows.

[8] "I tell you, whoever publicly acknowledges me, the Son of Man will also acknowledge before the angels of God. [9] But whoever publicly disowns me will be disowned before the angels of God. [10] And

---

everyone who speaks a word against the Son of Man will be forgiven, but anyone who blasphemes against the Holy Spirit will not be forgiven.

[11]"When you are brought before synagogues, rulers and authorities, do not worry about how you will defend yourselves or what you will say, [12]for the Holy Spirit will teach you at that time what you should say."

The Parable of the Rich Fool

[13]Someone in the crowd said to him, "Teacher, tell my brother to divide the inheritance with me."

[14]Jesus replied, "Man, who appointed me a judge or an arbiter between you?" [15]Then he said to them, "Watch out! Be on your guard against all kinds of greed; life does not consist in an abundance of possessions."

[16]And he told them this parable: "The ground of a certain rich man yielded an abundant harvest. [17]He thought to himself, 'What shall I do? I have no place to store my crops.'

[18]"Then he said, 'This is what I'll do. I will tear down my barns and build bigger ones, and there I will store my surplus grain. [19]And I'll say to myself, "You have plenty of grain laid up for many years. Take life easy; eat, drink and be merry."'

[20]"But God said to him, 'You fool! This very night your life will be demanded from you. Then who will get what you have prepared for yourself?'

[21]"This is how it will be with those who store up things for themselves but are not rich toward God."

Do Not Worry

[22]Then Jesus said to his disciples: "Therefore I tell you, do not worry about your life, what you will eat; or about your body, what you will wear. [23]Life is more than food, and the body more than clothes. [24]Consider the ravens: They do not sow or reap, they have no storeroom or barn; yet God feeds them. And how much more valuable you are than birds! [25]Who of you by worrying can add a single hour to your life[a]? [26]Since you cannot do this very little thing, why do you worry about the rest?

[27]"Consider how the wild flowers grow. They do not labor or spin. Yet I tell you, not even Solomon in all his splendor was dressed like one of these. [28]If that is how God clothes the grass of the field, which is here today, and tomorrow is thrown into the fire, how much more will he clothe you—you of little faith! [29]And do not set your heart on what you will eat or drink; do not worry about it. [30]For the pagan world runs after all such things, and your Father knows that you need them. [31]But seek his kingdom, and these things will be given to you as well.

[32]"Do not be afraid, little flock, for your Father has been pleased to give you the kingdom. [33]Sell your possessions and give to the poor. Provide purses for yourselves that will not wear out, a treasure in heaven that will never fail, where no thief comes near and no moth destroys. [34]For where your treasure is, there your heart will be also.

atissue:fashion

12:27–34 *Clothes*—You shop for them, try to lose weight so you'll fit into them, worry about how you look in them, think about wearing them for a certain event. How much of your time, money and mental energy do you put into your wardrobe? While clothing is necessary, it's relatively unimportant in light of eternity. Your clothes will wear out, and you certainly can't take them with you. So why invest so much in them? Tenderly, Jesus tells us, his "little flock," to provide ourselves with timeless, spiritual treasures that will never go out of style.

Watchfulness

[35]"Be dressed ready for service and keep your lamps burning, [36]like servants waiting for their master to return from a wedding banquet, so that when he comes and knocks they can immediately open the door for him. [37]It will be good for those servants whose master finds them watching when he comes.

---

[a] 25 Or *single cubit to your height*

myth# 85 *"MY COMPANY WILL ALWAYS TAKE CARE OF ME."*

I was so in love.

With my job, that is. It was everything I'd ever wanted. The leadership was superb—personally and professionally. They were moving in a direction that I wholeheartedly agreed with, and I knew I could play a key role in our future. They assured me they would take care of me, especially if I would invest here long-term. And I was more than ready to do that. I was fulfilled, and for the first time in my life, I felt as though I was on my way to having a career, not just a job.

I gave it my all. I worked more hours than I was expected to. I volunteered to help with extra projects and mentored my new co-workers. I was just happy to work for such an amazing company. Not everyone loves their job, so I knew I had it good.

Recently, however, we were bought out. The first blow was losing that family feel. My boss was "downsized," and my new boss is remarkable—in a bad way, as in, remarkably lacking leadership skills. Now I dread going to work, and the rumor is that more job cuts are coming. I'm walking around with a pit in my stomach, but I don't know what to do. I've spent 11 years of my life here—how could I throw that away? At the same time, I don't want to be unemployed. I want my old job back. I really believed my company would always take care of me. What happened?

—Marguerite

HAVE YOU LEARNED

the lesson yet? Everyone has to face it eventually: We can never completely put our trust in anything here on earth. Every job has its share of problems, even religious or people-helping organizations. While it would be nice to think that a company will always take care of us, especially if we work hard, it just isn't true. We can be laid off, demoted, unappreciated, underpaid or forgotten as we get older. Consider Joseph, for example. Remember all that Joseph did for the nation of Egypt, how he led them through a severe famine and saved thousands of lives? "Then a new king, to whom Joseph meant nothing, came to power in Egypt" (Exodus 1:8), and Joseph's faithful service was forgotten and his people enslaved.

Only God can truly take care of us; he alone promises to faithfully care for us, and he delights in doing so (see Luke 12:22–31). When times at work get hard and you're not sure what to do, keep this in mind:

- You may feel betrayed when you've done great work and aren't respected or recognized. It's a natural reaction in hard times. Remember that God will never betray you.

- You are not powerless. Be proactive. Prepare yourself financially and emotionally if your job is insecure. Plan your next moves.

- Ask friends and family to listen, to support you, to give you a reality check when you need it and to pray for you.

- Take care of yourself in a healthy way—de-stress by praying, exercising, talking to others or taking up a hobby. If your job is terrible, try not to appropriate that feeling to your whole life.

- Make sure your identity isn't tied up in what you do. If it is, then if you feel you've failed at work, you will feel like you've failed as a person—and that's not true.

- Above all, trust that God will not fail you.

> "You aren't the only unemployed person around. Don't get down on yourself . . . Be able to share with God and other believers your feelings of loss, anger, depression and stress."
>
> —Larry Burkett

1493

> "THAT IS WHY WE LABOR AND STRIVE, BECAUSE WE HAVE PUT OUR HOPE IN THE LIVING GOD, WHO IS THE SAVIOR OF ALL PEOPLE, AND ESPECIALLY OF THOSE WHO BELIEVE."
>
> 1 TIMOTHY 4:10

SEE ALSO

Psalm 9:10
Psalm 138:8
Ephesians 6:5–9

For more on **Career** and **Disappointment**, check the index.

Truly I tell you, he will dress himself to serve, will have them recline at the table and will come and wait on them. ³⁸It will be good for those servants whose master finds them ready, even if he comes in the middle of the night or toward daybreak. ³⁹But understand this: If the owner of the house had known at what hour the thief was coming, he would not have let his house be broken into. ⁴⁰You also must be ready, because the Son of Man will come at an hour when you do not expect him."

⁴¹Peter asked, "Lord, are you telling this parable to us, or to everyone?"

⁴²The Lord answered, "Who then is the faithful and wise manager, whom the master puts in charge of his servants to give them their food allowance at the proper time? ⁴³It will be good for that servant whom the master finds doing so when he returns. ⁴⁴Truly I tell you, he will put him in charge of all his possessions. ⁴⁵But suppose the servant says to himself, 'My master is taking a long time in coming,' and he then begins to beat the other servants, both men and women, and to eat and drink and get drunk. ⁴⁶The master of that servant will come on a day when he does not expect him and at an hour he is not aware of. He will cut him to pieces and assign him a place with the unbelievers.

⁴⁷"The servant who knows the master's will and does not get ready or does not do what the master wants will be beaten with many blows. ⁴⁸But the one who does not know and does things deserving punishment will be beaten with few blows. From everyone who has been given much, much will be demanded; and from the one who has been entrusted with much, much more will be asked.

Not Peace but Division

⁴⁹"I have come to bring fire on the earth, and how I wish it were already kindled! ⁵⁰But I have a baptism to undergo, and what constraint I am under until it is completed! ⁵¹Do you think I came to bring peace on earth? No, I tell you, but division. ⁵²From now on there will be five in one family divided against each other, three against two and two against three. ⁵³They will be divided, father against son and son against father, mother against daughter and daughter against mother, mother-in-law against daughter-in-law and daughter-in-law against mother-in-law."

Interpreting the Times

⁵⁴He said to the crowd: "When you see a cloud rising in the west, immediately you say, 'It's going to rain,' and it does. ⁵⁵And when the south wind blows, you say, 'It's going to be hot,' and it is. ⁵⁶Hypocrites! You know how to interpret the appearance of the earth and the sky. How is it that you don't know how to interpret this present time?

⁵⁷"Why don't you judge for yourselves what is right? ⁵⁸As you are going with your adversary to the magistrate, try hard to be reconciled on the way, or your adversary may drag you off to the judge, and the judge turn you over to the officer, and the officer throw you into prison. ⁵⁹I tell you, you will not get out until you have paid the last penny."

Repent or Perish

13 Now there were some present at that time who told Jesus about the Galileans whose blood Pilate had mixed with their sacrifices. ²Jesus answered, "Do you think that these Galileans were worse sinners than all the other Galileans because they suffered this way? ³I tell you, no! But unless you repent, you too will all perish. ⁴Or those eighteen who died when the tower in Siloam fell on them—do you think they were more guilty than all the others living in Jerusalem? ⁵I tell you, no! But unless you repent, you too will all perish."

⁶Then he told this parable: "A man had a fig tree growing in his vineyard, and he went to look for fruit on it but did not find any. ⁷So he said to the man who took care of the vineyard, 'For three years now I've been coming to look for fruit on this fig tree and haven't found any. Cut it down! Why should it use up the soil?'

⁸"'Sir,' the man replied, 'leave it alone for one more year, and I'll dig around it and fertilize it. ⁹If it bears fruit next year, fine! If not, then cut it down.'"

Jesus Heals a Crippled Woman on the Sabbath

¹⁰On a Sabbath Jesus was teaching in one of the synagogues, ¹¹and a woman was there who had been crippled by a spirit for eighteen years. She was bent over and could not straighten up at all. ¹²When Jesus

saw her, he called her forward and said to her, "Woman,*a* you are set free from your infirmity." [13]Then he put his hands on her, and immediately she straightened up and praised God.

[14]Indignant because Jesus had healed on the Sabbath, the synagogue leader said to the people, "There are six days for work. So come and be healed on those days, not on the Sabbath."

[15]The Lord answered him, "You hypocrites! Doesn't each of you on the Sabbath untie your ox or donkey from the stall and lead it out to give it water? [16]Then should not this woman, a daughter of Abraham, whom Satan has kept bound for eighteen long years, be set free on the Sabbath day from what bound her?"

[17]When he said this, all his opponents were humiliated, but the people were delighted with all the wonderful things he was doing.

The Parables of the Mustard Seed and the Yeast

[18]Then Jesus asked, "What is the kingdom of God like? What shall I compare it to? [19]It is like a mustard seed, which a man took and planted in his garden. It grew and became a tree, and the birds perched in its branches."

[20]Again he asked, "What shall I compare the kingdom of God to? [21]It is like yeast that a woman took and mixed into about sixty pounds*b* of flour until it worked all through the dough."

The Narrow Door

[22]Then Jesus went through the towns and villages, teaching as he made his way to Jerusalem. [23]Someone asked him, "Lord, are only a few people going to be saved?"

He said to them, [24]"Make every effort to enter through the narrow door, because many, I tell you, will try to enter and will not be able to. [25]Once the owner of the house gets up and closes the door, you will stand outside knocking and pleading, 'Sir, open the door for us.'

"But he will answer, 'I don't know you or where you come from.'

[26]"Then you will say, 'We ate and drank with you, and you taught in our streets.'

[27]"But he will reply, 'I don't know you or where you come from. Away from me, all you evildoers!'

[28]"There will be weeping there, and gnashing of teeth, when you see Abraham, Isaac and Jacob and all the prophets in the kingdom of God, but you yourselves thrown out. [29]People will come from east and west and north and south, and will take their places at the feast in the kingdom of God. [30]Indeed there are those who are last who will be first, and first who will be last."

Jesus' Sorrow for Jerusalem

[31]At that time some Pharisees came to Jesus and said to him, "Leave this place and go somewhere else. Herod wants to kill you."

[32]He replied, "Go tell that fox, 'I will keep on driving out demons and healing people today and tomorrow, and on the third day I will reach my goal.' [33]In any case, I must press on today and tomorrow and the next day—for surely no prophet can die outside Jerusalem!

[34]"Jerusalem, Jerusalem, you who kill the prophets and stone those sent to you, how often I have longed to gather your children together, as a hen gathers her chicks under her wings, and you were not willing. [35]Look, your house is left to you desolate. I tell you, you will not see me again until you say, 'Blessed is he who comes in the name of the Lord.'*c*"

Jesus at a Pharisee's House

14 One Sabbath, when Jesus went to eat in the house of a prominent Pharisee, he was being carefully watched. [2]There in front of him was a man suffering from abnormal swelling of his body. [3]Jesus asked the Pharisees and experts in the law, "Is it lawful to heal on the Sabbath or not?" [4]But they remained silent. So taking hold of the man, he healed him and sent him on his way.

[5]Then he asked them, "If one of you has a child*d* or an ox that falls into a well on the Sabbath day, will you not immediately pull it out?" [6]And they had nothing to say.

[7]When he noticed how the guests picked the places of honor at the table, he told them this parable:

1495

---

a 12 The Greek for *Woman* does not denote any disrespect.   *b 21* Or about 27 kilograms   *c 35* Psalm 118:26   *d 5* Some manuscripts *donkey*

[8]"When someone invites you to a wedding feast, do not take the place of honor, for a person more distinguished than you may have been invited. [9]If so, the host who invited both of you will come and say to you, 'Give this person your seat.' Then, humiliated, you will have to take the least important place. [10]But when you are invited, take the lowest place, so that when your host comes, he will say to you, 'Friend, move up to a better place.' Then you will be honored in the presence of all the other guests. [11]For all those who exalt themselves will be humbled, and those who humble themselves will be exalted."

[12]Then Jesus said to his host, "When you give a luncheon or dinner, do not invite your friends, your brothers or sisters, your relatives, or your rich neighbors; if you do, they may invite you back and so you will be repaid. [13]But when you give a banquet, invite the poor, the crippled, the lame, the blind, [14]and you will be blessed. Although they cannot repay you, you will be repaid at the resurrection of the righteous."

The Parable of the Great Banquet

[15]When one of those at the table with him heard this, he said to Jesus, "Blessed are those who will eat at the feast in the kingdom of God."

[16]Jesus replied: "A certain man was preparing a great banquet and invited many guests. [17]At the time of the banquet he sent his servant to tell those who had been invited, 'Come, for everything is now ready.'

[18]"But they all alike began to make excuses. The first said, 'I have just bought a field, and I must go and see it. Please excuse me.'

[19]"Another said, 'I have just bought five yoke of oxen, and I'm on my way to try them out. Please excuse me.'

[20]"Still another said, 'I just got married, so I can't come.'

[21]"The servant came back and reported this to his master. Then the owner of the house became angry and ordered his servant, 'Go out quickly into the streets and alleys of the town and bring in the poor, the crippled, the blind and the lame.'

[22]"'Sir,' the servant said, 'what you ordered has been done, but there is still room.'

[23]"Then the master told his servant, 'Go out to the roads and country lanes and compel them to come in, so that my house will be full. [24]I tell you, not one of those who were invited will get a taste of my banquet.'"

The Cost of Being a Disciple

[25]Large crowds were traveling with Jesus, and turning to them he said: [26]"If anyone comes to me and does not hate father and mother, wife and children, brothers and sisters—yes, even life itself—such a person cannot be my disciple. [27]And whoever does not carry their cross and follow me cannot be my disciple.

[28]"Suppose one of you wants to build a tower. Won't you first sit down and estimate the cost to see if you have enough money to complete it? [29]For if you lay the foundation and are not able to finish it, everyone who sees it will ridicule you, [30]saying, 'This person began to build and wasn't able to finish.'

[31]"Or suppose a king is about to go to war against another king. Won't he first sit down and consider whether he is able with ten thousand men to oppose the one coming against him with twenty thousand? [32]If he is not able, he will send a delegation while the other is still a long way off and will ask for terms of peace. [33]In the same way, those of you who do not give up everything you have cannot be my disciples.

[34]"Salt is good, but if it loses its saltiness, how can it be made salty again? [35]It is fit neither for the soil nor for the manure pile; it is thrown out.

"Whoever has ears to hear, let them hear."

1496

conversations

owning your own business «» 14:28–30

1» To whom can you turn for wise business and financial advice?

2» Do you usually finish projects you begin? If not, what hinders you?

3» What steps do you need to take in order to accomplish your business goals?

For more on owning your own business, check the index.
For the next Conversations, go to p. 1505.

The Parable of the Lost Sheep

15 Now the tax collectors and sinners were all gathering around to hear Jesus. ²But the Pharisees and the teachers of the law muttered, "This man welcomes sinners and eats with them."

³Then Jesus told them this parable: ⁴"Suppose one of you has a hundred sheep and loses one of them. Doesn't he leave the ninety-nine in the open country and go after the lost sheep until he finds it? ⁵And when he finds it, he joyfully puts it on his shoulders ⁶and goes home. Then he calls his friends and neighbors together and says, 'Rejoice with me; I have found my lost sheep.' ⁷I tell you that in the same way there will be more rejoicing in heaven over one sinner who repents than over ninety-nine righteous persons who do not need to repent.

HE IS: running

15:11–24 We learn so much about who God is from Jesus' parables. In Jesus' story of the lost son, one powerful little word sticks out. Staring off into the distance, the father sees his son, *runs* to him, and throws his arms around him to welcome him home.

When you come back to the Father, his welcome isn't begrudging or slow. It's impulsive, spontaneous, decisive and full of grace. He isn't waiting, walking or jogging out to meet you. He is all-out *running* to receive you back to him. What does that tell you about how he feels about your coming home?

1497

For the next He Is, go to p. 1500.

The Parable of the Lost Coin

⁸"Or suppose a woman has ten silver coins*a* and loses one. Doesn't she light a lamp, sweep the house and search carefully until she finds it? ⁹And when she finds it, she calls her friends and neighbors together and says, 'Rejoice with me; I have found my lost coin.' ¹⁰In the same way, I tell you, there is rejoicing in the presence of the angels of God over one sinner who repents."

The Parable of the Lost Son

¹¹Jesus continued: "There was a man who had two sons. ¹²The younger one said to his father, 'Father, give me my share of the estate.' So he divided his property between them.

¹³"Not long after that, the younger son got together all he had, set off for a distant country and there squandered his wealth in wild living. ¹⁴After he had spent everything, there was a severe famine in that whole country, and he began to be in need. ¹⁵So he went and hired himself out to a citizen of that country, who sent him to his fields to feed pigs. ¹⁶He longed to fill his stomach with the pods that the pigs were eating, but no one gave him anything.

¹⁷"When he came to his senses, he said, 'How many of my father's hired servants have food to spare, and here I am starving to death! ¹⁸I will set out and go back to my father and say to him: Father, I have sinned against heaven and against you. ¹⁹I am no longer worthy to be called your son; make me like one of your hired servants.' ²⁰So he got up and went to his father.

"But while he was still a long way off, his father saw him and was filled with compassion for him; he ran to his son, threw his arms around him and kissed him.

²¹"The son said to him, 'Father, I have sinned against heaven and against you. I am no longer worthy to be called your son.'

²²"But the father said to his servants, 'Quick! Bring the best robe and put it on him. Put a ring on his finger and sandals on his feet. ²³Bring the fattened calf and kill it. Let's have a feast and celebrate. ²⁴For this son of mine was dead and is alive again; he was lost and is found.' So they began to celebrate.

²⁵"Meanwhile, the older son was in the field. When he came near the house, he heard music and dancing. ²⁶So he called one of the servants and asked him what was going on. ²⁷'Your brother has come,' he replied, 'and your father has killed the fattened calf because he has him back safe and sound.'

---

a 8 Greek ten drachmas, each worth about a day's wages

[28] "The older brother became angry and refused to go in. So his father went out and pleaded with him. [29] But he answered his father, 'Look! All these years I've been slaving for you and never disobeyed your orders. Yet you never gave me even a young goat so I could celebrate with my friends. [30] But when this son of yours who has squandered your property with prostitutes comes home, you kill the fattened calf for him!'

[31] "'My son,' the father said, 'you are always with me, and everything I have is yours. [32] But we had to celebrate and be glad, because this brother of yours was dead and is alive again; he was lost and is found.'"

The Parable of the Shrewd Manager

16 Jesus told his disciples: "There was a rich man whose manager was accused of wasting his possessions. [2] So he called him in and asked him, 'What is this I hear about you? Give an account of your management, because you cannot be manager any longer.'

[3] "The manager said to himself, 'What shall I do now? My master is taking away my job. I'm not strong enough to dig, and I'm ashamed to beg— [4] I know what I'll do so that, when I lose my job here, people will welcome me into their houses.'

[5] "So he called in each one of his master's debtors. He asked the first, 'How much do you owe my master?'

[6] "'Nine hundred gallons*ⁿ of olive oil,' he replied.

"The manager told him, 'Take your bill, sit down quickly, and make it four hundred and fifty.'

[7] "Then he asked the second, 'And how much do you owe?'

"'A thousand bushels*ᵇ of wheat,' he replied.

"He told him, 'Take your bill and make it eight hundred.'

[8] "The master commended the dishonest manager because he had acted shrewdly. For the people of this world are more shrewd in dealing with their own kind than are the people of the light. [9] I tell you, use worldly wealth to gain friends for yourselves, so that when it is gone, you will be welcomed into eternal dwellings.

[10] "Whoever can be trusted with very little can also be trusted with much, and whoever is dishonest with very little will also be dishonest with much. [11] So if you have not been trustworthy in handling worldly wealth, who will trust you with true riches? [12] And if you have not been trustworthy with someone else's property, who will give you property of your own?

[13] "No one can serve two masters. Either you will hate the one and love the other, or you will be devoted to the one and despise the other. You cannot serve both God and Money."

[14] The Pharisees, who loved money, heard all this and were sneering at Jesus. [15] He said to them, "You are the ones who justify yourselves in the eyes of others, but God knows your hearts. What people value highly is detestable in God's sight.

Additional Teachings

[16] "The Law and the Prophets were proclaimed until John. Since that time, the good news of the kingdom of God is being preached, and people are forcing their way into it. [17] It is easier for heaven and earth to disappear than for the least stroke of a pen to drop out of the Law.

[18] "Anyone who divorces his wife and marries another woman commits adultery, and the man who marries a divorced woman commits adultery.

The Rich Man and Lazarus

[19] "There was a rich man who was dressed in purple and fine linen and lived in luxury every day. [20] At his gate was laid a beggar named Lazarus, covered with sores [21] and longing to eat what fell from the rich man's table. Even the dogs came and licked his sores.

[22] "The time came when the beggar died and the angels carried him to Abraham's side. The rich man also died and was buried. [23] In Hades, where he was in torment, he looked up and saw Abraham far away, with Lazarus by his side. [24] So he called to him, 'Father Abraham, have pity on me and send Lazarus to dip the tip of his finger in water and cool my tongue, because I am in agony in this fire.'

1498

ⁿ 6 Or about 3,000 liters   *ᵇ 7 Or about 30 tons*

²⁵"But Abraham replied, 'Son, remember that in your lifetime you received your good things, while Lazarus received bad things, but now he is comforted here and you are in agony. ²⁶And besides all this, between us and you a great chasm has been set in place, so that those who want to go from here to you cannot, nor can anyone cross over from there to us.'

²⁷"He answered, 'Then I beg you, father, send Lazarus to my family, ²⁸for I have five brothers. Let him warn them, so that they will not also come to this place of torment.'

²⁹"Abraham replied, 'They have Moses and the Prophets; let them listen to them.'

³⁰"'No, father Abraham,' he said, 'but if someone from the dead goes to them, they will repent.'

³¹"He said to him, 'If they do not listen to Moses and the Prophets, they will not be convinced even if someone rises from the dead.'"

Sin, Faith, Duty

17 Jesus said to his disciples: "Things that cause people to stumble are bound to come, but woe to anyone through whom they come. ²It would be better for you to be thrown into the sea with a millstone tied around your neck than for you to cause one of these little ones to stumble. ³So watch yourselves.

"If a brother or sister sins against you, rebuke them; and if they repent, forgive them. ⁴Even if they sin against you seven times in a day and seven times come back to you saying 'I repent,' you must forgive them."

⁵The apostles said to the Lord, "Increase our faith!"

⁶He replied, "If you have faith as small as a mustard seed, you can say to this mulberry tree, 'Be uprooted and planted in the sea,' and it will obey you.

⁷"Suppose one of you has a servant plowing or looking after the sheep. Will he say to the servant when he comes in from the field, 'Come along now and sit down to eat'? ⁸Won't he rather say, 'Prepare my supper, get yourself ready and wait on me while I eat and drink; after that you may eat and drink'? ⁹Will he thank the servant because he did what he was told to do? ¹⁰So you also, when you have done everything you were told to do, should say, 'We are unworthy servants; we have only done our duty.'"

at issue: forgiveness

17:3–4 Once again, your husband says something insensitive. Time after time, your mother-in-law criticizes your choices. Yet again, a friend you thought you could trust tells others what you told her in confidence. Though they apologize, each time it gets harder to forgive them. Isn't there a limit to forgiveness? Don't you have to set boundaries so you won't be hurt again? Isn't there a point when you can write them off? No, no and no. Depend on God to give you the grace to forgive others over and over again—the way he continually forgives you.

1499

Jesus Heals Ten Men With Leprosy

¹¹Now on his way to Jerusalem, Jesus traveled along the border between Samaria and Galilee. ¹²As he was going into a village, ten men who had leprosy*ᵃ* met him. They stood at a distance ¹³and called out in a loud voice, "Jesus, Master, have pity on us!"

¹⁴When he saw them, he said, "Go, show yourselves to the priests." And as they went, they were cleansed.

¹⁵One of them, when he saw he was healed, came back, praising God in a loud voice. ¹⁶He threw himself at Jesus' feet and thanked him—and he was a Samaritan.

¹⁷Jesus asked, "Were not all ten cleansed? Where are the other nine? ¹⁸Was no one found to return and give praise to God except this foreigner?" ¹⁹Then he said to him, "Rise and go; your faith has made you well."

The Coming of the Kingdom of God

²⁰Once, having been asked by the Pharisees when the kingdom of God would come, Jesus replied, "The coming of the kingdom of God is not something that can be observed, ²¹nor will people say, 'Here it is,' or 'There it is,' because the kingdom of God is in your midst."*ᵇ*

ᵃ 12 The Greek word traditionally translated leprosy was used for various diseases affecting the skin. ᵇ 21 Or is within you

²²Then he said to his disciples, "The time is coming when you will long to see one of the days of the Son of Man, but you will not see it. ²³People will tell you, 'There he is!' or 'Here he is!' Do not go running off after them. ²⁴For the Son of Man in his day^a will be like the lightning, which flashes and lights up the sky from one end to the other. ²⁵But first he must suffer many things and be rejected by this generation.

²⁶"Just as it was in the days of Noah, so also will it be in the days of the Son of Man. ²⁷People were eating, drinking, marrying and being given in marriage up to the day Noah entered the ark. Then the flood came and destroyed them all.

²⁸"It was the same in the days of Lot. People were eating and drinking, buying and selling, planting and building. ²⁹But the day Lot left Sodom, fire and sulfur rained down from heaven and destroyed them all.

³⁰"It will be just like this on the day the Son of Man is revealed. ³¹On that day no one who is on the housetop, with possessions inside, should go down to get them. Likewise, no one in the field should go back for anything. ³²Remember Lot's wife! ³³Whoever tries to keep their life will lose it, and whoever loses their life will preserve it. ³⁴I tell you, on that night two people will be in one bed; one will be taken and the other left. ^{35 [36]}Two women will be grinding grain together; one will be taken and the other left."

³⁷"Where, Lord?" they asked.

He replied, "Where there is a dead body, there the vultures will gather."

The Parable of the Persistent Widow

1500

18 Then Jesus told his disciples a parable to show them that they should always pray and not give up. ²He said: "In a certain town there was a judge who neither feared God nor cared what people thought. ³And there was a widow in that town who kept coming to him with the plea, 'Grant me justice against my adversary.'

⁴"For some time he refused. But finally he said to himself, 'Even though I don't fear God or care what people think, ⁵yet because this widow keeps bothering me, I will see that she gets justice, so that she won't eventually come and attack me!'"

⁶And the Lord said, "Listen to what the unjust judge says. ⁷And will not God bring about justice for his chosen ones, who cry out to him day and night? Will he keep putting them off? ⁸I tell you, he will see that they get justice, and quickly. However, when the Son of Man comes, will he find faith on the earth?"

HE IS: bringing justice

18:1–8 The parable of the persistent widow contrasts divine justice with an unjust judge's ruling. Jesus asked his listeners: If the unjust judge delivered justice under pressure, wouldn't God give even more justice to his chosen ones when they pray? The moral of the story—he is *bringing justice*, so keep praying.

If you've been mistreated and doubt God's justice, remember that he blends justice with mercy, giving offenders time to repent. But Jesus promised that God will in the end see that justice is done (see Romans 12:19). Leave vengeance to God, and in the meantime, ask for faith to wait on his timing.

For the next He Is, go to p. 1502.

The Parable of the Pharisee and the Tax Collector

⁹To some who were confident of their own righteousness and looked down on everyone else, Jesus told this parable: ¹⁰"Two men went up to the temple to pray, one a Pharisee and the other a tax collector. ¹¹The Pharisee stood by himself and prayed: 'God, I thank you that I am not like other people—robbers, evildoers, adulterers—or even like this tax collector. ¹²I fast twice a week and give a tenth of all I get.'

¹³"But the tax collector stood at a distance. He would not even look up to heaven, but beat his breast and said, 'God, have mercy on me, a sinner.'

---

^a *24* Some manuscripts do not have *in his day*.

[14] "I tell you that this man, rather than the other, went home justified before God. For all those who exalt themselves will be humbled, and those who humble themselves will be exalted."

The Little Children and Jesus

[15] People were also bringing babies to Jesus for him to place his hands on them. When the disciples saw this, they rebuked them. [16] But Jesus called the children to him and said, "Let the little children come to me, and do not hinder them, for the kingdom of God belongs to such as these. [17] Truly I tell you, anyone who will not receive the kingdom of God like a little child will never enter it."

The Rich and the Kingdom of God

[18] A certain ruler asked him, "Good teacher, what must I do to inherit eternal life?"

[19] "Why do you call me good?" Jesus answered. "No one is good—except God alone. [20] You know the commandments: 'You shall not commit adultery, you shall not murder, you shall not steal, you shall not give false testimony, honor your father and mother.'[a]"

[21] "All these I have kept since I was a boy," he said.

[22] When Jesus heard this, he said to him, "You still lack one thing. Sell everything you have and give to the poor, and you will have treasure in heaven. Then come, follow me."

[23] When he heard this, he became very sad, because he was very wealthy. [24] Jesus looked at him and said, "How hard it is for the rich to enter the kingdom of God! [25] Indeed, it is easier for a camel to go through the eye of a needle than for the rich to enter the kingdom of God."

[26] Those who heard this asked, "Who then can be saved?"

[27] Jesus replied, "What is impossible with human beings is possible with God."

[28] Peter said to him, "We have left all we had to follow you!"

[29] "Truly I tell you," Jesus said to them, "no one who has left home or wife or brothers or sisters or parents or children for the sake of the kingdom of God [30] will fail to receive many times as much in this age, and in the age to come eternal life."

Jesus Predicts His Death a Third Time

[31] Jesus took the Twelve aside and told them, "We are going up to Jerusalem, and everything that is written by the prophets about the Son of Man will be fulfilled. [32] He will be delivered over to the Gentiles. They will mock him, insult him and spit on him; [33] they will flog him and kill him. On the third day he will rise again."

[34] The disciples did not understand any of this. Its meaning was hidden from them, and they did not know what he was talking about.

A Blind Beggar Receives His Sight

[35] As Jesus approached Jericho, a blind man was sitting by the roadside begging. [36] When he heard the crowd going by, he asked what was happening. [37] They told him, "Jesus of Nazareth is passing by."

[38] He called out, "Jesus, Son of David, have mercy on me!"

[39] Those who led the way rebuked him and told him to be quiet, but he shouted all the more, "Son of David, have mercy on me!"

[40] Jesus stopped and ordered the man to be brought to him. When he came near, Jesus asked him, [41] "What do you want me to do for you?"

"Lord, I want to see," he replied.

[42] Jesus said to him, "Receive your sight; your faith has healed you." [43] Immediately he received his sight and followed Jesus, praising God. When all the people saw it, they also praised God.

Zacchaeus the Tax Collector

19 Jesus entered Jericho and was passing through. [2] A man was there by the name of Zacchaeus; he was a chief tax collector and was wealthy. [3] He wanted to see who Jesus was, but because he was short he could not see over the crowd. [4] So he ran ahead and climbed a sycamore-fig tree to see him, since Jesus was coming that way.

---

[a] 20 Exodus 20:12-16; Deut. 5:16-20

HE IS: looking for little people

19:1–10 A short man named Zacchaeus climbed a sycamore-fig tree to see Jesus. He probably enjoyed his bird's eye view, thinking, *I can see Jesus, but he can't see me.* But when Jesus reached the tree, he looked up and invited himself over to Zacchaeus's house.

Do you see yourself as too small or unimportant for Jesus to notice? He is *looking for little people.* He knows where you are and the things, big and small, that concern you. He wants to come into your home and your heart. When you invite him in, he will bring salvation to your house today.

For the next He Is, go to p. 1504.

⁵When Jesus reached the spot, he looked up and said to him, "Zacchaeus, come down immediately. I must stay at your house today." ⁶So he came down at once and welcomed him gladly.

⁷All the people saw this and began to mutter, "He has gone to be the guest of a sinner."

⁸But Zacchaeus stood up and said to the Lord, "Look, Lord! Here and now I give half of my possessions to the poor, and if I have cheated anybody out of anything, I will pay back four times the amount."

⁹Jesus said to him, "Today salvation has come to this house, because this man, too, is a son of Abraham. ¹⁰For the Son of Man came to seek and to save what was lost."

The Parable of the Ten Minas

¹¹While they were listening to this, he went on to tell them a parable, because he was near Jerusalem and the people thought that the kingdom of God was going to appear at once. ¹²He said: "A man of noble birth went to a distant country to have himself appointed king and then to return. ¹³So he called ten of his servants and gave them ten minas.ᵃ 'Put this money to work,' he said, 'until I come back.'

¹⁴"But his subjects hated him and sent a delegation after him to say, 'We don't want this man to be our king.'

¹⁵"He was made king, however, and returned home. Then he sent for the servants to whom he had given the money, in order to find out what they had gained with it.

¹⁶"The first one came and said, 'Sir, your mina has earned ten more.'

¹⁷"'Well done, my good servant!' his master replied. 'Because you have been trustworthy in a very small matter, take charge of ten cities.'

¹⁸"The second came and said, 'Sir, your mina has earned five more.'

¹⁹"His master answered, 'You take charge of five cities.'

²⁰"Then another servant came and said, 'Sir, here is your mina; I have kept it laid away in a piece of cloth. ²¹I was afraid of you, because you are a hard man. You take out what you did not put in and reap what you did not sow.'

²²"His master replied, 'I will judge you by your own words, you wicked servant! You knew, did you, that I am a hard man, taking out what I did not put in, and reaping what I did not sow? ²³Why then didn't you put my money on deposit, so that when I came back, I could have collected it with interest?'

²⁴"Then he said to those standing by, 'Take his mina away from him and give it to the one who has ten minas.'

²⁵"'Sir,' they said, 'he already has ten!'

²⁶"He replied, 'I tell you that to everyone who has, more will be given, but as for those who have nothing, even what they have will be taken away. ²⁷But those enemies of mine who did not want me to be king over them—bring them here and kill them in front of me.'"

Jesus Comes to Jerusalem as King

²⁸After Jesus had said this, he went on ahead, going up to Jerusalem. ²⁹As he approached Bethphage and Bethany at the hill called the Mount of Olives, he sent two of his disciples, saying to them, ³⁰"Go to

---

ᵃ *13* A mina was about three months' wages.

the village ahead of you, and as you enter it, you will find a colt tied there, which no one has ever ridden. Untie it and bring it here. ³¹If anyone asks you, 'Why are you untying it?' say, 'The Lord needs it.'"

³²Those who were sent ahead went and found it just as he had told them. ³³As they were untying the colt, its owners asked them, "Why are you untying the colt?"

³⁴They replied, "The Lord needs it."

³⁵They brought it to Jesus, threw their cloaks on the colt and put Jesus on it. ³⁶As he went along, people spread their cloaks on the road.

³⁷When he came near the place where the road goes down the Mount of Olives, the whole crowd of disciples began joyfully to praise God in loud voices for all the miracles they had seen:

³⁸"Blessed is the king who comes in the name of the Lord!"ᵃ

"Peace in heaven and glory in the highest!"

³⁹Some of the Pharisees in the crowd said to Jesus, "Teacher, rebuke your disciples!"

⁴⁰"I tell you," he replied, "if they keep quiet, the stones will cry out."

⁴¹As he approached Jerusalem and saw the city, he wept over it ⁴²and said, "If you, even you, had only known on this day what would bring you peace—but now it is hidden from your eyes. ⁴³The days will come on you when your enemies will build an embankment against you and encircle you and hem you in on every side. ⁴⁴They will dash you to the ground, you and the children within your walls. They will not leave one stone on another, because you did not recognize the time of God's coming to you."

Jesus at the Temple

⁴⁵When Jesus entered the temple courts, he began to drive out those who were selling. ⁴⁶"It is written," he said to them, "'My house will be a house of prayer'ᵇ; but you have made it 'a den of robbers.'ᶜ"

⁴⁷Every day he was teaching at the temple. But the chief priests, the teachers of the law and the leaders among the people were trying to kill him. ⁴⁸Yet they could not find any way to do it, because all the people hung on his words.

The Authority of Jesus Questioned

20 One day as Jesus was teaching the people in the temple courts and proclaiming the good news, the chief priests and the teachers of the law, together with the elders, came up to him. ²"Tell us by what authority you are doing these things," they said. "Who gave you this authority?"

³He replied, "I will also ask you a question. Tell me, ⁴John's baptism—was it from heaven, or of human origin?"

⁵They discussed it among themselves and said, "If we say, 'From heaven,' he will ask, 'Why didn't you believe him?' ⁶But if we say, 'Of human origin,' all the people will stone us, because they are persuaded that John was a prophet."

⁷So they answered, "We don't know where it was from."

⁸Jesus said, "Neither will I tell you by what authority I am doing these things."

The Parable of the Tenants

⁹He went on to tell the people this parable: "A man planted a vineyard, rented it to some farmers and went away for a long time. ¹⁰At harvest time he sent a servant to the tenants so they would give him some of the fruit of the vineyard. But the tenants beat him and sent him away empty-handed. ¹¹He sent another servant, but that one also they beat and treated shamefully and sent away empty-handed. ¹²He sent still a third, and they wounded him and threw him out.

¹³"Then the owner of the vineyard said, 'What shall I do? I will send my son, whom I love; perhaps they will respect him.'

¹⁴"But when the tenants saw him, they talked the matter over. 'This is the heir,' they said. 'Let's kill him, and the inheritance will be ours.' ¹⁵So they threw him out of the vineyard and killed him.

"What then will the owner of the vineyard do to them? ¹⁶He will come and kill those tenants and give the vineyard to others."

ᵃ *38* Psalm 118:26   ᵇ *46* Isaiah 56:7   ᶜ *46* Jer. 7:11

When the people heard this, they said, "God forbid!"

[17] Jesus looked directly at them and asked, "Then what is the meaning of that which is written:

> "'The stone the builders rejected
> has become the cornerstone'[a]?

[18] Everyone who falls on that stone will be broken to pieces, but anyone on whom it falls will be crushed."

[19] The teachers of the law and the chief priests looked for a way to arrest him immediately, because they knew he had spoken this parable against them. But they were afraid of the people.

Paying Taxes to Caesar

[20] Keeping a close watch on him, they sent spies, who pretended to be sincere. They hoped to catch Jesus in something he said so that they might hand him over to the power and authority of the governor. [21] So the spies questioned him: "Teacher, we know that you speak and teach what is right, and that you do not show partiality but teach the way of God in accordance with the truth. [22] Is it right for us to pay taxes to Caesar or not?"

[23] He saw through their duplicity and said to them, [24] "Show me a denarius. Whose image and inscription are on it?"

"Caesar's," they replied.

[25] He said to them, "Then give back to Caesar what is Caesar's, and to God what is God's."

[26] They were unable to trap him in what he had said there in public. And astonished by his answer, they became silent.

The Resurrection and Marriage

[27] Some of the Sadducees, who say there is no resurrection, came to Jesus with a question. [28] "Teacher," they said, "Moses wrote for us that if a man's brother dies and leaves a wife but no children, the man must marry the widow and raise up offspring for his brother. [29] Now there were seven brothers. The first one married a woman and died childless. [30] The second [31] and then the third married her, and in the same way the seven died, leaving no children. [32] Finally, the woman died too. [33] Now then, at the resurrection whose wife will she be, since the seven were married to her?"

[34] Jesus replied, "The people of this age marry and are given in marriage. [35] But those who are considered worthy of taking part in the age to come and in the resurrection from the dead will neither marry nor be given in marriage, [36] and they can no longer die; for they are like the angels. They are God's children, since they are children of the resurrection. [37] But in the account of the burning bush, even Moses showed that the dead rise, for he calls the Lord 'the God of Abraham, and the God of Isaac, and the God of Jacob.'[b] [38] He is not the God of the dead, but of the living, for to him all are alive."

[39] Some of the teachers of the law responded, "Well said, teacher!" [40] And no one dared to ask him any more questions.

---

[a] 17 Psalm 118:22   [b] 37 Exodus 3:6

HE IS: the God of the living

20:27–40 The Sadducees tried to trick Jesus into disavowing the resurrection of the dead. Cleverly, Jesus explained that the dead are alive spiritually. He is *the God of the living*, and his children will receive beautiful, ever-living bodies fit for eternity.

The Sadducees did not believe in life after death, but as a believer, you know your soul will live forever, and your dead body will be raised to life again (see 1 Thessalonians 4:13–14). Our God resurrects dead souls, dead bodies, dead hopes, dead dreams and dead emotions. Won't you trust *the God of the living* to resurrect whatever has died inside you?

For the next He Is, go to p. 1511.

Whose Son Is the Messiah?

[41] Then Jesus said to them, "Why is it said that the Messiah is the son of David? [42] David himself declares in the Book of Psalms:

> "'The Lord said to my Lord:
> "Sit at my right hand
> [43] until I make your enemies
> a footstool for your feet."'[a]

[44] David calls him 'Lord.' How then can he be his son?"

Warning Against the Teachers of the Law

[45] While all the people were listening, Jesus said to his disciples, [46] "Beware of the teachers of the law. They like to walk around in flowing robes and love to be greeted with respect in the marketplaces and have the most important seats in the synagogues and the places of honor at banquets. [47] They devour widows' houses and for a show make lengthy prayers. These men will be punished most severely."

The Widow's Offering

21 As Jesus looked up, he saw the rich putting their gifts into the temple treasury. [2] He also saw a poor widow put in two very small copper coins. [3] "Truly I tell you," he said, "this poor widow has put in more than all the others. [4] All these people gave their gifts out of their wealth; but she out of her poverty put in all she had to live on."

1505

The Destruction of the Temple and Signs of the End Times

[5] Some of his disciples were remarking about how the temple was adorned with beautiful stones and with gifts dedicated to God. But Jesus said, [6] "As for what you see here, the time will come when not one stone will be left on another; every one of them will be thrown down."

[7] "Teacher," they asked, "when will these things happen? And what will be the sign that they are about to take place?"

conversations

money «» 21:1–4

1 » Is Jesus saying here that it doesn't matter at all how much you give to God?

2 » What is the danger of comparing your gifts to the church with someone else's?

3 » How can you develop a give-it-all attitude like the widow's?

For more on **money**, check the index.
For the next Conversations, go to p. 1517.

[8] He replied: "Watch out that you are not deceived. For many will come in my name, claiming, 'I am he,' and, 'The time is near.' Do not follow them. [9] When you hear of wars and uprisings, do not be frightened. These things must happen first, but the end will not come right away."

[10] Then he said to them: "Nation will rise against nation, and kingdom against kingdom. [11] There will be great earthquakes, famines and pestilences in various places, and fearful events and great signs from heaven.

[12] "But before all this, they will lay hands on you and persecute you. They will deliver you to synagogues and prisons, and you will be brought before kings and governors, and all on account of my name. [13] And so you will bear testimony to me. [14] But make up your mind not to worry beforehand how you will defend yourselves. [15] For I will give you words and wisdom that none of your adversaries will be able to resist or contradict. [16] You will be betrayed even by parents, brothers, sisters, relatives and friends, and they will put some of you to death. [17] Everyone will hate you because of me. [18] But not a hair of your head will perish. [19] Stand firm, and you will win life.

[20] "When you see Jerusalem being surrounded by armies, you will know that its desolation is near. [21] Then let those who are in Judea flee to the mountains, let those in the city get out, and let those in the country not enter the city. [22] For this is the time of punishment in fulfillment of all that has been written. [23] How dreadful it will be in those days for pregnant women and nursing mothers! There will be great distress in the land and wrath against this people. [24] They will fall by the sword and will be taken as

---

[a] 43 Psalm 110:1

prisoners to all the nations. Jerusalem will be trampled on by the Gentiles until the times of the Gentiles are fulfilled.

²⁵"There will be signs in the sun, moon and stars. On the earth, nations will be in anguish and perplexity at the roaring and tossing of the sea. ²⁶People will faint from terror, apprehensive of what is coming on the world, for the heavenly bodies will be shaken. ²⁷At that time they will see the Son of Man coming in a cloud with power and great glory. ²⁸When these things begin to take place, stand up and lift up your heads, because your redemption is drawing near."

²⁹He told them this parable: "Look at the fig tree and all the trees. ³⁰When they sprout leaves, you can see for yourselves and know that summer is near. ³¹Even so, when you see these things happening, you know that the kingdom of God is near.

³²"Truly I tell you, this generation will certainly not pass away until all these things have happened. ³³Heaven and earth will pass away, but my words will never pass away.

³⁴"Be careful, or your hearts will be weighed down with dissipation, drunkenness and the anxieties of life, and that day will close on you suddenly like a trap. ³⁵For it will come on all those who live on the face of the whole earth. ³⁶Be always on the watch, and pray that you may be able to escape all that is about to happen, and that you may be able to stand before the Son of Man."

³⁷Each day Jesus was teaching at the temple, and each evening he went out to spend the night on the hill called the Mount of Olives, ³⁸and all the people came early in the morning to hear him at the temple.

Judas Agrees to Betray Jesus

22 Now the Festival of Unleavened Bread, called the Passover, was approaching, ²and the chief priests and the teachers of the law were looking for some way to get rid of Jesus, for they were afraid of the people. ³Then Satan entered Judas, called Iscariot, one of the Twelve. ⁴And Judas went to the chief priests and the officers of the temple guard and discussed with them how he might betray Jesus. ⁵They were delighted and agreed to give him money. ⁶He consented, and watched for an opportunity to hand Jesus over to them when no crowd was present.

The Last Supper

⁷Then came the day of Unleavened Bread on which the Passover lamb had to be sacrificed. ⁸Jesus sent Peter and John, saying, "Go and make preparations for us to eat the Passover."

⁹"Where do you want us to prepare for it?" they asked.

¹⁰He replied, "As you enter the city, a man carrying a jar of water will meet you. Follow him to the house that he enters, ¹¹and say to the owner of the house, 'The Teacher asks: Where is the guest room, where I may eat the Passover with my disciples?' ¹²He will show you a large room upstairs, all furnished. Make preparations there."

¹³They left and found things just as Jesus had told them. So they prepared the Passover.

¹⁴When the hour came, Jesus and his apostles reclined at the table. ¹⁵And he said to them, "I have eagerly desired to eat this Passover with you before I suffer. ¹⁶For I tell you, I will not eat it again until it finds fulfillment in the kingdom of God."

¹⁷After taking the cup, he gave thanks and said, "Take this and divide it among you. ¹⁸For I tell you I will not drink again of the fruit of the vine until the kingdom of God comes."

¹⁹And he took bread, gave thanks and broke it, and gave it to them, saying, "This is my body given for you; do this in remembrance of me."

²⁰In the same way, after the supper he took the cup, saying, "This cup is the new covenant in my blood, which is poured out for you. ²¹But the hand of him who is going to betray me is with mine on the table. ²²The Son of Man will go as it has been decreed. But woe to that man who betrays him!" ²³They began to question among themselves which of them it might be who would do this.

²⁴A dispute also arose among them as to which of them was considered to be greatest. ²⁵Jesus said to them, "The kings of the Gentiles lord it over them; and those who exercise authority over them call themselves Benefactors. ²⁶But you are not to be like that. Instead, the greatest among you should be like the youngest, and the one who rules like the one who serves. ²⁷For who is greater, the one who is at the table or the one who serves? Is it not the one who is at the table? But I am among you as one who serves.

[28] You are those who have stood by me in my trials. [29] And I confer on you a kingdom, just as my Father conferred one on me, [30] so that you may eat and drink at my table in my kingdom and sit on thrones, judging the twelve tribes of Israel.

[31] "Simon, Simon, Satan has asked to sift all of you as wheat. [32] But I have prayed for you, Simon, that your faith may not fail. And when you have turned back, strengthen your brothers."

[33] But he replied, "Lord, I am ready to go with you to prison and to death."

[34] Jesus answered, "I tell you, Peter, before the rooster crows today, you will deny three times that you know me."

[35] Then Jesus asked them, "When I sent you without purse, bag or sandals, did you lack anything?"

"Nothing," they answered.

[36] He said to them, "But now if you have a purse, take it, and also a bag; and if you don't have a sword, sell your cloak and buy one. [37] It is written: 'And he was numbered with the transgressors'[a]; and I tell you that this must be fulfilled in me. Yes, what is written about me is reaching its fulfillment."

[38] The disciples said, "See, Lord, here are two swords."

"That is enough," he replied.

Jesus Prays on the Mount of Olives

[39] Jesus went out as usual to the Mount of Olives, and his disciples followed him. [40] On reaching the place, he said to them, "Pray that you will not fall into temptation." [41] He withdrew about a stone's throw beyond them, knelt down and prayed, [42] "Father, if you are willing, take this cup from me; yet not my will, but yours be done." [43] An angel from heaven appeared to him and strengthened him. [44] And being in anguish, he prayed more earnestly, and his sweat was like drops of blood falling to the ground.[b]

[45] When he rose from prayer and went back to the disciples, he found them asleep, exhausted from sorrow. [46] "Why are you sleeping?" he asked them. "Get up and pray so that you will not fall into temptation."

Jesus Arrested

[47] While he was still speaking a crowd came up, and the man who was called Judas, one of the Twelve, was leading them. He approached Jesus to kiss him, [48] but Jesus asked him, "Judas, are you betraying the Son of Man with a kiss?"

[49] When Jesus' followers saw what was going to happen, they said, "Lord, should we strike with our swords?" [50] And one of them struck the servant of the high priest, cutting off his right ear.

[51] But Jesus answered, "No more of this!" And he touched the man's ear and healed him.

[52] Then Jesus said to the chief priests, the officers of the temple guard, and the elders, who had come for him, "Am I leading a rebellion, that you have come with swords and clubs? [53] Every day I was with you in the temple courts, and you did not lay a hand on me. But this is your hour—when darkness reigns."

Peter Disowns Jesus

[54] Then seizing him, they led him away and took him into the house of the high priest. Peter followed at a distance. [55] And when some there had kindled a fire in the middle of the courtyard and had sat down together, Peter sat down with them. [56] A servant girl saw him seated there in the firelight. She looked closely at him and said, "This man was with him."

[57] But he denied it. "Woman,[c] I don't know him," he said.

[58] A little later someone else saw him and said, "You also are one of them."

aussie:yielding to God

22:41–44 Sometimes God calls us to do things we do not want to do. To give up something or someone we love. To face our greatest fears. To embrace what we'd rather reject. Jesus knew that loving God required great sacrifice. In his honest prayer, we see his desire for a way around the pain he'd soon face, and we also see his greater desire to do God's will. We see that he cared more about yielding to God than seeking his own comfort. God calls each of us to difficult paths for the sake of his glory. Are you willing to yield to him?

1507

---

[a] 37 Isaiah 53:12   [b] 43,44 Some early manuscripts do not have verses 43 and 44.   [c] 57 The Greek for *Woman* does not denote any disrespect.

myth# 86 "I'LL HAVE TIME FOR MY FAMILY LATER."

When I was growing up, my parents always made me do my homework and chores before I could have free time to do what I wanted or go out with my friends. I hated their strict rules at the time, but now I see the tremendous self-discipline that taught me from an early age. Because of my hard work and sense of responsibility, I'm a successful small business owner, which I'm proud of.

The only problem is that sometimes I get complaints that I'm too hard-working. I know, I know—I tend to be "all work and no play." But I get a certain thrill from whittling down my task list every day. Most days, I barely finish everything I need to accomplish. Fortunately, my husband works from home, and his job gives him the flexibility to cover the bases on the home front. However, with my nutty schedule, I have no time to just sit down and relax. It also leaves me little time for my family. Don't get me wrong—I love the arrangement my husband and I have. I'm just a little jealous of the play days he has with our kids. My children are the most important priority in my life, although I'm not sure they always know that. My schedule is relentless.

I promise myself that when things slow down, I will spend quality time with my family. I know there will be time for vacations, leisurely days and quality talks later on. It's not that I'm necessarily choosing one over the other, but for now I have obligations that I just can't ignore.

—Selena

ONE THING THAT'S certain about life is that it's uncertain. We aren't promised a tomorrow. That's why it's crucial that we spend our time investing in what really matters today (see Ephesians 5:15–16). We must constantly remind ourselves of what is eternal and what is just temporary. Time clocks must be punched and laundry must be done, but *people* are far more important than running a business or having the perfect house. Our families are more precious than a finished "to do" list. While you are going through the daily routines of life, will you do the following?

- Remind yourself to enjoy and invest in your family. Take the time to plan a special afternoon outing or slow down for an unhurried talk together.

- Do the little things in life together. "Quality time" doesn't have to be an elaborate family vacation or evening out. Spend time together making dinner, cleaning the house, planting flowers, etc. Turn off your cell phone and the radio in the car so you can talk to your kids.

- Eliminate a commitment or two that takes you unnecessarily away from your family. Is there something you can drop from your schedule that will allow you to spend extra time with your friends and family?

- Set aside (and protect) family time. For example, many families commit to eating dinner together on certain days so they can have uninterrupted family time.

- Serve. Jesus served those he loved (see Luke 22:26–27). The simple acts of kindness will communicate to your family that you love them.

Quality time with your family won't just happen. It has to be planned, as any other thing worth doing. Will you get out your calendar and ruthlessly eliminate lesser commitments so that you can invest in what is most important? The sad reality is that kids grow up and

spouses drift apart while you're continually promising "later." Don't be someone who looks up one day to find that your children are grown, and you don't even know them, and your husband is a complete stranger to you. Cherish today for what it is, priceless and irreplaceable.

1509

"It isn't the ones who die with the most toys who win. It's those who've loved their families well and know the joy of having that love returned."

—R. Ruth Barton

"BE VERY CAREFUL, THEN, HOW YOU LIVE . . . MAKING THE MOST OF EVERY OPPORTUNITY, BECAUSE THE DAYS ARE EVIL."

EPHESIANS 5:15–16

SEE ALSO

Psalm 9:10
Psalm 138:8
Ephesians 6:5–9

For more on **Career** and **Family**, check the index.

"Man, I am not!" Peter replied.

⁵⁹About an hour later another asserted, "Certainly this fellow was with him, for he is a Galilean."

⁶⁰Peter replied, "Man, I don't know what you're talking about!" Just as he was speaking, the rooster crowed. ⁶¹The Lord turned and looked straight at Peter. Then Peter remembered the word the Lord had spoken to him: "Before the rooster crows today, you will disown me three times." ⁶²And he went outside and wept bitterly.

The Guards Mock Jesus

⁶³The men who were guarding Jesus began mocking and beating him. ⁶⁴They blindfolded him and demanded, "Prophesy! Who hit you?" ⁶⁵And they said many other insulting things to him.

Jesus Before Pilate and Herod

⁶⁶At daybreak the council of the elders of the people, both the chief priests and the teachers of the law, met together, and Jesus was led before them. ⁶⁷"If you are the Messiah," they said, "tell us."

Jesus answered, "If I tell you, you will not believe me, ⁶⁸and if I asked you, you would not answer. ⁶⁹But from now on, the Son of Man will be seated at the right hand of the mighty God."

⁷⁰They all asked, "Are you then the Son of God?"

He replied, "You say that I am."

⁷¹Then they said, "Why do we need any more testimony? We have heard it from his own lips."

23 Then the whole assembly rose and led him off to Pilate. ²And they began to accuse him, saying, "We have found this man subverting our nation. He opposes payment of taxes to Caesar and claims to be Messiah, a king."

³So Pilate asked Jesus, "Are you the king of the Jews?"

"You have said so," Jesus replied.

⁴Then Pilate announced to the chief priests and the crowd, "I find no basis for a charge against this man."

⁵But they insisted, "He stirs up the people all over Judea by his teaching. He started in Galilee and has come all the way here."

⁶On hearing this, Pilate asked if the man was a Galilean. ⁷When he learned that Jesus was under Herod's jurisdiction, he sent him to Herod, who was also in Jerusalem at that time.

⁸When Herod saw Jesus, he was greatly pleased, because for a long time he had been wanting to see him. From what he had heard about him, he hoped to see him perform a sign of some sort. ⁹He plied him with many questions, but Jesus gave him no answer. ¹⁰The chief priests and the teachers of the law were standing there, vehemently accusing him. ¹¹Then Herod and his soldiers ridiculed and mocked him. Dressing him in an elegant robe, they sent him back to Pilate. ¹²That day Herod and Pilate became friends—before this they had been enemies.

¹³Pilate called together the chief priests, the rulers and the people, ¹⁴and said to them, "You brought me this man as one who was inciting the people to rebellion. I have examined him in your presence and have found no basis for your charges against him. ¹⁵Neither has Herod, for he sent him back to us; as you can see, he has done nothing to deserve death. ¹⁶[¹⁷]Therefore, I will punish him and then release him."

¹⁸With one voice they cried out, "Away with this man! Release Barabbas to us!" ¹⁹(Barabbas had been thrown into prison for an insurrection in the city, and for murder.)

²⁰Wanting to release Jesus, Pilate appealed to them again. ²¹But they kept shouting, "Crucify him! Crucify him!"

²²For the third time he spoke to them: "Why? What crime has this man committed? I have found in him no grounds for the death penalty. Therefore I will have him punished and then release him."

²³But with loud shouts they insistently demanded that he be crucified, and their shouts prevailed. ²⁴So Pilate decided to grant their demand. ²⁵He released the man who had been thrown into prison for insurrection and murder, the one they asked for, and surrendered Jesus to their will.

The Crucifixion of Jesus

²⁶As the soldiers led him away, they seized Simon from Cyrene, who was on his way in from the country, and put the cross on him and made him carry it behind Jesus. ²⁷A large number of people followed

him, including women who mourned and wailed for him. ²⁸Jesus turned and said to them, "Daughters of Jerusalem, do not weep for me; weep for yourselves and for your children. ²⁹For the time will come when you will say, 'Blessed are the childless women, the wombs that never bore and the breasts that never nursed!' ³⁰Then

> "'they will say to the mountains, "Fall on us!"
> and to the hills, "Cover us!"'ᵃ

³¹For if people do these things when the tree is green, what will happen when it is dry?"

³²Two other men, both criminals, were also led out with him to be executed. ³³When they came to the place called the Skull, they crucified him there, along with the criminals—one on his right, the other on his left. ³⁴Jesus said, "Father, forgive them, for they do not know what they are doing."ᵇ And they divided up his clothes by casting lots.

³⁵The people stood watching, and the rulers even sneered at him. They said, "He saved others; let him save himself if he is God's Messiah, the Chosen One."

³⁶The soldiers also came up and mocked him. They offered him wine vinegar ³⁷and said, "If you are the king of the Jews, save yourself."

³⁸There was a written notice above him, which read: THIS IS THE KING OF THE JEWS.

³⁹One of the criminals who hung there hurled insults at him: "Aren't you the Messiah? Save yourself and us!"

⁴⁰But the other criminal rebuked him. "Don't you fear God," he said, "since you are under the same sentence? ⁴¹We are punished justly, for we are getting what our deeds deserve. But this man has done nothing wrong."

⁴²Then he said, "Jesus, remember me when you come into your kingdom.ᶜ"

⁴³Jesus answered him, "Truly I tell you, today you will be with me in paradise."

HE IS: in paradise

23:39–43 Jesus was crucified along with two criminals. One dying criminal insulted him. The other had a true "deathbed" conversion, coming to faith in the last moments of his life. Jesus assured the convert he would meet him that very day *in paradise*.

Even on the cross, Jesus was teaching us something. In his conversation with the criminal, he affirmed the reality of heaven and hell and emphasized the necessity of choosing between the two. The two criminals represent all of us humans, for all of us must choose one or the other. He is *in paradise* waiting for those who choose him.

For the next He Is, go to p. 1513.

The Death of Jesus

⁴⁴It was now about noon, and darkness came over the whole land until three in the afternoon, ⁴⁵for the sun stopped shining. And the curtain of the temple was torn in two. ⁴⁶Jesus called out with a loud voice, "Father, into your hands I commit my spirit."ᵈ When he had said this, he breathed his last.

⁴⁷The centurion, seeing what had happened, praised God and said, "Surely this was a righteous man." ⁴⁸When all the people who had gathered to witness this sight saw what took place, they beat their breasts and went away. ⁴⁹But all those who knew him, including the women who had followed him from Galilee, stood at a distance, watching these things.

The Burial of Jesus

⁵⁰Now there was a man named Joseph, a member of the Council, a good and upright man, ⁵¹who had not consented to their decision and action. He came from the Judean town of Arimathea, and he

---

ᵃ *30* Hosea 10:8   ᵇ *34* Some early manuscripts do not have this sentence.   ᶜ *42* Some manuscripts *come with your kingly power*   ᵈ *46* Psalm 31:5

himself was waiting for the kingdom of God. ⁵²Going to Pilate, he asked for Jesus' body. ⁵³Then he took it down, wrapped it in linen cloth and placed it in a tomb cut in the rock, one in which no one had yet been laid. ⁵⁴It was Preparation Day, and the Sabbath was about to begin.

⁵⁵The women who had come with Jesus from Galilee followed Joseph and saw the tomb and how his body was laid in it. ⁵⁶Then they went home and prepared spices and perfumes. But they rested on the Sabbath in obedience to the commandment.

Jesus Has Risen

24 On the first day of the week, very early in the morning, the women took the spices they had prepared and went to the tomb. ²They found the stone rolled away from the tomb, ³but when they entered, they did not find the body of the Lord Jesus. ⁴While they were wondering about this, suddenly two men in clothes that gleamed like lightning stood beside them. ⁵In their fright the women bowed down with their faces to the ground, but the men said to them, "Why do you look for the living among the dead? ⁶He is not here; he has risen! Remember how he told you, while he was still with you in Galilee: ⁷'The Son of Man must be delivered over to the hands of sinners, be crucified and on the third day be raised again.'" ⁸Then they remembered his words.

⁹When they came back from the tomb, they told all these things to the Eleven and to all the others. ¹⁰It was Mary Magdalene, Joanna, Mary the mother of James, and the others with them who told this to the apostles. ¹¹But they did not believe the women, because their words seemed to them like nonsense. ¹²Peter, however, got up and ran to the tomb. Bending over, he saw the strips of linen lying by themselves, and he went away, wondering to himself what had happened.

On the Road to Emmaus

¹³Now that same day two of them were going to a village called Emmaus, about seven miles*ᵃ* from Jerusalem. ¹⁴They were talking with each other about everything that had happened. ¹⁵As they talked and discussed these things with each other, Jesus himself came up and walked along with them; ¹⁶but they were kept from recognizing him.

¹⁷He asked them, "What are you discussing together as you walk along?"

They stood still, their faces downcast. ¹⁸One of them, named Cleopas, asked him, "Are you only a visitor to Jerusalem and do not know the things that have happened there in these days?"

¹⁹"What things?" he asked.

"About Jesus of Nazareth," they replied. "He was a prophet, powerful in word and deed before God and all the people. ²⁰The chief priests and our rulers handed him over to be sentenced to death, and they crucified him; ²¹but we had hoped that he was the one who was going to redeem Israel. And what is more, it is the third day since all this took place. ²²In addition, some of our women amazed us. They went to the tomb early this morning ²³but didn't find his body. They came and told us that they had seen a vision of angels, who said he was alive. ²⁴Then some of our companions went to the tomb and found it just as the women had said, but him they did not see."

²⁵He said to them, "How foolish you are, and how slow to believe all that the prophets have spoken! ²⁶Did not the Messiah have to suffer these things and then enter his glory?" ²⁷And beginning with Moses and all the Prophets, he explained to them what was said in all the Scriptures concerning himself.

²⁸As they approached the village to which they were going, Jesus continued on as if he were going farther. ²⁹But they urged him strongly, "Stay with us, for it is nearly evening; the day is almost over." So he went in to stay with them.

³⁰When he was at the table with them, he took bread, gave thanks, broke it and began to give it to them. ³¹Then their eyes were opened and they recognized him, and he disappeared from their sight. ³²They asked each other, "Were not our hearts burning within us while he talked with us on the road and opened the Scriptures to us?"

³³They got up and returned at once to Jerusalem. There they found the Eleven and those with them, assembled together ³⁴and saying, "It is true! The Lord has risen and has appeared to Simon." ³⁵Then the

---

ᵃ 13 Or about 11 kilometers

24:25–27 If Jesus' followers had fully grasped God's Word, they would have believed the accounts of his resurrection. But the two disciples walking to Emmaus couldn't quite believe all that had happened. So Jesus, the ever-patient Teacher, started at the beginning and explained to them all the Scriptures concerning himself.

Perhaps you readily believe *some* of what the Bible says, especially when it seems favorable. But are you reluctant to believe *all* of God's Word, especially when it foretells personal suffering? Jesus himself is *the fulfillment* of Scripture (see Acts 13:32–33). He is willing to walk beside you and give you insight into his Word.

For the next He Is, go to p. 1522.

two told what had happened on the way, and how Jesus was recognized by them when he broke the bread.

Jesus Appears to the Disciples

[36] While they were still talking about this, Jesus himself stood among them and said to them, "Peace be with you."

[37] They were startled and frightened, thinking they saw a ghost. [38] He said to them, "Why are you troubled, and why do doubts rise in your minds? [39] Look at my hands and my feet. It is I myself! Touch me and see; a ghost does not have flesh and bones, as you see I have."

[40] When he had said this, he showed them his hands and feet. [41] And while they still did not believe it because of joy and amazement, he asked them, "Do you have anything here to eat?" [42] They gave him a piece of broiled fish, [43] and he took it and ate it in their presence.

[44] He said to them, "This is what I told you while I was still with you: Everything must be fulfilled that is written about me in the Law of Moses, the Prophets and the Psalms."

[45] Then he opened their minds so they could understand the Scriptures. [46] He told them, "This is what is written: The Messiah will suffer and rise from the dead on the third day, [47] and repentance for the forgiveness of sins will be preached in his name to all nations, beginning at Jerusalem. [48] You are witnesses of these things. [49] I am going to send you what my Father has promised; but stay in the city until you have been clothed with power from on high."

The Ascension of Jesus

[50] When he had led them out to the vicinity of Bethany, he lifted up his hands and blessed them. [51] While he was blessing them, he left them and was taken up into heaven. [52] Then they worshiped him and returned to Jerusalem with great joy. [53] And they stayed continually at the temple, praising God.

john

1514

AUTHOR
The apostle John.

AUDIENCE
Followers of Jesus. John wrote to convince
unbelievers and the doubting.

DATE
About A.D. 85–90, before John's exile to the
island of Patmos.

SETTING
John's eyewitness account is presumably the
last Gospel written.

VERSE TO REMEMBER
"But these are written that you may believe
that Jesus is the Messiah, the Son of God, and
that by believing you may have life in his
name." (20:31)

THEME TO CONSIDER
By faith, we must accept the facts about Jesus.
He is the Son of God who gives eternal life.

The Word Became Flesh

1 In the beginning was the Word, and the Word was with God, and the Word was God. ²He was with God in the beginning. ³Through him all things were made; without him nothing was made that has been made. ⁴In him was life, and that life was the light of all people. ⁵The light shines in the darkness, and the darkness has not overcome*ᵃ* it.

⁶There was a man sent from God whose name was John. ⁷He came as a witness to testify concerning that light, so that through him all might believe. ⁸He himself was not the light; he came only as a witness to the light.

⁹The true light that gives light to everyone was coming into the world. ¹⁰He was in the world, and though the world was made through him, the world did not recognize him. ¹¹He came to that which was his own, but his own did not receive him. ¹²Yet to all who did receive him, to those who believed in his name, he gave the right to become children of God— ¹³children born not of natural descent, nor of human decision or a husband's will, but born of God.

¹⁴The Word became flesh and made his dwelling among us. We have seen his glory, the glory of the one and only ˌSonˌ, who came from the Father, full of grace and truth.

¹⁵(John testified concerning him. He cried out, saying, "This is he of whom I said, 'He who comes after me has surpassed me because he was before me.'") ¹⁶Out of his fullness we have all received grace in place of grace already given. ¹⁷For the law was given through Moses; grace and truth came through Jesus Christ. ¹⁸No one has ever seen God, but the one and only ˌSonˌ, who is himself God and*ᵇ* is in closest relationship with the Father, has made him known.

> **at issue: acceptance**
>
> **1:12–13** What do you have to do in order to win your boss's acceptance? Your husband's or boyfriend's? Your parents'? Your friends'? Each may have different criteria by which you measure yourself in order to feel accepted. What about God? Does it seem that, like everyone else, God has his own set of hoops for you to jump through so that he will accept you? These verses debunk that myth. Anyone who believes in Jesus and receives him becomes part of God's family—completely accepted as his child. That's all it takes. No hoop-jumping required.

1515

John the Baptist Denies Being the Messiah

¹⁹Now this was John's testimony when the Jewish leaders in Jerusalem sent priests and Levites to ask him who he was. ²⁰He did not fail to confess, but confessed freely, "I am not the Messiah."

²¹They asked him, "Then who are you? Are you Elijah?"

He said, "I am not."

"Are you the Prophet?"

He answered, "No."

²²Finally they said, "Who are you? Give us an answer to take back to those who sent us. What do you say about yourself?"

²³John replied in the words of Isaiah the prophet, "I am the voice of one calling in the wilderness, 'Make straight the way for the Lord.'"*ᶜ*

²⁴Now the Pharisees who had been sent ²⁵questioned him, "Why then do you baptize if you are not the Messiah, nor Elijah, nor the Prophet?"

²⁶"I baptize with*ᵈ* water," John replied, "but among you stands one you do not know. ²⁷He is the one who comes after me, the thongs of whose sandals I am not worthy to untie."

²⁸This all happened at Bethany on the other side of the Jordan, where John was baptizing.

John's Testimony About Jesus

²⁹The next day John saw Jesus coming toward him and said, "Look, the Lamb of God, who takes away the sin of the world! ³⁰This is the one I meant when I said, 'A man who comes after me has surpassed me

---

ᵃ 5 Or *understood*   *ᵇ 18* Some manuscripts *but the only Son, who*   *ᶜ 23* Isaiah 40:3   *ᵈ 26* Or *in*; also in verses 31 and 33 (twice) because he was before me.' [31]I myself did not know him, but the reason I came baptizing with water was that he might be revealed to Israel."

[32]Then John gave this testimony: "I saw the Spirit come down from heaven as a dove and remain on him. [33]And I myself did not know him, but the one who sent me to baptize with water told me, 'The man on whom you see the Spirit come down and remain is the one who will baptize with the Holy Spirit.' [34]I have seen and I testify that this is God's Chosen One."[a]

John's Disciples Follow Jesus

[35]The next day John was there again with two of his disciples. [36]When he saw Jesus passing by, he said, "Look, the Lamb of God!"

[37]When the two disciples heard him say this, they followed Jesus. [38]Turning around, Jesus saw them following and asked, "What do you want?"

They said, "Rabbi" (which means "Teacher"), "where are you staying?"

[39]"Come," he replied, "and you will see."

So they went and saw where he was staying, and they spent that day with him. It was about four in the afternoon.

[40]Andrew, Simon Peter's brother, was one of the two who heard what John had said and who had followed Jesus. [41]The first thing Andrew did was to find his brother Simon and tell him, "We have found the Messiah" (that is, the Christ). [42]And he brought him to Jesus.

Jesus looked at him and said, "You are Simon son of John. You will be called Cephas" (which, when translated, is Peter[b]).

Jesus Calls Philip and Nathanael

[43]The next day Jesus decided to leave for Galilee. Finding Philip, he said to him, "Follow me."

[44]Philip, like Andrew and Peter, was from the town of Bethsaida. [45]Philip found Nathanael and told him, "We have found the one Moses wrote about in the Law, and about whom the prophets also wrote—Jesus of Nazareth, the son of Joseph."

[46]"Nazareth! Can anything good come from there?" Nathanael asked.

"Come and see," said Philip.

[47]When Jesus saw Nathanael approaching, he said of him, "Here truly is an Israelite in whom there is no deceit."

[48]"How do you know me?" Nathanael asked.

Jesus answered, "I saw you while you were still under the fig tree before Philip called you."

[49]Then Nathanael declared, "Rabbi, you are the Son of God; you are the king of Israel."

[50]Jesus said, "You believe[c] because I told you I saw you under the fig tree. You will see greater things than that." [51]He then added, "Very truly I tell you,[d] you[d] will see 'heaven open, and the angels of God ascending and descending on'[e] the Son of Man."

Jesus Changes Water into Wine

2 On the third day a wedding took place at Cana in Galilee. Jesus' mother was there, [2]and Jesus and his disciples had also been invited to the wedding. [3]When the wine was gone, Jesus' mother said to him, "They have no more wine."

[4]"Woman,[f] why do you involve me?" Jesus replied. "My hour has not yet come."

[5]His mother said to the servants, "Do whatever he tells you."

[6]Nearby stood six stone water jars, the kind used by the Jews for ceremonial washing, each holding from twenty to thirty gallons.[g]

[7]Jesus said to the servants, "Fill the jars with water"; so they filled them to the brim.

[8]Then he told them, "Now draw some out and take it to the master of the banquet."

They did so, [9]and the master of the banquet tasted the water that had been turned into wine. He did not realize where it had come from, though the servants who had drawn the water knew. Then he called

---

the bridegroom aside ¹⁰and said, "Everyone brings out the choice wine first and then the cheaper wine after the guests have had too much to drink; but you have saved the best till now."

¹¹What Jesus did here in Cana of Galilee was the first of the signs through which he revealed his glory; and his disciples put their faith in him.

¹²After this he went down to Capernaum with his mother and brothers and his disciples. There they stayed for a few days.

Jesus Clears the Temple Courts

¹³When it was almost time for the Jewish Passover, Jesus went up to Jerusalem. ¹⁴In the temple courts he found people selling cattle, sheep and doves, and others sitting at tables exchanging money. ¹⁵So he made a whip out of cords, and drove all from the temple courts, both sheep and cattle; he scattered the coins of the money changers and overturned their tables. ¹⁶To those who sold doves he said, "Get these out of here! Stop turning my Father's house into a market!" ¹⁷His disciples remembered that it is written: "Zeal for your house will consume me."ᵃ

¹⁸The Jews then responded to him, "What sign can you show us to prove your authority to do all this?"

¹⁹Jesus answered them, "Destroy this temple, and I will raise it again in three days."

²⁰They replied, "It has taken forty-six years to build this temple, and you are going to raise it in three days?" ²¹But the temple he had spoken of was his body. ²²After he was raised from the dead, his disciples recalled what he had said. Then they believed the scripture and the words that Jesus had spoken.

²³Now while he was in Jerusalem at the Passover Festival, many people saw the signs he was performing and believed in his name.ᵇ ²⁴But Jesus would not entrust himself to them, for he knew all people. ²⁵He did not need human testimony about them, for he knew what was in them.

1517

Jesus Teaches Nicodemus

3 Now there was a Pharisee, a man named Nicodemus who was a member of the Jewish ruling council. ²He came to Jesus at night and said, "Rabbi, we know that you are a teacher who has come from God. For no one could perform the signs you are doing if God were not with him."

³Jesus replied, "Very truly I tell you, no one can see the kingdom of God without being born again.ᶜ"

⁴"How can anyone be born when they are old?" Nicodemus asked. "Surely they cannot enter a second time into their mother's womb to be born!"

⁵Jesus answered, "Very truly I tell you, no one can enter the kingdom of God without being born of water and the Spirit. ⁶Flesh gives birth to flesh, but the Spiritᵈ gives birth to spirit. ⁷You should not be surprised at my saying, 'Youᵉ must be born again.' ⁸The wind blows wherever it pleases. You hear its sound, but you cannot tell where it comes from or where it is going. So it is with everyone born of the Spirit."ᶠ

⁹"How can this be?" Nicodemus asked.

¹⁰"You are Israel's teacher," said Jesus, "and do you not understand these things? ¹¹Very truly I tell you, we speak of what we know, and we testify to what we have seen, but still you people do not accept our testimony. ¹²I have spoken to you of earthly things and you do not believe; how then will you believe if I speak of heavenly things? ¹³No one has ever gone into heaven except the one who came from heaven—the Son of Man.ᵍ ¹⁴Just as Moses lifted up the snake in the wilderness, so the Son of Man must be lifted up,ʰ ¹⁵that everyone who believes may have eternal life in him."ⁱ

¹⁶For God so loved the world that he gave his one and only Son, that whoever believes in him shall not perish but have eternal life. ¹⁷For God did not send his Son into the

conversations

salvation «» 3:16–17,36

1» What exactly does it mean to "believe in the Son"?

2» Do you believe Jesus is the only way to heaven? How would you defend your answer?

3» What effect does gaining eternal life have on the way you live your life now?

For more on **salvation**, check the index.
For the next Conversations, go to p. 1533.

ᵃ 17 Psalm 69:9   ᵇ 23 Or *in him*   ᶜ 3 The Greek for *again* also means *from above*; also in verse 7.   ᵈ 6 Or *but spirit*   ᵉ 7 The Greek is plural.   ᶠ 8 The Greek for *Spirit* is the same as that for *wind*.   ᵍ 13 Some manuscripts *Man, who is in heaven*   ʰ 14 The Greek for *lifted up* also means *exalted.*   ⁱ 15 Some interpreters end the quotation with verse 21.

world to condemn the world, but to save the world through him. [18]Whoever believes in him is not condemned, but whoever does not believe stands condemned already because they have not believed in the name of God's one and only Son. [19]This is the verdict: Light has come into the world, but people loved darkness instead of light because their deeds were evil. [20]All those who do evil hate the light, and will not come into the light for fear that their deeds will be exposed. [21]But those who live by the truth come into the light, so that it may be seen plainly that what they have done has been done in the sight of God.

John Testifies Again About Jesus

[22]After this, Jesus and his disciples went out into the Judean countryside, where he spent some time with them, and baptized. [23]Now John also was baptizing at Aenon near Salim, because there was plenty of water, and people were coming and being baptized. [24](This was before John was put in prison.) [25]An argument developed between some of John's disciples and a certain Jew over the matter of ceremonial washing. [26]They came to John and said to him, "Rabbi, that man who was with you on the other side of the Jordan—the one you testified about—look, he is baptizing, and everyone is going to him."

[27]To this John replied, "A person can receive only what is given from heaven. [28]You yourselves can testify that I said, 'I am not the Messiah but am sent ahead of him.' [29]The bride belongs to the bridegroom. The friend who attends the bridegroom waits and listens for him, and is full of joy when he hears the bridegroom's voice. That joy is mine, and it is now complete. [30]He must become greater; I must become less."[a]

[31]The one who comes from above is above all; the one who is from the earth belongs to the earth, and speaks as one from the earth. The one who comes from heaven is above all. [32]He testifies to what he has seen and heard, but no one accepts his testimony. [33]The person who has accepted it has certified that God is truthful. [34]For the one whom God has sent speaks the words of God, for God[b] gives the Spirit without limit. [35]The Father loves the Son and has placed everything in his hands. [36]Whoever believes in the Son has eternal life, but whoever rejects the Son will not see life, for God's wrath remains on them.

Jesus Talks With a Samaritan Woman

4 Now Jesus learned that the Pharisees had heard that he was gaining and baptizing more disciples than John— [2]although in fact it was not Jesus who baptized, but his disciples. [3]So he left Judea and went back once more to Galilee.

[4]Now he had to go through Samaria. [5]So he came to a town in Samaria called Sychar, near the plot of ground Jacob had given to his son Joseph. [6]Jacob's well was there, and Jesus, tired as he was from the journey, sat down by the well. It was about noon.

[7]When a Samaritan woman came to draw water, Jesus said to her, "Will you give me a drink?" [8](His disciples had gone into the town to buy food.)

[9]The Samaritan woman said to him, "You are a Jew and I am a Samaritan woman. How can you ask me for a drink?" (For Jews do not associate with Samaritans.[c])

[10]Jesus answered her, "If you knew the gift of God and who it is that asks you for a drink, you would have asked him and he would have given you living water."

[11]"Sir," the woman said, "you have nothing to draw with and the well is deep. Where can you get this living water? [12]Are you greater than our father Jacob, who gave us the well and drank from it himself, as did also his sons and his flocks and herds?"

atissue:prejudice

4:1–26 For a Jew to speak to a Samaritan was unheard of. For a man to speak to a woman violated cultural mores. For a Jewish teacher to speak to a well-known, sinful Samaritan woman was unbelievable. Jesus knew exactly who this woman was, and he boldly crossed a series of racial, social and economic lines in order to reach out to her. He knew what he had to offer was too important to be held back by tradition or customs. What lines might you need to cross to share the living water with those who may not even know they thirst for it?

---

[a] *30* Some interpreters end the quotation with verse 36.   [b] *34* Greek *he*   [c] *9* Or *do not use dishes Samaritans have used*

[13]Jesus answered, "Everyone who drinks this water will be thirsty again, [14]but those who drink the water I give them will never thirst. Indeed, the water I give them will become in them a spring of water welling up to eternal life."

[15]The woman said to him, "Sir, give me this water so that I won't get thirsty and have to keep coming here to draw water."

[16]He told her, "Go, call your husband and come back."

[17]"I have no husband," she replied.

Jesus said to her, "You are right when you say you have no husband. [18]The fact is, you have had five husbands, and the man you now have is not your husband. What you have just said is quite true."

[19]"Sir," the woman said, "I can see that you are a prophet. [20]Our ancestors worshiped on this mountain, but you Jews claim that the place where we must worship is in Jerusalem."

[21]"Woman,"[a] Jesus replied, "believe me, a time is coming when you will worship the Father neither on this mountain nor in Jerusalem. [22]You Samaritans worship what you do not know; we worship what we do know, for salvation is from the Jews. [23]Yet a time is coming and has now come when the true worshipers will worship the Father in the Spirit and in truth, for they are the kind of worshipers the Father seeks. [24]God is spirit, and his worshipers must worship in the Spirit and in truth."

[25]The woman said, "I know that Messiah" (called Christ) "is coming. When he comes, he will explain everything to us."

[26]Then Jesus declared, "I, the one speaking to you—I am he."

The Disciples Rejoin Jesus

[27]Just then his disciples returned and were surprised to find him talking with a woman. But no one asked, "What do you want?" or "Why are you talking with her?"

[28]Then, leaving her water jar, the woman went back to the town and said to the people, [29]"Come, see a man who told me everything I ever did. Could this be the Messiah?" [30]They came out of the town and made their way toward him.

[31]Meanwhile his disciples urged him, "Rabbi, eat something."

[32]But he said to them, "I have food to eat that you know nothing about."

[33]Then his disciples said to each other, "Could someone have brought him food?"

[34]"My food," said Jesus, "is to do the will of him who sent me and to finish his work. [35]Don't you have a saying, 'It's still four months until harvest'? I tell you, open your eyes and look at the fields! They are ripe for harvest. [36]Even now those who reap draw their wages, even now they harvest the crop for eternal life, so that the sower and the reaper may be glad together. [37]Thus the saying 'One sows and another reaps' is true. [38]I sent you to reap what you have not worked for. Others have done the hard work, and you have reaped the benefits of their labor."

Many Samaritans Believe

[39]Many of the Samaritans from that town believed in him because of the woman's testimony, "He told me everything I ever did." [40]So when the Samaritans came to him, they urged him to stay with them, and he stayed two days. [41]And because of his words many more became believers.

[42]They said to the woman, "We no longer believe just because of what you said; now we have heard for ourselves, and we know that this man really is the Savior of the world."

Jesus Heals the Official's Son

[43]After the two days he left for Galilee. [44](Now Jesus himself had pointed out that prophets have no honor in their own country.) [45]When he arrived in Galilee, the Galileans welcomed him. They had seen all that he had done in Jerusalem at the Passover Festival, for they also had been there.

[46]Once more he visited Cana in Galilee, where he had turned the water into wine. And there was a certain royal official whose son lay sick at Capernaum. [47]When this man heard that Jesus had arrived in Galilee from Judea, he went to him and begged him to come and heal his son, who was close to death.

[48]"Unless you people see signs and wonders," Jesus told him, "you will never believe."

---

[a] 21 The Greek for *Woman* does not denote any disrespect.

1519

⁴⁹The royal official said, "Sir, come down before my child dies."

⁵⁰"Go," Jesus replied, "your son will live."

The man took Jesus at his word and departed. ⁵¹While he was still on the way, his servants met him with the news that his boy was living. ⁵²When he inquired as to the time when his son got better, they said to him, "Yesterday, at one in the afternoon, the fever left him."

⁵³Then the father realized that this was the exact time at which Jesus had said to him, "Your son will live." So he and his whole household believed.

⁵⁴This was the second sign Jesus performed after coming from Judea to Galilee.

The Healing at the Pool

5 Some time later, Jesus went up to Jerusalem for one of the Jewish festivals. ²Now there is in Jerusalem near the Sheep Gate a pool, which in Aramaic is called Bethesda*a* and which is surrounded by five covered colonnades. ³[⁴]Here a great number of disabled people used to lie—the blind, the lame, the paralyzed.*b* ⁵One who was there had been an invalid for thirty-eight years. ⁶When Jesus saw him lying there and learned that he had been in this condition for a long time, he asked him, "Do you want to get well?"

⁷"Sir," the invalid replied, "I have no one to help me into the pool when the water is stirred. While I am trying to get in, someone else goes down ahead of me."

⁸Then Jesus said to him, "Get up! Pick up your mat and walk." ⁹At once the man was cured; he picked up his mat and walked.

The day on which this took place was a Sabbath, ¹⁰and so the Jewish leaders said to the man who had been healed, "It is the Sabbath; the law forbids you to carry your mat."

¹¹But he replied, "The man who made me well said to me, 'Pick up your mat and walk.'"

¹²So they asked him, "Who is this fellow who told you to pick it up and walk?"

¹³The man who was healed had no idea who it was, for Jesus had slipped away into the crowd that was there.

¹⁴Later Jesus found him at the temple and said to him, "See, you are well again. Stop sinning or something worse may happen to you." ¹⁵The man went away and told the Jewish leaders that it was Jesus who had made him well.

The Authority of the Son

¹⁶So, because Jesus was doing these things on the Sabbath, the Jewish leaders began to persecute him. ¹⁷In his defense Jesus said to them, "My Father is always at his work to this very day, and I too am working." ¹⁸For this reason they tried all the more to kill him; not only was he breaking the Sabbath, but he was even calling God his own Father, making himself equal with God.

¹⁹Jesus gave them this answer: "Very truly I tell you, the Son can do nothing by himself; he can do only what he sees his Father doing, because whatever the Father does the Son also does. ²⁰For the Father loves the Son and shows him all he does. Yes, and he will show him even greater works than these, so that you will be amazed. ²¹For just as the Father raises the dead and gives them life, even so the Son gives life to whom he is pleased to give it. ²²Moreover, the Father judges no one, but has entrusted all judgment to the Son, ²³that all may honor the Son just as they honor the Father. Whoever does not honor the Son does not honor the Father, who sent him.

²⁴"Very truly I tell you, whoever hears my word and believes him who sent me has eternal life and will not be judged but has crossed over from death to life. ²⁵Very truly I tell you, a time is coming and has now come when the dead will hear the voice of the Son of God and those who hear will live. ²⁶For as the Father has life in himself, so he has granted the Son also to have life in himself. ²⁷And he has given him authority to judge because he is the Son of Man.

²⁸"Do not be amazed at this, for a time is coming when all who are in their graves will hear his voice ²⁹and come out—those who have done what is good will rise to live, and those who have done what is

---

a 2 Some manuscripts Bethzatha; other manuscripts Bethsaida   b 3 Some later manuscripts and some ancient witnesses, wholly or in part, paralyzed—and they waited for the moving of the waters. ⁴From time to time an angel of the Lord would come down and stir up the waters. The first person into the pool after each such disturbance would be cured of whatever disease they had.

evil will rise to be condemned. ³⁰By myself I can do nothing; I judge only as I hear, and my judgment is just, for I seek not to please myself but him who sent me.

Testimonies About Jesus

³¹"If I testify about myself, my testimony is not true. ³²There is another who testifies in my favor, and I know that his testimony about me is true.

³³"You have sent to John and he has testified to the truth. ³⁴Not that I accept human testimony; but I mention it that you may be saved. ³⁵John was a lamp that burned and gave light, and you chose for a time to enjoy his light.

³⁶"I have testimony weightier than that of John. For the works that the Father has given me to finish— the very works that I am doing—testify that the Father has sent me. ³⁷And the Father who sent me has himself testified concerning me. You have never heard his voice nor seen his form, ³⁸nor does his word dwell in you, for you do not believe the one he sent. ³⁹You study*ᵃ* the Scriptures diligently because you think that in them you possess eternal life. These are the very Scriptures that testify about me, ⁴⁰yet you refuse to come to me to have life.

⁴¹"I do not accept glory from human beings, ⁴²but I know you. I know that you do not have the love of God in your hearts. ⁴³I have come in my Father's name, and you do not accept me; but if someone else comes in his own name, you will accept him. ⁴⁴How can you believe since you accept glory from one another but do not seek the glory that comes from the only God*ᵇ*?

⁴⁵"But do not think I will accuse you before the Father. Your accuser is Moses, on whom your hopes are set. ⁴⁶If you believed Moses, you would believe me, for he wrote about me. ⁴⁷But since you do not believe what he wrote, how are you going to believe what I say?"

1521

Jesus Feeds the Five Thousand

6 Some time after this, Jesus crossed to the far shore of the Sea of Galilee (that is, the Sea of Tiberias), ²and a great crowd of people followed him because they saw the signs he had performed by healing the sick. ³Then Jesus went up on a mountainside and sat down with his disciples. ⁴The Jewish Passover Festival was near.

⁵When Jesus looked up and saw a great crowd coming toward him, he said to Philip, "Where shall we buy bread for these people to eat?" ⁶He asked this only to test him, for he already had in mind what he was going to do.

⁷Philip answered him, "It would take almost a year's wages*ᶜ* to buy enough bread for each one to have a bite!"

⁸Another of his disciples, Andrew, Simon Peter's brother, spoke up, ⁹"Here is a boy with five small barley loaves and two small fish, but how far will they go among so many?"

¹⁰Jesus said, "Have the people sit down." There was plenty of grass in that place, and they sat down (about five thousand men were there). ¹¹Jesus then took the loaves, gave thanks, and distributed to those who were seated as much as they wanted. He did the same with the fish.

¹²When they had all had enough to eat, he said to his disciples, "Gather the pieces that are left over. Let nothing be wasted." ¹³So they gathered them and filled twelve baskets with the pieces of the five barley loaves left over by those who had eaten.

¹⁴After the people saw the sign Jesus performed, they began to say, "Surely this is the Prophet who is to come into the world." ¹⁵Jesus, knowing that they intended to come and make him king by force, withdrew again to a mountain by himself.

Jesus Walks on the Water

¹⁶When evening came, his disciples went down to the lake, ¹⁷where they got into a boat and set off across the lake for Capernaum. By now it was dark, and Jesus had not yet joined them. ¹⁸A strong wind was blowing and the waters grew rough. ¹⁹When they had rowed about three or three and a half miles,*ᵈ* they saw Jesus approaching the boat, walking on the water; and they were frightened. ²⁰But he said to them, "It is I; don't be afraid." ²¹Then they were willing to take him into the boat, and immediately the boat reached the shore where they were heading.

ᵃ 39 Or *39Study*   *ᵇ 44* Some early manuscripts *the Only One*   *ᶜ 7* Greek *take two hundred denarii*   *ᵈ 19* Or about 5 or 6 kilometers

²²The next day the crowd that had stayed on the opposite shore of the lake realized that only one boat had been there, and that Jesus had not entered it with his disciples, but that they had gone away alone. ²³Then some boats from Tiberias landed near the place where the people had eaten the bread after the Lord had given thanks. ²⁴Once the crowd realized that neither Jesus nor his disciples were there, they got into the boats and went to Capernaum in search of Jesus.

Jesus the Bread of Life

²⁵When they found him on the other side of the lake, they asked him, "Rabbi, when did you get here?"

²⁶Jesus answered, "Very truly I tell you, you are looking for me, not because you saw the signs I performed but because you ate the loaves and had your fill. ²⁷Do not work for food that spoils, but for food that endures to eternal life, which the Son of Man will give you. On him God the Father has placed his seal of approval."

²⁸Then they asked him, "What must we do to do the works God requires?"

²⁹Jesus answered, "The work of God is this: to believe in the one he has sent."

³⁰So they asked him, "What sign then will you give that we may see it and believe you? What will you do? ³¹Our ancestors ate the manna in the wilderness; as it is written: 'He gave them bread from heaven to eat.'ᵃ"

³²Jesus said to them, "Very truly I tell you, it is not Moses who has given you the bread from heaven, but it is my Father who gives you the true bread from heaven. ³³For the bread of God is the bread that comes down from heaven and gives life to the world."

³⁴"Sir," they said, "always give us this bread."

³⁵Then Jesus declared, "I am the bread of life. Whoever comes to me will never go hungry, and whoever believes in me will never be thirsty. ³⁶But as I told you, you have seen me and still you do not believe. ³⁷All whom the Father gives me will come to me, and whoever comes to me I will never drive away. ³⁸For I have come down from heaven not to do my will but to do the will of him who sent me. ³⁹And this is the will of him who sent me, that I shall lose none of all those he has given me, but raise them up at the last day. ⁴⁰For my Father's will is that everyone who looks to the Son and believes in him shall have eternal life, and I will raise them up at the last day."

⁴¹At this the Jews there began to grumble about him because he said, "I am the bread that came down from heaven." ⁴²They said, "Is this not Jesus, the son of Joseph, whose father and mother we know? How can he now say, 'I came down from heaven'?"

⁴³"Stop grumbling among yourselves," Jesus answered. ⁴⁴"No one can come to me unless the Father who sent me draws them, and I will raise them up at the last day. ⁴⁵It is written in the Prophets: 'They will all be taught by God.'ᵇ Everyone who has heard the Father and learned from him comes to me. ⁴⁶No one has seen the Father except the one who is from God; only he has seen the Father. ⁴⁷Very truly I tell you, whoever believes has eternal life. ⁴⁸I am the bread of life. ⁴⁹Your ancestors ate the manna in the wilderness, yet they died. ⁵⁰But here is the bread that comes down from heaven, which people may eat

---

ᵃ 31 Exodus 16:4; Neh. 9:15; Psalm 78:24,25   ᵇ 45 Isaiah 54:13

HE IS: the bread of life

6:48–51 God's miraculous provision of manna in the desert only sustained physical life for a time. But Jesus is *the bread of life* who provides eternal life. Jesus called himself the living bread that came down from heaven.

Are you allowing your worldly appetites to consume you? Such a lifestyle leads to disappointment, decay, disillusionment and death. Make *the bread of life* the whole of your diet. Unlike the fares of this world that never fully satisfy your appetite, you will taste and see that God is good (see Psalm 34:8) and that he fulfills you.

For the next He Is, go to p. 1527.

and not die. ⁵¹I am the living bread that came down from heaven. Whoever eats of this bread will live forever. This bread is my flesh, which I will give for the life of the world."

⁵²Then the Jews began to argue sharply among themselves, "How can this man give us his flesh to eat?"

⁵³Jesus said to them, "Very truly I tell you, unless you eat the flesh of the Son of Man and drink his blood, you have no life in you. ⁵⁴Whoever eats my flesh and drinks my blood has eternal life, and I will raise them up at the last day. ⁵⁵For my flesh is real food and my blood is real drink. ⁵⁶Whoever eats my flesh and drinks my blood remains in me, and I in them. ⁵⁷Just as the living Father sent me and I live because of the Father, so the one who feeds on me will live because of me. ⁵⁸This is the bread that came down from heaven. Your ancestors ate manna and died, but whoever feeds on this bread will live forever." ⁵⁹He said this while teaching in the synagogue in Capernaum.

Many Disciples Desert Jesus

⁶⁰On hearing it, many of his disciples said, "This is a hard teaching. Who can accept it?"

⁶¹Aware that his disciples were grumbling about this, Jesus said to them, "Does this offend you? ⁶²Then what if you see the Son of Man ascend to where he was before! ⁶³The Spirit gives life; the flesh counts for nothing. The words I have spoken to you—they are full of the Spirit[a] and life. ⁶⁴Yet there are some of you who do not believe." For Jesus had known from the beginning which of them did not believe and who would betray him. ⁶⁵He went on to say, "This is why I told you that no one can come to me unless the Father has enabled them."

⁶⁶From this time many of his disciples turned back and no longer followed him.

⁶⁷"You do not want to leave too, do you?" Jesus asked the Twelve.

⁶⁸Simon Peter answered him, "Lord, to whom shall we go? You have the words of eternal life. ⁶⁹We have come to believe and to know that you are the Holy One of God."

⁷⁰Then Jesus replied, "Have I not chosen you, the Twelve? Yet one of you is a devil!" ⁷¹(He meant Judas, the son of Simon Iscariot, who, though one of the Twelve, was later to betray him.)

1523

Jesus Goes to the Festival of Tabernacles

7 After this, Jesus went around in Galilee. He did not want[b] to go about in Judea because the Jewish leaders there were looking for a way to kill him. ²But when the Jewish Festival of Tabernacles was near, ³Jesus' brothers said to him, "Leave Galilee and go to Judea, so that your disciples there may see the works you do. ⁴No one who wants to become a public figure acts in secret. Since you are doing these things, show yourself to the world." ⁵For even his own brothers did not believe in him.

⁶Therefore Jesus told them, "My time is not yet here; for you any time will do. ⁷The world cannot hate you, but it hates me because I testify that its works are evil. ⁸You go to the festival. I am not[c] going up to this festival, because my time has not yet fully come." ⁹Having said this, he stayed in Galilee.

¹⁰However, after his brothers had left for the festival, he went also, not publicly, but in secret. ¹¹Now at the festival the Jewish leaders were watching for Jesus and asking, "Where is he?"

¹²Among the crowds there was widespread whispering about him. Some said, "He is a good man."

Others replied, "No, he deceives the people." ¹³But no one would say anything publicly about him for fear of the leaders.

Jesus Teaches at the Festival

¹⁴Not until halfway through the festival did Jesus go up to the temple courts and begin to teach. ¹⁵The Jews there were amazed and asked, "How did this man get such learning without having been taught?"

¹⁶Jesus answered, "My teaching is not my own. It comes from the one who sent me. ¹⁷Anyone who chooses to do the will of God will find out whether my teaching comes from God or whether I speak on my own. ¹⁸Whoever speaks on their own does so to gain personal glory, but he who seeks the glory of the one who sent him is a man of truth; there is nothing false about him. ¹⁹Has not Moses given you the law? Yet not one of you keeps the law. Why are you trying to kill me?"

²⁰"You are demon-possessed," the crowd answered. "Who is trying to kill you?"

---

[a] 63 Or are Spirit; or are spirit   [b] 1 Some manuscripts not have authority   [c] 8 Some manuscripts not yet

myth# 87 "IF I HAD HER LIFE, THEN I'D BE HAPPY."

I can't help it. Comparing myself to others just comes naturally for me. I've done it all my life. I remember in grade school comparing my thin, stick-straight hair to the thick, curly hair of the girl who sat in front of me. In high school, I compared my body to other girls' bodies, shamelessly in search of someone who was flatter than I was! Now I compare my whole life to other women's lives. What kind of clothes I have. My kids. Husband. House. In-laws. Everything.

Sometimes these thoughts even sabotage my desire to be friends with other women. I always seem to be envious of something about everyone. It seems that others I know have it so much easier than I do. They're prettier. Their husbands seem more loving and make more money. Their kids don't fight. Their houses are big and beautiful, unlike my home, the perpetual disaster zone. If my life could be more like theirs in some small way, it would ease this nagging dissatisfaction. I'd finally be at peace.

I've felt this even more acutely this past year, ever since I became friends with Tiffany. Talk about a woman with a good life! Her husband makes a killing in commercial real estate. She hires a decorator to furnish her beautiful, spacious home. When we shop together, she gives no thought to price. She's laidback and fun to be around. She's thin and doesn't struggle with her weight the way I do. She does private catering (did I mention she's a gourmet cook?) and works when she wants to. I can't tell whether I love her or I'm just in awe of her life. I feel so drab around her. I tried to be happy for her when she got a new car and announced she was pregnant. (Did I mention I drive a ten-year-old car and have been trying to conceive for a year?) It's hard for me not to want her life.

—Noelle

WOMEN ARE ESPECIALLY

susceptible to comparison. We either compare ourselves to others in a superior way that leads to pride. ("I'm glad I don't have her life.") Or we focus on someone else who seems to have the perfect life and let discontentment grow in our own hearts. ("I wish I had her life.") But you can break free from either extreme. Remind yourself that . . .

- **Envy is pointless.** Often the devil wants to distract you from what God has for your life by getting you to focus on someone else. Don't let him do that to you! Instead, focus on what God has for *you* and how he wants to use you.

- **You are unique.** You are not a victim in this life but a unique creation of God with a role he wants you to play in your world (see Psalm 139:14). If you spend all of your time trying to be someone else, you aren't fulfilling the role he designed for you.

- **You can choose to accept yourself and others.** Ask Jesus to change your focus from appearances to what really matters (see John 7:24) so that you can accept others—and yourself—just the way they (or you) are.

The secret to contentment is not having a perfect life with everything you want. Contentment is a learned attitude (see Philippians 4:11–13). When you are tempted to play the comparison game, flex your gratitude muscles instead. You may want to start a thankfulness journal in which you list blessings God has given you. Or you may simply want to name them off while you drive in the car or pray or take a shower. Choose to focus on Christ and his kingdom rather than others and the things of this world, and you will be amazed at how your perspective changes from comparison to contentment.

> "Envy germinates in our souls when we decide to plant the seeds of comparison."
>
> —Dennis Rainey

1525

> "I PRAISE YOU BECAUSE I AM FEARFULLY AND WONDERFULLY MADE; YOUR WORKS ARE WONDERFUL, I KNOW THAT FULL WELL."
>
> PSALM 139:14

SEE ALSO

Exodus 20:16
1 Timothy 6:6–10
James 3:13–18

For more on **Contentment**, check the index.

²¹Jesus said to them, "I did one miracle, and you are all amazed. ²²Yet, because Moses gave you circumcision (though actually it did not come from Moses, but from the patriarchs), you circumcise a boy on the Sabbath. ²³Now if a boy can be circumcised on the Sabbath so that the law of Moses may not be broken, why are you angry with me for healing a man's whole body on the Sabbath? ²⁴Stop judging by mere appearances, but instead judge correctly."

Division Over Who Jesus Is

²⁵At that point some of the people of Jerusalem began to ask, "Isn't this the man they are trying to kill? ²⁶Here he is, speaking publicly, and they are not saying a word to him. Have the authorities really concluded that he is the Messiah? ²⁷But we know where this man is from; when the Messiah comes, no one will know where he is from."

²⁸Then Jesus, still teaching in the temple courts, cried out, "Yes, you know me, and you know where I am from. I am not here on my own authority, but he who sent me is true. You do not know him, ²⁹but I know him because I am from him and he sent me."

³⁰At this they tried to seize him, but no one laid a hand on him, because his hour had not yet come. ³¹Still, many in the crowd put their faith in him. They said, "When the Messiah comes, will he perform more signs than this man?"

³²The Pharisees heard the crowd whispering such things about him. Then the chief priests and the Pharisees sent temple guards to arrest him.

³³Jesus said, "I am with you for only a short time, and then I go to the one who sent me. ³⁴You will look for me, but you will not find me; and where I am, you cannot come."

³⁵The Jews said to one another, "Where does this man intend to go that we cannot find him? Will he go where our people live scattered among the Greeks, and teach the Greeks? ³⁶What did he mean when he said, 'You will look for me, but you will not find me,' and 'Where I am, you cannot come'?"

³⁷On the last and greatest day of the festival, Jesus stood and said in a loud voice, "Let anyone who is thirsty come to me and drink. ³⁸Whoever believes in me, as Scripture has said, rivers of living water will flow from within them."^a ³⁹By this he meant the Spirit, whom those who believed in him were later to receive. Up to that time the Spirit had not been given, since Jesus had not yet been glorified.

⁴⁰On hearing his words, some of the people said, "Surely this man is the Prophet."

⁴¹Others said, "He is the Messiah."

Still others asked, "How can the Messiah come from Galilee? ⁴²Does not Scripture say that the Messiah will come from David's descendants and from Bethlehem, the town where David lived?" ⁴³Thus the people were divided because of Jesus. ⁴⁴Some wanted to seize him, but no one laid a hand on him.

Unbelief of the Jewish Leaders

⁴⁵Finally the temple guards went back to the chief priests and the Pharisees, who asked them, "Why didn't you bring him in?"

⁴⁶"No one ever spoke the way this man does," the guards replied.

⁴⁷"You mean he has deceived you also?" the Pharisees retorted. ⁴⁸"Have any of the rulers or of the Pharisees believed in him? ⁴⁹No! But this mob that knows nothing of the law—there is a curse on them."

⁵⁰Nicodemus, who had gone to Jesus earlier and who was one of their own number, asked, ⁵¹"Does our law condemn a man without first hearing him to find out what he has been doing?"

⁵²They replied, "Are you from Galilee, too? Look into it, and you will find that a prophet does not come out of Galilee."

[The earliest manuscripts and many other ancient witnesses do not have John 7:53-8:11.]

8 ⁵³*Then they all went home,* ¹*but Jesus went to the Mount of Olives.*

²*At dawn he appeared again in the temple courts, where all the people gathered around him, and he sat down to teach them.* ³*The teachers of the law and the Pharisees brought in a woman caught in adultery. They made her stand*

---

^a *37,38 Or me. And let anyone drink* ³⁸*who believes in me." As Scripture has said, "Out of him (or them) will flow rivers of living water."*

before the group ⁴and said to Jesus, "Teacher, this woman was caught in the act of adultery. ⁵In the Law Moses commanded us to stone such women. Now what do you say?" ⁶They were using this question as a trap, in order to have a basis for accusing him.

But Jesus bent down and started to write on the ground with his finger. ⁷When they kept on questioning him, he straightened up and said to them, "Let any one of you who is without sin be the first to throw a stone at her." ⁸Again he stooped down and wrote on the ground.

⁹At this, those who heard began to go away one at a time, the older ones first, until only Jesus was left, with the woman still standing there. ¹⁰Jesus straightened up and asked her, "Woman,ᵃ where are they? Has no one condemned you?"

¹¹"No one, sir," she said.

"Then neither do I condemn you," Jesus declared. "Go now and leave your life of sin."

Dispute Over Jesus' Testimony

¹²When Jesus spoke again to the people, he said, "I am the light of the world. Whoever follows me will never walk in darkness, but will have the light of life."

HE IS: the light of the world

8:1–12 Imagine the effect that Jesus had that morning in the temple courts. How appropriate his later words: I am *the light of the world*. The contrast between dark and light was magnified that day. The adulterous woman's actions were exposed, brought out of the dark night by the gracious, forgiving Light.

If you are hiding a dark sin, you may fear what the light of Jesus may do to you. He exposes your sin, but he also shines his forgiveness on you. This light thaws you, heals you and frees you from the prison of darkness (see 1 John 1:5). Turn to the Light.

For the next He Is, go to p. 1530.

¹³The Pharisees challenged him, "Here you are, appearing as your own witness; your testimony is not valid."

¹⁴Jesus answered, "Even if I testify on my own behalf, my testimony is valid, for I know where I came from and where I am going. But you have no idea where I come from or where I am going. ¹⁵You judge by human standards; I pass judgment on no one. ¹⁶But if I do judge, my decisions are true, because I am not alone. I stand with the Father, who sent me. ¹⁷In your own Law it is written that the testimony of two witnesses is true. ¹⁸I am one who testifies for myself; my other witness is the Father, who sent me."

¹⁹Then they asked him, "Where is your father?"

"You do not know me or my Father," Jesus replied. "If you knew me, you would know my Father also." ²⁰He spoke these words while teaching in the temple courts near the place where the offerings were put. Yet no one seized him, because his hour had not yet come.

Dispute Over Who Jesus Is

²¹Once more Jesus said to them, "I am going away, and you will look for me, and you will die in your sin. Where I go, you cannot come."

²²This made the Jews ask, "Will he kill himself? Is that why he says, 'Where I go, you cannot come'?"

²³But he continued, "You are from below; I am from above. You are of this world; I am not of this world. ²⁴I told you that you would die in your sins; if you do not believe that I am he, you will indeed die in your sins."

ᵃ *10* The Greek for *Woman* does not denote any disrespect.

²⁵"Who are you?" they asked.

"Just what I have been telling you from the beginning," Jesus replied. ²⁶"I have much to say in judgment of you. But he who sent me is trustworthy, and what I have heard from him I tell the world."

²⁷They did not understand that he was telling them about his Father. ²⁸So Jesus said, "When you have lifted up^a the Son of Man, then you will know that I am he and that I do nothing on my own but speak just what the Father has taught me. ²⁹The one who sent me is with me; he has not left me alone, for I always do what pleases him." ³⁰Even as he spoke, many put their faith in him.

Dispute Over Whose Children Jesus' Opponents Are

³¹To the Jews who had believed him, Jesus said, "If you hold to my teaching, you are really my disciples. ³²Then you will know the truth, and the truth will set you free."

³³They answered him, "We are Abraham's descendants and have never been slaves of anyone. How can you say that we shall be set free?"

³⁴Jesus replied, "Very truly I tell you, everyone who sins is a slave to sin. ³⁵Now a slave has no permanent place in the family, but a son belongs to it forever. ³⁶So if the Son sets you free, you will be free indeed. ³⁷I know you are Abraham's descendants. Yet you are looking for a way to kill me, because you have no room for my word. ³⁸I am telling you what I have seen in the Father's presence, and you are doing what you have heard from your father.^b"

³⁹"Abraham is our father," they answered.

"If you were Abraham's children," said Jesus, "then you would^c do what Abraham did. ⁴⁰As it is, you are looking for a way to kill me, a man who has told you the truth that I heard from God. Abraham did not do such things. ⁴¹You are doing the works of your own father."

"We are not illegitimate children," they protested. "The only Father we have is God himself."

⁴²Jesus said to them, "If God were your Father, you would love me, for I came from God and now am here. I have not come on my own; but he sent me. ⁴³Why is my language not clear to you? Because you are unable to hear what I say. ⁴⁴You belong to your father, the devil, and you want to carry out your father's desires. He was a murderer from the beginning, not holding to the truth, for there is no truth in him. When he lies, he speaks his native language, for he is a liar and the father of lies. ⁴⁵Yet because I tell the truth, you do not believe me! ⁴⁶Can any of you prove me guilty of sin? If I am telling the truth, why don't you believe me? ⁴⁷Whoever belongs to God hears what God says. The reason you do not hear is that you do not belong to God."

Jesus' Claims About Himself

⁴⁸The Jews answered him, "Aren't we right in saying that you are a Samaritan and demon-possessed?"

⁴⁹"I am not possessed by a demon," said Jesus, "but I honor my Father and you dishonor me. ⁵⁰I am not seeking glory for myself; but there is one who seeks it, and he is the judge. ⁵¹Very truly I tell you, whoever obeys my word will never see death."

⁵²At this they exclaimed, "Now we know that you are demon-possessed! Abraham died and so did the prophets, yet you say that whoever obeys your word will never taste death. ⁵³Are you greater than our father Abraham? He died, and so did the prophets. Who do you think you are?"

⁵⁴Jesus replied, "If I glorify myself, my glory means nothing. My Father, whom you claim as your God, is the one who glorifies me. ⁵⁵Though you do not know him, I know him. If I said I did not, I would be a liar like you, but I do know him and obey his word. ⁵⁶Your father Abraham rejoiced at the thought of seeing my day; he saw it and was glad."

⁵⁷"You are not yet fifty years old," they said to him, "and you have seen Abraham!"

⁵⁸"Very truly I tell you," Jesus answered, "before Abraham was born, I am!" ⁵⁹At this, they picked up stones to stone him, but Jesus hid himself, slipping away from the temple grounds.

Jesus Heals a Man Born Blind

9 As he went along, he saw a man blind from birth. ²His disciples asked him, "Rabbi, who sinned, this man or his parents, that he was born blind?"

---

^a 28 The Greek for lifted up also means exalted.   ^b 38 Or presence. Therefore do what you have heard from the Father.   ^c 39 Some early manuscripts "If you are Abraham's children," said Jesus, "then

³"Neither this man nor his parents sinned," said Jesus, "but this happened so that the works of God might be displayed in him. ⁴As long as it is day, we must do the works of him who sent me. Night is coming, when no one can work. ⁵While I am in the world, I am the light of the world."

⁶Having said this, he spit on the ground, made some mud with the saliva, and put it on the man's eyes. ⁷"Go," he told him, "wash in the Pool of Siloam" (this word means "Sent"). So the man went and washed, and came home seeing.

⁸His neighbors and those who had formerly seen him begging asked, "Isn't this the same man who used to sit and beg?" ⁹Some claimed that he was.

Others said, "No, he only looks like him."

But he himself insisted, "I am the man."

¹⁰"How then were your eyes opened?" they asked.

¹¹He replied, "The man they call Jesus made some mud and put it on my eyes. He told me to go to Siloam and wash. So I went and washed, and then I could see."

¹²"Where is this man?" they asked him.

"I don't know," he said.

The Pharisees Investigate the Healing

¹³They brought to the Pharisees the man who had been blind. ¹⁴Now the day on which Jesus had made the mud and opened the man's eyes was a Sabbath. ¹⁵Therefore the Pharisees also asked him how he had received his sight. "He put mud on my eyes," the man replied, "and I washed, and now I see."

¹⁶Some of the Pharisees said, "This man is not from God, for he does not keep the Sabbath."

But others asked, "How can a sinner perform such signs?" So they were divided.

¹⁷Then they turned again to the blind man, "What have you to say about him? It was your eyes he opened."

The man replied, "He is a prophet."

¹⁸They still did not believe that he had been blind and had received his sight until they sent for the man's parents. ¹⁹"Is this your son?" they asked. "Is this the one you say was born blind? How is it that now he can see?"

²⁰"We know he is our son," the parents answered, "and we know he was born blind. ²¹But how he can see now, or who opened his eyes, we don't know. Ask him. He is of age; he will speak for himself." ²²His parents said this because they were afraid of the Jewish leaders, who already had decided that anyone who acknowledged that Jesus was the Messiah would be put out of the synagogue. ²³That was why his parents said, "He is of age; ask him."

²⁴A second time they summoned the man who had been blind. "Give glory to God and tell the truth," they said. "We know this man is a sinner."

²⁵He replied, "Whether he is a sinner or not, I don't know. One thing I do know. I was blind but now I see!"

²⁶Then they asked him, "What did he do to you? How did he open your eyes?"

²⁷He answered, "I have told you already and you did not listen. Why do you want to hear it again? Do you want to become his disciples too?"

²⁸Then they hurled insults at him and said, "You are this fellow's disciple! We are disciples of Moses! ²⁹We know that God spoke to Moses, but as for this fellow, we don't even know where he comes from."

³⁰The man answered, "Now that is remarkable! You don't know where he comes from, yet he opened my eyes. ³¹We know that God does not listen to sinners. He listens to the godly person who does his will.

1529

³²Nobody has ever heard of opening the eyes of a man born blind. ³³If this man were not from God, he could do nothing."

³⁴To this they replied, "You were steeped in sin at birth; how dare you lecture us!" And they threw him out.

Spiritual Blindness

³⁵Jesus heard that they had thrown him out, and when he found him, he said, "Do you believe in the Son of Man?"

³⁶"Who is he, sir?" the man asked. "Tell me so that I may believe in him."

³⁷Jesus said, "You have now seen him; in fact, he is the one speaking with you."

³⁸Then the man said, "Lord, I believe," and he worshiped him.

³⁹Jesus said,ᵃ "For judgment I have come into this world, so that the blind will see and those who see will become blind."

⁴⁰Some Pharisees who were with him heard him say this and asked, "What? Are we blind too?"

⁴¹Jesus said, "If you were blind, you would not be guilty of sin; but now that you claim you can see, your guilt remains.

The Good Shepherd and His Sheep

10 "Very truly I tell you Pharisees, anyone who does not enter the sheep pen by the gate, but climbs in by some other way, is a thief and a robber. ²The one who enters by the gate is the shepherd of the sheep. ³The gatekeeper opens the gate for him, and the sheep listen to his voice. He calls his own sheep by name and leads them out. ⁴When he has brought out all his own, he goes on ahead of them, and his sheep follow him because they know his voice. ⁵But they will never follow a stranger; in fact, they will run away from him because they do not recognize a stranger's voice." ⁶Jesus used this figure of speech, but the Pharisees did not understand what he was telling them.

⁷Therefore Jesus said again, "Very truly I tell you, I am the gate for the sheep. ⁸All who have come before me are thieves and robbers, but the sheep have not listened to them. ⁹I am the gate; whoever enters through me will be saved.ᵇ They will come in and go out, and find pasture. ¹⁰The thief comes only to steal and kill and destroy; I have come that they may have life, and have it to the full.

¹¹"I am the good shepherd. The good shepherd lays down his life for the sheep. ¹²The hired hand is not the shepherd and does not own the sheep. So when he sees the wolf coming, he abandons the sheep and runs away. Then the wolf attacks the flock and scatters it. ¹³The man runs away because he is a hired hand and cares nothing for the sheep.

¹⁴"I am the good shepherd; I know my sheep and my sheep know me— ¹⁵just as the Father knows me and I know the Father—and I lay down my life for the sheep. ¹⁶I have other sheep that are not of this sheep pen. I must bring them also. They too will listen to my voice, and there shall be one flock and one shepherd. ¹⁷The reason my Father loves me is that I lay down my life—only to take it up again. ¹⁸No one

---

ᵃ *38,39* Some early manuscripts do not have verses 38 and 39a.   ᵇ *9* Or *kept safe*

HE IS: the Good Shepherd

10:11–18 Jesus spoke so that the common people of Israel could easily identify with him. When he portrayed himself as *the Good Shepherd*, the people understood that a shepherd so values his flock that he is willing to die for them.

Jesus wants you to personally identify him as your *Good Shepherd*, who will direct and protect you (see Psalm 23). You may not like the comparison, but you are like a helpless sheep, needing guidance to green pastures and defense against spiritual wolves. To stay safe, you must stay close to the shepherd. He knows his sheep—do you know him?

For the next He Is, go to p. 1532.

takes it from me, but I lay it down of my own accord. I have authority to lay it down and authority to take it up again. This command I received from my Father."

[19] The Jews who heard these words were again divided. [20] Many of them said, "He is demon-possessed and raving mad. Why listen to him?"

[21] But others said, "These are not the sayings of someone possessed by a demon. Can a demon open the eyes of the blind?"

Further Conflict Over Jesus' Claims

[22] Then came the Festival of Dedication[a] at Jerusalem. It was winter, [23] and Jesus was in the temple courts walking in Solomon's Colonnade. [24] The Jews who were there gathered around him, saying, "How long will you keep us in suspense? If you are the Messiah, tell us plainly."

[25] Jesus answered, "I did tell you, but you do not believe. The works I do in my Father's name testify about me, [26] but you do not believe because you are not my sheep. [27] My sheep listen to my voice; I know them, and they follow me. [28] I give them eternal life, and they shall never perish; no one will snatch them out of my hand. [29] My Father, who has given them to me, is greater than all[b]; no one can snatch them out of my Father's hand. [30] I and the Father are one."

[31] Again the Jews picked up stones to stone him, [32] but Jesus said to them, "I have shown you many good works from the Father. For which of these do you stone me?"

[33] "We are not stoning you for any good work," they replied, "but for blasphemy, because you, a mere man, claim to be God."

[34] Jesus answered them, "Is it not written in your Law, 'I have said you are "gods"'[c]? [35] If he called them 'gods,' to whom the word of God came—and Scripture cannot be broken— [36] what about the one whom the Father set apart as his very own and sent into the world? Why then do you accuse me of blasphemy because I said, 'I am God's Son'? [37] Do not believe me unless I do the works of my Father. [38] But if I do them, even though you do not believe me, believe the works, that you may know and understand that the Father is in me, and I in the Father." [39] Again they tried to seize him, but he escaped their grasp.

[40] Then Jesus went back across the Jordan to the place where John had been baptizing in the early days. Here he stayed [41] and many people came to him. They said, "Though John never performed a sign, all that John said about this man was true." [42] And in that place many believed in Jesus.

The Death of Lazarus

11 Now a man named Lazarus was sick. He was from Bethany, the village of Mary and her sister Martha. [2] (This Mary, whose brother Lazarus now lay sick, was the same one who poured perfume on the Lord and wiped his feet with her hair.) [3] So the sisters sent word to Jesus, "Lord, the one you love is sick."

[4] When he heard this, Jesus said, "This sickness will not end in death. No, it is for God's glory so that God's Son may be glorified through it." [5] Now Jesus loved Martha and her sister and Lazarus. [6] So when he heard that Lazarus was sick, he stayed where he was two more days, [7] and then he said to his disciples, "Let us go back to Judea."

[8] "But Rabbi," they said, "a short while ago the Jews there tried to stone you, and yet you are going back?"

[9] Jesus answered, "Are there not twelve hours of daylight? Those who walk in the daytime will not stumble, for they see by this world's light. [10] It is when people walk at night that they stumble, for they have no light."

[11] After he had said this, he went on to tell them, "Our friend Lazarus has fallen asleep; but I am going there to wake him up."

[12] His disciples replied, "Lord, if he sleeps, he will get better." [13] Jesus had been speaking of his death, but his disciples thought he meant natural sleep.

[14] So then he told them plainly, "Lazarus is dead, [15] and for your sake I am glad I was not there, so that you may believe. But let us go to him."

---

[a] 22 That is, Hanukkah   [b] 29 Many early manuscripts *What my Father has given me is greater than all*   [c] 34 Psalm 82:6

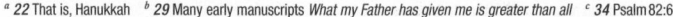

[16] Then Thomas (also known as Didymus[a]) said to the rest of the disciples, "Let us also go, that we may die with him."

Jesus Comforts the Sisters of Lazarus

[17] On his arrival, Jesus found that Lazarus had already been in the tomb for four days. [18] Now Bethany was less than two miles[b] from Jerusalem, [19] and many Jews had come to Martha and Mary to comfort them in the loss of their brother. [20] When Martha heard that Jesus was coming, she went out to meet him, but Mary stayed at home.

[21] "Lord," Martha said to Jesus, "if you had been here, my brother would not have died. [22] But I know that even now God will give you whatever you ask."

[23] Jesus said to her, "Your brother will rise again."

[24] Martha answered, "I know he will rise again in the resurrection at the last day."

[25] Jesus said to her, "I am the resurrection and the life. Anyone who believes in me will live, even though they die; [26] and whoever lives by believing in me will never die. Do you believe this?"

[27] "Yes, Lord," she told him, "I believe that you are the Messiah, the Son of God, who was to come into the world."

1532

HE IS: the resurrection and the life

11:17–27 Jesus had lingered a few days before answering Martha and Mary's summons to help their dying brother. When Jesus arrived, Martha offered a stinging statement of faith: If you'd been here, Lazarus wouldn't have died. Jesus brought Martha to deeper faith by revealing that he is *the resurrection and the life*.

Perhaps your faith needs a Martha transformation from *If you had only done this . . .* to *Yes, Lord, I believe*. When God seems to tarry, rather than saying *If only*, try, *I believe*. He is *the resurrection and the life*. His plans often involve greater works (like raising the dead) than you can imagine.

For the next He Is, go to p. 1539.

[28] After she had said this, she went back and called her sister Mary aside. "The Teacher is here," she said, "and is asking for you." [29] When Mary heard this, she got up quickly and went to him. [30] Now Jesus had not yet entered the village, but was still at the place where Martha had met him. [31] When the Jews who had been with Mary in the house, comforting her, noticed how quickly she got up and went out, they followed her, supposing she was going to the tomb to mourn there.

[32] When Mary reached the place where Jesus was and saw him, she fell at his feet and said, "Lord, if you had been here, my brother would not have died."

[33] When Jesus saw her weeping, and the Jews who had come along with her also weeping, he was deeply moved in spirit and troubled. [34] "Where have you laid him?" he asked.

"Come and see, Lord," they replied.

[35] Jesus wept.

[36] Then the Jews said, "See how he loved him!"

[37] But some of them said, "Could not he who opened the eyes of the blind man have kept this man from dying?"

Jesus Raises Lazarus From the Dead

[38] Jesus, once more deeply moved, came to the tomb. It was a cave with a stone laid across the entrance. [39] "Take away the stone," he said.

"But, Lord," said Martha, the sister of the dead man, "by this time there is a bad odor, for he has been there four days."

---

[a] *16 Thomas* (Aramaic) and *Didymus* (Greek) both mean *twin.* [b] *18* Or about 3 kilometers

⁴⁰Then Jesus said, "Did I not tell you that if you believe, you will see the glory of God?"

⁴¹So they took away the stone. Then Jesus looked up and said, "Father, I thank you that you have heard me. ⁴²I knew that you always hear me, but I said this for the benefit of the people standing here, that they may believe that you sent me."

⁴³When he had said this, Jesus called in a loud voice, "Lazarus, come out!" ⁴⁴The dead man came out, his hands and feet wrapped with strips of linen, and a cloth around his face.

Jesus said to them, "Take off the grave clothes and let him go."

conversations

emotions «» 11:33–36

1 » Do you view crying as a sign of weakness? Why or why not?

2 » Where is the balance between self-control and honestly expressing your emotions?

3 » Who in your life encourages you to be more open about how you feel?

For more on **emotions**, check the index.
For the next Conversations, go to p. 1537.

The Plot to Kill Jesus

⁴⁵Therefore many of the Jews who had come to visit Mary, and had seen what Jesus did, put their faith in him. ⁴⁶But some of them went to the Pharisees and told them what Jesus had done. ⁴⁷Then the chief priests and the Pharisees called a meeting of the Sanhedrin.

"What are we accomplishing?" they asked. "Here is this man performing many signs. ⁴⁸If we let him go on like this, everyone will believe in him, and then the Romans will come and take away both our temple and our nation."

⁴⁹Then one of them, named Caiaphas, who was high priest that year, spoke up, "You know nothing at all! ⁵⁰You do not realize that it is better for you that one man die for the people than that the whole nation perish."

⁵¹He did not say this on his own, but as high priest that year he prophesied that Jesus would die for the Jewish nation, ⁵²and not only for that nation but also for the scattered children of God, to bring them together and make them one. ⁵³So from that day on they plotted to take his life.

⁵⁴Therefore Jesus no longer moved about publicly among the Jews. Instead he withdrew to a region near the wilderness, to a village called Ephraim, where he stayed with his disciples.

⁵⁵When it was almost time for the Jewish Passover, many went up from the country to Jerusalem for their ceremonial cleansing before the Passover. ⁵⁶They kept looking for Jesus, and as they stood in the temple courts they asked one another, "What do you think? Isn't he coming to the festival at all?" ⁵⁷But the chief priests and the Pharisees had given orders that anyone who found out where Jesus was should report it so that they might arrest him.

Jesus Anointed at Bethany

12 Six days before the Passover, Jesus came to Bethany, where Lazarus lived, whom Jesus had raised from the dead. ²Here a dinner was given in Jesus' honor. Martha served, while Lazarus was among those reclining at the table with him. ³Then Mary took about a pint^a of pure nard, an expensive perfume; she poured it on Jesus' feet and wiped his feet with her hair. And the house was filled with the fragrance of the perfume.

⁴But one of his disciples, Judas Iscariot, who was later to betray him, objected, ⁵"Why wasn't this perfume sold and the money given to the poor? It was worth a year's wages.^b" ⁶He did not say this because he cared about the poor but because he was a thief; as keeper of the money bag, he used to help himself to what was put into it.

⁷"Leave her alone," Jesus replied. "It was intended that she should save this perfume for the day of my burial. ⁸You will always have the poor among you,^c but you will not always have me."

⁹Meanwhile a large crowd of Jews found out that Jesus was there and came, not only because of him but also to see Lazarus, whom he had raised from the dead. ¹⁰So the chief priests made plans to kill Lazarus as well, ¹¹for on account of him many of the Jews were going over to Jesus and putting their faith in him.

1533

---

^a *3* Or about half a liter   ^b *5* Greek *three hundred denarii*   ^c *8* See Deut. 15:11.

myth# 88

"IF THIS MARRIAGE DOESN'T WORK OUT, I CAN ALWAYS START OVER WITH SOMEONE ELSE."

WANTED:

Someone who understands me.

Someone who loves me even when I'm at my worst.

Someone who is crazy about me and thinks I'm the most beautiful woman in the world.

I've been looking a long time for this guy. I'd always assumed I would find him at college. When he wasn't there, I thought we'd meet at church. Now, I've concluded that I probably missed out on my perfect match. The closest I've found so far is Mike.

Mike may not be perfect, but he's kind and sweet to me (most of the time). We've had our share of rocky times this past year that we've been dating, but for the most part, we've done pretty well. I know he loves me—he really loves me. And I'm very attracted to him. We want most of the same things in life—kids, a house, careers, the usual. I think we're a pretty good match, but it's not as if he's the one true love I've always dreamed about. I've thought about breaking up with him, but I've already put so much work into this relationship. I'd hate to see it all be for nothing, and the thought of hurting him is too painful.

The wedding is two months away, and as excited as I am about it, a part of me still thinks maybe there is someone else better for me. What if I'm making a big mistake and my soul mate is still out there? I just keep telling myself that if it doesn't work out, I can always start over again. But for now, I'm willing to give it a try and hope for the best.

—Carolyn

IN OUR CULTURE, divorce seems like such a reasonable, obvious option when things aren't going the way we'd expected in a marriage. But we know there are no simple answers in life. While a divorce may seem like an easy, quick fix to a problem, it's not. Divorces are inherently painful. Divorce should always be a last resort, not an easy escape. Whether you're engaged, already married or hoping to be someday, keep this in mind:

- No relationship is perfect. There will always be some way you're incompatible with your potential spouse.

- Decide before you marry if the incompatibilities are manageable. When you marry, commit to managing them. After you marry, be true to your commitment.

- Before you get married, talk with each other about any reservations you have. Decide now how you can handle the problems that will inevitably come up.

- Agree to seek couples' counseling if necessary.

- Ask a close friend who's divorced about her experience and what she learned. Also talk to a friend who's been married for a while and find out what's kept them together.

- Center your marriage on God and your shared faith. A marriage becomes healthy, happy and lasting by the grace of God, so don't try to make your marriage work on your own apart from that grace!

Entering marriage with an "out" in the back of your mind can doom your relationship. You'll quickly revert to that proviso as soon as the relationship gets strained. Although Jesus "wanted out" on his way to the cross, he didn't take any shortcuts (see John 12:27–28). In fact, he asked God to glorify himself through his struggles. In the same way, marriage is about making and keeping a promise, not reserving an escape route.

"Nearly four out of five Americans (79 percent) want to have one marriage partner for life."
——Barna Research Group (2000)

1535

"WHEN YOU MAKE a VOW TO GOD, DO NOT DELAY TO FULFILL IT. HE HAS NO PLEASURE IN FOOLS; FULFILL YOUR VOW. IT IS BETTER NOT TO MAKE A VOW THAN TO MAKE ONE AND NOT FULFILL IT."

ECCLESIASTES 5:4–5

SEE ALSO

Mark 10:2–12
Galatians 6:7–9
James 1:5–8

For more on **Marriage** and **Divorce**, check the index.

Jesus Comes to Jerusalem as King

¹²The next day the great crowd that had come for the festival heard that Jesus was on his way to Jerusalem. ¹³They took palm branches and went out to meet him, shouting,

> "Hosanna!*ᵃ*"
>
> "Blessed is he who comes in the name of the Lord!"*ᵇ*
>
> "Blessed is the king of Israel!"

¹⁴Jesus found a young donkey and sat on it, as it is written:

> ¹⁵"Do not be afraid, Daughter Zion;
> see, your king is coming,
> seated on a donkey's colt."*ᶜ*

¹⁶At first his disciples did not understand all this. Only after Jesus was glorified did they realize that these things had been written about him and that these things had been done to him.

¹⁷Now the crowd that was with him when he called Lazarus from the tomb and raised him from the dead continued to spread the word. ¹⁸Many people, because they had heard that he had performed this sign, went out to meet him. ¹⁹So the Pharisees said to one another, "See, this is getting us nowhere. Look how the whole world has gone after him!"

Jesus Predicts His Death

²⁰Now there were some Greeks among those who went up to worship at the festival. ²¹They came to Philip, who was from Bethsaida in Galilee, with a request. "Sir," they said, "we would like to see Jesus." ²²Philip went to tell Andrew; Andrew and Philip in turn told Jesus.

²³Jesus replied, "The hour has come for the Son of Man to be glorified. ²⁴Very truly I tell you, unless a kernel of wheat falls to the ground and dies, it remains only a single seed. But if it dies, it produces many seeds. ²⁵Those who love their life will lose it, while those who hate their life in this world will keep it for eternal life. ²⁶Whoever serves me must follow me; and where I am, my servant also will be. My Father will honor the one who serves me.

²⁷"Now my soul is troubled, and what shall I say? 'Father, save me from this hour'? No, it was for this very reason I came to this hour. ²⁸Father, glorify your name!"

Then a voice came from heaven, "I have glorified it, and will glorify it again." ²⁹The crowd that was there and heard it said it had thundered; others said an angel had spoken to him.

³⁰Jesus said, "This voice was for your benefit, not mine. ³¹Now is the time for judgment on this world; now the prince of this world will be driven out. ³²And I, when I am lifted up*ᵈ* from the earth, will draw all people to myself." ³³He said this to show the kind of death he was going to die.

³⁴The crowd spoke up, "We have heard from the Law that the Messiah will remain forever, so how can you say, 'The Son of Man must be lifted up'? Who is this 'Son of Man'?"

³⁵Then Jesus told them, "You are going to have the light just a little while longer. Walk while you have the light, before darkness overtakes you. Those who walk in the dark do not know where they are going. ³⁶Put your trust in the light while you have the light, so that you may become children of light." When he had finished speaking, Jesus left and hid himself from them.

Belief and Unbelief Among the Jews

³⁷Even after Jesus had performed so many signs in their presence, they still would not believe in him. ³⁸This was to fulfill the word of Isaiah the prophet:

> "Lord, who has believed our message
> and to whom has the arm of the Lord been revealed?"*ᵉ*

³⁹For this reason they could not believe, because, as Isaiah says elsewhere:

ᵃ 13 A Hebrew expression meaning "Save!" which became an exclamation of praise   *ᵇ 13* Psalm 118:25,26   *ᶜ 15* Zech. 9:9   *ᵈ 32* The Greek for *lifted up* also means *exalted.*   *ᵉ 38* Isaiah 53:1

[40]"He has blinded their eyes
 and hardened their hearts,
so they can neither see with their eyes,
 nor understand with their hearts,
 nor turn—and I would heal them."[a]

[41]Isaiah said this because he saw Jesus' glory and spoke about him.

[42]Yet at the same time many even among the leaders believed in him. But because of the Pharisees they would not openly acknowledge their faith for fear they would be put out of the synagogue; [43]for they loved human glory more than the glory of God.

[44]Then Jesus cried out, "Those who believe in me do not believe in me only, but in the one who sent me. [45]When they look at me, they see the one who sent me. [46]I have come into the world as a light, so that no one who believes in me should stay in darkness.

[47]"As for those who hear my words but do not keep them, I do not judge them. For I did not come to judge the world, but to save the world. [48]There is a judge for those who reject me and do not accept my words; the very words I have spoken will condemn them at the last day. [49]For I did not speak on my own, but the Father who sent me commanded me to say all that I have spoken. [50]I know that his command leads to eternal life. So whatever I say is just what the Father has told me to say."

1537

Jesus Washes His Disciples' Feet

13 It was just before the Passover Festival. Jesus knew that the hour had come for him to leave this world and go to the Father. Having loved his own who were in the world, he loved them to the end.

[2]The evening meal was in progress, and the devil had already prompted Judas, the son of Simon Iscariot, to betray Jesus. [3]Jesus knew that the Father had put all things under his power, and that he had come from God and was returning to God; [4]so he got up from the meal, took off his outer clothing, and wrapped a towel around his waist. [5]After that, he poured water into a basin and began to wash his disciples' feet, drying them with the towel that was wrapped around him.

[6]He came to Simon Peter, who said to him, "Lord, are you going to wash my feet?"

[7]Jesus replied, "You do not realize now what I am doing, but later you will understand."

[8]"No," said Peter, "you shall never wash my feet."

Jesus answered, "Unless I wash you, you have no part with me."

[9]"Then, Lord," Simon Peter replied, "not just my feet but my hands and my head as well!"

[10]Jesus answered, "Those who have had a bath need only to wash their feet; their whole body is clean. And you are clean, though not every one of you." [11]For he knew who was going to betray him, and that was why he said not every one was clean.

[12]When he had finished washing their feet, he put on his clothes and returned to his place. "Do you understand what I have done for you?" he asked them. [13]"You call me 'Teacher' and 'Lord,' and rightly so, for that is what I am. [14]Now that I, your Lord and Teacher, have washed your feet, you also should wash one another's feet. [15]I have set you an example that you should do as I have done for you. [16]Very truly I tell you, servants are not greater than their master, nor are messengers greater than the one who sent them. [17]Now that you know these things, you will be blessed if you do them.

conversations

serving «» 13:14

1» In what ways have you been "served" by Jesus?

2» What acts of service could you do that would be the equivalent of washing another's feet?

3» Why is serving others so critical for your spiritual growth?

For more on serving, check the index.
For the next Conversations, go to p. 1538.

---

[a] *40* Isaiah 6:10

Jesus Predicts His Betrayal

[18] "I am not referring to all of you; I know those I have chosen. But this is to fulfill this passage of Scripture: 'He who shared my bread has lifted up his heel against me.'[a]

[19] "I am telling you now before it happens, so that when it does happen you will believe that I am who I am. [20] Very truly I tell you, whoever accepts anyone I send accepts me; and whoever accepts me accepts the one who sent me."

[21] After he had said this, Jesus was troubled in spirit and testified, "Very truly I tell you, one of you is going to betray me."

[22] His disciples stared at one another, at a loss to know which of them he meant. [23] One of them, the disciple whom Jesus loved, was reclining next to him. [24] Simon Peter motioned to this disciple and said, "Ask him which one he means."

[25] Leaning back against Jesus, he asked him, "Lord, who is it?"

[26] Jesus answered, "It is the one to whom I will give this piece of bread when I have dipped it in the dish." Then, dipping the piece of bread, he gave it to Judas, the son of Simon Iscariot. [27] As soon as Judas took the bread, Satan entered into him.

So Jesus told him, "What you are about to do, do quickly." [28] But no one at the meal understood why Jesus said this to him. [29] Since Judas had charge of the money, some thought Jesus was telling him to buy what was needed for the festival, or to give something to the poor. [30] As soon as Judas had taken the bread, he went out. And it was night.

Jesus Predicts Peter's Denial

[31] When he was gone, Jesus said, "Now is the Son of Man glorified and God is glorified in him. [32] If God is glorified in him,[b] God will glorify the Son in himself, and will glorify him at once.

[33] "My children, I will be with you only a little longer. You will look for me, and just as I told the Jews, so I tell you now: Where I am going, you cannot come.

[34] "A new command I give you: Love one another. As I have loved you, so you must love one another. [35] By this everyone will know that you are my disciples, if you love one another."

[36] Simon Peter asked him, "Lord, where are you going?"

Jesus replied, "Where I am going, you cannot follow now, but you will follow later."

[37] Peter asked, "Lord, why can't I follow you now? I will lay down my life for you."

[38] Then Jesus answered, "Will you really lay down your life for me? Very truly I tell you, before the rooster crows, you will disown me three times!

Jesus Comforts His Disciples

14 "Do not let your hearts be troubled. Trust in God[c]; trust also in me. [2] My Father's house has plenty of room; if that were not so, would I have told you that I am going there to prepare a place for you? [3] And if I go and prepare a place for you, I will come back and take you to be with me that you also may be where I am. [4] You know the way to the place where I am going."

Jesus the Way to the Father

[5] Thomas said to him, "Lord, we don't know where you are going, so how can we know the way?"

[6] Jesus answered, "I am the way and the truth and the life. No one comes to the Father except through me. [7] If you really know me, you will know[d] my Father as well. From now on, you do know him and have seen him."

conversations

stress «» 14:1

1» What troubles or concerns do you have on your mind right now?

2» Why is it so hard to trust God to take care of those things that stress you out?

3» How can you develop more trust in God?

For more on **stress**, check the index.
For the next Conversations, go to p. 1544.

---

[a] *18* Psalm 41:9   [b] *32* Many early manuscripts do not have *If God is glorified in him.*   [c] *1* Or *You trust in God*   [d] *7* Some manuscripts *If you really knew me, you would know*

HE IS: the way and the truth and the life

14:6–7 Thomas and the others wanted to follow Jesus but didn't know the way he was going. Jesus plainly stated that he is *the way and the truth and the life*. Rather than sermonizing about a complicated set of directions to reach the heavenly Father, Jesus made the way simple: *Really know me.*

When you are lost, would you rather look at a map or follow a person who knows the way? The same is true for coming to Jesus. What an unsaved person needs isn't a complicated explanation but someone to show her the way to *the way* himself (see also Acts 4:12).

For the next He Is, go to p. 1540.

1539

[8] Philip said, "Lord, show us the Father and that will be enough for us."

[9] Jesus answered: "Don't you know me, Philip, even after I have been among you such a long time? Anyone who has seen me has seen the Father. How can you say, 'Show us the Father'? [10] Don't you believe that I am in the Father, and that the Father is in me? The words I say to you I do not speak on my own authority. Rather, it is the Father, living in me, who is doing his work. [11] Believe me when I say that I am in the Father and the Father is in me; or at least believe on the evidence of the works themselves. [12] Very truly I tell you, all who have faith in me will do the works I have been doing, and they will do even greater things than these, because I am going to the Father. [13] And I will do whatever you ask in my name, so that the Father may be glorified in the Son. [14] You may ask me for anything in my name, and I will do it.

Jesus Promises the Holy Spirit

[15] "If you love me, keep my commands. [16] And I will ask the Father, and he will give you another advocate to help you and be with you forever— [17] the Spirit of truth. The world cannot accept him, because it neither sees him nor knows him. But you know him, for he lives with you and will be[a] in you. [18] I will not leave you as orphans; I will come to you. [19] Before long, the world will not see me anymore, but you will see me. Because I live, you also will live. [20] On that day you will realize that I am in my Father, and you are in me, and I am in you. [21] Whoever has my commands and keeps them is the one who loves me. Anyone who loves me will be loved by my Father, and I too will love them and show myself to them."

[22] Then Judas (not Judas Iscariot) said, "But, Lord, why do you intend to show yourself to us and not to the world?"

[23] Jesus replied, "Anyone who loves me will obey my teaching. My Father will love them, and we will come to them and make our home with them. [24] Anyone who does not love me will not obey my teaching. These words you hear are not my own; they belong to the Father who sent me.

[25] "All this I have spoken while still with you. [26] But the Advocate, the Holy Spirit, whom the Father will send in my name, will teach you all things and will remind you of everything I have said to you. [27] Peace I leave with you; my peace I give you. I do not give to you as the world gives. Do not let your hearts be troubled and do not be afraid.

[28] "You heard me say, 'I am going away and I am coming back to you.' If you loved me, you would be glad that I am going to the Father, for the Father is greater than I. [29] I have told you now before it happens, so that when it does happen you will believe. [30] I will not say much more to you, for the prince of this world is coming. He has no hold over me, [31] but he comes so that the world may learn that I love the Father and do exactly what my Father has commanded me.

"Come now; let us leave.

The Vine and the Branches

15 "I am the true vine, and my Father is the gardener. [2] He cuts off every branch in me that bears no fruit, while every branch that does bear fruit he prunes[b] so that it will be even more fruitful. [3] You are already clean because of the word I have spoken to you. [4] Remain in me, as I also remain in you. No

---

[a] *17* Some early manuscripts *and is*   [b] *2* The Greek for *he prunes* also means *he cleans*.

HE IS: the gardener

15:1–2 Using an agricultural metaphor, Jesus portrayed the integral relationship between the believer, Jesus and the Father. The believer (the branch) grows from Jesus (the true vine) the source of spiritual fruit. God *(the gardener)* wisely prunes even fruitful branches to produce more fruit.

God wants you to bear fruit. Just as a gardener trims a healthy plant to maximize growth, your divine *gardener* is willing to cut away even good things to focus energy on the best things. His use of the pruning shears doesn't mean he is displeased with your growth; it may mean he is generating greater growth in you.

For the next He Is, go to p. 1552.

1540

branch can bear fruit by itself; it must remain in the vine. Neither can you bear fruit unless you remain in me.

[5] "I am the vine; you are the branches. If you remain in me and I in you, you will bear much fruit; apart from me you can do nothing. [6] If you do not remain in me, you are like a branch that is thrown away and withers; such branches are picked up, thrown into the fire and burned. [7] If you remain in me and my words remain in you, ask whatever you wish, and it will be done for you. [8] This is to my Father's glory, that you bear much fruit, showing yourselves to be my disciples.

[9] "As the Father has loved me, so have I loved you. Now remain in my love. [10] If you keep my commands, you will remain in my love, just as I have kept my Father's commands and remain in his love. [11] I have told you this so that my joy may be in you and that your joy may be complete. [12] My command is this: Love each other as I have loved you. [13] Greater love has no one than this: to lay down one's life for one's friends. [14] You are my friends if you do what I command. [15] I no longer call you servants, because servants do not know their master's business. Instead, I have called you friends, for everything that I learned from my Father I have made known to you. [16] You did not choose me, but I chose you and appointed you so that you might go and bear fruit—fruit that will last—and so that whatever you ask in my name the Father will give you. [17] This is my command: Love each other.

The World Hates the Disciples

[18] "If the world hates you, keep in mind that it hated me first. [19] If you belonged to the world, it would love you as its own. As it is, you do not belong to the world, but I have chosen you out of the world. That is why the world hates you. [20] Remember what I told you: 'Servants are not greater than their master.'[a] If they persecuted me, they will persecute you also. If they obeyed my teaching, they will obey yours also. [21] They will treat you this way because of my name, for they do not know the one who sent me. [22] If I had not come and spoken to them, they would not be guilty of sin; but now they have no excuse for their sin. [23] Those who hate me hate my Father as well. [24] If I had not done among them the works no one else did, they would not be guilty of sin. As it is, they have seen, and yet they have hated both me and my Father. [25] But this is to fulfill what is written in their Law: 'They hated me without reason.'[b]

The Work of the Holy Spirit

[26] "When the Advocate comes, whom I will send to you from the Father—the Spirit of truth who goes out from the Father—he will testify about me. [27] And you also must testify, for you have been with me from the beginning.

16 "All this I have told you so that you will not fall away. [2] They will put you out of the synagogue; in fact, the hour is coming when those who kill you will think they are offering a service to God. [3] They will do such things because they have not known the Father or me. [4] I have told you this, so that when their hour comes you will remember that I warned you about them. I did not tell you this from the

a 20 John 13:16   b 25 Psalms 35:19; 69:4

beginning because I was with you, [5]but now I am going to him who sent me. None of you asks me, 'Where are you going?' [6]Rather, you are filled with grief because I have said these things. [7]But very truly I tell you, it is for your good that I am going away. Unless I go away, the Advocate will not come to you; but if I go, I will send him to you. [8]When he comes, he will prove the world to be in the wrong about sin and righteousness and judgment: [9]about sin, because people do not believe in me; [10]about righteousness, because I am going to the Father, where you can see me no longer; [11]and about judgment, because the prince of this world now stands condemned.

[12]"I have much more to say to you, more than you can now bear. [13]But when he, the Spirit of truth, comes, he will guide you into all the truth. He will not speak on his own; he will speak only what he hears, and he will tell you what is yet to come. [14]He will glorify me because it is from me that he will receive what he will make known to you. [15]All that belongs to the Father is mine. That is why I said the Spirit will receive from me what he will make known to you."

The Disciples' Grief Will Turn to Joy

[16]Jesus went on to say, "In a little while you will see me no more, and then after a little while you will see me."

[17]At this, some of his disciples said to one another, "What does he mean by saying, 'In a little while you will see me no more, and then after a little while you will see me,' and 'Because I am going to the Father'?" [18]They kept asking, "What does he mean by 'a little while'? We don't understand what he is saying."

[19]Jesus saw that they wanted to ask him about this, so he said to them, "Are you asking one another what I meant when I said, 'In a little while you will see me no more, and then after a little while you will see me'? [20]Very truly I tell you, you will weep and mourn while the world rejoices. You will grieve, but your grief will turn to joy. [21]A woman giving birth to a child has pain because her time has come; but when her baby is born she forgets the anguish because of her joy that a child is born into the world. [22]So with you: Now is your time of grief, but I will see you again and you will rejoice, and no one will take away your joy. [23]In that day you will no longer ask me anything. Very truly I tell you, my Father will give you whatever you ask in my name. [24]Until now you have not asked for anything in my name. Ask and you will receive, and your joy will be complete.

[25]"Though I have been speaking figuratively, a time is coming when I will no longer use this kind of language but will tell you plainly about my Father. [26]In that day you will ask in my name. I am not saying that I will ask the Father on your behalf. [27]No, the Father himself loves you because you have loved me and have believed that I came from God. [28]I came from the Father and entered the world; now I am leaving the world and going back to the Father."

[29]Then Jesus' disciples said, "Now you are speaking clearly and without figures of speech. [30]Now we can see that you know all things and that you do not even need to have anyone ask you questions. This makes us believe that you came from God."

[31]"Do you now believe?" Jesus replied. [32]"A time is coming and in fact has come when you will be scattered, each to your own home. You will leave me all alone. Yet I am not alone, for my Father is with me.

[33]"I have told you these things, so that in me you may have peace. In this world you will have trouble. But take heart! I have overcome the world."

Jesus Prays to Be Glorified

17 After Jesus said this, he looked toward heaven and prayed:

"Father, the hour has come. Glorify your Son, that your Son may glorify you. [2]For you granted him authority over

1541

atissue:peace

16:33 We all want peace— in our world, in our homes and in our lives. But the Christian life is difficult. It involves struggle and pain. If you think peace is the absence of problems, you will never find it. You may get snatches of that kind of peace, but they will be fleeting. The only way to experience true, lasting peace is to find it in Jesus. Knowing that he has conquered sin, death and the very problem you face enables you to have peace *in the midst of* your pain, not in spite of it or after it passes.

all people that he might give eternal life to all those you have given him. ³Now this is eternal life: that they know you, the only true God, and Jesus Christ, whom you have sent. ⁴I have brought you glory on earth by finishing the work you gave me to do. ⁵And now, Father, glorify me in your presence with the glory I had with you before the world began.

Jesus Prays for His Disciples

⁶"I have revealed you*ᵃ* to those whom you gave me out of the world. They were yours; you gave them to me and they have obeyed your word. ⁷Now they know that everything you have given me comes from you. ⁸For I gave them the words you gave me and they accepted them. They knew with certainty that I came from you, and they believed that you sent me. ⁹I pray for them. I am not praying for the world, but for those you have given me, for they are yours. ¹⁰All I have is yours, and all you have is mine. And glory has come to me through them. ¹¹I will remain in the world no longer, but they are still in the world, and I am coming to you. Holy Father, protect them by the power of*ᵇ* your name, the name you gave me, so that they may be one as we are one. ¹²While I was with them, I protected them and kept them safe by*ᶜ* that name you gave me. None has been lost except the one doomed to destruction so that Scripture would be fulfilled.

¹³"I am coming to you now, but I say these things while I am still in the world, so that they may have the full measure of my joy within them. ¹⁴I have given them your word and the world has hated them, for they are not of the world any more than I am of the world. ¹⁵My prayer is not that you take them out of the world but that you protect them from the evil one. ¹⁶They are not of the world, even as I am not of it. ¹⁷Sanctify them by*ᵈ* the truth; your word is truth. ¹⁸As you sent me into the world, I have sent them into the world. ¹⁹For them I sanctify myself, that they too may be truly sanctified.

atissue:identity

17:14–16 What does it mean to be Jesus' disciple? Jesus gives us some clues: You will be hated. You will be a target of the evil one. You will live with the pain and realities of life on this earth. And you will not belong here, as he did not belong here. Does your life fit his description? Ask yourself: Does anyone dislike you for your faith or how you live? Does your life stand out from the world? Are you suffering at all for your faith? Your life shouldn't be pain-free or 100 percent popular. If it is, are you truly his?

Jesus Prays for All Believers

²⁰"My prayer is not for them alone. I pray also for those who will believe in me through their message, ²¹that all of them may be one, Father, just as you are in me and I am in you. May they also be in us so that the world may believe that you have sent me. ²²I have given them the glory that you gave me, that they may be one as we are one— ²³I in them and you in me—so that they may be brought to complete unity. Then the world will know that you sent me and have loved them even as you have loved me.

²⁴"Father, I want those you have given me to be with me where I am, and to see my glory, the glory you have given me because you loved me before the creation of the world.

²⁵"Righteous Father, though the world does not know you, I know you, and they know that you have sent me. ²⁶I have made you known to them, and will continue to make you known in order that the love you have for me may be in them and that I myself may be in them."

Jesus Arrested

18 When he had finished praying, Jesus left with his disciples and crossed the Kidron Valley. On the other side there was a garden, and he and his disciples went into it.

²Now Judas, who betrayed him, knew the place, because Jesus had often met there with his disciples.

ᵃ 6 Greek your name; also in verse 26   ᵇ 11 Or Father, keep them faithful to   ᶜ 12 Or kept them faithful to   ᵈ 17 Or them to live in accordance with

³So Judas came to the garden, guiding a detachment of soldiers and some officials from the chief priests and the Pharisees. They were carrying torches, lanterns and weapons.

⁴Jesus, knowing all that was going to happen to him, went out and asked them, "Who is it you want?"

⁵"Jesus of Nazareth," they replied.

"I am he," Jesus said. (And Judas the traitor was standing there with them.) ⁶When Jesus said, "I am he," they drew back and fell to the ground.

⁷Again he asked them, "Who is it you want?"

"Jesus of Nazareth," they said.

⁸Jesus answered, "I told you that I am he. If you are looking for me, then let these men go." ⁹This happened so that the words he had spoken would be fulfilled: "I have not lost one of those you gave me."ᵃ

¹⁰Then Simon Peter, who had a sword, drew it and struck the high priest's servant, cutting off his right ear. (The servant's name was Malchus.)

¹¹Jesus commanded Peter, "Put your sword away! Shall I not drink the cup the Father has given me?"

¹²Then the detachment of soldiers with its commander and the Jewish officials arrested Jesus. They bound him ¹³and brought him first to Annas, who was the father-in-law of Caiaphas, the high priest that year. ¹⁴Caiaphas was the one who had advised the Jewish leaders that it would be good if one man died for the people.

Peter's First Denial

¹⁵Simon Peter and another disciple were following Jesus. Because this disciple was known to the high priest, he went with Jesus into the high priest's courtyard, ¹⁶but Peter had to wait outside at the door. The other disciple, who was known to the high priest, came back, spoke to the servant girl on duty there and brought Peter in.

¹⁷"You aren't one of this man's disciples too, are you?" she asked Peter.

He replied, "I am not."

¹⁸It was cold, and the servants and officials stood around a fire they had made to keep warm. Peter also was standing with them, warming himself.

The High Priest Questions Jesus

¹⁹Meanwhile, the high priest questioned Jesus about his disciples and his teaching.

²⁰"I have spoken openly to the world," Jesus replied. "I always taught in synagogues or at the temple, where all the Jews come together. I said nothing in secret. ²¹Why question me? Ask those who heard me. Surely they know what I said."

²²When Jesus said this, one of the officials nearby slapped him in the face. "Is this the way you answer the high priest?" he demanded.

²³"If I said something wrong," Jesus replied, "testify as to what is wrong. But if I spoke the truth, why did you strike me?" ²⁴Then Annas sent him bound to Caiaphas the high priest.

Peter's Second and Third Denials

²⁵Meanwhile, Simon Peter was still standing there warming himself. So they asked him, "You aren't one of his disciples too, are you?"

He denied it, saying, "I am not."

²⁶One of the high priest's servants, a relative of the man whose ear Peter had cut off, challenged him, "Didn't I see you with him in the garden?" ²⁷Again Peter denied it, and at that moment a rooster began to crow.

Jesus Before Pilate

²⁸Then the Jewish leaders took Jesus from Caiaphas to the palace of the Roman governor. By now it was early morning, and to avoid ceremonial uncleanness they did not enter the palace, because they wanted to be able to eat the Passover. ²⁹So Pilate came out to them and asked, "What charges are you bringing against this man?"

1543

ᵃ *9* John 6:39

³⁰"If he were not a criminal," they replied, "we would not have handed him over to you."

³¹Pilate said, "Take him yourselves and judge him by your own law."

"But we have no right to execute anyone," they objected. ³²This took place to fulfill what Jesus had said about the kind of death he was going to die.

³³Pilate then went back inside the palace, summoned Jesus and asked him, "Are you the king of the Jews?"

³⁴"Is that your own idea," Jesus asked, "or did others talk to you about me?"

³⁵"Am I a Jew?" Pilate replied. "Your own people and chief priests handed you over to me. What is it you have done?"

³⁶Jesus said, "My kingdom is not of this world. If it were, my servants would fight to prevent my arrest by the Jewish leaders. But now my kingdom is from another place."

³⁷"You are a king, then!" said Pilate.

Jesus answered, "You say that I am a king. In fact, the reason I was born and came into the world is to testify to the truth. Everyone on the side of truth listens to me."

³⁸"What is truth?" retorted Pilate. With this he went out again to the Jews gathered there and said, "I find no basis for a charge against him. ³⁹But it is your custom for me to release to you one prisoner at the time of the Passover. Do you want me to release 'the king of the Jews'?"

⁴⁰They shouted back, "No, not him! Give us Barabbas!" Now Barabbas had taken part in an uprising.

Jesus Sentenced to Be Crucified

19 Then Pilate took Jesus and had him flogged. ²The soldiers twisted together a crown of thorns and put it on his head. They clothed him in a purple robe ³and went up to him again and again, saying, "Hail, king of the Jews!" And they slapped him in the face.

⁴Once more Pilate came out and said to the Jews, "Look, I am bringing him out to you to let you know that I find no basis for a charge against him." ⁵When Jesus came out wearing the crown of thorns and the purple robe, Pilate said to them, "Here is the man!"

⁶As soon as the chief priests and their officials saw him, they shouted, "Crucify! Crucify!"

But Pilate answered, "You take him and crucify him. As for me, I find no basis for a charge against him."

⁷The Jews insisted, "We have a law, and according to that law he must die, because he claimed to be the Son of God."

⁸When Pilate heard this, he was even more afraid, ⁹and he went back inside the palace. "Where do you come from?" he asked Jesus, but Jesus gave him no answer. ¹⁰"Do you refuse to speak to me?" Pilate said. "Don't you realize I have power either to free you or to crucify you?"

¹¹Jesus answered, "You would have no power over me if it were not given to you from above. Therefore the one who handed me over to you is guilty of a greater sin."

¹²From then on, Pilate tried to set Jesus free, but the Jews kept shouting, "If you let this man go, you are no friend of Caesar. Anyone who claims to be a king opposes Caesar."

¹³When Pilate heard this, he brought Jesus out and sat down on the judge's seat at a place known as the Stone Pavement (which in Aramaic is Gabbatha). ¹⁴It was the day of Preparation of the Passover; it was about noon.

"Here is your king," Pilate said to the Jews.

¹⁵But they shouted, "Take him away! Take him away! Crucify him!"

"Shall I crucify your king?" Pilate asked.

conversations

salvation «» 19:1–37

1» Was it necessary for Jesus to suffer before he died? If so, why?

2» Like each person surrounding Jesus, what difficulties must you face in accepting his sacrifice?

3» How does understanding the pain Jesus suffered help you appreciate your salvation more?

For more on **salvation**, check the index. For the next Conversations, go to p. 1565.

"We have no king but Caesar," the chief priests answered.

[16] Finally Pilate handed him over to them to be crucified.

The Crucifixion of Jesus

So the soldiers took charge of Jesus. [17] Carrying his own cross, he went out to the place of the Skull (which in Aramaic is called Golgotha). [18] Here they crucified him, and with him two others—one on each side and Jesus in the middle.

[19] Pilate had a notice prepared and fastened to the cross. It read: JESUS OF NAZARETH, THE KING OF THE JEWS. [20] Many of the Jews read this sign, for the place where Jesus was crucified was near the city, and the sign was written in Aramaic, Latin and Greek. [21] The chief priests of the Jews protested to Pilate, "Do not write 'The King of the Jews,' but that this man claimed to be king of the Jews."

[22] Pilate answered, "What I have written, I have written."

[23] When the soldiers crucified Jesus, they took his clothes, dividing them into four shares, one for each of them, with the undergarment remaining. This garment was seamless, woven in one piece from top to bottom.

[24] "Let's not tear it," they said to one another. "Let's decide by lot who will get it."

This happened that the scripture might be fulfilled that said,

> "They divided my clothes among them
> and cast lots for my garment."[a]

So this is what the soldiers did.

[25] Near the cross of Jesus stood his mother, his mother's sister, Mary the wife of Clopas, and Mary Magdalene. [26] When Jesus saw his mother there, and the disciple whom he loved standing nearby, he said to her, "Woman,[b] here is your son," [27] and to the disciple, "Here is your mother." From that time on, this disciple took her into his home.

The Death of Jesus

[28] Later, knowing that everything had now been finished, and so that Scripture would be fulfilled, Jesus said, "I am thirsty." [29] A jar of wine vinegar was there, so they soaked a sponge in it, put the sponge on a stalk of the hyssop plant, and lifted it to Jesus' lips. [30] When he had received the drink, Jesus said, "It is finished." With that, he bowed his head and gave up his spirit.

[31] Now it was the day of Preparation, and the next day was to be a special Sabbath. Because the Jewish leaders did not want the bodies left on the crosses during the Sabbath, they asked Pilate to have the legs broken and the bodies taken down. [32] The soldiers therefore came and broke the legs of the first man who had been crucified with Jesus, and then those of the other. [33] But when they came to Jesus and found that he was already dead, they did not break his legs. [34] Instead, one of the soldiers pierced Jesus' side with a spear, bringing a sudden flow of blood and water. [35] The man who saw it has given testimony, and his testimony is true. He knows that he tells the truth, and he testifies so that you also may believe. [36] These things happened so that the scripture would be fulfilled: "Not one of his bones will be broken," [c] [37] and, as another scripture says, "They will look on the one they have pierced." [d]

The Burial of Jesus

[38] Later, Joseph of Arimathea asked Pilate for the body of Jesus. Now Joseph was a disciple of Jesus, but secretly because he feared the Jewish leaders. With Pilate's permission, he came and took the body away. [39] He was accompanied by Nicodemus, the man who earlier had visited Jesus at night. Nicodemus brought a mixture of myrrh and aloes, about seventy-five pounds.[e] [40] Taking Jesus' body, the two of them wrapped it, with the spices, in strips of linen. This was in accordance with Jewish burial customs. [41] At the place where Jesus was crucified, there was a garden, and in the garden a new tomb, in which no one had ever been laid. [42] Because it was the Jewish day of Preparation and since the tomb was nearby, they laid Jesus there.

1545

---

[a] 24 Psalm 22:18 [b] 26 The Greek for *Woman* does not denote any disrespect. [c] 36 Exodus 12:46; Num. 9:12; Psalm 34:20 [d] 37 Zech. 12:10 [e] 39 Or about 34 kilograms

The Empty Tomb

20 Early on the first day of the week, while it was still dark, Mary Magdalene went to the tomb and saw that the stone had been removed from the entrance. ²So she came running to Simon Peter and the other disciple, the one Jesus loved, and said, "They have taken the Lord out of the tomb, and we don't know where they have put him!"

³So Peter and the other disciple started for the tomb. ⁴Both were running, but the other disciple out-ran Peter and reached the tomb first. ⁵He bent over and looked in at the strips of linen lying there but did not go in. ⁶Then Simon Peter came along behind him and went straight into the tomb. He saw the strips of linen lying there, ⁷as well as the cloth that had been wrapped around Jesus' head. The cloth was still lying in its place, separate from the linen. ⁸Finally the other disciple, who had reached the tomb first, also went inside. He saw and believed. ⁹(They still did not understand from Scripture that Jesus had to rise from the dead.) ¹⁰Then the disciples went back to where they were staying.

Jesus Appears to Mary Magdalene

¹¹Now Mary stood outside the tomb crying. As she wept, she bent over to look into the tomb ¹²and saw two angels in white, seated where Jesus' body had been, one at the head and the other at the foot.

¹³They asked her, "Woman,ᵃ why are you crying?"

"They have taken my Lord away," she said, "and I don't know where they have put him." ¹⁴At this, she turned around and saw Jesus standing there, but she did not realize that it was Jesus.

¹⁵He asked her, "Woman, why are you crying? Who is it you are looking for?"

Thinking he was the gardener, she said, "Sir, if you have carried him away, tell me where you have put him, and I will get him."

¹⁶Jesus said to her, "Mary."

She turned toward him and cried out in Aramaic, "Rabboni!" (which means "Teacher").

¹⁷Jesus said, "Do not hold on to me, for I have not yet ascended to the Father. Go instead to my brothers and tell them, 'I am ascending to my Father and your Father, to my God and your God.'"

¹⁸Mary Magdalene went to the disciples with the news: "I have seen the Lord!" And she told them that he had said these things to her.

Jesus Appears to His Disciples

¹⁹On the evening of that first day of the week, when the disciples were together, with the doors locked for fear of the Jewish leaders, Jesus came and stood among them and said, "Peace be with you!" ²⁰After he said this, he showed them his hands and side. The disciples were overjoyed when they saw the Lord.

²¹Again Jesus said, "Peace be with you! As the Father has sent me, I am sending you." ²²And with that he breathed on them and said, "Receive the Holy Spirit. ²³If you forgive the sins of anyone, their sins are forgiven; if you do not forgive them, they are not forgiven."

Jesus Appears to Thomas

²⁴Now Thomas (also known as Didymusᵇ), one of the Twelve, was not with the disciples when Jesus came. ²⁵So the other disciples told him, "We have seen the Lord!"

But he said to them, "Unless I see the nail marks in his hands and put my finger where the nails were, and put my hand into his side, I will not believe."

²⁶A week later his disciples were in the house again, and

1546

atissue:doubt

20:24–29 Like doubting Thomas, most of us prefer to put our faith in what we can feel and see. It's easier to trust in other people, material things or our own strength. They feel more real to us than a God we can't see or touch. But as Christians, we choose to live by faith, not by what we can see. Though it's a harder road, it's worth it. God rewards our faith with more spiritual blessings than we can count in a lifetime. At the end of the day, nothing we can see or touch is as trustworthy as our unseen God.

ᵃ 13 The Greek for *Woman* does not denote any disrespect; also in verse 15.   ᵇ 24 *Thomas* (Aramaic) and *Didymus* (Greek) both mean *twin*.

ASKmeanyTHING

What was your relationship with Jesus?

I owed him my life—literally. I know a lot of people would say that, including many of the other disciples. But my case was clearly one where if I hadn't met Jesus, I wouldn't have had a life. You see, Jesus cast seven demons out of me. Before I met him, I was tortured continually—physically and spiritually. When he healed me, my one overwhelming emotion was *gratitude*. So I chose to follow him and support his ministry.

But then you lost him. How did you handle that?

The day Jesus was killed, I felt as if my life and hope had been extinguished. I felt so helpless—what could I do for my Lord, who was being laughed at and tortured right in front of my eyes? Many of the other disciples fled, but I felt rooted to the spot. He had saved me; the least I could do was stay with him. I watched him die.

The next day only got worse. Because it was the Sabbath, we weren't allowed to do any work, so I couldn't do anything to take my mind off the horrors. I just sat and cried. I grieved for all he had been to me—my healer, teacher, leader and friend. I had no hope. Of course, I didn't know then what would come to pass the next morning.

What happened?

The next morning I went to the tomb with a few of the other women to anoint Jesus' body for burial. But as if things weren't bad enough, when we got there, we discovered that his body was missing. We ran to tell the disciples the unbelievable news. After Peter and John came to see, I was left alone, crying by his empty tomb. I saw two men dressed in white sitting in Jesus' tomb, and told them that I was crying because Jesus was gone. Then I turned and saw a man—the gardener, I thought. But then he said my name, and I knew it was Jesus! He was alive!

So what can we learn from your life?

That there's always hope. Our Lord has conquered death, so this life is not the end! Have you lost someone you love? Do you feel as if your own life is over? That's how I felt. I didn't know what to do with myself if I couldn't follow Jesus. But Jesus had something different for me. Yes, I missed Jesus every day of my life. But he gave me the hope to go on.

1547

FOR MORE INSIGHT: The Bible tells us only a few facts about Mary Magdalene (see Matthew 27:55–56; Luke 23:55—24:11). Despite negative depictions in some popular films and books, there is no Biblical or credible historical evidence that Mary's relationship with Jesus was anything other than a grateful disciple to her teacher and Lord.

To see how Jesus dealt with grief, read Matthew 14:1–13; and John 11:33–35. For more on comfort, read Psalm 55:16–23; and 2 Corinthians 1:3–7.

Thomas was with them. Though the doors were locked, Jesus came and stood among them and said, "Peace be with you!" [27] Then he said to Thomas, "Put your finger here; see my hands. Reach out your hand and put it into my side. Stop doubting and believe."

[28] Thomas said to him, "My Lord and my God!"

[29] Then Jesus told him, "Because you have seen me, you have believed; blessed are those who have not seen and yet have believed."

The Purpose of John's Gospel

[30] Jesus performed many other signs in the presence of his disciples, which are not recorded in this book. [31] But these are written that you may believe[a] that Jesus is the Messiah, the Son of God, and that by believing you may have life in his name.

Jesus and the Miraculous Catch of Fish

21 Afterward Jesus appeared again to his disciples, by the Sea of Galilee.[b] It happened this way: [2] Simon Peter, Thomas (also known as Didymus[c]), Nathanael from Cana in Galilee, the sons of Zebedee, and two other disciples were together. [3] "I'm going out to fish," Simon Peter told them, and they said, "We'll go with you." So they went out and got into the boat, but that night they caught nothing.

[4] Early in the morning, Jesus stood on the shore, but the disciples did not realize that it was Jesus.

[5] He called out to them, "Friends, haven't you any fish?"

"No," they answered.

[6] He said, "Throw your net on the right side of the boat and you will find some." When they did, they were unable to haul the net in because of the large number of fish.

[7] Then the disciple whom Jesus loved said to Peter, "It is the Lord!" As soon as Simon Peter heard him say, "It is the Lord," he wrapped his outer garment around him (for he had taken it off) and jumped into the water. [8] The other disciples followed in the boat, towing the net full of fish, for they were not far from shore, about a hundred yards.[d] [9] When they landed, they saw a fire of burning coals there with fish on it, and some bread.

[10] Jesus said to them, "Bring some of the fish you have just caught."

[11] Simon Peter climbed aboard and dragged the net ashore. It was full of large fish, 153, but even with so many the net was not torn. [12] Jesus said to them, "Come and have breakfast." None of the disciples dared ask him, "Who are you?" They knew it was the Lord. [13] Jesus came, took the bread and gave it to them, and did the same with the fish. [14] This was now the third time Jesus appeared to his disciples after he was raised from the dead.

Jesus Reinstates Peter

[15] When they had finished eating, Jesus said to Simon Peter, "Simon son of John, do you love me more than these?"

"Yes, Lord," he said, "you know that I love you."

Jesus said, "Feed my lambs."

[16] Again Jesus said, "Simon son of John, do you love me?"

He answered, "Yes, Lord, you know that I love you."

Jesus said, "Take care of my sheep."

[17] The third time he said to him, "Simon son of John, do you love me?"

at issue: second chances

21:15–19 Three times Peter denied Christ. He renounced the person he had vowed to follow regardless of the cost. Have you ever been in Peter's place? Have you turned your back on God? Have you experienced the pain and shame of realizing your betrayal? Take heart! God is a God of second chances. Note Jesus' response to Peter's failure. Three times he gave Peter the opportunity to affirm his love. He restored their relationship, reinstated Peter and assigned him a special task to do. If you've failed God, he wants to restore you, too. Come back to him, and know that you're forgiven, accepted and loved.

1548

---

[a] 31 Or may continue to believe   [b] 1 Greek Tiberias   [c] 2 Thomas (Aramaic) and Didymus (Greek) both mean twin.   [d] 8 Or about 90 meters

Peter was hurt because Jesus asked him the third time, "Do you love me?" He said, "Lord, you know all things; you know that I love you."

Jesus said, "Feed my sheep. [18]Very truly I tell you, when you were younger you dressed yourself and went where you wanted; but when you are old you will stretch out your hands, and someone else will dress you and lead you where you do not want to go." [19]Jesus said this to indicate the kind of death by which Peter would glorify God. Then he said to him, "Follow me!"

[20]Peter turned and saw that the disciple whom Jesus loved was following them. (This was the one who had leaned back against Jesus at the supper and had said, "Lord, who is going to betray you?") [21]When Peter saw him, he asked, "Lord, what about him?"

[22]Jesus answered, "If I want him to remain alive until I return, what is that to you? You must follow me." [23]Because of this, the rumor spread among the believers that this disciple would not die. But Jesus did not say that he would not die; he only said, "If I want him to remain alive until I return, what is that to you?"

[24]This is the disciple who testifies to these things and who wrote them down. We know that his testimony is true.

[25]Jesus did many other things as well. If every one of them were written down, I suppose that even the whole world would not have room for the books that would be written.

1549

acts

1550

AUTHOR
Luke.

AUDIENCE
Specifically, Theophilus, whose name means
"dear friend who loves God." He is the same
high official for whom the book of Luke was
written (see Luke 1:1).

DATE
Probably about A.D. 63.

SETTING
The gospel is spreading to all parts of the
Roman Empire.

VERSE TO REMEMBER
"But you will receive power when the Holy
Spirit comes on you; and you will be my wit-
nesses in Jerusalem, and in all Judea and
Samaria, and to the ends of the earth." (1:8)

THEME TO CONSIDER
The Holy Spirit fuels believers' passion and
faith, strengthens the church and performs
miracles. Apart from the Spirit's work, there
would be no church today.

Jesus Taken Up Into Heaven

1 In my former book, Theophilus, I wrote about all that Jesus began to do and to teach ²until the day he was taken up to heaven, after giving instructions through the Holy Spirit to the apostles he had chosen. ³After his suffering, he presented himself to them and gave many convincing proofs that he was alive. He appeared to them over a period of forty days and spoke about the kingdom of God. ⁴On one occasion, while he was eating with them, he gave them this command: "Do not leave Jerusalem, but wait for the gift my Father promised, which you have heard me speak about. ⁵For John baptized with* water, but in a few days you will be baptized with* the Holy Spirit."

⁶So when they met together, they asked him, "Lord, are you at this time going to restore the kingdom to Israel?"

⁷He said to them: "It is not for you to know the times or dates the Father has set by his own authority. ⁸But you will receive power when the Holy Spirit comes on you; and you will be my witnesses in Jerusalem, and in all Judea and Samaria, and to the ends of the earth."

⁹After he said this, he was taken up before their very eyes, and a cloud hid him from their sight.

¹⁰They were looking intently up into the sky as he was going, when suddenly two men dressed in white stood beside them. ¹¹"Men of Galilee," they said, "why do you stand here looking into the sky? This same Jesus, who has been taken from you into heaven, will come back in the same way you have seen him go into heaven."

Matthias Chosen to Replace Judas

¹²Then the apostles returned to Jerusalem from the hill called the Mount of Olives, a Sabbath day's walk*b* from the city. ¹³When they arrived, they went upstairs to the room where they were staying. Those present were Peter, John, James and Andrew; Philip and Thomas, Bartholomew and Matthew; James son of Alphaeus and Simon the Zealot, and Judas son of James. ¹⁴They all joined together constantly in prayer, along with the women and Mary the mother of Jesus, and with his brothers.

¹⁵In those days Peter stood up among the believers (a group numbering about a hundred and twenty) ¹⁶and said, "Brothers and sisters, the Scripture had to be fulfilled in which the Holy Spirit spoke long ago through David concerning Judas, who served as guide for those who arrested Jesus. ¹⁷He was one of our number and shared in our ministry."

¹⁸(With the reward he got for his wickedness, Judas bought a field; there he fell headlong, his body burst open and all his intestines spilled out. ¹⁹Everyone in Jerusalem heard about this, so they called that field in their language Akeldama, that is, Field of Blood.)

²⁰"For," said Peter, "it is written in the Book of Psalms:

> "'May his place be deserted;
> let there be no one to dwell in it,'*c*

and,

> "'May another take his place of leadership.'*d*

²¹Therefore it is necessary to choose one of the men who have been with us the whole time the Lord Jesus went in and out among us, ²²beginning from John's baptism to the time when Jesus was taken up from us. For one of these must become a witness with us of his resurrection."

²³So they proposed the names of two men: Joseph called Barsabbas (also known as Justus) and Matthias. ²⁴Then they prayed, "Lord, you know everyone's heart. Show us which of these two you have chosen ²⁵to take over this apostolic ministry, which Judas left to go where he belongs." ²⁶Then they cast lots, and the lot fell to Matthias; so he was added to the eleven apostles.

The Holy Spirit Comes at Pentecost

2 When the day of Pentecost came, they were all together in one place. ²Suddenly a sound like the blowing of a violent wind came from heaven and filled the whole house where they were sitting. ³They saw what seemed to be tongues of fire that separated and came to rest on each of them. ⁴All of

---

HE IS: the Holy Spirit

2:1–4 On the day of Pentecost, an amazing thing happened—*all* of Jesus' followers were filled with the Holy Spirit. Before this time, the Holy Spirit had come upon only a few, select individuals to do God's work. From now on, the Holy Spirit would fill *all* believers (see Joel 2:28–29).

If you are a follower of Christ, then God himself lives within you. He comes to comfort you, teach you and enable you to help build God's kingdom on earth. Ask *the Holy Spirit*, who is always with you, to empower you to fulfill his purpose.

For the next He Is, go to p. 1564.

1552

them were filled with the Holy Spirit and began to speak in other tongues[a] as the Spirit enabled them.

[5] Now there were staying in Jerusalem God-fearing Jews from every nation under heaven. [6] When they heard this sound, a crowd came together in bewilderment, because each one heard their own language being spoken. [7] Utterly amazed, they asked: "Aren't all these who are speaking Galileans? [8] Then how is it that each of us hears them in our native language? [9] Parthians, Medes and Elamites; residents of Mesopotamia, Judea and Cappadocia, Pontus and Asia,[b] [10] Phrygia and Pamphylia, Egypt and the parts of Libya near Cyrene; visitors from Rome [11] (both Jews and converts to Judaism); Cretans and Arabs—we hear them declaring the wonders of God in our own tongues!" [12] Amazed and perplexed, they asked one another, "What does this mean?"

[13] Some, however, made fun of them and said, "They have had too much wine."

Peter Addresses the Crowd

[14] Then Peter stood up with the Eleven, raised his voice and addressed the crowd: "Fellow Jews and all of you who live in Jerusalem, let me explain this to you; listen carefully to what I say. [15] These people are not drunk, as you suppose. It's only nine in the morning! [16] No, this is what was spoken by the prophet Joel:

> [17] "'In the last days, God says,
> I will pour out my Spirit on all people.
> Your sons and daughters will prophesy,
> your young men will see visions,
> your old men will dream dreams.
> [18] Even on my servants, both men and women,
> I will pour out my Spirit in those days,
> and they will prophesy.
> [19] I will show wonders in the heaven above
> and signs on the earth below,
> blood and fire and billows of smoke.
> [20] The sun will be turned to darkness
> and the moon to blood
> before the coming of the great and glorious day of the Lord.
> [21] And everyone who calls
> on the name of the Lord will be saved.'[c]

[22] "People of Israel, listen to this: Jesus of Nazareth was a man accredited by God to you by miracles, wonders and signs, which God did among you through him, as you yourselves know. [23] This man was handed over to you by God's deliberate plan and foreknowledge; and you, with the help of wicked men,[d]

---

[a] *4* Or *languages;* also in verse 11   [b] *9* That is, the Roman province by that name   [c] *21* Joel 2:28-32   [d] *23* Or *of those not having the law* (that is, Gentiles)

put him to death by nailing him to the cross. ²⁴But God raised him from the dead, freeing him from the agony of death, because it was impossible for death to keep its hold on him. ²⁵David said about him:

> "'I saw the Lord always before me.
>   Because he is at my right hand,
>   I will not be shaken.
> ²⁶Therefore my heart is glad and my tongue rejoices;
>   my body also will rest in hope,
> ²⁷because you will not abandon me to the realm of the dead,
>   you will not let your holy one see decay.
> ²⁸You have made known to me the paths of life;
>   you will fill me with joy in your presence.'ᵃ

²⁹"Brothers and sisters, we all know that the patriarch David died and was buried, and his tomb is here to this day. ³⁰But he was a prophet and knew that God had promised him on oath that he would place one of his descendants on his throne. ³¹Seeing what was to come, he spoke of the resurrection of the Messiah, that he was not abandoned to the realm of the dead, nor did his body see decay. ³²God has raised this Jesus to life, and we are all witnesses of the fact. ³³Exalted to the right hand of God, he has received from the Father the promised Holy Spirit and has poured out what you now see and hear. ³⁴For David did not ascend to heaven, and yet he said,

> "'The Lord said to my Lord:
>   "Sit at my right hand
> ³⁵until I make your enemies
>   a footstool for your feet."'ᵇ

1553

³⁶"Therefore let all Israel be assured of this: God has made this Jesus, whom you crucified, both Lord and Messiah."

³⁷When the people heard this, they were cut to the heart and said to Peter and the other apostles, "Brothers, what shall we do?"

³⁸Peter replied, "Repent and be baptized, every one of you, in the name of Jesus Christ for the forgiveness of your sins. And you will receive the gift of the Holy Spirit. ³⁹The promise is for you and your children and for all who are far off—for all whom the Lord our God will call."

⁴⁰With many other words he warned them; and he pleaded with them, "Save yourselves from this corrupt generation." ⁴¹Those who accepted his message were baptized, and about three thousand were added to their number that day.

The Fellowship of the Believers

⁴²They devoted themselves to the apostles' teaching and to fellowship, to the breaking of bread and to prayer. ⁴³Everyone was filled with awe at the many wonders and signs performed by the apostles. ⁴⁴All the believers were together and had everything in common. ⁴⁵They sold property and possessions to give to anyone who had need. ⁴⁶Every day they continued to meet together in the temple courts. They broke bread in their homes and ate together with glad and sincere hearts, ⁴⁷praising God and enjoying the favor of all the people. And the Lord added to their number daily those who were being saved.

Peter Heals a Lame Beggar

3 One day Peter and John were going up to the temple at the time of prayer—at three in the afternoon. ²Now a man who was lame from birth was being carried to the temple gate called Beautiful, where he was put every day to beg from those going into the temple courts. ³When he saw Peter and John about to enter, he asked them for money. ⁴Peter looked straight at him, as did John. Then Peter said, "Look at us!" ⁵So the man gave them his attention, expecting to get something from them.

⁶Then Peter said, "Silver or gold I do not have, but what I do have I give you. In the name of Jesus Christ of Nazareth, walk." ⁷Taking him by the right hand, he helped him up, and instantly the man's feet

---

ᵃ 28 Psalm 16:8-11 (see Septuagint)   ᵇ 35 Psalm 110:1

myth# 89 "IT'S OK IF I'M NOT COMMITTED TO A CHURCH AS LONG AS MY RELATIONSHIP WITH GOD IS HEALTHY."

I stopped going to church in college. I don't remember making a conscious choice not to go; it just sort of happened over time. My friends and I were always out late on the weekends, so when my alarm would go off early on Sunday morning, I'd hit snooze for an hour or so and then just give up. I needed those few hours of sleep more than I needed to sleep through another dull sermon.

Then I got out of college and started grad school, and things didn't get any easier. Now that I'm in banking, any free time I have is dedicated to my family and my bed. In that order. By the time the weekend rolls around, I feel exhausted. I pry myself out of bed each Saturday morning to take the kids to swim practice, and that just makes my Sunday morning sleep vigil all the more essential. Sometimes we go on little weekend getaways, too, so we'd miss church anyway.

Occasionally I feel guilty about not going. My parents kind of ingrained in me that I should go to church every Sunday. When I hear one of the women in my office, Susanne, talk about serving in the high school ministry at her church, I feel a twinge of guilt. I wish I could explain to her that going to church is not what gets you saved. It's your personal relationship with Jesus that matters, and church has nothing to do with that. I still pray. As long as I'm right with God, then church can wait. I'll get back eventually. I know I should someday for my kids' sake.

—Lindsay

NO, CHURCH ATTENDANCE

doesn't save you. But the church does matter to God. *So what?* you may ask. Consider this:

- Church wasn't your pastor's idea or your mother's idea. It was God's idea. Because the church matters to God, it should matter to you too. Paul calls the church "God's household, which is the church of the living God" (1 Timothy 3:15).

- Sometimes we approach church with a fast-food attitude—wanting to zip through the drive-through window, get what we want in minutes and not have to interact with other people. Instead, we can transform our attitudes about church by approaching it as a place to give, to know and be known, to invest our time, to develop intentional relationships and to slow down and truly worship.

- While your personal relationship with Christ is what saves you, the Bible also emphasizes that you are a part of a body with many parts (see 1 Corinthians 12). It's impossible to be a healthy Christian apart from the life-giving local body.

- We were not designed to live in isolation, plowing through life alone. God intended for Christians to do life together. To raise our families together and meet each others' needs (see Acts 2:42). To roll up our sleeves and work together. To support each other through the good and bad times in life. While the church isn't perfect, it is the most amazing institution on earth and one worth investing in—both for what you can give and for what you can get.

"From high school graduation to age 25 there is a 42 percent drop in weekly church attendance and a 58 percent decline from age 18 to age 29. That represents about 8 million twentysomethings alive today who were active church-goers as teenagers but who will no longer be active in a church by their 30th birthday."

—Barna Research Group (2003)

"SPUR ONE ANOTHER ON TOWARD LOVE AND GOOD DEEDS, NOT GIVING UP MEETING TOGETHER, AS SOME ARE IN THE HABIT OF DOING, BUT encouraging one another."

HEBREWS 10:24–25

SEE ALSO

Romans 12:1–8
Ephesians 5:25–27
James 4:7–10

For more on **Church**, check the index.

and ankles became strong. ⁸He jumped to his feet and began to walk. Then he went with them into the temple courts, walking and jumping, and praising God. ⁹When all the people saw him walking and praising God, ¹⁰they recognized him as the same man who used to sit begging at the temple gate called Beautiful, and they were filled with wonder and amazement at what had happened to him.

Peter Speaks to the Onlookers

¹¹While the man held on to Peter and John, all the people were astonished and came running to them in the place called Solomon's Colonnade. ¹²When Peter saw this, he said to them: "People of Israel, why does this surprise you? Why do you stare at us as if by our own power or godliness we had made this man walk? ¹³The God of Abraham, Isaac and Jacob, the God of our fathers, has glorified his servant Jesus. You handed him over to be killed, and you disowned him before Pilate, though he had decided to let him go. ¹⁴You disowned the Holy and Righteous One and asked that a murderer be released to you. ¹⁵You killed the author of life, but God raised him from the dead. We are witnesses of this. ¹⁶By faith in the name of Jesus, this man whom you see and know was made strong. It is Jesus' name and the faith that comes through him that has completely healed him, as you can all see.

¹⁷"Now, brothers and sisters, I know that you acted in ignorance, as did your leaders. ¹⁸But this is how God fulfilled what he had foretold through all the prophets, saying that his Messiah would suffer. ¹⁹Repent, then, and turn to God, so that your sins may be wiped out, that times of refreshing may come from the Lord, ²⁰and that he may send the Messiah, who has been appointed for you—even Jesus. ²¹Heaven must receive him until the time comes for God to restore everything, as he promised long ago through his holy prophets. ²²For Moses said, 'The Lord your God will raise up for you a prophet like me from among your own people; you must listen to everything he tells you. ²³Anyone who does not listen to him will be completely cut off from their people.'ᵃ

²⁴"Indeed, beginning with Samuel, all the prophets who have spoken have foretold these days. ²⁵And you are heirs of the prophets and of the covenant God made with your fathers. He said to Abraham, 'Through your offspring all peoples on earth will be blessed.'ᵇ ²⁶When God raised up his servant, he sent him first to you to bless you by turning each of you from your wicked ways."

3:19–20 Have you ever felt the weight of guilt pulling you down? It feels like a burden that you're forced to carry. It becomes an unwanted, but unavoidable, part of who you are. But it doesn't have to be that way. All you have to do is repent and turn to God. Turn away from your sin and turn to him, and your sin will be "wiped out"—not cut in half, not slightly smudged—it will be completely removed, gone forever. Then times of refreshing will come. Don't you want sweet refreshment for your soul to replace that bitter weight you've carried?

a:issue:guilt over sin

Peter and John Before the Sanhedrin

4 The priests and the captain of the temple guard and the Sadducees came up to Peter and John while they were speaking to the people. ²They were greatly disturbed because the apostles were teaching the people, proclaiming in Jesus the resurrection of the dead. ³They seized Peter and John, and because it was evening, they put them in jail until the next day. ⁴But many who heard the message believed; so the number of men who believed grew to about five thousand.

⁵The next day the rulers, the elders and the teachers of the law met in Jerusalem. ⁶Annas the high priest was there, and so were Caiaphas, John, Alexander and others of the high priest's family. ⁷They had Peter and John brought before them and began to question them: "By what power or what name did you do this?"

⁸Then Peter, filled with the Holy Spirit, said to them: "Rulers and elders of the people! ⁹If we are being called to account today for an act of kindness shown to a man who was lame and are being asked how he was healed, ¹⁰then know this, you and all the people of Israel: It is by the name of Jesus Christ of

Nazareth, whom you crucified but whom God raised from the dead, that this man stands before you healed. ¹¹Jesus is

> "'the stone you builders rejected,
> which has become the cornerstone.'ᵃ

¹²Salvation is found in no one else, for there is no other name given under heaven by which we must be saved."

¹³When they saw the courage of Peter and John and realized that they were unschooled, ordinary men, they were astonished and they took note that these men had been with Jesus. ¹⁴But since they could see the man who had been healed standing there with them, there was nothing they could say. ¹⁵So they ordered them to withdraw from the Sanhedrin and then conferred together. ¹⁶"What are we going to do with these men?" they asked. "Everyone living in Jerusalem knows they have performed a notable sign, and we cannot deny it. ¹⁷But to stop this thing from spreading any further among the people, we must warn them to speak no longer to anyone in this name."

¹⁸Then they called them in again and commanded them not to speak or teach at all in the name of Jesus. ¹⁹But Peter and John replied, "Which is right in God's eyes: to listen to you, or to him? You be the judges! ²⁰As for us, we cannot help speaking about what we have seen and heard."

²¹After further threats they let them go. They could not decide how to punish them, because all the people were praising God for what had happened. ²²For the man who was miraculously healed was over forty years old.

The Believers' Prayer

²³On their release, Peter and John went back to their own people and reported all that the chief priests and the elders had said to them. ²⁴When they heard this, they raised their voices together in prayer to God. "Sovereign Lord," they said, "you made the heaven and the earth and the sea, and everything in them. ²⁵You spoke by the Holy Spirit through the mouth of your servant, our father David:

> "'Why do the nations rage
> and the peoples plot in vain?
> ²⁶The kings of the earth rise up
> and the rulers band together
> against the Lord
> and against his anointed one.'ᵇ,ᶜ

²⁷Indeed Herod and Pontius Pilate met together with the Gentiles and the people of Israel in this city to conspire against your holy servant Jesus, whom you anointed. ²⁸They did what your power and will had decided beforehand should happen. ²⁹Now, Lord, consider their threats and enable your servants to speak your word with great boldness. ³⁰Stretch out your hand to heal and perform signs and wonders through the name of your holy servant Jesus." ³¹After they prayed, the place where they were meeting was shaken. And they were all filled with the Holy Spirit and spoke the word of God boldly.

---

atissue:education

4:13 In our society, education is the key that opens many doors. Most jobs require at least a high school diploma, and many require a college degree, graduate degree or specialized training. But in the kingdom of God, you don't need a degree to get a job. You just need to know Jesus. God often chooses to use simple people, simple words and a simple message to communicate the awesome wonder of who he is and what he's done. Whether you have a degree or not, God can accomplish great things in his kingdom through *you*.

1557

ᵃ *11* Psalm 118:22   ᵇ *26* That is, Messiah or Christ   ᶜ *26* Psalm 2:1,2

The Believers Share Their Possessions

³²All the believers were one in heart and mind. No one claimed that any of their possessions was their own, but they shared everything they had. ³³With great power the apostles continued to testify to the resurrection of the Lord Jesus. And God's grace was so powerfully at work in them all ³⁴that there were no needy persons among them. For from time to time those who owned land or houses sold them, brought the money from the sales ³⁵and put it at the apostles' feet, and it was distributed to anyone who had need.

³⁶Joseph, a Levite from Cyprus, whom the apostles called Barnabas (which means "son of encouragement"), ³⁷sold a field he owned and brought the money and put it at the apostles' feet.

Ananias and Sapphira

5 Now a man named Ananias, together with his wife Sapphira, also sold a piece of property. ²With his wife's full knowledge he kept back part of the money for himself, but brought the rest and put it at the apostles' feet.

³Then Peter said, "Ananias, how is it that Satan has so filled your heart that you have lied to the Holy Spirit and have kept for yourself some of the money you received for the land? ⁴Didn't it belong to you before it was sold? And after it was sold, wasn't the money at your disposal? What made you think of doing such a thing? You have not lied just to human beings but to God."

⁵When Ananias heard this, he fell down and died. And great fear seized all who heard what had happened. ⁶Then some young men came forward, wrapped up his body, and carried him out and buried him.

⁷About three hours later his wife came in, not knowing what had happened. ⁸Peter asked her, "Tell me, is this the price you and Ananias got for the land?"

"Yes," she said, "that is the price."

⁹Peter said to her, "How could you conspire to test the Spirit of the Lord? Listen! The feet of those who buried your husband are at the door, and they will carry you out also."

¹⁰At that moment she fell down at his feet and died. Then the young men came in and, finding her dead, carried her out and buried her beside her husband. ¹¹Great fear seized the whole church and all who heard about these events.

atissue:lying

5:1–11 It's bad enough when someone wrongs us, but it's even worse when that person lies about it. Most of us would prefer to hear the truth, even if it's a hard truth to handle. Being lied to feels like a personal betrayal. Did you know that every lie is also a betrayal against God? God is all about truth. And he has sacrificed greatly to free us from sin so that we can know and love and embrace the truth for ourselves. Loving God means loving the truth.

The Apostles Heal Many

¹²The apostles performed many signs and wonders among the people. And all the believers used to meet together in Solomon's Colonnade. ¹³No one else dared join them, even though they were highly regarded by the people. ¹⁴Nevertheless, more and more men and women believed in the Lord and were added to their number. ¹⁵As a result, people brought the sick into the streets and laid them on beds and mats so that at least Peter's shadow might fall on some of them as he passed by. ¹⁶Crowds gathered also from the towns around Jerusalem, bringing their sick and those tormented by evilᵃ spirits, and all of them were healed.

The Apostles Persecuted

¹⁷Then the high priest and all his associates, who were members of the party of the Sadducees, were filled with jealousy. ¹⁸They arrested the apostles and put them in the public jail. ¹⁹But during the night

---

ᵃ *16* Greek *unclean*

an angel of the Lord opened the doors of the jail and brought them out. [20]"Go, stand in the temple courts," he said, "and tell the people all about this new life."

[21]At daybreak they entered the temple courts, as they had been told, and began to teach the people.

When the high priest and his associates arrived, they called together the Sanhedrin—the full assembly of the elders of Israel—and sent to the jail for the apostles. [22]But on arriving at the jail, the officers did not find them there. So they went back and reported, [23]"We found the jail securely locked, with the guards standing at the doors; but when we opened them, we found no one inside." [24]On hearing this report, the captain of the temple guard and the chief priests were puzzled, wondering what this might lead to.

[25]Then someone came and said, "Look! The men you put in jail are standing in the temple courts teaching the people." [26]At that, the captain went with his officers and brought the apostles. They did not use force, because they feared that the people would stone them.

[27]The apostles were brought in and made to appear before the Sanhedrin to be questioned by the high priest. [28]"We gave you strict orders not to teach in this name," he said. "Yet you have filled Jerusalem with your teaching and are determined to make us guilty of this man's blood."

[29]Peter and the other apostles replied: "We must obey God rather than human beings! [30]The God of our ancestors raised Jesus from the dead—whom you killed by hanging him on a cross. [31]God exalted him to his own right hand as Prince and Savior that he might bring Israel to repentance and forgive their sins. [32]We are witnesses of these things, and so is the Holy Spirit, whom God has given to those who obey him."

[33]When they heard this, they were furious and wanted to put them to death. [34]But a Pharisee named Gamaliel, a teacher of the law, who was honored by all the people, stood up in the Sanhedrin and ordered that the men be put outside for a little while. [35]Then he addressed the Sanhedrin: "Men of Israel, consider carefully what you intend to do to these men. [36]Some time ago Theudas appeared, claiming to be somebody, and about four hundred men rallied to him. He was killed, all his followers were dispersed, and it all came to nothing. [37]After him, Judas the Galilean appeared in the days of the census and led a band of people in revolt. He too was killed, and all his followers were scattered. [38]Therefore, in the present case I advise you: Leave these men alone! Let them go! For if their purpose or activity is of human origin, it will fail. [39]But if it is from God, you will not be able to stop these men; you will only find yourselves fighting against God."

[40]His speech persuaded them. They called the apostles in and had them flogged. Then they ordered them not to speak in the name of Jesus, and let them go.

[41]The apostles left the Sanhedrin, rejoicing because they had been counted worthy of suffering disgrace for the Name. [42]Day after day, in the temple courts and from house to house, they never stopped teaching and proclaiming the good news that Jesus is the Messiah.

The Choosing of the Seven

6 In those days when the number of disciples was increasing, the Hellenistic Jews[a] among them complained against the Hebraic Jews because their widows were being overlooked in the daily distribution of food. [2]So the Twelve gathered all the disciples together and said, "It would not be right for us to neglect the ministry of the word of God in order to wait on tables. [3]Brothers and sisters, choose seven men from among you who are known to be full of the Spirit and wisdom. We will turn this responsibility over to them [4]and will give our attention to prayer and the ministry of the word."

[5]This proposal pleased the whole group. They chose Stephen, a man full of faith and of the Holy Spirit; also Philip, Procorus, Nicanor, Timon, Parmenas, and Nicolas from Antioch, a convert to Judaism. [6]They presented them to the apostles, who prayed and laid their hands on them.

[7]So the word of God spread. The number of disciples in Jerusalem increased rapidly, and a large number of priests became obedient to the faith.

Stephen Seized

[8]Now Stephen, a man full of God's grace and power, performed great wonders and signs among the people. [9]Opposition arose, however, from members of the Synagogue of the Freedmen (as it was called)—

---

[a] 1 That is, Jews who had adopted the Greek language and culture

myth# 90

"NO ONE WILL EVER KNOW."

It's not as if I do it all that often. I just feel so fat sometimes; this way, I feel in control. After I've eaten more than I should, I just get rid of some of it. It can't be any worse than letting all those extra calories and all that greasy fat stay in my body.

What's depressing is that even when my stomach is full, I still feel so empty inside. It's an aching loneliness that won't go away, no matter what. I eat to try to fill this void, but then I eat so much I feel sick. Then I feel so disgusted and angry at myself. I hate my body and everything in it. So I purge. I throw up. And I'm back to feeling empty again. The whole process is so familiar. It helps me forget about feeling empty, but it never seems to satisfy me.

When I was in college, I know that a lot of my girlfriends purged. It's not like we openly admitted it, but I could tell. Some of the girls did it every day. I never did it that much, only a couple of times a week, after an especially bad binge. I was careful not to let other people know what I was doing. My family never knew, though I'm sure a few of my close friends must have suspected.

So what if I still do it? It's quick and easy, and I'm always discreet. It's a good way to counteract my food indulgences. I usually eat a healthy diet and I try to exercise when I can, so I know I'm not doing much damage to my body. The Bible doesn't say anything about it, so I'm not too worried. Besides, no one will ever know. It's my little secret.

—Anya

ANYA'S STORY IS as old as time.

Since the Garden of Eden, we humans have been trying to hide our secret sins from God. We see this in the early church as well—when Ananias and Sapphira thought they could get away with hiding something from God (see Acts 5:1–11). But our cover stories never work.

In Anya's case, her struggles with eating likely represent much more than an unhealthy relationship with food. Anya may be dealing with low self-esteem or a need for control. Her problems are compounded by the fact that she keeps her struggle a secret. Without help, her problems could continue for a long time. Are you hiding a secret sin from others and from God? Consider this:

- Secret sins come in every shape and form. Yours could be anything from habitual lying to alcoholism to gambling to an eating disorder to vanity. These sins hurt us in many ways—spiritually they strain our relationship with God; they can also damage our bodies; and they can sever our relationships with others. Secret sins are especially destructive because we feel like we can't admit them, so we try to fight them alone.

- Satan loves a juicy secret. He wants us to hide in the darkness. In contrast, God wants us to bring everything to light. God offers us freedom from sin and freedom from living a lie (see John 8:34–36).

- No matter how stuck in your sin you feel, God can give you the strength to overcome that struggle. Ask God to set you free and then reach out for help. It takes humility to admit a secret sin, yet this is the first step toward hope and healing. Consider talking with a Christian counselor or pastor to begin that process.

"Alcohol Health & Research World, a study of women who attend church, indicates that . . . out of the eight women who form the committee to plan the annual church dinner, two have an abusive relationship with food."

—Sharon Hersh

1561

"WOULD NOT GOD HAVE DISCOVERED IT, SINCE HE KNOWS THE SECRETS OF THE HEART?"

PSALM 44:21

SEE ALSO
Psalm 139:1–4,23–24
1 Corinthians 10:13
1 John 1:9–10

For more on **Eating Disorders** and **Secret Sin**, check the index.

Jews of Cyrene and Alexandria as well as the provinces of Cilicia and Asia—who began to argue with Stephen. [10]But they could not stand up against the wisdom the Spirit gave him as he spoke.

[11]Then they secretly persuaded some men to say, "We have heard Stephen speak blasphemous words against Moses and against God."

[12]So they stirred up the people and the elders and the teachers of the law. They seized Stephen and brought him before the Sanhedrin. [13]They produced false witnesses, who testified, "This fellow never stops speaking against this holy place and against the law. [14]For we have heard him say that this Jesus of Nazareth will destroy this place and change the customs Moses handed down to us."

[15]All who were sitting in the Sanhedrin looked intently at Stephen, and they saw that his face was like the face of an angel.

Stephen's Speech to the Sanhedrin

7 Then the high priest asked Stephen, "Are these charges true?"

[2]To this he replied: "Brothers and fathers, listen to me! The God of glory appeared to our father Abraham while he was still in Mesopotamia, before he lived in Harran. [3]'Leave your country and your people,' God said, 'and go to the land I will show you.'[a]

[4]"So he left the land of the Chaldeans and settled in Harran. After the death of his father, God sent him to this land where you are now living. [5]He gave him no inheritance here, not even enough ground to set his foot on. But God promised him that he and his descendants after him would possess the land, even though at that time Abraham had no child. [6]God spoke to him in this way: 'For four hundred years your descendants will be strangers in a country not their own, and they will be enslaved and mistreated. [7]But I will punish the nation they serve as slaves,' God said, 'and afterward they will come out of that country and worship me in this place.'[b] [8]Then he gave Abraham the covenant of circumcision. And Abraham became the father of Isaac and circumcised him eight days after his birth. Later Isaac became the father of Jacob, and Jacob became the father of the twelve patriarchs.

[9]"Because the patriarchs were jealous of Joseph, they sold him as a slave into Egypt. But God was with him [10]and rescued him from all his troubles. He gave Joseph wisdom and enabled him to gain the good-will of Pharaoh king of Egypt. So Pharaoh made him ruler over Egypt and all his palace.

[11]"Then a famine struck all Egypt and Canaan, bringing great suffering, and our people could not find food. [12]When Jacob heard that there was grain in Egypt, he sent our ancestors on their first visit. [13]On their second visit, Joseph told his brothers who he was, and Pharaoh learned about Joseph's family. [14]After this, Joseph sent for his father Jacob and his whole family, seventy-five in all. [15]Then Jacob went down to Egypt, where he and our ancestors died. [16]Their bodies were brought back to Shechem and placed in the tomb that Abraham had bought from the sons of Hamor at Shechem for a certain sum of money.

[17]"As the time drew near for God to fulfill his promise to Abraham, the number of our people in Egypt had greatly increased. [18]Then 'a new king, to whom Joseph meant nothing, came to power in Egypt.'[c] [19]He dealt treacherously with our people and oppressed our ancestors by forcing them to throw out their newborn babies so that they would die.

[20]"At that time Moses was born, and he was no ordinary child.[d] For three months he was cared for in his parents' home. [21]When he was placed outside, Pharaoh's daughter took him and brought him up as her own son. [22]Moses was educated in all the wisdom of the Egyptians and was powerful in speech and action.

[23]"When Moses was forty years old, he decided to visit his own people, the Israelites. [24]He saw one of them being mistreated by an Egyptian, so he went to his defense and avenged him by killing the Egyptian. [25]Moses thought that his own people would realize that God was using him to rescue them, but they did not. [26]The next day Moses came upon two Israelites who were fighting. He tried to reconcile them by saying, 'Men, you are brothers; why do you want to hurt each other?'

[27]"But the man who was mistreating the other pushed Moses aside and said, 'Who made you ruler

---

[a] 3 Gen. 12:1   [b] 7 Gen. 15:13,14   [c] 18 Exodus 1:8   [d] 20 Or was fair in the sight of God

and judge over us?[28] Are you thinking of killing me as you killed the Egyptian yesterday?'[a] [29] When Moses heard this, he fled to Midian, where he settled as a foreigner and had two sons.

[30] "After forty years had passed, an angel appeared to Moses in the flames of a burning bush in the desert near Mount Sinai. [31] When he saw this, he was amazed at the sight. As he went over to get a closer look, he heard the Lord say: [32] 'I am the God of your fathers, the God of Abraham, Isaac and Jacob.'[b] Moses trembled with fear and did not dare to look.

[33] "Then the Lord said to him, 'Take off your sandals, for the place where you are standing is holy ground. [34] I have indeed seen the oppression of my people in Egypt. I have heard their groaning and have come down to set them free. Now come, I will send you back to Egypt.'[c]

[35] "This is the same Moses they had rejected with the words, 'Who made you ruler and judge?' He was sent to be their ruler and deliverer by God himself, through the angel who appeared to him in the bush. [36] He led them out of Egypt and performed wonders and signs in Egypt, at the Red Sea and for forty years in the wilderness.

[37] "This is the Moses who told the Israelites, 'God will send you a prophet like me from your own people.'[d] [38] He was in the assembly in the wilderness, with the angel who spoke to him on Mount Sinai, and with our ancestors; and he received living words to pass on to us.

[39] "But our ancestors refused to obey him. Instead, they rejected him and in their hearts turned back to Egypt. [40] They told Aaron, 'Make us gods who will go before us. As for this fellow Moses who led us out of Egypt—we don't know what has happened to him!'[e] [41] That was the time they made an idol in the form of a calf. They brought sacrifices to it and reveled in what their own hands had made. [42] But God turned away from them and gave them over to the worship of the sun, moon and stars. This agrees with what is written in the book of the prophets:

> "'Did you bring me sacrifices and offerings
>   forty years in the wilderness, house of Israel?
> [43] You have taken up the tabernacle of Molek
>   and the star of your god Rephan,
>   the idols you made to worship.
> Therefore I will send you into exile'[f] beyond Babylon.

[44] "Our ancestors had the tabernacle of the covenant law with them in the wilderness. It had been made as God directed Moses, according to the pattern he had seen. [45] Having received the tabernacle, our ancestors under Joshua brought it with them when they took the land from the nations God drove out before them. It remained in the land until the time of David, [46] who enjoyed God's favor and asked that he might provide a dwelling place for the God of Jacob.[g] [47] But it was Solomon who built a house for him.

[48] "However, the Most High does not live in houses made by human hands. As the prophet says:

> [49] "'Heaven is my throne,
>   and the earth is my footstool.
> What kind of house will you build for me?
>
>   says the Lord.
>
> Or where will my resting place be?
> [50] Has not my hand made all these things?'[h]

[51] "You stiff-necked people! Your hearts and ears are still uncircumcised. You are just like your ancestors: You always resist the Holy Spirit! [52] Was there ever a prophet your ancestors did not persecute? They even killed those who predicted the coming of the Righteous One. And now you have betrayed and murdered him— [53] you who have received the law that was given through angels but have not obeyed it."

The Stoning of Stephen

[54] When the members of the Sanhedrin heard this, they were furious and gnashed their teeth at him. [55] But Stephen, full of the Holy Spirit, looked up to heaven and saw the glory of God, and Jesus standing

at the right hand of God. ⁵⁶"Look," he said, "I see heaven open and the Son of Man standing at the right hand of God."

⁵⁷At this they covered their ears and, yelling at the top of their voices, they all rushed at him, ⁵⁸dragged him out of the city and began to stone him. Meanwhile, the witnesses laid their coats at the feet of a young man named Saul.

⁵⁹While they were stoning him, Stephen prayed, "Lord Jesus, receive my spirit." ⁶⁰Then he fell on his knees and cried out, "Lord, do not hold this sin against them." When he had said this, he fell asleep.

 standing at the right hand of God

7:55–58 At his trial, Stephen defended his faith in Jesus to the powerful Jewish Sanhedrin. As Stephen was standing up for Jesus just before he was killed by stoning, he saw Jesus himself, *standing at the right hand of God,* a place of the utmost power and honor.

If people begin to throw "stones" of derision at you because of your faith, be encouraged by the way Jesus honored his servant Stephen. You have Jesus' full attention, and you can trust that he is *standing at the right hand of God* to strengthen you and applaud your faithfulness (see also Romans 8:34).

For the next He Is, go to p. 1569.

8 And Saul approved of their killing him.

The Church Persecuted and Scattered

On that day a great persecution broke out against the church in Jerusalem, and all except the apostles were scattered throughout Judea and Samaria. ²Godly men buried Stephen and mourned deeply for him. ³But Saul began to destroy the church. Going from house to house, he dragged off both men and women and put them in prison.

Philip in Samaria

⁴Those who had been scattered preached the word wherever they went. ⁵Philip went down to a city in Samaria and proclaimed the Messiah there. ⁶When the crowds heard Philip and saw the signs he performed, they all paid close attention to what he said. ⁷With shrieks, evil*ᵃ* spirits came out of many, and many who were paralyzed or lame were healed. ⁸So there was great joy in that city.

Simon the Sorcerer

⁹Now for some time a man named Simon had practiced sorcery in the city and amazed all the people of Samaria. He boasted that he was someone great, ¹⁰and all the people, both high and low, gave him their attention and exclaimed, "This man is rightly called the Great Power of God." ¹¹They followed him because he had amazed them for a long time with his sorcery. ¹²But when they believed Philip as he proclaimed the good news of the kingdom of God and the name of Jesus Christ, they were baptized, both men and women. ¹³Simon himself believed and was baptized. And he followed Philip everywhere, astonished by the great signs and miracles he saw.

¹⁴When the apostles in Jerusalem heard that Samaria had accepted the word of God, they sent Peter and John to Samaria. ¹⁵When they arrived, they prayed for the new believers there that they might receive the Holy Spirit, ¹⁶because the Holy Spirit had not yet come on any of them; they had simply been baptized into*ᵇ* the name of the Lord Jesus. ¹⁷Then Peter and John placed their hands on them, and they received the Holy Spirit.

¹⁸When Simon saw that the Spirit was given at the laying on of the apostles' hands, he offered them money ¹⁹and said, "Give me also this ability so that everyone on whom I lay my hands may receive the Holy Spirit."

ᵃ 7 Greek unclean ᵇ 16 Or in

conversations

bitterness «» 8:20–23

1» Are you holding on to any hidden bitterness? If so, what?

2» In what form does bitterness show itself to others?

3» How can you be released from long-held bitterness?

For more on **bitterness**, check the index.
For the next Conversations, go to p. 1570.

[20]Peter answered: "May your money perish with you, because you thought you could buy the gift of God with money! [21]You have no part or share in this ministry, because your heart is not right before God. [22]Repent of this wickedness and pray to the Lord in the hope that he may forgive you for having such a thought in your heart. [23]For I see that you are full of bitterness and captive to sin."

[24]Then Simon answered, "Pray to the Lord for me so that nothing you have said may happen to me."

[25]After they had further proclaimed the word of the Lord and testified about Jesus, Peter and John returned to Jerusalem, preaching the gospel in many Samaritan villages.

1565

Philip and the Ethiopian

[26]Now an angel of the Lord said to Philip, "Go south to the road—the desert road—that goes down from Jerusalem to Gaza." [27]So he started out, and on his way he met an Ethiopian[a] eunuch, an important official in charge of all the treasury of the Kandake (which means "queen of the Ethiopians"). This man had gone to Jerusalem to worship, [28]and on his way home was sitting in his chariot reading the Book of Isaiah the prophet. [29]The Spirit told Philip, "Go to that chariot and stay near it."

[30]Then Philip ran up to the chariot and heard the man reading Isaiah the prophet. "Do you understand what you are reading?" Philip asked.

[31]"How can I," he said, "unless someone explains it to me?" So he invited Philip to come up and sit with him.

[32]This is the passage of Scripture the eunuch was reading:

> "He was led like a sheep to the slaughter,
>   and as a lamb before its shearer is silent,
>   so he did not open his mouth.
> [33]In his humiliation he was deprived of justice.
>   Who can speak of his descendants?
>   For his life was taken from the earth."[b]

[34]The eunuch asked Philip, "Tell me, please, who is the prophet talking about, himself or someone else?" [35]Then Philip began with that very passage of Scripture and told him the good news about Jesus.

[36][37]As they traveled along the road, they came to some water and the eunuch said, "Look, here is water. What can stand in the way of my being baptized?"[c] [38]And he gave orders to stop the chariot. Then both Philip and the eunuch went down into the water and Philip baptized him. [39]When they came up out of the water, the Spirit of the Lord suddenly took Philip away, and the eunuch did not see him again, but went on his way rejoicing. [40]Philip, however, appeared at Azotus and traveled about, preaching the gospel in all the towns until he reached Caesarea.

Saul's Conversion

9 Meanwhile, Saul was still breathing out murderous threats against the Lord's disciples. He went to the high priest [2]and asked him for letters to the synagogues in Damascus, so that if he found any there who belonged to the Way, whether men or women, he might take them as prisoners to Jerusalem. [3]As he neared Damascus on his journey, suddenly a light from heaven flashed around him. [4]He fell to the ground and heard a voice say to him, "Saul, Saul, why do you persecute me?"

---

[a] *27* That is, from the southern Nile region   [b] *33* Isaiah 53:7,8 (see Septuagint)   [c] *36* Some late manuscripts *baptized?" [37]Philip said, "If you believe with all your heart, you may." The eunuch answered, "I believe that Jesus Christ is the Son of God."*

⁵"Who are you, Lord?" Saul asked.

"I am Jesus, whom you are persecuting," he replied. ⁶"Now get up and go into the city, and you will be told what you must do."

⁷The men traveling with Saul stood there speechless; they heard the sound but did not see anyone. ⁸Saul got up from the ground, but when he opened his eyes he could see nothing. So they led him by the hand into Damascus. ⁹For three days he was blind, and did not eat or drink anything.

¹⁰In Damascus there was a disciple named Ananias. The Lord called to him in a vision, "Ananias!"

"Yes, Lord," he answered.

¹¹The Lord told him, "Go to the house of Judas on Straight Street and ask for a man from Tarsus named Saul, for he is praying. ¹²In a vision he has seen a man named Ananias come and place his hands on him to restore his sight."

¹³"Lord," Ananias answered, "I have heard many reports about this man and all the harm he has done to your people in Jerusalem. ¹⁴And he has come here with authority from the chief priests to arrest all who call on your name."

¹⁵But the Lord said to Ananias, "Go! This man is my chosen instrument to proclaim my name to the Gentiles and their kings and to the people of Israel. ¹⁶I will show him how much he must suffer for my name."

¹⁷Then Ananias went to the house and entered it. Placing his hands on Saul, he said, "Brother Saul, the Lord—Jesus, who appeared to you on the road as you were coming here—has sent me so that you may see again and be filled with the Holy Spirit." ¹⁸Immediately, something like scales fell from Saul's eyes, and he could see again. He got up and was baptized, ¹⁹and after taking some food, he regained his strength.

Saul in Damascus and Jerusalem

Saul spent several days with the disciples in Damascus. ²⁰At once he began to preach in the synagogues that Jesus is the Son of God. ²¹All those who heard him were astonished and asked, "Isn't he the man who raised havoc in Jerusalem among those who call on this name? And hasn't he come here to take them as prisoners to the chief priests?" ²²Yet Saul grew more and more powerful and baffled the Jews living in Damascus by proving that Jesus is the Messiah.

²³After many days had gone by, there was a conspiracy among the Jews to kill him, ²⁴but Saul learned of their plan. Day and night they kept close watch on the city gates in order to kill him. ²⁵But his followers took him by night and lowered him in a basket through an opening in the wall.

²⁶When he came to Jerusalem, he tried to join the disciples, but they were all afraid of him, not believing that he really was a disciple. ²⁷But Barnabas took him and brought him to the apostles. He told them how Saul on his journey had seen the Lord and that the Lord had spoken to him, and how in Damascus he had preached fearlessly in the name of Jesus. ²⁸So Saul stayed with them and moved about freely in Jerusalem, speaking boldly in the name of the Lord. ²⁹He talked and debated with the Hellenistic Jews,^a but they tried to kill him. ³⁰When the believers learned of this, they took him down to Caesarea and sent him off to Tarsus.

³¹Then the church throughout Judea, Galilee and Samaria enjoyed a time of peace and was strengthened. Living in the fear of the Lord and encouraged by the Holy Spirit, it increased in numbers.

Aeneas and Dorcas

³²As Peter traveled about the country, he went to visit the Lord's people who lived in Lydda. ³³There he found a man named Aeneas, who was paralyzed and had been bedridden for eight years. ³⁴"Aeneas," Peter said to him, "Jesus Christ heals you. Get up and roll up your mat." Immediately Aeneas got up. ³⁵All those who lived in Lydda and Sharon saw him and turned to the Lord.

³⁶In Joppa there was a disciple named Tabitha (in Greek her name is Dorcas); she was always doing good and helping the poor. ³⁷About that time she became sick and died, and her body was washed and placed in an upstairs room. ³⁸Lydda was near Joppa; so when the disciples heard that Peter was in Lydda, they sent two men to him and urged him, "Please come at once!"

---

^a 29 That is, Jews who had adopted the Greek language and culture

³⁹Peter went with them, and when he arrived he was taken upstairs to the room. All the widows stood around him, crying and showing him the robes and other clothing that Dorcas had made while she was still with them.

⁴⁰Peter sent them all out of the room; then he got down on his knees and prayed. Turning toward the dead woman, he said, "Tabitha, get up." She opened her eyes, and seeing Peter she sat up. ⁴¹He took her by the hand and helped her to her feet. Then he called for the believers, especially the widows, and presented her to them alive. ⁴²This became known all over Joppa, and many people believed in the Lord. ⁴³Peter stayed in Joppa for some time with a tanner named Simon.

Cornelius Calls for Peter

10 At Caesarea there was a man named Cornelius, a centurion in what was known as the Italian Regiment. ²He and all his family were devout and God-fearing; he gave generously to those in need and prayed to God regularly. ³One day at about three in the afternoon he had a vision. He distinctly saw an angel of God, who came to him and said, "Cornelius!"

⁴Cornelius stared at him in fear. "What is it, Lord?" he asked.

The angel answered, "Your prayers and gifts to the poor have come up as a memorial offering before God. ⁵Now send men to Joppa to bring back a man named Simon who is called Peter. ⁶He is staying with Simon the tanner, whose house is by the sea."

⁷When the angel who spoke to him had gone, Cornelius called two of his servants and a devout soldier who was one of his attendants. ⁸He told them everything that had happened and sent them to Joppa.

Peter's Vision

⁹About noon the following day as they were on their journey and approaching the city, Peter went up on the roof to pray. ¹⁰He became hungry and wanted something to eat, and while the meal was being prepared, he fell into a trance. ¹¹He saw heaven opened and something like a large sheet being let down to earth by its four corners. ¹²It contained all kinds of four-footed animals, as well as reptiles and birds. ¹³Then a voice told him, "Get up, Peter. Kill and eat."

¹⁴"Surely not, Lord!" Peter replied. "I have never eaten anything impure or unclean."

¹⁵The voice spoke to him a second time, "Do not call anything impure that God has made clean."

¹⁶This happened three times, and immediately the sheet was taken back to heaven.

¹⁷While Peter was wondering about the meaning of the vision, the men sent by Cornelius found out where Simon's house was and stopped at the gate. ¹⁸They called out, asking if Simon who was known as Peter was staying there.

¹⁹While Peter was still thinking about the vision, the Spirit said to him, "Simon, three^a men are looking for you. ²⁰So get up and go downstairs. Do not hesitate to go with them, for I have sent them."

²¹Peter went down and said to the men, "I'm the one you're looking for. Why have you come?"

²²The men replied, "We have come from Cornelius the centurion. He is a righteous and God-fearing man, who is respected by all the Jewish people. A holy angel told him to ask you to come to his house so that he could hear what you have to say." ²³Then Peter invited the men into the house to be his guests.

atissue:prejudice

1567

10:1–48 Like any good Jew of his day, Peter believed that God's salvation was for the Jews only. But God showed Peter that he had no right to call others impure, unclean or unworthy of the message of the gospel. Do you have your own "unclean" list? Who's on your list? Homosexuals, alcoholics, pro-choice advocates, prostitutes, people of other races, nationalities or religions? Deep down do you consider yourself better? Remember that we are all recipients of God's grace—*through no merit of our own.* If God doesn't show favoritism in accepting people into his kingdom, who are we to turn away from them?

^a *19* One early manuscript *two*; other manuscripts do not have the number.

Peter at Cornelius's House

The next day Peter started out with them, and some of the believers from Joppa went along. [24] The following day he arrived in Caesarea. Cornelius was expecting them and had called together his relatives and close friends. [25] As Peter entered the house, Cornelius met him and fell at his feet in reverence. [26] But Peter made him get up. "Stand up," he said, "I am only human myself."

[27] While talking with him, Peter went inside and found a large gathering of people. [28] He said to them: "You are well aware that it is against our law for a Jew to associate with Gentiles or visit them. But God has shown me that I should not call anyone impure or unclean. [29] So when I was sent for, I came without raising any objection. May I ask why you sent for me?"

[30] Cornelius answered: "Three days ago I was in my house praying at this hour, at three in the afternoon. Suddenly a man in shining clothes stood before me [31] and said, 'Cornelius, God has heard your prayer and remembered your gifts to the poor. [32] Send to Joppa for Simon who is called Peter. He is a guest in the home of Simon the tanner, who lives by the sea.' [33] So I sent for you immediately, and it was good of you to come. Now we are all here in the presence of God to listen to everything the Lord has commanded you to tell us."

[34] Then Peter began to speak: "I now realize how true it is that God does not show favoritism [35] but accepts those from every nation who fear him and do what is right. [36] You know the message God sent to the people of Israel, announcing the good news of peace through Jesus Christ, who is Lord of all. [37] You know what has happened throughout the province of Judea, beginning in Galilee after the baptism that John preached— [38] how God anointed Jesus of Nazareth with the Holy Spirit and power, and how he went around doing good and healing all who were under the power of the devil, because God was with him.

[39] "We are witnesses of everything he did in the country of the Jews and in Jerusalem. They killed him by hanging him on a cross, [40] but God raised him from the dead on the third day and caused him to be seen. [41] He was not seen by all the people, but by witnesses whom God had already chosen—by us who ate and drank with him after he rose from the dead. [42] He commanded us to preach to the people and to testify that he is the one whom God appointed as judge of the living and the dead. [43] All the prophets testify about him that everyone who believes in him receives forgiveness of sins through his name."

[44] While Peter was still speaking these words, the Holy Spirit came on all who heard the message. [45] The circumcised believers who had come with Peter were astonished that the gift of the Holy Spirit had been poured out even on Gentiles. [46] For they heard them speaking in tongues[a] and praising God.

Then Peter said, [47] "Surely no one can stand in the way of their being baptized with water. They have received the Holy Spirit just as we have." [48] So he ordered that they be baptized in the name of Jesus Christ. Then they asked Peter to stay with them for a few days.

Peter Explains His Actions

11 The apostles and the believers throughout Judea heard that the Gentiles also had received the word of God. [2] So when Peter went up to Jerusalem, the circumcised believers criticized him [3] and said, "You went into the house of the uncircumcised and ate with them."

[4] Starting from the beginning, Peter told them the whole story: [5] "I was in the city of Joppa praying, and in a trance I saw a vision. I saw something like a large sheet being let down from heaven by its four corners, and it came down to where I was. [6] I looked into it and saw four-footed animals of the earth, wild beasts, reptiles and birds. [7] Then I heard a voice telling me, 'Get up, Peter. Kill and eat.'

[8] "I replied, 'Surely not, Lord! Nothing impure or unclean has ever entered my mouth.'

[9] "The voice spoke from heaven a second time, 'Do not call anything impure that God has made clean.' [10] This happened three times, and then it was all pulled up to heaven again.

[11] "Right then three men who had been sent to me from Caesarea stopped at the house where I was staying. [12] The Spirit told me to have no hesitation about going with them. These six brothers also went with me, and we entered the man's house. [13] He told us how he had seen an angel appear in his house and say, 'Send to Joppa for Simon who is called Peter. [14] He will bring you a message through which you and all your household will be saved.'

1568

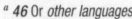

---

a 46 Or other languages

not exclusive

11:1–18 Some Jewish believers criticized Peter for associating with Gentiles. These Jews believed that uncircumcised Gentiles were disqualified from relationships with believers and even a relationship with Jesus. But God is *not exclusive*. He offers the same gift of salvation to all who believe in the Lord Jesus Christ.

When you're tempted to limit God's offer of salvation to those who fit your expectation of what a Christian should look like, remember that God is *not exclusive*. If you see an evangelist drawing an unlikely audience, don't judge—instead, rejoice. Who are you to stand in God's way?

For the next He Is, go to p. 1571.

¹⁵"As I began to speak, the Holy Spirit came on them as he had come on us at the beginning. ¹⁶Then I remembered what the Lord had said: 'John baptized with*ᵃ* water, but you will be baptized with*ᵃ* the Holy Spirit.' ¹⁷So if God gave them the same gift he gave us who believed in the Lord Jesus Christ, who was I to think that I could stand in God's way?"

¹⁸When they heard this, they had no further objections and praised God, saying, "So then, even to Gentiles God has granted repentance that leads to life."

The Church in Antioch

¹⁹Now those who had been scattered by the persecution that broke out when Stephen was killed traveled as far as Phoenicia, Cyprus and Antioch, spreading the word only among Jews. ²⁰Some of them, however, men from Cyprus and Cyrene, went to Antioch and began to speak to Greeks also, telling them the good news about the Lord Jesus. ²¹The Lord's hand was with them, and a great number of people believed and turned to the Lord.

²²News of this reached the ears of the church in Jerusalem, and they sent Barnabas to Antioch. ²³When he arrived and saw what the grace of God had done, he was glad and encouraged them all to remain true to the Lord with all their hearts. ²⁴He was a good man, full of the Holy Spirit and faith, and a great number of people were brought to the Lord.

²⁵Then Barnabas went to Tarsus to look for Saul, ²⁶and when he found him, he brought him to Antioch. So for a whole year Barnabas and Saul met with the church and taught great numbers of people. The disciples were called Christians first at Antioch.

²⁷During this time some prophets came down from Jerusalem to Antioch. ²⁸One of them, named Agabus, stood up and through the Spirit predicted that a severe famine would spread over the entire Roman world. (This happened during the reign of Claudius.) ²⁹The disciples, as each one was able, decided to provide help for the believers living in Judea. ³⁰This they did, sending their gift to the elders by Barnabas and Saul.

Peter's Miraculous Escape From Prison

12 It was about this time that King Herod arrested some who belonged to the church, intending to persecute them. ²He had James, the brother of John, put to death with the sword. ³When he saw that this met with approval among the Jews, he proceeded to seize Peter also. This happened during the Festival of Unleavened Bread. ⁴After arresting him, he put him in prison, handing him over to be guarded by four squads of four soldiers each. Herod intended to bring him out for public trial after the Passover.

⁵So Peter was kept in prison, but the church was earnestly praying to God for him.

⁶The night before Herod was to bring him to trial, Peter was sleeping between two soldiers, bound with two chains, and sentries stood guard at the entrance. ⁷Suddenly an angel of the Lord appeared and

---
ᵃ 16 Or in

a light shone in the cell. He struck Peter on the side and woke him up. "Quick, get up!" he said, and the chains fell off Peter's wrists.

[8] Then the angel said to him, "Put on your clothes and sandals." And Peter did so. "Wrap your cloak around you and follow me," the angel told him. [9] Peter followed him out of the prison, but he had no idea that what the angel was doing was really happening; he thought he was seeing a vision. [10] They passed the first and second guards and came to the iron gate leading to the city. It opened for them by itself, and they went through it. When they had walked the length of one street, suddenly the angel left him.

[11] Then Peter came to himself and said, "Now I know without a doubt that the Lord has sent his angel and rescued me from Herod's clutches and from everything the Jewish people were hoping would happen."

"conversations"

doubt ‹› 12:1–19

1» Why was Peter saved, but not James? Do you think this caused Peter to doubt God?

2» How can doubts sometimes imprison you more than your circumstances?

3» Do painful or disappointing experiences cause you to doubt God? Why or why not?

For more on doubt, check the index.
For the next Conversations, go to p. 1575.

[12] When this had dawned on him, he went to the house of Mary the mother of John, also called Mark, where many people had gathered and were praying. [13] Peter knocked at the outer entrance, and a servant named Rhoda came to answer the door. [14] When she recognized Peter's voice, she was so overjoyed she ran back without opening it and exclaimed, "Peter is at the door!"

[15] "You're out of your mind," they told her. When she kept insisting that it was so, they said, "It must be his angel."

[16] But Peter kept on knocking, and when they opened the door and saw him, they were astonished. [17] Peter motioned with his hand for them to be quiet and described how the Lord had brought him out of prison. "Tell James and the other brothers and sisters about this," he said, and then he left for another place.

[18] In the morning, there was no small commotion among the soldiers as to what had become of Peter. [19] After Herod had a thorough search made for him and did not find him, he cross-examined the guards and ordered that they be executed.

Herod's Death

Then Herod went from Judea to Caesarea and stayed there. [20] He had been quarreling with the people of Tyre and Sidon; they now joined together and sought an audience with him. Having secured the support of Blastus, a trusted personal servant of the king, they asked for peace, because they depended on the king's country for their food supply.

[21] On the appointed day Herod, wearing his royal robes, sat on his throne and delivered a public address to the people. [22] They shouted, "This is the voice of a god, not of a mere mortal." [23] Immediately, because Herod did not give praise to God, an angel of the Lord struck him down, and he was eaten by worms and died.

[24] But the word of God continued to increase and spread.

Barnabas and Saul Sent Off

[25] When Barnabas and Saul had finished their mission, they returned from[a] Jerusalem, taking with them John, also called Mark. [1] Now in the church at Antioch there were prophets and teachers: Barnabas, Simeon called Niger, Lucius of Cyrene, Manaen (who had been brought up with Herod the tetrarch) and Saul. [2] While they were worshiping the Lord and fasting, the Holy Spirit said, "Set apart for me Barnabas and Saul for the work to which I have called them." [3] So after they had fasted and prayed, they placed their hands on them and sent them off.

[a] 25 Some manuscripts to

On Cyprus

⁴The two of them, sent on their way by the Holy Spirit, went down to Seleucia and sailed from there to Cyprus. ⁵When they arrived at Salamis, they proclaimed the word of God in the Jewish synagogues. John was with them as their helper.

⁶They traveled through the whole island until they came to Paphos. There they met a Jewish sorcerer and false prophet named Bar-Jesus, ⁷who was an attendant of the proconsul, Sergius Paulus. The proconsul, an intelligent man, sent for Barnabas and Saul because he wanted to hear the word of God. ⁸But Elymas the sorcerer (for that is what his name means) opposed them and tried to turn the proconsul from the faith. ⁹Then Saul, who was also called Paul, filled with the Holy Spirit, looked straight at Elymas and said, ¹⁰"You are a child of the devil and an enemy of everything that is right! You are full of all kinds of deceit and trickery. Will you never stop perverting the right ways of the Lord? ¹¹Now the hand of the Lord is against you. You are going to be blind for a time, not even able to see the light of the sun."

Immediately mist and darkness came over him, and he groped about, seeking someone to lead him by the hand. ¹²When the proconsul saw what had happened, he believed, for he was amazed at the teaching about the Lord.

In Pisidian Antioch

¹³From Paphos, Paul and his companions sailed to Perga in Pamphylia, where John left them to return to Jerusalem. ¹⁴From Perga they went on to Pisidian Antioch. On the Sabbath they entered the synagogue and sat down. ¹⁵After the reading from the Law and the Prophets, the leaders of the synagogue sent word to them, saying, "Brothers, if you have a word of exhortation for the people, please speak."

¹⁶Standing up, Paul motioned with his hand and said: "People of Israel and you Gentiles who worship God, listen to me! ¹⁷The God of the people of Israel chose our ancestors; he made the people prosper during their stay in Egypt; with mighty power he led them out of that country; ¹⁸for about forty years he endured their conduct*a* in the wilderness; ¹⁹and he overthrew seven nations in Canaan, giving their land to his people as their inheritance. ²⁰All this took about 450 years.

"After this, God gave them judges until the time of Samuel the prophet. ²¹Then the people asked for a king, and he gave them Saul son of Kish, of the tribe of Benjamin, who ruled forty years. ²²After removing Saul, he made David their king. God testified concerning him: 'I have found David son of Jesse, a man after my own heart; he will do everything I want him to do.'

²³"From this man's descendants God has brought to Israel the Savior Jesus, as he promised. ²⁴Before the coming of Jesus, John preached repentance and baptism to all the people of Israel. ²⁵As John was completing his work, he said: 'Who do you suppose I am? I am not the one you are looking for. But there is someone coming after me whose sandals I am not worthy to untie.'

²⁶"Brothers and sisters from the children of Abraham and you God-fearing Gentiles, it is to us that this message of salvation has been sent. ²⁷The people of Jerusalem and their rulers did not recognize Jesus,

---

a 18 Some manuscripts *he cared for them*

HE IS: proclaimed

13:13–41 On their travels, the apostles would first share the Good News about Jesus in the synagogues with their own people, the Jews. In Pisidian Antioch, Paul preached the message that through Jesus the forgiveness of sins is *proclaimed*. Sadly, most of their Jewish brothers and sisters failed to believe.

Sometimes it's easier to tell strangers about Jesus than it is to witness to our closest friends and family, neighbors and co-workers. However, if you don't make sure he is *proclaimed* to your loved ones, who will (see Matthew 28:18–20)? While all may not accept the message, you'll know you've been a faithful messenger.

For the next He Is, go to p. 1586.

yet in condemning him they fulfilled the words of the prophets that are read every Sabbath. ²⁸Though they found no proper ground for a death sentence, they asked Pilate to have him executed. ²⁹When they had carried out all that was written about him, they took him down from the cross and laid him in a tomb. ³⁰But God raised him from the dead, ³¹and for many days he was seen by those who had traveled with him from Galilee to Jerusalem. They are now his witnesses to our people.

³²"We tell you the good news: What God promised our ancestors ³³he has fulfilled for us, their children, by raising up Jesus. As it is written in the second Psalm:

> "'You are my son;
> today I have become your father.'ᵃ

³⁴God raised him from the dead so that he will never be subject to decay. As God has said,

> "'I will give you the holy and sure blessings promised to David.'ᵇ

³⁵So it is also stated elsewhere:

> "'You will not let your holy one see decay.'ᶜ

³⁶"Now when David had served God's purpose in his own generation, he fell asleep; he was buried with his ancestors and his body decayed. ³⁷But the one whom God raised from the dead did not see decay.

³⁸"Therefore, my brothers and sisters, I want you to know that through Jesus the forgiveness of sins is proclaimed to you. ³⁹Through him everyone who believes is set free from every sin, a justification you were not able to obtain under the law of Moses. ⁴⁰Take care that what the prophets have said does not happen to you:

> ⁴¹"'Look, you scoffers,
> wonder and perish,
> for I am going to do something in your days
> that you would never believe,
> even if someone told you.'ᵈ"

⁴²As Paul and Barnabas were leaving the synagogue, the people invited them to speak further about these things on the next Sabbath. ⁴³When the congregation was dismissed, many of the Jews and devout converts to Judaism followed Paul and Barnabas, who talked with them and urged them to continue in the grace of God.

⁴⁴On the next Sabbath almost the whole city gathered to hear the word of the Lord. ⁴⁵When the Jews saw the crowds, they were filled with jealousy. They began to contradict what Paul was saying and heaped abuse on him.

⁴⁶Then Paul and Barnabas answered them boldly: "We had to speak the word of God to you first. Since you reject it and do not consider yourselves worthy of eternal life, we now turn to the Gentiles. ⁴⁷For this is what the Lord has commanded us:

> "'I have made youᵉ a light for the Gentiles,
> that youᵉ may bring salvation to the ends of the earth.'ᶠ"

⁴⁸When the Gentiles heard this, they were glad and honored the word of the Lord; and all who were appointed for eternal life believed.

⁴⁹The word of the Lord spread through the whole region. ⁵⁰But the Jewish leaders incited the God-fearing women of high standing and the leading men of the city. They stirred up persecution against Paul and Barnabas, and expelled them from their region. ⁵¹So they shook the dust off their feet as a warning to them and went to Iconium. ⁵²And the disciples were filled with joy and with the Holy Spirit.

In Iconium

14 At Iconium Paul and Barnabas went as usual into the Jewish synagogue. There they spoke so effectively that a great number of Jews and Greeks believed. ²But the Jews who refused to believe

ᵃ 33 Psalm 2:7   ᵇ 34 Isaiah 55:3   ᶜ 35 Psalm 16:10 (see Septuagint)   ᵈ 41 Hab. 1:5   ᵉ 47 The Greek is singular.   ᶠ 47 Isaiah 49:6

stirred up the other Gentiles and poisoned their minds against the brothers. ³So Paul and Barnabas spent considerable time there, speaking boldly for the Lord, who confirmed the message of his grace by enabling them to perform signs and wonders. ⁴The people of the city were divided; some sided with the Jews, others with the apostles. ⁵There was a plot afoot among both Gentiles and Jews, together with their leaders, to mistreat them and stone them. ⁶But they found out about it and fled to the Lycaonian cities of Lystra and Derbe and to the surrounding country, ⁷where they continued to preach the gospel.

In Lystra and Derbe

⁸In Lystra there sat a man who was lame. He had been that way from birth and had never walked. ⁹He listened to Paul as he was speaking. Paul looked directly at him, saw that he had faith to be healed ¹⁰and called out, "Stand up on your feet!" At that, the man jumped up and began to walk.

¹¹When the crowd saw what Paul had done, they shouted in the Lycaonian language, "The gods have come down to us in human form!" ¹²Barnabas they called Zeus, and Paul they called Hermes because he was the chief speaker. ¹³The priest of Zeus, whose temple was just outside the city, brought bulls and wreaths to the city gates because he and the crowd wanted to offer sacrifices to them.

¹⁴But when the apostles Barnabas and Paul heard of this, they tore their clothes and rushed out into the crowd, shouting: ¹⁵"Friends, why are you doing this? We too are only human, like you. We are bringing you good news, telling you to turn from these worthless things to the living God, who made heaven and earth and sea and everything in them. ¹⁶In the past, he let all nations go their own way. ¹⁷Yet he has not left himself without testimony: He has shown kindness by giving you rain from heaven and crops in their seasons; he provides you with plenty of food and fills your hearts with joy." ¹⁸Even with these words, they had difficulty keeping the crowd from sacrificing to them.

¹⁹Then some Jews came from Antioch and Iconium and won the crowd over. They stoned Paul and dragged him outside the city, thinking he was dead. ²⁰But after the disciples had gathered around him, he got up and went back into the city. The next day he and Barnabas left for Derbe.

The Return to Antioch in Syria

²¹They preached the gospel in that city and won a large number of disciples. Then they returned to Lystra, Iconium and Antioch, ²²strengthening the disciples and encouraging them to remain true to the faith. "We must go through many hardships to enter the kingdom of God," they said. ²³Paul and Barnabas appointed elders*a* for them in each church and, with prayer and fasting, committed them to the Lord, in whom they had put their trust. ²⁴After going through Pisidia, they came into Pamphylia, ²⁵and when they had preached the word in Perga, they went down to Attalia.

²⁶From Attalia they sailed back to Antioch, where they had been committed to the grace of God for the work they had now completed. ²⁷On arriving there, they gathered the church together and reported all that God had done through them and how he had opened a door of faith to the Gentiles. ²⁸And they stayed there a long time with the disciples.

The Council at Jerusalem

15 Certain individuals came down from Judea to Antioch and were teaching the believers: "Unless you are circumcised, according to the custom taught by Moses, you cannot be saved." ²This brought Paul and Barnabas into sharp dispute and debate with them. So Paul and Barnabas were appointed, along with some other believers, to go up to Jerusalem to see the apostles and elders about this question. ³The church sent them on their way, and as they traveled through Phoenicia and Samaria, they told how the Gentiles had been converted. This news made all the believers very glad. ⁴When they came to Jerusalem, they were welcomed by the church and the apostles and elders, to whom they reported everything God had done through them.

⁵Then some of the believers who belonged to the party of the Pharisees stood up and said, "The Gentiles must be circumcised and required to keep the law of Moses."

⁶The apostles and elders met to consider this question. ⁷After much discussion, Peter got up and addressed them: "Brothers, you know that some time ago God made a choice among you that the

---

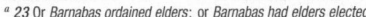

Gentiles might hear from my lips the message of the gospel and believe. [8]God, who knows the heart, showed that he accepted them by giving the Holy Spirit to them, just as he did to us. [9]He did not discriminate between us and them, for he purified their hearts by faith. [10]Now then, why do you try to test God by putting on the necks of Gentiles a yoke that neither we nor our ancestors have been able to bear? [11]No! We believe it is through the grace of our Lord Jesus that we are saved, just as they are."

[12]The whole assembly became silent as they listened to Barnabas and Paul telling about the signs and wonders God had done among the Gentiles through them. [13]When they finished, James spoke up. "Brothers," he said, "listen to me. [14]Simon[a] has described to us how God first intervened to choose a people for his name from the Gentiles. [15]The words of the prophets are in agreement with this, as it is written:

[16]"'After this I will return
 and rebuild David's fallen tent.
 Its ruins I will rebuild,
 and I will restore it,
[17]that the rest of humanity may seek the Lord,
 even all the Gentiles who bear my name,
 says the Lord, who does these things'[b]—
[18] things known from long ago.[c]

[19]"It is my judgment, therefore, that we should not make it difficult for the Gentiles who are turning to God. [20]Instead we should write to them, telling them to abstain from food polluted by idols, from sexual immorality, from the meat of strangled animals and from blood. [21]For the law of Moses has been preached in every city from the earliest times and is read in the synagogues on every Sabbath."

The Council's Letter to Gentile Believers

[22]Then the apostles and elders, with the whole church, decided to choose some of their own men and send them to Antioch with Paul and Barnabas. They chose Judas (called Barsabbas) and Silas, who were leaders among the believers. [23]With them they sent the following letter:

The apostles and elders, your brothers,

To the Gentile believers in Antioch, Syria and Cilicia:

Greetings.

[24]We have heard that some went out from us without our authorization and disturbed you, troubling your minds by what they said. [25]So we all agreed to choose some men and send them to you with our dear friends Barnabas and Paul— [26]men who have risked their lives for the name of our Lord Jesus Christ. [27]Therefore we are sending Judas and Silas to confirm by word of mouth what we are writing. [28]It seemed good to the Holy Spirit and to us not to burden you with anything beyond the following requirements: [29]You are to abstain from food sacrificed to idols, from blood, from the meat of strangled animals and from sexual immorality. You will do well to avoid these things.

Farewell.

[30]So they were sent off and went down to Antioch, where they gathered the church together and delivered the letter. [31]The people read it and were glad for its encouraging message. [32]Judas and Silas, who themselves were prophets, said much to encourage and strengthen the believers. [33] [34]After spending some time there, they were sent off by the believers with the blessing of peace to return to those who had sent them. [35]But Paul and Barnabas remained in Antioch, where they and many others taught and preached the word of the Lord.

Disagreement Between Paul and Barnabas

³⁶Some time later Paul said to Barnabas, "Let us go back and visit the believers in all the towns where we preached the word of the Lord and see how they are doing." ³⁷Barnabas wanted to take John, also called Mark, with them, ³⁸but Paul did not think it wise to take him, because he had deserted them in Pamphylia and had not continued with them in the work. ³⁹They had such a sharp disagreement that they parted company. Barnabas took Mark and sailed for Cyprus, ⁴⁰but Paul chose Silas and left, commended by the believers to the grace of the Lord. ⁴¹He went through Syria and Cilicia, strengthening the churches.

Timothy Joins Paul and Silas

16 Paul came to Derbe and then to Lystra, where a disciple named Timothy lived, whose mother was Jewish and a believer but whose father was a Greek. ²The believers at Lystra and Iconium spoke well of him. ³Paul wanted to take him along on the journey, so he circumcised him because of the Jews who lived in that area, for they all knew that his father was a Greek. ⁴As they traveled from town to town, they delivered the decisions reached by the apostles and elders in Jerusalem for the people to obey. ⁵So the churches were strengthened in the faith and grew daily in numbers.

Paul's Vision of the Man of Macedonia

⁶Paul and his companions traveled throughout the region of Phrygia and Galatia, having been kept by the Holy Spirit from preaching the word in the province of Asia. ⁷When they came to the border of Mysia, they tried to enter Bithynia, but the Spirit of Jesus would not allow them to. ⁸So they passed by Mysia and went down to Troas. ⁹During the night Paul had a vision of a man of Macedonia standing and begging him, "Come over to Macedonia and help us." ¹⁰After Paul had seen the vision, we got ready at once to leave for Macedonia, concluding that God had called us to preach the gospel to them.

1575

Lydia's Conversion in Philippi

¹¹From Troas we put out to sea and sailed straight for Samothrace, and the next day we went on to Neapolis. ¹²From there we traveled to Philippi, a Roman colony and the leading city of that district*ᵃ* of Macedonia. And we stayed there several days.

¹³On the Sabbath we went outside the city gate to the river, where we expected to find a place of prayer. We sat down and began to speak to the women who had gathered there. ¹⁴One of those listening was a woman from the city of Thyatira named Lydia, a dealer in purple cloth. She was a worshiper of God. The Lord opened her heart to respond to Paul's message. ¹⁵When she and the members of her household were baptized, she invited us to her home. "If you consider me a believer in the Lord," she said, "come and stay at my house." And she persuaded us.

conversations

trust «» 16:16–25

1» What can your faithful response to hard times communicate to non-Christians?

2» How do you *demonstrate* your trust in God?

3» In the midst of life's uncertainties, what remains certain about God?

For more on trust, check the index.
For the next Conversations, go to p. 1580.

Paul and Silas in Prison

¹⁶Once when we were going to the place of prayer, we were met by a female slave who had a spirit by which she predicted the future. She earned a great deal of money for her owners by fortune-telling. ¹⁷She followed Paul and the rest of us, shouting, "These men are servants of the Most High God, who are telling you the way to be saved." ¹⁸She kept this up for many days. Finally Paul became so annoyed that he turned around and said to the spirit, "In the name of Jesus Christ I command you to come out of her!" At that moment the spirit left her.

¹⁹When her owners realized that their hope of making money was gone, they seized Paul

ᵃ 12 The text and meaning of the Greek for the leading city of that district *are uncertain.*

and Silas and dragged them into the marketplace to face the authorities. [20]They brought them before the magistrates and said, "These men are Jews, and are throwing our city into an uproar [21]by advocating customs unlawful for us Romans to accept or practice."

[22]The crowd joined in the attack against Paul and Silas, and the magistrates ordered them to be stripped and beaten with rods. [23]After they had been severely flogged, they were thrown into prison, and the jailer was commanded to guard them carefully. [24]When he received these orders, he put them in the inner cell and fastened their feet in the stocks.

[25]About midnight Paul and Silas were praying and singing hymns to God, and the other prisoners were listening to them. [26]Suddenly there was such a violent earthquake that the foundations of the prison were shaken. At once all the prison doors flew open, and everyone's chains came loose. [27]The jailer woke up, and when he saw the prison doors open, he drew his sword and was about to kill himself because he thought the prisoners had escaped. [28]But Paul shouted, "Don't harm yourself! We are all here!"

[29]The jailer called for lights, rushed in and fell trembling before Paul and Silas. [30]He then brought them out and asked, "Sirs, what must I do to be saved?"

[31]They replied, "Believe in the Lord Jesus, and you will be saved—you and your household." [32]Then they spoke the word of the Lord to him and to all the others in his house. [33]At that hour of the night the jailer took them and washed their wounds; then immediately he and all his household were baptized. [34]The jailer brought them into his house and set a meal before them; he was filled with joy because he had come to believe in God—he and his whole household.

[35]When it was daylight, the magistrates sent their officers to the jailer with the order: "Release those men." [36]The jailer told Paul, "The magistrates have ordered that you and Silas be released. Now you can leave. Go in peace."

[37]But Paul said to the officers: "They beat us publicly without a trial, even though we are Roman citizens, and threw us into prison. And now do they want to get rid of us quietly? No! Let them come themselves and escort us out."

[38]The officers reported this to the magistrates, and when they heard that Paul and Silas were Roman citizens, they were alarmed. [39]They came to appease them and escorted them from the prison, requesting them to leave the city. [40]After Paul and Silas came out of the prison, they went to Lydia's house, where they met with the believers and encouraged them. Then they left.

In Thessalonica

17 When Paul and his companions had passed through Amphipolis and Apollonia, they came to Thessalonica, where there was a Jewish synagogue. [2]As was his custom, Paul went into the synagogue, and on three Sabbath days he reasoned with them from the Scriptures, [3]explaining and proving that the Messiah had to suffer and rise from the dead. "This Jesus I am proclaiming to you is the Messiah," he said. [4]Some of the Jews were persuaded and joined Paul and Silas, as did a large number of God-fearing Greeks and not a few prominent women.

[5]But other Jews were jealous; so they rounded up some bad characters from the marketplace, formed a mob and started a riot in the city. They rushed to Jason's house in search of Paul and Silas in order to bring them out to the crowd.[a] [6]But when they did not find them, they dragged Jason and some other believers before the city officials, shouting: "These men who have caused trouble all over the world have now come here, [7]and Jason has welcomed them into his house. They are all defying Caesar's decrees, saying that there is another king, one called Jesus." [8]When they heard this, the crowd and the city officials were thrown into turmoil. [9]Then they made Jason and the others post bond and let them go.

In Berea

[10]As soon as it was night, the believers sent Paul and Silas away to Berea. On arriving there, they went to the Jewish synagogue. [11]Now the Berean Jews were of more noble character than those in Thessalonica, for they received the message with great eagerness and examined the Scriptures every day to see if what Paul said was true. [12]Many of them believed, as did also a number of prominent Greek women and many Greek men.

a 5 Or the assembly of the people

¹³But when the Jews in Thessalonica learned that Paul was preaching the word of God at Berea, some of them went there too, agitating the crowds and stirring them up. ¹⁴The believers immediately sent Paul to the coast, but Silas and Timothy stayed at Berea. ¹⁵Those who escorted Paul brought him to Athens and then left with instructions for Silas and Timothy to join him as soon as possible.

In Athens

¹⁶While Paul was waiting for them in Athens, he was greatly distressed to see that the city was full of idols. ¹⁷So he reasoned in the synagogue with both Jews and God-fearing Greeks, as well as in the marketplace day by day with those who happened to be there. ¹⁸A group of Epicurean and Stoic philosophers began to debate with him. Some of them asked, "What is this babbler trying to say?" Others remarked, "He seems to be advocating foreign gods." They said this because Paul was preaching the good news about Jesus and the resurrection. ¹⁹Then they took him and brought him to a meeting of the Areopagus, where they said to him, "May we know what this new teaching is that you are presenting? ²⁰You are bringing some strange ideas to our ears, and we would like to know what they mean." ²¹(All the Athenians and the foreigners who lived there spent their time doing nothing but talking about and listening to the latest ideas.)

²²Paul then stood up in the meeting of the Areopagus and said: "People of Athens! I see that in every way you are very religious. ²³For as I walked around and looked carefully at your objects of worship, I even found an altar with this inscription: TO AN UNKNOWN GOD. So you are ignorant of the very thing you worship—and this is what I am going to proclaim to you.

²⁴"The God who made the world and everything in it is the Lord of heaven and earth and does not live in temples built by hands. ²⁵And he is not served by human hands, as if he needed anything. Rather, he himself gives everyone life and breath and everything else. ²⁶From one man he made all the nations, that they should inhabit the whole earth; and he marked out their appointed times in history and the boundaries of their lands. ²⁷God did this so that they would seek him and perhaps reach out for him and find him, though he is not far from any one of us. ²⁸'For in him we live and move and have our being.'^a As some of your own poets have said, 'We are his offspring.'^b

²⁹"Therefore since we are God's offspring, we should not think that the divine being is like gold or silver or stone—an image made by human design and skill. ³⁰In the past God overlooked such ignorance, but now he commands all people everywhere to repent. ³¹For he has set a day when he will judge the world with justice by the man he has appointed. He has given proof of this to everyone by raising him from the dead."

³²When they heard about the resurrection of the dead, some of them sneered, but others said, "We want to hear you again on this subject." ³³At that, Paul left the Council. ³⁴Some of the people became followers of Paul and believed. Among them was Dionysius, a member of the Areopagus, also a woman named Damaris, and a number of others.

In Corinth

18 After this, Paul left Athens and went to Corinth. ²There he met a Jew named Aquila, a native of Pontus, who had recently come from Italy with his wife Priscilla, because Claudius had ordered all Jews to leave Rome. Paul went to see them, ³and because he was a tentmaker as they were, he stayed

---

atissue:pride

17:24–28 Deep down many of us think (and live as if) God is somehow incomplete without us. Yet it's only because of him that we live and move and breathe. God is bigger than we are, larger than our churches, grander than our world. He doesn't need *anything*—including us. He's complete, entirely sufficient and perfectly content even without us. Yet he sacrificed his only Son so that we could enjoy a relationship with him. Let go of your pride. You have nothing to offer God that he needs. But you do have something he wants: your life, your love and your humble praise.

1577

---

^a 28 From the Cretan philosopher Epimenides   ^b 28 From the Cilician Stoic philosopher Aratus

myth#91 "I CAN DO ANY-THING I PUT MY MIND TO."

I'd always believed that I could do anything I put my mind to. From the time I was a little girl, my mama assured me that I could be anything I wanted to be, that I shouldn't let anyone stand in my way. I've applied that same determination to every challenge I've faced so far in life—getting a scholarship for college, running Division I track, winning academic honors, landing my dream job and then pursuing my man.

But now my strategy is failing me. David left me. Three weeks before our wedding, he called it off. It was humiliating. My parents had to call all our friends and family and tell them to cancel their plans. They had to call the florist, the reception hall, the dress store, the baker, the salon, the church . . . I was so humiliated that I wouldn't leave the house for weeks. I finally went back to work, but even I could tell that I was different. Deflated somehow. I wasn't the same confident woman I'd always been.

So I made up my mind to win David back. I knew that if I could just work a little harder—lose a few pounds, be a little more charming, convince him of how right we are for each other—that he'd see the light and beg me to take him back. I'd be aloof at first, making him see the pain he'd caused me, but then we'd be back together, forever. We'd do a small wedding this time, simple and elegant.

But my plan failed. David said he'd made up his mind. He asked me to stop calling him. He said he wanted to move on and heal from our relationship. He said we weren't right for each other—not now, not ever.

Now I don't know what to do. I've given this relationship everything I have; how can that still not be enough?

—Lynnette

"YOU CAN DO anything you put your mind to" is good advice for building a girl's self-esteem, but it's not a fail-proof maxim. Sometimes our talent, effort and determination are just not enough to help us reach our goals. There are factors beyond our control, such as other people's choices. At some point we must accept that we are not the mistresses of our own fates.

The real problem comes when we seek to become self-sufficient—when we attribute our successes to ourselves and believe that in our own strength we can do anything. In contrast, God tells us that *in Christ* we can do all this (see Philippians 4:13). But what "this" is he referring to? "This" is not a guarantee of success in human terms; it's a promise that Christ will get us through whatever situation we're facing. "This" is a very different type of promise and could take any number of forms in our lives.

- Being deserted by my fiancée—*I can't do this in my own strength, but Christ will somehow get me through.*

- Burying my child—*I can't do this in my own strength, but Christ will somehow get me through.*

- Being laid off yet trusting that God will provide for me—*I can't do this in my own strength, but Christ will somehow get me through.*

- Learning to be content, even when I am in a bad marriage or unfulfilling job—*I can't do this in my own strength, but Christ will somehow get me through.*

If you have a dream goal in life, there's no harm in working toward it, as long as you believe it's honoring to God. Often he is the one who gives you your heartfelt dreams and passions. You may find that along the way in life, your goals change. Be willing to adapt your goals so that they're realistic and align with God's plan for your life. Keep this brief advice in mind:

- Acknowledge your insufficiency and his all-sufficiency. God determined your life's scenarios (see Acts 17:26). Depend on God—not yourself—to help you succeed.

- Define success in God's terms.

- Find a mentor, someone who has followed a path similar to the one you want. Ask her how she got where she is today and what God taught her along the way.

1579

"A majority of lay church leaders (58 percent) believe that the Bible teaches, 'God helps those who help themselves.'"

—Barna Research Group (2000)

"I can Do all This THROUGH HIM WHO GIVes me STRENGTH."

PHILIPPIANS 4:13

SEE ALSO

1 Corinthians 2:1–5
2 Corinthians 12:9
Revelation 3:17–18

For more on **Self-Reliance**, check the index.

and worked with them. [4]Every Sabbath he reasoned in the synagogue, trying to persuade Jews and Greeks.

[5]When Silas and Timothy came from Macedonia, Paul devoted himself exclusively to preaching, testifying to the Jews that Jesus was the Messiah. [6]But when they opposed Paul and became abusive, he shook out his clothes in protest and said to them, "Your blood be on your own heads! I am innocent of it. From now on I will go to the Gentiles."

[7]Then Paul left the synagogue and went next door to the house of Titius Justus, a worshiper of God. [8]Crispus, the synagogue leader, and his entire household believed in the Lord; and many of the Corinthians who heard Paul believed and were baptized.

[9]One night the Lord spoke to Paul in a vision: "Do not be afraid; keep on speaking, do not be silent. [10]For I am with you, and no one is going to attack and harm you, because I have many people in this city." [11]So Paul stayed in Corinth for a year and a half, teaching them the word of God.

[12]While Gallio was proconsul of Achaia, the Jews of Corinth made a united attack on Paul and brought him to the place of judgment. [13]"This man," they charged, "is persuading the people to worship God in ways contrary to the law."

[14]Just as Paul was about to speak, Gallio said to them, "If you Jews were making a complaint about some misdemeanor or serious crime, it would be reasonable for me to listen to you. [15]But since it involves questions about words and names and your own law—settle the matter yourselves. I will not be a judge of such things." [16]So he drove them off. [17]Then the crowd there turned on Sosthenes the synagogue leader and beat him in front of the proconsul; and Gallio showed no concern whatever.

Priscilla, Aquila and Apollos

[18]Paul stayed on in Corinth for some time. Then he left the believers and sailed for Syria, accompanied by Priscilla and Aquila. Before he sailed, he had his hair cut off at Cenchreae because of a vow he had taken. [19]They arrived at Ephesus, where Paul left Priscilla and Aquila. He himself went into the synagogue and reasoned with the Jews. [20]When they asked him to spend more time with them, he declined. [21]But as he left, he promised, "I will come back if it is God's will." Then he set sail from Ephesus. [22]When he landed at Caesarea, he went up to Jerusalem and greeted the church and then went down to Antioch.

[23]After spending some time in Antioch, Paul set out from there and traveled from place to place throughout the region of Galatia and Phrygia, strengthening all the disciples.

[24]Meanwhile a Jew named Apollos, a native of

1580

aussie:making new friends

18:1–3 Priscilla and Aquila were forced to move from Italy to a new country. In Corinth they could have closed themselves off—pining for what they had left behind, scared to start again. If they had, they would have missed out on a life-changing friendship with Paul. (They become deeply involved in Paul's ministry and are fondly mentioned in his letters.) When you move somewhere new or even enter into a new community or job, it's difficult to embrace new challenges and relationships when all you want is the familiar comfort of your old life. But be open, reach out to new people and ask God to bring new friends into your life.

" conversations "

marriage «» 18:24–26

1» What unique ministry can you share with your husband?

2» What does your marriage teach others about God and God-honoring relationships?

3» How can you develop a deeper partnership with your husband?

For more on marriage, check the index.
For the next Conversations, go to p. 1583.

Alexandria, came to Ephesus. He was a learned man, with a thorough knowledge of the Scriptures. [25]He had been instructed in the way of the Lord, and he spoke with great fervor[a] and taught about Jesus accurately, though he knew only the baptism of John. [26]He began to speak boldly in the synagogue. When Priscilla and Aquila heard him, they invited him to their home and explained to him the way of God more adequately.

[27]When Apollos wanted to go to Achaia, the believers encouraged him and wrote to the disciples there to welcome him. When he arrived, he was a great help to those who by grace had believed. [28]For he vigorously refuted the Jews in public debate, proving from the Scriptures that Jesus was the Messiah.

Paul in Ephesus

19 While Apollos was at Corinth, Paul took the road through the interior and arrived at Ephesus. There he found some disciples [2]and asked them, "Did you receive the Holy Spirit when[b] you believed?"

They answered, "No, we have not even heard that there is a Holy Spirit."

[3]So Paul asked, "Then what baptism did you receive?"

"John's baptism," they replied.

[4]Paul said, "John's baptism was a baptism of repentance. He told the people to believe in the one coming after him, that is, in Jesus." [5]On hearing this, they were baptized into[c] the name of the Lord Jesus. [6]When Paul placed his hands on them, the Holy Spirit came on them, and they spoke in tongues[d] and prophesied. [7]There were about twelve men in all.

[8]Paul entered the synagogue and spoke boldly there for three months, arguing persuasively about the kingdom of God. [9]But some of them became obstinate; they refused to believe and publicly maligned the Way. So Paul left them. He took the disciples with him and had discussions daily in the lecture hall of Tyrannus. [10]This went on for two years, so that all the Jews and Greeks who lived in the province of Asia heard the word of the Lord.

[11]God did extraordinary miracles through Paul, [12]so that even handkerchiefs and aprons that had touched him were taken to the sick, and their illnesses were cured and the evil spirits left them.

[13]Some Jews who went around driving out evil spirits tried to invoke the name of the Lord Jesus over those who were demon-possessed. They would say, "In the name of the Jesus whom Paul preaches, I command you to come out." [14]Seven sons of Sceva, a Jewish chief priest, were doing this. [15]One day the evil spirit answered them, "Jesus I know, and I know about Paul, but who are you?" [16]Then the man who had the evil spirit jumped on them and overpowered them all. He gave them such a beating that they ran out of the house naked and bleeding.

[17]When this became known to the Jews and Greeks living in Ephesus, they were all seized with fear, and the name of the Lord Jesus was held in high honor. [18]Many of those who believed now came and openly confessed what they had done. [19]A number who had practiced sorcery brought their scrolls together and burned them publicly. When they calculated the value of the scrolls, the total came to fifty thousand drachmas.[e] [20]In this way the word of the Lord spread widely and grew in power.

[21]After all this had happened, Paul decided[f] to go to Jerusalem, passing through Macedonia and Achaia. "After I have been there," he said, "I must visit Rome also." [22]He sent two of his helpers, Timothy and Erastus, to Macedonia, while he stayed in the province of Asia a little longer.

The Riot in Ephesus

[23]About that time there arose a great disturbance about the Way. [24]A silversmith named Demetrius, who made silver shrines of Artemis, brought in no little business for the skilled workers there. [25]He called them together, along with the workers in related trades, and said: "You know, my friends, that we receive a good income from this business. [26]And you see and hear how this fellow Paul has convinced and led astray large numbers of people here in Ephesus and in practically the whole province of Asia. He says that gods made by human hands are no gods at all. [27]There is danger not only that our trade will lose its good name, but also that the temple of the great goddess Artemis will be discredited; and the

1581

---

a 25 Or *with fervor in the Spirit*   *b* 2 Or *after*   *c* 5 Or *in*   *d* 6 Or *other languages*   *e* 19 A drachma was a silver coin worth about a day's wages.
f 21 Or *decided in the Spirit*

goddess herself, who is worshiped throughout the province of Asia and the world, will be robbed of her divine majesty."

[28]When they heard this, they were furious and began shouting: "Great is Artemis of the Ephesians!" [29]Soon the whole city was in an uproar. The people seized Gaius and Aristarchus, Paul's traveling companions from Macedonia, and all of them rushed together into the theater. [30]Paul wanted to appear before the crowd, but the disciples would not let him. [31]Even some of the officials of the province, friends of Paul, sent him a message begging him not to venture into the theater.

[32]The assembly was in confusion: Some were shouting one thing, some another. Most of the people did not even know why they were there. [33]The Jews in the crowd pushed Alexander to the front, and they shouted instructions to him. He motioned for silence in order to make a defense before the people. [34]But when they realized he was a Jew, they all shouted in unison for about two hours: "Great is Artemis of the Ephesians!"

[35]The city clerk quieted the crowd and said: "People of Ephesus, doesn't all the world know that the city of Ephesus is the guardian of the temple of the great Artemis and of her image, which fell from heaven? [36]Therefore, since these facts are undeniable, you ought to calm down and not do anything rash. [37]You have brought these men here, though they have neither robbed temples nor blasphemed our goddess. [38]If, then, Demetrius and his associates have a grievance against anybody, the courts are open and there are proconsuls. They can press charges. [39]If there is anything further you want to bring up, it must be settled in a legal assembly. [40]As it is, we are in danger of being charged with rioting because of what happened today. In that case we would not be able to account for this commotion, since there is no reason for it." [41]After he had said this, he dismissed the assembly.

Through Macedonia and Greece

20 When the uproar had ended, Paul sent for the disciples and, after encouraging them, said goodby and set out for Macedonia. [2]He traveled through that area, speaking many words of encouragement to the people, and finally arrived in Greece, [3]where he stayed three months. Because some Jews had plotted against him just as he was about to sail for Syria, he decided to go back through Macedonia. [4]He was accompanied by Sopater son of Pyrrhus from Berea, Aristarchus and Secundus from Thessalonica, Gaius from Derbe, Timothy also, and Tychicus and Trophimus from the province of Asia. [5]These men went on ahead and waited for us at Troas. [6]But we sailed from Philippi after the Festival of Unleavened Bread, and five days later joined the others at Troas, where we stayed seven days.

Eutychus Raised From the Dead at Troas

[7]On the first day of the week we came together to break bread. Paul spoke to the people and, because he intended to leave the next day, kept on talking until midnight. [8]There were many lamps in the upstairs room where we were meeting. [9]Seated in a window was a young man named Eutychus, who was sinking into a deep sleep as Paul talked on and on. When he was sound asleep, he fell to the ground from the third story and was picked up dead. [10]Paul went down, threw himself on the young man and put his arms around him. "Don't be alarmed," he said. "He's alive!" [11]Then he went upstairs again and broke bread and ate. After talking until daylight, he left. [12]The people took the young man home alive and were greatly comforted.

Paul's Farewell to the Ephesian Elders

[13]We went on ahead to the ship and sailed for Assos, where we were going to take Paul aboard. He had made this arrangement because he was going there on foot. [14]When he met us at Assos, we took him aboard and went on to Mitylene. [15]The next day we set sail from there and arrived off Chios. The day after that we crossed over to Samos, and on the following day arrived at Miletus. [16]Paul had decided to sail past Ephesus to avoid spending time in the province of Asia, for he was in a hurry to reach Jerusalem, if possible, by the day of Pentecost.

[17]From Miletus, Paul sent to Ephesus for the elders of the church. [18]When they arrived, he said to them: "You know how I lived the whole time I was with you, from the first day I came into the province of Asia. [19]I served the Lord with great humility and with tears and in the midst of severe testing by the plots of the Jews. [20]You know that I have not hesitated to preach anything that would be helpful to you

but have taught you publicly and from house to house. ²¹I have declared to both Jews and Greeks that they must turn to God in repentance and have faith in our Lord Jesus.

²²"And now, compelled by the Spirit, I am going to Jerusalem, not knowing what will happen to me there. ²³I only know that in every city the Holy Spirit warns me that prison and hardships are facing me. ²⁴However, I consider my life worth nothing to me; my only aim is to finish the race and complete the task the Lord Jesus has given me—the task of testifying to the good news of God's grace.

"conversations"

discernment «» 20:25–31

1 » What kinds of threats do people in the church need to guard against?

2 » How can you discern between truth and a distortion of the truth?

3 » Has God given you a flock to oversee? If so, how can you teach them to discern the truth?

For more on **discernment**, check the index.
For the next Conversations, go to p. 1590.

²⁵"Now I know that none of you among whom I have gone about preaching the kingdom will ever see me again. ²⁶Therefore, I declare to you today that I am innocent of the blood of everyone. ²⁷For I have not hesitated to proclaim to you the whole will of God. ²⁸Keep watch over yourselves and all the flock of which the Holy Spirit has made you overseers. Be shepherds of the church of God,^a which he bought with his own blood. ²⁹I know that after I leave, savage wolves will come in among you and will not spare the flock. ³⁰Even from your own number some will arise and distort the truth in order to draw away disciples after them. ³¹So be on your guard! Remember that for three years I never stopped warning each of you night and day with tears.

1583

³²"Now I commit you to God and to the word of his grace, which can build you up and give you an inheritance among all those who are sanctified. ³³I have not coveted anyone's silver or gold or clothing. ³⁴You yourselves know that these hands of mine have supplied my own needs and the needs of my companions. ³⁵In everything I did, I showed you that by this kind of hard work we must help the weak, remembering the words the Lord Jesus himself said: 'It is more blessed to give than to receive.'"

³⁶When Paul had finished speaking, he knelt down with all of them and prayed. ³⁷They all wept as they embraced him and kissed him. ³⁸What grieved them most was his statement that they would never see his face again. Then they accompanied him to the ship.

On to Jerusalem

21 After we had torn ourselves away from them, we put out to sea and sailed straight to Kos. The next day we went to Rhodes and from there to Patara. ²We found a ship crossing over to Phoenicia, went on board and set sail. ³After sighting Cyprus and passing to the south of it, we sailed on to Syria. We landed at Tyre, where our ship was to unload its cargo. ⁴We sought out the disciples there and stayed with them seven days. Through the Spirit they urged Paul not to go on to Jerusalem. ⁵When it was time to leave, we left and continued on our way. All of them, including wives and children, accompanied us out of the city, and there on the beach we knelt to pray. ⁶After saying good-by to each other, we went aboard the ship, and they returned home.

⁷We continued our voyage from Tyre and landed at Ptolemais, where we greeted the believers and stayed with them for a day. ⁸Leaving the next day, we reached Caesarea and stayed at the house of Philip the evangelist, one of the Seven. ⁹He had four unmarried daughters who prophesied.

¹⁰After we had been there a number of days, a prophet named Agabus came down from Judea. ¹¹Coming over to us, he took Paul's belt, tied his own hands and feet with it and said, "The Holy Spirit says, 'In this way the Jewish leaders in Jerusalem will bind the owner of this belt and will hand him over to the Gentiles.'"

¹²When we heard this, we and the people there pleaded with Paul not to go up to Jerusalem. ¹³Then Paul answered, "Why are you weeping and breaking my heart? I am ready not only to be bound, but also

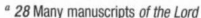

^a 28 Many manuscripts of the Lord

to die in Jerusalem for the name of the Lord Jesus." ¹⁴When he would not be dissuaded, we gave up and said, "The Lord's will be done."

¹⁵After this, we started on our way up to Jerusalem. ¹⁶Some of the disciples from Caesarea accompanied us and brought us to the home of Mnason, where we were to stay. He was a man from Cyprus and one of the early disciples.

Paul's Arrival at Jerusalem

¹⁷When we arrived at Jerusalem, the believers received us warmly. ¹⁸The next day Paul and the rest of us went to see James, and all the elders were present. ¹⁹Paul greeted them and reported in detail what God had done among the Gentiles through his ministry.

²⁰When they heard this, they praised God. Then they said to Paul: "You see, brother, how many thousands of Jews have believed, and all of them are zealous for the law. ²¹They have been informed that you teach all the Jews who live among the Gentiles to turn away from Moses, telling them not to circumcise their children or live according to our customs. ²²What shall we do? They will certainly hear that you have come, ²³so do what we tell you. There are four men with us who have made a vow. ²⁴Take these men, join in their purification rites and pay their expenses, so that they can have their heads shaved. Then everyone will know there is no truth in these reports about you, but that you yourself are living in obedience to the law. ²⁵As for the Gentile believers, we have written to them our decision that they should abstain from food sacrificed to idols, from blood, from the meat of strangled animals and from sexual immorality."

²⁶The next day Paul took the men and purified himself along with them. Then he went to the temple to give notice of the date when the days of purification would end and the offering would be made for each of them.

Paul Arrested

²⁷When the seven days were nearly over, some Jews from the province of Asia saw Paul at the temple. They stirred up the whole crowd and seized him, ²⁸shouting, "People of Israel, help us! This is the man who teaches everyone everywhere against our people and our law and this place. And besides, he has brought Greeks into the temple and defiled this holy place." ²⁹(They had previously seen Trophimus the Ephesian in the city with Paul and assumed that Paul had brought him into the temple.)

³⁰The whole city was aroused, and the people came running from all directions. Seizing Paul, they dragged him from the temple, and immediately the gates were shut. ³¹While they were trying to kill him, news reached the commander of the Roman troops that the whole city of Jerusalem was in an uproar. ³²He at once took some officers and soldiers and ran down to the crowd. When the rioters saw the commander and his soldiers, they stopped beating Paul.

³³The commander came up and arrested him and ordered him to be bound with two chains. Then he asked who he was and what he had done. ³⁴Some in the crowd shouted one thing and some another, and since the commander could not get at the truth because of the uproar, he ordered that Paul be taken into the barracks. ³⁵When Paul reached the steps, the violence of the mob was so great he had to be carried by the soldiers. ³⁶The crowd that followed kept shouting, "Get rid of him!"

Paul Speaks to the Crowd

³⁷As the soldiers were about to take Paul into the barracks, he asked the commander, "May I say something to you?"

"Do you speak Greek?" he replied. ³⁸"Aren't you the Egyptian who started a revolt and led four thousand terrorists out into the wilderness some time ago?"

³⁹Paul answered, "I am a Jew, from Tarsus in Cilicia, a citizen of no ordinary city. Please let me speak to the people."

⁴⁰Having received the commander's permission, Paul stood on the steps and motioned to the crowd.

22 When they were all silent, he said to them in Aramaic*ᵃ*: ¹"Brothers and fathers, listen now to my defense."

²When they heard him speak to them in Aramaic, they became very quiet.

ᵃ 40 Or possibly *Hebrew*; also in 22:2

Then Paul said: ³"I am a Jew, born in Tarsus of Cilicia, but brought up in this city. I studied under Gamaliel and was thoroughly trained in the law of our ancestors. I was just as zealous for God as any of you are today. ⁴I persecuted the followers of this Way to their death, arresting both men and women and throwing them into prison, ⁵as the high priest and all the Council can themselves testify. I even obtained letters from them to their associates in Damascus, and went there to bring these people as prisoners to Jerusalem to be punished.

⁶"About noon as I came near Damascus, suddenly a bright light from heaven flashed around me. ⁷I fell to the ground and heard a voice say to me, 'Saul! Saul! Why do you persecute me?'

⁸"'Who are you, Lord?' I asked.

"'I am Jesus of Nazareth, whom you are persecuting,' he replied. ⁹My companions saw the light, but they did not understand the voice of him who was speaking to me.

¹⁰"'What shall I do, Lord?' I asked.

"'Get up,' the Lord said, 'and go into Damascus. There you will be told all that you have been assigned to do.' ¹¹My companions led me by the hand into Damascus, because the brilliance of the light had blinded me.

¹²"A man named Ananias came to see me. He was a devout observer of the law and highly respected by all the Jews living there. ¹³He stood beside me and said, 'Brother Saul, receive your sight!' And at that very moment I was able to see him.

¹⁴"Then he said: 'The God of our ancestors has chosen you to know his will and to see the Righteous One and to hear words from his mouth. ¹⁵You will be his witness to all people of what you have seen and heard. ¹⁶And now what are you waiting for? Get up, be baptized and wash your sins away, calling on his name.'

¹⁷"When I returned to Jerusalem and was praying at the temple, I fell into a trance ¹⁸and saw the Lord speaking to me. 'Quick!' he said. 'Leave Jerusalem immediately, because the people here will not accept your testimony about me.'

¹⁹"'Lord,' I replied, 'these people know that I went from one synagogue to another to imprison and beat those who believe in you. ²⁰And when the blood of your martyrᵃ Stephen was shed, I stood there giving my approval and guarding the clothes of those who were killing him.'

²¹"Then the Lord said to me, 'Go; I will send you far away to the Gentiles.'"

Paul the Roman Citizen

²²The crowd listened to Paul until he said this. Then they raised their voices and shouted, "Rid the earth of him! He's not fit to live!"

²³As they were shouting and throwing off their cloaks and flinging dust into the air, ²⁴the commander ordered that Paul be taken into the barracks. He directed that he be flogged and interrogated in order to find out why the people were shouting at him like this. ²⁵As they stretched him out to flog him, Paul said to the centurion standing there, "Is it legal for you to flog a Roman citizen who hasn't even been found guilty?"

²⁶When the centurion heard this, he went to the commander and reported it. "What are you going to do?" he asked. "This man is a Roman citizen."

²⁷The commander went to Paul and asked, "Tell me, are you a Roman citizen?"

atissue:evangelism

22:1–21 Surely someone who hates Christians so much that he gladly watches them die is beyond God's redemption, right? Wrong! God is the master of the dramatic spiritual U–turn. He took Paul's passion in opposing Christ and converted it into a passion for serving Christ. Is there someone in your life who seems unlikely to ever follow God? Remember that no heart is too hard for God to soften. Target that tough person with your prayers and love. Pray for God to turn that person's life around, and keep showing that person how God changed the direction of your life.

1585

ᵃ 20 Or witness

"Yes, I am," he answered.

²⁸ Then the commander said, "I had to pay a lot of money for my citizenship."

"But I was born a citizen," Paul replied.

²⁹ Those who were about to interrogate him withdrew immediately. The commander himself was alarmed when he realized that he had put Paul, a Roman citizen, in chains.

Paul Before the Sanhedrin

³⁰ The commander wanted to find out exactly why Paul was being accused by the Jews. So the next day he released him and ordered the chief priests and all the members of the Sanhedrin to assemble. Then he brought Paul and had him stand before them.

23 Paul looked straight at the Sanhedrin and said, "My brothers, I have fulfilled my duty to God in all good conscience to this day." ² At this the high priest Ananias ordered those standing near Paul to strike him on the mouth. ³ Then Paul said to him, "God will strike you, you whitewashed wall! You sit there to judge me according to the law, yet you yourself violate the law by commanding that I be struck!"

⁴ Those who were standing near Paul said, "How dare you insult God's high priest!"

⁵ Paul replied, "Brothers, I did not realize that he was the high priest; for it is written: 'Do not speak evil about the ruler of your people.'ᵃ"

⁶ Then Paul, knowing that some of them were Sadducees and the others Pharisees, called out in the Sanhedrin, "My brothers, I am a Pharisee, descended from Pharisees. I stand on trial because of the hope of the resurrection of the dead." ⁷ When he said this, a dispute broke out between the Pharisees and the Sadducees, and the assembly was divided. ⁸ (The Sadducees say that there is no resurrection, and that there are neither angels nor spirits, but the Pharisees believe all these things.)

⁹ There was a great uproar, and some of the teachers of the law who were Pharisees stood up and argued vigorously. "We find nothing wrong with this man," they said. "What if a spirit or an angel has spoken to him?" ¹⁰ The dispute became so violent that the commander was afraid Paul would be torn to pieces by them. He ordered the troops to go down and take him away from them by force and bring him into the barracks.

¹¹ The following night the Lord stood near Paul and said, "Take courage! As you have testified about me in Jerusalem, so you must also testify in Rome."

HE IS: standing near

23:11 Paul was in a precarious position. In order to escape the persecuting Jews, he had to accept imprisonment by the powerful Romans. Yet in the midst of Paul's trials, God gave him a specific mission—to testify about Jesus in Rome, the capital of the world empire. Though the circumstances were dangerous, the Lord *stood near* Paul, encouraging him.

When you feel imprisoned by a relationship or persecuted for your faith, remember God's purpose in allowing the strain—so that you will testify about Jesus. Take courage! You are not alone in your trials (see 2 Timothy 4:17). He is *standing near* to give you strength.

For the next He Is, go to p. 1592.

The Plot to Kill Paul

¹² The next morning the Jews formed a conspiracy and bound themselves with an oath not to eat or drink until they had killed Paul. ¹³ More than forty men were involved in this plot. ¹⁴ They went to the chief priests and the elders and said, "We have taken a solemn oath not to eat anything until we have killed Paul. ¹⁵ Now then, you and the Sanhedrin petition the commander to bring him before you on the pretext of wanting more accurate information about his case. We are ready to kill him before he gets here."

ᵃ *5* Exodus 22:28

¹⁶But when the son of Paul's sister heard of this plot, he went into the barracks and told Paul.

¹⁷Then Paul called one of the centurions and said, "Take this young man to the commander; he has something to tell him." ¹⁸So he took him to the commander.

The centurion said, "Paul, the prisoner, sent for me and asked me to bring this young man to you because he has something to tell you."

¹⁹The commander took the young man by the hand, drew him aside and asked, "What is it you want to tell me?"

²⁰He said: "The Jews have agreed to ask you to bring Paul before the Sanhedrin tomorrow on the pretext of wanting more accurate information about him. ²¹Don't give in to them, because more than forty of them are waiting in ambush for him. They have taken an oath not to eat or drink until they have killed him. They are ready now, waiting for your consent to their request."

²²The commander dismissed the young man with this warning: "Don't tell anyone that you have reported this to me."

Paul Transferred to Caesarea

²³Then he called two of his centurions and ordered them, "Get ready a detachment of two hundred soldiers, seventy horsemen and two hundred spearmen^a to go to Caesarea at nine tonight. ²⁴Provide horses for Paul so that he may be taken safely to Governor Felix."

²⁵He wrote a letter as follows:

²⁶Claudius Lysias,

To His Excellency, Governor Felix:

Greetings.

²⁷This man was seized by the Jews and they were about to kill him, but I came with my troops and rescued him, for I had learned that he is a Roman citizen. ²⁸I wanted to know why they were accusing him, so I brought him to their Sanhedrin. ²⁹I found that the accusation had to do with questions about their law, but there was no charge against him that deserved death or imprisonment. ³⁰When I was informed of a plot to be carried out against the man, I sent him to you at once. I also ordered his accusers to present to you their case against him.

³¹So the soldiers, carrying out their orders, took Paul with them during the night and brought him as far as Antipatris. ³²The next day they let the cavalry go on with him, while they returned to the barracks. ³³When the cavalry arrived in Caesarea, they delivered the letter to the governor and handed Paul over to him. ³⁴The governor read the letter and asked what province he was from. Learning that he was from Cilicia, ³⁵he said, "I will hear your case when your accusers get here." Then he ordered that Paul be kept under guard in Herod's palace.

Paul's Trial Before Felix

24 Five days later the high priest Ananias went down to Caesarea with some of the elders and a lawyer named Tertullus, and they brought their charges against Paul before the governor. ²When Paul was called in, Tertullus presented his case before Felix: "We have enjoyed a long period of peace under you, and your foresight has brought about reforms in this nation. ³Everywhere and in every way, most excellent Felix, we acknowledge this with profound gratitude. ⁴But in order not to weary you further, I would request that you be kind enough to hear us briefly.

⁵"We have found this man to be a troublemaker, stirring up riots among the Jews all over the world. He is a ringleader of the Nazarene sect ⁶^[7]and even tried to desecrate the temple; so we seized him. ⁸By examining him yourself you will be able to learn the truth about all these charges we are bringing against him."

⁹The other Jews joined in the accusation, asserting that these things were true.

---

^a *23 The meaning of the Greek for this word is uncertain.*

[10]When the governor motioned for him to speak, Paul replied: "I know that for a number of years you have been a judge over this nation; so I gladly make my defense. [11]You can easily verify that no more than twelve days ago I went up to Jerusalem to worship. [12]My accusers did not find me arguing with anyone at the temple, or stirring up a crowd in the synagogues or anywhere else in the city. [13]And they cannot prove to you the charges they are now making against me. [14]However, I admit that I worship the God of our ancestors as a follower of the Way, which they call a sect. I believe everything that is in accordance with the Law and that is written in the Prophets, [15]and I have the same hope in God as these people themselves have, that there will be a resurrection of both the righteous and the wicked. [16]So I strive always to keep my conscience clear before God and all people.

[17]"After an absence of several years, I came to Jerusalem to bring my people gifts for the poor and to present offerings. [18]I was ceremonially clean when they found me in the temple courts doing this. There was no crowd with me, nor was I involved in any disturbance. [19]But there are some Jews from the province of Asia, who ought to be here before you and bring charges if they have anything against me. [20]Or these who are here should state what crime they found in me when I stood before the Sanhedrin— [21]unless it was this one thing I shouted as I stood in their presence: 'It is concerning the resurrection of the dead that I am on trial before you today.'"

[22]Then Felix, who was well acquainted with the Way, adjourned the proceedings. "When Lysias the commander comes," he said, "I will decide your case." [23]He ordered the centurion to keep Paul under guard but to give him some freedom and permit his friends to take care of his needs.

1588

[24]Several days later Felix came with his wife Drusilla, who was Jewish. He sent for Paul and listened to him as he spoke about faith in Christ Jesus. [25]As Paul talked about righteousness, self-control and the judgment to come, Felix was afraid and said, "That's enough for now! You may leave. When I find it convenient, I will send for you." [26]At the same time he was hoping that Paul would offer him a bribe, so he sent for him frequently and talked with him.

[27]When two years had passed, Felix was succeeded by Porcius Festus, but because Felix wanted to grant a favor to the Jews, he left Paul in prison.

Paul's Trial Before Festus

25 Three days after arriving in the province, Festus went up from Caesarea to Jerusalem, [2]where the chief priests and the Jewish leaders appeared before him and presented the charges against Paul. [3]They requested Festus, as a favor to them, to have Paul transferred to Jerusalem, for they were preparing an ambush to kill him along the way. [4]Festus answered, "Paul is being held at Caesarea, and I myself am going there soon. [5]Let some of your leaders come with me, and if the man has done anything wrong, they can press charges against him there."

[6]After spending eight or ten days with them, Festus went down to Caesarea. The next day he convened the court and ordered that Paul be brought before him. [7]When Paul came in, the Jews who had come down from Jerusalem stood around him. They brought many serious charges against him, but they could not prove them.

[8]Then Paul made his defense: "I have done nothing wrong against the Jewish law or against the temple or against Caesar."

[9]Festus, wishing to do the Jews a favor, said to Paul, "Are you willing to go up to Jerusalem and stand trial before me there on these charges?"

[10]Paul answered: "I am now standing before Caesar's court, where I ought to be tried. I have not done any wrong to the Jews, as you yourself know very well. [11]If, however, I am guilty of doing anything deserving death, I do not refuse to die. But if the charges brought against me by these Jews are not true, no one has the right to hand me over to them. I appeal to Caesar!"

[12]After Festus had conferred with his council, he declared: "You have appealed to Caesar. To Caesar you will go!"

Festus Consults King Agrippa

[13]A few days later King Agrippa and Bernice arrived at Caesarea to pay their respects to Festus. [14]Since they were spending many days there, Festus discussed Paul's case with the king. He said: "There is a man

here whom Felix left as a prisoner. [15]When I went to Jerusalem, the chief priests and the elders of the Jews brought charges against him and asked that he be condemned.

[16]"I told them that it is not the Roman custom to hand over anyone before they have faced their accusers and have had an opportunity to defend themselves against the charges. [17]When they came here with me, I did not delay the case, but convened the court the next day and ordered the man to be brought in. [18]When his accusers got up to speak, they did not charge him with any of the crimes I had expected. [19]Instead, they had some points of dispute with him about their own religion and about a dead man named Jesus who Paul claimed was alive. [20]I was at a loss how to investigate such matters; so I asked if he would be willing to go to Jerusalem and stand trial there on these charges. [21]But when Paul made his appeal to be held over for the Emperor's decision, I ordered him held until I could send him to Caesar."

[22]Then Agrippa said to Festus, "I would like to hear this man myself."

He replied, "Tomorrow you will hear him."

Paul Before Agrippa

[23]The next day Agrippa and Bernice came with great pomp and entered the audience room with the high-ranking military officers and the prominent men of the city. At the command of Festus, Paul was brought in. [24]Festus said: "King Agrippa, and all who are present with us, you see this man! The whole Jewish community has petitioned me about him in Jerusalem and here in Caesarea, shouting that he ought not to live any longer. [25]I found he had done nothing deserving of death, but because he made his appeal to the Emperor I decided to send him to Rome. [26]But I have nothing definite to write to His Majesty about him. Therefore I have brought him before all of you, and especially before you, King Agrippa, so that as a result of this investigation I may have something to write. [27]For I think it is unreasonable to send a prisoner on to Rome without specifying the charges against him."

26 Then Agrippa said to Paul, "You have permission to speak for yourself."

So Paul motioned with his hand and began his defense: [2]"King Agrippa, I consider myself fortunate to stand before you today as I make my defense against all the accusations of the Jews, [3]and especially so because you are well acquainted with all the Jewish customs and controversies. Therefore, I beg you to listen to me patiently.

[4]"The Jewish people all know the way I have lived ever since I was a child, from the beginning of my life in my own country, and also in Jerusalem. [5]They have known me for a long time and can testify, if they are willing, that I conformed to the strictest sect of our religion, living as a Pharisee. [6]And now it is because of my hope in what God has promised our ancestors that I am on trial today. [7]This is the promise our twelve tribes are hoping to see fulfilled as they earnestly serve God day and night. King Agrippa, it is because of this hope that the Jews are accusing me. [8]Why should any of you consider it incredible that God raises the dead?

[9]"I too was convinced that I ought to do all that was possible to oppose the name of Jesus of Nazareth. [10]And that is just what I did in Jerusalem. On the authority of the chief priests I put many of the Lord's people in prison, and when they were put to death, I cast my vote against them. [11]Many a time I went from one synagogue to another to have them punished, and I tried to force them to blaspheme. I was so obsessed with persecuting them that I even hunted them down in foreign cities.

[12]"On one of these journeys I was going to Damascus with the authority and commission of the chief priests. [13]About noon, King Agrippa, as I was on the road, I saw a light from heaven, brighter than the sun, blazing around me and my companions. [14]We all fell to the ground, and I heard a voice saying to me in Aramaic,*a* 'Saul, Saul, why do you persecute me? It is hard for you to kick against the goads.'

[15]"Then I asked, 'Who are you, Lord?'

"'I am Jesus, whom you are persecuting,' the Lord replied. [16]'Now get up and stand on your feet. I have appeared to you to appoint you as a servant and as a witness of what you have seen and will see of me. [17]I will rescue you from your own people and from the Gentiles. I am sending you to them [18]to open their eyes and turn them from darkness to light, and from the power of Satan to God, so that they may receive forgiveness of sins and a place among those who are sanctified by faith in me.'

---

a 14 Or *Hebrew*

[19]"So then, King Agrippa, I was not disobedient to the vision from heaven. [20]First to those in Damascus, then to those in Jerusalem and in all Judea, and then to the Gentiles, I preached that they should repent and turn to God and demonstrate their repentance by their deeds. [21]That is why some Jews seized me in the temple courts and tried to kill me. [22]But God has helped me to this very day; so I stand here and testify to small and great alike. I am saying nothing beyond what the prophets and Moses said would happen— [23]that the Messiah would suffer and, as the first to rise from the dead, would bring the message of light to his own people and to the Gentiles."

[24]At this point Festus interrupted Paul's defense. "You are out of your mind, Paul!" he shouted. "Your great learning is driving you insane."

[25]"I am not insane, most excellent Festus," Paul replied. "What I am saying is true and reasonable. [26]The king is familiar with these things, and I can speak freely to him. I am convinced that none of this has escaped his notice, because it was not done in a corner. [27]King Agrippa, do you believe the prophets? I know you do."

[28]Then Agrippa said to Paul, "Do you think that in such a short time you can persuade me to be a Christian?"

[29]Paul replied, "Short time or long—I pray to God that not only you but all who are listening to me today may become what I am, except for these chains."

conversations

witnessing «» 26:25–29

1» Is it a Christian's responsibility to "persuade" others to become Christians? Why or why not?

2» What is one way you can use your unique gifts and relationships to witness to others?

3» How can you become bolder in your witness for Christ?

For more on **witnessing**, check the index.
For the next Conversations, go to p. 1604.

[30]The king rose, and with him the governor and Bernice and those sitting with them. [31]After they left the room, they began saying to one another, "This man is not doing anything that deserves death or imprisonment."

[32]Agrippa said to Festus, "This man could have been set free if he had not appealed to Caesar."

Paul Sails for Rome

27 When it was decided that we would sail for Italy, Paul and some other prisoners were handed over to a centurion named Julius, who belonged to the Imperial Regiment. [2]We boarded a ship from Adramyttium about to sail for ports along the coast of the province of Asia, and we put out to sea. Aristarchus, a Macedonian from Thessalonica, was with us.

[3]The next day we landed at Sidon; and Julius, in kindness to Paul, allowed him to go to his friends so they might provide for his needs. [4]From there we put out to sea again and passed to the lee of Cyprus because the winds were against us. [5]When we had sailed across the open sea off the coast of Cilicia and Pamphylia, we landed at Myra in Lycia. [6]There the centurion found an Alexandrian ship sailing for Italy and put us on board. [7]We made slow headway for many days and had difficulty arriving off Cnidus. When the wind did not allow us to hold our course, we sailed to the lee of Crete, opposite Salmone. [8]We moved along the coast with difficulty and came to a place called Fair Havens, near the town of Lasea.

[9]Much time had been lost, and sailing had already become dangerous because by now it was after the Day of Atonement.[a] So Paul warned them, [10]"Men, I can see that our voyage is going to be disastrous and bring great loss to ship and cargo, and to our own lives also." [11]But the centurion, instead of listening to what Paul said, followed the advice of the pilot and of the owner of the ship. [12]Since the harbor was unsuitable to winter in, the majority decided that we should sail on, hoping to reach Phoenix and winter there. This was a harbor in Crete, facing both southwest and northwest.

The Storm

[13]When a gentle south wind began to blow, they saw their opportunity; so they weighed anchor and sailed along the shore of Crete. [14]Before very long, a wind of hurricane force, called the Northeaster,

---

[a] *9* That is, Yom Kippur

swept down from the island. [15]The ship was caught by the storm and could not head into the wind; so we gave way to it and were driven along. [16]As we passed to the lee of a small island called Cauda, we were hardly able to make the lifeboat secure, [17]so the men hoisted it aboard. Then they passed ropes under the ship itself to hold it together. Because they were afraid they would run aground on the sandbars of Syrtis, they lowered the sea anchor[a] and let the ship be driven along. [18]We took such a violent battering from the storm that the next day they began to throw the cargo overboard. [19]On the third day, they threw the ship's tackle overboard with their own hands. [20]When neither sun nor stars appeared for many days and the storm continued raging, we finally gave up all hope of being saved.

[21]After they had gone a long time without food, Paul stood up before them and said: "Men, you should have taken my advice not to sail from Crete; then you would have spared yourselves this damage and loss. [22]But now I urge you to keep up your courage, because not one of you will be lost; only the ship will be destroyed. [23]Last night an angel of the God whose I am and whom I serve stood beside me [24]and said, 'Do not be afraid, Paul. You must stand trial before Caesar; and God has graciously given you the lives of all who sail with you.' [25]So keep up your courage, men, for I have faith in God that it will happen just as he told me. [26]Nevertheless, we must run aground on some island."

The Shipwreck

[27]On the fourteenth night we were still being driven across the Adriatic[b] Sea, when about midnight the sailors sensed they were approaching land. [28]They took soundings and found that the water was a hundred and twenty feet[c] deep. A short time later they took soundings again and found it was ninety feet[d] deep. [29]Fearing that we would be dashed against the rocks, they dropped four anchors from the stern and prayed for daylight. [30]In an attempt to escape from the ship, the sailors let the lifeboat down into the sea, pretending they were going to lower some anchors from the bow. [31]Then Paul said to the centurion and the soldiers, "Unless these men stay with the ship, you cannot be saved." [32]So the soldiers cut the ropes that held the lifeboat and let it drift away.

[33]Just before dawn Paul urged them all to eat. "For the last fourteen days," he said, "you have been in constant suspense and have gone without food—you haven't eaten anything. [34]Now I urge you to take some food. You need it to survive. Not one of you will lose a single hair from his head." [35]After he said this, he took some bread and gave thanks to God in front of them all. Then he broke it and began to eat. [36]They were all encouraged and ate some food themselves. [37]Altogether there were 276 of us on board. [38]When they had eaten as much as they wanted, they lightened the ship by throwing the grain into the sea.

[39]When daylight came, they did not recognize the land, but they saw a bay with a sandy beach, where they decided to run the ship aground if they could. [40]Cutting loose the anchors, they left them in the sea and at the same time untied the ropes that held the rudders. Then they hoisted the foresail to the wind and made for the beach. [41]But the ship struck a sandbar and ran aground. The bow stuck fast and would not move, and the stern was broken to pieces by the pounding of the surf.

[42]The soldiers planned to kill the prisoners to prevent any of them from swimming away and escaping. [43]But the centurion wanted to spare Paul's life and kept them from carrying out their plan. He ordered those who could swim to jump overboard first and get to land. [44]The rest were to get there on planks or on other pieces of the ship. In this way everyone reached land safely.

Paul Ashore on Malta

28 Once safely on shore, we found out that the island was called Malta. [2]The islanders showed us unusual kindness. They built a fire and welcomed us all because it was raining and cold. [3]Paul gathered a pile of brushwood and, as he put it on the fire, a viper, driven out by the heat, fastened itself on his hand. [4]When the islanders saw the snake hanging from his hand, they said to each other, "This man must be a murderer; for though he escaped from the sea, the goddess Justice has not allowed him to live." [5]But Paul shook the snake off into the fire and suffered no ill effects. [6]The people expected him to swell up or suddenly fall dead; but after waiting a long time and seeing nothing unusual happen to him, they changed their minds and said he was a god.

---

[a] 17 Or the sails   [b] 27 In ancient times the name referred to an area extending well south of Italy.   [c] 28 Or about 37 meters   [d] 28 Or about 27 meters

⁷There was an estate nearby that belonged to Publius, the chief official of the island. He welcomed us to his home and showed us generous hospitality for three days. ⁸His father was sick in bed, suffering from fever and dysentery. Paul went in to see him and, after prayer, placed his hands on him and healed him. ⁹When this had happened, the rest of the sick on the island came and were cured. ¹⁰They honored us in many ways; and when we were ready to sail, they furnished us with the supplies we needed.

Paul's Arrival at Rome

¹¹After three months we put out to sea in a ship that had wintered in the island—it was an Alexandrian ship with the figurehead of the twin gods Castor and Pollux. ¹²We put in at Syracuse and stayed there three days. ¹³From there we set sail and arrived at Rhegium. The next day the south wind came up, and on the following day we reached Puteoli. ¹⁴There we found some believers who invited us to spend a week with them. And so we came to Rome. ¹⁵The believers there had heard that we were coming, and they traveled as far as the Forum of Appius and the Three Taverns to meet us. At the sight of these people Paul thanked God and was encouraged. ¹⁶When we got to Rome, Paul was allowed to live by himself, with a soldier to guard him.

Paul Preaches at Rome Under Guard

¹⁷Three days later he called together the local Jewish leaders. When they had assembled, Paul said to them: "My brothers, although I have done nothing against our people or against the customs of our ancestors, I was arrested in Jerusalem and handed over to the Romans. ¹⁸They examined me and wanted to release me, because I was not guilty of any crime deserving death. ¹⁹The Jews objected, so I was compelled to make an appeal to Caesar. I certainly did not intend to bring any charge against my own people. ²⁰For this reason I have asked to see you and talk with you. It is because of the hope of Israel that I am bound with this chain."

²¹They replied, "We have not received any letters from Judea concerning you, and none of our people who have come from there has reported or said anything bad about you. ²²But we want to hear what your views are, for we know that people everywhere are talking against this sect."

²³They arranged to meet Paul on a certain day, and came in even larger numbers to the place where he was staying. He witnessed to them from morning till evening, explaining about the kingdom of God, and from the Law of Moses and from the Prophets he tried to persuade them about Jesus. ²⁴Some were convinced by what he said, but others would not believe. ²⁵They disagreed among themselves and began to leave after Paul had made this final statement: "The Holy Spirit spoke the truth to your ancestors when he said through Isaiah the prophet:

²⁶"'Go to this people and say,
"You will be ever hearing but never understanding;
    you will be ever seeing but never perceiving."
²⁷For this people's heart has become calloused;

1592

HE IS: unhindered

28:28–31 Paul could have allowed innumerable obstacles to hinder his preaching: persecution, imprisonment, even shipwreck at sea. Yet he didn't let anything stop him—not even incarceration in Rome! Instead of worrying about his upcoming trial and his confinement to his rented house, Paul boldly proclaimed Jesus without hindrance.

Perhaps being confined to one location or being imprisoned by insecurities has left you feeling unable to share your faith. Take a lesson from Paul—in any situation, even imprisonment, you can boldly share the gospel with people, and some will listen! God is *unhindered* and can use even the most restricted circumstances to spread his Word.

For the next He Is, go to p. 1599.

they hardly hear with their ears,
    and they have closed their eyes.
Otherwise they might see with their eyes,
    hear with their ears,
    understand with their hearts
and turn, and I would heal them.'ᵃ

²⁸ ⁽²⁹⁾"Therefore I want you to know that God's salvation has been sent to the Gentiles, and they will listen!"

³⁰For two whole years Paul stayed there in his own rented house and welcomed all who came to see him. ³¹He proclaimed the kingdom of God and taught about the Lord Jesus Christ—with all boldness and without hindrance!

1593

1596	1617	1635	1648	1656
ROMANS	1 CORINTHIANS	2 CORINTHIANS	GALATIANS	EPHESIANS
1662	1669	1674	1681	1685
PHILIPPIANS	COLOSSIANS	1 THESSALONIANS	2 THESSALONIANS	1 TIMOTHY
1693	1698	1702	1704	1721
2 TIMOTHY	TITUS	PHILEMON	HEBREWS	JAMES
1728	1734	1738	1744	1746
1 PETER	2 PETER	1 JOHN	2 JOHN	3 JOHN
1748	1751			
JUDE	REVELATION			

the let
& reve

The rest of the New Testament is made up primarily of letters, or epistles. The books of Romans through Thessalonians are letters from the apostle Paul to particular churches and situations in the latter half of the first century A.D. These situations range from eating food sacrificed to idols and dealing with sexual purity to specific doctrine and teachings relevant to what the churches were facing.

The "pastoral epistles" are Paul's special instructions to Timothy and Titus as church leaders. Along with Philemon, these letters are addressed to individuals rather than churches (although they have wider intended audiences). It is in these books that we see Paul at his most personal and vulnerable.

The "general letters" are the books of Hebrews through Jude. These texts were written by various authors, generally follow a typical epistolary form (like other letters) and were addressed to specific situations. The book of Revelation might too be viewed as a kind of letter, as it begins with letters to the seven churches of Asia Minor (modern-day Turkey). However, it is also considered apocalyptic literature in which symbolism and vivid language are used to describe the cosmic conflict between good and evil.

romans

1596

AUTHOR
The apostle Paul.

AUDIENCE
Followers of Jesus; originally written to
Christians in Rome.

DATE
About A.D. 57.

SETTING
Paul wrote from Corinth regarding his pend-
ing visit to Rome via Jerusalem.

VERSE TO REMEMBER
"For the wages of sin is death, but the gift
of God is eternal life in Christ Jesus our
Lord." (6:23)

THEME TO CONSIDER
The gospel of Jesus Christ explains how
undeserving sinners become saints—that's
why it's called "Good News."

1 Paul, a servant of Christ Jesus, called to be an apostle and set apart for the gospel of God— [2]the gospel he promised beforehand through his prophets in the Holy Scriptures [3]regarding his Son, who as to his earthly life[a] was a descendant of David, [4]and who through the Spirit of holiness was appointed the Son of God in power[b] by his resurrection from the dead: Jesus Christ our Lord. [5]Through him we received grace and apostleship to call all the Gentiles to faith and obedience for his name's sake. [6]And you also are among those Gentiles who are called to belong to Jesus Christ.

[7]To all in Rome who are loved by God and called to be his holy people:

Grace and peace to you from God our Father and from the Lord Jesus Christ.

Paul's Longing to Visit Rome

[8]First, I thank my God through Jesus Christ for all of you, because your faith is being reported all over the world. [9]God, whom I serve in my spirit in preaching the gospel of his Son, is my witness how constantly I remember you [10]in my prayers at all times; and I pray that now at last by God's will the way may be opened for me to come to you.

[11]I long to see you so that I may impart to you some spiritual gift to make you strong— [12]that is, that you and I may be mutually encouraged by each other's faith. [13]I do not want you to be unaware, brothers and sisters, that I planned many times to come to you (but have been prevented from doing so until now) in order that I might have a harvest among you, just as I have had among the other Gentiles.

[14]I am obligated both to Greeks and non-Greeks, both to the wise and the foolish. [15]That is why I am so eager to preach the gospel also to you who are in Rome.

[16]I am not ashamed of the gospel, because it is the power of God that brings salvation to everyone who believes: first to the Jew, then to the Gentile. [17]For in the gospel the righteousness of God is revealed—a righteousness that is by faith from first to last,[c] just as it is written: "The righteous will live by faith."[d]

God's Wrath Against Sinful Humanity

[18]The wrath of God is being revealed from heaven against all the godlessness and wickedness of human beings who suppress the truth by their wickedness, [19]since what may be known about God is plain to them, because God has made it plain to them. [20]For since the creation of the world God's invisible qualities—his eternal power and divine nature—have been clearly seen, being understood from what has been made, so that people are without excuse.

[21]For although they knew God, they neither glorified him as God nor gave thanks to him, but their thinking became futile and their foolish hearts were darkened. [22]Although they claimed to be wise, they became fools [23]and exchanged the glory of the immortal God for images made to look like mortal human beings and birds and animals and reptiles.

[24]Therefore God gave them over in the sinful desires of their hearts to sexual impurity for the degrading of their bodies with one another. [25]They exchanged the truth about God for a lie, and worshiped and served created things rather than the Creator—who is forever praised. Amen.

[26]Because of this, God gave them over to shameful lusts. Even their women exchanged natural sexual relations for unnatural ones. [27]In the same way the men also abandoned natural relations with women and were inflamed with lust for

at issue: homosexuality

1:24–27 Those who defend, promote and live homosexual lifestyles have exchanged the truth of God for a lie. Many claim it's genetic or natural, so they expect others to accept this "alternative" lifestyle. But the truth is that God calls homosexuality *sin,* and with his help you always have a choice of whether or not to live in your sin (see Romans 8:1–17). Sadly, many Christians have also sinned by failing to love and reach out to those who struggle with or promote homosexuality and have treated them instead with contempt and fear. Let's learn how to love others even as we hold on to the truth.

---

[a] *3* Or *who according to the flesh*   [b] *4* Or *was declared with power to be the Son of God*   [c] *17* Or *is from faith to faith*   [d] *17* Hab. 2:4

one another. Men committed shameful acts with other men, and received in themselves the due penalty for their error.

[28] Furthermore, just as they did not think it worthwhile to retain the knowledge of God, so God gave them over to a depraved mind, so that they do what ought not to be done. [29] They have become filled with every kind of wickedness, evil, greed and depravity. They are full of envy, murder, strife, deceit and malice. They are gossips, [30] slanderers, God-haters, insolent, arrogant and boastful; they invent ways of doing evil; they disobey their parents; [31] they have no understanding, no fidelity, no love, no mercy. [32] Although they know God's righteous decree that those who do such things deserve death, they not only continue to do these very things but also approve of those who practice them.

God's Righteous Judgment

2 You, therefore, have no excuse, you who pass judgment on someone else, for at whatever point you judge another, you are condemning yourself, because you who pass judgment do the same things. [2] Now we know that God's judgment against those who do such things is based on truth. [3] So when you, a mere human, pass judgment on them and yet do the same things, do you think you will escape God's judgment? [4] Or do you show contempt for the riches of his kindness, forbearance and patience, not realizing that God's kindness is intended to lead you to repentance?

[5] But because of your stubbornness and your unrepentant heart, you are storing up wrath against yourself for the day of God's wrath, when his righteous judgment will be revealed. [6] God "will repay everyone according to what they have done."[a] [7] To those who by persistence in doing good seek glory, honor and immortality, he will give eternal life. [8] But for those who are self-seeking and who reject the truth and follow evil, there will be wrath and anger. [9] There will be trouble and distress for every human being who does evil: first for the Jew, then for the Gentile; [10] but glory, honor and peace for everyone who does good: first for the Jew, then for the Gentile. [11] For God does not show favoritism.

[12] All who sin apart from the law will also perish apart from the law, and all who sin under the law will be judged by the law. [13] For it is not those who hear the law who are righteous in God's sight, but it is those who obey the law who will be declared righteous. [14] (Indeed, when Gentiles, who do not have the law, do by nature things required by the law, they are a law for themselves, even though they do not have the law. [15] They show that the requirements of the law are written on their hearts, their consciences also bearing witness, and their thoughts now accusing, now even defending them.) [16] This will take place on the day when God judges everyone's secrets through Jesus Christ, as my gospel declares.

The Jews and the Law

[17] Now you, if you call yourself a Jew; if you rely on the law and boast in God; [18] if you know his will and approve of what is superior because you are instructed by the law; [19] if you are convinced that you are a guide for the blind, a light for those who are in the dark, [20] an instructor of the foolish, a teacher of infants, because you have in the law the embodiment of knowledge and truth— [21] you, then, who teach others, do you not teach yourself? You who preach against stealing, do you steal? [22] You who say that people should not commit adultery, do you commit adultery? You who abhor idols, do you rob temples? [23] You who boast in the law, do you dishonor God by breaking the law? [24] As it is written: "God's name is blasphemed among the Gentiles because of you."[b]

[25] Circumcision has value if you observe the law, but if you break the law, you have become as though you had not been circumcised. [26] If those who are not circumcised keep the law's requirements, will they not be regarded as though they were circumcised? [27] The one who is not circumcised physically and yet obeys the law will condemn you who, even though you have the[c] written code and circumcision, are a lawbreaker.

[28] A person is not a Jew who is one only outwardly, nor is circumcision merely outward and physical. [29] No, a person is a Jew who is one inwardly; and circumcision is circumcision of the heart, by the Spirit, not by the written code. Such a person's praise is not from other people, but from God.

---

[a] 6 Psalm 62:12; Prov. 24:12 [b] 24 Isaiah 52:5 (see Septuagint); Ezek. 36:20,22 [c] 27 Or who, by means of a

God's Faithfulness

3 What advantage, then, is there in being a Jew, or what value is there in circumcision? [2]Much in every way! First of all, the Jews have been entrusted with the very words of God.

[3]What if some were unfaithful? Will their unfaithfulness nullify God's faithfulness? [4]Not at all! Let God be true, and every human being a liar. As it is written:

> "So that you may be proved right when you speak
> and prevail when you judge."[a]

[5]But if our unrighteousness brings out God's righteousness more clearly, what shall we say? That God is unjust in bringing his wrath on us? (I am using a human argument.) [6]Certainly not! If that were so, how could God judge the world? [7]Someone might argue, "If my falsehood enhances God's truthfulness and so increases his glory, why am I still condemned as a sinner?" [8]Why not say—as we are being slanderously reported as saying and as some claim that we say—"Let us do evil that good may result"? Their condemnation is just!

No One Is Righteous

[9]What shall we conclude then? Do we have any advantage? Not at all! We have already made the charge that Jews and Gentiles alike are all under the power of sin. [10]As it is written:

> "There is no one righteous, not even one;
> [11] there is no one who understands;
> there is no one who seeks God.
> [12]All have turned away,
> they have together become worthless;
> there is no one who does good,
> not even one."[b]
> [13]"Their throats are open graves;
> their tongues practice deceit."[c]
> "The poison of vipers is on their lips."[d]
> [14] "Their mouths are full of cursing and bitterness."[e]
> [15]"Their feet are swift to shed blood;
> [16] ruin and misery mark their ways,
> [17]and the way of peace they do not know."[f]
> [18] "There is no fear of God before their eyes."[g]

[19]Now we know that whatever the law says, it says to those who are under the law, so that every mouth may be silenced and the whole world held accountable to God. [20]Therefore no one will be

---

[a] *4* Psalm 51:4 [b] *12* Psalms 14:1-3; 53:1-3; Eccles. 7:20 [c] *13* Psalm 5:9 [d] *13* Psalm 140:3 [e] *14* Psalm 10:7 (see Septuagint) [f] *17* Isaiah 59:7,8
[g] *18* Psalm 36:1

HE IS: made known

3:20–24 Understanding God's law doesn't free us from sin; it makes us more conscious of our sin. After reminding us that we're *all* lawbreakers, Paul wanted to make sure that we also knew something else: that God's righteousness has been *made known*. Paul revealed that we can only become right with God through faith in Jesus Christ.

You can't help being a lawbreaker; it's the plight of being human. Thankfully, the Law Giver *made known* the Law Keeper—Jesus Christ. When you are justified by him, God looks at you as if you had never sinned (see Isaiah 1:18).

For the next He Is, go to p. 1616.

declared righteous in God's sight by observing the law; rather, through the law we become conscious of our sin.

Righteousness Through Faith

[21]But now apart from the law the righteousness of God has been made known, to which the Law and the Prophets testify. [22]This righteousness is given through faith in[a] Jesus Christ to all who believe. There is no difference between Jew and Gentile, [23]for all have sinned and fall short of the glory of God, [24]and all are justified freely by his grace through the redemption that came by Christ Jesus. [25]God presented Christ as a sacrifice of atonement,[b] through the shedding of his blood—to be received by faith. He did this to demonstrate his justice, because in his forbearance he had left the sins committed beforehand unpunished— [26]he did it to demonstrate his justice at the present time, so as to be just and the one who justifies those who have faith in Jesus.

[27]Where, then, is boasting? It is excluded. Because of what law? The law that requires works? No, because of the "law" that requires faith. [28]For we maintain that a person is justified by faith apart from observing the law. [29]Is God the God of Jews only? Is he not the God of Gentiles too? Yes, of Gentiles too, [30]since there is only one God, who will justify the circumcised by faith and the uncircumcised through that same faith. [31]Do we, then, nullify the law by this faith? Not at all! Rather, we uphold the law.

Abraham Justified by Faith

4 What then shall we say that Abraham, the forefather of us Jews, discovered in this matter? [2]If, in fact, Abraham was justified by works, he had something to boast about—but not before God. [3]What does Scripture say? "Abraham believed God, and it was credited to him as righteousness."[c]

[4]Now to anyone who works, their wages are not credited to them as a gift, but as an obligation. [5]However, to anyone who does not work but trusts God who justifies the ungodly, their faith is credited as righteousness. [6]David says the same thing when he speaks of the blessedness of those to whom God credits righteousness apart from works:

> [7]"Blessed are those
>   whose transgressions are forgiven,
>   whose sins are covered.
> [8]Blessed are those
>   whose sin the Lord will never count against them."[d]

[9]Is this blessedness only for the circumcised, or also for the uncircumcised? We have been saying that Abraham's faith was credited to him as righteousness. [10]Under what circumstances was it credited? Was it after he was circumcised, or before? It was not after, but before! [11]And he received circumcision as a sign, a seal of the righteousness that he had by faith while he was still uncircumcised. So then, he is the father of all who believe but have not been circumcised, in order that righteousness might be credited to them. [12]And he is then also the father of the circumcised who not only are circumcised but who also follow in the footsteps of the faith that our father Abraham had before he was circumcised.

[13]It was not through the law that Abraham and his offspring received the promise that he would be heir of the world, but through the righteousness that comes by faith. [14]For if those who depend on the law are heirs, faith means nothing and the promise is worthless, [15]because the law brings wrath. And where there is no law there is no transgression.

[16]Therefore, the promise comes by faith, so that it may be by grace and may be guaranteed to all Abraham's offspring—not only to those who are of the law but also to those who have the faith of Abraham. He is the father of us all. [17]As it is written: "I have made you a father of many nations."[e] He is our father in the sight of God, in whom he believed—the God who gives life to the dead and calls into being things that were not.

[18]Against all hope, Abraham in hope believed and so became the father of many nations, just as it had been said to him, "So shall your offspring be."[f] [19]Without weakening in his faith, he faced the fact that

---

[a] 22 Or through the faithfulness of   [b] 25 The Greek for sacrifice of atonement refers to the atonement cover on the ark of the covenant (see Lev. 16:15,16).
[c] 3 Gen. 15:6; also in verse 22   [d] 8 Psalm 32:1,2   [e] 17 Gen. 17:5   [f] 18 Gen. 15:5

ASKMEanything

Tell us about yourself.

My husband, Ananias, and I were members of the church in Jerusalem. We got to meet and worship with the likes of Peter, James, John and the other apostles. Daily we witnessed the power of the Holy Spirit as more and more believers joined the church. It was thrilling to be part of that scene. It was like one big happy family—we all gave to the church and helped each other out.

But what happened when you and your husband decided to give some money?

I'd like to tell you that it was all Ananias's idea, but I knew exactly what he was going to do and was in agreement with him. You see, we had this little piece of property in Jerusalem that Ananias decided to sell so we could make a contribution. But rather than giving all the money to the church, he kept some of it for us.

1601

That wasn't the real problem, though, was it?

No. The real problem was that we told Peter and everyone that we had given *all* the money to the church. We lied to our church family. And we lied to God.

When you came to the church that day, did you have any idea what had happened to your husband just a few short hours before?

None. If I had known that Ananias had already been found out and judged, I never would have kept up the deception. It didn't seem like such a big deal to us. But obviously neither of us understood the seriousness of lying to the Holy Spirit. And I think there were probably a lot of shocked people in the church that day.

Your story hits us all a bit close to home. Why is that?

Well, if we're all completely honest, there probably are many in the church who are more like Ananias and me than they'd care to admit. A lot of Christians look good on the outside—being part of the church, worshiping every Sunday, giving money, even serving in ministry—but deep within they harbor secret thoughts or desires or sins. It's too late for me, but it's not too late for others to wake up and be 100 percent honest with God. Don't be fooled. God knows what's going on—inside and out.

FOR MORE INSIGHT: To see how much God values honesty and integrity, read Leviticus 19:35–36; Proverbs 11:1–3; 12:19; 16:8; Isaiah 33:15–16; and Colossians 3:9–10.

his body was as good as dead—since he was about a hundred years old—and that Sarah's womb was also dead. ²⁰Yet he did not waver through unbelief regarding the promise of God, but was strengthened in his faith and gave glory to God, ²¹being fully persuaded that God had power to do what he had promised. ²²This is why "it was credited to him as righteousness." ²³The words "it was credited to him" were written not for him alone, ²⁴but also for us, to whom God will credit righteousness—for us who believe in him who raised Jesus our Lord from the dead. ²⁵He was delivered over to death for our sins and was raised to life for our justification.

Peace and Hope

5 Therefore, since we have been justified through faith, we[a] have peace with God through our Lord Jesus Christ, ²through whom we have gained access by faith into this grace in which we now stand. And we[b] boast in the hope of the glory of God. ³Not only so, but we[c] also glory in our sufferings, because we know that suffering produces perseverance; ⁴perseverance, character; and character, hope. ⁵And hope does not put us to shame, because God's love has been poured out into our hearts through the Holy Spirit, who has been given to us.

⁶You see, at just the right time, when we were still powerless, Christ died for the ungodly. ⁷Very rarely will anyone die for a righteous person, though for a good person someone might possibly dare to die. ⁸But God demonstrates his own love for us in this: While we were still sinners, Christ died for us.

⁹Since we have now been justified by his blood, how much more shall we be saved from God's wrath through him! ¹⁰For if, while we were God's enemies, we were reconciled to him through the death of his Son, how much more, having been reconciled, shall we be saved through his life! ¹¹Not only is this so, but we also boast in God through our Lord Jesus Christ, through whom we have now received reconciliation.

Death Through Adam, Life Through Christ

¹²Therefore, just as sin entered the world through one man, and death through sin, and in this way death came to all people, because all sinned—

¹³To be sure, sin was in the world before the law was given, but sin is not charged against anyone's account where there is no law. ¹⁴Nevertheless, death reigned from the time of Adam to the time of Moses, even over those who did not sin by breaking a command, as did Adam, who is a pattern of the one to come.

¹⁵But the gift is not like the trespass. For if the many died by the trespass of the one man, how much more did God's grace and the gift that came by the grace of the one man, Jesus Christ, overflow to the many! ¹⁶Nor can the gift of God be compared with the result of one man's sin: The judgment followed one sin and brought condemnation, but the gift followed many trespasses and brought justification. ¹⁷For if, by the trespass of the one man, death reigned through that one man, how much more will those who receive God's abundant provision of grace and of the gift of righteousness reign in life through the one man, Jesus Christ!

¹⁸Consequently, just as one trespass resulted in condemnation for all people, so also one righteous act resulted in justification and life for all. ¹⁹For just as through the disobedience of the one man the many were made sinners, so also through the obedience of the one man the many will be made righteous.

²⁰The law was brought in so that the trespass might increase. But where sin increased, grace increased all the more, ²¹so that, just as sin reigned in death, so also grace might reign through righteousness to bring eternal life through Jesus Christ our Lord.

Dead to Sin, Alive in Christ

6 What shall we say, then? Shall we go on sinning so that grace may increase? ²By no means! We are those who have died to sin; how can we live in it any longer? ³Or don't you know that all of us who were baptized into Christ Jesus were baptized into his death? ⁴We were therefore buried with him through baptism into death in order that, just as Christ was raised from the dead through the glory of the Father, we too may live a new life.

⁵If we have been united with him in a death like his, we will certainly also be united with him in a res-

urrection like his. [6]For we know that our old self was crucified with him so that the body ruled by sin might be done away with,[a] that we should no longer be slaves to sin— [7]because anyone who has died has been set free from sin.

[8]Now if we died with Christ, we believe that we will also live with him. [9]For we know that since Christ was raised from the dead, he cannot die again; death no longer has mastery over him. [10]The death he died, he died to sin once for all; but the life he lives, he lives to God.

[11]In the same way, count yourselves dead to sin but alive to God in Christ Jesus. [12]Therefore do not let sin reign in your mortal body so that you obey its evil desires. [13]Do not offer any part of yourself to sin as an instrument of wickedness, but rather offer yourselves to God as those who have been brought from death to life; and offer every part of yourself to him as an instrument of righteousness. [14]For sin shall no longer be your master, because you are not under the law, but under grace.

Slaves to Righteousness

[15]What then? Shall we sin because we are not under the law but under grace? By no means! [16]Don't you know that when you offer yourselves to someone as obedient slaves, you are slaves of the one you obey—whether you are slaves to sin, which leads to death, or to obedience, which leads to righteousness? [17]But thanks be to God that, though you used to be slaves to sin, you have come to obey from your heart the pattern of teaching that has now claimed your allegiance. [18]You have been set free from sin and have become slaves to righteousness.

[19]I am using an example from everyday life because of your human limitations. Just as you used to offer yourselves as slaves to impurity and to ever-increasing wickedness, so now offer yourselves as slaves to righteousness leading to holiness. [20]When you were slaves to sin, you were free from the control of righteousness. [21]What benefit did you reap at that time from the things you are now ashamed of? Those things result in death! [22]But now that you have been set free from sin and have become slaves of God, the benefit you reap leads to holiness, and the result is eternal life. [23]For the wages of sin is death, but the gift of God is eternal life in[b] Christ Jesus our Lord.

atissue:freedom

6:11–18 *Your former identity: a slave to sin.* Once you've lived as a slave for many years, the taste of freedom is delicious. But it can also feel overwhelming to let go of the life you've always known—that comfortable sin pattern that fits you like a glove (pride, gossip, vanity, fear, alcoholism, etc.). Jesus didn't set us free so that we'd be our own little masters, and he sure didn't set us free so that we'd return to our slavery. He set us free so that we'd then turn our lives over to him. *Your new identity: a slave to righteousness.*

1603

Released From the Law, Bound to Christ

7 Do you not know, brothers and sisters—for I am speaking to those who know the law—that the law has authority over someone only as long as that person lives? [2]For example, by law a married woman is bound to her husband as long as he is alive, but if her husband dies, she is released from the law that binds her to him. [3]So then, if she marries another man while her husband is still alive, she is called an adulteress. But if her husband dies, she is released from that law and is not an adulteress if she marries another man.

[4]So, my brothers and sisters, you also died to the law through the body of Christ, that you might belong to another, to him who was raised from the dead, in order that we might bear fruit for God. [5]For when we were controlled by our sinful nature,[c] the sinful passions aroused by the law were at work in us, so that we bore fruit for death. [6]But now, by dying to what once bound us, we have been released from the law so that we serve in the new way of the Spirit, and not in the old way of the written code.

---

[a] 6 Or be rendered powerless   [b] 23 Or through   [c] 5 Or by the flesh

The Law and Sin

[7]What shall we say, then? Is the law sinful? Certainly not! Nevertheless, I would not have known what sin was had it not been for the law. For I would not have known what coveting really was if the law had not said, "You shall not covet."[a] [8]But sin, seizing the opportunity afforded by the commandment, produced in me every kind of coveting. For apart from the law, sin was dead. [9]Once I was alive apart from the law; but when the commandment came, sin sprang to life and I died. [10]I found that the very commandment that was intended to bring life actually brought death. [11]For sin, seizing the opportunity afforded by the commandment, deceived me, and through the commandment put me to death. [12]So then, the law is holy, and the commandment is holy, righteous and good.

[13]Did that which is good, then, become death to me? By no means! Nevertheless, in order that sin might be recognized as sin, it used what is good to bring about my death, so that through the commandment sin might become utterly sinful.

[14]We know that the law is spiritual; but I am unspiritual, sold as a slave to sin. [15]I do not understand what I do. For what I want to do I do not do, but what I hate I do. [16]And if I do what I do not want to do, I agree that the law is good. [17]As it is, it is no longer I myself who do it, but it is sin living in me. [18]I know that good itself does not dwell in me, that is, in my sinful nature.[b] For I have the desire to do what is good, but I cannot carry it out. [19]For I do not do the good I want to do, but the evil I do not want to do—this I keep on doing. [20]Now if I do what I do not want to do, it is no longer I who do it, but it is sin living in me that does it.

[21]So I find this law at work: Although I want to do good, evil is right there with me. [22]For in my inner being I delight in God's law; [23]but I see another law at work in me, waging war against the law of my mind and making me a prisoner of the law of sin at work within me. [24]What a wretched man I am! Who will rescue me from this body of death? [25]Thanks be to God, who delivers me through Jesus Christ our Lord!

So then, I myself in my mind am a slave to God's law, but in my sinful nature[c] a slave to the law of sin.

conversations

internet addiction «» 7:14–25

1» Do you consider your internet use to be out of control? Would others think so?

2» Are there sites that you feel consistently compelled to visit? Why?

3» Who can help you be more accountable for how you spend your time online?

For more on **internet addiction**, check the index. For the next Conversations, go to p. 1612.

Life Through the Spirit

8 Therefore, there is now no condemnation for those who are in Christ Jesus, [2]because through Christ Jesus the law of the Spirit who gives life has set you[d] free from the law of sin and death. [3]For what the law was powerless to do because it was weakened by the sinful nature,[e] God did by sending his own Son in the likeness of sinful humanity to be a sin offering.[f] And so he condemned sin in human flesh, [4]in order that the righteous requirement of the law might be fully met in us, who do not live according to the sinful nature but according to the Spirit.

[5]Those who live according to the sinful nature have their minds set on what that nature desires; but those who live in accordance with the Spirit have their minds set on what the Spirit desires. [6]The mind controlled by the sinful nature[g] is death, but the mind controlled by the Spirit is life and peace. [7]The sinful mind[h] is hostile to God; it does not submit to God's law, nor can it do so. [8]Those controlled by the sinful nature cannot please God.

[9]You, however, are not controlled by the sinful nature but are in the Spirit, if indeed the Spirit of God lives in you. And if anyone does not have the Spirit of Christ, they do not belong to Christ. [10]But if Christ is in you, then even though your body is subject to death because of sin, the Spirit gives life[i] because of

---

[a] 7 Exodus 20:17; Deut. 5:21   [b] 18 Or my flesh   [c] 25 Or in the flesh   [d] 2 The Greek is singular; some manuscripts me   [e] 3 Or the flesh; also in verses 4, 5, 8, 9, 12 and 13   [f] 3 Or humanity, for sin   [g] 6 Or mind set on the flesh   [h] 7 Or the mind set on the flesh   [i] 10 Or you, your body is dead because of sin, yet your spirit is alive

righteousness. ¹¹And if the Spirit of him who raised Jesus from the dead is living in you, he who raised Christ from the dead will also give life to your mortal bodies because of[a] his Spirit who lives in you.

¹²Therefore, brothers and sisters, we have an obligation—but it is not to the sinful nature, to live according to it. ¹³For if you live according to the sinful nature, you will die; but if by the Spirit you put to death the misdeeds of the body, you will live.

¹⁴For those who are led by the Spirit of God are the children of God. ¹⁵The Spirit you received does not make you slaves, so that you live in fear again; rather, the Spirit you received brought about your adoption to sonship.[b] And by him we cry, "Abba,[c] Father." ¹⁶The Spirit himself testifies with our spirit that we are God's children. ¹⁷Now if we are children, then we are heirs—heirs of God and co-heirs with Christ, if indeed we share in his sufferings in order that we may also share in his glory.

Present Suffering and Future Glory

¹⁸I consider that our present sufferings are not worth comparing with the glory that will be revealed in us. ¹⁹The creation waits in eager expectation for the children of God to be revealed. ²⁰For the creation was subjected to frustration, not by its own choice, but by the will of the one who subjected it, in hope ²¹that[d] the creation itself will be liberated from its bondage to decay and brought into the freedom and glory of the children of God.

²²We know that the whole creation has been groaning as in the pains of childbirth right up to the present time. ²³Not only so, but we ourselves, who have the firstfruits of the Spirit, groan inwardly as we wait eagerly for our adoption, the redemption of our bodies. ²⁴For in this hope we were saved. But hope that is seen is no hope at all. Who hopes for what they already have? ²⁵But if we hope for what we do not yet have, we wait for it patiently.

²⁶In the same way, the Spirit helps us in our weakness. We do not know what we ought to pray for, but the Spirit himself intercedes for us through wordless groans. ²⁷And he who searches our hearts knows the mind of the Spirit, because the Spirit intercedes for God's people in accordance with the will of God.

²⁸And we know that in all things God works for the good of those who love him, who[e] have been called according to his purpose. ²⁹For those God foreknew he also predestined to be conformed to the image of his Son, that he might be the firstborn among many brothers and sisters. ³⁰And those he predestined, he also called; those he called, he also justified; those he justified, he also glorified.

atissue:self-esteem

8:1–39 *Child of God. Co-heir with Christ. Free from condemnation. Given life and peace, freedom and glory and hope. Supplied with help in weakness. Called, justified and glorified. More than conquerors. Inseparable from God's love.* If you are a Christ-follower, then Paul is describing *you* in Romans 8! You need to camp on this passage. Live in it. Dwell on it. Let these truths transform how you perceive yourself. Read those phrases again—this time slowly, out loud. Find your value and worth in the things God declares here to be true about you.

1605

More Than Conquerors

³¹What, then, shall we say in response to these things? If God is for us, who can be against us? ³²He who did not spare his own Son, but gave him up for us all—how will he not also, along with him, graciously give us all things? ³³Who will bring any charge against those whom God has chosen? It is God who justifies. ³⁴Who then can condemn? No one. Christ Jesus who died—more than that, who was raised to life—is at the right hand of God and is also interceding for us. ³⁵Who shall separate us from the love of Christ? Shall trouble or hardship or persecution or famine or nakedness or danger or sword? ³⁶As it is written:

> "For your sake we face death all day long;
> we are considered as sheep to be slaughtered."[a]

[37]No, in all these things we are more than conquerors through him who loved us. [38]For I am convinced that neither death nor life, neither angels nor demons,[b] neither the present nor the future, nor any powers, [39]neither height nor depth, nor anything else in all creation, will be able to separate us from the love of God that is in Christ Jesus our Lord.

Paul's Anguish Over Israel

 I speak the truth in Christ—I am not lying, my conscience confirms it through the Holy Spirit— [2]I have great sorrow and unceasing anguish in my heart. [3]For I could wish that I myself were cursed and cut off from Christ for the sake of my people, those of my own race, [4]the people of Israel. Theirs is the adoption; theirs the divine glory, the covenants, the receiving of the law, the temple worship and the promises. [5]Theirs are the patriarchs, and from them is traced the human ancestry of the Messiah, who is God over all, forever praised![c] Amen.

God's Sovereign Choice

[6]It is not as though God's word had failed. For not all who are descended from Israel are Israel. [7]Nor because they are his descendants are they all Abraham's children. On the contrary, "It is through Isaac that your offspring will be reckoned."[d] [8]In other words, it is not the natural children who are God's children, but it is the children of the promise who are regarded as Abraham's offspring. [9]For this was how the promise was stated: "At the appointed time I will return, and Sarah will have a son."[e]

[10]Not only that, but Rebekah's children were conceived at the same time by our father Isaac. [11]Yet, before the twins were born or had done anything good or bad—in order that God's purpose in election might stand: [12]not by works but by him who calls—she was told, "The older will serve the younger."[f] [13]Just as it is written: "Jacob I loved, but Esau I hated."[g]

[14]What then shall we say? Is God unjust? Not at all! [15]For he says to Moses,

> "I will have mercy on whom I have mercy,
> and I will have compassion on whom I have compassion."[h]

[16]It does not, therefore, depend on human desire or effort, but on God's mercy. [17]For Scripture says to Pharaoh: "I raised you up for this very purpose, that I might display my power in you and that my name might be proclaimed in all the earth."[i] [18]Therefore God has mercy on whom he wants to have mercy, and he hardens whom he wants to harden.

[19]One of you will say to me: "Then why does God still blame us? For who is able to resist his will?" [20]But who are you, a mere human being, to talk back to God? "Shall what is formed say to the one who formed it, 'Why did you make me like this?'"[j] [21]Does not the potter have the right to make out of the same lump of clay some pottery for noble purposes and some for disposal of refuse?

[22]What if God, although choosing to show his wrath and make his power known, bore with great patience the objects of his wrath—prepared for destruction? [23]What if he did this to make the riches of his glory known to the objects of his mercy, whom he prepared in advance for glory— [24]even us, whom he also called, not only from the Jews but also from the Gentiles? [25]As he says in Hosea:

> "I will call them 'my people' who are not my people;
> and I will call her 'my loved one' who is not my loved one,"[k]

[26]and,

> "In the very place where it was said to them,
> 'You are not my people,'
> they will be called 'children of the living God.'"[l]

---

[a] 36 Psalm 44:22   [b] 38 Or nor heavenly rulers   [c] 5 Or Messiah, who is over all. God be forever praised! Or Messiah. God who is over all be forever praised!
[d] 7 Gen. 21:12   [e] 9 Gen. 18:10,14   [f] 12 Gen. 25:23   [g] 13 Mal. 1:2,3   [h] 15 Exodus 33:19   [i] 17 Exodus 9:16   [j] 20 Isaiah 29:16; 45:9   [k] 25 Hosea 2:23
[l] 26 Hosea 1:10

[27]Isaiah cries out concerning Israel:

> "Though the number of the Israelites be like the sand by the sea,
>> only the remnant will be saved.
> [28]For the Lord will carry out
>> his sentence on earth with speed and finality."[a]

[29]It is just as Isaiah said previously:

> "Unless the Lord Almighty
>> had left us descendants,
> we would have become like Sodom,
>> we would have been like Gomorrah."[b]

Israel's Unbelief

[30]What then shall we say? That the Gentiles, who did not pursue righteousness, have obtained it, a righteousness that is by faith; [31]but the people of Israel, who pursued the law as the way of righteousness, have not attained their goal. [32]Why not? Because they pursued it not by faith but as if it were by works. They stumbled over the stumbling stone. [33]As it is written:

> "See, I lay in Zion a stone that causes people to stumble
>> and a rock that makes them fall,
>> and the one who believes in him will never be put to shame."[c]

10 Brothers and sisters, my heart's desire and prayer to God for the Israelites is that they may be saved. [2]For I can testify about them that they are zealous for God, but their zeal is not based on knowledge. [3]Since they did not know the righteousness of God and sought to establish their own, they did not submit to God's righteousness. [4]Christ is the culmination of the law so that there may be righteousness for everyone who believes.

[5]Moses writes this about the righteousness that is by the law: "Whoever does these things will live by them."[d] [6]But the righteousness that is by faith says: "Do not say in your heart, 'Who will ascend into heaven?'"[e] (that is, to bring Christ down) [7]"or 'Who will descend into the deep?'"[f] (that is, to bring Christ up from the dead). [8]But what does it say? "The word is near you; it is in your mouth and in your heart,"[g] that is, the message concerning faith that we proclaim: [9]If you declare with your mouth, "Jesus is Lord," and believe in your heart that God raised him from the dead, you will be saved. [10]For it is with your heart that you believe and are justified, and it is with your mouth that you profess your faith and are saved. [11]As Scripture says, "Anyone who believes in him will never be put to shame."[h] [12]For there is no difference between Jew and Gentile—the same Lord is Lord of all and richly blesses all who call on him, [13]for, "Everyone who calls on the name of the Lord will be saved."[i]

[14]How, then, can they call on the one they have not believed in? And how can they believe in the one of whom they have not heard? And how can they hear without someone preaching to them? [15]And how can anyone preach unless they are sent? As it is written: "How beautiful are the feet of those who bring good news!"[j]

[16]But not all the Israelites accepted the good news. For Isaiah says, "Lord, who has believed our message?"[k] [17]Consequently, faith comes from hearing the message, and the message is heard through the word about Christ. [18]But I ask: Did they not hear? Of course they did:

> "Their voice has gone out into all the earth,
>> their words to the ends of the world."[l]

[19]Again I ask: Did Israel not understand? First, Moses says,

> "I will make you envious by those who are not a nation;
> I will make you angry by a nation that has no understanding."[m]

---

[a] *28* Isaiah 10:22,23 (see Septuagint)   [b] *29* Isaiah 1:9   [c] *33* Isaiah 8:14; 28:16   [d] *5* Lev. 18:5   [e] *6* Deut. 30:12   [f] *7* Deut. 30:13   [g] *8* Deut. 30:14   [h] *11* Isaiah 28:16 (see Septuagint)   [i] *13* Joel 2:32   [j] *15* Isaiah 52:7   [k] *16* Isaiah 53:1   [l] *18* Psalm 19:4   [m] *19* Deut. 32:21

²⁰And Isaiah boldly says,

> "I was found by those who did not seek me;
>> I revealed myself to those who did not ask for me."ᵃ

²¹But concerning Israel he says,

> "All day long I have held out my hands
>> to a disobedient and obstinate people."ᵇ

The Remnant of Israel

11 I ask then: Did God reject his people? By no means! I am an Israelite myself, a descendant of Abraham, from the tribe of Benjamin. ²God did not reject his people, whom he foreknew. Don't you know what Scripture says in the passage about Elijah—how he appealed to God against Israel: ³"Lord, they have killed your prophets and torn down your altars; I am the only one left, and they are trying to kill me"ᶜ? ⁴And what was God's answer to him? "I have reserved for myself seven thousand who have not bowed the knee to Baal."ᵈ ⁵So too, at the present time there is a remnant chosen by grace. ⁶And if by grace, then it cannot be based on works; if it were, grace would no longer be grace.

⁷What then? What the people of Israel sought so earnestly they did not obtain. The elect among them did, but the others were hardened, ⁸as it is written:

> "God gave them a spirit of stupor,
>> eyes that could not see
>> and ears that could not hear,
> to this very day."ᵉ

⁹And David says:

> "May their table become a snare and a trap,
>> a stumbling block and a retribution for them.
> ¹⁰May their eyes be darkened so they cannot see,
>> and their backs be bent forever."ᶠ

Ingrafted Branches

¹¹Again I ask: Did they stumble so as to fall beyond recovery? Not at all! Rather, because of their transgression, salvation has come to the Gentiles to make Israel envious. ¹²But if their transgression means riches for the world, and their loss means riches for the Gentiles, how much greater riches will their fullness bring!

¹³I am talking to you Gentiles. Inasmuch as I am the apostle to the Gentiles, I make much of my ministry ¹⁴in the hope that I may somehow arouse my own people to envy and save some of them. ¹⁵For if their rejection brought reconciliation to the world, what will their acceptance be but life from the dead? ¹⁶If the part of the dough offered as firstfruits is holy, then the whole batch is holy; if the root is holy, so are the branches.

¹⁷If some of the branches have been broken off, and you, though a wild olive shoot, have been grafted in among the others and now share in the nourishing sap from the olive root, ¹⁸do not consider yourself to be superior to those other branches. If you do, consider this: You do not support the root, but the root supports you. ¹⁹You will say then, "Branches were broken off so that I could be grafted in." ²⁰Granted. But they were broken off because of unbelief, and you stand by faith. Do not be arrogant, but tremble. ²¹For if God did not spare the natural branches, he will not spare you either.

²²Consider therefore the kindness and sternness of God: sternness to those who fell, but kindness to you, provided that you continue in his kindness. Otherwise, you also will be cut off. ²³And if they do not persist in unbelief, they will be grafted in, for God is able to graft them in again. ²⁴After all, if you were cut out of an olive tree that is wild by nature, and contrary to nature were grafted into a cultivated olive tree, how much more readily will these, the natural branches, be grafted into their own olive tree!

ᵃ *20* Isaiah 65:1   ᵇ *21* Isaiah 65:2   ᶜ *3* 1 Kings 19:10,14   ᵈ *4* 1 Kings 19:18   ᵉ *8* Deut. 29:4; Isaiah 29:10   ᶠ *10* Psalm 69:22,23

All Israel Will Be Saved

²⁵I do not want you to be ignorant of this mystery, brothers and sisters, so that you may not think you are superior: Israel has experienced a hardening in part until the full number of the Gentiles has come in, ²⁶and in this way*ᵃ* all Israel will be saved. As it is written:

> "The deliverer will come from Zion;
> he will turn godlessness away from Jacob.
> ²⁷And this is*ᵇ* my covenant with them
> when I take away their sins."*ᶜ*

²⁸As far as the gospel is concerned, they are enemies for your sake; but as far as election is concerned, they are loved on account of the patriarchs, ²⁹for God's gifts and his call are irrevocable. ³⁰Just as you who were at one time disobedient to God have now received mercy as a result of their disobedience, ³¹so they too have now become disobedient in order that they too may now*ᵈ* receive mercy as a result of God's mercy to you. ³²For God has bound everyone over to disobedience so that he may have mercy on them all.

Doxology

> ³³Oh, the depth of the riches of the wisdom and*ᵉ* knowledge of God!
> How unsearchable his judgments,
> and his paths beyond tracing out!
> ³⁴"Who has known the mind of the Lord?
> Or who has been his counselor?"*ᶠ*
> ³⁵"Who has ever given to God,
> that God should repay them?"*ᵍ*
> ³⁶For from him and through him and to him are all things.
> To him be the glory forever! Amen.

1609

A Living Sacrifice

12 Therefore, I urge you, brothers and sisters, in view of God's mercy, to offer your bodies as a living sacrifice, holy and pleasing to God—this is true worship. ²Do not conform to the pattern of this world, but be transformed by the renewing of your mind. Then you will be able to test and approve what God's will is—his good, pleasing and perfect will.

Humble Service in the Body of Christ

³For by the grace given me I say to every one of you: Do not think of yourself more highly than you ought, but rather think of yourself with sober judgment, in accordance with the faith God has distributed to each of you. ⁴For just as each of us has one body with many members, and these members do not all have the same function, ⁵so in Christ we, though many, form one body, and each member belongs to all the others. ⁶We have different gifts, according to the grace given to each of us. If your gift is prophesying, then prophesy in accordance with your*ʰ* faith; ⁷if it is serving, then serve; if it is teaching, then teach; ⁸if it is to encourage, then give encouragement; if it is giving, then give generously; if it is to lead,*ⁱ* do it diligently; if it is to show mercy, do it cheerfully.

at issue: body image

12:1–2 How would you describe your body? Would you use the words "living sacrifice"? Do you view your body as God's? Or do you compare your appearance to others' and worry about what others think of your body, primarily because you want to be noticed or to feel a sense of approval? The purpose of your body, in fact the purpose of your *life,* is to glorify God by loving him and loving others. It's not about you. It's *really* not about you. It's about laying down your life—heart, mind, soul *and* body—all for the sake of God's kingdom.

ᵃ *26* Or *and so*   ᵇ *27* Or *will be*   ᶜ *27* Isaiah 59:20,21; 27:9 (see Septuagint); Jer. 31:33,34   ᵈ *31* Some manuscripts do not have *now.*   ᵉ *33* Or *riches and the wisdom and the*   ᶠ *34* Isaiah 40:13   ᵍ *35* Job 41:11   ʰ *6* Or *the*   ⁱ *8* Or *to provide for others*

myth# 92 "I WILL LOVE ALL MY CHILDREN THE SAME."

When I was pregnant with our first daughter, Sophie, I was so nervous that I could barely even smile at my baby shower. What if I'm a bad mother? I wondered. What if I can't do it right? I remember having nightmares about accidentally leaving her at the mall or forgetting to feed her. Then she was born, and I adjusted to being a mother much better than I'd expected.

Then daughter number two arrived. Maggie was a surprise. My doctor had told me she doubted I'd ever be able to carry another child, let alone conceive again, so when Maggie arrived safely, I knew she was the Lord's gift to me. She couldn't have been an easier baby. Sophie had been fussy and didn't like to be held when she was a baby, but Maggie was a happy baby and wanted me to hold her all the time. From what my mother tells me, Maggie is a mini-replica of me as a child.

Sometimes I see that Sophie is jealous. After all, she was nine when Maggie was born. She's been in school for years now and is really just her own person, much more like her father. I can tell that she envies the time I spend with Maggie and how much I fuss over her. But I also know that I love my girls equally. I really do. It's just that Maggie is more responsive to me. She wants to be with me—we take naps together, she follows me around the house, she goes shopping with me. And she's a striking child. Complete strangers stare and compliment me on her soft brown curls and almond-shaped eyes. She is everything I'd ever dreamed a child could be.

—Stasia

AS PARENTS, WE may feel like we should love our children equally, yet we do ourselves a disservice if we set out to love our children *in the exact same way.* (Note the difference.) Children are individuals with different wants, needs and interests. The parenting methods that worked with child number one may completely fail on child number two. The same holds true for the ways we express love to our children—what works for one may or may not work for another. One child may feel loved when his parents spend time with him. Another child may feel loved when her parents praise her.

It's up to *parents* to discover how each child wants to be loved. Resist the urge to love your children in the way you prefer. Cater your style to each child. Don't feel guilty if you bond more or differently with each child, but make sure that each of your children knows that she is deeply loved, just as she is, with the same amount of love that you also show her siblings.

Here are some ways to invest in your children and communicate your love to them:

- Study your child. Watch how she responds to each style of love you show her. Read *The Five Love Languages of Children* by Dr. Gary Chapman for tips on how to discern your child's preferred method of receiving love.

- As your family grows and changes, think through in advance how each child will react to those changes. Set aside time and energy to devote to loving each child.

- Strive for fairness in how you treat your children (not favoring one or giving more gifts to one), yet be willing to tailor your style for each child (see Proverbs 22:6).

- Ask for advice from older parents who have sorted through these issues with their children. What tips can they give you?

- Remember that God created each of us to be unique, exquisite creations. As parents, we have the privilege and the responsibility to honor the special traits and gifts each child has, just as God honors uniqueness in each of us.

1611

"Keep in mind that you will always love each child differently, because they are different people. And you will not treat them the same because their needs are unique."

—Gayle Peterson, MSSW, Ph.D.

"Dear children, let us not love with words or tongue but with actions and in truth."

1 JOHN 3:18

SEE ALSO

Psalm 139:1–4

1 Corinthians 13:8

James 2:1

For more on **Parenting**, check the index.

Love in Action

[9]Love must be sincere. Hate what is evil; cling to what is good. [10]Be devoted to one another in love. Honor one another above yourselves. [11]Never be lacking in zeal, but keep your spiritual fervor, serving the Lord. [12]Be joyful in hope, patient in affliction, faithful in prayer. [13]Share with the Lord's people who are in need. Practice hospitality.

[14]Bless those who persecute you; bless and do not curse. [15]Rejoice with those who rejoice; mourn with those who mourn. [16]Live in harmony with one another. Do not be proud, but be willing to associate with people of low position.[a] Do not think you are superior.

[17]Do not repay anyone evil for evil. Be careful to do what is right in the eyes of everyone. [18]If it is possible, as far as it depends on you, live at peace with everyone. [19]Do not take revenge, my dear friends, but leave room for God's wrath, for it is written: "It is mine to avenge; I will repay,"[b] says the Lord. [20]On the contrary:

> "If your enemy is hungry, feed him;
>   if he is thirsty, give him something to drink.
> In doing this, you will heap burning coals on his head."[c]

[21]Do not be overcome by evil, but overcome evil with good.

Submission to Governing Authorities

13 Let everyone be subject to the governing authorities, for there is no authority except that which God has established. The authorities that exist have been established by God. [2]Consequently, whoever rebels against the authority is rebelling against what God has instituted, and those who do so will bring judgment on themselves. [3]For rulers hold no terror for those who do right, but for those who do wrong. Do you want to be free from fear of the one in authority? Then do what is right and you will be commended. [4]For the one in authority is God's servant for your good. But if you do wrong, be afraid, for rulers do not bear the sword for no reason. They are God's servants, agents of wrath to bring punishment on the wrongdoer. [5]Therefore, it is necessary to submit to the authorities, not only because of possible punishment but also as a matter of conscience.

[6]This is also why you pay taxes, for the authorities are God's servants, who give their full time to governing. [7]Give to everyone what you owe: If you owe taxes, pay taxes; if revenue, then revenue; if respect, then respect; if honor, then honor.

"conversations"

authority «» 13:1–5

1» Should you submit to a governing authority you disagree with? If so, why?

2» Is it ever OK for a Christian to rebel against an authority? If so, when?

3» What or who are the authorities in your life? How well do you submit to them?

For more on **authority**, check the index.
For the next Conversations, go to p. 1623.

Love Fulfills the Law

[8]Let no debt remain outstanding, except the continuing debt to love one another, for whoever loves others has fulfilled the law. [9]The commandments, "You shall not commit adultery," "You shall not murder," "You shall not steal," "You shall not covet,"[d] and whatever other command there may be, are summed up in this one command: "Love your neighbor as yourself."[e] [10]Love does no harm to its neighbor. Therefore love is the fulfillment of the law.

The Day Is Near

[11]And do this, understanding the present time. The hour has already come for you to wake up from your slumber, because our salvation is nearer now than when we first believed. [12]The night is nearly

---

[a] **16** Or *willing to do menial work*   [b] **19** Deut. 32:35   [c] **20** Prov. 25:21,22   [d] **9** Exodus 20:13-15,17; Deut. 5:17-19,21   [e] **9** Lev. 19:18

over; the day is almost here. So let us put aside the deeds of darkness and put on the armor of light. [13] Let us behave decently, as in the daytime, not in carousing and drunkenness, not in sexual immorality and debauchery, not in dissension and jealousy. [14] Rather, clothe yourselves with the Lord Jesus Christ, and do not think about how to gratify the desires of the sinful nature. [a]

The Weak and the Strong

14 Accept those whose faith is weak, without quarreling over disputable matters. [2] One person's faith allows them to eat everything, but another person, whose faith is weak, eats only vegetables. [3] The one who eats everything must not treat with contempt the one who does not, and the one who does not eat everything must not judge the one who does, for God has accepted that person. [4] Who are you to judge someone else's servant? To their own master they stand or fall. And they will stand, for the Lord is able to make them stand.

[5] Some consider one day more sacred than another; others consider every day alike. Everyone should be fully convinced in their own mind. [6] Those who regard one day as special do so to the Lord. Those who eat meat do so to the Lord, for they give thanks to God; and those who abstain do so to the Lord and give thanks to God. [7] For we do not live to ourselves alone and we do not die to ourselves alone. [8] If we live, we live to the Lord; and if we die, we die to the Lord. So, whether we live or die, we belong to the Lord. [9] For this very reason, Christ died and returned to life so that he might be the Lord of both the dead and the living.

[10] You, then, why do you judge your brother or sister? Or why do you treat your brother or sister with contempt? For we will all stand before God's judgment seat. [11] It is written:

> "'As surely as I live,' says the Lord,
> 'every knee will bow before me;
>   every tongue will confess to God.'" [b]

[12] So then, we will all give an account of ourselves to God.

[13] Therefore let us stop passing judgment on one another. Instead, make up your mind not to put any stumbling block or obstacle in the way of a brother or sister. [14] I am convinced, being fully persuaded in the Lord Jesus, that nothing is unclean in itself. But if anyone regards something as unclean, then for that person it is unclean. [15] If your brother or sister is distressed because of what you eat, you are no longer acting in love. Do not by your eating destroy your brother or sister for whom Christ died. [16] Therefore do not let what you know is good be spoken of as evil. [17] For the kingdom of God is not a matter of eating and drinking, but of righteousness, peace and joy in the Holy Spirit, [18] because anyone who serves Christ in this way is pleasing to God and receives human approval.

[19] Let us therefore make every effort to do what leads to peace and to mutual edification. [20] Do not destroy the work of God for the sake of food. All food is clean, but it is wrong for a person to eat anything that causes someone else to stumble. [21] It is better not to eat meat or drink wine or to do anything else that will cause your brother or sister to fall.

[22] So whatever you believe about these things keep between yourself and God. Blessed are those who do not condemn themselves by what they approve. [23] But those who have doubts are condemned if they eat, because their eating is not from faith; and everything that does not come from faith is sin.

atissue:alcohol

14:19–23 Ashley believes she has freedom in her spiritual life to drink alcohol, as long as she doesn't get drunk. In her opinion, Christians who won't touch alcohol are legalistic. Ashley loves to flaunt her freedom and argue her point. Anna also believes God gave her the freedom to drink in moderation. But she's aware she could cause others to stumble. Because she's more concerned about peace and building up others' faith, she exercises her freedom quietly. Addy chooses not to drink at all in order to be a witness to others, but she can't help but look down on those who do. Who's got it right?

1613

---

15 We who are strong ought to bear with the failings of the weak and not to please ourselves. [2]We should all please our neighbors for their good, to build them up. [3]For even Christ did not please himself but, as it is written: "The insults of those who insult you have fallen on me."[a] [4]For everything that was written in the past was written to teach us, so that through the endurance taught in the Scriptures and the encouragement they provide we might have hope.

[5]May the God who gives endurance and encouragement give you the same attitude of mind toward each other that Christ Jesus had, [6]so that with one mind and one voice you may glorify the God and Father of our Lord Jesus Christ.

[7]Accept one another, then, just as Christ accepted you, in order to bring praise to God. [8]For I tell you that Christ has become a servant of the Jews[b] on behalf of God's truth, so that the promises made to the patriarchs might be confirmed [9]and, moreover, that the Gentiles might glorify God for his mercy. As it is written:

> "Therefore I will praise you among the Gentiles;
>   I will sing the praises of your name."[c]

[10]Again, it says,

> "Rejoice, you Gentiles, with his people."[d]

[11]And again,

> "Praise the Lord, all you Gentiles;
>   let all the peoples extol him."[e]

[12]And again, Isaiah says,

> "The Root of Jesse will spring up,
>   one who will arise to rule over the nations;
>   in him the Gentiles will hope."[f]

[13]May the God of hope fill you with all joy and peace as you trust in him, so that you may overflow with hope by the power of the Holy Spirit.

Paul the Minister to the Gentiles

[14]I myself am convinced, my brothers and sisters, that you yourselves are full of goodness, filled with knowledge and competent to instruct one another. [15]Yet I have written you quite boldly on some points to remind you of them again, because of the grace God gave me [16]to be a minister of Christ Jesus to the Gentiles. He gave me the priestly duty of proclaiming the gospel of God, so that the Gentiles might become an offering acceptable to God, sanctified by the Holy Spirit.

[17]Therefore I glory in Christ Jesus in my service to God. [18]I will not venture to speak of anything except what Christ has accomplished through me in leading the Gentiles to obey God by what I have said and done— [19]by the power of signs and wonders, through the power of the Spirit of God. So from Jerusalem all the way around to Illyricum, I have fully proclaimed the gospel of Christ. [20]It has always been my ambition to preach the gospel where Christ was not known, so that I would not be building on someone else's foundation. [21]Rather, as it is written:

> "Those who were not told about him will see,
>   and those who have not heard will understand."[g]

[22]This is why I have often been hindered from coming to you.

Paul's Plan to Visit Rome

[23]But now that there is no more place for me to work in these regions, and since I have been longing for many years to visit you, [24]I plan to do so when I go to Spain. I hope to see you while passing through

1614

---

[a] *3* Psalm 69:9   [b] *8* Greek *circumcision*   [c] *9* 2 Samuel 22:50; Psalm 18:49   [d] *10* Deut. 32:43   [e] *11* Psalm 117:1   [f] *12* Isaiah 11:10 (see Septuagint)
[g] *21* Isaiah 52:15 (see Septuagint)

and to have you assist me on my journey there, after I have enjoyed your company for a while. ²⁵Now, however, I am on my way to Jerusalem in the service of the Lord's people there. ²⁶For Macedonia and Achaia were pleased to make a contribution for the poor among the Lord's people in Jerusalem. ²⁷They were pleased to do it, and indeed they owe it to them. For if the Gentiles have shared in the Jews' spiritual blessings, they owe it to the Jews to share with them their material blessings. ²⁸So after I have completed this task and have made sure that they have received this fruit, I will go to Spain and visit you on the way. ²⁹I know that when I come to you, I will come in the full measure of the blessing of Christ.

³⁰I urge you, brothers and sisters, by our Lord Jesus Christ and by the love of the Spirit, to join me in my struggle by praying to God for me. ³¹Pray that I may be kept safe from the unbelievers in Judea and that the contribution I take to Jerusalem may be favorably received by the Lord's people there, ³²so that by God's will I may come to you with joy and together with you be refreshed. ³³The God of peace be with you all. Amen.

Personal Greetings

16 I commend to you our sister Phoebe, a deacon*ᵃ* of the church in Cenchreae. ²I ask you to receive her in the Lord in a way worthy of his people and to give her any help she may need from you, for she has been the benefactor of many people, including me.

³Greet Priscilla*ᵇ* and Aquila, my co-workers in Christ Jesus. ⁴They risked their lives for me. Not only I but all the churches of the Gentiles are grateful to them.

⁵Greet also the church that meets at their house.

Greet my dear friend Epenetus, who was the first convert to Christ in the province of Asia.

⁶Greet Mary, who worked very hard for you.

⁷Greet Andronicus and Junia, my fellow Jews who have been in prison with me. They are outstanding among the apostles, and they were in Christ before I was.

⁸Greet Ampliatus, my dear friend in the Lord.

⁹Greet Urbanus, our co-worker in Christ, and my dear friend Stachys.

¹⁰Greet Apelles, whose fidelity to Christ has stood the test.

Greet those who belong to the household of Aristobulus.

¹¹Greet Herodion, my fellow Jew.

Greet those in the household of Narcissus who are in the Lord.

¹²Greet Tryphena and Tryphosa, those women who work hard in the Lord.

Greet my dear friend Persis, another woman who has worked very hard in the Lord.

¹³Greet Rufus, chosen in the Lord, and his mother, who has been a mother to me, too.

¹⁴Greet Asyncritus, Phlegon, Hermes, Patrobas, Hermas and the other brothers and sisters with them.

¹⁵Greet Philologus, Julia, Nereus and his sister, and Olympas and all the Lord's people who are with them.

¹⁶Greet one another with a holy kiss.

All the churches of Christ send greetings.

¹⁷I urge you, brothers and sisters, to watch out for those who cause divisions and put obstacles in your way that are contrary to the teaching you have learned. Keep away from them. ¹⁸For such people are not serving our Lord Christ, but their own appetites. By smooth talk and flattery they deceive the minds of naive people. ¹⁹Everyone has heard about your obedience, so I rejoice because of you; but I want you to be wise about what is good, and innocent about what is evil.

²⁰The God of peace will soon crush Satan under your feet.

The grace of our Lord Jesus be with you.

²¹Timothy, my co-worker, sends his greetings to you, as do Lucius, Jason and Sosipater, my fellow Jews.

²²I, Tertius, who wrote down this letter, greet you in the Lord.

_____
ᵃ 1 Or servant ᵇ 3 Greek Prisca, a variant of Priscilla

HE IS: the God of peace

16:17–20 Paul sent personal greetings to his friends in Rome and commended them for their obedience. He warned them against divisions and expressed his confidence that *the God of peace* would prove victorious over divisive disruptions within the church.

If Paul wrote a letter to your church, would he praise you by name? Would he have to scold you and your church for divisions and bickering? Or would he commend you for the way you get along together? Because we worship *the God of peace*, we are to be at peace with each other (see Hebrews 12:14).

For the next He Is, go to p. 1618.

²³ [24] Gaius, whose hospitality I and the whole church here enjoy, sends you his greetings.

Erastus, who is the city's director of public works, and our brother Quartus send you their greetings. *

²⁵ Now to him who is able to establish you in accordance with my gospel, the message I proclaim about Jesus Christ, in keeping with the revelation of the mystery hidden for long ages past, ²⁶ but now revealed and made known through the prophetic writings by the command of the eternal God, so that all the Gentiles might come to faith and obedience— ²⁷ to the only wise God be glory forever through Jesus Christ! Amen.

ᵃ 23 Some manuscripts *their greetings.* *²⁴May the grace of our Lord Jesus Christ be with all of you. Amen.*

1 corinthians

AUTHOR
The apostle Paul.

AUDIENCE
Followers of Jesus; originally written to the church in Corinth.

DATE
About A.D. 55.

SETTING
Paul wrote from Ephesus to the church in Corinth, a pagan cosmopolitan city in Greece. He started this church during his second missionary journey.

VERSES TO REMEMBER
"Do you not know that your bodies are temples of the Holy Spirit, who is in you, whom you have received from God? You are not your own; you were bought at a price. Therefore honor God with your bodies." (6:19–20)

THEME TO CONSIDER
Christians must stand out from the crowd when they choose to follow Jesus.

1617

1 corinthians 1:1

1 Paul, called to be an apostle of Christ Jesus by the will of God, and our brother Sosthenes,

²To the church of God in Corinth, to those sanctified in Christ Jesus and called to be his holy people, together with all those everywhere who call on the name of our Lord Jesus Christ—their Lord and ours:

³Grace and peace to you from God our Father and the Lord Jesus Christ.

Thanksgiving

⁴I always thank my God for you because of his grace given you in Christ Jesus. ⁵For in him you have been enriched in every way—with all kinds of speech and with all knowledge— ⁶God thus confirming our testimony about Christ among you. ⁷Therefore you do not lack any spiritual gift as you eagerly wait for our Lord Jesus Christ to be revealed. ⁸He will also keep you firm to the end, so that you will be blameless on the day of our Lord Jesus Christ. ⁹God is faithful, who has called you into fellowship with his Son, Jesus Christ our Lord.

HE IS: faithful

1:5–9 Paul reminded the Corinthians that they didn't lack anything, that God would keep them firm to the end, that God would make them blameless, that God called them into fellowship with Jesus. The Corinthians' salvation did not depend on them; it depended on God, and he is *faithful*.

When you feel poorly equipped to live a life that's pleasing to God or to endure a particular trial, remember that your salvation doesn't depend on you. True faith is not based on your ability to come through for God but on his faithfulness to keep his promises—which he'll always do because he's *faithful*.

For the next He Is, go to p. 1620.

A Church Divided Over Leaders

¹⁰I appeal to you, brothers and sisters, in the name of our Lord Jesus Christ, that all of you agree with one another in what you say and that there be no divisions among you, but that you be perfectly united in mind and thought. ¹¹My brothers and sisters, some from Chloe's household have informed me that there are quarrels among you. ¹²What I mean is this: One of you says, "I follow Paul"; another, "I follow Apollos"; another, "I follow Cephas*"; still another, "I follow Christ."

¹³Is Christ divided? Was Paul crucified for you? Were you baptized into*ᵇ* the name of Paul? ¹⁴I thank God that I did not baptize any of you except Crispus and Gaius, ¹⁵so no one can say that you were baptized into my name. ¹⁶(Yes, I also baptized the household of Stephanas; beyond that, I don't remember if I baptized anyone else.) ¹⁷For Christ did not send me to baptize, but to preach the gospel—not with wisdom and eloquence, lest the cross of Christ be emptied of its power.

Christ Crucified Is God's Power and Wisdom

¹⁸For the message of the cross is foolishness to those who are perishing, but to us who are being saved it is the power of God. ¹⁹For it is written:

> "I will destroy the wisdom of the wise;
> the intelligence of the intelligent I will frustrate."*ᶜ*

²⁰Where are the wise? Where is the teacher of the law? Where is the philosopher of this age? Has not God made foolish the wisdom of the world? ²¹For since in the wisdom of God the world through its wisdom did not know him, God was pleased through the foolishness of what was preached to save those who believe. ²²Jews demand signs and Greeks look for wisdom, ²³but we preach Christ crucified: a stum-

---

ᵃ 12 That is, Peter   ᵇ 13 Or in; also in verse 15   ᶜ 19 Isaiah 29:14 bling block to Jews and foolishness to Gentiles, [24]but to those whom God has called, both Jews and Greeks, Christ the power of God and the wisdom of God. [25]For the foolishness of God is wiser than human wisdom, and the weakness of God is stronger than human strength.

[26]Brothers and sisters, think of what you were when you were called. Not many of you were wise by human standards; not many were influential; not many were of noble birth. [27]But God chose the foolish things of the world to shame the wise; God chose the weak things of the world to shame the strong. [28]God chose the lowly things of this world and the despised things—and the things that are not—to nullify the things that are, [29]so that no one may boast before him. [30]It is because of him that you are in Christ Jesus, who has become for us wisdom from God—that is, our righteousness, holiness and redemption. [31]Therefore, as it is written: "Let those who boast boast in the Lord."[a]

2 And so it was with me, brothers and sisters. When I came to you, I did not come with eloquence or human wisdom as I proclaimed to you the testimony about God.[b] [2]For I resolved to know nothing while I was with you except Jesus Christ and him crucified. [3]I came to you in weakness with great fear and trembling. [4]My message and my preaching were not with wise and persuasive words, but with a demonstration of the Spirit's power, [5]so that your faith might not rest on human wisdom, but on God's power.

God's Wisdom Revealed by the Spirit

[6]We do, however, speak a message of wisdom among the mature, but not the wisdom of this age or of the rulers of this age, who are coming to nothing. [7]No, we declare God's wisdom, a mystery that has been hidden and that God destined for our glory before time began. [8]None of the rulers of this age understood it, for if they had, they would not have crucified the Lord of glory. [9]However, as it is written:

> "What no eye has seen,
>   what no ear has heard,
> and what no human mind has conceived—
>   these things God has prepared for those who love him"[c]—

[10]for God has revealed them to us by his Spirit.

The Spirit searches all things, even the deep things of God. [11]For who knows a person's thoughts except that person's own spirit within? In the same way no one knows the thoughts of God except the Spirit of God. [12]We have not received the spirit of the world but the Spirit who is from God, that we may understand what God has freely given us. [13]This is what we speak, not in words taught us by human wisdom but in words taught by the Spirit, explaining spiritual realities with Spirit-taught words.[d] [14]The person without the Spirit does not accept the things that come from the Spirit of God but considers them foolishness, and cannot understand them because they are discerned only through the Spirit. [15]The person with the Spirit makes judgments about all things, but such a person is not subject to merely human judgments, [16]for,

> "Who has known the mind of the Lord
>   so as to instruct him?"[e]

But we have the mind of Christ.

The Church and Its Leaders

3 Brothers and sisters, I could not address you as spiritual but as worldly—mere infants in Christ. [2]I gave you milk, not solid food, for you were not yet ready for it. Indeed, you are still not ready. [3]You are still worldly. For since there is jealousy and quarreling among you, are you not worldly? Are you not acting like mere human beings? [4]For when one says, "I follow Paul," and another, "I follow Apollos," are you not mere human beings?

[5]What, after all, is Apollos? And what is Paul? Only servants, through whom you came to believe—as the Lord has assigned to each his task. [6]I planted the seed, Apollos watered it, but God has been

1619

---

[a] 31 Jer. 9:24   [b] 1 Some manuscripts as I proclaimed to you God's mystery   [c] 9 Isaiah 64:4   [d] 13 Or Spirit, interpreting spiritual truths to those who are spiritual   [e] 16 Isaiah 40:13

making it grow. ⁷So neither the one who plants nor the one who waters is anything, but only God, who makes things grow. ⁸The one who plants and the one who waters have one purpose, and they will each be rewarded according to their own labor. ⁹For we are God's co-workers; you are God's field, God's building.

¹⁰By the grace God has given me, I laid a foundation as a wise builder, and someone else is building on it. But each one should build with care. ¹¹For no one can lay any foundation other than the one already laid, which is Jesus Christ. ¹²If anyone builds on this foundation using gold, silver, costly stones, wood, hay or straw, ¹³their work will be shown for what it is, because the Day will bring it to light. It will be revealed with fire, and the fire will test the quality of each person's work. ¹⁴If what has been built survives, the builder will receive a reward. ¹⁵If it is burned up, the builder will suffer loss but yet will be saved—even though only as one escaping through the flames.

HE IS: testing your work

3:10–15 Paul, the expert builder, made sure that he always laid his work on the only sure foundation: Jesus himself. Paul warned believers against building their work on any lesser foundation or with inferior materials. Someday when Christ *tests our work*, anything that's not built on him will be burned away.

Do you want your ministry to count for eternity? Then make sure that it's always built on Jesus and that your motives are sincere. Don't build your work on anything else—on a clever program, on relationships or on human principles. When Jesus tests your work with fire, what will be left (see 1 Peter 1:7)?

For the next He Is, go to p. 1638.

¹⁶Don't you know that you yourselves are God's temple and that God's Spirit dwells in your midst? ¹⁷If anyone destroys God's temple, God will destroy that person; for God's temple is sacred, and you together are that temple.

¹⁸Do not deceive yourselves. If any of you think you are wise by the standards of this age, you should become "fools" so that you may become wise. ¹⁹For the wisdom of this world is foolishness in God's sight. As it is written: "He catches the wise in their craftiness"ᵃ; ²⁰and again, "The Lord knows that the thoughts of the wise are futile."ᵇ ²¹So then, no more boasting about human leaders! All things are yours, ²²whether Paul or Apollos or Cephasᶜ or the world or life or death or the present or the future—all are yours, ²³and you are of Christ, and Christ is of God.

The Nature of True Apostleship

4 This, then, is how you ought to regard us: as servants of Christ and as those entrusted with the mysteries God has revealed. ²Now it is required that those who have been given a trust must prove faithful. ³I care very little if I am judged by you or by any human court; indeed, I do not even judge myself. ⁴My conscience is clear, but that does not make me innocent. It is the Lord who judges me. ⁵Therefore judge nothing before the appointed time; wait till the Lord comes. He will bring to light what is hidden in darkness and will expose the motives of people's hearts. At that time each will receive their praise from God.

⁶Now, brothers and sisters, I have applied these things to myself and Apollos for your benefit, so that you may learn from us the meaning of the saying, "Do not go beyond what is written." Then you will not be puffed up in being a follower of one of us over against the other. ⁷For who makes you different from anyone else? What do you have that you did not receive? And if you did receive it, why do you boast as though you did not?

ᵃ *19* Job 5:13   ᵇ *20* Psalm 94:11   ᶜ *22* That is, Peter

[8] Already you have all you want! Already you have become rich! You have begun to reign—and that without us! How I wish that you really had begun to reign so that we also might reign with you! [9] For it seems to me that God has put us apostles on display at the end of the procession, like those condemned to die in the arena. We have been made a spectacle to the whole universe, to angels as well as to human beings. [10] We are fools for Christ, but you are so wise in Christ! We are weak, but you are strong! You are honored, we are dishonored! [11] To this very hour we go hungry and thirsty, we are in rags, we are brutally treated, we are homeless. [12] We work hard with our own hands. When we are cursed, we bless; when we are persecuted, we endure it; [13] when we are slandered, we answer kindly. We have become the scum of the earth, the garbage of the world—right up to this moment.

Paul's Appeal and Warning

[14] I am writing this not to shame you but to warn you as my dear children. [15] Even if you had ten thousand guardians in Christ, you do not have many fathers, for in Christ Jesus I became your father through the gospel. [16] Therefore I urge you to imitate me. [17] For this reason I have sent to you Timothy, my son whom I love, who is faithful in the Lord. He will remind you of my way of life in Christ Jesus, which agrees with what I teach everywhere in every church.

[18] Some of you have become arrogant, as if I were not coming to you. [19] But I will come to you very soon, if the Lord is willing, and then I will find out not only how these arrogant people are talking, but what power they have. [20] For the kingdom of God is not a matter of talk but of power. [21] What do you prefer? Shall I come to you with a rod of discipline, or shall I come in love and with a gentle spirit?

Dealing With a Case of Incest

5 It is actually reported that there is sexual immorality among you, and of a kind that even pagans do not tolerate: A man has his father's wife. [2] And you are proud! Shouldn't you rather have gone into mourning and have put out of your fellowship the man who has been doing this? [3] For my part, even though I am not physically present, I am with you in spirit. As one who is present with you in this way, I have already passed judgment in the name of our Lord Jesus on the one who has been doing this. [4] So when you are assembled and I am with you in spirit, and the power of our Lord Jesus is present, [5] hand this man over to Satan for the destruction of the sinful nature[a] so that his spirit may be saved on the day of the Lord.

[6] Your boasting is not good. Don't you know that a little yeast leavens the whole batch of dough? [7] Get rid of the old yeast, so that you may be a new unleavened batch—as you really are. For Christ, our Passover lamb, has been sacrificed. [8] Therefore let us keep the Festival, not with the old bread leavened with malice and wickedness, but with the unleavened bread of sincerity and truth.

[9] I wrote to you in my letter not to associate with sexually immoral people— [10] not at all meaning the people of this world who are immoral, or the greedy and swindlers, or idolaters. In that case you would have to leave this world. [11] But now I am writing to you that you must not associate with any who claim to be fellow believers but are sexually immoral or greedy, idolaters or slanderers, drunkards or swindlers. With such persons do not even eat.

[12] What business is it of mine to judge those outside the church? Are you not to judge those inside? [13] God will judge those outside. "Expel the wicked person from among you."[b]

Lawsuits Among Believers

6 If any of you has a dispute with another, do you dare to take it before the ungodly for judgment instead of before the Lord's people? [2] Or do you not know that the Lord's people will judge the world? And if you are to judge the world, are you not competent to judge trivial cases? [3] Do you not know that we will judge angels? How much more the things of this life! [4] Therefore, if you have disputes about such matters, do you ask for a ruling from those whose way of life is scorned in the church? [5] I say this to shame you. Is it possible that there is nobody among you wise enough to judge a dispute between believers? [6] But instead, one brother goes to law against another—and this in front of unbelievers!

[7] The very fact that you have lawsuits among you means you have been completely defeated already.

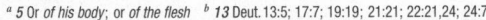

[a] *5* Or *of his body; or of the flesh* [b] *13* Deut. 13:5; 17:7; 19:19; 21:21; 22:21,24; 24:7

Why not rather be wronged? Why not rather be cheated? ⁸Instead, you yourselves cheat and do wrong, and you do this to your brothers and sisters. ⁹Or do you not know that wrongdoers will not inherit the kingdom of God? Do not be deceived: Neither the sexually immoral nor idolaters nor adulterers nor male prostitutes nor practicing homosexuals ¹⁰nor thieves nor the greedy nor drunkards nor slanderers nor swindlers will inherit the kingdom of God. ¹¹And that is what some of you were. But you were washed, you were sanctified, you were justified in the name of the Lord Jesus Christ and by the Spirit of our God.

Sexual Immorality

¹²"I have the right to do anything," you say—but not everything is beneficial. "I have the right to do anything"—but I will not be mastered by anything. ¹³You say, "Food for the stomach and the stomach for food, and God will destroy them both." The body, however, is not meant for sexual immorality but for the Lord, and the Lord for the body. ¹⁴By his power God raised the Lord from the dead, and he will raise us also. ¹⁵Do you not know that your bodies are members of Christ himself? Shall I then take the members of Christ and unite them with a prostitute? Never! ¹⁶Do you not know that he who unites himself with a prostitute is one with her in body? For it is said, "The two will become one flesh."ᵃ ¹⁷But whoever is united with the Lord is one with him in spirit.ᵇ

at issue: sexual sin

6:9–20 Satan is big into recycling—telling the same lies to every generation. He had Christians in Corinth believing their bodies were created for sex and should be satisfied in every possible way, the same way a stomach's designed for food and should always be fed. It was a lie then and it's a lie now. Your body was created to honor God. It doesn't belong to you; it belongs to him. Whatever sexual sin is in your past—premarital sex, adultery, homosexuality, incest, promiscuity—God has washed you clean from its filth. Don't go back there! Keep fleeing to God instead.

¹⁸Flee from sexual immorality. All other sins people commit are outside their bodies, but those who sin sexually sin against their own bodies. ¹⁹Do you not know that your bodies are temples of the Holy Spirit, who is in you, whom you have received from God? You are not your own; ²⁰you were bought at a price. Therefore honor God with your bodies.

Concerning Married Life

7 Now for the matters you wrote about: "It is good for a man not to have sexual relations with a woman." ²But since sexual immorality is occurring, each man should have sexual relations with his own wife, and each woman with her own husband. ³The husband should fulfill his marital duty to his wife, and likewise the wife to her husband. ⁴The wife does not have authority over her own body but yields it to her husband. In the same way, the husband does not have authority over his own body but yields it to his wife. ⁵Do not deprive each other except perhaps by mutual consent and for a time, so that you may devote yourselves to prayer. Then come together again so that Satan will not tempt you because of your lack of self-control. ⁶I say this as a concession, not as a command. ⁷I wish that all of you were as I am. But each of you has your own gift from God; one has this gift, another has that.

⁸Now to the unmarriedᶜ and the widows I say: It is good for them to stay unmarried, as I do. ⁹But if they cannot control themselves, they should marry, for it is better to marry than to burn with passion.

¹⁰To the married I give this command (not I, but the Lord): A wife must not separate from her husband. ¹¹But if she does, she must remain unmarried or else be reconciled to her husband. And a husband must not divorce his wife.

¹²To the rest I say this (I, not the Lord): If any brother has a wife who is not a believer and she is willing to live with him, he must not divorce her. ¹³And if a woman has a husband who is not a believer and he is willing to live with her, she must not divorce him. ¹⁴For the unbelieving husband has been sanctified through his wife, and the unbelieving wife has been sanctified through her believing husband.

ᵃ *16* Gen. 2:24 ᵇ *17* Or *in the Spirit* ᶜ *8* Or *widowers*

Otherwise your children would be unclean, but as it is, they are holy.

¹⁵But if the unbeliever leaves, let it be so. The brother or sister is not bound in such circumstances; God has called us to live in peace. ¹⁶How do you know, wife, whether you will save your husband? Or, how do you know, husband, whether you will save your wife?

Concerning Change of Status

¹⁷Nevertheless, each of you should live as a believer in whatever situation the Lord has assigned to you, just as God has called you. This is the rule I lay down in all the churches. ¹⁸Was a man already circumcised when he was called? He should not become uncircumcised. Was a man uncircumcised when he was called? He should not be circumcised. ¹⁹Circumcision is nothing and uncircumcision is nothing. Keeping God's commands is what counts. ²⁰Each of you should remain in the situation you were in when God called you.

²¹Were you a slave when you were called? Don't let it trouble you—although if you can gain your freedom, do so. ²²For those who were slaves when called to faith in the Lord are the Lord's freed people; similarly, those who were free when called are Christ's slaves. ²³You were bought at a price; do not become slaves of human beings. ²⁴Brothers and sisters, all of you, as responsible to God, should remain in the situation in which God called you.

Concerning the Unmarried

²⁵Now about virgins: I have no command from the Lord, but I give a judgment as one who by the Lord's mercy is trustworthy. ²⁶Because of the present crisis, I think that it is good for a man to remain as he is. ²⁷Are you pledged to a woman? Do not seek to be released. Are you free from such a commitment? Do not look for a wife. ²⁸But if you do marry, you have not sinned; and if a virgin marries, she has not sinned. But those who marry will face many troubles in this life, and I want to spare you this.

²⁹What I mean, brothers and sisters, is that the time is short. From now on those who are married should live as if they were not; ³⁰those who mourn, as if they did not; those who are happy, as if they were not; those who buy something, as if it were not theirs to keep; ³¹those who use the things of the world, as if not engrossed in them. For this world in its present form is passing away.

³²I would like you to be free from concern. An unmarried man is concerned about the Lord's affairs—how he can please the Lord. ³³But a married man is concerned about the affairs of this world—how he can please his wife— ³⁴and his interests are divided. An unmarried woman or virgin is concerned about the Lord's affairs: Her aim is to be devoted to the Lord in both body and spirit. But a married woman is concerned about the affairs of this world—how she can please her husband. ³⁵I am saying this for your own good, not to restrict you, but that you may live in a right way in undivided devotion to the Lord.

atissue:marriage

7:12–16 In a world corrupted by sin and far from ideal, issues of morality get tricky. Paul was a Christian "Dear Abby" of sorts for the early church—giving advice about sticky situations the church faced.

Question: If one is married to a non-Christian, what should he or she do? After all, God wants believers to be married to other believers, but he also hates divorce.

Answer: Depends on the unbelieving spouse. If the spouse wants to stay together, then you stay. If the spouse wants to leave, let him or her go.

Now, keep reading to find out the rest of Paul's advice.

1623

"conversations

singleness «» 7:29–35

1» What has shaped your attitude toward singleness?

2» What are the advantages of being a Christian single?

3» Married or single, how can you develop "undivided devotion to the Lord"?

For more on **singleness**, check the index.
For the next Conversations, go to p. 1629.

myth# 93 "MARRIAGE WILL FULFILL ALL MY DREAMS."

From the time I was a little girl, I have collected bridal magazines, savoring ideas for my special day. Even now I find my mind drifting off to a lovely chapel, planning the details of the perfect wedding in my head. I'm a hopeless romantic and love the fairy-tale idea of a handsome prince riding up on a white horse and whisking me away to live happily ever after.

But I'm a realist too. I know we'll have to divvy up the chores, and we might even have an argument or disagreement here and there. I realize marriage is hard work. But I also know it will finally fulfill my most important dreams.

I can't wait to get married so that I will never have to be alone again. I won't be by myself on holidays, and I'll always have someone to eat dinner with on weekends. I'll never have those ugly and unloved feelings again when I really need someone to love me unconditionally and comfort me. I know that having a husband will make me feel whole and happy.

In many ways, I feel as if my life is "on hold" until I meet that one special person. I find myself waiting to take trips until I am married and can travel with my husband. I know they would be so much more fun with him than with my single girlfriends or family. I wait to purchase special items for myself, thinking that one day someone will buy them for me. I'm in preparation mode now (even though that period is stretching way past my original cut-off date). I can't wait for God to bring me a wonderful person who will make all of my dreams come true.

—Brandi

WHILE MARRIAGE IS

a wonderful gift from God, it is certainly not a guarantee that you will always be happy. In fact, Paul considered singleness preferable to marriage (see 1 Corinthians 7:8,34). Any woman who goes into marriage expecting her husband to make all her dreams come true is sure to be disappointed. No one person, no matter how wonderful or godly he is, can fulfill all of your dreams or meet all your needs. It's impossible. He is just a man, as you are just a woman. There is only one perfect Bridegroom who will never let you down.

When you look to God to meet your primary needs for love, affection and acceptance, you can then freely enjoy your other relationships. On the other hand, if you're always looking to people to meet the needs in you that only God can meet, you'll never find true fulfillment. If you need some help in this area, keep the following in mind:

- Single women often make the mistake of thinking their lives will really start when they get married. Instead of living in the moment, they fantasize about *someday*. Are there ways you have put your life on "pause," waiting for a man to come along and fulfill your dreams? If so, press "play" and start living in the moments God has given you to enjoy today.

- Single women often believe that after they marry, they will never be lonely again. This simply isn't true. Even women in the best of marriages feel lonely and sad at times. The key is not whether you're married or single; it's where you look to get your needs met (see Psalm 142:5). Do you look to God to meet your primary love needs?

- Are you content in the situation God has placed you in now? Did you know that contentment is a learned behavior (see Philippians 4:11)? It doesn't come when you get everything you want but when you choose to be thankful for what you do have.

When you're tempted to put all of your hopes into the dream of marriage, stop to count your blessings now. Then enjoy the most wonderful love relationship possible—with your Lord Jesus. If God should bring a husband to you someday, you'll be able to enjoy him out of a content and full heart.

> "The belief in a happily-ever-after marriage is one of the most widely held, destructive marriage myths. But it's only the tip of the marital-myth iceberg. Every difficult marriage is plagued by misconceptions about what marriage should be."
>
> —Les and Leslie Parrott

1625

> "I am not saying this because I am in need, for I have learned to be content whatever the circumstances."
>
> PHILIPPIANS 4:11

SEE ALSO

Psalm 62:8

Psalm 139:23–24

1 Corinthians 7:1–40

For more on **Marriage**, check the index.

³⁶If anyone is worried that he might not be acting honorably toward the virgin he is engaged to, and if she is getting beyond the usual age for marrying*a* and he feels he ought to marry, he should do as he wants. He is not sinning. They should get married. ³⁷But the man who has settled the matter in his own mind, who is under no compulsion but has control over his own will, and who has made up his mind not to marry the virgin—this man also does the right thing. ³⁸So then, he who marries the virgin does right, but he who does not marry her does better.*b*

³⁹A woman is bound to her husband as long as he lives. But if her husband dies, she is free to marry anyone she wishes, but he must belong to the Lord. ⁴⁰In my judgment, she is happier if she stays as she is—and I think that I too have the Spirit of God.

Concerning Food Sacrificed to Idols

8 Now about food sacrificed to idols: We know that "We all possess knowledge." But knowledge puffs up while love builds up. ²Those who think they know something do not yet know as they ought to know. ³But whoever loves God is known by God.*c*

⁴So then, about eating food sacrificed to idols: We know that "An idol is nothing at all in the world" and that "There is no God but one." ⁵For even if there are so-called gods, whether in heaven or on earth (as indeed there are many "gods" and many "lords"), ⁶yet for us there is but one God, the Father, from whom all things came and for whom we live; and there is but one Lord, Jesus Christ, through whom all things came and through whom we live.

⁷But not everyone possesses this knowledge. Some people are still so accustomed to idols that when they eat sacrificial food they think of it as having been sacrificed to a god, and since their conscience is weak, it is defiled. ⁸But food does not bring us near to God; we are no worse if we do not eat, and no better if we do.

⁹Be careful, however, that the exercise of your rights does not become a stumbling block to the weak. ¹⁰For if anyone with a weak conscience sees you, with all your knowledge, eating in an idol's temple, won't they be emboldened to eat what is sacrificed to idols? ¹¹So this weak brother or sister, for whom Christ died, is destroyed by your knowledge. ¹²When you sin against them in this way and wound their weak conscience, you sin against Christ. ¹³Therefore, if what I eat causes my brother or sister to fall into sin, I will never eat meat again, so that I will not cause them to fall.

Paul's Rights as an Apostle

9 Am I not free? Am I not an apostle? Have I not seen Jesus our Lord? Are you not the result of my work in the Lord? ²Even though I may not be an apostle to others, surely I am to you! For you are the seal of my apostleship in the Lord.

³This is my defense to those who sit in judgment on me. ⁴Don't we have the right to food and drink? ⁵Don't we have the right to take a believing wife along with us, as do the other apostles and the Lord's brothers and Cephas*d*? ⁶Or is it only I and Barnabas who don't have the right not to work for a living?

⁷Who serves as a soldier at his own expense? Who plants a vineyard and does not eat of its grapes? Who tends a flock and does not drink of the milk? ⁸Do I say this merely on human authority? Doesn't the Law say the same thing? ⁹For it is written in the Law of Moses: "Do not muzzle an ox while it is treading out the grain."*e* Is it about oxen that God is concerned? ¹⁰Surely he says this for us, doesn't he? Yes, this was written for us, because when farmers plow and thresh, they should be able to do so in the hope of sharing in the harvest. ¹¹If we have sown spiritual seed among you, is it too much if we reap a material harvest from you? ¹²If others have this right of support from you, shouldn't we have it all the more?

But we did not use this right. On the contrary, we put up with anything rather than hinder the gospel of Christ.

¹³Don't you know that those who serve in the temple get their food from the temple, and that those

1626

---

a **36** Or *if his (or her) passions are too strong*   *b* **36-38** Or ³⁶*If anyone thinks he is not treating his daughter properly, and if she is getting along in years (or if her passions are too strong), and he feels she ought to marry, he should do as he wants. He is not sinning. He should let her get married.* ³⁷*But the man who has settled the matter in his own mind, who is under no compulsion but has control over his own will, and who has made up his mind to keep the virgin unmarried— this man also does the right thing.* ³⁸*So then, he who gives his virgin in marriage does right, but he who does not give her in marriage does better.*   *c* **2,3** An early manuscript and another ancient witness *think they have knowledge do not yet know as they ought to know.* ³*But whoever loves truly knows.*   *d* **5** That is, Peter   *e* **9** Deut. 25:4

1627

who serve at the altar share in what is offered on the altar? [14]In the same way, the Lord has commanded that those who preach the gospel should receive their living from the gospel.

[15]But I have not used any of these rights. And I am not writing this in the hope that you will do such things for me, for I would rather die than allow anyone to deprive me of this boast. [16]For when I preach the gospel, I cannot boast, since I am compelled to preach. Woe to me if I do not preach the gospel! [17]If I preach voluntarily, I have a reward; if not voluntarily, I am simply discharging the trust committed to me. [18]What then is my reward? Just this: that in preaching the gospel I may offer it free of charge, and so not misuse my rights as a preacher of the gospel.

Paul's Use of His Freedom

[19]Though I am free and belong to no one, I have made myself a slave to everyone, to win as many as possible. [20]To the Jews I became like a Jew, to win the Jews. To those under the law I became like one under the law (though I myself am not under the law), so as to win those under the law. [21]To those not having the law I became like one not having the law (though I am not free from God's law but am under Christ's law), so as to win those not having the law. [22]To the weak I became weak, to win the weak. I have become all things to all people so that by all possible means I might save some. [23]I do all this for the sake of the gospel, that I may share in its blessings.

The Need for Self-Discipline

[24]Do you not know that in a race all the runners run, but only one gets the prize? Run in such a way as to get the prize. [25]Everyone who competes in the games goes into strict training. They do it to get a crown that will not last; but we do it to get a crown that will last forever. [26]Therefore I do not run like someone running aimlessly; I do not fight like a boxer beating the air. [27]No, I strike a blow to my body and make it my slave so that after I have preached to others, I myself will not be disqualified for the prize.

Warnings From Israel's History

10 For I do not want you to be ignorant of the fact, brothers and sisters, that our ancestors were all under the cloud and that they all passed through the sea. [2]They were all baptized into Moses in the cloud and in the sea. [3]They all ate the same spiritual food [4]and drank the same spiritual drink; for they drank from the spiritual rock that accompanied them, and that rock was Christ. [5]Nevertheless, God was not pleased with most of them; their bodies were scattered in the wilderness.

[6]Now these things occurred as examples to keep us from setting our hearts on evil things as they did. [7]Do not be idolaters, as some of them were; as it is written: "The people sat down to eat and drink and got up to indulge in revelry."[a] [8]We should not commit sexual immorality, as some of them did—and in one day twenty-three thousand of them died. [9]We should not test Christ,[b] as some of them did—and were killed by snakes. [10]And do not grumble, as some of them did—and were killed by the destroying angel.

[11]These things happened to them as examples and were written down as warnings for us, on whom the culmination of the ages has come. [12]So, if you think you are standing firm, be careful that you don't fall! [13]No temptation[c] has overtaken you except what is common to us all. And God is faithful; he

atissue:addiction

10:12–13 *Watch out!* If you think you're standing firm in the face of that oh-so-familiar temptation, be careful. As soon as you let down your guard, you're likely to fall again. Recognize that the pull of any addiction is strong, but God's power and love are stronger. He'll never let you be tempted beyond your limit. He always provides a way out so you can endure it—but it's up to you to take those God-given escape routes. Remind yourself that you are not alone. Others have wrestled with this same sin, so enlist someone else to help in your struggle.

---

[a] *7* Exodus 32:6   [b] *9* Some manuscripts *test the Lord*   [c] *13* The Greek for *temptation* and *tempted* can also mean *testing* and *tested.*

will not let you be tempted[a] beyond what you can bear. But when you are tempted,[a] he will also provide a way out so that you can endure it.

Idol Feasts and the Lord's Supper

[14]Therefore, my dear friends, flee from idolatry. [15]I speak to sensible people; judge for yourselves what I say. [16]Is not the cup of thanksgiving for which we give thanks a participation in the blood of Christ? And is not the bread that we break a participation in the body of Christ? [17]Because there is one loaf, we, who are many, are one body, for we all partake of the one loaf.

[18]Consider the people of Israel: Do not those who eat the sacrifices participate in the altar? [19]Do I mean then that food sacrificed to an idol is anything, or that an idol is anything? [20]No, but the sacrifices of pagans are offered to demons, not to God, and I do not want you to be participants with demons. [21]You cannot drink the cup of the Lord and the cup of demons too; you cannot have a part in both the Lord's table and the table of demons. [22]Are we trying to arouse the Lord's jealousy? Are we stronger than he?

The Believer's Freedom

[23]"I have the right to do anything," you say—but not everything is beneficial. "I have the right to do anything"—but not everything is constructive. [24]No one should seek their own good, but the good of others.

[25]Eat anything sold in the meat market without raising questions of conscience, [26]for, "The earth is the Lord's, and everything in it."[b]

[27]If an unbeliever invites you to a meal and you want to go, eat whatever is put before you without raising questions of conscience. [28]But if someone says to you, "This has been offered in sacrifice," then do not eat it, both for the sake of the one who told you and for the sake of conscience. [29]I am referring to the other person's conscience, not yours. For why is my freedom being judged by another's conscience? [30]If I take part in the meal with thankfulness, why am I denounced because of something I thank God for?

[31]So whether you eat or drink or whatever you do, do it all for the glory of God. [32]Do not cause anyone to stumble, whether Jews, Greeks or the church of God— [33]even as I try to please everyone in every way. For I am not seeking my own good but the good of many, so that they may be saved. [1]Follow my example, as I follow the example of Christ.

On Covering the Head in Worship

[2]I praise you for remembering me in everything and for holding to the traditions just as I passed them on to you. [3]But I want you to realize that the head of every man is Christ, and the head of the woman is man,[c] and the head of Christ is God. [4]Every man who prays or prophesies with his head covered dishonors his head. [5]But every woman who prays or prophesies with her head uncovered dishonors her head—it is the same as having her head shaved. [6]For if a woman does not cover her head, she might as well have her hair cut off; but if it is a disgrace for a woman to have her hair cut off or her head shaved, then she should cover her head.

[7]A man ought not to cover his head, since he is the image and glory of God; but woman is the glory of man. [8]For man did not come from woman, but woman from man; [9]neither was man created for woman, but woman for man. [10]It is for this reason that a woman ought to have authority over her own[d] head, because of the angels. [11]Nevertheless, in the Lord woman is not independent of man, nor is man independent of woman. [12]For as woman came from man, so also man is born of woman. But everything comes from God.

[13]Judge for yourselves: Is it proper for a woman to pray to God with her head uncovered? [14]Does not the very nature of things teach you that if a man has long hair, it is a disgrace to him, [15]but that if a woman has long hair, it is her glory? For long hair is given to her as a covering. [16]If anyone wants to be contentious about this, we have no other practice—nor do the churches of God.

---

[a] 13 The Greek for *temptation* and *tempted* can also mean *testing* and *tested.*   [b] 26 Psalm 24:1   [c] 3 Or *of the wife is her husband*   [d] 10 Or *have a sign of authority on her*

Correcting an Abuse of the Lord's Supper

¹⁷In the following directives I have no praise for you, for your meetings do more harm than good. ¹⁸In the first place, I hear that when you come together as a church, there are divisions among you, and to some extent I believe it. ¹⁹No doubt there have to be differences among you to show which of you have God's approval. ²⁰So then, when you come together, it is not the Lord's Supper you eat, ²¹for when you are eating, some of you go ahead with your own private suppers. As a result, one person remains hungry and another gets drunk. ²²Don't you have homes to eat and drink in? Or do you despise the church of God by humiliating those who have nothing? What shall I say to you? Shall I praise you? Certainly not in this matter!

²³For I received from the Lord what I also passed on to you: The Lord Jesus, on the night he was betrayed, took bread, ²⁴and when he had given thanks, he broke it and said, "This is my body, which is for you; do this in remembrance of me." ²⁵In the same way, after supper he took the cup, saying, "This cup is the new covenant in my blood; do this, whenever you drink it, in remembrance of me." ²⁶For whenever you eat this bread and drink this cup, you proclaim the Lord's death until he comes.

²⁷So then, whoever eats the bread or drinks the cup of the Lord in an unworthy manner will be guilty of sinning against the body and blood of the Lord. ²⁸Everyone ought to examine themselves before they eat of the bread and drink of the cup. ²⁹For those who eat and drink without discerning the body of Christ eat and drink judgment on themselves. ³⁰That is why many among you are weak and sick, and a number of you have fallen asleep. ³¹But if we were more discerning with regard to ourselves, we would not come under such judgment. ³²Nevertheless, when we are judged in this way by the Lord, we are being disciplined so that we will not be finally condemned with the world.

³³So then, my brothers and sisters, when you gather to eat, you should all eat together. ³⁴Those who are hungry should eat something at home, so that when you meet together it may not result in judgment.

And when I come I will give further directions.

Concerning Spiritual Gifts

12 Now about the gifts of the Spirit, brothers and sisters, I do not want you to be uninformed. ²You know that when you were pagans, somehow or other you were influenced and led astray to mute idols. ³Therefore I want you to know that no one who is speaking by the Spirit of God says, "Jesus be cursed," and no one can say, "Jesus is Lord," except by the Holy Spirit.

⁴There are different kinds of gifts, but the same Spirit distributes them. ⁵There are different kinds of service, but the same Lord. ⁶There are different kinds of working, but in all of them and in everyone it is the same God at work.

⁷Now to each one the manifestation of the Spirit is given for the common good. ⁸To one there is given through the Spirit a message of wisdom, to another a message of knowledge by means of the same Spirit, ⁹to another faith by the same Spirit, to another gifts of healing by that one Spirit, ¹⁰to another miraculous powers, to another prophecy, to another distinguishing between spirits, to another speaking in different kinds of tongues,ᵃ and to still another the interpretation of tongues.ᵃ ¹¹All these are the work of one and the same Spirit, and he distributes them to each one, just as he determines.

Unity and Diversity in the Body

¹²Just as a body, though one, has many parts, but all its many parts form one body, so it is with Christ. ¹³For we were all baptized byᵇ one Spirit so as to form one body—whether Jews or Gentiles, slave or free—and we were all given the one Spirit to drink. ¹⁴Even so the body is not made up of one part but of many.

¹⁵Now if the foot should say, "Because I am not a hand,

conversations
giftedness «» 12:14–31

1» What spiritual gifts has God given you?

2» How are you using your gifts? Do you feel you could use your gifts more?

3» Are there spiritual gifts you consider more important than others? If so, why?

For more on **giftedness**, check the index. For the next Conversations, go to p. 1643.

ᵃ 10 Or languages; also in verse 28 ᵇ 13 Or with; or in

I do not belong to the body," it would not for that reason cease to be part of the body. [16]And if the ear should say, "Because I am not an eye, I do not belong to the body," it would not for that reason cease to be part of the body. [17]If the whole body were an eye, where would the sense of hearing be? If the whole body were an ear, where would the sense of smell be? [18]But in fact God has placed the parts in the body, every one of them, just as he wanted them to be. [19]If they were all one part, where would the body be? [20]As it is, there are many parts, but one body.

[21]The eye cannot say to the hand, "I don't need you!" And the head cannot say to the feet, "I don't need you!" [22]On the contrary, those parts of the body that seem to be weaker are indispensable, [23]and the parts that we think are less honorable we treat with special honor. And the parts that are unpresentable are treated with special modesty, [24]while our presentable parts need no special treatment. But God has put the body together, giving greater honor to the parts that lacked it, [25]so that there should be no division in the body, but that its parts should have equal concern for each other. [26]If one part suffers, every part suffers with it; if one part is honored, every part rejoices with it.

[27]Now you are the body of Christ, and each one of you is a part of it. [28]And God has placed in the church first of all apostles, second prophets, third teachers, then miracles, then gifts of healing, of helping, of guidance, and of different kinds of tongues. [29]Are all apostles? Are all prophets? Are all teachers? Do all work miracles? [30]Do all have gifts of healing? Do all speak in tongues[a]? Do all interpret? [31]Now eagerly desire[b] the greater gifts.

1630

Love Is Indispensable

And yet I will show you the most excellent way.

13 If I speak in human or angelic tongues,[c] but do not have love, I am only a resounding gong or a clanging cymbal. [2]If I have the gift of prophecy and can fathom all mysteries and all knowledge, and if I have a faith that can move mountains, but do not have love, I am nothing. [3]If I give all I possess to the poor and give over my body to hardship, that I may boast,[d] but do not have love, I gain nothing.

[4]Love is patient, love is kind. It does not envy, it does not boast, it is not proud. [5]It does not dishonor others, it is not self-seeking, it is not easily angered, it keeps no record of wrongs. [6]Love does not delight in evil but rejoices with the truth. [7]It always protects, always trusts, always hopes, always perseveres.

[8]Love never fails. But where there are prophecies, they will cease; where there are tongues, they will be stilled; where there is knowledge, it will pass away. [9]For we know in part and we prophesy in part, [10]but when completeness comes, what is in part disappears. [11]When I was a child, I talked like a child, I thought like a child, I reasoned like a child. When I became a man, I put the ways of childhood behind me. [12]For now we see only a reflection as in a mirror; then we shall see face to face. Now I know in part; then I shall know fully, even as I am fully known.

[13]And now these three remain: faith, hope and love. But the greatest of these is love.

at•issue:marriage

13:4–7 Perhaps your marriage isn't delivering the fairy-tale life you'd dreamed of. Your prince devotes all his time and energy to work, sports, the computer, the car, the yard—anything but you. He's more like a roommate than the soul-mate you'd hoped for. And you're starting to wonder if it's worth staying or if you should just give up. But real life isn't a fairy tale, and real love isn't a fuzzy feeling—it's a choice God calls you to make each moment of each day. *Choose* to love your husband with the same unconditional love God continually shows you.

Intelligibility in Worship

14 Follow the way of love and eagerly desire spiritual gifts, especially the gift of prophecy. [2]For those who speak in a tongue[e] do not speak to other people but to God. Indeed, no one understands

---

[a] *30 Or other languages* [b] *31 Or But you are eagerly desiring* [c] *1 Or languages* [d] *3 Some manuscripts body to the flames* [e] *2 Or in another language; also in verses 4, 13, 14, 19, 26 and 27*

them; they utter mysteries by the Spirit. ³But those who prophesy speak to people for their strengthening, encouragement and comfort. ⁴Those who speak in a tongue edify themselves, but those who prophesy edify the church. ⁵I would like every one of you to speak in tongues,*a* but I would rather have you prophesy. Those who prophesy are greater than those who speak in tongues,*a* unless they interpret, so that the church may be edified.

⁶Now, brothers and sisters, if I come to you and speak in tongues, what good will I be to you, unless I bring you some revelation or knowledge or prophecy or word of instruction? ⁷Even in the case of lifeless things that make sounds, such as the pipe or harp, how will anyone know what tune is being played unless there is a distinction in the notes? ⁸Again, if the trumpet does not sound a clear call, who will get ready for battle? ⁹So it is with you. Unless you speak intelligible words with your tongue, how will anyone know what you are saying? You will just be speaking into the air. ¹⁰Undoubtedly there are all sorts of languages in the world, yet none of them is without meaning. ¹¹If then I do not grasp the meaning of what someone is saying, I am a foreigner to the speaker, and the speaker is a foreigner to me. ¹²So it is with you. Since you are eager for gifts of the Spirit, try to excel in those that build up the church.

¹³For this reason those who speak in a tongue should pray that they may interpret what they say. ¹⁴For if I pray in a tongue, my spirit prays, but my mind is unfruitful. ¹⁵So what shall I do? I will pray with my spirit, but I will also pray with my understanding; I will sing with my spirit, but I will also sing with my understanding. ¹⁶Otherwise when you are praising God in the Spirit, how can the others, who are now put in the same situation as an inquirer,*b* say "Amen" to your thanksgiving, since they do not know what you are saying? ¹⁷You are giving thanks well enough, but the others are not edified.

¹⁸I thank God that I speak in tongues more than all of you. ¹⁹But in the church I would rather speak five intelligible words to instruct others than ten thousand words in a tongue.

²⁰Brothers and sisters, stop thinking like children. In regard to evil be infants, but in your thinking be adults. ²¹In the Law it is written:

> "With other tongues
>   and through the lips of foreigners
> I will speak to this people,
>   but even then they will not listen to me,
>
> says the Lord."*c*

²²Tongues, then, are a sign, not for believers but for unbelievers; prophecy, however, is not for unbelievers but for believers. ²³So if the whole church comes together and everyone speaks in tongues, and inquirers or unbelievers come in, will they not say that you are out of your mind? ²⁴But if an unbeliever or an inquirer comes in while everyone is prophesying, they are convicted of sin and are brought under judgment by all, ²⁵as the secrets of their hearts are laid bare. So they will fall down and worship God, exclaiming, "God is really among you!"

Good Order in Worship

²⁶What then shall we say, brothers and sisters? When you come together, each of you has a hymn, or a word of instruction, a revelation, a tongue or an interpretation. Everything must be done so that the church may be built up. ²⁷If anyone speaks in a tongue, two—or at the most three—should speak, one at a time, and someone must interpret. ²⁸If there is no interpreter, the speaker should keep quiet in the church; let them speak to themselves and to God.

²⁹Two or three prophets should speak, and the others should weigh carefully what is said. ³⁰And if a revelation comes to someone who is sitting down, the first speaker should stop. ³¹For you can all prophesy in turn so that everyone may be instructed and encouraged. ³²The spirits of prophets are subject to the control of prophets. ³³For God is not a God of disorder but of peace—as in all the congregations of the Lord's people.

³⁴Women should remain silent in the churches. They are not allowed to speak, but must be in

1631

---

a 5 Or *in other languages*; also in verses 6, 18, 22, 23 and 39 *b 16* The Greek word for *inquirer* is a technical term for someone not fully initiated into a religion; also in verses 23 and 24. *c 21* Isaiah 28:11,12 submission, as the law says. [35] If they want to inquire about something, they should ask their own husbands at home; for it is disgraceful for a woman to speak in the church.[a]

[36] Or did the word of God originate with you? Or are you the only people it has reached? [37] If any think they are prophets or otherwise gifted by the Spirit, let them acknowledge that what I am writing to you is the Lord's command. [38] Those who ignore this will themselves be ignored.[b]

[39] Therefore, my brothers and sisters, be eager to prophesy, and do not forbid speaking in tongues. [40] But everything should be done in a fitting and orderly way.

The Resurrection of Christ

15 Now, brothers and sisters, I want to remind you of the gospel I preached to you, which you received and on which you have taken your stand. [2] By this gospel you are saved, if you hold firmly to the word I preached to you. Otherwise, you have believed in vain.

[3] For what I received I passed on to you as of first importance[c]: that Christ died for our sins according to the Scriptures, [4] that he was buried, that he was raised on the third day according to the Scriptures, [5] and that he appeared to Cephas,[d] and then to the Twelve. [6] After that, he appeared to more than five hundred of the brothers and sisters at the same time, most of whom are still living, though some have fallen asleep. [7] Then he appeared to James, then to all the apostles, [8] and last of all he appeared to me also, as to one abnormally born.

[9] For I am the least of the apostles and do not even deserve to be called an apostle, because I persecuted the church of God. [10] But by the grace of God I am what I am, and his grace to me was not without effect. No, I worked harder than all of them—yet not I, but the grace of God that was with me. [11] Whether, then, it is I or they, this is what we preach, and this is what you believed.

The Resurrection of the Dead

[12] But if it is preached that Christ has been raised from the dead, how can some of you say that there is no resurrection of the dead? [13] If there is no resurrection of the dead, then not even Christ has been raised. [14] And if Christ has not been raised, our preaching is useless and so is your faith. [15] More than that, we are then found to be false witnesses about God, for we have testified about God that he raised Christ from the dead. But he did not raise him if in fact the dead are not raised. [16] For if the dead are not raised, then Christ has not been raised either. [17] And if Christ has not been raised, your faith is futile; you are still in your sins. [18] Then those also who have fallen asleep in Christ are lost. [19] If only for this life we have hope in Christ, we are to be pitied more than all others.

[20] But Christ has indeed been raised from the dead, the firstfruits of those who have fallen asleep. [21] For since death came through a human being, the resurrection of the dead comes also through a human being. [22] For as in Adam all die, so in Christ all will be made alive. [23] But in this order: Christ, the firstfruits; then, when he comes, those who belong to him. [24] Then the end will come, when he hands over the kingdom to God the Father after he has destroyed all dominion, authority and power. [25] For he must reign until he has put all his enemies under his feet. [26] The last enemy to be destroyed is death. [27] For he "has put everything under his feet."[e] Now when it says that "everything" has been put under him, it is clear that this does not include God himself, who put everything under Christ. [28] When he has done this, then the Son himself will be made subject to him who put everything under him, so that God may be all in all.

[29] Now if there is no resurrection, what will those do who are baptized for the dead? If the dead are not raised at all, why are people baptized for them? [30] And as for us, why do we endanger ourselves every hour? [31] I face death every day—yes, just as surely as I boast about you in Christ Jesus our Lord. [32] If I fought wild beasts in Ephesus with no more than human hopes, what have I gained? If the dead are not raised,

> "Let us eat and drink,
> for tomorrow we die."[f]

---

[a] *34,35* In some manuscripts these verses come after verse 40.   [b] *38* Some manuscripts *Those who are ignorant of this will be ignorant*   [c] *3* Or *you at the first*   [d] *5* That is, Peter   [e] *27* Psalm 8:6   [f] *32* Isaiah 22:13

³³Do not be misled: "Bad company corrupts good character."*ᵃ ³⁴Come back to your senses as you ought, and stop sinning; for there are some who are ignorant of God—I say this to your shame.

The Resurrection Body

³⁵But someone will ask, "How are the dead raised? With what kind of body will they come?" ³⁶How foolish! What you sow does not come to life unless it dies. ³⁷When you sow, you do not plant the body that will be, but just a seed, perhaps of wheat or of something else. ³⁸But God gives it a body as he has determined, and to each kind of seed he gives its own body. ³⁹All flesh is not the same: Human beings have one kind of flesh, animals have another, birds another and fish another. ⁴⁰There are also heavenly bodies and there are earthly bodies; but the splendor of the heavenly bodies is one kind, and the splendor of the earthly bodies is another. ⁴¹The sun has one kind of splendor, the moon another and the stars another; and star differs from star in splendor.

⁴²So will it be with the resurrection of the dead. The body that is sown is perishable, it is raised imperishable; ⁴³it is sown in dishonor, it is raised in glory; it is sown in weakness, it is raised in power; ⁴⁴it is sown a natural body, it is raised a spiritual body.

If there is a natural body, there is also a spiritual body. ⁴⁵So it is written: "The first Adam became a living being"ᵇ; the last Adam, a life-giving spirit. ⁴⁶The spiritual did not come first, but the natural, and after that the spiritual. ⁴⁷The first man was of the dust of the earth; the second man is of heaven. ⁴⁸As was the earthly man, so are those who are of the earth; and as is the heavenly man, so also are those who are of heaven. ⁴⁹And just as we have borne the image of the earthly man, so shall weᶜ bear the image of the heavenly man.

⁵⁰I declare to you, brothers and sisters, that flesh and blood cannot inherit the kingdom of God, nor does the perishable inherit the imperishable. ⁵¹Listen, I tell you a mystery: We will not all sleep, but we will all be changed— ⁵²in a flash, in the twinkling of an eye, at the last trumpet. For the trumpet will sound, the dead will be raised imperishable, and we will be changed. ⁵³For the perishable must clothe itself with the imperishable, and the mortal with immortality. ⁵⁴When the perishable has been clothed with the imperishable, and the mortal with immortality, then the saying that is written will come true: "Death has been swallowed up in victory."ᵈ

⁵⁵"Where, O death, is your victory?
   Where, O death, is your sting?"ᵉ

⁵⁶The sting of death is sin, and the power of sin is the law. ⁵⁷But thanks be to God! He gives us the victory through our Lord Jesus Christ.

⁵⁸Therefore, my dear brothers and sisters, stand firm. Let nothing move you. Always give yourselves fully to the work of the Lord, because you know that your labor in the Lord is not in vain.

---

atissue:facing death

15:50–57 Death seems so final, but it's not. It seems like the end, but it's actually just the beginning. Death seems to conquer us all, but over those who believe in Jesus it gains no victory. When Christ died on the cross then came back to life through the power of God, he triumphed over sin and death. Our earthly bodies are temporary, and they will pass away, but our souls can live forever with God because of Jesus. And so the sting of death is removed. For those who know God, death is nothing to fear.

The Collection for the Lord's People

16 Now about the collection for the Lord's people: Do what I told the Galatian churches to do. ²On the first day of every week, each one of you should set aside a sum of money in keeping with your income, saving it up, so that when I come no collections will have to be made. ³Then, when I arrive, I will give letters of introduction to the men you approve and send them with your gift to Jerusalem. ⁴If it seems advisable for me to go also, they will accompany me.

ᵃ *33* From the Greek poet Menander   ᵇ *45* Gen. 2:7   ᶜ *49* Some early manuscripts *so let us*   ᵈ *54* Isaiah 25:8   ᵉ *55* Hosea 13:14

Personal Requests

[5]After I go through Macedonia, I will come to you—for I will be going through Macedonia. [6]Perhaps I will stay with you for a while, or even spend the winter, so that you can help me on my journey, wherever I go. [7]For I do not want to see you now and make only a passing visit; I hope to spend some time with you, if the Lord permits. [8]But I will stay on at Ephesus until Pentecost, [9]because a great door for effective work has opened to me, and there are many who oppose me.

[10]When Timothy comes, see to it that he has nothing to fear while he is with you, for he is carrying on the work of the Lord, just as I am. [11]No one, then, should treat him with contempt. Send him on his way in peace so that he may return to me. I am expecting him along with the brothers.

[12]Now about our brother Apollos: I strongly urged him to go to you with the brothers. He was quite unwilling to go now, but he will go when he has the opportunity.

[13]Be on your guard; stand firm in the faith; be courageous; be strong. [14]Do everything in love.

[15]You know that the household of Stephanas were the first converts in Achaia, and they have devoted themselves to the service of the Lord's people. I urge you, brothers and sisters, [16]to submit to such as these and to everyone who joins in the work and labors at it. [17]I was glad when Stephanas, Fortunatus and Achaicus arrived, because they have supplied what was lacking from you. [18]For they refreshed my spirit and yours also. Such men deserve recognition.

Final Greetings

[19]The churches in the province of Asia send you greetings. Aquila and Priscilla[a] greet you warmly in the Lord, and so does the church that meets at their house. [20]All the brothers and sisters here send you greetings. Greet one another with a holy kiss.

[21]I, Paul, write this greeting in my own hand.

[22]If anyone does not love the Lord, let that person be cursed! Come, Lord[b]!

[23]The grace of the Lord Jesus be with you.

[24]My love to all of you in Christ Jesus. Amen.[c]

2corinthians

AUTHOR
The apostle Paul.

AUDIENCE
Followers of Jesus; originally written to the church in Corinth.

DATE
About A.D. 55.

SETTING
False teachers in the church at Corinth were denying Paul's authority over them as an apostle.

VERSE TO REMEMBER
"But he said to me, 'My grace is sufficient for you, for my power is made perfect in weakness.' Therefore I will boast all the more gladly about my weaknesses, so that Christ's power may rest on me." (12:9)

THEME TO CONSIDER
God uses ordinary humans—despite our weaknesses—in extraordinary ways.

1 Paul, an apostle of Christ Jesus by the will of God, and Timothy our brother,

To the church of God in Corinth, together with all his holy people throughout Achaia:

²Grace and peace to you from God our Father and the Lord Jesus Christ.

Praise to the God of All Comfort

³Praise be to the God and Father of our Lord Jesus Christ, the Father of compassion and the God of all comfort, ⁴who comforts us in all our troubles, so that we can comfort those in any trouble with the comfort we ourselves receive from God. ⁵For just as we share abundantly in the sufferings of Christ, so also our comfort abounds through Christ. ⁶If we are distressed, it is for your comfort and salvation; if we are comforted, it is for your comfort, which produces in you patient endurance of the same sufferings we suffer. ⁷And our hope for you is firm, because we know that just as you share in our sufferings, so also you share in our comfort.

⁸We do not want you to be uninformed, brothers and sisters, about the troubles we experienced in the province of Asia. We were under great pressure, far beyond our ability to endure, so that we despaired of life itself. ⁹Indeed, we felt we had received the sentence of death. But this happened that we might not rely on ourselves but on God, who raises the dead. ¹⁰He has delivered us from such a deadly peril, and he will deliver us again. On him we have set our hope that he will continue to deliver us, ¹¹as you help us by your prayers. Then many will give thanks on our behalf for the gracious favor granted us in answer to the prayers of many.

atissue:suffering

1:3–7 When you suffer, God heaps his compassion on you. He embraces you in your time of trouble. And he pours so much comfort into your life that it will spill over you, so that you have more than enough to pass along. When you are in pain, it can be hard to see how any good can possibly come from it. But God assures you that he loves you and comforts you as only he can. One day, you will have the opportunity to share with someone else the amazing compassion and comfort that can only come from God.

Paul's Change of Plans

¹²Now this is our boast: Our conscience testifies that we have conducted ourselves in the world, and especially in our relations with you, with integrity*ᵃ* and godly sincerity. We have done so, relying not on worldly wisdom but on God's grace. ¹³For we do not write you anything you cannot read or understand. And I hope that, ¹⁴as you have understood us in part, you will come to understand fully that you can boast of us just as we will boast of you in the day of the Lord Jesus.

¹⁵Because I was confident of this, I wanted to visit you first so that you might benefit twice. ¹⁶I wanted to visit you on my way to Macedonia and to come back to you from Macedonia, and then to have you send me on my way to Judea. ¹⁷Was I fickle when I intended to do this? Or do I make my plans in a worldly manner so that in the same breath I say both "Yes, yes" and "No, no"?

¹⁸But as surely as God is faithful, our message to you is not "Yes" and "No." ¹⁹For the Son of God, Jesus Christ, who was preached among you by us—by me and Silas*ᵇ* and Timothy—was not "Yes" and "No," but in him it has always been "Yes." ²⁰For no matter how many promises God has made, they are "Yes" in Christ. And so through him the "Amen" is spoken by us to the glory of God. ²¹Now it is God who makes both us and you stand firm in Christ. He anointed us, ²²set his seal of ownership on us, and put his Spirit in our hearts as a deposit, guaranteeing what is to come.

²³I call God as my witness—and I stake my life on it—that it was in order to spare you that I did not return to Corinth. ²⁴Not that we lord it over your faith, but we work with you for your joy, because

2 it is by faith you stand firm. ¹So I made up my mind that I would not make another painful visit to you. ²For if I grieve you, who is left to make me glad but you whom I have grieved? ³I wrote as I did, so that when I came I would not be distressed by those who should have made me rejoice. I had confidence in all of you, that you would all share my joy. ⁴For I wrote you out of great distress and anguish of heart and with many tears, not to grieve you but to let you know the depth of my love for you.

Forgiveness for the Offender

⁵If anyone has caused grief, he has not so much grieved me as he has grieved all of you to some extent—not to put it too severely. ⁶The punishment inflicted on him by the majority is sufficient. ⁷Now instead, you ought to forgive and comfort him, so that he will not be overwhelmed by excessive sorrow. ⁸I urge you, therefore, to reaffirm your love for him. ⁹Another reason I wrote you was to see if you would stand the test and be obedient in everything. ¹⁰Anyone you forgive, I also forgive. And what I have forgiven—if there was anything to forgive—I have forgiven in the sight of Christ for your sake, ¹¹in order that Satan might not outwit us. For we are not unaware of his schemes.

Ministers of the New Covenant

¹²Now when I went to Troas to preach the gospel of Christ and found that the Lord had opened a door for me, ¹³I still had no peace of mind, because I did not find my brother Titus there. So I said good-by to them and went on to Macedonia.

¹⁴But thanks be to God, who always leads us as captives in Christ's triumphal procession and uses us to spread the aroma of the knowledge of him everywhere. ¹⁵For we are to God the pleasing aroma of Christ among those who are being saved and those who are perishing. ¹⁶To the one we are an aroma that brings death; to the other, an aroma that brings life. And who is equal to such a task? ¹⁷Unlike so many, we do not peddle the word of God for profit. On the contrary, in Christ we speak before God with sincerity, as those sent from God.

3 Are we beginning to commend ourselves again? Or do we need, like some people, letters of recommendation to you or from you? ²You yourselves are our letter, written on our hearts, known and read by everyone. ³You show that you are a letter from Christ, the result of our ministry, written not with ink but with the Spirit of the living God, not on tablets of stone but on tablets of human hearts.

⁴Such confidence we have through Christ before God. ⁵Not that we are competent in ourselves to claim anything for ourselves, but our competence comes from God. ⁶He has made us competent as ministers of a new covenant—not of the letter but of the Spirit; for the letter kills, but the Spirit gives life.

The Greater Glory of the New Covenant

⁷Now if the ministry that brought death, which was engraved in letters on stone, came with glory, so that the Israelites could not look steadily at the face of Moses because of its glory, transitory though it was, ⁸will not the ministry of the Spirit be even more glorious? ⁹If the ministry that brought condemnation was glorious, how much more glorious is the ministry that brings righteousness! ¹⁰For what was glorious has no glory now in comparison with the surpassing glory. ¹¹And if what was transitory came with glory, how much greater is the glory of that which lasts!

¹²Therefore, since we have such a hope, we are very bold. ¹³We are not like Moses, who would put a veil over his face to prevent the Israelites from seeing the end of what was passing away. ¹⁴But their minds were made dull, for to this day the same veil remains when the old covenant is read. It has not been removed, because only in Christ is it taken away. ¹⁵Even to this day when Moses is read, a veil covers their hearts. ¹⁶But whenever anyone turns to the Lord, the veil is taken away. ¹⁷Now the Lord is the Spirit, and where the Spirit of the Lord is, there is freedom. ¹⁸And we all, who with unveiled faces contemplate*ᵃ* the Lord's glory, are being transformed into his image with ever-increasing glory, which comes from the Lord, who is the Spirit.

Present Weakness and Resurrection Life

4 Therefore, since through God's mercy we have this ministry, we do not lose heart. ²Rather, we have renounced secret and shameful ways; we do not use deception, nor do we distort the word of God.

ᵃ 18 Or reflect

HE IS: transforming

For the next He Is, go to p. 1639.

3:12–18 After Moses spent time with God, he wore a veil to shield the people from God's glory, which was reflected on his face. Over time, that glory faded away. Through Christ, however, we reflect God's glory constantly, as he is at work *transforming* us.

Transforming yourself is hard work—ask anyone who's ever tried to lose weight or go back to school. Yet God changes people from the inside out, forever. Slowly but surely, he's transforming you into his likeness (see Colossians 3:9–10). You may not be aware of the process or see instant results, but as you look back on your life, you'll see how much he has been *transforming* you all along.

On the contrary, by setting forth the truth plainly we commend ourselves to everyone's conscience in the sight of God. ³And even if our gospel is veiled, it is veiled to those who are perishing. ⁴The god of this age has blinded the minds of unbelievers, so that they cannot see the light of the gospel that displays the glory of Christ, who is the image of God. ⁵For what we preach is not ourselves, but Jesus Christ as Lord, and ourselves as your servants for Jesus' sake. ⁶For God, who said, "Let light shine out of darkness,"*ᵃ* made his light shine in our hearts to give us the light of the knowledge of God's glory displayed in the face of Christ.

⁷But we have this treasure in jars of clay to show that this all-surpassing power is from God and not from us. ⁸We are hard pressed on every side, but not crushed; perplexed, but not in despair; ⁹persecuted, but not abandoned; struck down, but not destroyed. ¹⁰We always carry around in our body the death of Jesus, so that the life of Jesus may also be revealed in our body. ¹¹For we who are alive are always being given over to death for Jesus' sake, so that his life may also be revealed in our mortal body. ¹²So then, death is at work in us, but life is at work in you.

¹³It is written: "I believed; therefore I have spoken."*ᵇ* Since we have that same spirit of*ᶜ* faith, we also believe and therefore speak, ¹⁴because we know that the one who raised the Lord Jesus from the dead will also raise us with Jesus and present us with you to himself. ¹⁵All this is for your benefit, so that the grace that is reaching more and more people may cause thanksgiving to overflow to the glory of God.

¹⁶Therefore we do not lose heart. Though outwardly we are wasting away, yet inwardly we are being renewed day by day. ¹⁷For our light and momentary troubles are achieving for us an eternal glory that far outweighs them all. ¹⁸So we fix our eyes not on what is seen, but on what is unseen, since what is seen is temporary, but what is unseen is eternal.

Awaiting the New Body

5 For we know that if the earthly tent we live in is destroyed, we have a building from God, an eternal house in heaven, not built by human hands. ²Meanwhile we groan, longing to be clothed with our heavenly dwelling, ³because when we are clothed, we will not be found naked. ⁴For while we are in this tent, we groan and are burdened, because we do not wish to be unclothed but to be clothed with our heavenly dwelling, so that what is mortal may be swallowed up by life. ⁵Now the one who has fashioned us for this very purpose is God, who has given us the Spirit as a deposit, guaranteeing what is to come.

⁶Therefore we are always confident and know that as long as we are at home in the body we are away from the Lord. ⁷We live by faith, not by sight. ⁸We are confident, I say, and would prefer to be away from the body and at home with the Lord. ⁹So we make it our goal to please him, whether we are at home in the body or away from it. ¹⁰For we must all appear before the judgment seat of Christ, that everyone may receive what is due them for the things done while in the body, whether good or bad.

ᵃ 6 Gen. 1:3   ᵇ 13 Psalm 116:10 (see Septuagint)   ᶜ 13 Or Spirit-given

The Ministry of Reconciliation

[11] Since, then, we know what it is to fear the Lord, we try to persuade people. What we are is plain to God, and I hope it is also plain to your conscience. [12] We are not trying to commend ourselves to you again, but are giving you an opportunity to take pride in us, so that you can answer those who take pride in what is seen rather than in what is in the heart. [13] If we are "out of our mind," as some say, it is for God; if we are in our right mind, it is for you. [14] For Christ's love compels us, because we are convinced that one died for all, and therefore all died. [15] And he died for all, that those who live should no longer live for themselves but for him who died for them and was raised again.

HE IS: compelling

5:14–15 What drove Paul to continue in ministry through trials and tribulations? Was he motivated by the number of churches he planted? By the praise of people? By the hope of material gain? None of these selfish factors motivated the apostle Paul. He made it clear that what compelled him was Christ's love alone.

Do you keep a mental record of people you've helped? Do you long for people's praise? Do you hope for recognition or material rewards? These are indications that you're driven by selfish motives. But if Christ's love is *compelling* you, you won't live for yourself—you'll live for him.

For the next He Is, go to p. 1650.

1639

[16] So from now on we regard no one from a worldly point of view. Though we once regarded Christ in this way, we do so no longer. [17] Therefore, if anyone is in Christ, the new creation has come: The old has gone, the new is here! [18] All this is from God, who reconciled us to himself through Christ and gave us the ministry of reconciliation: [19] that God was reconciling the world to himself in Christ, not counting people's sins against them. And he has committed to us the message of reconciliation. [20] We are therefore Christ's ambassadors, as though God were making his appeal through us. We implore you on Christ's behalf: Be reconciled to God. [21] God made him who had no sin to be sin[a] for us, so that in him we might become the righteousness of God.

6 As God's co-workers we urge you not to receive God's grace in vain. [2] For he says,

> "In the time of my favor I heard you,
> and in the day of salvation I helped you."[b]

I tell you, now is the time of God's favor, now is the day of salvation.

Paul's Hardships

[3] We put no stumbling block in anyone's path, so that our ministry will not be discredited. [4] Rather, as servants of God we commend ourselves in every way: in great endurance; in troubles, hardships and distresses; [5] in beatings, imprisonments and riots; in hard work, sleepless nights and hunger; [6] in purity, understanding, patience and kindness; in the Holy Spirit and in sincere love; [7] in truthful speech and in the power of God; with weapons of righteousness in the right hand and in the left; [8] through glory and dishonor, bad report and good report; genuine, yet regarded as impostors; [9] known, yet regarded as unknown; dying, and yet we live on; beaten, and yet not killed; [10] sorrowful, yet always rejoicing; poor, yet making many rich; having nothing, and yet possessing everything.

[11] We have spoken freely to you, Corinthians, and opened wide our hearts to you. [12] We are not withholding our affection from you, but you are withholding yours from us. [13] As a fair exchange—I speak as to my children—open wide your hearts also.

---

[a] 21 Or *be a sin offering*   [b] 2 Isaiah 49:8

myth# 94 "SEXUAL ABUSE IS AT LEAST PARTLY THE VICTIM'S FAULT."

I remember it as if it were yesterday, even though it's been over 20 years. I wanted to be invisible then, and the same feeling sometimes overcomes me today without warning. I try to imagine myself covered with heavy clothes and blankets. Safe and secure in the closet . . . until the next time.

It wasn't very often. Just when he came home drunk. The first time it happened, I thought he was coming to say goodnight and tuck me in. Instead, he got into bed with me and started touching me. I knew he shouldn't be doing what he was doing, but I felt paralyzed. Each time after he finished, he would tell me that he loved me and that if I told anyone, he would hate me. I wanted him to love me. On the other hand, I hated what he was doing.

When I got older, I learned how to avoid him. I slept over at someone else's house or hid in the closet when he came home late. Always being on your guard in your own home is a terrible way to live. I did some counseling in college, and I've told myself repeatedly that it wasn't my fault. Even though I know that intellectually, I still feel so ashamed. Surely I could have done something more to stop it. Maybe I should have told someone. Or I should have fought him. At the least, I should have been able to see it coming. If only I'd known what to do, it wouldn't have happened, and I could have a normal life.

—Hope

SEXUAL ABUSE IS a terrible violation of a person's body and emotions. Some of the complex emotions that may result from sexual abuse include the following:

Making excuses for the perpetrator. Although a sexual abuse victim may wish to rationalize her abuse, there is never an instance when it is "OK" or "just a mistake." The perpetrator is always responsible, even if alcohol or some other factor comes into play. When a person is sexually abused, it is never her fault. Period.

Conflicting emotions. A sexual abuse victim may love the perpetrator but hate what the perpetrator does. A child's brain is not designed to hold two intense, conflicting emotions at the same time. This often leads to depression and stress.

"If only . . ." Abused women often feel they could or should have done something to stop the abuse. However, it is a very rare instance when the victim could have changed her situation. Often the perpetrator is bigger, stronger and more powerful (physically and emotionally). A child should never be asked to defend herself against abuse.

Guilt. Women who have been sexually abused often feel guilty about what happened. They feel damaged and that their lives are permanently tainted because of something they could not control.

Sometimes the worst consequence of abuse is feeling you will never be whole again. However, if you belong to Jesus, then you are a brand new creation (see 2 Corinthians 5:17), regardless of what happened to you in the past. The journey toward healing may be long, but the Holy Spirit is always with you, guiding and loving you, no matter what. Trust that God will give you all you need on your journey.

Many people who care about sexual abuse victims are committed to helping them find healing for these complex emotions and painful memories. Go to a Christian counselor, a rape-counseling center or a domestic violence agency. You are not alone. Why not take the first steps toward healing today?

"1 in 4 girls and 1 in 6 boys will be sexually abused before they turn 16.
75–95 percent of these victims know their offender."

—FBI (1990)

1641

"THEREFORE, IF ANYONE IS IN CHRIST, THE NEW CREATION HAS COME: THE OLD HAS GONE, THE NEW IS HERE!"

2 CORINTHIANS 5:17

SEE ALSO

Psalm 147:3–6
Isaiah 43:18–19
Romans 8:28,38–39

For more on **Guilt** and **Sexual Abuse**, check the index.

Warning Against Idolatry

[14]Do not be yoked together with unbelievers. For what do righteousness and wickedness have in common? Or what fellowship can light have with darkness? [15]What harmony is there between Christ and Belial[a]? Or what does a believer have in common with an unbeliever? [16]What agreement is there between the temple of God and idols? For we are the temple of the living God. As God has said:

> "I will live with them
> and walk among them,
> and I will be their God,
> and they will be my people."[b]

[17]Therefore,

> "Come out from them
> and be separate,
>   says the Lord.
> Touch no unclean thing,
> and I will receive you."[c]

[18]And,

> "I will be a Father to you,
> and you will be my sons and
> daughters,
>   says the Lord Almighty."[d]

atissue:dating

6:14—7:1 A wooden yoke was used to bind together two animals and force them to work together, typically pulling a plow or cart. If both animals were of the same mind, they accomplished more together than apart. But if the two tried to pull in different directions, they went nowhere and accomplished little. When you follow God, he takes your life in one direction. Yoking yourself to someone who doesn't follow God means you'll continually be pulled in an opposing direction. It's worth waiting for God to bring a man into your life who will pull with you, not against you.

7 Therefore, since we have these promises, dear friends, let us purify ourselves from everything that contaminates body and spirit, perfecting holiness out of reverence for God.

Paul's Joy Over the Church's Repentance

[2]Make room for us in your hearts. We have wronged no one, we have corrupted no one, we have exploited no one. [3]I do not say this to condemn you; I have said before that you have such a place in our hearts that we would live or die with you. [4]I have spoken to you with great frankness; I take great pride in you. I am greatly encouraged; in all our troubles my joy knows no bounds.

[5]For when we came into Macedonia, this body of ours had no rest, but we were harassed at every turn—conflicts on the outside, fears within. [6]But God, who comforts the downcast, comforted us by the coming of Titus, [7]and not only by his coming but also by the comfort you had given him. He told us about your longing for me, your deep sorrow, your ardent concern for me, so that my joy was greater than ever.

[8]Even if I caused you sorrow by my letter, I do not regret it. Though I did regret it—I see that my letter hurt you, but only for a little while— [9]yet now I am happy, not because you were made sorry, but because your sorrow led you to repentance. For you became sorrowful as God intended and so were not harmed in any way by us. [10]Godly sorrow brings repentance that leads to salvation and leaves no regret, but worldly sorrow brings death. [11]See what this godly sorrow has produced in you: what earnestness, what eagerness to clear yourselves, what indignation, what alarm, what longing, what concern, what readiness to see justice done. At every point you have proved yourselves to be innocent in this matter. [12]So even though I wrote to you, it was neither on account of the one who did the wrong nor on account of the injured party, but rather that before God you could see for yourselves how devoted to us you are. [13]By all this we are encouraged.

In addition to our own encouragement, we were especially delighted to see how happy Titus was,

---

[a] 15 Greek *Beliar*, a variant of *Belial*   [b] 16 Lev. 26:12; Jer. 32:38; Ezek. 37:27   [c] 17 Isaiah 52:11; Ezek. 20:34,41   [d] 18 2 Samuel 7:14; 7:8

because his spirit has been refreshed by all of you. ¹⁴I had boasted to him about you, and you have not embarrassed me. But just as everything we said to you was true, so our boasting about you to Titus has proved to be true as well. ¹⁵And his affection for you is all the greater when he remembers that you were all obedient, receiving him with fear and trembling. ¹⁶I am glad I can have complete confidence in you.

The Collection for the Lord's People

8 And now, brothers and sisters, we want you to know about the grace that God has given the Macedonian churches. ²In the midst of a very severe trial, their over-flowing joy and their extreme poverty welled up in rich generosity. ³For I testify that they gave as much as they were able, and even beyond their ability. Entirely on their own, ⁴they urgently pleaded with us for the privilege of sharing in this service to the Lord's people. ⁵And they went beyond our expectations; having given themselves first of all to the Lord, they gave themselves by the will of God also to us. ⁶So we urged Titus, just as he had earlier made a beginning, to bring also to completion this act of grace on your part. ⁷But since you excel in everything—in faith, in speech, in knowledge, in complete earnestness and in the love we have kindled in you*a*—see that you also excel in this grace of giving.

conversations

money «» 8:1–15

1» As you read Paul's money advice, what tips can you pick up for your own finances?

2» Why is your *desire* to give as important as your actual giving?

3» How can you promote financial equality within the church (see v.v. 13–15)?

1643

For more on **money**, check the index.
For the next Conversations, go to p. 1646.

⁸I am not commanding you, but I want to test the sincerity of your love by comparing it with the earnestness of others. ⁹For you know the grace of our Lord Jesus Christ, that though he was rich, yet for your sake he became poor, so that you through his poverty might become rich.

¹⁰And here is my judgment about what is best for you in this matter. Last year you were the first not only to give but also to have the desire to do so. ¹¹Now finish the work, so that your eager willingness to do it may be matched by your completion of it, according to your means. ¹²For if the willingness is there, the gift is acceptable according to what one has, not according to what one does not have.

¹³Our desire is not that others might be relieved while you are hard pressed, but that there might be equality. ¹⁴At the present time your plenty will supply what they need, so that in turn their plenty will supply what you need. The goal is equality, ¹⁵as it is written: "The one who gathered much did not have too much, and the one who gathered little did not have too little."*b*

Titus Sent to Receive the Collection

¹⁶Thanks be to God, who put into the heart of Titus the same concern I have for you. ¹⁷For Titus not only welcomed our appeal, but he is coming to you with much enthusiasm and on his own initiative. ¹⁸And we are sending along with him the brother who is praised by all the churches for his service to the gospel. ¹⁹What is more, he was chosen by the churches to accompany us as we carry the offering, which we administer in order to honor the Lord himself and to show our eagerness to help. ²⁰We want to avoid any criticism of the way we administer this liberal gift. ²¹For we are taking pains to do what is right, not only in the eyes of the Lord but also in the eyes of others.

²²In addition, we are sending with them our brother who has often proved to us in many ways that he is zealous, and now even more so because of his great confidence in you. ²³As for Titus, he is my partner and co-worker among you; as for our brothers, they are representatives of the churches and an honor to Christ. ²⁴Therefore show these men the proof of your love and the reason for our pride in you, so that the churches can see it.

9 There is no need for me to write to you about this service to the Lord's people. ²For I know your eagerness to help, and I have been boasting about it to the Macedonians, telling them that since last year you in Achaia were ready to give; and your enthusiasm has stirred most of them to action. ³But I am sending the brothers in order that our boasting about you in this matter should not prove hollow, but

---

a 7 Some manuscripts *and in your love for us*   *b* 15 Exodus 16:18

that you may be ready, as I said you would be. [4]For if any Macedonians come with me and find you unprepared, we—not to say anything about you—would be ashamed of having been so confident. [5]So I thought it necessary to urge the brothers to visit you in advance and finish the arrangements for the generous gift you had promised. Then it will be ready as a generous gift, not as one grudgingly given.

Generosity Encouraged

[6]Remember this: Whoever sows sparingly will also reap sparingly, and whoever sows generously will also reap generously. [7]Each of you should give what you have decided in your heart to give, not reluctantly or under compulsion, for God loves a cheerful giver. [8]And God is able to bless you abundantly, so that in all things at all times, having all that you need, you will abound in every good work. [9]As it is written:

> "They have scattered abroad their gifts to the poor;
> their righteousness endures forever."[a]

[10]Now he who supplies seed to the sower and bread for food will also supply and increase your store of seed and will enlarge the harvest of your righteousness. [11]You will be made rich in every way so that you can be generous on every occasion, and through us your generosity will result in thanksgiving to God.

[12]This service that you perform is not only supplying the needs of the Lord's people but is also overflowing in many expressions of thanks to God. [13]Because of the service by which you have proved yourselves, people will praise God for the obedience that accompanies your confession of the gospel of Christ, and for your generosity in sharing with them and with everyone else. [14]And in their prayers for you their hearts will go out to you, because of the surpassing grace God has given you. [15]Thanks be to God for his indescribable gift!

Paul's Defense of His Ministry

10 By the meekness and gentleness of Christ, I appeal to you—I, Paul, who am "timid" when face to face with you, but "bold" toward you when away! [2]I beg you that when I come I may not have to be as bold as I expect to be toward some people who think that we live by the standards of this world. [3]For though we live in the world, we do not wage war as the world does. [4]The weapons we fight with are not the weapons of the world. On the contrary, they have divine power to demolish strongholds. [5]We demolish arguments and every pretension that sets itself up against the knowledge of God, and we take captive every thought to make it obedient to Christ. [6]And we will be ready to punish every act of disobedience, once your obedience is complete.

[7]You are judging by appearances.[b] If anyone is confident that they belong to Christ, they should consider again that we belong to Christ just as much as they do. [8]So even if I boast somewhat freely about the authority the Lord gave us for building you up rather than tearing you down, I will not be ashamed of it. [9]I do not want to seem to be trying to frighten you with my letters. [10]For some say, "His letters are weighty and forceful, but in person he is unimpressive and his speaking amounts to nothing." [11]Such people should realize that what we are in our letters when we are absent, we will be in our actions when we are present.

[12]We do not dare to classify or compare ourselves with some who commend themselves. When they measure themselves by themselves and compare themselves with themselves, they are not wise. [13]We, however, will not boast beyond proper limits, but will confine our boasting to the sphere of service God himself has assigned to us, a sphere that also includes you. [14]We are not going too far in our boasting, as would be the case if we had not come to you, for we did get as far as you with the gospel of Christ. [15]Neither do we go beyond our limits by boasting of work done by others. Our hope is that, as your faith continues to grow, our sphere of activity among you will greatly expand, [16]so that we can preach the gospel in the regions beyond you. For we do not want to boast about work already done in someone else's territory. [17]But, "Let those who boast boast in the Lord."[c] [18]For it is not those who commend themselves who are approved, but those whom the Lord commends.

a 9 Psalm 112:9   *b 7* Or *Look at the obvious facts*   *c 17* Jer. 9:24

Paul and the False Apostles

11 I hope you will put up with me in a little foolishness. Yes, please put up with me! [2] I am jealous for you with a godly jealousy. I promised you to one husband, to Christ, so that I might present you as a pure virgin to him. [3] But I am afraid that just as Eve was deceived by the serpent's cunning, your minds may somehow be led astray from your sincere and pure devotion to Christ. [4] For if someone comes to you and preaches a Jesus other than the Jesus we preached, or if you receive a different spirit from the Spirit you received, or a different gospel from the one you accepted, you put up with it easily enough.

[5] I do not think I am in the least inferior to those "super-apostles."[a] [6] I may indeed be untrained as a speaker, but I do have knowledge. We have made this perfectly clear to you in every way. [7] Was it a sin for me to lower myself in order to elevate you by preaching the gospel of God to you free of charge? [8] I robbed other churches by receiving support from them so as to serve you. [9] And when I was with you and needed something, I was not a burden to anyone, for the brothers and sisters who came from Macedonia supplied what I needed. I have kept myself from being a burden to you in any way, and will continue to do so. [10] As surely as the truth of Christ is in me, nobody in the regions of Achaia will stop this boasting of mine. [11] Why? Because I do not love you? God knows I do!

[12] And I will keep on doing what I am doing in order to cut the ground from under those who want an opportunity to be considered equal with us in the things they boast about. [13] For such persons are false apostles, deceitful workers, masquerading as apostles of Christ. [14] And no wonder, for Satan himself masquerades as an angel of light. [15] It is not surprising, then, if his servants also masquerade as servants of righteousness. Their end will be what their actions deserve.

Paul Boasts About His Sufferings

[16] I repeat: Let no one take me for a fool. But if you do, then tolerate me just as you would a fool, so that I may do a little boasting. [17] In this self-confident boasting I am not talking as the Lord would, but as a fool. [18] Since many are boasting in the way the world does, I too will boast. [19] You gladly put up with fools since you are so wise! [20] In fact, you even put up with any who enslave you or exploit you or take advantage of you or push themselves forward or slap you in the face. [21] To my shame I admit that we were too weak for that!

Whatever anyone else dares to boast about—I am speaking as a fool—I also dare to boast about. [22] Are they Hebrews? So am I. Are they Israelites? So am I. Are they Abraham's descendants? So am I. [23] Are they servants of Christ? (I am out of my mind to talk like this.) I am more. I have worked much harder, been in prison more frequently, been flogged more severely, and been exposed to death again and again. [24] Five times I received from the Jews the forty lashes minus one. [25] Three times I was beaten with rods, once I was pelted with stones, three times I was shipwrecked, I spent a night and a day in the open sea, [26] I have been constantly on the move. I have been in danger from rivers, in danger from bandits, in danger from my own people, in danger from Gentiles; in danger in the city, in danger in the country, in danger at sea; and in danger from false believers. [27] I have labored and toiled and have often gone without sleep; I have known hunger and thirst and have often gone without food; I have been cold and naked. [28] Besides everything else, I face daily the pressure of my concern for all the churches. [29] Who is weak, and I do not feel weak? Who is led into sin, and I do not inwardly burn?

[30] If I must boast, I will boast of the things that show my weakness. [31] The God and Father of the Lord Jesus, who is to be praised forever, knows that I am not lying. [32] In Damascus the governor under King Aretas had the city of the Damascenes guarded in order to arrest me. [33] But I was lowered in a basket from a window in the wall and slipped through his hands.

Paul's Vision and His Thorn

12 I must go on boasting. Although there is nothing to be gained, I will go on to visions and revelations from the Lord. [2] I know a man in Christ who fourteen years ago was caught up to the third heaven. Whether it was in the body or out of the body I do not know—God knows. [3] And I know that this man—whether in the body or apart from the body I do not know, but God knows— [4] was caught up to

a 5 Or *to the most eminent apostles*

paradise and heard inexpressible things, things that no one is permitted to tell. [5]I will boast about someone like that, but I will not boast about myself, except about my weaknesses. [6]Even if I should choose to boast, I would not be a fool, because I would be speaking the truth. But I refrain, so no one will think more of me than is warranted by what I do or say, [7]or because of these surpassingly great revelations. Therefore, in order to keep me from becoming conceited, I was given a thorn in my flesh, a messenger of Satan, to torment me. [8]Three times I pleaded with the Lord to take it away from me. [9]But he said to me, "My grace is sufficient for you, for my power is made perfect in weakness." Therefore I will boast all the more gladly about my weaknesses, so that Christ's power may rest on me. [10]That is why, for Christ's sake, I delight in weaknesses, in insults, in hardships, in persecutions, in difficulties. For when I am weak, then I am strong.

1646

conversations

failure «» 12:9

1» Do you have a failure that continues to haunt you?

2» How can "God's power be made perfect" in that failure?

3» If you begin to think of your personal failure the way Paul did, how will your outlook on that failure change?

For more on failure, check the index.
For the next Conversations, go to p. 1654.

Paul's Concern for the Corinthians

[11]I have made a fool of myself, but you drove me to it. I ought to have been commended by you, for I am not in the least inferior to the "super-apostles,"[a] even though I am nothing. [12]I persevered in demonstrating among you the marks of a true apostle, including signs, wonders and miracles. [13]How were you inferior to the other churches, except that I was never a burden to you? Forgive me this wrong!

[14]Now I am ready to visit you for the third time, and I will not be a burden to you, because what I want is not your possessions but you. After all, children should not have to save up for their parents, but parents for their children. [15]So I will very gladly spend for you everything I have and expend myself as well. If I love you more, will you love me less? [16]Be that as it may, I have not been a burden to you. Yet, crafty fellow that I am, I caught you by trickery! [17]Did I exploit you through any of the men I sent to you? [18]I urged Titus to go to you and I sent our brother with him. Titus did not exploit you, did he? Did we not walk in the same footsteps by the same Spirit?

[19]Have you been thinking all along that we have been defending ourselves to you? We have been speaking in the sight of God as those in Christ; and everything we do, dear friends, is for your strengthening. [20]For I am afraid that when I come I may not find you as I want you to be, and you may not find me as you want me to be. I fear that there may be quarreling, jealousy, outbursts of anger, factions, slander, gossip, arrogance and disorder. [21]I am afraid that when I come again my God will humble me before you, and I will be grieved over many who have sinned earlier and have not repented of the impurity, sexual sin and debauchery in which they have indulged.

Final Warnings

13 This will be my third visit to you. "Every matter must be established by the testimony of two or three witnesses."[b] [2]I already gave you a warning when I was with you the second time. I now repeat it while absent: On my return I will not spare those who sinned earlier or any of the others, [3]since you are demanding proof that Christ is speaking through me. He is not weak in dealing with you, but powerful among you. [4]For to be sure, he was crucified in weakness, yet he lives by God's power. Likewise, we are weak in him, yet by God's power we will live with him in our dealing with you.

[5]Examine yourselves to see whether you are in the faith; test yourselves. Do you not realize that Christ Jesus is in you—unless, of course, you fail the test? [6]And I trust that you will discover that we have not failed the test. [7]Now we pray to God that you will not do anything wrong. Not that people will see that we have stood the test but that you will do what is right even though we may seem to have failed. [8]For we cannot do anything against the truth, but only for the truth. [9]We are glad whenever we are weak but

you are strong; and our prayer is that you may be fully restored. ¹⁰This is why I write these things when I am absent, that when I come I may not have to be harsh in my use of authority—the authority the Lord gave me for building you up, not for tearing you down.

Final Greetings

¹¹Finally, brothers and sisters, rejoice! Strive for full restoration, encourage one another, be of one mind, live in peace. And the God of love and peace will be with you.

¹²Greet one another with a holy kiss. ¹³All God's people here send their greetings.

¹⁴May the grace of the Lord Jesus Christ, and the love of God, and the fellowship of the Holy Spirit be with you all.

1647

What was so "astonishing" to Paul? >> (1:6–10)

Are you living as if Christ died for nothing? >> (2:20–21)

What are the fruit of the Spirit? >> (5:22–26)

Can God be mocked? >> (6:7–10)

galatians

AUTHOR
The apostle Paul.

AUDIENCE
Followers of Jesus; originally written to the churches in Galatia.

DATE
About A.D. 50.

SETTING
Judaizers were falsely telling Gentiles that they had to obey the Jewish laws in order to be saved by Christ.

VERSE TO REMEMBER
"It is for freedom that Christ has set us free. Stand firm, then, and do not let yourselves be burdened again by a yoke of slavery." (5:1)

THEME TO CONSIDER
Salvation is God's undeserved gift to us—not something we can earn by good behavior.

1 Paul, an apostle—sent not with a human commission nor by human authority, but by Jesus Christ and God the Father, who raised him from the dead— [2] and all the brothers and sisters with me,

To the churches in Galatia:

[3] Grace and peace to you from God our Father and the Lord Jesus Christ, [4] who gave himself for our sins to rescue us from the present evil age, according to the will of our God and Father, [5] to whom be glory for ever and ever. Amen.

No Other Gospel

[6] I am astonished that you are so quickly deserting the one who called you by the grace of Christ and are turning to a different gospel— [7] which is really no gospel at all. Evidently some people are throwing you into confusion and are trying to pervert the gospel of Christ. [8] But even if we or an angel from heaven should preach a gospel other than the one we preached to you, let that person be under God's curse! [9] As we have already said, so now I say again: If anybody is preaching to you a gospel other than what you accepted, let that person be under God's curse!

[10] Am I now trying to win human approval, or God's approval? Or am I trying to please people? If I were still trying to please people, I would not be a servant of Christ.

Paul Called by God

[11] I want you to know, brothers and sisters, that the gospel I preached is not of human origin. [12] I did not receive it from any human source, nor was I taught it; rather, I received it by revelation from Jesus Christ.

[13] For you have heard of my previous way of life in Judaism, how intensely I persecuted the church of God and tried to destroy it. [14] I was advancing in Judaism beyond many of my own age among my people and was extremely zealous for the traditions of my fathers. [15] But when God, who set me apart from birth[a] and called me by his grace, was pleased [16] to reveal his Son in me so that I might preach him among the Gentiles, my immediate response was not to consult any human being. [17] I did not go up to Jerusalem to see those who were apostles before I was, but I went into Arabia. Later I returned to Damascus.

[18] Then after three years, I went up to Jerusalem to get acquainted with Cephas[b] and stayed with him fifteen days. [19] I saw none of the other apostles—only James, the Lord's brother. [20] I assure you before God that what I am writing you is no lie.

[21] Then I went to Syria and Cilicia. [22] I was personally unknown to the churches of Judea that are in Christ. [23] They only heard the report: "The man who formerly persecuted us is now preaching the faith he once tried to destroy." [24] And they praised God because of me.

Paul Accepted by the Apostles

2 Then after fourteen years, I went up again to Jerusalem, this time with Barnabas. I took Titus along also. [2] I went in response to a revelation and, meeting privately with those esteemed as leaders, I set before them the gospel that I preach among the Gentiles. I wanted to be sure I was not running and had not been running my race in vain. [3] Yet not even Titus, who was with me, was compelled to be circumcised, even though he was a Greek. [4] This matter arose because some false believers had infiltrated our ranks to spy on the freedom we have in Christ Jesus and to make us slaves. [5] We did not give in to them for a moment, so that the truth of the gospel might remain with you.

atissue:dieting

1:10 Paul was intent on pleasing God—not others—so he didn't change his message to please the crowds. What does this have to do with dieting? Just hold on. Why do many of us diet? Because we like how it feels when people notice and say we look good . . . so others will find us more attractive . . . so we can *win their approval*. But God wants us to focus on pleasing him. Women diet for many reasons. Ask yourself: When I diet, is my goal to gain human approval or to please God by improving my health?

1649

---

[a] *15 Or from my mother's womb*   [b] *18 That is, Peter*

[6]As for those who were held in high esteem—whatever they were makes no difference to me; God does not show favoritism—they added nothing to my message. [7]On the contrary, they saw that I had been entrusted with the task of preaching the gospel to the Gentiles,[a] just as Peter had been to the Jews.[b] [8]For God, who was at work in Peter as an apostle to the Jews, was also at work in me as an apostle to the Gentiles. [9]James, Cephas[c] and John, those esteemed as pillars, gave me and Barnabas the right hand of fellowship when they recognized the grace given to me. They agreed that we should go to the Gentiles, and they to the Jews. [10]All they asked was that we should continue to remember the poor, the very thing I had been eager to do all along.

Paul Opposes Cephas

[11]When Cephas came to Antioch, I opposed him to his face, because he stood condemned. [12]For before certain people came from James, he used to eat with the Gentiles. But when they arrived, he began to draw back and separate himself from the Gentiles because he was afraid of those who belonged to the circumcision group. [13]The other Jews joined him in his hypocrisy, so that by their hypocrisy even Barnabas was led astray.

[14]When I saw that they were not acting in line with the truth of the gospel, I said to Cephas in front of them all, "You are a Jew, yet you live like a Gentile and not like a Jew. How is it, then, that you force Gentiles to follow Jewish customs?

[15]"We who are Jews by birth and not sinful Gentiles [16]know that a person is not justified by observing the law, but by faith in Jesus Christ. So we, too, have put our faith in Christ Jesus that we may be justified by faith in[d] Christ and not by observing the law, because by observing the law no one will be justified.

[17]"But if, in seeking to be justified in Christ, we Jews find ourselves also among the sinners, doesn't that mean that Christ promotes sin? Absolutely not! [18]If I rebuild what I destroyed, then I really would be a lawbreaker.

[19]"For through the law I died to the law so that I might live for God. [20]I have been crucified with Christ and I no longer live, but Christ lives in me. The life I now live in the body, I live by faith in the Son of God, who loved me and gave himself for me. [21]I do not set aside the grace of God, for if righteousness could be gained through the law, Christ died for nothing!"[e]

HE IS: in me

2:20 One of the Bible's greatest paradoxes is that death can bring life. Paul looked upon his past life as dead and considered the old Paul (Saul, the purebred Pharisee) crucified with Christ. With confidence he could say, "Christ now lives *in me*."

Have you crucified your old life so that your new, spiritual life can begin? Have you let go of the person you used to be, along with the bragging rights or baggage that went along with it? It's time for you to let go of your past self and give Christ full freedom to live and reign *in you*.

For the next He Is, go to p. 1657.

Faith or Observance of the Law

3 You foolish Galatians! Who has bewitched you? Before your very eyes Jesus Christ was clearly portrayed as crucified. [2]I would like to learn just one thing from you: Did you receive the Spirit by observing the law, or by believing what you heard? [3]Are you so foolish? After beginning with the Spirit, are you now trying to finish by human effort? [4]Have you experienced[f] so much in vain—if it really was in vain? [5]Does God give you his Spirit and work miracles among you by your observing the law, or by

---

[a] 7 Greek *uncircumcised*   [b] 7 Greek *circumcised*; also in verses 8 and 9   [c] 9 That is, Peter; also in verses 11 and 14   [d] 16 Or *but through the faithfulness of … justified on the basis of the faithfulness of*   [e] 21 Some interpreters end the quotation after verse 14.   [f] 4 Or *suffered*

ASKmeanyTHING

the samaritan woman

John 4:4–42

Tell us what your life was like when you first met Jesus.

Basically, I lived on the fringe of society, just above the status of a leper, you could say. I'm a Samaritan woman—the most disdained group in everyone's eyes, especially Jews'. Plus I had made some bad choices. That's three strikes against me. Why Jesus ever stopped to talk with me I will never understand.

What do you mean by "bad choices"?

I mean I was a relational disaster. I'd had five husbands, but they didn't last long. And the man I was currently with didn't want to marry me and become number six. He probably wondered what the point of an official marriage would be.

1651

Tell us what happened the day you met Jesus.

I deliberately went to the well at noon to avoid meeting anyone I knew. My reputation was no secret to the people of Sychar, and I didn't need another disparaging look or sarcastic remark. So I was shocked to see a man already there—a *Jew*, no less. I braced myself for the inevitable cold shoulder. I really wanted to hide and wait till he was gone. But there was something in the way he looked at me and in how he spoke to me that caused me to stay.

What do you mean?

This man knew me. He knew all about me—why I was there at the well at that time, everything. He told me my entire history, yet he didn't condemn me. Instead he offered me—*me!*—"living water," a chance for a new life. After that I knew he was no ordinary man. He was the Messiah we had been waiting for.

So you had another choice to make.

Yes, and finally, I made the right one. I grabbed on to the love that this man offered me—true, real love—and I ran to tell as many people as I could. "Look, here is someone who is able to peer deep inside you, see all the ruin in your life, yet still offer you love and compassion and a new life!" I would have been a fool to walk away from that.

What can we learn from your experience?

Don't let your past keep you away from the one who offers you a real future. Don't think you need to have it all together in order to come to Jesus. He is already waiting, with open arms, no matter what you've done, where you've been or how you feel about yourself.

FOR MORE INSIGHT: For more on the new life that Jesus offers to us, read John 1:12–13; 3:36; 2 Corinthians 5:17; Galatians 2:20; and 1 John 5:11–12.

your believing what you heard? ⁶So also Abraham "believed God, and it was credited to him as righteousness."ᵃ

⁷Understand, then, that those who have faith are children of Abraham. ⁸Scripture foresaw that God would justify the Gentiles by faith, and announced the gospel in advance to Abraham: "All nations will be blessed through you."ᵇ ⁹So those who rely on faith are blessed along with Abraham, the man of faith.

¹⁰All who rely on observing the law are under a curse, for it is written: "Cursed is everyone who does not continue to do everything written in the Book of the Law."ᶜ ¹¹Clearly no one is justified before God by the law, because "the righteous will live by faith."ᵈ ¹²The law is not based on faith; on the contrary, it says, "Whoever does these things will live by them."ᵉ ¹³Christ redeemed us from the curse of the law by becoming a curse for us, for it is written: "Cursed is everyone who is hung on a pole."ᶠ ¹⁴He redeemed us in order that the blessing given to Abraham might come to the Gentiles through Christ Jesus, so that by faith we might receive the promise of the Spirit.

The Law and the Promise

¹⁵Brothers and sisters, let me take an example from everyday life. Just as no one can set aside or add to a human covenant that has been duly established, so it is in this case. ¹⁶The promises were spoken to Abraham and to his seed. Scripture does not say "and to seeds," meaning many people, but "and to your seed,"ᵍ meaning one person, who is Christ. ¹⁷What I mean is this: The law, introduced 430 years later, does not set aside the covenant previously established by God and thus do away with the promise. ¹⁸For if the inheritance depends on the law, then it no longer depends on the promise; but God in his grace gave it to Abraham through a promise.

¹⁹What, then, was the purpose of the law? It was added because of transgressions until the Seed to whom the promise referred had come. The law was given through angels and entrusted to a mediator. ²⁰A mediator, however, implies more than one party; but God is one.

²¹Is the law, therefore, opposed to the promises of God? Absolutely not! For if a law had been given that could impart life, then righteousness would certainly have come by the law. ²²But Scripture has locked up everything under the control of sin, so that what was promised, being given through faith in Jesus Christ, might be given to those who believe.

Children of God

²³Before the coming of this faith,ʰ we were held in custody under the law, locked up until the faith that was to come would be revealed. ²⁴So the law was put in charge of us until Christ came that we might be justified by faith. ²⁵Now that this faith has come, we are no longer under the supervision of the law.

²⁶So in Christ Jesus you are all children of God through faith, ²⁷for all of you who were baptized into Christ have clothed yourselves with Christ. ²⁸There is neither Jew nor Gentile, neither slave nor free, neither male nor female, for you are all one in Christ Jesus. ²⁹If you belong to Christ, then you are Abraham's seed, and heirs according to the promise.

4 What I am saying is that as long as heirs are underage they are no different from slaves, although they own the whole estate. ²They are subject to guardians and trustees until the time set by their fathers. ³So also, when we were underage, we were in slavery under the elemental spiritual forcesⁱ of the world. ⁴But when the set time had fully come, God sent his Son, born of a woman, born under the law, ⁵to redeem those under the law, that we might receive adoption to sonship.ʲ ⁶Because you are his sons, God sent the Spirit of his Son into our hearts, the Spirit who calls out, "Abba,ᵏ Father." ⁷So you are no longer slaves, but God's children; and since you are his children, he has made you also heirs.

Paul's Concern for the Galatians

⁸Formerly, when you did not know God, you were slaves to those who by nature are not gods. ⁹But now that you know God—or rather are known by God—how is it that you are turning back to those weak and miserable forcesˡ? Do you wish to be enslaved by them all over again? ¹⁰You are observing special days and months and seasons and years! ¹¹I fear for you, that somehow I have wasted my efforts on you.

1652

ᵃ 6 Gen. 15:6   ᵇ 8 Gen. 12:3; 18:18; 22:18   ᶜ 10 Deut. 27:26   ᵈ 11 Hab. 2:4   ᵉ 12 Lev. 18:5   ᶠ 13 Deut. 21:23   ᵍ 16 Gen. 12:7; 13:15; 24:7
ʰ 22,23 Or through the faithfulness of Jesus.... ²³Before faith came   ⁱ 3 Or under the basic principles   ʲ 5 The Greek word for adoption to sonship is a legal term referring to the full legal standing of an adopted male heir in Roman culture.   ᵏ 6 Aramaic for Father   ˡ 9 Or principles

¹²I plead with you, brothers and sisters, become like me, for I became like you. You have done me no wrong. ¹³As you know, it was because of an illness that I first preached the gospel to you. ¹⁴Even though my illness was a trial to you, you did not treat me with contempt or scorn. Instead, you welcomed me as if I were an angel of God, as if I were Christ Jesus himself. ¹⁵What has happened to all your joy? I can testify that, if you could have done so, you would have torn out your eyes and given them to me. ¹⁶Have I now become your enemy by telling you the truth?

¹⁷Those people are zealous to win you over, but for no good. What they want is to alienate you from us, so that you may have zeal for them. ¹⁸It is fine to be zealous, provided the purpose is good, and to be so always, not just when I am with you. ¹⁹My dear children, for whom I am again in the pains of childbirth until Christ is formed in you, ²⁰how I wish I could be with you now and change my tone, because I am perplexed about you!

Hagar and Sarah

²¹Tell me, you who want to be under the law, are you not aware of what the law says? ²²For it is written that Abraham had two sons, one by the slave woman and the other by the free woman. ²³His son by the slave woman was born as the result of human effort,ᵃ but his son by the free woman was born as the result of a divine promise.

²⁴I am taking these things figuratively, for the women represent two covenants. One covenant is from Mount Sinai and bears children who are to be slaves: This is Hagar. ²⁵Now Hagar stands for Mount Sinai in Arabia and corresponds to the present city of Jerusalem, because she is in slavery with her children. ²⁶But the Jerusalem that is above is free, and she is our mother. ²⁷For it is written:

> "Be glad, barren woman,
>   you who never bore a child;
> shout for joy and cry aloud,
>   you who were never in labor;
> because more are the children of the desolate woman
>   than of her who has a husband."ᵇ

²⁸Now you, brothers and sisters, like Isaac, are children of promise. ²⁹At that time the son born by human effort persecuted the son born by the power of the Spirit. It is the same now. ³⁰But what does Scripture say? "Get rid of the slave woman and her son, for the slave woman's son will never share in the inheritance with the free woman's son."ᶜ ³¹Therefore, brothers and sisters, we are not children of the slave woman, but of the free woman.

Freedom in Christ

5 It is for freedom that Christ has set us free. Stand firm, then, and do not let yourselves be burdened again by a yoke of slavery.

²Mark my words! I, Paul, tell you that if you let yourselves be circumcised, Christ will be of no value to you at all. ³Again I declare to every man who lets himself be circumcised that he is obligated to obey the whole law. ⁴You who are trying to be justified by the law have been alienated from Christ; you have fallen away from grace. ⁵But by faith we eagerly await through the Spirit the righteousness for which we hope. ⁶For in Christ Jesus neither circumcision nor uncircumcision has any value. The only thing that counts is faith expressing itself through love.

⁷You were running a good race. Who cut in on you to keep you from obeying the truth? ⁸That kind of persuasion does not come from the one who calls you. ⁹"A little yeast works through the whole batch of dough." ¹⁰I am confident in the Lord that you will take no other view. The one who is throwing you into confusion will have to pay the penalty, whoever that may be. ¹¹Brothers and sisters, if I am still preaching circumcision, why am I still being persecuted? In that case the offense of the cross has been abolished. ¹²As for those agitators, I wish they would go the whole way and emasculate themselves!

ᵃ 23 Or born according to the flesh; also in verse 29 ᵇ 27 Isaiah 54:1 ᶜ 30 Gen. 21:10

Life by the Spirit

[13] You, my brothers and sisters, were called to be free. But do not use your freedom to indulge the sinful nature[a]; rather, serve one another humbly in love. [14] For the entire law is fulfilled in keeping this one command: "Love your neighbor as yourself."[b] [15] If you keep on biting and devouring each other, watch out or you will be destroyed by each other.

[16] So I say, walk by the Spirit, and you will not gratify the desires of the sinful nature. [17] For the sinful nature desires what is contrary to the Spirit, and the Spirit what is contrary to the sinful nature. They are in conflict with each other, so that you are not to do whatever[c] you want. [18] But if you are led by the Spirit, you are not under the law.

[19] The acts of the sinful nature are obvious: sexual immorality, impurity and debauchery; [20] idolatry and witchcraft; hatred, discord, jealousy, fits of rage, selfish ambition, dissensions, factions [21] and envy; drunkenness, orgies, and the like. I warn you, as I did before, that those who live like this will not inherit the kingdom of God.

[22] But the fruit of the Spirit is love, joy, peace, patience, kindness, goodness, faithfulness, [23] gentleness and self-control. Against such things there is no law. [24] Those who belong to Christ Jesus have crucified the sinful nature with its passions and desires. [25] Since we live by the Spirit, let us keep in step with the Spirit. [26] Let us not become conceited, provoking and envying each other.

Doing Good to All

6 Brothers and sisters, if someone is caught in a sin, you who live by the Spirit should restore that person gently. But watch yourselves, or you also may be tempted. [2] Carry each other's burdens, and in this way you will fulfill the law of Christ. [3] If any of you think you are something when you are nothing, you deceive yourselves. [4] Each of you should test your own actions. Then you can take pride in yourself, without comparing yourself to somebody else, [5] for each of you should carry your own load. [6] Nevertheless, those who receive instruction in the word should share all good things with their instructor.

[7] Do not be deceived: God cannot be mocked. People reap what they sow. [8] Those who sow to please their sinful nature, from that nature[d] will reap destruction; those who sow to please the Spirit, from the Spirit will reap eternal life. [9] Let us not become weary in doing good, for at the proper time we will reap a harvest if we do not give up. [10] Therefore, as we have opportunity, let us do good to all people, especially to those who belong to the family of believers.

Not Circumcision but the New Creation

[11] See what large letters I use as I write to you with my own hand!

"conversations"

attitude «» 5:19–23

1 » Is your attitude toward life characterized by the fruit of the Spirit? Would your friends agree?

2 » Why do the lists in these verses focus as much on attitudes as they do on actions?

3 » How does your attitude help or hinder the Holy Spirit's work in your life?

For more on **attitude**, check the index. For the next Conversations, go to p. 1660.

1654

---

at issue: serving

6:7–10 Plant corn seeds and you get corn. Plant kernels of wheat and you get wheat. Sow to please the Holy Spirit and you get eternal blessings. It's true: You reap what you sow. How do you sow to please the Spirit? Do good to all people, especially other believers. Don't give up—even when you've been serving in the same way for years. Even if no one notices. Even if some take advantage of you. Even if you receive more criticism than praise. Even if it doesn't seem to make a difference. Remember, the harvest *will* come. So keep planting!

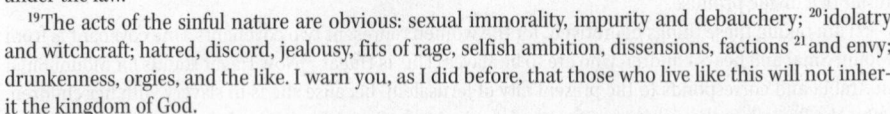

a 13 Or the flesh; also in verses 16, 17, 19 and 24   *b 14 Lev. 19:18*   *c 17 Or you do not do what*   *d 8 Or their flesh, from the flesh*

¹²Those who want to impress others by means of the flesh are trying to compel you to be circumcised. The only reason they do this is to avoid being persecuted for the cross of Christ. ¹³Not even those who are circumcised keep the law, yet they want you to be circumcised that they may boast about your circumcision in the flesh. ¹⁴May I never boast except in the cross of our Lord Jesus Christ, through which *a* the world has been crucified to me, and I to the world. ¹⁵Neither circumcision nor uncircumcision means anything; what counts is the new creation. ¹⁶Peace and mercy to all who follow this rule—to *b* the Israel of God.

¹⁷From now on, let no one cause me trouble, for I bear on my body the marks of Jesus.

¹⁸The grace of our Lord Jesus Christ be with your spirit, brothers and sisters. Amen.

ephesians

1656

AUTHOR
The apostle Paul.

AUDIENCE
Followers of Jesus; originally written to the
church in Ephesus.

DATE
About A.D. 60.

SETTING
Paul penned this letter from a Roman prison
to encourage all the Christians in Ephesus and
other areas.

VERSE TO REMEMBER
"There is one body and one Spirit, just as you
were called to one hope when you were
called." (4:4)

THEME TO CONSIDER
Christians practice unity when they agree to
disagree without dishonoring one another.

1 Paul, an apostle of Christ Jesus by the will of God,

To God's holy people in Ephesus,*a* the faithful in Christ Jesus:

²Grace and peace to you from God our Father and the Lord Jesus Christ.

Praise for Spiritual Blessings in Christ

³Praise be to the God and Father of our Lord Jesus Christ, who has blessed us in the heavenly realms with every spiritual blessing in Christ. ⁴For he chose us in him before the creation of the world to be holy and blameless in his sight. In love ⁵he*b* predestined us for adoption to sonship*c* through Jesus Christ, in accordance with his pleasure and will— ⁶to the praise of his glorious grace, which he has freely given us in the One he loves. ⁷In him we have redemption through his blood, the forgiveness of sins, in accordance with the riches of God's grace ⁸that he lavished on us. With all wisdom and understanding, ⁹he*d* made known to us the mystery of his will according to his good pleasure, which he purposed in Christ, ¹⁰to be put into effect when the times reach their fulfillment—to bring unity to all things in heaven and on earth under Christ.

HE IS: lavish

1657

1:7–8 The Ephesian believers were surrounded by the industry of idolatry. Many unbelievers made huge profits in the nearby temple of Diana. So Paul reminded the faithful Christians of the spiritual treasures God had lavished on them: redemption through his blood, forgiveness of sins and the riches of God's grace.

If unbelievers in our materialistic society seem to flourish while you falter financially, don't question God's love for you. Remember that he doesn't always give his children earthly riches, fame or glory. He is a *lavish* giver, but his best gifts are often invisible: redemption, forgiveness and grace (see 1 John 3:1).

For the next He Is, go to p. 1665.

---

¹¹In him we were also chosen,*e* having been predestined according to the plan of him who works out everything in conformity with the purpose of his will, ¹²in order that we, who were the first to put our hope in Christ, might be for the praise of his glory. ¹³And you also were included in Christ when you heard the word of truth, the gospel of your salvation. When you believed, you were marked in him with a seal, the promised Holy Spirit, ¹⁴who is a deposit guaranteeing our inheritance until the redemption of those who are God's possession—to the praise of his glory.

Thanksgiving and Prayer

¹⁵For this reason, ever since I heard about your faith in the Lord Jesus and your love for all his people, ¹⁶I have not stopped giving thanks for you, remembering you in my prayers. ¹⁷I keep asking that the God of our Lord Jesus Christ, the glorious Father, may give you the Spirit*f* of wisdom and revelation, so that you may know him better. ¹⁸I pray that the eyes of your heart may be enlightened in order that you may know the hope to which he has called you, the riches of his glorious inheritance in his people, ¹⁹and his incomparably great power for us who believe. That power is the same as the mighty strength ²⁰he exerted when he raised Christ from the dead and seated him at his right hand in the heavenly realms, ²¹far above all rule and authority, power and dominion, and every name that can be invoked, not only in the present age but also in the one to come. ²²And God placed all things under his feet and appointed him to be head over everything for the church, ²³which is his body, the fullness of him who fills everything in every way.

---

a 1 Some early manuscripts do not have *in Ephesus.* *b* 4,5 Or *sight in love.* ⁵*He* *c* 5 The Greek word for *adoption to sonship* is a legal term referring to the full legal standing of an adopted male heir in Roman culture. *d* 8,9 Or *us with all wisdom and understanding.* ⁹*And he* *e* 11 Or *were made heirs* *f* 17 Or *a spirit*

Made Alive in Christ

2 As for you, you were dead in your transgressions and sins, [2] in which you used to live when you followed the ways of this world and of the ruler of the kingdom of the air, the spirit who is now at work in those who are disobedient. [3] All of us also lived among them at one time, gratifying the cravings of our sinful nature[a] and following its desires and thoughts. Like the rest, we were by nature deserving of wrath. [4] But because of his great love for us, God, who is rich in mercy, [5] made us alive with Christ even when we were dead in transgressions—it is by grace you have been saved. [6] And God raised us up with Christ and seated us with him in the heavenly realms in Christ Jesus, [7] in order that in the coming ages he might show the incomparable riches of his grace, expressed in his kindness to us in Christ Jesus. [8] For it is by grace you have been saved, through faith—and this is not from yourselves, it is the gift of God— [9] not by works, so that no one can boast. [10] For we are God's handiwork, created in Christ Jesus to do good works, which God prepared in advance for us to do.

Jew and Gentile Reconciled Through Christ

[11] Therefore, remember that formerly you who are Gentiles by birth and called "uncircumcised" by those who call themselves "the circumcision" (which is done in the body by human hands)— [12] remember that at that time you were separate from Christ, excluded from citizenship in Israel and foreigners to the covenants of the promise, without hope and without God in the world. [13] But now in Christ Jesus you who once were far away have been brought near by the blood of Christ.

[14] For he himself is our peace, who has made the two one and has destroyed the barrier, the dividing wall of hostility, [15] by setting aside in his flesh the law with its commands and regulations. His purpose was to create in himself one new humanity out of the two, thus making peace, [16] and in one body to reconcile both of them to God through the cross, by which he put to death their hostility. [17] He came and preached peace to you who were far away and peace to those who were near. [18] For through him we both have access to the Father by one Spirit.

[19] Consequently, you are no longer foreigners and strangers, but fellow citizens with God's people and also members of his household, [20] built on the foundation of the apostles and prophets, with Christ Jesus himself as the chief cornerstone. [21] In him the whole building is joined together and rises to become a holy temple in the Lord. [22] And in him you too are being built together to become a dwelling in which God lives by his Spirit.

God's Marvelous Plan for the Gentiles

3 For this reason I, Paul, the prisoner of Christ Jesus for the sake of you Gentiles— [2] Surely you have heard about the administration of God's grace that was given to me for you, [3] that is, the mystery made known to me by revelation, as I have already written briefly. [4] In reading this, then, you will be able to understand my insight into the mystery of Christ, [5] which was not made known to people in other generations as it has now been revealed by the Spirit to God's holy apostles and prophets. [6] This mystery is that through the gospel the Gentiles are heirs together with Israel, members together of one body, and sharers together in the promise in Christ Jesus.

[7] I became a servant of this gospel by the gift of God's grace given me through the working of his power. [8] Although I am less than the least of all the Lord's people, this grace was given me: to preach to the Gentiles the boundless riches of Christ, [9] and to make plain to everyone the administration of this mystery, which for ages past was kept hidden in God, who created all things. [10] His intent was that now, through the church, the manifold wisdom of God should be made known to the rulers and authorities in the heavenly realms, [11] according to his eternal purpose that he accomplished in Christ Jesus our Lord. [12] In him and through faith in him we may approach God with freedom and confidence. [13] I ask you, therefore, not to be discouraged because of my sufferings for you, which are your glory.

A Prayer for the Ephesians

[14] For this reason I kneel before the Father, [15] from whom every family[b] in heaven and on earth derives its name. [16] I pray that out of his glorious riches he may strengthen you with power through his Spirit in

your inner being, ¹⁷so that Christ may dwell in your hearts through faith. And I pray that you, being rooted and established in love, ¹⁸may have power, together with all the Lord's people, to grasp how wide and long and high and deep is the love of Christ, ¹⁹and to know this love that surpasses knowledge—that you may be filled to the measure of all the fullness of God.

²⁰Now to him who is able to do immeasurably more than all we ask or imagine, according to his power that is at work within us, ²¹to him be glory in the church and in Christ Jesus throughout all generations, for ever and ever! Amen.

Unity and Maturity in the Body of Christ

4 As a prisoner for the Lord, then, I urge you to live a life worthy of the calling you have received. ²Be completely humble and gentle; be patient, bearing with one another in love. ³Make every effort to keep the unity of the Spirit through the bond of peace. ⁴There is one body and one Spirit, just as you were called to one hope when you were called; ⁵one Lord, one faith, one baptism; ⁶one God and Father of all, who is over all and through all and in all.

⁷But to each one of us grace has been given as Christ apportioned it. ⁸This is why it*ᵃ* says:

> "When he ascended on high,
> he took many captives
> and gave gifts to his people."*ᵇ*

⁹(What does "he ascended" mean except that he also descended to the lower, earthly regions*ᶜ*? ¹⁰He who descended is the very one who ascended higher than all the heavens, in order to fill the whole universe.) ¹¹So Christ himself gave the apostles, the prophets, the evangelists, the pastors and teachers, ¹²to equip his people for works of service, so that the body of Christ may be built up ¹³until we all reach unity in the faith and in the knowledge of the Son of God and become mature, attaining to the whole measure of the fullness of Christ.

¹⁴Then we will no longer be infants, tossed back and forth by the waves, and blown here and there by every wind of teaching and by the cunning and craftiness of people in their deceitful scheming. ¹⁵Instead, speaking the truth in love, we will in all things grow up into him who is the head, that is, Christ. ¹⁶From him the whole body, joined and held together by every supporting ligament, grows and builds itself up in love, as each part does its work.

Instructions for Christian Living

¹⁷So I tell you this, and insist on it in the Lord, that you must no longer live as the Gentiles do, in the futility of their thinking. ¹⁸They are darkened in their understanding and separated from the life of God because of the ignorance that is in them due to the hardening of their hearts. ¹⁹Having lost all sensitivity, they have given themselves over to sensuality so as to indulge in every kind of impurity, and they are full of greed.

²⁰That, however, is not the way of life you learned ²¹when you heard about Christ and were taught in him in accordance with the truth that is in Jesus. ²²You were taught, with regard to your former way of life, to put off your old self, which is being corrupted by its deceitful desires; ²³to be made new in the attitude of your minds; ²⁴and to put on the new self, created to be like God in true righteousness and holiness.

²⁵Therefore each of you must put off falsehood and speak truthfully to your neighbor, for we are all

an issue: journey on burnout

3:14–21 Feeling burnt out, disillusioned, exhausted or lonely? At some point on the road of life we all hit "empty." When it happens to you, it's time to pray Paul's prayer here—and expect God to answer it. Ask God to strengthen your inner self—because only Christ can fill the emptiness in your heart. Ask God to help you grasp a measure of his immeasurable love for you—to experience it yourself so that you may be filled with the fullness of God. His unfathomable love is always the renewing antidote for burnout. It may take time, but God *will* answer.

1659

ᵃ 8 Or *God*   *ᵇ 8* Psalm 68:18   *ᶜ 9* Or *the depths of the earth* members of one body. [26]"In your anger do not sin"[a]: Do not let the sun go down while you are still angry, [27]and do not give the devil a foothold. [28]Those who have been stealing must steal no longer, but must work, doing something useful with their own hands, that they may have something to share with those in need.

[29]Do not let any unwholesome talk come out of your mouths, but only what is helpful for building others up according to their needs, that it may benefit those who listen. [30]And do not grieve the Holy Spirit of God, with whom you were sealed for the day of redemption. [31]Get rid of all bitterness, rage and anger, brawling and slander, along with every form of malice. [32]Be kind and compassionate to one another, forgiving each other, just as in Christ God forgave you.

conversations
anger «» 4:26–27

1 » When does anger become sin?

2 » Why is it important not to let the sun go down while you're still angry? Do you do that?

3 » What makes lingering anger so dangerous?

For more on anger, check the index.
For the next Conversations, go to p. 1668.

1660

5 [1]Follow God's example, therefore, as dearly loved children [2]and walk in the way of love, just as Christ loved us and gave himself up for us as a fragrant offering and sacrifice to God.

[3]But among you there must not be even a hint of sexual immorality, or of any kind of impurity, or of greed, because these are improper for the Lord's people. [4]Nor should there be obscenity, foolish talk or coarse joking, which are out of place, but rather thanksgiving. [5]For of this you can be sure: No immoral, impure or greedy person—such a person is an idolater—has any inheritance in the kingdom of Christ and of God.[b] [6]Let no one deceive you with empty words, for because of such things God's wrath comes on those who are disobedient. [7]Therefore do not be partners with them.

[8]For you were once darkness, but now you are light in the Lord. Live as children of light [9](for the fruit of the light consists in all goodness, righteousness and truth) [10]and find out what pleases the Lord. [11]Have nothing to do with the fruitless deeds of darkness, but rather expose them. [12]It is shameful even to mention what the disobedient do in secret. [13]But everything exposed by the light becomes visible— and everything that is illuminated becomes a light. [14]This is why it is said:

> "Wake up, sleeper,
>   rise from the dead,
>   and Christ will shine on you."

[15]Be very careful, then, how you live—not as unwise but as wise, [16]making the most of every opportunity, because the days are evil. [17]Therefore do not be foolish, but understand what the Lord's will is. [18]Do not get drunk on wine, which leads to debauchery. Instead, be filled with the Spirit, [19]speaking to one another with psalms, hymns and songs from the Spirit. Sing and make music from your heart to the Lord, [20]always giving thanks to God the Father for everything, in the name of our Lord Jesus Christ.

Instructions for Christian Households

[21]Submit to one another out of reverence for Christ.

[22]Wives, submit yourselves to your own husbands as you do to the Lord. [23]For the husband is the head of the wife as Christ is the head of the church, his body, of which he is the Savior. [24]Now as the church submits to Christ, so also wives should submit to their husbands in everything.

[25]Husbands, love your wives, just as Christ loved the church and gave himself up for her [26]to make her holy, cleansing[c] her by the washing with water through the word, [27]and to present her to himself as a radiant church, without stain or wrinkle or any other blemish, but holy and blameless. [28]In this same way, husbands ought to love their wives as their own bodies. He who loves his wife loves himself. [29]After

---

[a] 26 Psalm 4:4 (see Septuagint)   [b] 5 Or *kingdom of the Christ and God*   [c] 26 Or *having cleansed*

all, people have never hated their own bodies, but they feed and care for them, just as Christ does the church— ³⁰for we are members of his body. ³¹"For this reason a man will leave his father and mother and be united to his wife, and the two will become one flesh."ᵃ ³²This is a profound mystery—but I am talking about Christ and the church. ³³However, each one of you also must love his wife as he loves himself, and the wife must respect her husband.

6 Children, obey your parents in the Lord, for this is right. ²"Honor your father and mother"—which is the first commandment with a promise— ³"so that it may go well with you and that you may enjoy long life on the earth."ᵇ

⁴Fathers,ᶜ do not exasperate your children; instead, bring them up in the training and instruction of the Lord.

⁵Slaves, obey your earthly masters with respect and fear, and with sincerity of heart, just as you would obey Christ. ⁶Obey them not only to win their favor when their eye is on you, but as slaves of Christ, doing the will of God from your heart. ⁷Serve wholeheartedly, as if you were serving the Lord, not people, ⁸because you know that the Lord will reward each one of you for whatever good you do, whether you are slave or free.

⁹And masters, treat your slaves in the same way. Do not threaten them, since you know that he who is both their Master and yours is in heaven, and there is no favoritism with him.

The Armor of God

¹⁰Finally, be strong in the Lord and in his mighty power. ¹¹Put on the full armor of God, so that you can take your stand against the devil's schemes. ¹²For our struggle is not against flesh and blood, but against the rulers, against the authorities, against the powers of this dark world and against the spiritual forces of evil in the heavenly realms. ¹³Therefore put on the full armor of God, so that when the day of evil comes, you may be able to stand your ground, and after you have done everything, to stand. ¹⁴Stand firm then, with the belt of truth buckled around your waist, with the breastplate of righteousness in place, ¹⁵and with your feet fitted with the readiness that comes from the gospel of peace. ¹⁶In addition to all this, take up the shield of faith, with which you can extinguish all the flaming arrows of the evil one. ¹⁷Take the helmet of salvation and the sword of the Spirit, which is the word of God.

¹⁸And pray in the Spirit on all occasions with all kinds of prayers and requests. With this in mind, be alert and always keep on praying for all the Lord's people. ¹⁹Pray also for me, that whenever I speak, words may be given me so that I will fearlessly make known the mystery of the gospel, ²⁰for which I am an ambassador in chains. Pray that I may declare it fearlessly, as I should.

Final Greetings

²¹Tychicus, the dear brother and faithful servant in the Lord, will tell you everything, so that you also may know how I am and what I am doing. ²²I am sending him to you for this very purpose, that you may know how we are, and that he may encourage you.

²³Peace to the brothers and sisters, and love with faith from God the Father and the Lord Jesus Christ. ²⁴Grace to all who love our Lord Jesus Christ with an undying love.ᵈ

1661

at issue : submission

5:21–33 Contrary to popular belief, submission in marriage is not a curse inflicted on women. Submitting to your husband doesn't mean you're inferior, weak or unimportant. Submission is God's call to wives *and* husbands to yield to each other in love. God desires our reverence for him to translate into love and respect for each other. So he gives a husband and wife unique ways to put the other first in marriage—which promotes harmony and ultimately brings God glory. Your role differs from your husband's, but it's equally valuable. Consider it a privilege, not a curse, and remember your motive—your reverence for Christ.

ᵃ 31 Gen. 2:24   ᵇ 3 Deut. 5:16   ᶜ 4 Or *Parents*   ᵈ 24 Or *Grace and immortality to all who love our Lord Jesus Christ.*

1662

philippians

AUTHOR
The apostle Paul.

AUDIENCE
The church in Philippi and all followers
of Jesus.

DATE
About A.D. 61.

SETTING
Under house arrest in Rome, Paul writes a
letter to the believers in Philippi, the location
of the first European church.

VERSE TO REMEMBER
"I want to know Christ—yes, to know the
power of his resurrection and participation
in his sufferings, becoming like him in his
death." (3:10)

THEME TO CONSIDER
Knowing Christ is the supreme goal of life.

1 Paul and Timothy, servants of Christ Jesus,

To all God's holy people in Christ Jesus at Philippi, together with the overseers and deacons:

²Grace and peace to you from God our Father and the Lord Jesus Christ.

Thanksgiving and Prayer

³I thank my God every time I remember you. ⁴In all my prayers for all of you, I always pray with joy ⁵because of your partnership in the gospel from the first day until now, ⁶being confident of this, that he who began a good work in you will carry it on to completion until the day of Christ Jesus.

⁷It is right for me to feel this way about all of you, since I have you in my heart and, whether I am in chains or defending and confirming the gospel, all of you share in God's grace with me. ⁸God can testify how I long for all of you with the affection of Christ Jesus.

⁹And this is my prayer: that your love may abound more and more in knowledge and depth of insight, ¹⁰so that you may be able to discern what is best and may be pure and blameless for the day of Christ, ¹¹filled with the fruit of righteousness that comes through Jesus Christ—to the glory and praise of God.

Paul's Chains Advance the Gospel

¹²Now I want you to know, brothers and sisters, that what has happened to me has actually served to advance the gospel. ¹³As a result, it has become clear throughout the whole palace guard*ᵃ* and to everyone else that I am in chains for Christ. ¹⁴And because of my chains, most of the brothers and sisters have become confident in the Lord and dare all the more to proclaim the gospel without fear.

1663

¹⁵It is true that some preach Christ out of envy and rivalry, but others out of goodwill. ¹⁶The latter do so out of love, knowing that I am put here for the defense of the gospel. ¹⁷The former preach Christ out of selfish ambition, not sincerely, supposing that they can stir up trouble for me while I am in chains. ¹⁸But what does it matter? The important thing is that in every way, whether from false motives or true, Christ is preached. And because of this I rejoice.

Yes, and I will continue to rejoice, ¹⁹for I know that through your prayers and God's provision of the Spirit of Jesus Christ what has happened to me will turn out for my deliverance.*ᵇ* ²⁰I eagerly expect and hope that I will in no way be ashamed, but will have sufficient courage so that now as always Christ will be exalted in my body, whether by life or by death. ²¹For to me, to live is Christ and to die is gain. ²²If I am to go on living in the body, this will mean fruitful labor for me. Yet what shall I choose? I do not know! ²³I am torn between the two: I desire to depart and be with Christ, which is better by far; ²⁴but it is more necessary for you that I remain in the body. ²⁵Convinced of this, I know that I will remain, and I will continue with all of you for your progress and joy in the faith, ²⁶so that through my being with you again your boasting in Christ Jesus will abound on account of me.

Life Worthy of the Gospel

²⁷Whatever happens, as citizens of heaven live in a manner worthy of the gospel of Christ. Then, whether I come and see you or only hear about you in my absence, I will know that you stand firm in the one Spirit,*ᶜ* striving together with one accord for the faith of the gospel ²⁸without being frightened in any way by those who oppose you. This is a sign to them that they will be destroyed, but that you will be saved—and that by God. ²⁹For it has been granted to you on behalf of Christ not only to believe on him, but also to suffer for him, ³⁰since you are going through the same struggle you saw I had, and now hear that I still have.

Imitating Christ's Humility

2 Therefore if you have any encouragement from being united with Christ, if any comfort from his love, if any common sharing in the Spirit, if any tenderness and compassion, ²then make my joy complete by being like-minded, having the same love, being one in spirit and of one mind. ³Do nothing out of selfish ambition or vain conceit. Rather, in humility value others above yourselves, ⁴not looking to your own interests but each of you to the interests of the others.

ᵃ 13 Or whole palace ᵇ 19 Or vindication; or salvation ᶜ 27 Or in one spirit

⁵In your relationships with one another, have the same attitude of mind Christ Jesus had:

⁶Who, being in very nature*ᵃ* God,
did not consider equality with God
something to be used to his own
advantage;
⁷rather, he made himself nothing
by taking the very nature*ᵇ* of a
servant,
being made in human likeness.
⁸And being found in appearance as a
human being,
he humbled himself
by becoming obedient to death—
even death on a cross!

⁹Therefore God exalted him to the
highest place
and gave him the name that is above
every name,
¹⁰that at the name of Jesus every knee
should bow,
in heaven and on earth and under the
earth,
¹¹and every tongue acknowledge that
Jesus Christ is Lord,
to the glory of God the Father.

2:1–11 Every woman has her own personal "Bill of Rights." Yours might read: "I have the right to a hot bath at least once a week. I have the right to spend time and money on my hobbies. I have the right to decide my husband's free time." But Paul points out that clinging to your rights won't cultivate the unity God desires. Just as Jesus humbled himself in order to serve us, you also are called to set aside your rights and look after your husband's interests. This *may* promote harmony in your relationship with your husband; it *will* please Jesus.

at issue: marriage

1664

Do Everything Without Grumbling

¹²Therefore, my dear friends, as you have always obeyed—not only in my presence, but now much more in my absence—continue to work out your salvation with fear and trembling, ¹³for it is God who works in you to will and to act in order to fulfill his good purpose.

¹⁴Do everything without grumbling or arguing, ¹⁵so that you may become blameless and pure, "children of God without fault in a warped and crooked generation."*ᶜ* Then you will shine among them like stars in the sky ¹⁶as you hold firmly to the word of life. And then I will be able to boast on the day of Christ that I did not run or labor in vain. ¹⁷But even if I am being poured out like a drink offering on the sacrifice and service coming from your faith, I am glad and rejoice with all of you. ¹⁸So you too should be glad and rejoice with me.

Timothy and Epaphroditus

¹⁹I hope in the Lord Jesus to send Timothy to you soon, that I also may be cheered when I receive news about you. ²⁰I have no one else like him, who will show genuine concern for your welfare. ²¹For everyone looks out for their own interests, not those of Jesus Christ. ²²But you know that Timothy has proved himself, because as a son with his father he has served with me in the work of the gospel. ²³I hope, therefore, to send him as soon as I see how things go with me. ²⁴And I am confident in the Lord that I myself will come soon.

²⁵But I think it is necessary to send back to you Epaphroditus, my brother, co-worker and fellow soldier, who is also your messenger, whom you sent to take care of my needs. ²⁶For he longs for all of you and is distressed because you heard he was ill. ²⁷Indeed he was ill, and almost died. But God had mercy on him, and not on him only but also on me, to spare me sorrow upon sorrow. ²⁸Therefore I am all the

---
ᵃ 6 Or *in the form of* *ᵇ 7* Or *the form* *ᶜ 15* Deut. 32:5

more eager to send him, so that when you see him again you may be glad and I may have less anxiety. [29]Welcome him in the Lord with great joy, and honor people like him, [30]because he almost died for the work of Christ. He risked his life to make up for the help you yourselves could not give me.

No Confidence in the Flesh

3 Further, my brothers and sisters, rejoice in the Lord! It is no trouble for me to write the same things to you again, and it is a safeguard for you. [2]Watch out for those dogs, those evildoers, those mutilators of the flesh. [3]For it is we who are the circumcision, we who serve God by his Spirit, who boast in Christ Jesus, and who put no confidence in the flesh— [4]though I myself have reasons for such confidence.

If others think they have reasons to put confidence in the flesh, I have more: [5]circumcised on the eighth day, of the people of Israel, of the tribe of Benjamin, a Hebrew of Hebrews; in regard to the law, a Pharisee; [6]as for zeal, persecuting the church; as for righteousness based on the law, faultless.

[7]But whatever were gains to me I now consider loss for the sake of Christ. [8]What is more, I consider everything a loss because of the surpassing worth of knowing Christ Jesus my Lord, for whose sake I have lost all things. I consider them garbage, that I may gain Christ [9]and be found in him, not having a righteousness of my own that comes from the law, but that which is through faith in*a* Christ—the righteousness that comes from God on the basis of faith. [10]I want to know Christ—yes, to know the power of his resurrection and participation in his sufferings, becoming like him in his death, [11]and so, somehow, attaining to the resurrection from the dead.

[12]Not that I have already obtained all this, or have already arrived at my goal, but I press on to take hold of that for which Christ Jesus took hold of me. [13]Brothers and sisters, I do not consider myself yet to have taken hold of it. But one thing I do: Forgetting what is behind and straining toward what is ahead, [14]I press on toward the goal to win the prize for which God has called me heavenward in Christ Jesus.

Following Paul's Example

[15]All of us, then, who are mature should take such a view of things. And if on some point you think differently, that too God will make clear to you. [16]Only let us live up to what we have already attained.

[17]Join together in following my example, brothers and sisters, and just as you have us as a model, keep your eyes on those who live as we do. [18]For, as I have often told you before and now tell you again even with tears, many live as enemies of the cross of Christ. [19]Their destiny is destruction, their god is their stomach, and their glory is in their shame. Their mind is set on earthly things. [20]But our citizenship is in heaven. And we eagerly await a Savior from there, the Lord Jesus Christ, [21]who, by the power that enables him to bring everything under his control, will transform our lowly bodies so that they will be like his glorious body.

1665

---

a 9 Or *through the faithfulness of*

HE IS: in control

3:19–21 Many professing Christians pursue earthly things, allowing their appetites to hold sway over their lives. So Paul wrote to remind true believers that their citizenship is in heaven. For residents of God's kingdom, Christ will one day bring everything under his control.

Your driver's license specifies your home state; your passport shows your national residence. But the things that control you reveal your spiritual citizenship. If earthly pleasures are your focus, then you're at home in this world. If you're preoccupied with heavenly things, then Jesus is *in control* of your life, and you're a citizen of his divine kingdom

For the next He Is, go to p. 1670.

myth# 95 "THE PERFECT CHURCH IS OUT THERE."

For the past six months there's been an undercurrent of tension at my church. Everyone's talking about one of our associate pastors who's about to leave and start a new church. Some of the members of our congregation are going with him to help with the church plant. Rumor has it that he's had some philosophical disagreements with our senior pastor. I'm not sure if that's true or not.

Some of our friends here are really angry and vocal about it. They say we need to discuss the matter openly with the senior pastor since he seems to be hiding the truth. Frankly, I don't know what to believe.

Matt and I came to this church five years ago, still reeling from the split that occurred in our last church, a church we'd attended ever since we were married ten years before. The split was over money issues. Now that I look back, it seems so trivial. Why couldn't we resolve those issues?

Regardless, that split was really painful. That's why this church seemed like a gift from God. He really met us here. I experienced some much-needed healing, and I know Matt did too. The worship is outstanding and being involved in the community has been great—well, it was great until the rumors about the disagreement between the pastors began.

Matt and I have talked this through, and we're wondering if we need to find another church. Maybe we've been settling all along. Maybe we became involved with this church while we were "on the rebound" from our other church. I've heard of churches that don't have these ridiculous splits, and I know the right church for us is out there. We just have to find it.

—Myra

MANY PEOPLE WHO

have gone through difficult relationships dream of "the perfect person" out there somewhere—the one who will solve all their problems and complement them perfectly. The same wistful thoughts are sometimes applied to churches. When problems occur, the belief that "the perfect church is out there somewhere" provides a sense of comfort, albeit a false one.

You've probably heard the old joke about finding the perfect church. Once you join, it ceases to be perfect. The church—the body of Christ—is made up of imperfect people; thus, it could not possibly be the "perfect" church. But the Holy Spirit is the glue that perfectly bonds the church and keeps this "body" attached to the perfect head—Jesus.

Sooner or later, all churches face conflicts of some kind. How they handle these times of disagreement shows their level of unity and commitment (or lack thereof). It also shows their level of trust in God and his ability, ultimately, to help his people work through problems. Rather than growing disillusioned with your church and jumping ship, try the following:

- Accept that no church is perfect—yours included.

- Pray (often and hard)—for unity in your church; for the Holy Spirit to lead and to bring peace; for humility and patience; and for God to work in your church.

- Be a peacemaker—cover over others' sins with love and help bring the factions together. Listen to each other, and be open to hearing others' ideas.

- Be immovable on the essentials (see 2 Thessalonians 2:15) and flexible on the non-essentials (see 1 Corinthians 8:8–13). Take a strong stand when you need to (e.g., the deity and supremacy of Christ), and humbly let go of the issues that don't truly matter (e.g., the church's carpet color).

- Stay committed. If your church starts preaching false doctrine, by all means, leave. But if the disagreement isn't heretical and the Lord is leading you to stay and to help bring peace, try to choose that road, even though it's a hard one.

Remember, perfect people don't have any problems. Imperfect people do. That's why the perfect church isn't out there somewhere. But the perfect God is.

1667

"A majority of Americans did not rate their church as 'excellent' in any aspect of ministry."
—Barna Research Group (1991)

"over all these virtues put on love, which binds them all together in perfect unity."

COLOSSIANS 3:14

SEE ALSO

1 Corinthians 12:12–13
Colossians 1:17–18
Hebrews 10:24–25

For more on **Church**, check the index.

philippians 4:1

Closing Appeal for Steadfastness and Unity

4 Therefore, my brothers and sisters, you whom I love and long for, my joy and crown, stand firm in the Lord in this way, dear friends!

²I plead with Euodia and I plead with Syntyche to be of the same mind in the Lord. ³Yes, and I ask you, my true companion, help these women since they have contended at my side in the cause of the gospel, along with Clement and the rest of my co-workers, whose names are in the book of life.

Final Exhortations

⁴Rejoice in the Lord always. I will say it again: Rejoice! ⁵Let your gentleness be evident to all. The Lord is near. ⁶Do not be anxious about anything, but in every situation, by prayer and petition, with thanksgiving, present your requests to God. ⁷And the peace of God, which transcends all understanding, will guard your hearts and your minds in Christ Jesus.

⁸Finally, brothers and sisters, whatever is true, whatever is noble, whatever is right, whatever is pure, whatever is lovely, whatever is admirable—if anything is excellent or praiseworthy—think about such things. ⁹Whatever you have learned or received or heard from me, or seen in me—put it into practice. And the God of peace will be with you.

Thanks for Their Gifts

¹⁰I rejoiced greatly in the Lord that at last you renewed your concern for me. Indeed, you were concerned, but you had no opportunity to show it. ¹¹I am not saying this because I am in need, for I have learned to be content whatever the circumstances. ¹²I know what it is to be in need, and I know what it is to have plenty. I have learned the secret of being content in any and every situation, whether well fed or hungry, whether living in plenty or in want. ¹³I can do all this through him who gives me strength.

¹⁴Yet it was good of you to share in my troubles. ¹⁵Moreover, as you Philippians know, in the early days of your acquaintance with the gospel, when I set out from Macedonia, not one church shared with me in the matter of giving and receiving, except you only; ¹⁶for even when I was in Thessalonica, you sent me aid more than once when I was in need. ¹⁷Not that I desire your gifts; what I desire is that more be credited to your account. ¹⁸I have received full payment and have more than enough. I am amply supplied, now that I have received from Epaphroditus the gifts you sent. They are a fragrant offering, an acceptable sacrifice, pleasing to God. ¹⁹And my God will meet all your needs according to the riches of his glory in Christ Jesus.

²⁰To our God and Father be glory for ever and ever. Amen.

Final Greetings

²¹Greet all God's people in Christ Jesus. The brothers and sisters who are with me send greetings. ²²All the Lord's people here send you greetings, especially those who belong to Caesar's household.

²³The grace of the Lord Jesus Christ be with your spirit. Amen.ᵃ

"conversations"

dissatisfaction «» 4:11

1» With what aspects of your life do you feel dissatisfied?

2» How can feelings of dissatisfaction rob you of God's blessing?

3» What do you think it means to "learn" to be content?

For more on **dissatisfaction**, check the index.
For the next Conversations, go to p. 1673.

1668

Any doubts that Jesus was fully
God and fully human? ≫ (1:15–20; 2:9–10)

Are you an unwitting captive? ≫ (2:8)

Would Jesus ever make a public
spectacle of someone? ≫ (2:13–15)

What's the flavor of your conversations? ≫ (4:6)

What did Paul mean by his cryptic closing? ≫ (4:18)

colossians

AUTHOR
The apostle Paul.

AUDIENCE
The church in Colosse (a city in what is
modern-day Turkey) and all followers
of Jesus.

DATE
About A.D. 60.

SETTING
Paul writes from house arrest in Rome to
dispel false teachings in Colosse.

VERSE TO REMEMBER
"He is before all things, and in him all
things hold together." (1:17)

THEME TO CONSIDER
Jesus Christ is Lord of all; is he also Lord
of you?

1 Paul, an apostle of Christ Jesus by the will of God, and Timothy our brother,

²To God's holy people in Colossae, the faithful brothers and sisters in Christ:

Grace and peace to you from God our Father.ᵃ

Thanksgiving and Prayer

³We always thank God, the Father of our Lord Jesus Christ, when we pray for you, ⁴because we have heard of your faith in Christ Jesus and of the love you have for all his people— ⁵the faith and love that spring from the hope stored up for you in heaven and about which you have already heard in the true word of the gospel ⁶that has come to you. In the same way, the gospel is bearing fruit and growing throughout the whole world— just as it has been doing among you since the day you heard it and truly understood God's grace. ⁷You learned it from Epaphras, our dear fellow servant,ᵇ who is a faithful minister of Christ on ourᶜ behalf, ⁸and who also told us of your love in the Spirit.

⁹For this reason, since the day we heard about you, we have not stopped praying for you. We continually ask God to fill you with the knowledge of his will through all the wisdom and understanding that the Spirit gives,ᵈ ¹⁰so that you may live a life worthy of the Lord and please him in every way: bearing fruit in every good work, growing in the knowledge of God, ¹¹being strengthened with all power according to his glorious might so that you may have great endurance and patience, ¹²and giving joyful thanks to the Father, who has qualified youᵉ to share in the inheritance of his people in the kingdom of light. ¹³For he has rescued us from the dominion of darkness and brought us into the kingdom of the Son he loves, ¹⁴in whom we have redemption, the forgiveness of sins.

The Supremacy of the Son of God

¹⁵The Son is the image of the invisible God, the firstborn over all creation. ¹⁶For in him all things were created: things in heaven and on earth, visible and invisible, whether thrones or powers or rulers or authorities; all things have been created through him and for him. ¹⁷He is before all things, and in him all things hold together. ¹⁸And he is the head of the body, the church; he is the beginning and the firstborn from among the dead, so that in everything he might have the supremacy. ¹⁹For God was pleased to have all his fullness dwell in him, ²⁰and through him to reconcile to himself all things, whether things on earth or things in heaven, by making peace through his blood, shed on the cross.

HE IS: supreme

1:16–18 False teachers in Colosse taught that other things—in heaven and on earth, visible and invisible—were as significant as Christ. Paul corrected this deceptive doctrine, reminding the Colossians that Jesus is *supreme* in every way. Any teaching that questions Christ's supremacy is a sham.

Jesus wants—and deserves—supremacy in everything. Have you given it to him? To make Christ *supreme* in your life means to give him the first place and his rightful authority in your thoughts, your actions, your work, your motives, your plans. Does he come before all things in your life? He's the one holding your life together.

For the next He Is, go to p. 1675.

²¹Once you were alienated from God and were enemies in your minds because ofᶠ your evil behavior. ²²But now he has reconciled you by Christ's physical body through death to present you holy in his sight, without blemish and free from accusation— ²³if you continue in your faith, established and firm, and do not move from the hope held out in the gospel. This is the gospel that you heard and that has been proclaimed to every creature under heaven, and of which I, Paul, have become a servant.

ᵃ *2* Some manuscripts *Father and the Lord Jesus Christ*   ᵇ *7* Or *slave*   ᶜ *7* Some manuscripts *your*   ᵈ *9* Or *all spiritual wisdom and understanding*   ᵉ *12* Some manuscripts *us*   ᶠ *21* Or *minds, as shown by*

Paul's Labor for the Church

²⁴Now I rejoice in what I am suffering for you, and I fill up in my flesh what is still lacking in regard to Christ's afflictions, for the sake of his body, which is the church. ²⁵I have become its servant by the commission God gave me to present to you the word of God in its fullness— ²⁶the mystery that has been kept hidden for ages and generations, but is now disclosed to the Lord's people. ²⁷To them God has chosen to make known among the Gentiles the glorious riches of this mystery, which is Christ in you, the hope of glory.

²⁸We proclaim him, admonishing and teaching everyone with all wisdom, so that we may present everyone fully mature in Christ. ²⁹To this end I strenuously contend with all the energy Christ so powerfully works in me.

2 I want you to know how hard I am contending for you and for those at Laodicea, and for all who have not met me personally. ²My goal is that they may be encouraged in heart and united in love, so that they may have the full riches of complete understanding, in order that they may know the mystery of God, namely, Christ, ³in whom are hidden all the treasures of wisdom and knowledge. ⁴I tell you this so that no one may deceive you by fine-sounding arguments. ⁵For though I am absent from you in body, I am present with you in spirit and delight to see how disciplined you are and how firm your faith in Christ is.

Spiritual Fullness in Christ

⁶So then, just as you received Christ Jesus as Lord, continue to live your lives in him, ⁷rooted and built up in him, strengthened in the faith as you were taught, and overflowing with thankfulness.

⁸See to it that no one takes you captive through hollow and deceptive philosophy, which depends on human tradition and the elemental spiritual forces*ᵃ* of this world rather than on Christ.

⁹For in Christ all the fullness of the Deity lives in bodily form, ¹⁰and in Christ you have been brought to fullness. He is the head over every power and authority. ¹¹In him you were also circumcised with a circumcision not performed by human hands. Your sinful nature*ᵇ* was put off when you were circumcised by*ᶜ* Christ, ¹²having been buried with him in baptism, in which you were also raised with him through your faith in the working of God, who raised him from the dead.

¹³When you were dead in your sins and in the uncircumcision of your sinful nature,*ᵇ* God made you*ᵈ* alive with Christ. He forgave us all our sins, ¹⁴having canceled the charge of our legal indebtedness, which stood against us and condemned us; he has taken it away, nailing it to the cross. ¹⁵And having disarmed the powers and authorities, he made a public spectacle of them, triumphing over them by the cross.*ᵉ*

Freedom From Human Rules

¹⁶Therefore do not let anyone judge you by what you eat or drink, or with regard to a religious festival, a New Moon celebration or a Sabbath day. ¹⁷These are a shadow of the things that were to come; the reality, however, is found in Christ. ¹⁸Do not let anyone who delights in false humility and the worship of angels disqualify you. Such people also go into great detail about what they have seen, and their unspiritual minds puff them up with idle notions. ¹⁹They have lost connection with the head, from whom the whole body, supported and held together by its ligaments and sinews, grows as God causes it to grow.

²⁰Since you died with Christ to the elemental spiritual forces of this world, why, as though you still belonged to the world, do you submit to its rules: ²¹"Do not handle! Do not taste! Do not touch!"? ²²These rules, which have to do with things that are all destined to perish with use, are based on merely human commands and teachings. ²³Such regulations indeed have an appearance of wisdom, with their self-imposed worship, their false humility and their harsh treatment of the body, but they lack any value in restraining sensual indulgence.

Living as Those Made Alive in Christ

3 Since, then, you have been raised with Christ, set your hearts on things above, where Christ is seated at the right hand of God. ²Set your minds on things above, not on earthly things. ³For you died,

---

ᵃ 8 Or the basic principles; also in verse 20   ᵇ 11,13 Or Your flesh   ᶜ 11 Or put off in the circumcision of   ᵈ 13 Some manuscripts us   ᵉ 15 Or them in him
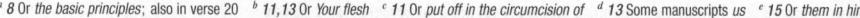

and your life is now hidden with Christ in God. [4]When Christ, who is your[a] life, appears, then you also will appear with him in glory.

[5]Put to death, therefore, whatever belongs to your earthly nature: sexual immorality, impurity, lust, evil desires and greed, which is idolatry. [6]Because of these, the wrath of God is coming.[b] [7]You used to walk in these ways, in the life you once lived. [8]But now you must also rid yourselves of all such things as these: anger, rage, malice, slander, and filthy language from your lips. [9]Do not lie to each other, since you have taken off your old self with its practices [10]and have put on the new self, which is being renewed in knowledge in the image of its Creator. [11]Here there is no Gentile or Jew, circumcised or uncircumcised, barbarian, Scythian, slave or free, but Christ is all, and is in all.

[12]Therefore, as God's chosen people, holy and dearly loved, clothe yourselves with compassion, kindness, humility, gentleness and patience. [13]Bear with each other and forgive one another if any of you has a grievance against someone. Forgive as the Lord forgave you. [14]And over all these virtues put on love, which binds them all together in perfect unity.

[15]Let the peace of Christ rule in your hearts, since as members of one body you were called to peace. And be thankful. [16]Let the message of Christ dwell among you richly as you teach and admonish one another with all wisdom through psalms, hymns and songs from the Spirit, singing to God with gratitude in your hearts. [17]And whatever you do, whether in word or deed, do it all in the name of the Lord Jesus, giving thanks to God the Father through him.

1672

at issue : swearing

3:5–14 Is occasional swearing a big deal? Think of it this way: Remember that hideous outfit you wore ten years ago (that seemed cool at the time) and the hideous earrings you wore to match? If you changed your clothes, the earrings would still be hideous. When you're a Christian, you change your spiritual wardrobe. Why wear the hideous earrings? They're a small accessory, but they clash noticeably! Get rid of everything that belongs to your old sin nature and live as the new person God made you. Filthy language has no place in your new wardrobe; refuse to put it back on.

Instructions for Christian Households

[18]Wives, submit yourselves to your husbands, as is fitting in the Lord.

[19]Husbands, love your wives and do not be harsh with them.

[20]Children, obey your parents in everything, for this pleases the Lord.

[21]Fathers,[c] do not embitter your children, or they will become discouraged.

[22]Slaves, obey your earthly masters in everything; and do it, not only when their eye is on you and to curry their favor, but with sincerity of heart and reverence for the Lord. [23]Whatever you do, work at it with all your heart, as working for the Lord, not for human masters, [24]since you know that you will receive an inheritance from the Lord as a reward. It is the Lord Christ you are serving. [25]Those who do wrong will be repaid for their wrongs, and there is no favoritism.

4 Masters, provide your slaves with what is right and fair, because you know that you also have a Master in heaven.

Further Instructions

[2]Devote yourselves to prayer, being watchful and thankful. [3]And pray for us, too, that God may open a door for our message, so that we may proclaim the mystery of Christ, for which I am in chains. [4]Pray that I may proclaim it clearly, as I should. [5]Be wise in the way you act toward outsiders; make the most of every opportunity. [6]Let your conversation be always full of grace, seasoned with salt, so that you may know how to answer everyone.

---

[a] 4 Some manuscripts *our*   [b] 6 Some early manuscripts *coming on those who are disobedient*   [c] 21 Or *Parents*

Final Greetings

[7]Tychicus will tell you all the news about me. He is a dear brother, a faithful minister and fellow servant[a] in the Lord. [8]I am sending him to you for the express purpose that you may know about our[b] circumstances and that he may encourage your hearts. [9]He is coming with Onesimus, our faithful and dear brother, who is one of you. They will tell you everything that is happening here.

[10]My fellow prisoner Aristarchus sends you his greetings, as does Mark, the cousin of Barnabas. (You have received instructions about him; if he comes to you, welcome him.) [11]Jesus, who is called Justus, also sends greetings. These are the only Jews[c] among my co-workers for the kingdom of God, and they have proved a comfort to me. [12]Epaphras, who is one of you and a servant of Christ Jesus, sends greetings. He is always wrestling in prayer for you, that you may stand firm in all the will of God, mature and fully assured. [13]I vouch for him that he is working hard for you and for those at Laodicea and Hierapolis. [14]Our dear friend Luke, the doctor, and Demas send greetings. [15]Give my greetings to the brothers and sisters at Laodicea, and to Nympha and the church in her house.

[16]After this letter has been read to you, see that it is also read in the church of the Laodiceans and that you in turn read the letter from Laodicea.

[17]Tell Archippus: "See to it that you complete the work you have received in the Lord."

[18]I, Paul, write this greeting in my own hand. Remember my chains. Grace be with you.

" conversations "

friendship with non-christians «» 4:5–6

1» Who are your non-Christian friends? What's beneficial about those friendships (to you and to them)?

2» How can you make the most of every opportunity with your non-Christian friends?

3» How can you keep your conversations full of grace and seasoned with salt?

For more on friendship with non-christians, check the index. For the next Conversations, go to p. 1679.

1673

1 thessalonians

1674

AUTHOR
The apostle Paul.

AUDIENCE
The church in Thessalonica (in the area of
modern-day northern Greece) and all followers
of Jesus.

DATE
About A.D. 51.

SETTING
Paul wrote from Corinth to encourage the
persecuted Christians in Thessalonica.

VERSE TO REMEMBER
"For the Lord himself will come down from
heaven, with a loud command, with the voice
of the archangel and with the trumpet call of
God, and the dead in Christ will rise first."
(4:16)

THEME TO CONSIDER
Take courage when you're suffering—Jesus is
coming again soon!

1

Paul, Silas*a* and Timothy,

To the church of the Thessalonians in God the Father and the Lord Jesus Christ:

Grace and peace to you.

Thanksgiving for the Thessalonians' Faith

²We always thank God for all of you and continually mention you in our prayers. ³We remember before our God and Father your work produced by faith, your labor prompted by love, and your endurance inspired by hope in our Lord Jesus Christ.

⁴For we know, brothers and sisters loved by God, that he has chosen you, ⁵because our gospel came to you not simply with words but also with power, with the Holy Spirit and deep conviction. You know how we lived among you for your sake. ⁶You became imitators of us and of the Lord, for you welcomed the message in the midst of severe suffering with the joy given by the Holy Spirit. ⁷And so you became a model to all the believers in Macedonia and Achaia. ⁸The Lord's message rang out from you not only in Macedonia and Achaia—your faith in God has become known everywhere. Therefore we do not need to say anything about it, ⁹for they themselves report what happened when we visited you. They tell how you turned to God from idols to serve the living and true God, ¹⁰and to wait for his Son from heaven, whom he raised from the dead—Jesus, who rescues us from the coming wrath.

1675

Paul's Ministry in Thessalonica

2

You know, brothers and sisters, that our visit to you was not without results. ²We had previously suffered and been treated outrageously in Philippi, as you know, but with the help of our God we dared to tell you his gospel in the face of strong opposition. ³For the appeal we make does not spring from error or impure motives, nor are we trying to trick you. ⁴On the contrary, we speak as those approved by God to be entrusted with the gospel. We are not trying to please people but God, who tests our hearts. ⁵You know we never used flattery, nor did we put on a mask to cover up greed—God is our witness. ⁶We were not looking for praise from any human being, not from you or anyone else, even though as apostles of Christ we could have asserted our prerogatives. ⁷Instead, we were like young children among you.

Just as a nursing mother cares for her children, ⁸so we cared for you. Because we loved you so much, we were delighted to share with you not only the gospel of God but our lives as well. ⁹Surely you remember, brothers and sisters, our toil and hardship; we worked night and day in order not to be a burden to anyone while we preached the gospel of God to you.

¹⁰You are witnesses, and so is God, of how holy, righteous and blameless we were among you who believed. ¹¹For you know that we dealt with each of you as a father deals with his own children, ¹²encouraging, comforting and urging you to live lives worthy of God, who calls you into his kingdom and glory.

¹³And we also thank God continually because, when you received the word of God, which you heard

---

a *1* Greek *Silvanus*, a variant of *Silas*

HE IS: at work

2:13 The Thessalonian church was a healthy church because the people had received God's Word and accepted it as divine truth. They had opened their hearts to God's message and had allowed it to work in them. God was *at work* in their lives.

Have you followed the Thessalonian workout plan? If you've received God's Word, diligently studied Scripture for yourself and accepted that the Bible is not merely a human word but a relevant and timely message from God, then you can be sure he is *at work* in you (see Philippians 2:12–13).

For the next He Is, go to p. 1682.

myth# 96 "I DON'T HAVE ANYTHING USEFUL TO CONTRIBUTE."

I can't sing—well, not in a way that anyone would want to hear. I definitely can't preach, and as far as teaching is concerned, well, I don't do that well either. Evangelism? Not good at it. I tried to tell a friend about Jesus once and felt so tongue-tied. No wonder she never became a believer.

Let's see. What else? I don't have a lot of money to give to others. I wish I did. I'm not very organized (which is why I'm never asked to head up committees and such).

So, what do I have to contribute to the church? I'm not sure. I'm not out-going. Most people don't notice me at church (and I've attended the same church for 12 years). I just quietly come and go, occasionally helping to sort clothes for the clothing ministry or hand out food at our church's homeless shelter. I also deliver meals to shut-ins. I know I'm not as important to the church as a minister or a teacher.

I sometimes wish I were like my good friend Jeanette, who has a beautiful voice. She receives a lot of invitations to sing and speak at women's retreats. She's quite a powerful speaker. After attending her last concert, I wondered what I'm contributing to the body. What, if anything, is my legacy? I haven't made any disciples. Am I disappointing God somehow?

—Ginger

WHO ARE THE movers and shakers in our society? People with abilities that place them in the public eye might seem more useful and important. The rest of us covet their abilities because of the attention they receive.

That same bias crops up in the thoughts of many Christians. Despite the fact that the Holy Spirit gives all believers at least one spiritual gift (see 1 Corinthians 12:4–11 and Ephesians 4:4–13), some gifts are viewed as more important than others because they place a believer in the limelight.

When you think of truly "useful" members of your church, who comes to mind? Probably worship leaders, evangelists, teachers, pastors and missionaries. But what about those who help in less visible ways?

The women who anointed Jesus' feet with perfume and tears (see Matthew 26:6–13; Luke 7:36–38; John 12:1–8) weren't highly visible members of the body. In fact, a watching Pharisee and some of Jesus' disciples disdained their contributions. Yet Jesus was deeply moved by their simple acts of love.

Paul reminds us, "We do not dare to classify or compare ourselves with some who commend themselves" (2 Corinthians 10:12). The belief that "I have nothing useful to contribute" is a subtle comparison with others—one that seldom makes us feel any better. Yet the same Holy Spirit who doled out the spiritual gifts is at work in all Christians—those who preach and those who clean the offices of the ones who preach; those who teach and those who write the curriculum to enable those who teach and those who photocopy that curriculum for the class. Our abilities, when used together, keep the body of Christ functioning.

Tempted to think you have nothing useful to contribute? Remember the widow's offering in Luke 21:1–4. What pleases Jesus isn't the amount or "impressiveness" of our gifts, but that we give him all we have.

"Sitting in the pews of churches across America are literally millions of [Christians] who are God's gift to a hurting nation... 98 percent of [them] are not ordained ministers, but their callings to ministry are just as important as the pastor's calling."

—Frank Tillapaugh and Richard Hurst

1677

"GOD HAS PUT THE BODY TOGETHER, GIVING GREATER HONOR TO THE PARTS THAT LACKED IT,... ITS PARTS SHOULD HAVE EQUAL CONCERN FOR EACH OTHER."

1 CORINTHIANS 12:24–25

SEE ALSO

Matthew 10:42; 25:35–40
1 Corinthians 12:4–31
Ephesians 4:7–16

For more on **Serving**, check the index.

from us, you accepted it not as a human word, but as it actually is, the word of God, which is indeed at work in you who believe. [14]For you, brothers and sisters, became imitators of God's churches in Judea, which are in Christ Jesus: You suffered from your fellow citizens the same things those churches suffered from the Jews, [15]who killed the Lord Jesus and the prophets and also drove us out. They displease God and are hostile to everyone [16]in their effort to keep us from speaking to the Gentiles so that they may be saved. In this way they always heap up their sins to the limit. The wrath of God has come upon them at last.[a]

Paul's Longing to See the Thessalonians

[17]But, brothers and sisters, when we were orphaned by being separated from you for a short time (in person, not in thought), out of our intense longing we made every effort to see you. [18]For we wanted to come to you—certainly I, Paul, did, again and again—but Satan blocked our way. [19]For what is our hope, our joy, or the crown in which we will glory in the presence of our Lord Jesus when he comes? Is it not you? [20]Indeed, you are our glory and joy.

3 So when we could stand it no longer, we thought it best to be left by ourselves in Athens. [2]We sent Timothy, who is our brother and co-worker in God's service in spreading the gospel of Christ, to strengthen and encourage you in your faith, [3]so that no one would be unsettled by these trials. You know quite well that we are destined for them. [4]In fact, when we were with you, we kept telling you that we would be persecuted. And it turned out that way, as you well know. [5]For this reason, when I could stand it no longer, I sent to find out about your faith. I was afraid that in some way the tempter had tempted you and that our labors might have been in vain.

Timothy's Encouraging Report

[6]But Timothy has just now come to us from you and has brought good news about your faith and love. He has told us that you always have pleasant memories of us and that you long to see us, just as we also long to see you. [7]Therefore, brothers and sisters, in all our distress and persecution we were encouraged about you because of your faith. [8]For now we really live, since you are standing firm in the Lord. [9]How can we thank God enough for you in return for all the joy we have in the presence of our God because of you? [10]Night and day we pray most earnestly that we may see you again and supply what is lacking in your faith.

[11]Now may our God and Father himself and our Lord Jesus clear the way for us to come to you. [12]May the Lord make your love increase and overflow for each other and for everyone else, just as ours does for you. [13]May he strengthen your hearts so that you will be blameless and holy in the presence of our God and Father when our Lord Jesus comes with all his holy ones.

Living to Please God

4 As for other matters, brothers and sisters, we instructed you how to live in order to please God, as in fact you are living. Now we ask you and urge you in the Lord Jesus to do this more and more. [2]For you know what instructions we gave you by the authority of the Lord Jesus.

[3]It is God's will that you should be sanctified: that you should avoid sexual immorality; [4]that each of you should learn to control your own body[b] in a way that is holy and honorable, [5]not in passionate lust like the pagans, who do

atissue:lust

4:1–8 Men don't have the monopoly on lust. Women may phrase it or express it differently—but we still struggle with lust. You know the experience of seeing a really good-looking man and feeling that churning inside. Lust causes you to flirt shamelessly or buy revealing clothes. It causes you to act in a way the world calls harmless, but God defines as less than holy. Don't reject God's instruction on this. Let your body—and your mind—be controlled by his Spirit rather than your own desires.

---

[a] 16 Or them fully   [b] 4 Or learn to live with his own wife; or learn to acquire a wife

not know God; [6]and that in this matter no one should wrong or take advantage of a brother or sister. The Lord will punish all those who commit such sins, as we told you and warned you before. [7]For God did not call us to be impure, but to live a holy life. [8]Therefore, anyone who rejects this instruction does not reject a human being but God, the very God who gives you his Holy Spirit.

[9]Now about your love for one another we do not need to write to you, for you yourselves have been taught by God to love each other. [10]And in fact, you do love all the brothers and sisters throughout Macedonia. Yet we urge you, dear friends, to do so more and more, [11]and to make it your ambition to lead a quiet life: You should mind your own business and work with your hands, just as we told you, [12]so that your daily life may win the respect of outsiders and so that you will not be dependent on anybody.

Believers Who Have Died

[13]Brothers and sisters, we do not want you to be uninformed about those who sleep in death, so that you do not grieve like the rest, who have no hope. [14]We believe that Jesus died and rose again, and so we believe that God will bring with Jesus those who have fallen asleep in him. [15]According to the Lord's word, we tell you that we who are still alive, who are left till the coming of the Lord, will certainly not precede those who have fallen asleep. [16]For the Lord himself will come down from heaven, with a loud command, with the voice of the archangel and with the trumpet call of God, and the dead in Christ will rise first. [17]After that, we who are still alive and are left will be caught up together with them in the clouds to meet the Lord in the air. And so we will be with the Lord forever. [18]Therefore encourage one another with these words.

1679

The Day of the Lord

5 Now, brothers and sisters, about times and dates we do not need to write to you, [2]for you know very well that the day of the Lord will come like a thief in the night. [3]While people are saying, "Peace and safety," destruction will come on them suddenly, as labor pains on a pregnant woman, and they will not escape.

[4]But you, brothers and sisters, are not in darkness so that this day should surprise you like a thief. [5]You are all children of the light and children of the day. We do not belong to the night or to the darkness. [6]So then, let us not be like others, who are asleep, but let us be awake and sober. [7]For those who sleep, sleep at night, and those who get drunk, get drunk at night. [8]But since we belong to the day, let us be sober, putting on faith and love as a breastplate, and the hope of salvation as a helmet. [9]For God did not appoint us to suffer wrath but to receive salvation through our Lord Jesus Christ. [10]He died for us so that, whether we are awake or asleep, we may live together with him. [11]Therefore encourage one another and build each other up, just as in fact you are doing.

" conversations "

drugs «» 5:1–8

1 » How might drug use or drunkenness make you less "awake and sober"?

2 » How do you feel about using caffeine, nicotine, or alcohol (socially acceptable drugs)?

3 » Why do you think God values sobriety?

For more on drugs, check the index.
For the next Conversations, go to p. 1683.

Final Instructions

[12]Now we ask you, brothers and sisters, to acknowledge those who work hard among you, who care for you in the Lord and who admonish you. [13]Hold them in the highest regard in love because of their work. Live in peace with each other. [14]And we urge you, brothers and sisters, warn those who are idle and disruptive, encourage the disheartened, help the weak, be patient with everyone. [15]Make sure that nobody pays back wrong for wrong, but always strive to do what is good for each other and for everyone else.

[16]Rejoice always, [17]pray continually, [18]give thanks in all circumstances; for this is God's will for you in Christ Jesus.

[19]Do not put out the Spirit's fire. [20]Do not treat prophecies with contempt [21]but test them all; hold on to what is good, [22]reject whatever is harmful.

[23]May God himself, the God of peace, sanctify you through and through. May your whole spirit, soul

and body be kept blameless at the coming of our Lord Jesus Christ. ²⁴The one who calls you is faithful, and he will do it.

²⁵Brothers and sisters, pray for us. ²⁶Greet all God's people with a holy kiss. ²⁷I charge you before the Lord to have this letter read to all the brothers and sisters.

²⁸The grace of our Lord Jesus Christ be with you.

What do we know about the nefarious
"man of lawlessness"? ➤➤ (2:1–12)

Which are you—*busy* or a *busybody*? ➤➤ (3:11–13)

2thessalonians

AUTHOR
The apostle Paul.

AUDIENCE
The church in Thessalonica and all followers of Jesus.

DATE
About A.D. 51 or 52, six months after the
writing of 1 Thessalonians.

SETTING
The Christians in Thessalonica thought
that Christ would return immediately. They
became confused and disappointed when
he didn't return on their timetable.

VERSE TO REMEMBER
"And as for you, brothers and sisters, never
tire of doing what is good." (3:13)

THEME TO CONSIDER
Don't waste time while you wait for Jesus
to return.

1 Paul, Silas*a* and Timothy,

To the church of the Thessalonians in God our Father and the Lord Jesus Christ:

²Grace and peace to you from God the Father and the Lord Jesus Christ.

Thanksgiving and Prayer

³We ought always to thank God for you, brothers and sisters, and rightly so, because your faith is growing more and more, and the love all of you have for one another is increasing. ⁴Therefore, among God's churches we boast about your perseverance and faith in all the persecutions and trials you are enduring.

⁵All this is evidence that God's judgment is right, and as a result you will be counted worthy of the kingdom of God, for which you are suffering. ⁶God is just: He will pay back trouble to those who trouble you ⁷and give relief to you who are troubled, and to us as well. This will happen when the Lord Jesus is revealed from heaven in blazing fire with his powerful angels. ⁸He will punish those who do not know God and do not obey the gospel of our Lord Jesus. ⁹They will be punished with everlasting destruction and shut out from the presence of the Lord and from the glory of his might ¹⁰on the day he comes to be glorified in his holy people and to be marveled at among all those who have believed. This includes you, because you believed our testimony to you.

1682

HE IS: just

1:4–7 Believers in Thessalonica were experiencing unfair persecution. Paul wrote to encourage them that their suffering wasn't a sign of God's displeasure; it was evidence of his work in their lives. Paul reminded them that while people are often unjust, God is always perfectly *just*.

When you suffer, remember that your suffering doesn't mean that God is unhappy with you. On the contrary, he is developing perseverance and faith in you. Because God is perfectly just, he will one day judge those who have been unfair to you (see Romans 12:19). You can let go of those injustices and wait for your just judge to make things right.

For the next He Is, go to p. 1686.

¹¹With this in mind, we constantly pray for you, that our God may make you worthy of his calling, and that by his power he may bring to fruition your every desire for goodness and your every deed prompted by faith. ¹²We pray this so that the name of our Lord Jesus may be glorified in you, and you in him, according to the grace of our God and the Lord Jesus Christ.*b*

The Man of Lawlessness

2 Concerning the coming of our Lord Jesus Christ and our being gathered to him, we ask you, brothers and sisters, ²not to become easily unsettled or alarmed by the teaching allegedly from us— whether by a prophecy or by word of mouth or by letter—asserting that the day of the Lord has already come. ³Don't let anyone deceive you in any way, for that day will not come until the rebellion occurs and the man of lawlessness*c* is revealed, the man doomed to destruction. ⁴He will oppose and will exalt himself over everything that is called God or is worshiped, so that he sets himself up in God's temple, proclaiming himself to be God.

⁵Don't you remember that when I was with you I used to tell you these things? ⁶And now you know what is holding him back, so that he may be revealed at the proper time. ⁷For the secret power of lawlessness is already at work; but the one who now holds it back will continue to do so till he is taken out

---

a 1 Greek *Silvanus,* a variant of *Silas*   *b 12* Or *God and Lord, Jesus Christ*   *c 3* Some manuscripts *sin*

conversations

loyalty «»» 2:15

1 » Which core Christian teachings do you hold fast to at all costs?

2 » What might threaten your loyalty to these truths?

3 » How do you show loyalty in the context of an imperfect and sometimes inconsistent church?

For more on **loyalty**, check the index.
For the next Conversations, go to p. 1691.

of the way. [8]And then the lawless one will be revealed, whom the Lord Jesus will overthrow with the breath of his mouth and destroy by the splendor of his coming. [9]The coming of the lawless one will be in accordance with how Satan works. He will use all sorts of displays of power through signs and wonders that serve the lie, [10]and all the ways that wickedness deceives those who are perishing. They perish because they refused to love the truth and so be saved. [11]For this reason God sends them a powerful delusion so that they will believe the lie [12]and so that all will be condemned who have not believed the truth but have delighted in wickedness.

Stand Firm

[13]But we ought always to thank God for you, brothers and sisters loved by the Lord, because God chose you as firstfruits[a] to be saved through the sanctifying work of the Spirit and through belief in the truth. [14]He called you to this through our gospel, that you might share in the glory of our Lord Jesus Christ.

[15]So then, brothers and sisters, stand firm and hold fast to the teachings[b] we passed on to you, whether by word of mouth or by letter.

[16]May our Lord Jesus Christ himself and God our Father, who loved us and by his grace gave us eternal encouragement and good hope, [17]encourage your hearts and strengthen you in every good deed and word.

Request for Prayer

3 As for other matters, brothers and sisters, pray for us that the message of the Lord may spread rapidly and be honored, just as it was with you. [2]And pray that we may be delivered from wicked and evil people, for not everyone has faith. [3]But the Lord is faithful, and he will strengthen you and protect you from the evil one. [4]We have confidence in the Lord that you are doing and will continue to do the things we command. [5]May the Lord direct your hearts into God's love and Christ's perseverance.

Warning Against Idleness

[6]In the name of the Lord Jesus Christ, we command you, brothers and sisters, to keep away from every believer who is idle and disruptive and does not live according to the teaching[c] you received from us. [7]For you yourselves know how you ought to follow our example. We were not idle when we were with you, [8]nor did we eat anyone's food without paying for it. On the contrary, we worked night and day, laboring and toiling so that we would not be a burden to any of you. [9]We did this, not because we do not have the right to such help, but in order to offer ourselves as a model for you to imitate. [10]For even when we were with you, we gave you this rule: "Anyone who is unwilling to work shall not eat."

anissue:laziness

3:6–13 Laziness isn't akin to relaxing (which many of us need to do more). Laziness is related to idleness—frittering away our time on things that won't last. Some of the Thessalonians were masters of this. Expecting Jesus to reappear at any moment, they essentially sat in their lawn chairs, stared at the sky and expected others to provide for them. Like many of us, they'd forgotten that life is short. We can translate Paul's advice to them into some practical reminders for us today: Be intentional in your relationships. Be purposeful in how you approach each day God gives you. Be industrious in your work.

1683

---

[a] 13 Some manuscripts *because from the beginning God chose you* [b] 15 Or *traditions* [c] 6 Or *tradition*

[11] We hear that some among you are idle and disruptive. They are not busy; they are busybodies. [12] Such people we command and urge in the Lord Jesus Christ to settle down and earn the bread they eat. [13] And as for you, brothers and sisters, never tire of doing what is good.

[14] Take special note of those who do not obey our instruction in this letter. Do not associate with them, in order that they may feel ashamed. [15] Yet do not regard them as enemies, but warn them as fellow believers.

Final Greetings

[16] Now may the Lord of peace himself give you peace at all times and in every way. The Lord be with all of you.

[17] I, Paul, write this greeting in my own hand, which is the distinguishing mark in all my letters. This is how I write.

[18] The grace of our Lord Jesus Christ be with you all.

1 timothy

1685

AUTHOR
The apostle Paul.

AUDIENCE
Timothy, Paul's young protégé, young
church leaders and all believers everywhere.

DATE
About A.D. 64, probably between Paul's first
and second imprisonments in Rome.

SETTING
Timothy, the young pastor of the church of
Ephesus, receives instructions from Paul
on church management.

VERSE TO REMEMBER
"Don't let anyone look down on you because
you are young, but set an example for the
believers in speech, in conduct, in love, in
faith and in purity." (4:12)

THEME TO CONSIDER
God loves the church and gives us instructions on how it should function.

1 Paul, an apostle of Christ Jesus by the command of God our Savior and of Christ Jesus our hope,

²To Timothy my true son in the faith:

Grace, mercy and peace from God the Father and Christ Jesus our Lord.

Timothy Charged to Oppose False Teachers

³As I urged you when I went into Macedonia, stay there in Ephesus so that you may command certain persons not to teach false doctrines any longer ⁴or to devote themselves to myths and endless genealogies. Such things promote controversial speculations rather than advancing God's work—which is by faith. ⁵The goal of this command is love, which comes from a pure heart and a good conscience and a sincere faith. ⁶Some have departed from these and have turned to meaningless talk. ⁷They want to be teachers of the law, but they do not know what they are talking about or what they so confidently affirm.

⁸We know that the law is good if one uses it properly. ⁹We also know that the law is made not for the righteous but for lawbreakers and rebels, the ungodly and sinful, the unholy and irreligious, for those who kill their fathers or mothers, for murderers, ¹⁰for the sexually immoral, for those practicing homosexuality, for slave traders and liars and perjurers. And it is for whatever else is contrary to the sound doctrine ¹¹that conforms to the gospel concerning the glory of the blessed God, which he entrusted to me.

The Lord's Grace to Paul

¹²I thank Christ Jesus our Lord, who has given me strength, that he considered me trustworthy, appointing me to his service. ¹³Even though I was once a blasphemer and a persecutor and a violent man, I was shown mercy because I acted in ignorance and unbelief. ¹⁴The grace of our Lord was poured out on me abundantly, along with the faith and love that are in Christ Jesus.

¹⁵Here is a trustworthy saying that deserves full acceptance: Christ Jesus came into the world to save sinners—of whom I am the worst. ¹⁶But for that very reason I was shown mercy so that in me, the worst of sinners, Christ Jesus might display his immense patience as an example for those who would believe in him and receive eternal life. ¹⁷Now to the King eternal, immortal, invisible, the only God, be honor and glory for ever and ever. Amen.

HE IS: patient

1:13–17 Calling himself the worst of sinners, Paul pointed to Jesus' unlimited patience with those who rebel. Jesus not only forgave Paul, but he also changed the whole course of his life. The hardened Jesus-hater became a sold-out servant of the very one whom he had offended.

Because of his infinite patience, Jesus isn't giving up on you either (see 2 Peter 3:9). Not now. Not ever. So, don't give up on yourself, thinking you can never change. Tomorrow is a chance for him to make you more than you are today. It doesn't matter how long it takes. He's at work—and he is *patient*.

For the next He Is, go to p. 1694.

The Charge to Timothy Renewed

¹⁸Timothy, my son, I am giving you this command in keeping with the prophecies once made about you, so that by recalling them you may fight the battle well, ¹⁹holding on to faith and a good conscience, which some have rejected and so have suffered shipwreck with regard to the faith. ²⁰Among them are Hymenaeus and Alexander, whom I have handed over to Satan to be taught not to blaspheme.

Instructions on Worship

2 I urge, then, first of all, that petitions, prayers, intercession and thanksgiving be made for everyone— ²for kings and all those in authority, that we may live peaceful and quiet lives in all godliness and holiness. ³This is good, and pleases God our Savior, ⁴who wants all people to be saved and to come to a knowledge of the truth. [5]For there is one God and one mediator between God and human beings, Christ Jesus, himself human, [6]who gave himself as a ransom for all people. This has now been witnessed to at the proper time. [7]And for this purpose I was appointed a herald and an apostle—I am telling the truth, I am not lying—and a true and faithful teacher of the Gentiles.

[8]Therefore I want the men everywhere to pray, lifting up holy hands without anger or disputing. [9]I also want the women to dress modestly, with decency and propriety, adorning themselves, not with elaborate hairstyles or gold or pearls or expensive clothes, [10]but with good deeds, appropriate for women who profess to worship God.

[11]A woman[a] should learn in quietness and full submission. [12]I do not permit a woman to teach or to assume authority over a man;[b, c] she must be quiet. [13]For Adam was formed first, then Eve. [14]And Adam was not the one deceived; it was the woman who was deceived and became a sinner. [15]But women[d] will be saved through childbearing—if they continue in faith, love and holiness with propriety.

Qualifications for Overseers and Deacons

3 Here is a trustworthy saying: Whoever aspires to be an overseer desires a noble task. [2]Now the overseer is to be above reproach, faithful to his wife, temperate, self-controlled, respectable, hospitable, able to teach, [3]not given to drunkenness, not violent but gentle, not quarrelsome, not a lover of money. [4]He must manage his own family well and see that his children obey him, and he must do so in a manner worthy of full[e] respect. [5](If anyone does not know how to manage his own family, how can he take care of God's church?) [6]He must not be a recent convert, or he may become conceited and fall under the same judgment as the devil. [7]He must also have a good reputation with outsiders, so that he will not fall into disgrace and into the devil's trap.

[8]In the same way, deacons are to be worthy of respect, sincere, not indulging in much wine, and not pursuing dishonest gain. [9]They must keep hold of the deep truths of the faith with a clear conscience. [10]They must first be tested; and then if there is nothing against them, let them serve as deacons.

[11]In the same way, the women[f] are to be worthy of respect, not malicious talkers but temperate and trustworthy in everything.

[12]A deacon must be faithful to his wife and must manage his children and his household well. [13]Those who have served well gain an excellent standing and great assurance in their faith in Christ Jesus.

Reasons for Paul's Instructions

[14]Although I hope to come to you soon, I am writing you these instructions so that, [15]if I am delayed, you will know how people ought to conduct themselves in God's household, which is the church of the living God, the pillar and foundation of the truth. [16]Beyond all question, the mystery from which true godliness springs is great:

> He appeared in a body,
>   was vindicated by the Spirit,[g]
> was seen by angels,
>   was preached among the nations,
> was believed on in the world,
>   was taken up in glory.

4 The Spirit clearly says that in later times some will abandon the faith and follow deceiving spirits and things taught by demons. [2]Such teachings come through hypocritical liars, whose consciences have been seared as with a hot iron. [3]They forbid people to marry and order them to abstain from certain foods, which God created to be received with thanksgiving by those who believe and who know the truth. [4]For everything God created is good, and nothing is to be rejected if it is received with thanksgiving, [5]because it is consecrated by the word of God and prayer.

[6]If you point these things out to the brothers and sisters, you will be a good minister of Christ Jesus, nourished on the truths of the faith and of the good teaching that you have followed. [7]Have nothing to

---

[a] 11 Or wife; also in verse 12   [b] 12 Or teach a man in a domineering way; or teach or to exercise (or have) authority over a man   [c] 12 Or over her husband
[d] 15 Greek she   [e] 4 Or him with proper   [f] 11 Probably women who are deacons, or possibly deacons' wives   [g] 16 Or vindicated in spirit

myth# 97

"A GOOD MARRIAGE IS ALWAYS EXCITING."

Our friends would say that Mel and I have a good marriage. We've been married for 12 years. Up till a year ago, I would have agreed that our marriage was good. But lately, one word sums up how I've been feeling about it: bored. It's not that I don't love Mel. I do. But I miss how exciting our marriage used to be—used to be.

Oh, I know the drill. I have a lot to be thankful for, and I need to remind myself of that, right? My well-meaning friends tell me how lucky I am to have a loving husband, four great kids, a beautiful home, no major money problems and wonderful in-laws. What would I have to complain about?

Well, I'm not exactly complaining. I'm just . . . bored. And I could never tell Mel that.

The other day I looked through pictures of us when we were dating and in the first few years of marriage. I had this ache inside when I thought about how incredibly in love we were then. Every day seemed exciting. We couldn't get enough of each other.

When our son was born, everyone said that we should expect to feel less "crazy in love." But the excitement continued for us. I felt even more in love with Mel.

But around year ten of our marriage, we seemed to get busier and busier, especially with the kids starting to get more involved in school. Soon all of life fell into a routine. Mel and I tried to schedule time with each other. But after awhile, even sex began to seem routine.

If I'm bored, how can I truly say that my marriage is good?

—Marliss

HOW MANY MOVIES have you seen depicting the excitement of being in love? Probably dozens, right? They portray the romantic highs of love and reinforce the fallacy that the "in-love" feeling will last forever. And if it doesn't . . . well, perhaps it's time to move on to a "better" relationship. Then the in-love cycle starts all over again.

In relationships feelings ebb and flow like the tides of an ocean. When you first fall in love with someone, your excitement level is high. Even everyday activities can seem exciting. Yet the "in-love" feeling can be addictive. For this reason, so many people bounce from relationship to relationship. Once the excitement wears off, like the flavor of bubble gum after several chews, the good times seem to be over.

Yet real love isn't based on changeable feelings. Instead, it's an act of the will, a choice to honor your commitment to another person. This is the kind of love that Jesus had as he determined to go through the agony of the cross.

The quality of a marriage isn't measured by the excitement level. Rather, a good marriage is one in which the spouses love each other enough to stay together even after the "flavor" seems to have worn off. In a good marriage, spouses . . .

- Choose to adjust false expectations. Unrealistic expectations ("he should meet all of my needs" or "I should feel excited 24/7") can take a toll on a marriage.

- Keep the lines of communication open. They don't live under the expectation that their spouse is a mind-reader.

- Stay individually connected with God, seeking his help with their marriage and trusting that he's the glue to bind them together.

- Serve one another. They choose to "serve one another humbly in love" (Galatians 5:13).

The choice to remain together and work through problems often results in a renewed passion for each other and helps an OK marriage grow into a great marriage.

"Being in love is something you do."

—C. S. Lewis

"Be Devoted To one another in Love. Honor one another above yourselves."

ROMANS 12:10

SEE ALSO

Proverbs 5:18–19
1 Corinthians 7:27
1 Corinthians 13:4–7
1 Peter 1:6–7

For more on **Marriage,** check the index.

do with godless myths and old wives' tales; rather, train yourself to be godly. [8]For physical training is of some value, but godliness has value for all things, holding promise for both the present life and the life to come. [9]This is a trustworthy saying that deserves full acceptance. [10]That is why we labor and strive, because we have put our hope in the living God, who is the Savior of all people, and especially of those who believe.

[11]Command and teach these things. [12]Don't let anyone look down on you because you are young, but set an example for the believers in speech, in conduct, in love, in faith and in purity. [13]Until I come, devote yourself to the public reading of Scripture, to preaching and to teaching. [14]Do not neglect your gift, which was given you through prophecy when the body of elders laid their hands on you.

[15]Be diligent in these matters; give yourself wholly to them, so that everyone may see your progress. [16]Watch your life and doctrine closely. Persevere in them, because if you do, you will save both yourself and your hearers.

Widows, Elders and Slaves

5 Do not rebuke an older man harshly, but exhort him as if he were your father. Treat younger men as brothers, [2]older women as mothers, and younger women as sisters, with absolute purity.

[3]Give proper recognition to those widows who are really in need. [4]But if a widow has children or grandchildren, these should learn first of all to put their religion into practice by caring for their own family and so repaying their parents and grandparents, for this is pleasing to God. [5]The widow who is really in need and left all alone puts her hope in God and continues night and day to pray and to ask God for help. [6]But the widow who lives for pleasure is dead even while she lives. [7]Give the people these instructions, so that no one may be open to blame. [8]Anyone who does not provide for their relatives, and especially for their own household, has denied the faith and is worse than an unbeliever.

[9]No widow may be put on the list of widows unless she is over sixty, has been faithful to her husband, [10]and is well known for her good deeds, such as bringing up children, showing hospitality, washing the feet of the Lord's people, helping those in trouble and devoting herself to all kinds of good deeds.

[11]As for younger widows, do not put them on such a list. For when their sensual desires overcome their dedication to Christ, they want to marry. [12]Thus they bring judgment on themselves, because they have broken their first pledge. [13]Besides, they get into the habit of being idle and going about from house to house. And not only do they become idlers, but also busybodies who talk nonsense, saying things they ought not to. [14]So I counsel younger widows to marry, to have children, to manage their homes and to give the enemy no opportunity for slander. [15]Some have in fact already turned away to follow Satan.

[16]If any woman who is a believer has widows in her care, she should continue to help them and not let the church be burdened with them, so that the church can help those widows who are really in need.

[17]The elders who direct the affairs of the church well are worthy of double honor, especially those whose work is preaching and teaching. [18]For Scripture says, "Do not muzzle an ox while it is treading out the grain,"[a] and "Workers deserve their wages."[b] [19]Do not entertain an accusation against an elder unless it is brought by two or three witnesses. [20]But those elders who are sinning you are to reprove before

1690

atissue:godliness

4:7–8 Do you have to dust your treadmill? Does your gym membership go unused? Or are you someone who wouldn't miss your morning run unless you broke a leg? Make no mistake—physical training *is* important. Exercise gives you energy and strength to serve God each day. But its value doesn't begin to compare with the value of godliness. We need to exercise our spiritual muscles each day in order to train ourselves to be godly (and to prevent atrophy). Physical training benefits you in this short life on earth, but godliness has eternal benefits. So, how's your spiritual workout regimen?

[a] 18 Deut. 25:4   [b] 18 Luke 10:7

everyone, so that the others may take warning. ²¹I charge you, in the sight of God and Christ Jesus and the elect angels, to keep these instructions without partiality, and to do nothing out of favoritism.

²²Do not be hasty in the laying on of hands, and do not share in the sins of others. Keep yourself pure.

²³Stop drinking only water, and use a little wine because of your stomach and your frequent illnesses.

²⁴The sins of some are obvious, reaching the place of judgment ahead of them; the sins of others trail behind them. ²⁵In the same way, good deeds are obvious, and even those that are not obvious cannot remain hidden forever.

6 All who are under the yoke of slavery should consider their masters worthy of full respect, so that God's name and our teaching may not be slandered. ²Those who have believing masters should not show them disrespect just because they are fellow believers. Instead, they should serve them even better because their masters are dear to them as fellow believers and are devoted to the welfare*a* of their slaves.

False Teachers and the Love of Money

These are the things you are to teach and insist on. ³If anyone teaches otherwise and does not agree to the sound instruction of our Lord Jesus Christ and to godly teaching, ⁴they are conceited and understand nothing. They have an unhealthy interest in controversies and quarrels about words that result in envy, strife, malicious talk, evil suspicions ⁵and constant friction between people of corrupt mind, who have been robbed of the truth and who think that godliness is a means to financial gain.

⁶But godliness with contentment is great gain. ⁷For we brought nothing into the world, and we can take nothing out of it. ⁸But if we have food and clothing, we will be content with that. ⁹Those who want to get rich fall into temptation and a trap and into many foolish and harmful desires that plunge people into ruin and destruction. ¹⁰For the love of money is a root of all kinds of evil. Some people, eager for money, have wandered from the faith and pierced themselves with many griefs.

atissue:money

6:6–10 We all want more, more, MORE! But when you truly don't have much, such feelings seem more justified. It's tempting to covet your friends' homes, their vacations or their ability to eat out. It's easy to feel discontent when you can barely pay your bills, let alone afford the luxuries of life. When you feel yourself growing discontent, remind yourself that pursuing money is a dead-end prospect. Remind yourself that while God won't supply all your wants, he will supply your needs. Then let love for God—rather than love for money—rule your heart, and you will discover that you have true riches.

1691

conversations

money «» 6:3–10

1 » Is it ever OK for a Christian to desire wealth?

2 » What other temptations often go hand in hand with greed?

3 » What are practical ways for you to avoid the love of money?

For more on **money**, check the index.
For the next Conversations, go to p. 1697.

Final Charge to Timothy

¹¹But you, man of God, flee from all this, and pursue righteousness, godliness, faith, love, endurance and gentleness. ¹²Fight the good fight of the faith. Take hold of the eternal life to which you were called when you made your good confession in the presence of many witnesses. ¹³In the sight of God, who gives life to everything, and of Christ Jesus, who while testifying before Pontius Pilate made the good confession, I charge you ¹⁴to keep this command without spot or blame until the appearing of our Lord Jesus Christ, ¹⁵which God will bring about in his own time—God, the blessed and only Ruler, the King of kings and Lord of lords,

---

a 2 Or and benefit from the service

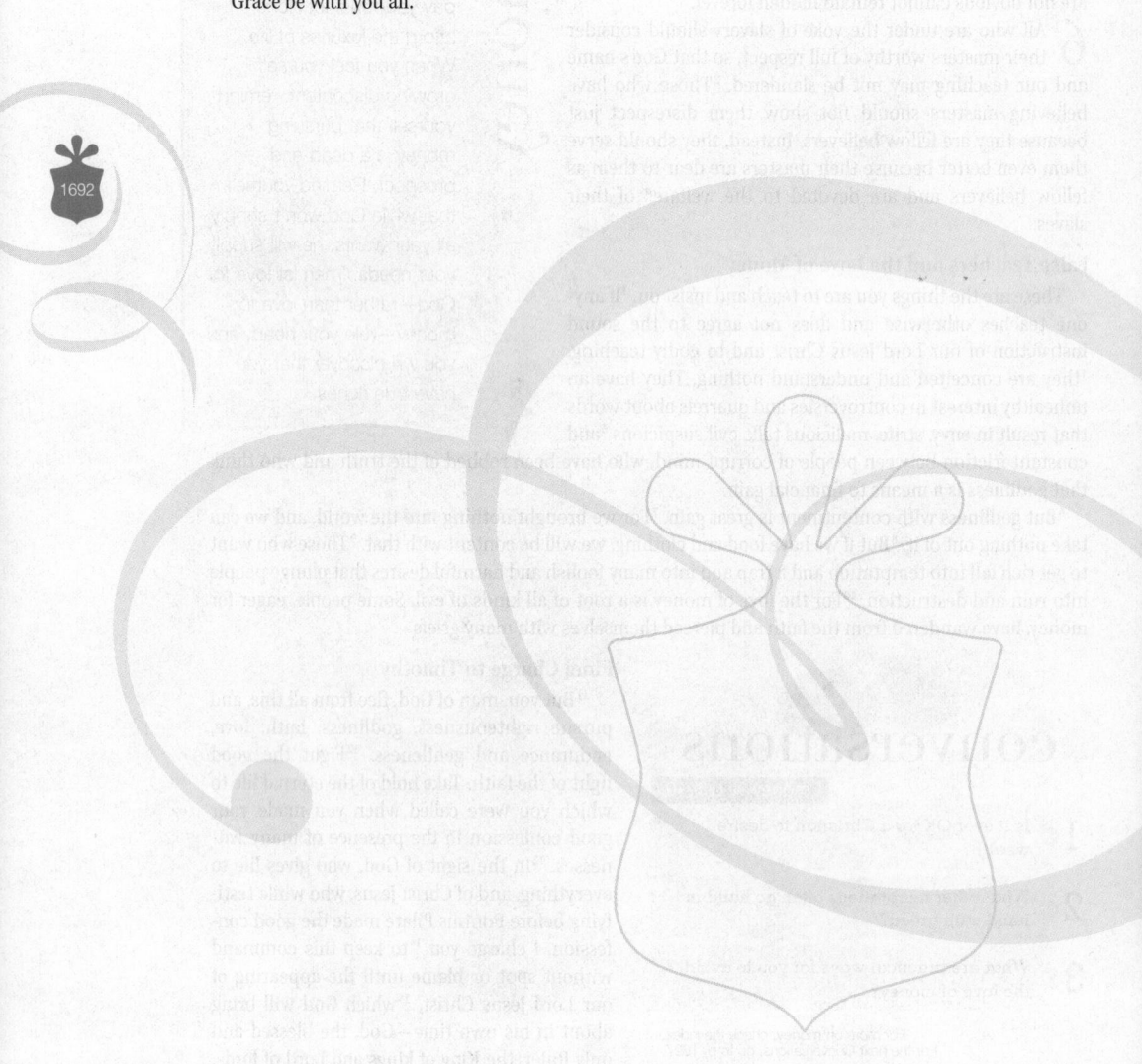

1 timothy 6:16

¹⁶who alone is immortal and who lives in unapproachable light, whom no one has seen or can see. To him be honor and might forever. Amen.

¹⁷Command those who are rich in this present world not to be arrogant nor to put their hope in wealth, which is so uncertain, but to put their hope in God, who richly provides us with everything for our enjoyment. ¹⁸Command them to do good, to be rich in good deeds, and to be generous and willing to share. ¹⁹In this way they will lay up treasure for themselves as a firm foundation for the coming age, so that they may take hold of the life that is truly life.

²⁰Timothy, guard what has been entrusted to your care. Turn away from godless chatter and the opposing ideas of what is falsely called knowledge, ²¹which some have professed and in so doing have departed from the faith.

Grace be with you all.

2 timothy

AUTHOR
The apostle Paul.

AUDIENCE
Timothy and Christians everywhere.

DATE
About A.D. 66 or 67.

SETTING
Paul wrote this, his last letter, from a Roman
dungeon shortly before he was executed for
his faith.

VERSE TO REMEMBER
"That is why I am suffering as I am. Yet this
is no cause for shame, because I know
whom I have believed, and am convinced
that he is able to guard what I have entrusted to him until that day." (1:12)

THEME TO CONSIDER
Suffering comes as no surprise to those
following in the footsteps of Jesus.

1 Paul, an apostle of Christ Jesus by the will of God, in keeping with the promise of life that is in Christ Jesus,

²To Timothy, my dear son:

Grace, mercy and peace from God the Father and Christ Jesus our Lord.

Thanksgiving

³I thank God, whom I serve, as my ancestors did, with a clear conscience, as night and day I constantly remember you in my prayers. ⁴Recalling your tears, I long to see you, so that I may be filled with joy. ⁵I am reminded of your sincere faith, which first lived in your grandmother Lois and in your mother Eunice and, I am persuaded, now lives in you also.

Appeal for Loyalty to Paul and the Gospel

⁶For this reason I remind you to fan into flame the gift of God, which is in you through the laying on of my hands. ⁷For the Spirit God gave us does not make us timid, but gives us power, love and self-discipline. ⁸So do not be ashamed of the testimony about our Lord or of me his prisoner. But join with me in suffering for the gospel, by the power of God, ⁹who has saved us and called us to a holy life—not because of anything we have done but because of his own purpose and grace. This grace was given us in Christ Jesus before the beginning of time, ¹⁰but it has now been revealed through the appearing of our Savior, Christ Jesus, who has destroyed death and has brought life and immortality to light through the gospel. ¹¹And of this gospel I was appointed a herald and an apostle and a teacher. ¹²That is why I am suffering as I am. Yet this is no cause for shame, because I know whom I have believed, and am convinced that he is able to guard what I have entrusted to him until that day.

HE IS: death's destroyer

1:8-10 It was a dark time in Paul's life. Imprisoned and knowing his time on earth was drawing to a close, Paul reminded the church that physical death is not the end. Through his sacrificial death and resurrection, Jesus destroyed death, bringing life and immortality to us mortals.

When you face death, whether it's your own or a loved one's, remember to whom you've entrusted your eternity—*death's destroyer* himself. He has resoundingly defeated your sworn, overpowering enemy. With Christ as your Savior, you can be confident that death is only the beginning of eternal life with him (see 1 Corinthians 15:54–57).

For the next He Is, go to p. 1700.

¹³What you heard from me, keep as the pattern of sound teaching, with faith and love in Christ Jesus. ¹⁴Guard the good deposit that was entrusted to you—guard it with the help of the Holy Spirit who lives in us.

Examples of Disloyalty and Loyalty

¹⁵You know that everyone in the province of Asia has deserted me, including Phygelus and Hermogenes.

¹⁶May the Lord show mercy to the household of Onesiphorus, because he often refreshed me and was not ashamed of my chains. ¹⁷On the contrary, when he was in Rome, he searched hard for me until he found me. ¹⁸May the Lord grant that he will find mercy from the Lord on that day! You know very well in how many ways he helped me in Ephesus.

The Appeal Renewed

2 You then, my son, be strong in the grace that is in Christ Jesus. ²And the things you have heard me say in the presence of many witnesses entrust to reliable people who will also be qualified to teach others. ³Join with me in suffering, like a good soldier of Christ Jesus. ⁴No one serving as a soldier gets

involved in civilian affairs; rather, they try to please their commanding officer. ⁵Similarly, anyone who competes as an athlete does not receive the victor's crown except by competing according to the rules. ⁶The hardworking farmer should be the first to receive a share of the crops. ⁷Reflect on what I am saying, for the Lord will give you insight into all this.

⁸Remember Jesus Christ, raised from the dead, descended from David. This is my gospel, ⁹for which I am suffering even to the point of being chained like a criminal. But God's word is not chained. ¹⁰Therefore I endure everything for the sake of the elect, that they too may obtain the salvation that is in Christ Jesus, with eternal glory.

ASKmeanyTHING

eunice — Acts 16:1; 2 Timothy 1:5

1695

Tell us about your marriage.

My husband and I had different faiths. My mother, Lois, and my son, Timothy, both believed in Jesus, like I did, and I thought and dreamed that someday my husband would join us in our faith. But he never did. I know I'm not the first woman to find herself married to an unbeliever, and I won't be the last. But it's hard. I'd never imagined just how hard it could be.

Did it affect how you raised your son?

Well, my husband and I had different priorities, different goals for Timothy. I knew there would be two conflicting influences in our home, so I made sure Timothy knew the Scriptures from a young age. I was so proud of him when the other Christians in our town spoke well of our son. But can you imagine how I felt when Paul—yes, the apostle *Paul*—invited Timothy to travel with him? I gave him my blessing and let him go. It was such an honor! But of course my husband was mystified by Timothy's desire to become a pastor.

What advice do you have for women who are married to non-Christians?

It's not easy. My heart goes out to you. First, I think you really need to find the support of other women in the church to pray for you *and* for your husband. It's important also to remember Paul's instructions that we should not divorce our unbelieving husbands as long as they're willing to live with us. And then, as Peter advises, we are to live out our faith as a beautiful example to our husbands so that they may be won over to believe God's Word. Most of all, I'd remind women that if your husband comes to Christ, it will be in his time. Don't push him, but do pray for him.

Can I also say a word to single women? Take God's Word seriously about not marrying unbelievers, hoping against hope that they'll change. It will save you and your future children heartache, pain and stress.

FOR MORE INSIGHT: While the Bible doesn't say if Eunice's husband ever came to Christ, we know her legacy of faith lived on in her son, Timothy, who became the apostle Paul's protégé. Read 1 Corinthians 7:12–17; 2 Corinthians 6:14–16; and 1 Peter 3:1–6 for more on the topic of being married to a non-Christian.

[11] Here is a trustworthy saying:

> If we died with him,
> we will also live with him;
> [12] if we endure,
> we will also reign with him.
> If we disown him,
> he will also disown us;
> [13] if we are faithless,
> he remains faithful,
> for he cannot disown himself.

Dealing With False Teachers

[14] Keep reminding God's people of these things. Warn them before God against quarreling about words; it is of no value, and only ruins those who listen. [15] Do your best to present yourself to God as one approved, a worker who does not need to be ashamed and who correctly handles the word of truth. [16] Avoid godless chatter, because those who indulge in it will become more and more ungodly. [17] Their teaching will spread like gangrene. Among them are Hymenaeus and Philetus, [18] who have departed from the truth. They say that the resurrection has already taken place, and they destroy the faith of some. [19] Nevertheless, God's solid foundation stands firm, sealed with this inscription: "The Lord knows those who are his," and, "Everyone who confesses the name of the Lord must turn away from wickedness."

[20] In a large house there are articles not only of gold and silver, but also of wood and clay; some are for noble purposes and some for disposal of refuse. [21] Those who cleanse themselves from the latter will be instruments for noble purposes, made holy, useful to the Master and prepared to do any good work.

[22] Flee the evil desires of youth and pursue righteousness, faith, love and peace, along with those who call on the Lord out of a pure heart. [23] Don't have anything to do with foolish and stupid arguments, because you know they produce quarrels. [24] And the Lord's servant must not be quarrelsome but must be kind to everyone, able to teach, not resentful. [25] Opponents must be gently instructed, in the hope that God will grant them repentance leading them to a knowledge of the truth, [26] and that they will come to their senses and escape from the trap of the devil, who has taken them captive to do his will.

---

atissue:purpose

2:22 We all chase after something. What are you chasing? Mr. Right? The perfect job? An incredible bargain at the 12-hour sale-of-the-century? Or are you chasing the things God calls you to pursue—righteousness, faith, love and peace? There's only one way to "catch" them—by calling on the Lord out of a pure heart, by running from evil and seeking God wholeheartedly. The more you get to know and love him, the more your life will reflect the righteousness, faith, love and peace that are an integral part of who he is.

---

3 But mark this: There will be terrible times in the last days. [2] People will be lovers of themselves, lovers of money, boastful, proud, abusive, disobedient to their parents, ungrateful, unholy, [3] without love, unforgiving, slanderous, without self-control, brutal, not lovers of the good, [4] treacherous, rash, conceited, lovers of pleasure rather than lovers of God— [5] having a form of godliness but denying its power. Have nothing to do with such people.

[6] They are the kind who worm their way into homes and gain control over gullible women, who are loaded down with sins and are swayed by all kinds of evil desires, [7] always learning but never able to come to a knowledge of the truth. [8] Just as Jannes and Jambres opposed Moses, so also these teachers oppose the truth. They are men of depraved minds, who, as far as the faith is concerned, are rejected. [9] But they will not get very far because, as in the case of those men, their folly will be clear to everyone.

conversations

discernment «» 3:1–9

1» How do you protect yourself from subtle, harmful influences around you?

2» How can you balance the desire to reach out to non-Christians with the desire to guard yourself against temptation?

3» What does it mean to have a "form of godliness" (v. 5)?

For more on **discernment**, check the index.
For the next Conversations, go to p. 1700.

A Final Charge to Timothy

[10]You, however, know all about my teaching, my way of life, my purpose, faith, patience, love, endurance, [11]persecutions, sufferings—what kinds of things happened to me in Antioch, Iconium and Lystra, the persecutions I endured. Yet the Lord rescued me from all of them. [12]In fact, everyone who wants to live a godly life in Christ Jesus will be persecuted, [13]while evildoers and impostors will go from bad to worse, deceiving and being deceived. [14]But as for you, continue in what you have learned and have become convinced of, because you know those from whom you learned it, [15]and how from infancy you have known the Holy Scriptures, which are able to make you wise for salvation through faith in Christ Jesus. [16]All Scripture is God-breathed and is useful for teaching, rebuking, correcting and training in righteousness, [17]so that all God's people[a] may be thoroughly equipped for every good work.

1697

4 In the presence of God and of Christ Jesus, who will judge the living and the dead, and in view of his appearing and his kingdom, I give you this charge: [2]Preach the word; be prepared in season and out of season; correct, rebuke and encourage—with great patience and careful instruction. [3]For the time will come when people will not put up with sound doctrine. Instead, to suit their own desires, they will gather around them a great number of teachers to say what their itching ears want to hear. [4]They will turn their ears away from the truth and turn aside to myths. [5]But you, keep your head in all situations, endure hardship, do the work of an evangelist, discharge all the duties of your ministry.

[6]For I am already being poured out like a drink offering, and the time for my departure is near. [7]I have fought the good fight, I have finished the race, I have kept the faith. [8]Now there is in store for me the crown of righteousness, which the Lord, the righteous Judge, will award to me on that day—and not only to me, but also to all who have longed for his appearing.

Personal Remarks

[9]Do your best to come to me quickly, [10]for Demas, because he loved this world, has deserted me and has gone to Thessalonica. Crescens has gone to Galatia, and Titus to Dalmatia. [11]Only Luke is with me. Get Mark and bring him with you, because he is helpful to me in my ministry. [12]I sent Tychicus to Ephesus. [13]When you come, bring the cloak that I left with Carpus at Troas, and my scrolls, especially the parchments.

[14]Alexander the metalworker did me a great deal of harm. The Lord will repay him for what he has done. [15]You too should be on your guard against him, because he strongly opposed our message.

[16]At my first defense, no one came to my support, but everyone deserted me. May it not be held against them. [17]But the Lord stood at my side and gave me strength, so that through me the message might be fully proclaimed and all the Gentiles might hear it. And I was delivered from the lion's mouth. [18]The Lord will rescue me from every evil attack and will bring me safely to his heavenly kingdom. To him be glory for ever and ever. Amen.

Final Greetings

[19]Greet Priscilla[b] and Aquila and the household of Onesiphorus. [20]Erastus stayed in Corinth, and I left Trophimus sick in Miletus. [21]Do your best to get here before winter. Eubulus greets you, and so do Pudens, Linus, Claudia and all the brothers and sisters.

[22]The Lord be with your spirit. Grace be with you all.

---

[a] *17* Or *that the servant of God*   [b] *19* Greek *Prisca*, a variant of *Priscilla*

You claim to know God; what
do your actions say? ≫ (1:16)

Want some tips from God
himself on mentoring? ≫ (2:3–5)

Why are you trying to pick a fight? ≫ (3:9–11)

titus

1698

AUTHOR
The apostle Paul.

AUDIENCE
Titus, a Greek Christian, and followers of
Jesus everywhere.

DATE
Probably about A.D. 64.

SETTING
Paul left Titus in charge of the churches on the
Mediterranean island of Crete.

VERSES TO REMEMBER
"For the grace of God has appeared that offers
salvation to all people. It teaches us to say
'No' to ungodliness and worldly passions, and
to live self-controlled, upright and godly lives
in this present age." (2:11–12)

THEME TO CONSIDER
Character matters when it comes to Christian
leadership.

1 Paul, a servant of God and an apostle of Jesus Christ to further the faith of God's elect and their knowledge of the truth that leads to godliness— ²in the hope of eternal life, which God, who does not lie, promised before the beginning of time, ³and which now at his appointed season he has brought to light through the preaching entrusted to me by the command of God our Savior,

⁴To Titus, my true son in our common faith:

Grace and peace from God the Father and Christ Jesus our Savior.

Appointing Elders Who Love What Is Good

⁵The reason I left you in Crete was that you might put in order what was left unfinished and appoint*ᵃ* elders in every town, as I directed you. ⁶An elder must be blameless, faithful to his wife, a man whose children believe and are not open to the charge of being wild and disobedient. ⁷Since an overseer manages God's household, he must be blameless—not overbearing, not quick-tempered, not given to drunkenness, not violent, not pursuing dishonest gain. ⁸Rather, he must be hospitable, one who loves what is good, who is self-controlled, upright, holy and disciplined. ⁹He must hold firmly to the trust-worthy message as it has been taught, so that he can encourage others by sound doctrine and refute those who oppose it.

Rebuking Those Who Fail to Do Good

¹⁰For there are many rebellious people, full of meaningless talk and deception, especially those of the circumcision group. ¹¹They must be silenced, because they are disrupting whole households by teaching things they ought not to teach—and that for the sake of dishonest gain. ¹²One of Crete's own prophets has said it: "Cretans are always liars, evil brutes, lazy gluttons."*ᵇ* ¹³He has surely told the truth! Therefore rebuke them sharply, so that they will be sound in the faith ¹⁴and will pay no attention to Jewish myths or to the merely human commands of those who reject the truth. ¹⁵To the pure, all things are pure, but to those who are corrupted and do not believe, nothing is pure. In fact, both their minds and consciences are corrupted. ¹⁶They claim to know God, but by their actions they deny him. They are detestable, disobedient and unfit for doing anything good.

Doing Good for the Sake of the Gospel

2 You, however, must teach what is appropriate to sound doctrine. ²Teach the older men to be temperate, worthy of respect, self-controlled, and sound in faith, in love and in endurance.

³Likewise, teach the older women to be reverent in the way they live, not to be slanderers or addicted to much wine, but to teach what is good. ⁴Then they can urge the younger women to love their husbands and children, ⁵to be self-controlled and pure, to be busy at home, to be kind, and to be subject to their husbands, so that no one will malign the word of God.

⁶Similarly, encourage the young men to be self-controlled. ⁷In everything set them an example by doing what is good. In your teaching show integrity, seriousness ⁸and soundness of speech that cannot be condemned, so that those who oppose you may be ashamed because they have nothing bad to say about us.

1699

atissue:mentors

2:3–5 *Out with the old; in with the new.* That philosophy characterizes the mindset of many in our generation. We don't always appreciate or respect anything that isn't "updated" or "new." Consequently, we often fail to make the most of an important resource God has given us—older, godly women. Older women are a treasure! What older women do you know who could be mentors to you? Spend time with them and learn from them. Cultivate relationships with them. You have much to gain from their experience, wisdom and knowledge. And remember, regardless of your age, there's always someone younger you can be mentoring, too.

ᵃ 5 Or ordain ᵇ 12 From the Cretan philosopher Epimenides

⁹Teach slaves to be subject to their masters in everything, to try to please them, not to talk back to them, ¹⁰and not to steal from them, but to show that they can be fully trusted, so that in every way they will make the teaching about God our Savior attractive.

¹¹For the grace of God has appeared that offers salvation to all people. ¹²It teaches us to say "No" to ungodliness and worldly passions, and to live self-controlled, upright and godly lives in this present age, ¹³while we wait for the blessed hope—the appearing of the glory of our great God and Savior, Jesus Christ, ¹⁴who gave himself for us to redeem us from all wickedness and to purify for himself a people that are his very own, eager to do what is good.

¹⁵These, then, are the things you should teach. Encourage and rebuke with all authority. Do not let anyone despise you.

conversations

emotions «» 2:12–14

1» What areas in your life are controlled by your emotions?

2» How can you say "No" to worldly passions when your emotions seem to overwhelmingly lead you to them?

3» What makes you feel eager to do what's good?

For more on **emotions**, check the index.
For the next Conversations, go to p. 1703.

1700

Saved in Order to Do Good

3 Remind the people to be subject to rulers and authorities, to be obedient, to be ready to do whatever is good, ²to slander no one, to be peaceable and considerate, and always to be gentle toward everyone.

³At one time we too were foolish, disobedient, deceived and enslaved by all kinds of passions and pleasures. We lived in malice and envy, being hated and hating one another. ⁴But when the kindness and love of God our Savior appeared, ⁵he saved us, not because of righteous things we had done, but because of his mercy. He saved us through the washing of rebirth and renewal by the Holy Spirit, ⁶whom he poured out on us generously through Jesus Christ our Savior, ⁷so that, having been justified by his grace, we might become heirs having the hope of eternal life. ⁸This is a trustworthy saying. And I want you to stress these things, so that those who have trusted in God may be careful to devote themselves to doing what is good. These things are excellent and profitable for everyone.

HE IS: merciful

3:4–7 Remember Christ's mercy, Paul said. Christ's mercy is so miraculous because it is undeserved—we by no means earned it. His mercy is so meaningful because it cost so much—he purchased our pardon with his very life.

Because Jesus is so *merciful* (and we are so undeserving), we ought to be merciful too. How can you show mercy to someone else today? By helping an overworked co-worker? By forgiving an offense? By being generous to someone in need? Nothing you do deserves his mercy, but everything you do can display his mercy to those you encounter each day.

For the next He Is, go to p. 1705.

⁹But avoid foolish controversies and genealogies and arguments and quarrels about the law, because these are unprofitable and useless. ¹⁰Warn divisive people once, and then warn them a second time. After that, have nothing to do with them. ¹¹You may be sure that such people are warped and sinful; they are self-condemned.

Final Remarks

[12] As soon as I send Artemas or Tychicus to you, do your best to come to me at Nicopolis, because I have decided to winter there. [13] Do everything you can to help Zenas the lawyer and Apollos on their way and see that they have everything they need. [14] Our people must learn to devote themselves to doing what is good, in order to provide for urgent needs and not live unproductive lives.

[15] Everyone with me sends you greetings. Greet those who love us in the faith.

Grace be with you all.

How did Paul respectfully ask for what
he could have rightfully demanded? »» (8–10)

Why is it human nature to want justice
for others but mercy for ourselves? »» (12–21)

Would you say, "Blame me! I'll pay his debt"? »» (17–19)

philemon

AUTHOR
The apostle Paul.

AUDIENCE
Philemon, who was likely a member of the
Colossian church, and all followers of Jesus.

DATE
About A.D. 60.

SETTING
Paul wrote to his friend, Philemon, asking him
to forgive a runaway slave, Onesimus.

VERSES TO REMEMBER
"Perhaps the reason he was separated from
you for a little while was that you might have
him back forever—no longer as a slave, but
better than a slave, as a dear brother. He is
very dear to me but even dearer to you, both as
a fellow man and as a brother in the Lord."
(15–16)

THEME TO CONSIDER
Christians are to demonstrate unexpected
kindness to all.

¹Paul, a prisoner of Christ Jesus, and Timothy our brother,

To Philemon our dear friend and fellow worker— ²also to Apphia our sister and Archippus our fellow soldier—and to the church that meets in your home:

³Grace and peace to you*a* from God our Father and the Lord Jesus Christ.

Thanksgiving and Prayer

⁴I always thank my God as I remember you in my prayers, ⁵because I hear about your love for all his people and your faith in the Lord Jesus. ⁶I pray that your partnership with us in the faith may be effective in deepening your understanding of every good thing we share for the sake of Christ. ⁷Your love has given me great joy and encouragement, because you, brother, have refreshed the hearts of the Lord's people.

Paul's Plea for Onesimus

⁸Therefore, although in Christ I could be bold and order you to do what you ought to do, ⁹yet I prefer to appeal to you on the basis of love. It is as none other than Paul—an old man and now also a prisoner of Christ Jesus— ¹⁰that I appeal to you for my son Onesimus,*b* who became my son while I was in chains. ¹¹Formerly he was useless to you, but now he has become useful both to you and to me.

¹²I am sending him—who is my very heart—back to you. ¹³I would have liked to keep him with me so that he could take your place in helping me while I am in chains for the gospel. ¹⁴But I did not want to do anything without your consent, so that any favor you do would not seem forced but would be voluntary. ¹⁵Perhaps the reason he was separated from you for a little while was that you might have him back forever— ¹⁶no longer as a slave, but better than a slave, as a dear brother. He is very dear to me but even dearer to you, both as a fellow man and as a brother in the Lord.

¹⁷So if you consider me a partner, welcome him as you would welcome me. ¹⁸If he has done you any wrong or owes you anything, charge it to me. ¹⁹I, Paul, am writing this with my own hand. I will pay it back—not to mention that you owe me your very self. ²⁰I do wish, brother, that I may have some benefit from you in the Lord; refresh my heart in Christ. ²¹Confident of your obedience, I write to you, knowing that you will do even more than I ask.

²²And one thing more: Prepare a guest room for me, because I hope to be restored to you in answer to your prayers.

²³Epaphras, my fellow prisoner in Christ Jesus, sends you greetings. ²⁴And so do Mark, Aristarchus, Demas and Luke, my fellow workers.

²⁵The grace of the Lord Jesus Christ be with your spirit.

at issue: forgiveness

1–25 When someone hurts you, do you try to punish that person by refusing to forgive? Know that the only person your bitterness truly hurts is you. Unforgiveness cripples your spirit and chains your heart; only forgiveness can set you free. Paul urged Philemon to forgive his runaway slave, Onesimus, for the wrongs that Onesimus had committed—just as much for Philemon's sake as for Onesimus's sake. Paul wanted Philemon to know the freedom that comes from choosing to forgive others the way God forgives us—freely, undeservedly, without payment. Do you need to let go of your anger against someone and choose to forgive?

1703

conversations

conflict «» 12–21

1 » Do you tend to avoid conflict or confront it head-on? Why do you think you handle conflict this way?

2 » What can you learn from Paul's approach to Philemon in this emotionally charged situation?

3 » When you're resolving a conflict, why can validating the other person's emotions be so important?

For more on **conflict**, check the index.
For the next Conversations, go to p. 1707

a **3** The Greek is plural; also in verses 22 and 25; elsewhere in this letter "you" is singular.   *b* **10** *Onesimus* means *useful.*

hebrews

1704

AUTHOR
Unknown.

AUDIENCE
Hebrew Christians and all followers of Jesus.

DATE
Sometime before the destruction of the temple
in Jerusalem in A.D. 70.

SETTING
Jewish Christians were being persecuted,
probably by both Jews and Romans, and were
growing weary.

VERSES TO REMEMBER
"Let us run with perseverance the race marked
out for us, fixing our eyes on Jesus, the pioneer
and perfecter of faith. For the joy set before
him he endured the cross, scorning its shame,
and sat down at the right hand of the throne
of God." (12:1b–2)

THEME TO CONSIDER
Is it worth it to follow Christ, or is there some-
thing better? The Bible reassures us that
Christ is sufficient and supreme.

God's Final Word: His Son

1 In the past God spoke to our ancestors through the prophets at many times and in various ways, ²but in these last days he has spoken to us by his Son, whom he appointed heir of all things, and through whom also he made the universe. ³The Son is the radiance of God's glory and the exact representation of his being, sustaining all things by his powerful word. After he had provided purification for sins, he sat down at the right hand of the Majesty in heaven. ⁴So he became as much superior to the angels as the name he has inherited is superior to theirs.

HE IS: the exact representation

1:1–3 God made it clear that no one could see him and live (see Exodus 33:20). Yet God made a way for humans to see him. Jesus Christ is God's *exact representation*. If you want to see God, just look at Jesus.

What is God like? we wonder. *What does God think of suffering?* Look at Jesus—as seen in his life, suffering is sometimes necessary. *Of hypocrisy?* Look at how Jesus responded to hypocrites. *Of people?* He clearly loved them. *Of sin?* It's serious—ours cost him his life. You want to know what God is like and what he thinks about something? Look at his *exact representation*.

For the next He Is, go to p. 1708.

The Son Superior to Angels

⁵For to which of the angels did God ever say,

> "You are my Son;
> today I have become your Father"ᵃ?

Or again,

> "I will be his Father,
> and he will be my Son"ᵇ?

⁶And again, when God brings his firstborn into the world, he says,

> "Let all God's angels worship him."ᶜ

⁷In speaking of the angels he says,

> "He makes his angels spirits,
> and his servants flames of fire."ᵈ

⁸But about the Son he says,

> "Your throne, O God, will last for ever and ever;
> a scepter of justice will be the scepter of your kingdom.
> ⁹You have loved righteousness and hated wickedness;
> therefore God, your God, has set you above your companions
> by anointing you with the oil of joy."ᵉ

¹⁰He also says,

> "In the beginning, Lord, you laid the foundations of the earth,
> and the heavens are the work of your hands.
> ¹¹They will perish, but you remain;

ᵃ *5* Psalm 2:7   ᵇ *5* 2 Samuel 7:14; 1 Chron. 17:13   ᶜ *6* Deut. 32:43 (see Dead Sea Scrolls and Septuagint)   ᵈ *7* Psalm 104:4   ᵉ *9* Psalm 45:6,7

they will all wear out like a garment.
¹²You will roll them up like a robe;
like a garment they will be changed.
But you remain the same,
and your years will never end."ᵃ

¹³To which of the angels did God ever say,

"Sit at my right hand
until I make your enemies
a footstool for your feet"ᵇ?

¹⁴Are not all angels ministering spirits sent to serve those who will inherit salvation?

Warning to Pay Attention

2 We must pay the most careful attention, therefore, to what we have heard, so that we do not drift away. ²For since the message spoken through angels was binding, and every violation and disobedience received its just punishment, ³how shall we escape if we ignore so great a salvation? This salvation, which was first announced by the Lord, was confirmed to us by those who heard him. ⁴God also testified to it by signs, wonders and various miracles, and by gifts of the Holy Spirit distributed according to his will.

Jesus Made Like His Brothers and Sisters

⁵It is not to angels that he has subjected the world to come, about which we are speaking. ⁶But there is a place where someone has testified:

"What are mere mortals that you are mindful of them,
human beings that you care for them?
⁷You made them a little lower than the angels;
you crowned them with glory and honor
⁸ and put everything under their feet."ᶜ

In putting everything under them,ᵈ God left nothing that is not subject to them.ᵉ Yet at present we do not see everything subject to them.ᶠ ⁹But we do see Jesus, who was made lower than the angels for a little while, now crowned with glory and honor because he suffered death, so that by the grace of God he might taste death for everyone.

¹⁰In bringing many sons and daughters to glory, it was fitting that God, for whom and through whom everything exists, should make the pioneer of their salvation perfect through what he suffered. ¹¹Both the one who makes people holy and those who are made holy are of the same family. So Jesus is not ashamed to call them brothers and sisters. ¹²He says,

"I will declare your name to my brothers and sisters;
in the assembly I will sing your praises."ᵍ

¹³And again,

"I will put my trust in him."ʰ

And again he says,

"Here am I, and the children God has given me."ⁱ

¹⁴Since the children have flesh and blood, he too shared in their humanity so that by his death he might break the power of him who holds the power of death—that is, the devil— ¹⁵and free those who all their lives were held in slavery by their fear of death. ¹⁶For surely it is not angels he helps, but

ᵃ 12 Psalm 102:25-27 ᵇ 13 Psalm 110:1 ᶜ 6-8 Psalm 8:4-6; or "What is a human being that you are mindful of him, / the son of man that you care for him?/ ⁷You made him lower than the angels for a little while; / you crowned him with glory and honor/ ⁸and put everything under his feet." ᵈ 8 Or him ᵉ 8 Or him ᶠ 8 Or him ᵍ 12 Psalm 22:22 ʰ 13 Isaiah 8:17 ⁱ 13 Isaiah 8:18

Abraham's descendants. [17] For this reason he had to be made like his brothers and sisters in every way, in order that he might become a merciful and faithful high priest in service to God, and that he might make atonement for the sins of the people. [18] Because he himself suffered when he was tempted, he is able to help those who are being tempted.

conversations

priorities «» 3:1

1 What does it mean to "fix your thoughts on Jesus" each day? How do you do that?

2 If you make Jesus your highest priority, how does that affect your other choices in life?

3 Would you consider Jesus the true leader of your life? Why or why not?

For more on **priorities**, check the index.
For the next Conversations, go to p. 1719.

Jesus Greater Than Moses

3 Therefore, holy brothers and sisters, who share in the heavenly calling, fix your thoughts on Jesus, whom we acknowledge as our apostle and high priest. [2] He was faithful to the one who appointed him, just as Moses was faithful in all God's house. [3] Jesus has been found worthy of greater honor than Moses, just as the builder of a house has greater honor than the house itself. [4] For every house is built by someone, but God is the builder of everything. [5] "Moses was faithful as a servant in all God's house,"[a] bearing witness to what would be spoken by God in the future. [6] But Christ is faithful as the Son over God's house. And we are his house, if indeed we hold firmly to our confidence and the hope in which we glory.

1707

Warning Against Unbelief

[7] So, as the Holy Spirit says:

"Today, if you hear his voice,
[8]   do not harden your hearts
as you did in the rebellion,
    during the time of testing in the wilderness,
[9] where your ancestors tested and tried me,
    though for forty years they saw what I did.
[10] That is why I was angry with that generation;
I said, 'Their hearts are always going astray,
and they have not known my ways.'
[11] So I declared on oath in my anger,
'They shall never enter my rest.'"[b]

[12] See to it, brothers and sisters, that none of you has a sinful, unbelieving heart that turns away from the living God. [13] But encourage one another daily, as long as it is called "Today," so that none of you may be hardened by sin's deceitfulness. [14] We have come to share in Christ, if indeed we hold firmly till the end our original conviction. [15] As has just been said:

"Today, if you hear his voice,
do not harden your hearts
as you did in the rebellion."[c]

[16] Who were they who heard and rebelled? Were they not all those Moses led out of Egypt? [17] And with whom was he angry for forty years? Was it not with those who sinned, whose bodies perished in the wilderness? [18] And to whom did God swear that they would never enter his rest if not to those who disobeyed? [19] So we see that they were not able to enter, because of their unbelief.

---

[a] *5* Num. 12:7 [b] *11* Psalm 95:7-11 [c] *15* Psalm 95:7,8

A Sabbath-Rest for the People of God

4 Therefore, since the promise of entering his rest still stands, let us be careful that none of you be found to have fallen short of it. ²For we also have had the good news proclaimed to us, just as they did; but the message they heard was of no value to them, because they did not share the faith of those who obeyed.ᵃ ³Now we who have believed enter that rest, just as God has said,

> "So I declared on oath in my anger,
> 'They shall never enter my rest.'"ᵇ

And yet his work has been finished since the creation of the world. ⁴For somewhere he has spoken about the seventh day in these words: "On the seventh day God rested from all his work."ᶜ ⁵And again in the passage above he says, "They shall never enter my rest."

⁶Therefore since it still remains for some to enter that rest, and since those who formerly had the good news proclaimed to them did not go in because of their disobedience, ⁷God again set a certain day, calling it "Today." This he did when a long time later he spoke through David, as in the passage already quoted:

> "Today, if you hear his voice,
> do not harden your hearts."ᵈ

⁸For if Joshua had given them rest, God would not have spoken later about another day. ⁹There remains, then, a Sabbath-rest for the people of God; ¹⁰for those who enter God's rest also rest from their own work, just as God did from his. ¹¹Let us, therefore, make every effort to enter that rest, so that no one will perish by following their example of disobedience.

¹²For the word of God is alive and active. Sharper than any double-edged sword, it penetrates even to dividing soul and spirit, joints and marrow; it judges the thoughts and attitudes of the heart. ¹³Nothing in all creation is hidden from God's sight. Everything is uncovered and laid bare before the eyes of him to whom we must give account.

Jesus the Great High Priest

¹⁴Therefore, since we have a great high priest who has ascended into heaven,ᵉ Jesus the Son of God, let us hold firmly to the faith we profess. ¹⁵For we do not have a high priest who is unable to empathize with our weaknesses, but we have one who has been tempted in every way, just as we are—yet he did not sin. ¹⁶Let us then approach God's throne of grace with confidence, so that we may receive mercy and find grace to help us in our time of need.

ᵃ *2 Some manuscripts* because those who heard did not combine it with faith   ᵇ *3 Psalm 95:11; also in verse 5*   ᶜ *4 Gen. 2:2*   ᵈ *7 Psalm 95:7,8*   ᵉ *14 Greek has gone through the heavens*

HE IS: approachable

4:15–16 God is not some detached deity far away in the heavens, unable to relate to human frailty and emotions. God's son, Jesus, came to earth and was tempted in every way in order to empathize with our weaknesses.

Because of Jesus' firsthand experience as a human, he can relate to us. He knows what it's like to struggle and to be tempted. What an *approachable* Savior! When you're tempted, turn to Jesus—he's also been tempted. When you're discouraged, depend on him—he understands that feeling all too well. When you're tired, lean on him—he knows exactly how you feel.

For the next He Is, go to p. 1727.

5 Every high priest is selected from among the people and is appointed to represent them in matters related to God, to offer gifts and sacrifices for sins. ²He is able to deal gently with those who are ignorant and are going astray, since he himself is subject to weakness. ³This is why he has to offer sacrifices for his own sins, as well as for the sins of the people. ⁴And no one takes this honor on himself, but he receives it when called by God, just as Aaron was.

⁵In the same way, Christ did not take on himself the glory of becoming a high priest. But God said to him,

> "You are my Son;
>   today I have become your Father."*ᵃ*

⁶And he says in another place,

> "You are a priest forever,
>   in the order of Melchizedek."*ᵇ*

⁷During the days of Jesus' life on earth, he offered up prayers and petitions with fervent cries and tears to the one who could save him from death, and he was heard because of his reverent submission. ⁸Son though he was, he learned obedience from what he suffered ⁹and, once made perfect, he became the source of eternal salvation for all who obey him ¹⁰and was designated by God to be high priest in the order of Melchizedek.

Warning Against Falling Away

¹¹We have much to say about this, but it is hard to make it clear to you because you no longer try to understand. ¹²In fact, though by this time you ought to be teachers, you need someone to teach you the elementary truths of God's word all over again. You need milk, not solid food! ¹³Anyone who lives on milk, being still an infant, is not acquainted with the teaching about righteousness. ¹⁴But solid food is for the mature, who by constant use have trained themselves to distinguish good from evil.

6 Therefore let us move beyond the elementary teachings about Christ and be taken forward to maturity, not laying again the foundation of repentance from acts that lead to death,*ᶜ* and of faith in God, ²instruction about cleansing rites,*ᵈ* the laying on of hands, the resurrection of the dead, and eternal judgment. ³And God permitting, we will do so.

⁴It is impossible for those who have once been enlightened, who have tasted the heavenly gift, who have shared in the Holy Spirit, ⁵who have tasted the goodness of the word of God and the powers of the coming age ⁶and who have fallen*ᵉ* away, to be brought back to repentance. To their loss they are crucifying the Son of God all over again and subjecting him to public disgrace. ⁷Land that drinks in the rain often falling on it and that produces a crop useful to those for whom it is farmed receives the blessing of God. ⁸But land that produces thorns and thistles is worthless and is in danger of being cursed. In the end it will be burned.

⁹Even though we speak like this, dear friends, we are convinced of better things in your case—the things that have to do with salvation. ¹⁰God is not unjust; he will not forget your work and the love you have shown him as you have helped his people and continue to help them. ¹¹We want each of you to show this same diligence to the very end, in order to make your hope sure. ¹²We do not want you to become lazy, but to imitate those who through faith and patience inherit what has been promised.

The Certainty of God's Promise

¹³When God made his promise to Abraham, since there was no one greater for him to swear by, he swore by himself, ¹⁴saying, "I will surely bless you and give you many descendants."*ᶠ* ¹⁵And so after waiting patiently, Abraham received what was promised.

¹⁶People swear by someone greater than themselves, and the oath confirms what is said and puts an end to all argument. ¹⁷Because God wanted to make the unchanging nature of his purpose very clear to the heirs of what was promised, he confirmed it with an oath. ¹⁸God did this so that, by two unchangeable things in which it is impossible for God to lie, we who have fled to take hold of the hope set before

ᵃ 5 Psalm 2:7   ᵇ 6 Psalm 110:4   ᶜ 1 Or from useless rituals   ᵈ 2 Or about baptisms   ᵉ 6 Or age, ⁶if they fall   ᶠ 14 Gen. 22:17 us may be greatly encouraged. [19]We have this hope as an anchor for the soul, firm and secure. It enters the inner sanctuary behind the curtain, [20]where our forerunner, Jesus, has entered on our behalf. He has become a high priest forever, in the order of Melchizedek.

Melchizedek the Priest

7 This Melchizedek was king of Salem and priest of God Most High. He met Abraham returning from the defeat of the kings and blessed him, [2]and Abraham gave him a tenth of everything. First, the name Melchizedek means "king of righteousness"; then also, "king of Salem" means "king of peace." [3]Without father or mother, without genealogy, without beginning of days or end of life, resembling the Son of God, he remains a priest forever.

[4]Just think how great he was: Even the patriarch Abraham gave him a tenth of the plunder! [5]Now the law requires the descendants of Levi who become priests to collect a tenth from the people—that is, from their kindred—even though their kindred are descended from Abraham. [6]This man, however, did not trace his descent from Levi, yet he collected a tenth from Abraham and blessed him who had the promises. [7]And without doubt the lesser is blessed by the greater. [8]In the one case, the tenth is collected by those who die; but in the other case, by him who is declared to be living. [9]One might even say that Levi, who collects the tenth, paid the tenth through Abraham, [10]because when Melchizedek met Abraham, Levi was still in the body of his ancestor.

Jesus Like Melchizedek

[11]If perfection could have been attained through the Levitical priesthood—and indeed the law given to the people established that priesthood—why was there still need for another priest to come, one in the order of Melchizedek, not in the order of Aaron? [12]For when the priesthood is changed, the law must be changed also. [13]He of whom these things are said belonged to a different tribe, and no one from that tribe has ever served at the altar. [14]For it is clear that our Lord descended from Judah, and in regard to that tribe Moses said nothing about priests. [15]And what we have said is even more clear if another priest like Melchizedek appears, [16]one who has become a priest not on the basis of a regulation as to his ancestry but on the basis of the power of an indestructible life. [17]For it is declared:

> "You are a priest forever,
>   in the order of Melchizedek."[a]

[18]The former regulation is set aside because it was weak and useless [19](for the law made nothing perfect), and a better hope is introduced, by which we draw near to God.

[20]And it was not without an oath! Others became priests without any oath, [21]but he became a priest with an oath when God said to him:

> "The Lord has sworn
>   and will not change his mind:
>   'You are a priest forever.'"[a]

[22]Because of this oath, Jesus has become the guarantor of a better covenant.

[23]Now there have been many of those priests, since death prevented them from continuing in office;

1710

---
[a] 17,21 Psalm 110:4

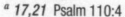

[24] but because Jesus lives forever, he has a permanent priesthood. [25] Therefore he is able to save completely[a] those who come to God through him, because he always lives to intercede for them.

[26] Such a high priest truly meets our need—one who is holy, blameless, pure, set apart from sinners, exalted above the heavens. [27] Unlike the other high priests, he does not need to offer sacrifices day after day, first for his own sins, and then for the sins of the people. He sacrificed for their sins once for all when he offered himself. [28] For the law appoints as high priests men in all their weakness; but the oath, which came after the law, appointed the Son, who has been made perfect forever.

The High Priest of a New Covenant

8 Now the main point of what we are saying is this: We do have such a high priest, who sat down at the right hand of the throne of the Majesty in heaven, [2] and who serves in the sanctuary, the true tabernacle set up by the Lord, not by a mere human being.

[3] Every high priest is appointed to offer both gifts and sacrifices, and so it was necessary for this one also to have something to offer. [4] If he were on earth, he would not be a priest, for there are already priests who offer the gifts prescribed by the law. [5] They serve at a sanctuary that is a copy and shadow of what is in heaven. This is why Moses was warned when he was about to build the tabernacle: "See to it that you make everything according to the pattern shown you on the mountain."[b] [6] But in fact the ministry Jesus has received is as superior to theirs as the covenant of which he is mediator is superior to the old one, since the new covenant is established on better promises.

[7] For if there had been nothing wrong with that first covenant, no place would have been sought for another. [8] But God found fault with the people and said[c]:

> "The days are coming, declares the Lord,
>   when I will make a new covenant
> with the house of Israel
>   and with the house of Judah.
> [9] It will not be like the covenant
>   I made with their ancestors
> when I took them by the hand
>   to lead them out of Egypt,
> because they did not remain faithful to my covenant,
>   and I turned away from them,
>   declares the Lord.
> [10] This is the covenant I will establish with the house of Israel
>   after that time, declares the Lord.
> I will put my laws in their minds
>   and write them on their hearts.
> I will be their God,
>   and they will be my people.
> [11] No longer will they teach their neighbors,
>   or say to one another, 'Know the Lord,'
> because they will all know me,
>   from the least of them to the greatest.
> [12] For I will forgive their wickedness
>   and will remember their sins no more."[d]

[13] By calling this covenant "new," he has made the first one obsolete; and what is obsolete and outdated will soon disappear.

Worship in the Earthly Tabernacle

9 Now the first covenant had regulations for worship and also an earthly sanctuary. [2] A tabernacle was set up. In its first room were the lampstand and the table with its consecrated bread; this was

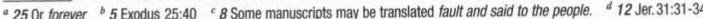

called the Holy Place. [3]Behind the second curtain was a room called the Most Holy Place, [4]which had the golden altar of incense and the gold-covered ark of the covenant. This ark contained the gold jar of manna, Aaron's staff that had budded, and the stone tablets of the covenant. [5]Above the ark were the cherubim of the Glory, overshadowing the atonement cover. But we cannot discuss these things in detail now.

[6]When everything had been arranged like this, the priests entered regularly into the outer room to carry on their ministry. [7]But only the high priest entered the inner room, and that only once a year, and never without blood, which he offered for himself and for the sins the people had committed in ignorance. [8]The Holy Spirit was showing by this that the way into the Most Holy Place had not yet been disclosed as long as the first tabernacle was still functioning. [9]This is an illustration for the present time, indicating that the gifts and sacrifices being offered were not able to clear the conscience of the worshiper. [10]They are only a matter of food and drink and various ceremonial washings—external regulations applying until the time of the new order.

The Blood of Christ

[11]But when Christ came as high priest of the good things that are now already here,[a] he went through the greater and more perfect tabernacle that is not made with human hands, that is to say, is not a part of this creation. [12]He did not enter by means of the blood of goats and calves; but he entered the Most Holy Place once for all by his own blood, thus obtaining[b] eternal redemption. [13]The blood of goats and bulls and the ashes of a heifer sprinkled on those who are ceremonially unclean sanctify them so that they are outwardly clean. [14]How much more, then, will the blood of Christ, who through the eternal Spirit offered himself unblemished to God, cleanse our consciences from acts that lead to death,[c] so that we may serve the living God!

[15]For this reason Christ is the mediator of a new covenant, that those who are called may receive the promised eternal inheritance—now that he has died as a ransom to set them free from the sins committed under the first covenant.

[16]In the case of a will,[d] it is necessary to prove the death of the one who made it, [17]because a will is in force only when somebody has died; it never takes effect while the one who made it is living. [18]This is why even the first covenant was not put into effect without blood. [19]When Moses had proclaimed every command of the law to all the people, he took the blood of calves, together with water, scarlet wool and branches of hyssop, and sprinkled the scroll and all the people. [20]He said, "This is the blood of the covenant, which God has commanded you to keep."[e] [21]In the same way, he sprinkled with the blood both the tabernacle and everything used in its ceremonies. [22]In fact, the law requires that nearly everything be cleansed with blood, and without the shedding of blood there is no forgiveness.

[23]It was necessary, then, for the copies of the heavenly things to be purified with these sacrifices, but the heavenly things themselves with better sacrifices than these. [24]For Christ did not enter a sanctuary made with human hands that was only a copy of the true one; he entered heaven itself, now to appear for us in God's presence. [25]Nor did he enter heaven to offer himself again and again, the way the high priest enters the Most Holy Place every year with blood that is not his own. [26]Otherwise Christ would have had to suffer many times since the creation of the world. But he has appeared once for all at the culmination of the ages to do away with sin by the sacrifice of himself. [27]Just as people are destined to die once, and after that to face judgment, [28]so Christ was sacrificed once to take away the sins of many; and he will appear a second time, not to bear sin, but to bring salvation to those who are waiting for him.

Christ's Sacrifice Once for All

10 The law is only a shadow of the good things that are coming—not the realities themselves. For this reason it can never, by the same sacrifices repeated endlessly year after year, make perfect those who draw near to worship. [2]Otherwise, would they not have stopped being offered? For the worshipers would have been cleansed once for all, and would no longer have felt guilty for their sins. [3]But

[a] 11 Some early manuscripts *are to come*   [b] 12 Or *blood, having obtained*   [c] 14 Or *from useless rituals*   [d] 16 Same Greek word as *covenant*; also in verse 17
[e] 20 Exodus 24:8

those sacrifices are an annual reminder of sins. ⁴It is impossible for the blood of bulls and goats to take away sins.

⁵Therefore, when Christ came into the world, he said:

> "Sacrifice and offering you did not desire,
>   but a body you prepared for me;
> ⁶with burnt offerings and sin offerings
>   you were not pleased.
> ⁷Then I said, 'Here I am—it is written about me in the scroll—
>   I have come to do your will, my God.'"ᵃ

⁸First he said, "Sacrifices and offerings, burnt offerings and sin offerings you did not desire, nor were you pleased with them"—though they were offered in accordance with the law. ⁹Then he said, "Here I am, I have come to do your will." He sets aside the first to establish the second. ¹⁰And by that will, we have been made holy through the sacrifice of the body of Jesus Christ once for all.

¹¹Day after day every priest stands and performs his religious duties; again and again he offers the same sacrifices, which can never take away sins. ¹²But when this priest had offered for all time one sacrifice for sins, he sat down at the right hand of God, ¹³and since that time he waits for his enemies to be made his footstool. ¹⁴For by one sacrifice he has made perfect forever those who are being made holy.

¹⁵The Holy Spirit also testifies to us about this. First he says:

> ¹⁶"This is the covenant I will make with them
>   after that time, says the Lord.
> I will put my laws in their hearts,
>   and I will write them on their minds."ᵇ

¹⁷Then he adds:

> "Their sins and lawless acts
>   I will remember no more."ᶜ

¹⁸And where these have been forgiven, sacrifice for sin is no longer necessary.

A Call to Persevere in Faith

¹⁹Therefore, brothers and sisters, since we have confidence to enter the Most Holy Place by the blood of Jesus, ²⁰by a new and living way opened for us through the curtain, that is, his body, ²¹and since we have a great priest over the house of God, ²²let us draw near to God with a sincere heart in full assurance of faith, having our hearts sprinkled to cleanse us from a guilty conscience and having our bodies washed with pure water. ²³Let us hold unswervingly to the hope we profess, for he who promised is faithful. ²⁴And let us consider how we may spur one another on toward love and good deeds, ²⁵not giving up meeting together, as some are in the habit of doing, but encouraging one another—and all the more as you see the Day approaching.

²⁶If we deliberately keep on sinning after we have received the knowledge of the truth, no sacrifice for sins is left, ²⁷but only a fearful expectation of judgment and of raging fire that will consume the enemies of God. ²⁸Anyone who rejected the law of Moses died without mercy on the testimony of two or

1713

a tissue: access to God

10:19–23 Before Jesus' death, the average person didn't have direct access to God and couldn't enter the Most Holy Place, where God's presence was; only the high priest could do that. (And then only one day a year!) But Jesus changed everything. His blood covered the sin that separated us from God. Now we are purified and can come before God *at any moment of every day.* If you've come to Jesus to be forgiven, no matter who you are or what you've done, you can now approach God with confidence. What are you waiting for? Draw near to God, and enjoy that direct access you have to God himself.

ᵃ 7 Psalm 40:6-8 (see Septuagint)   ᵇ 16 Jer. 31:33   ᶜ 17 Jer. 31:34

three witnesses. [29]How much more severely do you think those deserve to be punished who have trampled the Son of God underfoot, who have treated as an unholy thing the blood of the covenant that sanctified them, and who have insulted the Spirit of grace? [30]For we know him who said, "It is mine to avenge; I will repay,"[a] and again, "The Lord will judge his people."[b] [31]It is a dreadful thing to fall into the hands of the living God.

[32]Remember those earlier days after you had received the light, when you endured in a great conflict full of suffering. [33]Sometimes you were publicly exposed to insult and persecution; at other times you stood side by side with those who were so treated. [34]You suffered along with those in prison and joyfully accepted the confiscation of your property, because you knew that you yourselves had better and lasting possessions. [35]So do not throw away your confidence; it will be richly rewarded.

[36]You need to persevere so that when you have done the will of God, you will receive what he has promised. [37]For,

> "In just a little while,
> he who is coming will come
> and will not delay."[c]

[38]And,

> "But my righteous one[d] will live by faith.
> And I take no pleasure
> in the one who shrinks back."[e]

[39]But we are not of those who shrink back and are destroyed, but of those who believe and are saved.

Faith in Action

11 Now faith is being sure of what we hope for and certain of what we do not see. [2]This is what the ancients were commended for.

[3]By faith we understand that the universe was formed at God's command, so that what is seen was not made out of what was visible.

[4]By faith Abel brought God a better offering than Cain did. By faith he was commended as righteous, when God spoke well of his offerings. And by faith Abel still speaks, even though he is dead.

[5]By faith Enoch was taken from this life, so that he did not experience death: "He could not be found, because God had taken him away."[f] For before he was taken, he was commended as one who pleased God. [6]And without faith it is impossible to please God, because anyone who comes to him must believe that he exists and that he rewards those who earnestly seek him.

[7]By faith Noah, when warned about things not yet seen, in holy fear built an ark to save his family. By his faith he condemned the world and became heir of the righteousness that is in keeping with faith.

[8]By faith Abraham, when called to go to a place he would later receive as his inheritance, obeyed and went, even though he did not know where he was going. [9]By faith he made his home in the promised land like a stranger in a foreign country; he lived in tents, as did Isaac and Jacob, who were heirs with him of the same promise. [10]For he was looking forward to the city with foundations, whose architect and builder is God. [11]And by faith even Sarah, who was past childbearing age, was enabled to bear children because she[g] considered him faithful who had made the promise. [12]And so from this one man, and he as good as dead, came descendants as numerous as the stars in the sky and as countless as the sand on the seashore.

[13]All these people were still living by faith when they died. They did not receive the things promised; they only saw them and welcomed them from a distance, admitting that they were foreigners and strangers on earth. [14]People who say such things show that they are looking for a country of their own. [15]If they had been thinking of the country they had left, they would have had opportunity to return. [16]Instead, they were longing for a better country—a heavenly one. Therefore God is not ashamed to be called their God, for he has prepared a city for them.

¹⁷By faith Abraham, when God tested him, offered Isaac as a sacrifice. He who had embraced the promises was about to sacrifice his one and only son, ¹⁸even though God had said to him, "It is through Isaac that your offspring will be reckoned."ᵃ ¹⁹Abraham reasoned that God could even raise the dead, and so in a manner of speaking he did receive Isaac back from death.

²⁰By faith Isaac blessed Jacob and Esau in regard to their future.

²¹By faith Jacob, when he was dying, blessed each of Joseph's sons, and worshiped as he leaned on the top of his staff.

²²By faith Joseph, when his end was near, spoke about the exodus of the Israelites from Egypt and gave instructions concerning the burial of his bones.

²³By faith Moses' parents hid him for three months after he was born, because they saw he was no ordinary child, and they were not afraid of the king's edict.

²⁴By faith Moses, when he had grown up, refused to be known as the son of Pharaoh's daughter. ²⁵He chose to be mistreated along with the people of God rather than to enjoy the fleeting pleasures of sin. ²⁶He regarded disgrace for the sake of Christ as of greater value than the treasures of Egypt, because he was looking ahead to his reward. ²⁷By faith he left Egypt, not fearing the king's anger; he persevered because he saw him who is invisible. ²⁸By faith he kept the Passover and the application of blood, so that the destroyer of the firstborn would not touch the firstborn of Israel.

²⁹By faith the people passed through the Red Sea as on dry land; but when the Egyptians tried to do so, they were drowned.

³⁰By faith the walls of Jericho fell, after the army had marched around them for seven days.

³¹By faith the prostitute Rahab, because she welcomed the spies, was not killed with those who were disobedient.ᵇ

³²And what more shall I say? I do not have time to tell about Gideon, Barak, Samson and Jephthah, about David and Samuel and the prophets, ³³who through faith conquered kingdoms, administered justice, and gained what was promised; who shut the mouths of lions, ³⁴quenched the fury of the flames, and escaped the edge of the sword; whose weakness was turned to strength; and who became powerful in battle and routed foreign armies. ³⁵Women received back their dead, raised to life again. There were others who were tortured, refusing to be released so that they might gain an even better resurrection. ³⁶Some faced jeers and flogging, and even chains and imprisonment. ³⁷They were put to death by stoning;ᶜ they were sawed in two; they were killed by the sword. They went about in sheepskins and goatskins, destitute, persecuted and mistreated— ³⁸the world was not worthy of them. They wandered in deserts and mountains, and in caves and holes in the ground.

³⁹These were all commended for their faith, yet none of them received what had been promised. ⁴⁰God had planned something better for us so that only together with us would they be made perfect.

12 Therefore, since we are surrounded by such a great cloud of witnesses, let us throw off everything that hinders and the sin that so easily entangles. And let us run with perseverance the race marked out for us, ²fixing our eyes on Jesus, the pioneer and perfecter of faith. For the joy set before him he endured the cross, scorning its shame, and sat down at the right hand of the throne of God. ³Consider him who endured such opposition from sinners, so that you will not grow weary and lose heart.

atissue:sacrifice

11:23–28 What's remarkable about this list of "Who's Who of the Faith" is that these were ordinary people—completely transformed by faith. Each person has a great deal to teach us. Take Moses. He decided to give up his privileged life as an Egyptian prince and chose instead to suffer with God's people. Why? Because he valued eternal reward more than the fleeting pleasures of this world. Will you also turn your back on the temporary enjoyment of sin and the "fun" of this world and look with faith to a greater reward? Moses would say that the sacrifice is definitely worth it.

1715

ᵃ 18 Gen. 21:12 ᵇ 31 Or unbelieving ᶜ 37 Some early manuscripts stoning; they were put to the test;

myth# 98

"I SHOULDN'T HAVE DOUBTS ABOUT MY FAITH."

If I had to pick a year to live over again, I certainly wouldn't pick this one. It's been a terrible year, one that started with my stepfather's sudden death (we were really close), my job loss and the end of a serious relationship that I'd held dear.

I've felt hammered by life on the one hand and abandoned by God on the other. He seems silent these days, silent in the face of my pain. To top it all off, I've felt so guilty about doubting him. I feel phony every time I try to pray. And I feel so miserable right now that prayer seems like a chore.

Recently, I had a conversation with a friend from church. I was just sharing some of my struggles with her, letting her into my world. I was tired of always generating the "I'm fine" response. I even told her, "Sometimes, I wonder if God is really there for me." When she immediately launched into a shocked, "I can't believe you would question God's existence" (I wasn't), she simply confirmed what I'd always believed— that I shouldn't doubt (or at least I should never admit it).

I was raised to believe that you shouldn't doubt your faith. "You should know that you know that you know"—that's what my grandmother always said. Those who doubt God probably don't know him.

Maybe I don't really know God. If I really knew him, would I doubt that he cares about me right now?

—Amy

WHEN YOU THINK of Thomas, one of Jesus' 12 disciples, what's the first thing that pops into your mind? If you're like many, the nickname "Doubting Thomas" comes to mind, the name he's been saddled with for generations because of his doubts about Jesus' resurrection (see John 20:24–28).

John the Baptist—considered one of the greatest prophets of all time (see Matthew 11:11) had doubts about Jesus. While in prison, John sent some of his disciples to ask Jesus, "Are you the one who was to come, or should we expect someone else?" (Matthew 11:3). Instead of rebuking him for his doubts, Jesus responded with his résumé: "Go back and report to John what you hear and see: The blind receive sight, the lame walk, those who have leprosy are cleansed, the deaf hear, the dead are raised, and the good news is proclaimed to the poor" (Matthew 11:4–5). Basically, "John, check out what I've done; that'll tell you who I am."

Pain, exhaustion and disillusionment often lead us to confront doubts long hidden. Some of God's greatest prophets were not exempt from doubt or despair. Elijah had moments of doubt after a spiritual high. A death threat from Jezebel sent the soaring prophet into a tailspin of depression (see 1 Kings 18:16—19:18). And let's not forget Peter, whose fear and doubt caused him to sink after walking on water (see Matthew 14:25–31).

No one wants to be thought of as a "Doubting Thomas" or a "Sinking Peter" because of the negative connotation of doubt. Yet doubt can be the lever that launches us to a deeper faith in God. The point is not so much that we doubt. What matters is that we keep moving forward in our search for answers. That's growth. That's faith.

God isn't intimidated or disappointed that we doubt. He can handle any doubt. He would prefer that we not have faith in our faith. He wants us to have faith in him.

"One of the facets of a sound Christian faith is to level with God about your doubts or disbelief, your lack of wisdom or strength. God can withstand tough, honest prayers. I try to face my doubts and fears forcefully with confidence that God will forgive me."

—Former President Jimmy Carter

1717

"BE MERCIFUL TO THOSE WHO DOUBT."

JUDE 22

SEE ALSO
Luke 22:31–32

1 Corinthians 2:1–5

2 Corinthians 5:7

For more on **Doubt**, check the index.

God Disciplines His Children

[4]In your struggle against sin, you have not yet resisted to the point of shedding your blood. [5]And have you completely forgotten this word of encouragement that addresses you as children? It says,

> "My son, do not make light of the Lord's discipline,
> and do not lose heart when he rebukes you,
> [6]because the Lord disciplines those he loves,
> and he chastens everyone he accepts as his child."[a]

[7]Endure hardship as discipline; God is treating you as his children. For what children are not disciplined by their father? [8]If you are not disciplined—and everyone undergoes discipline—then you are not legitimate children at all. [9]Moreover, we have all had parents who disciplined us and we respected them for it. How much more should we submit to the Father of spirits and live! [10]Our parents disciplined us for a little while as they thought best; but God disciplines us for our good, that we may share in his holiness. [11]No discipline seems pleasant at the time, but painful. Later on, however, it produces a harvest of righteousness and peace for those who have been trained by it. [12]Therefore, strengthen your feeble arms and weak knees. [13]"Make level paths for your feet,"[b] so that the lame may not be disabled, but rather healed.

1718

at issue: boredom

12:1–3 Same places. Same tasks. Been there, done that. Do you ever feel that you spend your days doing the same old things over and over again, like bad reruns on TV? The Bible says that God has marked out a "race" for our lives. You may feel as if you've been running forever, yet the finish line is still out of sight. These are the moments when you most need to persevere. The finish line *is* ahead, and you'll experience indescribable joy when you reach it. When you feel bored with the tedium of the race, focus on Jesus and know that he'll give you strength for the rest of the race.

Warning and Encouragement

[14]Make every effort to live in peace with everyone and to be holy; without holiness no one will see the Lord. [15]See to it that no one falls short of the grace of God and that no bitter root grows up to cause trouble and defile many. [16]See that no one is sexually immoral, or is godless like Esau, who for a single meal sold his inheritance rights as the oldest son. [17]Afterward, as you know, when he wanted to inherit this blessing, he was rejected. Even though he sought the blessing with tears, he could not change what he had done.

The Mountain of Fear and the Mountain of Joy

[18]You have not come to a mountain that can be touched and that is burning with fire; to darkness, gloom and storm; [19]to a trumpet blast or to such a voice speaking words that those who heard it begged that no further word be spoken to them, [20]because they could not bear what was commanded: "If even an animal touches the mountain, it must be stoned to death."[c] [21]The sight was so terrifying that Moses said, "I am trembling with fear."[d]

[22]But you have come to Mount Zion, to the city of the living God, the heavenly Jerusalem. You have come to thousands upon thousands of angels in joyful assembly, [23]to the church of the firstborn, whose names are written in heaven. You have come to God, the Judge of all, to the spirits of the righteous made perfect, [24]to Jesus the mediator of a new covenant, and to the sprinkled blood that speaks a better word than the blood of Abel.

[25]See to it that you do not refuse him who speaks. If they did not escape when they refused him who warned them on earth, how much less will we, if we turn away from him who warns us from heaven? [26]At that time his voice shook the earth, but now he has promised, "Once more I will shake not only the

---

[a] 5,6 Prov. 3:11,12 (see Septuagint)   [b] 13 Prov. 4:26   [c] 20 Exodus 19:12,13   [d] 21 See Deut. 9:19.

earth but also the heavens."*a* [27] The words "once more" indicate the removing of what can be shaken—that is, created things—so that what cannot be shaken may remain.

[28] Therefore, since we are receiving a kingdom that cannot be shaken, let us be thankful, and so worship God acceptably with reverence and awe, [29] for our "God is a consuming fire."*b*

conversations

marriage «» 13:4

1» What does it mean to honor marriage—your own or others'?

2» If that attitude were widespread, how would that help prevent affairs?

3» Why is purity vital for a strong marriage?

For more on **marriage**, check the index.
For the next Conversations, go to p. 1722.

Concluding Exhortations

13 Keep on loving one another as brothers and sisters. [2] Do not forget to show hospitality to strangers, for by so doing some people have shown hospitality to angels without knowing it. [3] Continue to remember those in prison as if you were together with them in prison, and those who are mistreated as if you yourselves were suffering.

[4] Marriage should be honored by all, and the marriage bed kept pure, for God will judge the adulterer and all the sexually immoral. [5] Keep your lives free from the love of money and be content with what you have, because God has said,

1719

> "Never will I leave you;
> never will I forsake you."*c*

[6] So we say with confidence,

> "The Lord is my helper; I will not be afraid.
> What can human beings do to me?"*d*

[7] Remember your leaders, who spoke the word of God to you. Consider the outcome of their way of life and imitate their faith. [8] Jesus Christ is the same yesterday and today and forever.

[9] Do not be carried away by all kinds of strange teachings. It is good for our hearts to be strengthened by grace, not by the eating of ceremonial foods, which is of no benefit to those who observe such rituals. [10] We have an altar from which those who minister at the tabernacle have no right to eat.

[11] The high priest carries the blood of animals into the Most Holy Place as a sin offering, but the bodies are burned outside the camp. [12] And so Jesus also suffered outside the city gate to make the people holy through his own blood. [13] Let us, then, go to him outside the camp, bearing the disgrace he bore. [14] For here we do not have an enduring city, but we are looking for the city that is to come.

[15] Through Jesus, therefore, let us continually offer to God a sacrifice of praise—the fruit of lips that openly profess his name. [16] And do not forget to do good and to share with others, for with such sacrifices God is pleased.

[17] Have confidence in your leaders and submit to their authority, because they keep watch over you as those who must give an account. Do this so that their work will be a joy, not a burden, for that would be of no benefit to you.

[18] Pray for us. We are sure that we have a clear conscience and desire to live honorably in every way. [19] I particularly urge you to pray so that I may be restored to you soon.

Benediction and Final Greetings

[20] Now may the God of peace, who through the blood of the eternal covenant brought back from the dead our Lord Jesus, that great Shepherd of the sheep, [21] equip you with everything good for doing his will, and may he work in us what is pleasing to him, through Jesus Christ, to whom be glory for ever and ever. Amen.

---

a **26** Haggai 2:6   *b* **29** Deut. 4:24   *c* **5** Deut. 31:6   *d* **6** Psalm 118:6,7

²²Brothers and sisters, I urge you to bear with my word of exhortation, for in fact I have written to you quite briefly.

²³I want you to know that our brother Timothy has been released. If he arrives soon, I will come with him to see you.

²⁴Greet all your leaders and all the Lord's people. Those from Italy send you their greetings.

²⁵Grace be with you all.

james

1721

AUTHOR
James, the brother of Jesus.

AUDIENCE
Early Jewish Christians scattered because
of persecution and all followers of Jesus.

DATE
About A.D. 49.

SETTING
James encouraged the former members of
the Jerusalem church, now scattered to various places because of persecution.

VERSE TO REMEMBER
"In the same way, faith by itself, if it is not
accompanied by action, is dead." (2:17)

THEME TO CONSIDER
Faith without action isn't real faith at all.

1 James, a servant of God and of the Lord Jesus Christ,

To the twelve tribes scattered among the nations:

Greetings.

Trials and Temptations

²Consider it pure joy, my brothers and sisters, whenever you face trials of many kinds, ³because you know that the testing of your faith produces perseverance. ⁴Let perseverance finish its work so that you may be mature and complete, not lacking anything. ⁵If any of you lacks wisdom, you should ask God, who gives generously to all without finding fault, and it will be given to you. ⁶But when you ask, you must believe and not doubt, because the one who doubts is like a wave of the sea, blown and tossed by the wind. ⁷Those who doubt should not think they will receive anything from the Lord; ⁸they are double-minded and unstable in all they do.

⁹Believers in humble circumstances ought to take pride in their high position. ¹⁰But the rich should take pride in their humiliation—since they will pass away like a wild flower. ¹¹For the sun rises with scorching heat and withers the plant; its blossom falls and its beauty is destroyed. In the same way, the rich will fade away even while they go about their business.

¹²Blessed are those who persevere under trial, because when they have stood the test, they will receive the crown of life that God has promised to those who love him.

¹³When tempted, no one should say, "God is tempting me." For God cannot be tempted by evil, nor does he tempt anyone; ¹⁴but each of you is tempted when you are dragged away by your own evil desire and enticed. ¹⁵Then, after desire has conceived, it gives birth to sin; and sin, when it is full-grown, gives birth to death.

¹⁶Don't be deceived, my dear brothers and sisters. ¹⁷Every good and perfect gift is from above, coming down from the Father of the heavenly lights, who does not change like shifting shadows. ¹⁸He chose to give us birth through the word of truth, that we might be a kind of firstfruits of all he created.

1722

conversations

conflict at work ‹» 1:19

1 How would your workplace be altered if you were quick to listen and slow to speak?

2 How can you be humble at work without inviting (or enabling) others to take advantage of you?

3 Have unresolved anger and bitterness hindered your work relationships? If so, how?

For more on **conflict at work**, check the index. For the next Conversations, go to p. 1731.

Listening and Doing

¹⁹My dear brothers and sisters, take note of this: Everyone should be quick to listen, slow to speak and slow to become angry, ²⁰because our anger does not produce the righteousness that God desires. ²¹Therefore, get rid of all moral filth and the evil that is so prevalent and humbly accept the word planted in you, which can save you.

²²Do not merely listen to the word, and so deceive yourselves. Do what it says. ²³Those who listen to the word but do not do what it says are like people who look at their faces in a mirror ²⁴and, after looking at themselves, go away and immediately forget what they look like. ²⁵But those who look intently into the perfect law that gives freedom and continue in it—not forgetting what they have heard but doing it—they will be blessed in what they do.

²⁶Those who consider themselves religious and yet do not keep a tight rein on their tongues deceive themselves, and their religion is worthless. ²⁷Religion that God our Father accepts as pure and faultless is this: to look after orphans and widows in their distress and to keep oneself from being polluted by the world.

Favoritism Forbidden

2 My brothers and sisters, believers in our glorious Lord Jesus Christ must not show favoritism. ²Suppose someone comes into your meeting wearing a gold ring and fine clothes, and a poor person in filthy old clothes also comes in. ³If you show special attention to the one wearing fine clothes and say, "Here's a good seat for you," but say to the one who is poor, "You stand there" or "Sit on the floor by

my feet," ⁴have you not discriminated among yourselves and become judges with evil thoughts?

⁵Listen, my dear brothers and sisters: Has not God chosen those who are poor in the eyes of the world to be rich in faith and to inherit the kingdom he promised those who love him? ⁶But you have dishonored the poor. Is it not the rich who are exploiting you? Are they not the ones who are dragging you into court? ⁷Are they not the ones who are blaspheming the noble name of him to whom you belong?

⁸If you really keep the royal law found in Scripture, "Love your neighbor as yourself,"ᵃ you are doing right. ⁹But if you show favoritism, you sin and are convicted by the law as law-breakers. ¹⁰For whoever keeps the whole law and yet stumbles at just one point is guilty of breaking all of it. ¹¹For he who said, "You shall not commit adultery,"ᵇ also said, "You shall not murder."ᶜ If you do not commit adultery but do commit murder, you have become a lawbreaker.

¹²Speak and act as those who are going to be judged by the law that gives freedom, ¹³because judgment without mercy will be shown to anyone who has not been merciful. Mercy triumphs over judgment.

Faith and Deeds

¹⁴What good is it, my brothers and sisters, if people claim to have faith but have no deeds? Can such faith save them? ¹⁵Suppose a brother or sister is without clothes and daily food. ¹⁶If one of you says to them, "Go in peace; keep warm and well fed," but does nothing about their physical needs, what good is it? ¹⁷In the same way, faith by itself, if it is not accompanied by action, is dead.

¹⁸But someone will say, "You have faith; I have deeds."

Show me your faith without deeds, and I will show you my faith by what I do. ¹⁹You believe that there is one God. Good! Even the demons believe that—and shudder.

²⁰You foolish person, do you want evidence that faith without deeds is uselessᵈ? ²¹Was not our father Abraham considered righteous for what he did when he offered his son Isaac on the altar? ²²You see that his faith and his actions were working together, and his faith was made complete by what he did. ²³And the scripture was fulfilled that says, "Abraham believed God, and it was credited to him as righteousness,"ᵉ and he was called God's friend. ²⁴You see that people are justified by what they do and not by faith alone.

²⁵In the same way, was not even Rahab the prostitute considered righteous for what she did when she gave lodging to the spies and sent them off in a different direction? ²⁶As the body without the spirit is dead, so faith without deeds is dead.

Taming the Tongue

3 Not many of you should presume to be teachers, my brothers and sisters, because you know that we who teach will be judged more strictly. ²We all stumble in many ways. Those who are never at fault in what they say are perfect, able to keep their whole body in check.

³When we put bits into the mouths of horses to make them obey us, we can turn the whole animal. ⁴Or take ships as an example. Although they are so large and are driven by strong winds, they are steered by a very small rudder wherever the pilot wants to go. ⁵Likewise, the tongue is a small part of the body, but it makes great boasts. Consider what a great forest is set on fire by a small spark. ⁶The tongue also is a fire, a world of evil among the parts of the body. It corrupts the whole person, sets the whole course of one's life on fire, and is itself set on fire by hell.

---

atissue:adoption

1:27 You probably resemble your earthly parents in some way—your father's nose, your mother's mannerisms. Do you also resemble your heavenly Father? If you're going to be like your heavenly Dad, you'll show love and compassion for the oppressed in your world. One way of doing that is by adopting an orphaned or needy child and showing that child the kind of love God has shown you. God gave you an identity, a family and a home when he adopted you as his child. Perhaps God would also have you open your heart and home to a child in need of love and care.

1723

---

myth# 99 "I CAN NEVER TELL SOMEONE THAT I STRUGGLE WITH ..."

I don't know how this happened exactly, but I seem to have developed this reputation for true dependability. That's why I'm on two different committees at church. I teach Sunday school and am one of the youth leaders. So many people depend on me. They think I'm incredibly disciplined and put together. That's why I can never tell anyone that I struggle with sexual purity—at age 29. I know everyone would be shocked—and disappointed.

Jeff and I have been dating for two years. We met at church, and we just seemed to click. He's funny and sincere, and he's also in a men's Bible study, so I know he's serious about his faith. But he's in the middle of starting his own business and also taking some classes, so he doesn't want to get married until life settles down a little. He's promised me that we'll get married next year when he's finished his degree. I feel like we're as good as married. It's just a matter of time . . . which is why it's so easy to justify sleeping together. And also we're almost 30! We're not some silly kids, messing around. We are committed adults, and we know what we're doing . . . but obviously no one else can know.

I've tried to convince Jeff that we need to stop what we're doing. He agrees, and for awhile we'll do really well. But then we fail again, and that leads to a fight. How are we supposed to go back to a life of holding hands and good-night kisses? It's only another year, and then we'll be safe.

Some of the girls in the youth group look up to me, and I talk to them about remaining pure. I tell them that they need to save themselves for the man they will someday marry. And I know that I'm the biggest hypocrite in the church.

That's why I could never tell anyone about what Jeff and I are doing. Not with me in so many important leadership positions. I've thought about mentioning something to one of the other youth leaders. She's older than me and married, and I really respect her. But then I imagine the look on her face if I were to say something about Jeff and me struggling. What would she think of me?

I don't know what to do anymore. I don't want to live a lie. But I can't tell anyone the truth. Do I just keep hiding what I'm doing? I feel so alone.

—Camille

MANY PEOPLE—those who don't appear on talk shows, that is—struggle with how much of themselves to reveal to others. Although the Bible tells us to "share the load" with others (see James 5:16), we don't often feel safe doing that, especially if our confidence has been betrayed in the past. Or, we might fear that others will judge us.

Yet when we struggle with things in secret, we often have to keep up a façade so people won't discover that secret. After all, do we really need to drag our dirty laundry out in public? Aren't there some weaknesses we need to keep to ourselves? If you're wondering if you should reveal a hidden struggle . . .

- Ask God to give you wisdom to know what to share and with whom. "There is a time for everything" (Ecclesiastes 3:1). Some times are appropriate for sharing, and some are inappropriate. For example, sharing your hidden struggle with an impressionable teenage girl might overwhelm her or make her feel disillusioned.

- Ask God to give you wisdom about how much to reveal to whom. Paul talked openly about a "thorn" in his flesh and how he made a fool of himself (see 2 Corinthians 12:7,11). Yet Paul didn't give many specifics about the thorn in this rather public letter. He simply admitted to being weak, rather than relying on the façade of strength. God has used Paul's revelation of weakness to encourage believers for centuries.

- Ask God to give you the right motives for revealing your struggle. A subtle desire for attention or bragging about your "past" isn't the right reason to share. The desire for freedom, true support and accountability is the right reason to share.

- Ask God for the courage to tell someone. Choose someone you trust, such as a Christian girlfriend or a wise mentor.

You will find freedom when you share your struggle. Simply stating your hidden sin out loud breaks some of its power over you.

Being vulnerable can be costly. But the results—genuine intimacy with others; the freedom of living a transparent life before others; the bond that comes from a shared burden—can be transforming.

"You may think you are hiding your sin from other people, but God knows . . . You may not realize it now, but that sin could be causing you to miss great blessings . . . Confess it today, and receive God's loving restoration."
—Michael Ullrich

"CONFESS YOUR SINS TO EACH OTHER AND PRAY FOR EACH OTHER SO THAT YOU MAY BE HEALED. THE PRAYER OF A RIGHTEOUS PERSON IS POWERFUL AND EFFECTIVE."

JAMES 5:16

SEE ALSO

Psalm 90:8
Proverbs 2:11
Ecclesiastes 4:9–12
Galatians 6:2

For more on **Purity, Sex, and Hidden Sin**, check the index.

[7]All kinds of animals, birds, reptiles and sea creatures are being tamed and have been tamed by human beings, [8]but no one can tame the tongue. It is a restless evil, full of deadly poison.

[9]With the tongue we praise our Lord and Father, and with it we curse human beings, who have been made in God's likeness. [10]Out of the same mouth come praise and cursing. My brothers and sisters, this should not be. [11]Can both fresh water and salt water flow from the same spring? [12]My brothers and sisters, can a fig tree bear olives, or a grapevine bear figs? Neither can a salt spring produce fresh water.

Two Kinds of Wisdom

[13]Who is wise and understanding among you? Let them show it by their good life, by deeds done in the humility that comes from wisdom. [14]But if you harbor bitter envy and selfish ambition in your hearts, do not boast about it or deny the truth. [15]Such "wisdom" does not come down from heaven but is earthly, unspiritual, demonic. [16]For where you have envy and selfish ambition, there you find disorder and every evil practice.

[17]But the wisdom that comes from heaven is first of all pure; then peace-loving, considerate, submissive, full of mercy and good fruit, impartial and sincere. [18]Peacemakers who sow in peace reap a harvest of righteousness.

Submit Yourselves to God

4 What causes fights and quarrels among you? Don't they come from your desires that battle within you? [2]You desire but do not have, so you kill. You covet but you cannot get what you want, so you quarrel and fight. You do not have because you do not ask God. [3]When you ask, you do not receive, because you ask with wrong motives, that you may spend what you get on your pleasures.

[4]You adulterous people, don't you know that friendship with the world means enmity against God? Anyone who chooses to be a friend of the world becomes an enemy of God. [5]Or do you think Scripture says without reason that he jealously longs for the spirit he has caused to dwell in us?[a] [6]But he gives us more grace. That is why Scripture says:

> "God opposes the proud
> but shows favor to the humble and oppressed."[b]

[7]Submit yourselves, then, to God. Resist the devil, and he will flee from you. [8]Come near to God and he will come near to you. Wash your hands, you sinners, and purify your hearts, you double-minded. [9]Grieve, mourn and wail. Change your laughter to mourning and your joy to gloom. [10]Humble yourselves before the Lord, and he will lift you up.

[11]Brothers and sisters, do not slander one another. Anyone who speaks against a brother or sister or judges them speaks against the law and judges it. When you judge the law, you are not keeping it, but sitting in judgment on it. [12]There is only one Lawgiver and Judge, the one who is able to save and destroy. But you—who are you to judge your neighbor?

Boasting About Tomorrow

[13]Now listen, you who say, "Today or tomorrow we will go to this or that city, spend a year there, carry on business and make money." [14]Why, you do not even know what will happen tomorrow. What is your

at issue: power of words

3:1–12 Did you realize you have *superpowers?* You may not be Wonder Woman or Bat Girl, but you have an incredible weapon in your personal arsenal—your tongue. Though small, it holds astonishing power. It can encourage, strengthen and brighten another's day. Or it can tear down, wound and crush other people. Every day you face a choice: Will you use your superpowers for good or for evil? When you praise God with the same tongue that you curse the people he created, you've made the wrong choice. Respect the power of words and learn to use them to encourage and strengthen others.

[a] *5 Or that the spirit he caused to dwell in us envies intensely; or that the Spirit he caused to dwell in us longs jealously*   [b] *6 Prov. 3:34*

HE IS: nearby

4:8 Double-minded people are torn between God and the world. They can't quite decide which to commit to. James urged these double-minded people to purify their hearts and come near to God. In return, James promised, "he will come near to you."

Do you feel far from God? He hasn't moved. He's exactly the same yesterday, today and forever (see Hebrews 13:8). If you feel far from God, then you are the one who's been wandering or hiding. He's *nearby*, waiting for you. Come back to God with single-minded focus, and you'll find that he's right there beside you.

For the next He Is, go to p. 1730.

life? You are a mist that appears for a little while and then vanishes. ¹⁵Instead, you ought to say, "If it is the Lord's will, we will live and do this or that." ¹⁶As it is, you boast in your arrogant schemes. All such boasting is evil. ¹⁷So then, if you know the good you ought to do and don't do it, you sin.

Warning to Rich Oppressors

5 Now listen, you rich people, weep and wail because of the misery that is coming on you. ²Your wealth has rotted, and moths have eaten your clothes. ³Your gold and silver are corroded. Their corrosion will testify against you and eat your flesh like fire. You have hoarded wealth in the last days. ⁴Look! The wages you failed to pay the workers who mowed your fields are crying out against you. The cries of the harvesters have reached the ears of the Lord Almighty. ⁵You have lived on earth in luxury and self-indulgence. You have fattened yourselves in the day of slaughter.*ᵃ* ⁶You have condemned and murdered the innocent one, who was not opposing you.

Patience in Suffering

⁷Be patient, then, brothers and sisters, until the Lord's coming. See how the farmer waits for the land to yield its valuable crop, patiently waiting for the autumn and spring rains. ⁸You too, be patient and stand firm, because the Lord's coming is near. ⁹Don't grumble against one another, brothers and sisters, or you will be judged. The Judge is standing at the door!

¹⁰Brothers and sisters, as an example of patience in the face of suffering, take the prophets who spoke in the name of the Lord. ¹¹As you know, we count as blessed those who have persevered. You have heard of Job's perseverance and have seen what the Lord finally brought about. The Lord is full of compassion and mercy.

¹²Above all, my brothers and sisters, do not swear—not by heaven or by earth or by anything else. All you need to say is a simple "Yes" or "No." Otherwise you will be condemned.

The Prayer of Faith

¹³Is anyone among you in trouble? Let them pray. Is anyone happy? Let them sing songs of praise. ¹⁴Is anyone among you sick? Let them call the elders of the church to pray over them and anoint them with oil in the name of the Lord. ¹⁵And the prayer offered in faith will make them well; the Lord will raise them up. If they have sinned, they will be forgiven. ¹⁶Therefore confess your sins to each other and pray for each other so that you may be healed. The prayer of a righteous person is powerful and effective.

¹⁷Elijah was a human being, even as we are. He prayed earnestly that it would not rain, and it did not rain on the land for three and a half years. ¹⁸Again he prayed, and the heavens gave rain, and the earth produced its crops.

¹⁹My brothers and sisters, if one of you should wander from the truth and someone should bring them back, ²⁰remember this: Whoever turns a sinner from the way of error will save them from death and cover over a multitude of sins.

ᵃ 5 Or yourselves as in a day of feasting

1peter

AUTHOR
The apostle Peter.

AUDIENCE
Early Jewish Christians scattered because of
persecution and all followers of Jesus.

DATE
About A.D. 62–64, possibly written from Rome.

SETTING
The Roman Emperor Nero was leading severe
persecution of Christians.

VERSE TO REMEMBER
" 'He himself bore our sins' in his body on the
cross, so that we might die to sins and live for
righteousness; 'by his wounds you have been
healed.' " (2:24)

THEME TO CONSIDER
In life, pain is inevitable. Being miserable is
optional.

1 Peter, an apostle of Jesus Christ,

To God's elect, exiles scattered throughout the provinces of Pontus, Galatia, Cappadocia, Asia and Bithynia, [2] who have been chosen according to the foreknowledge of God the Father, through the sanctifying work of the Spirit, to be obedient to Jesus Christ and sprinkled with his blood:

Grace and peace be yours in abundance.

Praise to God for a Living Hope

[3] Praise be to the God and Father of our Lord Jesus Christ! In his great mercy he has given us new birth into a living hope through the resurrection of Jesus Christ from the dead, [4] and into an inheritance that can never perish, spoil or fade. This inheritance is kept in heaven for you, [5] who through faith are shielded by God's power until the coming of the salvation that is ready to be revealed in the last time. [6] In all this you greatly rejoice, though now for a little while you may have had to suffer grief in all kinds of trials. [7] These have come so that your faith—of greater worth than gold, which perishes even though refined by fire—may be proved genuine and may result in praise, glory and honor when Jesus Christ is revealed. [8] Though you have not seen him, you love him; and even though you do not see him now, you believe in him and are filled with an inexpressible and glorious joy, [9] for you are receiving the end result of your faith, the salvation of your souls.

[10] Concerning this salvation, the prophets, who spoke of the grace that was to come to you, searched intently and with the greatest care, [11] trying to find out the time and circumstances to which the Spirit of Christ in them was pointing when he predicted the sufferings of Christ and the glories that would follow. [12] It was revealed to them that they were not serving themselves but you, when they spoke of the things that have now been told you by those who have preached the gospel to you by the Holy Spirit sent from heaven. Even angels long to look into these things.

Be Holy

[13] Therefore, with minds that are alert and fully sober, set your hope on the grace to be brought to you when Jesus Christ is revealed at his coming. [14] As obedient children, do not conform to the evil desires you had when you lived in ignorance. [15] But just as he who called you is holy, so be holy in all you do; [16] for it is written: "Be holy, because I am holy."[a]

[17] Since you call on a Father who judges each person's work impartially, live out your time as foreigners here in reverent fear. [18] For you know that it was not with perishable things such as silver or gold that you were redeemed from the empty way of life handed down to you from your ancestors, [19] but with the precious blood of Christ, a lamb without blemish or defect. [20] He was chosen before the creation of the world, but was revealed in these last times for your sake. [21] Through him you believe in God, who raised him from the dead and glorified him, and so your faith and hope are in God.

[22] Now that you have purified yourselves by obeying the truth so that you have sincere love for each other, love one another deeply, from the heart.[b] [23] For you have been born again, not of perishable seed, but of imperishable, through the living and enduring word of God. [24] For,

> "All people are like grass,
>   and all their glory is like the flowers of the field;
> the grass withers and the flowers fall,
> [25]   but the word of the Lord endures forever."[c]

And this is the word that was preached to you.

2 Therefore, rid yourselves of all malice and all deceit, hypocrisy, envy, and slander of every kind. [2] Like newborn babies, crave pure spiritual milk, so that by it you may grow up in your salvation, [3] now that you have tasted that the Lord is good.

[a] 16 Lev. 11:44,45; 19:2 [b] 22 Some early manuscripts from a pure heart [c] 25 Isaiah 40:6-8 (see Septuagint)

HE IS: the living Stone

2:4–5 The church is not a building constructed by humans but a divine institution, built on *the living Stone*, Jesus. He's the strong, foundational building block of the church, and his followers are living stones who are being built into a spiritual house (see Ephesians 2:19–22).

As one of the many little living stones in the church, remember that each diverse stone has great worth to Jesus and to his body. When you're tempted to ignore your need for others or to discount those who aren't like you, remember that each stone is balanced by all those around it, and all rest on *the living Stone* himself.

For the next He Is, go to p. 1735.

1730

The Living Stone and a Chosen People

⁴As you come to him, the living Stone—rejected by human beings but chosen by God and precious to him— ⁵you also, like living stones, are being built into a spiritual house*ᵃ* to be a holy priesthood, offering spiritual sacrifices acceptable to God through Jesus Christ. ⁶For in Scripture it says:

> "See, I lay a stone in Zion,
> a chosen and precious cornerstone,
> and the one who trusts in him
> will never be put to shame."*ᵇ*

⁷Now to you who believe, this stone is precious. But to those who do not believe,

> "The stone the builders rejected
> has become the cornerstone,"*ᶜ*

⁸and,

> "A stone that causes people to stumble
> and a rock that makes them fall."*ᵈ*

They stumble because they disobey the message—which is also what they were destined for.

⁹But you are a chosen people, a royal priesthood, a holy nation, God's special possession, that you may declare the praises of him who called you out of darkness into his wonderful light. ¹⁰Once you were not a people, but now you are the people of God; once you had not received mercy, but now you have received mercy.

Living Godly Lives in a Pagan Society

¹¹Dear friends, I urge you, as foreigners and exiles, to abstain from sinful desires, which war against your soul. ¹²Live such good lives among the pagans that, though they accuse you of doing wrong, they may see your good deeds and glorify God on the day he visits us.

¹³Submit yourselves for the Lord's sake to every human authority: whether to the emperor, as the supreme authority, ¹⁴or to governors, who are sent by him to punish those who do wrong and to commend those who do right. ¹⁵For it is God's will that by doing good you should silence the ignorant talk of the foolish. ¹⁶Live as free people, but do not use your freedom as a cover-up for evil; live as God's slaves. ¹⁷Show proper respect to everyone, love your fellow believers, fear God, honor the emperor.

¹⁸Slaves, in reverent fear of God submit yourselves to your masters, not only to those who are good and considerate, but also to those who are harsh. ¹⁹For it is commendable if you bear up under the pain of unjust suffering because you are conscious of God. ²⁰But how is it to your credit if you receive a beating for doing wrong and endure it? But if you suffer for doing good and you endure it, this is commend-

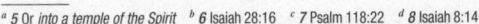

ᵃ 5 Or into a temple of the Spirit   ᵇ 6 Isaiah 28:16   ᶜ 7 Psalm 118:22   ᵈ 8 Isaiah 8:14 able before God. [21] To this you were called, because Christ suffered for you, leaving you an example, that you should follow in his steps.

> [22] "He committed no sin,
>> and no deceit was found in his mouth."[a]

[23] When they hurled their insults at him, he did not retaliate; when he suffered, he made no threats. Instead, he entrusted himself to him who judges justly. [24] "He himself bore our sins" in his body on the cross, so that we might die to sins and live for righteousness; "by his wounds you have been healed." [25] For "you were like sheep going astray,"[b] but now you have returned to the Shepherd and Overseer of your souls.

3 Wives, in the same way submit yourselves to your own husbands so that, if any of them do not believe the word, they may be won over without words by the behavior of their wives, [2] when they see the purity and reverence of your lives. [3] Your beauty should not come from outward adornment, such as elaborate hairstyles and the wearing of gold jewelry and fine clothes. [4] Rather, it should be that of your inner self, the unfading beauty of a gentle and quiet spirit, which is of great worth in God's sight. [5] For this is the way the holy women of the past who put their hope in God used to adorn themselves. They submitted themselves to their own husbands, [6] like Sarah, who obeyed Abraham and called him her lord. You are her daughters if you do what is right and do not give way to fear.

[7] Husbands, in the same way be considerate as you live with your wives, and treat them with respect as the weaker partner and as heirs with you of the gracious gift of life, so that nothing will hinder your prayers.

Suffering for Doing Good

[8] Finally, all of you, be like-minded, be sympathetic, love one another, be compassionate and humble. [9] Do not repay evil with evil or insult with insult. On the contrary, repay evil with blessing, because to this you were called so that you may inherit a blessing. [10] For,

> "Whoever among you would love life
>> and see good days
> must keep your tongue from evil
>> and your lips from deceitful speech.
> [11] Turn from evil and do good;
>> seek peace and pursue it.
> [12] For the eyes of the Lord are on the righteous
>> and his ears are attentive to their prayer,
> but the face of the Lord is against those
>> who do evil."[c]

[13] Who is going to harm you if you are eager to do good? [14] But even if you should suffer for what is right, you are

---

at issue: marriage

3:1–6 You love God. You also love your husband. But if your husband doesn't love or follow God, you find yourself with a definite conflict of interest. Your natural instinct is to cajole, coerce, nag and otherwise manipulate your husband into a change of heart towards God. But only *God* can change your husband's heart—and your words are likely to hurt more than help. Rather than trying to persuade your husband, choose instead to live your life with reverence and love for God, which spills over into love and respect for your husband. Your actions will communicate more clearly than your words ever could.

1731

---

conversations

appearance «» 3:3–4

1» Is it OK for Christian women to care about their appearance? If so, are there any limits?

2» Would you consider the time you spend caring for your inner and outer self balanced? Why?

3» What does God see when he looks at you?

For more on **appearance**, check the index.
For the next Conversations, go to p. 1737.

---

[a] *22* Isaiah 53:9   [b] *24,25* Isaiah 53:4,5,6 (see Septuagint)   [c] *12* Psalm 34:12-16

blessed. "Do not fear their threats; do not be frightened."[a] [15]But in your hearts revere Christ as Lord. Always be prepared to give an answer to everyone who asks you to give the reason for the hope that you have. But do this with gentleness and respect, [16]keeping a clear conscience, so that those who speak maliciously against your good behavior in Christ may be ashamed of their slander. [17]It is better, if it is God's will, to suffer for doing good than for doing evil. [18]For Christ also suffered once for sins, the righteous for the unrighteous, to bring you to God. He was put to death in the body but made alive in the Spirit. [19]In that state[b] he went and made proclamation to the imprisoned spirits— [20]to those who were disobedient long ago when God waited patiently in the days of Noah while the ark was being built. In it only a few people, eight in all, were saved through water, [21]and this water symbolizes baptism that now saves you also—not the removal of dirt from the body but the pledge of a clear conscience toward God.[c] It saves you by the resurrection of Jesus Christ, [22]who has gone into heaven and is at God's right hand— with angels, authorities and powers in submission to him.

Living for God

4 Therefore, since Christ suffered in his body, arm yourselves also with the same attitude, because those who have suffered in their bodies are done with sin. [2]As a result, they do not live the rest of their earthly lives for evil human desires, but rather for the will of God. [3]For you have spent enough time in the past doing what pagans choose to do—living in debauchery, lust, drunkenness, orgies, carousing and detestable idolatry. [4]They are surprised that you do not join them in their reckless, wild living, and they heap abuse on you. [5]But they will have to give account to him who is ready to judge the living and the dead. [6]For this is the reason the gospel was preached even to those who are now dead, so that they might be judged according to human standards in regard to the body, but live according to God in regard to the spirit.

[7]The end of all things is near. Therefore be alert and of sober mind so that you may pray. [8]Above all, love each other deeply, because love covers over a multitude of sins. [9]Offer hospitality to one another without grumbling. [10]Each of you should use whatever gift you have received to serve others, as faithful stewards of God's grace in its various forms. [11]If you speak, you should do so as one who speaks the very words of God. If you serve, you should do so with the strength God provides, so that in all things God may be praised through Jesus Christ. To him be the glory and the power for ever and ever. Amen.

Suffering for Being a Christian

[12]Dear friends, do not be surprised at the fiery ordeal that has come on you to test you, as though something strange were happening to you. [13]But rejoice inasmuch as you participate in the sufferings of Christ, so that you may be overjoyed when his glory is revealed. [14]If you are insulted because of the name of Christ, you are blessed, for the Spirit of glory and of God rests on you. [15]If you suffer, it should not be as a murderer or thief or any other kind of criminal, or even as a meddler. [16]However, if you suffer as a Christian, do not be ashamed, but praise God that you bear that name. [17]For it is time for judgment to begin with God's household; and if it begins with us, what will the outcome be for those who do not obey the gospel of God? [18]And,

> "If it is hard for the righteous to be saved,
>   what will become of the ungodly and the sinner?"[d]

[19]So then, those who suffer according to God's will should commit themselves to their faithful Creator and continue to do good.

To the Elders and the Flock

5 To the elders among you, I appeal as a fellow elder and a witness of Christ's sufferings who also will share in the glory to be revealed: [2]Be shepherds of God's flock that is under your care, watching over them—not because you must, but because you are willing, as God wants you to be; not pursuing dishonest gain, but eager to serve; [3]not lording it over those entrusted to you, but being examples to the

---

[a] 14 Isaiah 8:12   [b] 18,19 Or alive in the spirit, [19]in which also   [c] 21 Or but an appeal to God for a clear conscience   [d] 18 Prov. 11:31 (see Septuagint)

flock. [4]And when the Chief Shepherd appears, you will receive the crown of glory that will never fade away.

[5]In the same way, you who are younger, submit yourselves to your elders. All of you, clothe yourselves with humility toward one another, because,

> "God opposes the proud
> but shows favor to the humble and
> oppressed."[a]

[6]Humble yourselves, therefore, under God's mighty hand, that he may lift you up in due time. [7]Cast all your anxiety on him because he cares for you.

[8]Be alert and of sober mind. Your enemy the devil prowls around like a roaring lion looking for someone to devour. [9]Resist him, standing firm in the faith, because you know that your fellow believers throughout the world are undergoing the same kind of sufferings.

[10]And the God of all grace, who called you to his eternal glory in Christ, after you have suffered a little while, will himself restore you and make you strong, firm and steadfast. [11]To him be the power for ever and ever. Amen.

Final Greetings

[12]With the help of Silas,[b] whom I regard as a faithful brother, I have written to you briefly, encouraging you and testifying that this is the true grace of God. Stand fast in it.

[13]She who is in Babylon, chosen together with you, sends you her greetings, and so does my son Mark. [14]Greet one another with a kiss of love.

Peace to all of you who are in Christ.

---

atissue:fear of relapse

5:7 When you go fishing, you cast your line into the water, only to reel it in again and again. That's not the kind of "casting" this verse intends. God doesn't want you to cast your anxiety on him only to take it back again. Instead he wants you to toss him the entire fishing pole. If someone you love is recovering from an addiction (to alcohol, drugs, pornography, etc.), it's natural to worry that he or she will relapse. God wants you to cast that worry on him— pole and all. Let go and trust God no matter what happens.

1733

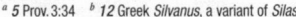

[a] 5 Prov. 3:34   [b] 12 Greek *Silvanus*, a variant of *Silas*

1734

2peter

AUTHOR
The apostle Peter.

AUDIENCE
All followers of Jesus.

DATE
About A.D. 67.

SETTING
Shortly before his death, Peter wrote this letter to warn believers about false teachers.

VERSE TO REMEMBER
"So then, dear friends, since you are looking forward to this, make every effort to be found spotless, blameless and at peace with him." (3:14)

THEME TO CONSIDER
Beware of those who have a full grasp on half-truths.

1 Simon Peter, a servant and apostle of Jesus Christ,

To those who through the righteousness of our God and Savior Jesus Christ have received a faith as precious as ours:

[2]Grace and peace be yours in abundance through the knowledge of God and of Jesus our Lord.

Confirming One's Calling and Election

[3]His divine power has given us everything we need for a godly life through our knowledge of him who called us by his own glory and goodness. [4]Through these he has given us his very great and precious promises, so that through them you may participate in the divine nature, having escaped the corruption in the world caused by evil desires.

HE IS: everything you need

1:3 Peter left everything to follow Jesus: his home, business, friends and family. Yet when he wrote this letter near the end of his life, he could confidently say that God had given him everything he needed. He understood that knowing Jesus was more valuable than material possessions or earthly concerns.

What do you think you need? If you think you must acquire things in order to be happy, then you'll never be satisfied. But if you discover that true contentment comes from your intimate knowledge of a person—Jesus Christ—then you'll understand that he is *everything you need.*

1735

For the next He Is, go to p. 1743.

[5]For this very reason, make every effort to add to your faith goodness; and to goodness, knowledge; [6]and to knowledge, self-control; and to self-control, perseverance; and to perseverance, godliness; [7]and to godliness, mutual affection; and to mutual affection, love. [8]For if you possess these qualities in increasing measure, they will keep you from being ineffective and unproductive in your knowledge of our Lord Jesus Christ. [9]But if any of you do not have them, you are nearsighted and blind, and you have forgotten that you have been cleansed from your past sins.

[10]Therefore, my brothers and sisters, make every effort to confirm your calling and election. For if you do these things, you will never stumble, [11]and you will receive a rich welcome into the eternal kingdom of our Lord and Savior Jesus Christ.

Prophecy of Scripture

[12]So I will always remind you of these things, even though you know them and are firmly established in the truth you now have. [13]I think it is right to refresh your memory as long as I live in the tent of this body, [14]because I know that I will soon put it aside, as our Lord Jesus Christ has made clear to me. [15]And I will make every effort to see that after my departure you will always be able to remember these things.

[16]For we did not follow cleverly devised stories when we told you about the coming of our Lord Jesus Christ in power, but we were eyewitnesses of his majesty. [17]He received honor and glory from God the Father when the voice came to him from the Majestic Glory, saying, "This is my Son, whom I love; with him I am well pleased."[a] [18]We ourselves heard this voice that came from heaven when we were with him on the sacred mountain.

[19]We also have the prophetic message as something completely reliable, and you will do well to pay attention to it, as to a light shining in a dark place, until the day dawns and the morning star rises in your hearts. [20]Above all, you must understand that no prophecy of Scripture came about by the

a 17 Matt. 17:5; Mark 9:7; Luke 9:35

prophet's own interpretation of things. ²¹For prophecy never had its origin in the human will, but prophets, though human, spoke from God as they were carried along by the Holy Spirit.

False Teachers and Their Destruction

2 But there were also false prophets among the people, just as there will be false teachers among you. They will secretly introduce destructive heresies, even denying the sovereign Lord who bought them—bringing swift destruction on themselves. ²Many will follow their depraved conduct and will bring the way of truth into disrepute. ³In their greed these teachers will exploit you with fabricated stories. Their condemnation has long been hanging over them, and their destruction has not been sleeping.

⁴For if God did not spare angels when they sinned, but sent them to hell,ᵃ putting them in chains of darknessᵇ to be held for judgment; ⁵if he did not spare the ancient world when he brought the flood on its ungodly people, but protected Noah, a preacher of righteousness, and seven others; ⁶if he condemned the cities of Sodom and Gomorrah by burning them to ashes, and made them an example of what is going to happen to the ungodly; ⁷and if he rescued Lot, a righteous man, who was distressed by the depraved conduct of the lawless ⁸(for that righteous man, living among them day after day, was tormented in his righteous soul by the lawless deeds he saw and heard)— ⁹if this is so, then the Lord knows how to rescue the godly from trials and to hold the unrighteous for punishment on the day of judgment. ¹⁰This is especially true of those who follow the corrupt desire of the sinful natureᶜ and despise authority.

Bold and arrogant, they are not afraid to heap abuse on celestial beings; ¹¹yet even angels, although they are stronger and more powerful, do not heap abuse on such beings when bringing judgment on them fromᵈ the Lord. ¹²But these people blaspheme in matters they do not understand. They are like unreasoning animals, creatures of instinct, born only to be caught and destroyed, and like animals they too will perish.

¹³They will be paid back with harm for the harm they have done. Their idea of pleasure is to carouse in broad daylight. They are blots and blemishes, reveling in their pleasures while they feast with you.ᵉ ¹⁴With eyes full of adultery, they never stop sinning; they seduce the unstable; they are experts in greed— an accursed brood! ¹⁵They have left the straight way and wandered off to follow the way of Balaam son of Bezer,ᶠ who loved the wages of wickedness. ¹⁶But he was rebuked for his wrongdoing by a donkey— an animal without speech—who spoke with a human voice and restrained the prophet's madness.

¹⁷These people are springs without water and mists driven by a storm. Blackest darkness is reserved for them. ¹⁸For they mouth empty, boastful words and, by appealing to the lustful desires of sinful human nature, they entice people who are just escaping from those who live in error. ¹⁹They promise them freedom, while they themselves are slaves of depravity—for "people are slaves to whatever has mastered them." ²⁰If they have escaped the corruption of the world by knowing our Lord and Savior Jesus Christ and are again entangled in it and are overcome, they are worse off at the end than they were at the beginning. ²¹It would have been better for them not to have known the way of righteousness, than to have

atissue:discernment

2:1–3 Remember the wolf in grandma's clothing in the story of *Little Red Riding Hood?* At first the wolf seemed harmless—maybe a bit eccentric, but harmless nonetheless. Peter warns us against such disguised wolves, false teachers masquerading as spiritual experts who really have malevolent intentions. These people introduce "creative" theology and make God's message "more appealing." Be on the lookout for these false teachers. You'll recognize them by two main clues: First, they deny (or maybe just downplay) Jesus and his work on the cross. Second, they contradict God's Word. Don't be taken in by the lies they peddle.

1736

known it and then to turn their backs on the sacred command that was passed on to them. ²²Of them the proverbs are true: "A dog returns to its vomit,"ᵃ and, "A sow that is washed returns to her wallowing in the mud."

The Day of the Lord

3 Dear friends, this is now my second letter to you. I have written both of them as reminders to stimulate you to wholesome thinking. ²I want you to recall the words spoken in the past by the holy prophets and the command given by our Lord and Savior through your apostles.

³Above all, you must understand that in the last days scoffers will come, scoffing and following their own evil desires. ⁴They will say, "Where is this 'coming' he promised? Ever since our ancestors died, everything goes on as it has since the beginning of creation." ⁵But they deliberately forget that long ago by God's word the heavens came into being and the earth was formed out of water and by water. ⁶By these waters also the world of that time was deluged and destroyed. ⁷By the same word the present heavens and earth are reserved for fire, being kept for the day of judgment and destruction of the ungodly.

⁸But do not forget this one thing, dear friends: With the Lord a day is like a thousand years, and a thousand years are like a day. ⁹The Lord is not slow in keeping his promise, as some understand slowness. Instead he is patient with you, not wanting anyone to perish, but everyone to come to repentance.

¹⁰But the day of the Lord will come like a thief. The heavens will disappear with a roar; the elements will be destroyed by fire, and the earth and everything done in it will be laid bare.ᵇ

¹¹Since everything will be destroyed in this way, what kind of people ought you to be? You ought to live holy and godly lives ¹²as you look forward to the day of God and speed its coming.ᶜ That day will bring about the destruction of the heavens by fire, and the elements will melt in the heat. ¹³But in keeping with his promise we are looking forward to a new heaven and a new earth, where righteousness dwells.

¹⁴So then, dear friends, since you are looking forward to this, make every effort to be found spotless, blameless and at peace with him. ¹⁵Bear in mind that our Lord's patience means salvation, just as our dear brother Paul also wrote you with the wisdom that God gave him. ¹⁶He writes the same way in all his letters, speaking in them of these matters. His letters contain some things that are hard to understand, which ignorant and unstable people distort, as they do the other Scriptures, to their own destruction.

¹⁷Therefore, dear friends, since you have been forewarned, be on your guard so that you may not be carried away by the error of the lawless and fall from your secure position. ¹⁸But grow in the grace and knowledge of our Lord and Savior Jesus Christ. To him be glory both now and forever! Amen.

conversations

patience «» 3:9

1» How can your impatience cause you to miss God's larger plan?

2» When has God been patient with you?

3» Who in your life needs some patient grace from you?

For more on **patience**, check the index.
For the next Conversations, go to p. 1742.

1737

ᵃ 22 Prov. 26:11   ᵇ 10 Some manuscripts *be burned up*   ᶜ 12 Or *as you wait eagerly for the day of God to come*

Think you can fill this tall order? >> (2:6)

Do you have to love that person who gossiped about you at church, got to chair the committee (when you deserved it) or gloated over you? >> (2:9–11; 3:11–18)

Is it OK to own Prada? >> (2:15–17)

Is Jesus one of many options God gives us? >> (4:2–3,14–15)

Will God ever stop loving you? >> (4:16–19)

1john

AUTHOR
The apostle John.

AUDIENCE
All the early churches and every follower of Jesus.

DATE
Between A.D. 85–95.

SETTING
Now an old man, this beloved disciple and close friend of Jesus writes to encourage the early churches.

VERSES TO REMEMBER
"Dear friends, let us love one another, for love comes from God. Everyone who loves has been born of God and knows God. Whoever does not love does not know God, because God is love."
(4:7–8)

THEME TO CONSIDER
Love one another—so simple yet so hard; so timely yet so timeless; so gentle yet so transforming. Love is the greatest force in the world.

The Incarnation of the Word of Life

1 That which was from the beginning, which we have heard, which we have seen with our eyes, which we have looked at and our hands have touched—this we proclaim concerning the Word of life. [2]The life appeared; we have seen it and testify to it, and we proclaim to you the eternal life, which was with the Father and has appeared to us. [3]We proclaim to you what we have seen and heard, so that you also may have fellowship with us. And our fellowship is with the Father and with his Son, Jesus Christ. [4]We write this to make our[a] joy complete.

Light and Darkness, Sin and Forgiveness

[5]This is the message we have heard from him and declare to you: God is light; in him there is no darkness at all. [6]If we claim to have fellowship with him and yet walk in the darkness, we lie and do not live out the truth. [7]But if we walk in the light, as he is in the light, we have fellowship with one another, and the blood of Jesus, his Son, purifies us from all[b] sin.

[8]If we claim to be without sin, we deceive ourselves and the truth is not in us. [9]If we confess our sins, he is faithful and just and will forgive us our sins and purify us from all unrighteousness. [10]If we claim we have not sinned, we make him out to be a liar and his word is not in us.

2 My dear children, I write this to you so that you will not sin. But if anybody does sin, we have an advocate with the Father—Jesus Christ, the Righteous One. [2]He is the atoning sacrifice for our sins, and not only for ours but also for the sins of the whole world.

1739

Love and Hatred for Fellow Believers

[3]We know that we have come to know him if we keep his commands. [4]Those who say, "I know him," but do not do what he commands are liars, and the truth is not in them. [5]But if anyone obeys his word, love for God[c] is truly made complete in them. This is how we know we are in him: [6]Whoever claims to live in him must live as Jesus did.

[7]Dear friends, I am not writing you a new command but an old one, which you have had since the beginning. This old command is the message you have heard. [8]Yet I am writing you a new command; its truth is seen in him and in you, because the darkness is passing and the true light is already shining.

[9]Those who claim to be in the light but hate a fellow believer are still in the darkness. [10]Those who love their fellow believers live in the light, and there is nothing in them to make them stumble. [11]But those who hate a fellow believer are in the darkness and walk around in the darkness; they do not know where they are going, because the darkness has blinded them.

Reasons for Writing

[12]I am writing to you, dear children,
    because your sins have been forgiven on account of his name.
[13]I am writing to you, fathers,
    because you know him who is from the beginning.
I am writing to you, young people,
    because you have overcome the evil one.

[14]I write to you, dear children,
    because you know the Father.
I write to you, fathers,
    because you know him who is from the beginning.
I write to you, young people,
    because you are strong,
    and the word of God lives in you,
    and you have overcome the evil one.

On Not Loving the World

[15]Do not love the world or anything in the world. If you love the world, love for the Father[d] is not in you. [16]For everything in the world—the cravings of sinful people, the lust of their eyes and their

---

[a] 4 Some manuscripts *your* [b] 7 Or *every* [c] 5 Or *word, God's love* [d] 15 Or *world, the Father's love*

boasting about what they have and do—comes not from the Father but from the world. [17]The world and its desires pass away, but whoever does the will of God lives forever.

Warnings Against Denying the Son

[18]Dear children, this is the last hour; and as you have heard that the antichrist is coming, even now many antichrists have come. This is how we know it is the last hour. [19]They went out from us, but they did not really belong to us. For if they had belonged to us, they would have remained with us; but their going showed that none of them belonged to us.

[20]But you have an anointing from the Holy One, and all of you know the truth.[a] [21]I do not write to you because you do not know the truth, but because you do know it and because no lie comes from the truth. [22]Who is the liar? It is whoever denies that Jesus is the Messiah.[b] Such a person is the antichrist—denying the Father and the Son. [23]No one who denies the Son has the Father; whoever acknowledges the Son has the Father also.

[24]As for you, see that what you have heard from the beginning remains in you. If it does, you also will remain in the Son and in the Father. [25]And this is what he promised us—eternal life.

[26]I am writing these things to you about those who are trying to lead you astray. [27]As for you, the anointing you received from him remains in you, and you do not need anyone to teach you. But as his anointing teaches you about all things and as that anointing is real, not counterfeit—just as it has taught you, remain in him.

God's Children and Sin

[28]And now, dear children, continue in him, so that when he appears we may be confident and unashamed before him at his coming.

[29]If you know that he is righteous, you know that everyone who does what is right has been born of him.

3 See what great love the Father has lavished on us, that we should be called children of God! And that is what we are! The reason the world does not know us is that it did not know him. [2]Dear friends, now we are children of God, and what we will be has not yet been made known. But we know that when Christ appears,[c] we shall be like him, for we shall see him as he is. [3]All who have this hope in him purify themselves, just as he is pure.

[4]Everyone who sins breaks the law; in fact, sin is lawlessness. [5]But you know that he appeared so that he might take away our sins. And in him is no sin. [6]No one who lives in him keeps on sinning. No one who continues to sin has either seen him or known him.

[7]Dear children, do not let anyone lead you astray. The one who does what is right is righteous, just as he is righteous. [8]The one who does what is sinful is of the devil, because the devil has been sinning from the beginning. The reason the Son of God appeared was to destroy the devil's work. [9]Those who are born of God will not continue to sin, because God's seed remains in them; they cannot go on sinning, because they have been born of God. [10]This is how we know who the children of God are and who the children of the devil are: Those who do not do what is right are not God's children; nor are those who do not love their brothers and sisters.

atissue:shopping

2:15–17 Do you ever find that once you start shopping, you discover all these items you "need"? It's all too easy to become fixated on *stuff*. Yet those fixations can crowd out your thoughts for God. Instead of thinking about what God wants for you or how to introduce his name in conversation, you may be distracted by how you want to arrange your new living room furniture or what kind of shoes you want for your new outfit. That's the danger implicit in the stuff of this world—not that the things themselves are innately wrong, but obsession with them is.

---

[a] 20 Some manuscripts *and you know all things*   [b] 22 Greek *Christ*   [c] 2 Or *when it is made known*

martha

Luke 10:38–42

1741

How would you describe yourself?

Well, no one likes to admit this about herself, but I tend to be something of a control freak. I like things to be done a certain way—basically, *my* way—and I want everything to be perfect. I don't like to be surprised, and I definitely don't like last-minute changes that disrupt my entire day.

So when Jesus came to visit, it was a big deal.

Yes. He came to our house frequently, but still, every time he came it was an exciting event. I loved Jesus, I really did, and I wanted everything to be perfect for him and his disciples. He was always on the road, and I knew he could really use a good home-cooked meal and a place to rest without the crowds bothering him. And that's exactly what I wanted to give him. I had in my mind what I wanted to serve, how I wanted the house to look and how the evening would flow. But I couldn't do it all myself. And where was my sister Mary? Just sitting with Jesus!

What did you do?

When I couldn't get Mary's attention (she was so caught up in Jesus' every word), I went straight to Jesus. Certainly if Jesus asked her to help me, she would.

And what happened?

[shakes her head] Instead of telling *Mary* what to do, Jesus told *me* what to do.

And that was . . . ?

Basically, to rethink my priorities. There was my Lord, sitting in my living room, and all I could think of was getting the bread baked exactly right. I was missing out on the most important thing—*being* with Jesus.

What can we learn from your life?

My story carries a big lesson—especially for those women who, like me, try to do it all. The lesson is this: Just let it go. If all that *doing* takes you away from *being* with Jesus, then sit down and redo your list. Better yet, tear up your list and start a new one. Put JESUS at the top. You can bet that he has your name at the top of his list.

FOR MORE INSIGHT: Take a look at the following for more on priorities: Matthew 6:33–34; 13:44–46; and Mark 12:28–31.

More on Love and Hatred

[11] For this is the message you heard from the beginning: We should love one another. [12] Do not be like Cain, who belonged to the evil one and murdered his brother. And why did he murder him? Because his own actions were evil and his brother's were righteous. [13] Do not be surprised, my brothers and sisters, if the world hates you. [14] We know that we have passed from death to life, because we love each other. Anyone who does not love remains in death. [15] Anyone who hates a fellow believer is a murderer, and you know that no murderers have eternal life in them.

[16] This is how we know what love is: Jesus Christ laid down his life for us. And we ought to lay down our lives for one another. [17] If any one of you has material possessions and sees a brother or sister in need but has no pity on them, how can the love of God be in you? [18] Dear children, let us not love with words or tongue but with actions and in truth.

[19] This is how we know that we belong to the truth and how we set our hearts at rest in his presence: [20] If our hearts condemn us, we know that God is greater than our hearts, and he knows everything. [21] Dear friends, if our hearts do not condemn us, we have confidence before God [22] and receive from him anything we ask, because we keep his commands and do what pleases him. [23] And this is his command: to believe in the name of his Son, Jesus Christ, and to love one another as he commanded us. [24] Those who keep his commands live in him, and he in them. And this is how we know that he lives in us: We know it by the Spirit he gave us.

conversations

materialism «» 3:16–20

1. Do you have material things that you value above relationships?

2. What possession could you could give away to someone who has a current need?

3. Why is materialism such an easy sin for us to unwittingly fall into?

For more on **materialism**, check the index.
For the next Conversations, go to p. 1745.

On Denying the Incarnation

[4] Dear friends, do not believe every spirit, but test the spirits to see whether they are from God, because many false prophets have gone out into the world. [2] This is how you can recognize the Spirit of God: Every spirit that acknowledges that Jesus Christ has come in the flesh is from God, [3] but every spirit that does not acknowledge Jesus is not from God. This is the spirit of the antichrist, which you have heard is coming and even now is already in the world.

[4] You, dear children, are from God and have overcome them, because the one who is in you is greater than the one who is in the world. [5] They are from the world and therefore speak from the viewpoint of the world, and the world listens to them. [6] We are from God, and whoever knows God listens to us; but whoever is not from God does not listen to us. This is how we recognize the Spirit[a] of truth and the spirit of falsehood.

God's Love and Ours

[7] Dear friends, let us love one another, for love comes from God. Everyone who loves has been born of God and knows God. [8] Whoever does not love does not know God, because God is love. [9] This is how God showed his love among us: He sent his one and only Son into the world that we might live through him. [10] This is love: not that we loved God, but that he loved us and sent his Son as an atoning sacrifice for our sins. [11] Dear friends, since God so loved us, we also ought to love one another. [12] No one has ever seen God; but if we love one another, God lives in us and his love is made complete in us.

[13] This is how we know that we live in him and he in us: He has given us of his Spirit. [14] And we have seen and testify that the Father has sent his Son to be the Savior of the world. [15] If anyone acknowledges that Jesus is the Son of God, God lives in them and they in God. [16] And so we know and rely on the love God has for us.

God is love. Whoever lives in love lives in God, and God in them. [17] This is how love is made complete

1742

---

a 6 Or *spirit*

among us so that we will have confidence on the day of judgment: In this world we are like Jesus. [18]There is no fear in love. But perfect love drives out fear, because fear has to do with punishment. The one who fears is not made perfect in love.

[19]We love because he first loved us. [20]If we say we love God yet hate a brother or sister, we are liars. For if we do not love a fellow believer, whom we have seen, we cannot love God, whom we have not seen. [21]And he has given us this command: Those who love God must also love one another.

HE IS: love

4:16–19 How appropriate that John, the disciple Jesus loved (see John 20:2), reveals the simple yet profound truth that God is *love*. God sent humanity the greatest love letter ever written, the Bible. He demonstrated his love by dying for those he loved. It is his very nature to love.

Because God is love, we too are learning to love—not because it's our nature, for human love is fickle and failing, but because he loved us first. Because God is love, he commands us to love our brothers and sisters, neighbors and friends, and even our enemies—those people we find hardest to love.

For the next He Is, go to p. 1752.

Faith in the Incarnate Son of God

5 Everyone who believes that Jesus is the Messiah is born of God, and everyone who loves the father loves his child as well. [2]This is how we know that we love the children of God: by loving God and carrying out his commands. [3]In fact, this is love for God: to keep his commands. And his commands are not burdensome, [4]for everyone born of God overcomes the world. This is the victory that has overcome the world, even our faith. [5]Who is it that overcomes the world? Only the one who believes that Jesus is the Son of God.

[6]This is the one who came by water and blood—Jesus Christ. He did not come by water only, but by water and blood. And it is the Spirit who testifies, because the Spirit is the truth. [7]For there are three that testify: [8]the[a] Spirit, the water and the blood; and the three are in agreement. [9]We accept human testimony, but God's testimony is greater because it is the testimony of God, which he has given about his Son. [10]Whoever believes in the Son of God accepts this testimony. Whoever does not believe God has made him out to be a liar, because they have not believed the testimony God has given about his Son. [11]And this is the testimony: God has given us eternal life, and this life is in his Son. [12]Whoever has the Son has life; whoever does not have the Son of God does not have life.

Concluding Affirmations

[13]I write these things to you who believe in the name of the Son of God so that you may know that you have eternal life. [14]This is the confidence we have in approaching God: that if we ask anything according to his will, he hears us. [15]And if we know that he hears us—whatever we ask—we know that we have what we asked of him.

[16]If you see any brother or sister commit a sin that does not lead to death, you should pray and God will give them life. I refer to those whose sin does not lead to death. There is a sin that leads to death. I am not saying that you should pray about that. [17]All wrongdoing is sin, and there is sin that does not lead to death.

[18]We know that anyone born of God does not continue to sin; the One who was born of God keeps them safe, and the evil one cannot harm them. [19]We know that we are children of God, and that the whole world is under the control of the evil one. [20]We know also that the Son of God has come and has given us understanding, so that we may know him who is true. And we are in him who is true by being in his Son Jesus Christ. He is the true God and eternal life.

[21]Dear children, keep yourselves from idols.

---

[a] *7,8* Late manuscripts of the Vulgate *testify in heaven: the Father, the Word and the Holy Spirit, and these three are one.* [8]*And there are three that testify on earth: the* (not found in any Greek manuscript before the fourteenth century)

2john

1744

AUTHOR
The apostle John.

AUDIENCE
All the early churches and every follower
of Jesus.

DATE
Between A.D. 85–95.

SETTING
John addressed his letter to the "lady chosen
by God and to her children," who may have
been a personal friend of John's, or a metaphor
for a church and its members.

VERSE TO REMEMBER
"And this is love: that we walk in obedience
to his commands. As you have heard from
the beginning, his command is that you walk
in love." (6)

THEME TO CONSIDER
Love one another, plain and simple. (Sound
familiar?)

¹The elder,

To the lady chosen by God and to her children, whom I love in the truth—and not I only, but also all who know the truth— ²because of the truth, which lives in us and will be with us forever:

³Grace, mercy and peace from God the Father and from Jesus Christ, the Father's Son, will be with us in truth and love.

⁴It has given me great joy to find some of your children walking in the truth, just as the Father commanded us. ⁵And now, dear lady, I am not writing you a new command but one we have had from the beginning. I ask that we love one another. ⁶And this is love: that we walk in obedience to his commands. As you have heard from the beginning, his command is that you walk in love.

⁷Many deceivers, who do not acknowledge Jesus Christ as coming in the flesh, have gone out into the world. Any such person is the deceiver and the antichrist. ⁸Watch out that you do not lose what we*a* have worked for, but that you may be rewarded fully. ⁹Anyone who runs ahead and does not continue in the teaching of Christ does not have God; whoever continues in the teaching has both the Father and the Son. ¹⁰If anyone comes to you and does not bring this teaching, do not take them into your house or welcome them. ¹¹Anyone who welcomes them shares in their wicked work.

¹²I have much to write to you, but I do not want to use paper and ink. Instead, I hope to visit you and talk with you face to face, so that our joy may be complete.

¹³The children of your sister, who is chosen by God, send their greetings.

at issue : obedience

6 When God speaks of love and obedience, it's as though he's describing two inseparable friends who walk arm-in-arm through the pages of Scripture. True love for God produces obedience. And true obedience to God is motivated by love for him. Don't make the mistake of trying to separate the two. Invite them to walk arm-in-arm in your life. If you're struggling to obey God in a particular area, remember his amazing love for you, and let your love for him motivate you to obey. And if you say you love God, demonstrate it by your obedience to his commands.

1745

conversations

discernment «» 7

1» How can you be discerning without being judgmental?

2» What distortions of the gospel are popular today?

3» How do you recognize a godly leader?

For more on **discernment**, check the index.
For the next Conversations, go to p. 1747.

a 8 Some manuscripts *you*

When was the last time you welcomed
a Christian worker into your home? ➤➤ (6–8)

Why do we insist on being so original? ➤➤ (11)

3john

AUTHOR
The apostle John.

AUDIENCE
Members of all the early churches, specifically
a friend named Gaius, and all followers of
Jesus.

DATE
Between A.D. 85–95.

SETTING
Traveling pastors relied on church members'
hospitality.

VERSE TO REMEMBER
"We ought therefore to show hospitality to
such people so that we may work together for
the truth." (8)

THEME TO CONSIDER
Christians depend on one another to finish the
work Jesus gave us to do.

conversations

children «» 4

1 What responsibilities do you have for your children's spirituality?

2 Where should that responsibility end?

3 Whose spiritual child are you? Do you have spiritual children? If so, who?

For more on **children**, check the index.
For the next Conversations, go to p. 1754.

¹The elder,

To my dear friend Gaius, whom I love in the truth.

²Dear friend, I pray that you may enjoy good health and that all may go well with you, even as your soul is getting along well. ³It gave me great joy to have some believers come and testify to your faithfulness to the truth, telling how you continue to walk in it. ⁴I have no greater joy than to hear that my children are walking in the truth.

⁵Dear friend, you are faithful in what you are doing for the brothers and sisters, even though they are strangers to you. ⁶They have told the church about your love. You will do well to send them on their way in a manner worthy of God. ⁷It was for the sake of the Name that they went out, receiving no help from the pagans. ⁸We ought therefore to show hospitality to such people so that we may work together for the truth.

⁹I wrote to the church, but Diotrephes, who loves to be first, will have nothing to do with us. ¹⁰So when I come, I will call attention to what he is doing, spreading malicious nonsense about us. Not satisfied with that, he refuses to welcome other believers. He also stops those who want to do so and puts them out of the church.

¹¹Dear friend, do not imitate what is evil but what is good. Anyone who does what is good is from God. Anyone who does what is evil has not seen God. ¹²Demetrius is well spoken of by everyone—and even by the truth itself. We also speak well of him, and you know that our testimony is true.

¹³I have much to write you, but I do not want to do so with pen and ink. ¹⁴I hope to see you soon, and we will talk face to face.

Peace to you. The friends here send their greetings. Greet the friends there by name.

1747

atissue:purity

11 Have you noticed how close friends tend to pick up each other's mannerisms? The more time they spend together, the more they use the same words and expressions. The same is true in close families. It's natural to unconsciously imitate your family and friends, just as you would expect to pick things up from what you watch or listen to. God wants you to be careful about the influences you invite into your heart and mind. Be purposeful about emulating him, so that you imitate only what is good rather than what's evil. Your mannerisms betray who or what is truly influencing you.

jude

AUTHOR
Jude, the brother of James and Jesus.

AUDIENCE
Jewish Christians and all followers of Jesus.

DATE
About A.D. 65.

SETTING
Jude issued a warning about false teachers
who lead people astray.

VERSE TO REMEMBER
"Keep yourselves in God's love as you wait for
the mercy of our Lord Jesus Christ to bring you
to eternal life." (21)

THEME TO CONSIDER
Test what you are taught; search the
Scriptures for yourself.

¹Jude, a servant of Jesus Christ and a brother of James,

To those who have been called, who are loved in God the Father and kept for *a* Jesus Christ:

²Mercy, peace and love be yours in abundance.

The Sin and Doom of Ungodly People

³Dear friends, although I was very eager to write to you about the salvation we share, I felt compelled to write and urge you to contend for the faith that the Lord has once for all entrusted to us, his people. ⁴For certain individuals whose condemnation was written about *b* long ago have secretly slipped in among you. They are ungodly people, who pervert the grace of our God into a license for immorality and deny Jesus Christ our only Sovereign and Lord.

⁵Though you already know all this, I want to remind you that the Lord *c* at one time delivered his people out of Egypt, but later destroyed those who did not believe. ⁶And the angels who did not keep their positions of authority but abandoned their proper dwelling—these he has kept in darkness, bound with everlasting chains for judgment on the great Day. ⁷In a similar way, Sodom and Gomorrah and the surrounding towns gave themselves up to sexual immorality and perversion. They serve as an example of those who suffer the punishment of eternal fire.

⁸In the very same way, on the strength of their dreams these ungodly people pollute their own bodies, reject authority and heap abuse on celestial beings. ⁹But even the archangel Michael, when he was disputing with the devil about the body of Moses, did not himself dare to condemn him for slander but said, "The Lord rebuke you!" *d* ¹⁰Yet these people speak abusively against whatever they do not understand; and what things they do understand by instinct, like unreasoning animals—these are the very things that destroy them.

¹¹Woe to them! They have taken the way of Cain; they have rushed for profit into Balaam's error; they have been destroyed in Korah's rebellion.

¹²These people are blemishes at your love feasts, eating with you without the slightest qualm—shepherds who feed only themselves. They are clouds without rain, blown along by the wind; autumn trees, without fruit and uprooted—twice dead. ¹³They are wild waves of the sea, foaming up their shame; wandering stars, for whom blackest darkness has been reserved forever.

¹⁴Enoch, the seventh from Adam, prophesied about them: "See, the Lord is coming with thousands upon thousands of his holy ones ¹⁵to judge everyone, and to convict all the ungodly of all the ungodly acts they have done in an ungodly way, and of all the defiant words ungodly sinners have spoken against him." *e* ¹⁶These people are grumblers and faultfinders; they follow their own evil desires; they boast about themselves and flatter others for their own advantage.

A Call to Persevere

¹⁷But, dear friends, remember what the apostles of our Lord Jesus Christ foretold. ¹⁸They said to you, "In the last times there will be scoffers who will follow their own ungodly desires." ¹⁹These are the people who divide you, who follow mere natural instincts and do not have the Spirit.

atissue: facing judgment

24–25 If you've ever gone to court and stood before a judge, you know how scary that experience is. One day you will be brought before the Judge of all heaven and earth. If you belong to God, then Jesus already served your sentence, and you'll be found innocent. Though we may be grieved by our sins and the ways we hurt the one who loves us so deeply, we need not fear punishment. We'll experience joy at seeing our Savior who sacrificed so much for us, and we'll be with him forever. Our "day in court" will actually be cause for great celebration!

---

a 1 Or *by; or in*   *b* 4 Or *individuals who were marked out for condemnation*   *c* 5 Some early manuscripts *Jesus*   *d* 9 Jude is alluding to the Jewish *Testament of Moses* (approximately the first century A.D.).   *e* 14,15 From the Jewish *First Book of Enoch* (approximately the first century B.C.)

²⁰But you, dear friends, by building yourselves up in your most holy faith and praying in the Holy Spirit, ²¹keep yourselves in God's love as you wait for the mercy of our Lord Jesus Christ to bring you to eternal life.

²²Be merciful to those who doubt; ²³save others by snatching them from the fire; to others show mercy, mixed with fear—hating even the clothing stained by corrupted flesh.^a

Doxology

²⁴To him who is able to keep you from stumbling and to present you before his glorious presence without fault and with great joy— ²⁵to the only God our Savior be glory, majesty, power and authority, through Jesus Christ our Lord, before all ages, now and forevermore! Amen.

---

^a 22,23 The Greek manuscripts of these verses vary at several points.

revelation

AUTHOR
The apostle John.

AUDIENCE
Seven churches in Asia and all followers of
Jesus.

DATE
About A.D. 95.

SETTING
John wrote about a vision he had while
exiled on the island of Patmos near the end
of his life.

VERSE TO REMEMBER
"He who testifies to these things says, 'Yes, I
am coming soon.' Amen. Come, Lord Jesus."
(22:20)

THEME TO CONSIDER
Knowing life's future outcome should give
you hope in the present.

Prologue

1 The revelation from Jesus Christ, which God gave him to show his servants what must soon take place. He made it known by sending his angel to his servant John, ²who testifies to everything he saw—that is, the word of God and the testimony of Jesus Christ. ³Blessed is the one who reads aloud the words of this prophecy, and blessed are those who hear it and take to heart what is written in it, because the time is near.

Greetings and Doxology

⁴John,

To the seven churches in the province of Asia:

Grace and peace to you from him who is, and who was, and who is to come, and from the seven spirits*ᵃ* before his throne, ⁵and from Jesus Christ, who is the faithful witness, the firstborn from the dead, and the ruler of the kings of the earth.

To him who loves us and has freed us from our sins by his blood, ⁶and has made us to be a kingdom and priests to serve his God and Father—to him be glory and power for ever and ever! Amen.

1752

> ⁷"Look, he is coming with the clouds,"*ᵇ*
>   and "every eye will see him,
>   even those who pierced him";
>   and all peoples on earth "will mourn because of him."*ᶜ*

So shall it be! Amen.

⁸"I am the Alpha and the Omega," says the Lord God, "who is, and who was, and who is to come, the Almighty."

HE IS: the Alpha and the Omega

1:8 When Jesus announced that he is *the Alpha and the Omega*, which are the first and last letters of the Greek alphabet, he revealed that he is the beginning and end of all things. He's the beginning and end in time—for he created all things—and in power—for in him all things hold together (see Colossians 1:16–17).

He who started all things will finish his work—including his work in you (see Philippians 1:6). If you feel spiritually stuck, remember that he who started that good work in your life (past) is still at work in you (present) and will finish what he started (future).

For the next He Is, go to p. 1756.

John's Vision of Christ

⁹I, John, your brother and companion in the suffering and kingdom and patient endurance that are ours in Jesus, was on the island of Patmos because of the word of God and the testimony of Jesus. ¹⁰On the Lord's Day I was in the Spirit, and I heard behind me a loud voice like a trumpet, ¹¹which said: "Write on a scroll what you see and send it to the seven churches: to Ephesus, Smyrna, Pergamum, Thyatira, Sardis, Philadelphia and Laodicea."

¹²I turned around to see the voice that was speaking to me. And when I turned I saw seven golden lampstands, ¹³and among the lampstands was someone like a son of man,*ᵈ* dressed in a robe reaching down to his feet and with a golden sash around his chest. ¹⁴The hair on his head was white like wool, as white as snow, and his eyes were like blazing fire. ¹⁵His feet were like bronze glowing in a furnace, and his voice was like the sound of rushing waters. ¹⁶In his right hand he held seven stars, and coming out of his mouth was a sharp, double-edged sword. His face was like the sun shining in all its brilliance.

ᵃ *4* That is, the sevenfold Spirit   ᵇ *7* Daniel 7:13   ᶜ *7* Zech. 12:10   ᵈ *13* See Daniel 7:13.

[17]When I saw him, I fell at his feet as though dead. Then he placed his right hand on me and said: "Do not be afraid. I am the First and the Last. [18]I am the Living One; I was dead, and now look, I am alive for ever and ever! And I hold the keys of death and Hades.

[19]"Write, therefore, what you have seen: both what is now and what will take place later. [20]The mystery of the seven stars that you saw in my right hand and of the seven golden lampstands is this: The seven stars are the angels[a] of the seven churches, and the seven lampstands are the seven churches.

To the Church in Ephesus

2 "To the angel[b] of the church in Ephesus write:

These are the words of him who holds the seven stars in his right hand and walks among the seven golden lampstands. [2]I know your deeds, your hard work and your perseverance. I know that you cannot tolerate wicked people, that you have tested those who claim to be apostles but are not, and have found them false. [3]You have persevered and have endured hardships for my name, and have not grown weary.

[4]Yet I hold this against you: You have forsaken the love you had at first. [5]Consider how far you have fallen! Repent and do the things you did at first. If you do not repent, I will come to you and remove your lampstand from its place. [6]But you have this in your favor: You hate the practices of the Nicolaitans, which I also hate.

[7]Whoever has ears, let them hear what the Spirit says to the churches. To those who are victorious, I will give the right to eat from the tree of life, which is in the paradise of God.

To the Church in Smyrna

[8]"To the angel of the church in Smyrna write:

These are the words of him who is the First and the Last, who died and came to life again. [9]I know your afflictions and your poverty—yet you are rich! I know about the slander of those who say they are Jews and are not, but are a synagogue of Satan. [10]Do not be afraid of what you are about to suffer. I tell you, the devil will put some of you in prison to test you, and you will suffer persecution for ten days. Be faithful, even to the point of death, and I will give you life as your victor's crown.

[11]Whoever has ears, let them hear what the Spirit says to the churches. Those who are victorious will not be hurt at all by the second death.

To the Church in Pergamum

[12]"To the angel of the church in Pergamum write:

These are the words of him who has the sharp, double-edged sword. [13]I know where you live—where Satan has his throne. Yet you remain true to my name. You did not renounce your faith in me, not even in the days of Antipas, my faithful witness, who was put to death in your city—where Satan lives.

[14]Nevertheless, I have a few things against you: There are some among you who hold to the teaching of Balaam, who taught Balak to entice the Israelites to sin so that they ate food sacrificed to idols and committed sexual immorality. [15]Likewise, you also have those who hold to the teaching of the Nicolaitans. [16]Repent therefore! Otherwise, I will soon come to you and will fight against them with the sword of my mouth.

[17]Whoever has ears, let them hear what the Spirit says to the churches. To those who are victorious, I will give some of the hidden manna. I will also give each of them a white stone with a new name written on it, known only to the one who receives it.

To the Church in Thyatira

[18]"To the angel of the church in Thyatira write:

These are the words of the Son of God, whose eyes are like blazing fire and whose feet are like burnished bronze. ¹⁹I know your deeds, your love and faith, your service and perseverance, and that you are now doing more than you did at first.

²⁰Nevertheless, I have this against you: You tolerate that woman Jezebel, who calls herself a prophet. By her teaching she misleads my servants into sexual immorality and the eating of food sacrificed to idols. ²¹I have given her time to repent of her immorality, but she is unwilling. ²²So I will cast her on a bed of suffering, and I will make those who commit adultery with her suffer intensely, unless they repent of her ways. ²³I will strike her children dead. Then all the churches will know that I am he who searches hearts and minds, and I will repay each of you according to your deeds. ²⁴Now I say to the rest of you in Thyatira, to you who do not hold to her teaching and have not learned Satan's so-called deep secrets, 'I will not impose any other burden on you, ²⁵except to hold on to what you have until I come.'

²⁶To those who are victorious and do my will to the end, I will give authority over the nations— ²⁷they 'will rule them with an iron scepter and will dash them to pieces like pottery'ᵃ—just as I have received authority from my Father. ²⁸I will also give them the morning star. ²⁹Whoever has ears, let them hear what the Spirit says to the churches.

conversations

sex «» 2:20

1» How does sexual immorality in the church hurt the whole body of Christ?

2» In what ways does the church tolerate sexual immorality?

3» How can you be on your guard against any kind of sexual temptation?

For more on **sex**, check the index.
For the next Conversations, go to p. 1760.

1754

To the Church in Sardis

3 "To the angelᵇ of the church in Sardis write:

These are the words of him who holds the seven spiritsᶜ of God and the seven stars. I know your deeds; you have a reputation of being alive, but you are dead. ²Wake up! Strengthen what remains and is about to die, for I have found your deeds unfinished in the sight of my God. ³Remember, therefore, what you have received and heard; hold it fast, and repent. But if you do not wake up, I will come like a thief, and you will not know at what time I will come to you.

⁴Yet you have a few people in Sardis who have not soiled their clothes. They will walk with me, dressed in white, for they are worthy. ⁵Those who are victorious will, like them, be dressed in white. I will never blot out their names from the book of life, but will acknowledge their names before my Father and his angels. ⁶Whoever has ears, let them hear what the Spirit says to the churches.

To the Church in Philadelphia

⁷"To the angel of the church in Philadelphia write:

These are the words of him who is holy and true, who holds the key of David. What he opens no one can shut, and what he shuts no one can open. ⁸I know your deeds. See, I have placed before you an open door that no one can shut. I know that you have little strength, yet you have kept my word and have not denied my name. ⁹I will make those who are of the synagogue of Satan, who claim to be Jews though they are not, but are liars—I will make them come and fall down at your feet and acknowledge that I have loved you. ¹⁰Since you have kept my command to endure patiently, I will also keep you from the hour of trial that is going to come on the whole world to test those who live on the earth.

¹¹I am coming soon. Hold on to what you have, so that no one will take your crown. ¹²Those who are victorious I will make pillars in the temple of my God. Never again will they leave it. I will write on them the name of my God and the name of the city of my God, the new Jerusalem, which is com-

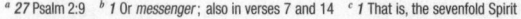

ᵃ *27* Psalm 2:9 ᵇ *1* Or *messenger*; also in verses 7 and 14 ᶜ *1* That is, the sevenfold Spirit ing down out of heaven from my God; and I will also write on them my new name. ¹³Whoever has ears, let them hear what the Spirit says to the churches.

To the Church in Laodicea

¹⁴"To the angel of the church in Laodicea write:

These are the words of the Amen, the faithful and true witness, the ruler of God's creation. ¹⁵I know your deeds, that you are neither cold nor hot. I wish you were either one or the other! ¹⁶So, because you are lukewarm—neither hot nor cold—I am about to spit you out of my mouth. ¹⁷You say, 'I am rich; I have acquired wealth and do not need a thing.' But you do not realize that you are wretched, pitiful, poor, blind and naked. ¹⁸I counsel you to buy from me gold refined in the fire, so you can become rich; and white clothes to wear, so you can cover your shameful nakedness; and salve to put on your eyes, so you can see.

¹⁹Those whom I love I rebuke and discipline. So be earnest, and repent. ²⁰Here I am! I stand at the door and knock. If anyone hears my voice and opens the door, I will come in and eat with them, and they with me.

²¹To those who are victorious, I will give the right to sit with me on my throne, just as I was victorious and sat down with my Father on his throne. ²²Whoever has ears, let them hear what the Spirit says to the churches."

The Throne in Heaven

4 After this I looked, and there before me was a door standing open in heaven. And the voice I had first heard speaking to me like a trumpet said, "Come up here, and I will show you what must take place after this." ²At once I was in the Spirit, and there before me was a throne in heaven with someone sitting on it. ³And the one who sat there had the appearance of jasper and ruby. A rainbow that shone like an emerald encircled the throne. ⁴Surrounding the throne were twenty-four other thrones, and seated on them were twenty-four elders. They were dressed in white and had crowns of gold on their heads. ⁵From the throne came flashes of lightning, rumblings and peals of thunder. Before the throne, seven lamps were blazing. These are the seven spirits*a* of God. ⁶Also before the throne there was what looked like a sea of glass, clear as crystal.

In the center, around the throne, were four living creatures, and they were covered with eyes, in front and in back. ⁷The first living creature was like a lion, the second was like an ox, the third had a face like a man, the fourth was like a flying eagle. ⁸Each of the four living creatures had six wings and was covered with eyes all around, even under its wings. Day and night they never stop saying:

> "'Holy, holy, holy
> is the Lord God Almighty,'*b*
> who was, and is, and is to come."

⁹Whenever the living creatures give glory, honor and thanks to him who sits on the throne and who lives for ever and ever, ¹⁰the twenty-four elders fall down before him who sits on the throne and worship him who lives for ever and ever. They lay their crowns before the throne and say:

---

at issue : self-reliance

3:14–20 Though many Christians use these verses in evangelism, this scolding was actually intended for those who already believed yet had grown self-sufficient. Could that be you? Over the years have you grown self-reliant? Have you forgotten how much you desperately need Jesus? Have your prayers dwindled? Do you think you're rich—though you truly have nothing? Jesus takes these offenses personally. Just as there's nothing satisfying about a lukewarm beverage, so there's nothing satisfying (or persuasive) about a lukewarm Christian. Ask yourself: What's the temperature of my faith? Does Christ want to vomit me out? Have I forgotten just how much I need him?

1755

---

[11]"You are worthy, our Lord and God,
  to receive glory and honor and power,
for you created all things,
  and by your will they were created
  and have their being."

The Scroll and the Lamb

5 Then I saw in the right hand of him who sat on the throne a scroll with writing on both sides and sealed with seven seals. [2]And I saw a mighty angel proclaiming in a loud voice, "Who is worthy to break the seals and open the scroll?" [3]But no one in heaven or on earth or under the earth could open the scroll or even look inside it. [4]I wept and wept because no one was found who was worthy to open the scroll or look inside. [5]Then one of the elders said to me, "Do not weep! See, the Lion of the tribe of Judah, the Root of David, has triumphed. He is able to open the scroll and its seven seals."

[6]Then I saw a Lamb, looking as if it had been slain, standing in the center before the throne, encircled by the four living creatures and the elders. The Lamb had seven horns and seven eyes, which are the seven spirits[a] of God sent out into all the earth. [7]He went and took the scroll from the right hand of him who sat on the throne. [8]And when he had taken it, the four living creatures and the twenty-four elders fell down before the Lamb. Each one had a harp and they were holding golden bowls full of incense, which are the prayers of God's people. [9]And they sang a new song, saying:

the Lion and the Lamb

5:5–6 In his vision, John saw Jesus as he would reveal himself on his earthly visitations. First John saw Jesus as *the Lion*, the conquering King of the second coming. Next he saw Jesus as *the Lamb*, sacrificed for our sins during his first coming (see John 1:29).

Jesus is both of these to us: *the Lion*, the powerful ruler, and *the Lamb*, the gentle sacrifice. If you only know Jesus as one or the other, then you've only glimpsed a part of who he is. *The Lion* demands your respect, allegiance and surrender. *The Lamb* demands your gratitude, worship and love.

For the next He Is, go to p. 1773.

"You are worthy to take the scroll
  and to open its seals,
because you were slain,
  and with your blood you purchased for God
  members of every tribe and language and people and nation.
[10]You have made them to be a kingdom and priests to serve our God,
  and they will reign[b] on the earth."

[11]Then I looked and heard the voice of many angels, numbering thousands upon thousands, and ten thousand times ten thousand. They encircled the throne and the living creatures and the elders. [12]In a loud voice they were saying:

"Worthy is the Lamb, who was slain,
  to receive power and wealth and wisdom and strength
  and honor and glory and praise!"

[13]Then I heard every creature in heaven and on earth and under the earth and on the sea, and all that is in them, saying:

---

[a] 6 That is, the sevenfold Spirit   [b] 10 Some manuscripts *they reign*

> "To him who sits on the throne and to the Lamb
> be praise and honor and glory and power,
> for ever and ever!"

¹⁴The four living creatures said, "Amen," and the elders fell down and worshiped.

The Seals

6 I watched as the Lamb opened the first of the seven seals. Then I heard one of the four living creatures say in a voice like thunder, "Come!" ²I looked, and there before me was a white horse! Its rider held a bow, and he was given a crown, and he rode out as a conqueror bent on conquest.

³When the Lamb opened the second seal, I heard the second living creature say, "Come!" ⁴Then another horse came out, a fiery red one. Its rider was given power to take peace from the earth and to make people slay each other. To him was given a large sword.

⁵When the Lamb opened the third seal, I heard the third living creature say, "Come!" I looked, and there before me was a black horse! Its rider was holding a pair of scales in his hand. ⁶Then I heard what sounded like a voice among the four living creatures, saying, "Two pounds*a* of wheat for a day's wages,*b* and six pounds*c* of barley for a day's wages,*d* and do not damage the oil and the wine!"

⁷When the Lamb opened the fourth seal, I heard the voice of the fourth living creature say, "Come!" ⁸I looked, and there before me was a pale horse! Its rider was named Death, and Hades was following close behind him. They were given power over a fourth of the earth to kill by sword, famine and plague, and by the wild beasts of the earth.

⁹When he opened the fifth seal, I saw under the altar the souls of those who had been slain because of the word of God and the testimony they had maintained. ¹⁰They called out in a loud voice, "How long, Sovereign Lord, holy and true, until you judge the inhabitants of the earth and avenge our blood?" ¹¹Then each of them was given a white robe, and they were told to wait a little longer, until the full number of their fellow servants and brothers and sisters were killed just as they had been.

¹²I watched as he opened the sixth seal. There was a great earthquake. The sun turned black like sackcloth made of goat hair, the whole moon turned blood red, ¹³and the stars in the sky fell to earth, as figs drop from a fig tree when shaken by a strong wind. ¹⁴The sky receded like a scroll, rolling up, and every mountain and island was removed from its place.

¹⁵Then the kings of the earth, the princes, the generals, the rich, the mighty, and everyone else, both slave and free, hid in caves and among the rocks of the mountains. ¹⁶They called to the mountains and the rocks, "Fall on us and hide us*e* from the face of him who sits on the throne and from the wrath of the Lamb! ¹⁷For the great day of their*f* wrath has come, and who can withstand it?"

144,000 Sealed

7 After this I saw four angels standing at the four corners of the earth, holding back the four winds of the earth to prevent any wind from blowing on the land or on the sea or on any tree. ²Then I saw another angel coming up from the east, having the seal of the living God. He called out in a loud voice to the four angels who had been given power to harm the land and the sea: ³"Do not harm the land or the sea or the trees until we put a seal on the foreheads of the servants of our God." ⁴Then I heard the number of those who were sealed: 144,000 from all the tribes of Israel.

⁵ From the tribe of Judah 12,000 were sealed,
from the tribe of Reuben 12,000,
from the tribe of Gad 12,000,
⁶ from the tribe of Asher 12,000,
from the tribe of Naphtali 12,000,
from the tribe of Manasseh 12,000,
⁷ from the tribe of Simeon 12,000,
from the tribe of Levi 12,000,

1757

---

a 6 Or about 1 kilogram   *b 6* Greek *a denarius*   *c 6* Or about 3 kilograms   *d 6* Greek *a denarius*   *e 16* See Hosea 10:8.   *f 17* Some manuscripts *his*

myth# 100 "I CAN MAKE THIS BLENDED FAMILY WORK."

Activities this week:

Becca—violin recital

Jason—band and yearbook

Danni—dance

Drew—science fair

I'm going to marry Dennis in three months, seven days and approximately ten hours. I seriously love this guy. That's why I'm going to do everything in my power to make our blended family work. I know I can do this.

Dennis has a son, Tyler (age 13), and a daughter, Becca (age 10). I have a 15-year-old (Jason), a 10-year-old (Drew) and a 6-year-old (Danielle, or Danni). Becca and Danni don't get along sometimes. Tyler isn't quite reconciled to the idea of us moving into "his" house.

On top of that, Jason thinks that sullenness is the train that can derail this marriage. When I first began seeing Dennis two years ago (four years after my divorce), he was sullen. Dennis slowly won him over. But now that we're getting married, he's sullen again. He has this sliver of hope that his father and I will get back together, which is not happening. Sigh.

And Becca. What to do about her, I wonder. She's sweet most of the time, but she still has a hard time trusting me because her mom abandoned her. She expects that I'm going to leave them, so she won't open up to me about anything.

These are all just hurdles I need to cross to make this family work. I've just got to stay organized and focused. The kids have so many activities. I need to attend as many as I can. If I stay on top of things, I'm sure God will bring about a miracle. And, even though I'm just the fiancée for now, I still want all the kids—especially Dennis's children—to know how important they are.

I'm not asking our family to be the Von Trapps, singing and laughing in matching outfits. I just want us to be a family—not a "blended" family, but a family, period.

—Leanne

EVER THINK YOU could make a relationship work by the sheer force of your will? Many of us have, especially when we determine not to repeat past mistakes as we begin new relationships. We tell ourselves, "It must work. It *will* work." Yet in reality, we have very little control over circumstances, schedules and other people, who have wills of their own.

Because of the high percentage of divorce in our society, many families are blended. Do you find yourself in the midst of a soon-to-be blended family? Have you confronted your expectations? Consider these expectations and the reality behind them:

Expectation 1: Since we love each other, living together shouldn't be too difficult if we're all willing to work at it.

Reality: This expectation seems reasonable, yet many relationships, particularly those in blended families, involve people with wounded emotions and bad memories, some of which require healing. All relationships have challenges. For a family to really gel takes about three to five years. Remember that this process is going to take time.

Expectation 2: I have to establish the relationship boundaries with my stepchildren right off the bat.

Reality: Many experts agree that the stepchild is the one to establish the boundaries. But as for setting goals in the relationship, the stepparent and the spouse (the biological parent) need to work together. Expecting intimacy too quickly usually leads to disappointment.

Expectation 3: I am in this alone. I can't expect others to do my part to make this family work.

Reality: Sure, no one else can walk in your shoes. But you're not alone. God is always with you, just waiting for you to ask for help.

Only the Holy Spirit can truly blend a family. Think of the church: a group of disparate individuals united by the love of God. He offers the fruit of the Spirit (see Galatians 5:22–23) and—more importantly—his presence. He also offers wisdom (see James 1:5) and assures us that we're not in this alone.

1759

"Trends suggest that within the next few years, 50 percent of American families with children under the age of 18 will be blended families."
—Linda Schertz, Ph.D.

"MANY ARE THE PLANS IN A HUMAN HEART, BUT IT IS THE LORD'S PURPOSE THAT PREVAILS."

PROVERBS 19:21

SEE ALSO

Proverbs 31:26–29
Romans 12:3,9–21
Philippians 4:5,13

For more on **Blended Families**, check the index.

from the tribe of Issachar 12,000,
⁸from the tribe of Zebulun 12,000,
from the tribe of Joseph 12,000,
from the tribe of Benjamin 12,000.

The Great Multitude in White Robes

⁹After this I looked, and there before me was a great multitude that no one could count, from every nation, tribe, people and language, standing before the throne and in front of the Lamb. They were wearing white robes and were holding palm branches in their hands. ¹⁰And they cried out in a loud voice:

> "Salvation belongs to our
> God,
> who sits on the throne,
> and to the Lamb."

¹¹All the angels were standing around the throne and around the elders and the four living creatures. They fell down on their faces before the throne and worshiped God, ¹²saying:

> "Amen!
> Praise and glory
> and wisdom and thanks and honor
> and power and strength
> be to our God for ever and ever.
> Amen!"

¹³Then one of the elders asked me, "These in white robes—who are they, and where did they come from?"

¹⁴I answered, "Sir, you know."

And he said, "These are they who have come out of the great tribulation; they have washed their robes and made them white in the blood of the Lamb. ¹⁵Therefore,

> "they are before the throne of God
>   and serve him day and night in his temple;
> and he who sits on the throne
>   will spread his tent over them.
> ¹⁶'Never again will they hunger;
>   never again will they thirst.
> The sun will not beat down on them,'ᵃ
>   nor any scorching heat.
> ¹⁷For the Lamb at the center before the throne
>   will be their shepherd;
> 'he will lead them to springs of living water.'ᵇ
>   'And God will wipe away every tear from their eyes.'ᶜ"

The Seventh Seal and the Golden Censer

8 When he opened the seventh seal, there was silence in heaven for about half an hour.

²And I saw the seven angels who stand before God, and seven trumpets were given to them.

³Another angel, who had a golden censer, came and stood at the altar. He was given much incense to

"conversations

racism «» 7:9

1» Does God value any race of people more than others?

2» Where do you see subtle hints of racism in your church, home or workplace?

3» How can you encourage here on earth this multi-ethnic picture of heaven?

For more on **racism**, check the index.
For the next Conversations, go to p. 1765.

1760

ᵃ *16* Isaiah 49:10   ᵇ *17* Isaiah 49:10   ᶜ *17* Isaiah 25:8

offer, with the prayers of all God's people, on the golden altar before the throne. ⁴The smoke of the incense, together with the prayers of God's people, went up before God from the angel's hand. ⁵Then the angel took the censer, filled it with fire from the altar, and hurled it on the earth; and there came peals of thunder, rumblings, flashes of lightning and an earthquake.

The Trumpets

⁶Then the seven angels who had the seven trumpets prepared to sound them.

⁷The first angel sounded his trumpet, and there came hail and fire mixed with blood, and it was hurled down on the earth. A third of the earth was burned up, a third of the trees were burned up, and all the green grass was burned up.

⁸The second angel sounded his trumpet, and something like a huge mountain, all ablaze, was thrown into the sea. A third of the sea turned into blood, ⁹a third of the living creatures in the sea died, and a third of the ships were destroyed.

¹⁰The third angel sounded his trumpet, and a great star, blazing like a torch, fell from the sky on a third of the rivers and on the springs of water— ¹¹the name of the star is Wormwood.ᵃ A third of the waters turned bitter, and many people died from the waters that had become bitter.

¹²The fourth angel sounded his trumpet, and a third of the sun was struck, a third of the moon, and a third of the stars, so that a third of them turned dark. A third of the day was without light, and also a third of the night.

¹³As I watched, I heard an eagle that was flying in midair call out in a loud voice: "Woe! Woe! Woe to the inhabitants of the earth, because of the trumpet blasts about to be sounded by the other three angels!"

9 The fifth angel sounded his trumpet, and I saw a star that had fallen from the sky to the earth. The star was given the key to the shaft of the Abyss. ²When he opened the Abyss, smoke rose from it like the smoke from a gigantic furnace. The sun and sky were darkened by the smoke from the Abyss. ³And out of the smoke locusts came down on the earth and were given power like that of scorpions of the earth. ⁴They were told not to harm the grass of the earth or any plant or tree, but only those people who did not have the seal of God on their foreheads. ⁵They were not allowed to kill them but only to torture them for five months. And the agony they suffered was like that of the sting of a scorpion when it strikes. ⁶During those days people will seek death but will not find it; they will long to die, but death will elude them.

⁷The locusts looked like horses prepared for battle. On their heads they wore something like crowns of gold, and their faces resembled human faces. ⁸Their hair was like women's hair, and their teeth were like lions' teeth. ⁹They had breastplates like breastplates of iron, and the sound of their wings was like the thundering of many horses and chariots rushing into battle. ¹⁰They had tails with stingers, like scorpions, and in their tails they had power to torment people for five months. ¹¹They had as king over them the angel of the Abyss, whose name in Hebrew is Abaddon and in Greek is Apollyon (that is, Destroyer).

¹²The first woe is past; two other woes are yet to come.

¹³The sixth angel sounded his trumpet, and I heard a voice coming from the four horns of the golden altar that is before God. ¹⁴It said to the sixth angel who had the trumpet, "Release the four angels who are bound at the great river Euphrates." ¹⁵And the four angels who had been kept ready for this very hour and day and month and year were released to kill a third of the world's people. ¹⁶The number of the mounted troops was two hundred million. I heard their number.

¹⁷The horses and riders I saw in my vision looked like this: Their breastplates were fiery red, dark blue, and yellow as sulfur. The heads of the horses resembled the heads of lions, and out of their mouths came fire, smoke and sulfur. ¹⁸A third of the people were killed by the three plagues of fire, smoke and sulfur that came out of their mouths. ¹⁹The power of the horses was in their mouths and in their tails; for their tails were like snakes, having heads with which they inflict injury.

²⁰The rest of the people who were not killed by these plagues still did not repent of the work of their hands; they did not stop worshiping demons, and idols of gold, silver, bronze, stone and wood—idols

---

ᵃ *11* Wormwood is a bitter substance.

that cannot see or hear or walk. [21] Nor did they repent of their murders, their magic arts, their sexual immorality or their thefts.

The Angel and the Little Scroll

10 Then I saw another mighty angel coming down from heaven. He was robed in a cloud, with a rainbow above his head; his face was like the sun, and his legs were like fiery pillars. [2] He was holding a little scroll, which lay open in his hand. He planted his right foot on the sea and his left foot on the land, [3] and he gave a loud shout like the roar of a lion. When he shouted, the voices of the seven thunders spoke. [4] And when the seven thunders spoke, I was about to write; but I heard a voice from heaven say, "Seal up what the seven thunders have said and do not write it down."

[5] Then the angel I had seen standing on the sea and on the land raised his right hand to heaven. [6] And he swore by him who lives for ever and ever, who created the heavens and all that is in them, the earth and all that is in it, and the sea and all that is in it, and said, "There will be no more delay! [7] But in the days when the seventh angel is about to sound his trumpet, the mystery of God will be accomplished, just as he announced to his servants the prophets."

[8] Then the voice that I had heard from heaven spoke to me once more: "Go, take the scroll that lies open in the hand of the angel who is standing on the sea and on the land."

[9] So I went to the angel and asked him to give me the little scroll. He said to me, "Take it and eat it. It will turn your stomach sour, but 'in your mouth it will be as sweet as honey.'[a]" [10] I took the little scroll from the angel's hand and ate it. It tasted as sweet as honey in my mouth, but when I had eaten it, my stomach turned sour. [11] Then I was told, "You must prophesy again about many peoples, nations, languages and kings."

The Two Witnesses

11 I was given a reed like a measuring rod and was told, "Go and measure the temple of God and the altar, with its worshipers. [2] But exclude the outer court; do not measure it, because it has been given to the Gentiles. They will trample on the holy city for 42 months. [3] And I will appoint my two witnesses, and they will prophesy for 1,260 days, clothed in sackcloth." [4] They are "the two olive trees" and the two lampstands, and "they stand before the Lord of the earth."[b] [5] If anyone tries to harm them, fire comes from their mouths and devours their enemies. This is how anyone who wants to harm them must die. [6] They have power to shut up the sky so that it will not rain during the time they are prophesying; and they have power to turn the waters into blood and to strike the earth with every kind of plague as often as they want.

[7] Now when they have finished their testimony, the beast that comes up from the Abyss will attack them, and overpower and kill them. [8] Their bodies will lie in the public square of the great city, which is figuratively called Sodom and Egypt, where also their Lord was crucified. [9] For three and a half days many from every people, tribe, language and nation will gaze on their bodies and refuse them burial. [10] The inhabitants of the earth will gloat over them and will celebrate by sending each other gifts, because these two prophets had tormented those who live on the earth.

[11] But after the three and a half days the breath[c] of life from God entered them, and they stood on their feet, and terror struck those who saw them. [12] Then they heard a loud voice from heaven saying to them, "Come up here." And they went up to heaven in a cloud, while their enemies looked on.

[13] At that very hour there was a severe earthquake and a tenth of the city collapsed. Seven thousand people were killed in the earthquake, and the survivors were terrified and gave glory to the God of heaven.

[14] The second woe has passed; the third woe is coming soon.

The Seventh Trumpet

[15] The seventh angel sounded his trumpet, and there were loud voices in heaven, which said:

> "The kingdom of the world has become
> the kingdom of our Lord and of his Messiah,
> and he will reign for ever and ever."

[a] *9* Ezek. 3:3   [b] *4* See Zech. 4:3,11,14.   [c] *11* Or *Spirit* (see Ezek. 37:5,14)

¹⁶ And the twenty-four elders, who were seated on their thrones before God, fell on their faces and worshiped God, ¹⁷ saying:

> "We give thanks to you, Lord God Almighty,
>   the One who is and who was,
> because you have taken your great power
>   and have begun to reign.
> ¹⁸ The nations were angry,
>   and your wrath has come.
> The time has come for judging the dead,
>   and for rewarding your servants the prophets
> and your people who revere your name,
>   both great and small—
> and for destroying those who destroy the earth."

¹⁹ Then God's temple in heaven was opened, and within his temple was seen the ark of his covenant. And there came flashes of lightning, rumblings, peals of thunder, an earthquake and a great hailstorm.

The Woman and the Dragon

12 A great and wondrous sign appeared in heaven: a woman clothed with the sun, with the moon under her feet and a crown of twelve stars on her head. ² She was pregnant and cried out in pain as she was about to give birth. ³ Then another sign appeared in heaven: an enormous red dragon with seven heads and ten horns and seven crowns on its heads. ⁴ Its tail swept a third of the stars out of the sky and flung them to the earth. The dragon stood in front of the woman who was about to give birth, so that it might devour her child the moment he was born. ⁵ She gave birth to a son, a male child, who "will rule all the nations with an iron scepter."ᵃ And her child was snatched up to God and to his throne. ⁶ The woman fled into the wilderness to a place prepared for her by God, where she might be taken care of for 1,260 days.

⁷ And there was war in heaven. Michael and his angels fought against the dragon, and the dragon and his angels fought back. ⁸ But he was not strong enough, and they lost their place in heaven. ⁹ The great dragon was hurled down—that ancient serpent called the devil, or Satan, who leads the whole world astray. He was hurled to the earth, and his angels with him.

¹⁰ Then I heard a loud voice in heaven say:

> "Now have come the salvation and the power
>   and the kingdom of our God,
>   and the authority of his Messiah.
> For the accuser of our brothers and sisters,
>   who accuses them before our God day and night,
>   has been hurled down.
> ¹¹ They triumphed over him
>   by the blood of the Lamb
>   and by the word of their testimony;
> they did not love their lives so much
>   as to shrink from death.
> ¹² Therefore rejoice, you heavens
>   and you who dwell in them!
> But woe to the earth and the sea,
>   because the devil has gone down to you!
> He is filled with fury,
>   because he knows that his time is short."

ᵃ 5 Psalm 2:9

[13]When the dragon saw that he had been hurled to the earth, he pursued the woman who had given birth to the male child. [14]The woman was given the two wings of a great eagle, so that she might fly to the place prepared for her in the wilderness, where she would be taken care of for a time, times and half a time, out of the serpent's reach. [15]Then from his mouth the serpent spewed water like a river, to overtake the woman and sweep her away with the torrent. [16]But the earth helped the woman by opening its mouth and swallowing the river that the dragon had spewed out of his mouth. [17]Then the dragon was enraged at the woman and went off to make war against the rest of her offspring—those who keep God's commands and hold fast their testimony about Jesus.

The Beast out of the Sea

13 The dragon[a] stood on the shore of the sea. And I saw a beast coming out of the sea. It had ten horns and seven heads, with ten crowns on its horns, and on each head a blasphemous name. [2]The beast I saw resembled a leopard, but had feet like those of a bear and a mouth like that of a lion. The dragon gave the beast his power and his throne and great authority. [3]One of the heads of the beast seemed to have had a fatal wound, but the fatal wound had been healed. The whole world was filled with wonder and followed the beast. [4]People worshiped the dragon because he had given authority to the beast, and they also worshiped the beast and asked, "Who is like the beast? Who can make war against it?"

[5]The beast was given a mouth to utter proud words and blasphemies and to exercise its authority for forty-two months. [6]It opened its mouth to blaspheme God, and to slander his name and his dwelling place and those who live in heaven. [7]It was given power to make war against God's people and to conquer them. And it was given authority over every tribe, people, language and nation. [8]All inhabitants of the earth will worship the beast—all whose names have not been written in the Lamb's book of life, the Lamb who was slain from the creation of the world.[b]

[9]Whoever has ears, let them hear.

> [10]"If anyone is to go into captivity,
>   into captivity they will go.
> If anyone is to be killed[c] with the sword,
>   with the sword they will be killed."[d]

This calls for patient endurance and faithfulness on the part of God's people.

The Beast out of the Earth

[11]Then I saw another beast, coming out of the earth. It had two horns like a lamb, but it spoke like a dragon. [12]It exercised all the authority of the first beast on its behalf, and made the earth and its inhabitants worship the first beast, whose fatal wound had been healed. [13]And it performed great signs, even causing fire to come down from heaven to the earth in full view of everyone. [14]Because of the signs it was given power to perform on behalf of the first beast, it deceived the inhabitants of the earth. It ordered them to set up an image in honor of the beast who was wounded by the sword and yet lived. [15]It was given power to give breath to the image of the first beast, so that it could speak and cause all who refused

1764

a t issue : sacrifice

12:17 Say you want a new pair of shoes. They're cute and comfortable and would look incredible with your favorite dress. But they're expensive. Are they worth it? To decide, you'd have to think through the cost and evaluate what you get for it. Let's consider now something infinitely more important: As Christians, we also have to consider the cost. Following Jesus *will* cost us something—perhaps a great deal of sacrifice and suffering. And we will have to decide, are keeping God's commands and holding on to our testimony about Jesus worth the cost?

---

[a] 1 Some manuscripts *And I*   [b] 8 Or *written from the creation of the world in the book of life belonging to the Lamb who was slain*   [c] 10 Some manuscripts *anyone kills*   [d] 10 Jer. 15:2

to worship the image to be killed. [16]It also forced all people, great and small, rich and poor, free and slave, to receive a mark on their right hands or on their foreheads, [17]so that they could not buy or sell unless they had the mark, which is the name of the beast or the number of its name.

[18]This calls for wisdom. Let those who have insight calculate the number of the beast, for it is the number of a man.[a] That number is 666.

The Lamb and the 144,000

14 Then I looked, and there before me was the Lamb, standing on Mount Zion, and with him 144,000 who had his name and his Father's name written on their foreheads. [2]And I heard a sound from heaven like the roar of rushing waters and like a loud peal of thunder. The sound I heard was like that of harpists playing their harps. [3]And they sang a new song before the throne and before the four living creatures and the elders. No one could learn the song except the 144,000 who had been redeemed from the earth. [4]These are those who did not defile themselves with women, for they remained virgins. They follow the Lamb wherever he goes. They were purchased from among the human race and offered as firstfruits to God and the Lamb. [5]No lie was found in their mouths; they are blameless.

The Three Angels

[6]Then I saw another angel flying in midair, and he had the eternal gospel to proclaim to those who live on the earth—to every nation, tribe, language and people. [7]He said in a loud voice, "Fear God and give him glory, because the hour of his judgment has come. Worship him who made the heavens, the earth, the sea and the springs of water."

[8]A second angel followed and said, "'Fallen! Fallen is Babylon the Great,'[b] which made all the nations drink the maddening wine of her adulteries."

[9]A third angel followed them and said in a loud voice: "If anyone worships the beast and its image and receives its mark on their forehead or on their hand, [10]they, too, will drink of the wine of God's fury, which has been poured full strength into the cup of his wrath. They will be tormented with burning sulfur in the presence of the holy angels and of the Lamb. [11]And the smoke of their torment will rise for ever and ever. There will be no rest day or night for those who worship the beast and its image, or for anyone who receives the mark of its name." [12]This calls for patient endurance on the part of the people of God who keep his commands and remain faithful to Jesus.

[13]Then I heard a voice from heaven say, "Write: Blessed are the dead who die in the Lord from now on."

"Yes," says the Spirit, "they will rest from their labor, for their deeds will follow them."

1765

conversations

patience «» 14:12

1 » What kind of patient endurance do you need to get through a day? Through a time of suffering?

2 » How patient are you with others when they are suffering?

3 » Have you experienced a time of trial because of your faith? Explain.

For more on **patience**, check the index.

Harvesting the Earth and Trampling the Winepress

[14]I looked, and there before me was a white cloud, and seated on the cloud was one like a son of man[c] with a crown of gold on his head and a sharp sickle in his hand. [15]Then another angel came out of the temple and called in a loud voice to him who was sitting on the cloud, "Take your sickle and reap, because the time to reap has come, for the harvest of the earth is ripe." [16]So he who was seated on the cloud swung his sickle over the earth, and the earth was harvested.

[17]Another angel came out of the temple in heaven, and he too had a sharp sickle. [18]Still another angel, who had charge of the fire, came from the altar and called in a loud voice to him who had the sharp sickle, "Take your sharp sickle and gather the clusters of grapes from the earth's vine, because its grapes are

---

[a] 18 Or is humanity's number   [b] 8 Isaiah 21:9   [c] 14 See Daniel 7:13.

ripe." ¹⁹The angel swung his sickle on the earth, gathered its grapes and threw them into the great wine-press of God's wrath. ²⁰They were trampled in the winepress outside the city, and blood flowed out of the press, rising as high as the horses' bridles for a distance of 1,600 stadia.ᵃ

Seven Angels With Seven Plagues

15 I saw in heaven another great and marvelous sign: seven angels with the seven last plagues—last, because with them God's wrath is completed. ²And I saw what looked like a sea of glass glowing with fire and, standing beside the sea, those who had been victorious over the beast and its image and over the number of its name. They held harps given them by God ³and sang the song of God's servant Moses and of the Lamb:

> "Great and marvelous are your deeds,
>   Lord God Almighty.
> Just and true are your ways,
>   King of the nations.ᵇ
> ⁴Who will not fear you, Lord,
>   and bring glory to your name?
> For you alone are holy.
> All nations will come
>   and worship before you,
> for your righteous acts have been revealed."ᶜ

⁵After this I looked, and I saw in heaven the temple—that is, the tabernacle of the covenant law—and it was opened. ⁶Out of the temple came the seven angels with the seven plagues. They were dressed in clean, shining linen and wore golden sashes around their chests. ⁷Then one of the four living creatures gave to the seven angels seven golden bowls filled with the wrath of God, who lives for ever and ever. ⁸And the temple was filled with smoke from the glory of God and from his power, and no one could enter the temple until the seven plagues of the seven angels were completed.

The Seven Bowls of God's Wrath

16 Then I heard a loud voice from the temple saying to the seven angels, "Go, pour out the seven bowls of God's wrath on the earth."

²The first angel went and poured out his bowl on the land, and ugly, festering sores broke out on the people who had the mark of the beast and worshiped its image.

³The second angel poured out his bowl on the sea, and it turned into blood like that of a dead person, and every living thing in the sea died.

⁴The third angel poured out his bowl on the rivers and springs of water, and they became blood. ⁵Then I heard the angel in charge of the waters say:

> "You are just in these judgments,
>   you who are and who were, the Holy One,
>   because you have so judged;
> ⁶for they have shed the blood of your people and your prophets,
>   and you have given them blood to drink as they deserve."

⁷And I heard the altar respond:

> "Yes, Lord God Almighty,
>   true and just are your judgments."

⁸The fourth angel poured out his bowl on the sun, and the sun was allowed to scorch people with fire. ⁹They were seared by the intense heat and they cursed the name of God, who had control over these plagues, but they refused to repent and glorify him.

ᵃ *20* That is, about 180 miles or about 300 kilometers   ᵇ *3* Some manuscripts *ages*   ᶜ *3,4* Phrases in this song are drawn from Psalm 111:2,3; Deut. 32:4; Jer. 10:7; Psalms 86:9; 98:2.

¹⁰The fifth angel poured out his bowl on the throne of the beast, and its kingdom was plunged into darkness. People gnawed their tongues in agony ¹¹and cursed the God of heaven because of their pains and their sores, but they refused to repent of what they had done.

¹²The sixth angel poured out his bowl on the great river Euphrates, and its water was dried up to prepare the way for the kings from the East. ¹³Then I saw three evil*ᵃ* spirits that looked like frogs; they came out of the mouth of the dragon, out of the mouth of the beast and out of the mouth of the false prophet. ¹⁴They are demonic spirits that perform signs, and they go out to the kings of the whole world, to gather them for the battle on the great day of God Almighty.

¹⁵"Look, I come like a thief! Blessed are those who stay awake and keep their clothes on, so that they may not go naked and be shamefully exposed."

¹⁶Then they gathered the kings together to the place that in Hebrew is called Armageddon.

¹⁷The seventh angel poured out his bowl into the air, and out of the temple came a loud voice from the throne, saying, "It is done!" ¹⁸Then there came flashes of lightning, rumblings, peals of thunder and a severe earthquake. No earthquake like it has ever occurred since the human race has been on earth, so tremendous was the quake. ¹⁹The great city split into three parts, and the cities of the nations collapsed. God remembered Babylon the Great and gave her the cup filled with the wine of the fury of his wrath. ²⁰Every island fled away and the mountains could not be found. ²¹From the sky huge hailstones, each weighing about a hundred pounds,*ᵇ* fell on people. And they cursed God on account of the plague of hail, because the plague was so terrible.

1767

Babylon, the Prostitute on the Beast

17 One of the seven angels who had the seven bowls came and said to me, "Come, I will show you the punishment of the great prostitute, who sits by many waters. ²With her the kings of the earth committed adultery, and the inhabitants of the earth were intoxicated with the wine of her adulteries."

³Then the angel carried me away in the Spirit into a wilderness. There I saw a woman sitting on a scarlet beast that was covered with blasphemous names and had seven heads and ten horns. ⁴The woman was dressed in purple and scarlet, and was glittering with gold, precious stones and pearls. She held a golden cup in her hand, filled with abominable things and the filth of her adulteries. ⁵This title was written on her forehead:

MYSTERY

BABYLON THE GREAT

THE MOTHER OF PROSTITUTES

AND OF THE ABOMINATIONS OF THE EARTH.

⁶I saw that the woman was drunk with the blood of God's people, the blood of those who bore testimony to Jesus.

When I saw her, I was greatly astonished. ⁷Then the angel said to me: "Why are you astonished? I will explain to you the mystery of the woman and of the beast she rides, which has the seven heads and ten horns. ⁸The beast, which you saw, once was, now is not, and will come up out of the Abyss and go to its destruction. The inhabitants of the earth whose names have not been written in the book of life from the creation of the world will be astonished when they see the beast, because it once was, now is not, and yet will come.

⁹"This calls for a mind with wisdom. The seven heads are seven hills on which the woman sits. ¹⁰They are also seven kings. Five have fallen, one is, the other has not yet come; but when he does come, he must remain for a little while. ¹¹The beast who once was, and now is not, is an eighth king. He belongs to the seven and is going to his destruction.

¹²"The ten horns you saw are ten kings who have not yet received a kingdom, but who for one hour will receive authority as kings along with the beast. ¹³They have one purpose and will give their power and authority to the beast. ¹⁴They will make war against the Lamb, but the Lamb will triumph over them

---

ᵃ 13 Greek *unclean*   *ᵇ 21* Or *about 40 kilograms*

because he is Lord of lords and King of kings—and with him will be his called, chosen and faithful followers."

¹⁵Then the angel said to me, "The waters you saw, where the prostitute sits, are peoples, multitudes, nations and languages. ¹⁶The beast and the ten horns you saw will hate the prostitute. They will bring her to ruin and leave her naked; they will eat her flesh and burn her with fire. ¹⁷For God has put it into their hearts to accomplish his purpose by agreeing to give the beast their power to rule, until God's words are fulfilled. ¹⁸The woman you saw is the great city that rules over the kings of the earth."

Lament Over Fallen Babylon

18 After this I saw another angel coming down from heaven. He had great authority, and the earth was illuminated by his splendor. ²With a mighty voice he shouted:

> "'Fallen! Fallen is Babylon the Great!'*ᵃ*
>   She has become a dwelling for demons
> and a haunt for every evil*ᵇ* spirit,
>   a haunt for every unclean bird,
>   a haunt for every unclean and detestable animal.
> ³For all the nations have drunk
>   the maddening wine of her adulteries.
> The kings of the earth committed adultery with her,
>   and the merchants of the earth grew rich from her excessive luxuries."

Warning to Escape Babylon's Judgment

⁴Then I heard another voice from heaven say:

> "'Come out of her, my people,'*ᶜ*
>   so that you will not share in her sins,
>   so that you will not receive any of her plagues;
> ⁵for her sins are piled up to heaven,
>   and God has remembered her crimes.
> ⁶Give back to her as she has given;
>   pay her back double for what she has done.
>   Pour her a double portion from her own cup.
> ⁷Give her as much torment and grief
>   as the glory and luxury she gave herself.
> In her heart she boasts,
>   'I sit enthroned as queen.
> I am not a widow;*ᵈ*
>   I will never mourn.'
> ⁸Therefore in one day her plagues will overtake her:
>   death, mourning and famine.
> She will be consumed by fire,
>   for mighty is the Lord God who judges her.

Threefold Woe Over Babylon's Fall

⁹"When the kings of the earth who committed adultery with her and shared her luxury see the smoke of her burning, they will weep and mourn over her. ¹⁰Terrified at her torment, they will stand far off and cry:

> "'Woe! Woe to you, great city,
>   you mighty city of Babylon!
> In one hour your doom has come!'

ᵃ 2 Isaiah 21:9   *ᵇ* 2 Greek *unclean*   *ᶜ* 4 Jer. 51:45   *ᵈ* 7 See Isaiah 47:7,8.

1768

¹¹"The merchants of the earth will weep and mourn over her because no one buys their cargoes anymore— ¹²cargoes of gold, silver, precious stones and pearls; fine linen, purple, silk and scarlet cloth; every sort of citron wood, and articles of every kind made of ivory, costly wood, bronze, iron and marble; ¹³cargoes of cinnamon and spice, of incense, myrrh and frankincense, of wine and olive oil, of fine flour and wheat; cattle and sheep; horses and carriages; and human beings sold as slaves.

¹⁴"They will say, 'The fruit you longed for is gone from you. All your luxury and splendor have vanished, never to be recovered.' ¹⁵The merchants who sold these things and gained their wealth from her will stand far off, terrified at her torment. They will weep and mourn ¹⁶and cry out:

> "'Woe! Woe to you, great city,
>> dressed in fine linen, purple and scarlet,
>> and glittering with gold, precious stones and pearls!
> ¹⁷In one hour such great wealth has been brought to ruin!'

"Every sea captain, and all who travel by ship, the sailors, and all who earn their living from the sea, will stand far off. ¹⁸When they see the smoke of her burning, they will exclaim, 'Was there ever a city like this great city?' ¹⁹They will throw dust on their heads, and with weeping and mourning cry out:

> "'Woe! Woe to you, great city,
>> where all who had ships on the sea
>> became rich through her wealth!
> In one hour she has been brought to ruin!'

> ²⁰"Rejoice over her, you heavens!
>> Rejoice, you people of God!
>> Rejoice, apostles and prophets!
> For God has judged her
>> with the judgment she imposed on you."

The Finality of Babylon's Doom

²¹Then a mighty angel picked up a boulder the size of a large millstone and threw it into the sea, and said:

> "With such violence
>> the great city of Babylon will be thrown down,
>> never to be found again.
> ²²The music of harpists and musicians, pipers and trumpeters,
>> will never be heard in you again.
> No worker of any trade
>> will ever be found in you again.
> The sound of a millstone
>> will never be heard in you again.
> ²³The light of a lamp
>> will never shine in you again.
> The voice of bridegroom and bride
>> will never be heard in you again.
> Your merchants were the world's important people.
>> By your magic spell all the nations were led astray.
> ²⁴In her was found the blood of prophets and of God's people,
>> of all who have been slaughtered on the earth."

Threefold Hallelujah Over Babylon's Fall

19 After this I heard what sounded like the roar of a great multitude in heaven shouting:

> "Hallelujah!
> Salvation and glory and power belong to our God,

1769

² for true and just are his judgments.
He has condemned the great prostitute
who corrupted the earth by her adulteries.
He has avenged on her the blood of his servants."

³And again they shouted:

"Hallelujah!
The smoke from her goes up for ever and ever."

⁴The twenty-four elders and the four living creatures fell down and worshiped God, who was seated on the throne. And they cried:

"Amen, Hallelujah!"

⁵Then a voice came from the throne, saying:

"Praise our God,
all you his servants,
you who fear him,
both great and small!"

⁶Then I heard what sounded like a great multitude, like the roar of rushing waters and like loud peals of thunder, shouting:

"Hallelujah!
For our Lord God Almighty reigns.
⁷Let us rejoice and be glad
and give him glory!
For the wedding of the Lamb has come,
and his bride has made herself ready.
⁸Fine linen, bright and clean,
was given her to wear."

(Fine linen stands for the righteous acts of God's people.)

⁹Then the angel said to me, "Write: 'Blessed are those who are invited to the wedding supper of the Lamb!'" And he added, "These are the true words of God."

¹⁰At this I fell at his feet to worship him. But he said to me, "Don't do that! I am a fellow servant with you and with your brothers and sisters who hold to Jesus' testimony. Worship God! For the testimony of Jesus is the Spirit of prophecy."

The Heavenly Warrior Defeats the Beast

¹¹I saw heaven standing open and there before me was a white horse, whose rider is called Faithful and True. With justice he judges and makes war. ¹²His eyes are like blazing fire, and on his head are many crowns. He has a name written on him that no one knows but he himself. ¹³He is dressed in a robe dipped in blood, and his name is the Word of God. ¹⁴The armies of heaven were following him, riding on white horses and dressed in fine linen, white and clean. ¹⁵Coming out of his mouth is a sharp sword with which to strike down the nations. "He will rule them with an iron scepter."ᵃ He treads the winepress of the fury of the wrath of God Almighty. ¹⁶On his robe and on his thigh he has this name written:

KING OF KINGS AND LORD OF LORDS.

¹⁷And I saw an angel standing in the sun, who cried in a loud voice to all the birds flying in midair, "Come, gather together for the great supper of God, ¹⁸so that you may eat the flesh of kings, generals, and the mighty, of horses and their riders, and the flesh of all people, free and slave, great and small."

ᵃ 15 Psalm 2:9

¹⁹Then I saw the beast and the kings of the earth and their armies gathered together to make war against the rider on the horse and his army. ²⁰But the beast was captured, and with him the false prophet who had performed the signs on his behalf. With these signs he had deluded those who had received the mark of the beast and worshiped his image. The two of them were thrown alive into the fiery lake of burning sulfur. ²¹The rest were killed with the sword coming out of the mouth of the rider on the horse, and all the birds gorged themselves on their flesh.

The Thousand Years

20 And I saw an angel coming down out of heaven, having the key to the Abyss and holding in his hand a great chain. ²He seized the dragon, that ancient serpent, who is the devil, or Satan, and bound him for a thousand years. ³He threw him into the Abyss, and locked and sealed it over him, to keep him from deceiving the nations anymore until the thousand years were ended. After that, he must be set free for a short time.

⁴I saw thrones on which were seated those who had been given authority to judge. And I saw the souls of those who had been beheaded because of their testimony about Jesus and because of the word of God. They had not worshiped the beast or his image and had not received his mark on their foreheads or their hands. They came to life and reigned with Christ a thousand years. ⁵(The rest of the dead did not come to life until the thousand years were ended.) This is the first resurrection. ⁶Blessed and holy are those who have part in the first resurrection. The second death has no power over them, but they will be priests of God and of Christ and will reign with him for a thousand years.

The Judgment of Satan

⁷When the thousand years are over, Satan will be released from his prison ⁸and will go out to deceive the nations in the four corners of the earth—Gog and Magog—and to gather them for battle. In number they are like the sand on the seashore. ⁹They marched across the breadth of the earth and surrounded the camp of God's people, the city he loves. But fire came down from heaven and devoured them. ¹⁰And the devil, who deceived them, was thrown into the lake of burning sulfur, where the beast and the false prophet had been thrown. They will be tormented day and night for ever and ever.

The Judgment of the Dead

¹¹Then I saw a great white throne and him who was seated on it. The earth and the heavens fled from his presence, and there was no place for them. ¹²And I saw the dead, great and small, standing before the throne, and books were opened. Another book was opened, which is the book of life. The dead were judged according to what they had done as recorded in the books. ¹³The sea gave up the dead that were in it, and death and Hades gave up the dead that were in them, and everyone was judged according to what they had done. ¹⁴Then death and Hades were thrown into the lake of fire. The lake of fire is the second death. ¹⁵All whose names were not found written in the book of life were thrown into the lake of fire.

A New Heaven and a New Earth

21 Then I saw "a new heaven and a new earth,"^a for the first heaven and the first earth had passed away, and there was no longer any sea. ²I saw the Holy City, the new Jerusalem, coming down out of heaven from God, prepared as a bride beautifully dressed for her husband. ³And I heard a loud voice from the throne saying, "Look! God's dwelling place is now among the people, and he will dwell with them. They will be his people, and God himself will be with them and be their God. ⁴He will wipe every tear from their eyes. There will be no more death'^b or mourning or crying or pain, for the old order of things has passed away."

⁵He who was seated on the throne said, "I am making everything new!" Then he said, "Write this down, for these words are trustworthy and true."

⁶He said to me: "It is done. I am the Alpha and the Omega, the Beginning and the End. To the thirsty I will give water without cost from the spring of the water of life. ⁷Those who are victorious will inherit all this, and I will be their God and they will be my children. ⁸But the cowardly, the unbelieving, the vile,

^a 1 Isaiah 65:17   ^b 4 Isaiah 25:8

the murderers, the sexually immoral, those who practice magic arts, the idolaters and all liars—they will be consigned to the fiery lake of burning sulfur. This is the second death."

The New Jerusalem, the Bride of the Lamb

[9] One of the seven angels who had the seven bowls full of the seven last plagues came and said to me, "Come, I will show you the bride, the wife of the Lamb." [10] And he carried me away in the Spirit to a mountain great and high, and showed me the Holy City, Jerusalem, coming down out of heaven from God. [11] It shone with the glory of God, and its brilliance was like that of a very precious jewel, like a jasper, clear as crystal. [12] It had a great, high wall with twelve gates, and with twelve angels at the gates. On the gates were written the names of the twelve tribes of Israel. [13] There were three gates on the east, three on the north, three on the south and three on the west. [14] The wall of the city had twelve foundations, and on them were the names of the twelve apostles of the Lamb.

[15] The angel who talked with me had a measuring rod of gold to measure the city, its gates and its walls. [16] The city was laid out like a square, as long as it was wide. He measured the city with the rod and found it to be 12,000 stadia[a] in length, and as wide and high as it is long. [17] He measured its wall and it was 144 cubits[b] thick,[c] by human measurement, which the angel was using. [18] The wall was made of jasper, and the city of pure gold, as pure as glass. [19] The foundations of the city walls were decorated with every kind of precious stone. The first foundation was jasper, the second sapphire, the third agate, the fourth emerald, [20] the fifth onyx, the sixth ruby, the seventh chrysolite, the eighth beryl, the ninth topaz, the tenth turquoise, the eleventh jacinth, and the twelfth amethyst.[d] [21] The twelve gates were twelve pearls, each gate made of a single pearl. The great street of the city was of gold, as pure as transparent glass.

[22] I did not see a temple in the city, because the Lord God Almighty and the Lamb are its temple. [23] The city does not need the sun or the moon to shine on it, for the glory of God gives it light, and the Lamb is its lamp. [24] The nations will walk by its light, and the kings of the earth will bring their splendor into it. [25] On no day will its gates ever be shut, for there will be no night there. [26] The glory and honor of the nations will be brought into it. [27] Nothing impure will ever enter it, nor will anyone who does what is shameful or deceitful, but only those whose names are written in the Lamb's book of life.

Eden Restored

22 Then the angel showed me the river of the water of life, as clear as crystal, flowing from the throne of God and of the Lamb [2] down the middle of the great street of the city. On each side of the river stood the tree of life, bearing twelve crops of fruit, yielding its fruit every month. And the leaves of the tree are for the healing of the nations. [3] No longer will there be any curse. The throne of God and of the Lamb will be in the city, and his servants will serve him. [4] They will see his face, and his name will be on their foreheads. [5] There will be no more night. They will not need the light of a lamp or the light of the sun, for the Lord God will give them light. And they will reign for ever and ever.

John and the Angel

[6] The angel said to me, "These words are trustworthy and true. The Lord, the God who inspires the prophets, sent his angel to show his servants the things that must soon take place."

1772

a tissue:your future

21:1–27 Although it defies imagination, try anyway. Read this chapter and try to imagine what John describes: A place where God will live with us and we'll know him fully. No death or pain. This tired old world will be gone, and everything will be fresh and new. The thirst of your soul quenched. A glorious home. When the pain of life overwhelms you, find hope in these truths about your future and what God has in store for you. And remember that life on earth—even at its best—can't begin to compare with the glory of what waits for you in heaven.

---

[a] *16* That is, about 1,400 miles or about 2,200 kilometers   [b] *17* That is, about 200 feet or about 65 meters   [c] *17* Or *high*   [d] *20* The precise identification of some of these precious stones is uncertain.

[7]"Look, I am coming soon! Blessed are those who keep the words of the prophecy in this scroll."

[8]I, John, am the one who heard and saw these things. And when I had heard and seen them, I fell down to worship at the feet of the angel who had been showing them to me. [9]But he said to me, "Don't do that! I am a fellow servant with you and with your fellow prophets and with all who keep the words of this scroll. Worship God!"

[10]Then he told me, "Do not seal up the words of the prophecy of this scroll, because the time is near. [11]Let those who do wrong continue to do wrong; let those who are vile continue to be vile; let those who do right continue to do right; and let those who are holy continue to be holy."

Epilogue: Invitation and Warning

[12]"Look, I am coming soon! My reward is with me, and I will give to everyone according to what they have done. [13]I am the Alpha and the Omega, the First and the Last, the Beginning and the End.

[14]"Blessed are those who wash their robes, that they may have the right to the tree of life and may go through the gates into the city. [15]Outside are the dogs, those who practice magic arts, the sexually immoral, the murderers, the idolaters and everyone who loves and practices falsehood.

[16]"I, Jesus, have sent my angel to give you[a] this testimony for the churches. I am the Root and the Offspring of David, and the bright Morning Star."

[17]The Spirit and the bride say, "Come!" And let those who hear say, "Come!" Let those who are thirsty come; and let all who wish take the free gift of the water of life.

[18]I warn everyone who hears the words of the prophecy of this scroll: If anyone of you adds anything to them, God will add to you the plagues described in this scroll. [19]And if anyone of you takes words away from this scroll of prophecy, God will take away from you your share in the tree of life and in the Holy City, which are described in this scroll.

[20]He who testifies to these things says, "Yes, I am coming soon."

Amen. Come, Lord Jesus.

[21]The grace of the Lord Jesus be with God's people. Amen.

HE IS: coming soon

22:20–21 John saw horrible visions of the future—dreadful plagues, cosmic disturbances, vicious wars and an evil ruler. The greatest comfort in the midst of these horrendous predictions was Christ's simple promise: "Yes, I am *coming soon.*"

Though "soon" may feel relatively far-off and safe to you, it's nearer than you think. Are you ready for Christ's return? Are you right with God? Is your life pleasing to him? Have you told others in your life the Good News about Jesus? He is *coming soon!* If you are ready for his return, then let this be your prayer of comfort: "Come, Lord Jesus!"

appendix I

TABLE OF
WEIGHTS AND MEASURES

	BIBLICAL UNIT	APPROXIMATE AMERICAN EQUIVALENT	APPROXIMATE METRIC EQUIVALENT
WEIGHTS	talent (60 minas)	75 pounds	34 kilograms
	mina (50 shekels)	1¹/₄ pounds	0.6 kilogram
	shekel (2 bekas)	²/₅ ounce	11.5 grams
	pim (²/₃ shekel)	¹/₃ ounce	9.5 grams
	beka (10 gerahs)	¹/₅ ounce	5.5 grams
	gerah	¹/₅₀ ounce	0.6 gram
LENGTH	cubit	18 inches	0.5 meter
	span	9 inches	23 centimeters
	handbreadth	3 inches	8 centimeters
CAPACITY *Dry Measure*	cor [homer] (10 ephahs)	6 bushels	220 liters
	lethek (5 ephahs)	3 bushels	110 liters
	ephah (10 omers)	³/₅ bushel	22 liters
	seah (¹/₃ ephah)	7 quarts	7.7 liters
	omer (¹/₁₀ ephah)	2 quarts	2 liters
	cab (¹/₁₈ ephah)	1 quart	1 liter
Liquid Measure	bath (1 ephah)	6 gallons	22 liters
	hin (¹/₆ bath)	4 quarts	4 liters
	log (¹/₇₂ bath)	¹/₃ quart	0.3 liter

The figures of the table are calculated on the basis of a shekel equaling 11.5 grams, a cubit equaling 18 inches and an ephah equaling 22 liters. The quart referred to is either a dry quart (slightly larger than a liter) or a liquid quart (slightly smaller than a liter), whichever is applicable. The ton referred to in the footnotes is the American ton of 2,000 pounds. Since most readers are more familiar with dry measures being given in weight rather than capacity (bushel, quart), dry measures have been converted in the footnotes to approximate weights.

This table is based upon the best available information, but it is not intended to be mathematically precise; like the measurement equivalents in the footnotes, it merely gives approximate amounts and distances. Weights and measures differed somewhat at various times and places in the ancient world. There is uncertainty particularly about the ephah and the bath; further discoveries may shed more light on these units of capacity.

appendix II
revised spelling of proper names

1775

revised spelling of proper names

1776

contents

subject index

This subject index will help you find information about a particular topic. Look through the list; you'll probably find something you want to read about!

subject index

1781

subject index

1783

subject index

1784

subject index

subject index

reading
plans

reading plans

60-day overview of the Bible

1790

1791

30 days with Jesus

Day	Description	Passage
1	Jesus' coming is predicted.	Isaiah 7:14; 9:1–9; Luke 1:26–38
2	Jesus is born.	Matthew 1:18—2:23; Luke 2:1–20
3	Jesus is baptized by John the Baptist.	Matthew 3:1–17
4	Jesus begins his public ministry.	Matthew 4:1–17; Luke 4:14–44
5	Jesus calls his disciples.	Luke 5:1–11; 6:12–16; John 1:35–51
6	Jesus talks to a Pharisee and a Samaritan.	John 3:1—4:42
7	Jesus delivers the Sermon on the Mount.	Matthew 5:1—7:29
8	Jesus heals people in need.	Matthew 8:1—9:8
9	Jesus tangles with the Pharisees.	Matthew 12:1–45
10	Jesus teaches his disciples using parables.	Matthew 13:1–52
11	Jesus demonstrates his power over nature.	Mark 6:45–52; Luke 8:22–25
12	Jesus heals many.	Mark 5:1–43
13	Jesus feeds 5,000 followers.	John 6:1–15
14	Jesus is identified as the Christ.	Matthew 16:13—17:13
15	Jesus casts out an evil spirit.	Mark 9:14–32
16	Jesus teaches on forgiveness.	Matthew 18:15–35
17	Jesus teaches on the kingdom of heaven.	Matthew 13:24–52
18	Jesus confronts the rich young man.	Mark 10:17–31
19	Jesus sends out his disciples.	Luke 10:1–24
20	Jesus teaches how to love and pray.	Luke 10:25—11:13
21	Jesus teaches about himself.	John 10:1–42
22	Jesus raises Lazarus from the dead.	John 11:1–44
23	Jesus travels to Jerusalem.	Matthew 21:1–27
24	Jesus eats the Last Supper.	Matthew 26:17–30; John 13:1–17
25	Jesus comforts his disciples.	John 14:1—16:33
26	Jesus is arrested.	Matthew 26:36–75
27	Jesus is put on trial.	John 18:19—19:16
28	Jesus is crucified and buried.	John 19:17–42
29	Jesus rises from the dead.	John 20:1—21:25
30	Jesus ascends to heaven.	Matthew 28:16–20; Luke 24:36–53

30 days of "ask me anything"

meet the women of the Bible

Day	Meet	Passage
1	Eve	Genesis 2:19—4:2
2	Sarah	Genesis 12:1–9; 17:15—18:15; 21:1–7
3	Hagar	Genesis 16:1–16
4	Lot's wife	Genesis 19:1–26
5	Rebekah	Genesis 24:1–67
6	Leah	Genesis 29:1–35
7	Rachel	Genesis 29:14—30:24; 35:16–20
8	Miriam	Exodus 2:1–10; 15:19–21; Numbers 12:1–15
9	Rahab	Joshua 2:1–24
10	Deborah	Judges 4:1—5:31
11	Naomi	Ruth 1:1—4:22
12	Ruth	Ruth 1:1—4:22
13	Hannah	1 Samuel 1:1—2:11
14	Abigail	1 Samuel 25:1–44
15	Michal	2 Samuel 6:1–23
16	Bathsheba	2 Samuel 11:1–27
17	Tamar	2 Samuel 13:1–22
18	Queen of Sheba	1 Kings 10:1–13; 2 Chronicles 9:1–12
19	Esther	Esther 2:1–18; 4:1–17; 7:1–10
20	Job's wife	Job 1:1—2:10
21	Gomer	Hosea 1:1–11; 3:1–5
22	Salome	Matthew 27:55–56; Mark 15:40—16:8
23	Mary Magdalene	Luke 8:1–3; John 19:25; 20:1–18
24	Elizabeth	Luke 1:5–80
25	Mary, Jesus' mother	Luke 1:26–56; 2:1–20
26	Anna	Luke 2:36–38
27	Martha	Luke 10:38–42; John 11:1–44
28	The Samaritan woman	John 4:4–42
29	Sapphira	Acts 5:1–10
30	Eunice	Acts 16:1; 2 Timothy 1:5

30 days of "conversations"

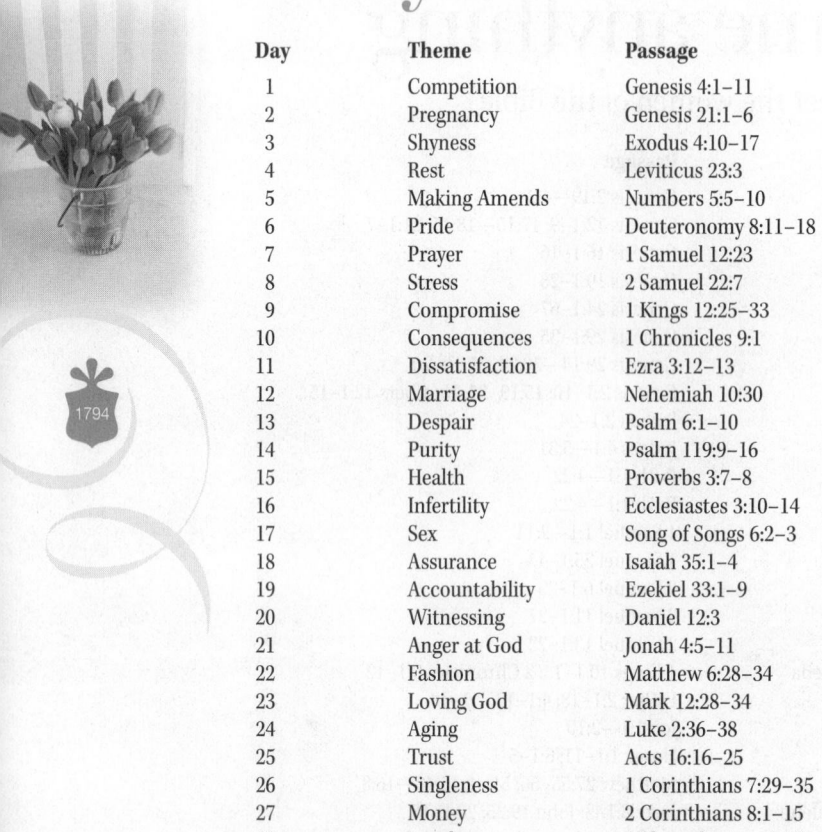

Day	Theme	Passage
1	Competition	Genesis 4:1–11
2	Pregnancy	Genesis 21:1–6
3	Shyness	Exodus 4:10–17
4	Rest	Leviticus 23:3
5	Making Amends	Numbers 5:5–10
6	Pride	Deuteronomy 8:11–18
7	Prayer	1 Samuel 12:23
8	Stress	2 Samuel 22:7
9	Compromise	1 Kings 12:25–33
10	Consequences	1 Chronicles 9:1
11	Dissatisfaction	Ezra 3:12–13
12	Marriage	Nehemiah 10:30
13	Despair	Psalm 6:1–10
14	Purity	Psalm 119:9–16
15	Health	Proverbs 3:7–8
16	Infertility	Ecclesiastes 3:10–14
17	Sex	Song of Songs 6:2–3
18	Assurance	Isaiah 35:1–4
19	Accountability	Ezekiel 33:1–9
20	Witnessing	Daniel 12:3
21	Anger at God	Jonah 4:5–11
22	Fashion	Matthew 6:28–34
23	Loving God	Mark 12:28–34
24	Aging	Luke 2:36–38
25	Trust	Acts 16:16–25
26	Singleness	1 Corinthians 7:29–35
27	Money	2 Corinthians 8:1–15
28	Loyalty	2 Thessalonians 2:15
29	Discernment	2 Timothy 3:1–9
30	Patience	Revelation 13:10; 14:12

30 days of "he is"

getting to know God

Day	Title	Passage
1	He Is: Creator	Genesis 1:1
2	He Is: All-Powerful	Exodus 8:19
3	He Is: The Purifier	Leviticus 16:29–30
4	He Is: The Appointer	Numbers 3:5–10
5	He Is: Encouraging	Deuteronomy 31:6
6	He Is: Unbiased	Judges 11:1–29
7	He Is: The Secret Weapon	1 Samuel 17:45–47
8	He Is: Approachable	2 Samuel 21:1
9	He Is: Uncontainable	1 Kings 8:27–30
10	He Is: Worthy of Praise	1 Chronicles 16:34
11	He Is: Unifying	2 Chronicles 5:13–14
12	He Is: My Friend	Job 16:18–27
13	He Is: My Shepherd	Psalm 23:1–6
14	He Is: Worth Considering	Psalm 77:12–13
15	He Is: A Fountain of Life	Proverbs 14:26–27
16	He Is: Listening	Ecclesiastes 5:4–7
17	He Is: My Everything	Isaiah 9:6–7
18	He Is: Vindicating	Jeremiah 51:1–10
19	He Is: High Above	Ezekiel 1:26–28
20	He Is: The Ancient of Days	Daniel 7:9–10
21	He Is: Slow to Anger	Nahum 1:2–3
22	He Is: God with Us	Matthew 1:22–23
23	He Is: The Messiah	Mark 8:27–29
24	He Is: The Resurrection and the Life	John 11:17–27
25	He Is: Not Exclusive	Acts 11:1–18
26	He Is: Testing Your Work	1 Corinthians 3:10–15
27	He Is: In Me	Galatians 2:20
28	He Is: In Control	Philippians 3:19–21
29	He Is: Death's Destroyer	2 Timothy 1:8–10
30	He Is: The Alpha and the Omega	Revelations 1:8

articles

table for two

Enjoying Intimacy With God

For many of us, having consistent time with God is a noble but elusive goal. We race through life, busy with our work, relationships, volunteering, while our spiritual life is often at the bottom of our to-do lists. We picture quiet time with God as an unavoidable duty, a mandatory time-out, a failed assignment, a ritual, even an impossible task. The magic formula—pray, read, journal, repeat—seems easy enough. But we settle for hit or miss, emphasis on *miss*.

Yet God invites you to enjoy intimacy with him every day. The heaven-sent invitation reads simply, "Come to me" (see Matthew 11:28). Even if you are spiritually starving and seriously underdressed, God nevertheless beckons you to an elegant, reserved table for two. This is a place where you can settle into your chair late and bedraggled and still hear, "Welcome! I'm so glad you're here."

If you're ready to accept God's invitation, remember the following:

- **Today.** That's all you can focus on. You can have time with God *today*. Don't make empty promises about tomorrow's faithfulness. Today's faithfulness gives you a good chance for tomorrow's success.

- **Packing light.** Bring your Bible, a pen, a journal and a cup of coffee. Don't feel obligated to lug around a dense commentary or a dozen extra resources.

- **Ambience.** Choose a quiet spot. If possible, meet God in the same special place each time—make it *your* spot. Find out what time of day is most conducive to your getting away.

- **Writing.** Journal your prayers and note God's provisions with specific dates. Record what you're learning in the Bible and look for common themes. Look back at what you've written so that you can thank him for his faithfulness.

- **Short accounts.** If you miss a day (or two or three), don't quit coming altogether. Don't allow yourself to get stuck on feeling guilty.

- **Fasting.** Fasting brings focus to your time together and a heightened sensitivity to what your dinner Companion is saying.

- **Timing.** Sometimes the table for two is set for a long, enjoyable meal. Sometimes there are to-go boxes waiting. Some of your times together are more meaningful than others—not every day is a spiritual high. God, aware of your season of life, honors your time together regardless of its length.

six degrees of separation

You May Be Closer to Encouraging Others Than You Realize

You may have heard that every person in the world is separated from anyone else by no more than six degrees of separation—six friends of friends of friends. The point is that we are all more connected than we realize.

When it comes to mentoring, it's all about discovering those connections. When you begin to look intentionally for connections with others (not necessarily friends of friends, but universal experiences you may share with another person, such as dealing with depression or loneliness, making choices about a career, or striving for personal fulfillment), you'll realize you have much in common. In any given conversation, relationship or scenario, you are only a few degrees away from an opportunity to influence another person. *If only you'll be intentional.*

Consider the following creative twists on living a life of influence wherever you go.

- **Inventory your life experiences.** You don't have to dig too deep into your basic life experiences to find something that could benefit another person. Have you ever applied for a job? Many single mothers are doing this for the first time and would appreciate hearing about your experiences. Have you graduated from college? Many young women need someone to walk them through the application process. On a deeper level, have you experienced infertility or infidelity? Marital difficulties or miscarriages? Bankruptcy or breast cancer? Many women undergoing the same things would cherish hearing from someone who has already been there. Let your pastor know your willingness to talk about these subjects with other women.

- **E-mail.** Many informal mentoring relationships take place over the phone or in e-mail conversations. Your goal is to establish a spiritual or emotional touchpoint with another woman. For example, as a mother of teenagers, you may have noticed a mother with toddlers in your church. Remember how stressful that time was, and offer to e-mail her encouraging verses once a week. Building on that, you may call her once a week to talk about pediatricians, discipline, etc.

- **Use your personal testimony.** You don't have to sit down for an hour with someone in order to share your testimony. Instead, share with someone you see on a regular basis—your hair stylist, grocery clerk or UPS driver—and simply make a comment or two that incorporates part of your testimony. Strike up a conversation, and share how your experiences relate. "So you're stressed about your work schedule? I was stressed at work, too, but I found a way to deal with it that really works." The next time you see that person, pick up where you last left off.

- **Offer to pray.** Look for those who are hurting. Every person you meet is fighting a battle of some kind. She may be sitting beside you on the bus or alone at church. Simply say, "I noticed you seemed [sad, lonely, upset, etc.]. May I pray for you this week?" You don't have to pray right then and there, but take the initiative—it may be a divine appointment.

mentoring
101

What are women looking for in a mentor today?

A friend. Authenticity. A relationship based on grace. Help in how to be a better wife, daughter, friend, mother, co-worker. Guidance on time management. Practical advice on how to study the Bible.

Titus 2:3–5 tells us that mentoring is how life skills are passed down generation to generation. It allows a woman who might not have learned life skills from her family of origin to acquire them through the body of Christ.

Does every woman need a mentor?

Every woman would benefit from a mentor. Most women have at least one mentor, whether they recognizes it as a mentor relationship or not. As relational beings, we seek input and affirmation from other women in our lives. We may admire a woman's marriage and want to know her "secret." Or we may value someone's feedback on a particular problem and seek her advice in a crisis.

How do I know if I'm ready to be a mentor?

If you are a Christian, then you are ready. The question is not, "Am I ready?" The question is, "Who around me is ready to be mentored?" A mentor only has to be one step ahead of the mentee, not a seminary graduate or an expert on life.

How do I start mentoring?

First, tell God your desire to mentor. Then inform your pastor that you are available to mentor another woman. God will show you who—the women you will end up mentoring are most likely already in your life.

Start where your passions are. If your passion is praying, you can meet to pray with someone. If your passion is sharing what you're learning in the Bible, you may consider doing a study with another woman.

Why is mentoring so powerful?

Studies have scientifically proven the value of relationships between women. An actual therapeutic, biochemical change occurs when women talk together. Their stress and adrenaline decrease and healthy hormones increase. Women relax in the presence of other women.

Make yourself available to encourage and walk beside another woman. You can make a life-changing difference in another woman's life.

your most powerful possession

Using Your Personal Testimony to Touch Others

"Always be prepared to give an answer to everyone who asks you to give the reason for the hope that you have" (1 Peter 3:15).

How many opportunities have you missed because you were unprepared or unwilling to share your faith? For many people, the answer is "too many."

The most powerful evangelistic tool you have is within your grasp. It's not a seminary degree—it's your personal testimony. Why? Because *you* are the expert on what happened in your life. People may debate the reliability of the Bible, but they cannot refute your personal experience. Your testimony can be a spiritual tie-in at any point in a conversation. But you must be prepared. You should be able to tell your testimony in a short version (less than one minute) and in a longer version (three minutes max).

There are three parts to a personal testimony:

- *Life before Christ.* Choose a descriptive word for your life before Christ. If you were a child when you became a Christian, think how your life might have turned out without Christ. Your word might be *empty, boring* or *purposeless.*

- *How you became a Christian.* Where were you? (At church, at camp, at home?) How did you become a Christian?

- *Life after you met Christ.* Choose another descriptive word of your life as a Christian. You might say something like *meaningful, fulfilled* or *exciting.* Describe some tangible benefit that God brings to your life today.

For example, you might put these simple cue-words into a paragraph like this:

I grew up in a Christian home. Even though I attended church every Sunday with my family, my life still seemed **empty.** **When I was sixteen years old,** *I attended a* **church camp** *and heard the Gospel in a fresh way. I talked with my pastor one day at camp and told him I was ready to receive Christ as my Savior and Lord. He helped me* **say a prayer to God** *to ask him to forgive me of my sins and to come into my heart. Since that time, my life has been* **complete.** *Now that Jesus is with me, I no longer feel lonely, as I once did.*

Many people make the mistake of over-emphasizing part one, life before Christ. It is especially tempting to camp out in this part of your story if you had a rebellious past. The most important and powerful part of your testimony is not what your life was like before Christ—*it is the difference he makes in your life now.* This should be the longest part of your testimony, and it is what will appeal to people. Because God is always at work in your life, keep your testimony fresh and updated. Look for opportunities to tie your testimony into everyday conversations. With practice, you'll become more confident sharing your faith and even more aware of the many people you encounter who will be changed by your story.

True Identity

Project Management and Editorial
Shari Vanden Berg

Editorial Assistance
Amy Ballor
Julie Zahm

Theological Review
Jordan Ballor, M.T.S., Th.M., Calvin Theological Seminary

Production Management
Phil Herich

Art Direction
Jamie DeBruyn

Cover Design
Jamie DeBruyn

Interior Design
Kirk Luttrell and Jeff James

Proofreading
Peachtree Editorial and Proofreading Service, Peachtree, GA

Interior Typesetting
The Livingstone Corporation, Carol Stream, IL

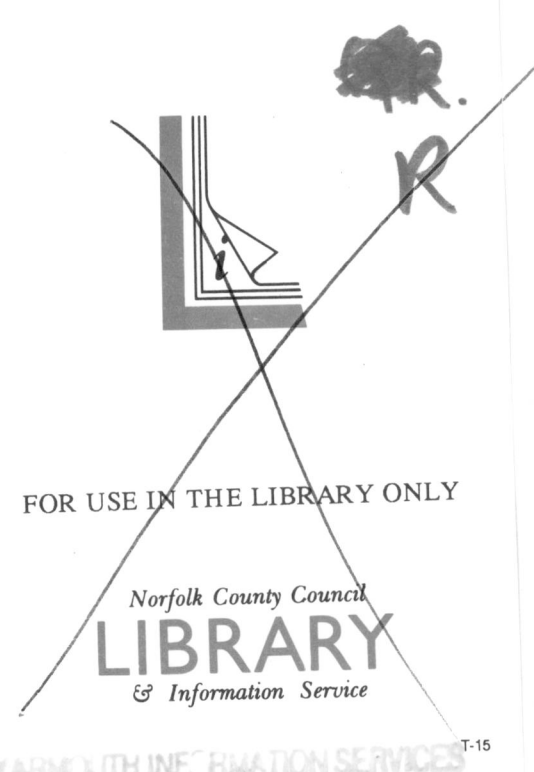

LAROUSSE

Dictionary of

WRITERS

LAROUSSE

Dictionary of

WRITERS

Editor
Rosemary Goring

LAROUSSE

LAROUSSE
Larousse plc
43–45 Annandale Street, Edinburgh EH7 4AZ
Larousse Kingfisher Chambers Inc.,
95 Madison Avenue, New York, New York 10016

First published by Larousse 1994

10 9 8 7 6 5 4 3 2 1

British Library Cataloging in Publication Data
for this book is available from the British Library

Library of Congress Catalog Card Number: 94-75741

ISBN 0-7523-0006-7

The publisher would like to thank Peter Dollard, Library Director
at Alma College, Michigan, for his invaluable assistance in reviewing
the material for this volume.

Cover illustration: Reading by Yula Bencur
Illustration provided by e. t. archive

Typeset from author-generated disks by BPC Digital Data Ltd
Printed in Great Britain by Clays Ltd, St Ives plc

Contents

Contributors

Dr Colin Affleck

Stuart Bathgate

Fran Cannon

Anne Collett

Richard Cook

Dr Jo M Evans

Dr Helena Forsås-Scott

Iain Grant

Peter Graves

Allan Hunter

Dr Jeremy Idle

Robert Irwin

Mechthild Krüger

Arne Kruse

Huw Aled Lewis

Dr Christopher Little

Henry Maas

Deirdre Maclean

Heidi Macpherson

Kenny Mathieson

Julie Morris

Brian Morton

Helen E Mundler

Hayden Murphy

Jim Orton

Greig Proctor

Dr David Reid

Dr Mario Relich

Susan Rennie

Dr Anita Shanley

Dr Berthold Schoene

Martin Seymour-Smith

Alan Taylor

Gunilla Blom Thomsen

Bjarne Thorup Thomsen

Michael Thorn

Peter Whitebrook

Karina Williamson

Introduction

In many respects this dictionary is like a well-stocked bookshop. In a relatively small space it gathers together an enormous range of authors, from the familiar names of school and university English courses to some of the most neglected figures in world literature. As in a bookshop a Bloomsbury classic may be flanked by an arresting science-fiction title, which in turn is only a short distance from a quiet enclave of women's writing, where the intriguing titles of 18th-century gentlewomen peer out from the shade of their neighbours.

We hope the *Larousse Dictionary of Writers* will be used as the first place to look when trying to find out about an author, and the aim has been to cover as widely as possible the diversity of creative writers across the world, from all periods and all countries. The basis of selection has largely been confined to novelists, short-story writers, essayists, poets, playwrights, dramatists and travel writers, plus the most notable of screen and television writers. However, we also include some names that do not fall strictly into the literary camp, but whose influence on the nature of creative writing has been immense; into this category fall such psychological theorists as Freud and Jung; critics like F R and Q D Leavis; and philosophers such as Rudolf Steiner and Gurdjieff. Also included are those who have achieved a notable literary 'first', such as Hannah Adams, the earliest professional woman writer in the United States.

Although literary merit forms the basis for the majority of the entries included, it has not been the only touchstone for selection. We have, for example, included the top best-selling authors — Jackie Collins, Jeffrey Archer, Robert Ludlum — without whom no bookshop would be complete (or as profitable). Nor would it be fully stocked without the best of the genre writers — the doyens of historical novels, romances and westerns; of detective, thriller and crime fiction; and the leaders of science and fantasy fiction.

While fame and reputation have been important indicators of whom to include, we have also strayed into less familiar territory to cover writers who are known only in their own countries, largely because they have not yet been translated, but whose talent emphatically deserves a wider public. At the other end of the spectrum are those relatively minor names who, nevertheless, remain an established part of the literary firmament, and thus are given a mention.

Inevitably there is a British and American bias to our selection, but as far as possible we have tried to cover the most significant writers from every country, and to give fair attention to those from marginalized cultures or languages, such as Native Americans, Basques, Bretons and Gaels.

Within the scope of thumbnail sketches we give a brief outline of an author's life and point to what we consider are his or her most representative works. In many cases we have attempted to place a writer in context, sometimes by making reference to other writers (referred to in bold type if they also have an entry, unless their name falls within a quotation), and to give an indication of his or her major themes and style.

To help with this we have, where feasible, given rough translations of foreign-language titles. In some cases, though, to attempt even an approximate translation might misrepresent the work, and in such instances we have left well alone. Where the foreign title is a proper name, we have not repeated this; similarly, where a published English translation is identical to the original, we have simply given the date of the translation. Also, where there has been more than one English translation, we have generally cited the earliest.

Although it may seem like stating the obvious, it is worth adding that the length of an entry is not necessarily an indicator of the subject's importance. Some authors can be dealt with succinctly, while others have had such complicated or varied careers that to give a bare outline takes several lines; some writers' works need greater elucidation, others' are relatively self-explanatory.

As a pointer towards further reading, at the end of many entries we list one or two biographies or essays about the writer. This selection has been based on the works we believe are most useful, rather than necessarily those most recently published. Where no author is given for a bibliographical reference, this is because the work cited is by the writer whose entry it is attached to, and is usually an autobiography or memoir.

Reference books stand or fall by their reliability, and every effort has been made to use the most trustworthy sources. Inevitably, though, some errors will have found their way into this work and we would be most grateful for being advised of any mistakes where they occur.

In his *Life of Schiller*, Carlyle commented that there is 'no more sickening reading than the biographies of authors'. With this dictionary we hope to prove him wrong.

Rosemary Goring
May 1994

Acknowledgements

Foremost I would like to thank Martin Seymour-Smith for the advice and knowledge he has offered throughout the compilation of this book. The suggestions he has put forward have helped substantially to shape this work, and I am hugely grateful for his perspective. I would also like to thank Kenny Mathieson, Brian Morton, Jim Orton and Peter Whitebrook for being so generous with their help; likewise Dr J G D Kerr, Alan Taylor of *Scotland on Sunday*, Sally Craighead of Thins Bookshop, Edinburgh and Catherine Schwarz. Thanks are also due to Peter Dollard, Library Director at Alma College, Michigan, the staff at Auckland Central Library, the Reference Department staff at Edinburgh Central Library, Faith Pullen at the University of Edinburgh, Catherine Lockerbie of *The Scotsman* and Giles Foden at the *Times Literary Supplement*. For help with translations I am most grateful to George Davidson, Ilona Morison, Liam Roger, Berthold Schoene and Anne Seaton. Many thanks also to my colleagues at Chambers Larousse for their unfailing encouragement and wit.

A

AAKJAER, Jeppe
(1865–1930)
Danish dramatist, novelist, poet and translator (of **Burns**), born in the Jutland village bearing his name. He was most famous for his radical novel *Vredens Born* (1904, 'Children of Rage'), a vivid protest against the exploitation of farm labourers by their wealthy masters. He is now, however, chiefly remembered for his folk-like poetry.

AARESTRUP, Emil
(1800–56)
Danish poet. A graduate in medicine, he combined a successful professional career—first as a general practitioner in the Southern Isles, then as a health inspector in Odense—with a mainly private poetic production that was to break new ground for Danish erotic poetry. With only one collection, *Digte* (1838, 'Poems'), published in his lifetime, Aarestrup was largely unimpeded by the literary conventions of his day and created a poetic universe distinctive for its bold concentration on sexual desire and fulfilment. By means of a masterly, fluid verse technique, his short texts outline a world of beauty centred on nature and the female body. Although focusing on pleasure, the poems frequently contain overtones of dread and death, conveying insights into the complex nature of desire that anticipated those of **Sigmund Freud** and many modernists.
▷ K Zeruneith, *Den frigjorte. Emil Aarestrup i digtning og samtid. En biografi* (1981)

ABBAS, (Khwaja) Ahmad
(1914–)
Indian novelist, short-story writer, filmmaker and journalist, whose Muslim background, prolific output and choice of English as his literary language have tended to marginalize him in his native country. A Gandhian nationalist, Abbas has dealt sharply with the anglophile intellectual middle class, attacking it in his first collection of short stories *Not All Lies!* (1945). A sophisticated awareness of the relationship between personal and political forces is also shown in his first novel *Tomorrow is Ours!* (1943), which anticipates some of the concerns of **Salman Rushdie**'s *Midnight's Children*. In his masterpiece, *Inqilab* (1955, 'Revolution'), he creates a deracinated and culturally displaced protagonist in order to gauge the human implications of major events in Indian history, from the Amritsar massacre to the Congress's 'Quit India' resolution of 1942. Abbas has also written perceptively about Jawaharlal Nehru, his daughter Indira Gandhi, Mao Zedong, and the Maoist Naxalite revolutionaries.
▷ *I Am Not an Island: An Experiment in Autobiography* (1977)

ABBOTT, George Francis
(1887–)
American dramatist, director, producer and actor, born in Forestville, New York State. He studied drama at the celebrated 47 Workshop at Harvard, where he began writing. His first major hit came with *Broadway* (1926), the first of a number of successful melodramas, farces and musical comedies which he either co-wrote, staged, or both. He was awarded the Pulitzer Prize for Drama in 1960 for the hit musical *Fiorello!* (1959), along with co-writer **Jerome Weidman**, lyricist Sheldon Harnick (1924–) and composer Jerry Bock (1928–). He is widely regarded as an important innovator in the staging of musicals.

ABD AL-MALIK NURI
(1914–)
Iraqi short-story writer, whose *Nasid al-ard* (1954, 'Song of the Earth') shows the influence of European techniques. He is known as a gloomy and pessimistic writer.
▷ I J Boullata (ed), *Critical Perspectives in Modern Arabic Literature* (1980)

ABD-UL-LATIF
(1162–1231)
Arabian writer, born in Baghdad. He taught medicine and philosophy at Cairo and Damascus. His best-known book is a work on Egypt.
▷ T Clabert, *Latifi, oder biografische Nachrichten von vorzuglichen turkische Dichtern* (1800)

ABDÜLLHAK HAMID TARHAN
(1852–1937)
Turkish dramatist, born in Bebek. He belonged to the Tanzimat ('Transformation') school of writers, who sought to bring Turkey into Europe. His model was **Racine**, but he

had read **Shakespeare**. His bold verse plays, usually on themes from Islamic history, are genuinely stirring as well as intelligently conceived. His influence on the Turkish theatre cannot be over-estimated.

ABE Kobo
(1924–93)

Japanese novelist and playwright, born in Tokyo. He trained as a doctor, but turned to literature after graduating. Recognition in Japan came with the award of the Akutagawa Prize for *The Wall* in 1951. His international reputation is often linked with that of writers like **Junichiro Tanizaki**, **Yasunari Kawabata**, and **Yukio Mishima**, but unlike them he stands outside the great tradition of Japanese literature. His predominant theme of alienation is explored in a series of novels and plays, his early work set in the wasteland of Manchuria and post-war Japan; in later books he focused on an urban, industrialized society on the brink of explosive economic growth. His novels include *Daiyon Kampyoki* (1959, Eng trans *Inter Ice Age Four*, 1971), *Suna no onna* (1962, Eng trans *The Woman in the Dunes*, 1965) and *Mikkai* (1977, Eng trans *Secret Rendezvous*, 1980).
▷H Yamaanouchi, *The Search for Authenticity in Modern Japanese Literature* (1978)

À BECKETT, Gilbert Abbott
(1811–56)

English humorist, born in London. He was educated at Westminster and in 1841 was called to the Bar. In 1849 he became a metropolitan police magistrate. As well as writing for *Punch* and *The Times*, he was the author of *The Comic Blackstone* (1846), and comic histories of England and Rome.
▷A A'Beckett, *The A'Becketts of Punch: memoirs of fathers and sons* (1903)

ABELL, Kjeld
(1901–61)

Danish playwright, born in Ribe, the leading modernizer of 20th-century Danish drama. After graduating in Politics, and working as a scene painter and dress designer at theatres in Paris and London, he experienced his breakthrough as a playwright in Copenhagen with the activating, revue-style play *Melodien der blev v'k* (1935, 'The Melody that got Lost'). It tells the story of the liberation of Larsen, a white-collar worker who has lost his 'melody' under the constraints of a conventional working and married life—a topical theme in European literature of the 1930s. Abell broke emphatically away from the naturalistic 'drawing-room drama' in the tradition of **Ibsen** and **Bjørnson**: he placed actors among the audience, brought the stage decorations to life, blended speech and song, and used long addresses to the audience. In *Anna Sophie Hedvig* (1939), the title hero is a mousy schoolmistress who kills her tyrannical colleague. The play makes a political statement about the need for the individual to stand up against authoritarian ideologies. This theme was developed further in *Silkeborg*, written during World War II, but first performed in 1946. After the war, Abell continued his experimentation with plays such as *Dage på en sky* (1947, 'Days on a Cloud'), *Den blå pekingeser* (1954, 'The Blue Pekinese') and *Skriget* (1961, 'The Scream').
▷*Fodnoten i støvet* (1951); F J Marker, *Kjeld Abell* (1976)

ABERCROMBIE, Lascelles
(1881–1938)

English poet and critic, born in Ashton-on-Mersey. Educated at Malvern College and Victoria University, Manchester, he became Professor of English at Leeds (1922) and London (1929), and Reader at Oxford (1935). His works include *Romanticism* (1926) and *Principles of Literary Criticism* (1932). He published several volumes of Georgian-style poetry, collected as *The Poems of Lascelles Abercrombie* (1930). A posthumous collection of *Lyrics and Unfinished Poems* appeared in 1940. A few contemporary critics have found his poetry well above the general run of the Georgians.
▷O Ellon, *Lascelles Abercrombie, 1881–1938* (1939)

ABISH, Walter
(1931–)

American novelist, short-story writer and poet, he was born in Vienna and raised in China, before moving to the USA, where he took citizenship in 1960. After teaching at Columbia University in New York for more than 10 years, he made his name with the experimental novel *Alphabetical Africa* (1974), in which the opening chapter consists only of words beginning with A, the second of words beginning with A and B, and so on until the 26th chapter, when the process reverses. A witty linguistic device allows him to explore ideas about cultural identity in the outwardly more conventional *How German Is It* (1980), in which the central character's father has been a conspirator in the 'July Plot' to kill Hitler, but who has himself been forced to betray fellow members of a terrorist group. His later *99: The New Meaning* (1990) is also experimental in form, but with a more conventional structure, as is *Eclipse Fever* (1993). Abish's short stories are collected in *Minds*

Meet (1975) and *In the Future Perfect* (1977), his verse in *Duel Site* (1970).
▷R Martin, 'Walter Abish: Perfect Unfamiliarity, Familiar Imperfections', in *Journal of American Studies*, vol 17 (1983)

ABOUT, Edmond François Valentin
(1828–85)

French journalist and novelist, born in Dieuze, in Lorraine. After schooling in Paris, he studied archaeology in Athens. On returning to Paris, he devoted himself to a literary career. He was a sceptical, crusading journalist, and founded the journal *Le XIX Siècle* ('The Nineteenth Century'). His fiction includes *Le Roi des montagnes* (1856, 'The King of the Mountains'), *Madelon* (1863), *Alsace* (1872), which cost him a week's imprisonment at the hands of the Germans, and *Le Roman d'un brave homme* (1880, 'The Story of a Good Man').

ABRAHAMS, Peter
(1919–)

South African novelist and polemicist, son of an Ethiopian father and a 'coloured' woman (ie he was then designated as 'of mixed race'). He began as a protest poet (*A Blackman Speaks of Freedom*, 1938), then graduated to novels and stories. He left South Africa at the age of 20 to become a merchant seaman, lived in England for a time, and settled in Jamaica as a journalist. His most famous, subtle and successful novel was *A Wreath for Udomo* (1956), which dealt with the problem of what would happen when newly independent Black nations were confronted with the choice between collaborating with white imperialists for financial advantage, and their moral imperative to support other liberation movements. His work is still eagerly discussed, but after *This Island Now* (1967), on a Caribbean dictatorship, he wrote less fiction. *Tell Freedom* (1954) is a moving and widely read autobiography.
▷W Cartey, *Whispers from a Continent* (1969)

ABRAMOV, Fyodor Aleksandrovich
(1920–)

Russian novelist and story-writer, born in Verkola, in the Archangel region, which forms the background to his fiction (none of which has been translated). He has steeped himself in the history and culture of his region, and his dialogue is closely modelled on peasant usage. His main theme, which nonetheless never obtrudes, is the artificial circumstances brought about by collectivization, with its unrealistic demands.

ABREU, Casimiro José Marques de
(1839–60)

Brazilian romantic poet, born near Rio de Janeiro. Doomed to die young from consumption, his ingenuous verse has charmed most modern Brazilian readers, who also admire his dramatic fragment *Camões* (1854). He has always been the 'favourite of the folk'.

ABSE, Dannie
(1923–)

Welsh writer and physician, born in Cardiff. Educated at the Welsh National School of Medicine, King's College, London and Westminster Hospital, he has been senior specialist in the chest clinic at the Central Medical Establishment, London, since 1954. His literary output includes nine volumes of poetry, two novels and half a dozen plays. His autobiographical volumes are *A Poet in the Family* (1974) and *A Strong Dose of Myself* (1982), and the autobiographical novel *Ash on a Young Man's Sleeve* (1954).

ABUL-ALA, Ahmed ibn Adullah, al-Maarri
(973–1057)

Arabic poet, born, as his name signifies, at Mararra, near Aleppo in Syria. He was blind from early childhood, and spent most of his life in seclusion in his home town. He stands apart from all other Arab poets in what has been called his atheism and harsh judgement of the world. His most famous work, *Risalat al-Ghufran* (Eng trans *The Epistle of Forgiveness*, 1943), has been compared to the *Divine Comedy* of **Dante**, who may have heard of it (even if he never read it). The story of a journey through heaven and hell, it is one of the most original and perplexing of all long Arabic poems.
▷H Baerlin, *Abdul Ala the Syrian* (1914); R A Nicolson, *Studies in Islamic Poetry* (1921)

ABU NUWAS
(c.760–c.813–815)

Arab poet, considered one of the greatest poets of the 'Abbasid period. He abandoned older, traditional forms for erotic and witty lyrics. He was a favourite at the court of the caliph Hārūn al-Raschīd in Baghdad, and figures in the *Arabian Nights*.
▷W H Ingrams, *Abu Nuwas in Life and Legend* (1933)

ABU TAMMAM, Habib ibn Aus
(807–c.850)

Arabian poet, born near Lake Tiberias, the son of a Christian. He rose to favour under the caliphs al-Ma'mūn and al-Mu'tasim as a composer of panegyrics. He travelled extensively and towards the end of his life he discovered a private library of desert poetry at Hamadhan. From this he compiled a celebrated anthology of early Arab poetry, the *Hamasu*.

▷F Ruckert, *Hamasa oder des altesten arabischen Volkslieder gesammelt von Abu Tammam* (1846)

ACEDEVO DÍAZ, Edourdo
(1851–1924)

Uruguayan novelist, born in La Unión, in many respects 'the father of the modern Uruguayan novel'. His son, also called Edourdo (1882–1978), was himself an Argentinian novelist of some small distinction, who wrote a book on his father (1941). Acedevo Díaz, modelling himself on **Pérez Galdós**, wrote a famous and illuminating trilogy on the history of Uruguay, *Himno de Sangre* (1888–93, 'Hymn of Blood'); but his most famous book was *Soledad* (1894), an exemplary gauchesque novel about an outlawed minstrel who falls in love with a girl on a ranch. He founded the daily newspaper *El National* in 1896.

ACHARD, Marcel, originally Marcel Auguste Ferréol
(1901–74)

French playwright, a member of the Académie française, who charmed audiences in Paris and New York with his witty comedies and fantasies. His character Charlemagne, a vagabond, was first introduced in *La Vie est belle* (1918, 'Life is Beautiful'). Many plays were adapted for the American stage, eg *I Know My Love* (1949), from *Auprès de ma blonde* (1946).

ACHEBE, Chinua, originally Albert Chinualumogo
(1930–)

Nigerian novelist, poet and essayist, born in Ogidi, the son of a mission teacher. He was educated at the University College of Ibadan, and his early career was in broadcasting, but the publication of his first novel *Things Fall Apart* (1958) at once heralded the emergence of a unique voice in African literature. Set in the second half of the 19th century and presenting an unsentimentalized picture of the Ibo tribe, it has since been translated into 40 languages. Writing exclusively in English, he confirmed his early promise with four more novels, *No Longer At Ease* (1960), *Arrow of God* (1964), *A Man of the People* (1966) and *Anthills of the Savanna* (1987), which was shortlisted for the Booker Prize. An overtly political writer, he has taught at

the universities of Massachusetts and Connecticut, and at the University of Nigeria at Nsukka.

▷D Carroll, *Chinua Achebe* (1970); G D Skillan, *The Novels of Chinua Achebe* (1969)

ACHILLES, Tatius
(?3rd century)

Greek writer. A rhetorician at Alexandria, he wrote the romance *Leucippe and Cleitophon*.

ACHILLINI, Claudio
(1574–1640)

Italian Baroque poet, born in Bologna. A minor follower of **Marino**, he is now celebrated for his almost comic bombast and convolutedness: **Manzoni** quotes him, with notable irony, in *I promessi sposi* (Chapter XXXVII).

ACHTERBERG, Gerrit
(1905–62)

Dutch poet, born in Langbroek. He is one of the few modern poets literally to have 'acted out' his deepest and most murderous impulses: on 15 December 1937 he shot and killed his landlady; he also shot at her young daughter, who was not killed. The major theme in the two collections of poetry he had already published had been his desire to be united with a beloved in death. He did not turn the gun on himself, however, but spent six years in a psychiatric hospital before marrying, and intensifying 'his earlier struggle to write'. Despite or because of this Achterberg was a major—indeed, a unique—poet, although not one who has yet attracted even adequate criticism. He is the key figure in Netherlandic poetry, whose character it is impossible to conceive without reference to him. He is the **Jung**ian 'shadow', envied by all his male successors, for whom he seems to be the hero who actually murdered his beloved. His poetry opposes a fanatically close observance of traditional form—seen by the poet as the puritanical 'control' he exercised over his life after his release—to an extreme, and deliberately psychotic, violence of content. In his most famous poem, *De ballade van de gasfitter* (1953, Eng trans in *A Tourist Does Golgotha*, 1972), a series of 14 strict sonnets themselves making up a 'macrocosmic sonnet', he presents the reader with a confused gas worker whose job is to fill holes (*dichter* in Dutch, means 'poet', 'closer of holes', and 'closer to'), and who repairs gas lines even when they do not need it; he is a 'self-mocking Orpheus': 'God is the hole' which needs filling. Achterberg is a compelling poet, and one of great power, although also one of somewhat sinister humourlessness. A critic has said of what has been described as his 'masterwork', the sequence *Spel van de wilde jacht* (1957, 'Play of the Wild Chase'), that 'the definitive interpretation has not yet appeared'; the world may have to wait for this.

▷ *Odyssey*, 1 (1961)

ACKER, Kathy
(1948–)

American novelist and short-story writer, with a visceral, 'punk' approach influenced by **William Burroughs**'s drug imagery and rhetorically violent 'cut-ups'. She also draws on rock music lyrics and pornography, as in *I Dreamt I Was a Nymphomaniac: Imagining* (1974). Her first novel, *The Childlike Life of the Black Tarantula* (1975), was published under the pseudonym Black Tarantula, while *Kathy Goes to Haiti* (1978) deliberately evokes American 'teen' movies of the fifties. *Great Expectations* (1982) and *Don Quixote* (1986) recall **Jorge Luis Borges**'s 'intertextual' adaptations of literary classics. Perhaps her best work is to be found in *Blood and Guts in High School* (1984), shorter fictions of a vividness not found in the more laboured *Empire of the Senseless* (1988) and *In Memoriam to Identity* (1990).

ACKERLEY, Joseph Randolph
(1896–1967)

English author, born in Herne Hill, Kent. His post-university acquaintance with **E M Forster** resulted in his appointment as private secretary to the Maharajah of Chhokrapur, from which experience he wrote *Hindoo Holiday* (1932), an intelligent and amusing log of his five-month sojourn in India. From 1935 to 1959 he was literary editor of *The Listener*. In 1956 he published *My Dog Tulip*, eulogized by **Christopher Isherwood** as 'one of the greatest masterpieces of animal literature', and, in 1960, his only novel, *We Think the World of You*, in which an Alsatian dog plays a lead role. His other books include the autobiographical *My Father and Myself* (1968) and *My Sister and Myself; The Diaries of J R Ackerley* (1982), both published posthumously.

▷ N Braybrooke (ed), *The Letters of J.R. Ackerley* (1975)

ACKROYD, Peter
(1949–)

English novelist, biographer and critic, born in London. He was educated at Clare College, Cambridge, and Yale University, and was literary editor of *The Spectator* (1973–7), and later television critic of *The Times*. His polemical interest in Modernism is reflected in *Notes for a New Culture* (1976), *Ezra Pound and His World* (1981) and *T.S. Eliot* (1984).

His novels are erudite, playful, and complex, and draw on literary and historical sources in fulfilment of his belief that writing springs from other writing. *The Great Fire of London* (1982), for example, has modern echoes of **Dickens**, while *Chatterton* (1987) draws on the life of its subject. *English Music* (1992) is an ambitious study of English culture seen through the trance-consciousness of its narrator, while *The House of Doctor Dee* (1993) explores history through the character of the 16th-century alchemist.

ACORN, Milton
(1923–)

Canadian poet, born on Prince Edward Island. Acorn calls himself a 'revolutionary poet' and writes in craggy solidarity with the working man. He himself has worked as a carpenter, freight handler and longshoreman, and served with Canadian forces in World War II. He was one of the mainstays of the Toronto coffee-house circuit in the 1960s and was the first recipient of the Canadian Poets Award in 1970. There have been two volumes of selected poems, *I've Tasted My Blood: Poems 1956–68* (1969), and *Dig Up My Heart: Selected Poems 1952–83* (1983).

ACOSTA DE SAMPER, Soledad
(1833–1903)

Colombian historian, editor and novelist, born in Bogotá. A pioneer feminist, she edited *La Mujer* (1878–82, 'Woman'). She is most famous for her *Los piratas en Cartegena* (1885, 'Pirates in Carthage'), a vivid, capable and psychologically convincing historical novel.

ACUÑA, Hernando de
(c.1520–c.1580)

Spanish poet, soldier and diplomat of Portuguese extraction, who wrote in Spanish. He put into verse, under the title *El caballero determinado*, a translation by Charles V of a French romance, *Le Chevalier délibéré* ('The determined knight') by Olivier de la Marche (1486). Other poems, Italian in style, were published in 1591 by his widow.

▷ N Alonso Cortes, *Don Hernando de Acuña. Noticas biograficos* (1913)

ACUÑA, Manuel
(1849–73)

Mexican poet, born in Saltillo, Coahuila. His life was by all accounts unhappy, and his congenital poor health and thwarted love affairs drove him to commit suicide at an early age. He was both an avowed atheist and a literary Romantic, and his poetry is unusual for the period in its emphasis on materialism, while its dark, bitter moods contrast with the prevailing lyricism and optimism of the Romantic temperament. In addition to poetry, he also left *El Pasado* (1872, 'The Past'), a fiery play denouncing what he saw as the outrages of Christian society and religious extremism.

ADAM OF ST VICTOR
(fl.1140)

French poet. A monk of the Augustinian order, living at the Abbey of St Victor in Paris, he was one of the supreme religious poets of the period. His Latin is beautifully polished, and his *Sequentiae* ('Sequences', the common mode for the expression of religious themes at the time) are amongst the finest examples of the genre.

ADAM, Helen Douglas
(1909–)

Scottish-born American poet. Born in Glasgow, she was raised in Scotland's rural northeast, before taking up journalism in Edinburgh and London. She moved to the USA at the onset of World War II, and took citizenship in 1977. Her debut collections were two volumes of quirky lyrics about the 'Elfin Pedlar' (1923, 1924), in which dialect and archaic forms tended to mask a concern with female sexuality and its buried power. There was a long gap between *Shadow of the Moon* (1929) and *The Queen o' Crow Castle* (1958), but the later volume drew the admiration of younger poets in California (where she had settled), and *Selected Poems and Ballads* (1974) established her as a significant outsider.

ADAM, Paul Auguste Marie
(1862–1920)

French novelist and essayist, born in Paris. Among his numerous novels are *Chair Molle* (1885, 'Weak Flesh'), *Le Mystère des foules* (1895, 'The Mystery of the Masses'), *Lettres de Malaisie* (1879, 'Letters from Malaysia'), and *La Force* (1899, 'The Power'). He was co-founder of *Symboliste* and other French literary periodicals.
▷F Jean-Desthieux, *Paul Adam: le dernier des encyclopédistes* (1928)

ADAMIC, Louis
(1899–1951)

Yugoslav-born American writer, born in Blato, Dalmatia. The son of Slovene peasants, he emigrated to the USA in 1913. He served in the American army, and became naturalized in 1918. He began writing short stories in the early twenties, utilizing his experiences and personal observations in his books— as in *Laughing in the Jungle* (1932), about an immigrant. Other works include

Dynamite: the Story of Class Violence in America (1931); an autobiographical survey, *My America 1928–38* (1938); *From Many Lands* (1940); *Dinner at the White House* (1946) and *The Eagle and the Root* (1950).
▷H A Christian, *Louis Adamic: a checklist* (1971)

ADAMNAN, St
(624–704)

Scottish or Irish biographer and cleric. He was the eighth abbot of Iona, and his great literary work, which, in its day, was read right across Europe, is a biography of the first abbot, **St Columba**. Written in church Latin, the work is an account of Columba's childhood in Ireland, with portents of his subsequent career and instances of his miraculous powers (a field is sown and harvested in one month; a demon is driven out of a milk pail; a lump of salt, blessed by him, is found to be indestructible). There is also a lengthy account of the founding of Iona. The classic, and still the best, translation of the work is *Life of St Columba, Founder of Hy*, ed W Reeves (1874).

ADAMOV, Arthur
(1908–70)

Russian dramatist, born in Kislovodsk in the Caucasus, brought up in France and educated in Switzerland and Germany. Before turning to drama he wrote *L'Aveu* ('The Confession'), about his despair at life's meaninglessness; his first play, *La Parodie* (1950), sees two men infatuated with the same girl, Lili, who is unable to tell them apart. Further plays such as *L'invasion* (1950) and *Le Professeur Taranne* (1951) continue the themes of bad communication and loss of identity. In the words of critic Martin Esslin, his plays depict 'a senseless and brutal nightmare world'. With *Paolo Paoli* (1957) he abandoned the Absurd, and his distinctive talent, for **Brecht**ian Epic Theatre. His death from overdosing was probably suicide.
▷M Esslin, 'Arthur Adamov: The Curable and the Incurable', in *The Theatre of the Absurd* (1983)

ADAMS, Alice
(1926–)

American novelist and short-story writer, born in Virginia and raised in North Carolina, which is the setting of *Families and Survivors* (1975). Her debut novel was *Careless Love* (1966, published in the UK as *The Fall of Daisy Duke*), which established as one of her central themes the dilemmas of women in marginal social and economic positions; she moved up the social scale with *Rich Rewards* (1980). *Listening to Billie* (1978) uses the jazz singer Billie Holiday's life as a touchstone for contemporary women. In *Superior Women* (1984) she returns to her Radcliffe education, class of '46, in a latter-day (but more formulaic) version of **Mary McCarthy**'s *The Group*. The best of Adams's short stories are collected in *To See You Again* (1982), *Return Trips* (1985), and the magnificent *After You've Gone* (1989).

ADAMS, Arthur H(enry)
(1872–1936)

New Zealand journalist and writer, born in Lawrence, Otago. After *Maoriland: and Other Verses* (1899) he visited China to report the Boxer Rebellion for a Sydney newspaper. In London he wrote one novel, *Tussock Land* (1904) and more verse, *London Streets* (1906). Returning to Sydney as editor on the periodicals *Bulletin* and *Lone Hand* he championed the work of Australian playwrights. Following publication of *The Collected Verses of Arthur H Adams* (1913) he turned again to writing novels, some under the name 'Henry Henry James', with a flavour of picaresque whimsy and a sympathy for the 'under-dog'. Adams wrote several plays, the most significant of which was *Mrs Pretty and the Premier* (1914), later included in his *Three Plays for the Australian Stage* (1914).

ADAMS, Douglas Noel
(1952–)

English novelist and scriptwriter, born in Cambridge. He was educated at Cambridge, and was script editor on the popular television series *Doctor Who* (1978–80). He is best known for a sequence of novels: *The Hitch-Hiker's Guide to the Galaxy* (1979) and *The Restaurant at the End of the Universe* (1980), *Life, The Universe and Everything* (1982) and *So Long, and Thanks for All The Fish* (1984). A further novel, *Mostly Harmless*, was added in 1992. The zany, free-wheeling satire on the nature of human evolution grew increasingly dark as the sequence progressed, a mood also evident in two linked novels, *Dirk Gently's Holistic Detective Agency* (1987) and *The Long Dark Tea-Time of the Soul* (1988).

ADAMS, Hannah
(1755–1831)

American historian and memoirist, born in Medfield, Massachusetts, whose posthumous autobiography (1832) is a vital document in the history of the young republic. Adams has often been described as the first professional female author to emerge in the United States. She grew up during the independence era and published her first important book, the *Alphabetical Compendium of the Various Sects* (1784), at the age of 29. Remarkably, it covered schisms and doctrinal disputes from the Early Fathers to the present day. Her range of scholarship was also visible in *A Summary History of New England* (1799), one of the best available accounts of the pre- and post-Revolutionary north-eastern states. Later works were more devotional, but *The History of the Jews* (1812) is rather remarkable for its bluntness.

ADAMS, Henry Brooks
(1838–1918)

American historian, born in Boston, son of Charles Francis Adams (1807–86) and grandson of John Quincy Adams, 6th President of the USA. Educated at Harvard, he acted as his father's secretary in Washington (1860–1) and England (1861–8), then worked as a journalist in Washington (1868–70) before teaching medieval and American history at Harvard (1870–7). He edited the *North American Review* (1870–6) and wrote two novels, *Democracy* (1880) and *Esther* (1884) before embarking on important historical works. *Mont Saint Michel and Chartres* (1904) is a major study of the unity of art and religion in the middle ages. He also wrote a monumental *History of the United States during the Administrations of Jefferson and Madison* (9 vols, 1870–7); and a classic autobiography, *The Education of Henry Adams* (1907), which was awarded the Pulitzer Prize in 1919.
▷ E Samuels, *The Young Adams, Adams: The Middle Years, Adams: The Major Phase*, (1948–64); L Auchincloss, *Adams* (1971)

ADAMS, Perseus, pseud of Peter Robert Charles Adams
(1933–)

South African lyric poet, born in Cape Town. Much of his work (and he has not been unduly prolific) has been inspired by the natural scene; *The Land at My Door* (1965) is an almost **Wordsworth**ian response to the South African countryside. What pressures and contradictions there are in the verse, which is free but musically structured, are not overtly political. There is, however, a didactic strain which has largely disappeared in the later *Grass for the Unicorn* (1975), a tauter and more disciplined collection, in which the line has become shorter and less deliberately musical.

ADAMS, Richard George
(1920–)

English novelist, born in Berkshire. He was educated at Worcester College, Oxford, and after wartime service in the army he worked as a civil servant with the department of the environment (1948–74). He made his name as a writer with the bestselling *Watership Down*

(1972), an epic tale of a community of rabbits. Later books have included *Shardik* (1974), *The Plague Dogs* (1977), *The Iron Wolf* (1980), *The Girl in a Swing* (1980), *Maia* (1984) and *The Bureaucats* (1985).

▷ *The Day Gone By* (1990)

ADAMSON, Robert
(1943–)

Australian poet and editor, born in Maryborough, Victoria. A proponent of the 'New Australian School', he is known for changing the direction of the Poetry Society of Australia and its *Poetry Magazine*. After a bitter dispute concerning the amount of non-Australian verse in its pages, the magazine ceased and was replaced by *New Poetry* which, under Adamson's direction, published much overseas experimental work. His own early verse was strongly centred on his own experiences of prison life and drug abuse, but some of *Canticles on the Skin* (1970) and *The Rumour* (1971) was later revised for his *Selected Poems* (1977). *Where I Come From*, also partly autobiographical, appeared in 1979.

ADCOCK, (Kareen) Fleur
(1934–)

New Zealand poet, born in Papakura, Auckland. She was educated and then (from 1963) resident in the UK, working with the Foreign and Commonwealth Office from 1963 to 1979. She writes in a lucid, mostly narrative manner, preferring invented situations to autobiographical inscape. Her poems are mostly ironic in tone, often as a means to camouflaging fear or anxiety, and thus very English, though she is most successful when writing about apparently marginal or peripheral locations: New Zealand, Ulster, the English Lakes. This detachment is evident in her (aptly titled) first collection *The Eye of the Hurricane* (1964), but also in the excellent *In Focus* (1977) and among the **Words-worth**ian echoes of her Lake District sequence *Below Loughrigg* (1977). Her *Selected Poems* appeared in 1983, shortly after her editorship of the influential *Oxford Book of Contemporary New Zealand Poetry* (1982), which re-affirmed links with her country of birth. She was married to the Maori poet **Alistair Te Ariki Campbell** and her sister is the novelist **Marilyn Duckworth**.

ADDISON, Joseph
(1672–1719)

English essayist and politician, born in Milston, Wiltshire, eldest son of Lancelot Addison (1632–1703), dean of Lichfield. He was educated at Amesbury, Lichfield, then Charterhouse (where one of his school fellows was **Richard Steele**), and Queen's College and Magdalen College, Oxford, of which he became a fellow. A distinguished classical scholar, he began his literary career in 1693 with a poetical address to **Dryden**. Next year appeared his *Account of the Greatest English Poets*, and a translation of the fourth book of the *Georgics*. In 1699 he obtained a pension to train for the diplomatic service and spent four years in France, Italy, Austria, Germany, and Holland, during which he wrote his *Letter to Lord Halifax*, and made notes for his *Remarks on Italy*, and his *Dialogue on Medals*. *The Campaign*, a poem commissioned by Charles Montagu, 1st Earl of Halifax to celebrate the victory of Blenheim (1704), secured for him a commissionership of Excise. As an under secretary of state (1705–8) he produced his opera *Rosamond* (1706) and in 1707 he went with Lord Halifax to Hanover. Elected to parliament for Malmesbury in (1708), he kept the seat for life. In 1709 he went to Ireland as chief secretary to Lord Wharton, the lord lieutenant, where he formed a warm friendship with **Jonathan Swift**. Returning to England in 1710 at the fall of the Whig ministry, he became a member of the Kitcat Club, and contributed to the *Tatler*, started by his friend Steele in 1709. In March 1711 he and Steele founded the *Spectator*, 274 numbers of which (those signed with one of the letters C L I O), were the work of Addison. In 1711 he purchased the estate of Bilton, near Rugby. His blank-verse tragedy *Cato* (1713) aroused such vehement party enthusiasm that it was performed for 35 nights. In the Whig interest, he attacked the Treaty of Utrecht in *The Late Trial and Conviction of Count Tariff*. After the accession of George I (1714), he became once more, for about a year, secretary to the Earl of Sunderland as lord-lieutenant of Ireland. In 1715 his prose comedy, *The Drummer*, failed. In 1716 he became a lord commissioner of trade, and married Charlotte, Countess of Warwick. In the Hanoverian cause, he issued (1715–16) a political newspaper, the *Freeholder*, which cost him many of his old friends, and he was satirized by **Pope** as 'Atticus'. In 1717 he was appointed secretary of state under Sunderland, but resigned his post, owing to failing health, in March 1718. Almost his last literary undertaking was unfortunately a paper war, on the Peerage Bill of 1719, with his old friend Steele. He was buried in Westminster Abbey.

▷ N Ogle, *The Life of Addison* (1826); P Smithers, *The Life of Joseph Addison* (1954)

ADLER, Renata
(1938–)

American novelist and journalist. She was born in Milan, where her German family had gone to escape the Nazis. Educated at Bryn

Mawr, Harvard and the Sorbonne, she joined the *New Yorker* in 1962, and served as film critic for the *New York Times* during 1968–9, a stint recorded in *A Year in the Dark* (1969); other journalism was collected in *Toward a Radical Middle* (1970), titles that perhaps reflect some of the concerns of her two novels to date. *Speedboat* (1976), which won the **Ernest Hemingway** Award, is a series of filmic scenes about loss and abandonment, linked by a compulsive need to tell stories. In technique *Pitch Dark* (1983) recalls the suggestion that to see something clearly at night one looks slightly away, not directly at it. Adler's prose is oblique but precise, as demonstrated by her investigative reporting on Watergate and her account of Vietnam commander General Westmoreland's libel litigation against CBS, *Reckless Disregard* (1986).

ADONIAS FILHO
(1915–)

Brazilian novelist, critic and librarian, born near Bahia. His novels, not quite in the top flight of modern Brazilian fiction, but notably well observed and highly respected, all deal with cocoa production in the harsh north east of the country. He is unlucky not to have found a translator, since his depiction of brutality and reckless lawlessness in such novels as *Memorias de Lázaro* (1946) is powerful and innovative.

ADUNIS, pseud of Ali Ahmed Said
(1930–)

Syrian–Lebanese poet and critic, a leading Arabic poet of his generation. He was born in Syria but left it in 1956 for political reasons, and became a Lebanese citizen. In Lebanon he has been a prominent editor and polemicist, and has translated **Saint-John Perse** into Arabic. Poetry is to him a 'leap outside established concepts'. While some regard him as the major Arabic poet of his generation, others have attacked his work, much influenced by modern French poets, as impenetrably obscure. But few deny that the best of it is characterized by a haunting visionary beauty. Poetry in translation includes *The Blood of Adonis* (1971).
▷M Badawi, *A Critical Introduction to Modern Arabic Poetry* (1975)

ADY, Endre
(1877–1919)

Hungarian poet and journalist, who changed the direction of his country's poetry, and remains its leading literary figure. Much of his poetry was polemical, and is therefore now outdated, but the best of his work, though not yet well known outside Hungary (but **Edmund Wilson** learned Hungarian to read him), is of the highest international standard. He is certainly one of the world's great poets; no one who has taken the trouble to study him has disagreed. He went to Paris in the wake of his Jewish mistress, Adèle Brüll, 'Leda'—with whom he conducted his affair in public—and was there stimulated by Symbolist procedures (as he understood them) to break away from the prevailing Hungarian conservative poetics. But he was not an intellectual, and did not even know French well. Nonetheless, *Új versek* (1906, 'New Verses'), was the most incisive collection of poetry ever published in Hungary, and around it and Ady himself there coalesced a group of eager young radical writers such as **Mihály Babits**. By the end of the war, and the short-lived Bela Kun government, Ady was fatally ill with syphilis (one of his self-acknowledged muses) and alcoholism; but he had started something in Hungarian poetry which is still going on, and which was partially fulfilled in the tragic poetry of **Attila József**. There is a selection of his work in English in *Poems* (1969).

AESCHYLUS
(c.525–c.456 BC)

Greek tragedian, born in Eleusis, the town of the Mysteries, near Athens. He served in the Athenian army in the Persian Wars, was wounded at Marathon (490) and probably fought at Salamis (480). His first victory as a poet was gained in the dramatic competitions of 484 BC and he won 13 first prizes in tragic competitions before losing to **Sophocles** in 468 BC. He paid two visits to Sicily. During the second, he staged a new version of the *Persians*, and died at Gela. His last great success on the Athenian stage was with the *Oresteia* trilogy in 458 BC. Out of some 60 plays ascribed to him, only seven are extant: the *Persians*, the *Seven against Thebes*, the *Prometheus Bound*, the *Suppliants*, and the *Oresteia*, which comprises three plays on the murder of Agamemnon and its consequences (the *Agamemnon*, the *Choephoroe* and the *Eumenides*). He was the first great writer of tragedy and must be credited with devising its classical form and presentation. His verse is marked by the grandeur of its diction, as his thought is by the great scope of his themes (the conflict between human and divine law, free will and fate, retribution and forgiveness). Aeschylus was regarded in antiquity as the father of tragedy and the exemplar of his two great successors, Sophocles and **Euripides**.
▷G Murray, *Aeschylus: the Inventor of Tragedy* (1940); T Rosenmeyer, *The Art of Aeschylus* (1982)

AESOP

Legendary Greek author of fables. Tradition represents him as a slave in sixth-century Samos. The fables attributed to him are simple tales, often of animals, devised to illustrate moral lessons, and are probably derived from many sources. They were popularized by the Roman poet **Phaedrus** in the 1st century AD, and served as models for the verse fables of **La Fontaine** (published 1668–94).
▷B E Perry, *The Text Tradition of the Greek Life of Aesop* (1970)

AFFORD, Max
(1906–54)

Australian dramatist and scriptwriter, mainly for radio, born in Parkside, Adelaide. From 1932 he wrote for the Australian Broadcasting Commission over 50 plays and radio serials. One serial, *Hagen's Circus*, ran for 800 episodes; two others, *First Light Fraser* and *Danger Unlimited*, ran for over 600. He also adapted **Jon Cleary**'s *The Sundowners* as a serial. Three of his stage works and two radio plays were later collected in *Mischief in the Air* (1974), and he also wrote four popular thrillers between 1936 and 1942.

AFINOGENOV, Aleksandr Nikolaevich
(1904–41)

Russian dramatist, born in Skopin. At first a crude if always skilled communist 'proletcult' playwright, Afinogenov developed into one of the more interesting dramatists to come out of the Stalinist era. His *Strakh* (1930, Eng trans *Fear*, in *Six Soviet Plays*, ed E Lyons, 1934), on the subject of government interference with individual conscience and genius, did toe the Party line—but not before it had overstepped it. Further interesting plays by him are translated in *Soviet Scene: Six Plays of Russian Life* (1946, ed H Bashky), and in *Seven Soviet Plays* (1946, ed H W L Dana). He was killed in an air raid.

AGARD, John
(1949–)

Guyanese writer of children's and adult verse, resident in Britain since 1977. For several years he worked for the Commonwealth Institute as a travelling speaker, but now writes full-time. During 1993 he was writer-in-residence at London's South Bank centre. He has identified John Arlott's cricket commentary as an early influence, but the predominant strains of his children's verse, which really requires the medium of one of his extraordinarily exciting public readings to be fully appreciated, are West Indian raps and riddles. *Laughter Is An Egg* (1990) is a representative collection. His adult verse, currently overshadowed by his renown as a children's poet, is, at its best, a witty conflation of English and Caribbean idioms.

AGEE, James
(1909–55)

American novelist, poet, film critic and screen writer, born in Knoxville, Tennessee. Educated at Harvard, he worked for several magazines before being commissioned to rove the southern states with the photographer Walker Evans, an assignment that produced *Let Us Now Praise Famous Men* (1941). He became a literary celebrity and was wooed by Hollywood, for whom he wrote classic film scripts including *The African Queen* (1951) and *The Night of the Hunter* (1955). His only novel, the transparently autobiographical *A Death in the Family* (1957), was unfinished at the time of his death, and was awarded a posthumous Pulitzer Prize.
▷L Bergreen, *Agee: a Life* (1984)

AGNON, Shmuel Yosef (Shmuel Josef Czaczkes)
(1888–1970)

Israeli novelist, co-winner of the Nobel Prize for literature. Born in Buczacz, Galicia (now Poland), he went to Palestine in 1907, studied in Berlin (1913–24), then settled permanently in Jerusalem and changed his surname to Agnon. He wrote an epic trilogy of novels on Eastern Jewry in the early 20th century: *Hakhnasath Kallah* (1931, Eng trans *The Bridal Canopy*, 1937), *Ore-ah Nata Lalun* (1939, Eng trans *A Guest for the Night*, 1968) and *Tmol Shilshom* (1945, 'The Day Before Yesterday') as well as several volumes of short stories. He is considered the greatest writer in modern Hebrew, and became the first Israeli to win the Nobel Prize for literature, jointly with the Swedish author **Nelly Sachs**, in 1966.
▷A J Band, *Nostalgia and Nightmare: a study in the fiction of Agnon* (1968); S Sneh, *Schmuel Iosef Agnon* (1970)

AGUILERA MALTA, Demetrio
(1909–81)

Ecuadorean novelist, dramatist, poet, journalist and film director, born in Guayaquil into a middle-class family. He made his mark in 1930, when the so-called *Grupo de Guayaquil* brought out a story anthology in which he had eight stories. His colleagues were **Gil Gilbert**, Gallegos Lara, **Pareja Diez-Canseco** and **José de la Cuadra**. He was a reporter in the Spanish Civil War, and wrote two books about it, severely critical of Franco. Aguilera became one of the leading playwrights, as well as story-writers, of Ecuador. But his chief work was done in the novel:

his two masterpieces are: *Siete lunas y siete serpientes* (1970, Eng trans *Seven Serpents and Seven Moons*, 1979) and *El sequestro del general* (1973, Eng trans *Babelandia*, 1985). Both of these books appeared during the so-called 'boom' in Latin-American fiction, and both have been classified as 'magic realist'. Aguilera employed in both of them a well tried Latin-American procedure: by blurring the line between what is normally regarded as the 'real', and the allegedly 'fantastic', he was able to give his reader a glimpse of the reality of his characters' inner lives. Colonel Candelario Mariscal, a character in the first book, thus really is a crocodile as well as a rapist and murderer. The basis of the books is not 'reality' in the banal sense, but the richer reality of the inner life. Both books are as worthy of attention as the better-known ones of **García Márquez**, **Fuentes** and **Cortázar** (than whom Aguilera is less cerebral). *Babelandia* in particular, a mock-epic embodying both the best elements of political conscience and magic in popular culture, is a seminal book. For a long period he was forbidden to enter the USA on account of his description of its policies in Panama in the novel *Canal Zone* (1935).

▷V Carrabino (ed), *The Power of Myth in Literature and Film* (1981)

AGUIRRE, Domingo
(1864–1920)

Basque novelist whose *Garoa* (1912), a nostalgic portrait of a village, was the best known of all Basque novels, and was even translated into Castilian, as *El helecho* ('The Fern').

AGUIRRE, Nataniel
(1843–88)

Bolivian novelist and liberal politician, whose single novel, *Juan de la Rosa* (1885), records the struggle for independence, and is the outstanding Bolivian fiction of its century.

AGUSTÍ, Ignacio
(1913–74)

Spanish (and Catalan) novelist and poet, born near Barcelona. He was the founder and editor of the weekly *Destino* (1944–58). His novels about Barcelona, of which *Maiona Rebull* (1944) is the most famous, give a conventionally realistic, competent picture of the history of the city in modern times. The series as a whole was called *La ceniza fue arból* ('The Ashes Were Once a Tree').

AGUSTINI, Delmira
(1886–1914)

Uruguayan *modernista* poet, born in Montevideo, whose erotic poems took her country by storm, and who was murdered by her estranged husband, who then killed himself.

There is still much interest in her work: her poems were collected in 1954, and then her *Correspondencia íntima* (1969, 'Intimate Correspondence').

▷R B Amigo, *Delmira Agustini en la vida y en la poesía* (1964)

AHLGREN, Ernst, pseud of Victoria Benedictson
(1850–88)

Swedish novelist, born into a farmer's family in Scania in the south of Sweden. Besides **Strindberg**, she was considered to be the greatest talent of her time. Disappointed at not being allowed, despite her father's promise, to train as an artist, she threw herself into an ill-matched marriage to an older widower with five children. Her first novel, *Pengar* (1885, 'Money'), is a discussion of marriage and the emancipation of women based on her own experience. Her other novel, *Fru Marianne* (1887, 'Mrs Marianne'), in which a novel-reading young woman becomes a model country housewife, represents her dream of an ideal marriage, one in which literary interests and traditional women's work are combined. Benedictson's acquaintance with the leading Scandinavian critic of the time, Georg Brandes, developed into a passionate love on her part; when met with only chilly flirtation and scornful remarks about her writing, she committed suicide in a Copenhagen hotel. *Stora Boken* (3 vols, 1978–85, 'The Great Book'), published after her death, contains autobiographical fragments and is a significant document of the period she lived in and of her own struggle for personal liberation.

▷M Sjögren, *Rep Utan Knutar* (1979)

AHLIN, Lars
(1915–)

Swedish novelist and story-writer, born in Sundsvall. Owing to his family's poverty he had to leave school at 13 in order to work. Like many Scandinavian writers, Ahlin began as a communist and a member of the group loosely called 'proletarian'. But he is not properly of this group, since he early became interested in theology—in particular in Luther and Kierkegaard. He owes a debt to his compatriot **Pär Lagerkvist** and to **Dostoyevsky**. Thus his early (and enthralling) *Fromma mord* (1952, 'Pious Murders') is reminiscent of **Georges Duhamel**'s *Salavin*, in that it presents a protagonist who wants to be a saint but cannot prevent himself from damaging everyone with whom he comes into contact. In *Stora glömskan* (1954, 'The Great Forgetting') he created a memorable adolescent character called Zackarias.

▷A Guslafson, *A History of Swedish Literature* (1961)

AHO, Juhani, pseud of **Johannes Brofeldt**
(1861–1921)

Finnish novelist, dramatist and story-writer, born in Lapinlahti. He was a leading member of the Nuori Suomi ('Young Finland') movement, which was responsible for modernizing—mainly through French sources—Finnish literature in the last years of the 19th century. Although always a romantic at heart, he infused his work with a tough realism, for which it is still read and remembered today. He was much influenced by **Selma Lagerlöf**. *Panu* (1897, Eng trans 1899) is a historical novel set in 17th-century Finland. Some of his best and most vivid writing is contained in *Hellmanin herra* (1886, Eng trans *Squire Hellman and Other Stories*, 1893).
▷G Castren, *Juhani Aho* (1922, in Finnish)

AI CHING, pseud of **Chaing Hai-Chen**
(1910–)

Chinese poet, born in I-wu, Chekiang. He spent three years in Paris studying European art and poetry; on his return to Shanghai (1932) he was imprisoned (by the French) for three years as a 'radical'. In prison he wrote his first collection, *The Dyke River*. He was very popular as a patriotic (but never 'jingoist') poet during the war with Japan. In 1941 he threw in his lot with Mao, and over the succeeding years produced flat — but never abject, and sometimes brilliantly descriptive — polemic verse. Then in 1957 he was charged with being a 'rightist', and had to 'confess his faults'. In 1977 he was 'rehabilitated', whereupon he went to America. Translations are in K-Y Hsu's *Twentieth Century Chinese Poetry* (1963).
▷J C Lin, *Modern Chinese Poetry* (1972)

AI QING
(1910–)

Chinese poet, born into a wealthy land-owning family in Jinhua County, Shejiang Province. He studied painting in France (1928–31), but returned to China when the Japanese invaded, and was arrested for leftist activities and imprisoned (1932–5). His first published poem, 'Dayanhe' (1934), named after his wet-nurse, and his collection of poetry, *Ta-yen-ho* (1936), marked him out as a socially conscious writer and brought him fame; but his later work was not considered comparable. In 1941 he joined the communists at Yenan. After the communist take-over in 1949 he became associate editor, with **Mao Dun**, of the *People's Literature* journal. He was an active propagandist for communist-controlled literature, but at the time of the 'Hundred Flowers Campaign' (1956–7) he was accused of revisionism and stripped of his party membership. In 1959 he was exiled to a remote district in the desert area of Zinjiang for 17 years.

AICHINGER, Ilse
(1921–)

Austrian short-story writer and novelist, born and brought up in Vienna, where she studied medicine. Her novel *Die Grössere Hoffnung* (1948) made its mark as one of the first works in German to deal with the fate of Jews under the Third Reich. Although she has also published essays, poems, radio plays (such as *Auckland*, 1968) and sketches, it is on her short stories that her reputation rests; they range in tone from the light and capricious to the dark depression of Absurdism. In 1953 she married the poet **Günter Eich**; since his death in 1972 she has lived near Salzburg.

AIDOO, Christina Ama Ata
(1942–)

Ghanian story writer and poet, whose work first appeared in the magazine *Black Orpheus*. Her story 'The Message' is in *African Writing Today* (1967).

AIKEN, Conrad Potter
(1889–1973)

American poet and novelist, born in Savannah, Georgia. He was educated at Harvard, where his room mate was **T S Eliot** and his contemporaries were **Robert Benchley** and Walter Lippmann. He made his name with his first collection of verse, *Earth Triumphant* (1914), followed by a string of further volumes including *Turns and Intervals* (1917), *Punch, the Immortal Liar* (1921) and *Senlin* (1925). His *Selected Poems* won the 1930 Pulitzer Prize. He also wrote short stories and novels, including *Blue Voyage* (1927), the autobiographical *Great Circle* (1933), *King Coffin*, and another autobiographical novel, *Ushant* (1952). The novelist **Joan Aiken** is his daughter.
▷J Martin, *Conrad Aiken: a life of his art* (1962)

AIKEN, Joan Delano
(1924–)

English novelist and children's writer, born in Rye, Sussex, the daughter of the poet **Conrad Aiken**. She worked for the BBC, and for the UN Information Centre, and was a sub-editor and contributor on the literary journal *Argosy*. She is best known for her many books for children, the most famous of which are the historical adventures *Wolves of Willoughby Chase* (1962) and *The Stolen Lake*

(1981). She is a prolific and imaginative writer in that medium, and uses both historical and fantastic settings to good effect. Her books for adults include romantic thrillers as well as some poetry and plays.

AIMARD, Gustave, pseud of Olivier Gloux
(1818–83)

French novelist and adventurer, known as the French **James Fenimore Cooper**, born in Paris. He sailed as a cabin boy to America, and spent 10 years of adventure in Arkansas and Mexico. He travelled also in Spain, Turkey, and the Caucasus. In Paris, he served as an officer of the Garde Mobile (1848) and organized the Francs-tireurs de la Presse (1870–1). His numerous adventure stories include *La Grande Filibuste* (1860, 'The Great Piracy') and *La Forêt vierge* (1873, 'The Virgin Forest').

AINGER, Alfred
(1837–1904)

English biographer and essayist, born in London. He was educated with **Charles Dickens's** sons, and much influenced by him. He abandoned his family's Unitarianism for the Anglican Church, and was master of the Temple from 1894. He is best known as the biographer and editor of **Charles Lamb** and **Charles/Thomas Hood**, and also wrote a biography of **George Crabbe**. His *Lectures and Essays* were collected in 1905.

AINSWORTH, William Harrison
(1805–82)

English historical novelist, born in Manchester. He is chiefly remembered for popularizing the story of the highwayman Dick Turpin in *Rookwood* (1834) and the legend of Herne the Hunter in *Windsor Castle* (1843). A solicitor's son, he studied for the law but married a publisher's daughter and began a literary career instead. He edited *Bentley's Miscellany* (1840–2), *Ainsworth's Magazine* (1842–54) and *New Monthly Magazine*. *Rookwood* was his first major success; but he wrote no fewer than 39 popular historical romances, seven of which were illustrated by the cartoonist George Cruikshank.

AKAHITO Yamabe no
(early 8th century)

Major Japanese poet. A minor official at the Imperial Court, he seems to have kept his position largely through his poetic ability. His impression of snow-capped Mount Fuji is a famous example of his work. He is known as one of the 'twin stars'—Hitomaro being the other—of the great anthology of classical Japanese poetry known as the *Man'yōshū*

(completed in 759, 'Collection of a Myriad Leaves', translated by J L Pierson, 1929–49).

ÅKESSON, Sonja
(1926–77)

Swedish poet, born in Buttle, on the island of Gotland. Having left school early and tried a variety of jobs, she began to attend evening classes and courses in creative writing in the mid-1950s, and her first book of poetry was published in 1957. Her later collection *Husfrid* (1963, 'Domestic Peace') established her reputation, with some of the poems also winning the acclaim of the new women's movement. She combines an innovative, often colloquial, language with ready-mades from advertising and women's weeklies, creating a world which is frequently grotesque yet mellowed by a black sense of humour. She has successfully written songs and monologues for the stage, and a number of her poems have been set to music.
▷E Lilja, *Den dubbla tungan. En studie i Sonja Åkessons poesi* (1991)

AKHMADULINA, Bella
(1937–)

Russian poet and translator (mainly of Georgian poetry), born in Moscow into a family of mixed Italian-Russian-Tatar origin. She married, but divorced, **Yevgeni Yevtushenko**. She follows in the intense and candid tradition of **Tsvetayeva**, but does not possess the latter's driven quality, and is not up to the standard established by her, by **Akhmatova** and by **Gippius**. Nonetheless, she is a minor lyric poet of high quality, who has impressed with her fine readings of her poetry, given all over Europe and in New York, and whose first collection, *Struna* (1962, 'String'), attracted much attention. Available in English translation is *Fever* (1969).

AKHMATOVA, Anna, pseud of Anna Andreeyevna Gorenko
(1888–1966)

Russian poet, born in Odessa. The daughter of a naval officer, she studied in Kiev before moving to St Petersburg (Leningrad). In 1910 she married **Nikolai Gumilev**, who at first considerably influenced her style, and with him she started the neo-classicist Acmeist movement. After her early collections of terse but lyrical poems, including *Vecher* (1912, 'Evening'), *Chokti* (1913, 'The Rosary') and *Belaya Staya* (1917, 'The White Flock'), she developed an impressionist technique. She remained as far as possible neutral to the Revolution. Her husband, from whom she had parted, was shot as a counter-revolutionary in 1921. After the publication of *Anno Domini MCMXXI* (1922), she was officially silenced until 1940 when she published *Iz checti knig*. But in 1946 her verse, which previously had been acceptable, was banned as being 'too remote from socialist reconstruction'. She was 'rehabilitated' in the 1950s, and received official tributes on her death. Her later works include *Poema bez geroya* ('Poem without a Hero') and the banned *Rekviem* ('Requiem', Munich, 1963), a moving cycle of poems on the Stalin purges, during which her only son was arrested. *The Complete Poems of Anna Akhmatova* was published in 1993.

▷S Driver, *Anna Akhmatova* (1972)

AKILON, pseud of **P Vathalingam Akilandam**
(1923–)
Tamil novelist and story writer, author of *Pon malar* (1978, Eng trans *Flower of Gold*, 1978), described as 'the most awesomely realistic and relentless analysis of a woman's self-sacrifice in fiction'.

AKINS, Zoë
(1886–1958)
American dramatist, novelist and poet, born in Humansville, Montana. Moving to New York, where she trained as an actress, in 1912 she published *Interpretations*, a collection of poetry. Later, she concentrated on writing plays. Her most popular were *Déclassée* (1919), a society melodrama; *Daddy's Gone A-Hunting* (1921), a sentimental portrayal of a failing marriage, and *The Greeks had a Word for It* (1930), a comedy about the Ziegfield showgirls. Her best plays are witty and light, but not without irony or shrewd observation of middle-class women. In 1935, Akins was awarded the Pulitzer Prize for her dramatization of **Edith Wharton**'s novel, *The Old Maid*. Among her other works are a contribution to the screen adaptation of the musical, *Showboat*, and two novels, *Forever Young* (1941) and *Cake upon the Water* (1951).

AKSAKOV, Sergei Timofeyevitch
(1791–1859)
Russian novelist, born in Ufa in Orenburg. The son of a wealthy landowner, he held government posts in St Petersburg and Moscow before a meeting with **Nikolai Gogol** in 1832 turned him to literature. His house became the centre of a Gogol cult. He wrote *Metel* (1834, 'The Blizzard'), *Semeïnaya Khronika* (1846–56, 'A Family Chronicle'), *Detskie gody Bagrova-vnuka* (1858, 'Childhood Years of Bagrov-grandchild'). His writing shows his love of country sports and deep feeling for nature, and conveys a vivid impression of the rural, serf-owning society of the period.

▷S I Mashinksy, *Sergei Timofeyevitch Aksakov* (1973)

AKSYONOV, Vasily Pavlovich
(1932–)
Russian novelist, son of a communist official, born in Kazan, who (eventually) abandoned medicine for a literary career. His mother, Yevgeniya Ginzburg, wrote the widely-read *Krutoy marshrut* (1947, Eng trans *Journey into the Whirlwind*, 1967), an account of her husband's murder and her own incarceration in a Stalinist concentration camp. Aksyonov published the novel *Kollegi* (1960, Eng trans *Colleagues*, 1962), about doctors, and then, most notably, a study of adolescence in Moscow, and on the coast of the Baltic Sea, called *Zvyozdny bilet* (1961, Eng trans *A Starry Ticket*, 1962).

AKUTAGAWA Ryunosuke
(1892–1927)
Japanese writer, born in Tokyo, into a wealthy middle-class family, and educated there. Though an *habitué* of literary circles, Akutagawa seems not to have written anything until he was about 25, when he began to produce work prolifically. His novel *Shogun* (1922) is a liberal and (in the circumstances) quite daring counterblast to the rising tide of militarism in Japanese society. His bourgeois liberalism was to inform his other work, the best of which is available in translation as *Kappa* (1927), which is a social satire, and *Rashomon* (1916), a charming collection of stories. He thought of himself primarily as a poet and published several collections of verse. His later years were marked by a decline into a depressive mental illness—recorded in his verse collection *Koshibito* (1926)—culminating in his suicide at the age of 35.

▷N M Lippit, *Reality and Fiction in Japanese Literature* (1980)

ALABASTER, William
(1567–1640)
English poet and theologian. Educated at Westminster and Cambridge, he was the author of a Latin tragedy, *Roxana* (1632), a number of theological works (one of which was proscribed by the Inquisition) and some religious poetry written exclusively in sonnets. Strongly devotional, they are perhaps a little too earnest for the modern reader: 'Jesu, thy love within me is so main/And my poor heart so narrow of content/That within thy love my heart is wellnigh rent/And yet I love to bear such loving pain' is a typical opening passage.

ALAIN, pseud of **Émile-Auguste Chartier**
(1868–1951)
French philosopher and lecturer, born in Mortagne, Normandy. He studied at the École Normale Supérieure, became a philosophy teacher, exerting a formative influence on the succeeding generation of *littérateurs*, then fought as a private in World War I. His 'Propos d'un Normand' column in the *Dépêche de Rouen* newspaper dealt with politics, education and a wide range of moral issues. His own philosophy was similarly eclectic, being influenced by most of the great western thinkers, from **Plato** to Hegel. His *Histoire de mes Pensées* (1936) explains the development of his thought. Other important works include *Les Dieux* (1934) and *Vingt Leçons sur les Beaux-Arts* (1931).
▷A Maurois, *Alain* (1950)

ALAIN-FOURNIER, pseud of **Henri-Alban Fournier**
(1886–1914)
French writer, born in La Chapelle d'Angillon, the son of a country schoolmaster. He became a literary journalist in Paris, and was killed at St Remy soon after the outbreak of World War I. He left a semi-autobiographical fantasy novel, *Le Grand Meaulnes* (1913, Eng trans in the USA *The Wanderer*, 1958, in UK *The Lost Domain*, 1966), now considered a modern classic, and a few short stories, collected in *Miracles* (1924). His voluminous family correspondence was published posthumously.
▷R D D Gibson, *The Quest of Alain-Fournier* (1953)

ALAMANNI, Luigi
(1495–1556)
Italian poet, born in Florence. He died at Amboise a political refugee, having been employed as a diplomat by Francis I in France. He drew heavily on classical forms in his work, the best of which is *La coltivazione* (1546, 'Farming'), a didactic poem in the style of **Virgil**'s *Georgics*.
▷H Hauvette, *Un exile florentin à la cour de France au XVIème siècle* (1903)

ALARCÓN, Pedro Antonio de
(1833–91)
Spanish writer, born in Guadic. He served with distinction in the African campaign of 1859–60, and became a radical journalist. At the Restoration in 1874, however, he became a Conservative, and served as minister to Stockholm, and councillor of state. He published a vivid war diary, travel notes and poems, but is best known for his novels, particularly *Sombrero de tres picos* (1874), on

which Manuel de Falla based his ballet, *The Three-Cornered Hat*.
▷R Carrasco, *Pedro Antonio de Alarcón autor dramatico* (1933)

ALAS, Leopoldo
(1852–1901)
Spanish author, born in Zamora, he also wrote under the pseudonym of Clarin, meaning 'bugle'. He was Professor of Law at Oviedo, but is better known as a literary figure. He published short stories (*Cuentos morales*, 1896, 'Moral Stories'), a social drama, *Teresa* (1895), and several novels, including *La Regenta* (1884–5, 'The Regent's Wife'). He also wrote treatises on law and economics. His writing is objective, sometimes cold, but always powerful and sincere.
▷M Goyanes Baquero, *'Clarin' creador del cuento español* (1949)

ALBEE, Edward Franklin, III
(1928–)
American dramatist, born in Virginia and adopted by a rich theatre-owning family. He was educated in Connecticut and then had various jobs in New York. His play *The Zoo Story* (1958) was influenced by the Theatre of the Absurd and began his attack on the complacency of the American middle class. He continued this in further one-act plays, such as *The American Dream* (1960), a hilarious parody of family life. He had an enormous success with *Who's Afraid of Virginia Woolf?* (1962), which, with caustic wit, exposes a marriage built on illusions, and then used his new-found influence to help other writers. The bizarrely plotted *Tiny Alice* (1964) was denounced as obscure by many American theatre critics—of whom Albee has a famously low opinion. *A Delicate Balance* (1966) deals with another unhappy family. Albee's interest in experimental dramatic forms is particularly evident in *Box* and *Quotations from Chairman Mao Tse-Tung* (both 1968). His later plays, such as the brilliant allegory *The Man Who Had Three Arms* (1982), again displayed great poetic intelligence and masterly dialogue, but were not commercially successful. His dramatizations include *Malcolm* (1965) and *Lolita* (1981).
▷C W E Bigsby, *Albee* (1969); G McCarthy, *Edward Albee* (1987)

ALBERTI, Rafael
(1902–)
Spanish poet and dramatist, a member of the great 'Generation of '27', which included **Lorca**, **Louis Cernuda** and **Pedro Salinas**. He began as a painter, and has always alluded to painting in his poetry. He fought against

Franco and in 1939 went into exile to Argentina, and then to Rome. After Franco's death he returned to Spain as the most honoured of all its literary veterans. It is generally conceded that his supreme poetry is in his astonishing fifth collection *Sobre los ángeles* (1929, English version, *Concerning the Angels*, 1967). This work shows the influences of Surrealism and of the critical views of the Spanish critic **Ortega y Gasset**, but far transcends the genre of Surrealism in its visionary qualities and the power of its expression of the conflict between innocence and 'authenticity', and the dehumanizing effects of Positivism. But the strain—and natural anger at injustice—proved too much for Alberti, and he retreated into more simplistic communist verse. Later, however, in the bitterness of exile, his poetry once again reverted to its old and less certain self, so that his output as a whole deserves even more close study than it gets. In general he has not yet been dealt with adequately in English-language criticism. Other poetry in English translation: *Selected Poems* (1966); *The Owl's Insomnia* (1973).

ALCAEUS
(c.620–after 580 BC)

One of the great Greek lyric poets. He lived at Mytilene on the island of Lesbos, where he was a contemporary of **Sappho**. He wrote in a variety of metres, including the four-line alcaic stanza named after him and used notably (in Latin) by **Horace**. A bluff, blustering extrovert, he composed a host of drinking songs, hymns, political odes and love songs, of which only fragments now remain.

ALCÁNTARA MACHADO, Antonio de
(1901–35)

Brazilian story writer and essayist, prominent amongst the modernist group. His laconic, ironic, pointillist collection *Brás, Bexiga e Barra-Funda* (1927), named after three poor districts of São Paulo, made his reputation. *Mana María* (1936) is an unfinished novel, also about São Paulo.

ALCIPHRON
(fl.180)

Greek writer. He wrote 118 fictitious letters from ordinary people (farmers, fisherman, etc) affording glimpses into everyday life in 4th century BC Athens.

ALCMAN
(fl.c.630 BC)

Greek lyric poet. Born, according to one tradition, in Asia Minor, he lived in Sparta. He wrote six books of poems. Of one, a choral hymn, about half survives; otherwise there are only short fragments, mostly written in the Doric dialect. His subjects include animals, food, night and sleep.

ALCOTT, Louisa May
(1832–88)

American writer, and author of the children's classic *Little Women*. The daughter of the Transcendentalist Amos Bronson Alcott, she was born in Germantown, Philadelphia. She was a nurse in a Union hospital during the Civil War, and published her letters from this period as *Hospital Sketches* in 1864. In 1868 she achieved enormous success with *Little Women*, which drew on her own home experiences, and a second volume, *Good Wives*, in 1869, followed by *An Old Fashioned Girl* (1870), *Little Men* (1871) and *Jo's Boys* (1886).
▷M Saxton, *Louisa May: a modern biography of Alcott* (1977)

ALCOVER, Joan
(1854–1926)

Spanish poet, born in Palma, Majorca. Although his first writings were in the Castilian language, he is chiefly known as a poet in Catalan. He presided over a literary *salon* in Majorca, where he was known as a precise literary critic and brilliant talker. His poetry reflects the tragedy of his private life (he lost his wife and four children in rapid succession) and a deep feeling for his native landscape. He published *Poesias* (1887), *Metereos* (1901) and *Poèmes Biblics* (1919).
▷J Arus, *Tres poetas: Maragall, Alcover, Guesch* (1970)

ALCUIN
(c.735–804)

Northumbrian scholar, and adviser to Emperor Charlemagne, born in York and educated at the cloister school, of which in 778 he became master. He is also known as Albinus, and his Anglo-Saxon name is Ealhwine. In 781, returning from Rome, he met Charlemagne at Parma, and on his invitation attached himself to the court at Aix-la-Chapelle (Aachen). Here he devoted himself first to the education of the royal family, but through his influence the court became a school of culture for the Frankish empire, inspiring the Carolingian renaissance. In 796 he settled at Tours as abbot; and the school here soon became one of the most important in the empire. Till his death he still corresponded constantly with Charlemagne. His works comprise poems; works on grammar, rhetoric, and dialectics; theological and ethical treatises; biographies of several saints; and over 200 letters.
▷E M W Buxton, *Alcuin* (1922)

ALDANA, Francisco de
(1537–78)

Spanish poet of noble family from Extremadura, probably born in the kingdom of Naples. He spent his youth in Florence under the protection of the Medici. Neoplatonism was a marked influence on him, as was the paganism of **Horace** and **Virgil**. Aldana was an unusual weave of various strands; while he wrote the usual courtly verses, they were underpinned by an unabashed sensuality far removed from the rigidity of idealized love. He also wrote military, religious and erotic poetry; 45 sonnets are preserved as well as long narrative or doctrinal poems ('Fabula de Factarte' being one), and six epistles, mainly of a moral character. Although highly regarded by **Cervantes** among others, he later fell into oblivion. Aldana disappeared in the battle of Alcazarquivir, the king of Portugal's quixotic attempt to defeat the Moors.

ALDINGTON, Richard, originally Edward Godfree
(1892–1962)

English poet, novelist, editor and biographer, born in Hampshire. He was educated at London University, and in 1913 became editor of *Egoist*, the periodical of the Imagist school, to which he belonged. His experiences in World War I left him ill and bitter, and this led to his novel *Death of a Hero* (1929). As well as other novels, such as *The Colonel's Daughter* (1931), he published several volumes of poetry, including *A Fool i' the Forest* (1925) and *A Dream in the Luxembourg* (1930). At the beginning of World War II he went to the USA, where he published his *Poetry of the English-Speaking World* (1941) and many biographies, including *Wellington* (1946), which was awarded the James Tait Black Memorial Prize, a study of **D H Lawrence** (1950), a controversial and embittered study of *Lawrence of Arabia* (1955), and a study of **Robert Louis Stevenson** (1957). He married **Hilda Doolittle**, also a poet; in 1913, they were divorced in 1937. He published his autobiography, *Life for Life's Sake*, in 1940, and his correspondence with **Lawrence Durrell**, *Literary Lifelines*, appeared in 1981.
▷A Kershaw and F J Temple, *Richard Aldington: an intimate portrait* (1965)

ALDISS, Brian Wilson
(1925–)

English science-fiction writer and novelist, born in Dereham, Norfolk and educated at Framlingham College. After a career in bookselling, he embarked on a prolific career of writing with his first novel, *The Brightfount Diaries*, in 1955. He was literary editor of the *Oxford Mail* (1958–69), and had considerable success with *The Hand-Reared Boy* (1970) and *A Soldier Erect* (1971). He is best known, however, as a writer of science fiction, such as *Non-Stop* (1958, entitled *Starship* in the USA), *Hothouse* (1962), *The Saliva Tree* (1966), *The Moment of Eclipse* (1971), *Frankenstein Unbound* (1973), *Helliconia Spring* (1982), *Helliconia Summer* (1983), *Helliconia Winter* (1985) and *Dracula Unbound* (1991). His more experimental works in the genre include *Report on Probability A* (1964) and *Barefoot in the Head* (1969). He also writes graphic novels, has edited many books of short stories, and produced histories of science fiction such as *Billion Year Spree* (1973) and *Trillion Year Spree* (1986).
▷*Bury My Heart at W. H. Smith's* (1990)

ALDRICH, Thomas Bailey
(1836–1907)

American writer, born in Portsmouth, New Hampshire. He was Editor of the *Atlantic Monthly* (1881–90), and the author of numerous short stories and novels, and several volumes of poetry. His most successful book, *The Story of a Bad Boy* (1870) was an autobiographical novel about his boyhood. *Prudence Palfrey* (1874) and *The Queen of Sheba* (1877) were more romantic. *The Stillwater Tragedy* (1880) is a detective story.
▷C Samuels, *Thomas Bailey Aldrich* (1965)

ALDRIDGE, (Harold Edward) James
(1918–)

Australian-born British journalist and writer of popular fiction, born in White Hills, Victoria. Based in England since before World War II, during which he served as a war correspondent in Europe, his first books drew upon that experience. *Signed with Their Honour* (1942) was followed by *The Sea Eagle* (1944) and *Of Many Men* (1946). Later he turned to the political turmoil in Europe and the Near East in such books as *The Diplomat* (1950) and *The Last Exile* (1961), in which his left-wing views colour the scene. A follower of the **Hemingway** school, he paid his dues in *One Last Glimpse* (1977) in which Papa (Hemingway), **Zelda** and **F Scott Fitzgerald** and other real-life characters of the period make their appearance.

ALECSANDRI, Vasile
(1821–90)

Romanian poet and dramatist, born in Bacau. He began as a Paris-educated theatre director who was obliged to create a repertory of his own as there were no plays in his own language. He wrote polite and well-crafted farces and historical dramas. Later he became interested in folk poetry, and his understanding of it produced his most vital work:

subtle nature and landscape poems of great mellifluousness. His patriotic poetry was popular.

ALEGRÍA, Ciro
(1909–67)

Peruvian novelist, born in Sartimbamba; both his parents were of the Lynch family—that of the Argentinian novelist **Benito Lynch**. Alegría had the privilege of having been taught at school by **César Vallejo**. He worked with the forbidden APRA party of Haya de la Torre until 1931, when he was imprisoned. He was forced out of his own country in 1934, and settled down to writing in Santiago de Chile. The success of *La serpiente de oro* (1935, Eng trans *The Golden Serpent*, 1943), *Los perros hambrientes* (1938, Eng trans of an excerpt in G Arciniegas, ed, *The Green Continent*, 1944) and of the novel which gave him an international reputation, *El mundo es ancho y acheno* (1941, Eng trans *Broad and Alien Is the World*, 1941), enabled him to live and work in the United States. After he returned to Peru he became an MP, with links to the Popular Action Party. *Broad and Alien is the World*, about the Native Americans, was long taken to be his best novel, and certainly it familiarized many readers all over the world with these oppressed peoples in Peru. But more recent criticism has preferred *The Golden Serpent*, and has also pointed out that the Native Americanism is anthropologically flawed—and that the real nature of Native American peoples is better conveyed in the more poetic fiction of **José María Arguedas**.
▷J Early, *Joy in Exile: Ciro Alegría's Narrative Art* (1980)

ASCH, Sholem
(1880–1957)

Jewish writer, born in Kutno in Poland, who emigrated to America in 1914 and became naturalized in 1920. His prolific output of novels and short stories, most of them originally in Yiddish but many since translated, includes *The Mother* (1930), *The War Goes On* (1936), *The Nazarene* (1939), *The Apostle* (1943), *East River* (1946) and *Moses* (1951), mostly concerned with the fate of modern Jewry. His early work includes the plays *Mottke the Thief* (1917) and *The God of Vengeance* (1918).
▷C Lieberman, *The Christianity of Sholem Asch* (1953)

ALEIXANDRE, Vicente
(1898–1984)

Spanish poet, and winner of the Nobel Prize for literature. Born in Seville, the son of a railway engineer, he suffered from renal tuberculosis in his youth, which forced him to remain in Spain after the Civil War despite his Republican sympathies. Among his early works were *Ambito* (1928, 'Ambit'), *La Destrucción o el amor* (1935, 'Destruction or Love') and *Pasión de la Tierra* (1935, 'Passion of the World'), but it was the appearance of his collected poems, *Mis Poemas Mejores*, in 1937, that established his reputation as a major poet. His later publications include *En un vasto dominio* (1962), *Presencias* (1965, 'Presences'), and *Antologia Total* (1976, 'Complete Works'). He was awarded the Nobel Prize for literature in 1977.
▷K Schwartz, *Vicente Aleixandre* (1970)

ALEMÁN, Mateo
(1547–1610 or 1620)

Spanish novelist, born in Seville. He led a disorderly, poverty-stricken life in Spain, and ultimately emigrated to Mexico in 1608. His great work is the important picaresque novel *Guzmán de Alfarache* (1599), in which the decline and ultimate repentence of a runaway boy mirrors the sinful and corrupt state of Spain.
▷E Cros, *Mateo Alemán: introduccion a su vida y su obras* (1971)

ALENCAR, José Martiniano de
(1829–77)

Brazilian novelist, born in Mecejana, Ceará. He was Minister of Justice before he retired to devote himself to fiction in 1870. He was an early 'Indianist', seeing—largely under the influence of **Chateaubriand**, but also of **Scott** and **Fenimore Cooper**—in the Brazilian Native American the apotheosis of nobility. Conversely, he attacked the commercial greed of the white man and the obscurantism of the clergy. His romantic novel *Iracema* (1865, Eng trans *Iracema, the Honey-Lips, a Legend of Brazil*, 1886) concerns a Portuguese officer who is led into purity by the example of a lovely Native American maiden.
▷D M Driver, *The Indian in Brazilian Literature* (1942)

ALERAMO, Sibilla, pseud of **Rina Faccio**
(1876–1960)

Italian novelist, poet and memoirist (*Dal mio diario*, 1945, 'From My Diary'), born in Alesandria. She was the lover of a number of poets, including the great **Campana** and **Cardelli**. Always a socialist, she joined the communists after World War II. She was a woman of great but underrated gifts, whose feminist viewpoint is most poignantly evoked in *Una donna* (1906, Eng trans *A Woman at Bay*, 1908), an early and acute description of the manner in which men, while pretending to celebrate and love women, really treat them as objects; but other work shows that she understood the poignancy of those men who wanted to be exceptional. This has yet to be re-discovered in the English-speaking world. There is a moving collection of the letters between her and Campana: *Dino Campana-Sibilla Aleramo: Lettere* (1952). Her *Amo, dunque sono* (1927, 'I Love, Therefore I Am') is yet another of her remarkable books awaiting rediscovery. It has been said that 'if men really want to understand women they must read Aleramo'.

ALEXANDER, Cecil Frances, née Humphreys
(1818–95)

Irish poet and hymn writer, born in County Wicklow, the daughter of a captain in the Royal Marines, and wife of Bishop William Alexander. She published her *Verses for Holy Seasons* in 1846, and two years later her immensely popular *Hymns for Little Children*, which included the well known 'All things bright and beautiful', 'Once in Royal David's city', and 'There is a green hill far away'. She also wrote ballads on Irish history.

ALEXANDER, Sir William
(1567–1640)

Scottish poet, born in Menstrie, Clackmannanshire. He was educated at Glasgow and Leiden universities, and became a courtier to James VI in Edinburgh, and later in London, and to Charles I. He was created Earl of Stirling in 1633, and although a powerful political figure, he ultimately died in poverty. Most of his work does not appeal to modern tastes, as in the case of the tedious verse-dramas *The Monarchick Tragedies* (1603–7), his 'Elegy on the Death of Prince Henry' (1612), and the long religious poem *Doomesday* (1614). The songs, sonnets and elegies collected in *Aurora* (1604) have fared rather better, and are now the only works by which he is likely to be remembered.

ALEXANDER, William
(1826–94)

Scottish novelist, born in Chapel of Garioch, Aberdeenshire. He worked as a ploughman until losing a leg in an accident, after which he turned to journalism. He wrote a novel in racy dialect, *Johnny Gibb of Gushetneuk* (1871), a series of realistic sketches of the remote country folk and places of north-eastern Scotland, which was serialized in the *Aberdeen Free Press*, of which he later became editor.

ALEXIS, Jacques-Stéphen
(1922–61)

Haitian novelist whose *Les Arbes musiciens* (1957, 'The Musical Trees'), is the first Haitian novel to analyse in depth the national character. He was murdered at the instructions of the dictator Duvalier.

ALFIERI, Vittorio, Count
(1749–1803)

Italian poet and dramatist, born in Asti, near Piedmont. His political writings identify him as a precursor of the Risorgimento. He inherited a vast fortune at the age of 14, and travelled throughout Europe before turning his hand to writing, achieving great success with his first play, *Cleopatra*, in 1775. In Florence in 1777 he met the Countess of Albany, the estranged wife of Prince Charles Edward Stewart; after separating from her husband, she became his mistress. He wrote more than a score of tragedies, six comedies, and a 'tramelogedia', *Abele*, a mixture of opera and tragedy. His ashes, and those of his mistress, are kept in the church of S Croce, in Florence, between the tombs of Michelangelo and **Machiavelli**.
▷G Megaro, *Alfieri: Forerunner of Italian Nationalism* (1930)

ALFRED, the Great
(849–99)

Anglo-Saxon King of Wessex, born at Wantage in Berkshire, the fifth and youngest son of King Æthelwulf. His importance within a literary context lies in his role in restoring scholarship and learning in England in the wake of the Viking invasions; through his encouragement of translation and his emphasis on idiomatic translation, he laid the foundations of English prose. A noted scholar himself, his works include translations of Gregory the Great's *Cura Pastoralis*, **Boethius**'s *De Consolatione Philosophiae*, and Augustine's *Soliloquia*, as well as works by **Bede** and **Orosius**. It has also been suggested that it was he who inspired the production of the *Anglo-Saxon Chronicle*, the earliest historical record in the English language.
▷E S Duckett, *Alfred the Great and his England* (1961)

ALGER, Horatio, Jr
(1832–99)

American writer and clergyman, born in Revere, Massachusetts. He was educated at Harvard, became a Unitarian minister, and wrote boys' adventure stories on the 'poor boy makes good' theme, such as *Ragged Dick* (1867) and *From Canal Boy to President*

(1881). His own life was mythicized by early biographers.

▷F Gruber, *Alger: A Biography and Bibliography* (1961)

ALGREN, Nelson
(1909–81)

American novelist, born in Detroit. He moved early to Chicago, where he trained as a journalist at the University of Illinois, before becoming a migrant worker during the Depression. In Chicago again from 1935, he became a leading member of the 'Chicago school of realism'. He produced a series of uncompromising, powerful but baggy novels which include *Somebody in Boots* (1935), *Never Come Morning* (1942) and *The Man with the Golden Arm* (1949), a novel about drug addiction regarded by some as his best work. He had a transatlantic affair with **Simone de Beauvoir**, which is described in her novel *Les Mandarins* (1954) and in her autobiography.

▷M Cox and W Chatterton, *Nelson Algren* (1975)

AL-HAKIM, Tawfik
(1898–1987)

Egyptian playwright and novelist, born in Alexandria. He studied law in Cairo and Paris. One of his best novels, *Maze of Justice: Diary of a Country Prosecutor* (1947), was translated into English by Abba Eban, and originally published in 1937. **P H Newby** called this bitter comedy about the stunted lives of Egyptian peasants (*fellahin*), oppressed by bureaucrats, 'blacker than anything by Gogol or Dickens'. Al-Hakim's often astringently comic plays pioneered modern Arabic drama. English translations include *The Tree Climber* (1966), *Fate of a Cockroach and Other Plays* (1973), both translated by Denys Johnson-Davies, and *Plays, Prefaces and Postcripts* (1981, 1984), in two volumes, translated by William M Hutchins.

AL-HALLAJ, Husayn ibn Mansur
(c.858–922)

Persian mystic, born in the Iranian province of Fars, one of Islam's most famous Sufi teachers. He travelled widely in the East before settling in Baghdad. In his teaching he stressed the soul's need to attain unity with God through love. Some critics have detected Christian and Gnostic strains in his thought. A God-intoxicated man, he was alleged to have declared 'I am the Truth'. He attracted the hostility of certain Islamic jurists and politicians and was tried for heresy. After eight years in prison, he was put to death by crucifixion. His scrappy rhymed prose treatise, the *Kitab al-tawasin*, perhaps written in prison, deals with divine unity and the status of God's prophets. His *Akhbar* ('Reports') consist of anecdotes about him as well as sayings and verses by him collected by his disciples and posthumously written down.

▷L Massignon, *The Passion of al-Hallaj* (4 vols, 1982)

AL-HAMADHANI
(969–1007)

Arabic creator of the *maqamah*, the short story written out in rhymed prose. Two characters feature in his inventions, the *rawi* or narrator, and the unscrupulous wanderer or vagabond—one of the earliest representations of the trickster in post-classical literature. Al-Hamadhani's creations in the *Maqamat* (Eng trans 1913–17) played their part in the genesis of the picaresque novel.

ALI, Ahmed
(1912–)

Pakistani story writer and novelist who writes in Urdu and in English, and was in his youth a member of the Progressive Writers' Association and an active socialist. His stories, well known in India, are in Urdu; his novels, including the historical *Twilight in Delhi* (1940, about early 20th-century Delhi Muslims), and *Ocean of Night* (1964), are in English. He is also a poet, and his anthology *The Falcon and the Hunted Bird* (1950) gives some exquisite translations into English of classical Urdu poets.

ALIGER, Margarita Iosifovna
(1915–)

Russian poet, born in Odessa and educated in Moscow. She worked as a war correspondent during World War II and *Vesna v Leningrade* (1942), containing poems about the effect on the civilian population of the blockade on Leningrad, is one of the enduring poetic achievements of the war, as is *Zoya* (1942), a long poem about a Moscow schoolgirl tortured to death by the Germans. After the war she managed to tread the line between personal integrity and the expectations of the state. She wrote a patriotic hymn for the construction of the new Moscow University, but in general her territory is small-scale and sombre.

AL-JAHIZ, Abu 'Uthman 'Amr ibn Bahr al-Kinani al-Fuqaimi al-Basri
(c.776–868)

Essayist, writing in Arabic, possibly of African descent, though born in Basra, Iraq. Allegedly al-Jahiz ('the Goggle-Eyed') wrote 231 treatises, mostly of a belle-lettristic nature. His most famous work, the *Kitab al-Hayawan* ('Book of Beasts'), took as its pretext a debate about the respective merits of the cock and the dog. However, the work (which is full of digressions on the most bizarre subjects) was chiefly concerned to show that the Arabs' knowledge of natural history was not inferior to that of the Greeks. Other works discussed, among other subjects, rhetoric, singing slave girls, passion, cripples, the culture of bureaucrats, the superiority of blacks to whites, the respective merits of the back and the belly, Turks, misers, etiquette and cities. Al-Jahiz was a polemical and ironical stylist who rarely resisted an opportunity for intellectual clowning.

▷C Pellat, *The Life and Works of Jahiz* (1969)

AL-KHANSA

(fl.first part of 7th century)

Arabic poet, famous for the perfection of her dirges for her dead brothers.

▷G Gabrieli, *I tempi, la vita e il canzoniere della poetessa Al-Hansa* (1899)

ALLEN, (William) Hervey

(1889–1949)

American author, born in Pittsburg. He trained for the American navy, in which he became a midshipman. In World War I, however, he fought with distinction as a lieutenant in the army, and later (1926) published his war diary, *Towards the Flame*. His best-known novel *Anthony Adverse* (1933) sold a million and a half copies; others are *Action at Aquila* (1938), *The Forest and the Fort* (1943), *Bedford Village* (1945) and *The City of the Dawn* which was unfinished at his death. Allen also wrote a study of **Edgar Allan Poe** under the title *Israfel* (1926).

ALLEN, James Lane

(1849–1925)

American novelist, born in Kentucky. He wrote *The Kentucky Cardinal* (1895), *Aftermath* (1896), *The Choir Invisible* (1897–8), and other novels of a romantic sort, admired for their local colour.

▷W K Bottorff, *James Lane Allen* (1964)

ALLEN, Walter Ernest

(1911–)

English novelist and critic, born in Birmingham. After working as a schoolmaster and university lecturer in the USA, he became a journalist. His first novel, *Innocence is Drowned*, was published in 1938, and he scored a considerable success with *Dead Man over All* in 1950. His other novels include *Rogue Elephant* (1946) and *All In A Lifetime* (1959). He has written several critical works, including *The English Novel—A short critical history* (1954) and *Tradition and Dream* (1964).

ALLEN, Woody, properly Allen Stewart Konigsberg

(1935–)

American screenwriter, actor, director, short-story writer and occasional jazz clarinettist. He was born in Brooklyn, New York, and launched his career as a comedian in clubs and on television, developing the self-deprecating neurosis and 'genetic dissatisfaction with everything' that were to become his stock-in-trade. He made his film debut scripting and acting in *What's New, Pussycat?* (1965). Later movie projects—often co-scripted with Marshall Brickman—were more obviously vehicles for his stand-up routines: *Bananas* (1971), *Everything You Always Wanted to Know About Sex … But Were Afraid to Ask* (1972), *Sleeper* (1973) and *Love and Death* (1973). After *Annie Hall* (1977) and *Manhattan* (1979), his films took on a more fictive and structured aspect (in the eyes of detractors, they were simply less funny), as in *Stardust Memories* (1980), *Broadway Danny Rose* (1984), *Hannah and Her Sisters* (1986) and *Crimes and Misdemeanours* (1989). Allen's interest in modern literature and in the curiously compressed and ironic impact of contemporary culture is reflected in his books of stories and sketches: *Getting Even* (1971), *Without Feathers* (1975), *Side Effects* (1980) and *The Floating Light Bulb* (1982).

▷E Lax, *Woody Allen* (1991)

ALLENDE, Isabel

(1942–)

Chilean novelist, born in Lima, Peru, niece and god-daughter of Salvador Allende, the former President of Chile. Several months after the overthrow of Chile's coalition government in 1973 by the forces of a junta headed by General Augusto Pinochet Ugarte, she and her family fled Chile, Isabel seeking sanctuary in Venezuela. Her first novel, *Casa de los espíritus* (Eng trans *The House of the Spirits*, 1985), arose directly out of her exile and her estrangement from her family, in particular her aged grandfather, who remained in Chile. It became a worldwide bestseller and achieved critical success, and Allende was heralded as the most exciting talent to emerge from Latin America since **Gabriel García Márquez**. In 1987 she published *De Amor y de Sombra* (Eng trans *Of Love and Shadows*, 1987), and in 1993 *El Plan infinito* (Eng trans *The Infinite Plan*, 1993).

ALLEY, Rewi

(1897–1987)

New Zealand poet, born in Springfield, Canterbury, who spent most of his working life in China. After service in World War I he returned to New Zealand but, after a failed sheep-farming venture, went to Shanghai in 1927. There he became involved in flood and famine relief work and later organized industrial co-operatives. He published 16 volumes of poetry from *Gung Ho!* (1948) to *Today and Tomorrow* (1975), mainly set in China, though one, *Poems for Aotearoa* (1972), looks back to his homeland. Alley also translated and published over 30 volumes of Maoist verse and a book on western imperialism.

ALLFREY, Phyllis Byam, née Shand
(1915–86)

Dominican poet and novelist, daughter of the Crown Attorney and descendant of generations of white settlers. Educated at home and in Europe, she lived in England as a young woman, returning to Dominica after the war with her English husband. She was prominent in public affairs, founding the Dominican Labour Party, serving as Minister for Labour and Social Affairs in the federal government (1958–62), and editing two newspapers. She published four books of poems, a novel, *The Orchid House* (1953), and many short stories. Her writings powerfully convey the steamy atmosphere, beauty and decadence, and inbred social and political life of Dominica.
▷E Campbell, in *Fifty Caribbean Writers*, ed D C Dance (1986)

ALLINGHAM, Margery Louise
(1904–66)

English detective-story writer, and creator of the fictional detective Albert Campion. Born in London, she wrote a string of elegant and witty novels, including *Crime at Black Dudley* (1928), *Police at the Funeral* (1931), *Flowers for the Judge* (1936), *More Work for the Undertaker* (1949), *The Tiger in the Smoke* (1952), *The China Governess* (1963) and *The Mind Readers* (1965).

ALLINGHAM, William
(1824–89)

Irish poet, born in Ballyshannon, County Donegal. He was in the Irish Customs (1846–70), and in 1874 succeeded James Froude as Editor of *Fraser's Magazine*. In 1874 he married Helen Paterson (1848–1926), who, born near Burton-on-Trent, made a name by her book illustrations and water colours, and edited his *Diary* (1907), a rich recollection of Victorian literary life. His works include *Day and Night Songs* (1855), illustrated by **Dante Gabriel Rossetti** and Sir John Millais; *Laurence Bloomfield in Ireland* (1864), *Irish Songs and Poems* (1887), and *Collected Poems* (1888–93).

▷H Kropf, *William Allingham und seine Dichtung* (1928)

ALMADA-NEGREIROS, José de
(1893–1970)

Portuguese poet and writer of fiction, born on São Tome, off the west African (Gabon) coast. He spent most of his life in Lisbon. His minor poetry is lively, surreal, primitivistic, naive, striving always to express the joy in living. He wrote a novel, *Nome de Guerra* (1938, 'Pseudonym').
▷*Colóquio*, 60 (1970, in Portuguese)

ALMAFUERTE, pseud of Pedro Bonifacio Palacios
(1854–1917)

Argentinian minor poet whose too often vituperative work is, mainly, spoiled by his overly self-conscious cultivation of what he considered to be bad taste. He was by profession a self-educated village schoolmaster, who did good work in his own life, but a few Argentinian critics have found in his works what they take to be innovations. His autobiography, *La hora trágica* (1906, 'The Tragic Hour'), is in parts moving; it is also packed with interesting information. His works were collected and introduced by R Brughetti in an edition of 1954 called *Obras de Almafuerte*.

AL-MALAKAI, Nazik
(1923–)

Iraqi poet and critic, whose work has been deeply influenced by European models. Her poetry is subjective, and, in Western terms, would be called 'hermetic'. However, as a nationalist poet she is more conventional. One of her best-known collections is *Li al-salah wa al-thawra* (1978, 'To Prayer and Revolution').
▷M M Badawi, *Critical Introduction to Modern Arabic Poetry* (1975)

ALMEDINGEN, E M (Martha Edith von)
(1898–1971)

Russian-born British novelist, biographer, autobiographer and historian, born in St Petersburg. Settling in England, she became a distinguished academic historian. She was the author of over 60 books, including novels, but is best remembered for her biographies, both for adult and younger readers. These provide a highly readable and atmospheric account of Russia's turbulent history. *A Study of Emperor Paul I of Russia: 1754–1801* (1959), and *Catherine the Great: A Portrait* (1963), drawing upon letters and memoirs, are particularly vivid and politically balanced.
▷*Tomorrow Will Come* (1941); *The Almond Tree* (1947); *Late Arrival* (1952)

ALMEIDA, Guilherme de
(1890–1969)

Brazilian minor poet, remarkable for his delicacy of touch, born in the state of São Paulo. He was active in the Brazilian avant garde, and promoted the work of many younger poets, including **Bandeira**. He made a particularly prized translation of **Villon**.

ALMEIDA, José Américo de
(1887–1976)

Brazilian novelist, born in Areia, Paraiba. Almeida was the pioneer of Brazil's northeastern novel. Called a 'liberal politician' by some, and by others 'a servant of Brazilian politics' (he served the dictator Vargas twice), his one important book is the novel *A bagaceira* (1928, Eng trans *Cane Trash*, 1978), a crude, paternalistic but vivid and in certain respects truthful account of conditions on the cane plantations in the first years of the 20th century. As readable as it is stylistically inept and melodramatic, it turned serious people's attention towards an intractable problem.
▷F Ellison, *Brazil's New Novel* (1954)

ALMEIDA, Manuel Antônio de
(1831–61)

Brazilian novelist and journalist, born in Rio de Janeiro. He is best remembered for one anti-romantic, almost picaresque novel, which few of its first readers could really appreciate. *Memórias de um Sargento de Milicias* (1854–5, Eng trans *Memoirs of a Militia Sergeant*, 1959), the story of an illegitimate boy and his rise in fortune under the tutelage of several women, is not only an invaluable source book for life in Rio at the beginning of the 19th century, but also a work of very considerable literary worth.

ALMEIDA-GARRETT, João Baptista da Silva Leitão
(1799–1854)

Portuguese author and politician, born in Oporto. He was brought up in the Azores, and was exiled after the 1820 revolt, but returned and supported Pedro I and became Minister of the Interior. A pioneer of the romantic movement and of modern Portuguese drama, he wrote the historical play *Gil Vicente* (1838), the epic *Camões* (1825), and many ballads.
▷R B Lawton, *Almeida-Garrett, L'intime contrainte* (1966)

ALMQUIST, Carl Jonas Love
(1793–1866)

Swedish author, born in Stockholm. He had a bizarrely chequered career; a clergyman and teacher, he was accused of forgery and attempted murder, and fled to the USA.

Returning to Europe, he spent the last year of his life in Bremen under the assumed name of 'Professor Carl Westermann'. A prolific essayist and philosopher, his worked ranged from Swedenborgian mysticism to social realism, and included novels, plays, poems and essays. The 17-volume series *Törnrosensbok* (1833–40, 'The Book of the Wild Rose') was an eclectic summation of his earlier vision.
▷G Balgård, *Carl Jonas Love Almqvist: samhallsvisignaren* (1973)

AL-MUWAILIHI, Muhammad
(1858–1930)

Egyptian novelist and essayist. His *Hadith Isa ibn Hisham* (1898–1902, Eng trans 1974) was one of the most important books of its time. It offered a brilliant and satirical exposé of the faults of Egyptian society, and of the British administration.

ALONI, Nissim
(1926–)

Israeli dramatist, story writer and translator, born in Tel-Aviv. He fought in the War of Independence (1947–9), lived in Paris for a few years, and began as an author with stories of his youth in Tel Aviv. Two of his plays have received much attention. The first, *Achzar mikol hamelech* (1953, 'The Cruellest Of All—the King'), deals with the problems of the young Israel by means of biblical symbolism: the story is that of the revolt of Jeroboam, and Aloni thus is able to present Israel's conflict between its religious and its secular role. The second, *Bigdai hamelech* (1961, 'The King's Clothes'), based on **Hans Christian Andersen**'s 'The Emperor's Clothes', examines revolutionary pretences in the modern world. Aloni runs a theatre group for which he has written such plays as *Arlekino* (1963, 'Harlequin'), and much topical satire.
▷*Ariel: A Quarterly Review of Literature and the Arts in Israel*, 32 (1973)

ALONSO, Dámaso
(1898–1990)

Spanish poet and philologist, born in Madrid, where he studied under Ramon Menéndez Pidal before travelling widely in Europe and America as teacher and lecturer. He became Professor of Romance Philology at Madrid University, and established his reputation as an authority on **Góngora y Argote**. He also published poetry, of which *Hijos de la Ira* (1970, Eng trans *Children of Wrath*, 1970) is the best known. It is religious in inspiration, powerful and emotional in expression.
▷E Alvarado de Ricord, *La Obra poetica di Dámaso Alonso* (1968)

AL-RUSAFI, Maruf
(1875–1945)

Iraqi Arabic poet, mystic and critic. He was a Sufi who wrote a long mystical work which cannot be published before the year 2000. His poetry, however, was not always religious, but addressed itself to social and national issues in a boldly rebellious spirit.

AL-SHARQAWI, Abd al Rahman
(1920–)

Egyptian poet, radical verse playwright and novelist. *Thar Allah* (1969, 'God's Revenge'), is typical of his stage work. His novel *Al-Ard* (1954, Eng trans *Egyptian Earth*, 1962) is regarded as a 'realistic and obviously committed view of the Egyptian peasant'.
▷H Kilpatrick, *The Modern Eygptian Novel* (1974)

ALTERMAN, Nathan
(1910–70)

Polish–Jewish Hebrew poet, dramatist and translator, who moved to Palestine in his boyhood. He was a curious writer in that, while his poetry is wild and apparently uncontrolled (a critic spoke of 'an inoccuous alcoholic element' in it), his drama, which played an important part in the Hebrew theatrical revival, was carefully conceived and planned. He translated **Molière**, **Shakespeare**'s *Othello*, and others, and wrote a number of original plays. Some of his poetry is translated in *Selected Poems* (1968).

ALTHER, Lisa, née Reed
(1944–)

American novelist, born in Kingsport, Tennessee. She was educated at Wellesley College, Massachusetts, and although the Tennessee setting of much of her work has led to her being identified as a regional writer, it is more wide-ranging than that implies. Her characteristic theme is the evolution of personal and sexual identity, which was readily evident in her often comic first novel, *Kinflicks* (1976). *Original Sins* (1981) explored the fragmentation of a group of children as they were exposed to the social, racial and sexual pressures of adult life. *Other Women* (1985) is centred on the developing relationship between a woman and her female therapist, while *Bedrock* (1990) again focuses on her persistent concern with personal development and self-awareness.

ALTIMIRANO, Ignacio Manuel
(1834–93)

Mexican novelist and editor, of pure Native American blood, born in Tixtla. He wrote initially in the Spanish *costumbrista* tradition. His unusual *El Zarco* (1901, Eng trans *Zarco the Bandit*, 1957), presents a 'white' bandit and a 'dark' hero, and is an important part of early *indigenista* literature; but it possesses little merit as a story.

ALUKO, T M
(1918–)

Nigerian novelist whose *One Man, One Wife* (1959) was the first genuine Anglophone novel to be published in Nigeria. Accused of frivolity for his later and more broadly comic work, such as *Chief the Honourable Minister* (1970), he excelled at satirizing the more absurd aspects of native life, although always depicting these within the imperialist context.
▷A Tibble, *African/English Literature* (1965)

ALVARENGA, Manuel Inâcio da Silva
(1749–1814)

Brazilian poet, born in the Minas Gerais region. He was educated in Coimbra in Portugal. He was for a long time imprisoned, although not in harsh conditions, for his sympathy with the French Revolution. His poetry is more mellifluous and well wrought than interesting in its content, but he made technical innovations.

ALVAREZ, A(lfred)
(1929–)

English literary critic and novelist, perhaps unfortunately best known for an over-publicized affair with **Sylvia Plath**, which he documented in his own powerful study of suicide and the self-destructive impulse, *The Savage God* (1971). After graduating from Corpus Christi, Oxford, he went to the USA, out of which came his first critical book, *The Shaping Spirit* (1958, published in the USA as *Stewards of Excellence*), and somewhat later the interviews and essays in *Under Pressure* (1965), which examined the different constraints imposed on writers under state capitalism and communism. The essays in *Beyond All This Fiddle* (1968) suggested a sturdy critical consciousness largely undazzled by the trendier philosophies of the time. Unfortunately, the same could not be said about Alvarez's two novels, *Hers* (1974) and *Hunt* (1978), which are shallow and predictable. He is, however, a fine literary journalist, closely associated with *The Observer* newspaper, the *New Statesman*, and with the influential Penguin Modern European Poets in Translation series.
▷I Hamilton, interview with Alvarez in *New Review* (March 1978)

ÁLVAREZ QUINTERO, Serafín
(1871–1938)
ÁLVAREZ QUINTERO, Joaquín
(1873–1944)

Spanish playwrights, both born in Utrera. These brothers were the joint authors of well over a hundred modern Spanish plays, all displaying a characteristic gaiety and sentiment, although they are sometimes accused of being a little too stagily Spanish. Some are well known in the translations of Helen and **Harley Granville-Barker**: *Fortunato*, *The Lady from Alfaqueque*, and *A Hundred Years Old* (all produced in 1928), and *Don Abel Writes a Tragedy* (1933). In addition may be mentioned *El patio* (1900), *Las flores* (1901, 'The Flowers'), *El genio alegre* (1906, 'The Happy Spirit/Genius'), and *Pueblo de mujeres* (1912, 'Nation of Women').
▷ J Losada de la Torre, *Perfil de los hermanos Alvarez Quintero* (1945); D Diaz Hierro, *Huelva y los hermanos Alvarez Quintero* (1972)

ALVARO, Corrado
(1895–1956)

Italian novelist and journalist, born in Reggio. Sometime Editor of *Il Mondo*, he was the author of several novels and collections of essays. His best novels are *I maestri del diluvio* (1935, 'The Masters of the Flood') and *L'Uomo è forte* (1934, 'The Strong Man'), both set in Soviet Russia, though he declared that his criticisms were of fascist and not communist society. The deeply-felt disparity between town and country, his own sophisticated life as a cultivated man and a vision of an impossibly idealized memory of his native south, are recurring themes in his work.
▷ L Alessandrini, *Corrado Alvaro* (1968)

ALVER, Betti, pseud of Elisabet Lepik
(1906–)

Estonian lyrical poet. She was the wife of the poet Heiti Talvik, who was sent to Siberia and died there in 1945. She was a leading light in the *Arbujad* ('Magicians') circle of poets, which sought in the late 1930s to create a poetry independent of politics. She was silent for many years, but then began to publish again in the 1960s, when her collections sold out.
▷ W K Matthew (ed), *A Book of Modern Estonian Poetry* (1955)

AMADI, Elechi
(1934–)

Nigerian novelist and playwright, born in Aluu and educated at Ibadan. Unfashionably resistant to anti-colonial ideology and rhetoric, Amadi returned in his fiction to a pre-European African past, detailing village life as an organic, self-sufficient system. *The Concubine* (1966) was published by Heinemann in London and, despite its striking refusal to suggest political alternatives to white rule, was a marshalling point for black writers who sought to work outside white European models. *The Great Ponds* (1969) and *The Slave* (1978) were weaker, and the more recent *Estrangement* (1986) betrays some symptoms of artificiality. Like many of his compatriots, Amadi writes dramatically rather than discursively and has created a small but significant body of work for the stage, the best of it collected in *Peppersoup, and The Road to Ibadan* (1977). His *Sunset in Biafra: A Civil War Diary* (1973) is a strong-minded account of Nigeria's national tragedy.
▷ A Niven, *The Concubine: a Critical View* (1981)

AMADO, Jorge
(1912–)

Brazilian novelist, born on a cocoa plantation in Ilhéus, Bahia. His early fictions are pervaded with social and political themes. He was imprisoned for his political beliefs in 1935 and latterly spent several years in exile, though he was a communist deputy of the Brazilian parliament (1946–7). His first novel, *O país do carnaval* (1932, 'The Country of the Carnival'), is typically a young man's and follows a youthful member of the intelligentsia seeking political answers in the wake of the revolution of 1930. His next few novels outlined his personal manifesto and highlighted the cause of various exploited groups in society. With the publication of *Gabriela, cravo e canela* (1952, Eng trans *Gabriela, Clove and Cinnamon*, 1962) he showed a marked change in style and emphasis, Technicolor supplanting black and white. This second phase of the writer's career has been marked by books like *O gato malhado e a andorinha sinha* (1976, Eng trans *The Swallow and the Tom Cat*, 1982) and *Dona Flor e seus dois maridos: História moral e de amor* (1966, Eng trans *Dona Flor and Her Two Husbands*, 1969) which, while not lacking in social awareness or compassion, use irony to charming effect.

AMBLER, Eric
(1909–)

English novelist and playwright, born in London. Educated at Colfe's Grammar School and London University, he served an apprenticeship in engineering and worked as an advertising copy-writer before turning to writing thrillers, invariably with an espionage

25

background. He has done much to legitimize what has too glibly been dismissed as the stuff of pot-boilers. Considered by **Graham Greene** to be Britain's best thriller writer, he published his first novel, *The Dark Frontier*, in 1936. Niggardly with words and a skilful constructor of plots, he creates a world of shadows. His best-known books are *Epitaph for a Spy* (1938), *The Mask of Dimitrios* (1939), *Dirty Story* (1967) and *The Intercom Conspiracy* (1970). He has co-authored novels with Charles Rodda under the pseudonym Eliot Reed and has received the Crime Writers' Association Award four times, and the **Edgar Allan Poe** Award (1964). He has also written a number of screenplays.
▷ *Here Lies: An Autobiography* (1985).

AMES, Jennifer see GREIG, Maysie Coucher

AMICIS, Edmondo de
(1846–1908)

Italian novelist, born in Oneglia. Although he intended to pursue a career in the army, and became director of the Italia Militare, Florence, in 1867, he turned to literature and recorded his experiences as a soldier in *La vita militare* (1868, 'The Military Life'). He is chiefly remembered for his alliance with **Alessandro Manzoni** in an attempt to 'purify' the Italian language. *L'Idioma gentile* (1905, 'The Gentle Language') presents his views on this subject. His most popular work is the sentimental *Il Cuore* (1886), translated into English as *An Italian Schoolboy's Journal* and into more than 25 other languages. His interest in education is reflected in *Il romanzo d'un maestro* (1890, 'A School-teacher's Novel'), and he also travelled widely, producing several books about his adventures.
▷ V Chialant, *Edmondo de Amicis, educatore e artista* (1911)

AMIEL, Denys, pseud of Guillaume Roche
(1884–1977)

French playwright, best known for his collaboration with **André Obey** on the popularly experimental *La Souriante Mme Beudet* (1921), produced in New York as *The Wife with a Smile*. This stiffly 'presentational' work (ie drawing deliberate attention to the artificial devices of the theatre) in the up-market fashion of the time, was a variation on the 'Bovary' theme, but with a 'happy ending'. It was filmed with Germaine Dermoz in 1922. Amiel wrote many more successful 'tragicomedies of ordinary life', at which he excelled.

AMIHAI, Yehudah
(1924–)

German-born Israeli poet and novelist, born in Würzberg. He emigrated to Palestine with his family in 1936. He is thought of as having brought a much-needed 'matter-of-fact tone' into Hebrew poetry and has been much translated, eg in *Selected Poems* (1971), *Songs of Jerusalem and Myself* (1973), *Amen* (1977) and *Time* (1979).

AMIS, Sir Kingsley
(1922–)

English novelist and poet, born in London. He was educated at the City of London School and at St John's College, Oxford, and was a lecturer in English Literature at University College, Swansea (1948–61) and fellow of Peterhouse, Cambridge (1961–3). He achieved huge success with his first novel, *Lucky Jim* (1954), the story of a comic anti-hero in a provincial university; 'Jim' appeared again as a small-town librarian in *That Uncertain Feeling* (1956), and as a provincial author abroad in *I Like It Here* (1958). After the death of **Ian Fleming**, he wrote a James Bond novel, *Colonel Sun* (1968), under the pseudonym of Robert Markham, as well as *The James Bond Dossier* (1965). His later novels include *I Want It Now* (1968), *Ending Up* (1974), *Jake's Thing* (1978), *Stanley and the Women* (1984), *The Old Devils* (1986, Booker Prize), *The Folks That Live On The Hill* (1990), and *The Russian Girl* (1992). He has also published four books of poetry, and written non-fiction works, including one on the history of science fiction. He was married (1965–83) to the novelist **Elizabeth Jane Howard**. His son is **Martin Amis**.
▷ *Memoirs* (1991); R Rabinowitz, *The Reaction Against Experiment in the English Novel* (1967)

AMIS, Martin Louis
(1949–)

English novelist and journalist, born in Oxford, the son of **Kingsley Amis**. He was educated at Exeter College, Oxford, and acted in the film *A High Wind in Jamaica* (1965). He worked for the *Times Literary Supplement* and *New Statesman*, but has been a full-time writer since 1979. He began precociously with his first novel, *The Rachel Papers* (1973), and followed it with two more witty and pungent socio-cultural satires, *Dead Babies* (1975) and *Success* (1978). Subsequent novels include the nightmarish *Other People* (1981), *Einstein's Monsters* (1986)—a short-story collection on the theme of nuclear destruction—and *Time's Arrow* (1991), which plays with concepts of time and history.

AMMONS, A(rchie) R(andolph)
(1926–)

American poet, born in Whiteville, North Carolina. A romantic in the line of the New England Transcendentalists, but with something of **Wallace Stevens**'s agnostic insistence on the imagination as a non-transcendent sufficiency, he draws his subject-matter and his prosodic rhythms direct from nature. His first book, *Ommateum, with Doxology* (1955), wore both influences too publicly although later works were more self-possessed. *Corsons Inlet* (1965) is a major statement of his mature style, which developed in the subsequent *Tape for the Turn of the Year* (1965) and *Northfield Poems* (1966). A *Collected Poems* appeared in 1972, an updated *Selected* in 1977, and the important *Selected Longer Poems*, representing his gift for long forms, in 1980. Ammons has been Goldwin Smith Professor of English at Cornell University since 1973.
▷A Holder, *A R Ammons* (1978)

AMORIM, Enrique
(1900–60)

Passionate Uruguayan novelist, poet and story writer, born in Salta (the home town, also, of **Horacio Quiroga**). His father was of Portuguese descent, his ardently feminist mother, herself a poet, of Basque. His literary career was built up in Argentina. His compatriot, the novelist and historian of Uruguayan literature, **Mario Benedetti**, wrote of his prolific works (also praised by **Borges**): 'a writer of extraordinary fragments, of stupendous pages, of magnificent serendipity, but also of great stylistic holes, of evident structural blunders, of overstuffed chapters'. All Amorim's novels are worthy of study, but the most famous, and his own favourites, are *La carreta* (1929, 'The Cart'), *El paisano Aguilar* (1934, 'The Peasant Aguilar') and *El caballo y su sombra* (1941, Eng trans *The Horse and His Shadow*, 1943). *Coral abierto* (1955, 'The Open Yard') is a notable tale of juvenile delinquency. With some qualities in common with **Dreiser** and **Hardy**, Amorim was a great and sometimes intemperate protester against injustice; his standing is hardly secure, and perhaps never can be—but he is widely read and much loved. Many of the allegedly gloomy conclusions he draws from his depictions of landowners and peasants have been confirmed by sociologists.
▷*Books Abroad*, 34 (1960)

AMORY, Thomas
(c.1691–1788)

Irish author and eccentric, born in Dublin. He studied medicine at Trinity College, Dublin, but was wealthy enough to adopt the life of a gentleman of leisure in London, where he lived a very secluded life, and seldom went out until dark. His chief works include *Memoirs of Several Ladies of Great Britain* (1755), *A History of Antiquities*, *Productions of Nature* (1755), and the *Life of John Buncle* (2 vols, 1756–66), an odd combination of autobiography, fantastic descriptions of scenery, deistical theology, and sentimental rhapsody.
▷*Memoirs of the Life, Character and Writings of the Author* (1764)

ANACREON
(c.570–?c.475 BC)

Greek lyric poet, from Teos in Asia Minor. He helped to found the Greek colony of Abdera in Thrace (c.540 BC) in the face of threatened attack by the Persians. He was invited to Samos by Polycrates to tutor his son. After the tyrant's downfall, he was brought to Athens by Hipparchus, son of the tyrant Pisistratus, and later went to Thessaly. His work, which survives only in fragments, includes convivial poems in honour of love and wine, satires, dedications and epitaphs. It served as a model for the Latin lyric poets and was widely imitated by French and English poets of the Renaissance.
▷V Martin, *Quatre Figures de la Poésie Grecque* (1931)

ANAND, Mulk Raj
(1905–)

Indian novelist and critic, born in Peshawar. His early life was fraught with tragedy and familial strife and he left India for Britain, where he was beaten up for blacklegging during the General Strike (1926). His first novel, *Untouchable* (1935), was rejected by 19 publishers, the 20th agreeing to take it on if **E M Forster** would write a preface. This he did, sparking off a remarkable career for Anand which has included novels, short stories, cookery books, philosophical exegeses, tales for children and writings on art. His novels, such as *The Coolie* (1936), *Two Leaves and a Bud* (1937) and *The Village* (1939, the first of a trilogy), promote the underdog in society, his approach being that of a humanist rather than a communist. They are uneven in quality but consistent in their depiction of life in the poverty-stricken Punjab. More recently he has concentrated on an ambitious seven-volume autobiographical work of fiction, *The Seven Ages of Man*, which began with *Seven Summers: The Story of an Indian Childhood* (1951).
▷M Berry, *Mulk Raj Anand: the man and the novelist* (1971)

ANCHIETA, Padre José de
(1534–97)

Spanish (Canary Islands) Jesuit, born in Tenerife. He was educated at Coimbra in Portugal, and went to Brazil in 1553, where he played an important priestly role. He wrote a Tupi (Brazilian Native American) grammar. He is not an important poet in any of the languages he employed for his religious verse (Tupi, Latin, Spanish, Portuguese), but he was a versatile man whose historical work is invaluable, notably his *Fragmentos Históricos* (1584–6), which is an important source book. ▷D L Hamilton, *A Vida e a Obras de José de Anchieta* (1942)

AN CRAOIBHIN AOIBHINN *see* HYDE, Douglas

ANDAY, Melih Cedvat
(1915–)

Turkish poet, dramatist, critic, novelist and translator (**Molière**, **Gogol**), born in Istanbul. He has served on many Istanbul papers as a cultural columnist. With other poets he initiated, just after the end of World War II, the 'Garip' ('Strange') movement in Turkish poetry: the aims were to get rid of all conventions (there was therefore a later reaction), to bring the colloquial into poetry, and to write of social concerns. But Anday, too, reacted, and his poetry became more metaphysical and less overtly left-wing. His poetry is collected as *Sözcükler* (1978, 'Words'). There are English versions in *On the Nomad Sea* (1974) and *Rain One Step Away* (1980). ▷*Books Abroad*, 39 (1965)

ANDERSCH, Alfred
(1914–)

German novelist and critic, born in Munich. Imprisoned in Dachau by the Nazis for communist activity, Andersch was closely associated with Gruppe '47—the band of disparate friends who joined together to encourage a liberal and imaginative literature in a war-torn Germany. He eventually turned his back on his communism in favour of a still liberal but individual outlook. His major novel, *Sansibar, oder, der letze Grund* (1957, Eng trans *Flight to Afar*, 1958), exemplified this change.

ANDERSEN, Hans Christian
(1805–75)

Danish author, one of the world's great storytellers. He was born in Odense, the son of a poor but educated shoemaker. After his father's death, he worked in a factory, but soon displayed a talent for poetry. At 14 he went to Copenhagen, but failed to find a job in the theatre. His writing, however, attracted the attention of influential men and, application having been made to the king, he was placed at an advanced school. In 1829 he established his reputation with 'A Walk from the Holmen Canal to the Easternmost Point of Amager', a literary satire in the form of a humorous narrative. The following year, he published the first collected volume of his poems, and in 1831 a second. A travelling pension from the king in 1833 resulted in a volume of prose sketches of a tour in the Harz mountains, *Agnete og Havmanden* ('Agnete and the Merman'), which was completed in Switzerland, and *Improvisatoren* (Eng trans *The Improvisatore; or Life in Italy*, 1845), a series of scenes inspired by Rome and Naples. In 1835 he began publishing the tiny pamphlets of fairy tales which are his greatest work; there are more than 150 of them, including 'The Tin Soldier', 'The Emperor's New Clothes', 'The Tinderbox', 'The Snow Queen', and 'The Ugly Duckling'. He also wrote *O.T.* (1836), a novel containing vivid pictures of northern scenery and manners, *Kun en Spillemand* (1837, 'Only a Fiddler'), and an autobiography *Mit Livs Eventyr* (1855, rev edn 1870), translated by **Mary Howitt** as *The True Story of My Life* (1847). ▷R Bain, *Hans Christian Andersen: a biography* (1895)

ANDERSON, Ethel
(1883–1958)

English-born Australian writer, born in Leamington, Warwickshire, and a friend of the Keynes, Darwin, and Vulliamy families and of the poet **Frances Cornford**. She married an army officer and lived for some time in India. She wrote two books of verse, *Squatter's Luck* (1942) and *Sunday at Yarralumla* (1947), some essays, and two books of short stories, *Indian Tales* (1948) and *The Little Ghosts* (1959), delicate tales based on her Indian experiences. Her best-known book, *At Parramatta* (1956), turns vignettes of Australian middle-class life in the 1850s into a microcosm of the Seven Deadly Sins. She also wrote an oratorio, *The Song of Hagar* (1958), set to music by the composer John Antill.

ANDERSON, Jessica Margaret
(c.1918–)

Australian novelist, born in Brisbane but living mainly in Sydney. Her first book, *An Ordinary Lunacy* (1963), was not written until she was 40, and her reputation was only established in 1978 with *Tirra Lirra by the River*, a winner of the **Miles Franklin** Award, in which she recounts Nora Porteous's lifelong search for herself. Stories of her Brisbane childhood contrast with sophisticated Sydney in the 1980s in *Stories from the Warm Zone and Sydney Stories* (1987) and demonstrate a command of diverse moods. In her psychological crime story *The Last Man's Head* (1970) Anderson returns to the detective genre of her first novel. A historical novel *The Commandant* (1975), based on the true story of an early commander of the Moreton Bay (later Brisbane) penal settlement, was less successful.

ANDERSON, Maxwell
(1888–1959)

American historical dramatist, born in Atlantic, Pennsylvania, the son of a Baptist minister. A verse playwright, he was in vogue in the late 1920s to the early 1940s with numerous plays which included *Elizabeth the Queen* (1930), *Mary of Scotland* (1933), *Winterset* (1935), *Key Largo* (1939) and *The Eve of St Mark* (1942). Commercially successful, his plays tended to be centred on a strong, highly-focused idea, usually in keeping with a firm commitment to democratic humanism. He also wrote screenplays, most notably that from **Erich Maria Remarque**'s novel *All Quiet on the Western Front* (1930). He won a Pulitzer Prize for *Both Your Houses* in 1933.
▷M D Bailey, *Maxwell Anderson: the playwright as prophet* (1957)

ANDERSON, Patrick
(1915–)

English poet, born in Surrey and educated at Oxford University. He is regarded by some as a Canadian writer, having lived, taught and been anthologized there. Multi-faceted, he has produced poetry such as *The Colour as Naked* (1953) with experimental verse forms and overt, dialectical intellectualism, and *On This Side Nothing* (1948), which is more interested in ordinary nature such as wind, earth and trees. *A Visiting Distance* (1976), a selection of revised and new material, engagingly covers both the interest in what he finds in his own garden and what he finds on the other side of the world; his interest in travel shows itself also in *Over the Alps* (1969), which analyses the travel writing of **William Beckford**, **Byron** and **Boswell**.

ANDERSON, Poul William
(1926–)

American science-fiction writer, born in Pennsylvania of Swedish descent. He was educated at the University of Minnesota, and published his first short story in 1947. Most of his work is 'hard' science fiction, and he is a major figure in the genre, although he has also written fantasy and adaptations of mythological subjects. Many of his books can be grouped into loose sequences, of which the most important are the Technic History series (sub-divided into the 'Nicholas van Rijn' and

'Dominic Flandry' streams), and the smaller Psychotechnic League series. His characterization, dialogue and plotting can all be perfunctory, but he is rarely less than inventive. Important titles include *Brain Wave* (1953), *The High Crusade* (1960), *Tau Zero* (1970) and *The Book of a Million Years* (1989).

ANDERSON, Robert Woodruff
(1917–)

American dramatist, born in New York. Woodruff served as an intelligence officer in the US Navy during World War II and was awarded a Bronze Star. *Come Marching Home* (1945), a play about the return of a war hero, won an Army–Navy playwriting competition, but his reputation as a dramatist in the mould of **Tennessee Williams** was established with *Tea and Sympathy* (1953), a play about a schoolboy accused of homosexuality. (Anderson turned this into a precious and unsuccessful screenplay - much better is the screenplay he produced from someone else's book for *The Nun's Story*, 1959.) Subsequent productions have shown Anderson to be more sentimental and less subtle than Williams.

ANDERSON, Sherwood
(1876–1941)

American author, born in Camden, Ohio. He left his family and his lucrative position as manager of a paint factory to devote his entire time to writing. His first novel was *Windy McPherson's Son* (1916), but his best-known work is *Winesburg, Ohio* (1919), which portrayed the 'secret lives' of marginal characters and the sensibilities of the young artist who observes them and then escapes. *Poor White* (1920) is a strongly felt account of life under industrialization.
▷I Howe, *Sherwood Anderson: A Biography* (1951)

ANDERSSON, Dan(iel)
(1888–1920)

Swedish poet and novelist. One of Sweden's foremost writers in his time, he treated religious and metaphysical themes in his novels, like the autobiographical *De tre hemlösa* (1918, 'Three Homeless Ones'). His poems about traditional charcoal-burners in *Kolarhistorier* (1914) and *Kolvakterens visor* (1915) turned them into national folk-figures.
▷G Agren, *Dan Anderssons vag* (1970)

ANDRADE, DRUMMOND DE, Carlos
(1902–87)

Brazilian poet and short-story writer, born in Itabira, Minas Gerais. He graduated in pharmacy and worked as a journalist and teacher before moving to Rio de Janeiro in 1933. By that time his first volume, *Alguma poesia* (1930, 'Some Poetry'), had appeared, forging his links with the 'modernista' group. The spare, detached and accessible verse of *Alguma poesia* was succeeded, in 1940, by the altogether more sombre *Sentimento do mund* ('Feeling for the World'), over which looms the shadow of world war. From the end of the war onwards, his political concerns came to be more explicitly expressed in his poetry. Such collections as *A rosa do povo* (1945, 'The rose of the people'), however, remain firmly on the right side of the divide between committed art and overt propaganda.

ANDRADE, Mário de
(1893–1945)

Brazilian poet and novelist, born in São Paulo. He began by studying music, but devoted himself to writing after the publication of his first book of poems in 1917. He was a leading figure in the Brazilian modernist movement, and his avant-garde poems about his native city in *Paulicéia desvairada* (1922, Eng trans *Hallucinated City*, 1968) was influential in form and subject. His major prose work was the novel *Mucanaima* (1928), a complex, opaque work about a mythical Amazonian emperor whose adventures include a visit to 20th-century São Paulo, which carried a subtitle meaning 'hero without a character'. A *Complete Works* appeared in Portuguese in 1966.

ANDRADE, Olegario Victor
(1841–82)

Argentinian popular patriotic poet—a humble official until he suddenly became famous in the late 1870s—born in Alegrete, Brazil. Using **Hugo** (to whom he devoted a poem) as his model, he exalted the superiority of the Latin races in his technically capable, but perfervid and grandiose poems—not unlike **Swinburne** at his worst—from which there is now little to rescue except a genuine vision of a unified Latin America.

ANDRADE, Oswald de
(1890–1954)

Brazilian poet, novelist, literary publicist and founder-leader of the Brazilian *Modernista* movement (an urban and avant-garde movement, in which Andrade was associated with his namesake **Mário de Andrade** and the painter Anita Malfatti). He has been described as 'the enduring playboy of Brazilian letters'. His poetry is in itself trivial, although there has been an attempt by Brazilian critics, in recent years, to rehabilitate it, on the grounds of the 'economy with which he presents the complexity of Brazil'.

▷J Nist, *The Modernist Movement in Brazil* (1967)

ANDREAS-SALOMÉ, Lou
(1861–1937)

German novelist and thinker, loved by **Nietzsche** and the lover of **Rilke** and perhaps **Freud**, born in Russia. Lou, as she is always called, was one of the greatest women of the century. She became a lay analyst after studying with Freud. She wrote shrewdly and generously of the efforts of **Ibsen** to portray women, gave a piercing account of Nietzsche, and was responsible for releasing much poetry in Rilke, whom she understood better than any other woman in his life. Her *Die Erotik* (1910) is a key text, although it has been ignored by latter-day feminists. Her psychological and religious novels are now due for revival, as are her work and thought. Her *Rainer Maria Rilke* (1928) remains a seminal work on the poet.

▷H F Peters, *My Sister, My Spouse* (1962); L Binion, *Frau Lou* (1968)

ANDRES, Stefan
(1906–70)

German Roman Catholic novelist and poet, born in the Mosel country. He first studied for the priesthood, but abandoned this for art and then writing. His best-known novel is *Wir sind Utopia* (1942, Eng trans *We Are Utopia*, 1954), about a monk who finds himself imprisoned in the monastery he had once abandoned in order to fight against Franco. This was praised by **Graham Greene**, and its attitudes have been compared to his. He continued to write thoughtful and accomplished novels until his death.

ANDREWS, Virginia
(1933–86)

American novelist, born in West Virginia. Since her death the name has become a trademark of the Virginia C. Andrews Trust. The real Andrews lived in Portsmouth, Virginia, and was the author of four melodramatic novels about the Dollenganger family. The sequence began with *Flowers in the Attic* (1979), in which children have been locked away by their mother, and ends with *Seeds of Yesterday* (1984). Andrews' commercial success, combined with the unpublished work which she left at her death, led to the unprecedented posthumous use of her name in novels such as *Midnight Whispers* (1991), part of the Cutler family saga. Although some of the work now put out in her name is a revised and augmented version of something she started, other publications are only in the style of the original author.

ANDREYEV, Leonid Nikolayevich
(1871–1919)

Russian writer and artist, born in Orel. He suffered much from poverty and ill-health as a student, and attempted suicide, before taking to writing and portrait painting. He enjoyed a period of fame after the success of *Zhili-byli* (1901, 'Once Upon a Time'). His style is over-rhetorical, but his best works overcome that weakness, notably *Gubernator* (1906, Eng trans *His Excellency the Governor*, 1921). He is most famous, however, for his terrifyingly effective drama, *Tot, kto poluchaet poshchochiny* (1915, Eng trans, *He Who Gets Slapped*, 1915). He died in exile after fleeing the 1917 revolution.
▷L N Afonin, *Leonid Andreyev* (1959)

ANDRIĆ, Ivo
(1892–1975)

Serbian author and diplomat, winner of the Nobel Prize for literature, born near Travnik. He was interned by the Austrian government as a Yugoslav nationalist during World War I, and a sense of isolation haunts his writing. He joined the diplomatic service, and was minister in Berlin at the outbreak of war in 1939. His chief works, *Na Drini Ćuprija* (1945, Eng trans *The Bridge on the Drina*, 1959) and *Travnička hronika* (1945, Eng trans *Bosnian Story*, 1958), earned him the 1961 Nobel Prize for literature and the nickname 'the Yugoslav Tolstoy'.
▷E C Hawkesworth, *Andrić: a bridge between East and West* (1984)

ANDRZEJEWSKI, Jerzy
(1909–83)

Polish novelist, one of the country's most famous, who was always controversial amongst his countrymen. He began as a somewhat right-wing Catholic writer in the tradition of **Mauriac**. He became internationally famous with *Popiol i diament* (1948, Eng trans *Ashes and Diamonds*, 1968), which was made into a famous movie: it is an analysis of an unnamed Polish town and its sufferings under the Nazis, and is likely to be judged his finest novel. At first he tried to accommodate himself to the communist regime as a 'social realist', and got himself into severe trouble with such Poles as **Czeslaw Milosz**; he became critical of the regime in modernist novels such as *Ciemnósci kryja ziemie* (1957, Eng trans *The Inquisitors*, 1960), but still not in a way that satisfied everyone. Since his death his reputation has tended to fall: his work had, a critic wrote, '*longeurs* which are hard to explain away'.

ANEIRIN, or ANEURIN
(fl.late 6th century)

Ancient British poet, creator of the oldest surviving poetry composed in Scotland. He was Bard of Gododdin, the kingdom south of the Firth of Forth whose citadel was Din Eidyn (Edinburgh) until its capture by the Angles in 638, when the kingdom ended. Nennius speaks of him, together with **Taliesin**, as a poet in the Old North, while an earlier Triad speaks of him as 'Aneirin of flowing verse, prince of poets'. The great *Y Gododdin* ascribed to him describes the ill-fated expedition of a band of warriors defeated and destroyed after a march to Catterick in Yorkshire under the leadership of Mynyddawg Mwynfawr in c. AD600. It extols the martial virtues and generosity of the dead heroes, and contains one of the earliest extant references to King Arthur. Its initial composition was evidently oral and it was apparently transferred down the generations in that form for some 300 years. As a poet Aneirin proves himself a loyal follower of exceptional devotion.
▷S Turner, *A Vindication of the Genuineness of the Ancient British Poems of Aneurin, etc* (1803)

ANGEL, Albalucía
(1939–)

Colombian short-story writer and poet, born in Bogotá, one of the new wave of feminist writers to emerge in Latin America. Her fictional works tend to be experimental and, according to some critics, unusually difficult to read because of unexpected narrator changes, manipulations of structure, and verbal fireworks. Angel is also involved in film-making and journalism; she has produced a number of documentaries and written extensively on art. Her most famous work is *Estaba la pájara pinta sentada en el verde limón* ('The Painted Bird was Sitting on the Green Lemon Tree'), a female *Bildungsroman* dealing with the sexual and political awakening of the protagonist.

ANGELOU, Maya
(1928–)

American writer, singer, dancer, performer and Black activist, born in St Louis, Missouri. After the break-up of her parents' marriage, she and her brother lived with their grandmother in Stamps, Arkansas. She was raped by her mother's boyfriend when she was eight and for the next five years was mute. In her teens she moved to California to live with her mother, and at 16 gave birth to her son, Guy. She has had a variety of occupations in what she describes as 'a roller-coaster life'. In her twenties she toured Europe and Africa in the musical *Porgy and Bess*. In New York she joined the Harlem Writers Guild and continued to earn her living singing in night-clubs

and performing in **Jean Genet**'s *The Blacks*.
In the 1960s she was involved in Black strug-
gles and then spent several years in Ghana as
Editor of *African Review*. Her multi-volume
autobiography, commencing with *I Know
Why the Caged Bird Sings* (1970), was a critical and popular success, imbued with optimism, humour and homespun philosophy.
She has published several volumes of verse,
including *And Still I Rise* (1987), and is the
Reynolds Professor of American Studies at
Wake Forest University in North Carolina.
In 1994 she published a collection of personal
reflections, *Wouldn't take nothing for my journey now*.

ANGELUS SILESIUS, pseud (meaning 'Silesian Messenger') of Johann Scheffler
(1624–77)

German poet, who was born and died in Breslau (Wrocław). A physician, he became a
mystic through the impact upon him, in
youth, of Abraham von Franckenberg, who
introduced him to the works of **Jakob Böhme**.
He had been brought up a zealous Protestant,
but his translation of Catholic mystical works
caused the Lutherans to criticize him: he was
a Catholic priest by 1661. He therefore
became involved in the letters and theology of
the Counter-Reformation. His poetry, which
had a debt to that of Daniel von Czepko, is
most prized, not for its originality of thought,
but for the concise and passionate expression
of the manner in which the mystic (Protestant
or Catholic) loves Christ—this is often stated
in metaphorical, 'bride–Christ' terms. His
poems were collected under the title *Der
Cherubinische Wandersmann* (1674, 'The
Cherubinic Wanderer').
▷ J C E Flitch, *Selections from the Cherubinic
Wanderer*, with introduction (1932)

ANGIOLIERI, Cecco
(c.1260–c.1312)

Italian poet, born in Siena. Nothing is known
of his life except from his sonnets, the only
kind of verse he wrote, which reveal a drinker,
lecher and gambler with a cynical, sardonic
character and a heartless wit. He attacked
Dante in three poems.
▷ F Figurelli, *La Musa Bizarra de Cecco
Angiolieri* (1950)

ANGUS, Marion
(1866–1946)

Scottish poet, born in Aberdeen, the daughter
of a Church of Scotland minister. She grew
up in Arbroath, and later lived in Aberdeen,
Edinburgh and Helensburgh. Her volumes of
verse, mostly in Scots, include *The Lilt and*

Other Verses (1922), *Sun and Candlelight*
(1927), *The Singin' Lass* (1929) and *Lost
Country* (1937). Her best-known poem is a
lament for Mary, Queen of Scots, 'Alas, Poor
Queen'.

ANKER, Nini Roll
(1873–1942)

Norwegian novelist and playwright, born in
Molde. She became involved in the women's
rights movement and in radical politics, and
the conflict between feminine self-realization
and the traditional feminine roles set out by
the Lutheran Church is explored in *Det svake
Kjøon* (1915, 'The Weaker Sex'). The 'Stam-
pe' trilogy (1923–7) is an ambitious historical
novel, while *Den som henger i en tråd* (1935,
'Hanging by a Thread') highlights the plight
of women employed in the textile industry
and their joint efforts to improve their situation. *Kvinnen og den svarte fuglen* (completed
in 1942, published posthumously in 1945,
'The Woman and the Black Bird') is a powerful feminist–pacifist novel, underlining the
need for women to play an active social and
political role.
▷ 'Nini Roll Anker', in I Engelstad et al (eds),
Norsk kvinnelitteraturhistorie, vol 2 (1989)

ANNENSKY, Innocenty
(1856–1909)

Russian poet, dramatist, critic, translator and
classicist, born in Omsk. When **Gumilev**, **Akhmatova** and others founded the important
Acmeist school of poets, they called Annen-
sky their mentor. He really belonged to, and
certainly contributed to, the Symbolist movement in Russian poetry, but when his very
late first collection, *Tikiye pesni* (1904, 'Quiet
Nights'), was harshly and unfairly reviewed
by the leading Symbolist **Blok**, he was mor-
tified. His own mentors were **Verlaine** and
Mallarmé, and he brought the former's 'decadence', which was congenial to him, into Russian poetry. At his best, in his second,
posthumous collection, the unique *Kiparisovy
larets* (1910, 'The Cypress Chest'), he embodies the essence of fragrant decay and hopelessness. All he wrote, it has been said, is
pervaded with *toska*, 'anxiety', a kind of ever-
tremblingness in the face of his fragile circumstances; he had a weak heart, and died
while on the very verge of greater success and
recognition. He still seems a very 'modern'
poet. His criticism was superb and penetrating, his tragedies interestingly unplayable, his
translations (eg of the whole of *Euripides*)
learned. The 'flawless beauty' of his lyrics,
even now not well enough known outside
Russia, deeply influenced **Pasternak** and have
always been much loved by connoisseurs of

Russian poetry. There are English translations in: V Markov and M Sparks, *Modern Russian Poetry* (1967).

ANNO Mitsumasa
(1926–)

Japanese children's author and illustrator, born in Tsuwano. He is renowned for his visual puzzles, and his best work can be seen in *Fushigi na E* (1968, Eng trans *Topsy-Turvies: Pictures to Stretch the Imagination*, 1970) and *ABC no Hon* (1974, Eng trans *Anno's Alphabet*, 1975), which won a special Kate Greenaway Medal.

ANOUILH, Jean
(1910–87)

French dramatist, born in Bordeaux of French and Basque parentage. He began his career as a copywriter and as a gag-man in films. His first play, *L'Hermine* (1931, Eng trans *The Ermine*, 1955), was not a success, but his steady output soon earned him recognition as one of the leading dramatists of the contemporary theatre. He was influenced by the Neo-classical fashion inspired by **Giraudoux**, but his very personal approach to the re-interpretation of Greek myths was less poetic, and more in tune with the contemporary taste for artifice and stylization. Among his many successful plays are *Le Voyageur sans bagage* (1937, Eng trans *Traveller without Luggage*, 1959), *Le Bal des voleurs* (1938, Eng trans *Thieves' Carnival*, 1952), *La Sauvage* (1938, Eng trans *The Restless Heart*, 1957), *Eurydice* (1942, Eng trans *Point of Departure*, 1950), *Antigone* (1946, prod in English, New York 1946, London 1949), *Médée* (1946, Eng trans *Medea*, 1956), *L'Invitation au château* (1948, adapted by **Christopher Fry** as *Ring Round the Moon*, 1950), *L'Alouette* (1953, Eng trans *The Lark*, 1955), *Becket* (1959, first performed in London, 1961), *Pauvre Bitos* (1956, Eng trans *Poor Bitos*, 1963), *Cher Antoine* (1969, Eng trans *Dear Antoine*, 1971), *Ne Réveillez Pas Madame* (1970, 'Don't Wake Her Up'), *L'Arrestation* (1974, Eng trans *The Arrest*, 1974), *Vive Henri IV* (1977, 'Long Live Henry IV') and *La Culotte* (1978, 'The Breeches').
▷A D Fazia, *Jean Anouilh* (1972); J Harvey, *Jean Anouilh: a study in theatrics* (1964)

ANSTEY, Christopher
(1724–1805)

English writer, born in Brinkley, Cambridgeshire. He was educated at Bury St Edmunds, Eton, and King's College, Cambridge, of which he was a fellow (1745–54). In 1766 he wrote the *New Bath Guide*, an epistolary novel in verse setting out the

exploits of Squire Blunderhead and his family in Bath, which achieved great popularity.
▷W C Powell, *Christopher Anstey: Bath Laureate* (1944)

ANSTEY, F, pseud of **Thomas Anstey Guthrie**
(1856–1934)

English writer, born in London. He studied at Trinity Hall, Cambridge, and in 1880 was called to the Bar. A whimsical humorist he wrote *Vice Versa* (1882), *The Tinted Venus* (1885), *The Brass Bottle* (1900), and many other novels and dialogues. He was on the staff of *Punch* from 1887 to 1930.
▷M J Turner, *A Bibliography of the Writings of F. Anstey, T.A. Guthrie, etc* (1931)

ANTAR, more fully **l'Antarah Ibn Shaddād Al-'Absi**
(6th century)

Arab poet and warrior, born of a Bedouin chieftain and a black slave somewhere in the desert near Medina, Saudi Arabia. The author of one of the seven Golden Odes of Arabic literature, and the subject of the 10th-century *Romance of Antar*, he is regarded as the model of Bedouin heroism and chivalry and by some as 'the father of knights'.
▷V E Menil, *Disputatio philologica de Antar ejusque poemate arabico Moallakah* (1814)

ANTHONY, Frank S
(1891–1927)

New Zealand writer of humorous short stories. His experiences of farming a 'section' (of government-allocated land) produced some of the earliest natural writing of New Zealand country life; his sketches of life among the dairy farmers of Taranaki were widely published in periodicals during the 1920s. Meanwhile, in the hope of developing his writing, he had moved to London, but his early death there cut short a promising career as a humorous commentator on life. None of his books was published during his lifetime; his novel *Follow the Call* was issued in 1936 by his mother, and included a short memoir. The Taranaki stories appeared in book form as *Me and Gus* in 1938. A revised edition appeared in 1951 and, with two sequels, was reissued as *The Complete Me and Gus* in 1963.

ANTHONY, Michael
(1932–)

Trinidadian novelist, born in Mayaro. His first novel, *The Games Are Coming* (1963), added a new and distinctive voice to West Indian fiction, with its finely realized culmination in a cycle race. He lived in London and Brazil before returning to Trinidad in 1970. His later novels have seemed, to many

critics, to be less vivid than the earlier, in which he recreated the Trinidad of his youth.
▷K Ramchand, *The West Indian Novel and Its Background* (1970)

ANTHONY, Piers, pseud of **Piers Anthony Dillingham Jacob**
(1934–)
English-born American science-fiction and fantasy writer. He moved to the USA as a child in 1940, and became a US citizen in 1958. He made a positive impression at the start of his career with *Chthon* (1967) and the ambitious *Macroscope* (1969), still regarded by many as his best book, and one which transcends its space-adventure framework. His later work generally focused on multi-volume sequences, some of which also addressed larger issues, as in the *Cluster* (1977–82), *Tarot* (1979–80), *Bio of a Space Tyrant* (1983–6) or *Incarnations of Immortality* (1983–90) sequences, while others were more conventional action works. He is a prolific writer and a combative commentator.
▷ *Bio of an Ogre* (1988)

ANTIN, David
(1932–)
American prose poet, born in Brooklyn, New York, and educated there at City College and New York University. Antin's verbal improvisations are pure, plotless narrative, observing few of the rules of conventional storytelling and almost none of the prosodic or metaphoric organizational principles that usually distinguish lyric poetry. Early works such as *Definitions* and *Autobiography* (both 1967) suggest more formal tampering but less imaginative control than *Talking at the Boundaries* (1976), in which Antin abandons all remaining references to poetic form and writes almost entirely in unresolved or incomplete syntactic structures. A one-time science editor, he has also published on mathematics and physics.
▷S Paul, *So to Speak: Re-reading David Antin* (1982)

ANTOKOLSKY, Pavel
(1896–1978)
Russian poet and theatrical producer, born in St Petersburg. Antokolsky was a very capable and technically gifted poet who may have limited his achievement by his tendency to follow the wind. He was an actor in his youth. Competent romantic verse was succeeded by poems praising Russian industrialization; the so-called 'Thaw' under Kruschev produced poems in praise of freedom, and these were followed by ones on 'approved themes'. All he wrote was readable and skilfully executed,

and none of his 'dutiful' verse is ludicrous in the manner of some of his contemporaries.

ANTONINUS, Brother *see* **EVERSON, William**

APOLLINAIRE, Guillaume, originally **Apollinaris Kostrowitzky**
(1880–1918)
French poet, born in Rome of Polish descent. He settled in Paris in 1900, and became a leader of the movement rejecting poetic traditions in outlook, rhythm, and language. His work often reveals a basic lyricism at its roots, but its bizarre, Symbolist and fantastic elements have affinities with the Cubist school in painting. They include *L'Enchanteur pourrissant* (1909, 'The Decaying Magician'), *Le Bestiaire* (1911, Eng trans 1977), *Alcools* (1913, Eng trans 1964) and *Calligrammes* (1918). He was wounded in World War I, and during his convalescence wrote the play *Les Mamelles de Tirésias* (1918, 'The Breasts of Tiresias'), for which he coined the term 'surrealist', and the Modernist manifesto *L'Esprit nouveau et les poètes* (1946, 'The New Spirit and the Poets'.
▷P M Adema, *Guillaume Apollinaire: le mal-aimé* (1952); S Bates, *Guillaume Apollinaire* (1967)

APOLLONIUS RHODIUS
(b.c.295 BC)
Greek poet and literary scholar, born in Alexandria (or possibly Naucratis). A pupil of **Callimachus**, he was head of the Alexandrian library c.260–247 BC, before retiring to Rhodes. His great (and only surviving) work is the *Argonautica*, an epic poem on the Homeric model describing the voyage of Jason and the *Argo* to recover the Golden Fleece. It was much studied and admired in antiquity, its narrative of the love of Jason and Medea serving **Virgil** as a model for the story of Aeneas and Dido in Book IV of the *Aeneid*.

APTE, Hari Narayan
(1864–1919)
Indian (Marathi) novelist who introduced the novel proper into his language. Influenced by Sir **Walter Scott** and **Dickens**, he contributed readable and intelligent episodes from the history of the Maratha empire to its literature.

APULEIUS, Lucius
(2nd century)
Roman writer, satirist and rhetorician, born in Madaura, in Numidia in Africa. Educated at Carthage and Athens, he used the fortune bequeathed him by his father to travel; he visited Italy and Egypt, where it is likely that he was initiated into the mystery religion of

Isis and Osiris. The knowledge which he thus acquired of the priestly fraternities he put to use afterwards in his novel, the *Metamorphoses* (Eng trans *The Golden Ass*, 1566). Having married a wealthy, middle-aged widow, Aemilia Pudentilla, who nursed him in Alexandria, he was charged by her relations with having employed magic to gain her affections. His *Apologia*, still extant, was an eloquent speech in his defence. He settled in Carthage, where he devoted himself to literature, philosophy and rhetoric. *Metamorphoses* is a tale of adventure containing elements of magic, satire and romance, notably the story of Cupid and Psyche.
▷E H Haight, *Apuleius and his Influence* (1927)

ARAGON, Louis
(1897–1983)

French writer and political activist, born in Paris. One of the most brilliant of the Surrealist group, he co-founded the journal *Littérature* with **André Breton** in 1919. He published two volumes of poetry, *Feu de joie* (1920, 'Bonfire') and *Le Mouvement perpétuel* (1925, 'Perpetual Motion'), and a Surrealist novel, *Le Paysan de Paris* (1926, 'The Peasant of Paris'). After a visit to the Soviet Union in 1930 he became a convert to communism. Thereafter he wrote social-realistic novels in a series entitled *Le Monde Réel* (1933–51, 'The Real World'), and war poems, including *Le Crève-Coeur* (1941, 'Heartbreak') and *Les Yeux d'Elsa* (1942, 'Elsa's Eyes'), about his lifelong partner, the writer Elsa Triolet. The novel *La semaine sainte* (1958, 'Holy Week') attempted a Marxist analysis of the events of 1815. He was an important editor of left-wing publications, and an influential essayist.
▷A Hurant, *Louis Aragon: prisonnier politique* (1970)

ARANHA, José Pereira da Graça
(1868–1931)

Brazilian novelist and, at the end of his life, embracer of the avant-garde Brazilian modernist movement (the nativism of which, however, he rejected). He was born in Maranhao in the north-east of Brazil. A diplomat by profession, he maintained a European outlook throughout his life. His most important novel is *Chanaan* (1902, Eng trans, *Canaan*, 1920), about two German immigrants to Brazil who become members of a community which has settled in the interior. Whatever the worth of this still controversial novel, it succeeds in conveying the impact of the mysterious interior on the European sensibility.
▷M de L Teixeira, *Graça Aranha* (1952, in Portuguese)

ARANY, János
(1817–82)

Hungarian poet, born in Nagy-Szalonta of peasant stock. With **Sandor Petöfi** he was a leader of the popular national school, and is regarded as one of the greatest and most characteristic of Hungarian poets. He was chief secretary of the Academy from 1870 to 1879. His satire *The Lost Constitution* (1845) won the Kisfaludy Society Prize, but his chief work is the *Toldi* trilogy (1847–54), the story of the adventures of a murderously quick-tempered young peasant in the 14th century Hungarian court. He also published successful translations of **Aristophanes** and **Shakespeare**.
▷D Kevesztury, *Arany János* (1971)

ARATOR
(fl.540)

Poet, born in what is now Italy but what was then the kingdom of the Ostrogoths. He was employed at the court of King Athalric before moving to the papal Curia under Pope Vigilius. His poetry is a fine example of the epic religious tradition of the early church in which the forms and measures of classical Latin poetry are adapted and employed for exploring religious themes. Arator is recorded in church annals as having read aloud his epic account of the Acts of the Apostles in Rome in 544.

ARCHER, Jeffrey Howard, Baron
(1940–)

Bestselling British author and former parliamentarian, educated at Wellington School and Brasenose College, Oxford, where he won Blues for athletics and gymnastics. He sat as Conservative MP for the constituency of Louth from 1969 to 1974, but resigned from the House of Commons after a financial disaster that led to bankruptcy. In order to pay his debts in full he turned to writing fiction; his first book, *Not a Penny More, Not a Penny Less* (1975), based on his own unfortunate experiences in the financial world, was an instant bestseller, which he followed up with other blockbusters like *Shall We Tell the President?* (1976), *Kane and Abel* (1979), which was dramatized on television, and *First Among Equals* (1984), which was also televised. Despite critical reservations about their literary merits, his books continue to sell in vast numbers. In 1987 he wrote a thriller for the stage, *Beyond Reasonable Doubt*, and in 1988 capped his lifelong interest in the theatre by buying one outright—the Playhouse, London. In 1990 he wrote *Exclusive*, a play. He was Deputy Chairman of the Conservative Party 1985–6, but resigned following allegations over which he later cleared his name in a successful libel action against the *Daily Star*. He was made a life peer in 1992, taking the title Baron Archer of Weston-Super-Mare. Recent titles include *Honour Among Thieves* (1993) and *Twelve Red Herrings* (1994).

ARCHILOCHUS OF PAROS
(8th–7th century BC)

Early Greek lyric and elegiac poet. He was ranked by the ancients with **Homer** and **Pindar**, and **Plato** calls him 'the very wise', but much of his renown is for vituperative satire. Only fragments of his work are extant. He died in battle.

▷T Breitenstein, *Hésiode et Archiloque* (1971)

ARCHPOET, the
(d.c.1165)

German Latin poet whose career in many ways mirrors that of his contemporary and fellow satirist **Hugh Primas**. His real name is not known, but we know from his verse that he was of gentle birth and well educated, though impoverished. His one great patron was Rainald of Dassel, arch-chancellor to Emperor Frederick Barbarossa, who was impressed with his witty images and nicely turned phrases. However, after a falling-out between them (documented in verse), the archpoet disappeared into obscurity and, presumably, poverty.

ARDEN, John
(1930–)

British playwright, born in Barnsley, Yorkshire, and educated at Sedbergh School, King's College, Cambridge, and the Edinburgh College of Art. It was in Edinburgh, while he was completing his architectural training, that the College Dramatic Society produced his first play, a romantic comedy entitled *All Fall Down*, in 1955. *Live Like Pigs* (1958), with its **Rabelais**ian realism and humour, broke new ground in theatrical presentation. His aggressive awareness of the north of England is particularly evident in *The Workhouse Donkey* (1963), a caricature of northern local politics; in *Sergeant Musgrave's Dance* (1959), very much following the tradition of Brecht in its staging, the universality of the folk idiom reveals layers of political relevance beyond the simple tale of a group of soldiers returning to a northern town, bringing home with them the realities of war. In *Armstrong's Last Goodnight* (1964) the use of ballads and formal staging are particularly successful as Arden embodies contemporary political themes in a tale of the

16th-century Scottish borders. Arden has continually experimented with dramatic form and theatrical technique, both in the plays he has written alone and in the many pieces in which he has collaborated with his wife, Margaretta D'Arcy. *The Happy Haven* (1961) followed the commedia dell'arte tradition, the nativity play *The Business of Good Government* (1960) uses medieval stage techniques, *The Hero Rises Up* (1968) is a ballad opera about Nelson, and *The Ballygombeen Bequest* (1972) uses vaudeville on the theme of the political and class conflict in Ireland. Arden admits that he is not happy within the framework of the modern theatre. His plays also include *Ironhand* (1963), an adaptation of **Goethe**'s *Goetz von Berlichingen*; *Left-Handed Liberty*, commissioned in 1965 for the 750th anniversary of Magna Carta; a version of the Arthurian legend, *The Island of the Mighty* (1972), and *Vandaleur's Folly* (1978). He has also written television scripts, a volume of essays, and a novel, *Silence Among the Weapons* (1982). Since *The Island of the Mighty*, Arden has not produced a major new stage play but has written increasingly for radio, including a nine-part series, *Whose Is the Kingdom?* (1988). A second novel, *The Book of Bale*, appeared the same year, and continues Arden's theme of using early history to look closely at timeless moral issues.

▷J R Brown, *Theatre Language: a study of Arden, Osborne, Pinter and Wesker* (1972)

ARDERÍUS, Joaquín
(1890–1969)

Spanish experimental novelist, an isolated and highly original writer in whom there is now some new critical interest in Spain. He influenced many anti-Franco modernist and post-modernist novelists, such as **Juan Benet**. He wrote surrealistic and then, later, more idiosyncratic novels, such as *Yo y tres mujeres* ('I and Three Women'), a highly original and sophisticated erotic novel, and *Justo* (1929), a satire on pious official Roman Catholicism. His work was generally too difficult for it to have had commercial success, but it is now being studied as pioneering and influential.

ARENAS, Reinaldo
(1943–)

Cuban novelist, born in a small rural town in the province of Oriente, who has risen to international stature for his poetic vision of life in Castro's Cuba. Upon moving to Havana, he studied briefly at the university there and took a job at the National Library. His first book, *Celestino antes del Alba* (1967, 'Celestino Before Dawn'), is the first of five semi-autobiographical novels which describe Arena's fantastic vision of Cuba after the

Revolution. Because of the disenchantment with the Revolution expressed in his novels and also because of his homosexuality, he was placed in a re-education camp, imprisoned, and his works banned. In 1980, he left Cuba in the Mariel Boat Lift, and now lives in exile in New York, teaching and lecturing. Though mainly a novelist, he has also written brilliant short stories, a book of articles, a number of experimental theatre pieces, and is presently working on memoirs. He has won various awards, including a Guggenheim Fellowship.

ARETINO, Pietro
(1492–1557)

Italian poet, born in Arezzo, Tuscany, the illegitimate son of a nobleman named Luigi Bacci. Banished from his native town, he went to Perugia, where he worked as a bookbinder, and afterwards wandered through Italy in the service of various noblemen. In Rome (1517–27) he distinguished himself by his wit, impudence, and talents, and secured papal favour, which he subsequently lost by writing his salacious *Sonetti Lussuriosi* ('Lustful Sonnets'). He won the friendship of Giovanni de Medici and gained an opportunity of ingratiating himself with Francis I at Milan in 1524. He later settled in Venice, and again acquired powerful friends. It is said that while laughing heartily at a droll adventure of one of his sisters, he fell from a stool, and was killed on the spot. His poetical works include five witty comedies, and a tragedy of some merit.
▷F Berni, *La Vita di Pietro Aretino* (1939)

ARÉVALO MARTINEZ, Rafael
(1884–1975)

Guatemalan poet, story-writer and novelist, inventor of 'psychozoological fiction' in his tale *El hombre que paraci un caballo* (1914, 'The Man Who Looked Like a Horse'), about the legendary homosexual Colombian poet **Porfirio Barba Jacob**, born in Guatemala City. Classified as an 'extraordinary case', Arévalo has yet to be discovered and understood outside Latin America.

ARGENSOLA, Bartolomé Leonardo de
(1562–1631)
ARGENSOLA, Lupercio de
(1559–1613)

Spanish poets, born in Barbastro. They were both educated at Huesca University and both entered the service of Maria of Austria. Their poems led them to be styled the 'Spanish Horaces', but they were also official historians of Aragon. Lupercio also wrote some tragedies.
▷J A Molina, *Los Argensola* (1939)

ARGHEZI, Tudor, pseud of Ion N Theodorescu
(1880–1967)

Romanian poet, fiction-writer and translator—always the centre of violent controversy—more than once described as Romania's 'outstanding poet of the twentieth century'. He began as a monk (1899–1904), then became a communist. He was interned for part of World War II for ridiculing the Nazi ambassador to Romania. His final poetry, some of it socialist realist, is unconvincing. But earlier, as the non-intellectual but **Baudelaire**-inspired poet of the dark side of the environment, he reached major proportions. He made translations of Baudelaire and wrote fiction (1930) about his experiences in a monastery and in prison—always almost unreasonably wild in his polemic, he got himself charged after World War I with collaborating with a German newspaper. He was, a critic wrote, 'in search of ... apocalyptic visions of a putrescent world'. He was widely recognized throughout Europe, being translated by no less than **Salvatore Quasimodo** and **Rafael Alberti**; but *Selected Poems* (1976), in English, is not quite so effective at conveying his worth. At heart, and at his greatest, he is a religious poet.
▷D Micu, *The Work of Tudor Arghezi* (1965)

ARGUEDAS, Alcides
(1879–1946)

Bolivian novelist and historian, born in La Paz. As a historian and a sociologist, Arguedas exalted the European, and emphasized (too greatly, in some modern views) the influence of the environment. As a novelist, notably in *Raza de bronce* (1919, 'The Bronze Race', a radical re-working of an earlier novel of 1904, *Wata-Wara*), he was an avid defender of the Almairá Native Americans, showing them as exploited and despoiled by arrogant, greedy priests and clerks. Although its picture of the Native Americans is comprised of more fantasy than fact, the book is powerful, was influential—and was one of the first really good novels to be published in Bolivia. He wrote a rather stuffy, but invaluable, history of Bolivia (1922).
▷F Reinaga, *Alcides Arguedas* (1960, in Spanish)

ARGUEDAS, José María
(1911–69)

Peruvian novelist, born in a small provincial town. His life was spent working in literature and anthropology in order to champion the cause of the indigenous peoples of Peru. His literary works combine Quechua words and syntax with Spanish to illustrate the combination of cultures which characterizes his country. He is an important Regionalist writer, author of *Los ríos profundos* (1958, 'Deep Rivers'), a literary landmark which signalled the transition to the New Novel. His other major novels are *Yawar Fiesta* (1941, 'Yawar Festival') and *Todas las sangres* (1964, 'Everyone's Blood').

ARIBAU, Bonaventura Carles
(1798–1862)

Spanish economist and writer, born in Barcelona. He became a banker in Madrid, and was appointed director of the Mint and of the Spanish Treasury (1847). He was also decorated by the Prince Consort for his work on the industrial section of the Great Exhibition of 1851. He was editor of the *Biblioteca de autores españoles* ('Library of Spanish Writers'), and was the author of the *Oda a la Patria* (1833, 'Ode to the Motherland'), one of the earliest and best modern poems in Catalan, which had a tremendous influence on contemporary Catalan writers.
▷M de Montoliu, *Los grans personalitats de la litteratura catalana* (1936)

ARINOS, Affonso
(1868–1916)

Brazilian novelist, born in the Minas Gerais region. His books are interesting for their slight anticipations of **da Cunha**: both *Os Jagunços* and *Pelo Sertão* (both 1898) are about the backlands of the North East.

ARIOSTO, Ludovico
(1474–1533)

Italian poet, born in Reggio Emilia. He intended to take up law, but abandoned it for poetry. In 1503 he was introduced to the court of the Cardinal Ippolito d'Este at Ferrara, who employed him in many negotiations, but was extremely niggardly in his rewards. Here, in the space of 10 years, Ariosto produced his great poem, *Orlando Furioso* (1516, 'Orlando Enraged'), which takes up the epic tale of Roland (as Orlando) from the French *chansons de geste* and forms a continuation of **Boiardo**'s *Orlando Innamorato* ('Orlando in Love'). When the cardinal left Italy (1518), the duke, his brother, invited the poet to his service, and treated him with comparative liberality. In 1522 he was commissioned to suppress an insurrection in the wild mountain district of Garfagnana, an arduous task which he successfully accomplished; and after remaining there three years as governor of the province, he returned to Ferrara, where he composed his comedies, and finished

Orlando, which appeared in a third edition, enlarged to its present dimensions, in 1532. He was buried in the church of San Benedetto, at Ferrara, where a magnificent monument marks his resting place. Besides his great work, he wrote comedies, satires, sonnets, and a number of Latin poems. Of these the sonnets alone show the genius of the poet. His Latin poems are mediocre, and his comedies, besides lacking interest, are disfigured by licentious passages.
▷C P Brand, *Ludovico Ariosto: an introduction to the Orlando Furioso* (1974)

ARISTOPHANES
(c.448–c.385 BC)

Greek comic playwright. He wrote some 50 plays, but only 11 are extant. The best-known of his earlier works, in which the satire is largely political, are *Hippeis* (424, 'Knights'), *Nephelai* (423, 'Clouds') and *Sphekes* (422, 'Wasps') (named from their respective choruses), and *Eirene* (421, 'Peace'). These were followed by *Ornithes* (414, 'Birds'), *Lysistrata* (411, 'Destroyer of Armies'), *Thesmophoriazusae* (411, 'The Women attending the Thesmophoria') and *Batrachoi* (405, 'Frogs', which contains a burlesque poetic contest between **Aeschylus** and **Euripides**). Later come *Ecclesiazusae* (392, 'Women in Parliament') and *Plutus* (388). In the last, the themes are personal, and the chorus plays only a marginal role. Aristophanes is the only writer of Old Comedy of whom complete plays survive. The objects of his often savage satire are social and intellectual pretension; the plots of his plays show a genius for comic and often outrageous invention; his humour is usually good-natured; and the verse in his choruses marks him out as a notable poet.
▷L E Lord, *Aristophanes: his plays and influence* (1925)

ARLAND, Marcel
(1899–)

French fiction writer and critic, neglected outside his own country, a member of the Académie française since 1968. He was born in Varenne-sur-Amance. From 1953, at first with Jean Paulhan, he edited *La Nouvelle Revue Française*. He was involved in the Dada movement, but abandoned it to cultivate a precise style much influenced by his friend **André Gide**. Notable amongst his works are an influential anthology of French poetry (1941), the novel *L'Ordre* (1929, 'The Order'), and, above all, his tales of his own village, in such collections as *Il faut de tout pour faire un monde* (1946, 'It Takes Everything to Make a

World'), in which adults are seen through the eyes of a sensitive teenager.

ARLEN, Michael, originally Dikran Kouyoumdjian
(1895–1956)

British novelist, born in Ruschuk, Bulgaria, of Armenian parents. He was educated in England and naturalized in 1922, but lived in France from 1928 until World War II, and settled in the USA after the war. He made his reputation with *Piracy* (1922), *The Green Hat* (1924), and his short-story collections, *The Romantic Lady* (1921) and *These Charming People* (1923). His last novel was *The Flying Dutchman* (1939).
▷ M J Arlen, *Exiles* (1971)

ARLT, Roberto
(1900–42)

Argentinian novelist and dramatist, born in Buenos Aires of a German emigrant father and a Swiss–Italian mother. Arlt, initially reproached for his syntax (which was poor—and, worse, as they alleged, it was 'insulting'), was the most poetic of the urban realist Latin-American novelists of his century, with the exception of the Uruguayan **Juan Carlos Onetti**, who has acknowledged his own debt. Karl Arlt, 'the black father' (as Roberto called him), a professional failure, mocked his son throughout his childhood with 'sadistic machismo'; his mother was devoted to romantic pulp fiction. 'From the age of 15 to 20 I practised all the professions,' he wrote. 'They kicked me out everywhere for uselessness.' But then he taught himself to write, and started to compose 'crime spots' in the newspapers. His major work followed: four novels, and about 50 short stories. In the 1930s he devoted himself to theatre, which, although excellent, is not on such a high level. Of his work only *Los siete locos* (1929, Eng trans *The Seven Madmen*, 1984) has ever been translated. In *Los siete locos* and its sequel *Los lanzallamas* (1931, 'The Flame Throwers')—these are, with certain stories, his masterpieces—a group of madmen led by Erdosain, who seeks (like the Jewish 'false messiahs') 'holiness in sin', set out to destroy the capitalist world. The phantasmagorical world these novels conjure up can only be matched by the Argentinian political scene which formed their background: they are perhaps the blackest novels of the century. Yet Arlt's last novel, *El Amor Brujo* (1932, 'Love the Magician'), tells of frustrated love. His pieces for the newspaper *El Mundo* have been collected as *Aguafuertes* in two volumes (1950–3). His daughter Mirta edited his complete novels and stories (1963).
▷ K Schwartz, *A New History of Spanish-American Fiction* (1971)

ARNÉR, Sivar
(1909–)

Swedish novelist, short-story writer and dramatist. Born near Kalmar, he studied at the University of Lund and became a schoolteacher. An early novel such as *Plånbok borttappad* (1943, 'The Lost Wallet') reflects a **Nietzsche**an nihilism, tempered, in later novels such as *Fyra som var bröder* (1955, 'The Four who were Brothers'), by the influence of woman. Several texts offer psychological analyses of marital relationships, among them *Verandan* (1947, 'The Veranda'), a book of short stories, and *Egil* (1948), a novel. His works from the 1950s often reflect a mystical search for unity; and in the novel *Tvärbalk* (1963, 'The Cross-Beam') this quest results in a subtle critique of contemporary Swedish society. He is the author of numerous successful radio dramas.
▷ B Sjöberg, *Sivar Arnér—den livsbejakande nihilisten* (1993)

ARNICHES Y BARRERA, Carlos
(1866–1943)

Spanish playwright, born in Alicante. He moved while young to Madrid and there became so entrenched in the life of the capital that he was inextricably identified with it. After starting off in journalism, he turned his hand to play-writing, at first in collaboration. He excelled in the 'sainete', a short comedy or one-act farce reflecting everyday life. Originally it was an entr'acte made famous by **Ramon de la Cruz**. This kind of popular, comic work was at first rather scorned by critics but popular with audiences, who found the characters instantly recognizable. Some of the most famous works, from an output of over 300 pieces, were *El Santo de la Isidra* (1898, 'The Saint of Isidra') and *El Puñao de Rosas* (1902, 'The Bunch of Roses'), which were comedies, and *Los Caciques* (1919), a social criticism which finally won him critical acclaim. While never patronizing his audience, he maintained a common code of morality in his well-constructed slices of 'madrileño' life.

ARNIM, Achim von, real name Karl Joachim Friedrich Ludwig von Arnim
(1781–1831)

German writer of fantastic but original romances. He stirred up a warm sympathy for old popular poetry and folk-tales, and published over 20 volumes, mainly tales and novels, including the folk-song collections *Des Knaben Wunderhorn* (1806, 'The Boy's Magic Horn') with **Clemens von Brentano**. His writing is overtly moralistic and his most ambitious work is the unfinished novel *Die Kronenwächter* (1817, 'The Crown Minder').

39

His wife, Bettina (1785–1859), Brentano's sister, was as a girl infatuated with **Goethe**, and afterwards published a (largely fictitious) *Correspondence* with him, as well as 10 volumes of tales and essays.

▷H Liedke, *Literary Criticism and Romantic Theory in the Works of Achim von Arnim* (1927)

ARNIM, Bettina von, née von Brentano
(1785–1859)

German writer, sister to **Clemens von Brentano**, who was friendly with **Goethe** (who eventually severed connections with her owing to her treatment of his wife). Her books, such as one about Goethe and another about her brother, are not novels but somewhat fanciful—yet intelligent—accounts, or 'documentary' fabrications.

ARNOLD, Sir Edwin
(1832–1904)

English poet and journalist, born in Gravesend. He won the Newdigate Prize for poetry at Oxford in 1852 for his poem 'Belshazzar's Feast', taught at King Edward's School, Birmingham, and in 1856 became principal of Deccan College, Poona. Returning in 1861, he joined the staff of *The Daily Telegraph*, of which he became Editor in 1863. He wrote *The Light of Asia* (1879) on Buddhism, and other poems coloured by his experience of the East. A later volume, *The Light of the World* (1891), did not achieve the popularity of his earlier work. He also published translations from Eastern languages.

▷*Aspects of Life* (1893)

ARNOLD, Matthew
(1822–88)

English poet and critic, born in Laleham, near Staines, the eldest son of Dr Thomas Arnold of Rugby. He was educated at Winchester, Rugby, and Balliol College, Oxford. He won the Newdigate Prize with a poem on Cromwell (1843), and in 1845 was elected a fellow of Oriel College. After acting for four years as private secretary to Lord Lansdowne (1847–51), he was appointed one of the lay inspectors of schools in 1851, an office from which he retired in 1886. From 1857 to 1867 he was Professor of Poetry at Oxford. He was frequently sent by the government to inquire into the state of education on the Continent, especially in France, Germany, and Holland; and his masterly reports, with their downright statement of English deficiencies, attracted much attention in England. So, too, did his audacious application to scripture of the methods of literary criticism. In 1883 he received a pension of £250, and in the same year he lectured in the USA. He was buried at Laleham. His early volumes of poetry, *The Strayed Revelles and Other Poems* (1849), which contained 'The Forsaken Merman', and *Empedocles on Etna* (1852), which contained 'Tristram and Iseult', both failed, but he made his mark with *Poems: A New Edition* (1853–4), which contained 'The Scholar Gipsy' and 'Sohrab and Rustum', and confirmed his standing as a poet with *New Poems* (1867), which contained 'Dover Beach' and 'Thyrsis'. He published several distinguished works of criticism including *Essays in Criticism* (1865, 1888), *On the Study of Celtic Literature* (1867), *Culture and Anarchy* (1869), *St Paul and Protestantism* (1870), *Literature and Dogma* (1872), *Last Essays on Church and Religion* (1877), *Mixed Essays* (1879), *Irish Essays* (1882), and *Discourses on America* (1885).

▷L Trilling, *Matthew Arnold* (1939); M Thorpe, *Matthew Arnold* (1969)

ARP, Hans or Jean
(1887–1966)

Alsation sculptor, graphic artist and poet, born in Strasbourg, who had a command of three languages: French, German and Alsatian. He was the outstanding poet of the Dada movement, inaugurated (1916) by **Hugo Ball** in Zurich. Critic **Martin Seymour-Smith** has said of him that his poetry 'was a necessary means of expressing his essentially playful ... response to existence: childlike, spontaneous, cheerfully and mockingly aleatory in the face of a supremely confident assumption of the absurdity of everything'.

▷R W Last, *Hans Arp* (1969)

ARRABAL, Fernando
(1932–)

Spanish dramatist and novelist, born in Melilla, Spanish Morocco. His childhood was disrupted by the opposing political convictions of his parents during the Civil War. His strongly Catholic mother led him to believe that his father, who had escaped and disappeared in 1941 after being imprisoned for his Republican sympathies, was dead. He studied law in Madrid and drama in Paris in 1954, and then settled permanently in France. His first play, *Pique-nique en campagne* (1959, Eng trans *Picnic on the Battlefield*, 1964), established him in the tradition of the Theatre of the Absurd, greatly influenced by **Samuel Beckett**. He coined the term 'Panic theatre', intended to shock the senses, employing sadism and blasphemy to accomplish its aims. In *Le Cimetière des voitures* (1958, Eng trans as *The Car Cemetery*, 1969) life is seen as a used car dump, and in *Le grand cérémonial* (1965, 'The Grand Ceremonial') and *Cérémonie* *pour un noir assassiné* (1965, Eng trans *Ceremony for a Murdered Black*, 1972), ceremonial rites are used to play out sadistic fantasies. He writes in Spanish, his work being translated into French by his wife. In 1967 he was charged by a Spanish court with blasphemy and anti-patriotism, and his *Et ils passèrent des menottes aux fleurs* (1969, Eng trans *And They Put Handcuffs on the Flowers*, 1971), based on conversations with Spanish political prisoners, was eventually banned in France and Sweden while becoming his first major success in America in 1971. As well as his many plays he has published poetry—*La Pierre de la folie* (1963, 'The Stone of Stupidity') and *100 sonnets* (1966)—and novels including *Baal Babylone* (1959, Eng trans 1961).

▷A Schifres, *Entretiens avec Arrabal* (1969)

ARREOLA, Juan José
(1918–)

Mexican satirical story writer and dramatist, born in Cuidad Guzmán—one of Mexico's most unusual and original writers of his century. He was helped, in 1945, by the great French actor Louis Jouvet to obtain a scholarship so that he could study drama in Paris. He was later helped in his literary career by **Alfonso Reyes**. His best and most famous work, the much revised and unclassifiable *Confabulario* (1952, revised as *Confabulario y Varia invención*, 1954, Eng trans *Confabulario and Other Inventions*, 1964—the final Spanish revision is *Confabulario total*, 1962), consists of fables or parables, marked by a neurasthenic fear and hatred of women—a feature that has made Arreola's work unpalatable to some critics. He later became a television personality, and his work, often in the same vein as the *Confabulario*, is generally taken to have declined in power. *La feria* (1963, Eng trans *The Fair*, 1977) is a patchwork novel about his childhood in Zapotlán el Grande.

▷Y M Washburn, *Juan José Arreola* (1983)

ARTAUD, Antonin Marie Joseph
(1896–1948)

French dramatist, actor, director and theorist, born in Marseilles. A Surrealist in the 1920s, he published a volume of verse (*L'Ombilic des limbes*, 1925, 'The Umbilicus of Limbo'), and in 1927 co-founded the Théâtre Alfred Jarry. He propounded a theatre that dispensed with narrative and psychological realism but which returned instead to theatre as primitive rite, and the mythology of the human mind as expressed in dreams and interior obsessions. The function of drama was to give expression, through movement and gesture, to the inexpressible and irrational locked within the consciousness. His main theoretical work is the book, *Le Théâtre et son double* (1938, Eng trans *The Theatre and its Double*, 1958). As the creator of what has been termed the Theatre of Cruelty, his influence on post-war theatre was profound. A manic-depressive, his last years were spent in a mental institution, from where he continued to write. His *Collected Works* appeared in English in 1968–74 (4 vols).

ARTHUR, Timothy Shay
(1809–85)

American novelist and editor, born in Newburgh, New York, and educated in Baltimore. Hugely prolific, he wrote unashamedly didactic fiction, including the classic *Ten Nights in a Barroom and What I Saw There* (1854), an influential prohibitionist tract. It was dramatized (1958) by William W Pratt and became a long-running staple of popular theatre, memorable for little Mary's plangent song to her drunken father. No teetotaller himself, Arthur also wrote moralistic advice books like *Strong Drink: The Curse and the Cure* (1877, also published as *Grappling with the Monster*). He contributed to *Godey's Lady's Book* and founded what became *Arthur's Home Magazine* (1845–85), an 'improving' monthly dedicated to exposing the evils of alcoholism and gambling and reinforcing 'family values' and the sanctity of marriage. *The Three Eras of a Woman's Life* (1848, comprising *The Maiden*, *The Wife*, *The Mother*) was among his more ambitious works.

ARTMANN, H(ans) C(arl)
(1921–)

Austrian writer of the avant-garde, born in St Achatz am Walde. From 1952 to 1958 he was associated with the Wiener Gruppe, a coterie of avant-garde writers. He is a 'concrete' poet, interested in destroying old concepts and replacing them with entirely new ones; he is also a writer of dialect poems; he has been a dominant figure in Austria, but is otherwise known only in circles of experimental writers. One of his poems is translated in **Middleton** and **Hamburger**'s *Modern German Poetry 1910–1960* (1962).

ARTZYBASHEV, Mikhail Petrovich
(1878–1927)

Russian author. His liberalist novel *Sanin* (1907) had an international reputation at the turn of the century. It was translated by P Pinkerton in 1907, who also translated *Breaking Point* (1915), and with I Ohzol, *Tales of Revolution* (1918).

▷B N Lebedev, *Mikhail Artzybashev* (1908)

ARUNDEL, Honor
(1919–73)

British author of teenage fiction, born in
Wales, but living for much of her adult life in
Edinburgh. She was on the editorial staff of
the *Daily Worker*, and stood as a communist
candidate at the 1966 General Election. She
wrote several plays, worked as a critic, and
was married to the Scottish actor Alex
McCrindle. Her first children's book, *Green
Street* (1966), was written in response to her
daughters' request for stories about ordinary
people. Her work may seem a little dated to
today's young readers, but during the late
sixties and the seventies she was an important
force in establishing teenage fiction as a genre.
Her robust but sympathetic narratives are set
in Scotland and revolve around adolescent
heroines whose experiences reflect the
emotional, social and moral difficulties facing
girls growing up during a time of changing
values.

ASH, John
(1948–)

English poet, born in Manchester and educated at Birmingham University. His early
interest in the aesthetics and lifestyle of the
Symbolists and Decadents has given place to
an oblique and highly individual style that
occasionally suggests **John Ashbery**'s poetics
of omission. Ash's most important work to
date is *The Branching Stairs* (1984), which
demonstrates his ability to give tangible form
to quite ambiguous and only intermittently
specific images. Earlier collections—*The Bed*
(1981) and *The Goodbyes* (1982)—were less
successful because their surrealism seemed
more forced and their variations of voice
more mannered. In the dislocations of *The
Branching Stairs*, Ash created a highly personal voice and established himself as one of
the most important poets of his generation.

ASHBERY, John Lawrence
(1927–)

American poet, critic and novelist, born in
Rochester, New York, the son of a farmer.
Since attending Harvard, where he became
close friends with the poets **Kenneth Koch**
and **Frank O'Hara**, he has been associated
with the highly visual, almost Abstract Expressionist language of the 'New York' school.
He published his first volume, a chapbook,
Turandot and Other Poems, in 1953, but it
was not until the publication of *Some Trees*
in 1956 that he began to attract critical
attention. Influenced by **W H Auden**, he
inspires ardent admiration and bemused
antipathy in almost equal measure, and has
frequently been charged with obscurity. His

reputation is international and in 1976 his
twelfth collection, *Self-Portrait in a Convex
Mirror*, won the National Book Critics Circle
Prize, the National Book Award for poetry,
and the Pulitzer Prize for poetry. Other volumes include *The Tennis Court Oath* (1962),
Rivers and Mountains (1966), *Houseboat Days*
(1977) and *Shadow Train* (1982). His only
novel is *A Nest of Ninnies* (1969), co-authored
with **James Schuyler**.
▷D Shapiro, *John Ashbery: An Introduction
to the Poetry* (1979)

ASHFORD, Daisy (Margaret Mary)
(1881–1972)

English author, born in Petersham, Surrey.
She is famous for a story she wrote as a child,
but wrote nothing as an adult, apparently
content to run a market garden with her husband, whom she married in 1920. Thirty years
previously, in 1890, when she was nine years
old, she composed *The Young Visiters, or Mr
Salteena's Plan*, in which Bernard Clark and
Mr Salteena ('not quite a gentleman') vie for
the hand of 17-year-old Ethel Monticue. Ashford discovered her imperfectly spelled manuscript in 1919, and on its publication it
became both a bestseller and a talking point.
The following year *The Young Visiters*
became a successful play and in 1968 provided the basis of musical, albeit with a score
which caused one critic to describe it as 'amiably pointless'. Other juvenile Ashford writings appeared in *DA: Her Book* (1920).
▷R M Malcolmson, *Daisy Ashford* (1984)

ASHTON-WARNER, Sylvia
(1908–84)

New Zealand novelist and schoolteacher
whose account of her teaching life, *Teacher*,
was at first rejected. She recast it as fiction
and it appeared, to considerable acclaim, as
Spinster (1958); through the success of that
book *Teacher* finally appeared in 1963. In
Spinster the heroine is typical of Ashton-
Warner's strong feminine characters who
fight against suffocating New Zealand pro-
vinciality. Other novels are *Incense to Idols*
(1960), *Bell Call* (1964), *Greenstone* (1966)
and *Three* (1971), a closely observed power
struggle between mother and daughter-in-
law, set in London. Her autobiographical
I Passed This Way (1979) highlights a sense
of alienation from her homeland.
▷L Hood, *Sylvia!: The Biography of Sylvia
Ashton-Warner* (1988)

ASIMOV, Isaac
(1920–92)

Russian-born American novelist, critic and
popular scientist. Born in Petrovichi, he was

brought to the USA when he was three. He took a PhD in chemistry at Columbia University and his career as an academic biochemist was as distinguished and precocious as that as a science-fiction writer. In a prodigious body of work the titles that stand out include the 'Foundation' novels—*Foundation* (1951), *Foundation and Empire* (1952) and *Second Foundation* (1953); the so-called 'Robot' novels —*The Caves of Steel* (1954) and *The Naked Sun* (1957), and the short stories which form the collection *I, Robot* (1950). A leading spokesman for science fiction, he became ubiquitous on television and on the lecturing circuit as well as being an untiring contributor to newspapers and magazines. Increasingly regarded as a scientific seer, he added the term 'robotics' to the language.

▷N Goble, *Asimov Analyzed* (1972)

ASTLEY, Thea Beatrice May
(1925–)

Australian novelist and poet, born in Brisbane, three times winner of the **Miles Franklin** Award. Her first novel, *Girl with a Monkey* (1958), was followed by *A Descant for Gossips* (1960). *The Slow Natives* (1965) became Australian 'Best Novel of the Year' and established her reputation as a satiric and iconoclastic commentator on small-town Australian life. In *A Kindness Cup* (1974) she denounces aboriginal treatment in 19th-century Queensland. A collection of wrily humorous short stories, *Hunting the Wild Pineapple* (1979), is mostly narrated by a character from *The Slow Natives*, a favourite device of Astley.

ASTURIAS, Miguel Angel
(1899–1974)

Guatemalan fiction writer and poet, winner of the Nobel Prize for literature. A law graduate from the National University, he spent many years in exile, particularly in Paris, where he studied anthropology and translated the Mayan sacred book *Popul Vuh*, written in the Quiche language, into Spanish. This was to have an enduring influence on his fiction, though his most successful novel, *El Señor Presidente* (1946, Eng trans *The President*, 1963), reveals the Indian mythical influences only obliquely. Other books included *Hombres de maiz* (1949, Eng trans *Men of Maize*, 1975) and a trilogy on the foreign exploitation of the banana trade. A difficult, experimental and ambitious writer, he flirted with 'automatic writing' as a route into the unconscious. He was awarded the Nobel Prize for literature in 1967. In the Gua-

temalan civil service from 1946, he was ambassador to France, 1966–70.

▷R J Callan, *Miguel Angel Asturias* (1970)

ATHENAEUS
(2nd century)

Greek writer, born in Naucratis in Egypt. He lived first in Alexandria and later in Rome about the close of the 2nd century. He wrote the *Deipnosophistae* ('Banquet of the Learned'), a collection of anecdotes and excerpts from ancient authors arranged as scholarly dinner-table conversation. Thirteen of its 15 books survive more or less complete, together with a summary of the other two.

ATHERTON, Gertrude Franklin, née Horn
(1857–1948)

American novelist, born in San Francisco. Left a widow in 1887, she travelled extensively, living in Europe most of her life and using the places she visited as backgrounds for her novels—which range from ancient Greece to California and the West Indies. She was made Chevalier of the Legion of Honour for her relief work during World War I and in 1934 became President of the American National Academy of Literature. The most popular of her many novels are *The Conqueror* (1902), a fictional biography of Alexander Hamilton, and *Black Oxen* (1923), which is concerned with the possibility of rejuvenation.

▷J H Jackson, *Gertrude Atherton* (1940)

ATTAWAY, William
(1911–)

American black 'proletarian' novelist, born in Mississippi. He wrote *Let Me Breathe Thunder* (1939), about two white tramps, and *Blood on the Forge* (1941), about black farmers trying to get jobs in Pennsylvania steel mills.

ATTERBOM, Per Daniel Amadeus
(1790–1855)

Swedish poet, born in Östergötland. A leading member of the Uppsala Romantics clustered around the revolutionary journal *Phosphorus*, he was much influenced by German aesthetic theory, particularly the writings of Friedrich Schelling. Atterbom's lyrical talent with its descriptive sensitivity and pantheistic wonder is best seen in the 40 poems of the cycle *Blommorna* (1812, 'The Flowers'). In his poetic drama *Lycksalighetens ö* (1824–7, 'The Isle of the Blessed') he dresses the conflict between beauty and duty in a cloak of myth and symbolism and, in one part, caricatures the emergent liberal ideas of the day. His *Svenska siare*

och skalder 1–6 (1841–55, 'Swedish Seers and Poets') was the first real study of Swedish literary history.
▷H Frykenstedt, *Atterboms livs—och världsåskådning* (1951–2)

ATWOOD, Margaret Eleanor
(1939–)
Canadian novelist, short-story writer, poet and critic, described by one commentator as 'a staunch moralist' who insists 'that modern man must reinvent himself'. Born in Ottawa, she spent her early years in northern Ontario and Quebec bush country. After graduating from the University of Toronto and Radcliffe College, she held a variety of jobs ranging from waitress and summer-camp counsellor to lecturer in English literature and writer-in-residence. Her first published work, a collection of poems entitled *The Circle Game* (1966), won the Governor-General's Award. Since then she has published several volumes of poetry, collections of short stories—*Dancing Girls* (1977) and *Bluebeard's Egg* (1987)—and *Survival* (1972), an acclaimed study of Canadian literature. She is best known, however, as a novelist. *The Edible Woman* (1969) dealt with emotional cannibalism and provoked considerable controversy within and beyond the women's movement. It was followed by *Surfacing* (1972), *Lady Oracle* (1976), *Life Before Man* (1979) and *Bodily Harm* (1982), each in some way exploring the place of mythology on an individual's life. In 1985, *The Handmaid's Tale* was shortlisted for the Booker Prize, as was *Cat's Eye* in 1989. Her most recent novel, *The Robber Bride*, was published in 1993.
▷S Grace, *A Violent Duality* (1979); J H Rosenberg, *Margaret Atwood* (1984)

AUB, Max
(1903–72)
Spanish novelist, dramatist and literary hoaxer who is somewhat isolated in the literature of his country—unsurprisingly, because he was born in Paris of a German father and a French mother, and was not taken to Spain until he was 11 years old. He had written some poetic narratives before the Civil War, but it was that event which moved him to his best work. His cycle of novels about this war (of some of which there is a French translation), *El laberinto mágico* (1943–68, 'The Magic Labyrinth'), rivals the narratives of **Arturo Barea**. His *Josep Torres Campalans* (1958) was an illustrated and well documented biography of a Catalan painter and friend of Picasso; many claimed to have known him well, but he did not exist. Full critical appreciation of Aub is yet to come. From 1939 onwards he lived and worked in Mexico, from which he published the humorous story collection *La verdadera historia de la muerte de Francisco Franco* (1960, 'The True History of the Death of Francisco Franco'), which displeased its subject. His plays, never successful except in small theatres, were correspondingly remarkable.

AUBANEL, Théodore
(1829–86)
Provençal poet and playwright, born in Avignon. He was described by **Paul Ambroise Valery** as the only true Provençal poet, but was disowned in his lifetime by his native region because of the sensual and carnal subject-matter of his work. He produced three volumes of poetry: *La Grenade Entr' Ouverte* (1860, 'The Ripening Pomegranite'); *Les Filles d'Avignon* ('Daughters of Avignon', 300 copies privately circulated in 1885 and quickly banned by the archbishop); and *Le Soleil d'Outre-Tombe* ('The Sun from beyond the Tomb', published posthumously in 1899). Between 1861 and 1866 he also wrote the plays *Le Rapt* ('The Abduction') and *Le Berger* ('The Shepherd'), published in 1928 and 1944 respectively. In spite of a blissful marriage (1861) to Josephine Mazon, Aubanel dealt extensively with adultery in his work; he nonetheless professed a staunch Catholicism, and died, of apoplexy, with a crucifix pressed to his chest.

AUCHINCLOSS, Louis Stanton
(1917–)
American novelist, short-story writer and critic, born in Lawrence, New York. He trained as a lawyer and was admitted to the New York Bar in 1941. He is a novelist of manners, at home with old money and a highly codified, traditional society. He has nonetheless a fine sense of intrigue. His first novel, *The Indifferent Children* (1947), appeared under the pseudonym Andrew Lee, but subsequent books have appeared under his own name, the best of them being *Pursuit of the Prodigal* (1960), *Portrait in Brownstone* (1962), *The Embezzler* (1966) and *A World of Profit* (1963). His later novels have attracted less critical acclaim.
▷C C Dahl, *Louis Auchincloss* (1986)

AUDEN, W(ystan) H(ugh)
(1907–73)
Anglo–American poet and essayist. Born in York, he was educated at Gresham's School, Holt, and Christ Church, Oxford, and was naturalized as an American citizen in 1946. In the 1930s he wrote passionately on social problems from a far-Left standpoint, especially in his collection of poems *Look, Stranger!* (1936). He went to Spain as a civ-

ilian in support of the Republican side and reported on it in *Spain* (1937), followed by a verse commentary (with prose reports by **Christopher Isherwood**) on the Sino–Japanese war in *Journey to a War* (1939). He also collaborated with Isherwood in three plays: *The Dog Beneath the Skin* (1935), *The Ascent of F6* (1936) and *On the Frontier* (1938). He collaborated with **Louis MacNeice** in *Letters from Iceland* (1937) and wrote the libretto for *Ballad of Heroes* by Benjamin Britten in 1939. He emigrated to New York early in 1939 and was appointed associate professor at Michigan University, and Professor of Poetry at Oxford University in 1956. In America he became converted to Anglicanism, tracing his conversion in *The Sea and the Mirror* (1944) and *For the Time Being* (1944). His later works include *Nones* (1951), *The Shield of Achilles* (1955), *Homage to Clio* (1960) and *City Without Walls* (1969). He is best remembered today as the 'Poet of the Thirties', for his prodigious verbal dexterity, and for his essays of literary criticism. He met his lifelong partner, Chester Kallman, in New York, but he was also married to the writer Erika Mann, daughter of the German novelist **Thomas Mann**, in 1935; his most important relationship, however, was with Kallman, his lover and collaborator. He returned to England in 1972 but divided his time between Oxford and a second home in Kirchstetten in Austria, where he died.

▷H Carpenter, *W H Auden: A Biography* (1981)

AUDIBERTI, Jacques
(1899–1965)

French poet, playwright and novelist, born in Antibes. He wrote 15 novels, some distinguished poetry, and, above all, plays. He was a Surrealist who reacted against the confusions of Surrealism, and so tried to bring a classical order into his writings—but without suppressing any of his originally unconscious impulses. He was most influenced by **Antonin Artaud** and by the latter's theories of the 'theatre of cruelty'; but he was gifted with a sense of humour, which often went unnoticed. Essentially his project was to demonstrate that human beings tend to become, in **Wyndham Lewis**'s phrase, 'hallucinated automata', if they reject or ignore their atavistic origins, instead of coming to terms with them. He may therefore be characterized as having taken a **Jung**ian approach—but he puzzled interviewers by talking to them, not about his philosophy, but about Humphrey Bogart. His most famous play is *Quoat-Quoat* (1946), in which the rescuing stone of the Mexican God is rejected by a spy who falls in love with a ship captain's daughter under sentence of death. He has fascinated certain critics, but the time for a more general acceptance of his message lies in the future.

▷L E Pronko, *Avant-Garde* (1962); G E Wellwarth, *The Theatre of Protest and Paradox* (1964); J Guicharnaud, *Modern French Theatre* (1967)

AUEL, Jean Marie
(1936–)

American fantasy writer, born in Chicago. Her reputation rests on the sequence of novels known as *Earth's Children*, which began with *The Clan of the Cave Bear* (1980), followed by *The Valley of Horses* (1982), *The Mammoth Hunters* (1985) and *The Plains of Passage* (1990). They are a mixture of plausible anthropology and fantastic romance set in prehistoric times, and trace the story of the orphaned Cro-Magnon girl Ayla in the matriarchal Neanderthal tribe which adopts her.

AUERBACH, Berthold, originally Moses Baruch Auerbacher
(1812–82)

German novelist, born in Nordstetten in the Black Forest. He studied at the universities of Tübingen, Munich, and Heidelberg, and in 1836 was imprisoned as a member of the students' Burschenschaft. Destined for the synagogue, he abandoned theology for law, then law for history and philosophy, especially that of Spinoza, on whose life he based a novel of that name (1837), and whose works he translated (1841). In *Schwarzwälder Dorfgeschichten* (1843, 'Black Forest Village Tales'), on which his fame chiefly rests, he gives charming pictures of Black Forest life. Of his longer works the best known are *Barfüssele* (1856, 'Little Barefoot') and *Auf der Höhe* (1865, 'On the Summit').

▷L Stein, *Berthold Auerbach und das Judenthum* (1882)

AUERSPERG, Anton Alexander, Graf von, pseud Anastasius Grün
(1806–76)

Austrian poet. He was distinguished by his Liberalism and ultra-German sympathies. He was one of the German epic and lyrical poets, among whom he holds a high rank.

▷E Schatzmayer, *Anastasius Grüns Dichtungen* (1865)

AUGIER, Guillaume Victor Émile
(1820–89)

French dramatist, born in Valence. His *Théâtre complet* (1890, 'Complete Plays') fills seven volumes, and includes fine social comedies, such as *Le Gendre de M. Poirier* (1854, with Sandea, 'Mr Poirier's Son-in-Law') and *Les Fourchambault* (1878).

▷A Denoist, *Essais de critique dramatique* (1898)

AUGUSTINE, St (Aurelius Augustinus),
also known as **Augustine of Hippo**
(354–430)

The greatest of the Latin Church fathers, born in Tagaste in Numidia (modern Tunisia). His father was a pagan, but he was brought up a Christian by his devout mother, Monica. He went to Carthage to study and had a son, Adeonatus, by a mistress there. Carthage was a metropolitan centre, and he was exposed there to many new intellectual fashions and influences. He became deeply involved in Manicheanism, which seemed to offer a solution to the problem of evil, a theme which was to preoccupy him throughout his life. In 383 he moved to teach at Rome, then at Milan, and became influenced by scepticism and then by Neoplatonism. After the dramatic spiritual crises described in his *Confessiones*, he finally became converted to Christianity and was baptized (together with his son) by St Ambrose in 386. He returned to North Africa and in 395 became bishop of Hippo, where he was a relentless antagonist of the heretical schools of Donatists, Pelagians and Manicheans and champion of orthodoxy. He remained at Hippo until his death in 430, as the Vandals were besieging the gates of the city. He was an unusually productive writer and much of his work is marked by personal spiritual struggle. The *Confessiones* (400) is a classic of world literature and a spiritual autobiography as well as an original work of philosophy (with a famous discussion on the nature of time). *De civitate Dei* (413–26, Eng trans *The City of God*, 1957–72) is a monumental work of 22 books which presents human history in terms of the conflict between the spiritual and the temporal, which will end in the triumph of the City of God, whose manifestation on earth is the church.
▷R O'Connell, *St Augustine's Confessions: an odyssey of soul* (1969); J J O'Meara, *The Young Augustine* (1954)

AUKRUST, Olav Lom
(1883–1929)

Norwegian poet. He was a schoolmaster who wrote large quantities of religious and patriotic verse. *Himmelvarden* (1916) consists of three long cycles in New Norwegian containing many passages of great lyric power. *Hamar i Hellom* (1926), of which the chief poem is *Emme*, summons the people of Norway to use the power of their great traditions to achieve present security and progress. His final collection of poems, *Solrenning*, is incomplete and was published posthumously in 1930.
▷I Krokann, *Olav Aukrust* (1933)

AULNOY, Marie Catherine Jumelle de Barneville, Comtesse d'
(c.1650–1705)

French writer. She wrote romances of court life, but is mainly remembered for her charming fairy-tales, *Contes de Fées* (1698).

AURELIUS, Marcus Aurelius Antoninus,
originally **Marcus Annius Verus**
(121–80)

One of the most respected emperors in Roman history, the son of Annius Verus and Domita Calvilla, born in Rome. When only 17, he was adopted by Antoninus Pius, who had succeeded Hadrian and whose daughter Faustina was selected for his wife. From 140, when he was made consul, till the death of Antoninus in 161, he discharged his public duties with the utmost conscientiousness, and maintained the friendliest relations with the Emperor. At the same time he still devoted himself to the study of law and philosophy, especially Stoicism. On his accession, with characteristic magnanimity he voluntarily divided the government with his brother by adoption, Lucius Aurelius Verus, who in 161 was sent to take command against the Parthians. Despite the self-indulgence and dilatoriness of Verus, the generals were victorious, but the army brought back from the East a plague that ravaged the empire. Peaceful by temperament, Marcus Aurelius was nevertheless throughout his reign destined to suffer from constant wars, and though in Asia, Britain, and on the Rhine the barbarians were checked, permanent peace was never secured. At Athens he founded chairs of philosophy for each of the chief schools: Platonic, Stoic, Peripatetic, and Epicurean. One of the few Roman Emperors whose writings have survived, his 12 books of *Meditations* (*ta eis heauton*) record his innermost thoughts and are a unique document. They reveal his affinity with Stoicism, and show both his loneliness and the fact that he did not allow himself to be embittered by his experiences of life. His death was felt to be a national calamity, and he was retrospectively idealized as the model of the perfect Emperor.
▷A R Bailey, *Marcus Aurelius* (1966)

AUSONIUS, Decius Magnus
(c.309–392)

Latin poet, born in Burdigala (Bordeaux), the son of a physician. He taught rhetoric there for 30 years, and was then appointed by the Emperor Valentinian I tutor to his son Gratian; he afterwards held the offices of quaestor, prefect of Latium and consul of Gaul. On the death of Gratian, Ausonius retired to his estate at Bordeaux, where he occupied himself with literature and rural pursuits. His works, which show great versatility, include epigrams, poems on his deceased relatives and on his colleagues, epistles in verse and prose, and idylls.

▷C Aymonier, *Ausone et ses amis* (1935)

AUSTEN, Jane
(1775–1817)

English novelist, born in Steventon, Hampshire. She was the sixth of seven children of a country rector; her father was an able scholar who also served as her tutor. She spent the first 25 years of her life in Steventon, and the last eight in nearby Chawton, and did almost all her writing in those two places, writing virtually nothing in the intervening years in Bath, which appears to have been an unsettled time in her otherwise ordered and rather uneventful life. She never married, although she had a number of suitors, and wrote percipiently on the subjects of courtship and marriage in her novels. She began to write at an early age to amuse her family, and by 1790 had completed a burlesque on popular fiction in the manner of **Richardson**, entitled *Love and Friendship*, and ridiculed the taste for Gothic fiction in *Northanger Abbey*, which was written at this time, but only published in 1818. Her characteristic subject was the closely observed and often ironically depicted morals and mores of country life, and she rendered it with genius. Her best-known works in this vein are *Sense and Sensibility* (1811), *Pride and Prejudice* (1813), *Emma* (1816), and the posthumously published *Persuasion* (1817). *Mansfield Park* (1814) is a darker and more serious dissection of her chosen fictional territory, and although never as popular, is arguably her masterpiece. Modern research has seen the publication of the fragment of an unfinished novel she was writing when she died, called *Sanditon*, and some very early pieces, including *Lady Susan*, a juvenile work in epistolary form. Her own letters, although carefully filleted by her sister Cassandra after her death, are one of the few revealing documentary sources on her life. Her greatness has been clearer to subsequent generations than to her own, although Sir **Walter Scott** praised the delicate observation and fine judgement in her work, which she herself characterized as 'the little bit (two inches wide) of Ivory on which I work with so fine a Brush, as produces little effect after much labour'. If she chose a small stage for her labours, however, she worked upon it with exquisite understanding.

▷E Jenkins, *Jane Austen: a biography* (1938); J R Liddell, *The Novels of Jane Austen* (1974)

AUSTER, Paul
(1947–)

American novelist and poet, born in Newark, New Jersey. His varied occupations have included merchant seaman, census-taker, and teacher of creative writing. He wrote his first novel, *Squeeze Play* (1982), as 'Paul Benjamin', by which time he had already produced several volumes of poetry, a selection of which appeared with some essays in *Ground Work* (1990). The cerebral mystery novels which make up *The New York Trilogy* (1985–7) were followed by *In the Country of Last Things* (1987), a nightmare vision of a society trapped in terminal social disintegration. His novels share an ironic awareness of the limitations of language in apprehending reality, but reality itself is rendered mysterious in his evocative masterpiece *The Music of Chance* (1991).

AUSTIN, Alfred
(1835–1913)

English poet, born of Catholic parents in Leeds. He was educated at Stonyhurst and Oscott College, graduated from London University in 1853, and was called to the Bar in 1857, but abandoned law for literature. He was a strong supporter of **Benjamin Disraeli**, and an ardent imperialist. He published *The Season; a Satire* (1861), *The Human Tragedy* (1862), *The Conversion of Winckelmann* (1862) and a dozen more volumes of poems, and an autobiography (1911). Between 1883 and 1893 he edited the *National Review*; in 1896 he became poet laureate, an appointment which brought him more derision than honours from the literary community.

AUSTIN, Mary
(1868–1934)

American novelist and essayist, born in Carlinville, Illinois and educated at Blackburn College. A move to California in 1888 directly influenced her writing: Indians and the western environ figure prominently in her work, and her first book, *The Land of Little Rain* (1903), won acclaim as a western classic. Subsequent work addressed women's issues as Austin became involved in the suffrage movement and other feminist causes; other themes highlighted in her work include mysticism, Christ, and 'the individual'. A prolific writer, Austin produced 200 articles and 32 books in her lifetime. She is best known for her play *The Arrow Maker* (1911).

▷E Stineman, *Mary Austin: Song of a Maverick* (1990)

AVERY, Gillian Elise
(1926–)

English novelist, author of children's stories and sociological studies, born in Reigate, Surrey. Her adult novels include *The Lost Railway* (1980) and *Onlookers* (1983), but she is more widely known for her children's books, such as *The Warden's Niece* (1957) and *Huck and Her Time Machine* (1977). Her non-fiction work includes pioneering surveys of education and literature for young people. *Nineteenth Century Children: Heroes and Heroines in English Children's Stories 1700–1900*, written with Angela Bull, appeared in 1965, and *The Echoing Green: Memories of Victorian and Regency Youth*, in 1974. Her authoritative study of girls' independent schools in Britain, *The Best Type of Girl* (1991), vividly charts the changing social and cultural importance of girls' private schools, and confronts issues such as social class and educational privilege entirely without bias.

AVICEBRON, Arabic name Solomon ibn Gabirol
(c.1020–c.1070)

Jewish poet and philosopher in the Jewish 'Golden Age' in Spain, born in Malaga. Most of his prose work is lost but an ethical treatise in Arabic survives, as does a Latin translation of his most famous work, *Fons vitae* ('The Fount of Life'). This latter is a dialogue on the nature of matter and the soul, which is Neoplatonist in character, and was very influential among later Christian scholastics. His poetry became part of the mystical tradition of the Kabbalah.
▷F Brunner, *Platonisme et Aristotelisme* (1965)

AVIENUS, Rufus Festus
(fl. c.375)

Latin poet, a native of Vulsinii (Bolsena). He wrote on natural and geographical topics, and translated the *Phainomena* of Aratus of Sicyon. He also wrote a paraphrase of a description of the world, *Descriptio Orbis Terrae*.

AVISON, Margaret Kirkland
(1918–)

Canadian poet, born in Galt, Ontario and educated at the University of Toronto. She has worked as a librarian, a lecturer at the University of Toronto, and a social worker. Though she began writing in the 1950s, she did not publish her first book of poetry, *The Winter Sun*, until 1960, and has since published only two more volumes, *The Dumbfounding* (1966) and *Sunblue* (1978). She has, however, had her poems published in many periodicals. Her work has been influenced by her conversion to Christianity and contains elements of metaphysics. In 1990 a new edition of her first two books of poetry was published, for which she received a Governor General's Award.
▷D Kent, *Margaret Avison and Her Works* (1989)

AVITUS, Alcimus Edicus
(fl.490)

Gaulish Latin poet, born into an aristocratic family in Vienne (now in France) during the decline of the Roman Empire. He became Bishop of Vienne in 490. His poetry is in the religious epic tradition of the early church, setting out religious themes in classical form.

AWDRY, W(ilbert) V(ere)
(1911–)

English author and Church of England clergyman, born in Ampfield, Hampshire, whose railway stories for young people, especially those featuring Thomas The Tank Engine, have delighted generations of small children. The first, *The Three Railway Engines*, appeared in 1945, and *Thomas, the Tank Engine*, a year later. Over 25 books followed, each based on a real experience, until *Tramway Engines* in 1972, after which Awdry's son, Christopher, succeeded to the authorship. The passing of the age of steam has done nothing to diminish the appeal of Thomas or of his friends James the Red Engine and Henry the Green Engine, even to those who have never seen a steam locomotive. Together with their drivers and porters, the engines both inhabit and represent a comforting world, one which suffers from small divisions, but which, more importantly, has its reconciliations.

AWOONOR, Kofi
(1935–)

Arguably the leading Ghanaian poet of his generation, he combines traditional forms derived from Ewe oral poetry with a use of English that frequently recalls **T S Eliot** and **Ezra Pound**. Born in Wheta and educated in Ghana, London and New York, he has studied and been closely involved in Ghanaian culture and politics. *Rediscovery* (1964) marked a double journey back into 'the tradition' of African verse and into the poet's own divided consciousness. *Night of My Blood* (1971) and *Ride Me, Memory* (1973) were more obviously aimed at an international readership. His one novel, *This Earth, Mr Brother* ... (1972), was a rather lame and prosey attempt at similar themes. He has edited important anthologies of Ghanaian verse and folktales.

AXULAR, Pedro de

(b.1556)

Basque writer, born in Navarre, the most important of a group of early clerics writing in the language, and author of *Guero* (1643), a tract on the need for repentance which, while didactic and rhetorical, is also humane and readable.

▷R Gallop, *A Book of the Basques* (1930); L Michelena, *Historia de la literatura vasca* (1960)

AYALA, Francisco

(1906–)

Spanish novelist and sociologist, born in Granada, who, after serving the legal government, went into exile in 1939, but returned in 1973 when the regime made it possible. He was originally a professor of law at Madrid University. He wrote three promising early novels, much in the style of the times, but then in 1930 abandoned the form; in 1944 he took it up again, but in an entirely different spirit. His best-known books, and his best, are *Muertes de perro* (1958, Eng trans *Death as A Way of Life*, 1964) and its sequel *El fondo del vaso* (1962, 'The Dregs'), in which he rewrites for himself and his own time **Ramón Valle-Inclán**'s novel *El tirano Banderos*: the life and aftermath of the type of the paradigmatic and mad South American tyrant of that book. Ayala has written much intelligent and ironic criticism, and is a notable exposer of the evils of bureaucracy. He investigates the nature of power, and concludes that whoever has power over others is a 'usurper'.

AYCKBOURN, Alan

(1939–)

English playwright. Born in London, he began his theatrical career as an acting stage manager in repertory before joining Stephen Joseph's Theatre-in-the-Round company at Scarborough. A founder-member of the Victoria Theatre, Stoke-on-Trent in 1962, he returned in 1964 as producer to Scarborough, where most of his plays have been premiered. His first of a torrent of west-end successes was *Relatively Speaking* in 1967, and he was quickly established as a master of farce, basing his plays in traditional manner on a single idea, usually a mistake or a confusion, from which the whole plot derives. His plays often contain shrewd observation of the English class-structure, but it is in sheer mechanical ingenuity that he excels. He has made considerable experiments with staging and dramatic structure: *The Norman Conquests* (1974) is a trilogy in which each play takes place at the same time in a different part of the setting, and *Way Upstream* (1982) is set on and around a boat and necessitates the flooding of the stage. Among his most successful farces are *Time and Time Again* (1972), *Absurd Person Singular* (1973), *Bedroom Farce* (1977) and *Joking Apart* (1979). He has written two musicals, *Jeeves* (with Andrew Lloyd Webber, 1975) and *Making Tracks* (with Paul Todd, 1981), and was a BBC radio drama producer (1964–70). His later plays, including *Woman in Mind* (1985) and *Henceforward* (1987), reflect an increasingly bleak vision of society. Ayckbourn's techniques have become simpler and his characters more complex as he reveals himself to be not only a master farceur but a savage social commentator. He is now also recognized as a distinguished director, not only of his own work, but of plays by such authors as **Arthur Miller**.

AYGI, Gennady

(1934–)

Chuvash (originally Soviet) poet and translator, born in Shaymurino in the Chuvash republic, whose early work was in Chuvash, but who from 1960 wrote his poetry in Russian. For many years this could only be circulated in *samidzat* ('do-it-yourself publishing') form, but this changed with the collapse of the USSR. Essentially his poetry is in the tradition of his mentor, **Pasternak**, but it has also been influenced by the Czech **Wolker**, and has become markedly original, especially in technique, which breaks with conventional forms. His *Stikhi 1954–1971* ('Poems') appeared in Germany in 1975, with some notes by himself, but his work is not yet available in English.

ARMAH, Ayi Kwei

(1939–)

Ghanaian novelist, born in Accra and educated at Harvard and the University of Ghana. His first major work was *The Beautyful Ones are Not Yet Born* (1968), which explored the corruption of West African politics and the alienation of young intellectuals. Later works were less pessimistic; they include *Fragments* (1970), *Are We So Blest* (1971) and *The Healers* (1979).

▷R Fraser, *Armah* (1980)

AYMÉ, Marcel

(1902–67)

French novelist, story writer and playwright, born in Joigny. Writing in the tradition of **Rabelais**, and at heart an anarchist, his first success was his comic *La Jument vert* (1933, Eng trans *The Green Mare*, 1955), an account of the goings-on in a provincial community. He was a friend to **Louis-Ferdinand Céline**, and his fiction became increasingly informed with the latter's extreme bitterness and habit of ridicule—but he retained his popular audience, since his methods were traditional: strong plot, accurate characterization, satire of all organizations of whatever persuasion. Plays such as *Clérembard* (1950, Eng trans 1952), are unrestrained in their ridicule of pretences, hypocrisies and illusions, and have been called excessive, but they were for the most part successful with audiences.

▷D Brodin, *The Comic World of Marcel Aymé* (1964)

AYRER, Jacob
(c.1540–1625)

German dramatist, one of the most prolific of the 16th century, with over a hundred plays of all kinds, including a number of *Singspiele*, or musical plays. He was a citizen of Nuremberg in 1594, and procurator in the courts of law.

▷W Kozumplik, *The Phonology of Jacob Ayrer's Language* (1942)

AYRTON, Michael
(1921–75)

English painter, sculptor, illustrator, art critic, translator and novelist. His astonishing, polymathic gifts came in part from a cultured and intellectual family which included scientists and engineers, writers and politicians. In the early 1940s, he was the youngest ever guest on BBC radio's influential *The Brains Trust*. Though a visual artist first and foremost, Ayrton was profoundly influenced by literature and mythology; he produced a huge number of now highly prized book illustrations, including **Thomas Nashe**'s *The Unfortunate Traveller*. His book *British Drawings* (1946) had an impact on the reception of the neo-Romantics. His skittish *Tittivulus, the Verbiage Collector* (1953) was a satire on bureaucracy and the critical establishment. *The Maze Maker* (1967) was a novel based on the Daedalus story, which he had also explored in sculpture and in the prose *Testament of Daedalus* (1962). A second novel, *The Midas Consequence*, was published in 1974. He translated and illustrated **Archilochos of Paros**, wrote a study of the sculptor Giovanni Pisano, and published collections of essays. *Fabrications* (1972) summed up many of his varied concerns.

▷M Yorke, in *The Spirit of Place* (1988)

AYTMATOV, Chïngïz
(1928–)

Kirgiz novelist and dramatist, writing mainly in Russian, born in Sheker. Trained as a veterinarian, and always dedicated to animals and their welfare, as a writer he was described as 'the Soviet Union's most distinguished non-Russian author writing in Russian'—but he would never have used Russian had this not been made almost obligatory by Stalinist 'cultural organizers'. Thus, his first and greatest novel, *Proshchay, Gulsary!* (1966, Eng trans *Farewell, Gulsary!*, 1970), while set in Kirgizia, was published in Russian. Gulsary is the horse of a decent old-guard communist, whose losing struggle with Stalinist officials is the theme of the book. Aytmatov was attacked for ignoring the tenets of socialist realism in this and other novels, including the moving *Bely parakhod* (1970, Eng trans *The White Steamship*, 1972), about a boy who drowns himself when he perceives the nature of the world he is growing up into.

AYTON, Sir Robert
(1570–1638)

Scottish poet and courtier, born in Kinaldie, near St Andrews. He was educated at St Andrews University, studied law in Paris, and became a courtier of James VI and I in London, and was a friend of **Ben Jonson** and Thomas Hobbes. He wrote lyrics in English and Latin, and is credited with the prototype of 'Auld Lang Syne'.

▷A Johnson, *Delitiae poetarum scotorum* (1637)

AYTOUN, William Edmonstoune
(1818–65)

Scottish poet and humorist, born in Edinburgh, the son of a lawyer. Educated at The Edinburgh Academy and Edinburgh University, he was called to the Bar in 1840. He published a collection of romantic pastiches, *Poland, Homer and Other Poems* (1832), and in 1836 began a lifelong connection with *Blackwood's Magazine*, to which he contributed countless parodies and burlesque reviews. In 1845 he was appointed Professor of Rhetoric and Belles-Lettres at Edinburgh University, and in five years quintupled the number of his students. In 1849 he married a daughter of **John Wilson** ('Christopher North'). In 1852 was made Sheriff of Orkney. His works include *Lays of the Scottish Cavaliers* (1848); *Firmilian, a Spasmodic Tragedy* (1854); *Bon Gaultier Ballads* (1855), and *Poems of Goethe* (1858), conjunctly with **Theodore Martin**; *Bothwell* (1856); and *Norman Sinclair* (1861), a semi-autobiographical novel.

▷M E Weinstein, *William Aytoun and the Spasmodic Controversy* (1968)

AZEVEDO, Aluisio de
(1857–1913)

Brazilian novelist, diplomat and journalist. He was greatly influenced, in his 11 novels, by the naturalistic movement in Europe, and by **Zola** in particular. *O Homen* (1887, 'The

Man') was sensational in its time for its clear depiction of a case of sexual frustration. *O Cortiço* (1890, Eng trans *The Tenement*, 1928), about a 'Rachmanite' landlord, was vivid in its realism, and is still eminently readable and informative about Rio life in the latter part of the 19th century. All his works were reprinted in the 1950s, and have been the subject of discussion since then.

AZORÍN, pseud of **José Martinez Ruiz** (1873–1967)

Spanish novelist and critic. Born in Monóvar and educated at Valencia, he belongs to the generation of **Baroja** and **Unamuno**, and his early novel *La voluntad* (1902, 'Willpower') reflects their pessimism. His lucid essays rebelled against the prevailing florid manner, but they are uneven in their insights. His other novels include *Don Juan* (1922) and *Dona Inés* (1925).
▷L A LaJohn, *Azorín and the Spanish Stage* (1961)

AZUELA, Mariano (1873–1952)

Mexican novelist, born in Lagos de Moreno, Jalisco. Azuela has often been called 'the Mexican novelist of the Revolution', and certainly he was the first. As a medical student and young doctor he began to write novels (his first, *María Luisa*, appeared in 1907), and by the time he joined Pancho Villa's army as

a doctor had published five of them, including *Mala yerba* (1909, Eng trans *Marcela: A Mexican Love Story*, 1932). In 1916 came what many consider to be his masterpiece, *Los de abajos* (1916, Eng trans *The Underdogs*, 1929, and in *Three novels by Mariano Azuela*, 1979), which he sold for $20 to a newspaper in El Paso, Texas, where he had taken refuge. But, great novel though this account of the barbaric side of the Revolution is, the view of Azuela as having passed his peak after it is now often considered to be jejune. He remained devoted, always, to his own profession, eschewing politics, but bringing his developing satirical techniques to bear upon the political gangs (*chusma liderista*) and opportunists (*moscas*) which even now plague Mexican life. Thus, although **Reveultas** and **Yañez** have usually been taken to be the leading modernists of Mexican fiction, similar claims may be made for Azuela, especially for his book about a mad doctor and his dog, Lenin, and an underworld girl who cannot go straight: *La malhora* (1923, 'The Evil Hour'). He wrote many more novels, novellas and plays, including, in *Two Novels of Mexico* (1957), *Los caciques* (1917, 'The Bosses'), and *Las moscas* (1918, 'The Flies'), and *Las tribulaciones de una familia decente* ('Trials of a Respectable Family' with 'The Underdogs', and *La luciérnaga*, 'The Fireflies', in *Three Novels of Mariano Azuela*).
▷L Leal, *Mariano Azuela*; J S Brushwood, *Mexico in Its Novel* (1966)

B

BA JIN, pseud of Li Feigan
(1904–)

Chinese writer, born into a wealthy family in Chengdu, Sichuan. Educated in the traditional classical style in Shanghai and Nanjing, he also studied in France (1927–9), and became an enthusiastic anarchist. His major trilogy (*Family*, 1931, *Spring*, 1938, *Autumn*, 1940) attacked the traditional family system, and was immensely popular with the younger generation. Several other novels confirmed his standing as one of China's foremost patriotic writers. Although never a member of the Communist Party, he held important literary positions in the communist regime after renouncing his earlier anarchism. During the Cultural Revolution (1966–76) he was purged and punished, and compelled to do manual work. He re-emerged in 1977, and published a collection of essays about his experience, entitled *Random Thoughts* (1979).

BABEL, Isaac Emmanuilovich
(1894–?1941)

Russian short-story writer, a protégé of **Maxim Gorky**, born in the Jewish ghetto of Odessa. He worked as a journalist in St Petersburg, served in the Tsar's army on the Romanian front and, after the Revolution, in various Bolshevik campaigns as a Cossack supply officer. He is remembered for his stories of the Jews in Odessa in *Odesskie rasskazy* (1916, Eng trans *Odessa Tales*, 1924), and stories of war in *Konarmiya* (1926, Eng trans *Red Cavalry*, 1929), but also wrote plays, albeit less successfully. He was exiled to Siberia in the mid-1930s, and died in a concentration camp there in 1940 or 1941.
▷R W Hallett, *Isaac Babel* (1973)

BABITS, Mihály
(1883–1941)

Hungarian poet of the 20th-century literary renaissance. He was a schoolmaster, but devoted himself to writing from 1917. He was also a novelist and essayist, and a distinguished translator of **Dante**, **Shakespeare**, and the Greek classics.
▷M Becedek, *Babits Mihály* (1969)

BABRIUS

Greek writer of fables. Little is known of him except that he collected **Aesop**ic fables, which he turned into popular verse. Almost all of these were thought to have been lost, but in 1841 a Greek discovered 123 of them at Mount Athos.
▷J Werner, *Questiones Babrianae* (1892)

BACCHELLI, Riccardo
(1891–1985)

Italian novelist, born in Bologna. He wrote works in a large number of different genres and mediums, but is best known for his novels, and especially his historical novels. His works include *Il diavolo al Pontelungo* (1927, 'The Devil at Pontelungo'), a humorous tale of Bakunin's efforts to introduce socialism into Italy, the three-volume family chronicle of the Risorgimento, *Il mulino del Po* (1938–40, 'The Mill on the Po'), and *Bellezza e Unamità* (1972, 'Beauty and Humanity').
▷M Saccenti, *Riccardo Bacchelli* (1973)

BACCHYLIDES
(5th century BC)

Greek poet from Iulis on the island of Ceos (Kéa) and nephew of **Simonides**. Like his contemporary, **Pindar**, he specialized in odes commissioned to celebrate victories in the great athletic contests. Early in his career he worked in Thessaly; later he was in Athens, and in the 470s accompanied Simonides to the court of Hiero I, King of Syracuse, where they became rivals to Pindar. Towards the end of his life, he spent a period of exile in the Peloponnese where, according to Plutarch, he wrote some of his best work. His poems survived only in brief fragments until the discovery in 1896 of an Egyptian papyrus containing the text of 14 victory odes and six dithyrambs (short narrative poems). Though overshadowed by Pindar, Bacchylides's work has the merits of clarity and metrical simplicity, and he was regarded by Alexandrian critics as one of the canonical lyric poets.

BACHMANN, Ingeborg
(1926–73)

Austrian poet, short-story writer and novelist. Born in Klagenfurt and educated at several Austrian universities, she was strongly influenced by Heidegger's existentialism and

Wittgenstein's positivism. Her first two volumes of poetry, *Die gestundete Zeit* (1953) and *Anrufung des großen Bären* (1956) show the imperative unsentimentality of her voice, and combine succinct philosophical precision with the lyrical playfulness of a highly suggestive, but rationally irresolvable imagery. In her prose (*Das dreißigste Jahr*, 1961, 'The Thirtieth Birthday'; *Malina*, 1971; *Simultan*, 1972, 'Simultaneous') she likewise stresses the importance of human courage and initiative. Her mytho-magical radio plays, *Die Zikaden* (1954, 'The Cicadas') and *Der gute Gott von Manhattan* (1958, 'The Good God of Manhattan'), are dream-like parables exploring the dynamics of the human mind within the order of an inexorable outside world. In one of them, God is in the dock for having tried to assassinate two lovers whose unconditional love was believed a security risk.

▷A Hapkemeyer, *Ingeborg Bachmann. Entwicklungslinien in Werk und Leben* (1990)

BACON, Delia Salter
(1811–59)

American authoress, born in Tallmadge, Ohio, sister of **Leonard Bacon**. She spent the years 1853–8 in England trying to prove the theory that **Shakespeare**'s plays were written by Francis Bacon, Walter Raleigh, **Edmund Spenser**, and others. She did not originate the idea herself, but was the first to give it currency in her *Philosophy of the Plays of Shakspere Unfolded* (1857), with a preface by **Nathaniel Hawthorne**.

▷V C Hopkins, *Prodigal Puritan: a life of Delia Bacon* (1959)

BACON, Leonard
(1887–1954)

American poet, born in Solway, New York State, brother of **Delia Bacon**. He became Professor of English at the University of California in 1910, but resigned in 1923 to concentrate on writing. His collections of poems, which are often satirical in tone and content, include *Ulug Beg* (1923), *The Legend of Quincibald* (1928), *Rhyme and Punishment* (1936), and the wartime lyrics *Days of Fire* (1943). He won a Pulitzer Prize for Poetry in 1941 for his collection *Sunderland Capture* (1940). He also wrote an autobiographical volume, *Semi-centennial* (1939).

BACOVIA, George, pseud of G Vasiliu
(1881–1957)

Romanian poet, claimed by a few critics as the country's greatest of the 20th century, and certainly one who is now more universally admired than any other. His poetry, for once

beautifully translated into English in the bilingual *Plumb* (1980), is elegant, much influenced (initially) by **Laforgue** and (later) by **Fargue**, melancholy, and as word-perfect as any modern poet's. He was a manic-depressive and an alcoholic who captured, to a sometimes almost unbearable extent, the sad but excited nature of his fugitive and poverty-stricken existence. He exercised a great influence upon his younger contemporaries; that he was able to write at all was owing to his wife, Agatha Grigorescu, who, herself a poet, fully understood him. Much has been written about his affinities to the Symbolist movement, and assuredly he was part of the Romanian Symbolist movement; but essentially he was a law unto himself.

▷M Seymour-Smith, *Who's Who in Twentieth Century Literature* (1976)

BAGE, Robert
(1728–1801)

English novelist, born near Derby and educated at a local school. Trained by his father as a papermaker, he married in 1751 and bought a papermill in Staffordshire. He studied music, French, Italian and mathematics, and joined the Derby Philosophical Society, a group of political radicals. He turned to writing only after the failure of his business in 1780, but the mixture of humour, liberal ideas and good storytelling made his six novels an immediate success. They were admired particularly by Sir **Walter Scott**. *Hermsprong, or Man as He is not* (1796), his most original work, tells of a man reared among Native Americans whose entry into English society is used to highlight the conflict between 'natural' and 'civilized' values.

▷P Faulkner, *Robert Bage* (1979); G Kelly, *The English Jacobin Novel* (1976).

BAGGESEN, Jens
(1764–1826)

Danish poet and satirical humorist, he was born in Korsør, but spent much of his life abroad and wrote extensively in German. In 1785 he launched a long-standing feud with the Romantics, though he later became a follower of **Rousseau**. He was author of *Komiske Fortaelling* (1785, 'Comical Tales') and the more emotional *Labyrinten* (1792–3).

▷L L Albertsen, *Odins mjod. En studie i Baggesens mystike poetik* (1969)

BAGLEY, Desmond
(1923–83)

English thriller writer, a leader in his field. Born in Kendal, he received an elementary education only, and worked in the aircraft industry during the war years, before moving to Africa, where his writing career developed. Moving to Johannesburg in 1950, he was film critic for the *Rand Daily Mail* for nearly five years and scripted shorts until the success of his first novel, *The Golden Keel* (1963), allowed him to concentrate on his own writing. Bagley's great strength was the interaction of character (most often a first-person narrator) and physical environment. His settings were meticulously researched and ranged from the Andes in *High Citadel* (1965, his most successful book), to Mexico in *The Vivero Letter* (1968) and Iceland in *Running Blind* (1970), which introduced his series character, Slade. Among his other novels were the atmospheric *Wyatt's Hurricane* (1966), *The Tightrope Men* (1973) and *The Snow Tiger* (1975). *Night of Error* was published posthumously in 1984 and suggested that Bagley's talent was far from exhausted.

BAGNOLD, Enid
(1889–1981)

English novelist, playwright and children's writer. Throughout her life she balanced between 'society' and the world of artists and intellectuals; **Virginia Woolf** took an instant dislike to her, and **Nancy Mitford** described her as 'a sort of fearfully nice gym mistress'. She published *Serena Blandish* (1924, an English upper-class version of **Anita Loos**'s *Gentlemen Prefer Blondes*) under the pseudonym 'A Lady of Quality' to spare her father's feelings, and based *The Loved and the Envied* (1951) on an amalgam of her life and that of Lady Diana Cooper. She is best known, however, for *National Velvet* (1935), the skilfully-told story of a girl who wins the Grand National on a piebald horse won in a raffle, the bowdlerized film version of which provided Elizabeth Taylor with her first lead role. Of her plays, only *The Chalk Garden* (1955) was a hit, and solely in New York. Her *Autobiography* (1969) is a lively, impressionistic tumble through a life lived to the full.

BAGRITSKY, Eduard, pseud of **Eduard Dzyubin**
(1895–1934)

Russian poet and translator (of **Robert Burns** and Sir **Walter Scott**), from Odessa. Although always sickly, he worked for the police in Odessa and then fought on the Persian front. He began as a Futurist poet, in the manner of such Acmeist poets as **Gumilev**, but then came more under the revolutionary influence of **Mayakovsky**. However, in his last, most original and best phase he wrote *Duma pro Opanasa* (1926, 'The Lay of Opanas'), which was in the tradition of his native Ukrania, and deliberately echoed the style of the great Ukranian poet **Taras Shevchenko**. Criticism of him by Soviet culture-clerks at first drove

him into a defiant romanticism, then, finally, when he was weak and ill, into an attempt to come to terms with them. His final work, while interesting for what it contains despite himself, hardly counts in his development.
▷M Slonim, *Soviet Russian Literature* (1977)

BAGRYANA, Elisaveta, pseud of **Elisaveta Belcheva**
(1893–)

Bulgarian poet and editor, born in Sliven. Her first collection appeared in 1927. She was an aggressive and Bohemian personality, an urgent advocate of the emancipation of women, who shocked (and enjoyed shocking) the middle classes of inter-war Bulgaria, travelling much abroad, and announcing that she had 'a husband in every country'. She wrote 'official verse' under communism, but was clearly uneasy about it, and was finally able to give it up. Unfortunately none of her vigorous verse, most of the best of it passionate love poetry, has found a translator.
▷C A Moser, *A History of Bulgarian Literature* (1972)

BAHR, Hermann
(1863–1934)

Austrian dramatist, novelist, and critic, born in Linz. He studied in Vienna and Berlin, and took a leading part in the successive literary movements of Naturalism, neo-Romanticism and Expressionism. His 'decadent' novel *Die gute Schule* (1890, 'The Good School') is highly regarded. He published social novels such as *Die schöne Frau* (1899, 'The Beautiful Woman') and comedies such as *Die gelbe Nachtigall* (1907, 'The Yellow Nightingale') and the theatrical farce *Das Konzert* (1909, 'The Concert'). He was appointed manager of the Deutsches Theater, Berlin (1903), and the Burgtheater, Vienna (1918).
▷E Widder, *Hermann Bahr: sein Weg zum Glauben* (1963)

BAÏF, Jean Antoine de
(1532–89)

French poet, born in Venice. He was a member of the Pléiade, a group of seven poets gathered around **Pierre de Ronsard**. His works include *Amours* (1552, 'Love Poems') and *Passe Temps* (in *Oeuvres en rime*, 1573, 'Pastime'), as well as translations from the Greek. He attempted to introduce blank verse into French poetry, and experimented with combinations of poetry and music.
▷M Auge-Chignet, *La vie, les idées et l'oeuvre de Jean Antoine de Baïf* (1909)

BAIL, Murray
(1941–)

Australian experimental novelist and short-story writer, born in Adelaide. The strangely titled collection *Contemporary Portraits and Other Stories* (1975) showed the way his fiction was to develop. In *Homesickness* (1980) Bail describes the interplay of a group of tourists visiting museums round the world, each museum reflecting an aspect of their existence. *Holden's Performance* (1987) is a satire playing on the name of the hero and of Australia's popular car. Bail edited *The Faber Book of Contemporary Australian Short Stories* (1988).

BAILEY, Paul Peter Harry
(1937–)

English novelist, born in London into a working-class family. He went to grammar school in London, and later to the Central School of Speech and Drama, but did not fulfil his ambition to become an actor. He turned instead to writing, and made a striking debut with *At the Jerusalem* (1967), a novel about old age and its attendant isolation and disintegration, perennial themes in his work. His spare, allusive, concentrated style is found in more expansive form in the lighter *Peter Smart's Confessions* (1977), but he returned to old age in *Old Soldiers* (1980). *Gabriel's Lament* (1986) and *Sugar Cane* (1993) are linked by theme and characters. *An Immaculate Mistake* (1990) is a memoir which focuses on growing up as a homosexual.

BAILEY, Philip James
(1816–1902)

English poet, born in Basford, Nottingham, the son of the historian of Nottinghamshire, Thomas Bailey (1785–1856). After studying at Glasgow University, he was called to the English Bar in 1840, but never practised. Associated with the 'spasmodic' school, he was the author of *Festus: a Poem* (1839), his own version of the Faust legend, which reached, greatly altered, an 11th (Jubilee) edition in 1889. His reputation was high among his contemporaries.
▷J Ward, *Philip James Bailey, author of Festus: personal recollections* (1905)

BAILLIE, Grizel, Lady, née Hume
(1665–1746)

Scottish poet, daughter of the Covenanter Sir Patrick Hume. In 1684 she supplied him with food during his concealment in the vault beneath Polwarth Church, and helped shelter the Covenanting scholar, Robert Baillie of Jerviswood (1634–84), whose son, George, she married in 1692. She is remembered by her songs, particularly 'And werena my heart licht I wad dee'. In 1911 her domestic notebook was published as *The Household Book*, giving a fascinating, detailed insight into the trivia of daily household management.
▷Countess Ashburnham, *Lady Grisell Baillie: a sketch of her life* (1893)

BAILLIE, Joanna
(1762–1851)

Scottish playwright and poet. Daughter of the manse of Boswell in Lanarkshire, she moved to Hampstead in 1791 and, on being revealed as the author of the anonymous *Plays on the Passions* (1798, 1802 and 1812), was welcomed into London literary society. Sir **Walter Scott** especially admired her work. Written mainly in verse, and published as scripts before they were staged, the plays, particularly 'De Montfort' and 'Basil', now seem melodramatic, but were considered to contain striking treatments of the female character. Her *Fugitive Verses* (1790) echo the rhythms of Scottish folk song. Always retiring by nature, in later life she concerned herself with religious and philanthropic projects.

BAILLON, André
(1875–1932)

Belgian novelist, undeservedly neglected outside his own country and in France. In certain respects the **Gissing** of Belgium, Baillon was born in Antwerp. Orphaned at six, he was brought up by a pious and sadistic aunt, an experience he recollected in *Le Neveu de Mademoiselle Autorité* (1932, 'Miss Authority's Nephew'). His most famous book was *Histoire d'une Marie* (1921, 'The Story of a Mary'), a classic which for some inexplicable reason went untranslated; but his greatest works were to come. Set up in Paris as a writer, with the support of his wife and of various writers including **Vildrac**, Baillon fell victim to a mysterious and terrible depression. But, before he killed himself, he left an invaluable and extraordinary record of it, in such books as the epoch-making *Délires* (1927, 'Deliriums'). The discovery in English-speaking countries of this strange writer, with his mania for precise self-analysis, can only be a matter of time. Of *Délires* a Belgian critic has written: 'as rhythmic as a logical hallucination, this strange prose poem is the summit of an art founded on concision and the ultimate limit of experience'.

BAINBRIDGE, Beryl Margaret
(1934–)

English novelist, born in Liverpool. She attended ballet school in Tring, and was a repertory actress (1949–60), then a clerk for her eventual publisher, Duckworth (1961–73). Her novels, beginning with *A Weekend with Claude* (1967, rev edn 1981), are marked by concision, caustic wit, and carefully turned prose. Her family provided raw material for *A Quiet Life* (1976), just as her experience working as a cellar-woman fed into *The Bottle Factory Outing* (1975). *The Dressmaker* (1973), *Sweet William* (1976) and *Injury Time* (1978) are typical works. *Young Adolf* (1978) speculates on Hitler's reputed visit to Liverpool. She has also written a number of television plays.

BAIRD, Irene
(1901–81)

Canadian novelist. She moved to Canada from England at the age of 18, working as a reporter for the Vancouver *Sun* and the *Daily Province*, then for the National Film Board, later becoming a civil servant for a time. Her novels include: *John* (1937), her first; *Waste Heritage*, written two years later, which describes the Depression; and *The Climate of Power* (1971), which describes the government bureaucracy she became familiar with as a civil servant.

BAKER, Dorothy
(1907–68)

American novelist, born in Montana, most famous for her *Young Man with a Horn* (1938), a novel based on the character of the jazz trumpeter Bix Biederbecke, and for *Cassandra at the Wedding* (1962), an outstanding study of a young college woman. She has been likened to **Hemingway**, but the comparison is facile and misleading, since her main virtue lies in her ability to characterize her female characters.

BAKER, Elliott
(1922–)

American novelist and scriptwriter, born in Buffalo, New York. His first and best novel, *A Fine Madness* (1964, subsequently filmed to Baker's own screenplay), satirizes US society's desire to normalize and 'cure' the artist of the very turbulent and anarchic drives that fuel his creative instincts. *The Penny Wars* (1968) anatomizes a rebellious but sensitive young man facing up to fascism, war and nascent sexuality, an adolescent version of the interlinked dramas of *Unrequited Loves* (1974), in which one 'Elliott Baker' enlists in the rather more expensive conflicts of the sex war. In *Klynt's Law* (1976), Baker combines elements of **Bernard Malamud**'s academic novel-of-awakening *A New Life* with the knockabout humour of *A Fine Madness*, not always successfully. In *And We Were Young* (1979) he uses a stock reunion of army comrades to explore the long-term impact of war and corroded hopes. *Viva Max* (1970) is the best known of his screenplays.

BAKER, Louisa Alice
(1858–1926)

New Zealand romantic novelist who wrote, under the pen-name 'Alien', 16 tales of sacrifice, renunciation and the sanctity of marriage. Despite the approbation of the religious press, some contemporary critics believed that Baker dwelt perhaps a little too lovingly on the 'regrettable incidents' in her narratives. Her first book was *A Daughter of the King* (1894), followed by *The Majesty of Man* (1895). The moral point of *His Neighbour's Landmark* (1907) is heightened by the 1886 eruption of Mt Tarawera. Her last book was *A Double Blindness* (1910).

BALABAKKI, Layla
(1936–)

Lebanese writer of feminist novels of social and sexual revolt; there has been interest in her work in France, where one of her novels has been translated.

BALAGUER Y CIRERA, Victor
(1824–1901)

Spanish poet, politician and historian. A leading figure of the Catalan renaissance, he wrote a *History of Catalonia*, a *Political and Literary History of the Troubadours*, and poems in both Catalan and Spanish.

BALASSI, or BALASSA, Bálint
(1554–94)

Hungarian knight, adventurer and lyric poet, born in Kékkö. He died fighting the Turkish invaders. His poetry was inspired by military heroism, his love for the idealized figure of beauty and happiness he named 'Julia', and religion. He also experimented in drama (*Credulus and Julia*). He wrote *Little Garden for Diseased Minds* (1572). He experimented with verse forms, one of which is still known as the 'Balassi stanza'.
▷S Eckhardt, *Balassa Bálint* (1941)

BALBUENA, Bernardo de
(1568–1627)

Spanish poet and prelate, born in Valdepeñas. He spent his working life in Central America, where all his poetry was written, and became Bishop of Puerto Rico in 1620. He wrote an epic on the national hero, Bernardo del Capio, in *El Bernardo o la victoria de Roncesvalles* (1624, 'Bernardo, or the Victory of Roncesvalles'), which is excellently constructed, and full of allegory.
▷J Roja Garciduenas, *Bernardo de Balbuena* (1958)

BALCHIN, Nigel
(1908–70)

English novelist and screenwriter, born in Potterne, Wiltshire. He is best remembered for two of his several novels, *The Small Back Room* (1943) and *Mine Own Executioner* (1946). The first is an amiably satirical attack upon Civil Service bureaucracy and is based on the author's experiences while working in a government department during World War II. The second is a psychological thriller. Among Balchin's screenplays are *The Man Who Never Was* (1956), an excellent war-time espionage drama; *The Blue Angel* (1959), and *Barabbas* (1961).

BALDI, Bernardino
(1553–1617)

Italian Renaissance author, born in Urbino. He was secretary to various prelates and to the Duke of Urbino, and became abbot of Guastalla. He wrote eclogues, a didactic poem on seafaring called *La nautica* (1590), and prose dialogues.
▷G Zaccagnini, *Bernardino Baldi nella vita e nelle opere* (1908)

BALDINI, Antonio
(1889–1962)

Italian aesthete and writer, born in Rome. *Nostro purgatorio* (1918, 'Our Purgatory') recounts his war experiences, but his most characteristic works are *Michelaccio* (1924, 'Michael'), *La dolce calamità* (1929, 'Sweet Calamity'), and *Amici allo spiedo* (1932, 'Friends on the Spit'). He was a founder of *La Ronde*, a journal dedicated to high artistic taste and stylistic refinement, and later became Editor of the *Nuova Antologia* in 1931.
▷C di Bicse, *Antonio Baldini* (1973)

BALDWIN, Faith
(1893–1978)

American novelist, born in New Rochelle, New York. She wrote almost 100 works, mostly romantic and light novels, but also children's books and two volumes of poetry. Many were written during the Depression and World War II in the attempt to escape oppressive reality. Her early stories and serials having appeared in a variety of magazines, she was already known to a wide readership when she published her first novel, *Mavis of Green Hill*, in 1921. A string of best-sellers followed, including *Alimony* (1928), *Office Wife* (1930) and *The American Family* (1934), several of which were made into films. Her traditional, straightforward, sentimental fictions reasserted the strength of domestic US values at a time when they appeared most under threat.

BALDWIN, James Arthur
(1924–87)

American black writer, born and brought up in a poor section of Harlem, New York. After a variety of jobs he moved to Europe, where he lived (mainly in Paris) from 1948 to 1957, before returning to the USA as a civil-rights activist. His novels are often strongly auto-biographical but marked by a **Flaubert**ian attention to form. *Go Tell it on the Mountain* (1954) reflects his evangelical upbringing. *Giovanni's Room* (1957) is a study of gay relationships, *Another Country* (1963) examines the sexual dynamics of American racism. Others include *Tell Me How Long The Train's Been Gone* (1968), and *Just Above My Head* (1979). His journalism has been extremely influential and controversial. *Notes of a Native Son* (1955) is an ironic response to cultural and racial politics. Other works include *The Fire Next Time* (1963), and the plays *The Amen Corner* (1955), *Blues for Mr Charlie* (1964), and *The Women at the Well* (1972).
▷J Campbell, *Talking at the Gates: a life of James Baldwin* (1991); W J Weatherby, *James Baldwin: artist on fire* (1989)

BALE, John
(1495–1563)

English cleric and dramatist, born in Cove, near Dunwich. A Carmelite by training, he turned Protestant in 1533 and obtained the Suffolk living of Thorndon. In 1540 he had to flee to Germany. Recalled by Edward VI, he was made bishop of Ossory in Leinster. Here 'Bilious Bale' made himself so obnoxious to Catholics with his polemical writings that they attacked his house and killed five servants. On Queen Elizabeth's accession he was made a prebendary of Canterbury. He wrote a Latin history of 'British' authors (from Adam and Seth onwards!), and several plays. Most of these were in the form of traditional morality plays, but the last, *King John*, is considered the first English historical play for its realistic portrayal of the principal characters.
▷J W Harris, *John Bale: a study in the minor literature of the Reformation* (1940)

BALL, Hugo
(1886–1927)

German poet, born in Pirmasens, near the French border, the inaugurator of the Dada-ist movement at the Café **Voltaire** in Zurich. He contributed minor nonsense poems, but within a year had repudiated his activity on the grounds that it was negative and egoistic. He wrote acutely about his friend **Hermann Hesse**.

BALLANTINE, James
(1808–77)

Scottish artist and poet, born in Edinburgh. Originally a housepainter, he learned drawing under Sir William Allan, and was one of the first to revive the art of glass-painting. Two of his volumes of prose and verse, *The Gaberlunzie's Wallet* (1843) and *Miller of Deanhaugh* (1845), contain some of his best-known songs and ballads. He also wrote *Lilias Lee* (1871), a tale after the manner of **Spenser**.

BALLANTYNE, David Watt
(1924–86)

New Zealand journalist and writer, born in Auckland, who worked on the *Auckland Star* and, between 1955 and 1965, the London *Evening News* and *Evening Standard*. His first novel, *The Cunninghams*, was published in the USA in 1948. Other books include *The Last Pioneer* (1963); a biting satire on New Zealand business ethics in *A Friend of the Family* (1966); and the Gothic story of one hot summer at a beach 'on the edge of the world' in *Sydney Bridge Upside Down* (1968). Works for television include the award-winning *Passing Through* (1961). He modelled his approach on **James T Farrell**, adopting the pose of 'disinterested observer' the better to capture the minutiae of his characters' lives.

BALLANTYNE, Robert Michael
(1825–94)

Scottish author of boys' books, born in Edinburgh, a nephew of James and John Ballantyne, the printer and publisher of Sir **Walter Scott**. Educated at The Edinburgh Academy, he joined the Hudson's Bay Company in 1841, and worked as a clerk at the Red River Settlement in the backwoods of northern Canada until 1847, before returning to Edinburgh in 1848. He wrote his first stories about his experiences in Canada, with books such as *The Young Fur Traders* (1856). *Coral Island* (1858) is his most famous work, but he was a prolific writer; his other adventures included *Martin Rattler* (1859), *The Dog Crusoe* (1861) and *The Rover of the Andes* (1885). He published an autobiography, *Personal Reminiscences in Book-Making*, in 1893.
▷E Quayle, *Ballantyne the Brave* (1967)

BALLARD, J(ames) G(raham)
(1930–)

British fiction writer, born in Shanghai, China, and educated at Cambridge. He has commented that 'science fiction is the authentic literature of the 20th century, the only fiction to respond to the transforming nature of science and technology'. Until recently he was better known for his work in that genre, fashioning a series of novels at once inventive, experimental and, in several cases, bizarre. His early novels, including his first, *The Drowned World* (1962), offer a view of the world beset by elemental catastrophe, a theme also taken up in *The Drought* (1965) and *The Day of Creation* (1985). The more experimental side of his fiction is seen in the 'fragmented novels', like *The Atrocity Exhibition* (1970) and *Crash* (1973). He has been admired for his short stories, particularly those included in such collections as *The Terminal Beach* (1964), *The Disaster Area* (1967), *Vermilion Sands* (1973) and *War Fever* (1990); *Empire of the Sun* (1984), a mainstream novel which is portentously autobiographical, was shortlisted for the Booker Prize. Its sequel, *The Kindness of Women* (1991), is also autobiographical. He won the Guardian Fiction Prize in 1984 and the James Tait Black Memorial Prize in 1985.

BALMONT, Konstantin Dmitryevitch
(1867–1943)

Russian poet, translator and essayist, born in Gumische, Vladimir province, one of the greatest of the Russian symbolists. His work was coloured by the wide travelling he did during his periodic exiles, which added a vein of exoticism to his writing.
▷L L Kobuilinksy, *Russian Symbolists* (1972)

BALZAC, Honoré de
(1799–1850)

French novelist, born in Tours. He was educated at the Collège de Vendôme, and studied law at the Sorbonne. His father wished him to become a notary, but he left Tours in 1819 to seek his fortune as an author in Paris. From 1819 to 1830 he led a life of frequent privation and incessant industry, and incurred—mainly through unlucky business speculations—a heavy burden of debt, which harassed him to the end of his career. He first tasted success with *Le Dernier Chouan* (1829, Eng trans *The Chouans*, 1893), which was followed in the same year by *Le Peau de chagrin* (Eng trans *The Magic Skin*, 1888). After writing several other novels, he formed the idea of presenting in the *Comédie humaine* (1842–53, 'The Human Comedy') a complete picture of modern civilization. Among the masterpieces which form part of Balzac's vast scheme are *Le Père Goriot* (1835, Eng trans *Pere Goriot*, 1886), *Les Illusions perdues* (1837–43, 3 vols, Eng trans *Lost Illusions*, 1893), *Les Paysans* (1855, completed by his wife, Eng trans *Sons of the Soil*, 1890), *La Femme de trente ans* (1831–4, 'The Thirty-year-old Woman') and *Eugénie Grandet* (1833, Eng trans 1859) in which meticulously observed detail and imagination are the main features. The *Contes drolatiques* (1832–7,

'Droll Tales'), a series of **Rabelais**ian stories, stand by themselves. Balzac's industry was phenomenal. He worked regularly for 15 and even 18 hours a day, and wrote 85 novels in 20 years, sometimes correcting his own proofs in legendary shambolic fashion. His work did not bring him wealth; his yearly income rarely exceeded 12 000 francs, which may help account for his obsession with the workings of money in the novels. During his later years he lived principally in his villa at Sèvres. In 1849, when his health had broken down, he travelled to Poland to visit Eveline Hanska, a rich Polish lady, with whom he had corresponded for more than 15 years. In 1850, only three months before his death, she became his wife.

▷A Maurois, *Promethée, ou La vie de Balzac* (1965); Eng translation N Denny (1965); G Robb, *Balzac* (1994)

BAMM, Peter, pseud of Curt Emmrich
(1897–1975)

German novelist, essayist and writer of miscellaneous books. He was an effective, and ironical, popular novelist, especially with *Die unsichtbare Flagge* (1962, Eng trans *The Invisible Flag*, 1936), about his experiences as a surgeon on the Russian front during World War II.

BANCHS, Enrique
(1888–1968)

Argentinian poet, born in Buenos Aires. Largely a law unto himself in Argentinian poetry, Banchs was a neoclassicist writing under the direct influence of French poets such as **Valéry**; he was also indebted to French theories of 'pure poetry'. He did not publish a collection after *La Urna* (1911), consisting of 100 sonnets. Typical of him are such lines from one of these, describing the 'favourite dwelling of his soul': 'preferring lofty ruins to the waning palm of today'.

BANDEIRA, Manuel
(1886–1968)

Brazilian poet, translator (**Schiller**, **Shakespeare**) and critic, born in Recife, Pernambuco. As a critic has declared, Bandeira belongs 'to two worlds—the 19th century and [Brazilian] Modernismo'. While recovering from tuberculosis in a Swiss sanatorium at Davos he met **Éluard**, which had a decisive but delayed effect on him. His first book was *A Cinza das horas* (1917, 'The Dust of the Hours'), fairly conventional in form although playfully melancholy in content. His later poetry was seldom without the fin de siècle air which he established in this volume. But

he felt the full impact of the violent and iconoclastic *Modernismo* (the Brazilian movement), and helped to usher it in with collections such as *O Ritmo Dissoluto* (1924, 'Dissolved Rhythm'). In *Libertinagem* (1930, 'Libertinism'), he found his own voice, and demonstrated his mastery of free verse—something he had always struggled to achieve. He edited important anthologies, generously promoted the work of other poets, and became the grand old man of Brazilian letters. Minor in international terms, he was perhaps his country's most fulfilled 20th-century poet.

▷S Burnshaw (ed), *The Poem Itself* (1964, poems translated and analysed in depth)

BANDELLO, Matteo
(c.1485–1561)

Italian cleric and writer of *novelle* or tales, born in Castelnuovo in Piedmont. For a while a Dominican, he was driven from Milan by the Spaniards after the battle of Pavia (1525), and settling in France was in 1550 made Bishop of Agen. His 214 tales (1554–73), collected as *Novelliere*, have no over-arching narrative framework, but were used as source material by **Shakespeare**, **Philip Massinger**, and others, and are valuable (if perhaps a little unreliable) for the social history of the period.

▷K H Hartley, *Bandello and the Heptameron* (1960)

BANERJI, Bibhuti Bhusan
(1894–1950)

Indian (Bengali) author of a single masterpiece (though he wrote other good fiction) made famous by Saytajit Ray's great trilogy of movies of the same title, *Pather Panchali* (1928–9, translated into English, 1969). This book, whose title means 'Chronicle of the Street', unforgettably depicts the rural Bengal of the turn of the century: it is the tale of a boy, Opu, his sister Durga (who dies), and their parents; the father, a priest and singer, is too feckless to preserve them from poverty. It is a classic by any standards, and of it **Tagore** wrote: 'it helps one to see things—trees and shrubs … men and women … their joys and woes'. It was essentially the story of the author's own childhood, and the movies reflect it with an authenticity almost unique in the history of the translation of books to cinema.

BANG, Hermann Joachim
(1857–1912)

Danish novelist, born in Adserballe, Isle of Als. A homosexual, he wrote impressionistic novels about loneliness and failure, of which

his debut *Haabløse Slaegter* (1880, 'Lost Generations') is typical. His short stories *Ekcentriske Noveller* (1885) and *Stille Eksistenser* (1886) show the influence of **Jonas Lie**.
▷H Jacobsen, *Hermann Bang. Nye studier* (1974)

BANGS, John Kendrick
(1862–1922)

American humorous writer, lecturer and editor (of *Puck*). He was the author of the farcical *A Houseboat on the Styx* (1896), which features famous characters from the past—Diogenes, **Shakespeare**, George Washington—and facetiously but agreeably follows up the absurd situations which consequently develop.

BANIM, John
(1798–1842)
BANIM, Michael
(1796–1874)

Irish novelist brothers, born in Kilkenny. John studied art at Dublin and became a miniature painter; Michael, a postmaster. Having achieved some success as a playwright when a tragedy was produced at Covent Garden in 1821, John, with the collaboration of Michael, published such novels as the *Tales of the O'Hara Family* (1826), characterized by a faithful portrayal of humble Irish folk. John's illness and poverty were alleviated by a state pension. Michael's other novels include *The Croppy* (1828) and *The Town of the Cascades* (1864).
▷P J Murray, *The Life of John Banim* (1857)

BANKS, Iain Menzies
(1954–)

Scottish novelist and science-fiction writer, born in Dunfermline. He was educated at Gourock and Greenock High Schools, and the University of Stirling. He made a major impact with his controversial first novel, *The Wasp Factory* (1984), a study of insanity which shifted between psychological acuity and grotesque fantasy. *Walking on Glass* (1985), *The Bridge* (1986) and *Canal Dreams* (1989) drew more directly on science fiction and fantasy in multi-layered narratives. *The Crow Road* (1992) incorporated familiar motifs and themes of Scottish writing, viewed from a slightly displaced perspective. He writes science-fiction novels using the name Iain M Banks, and is highly regarded within that genre. Works in this vein include *Consider Phlebas* (1987), *The State of the Art* (1989, rev edn 1991) and *Against a Dark Background* (1993). His other works include *Cleaning Up* (1987) and *Complicity* (1993).

BANKS, John
(c.1650–c.1700)

English playwright, for whom biographical details are sketchy. His brand of historical tragedy was most successful in his day, though it has been neglected ever since. His first success was *The Unhappy Favourite: Or the Earl of Essex* (1681), which ran in London for several years despite Banks's (undeserved) critical reputation as a poor writer. He may be due for a revival because, like *The Unhappy Favourite*, his other major works *Virtue Betray'd, or Anna Bullen* (1682), *The Innocent Usurper* (about Lady Jane Grey), and *Albion Queens* (1684, about Elizabeth I and Mary, Queen of Scots) all have major, and rewarding, roles for women. Banks is perhaps a victim of the political turmoil of his own time (the English Revolution and its aftermath): the last two of these plays, both about Catholics attempting to usurp the throne, were banned by the Lord Chamberlain because of their political content.

BANKS, Lynne Reid
(1929–)

English novelist, born in London. She trained at RADA and worked as an actress and journalist before turning to writing. She was widely acclaimed for *The L-Shaped Room* (1960); *The Backward Shadow* (1970) and *Two Is Lonely* (1974), complete the trilogy. The first is particularly important, and not only because the heroine, a pregnant single woman, defied the social conventions of her class and time by refusing to undergo an abortion. It is significant because it added a female perspective to other novels being published at the time, which similarly dealt with young working- and lower middle-class people coming to terms with sexuality and family life in a grim post-war Britain. Although Banks has continued to write novels, it is her earlier books which have earned her a place in literary history.

BANKS, Russell Earl
(1940–)

American novelist and short-story writer, born in Newton, Massachusetts. A native New Englander recording the lives of the deprived, Banks is nevertheless fascinated by the warmth and light of the Caribbean, celebrated in his novel, *The Book of Jamaica* (1981). Other works are set in New Hampshire, as, for example, in the short-story collection *Trailerpark* (1981), where the lives of those living in trailer vans are recorded. *Continental Drift* (1985), his finest novel, is a story of two people attempting to begin new lives: a Haitian woman resolves to emigrate to the USA, while a troubled oil-burner repair man considers moving from New Hampshire to Florida. Banks frequently uses the device of a narrator who steps back from the main action in order to confide in the reader.

BANNERMAN, Helen Brodie, née Boog Watson
(1862–1946)

Scottish children's writer and illustrator, born in Edinburgh, the daughter of a Free Church minister. Her husband was a doctor in the Indian Medical Service and she spent much of her life in India, where she produced the children's classic, *The Story of Little Black Sambo* (1899), the tale of a black boy and his adventures with the tigers, based on illustrated letters she had written to her children. Phenomenally popular when it first appeared, it was judged by some after her death to be racist and demeaning to blacks. She wrote several other illustrated books for children.

BANNING, Lex (Arthur Alexander)
(1921–65)

Australian poet, born in St Leonards, Sydney, of a Belgian father and Scottish/Swedish mother. He published only three collections, *Everyman His Own Hamlet* (1951), *The Instant's Clarity* (1952) and *Apocalypse in Springtime* (1956), in each of which his own spastic condition underlies his conflict between hope and disillusion.

BANVILLE, John
(1945–)

Irish novelist, born in Wexford. He became a journalist, and has been the literary editor of the *Irish Times* since 1989. He writes in a highly compacted, allusive, and poetic manner. Much of his work is concerned with the nature of the fictionalizing process itself, and is filled with oblique literary references. His first book was a story collection, *Long Lankin* (1970). His tetralogy of novels on scientific figures, *Doctor Copernicus* (1976), *Kepler* (1981), *The Newton Letter* (1982) and *Mefisto* (1986), is highly metafictional in intent. The oblique crime story *The Book of Evidence* (1989) and its successor *Ghosts* (1993) are thematically linked.

BANVILLE, Théodore Faullin de
(1823–91)

French poet and dramatist, born in Moulins. From *Les Cariatides* (1841, 'The Caryatids') to *Dans la fournaise* (1892, 'In the Furnace'),

he showed himself one of the most musical of lyricists, and one of the wittiest of parodists. The title 'roi des rimes' was given him from his ingenuity in handling the most difficult forms of verse—the medieval ballades and rondels. His *Gringoire* (1866) holds an established place in French repertory.
▷A Carel, *Histoire anecdotique des contemporains* (1885)

BARAKA, Amiri, adopted name of LeRoi (Everett LeRoy) Jones
(1934–)

American poet, playwright, prose writer and essayist, born in Newark, New Jersey, into a middle-class black family. His politicization took him away from the bourgeois certainties of his roots into black nationalism (he took the name 'Amiri Baraka' in 1967) and later Marxism–Leninism. Although a prolific poet and dramatist with over 50 titles to his name, his best-known work dates from the early 1960s, when his cultural and racial anger spilled out in poetry collections like *Preface to a Twenty Volume Suicide Note* (1961), *The Dead Lecturer* (1964), *Black Magic* (1967), and in plays like *The Toilet*, *Dutchman* and *The Slave* (all 1964). His other works include a volume of stories, *Tales* (1967) and a seminal study of the social significance of black music, *Blues People* (1963).
▷*The Autobiography of LeRoi Jones/Amiri Baraka* (1984)

BARATYNSKI, Evgeny Abramovich, properly Boratynsky
(1800–44)

Russian lyric poet, born into a noble family. He was disgraced for his part in a theft as a cadet, but re-enlisted and served as a soldier until he was pardoned and made an officer in 1825. He resigned shortly after, and married an heiress. He wrote melancholy, tender, but pessimistic verse, at first under the overt influence of **Pushkin**, but later in more distinctive manner. His works include *Tsiganka* ('The Gypsy Girl'), *Bal* ('The Ball') and *Piroskaf* ('The Steamboat').
▷B Dees, *Evgeny Abramavitch Baratynski* (1972)

BARBA JACOB, Porfirio, pseud of Miguel Angel Osorio Benítez
(1883–1942)

Colombian poet, born in Santa Rose de Osos, Antioquia. Benítez was a legendary wandering figure in Latin-American literature, not unlike Baron Corvo (**Frederick William Rolfe**), but more gifted—for his haphazardly published, lyrical poetry has hardly been studied in the depth it deserves. He began in the *modernista* style established by **Darío**, and used it as a framework ever afterwards; but he was never a *modernista* poet. He is the 'man who turned into a horse' of the famous story of that title by **Arévalo Martínez**. He was homosexual, had other pseudonyms, and modelled his conduct on that of various European *poètes maudits*, 'often causing scandal by his riotous behaviour'. His most famous line is: 'En nada creo, en nada' ('I believe in nothing, nothing'), from 'La reina', a translation of which may be found in the *Penguin Book of Latin American Verse* (1971, ed E Curacciolo-Trejo). His poetry was collected in *Poesías completas* (1960), and his complete works of 1962 contains his untruthful and entertaining autobiography, *La divina tragedia* ('The Divine Tragedy').

BARBAULD, Anna Laetitia, née Aikin
(1743–1825)

English author, born in Kibworth-Harcourt, Leicestershire. Encouraged by the success of her *Poems* (1773), she in the same year, jointly with her brother, John Aikin, published *Miscellaneous Pieces in Prose*. She married a dissenting minister, Rochemont Barbauld, in 1774, and during the next 10 years published her best work, including *Early Lessons for Children* and *Hymns in Prose for Children*. Also with her brother she began the well-known series *Evenings at Home* in 1792.
▷*A Memoir by Lucy Aikin* (1825)

BARBEY D'AUREVILLY, Jules
(1808–89)

French Romantic writer, born in St Sauveur-le-Vicomte. He was extreme in his rejection of 18th-century values. His best-known novels were *La Vieille Maîtresse* (1851, 'The Old Mistress') and *L'Ensorcelée* (1854, 'The Bewitched Woman'), and he also published poetry and literary criticism.
▷J Canu, *Barbey D'Aurevilly* (1965)

BARBIER, Henri Auguste
(1805–82)

French poet, born in Paris. He was famous for a time for satirizing prominent social types for their efforts to procure favour after the July revolution. He wrote a number of collections of poems, including *Iambes* (1831), *Il pianto* (1833), and *Lazare* (1837), and was an influence on **Victor Hugo**.

BARBIER, Paul Jules
(1825–1901)

French dramatist, born in Paris. He wrote the libretto for Offenbach's *Tales of Hoffmann*.
▷M Carré, *L'amour mouillé, comédie vaudeville* (1849)

BARBOUR, John
(c.1320–1396)

Scottish poet, prelate and scholar, known as the 'father of Scottish poetry and history'. He was probably born in Aberdeen, and was Archdeacon of Aberdeen from 1357, or earlier, till his death. He studied at Oxford and Paris, and in 1372 was appointed Clerk of Audit for King Robert II. His national epic, *The Brus*, written in the 1370s and first printed at Edinburgh in 1571, is a narrative poem on the life and deeds of King Robert I, the Bruce, having as its climax the Battle of Bannockburn, and preserving many oral traditions. He also wrote two lost epics, *The Brut* (a history of the Britons) and *The Stewartis Original* (a fictitious pedigree of the kings of Scotland).
▷G Neilson, *John Barbour: poet and translator* (1900)

BARBU, Ion, pseud of Don Barbilian
(1895–1961)

Romanian poet who was also a gifted mathematician—he was Professor of Mathematics at the University of Bucharest. The chief initial influences upon him, as upon most modern Romanian poets, were French writers, in his case **Mallarmé**, and, to a lesser extent, **Valéry**. He was known amongst his friends and enemies as a 'priapic vandal', yet his poetry is deliberately cold and exact in its forms and expression: he called it 'passion on ice'. There are a few translations from his poems in *Modern Rumanian Poetry* (1967, ed D Caminescu).

BARBUSSE, Henri
(1873–1935)

French novelist, born of an English mother in Asnières. He fought as a volunteer in World War I, which inspired his masterpiece, *Le Feu* (1916, Eng trans *Under Fire*, 1917) in which a powerful realism is accompanied by a deep feeling for all human suffering. Other works include *Le Couteau entre les Dents* (1921, 'Knife Between the Teeth') and *Le Judas de Jésus* (1927, 'Jesus's Judas'). A noted pacifist, and an increasingly militant communist, he later settled in the Soviet Union.
▷J Duclos and J Freville, *Henri Barbusse* (1946)

BARCLAY, Alexander
(?1475–1552)

Scottish poet and author. He was most probably born in Scotland, may have studied at universities in England, France and Italy, and in 1508 was Chaplain of Ottery St Mary, Devon. Perhaps about 1511 he became a monk of the Benedictine monastery of Ely; he later became a Franciscan. His famous poem, *The Shyp of Folys of the Worlde* (1509), is partly a translation and partly an imitation of the German *Narrenschiff* by Sebastian Brant. He also published *Egloges* (Eclogues), an early example of English pastoral verse, and a number of translations, including Sallust's *Jugurthine War*.

▷ A Koelbing, in *Cambridge History of English History*, Volume 3 (1909)

BARCLAY, John
(1582–1621)

Scottish satirical writer, the son of a Scots father and a French mother, born in Pont-à-Mousson in Lorraine. He lived in London and Rome, and wrote mostly in Latin. His principal works are *Euphormionis Satyricon* (1603–7), a picaresque satire on the Jesuits, and *Argenis* (1621), an allegorical romance set in his own time.

▷ E Bensby, in *Cambridge History of English History*, Volume 4 (1909)

BARDIN, John Franklin
(1916–81)

American writer of bizarre detective fiction, who achieves his effect through the use of abnormal psychology, narrative non-logic and sheer freakishness. Though Bardin published his last novel in 1978, the three novels which established his cult following (stronger in Britain than in the USA) were published 30 years earlier, and his writing career was virtually over by 1955. His debut was *The Deadly Percheron* (1946). Like its successors, *The Last of Philip Banter* (1947) and *Devil Take the Blue-Tail Fly* (UK 1948, USA 1967), it is mechanical in construction but distinguished by an air of almost metaphysical menace, in which the stagey conventions of European Gothic are updated and assimilated to a topical concern for the disintegration of personality. Bardin was largely self-educated and came at his curious style independently rather than by reading others. In his fifties he was a senior editor with Coronet, and later edited the American Bar Association magazine.

BAREA, Arturo
(1897–1957)

Spanish novelist and critic, born in Madrid. He is most famous for what is undoubtedly his masterpiece, the trilogy *The Forging of a rebel* (1946), which first appeared in English in a translation by his Austrian wife, Lisa Barea: *La forja* ('The Forge'), *La ruta* ('The Route') and *La llama* ('The Flame'). The English edition is the relevant one, since the Spanish, published after it, was badly put into Spanish from it. It is an unforgettable account of Barea's experiences as a child in Madrid, as soldier in Morocco, and, finally and most memorably, of the siege of Madrid by Franco, and of the spirit of the resistance to him. Barea's novel *La raiz rota* (in Spanish 1955, after the English translation, *The Broken Root*, 1952), about an anti-fascist who visits Franco's Spain in secret, is a sound study of the tyranny, but is unsuccessful as a novel.

BARFOOT, Joan
(1946–)

Canadian novelist, born in the province of Ontario. She is a journalist in London, Ontario. She published her first novel, *Abra*, in 1978 (reissued as *Gaining Ground* in the UK, 1980). It has been followed by *Dancing in the Dark* (1982), *Duet for Three* (1985) and *Family News* (1990). Her general theme, explored in a variety of settings, is that of a woman's search for self-identity in a society which seems to offer no palatable role, and her work has attracted comparison with that of her fellow Canadian writer, **Margaret Atwood**.

BARHAM, Richard Harris
(1788–1845)

English humorist, born in Canterbury. In 1795 he succeeded to the manor of Tappington, and in 1802 he met with an almost fatal coach accident while on his way to St Paul's School, which partially crippled his right arm for life. He entered Brasenose College, Oxford (1807), was ordained (1813), and in 1821 received a minor canonry of St Paul's Cathedral. After unsuccessful attempts at novel writing, in 1837 he began his series of burlesque metrical tales under the pen-name of Thomas Ingoldsby, which, collected under the title of *The Ingoldsby Legends* (3 vols, 1840–7), at once became popular for their droll humour, fine irony and esoteric learning. His lyrics were published in 1881.

▷ W G Lane, *Richard Harris Barham* (1968)

BARKE, James
(1905–58)

Scottish novelist, born in Torwoodlee, Selkirk. He retired from his position as chief cost accountant with a ship-building company to devote himself to writing. His novels include *The World his Pillow* (1933), *Major Operation* (1936) and *The Land of the Leal* (1939), but he is chiefly remarkable for his devoted research on the life of **Robert Burns**, resulting in a five-volume cycle of novels (1946–54) collected as *The Immortal Memory*, an edition of *Poems and Songs of Robert Burns* (1955) and the posthumous *Bonnie Jean*, about Burns and Jean Armour.

▷ Moira Burgess, *The Glasgow Novel, 1870–1970* (1972)

BARKER, A(udrey) L(ilian)
(1918–)

English novelist and short-story writer, born in Beckenham, Kent. A former producer for the BBC, she published *Innocents*, her first volume of short stories, in 1947. The book won the first **Somerset Maugham** Award. Her other collections include *Elements of Doubt* (1992), a book of ghost stories. A writer whose work is distinguished by compassionate insight into private sadnesses, her novels include *Apology for a Hero* (1950), *A Case Examined* (1965) and *A Source of Embarrassment* (1974). *John Brown's Body* (1969) was shortlisted for the Booker Prize.

BARKER, George Granville
(1913–91)

English poet, novelist, playwright and scriptwriter, born in Loughton, Essex. He lived much abroad, in the USA and Italy. Throughout a long, prolific career from 1933 he suffered by association with **Dylan Thomas**, and by the inference that he was a member of the pre-war New Apocalyptics. He was, however, a more individual poet than these associations would suggest and though often playful and self-indulgent, his best writing is energetic and eloquent. His publications culminated in the stout *Collected Poems* (1987). *Street Ballads* was published posthumously in 1992.
▷M H Fodaski, *George Barker* (1969)

BARKER, Howard
(1946–)

English dramatist. His first play, *Cheek*, was produced at the Royal Court Theatre in London in 1970. He has written over 20 plays, and his themes are ambitiously large-scale: the nature of history, the degradation of political morality and the need to re-shape society according to finer values. His plays include *Stripwell* (1975), *The Hang of the Gaol* (1978), *Victory* (1983), *Crimes in Hot Countries* (1983), *The Power of the Dog* (1984), *The Castle*, *Downchild* (both 1985), *Possibilities* (1988) and *Golgo* (1990). Some, such as *Scenes from an Execution* (1984, staged 1990) and *A Hard Heart* (1992), were written for radio and then adapted for stage. His poetry includes *The Ascent of Monte Grappa* (1991).

BARLACH, Ernst
(1870–1938)

German Expressionist sculptor, playwright, and poet, born in Wedel. He was identified with the German Expressionist school of both art and drama. While he was best known as a sculptor in wood (his work in this medium being influenced by Gothic sculpture and Russian folk-carving), his greatest achievement was his war memorial at Güstrow Cathedral, a great bronze Angel of Death, which was removed by Hitler as 'degenerate'. Barlach's plays include *Der tote Tag* (1912, 'The Dead Day'), *Der arme Vetter* (1918, 'The Poor Cousin') and *Die Sündflut* (1924, 'The Flood'). He also wrote fiction which, like his plays, is still read and studied in Germany.
▷E M Chick, *Ernst Barlach* (1967)

BARLOW, Joel
(1754–1812)

American poet and politician, born in Redding, Connecticut. His *Columbiad* (1807) is a historical review of events from the time of Columbus to the French Revolution. Other works include the would-be humorous poem, 'Hasty Pudding' (1796).
▷J Woodress, *A Yankee's Odyssey: the life of Barlow* (1958)

BARNARD, Marjorie Faith
(1897–1987)

Australian novelist, critic, historian and biographer, born in Sydney. She wrote many books in conjunction with Flora Eldershaw as 'M Barnard Eldershaw'. Best known are *A House is Built* (1929) and the anti-Utopian novel *Tomorrow and Tomorrow* (1947, eventually published in unexpurgated form as *Tomorrow and Tomorrow and Tomorrow*, 1983). Her historical writing includes *Macquarie's World* (1941) and the impressive and scholarly one-volume *A History of Australia* (1962). Her subsequent solo writings include two collections of short stories, biographies of convict-architect Francis Greenaway and Governor Lachlan Macquarie, and a critical study of her friend **Miles Franklin**. She won many prizes, including the **Patrick White** Literary Award in 1983.
▷L E Rorabacher, *Marjorie Barnard and M. Barnard Eldershaw* (1973)

BARNES, Barnabe
(c.1570–1609)

English poet and playwright, born in Durham, where his father was bishop. His career was extremely eventful: a member of the Earl of Essex's retinue, he took part in the campaign against the Duke of Parma in 1591. In 1598 he was accused of trying to murder the recorder of Berwick by poisoning his claret, but managed to avoid being sentenced. His best poetic work, mainly bucolic in tone, is to be found in *Pathenopil and Parthenope* (1594) and *A Divine Century of Spiritual Sonnets* (1595), but he is perhaps more memorable for the colourful life he led than for the quality of his work.

BARNES, Djuna
(1892–1982)

American novelist, poet and illustrator, born in Cornwall-on-Hudson, New York. She began her career as reporter and illustrator for magazines, then became a writer of one-act plays and short stories, published in a variety of magazines and anthologies. Her works, many of which she has illustrated, range from the outstanding novel *Nightwood* (1936) to her verse play *The Antiphon* (1958), both included in *Selected Works* (1962). Although little known to the general public, her brilliant literary style has been acclaimed by many critics, including **T S Eliot**.
▷A Field, *The Formidable Miss Barnes* (1973)

BARNES, Julian Patrick
(1946–)

English novelist, born in Leicester. The crisp precision of Barnes's prose is partly explained by his having worked both as a journalist and as a lexicographer on the *Oxford English Dictionary Supplement*. His intellect, wit, and love of France are reflected in *Flaubert's Parrot* (1984), his third novel, in which a retired English doctor discovers in the Museum of Rouen the stuffed parrot said to have stood upon **Flaubert**'s desk during the writing of *Un Coeur Simple*. This precipitates a meditation upon the nature of biography. Speculation upon the historical process forms the backbone of *A History of the World in 10½ Chapters* (1989), a confection of fictional narrative, philosophical deliberation and art criticism, while *Talking It Over* (1991), written wholly in the words of its three lover-protagonists, deals with love, sorrow and emotional dignity. Barnes does not judge his characters, not even the vulgar Eastern European communist dictator or his state prosecutor, the central characters of *The Porcupine* (1992).

BARNES, Peter
(1931–)

English dramatist and author of screenplays. His only major commercial success has been *The Ruling Class* (1968), a play in which a madman inherits an earldom, believes he is God, and is only assumed to have been successfully rehabilitated when he makes a rampagingly right-wing speech in a decrepit House of Lords. His other plays have not shared its success. They include *Sclerosis*

(1965), *The Bewitched* (1974), *Laughter* (1978), *Red Noses* (1985), *Sunsets and Glories* (1990), and the screenplay *Enchanted April* (1991).

BARNES, William
(1801–86)

English pastoral poet, born in Rushay near Sturminster-Newton, the son of a farmer. After some time in a solicitor's office, he founded his own school, first in Wiltshire and then in Dorchester. He took time off to go to St John's College, Cambridge and take holy orders. He became curate of Whitcombe in 1847, and rector of Winterborne Came, Dorset, in 1862. Meantime he had become widely known—and greatly admired—for his fine idyllic poetry in the Dorset dialect, 'the bold and broad Doric of England'. His three volumes of poetry were collected in 1879 as *Poems of Rural Life in the Dorset Dialect*. He also wrote several philological works, and some poetry in standard English.
▷W D Jacobs, *William Barnes: linguist* (1952)

BARNFIELD, Richard
(1574–1627)

English poet, born in Norbury, Shropshire. He studied at Brasenose College, Oxford, and died a country gentleman. He is known for his pastoral poems like *The Affectionate Shepherd* (1594), which describes the love of Daphnis for Ganymede, and *Cynthia, with certain Sonnets* (1595).

BAROJA Y NESSI, Pío
(1872–1956)

Major Spanish writer, born in San Sebastian. He wrote more than 70 volumes of novels and essays, distinguished by an often violent humour and a vivid style in part derived from 19th-century Russian and French writers. He exercised a substantial influence upon his successors, in particular **Camilo Hosé Cela**.
▷B P Patt, *Pío Baroja* (1971)

BARRÈS, (Auguste) Maurice
(1862–1923)

French novelist and politician, born in Charmes-sur-Moselle. A member of the Chamber of Deputies (1889–93), he was an apostle of nationalism, individualism, provincial patriotism and national energy. He wrote a trilogy on his own self-analysis (*Le Culte du Moi*, 1888–91, 'The Cult of the Self'), and a nationalistic trilogy that included *L'Appel au Soldat* (1906, 'The Call to the Soldier'), and many other works, including *Colette Baudoche* (1909).

▷F Mauriac, *La rencontre avec Barrès* (1945)

BARRETO, Affonso Henriques de Lima
(1881–1922)

Brazilian mulatto novelist who sharply criticized the society of Rio de Janeiro. The most remarkable of his works is *Triste Fim de Policarpo Quaresma* (1915, 'The Sad End of Policarp Quaresma'), the story of a decent army officer, betrayed at every turn by ambitious men. (Barreto worked in the civil service and well understood treachery.) His work is now the subject of much critical enquiry and revaluation.

▷F de A Barbosa, *Vida de Lima Barreto* (1959, in Portuguese)

BARRIE, J M (Sir James Matthew)
(1860–1937)

Scottish novelist and dramatist, born in Kirriemuir, Angus, the son of a weaver. He was educated there and at Dumfries Academy, graduating at Edinburgh University in 1882. After a year and a half as a journalist in Nottingham he settled in London, and became a regular contributor to the *St James's Gazette* and *British Weekly* (as 'Gavin Ogilvy'). He wrote a series of autobiographical prose works, including *A Window in Thrums* (1889) and *The Little Minister* (1891, dramatized 1897), set in his native village disguised as 'Thrums'. From 1890 onwards he wrote for the theatre, works including the successful *Walker, London* (1892), *Quality Street* (1902) and *The Admirable Crichton* (1902), a good-humoured social satire. These established his reputation, but it is as the creator of *Peter Pan* (1904) that he will be chiefly remembered. Aware of the popular demand for dramatic sentimentality on the London stage, Barrie provided surface romance within dramatic structures which used indirect poetic methods to suggest a bleaker vision of life. He continued his excursions into faeryland in such later plays as *Dear Brutus* (1917) and *Mary Rose* (1920), and in his last play, *The Boy David* (1936), tried a biblical theme which, despite containing some of his finest writing, won no laurels in the theatre.

▷J Dunbar, *Barrie: the man behind the image* (1970); Harry Geduld, *J M Barrie* (1971)

BARRIOS, Edourdo
(1884–1963)

Major Chilean novelist and dramatist, born in Valparaíso, of a Chilean father and a Peruvian mother. Barrios, an unstable man (he was an unpopular Minister of Education in the government of the dictator Ibáñez del Campo, but also a weight-lifter, officer cadet, nitrate company accountant, academic and acrobat), was one of the earliest uncompromisingly psychological novelists of South America: his *El niño que enloqueció de amor* (1915, 'The Boy Who Went Mad for Love'), is often cited as the first novel of this kind. His avowed subject was 'the strange case', usually sexual; he was a student of the perverse. *El hermano asno* (1922, Eng trans as *Brother Ass* in *Fiesta in November*, 1942), often taken to be his best novel, is about two friars, one of whom is aware of his sexual urges, while the other is not. His attempt at a major novel, *Gran señor y rajadiablos* (1948, 'Gentleman and Hell Raiser'), set in the 19th century and written in a new, almost picaresque style, has not outlasted its initial popularity. *Los hombres de hombre* (1950, 'The Men of the Man'), seems, since it splits a man up into his component 'personalities', to have been written under the influence of **Gurdjieff** or one of his followers.

▷N J Davison, *Edourdo Barrios* (1970)

BARRY, Philip
(1896–1949)

American dramatist, born in Rochester, New York. While his first professional production, *You and I* (1923), enjoyed some success, he is now remembered for such plays as *The Philadelphia Story* (1939), a bright comedy of manners and a great hit for the actress Katherine Hepburn. *Holiday* (1929), a study of the generation gap, and *The Animal Kingdom* (1932), which transposes the conventional roles of a wife and mistress by making the latter the 'true love' and therefore more 'deserving', are much sharper satire but still, at heart, affectionate comedies. His genuinely more serious work, including the psychological dramas, *Hotel Universe* (1930) and *Here Come the Clowns* (1938), were not as successful.

BARSTOW, Stan(ley)
(1928–)

English novelist, born in Yorkshire. The mining communities of his youth provided much material for his fiction, which is firmly based in the entanglements and difficulties of everyday experience. He achieved a major success with his first novel, *A Kind of Loving* (1960), which later grew into a trilogy about its working-class protagonist Vic Brown, with *The Watchers on the Shore* (1966) and *The Right True End* (1976). *Joby* (1964) is a delicate evocation of childhood trauma; other novels include *A Raging Calm* (1968), *Just You Wait and See* (1986), *Give Us This Day* (1989) and *Next of Kin* (1991). He has also written short novels, stories, and plays for theatre, radio and television.

BARTAS, Guillaume de Salluste du
(1544–90)

French soldier, diplomat and poet, born in Montfort in Armagnac. A Huguenot, he fought in the religious wars, went on missions to the English court, and died of wounds received at the battle of Ivry. His chief poem, *La semaine* (1578, 'The Week'), gives an account of the creation, and is said to have influenced **Milton**'s *Paradise Lost*. He also wrote a biblical epic, *Judith* (1574), and an unfinished history from the birth of Christ, *La seconde semaine* ('The Second Week').
▷G Pelissie, *La vie et les oeuvres de Bartas* (1883)

BARTH, John Simmons
(1930–)

American novelist and short-story writer, born in Cambridge, Maryland. Educated at Johns Hopkins, he was a professional drummer before turning to literature and teaching. His earliest novels—*The Floating Opera* (1956), *End of the Road* (1958), *The Sot-Weed Factor* (1960) and *Giles Goat-Boy* (1966)—combined realism, formidable learning and fantastic humour in an attempt to make 'a transcension of the antithesis between the modern and the pre-modern which would revitalise fiction'. His later novels, *Letters* (1979), *Sabbatical* (1982), *Tidewater Tales* (1988) and *The Seventh Voyage of Sinbad the Sailor* (1991), are prolix and less assured.
▷C B Harris, *Passionate Virtuosity: the fiction of Barth* (1983)

BARTHELME, Donald
(1931–89)

American novelist and short-story writer, born in Philadelphia, Pennsylvania, the son of a Professor of Architecture, and brother of **Frederick Barthelme**. He worked as a journalist and magazine editor before turning to fiction. An experimentalist who rejected the traditions of the conventional novel form and was inventive in his use of language, he was associated with the mid-1960s avant-garde. The short stories in *Come Back, Dr Caligari* (1964) and *Unspeakable Practices, Unnatural Acts* (1968) are regarded as his most characteristic work; other collections include *City Life* (1970) and *Sadness* (1972) and are marked by the broader humour of the novels *Snow White* (1967) and *The Dead Father* (1975). He won the National Book Award in 1972.
▷M Couturier and R Durand, *Barthelme* (1982)

BARTHELME, Frederick
(1943–)

American novelist and short-story writer, he is the younger brother of **Donald Barthelme**.

His career has been slightly staccato. A brief stint in the 'family trade' of architecture interrupted his academic progress. His early fiction, the short-story collection *Rangoon* (1970) and the novel *War and War* (1971), were mannered and self-consciously experimental. Barthelme spent most of the seventies in advertising before re-emerging as a fiction writer with another story collection *Moon Deluxe* (1983) whose bald, uninflected prose offered a bleakly funny portrayal of the upper middle-class in America. *Second Marriage* (1984) and *Natural Selection* (1990) cover the same territory at greater length, but, like his brother, Barthelme is less satisfying when he makes the jump to a full-scale novel.

BARTON, Bernard
(1784–1849)

English Quaker poet, born in Carlisle. A bank clerk in Woodbridge in Suffolk throughout his life, he was a friend of **Charles Lamb**, and his *Metrical Effusions* (1812) interested **Robert Southey**. His *Poems* (1820) include devotional lyrics in the style of **George Herbert**. A biography of him was written by **Edward Fitzgerald**, who married his daughter.
▷E V Lucas, *Bernard Barton and his Friends* (1983)

BASHO, pseud of **Matsuo Munefusa**
(1644–94)

Japanese poet, he took his pen-name from the banana tree, after settling down in his hermitage near Tokyo; he was born further west, near Kyoto. He was responsible for turning the 17-syllable *haiku* from a light-hearted diversion into a serious art form. He improvised long stanzaic sequences (*renga* or *renku*), modulating the mood and prosody of this most restrictive of forms with apparently intuitive brilliance. After being apprenticed to a *samurai*, he led a wandering life, partly documented in *Oku no hosomichi* ('The Narrow Road to the Deep North', Eng trans *Noboyuki Yuasa*, 1966). As well as formal elegance, Basho's verse has a modern and almost existential quality, which guaranteed him a receptive audience when his *haiku* appeared in R H Blyth's English translation (1949–52), though he had already made an impact on **Ezra Pound** and the Imagists.
▷M Ueda, *Basho* (1970)

BASILE, Giambattista, pseud of **Gian Alesion Abbattutis**
(1575–1632)

Italian soldier and writer, born in Naples. He is now remembered for the *Pentamerone* (1637), a collection of 50 extravagant fairy tales written in Neapolitan dialect, which were edited by Felix Liebrecht and translated by Sir **Richard Burton** (1893).

BASIR, Vaikkam
(1910–)

Indian (Malayalam) comic novelist, a Muslim with great resources and well educated in Hindu customs. He wrote *Nruppuppak-koranentannu!* (1951, 'Me Grandad 'ad an Elephant'), a tender love-story not actually featuring an elephant but haunted by the spirit of Ganesha, the elephant-headed son of Siva the Destroyer. A maddened elephant *does* figure in the pages of *A Bhagavadgita and Some Breasts* (1967). Basir is a learned, subtle and unique writer, much admired by his only living rival, **Takazi**.

BASSANI, Giorgio
(1916–)

Italian novelist and poet, born in Bologna, the son of a physician. He lived until 1943 in Ferrara, where much of his fiction is set. *Cinque storie ferraresi* ('Five Stories of Ferrara') appeared in 1956, most of them composed in the aftermath of World War II. A sensitive chronicler of Italian Jews and their suffering under fascism, he is a realist who writes elegiacally. One of the outstanding Italian novelists of the 20th century, he is at his most exquisite in *Gli Occhiai d'Oro* (1960, 'The Gold-Rimmed Spectacles') and *Il Giardino dei Finnzi-Contini* (1965, 'The Garden of the Finzi-Continis').
▷G Varanini, *Bassani* (1970)

BASSO, Hamilton
(1904–64)

American novelist, born in New Orleans, most of whose books are set in the South. Outstanding amongst his novels is *The View from Pompey's Head* (1954), about a New York attorney from the South who is called back to his native town by a case, and reappraises his past. *Sun in Capricorn* (1942) was suggested by the career of the crypto-fascist governor of Louisiana, Huey Long.

BASTOS, Augustos Roa *see* ROA
BASTOS, Augustos

BATAILLE, Félix Henry
(1872–1922)

French poet and dramatist, born in Nîmes. The predominant theme in his melodramatic plays is inner conflict, and especially sexual or erotic conflict, as in *Maman Colibri* (1904, 'Mother Colibri'), which enjoyed some notoriety at the time, and *La Marche nuptiale* (1905, 'The Wedding March'). A number of his works focused on well-known social scandals involving eminent figures of the day, including the composer Debussy.
▷G de Catalogne, *Henry Bataille ou le romantisme de l'instinct* (1925)

BATES, H(erbert) E(rnest)
(1905–74)

English novelist, playwright, and short-story writer, born in Rushden, Northamptonshire. He began his working life as a solicitor's clerk, provincial journalist and warehouse clerk. His first play, *The Last Bread*, and his first novel, *The Two Sisters*, appeared in 1926. In his early days he benefited from the advice of **Edward Garnett** and was later influenced by **Stephen Crane**. He is one of the greatest exponents of the short-story form. His essay in literary criticism, *The Modern Short Story*, is regarded as a classic. His best-known works are *Fair Stood the Wind for France* (1944), *The Jacaranda Tree* (1949) and *The Darling Buds of May* (1958).
▷*An Autobiography* (1969–72)

BATES, Ralph
(1899–)

English novelist, born in Swindon, who later worked at the railway factory there. Politically alert, he left for Spain in 1930, and fought with the Republican International Brigade during the Civil War. His first novel, *Sierra*, set in Spain, appeared in 1933. His finest novels, *Lean Man* and *The Olive Field*, were published in 1934 and 1936. In the first, the Englishman Francis Charing debates the morality of his 'necessary murder' of an anarchist, while the second is set during the uprising of Asturian miners. Both novels see revolutionary struggle as inevitable in the modern world. In 1937 Bates left for the USA and became Professor of English Literature at New York University. He also published a biography of Franz Schubert (1934).

BATYUSHKOV, Konstantin Nikolaievitch
(1787–1855)

Russian poet, born in Vologda. He served in the Napoleonic wars, but became insane in 1821 and was confined in an asylum for the remaining 34 years of his life. Profoundly influenced by French and Italian writers, his work was much admired by **Alexander Pushkin**. His most important work was *Ymerayushi Tass* ('The Death of Tasso').
▷I Serman, *Konstantin Batyushkov* (1974)

BAUDELAIRE, Charles Pierre
(1821–67)

French Symbolist poet, born in Paris. After an unhappy childhood quarrelling with his soldier-diplomat stepfather, Colonel Aupick,

he was sent off on a voyage to India. He stopped off at Mauritius, where Jeanne Duval, a half-caste, became his mistress and inspiration. On his return to Paris in 1843 he spent much of his time in the studios of Delacroix and Daumier, and wrote art criticisms in *Le Salon de 1845* and *Le Salon de 1846*. In 1847 he published an autobiographical novel, *La Fanfarlo*. By nature aristocratic and Catholic, he sided with the revolutionaries in 1848. His masterpiece is a collection of poems, *Les Fleurs du mal* (1857, Eng trans *Flowers of Evil*, 1909), for which author, printer, and publisher were prosecuted for impropriety in 1864, but which earned the praise of critics and was to exert an influence far into the 20th century. Later works include *Les Paradis artificiels* (1860, 'Artificial Paradises') and *Petits Poèmes en prose* (1869, 'Little Poems in Prose'). He was greatly attracted by **Thomas De Quincey** and **Edgar Allan Poe**, whose works he translated (1856–65). His Satanism, his preoccupation with the macabre, the perverted, and the horrid, and with previously proscribed areas of human experience of perversity, were essential features of his work. Having written a critical work on his literary associates **Honoré de Balzac**, **Théophile Gautier**, and **Gérard de Nerval**, published posthumously in 1880, he took to drink and opium, and was struck down with paralysis. He died in poverty.
▷H Peyre, *Connaissance de Baudelaire* (1951); E Starkie, *Baudelaire* (1957)

BAUGHAN, Blanche Edith
(1870–1958)
English-born New Zealand poet, born in London, where she had published *Verses* in 1898. Her first New Zealand work appeared in *Reuben* (1903) but she considered *Shingle-Short* (1908) to contain her first true local verse; it was followed by *Poems from the Port Hills* (1923). In a collection of short stories, *Brown Bread from a Colonial Oven*, she describes herself as chronicler of 'a phase of New Zealand life that is already passing ...'.

BAUM, L(yman) Frank
(1856–1919)
American juvenile author, most famous for the perennially popular *The Wonderful Wizard of Oz*, which was first successful in its dramatized form (1901). Although without much strictly literary merit, this book remains a classic because of its appealing plot. It has been most famous in its movie version, starring the young Judy Garland.

BAUM, Vicki, originally Hedvig
(1888–1960)
Austrian-born American novelist, born in Vienna. After writing several novels and short stories in German, she made her name with *Grand Hotel* (1930), which became a bestseller and a popular film. She emigrated to the USA in 1931, where her later novels incuded *Falling Star* (1934), *Headless Angel* (1948) and *The Mustard Seed* (1953).

BAUMBACH, Jonathan
(1933–)
American novelist and short-story writer, born and educated in New York City. He set the terms for his innovative fiction with an important critical work, *The Landscape of Nightmare* (1965), in which he argued that the methods of realism are insufficient to grasp contemporary reality. The protagonist of his first novel, *A Man to Conjure With* (1965), moves freely in time and becomes known in discrete, almost dream-like images which are closer to collage technique than to conventional narrative. Baumbach's conviction that character psychology cannot be conveyed in logical sequential prose is also asserted in the ironically titled *What Comes Next* (1968), while in *Reruns* (1974), his best book, he turns to the imagistic abstractions of experimental cinema and abandons narrative altogether, although only temporarily, for later books return to a more approachable, tale-spinning approach. *Babble* (1976) is a collection of stories told by the author's baby son, while in *Chez Charlotte and Emily* (1979), he transcribes husband/wife dialogues. In the eighties Baumbach turned increasingly to short fiction; 'From the Life of the President' (1982, *Seattle Review*) and 'Children of Divorced Parents' (1983, *Fiction International*) are perhaps the best.
▷J Klinkowitz, *The Life of Fiction* (1977)

BAWDEN, Nina
(1925–)
English novelist for adults and young people, born in London. Many of her adult novels delve into the domestic and emotional turbulence of the middle-classes: their friendships, marriages, divorces and the resulting expanding and contracting families. *Anna Apparent* (1972) is a study of an illegitimate child evacuee, spanning from the London blitz to her life as a wife and mistress, while the middle-aged narrator of *Afternoon of a Good Woman* (1976) reflects on a life of disappointment and emotional betrayal before turning to face her future with renewed resilience. *The Ice House* (1983) casts a discriminating eye on a thirty-year female friendship, with all its confidences and rivalries. The implication in her adult work that the feelings and thoughts of children are too often overlooked becomes a dominant note in her novels for younger readers. In *Carrie's*

War (1973), Carrie's response to being evacuated to Wales during World War II is sharply and sympathetically observed.

BAX, Clifford
(1886–1962)

English playwright, born in London and educated at the Slade School of Art, Heatherly Art School and in Munich. He was editor of the verse journal *Orpheus Quarterly* from 1909 to 1914. His plays are generally light entertainment; first performed was *The Poetasters of Ispahan* (1912) followed by over 50 more before *Circe* (1949). Bax shows a taste for historical settings: *Socrates* (1930) shows its pre-hemlock hero in breezy and brilliant mood; *The Rose without a Thorn* (1931) attempts to depict Henry VIII's court, and *The Immortal Lady* is set in London in the year 1716. His slangy upper-class dialogue, however, has the effect of trivializing history, and his originally popular work leaves little of lasting value.

BAXTER, James Keir
(1926–72)

New Zealand poet, dramatist and critic, born in Dunedin. He worked as a labourer, journalist and teacher and led a bohemian life until he was converted to Roman Catholicism. Subsequently he founded a religious community on the Wanganui River. He published more than 30 books of poetry, his first volume, *Beyond the Palisade* (1944), appearing when he was 18. The poems he wrote before his conversion are collected in *In Fires of No Return* (1958). Latterly he was less productive but his appointment to the Burns Fellowship at the Universiy of Otago in 1966 inspired him, and *Howrah Bridge and Other Poems* (1961) and *Autumn Testament* (1972) are among his best work. His *Collected Poems* (1979) was edited by J E Weir who, since Baxter's death, has brought together editions of previously unpublished verse. His plays include *The Band Rotunda* (1967), *The Sore-Footed Man* (1967) and *The Temptation of Oedipus* (1967).
▷ J E Weir, *The Poetry of James Keir Baxter* (1970)

BAYBARS, Taner
(1936–)

Turkish Cypriot poet, resident in the UK, having previously served in the Royal Air Force. After a career in book production, since 1983 he has worked for the British Council. His first English-language collection, *To Catch a Falling Man* (1963), consists of brief, autobiographical images captured in vivid language that infuses them with a mysterious and sometimes sinister quality.

Susila in the Autumn Woods (1974) and *Narcissus in a Dry Pool* (1978) are progressively more complex in vision and rhetorical in approach, and are most successful when exploring his young daughter Susila's developing awareness of her surroundings. Baybars has also written a novel, *A Trap for the Burglar* (1965), and has translated three volumes of poetry from the Turkish of **Nazim Hikmet**.
▷ *Plucked in a Far-Off Land: Images in Self Biography* (1970)

BAYLEBRIDGE, William
(1883–1942)

Australian poet and writer, born in Brisbane, whose thoughts of mankind as a culmination of a **Nietzsche**an life-force led him close to a totalitarian philosophy. He published his early verse privately in a series of booklets including *Songs o' the South* (1908) and *Moreton Miles* (1910), love poems set around his birthplace. The best of his early verse was collected as *Selected Poems* (1919); he later wrote a series of sonnets, *Love Redeemed* (1934). In his major work, *This Vital Flesh* (1939, Memorial Edition 1961), he attempted to establish the foundations of Australian nationalism. He travelled in Europe and the Middle East from 1908, returning to Australia after World War I, during which he is supposed to have worked for Allied Intelligence; he later published *An ANZAC Muster* (1921), essays and stories on the Gallipoli campaign. In memory of a close relative he established the Grace Leven Prize for Poetry.

BAYNTON, Barbara Janet Ainsleigh
(1857–1929)

Australian writer and socialite, born in Scone, New South Wales. Her father was a carpenter of Irish stock, and Baynton afterwards fantasized about her origins. While working as a governess she married a son of the house who later left her for one of her servants. She then married a 70-year-old retired surgeon, Thomas Baynton, and entered a life of leisure and culture. She began to write stories for the popular periodical *The Bulletin* and became a close friend of its editor A G Stephens. In search of a publisher for her stories, she visited London in 1902 and was befriended by **Edward Garnett**. When Baynton died in 1904, leaving her wealthy, she returned to London, made profitable investments on the stock exchange, and lived in a series of increasingly grand houses surrounded by choice antiques. She travelled frequently between England and Australia, and in 1921 married the fifth Lord Headley, from whom she soon separated. She wrote one novel, *Human Toll* (1907), and a number of short stories first collected in *Bush Studies*

(1902) and, with two more stories, as *Cobbers* (1917). In all her writing the grime and squalor of the real bush, as seen and endured by women and the underprivileged, contrasts hugely with the romanticized male 'mateship' of **Henry Lawson** and his followers.

BAZAN, Emilia Pardo *see* PARDO BAZAN, Emilia

BAZHAN, Mykola
(1904–)

Ukrainian poet, born in Kamenets-Podolski. His incisive, dramatic and strident early work was written under the influence of Futurism and of **Mayakovsky**; subjected to official criticism, he became an avowed socialist realist, and his poetry lost force.

BAZIN, René
(1853–1932)

French novelist, born in Angers. He depicted with charm and colour the life of peasant folk in the various French provinces, and in some of his novels, such as *Les Oberlé* (1901, 'The Oberlé Family'), dealt with the social problems of his time.
▷G Duhamelet, *René Bazin, romancier catholique* (1935)

BEAGLE, Peter S(oyer)
(1939–)

American writer of fantasy fiction, born in New York City but quintessentially Californian in outlook. His best-known book is *The Last Unicorn* (1968), a love-generation fable whose overtones of **T S Eliot**'s *The Waste Land* pick up on ideas of rebirth and regeneration first explored in his underrated debut novel, *A Fine and Private Place* (1960). His second book, *I See By My Outfit* (1965), is a mild, search-for-America chronicle, reminiscent of Beat writing. Beagle has also written a notably sunny travel book, *The California Feeling* (1969), and an equally untroubled study of Hieronymus Bosch, *The Garden of Earthly Delights* (1982).
▷R Olderman, *Beyond the Waste Land* (1977)

BEAN, Charles Edwin Woodrow
(1879–1968)

Australian journalist and war historian, born in Bathurst, New South Wales and educated at Oxford University. He was London correspondent for the *Sydney Morning Herald* and became official correspondent to the Australian Imperial Forces. Landing at Gallipoli in 1915, Bean was wounded in that campaign but stayed at the front throughout. He then accompanied the troops to France where he served until the end of the war. On being appointed Australia's Official War Historian, Bean returned to Gallipoli in 1919 to research the campaign. He wrote a number of books including *On the Wool Track* (1910), the standard account of Australia's earlier dependence on sheep, and *Flagships Three* (1913). His memorial is the 12-volume *Official History of Australia in the War of 1914–18* (1921–42), in which Bean takes much credit for the creation of the ANZAC legend. He wrote six of the 12 volumes and edited the others, and in 1946 published his own single-volume abridgement, *Anzac to Amiens*.
▷K Fewster, *The Frontline Diary of C. E. W. Bean* (1983); D McCarthy, *Gallipoli to the Somme* (1983)

BEATTIE, Ann
(1947–)

American novelist, born in Washington DC, and educated at American University and the University of Connecticut. She has worked as a visiting lecturer at the University of Virginia and at Harvard University. She received a Guggenheim Fellowship in 1977 and has several novels and collections of short stories to her name, most of which focus on disaffected families or individuals. Both comic and detached, her work presents the theme of contemporary alienation in a minimalist manner. Her novel, *Picturing Will* (1990), uses photographic imagery to examine the issues her earlier novels and short stories explored through language.

BEATTIE, James
(1735–1803)

Scottish poet and essayist, born in Laurencekirk, Kincardineshire, the son of a shopkeeper. He was educated at the village school and at Marischal College, Aberdeen, and after some years as a schoolmaster in Fordoun he became a master at Aberdeen Grammar School, and then in 1760 became Professor of Moral Philosophy at Aberdeen. His overrated *Essay on Truth* (1770) attacked the philosopher David Hume, but he is chiefly remembered for his long poem, *The Minstrel* (1771–4), a forerunner of Romanticism.
▷M Forbes, *Beattie and His Friends* (1964)

BEAUMARCHAIS, Pierre Augustin Caron de
(1732–99)

French playwright, the greatest French comic dramatist, born in Paris, the son of a watchmaker named Caron. Brought up in his father's trade, he invented, at 21, a new escapement which was pirated by a rival. The affair brought him to notice at court, where his good looks and fine speech and manners quickly procured him advancement. He was

engaged to teach the harp to Louis XV's daughters, and in 1756 he married the wealthy widow of a court official, and assumed his title. Profitable speculation with Duverney, a rich Parisan banker, and another prudent marriage with a wealthy widow in 1768, increased his fortune. His first plays, *Eugénie* (1767, Eng trans *The School for Rakes*, 1769) and *Les Deux Amis* (1770, Eng trans *The Two Friends*, 1800), scored only a moderate success. The death of Duverney in 1770 involved him in a long lawsuit with his heir, Count Lablache, in the course of which he became the idol of the people, as the supposed champion of popular rights against the corrupt tribunals of the old regime. Beaumarchais appealed to the public by publishing his famous *Mémoires du Sieur Beaumarchais par lui-même* (1774–8, 'Autobiography'), a work which united the bitterest satire with the sharpest logic, and made his reputation. The same brilliant satire burns in his two famous comedies, *Le Barbier de Séville* (1775, Eng trans *The Barber of Seville*, 1776) and *La Folle Journée ou le mariage de Figaro* (1784, Eng trans *The Follies of a Day; or, The Marriage of Figaro*, 1785). The latter had a most unprecedented success; and both are still popular plays in France, but in Britain are chiefly known through Mozart's and Rossini's operatic adaptations. The Revolution cost Beaumarchais his vast fortune, and, suspected of an attempt to sell arms to the *émigrés*, he had to take refuge in Holland and England (1793).
▷R Pomeau, *Beaumarchais, l'homme et l'oeuvre* (1956)

BEAUMONT, Francis
(c.1584–1616)

English Elizabethan dramatist, born in Gracedieu, Leicestershire, the third son of a judge, and brother of Sir **John Beaumont**. He was educated at Broadgates Hall (now Pembroke College), Oxford, and entered the Inner Temple in 1600. He soon became a friend of **Ben Jonson** and the other men of genius who met at the Mermaid Tavern, among them **John Fletcher**. With the latter, Beaumont was to be associated closely until he married Ursula Isley (1613) and retired from the theatre. They are said to have shared everything: work, lodgings, and even clothes. Their dramatic works, compiled in 1647, contained 35 pieces; another folio, published in 1679, 52 works. Modern research finds Beaumont's hand in only about 10 plays, which include, however, the masterpieces. Fletcher's verse avoids enjambment, rhyme and prose while Beaumont uses all three devices. *The Woman Hater* (1607) is attributed solely to Beaumont, and he had the major share in *The*

Knight of the Burning Pestle (1609), a burlesque of knight errantry and a parody of **John Heywood**'s *Four Prentices of London. Philaster, The Maid's Tragedy* and *A King and no King* established their joint popularity. Other works include *The Scornful Lady* and *Cupid's Revenge. The Masque of the Inner Temple* was written by Beaumont in honour of the marriage of the Elector Palatinate Frederick V and the princess Elizabeth (1613). He was buried in Westminster Abbey.
▷W W Appleton, *Beaumont and Fletcher: a critical study* (1956)

BEAUMONT, Sir John
(1582–1627)

English poet, elder brother of **Francis Beaumont**. His best-known work is *Bosworth Field*, in which the heroic couplet makes its first appearance in English poetry.
▷A Chalmers, in *The Works of Early English Poets* (1910)

BEAUMONT, Joseph
(1616–99)

English poet, born in Hadleigh, Suffolk. From 1663 he was master of Peterhouse, Cambridge. He wrote the long epic poem *Psyche* (1648).
▷R Wrench, *A Biographical and Critical Sketch* (1859)

BEAVER, Bruce
(1928–)

Australian poet, born in Manly, New South Wales. His first collection, entitled *Under the Bridge* (1961), was followed by six more, the most significant of which was *Letters to Live Poets* (1969). In *Lauds and Plaints* (1974) he turned from semi-autobiographical subjects to a more outward vision. *Selected Poems* appeared in 1979, as did his return to personal themes in *As It Was*, an extended prose-poem. He received the **Patrick White** Literary Award in 1982.

BECK, Béatrix
(1914–)

Belgian (Francophone) novelist, born in Switzerland, herself daughter of a novelist, Christian Beck. She was for a time secretary to **André Gide**. In her novel *Barny* (1948) she introduces her perennial character who sees everything through the eyes of her insane mother. *Léon Morin, Prêtre* (1952, Eng trans *The Priest*, 1953), her most celebrated novel, deals in an acute manner with the theme of the 'leftist' priest. An unusual writer, Beck belongs essentially to the Catholic tradition in French literature—she has hardly had her due outside French-speaking countries.

▷H J G Godin, *The Creative Process in French Literature* (1974)

BECKE, Louis (George Lewis)
(1855–1913)

Australian writer of adventure fiction. Becke's early years under sail in the Pacific form the background for over 30 collections of 'yarns' in the style of **Melville**, whom he admired, and of **Conrad**, who admired Becke. *By Reef and Palm* (1894) set the pattern for those that followed, such as *His Native Wife* (1895), *The Ebbing of the Tide* (1896) and *Pacific Tales* (1897). Many of the stories rework popular themes of mixed love, mutiny and the degenerate white settler. Although Becke soon began to write to a pattern, all his tales show somebody who spoke from his hard-gained experience.

BECKER, Nikolaus
(1809–45)

German poet. He wrote the *Rheinlied* ('Rhine Song') ('Sie sollen ihn nicht haben', 'You shall not have it') in 1840, which prompted **Alfred de Musset**'s answer ('Nous l'avons eu, votre Rhin allemand', 'We have taken it, your German Rhine').
▷L Waeles, *Nikolaus Becker 'der Dichter des Rheinliedes'* (1896)

BECKETT, Samuel Barclay
(1906–89)

Irish author and playwright, winner of the Nobel Prize for literature, born in Dublin. He became a lecturer in English at the École Normale Supérieure in Paris and later in French at Trinity College, Dublin. From 1932 he lived mostly in France and was, for a time, secretary to **James Joyce**, with whom he shared the same tantalizing preoccupation with language, with the failure of human beings to communicate successfully mirroring the pointlessness of life which they strive to make purposeful. His early poetry and first two novels, *Murphy* (1938) and *Watt* (1953), were written in English, but not the trilogy *Molloy, Malone Meurt* and *L'Innommable* (translated in 1955, 1956 and 1958), or the plays *En attendant Godot* (1953, Eng trans *Waiting for Godot*, 1956), which took London by storm, and *Fin de partie* (1957, Eng trans *End Game*, 1958), all of which first appeared in French. *Godot* best exemplifies the Beckettian view of the human predicament, the poignant bankruptcy of all hopes, philosophies, and endeavours. His later works include *Happy Days* (1961), *Not I* (1973) and *Ill Seen Ill Said* (1981). He was awarded the 1969 Nobel Prize for literature. Although there were one or two increasingly short pieces in later years—*Breath* (1970) shows a heap of rubbish on the stage and has a soundtrack which consists of a single breath—he wrote very infrequently towards the end.
▷R Hayman, *Samuel Beckett* (1968); A Alvarez, *Beckett* (1973); Deirdrie Bair, *Samuel Beckett: A Biography* (1978)

BECKFORD, William Thomas
(1759–1844)

English writer and art collector, son of William Beckford, born in Fonthill, Wiltshire. In 1770 he inherited his father's fortune. As a young man of 16 he revealed remarkable intellectual precocity in his satirical *Memoirs of Extraordinary Painters*. From 1777 he spent much time on the Continent, meeting **Voltaire** in 1778, and later making a grand tour in Flanders, Germany, and Italy. In 1784 he entered parliament, but he became involved in a scandal and was excluded from society. He wrote, in French, *Vathek*, an Arabian tale of gloomy imaginative splendour modelled on Voltaire's style, which was published in France in 1787 and in an unauthorized English version in 1786. Revisiting Portugal in 1793, he settled in that 'paradise' near Cintra which **Byron** commemorates in *Childe Harold*. He returned to England in 1796, and proceeded to erect a new palace, Fonthill Abbey, designed by James Wyatt. Its chief feature was a tower, which fell in 1800, but was rebuilt (276 feet high). He lived there in mysterious seclusion until 1822, when he sold Fonthill Abbey, moved to Bath, and there built Lansdown Tower. In 1834 he published *Italy, with Sketches of Spain and Portugal* (incorporating, in modified form, *Dreams, Waking Thoughts*, and *Incident*, suppressed in 1783), and in 1835 another volume of *Recollections* of travel.
▷G Chapman, *Beckford* (1952)

BECKMANN, Gunnel
(1910–)

Swedish writer for children and teenagers, born in Falköping and educated at the University of Göteborg. For her first children's books, considered conventional and too idyllic by critics, she drew inspiration from her own large family. She came to notice with a novel for teenagers, *Tillträde till festen* (1969, *Nineteen is too young to die*, 1971), about a young girl who thinks she is going to die of leukemia. In subsequent novels she further develops the theme of women's growth towards awareness and independence. *Tre veckor över tiden* (1973, 'Three Weeks Late'), becomes a literary platform for the topical discussion of early pregnancy and abortion. In dealing with the generation gap, she manages to portray each generation sympathetically, as achieved in *Att trösta Fanny* (1981, 'Comforting Fanny'), where a shift of perspective is used and a young girl's problems with her divorced parents are reflected through the eyes of her grandmother.

BECQUE, Henry
(1837–99)

French dramatist, born in Paris. He is known for two naturalistic plays, *Les Corbeaux* (1882, 'The Crows') and *La Parisienne* (1885), both dramatic portrayals of bourgeois life and character.
▷L B Hyslop, *Henry Becque* (1972)

BÉCQUER, Gustavo Adolfo
(1836–70)

Spanish romance writer and lyric poet, born in Seville. His *Legends* are written in a weirdly musical prose, but he is best known for his troubadour love verses, although his poems in *Rimas* (1871) have been seen as crucial precursors of modern Spanish poetry.
▷R Benitez, *Bécquer, traditionalista* (1971)

BEDDOES, Thomas Lovell
(1803–49)

English poet and physiologist, born in Clifton (Bristol), eldest son of Thomas Beddoes (1760–1808). He was educated at Charterhouse and Oxford. In 1822 he published *The Bride's Tragedy*, a sombre murder drama. In 1825 he went to Göttingen to study medicine, and then led a strange wandering life as doctor and democrat, in Germany and Switzerland, with occasional visits to England. From 1825 he was engaged in the composition of a Gothic–Romantic drama in blank verse, *Death's Jest-book*, which appeared in 1850, a year after his suicide.
▷*The Letters of Thomas Lovell Beddoes* (1894); H W Donner, *Thomas Lovell Beddoes: the making of a poet* (1935)

BEDE, the Venerable, St
(c.673–735)

Anglo-Saxon scholar, theologian and historian, born near Monkwearmonth, Durham. At the age of seven he was placed in the care of Benedict Biscop at the monastery of Wearmouth, and in 682 moved to the new monastery of Jarrow in Northumberland, where he was ordained priest in 703 and remained a monk for the rest of his life, studying and teaching. His devotion to church discipline was exemplary and his industry enormous. Besides Latin and Greek, classical as well as patristic, literature, he studied Hebrew, medicine, astronomy and prosody. He wrote homilies, biographies of saints, biographies of abbots (*Historia abbatum*), hymns, epigrams, works on chronology (*De Temporum Ratione*, prompted by the debate over the date of Easter, and *De sex Aetatibus Mundi*, 'On the Six Ages of the World'), grammar and physical science (*De natura rerum*, 'On the Nature of the Universe'), and commentaries on the Old and New Testaments; and he translated the Gospel of St John into Anglo-Saxon just before his death. His greatest work was his Latin *Historia Ecclesiastica Gentis Anglorum* ('Ecclesiastical History of the English People'), which he finished in 731, and is the single most valuable source for early English history. It was later translated into Anglo-Saxon by, or under, King **Alfred**. He was canonized in 1899; his Feast day is 27 May.
▷P H Blair, *The World of Bede* (1970)

BEDFORD, (George) Randolph
(1868–1941)

Australian journalist, writer and politician, born in Camperdown, Sydney, who worked on newspapers in various towns and then in 1897, with **Norman Lindsay** established a literary and mining journal *The Clarion* through which he entered the literary circle of **Louis Esson**. He became wealthy through speculation in mining ventures, went to Europe in 1901 and, in London, published two partly autobiographical novels, *True Eyes and the Whirlwind* (1903) and *The Snare of Strength* (1905). He was a strong 'White Australia' advocate and made many unsuccessful attempts to enter politics from 1897 before being nominated to the Queensland Legislative Council in 1917; from then until 1941 he held a position in one or other of the state chambers. A character much larger than life, called 'The Man in the Big Hat', for the slouch hat which invariably covered his baldness, he had meanwhile continued to write novels including *Billy Pagan, Mining Engineer* (1911) and *The Silver Star* (1917), short stories, verse and descriptive books such as *Explorations in Civilization* (1914) on his travels in Italy.
▷*Naught to Thirty-Three* (1944, posthumous)

BEDFORD, Ruth Marjory
(1882–1963)

Australian writer, born in Petersham, Sydney. In collaboration with **Dorothea Mackellar** she wrote two novels, *The Little Blue Devil* (1912) and *Two's Company* (1914). She also produced collections of verse for children as well as stage and radio plays. *Who's Who in Verse* appeared in 1948 and, in 1952, *Think of Stephen: A Family Chronicle*, an affectionate portrait of family life in the mid-Victorian Sydney household of a past Chief Justice.

BEDFORD, Sybille, née von Schoenebeck
(1911–)

German-born British novelist, biographer, journalist and travel writer, born in Charlottenburg, Brandenburg, now part of Berlin; by the mid-1920s she had settled in London. Her biography of **Aldous Huxley** (1973–4) is both scholarly and vivid. As a journalist, she has written penetratingly on the Auschwitz trial at Frankfurt, the *Lady Chatterley's Lover* trial and that of John Bodkin Adams, an Eastbourne doctor tried (but acquitted) of poisoning one of his patients. Several of her novels take up the themes of political and emotional family inheritance. Some are based upon her own experiences, such as *A Legacy* (1956), a study and satirical portrait of the wealthy middle-class of pre-World War I Germany. Echoes of her own family sound again in *Jigsaw: An Unsentimental Education*, a 'biographical novel' published in 1989.

BEER, Johann
(1655–1700)

Austrian-born German novelist and composer of music, born in St Georgen. He emigrated, with his Lutheran parents, to Regensberg. After giving up theology in order to become the court musician at Weissenfels he began to publish, under various pseudonyms (as was the fashion at that time), such as 'Jan Rebhu', a series of novels—there were 20 in all. He was a rich character, whose not very literary fiction has continued to offend certain critics, until the present, for its 'obscenity'—they were so lively that many believe he was second only to **Grimmelshausen**, to whose fictional character Simplicissimus he attributed some of his own stories. His authorship of them all was not established until 1932.
▷ R Alewyn, *Johann Beer* (1932)

BEER, Patricia
(1924–)

English poet, born in Exmouth, Devon. Her work is characterized by an unhurried, West Country address and brilliantly intuitive matching of form to substance that is closer to **Thomas Hardy** than to her avowed most important influence, **W B Yeats**. Her first collections, *The Loss of the Magyar and Other Poems* (1959), *The Survivors* (1963) and *Just Like the Resurrection* (1967), were brisk and assured but lacked the personal focus of later work, a change Beer attributes to writing her autobiography, aged just over 40. *The Estuary* (1971) and *Driving West* (1975) were closer to the existential mode of the American 'confessional' poets, but **Ted Hughes**'s mythic self-plumbing was probably the most direct influence. *Selected Poems* appeared in 1980,

and was followed by a further imaginative reorganization which resulted in her finest book to date, *The Lie of the Land* (1983). Beer has also published an introduction to the Metaphysical poets (1972) and the deeply felt *Reader, I Married Him* (1974).
▷ *Mrs Beer's House* (1968)

BEERBOHM, Sir (Henry) Max(imilian)
(1872–1956)

Known as 'the Incomparable Max', English writer and caricaturist, born in London, the son of a Lithuanian corn merchant, and half-brother of Sir Herbert Beerbohm Tree. He was educated at Charterhouse and Merton College, Oxford. He published his first volume of essays under the ironic title *The Works of Max Beerbohm* (1896), some of which had appeared in the *Yellow Book*. He succeeded **George Bernard Shaw** as drama critic of *The Saturday Review*, until 1910, when he married an American actress, Florence Kahn (d.1951), and went to live, except during the two World Wars, in Rapallo, Italy. His delicate, unerring, aptly-captioned caricatures were collected in various volumes beginning with *Twenty-five Gentlemen* (1896) and *Poet's Corner* (1904). Further volumes of parodying essays appeared, including *The Happy Hypocrite* (1897) and *A Christmas Garland* (1912), full of gentle humour, elegance, and rare wit, and ending with *And Even Now* (1920). His best-known work was his only novel, *Zuleika Dobson* (1912), an ironic romance of Oxford undergraduate life. His broadcast talks from 1935 were another of his singularly brilliant stylistic accomplishments. A month before his death he married Elizabeth Jungmann, who had been his late wife's greatest friend.
▷ Lord Edward C D G Cecil, *Max: a biography* (1964)

BEER-HOFMANN, Richard
(1866–1945)

Austrian novelist, dramatist and poet, born in Vienna into a Jewish family. He was a prominent member of the Jungwein ('Young Vienna') circle—which included **Hofmannsthal** and **Schnitzler**—and, more sharply than any of his contemporaries, brought into German literature the influences of **Flaubert** and **Maupassant**, with *Novellen* (1903). He wrote one poem still famous in Austria: 'Schlaflied für Miriam' ('Lullaby for Miriam'). He is now best known for his plays, which include his impressive adaptation of *The Fatal Dowry* by **Philip Massinger**, *Der Graf von Charolais* (1905), and, most famous of all, and much played in the inter-war period, *Jaakobs Traum* (1918, Eng trans *Jacob's Dream*, 1946), in which he draws on the book which influenced him most of all, the Bible. After

BEETS, Nicolaas

the Anschluss Beer-Hofmann's friends rescued him from Nazi wrath: he went to Switzerland and from there to New York, where he died. His finest work may well be his single novel, *Der Tod Georgs* (1900, 'George's Death'), a work transitional between the author's 'decadence' and his noble attempt to clarify the meaning of Jewishness: the use of interior monologue in this masterpiece is especially fruitful.

▷ S Liptzin, *Richard Beer-Hofmann* (1936)

BEETS, Nicolaas
(1814–1903)

Dutch poet and writer, born in Haarlem. Professor of theology at Utrecht, he published under the pseudonym 'Hildebrand' *Camera Obscura* (1839), a series of quietly humorous sketches of everyday Dutch life, and *Volksliedjes* (1842, 'Little Folksongs'), a collection of simple verses.

▷ J J Dupoix, *Nicolaas Beets et la littérature hollandaise* (1907)

BEHAN, Brendan
(1923–64)

Irish author, born in a slum district in Dublin, brother of **Dominic Behan**. He left school at 14 to become a house painter, and soon joined the IRA. In 1939 he was sentenced to three years in Borstal for attempting to blow up a Liverpool shipyard, and soon after his release given 14 years by a Dublin military court for the attempted murder of two detectives, but was released by a general amnesty (1946). He was in prison again in Manchester (1947) and was deported in 1952. In prison he had learned to speak Irish from fellow IRA detainees, and read voraciously. His first play, *The Quare Fellow* (1956; filmed 1962), starkly dramatized the prison atmosphere prior to a hanging. His exuberant Irish wit, spiced with balladry and bawdry and a talent for fantastic caricature, found scope in his next play, *The Hostage* (1958, first produced in Irish as *An Giall*). It is also evident in the autobiographical novel, *Borstal Boy* (1958), and in *Brendan Behan's Island* (1963).

▷ D Behan, *My Brother Bernard* (1965)

BEHAN, Dominic
(1928–89)

Irish novelist and folklorist, born in Dublin, brother of **Brendan Behan**. He adapted old airs and poems into contemporary Irish Republican material, notably in *The Patriot Game*. Resentfully overshadowed for much of his life by the legend of his brother, he lived largely outside Ireland from 1947 as a journalist and singer. He ultimately settled in Scotland where for the first time he won acceptance in his own right as a writer, and

as an Irish and Scottish nationalist. His only novel, *The Public Life of Parable Jones*, was published just before his death.

▷ *Teems of Times and Happy Returns* (1961)

BEHN, Aphra, née Amis
(1640–89)

English writer and adventuress, born in Wye, Kent. She was brought up in Surinam, where she made the acquaintance of the enslaved negro prince Oroonoko, the subject afterwards of one of her novels, in which she anticipated **Rousseau**'s 'noble savage'. Returning to England in 1663, she married a merchant called Behn, who died within three years. She then turned professional spy at Antwerp, sent back political and naval information, but received little thanks, and on her return was imprisoned for debt. She turned to writing, as perhaps the first professional woman author in England, and wrote many coarse but popular Restoration plays, especially *The Forced Marriage* (1670), *The Rover* (1678), and *The Feigned Courtizans* (1678), and later published *Oroonoko* (1688). She was buried in Westminster Abbey.

▷ G Woodcock, *The Incomparable Aphra* (1948)

BEHRMAN, Samuel Nathaniel
(1893–1973)

American playwright, screenwriter and journalist, born in Worcester, Massachusetts. The production of a sophisticated comedy, *The Second Man* (1927), made him famous but despite being tagged the American **Noël Coward** his comedies of manners foundered on the harsh realities of Depression and war. However, his anecdotal portrait of the great art collector *Duveen* (1952) and *The Worcester Account* (1954), about his boyhood, retain their freshness and are reckoned to contain his best work. He co-wrote the screenplays *Queen Christina* (1933) and *Anna Karenina* (1935) for Greta Garbo.

▷ *Tribulations and Laughter: a memoir* (1972)

BEILBY, Richard Courtney
(1918–)

Australian novelist, born in Malacca (now Melaka), Malaysia. His service in Greece and Crete during World War II provided the background for his novels *No Medals for Aphrodite* (1970) and *Gunner* (1977), though his first, *The Sword and the Myrtle* (1968), is set in an earlier conflict, the Greece of 480BC at the battle of Thermopylae. *The Brown Land Crying* (1975) looks at the half-caste aborigine trapped between cultures.

BELASCO, David
(1853–1931)

American playwright, director and theatre-manager, born in San Francisco. As one of the most powerful figures on Broadway, he owned the Belasco Theatre where, from 1906 until his death, he directed numerous plays, usually heroic melodramas, which often incorporated sensational stage effects. Surprisingly, Belasco, the 'Bishop of Broadway', also found time to write—both alone and in collaboration—over 50 plays, mostly sentimental domestic and historical dramas. *Hearts of Oak* (with James A Herne) appeared in 1879, and the Civil War play, *The Heart of Maryland*, in 1895. As an author, though, he is chiefly remembered for writing *Madame Butterfly* (with John L Long, 1900), and *The Girl of the Golden West* (1905). Both were transformed into operas by Puccini, the former becoming one of the composer's most celebrated works, the latter one of his most neglected.
▷L L Marker, *David Belasco* (1975)

BELL, J(ohn) J(oy)
(1871–1934)

Scottish journalist and humorous writer. He is best known for his *Wee MacGreegor* (1902), an amusing, poignant evocation of boyhood in Glasgow in the days before World War I. Dramatized in 1911, it has been described as Scotland's equivalent of *Huckleberry Finn* and *Just William*. It is still in print.
▷*Do You Remember?* (1934)

BELL, Julian
(1908–37)

English poet, born in London, the elder son of the art historian and critic Clive Bell and the painter Vanessa Bell. In 1930, while still at Cambridge University, he published his first collection, *Winter Movement*, which was generally highly praised, although his aunt, **Virginia Woolf**, confided to her diary that 'for all his admirable good sense & observation & love of country life, he is no poet ... Common sense and Cambridge are not enough.' Although editing *We Did Not Fight* (1935), a volume of essays written by conscientious objectors, Bell later admitted that some situations demanded force and left to fight against the fascists in Spain, where he was killed. His writings were gathered in a posthumous volume, *Julian Bell: Essays, Poems and Letters* (1938).
▷P Stansky and W Abrahams, *Journey to the Frontier* (1966)

BELL, Madison Smartt
(1957–)

American novelist, described by one reviewer as 'a writer to be admired rather than loved'. He was born on a farm in Tennessee and went to school in Nashville. After graduating from Princeton in 1979 he worked variously as sound man for a film unit, as clerk at the Franklin Library and as a freelance writer. His novel *The Year of Silence* (1987), about the disappearance of a pianist's brother, is written in the slickly uncompassionate style which has become his forte. The start of an earlier novel, *Straight Cut* (1986), is typically arresting. The first heading is 'The Day I Shot My Dog'. Bell has his followers, who enjoy the philosophical subtexts in his essentially thriller-grade fictions.

BELLAMY, Edward
(1850–98)

American novelist, born in Chicopee Falls, Massachusetts. He achieved immense popularity with his Utopian romance *Looking Backward 2000–1887* (1888), a work which predicted a new social order and influenced economic thinking in the USA and Europe. The sequel *Equality* (1897) was much less acclaimed.
▷A E Morgan, *Edward Bellamy* (1944)

BELLAY, Joachim du
(1522–60)

French poet and prose writer, born in Lire in Anjou. After his friend and fellow-student, **Pierre de Ronsard**, he was the most important member of the Pléiade. His *Deffence et Illustration de la langue françoise* (1549, 'Defense and Illustration of the French Language'), the manifesto of the Pléiade, advocating the rejection of medieval linguistic traditions and a return to classical and Italian models, had a considerable influence at the time. It was accompanied by an example in the form of a set of **Petrarch**an sonnets, *l'Olive*, dedicated to an unknown lady. He went to Rome in 1533 as secretary to his kinsman, Cardinal du Bellay, but was not a success as a diplomat, though the visit inspired more sonnets, including the collections *Les Antiquités de Rome* ('Roman Antiquities') and *Les Regrets* (1558).

BELLEAU, Rémy
(1528–77)

French poet, born in Nogent le Rotrou. He was a member of the Pléiade and published in 1556 a translation of **Anacreon** that was at first believed to be an original imitation. *Bergerie* (1565, 'Pastoral', 2nd edition 1572) is a medley of delicately descriptive prose and verse, of which *Avril* ('April') still appears in anthologies. *Amours* (1576, 'Love Poems') is a collection of poems concerned with the appearance and arcane powers of precious stones.

▷S Eckhardt, *Rémy Belleau, sa vie, sa 'Berg-erie'* (1917)

BELLENDEN, or BALLANTYNE, John
(d.1587)

Scottish ecclesiastic and writer, born towards the close of the 15th century. In 1508 he matriculated from St Andrews and completed his theological studies at the Sorbonne. His translations in 1533 of Boece's *Historia Gentis Scotorum*, and of the first five books of Livy, are interesting as vigorous specimens of early Scottish prose. The *Croniklis of Scotland* is a very free translation, and contains numerous passages not found in Boece, so that it is in some respects almost an original work. Bellenden enjoyed great favour at the court of James V, at whose request the translations were made. As a reward, he received considerable grants from the Treasury, and afterwards was made Archdeacon of Moray and Canon of Ross. Becoming involved, however, in ecclesiastical controversy, he went to Rome.
▷R W Chambers and W W Seton, *Bellenden's Translation of the History of Hector Boece* (1919)

BELLI, Carlos Germán
(1927–)

Peruvian poet, born in Lima, who has looked to the Spanish past, and in particular to **Quevedo**, for his inspiration. Elegant but deeply felt, his poetry is also influenced by that of **Vallejo**. Some of his poems were translated in a collection, *Carlos Germán Belli*, in 1988.
▷F Cairns, *The Poet in Peru: Alienation and the Quest for A Super-reality* (1982)

BELLIDO, José María
(1922–)

Spanish dramatist, born (a Basque) in San Sebastián. He is a trained lawyer and a linguist, most of whose plays written while Franco was in power were banned and had to appear abroad in translation—chiefly in *Modern Spanish Theatre* (1968, M Benedikt and G E Wellwarth eds) and *The New Wave Spanish Drama* (1970, ed G E Wellwarth). His *La suite fantastica*, as he calls his series of a score and more short plays (*temblores*: 'quiverings'), are a genre unto themselves: spontaneous pieces written apparently without heed to form, but in fact exceedingly skilful. They could be classed as Theatre of the Absurd. *Futbol* (1963, Eng trans *Football*, in *Modern Spanish Theatre*) did get past Franco's censors, because they did not realize that it was not about a football team but a series of strutting fascists. Bellido has also written for the commercial theatre, as in *Rubio cordero* (1970, 'Blond Lamb'); but this account of

kidnapped diplomats also has its jokes for the initiated.
▷G E Wellwarth, *Spanish Underground Drama* (1972)

BELLMANN, Carl Michael
(1740–95)

Swedish poet and writer of popular songs, born in Stockholm. In 1757 he entered banking, but had to flee to Norway six years later to escape his creditors. In 1776 he was brought back as a protegé of King Gustav III, who gave him a sinecure as secretary of the national lottery. He founded a drinking club, the *Bacci orden* or 'Knights of Bacchus', and put in verse his impressions of his friends and others. His most important collections are the *Songs of Fredman* (1790) and *Epistles of Fredman* (1791), which combine burlesque with biblical parody and minute observation of Swedish life. There is a long-standing Bellmann Society in Sweden devoted to his memory.
▷P B Austin, *Life and Songs of Carl Michael Bellmann* (1967)

BELLO, Andrés
(1781–1865)

Venezuelan poet, translator (**Byron, Hugo**), philosopher and scholar—he was also a tutor to Simon Bolívar. He lived for many years in London (1810–29), where he prepared an important edition of the poem *El Cid*. In 1829 he emigrated to Chile, where he founded the National University. His grammar of the Castilian language (1847) is a landmark. In *Filosofia del entendimiento* (1881, 'Philosophy of Understanding'), he introduced the ideas of Locke, Berkeley and Mill into Latin America. His debate with **Domingo Sarmiento**, a convinced romantic, whereas Bello was at heart a classical humanist, stimulated South American thinking. The most famous of his artificial but technically flawless poems is *La agricultura de la zona torrida* (1826, 'The Agriculture of the Torrid Zone'), part of which is translated into prose in the *Penguin Book of Latin American Verse* (1971, ed E Curacciolo-Trejo).
▷E R Monmegal, *Este otro Andrés Bello* (1969)

BELLOC, (Joseph) Hilaire Pierre
(1870–1953)

French-born British writer and poet, born in St Cloud near Paris, the son of a French barrister, Louis Belloc, and his English wife. His sister was **Marie Belloc**. The family moved to England during the Franco–Prussian war, and settled there in 1872. He was educated at the Oratory School, Birmingham, under **Newman**, and Balliol College, Oxford, but did military service in the French army. He became a naturalized British subject in 1902, and became Liberal MP in 1906, but, disillusioned with politics, did not seek re-election in 1910. Disapproving of modern industrial society and socialism, he wrote *The Servile State* (1912), advocating a return to the system of medieval guilds. He was a close friend of **G K Chesterton**, who illustrated many of his books. He is best known, however, for his delightfully nonsensical verse for children: *The Bad Child's Book of Beasts* (1896) and the *Cautionary Tales* (1907); his numerous travel books, including *Path to Rome* (1902) and *The Old Road* (1910), reconstructing the Pilgrim's Way; his historical studies *Robespierre* (1901), *Marie Antoinette* (1910), *Richelieu* (1929), *Wolsey* (1930), and *Napoleon* (1932); and his religious books, including *Europe and the Faith* (1920) and *The Great Heresies* (1938). An energetic Roman Catholic apologist, he was fearlessly, sometimes fanatically, outspoken.

BELLOC, Marie Adelaide
(1868–1947)

French-born English novelist, playwright and short-story writer, the sister of **Hilaire Belloc**. She wrote over 40 novels, mostly atmospheric, deftly-plotted crime and mystery stories, and many involving a sharp moral dilemma. The most famous is *The Lodger* (1913), in which a landlady discovers that her tenant, an outwardly dignified and respectable man, is none other than Jack the Ripper, the notorious murderer of prostitutes in the east end of London. Despite her consternation, Mrs Bunting is unable to report her discovery to the police.

BELLOC LOWNDES, Mrs *see* BELLOC, Marie Adelaide

BELLOW, Saul
(1915–)

Canadian-born American writer, winner of the Nobel Prize for literature, born in Lachine in Quebec, the son of immigrant Russian parents. He spent his childhood in Montreal; in 1924 his family moved to Chicago. He attended university there, and at Northwestern in Evanston, Illinois. He abandoned his post-graduate studies at Wisconsin University to become a writer, and his first novel, *The Dangling Man*, a study of a man in pre-draft limbo, appeared in 1944. He became an associate professor at Minnesota University, and after being awarded a Guggenheim Fellowship in 1948 travelled to Paris and Rome. Other works include *The Victim* (1947), *The Adventures of Augie March* (1953), *Henderson the Rain King* (1959), *Herzog* (1964), *Mr Sammler's Planet* (1970), *Humboldt's Gift*

(1975) and *The Dean's December* (1982). Most are concerned with the fate of liberal humanism in a violent and absurd environment which has severed the present from an intellectually and emotionally nourishing past. In 1962 he was appointed a professor at Chicago University, and in 1976 was awarded the Nobel Prize for literature.

▷M Bradbury, *Bellow* (1982); J Braham, *A Sort of Columbus: The American Voyages of Bellow's Fiction* (1984)

BELLOY, Dormont de, properly Pierre Laurent Buyrette
(1727–75)

French dramatist. He was one of the first to introduce on the French stage native instead of classical heroes. His first success, *Zelmire* (1762), was followed by *Le Siège de Calais* (1765), *Gaston et Bayard* (1771) and *Pierre le cruel* (1772).

BELY, Andrei, pseud of Boris Nikolayevich Bugayev
(1880–1934)

Russian novelist, poet and critic, born in Moscow. A leading Symbolist writer, he early met **Vladimir Soloviev**, the religious philosopher, and fell under his influence. While at Moscow University he wrote Decadent poetry which he published in *Sinfoniya (2-aya, dramaticheskaya)* (1902, 'Symphony (Second, Dramatic)'). His poetry, however, was criticized mercilessly, and his reputation rests on his prose. *Serebryany golub* (1909, Eng trans *The Silver Dove*, 1974) was his first and most accessible novel, and was followed by *Petersburg* (1916, Eng trans *St Petersburg*, 1959), his masterpiece, in which the action centres on a bomb camouflaged as a tin of sardines. The autobiographical *Kotik Letayev* (1922, Eng trans *Kotik Letaev*, 1971) is Bely's most original work, a stream-of-consciousness attempt to show how children become aware of what is going on in the world. His later novels, written after a second sojourn in Berlin (1921–3), are more overtly satirical of the pre-revolutionary Russian scene but are still highly experimental. He is regarded as one of the most important Russian writers of the 1920s.

▷J D Elsworth, *Andrei Bely* (1972)

BEMELMENS, Ludwig
(1898–1963)

American humorous memoirist, novelist and painter, born in Austria of a Belgian father and a Bavarian mother. Much of his best writing appeared in the *New Yorker*. His work has now dated, but in their day such books as *Hotel Splendide* (1941), about his years as a waiter, and *Dirty Eddie* (1947), a novel about a pig movie-star, were much read. He was at his best when he could keep sentimentality out of his irreverent writing, and concentrate on his capacity for satire.

BENAVENTE, Jacinto
(1866–1954)

Spanish dramatist, born in Madrid. He intended to enter the legal profession but turned to literature. After publishing some poems and short stories he won recognition as a playwright with his *El nido ajeno* (1893, 'The Other Nest'), which was followed by some brilliantly satirical society comedies. His masterpiece is *Los intereses creados* (1907, 'Human Concerns'), an allegorical play in the *commedia dell'arte* style. He also wrote some excellent children's plays.
▷M Penuelas, translated by K Englev, *Jacinto Benavente* (1968)

BEN-AVIGDOR, pseud of Arieh Leib Shalkovitz
(1866–1921)

Hebrew story writer, Zionist, and influential advocate of the reform of the Hebrew language, born near Vilna. He was a notable publisher (he founded Ahiahsaf, and then Tushia), who wrote stories of proletarian Jews and a long historical novel set in 15th-century Spain; his work has not found a translator.

BENCHLEY, Robert Charles
(1889–1945)

American humorist, critic and parodist, born in Worcester, Massachusetts. **E B White** and **James Thurber** thought him a finer humorist even than **Mark Twain**; he was described by **Dorothy Parker** as 'a kind of saint'. At Harvard he edited the *Lampoon* and starred in the Hasty Pudding shows. He met Parker at *Vanity Fair*; together with **Robert Sherwood**, Thurber, **George Kaufman** and Franklin D Adams, they formed the notorious Algonquin Round Table. Subsequently he worked as a drama critic for *Life* (1920–29) and the *New Yorker* (1929–40) but was fired for excessive drinking. He was at his most brilliant writing sketches, which surfaced in several collections including *20,000 Leagues under the Sea, or, David Copperfield* (1928), *From Bed to Worse* (1934) and *My Ten Years in a Quandary, and How They Grew* (1936). His humour derives from the predicament of the 'Little Man', himself writ large, beset on all sides by the complexity of existence in the modern world. A chronic worrier, minor problems (leaving a party, curing hiccoughs) assumed epic proportions. He also appeared in cameo roles in many films.
▷N W Yates, *Robert Benchley* (1968)

BENDA, Julien
(1867–1956)

French philosopher and essayist, born in Paris and educated at the university there. After initial fame writing against **Henri Bergson** just prior to World War I, he caused a sensation in 1927 with *La Trahison des clercs* ('The Treachery of the Intellectuals') in which he accuses modern thinkers of abandoning philosophical neutrality to support doctrines of class and race hatred, such as Marxism and fascism, going on to attempt to 'restore the primacy of the spiritual'. He published little during the German occupation of France but much afterwards including idiosyncratic criticisms of then fashionable thought in *Tradition du Existentialisme* (1947) and *La Dialectique Materialiste* (1948). He wrote two novels, *L'Ordination* (1911) and *Les Amorandes* (1922).
▷ *La Jeunesse d'un clerc* (1936)

BENEDETTI, Mario
(1920–)

Uruguayan novelist, short-story writer and poet, born in Paso de los Toros. His early stories, included in *Esta Mañana* (1949, 'This Morning') and *El Último Viaje y otros cuentos* (1951, 'The Last Journey and other stories'), are disciplined depictions of the frustrations of mass existence in the cities. His novels, such as *Quién de Nosotros* (1955, 'Which One of Us'), expand on that theme, but his poetry, although at times it has a political subject-matter, can also engage in more abstract notions, as is the case with the collection *Noción de la Patria* (1963, 'Concept of the Homeland'). He has written several volumes of literary criticism, lively, eclectic and opinionated, including *Literatura Uruguayo siglo XX* (1963, rev edn 1969).

BENEDIKTSSON, Einar
(1864–1940)

Icelandic poet and entrepreneur, born at Ellíavatan, near Reykjavík. His mother was a fine poet; his father was a Supreme Court judge, from whom Benediktsson acquired his legal interests and nationalist sympathies. He himself became a country magistrate, but devoted many years to touring Europe, seeking capital (unsuccessfully) for ambitious industrial schemes to exploit Iceland's natural resources, notably fishing and hydro-electric power. His literary output reflected his patriotic concerns. He published five volumes of ornate poetry that harked back to the skaldic tradition of intricate metaphor and vocabulary, but which he modernized considerably.
▷S J Nordal, *Einar Benediktsson* (1971)

BENELLI, Sem
(1877–1949)

Italian dramatist, born in Prato, Tuscany. He wrote plays in prose and verse. His outstanding successes were *Tignola*, a light comedy, and *La cena della beffe* ('The Mocking Dinner'), a powerful tragedy in verse.
▷C Lavi, *Sem Benelli, il suo teatro e la sua compagnia* (1928)

BENET, Juan
(1927–93)

Spanish novelist and dramatist, a civil engineer by profession. His work, not unlike that of the French novelist **Michel Butor**, but most influenced by **Faulkner**, is immensely complex, 'hermetic' and allusive to a myriad of other writers, and for that reason has not yet been very widely read outside Spain, except by a band of critics devoted to it. But his successful novel, *Una Meditación* (1970), was translated as *A Meditation* in 1982. Benet's 'baroque prose poses substantial and sometimes insoluble problems for the reader', wrote a critic; but he added that his 'criticism [of human situations, particularly of the repressive Franco regime] is given life in a narrative that on the surface seems remote from conditions in … Spain'. As a journalist Benet was notably lucid.
▷D K Herzberger, *The Novelistic World of Juan Benet* (1977)

BENÉT, Laura
(1884–1979)

American poet and biographer, elder sister of **William** and **Stephen Benét**. She was born at Fort Hamilton, New York. Her verse, much of it written with a young readership in mind, occasionally recalls **Christina Rossetti**, but is often more robust metrically. Her most distinctive volumes are *Fairy Bread* (1921), *Basket for a Fair* (1934) and the very late *Bridge of a Single Hair* (1974), which marked a startling return to form. She also wrote literary biography for the young and a rather blowsy novel, *Come Slowly, Eden* (1942).
▷*When William Rose, Stephen Vincent and I Were Young* (1976)

BENÉT, Stephen Vincent
(1898–1943)

American poet and novelist, born in Bethlehem, Pennsylvania. He was the son of an Army Officer and brother of **William Rose Benét**. He was educated at Yale, and had published two volumes of poetry before graduating in 1919. His college novel, *The Beginning of Wisdom*, appeared in 1921. His main subject was the nature of the American national experience and character, and his most famous explorations of it are the long poems *John Brown's Body* (1928), on the Civil War, and *Western Star* (1943), which was part of a projected epic on American history. He wrote several volumes of evocative, well-crafted poems, including a collection, *Ballads and Poems 1915–30* (1931), and *Burning City* (1936), all of which are traditional in form. His other writings include four more novels, short stories, and two one-act folk operas.
▷C Fenton, *Stephen Vincent Benét* (1958)

BENÉT, William Rose
(1886–1950)

American poet, editor, novelist and playwright, born in Fort Hamilton, New York, brother of **Laura** and **Stephen Benét**. His main claim to fame is as a poet and he published many collections, among them *Merchants from Cathay* (1913), *Moons of Grandeur* (1920) and *The Stairway of Surprise* (1947), but his career was largely eclipsed by the success of his wife **Elinor Wylie** and his brother.
▷*My Brother Steve* (1943)

BENGTSSON, Frans G
(1894–1954)

Swedish essayist, novelist and poet. Born at Rösjöholm in Skåne, he studied at the University of Lund. He made his debut as a poet in 1923, his verses reflecting an exclusive aestheticism which was to pervade his work. His breakthrough with the reading public came with his collections of essays, among them *Litteratörer och militärer* (1929, 'Penmen and Military Men') and *De långhåriga merovingerna* (1933, 'The Long-Haired Merovingians'). He exploits his encyclopedic knowledge with notable artistic skill and a conspicuous sense of humour, the elegant complexity of his texts influenced by British essayists. His two-volume novel *Röde Orm* (1941–5, Eng trans *The Long Ships*, 1954), which is set in the age of the Vikings, is at once scholarly and humorous and brought him considerable international fame.
▷G Hägg, 'Esteten som underhållare. Frans G. Bengtssons essäform', in *Övertalning och underhållning. Den svenska essäistiken 1890–1930* (1978)

BENJAMIN, Walter
(1892–1940)

German, Marxist, literary and cultural critic, born in Berlin, to an assimilated Jewish family; he believed himself to be a descendant of the poet **Heinrich Heine**. He was educated at the Kaiser Friedrich School, and at the Friedrich-Wilhelm Gymnasium in Thuringia. His earliest influence was the Cabbalistic tradition, which he brought to bear on the philosophical legacy of Immanuel Kant. He set out his ideas in the notoriously difficult prologue

to his 1925 study of *Trauerspiel* (Eng trans *The Origin of German Tragic Drama*, 1977). This attempt to understand the 17th century from the standpoint of Germany was later followed by the so-called 'Arcades Project', which had post-Napoleonic France as its focus. Towards the end of the 1920s, Benjamin began to turn towards Marxian materialism, encouraged by his encounter with **Bertolt Brecht**: Benjamin later claimed that his best-known essay, 'The Work of Art in an Age of Mechanical Reproduction' (1936), had been deliberately written to outdo Brecht's materialism. This essay and the equally important 'Theses on the Philosophy of History' are included in a posthumous translated collection called *Illuminations* (1969), edited by Hannah Arendt. Together with the aphoristic and autobiographical writings in *Reflections* (published first in English, 1978), this effectively revived Benjamin's reputation, making him a central figure in neo-Marxist and materialist criticism, and an icon of heroic resistance against totalitarianism. In September 1940, believing that he was about to be denied asylum, he committed suicide on the Franco–Spanish border; in the words of Brecht, who composed a threnody, having encountered one impassable frontier, he willingly crossed the only passable one left available to him.
▷P Wolin, *Walter Benjamin: An Aesthetic of Redemption* (1982)

BENLOWES, Edward
(1602–76)

English religious poet. Having been brought up a staunch Roman Catholic, Benlowes scandalized his family in 1627 by changing his faith. In the eyes of some, he took another irretrievably wrong turning during the Civil War, when he became a passionate Royalist. *Theophila, or, Love's Sacrifice*, a sprawling spiritual romance completed in 1652, is his best-known work, but one with so many oddities of imagery and expression that it continues to perplex as well as intrigue scholars.

BENN, Gottfried
(1886–1956)

German poet, born in Mansfeld in West Prussia. Though the son of a clergyman he embraced the philosophy of Nihilism as a young man, but later became one of the few intellectuals to favour Nazi doctrines, although his poems were banned by the Nazis in 1938 (ironically, they were banned again by the Allies in 1945 for his earlier pro-Nazi sympathies). Trained in medicine as a venereologist, he began writing Expressionist verse that dealt with the uglier aspects of his profession, such as *Morgue* (1912). Later his outlook became more mature and his poetry

more versatile, though still pessimistic. After 1945, the cerebral, intellectually rigorous cast of his post-war poetry, and its mood of despondency in defeat, became influential and won him a place among the leading poets of the century.
▷E Buddeburg, *Gottfried Benn* (1961)

BENNETT, Alan
(1934–)

English dramatist, actor and director, born in Leeds. He came to prominence as a writer and performer in *Beyond the Fringe*, a revue performed at the Edinburgh Festival in 1960, and wrote a television series, *On The Margin* (1966), before his first stage play, *Forty Years On* (1968). Essentially a humanist, noted for his wry, self-deprecating humour, which combines a comic-tragic view of life, his subsequent plays include *Getting On* (1971, about a Labour MP), *Habeas Corpus* (1973), *The Old Country* (1977), a double bill, *Single Spies* (1988) and *The Madness of George III* (1991). He has also written much for television, including *An Englishman Abroad* (1983), *The Insurance Man* (1986), and a series of six monologues, *Talking Heads* (1988).

BENNETT, (Enoch) Arnold
(1867–1931)

English novelist, born near Hanley, Staffordshire, in the heart of 'the Potteries', the son of a solicitor. Educated locally and at London University, he became a solicitor's clerk in London, but quickly transferred to journalism, and in 1893 became assistant editor (editor in 1896) of the journal *Woman*. He published his first novel, *The Man from the North*, in 1898. In 1902 he moved to Paris for 10 years and from then on he was engaged exclusively in writing, journalistic and creative. His claims to recognition as a novelist rest mainly on the early *Anna of the Five Towns* (1902), the more celebrated *The Old Wives' Tale* (1908), and the *Clayhanger* series—*Clayhanger* (1910), *Hilda Lessways* (1911), *These Twain* (1916), subsequently issued (1925) as *The Clayhanger Family*—in all of which novels the 'Five Towns', centres of the pottery industry, feature not only as background, but almost as *dramatis personae*. He excels again with *Riceyman Steps* (1923), a picture of drab life in London, and his genial, humorous streak shows in works like *The Card* (1911), *The Grand Babylon Hotel* (1902), *Imperial Palace* (1930), and the play *The Great Adventure* (1913). *Lord Raingo* (1926) is a political novel. The play *Milestones* (1912), written in collaboration with Edward Knoblock, was much performed. He was a sound and influential critic, and as 'Jacob Tonson' on *The New Age* he was a discerning reviewer. His *Journals*, written in the manner of the

brothers **Edmond** and **Jules de Goncourt**, were published posthumously.
▷M Drabble, *Arnold Bennett: a biography* (1974)

BENNETT, Louise Simone
(1919–)
Jamaican poet, born in Kingston, and educated at Excelsior High School. She studied journalism by correspondence course before going to the Royal Academy of Dramatic Art in London in 1945. After graduating she taught drama in Jamaica, performed in theatres in Britain and America, and lectured widely on Jamaican folklore and music. She married the Jamaican actor and impresario, Eric Coverley, in 1954. Her numerous books include retellings of Jamaican folk stories and collections of her own ballads and verse monologues. Her use of Jamaican dialect and speech rhythms, humour and satirical wit for the purposes of social and political comment have made her one of the outstanding performance poets of the 20th century.
▷*Jamaican Labrish* (poetry collection, ed with introduction by R Nettleford, 1966); M Morris, in *Fifty Caribbean Writers*, ed D C Dance (1986)

BENOIT DE SAINTE-MAURE
(fl.c.1150)
French poet, born in either Sainte-Maure near Poitiers or Sainte-More near Tours. His vast romance *Roman de Troie* ('Tale of Troy') was a source book to many later writers, notably **Boccaccio**, who in turn inspired **Chaucer** and **Shakespeare** to use Benoit's episode of Troilus and Cressida.

BENSERADE, Isaac de
(1613–91)
French poet and dramatist, born in Paris His is remembered as the librettist for Lully's ballets and as the author of a sonnet, *Job*.
▷C I Silin, *Benserade and his Ballets de cour* (1940)

BENSON, Arthur Christopher
(1862–1925)
English author, son of Edward White Benson and brother of **Edward Frederic Benson** and **Robert Hugh Benson**. He was master of Magdalene College, Cambridge, and wrote studies of **Dante Gabriel Rossetti**, **Fitzgerald**, **Walter Pater**, **Tennyson**, and **John Ruskin**, a memoir of Robert Hugh Benson, and a biography of Edward White Benson. His poems include *Land of Hope and Glory* (1902).
▷*The Diary* (1926)

BENSON, E(dward) F(rederic)
(1867–1940)
English author, son of Edward White Benson and brother of **Arthur Christopher Benson** and **Robert Hugh Benson**. He was educated at Wellington and King's College, Cambridge. After some archaeological research in Greece and Egypt (1892–95) he published several light novels including *Dodo* (1893) and *Queen Lucia* (1920) as well as three autobiographical studies of Edwardian and Georgian society.
▷*Final Edition: informal autobiography* (1940)

BENSON, Robert Hugh
(1871–1914)
English author and clergyman, son of Edward White Benson and brother of **Arthur Christopher Benson** and **Edward Frederic Benson**. Educated at Eton and Trinity College, Cambridge, he took Anglican orders but turned Roman Catholic in 1903 and rose to private chamberlain to Pope Pius X (1911). A dynamic preacher and prolific author, he wrote such novels as *Come Rack! Come Rope!* (1912).
▷A C Benson, *Hugh: memoirs of a brother* (1915)

BENSON, Stella
(1892–1933)
English novelist, poet and short-story writer, born in Much Wenlock, Shropshire. Her first novel, *I Pose* (1915), is about the suffragette movement, and contains autobiographical elements; her second, *The Poor Man* (1932), is a witty, often introspective tale. Ill health forced her to travel, and she visited Switzerland, the West Indies and California, as well as spending many years in China; some of those visits are recounted in *The Little World* (1925) and *Worlds Within Worlds* (1928). Her diary, not published until decades after her death from tuberculosis, is both a more revealing and perhaps more enduring work than her fiction.

BENTLEY, Edmund Clerihew
(1875–1956)
English journalist and novelist, born in London. He worked on the *Daily News* (1901–12) and *The Daily Telegraph* (1912–34). He is chiefly remembered as the author of *Trent's Last Case* (1913), which is regarded as a milestone in the transformation of the detective novel. A close friend of **G K Chesterton**, he originated and gave name to the type of humorous verse-form known as the 'clerihew'.
▷*Those Days* (1940)

BENTLEY, Phyllis
(1894–1977)

English novelist, born in Halifax. Love of her native Yorkshire is reflected in over 20 novels, including her first, *Environment* (1915), *Carr* (1929), and her best-known, *Inheritance* (1932). Several of her books, including *Inheritance*, are partly autobiographical, drawing on her own family experiences to present a vivid evocation of the local textile trade. Her novels are realistic and strong on character; they are also sometimes sentimental, even though sentiment was something she strove hard to avoid. Continuing the Yorkshire theme, she wrote three critical studies of the **Brontë** sisters, and in 1949 edited an edition of their works.
▷ *O Dreams, O Destinations* (1962)

BEN-ZION, Simcha, pseud of Simcha Alter Gutmann
(1870–1932)

Hebrew novelist and translator (of, for example, **Goethe**'s *Hermann and Dorothea*), born in Teleneshte, Bessarabia. The son of a very pious father, he had to educate himself in secular matters in secret. A now neglected master, his subjects are the Jews of the small towns of Bessarabia and their insoluble economic problems, their courage, and their resourcefulness.
▷ M Waxman, *A History of Jewish Literature* (1960)

BÉRANGER, Pierre Jean de
(1780–1857)

French poet, born in Paris. After a scanty education he left regular employment as a clerk at the University of Paris for an impecunious literary life in 1798. His lyrics were coloured by his politics, a curious compound of republicanism and Bonapartism, and led to spells of imprisonment in 1821 and 1828, but their vivacity, satire, and wit endeared them to the masses.
▷ E de Pompery, *Béranger: sa biographie* (1865)

BERCEO, Gonzalo de
(c.1180–c.1246)

Spanish poet, born in Verceo, the earliest known Castilian poet. He became a deacon and wrote more than 13 000 verses on devotional subjects, of which the best is a biography of St Oria. He was also the author of *Milagros de la Virgen*, a collection of legends of the Virgin's appearances on earth. His poems were not discovered and published until the late 18th century.
▷ J E Keller, *Gonzalo de Berceo* (1972)

BERCHET, Giovanni
(1783–1851)

Italian poet, born in Milan. He began by translating foreign, especially English, literature, and through his translation of *The Vicar of Wakefield* (1809) became interested in ballads. In 1816 he published a pamphlet, *Lettera semiseria di Grisostomo* ('Grisostomo's Semi-serious Letter'), which became a manifesto of the Romantic movement in Italy. In 1821 he left Italy to avoid arrest, and lived in exile, mainly in England, until the abortive Revolution of 1848. He was received in Milan with enthusiasm and made director of education, but had to flee again to Piedmont. His best-known works are *I Profughi di Parga* (1821, 'The Refugees of Parga'), *Il Romito del Cenisio* ('The Hermit of Cenisio') and *Il Trovatore* ('The Troubadour').
▷ C Rosa, *Giovanni Berchet. Studio critico biografico* (1872)

BERENT, Wacklaw, pseud of W Rawicz
(1873–1940)

Polish novelist and translator of **Nietzsche**. He came to prominence in the so-called 'Young Poland' period (1895–1914), in which writers reacted, on the whole in neo-romantic fashion, against the positivism of their predecessors. Berent, a marine biologist who studied in Germany, is still one of Poland's more important novelists, and one who came very early not only to modernism but also to what is now called post-modernism. His first novel, *Fachowiec* (1895, 'The Expert'), satirized positivist optimism in a poker-faced and ironic, but not romantic, manner. His relatively few novels became progressively more disillusioned with the fictional mode, until he came to disbelieve in it altogether. His novels, in particular *Zywe Kamienie* (1918, 'Living Stones'), set in medieval times, await translation into English.

BERESFORD-HOWE, Constance
(1922–)

Canadian novelist and short-story writer, born in Montreal. With the exception of the historical romance *My Lady Greensleeves* (1955), her novels deal with contemporary women, her first three: *The Unreasoning Heart* (1946), *Of This Day's Journey* (1947) and *The Invisible Gate* (1949), focusing on young women at critical stages of their worldly development. Of her later books, *A Population of One* (1977) follows a single woman's plunge into the academic world, while *Night Studies* (1985) records the dismal lives of the students and staff at an urban college of further education. Her most famous novel, however, is *A Book of Eve* (1973), in which the eponymous protagonist, a woman in her mid-sixties, leaves her husband of 40 years to start a new life alone on the other side of Montreal. Like her other novels, it is compassionate, witty and gently effective.

BERG, Leila

(1917–)

English children's writer and editor, born in Salford, Lancashire. Her *Look At Kids* (1972), illustrated with unsentimental black and white photographs of urban life, was as influential, in its way, as the Plowden report. While she was an editor for Macmillan, she launched the 'Nippers' series of primary-school readers, many of which she wrote herself. These were criticized for the stereotyped portrait they drew of working-class life and have become museum pieces of the seventies. As a story-teller her work is longer-lasting. *A Box For Benny* (1958) is still enjoyed.

BERGELSON, David

(1884–1952)

Russian (Yiddish) novelist and story writer, and one of the leaders of the Yiddish generation which followed immediately after the 'classical' period of **Scholem Aleichem**. He was born in the Ukraine into a prosperous family of timber merchants, but their fortunes declined, and he knew poverty at first hand. He differed from his predecessors in two ways: his style developed (sometimes abruptly), and he put an unforgettable emphasis upon the social decline of the period through which he lived. *Nokh alemen* (1913, Eng trans *When All is Said and Done*, 1977), features the 'first authentic heroine of Yiddish fiction'. Bergelson lived in Berlin for a while, and struggled against communist dictation of artistic creation, but eventually he submitted, returned to Russia and became a socialist realist. Yet even his fiction of that period, such as *Midas hadin* (1925, 'Full Severity of the Law'), has its power and attraction. He was executed by Stalin on a trumped-up charge after he had turned back, as well as he could, to Jewish themes. *Baym Dnieper* (1932–40, 'Along the Dnieper'), is one of the most remarkable novels written under Stalinist oppression, and awaits translation.
▷ C A Madison, *Yiddish Literature* (1968)

BERGENGRUEN, Werner

(1892–1962)

German novelist, critic (eg of **E T A Hoffmann**) and poet, born in Riga (his father was a member of the German colony there, but returned to Germany early in Bergengruen's life), who fell foul of the Nazis and was expelled from the Academy of Writers in 1937. He was converted to Roman Catholicism in 1936. A conscientious, prolific, gifted and still much heeded writer (he was particularly popular after the end of World War II), he was at his best in the tradition of **Kleist** and **C F Meyer**, and it is by his historical novels that he will perhaps be best remembered, particularly for *Der Grosstyrann und das Gericht* (1935, Eng trans *A Matter of Conscience*, 1952), set in Renaissance Italy; this is a masterful and exciting allegorical arraignment of the Nazis, whose censor allowed it through. Also notable are Bergengruen's short stories, and his novels set in modern times. His poetry, although a few hymns have survived, is less effective, but has its champions.

BERGER, John Peter

(1926–)

English novelist, playwright and art critic, born in London. After studying at the Central and Chelsea Schools of Art he began his working life as a painter and a drawing teacher but soon turned to writing. His novels have a sensual awareness that is not entirely visual, but his Marxism and artistic background are ever present. Each of his novels has been well-received; they include *A Painter of Our Time* (1958), *The Foot of Clive* (1962) and *Corker's Freedom* (1964). His fame was enhanced with the publication of *G* (1972), a story of migrant workers in Europe, which won the Booker Prize; in his acceptance speech, Berger denounced the sponsors and announced that he would donate half of the prize money to the (now defunct) Black Panthers. Among his other writings the best known are *Ways of Seeing* (1972), on the visual arts, and *Pig Earth* (1979), a collection of short stories of French peasant life, and the first of the *Into Their Labours* trilogy, which was followed by *Once in Europa* (1989) and *Lilac and Flag* (1991). In 1992 he published *Keeping a Rendezvous*, a collection of essays and poems.

BERGER, Thomas Louis

(1924–)

American novelist, noted for what one critic characterized as 'bitter comedy'. Born in Cincinnati, he was educated in New York City and after military service worked as an academic librarian and editor. His sequence of novels about Carlo Reinhart spans four decades: *Crazy in Berlin* (1958) is set in occupied Germany at the end of World War II; Reinhart later studies the GI Bill (*Reinhart in Love*, 1962), and then slides inexorably through the holes in the American Dream (*Vital Parts*, 1970), before achieving a measure of chastened peace in *Reinhart's Women* (1981).

Berger's career as a novelist has been somewhat overshadowed by the movie of *Little Big Man* (1964), which tended to iron out the ambiguity of his protean hero Jack Crabb and his perspective on American life from both sides of the cowboys-and-indians, success-and-failure divide. *Who is Teddy Villanova?* (1977) and *Nowhere* (1985) parody detective and spy fiction but are again concerned with the shifting nature of identity in contemporary society.

BERGGOLTS, Olga
(1910–75)

Russian poet, born in St Petersburg. She married the poet **Boris Kornilov**, who was murdered by Stalin in the Purges (1937); she was herself imprisoned. Although she had published her first book in 1934, she became well known only when she organized resistance, and made highly effective daily broadcasts in Leningrad when it was besieged by the Nazis throughout World War II. Her lyrical prose effusion *Dnevnye zvyozdy* (1959, 'Stars in Daytime'), received high praise; her poetry is workmanlike and poignant in its sincerity.

BERGMAN, Bo Hjalmar
(1869–1967)

Swedish lyric poet, born in Stockholm. He studied law at Uppsala and later became a literary critic. The pessimism of his early poetry, as in *Marionetterna* (1903, 'Puppets'), gradually gave way to the optimistic humanism of *En människa* (1908, 'A Member of the Race'), which was frequently in opposition to the growing totalitarianism of modern society. His varied output includes novels, short stories, and two volumes of memoirs.
▷K Asplund, *Bo Bergman. Manniskan och diktaren* (1970)

BERGMAN, Hjalmar Fredrik Elgérus
(1883–1931)

Swedish novelist, poet and playwright, born in Örebro, a place he frequently satirized in later life, taking revenge for the humiliation he had suffered as a stout and painfully shy youth. His work ranges from a dark psychological vision, evident in *En döds memoarer* (1918–19, 'The Memoirs of a Dead Man'), to an almost Symbolist underpinning of conventional realism, as in *Murkurells i Wadköping* (1919, Eng trans *God's Orchid*, 1924), and to the lighter comic touch of plays like *Swedenhielms* (1925, 'The Swedenhielms') and *Patrasket* (1928, 'The Rabble').
▷E Linder, translated by Catherine Djurklou, *Hjalmar Bergman* (1975)

BERGNER, Herz
(1907–)

Polish-born Australian novelist and short-story writer, who emigrated to Australia before World War I. His first stories, all originally published in Yiddish, told of the immigrant experience in Australia. The novels *Between Sky and Sea* (1946) and *Light and Shadow* (1960), and the collection of short stories *Where the Truth Lies* (1965) all won significant awards upon publication.

BERGROTH
(1886–1966)

Finnish novelist, critic and playwright, who wrote in Swedish until 1920, but then turned to Finnish. She was a student of the anthroposophy of **Rudolph Steiner**. She has received little attention from critics.

BERGSON, Henri
(1859–1941)

French philosopher, born in Paris, son of a Polish Jewish musician and an English mother, and winner of the Nobel Prize for literature. He became professor at the Collège de France (1900–24), and was a highly original thinker who became something of a cult figure. He contrasted the fundamental reality of the dynamic flux of consciousness with the inert physical world of discrete objects, which was a convenient fiction for the mechanistic descriptions of science. The *élan vital*, or 'creative impulse', not a deterministic natural selection, is at the heart of evolution, and intuition, not analysis, reveals the real world of process and change. His own writings are literary, suggestive and analogical rather than philosophical in the modern sense, and he greatly influenced such writers as **Marcel Proust** (to whom he was connected by marriage), **Georges Sorel** and **Samuel Butler**. His most important works were *Essai sur les Données Immédiates de la Conscience* (1889, Eng trans *Time and Freewill*, 1910), *Matière et Memoire* (1896, Eng trans *Matter and Memory*, 1911), and *L'Evolution Créatrice* (1907, Eng trans *Creative Evolution*, 1911). He was awarded the Nobel Prize for literature in 1927.

BERKOFF, Steven
(1937–)

English dramatist, actor and director. After studying at the École Jacques Lecoq in Paris, he founded the London Theatre Group, for whom he directed his own adaptations from the classics, including **Franz Kafka**'s *Metamorphosis* (1969), in which he himself played the role of the young man who finds himself transformed into a beetle. His own plays include *Greek* (1979), a variant of the Oedipal myth transferred to contemporary London, and *West* (1983), an adaptation of the Beowulf legend; *Decadence* (1981) counterpoints the sexual and social activities of an upper-class couple with that of a working-class woman and a private detective. Other plays and adaptations include *The Penal Colony* (1968), *The Trial* (1970), *Agamemnon* (1963), *The Fall of the House of Usher* (1974), *Sink the Belgrano* (1986) and *Brighton Beach Scumbags* (1991).

BERMANT, Chaim Icyk
(1929–)

British novelist and journalist. He was born in Breslev, Poland, and educated at rabbinical college in Glasgow. After Glasgow University and the London School of Economics he worked as an economist and television scriptwriter before publishing his first novel in 1964, *Jericho Sleep Alone*, an autobiographical account of Orthodox Jewish life in Glasgow. In *Berl Make Tea* and *Ben Preserve Us* (both 1965) he strives too hard for an ironic tone; however, his gift for compassionate observation reappears in the slight but moving *Diary of an Old Man* (1967). In *The Last Supper* (1973), he dissects the tensions and aspirations of a well-off family as it mourns the dead mother. *The House of Women* (1983) stands aside from his usual constituency and analyses another upper middle-class family without the ideological and rhetorical props they and he were accustomed to use in the more overtly Jewish books. Bermant is a close observer of British Jewry, particularly of its upper echelons; *The Cousinhood* (1971) and *The Walled Garden* (1974) are clear-sighted contributions to the sociology of religion and race.

BERNA, Paul (Jean Sabran)
(1910–94)

French children's writer, born in Hyères, and author of the classic *Le Cheval sans tête* (1955, Eng trans *A Hundred Million Francs*, 1957), set in the backstreets of Paris. He worked in administrative jobs in a bank and the Post Office but his children's books are marked by an emphasis on open-air adventure. Most of his stories involve gangs of boys and girls, usually of mixed ages, pitted against a criminal element. Unlike many adventure novels written for the young they have retained their freshness and sense of excitement.

BERNANOS, Georges
(1888–1948)

French writer, born in Paris. He did not begin to write seriously until he was 37 and had taken degrees in law and letters. A Catholic polemicist, he attacked indifference and was preoccupied with problems of sin and grace. His most memorable novels are *Sous le soleil de Satan* (1926, 'Under Satan's Sun') and *Le Journal d'un curé de campagne* (1936, 'The Diary of a Country Priest'). He also wrote a play, *Dialogues des Carmélites* (1949), and *Les grands cimetières sous la lune* (1938, Eng trans *The Fearless Heart*, 1952).
▷G Blumenthal, *The Poetic Imagination of Georges Bernanos* (1965)

BERNARD, Jean-Jacques
(1888–1972)

French novelist and dramatist, born in Enghien-les-Bains, the son of Tristan Bernard (1866–1947), humorist and playwright. Jean-Jacques was the leading exponent of the so-called 'Theatre of Silence', which drew its inspiration from the plays of **Maurice Maeterlinck**. His most famous play was *Le feu qui reprend mal* (1921, Eng trans with four more plays, in *The Sulky Fire*, 1939). In it a soldier returns from the war to a wife grown cold to him—but she remains with him out of pity. He was a classical, anti-rhetorical dramatist, whose work played well and was moderately successful. In France his most highly regarded play is *Martine* (1922, Eng trans 1927, and in *The Sulky Fire*, 1939), about a girl who is seduced and then betrayed by a slick city man. This was memorably filmed in 1944 by Jacques Remy, with a script by **Jules Supervielle**, with Nora Gregor as the unhappy but radiant girl. Bernard wrote a life of his *farceur* father, several good novels and stories, and a moving memory of those French Jews who were imprisoned in the concentration camp at Compiègne: *Le Camp de la morte lente* (1945, 'The Camp of Slow Death'). He was a dramatist whose best (earlier) plays are likely to be revived on a quite large scale.
▷M Daniels, *French Drama of the Unspoken* (1953)

BERNARD, Tristan, originally Paul
(1866–1947)

French novelist and dramatist, born in Besançon. His first success came with the novel, *Les Mémoires d'un jeune homme rangé* (1899, 'Memoirs of a Dutiful Young Man'). In the same year he wrote a comedy, *L'Anglais tel qu'on le parle* ('English as it is Spoken'), and from then on produced a number of light-hearted pieces with stock comic situations, which proved very popular, including *Daisy* (1902), *Triplipatte* (1905), *Le Petit Café* (1911, 'The Small Café') and *Le Prince Charmant* (1921, 'Prince Charming').
▷J J Bernard, *Mon père Tristan Bernard* (1955)

BERNARDES, Diogo
(1532–c.1596)

Portuguese poet, who was with King Sebastian's Moroccan expedition (1578); he was a captive in North Africa until ransomed. A distinguished and influential representative of the Renaissance period, the bulk of his work now has little appeal except to the scholar or historian. However, some of his devotional poetry is exceptional, and he is still much anthologized in his own country.

BERNARDEZ, Francisco Luis
(1900–)

Argentinian poet, who spent his youth in Spain, where he picked up a certain type of *modernista* style. Later he developed into an altogether more interesting poet, a kind of Latin-American **Claudel**, whose techniques and perfervid Catholicism he has imported into Argentinian poetry.

BERNARI, Carlo, pseud of Carlo Bernardi
(1909–)

Italian novelist from Naples, whose views were originally formed under the influence of **Croce**. He was thrown out of school for his anti-fascist attitude. A sojourn with Surrealists such as **André Breton** in Paris in 1930 did not signify a real change of direction. His most important and influential book was the novel *Tre operi* (1934, 'Three Factory Workers'), an anti-fascist study of three workers (two men and a woman), whose real hero, it has been stated, is the Neapolitan language. This, a precursor of the Italian 'neorealistic' movement, was disliked by Mussolini's censors, but not banned. Later Bernari wrote *Speranzella* (1949), a novel of Neapolitan life which won the Viareggio Prize. His journalism has been influential.

BERNART DE VENTADORN, or DE VENTADOUR)
(c.1140–c.1190)

French poet and troubadour, born in Ventadorn, who became the leading *trouvere* of his day. He served in various noble houses, notably that of Eleanor of Aquitaine (who took him to England and knighted him) and that of Count Raimon V of Toulouse. Around 45 of his long poems in Old French survive, several with the melodies to which they were originally sung. He ended his days in a monastery in the Dordogne.

BERNHARD, Thomas
(1931–90)

Austrian novelist and dramatist, born in the Netherlands but raised in Austria by his grandfather, who was a highly eccentric writer called Johannes Freumbichler. Bernhard was unique in world letters, although he had debts to, or affinities with, **Louis-Ferdinand Céline** in particular and, for the construction of his novels, to 12-tone musical theory—of which he made brilliant use. He came very close to death from a lung illness in 1949, but just survived. He was the literary scourge of an Austria which elected the ex-Nazi intelligence officer Kurt Waldheim to its presidency (for which, although no leftist or even democrat, he castigated it), and yet won virtually every prize that could be offered. His misanthropy (which concealed a wistful tenderness) is reminiscent only of Céline, as is his humour. His technique, basically consisting of interior monologues embedded within interior monologues, is very complex, yet his books are compulsively readable. They are all more or less autobiographical. *Frost* (1963), his first success, is an account, by a cantankerous writer very like Bernhard, to a young medical student, of his impressions of the mountain valley to which he has fled. In *Korrektur* (1975, Eng trans *Corrections*, 1979), the protagonist character, Roithamer, is based on the philosopher Ludwig Wittgenstein, whose nephew Paul—who went mad—Bernhard knew well. His, essentially expressionistic, drama, is less profound, but his plays acted as useful shocks to Austrian audiences, who on at least one occasion rioted in order to show their displeasure. The trilogy of autobiographical volumes, *Die Ursache* (1975, 'The Cause'), *Der Keller* (1976, 'The Cellar'), and *Der Atem* (1978, 'The Breath'), is revelatory in its explanation of what has been called his pessimism.

BERNI, or BERNIA, Francesco
(c.1497–1535)

Italian poet, born in Lamporecchio in Tuscany. In 1517 he went from Florence to Rome, where he entered successively the service of his uncle, Cardinal Bibbiena, of Ghiberti, Chancellor to Clement VII, and in 1532 of Cardinal Ippolito de Medici. This he left a year later, and went to Florence, where, refusing to poison Cardinal Salviati, he was himself poisoned. His recast or *rifacimento* of **Boiardo**'s *Orlando Innamorato* (1542) is still read in Italy in preference to the original. He played a large part in establishing Italian as a literary language.
▷A Virgil, *Francesco Berni* (1981)

BERNSTEIN, Henry
(1876–1953)

French writer of initially successful, and sensational, plays, such as *Le Voleur* (1906, 'The Thief'), a thriller with clever and topical dialogue. Later he turned to the portrayal of character, and anticipated **Galsworthy**'s play

Loyalties in *Israel* (1908), an exposure of polite anti-Semitism. He went on writing until his death, but lost favour with his boulevard audiences.

▷B H Clark, *Contemporary French Dramatists* (1916)

BERRY, James
(1924–)

Jamaican-born poet, who moved to Britain in 1948. As an author and anthologist he has made a considerable impact on British poetry while simultaneously establishing himself as a respected authority on Caribbean culture. Collections of his own work include *Fractured Circles* (1979), *Lucy's Letters and Loving* (1982) and *Chain of Days* (1985). His anthologies include *Bluefoot Traveller: An Anthology of West Indian Poets of Britain* (1976) and *News for Babylon* (1984). He has a fine ear for speech rhythms, particularly those of the Caribbean vernacular. His own poetry, while often humorous, is compassionate and moving. He also writes for young people, his collection of stories for children, *A Thief in the Village* (1987), being especially acclaimed.

BERRY, Mary, née Seton
(1763–1852)

English dramatist and woman of letters, born in Kirkbridge in Yorkshire. Her comedy *Fashionable Friends* (1801) was played in Drury Lane, but had only small success. She held conventional opinions, but her *Journals* (edited in 1865) are of interest for the background they provide.

BERRY, Wendell
(1934–)

American poet, novelist and essayist. Growing up in Henry County, Kentucky, he quickly grasped the economic, cultural and racial contradictions of middle America. These form the substance of his finest book, *A Place on Earth* (1967, rev edn 1983) which is set in Kentucky just after World War II, but the unsentimental pastoral strain in his work is even more clearly seen in his verse, notably in *The Broken Ground* (1964), *Farming: A Handbook* (1970), *The Country of Marriage* (1973), the significantly titled *A Part* (1980) and *The Wheel* (1982). All of his verse up to that point was harvested in a *Collected Poems* (1985). *Nathan Coulter* (1960) established the retrospective style of his fiction, sustained in *The Memory of Old Jack* (1974) and *Remembering* (1988), though the latter was less focused than usual. *The Unsettling of America* (1977) gave a straightforward account of the status of US agriculture, but completely avoided bland discursiveness or reactionary pastoralism.

▷*The Hidden Wound* (1970)

BERRYMAN, John
(1914–72)

American poet, biographer, novelist and academic. Born John Allyn Smith in McAlester, Oklahoma, he adopted his stepfather's name at the age of 12. Educated at Columbia University and Clare College, Cambridge, he taught at Wayne State University, Harvard, Princeton, the University of Washington, the University of Connecticut, and University of Minnesota, where he was Regents Professor of Humanities (1955–72). His biography of **Stephen Crane** (1950) is rated highly but his reputation rests on his poetry. Often pigeonholed as a confessional poet he disparaged the label. His first collection, *Poems*, appeared in 1942. This was followed by *The Dispossessed* (1948) and *Homage to Mistress Bradstreet* (1956), inspired by the first New England poet, **Anne Bradstreet**, which established his reputation. His major work is his *Dream Songs*, which he began in 1955: *77 Dream Songs* (1964) won the Pulitzer Prize in 1965; *His Toy, His Dream, His Rest: 308 Dream Songs* (1968) received the National Book Award in 1969. The complete sequence was published in 1969. His other books include the novel *Recovery* (1973), which concerned alcoholism. He acknowledged his illness but could not overcome either it or his increasingly severe mental disturbances. He took his own life in Minneapolis.

▷J Haffenden, *John Berryman* (1982)

BERSHADSKY, Isaiah, pseud of Isaiah Domachevitsky
(1872–1910)

Hebrew novelist, born in Samoscha, who wrote the first truly realistic fiction in the language. He became editor of an important periodical in Vilna. Despite the fame of his work amongst Jewish readers, and its power and psychological acumen, he has not yet found a translator.

▷M Waxman, *A History of Jewish Literature* (1960)

BERTO, Guiseppe
(1914–78)

Italian novelist and dramatist from Mogliano Veneto, near Venice. He fought in World War II and was captured and spent 30 months as a prisoner of war in Texas. His first big success—which he wrote in captivity—was *Il cielo è rossi* (1947, Eng trans *The Sky is Red*, 1948), about the courage and recuperative powers of four children subjected to terrible

bombing raids. This fulfilled all the expectations of the so-called 'neorealistic' novel: it was indebted to American novelists such as **Faulkner**, and it dealt directly with World War II. Later Berto changed direction: *Il male oscuro* (1964, Eng trans *Incubus*, 1966), is about a neurotic who seeks a cure by free association, and is written in a notably avant-garde manner.
▷D Heiney, *America in Modern Italian Literature* (1964)

BERTRAND, Aloysius *see* BERTRAND, Jacques-Louis Napoléon

BERTRAND, Jacques-Louis Napoléon
(1807–41)

French poet, more generally known as Aloysius Bertrand. He was born in Ceva, but his family later settled in Dijon (1815). He is considered a highly significant figure in the development of the French prose poem; *Gaspard de la Nuit* (1842, posthumous) was to influence **Baudelaire**, **Mallarmé**, **Rimbaud** and **Apollinaire**, with its innovative form, and treatment of quintessential Romantic themes such as heightened sensibility, the medieval and the Gothic, and the opposition of the sentimental and the grotesque. Bertrand edited and directed various periodicals between 1828 and 1831, moved to Paris in 1833 and published a volume of poetry, *La Volupté*, in 1834.

BERTRAND, Louis Marie Émile
(1866–1941)

French author, born in Spincourt. He spent some years in Algeria, which provides a setting for *Sang des races* (1898, 'Blood of the People'), *La Cina* (1900), and other realistic novels and travel books. He also wrote historical novels and biographical studies of **Gustave Flaubert** and Louis XIV.

BERTRAND DE BORN
(c.1140–c.1215)

French troubadour and political intriguer, probably born and brought up in Guyenne. His poems encouraged Prince Henry to break with his father, King Henry II of England. Then, following the death of the prince, he supported Henry II and Richard I the Lionheart against the French king, Philippe II. Principally because of his original support for Prince Henry, he is placed by **Dante**, in Canto XXVIII of the *Inferno*, among the 'sowers of schism'.

BERZSENYI, Daniel
(1776–1836)

Hungarian lyric poet, born in Heteny. Educated by his father, he won fame as a patriotic poet with his *Ode to Magyarokhoz*, inspired by the Magyar nobility's successful opposition to Napoleon on the Styrian Alps. Collections of his verse appeared in 1813 and 1830.
▷O Merenyi, *Berzsenyi Daniel* (1966)

BESANT, Sir Walter
(1836–1901)

English novelist and social reformer, brother-in-law of Annie Besant. Born in Portsmouth, he studied at King's College, London, and at Christ's College, Cambridge. After a few years as a professor in Mauritius, he devoted himself to literature. His first work, *Studies in French Poetry*, appeared in 1868. In 1871 he entered into a literary partnership with **James Rice** (1844–82), who was editor of *Once a Week*. Together they produced many novels, including *Ready-Money Mortiboy* (1872), *The Golden Butterfly* (1876) and *The Steamy Side* (1881). He himself wrote *All Sorts and Conditions of Men* (1882) and *Children of Gibeon* (1886), describing conditions in the slums of the east end of London, and other novels advocating social reform, resulting in the establishment of the People's Palace (1887) for popular recreation. He was also the author of biographical studies and works on the history of London. He was secretary of the Palestine Exploration Fund and first chairman of the Incorporated Society of Authors (1884).
▷F W Sage, *Sir Walter Besant, novelist* (1956)

BESTALL, A(lfred) E(dmeades)
(1892–1986)

English illustrator and author, born in Manderlay, Burma. Although Bestall's drawings appeared in many books, including four volumes of the *Boys and Girls Annual* (1935–6), and several issues of the *Tatler* and *Punch*, he is mainly remembered for having illustrated and written the Rupert Bear picture strip in the *Daily Express* newspaper for 30 years (1935–65), taking over from Rupert's creator, **Mary Tourtel**. He also illustrated and wrote 41 volumes of the *Rupert Bear Annual* (1936–76). Rupert's inquisitive, white furry face, red pullover and yellow check trousers and scarf are known to millions through Bestall's drawings.
▷A Bestall and G Perry, *Rupert: A Bear's Life* (1985)

BESTER, Alfred
(1913–87)

American writer, born in New York. He was educated at the University of Pennsylvania, where he studied both humanities and sciences. He won a writing competition with his first science-fiction story, 'The Broken Axiom' (1939). He wrote scripts for radio serials and comic books in the 1940s, and returned to science fiction in 1950. His first novel, *The Demolished Man* (1953), was followed by his classic *Tiger, Tiger* (1956), retitled as *The Stars My Destination* in the USA, a psychologically powerful account of a man driven by inner demons and lust for revenge in a distintegrating 25th-century world. His short stories, collected in four volumes, and novels reveal an unusual degree of psychological and formal complexity for the genre, and he is one of the most individual voices working in science fiction.

BÉSUS, Roger
(1915–)

French novelist and playwright (he wrote a single play: *Savonarole*, 1954) in the tradition of **Bernanos**, born in Bayeux. He is a Catholic, and his characters, usually Normans like himself, are souls torn apart by the battle between good and evil as seen in the novels of Bernanos or **Marcel Jouhandeau**. He is a little neglected both within and outside France (there are no translations); of his work at least *Cet Homme qui vous aimait* (1953, 'That Man You Love') deserves consideration for its psychological penetration of a lacerated Catholic soul.

BETHELL, (Mary) Ursula
(1874–1945)

New Zealand poet, born in England, who started writing in her fifties with verses describing her domestic situation in letters to English friends, published as *From a Garden in the Antipodes* (1929). Her other collections were *Time and Place* (1936) and *Day and Night: Poems 1924–1935* (1939). The posthumous *Collected Poems* (1950) was followed later by a more complete *Collected Poems* ed **Vincent O'Sullivan** (1985). Her work shows a love of nature's delicate detail and a joy in fine words.

BETI, Mongo, pseud of Alexandre Biyidi
(1931–)

French Cameroonian Francophone novelist and essayist. He published his earliest work under the name of Eza Boto. He left his country in 1959, to become a schoolteacher in Rouen; in 1972 he wrote a polemic against its government, which he considered to be the servant of French colonial interests. His first novel to gain attention, and still his best-known work, was *Le pauvre Christ de Bomba* (1956, Eng trans *The Poor Christ of Bomba*, 1971), a vigorous and ironic exposure of colonialism. Beti has since become less overtly political; yet such subtler novels as *La ruine*

presque cocasse d'un polichinelle (1979, 'The Nearly Laughable Fall of a Buffoon'), dramatize oppression and liberation in an ultimately political manner.
▷A C Brench, *The Novelists' Inheritance in French Africa* (1967); W Cartey, *Whispers from a Continent* (1969)

BETJEMAN, Sir John
(1906–84)

English poet, broadcaster and writer on architecture, born in Highgate, London. The son of a Dutch-descended manufacturer of household objects, he was educated at Marlborough College and Magdalen College, Oxford, a period covered by his blank-verse autobiography, *Summoned by Bells* (1960). Incorrigibly indolent, he left university without a degree. He marked time as a cricket master in a preparatory school and was sacked as the *Evening Standard*'s film critic before beginning to write for the *Architectural Review* and becoming general editor of the *Shell Guides* in 1934. He published the bleak 'Death in Leamington' in the *London Mercury* in 1930 and a year later his first collection of verse, *Mount Zion; or In Touch with the Infinite* appeared. Other collections include *Continual Dew; A Little Book of Bourgeois Verse* (1937), *Old Lights for New Chancels* (1940), *New Bats in Old Belfries* (1945), *A Few Late Chrysanthemums* (1954) and *Collected Poems* (1958), of which 100 000 copies were sold of the first edition. Later (but lesser) volumes are *A Nip in the Air* (1972) and *High and Low* (1976). He is the quintessential poet of the suburbs, particular, jolly, nostalgic and wary of change, preferring the countryside to the city. Inveterately self-deprecatory, he described himself as 'the **Ella Wheeler Wilcox** de nos jours', and, in *Who's Who*, as a 'poet and hack'. He was an astute and sensitive social critic, impassioned in his abhorrence of modern architecture and town planning ('Come, friendly bombs, and fall on Slough. It isn't fit for humans now'), and beneath the froth lies a poet undeniably melancholic and serious. A national institution, he succeeded **Cecil Day-Lewis** as poet laureate in 1972.
▷D Stanford, *John Betjeman: a study* (1961)

BETOCCHI, Carlo
(1899–1987)

Italian poet and editor, born in Turin and raised in Florence, whose standing has increased since his death—some have even raised him to the same status of Italy's four greatest modern poets, **Montale**, **Saba**, **Quasimodo** and **Ungaretti**. He worked as an engineer, but was always at the centre of Italian literary life, and acted for many years as editor of the Florentine magazine *Il frontispizio*. He was close personally to **Rébora**, and drew his first inspiration from the 'crepuscular' poetry of **Gozzano**. His debts to Ungaretti and other more modern Italian poets have been much exaggerated, but, a man of broad sensibilities and reading, he was indebted to English poets such as **Shelley** and **Hopkins**. Betocchi's achievement, which received belated acknowledgement with the award of the Viareggio Prize (1955), was highly original within its Italian context. His poetry, deceptively simple, is religious, supple and dedicated to the communication of primary experience: 'his work glows with an inner certainty', a critic has written. There is an English translation in *Selected Poems* (1964).

BETTI, Ugo
(1892–1953)

Italian dramatist and poet, born in Camerino. He studied law and became a judge in Rome (1930–44) and librarian of the Ministry of Justice (1944–53). His collections of verse include *Re pensieroso* (1922, 'The Meditative King'), of short stories *Caino* (1929, 'Cain') and *Le Case* (1937, 'Houses'); in the best of his plays, *La Padrona* (1929), life appears symbolically in the person of a cynical, masterful and attractive woman. His own profession was not spared in *Corruzione al Palazzo di Giustizia* (1944, Eng trans *Corruption in the Palace of Justice*, 1957), and *La fuggitava* (1953, 'The Fugitive').
▷G Moro, *Il teatro di Ugo Betti* (1973)

BEYATLI, Yahya Kemal
(1884–1958)

Turkish poet and critic, a giant in terms of his country's literature, born in Skopje (later Yugoslavia). He was a diplomat and member of parliament. Before the modern era he gained a reputation as a neoclassical poet of great technical excellence; he remained active in Turkish literature until his death, when he was given a massive state funeral.
▷A H Tanipar, *Yayha Kemal* (1962)

BEZA, Theodorus, or THÉODORE DE BÈZE
(1519–1605)

French religious reformer, born of the noble family of De Besze at Vézelay, in Burgundy. He studied Greek and law at Orléans. He became known as a writer of witty (but indecent) verses in *Juvenilia* (1548), settled with brilliant prospects in Paris, and lived for a time in fashionable dissipation. But after an illness, he took a serious view of life, and, marrying his mistress, in 1548 went with her to Geneva, where he joined Calvin; and from 1549 to 1554 was Greek Professor at Lausanne, publishing his only important literary work, a drama on *The Sacrifice of Abraham*. In 1559, with Calvin, he founded the academy at Geneva and became Professor of Theology and first rector there. In 1563 he returned to Geneva from France, and on Calvin's death (1564) the care of the Genevese church fell upon Beza's shoulders. He presided over the synods of French reformers held at La Rochelle in 1571 and at Nîmes in 1572. His best-known work is the Latin New Testament.
▷P F Geisendorf, *Théodore de Bèze* (1949)

BEZRUC, Petr, pseud of Vladimir Vasek
(1867–1958)

Czech workers' poet and (on occasion) revolutionary, whose adopted name means 'Peter Without Hands'; he wrote only one collection, but continually revised it (for, critics say, the worse). A mild postal official by profession, his literary persona was of a rough coal-worker. His regional verse is unusually effective for what it is: a protest on behalf of the Silesian miners and peasants at the way they were being treated. There is a selection of his work by I Milner in *Silesian Songs* (1966).

BHARATI, C Subramania, pseud of C Subramania Iyer
(1882–1921)

Indian (Tamil) translator, seminal essayist, story writer and poet, his language's greatest in modern times. His work is well represented in English translation, but will undoubtedly be reappraised and rendered again. He was the sole Tamil poet of the 20th century to understand that the earlier traditions of Tamil literature must be preserved, but that mere imitation would not do. He was for the last years of his life virtually in exile at Pondicherry (controlled by the French) because of his activities on behalf of the Congress Party. Like **Hagiwara** in Japan, and other similar pioneer poets of other nations, he was the first to enrich his language with the vernacular idiom, without violating its essence. He excelled in the long poem. There are selected translations by himself, with some work composed in English, in *Agni* (1937), and others in *The Voice of a Poet* (1951) and *Selected Verse* (1958); *Poems* (1977) contains his three long poems: *Kannan pattu* (1917, 'The Krishna Songs'), *Pancali capatam* (1912, 'Panchali's Vow') and *Kuyil pattu* (1912, 'Kuyil's Song'), this last being the lyrical dream of a poet who listens to stories told to him by a cuckoo. He translated some of **Tagore** into Tamil.

BHARTRIHARI
(fl.7th century)

Hindu poet and philosopher. He was the author of three *satakas* (centuries) of stanzas

on practical conduct, love, and renunciation of the world, and a Sanskrit grammarian.
▷ *The Proverbial Philosophy of Bhartrihari* (1890)

BHASA
(fl.3rd century)
Sanskrit dramatist. He was the author of plays on religious and legendary themes.
▷ A D Pusalkar, *Bhasa: a study* (1940)

BHATTACHARYA, Bhabani
(1906–)
Indian (Bengali) novelist, educated in Patna and in England, who was much influenced by Gandhi, and wrote a book on him. His best-known and most powerful novel, in English, is *He Who Rides a Tiger* (1954), about an untouchable who poses as a holy man, and who finds success. Critics of an imperialist or conservative cast of mind tried to dismiss Bhattacharya as merely a 'documentary' writer, but may well have been aware of the sharpness of his indictments of British and other governmental corruption. *A Goddess Named Gold* (1960) is a later novel.

BHATTACHARYA, Birendra Kumar
(1924–)
Indian novelist from the Brahmaputra valley, whose Assamese novel *Iyanvingam* (1961) gives a powerful view of events in eastern India prior to and including World War II.

BHAVABHÛTI, surnamed 'Srî-Kantha'
A great Indian dramatist, who flourished in 730.
▷ Vimla Gera, *The Mind and Art of Bhavabhûti* (1973)

BIALIK, Chaim Nachman
(1873–1934)
Hebrew poet, the outstanding figure of his age, born in the Ukraine. After studying the Talmud and becoming a follower of **Mendele Mocher Seforim** in Odessa, he returned to his home near Zhitomir and became a wood merchant, at which he failed disastrously. **Maxim Gorky** helped him to emigrate in 1921 to Berlin, where he established the Devir publishing house. When he went to Palestine in 1924 he took this with him. His poetry is always cast in a personal form, and is often uninhibitedly erotic. He made an influential anthology of the *Aggadah* (folk poetry), and was always looked up to as the natural leader of Hebrew poetry. In translation there is the first volume (only) of *Complete Poetic Works* (1948), and a *Selected Poems* (1965). *Aftergrowth* is a selection of stories.
▷ M Waxman, *A History of Jewish Literature* (1947)

BIALOSZEWSKI, Miron
(1922–)
Polish poet, playwright, memoirist, essayist, whose work resists categorization. As an essayist he is against 'aesthetic values'. His plays were performed, mainly, in his own primitive apartment. 'He is', the sympathetic but perhaps impatient **Czeslaw Milosz** comments, 'fascinated by ugly sibilants and ridiculously jarring sounds.' The following remark exactly sums up his effect upon his superiors: 'in another kind of world he would have won the Nobel prize, but then in such a world there would be no Nobel prizes, since that kind of ' 'hopeless' ' honour would be mocked'. He wishes to return to the 'hopelessness' (again) of medieval Polish. He is a poet of undignified objects, 'dusty staircases, rusty pipes, old stoves, kitchen utensils, mouldy walls'. In one of his (untranslated) plays the characters are 10 fingers intimidated by a comb above them which appears to threaten their existence. They engage in dialogue which mocks philosophical niceties. Yet it is well acknowledged that his anti-eloquent accounts of the Warsaw uprising, through which he lived, are the most poignant and potent of all. Versions of some of his poems are in Milosz's *Post-War Polish Poetry* (1965).

BICHSEL, Peter
(1935–)
Swiss story writer (writing in German), born in Olten. He was given a prize by the German literary circle, Gruppe '47, in 1965. His collection *Frau Blum den Milchmann kenneriernen* (1964, Eng trans *And Really Frau Blum Would Very Much Like to Meet the Milkman*, 1969), consists of tiny stories, as does *Kindergeschichten* (1969, Eng trans *There Is No Such Place as America*, 1970). There is a limit to the interest that can be generated by such miniscule tales, all of whose detail revolves around choice of words, but Bichsel's minimalism and his outspoken criticism of his own people are based on an intelligent and sincere appraisal of what he sees around him.

BICKERSTAFFE, Isaac
(c.1735–c.1812)
Irish playwright, born in Dublin. He was page to Lord Chesterfield, the lord-lieutenant. Later he was an officer of marines, but was dismissed from the service, and in 1772 had to flee the country. Of his numerous pieces, produced between 1760 and 1771, the best known is *The Maid of the Mill*, and he is credited with establishing the comic opera in the English theatre. His musical collaborators included Thomas Arne and Samuel Arnold.

▷P A Tasch, *The Dramatic Cobbler* (1971)

BIELER, Manfred
(1934–)
German novelist, born in Zerbst, in the former East German Republic. He left in 1967 for Munich. His greatest achievement is the picaresque comic novel *Bonifaz* (1963, Eng trans *Bonifaz, or the Sailor in the Bottle*, 1966), about a 'ridiculous man', plainly modelled after the Schweyk of **Hašek**.

BIERBAUM, Otto Julius
(1865–1910)
German novelist, editor (of the influential art magazine *Pan*, which he co-founded, and of a magazine which became the famous publishing house Insel Verlag) and poet, born in Grünberg. His verse, a mixture of the traditional and the light-modern, is now remembered mainly as an important influence upon **Brecht** and other successors of like mind.

BIERCE, Ambrose Gwinnett
(1842–1914)
American short-story writer and journalist, and the **Dr Johnson** of cynicism, compiling the much-quoted *Cynic's Word Book* (published in book form 1906), now better known as *The Devil's Dictionary*. Bierce grew up in Indiana, and fought for the Union in the Civil War, an experience that provided the material for his finest stories. He lived in Britain for three years (1872–5), writing copy for *Fun* and other magazines. He published his first books, collections of brief stories and sketches, under the pseudonym 'Dod Grile'. In 1887, he joined William Randolph Hearst's *San Francisco Examiner* to write the 'Prattle' column, which honed his already sharp style. His most important collection of stories, *Tales of Soldiers and Civilians* (1892), was published at a time of great personal turmoil, during which he divorced, and his son was killed in a gunfight. The most celebrated story, 'An Occurrence at Owl Creek Bridge', is a haunted, near-death fantasy of escape, influenced by **Poe** and in turn influencing **Stephen Crane** and **Hemingway**. Hearst used Bierce as a lobbyist, and Bierce moved to Washington, DC, continuing to work as a journalist there. In 1913 he went to Mexico to report on Pancho Villa's army at first hand. Though the date of his death has been the subject of much romantic uncertainty, it seems probable that he was killed at or shortly after the battle of Ojinaga in January 1914.
▷R O'Connor, *Bierce: A Biography* (1967)

BIERMANN, Wolf
(1936–)
German poet, singer and playwright. He grew up in Hamburg in a socialist family which emigrated to East Germany in 1953. Biermann attended Humboldt University and joined the **Brecht**ian Berliner Ensemble. His own early verse reflected Brecht's militant aesthetics. In 1965 he was censured by the East German authorities and forbidden to perform in public or publish, guaranteeing him a sympathetic audience in the West. His best-known books are *The Wire Harp* (published in English in 1968) and the later and darker *Poems and Ballads* (published in English in 1977).

BIGELOW, John
(1817–1911)
American writer and diplomat, born in Malden, New York. He was co-owner and managing editor of the New York *Evening Post* from 1850 to 1861, when he went as consul to Paris. From 1865 to 1866 he was American minister in France. In 1875 he was elected secretary of state for New York. He published a biography of **Benjamin Franklin** (1874) and edited his works. His son, Poultney (1855–1954), was an international journalist and traveller, and friend of Kaiser Wilhelm II.
▷M A Clapp, *Forgotten First Citizen* (1968)

BIGGERS, Earl Derr
(1884–1933)
American novelist and playwright, born in Warren, Ohio. He was educated at Harvard, and entered journalism as a staff writer on the Boston *Traveller*. He introduced the famous character Charlie Chan in a series of detective novels starting with *The House without a Key* (1925), continuing until *Keeper of the Keys*, which appeared a year before Biggers's death.

BIGONGIARI, Piero
(1914–)
Italian poet, translator (**Ronsard**, **Rilke**, **Conrad**) and critic, born near Pisa. He was one of the minor promoters of Hermeticism, the movement so christened by the critic Francisco Flora. His own poetry has not received a great deal of attention, but, like his first collection, *La figlia di Babilonia* (1942, 'The Daughter of Babylon'), it is programmatically hermetic, and elegantly sealed from the reader.

BIJNS, Anna
(1493–1575)
Dutch poet, from Antwerp in what is now Belgium. Bijns was a schoolteacher and a strongly religious woman who took up writing verse at the behest of the Catholic Church. Many of her poems are responses to the spread of Protestantism in the northern Netherlands, others are simply devotional,

and a few are more earthly love poems. She was the first major woman poet writing in Dutch or Flemish, and is still very highly regarded in Holland and Belgium. *Schoon Ende suverlijc boecken inhoudende veel— constige refereinen* (1987) is a superb facsimile edition, with the original woodcuts and a modern commentary, of her 1528 original.

BILAC, Olavo Braes
(1865–1918)

Brazilian poet, educator and newspaper essayist, born in Rio de Janeiro. In his lush, beautifully executed, highly artificial poetry he crossed Portuguese traditionalism with French Parnassianism. Two of his poems are translated in the *Penguin Book of Latin American Verse* (1971, ed E Curacciolo-Trejo).

BILDERDIJK, Willem
(1756–1831)

Dutch poet and philologist, born in Amsterdam. Crippled as a child, he had talent and intellect, albeit marred by an egotistic, rather than unbalanced, temperament. His voluminous poetry, a blend of rhapsody and neoclassical style, ranges from light verse to epic.
▷H Bavinck, *Bilderdijk als denker en dichter* (1906)

BILLETDOUX, François
(1927–)

French actor and dramatist, born in Paris. His one unequivocal success with critics was *Tchin-Tchin* (1959, Eng trans *Chin-Chin*, 1963), about a couple of betrayed spouses who have an alcoholic affair. This touching play, which has been called both **Chekhov**ian and Absurdist, was successful in London and New York as well as Paris. His later plays, such as *Va donc chez Törpe* (1961, Eng trans *Chez Törpe*, 1963), and the **Brecht**ian exercise *Comment va le Monde, Mòssieu? Il tourne, Mòssieu!* (1964, 'How Goes the World, Mister? It Revolves, Mister!'), have been described variously, as 'pretentious', 'didactic', 'crude' and 'curiously haunting'.
▷J Guicharnaud, *Modern French Theatre* (1967)

BILLINGER, Richard
(1893–1965)

Austrian poet, born in St Marienkirchen. He was the author of collections of lyrics, as well as novels coloured by peasant life in Upper Austria.

BILLINGS, Josh, pseud of Henry Wheeler Shaw
(1818–85)

American humorous writer, born in Lanesboro, Massachusetts. A land agent in Poughkeepsie, New York, he published facetious almanacs and collections of witticisms, relying heavily on deliberate misspelling. The first of these was *Josh Billings, His Sayings* (1866).
▷C Clemens, *Josh Billings, Yankee Humorist* (1932)

BINCHY, Maeve
(1940–)

Irish novelist, playwright and short-story writer, born in Dublin and educated at University College, Dublin. She worked as a teacher and part-time travel writer before joining the *Irish Times* in 1969, later becoming the paper's London correspondent. She has had plays staged in Dublin and won awards in Ireland and Prague for her TV play *Deeply Regretted By* (1979). Her collections of short stories include observations on the lives of Londoners in *Victoria Line, Central Line* (1987) and Dubliners in *Dublin 4* (1982). Her novels include *Light a Penny Candle* (1982), *Firefly Summer* (1987) and *The Copper Beech* (1992). Binchy excels at exploring the private ambitions, joys and anguish of ordinary individuals and families and at evoking everyday life in small communities. Her writing is memorable for its strong female characters and for the depiction of friendships between women.

BINYON, (Robert) Laurence
(1869–1943)

English poet and art critic, born in Lancaster. On leaving Oxford, where he won the Newdigate Prize for poetry, he took a post in the British Museum printed-books department and from 1913 to 1933 was in charge of Oriental prints and paintings. His study *Painting in the Far East* (1908) was the first European treatise on the subject. *Japanese Art* followed in 1909, while other titles, such as *Botticelli* (1913) and *Drawings and Engravings of William Blake* (1922), show the wide range of his cultural interests. Meanwhile he had achieved a reputation as a poet untouched by *fin de siècle* ideas, but strongly in the tradition of **Wordsworth** and **Matthew Arnold**. Beginning with *Lyric Poems* (1894), he issued volumes at intervals up to his *Collected Poems* (1931). His *Odes* (1901) contains some of his best work, challenging comparison with major poets, especially 'The Sirens' and 'The Idols'. He also wrote plays—*Paris and Oenone, Attila, Arthur*—which had successful runs, and his one-act pieces are frequently performed by amateurs. He translated **Dante**'s *Divine Comedy* into terza rima (1933–43), and this discipline shows in his later work. He was Norton Professor of Poetry at Harvard in 1933–4. The poet of affecting melancholy and imaginative reflection, he is forever himself commemorated in his elegy 'For the Fallen' (set to music by Elgar), extracts from which adorn war memorials throughout the British commonwealth.

▷ *A Laurence Binyon Anthology* (1927)

BION
(fl.c.100BC)

Greek poet from Phlossa near Smyrna. He lived in Sicily and wrote 'bucolic' (pastoral) poems traditionally associated with those of **Theocritus** and **Moschus**. His best-known and only substantial extant work (attributed to him in a *Lament for Bion* written by one of his followers) is the 98-line *Lament for Adonis*, a highly emotional elegy in hexameters describing the grief of Aphrodite at the death of her lover. Apart from the *Lament*, only 17 of Bion's pastoral poems have survived, and nothing is known of his life.

BIOY CASARES, Adolfo
(1914–)

Argentinian writer, born in Buenos Aires. His first novel, *Prólogo* (1929, 'Prologue'), established the surreal and metaphysical game-playing with genre forms which has informed his work. He met **Jorge Luis Borges** in 1932, and they collaborated on the stories in *Seis problemas para Don Isidro Parodi* (1942, Eng trans *Six Problems for Don Isidro Parodi*, 1981), writing as 'H Bustos Domecq'. His best-known book is *La invención de Morel* (1940, Eng trans *The Invention of Morel*, 1964), centred upon a search for immortality. A supernatural intervention is at the heart of his novel *El sueño del los héroes* (1954, Eng trans *The Death of the Heroes*, 1973). Other titles include *Plan de evasión* (1945, Eng trans *A Plan for Escape*, 1975) and *Dormir al sol* (1973, Eng trans *Asleep in the Sun*, 1978).

BIRD, Robert Montgomery
(1806–54)

American author, born in Newcastle, Delaware and originally trained as a physician. As well as two successful tragedies, he wrote *Calavar, a Mexican Romance* (1834), *Nick of the Woods* (1837), and other novels.

▷ M M Bird, *The Life of Robert Montgomery Bird* (1945)

BIRGITTA, or BRIDGET, St
(c.1303–c.1373)

One of Sweden's earliest authors. Born in Finsta, Uppland, she was married at the age of 13, gave birth to eight children, and gained considerable political insight through travel and service at the Swedish court. She undertook several pilgrimages, to Trondheim (1338), Santiago de Compostela (1341), and Palestine (1372). Widowed in 1344, she subsequently moved to Rome. Her monastery at Vadstena in Sweden was founded towards the end of her life, and she was canonized in 1391. Her numerous revelations were recorded by her confessors and published in Latin after her death as *Revelationes coelestes* (there is also a 14th-century translation into Swedish). They are characterized by vivid realistic detail and an abundant imagery, frequently inspired by her experiences as a mother, and the *Revelationes* enjoyed a huge international reputation.

▷ 'Själen är av långt bättre natur än kroppen. Om Birgitta av Vadstena', in E Møller Jensen (ed), *Nordisk kvinnolitteraturhistoria*, vol I, *I Guds namn* (1993)

BIRNEY, Earle
(1904–)

Canadian poet, born in Calgary, North West Territories (now Alberta). He was educated at the universities of British Columbia and Toronto. He won the Governor General's Award for two volumes of his poetry, *David* (1942) and *Now is Time* (1945). A collection of his poems was published in 1975, and another, *Ghost in the Wheels* (1977), includes a selection of his work from 1920–76, but neither is definitive, as Birney refutes the notion of poetic finality, often revising extensively with every new imprint: poetry, he observes, is 'an oral entertainment and a visual notation'; a notation which it would seem must reflect the fluidity and mutability of spoken language. In addition to poetry, Birney has written plays, novels, short stories and essays, and is literary editor of a number of Canadian periodicals.

▷ J David (ed), 'Earle Birney Issue' of *Essays on Canadian Writing* (1981); *Perspectives on Earle Birney* (1981)

BIRO, Val (Balint Stephen Biro)
(1921–)

Hungarian-born British illustrator and author for children, born in Budapest. Although Biro's illustrations have brightened many books and dust-jackets, it was not until 1966 that he created his own children's character, that of a vintage car named Gumdrop, modelled on his own 1926 Austin. He made his first appearance in *Gumdrop: the Adventures of a Vintage Car* (1966), and has reappeared in numerous books since, including *Gumdrop Finds A Friend* (1973), in which the car, his owner Mr Oldcastle and his new friend Horace, foil a gang of desperate smugglers.

BIRRELL, Augustine
(1850–1933)

English politician and writer, born in Waver-tree, Liverpool. Educated at Amersham and Trinity Hall, Cambridge, he was called to the Bar in 1875 and was Liberal MP for West Fife (1889–1900) and Bristol North (1906–18). He was President of the Board of Education (1905–7) and put through the 1906 Education Act, was chief secretary for Ireland (1907–16), and founded the National University of Ireland (1908); he resigned after the Easter Rising of 1916. He was the author of delightful volumes of essays, *Obiter Dicta* (1884–7) and *More Obiter Dicta* (1924), whose charm and unobtrusive scholarship inspired the verb 'to birrell' meaning to comment on life gently and allusively, spicing good nature with irony. He also wrote biographies of **Charlotte Brontë** (1887), **William Hazlitt** (1902), and **Andrew Marvell** (1905) for the English Men of Letters series.
▷ *Things Past Redress* (1937)

BISHOP, Elizabeth
(1911–79)

American poet, born in Worcester, Massachusetts. A graduate of Vassar College, she was noted for the precision, elegance and imaginative power of her verse, which often evokes images of nature. She received a Pulitzer Prize for each of her first two collections, *North and South* (1946) and *Cold Spring* (1955). She lived in Brazil from 1952 to 1967, and taught at Harvard from 1970. A *Complete Poems* was published in 1979.
▷ A Stevenson, *Elizabeth Bishop* (1966)

BISHOP, John Peale
(1892–1944)

American poet, fiction writer and essayist, born in Charles Town, West Virginia. He was managing editor of *Vanity Fair* after World War I but joined the exodus of American literati to Paris in 1922. In debt to the 17th-century metaphysical poets, his collections include *Green Fruit* (1917), *Now with His Love* (1933) and *Minute Particulars* (1936). His *Collected Poems* was published in 1948. A year before he died he was appointed consultant in comparative literature at the Library of Congress.
▷ E C Spindler, *John Peale Bishop: a biography* (1980)

BISSETT, bill
(1939–)

Canadian poet, who spells his name in lower case, born in Halifax, Nova Scotia, and educated at Dalhousie University and the University of British Columbia. He is primarily associated with the 'West Coast 60s', the non-conformity of his spelling and grammar and his graphic poetics reflecting his rejection of social restraint and his celebration of the imaginative freedom of the individual. His first collection was *we sleep inside each other all* (1966). Later works include *Selected poems: nobody owns th earth* (sic, 1971) and *beyond even faithful legends* (1980). He has experimented with visual and oral poetic representation, developing a sound poetry that has a mesmeric, meditative effect and an orthographic approach in which line ending is determined by visual rather than rhythmic measure.

BITZIUS, Albert, pseud of Jeremias Gotthelf
(1797–1854)

Swiss author, born in Morat, in Freiburg canton. He studied at Berne, and in 1832 became pastor of Lützelfluh, in Emmenthal, and wrote many novels of Swiss village life, including *Käthi* (1847) and *Uli der Knecht* (1841, Eng trans *Ulric, the Farm Servant*, 1885).
▷ C Guggisberg, *Albert Bitzius* (1935)

BIZCARRONDO, Indalecio
(1831–76)

Basque poet, born in Donostiarra. He used the pseudonym 'Villinch'. He had little education, and so his spontaneity was never impeded. He died in an accident, and his collections of wry, satirical poetry only appeared long after his death.
▷ *El Dia* (1931)

BJELKE-PETERSEN, Marie Caroline
(1874–1969)

Danish-born Australian writer of romantic novels, born in Jagtvejen, Copenhagen. She went to Tasmania with her parents in 1891 and, after some early writing, received attention for her *The Captive Singer* (1917) which was followed by *The Immortal Flame* (1919), *Jewelled Nights* (1924) and much more in a similar vein of romantic religiosity. The latter title was filmed in 1925, starring the Australian actress Louise Lovely, with location scenes shot in Tasmania. Subsequently Bjelke-Petersen's romances became very popular in the USA for their florid style.

BJØRNEBOE, Jens Ingvald
(1920–76)

Norwegian novelist, playwright, poet and essayist, born in Kristiansand. Educated as a painter, he was for many years a teacher at the **Rudolph Steiner** School in Oslo. A main topic throughout his authorship is to unveil and attack authoritarian figures wherever they are to be found; in court, church, prison and school. He does this by consciously using starkly contrasting characters, as in *Jonas* (1955, Eng trans *The Least of These*, 1959), a harsh attack on the Norwegian school system, and in his plays, which in their form show the marked influence of **Brecht**. His main work is usually considered to be the trilogy referred to as *The History of Bestiality*, of which the first volume is *Frihetens øyeblikk* (1966, Eng trans *Moment of Freedom*, 1975). Here Bjørneboe deals—in minute and often nauseating detail—with the problem of evil throughout history.

▷ J Garton, *Jens Bjørneboe—Prophet without Honour* (1985)

BJØRNSON, Bjørnstjerne Martinius
(1832–1910)

Norwegian writer and statesman, winner of the Nobel Prize for literature, born in Kvikne in Österdalen, the son of a pastor. Educated at Molde, Christiania (now Oslo) and Copenhagen, he was a playwright and novelist of wide-ranging interests, a lifelong champion of liberal causes and constantly active politically as a Home Ruler and republican. His first successful drama was *Mellem Slagene* (1856, 'Between Blows'), about the Norwegian civil wars. An ardent patriot, he sought to free the Norwegian theatre from Danish influence and revive Norwegian as a literary language; he worked as a newspaper editor simultaneously with being director of Bergen's Ole Bull theatre (1857–9) and of the Oslo Theatre (1863–7), where he recreated Norway's epic past in saga-inspired dramas such as *Kong Sverre* (1861) and his trilogy about the pretender *Sigurd Slembe* (1862). He was named Norway's national poet, and his poem, *Ja, vi elsker dette landet* (1870, 'Yes, We Love This Land of Ours') became the national anthem. His other major works include the novel *Fiskerjenten* (1868, 'The Fisher Girl'), the epic poem *Arnljot Gelline* (1870), and his greatest plays, *Over Evne I and II* (1893, 1895, 'Beyond One's Powers'), about a clergyman capable of working miracles but incapable of responding to his wife's love. He was awarded the 1903 Nobel Prize for literature.

▷ O Anker, *Bjørnstjerne Bjørnson: the man and his work* (1955)

BJORNVIG, Thorkild
(1918–)

Danish poet, translator (**Rilke**) and critic, born in Århus, Jutland. Influenced by **T S Eliot** and Rilke, he has been thought of as Denmark's 'foremost stylist'. He was the joint editor of one of the country's most important post-war magazines, *Heretica* (1948–50). He also wrote a revealing study of his friend **Karen Blixen**. His poetry is dense and complex, and perhaps a little more concerned with developing procedures than with making statements. Many have found his first volume, *Figur og ild* (1947, 'Figure and Fire') his most urgent.

BLACK, William
(1841–98)

Scottish novelist, born in Glasgow. Educated at the Glasgow School of Art, he moved to London as a journalist and was a war correspondent during the Austro–Prussian War (1866) and the Franco–Prussian War of 1870–1. An early member of the 'Kailyard School', his first success was *A Daughter of Heth* (1871), followed by a succession of stereotypical novels, usually with Highland settings involving an outsider marrying into the community. The landscape and natural phenomena of the region are evoked in colourfully overwritten prose.

▷ Sir Thomas Reid, *William Black, novelist* (1902)

BLACKMORE, Richard Doddridge
(1825–1900)

English novelist, born in Longworth, Berkshire. Educated at Blundell's School, Tiverton, and Exeter College, Oxford, he was called to the Bar at the Middle Temple in 1852, and practised for a while, but poor health made him take to market gardening and literature in Teddington. After publishing several collections of poetry, he found his real bent in fiction. *Clara Vaughan* (1864) was the first of 15 novels, mostly with a Devonshire background, of which *Lorna Doone* (1869) is his masterpiece and an accepted classic of the West Country. Other novels include *The Maid of Sker* (1872), *Alice Lorraine* (1875) and *Tommy Upmore* (1884).

▷ K G Budd, *The Last Victorian* (1960)

BLACKWOOD, Algernon Henry
(1869–1951)

English novelist, born in Kent. He was educated at Wellington and Edinburgh University before working his way through Canada and the USA, as related in his *Episodes before Thirty* (1923). His novels, which reflect his taste for the supernatural and the occult, include *John Silence* (1908), *The Human Chord* (1910), *The Wave* (1916), *Tongues of Fire* (1924), and a volume of short stories, *Tales of the Uncanny and Supernatural* (1949).

BLACKWOOD, Caroline Maureen
(1931–)

Irish writer, born into an aristocratic family in Northern Ireland. An occasional journalist and the co-author (with Anna Haycraft, alias

Alice Thomas Ellis) of a cookery book, *Darling, You Shouldn't Have Gone to So Much Trouble* (1980), she is best known for her complex and often psychologically disturbing novels. *The Stepdaughter* (1976) examines the convoluted relationship between a stepdaughter and a woman whose husband has recently left her, and who discovers that the girl was not, after all, his child. *The Fate of Mary Rose* (1981) is a dark study of the effect of murder on a small rural community. Her characters sometimes appear more than a little eccentric, yet many are genuinely searching for redemption, such as the criminal posing as a disabled charity worker in *Corrigan* (1984), in many ways Blackwood's most haunting book.

▷ M Crosland, *Beyond the Lighthouse: English Women Novelists in the Twentieth Century* (1981)

BLAGA, Lucien
(1895–1961)

Romanian poet and dramatist (translator of **Shakespeare**'s *Richard III* and **Goethe**'s *Faust*) who, unusually in his context, found his initial inspiration in German rather than French poetry: in **Rilke** and **Stefan George**. He was by profession a philosopher. His ironic poetry was metaphysical in style, based on a complex philosophical system in which the 'paradise' of Aristotelian logic was contrasted with an exploration of the 'Luciferian' elements in a 'topography of mysteries'. He would not conform to the socialist realism of the communist regime, and devoted the last years of his life to translation. Now he is much read and discussed.

BLAIR, Robert
(1699–1746)

Scottish poet and preacher, born in Edinburgh. Educated at Edinburgh University, in 1731 he was ordained minister of Athelstaneford, East Lothian. He is best known as the author of *The Grave* (1743), a blank-verse poem which heralded the 'churchyard school' of poetry. The 1808 edition was finely illustrated with rare imaginative power by **William Blake**.

▷ W Row, *The Life of Mr Robert Blair* (1848, ed T McCrie)

BLAIS, Marie-Claire
(1939–)

Francophone Canadian novelist and poet. She wrote her first novel at 18; *La Belle Bête* (1959, Eng trans *Mad Shadows*, 1960) was a sometimes nightmarish portrayal of a stultified childhood in her native Quebec, though the actual location was, typically, ambiguous. *Tête blanche*, which followed (1960), was

more conventional, but *Une saison dans la vie d'Emmanuel* (1965) returned to the darkly lyrical strain. **Edmund Wilson** gave Blais's career a significant boost with a sensitive appreciation in his pioneering *O Canada* (1967). In the later sixties, she published a further sequence of novels with an autobiographical theme: *Manuscrits de Pauline Archange* (1968), *Vivre! Vivre!* (1969, published together as *The Manuscripts of Pauline Archange*, 1970) and *Les Apparances* (1970, Eng trans *Dürer's Angel*, 1976). Later novels have concentrated on the theme of gay and lesbian sexuality, and include the very fine *Les Nuits d'underground* (1978, Eng trans *Nights in the Underground*, 1979). Her verse was published in *Pays voilés* (1963) and *Existences* (1964, translated and collected as *Veiled Countries/Lives*, 1984).

▷ E Wilson, *O Canada: An American's Notes on Canadian Culture* (1967)

BLAKE, William
(1757–1827)

English poet, painter, engraver, and mystic, born in London, the son of an Irish hosier. In 1771 he was apprenticed to James Basire, the engraver, and after studying at the Royal Academy School he began to produce watercolour figure subjects and to engrave illustrations for magazines. His first book of poems, *Poetical Sketches* (1783), was followed by *Songs of Innocence* (1789) and *Songs of Experience* (1794), which include some of the purest lyrics in the English language and express his ardent belief in the freedom of the imagination and his hatred of rationalism and materialism. His mystical and prophetical works include the *Book of Thel* (1789), *The Marriage of Heaven and Hell* (1791), *The French Revolution* (1791), *The Song of Los* (1795), *Vala* and many others, which mostly have imaginative designs interwoven with their text, printed from copper treated by a peculiar process, and coloured by his own hand or that of his wife, Catherine Boucher. Among his designs of poetic and imaginative figure subjects are a superb series of 537 coloured illustrations to **Edward Young**'s *Night Thoughts* (1797) and 12 to **Robert Blair**'s *The Grave* (1808). Among the most important of his paintings are *The Canterbury Pilgrims*, which the artist himself engraved; *The Spiritual Form of Pitt guiding Behemoth* (now in the National Gallery); *Jacob's Dream*; and *The Last Judgment*. Blake's finest artistic work is to be found in the *21 Illustrations to the Book of Job* (1826), completed when he was almost 70, but unequalled in modern religious art for imaginative force and visionary power. At his death he was employed on the illustrations to **Dante**. He is also known as a wood engraver. During his life he met

with little encouragement from the public; but **William Hayley**, John Flaxman, and Samuel Palmer were faithful friends, and by John Linnell's generosity he was in his last days saved from financial worry. All through his life he was upheld by the most real and vivid faith in the unseen, guided and encouraged—as he believed—by perpetual visitations from the spirit-world.
▷J Bronowski, *Blake and the Age of Revolution* (1960); John Beer, *Blake's Visionary Universe* (1969)

BLANCHOT, Maurice
(1907–)

French novelist and essayist, born in Paris. A precursor of the *nouveau roman*, he has written works both of fiction and criticism which espouse an essentially absurdist view of existence. His novels include *Thomas l'Obscur* (1941, rev edn 1950), *L'Arret de Mort* (1948, 'Death Sentence') and *Le dernier Homme* (1957, 'The Last Man'). *L'Espace Littéraire* (1955, 'Literary Space') and *Le Livre a venir* (1959, 'The Book to Come') express his critical outlook on literature in general and the novel in particular. *The Sirens' Song* (1982) and *The Gaze of Orpheus* (1981) are English translations of his essays.

BLANCO FOMBANA, Rufino
(1874–1944)

Venezuelan novelist, politician, publisher (of Latin-American classics in Madrid, while he was in exile) and castigator of North American colonialism. He was imprisoned by the dictator Gómez, and had to leave the country until his death (1935). Called 'mediocre' by critics attached to North American policy towards Venezuela, Blanco Fombana's novels such as *El hombre de oro* (1916, 'The Golden Man'), unfavourably portraying the ruling elite in Venezuela, have also been found excellent—for example, by **Gabriel García Márquez**. *La mitra en el mano* (1927, 'The Mitre in the Hand'), is a novel that offended many Roman Catholics by the outspoken manner in which it portrayed the rise of a crooked and ambitious priest. He was a valuable literary critic, and edited the letters of Bolívar.

BLANCO WHITE, Joseph
(1775–1841)

Spanish poet, editor, writer and, initially, Catholic priest, born in Seville, the son of an Irishman who had practically become a Spaniard. White lost his faith and moved to England to edit a Spanish paper, *El Español* (1810–14), which was intended to stir up feeling against the French, who were then in Spain. He was the author of the famous poem

so admired by **Coleridge**, and still in most school anthologies, 'Sonnet to Night' (1828). White became an Anglican priest and an intimate of **Newman** and Pusey, who learned much from him. He ended as a unitarian. His prose writings have recently been revived by **Juan Goytisolo** and much praised for their understanding of the Moors in Spain. His important and fascinating *Autobiography* appeared in 1845.

BLAUMANIS, Rudolfs
(1863–1908)

Latvian author, born in Latvia, but who died in a Finnish sanatorium of the great scourge of the Baltic of that period, tuberculosis. At first a businessman, whose few writings had been in German, he started to write in Latvian in the early 1890s while working on a Riga newspaper. At the time of his death he had become a leading writer, prized for his delicate stories, poems and rural comedies.
▷V Kalve, *Latvian Literature* (1954)

BLEASDALE, Alan
(1946–)

English dramatist, born in Liverpool. His television play *The Blackstuff* (1980), and the ensuing television series *The Boys From the Blackstuff* (1982), about a group of unemployed Liverpudlians, were an enormous success, and established his reputation for hard-hitting social dramas with a blackly comic, even surreal, edge. *The Monocled Mutineer*, a television series set during World War I, followed in 1986 but was less well received. He enjoyed another success with *GBH* (1990), a TV drama about corruption in local politics. He has written several stage plays, including *Are You Lonesome Tonight?* (1985), a respectful musical about Elvis Presley, and *On The Ledge* (1993), a savage social drama about life in high-rise flats in Liverpool.

BLESSINGTON, Marguerite, née Power, Countess of
(1789–1849)

Irish journalist, novelist, literary hostess and adventuress, born at Knockbrit, County Tipperary. She abandoned her husband, to whom she was sold at 14 by her dissolute father, and when her spouse fell to his death from a window, married the Earl of Blessington, with whom she had been living for some time. After his death from apoplexy in 1829, she became one of Mayfair's most vivacious hostesses, a prolific author, and dreadful debtor. Her entertaining *Journal of Conversations with Lord Byron* appeared in 1832; two travel books, *The Idler in Italy* and *The Idler in France*, followed in 1839 and

1841. She also produced several intermittently engaging three-volume novels of upper middle-class manners, and edited such annual publications as *The Keepsake* and the *Book of Beauty*, volumes containing decorous social advice for young ladies.

BLEST GANA, Alberto
(1830–1920)

Chilean novelist, born in Santiago de Chile. His father was Irish. Despite his poor, often cliché-ridden style and his failure to achieve the stature of his avowed master, **Balzac**, he deserves to be called a master within the context of his country's novel. After a false start with some romantic novels, he published *Martín Rivas* (1862, Eng trans 1918), set in Santiago. He wrote little after 1886, when he took up diplomatic posts abroad—he was Chile's ambassador to both France and England—until 1904, when he published his best novel, *Los transplantados* ('The Transplanted'), about a Chilean girl deceived into marrying an impoverished aristocrat, and taking her own life as a consequence.

BLICHER, Steen Steensen
(1782–1848)

Danish poet and novelist, born in Jutland near Viborg, which forms the background of much of his work. He became a teacher and clergyman, was unhappily married, and took a great interest in the social and spiritual problems of his day. His collection *Traekfuglene* (1838, 'The Migratory Birds'), ranks among the purest of Danish lyrical poetry, with its pervasive note of resignation and sorrow. His short stories, often in dialect, such as 'E Bindstouw', are among the gems of Danish literature.
▷H P B Poulsen, *Steen Steensen Blicher* (1952)

BLIGHT, (Frederick) John
(1913–)

Australian poet, born in Unley, Adelaide. His *A Beachcomber's Diary* (1963) and *Beachcombing Days* (1968) gave him a reputation as 'a poet of the sea'. His complex lyrics capture the landscape and people of his adopted Queensland, such as *The Old Pianist* (1945) and *The Two Suns Met* (1954), but his verse is not restricted to concrete imagery; in *Pageantry for a Lost Empire* (1977) he explores themes such as urban life and the disappointments of age. His *Selected Poems* (1976) won a National Book Council award, and other recognition includes the **Patrick White** Literary Award in 1976.

BLIND HARRY
(fl.1440–92)

Scottish poet, said to have been blind from birth but that assertion has been challenged on the grounds of the pictorial vigour and precise topographical description in his work. He lived by telling tales, and from 1490 to 1492 was at the court of James IV, where he received occasional small gratuities. His major known work is the *Wallace*, on the life of the Scottish patriot William Wallace, written in rhyming couplets. The language is frequently obscure, but the work is written with vigour, and sometimes breaks into poetry. The author appears to have been familiar with the metrical romances, and represents himself as being indebted to the Latin Life of Wallace by Master John Blair, Wallace's chaplain, and to another by Sir Thomas Gray, parson of Liberton. The poem attributes to its hero some of the achievements of Robert Bruce, and contains many mistakes or misrepresentations, but much of the narrative can bear the test of historical criticism.

BLISH, James Benjamin
(1921–75)

American science-fiction writer, born in New York. He was educated at Rutgers University, where he studied microbiology, and later read zoology at Columbia University, but gave up to concentrate on writing. He was active in the science-fiction fan community in his youth, but his writing, while very centrally of the genre, is marked by an unusual seriousness of purpose. His best work includes the 'Okie' stories, collected as *Cities in Flight* (1970), in which mankind seeks a future among the stars, and the metaphysical 'After Such Knowledge' trilogy. His interest in 'soft' sciences is also reflected in the biological and genetic themes of *The Seedling Stars* (1957). He wrote a number of novelizations in the *Star Trek* series, and was an important critic and theorist as well as practitioner of science fiction.
▷D Ketterer, *Imprisoned in the Tesseract: The Life and Work of James Blish* (1988)

BLIXEN, Karen, Baroness, pseud Isak Dinesen
(1885–1962)

Danish story-teller and novelist, born in Rungsted. She was educated at home and in France, Switzerland and England and she adopted English as her main literary language, translating some of her most important works back into Danish. In 1914 she married her cousin, Baron Bror Blixen Finecke, from whom she contracted syphilis. Their life on an unproductive coffee plantation in Kenya is recounted in *Den Afrikanske Farm* (1937,

Eng trans *Out of Africa*, 1938), which was also the basis of a Hollywood film. After her divorce and the death of her lover Denys Finch-Hatton in a plane crash, she returned to Denmark and began writing the brooding, existential tales for which she is best known. Like the singer in 'The Wide-Travelling Lioness' (*Seven Gothic Tales*, 1934, Danish translation, 1935) they are usually concerned with identity and personal destiny, and are markedly artistocratic in spirit. This is confirmed in *Winter's Tales* (1942), *Last Tales* (1957) and *Anecdotes of Destiny* (1958) 'Babett's Feast' (1950), also successfully filmed, shows a lighter side to her artistic nature.
▷J Thurman, *Isak Dinesen: the Life of a Storyteller* (1982)

BLOCH, Jean-Richard
(1884–1947)

French novelist, playwright and critic. A polemicist for communism, his reputation is based on his novel *Et Compagnie* (1918, '& Co.'), which belongs to the school of realistic writing derived from **Émile Zola** and **Pierre Hamp**.
▷P Abraham, *Les trois frères* (1971)

BLOCH, Robert Albert
(1917–92)

American writer of suspense and science fiction, whose authorship of *Psycho* (1959) has largely been eclipsed by Alfred Hitchcock's auteurism. Bloch's early work was influenced by the highly mannered macabre tone of **H P Lovecraft**, but gradually became more relaxed and paced. His first novel, *The Scarf* (1947, also published as *The Scarf of Passion*, 1948), was the chillingly plain monologue of a serial strangler. He published no more books until *The Kidnapper* (1954), another impressively internalized tale of violence. *Psycho* established his reputation and has retained its power to shock, even though its effects work more slowly than Hitchcock's heart-stopping *coups de cinema*. In the sixties, Bloch continued to explore criminal and aberrant minds, with a style now unashamedly tailored to a movie audience. *Psycho II* (1982) was inevitably a disappointment, and *American Gothic* (1974) and *The Night of the Ripper* (1984) seemed to return to Lovecraftian material without the elaborate word-play.

BLOEM, Jacobus Cornelis
(1887–1966)

Dutch poet and critic, born in Oudshoorn. His pessimistic and well-made poetry, reminiscent of **Housman**, is treated with great respect in Holland. Rather too much the craftsman at the expense of breadth of theme,

Bloem was a gifted essayist and exponent of the work of other Dutch poets.

BLOK, Alexander Alexandrovich
(1880–1921)

Russian poet, born in St Petersburg. In 1903 he married the daughter of the famous chemist, Mendeleyev. His first book of poems, *Stikhi o Prekrasnoy Dame* (1904, 'Songs about the Lady Fair'), was influenced by the mysticism of **Vladimir Soloviev**, a **Tolstoy**an vision of reality beyond appearances, where truth is embodied in ideal womanhood. In *Nochnye Chasy* (1911, 'Nocturnal Hours') the ideal has given way to the realism of city squalor. He welcomed the 1917 Revolution and in 1918 wrote two poems, *Dvenadtsat* (Eng trans *The Twelve*, 1920), a symbolic sequence of revolutionary themes, and *Skify* ('The Scythians'), an ode, inciting Europe to follow Russia. He was soon disillusioned, however, and suffered greatly in the hard times which followed the Revolution. Other works include the romantic verse drama *Roza i Krest* (1922, 'The Rose and the Cross').
▷A Ashukin, *Aleksandr Blok* (1923)

BLOOM, Ursula
(20th century)

English novelist, born in London. Whether published under her own name or the pseudonym Deborah Mann, her output tends to be traditional, written from the viewpoint of a particular female character; it often verges on mainstream romance, but is informed by a more subtle sensibility than generally typifies the genre. *A Woman Called Mary* (1966), originally published under the pseudonym, is a version of the Gospel events through the eyes of Mary Magdalene. The 1976 publication *The Turn of Life's Tide* ('Madeleine would never forget the mixed emotions of that strange day when her husband died') is a contemporary account of one woman's reaction to bereavement.

BLOOMFIELD, Robert
(1766–1823)

English poet, born in Honington, near Bury St Edmunds, the son of a farm worker. A shoemaker's apprentice, he wrote *The Farmer's Boy* in a garret. Published in 1800 with the assistance of Capell Lofft, it proved very popular. He subsequently published *Rural Tales* (1802) and *Wild Flowers* (1806), was given a small allowance by the Duke of Grafton, but half-blind, died in poverty.
▷W Wickett and N Duval, *The Farmer's Boy* (1971)

BLOUET, Paul, pseud **Max O'Rell**
(1848–1903)

French author, born in Brittany. He served in the Franco–German war and fought against the Commune, being severely wounded. In 1873 he went to England as a newspaper correspondent, and was French master at St Paul's School (1876–84). From 1887 he lectured in Britain, the USA, and the British colonies. His works include *John Bull et son île* (1883, Eng trans *John Bull and his Island*, 1884) and *Un Français en Amérique* (1891, Eng trans *A Frenchman in America*, 1891)— both translations published under the author's pseudonym.

BLOY, Léon Marie
(1846–1917)

French author, born in Périgeux. He wrote novels, essays, and religious and critical studies with a strong Roman Catholic bias, containing bitter castigation of political and social institutions. This made him unpopular in his day but has contributed to the revival of interest in his works in the second half of the 20th century. His *Le Désespéré* (1886, 'The Desperate Man') and *La Femme pauvre* (1897, 'The Poor Woman') are autobiographical; other books include *Le Pélerin de l'absolu* (1914, 'On a Pilgrimage to the Absolute'). His journal, which relates the spiritual and mystical conversions of his later life, was published in 1924.
▷R Heppenstall, *Léon Bloy* (1953)

BLUEBUSH *see* **BOURKE, John Philip**

BLUM, Léon
(1872–1950)

French statesman, several times socialist prime minister of his country, who began his career as a literary critic of some influence. Blum was born in Paris into a Jewish family. He worked on magazines with **Proust** and most of the other leading authors and editors of his day. He wrote a play, *La Colère* (1902, 'Anger'), and as a theatre critic took up the cause of contemporary theatrical innovators. His *Nouvelles Conversations de Goethe avec Eckermann* (1901, 'New Conversations Between Goethe and Eckermann'), published anonymously, was his most influential work. In it he elevated the role of the non-creative critic, as a fruitful synthesizer of ideas. After World War I he turned to political writings. His literary importance lay in his transmission, to French writers, of the humanist ideas of Lucien Herr (librarian at the École Normale), who had helped convert Blum's mentor **Jean Jaurès** to socialism.

BLUME, Judy
(1938–)

American novelist. Perhaps the most controversial and certainly the most popular contemporary American writer for teenagers, she was born in New Jersey. Her first published book was *The One in the Middle is the Green Kangaroo* (1969), but her third book, *Are You There, God It's Me, Margaret* (1970), brought acclaim for her candid approach to the onset of puberty and for her natural, if unsubtle, style. As with subsequent books, attempts were made to restrict its circulation. Her explicitness brought her into conflict with parents, but she has a remarkable rapport with her readers and dares to confront subjects which previously were ignored. Her books include *Then Again, Maybe I Won't* (1971), *It's not the End of the World* (1972), *Deenie* (1973), *Blubber* (1974) and *Forever* (1975).

BLUNCK, Hans Friedrich
(1888–1961)

German novelist, poet and folklorist, born in Altona. After studying law he was successively propagandist, university official and farmer. Steeped in the folklore of the North German plain, Blunck's writings lent colour to the racial theories of National Socialism. His poetical works include *Sturm überm Land* (1915, 'Storm Over the Land'), *Der Wanderer* (1925, 'The Wanderer'), *Erwartung* (1936, 'Expectation'), and his novels *Werwendes Volk* (1933) and *Die Urvätersaga* (1934, 'Saga of the Forefathers'). He published his autobiographical *Unwegsame Zeiten* ('Pathless Times') in 1953.
▷C Jenssen, *Hans Friedrich Blunck* (1935)

BLUNDEN, Edmund Charles
(1896–1974)

English poet and critic, born in London. His family soon moved to Kent, and he was educated at Christ's Hospital and Queen's College, Oxford. He served in France in World War I and won the MC. He was Professor of English Literature at Tokyo (1924–7), fellow of Merton College, Oxford, from 1931, joined the staff of the *Times Literary Supplement* in 1943, returned to the Far East and from 1953 lectured at the University of Hong Kong. He was professor at Oxford from 1966 to 1968. A lover of the English countryside, he is essentially a nature poet, as is evident in *Pastorals* (1916) and *The Waggoner and Other Poems* (1920), but his prose work *Undertones of War* (1928) is perhaps his best. Other works include *The Bonadventure* (1922), on his visit to America, a biography of Leigh Hunt, and books on **Charles Lamb** and **Keats**. He also edited **John Clare**, **Christopher Smart**, **Shelley**, **Keats** and **Collins**.

BLUNT, Wilfrid Scawen
(1840–1922)

English poet and traveller, born in Petworth, Sussex. Educated at Stonyhurst and Oscott, he served in the diplomatic service (1859–70), and published his first volume of poems, *Sonnets and Songs by Proteus* (1875). He travelled in the Near and Middle East, espoused the cause of Arabi Pasha and Egyptian nationalism (1882), stood for parliament and was imprisoned in 1888 for activity in the Irish Land League. While in prison, he wrote the sonnet sequence *In Vinculis* (1899). He wrote fierce political verse and charming love poems, and bred Arab horses. In 1858 he married Lady Anne Isobel Noel, who shared his travels and love of Arab horses.
▷M J Reinehr, *The Writings of Wilfrid Scawen Blunt* (1940)

BLY, Robert
(1926–)

American poet, critic, translator and editor, born in Madison, Minnesota. As a critic he is caustic, but his targets are legitimate. For a man so aware of foreign literature (he has translated **Pablo Neruda**, **Knut Hamsun** and **Selma Lagerlöf**, among others), his poetry is surprisingly American in tone and locale, often dealing with the space and silences of his home state. His first collection was *Silence in the Snowy Fields* (1962), followed by *The Shadow-Mothers* (1970), *Sleepers Joining Hands* (1972) and *Talking All Morning* (1980). In 1991 he published a controversial study of maleness and its discontents, called *Iron John*.
▷H Nelson, *Robert Bly: An Introduction to the Poetry* (1984)

BLYTON, Enid Mary
(1897–1968)

English children's author, born in London. She trained as a Froebel kindergarten teacher, then became a journalist, specializing in educational and children's publications. In 1922 she published her first book, *Child Whispers*, a collection of verse, but it was in the late 1930s that she began writing her many children's stories featuring such characters as Noddy, the Famous Five, and the Secret Seven. She edited various magazines, including *Sunny Stories* and *Pictorial Knowledge* for children, and *Modern Teaching*, and was part-author of *Two Years in the Infant School*. She identified closely with children, and always considered her stories highly educational and moral in tone, but has recently been criticized for racism, sexism and snobbishness, as well as stylistic inelegance and over-simplicity. She published over 600 books, and is one of the most translated British authors. Her works also include school readers and books on nature and religious study.
▷B Stoney, *Enid Blyton: a biography* (1974)

BOBROWSKI, Johannes
(1917–65)

German short-story writer, novelist and poet, born in Tilsit and brought up in Memel (now Sovetsk and Klaipeda respectively, both in Lithuania). The land of his youth saw the harmonious intermingling of ethnic groups, and the bulk of his work expresses a longing for that past. A soldier on the eastern front during World War II, he was captured by the Soviets and remained a prisoner of war until 1949, when he went to live in East Berlin. His novels *Levins Mühle* (1964, 'Levin's Mill') and *Litauische Klaviere* (1966, 'Lithuanian Pianos') are both examinations of that intractable problem, the nature of German nationalism.

BOCAGE, Manoel Barbosa du
(1765–1805)

Portuguese lyric poet, born in Setubal. He served in the army and the navy, sailed in 1786 to India and China, returning to Lisbon in 1790, where, recognized as a poet, he joined the literary coterie *Nova Arcadia*, only to be expelled from their number in 1794 for his unorthodox views. He was jailed for anticlericalism in 1797, and released two years later after 'treatment' at the hands of the Inquisition. He is essentially a romantic, but his sonnets are classical in form. He often satirizes, as in *Pina de Talião* ('Talião's Pine Cone').
▷R Correia, *Bocage: cronica dramatica e grotesca* (1965)

BOCCACCIO, Giovanni
(1313–75)

Italian writer, born in Tuscany or Paris. He was the illegitimate son of a merchant of Certaldo, who launched him on a commercial career. He soon abandoned commerce and the study of canon law, and at Naples (1328) he turned to story-writing in verse and prose, mingled in courtly society, and fell in love with the noble lady whom he made famous under the name of Fiammetta. Until 1350 he lived alternately in Florence and Naples, producing prose tales, pastorals, and poems. The *Teseide* ('Book of Theseus') is a graceful version in *ottava rima* of the medieval romance of Palamon and Arcite, which was partly translated by **Chaucer** in the *Knight's*

Tale. The *Filostrato*, likewise in *ottava rima*, deals with the loves of Troilus and Cressida, also in great part translated by Chaucer. After 1350 he became a diplomat entrusted with important public affairs, and a scholar devoted to the cause of the new learning. During this period, in which he formed a lasting friendship with **Petrarch**, he visited Rome, Ravenna, Avignon, and Brandenburg as Florentine ambassador. In 1358 he completed his great work, the *Decameron*, begun some 10 years before. Boccaccio selected the plots of his stories from the floating popular fiction of the day, and especially from the *fabliaux* which had passed into Italy from France, the matter being medieval, while the form is classical. Boccaccio's originality lies in his consummate narrative skill, and in the rich poetical sentiment which transforms his borrowed materials. For some time he held a chair founded to expound the works of **Dante**, on whose *Divina Commedia* he produced a commentary. During his last years he lived principally in retirement at Certaldo, and would have entered into holy orders, moved by repentance for the follies of his youth, had he not been dissuaded by Petrarch. He wrote in Latin an elaborate work on mythology, *De genealogia deorum gentilium* ('The Genealogies of the Gentile Gods'), and treatises such as *De claris mulieribus* ('Famous Women') and *De Montibus* ('On Mountains').

▷ V Branca, *Boccaccio: the man and his works* (1976)

BOCCAGE, Marie Anne Fiquet du, née Le Page
(1710–1802)

French poet, born in Rouen. Her *Paradis terrestre* (1748, 'Earthly Paradise'), an imitation of **Milton**, and *La Colombiade* (1756), gave her an exaggerated fame, perhaps on account of their author's great beauty, but her letters to her sister, written while travelling through England, Holland, and Italy, have historical interest.

BOCK, Jerry *see* ABBOTT, George Francis

BODELSEN, Anders
(1937–)

Danish novelist and journalist, born in Copenhagen, where he later attended university. A prolific author, he has put the suspense novel firmly on the literary agenda as a forum for social, psychological and moral investigation, and his skill in depicting the climate of post-war Denmark has secured him large audiences. The thriller *Tænk på et tal* (1968, 'Think of a Number') gave him his popular breakthrough and has been filmed and translated into many languages. It elegantly narrates the story of a bank clerk who aims to cheat a bank robber, thus raising the question of who is the victim and who is the culprit— a theme central in Bodelsen's crime fiction. He frequently focuses on the paradoxical attachment and similarity between the hunter and the hunted, the blackmailer and the blackmailed, as in, for example, *Pengene og livet* (1976, 'Money and Life') and *Mørklægning* (1988, 'Blackout'). A 'state-of-the-nation' novelist, Bodelsen has frequently chosen to set his novels in the Denmark of the 1960s and beyond, but has also taken on all decades from the 1930s onwards, and even reflected on the future, with the science-fiction novel *Frysepunktet* (1971, 'Freezing Point').

BODENHEIM, Maxwell
(1893–1954)

American poet and novelist. After moving to Chicago and then New York, he was jailed for desertion from the army, and later was suspected of Communist Party membership. He never fulfilled his potential, though his verse is often powerful and his fiction powerfully advocated. Supporting Modernism in his criticism of the early 1920s, he wrote in a highly coloured style that combined strong images with a genuine feel for social problems. *Introducing Irony* (1922) was a collection of stories and poems; *Against This Age* and *The Sardonic Arm* (both 1923) marked his peak as a poet. Later, he managed to write a novel a year, the best of them being *Ninth Avenue* (1926), *Georgie May* (1928), the story of a run-down prostitute, and *Slow Vision* (1934), a much under-rated novel of the Depression which was to be his last prose book. He experimented with jazz forms in verse, but his *Selected Poems, 1914–1944* (1946) shows little tendency to fall prey to literary fashions. Inactive long before his death, he became a personage rather than a creator, and Sam Roth's ghosted *My Life and Loves in Greenwich Village* (1954) fed the myth posthumously. In February 1954, Bodenheim and his third wife were murdered.

▷ J B Moore, *Bodenheim* (1970)

BODENSTEDT, Friedrich Martin von
(1819–92)

German writer, born in Peine in Hanover. He lived for a while in Moscow, travelled in the Middle East, was a professor at Munich University (from 1854) and director of the Meiningen court theatre (1867–73). He translated into German many Russian, English, and Persian texts, and published poetry. His best-known work is *Lieder des Mirza Schaffy*

(1851, 'Songs of Mirza Schaffy'), alleged to be a translation from the Tartar.

BODTCHER, Ludvig Adolph
(1793–1874)

Danish poet, born in Copenhagen. He lived for 11 years in Rome, where he associated with Danish artists, especially the sculptor Bertel Thorvaldsen. He was a graceful minor romantic poet, whose work in *Digte* (1856, 'Poems') is still read.

BOETHIUS, Anicius Manlius Severinus
(c.480–524)

Roman philosopher and statesman, sometimes described as 'the last of the Roman philosophers, the first of the scholastic theologians'. Born of a patrician Roman family, he studied at Athens and there gained the knowledge which later enabled him to produce the translations of and commentaries on Aristotle and Porphyry that became the standard textbooks on logic in medieval Europe. He became consul in 510 during the Gothic occupation of Rome and later chief minister to the ruler Theodoric; but in 523 he was accused of treason and after a year in prison at Pavia was executed. It was during his imprisonment that he wrote the famous *De consolatione philosophiae*, in which Philosophy personified solaces the distraught author by explaining the mutability of all earthly fortune and demonstrating that happiness can be attained only by virtue, that is by being like God. The *Consolation* was for the next millennium probably the most widely read book after the Bible.
▷H H Patch, *The Tradition of Boethius* (1935)

BÖEX, Joseph and Séraphin *see* ROSNY

BOGAN, Louise
(1897–1970)

American poet and short-story writer, born in Livermore, Maine. She began writing in high school and first published a collection of verse, *Body of this Death*, in 1923. She published comparatively few works, but enough of sufficient quality to be considered a 'poet's poet'. Her writing is a sometimes erotic celebration of, and often disillusioned lament for, romantic love. Her two marriages and other relationships with men led her to believe that love almost always ends in acrimony and betrayal. While editions of her collected poetry were published in 1941 and 1954, *The Blue Estuaries* (1968) is the definitive volume, all 105 poems having been selected by the author herself as those by which she wished to be remembered.
▷*Journey Around My Room* (ed R Limmer, 1980)

BÖHME, Jakob
(1575–1624)

German mystical writer and alchemical thinker, born near Görlitz. For many years a cobbler, he exercised as incalculable an influence on literature—in particular on **Goethe**, and on romantic thinkers such as Hamann, Hegel, Schelling and, later, **Jung**—as he did on the course of individualistic religion. Isaac Newton too studied his writings. He has been called both dualist and pantheistic, and there are, quite certainly, profoundly gnostic elements in his wild but seminal thinking. He was therefore persecuted, and from 1618 forbidden to publish (that is, to circulate his writings). He is the chief heir of **Meister Eckhart**, and of Paracelsus. Creation, for Böhme, arises from 'Nothing', which directs its will to 'Everything'. He regarded God, 'Nichts' and 'Ungrund' ('Nothing' and 'bottomlessness'), as possessing both love and anger, and therefore as containing the seeds of both good and evil: God dwells in nature as the soul lives in the body of man. Man's character is determined by the map of the heavens at the time at which his body is formed. His style (like that of Jung) is, because he dealt in paradoxes, obscure and even confused, but vigorous and spiritually provocative. His influence is most directly seen in the poetry of **Angelus Silesius**. All his writings have been translated, some of them many times.
▷S Hobhouse, *Jakob Böhme, His Life and Teaching* (1950)

BOIARDO, Matteo Maria, Count of Scandiano
(?1441–1494)

Italian poet, born in Scandiano, a village at the foot of the Lombard Apennines. He studied at Ferrara, and in 1462 married the daughter of the Count of Norellara. He lived at the court of Ferrara on intimate terms with Dukes Borso and Ercole; by the latter he was employed on diplomatic missions, and was appointed governor in 1481 of Modena, and in 1487 of Reggio. As an administrator he was distinguished for his clemency, and opposition to capital punishment. Boiardo has been called the 'Flower of Chivalry'. His early lyric poems in *Canzioniere* were inspired by a woman, Antonia Caprara, whom he met in 1469. His fame rests on the unfinished *Orlando Innamorato* (1486), a long narrative poem in which the Charlemagne romances are recast into *ottava rima*. His other works comprise Latin eclogues, a versification of **Lucian**'s *Timon*, translations of **Herodotus**, the *Ass* of Lucian, and the *Golden Ass* of

Apuleius, and a series of sonnets and *Canzoni* (1499).

▷G Reichenbach, *Matteo Maria Boiardo* (1929)

BOILEAU, or BOILEAU DESPRÉAUX, Nicolas
(1636–1711)

French poet and critic, born in Paris. He studied law and theology at Beauvais, but as a man of means devoted himself to literature. His first publications (1660–6) were satires, some of which got him into trouble. In 1677 the king appointed him, along with **Racine**, official royal historian. *L'Art poétique* ('The Art of Poetry'), imitated by **Pope** in the *Essay on Criticism*, was published in 1674, along with the first part of the clever serio-comic *Lutrin* ('Lectern'). Between 1669 and 1677 he published nine epistles, written, like his satires, on the Horatian model. In his last years he returned to Auteuil. His works include several critical dissertations, a collection of epigrams, a translation of Longinus's *On the Sublime*, a *Dialogue des héros de roman* ('A Conversation between the Heroes of Novels'), and a series of letters (many to Racine). His influence as a critic has been profound. He set up good sense, sobriety, elegance, and dignity of style as the cardinal literary virtues.

▷J E White, *Nicolas Boileau* (1969)

BOISROBERT, François de Métel, Sieur de
(1592–1662)

French dramatist, translator and professional buffoon, born in Caen. He was employed by the French prelate and statesman Cardinal Richelieu to provide entertainment at court. The author of the play *La Belle Plaideuse* (1654, 'The Beautiful Litigant'), which provided **Molière** with a scene, he was also—like **Corneille**—one of Richelieu's *cinq auteurs*, employed by the Cardinal to put his own ambitious theatrical theories into practice, and an original member of the Académie française.

BOITO, Arrigo
(1842–1918)

Italian composer and poet, born in Padua. He studied at the Milan Conservatory. His first important work was the opera *Mefistofele* (1868), which survived its initial failure and later grew in popularity. Thereafter he concentrated mainly on writing libretti, the best-known of which are those for Verdi's *Otello* and *Falstaff*. Another opera, *Nerone*, written in 1916, was not produced till 1924.

▷P Nardi, *Vita di Arrigo Boito* (1944)

BOJER, Johan
(1872–1959)

Norwegian novelist, playwright and short-story writer, he grew up in a poor rural family at Orkdalsøyra, and though he maintained great affection for that background, he became a lifelong progressive. *Den store hunger* (1916, Eng trans *The Great Hunger*, 1918) holds up technological development as the key to survival, but then recognizes the need for a supra-rational dimension to life. His novels of the 1920s recount the struggles of the rural poor; *Den siste viking* (1921, Eng trans *Last of the Vikings*, 1923) is the best, but *Vor egen stamme* (1924, Eng trans *The Emigrants*, 1925) and *Folk ved sjøen* (1929, Eng trans *Folk by the Sea*, 1931) are almost equally strong. The use of dialect established him as an important national figure.

▷C Gad, *Johan Bojer: The Man and His Works* (1974)

BOKER, George Henry
(1823–90)

American poet, playwright, and diplomat, born in Philadelphia. He won belated recognition for his 400 sonnets and for *Francesca da Rimini* (1855), a romantic verse tragedy and the best American play before the Civil War. His propaganda for the North secured him the post of minister to Turkey (1871–5) and Russia (1875–8).

▷E S Bradley, *George Henry Boker: poet and patriot* (1927)

BOLAND, Eavan
(1944–)

Irish poet and critic, born in Dublin and educated there, in London and in New York. From *New Territory* (1967) onwards she became a poetic commentator on the 'frail compasses and trenchant constellations' that she sees as constituting suburban Irish lives in the style-conscious second half of the 20th century. Her experience of motherhood lent deep emotion to *Night Feed* (1982) and her subsequent combination of intellectualism and feminism led to the award-winning *Outside History* (1990), which represented a significant step forward for women writing from within a male-dominated Irish culture.

BOLD, Alan
(1943–)

Scottish poet, biographer, critic and editor, born in Edinburgh. He was educated at Broughton High School, where he showed signs of the rebelliousness which was to mark his early poetry, and went on to Edinburgh University. After a variety of jobs, including journalism, he became a full-time writer in 1967. A prolific writer and anthologizer, he has been a particularly influential commentator on **Hugh MacDiarmid**, and his biography of the poet won the McVitie Scottish Writer of the Year Award in 1989. He has published several volumes of poetry in both English and Scots, including *In this Corner: Selected Poems 1963–83*, which traces the development in his work from an initial angry humanism into a more cooly-observed scrutiny of the natural world and of the society which surrounds him. He is a trenchant and combative literary commentator.

BOLDREWOOD, Rolf, pseud of **Thomas Alexander Browne**
(1826–1915)

Australian novelist, born in London. His family emigrated to Australia in 1830. He was educated in Sydney, and became a squatter in Victoria. After a series of misadventures and some years as an inspector of goldfields, he started writing serials for Australian periodicals in order to pay his debts. One, 'The Squatter's Dream' (1875), echoed Boldrewood's own misfortunes and was published as *Ups and Downs* (1878, rev edn *The Squatter's Dream*, 1890). His success was confirmed by *Robbery Under Arms*, the bushranging adventure with which his name is permanently associated. Serialized in the *Sydney Morning Herald* in 1882, it was not published until 1888 (rev edn 1889). There followed in the next 20 years a considerable number of novels in similar vein, set in Australia or New Zealand, many written from personal experience, among which were *A Colonial Reformer* (1890), *A Sydney-Side Saxon* (1891) and *A Romance of Canvas Town* (1898).
▷A Brissenden, *Rolf Boldrewood* (1972)

BOLGER, Dermot
(1959–)

Irish novelist and playwright, born in Dublin, the city which provides the background to much of his work. His first novel, *Night Shift* (1986), was quickly followed by *The Woman's Daughter* (1987), *The Journey Home* (1990) and *Emily's Shoes* (1992). His plays include *The Lament for Arthur Cleary* (1989). Bolger is in the forefront of younger Irish writers who, rather than present Dublin as a place of amiable eccentrics and affable rogues, portray it as a mean, often violent city, corrupted and degraded by drugs and by political and criminal rivalries. In his work it appears as a place where love and compassion are coarsened, thriving only in those tenacious enough to overcome the odds against them.

BOLITHO, Hector
(1898–1974)

New Zealand biographer, novelist and historian, who moved to England at the age of 24, having struck up an acquaintance with the then Prince of Wales. Self-characterized as 'second-rate', he was an unofficial 'court biographer' who wrote more than a score of polite accounts of royalty, of which the most successful was the pallid and inaccurate *Edward VIII: His Life and Reign* (1937). He was selected by the daughter of **Rudyard Kipling** to write his 'official' biography, but could not abide her terms. His novels include *Solemn Boy* (1927).

BOLITHO, William, pseud of **William Bolitho Ryall**
(1890–1930)

South African author, a much-prized—and still reprinted—writer on crime, famous for his acerbic and ironic style. He served in World War I, and his health was shattered by it. *Murder for Profit* (1926) studies mass murderers. His wife Sybil Bolitho told his as well as her own story in her novel *My Shadow As I Pass* (1931).

BÖLL, Heinrich
(1917–85)

German writer, winner of the Nobel Prize for literature, born in Cologne. He served as an infantryman in World War II before becoming a full-time writer. His first novel, *Der Zug war pünktlich* (Eng trans *The Train was on Time*, 1956), was published in 1949. A trilogy, *Und sagte kein einziges Worte* (1953, Eng trans *Acquainted with the Night*, 1954), *Haus ohne Hüter* (1954, Eng trans *The Unguarded House*, 1957) and *Das Brot der frühen Jahre* (1955, Eng trans *The Bread of our Early Years*, 1957), depicting life in Germany during and after the Nazi regime, gained him a worldwide reputation. His later novels, characteristically satirizing modern German society, included *Gruppenbild mit Dame* (1971, Eng trans *Group Portrait with Lady*, 1973) and *Die vorlorene Ehre der Katherina Blum* (1974, Eng trans *The Lost Honour of Katherina Blum*, 1975). He also wrote a number of plays, and a volume of poems. He was awarded the 1972 Nobel Prize for literature.
▷J H Reid, *Heinrich Böll: withdrawal and re-emergence* (1973); Charlotte W Ghurye, *The Writer and Society: studies in the fiction of Günter Grass and Heinrich Böll* (1976)

BOLT, Carol
(1941–)

Canadian playwright, born in Winnipeg, Manitoba, and educated at the University of British Columbia, Vancouver. A prolific writer, she has written over 20 plays, including three for television, and is noted for her frequent collaborations with other writers.

Her plays combine an understanding of Canadian life and culture with musical comedy, mythic characters, and epic romance. Much of her work is overtly political, though she also writes for children. Her best-known works are *Buffalo Jump* (1972), a play about the riots which occurred during the Depression, and *Red Emma: Queen of Anarchists* (1973), about Emma Goldman, a New York anarchist.

BOLT, Robert Oxton
(1924–)

English playwright, born in Manchester. He was educated at Manchester University, and worked as a schoolmaster until the success of his first play, *Flowering Cherry* (1957), a domestic drama about a frustrated insurance salesman. His best-known work is *A Man For All Seasons* (1960), a play about the moral courage of Sir Thomas More in refusing to recant on his beliefs, even to save his life. His writings are generally politically overt, and often return to the theme of the private conscience in conflict with public demands. Other historical works include *Vivat! Vivat! Regina* (1970), about Elizabeth I and Mary, Queen of Scots, and *State of Revolution* (1977), on Lenin, Trotsky, and the fate of the Russian Revolution. He wrote the screenplay for the film *Lawrence of Arabia* (1962). The conventional formal aspects of his work have made him more popular with theatre-goers than with critics.

BOMBAL, María Luisa
(1910–80)

Chilean novelist, born in Viña del Mar. She spent much of her youth in Paris, and acquired a degree from the Sorbonne. Back in Chile, she fell in love with the aviator Eugolio Sánchez; but he did not love her, and so, after failing to kill herself, she shot him. Luckily she did not kill him, and under the wing of **Neruda** and other friends, she was able to get to Buenos Aires. There she wrote her first and most famous novel, *La última niebla* (1935, Eng trans *House of Mist*, 1947—but this is taken from a re-working of the original). This, and her second book, *La amortajada* (1938, Eng trans *The Shrouded Woman*, 1948), have been said to have marked a turning point in Latin-American fiction: hallucinated, often unintelligible, they are (or have been taken to be) the first truly feminist books in Chilean literature. **Borges** greatly admired the second of them, about a corpse which can hear what is going on around it. She was in the news again in 1940, when she took a pistol shot at her husband—who was alleged to have been intent on killing her—but missed. She became involved in the film world, wrote a few more stories (collected in

New Island, 1982), and on the death of her second husband, a French financier, returned to Chile, where she died in near poverty. Chronic alcoholism prevented her from carrying out many of the projects she had planned. The degree of her achievement has not yet been decided: the charge that she did little more in her novels than render, in words, some notion of the cinematic achievement of Luis Buñuel, is hard to counter; unlike Buñuel, she displayed no sense of humour. However, feminists have pointed to her as a great writer.
▷ M I Adams, *Three Authors of Alienation* (1975)

BONALD, Louis Gabriel Ambroise, Vicomte de
(1754–1840)

French writer. He emigrated to Heidelberg during the French Revolution and wrote *Théorie du pouvoir politique et religieux* (1796, 'Theory of Political and Religious Power'), advocating the system of monarchy and prophesying the return of the Bourbons. He was appointed by Napoleon Minister of Instruction in 1808, in 1815 ennobled by Louis XVIII. His son, Louis Jacques Maurice (1787–1870), became Archbishop of Lyons in 1839, and Cardinal in 1841.
▷ M H Quinlan, *The Historical Thought of the Vicomte de Bonald* (1953)

BOND, Edward
(1934–)

English dramatist and director, born in London. A left-wing writer whose work uses a variety of metaphors for the corruption of capitalist society, his first play, *The Pope's Wedding*, was given a Sunday night reading at the Royal Court Theatre, London, in 1962 and aroused great controversy. *Saved* (1965) achieved notoriety through a scene in which a baby in a pram is stoned to death. Both of these plays were set in contemporary England, although later plays such as *Narrow Road to the Deep North* (1968) use historical themes to look at broad contemporary issues. Other plays include *Lear* (1971), a reworking of **Shakespeare**'s play; *The Fool* (1976), based on the life of the 'peasant poet', **John Clare**; *The Woman* (1978), in which the characters are drawn from Greek tragedy; *The Worlds* (1979); a trilogy, *The War Plays* (1985); and, for television, *Olly's Prison* (1992).

BOND, (Thomas) Michael
(1926–)

English author of children's books, born in Newbury, Berkshire, who worked for many years as a BBC cameraman. He is the creator of several fictional animal characters, each of which appears in a series of stories. The adventures of Thursday, an orphan mouse, are recorded in *Here Comes Thursday* (1966), and others, while Olga da Polga, a guinea-pig, features in *The Tales of Olga da Polga* (1971), and further stories. Bond's most popular creation, however, is Paddington Bear, a small bear so named because he was discovered at Paddington Station. He wears a sou'wester, wellington boots and a duffle-coat, from a toggle of which hangs a luggage label bearing the words, 'Please look after this bear'. Hapless, vulnerable and good-natured, Paddington has so far been the hero of almost 40 stories since his first appearance in *A Bear Called Paddington* (1958); his enormous popularity shows no sign of waning.

BONER, Ulrich
(1300–49)
Swiss writer of fables. A Dominican friar in Bern from 1324, his *Edelstein* ('Precious Stone'), a collection of fables and jokes, was one of the first German books printed, in 1461.
▷ J J Oberlin, *Bonerii gemma* (1782)

BONNARD, Abel
(1883–1968)
French poet, novelist, and essayist, born in Poitiers. He won the National Poetry Prize with his first collection of poems, *Les Familiers* (1906, 'The Familiars'). He took up the psychological novel with *La Vie et l'amour* (1913, 'Life and Love'), and later published travel books and collections of essays. He was Minister of Education in the Vichy government (1942–4), fled to Spain and was sentenced to death in his absence (1945). He returned to France (1958) and was banished (1960).
▷ R Brasillach, *Abel Bonnard* (1971)

BONNEVILLE, Nicholas de
(1760–1828)
French writer. He was appointed president of a Paris district during the French Revolution (1789). A student of English and German literature, he translated **Shakespeare**, founded several newspapers, and wrote a history of modern Europe (1792).

BONTEMPELLI, Massimo
(1878–1960)
Italian novelist, playwright and journalist, born in Como. He was one of the most important of European writers, but his achievements have been passed over except in his own country. His as yet untranslated novel *La scacchiera davanti allo specchio* (1922, 'The Chess Board Before the Mirror'), bids fair to be regarded as one of the first novels of magical realism, although that term, outside painting (in which connection it was coined, by Franz Roh, in 1925—it was also coined, independently, by Bontempelli in his critical work of 1938, *L'avventura novecentista*, 'Twentieth Century Adventure'), is too often employed as applying only to German or Latin-American novels. Later Bontempelli wrote the majestic and neglected novels *Il figlio di due madri* (1929, 'The Son of Two Mothers') and *Vita e morte do Adria e suoi figli* (1930, 'The Life and Death of Adria and Her Two Sons'), both again in the 'magical realist' mode. He usually went along with fascism, although unhappily, and initially acted as a propagandist for it; but he was suspended from the party for two years from 1938, and he refused to accept a university chair offered to him after its occupier had been deprived of it because he was a Jew. But when he was elected a senator on a communist ticket after World War II, he was not able to take it up owing to his past. His Pirandellian play *Nostra Dea* (1925, 'Our Goddess') is notable.
▷ F Tempesti, *Bontempelli* (1974, in Italian)

BONTEMPS, Arna Wendell
(1902–73)
American writer and educator, born in Louisiana, associated with the so-called Harlem Renaissance. His work delves into the history and folklore of Afro-Americans: a jockey in *God Sends Sunday* (1931, later dramatized as *St Louis Woman*, 1946, in collaboration with **Countee Cullen**); slave uprisings in the very fine *Black Thunder* (1935) and *Drums at Dusk* (1939), the latter set in Haiti. In *Father of the Blues* (1941) Bontemps edited W C Handy's compositions; he later collaborated with **Langston Hughes** on *The Poetry of the Negro* (1949) and *The Book of Negro Folklore* (1958). His characteristic tone is rational, tending to mildness, and he was largely repudiated in the black nationalist atmosphere of the 1960s.
▷ R A Bone, *The Negro Novel in America* (1958)

BOON, Louis Paul
(1912–79)
Belgian (Flemish) novelist, poet, journalist and painter, born in Aalst (where he lived for most of his life), one of the outstanding writers of his day. He was the first Dutch-language author—he made a point of sticking to Flemish dialect—to employ the set of techniques first practised by **John Dos Passos** in the trilogy *U.S.A.*. Another powerful influence was that of **Louis Ferdinand Céline**, this time in the delivery of streams of bitter, colloquial invective. But he was highly original, and *Kapellekensbaan* (1953, Eng trans *Chapel*

Road, 1972), which brilliantly interweaves and counterpoints three separate tales, tells the story of the rise and fall of Belgian socialism in imaginative terms. *Abel Gholaerts* (1944) is an interesting autobiographical novel in which the author refers to the unhappy life of the painter Van Gogh.
▷ R P Meijer, *Literature of the Low Countries* (1971)

BOOTH, Martin
(1944–)

English poet and critic, born in Lancashire. He trained and worked as a teacher, but has managed to produce a substantial body of verse and of highly intelligent literary journalism, of which *Driving Through the Barricades: British Poetry 1964–1984* (1985) is the most developed example. He has tended to work best in longer or cycle forms, particularly where dream-like displacements of time are involved. This was evident in collections like *The Crying Embers* (1971) and his eleventh book, *Coronis* (1973), but his interest in the imaginative pull of the past reached its peak with *The Knotting Sequence* (1977) and *Winter's Night, Knotting* (1979), named after his home village in Bedfordshire, and *The Cnot Dialogues* (1979), named after its founder. In later work, he devises a historical perspective which differs sharply from that of **Geoffrey Hill** and other guardians of the national mythology. Recent collections include a sequence inspired by America, *Looking for the Rainbow* (1983). Booth has also edited an important textbook anthology of *Contemporary British and North American Verse* (1981), which bears witness to his instincts as a teacher.

BOOTHBY, Guy Newell
(1867–1905)

Australian novelist, born in Adelaide, where he was sometime secretary to the mayor. His early work included librettos for two operas to music by Cecil Sharp, the folk-song collector, and *On the Wallaby* (1894), an account of a journey across Australia with his brother. His first novel, *In Strange Company* (1894), was a mélange of espionage and revolution in a South American state, and set the style for his melodramatic fiction; within the next 10 years he had published over 50 novels of adventure, often in exotic settings. His third book introduced the sinister Dr Nikola, a Mephistophelian character who appeared in several of his tales.

BOOTHE, Clare, also known by her married name of Clare Boothe Luce
(1903–87)

American writer, socialite and wit, born in New York City. Married to the millionaire publisher Henry Luce at 20, she was made associate editor of *Vogue* (1930), was elected to the House of Representatives as a Republican in 1942, was American Ambassador to Italy (1953–7) and was the author of several Broadway successes, including *The Women* (1936) and *Kiss the Boys Goodbye* (1938).
▷ A P Hatch, *Clare Boothe Luce: ambassador extraordinary* (1956)

BOPP, Raul
(1898–)

Brazilian poet, known mainly for his 'cannibalist' poem *Cobrata Norato* (1931, 'Norato the Snake'): 'the equivalent of the tragedy of fever', it is a lively and brilliant trip through the jungle—a true tour de force.

BORATYNSKY, Yevgeni
(1800–44)

Russian poet, born in Mara, regarded as the outstanding member of the so-called 'Pushkin Pléiade'—he was thought of by critics as **Pushkin**'s leading rival. His name, wrongly spelled as 'Baratynsky', has passed into common usage and is thus often found in many dictionaries and indices. He was a precise, aristocratic, philosophical poet, with an astringent quality which was never truly popular in his own day, but which is now increasingly valued. A few of his poems are translated into prose in the *Penguin Book of Russian Verse* (1965, ed Dimitry Obolensky).
▷ R Poggioli, *Poets of Russia* (1960)

BORCHARDT, Rudolf
(1877–1945)

German poet and essayist, born in Königsberg, and living most of his life in Italy. Borchardt was an outstanding speaker whose reputation rests predominantly on his criticism, essays, translations and anthologies. As a poet he has been described as a revolutionary conservatist, because of his attempt to reanimate everyday speech by using archaic forms—the result is a poetry as extravagantly formal as **Swinburne**'s, whose work Borchardt translated in *Swinburne Deutsch* (1919). *Jugendgedichte* (1913) contains some of Borchardt's most enduring verse.

BORCHERT, Wolfgang
(1921–47)

German short-story writer, playwright and poet, born in Hamburg. Conscripted in 1941, Borchert, not the most compliant of Wehrmacht soldiers, was imprisoned on several occasions under the Third Reich, and the privations he suffered in prison contributed to his early death. The quest for meaning in an apparently God-forsaken world underlies both his stories, such as the collection *Die Hundeblume* (1947, 'The Dogflower'), and his only play, *Draussen vor der Tür* ('Outside in front of the Door'), which was premiered the day after his death.

BORDEAUX, Henri
(1870–1963)

French novelist, born in Thonon. He studied law before he took to writing novels concerned with the defence of family life, often with a Savoy background, such as *La Peur de vivre* (1902, 'Fear of Living'), *Les Roquevillard* (1906), and *La Maison* (1913, 'The House').
▷ E Mariotte, *L'Enigme de la vie* (1909)

BORDEWIJK, Ferdinand
(1884–1965)

Dutch poet, fiction writer and playwright, born in Amsterdam. One of Holland's finest writers of the 20th century, he did not find himself until middle age, when he produced *Blokken* (1931, 'Blocks'), one of the most chilling and prophetic of all depictions of totalitarian societies, and worthy to rank with **Orwell**'s *1984* and the *We* of **Zamyatin**. Before that he had written decadent poetry and stories influenced by **Poe** and **Couperus**, but these had not attracted more than cursory attention. *Bint* (1934), a similar novel about a fascistic school, employs staccato techniques imported from the last phase of German Expressionism. *Karakter* (1938, Eng trans *Character*, 1966) develops his gifts still further: in this variation on the theme of *The Ordeal of Richard Feverel* by **George Meredith**, a father destroys his son by trying to educate him by psychoanalytical methods.
▷ R P Meijer, *Literature of the Low Countries* (1978)

BOREL (D'HAUTERIVE), Petrus
(1809–59)

French poet, translator (of **Defoe**'s *Robinson Crusoe*) and novelist, self-styled 'the Lycanthrope' (werewolf) on the grounds that 'man was a wolf to man'; he was born in Lyons. One of the least distinguished in the French misanthropic tradition which ran through **Vallés** and culminated in the great **Céline**, Borel became a leader of the ultra-romantic post-1831 Revolution group (its average age was 20) called 'Bousingo', after the wide-brimmed hat its members affected (*bousingo* is derived from the English word 'booze'). Another leader was **Gautier**, but, while he went on to better things, Borel produced sensationalist horror novels of no merit, and some bad poetry of hatred—although this is not, however, technically poor. He made some amends by joining the colonial service in Algeria; then, having been dismissed for inefficiency, became Mayor of Blad-Touaria.
▷ E Starkie, *Petrus Borel* (1954)

BOREMAN, Yokutiel
(1825–90)

Hebrew novelist, born in Russia, whose books, written in a highly ornate and rhetorical style, deal with the pogroms, and are said to be brilliantly plotted. Unfortunately, as yet untranslated they are lost to English-speaking readers, for whom they would have been full of fascinating information, unobtainable elsewhere.
▷ M Waxman, *A History of Jewish Literature* (1960)

BORGEN, Johan
(1902–79)

Norwegian novelist, playwright, critic and journalist, born in Oslo into a protective, bourgeois family—a milieu he later used as setting for the novel *Lillelord* (1955, Eng trans 1982), which was to become his literary breakthrough. One of Norway's most significant writers of this century, Borgen is also a very innovative and experimental playwright and novelist. Some of his plays are examples of early abstract theatre. In his novels and short stories he rather consistently concentrates on the existential conflict between psychological identity and social participation. The theme is given an experimental form in the novel *Jeg* (1959, Eng trans *The Scapegoat*, 1992).
▷ R Birn, *Johan Borgen* (1974)

BORGES, Jorge Luis
(1899–1986)

Argentinian writer, born in Buenos Aires. He was educated there and at Geneva and Cambridge. From 1918 he was in Spain, where he was a member of the avant-garde Ultraist literary group, returning to Argentina in 1921. His first book of poems, *Fervor de Buenos Aires*, was published in 1923. He continued publishing poems and essays, and in 1941 appeared the first collection of the intricate and fantasy-woven short stories for which he is famous. Later collections include *Ficciónes* (1944 and 1956, Eng trans in US *Ficciones*, 1962, Eng trans in UK *Fictions*, 1965), *El Aleph* (1949, Eng trans *The Aleph and Other Stories 1933–1969*, 1970 (US); 1973 (UK)), *La Muerta y la Brújula* ('Death and the Compass', 1951) and the verse collection *El Hacedor* (1960, Eng trans *Dreamtigers*, 1963). Some stories from *El Aleph* appear in the collection of translations, *Labyrinths* (1962). He became director of the National Library in 1955, after losing his sight. His last book was *Atlas* (1986), written in collaboration with his companion, Maria Kodama, whom he married a month before his death.

▷ J M Cohen, *Jorge Luis Borges* (1973); J Sturrock, *The Ideal Fictions of Jorge Luis Borges* (1977)

BORGESE, Giuseppe
(1882–1952)

Italian critic, novelist, political activist and teacher, born near Palermo, Sicily. His career began with his *Storia della critica romantica in Italia* (1905, 'History of Romantic Criticism in Italy'). This was directly influenced by **Croce**, who praised it highly. Borgese coined the term 'Crepusculari' ('twilight' poets) to describe **Gozzano**, **Moretti**, and others, discovered **Tozzi**, and encouraged many other major writers, such as **Moravia**. His chief novel is the prophetic and Pirandellian *Rubè* (1921, Eng trans 1923), about an anti-hero torn between the two extremes of fascism and communism. He left Italy, refusing to sign an oath of loyalty to Mussolini as all academics were required to do, and went to the USA to teach (1931–47). He repudiated Croce, but it has been well said that 'although he sided with the classicists, he continued to be an irrepressible romantic'.

▷ S Pacifici, *The Modern Novel from Capuana to Tozzi* (1973)

BORROW, George Henry
(1803–81)

English author, born in East Dereham, Norfolk, the son of an army recruiting officer. He went to school at the High School in Edinburgh and at Norwich Grammar School (1816–18), and for the next five years was articled to a firm of solicitors. He turned to literature, and edited six volumes of *Celebrated Trials and Remarkable Cases of Criminal Jurisprudence* (1825). Already an accomplished linguist, from 1825 to 1832 he travelled on foot through England, France and Germany, studying the languages of the countries he visited. As an agent for the Bible Society he visited St Petersburg (1833–5), Portugal, Spain, and Morocco (1835–9). In 1840 he married a well-to-do widow, Mary Clarke, and settled down on a small estate of hers at Oulton, near Lowestoft, where, after travels in southeastern Europe (1844), a tour in Wales (1854), and a residence of some years in London, he ended his days a lonely man, sensitive to criticism. He wrote numerous books in which romantic fiction and autobiography often overlapped: *The Zincali or an Account of the Gypsies of Spain* (1840); *The Bible in Spain* (1843), which was an instant success as a travel book; *Lavengro* (1851) and its sequel, *The Romany Rye* (1857), novels

about his own gypsy life (the word 'Lavengro' means 'word-master'); *Wild Wales* (1862); and *Romano Lavo-Lil, or Word-book of the English-Gypsy Language* (1874).

▷ M D Armstrong, *George Borrow* (1950)

BOSBOOM-TOUSSAINT, Anna Louisa Geetruida
(1812–86)

Dutch novelist, born in Alkmaar. Her first novels were able and readable imitations of **Scott**. Her later novels were on contemporary themes: *Majoor Frans* (1874, Eng trans 1885) seems to be her only novel which reached an English-speaking audience.

BOSCO, Henri
(1888–1976)

French regionalist novelist and minor poet, born in Avignon, and throughout his work identified with the countryside of Provence. A classics teacher by profession, he did not publish his first novel until he was 36; and became famous only in 1945, when he published *Le Mas Théotime* (Eng trans *The Farm Théotime*, 1947), almost a detective story in form (although the murder in it is accidental), but far more artistic than most detective stories. He had a feeling for mysteries hidden beneath the surface, and produced more novels at this high level of accomplishment, including *Un Rameau de la nuit* (1950, Eng trans *The Dark Bough*, 1955).

▷ R T Sussex, *Henri Bosco, Poet-Novelist* (1966)

BOSTOCK, Gerald
(1942–)

Australian aboriginal poet and playwright, born in Grafton, New South Wales, who, after serving with the army in South-East Asia, became involved in the history of aboriginals. He set up the Black Theatre in Sydney where his play *Here Comes the Nigger*, calling for aboriginal nationalism, was produced in 1976. He has worked in film and co-produced *Lousy Little Sixpence* (1983), a documentary of the exploitation of aboriginal labour in the early 1900s. *Black Man Coming* (1980) is a powerful collection of poetry on the same themes.

BOSWELL, James
(1740–95)

Scottish writer and biographer of **Dr Johnson**, born in Edinburgh, the eldest son of a judge, Lord Auchinleck. He was educated privately in Edinburgh and at the University of Edinburgh. He then studied civil law at Glasgow, but his true goal was literary fame and the friendship of the famous. At the age of 18 he began to keep an astonishingly frank and self-probing journal. In spring 1760 he ran away to London and turned Catholic. To discourage such religious fervour, Lord Eglinton, a London-based friend of Boswell's father, saw to it that Boswell became more of a libertine than ever and he reverted to his original faith. Young Boswell hobnobbed with the young Duke of York, with **Sheridan**'s father, made plans to join the army, and skilfully resisted all attempts to lure him into matrimony. He first met Dr Johnson on his second visit to London, on 16 May 1763, at Tom Davies's bookshop in Russell Street. By the following year they were on such cordial terms that Johnson accompanied him as far as Harwich. Boswell was on his way to Utrecht to continue his legal studies, but stayed only for the winter and then toured Germany, France, Switzerland, and Italy. By an astounding process of literary gatecrashing he introduced himself to **Voltaire** and **Rousseau**. From Rousseau he procured an introduction to Paoli, the hero of Corsica, whom he 'Boswellized' in *Account of Corsica* (1768), which had an immediate success and was translated into several languages. Boswell had many love affairs. There was the serious and high-minded affair with 'Zélide' of Utrecht, and liaisons with the Irish Mary Anne Montgomery, and with numerous others in London, Rome and elsewhere, including a disreputable episode with Rousseau's mistress, Thérèse Le Vasseur. He finally married in 1769 a cousin, Margaret Montgomerie, a prudent, amiable woman who put up with his shortcomings. He returned from the Continent in 1766, was admitted advocate, then in 1773 was elected to Johnson's famous literary club, and took the great doctor on a memorable journey to the Hebrides. A major literary enterprise (1777–83) was a series of 70 monthly contributions to the *London Magazine* under the pseudonym 'The Hypochondriak'. After Johnson's death appeared *The Journal of the Tour of the Hebrides* (1785). Its great success made Boswell plan his masterpiece, the *Life of Samuel Johnson* (1791), of which *The Journal* served as a first instalment. Meanwhile Boswell had entered the Inner Temple and had been called to the English Bar in 1786. He hardly practised, however, except to publish anonymously *Dorando, a Spanish Tale* (1767), a thinly disguised summary of a topical case which, at the time of publication, was still *sub judice*. Boswell's wife died in 1789, leaving him six children, and his drinking habits got the better of him. His work is that of a conscious artist, a born journalist, and a biographical researcher. The discoveries of Boswell's manuscripts, at Malahide Castle in Ireland in 1927 and at Fettercairn House in Scotland in 1930, which have been assembled by Yale University, are proof of his literary industry and integrity.

▷I Finlayson, *The Moth and the Candle: a life of James Boswell* (1985)

BOTELHO GOSÁLVEZ, Raúl
(1917–)

Bolivian novelist and critic, born in La Paz. He fought in the disastrous Chaco War, and later showed his solidarity with the Aymara Indians by going to live amongst them for a year. He became a diplomat, then a politician, and even served as interim president (1979) under a military junta which was returning the country to democratic rule. *Altiplano* (1945), his most powerful novel, deals in great and profound detail with the plight of a whole community left to its fate in the Bolivian highlands. Botelho Gosálvez has written much about **Jaimes Freyre**, whose example he believes to have been vital not only to Bolivia but also to Latin America.

▷J S Guevara, *La cien obras capitales de la literature boliviana* (1975)

BOTEV, Hristo
(1847–76)

Bulgarian poet who was educated in Odessa, where he picked up the progressive ideas of the Russian intelligentsia. Just as Hungary has its Petofi (killed in battle against Russians) and Romania its **Mihail Eminescu** (died mad), so Bulgaria has its Botev: like them, he was a poet-revolutionary who perished young. He died fighting the Turks in the abortive rising at Mount Vola, Vratsa. Mostly he wrote polemical journalism; but his few poems, based on folk song and celebrating the tradition of the *haydutin*, or guerrillas, vividly catch and preserve the spirit of Bulgarian romantic independence.

▷C Manning and R Smal-Stocki, *The History of Modern Bulgarian Literature* (1960)

BOTTO, Ján
(1829–81)

Slovak nationalist poet whose work will doubtless gain even more attention in the new republic. He brought the influences of Serbian and, especially, Polish epic and folk poetry to bear on Slovak poetry: his masterpiece, *Smrt' Jánosikva* (1862, 'Jánosik's Death'), is probably untranslatable, since it builds on Slovak folk elements that cannot be transferred to another language. Jánosik is the Slovak Robin Hood figure.

BOTTOME, Phyllis
(1884–1963)

American novelist and biographer, born in Rochester, Kentucky. She travelled extensively, both during her formative years and later, after her marriage, and her novels reflect the differing environments in which she found herself. *The Dark Tower* (1916), for example, derives from her work with the Ministry of Information in London during World War I, while *Old Wine* (1925) examines life in Vienna, where her husband was working at the time of writing. *The Mortal Storm* (1937) is based upon her experiences in Munich during the early thirties, when she observed the Nazis take political power. She had earlier (1934) written an anti-war novel, *Private Worlds*. She is also the author of several biographical studies and a biography of the Austrian psychiatrist, *Alfred Adler: Apostle of Freedom* (1939).

▷ *Search for a Soul* (1947); *The Challenge* (1952); *The Goal* (1962)

BOTTOMLEY, Gordon
(1874–1948)

English poet and playwright, born in Keighley, Yorkshire. His interest in Celtic folklore emerged in much of his work, including his first collection of verse, *The Mickle Drede* (1896). He is best remembered for his *Poems of Thirty Years* (1925) and his collections of plays, including *King Lear's Wife and Other Plays* (1920), which, although they mostly constituted an unhappy blend of poetry and rhetoric, won critical approval. His poetry anticipated Imagism.

▷ *Poet and Painter: the correspondence of Gordon Bottomley and Paul Nash* (1955)

BOTTRALL, (Francis James) Ronald
(1906–)

English poet of diverse interests. His work has ranged very widely, experimenting with most of the major prosodic types. His early poetry was published in *The Loosening* (1931), *Festivals of Fire* (1934) and *The Turning Path* (1939) and attracted the attention of T S Eliot and G S Fraser. He began to develop a new and more allusive voice after the war, beginning with *Farewell and Welcome* (1945), but reaching a new level of sophistication and confidence in *The Palisades of Fear* (1949) and in his best book, *Adam Unparadised* (1954). There have been three important collections: *The Collected Poems* appeared in 1961; *Poems 1953–1973* (1974) was complementary, and *Against a Setting Sun* (1984) brought his work up to date.

▷ G S Fraser, *The Modern Writer and His World* (1953)

BOUCICAULT, Dion(ysius Lardner)
(?1820–1890)

Dramatist and actor, born in Dublin. He was educated at University College School, London. He scored an early success on the London stage with *London Assurance* (1841), a comedy written under the pseudonym 'Lee Morton'. He adapted a number of French plays into English, then emigrated to the USA in 1853, where his successful melodramas included *The Colleen Bawn* (1860) and *The Octoroon* (1861). He was a major figure in the theatre of his day, but his reputation is now much diminished.

▷ R G Hogan, *Dion Boucicault* (1969)

BOUILHET, Louis
(1821–69)

French poet and dramatist, born in Cany in Seine Inférieure. He is best known as a lifelong friend of **Gustave Flaubert**. In his *Fossiles* (1856), he attempted to use science as a subject for poetry and also wrote on historical subjects. Of his many plays, *Madame de Montarcy* (1856) and *Conjuration d'Amboise* (1866, 'The Amboise Conspiracy') met with success.

BOULLE, Pierre
(1912–94)

French novelist and short-story writer, born in Avignon. He is best known in the English-speaking world as the author of two novels which subsequently, and—at least in box-office terms—successfully, became films: *Le Pont Sur la Rivière Kwai* (1952, Eng trans *The Bridge on the River Kwai*, 1954), the tale of a group of Allied soldiers held prisoner by the Japanese; and *La Planete des Singes* (1959, Eng trans *Planet of the Apes*, 1963), an allegory of oppression and racial hatred set on a future Earth in which chimpanzees have become the dominant species. Not nearly so well known as the two novels, his short stories—particularly the collections *Contes de l'Absurde* (1953, 'Tales of the Absurd') and *E = MC2* (1957), which were translated jointly as *Time Out of Mind* (1966)—tend to be lighter, more subtle expressions of his gentle, humane humour.

BOURDET, Édouard
(1887–1945)

French playwright, born in Saint-Germain-en-Laye. He administered the Comédie-Française from 1936 until 1940. He was a highly skilled popular dramatist, who managed to treat serious subjects, such as homosexuality, without trivializing them. *La Prisonnière* (1926, 'The Captive'), is a quite serious study of lesbianism. He also wrote in a lighter and more farcical vein. **Louis Bromfield** adapted his satirical *Les Temps difficiles* (1934) as *Times Have Changed* (1935).

BOURGES, Elémir
(1852–1925)

French novelist who is now more studied by critics than read, but whose grandiloquent works continue to arouse interest. After neglect, he is coming to be appreciated for his anticipations of modernist techniques—a kind of prose **Mallarmé**, who was his friend. He had few other literary connections (although he had a correspondence with Paule Régnier). He reacted against such naturalists as **Zola**, and, much influenced by the English Elizabethan dramatists, and by **Shelley**, **Goethe** and Wagner, he tried, in such massive volumes as *Le Crépuscule des dieux* (1884, Eng trans *The Chains of Destiny*, 1928), to present a less degraded picture of man; this novel has been called 'one of the masterpieces of symbolist fiction'. *La Nef* (1904–22), 'The Ship'), is a huge two-part closet play or prose-poem, fascinating but weighed down by its erudition and operatic earnestness.

BOURGET, Paul
(1852–1935)

French poet, essayist and novelist, born in Amiens. He first wrote striking verse: *La Vie inquiète* (1875, 'The Anxious Life'), *Edel* (1878), and *Les Aveux* (1881, 'Confessions'). His *Essais* (1883) indicated his true strength; the second series, *Nouveaux Essais de psychologie contemporaine* (1886, 'New Essays on Contemporary Psychology'), was a subtle inquiry into the causes of pessimism in France. His first novel, *L'Irréparable* (1884), was followed by a steady stream of works which placed him in the front rank of modern French novelists. *L'Étape* (1902, 'The Halting-Place') marked the crystallization of his talent. His works after 1892 showed a marked reaction from realism and scepticism towards mysticism.
▷G Bennoville, *Paul Bourget* (1936)

BOURJAILY, Vance Nye
(1922–)

American novelist, raised in Ohio. His first novel, *The End of My Life* (1947), like the later *The Violated* (1958), was a conventionally autobiographical account of the collapse of liberal values in the face of war; it drew on Bourjaily's experience as an ambulance driver in the Mediterranean theatre. In *The Hound of Earth* (1955), he focused on a character troubled by his role in developing the atomic bomb. *Confessions of a Spent Youth* (1960) established him as a wry commentator on the making of the counterculture. He continued the thread in *The Man Who Knew Kennedy* (1967), a latter-day version of **Sinclair Lewis**'s *The Man Who Knew Coolidge* (1928), and in the romping *Brill*

Among the Ruins (1971). Later novels have been less successful, perhaps because too self-consciously targeted on cultural change, but *Old Soldier* (1990) was a welcome return to form, a 'green' book written without cant or editorializing. During the fifties, Bourjaily also edited the short-lived but influential journal *Discovery* (1953–5), which very accurately named the contenders for literary fame in the second half of the decade.

BOURKE, John Philip, pseud Bluebush
(1857–1914)

Australian bush poet, born in Nundle, New South Wales. His vigorous verse descriptions of the Western Australian gold diggings in the 1890s and of the outback earned him the praise of A G Stephens, editor of the *Bulletin*; After Bourke's death Stephens edited a collection of his verse in *Off the Bluebush: Verses for Australians, West and East* (1915).

BOUTENS, Pieter
(1870–1943)

Dutch poet, translator and classicist, born on the island of Walcheren. He was initially associated with De Nieuwe Gids, the 'Men of the Eighties', the individualistic Dutch poetic movement which took its bearings from contemporary French poets such as **Verlaine**. His later poetry is elaborately Symbolist, somewhat cold, perfectly rendered, and artificial.
▷H J Grierson, *Two Dutch Poets* (1936)

BOWEN, Elizabeth Dorothea Cole
(1899–1973)

Irish novelist and short-story writer, born in County Cork, the daughter of a wealthy barrister and land-owner, and brought up in Dublin. Educated in England at Downe House School in Kent, she married in 1923 and in the same year published her first collection of short stories, *Encounters*, followed by *Anne Lee's* (1926). Her first novel, *The Hotel* (1927), began a string of delicately-written explorations of personal relationships, of which *The Death of the Heart* (1938) and *The Heat of the Day* (1949), a war story, are the best known. She was also a perceptive literary critic, and published *English Novelists* (1942) and *Collected Impressions* (1950).
▷J Brooke, *Elizabeth Bowen* (1952); A E Austin, *Elizabeth Bowen* (1971)

BOWEN, John Griffith
(1924–)

English playwright, television scriptwriter and novelist, born in Calcutta, India. Athough also writing novels and stage plays during the 1950s and 1960s, Bowen's association since 1960 with such successful television series as *The Power Game*, *The Guardians* and *The Villains* resulted in his becoming widely-known as an author for the small screen. His most successful stage plays remain *After the Rain* (1966; adapted from his 1958 novel of the same title) and *Little Boxes* (1968). Both are sympathetic studies of human nature. The second piece comprises two one-act plays, one of which, *Trevor*, deals with a young lesbian couple who attempt to keep their relationship secret from their respective parents.

BOWERING, George
(1938–)
Canadian poet, novelist, essayist and academic, born in British Columbia. Bowering set himself up as an arch-enemy of the confessional school, saying that he would rather read baseball scores than personal poetry which is too disclosing. It has been said, quite accurately, that his own work 'has more tone than taste'. He is exceptionally prolific, in both prose and verse, and correspondingly uneven. The size of his bibliography is matched by his ego: 'I was all those things that other poets always are on the dust jackets before they became poets,' he has boasted.
▷G Bowering, (Introduction to) *Touch: Selected Poems* (1971)

BOWLES, Jane Auer
(1918–73)
American fiction writer and playwright. For many years she suffered from acute ill-health and her literary output was consequently slim. An original writer, she has been linked with **Gertrude Stein** whose influence is apparent but not destructive. *In the Summer House* (1953), a play, is her most accessible work. Her *Collected Works* appeared in 1967. She married **Paul Bowles** in 1939.
▷I Finlayson, in *Tangier: the city of the dream* (1991)

BOWLES, Paul Frederick
(1910–)
American novelist, composer, poet, travel writer and translator, born in New York City. After studying at the University of Virginia, he went to Europe in 1931 to study music with Aaron Copland in Paris, and became a composer and music critic. He did not devote himself to writing until after World War II. His first novel, *The Sheltering Sky*, set in Morocco, appeared in 1949 and was immediately influential, sparking off an American literary exodus to Tangier, of which he became a resident in 1952. He wrote three

other novels, *Let It Come Down* (1952), *The Spider's House* (1955) and *Up Above the World* (1966), as well as several collections of short stories, including *Pages from Cold Point* (1968) and *Midnight Mass* (1981). He was married to the writer **Jane Bowles**.
▷*Without Stopping* (1972)

BOWLES, William Lisle
(1762–1850)
English clergyman and poet, born in King's Sutton vicarage, Northamptonshire. Educated at Winchester and Trinity College, Oxford, he became vicar of Bremhill in Yorkshire and prebendary of Salisbury in 1804, and later chaplain to the Prince Regent (1818). In his poetry he was a forerunner of the Romantic movement in English poetry. His *Fourteen Sonnets, written chiefly on Picturesque Spots during a Journey* (1789), published anonymously, had **Coleridge**, **Wordsworth** and **Robert Southey** among their enthusiastic admirers. His best poetical work is *The Missionary of the Andes*. In 1806 he published an edition of **Pope**, and an opinion which he expressed on Pope's poetical merits led to a memorable controversy (1809–25) in which **Thomas Campbell** and **Byron** were his antagonists.
▷G Gilfillan, *A Critical Dissertation by the Rev. Geo Gilfillan* (1855)

BOYD, James
(1888–1944)
American novelist, born in Pennsylvania and raised in North Carolina. His fiction delves back into the historical past. *Drums* (1925) is set in the War of Independence, and *Marching On* (1927) during the Civil War. He was not a localist, or a 'historical novelist' in any conventional sense, but used the past as a point of entry for examining contemporary issues and tensions. Other novels, less well known, include the very fine *Roll River* (1935) and *Bitter Creek* (1939). A collection of verse was published after his death.

BOYD, Martin à Beckett
(1893–1972)
Australian novelist and poet, born in Lucerne, Switzerland, son of Arthur Merric Boyd. Brought up in Melbourne, he lived for much of his life in Britain. After World War I he tried journalism for a time. His first three novels, *Love Gods* (1925), *Brangane: A Memoir* (1926) and *The Montforts* (1928) appeared under a pseudonym, 'Martin Mills', as did his fourth, *Dearest Idol* (1929), for which he adopted the name 'Walter Beckett'. Thereafter he acknowleged his authorship and produced his best work, to be seen in

what is now referred to as the Langton tetralogy: *The Cardboard Crown* (1952), *A Difficult Young Man* (1955), *Outbreak of Love* (1957) and *When Blackbirds Sing* (1962). He wrote two autobiographies; the earlier, *A Single Flame* (1938) was superceded by *Day of My Delight: An Anglo-Australian Memoir* (1965) in which he casts light on his fiction and its characters, and on the multi-talented Boyd family.

▷ B Niall, *Martin Boyd* (1974)

BOYD, William Andrew Murray
(1952–)

Scottish novelist, born in Ghana, West Africa. He was educated at Gordonstoun School, and at the universities of Nice, Glasgow and Oxford. He lectured in English at Oxford (1980–3) and wrote television criticism for the *New Statesman*, before concentrating on fiction. His first book was the novel *A Good Man in Africa* (1981), which drew on the experiences of his formative years, and introduced the character of Morgan Leafy, a minor diplomat in an insignificant West African state who keeps boredom at bay by resorting to sex and alcohol. For this Boyd was hailed for his comic touch and likened to **Kingsley Amis**. His next book was a collection of stories, *On the Yankee Station* (1981), in which Leafy reappeared; then came *An Ice-Cream War* (1982), set in East Africa during World War I. In *Stars and Bars* (1984) the tone is conspicuously lighter as Henderson Dores, an English art expert, grapples with the shock of the New World. In *The New Confessions* (1987) Boyd introduced another memorable character, John James Todd, a Scottish filmmaker. *Brazzaville Beach* marked a return to Africa and the theme of conflict—professional, personal and political—as Hope Clearwater, an idealist anthropologist, studies a colony of apes against a backdrop of civil unrest and academic backstabbing. He has also written a number of screenplays and adaptations; another novel, *The Blue Afternoon*, appeared in 1993.

BOYE, Karin Maria
(1900–41)

Swedish poet and novelist, born in Gothenburg. She studied at Uppsala University and worked for a time as a teacher and journalist. In 1925 she abandoned Christianity in favour of the socialist *Clarté* group, but seems to have been more directly affected by psychoanalytic ideas than by Marxism. Sexually ambivalent, she was profoundly concerned about the relationship between instinct and social convention. Much of her poetry appeared in the modernist journal *Spektrum* which she founded and edited from

1931, and in which she also published translations of **T S Eliot**. Her collections include *Moln* (1922, 'Cloud'), *För trädets skull* (1935, 'For the Tree's Sake') and the posthumous *De sju dödssynderna* (1941, 'The Seven Deadly Sins'), published after her suicide. Despite the lyrical simplicity of this last volume, Boye had for some time been profoundly depressed about the rise of totalitarianism; this concern is explored in her novels *Kris* (1934, 'Crisis') and *Kallocain* (1940). She committed suicide.

▷ M Adenius and O G H Lagercrantz, *Karin Boye* (1942)

BOYESEN, H(jalmar) H(jorth)
(1848–95)

Born and raised in Scandinavia, he is, after **Ole Rølvaag**, the most important Norwegian –American writer. He first visited the USA in 1869, and was persuaded to stay by **William Dean Howells**'s enthusiasm for his novel *Gunnar* (1874), which first appeared in the *Atlantic Monthly*. Boyesen wrote ground-breaking *Essays on Scandinavian Literature* (1895) which, along with the autobiographical *Boyhood in Norway* (1892), written for teenagers, helped shape American awareness of Nordic culture. Later in his career, he wrote realistic but somewhat schematic novels of modern life: *The Mammon of Unrighteousness* (1891), *The Golden Calf* (1892) and *The Social Strugglers* (1893) reflect an outsider's view of American materialism.

BOYLAN, Clare
(1948–)

Irish novelist and short-story writer and journalist, born in Dublin. Her first novel, *Holy Pictures*, appeared in 1983 and her first collection of short stories, *A Nail on the Head*, later the same year. They share a common theme in loss of innocence and the human capacity for self-deception. *Holy Pictures* looks at the adult world through the eyes of two young Catholic sisters, Nan and Mary Cantwell, while in *Black Baby* (1988), an elderly Irish woman finds her way of life unexpectedly revived when she offers shelter to a young and vivacious black woman.

BOYLE, John, 5th Earl of Cork and of Orrery
(1707–62)

Irish writer, son of Charles Boyle, the 4th Earl. An intimate of **Swift**, **Pope** and **Dr Johnson**, he is remembered more by his rancorous *Remarks on the Life and Writings of Dr Jonathan Swift* (1751) than by an excellent translation of the *Letters of Pliny* (1751).

BOYLE, Kay
(1902–92)

American novelist, short-story writer, poet and essayist. Born in St Paul, Minnesota, she was brought up and educated in the USA, studying music and architecture, then lived in Europe for 30 years as part of the literary expatriate fraternity of Paris's Left Bank in the 1920s and latterly as the *New Yorker*'s foreign correspondent (1945–53). Influenced by **Henry James**, she has used her experience of expatriation most effectively in *Plagued by the Nightingale* (1931) and *Generation Without Farewell* (1960), but her novels are generally inferior to her stories, which are amassed in several volumes including *The Smoking Mountain* (1951). Her poems, indebted to **William Carlos Williams** and **Pádraic Colum**, were collected in 1962.
▷ S W Spanier, *Kay Boyle: Artist and Activist* (1986)

BOYLESVE, properly Tardivaux, René
(1867–1926)

French novelist, born and brought up in La Haye-Descartes. He studied in Paris, and established his reputation as a portrayer of provincial life with *Le Parfum des îles Borrommées* (1898, 'The Scent of the Borrommee Islands') and *Mademoiselle Cloque* (1899).
▷ A Bourgeois, *La vie de Boylesve* (1910)

BOZIĆ, Mirko
(1919–)

Croatian novelist and playwright, born in Sinj. He was a lawyer; then, in 1943, he joined Tito's partisans. He was active in the Croatian National Theatre in Zagreb, but his finest work is the novel *Kurlani* (1952, 'The Kurlans'), about peasants living in his native Dalmatia.

BRAATEN, Oskar
(1891–1939)

Norwegian dramatist and novelist, born into a poverty-stricken family in the slums of Oslo, in which two of his best novels are set: *Ulvehiet* (1919, 'The Wolf's Lair') and *Matilde* (1920). His folk comedy, *Ungen* (1911, 'The Child') was a huge success, as was his lively play about Oslo factory girls, *Den store barnedåpen* (1925, 'The Great Christening').
▷ A Lind, *Oskar Braaten* (1962, in Norwegian)

BRACE, Gerald Warner
(1901–78)

American novelist, teacher and critic, born in Islip, New York. Brace published his first book, *The Islands*, in 1936 while a professor at Boston University. Although he went on to greater academic eminence and published

a further 10 perceptive novels, many critics believe he has not been given the recognition he deserves. *The Department* (1968) in particular is an excellent novel of academic life, written in the unobtrusively effective prose for which Brace is noted.
▷ *Days That Were* (1976)

BRACKEN, Thomas
(1843–98)

Irish-born New Zealand poet, born in County Monaghan. His work is characterized by a sentimental Victorian attachment to nature and was written primarily for a readership 'back home', as in his *Lays of the Land of the Maori and Moa* (1884), *Lays and Lyrics: God's Own Country and Other Poems* (1893) and *Musings in Maoriland* (1890); this last was dedicated to his friend Lord **Alfred Tennyson** and bore a preface by the New Zealand governor-general. Regarded in his day as the 'poet laureate' of his adopted land, he wrote the words to New Zealand's national song 'God Defend New Zealand', and was perhaps at his best in the 'public' verse of the time. *Not Understood* (1905) went through many editions, the last as recent as 1956; the title poem, '… we wonder/Why life is life: and then we fall asleep/Not understood' has entered folk memory.

BRACKENRIDGE, Hugh Henry
(1748–1816)

Scottish-born American author of the satirical romance *Modern Chivalry*, he grew up near Campbeltown in Kintyre, Argyll, and emigrated to the USA in 1753, receiving an education at what became Princeton University. He was admitted to the Philadelphia Bar in 1780, and founded the newspaper *Tree of Liberty*, before moving to Pittsburgh to practise. His main literary achievement, *Modern Chivalry*, was originally published in four volumes between 1792 and 1797, extended (perhaps with contributions from other hands) in 1804–5, and then revised in 1815. Loosely modelled on *Don Quixote*, it recounts the adventures of Captain John Farrago and his Irish servant Teague O'Regan. Loose, episodic and shapeless, it hardly qualifies as a novel, but was nonetheless brilliantly written and remains an important source of social commentary on pre-Jeffersonian America. *Father Bembo's Pilgrimage to Mecca* (1770) was a fictional collaboration with **Philip Freneau** who also contributed to the epical *A Poem on the Rising Glory of America* (1772). Brackenridge also wrote political discourses and legal miscellanies.
▷ C M Newlin, *The Life and Writings of Hugh Henry Brackenridge* (1932)

BRADBURY, Malcolm Stanley
(1932–)

English novelist, literary critic and university teacher. Born in Sheffield, he graduated from University College, Leicester, before taking undergraduate courses in London and the USA. Since 1965, he has taught at the University of East Anglia. Promoted to a professorship in 1970, he is a pioneer of American Studies in the UK, and also of the university's much-discussed creative writing programme, which he founded with **Angus Wilson**. His first novels, *Eating People is Wrong* (1959) and *Stepping Westward* (1965), established a satirical style which nonetheless contained the germ of a darker, more fabulatory approach. This began to surface in *The History Man* (1975, subsequently adapted for television), in which Bradbury's essential subject, the slow collapse of liberal humanism, received its definitive expression. *Rates of Exchange* (1983) was set in the imaginary Iron Curtain country of Slaka and was more experimental in tone. His most recent novel is *Dr Criminale* (1992). Of his literary criticism, *The Social Context of Modern English Literature* (1971) and *Possibilities: Essays on the State of the Novel* (1973) are perhaps the most important.
▷J Haffenden, *Novelists in Interview* (1985)

BRADBURY, Ray(mond Douglas)
(1920–)

American writer of science fiction, born in Waukegan, Illinois. An avid reader of sensational fiction and comics, he began early to contribute to pulp magazines, graduating to better quality magazines and short-story anthologies. While he has written notable novels—*Fahrenheit 451* (1953), *Dandelion Wine* (1957) and *Death is a Lonely Business* (1985)—he is primarily a short-story writer and has created some of the finest examples in the genre: 'The Day It Rained Forever', 'R Is for Rocket' and those included in *The Martian Chronicles* (1950). A prolific writer, he ranges widely and has been the recipient of numerous awards.
▷J L Garci, *Ray Bradbury humanista del futuro* (1971)

BRADDON, Mary Elizabeth
(1835–1915)

English novelist, born in London. She attained fame with a Victorian thriller, *Lady Audley's Secret* (1862), the story of a golden-haired murderess. Of some 75 popular novels, perhaps the best is *Ishmael* (1884). Her *The Doctor's Wife* (1864) is an adaptation of the theme of **Flaubert**'s *Madame Bovary*.

BRADDON, Russell Reading
(1921–)

Australian author, playwright and film and television scriptwriter, born in Sydney, the great-grandson of Sir Edward Braddon, premier of Tasmania (1894–9). Educated at Sydney University, during World War II he was a prisoner of the Japanese for four years, at the notorious Changi Jail, Singapore, and worked on the Burma Railway. His experiences were published as *The Naked Island* (1952, dramatized 1961) and *End of a Hate* (1958). A string of popular novels followed, including *End Play* (1972, filmed 1976) and *The Year of the Angry Rabbit* (1964, filmed as *Night of the Lepus*, 1972), but he is perhaps best known for his biographies, such as those of wartime hero Leonard Cheshire, *Cheshire VC* (1954) and the resistance heroine *Nancy Wake* (1956).

BRADFORD, Barbara Taylor
(1933–)

English novelist, born in Leeds. After working as a journalist specializing in interior design, she left for the USA, where she now lives. Her early publications, books of domestic advice such as *How to Solve Your Decorating Problems* and three volumes of *How to be a Perfect Wife*, appeared during the 1960s and 70s. She is internationally known, though, for such bestselling novels of money and romance as *A Woman of Substance* (1979), a heady, rags to riches story taking Emma Harte from obscurity in Yorkshire to a new life as the founder of a retail empire. *Hold the Dream* (1985) and *To Be the Best* (1988) continue the saga. Bradford writes about strong, adaptable, sexy women who triumph in a man's world because of their intellect and indomitable spirit.

BRADFORD, Roark
(1896–1948)

American author and newspaperman, born in Lauderdale County, Tennessee, near the Mississippi. He wrote about Blacks in his first collection, *Ol' Man Adam an' His Chillun* (1928), drawn from his contributions to the New York *World*. This was turned by **Marc Connelly** into the famous and successful play *Green Pastures*. Bradford continued in this vein, regarded by many as patronizing, in further collections.

BRADFORD, William
(1590–1656)

American colonist and religious leader, one of the Pilgrim Fathers, born in Austerfield near Doncaster. A nonconformist from boyhood, he joined a separatist group in 1606 and went with them to Holland in 1609, seeking

freedom of worship. In Leiden he became a tradesman and read widely. One of the moving spirits in the Pilgrim Fathers' expedition to the New World in 1620, he sailed on the *Mayflower*, signed the Mayflower Compact, and in 1621 took over from John Carver as elected governor of Plymouth colony. He was re-elected governor 30 times between 1622 and 1656, and guided the fledgling colony with exemplary fairness and firmness. He wrote a *History of Plimmoth Plantation* (completed c.1651, printed in 1856), a long descriptive poem (1654), a letter-book (1624–30) and a *Dialogue between some young men born in New England and sundry ancient men that came out of Holland.*
▷B Smith, *Bradford of Plymouth* (1951)

BRADLEY, Edward, pseud Cuthbert Bede
(1827–89)

English author and clergyman, born in Kidderminster. He was educated at Durham University. His facetious description of Oxford undergraduate life in *Adventures of Mr Verdant Green* (1853–7) was the first and most popular of 26 works. He was also an illustrator, and drew for *Punch* as well as his own works.

BRADSTREET, Anne, née Dudley
(1612–72)

English-born American Puritan poet, born probably in Northampton. In 1628 she married a Nonconformist minister, Simon Bradstreet (1603–97), who later became Governor of Massachusetts. In 1630 they emigrated to New England. Her first volume of poems, *The Tenth Muse lately sprung up in America*, written in the style of **Phineas Fletcher**, was published by her brother-in-law in London in 1650 without her knowledge. She is considered the first English poet in America.
▷E W White, *Anne Bradstreet: the tenth muse* (1971); Wendy Martin, *An American Triptych: Anne Bradstreet, Emily Dickinson, Adrienne Rich* (1986)

BRADY, Edwin James
(1869–1952)

Australian journalist, poet and writer, born in Carcoar, New South Wales. Early work on the wharfs around Sydney led to a strong bond with the sailing fraternity, and it is for his sea ballads that he is especially remembered. His first collection of verse was *The Ways of Many Waters* (1899); other collections were *Bush-land Ballads* (1910), *Bells and Hobbles* (1911) and *Wardens of the Seas* (1933). His travels around Australia are recounted in *The King's Caravan: Across Australia in a Wagon* (1911), and a journey down the Murray River in *River Rovers* (1911). His

other writings include books for children, short stories and the tale of his Irish father's experiences in the American Civil War.
▷*Life's Highway*, published posthumously in the quarterly journal *Southerly* (1952–5)

BRAGA, Rubem
(1913–)

Brazilian humorous writer, publisher and translator. Braga is a minor writer who takes an irreverent look at Brazilian life. He is best known for his *chrônicas*, short pieces which take a whimsical look at life in Rio de Janeiro.

BRAGG, Melvyn
(1939–)

English novelist and television arts presenter, born in Carlisle and educated at Wadham College, Oxford. Bragg's skill as a novelist only emerged fully with his third book, *Without a City Wall* (1968), which sets the oppositions of city (London) and country (Cumberland), centre and periphery, in terms of a powerful sexual struggle. The same themes emerge strongly in *The Silken Net* (1974), but *The Nerve* (1971), written at the time of his first wife's death, powerfully internalizes them and avoids many of the other books' tendency to schematicism. Perhaps more comfortable with set-pieces and images than straight prose, he has been an effective collaborator on film and television projects, notably with Ken Russell. Until a controversial television adaptation of his own *A Time to Dance* (1990) reawakened interest in his fiction, Bragg was better known as the front man (since 1978) of the South Bank Show, made by London Weekend Television, where he has also been Head of Arts. Previously, he was presenter of the BBC's *Second House* (1973–7) and the books programme, *Read All About It* (1976–7).

BRAINE, John Gerard
(1922–86)

English novelist, born in Bradford. He was educated at St Bede's Grammar School and had various jobs, including service in the Royal Navy, before following his mother's profession of librarian. In 1951 he went to London to become a full-time writer, but returned north the same year, after his mother's death in a road accident. He then spent 18 months in hospital suffering from tuberculosis, and it was during this period of enforced rest that he began to write his first successful novel, *Room at the Top*. He went back to library work until the publication of the book in 1957, and its success enabled him to embark again on a full-time career as a novelist. The theme of aggressive ambition and determination to break through rigid social barriers identified him with the 'angry young men' of the 1950s. His novels include *Life at the Top* (1962), a sequel to *Room at the Top*, *The Jealous God* (1964), *The Crying Game* (1964), *The Queen of a Distant Country* (1972), *The Vodi* (1959), *Stay with Me Till Morning* (1968), *Finger of Fire* (1977) and *One and Last Love* (1981).

▷J W Lee, *John Braine* (1973)

BRAITHWAITE, Edward Kamau
(1930–)

West Indian poet and historian, born in Bridgetown, Barbados. Described as 'one of the finest living poets of the Western hemisphere', he made his reputation with the three long poems reprinted together in 1973 as *The Arrivants: A New World Trilogy*. Each of the three — *Rights of Passage* (1967), *Masks* (1968) and *Islands* (1969) — analyses a different aspect of West Indian blacks' dispossession and their attempts to reconstitute an African-cum-Caribbean culture. His historical researches, for works such as *The Folk Culture of the Slaves of Jamaica* (1970), have complemented his creative output, which has continued with *Mother Poem* (1977) and *Sun Poem* (1982), both celebrations of his home island.

▷L Brown, 'The Cyclical Vision of Braithwaite' in *West Indian Poetry* (1978)

BRAITHWAITE, William Stanley Beaumont
(1878–1962)

Black American poet and editor, born in Boston. He was well known for his annual *Anthology of Magazine Verse* (1913–29). His own verse, full of what **Conrad Aiken** called 'chaste, romantic awe', is no longer much read.

BRAMAH, Ernest, pseud of Ernest Bramah Smith
(1868–1942)

English short-story writer and novelist. Little is known about his life beyond the fact that he was born and educated in Manchester and worked on the land—a period covered in *English Farming and Why I Turned It Up* (1894)—before turning to journalism. He was **Jerome K Jerome**'s secretary, and worked on Jerome's *Today* magazine. In 1895 and 1896, he edited the London journal *The Minster*. He is known primarily for the Kai Lung stories, elegant chinoiseries which enjoyed a vogue but are now little read; the first of these, *The Wallet of Kai Lung* (1900), is perhaps the best. In 1914 Bramah unveiled the detective Max Carrados, who featured in four collections of stories: *Max Carrados* (1914), *The Eyes of Max Carrados* (1923), *The Specimen Case* (1924) and *Max Carrados Mysteries* (1927), also in one novel, *The Bravo of London* (1934). What distinguishes Carrados from any other fictional detective is that he is blind. His manservant Parkinson acts as his Watson, making up the sensory deficit as the plots demand.

▷W White, 'A Bramah Biographer's Dilemma', in *American Book Collector*, vol 15 (1965)

BRANCATI, Vitaliano
(1907–54)

Italian novelist, dramatist and journalist, born in Pachino, Sicily. At first an ardent fascist and an adherent of the proto-fascist **Gabriele D'Annunzio**, he broke with the Party in 1934 when they objected to a novel he had written (he claimed to have broken with them a year earlier, 'privately', but some doubted this). Later he certainly moved over to the left, but also—and more decisively—switched from praise of the brutal man of action to biting criticism of him and of his motives. His first novel to signify his new direction was *Gli anni perduti* (1935, 'The Lost Years'); in *Don Giovanni in Sicilia* (1942, 'Don Giovanni in Sicily'), he reached his main theme: homosexuality and impotence posing as heterosexual boastfulness—*gallismo*, as he called it. His best novel is reckoned to be *Il bell'Antonio* (1949, Eng trans *Bell'Antonio*, 1978), again about a man doomed to a (this time figurative) impotence. In his final years Brancati was beset by many difficulties, and, perhaps rightly, felt that he had failed to do full justice to his gifts.

BRAND, Dionne
(1953–)

Trinidadian-born poet, now settled in Canada, where she has worked as a teacher and counsellor in the black community. Her poems, which have been described by one critic as 'heavy stuff', are longer than most contemporary poems and attempt to deal with a wider perspective than the purely personal. *Chronicles of the Hostile Sun* (1984) is an example of her attempt to write historical verse of immediate urgency. It reflects a period of residency in Grenada, where she stayed up to the moment of the US invasion. *Sans Souci* (1989) contains short stories.

▷D Cumberdance (ed), *Fifty Caribbean Writers* (1986)

BRAND, Max, pseud of Frederick Schiller Faust
(1892–1944)

American novelist and short-story writer, born in Seattle. An orphan by 13, he had a nomadic youth as an agricultural worker, then paid his own way through university. In 1918 he became a Western writer, contributing stories to around two dozen pulp magazines using almost as many pseudonyms. The following year his first novel, *The Untamed*, appeared under the Brand name. Other notable works in a prolific career include *Trailin'* (1919, a tale of Oedipal conflict), and *Destry Rides Again* (1930). A classicist and a Europhile, he regarded the West of which he wrote as dirty and brutish. He spent more than a decade (1926–37) in a Florentine villa, and died in Italy, where he was serving as a war correspondent with the US 88th Infantry Division.

▷R Easton, *Max Brand: The Big Westerner* (1970)

BRANDAO, Raúl
(1867–1930)

Portuguese novelist, memoirist and playwright. He began under the influence of **Zola** as a simple naturalist, but later wrote more complex novels, such as his last, and perhaps most powerful of all, *Pobre de pedir* (1931, 'Reduced to Begging'), a vivid picture of poverty and brutality redeemed only by the compassion which pervades all his work.

BRANNER, H(ans) C(hristian)
(1903–66)

Danish novelist, short-story writer and playwright, born in Ordrup. A former actor and publisher, he wrote a number of psychologically realistic novels, beginning with *Legetøj* (1936, 'Toys'), which expressed his fears about fascism. Later works were less socially grounded and bear the mark of French existentialism: *Drømmen om en kvinde* (1949, 'A Woman's Dream'), and the later *Ingen kender Natten* (1955, 'Nobody Knows the Night'), which returns to the Nazi occupation for its material. His ability to capture the inner life was also evident in the **Joyce**an short stories of *To Minutters Stilhed* (1944, 'Two Minutes of Silence'), and his remarkable plays for radio.

▷T L Markey, *Hans Christian Branner* (1973)

BRANT, Sebastian
(1458–1521)

German poet and humanist, born in Strasbourg. He studied and lectured at Basel. His *Narrenschiff* (1494, 'Ship of Fools'), an important vernacular satire on the follies and vices of his times, is not very poetical, but is full of sound sense and good moral teaching, and enjoyed immense popularity. It was translated into English by **Alexander Barclay** and Henry Watson, both in 1509. His other writings include biographies of the Saints and translations from Latin texts.

▷E H Teydal, *Sebastian Brant* (1967)

BRANTENBERG, Gerd
(1941–)

Norwegian novelist, born in Oslo. She studied at Oslo University, and had her first novel published in 1973: *Opp alle jordens homofile* (Eng trans *What Comes Naturally*, 1986) explores the complexities of being lesbian in Oslo in the 1960s, the humorous style tackling conventional prejudices head on. *Egalias døtre* (1977, Eng trans *The Daughters of Egalia*, 1985) exposes the absurdities of patriarchal society by inverting its norms, and has enjoyed considerable international success. *Favntak* (1983, 'Embraces') depicts lesbian love, while *Sangen om St. Croix* (1979, 'The Song of St Croix'), *Ved fergestedet* (1985, 'At the Ferry Crossing') and *For alle vinder* (1989, 'To the Winds') is a realist trilogy focusing on differences of class and sex.

▷J Garton, 'Gerd Brantenberg', in *Norwegian Women's Writing 1850–1990* (1993)

BRANTÔME, Pierre de Bourdeilles, Seigneur de
(c.1540–1614)

French soldier and author, born in Périgord. He was educated at Paris and at Poitiers. In his sixteenth year he was given the abbacy of Brantôme, but he never took orders, and spent most of his life as a courtier and soldier. In 1561 he accompanied Mary, Queen of Scots to Scotland, and in 1565 he joined the expedition sent to Malta to assist the Knights of St John against the sultan. He served in Italy under the Maréchal de Brissac, in Africa under the Spaniards, and in Hungary as a volunteer against the Turks. He was made chamberlain to Charles IX and Henri III, and fought against the Huguenots. He was injured after a fall from a horse in about 1594, and he began to write his memoirs, and from then on lived in retirement. His works, first published in 1665–6, comprise *Vies des grands capitaines* ('Lives of the Great Captains'), *Vies des dames galantes* ('Lives of the Lady Courtesans') and *Vies des dames illustres* ('Lives of the Illustrious Ladies'), and provide a detailed picture of the Valois court. Their literary merit and historical interest are considerable. Their matter is often of the most scandalous nature, but they give a wonderfully vivid picture of his times.

▷R D Cottrell, *Brantôme: the writer as portraitist of his age* (1970)

BRASCH, Charles Orwell
(1909–73)

New Zealand poet, critic and editor, born in Dunedin. In 1947 he established *Landfall*, a

123

periodical of art, literature and politics, and was its editor for 20 years, exercising great influence on the form and direction of contemporary New Zealand poets. In 1962 he edited a selection of verse, *Landfall Country: Work from Landfall, 1947–1961*. His own verse is collected in *The Land and the People* (1939), *Disputed Ground: Poems 1939–1945* (1948), *The Estate* (1957), which collected poems written after 1945, *Ambulando* (1964), *Not Far Off* (1969) and the posthumous *Home Ground* (1974), ed Alan Roddick, who also edited *Collected Poems* (1984).
▷*Indirections: A Memoir 1909–1947* (1980), ed J Bertram

BRASILLACH, Robert
(1909–45)

French novelist and journalist, born in Perpignan. His early work includes studies of **Virgil**, **Corneille**, and the French revolutionary André Chenier. His fascist sympathies became increasingly evident as the 1930s wore on, and his novel *Les Sept Couleurs* (1939, 'The Seven Colours') has as its hero a man who becomes a Legionnaire, an admirer of Hitler, and finally one of Franco's soldiers. Under the German occupation, as editor of the fascist weekly *Je Suis Partout* ('I Am Everywhere'), Brasillach demanded the summary execution of imprisoned communists. With the liberation of the city, he was arrested—most other fascist writers had long since fled the capital—and sentenced to death as a collaborator. His trial became a focus for the debate on how collaborators should be treated in post-war France. Forty-five writers, including **Albert Camus**, signed a plea for clemency; others, among them **Simone de Beauvoir**, refused to lend their names to the appeal. The sentence was not commuted, and Brasillach was killed by firing squad.

BRATHWAITE, Errol Freeman
(1924–)

New Zealand novelist, born in Clive, Hawkes Bay. His service during World War II with the Royal New Zealand Air Force provided themes for his first novels, *Fear in the Night* (1959) concerning a crashed aircrew trapped behind Japanese lines, *An Affair of Men* (1962) and *Long Way Home* (1964). Next came a trilogy of historical novels on the New Zealand Land Wars of the 1860s: *The Flying Fish* (1964); *The Needle's Eye* (1965) and *The Evil Day* (1967). He has written topographical books including *Companion Guides* to the North and South Islands: *New Zealand and its People* (1974) and *The Beauty of New Zealand* (4 vols, 1974–82).

BRAUN, Lili, née von Kretschmann
(1865–1916)

German socialist authoress and feminist, born in Halberstadt. She married the socialist writer and politician Heinrich Braun (1854–1927). Her best-known book is *Im Schatten der Titanen* (1908, 'In the Shadow of the Titans'), and she is known for her novel *Liebesbriefe der Marquise* (1912, 'Love Letters of the Marquis'), and her *Memoiren einer Sozialistin* (1909–11, 'Memoirs of a Woman Socialist').
▷J Vogelstein, biographical note in *Gesammelte Werke* (1923)

BRAUTIGAN, Richard
(1935–84)

American fabulist and poet. Born in Tacoma, Washington, he is identified strongly with the Far West sensibility and hippy ethos of writers like **Ken Kesey**. Rejecting social fiction, Brautigan wrote brief surreal fantasies, outwardly naive, but often laden with unexpected cultural references. His finest work, *Trout Fishing in America* (1967), masquerades as a 'how-to' book; Brautigan's search for the ideal trout stream is, however, a purely rhetorical one, in which Trout Fishing in America becomes a verbal cipher or 'character' that can be placed in any context. Brautigan interweaves references to literary pastoral, American materialism and waste, and political totalitarianism; the 'novel' is also a satirical gloss on *Moby-Dick*. Other books include *In Watermelon Sugar* (1964), *A Confederate General from Big Sur* (1965) and the best of his verse collections, *The Pill Versus the Springhill Mine Disaster* (1968). After *The Abortion: An Historical Romance* (1971) he increasingly satirized popular literary genre and his books became marked by a dark thread of melancholy and loneliness. He committed suicide.
▷M Chénetier, *Richard Brautigan* (1982)

BRAZIL, Angela
(1868–1947)

English writer of girls' school stories, born in Preston. She was a governess for some years before beginning to write tales. She never married, and lived with her brother and sister, describing her adult self as 'an absolute schoolgirl'. Her stories of school life are heavily moralistic, and are notable for their healthy realism. Her best books include *The New Girl at St Chad's*, *A Fourth Form Friendship* and *Captain Peggie*.

BRECHT, Bertolt Eugen Friedrich
(1898–1956)

German playwright and poet, born in Augsburg, perhaps Germany's greatest dramatist.

He studied medicine and philosophy at Munich and Berlin Universities, and served briefly as a medical orderly in 1918. He won the **Kleist** Drama Prize in 1922 for his first two Expressionist plays, *Trommeln in der Nacht* (1922, Eng trans *Drums in the Night*, 1966), and *Baal* (1922, Eng trans 1964), followed by *Mann ist Mann* (1926, Eng trans *A Man's a Man*, 1964) with its clownish, inhuman soldiery. He was keenly interested in the effects produced by combining drama and music, and consequently collaborated with Kurt Weill, Eisler and Dessau in his major works. It was the *Dreigroschenoper* (1928, Eng trans *The Threepenny Opera*, 1958), an adaptation of **John Gay**'s *Beggar's Opera* in a sham Victorian London setting, with music by Kurt Weill, that established Brecht's reputation. A Marxist, he regarded his plays as social experiments, requiring detachment, not passion, from the observing audience. To achieve this, he introduced the 'epic' theatre, where the audience is required to see the stage as a stage, actors as actors, and not the traditional make-believe of the theatre. Thus, to prevent the audience from identifying themselves with a principal actor, the camp-following title character in *Mutter Courage und ihre Kinder* (1941, Eng trans *Mother Courage and her Children*, 1961) is deliberately made to muff her lines, and *Puntilla* (1940) is given an increasingly ugly make-up. With Hitler's rise to power in 1933, Brecht sought asylum in Denmark, Sweden, and Finland, journeyed across Russia and Persia, and in 1941 settled in Hollywood. His abiding hatred of Nazi Germany found expression in a series of short, episodic plays and poems collected under the title of *Furcht und Elend des dritten Reiches* (1945, 'Fear and Loathing under the Third Reich'), and *Der aufhaltsame Aufstieg des Arturo Ui* (1957, Eng trans *The Resistible Rise of Arturo Ui*, 1976). He denied membership of the Communist Party before a Senate sub-committee on un-American activities in 1946, and in 1948 accepted the East German government's offer of a theatre in East Berlin. The *Berliner Ensemble* was founded, producing under his direction his later plays, such as *Der kaukasische Kreidekreis* (1947, Eng trans *The Caucasian Chalk Circle*, 1948), and *Der gute Mensch von Sezuan* (1943, Eng trans *The Good Woman of Setzuan*, 1948), as well as touring in Western Europe, and visiting London shortly after his death with Helene Weigel, his widow, as the company's leading actress. Although apparently antipathetic towards the East German anti-communist uprising in 1953 and a recipient of the Stalin Peace Prize (1954), he proved as artist and thinker to be an embarrassment to the East German authorities. His opera *Lukullus* (1932–51), in which the Roman general has to account for his deeds before a tribunal-of-the-shadows, was withdrawn by order after the first night. *Galileo* (1938) underlined the moral that, however much the intellect may be oppressed, truth will out.
▷M Esslin, *Bertolt Brecht* (1969); K Volker, *Bertolt Brecht: a biography* (1979)

BREDERODE, or BREDERO, Gerbrand Adriaenz
(1585–1618)

Major Dutch poet and dramatist, who was also a painter, born in Amsterdam. He is best known for his strident hatred of affectation, his lyrical poetry, and his stage comedies. *Spaanschen Brabander* (1618) is his play based on the great anonymous Spanish picaresque novel *Lazarillo de Tormes* (1554), which he sets in a vibrant Amsterdam.
▷J A N Knuttel, *Bredero* (1949, in Dutch)

BREMER, Fredrika
(1801–65)

Swedish novelist, born near Åbo in Finland, and brought up near Stockholm. Her stories *Teckningar utur hvardagslifvet* (1828, 'Scenes from Everyday Life') were immediately successful and helped bring about realistic family fiction in Sweden; *Familjen H* (1831, 'The H Family'), and *Hemmet* (1839, 'The Home') developed the strain considerably. Novels like *Hertha* (1856) and *Fader och dotter* (1858, 'Father and Daughter') express her interest in female education and political emancipation, ideas she had absorbed on visits to Britain and the USA. She travelled widely elsewhere in Europe and the Levant and published two volumes of impressions.
▷E Ehrnach, *Fredrika Bremer* (1955)

BRENAN, Gerald
(1894–1987)

English travel writer, Hispanophile and novelist, born in Malta, the son of an officer in an Irish regiment. After an itinerant boyhood he debunked with a donkey, drifting his way across Europe to the Balkans and back again. He went to Spain and settled in Yegen, an isolated village which became the focus of his classic *South from Granada* (1957). This was preceded by his best-known book, *The Spanish Labyrinth* (1943), still regarded as one of the most profound and perceptive studies of modern Spain. Other books include two volumes of memoirs, *A Life of One's Own* (1962) and *Personal Record* (1974), *The Literature of the Spanish People* (1951) and a novel, *Thoughts in a Dry Season* (1978).

BRENNAN, Christopher John
(1870–1932)

Australian poet, academic and critic, born in Sydney of a Catholic family. Intended for the

priesthood, after entering Sydney University he turned to the classics and philosophy. Going to Berlin University in 1892 to read philosophy, he was distracted by the exciting social and cultural life, and by French Symbolist poetry, which influenced his future writing. Returning to Sydney University in 1894, he was appointed Associate Professor of German Literature in 1920, but his intemperate and iconoclastic nature led to his dismissal five years later. He published only a select number of volumes of verse, the best of which was written before 1900 and issued as *Poems* (1913). The sequence of verse, 'The Wanderer' suggests the torment of Brennan's own life. A later collection was *A Chant of Doom and Other Verses* (1918). Some of his verse was published posthumously, and his criticism appeared mainly in journals, but he is also known for his co-editing of the standard college anthology *From Blake to Arnold* (1900), which contains much of his critical work.
▷ J P McAuley, *Christopher Brennan* (1973)

BRENNER, Joseph Chaim
(1881–1921)

Hebrew novelist, story writer and translator (of **Dostoyevsky**'s *Crime and Punishment*), born in the ghetto in Novi Malini, Bulgaria. He studied in a Talmudic College (Yeshivah), then served in the Russian army, but in 1905 moved to London, where he lived in poverty as editor of a Hebrew periodical. He became a Zionist, and settled in Palestine in 1908—he died in the Arab riots in Jaffa. His novels and stories are very harshly realistic, but—as is so often the case with the Jewish writers of this era—unavailable in English translation.
▷ M Waxman, *A History of Jewish Literature* (1960)

BRENTANO, Clemens von
(1778–1842)

German poet, novelist and dramatist, born in Ehrenbreitstein. After a somewhat irresponsible early life, he became a Roman Catholic in 1818 and withdrew to the monastery of Dülmen, near Münster (1818–24), where he recorded the revelations of the nun, Anna Katharina Emmerich. Thereafter he led a restless life, and showed plain signs of derangement some years before his death. In his earliest poems the peculiarities of the Romantic school are carried to excess. His dramatic productions, the best of which is *Die Gründung Prags* ('The Founding of Prague'), are characterized by great dramatic power, and a wonderful humour. He was mostly successful in his novellas, particularly in the *Geschichte vom braven Kasperl* ('Tale of Honest Kasper'), and with his brother-in-law **Achim von Arnim** he edited *Des Knaben Wunderhorn* ('The Boy's Magic Horn'), a collection of folk songs.
▷ J B Heinreise, *Clemens von Brentano* (1878)

BRENT-DYER, Elinor M(ary)
(1894–1969)

English author of the 'Chalet School' girls' stories, born in South Shields. Educated at Leeds University, she became a schoolmistress, and later headmistress of the Margaret Roper Girls' School in Hereford. Her first schoolgirl novel, *Gerry Goes to School*, appeared in 1922, inaugurating her 98 titles. Her fourth book, *The School at the Chalet* (1925), established her famous series by showing the 24-year-old Madge Bettany's successful attempt to found an English school in the Austrian Tyrol, to which Austrian as well as English parents were attracted. Centred on Jo Bettany, Madge's younger sister, the series sought to evangelize against English parochialism and xenophobia. Perhaps the best single title was *The Chalet School in Exile* (1940), a horrific if judicious account of the school's flight from Nazi rule with a grimly realistic depiction of homicidal persecution of Jews. Later stories were set in the Channel Islands, in Wales, and in the Bernese Oberland: the inevitable decline was offset for many years by the creation of another memorable character, the impetuous and gloriously frank Mary-Lou Trelawney. The final book in the series, *Prefects of the Chalet School*, was published posthumously in 1970.

BRENTON, Howard
(1942–)

English dramatist, born in Portsmouth. He wrote for fringe theatre companies during the late 1960s, and was resident dramatist at the Royal Court Theatre, London, from 1972 to 1973, where his play *Magnificence*, dealing with urban terrorism, was staged. *The Churchill Play* (1974), a bleak look at a future Britain governed by hard-liners using troops to brutalize trade unionists, was produced at the Nottingham Playhouse. *Weapons of Happiness* (1976) became the first new play to be produced at the National Theatre's recently-opened South Bank building. *The Romans in Britain* was premiered at the National Theatre in 1980, and *The Genius*, on the nuclear arms race, at the Royal Court in 1983. He has also collaborated with **David Hare** on a number of projects, the most outstanding being *Pravda* (1985), a furiously ebullient satire on the cravenness of the national press. He has also written a political thriller, *Diving for Pearls* (1989).

BRETON, André
(1896–1966)

French poet, essayist and critic, born in Tinchebray, Normandy. In 1916 he joined the Dadaist group and was co-founder of the Dada magazine *Littérature* (1919), and collaborated with Philippe Soupault to write *Les Champs magnétiques* (1920, 'Magnetic Fields'), which was described as 'an experiment in automatic writing'. In 1922 he turned to Surrealism, and in 1924 he published his first Surrealist manifesto (he developed his ideas more fully in 1930 and 1942) and *Le Poissonsoluble* ('Solublefish'), and became Editor of *La Révolution surréaliste*. His major novel, *Nadja*, which mingles the irrational and the everyday, was published in 1928 (Eng trans 1960). In 1930 he joined the Communist Party for a time. He spent the war years in the USA. His writings also include *Qu'est-ce que le surréalisme?* (1934, Eng trans *What is Surrealism?*, 1936), and he continued his highly personal, poetic exploration of Surrealism and the unconscious in his post-war writings.
▷M A Caws, *André Breton* (1971)

BRETON, Nicholas
(c.1555–c.1626)

English poet, born in London, the son of a merchant, and stepson of **George Gascoigne**. Educated at Oxford, he became a prolific writer of all kinds of verse, prose and pamphlets. His best-known poem is *The Passionate Shepheard* (1604). His prose *Wits Trenchmour* (1597) is a fishing idyll on which **Izaak Walton** drew for *The Compleat Angler*. He also wrote a prose romance, *The Strange Fortune of Two Excellent Princes* (1600), and a collection of character observations, *Fantasticks* (1626).
▷G A Tannenbaum, *Elizabethan Bibliographies* (1937)

BRETÓN DE LOS HERREROS, Don Manuel
(1796–1873)

Spanish dramatist. He is the author of some 150 plays, most of which are social comedies concerned with middle-class manners and mores, in which caricature rather than character is portrayed. Many of his works were translations and adaptations. He also wrote poetry, and was a popular figure in his day.
▷G le Gentil, *La poète Manuel Bretón de los Herreros* (1903)

BREWSTER, Elizabeth
(1922–)

Canadian poet, born in Chipman, New Brunswick, she has been a university teacher of English. Her poems are quiet, meditative, and, in her own words, attempt to dramatize 'the struggle to lead a human rational life in a world which is increasingly inhuman and irrational'. Her *Selected Poems 1944–84* appeared in two volumes in 1985.
▷*Canadian Literature* (Autumn, 1974)

BŘEZINA, Otakar, properly Václav Jebavý
(1868–1929)

Czech poet, born in Pocatky. He was a school-teacher, and lived as a bachelor recluse in a small country town. His work, which consists of five books of poems and one of philosophical essays, attempted an ambitious synthesis of philosophical and mystical elements. He was a leading exponent of a richly evocative Symbolism in Czech poetry in his collections *Vrěy od pólő* (1897, 'Polar Winds'), *Stavitelé chramu* (1899, 'Temple Builders'), *Ruce* (1901, 'The Hands'), and others.
▷P Selver, *Otakar Březina: a study in Czech literature* (1921)

BRICKHILL, Paul Chester Jerome
(1916–91)

Australian author, born in Melbourne. Educated at Sydney University, he worked in journalism before serving with the Royal Australian Air Force during World War II. Shot down in North Africa, he was for two years a prisoner-of-war in Germany, in Stalag Luft III from which the intrepid escape was made, later described by him in *The Great Escape* (1951, filmed 1963). His first published book, *Escape to Danger* (1946), collected many stories of prison-camp life. He went on to become the most successful non-fiction writer of the post-war period, with *The Dam Busters* (1951, filmed 1956), *Escape—or Die* (1952), and the story of the legless air ace Douglas Bader, *Reach for the Sky* (1954, filmed 1956).

BRIDGES, Robert Seymour
(1844–1930)

English poet and critic, born in Walmer, Kent. Educated at Eton and Corpus Christi College, Oxford, he then studied medicine at St Bartholomew's Hospital and practised until 1881. At university he met **Gerard Manley Hopkins**, with whom he became friendly, arranging for the posthumous publication of his poems in 1918. His first collection, *Poems*, appeared in 1873, and was followed by *The Growth of Love* (1876), a sequence of sonnets which was a popular success. He followed this with two long poems, *Prometheus the Firegiver* (1883) and *Eros and Psyche* (1885), but for the next decade he concentrated on plays and wrote eight, only one of which was

performed in his lifetime. He made important contributions to criticism, with studies of **Milton** (1893) and **Keats** (1895), and wrote poems set to music by Charles Parry, as well as *A Practical Discourse on Hymn Singing* (1901). In 1912 he published his *Collected Poems* to wide public acclaim and in 1913 he was surprisingly appointed poet laureate, and produced *The Spirit of Man* (1916), an idiosyncratic anthology of prose and verse designed to lift the nation's spirits during World War I. After the war, he published *October and Other Poems* (1920) and, in his 85th year, *The Testament of Beauty*, a long poem in four parts whose philosophy is expressed in its title.
▷L P Smith, *Robert Bridges: recollections* (1931)

BRIDIE, James, pseud of **Osborne Henry Mavor**
(1888–1951)

Scottish dramatist, born in Glasgow, son of the pioneering electrical engineer Henry Mavor. He qualified as a doctor at Glasgow University and became a successful general practitioner and consultant. Always interested in theatre, he seized his chance when the Scottish National Players produced his *Sunlight Sonata* in 1928 under the pseudonym of Mary Henderson. After that, he wrote a stream of plays, among them *The Anatomist* (1931), *A Sleeping Clergyman* (1933), *Mr Bolfry* (1943) and *Dr Angelus* (1947). He served in both world wars in the Royal Army Medical Corps and after the second he became Head of the Scottish Committee of CEMA. He founded the Citizens' Theatre in Glasgow in 1943.
▷H Luyben, *James Bridie: clown and philosopher* (1965)

BRIEUX, Eugène
(1858–1932)

French dramatist and Academician, born in Paris of poor parents. He experienced many of the social evils which his powerful, didactic plays, leavened by wit, expose. His works include *L'Engrenage* (1894, Eng trans *The Evasion*, 1896) and *Maternité* (1903, Eng trans *Maternity*, 1907). His attack on the judiciary in *La Robe Rouge* (1900, 'The Red Dress'), and his use of the effects of syphilis in *Les Avariés* (1901, Eng trans *Damaged Goods*, 1914), both aroused public controversies.
▷W H Scheifley, *Brieux and contemporary French society* (1917)

BRIGGS, Raymond (Redvers)
(1934–)

English children's illustrator and author, born in London, the son of a milkman. His early publications were conventional, such as *Midnight Adventure* (1961), but in 1966 his *Mother Goose Treasury* appeared with over 900 pictures, and his talent for eccentric comedy was established, winning him the Kate Greenaway Medal. *Father Christmas* (1973), another distinctive work, uses the comic-strip format, featuring a grumpy, expletory Santa, reluctantly braving the wintry elements. For this he was awarded his second Greenaway Medal. *Fungus the Bogeyman* (1977) brought him love and loathing, and *The Snowman* (1979) enchanted adults and children alike. A provocative as well as an entertaining artist, his anxiety for the future well-being of the planet is expressed in *When the Wind Blows* (1982), while *The Tin Pot Foreign General and the Old Iron Woman* (1983) was an attack on the political manipulation of the Falklands War. In 1992 he was awarded the Kurt Maschler Award for *The Man*.

BRIGHOUSE, Harold
(1882–1958)

English playwright, born near Manchester, one of the first 20th-century English authors to write plays that were both popular and set beyond the metropolitan and country-house world of the fashionable and wealthy. Brighouse was working at a local cotton mill when Annie Horniman (the heiress of the tea empire) took over the Manchester Gaiety Theatre in 1908. He was one of several hopefuls who answered her call for new writers, and between 1909 and his death he completed over 70 plays, many of them amiably folksy one-act comedies set in Lancashire. Some of the full-length plays, such as *Lonesome-Like* (1911) and *The Odd Man Out* (1912), might profitably be revived today, but are overlooked, Brighouse's reputation depending, unfortunately, on only one play, *Hobson's Choice* (1915). In this work, the pragmatic and determined Maggie Hobson, supposedly on the shelf at 30, coerces the talented but timid bootmaker Willie Mossop into marriage, makes him her business partner and successfully takes over her domineering father's boot and shoe business. Highly popular at the time, it is frequently revived.

BRINK, André
(1935–)

South African novelist, short-story writer, playwright, critic and translator, born in Vrede, Orange Free State. An Afrikaaner dissident, he has produced a prodigious body of work of uneven quality and has, almost single-handedly, contemporized Afrikaans novel writing. He emerged as a writer in the 1950s but it was not until his seventh novel, *Kennis van die aand* (1973)—which he later

translated into English as *Looking on Darkness* (1974)—was banned by the South African authorities that he began to attract international attention. Relating the story of a coloured actor who makes good in London and returns to South Africa to confront the apartheid regime, it won the author admiration, though more for his courage than his style. Subsequent books have been criticized for their sentimentality and sensationalism but the best—*Rumours of Rain* (1978), *A Chain of Voices* (1982) and *States of Emergency* (1988)—are powerful narratives which highlight conditions in South Africa without resorting to propaganda. He received the Martin Luther King Memorial Prize and the French Prix Medicis Étranger in 1980, has thrice won the CNA Award, South Africa's most prestigious commendation, and has twice been runner-up for the Booker Prize.
▷ *Pot Pourri: Skatse uit parys* (1962)

BRINSMEAD, Hesba Fay
(1922–)

Australian writer, born in Bilpin, Blue Mountains, New South Wales. The author of award-winning fiction, she was one of the first writers of 'transitional' books which give adult perspectives within an adolescent frame of reference. Her first work, *Pastures of the Blue Crane* (1964), achieved immediate success, winning two awards and becoming a popular television series in the 1970s. Many of her adolescent romances are set in country areas, such as the Tasmania of *Season of the Briar* (1965), but she is aware of the social and racial tensions which affect young people, as in *Beat of the City* (1966). *Longtime Passing* (1971) won the Children's Book of the Year Award, and was followed by *Longtime Dreaming* in 1982.

BRITTAIN, Vera Mary
(1893–1970)

English writer, born in Newcastle-under-Lyme. After studying at Oxford she served as a nurse in World War I, recording her experiences with war-found idealism in *Testament of Youth* (1933). As well as writing a number of novels, she made several lecture tours in the USA, promoting feminism and pacifism. In 1925 she married George Catlin, Professor of Politics at Cornell, and wrote the sequels, *Testament of Friendship* (1940) and *Testament of Experience* (1957). Her daughter is the English politician Shirley Williams.
▷ V Brittain and J S Reid (eds), *Selected Letters of Winifred Holtby and Vera Brittain* (1960)

BRITTING, Georg
(1891–1964)

German poet, born in Regensburg. He was severely wounded during World War I and afterwards settled in Munich. He wrote one novel, *Lebenslauf eines dicken mannes, der Hamlet hieβ* (1932), a bizarre adaptation of the Hamlet story. His poetry, as found in the collections *Michael und das Fräulein* (1927) or *Der bekränzte Weiher* (1937, 'The Garlanded Pond'), is marked by colourful vocabulary and a precise technique.

BRIZEUX, Julien Auguste Pélage
(1803–58)

French poet, born in Lorient. Much of his work, including a translation of **Dante**'s *Divina Commedia*, was influenced by Italian styles, but his verse also incorporated the folklore and dialect of Britanny.
▷ C Levigne, *Brizeux et ses oeuvres* (1898)

BROCH, Hermann
(1886–1951)

Austrian novelist and essayist, born in Vienna. He spent his early adult life working in his father's textile business and was over 40 when he went to Vienna University to study philosophy and mathematics. When the Nazis invaded Austria in 1938 he was imprisoned, but influential friends, including **James Joyce**, obtained his release and facilitated his emigration to America in 1940, where he remained until he died in abject surroundings. He is regarded as one of the greatest German writers of the 20th century, though he was a reluctant writer and his books reward only readers with perseverance. His masterpiece is *The Death of Virgil* (1946). Other notable books include *The Sleepwalkers* (3 vols, 1931–2), *The Unknown Quantity* (1935) and *The Spell*, published posthumously and first translated into English in 1987.
▷ D C Cohn, *The Sleepwalkers: elucidations* (1966)

BROCKES, Barthold Heinrich
(1680–1747)

German poet, translator (**Pope**, **James Thomson**) and politician (he was Senator of Hamburg and then Mayor of Ritzbüttel, but more to do people a favour than out of ambition). He was born in Hamburg. Both Handel and Telemann set to music his somewhat florid verses, written in the Baroque manner. Most of his poetry is pedestrian, though it is technically adept; he was also a keen observer of the natural scene, adding to German poetry what one critic has called 'a new world of exact perception'.
▷ A Brandl, *Barthold Heinrich Brockes* (1878, in German)

129

BROD, Max
(1884–1968)

Austrian novelist, biographer, essayist, poet and dramatist, born in Prague. He became a Zionist and emigrated to Palestine (Israel) in 1939, where he became the literary director of the Habimah Theatre in Tel Aviv. Although he is known in the English-speaking world as the long-time friend, editor and biographer of **Franz Kafka**, he was a versatile and prolific writer in his own right. His work includes novels on religious and social themes, plays, autobiographical writings, and literary criticism.

▷M Pazi, *Max Brod, Werk und Persönlichkeit* (1970)

BRODBER, Erna
(1940–)

Jamaican novelist, born in St Mary and educated at the University of West Indies. She is a respected sociologist/social historian and has published extensively in these fields. Her fiction draws on this knowledge and gives a strong sense of the importance of oral history in transmitting traditional wisdom and an appreciation of African ancestry. Her first novel, *Jane and Louisa Will Soon Come Home* (1981), is a semi-autobiographical prose-poem centring on the character Nellie's search for identity. In both this work and in *Myal* (1989), a lyrical, amusing novel which scrutinizes the educational and religious institutions derived from a colonial past, the acceptance of the varied strands of a multi-racial past is shown to be essential for the renewal of individual and society.

▷E O'Callaghan, 'Engineering the Female Subject: Erna Brodber's *Myal*', in *Kunapipi*, Vol XII, No.3 (1990)

BRODERICK, Damien
(1944–)

Australian science-fiction writer, born in Melbourne, whose *The Dreaming Dragons: A Time Opera* (1980) was runner-up for the international **John W Campbell** Award in 1981. With *The Judas Mandala* (1982, rev edn 1990), *Transmitters* (1984), *The Black Grail* (1986), *Striped Holes* (1988) and *The Sea's Furthest End* (1993) it comprises the thematically cross-linked *Faustus Hexagram* sequence. Short-story collections are *A Man Returned* (1965) and *The Dark Between the Stars* (1991). He has edited anthologies of Australian science fiction and writes critically on science and fiction; *The Lotto Effect* (1992) is a study of parapsychology, and recent titles are *Reading by Starlight: The Semiotics of Modern and Postmodern Science Fiction* (1994) and *The Architecture of Babel: Discourses of Literature and Science* (1994). His

novels have been translated into German, Portuguese and Polish.

BRODKEY, Harold Roy
(1930–)

American short-story writer and novelist, born in Staunton, Illinois. Originally called Harold Weintraub, he took his name from the family who adopted him. His debut as a short-story writer, *First Love and Other Sorrows* (1957), led to widespread belief that he was an author of substantial promise. His output since, however, has been sparse to say the least: a gap of almost 30 years followed before his next collection, *Women and Angels*, appeared in 1985. His novel *The Runaway Soul*, also some three decades in the making, appeared in 1991; like the rest of his writing it contains a strong autobiographical thread, but is strangely devoid of vitality and verve.

BRODSKY, Iosef
(1940–)

Russian poet, translator and critic, winner of the Nobel Prize for literature, born in Leningrad, who was tried as a 'social parasite' in 1964, and sent into exile. Although he was hardly known to general readers in Russia, his poetry circulated in *samizdat* form, and various critics and poets interceded on his behalf. His cause was taken up in the USA, but in 1972 he was expelled from Russia. In 1977 he became an American citizen, and in 1987 he was awarded the Nobel Prize. He has latterly written in English and translated his own Russian poems into English; but it is for his earlier poetry that he is most valued. Often dismissed in contemporary Russia as merely a charming minor voice, he is a scholarly poet, who introduced into Russian poetry the influences of the English metaphysical poets, of **Yeats** and **Eliot**, and of his personal mentor, **W H Auden**. He is, after **Seferis**, perhaps the best of the European synthetic poets—that is, highly artificial, ornate, earnest, mannerist, learned, unspontaneous. His collections include *Stikhotvoreniia i Poemy* (1965, 'Longer and Shorter Poems'), and *Uraniia: Novaia Kniga Stikhov* (1985, 'Urania: A New Book of Poems', later reissued in English as *To Urania: Selected Poems 1965–1985*, 1988). His translations of **Donne** and **Marvell** into Russian are particularly prized. There are English translations of his work in *Selected Poems* (1973) and *Less Than One* (prose essays, 1980).

▷*A Part of Speech* (1979)

BRÓDY, Sándor
(1863–1924)

Hungarian novelist, story writer, dramatist and journalist, born in Budapest. He was extremely influential and popular in Hungarian literature for many years, but now has his sharp (mainly academic) detractors, who accuse him of sentimentality and indulgence in mediocre writing. However, he possessed a remarkable vitality, and what he took from his two chief mentors, the historical novelist **Mór Jókai** and **Zola**, was worth adopting. His stories about Rembrandt were translated in 1928; and one of his greatest stories, 'The Jest', is translated in *Hungarian Short Stories* (1962).

BRØGGER, Suzanne
(1944–)

Danish novelist, critic and playwright, born in Copenhagen, who spent long periods abroad as a child and adolescent; among her major literary influences are writers such as **Anaïs Nin** and **Henry Miller** as well as **Karen Blixen**. Her first book, *Fri os fra kærligheden* (1973, Eng trans *Deliver Us from Love*, 1977), characteristically transcends the conventional genres to formulate a critique of marriage and the nuclear family which culminates in a celebration of the free unfolding of female eroticism. *Creme Fraiche* (1978) is a fictive autobiography focusing on erotic exploits, while *Brøg* (1980, 'Brew'), a collection of articles and essays, demonstrates the scope of her cultural criticism. The ambitious novel *JA* (1984, 'YES') opens up new perspectives on *Creme Fraiche*; and the play entitled *Efter Orgiet* (1991, 'After the Orgy') offers a critical view of the 'sexual liberation' of the 1960s.
▷M Schack, 'Suzanne Brøgger', in T Brostrøm and M Winge (eds), *Danske digtere i det 20. århundrede*, vol V (1982)

BROME, Richard
(c.1590–1652)

English dramatist, of whom little is known except that he had been in his earlier days servant to **Ben Jonson**, and that he wrote as many as 24 popular plays, the best being *The Northern Lass* and *The Jovial Crew*.
▷R J Kaufman, *Richard Brome, Caroline playwright* (1961)

BROMFIELD, Louis
(1896–1956)

American novelist, born in Mansfield, Ohio, the son of a farmer. Educated at Cornell Agricultural College and Columbia University, he joined the French army in 1914, was awarded the *Croix de Guerre*, and returned to journalism in America. His novels include *The Green Bay Tree* (1924), *Early Autumn* (1926, Pulitzer Prize), *The Strange Case of Miss Annie Spragge* (1928), *The Rains Came* (1937), *Until the Day Break* (1942), *Colorado*

(1947), and *Mr Smith* (1951). His short stories include *Awake and Rehearse* (1929), and his plays *The House of Women* (1927).
▷D D Anderson, *Louis Bromfield* (1964)

BRONTË, originally Brunty or Prunty,

The name of three sisters, **Anne, Charlotte** and **Emily**, remarkable in English literary history, born in Thornton, Yorkshire. They were the daughters of Patrick Brontë (1777–1861), a clergyman of Irish descent and his Cornish wife, Maria (1783–1821), and sisters of Maria and Elizabeth, who both died in childhood, and Branwell (1817–48), a brother who squandered his many talents. The family moved to Haworth, now part of Keighley, in 1820 when their father became rector there. After the mother's death from cancer, her sister came to look after the children. Their childhood, spent in the sole companionship of one another on the wild Yorkshire moors, was happy enough. Branwell's 12 toy soldiers inspired them to construct two fantasy worlds of their own, *Gondal* and *Angria*, which contained all the exotic places and was peopled by all the great figures they had read about. Incidents in these were described by the children in verse and prose in rival collections of notebooks. Such escapism did not prepare them for their harsh schooling at Cowan Bridge, but Roe Head, their second school, proved more amenable. Branwell's debts caused them to leave home and find employment, but they always returned to their beloved Haworth.
▷W Gerin, *The Brontës* (1973–4)

BRONTË, Anne, pseud Acton Bell
(1820–49)

She went as governess to the Inghams at Blake Hall in 1839 and to the Robinsons at Thorpe Green (1841–5), a post she had to leave because of Branwell's unfortunate love for Mrs Robinson. She shared in the joint publication, under pseudonyms, of the three sisters' *Poems* (1846), only two volumes of which were sold. Her two novels, *Agnes Grey* (1845) and *The Tenant of Wildfell Hall* (1848), although unsuccessful at the time, show a decided talent, if less vivid than that of her sisters.
▷W Gerin, *Anne Brontë* (1959); *The Brontës* (1973–4)

BRONTË, Charlotte, pseud Currer Bell
(1816–55)

She returned in 1835 to her old school, Roe Head, as teacher, but gave up this post and two others, both as governess. Back at Haworth, the three sisters planned to start a school of their own and, to augment their qualifications, Charlotte and Emily attended

the Héger Pensionat in Brussels (1842). Their plans foundered, however, and Charlotte returned to Brussels as an English teacher (1843–4) and formed an unreciprocated attachment to the married M Héger, whom she later scornfully satirized in *Villette* (1852). Her chance discovery of Emily's remarkable poems in 1845 led to the abortive joint publication, under pseudonyms, of the three sisters' *Poems* (1846). This provoked them all to novel-writing. *The Professor*, which did not achieve publication until Charlotte's death, dwells on the theme of moral madness, possibly inspired by Branwell's degeneration. It was rejected by her publisher, but with sufficient encouragement for her to complete her masterpiece, *Jane Eyre* (1847). This in essence, through the master-pupil love relationship between Rochester and Jane, constituted a magnificent plea for feminine equality with men in the avowal of their passions. It was followed in 1849 by *Shirley*, a novel set in the background of the Luddite riots. By now her brother and two sisters were dead, and she was left alone at Haworth with her father. *Villette*, founded on her memories of Brussels, was published in 1853. She married her father's curate, Arthur Bell Nicholls, in 1854 and died during pregnancy in the following year, leaving the fragment of another novel, *Emma*. Two stories, *The Secret* and *Lily Hart*, were published for the first time in 1978.
▷E Gaskell, *The Life of Charlotte Brontë* (1860); W Gerin, *The Brontës* (1973–4)

BRONTË, Emily Jane, pseud Ellis Bell
(1818–48)

In 1837 she became a governess in Halifax. She attended the Héger Pensionat in Brussels with Charlotte and in 1845 embarked upon a joint publication of poems after the discovery by the latter of her *Gondal* verse, including such fine items as *To Imagination*, *Plead for Me*, and *Last Lines*. Her single novel, *Wuthering Heights* (1847), an intense and powerful tale of love and revenge set in the remote wilds of 18th-century Yorkshire, has much in common with Greek tragedy, and has no real counterpart in English literature.
▷W Gerin, *Emily Brontë: a biography* (1971); *The Brontës* (1973–4)

BROOKE, Frances
(1723–89)

English novelist and playwright. After establishing herself in the literary circles of London, she spent five years in Canada and she is primarily recognized as the author of 'Canada's first novel', *The History of Emily Montague* (1769). Set in Quebec during the 1760s, the novel explores the differences of a 'woman's place' in England and Canada, the complexity of French–English relations, and details many features of the pioneer settler's life in Canada. In addition to three novels, she wrote and staged a number of dramatic works, edited her own periodical, *The Old Maid*, and translated a number of texts from Italian and French. Her work has been reassessed in the light of more recent gender studies.
▷L McMullen, in R Lecker, J David and E Quigley (eds), *Canadian Writers and Their Work: Fiction Series: Vol.I* (1983)

BROOKE, Henry
(c.1703–1783)

Irish dramatist and novelist, born in Rantavan, County Cavan. He became the friend of **Pope** and married his cousin and ward. His poem *Universal Beauty* (1735) is supposed to have suggested Erasmus Darwin's *Botanic Garden*. His novel, *The Fool of Quality* (1766), is the only one of his numerous works to have retained some reputation.
▷C H Wilson (ed), *Brookiana* (1804)

BROOKE, (Bernard) Jocelyn
(1908–66)

English novelist, poet and amateur botanist, born in Kent. After running away from boarding school twice he settled at Bedales before going to Worcester College, Oxford, emerging without distinction. He tried various occupations before joining the family wine firm. During World War II he enlisted in the Royal Army Medical Corps, and re-enlisted after the war; but the army in peacetime was not to his liking and following the critical success of *The Military Orchid* (1948) he bought himself out and thereafter devoted himself to writing. He followed this with the second and third parts of the overtly autobiographical trilogy (known subsequently as *The Orchid Trilogy*), *A Mine of Serpents* (1949) and *The Goose Cathedral* (1950), the former drawing heavily on his obsession with pyrotechnics. His works also include two volumes of poetry, *December Spring* (1946) and *The Elements of Death* (1952); a **Kafka**esque novel, *The Image of a Drawn Sword* (1950), and botanical books.

BROOKE, Rupert Chawner
(1887–1915)

English poet, born in Rugby. Educated at King's College, Cambridge, he travelled in Germany and visited the USA and Tahiti. He died a commissioned officer on Skyros on his way to the Dardanelles and was buried there. His *Poems* appeared in 1911, *1914 and Other Poems* in 1915, after his death. If lacking the insight of a maturer poet, his poetry was characterized by a youthful, self-probing honesty, a fresh perception, a gentle lyricism and comedy. These, together with his handsome appearance and untimely death, made him a favourite poet among young people in the inter-war period.

▷C Hassall, *Rupert Brooke, a biography* (1972)

BROOKE-ROSE, Christine
(1926–)

British experimental novelist and literary critic, she was born in Geneva to a Swiss-American mother and English father, and has lived much of her life in France. Her fiction draws heavily on the *nouveau roman*, but with a quirkiness that is quintessentially English. Early novels like *The Languages of Love* (1957) are reminiscent of **Ivy Compton-Burnett** and it was only with her fifth novel *Out* (1964) that she began to experiment with a version of **Alain Robbe-Grillet**'s 'dogmatic realism'. *Such* (1966) captures a three-minute flow of consciousness in a man who is being revived following a heart seizure. *Thru* (1975) is more playful, but it was to be Brooke-Rose's last novel for nearly a decade. She broke her silence with *Amalgamemnon* (1984), a novel about a university teacher who is made redundant; written entirely in unresolved tenses, it has a shimmering, uncertain quality that is appropriate to a theme also taken up in the computer fantasy *Xorandor* (1986), in which a computer begins to address two young children, and continued in *Verbivore* (1990) and *Textermination* (1991). Brooke-Rose's criticism includes *A Grammar of Metaphor* (1958) and *A Rhetoric of the Unreal* (1981). She was married to the novelist **Jerzy Peterkiewicz**.

BROOKNER, Anita
(1928–)

English novelist and art historian, born in London. An authority on 18th-century painting, she was the first woman Slade Professor at Cambridge University (1967–8), and has been a reader at the Courtauld Institute of Art since 1977. She is the author of *Watteau* (1968), *The Genius of the Future* (1971) and *Jacques-Louis David* (1981). As a novelist she was a late starter, but in eight years (1981–8) she published as many novels, elegant, witty and imbued with cosmopolitan melancholy. Invariably, her main characters are women, self-sufficient in all but love. By winning the Booker Prize, *Hôtel du Lac* (1984) has become her best-known novel and is regarded by many as her most accomplished. Her other titles include *Family and Friends* (1985) and *Friends from England* (1987).

BROOKS, Gwendolyn
(1917–)

American poet and novelist, born in Topeka, Kansas, and brought up in the slums of Chicago. An active writer from an early age, she was 13 when her first poem was published. She has taught English in a number of colleges, and was Publicity Director of the NAACP (National Association for the Advancement of Colored People) for a time in the 1930s. Her first collection, *A Street in Bronzeville* (1945), chronicles the cares of city-dwelling black Americans, while *Annie Allen* (1949) traces the growth to maturity of a black woman amid the spiritual and social ills of her race and earned her a Pulitzer Prize, of which she was the first black winner. Subsequent works in both poetry and prose have focused on the life and politics of the USA's black community, and have been increasingly radical in tone, as in *Riot* (1969) and *Blacks* (1987). Other works include the novel *Maud Martha* (1953), about one woman's growing personal and political maturity; *Report From Part One* (1972), an autobiography, may be said to account for the same process in Brooks herself.

▷G E Kent, *A Life of Gwendolyn Brooks* (1990)

BROOKS, Van Wyck
(1886–1963)

American author and critic, born in Plainfield, New Jersey. His major achievement was the thesis, first expressed in *The Wine of the Puritans* (1909), that the Puritan tradition had held back free creative expression in America. In related vein, he wrote biographical studies of **Mark Twain** (1920), **Henry James** (1925) and **Ralph Waldo Emerson** (1932), attacked American materialism, and won the Pulitzer Prize with his *Flowering of New England* (1936).

▷W Wasserstrom, *Van Wyck Brooks* (1968)

BROPHY, Brigid Antonia
(1929–)

English novelist, essayist and critic, born in London. Her first novel, *Hackenfeller's Ape*, appeared in 1953, revealing her social, ethical and philosophical concerns, and especially her opposition to vivisection. Other novels, such as *The Finishing Touch* (1963) and *In Transit* (1969), look at lesbianism and transsexuality, while in *Palace Without Chairs* (1978), the lesbian life-force bursts through a bleak Absurdist nightmare. Brophy describes her novels as 'baroque'. Her critical works include *Mozart the Dramatist: A New View of Mozart, His Operas and His Age* (1964), studies of Aubrey Beardsley (1968), censorship (1972) and a vivacious defence of the work of **Ronald Firbank** (*Prancing Novelist*, 1973).

▷'A Case Historical Fragment of Autobiography', in *Baroque-'n'-Roll and Other Essays* (1987)

BROWN, Carter, pseud of **Alan Geoffrey Yates**
(1923–85)

English-born Australian thriller writer, born in London, who served in the Royal Navy during World War II and moved to Australia in 1948. It is estimated that he wrote an average of six books a year, novels of horror, romance, science fiction and westerns, under a variety of names. In 1950 he began writing a series of 'hard-boiled' thrillers, aimed at the US market, under the pseudonym Carter Brown, which he estimated in the mid-1980s to have reached over 150 titles. An Australian radio series *The Carter Brown Mystery Theatre* ran between 1956 and 1958.

▷*Ready When You Are, CB* (1983)

BROWN, Charles Brockden
(1771–1810)

American novelist, born of Quaker ancestry in Philadelphia. He was the first professional American writer making use of English models in a highly distinctive way. *Wieland* (1798), *Ormund* (1799) and *Jane Talbot* (1804), among many others, are Gothic romances, full of incident and subtle analysis, but extravagant in style.

▷A Axelrod, *Charles Brockden Brown: an American tale* (1983)

BROWN, Frederic William
(1906–72)

American novelist and journalist, born in Cincinnati, Ohio. He worked mainly in the science-fiction and detective genres, and brought an unusual degree of humour to his work in them. His first success was with a detective novel, *The Fabulous Clipjoint* (1947), followed by his science-fiction novel, *What Mad Universe* (1949). Other novels include *Martians, Go Home* (1955), on a comic invasion theme, and *The Mind Thing* (1961). He is best known for his short stories, and several of them, such as 'Etaoin Shrdlu' (1942) and 'Arena' (1944), are regarded as idiosyncratic classics of the science-fiction genre.

BROWN, George Douglas
(1869–1902)

Scottish writer, born in Ochiltree, Ayrshire, the illegitimate son of a farmer. Educated at the village school and Ayr Academy, he went to Glasgow University and Balliol College, Oxford, on a scholarship. He settled in London as a journalist, published a boys' adventure book, *Love and Sword* (1899), but made his name, under the pseudonym 'George Douglas', with *The House with the Green Shutters* (1901), a powerfully realistic novel and an antidote to the 'Kailyard School'. He died of pneumonia before he was able to complete two other novels.

▷F R Hart, *The Scottish Novel* (1978)

BROWN, George Mackay
(1921–)

Scottish poet, novelist and short-story writer, born in Stromness, Orkney, the 'Hamnavoe' of his stories and poems. Suffering from tuberculosis, he was unable to work when he left school. In 1957 he went to Newbattle Abbey College, where **Edwin Muir** was warden. Encouraged in his poetry by his mentor and fellow-Orcadian, Brown was introduced by Muir to a London publisher. His first collection was *The Storm* (1954), followed five years later by *Loaves and Fishes*. Though illness prevented him from completing the course at Newbattle, he went on to Edinburgh University where he did postgraduate work on **Gerard Manley Hopkins**. In 1964 he returned to Stromness, and he has since rarely left it. A prolific and easily identifiable writer, his best work is ruggedly elemental, drawing on old sea yarns, myths, Scandinavian sagas and the folklore of Orkney. His conversion to Catholicism in 1961 brought into relief his concern with religion. A lyrically intense, poetic writer, his popularity lies in his stories and novels. Published in 1967, *A Calendar of Love*, a collection of stories, was the first trickle in what has become a dam-burst of fiction. *A Time to Keep* (1969), widely regarded as his best collection of stories, is the closest he comes to confronting contemporary life. His first novel was *Greenvoe* (1972), which describes the last days of an island community on 'Hellya' in the 1960s. *Magnus* (1973), its unconventional successor, is more a meditation on the eponymous saint than a novel, but is no less effective. His *Selected Poems* were published in 1991.

▷R Fulton, *Contemporary Scottish Poetry* (1974)

BROWN, Harry
(1917–86)

American novelist and dramatist, born in Portland, Maine. He worked for the *New Yorker*, and then, after joining the army, for *Yank* magazine. His greatest success was his war novel *A Walk in the Sun* (1944), made into a film by Lewis Milestone. Thereafter he worked in Hollywood, wrote more fiction—which was adjudged of less account—and devoted himself to film work and to hunting, his grand passion. His verse, collected in *The Beast in his Hunger* (1949) and elsewhere, attracted little attention.

BROWN, John
(1810–82)

Scottish physician and essayist, born in Biggar, Lanarkshire. He attended the High School of Edinburgh and studied medicine at Edinburgh University. He wrote *Horae subsecivae* (1858–61, 'Leisure Hours') and *John Leech and other Papers* (1882). Humour and pathos are the chief features of his style, as exemplified in his essay on the human nature of dogs in 'Rab and his Friends' and 'Pet Marjorie', an essay on the child writer **Margaret Fleming**.
▷J Brown (jr) and D W Forrest (eds), *Letters of Dr John Brown* (1907, with a biographical note by E McLaren)

BROWN, Oliver Madox
(1855–74)

English author and artist, born in Finchley, son of Ford Madox Brown. At 12 he painted a watercolour of considerable merit. In 1871 he wrote his first novel, *Gabriel Denver*, reprinted in his *Literary Remains* (1876) under its first title *The Black Swan*. He died of food poisoning.
▷J H Ingram, *Oliver Madox Brown* (1893)

BROWN, Sterling A(llen)
(1901–89)

American poet and critic, born in Washington DC. Brown was an authority on the literature of his fellow blacks, edited several anthologies and wrote about fiction and drama as well as poetry. He made full use of folk imagery and black idiom in his own work. *A Collected Poems* was published in 1980.

BROWN, Thomas
(1663–1704)

English satirist, born possibly in Shifnal or, more probably, Newport, Shropshire. As a student at Christ Church, Oxford, he produced his famous extempore adaptation of **Martial**'s 33rd epigram, 'Non amo te, Sabidi', at the demand of Dr John Fell, the dean: 'I do not love thee, Dr Fell'. After teaching at Kingston-on-Thames, he settled in London, where he made an uncertain living by writing scurrilous satirical poems and pamphlets, and published *Amusements Serious and Comical* (1700). He was buried in the Westminster cloisters near his friend, Mrs **Aphra Behn**.

BROWN, Wayne Vincent
(1944–)

Trinidadian poet, educated at the University of the West Indies and Gregory Fellow in Poetry at the University of Leeds. His first volume of poetry, *On the Coast* (1972), which won the Commonwealth Prize for Poetry, was dedicated to **Derek Walcott** and the diaspora of the Caribbean people. The title poem declares: '... I am an orphaned islander,/in a winter/of bays. I have no home.' Yet the home of memory is Caribbean sun and sea.

BROWN, William Hill
(1765–93)

American novelist and essayist, born in Boston. Related to the Mather dynasty of Puritan divines, Brown can hardly be said to have followed in his forebears' footsteps. He has been called the first American novelist, on the basis of *The Power of Sympathy* (1789), a fictional treatment of a scandal affecting the family of the poet Sarah Wentworth Morton. While Brown was alive the book was thought to have been written by Morton, whose husband was implicated in the scandal. Brown died at the age of 28, the victim of a local epidemic. He had been a prolific contributor to magazines, using the pseudonyms Pollio and The Yankee. A number of works appeared after his death, including *West Point Preserved* (1797), a drama based on the life of Major André.

BROWN, William Wells
(c.1816–1884)

American writer, born into slavery in Kentucky. He was raised in St Louis, but after gaining his freedom, helped runaway slaves in Ohio. He achieved fame with his autobiographical *Narrative of William W Brown, a Fugitive Slave* (1847), and became a leading black advocate of abolition. He published a collection of poems, *The Anti-Slavery Harp* (1848), and an account of his travels in Europe, but is best known for his novel *Clotelle; or, The President's Daughter* (1853), the story of an illegitimate mulatto girl born to President Jefferson's housekeeper. It was published in London, and subsequently appeared in the US (1864) with all references to the president omitted. His other works were a play, *The Escape* (1858), and an account of the history and culture of *The Black Man* (1863), later expanded as *The Rising Son* (1874).

BROWNE, William
(1591–1643)

English pastoral poet, born in Tavistock, Devon. Educated at Exeter College, Oxford, he entered the Inner Temple, and was then tutor to Robert Dormer, the future Earl of Carnarvon. His finest poetry is to be found in the three-volumed *Britannia's Pastorals* (1613–52) and in the *Inner Temple Masque* (1615).

▷F W Moorman, *William Browne; his Britannia's Pastorals and the pastoral poetry of the Elizabethan age* (1897)

BROWNING, Elizabeth, née **Barrett**
(1806–61)

English poet, born in Coxhoe Hall, Durham, wife of **Robert Browning**. She spent her girlhood mostly on her father's estate, at Hope Hill in Herefordshire. At 10 she read **Homer** in the original, and at 14 wrote an epic on *The Battle of Marathon*. In her teens she developed a tubercular complaint that damaged her spine, and was an invalid for a long time. The family ultimately settled in 50 Wimpole Street, London, in 1837. Her *Essay on Mind, and Other Poems*, was published in 1826 when she was 19. In 1833 she issued a translation of **Aeschylus'** *Prometheus Bound*. This was succeeded by *The Seraphim, and Other Poems* (1838), in which volume was republished the fine poem on **William Cowper**'s grave. When she was staying at Torquay, her brother and a party of friends were drowned there in a boating expedition, and the shock confined her for many years to the sickroom. In 1844 appeared *Poems*, which contained 'The Cry of the Children', an outburst against the employment of young children in factories. In 1845 she first met Robert Browning, six years her junior, who freed her from her sickroom and a possessive father by marrying her the following year. They settled in Pisa (1846), and then Florence (1847), where their son Robert was born in 1849. They became the centre of a brilliant literary circle there. The *Poems* of 1850 contained an entirely new translation of the *Prometheus Bound*. In *Casa Guidi Windows* (1851) she expressed her sympathy with the regeneration of Italy. *Aurora Leigh* (1856) is a long narrative poem into which all the treasures of its writer's mind and heart have been poured. In *Poems before Congress* (1860) she again manifested her interest in Italian freedom. Her so-called *Sonnets from the Portuguese* (published in the *Poems* of 1850) are not translations at all, but express her own love for the country ('my little Portuguese' was Browning's pet name for her). Her *Last Poems* were published the following year.

▷D Hewlett, *Elizabeth Barrett Browning* (1953)

BROWNING, Robert
(1812–89)

English poet, and husband of **Elizabeth Browning**, born in Camberwell, the only son of a Bank of England clerk. He attended lectures briefly at University College, London and then travelled abroad. *Pauline*, a dramatic poem, written at the age of 20, was published anonymously in 1833. He made a visit to St Petersburg (Leningrad), and on his return *Paracelsus* (1835) won him some recognition in literary circles; but *Sordello* (1840) was a failure. He wrote several dramas and dramatic poems, which were published as 'Bells and Pomegranates' in *Dramatic Romances and Lyrics*, which also contained 'My Last Duchess' 'Soliloquy of the Spanish Cloister', 'The Pied Piper of Hamelin', 'Home Thoughts from Abroad', and many other familiar and much loved poems. In 1846 he married Elizabeth Barrett, and with her settled first in Pisa (1846) and then in Florence (1847); their son, Robert Barrett (1849–1912), who became a sculptor, was born there. In 1855 he published *Men and Women*, which contained such poems as 'Fra Lippo Lippi', 'Childe Roland to the Dark Tower Came', and 'Andrea del Sarte'. After the death of his wife (1861) he settled permanently in London with his son. His masterpiece, *The Ring and the Book*, published in four volumes (1868–9), is an epic dealing searchingly with passions of humanity, and has for its basis the narrative of a murder by an Italian count, as related by the various persons concerned. Browning's poetry is distinguished by its depth of spiritual insight and power of psychological analysis; and he invented new kinds of narrative structure which have taken the place of the epic and the pastoral. In his play, *Pippa Passes* (1841), for example, a girl's song binds together a variety of scenes. His other chief works are *Dramatis Personae* (1864), *Fifine at the Fair* (1872), *The Inn Album* (1875), *Pacchiarotto* (1876) and *Asolando* (1889).

▷A Maurois, *Robert and Elizabeth Browning* (1955); T E F Blackburn, *Robert Browing: a study of his poetry* (1973)

BRU, Hedin, pseud of **Hans Jacob Jacobsen**
(1901–)

Faeroese novelist, story writer and translator, whose language resembles Icelandic. He was born in Skálavik. Bru has also translated **Shakespeare**'s works into Faeroese, making brilliant use of old dialects. His leading novel, about the Faeroes in the 1930s, is the richly comic and ironic *Fedgar á fero* (1940, Eng trans *The Old Man and his Sons*, 1970).

BRUCE, Mary Grant
(1878–1958)

Australian novelist, born in Sale, Victoria. She began writing as a child, but moved to Melbourne in 1898 where she ran the 'Children's Page' of the *Leader* weekly newspaper, in which some of her stories were serialized as *A Little Bush Maid* and later published in book form in 1910. In a long career she published a book nearly every year until 1942, as well as much short fiction and numerous contributions to newspapers and periodicals. Though she is considered today mainly as a children's writer, her novels were at the time widely read by adults and were so reviewed. Her fame lies mainly in the *Billabong* series of novels of Australian pastoral life and their heroine Norah Linton, perhaps the first Australian female character drawn in an unpatronizing and realistic light.

BRUCKNER, Ferdinand, pseud of **Theodor Tagger**
(1891–1958)

Austrian dramatist and poet who made his reputation under his given name as an expressionist poet in Berlin, where he was also a theatrical director, and where he edited a journal, *Marsyas*; he was born in Sofia while his mother was en route from Constantinople to Vienna. Wishing to make a new start with his play *Krankheit der Jugend* (1926, 'Sickness of Youth'), which was more serious than anything he had attempted hitherto, he circulated it anonymously. It was a success, and he commenced writing under a pseudonym, chosen because it combined his admiration for a dramatist, Ferdinand Raimund, and for the composer Anton Bruckner. He did not reveal his true identity for many years. When Max Reinhart produced *Die Verbrecher* (1928, 'The Criminals'), he became well known. This play, technically very brilliant, with three plots presented simultaneously, blames society for individual crimes. The more conventional *Elizabeth von England* (1930, 'Elizabeth of England'), again technically brilliant, had long runs in various capitals, and established him as a leading international dramatist. In 1933 he left Germany in protest against the Nazis, and lived in France and New York until 1947. On his return he played a large part in the West German post-war revival; he wrote well-constructed plays, some of them in turgid verse, but failed to re-establish himself. He had been caught by Hitler at the height of his powers, and never regained them.
▷H F Garten, *Modern German Drama* (1964)

BRUNET, Marta
(1897–1967)

Chilean novelist of Catalan extraction, born in Chillán. A sickly child, she was cured by a long series of mystical experiences. A traditional writer in the *costumbista* (regional) style, she gradually acquired popularity with her tales of rural life. Her chief work is the novel *Soledad de la sangre* (1948, 'Lonely Blood'). She died in Montevideo, where she had been serving as Chilean cultural attaché.

BRUNHOFF, Jean de
(1899–1937)

French writer and illustrator of children's books, born in Paris. His creation Babar the Elephant is one of the most enduring and, to some, endearing characters of 20th-century children's literature. The pachyderm possessed of a peculiarly Gallic charm and hauteur made his debut in *L'Histoire de Babar, le petit elephant* (1931, Eng trans *The Story of Babar the Little Elephant*, 1934), which de Brunhoff both wrote and illustrated. *Les Voyages de Babar* ('Babar's Travels') came out in France in 1932, and three years later in Britain, but the books' relative success in the UK meant that the English versions were being published first by the time of *Babar and Father Christmas* (1940, French edition 1941). He wrote seven Babar books in all, three of which were published posthumously. His son, Laurent de Brunhoff, continued the success of the stories after World War II.

BRUNNER, John Kilian Houston
(1934–)

English science-fiction writer, born in Preston Crowmarsh, Oxfordshire. He was educated at Cheltenham College, served in the RAF (1953–5), and worked as a book editor (1956–8). He had written over 30 science-fiction adventure novels by 1968, but his work was becoming increasingly serious in tone and experimental in form, as in *Squares of the City* (1965), based on a chess game. His major works in this new phase, which placed him among the most significant voices in the genre, are four dystopian visions of future chaos, *Stand On Zanzibar* (1969), *The Jagged Orbit* (1969), *The Sheep Look Up* (1972) and *The Shockwave Rider* (1975). The most important of his later books are *The Crucible of Time* (1983), *The Tides of Time* (1984) and *Children of the Thunder* (1989).

BRUNTON, Mary, née **Balfour**
(1778–1818)

Scottish novelist, born in Orkney, the daughter of an army officer. In 1798 she married the Reverend Alexander Brunton, whom she called 'my companion and instructor', and they settled in the parish of Bolton, East Lothian. Between 1803 and her death she lived in Edinburgh where her husband was minister of the Tron Kirk and Professor of Oriental Languages at Edinburgh University. She made her name with her first novel *Self Control* (1810), which she dedicated to her close friend **Joanna Baillie**, and which **Jane**

Austen called an 'elegantly written work, without anything of nature or probability in it'. Her next novel was *Discipline* (1814). Both were so-called improving works, very popular in their day, and she was included in the school of 'improver-satirists' along with **Susan Ferrier** and Elizabeth Hamilton. After a visit to England in 1815 she planned a series of domestic sketches on middle-class manners, but only one, *Emmeline* (1819), was completed before her death in childbirth.

BRUST, Alfred
(1891–1934)

German playwright from East Prussia whose *Der singende Fisch* (1922, 'The Singing Fish'), about a man's spirit becoming divorced from his body, made a sensation when Max Reinhart produced it. *Die Wolfë* (Eng trans *The Wolves*, in *Seven Expressionistic Plays*, 1968), part of a trilogy of 1924, depicts a woman being killed just as she is about to be sodomized by a wolf. Brust also wrote comedies, and exercised some short-lived influence.

BRUTUS, Dennis Vincent
(1924–)

South African poet, exiled in the USA and UK. He was born in Salisbury, Rhodesia, and educated at Witwatersrand University in Johannesburg. Despite committed opposition to the South African system (he was jailed for 18 months on the notorious Robben Island) he insists that anti-apartheid protest is simply one element among many in what is essentially lyric poetry. Few poets confronted with political violence have been able to invest it with such chastened calm. His first volume, *Sirens, Knuckles, Boots* (1963), expresses something like **W B Yeats**'s 'terrible beauty'. The prison poems in *Letters to Martha* (1968) are without rancour. Later in his career, Brutus began to take up the postcolonial cause of other Third World nations, and in *Salutes and Censures* (1982) to examine large-scale environmental and disarmament issues. In 1983, following a forceful campaign on his behalf, he avoided deportation from the USA.
▷D Herdeck, *African Authors* (1973)

BRYANT, William Cullen
(1794–1878)

American poet and journalist, born in Cummington, Massachusetts. He graduated in law and practised in Great Barrington, Massachusetts, from 1816, but in 1817 the majestic blank verse of *Thanatopsis* appeared. He continued to practise at the Bar until 1825, but more and more turned to journalism in both prose and verse, becoming co-owner and Editor of the New York *Evening Post* in 1829. The paper was Democratic, but, having anti-

slavery views, assisted in 1856 in forming the Republican party. Bryant's public addresses and letters to his paper on his visits to Europe and the West Indies were published in book form as *Letters of a Traveller* (1850), and he also published volumes of his poetry.
▷P Godwin, *A Biography of Willian Cullen Bryant* (1883)

BRYHER, pseud of Annie Winnifred Ellerman
(1894–1983)

English novelist, poet and autobiographer, born in Margate, the daughter of a rich shipping owner. Lover and protector of the American poet **Hilda Doolittle** (HD), Bryher helped to bring psychoanalysis to Great Britain, and to arrange for HD's analysis with **Freud**. She made two marriages of convenience. Her novels and poetry were interesting but lacked the robustness to stand the test of time, although her autobiographies *The Heart to Artemis* (1962) and *The Days of Mars 1940–1946* (1972) are illuminating.
▷N Riley-Fitch, *Sylvia Beach and the Lost Generation* (1983)

BRYUSSOV, Valery Yakovlevich
(1873–1924)

Russian poet, critic, editor and translator, born in Moscow. He was one of the leaders of the Russian Symbolist movement which looked to France for its inspiration. Like **Konstantin Balmont**, his best work was done before 1910, but unlike him his technique remained unimpaired to the last. He translated many of the major modernist writers in Europe, including **Paul Verlaine**, **Stéphane Mallarmé**, **Maurice Maeterlinck** and **Gabriele D'Annunzio**. He became an enthusiastic Bolshevist in 1917 and worked tirelessly for that cause until his death. His best-known prose works are the two novels *Ognennyy Angel* (1907–8), which provided the basis of Prokofiev's opera *The Fiery Angel*, and *Altar pobedy* (1911–12, 'The Altar of Victory').

BUBER, Martin
(1878–1965)

Austrian religious philosopher, mystic, folklorist and novelist, born in Vienna, who has had an immense—although often subterranean—influence on European and American literature. This influence has arisen from his famous 'I–Thou' philosophy, and from his reworkings into a modern idiom of Hasidic tales, collected in English translation in *The Legend of the Baal-Shem* (1955), *Tales of Rabbi Nachman* (1956), and elsewhere. His earlier thinking was much influenced by his radical reinterpretation of **Nietzsche**: man must respond creatively to the challenge made to him by God. He found, in *Ich und*

Du (1922, Eng trans *I and Thou*, 1958), that an I–Thou rather than an I–It relationship could exist between human beings: 'There is no "I" except he responds to his "Thou"'. But I–It is the 'ordinary' currency of science, politics and economics. His only novel, persistently underrated, is *Gog and Magog* (1943, in Hebrew translation, English translation *For the Sake of Heaven*, 1945—original German text, 1949), about the Hasidic world in Napoleonic times.
▷R Horwitz, *Buber's Way to 'I and Thou'* (1978); M Seymour-Smith, *Who's Who in Twentieth Century Literature* (1976)

BUCHAN, John, 1st Baron Tweedsmuir
(1875–1940)

Scottish author and statesman, born in Perth, the son of a Free Church minister. He was educated at Hutcheson's Grammar School and Glasgow University and at Brasenose College, Oxford, where he won the Newdigate Prize for Poetry in 1898. In 1901 he was called to the Bar and became Private Secretary to Lord Milner, High Commissioner for South Africa. He returned in 1903 to become a director of Nelson's the publishers. During World War I he served on HQ staff until 1917, when he became Director of Information. He wrote *Nelson's History of the War* (1915–19), and became President of the Scottish History Society (1929–32). He was MP for the Scottish Universities (1927–35), and was raised to the peerage in 1935, when he became Governor-General of Canada. In 1937 he was made a Privy Councillor, and Chancellor of Edinburgh University. Despite his busy public life, Buchan wrote over 50 books, beginning with a series of essays, *Scholar Gipsies* (1896). His strength as a writer was for fast-moving adventure stories, which included *Prester John* (1910), *Huntingtower* (1922) and *Witch Wood* (1927). He became best known, however, for his spy thrillers featuring Richard Hannay: *The Thirty-Nine Steps* (1915), *Greenmantle* (1916), *The Three Hostages* (1924), and others. He also wrote biographies, including *Montrose* (1928) and *Sir Walter Scott* (1932).
▷J Adam Smith, *John Buchan* (1965)

BUCHANAN, George
(c.1506–1582)

Scottish scholar and humanist, born near Killearn, Stirlingshire. Because of straitened family circumstances he attended the local grammar school, but at the age of 14 was sent by an uncle to study Latin at the University of Paris. He returned to Scotland in 1523, and did service in the army of the Duke of Albany (the future King James V). Thereafter he was enrolled at St Andrews as a poor student, before returning to Paris, where he taught at the College of Sainte Barbe (1528–37). In 1537 King James appointed him tutor to one of his illegitimate sons, the future Earl of Moray, but he was soon charged with heresy at St Andrews after writing *Franciscanus*, a satirical poem about friars, which offended Cardinal Beaton. He fled to France, where he taught at Bordeaux (1539–42), with Montaigne as one of his pupils, and wrote two tragedies in Latin, *Jeptha* and *Baptistes*. In 1547 he went to teach at Coimbra in Portugal, where he was arrested by the Inquisition as a suspected heretic. During his confinement (1547–53) he made a Latin paraphrase of the Psalms, which was published in 1566 with a dedication to Mary, Queen of Scots. He returned to Scotland in 1561 and was appointed classical tutor to the 19-year-old queen, despite his acknowledged leanings towards Protestantism. The queen awarded him a handsome pension, and in 1566 he was appointed Principal of St Leonard's College at St Andrews. He abandoned the queen's cause after the murder of Lord Darnley in 1567, and charged her with complicity in a scurrilous pamphlet, *Ane Detectioun of the Duings of Mary Quene* (1571). In 1567 he was elected Moderator of the newly-formed General Assembly of the Church of Scotland, and was later appointed Keeper of the Privy Seal of Scotland, and tutor to the four-year-old King James VI of Scotland (1570–8). He proved a hard taskmaster, ensuring that the king learned his classics thoroughly. Buchanan's main works were *De juri regni apud Scotos* (1579), an attack on the divine right of monarchs and a justification for the deposition of Mary, and a monumental but unreliable history of Scotland, *Rerum scoticarum historia* (20 vols), which he completed shortly before his death.
▷I D McFarlane, *Buchanan* (1981)

BUCHANAN, Robert Williams
(1841–1901)

English poet, novelist and playwright, born in Caverswall, Staffordshire. He was educated at Glasgow High School and University, where his closest friend was **David Gray**, with whom he set out for London in 1860. They found life hard in London and success came too late for Buchanan. He is noted for his attack in the *Spectator* on **Algernon Charles Swinburne**, whom he called unclean, morbid and sensual, and on the pre-Raphaelites under the pseudonym of 'Thomas Maitland' in another article entitled 'The Fleshly School of Poetry' (1871). *London Poems* (1866) was his first distinct success. He also wrote many now-forgotten novels and plays.
▷A Walker, *Robert Buchanan, the poet of modern revolt* (1901)

BÜCHNER, Georg
(1813–37)

German dramatist and pioneer of Expressionist theatre, born in Goddelau near Darmstadt. He studied medicine and science, became involved in revolutionary politics and fled to Zürich where he died of typhoid at the age of 24. His best-known works are the poetical dramas *Dantons Tod* (1835, Eng trans *Danton's Death*, 1958) and *Woyzeck* (1837, Eng trans 1979, of which he left many unfinished manuscript versions), the true story of an uneducated and mentally-backward army private who killed his girlfriend in a fit of jealousy. It was used by Alban Berg as the basis for his opera *Wozzeck*. His sister Louise (1821–77) was also a poet and novelist.

▷ R Hauser, *Georg Büchner* (1974)

BUCK, Pearl S, née Sydenstricker
(1892–1973)

American novelist, winner of the Nobel Prize for literature, born in Hillsboro, West Virginia. The daughter of Presbyterian missionaries, she lived in China from childhood, went to the USA for her education, but returned to China as a missionary and teacher in 1921. She married another missionary, John Lossing Buck, in 1917, and divorced in 1934. Her earliest novels are coloured by her experiences while living in China. *The Good Earth* (1931) was a runaway bestseller. In 1935 she returned to America, and most of her output after that date was concerned with the contemporary American scene. She was awarded the 1938 Nobel Prize for literature. Her other novels on China include *Sons* (1932), *A House Divided* (1935), *Dragon Seed* (1942) and *Imperial Woman* (1956), and amongst other works are *What America Means to Me* (1944) and *My Several Worlds* (1955).

▷ T F Hariss, *Pearl S Buck* (1969, 1971)

BUCKERIDGE, Anthony
(1912–)

English author of schoolboy fiction, born in London. Buckeridge created the characters of Jennings and Darbishire while a master at a boys' preparatory school. His first book, *Jennings Goes to School*, appeared in 1950, and by the time *Jennings at Large* was published in 1977, there were 23 in the series. The inferior *Jennings Again* followed in 1991. Jennings, an impulsive natural leader, and his great friend, the bespectacled, logical, retiring Darbishire, are 11-year-old third formers at Linbury Court Preparatory School in Sussex. The stories are zestful, full of incident and are the finest schoolboy fiction since **Richmal**

Crompton's *Just William* series. Buckeridge also had a muted success with his Rex Milligan stories (1953–61).

BUCKLER, Ernest
(1908–)

Canadian novelist, born in Dalhousie. Buckler has written many books, stories and radio plays, but is most famous for one novel, his first, *The Mountain and the Valley* (1952). This is a rich study of a doomed, artistic boy, set in Nova Scotia's Annapolis Valley, distinguished less by its plot than by the intricate and convincing picture it gives of country life in its setting. Buckler's second novel, *The Cruellest Month* (1963), again set in Nova Scotia, fared less well at the time of its publication, but has never been forgotten. *The Rebellion of Young David* (1975) is a collection of stories.

▷ G M Cook (ed), *Ernest Buckler* (1972); A Young, *Ernest Buckler* (1976)

BUCKLEY, Vincent
(1925–88)

Australian poet, critic and editor of Irish descent, born in Romsey, Victoria; a strong Catholic faith and emotional ties to his 'source-country' coloured much of his writing. His first book of verse was *The World's Flesh* (1954); he published five more volumes before *Selected Poems* in 1982. His critical work includes *Essays in Poetry: Mainly Australian* (1957) and a study of **Henry Handel Richardson** (1961). Between 1958 and 1964 he edited *Prospect*, a quarterly journal, and was poetry editor of the *Bulletin* (1961–3). He published his memoirs *Cutting Green Hay* in 1983, telling of his lifelong involvement with Irish Catholic and Republican movements, themes evinced strongly in *The Pattern* (1979), a series of poems which link Irish history with the 'Troubles' of today and with the country life. In *Late-Winter Child* (1979) he turned to intensely personal matters in celebrating the birth of his daughter.

BUCKLEY, William F(rank), Jr
(1925–)

American journalist, novelist and freelance conservative. Having served in the military and the Central Intelligence Agency, he dedicated himself to combating creeping liberalism in American life. In 1955, he founded *National Review*, an influential conduit for conservative ideas. He has taught at the New School for Social Research (1967–8) and stood as Conservative Party candidate for the mayoralty of New York City, a campaign detailed in *The Unmaking of a Mayor* (1966). *Up From Liberalism* (1959) was a strong statement of his political position, but his most effective writing has been in a syndicated gadfly column called 'On the Right'. He brings the same acerbity to a television show, *Firing Line*. In 1976, Buckley introduced his fictional CIA hero, Blackford Oakes; the plot of *Saving the Queen* was part conventional thriller and part elaborate revenge for English snobbism (which Buckley had experienced as a public schoolboy); it was controversial for a sex scene involving the reigning Queen of England. Later Oakes novels, *Stained Glass* (1978), *Who's On First?* (1980) and *Marco Polo, If You Can* (1982) were subtler and more ambiguous in their portrayal of Cold War camaraderie.

▷ *Overdrive: a Personal Documentary* (1983)

BUCKSTONE, John Baldwin
(1802–79)

English comedian, actor-manager and playwright, born in Hoxton. He played at the Surrey, Adelphi, Drury Lane, and Lyceum theatres, mostly as a comedian, and visited the USA in 1840 and then played at the Haymarket, where he was actor-manager (1853–78). He wrote 150 pieces for the stage, including *Luke the Labourer* (1826), *Married Life* (1834) and *The Flowers of the Forest* (1847).

BUDGELL, Eustace
(1686–1737)

English writer, born in Exeter. He was a cousin of **Joseph Addison**, and contributed miscellaneous essays to the *Spectator*. He was the butt of **Pope**'s mockery in *The Dunciad*. After losing a fortune in the South Sea Company collapse (1720) he degenerated to a Grub Street writer. He drowned himself in the Thames.

▷ *A Vindication of Eustace Budgell Esq, by William Wilson* (1733)

BUDRYS, Algis (Algirdas)
(1931–)

Lithuanian–American science-fiction novelist and short-story writer, born in Konigsberg, Germany. An infant refugee, he moved with his family to the USA, and publicized the plight of his Baltic homeland throughout the long night of Soviet rule. *Who?* (1958), the book which made his reputation, is concerned with the dehumanizing effect of the Cold War. *Rogue Moon* (1960), superficially a genre action novel, but more deeply philosophical than this, is the best work to come out of his first period. *Michaelmas* (1977), which followed a decade of silence, has as its central hero one Laurent Michaelmas, the unacknowledged legislator, the secret president of the world. In its contention that great

power need not corrupt it is a profoundly optimistic book.

BUECHNER, (Carl) Frederick
(1926–)

American novelist and Presbyterian clergyman, born in New York City. After graduating from Princeton University, he taught English at Lawrenceville School, New Jersey, and worked in a Harlem employment office before studying at Union Theological Seminary. After his ordination he taught and later headed the religion department at Phillips Academy in New Hampshire, leaving to write full-time in 1967. Religion plays an inevitably powerful role in his fiction, providing the underlying moral and philosophical structure that is missing from the early *A Long Day's Dying* (1950), an elaborate and somewhat overwrought story of sexual deception. *The Final Beast* (1965) and *The Entrance to Porlock* (1970) are religious romances, and *Lion Country* (1971), perhaps his most characteristic novel, examines the state of the contemporary church. Buechner's sermons have been published in several volumes.

▷ *The Sacred Journey* (1982)

BUERO VALLEJO, Antonio
(1916–)

Spanish playwright, born in Guadalajara, who was sentenced to death (for being a medical aide to the forces of the legal government) by Franco, but 'exonerated' in 1945. He thus spent six years in prison. He did well, under Franco's censorship, to present well-made and successful plays on humane themes. His plays were not often produced, but with **Alfonso Sastre** he nevertheless dominated the Spanish theatre during the Franco years. He has not been a conventional dramatist, since he eschews 'happy endings' and wooing of audiences in search of easy pleasure. Influenced by the earlier plays of **Gerhart Hauptmann**, he mixes the naturalism of the latter with playful surrealism and attention to Spanish legend. His play *La tejedora de sueños* (1952) is translated as *The Dream Weaver* in *Masterpieces of Modern Spanish Theatre* (1967, ed Robert W Corrigan), together with his own notes.

BUKOWSKI, Charles
(1920–94)

German-born American poet, short-story writer and novelist, born in Andernach. As befits an underground writer, his world is one frequented by low lifers which he evokes, as one critic has said, in 'words nailed to the page'. His pared style, revealing an affinity with **Hemingway**, has been employed to effect in four novels, half a dozen collections of

short stories and many volumes of verse. A
cult figure who did not achieved popular success, he had a sardonic sense of humour and
a liking for long titles, such as *Play the Piano
Drunk Like a Percussion Instrument until the
Fingers Begin to Bleed a Bit* (1979).
▷H Fox, *Charles Bukowski: a biographical
study* (1968)

BULATOVIĆ, Miodrag
(1930–)

Yugoslav (Montenegran) fiction writer, born
near Bijelo Polje. His father was a forest
ranger whom, when Bulatović was 11, he saw
murdered by a relative over a land dispute.
Bulatović was in the 1960s and 1970s the best-
known and most translated in the West of the
Yugoslav younger writers. He was influenced
as much by **Beckett** and **Joyce** as by native
writers. He lived in Belgrade, but then moved
to Slovenia. His novels, such as *Crveni petao
leti prema nebu* (1959, Eng trans *The Red
Cockerel*, 1962) and *Rat je bio bolji* (1970,
Eng trans *The War Was Better*, 1972), reflect
his belief that 'dislocation is the norm' and
that the world is 'far worse' than even Beckett
saw it.

BULGAKOV, Mikhail Afanas'evich
(1891–1940)

Russian novelist and dramatist, born in Kiev.
His father was a professor of divinity, and he
studied at Kiev Theological Academy and
Kiev University, and practised as a country
doctor for a short time. He settled in Moscow
in 1921, and began a stormy association with
the Moscow Art Theatre when he adapted
part of his novel *Belaya gvardiya* (1925, Eng
trans *The White Guard*, 1971) for the stage in
1926. His political attitudes in that play, and
in others like *Beg* (1928, 'The Flight'),
brought him much criticism, and only a personal appeal to Stalin restored him to some
favour. He gained success with a play (1930)
about **Molière**, on whom he wrote an imaginative biography. He described his tribulations
with the theatre in *Tetralnyi roman* (1965,
Eng trans *Black Show, a Theatrical Novel*,
1967). His masterpiece is the novel *Master i
Margarita* (1966, Eng trans *The Master and
Margarita*, 1967), a remarkable multi-level
fantasy. Although he died in obscurity with
much of his work unpublished, his posthumous reputation has flourished.

BULGARIN, Thaddeus
(1789–1859)

Russian author and journalist. He was a zeal-
ous supporter of reaction and of absolutism.
His best novel is *Ivan Vyzhigin* (1829).
▷E von Reinthal and H Clemenz, *Bulgarin,
Memoiren* (1859–60)

BULL, Olaf Jacob Martin Luther
(1883–1933)

Norwegian poet and bohemian, born in Christiania (now Oslo). He rejected his family's
robustly altruistic Christianity in favour of a
life of wandering and self-examination. His
poetry, from the early *Digte* (1909, 'Poems')
onwards, combines a strongly Romantic and
quasi-Symbolist treatment of great themes
like love and the natural world, with Bull's
interest in the creative act itself. His style is
compacted, almost private, but highly varied.
He found his true voice early but continually
experimented with styles. Among his more
important later collections were *De hundrede
år* (1928) and *Oinos og Eros* (1930). Still little-
known outside Norway and France, he
posthumously won the admiration of the
American poet **Robert Bly**.
▷T Greiff, *Olaf Bull: Taper og seirer* (1952)

BULLEN, Frank Thomas
(1857–1915)

English writer. He was a sailor till 1883, and
made notable additions to the literature of
the sea, including *Cruise of the Cachalot*
(1898). He also wrote *Recollections* (1915).
▷*With Christ at Sea: a religious autobiography* (1900)

BULLETT, Gerald
(1893–1958)

English author, born in London. Educated
at Jesus College, Cambridge, from 1914 his
published work included fiction, poems,
essays, biographies, anthologies, children's
books, literary criticism, and plays. His novels include *The Pandervils*, *The Jury* and *The
Snare of the Fowler*.
▷*Modern English Fiction: a personal view*
(1926)

BULLINS, Ed
(1935–)

American playwright, fiction writer and cultural activist. Born in Philadelphia, he was
educated largely in California and became
involved in ghetto drama projects in San
Francisco, acting as a cultural adviser for the
Black Panthers. Between 1968 and 1973, he
edited the journal *Black Theatre*. His first
major play was *Clara's Old Man* (1965), followed by *In Wine Time*, *A Son, Come Home*
and his best-known work, *The Electronic
Nigger*, all from 1968. Many of his plays are
linked into a huge cycle about the lives of
American blacks in the 20th century, projecting forward to the year 1999. Despite this,
Bullins's approach has been markedly different from that of **Amiri Baraka** (Leroi Jones),

attempting to work (just) within realist conventions. His angry 'Dynamite Plays' fall outside the cycle and are more ephemeral. He has also written a novel, *The Reluctant Rapist* (1973).

BULWER-LYTTON, Edward George Lytton, 1st Baron Lytton
(1803–73)

English novelist, playwright, essayist, poet and politician, born in London. He was the youngest son of General Earle Bulwer (1776–1807) by Elizabeth Barbara Lytton (1773–1843), the heiress of Knebworth in Hertfordshire. He took early to poetry and in 1820 published *Ismael and other Poems*. At Trinity Hall, Cambridge (1822–5) he won the Chancellor's Medal for a poem upon 'Sculpture', but left with only a pass degree. His unhappy marriage (1827), against his mother's wishes, to the Irish beauty Rosina Wheeler, ended in separation (1836), but called forth a marvellous literary activity, for the temporary estrangement from his mother threw him almost wholly on his own resources. His enormous output, vastly popular during his lifetime, but now forgotten, includes *Eugene Aram* (1832), *The Last Days of Pompeii* (1834) and *Harold* (1843). Among his plays are *The Lady of Lyons* (1838), *Richelieu* (1839) and *Money* (1840), and his poetry includes an epic, *King Arthur* (1848–9). MP for St Ives (1831–41), he was created a baronet in 1838, and in 1843 he succeeded to the Knebworth estate and assumed the surname of Lytton. He re-entered parliament as member for Hertfordshire in 1852, and in the Derby government (1858–9) was colonial secretary. In 1866 he was raised to the peerage. His son Edward (1831–91) was a successful diplomat and minor poet.
▷J Campbell, *Edward Bulwer-Lytton* (1986)

BUNIN, Ivan Alexeievich
(1870–1953)

Russian author, winner of the Nobel Prize for literature, born in Voronezh. He wrote lyrics and novels about the decay of the Russian nobility and of peasant life, and the disintegration of traditional rural patterns of life under the pressure of a changing world. They include *Derevnia* (1910, Eng trans *The Village* 1923), *Gospodin iz San-Frantsisko* (1914, Eng trans *The Gentleman from San Francisco*, 1922), his best-known work, which has the vanity of all things earthly as its theme, and the autobiographical *The Well of Days* (1933, trans 1946). He lived in Paris after the Russian Revolution, and received the 1933 Nobel Prize for literature. His work belongs in the great Russian realist tradition of **Turgenev**, **Tolstoy** and **Chekhov**.
▷A Poggioli, *The Art of Ivan Bunin* (1953)

BUNTING, Basil
(1900–85)

English poet, born in Northumberland. His career was one of neglect, and until the publication of *Loquitur* (1965) **Ezra Pound** seemed to be his sole aficionado. That, however, encouraged the growth of a cult following and Bunting attracted more admirers with his long poem, *Briggflatts* (1966). He assisted **Ford Madox Ford** with *The Transatlantic Review* in Paris but he largely shunned literary society. His admirers have included **Piers Paul Read**, **Henry Tomlinson**, **Hugh MacDiarmid** and **Robert Creeley**, but he has a greater following in the USA than in Britain despite attempts to revive interest. His *Collected Poems* appeared in 1968.
▷R Guedalla, *Basil Bunting: a bibliography of works and criticism* (1973); 'Basil Bunting Issue', *Poetry Information* (1978)

BUNTLINE, Ned, pseud of E Z C Judson
(1823–86)

American dime novelist (he more or less invented the genre) and organizer of the anti-Catholic Know-Nothing Party, who (with Prentiss Ingraham) helped to invent the largely fictitious exploits of 'Buffalo Bill' (ie, William Cody), himself a noted liar and showman. But Judson's own life really was an incredible one: after killing the husband of his mistress in a duel, he was actually lynched, being rescued only at the last minute; dismissed from the Union army for drunkenness, he afterwards claimed to have been a colonel, Chief of Scouts for the Army of the Potomac. Hymn-writer and temperance preacher, he wrote a 600-page novel in less than three days.
▷J Monaghan, *The Great Rascal* (1952)

BUNYAN, John
(1628–88)

English writer and preacher, born in Elstow near Bedford, son of a 'brasever' or tinker. In 1644 he was drafted into the army, in June 1645 he returned to Elstow, and there about 1649 married a poor girl who brought with her two books which had belonged to her father, the *Plain Man's Pathway to Heaven* and the *Practice of Piety*. About this time Bunyan began to experience those deep religious experiences which he has described so vividly in his *Grace Abounding* (1666). In 1653 he joined a Christian fellowship which had been organized by a converted royalist major, and about 1655 he was asked by the brethren to address them. This led to his preaching in the villages round Bedford; and in 1656 he was brought into discussions with the followers of George Fox, which led to

143

his first book, *Some Gospel Truths Opened* (1656), a vigorous attack on Quakerism. To this Edward Burrough, the Quaker, replied, and Bunyan replied in *A Vindication of Gospel Truths Opened* (1657). In November 1660 he was arrested while preaching in a farmhouse near Ampthill. During the 12 years' imprisonment in Bedford county jail which followed, Bunyan wrote *Profitable Meditations* (1661), *I Will Pray with the Spirit* (1663), *Christian Behaviour* (1663), *The Holy City* (1665), *The Resurrection of the Dead* (1665), *Grace Abounding* (1666) and some other works. He was released after the Declaration of Indulgence of 1672, under which he became a licensed preacher, and pastor of the church to which he belonged. In February 1673, however, the Declaration of Indulgence was cancelled, and on 4 March, a warrant, signed by 13 magistrates, was issued for his arrest. Brought to trial under the Conventicle Act, Bunyan was sent to prison for six months in the town gaol. It was during this later and briefer imprisonment that he wrote the first part of *The Pilgrim's Progress*. When first issued in 1678 it contained no Mr Worldly Wiseman, and many passages were added in the second and third editions (1679). It is essentially a vision of life recounted allegorically as the narrative of a journey. There followed the *Life and Death of Mr Badman* (1680), the *Holy War* (1682), and *The Pilgrim's Progress, Second Part* (1684), containing the story of Christiana and her children. Bunyan became pastor at Bedford for 16 years until his death after a ride through the rain from Reading to London. He was buried in Bunhill Fields, the *Campo Santo* of the Nonconformists.
▷ R Sharrock, *John Bunyan* (1954)

BÜRGER, Gottfried August
(1747–94)

German lyric poet and writer of ballads, born in Molmerswende, near Halberstadt, the son of Lutheran pastor. In boyhood he displayed no inclination to study, but showed a relish for verse. In 1764 he began to study theology, but in 1768 he migrated to Göttingen, and entered on a course of jurisprudence. His life there was wild and extravagant, and he might have sunk into obscurity but for the friendship which he happily formed with **Johann Heinrich Voss**, the two **Stolbergs**, and others. He studied closely the ancient and modern classics and translated Percy's *Reliques*. His most important work lay in reviving the ballad tradition, and he wrote many, including *Lenore* (1774), which was translated (*William and Helen*, 1797) by Sir **Walter Scott**. He married unhappily three times, speculated unwisely, and although a favourite poet of the German nation, he was left to earn his

livelihood by translations and similar hackwork.
▷ W A Little, *Gottfried August Bürger* (1974)

BURGESS, Anthony, pseud of John Anthony Burgess Wilson
(1917–93)

English novelist, critic and composer, born in Manchester into a Catholic family of predominantly Irish background. His grandfather was a publican and his father ran a tobacconist's shop. His mother was of Scottish extraction, a singer and dancer, who died in the influenza epidemic of 1919. Educated at the Xaverian College, Manchester, he did odd jobs before going to the University of Manchester where he studied language and literature. He also taught himself music, and composed a large number of works. In World War II he served in the Royal Army Medical Corps and entertained the troops with his compositions and piano-playing. He married in 1942, and after the war he taught in England before going to Malaya in 1954 where he trained teachers. He wrote his first novel, *A Vision of Battlements*, in 1953, but it was not published until 1965. In the far east he wrote the three novels which became *The Long Day Wanes: Time for a Tiger* (1956), *The Enemy in the Blanket* (1958), and *Beds in the East* (1959). Invalided out of the Colonial Service with a suspected brain tumour, he was given a year to live and wrote five novels in a year to provide for his prospective widow. But it was she who died first. In 1968 he married the Contessa Pasi and, beleaguered by death duties, went to live abroad, where he spent the rest of his life, first in Italy, latterly in Monte Carlo and Switzerland. Among his many novels are his dark and violent vision of the future, *A Clockwork Orange* (1962), *Inside Mr Enderby* (1963), *Napoleon Symphony* (1974), *Earthly Powers* (1980), *Kingdom of the Wicked* (1985) and *Any Old Iron* (1989). He was fascinated by language, as his various works of exegesis demonstrate. He also wrote biographies, books for children, and libretti.
▷ *Little Wilson and Big God* (1987); *You've Had Your Time* (1990)

BURKE, Edmund
(1729–97)

Irish essayist and politician, born in Dublin. A political writer of enormous influence, Burke began as a liberal and defender of the rights of minorities and the oppressed, but, with with advent of the French Revolution, became alarmed, and wrote the famous, and rigidly conservative, *Reflections on the Revolution in France* (1790), a vital document in modern conservatism. But Burke's greatest work, which influenced Kant and many

others, is the earlier essay *A Philosophical Enquiry into the Origin of our Ideas of the Sublime and the Beautiful* (1756), a profound investigation into its subject. **Oliver Goldsmith**'s comment upon him cannot be bettered: 'Who, born for the Universe, narrowed his mind/And to party gave up what was meant for mankind'. Burke remains one of Britain's greatest literary critics and aestheticians, and his political theory, although flawed by its shortness on facts and its excess of rhetoric, is still potent.
▷T W Copeland, *Our Eminent Friend Edmund Burke* (1949)

BURKE, Kenneth Duva
(1897–1992)

American philosopher, critic, poet, and 20th-century Renaissance mage. Born in Pittsburgh, he was educated in Ohio and at Columbia University in New York City. He served as music critic for *The Dial* and *The Nation* during the 1920s, but gradually developed critical-theoretical constructs which put heavy emphasis on 'rhetoric' as a means of revealing psychological, literary and cultural motives. His most important criticism is contained in *Counterstatement* (1931), *The Philosophy of Literary Form* (1941), *A Grammar of Motives* (1945) and *A Rhetoric of Motives* (1950). He gave currency to the expression 'failure of nerve' to describe the intellectual climate that followed the collapse of utopian and chiliastic hopes when fellow-travellers began to retreat towards the US political centre in the 1950s. Burke's verse was collected in 1968. He also wrote short fiction, notably *The White Oxen* (1924), and a single, experimental novel, *Towards a Better Life* (1932), which he revised nearly 35 years after first publication.
▷M E Brown, *Kenneth Burke* (1969)

BURKE, Thomas
(1886–1945)

English writer, born in London. He is best known for his *Limehouse Nights* (1916), but he was the author of about 30 books, mostly on aspects of London or about inns. These include *Nights in Town* (1915), *The Streets of London* (1941) and *The English Inn* (1930). He also made a fine reconstruction of the Thurtell and Hunt case in *Murder at Elstree* (1936). He published an autobiography, *The Wind and the Rain*, in (1924).
▷*Son of London* (1946)

BURNAND, Sir Francis Cowley
(1836–1917)

English dramatist and journalist. He was called to the Bar in 1862, but the success

of some early dramatic ventures altered his plans. He helped to start *Fun*, but in 1863 left that paper for *Punch*, of which he was Editor (1880–1906). He wrote many burlesques, including *Black-Eyed Susan* (1866) and *Cox and Box* (1867), with music by Arthur Sullivan (1867).
▷*Records and Reminiscences* (1917)

BURNETT, Frances Eliza, née Hodgson
(1849–1924)

English-born American novelist, born in Manchester, the daughter of a manufacturer. In 1865 she emigrated with her parents to Knoxville, Tennessee, turning to writing to help out the family finances. She married Dr Swan Moses Burnett in 1873 (divorced in 1898). There is speculation that her second marriage was made under the threat of blackmail; an unhappy alliance, it did much to cloud her later life. Her first literary success was *That Lass o' Lowrie's* (1877). Later works included plays and her most popular story *Little Lord Fauntleroy* (1886), *The One I Knew Best of All* (1893, autobiographical), *The Little Princess* (1905) and *The Secret Garden* (1909), still one of the best-loved classics of children's literature. In her lifetime she was rated one of America's foremost writers, and was a friend of **Henry James**.
▷A Thwaite, *Waiting for the Party: a life of Frances Hodgson Burnett* (1974)

BURNEY, Fanny, originally **Frances**, later **Madame D'Arblay**
(1752–1840)

English novelist and diarist, daughter of Charles Burney, born in King's Lynn. She educated herself by reading English and French literature and observing the distinguished people who visited her father. By 10 she had begun her incessant scribbling of stories, plays, and poems; on her 15th birthday, in a fit of repentance for such waste of time, she burned all her papers, but she could not forget the plot of *Evelina*, her first and best novel, published anonymously in 1778, which describes the entry of a country girl into the gaieties of London life. Her father at once recognized his daughter's talent, and confided the secret to Mrs Thrale, who, as well as **Dr Johnson**, championed the gifted young authoress. *Cecilia* (1782), though more complex, is less natural, and her style gradually declined in *Camilla* (1796) and *The Wanderer* (1814). She was appointed a second Keeper of the robes to Queen Charlotte in 1786, but her health declined; she retired on a pension and married a French émigré General d'Arblay, in 1793. Her *Letters and Diaries* (1846) show her skill in reporting dramatically. As a portrayer of the domestic scene she was a forerunner of **Jane Austen**, whom she influenced.

▷M E Adelstein, *Fanny Burney* (1968)

BURNINGHAM, John
(1936–)

English illustrator and writer for children, born in Farnham, Surrey, and educated at A S Neill's Summerhill and the Central School for Arts and Crafts, London. Popular and amusing, he draws children with round, cherubic faces which belie their highly-aware resourcefulness as seen in, say, *The Shopping Basket* (1982), where young Stephen fools a number of talking animals who try to rob him of his groceries. Distinctions include illustrating **Ian Fleming**'s *Chitty Chitty Bang Bang* (1964) and receiving the Kate Greenaway Award for *Borka* (1964) and *Mr Gumpy's Outing* (1970).

BURNS, Alan
(1929–)

English writer of experimental fiction. He was born in London; after Merchant Taylor's School, he served articles in Middle Temple and was called to the Bar in 1956, practising as a barrister until 1959, when he became legal manager at Beaverbrook Newspapers. He was the first Henfield Fellow in Creative Writing at the University of East Anglia in 1971, having published his first novel, the bleak *Europe after the Rain*, in 1965. It was followed by *Celebrations* (1967) and *Babel* (1969), a violent collage owing something to **William Burroughs**'s 'cut-up' technique but rather more to the nihilism of **J G Ballard**. Many readers took *The Angry Brigade* (1973) at face value, believing that the reminiscences of a group of alienated urban guerrillas were transcriptions of actual interviews; in fact the 'documentary' aspect was entirely fictional. In 1977, Burns moved to the USA, where he taught at the University of Minnesota. After a break of nearly a decade, he returned to fiction with *The Day Daddy Died* (1981). In 1993 he became Head of Creative Writing at Lancaster University.

BURNS, John Horne
(1916–53)

American novelist. Born in Massachusetts, he was educated at Phillips Academy and Harvard. During World War II he served in Italy and North Africa, an experience that strongly influenced his first and best novel *The Gallery* (1947), one of a group of works published around this time that explored the ambiguous nature of US values on a world stage. It was followed by *Lucifer with a Book* (1949), which drew on his pre-war job in a boys' boarding school. *A Cry of Children* (1952), completed in the year before his death,

suggested that he was working towards a new, more sophisticated vision.

BURNS, Robert
(1759–96)

Scottish poet, born in Alloway near Ayr, the son of a farmer. His education, begun at a school at Alloway Mill, and continued by a tutor called John Murdoch, was thoroughly literary. Among early influences were the popular tales, ballads and songs of Betty Davidson, an old woman who lived with the poet's family. He read **Allan Ramsay**, and began to write a little. Acquaintance with sailors and smugglers broadened his outlook, and his interest in women made him a kind of rural Don Juan. The death of Burns's father in 1784 left him to try to farm for himself. Burns's husbandry at Mossgiel near Mauchline went badly; the entanglement with Jean Armour (1767–1834) began; and out of his poverty, his passion, his despair and his desperate mirth, came the extraordinary poetic harvest of 1785. To this year belong the 'Epistle to Davie', 'Death and Dr Hornbook', 'The Twa Herds', 'The Jolly Beggars', 'Halloween', 'The Cotter's Saturday Night', 'Holy Willie's Prayer', 'The Holy Fair', and 'The Address to a Mouse'. The next year produced yet more excellent work, though much of the verse is satirical. 'The Twa Dogs' is a masterpiece of humour, and 'The Lament' and 'Despondency' are fine works. In this year there was abundant trouble with Jean Armour, and there was a love episode involving 'Highland Mary' (Mary Campbell) and her subsequent death. Looking about for money to emigrate to Jamaica, Burns published the famous Kilmarnock edition of his poems (1786). Their fame spread, and with the money he received he decided to leave Scotland for good. He was just about to sail when the praises and promises of admirers induced him to stay in Scotland. That winter he went to Edinburgh and was greeted with acclaim. On returning to the country, he 'fell to his old love again', Jean Armour; then, after a Highland tour, went back to Edinburgh, and began the epistolary flirtations with 'Clarinda' (Agnes Maclehose). By this time James Johnson had set about publishing his *Scots Musical Museum*, which contains all that is briefest and brightest of Burns. He contributed an astonishing number of the most beautiful, tender, passionate and vivacious songs in any language, chiefly adapted to old Scottish airs, and moulded now and then on old Scots words. In 1788 he married Jean Armour. He took a lease of Ellisland farm, on the Nith, above Dumfries, and next year became an excise officer. 'Tam o'Shanter' (1790) was written in one day; by this time Ellisland had proved a failure. Burns left his farm, withdrew to Dumfries, flirted with the French Revolution, drank, wrote songs, expressed opinions then thought radical, and made himself unpopular with the local lairds. However, in 1795 he turned patriot again. He died of endocarditis consequent on rheumatic fever, and is buried in Dumfries. His humble origin and his identification with the Scottish folk tradition, which he rescued, refurbished and in part embellished, are factors that help to explain his unwaning popularity as the national poet of Scotland.

▷ C Carswell, *The Life of Robert Burns* (1930)

BURROUGHS, Edgar Rice
(1875–1950)

American popular author, creator of Tarzan, born in Chicago. He served in the US cavalry and fought against the Apache Indians but was discharged when it was discovered he was under age. Thereafter he had several colourful occupations before he took to writing, his aim being to improve on the average dime novel. *Tarzan of the Apes* (1914) was his first book to feature the eponymous hero, the son of a British aristocrat, abandoned in the African jungle and brought up by apes. It spawned many sequels, films (Tarzan played, most memorably, by Johnny Weismuller), radio programmes and comic strips, making Burroughs a millionaire.

▷ R A Lopoff, *Edgar Rice Burroughs, master of adventure* (1965)

BURROUGHS, William S(eward)
(1914–)

American author, born to a wealthy family in St Louis, Missouri. He graduated from Harvard in 1936 and wandered throughout the USA and Europe. In 1944 he became a heroin addict while doing odd jobs in New York. In 1953 he published *Junkie*, an account of this experience, and his novels *The Naked Lunch* (1959) and *The Soft Machine* (1961) established him as a leading figure of the Beat movement, though one who stood somewhat apart. Intensely interested in the juxtaposition of apparently random ideas and observations, his later work is concerned with innovations in the novel form, such as the techniques of 'cut-up' and 'fold-in', in which words and phrases are either cut out and pasted together or formed by cross-column reading. Other works include *The Experimentor* (1960, with Bryon Gysin), *The Ticket that Exploded* (1962), *The Yage Letters* (1963, with **Allen Ginsberg**), *Dead Fingers Talk* (1963), *Nova Express* (1964), *The Wild Boys* (1971), *Exterminator!* (1973), *The Last Words of Dutch Schultz* (1975), *Ah, Pook is Here* (1971) and *Cities of the Red Night* (1981). He has lived mainly abroad, in Tangier and Paris. His autobiography appeared in 1973.

▷ E Mottram, *The Algebra of Need* (1971)

BURTON, Sir Richard Francis
(1821–90)

English linguist, explorer, travel writer, diplomat and adventurer, born in Torquay. A flamboyant character, largely self-educated, he won a place at Oxford, where he began (without the benefit of a tutor) to study Arabic. He is said eventually to have mastered approximately 30 languages, many with various tributaries of dialect. While in India, he contributed to government reports, often masquerading as a native in order to gather information. Commissioned by the Foreign Office to search for the sources of the Nile, he was one of a party which, in 1858, discovered Lake Tanganyika. His most important books include *First Footsteps in East Africa* (1851), *The Pilgrimage to Al-Medinah and Meccah* (1855) and *The Lake Region of Central Africa* (1860). His most famous and enduring work is his translation of *The Arabian Nights* (1885–8).

▷ Lady Burton, *Life of Sir Richard Burton* (1893)

BURTON, Robert
(1577–1640)

English writer and clergyman, author of the *Anatomy of Melancholy*, born in Lindley, Leicestershire. Educated at Nuneaton, Sutton Coldfield, and Brasenose College, Oxford, in 1599 he was elected a student of Christ Church. In 1616 he was presented to the Oxford vicarage of St Thomas, and about 1630 to the rectory of Segrave. Both livings he kept, but spent his life at Christ Church, where he died. The first edition of *Anatomy of Melancholy*, written under the pseudonym 'Democritus Junior', appeared in quarto in 1621. Four more editions in folio were published within the author's lifetime, each with successive alterations and additions; the final version of the book was the sixth edition (1651–2). One of the most interesting parts is the long preface, 'Democritus to the Reader', in which Burton gives indirectly an account of himself and his studies. This strange book is a vast and witty compendium of Jacobean knowledge about the 'disease' of melancholy, gathered from even the most out-of-the-way classical and medieval writers, as well as folklore and superstition.

▷ B Evans, *The Psychiatry of Robert Burton* (1944)

BURY, Lady Charlotte Susan Maria
(1775–1861)

Scottish novelist, youngest child of the 5th Duke of Argyll, born in London. She married in 1796 Colonel John Campbell (d.1809), and in 1818 the Rev Edward John Bury (1790–1832). She briefly became lady-in-waiting to Princess Caroline of Wales (1809). Beautiful and accomplished, she published 16 novels, including *Flirtation* and *Separation*, and was reputedly the anonymous author of the spicy *Diary illustrative of the Times of George IV* (1838).

BUSCH, Frederick Matthew
(1941–)

American novelist and short-story writer. He was born in Brooklyn, educated largely at Columbia University, and has worked as a college professor. His fiction is remarkably of a piece, largely concerned with the relationships of fathers and sons, with an unusual awareness of both roles. *I Wanted a Year Without Fall* (1971) is perhaps the best example of this, but the best known is *The Mutual Friend* (1978), a semi-documentary study of episodes in **Charles Dickens**'s life, in which the aftershocks of childhood traumas and oedipal fears are explored. His prose is rhythmic, occasionally terse and ironic, his style demanding but rewarding. Other novels include *Take This Man* (1981), *Sometimes I Live in the Country* (1986) and *Harry and Catherine* (1990). *Domestic Particulars* (1976) is a family chronicle cast in the form of a short-story collection. *When People Publish* (1986) brings together the best of his essays.

BUSCH, Wilhelm
(1832–1908)

German cartoonist and writer, born near Hanover. He worked as an illustrator for the comic weekly *Fliegende Blätter* (1859–71), and wrote satirical verse-stories with his own illustrations, such as *Max und Moritz* (1865, the prototypes for Rudolph Dirks' *Katzenjammer Kids*), and *Herr und Frau Knopp* (1876). He also wrote serious poetry, but is remembered for his 'non-sense' works.
▷F Bohme, *Wilhelm Busch, Leben, Werk, Schicksal* (1958)

BUSI, Aldo
(1948–)

Italian novelist and translator, born and educated in Montichiari, west of Verona. His fiction is lively, funny and fantastical. He remains best known to an English-speaking readership for *Vita standard di un venditore di collant* (1985, Eng trans *The Short Life of a Temporary Pantyhose Salesman*, 1988), but in Italy he is highly regarded as an interpreter of English and American literature. He has translated work by **John Ashbery** and **Christina Stead**, and has prepared an Italian version of **Lewis Carroll**'s *Alice's Adventures in Wonderland*.

BUSTA, Christine, pseud C Dimt
(1915–87)

Austrian poet, born in Vienna, where she worked as a librarian. Her collections, which include *Jahr um Jahr* (1950), *Lampe und Delphin* (1955) and *Unterwegs zu älteren Feuern* (1965), all display a deep but lightly rendered religious belief. In her subject-matter and traditional craftsmanship she is similar to the English poet, **Ruth Pitter**. Busta also wrote for children.

BUTLER, Guy
(1918–)

South African poet and critic who pursued an academic career in his native country, but was opposed to its policies until the early 1990s. Although somewhat neglected outside South Africa, he is often regarded as the most considerable poet writing in it: his poetry appears to be old-fashioned, but, it has been said, often takes risks 'with rhyme, rhythm, intricate verse and image patterns, colloquialisms, cliché, plain statement, or rhetorically splendid utterance'. He has written plays, a novel and much useful criticism. The most representative volume is *Selected Poems* (1989).
▷M van Wyk Smith and D Maclennan (eds), *Olive Schreiner and After: Essays on South African Literature in Honour of Guy Butler* (1983)

BUTLER, Robert Olen
(1945–)

American novelist, born in Granite City, Illinois. His educational qualifications include an MA in playwriting from the University of Iowa. He served in Vietnam from 1969 to 1972, an experience which re-emerges in his fiction. He edited *Energy Users News* from 1975 to 1985, then joined the faculty of McNeese State University at Lake Charles in Louisiana, where he teaches creative writing. His first novel was *The Alleys of Eden* (1981), and he published four more in the ensuing decade, along with the short-story collection *The Deuce* (1989). His most successful novel to date is *A Good Scent from A Strange Mountain* (1992), which was awarded the Pulitzer Prize in 1993. It was followed by *They Whisper* (1994), a novel about sexual obsession, set in Vietnam.

BUTLER, Samuel
(1835–1902)

English author, painter and musician, born in Langar Rectory, near Bingham, Nottinghamshire. He was educated at Shrewsbury and St John's College, Cambridge. Always quarrelling with his clergyman father, he gave up the idea of taking orders and

became instead a sheep farmer in New Zealand. Passages from his *A First Year in Canterbury Settlement* (1863) reappeared in *Erewhon* (1872), a Utopian satire in which many of the conventional practices and customs are reversed. For example, crime is treated as an illness and illness as a crime, and machines have been abolished for fear of their mastery over men's minds. The dominant theme of its supplement, *Erewhon Revisited* (1901), is the origin of religious belief. Butler was greatly influenced by Charles Darwin's *Origin of Species*, and accepted the latter's theory of evolution, but not of natural selection. He returned to Britain in 1864, and from then on lived in London. For a time he studied painting, and his picture *Mr Heatherley's Holiday* is in the Tate Gallery. In a series of writings he tried to revive the 'vitalist' or 'creative' view of evolution, as in *Luck or Cunning* (1886), in opposition to Darwin's doctrine of natural selection. He loved music, especially Handel's, and composed two oratorios, gavottes, minuets, fugues, and a cantata. In his later years he turned to scholarship and published translations of the *Iliad* (1898) and the *Odyssey* (1900). His essay *The Humour of Homer* (1892) is a remarkable piece of literary criticism. He is best known, however, for his autobiographical novel *The Way of All Flesh*, published posthumously in 1903, a work of moral realism on the causes of strife between different generations which left its mark on **George Bernard Shaw** and much 20th-century literature.
▷ *The Life and Letters of Dr Samuel Butler* (1856); P N Furbank, *Samuel Butler* (1948)

BUTLER, Sir William Francis
(1838–1910)

Irish soldier and author, born in Suirville, Tipperary. He joined the British army in 1858, and served in Canada from 1867 to 1873, where his experiences provided the material for his popular book, *The Great Lone Land* (1872). He served on the Red River expedition (1870–1), on the Ashanti expedition (1873), in the Sudan (1884–5), and in South Africa (1888–99). He published biographies of Gordon and Sir Charles Napier, and several travel books. In 1877 he married Elizabeth Southerden Thompson (1850–1933), a battle-painter, born in Lausanne, who made her reputation with the *Roll Call* (1874) and *Inkermann* (1877).
▷ *Remember Butler* (1967)

BUTOR, Michel Marie François
(1926–)

French writer, born in Mons-en-Baroeul. He taught in Egypt, England, Greece, Switzerland and the USA, and in French universities. He is 'professor extraordinaire' at the University of Geneva. He came to the fore in the 1950s, together with **Alain Robbe-Grillet**, **Nathalie Sarraute**, **Claude Simon** and others who were known collectively as the New Novelists. His novels include *Passage de Milan* (1954), *L'emploi du temps* (1956, Eng trans *Passing Time*, 1960), *Degrés* (1960, Eng trans *Degrees*, 1961 (US); 1962 (UK)), *Le génie du Lieu* (1960, 'The Spirit of the Place') and *Mobile* (1963), which extended the experimental nature of his texts. He wrote a series of critical volumes under the title *Répertoire 1–4* (1960–74), and other critical and non-fiction works, and is also known as a writer of poetry and drama, and has collaborated with the Belgian composer Henri Pousseur in an opera, *Votre Faust* (1968). His later fiction includes *Matière de rêves* (4 vols 1975–7, 'The Stuff of Dreams') and *Vanité: Conversation dans les Alpes-Maritimes* (1980, 'Vanitas: A Conversation in the Alpes-Maritimes').
▷ M C Spencer, *Michel Butor* (1974)

BUYSSE, Cyriel
(1859–1932)

Belgian (Flemish) novelist and dramatist, born in Nevele; he was a close friend of **Maurice Maeterlinck**, Belgium's foremost writer of the period. At first he represented the naturalist strain in Flemish literature, with such novels as his first, *Het recht van de sterkst* (1893, 'The Law of the Strongest'), about a farmer's struggle for survival. Later the tone of his work deepened, and in *De Schandpaal* (1928, 'The Pillory'), there is psychological penetration as well as his naturally pessimistic attitude. His plays include *Het gezin Van Paemel* (1903, 'The Van Paemal Family'), a sombre work about the struggle between peasants and aristocrats.
▷ S Lilar, *The Belgian Theatre Since 1890* (1962)

BUZO, Alexander
(1944–)

Australian playwright, born in Sydney, who first came to notice with *Norm and Achmed* (1968) through prosecutions for obscenity which followed its first productions. *Rooted* was produced in 1969 and was the first of his plays to receive an overseas production. In more serious vein, Buzo was awarded the Australian Literature Society's Gold Medal for *Macquarie* (1972), a study of an early governor of New South Wales, and *Tom* (1972). His plays cast a wry light on human affairs where the Australian setting is merely incidental to the drama, though a more exotic backdrop, a tropical seaport, is the setting of *Makassar Reef* (1978). Buzo's interest in the tools of his trade has resulted in three entertaining books, *Tautology* (1981), *Tautology Too* (1982), and *Glancing Blows: Life and*

Language in Australia (1987). His first novel, a humorous detective story, *The Search for Harry Allfay*, was published in 1985.

BUZZATI, Dino
(1906–72)

Italian novelist and short-story writer, born in the mountainous north-east of Italy, an area which inspired the remote, mysterious settings of much of his work. After university in Milan, he became a journalist on the *Corriere della Sera*, and continued to work for the paper, as reporter, critic and Africa correspondent, throughout his literary career. His first novellas were reminiscent of Nordic myths, and his great novel, *Il deserto dei tartari* (1940), has a mystic, allegorical power in its story of a lieutenant stationed in a border fort, awaiting a Tartar attack that never materializes. A sense of the surreal and the macabre haunts his best work, notably the short stories collected in *Sessanta racconti* (1958), which won the Strega Prize for Literature. His later writing ranged widely, from a science-fiction novel to a comic-strip version of *Orpheus and Eurydice*.

B V *see* THOMSON, James

BYARS, Betsy Cromer
(1928–)

American children's novelist, born in Charlotte, North Carolina. She began to write in the 1960s but had no great impact until *The Summer of the Swans* (1970), the story of a girl and her retarded brother, which was awarded the **Newbery** Medal. Specializing in kitchen-sink drama—contemporary realism—she produced a number of popular novels, at times perceptive and inventive, at others predictable and reminiscent of soap opera. Her titles include *The Eighteenth Emergency* (1973), *Goodbye, Chicken Little* (1979) and *The Animal, The Vegetable, and John D Jones* (1982).

BYATT, A(ntonia) S(usan)
(1938–)

English novelist and critic, born in Sheffield, elder sister of **Margaret Drabble**. She taught with Westminster Tutors (1962–5), and at the Central School of Art and Design (1965–9) before joining the extra-mural faculty at Uniersity College London (1971); she has subsequently been senior lecturer in English. In 1965 she published *Degrees of Freedom*, the first full-length study of **Iris Murdoch**'s novels, whose philosophical style has influenced her own; in 1976 she added a shorter monograph, *Iris Murdoch*. Highly respected as a critic, she made her reputation as a novelist with her third novel, *The Virgin in the Garden* (1978). This was followed by *Still Life* (1985), and in 1990 she won the Booker Prize with *Possession* (1990), in which two young academics research the lives of a fictitious mid-Victorian poet, Randolph Henry Ash, and his contemporary, Christabel LaMotte. An excellent example of her style, it is part literary detective story, part romance, part a satirical comedy of English and American academia. Byatt has also written on **Ford Madox Ford** and on 18th- and 19th-century poetry: *Unruly Times: Wordsworth and Coleridge in their Time* (1970). Her interests extend to art and art history, literary and social history, and philosophy, all of which feature in her novels.

BYNNER, (Harold) Witter
(1881–1968)

American poet, playwright and translator, the nephew of a once-popular novelist, Edwin Lassetter Bynner. He grew up in Brooklyn, New York, and was educated at Harvard, to which he wrote a celebrated *Ode* (1907; as *Young Harvard*, 1925). After graduation, he made his way as an editor and playwright, before travelling and researching in the Far East, where he became a passionate propagandist for oriental life and culture; *The Jade Mountain* (1929) is an account of his travels. His other well-known book is *Journey With Genius* (1951), a memoir of his stay at Taos, New Mexico, with **D H Lawrence**, who anticipated the compliment by including Bynner as a character in *The Plumed Serpent* (1926). Bynner's main claim to fame, however, is an elaborate poetic hoax in which, with Arthur Davis Ficke, he published a volume called *Spectra* (1916) under the names 'Emmanuel Morgan' and 'Anne Knish', a book of supposed 'poetic experiments' that were then talked into brief vogue by glowing reviews from him and Ficke. The deception lasted somewhat longer than the 'Ern Malley' stunt in Australia, which shared many of its sincere critical motives. Sadly, Bynner's own verse, particularly those in *New Poems* (1960), have been much undervalued as a result.

BYRNE, Donn, pseud of Brian Oswald Donn-Byrne
(1889–1928)

Irish–American novelist and short-story writer, born in Brooklyn. He was educated at Dublin, the Sorbonne, and at Leipzig. A cowpuncher in South America and garage hand in New York, his works include *Messer Marco Polo* (1921) and *Hangman's House* (1926).
▷T McCauley, *Donn Byrne, Bard of Armagh* (1929)

BYRNE, John
(1940–)

Scottish dramatist and stage designer, born in Paisley. He had designed plays for the 7:84 Theatre Company before writing his first play, *Writer's Cramp*, produced at the Edinburgh Festival Fringe (1977). *The Slab Boys* (1978), concerning the lives of the employees of a carpet factory, grew into a trilogy with *Cuttin' A Rug* (1980) and *Still Life* (1983). Other plays include *Normal Service* (1979) and *Cara Coco* (1982). He wrote the highly acclaimed *Tutti Frutti* (1987), a BBC Scotland television series about an ageing pop group, and followed it with the less universally-acclaimed *Your Cheatin' Heart* (1989). He returned to writing for the stage in 1992 with *Colquhoun and MacBryde*, a play based on the lives of two Scottish artists. He has designed stage sets for most of his own work and many other productions.

BYRON, George Gordon, 6th Baron Byron of Rochdale
(1788–1824)

English poet of Scottish antecedents, born in London, son of the irresponsible and eccentric Captain 'Mad Jack' Byron (1756–91) and Catherine Gordon of Gight, Aberdeen, a Scottish heiress. His grandfather was admiral John Byron. His first 10 years were spent in his mother's lodgings in Aberdeen, her husband having squandered her fortune in France. Byron was lame from birth, and the shabby surroundings and the violent temper of his foolish, vulgar and deserted mother produced a repression in him which explains many of his later actions. In 1798 he succeeded to the title on the death of 'the wicked lord', his great-uncle. He was educated at Aberdeen Grammar School, then privately at Dulwich and at Harrow School, proceeding to Trinity College, Cambridge, in 1805, where he read much, swam and boxed, and led a dissipated life. An early collection of poems under the title of *Hours of Idleness* was reprinted with alterations in 1807 and was 'savagely cut up' by the *Edinburgh Review* in 1808. Byron replied with his powerful Popian satire *English Bards and Scotch Reviewers* (1809), and set out on his grand tour, visiting Spain, Malta, Albania, Greece, and the Aegean, returning after two years with 'a great many stanzas in Spenser's measure relative to the countries he had visited', which appeared under the title of *Childe Harold's Pilgrimage* in 1812 and were widely popular. This was followed by a series of oriental pieces such as the *Giaour* (1813), *Lara* (1814), and the *Siege of Corinth* (1816). During this time he dramatized himself as a man of mystery, a gloomy romantic figure, derived from the popular fiction of the day and not

least from *Childe Harold*. He became the darling of London society, and lover of Lady Caroline Lamb, and gave to Europe the concept of the 'Byronic hero'. In 1815 he married an heiress, Anne Isabella Milbanke, who left him in 1816 after the birth of a daughter, Ada (later Countess of Lovelace). He was also suspected of a more than brotherly love for his half-sister, Augusta Leigh, and was ostracized. He left for the continent, travelled through Belgium and the Rhine country to Switzerland, where he met **Shelley**, and on to Venice and Rome, where he wrote the last canto of *Childe Harold* (1817). He spent two years in Venice and met the Countess Teresa Guiccioli, who became his mistress. Some of his best works belong to this period, including *Beppo* (1818), *A Vision of Judgment* (1822), and *Don Juan* (1819–24), written in a new metre (ottava rima) and in an informal conversational manner which enabled him to express the whole of his complex personality. He gave active help to the Italian revolutionaries and founded with Leigh Hunt a short-lived journal, *The Liberal*. In 1823 he joined the Greek insurgents who had risen against the Turks, and died of marsh fever at Missolonghi. His body was brought back to England and buried at Hucknall Torkard in Nottingham. His reputation declined after his death despite the championship of **Matthew Arnold**. On the continent his influence was far-reaching both as the creator of the 'Byronic hero' and as the champion of political liberty, leaving his mark on such writers as **Victor Hugo**, **Paul De Musset**, **Giacomo Leopardi**, **Heinrich Heine**, **José de Espronceda**, **Alexander Pushkin**, and **Mikhail Lermontov**.
▷P Quennell, *Byron* (1934–51)

BYRON, H(enry) J(ames)
(1834–84)

English actor, prolific comic dramatist and occasional editor of humorous papers, born in Manchester. Byron notched up over 150 works, liberally laced with puns and borrowing themes from opera, contemporary political and social events, mythology and even children's stories. The dominant dramatic form of his day was melodrama and burlesque, and Byron enjoyed a considerable reputation, especially during the mid-1850s until the late 1860s, by writing burlesques of popular melodrama, of which *The Maid and the Magpie* (1858), *Blue Beard from a New Point of Hue* (1860), and *Ali Baba or, The Thirty-Nine Thieves* (1863), are among the more notable examples. A comedy, *Our Boys* (1875), ran for four years at the Vaudeville Theatre in London.
▷J Davis, *Plays by H. J. Byron* (1984)

BYRON, Robert
(1905–41)

English writer on travel and architecture, Byzantinist and aesthete. Born in Wiltshire, he was educated at Eton and Merton College, Oxford, where he collected Victoriana. A visit to Mount Athos led to *The Station* (1928), which was followed by *The Byzantine Achievement* (1929) and *The Appreciation of Architecture* (1932). He is best-remembered, however, for his vivacious and erudite travelogues, which include *First Russia, Then Tibet* (1933) and *The Road to Oxiana* (1937), a minor masterpiece conceived as a collection of diary jottings. Typically aggressive in its assertions, it is suffused with humour and sensibility, and won *The Sunday Times* Literary Award. A combative personality, his life was infused with passionate antagonisms and furious enthusiasms. He died during World War II when his ship was torpedoed.

C

CABALLERO, Fernán, pseud of Cecilia Francesca de Arrom
(1797–1877)

Spanish novelist, born in Morges in Switzerland. She was the daughter of Nikolaus Böhl von Faber (1770–1836), a German merchant in Spain. She spent most of her childhood in Germany, but returned to Spain in 1813. She wrote on the history of Spanish literature and introduced in Spain the picturesque local-colour novel. The first of her 50 romances was *La Gaviota* (1849, 'The Seagull'); others include *Clemencia* (1852), *Un servilón y un liberalito* (1855, 'A Groveller and a Little Liberal') and *La Familia de Alvareda* (1856). She also collected Spanish folk tales.
▷L H Klibbe, *Fernán Caballero* (1973)

CABALLERO CALDERON, Eduardo
(1910–)

Colombian writer, politician and diplomat. He ran the daily newspaper *El Tiempo* in Bogotá (1939–43), besides being a diplomat in Peru, Argentina and Spain before finally becoming a permanent representative of UNESCO. His first novels are vivid, descriptive reminiscences with a strong Creole element, a feel for colloquial speech and brutal scenes, with titles such as *Siervo Sin Tierra* (1954, 'Slave without Land') and *Manuel Pacho* (1964). His best-known work is *El Cristo de Espaldas* (1953, 'Christ with His Back Turned'), about the moral crisis of a young rural priest involved in political conflict.

CABANILLOS, Ramón
(1873–1959)

Spanish poet and dramatist writing in Galician, born in Cambados, Pontreveda. He was one of the foremost Gallegan poets of the 20th century, and also one of the most original and wide-ranging. Gallegan poetry is as much (or more) Portuguese as Spanish, and thus partakes far more of the *saudade* (nostalgic longing). But Cabanillos was influenced by the Spanish–American *modernismo*, and expanded the horizons of his poetry. He was in his way a brilliant figure who deserved, like **Eduardo Pondal**, a wider exposure than his minority language enabled him to gain.

CABELL, James Branch
(1879–1958)

American novelist and critic, born in Richmond, Virginia. He made his name with his romance *Jurgen* (1919), the best known of a sequence of 18 novels, collectively known as *Biography of Michael*, set in the imaginary medieval kingdom of Poictesme and written in an elaborate, sophisticated style showing the author's fondness for archaisms. He also published a book of criticism, *Preface to the Past* (1936).
▷C van Doren, *James Branch Cabell* (1926)

CABLE, George Washington
(1844–1925)

American author, born in New Orleans. At the age of 19 he volunteered as a Confederate soldier. After the war he earned a precarious living in New Orleans, before taking up a literary career in 1879. In 1884 he went to New England. His Creole sketches in *Scribner's* made his reputation. Among his books are *Old Creole Days* (1879), *The Grandissimes* (1880, this is his finest work, a profound study of colour and caste in New Orleans at the time of the Louisiana Purchase), *The Silent South* (1885), *Bylow Hill* (1902), *Kincaid's Battery* (1908) and *Lovers of Louisiana* (1918).
▷A Turner, *George Washington Cable: biography* (1956)

CABRAL DE MELO NETO, João
(1920–)

Brazilian poet and dramatist, born in Recife, Pernambuco. Cabral de Melo Neto is the leading poet of the group, known as 'the generation of '45', which first decisively reacted away from Brazilian *modernismo*. He took as his initial models **Jorge Guillén**, **Nicanor Parra** (in his capacity as deliberate 'anti-poet'), whose first collection had appeared in 1937, a cluster of Brazilian poets such as **Bandeira**, **Oswald de Andrade** and **Carlos Drummond de Andrade**—and, above all, the folk poetry and ballads of his own northeastern area of Brazil. Later he incorporated some of the techniques of the concrete poetry into his own work, but without accepting any of the trivial programmes of the concretists. His plays have been well received; there are translations of his work by **Elizabeth Bishop** in *An Anthology of Twentieth Century Brazilian Poetry* (1972). He has been the most widely imitated of the poets of his generation.
▷M Bandeira, *A Brief History of Brazilian Literature* (1958)

CABRERA INFANTE, Guillermo
(1929–)

Cuban-born British novelist, born in Gibara. Educated at Havana University, he emigrated to England in 1966. He is known chiefly for his fiction, particularly *Three Trapped Tigers* (1971), a highly experimental work, *A View of Dawn in the Tropics* (1978) and *Infante's Inferno* (1984), set in Havana during the 1940s and 1950s, which skilfully blurs the distinction between autobiography and fiction, in the process demythologizing the Don Juan legend in Hispanic culture. He translated **James Joyce**'s *Dubliners* into Spanish (1972), and has also written journalism, and, writing under the name Guillermo Cain, film criticism (collected in *A Twentieth Century Job*, 1991) and screenplays.

CADALSO VASQUEZ, José de
(1741–82)

Spanish writer, born in Cadiz. By profession an army officer, he wrote as a hobby. He is best known for his prose satire *Los eruditos a la violeta* (1772, 'The Scholars and the Violet'), which ridicules pedantry, and *Cartas marruecas* (1774, 'Moroccan Letters'), a work of social criticism in epistolary form. He was killed at the siege of Gibraltar.
▷R P Sebold, *Colonel Don José Cadalso* (1971)

CAEDMON
(7th century)

Anglo-Saxon poet, the earliest Christian English poet known by name. According to **Bede**, he was an unlettered herdsman who in his old age received a divine call in a dream to sing of the Creation. He then became a monk at Whitby under the rule of St Hilda, where he turned other biblical themes into vernacular poetry. But the original hymn of the Creation, a mere nine lines long, is the only extant poem that can be attributed to him with any certainty.
▷E Dobbie, *The MSS of Caedmon's Hymn and Bede's Death Song* (1937)

CAESAR, Gaius Julius
(100–44BC)

Roman general, statesman and historian. Caesar, by intrigue and bribery, got himself into a powerful position in Rome in 59; he spent the next nine years in Gaul. After winning a civil war (49–45) he became supreme ruler, but was assassinated in 44. His literary fame rests on his *Commentaries on the Gallic War* (Eng trans 1930), in seven books, and *On the Civil War* (Eng trans 1921), in three books. His style is famously straightforward and gripping, and guilefully clever at seeming objective (which it is not). He was a noted orator.
▷F E Adcock, *Caesar as a Man of Letters* (1956)

CAHAN, Abraham
(1860–1951)

Jewish–American novelist, born in Russia. He emigrated to the USA in 1882, and took up journalism as a career. He was the editor of the socialist newspaper the *Jewish Daily Forward* for many years. He wrote a number of works in Yiddish, but his best-known books are in English, and deal with the process of Americanization of Jewish immigrants. *Yekl: A Tale of the New York Ghetto* (1896) was the first of these, but his most celebrated and influential book was *The Rise of David Levinsky* (1917), which described the psychological and human price of assimilation, and remains a classic treatment of its subject. He wrote also *The Imported Bridegroom and Other Stories* (1898) and an *Autobiography* in five volumes (1916–36).

CAIN, James M(allahan)
(1892–1977)

American thriller writer, born in Annapolis, Maryland. Often associated with **Dashiell Hammett** and **Raymond Chandler**, his earliest ambition was to emulate his mother and become a professional singer. Music remained his favourite recreation and it forms the background of some of his stories. He tried various jobs, was a reporter for many years and also taught journalism, but he always hankered after 'the great American novel'. After moving to California he found the style which is his hallmark. It first emerged in *The Postman Always Rings Twice* (1934), in which an adulterous couple murder the woman's husband but betray each other, then in *Serenade* (1937), *Mildred Pierce* (1941), *Double Indemnity* (1943) and *The Butterfly* (1947). Several of his stories were filmed with what Cain described as 'legendary success', but the script credits went to others.
▷R Hoopes, *Cain: the biography* (1982)

CAINE, Sir (Thomas Henry) Hall
(1853–1931)

English novelist, born in Runcorn. He trained as an architect, and became secretary to **Dante Gabriel Rossetti** from 1881 to 1882, and later published *Recollections of Rossetti* (1882). He wrote a number of popular novels, many of them set in the Isle of Man, including *The Shadow of a Crime* (1885), *The Deemster* (1887), *The Bondman* (1890), *The Scapegoat* (1891), *The Manxman* (1894), *The Eternal City* (1901) and *The Prodigal Son* (1904). He also wrote a *Life of Christ* (1938), and published an early autobiography, *My Story* (1908).

▷C F Kenyon, *Hall Caine, the man and the novelist* (1901)

CAKS, Aleksandrs, pseud of **Aleksandrs Cadarainis**
(1901–50)
Innovatory and controversial Latvian poet and short-story writer. He studied medicine in Moscow, served in the Latvian Red Guards in the Revolution, then settled in Riga as a teacher. His highly dramatic, effective but somewhat inchoate early collections, influenced by **Mayakovsky**, broke with the pastoral traditions of Latvian poetry and caused scandal amongst both left and right elements by its frequent allusions to sexuality and drink. He later fell foul of the Soviet authorities; his poetry suffered through his unconvincing attempts to become a socialist realist. His death was passed over in silence, but he was 'rediscovered' in Latvia in 1966 and now has his rightful place as his country's leading modernist, who inspired poets both inside and outside Latvia. Poetry in translation includes *Let's Get Acquainted* (1973) and *Selected Poems* (1979).

CALDERÓN DE LA BARCA, Pedro
(1600–81)
Spanish dramatist, born of a prestigious family in Madrid. After schooling under the Jesuits, he studied law and philosophy at Salamanca (1613–19), and during 10 years' service in the Milanese and in Flanders saw much of men and manners that he afterwards utilized. On Vega Carpio's death in 1635 he was summoned by Philip IV to Madrid, and appointed a sort of master of the revels. In 1640 the rebellion in Catalonia made him return to the army; but in 1651 he entered the priesthood, and in 1653 withdrew to Toledo. Ten years later he was recalled to court and to the resumption of his dramatic activity, receiving, with other preferments, the post of chaplain of honour to Philip; and he continued to write for the court, the church, and the public theatres till his death. Castilian and Catholic to the backbone, Calderón wrote with perfect fidelity to the Spanish thought and manners of his age. His *autos sacramentales*, outdoor plays for the festival of Corpus Christi, number 72, and have been divided into seven classes—biblical, classical, ethical, 'cloak and sword plays', dramas of passion, and so forth; the finest of them is *El divino Orfeo* ('Divine Orpheus'). Of his regular dramas 118 are extant.

▷E W Hesse, *Calderón* (1967)

CALDWELL, Erskine
(1903–87)
American author, born in White Oak, Georgia. He worked amongst the 'poor whites' in the southern states, where he absorbed the background for his best-known work *Tobacco Road* (1932), of which the dramatized version by Jack Kirkland (1933) had a record run in New York. Other books include *God's Little Acre* (1933), *Sure Hand of God* (1947), *A Lamp for Nightfall* (1952), *Love and Money* (1954) and *Close to Home* (1962).

CALDWELL, (Janet) Taylor
(1900–85)
English-born American novelist, born in Manchester, of Scots descent. She moved with her family to the USA in 1906. Her debut, *Dynasty of Death* (1938), is the saga of a family of armaments manufacturers. It and its many sequels, such as *The Eagles Gather* (1940) and *Dear Glorious Physician* (1959), were bestsellers, impressing the reader by an accumulation of detail rather than by literary merit.

CALISHER, Hortense
(1911–)
American novelist and short-story writer, born in New York City. Her milieu is New York and her characters are usually drawn from the upper middle-class. A powerful and precise writer, her novels—*The New Yorkers* (1969), *Queenie* (1971), *The Bobby-Soxer* (1986)—though frequently of novella length are less successful than stories like 'In Greenwich There Are Many Gravelled Walks', which aspire to classic status.
▷ *Herself* (1972)

CALLAGHAN, Morley Edward
(1903–90)
Canadian novelist, short-story writer and memoirist, born in Toronto of Irish descent. One of Canada's premier novelists, he was educated at Toronto University, and when a cub reporter on the Toronto *Daily Star* was befriended by **Ernest Hemingway**. They met up again in Paris, where his boxing prowess earned him Hemingway's respect, and he wrote about his time there in one of his most appealing books, *That Summer in Paris* (1963). He had been called to the Bar in 1928, but Hemingway encouraged him to renounce law for literature and helped him get some of his stories published in expatriate literary magazines. In terms of publication, Callaghan's career was strikingly uneven, periods of productivity mirrored by prolonged silence. His first novel was *Strange Fugitive* (1928) and his first collection of stories *A Native Argosy* (1930). From the late

1920s to the late 1930s he wrote six novels, finishing with *More Joy in Heaven* (1937). He returned to Toronto in 1929. His later novels include *The Loved and the Lost* (1951), *The Many Colored Coat* (1960), *A Fine and Private Place* (1975) and *A Time for Judas* (1983).
▷A Conron, *Morley Callaghan* (1966)

CALLIMACHUS
(c.305–c.240 BC)

Hellenistic poet, grammarian and critic, of Alexandria, born in Cyrene in Libya. He became head of the Alexandrian library, and prepared a catalogue of it, in 120 volumes. He wrote numerous prose works and plays which have not survived, a number of *Hymns*, and a long elegiac poem, the *Aitia*. He excelled in the smaller forms, and some 60 of his epigrams are included in the Greek Anthology, to which he is one of the most distinguished contributors.
▷G Capovilla, *Callimaco* (1967)

CALLOW, Philip
(1924–)

English poet, novelist and biographer, born in Birmingham, whose recurring literary theme is family relationships and the emotional chasms between the sexes. His early trilogy, *Going to the Moon* (1968), *The Bliss Body* (1969), and *Flesh of Morning* (1971), which was republished as *Another Flesh* in 1989, examines the developing maturity of a young boy in the English Midlands, his adolescent drifting, his adult love affairs and gradual acceptance of his own nature. Among his more recent works, *Some Love* (1991) is a sharply-observed study of the relationship between a young, suspicious 14-year-old boy and a 30-year-old woman disenchanted by men. Callow's first collection of poetry was *The Turning Point*; later collections include *New York Insomnia and Other Poems* (1984). He has also written studies of **D H Lawrence** and Vincent van Gogh.

CALPRENÈDE, Gautier des Costes de la
(1610–63)

French author, officer of the guards and royal chamberlain of France. He wrote tragedies, tragi-comedies, and the clever but tedious 'heroic romances', *Cléopâtre*, *Cassandre*, and others.

CALPURNIUS SICULUS, Titus
(fl.mid 1st century)

Latin pastoral poet. He is best known for his seven surviving Eclogues.

CALVERLEY, Charles Stuart
(1831–84)

English poet and parodist, born in Martley, Worcestershire, the son of a clergyman. He was educated at Marlborough, Harrow, Oxford and Cambridge. In 1858 he was elected a fellow of Christ's College, Cambridge, and in 1865 called to the Bar, and settled in London. A fall on the ice in the winter of 1866–7 put an end to a brilliant career and his last years were spent as an invalid. One of the most gifted men of his time, he is remembered as a skilful parodist in his two little volumes, *Verses and Translations* (1862) and *Fly Leaves* (1872). His translation of **Theocritus** (1869) shows at once his scholarship and his mastery of English verse.
▷R B Ince, *Calverley and the Cambridge Wits of the 19th Century* (1929)

CALVINO, Italo
(1923–85)

Italian novelist, essayist and journalist, born in Santiago de las Vegas, Cuba, of Italian parents. He grew up in San Remo on the Italian Riviera and was educated at the University of Turin. In 1940 he was forced to join the Young Fascists. He was a reluctant participant in the Italian occupation of the French Riviera, but in 1943 he was able to join the Resistance, and until 1945 he was with the Partisan forces fighting the Nazis in Liguria. Throughout the 1940s he wrote for the communist paper *L'unità* and later he succeeded **Cesare Pavese** at Einaudi, the Turin-based publishers. His first novel, *Il sentiero dei nidi di ragno* (1947, Eng trans *The Path to the Nest of Spiders*, 1956), was dubbed Neorealist, but he became increasingly interested in fantasy, folk-tales and the nature of narrative. During the Cold War years of the 1950s he wrote three fantastic 'historical' novels, collectively titled *I nostri antenati* (1960, Eng trans *Our Ancestors*, 1980). A complete translation of his *Fiabe Italiane* (1956) was published as *Italian Folktales* in English in 1980. Regarded as one of the most inventive of the European modernists, he combined fantasy and surrealism with a hard, satirical wit and his later books are complex and profound. Seminal titles are *Le città invisibili* (1972, Eng trans *Invisible Cities*, 1974), *Il castello dei destini incrociati* (1973, Eng trans *The Castle of Crossed Destinies*, 1977), *Si una notte d'inverno un viaggiatore* (1979, Eng trans *If on a Winter's Night a Traveller*, 1981) and *Palomar* (1983). In 1973 he won the prestigious Italian literary award, the Premio Feltrinelli.
▷J Cannon, *Calvino: writer and society* (1981)

CAMBRIDGE, Ada
(1844–1926)

English-born Australian novelist and poet, born in Norfolk, the second of 10 children, her father was a gentleman farmer and she was educated privately. By the time she met and married George Cross at the age of 26, she had published short stories, poems and a book of hymns. They left almost immediately for Australia where her husband was to be a missionary priest, and settled eventually in Melbourne. In 1873 she began contributing to the *Australian* which, between 1875 and 1886, serialized nine novels, of which three were subsequently published: *In Two Years' Time* (1879), *A Mere Chance* (1882) and *The Three Miss Kings* (1891). A woman with a strong sense of class, her writing called attention to women's social position and encouraged them to think for themselves. She wrote 18 novels and attracted a wide English readership but was modest about her success, regarding herself fortunate to have been the first in the field. **Jane Austen** is the most obvious influence, and her best work is to be found in *A Marked Man* (1890), *The Three Miss Kings* (1891), *Not All In Vain* (1892), *Fidelis* (1895) and *Materfamilias* (1898).
▷ *Thirty Years in Australia* (1903); *The Retrospect* (1912)

CAMERON, (John) Norman
(1905–53)

Scottish poet and translator, born in Bombay. He published only three volumes of his own verse, and financed himself by working in the colonial service (Nigeria, 1929–31); as an advertising copywriter (1933–9), and as a writer of government propaganda during World War II. He lived for a time in Deya, Majorca, home also to **Robert Graves**. His second book, *Work In Hand* (1942), was a joint effort with Graves and Alan Hodge. He was, however, by no means a follower of Graves, having early formed his own formal, introspective vision, as is shown in *The Winter House and Other Poems* (1935). *Forgive Me, Sire* (1950) is restrained, almost repressed, in its narrowness of subject matter. His *Complete Poems* was published in 1985.

CAMOENS, or CAMÕES, Luis de
(1524–80)

Portuguese poet, born in Lisbon. He studied for the church as an 'honourable poor student' at Coimbra, but declined to take orders. His *Amphitriões* ('The Host') was acted before the university. Returning to Lisbon, probably in 1542, he fell in love with Donna Caterina Ataide, who returned his affection; but her father was against the marriage, and the poet had to content himself with passionate protestations in his *Rimas*—short poems after the model of the Italians. He was banished from Lisbon for a year, and joining a Portuguese force at Ceuta, served there for two years, losing his right eye because of a splinter. In 1550 he returned to Lisbon, where for the next three years he seems to have led a somewhat discreditable life; and having been thrown into prison for his share in a street brawl, was released only on his volunteering to go to India. At Goa (1553–5) he engaged in two military expeditions, but his bold denunciations of the Portuguese officials at length led to an honourable exile in a lucrative post at Macao (1556). Returning to Goa (1558) he was shipwrecked and lost everything except his poem, *Os Lusiadas* ('The Lusiads'). At Goa he was thrown into prison through the machinations of his former enemies; but at length, after an exile of 16 years, he returned to Portugal to spend the remainder of his life at Lisbon in poverty and obscurity. In 1572 he published *Os Lusiadas*, which had an immediate and brilliant success, but did little for the fortunes of its author, who died in a public hospital. In *Os Lusiadas* he did for the Portuguese language what **Chaucer** did for English and **Dante** for Italian, as well as making himself the interpreter of the deepest aspirations of the Portuguese nation. The Portuguese regard it as their national epic, while modern readers have learned to value its lyrical as well as its epic aspects.
▷W Freitas, *Camoens and his Epic: a Historic, Geographic and Cultural Background* (1963)

CAMPANA, Dino
(1885–1932)

Major Italian poet from Marradi near Florence. He was for the last 12 years of his life a patient in a mental hospital, a victim of the manic-depression which had dominated his life. He earned his living in many ways, and was often jailed as a tramp. But he was almost inordinately gifted as an incantatory and visionary poet, and his *Canti Orfici* (1914, Eng trans *Orphic Songs*, 1968), was fully recognized as a work of genius by Giovanni Papini, Ardengo Soffici (who lost the original manuscript, so that Campana had to reconstruct it from memory) and eventually by most other readers of poetry in Italy. His poetry was later collected, still under the title of his only publication. His work is highly original, influenced initially by **D'Annunzio**, but also anticipating every mode in Italian literature throughout the 20th century, inspired, frenzied, mostly coherent at a deeply visionary level. All his writing, including articles, was edited in *Opere e contributi* (2 vols, 1973).

CAMPBELL, Alistair Te Ariki
(1925–)

New Zealand poet and playwright, born in Rarotonga, Cook Islands, whose first collection of verse, *Mine Eyes Dazzle: Poems 1947–49* (1950, rev edns 1951, 1956) received immediate attention. His Polynesian ancestry responds to the pulse of land and sea, as in *Sanctuary of Spirits: Poems* (1963) and *Blue Rain: Poems* (1967). His later verse closely identifies with Maori myth and history, and his search for his Cook Islands roots is reflected in *The Dark Lord of Savaiki* (1980) and *Soul Traps: A Lyric Sequence* (1985). *Collected Poems, 1947–1981* came out in 1981. Much of his radio drama is unpublished; it brings out personal concerns through themes of mental illness or racial conflict.
▷ *Island to Island* (1984)

CAMPBELL, David Watt
(1915–79)

Australian poet, born on a remote station near Adelong, New South Wales. After serving with distinction in the Royal Australian Air Force in World War II, he returned to farming and in 1964 became poetry editor of the *Australian* newspaper. His first book of verse was *Speak with the Sun* (1949), much in the Australian ballad tradition, followed by *The Miracle of Mullion Hill* (1956). *Poems* (1962) turns more to universal themes and includes the pastoral sequence of 12 poems, 'Cocky's Calendar', which ranks alongside the best of the English 18th-century tradition. Four further volumes were followed by his last book, *The Man in the Honeysuckle* (posthumous, 1979). He edited two anthologies, *Australian Poetry* (1966) and *Modern Australian Poetry* (1970), and wrote short stories and translations of Russian poetry. He received the **Patrick White** Literary Award in 1975.

CAMPBELL, George
(1916–)

Jamaican poet, born in Panama and educated in Jamaica and New York. His *First Poems* (1945) had enormous influence on the generation of Caribbean poets that includes **Edward Kamau Brathwaite**—who describes him as 'one of the most important figures in the transition from colonial apprenticeship to a sense of the autochthonous and its expression'—and **Derek Walcott**, who acknowledges the exhilarating impact of *First*

Poems in *Another Life* (1973). Campbell's poetry celebrates the land and people of the Black Caribbean, demanding a humane and multicultural perspective.

CAMPBELL, John Wood, Jr
(1910–71)

American science-fiction writer and editor, born in Newark, New Jersey. He graduated in physics from Duke University in 1932. A science-fiction fan from the earliest days of the genre, he rivalled **E E 'Doc' Smith** in the galactic adventure stories known as 'space opera' in the early 1930s. From 1934 he published most of his fiction under the pseudonym 'Don A Stuart', and wrote little more after 1937. His chief claim to fame, though, was as the hugely influential editor of the magazine *Astounding Stories* (later *Astounding Science Fiction*, and still later *Analog*, 1937–71). The first decade of his editorship is remembered as a 'golden age' in which he discovered and encouraged a stable of writers who became major figures in the genre, including **Asimov**, **Del Ray**, **Heinlein**, **Van Vogt** and **Kuttner**.

CAMPBELL, (Ignatius) Roy Dunnachie
(1901–57)

South African poet, translator and critic, born in Durban, but who lived most of his life in Great Britain, and died in a car crash in Portugal. Campbell was a boisterous figure, given—as his biographer demonstrates—to lying about his exploits; the work of his middle and later period is badly flawed by over-aggressiveness or delight in violence. The consensus now, however, is that he wrote a few powerful lyrics which will outlast his self-spoiled reputation. He was an outdoors man, and much of his best poetry celebrates this. An effective satirist of apartheid and all sorts of pretension in his youth in his native South Africa, he later became the apotheosis of right-wing Catholicism, and even gave out that he had fought for Franco in the Spanish Civil War (which he had not). His defence of Franco in the long, maladroit poem *Flowering Rifle* (1939) greatly harmed his reputation, and it has not gained admirers even from the right. Among his great poems is the comparatively long 'Tristan da Cunha', written when he was a young man; many of his shorter lyrics have been anthologized. His books of poetry include *The Flamingo Terrapin* (1924), *The Wayzgoose* (1928), *Adamastor* (1930), *The Georgiad* (1931), *Mithraic Emblems* (1936), and *Flowering Rifle* (1939).
▷ *Collected Poems*, 3 vols (1949–60); *Light on a Dark Horse* (1951, autobiography); P Alexander, *Roy Campbell* (1982)

CAMPBELL, Thomas
(1777–1844)

Scottish poet and journalist, born and educated in Glasgow, the eleventh child of a tobacco merchant who was ruined by the American War of Independence. In 1797 he went to Edinburgh to study law, but was increasingly drawn to the reading and writing of poetry. *The Pleasures of Hope*, published in 1799, ran through four editions in a year. During a tour on the Continent (1800–1) he visited Hohenlinden, only just missing the battle there, fell in with the prototype of his 'Exile of Erin' at Hamburg, and sailed past the batteries of Copenhagen. In 1803 he married and settled in London, having refused the offer of a professorship at Wilna, and resolved to adopt a literary career. He contributed articles to *The Edinburgh Encyclopaedia*, and compiled *The Annals of Great Britain from George II to the Peace of Amiens*. In 1809 *Gertrude of Wyoming* appeared; in 1818 he visited Germany again, and on his return he published his *Specimens of the British Poets* (1819). In 1820 he delivered a course of lectures on poetry at the Surrey Institution, and from 1820 to 1830 he edited *The New Monthly Magazine*, contributing 'The Last Man' and other poems. He was buried in Westminster Abbey. 'Hohenlinden', 'Ye Mariners of England' and 'The Battle of the Baltic' are among his best-known poems.
▷W Beattie, *Life and Letters of Thomas Campbell* (1849)

CAMPBELL, William Wilfred
(1860–1919)

Canadian poet, born in Kitchener, Ontario. An Anglican clergyman, he joined the Canadian civil service in 1891. He was author of *Lake Lyrics* (1889) and other volumes of poetry, and was editor of the *Oxford Book of Canadian Verse* (1906).
▷C Klinck, *William Campbell, a study in late provincial Victorianism* (1942)

CAMPHUYSEN, Dirck Rafaelsz
(1586–1627)

Dutch religious poet and painter, born in Gorinchem. He studied painting, then became a priest, but was dismissed because of his Arminianism, for which he was persecuted. Thereafter he lived in poverty, making a meagre living as a flax dealer. Translations of his poetry are in *Batavian Anthology* (1824).
▷L A Rademaker, *Dirck Camphuysen* (1898, in Dutch)

CAMPION, Thomas
(1567–1620)

English poet and composer, one of the world's great song-writers. He was by profession a doctor. He wrote a treatise, *Observations in the Art of English Rhyme* (1602), which seemed to disparage rhyme; but his own songs use rhyme. Judged as poetry, his songs are slight; judged as songs, they are paramount.
▷M Kastendieck, *England's Musical Poet: Thomas Campion* (1938)

CAMPO, Estanislao del
(1834–80)

Argentinian *gaucho* poet, soldier and journalist, born in Buenos Aires. The *gaucho* poets were not nomadic cowboys, but city men who aped their dialect for sophisticated purposes—until the masterpiece of **José Hernández**, *Martin Fierro*, which was a real tribute. It is significant that his most famous and successful poem, *Fausto* (1866), angered Hernández for its mockery of its gaucho protagonist, who, having witnessed the opera *Faust*, believes he has seen a real instance of black magic. It, and Campo's other skilful and sometimes superficially amusing verse, are now of more historical than intrinsic interest.

CAMPOAMOR, Ramón de
(1817–1901)

Spanish poet, born in Navia. He studied medicine, almost became a Jesuit, and ultimately chose a career in politics and literature. He enjoyed some success during his lifetime, but his work is now neglected. His short, epigrammatic poems, including those in *Doloras* (1858, 'Laments'), *Pequeños poemas* (1871, 'Little Poems') and *Humoradas* (1890), represent his most significant literary contribution, but he also wrote larger poems, including *El drama universal* (1869, 'The Universal Drama') and *El tren expreso* (1874, 'The Express Train').
▷V Gaos, *La Poetica de Campoamor* (1955)

CAMUS, Albert
(1913–60)

French writer, winner of the Nobel Prize for literature, born in Mondovi, Algeria, the son of a farm labourer. He studied philosophy at Algiers and, interrupted by long spells of ill-health, became actor, schoolmaster, playwright and journalist there and in Paris. Active in the French Resistance during World War II, he became co-editor with **Jean-Paul Sartre** of the left-wing newspaper *Combat* after the liberation until 1948, when he broke with Sartre and 'committed' political writing. Having earned an international reputation with his Existentialist novel, *L'Étranger* (1942, Eng trans *The Outsider*, 1946), 'the study of an absurd man in an absurd world', he set himself in his subsequent work the aim of elucidating some values for man confronted with cosmic meaninglessness. The essays *Le Mythe de Sisyphe* (1942, Eng trans *The Myth of Sisyphus*, 1955), concerning suicide, and *L'Homme révolté* (1951, Eng trans *The Rebel*, 1954), on the harm done by surrendering to ideologies, the magnanimous letters to a German friend (1945), a second masterpiece *La Peste* (1947, Eng trans *The Plague*, 1948), in which the plague-stricken city Oran symbolizes man's isolation, were followed by a return to extreme ironical pessimism in *La Chute* (1956, Eng trans *The Fall*, 1957). *Le Malentendu* (1945, Eng trans *Cross Purpose*, 1947) and *Caligula* (1938, Eng trans 1947) are his best plays. His political writings are collected in *Actuelles I* (1950, 'Chronicles of Today I') and *II* (1953). He was awarded the 1957 Nobel Prize for literature. He died in a car accident.

▷P Thody, *Albert Camus 1913–1960* (1962); H Lottman, *Camus: a biography* (1979)

CANETTI, Elias
(1905–)

Bulgarian writer, winner of the Nobel Prize for literature, born in Rutschuk, Bulgaria, into a community of Spanish-speaking Jews. In his formative years he moved between England, Switzerland, Austria and Germany. Since 1938 he has lived in Britain. The works for which he is best known are his novel on the growth of totalitarianism, *Die Blendung* (1935–6, Eng trans *Auto-da-Fé*, 1946), and a speculative study of the psychology of mass behaviour, *Masse und Macht* (1960, Eng trans *Crowds and Power*, 1962). His autobiographies, *Die gerettete Zunge: Geschichte einer Jugenol* (1977, Eng trans *The Tongue Set Free*, 1979) and *Die Fachel im Ohr* (1980, Eng trans *The Torch in my Ear*, 1982), have emphasized the origins of and inspiration for his life's work. He was awarded the Nobel Prize for literature in 1981.

▷D Barnuow, *Canetti* (1979)

CANNING, Victor
(1911–86)

English author of suspense thrillers, mostly with an espionage background. Born in Plymouth, he served in the Royal Artillery during World War II. His first book, and first use of a series character, was *Mr Finchley Discovers His England* (1934), a mild and slightly ironic novel with overtones of **H G Wells**. Other Finchley books followed, but it was with *The Chasm* (1947) that Canning discovered his forte for fast-paced action leavened with dry humour. In *The Whip Hand* (1965) he introduced the private investigator and intelligence operative Rex Carver, who figured in four subsequent novels. A hugely prolific author, Canning's plots are as varied

as his settings and he scrupulously avoided formulaic situations. He also wrote short stories and drama. During the 1930s he sometimes published under the pseudonym Alan Gould.

CANSINOS-ASSÉNS, Rafael
(1883–1964)

Spanish novelist, translator (the complete works of **Dostoyevsky**), editor (*Cervantes*, which he founded in Madrid) and critic, born in Seville. He was Spain's best informed critic about other literatures; charges that he was 'excessively anecdotal' ignore the sheer amount of good reading he was able to recommend, and with great authority. As a novelist he was in many ways a small edition of his friend **Valle-Inclán**, at his best when at his most brief, as in *El eterno milagro* (1918, 'The Eternal Miracle'). His *La nueva literatura* (1917–27) remains invaluable. He was the leading expert on the contribution of the Sephardic Jews to Spanish literature, as seen in *España y los judios españoles* (1919, 'Spain and the Spanish Jews').

▷S Robles, *La novela corte en España* (1952)

CANTH, Minna, née Ulrika Vilhelmina Johnsson
(1844–97)

Finnish playwright and feminist, born in Tampere. She began writing at 40 after an intensive course of self-education in literary and social history. Her reading, and her experience as the single parent of seven children, turned her into a radical. A powerful exponent of the Realist school, her best-known plays are *Työmiehen vaimo* (1885, 'A Working-class Wife') and *Kovan onnen lapsia* (1888, 'The Hard Luck Kids'). Later she turned to psychological dramas about women, such as *Anna Liisa* (1895), which recalls **Tolstoy** and some elements of **Ibsen**.

▷G von Frenckell-Thesleff, *Minna Canth* (1943)

CANTÙ, Cesare
(1804–95)

Italian historian and novelist, born in Brivio in the Milanese territory. Imprisoned as a liberal in 1833, he described the sorrows of a prisoner in a historical romance, *Margherita Pusterla* (1838). As well as his monumental history of the world, *Storia universale* (35 vols, 1836–42, 'A History of the World'), he wrote a multitude of works on Italian history and literature, as well as lighter works, and *Manzoni: Reminiscinze* (2 vols, 1883, 'Manzoni: Reminiscences').

▷G Grabinski, *Cesare Cantù* (1896)

CAO YU, pseud of **Wan Jiabao**
(1910–)
Chinese playwright, born in Tianjin. The most significant 20th-century dramatist in China, he studied western literature at Qinghua University (1930–4), where he was profoundly influenced by **Ibsen** and **George Bernard Shaw** to attack the corruption of traditional society. His best-known work, *Thunderstorm*, was staged in 1935; his other major plays are *Sunrise* (1935), *Wilderness* (1936), *Metamorphosis* (1940), *Peking Man* (1940) and *Family* (1941), adapted from the novel by **Ba Jin**. He toured the USA in 1946, and after the foundation of the People's Republic in 1949 he was appointed to numerous official posts. In 1979 he wrote the play *The Consort of Peace*.

ČAPEK, Josef
(1887–1945)
Czech writer and painter, born in Schwadonitz, elder brother of **Karel Čapek**. His early literary works, written in collaboration with his brother, include the allegorical *Ze života hmyzu* (1921, Eng trans *The Insect Play*, 1923). From such anxious visions of the future he progressed to a philosophy of sceptical humanism which found expression in his novel, *Stín Kapradiny* (1930), and in his essays. He died in Belsen.
▷J Peirha, *Josef Čapek* (1961)

ČAPEK, Karel
(1890–1938)
Bohemian novelist and playwright, brother of **Josef Čapek**. He was born in Malé Svatoňovice, and educated in Prague, Paris and Berlin. He worked as a journalist and, in the early twenties, as stage director at the Vinograd Theatre in Prague. Several early works, including the novel *Zářivé hlubiny* (1916, *The Shining Depths*), were collaborations with his brother, but he came to international attention with the play *R.U.R.* (1920), a satirical vision of a dehumanized post-industrial society. The brothers later collaborated on *Ze života hmyzu* (1921, now best known as *The Insect Play*, 1923), which has a similar theme, as does the late novel *Válka s mloky* (1937), written as Czech independence was increasingly threatened by Nazi expansionism. Karel also wrote *Věc Makropulos* (1922), which formed the basis for his countryman Leoš Janáček's 1925 opera *The Makropulos Affair*. His style is dense, allusive and very Slavic, not always translating effectively, but his ideas and the robotic world of *R.U.R.* are still compelling.
▷W E Harkins, *Karel Čapek* (1962)

CAPOTE, Truman
(1924–84)
American author, born in New Orleans of Spanish descent. He spent much of his childhood in Alabama. He won several literary prizes while at school in New York but showed little ability in other subjects. His short story 'Miriam', published in the magazine *Mademoiselle*, was selected for the **O Henry** Memorial Award volume in 1946. *Other Voices, Other Rooms* (1948), his first novel, revealed his talent for sympathetic description of small-town life in the deep South and centres on the (homo)sexual awakenings of a young boy. *The Grass Harp* (1951) is a fantasy performed against a background of the Alabama of his childhood. Other works are *Breakfast at Tiffany's* (1958), which was highly successful as a film, *In Cold Blood* (1966), a 'non-fiction novel' about a murder in Kansas; latterly he published a collection of short pieces, *Music for Chameleons* and the long-promised but unfinished novel *Answered Prayers*.
▷W L Nance, *The Worlds of Truman Capote* (1970); Gerald Clarke, *Capote: a biography* (1987)

CAPPS, Ben(jamin Franklin)
(1922–)
American writer of Westerns, born in Texas, the son of a cowboy. Capps was most successful in the 1960s, winning the Spur Award and other prizes for *The Trail to Ogallala* (1964). *A Woman of the People* (1966), about a white girl captured and raised as an Indian by the Comanches, is regarded by Capps' admirers as an American classic. Since then his work has been too seriously historical to capture the popular audience of the genre. *The Heirs of Franklin Woodstock* (1989), set in present-day Texas, examines the death of the frontier spirit.

CAPUANA, Luigi
(1839–1915)
Italian novelist, story writer, poet and critic, born in Mineo (Catania), Sicily. He was a leading figure in Italian letters, and an important predecessor of **Pirandello**. He began as a folklorist and philological scholar, then graduated to drama critic in Rome (1864). In 1901 he published his major novel, *Il marchese di Roccaverdina* ('The Marquis of Roccaverdina'), which has its origins in its author's liaison with an illiterate Sicilian girl who bore him children. This book is Italy's worthy naturalist version of the *Crime and Punishment* of **Dostoyevsky**, was influenced by it, and has a plot resembling it. Capuana's short novels and criticism are also notable.

The former have been collected in *Racconti* (1973–4).

▷V Traverso, *Luigi Capuana* (1968)

CAPUS, (Vincent Marie) Alfred
(1858–1922)

French writer, born in Aix-en-Provence. He left engineering for journalism, and became political editor of *Le Figaro*. He wrote *Qui perd gagne* (1890, 'The Loser Wins') and other novels, but is best remembered for his comedies of the Parisian bourgeoisie such as *La Veine* (1901, 'Luck').

▷E Quet, *Alfred Capus* (1904)

CARAGIALE, Ion Luca
(1852–1912)

Romanian dramatist and short-story writer of Greek extraction who, owing to his quarrelsome and satirical nature, did not receive his full due in his lifetime. He removed himself and his family to Berlin, where he died, in 1904. **Mateiu Caragiale** was his illegitimate son. The communist regime favoured his work, pretending that it was Marxist in spirit. The Romanian theatre was lifeless in his day: he put life into it with ironic comedies such as *O scrisoare pierduta* (1884, Eng trans, with other plays, *The Lost Letter*, 1956), in which the bourgeois are mocked but in which the underlying theme of the human perils of 'modernization' remains potent. His sketches, usually very short, are unparalleled in their piercing accuracy and professionalism.

CARAGIALE, Mateiu
(1885–1936)

Romanian novelist and poet, illegitimate son of the famous dramatist **Ion Caragiale**, whose work was until quite recently largely unrecognized, even in his own country. *Remember* (1921)—the title is in English, but there is as yet no translation—is a strange story about the victimization of a homosexual, but bears signs of influence from 'decadent' French writers such as **Huysmans**. His masterpiece, *Craii de Curtea Veche* (1926–8, 'Knights of the Round Table'), however, is wholly original. It is said to have been in part inspired by his dislike of his father's 'straightforwardness', but this may be an oversimplification: his father, as an ironist, was hardly straightforward. It portrays, with great power and subtlety, a mad world of utterly degenerate aristocrats in a twilit Bucharest where East jostles with West. **Kafka**, could he have read it, would have revelled in it; but it is quintessentially Romanian. **Ion Barbu** was almost alone in his immediate recognition of its greatness.

CARCO, Francis, pseud of François Carcopino-Tusoli
(1886–1958)

French author, born in Nouméa in New Caledonia. He first gained recognition with his volume of poems *La Bohème et mon coeur* (1912, 'Bohemia and My Heart'), and added to his reputation with a series of novels chiefly set in Paris's Latin Quarter. He wrote a colourful account of his early life in *De Montmartre au Quartier latin* (1934, 'From Montmartre to the Latin Quarter').

▷S Weiner, *Francis Carco, career of a literary Bohemian* (1952)

CARDARELLI, Vincenzo, pseud of Nazareno Calderelli
(1887–1959)

Italian poet, critic and editor, born in Corneto Tarquinia (now Tarquinia). He was an influential and useful critic, always opting for a commonsense approach (in the theory-ridden Italian context), and insisting that form alone could not make good poetry: it had to have something interesting to say. He was an editor at *La ronda* (which he founded in Rome together with **Bacchelli** and **Cecchi**), and of the weekly *La fiera letteraria*. He was an active opponent of both the Futurist movement and of Hermeticism when it became a school (after the critic Flores had named it as one). His poetry, modelled on that of **Petrarch** and **Leopardi**, is unusually coherent for its time, and is chiefly meditative and concerned with the passage of time.

▷N J Perella, *Midday in Italian Literature* (1979)

CARDENAL, Ernesto
(1925–)

Nicaraguan poet, born in Granada. He was educated at the University of Mexico and Columbia University, New York. Later he became a Franciscan priest, and ran a small religious commune in the remote hinterlands of the country. His religious beliefs were a compound of Catholicism, native Indian myth and Buddhist precepts, and he was influenced by Jose Coronel Urtecho, an older Nicaraguan poet, and the American poet-priest **Thomas Merton**. His poetry is distinctly modernist in form and rhetorical in tone, and reflects both his religious and radical political commitments. He has published numerous collections, including *Epigramas: Poemas* (1961, 'Epigrams: Poems'), *Oracion por Marilyn Monroe* (1965, Eng trans *Marilyn Monroe*, 1975) and *Salmos* (1967, Eng trans *Psalms of Struggle and Liberation*, 1981). He also wrote a number of prose works, mainly on spiritual subjects.

CARDUCCI, Giosuè
(1835–1907)

Italian poet, winner of the Nobel Prize for literature, born in Valdicastello Pisa province, the son of a physician. In 1860 he became Professor of Italian literature at Bologna, and set a new standard in scholarship. In 1876 he was returned to the Italian parliament as a Republican, and in 1890 was nominated a senator. He published several volumes of verse, and was considered Italy's national poet for his patriotic vision of a revived Italy. He was awarded the Nobel Prize for literature in 1906.
▷J C Bailey, *Carducci* (1926)

CAREW, Jan
(1924–)

Guyanese novelist, who wrote vividly and with vigour of his own country, in *Black Midas* (1958) and *The Wild Coast* (1958), and of Harlem in *The Last Barbarian* (1961). He has also written outspoken travel books, such as *Moscow Is Not My Mecca* (1964).

CAREW, Thomas
(1595–1639)

English Cavalier poet, born in West Wickham, the son of a successful lawyer. He studied at Merton College, and entered the Inner Temple to study law in 1612. Between 1613 and 1616 he visited Holland as secretary to the ambassador, but was dismissed for slandering his employers. After three years in London he went to France in 1619–24, again as secretary to the ambassador. Afterwards he rose into high favour with Charles I. A friend of **Ben Jonson** and **John Donne**, he wrote polished lyrics in the Cavalier tradition, particularly the love poem 'Rapture'.

CAREY, Henry
(c.1690–1743)

English poet and musician, born in Yorkshire, believed to have been an illegitimate son of a member of the Savile family. He published his first volume of poems in 1713. He wrote innumerable songs, witty poems, burlesques, farces, and dramatic pieces, sometimes composing the accompanying music. His best-known poem is 'Sally in our Alley'.

CAREY, Peter
(1943–)

Australian novelist, born in Bacchus Marsh, Victoria. He attended Geelong Grammar School before beginning a career as an advertising copywriter, after which he lived for a spell in London. His first book, *The Fat Man in History* (1974), was a collection of short stories, and he was quickly regarded as an innovative force in Australian writing, breaking free from the mould of realism to experiment with modes as diverse as Absurdism, Surrealism, science fiction and fable. His next book, *Bliss* (1981), explored the advertising world. In 1985 he published *Illywhacker* (Australian slang for a trickster or conman), an imaginative tour de force which was shortlisted for the Booker Prize. He won the Booker Prize with *Oscar and Lucinda* (1988), an exuberant novel constructed on a Victorian scale, in which a compulsive gambler and a Sydney heiress fascinated with the manufacture of glass are bizarrely united. In 1991 he published *The Tax Inspector*.

CARLETON, William
(1794–1869)

Irish novelist, born in Prillisk, County Tyrone, of peasant birth, the youngest of 14 children. He became a tutor and writer in Dublin, contributing sketches to the *Christian Examiner*, republished as *Traits and Stories of the Irish Peasantry* (1830). A second series (1833) was just as well received. In 1839 he published a long novel, *Fardorougha the Miser*, which was followed by *The Black Prophet* (1847), about the Famine, *The Tithe Proctor* (1849), *The Squanders of Castle Squander* (1852), *The Evil Eye* (1860), and others.

CARLETON, Will(iam McKendree)
(1845–1912)

American poet, born in Hudson, Michigan. He graduated at Hillsdale College, Michigan, and wrote *Farm Ballads* (1875), *City Ballads* (1885) and other works.
▷B Kiely, *Poor Scholar: a study of the works and days of Will Carleton* (1947)

CARLYLE, Thomas
(1795–1881)

Scottish historian, essayist and sage, born in Ecclefechan, Dumfriesshire, the son of a stonemason (and later farmer). Brought up in a strictly Calvinist and Secessionist home, he was educated at Ecclefechan village school, Annan Academy and Edinburgh University, where he studied arts and mathematics. He then spent a year studying for the Secessionist Church in Edinburgh, but turned to teaching instead, initially at Annan Academy and then in Kirkcaldy (1816–18), where he met the revivalist minister Edward Irving, who became a lifelong friend. He moved back to Edinburgh in 1818 to study law, but turned to private tutoring. He wrote several articles for Sir David Brewster, Editor of the *Edinburgh Encyclopaedia*, and immersed himself in the study of German literature, publishing his first major essay, on **Goethe**'s *Faust*, in the

New Edinburgh Review (1822). He translated Legendre's *Elements of Geometry* from the French, and wrote an ambitious *Life of Schiller*, which was published in instalments in *The London Magazine* from October 1823 and in book form in 1825. His major work during this period was his translation of Goethe's *Wilhelm Meister*, which was published in 1824 and earned him the acquaintance of **Coleridge**, **Hazlitt**, **Thomas Campbell** and other literary figures in London. In 1825 he moved to the farm of Hoddam Hill in Dumfriesshire, where he prepared a four-volume collection of translations of various writers, *German Romance* (1827). In 1826 he married Jane Baillie Welsh, and settled in Edinburgh, where he wrote articles for Francis Jeffrey in the *Edinburgh Review*. However, in 1828 he moved to the estate of Craigenputtock, near Dumfries, which Jane had inherited. There he wrote articles for the *Edinburgh Review*, and a *History of German Literature* (subsequently published in a series of essays). He also wrote his first major work on social philosophy, *Sartor Resartus*, which was published in instalments in *Fraser's Magazine* in 1833–4; it was produced in book form in the USA in 1836 with an introduction by **Ralph Waldo Emerson**, who had visited Carlyle at Craigenputtock. It was partly a satirical discourse on the value of clothes by 'Professor Teufelsdröckh', and partly a semi-autobiographical discussion of creeds and human values. In 1834 the couple moved to London, where Carlyle spent the rest of his life. Here he completed his romantic history of *The French Revolution* (1837), despite the accidental burning of the manuscript of most of the first volume by John Stuart Mill's maidservant. He was now established as a man of letters, and engaged in a series of lectures, collected as *On Heroes, Hero Worship and the Heroic in History* (1841), which foreshadowed his advocacy of the view that a strong hero-figure as a nation's leader was the best remedy for society's ills. On this theme of strong, benevolent autocracy as the best form of protection of freedom he also wrote an important essay on *Chartism* (1839), and a major political essay, *Past and Present* (1843). In 1845 he published *Oliver Cromwell's Letters and Speeches*, which revolutionized contemporary attitudes to the Protector and his dictatorship. Another collection of essays, *Latter Day Pamphlets* (1850), highlighted his increasingly right-wing political attitudes, with their emphasis on duty, obedience and punishment. His most ambitious work was then published: a six-volume *History of...Frederick the Great* (1858–65), a compelling portrait of the practical autocrat as a heroic idealist. In 1866 Carlyle was installed as Lord Rector of Edinburgh University. His

wife died suddenly at this time, and he wrote little more except for a minor work, *The Early Kings of Norway* (1875). He edited and published his wife's letters and diaries in 1883, having already written an anguished memoir of her in his *Reminiscences* (1881). He refused an honour from **Disraeli**, and was buried at his own wish in Ecclefechan, not Westminster Abbey.

▷ J A Froude, *Thomas Carlyle: a history of his life* (1884)

CARMAN, (William) Bliss
(1861–1929)

Canadian poet, born in Fredericton, who left Canada as a student to study at Harvard, and later became a journalist in New York. His first volume, *Low Tide on Grand Pré*, appeared in 1893, after which he produced three books in collaboration with **Richard Hovey**. Carman's other books include *April Airs* (1916), *Far Horizons* (1925) and *Sanctuary* (1929). He also translated the lyrics of **Sappho** in 1904 and published several volumes of essays. Carman was considered an accessible and popular poet, although he appears less highly regarded now than he was during his lifetime.

CARMAN, Dulce
(1883–1970)

New Zealand author of popular romantic fiction, originally for periodicals, whose first book was *The Broad Stairway* (1924). Throughout her work (more than 20 books) the themes are generally simple; mixed blood, inheritance and the integration of Maoris into the Paheka (white settler) way of life are treated sympathetically but naively. Typical titles are *Neath the Maori Moon* (1948), *The Tapu Tree* (1954), *The Wailing Pool* (1961) and *The Maori Gateway* (1963).

CARMEN SYLVA, pseud of Elisabeth, Queen of Romania
(1843–1916)

The daughter of Prince Hermann of Wied Neuwied, she married King (then Prince) Carol I of Romania in 1869. Her only child, a daughter, died in 1874, and out of her sorrow arose her literary activity. Two poems, printed privately at Leipzig in 1880 under the name 'Carmen Sylva', were followed by *Stürme* (1881, 'Storms'), *Leidens Erdengang* (1882, Eng trans *Pilgrim Sorrow*, 1884), *Pensées d'une reine* (1882, 'Thoughts of a Queen'), *The Bard of Dimbovitza* (1891), *Meister Manole* (1892), and other works. In the war of 1877–8 she endeared herself to her people by her devotion to the wounded.

CARMI, T, pseud of **Charmi Charny**
(1925–)

American-born Israeli poet, educated at Yeshiva University and Columbia University, New York, afterwards at the Sorbonne in Paris. He emigrated to Israel in 1947 and began to write poetry that combined literary elements from the sacred tradition with demotic speech. His first collection, *Mum Vahalom* ('Tainted Vision'), appeared in 1951. During the fifties he worked in literary journalism and publishing, later (1971–4) editing the influential *Ariel*. *Nehash Hanehoshet* (1961) was the first to be translated into English (by **Dom Moraes** as the *Brass Serpent* in 1964); a *Selected Poems*, translated by Stephen Mitchell, appeared in London in 1976. Five years later, Carmi made an even greater impact on English-speaking readers and on international understanding of his cultural tradition when he edited the *Penguin Book of Hebrew Verse* (1981). He has adapted plays by **Shakespeare**, **Brecht**, **Christopher Fry**, **Tom Stoppard** and others.

CARNER, Josep
(1884–1970)

Catalan poet and essayist. He was born in Barcelona, and pursued a career as a diplomat until the advent of the Franco dictatorship, which he opposed. His masterpiece is the long narrative poem on the Jonah-and-the-Whale theme, *Nabí*, containing such magnificent lines as 'Goodbye, though, great clusters of greed and punishment!' Carner has not been translated, but it is often said that he is worth learning Catalan for. If any single man is responsible for the miraculous Catalan linguistic reintegration, then it is Carner, whose collected works were published in 1968. He died in exile in Brussels.
▷ A H Terry, *Catalan Literature* (1972)

CARO, José Eusebio
(1817–53)

Colombian poet, born in Ocaña, his country's outstanding representative of liberalism and romanticism. His son Miguel (1843–1909), also a writer, became President of Colombia. He was at first influenced by **Byron**, but then became a devout Christian. His poetry is now more valued for its technical proficiency than for its content.

CAROSSA, Hans
(1878–1956)

German writer and physician, born in Tölz. A doctor in Bavaria, he became prominent with *Eine Kindheit* (1922, 'A Childhood'), the first of an autobiographical sequence which also includes *Rumänisches Tagebuch* (1924,

'Romanian Journal'), a war diary, and *Verwandlungen einer Jugend* (1928, 'Transformations of a Youth'), which consciously echoed the life-affirming example of his literary master, **Goethe**. He wrote several novels, such as *Doktor Bürgers Ende* (1913, 'The End of Dr Bürger'), *Das Jahr der schönen Täuschungen* (1941, 'The Year of Beautiful Deceits') and *Ungleiche Welten* (1951, 'Different Worlds'), and some poems.
▷ A Haveis, *Hans Carossa* (1935)

CARPENTIER, Alejo
(1904–80)

Cuban novelist, born in Havana. For many years he lived in France and Venezuela but he returned to Cuba after the revolution and served in several official government posts, though some critics find the political messages in his novels at best ambiguous. One of the major Latin-American writers of this century, his numerous books include *El siglo de las luces* (1962, Eng trans *Explosion in a Cathedral*, 1963), *El reino de este mundo* (1949, Eng trans *The Kingdom of this World*, 1957) and *Los pasos perdidos* (1953, Eng trans *The Lost Steps*, 1956).
▷ R Gonzalez Echevarria, *Carpentier: the pilgrim at home* (1977)

CARR, Emily
(1871–1945)

Canadian 'autobiographical' writer, and painter, born in Victoria, British Columbia. She studied painting in San Francisco, London and Paris, and is best known for her representations of the West Coast Indian and British Columbian forest; her first book of short stories, *Klee Wyck* (1941), related her impressions of the West Coast Indians, and won a Governor General's Award. It was followed by a number of further 'autobiographical' writings, including *The Book of Small* (1942), *The House of All Sorts* (1944) and *Growing Pains* (1946). Selections from Carr's journals were published posthumously as *Hundreds and Thousands* (1966). She has been described as a 'Canadian cultural icon', and her writings have been used extensively to write further biography, but they have been neglected as literary texts in their own right.
▷ S H Elderkin, 'Recovering the Fictions of Emily Carr', *WLWE*, 17:2 (1992/3)

CARR, J(ames) L(loyd)
(1912–)

English novelist and publisher, born at Carlton Miniott, Yorkshire. A former teacher, wartime Intelligence Officer and headmaster (from 1951 to 1967, of a school in Northamptonshire), Carr's first novel, *A Day in Summer*, appeared in 1964. He has since published several novels casting a wry, sympathetic, often quirky and sometimes sorrowful eye on everyday life and personal tragedy. Titles include *How Steeple Sinderby Wanderers Won the FA Cup* (1975) and *The Battle of Pollocks Crossing* (1985). His finest work is the elegiac *A Month in the Country* (1980), set in a north of England village in the summer of 1920; in it Carr sensitively examines the relationship of two survivors of World War I: Birkin, who arrives to restore a wall painting in the local church, and Moon, an enigmatic character camping in the adjacent field.

CARR, John Dickson
(1905–77)

American novelist, born in Uniontown, Pennsylvania, an exponent of detective fiction during its so-called 'golden age', the 1930s and 40s. The author of over 70 novels, Carr pioneered the 'locked room' mystery, the principles of which are described in his first book, *It Walks By Night* (1929). The room in which the murder was committed had 'no secret entrances; the murderer was not hiding anywhere in the room; he did not go out by the window; he did not go out by the ... door ... Yet a murderer *had* beheaded his victim there'. Carr's finest novel is perhaps *The Hollow Man* (1931), featuring his most enduring detective, Dr Gideon Fell, a portly, learned, rather dandyish Edwardian figure, partly modelled on **G K Chesterton**. Under the name Carter Dickson, he wrote over 20 novels in which the detective is the more buffoonish Sir Henry Merrivale.

CARRASQUILLA, Tomás
(1858–1940)

Colombian novelist, born in Santodomingo, Antioquia. His racy, lively work, done for his own satisfaction rather than for that of the public, is distinguished by its lack of pompous moralizing and its profound insight into human beings represented as animals—he is one of the most important of all the many South American novelists, the substance of whose work has not yet been translated into English. His first book was *Frutos de mi tierra* (1896, Eng trans *Fruits of My Earth*, 1972), in which, within its framework of city men outsmarting innocent provincials, he develops his technique. His novels include the historical *La marquesa de Yolombó* (1926, 'The Marquesa of Yolombo'), and the long *Hace tiempos* (1935–6, 'Waiting'), which he dictated during a period of blindness and which is his greatest—but still most neglected—novel. It is now gradually being understood that a few of the characteristics of his writings which have been taken as faults—

digressions, apparent anachronisms, didacticisms—probably concealed a superior art. His collected works appeared in 1958.

▷K L Levy, *Vida y obras de Tomás Carrasquilla* (1958)

CARRERA ANDRADE, Jorge
(1903–78)

Ecuadorean poet, born in Quito. Called 'one of the most original Latin-American poets of the 20th century', and certainly one of the best known, Carrera Andrade was a diplomat by profession. His first poetry was in the *modernista* vein of **Darío**, but he soon broke with this 'world of artificial paradises', and his first collection, *Estanque inefable* (1922, 'Ineffable Pond'), consisted of mostly rural poems. He helped to found the Ecuadorean Socialist Party in 1926. In a long career as a diplomat, much of it spent abroad, Carrera Andrade absorbed the influences of **Pound**, **Williams** (who described his poetry as a 'sad pleasure but a great one') and French poets such as **Valéry**; he also adapted the Japanese haiku into Spanish. His poetry has been translated in *To the Bay Bridge* (1941), *Visitor of Mist* (1950), *Secret Country* (1946), and in (the most substantial) *Selected Poems* (1972). His *Reflections on Spanish American Poetry* appeared in the USA in 1972.

▷A Flores, *The Literature of Spanish America* (1966–9)

CARRIÈRE, Jean-Claude
(1931–)

French writer, actor and director, born in Colombières-sur-Orbes. An association with comedy director Pierre Étaix brought his first involvement with the cinema as co-director of the short films *Rupture* (1961) and *Heureux Anniversaire* (1961, 'Happy Anniversary'). *Le Journal D'Une Femme De Chambre* (1964, 'The Diary of a Chambermaid') was the first of six films he wrote in collaboration with Luis Buñuel that revealed a dry, dark humour and ability to dissect the social and sexual hypocrisies of the middle-classes. Their subsequent collaborations include *Belle De Jour* (1967), *Le Charme Discrèt De La Bourgeoisie* (1972, 'The Discreet Charm of the Bourgeoisie') and *Cet Obscur Objet Du Désir* (1977, 'That Obscure Object of Desire'). A prolific scenarist whose work is often laced with a sense of anti-authoritarianism and irony, his many screenplays include *The Tin Drum* (1979), *Danton* (1982), *The Unbearable Lightness Of Being* (1988) and *Cyrano De Bergerac* (1990). A novelist, he has also written for television and the theatre, most notably for Peter Brooks's company.

CARROLL, Lewis, pseud of Charles Lutwidge Dodgson
(1832–98)

English writer, nonsense versifier and mathematician, born in Daresbury, near Warrington, the third of 11 children. His pseudonym derived from his first two names: Lutwidge is the same as Lutwig, of which Lewis is the anglicized version, and Carroll is a form of Charles. Throughout his childhood, with his siblings he invented and played many board games, acrostics and other puzzles. He was educated at Rugby and Christ Church, Oxford, where he lectured in mathematics after 1855 and took orders in 1861. *Alice's Adventures in Wonderland* (1865), his most famous book, had its origin in a boat trip which he made with Alice Liddell and her sisters, Lorina and Edith, the daughters of the Dean of his college, Henry George Liddell, 'all in the golden afternoon' of 4 July 1862. Originally he intended calling it *Alice's Adventures Underground*. A sequel, *Through the Looking-Glass and What Alice Found There*, appeared in 1871. Illustrated by Sir John Tenniel, both are superficially similar: in each Alice meets a succession of fantastic characters (Tweedledee and Tweedledum, the White Rabbit and the March Hare, Humpty-Dumpty), and each ends grandly, one with a trial, the other with a banquet. Each has been translated into many languages and there have been innumerable editions, many illustrated by distinguished artists. Their success among Victorian children was doubtless due to the fact that Carroll eschewed moralizing. His other works include *Phantasmagoria and other poems* (1869), *The Hunting of the Snark* (1876), *Rhyme? and Reason?* (1883) and *Sylvie and Bruno* (1889 and 1893). Of his mathematical works *Euclid and his Modern Rivals* (1879) is still of interest. He was also a pioneer photographer, and took many portraits of young girls with whom he seemed to empathize particularly. *The Diaries of Lewis Carroll* appeared in 1953, and an edition of his letters in 1979.
▷D Hudson, *Lewis Carroll: a biography* (1952)

CARROLL, Paul Vincent
(1900–68)

Irish playwright, born in County Louth, who established his name when the Abbey Theatre put on his *Shadow and Substance* (1937). This was followed by *The White Steed* (1939). After these successes his career went rather into decline, and he became overshadowed by his compatriot **Sean O'Casey**. With **James Bridie** he founded the Glasgow Citizens' Theatre (1943). *Shadow and Substance*, his acknowledged masterpiece, memorably portrays Irish bigotry.

▷P Kavanagh, *The Story of the Abbey Theatre* (1950)

CARRUTH, Hayden
(1921–)

American poet and critic, born in Waterbury, Connecticut. Carruth's reputation as an editor and critic has sometimes overshadowed his eminence as a poet. He published his first collection, *The Crow and the Heart 1946–1959*, in 1959, and has published steadily since. His *Selected Poems* appeared in 1986. But while his supporters point to the precision and vitality of his verse, others contend that the body of his work is inconsistent. All are agreed, though, that his most powerful poetry draws upon personal experience. *The Bloomingdale Papers* (1975) is a long poem written during the 1950s while Carruth was confined to a mental hospital as a consequence of alcoholism and a nervous breakdown; one of his more personal compositions, it is also one of his more profound.

CARSTAIRS, John Paddy, real name John Keys
(1914–70)

British novelist, film director, filmscript writer and artist. He studied art at the Slade School, and painted several light-hearted landscapes in various media. His best-known novel is *Love and Ella Rafferty* (1947).
▷ *Honest Injun, a light hearted autobiography* (1942)

CARSWELL, Catherine Roxburgh, née Macfarlane
(1879–1946)

Scottish novelist and critic, born in Glasgow, the daughter of a merchant. Educated at the Park School, Glasgow, and in Frankfurt-am-Main, she became a socialist after reading Robert Blatchford at the age of 17, and went on to study English at Glasgow University. Her first marriage was annulled after her husband attempted to kill her. She married fellow journalist and critic Donald Carswell in 1917. She made her reputation as a dramatic and literary critic for the *Glasgow Herald* from 1907 to 1915 but lost this position when she wrote a review of **D H Lawrence**'s banned novel *The Rainbow*. Lawrence encouraged her to complete her autobiographical novel of Glasgow life *Open the Door* (1920), a work depicting a young woman's escape from the confinement of a middle-class, Calvinistic Glasgow family. Lawrence also encouraged her to emphasize Burns's passionate nature in her *The Life of Burns* (1930). She hoped to bring **Robert Burns** 'out of the mist they loved to keep about him', but the work was unfavourably received by Burns scholars in

Scotland. She also wrote biographies of Lawrence, *The Savage Pilgrim: A Narrative of D.H. Lawrence* (1932), and Boccaccio, *The Tranquil Heart* (1937), but is best remembered as a critic.

▷ *Lying Awake: an unfinished autobiography* (1952)

CARTER, Angela Olive, née **Stalker** (1940–92)

English novelist and essayist, born in Eastbourne. Educated at Bristol University, she taught Creative Writing in England, the USA and Australia, and lived in Japan for two years, an experience recorded in *Nothing Sacred* (1982). Her fiction is characterized by imaginative use of fantasy, surrealism, genre pastiche, vibrant humour and psychological symbolism. Novels include *The Magic Toyshop* (1967), *Heroes and Villains* (1969), *The Passion of New Eve* (1977), *Nights at the Circus* (1985) and *Wise Children* (1991), while her stories are collected in *Fireworks* (1974), *The Bloody Chamber* (1979), *Black Venus* (1985) and *American Ghosts & Old World Wonders* (1993). *The Sadeian Woman* (1979) is a feminist reinterpretation of the Marquis de **Sade**. She also wrote poetry, tales for children, radio plays, and translated fairy tales. She wrote the screenplay for the film *The Company of Wolves* (1984) with **Neil Jordan**.

CARTER, Martin Wylde (1927–)

Guyanese poet, born in Georgetown, British Guiana, and educated at Queen's College, Georgetown. He spent some time in prison for anti-colonial activities, which resulted in *Poems of Resistance* (1954). After Guyana became independent, he was prominent in the Forbes Burnham government as Minister of Public Information and Broadcasting. His frequent theme is the burning desire for liberation. In 'The Great Dark' he highlights the dilemma of the poet up against the fact that words alone cannot bring about a better world, 'caught as I am/in the great dark of the bright connection of words'. His principal collections include *Poems of Succession* (1977) and *Poems of Affinity* (1980).

CARTLAND, Dame (Mary) Barbara Hamilton (1901–)

English popular romantic novelist, born in Edgbaston, Birmingham, and step-grandmother of Diana, Princess of Wales. She published her first novel, *Jigsaw*, in 1923, and has since produced well over 400 bestselling books, mostly novels of chaste romantic love designed for women readers, but also including biographies and books on food, health and beauty, and several volumes of autobiography. She earned a place in the *Guinness Book of Records* for writing 26 books in the year 1983. An ardent advocate of health foods and fitness for the elderly, she has championed causes like the St John's Ambulance Brigade and the provision of camp-sites for Romany gipsies. She was appointed DBE in 1991.

▷ *The Years of Opportunity, 1939–1945* (1948)

CARTWRIGHT, William (1611–43)

English playwright, poet, and preacher, born in Northway, near Tewkesbury. He preached at Oxford, and wrote plays such as *The Royal Slave*, which was performed at Oxford before Charles I in 1636, and a play ridiculing Puritans, *The Ordinary*. He was one of the group of young playwrights known as the 'sons' of **Ben Jonson**.

▷ A Chalmers, 'A Life', in *The Works of Early English Poets* (1810)

CARVALHO, Vicente (1866–1924)

Brazilian poet, born in São Paulo. Carvalho was a traditional poet, a so-called 'Parnassian', who wrote one collection that has remained in print: *Poemas e Canções* (1906, 'Poems and Songs'). He is seldom included in anthologies of Brazilian poetry in translation.

▷ M Bandeira, *A Brief History of Brazilian Literature* (1958)

CARVER, Raymond (1939–88)

American poet and short-story writer, born in Clatskanie, Oregon. He married at 18 and struggled for many years to provide for a young family and further his career as a writer. He also fought against chronic alcoholism. His first published story, 'Pastoral', was accepted by the *Western Humanities Review*. His collections include *Will You Please Be Quiet, Please?* (1976), *What We Talk About When We Talk About Love* (1981) and *Cathedral* (1983). Both his fiction and his poetry are remarkable for their spare narratives, focusing on a society of the lower and middle classes and dealing with people in a state of transition: couples breaking up, people between jobs, between sleeping and wakefulness. He wrote no novels. He was a Guggenheim Fellow in 1979 and was twice awarded grants by the National Endowment for Arts. He taught at the University of Iowa, the University of Texas and the University of California. Other books include *Fire: Essays, Poems, Stories* (1984), and books of poems: *Where Water Comes Together with Other*

Water (1985) and *Ultramarine* (1985). *In A Marine Light: Selected Poems* and *Elephant and Other Stories* appeared in the year he died.

CARY, Alice
(1820–71)

American poet and novelist, born in Cincinnati, Ohio, and sister of Phoebe Cary, another noted poet, with whom she worked closely. She was first published in her early teens and went on to produce three volumes of poetry: *Lyra* (1852), *Poems* (1855) and *Ballads, Lyrics, Hymns* (1866). Abandoned or alienated women often figure in her poetry and a sense of despair pervades much of her work. In addition to her poetry, Cary wrote novels, sketches, and children's books. She is best remembered for her 'Clovernook' series of sketches (1852), which focus on farming communities. She and Phoebe established a literary salon which gained attention from many of the leading literary personalities of the era.

CARY, (Arthur) Joyce Lunel
(1888–1957)

English novelist, born in Londonderry of English parents. He was educated at Tunbridge Wells and Clifton College and later studied art in Edinburgh and Paris, graduating (1912) at Oxford. He then served with the Red Cross in the Balkan war of 1912–13 and was decorated by the King of Montenegro. In 1913 he joined the Nigerian Political Service and fought in a Nigerian regiment in World War I. War injuries and ill-health dictated his early retirement after the war to Oxford, where he took up writing. Out of his African experiences emerge such novels as *Aissa Saved* (1932), *African Witch* (1936) and *Mister Johnson* (1939), a high-spirited, richly humorous study of a native clerk. In 1941 he was awarded the James Tait Black Memorial Prize for *The House of Children*, and established himself with the trilogy, *Herself Surprised* (1940), *To be a Pilgrim* (1942) and *The Horse's Mouth* (1944), which explores the art world in memorably comic fashion. These were followed by *Moonlight* (1946) and *A Fearful Joy* (1949), and a later trilogy on the life of Chester Nimmo, a politician, *Prisoner of Grace* (1952), *Except the Lord* (1953) and *Not Honour More* (1955), and finally an unfinished novel with a religious theme, *The Captive and the Free* (1959).
▷W Allen, *Joyce Cary* (1953)

CASA, Giovanni della
(1503–56)

Italian author and prelate, born near Florence. He was appointed archbishop of Benevento in 1544. He is remembered for stylish lyric verse, and *Il Galateo ovvero De' Costumi* (1558, 'The Book of Etiquette or of Good Manners').
▷M Richter, *Giovanni della Casa in Francia nel seculo XVI* (1966)

CASACCIA, Gabriel
(1907–80)

Paraguayan novelist, dramatist and story writer, second in importance in his country only to **Roa Bastos** (who has called him 'a founding father'). He was born in Itacurubi, into an Italian immigrant family called Bibolini (which name he dropped when he began to publish in 1930). He studied law and then served the government until the end of the Chaco War, when he left Paraguay for Posadas (1935) in Argentina. From 1951 he lived in Buenos Aires, where he died. His stories—for example those collected in *El pozo* (1947, 'The Well')—have been compared to those of **Kafka**. But his novels, with *La babosa* (1952, 'The Slug') and *Los exiliados* (1966, 'The Exiles') outstanding amongst them, represent, as Roa Bastos has written, the foundations 'of the modern Paraguayan narrative'. He is unlucky to have escaped the attention of translators.
▷*Journal of Inter-American Studies and World Affairs* (1, 1970)

CASAL, Julián del
(1863–93)

Cuban poet, born in Havana. For most of his brief life—he suffered from tuberculosis—he lived in seclusion, modelling himself on the French Parnassian poets, such as **Heredia**, who influenced him immensely. In his context he is a precursor of *modernismo*, and he met **Darío** himself during his last year. His *fin de siècle* mood and his high accomplishment made a deep impression on his contemporaries and immediate successors. Two poems are translated in the *Penguin Book of Latin American Verse* (1971, ed E Curacciolo-Trejo).

CASEY, Gavin Stodart
(1907–64)

Australian novelist and short-story writer, born in Kalgoorlie, Western Australia. He published two collections, *It's Harder for Girls* (1942) and *Birds of a Feather* (1943). In the laconic and alcoholic mateship style of **Henry Lawson**, his tales draw much on his experiences as a newspaper reporter in the Kalgoorlie goldfields during the Depression, and were later reissued as *Short Shift Saturday and Other Stories* (1973). As a journalist he worked in New York and then returned to Canberra and Sydney where he wrote a couple of humorous books. More substantial

novels were *City of Men* (1950), a family saga of the West Australian goldfields; the conflict of half-caste aborigines and white inhabitants of a small town were dealt with in *Snowball* (1962) and *The Man Whose Name was Mud* (1963), again set in the goldfields.
▷D Casey, *Casey's Wife* (1982)

CASIA, or IKASIA
(fl.first half of 9th century)

Byzantine author of verse epigrams, born into a prestigious family. She spent most of her life in a convent, and was known for her harsh tongue.

CASONA, Alejandro, pseud of Alejandro Rodriguez Alvarez
(1903–65)

Spanish dramatist, who began as a poet, and then became director of the Teatro del Pueblo ('Theatre of the People') in 1931; he was born in the Asturias. His plays of the 1930s, grouped together as *teatro de evasión* ('theatre of evasion'), were influential—and, later, in the 1950s, were played all over eastern Europe. He fled to Buenos Aires in 1939, having angered the Falangists with his *Nuestro Natacha* (1936, 'Our Natacha'), about a reforming woman educator. He was allowed to return to Madrid in 1962. His famous and sarcastic *Prohibido suicidarse en primavera* (1937, 'It is forbidden to commit suicide in spring') is translated in *Masterpieces of Modern Spanish Theatre* (1967, ed Robert W Corrigan).

CASSILL, R(onald) V(erlin)
(1919–)

American novelist and short-story writer, born in Cedar Falls, Iowa. Educated at Iowa University, where he later taught creative writing, he published *Eagle on the Coin*, his first novel, in 1950. Cassill is a moralist with an instinctive sense of narrative, whose recurring themes are the nature of power and love, and the relationship between the private individual and the public event. *A Taste of Sin* (1956), *The President* (1964) and *Labors of Love* (1980) are representative works.

CASSOLA, Carlo
(1917–90)

Italian novelist from Rome. While still a student, Cassola already took up an anti-fascist position; after the fall of Mussolini he became a member of the extreme left. His early, almost minimalist stories of 1942 attracted some attention because they harked back to the 'crepuscular' tone of some 50 years earlier, and because by implication they rejected fascist and Futurist rhetoric. Two novels, *Fausto e Anna* (1952, rev edn 1958, Eng trans 1960) and *La ragazza di Bebo* (1960, Eng

trans *Bebo's Girl*, 1962), were considered to be 'neorealistic' because they dealt with World War II and because they reflected the influence of such Americans as **Hemingway** and **Faulkner**. His best novel has long been considered to be *Il taglio del bosco* (1950, Eng trans *The Cutting of the Woods*, 1960), which had its source in the author's grief over the loss of his wife in 1949. In his later work, generally thought to be somewhat inferior, Cassola tried to widen his range to include a fuller treatment of female characters.
▷*Italica 54* (1977)

CASTELLANOS, Juan de
(1522–1607)

Spanish poet, born in Alanís, Seville. He led the life of a soldier until, after taking holy orders, he settled down as prebendary of Tunja, in Colombia, amongst the Chubcha Indians. He is famous for the long epic *Elegías de Varones Illustres e Indias*, about the Spanish conquest and the conquistadores. It is an imitation of the *La Araucana* of **Alonso de Ercilla** and, while of great interest, is markedly inferior as poetry. It is to be found in Castellanos's *Obras completas* (1953, 'Complete Works').

CASTELLANOS, Rosario
(1925–74)

Mexican poet, novelist, story writer and translator, born in Mexico City, one of the great Latin-American writers of her century. Her early work, described by one influential critic, perhaps not insignificantly, as 'insubstantial and feminine', was in fact full of promise and interest; but she did not develop her full powers until *Poemas 1953–5* (1957), published at the height of her close involvement with the Native Americans of Chialas, where she had spent her childhood and adolescence: her theme, that in such conquered and suffering peoples lies the only residue of hope in a world 'civilized' in the name of barbarism, is movingly expressed. Several of these works are translated in *The Selected Poems of Rosario Castellanos* (1988). Many of her novels and stories have been translated, including *Balún-canán* (1957, Eng trans *The Nine Guardians*, 1958), about the break-up of the old ways under the impact of the reforms of Lázaro Cárdenas. Rosario Castellanos, on a visit to Israel, was electrocuted while trying to change a light bulb.
▷M Allgood, *A Rosario Castellanos Reader* 1988; D Meyer and M F Olmos (eds), *Contemporary Women Authors of Latin America: Introductory Essays* (1983)

CASTELLI, Ignaz Franz
(1781–1862)

Austrian poet, born in Vienna. He wrote *Kriegeslieder für die österreichische Armee*

(1809, 'War Songs for the Austrian Army'), which was banned by Napoleon.

CASTELO BRANCO, Camilo, Visconde de Correia Botelho
(1825–90)

Portuguese novelist. An illegitimate child whose love of literature and longing for adventure grew from his reading, he became one of the most important of modern Portuguese novelists, with a deep understanding of the life of his people. His work ranges from romances like *Mysterios de Lisboa* (1958, 'The Mysteries of Lisbon'), to closely observed, imaginative interpretations of the everyday Portuguese scene, such as *The Crime of Father Amara*. He was created viscount for his services to literature in 1885. He committed suicide.
▷A Pimentel, *O Torturado de Seide* (1921)

CASTI, Giambattista
(c.1721–1803)

Italian poet, born in Prato, Tuscany. He took holy orders, but in 1764 went to Vienna, where he became poet laureate. On Joseph II's death he returned to Florence, and in 1798 went to Paris. He wrote the *48 Novelle galanti* (1793), and *Gli animali parlanti* (1802, 'The Talking Animals'), a political satire.
▷H van den Bergh, *Giambattista Casti, l'homme et l'oeuvre* (1951)

CASTIGLIONE, Baldassare, Count
(1478–1529)

Italian courtier and writer, born near Mantua. In 1505 he was sent by the Duke of Urbino as envoy to Henry VII of England, who made him a knight, and was later Mantuan ambassador at the papal court in Rome (1513–24). Thereafter he was papal nuncio for Pope Clement VII in Spain, from 1524. His chief work, *Il Cortegiano* (1528, 'The Courtier'), is a manual for courtiers, in dialogue form, and was translated into English by Sir Thomas Hoby in 1561. His Italian and Latin poems are models of elegance. His Letters (1769–71) illustrate political and literary history.
▷J Cartwright, *Baldassare Castiglione, his life and letters* (1908)

CASTILHO, António Feliciano de
(1800–75)

Portuguese poet and translator, blind from the age of six, born in Lisbon. His soft, perhaps somewhat vacuous, neo-classical poetry still has a place in Portuguese poetry today. He was and is a controversial figure, since he became a virtual dictator in Portuguese letters. He made smooth translations of many classics, including one of **Goethe**'s *Faust*, which he took from a French version, and which bears no resemblance to the German original. His authority was finally broken by younger writers, in particular **Quental**: de Castilho had shown his preference for a long ultra-romantic poem called *D. Jaime* (by Thomaz Ribiero) over the *Lusiades* of **Camoens**, and in the so-called *Questão Coimbra* (Coimbra Dispute), of 1865, a complex pamphlet-row between younger and older poets about the virtues of romanticism, Quental tore him to pieces.
▷A F G Bell, *Portuguese Literature* (1922)

CASTILLEJO, Cristóbal de
(c.1490–1550)

Spanish poet, born in Ciudad Rodrigo. It is thought he became a Cistercian monk in 1515, later going into the service of the Archduke Ferdinand, which allowed him to travel throughout Spain and Europe on court business. However, although a monk, he was apparently not celibate and his poetry was often dedicated to women. In fact his first poetry to be printed (1573) had to be amended to avoid trouble with the Inquisition. His works were divided into three categories: those dealing with love ('de amor'), with conversation ('de conversación y pasatiempos'), and with morals and devotion ('de morales y de devoción'). Outstanding in the former is the 'Sermón de Amores' (1542) about one who loves and is not loved, and the bittersweetness of requited love. The 'Beatus Ille' is one of the best of the second category. He also wrote a misogynistic piece entitled the 'Dialogo de Mujeres' (1544, 'Dialogue of Women'). Castillejo's talent lay in successfully fusing medieval and Renaissance thought, adapting it to traditional moulds and forms of expression. His best poetry is considered as skilled as that of **Garcilaso de la Vega**.

CASTRO ALVES, Antônio de
(1847–71)

Brazilian poet, born in Muritiba, Bahia, the chief representative of *Condoreira* (a style symbolic of the condor's grandeur of flight). His life was as ultra-romantic as his poetry, which, influenced by that of **Hugo**, celebrated his loves and his fervent hatred of the slave trade. His degree of literary merit has been the subject of controversy; but his sincerity and burning resentment of injustice have endeared him to many modern readers. His best verse is direct and simple.
▷F P de Barros, *Poesia e vida de Castro Alves* (1962)

CASTRO, Eugenio de
(1869–1944)

Portuguese poet, born in Coimbra. He became Professor of Portuguese literature in his native town and travelled widely in Europe. In Paris he became interested in Symbolism, and introduced that movement to Portuguese writing in his poetry, beginning with *Oaristos* (1890). Although derided at first, his work eventually became influential, although his own later work reflected a return to more classical forms, and a growing fascination with folklore.

CASTRO, Guillén de
(1569–1631)

Spanish dramatist, born in Valencia. He commanded a Neapolitan fortress, but later lived in Madrid, and died in poverty. His early works were romantic comedies, before he turned to epic subjects, notably in *La Mocedades del Cid* (c.1600), which formed the basis for **Corneille**'s *Le Cid*. His other works include a realistic play about an unhappy marriage, *Los mal cascados de Valencia*, and dramatizations of works by **Cervantes**.
▷W E Wilson, *Guillén de Castro* (1973)

CASTRO, Rosalía de
(1837–85)

Spanish poet and novelist, born in Santiago de Compostela. Her earliest works, such as the poetry collection *La Flor* (1857, 'The Flower'), were written in Spanish, but it is on her later volumes in Galician that her fame rests. *Cantares Gallegos* (1863, 'Galician Songs') and the later *Follas Novas* (1880, 'New Leaves') place her among the most significant poets of the 19th century. Her novels, written in Spanish, brought her to the attention of a wider public; they include *La Hija del Mar* (1859, 'The Daughter of the Sea') and *Ruinas* (1867, 'Ruins'). Despite the currently perilous position of Galician—it receives official support, but the number of mother-tongue speakers is declining—de Castro's reputation as a poet appears secure.

CATALÀ, Victor, pseud of Caterina Albert i Paradís
(1869–1966)

Catalan writer. Born in L'Escala, a fishing village near the Catalan French border, Català published her first book, the poetry collection *El Cant del Mesos* ('Song of the Months'), in 1901. She followed this with several volumes of short stories and, in 1905, the psychological novel *Solitud*, a richly atmospheric story of a young bride's experiences and growing self-awareness in an isolated hermitage in the Pyrenees. Although continuing to write and publish—including a second novel, *Caires Vius* ('Living Aspects'), in 1907—Català largely withdrew from the public eye after the success of her first novel.

Unpublished during the Francoist suppression of Catalan writing, her work suffered critical neglect for many years, but she has recently begun to reattract attention as a pioneer of modernist literature, and her writing has been translated into many languages.

CATHER, Willa Sibert
(1873–1947)

American fiction writer, poet and journalist, born on a farm near Winchester, Virginia. Her formative years were spent in Nebraska, and after university there (1891–5), her career began with a well-written but not significant volume of poetry, *April Twilights* (1903). She moved to New York as Editor of *McClure's* magazine (1906–12). After her first novel, *Alexander's Bridge* (1912), she wrote three novels dealing with immigrants to the USA: *O Pioneers!* was published in 1913 and *The Song of the Lark* two years later. The third, *My Ántonia* (1918), is generally regarded as her best book. A homosexual who wrote primarily about independent women, she was a prolific writer, and other novels include *Death Comes for the Archbishop* (1927) and *One of Ours* (1922), which won the Pulitzer Prize.
▷P C Robinson, *Willa: the life of Cather* (1983)

CATLIN, George
(1796–1872)

American artist and author, born in Wilkes-Barre, Pennsylvania. He studied law, but soon turned to drawing and painting. During 1832–40 he was studying the Native Americans of the Far West, everywhere painting portraits (470 full length) and pictures illustrative of life and manners, now in the National Museum at Washington. He spent eight years in Europe with a Far West show; travelled (1852–7) in South and Central America; and again lived in Europe until 1871. His works include *Manners of the North American Indians* (2 vols, 1841), *The North American Portfolio* (1844), and *Last Rambles in the Rocky Mountains* (1868).
▷R Plate, *Palette and Tomahawk: the story of George Catlin* (1962)

CATO, Dionysius
(?4th century)

Traditional name of the Roman author of a volume of 164 moral precepts in Latin hexameters, known as *Dionysii Catonis disticha de moribus ad filium* ('Couplets on Morals, to his Son'), which was a great favourite during the Middle Ages. An English version by Benedict Burgh was printed by **William Caxton** before 1479.

▷Plutarch, *Life of Cato* in *Works*, D Wyttenbach (ed) (1795–1830)

CATO, Nancy Fotheringham
(1917–)
Australian novelist, poet and short-story writer, born in Adelaide. Her prime achievement is the trilogy of historical novels set along the banks of the Murray River, which forms a continuous counterpoint to her narrative. *All the Rivers Run* (1958) was followed by *Time, Flow Softly* (1959) and *But Still the Stream* (1962). These were later rewritten and published in 1978 under the title *All the Rivers Run* and became a popular television series. *Forefathers* (1983) follows the fortunes through seven generations of three interlinked families. Other significant novels are *North-West by South* (1964), on the last years of Arctic explorer Sir John Franklin, and a fey historical novel *Lady Lost in Time* (1985). She has also published poetry, a book for children, and, in *Mister Maloga* (1976, rev edn 1993), the biography of an aboriginal missionary.

CATS, Jacob
(1577–1660)
Enormously popular Dutch poet and statesman, born in the Hague. A lawyer by training, he was at various times the Dutch ambassador to England. Vader Cats ('Father Cats') was a homely Calvinist, whose often wildly unconventional poetry more or less ignored the Renaissance. He was a rich man through his ownership of drainage works in both Holland and England. He was not, as has been frequently emphasized by critics, a great poet—but he was much read. Although fussy and, by today's standards, often absurdly didactic, he was above all a born storyteller.
▷G Derudder, *Un poète néerlandais, Cats, sa vie et ses Oeuvres* (1898)

CATULLUS, Gaius Valerius
(c.84–c.54 BC)
Roman lyric poet, born in Verona, the son of a wealthy and well-connected family. He lived mainly in Rome, where he settled about 62 BC, and in his villas at Tibur and Sirmio. He began to write verses when a boy of 16. In Rome he became friendly with **Cicero**, the Metelli, Hortensius, and probably **Lucretius**; and in Rome he met 'Lesbia', a married woman to whom he addressed verses unequalled in the lyric poetry of passion. A final rupture seems to have happened in 57BC, and in that year he accompanied the governor, Memmius, to his province of Bithynia. A fiery, unscrupulous partisan, he assailed his enemies, including **Caesar**, with equal scurrility and wit. His extant works comprise 116 pieces (though three are spurious), many of them extremely brief, while the longest contains only some 400 lines. But in this body of poetry, there are, besides the magnificent love poems, graceful, playful verses of society, fierce, satiric poems, elaborate descriptive and mythological pieces (some of them adapted from the Greek), and the strange, wild, imaginative *Attis*. The text depends on a single manuscript discovered in the 14th century at Verona, inaccurately transcribed and subsequently lost.
▷K Quinn, *Catullus, an interpretation* (1972); and other works by Quinn

CAUSLEY, Charles
(1917–)
English poet and children's writer, whose close ties with his home town of Launceston in Cornwall provide him with a unique, rooted point of view on the world. His naval war experiences inspired his early verse, and *Farewell, Aggie Weston* (1951) broods on loss and innocence with the force of traditional ballad. His poetry has gradually become more conversational in style, yet his meditations on family memories, life, landscape and legend are far from simplistic. In his *Collected Poems 1951–1975* (1975) verse for adults sits easily beside that intended for children, both revealing the compassion and humour that make him a genuinely popular poet.
▷H Chambers (ed), *Causley at 70* (1987)

CAUTE, (John) David
(1936–)
English novelist and author of non-fiction, born in Alexandria, Egypt. In 1959 he published his first novel, *At Fever Pitch*, based upon his own adventures as an infantryman in the former Gold Coast, Africa, and thereafter for several years combined a career as a writer with that of an academic. His books deal with the relationship between the West, East and the Third World. His novel *The Decline of the West* (1966), a portrait of a fictional African state in turmoil during the years following independence, is both his most ambitious and most controversial. Among his non-fiction titles are *Under the Skin: The Death of White Rhodesia* (1983), his observations of the last days of white rule in Rhodesia and the nation's emergence as Zimbabwe.

CAVAFY, Constantine, pseud of
Konstantínos Pétron Kaváfis
(1863–1933)
Greek poet, born in Alexandria, Egypt, of a Greek merchant family. After his father's death in 1872 he was taken by his mother to

England for five years, and apart from three years in Istanbul (1882–5) he spent the rest of his life in Alexandria, where he worked as a civil servant, making it the setting, either physical or symbolic, of much of his poetry. His work tends to diverge into the erotic—in which he was one of the first modern writers to deal explicitly with homosexuality—and the historical, in which he recreates the world of Greece and Alexandria in the Hellenistic period. His view of life is essentially tragic. His first book, containing 14 poems, was privately published when he was 41, and reissued five years later with an additional seven poems. He published no further work during his lifetime, preferring to distribute his work among his friends, but in recent years he has come to be regarded as one of the finest and most influential modern Greek poets. Some of his early verse was written in English, but it was not until the 1950s that his work became available in English translation. His best-known poems are, perhaps, his earlier ones, such as *I Polis* ('The City') and *Perimenondas tous Varvarous* ('Waiting for the Barbarians'). His work has been translated into English as *Poems* (1951) and *Complete Poems* (1961).
▷ R Liddell, *Cavafy: a critical biography* (1974)

CAVALCANTI, Guido
(c.1240–1300)

Italian poet, and friend of **Dante**. He married a Ghibelline, and was banished by the Guelfs. He returned to Florence only to die within the year. His works, which included ballads, sonnets and *canzoni*, were translated by **Dante Gabriel Rossetti** and **Ezra Pound**. He is said to have been a studious man, if also an eccentric one, and much of his poetry reflects that intellectualism, although he is also vividly aware of the emotional depths of his usual subject, love.
▷ A Ribera, *Guido Cavalcanti* (1911); Ezra Pound, 'Cavalcanti', in *Literary Essays* (1954)

CAVENDISH, Margaret
(?1624–1674)

English author of poetry, plays, biography and miscellanea. She was a Maid of Honour at the court of Charles I and became the Duchess of Newcastle on her marriage in 1645. She spent the ensuing 15 years of the English Civil War with her exiled husband in Europe, and on her return suffered the ridicule of society for her eccentricities of behaviour and dress. Her *Poems and Fancies* (1653) contains charming fairy verses, and both her autobiography and the *Life* of her husband show restraint and good sense. Her later poetry is doggerel, her philosophy is pompous and naive, and **Pepys** described one of her plays as 'the most ridiculous thing that was ever wrote'.
▷ V Woolf, 'The Duchess of Newcastle', in *The Common Reader* (1938)

CAXTON, William
(c.1422–c.1491)

English printer and translator, born in Kent, important because he was the first English printer. He learned his craft in Europe, and set up his own press at Westminster in 1476, and from it issued about 100 books, including editions of **Chaucer**, **Gower** and his own translations from the French, which included a book by **Christine de Pisan**. His own prose was not outstanding, being somewhat over-elaborate and rambling; but it did contribute something to the 15th-century style. He was responsible, too, for the edition of **Malory** generally known until 1934.
▷ W Blades, *The Life and Typography of Caxton* (1861–3)

CAYROL, Jean
(1911–)

French Catholic novelist, poet, critic and film scriptwriter, from Bordeaux. He began with minor Surrealist poems. His later work is influenced by his experiences in a German concentration camp, where he was sent as a member of the wartime resistance. Much influenced by Emmanuel Mounier's Personalism—a Catholic movement blending **Bergson**ism with left-wing aspirations and proto-existentialism—his many novels and poems deal with problems of identity and guilt. Of them, *L'Espace d'une nuit* (1954, Eng trans *All in a Night*, 1957), and *Les Corps étrangers* (1959, Eng trans *Foreign Bodies*, 1960), have appeared in English. Because of his awareness of the limitations of language, he was regarded as on the edge of the *nouveau roman*, but is distinguished from it by his religious feelings. He has collaborated in films with the director Alain Resnais.

CECCHI, Emilio
(1884–1966)

Italian poet, critic, translator and essayist from Florence, who exercised a decisive influence upon the course of his country's poetry and prose. He introduced the essay, as a form, into this literature. His early attempts at poetry were a failure, but his critical work, influenced by **Croce** but always wary that Croce's idealism might undermine literature-as-history, and in particular *Peschi rossi* (1920, 'Goldfish'), succeeded (it has been asserted) in 'approximating the polyphonic essence of reality'. The short newspaper essays of *Peschi rossi* had an enormous influence, and encouraged Italians not to be afraid of making subjective investigations of reality. He based his style on that of two Englishmen, **Charles Lamb** and **Thomas De Quincey**. Those who have responded to his work include **Cesare Pavese** and **Elio Vittorini**.

CECCHI D'AMICO, Suso, originally Giovanna Cecchi
(1914–)

Italian screenwriter, born in Rome, the daughter of **Emilio Cecchi**. A student at Rome and Cambridge, she worked as a journalist and translator before writing the screenplay of the film *Mio Figlio Professore* (1946). An active figure in the school of Italian neo-realism that flourished after the war, she contributed to the screenplays of *Ladri Di Biciclette* (1948, 'Bicycle Thieves') and *Miracolo A Milano* (1950, 'Miracle in Milan'), but found some of her best opportunities working in collaboration with director Luchino Visconti, especially on a number of elegant literary adaptations, including *Il Gattopardo* (1963, 'The Leopard'), *Lo Straniero* (1967, 'The Stranger') and *L'Innocente* (1976, 'The Innocent'). Dedicated to indigenous Italian storytelling, she has provided many of her country's leading film-makers with expertly crafted and structured screenplays, tailored to the specific sensibility of the director. Among her finest work is *Salvatore Giuliano* (1961), *Jesus of Nazareth* (1977) and *Oci Ciornie* (1987, 'Dark Eyes').

CECH, Svatopluk
(1846–1908)

Czech novelist, poet, dramatist and satirist, born in Ostredek. He travelled widely, and was one of the leaders of the humane resistance to Austrian tyranny. His chief work, still as topical today as it was when it was written, is the novel *Hanuman* (1884, Eng trans 1894), about a civil war amongst apes. His poetry, much of it consisting of epics, was highly thought of in its day, but is not so much read now. He punished the bourgeoisie of his own country in a series of fine satirical novels, *The Excursions of Mr Broucek* (1886–92), two of which inspired Janáček to his famous 1917 opera.

CÉITINN, Séthrún
(1570–c.1650)

Irish poet and historian, born in County Tipperary. His chief work is a defensive outline of Irish history, *Foras Feasa ar Éirinn*: although a masterpiece of Gaelic prose, it has little value as a chronicle. A few of his eloquent poems are remembered.

CELA, Camilo José
(1916–)

Spanish novelist, winner of the Nobel Prize for literature, born in Iria Flavia, La Coruña. He attended Madrid University and served in Franco's forces; his work is frequently interpreted as an eloquent, aggressive, idiosyncratic reaction to that error of judgement. He has been the dominant novelist in Spain for over 40 years. His first novel, *La familia de Pascual Duarte* (1942, Eng trans *The Family of Pascual Duarte*, 1946), appeared in 1942 and was banned, having stunned readers with its seemingly gratuitous violence. The range of his work is vast and varied but he is best known for *La Colmena* (1951, Eng trans *The Hive*, 1953), which recreates daily life in Madrid in the aftermath of the Spanish Civil War with great sensitivity and feeling for the plight of ordinary people. Others worthy of note are *Viaje a la Alcarría* (1948, Eng trans *Journey to the Alcarria*, 1948) and *San Camilo 1936* (1970). Eccentric, even scatological, he is a candid, combative protagonist who says what he thinks regardless of popularity. A member of the Spanish Royal Academy, he holds a plethora of honorary doctorates. In 1989 he was awarded the Nobel Prize for literature.
▷D W MacPheeters, *Camilo José Cela* (1963)

CELAN, Paul, pseud of Paul Ancel or Antschel
(1920–70)

One of the greatest modern poets of the German language, born into the Jewish community at Czernowitz in Romania. He studied there and in France. His parents were murdered by the Nazis, but he survived a labour camp, later becoming a lecturer in German literature in Paris and taking French nationality. His second collection of poems, *Mohn und Gedächtnis* (1952, 'Poppy and Memory'), immediately established his reputation. It includes his most famous poem, 'Todesfuge' ('Death Fugue'), a beautiful and horrible evocation of the concentration camps. *Sprachgitter* (1959, Eng trans *Speech-Grille*, 1971) and *Die Niemandsrose* (1963, 'The No-One's Rose') reflect his ambiguous attitude to the Jewish God. The flowing lines and vivid images of his early work, influenced by the French Surrealists and **Yvan Goll**, later gave way to increasingly difficult and concentrated poems as Celan struggled to communicate the horror of his wartime experiences. He committed suicide by drowning himself in the Seine.
▷J Glenn, *Paul Celan* (1973)

CELAYA, Gabriel, pseud of Rafael Múgica Celaya
(1911–90)

Spanish poet and publisher (he founded *Norte*), who remained in Spain after 1939, and whose voice was muted for many years. He was prolific (over 50 books); the best of his poems, some of which, written in the 1930s, were calculatedly Absurdist or Surrealist, concern the woman, Amparo Gastón, who changed his pessimistic view of the world. He was regarded as Spain's leading 'social poet' of the Franco years; but his final poems, again 'absurdist' in form, return to pessimism.

▷ *Encounter*, 12, 2 (1959)

CÉLINE, Louis-Ferdinand, pseud of L F Destouches
(1894–1961)

French novelist, born in Paris, the son of a poor clerk and a lace seamstress. His education was rudimentary and he had various jobs until 1912, when he joined the cavalry. In the first year of World War I he was wounded in the head and shell-shocked in an action for which he was decorated. The suffering, both mental and physical, caused by his wounds dogged him to the end of his days. He was invalided out of the military, took a medical degree, worked as a staff surgeon at the Ford plant in Detroit and later ministered to the poor of Paris, the experience of which, he acknowledged, was invaluable to his literary endeavours. His first novel, *Voyage au bout de la nuit* (1932, rev edn 1952, Eng trans *Journey to the End of Night*, 1934), brought international acclaim, and his reputation was enhanced on the publication of his second novel, *Mort à Crédit* (1936, Eng trans *Death on the Installment Plan*, 1938). His use of the demotic and his insights into life among the lower classes have influenced many writers, among them **Jean-Paul Sartre**, **William Burroughs** and **Henry Miller**. In the late 1930s he was a declared anti-semite, and after the liberation of France (1944) he fled to Denmark. He was tried and sentenced to death *in absentia* but this was later reversed and he spent his last years in France, suffering from partial paralysis and tinnitus, and close to insanity. His final novels, *D'un Château à L'Autre* (1957, Eng trans *Castle to Castle*, 1968) and *Nord* (1960, Eng trans *North*, 1972), are ranked with his best.

▷ D O'Connell, *Céline* (1976)

CELSUS, Aulus Cornelius
(1st century)

Roman writer. He compiled an encyclopedia on medicine, rhetoric, history, philosophy, war, and agriculture. The only extant portion of the work is the *De Medicina*, one of the first medical works to be printed (1478).

▷ N Scalinci, *La Oftalmiatria di Aulo Cornelio Celso* (1940)

CENDRARS, Blaise, originally Frédéric Louis Sauser
(1887–1961)

Swiss novelist, poet and traveller, born in Chaux-de-Fonds, Switzerland. His mother was a Scot, and he regarded himself as a cosmopolitan. When he was 15 he ran away from home to work for a jewel merchant with whom he travelled through Russia, Persia and China. He later described this journey in a long poem, *Transsibérien* (1913). In 1910 he met **Guillaume Apollinaire**, by whom he was much influenced. He wrote his first long poem in America, *Pâques à New York* (1912, 'Easter in New York'), which, with *Transsibérien* and his third and last long poem, *Le Panama ou Les Aventures de mes Sept Oncles* (written in 1918, published as *Panama; or the Adventures of my Seven Uncles* in 1931 in a translation by **John Dos Passos**), was important in shaping the spirit of modern poetry. He was careless with the truth and was fond of apocryphal stories, but he did lose an arm fighting for the French Foreign Legion in World War I. A reluctant writer, his poetry is not particularly memorable but his best novels—*La Confession de Dan Yack* (1927–9; 1946; Eng trans *Antarctic Fugue*, 1948), *Moravagine* (1926, Eng trans 1969) and *L'Or* (1925, Eng trans *Sutter's Gold*, 1926)—are less well known than they ought to be.

▷ M A Caws, *The Inner Theatre of Recent French Poetry* (1932)

CENTLIVRE, Susannah, née Freeman
(c.1667– c.1723)

English dramatist, born probably in Holbeach, Lincolnshire. She was first married at 16 and twice widowed. In 1700 she produced a tragedy, *The Perjured Husband*, and subsequently appeared on the stage in Bath in her own comedy, *Love at a Venture* (1706). In 1706 she married her third husband, Joseph Centlivre, head cook to Queen Anne at Windsor. Her 18 plays also included *The Gamester* (1705), *The Busybody* (1709) and *A Bold Stroke for a Wife* (1717).

▷ J H Bowyer, *The Celebrated Mrs Centlivre* (1952)

CERNUDA, Luis
(1902–67)

Spanish poet and critic, and, according to many critics, the greatest of all the famous 'Generation of '27', which included **Lorca** and **Rafael Alberti**. Cernuda is also highly prized as, with **Cavafy** and **Sandro Penna**, one of the great homosexual poets of the 20th century. An anti-Francoist, he escaped from Madrid in 1938 and moved, first to Britain, as a Professor of Spanish Literature at Glasgow

University, then to America; he died in Mexico City. His poetry, as well as being as explicitly homosexual as it could be at the time he wrote it, is soaked in his Andalusian origins, and has all the sad and beautiful virtues of Mediterranean art: in it, bitterness at his fate is counterpointed with a sense of the impermanence of beauty; but he had a rare ability to express beauty. His project was to find 'dignity' in a fate he deplored: he had had a fierce and *macho* militaristic father, lucidly omnipresent in his developing poetry, as a symbol of the unavoidable, unlovable hostility of reality. All his 11 collections were finally published as *La realidad y el deseo* (1964, 'Reality and Desire'). He ended in a courageous, but, paradoxically, affirmative vision of absolute disgust with the world. His first teacher and mentor was **Pedro Salinas**. 'The public', he wrote: 'I do not know what it is.' In English translation are: *The Poetry of Luis Cernuda* (1971) and *Selected Poems of Luis Cernuda* (1977).
▷D Harris, *Luis Cernuda: A Study of the Poetry* (1973)

CERVANTES SAAVEDRA, Miguel de
(1547–1616)

Spanish novelist, and author of *Don Quixote*, born in Alcalá de Henares, the son of a poor medical practitioner. In 1569 he published his first known work, a collection of pieces on the death of the queen. He then travelled to Italy in the service of Cardinal Giulio Acquaviva, and enlisted as a soldier. At the battle of Lepanto a gunshot wound maimed his left hand. After further service against the Turks in Tunis, he was returning to Spain in 1575 when the galley he sailed in was captured by Algerian corsairs, and with his brother Rodrigo and others he was carried into Algiers, where he remained in captivity for five years, during which he made four daring attempts to escape. In 1580 he was ransomed by the efforts of Trinitarian monks, Algiers traders, and his devoted family. Finding no permanent occupation at home, he drifted to Madrid, and tried a literary career. In 1584 he married Catalina de Salazar y Palacios (1565–1626). The marriage was childless, but Cervantes had an illegitimate daughter, Isabel de Saavedra (c.1585–1652). His first important work was *La Galatea* (Eng trans 1867), a pastoral romance, printed at Alcalá in 1585. For some years he strove to gain a livelihood by writing plays, of which two only, *La Numancia* (1784, Eng trans 1870) and *El trato de Argel* (1798, Eng trans *The Commerce of Algiers*, 1870), have survived. In 1587 he became commissary to the fleet at Seville. In 1594 he was appointed as collector of revenues for the kingdom of Granada; but in 1597, failing to make up the sum due to

the treasury, he was sent to prison in Seville, released on giving security, but not reinstated. Local tradition maintains that he wrote *Don Quixote* in prison at Argamasilla in La Mancha. In September 1604 leave was granted to print the first part of *Don Quixote*, and early in January 1605 the book came out at Madrid. It was immediately popular, though **Lope de Vega** wrote sneeringly of it; but instead of giving his readers the sequel they asked for, Cervantes busied himself with writing for the stage and composing short tales, or 'exemplary novels' as he called them, which came out as *Novelas Ejemplares* (Eng trans *Exemplary Novels*, 1972) in 1613. His *Viage al Parnaso* (1614), a poem of over 3000 lines in *terza rima*, reviews the poetry and poets of the day. In 1614 a pseudonymous writer brought out a spurious second part of *Don Quixote*, with an insulting preface, which served to spur Cervantes to the completion of the genuine second part (1615). While it was in the press he revised his various plays and interludes, and a little before his death, he finished the romance of *Persiles y Sigismunda* (1617, Eng trans *The Travels of Persiles and Sigismunda*, 1619). For *Don Quixote*, Cervantes ranks as one of the great writers of the world; though it is the most carelessly written of all great books, it is widely regarded as being the genuine precursor of the modern novel, as well as a great comic epic in its own right.
▷W Byron, *Cervantes, a biography* (1978); Manuel Duran, *Cervantes* (1974)

CÉSAIRE, Aimé Fernand
(1913–)

West Indian poet and playwright, born in Basse-Point, Martinique. One of the best-known poets and playwrights in the Third World, his reputation is based on two plays, *La Tragédie du roi Christophe* (1963, Eng trans *The Tragedy of King Christophe*, 1970) and *Une Tempête: Adaptation pour un théâtre negre* (1969), an original adaptation of **Shakespeare**'s *The Tempest* for black actors. He is also noted for a long poem, the *Cahier d'un retour au pays natal* (1947, Eng trans *Notebook of a Return to my Native Land*, 1969), and for a biography of the Haitian revolutionary, Toussaint L'Ouverture (1960, rev edn 1962). A militant Marxist and anti-colonialist, he played a large role in rallying decolonized Africans in the 1950s.
▷L Kesteloot and B Kotchy, *Césaire: l'homme et l'oeuvre* (1973)

CHACEL, Rosa
(1898–)

Spanish novelist and poet, born in Valladolid. Having spent much time in Italy, she was almost unknown in Spain until 1970, when her novel *La sinrazón* (1960, 'The Wrong'), was reprinted in Barcelona. Now she is recognized as one of the more important novelists of her age. She has continued to live in Brazil. Her first novel *Estación, ida y vuelta* (1930, 'Station, Round Trip'), was more original than it seemed at that time: it was influenced by **Ortega y Gasset**, but anticipated the French *nouveau roman* far more clearly than apparently similar contemporaneous novels by such as **Francisco Ayala**. However, her insistence upon examining the inner life of her characters, at the apparent expense of the outer, only gave an impression of the 'dehumanization' then fashionable in Spanish fiction. *Memorias de Leticia Valle* (1945, 'Memoirs of Leticia Valle'), is a tour de force in which a young girl relates the effects upon her of her sexual attractiveness to her male teacher. It is a novel which has annoyed male critics, as it was perhaps intended to do, and, were it translated (a critic has suggested), might become a 'woman's *Lolita*'.

CHAGAS, António das, Frei, monastic name of António da Fonseca Soares
(1631–82)

Portuguese poet, religious writer and moralist, born in Vidigureira. In his early life Chagas was violent and swaggering: after fighting in the Wars of the Restoration he had to flee to Brazil because he had killed a love-rival in a duel. He even earned himself the nickname of 'Captain Daisy'. In 1663, some years after he had returned to military life in Portugal, he suddenly became a Franciscan monk, and soon became famous for his 'hell-fire' sermons preaching identification with Christ. But both his fervent *Gongorista* poetry written as a soldier (he committed much of it to the flames) and his prose *Cartes Espirituals* (1684–7, 'Spiritual Letters'), his main work written towards the end of his life, are informed by the same ardour and self-knowledge, so that, despite some artificialities typical of the time, almost everything he wrote reads genuinely.
▷A F G Bell, *Portuguese Literature* (1922)

CHAMBERLAIN, Houston Stewart
(1855–1927)

English-born German author and propagandist, son of an admiral. He settled in Dresden in 1885, and in 1908 he moved to Bayreuth and married, as his second wife, Eva, daughter of Richard Wagner, and wrote in German on music, Wagner, Kant and philosophy. A committed supporter of the dogmas of Aryan supremacy, he was naturalized as a German in 1916.
▷W Vollrath, *Houston Stewart Chamberlain und sein britisches Erbgut* (1939); and other works by Vollrath

CHAMBERLAYNE, William
(1619–89)

English poet. He practised as a physician at Shaftesbury, Dorset, and fought as a royalist at Newbury. His works are *Love's Victory, a Tragi-Comedy* (1658), and *Pharonnida, An Heroick Poem* (1659) in five books of rhymed couplets, recounting the adventures of the knight Argolia in quest of his beloved, Pharonnida.
▷G Saintsbury, *Minor Poets of the Caroline Period* (1905)

CHAMFORT, Sébastien-Roch Nicolas
(1741–94)

French writer. He made an entrance into the literary circles of Paris, and lived for years 'by his wit, if not by his wits'. He joined the Jacobins at the outbreak of the French Revolution (1789), but his remarks on the Terror brought him into disfavour. Threatened with arrest, he tried to commit suicide and died after several days' suffering. His works include tales, dramas, *éloges*, brilliant maxims and even more admirably observed anecdotes (published posthumously in 1795), which attack the corruption of the period.
▷P J Richard, *Aspects de Chamfort* (1959)

CHAMISSO, Adelbert von (Louis Charles Adelaide de)
(1781–1838)

French-born German poet and biologist, born in Champagne. The French Revolution drove his parents to Prussia, and he served in the Prussian army (1798–1807). In Geneva he joined the literary circle of **Madame de Staël** and later studied at Berlin. In 1815–18 he accompanied a Russian exploring expedition round the world as naturalist, and on his return was appointed Keeper of the Botanical Garden of Berlin. In 1819 he was the first to discover in certain animals what he called 'alternation of generations' (the recurrence in the life cycle of two or more forms). He wrote several works on natural history, but his fame rests partly on his poems, still more on his quaint and humorous *Peter Schlemihls wundersame Geschichte* (1813, 'Peter Schlemihl's Remarkable Story'), the story of a man who sells his shadow to the Devil for earthly rewards. His lyrical verses *Frauenliebe und Frauenleben* ('Women's Life and Women's Love') are now best known in Schumann's song-cycle.
▷C A Lentzner, *Chamisso: a sketch of his life and work* (1893)

CHAMPFLEURY, assumed name of Jules Fleury-Husson
(1821–89)

French author, born in Laon. He wrote several early pieces for the theatre, and a number of novels in Realist style, inspired by the example of Courbet in painting. He became head of the Porcelain Museum in Sèvres, and published important studies on the history of caricature, literature, art and pottery, and a manifesto, *Le réalisme* (1857).

▷ E de Mirecourt, *Champfleury* (1891)

CHAMSON, André
(1900–83)

French novelist, born in Nîmes. His early novels were realistic tales of life in the Cévennes, often dealing with the Huguenot traditions which were a part of his own family. An anti-fascist activist in the 1930s, he fought in the Resistance during World War II. His later novels illustrate this social and political commitment; they include *La Galère* (1939, 'The Galley'), *La Neige et la Fleur* (1951, 'The Snow and the Flower') and *La Superbe* (1967, 'The Superb'). He was elected to the Académie française in 1956.

CHANDLER, Raymond
(1888–1959)

American novelist, born in Chicago. He was brought up in England from the age of seven, educated at Dulwich College and in France and Germany, and worked as a freelance writer in London. In 1912 he went to California, and served in the Canadian army in France, and in the RAF during World War I. After a variety of jobs, during the Depression he began to write short stories and novelettes for the detective-story pulp magazines of the day. On such stories he based his subsequent full-length 'private eye' novels, *The Big Sleep* (1939), *Farewell, My Lovely* (1940), *The High Window* (1942) and *The Lady in the Lake* (1943), all of which were successfully filmed. Chandler himself went to Hollywood in 1943 and worked on film scripts. He did much to establish the conventions of his genre, particularly with his cynical but honest anti-hero, Philip Marlowe, who also appeared in such later works as *The Little Sister* (1949), *The Long Goodbye* (1953) and *Playback* (1958).

▷ P Knight, *Down these Mean Streets a Man Must Go: Chandler's Knight* (1963)

CHANG, Eileen, originally Chang Ai Ling
(1920–)

Taiwanese (originally Chinese) novelist, the leading writer of a branch of Chinese literature-in-exile. She left China in 1952, for Hong Kong, and later became domiciled in the United States, and taught (as a virulent anti-communist) in several universities. At first she made her living from women's romances (they have been praised for their 'intimate boudoir realism'). *The Rice Sprout Song*

(1954), which she translated herself into English in 1955, is about peasants being asked for more than they can pay towards the Korean War effort. She has not attracted the attention of serious critics, but had many admirers in the 1960s and 1970s.

CHANNING, William Ellery
(1780–1842)

American clergyman, born in Newport, Rhode Island. He graduated at Harvard in 1798, and in 1803 was ordained to the Congregational Federal Street Church in Boston, where his sermons were famous for their 'fervour, solemnity, and beauty'. He was ultimately the leader of the Unitarians. In 1822 he visited Europe, and made the acquaintance of **Wordsworth** and **Coleridge**. Among his Works (6 vols, 1841–6) were his *Essay on National Literature*, *Remarks on Milton*, *Character and Writings of Fénelon*, *Negro Slavery*, and *Self-culture*.

▷ R Hudspeth, *Ellery Channing* (1973)

CHAPELAIN, Jean
(1595–1674)

French poet and critic. An original member of the Académie française (1634), he had a high reputation as a critic, as well as considerable political influence, firstly with Richelieu, and later with Colbert. He also wrote *La Pucelle* (1656, 'The Maid of Orleans'), a poem in 24 long cantos on Joan of Arc, which was savaged by **Nicolas Boileau**.

▷ G Colas, *Un poète protecteur des lettres au XVI siècle* (1912)

CHAPMAN, George
(c.1559–1634)

English dramatist, born near Hitchin, Hertfordshire. He is thought to have had a university education, possibly at Oxford. He began to make a reputation in Elizabethan literary circles with his poems *The Shadow of the Night* (1594), and in 1595 saw the production of his earliest extant play, the popular comedy *The Blind Beggar of Alexandria*. His next comedy, *All Fools*, printed in 1605, was probably produced in 1599. In 1598 he wrote a continuation of **Christopher Marlowe**'s *Hero and Leander*. After partial translations from the *Iliad* in 1598 and 1610, the complete translation of *The Iliads of Homer, Prince of Poets*, appeared in 1611. Having finished the *Iliad*, he set to work on the *Odyssey* (1616), followed (about 1624) by the minor works. He joined **Ben Jonson** and **John Marston** in the composition of *Eastward Hoe* (1605), in which slighting references to the Scots earned the authors a jail sentence, and in 1606 published a graceful comedy, *The Gentleman Usher*. In 1607 appeared the tragedy *Bussy*

d'Ambois, and in 1613 *The Revenge of Bussy d'Ambois*. *The Conspiracie* and *Tragedie of Charles, Duke of Byron* (1608) are also undramatic, but are full of fine poetry. His other plays are *The May Day* (1611), *The Widow's Tears* (1612) and *Caesar and Pompey* (1631). Two posthumous tragedies (1654), *Alphonsus* and *Revenge for Honour*, bear his name, but it is doubtful that he wrote them. *The Ball*, a comedy, and *The Tragedie of Chabot* (1639) were the joint work of Chapman and **James Shirley**. Among Chapman's nondramatic works are the epic philosophical poem *Euthymiae & Raptus* (1609), *Petrarch's Seven Penitentiall Psalmes* (1612), *The Divine Poem of Musaeus* (1616) and *The Georgicks of Hesiod* (1618).
▷C K Spivack, *George Chapman* (1967)

CHAPONE, Hester, née **Mulso**
(1727–1801)

English essayist, born in Twywell, Northamptonshire. One of the 'blue-stocking' circle associated with Elizabeth Montagu, she published verse stories and wrote for the *Rambler* (No. 10), *Gentleman's Magazine* and other magazines; she is chiefly remembered for her *Letters on the Improvement of the Mind* (1772).
▷*An Account of Her Life and Character drawn up by her family* (1807)

CHAR, René
(1907–88)

Prolific French poet, born at L'Isle-sur-Sorgue, Vaucluse. He was educated in Avignon and Marseilles, and fought with the Resistance during the war. Originally associated with Surrealism, he rejected the movement's more doctrinaire aspects but drew from it a lasting belief in human individuality and the need to protest against convention. An admirer of Heraclitus, he attempted to register the flux of experience, particularly the sunny landscape and culture of the Mediterranean. In his most representative collection, *Fureur et Mystère* (1948, 'Madness and Mystery'), he claims a hermetic, almost magical role for poetry. His war journal *Feuillets d'Hypnos* (1946, Eng trans *Leaves of Hypnos*, 1973) was dedicated to **Camus**, whose emphasis on protest and southern neo-classicism he shared. Char's later work was more directly concerned with social issues, but still retains its essentially irrational emphasis.
▷M A Caws, *René Char* (1977)

CHARBONNEAU, Robert
(1911–67)

French–Canadian poet, novelist and critic, noted for his irony and in particular for his use of French techniques in such novels as

Les désirs et les jours (1948, 'Desires and Days'). The novelist who has mainly influenced him is François Mauriac.
▷M B Ellis, *Robert Charbonneau et la création romanesque* (1948)

CHARDONNE, Jacques, pseud of **Jacques Boutelleau**
(1884–1968)

French writer, born in Barbezieux. He wrote domestic novels mainly set in his native Charente, among them *Claire* (1931), *Les Destinées sentimentales* (1934–6, 'Sentimental Destinies') and *Romanesques* (1937). He also wrote essays, and a chronicle of the French collapse in 1940.
▷G Chardonne, *La Vie de Jacques Chardonne et son art* (1953)

CHARLWOOD, Don(ald Ernest Cameron)
(1915–)

Australian writer, born in Hawthorn, Melbourne, who served in the Royal Australian Air force during World War II. He achieved immediate success with *No Moon Tonight* (1956), his experiences in bombing sorties over Germany. He returned to this period of his life in a collection of partly autobiographical short stories, *Flight and Time* (1979). His other books include a history of Australian air-traffic control, in which the author worked from 1945, and two books of nautical history, *Wrecks and Reputations* (1977) and *Settlers under Sail* (1978). *The Long Farewell* (1981), based on authentic diaries, celebrates the spirit of 19th-century immigrants who made the long sea voyage to Australia.

CHARTERIS, Leslie, pseud of **Leslie Charles Bowyer Yin**
(1907–93)

British-born American crime story writer, born in Singapore, the son of an English mother and a Chinese father. Educated at Cambridge, he was author of a series of books featuring a criminal hero, Simon Templar, 'the Saint', starting with *Meet the Tiger* (1928) and *Enter the Saint* (1930). He moved to the USA in 1932 and worked in Hollywood as a screenwriter. He was naturalized in 1941.
▷W O G Lofts and D J Adley, *The Saint and Leslie Charteris* (1979)

CHARTIER, Alain
(c.1390–c.1440)

French writer and courtier, born in Bayeux. He was secretary to Charles VI and VII and went on diplomatic missions to Germany, Venice and Scotland (1425–8). His much imitated poem, *La belle dame sans merci* (1424,

'The Beautiful Woman with no Mercy'), is a piece of escapism in the midst of his preoccupation with the plight of France in the Hundred Years War. This forms the backcloth of his two best works, the *Livre des quatre dames* (1415–16, 'Book of Four Women'), in which four ladies on the day after Agincourt weep for their lost lovers, and the prose *Quadrilogue invectif* (1422, 'A Debate Between Four People, Containing Invective'), a debate apportioning the blame for France's ills between the people and the nobility. He also showed skill in handling the *ballade* and other lyrical forms.
▷D Delaunay, *Étude sur Alain Chartier* (1876)

CHARYN, Jerome
(1937–)

American novelist, born and educated in New York City, where he later taught at City College and City University. Since 1980 he has been lecturer in creative writing at Princeton University, New Jersey. His first three novels, *Once Upon a Droshky* (1964), *On the Darkening Green* (1965) and *Going to Jerusalem* (1967), were episodic picaresques, mostly concerned with rebellion against conformity, but containing elements of fantasy. *American Scrapbook* (1969) portrayed a Japanese family's internment during World War II, while *Eisenhower, My Eisenhower* (1971) reimagines New York as Bedlam and converts his customary Jewish characters into gypsies. In 1975, Charyn (whose brother is a New York police inspector) introduced his fictional detective Isaac Sidel in *Blue Eyes*, the first of a tetralogy, continuing with *Marilyn the Wild*, *The Education of Patrick Silver* (both 1976), *Secret Isaac* (1978), published in the UK as *The Isaac Quartet* (1984). In the mid-eighties, he returned to the style of the earlier books with *War Cries over Avenue C* (1985).

CHASE, James Hadley, pseud of René Raymond
(1906–85)

English novelist, born in London. He is a prolific author of mystery stories, almost all of which have an American setting derived from copious second-hand research, since he has rarely visited that country. He adopted the manner of the American 'hard-boiled' school, and had an immediate success with his first novel, *No Orchids for Miss Blandish* (1939), and continued in a similar vein. He has employed a number of different detectives in various series, but their hallmark is always an intricate plot, and a fast-moving, harshly realistic narrative.

CHASE, Mary Coyle
(1907–81)

American playwright, born in Colorado. She is chiefly remembered as the author of the play *Harvey* (1944), a comedy about a drunk whose closest companion is a huge, invisible rabbit. It won her a Pulitzer Prize for Drama in 1945, and was made into a highly successful film in 1950. She wrote a number of other plays, including *Now You've Done It* (1937), *Mrs McThing* (1952) and *Cocktails with Mum* (1974). She also wrote several books for children, in which field she should not be confused with the novelist and children's writer Mary Chase (1887–1973) of Maine, an academic who also achieved a considerable reputation as a writer of popular fiction.

CHASE, Mary Ellen
(1887–1973)

American novelist and essayist, born in Blue Hill, Maine. From 1936 until her retirement she taught English literature at Smith College. Her best-known, accomplished novels are *Mary Peters* (1934) and *Silas Crockett* (1935). They are in the regional, or 'local colour', tradition established by such writers as **Sarah Orne Jewett** and **Mary Wilkins Freeman**. *Silas Crockett* is set in the Maine herring industry, and vividly depicts the misery caused by the inhumanely handled introduction of steam-ships. *A Goodly Fellowship* (1939) is autobiographical.
▷P Westbrook, *Mary Ellen Chase* (1965)

CHASSIGNET, Jean-Baptiste
(c.1580–c.1635)

French poet, author of *Le Mespris de la vie et consolation contre la mort* (1594), a series of 434 sonnets, together with a number of other poems, which together constitute an argument (which can be inferred from the title of the work) that life and death are inseparable, that life should be lived bearing death in mind, and that death, when it comes, should be welcomed. The argument is based on Christian doctrine, and much of the imagery in this highly rhetorical but attractive work is drawn from the bible.

CHATEAUBRIAND, François René, Vicomte de
(1768–1848)

French writer and statesman, born of a noble Breton family in St Malo. He served for a short time as an ensign, and in 1791 sailed to North America, spending eight months in the travels recounted in his *Voyage en Amérique* (1827, Eng trans *Travels in America*, 1828). Returning to France, he married, but immediately joined the army of the émigrés, and was left for dead near Namur. From 1793

to 1800 he lived in London, teaching and translating. In 1797 he published an *Essai sur les Révolutions* ('Essay on Revolutions'). *Atala* (Eng trans 1802), an unfinished Romantic epic of Native American life (1801), established his literary reputation; and *Génie du christianisme* (1802, Eng trans *The Beauties of Christianity*, 1813), a vindication of the Church of Rome, raised him to the foremost position among the French men of letters of the day. In 1803 he was appointed secretary to the embassy in Rome, where he wrote his *Lettres sur l'Italie* ('Letters about Italy'), and in 1804 was sent as envoy to the little republic of Valais. But on the murder of the Duc d'Enghien, Chateaubriand refused to hold office under Napoleon. He set out for the East in 1806, visited Greece, Palestine and Egypt, and returned to France in 1807. Two years later he issued *Les Martyrs*, a prose epic of Diocletian's persecutions. From 1814 to 1824 he gave support to the Restoration monarchy. He was made a peer and minister, and in 1822–4 was ambassador extraordinary at the British court. Disappointed in his hope of becoming Prime Minister, from 1824 to 1830 he figured as a Liberal. On the downfall of Charles X he went back to the Royalists. During the reign of Louis-Philippe he occupied himself in writing his celebrated *Mémoires d'outre-tombe* ('Memoirs from Beyond the Grave'). Parts of this eloquent autobiography appeared before his death and were translated as *Memoirs* in three volumes in 1848; the whole, in six volumes, not till 1902. His writings also include the *Itinéraire de Paris à Jerusalem* (1811, Eng trans *Travels in Greece, Palestine, Egypt and Barbary*, 1812); *Les Natchez* (1827, Eng trans *The Natchez*, 1827), a prose epic dealing with Native American life; and two works of fiction, *René* (1802, Eng trans *René: A Tale*, 1813) and *Les Aventures du dernier des Abencérages* (1826, Eng trans *The Last of the Abencérages*, 1826), a tale of 16th-century Spain.
▷G Painter, *Chateaubriand: a biography* (1977)

CHATEAUBRIANT, Alphonse de
(1877–1951)

French novelist, associated particularly with the regions of Basse-Bretagne and La Brière. Born in Rennes, the son of a family particularly gifted in art and music, he won the Prix **Goncourt** with *Monsieur des Lourdines* in 1911. In spite of his Christian convictions, as revealed in the *Écrits de l'autre rive* (1950), Chateaubriant was an active supporter of Hitler's ideology, spending periods in Germany prior to World War II, openly collaborating with the Germans during the Occupation and editing the pro-Nazi journal *La Gerbe*. After the war he was exiled, and he ended his days in the monastery at Kitzbühel, Austria. Despite this retreat into mysticism towards the end of his life, Chateaubriant's work more typically reflects a belief in man's ability to redeem himself through the successful accomplishment of his dreams and aspirations.

CHATTERJEE, Bankim Chandra
(1838–94)

Indian writer, born in Katalpura, Bengal. One of the most influential figures in 19th-century Indian literature, his novels include *Durges Nandini* (1864) and *Anandamath* (1882), a novel of the Sannyasi rebellion of 1772, from which the Nationalist song *Bande Mataram* ('Hail to thee, Mother'), was taken.
▷M Lala Dasa, *Bankim Chatterjee, prophet of the Indian Renaissance* (1938)

CHATTERJI, Sarat Chandra
(1876–1936)

Indian (Bengali) novelist, most of whose fiction has been translated into English. He is thought of by the Indian public as being the greatest novelist of the continent; he was hardly that, by the highest literary standards, for he could be sentimental, and his plots were often highly artificial. But, rather like **Upton Sinclair** in the United States, he deserved his great popularity: like **Dickens**, he was appalled by poor living conditions; he was one of the first Indian writers to draw attention to the plight of women, and his style was unaffected. His feeling for women is well seen in the most famous of his many novels, *Srikanta*, part of which was translated in 1922. From a literary viewpoint, his finest work in translation is contained in a selection of stories: *The Eldest Sister* (1950).

CHATTERTON, Thomas
(1752–70)

English poet, born in Bristol. His father, a sub-chanter in the cathedral, and master of a charity school, died before the boy was born. The mother, a poor schoolmistress and needlewoman, brought up her son and his sister beneath the shadow of St Mary Redcliffe, where their forefathers had been sextons (more probably masons) since the days of Queen Elizabeth. He was a scholar of Colston's bluecoat hospital (1760–5), and then was apprenticed an attorney. Fascinated from boyhood by antiques, he wrote and published pseudo-archaic poems purporting to be the work of a 15th-century Bristol Monk, Thomas Rowley, a friend of a historical figure, a merchant called William Canynge.

In 1769 he sent a history of painting in England, allegedly by Rowley, to **Horace Walpole**, who was only temporarily deceived. He was released from his apprenticeship in 1770 and left for London, where he worked on innumerable satires, essays and epistles, and a burlesque opera, *The Revenge*. But later that year he poisoned himself with arsenic. His 'Rowley' poems, although soon exposed as forgeries, are considered to have genuine talent, and he became a romantic hero to later poets. His story was dramatized by Alfred de Vigny in 1835.

CHATWIN, Bruce
(1940–89)

English writer and traveller, born in Sheffield. He worked at Sotheby's as an expert on modern art for eight years until he temporarily went blind. To recuperate, he went to Africa and the Sudan. He was converted to a life of nomadic asceticism and began writing beguiling books which defy classification, combining fiction, anthropology, philosophy and travel. They include *In Patagonia* (1977), which won the Hawthornden Prize and the **E M Forster** Award of the American Academy of Letters; *The Viceroy of Ouidah* (1980); *On The Black Hill* (1982), winner of the Whitbread Award for the best first novel; *The Songlines* (1987), and *Utz* (1988), a novella which was shortlisted for the Booker Prize.

CHAUCER, Geoffrey
(c.1345–1400)

English poet, the son of John Chaucer, a vintner and tavern keeper in London, perhaps the John Chaucer who was deputy to the king's butler. In 1357 and 1358 he was a page in the service of the wife of Lionel, Duke of Clarence; he would seem to have been presently transferred to King Edward III's household. In 1359 he served in the campaign in France, and was taken prisoner at 'Retters' (Rethel), but was soon ransomed, the king contributing £16 towards the required amount. He returned home in 1360. In 1367 the king granted him a pension. He is described as 'our beloved yeoman', and as 'one of the yeomen of the king's chamber', and in 1368 he was one of the king's esquires. In 1369 he first appeared as a poet, with his *Book of the Duchess*, on the death of John of Gaunt's wife. In 1370 he went abroad on the king's service; in 1372–3 on a royal mission to Genoa, Pisa, Florence; in 1376, abroad again; in 1377, to Flanders and to France; in 1378, to Italy again. Meanwhile in 1374 he was appointed comptroller of the Customs and Subsidy of Wools, Skins, and Tanned Hides in the port of London; in 1382,

comptroller of the Petty Customs; and in 1385 he was allowed to nominate a permanent deputy. In 1374 the king granted him a pitcher of wine daily; and John of Gaunt conferred on him a pension of £10 for life. In 1375 he received from the crown the custody of lands that brought him in £104. In 1386 he was elected a knight of the shire for Kent. The following writings certainly belong to the period 1369–87: *The Parliament of Fowls*, *The House of Fame*, *Troilus and Cressida* and *The Legend of Good Women*; also what ultimately appeared as the Clerk's, Man of Law's, Prioress's, Second Nun's and Knight's Tales in the *Canterbury Tales*. Chaucer's earlier writings, including his translation of part of the *Roman de la Rose*, followed the current French trends, but the most important influence acting upon him during this middle period of his literary life was that of Italy. Much of his subject-matter he derived from his great Italian contemporaries, especially from **Boccaccio**, but it was the spirit, not the letter of these masters which he imitated. The crowning work of the middle period of his life is *Troilus and Cressida*—a work in which his immense power of human observation, his sense of humour, and his dramatic skill are lavishly displayed. *The Legend of Good Women* has an admirable prologue, but was never finished. His next great subject was the *Canterbury Tales*. But about the end of 1386 he lost his offices, possibly owing to the absence abroad of John of Gaunt, and fell upon hard times. In 1389 he was appointed clerk of the King's Works, but this did not last and he fell into debt. In 1394 King Richard II granted him a pension of £20 for life; but the advances of payment he applied for, and the issue of letters of protection from arrest for debt, indicate his condition. On the accession in 1399 of Henry IV, John of Gaunt, he was granted a pension of 40 marks (£26 13s 4d), and his few remaining months were spent in comfort. After his death he was laid in that part of Westminster Abbey which through his burial there came afterwards to be called the Poets' Corner. His greatest achievement is the Prologue (1387) to the *Tales*, which, as a piece of descriptive writing, is unique. Chaucer was the first great poet of the English race, and he established the southern English dialect as the literary language of England. Many works have been ascribed to Chaucer, and were long printed in popular editions, that are certainly not his—eg, *The Court of Love*, *Chaucer's Dream*, *The Complaint of the Black Knight*, *The Cuckoo and Nightingale*, *The Flower and the Leaf*, and much of the extant *Romaunt of the Rose*.

▷D S Brewer, *Chaucer* (1973, 3rd edn); I Robinson, *Chaucer and the English Tradition* (1972)

CHAUDHURI, Nirad C
(1897–)

Indian writer, born in Kishorganj, Bengal, and educated at Calcutta University. A prolific writer on Indian topics, he is best-known for *The Autobiography of an Unknown Indian* (1951), which chronicles his rural childhood and early life as a student during the British Raj. **V S Naipaul** hailed it as possibly 'the one great book to come out of the Indo–English encounter'. Acutely perceptive about the English, *A Passage to England* (1959) is an amusing account of his first visit to that country. *Thy Hand, Great Anarch! India 1921–1952* (1987) is a further, and probably final, instalment of epic autobiography.

CHAYEFSKY, Paddy (born **Sidney**)
(1923–81)

American stage and television playwright, born in New York City. He is best known for *Marty* (1953, television) and *The Bachelor Party* (1954, screenplay), sensitive and affecting plays about ordinary people.
▷ J M Clun, *Chayevsky* (1976)

CHAZAL, Malcolm de
(1902–)

French prose-poet living in mysterious isolation in Mauritius, who was discovered by **André Breton** and was put forward as an exponent of genuine Surrealism. His *Sens Plastique* (1948, 'Plastic Sense') excited Paris. His *La Bible du mal* (1952, 'Evil Bible'), published in St Louis, has been compared to **Blake**. All his work is about the sexual act: for him, nothing else exists.
▷ A Breton, *La Clé des champs* (1953)

CHÉDID, Andrée
1921–)

French novelist, poet and dramatist, of Lebanese origin, born in Cairo. She is mainly notable for her expressions of eastern myths in western, rationalist forms. She moved to Paris in 1946. She has published many volumes of poetry, and her novels *Le sixième jour* (1960) and *Le sommeil délivré* (1976) have been translated into English as, respectively, *The Sixth Day* (1962) and *From Sleep Unbound* (1983). Her play *Bérénice d'Egypt* was published in 1968. *The Sixth Day* was filmed.

CHEEVER, John William
(1912–82)

American short-story writer and novelist. Born in Quincy, Massachusetts, he began telling stories when he was eight or nine. He sold his first story, 'Expelled', to *The New Republic* after he was thrown out of Thayer Academy in South Braintree, Massachusetts, at the age of 17. By the time he was 22 the *New Yorker* was accepting his work and for years he contributed a dozen stories a year to it. His first collection of stories was published in 1943 when he was in the army. After the war he taught freshman English and wrote scripts for television, but in 1951 a Guggenheim Fellowship allowed him to devote his attention to writing, and a second collection, *The Enormous Radio and Other Stories*, came out in 1953. His first novel, *The Wapshot Chronicle* (1957), won the National Book Award and its sequel, *The Wapshot Scandal* (1964), was awarded the Howell's Medal for fiction. A steady stream of novels and stories followed, many of them focusing on the isolation and discontent of contemporary American life. Invariably funny and ironic, sad and sophisticated, these include *Bullet Park* (1969), *The World of Apples* (1973), *Falconer* (1977) and *The Stories of John Cheever*, winner of the Pulitzer Prize and the National Book Critics Award in 1979.
▷ *The Journals* (1990); S Cheever, *Home Before Dark* (1984)

CHEKHOV, Anton Pavlovich
(1860–1904)

Russian author, born in Taganrog, the son of an unsuccessful shopkeeper and the grandson of a serf. He studied medicine at Moscow University and qualified as a doctor in 1884. As a student, he had written articles for various comic papers, and his first book, *Pëstrye Rasskazy* ('Motley Stories'), appearing in 1886, was successful enough for him to think of writing as a profession. He continued to regard himself as a doctor rather than a writer, though he practised very little except during the cholera epidemic of 1892–3. His magazine articles led to an interest in the popular stage of vaudeville and French farce, and, after the failure of his first full-length play, *Ivanov* (1887, Eng trans 1912), he wrote several one-acters, such as *Medved* (1889, Eng trans *The Bear*, 1909) and *Predlozheniye* (1889, Eng trans *A Marriage Proposal*, 1914). In 1892 he settled on a farm estate at Melikhovo. His next full-length plays, *Leshy* (1889, Eng trans *The Wood Demon*, 1926) and *Chayka* (1896, Eng trans *The Seagull*, 1912), were also failures and Chekhov had decided to concentrate on his stories (which had introduced him to his admired **Tolstoy** and **Maxim Gorky**) when Nemirovich-Danchenko persuaded him to let the Moscow Art Theatre revive *Chayka* in 1898. Produced by Stanislavsky, who revealed its quality and originality, its reception encouraged him to write for the same company his masterpieces: *Dyadya Vanya* (1896, Eng trans *Uncle Vanya*, 1912), *Tri Sestry* (1901, Eng trans *The Three Sisters*, 1916) and *Vishnyovy Sad* (1904, Eng trans *The Cherry Orchard*, 1908). Meanwhile he continued to write short stories. In 1891 he wrote *Ostrov Sakhalin* (1895, 'Saghalien Island'), after a visit to a penal settlement which had a considerable effect on subsequent criminal legislation. In 1897 tuberculosis forced him to live either abroad or at Yalta in the Crimea. In 1900 he was elected fellow of the Moscow Academy of Science, but resigned when his fellow-member, Gorky, was dismissed by order of the tsar. In 1901 he married the actress Olga Knipper, who for many years after her husband's death was the admired exponent of female parts in his plays. Chekhov is perhaps the most popular Russian author outside his own country. His stories have strongly influenced many writers, and his plays are firmly established in the classical repertoires of Europe. His technique is impressionistic—almost *pointilliste*. In all his work he equates worldly success with loss of soul. It is the sensitive, hopefully struggling people, at the mercy of forces almost always too strong for them, who are his heroes. For this reason his work, though presenting a convincing picture of Russian middle-class life at the end of the 19th century, has a timeless quality, since it reflects the universal predicament of the 'little man'. Among his many short stories, the following are outstanding: *Step* ('The Steppe'), *Khoristka* ('The Chorus Girl'), *Duel* ('The Duel'), *Palata No. 6* ('Ward No 6'), *Dushetska* ('The Darling'), *Dama s sobachkoĭ* ('The Lady with the Dog') and *V ovrag'e* ('In the Ravine'). The bulk of his stories were translated in 13 volumes by Constance Garnett (1916–22).

▷ E J Simmons, *Chekhov: a biography* (1962)

CHÊNEDOLLÉ, Charles-Julien Lioult de
(1769–1833)

French poet, born in Vire. While living in Hamburg during the Revolution, he was a close friend to both **Rivarol** and **Klopstock**. Later he became a friend to **Constant de Rebecque**, and joined the circle of **Madame de Staël**. He became famous for his gigantic didactic poem *La Génie de l'Homme* (1807, 'The Genius of Man'). He is transitional between neo-classicism and romanticism. **Sainte-Beuve** introduced his collected works of 1864.

▷ L de Samie, *Chênedollé* (1922, in French)

CHÉNIER, (Marie) André
(1762–94)

French poet, born in Constantinople, the third son of the French consul-general and a Greek woman. At three he was sent to France, and at 12 was placed at the Collège de Navarre, Paris, where Greek literature was his special subject. At 20 he entered the army, and served for six months in Strasbourg; but disgusted with military life, returned to Paris and to strenuous study. To this period belong his famous idylls *Le Mendiant* ('The Beggar') and *L'Aveugle* ('The Blind Man'). His health giving way, he travelled in Switzerland, Italy and the Greek Islands. In 1786 he returned to Paris and began several ambitious poems, most of which remained fragments. The most noteworthy are *Suzanne*, *L'Invention* and *Hermès*, the last being an imitation of **Lucretius**. In 1787 he went to England as secretary to the French ambassador, but in 1790 he returned to Paris to find himself in the ferment of the Revolution, which at first he supported; but alarmed by its excesses he mortally offended Robespierre by political pamphlets supporting liberal monarchism. He was thrown into prison, and six months later was guillotined on 25 July—three days before the end of the Reign of Terror. Almost nothing was published in his lifetime, but the appearance of his collected poems in 1819 made a notable impression on subsequent French poetry.

▷ V Loggins, *André Chénier, his life, death and glory* (1965)

CHÉNIER, Marie-Joseph Blaise
(1764–1811)

French republican playwright, born in Constantinople. He studied at the Collège de Navarre in Paris before embarking on a military career at the age of 17. Active in the overthrow of the Ancien Régime, he saw theatre as a political weapon, publishing, in 1789, a pamphlet entitled *De la liberté du théâtre en France*. He was a successful tragedian, the period between 1791 and 1794 yielding *Jean Calas* (c.1791), which transmutes a celebrated contemporary episode of religious fanaticism into political terms, *Henri VIII* (1791), *Caius Gracchus* (1792), *Fénelon* (1793) and *Timoléon* (1794), as well as some poetry and prose. A man of irascible temperament, Chénier voted his own brother, André, to the scaffold in 1794.

CHERBULIEZ, Charles Victor
(1829–99)

Swiss-born French novelist and critic, born in Geneva. At Paris, Bonn and Berlin, he studied first mathematics, then philology and philosophy, after which he lived in Geneva as a teacher. In 1864 he went to Paris to join the staff of the *Revue des Deux Mondes*, writing under the pseudonym of G Valbert. He was elected to the Académie française in 1881. His novels include *Le Roman d'une honnête femme* (1866, 'The Story of an Honest Woman'), *Meta Holdenis* (1873), *Samuel Brohl et Cⁱᵉ* (1877, 'Samuel Brohl & Co.'), *L'Idée de Jean Têterol* (1878, 'Jean Teterol's Idea'), *Noirs et rouges* (1881, 'Blacks and Reds'), *La Vocation du Comte Ghislain* (1888, 'Count Ghislain's Calling') and *Le Secret du précepteur* (1893, 'The Tutor's Secret'). He also wrote many literary and political articles in the *Revue des Deux Mondes*.

CHERBULIEZ, Joel
(1806–70)

Swiss novelist and critic, born in Geneva, the son of a prosperous bookseller. He succeeded to his father's business, and edited the *Revue critique* from 1833. His *Lendemain du dernier jour d'un condamné* (1829, 'The Day After a Condemned Man's Last Day') was a clever burlesque on **Victor Hugo**'s well-known tour de force, while his *Genève* (1867) was a solid contribution to the history of the city.

CHERNYSHEVSKI, Nikolai Gavrilovich
(1828–89)

Russian critic and novelist. A follower of the French socialists, he wrote on political, economic and social matters such as Nihilism, and saw his literary works in a utilitarian light. A spokesman for the radical intelligentsia, he was imprisoned in Siberia from 1862 to 1883 for revolutionary activities. His *Esteticheski otnoshenia iskusstva k deïstvitelnosti* ('Aesthetic Relationship between Art and Reality') deals with his theory of the place of art in life, and his propagandist novel, *Shto delat'?* (1864, 'A Vital Question', also known as 'What Is To Be Done?'), was written during imprisonment, and is said to have in part provoked **Dostoyevsky**'s *Zapiski iz podpol'ya* ('Notes from Underground').
▷F B Randall, *Nikolai Gavrilovich Chernyshevsky* (1967)

CHESNUTT, Charles Wadell
(1858–1932)

American novelist and short-story writer, born in Cleveland, Ohio, where his family had taken refuge to escape the prejudice against free blacks in their native South. After the Civil War, they returned to North Carolina, where he was educated. He worked as a school teacher and a journalist, and came to national attention with two successful volumes of short stories on the issue of colour, *The Conjure Woman* (1899) and *The Wife of His Youth* (1899). He was an accomplished writer in this form, but his three subsequent novels dealing with racial issues were less successful. *The Marrow of Tradition* (1901), about the struggles facing black and white half-sisters, is the best of them. He also wrote regular essays and reviews in various journals.

CHESSEX Jacques
(1934–)

Swiss (Vaudois) novelist, poet and critic, whose work expresses his reaction to a very strict Calvinistic upbringing by a father who eventually killed himself. He has written much poetry, but his most important book is *La Confession du Pastor Burn* (1967, 'The Confession of Pastor Burn'), which has been compared, for the power of its self-analysis, to the work of **Constant de Rebecque**. He has written illuminatingly of the Vaud people, and of Swiss literature. For his novel *L'Ogre* (1973), whose subject is an overwhelming father (representing, a critic has suggested, the whole of the Vaud people), he received the Prix **Goncourt**.

CHESSMAN, Caryl Whittier
(1921–60)

American convict-author, born in St Joseph, Michigan. He was sentenced to death in 1948 on 17 charges of kidnapping, robbery and rape, but was granted eight stays of execution by the governor of California amounting to a record period of 12 years under sentence of death, without a reprieve. During this period he conducted a brilliant legal battle from prison, learnt four languages and wrote the bestselling, autobiographical books against capital punishment *Cell 2455 Death Row* (1954), *Trial by Ordeal* (1955) and *The Face of Justice* (1958). His ultimate execution provoked worldwide criticism of American judicial methods.

CHESTERTON, G(ilbert) K(eith)
(1874–1936)

English critic, novelist and poet, born in London. He was educated at St Paul's School and studied art at the Slade School, which he never practised professionally, although he contributed illustrations to the novels of his friend **Hilaire Belloc**. His first writings were for periodicals, and all through his life much of his best work went into essays and articles in *The Bookman, The Speaker, The Illustrated London News*, and his own *G.K's Weekly*, which was born in 1925 of the *New Witness* inherited from his brother a few years earlier. Tremendous zest and energy, with a mastery of paradox, a robust humour and forthright devotion characterize his entire output. He became a Roman Catholic in 1922, but this decision is clearly foreshadowed in his works, the best of which were published before that date. His two earliest books were the collections of poetry *The Wild Knight* and *Greybeards at Play* (both 1900); the works which followed include *The Napoleon of Notting Hill*

(1904), liberal and anti-Imperialist in outlook, also brilliant studies of **Robert Browning** (1903), **Dickens** (1906) and **Robert Louis Stevenson** (1907); and the provocative *Heretics* (1908) and *Orthodoxy* (1908). The amiable detective-priest Father Brown, who brought Chesterton popularity with a wider public, first appeared in *The Innocence of Father Brown* (1911). Soon after his conversion Chesterton published his well-known Life of St Francis of Assisi, also one of St Thomas Aquinas (1933). His *Collected Poems* appeared in 1933, and his *Autobiography* posthumously in 1936. An ebullient personality, with a figure of **Johnson**ian proportions, absent-minded but quick-witted, he will go down as one of the most colourful and provocative writers of his day. His brother, Cecil Edward (1879–1918), wrote anti-liberal books and started, with Hilaire Belloc, the anti-bureaucratic paper *New Witness* in 1912. He married Ada Elizabeth Jones, journalist and writer, who pioneered the Cecil Houses for London's homeless women.
▷P Braybrooke, *Gilbert Keith Chesterton* (1922); and other works by Braybrooke

CHETTLE, Henry
(c.1560–?1607)
English dramatist and pamphleteer, born in London, the son of a dyer. A printer by trade, he turned to writing when his printing-house failed. He edited **Robert Greene**'s *Groat's-worth of Wit* (1592), and in 1593 published a pamphlet, *Kind Harts Dreame*, apologizing for Greene's attack on **Shakespeare**. He wrote a picaresque romance, *Piers Plainnes Seven Yeres Prentiship* (1595), and from 1598 turned to writing plays for Philip Henslowe's Rose Theatre in Bankside, especially *The Tragedy of Hoffman* (1602). He collaborated on many others, including *Robin Hood, Patient Grisel, The Blind Beggar of Bednal-Green* (with **John Day**) and *Jane Shore*. He also wrote an elegy for Queen Elizabeth, *England's Mourning Garment* (1603).
▷H Jenkins, *The Life and Work of Henry Chettle* (1934)

CHEVALLIER, Gabriel
(1895–1969)
French novelist, born in Lyons. He won wide acclaim with his *Clochemerle* (1934, Eng trans 1936), an earthy satire on petty bureaucracy in a vividly evoked French town, after a series of less successful psychological novels. Other books include *La Peur* (1930, 'Fear'), *Clarisse Vernon* (1933), *Sainte-Colline* (1937), *Les*

Héritiers Euffe (1945, 'The Euffe Inheritance'), *Le Petit général* (1951, 'The Little General') and *Clochemerle Babylone* (1954).

CHEYNEY, Peter, pseud of **Reginald Shorthouse Cheyney**
(1896–1951)
English crime writer in a hard-boiled US idiom. His first novel, *This Man is Dangerous* (1936), introduced the FBI man Lemmy Caution, a character with some of the characteristics of **Mickey Spillane**'s Mike Hammer. Other series included Alonzo MacTavish (who featured in **Leslie Charteris**-style short stories), and the American private investigator Slim Callaghan, who first appeared in *The Urgent Hangman* (1938). Cheyney also wrote a group of tense wartime spy thrillers, beginning with *Dark Duet* (1942) and always featuring 'dark' in the title. His style here was dry, precise and unaffected. Cheyney also wrote under the name Harold Brust.
▷M Harrison, *Peter Cheyney, Prince of Hokum* (1954)

CHIABRERA, Gabriello
(1552–1637)
Italian poet, born in Savona. Educated at Rome, he served Cardinal Cornaro, but was obliged to leave for revenging himself upon a Roman nobleman. An enthusiastic student of Greek, he skilfully imitated **Pindar** and **Anacreon**, while his *Lettere Famigliari* ('Family Letters') introduced the poetical epistle into Italian.
▷E N Girardi, *Esperienza e poesia di Gabriello Chiabrera* (1950)

CHIARELLI, Luigi
(1884–1947)
Italian playwright, born in Trani. A journalist who took to the stage, he had his first play, *Vita intima* ('Inner Life'), performed in 1909. His great success was *La Maschera e il volta* (1916, 'The Mask and the Face'), a farcical comedy translated into nearly every European language.
▷M Lo Vecchio O Musti, *L'Opere di Luigi Chiarelli* (1942)

CHILD, Lydia Maria
(1802–80)
American social campaigner, essayist and novelist, born in Watertown, Massachusetts. A committed campaigner for social and political reform, Child was editor of the *National Anti-Slavery Standard* and published many essays on political and social issues. Her *The History of the Condition of Women in Various Ages and Nations* (1835) suggested women's equal capacity in the workplace, and *An Appeal in Favor of that Class of Americans*

Called Africans (1833) was particularly influential for the abolitionist cause. She published several novels, including *Hobomok* (1824), describing the conflict between the Puritans and Native American tribes in the Massachusetts Bay Colony, *The Rebels* (1825), a romance set during the American revolution, *Philothea* (1836), set in Ancient Greece at the time of Pericles, and *A Romance of the Republic* (1867), a 19th-century story which dramatized her anti-slavery convictions.

▷ W S Osborne, *Lydia Maria Child* (1980)

CHILDERS, (Robert) Erskine
(1870–1922)

Anglo-Irish writer and nationalist, born in London. Educated at Haileybury and Trinity College, Cambridge, he was a clerk in the House of Commons from 1895 to 1910. He served as a volunteer in the 2nd Boer War (1899–1902). A skilled yachtsman, in 1903 he wrote a popular spy novel about a German invasion of Britain, called *The Riddle of the Sands*. In 1910 he devoted himself to working for Irish Home Rule, and used his yacht, the 'Asgard', to bring German arms to the Irish volunteers in 1914. Nonetheless he served in the Royal Navy in World War I. In 1921 he became a Sinn Fein member of the Irish parliament for County Widelow and Minister for Propaganda. He opposed the treaty that established the Irish Free State, joined the IRA, but was captured by the Free State authorities and executed. One of his sons, Erskine Hamilton Childers (1905–74), became the 4th President (1973–4).

▷ A F B Williams, *Erskine Childers: 1870–1922* (1926)

CHIVERS, Thomas Holley
(1807/9–1858)

American poet, mystic and dramatist who finally became mad, but was reckoned by himself and some others as a potent influence on **Poe**, with whom he carried on a running quarrel over mutual charges of plagiarism. He was the son of a wealthy Georgian plantation owner. His biographer said that he possessed 'great genius but no talent', and that was, indeed, his unhappy fate. His most solid achievement was the invention of a machine which shredded fibre from silkworm cocoons. His poems, in one of which he compares his heart to a broken egg, are laughable and yet, in their aspirations, deeply touching. His chief philosophical work was *Search After Truth: or, A New Revelation of the Psycho-Physiological Nature of Man* (1848).

▷ S F Damon, *Thomas Holley Chivers: Friend of Poe* (1930)

CHOCANO, José Santos
(1875–1934)

Grandiloquent Peruvian poet, bigamist and murderer, supporter of Pancho Villa and then advisor to and apologist for the Guatemalan dictator Estrada Cabrera (the president of the *El presidente* of **Asturias**), almost executed on the latter's downfall, and finally assassinated on a Santiago tram by a madman. He spent the years 1925–7 in prison in his own country, for murdering a young critic, Edwin Elmore, who had failed to agree with him—and then left Peru in disgrace. Yet Chocano, born in Lima, was a gifted poet, whose achievement has been hailed by many—and who may have influenced **Neruda**. Though not a *modernista* poet, he introduced—as an arch opportunist—*modernismo* to Peru, and at one point his reputation rivalled that of **Darío** himself. At his best, as in *Oro de indias* (1940, 'Gold of the Indies'), Chocano is a genuinely autochthonous poet, with full sympathy for the Native Americans, who helped turn Latin-American poetry away from European models and towards its mysterious interior. Some of his poems are translated in *Spirit of the Andes* (1935), and in the *Penguin Book of Latin American Verse* (1971, ed E Curacciolo-Trejo).

▷ L A Sanchéz, *Aladino* (1960)

CHODOROV, Edward
(1904–)

American stage manager, dramatist and director, brother of **Jerome Chodorov**. His first play, *Wonder Boy* (1931), written with Arthur Barton (1904–36), satirized Hollywood. *Kind Lady* (1934) was a memorable chiller about a woman kidnapped in her own home by macabre villains.

CHODOROV, Jerome
(1911–)

American playwright and screenwriter, born in New York, brother of **Edward Chodorov**. Although Chodorov was a prolific and efficient author of light comedies on his own account, writing such plays as *Three Bags Full* (1966) and *A Community of Two* (1974), and such screenplays as *Two Girls on Broadway* (1939) and *Happy Anniversary* (1959), he is mainly known for his collaborations with Joseph Fields. These include *Anniversary Waltz* (1954). Their most famous collaboration, and the work for which Chodorov will probably be best remembered, is their adaptation of their own play, *My Sister Eileen* (1940), as the book for the musical, *Wonderful Town*, for which the score was composed by Leonard Bernstein. He also successfully adapted **Eudora Welty**'s *The Ponder Heart* (1956) for the stage.

CHOPIN, Katherine ('Kate'), née O'Flaherty
(1851–1904)

American novelist, short-story writer and poet, born in St Louis, Missouri, The daughter of an Irish immigrant and a French–Creole mother, she was well educated at the Sacred Heart convent, made her 'debut' in society and married Oscar Chopin, a Creole cotton trader from Louisiana. It was a happy marriage, scarred only by business failure. After her husband died of swamp fever (1882) she returned with their six children to St Louis where she began to compose sketches of her life in 'Old Natachitoches', such as *Bayou Folk* (1894) and *A Night in Acadie* (1897). This work gives no indication of the furore she aroused with the publication of a realistic novel of sexual passion, *The Awakening* (1899), which was harshly condemned by the public. Thereafter she wrote only a few poems and short stories. Interest in her work was revived by **Edmund Wilson**, and she has since been embraced by feminists as a *fin de siècle* iconoclast bravely articulating the plight of the 'lost' woman.
▷P Seyersted, *Kate Chopin, a critical biography* (1969)

CHOQUETTE, Robert
(1905–)

French–Canadian poet and novelist, born in the USA. **A J M Smith** has spoken of his 'boldness' and 'ability to create on a large scale': he cultivated, Smith suggested, a poetry 'that was to be at once national and filled with energy and thought'. Choquette has written much for radio and television. His chief mentor is **Hugo**, and in *Suite marine* (1953), an immense poem about the sea, he has created what Smith called 'a long and beautifully sustained poem'. *La Pension Leblanc* is the best of his novels.
▷A J M Smith, *The Oxford Book of Canadian Verse* (1960)

CHORELL, Walentin
(1912–)

Versatile Finland–Swedish dramatist and novelist, who has written all kinds of plays, from farces to high tragedies. They are often performed throughout Scandinavia and Germany. His *Madame* (1952) deals with the fantasies of a retired prima donna; the impressive *Gräset* (1958) treats the theme of incest.

CHOROMÁNSKI, Michał
(1904–72)

Polish novelist who was born and brought up in Russia, and lived there for the first 20 years of his life. He started as a translator of Polish works into Russian, and also put much Russian poetry into Polish. His best novels, highly anticipatory of modernist techniques (as is much Polish writing), are his earlier ones, chief of which is *Zazdość i medycyna* (1932, Eng trans *Jealousy and Medicine*, 1946), about a surgeon who relieves himself of his jealousies in the course of a phantasmal operation.

CHRÉTIEN DE TROYES
(d.c.1183)

French poet and troubadour, born in Troyes, in Champagne, and author of the earliest romances dealing with the King Arthur legend. The greatest of the French medieval poets, he was a member of the court of the Countess Marie de Champagne, daughter of Louis VII, and to whom he dedicated his metrical romance of courtly love, *Yvain et Lancelot*. His other romances were *Érec et Énide* (c.1160), *Cligès* (c.1164), and the unfinished *Perceval, ou Le Conte du Graal* (c.1180, 'Percival, or the Story of the Holy Grail'). His works enjoyed huge popularity throughout medieval Europe.
▷U T Holmes, *Chrétien de Troyes* (1970)

CHRISTENSEN, Inger
(1935–)

Danish poet, novelist and essayist. Born in Vejle, she trained as a teacher, and had her first book of poetry published in 1962. Her modernist texts locate the individual within structures that he or she simultaneously creates and is created by; her use of language and form highlight the inclusion of her own works in this process. The novel *Evighedsmaskinen* (1964, 'The Eternity Machine') is a modern version of the story of Christ, while her second novel, *Azorno* (1967), employs an elaborate series of experiments to explore the borderline between fiction and reality. *Det* (1969, 'It') is a book of poetry which has been characterized as a poetic drama. The magnificent poetic structure of *Alfabet* (1981, 'Alphabet') focuses on creativity and annihilation, adding a prominent ecological dimension. She was elected a member of the Danish Academy in 1978.
▷I Holk (ed), *Tegnverden. En bog om Inger Christensens forfatterskab* (1983)

CHRISTIANSEN, Sigurd Wesley
(1891–1947)

Norwegian novelist and dramatist. His first book was published in 1915, but his great breakthrough came in 1931 with the novel *To levende og en død* (Eng trans *Two Living and One Dead*, 1932), first prize-winner in an important Scandinavian competition. This novel, easier than most of his other works,

focuses on the ethical values recurrent in all Christiansen's writing. Although he is not an overtly Christian author, his typical themes, such as freedom versus responsibility and guilt, are often linked to Christian ethics. Intensive soul-searching for motives behind our actions is a hallmark of what is regarded as his greatest work, the trilogy *Drømmen og livet* (1935, 'Dream and Life'), *Det ensomme hjertet* (1939, 'The Lonely Heart') and *Menneskenes lodd* (1945, 'Man's Destiny'), dating from 1935 to 1945.
▷ E Kielland, *Sigurd Christiansen i liv og diktning* (1952)

CHRISTIE, Dame Agatha Mary Clarissa,
née **Miller**
(1890–1976)

English author, born in Torquay. Under the surname of her first husband (Colonel Christie, divorced 1928), she wrote more than 70 classic detective novels, featuring the Belgian detective, Hercule Poirot, or the village spinster, Miss Jane Marple. In 1930 she married Sir Max Mallowan (1904–1978), the noted archaeologist. Between December 1953 and January 1954, she achieved three concurrent West End productions, *The Spider's Web*, *Witness for the Prosecution* and *The Mousetrap*, which continued its record-breaking run into the 1990s. Her best-known novels are *The Mysterious Affair at Styles* (1920), first featuring the Belgian detective Poirot; *The Murder of Roger Ackroyd* (1926); *Murder at the Vicarage* (1930), introducing Miss Marple; *Murder on the Orient Express* (1934); *Death on the Nile* (1937); *And Then There Were Nine* (1941) and *Curtain* (1975), in which Poirot met his end. She also wrote under the pen-name 'Mary Westmacott'.
▷ R Barnard, *A Talent to Deceive* (1975)

CHRISTINE DE PISAN
(c.1364–1431)

French poet, born in Venice. She was daughter of an Italian who was court astrologer to Charles V. Brought up in Paris, in 1378 she married Étienne Castel, who became the king's secretary, but died in 1389. Left with three children and no money, she was obliged to call upon her literary talents and between 1399 and 1415 produced a number of brilliant works in both prose and verse, including a biography of Charles V for Philippe, Duke of Burgundy; *Cité des dames* ('City of Women'), a translation from **Boccaccio**; and *Livres des trois vertus* ('Books of the Three Virtues'), an educational and social compendium for women. Her love poems have grace and charm, but lack depth. Christine is noteworthy for her defence of the female sex, hitherto a target for satirists. Saddened by the misfortunes of the Hundred Years War she withdrew to a nunnery in about 1418 but lived to write in celebration of Joan of Arc's early successes in 1429.
▷ E M D Robineau, *Christine de Pisan. Sa vie, ses oeuvres* (1883)

CHRISTOPHER, John, pseud of **Samuel Youd**
(1922–)

English novelist and science-fiction writer, born in Knowseley, Cheshire. A hugely prolific writer, he has published a few novels, including his first, *The Winter Swan* (1949), under his real name. He has since emerged under several pseudonyms, including Peter Nichols, Peter Graaf, William Godfrey and Hilary Ford. He is best known as John Christopher, writing science fiction for adults and children. *No Blade of Grass* (1956) is a particularly highly regarded adult novel of fantasy. For young people, *The Tripods Trilogy* (1967–8) imagines that the consequences of an alien invasion and domination of Earth might be an imposed feudal society; *The Sword Trilogy* (1970–2) suggests that a series of natural disasters might precipitate a similar outcome, while *The Fireball Trilogy* (1981–6), considers a Europe governed by the Roman Empire.

CHUDLEIGH, Lady Mary, née **Lee**
(1656–1710)

English poet and essayist, born in Winslade, Devon. In 1674 she married George Chudleigh, who became baronet in 1691. Though confined to what she called the 'rough and unpolished life' of Devon, she read widely and corresponded with other writers. The influence of the feminist, Mary Astell, is apparent in her best-known work, *The Ladies Defence* (1701), a spirited verse-debate exposing male prejudices and the deficiencies of female education. She also published *Poems on Several Occasions* (1703) and *Essays upon Several Subjects in Verse and Prose* (1710).
▷ M Ferguson, (ed), *First Feminists: British Women Writers 1578–1799* (1985)

CHUKOVSKY, Korney, pseud of **Nikolay Vasilyevich Korneychuk**
(1882–1969)

Russian translator (**Whitman, Defoe, Dickens** and many others), critic and children's writer, born in St Petersburg. As a young man he lived in London, where he picked up an extensive knowledge and understanding of English literature. He was the leading editor and critic of **Nekrasov**.

CHUMACERO, Ali
(1918–)

Minor Mexican poet of a highly intellectual cast. One of his most impressive poems, 'Losa del Desconocido' ('Gravestone of an Unknown Man'), is translated in J M Cohen (ed), the *Penguin Book of Spanish Verse* (1956).

▷ R Xirau, *Poetas de México y España* (1962)

CHURCH, Richard
(1893–1972)

English novelist, poet and essayist, born in London. Until the age of 40 he financed his writing by working as a civil servant. This and subsequent periods of his life form the subject of his two autobiographical volumes, *Over the Bridge* (1955) and *The Golden Sovereign* (1957). *The Porch* (1937) was among the best received of his novels, and won the Femina Vie-Heureuse Prize. He also wrote for children. His poetry, as represented in *Collected Poems* (1948), is well disciplined and restrained in both form and content. Applauded as a polished craftsman in a more genteel era, he is wholly out of favour in our own age, in which the absence of rough edges appears to be regarded by some with suspicion and disdain.

CHURCHILL, Caryl
(1938–)

English dramatist. Her first play was *Light Shining* (1976), about the Levellers. Her greatest commercial success has been *Serious Money* (1987), satirizing the world of the young, get-rich-quick City financial brokers. Other plays include *Cloud Nine* (1979), *Top Girls* (1982), *Fen* (1983) and *Softcops* (1984), all of greater dramatic quality than *Serious Money*.

CHURCHILL, Charles
(1731–64)

English satirical poet, born in Westminster, the son of a curate. He was educated at Westminster School and went on to John's College, Cambridge, but ruined his academic career with a clandestine marriage at the age of 17. With his father's help he was ordained priest in 1756, and at his father's death in 1758 succeeded him as curate of St John's, Westminster. But after a bankruptcy, a formal separation from his wife and a course of unclerical dissipation, he gave up the church (1763). His *Rosciad* (1761) had already made him famous and a terror to actors. *The Apology* (also 1761) was a savage onslaught on his critics, particularly **Tobias Smollett**. In *Night* (1762) he lengthily replied to criticisms of his life. *The Ghost* (1762) ridiculed **Dr Johnson** and others in over 4000 lines. He next helped John Wilkes in the *North Briton*, and heaped ridicule upon the Scots in *The Prophecy of Famine* (1763), an admirable satire. For *The Epistle to Hogarth* (1763) the artist retaliated

with a savage caricature. Other works include *The Candidate* (1764), *Independence* (1794), and, unfinished, *The Journey* and the masterly *Dedication*. He died suddenly on a visit to Wilkes in France. He lacked the chief essential of true satire, a real insight into the heart of man, but possessed volubility in rhyming, boisterous energy, and an instinctive hatred of wrong.

▷ W C Brown, *Poet, rake and rebel* (1953)

CHURCHILL, Sir Winston
(1875–1965)

British statesman and writer, born in Blenheim Palace, and awarded the Nobel Prize for literature. This was grossly out of proportion to his merits as a writer, but, like **Caesar**, he was one of the select few soldier-statesmen who have had the gift of the written gab, although his finest efforts are the radio speeches he gave to the British people during the war with Hitler. His novel *Savrola* (1900) is of no account, but *Marlborough* (1933–8), written while he was out of office and the Nazis were being appeased by his party, is a valuable biography. His history of World War II, in six volumes (1948–54), is his best single work, written as it is from the inside.

CHURCHILL, Winston
(1871–1947)

American historical novelist, born in St Louis, Missouri. His works include *Richard Carvel* (1899) and *The Crisis* (1901), and show a significant insight into the workings of political life which Churchill knew at first hand as New Hampshire delegate to the Republican National Convention (1904) and Progressive Party candidate for governorship (1912).

▷ R W Schneider, *The Life and Thought of Churchill* (1976)

CHURCHYARD, Thomas
(1520–1604)

English soldier of fortune and writer, born in Shrewsbury. He served in Scotland, Ireland and the Low Countries under the Earl of Surrey and published many verse and prose pieces, the best-known being *The Legend of Shore's Wife* (1563, in *A Mirror for Magistrates*), and *Worthiness of Wales* (1587).

CHUTE, Anthony
(d.?1595)

Elizabethan poet, author of *Beawtie Dishonoured* (1593), largely plagiarized from **Thomas Churchyard**'s *Legend of Shore's Wife*. He was patronized by **Gabriel Harvey** and assailed by **Thomas Nashe** the satirist.

CIARDI, John

CIARDI, John
(1916–85)

American poet, translator (his version of the Divine Comedy of **Dante**, 1954–61, is one of the most highly esteemed of its time—'a shining deed in a bad age'), teacher and editor (of the poetry in the *Saturday Review*), born in Boston. Influenced mostly by **Yeats** in his own poetry, he aimed to steer a course between the 'Baroque' and ordinary 'poesy', being most successful in his lighter, colloquial vein.

▷ *As If, Poems New and Selected* (1955)

CICERO, Marcus Tullius
(106–43 BC)

Roman orator, statesman, and writer, born in Arpinum in Latium, of a wealthy family. At Rome he studied law and oratory, Greek philosophy, and Greek literature. He saw military service in the war of 90–88 BC under Pompeius Strabo, the father of Pompey the Great. His first important speech, in his twenty-sixth year, was the successful defence of a client against a favourite of the dictator Sulla. After a two-year stay in Athens and Rhodes, he was elected quaestor (76), and obtained an appointment in Sicily; at the request of the Sicilians he undertook his successful impeachment of the corrupt governor Gaius Verres in 70. In 63 he was consul, and foiled the plot of Catiline by carrying out the Senate's order to execute five of the conspirators. Hailed as 'father of his country' Cicero was for a brief space the great man of the day, but the tide soon turned. Faced with prosecution for the summary execution of the conspirators, he was condemned to exile. Though recalled in 57, he was no longer a power in politics, where the overriding question was the mounting rivalry between Pompey and **Caesar**. On the outbreak of the Civil War he joined Pompey's army in Greece, but after the defeat at Pharsalus (48) threw himself on Caesar's mercy. In 46–44 he wrote most of his chief works on rhetoric and philosophy, living in retirement and brooding over his disappointments. In 43, after Caesar's death, his famous speeches against Mark Antony, the *Philippics*, were delivered, and cost him his life. As soon as Antony, Octavian and Lepidus had leagued themselves in the triumvirate, they proscribed their enemies, and Cicero's name was on the fatal list. Old and feeble, he fled to his villa at Formiae, pursued by the soldiers of Antony, and was overtaken as he was being carried in a litter. With calm courage he put his head out of the litter and bade the murderers strike. He was in his sixty-fourth year. As orator and pleader Cicero stands in the first rank; of his speeches the most famous are those against Verres and Catiline. As a politician, though in the end defeated, he was one of the outstanding figures of the late Republic. He is best remembered as an essayist and letter-writer, especially for his essays *De Senectute* ('On Old Age') and *De Amicitia* ('On Friendship'). His voluminous correspondence is one of the principal sources of knowledge of the politics of his time, and his prose style was a model for the orators of the next four centuries.

▷ D Stockton, *Cicero: a political biography* (1971)

CICOGNANI, Bruno
(1879–1972)

Italian novelist, story writer and playwright, born in Florence into a family with literary connections (**Carducci**, **D'Annunzio**). He began in the high-romantic, decadent manner of D'Annunzio, but developed his own style in his psychological novels of Florentine life, in which he excelled in the portrayal of female characters: *La Velia* (1922) and *Villa Beatrice* (1931) are typically rich, precise masterpieces. His autobiographical works are often taken to be even better than these two novels; *L'omino che a spento i fochi* (1937, 'The Little Man Who Has Put Out the Fires') recollects his youth. His most successful play was *Yo, el rey* (1949, 'I, the King').

CISNEROS, Sandra
(1954–)

Mexican–American novelist and short-story writer, born and brought up 'rat poor' in Chicago. She was educated at Iowa University before returning home to work as an educator and arts administrator in the Latino community. In 1984 she published *The House on Mango Street*, a series of stories linked through the consciousness of a young girl. This was followed by a poetry collection, *My Wicked Ways* (1987), and another short-story collection, *Woman Hollering Creek* (1991). The foremost talent in a new wave of US Latina authors, her writing conveys the sensory textures of Chicano life with precise, prismatic brilliance, her polyphonic style capturing the *barrio*'s many diverse voices with vibrant immediacy.

CLARE, John
(1793–1864)

English peasant poet, born in Helpstone, near Peterborough, the son of a poor labourer. Though almost without schooling, he studied **James Thomson**'s *Seasons*, and began to cultivate verse writing as well as gardening. After serving in the Northamptonshire militia (1812–14), in 1817 he published *Proposals for Publishing a Collection of Trifles in Verse* at his own expense, but got no subscribers. It led, however, to the publication of his *Poems*

Descriptive of Rural Life (1820), which had a good reception; but though the Marquis of Exeter and other patrons secured him £45 a year, he continued to live in poverty, and went insane. His other published works were *Village Minstrel* (1821), *The Shepherd's Calendar* (1827) and *Rural Muse* (1835). He was committed to an asylum in Epping in 1837, and later in Northampton in 1841, where he died.
▷ J W Tibble and A Tibble, *John Clare: a life* (1972)

CLARETIE, Jules, properly **Arsène Arnaud** (1840–1913)
French novelist, born in Limoges. While a schoolboy in Paris he published a novel, and soon became a leading critic and political writer. His short story *Pierrille* (1863) was praised by **George Sand**. His novels also were generally popular. During the Franco–German war he sent a series of remarkable letters to the *Rappel* and *Opinion nationale*, and acquired the materials for a later series of bright and vigorous anti-German books of a historical character. He first made a hit on the stage with his Revolution plays, *Les Muscadins* (1874), *Le Régiment de Champagne* (1877) and *Les Mirabeau* (1878); in 1885 he became director of the Comédie Française.
▷ G de Cherville, *Jules Claretie* (1883, in French)

CLARÍN, pseud of **Leopoldo Alas y Ureña** (1852–1901)
Spanish novelist, critic and short-story writer, born in Zamora. In his teens he moved to Oviedo, where he studied law, eventually (1883) becoming a professor. His criticism, although lapsing on occasion into legalistic prolixity, brought a much-needed rigour to the Spanish literary scene of the late 19th century. Short-story volumes such as *Cuentos Morales* (1896, 'Moral Tales') display his mature style—more relaxed and less verbose—to best advantage. In the English-speaking world he is now known almost exclusively as the author of *La Regenta* (1884), an epic account, influenced by *Madame Bovary*, of the suffocating effect of small-city life on an intelligent, frustrated young woman.

CLARK, Charles Manning Hope (1915–91)
Australian historian and writer, born in Burwood, New South Wales, the son of a vicar. Educated at Melbourne and Oxford universities, in 1949 he became the first Professor of Australian History at the Australian National University, where he popularized the study of Australian history with his collections *Select Documents in Australian History* (1950–5) and *Sources of Australian History* (1957). Clark was never far from the centre of controversy on political issues, and his strong republican views colour his six-volume *A History of Australia* (1962–88). Although criticized by academics, it remains a considerable achievement and was successfully abridged into one volume by Michael Cathcart in 1993. His partly autobiographical fiction *Disquiet and Other Stories* (1969) was republished with additional material as *Manning Clark: Collected Short Stories* in 1986. He also wrote a contentious biographical essay *In Search of Henry Lawson* (1978). The first volume of a projected autobiography, *The Puzzles of Childhood*, was published in 1989, followed in 1990 by *The Quest for Grace*, a very personal odyssey 'in search of the unknowable'.

CLARK, Eleanor (1913–)
American novelist, non-fiction and short-story writer, born in Los Angeles, California and educated at Vassar College. She worked for a publishing firm and the US Office of Strategic Services before devoting herself to writing. She has twice received a Guggenheim Fellowship. In the 24 years between *The Bitter Box* (1946), her first novel, and *Baldur's Gate* (1970), her second, Clark wrote essays and longer non-fiction work, dominated by the themes of tradition, ecology, and the quest for values; *The Oysters of Locmariaquer* won the National Book Award for Non-Fiction in 1965. She has also published a collection of short stories and a children's book.
▷ Eleanor Clark issue of *The New England Review* (Winter 1979)

CLARK, John Pepper (1935–)
Nigerian poet, playwright and critic who, since his collection *State of the Union* (1985), has signed himself J P Clark Bekederemo. In 1964 he published an angry attack upon the America he knew, *Their America*; his Parvin Scholarship at Princeton was terminated on account of it. His lyrical poetry has been called over-diffuse even by his admirers, but plays, such as *Song of a Goat* (1961), have received more praise. His selected poems are in *A Decade of Tongues* (1981).
▷ R M Wren, *John Pepper Clark* (1984)

CLARK, Mavis Thorpe (?1912–)
Australian writer of books for older children, born in Melbourne. Educated at the Methodist Ladies College there, she attracted attention with *The Brown Land was Green* (1956),

the story of a pioneer family, which became a long-running serial on ABC radio, as did *Gully of Gold* (1958) and *They Came South* (1963). *The Min-Min* (1967) was Australian Children's Book of the Year. Australian settings are also prominent in such novels as *Spark of Opal* (1968) and *Iron Mountain* (1970). Later titles include *Young and Brave* (1984), *No Mean Destiny* (1986) and *Soft Shoe* (1988). She has also written a biography of *John Batman* (1962), the founder of Melbourne, and *Paster Doug* (1965), the autobiography of Sir Douglas Nicholls, the first aborigine to be knighted and to become a state governor.

CLARK, Walter van Tilburg
(1909–71)

American novelist and short-story writer. Born in East Orland, Maine, he moved to Nevada in childhood and was educated there before returning to New England. While teaching English (and basketball) at Cazenovia High School in New York City, he wrote his first and best novel, *The Ox-Bow Incident* (1940), a tense Western with an unmistakable allegorical subtext about the rise of fascism. Clark's belief that liberalism is powerless in the face of mob violence and charismatic leadership anticipates the themes of **Mailer**'s post-war *The Naked and the Dead*. Clark's next novel, *The City of Trembling Leaves* (1945, republished as *Tim Hazard*, 1951), was a disappointment, but his skill returned with *The Track of the Cat* (1949), a **Faulkner**-influenced account of a panther hunt, with an obsessive psychological undercurrent. Clark's short stories were collected in *The Watchful Gods* (1950), after which he published nothing more.
▷M Westbrook, *Walter van Tilburg Clark* (1969)

CLARKE, Arthur C(harles)
(1917–)

English writer of science fiction, born in Minehead, Somerset. He worked in scientific research before turning to fiction: he was a radar instructor in World War II, and originated the idea of satellite communication in a scientific article in 1945. A prolific writer and an unashamed entertainer, his themes are exploration—in both the near and distant future—and man's position in the hierarchy of the universe. His first book was *Prelude to Space* (1951) and while he is credited with some of the genre's best examples—*Rendezvous with Rama* (1973), *The Fountains of Paradise* (1979)—his name will always be associated first with *2001: A Space Odyssey* (1968), which, under the direction of Stanley Kubrick, became a highly successful film. He emigrated to Sri Lanka in the 1950s.

CLARKE, Austin
(1896–1974)

Irish poet and dramatist, born in Dublin where he was educated at the Jesuit Belvedere College and University College. He spent 15 years in England as a book reviewer and journalist before returning to Dublin in 1937. *The Vengeance of Fionn*, the first of 18 books of verse, was published in 1917. Like other earlier verse, it is markedly influenced by **W B Yeats** and his obsession with Irish mythology, but he shook this off and developed into a technically accomplished poet, sharply satirical, and critical, of Irish attitudes. *Collected Poems* was published in 1974. He was also a noted playwright and an adherent of verse drama which he promoted through the Dublin Verse-Speaking Society which he formed in 1941. His plays, drawing heavily on Irish legend, were collected in 1963. His first novel, *The Bright Temptation* (1932), was banned in Ireland until 1954. *Twice Round the Black Church* (1962) and *A Penny in the Clouds* (1968) are autobiographical.

CLARKE, Gillian
(1937–)

Welsh poet, born in Cardiff and educated at the city's University College. Her earliest collections of poems, *Snow on the Mountain* (1971) and *Sundial* (1978), were followed by the more widely-read *Letter from a Far Country* (1982). *Selected Poems* followed in 1985, then *Letting in the Rumour* (1989). She was editor of *The Anglo-Welsh Review* from 1976 to 1984, and since 1987 has been Chair of the Welsh Academy.

CLARKE, Marcus
(1846–81)

Australian novelist, born and educated in London. Collapse of the family fortunes having sent him to Australia where relatives had held high office, he contributed to the Melbourne press while working first as a bank clerk and then on sheep stations. As with many of his books, his first novel, *Long Odds* (1860), began life as a serial. He visited Tasmania to study its convict past; the subsequent articles were worked up into *Old Tales of a Young Country* (1871), and formed the basis for his best-known book, *His Natural Life* (1874, rev edn as *For the Term of His Natural Life*, 1882, under which title it was filmed and is now best known). Further financial problems were abated by his writing for the stage and contributing on various topics to newspapers and journals. He died destitute; most of his ephemeral work was subsequently collected in *The Selected Works of Marcus Clarke* (1890), and three books of

Australian tales published in 1896–7.
▷B Elliott, *Marcus Clarke* (1958)

CLARKE, Thomas Ernest Bennett
(1907–89)

English screenwriter and novelist, born in Watford, Hertfordshire. A graduate in law from Cambridge University, he lived in Australia and Argentina before returning to England, working as a reporter for the *Daily Sketch* and writing a series of novels, including *Go South—Go West* (1932) and *Cartwright Was A Cad* (1937). The wartime drama *For Those In Peril* (1944) marked his first work for the screen and he soon became one of the key creative figures at Ealing Studios, writing across a range of genres and creating a series of films that reflected the traditional English character with whimsical humour and affection. His best-known credits include *Hue and Cry* (1946), *Passport To Pimlico* (1948), *The Blue Lamp* (1949) and *The Lavender Hill Mob* (1951), for which he received an Oscar. His work away from Ealing was less distinctive, although he provided a notable adaptation of **D H Lawrence**'s *Sons and Lovers* (1960) for the cinema.
▷*This Is Where I Came In* (1974)

CLAUDEL, Paul
(1868–1955)

French poet, essayist and dramatist, born in Villeneuve-sur-Fère. Now regarded as one of the major figures in French Catholic literature, it was long before he was recognized, even by his countrymen. He joined the diplomatic service and held posts in many parts of the world. This experience, with the early influence of the Symbolists, adds quality and richness to his work. His dramas, of which the most celebrated are *L'Annonce faite à Marie* (1892, 'The Annunciation'), *Partage de Midi* (1905, Eng trans *Break of Noon*, 1960), *L'Otage* (1909, Eng trans *The Hostage*, 1917) and *Le Soulier de satin* (1921, Eng trans *The Satin Slipper*, 1931), have a Wagnerian grandeur and, in many cases, an anti-Protestant violence that make them too strong for popular taste. He wrote memorable poetry—*Cinq Grandes Odes* (1910, Eng trans *Five Great Odes*, 1967) and *Corona benignitatis anni dei* (1915, Eng trans *Coronal*, 1943)—and the libretti for two operas: *Jeanne d'Arc au bûcher* (1943, 'Joan of Arc at the Stake') by Honegger and *Christophe Colomb* (1929, Eng trans *Christopher Columbus*, 1930) by Milhaud. His later writings were mainly devoted to biblical exegesis.
▷H A Waters, *Paul Claudel* (1970)

CLAUDIAN (Claudius Claudianus)
(4th–5th century)

The last of the great Latin poets. He came from Alexandria to Rome in AD 395, and obtained patrician dignity by favour of Stilicho, whose fall (408) he seems not to have long survived. A pagan, he wrote first in Greek, though he was of Roman extraction. Several epic poems by him, including *The Rape of Proserpine*, panegyrics on Honorius, Stilicho and others, invectives against Rufinus and Eutropius, occasional poems, and a Greek fragment, *Gigantomachia*, are still extant.
▷J H E Crews, *Claudian as Historical Authority* (1908)

CLAUDIUS, Matthias
(1740–1815)

German poet and editor (of the *Der Wandsbecker Bote*, a local newspaper), born in Reinfeld, into the family of a pastor. He studied law and theology at Jena. He is often called the father of popular (serious) German journalism, and is famous for his euphemism for death: 'Freund Hein'. The part of his poetry that is not falsely hearty is perhaps as good as uninspired poetry can be: pastoral, simple, good-hearted.
▷I Rüttenhauer, *M. Claudius* (1952, in German)

CLAUS, Hugo Maurice Julien
(1929–)

Belgian dramatist, fiction writer, poet, and film-maker, writing in Dutch. He was born in Bruges and worked as a farm labourer, house painter and actor before turning to full-time writing. His essential subject is the conflict of the natural world with abstract reason. This is evident in his fine first novel *De metsiers* (1950, published in the USA as *The Duck Hunt*, 1965, in the UK as *Sister of Earth*, 1966), one of only a few of his works known in English, and also in the brilliant play *De dans vande reiger* (1962, 'The Heron's Dance', later adapted as a screenplay, 1966). His most remarkable poem is the long *Het teken van de hamster* (1979, 'At the Sign of the Hamster'). Claus wrote the libretto for the collaborative opera *Reconstructie* (1969), composed by Louis Andriessen, Reinbert de Leeuw, Misha Mengelberg, Peter Schat, and Jan van Vlijmen. He has won the Belgian State Prize for drama three times (1955, 1967, 1973) and for poetry (1971).
▷B Kooijman, *Hugo Claus* (1973)

CLAUSSEN, Sophus Niels Christen
(1865–1931)

Danish poet, born in Heletoft, the son of a farmer and rural politician. He gave up law to concentrate on journalism and writing and lived for many years in France, where he came

into contact with the symbolists, later translating **Baudelaire**, as well as **Heine** and **Shelley**. His best-known poem, 'Rejseminder' ('Recollections of a Journey'), establishes the characteristic tone of erotic reverie which runs through *Naturbørn* (1887, 'Children of Nature'), his first book. Later works were less realistic in detail and the poems in *Djaevlerier* (1904, 'Demonism') are overtly Symbolist and psychological. His complete works were published in seven volumes in 1910.
▷ E Frandsen, *Sophus Claussen* (1950)

CLAVELL, James du Maresq
(1924–)

Australian-born American novelist, film producer and director, born in Sydney. Now based in New York, his work in film includes scripting the epic war movies *The Great Escape* (1960, from the book by **Paul Brickhill**) and *633 Squadron* (1963). He served during World War II and was a prisoner-of-war in Changi Jail, Singapore. The clash of East and West runs through his Asian Saga, which covers three and a half centuries, beginning in the year 1600 with *Shogun* (1975), *Tai-Pan* (1966) and *Gai-Jin* (1983). *King Rat* (1962), *Noble House* (1980) and *Whirlwind* (1986) bring the story up to the year 1979. Clavell has also published an edition of Sun Tzu's 4th-century BC classic, *The Art of War*.

CLAYTON, Richard Henry Michael *see* HAGGARD, William

CLEARY, Jon Stephen
(1917–)

Australian novelist, born in Sydney, who served in the Middle East and New Guinea during World War II. His first book after the war was a collection of short stories, *These Small Glories* (1946). This was followed by *You Can't See Round Corners* (1947), which had won a newspaper competition the year before, the story of deserter and small-time crook Frankie McCoy and his descent into murder in wartime Sydney. *The Sundowners* (1952), set in the depressed Australia of the 1920s, was his first big success, and was followed by over 40 novels, of which some of the best known are *The Climate of Courage* (1954, filmed as *Naked in the Night*, 1963), *The Commissioner* (1966, filmed as *Nobody Runs Forever*, 1968) and *High Road to China* (1977, filmed 1982). Cleary's well-constructed plots and detailed research of settings lend themselves admirably to the large screen. In *The High Commissioner* Cleary introduced the character of Scobie Malone, a hybrid from **Dashiell Hammett**'s Sam Spade school, who returns in five other books including *Helga's Web* (1970, filmed as *Scobie Malone*, 1975) and *Babylon South* (1989).

CLELAND, John
(1709–89)

English novelist, born in London. He was educated at Westminster School, and after a spell in the consular service and in the East India Company, followed by vagrant travel in Europe, he published in 1750 a pornographic novel, *Fanny Hill, or the Memoirs of a Woman of Pleasure*, a bestseller in its time which achieved a second *succès de scandale* on its revival and subsequent prosecution under the Obscene Publications Act in 1963. He also wrote *Memoirs of a Coxcomb* (1751), and *The Surprises of Love* (1764).
▷ W H Epstein, *John Cleland: images of a life* (1974)

CLEMO, (Reginald) Jack (John)
(1916–91)

English poet, born in St Austell, Cornwall. The earlier poems, collected in *The Clay Verge* (1951) and *The Map of Clay* (1961), are largely descriptive of the Cornish clay-mining landscape. After he lost his sight in 1955, his work increasingly involved itself with an inner vision of sacramental love and suffering. Clemo pointed to the influence of **Francis Thompson** and **D H Lawrence**, but his rejection of bland nature mysticism and his preoccupation with original sin set him apart from the English Romantics. Nothing made a more immediate impact on his verse than the gospel rhythms of American evangelists like Billy Graham. With *The Echoing Tip* (1971), which followed his marriage, the sexual element in his verse becomes less prominent and in *Broad Autumn* (1975) he develops a more abstract and philosophical vision. The term is appropriate because Clemo always rejected interpretations based solely on his physical handicap.
▷ *Confession of a Rebel* (1949); *The Marriage of a Rebel: A Mystical Erotic Quest* (1980)

CLEVELAND, John
(1613–58)

English Cavalier poet, born in Loughborough, Leicestershire, son of a poor clergyman who was ousted by parliament from the living of Hinckley in 1645. In 1627 he entered Christ's College, Cambridge, graduated BA four years later, and then moved to St John's College, where he was elected to a fellowship in 1634 and lived nine years as 'the delight and ornament of the society'. He vigorously opposed Cromwell's election to the Long Parliament for Cambridge, and was for his loyalty himself ejected from his fellowship in 1645. He joined the Royalist army, and was appointed judge advocate at Newark, but was obliged to surrender with the garrison. In 1655 he was arrested at Norwich, but was released by Cromwell, who could admire the courageous manliness of the poor poet's letter addressed to him. In 1656 he published a volume containing 36 poems—elegies on Charles I, Strafford, Laud and Edward King, and also some stinging satires. Cleveland now went to live at Gray's Inn, where he died. In 1677 was published, with a short Life, *Clievelandi Vindiciae*. Extremely popular as a poet in his day, he is little read now.

▷B Morris, *John Cleveland, 1613–1658: a bibliography* (1967)

CLIFF, Michele
(1946–)

Jamaican writer, whose family left Jamaica to live in New York when Cliff was three years old. She has called her work a 'search into the diasporic experience'. In *Claiming An Identity They Taught Me To Despise* (1980) she charted a personal and political history in a miscellany of prose and poetry. She is a 'mixed blood Jamaican' and in both the novels *Abeno* (1984) and *No Telephone To Heaven* (1987) there is a light-skinned heroine, Clare Savage. Her poetry is included in the Caribbean anthology *Creation Fire* (1989, ed Espinet).

CLIFT, Charmian
(1923–69)

Australian novelist and essayist, born in Kiama, New South Wales, and associated with the novelist **George Johnston**, whom she married in 1947. They travelled to London and then, with their three children, lived in Greece for 10 years, providing the setting for much of Clift's best writing. She wrote three novels in collaboration with Johnston, *High Valley* (1949), *The Big Chariot* (1953) and *The Sponge Divers* (1955). Her own work included two novels, *Walk to the Paradise Gardens* (1960) and *Honour's Mimic* (1964), and accounts of their life in Greece in *Mermaid Singing* (1956) and *Peel me a Lotus* (1959). Johnston later edited two collections of Clift's essays, *Images in Aspic* (1965) and *The World of Charmian Clift* (1970).

CLOSSON, Herman
(1901–)

Belgian playwright, born in Brussels. His drama, deriving from that of his compatriots **Maeterlinck** and **Crommelynck**, deals with the notion of greatness. Thus, in *William ou La Comédie de l'aventure* (1938, 'William, or the Comedy of Adventure'), **Shakespeare** is tempted into sacrificing a play for the sake of slaking his lust in a fantastic modern setting. Other plays, which treat the same theme, include ones about Joan of Arc, Cesare Borgia and Godefroy de Bouillon.

▷D Grossvogel, *20th Century French Drama* (1961)

CLOUGH, Arthur Hugh
(1819–61)

English poet, born in Liverpool, the son of a cotton merchant who emigrated to Charleston, USA, in 1823. The boy was sent back to England in 1828 and entered Rugby, where he became Dr Thomas Arnold's most promising pupil and where he began his friendship with **Matthew Arnold**. Though he only got a 'second' at Balliol College, Oxford, in 1841, he was elected a fellow of Oriel College and there lived through the crisis which resulted in **Newman**'s conversion to Rome. His own difficulties with the Thirty-nine Articles led to his resignation in 1848. He became for a time principal of the new University Hall, attached to University College, Gower Street, which had a Unitarian bias little to Clough's liking ('the Sadducees', he called them). On his dismissal from University Hall he obtained an examinership in the education department. Before taking up that appointment he spent some months in Boston, Massachusetts, where he met the Boston Brahmins. Financial worries added to his religious troubles; in the year he got his fellowship at Oriel his father became a bankrupt. He seems not to have enjoyed much of a family life before his marriage to Blanche Smith in 1854. The last years of his short life were relatively happy. He enjoyed not only the friendship of the great Victorians, **John Ruskin**, Arnold and **Thomas Carlyle**, but also of distinguished Americans of the Boston connection. At Oriel he was the self-confident leader of a group, Members of the Decade, and conducted reading parties in vacations to the Lakes and to Scotland. The latter resulted in a 'Long-vacation pastoral' called *The Bothie of Tober-na-Vuolich* (1848), which delighted those of his friends whom it did not outrage. His only other long poems were *Amours de voyage*, written in Rome in 1849; and *Dipsychus*, 1850, both published posthumously. Arnold hesitated for 10 years to write his commemorative poem *Thyrsis*. The two-volume *Correspondence* published in 1957 shows that Clough's dilemma was not confined to the Thirty-nine Articles (to which after all he subscribed) but to the whole of what is now called the Establishment. He followed the revolutionary doctrines of **George Sand**, called himself a republican, disliked class distinction ('your aversion, the Gentleman') and the capitalist system. He left two more long poems, *Mari Magno* and *Adam and Eve*, unfinished.

▷W V Harris, *Arthur Hugh Clough* (1970); Evelyn B Grenberger, *Arthur Hugh Clough* (1970)

CLUNE, Frank (Francis Patrick)
(1893–1971)

Australian writer of biography, history and adventure, born in the dockside district of Woolloomooloo, Sydney, of Irish extraction. His early life was one of travel and adventure at sea, in Europe and America. He served with the Australian Imperial Forces in World War I and was wounded at Gallipoli. A vagabond life followed, and marriage, then a career in accountancy. At the age of 40, while recuperating from an ulcer, he decided to write the story of his early years; this was published as *Try Anything Once* (1933, which includes a hilarious account of his brief career with a touring opera company) and Clune was launched into a writing career. He wrote over 60 books, often in collaboration with P R ('Inky') Stephensen, and became one of Australia's bestselling writers. Of popular appeal, Clune's work such as *Rolling down the Lachlan* (1935), *Wild Colonial Boys* (1948) and *Ben Hall the Bushranger* (1947) aroused interest in stories of Australian history.
▷ *Try Nothing Twice* (1946); *Korean Diary* (1955); B Adamson, *Francis Clune, author and ethnological anachronism* (1944)

COATES, Robert M(yron)
(1897–1973)

American novelist, short-story writer, journalist, travel writer and art critic, born in New Haven, Connecticut. Although critically well-regarded for his atmospheric novels, such as *The Eater of Darkness* (1929), and books including *Hour after Westerly and other Stories* (1957), Coates is more widely known for the accounts of his Italian travels. *Beyond the Alps* (1961) and *South of Rome* (1965), are considered among the most lucid, evocative and informed volumes of travel writing.

COATSWORTH, Elizabeth (Jane)
(1893–1986)

American novelist, poet and writer for children. She grew up in Buffalo, New York, and spent much of her life in New England, which is the main setting for her work. Her best-known book is *The Cat Who Went to Heaven* (1930), a prize-winning piece of children's fiction and perhaps her best prose work. Her adult novels, *Here I Stay* (1938) and *The Trunk* (1941), tend to lack its imaginative freedom, but something of this is captured in the verse, notably in *Fox Footprints* (1923), *Country Poems* (1942) and *The Creaking Stair* (1942), which might be compared with the work of **Ruth Pitter** in England. Her understanding of country ways is evident in the

non-fiction *Country Neighbourhood* (1944). In a long life, she published well over 60 books.
▷ *Personal Geography* (1976)

COBBETT, William
(1763–1835)

English writer and champion of the poor, born in Farnham, Surrey, the son of a small farmer. In 1784 he enlisted in the 54th Foot, taught himself to read and write, and served as sergeant-major in New Brunswick (1785–91), meanwhile studying rhetoric, geometry, logic, French and fortification. He bought his discharge in 1791, and brought charges of corruption against several of his officers, but went to France when he was not even called to give evidence at the court-martial. After mastering the language he sailed for America (1792). In Philadelphia he taught English to French refugees, opened a bookshop and published a paper called *Porcupine's Gazette* (1797–9). Under the pseudonym 'Peter Porcupine' he wrote fierce onslaughts on Joseph Priestley, **Tom Paine** and the native Democrats. Twice he was prosecuted for libel, and in 1800 he returned to England. The Tories welcomed him with open arms and in 1802 he started his weekly *Cobbett's Political Register*, which, with a three-months' break in 1817, continued till his death. Tory at first, he altered its politics in 1804, till at last it became the most uncompromising champion of Radicalism. He initiated the publication of *Parliamentary Debate* (1806, later taken over by Luke Hansard) and *State Trials* (1809). A great lover of the country, he purchased a model farm at Botley in Hampshire. He got two years in Newgate (1810–12) for his strictures on flogging in the army. In 1817 money muddles and dread of a second imprisonment drove him once more across the Atlantic and he farmed in Long Island, published a *Grammar of the English Language* (1819) and, in 1819, ventured back to England. Botley had to be sold, but he started a seed-farm at Kensington and stood unsuccessfully for parliament in 1821 and 1826. In 1831 he defended himself against a charge of sedition, and in 1832, after the First Reform Bill, he entered parliament as member for Oldham. His celebrated *Rural Rides* (1830), a delightful picture of a vanishing world, were reprinted from the *Register*. He also published a savage *History of the Reformation* (1824–7), *The Woodlands* (1825), *Advice to Young Men* (1830), and 40 or 50 more works.
▷ G D H Cole, *The Life of Cobbett* (1924)

COBBING, Bob
(1920–)

English sound and concrete poet, born in Enfield, Middlesex, who rejects conventional verse in favour of diagrammatized forms, phonetic 'choreography' and improvisational contexts with jazz musicians and dancers. Cobbing has worked as a civil servant, farmer, teacher and publisher; most of his work has appeared under his own Writers Forum imprint, which he established in 1963. From a huge output, the most effective and representative collections are *Sound Poems: An ABC in Sound* (1965), *The Five Vowels* (1974) and *Bob Cob's Rag Bag* (1977). A festival favourite, alone and with his group abAna, much of his work has been recorded. *Concerning Concrete Poetry* (1978, with Peter Mayer) was the latest in a group of nondiscursive manifestos. His interest in printing technique and electronic synthesis by no means negates his essentially simple, even primitive, approach.

▷P Mayer (ed), *Bob Cobbing and Writers Forum* (1974)

COBLENTZ, Stanton A
(1896–1981)

American poet and writer, born in San Francisco. He was a popular poet of some skill and merit, whose best work is gathered in *Garnered Sheaves: Selected Poems* (1949).

COCKBURN, Alison or Alicia, née Rutherford
(1713–94)

Scottish poet, born in Selkirkshire. In 1731 she married Patrick Cockburn, an advocate, and for over 60 years she was a leading figure in Edinburgh society. Of her lyrics, the best known is the exquisite version of 'The Flowers of the Forest' ('I've seen the smiling of Fortune beguiling'), which commemorates a wave of calamity that swept over Ettrick Forest, and was first printed in 1765. In 1777 she discerned in **Walter Scott** 'the most extraordinary genius of a boy'; in 1786 she made **Robert Burns**'s acquaintance.

▷*Letters and Memoirs of Her Own Life* (1900)

COCTEAU, Jean
(1889–1963)

French poet, playwright and film director, born in Maisons-Lafitte, near Paris. Success came early with *La Lampe d'Aladin* (1909, 'Aladdin's Lamp'), and he exploited it. He postured and preened and ran the gamut of experience, first a spectacular conversion to Roman Catholicism through Jacques Maritain; a derisive repudiation of his mentor; recourse to opium; and search for salvation through solitude. Nevertheless he had astonishing success with whatever he touched. He figured as the sponsor of Picasso, Stravinsky, Giorgio de Chirico and the musical group known as *Les Six*, in complete accord with the Surrealist and Dadaist movements. He was actor, director, scenario writer, novelist, critic, artist, and all of his work was marked by vivacity and a pyrotechnic brilliance. He was elected to the Académie française in 1955. Significant works are his novels *Le Grand Écart* (1923, Eng trans *The Grand Escort*, 1925), *Thomas l'Imposteur* (1923, Eng trans *Thomas the Imposter*, 1925), *Les Enfants terribles* (1929, Eng trans *Enfants Terribles*, 1930), and plays: *Les Mariés de la Tour Eiffel* (1921, Eng trans *The Eiffel Tower Wedding Party*, 1963), *Orphée* (1926, Eng trans *Orpheus*, 1933) and *L'Aigle a deux têtes* (1946, Eng trans *The Eagle has Two Heads*, 1948). His films include *Le Sang d'un poète* (1930, 'The Blood of a Poet'), *La Belle et la bête* (1945, 'Beauty and the Beast'), *Orphée* (adapted from his play, 1949) and *Le Testament d'Orphée* (1960).

▷F Brown, *An Impersonation of Angels: a biography of Cocteau* (1968)

COETZEE, J(ohn) M(ichael)
(1940–)

South African novelist, born in Cape Town. The political situation in his native country provides him with the base from which to launch his allegories and fables, attacking colonialism and demythologizing historical and contemporary myths of imperialism. His first work of fiction was *Dusklands* (1974), followed by *In the Heart of the Country* (1977), *Waiting for the Barbarians* (1980), *Life and Times of Michael K* (1983), for which he was awarded the Booker Prize, and *Foe* (1986).

COFFEY, Brian
(1905–)

Irish poet, born in Dun Laoghaire, County Dublin; he studied with the French Catholic philosopher Jacques Maritan in Paris. A professor of philosophy in the USA for most of his life, Coffey reached a general public with his consistently experimental verse with *Selected Poems* (1971). A deep questioning of freedom, both personal and ethical, informs all his work and is seen to best effect in *Poems and Versions 1929–1990* (1991).

COFFEY, Brian see KOONTZ, Dean R(ay)

COFFIN, Robert Peter Tristram
(1892–1955)

American writer, born in Brunswick, Maine. He graduated from Bowdoin College in 1915, was a Rhodes Scholar at Oxford, and became Professor of English at Wells College in Aurora, New York State, in 1921, while also running two farms in Maine. He was a prolific author, but was best known for his robust pastoral poetry, collected in several volumes, beginning with *Golden Falcon* (1929). He won the Pulitzer Prize for Poetry in 1936 for *Strange Holiness* (1935), and a *Collected Poems* was published in 1948. He also wrote novels, biography, the autobiographical volume *Lost Paradise* (1934), and collections of essays ranging from literary criticism to family reminiscences and sketches of rural Maine life.

COHAN, George M(ichael)
(1878–1942)

American playwright, actor and theatre manager, born in New York. Among his plays, which were highly popular at the time, are *Johnny Jones* (1904) and *The Song and Dance Man* (1923). His songs include 'Over There', one of the best-loved numbers of American servicemen. Cohan is best known to a later generation through the 1942 film *Yankee Doodle Dandy*, in which he was played with grinning gusto by James Cagney. The autobiography *Twenty Years on Broadway* (1925) recalls his time atop the seething heap of New York's theatre world.

COHEN, Leonard Norman
(1934–)

Canadian poet, novelist and singer, whose work is valued strictly in that order in his native country, the opposite order almost everywhere else. Though his background is Jewish, he grew up in the predominantly Catholic city of Montreal, and the title of his first collection, *Let Us Compare Mythologies* (1956), offers an indication of how he has moved between traditions. *The Spice-Box of Earth* (1961) and *Flowers for Hitler* (1964) both examine aspects of the Jewish experience, but increasingly in the context of a Christianity somewhat eroticized and frequently ironic. A novel, *The Favorite Game* (1963), was written in London; *Beautiful Losers* (1966) was in the same verbosely surreal line. His recording contract with Columbia began with *The Songs of Leonard Cohen* in 1968, the same year as his *Selected Poems* appeared. Later volumes such as *The Energy of Slaves* (1972) seemed to document a rather thoughtful mid-life crisis, but with *Book of Mercy* (1984) Cohen began again to write lyrics with the strong metre and imagery of the Psalms and marked by his personal vision of redemption.
▷S Scobie, *Leonard Cohen* (1978)

COHEN, Matt(hew)
(1942–)

Canadian novelist, born in Kingston, Ontario, and educated in Ottawa and Toronto. He lectured in religion for two semesters at McMaster University, Hamilton, Ontario,

before the publication of his short novel *Korsoniloff* (1969), the diary of a self-divided academic whose very existence is a problem in philosophy. *Johnny Crackle Sings* (1971) is also concerned with self-awareness; its drug-taking rock-star hero has become an artefact, image rather than substance. Cohen takes up the theme again in his best book, *The Disinherited* (1974), which tackles a more generous social and temporal range than its predecessors. Later books are weaker, though *The Sweet Second Summer of Kitty Malone* (1979) has a gentle elegiac quality which, though different from Cohen's usual manner, is highly effective. His short stories are collected in *Night Flights* (1978) and *The Expatriate* (1981); later stories appeared in *Café le dog* (1983, published in the USA as *Life on This Planet*, 1985).

COIMIN, Mícheál
(1688–1760)

Irish poet from County Clare. He wrote of **Ossian** even as **Macpherson** was working in Scotland, and his *Laoidh Oisin ar Thir na nóg* was translated as *Lay of Oisin in the Land of Youth* in 1896.

COKAYNE, Sir Aston
(1608–84)

English minor poet, playwright and translator. The best-known of his very slight works is his version of the *Diana* of **Montemayor**.
▷*Poems by Sir Aston Cokayne* (1877); *Dramatic Works* (1965)

COLCORD, Lincoln (Ross)
(1883–1947)

American poet, novelist and mariner. Colcord was born at sea but settled in Maine, where he studied engineering and began to write. His first major work was a novel, *The Game of Life and Death* (1914), which merits comparison with **Dana**'s equally autobiographical *Two Years Before the Mast*. In the following year, with American involvement in World War I looming, he published the long poem *Vision of War*. His other notable novel was *An Instrument of the Gods* (1922).

COLEGATE, Isabel Diana
(1931–)

English novelist, born in Lincolnshire. Between 1952 and 1957 she worked as a literary agent. Her first novel, *The Blackmailer*, appeared in 1958, since when she has written several interlinked works, of which the most ambitious is the *Orlando* trilogy: *Orlando King* (1968), *Orlando at the Brazen Threshold* (1971) and *Agatha* (1973). These trace the rise of Orlando King, from his adoption by a Cambridge don, to his appointment as a Cabinet Minister at the outbreak of World War II, and eventually to his retiral in Italy. Colegate's most notable novel, *The Shooting Party* (1980), dealing with tragic events at a country house in the autumn of 1913, is a perceptive, affectionate but critical study of a social class whose lives were to be altered by war and its consequences.

COLERIDGE, Hartley

(1796–1849)

English writer, eldest son of **Samuel Taylor Coleridge**, born in Clevedon, Somerset. He was brought up by **Robert Southey** at Greta Hall, and educated at Ambleside school and Merton College, Oxford. His scholarship was great but unequal; his failures to win the Newdigate filled him with 'a passionate despondency'; and he forfeited an Oriel College fellowship by intemperance. He spent two years in London, tried taking pupils at Ambleside, occasionally writing for *Blackwood's Magazine*, lived for some time at Grasmere, and then went to live at Leeds with a publisher, for whom he wrote biographies, published under the titles of *Biographia Borealis* (1833) and *Worthies of Yorkshire and Lancashire* (1836). He subsequently lived at Grasmere, with two short intervals of teaching at Sedbergh. Provided for by an annuity, he continued to write poetry, and edited **John Ford** and **Philip Massinger**. His days were spent in fitful study, lonely reverie, and wanderings over the Lake Country, with occasional bouts of intemperance. His poetry is graceful, tender and sincere.

▷ Earl Griggs, *Hartley Coleridge, his life and work* (1929)

COLERIDGE, Samuel Taylor

(1772–1834)

English poet, son of a vicar of Ottery St Mary, Devon. The youngest of a very large family, he had an unhappy childhood, and was educated at Christ's Hospital and went to Jesus College, Cambridge, to study for the church. His university career was interrupted in 1793 by a runaway enlistment in the 15th Dragoons, from which he was rescued by his family. On a walking tour in 1794 he met **Robert Southey** at Balliol College, Oxford, with whom he shared Romantic and revolutionary views. Together they planned a 'pantisocracy' or communist society on the banks of the Susquehanna, in Pennsylvania, but the idea came to nothing. In 1795 he married Sarah Fricker, a friend of Southey's, while her sister Edith married Southey. He had contributed some verses to the *Morning Chronicle* in 1793, and now he wrote, with Southey, a historical play, *The Fall of Robespierre*. He now became immersed in lecturing and journalism in Bristol, interspersed with itinerant preaching at Unitarian chapels. The Bristol circle provided Coleridge with generous friends, notably Joseph Cottle the bookseller, who published his first book of poems, *Poems on Various Subjects* (1796), which contained the 'Ode to France'. In 1797 the Coleridges moved to a cottage at Nether Stowey, Somerset, and later that year met **William** and **Dorothy Wordsworth**. The result was momentous for English poetry—from their discussions emerged a new poetry which represented a revulsion from neo-classic artificiality and, as a consequence, the renovation of the language of poetry. *Lyrical Ballads* (1798), which opened with Coleridge's 'Ancient Mariner' and closed with Wordsworth's 'Tintern Abbey', was thus in the nature of a manifesto. A visit to Germany with the Wordsworths (1798–9) followed. German philosophy and criticism influenced him greatly and he published translations of **Schiller**'s *Piccolomini* and *Wallenstein*. In 1800 he moved to Keswick and for a time, with the Wordsworths at Grasmere and Southey already resident at Keswick, it looked as if a fruitful career was opening out for him, but his moral collapse, due partly to opium, made the next few years a misery to him and his friends. His 'Ode to Dejection' (1802) is both a recantation of Wordsworth's animistic view of Nature and a confession of failure. From then on his association with Wordsworth was strained; his relations with Dorothy continued only through her devotion to him. He had a sojourn in Malta as secretary to the Governor from 1804 to 1806. In 1809 he began a weekly paper, *The Friend*, which ran for 28 issues and was published as a book in 1818. In 1810 he finally broke with Wordsworth and settled in London, where he engaged in various activities, including miscellaneous writing and lecturing at the Royal Institution (his lectures on **Shakespeare** alone are extant). He also wrote a play, *Remorse* (1813), which had a mild success at Drury Lane. In 1816 he published 'Christabel' and the fragment, 'Kubla Khan', both written in his earlier period of inspiration. He had long relinquished the idea of renewing that inspiration and resigned himself, as he indicates in the close of 'Dejection', to philosophical speculation. His critical writing in these middle years is important also as the finest 'creative' criticism in the language, collected in *Biographia Literaria* (1817), *Aids to Reflection* (1825) and *Anima Poetae* (edited from his notebooks, 1895). He was a gifted poet and a writer of theological and politico-sociological works which have a relevance even today.

▷ J L Lowes, *The Road to Xanadu* (1927); T D Campbell, *Samuel Taylor Coleridge: a narrative of the events of his life* (1894)

COLET, Louise
(1810–76)

French poet, born in Aix-en-Provence and resident in Paris after marriage to Hippolyte Colet, a violin professor at the Conservatoire there. Her florid, passionate poetry, often on the theme of love's earth-shaking powers, is collected in *Fleurs du Midi* (1836), *Poesies* (1844) and *Ce qui est dans le coeur des femmes* (1852). She won the poetry prize of the Académie française four times, though according to some she had more beauty than writing talent. Infamous for violent behaviour and affairs with prominent writers such as **Flaubert** and **Alfred de Musset**, she gave the details in *Lui, roman contemporain* (1851, 'Him, A View of Him') which, in the words of critic Marilyn Gaddis Rose, involves 'skilful counterpointing of the personal and professional dilemmas of two women of letters in the 19th century'.
▷M Bood and S Grand, *L'indomptable Louise Colet* (1986)

COLETTE, Sidonie-Gabrielle
(1873–1954)

French novelist, born in Saint-Sauveur-en-Puisaye. Her early novels, the *Claudine* series, were published by her first husband, Henri Gauthier-Villars, under his pen-name 'Willy'. After their divorce in 1906 she appeared in music-halls in dance and mime, and out of this period came *L'Envers du music-hall* (1913, Eng trans *Music-Hall Sidelights*, 1957). Her work is characterized by an intense, almost entirely physical preoccupation with immediate sense experiences. Her novels include *Chéri* (1920, Eng trans 1929), *La Fin de Chéri* (1926, Eng trans *The Last of Chéri*, 1932), *La Chatte* (1933, Eng trans *The Cat*, 1936) and *Gigi* (1944, Eng trans 1953). She married Henri de Jouvenel in 1912, and in 1935, Maurice Goudeket.
▷J Richardson, *Colette* (1983)

COLIN MUSET
(b.c.1210)

French poet, from Champagne, of whom little is known except his poetry, from which he earned his living as a jongleur. He was a producer of light, happy verse, refreshingly free of the artifice beloved by so many of his contemporaries. Whereas they all discuss courtly love, Muset is content to talk of real emotions and real pleasures, souring this tone only with the occasional outburst against the cruelty and greed of his rich patrons. Around 15 of his poems survive, all of them short, some with their original simple musical settings.

COLLETT, (Jacobine) Camilla, née Wergeland
(1813–95)

Norwegian novelist, born in Kristiansand. She grew up in a much stricter environment than her brother, the poet **Hendrik Arnold Wergeland**, and in adult life she became a passionate champion of women's rights. Her novel *Amtmandens døttre* (1855, 'The Magistrate's Daughters') is notable for its sympathetic portrayal of young women trapped by stultifying convention. *I den lange naetter* (1862, 'Through the Long Nights') is an insomniac's pillow-book, reconstructing childhood scenes. Her occasional pieces were published in three volumes of *Sidtse blade* (1868, 1872, 1873).
▷A Collett, *Camilla Colletts livshistorie* (1911)

COLLIANDER, Tito
(1904–)

Finland–Swedish novelist and biographer (Ilya Repin), born in St Petersburg; he taught religion (Greek Orthodox) and art in schools, finally becoming a professor and writing a book about the problems of faith and everyday life (1951). His novels, none of which has been translated, trace mystical quests; they somewhat resemble those of **Mauriac**, but are less melodramatic and the viewpoint is Greek Orthodox.

COLLIER, Jeremy
(1650–1726)

Anglican Church historian and controversialist, born at Stow, Cambridgeshire, and educated at Ipswich and Cambridge. A non-juring bishop who opposed William and Mary, he was fierce in his polemics, which resulted in prison spells and temporary exile abroad as a political 'outlaw'. His *Ecclesiastical History of Great Britain* (1708–14) has considerable scholarly merit. He is best known, however, for *A Short View of the Immorality and Profaneness of the English Stage* (1698), a devastating attack on Restoration dramatists. Replies by **Dryden**, **Congreve**, **Vanbrugh** and others were generally considered to be ineffective. Collier's strictures did much ostensibly to reform, but actually tame, comic drama in the 18th century.
▷Sister Rose Anthony, *The Jeremy Collier Controversy* (1937)

COLLIER, John, known as 'Tim Bobbin'
(1708–86)

English poet, born in Urmston, near Manchester, the son of the curate of Stretford. From 1729 he was usher or master of a school at Milnrow, near Rochdale. His rhyming satire, *The Blackbird*, appeared in 1739, and

his *View of the Lancashire Dialect* (in humorous dialogue) in 1775.
▷J P Briscoe, *The Literature of Tim Bobbin* (1872)

COLLIER, Mary
(c.1690–c.1763)

English poet, born near Midhurst, Sussex to poor parents, she was taught to read at home. After her parents' death she earned her living by washing, brewing and field-work, later as housekeeper in Hampshire. Her best-known poem, 'The Woman's Labour' (1739), written in retort to **Stephen Duck**'s slighting reference to women's work in 'The Thresher's Labour', is forthright in expression and full of realistic detail. Labouring women, she protested, work even harder than men, for 'when we home are come,/Alas! we find our work has just begun'. She also published *Poems on Several Occasions* (1762). *The Thresher's Labour and The Woman's Labour*, ed M Ferguson was published in 1985.
▷D Landry, *Muses of Resistance* (1990)

COLLINS, Jackie
(1937–)

Bestselling English novelist, born in London. Expelled from school at 15, she moved to Hollywood in search of fame as a film actress. Instead, she has made a career out of writing fiction about the Hollywood set. Since the publication of her first novel, *The World is Full of Married Men*, in 1968, that career has been one of uninterrupted success. *The Stud* (1969) and *The Bitch* (1972) were both subsequently filmed starring her older sister, Joan Collins. *Hollywood Wives* (1983) is perhaps the archetypal Collins novel, being an engaging amalgam of young love, ageing lust, sex, shopping, glamour, grime, violence, drugs and rock'n'roll. And more sex. By 1994 she had sold in excess of 170 million copies of her books worldwide.

COLLINS, (William) Wilkie
(1824–89)

English novelist, elder son of the artist William Collins (1788–1847), born in London. He was educated partly at Highbury, but from 1836 to 1839 was with his parents in Italy. After his return he spent four years in business, and then was called to the Bar, but gradually turned to literature, his *Life* of his father (1848) being his earliest production. His first work of fiction was a novel about the fall of Rome, *Antonina* (1850). With *Basil* (1852) he turned his attention to mystery, suspense and crime. His best work was written in the 1860s when he produced *The Woman in White* (1860), *No Name* (1862), *Armadale* (1866) and *The Moonstone* (1868).

His popularity with the reading public declined after 1870, and his later novels, often driven by pressing social issues, are more uneven in quality.
▷K Robinson, *Wilkie Collins: a biography* (1951); William H Marshall, *Wilkie Collins* (1950)

COLLINS, William
(1721–59)

English poet, born in Chichester, the son of a hatter. He was educated at Winchester and Magdalen College, Oxford, but having been pronounced 'too indolent even for the army', and dissuaded from entering the church, as the sole alternative he came to London to make a living by literature. During this period he spent an inheritance, in advance of receiving it, and was forced to live on credit, reduced at times to the greatest straits; **Dr Johnson** once rescued him from the bailiffs by obtaining an advance from a bookseller on the promise of Collins to translate the *Poetics* of Aristotle. It was during this period, however, that he wrote his *Odes*, upon which his fame rests. They attracted no notice at the time of publication (1747), and were little valued even by **Thomas Gray** and Dr Johnson. On the death of an uncle in 1749, Collins inherited £2000, which enabled him to retire to Chichester, and apparently to pursue a regular course of study. It was about this time that he met **John Home**, the author of *Douglas*, and gave him his 'Ode on the Superstitions of the Highlands', a poem in which, says **James Lowell**, 'the whole Romantic School is foreshadowed'. His mental health broke down after a visit to France, and he died insane.
▷P L Carver, *The Life of a Poet: a biographical sketch* (1967)

COLLYMORE, Frank Appleton
(1893–1980)

Barbadian poet and story writer, educated at Combermere School, where he taught from 1910 to 1958. As founder and editor of the long-running literary magazine *Bim* from 1942 to 1975 he was a major force in the rise of modern West Indian literature. His short stories, published in *Bim* between 1942 and 1971, show a gift for strong characterization and insight into the dark recesses of the mind. He published five books of poems, notable chiefly for their evocation of the sea and Caribbean landscape and for a vein of social satire too seldom indulged. *Collected Poems* was published in 1959.
▷E Baugh, in *Fifty Caribbean Writers*, ed D C Dance (1986)

COLMAN, George, 'the Elder'
(1732–94)

English playwright and manager, born in Florence, the son of the English envoy. He was educated at Westminster and Oxford, and called to the Bar in 1755. In 1760 his first piece, *Polly Honeycombe*, was produced at Drury Lane with great success; next year came *The Jealous Wife*, and in 1766 *The Clandestine Marriage*, written in conjunction with Garrick. In 1767 he purchased, with three others, Covent Garden Theatre, and held the office of manager for seven years, until he sold his share. In 1776 he purchased the Haymarket Theatre from **Samuel Foote**, but was paralysed by a stroke from 1785.
▷E R Page, *George Colman the Elder* (1935)

COLMAN, George, 'the Younger'
(1762–1836)

English playwright, son of **George Colman 'the Elder'**. He was educated at Westminster, Oxford and Aberdeen. During his father's illness he acted as manager of the Haymarket and on his death the patent was transferred to him. As Examiner of Plays from 1824 he showed himself both arrogant and excessively precise. In industry he rivalled his father, and he made money by his *John Bull, Iron Chest, Heir at Law* and other comedies, and by songs like 'Mynheer Van Dunck'. He wrote *Random Records of My Life* (1830).
▷J F B Collins, *George Colman the Younger* (1946)

COLOMB, Catherine
(1899–1965)

Swiss (Vaudois) author of three novels which have been described as 'inexplicably neglected'. Paramount is *Les esprits de la terre* (1953, 'The Spirits of the Earth'), which deals with a leading family of wine-growers, and which fruitfully and convincingly employs such techniques as deliberate suppression of story-line and time-condensation; Colomb, claims a critic, 'possessed insights denied to the most of the "new novelists"'.

COLOMBO, John Robert
(1936–)

Canadian poet, translator, editor, journalist and sometime television personality ('Colombo's Quotes' series, 1978), born in Kitchener, Ontario. He is nationally known as the 'Master Gatherer' for his 'compilations of Canadiana' and has 'chosen not to live the life of the poet'. The essence of his poetry, much of it in free verse, has been summed up in his own lines: 'What is immensely important here is life itself: man/feeding on the world'. He has published more than 30 collections, including *Selected Poems* (1982).
▷*Canadian Literature* (Summer, 1966)

COLONNA, Vittoria
(1490–1547)

Italian poet from Marino. Born into a noble Roman family, she married the Marquis of Pescara, but saw little of him. The arranged marriage turned into one of love-in-absence, and on his death in battle at Pavi (1525), she devoted her life to good causes. Her religious thinking was profound, as were her objections to corruption in her church. She inspired her friend Michelangelo to some of his finest poetry. Her own lyric poetry—**Petrarch**an in style—is of the first order, and deserves even more extended study than it has already had. Many translations are included in M F Jerrold's *Vittora Colonna* (1906, reprinted 1969).

COLUM, Pádraic
(1881–1972)

Irish poet and playwright, born in County Longford, the son of the warden of a workhouse. He was educated at a school in Longford, and worked as a railway clerk in Dublin. He became a leader of the Irish literary revival, and wrote plays for the Abbey Theatre including *Broken Soil* (1903, later called *The Fiddler's House*), *The Land* (1905) and *Thomas Muskerry* (1910). He published his first collection of poems, *Wild Earth*, in 1907. In 1916 he was co-founder of the *Irish Review*. From 1914 he lived in the USA, where he and his wife (Molly Maguire) taught comparative literature at Columbia University. He published two studies on Hawaiian folklore (1924 and 1926), the result of government-sponsored research. He wrote several further volumes of verse, including the lyric *She Moved Through the Fair*. His novel *The Flying Swans* (1957) was followed by the memoir *Our Friend James Joyce* (1958).
▷Z R Brown, *Pádraic Colum* (1970)

COLUMBA, St, also known as Colmcille ('Colm of the Churches')
(521–97)

Irish apostle of Christianity in Scotland. According to his 7th-century biographer, Adomnán, he studied under St Finnian at Clonard with St Ciaran. In 546 he founded the monastery of Derry. In 561, however, he was accused of having been involved in the bloody Battle of Cuildreimhne, for which he was excommunicated and sentenced to exile. In 563, accompanied by 12 disciples, he set sail to do penance as a missionary, and found haven on the Hebridean island of Iona, where he founded a monastery that became the mother church of Celtic Christianity in Scotland. A formidably energetic administrator, he organized his monastery on Iona as a school for missionaries, and played a vig-

orous role in the politics of the country. Although he spent the last 34 years of his life in Scotland, he visited Ireland on occasions, and towards the end of his life he founded the monastery of Durrow in Ireland. He was renowned as a writer; he wrote hymns, and is credited with having transcribed 300 books with his own hand; but he was also revered as a warrior saint, and his supernatural aid was frequently invoked for victory in battle. He died on Iona and was buried in the abbey.
▷W D Simpson, *The Historical St Columba* (1927, rev edn 1963)

COLUMBAN, or COLUMBANUS, St
(543–615)

Irish missionary, 'the younger Columba', born in Leinster. He studied under St Comgall at Bangor in Down, and c.585 went to Gaul with 12 companions, and founded the monasteries of Anegray, Luxeuil and Fontaine in the Vosges country. His adherence to the Celtic Easter involved him in controversy; and the vigour with which he rebuked the vices of the Burgundian court led to his expulsion in 610. After a year or two at Bregenz, on Lake Constance, he went to Lombardy, and in 612 founded the monastery of Bobbio, in the Appenines, where he died. His writings, all in Latin, comprise a monastic rule, six poems on the vanity of life, 17 sermons and a commentary on the Psalms (1878).
▷C W Dispham, *Columban, Saint, Monk and Missionary* (1903)

COLUMELLA, Lucius Junius Moderatus
(1st century)

Roman writer on agriculture, born in Gades (Cadiz) in Spain. He wrote *De Re Rustica* (12 books), on arable and pasture lands, the culture of vines and olives, the care of domestic animals, and arboriculture. Book 10 (on gardening) is written in hexameters as an addendum to **Virgil**'s *Georgics*.
▷S Hedberg, *Contamination and Interpolation: a study of the 19th century MSS* (1968)

COMBE, William
(1741–1823)

English writer and adventurer, born in Bristol, renowned as the creator of *Dr Syntax*. The illegitimate son of a wealthy London alderman, he inherited a fortune in 1762 and led the life of an adventurer and spent much time in debtors' jails. Educated at Eton and Oxford, he wrote metrical satires like *The Diaboliad* (1776), but made his name with his three verse satires on popular travel-books. Illustrated with cartoons by Thomas Rowlandson, they recounted the adventures of a clergyman schoolmaster on his holidays (based on William Gilpin), in *Dr Syntax in search of the Picturesque* (1809), *The Second Tour of Dr Syntax in search of Consolation* (1820) and *The Third Tour of Dr Syntax in search of a Wife* (1821). He also wrote the text for Rowlandson's *Dance of Death* (1815–16), *Dance of Life* (1816) and *Johnny Quae Genus* (1822), and for *The Microcosm of London* (1808).
▷H Hamilton, *Doctor Syntax: a silhouette of William Combe Esq* (1969)

COMFORT, Alex(ander)
(1920–)

English biologist, gerontologist, social critic, poet and novelist of anarchist sensibilities, born in London. He is probably now best known for his 'gourmet guides' to lovemaking, *The Joy of Sex* (1972) and *More Joy of Sex* (1973). Educated at Trinity College, Cambridge, and at the London Hospital, he was lecturer in physiology (1945–51) and director of research on the biology of ageing (1966–73) at University College, London. In 1974 he started lecturing in psychiatry at Stanford University, California. His *Barbarism and Sexual Freedom* (1948) and *Sexual Behaviour in Society* (1950, revised as *Sex in Society*, 1963) were notable contributions to a libertarian understanding of sexuality, which functioned in dialectical opposition to the life-denying violence he observed in his war poems: *Elegies* (1944), *The Song of Lazarus* (1945), and *The Signal to Engage* (1947). After a gap of more than a decade, *Haste to the Wedding* (1962) signalled a more affirmative sensibility, and *All But a Rib* (1973) partially documented his reaction to the women's movement.
▷A E Salmon, *Alex Comfort* (1978)

COMPTON-BURNETT, Dame Ivy
(1892–1969)

English novelist, born in London. She graduated in classics from the Royal Holloway College, London University, and published her first novel, *Dolores*, in 1911. A prolific writer, her rather stylized novels have many features in common; they are often set in upper-class Victorian or Edwardian society, for example, and the characters usually belong to a large family, spanning several generations. She was noted for her skilful use of dialogue, not because the language is appropriate to character but because it conveys the secret thoughts and understanding of the characters. Her works include *Pastors and Masters* (1925), *Brothers and Sisters* (1929), *Parents and Children* (1941), *Mother and Son* (1955, James Tait Black Memorial Prize), *A Father*

and his Fate (1957), *The Mighty and their Fall* (1961) and *A God and His Gifts* (1963).
▷H Spurling, *Ivy Compton-Burnett* (2 vols, 1984–5)

CONDON, Richard
(1915–)

American novelist, born in New York City. He worked as a film-industry publicist for 21 years (1936–57), and saw service in the US merchant navy, before embarking on a literary career. He made his reputation with his second novel, *The Manchurian Candidate* (1959). It and *Winter Kills* (1974) are both political intrigues set amidst the paranoia of the Cold War. *Prizzi's Honor* (1982) was the first of a trilogy about the Prizzi crime family and their struggle to stay ahead of their rivals. Like the former two novels, it was subsequently filmed; Condon himself wrote the 1985 screenplay with Janet Roach. He describes himself as 'a professional entertainer'; his sales figures, sustained over more than 30 years, suggest he is a highly successful one.

CONGREVE, William
(1670–1729)

English dramatist and poet, born in Bardsey near Leeds. He was educated in Ireland at Kilkenny School and Trinity College, Dublin, where he was a fellow student of **Jonathan Swift**. In London he entered the Middle Temple to study law, but never practised. His first publication was *Incognita, or Love and Duty Reconciled* (1692), a novel of cross-purposes and disguises which was written in a fortnight. His translation of the eleventh satire of **Juvenal** came out soon after in **Dryden**'s *Juvenal and Persius*. In January 1693 his comedy *The Old Bachelor*, produced under Dryden's auspices, with the celebrated Anne Bracegirdle as heroine, achieved brilliant success at a time when the theatre had been suffering a slump. His second comedy, *The Double Dealer* (November 1693), was in every way stronger than *The Old Bachelor*, but the satire on the heartless sexual morals of the time was aimed too directly at the theatre's best customers, and it failed to please. *The Mourning Muse of Alexis* (1695), a poetic dialogue on the death of Queen Mary II, wife of William III, was full of artificial conceits. *Love for Love*, generally regarded as Congreve's stage masterpiece, was first produced in 1695. It is more satirical, more vital, and stronger in feeling than its predecessors; it also has a more coherent plot and truer characterization. In 1697 his only tragedy, *The Mourning Bride*, appeared, best remembered for the two overworked quotations 'music hath charms to soothe the savage breast' and 'hell hath no fury like a woman

scorned'. He was next occupied busily in the famous **Jeremy Collier** controversy, defending the morality of the new stage (1698). His last play, *The Way of the World*, was produced in 1700, but was not a success. He wrote no more for the stage, apart from the words of a masque of *The Judgment of Paris*, set to music by John Eccles for a musical competition in 1701, and the undistinguished libretto of *Semele*, also to the music of Eccles, but later used by Handel. He was now almost blind owing to cataracts, but his support of the Whig party brought him a few sinecures which enabled him to live comfortably, writing occasional poems, until his death after a coach accident. He was buried in Westminster Abbey.
▷E Goss, *The Life of William Congreve* (1888); M E Novak, *William Congreve* (1971)

CONLEY, Robert J
(1940–)

American writer, born in Cushing, Oklahoma. Of Cherokee descent, Conley has drawn inspiration for his work from Cherokee history and contemporary life. His first published work, *Twenty-one Poems* (1975), was followed by the short narrative history, *Adawosgi: Swimmer Wesley Snell, a Cherokee Memorial* (1980). The poems in *The Rattlesnake Band and Other Poems* (1984) and stories that comprise *The Witch of Goingsnake and Other Stories* (1988) are overlaid with a characteristically dark vision of the potential of evil to blight human life. Conley has also written westerns with a Native American slant; *Back to Malachi* (1986), for example, depicts the life of Cherokee outlaws in Indian Territory in the 19th century. He has recently begun a series of historical novels depicting pre-contact Cherokee life in the Southeastern US, beginning with *The Way of the Priests* and *The Dark Way* (1993).

CONNELL, Evan S(helby)
(1924–)

American novelist, short-story writer and poet, born in Kansas City and educated at the University of Kansas, but for long a resident of California. He is celebrated for two elegiac novels, *Mrs Bridge* (1959) and its companion piece *Mr Bridge* (1969), elegant studies of repressed gentlefolk, set against the Great Depression. *The Patriot* (1960) is more straightforwardly realistic, being the semi-autobiographical account of a young naval airman during World War II. *The Diary of a Rapist* (1966) is less gratuitous than the title suggests and considerably more insightful. His story collections include *St Augustine's Pigeon* (1980), while his calm, philosophical poetry can be found in *Notes from a Bottle Found on the Beach at Carmel* (1963), a minor classic of American writing, and *Points for a Compass Rose* (1973).

CONNELLY, Marc(us Cook)
(1890–1980)

American dramatist, born in McKeesport, Pennsylvania. As a journalist who took to the theatre, he achieved several outstanding successes in collaboration with **George Kaufman**, including *Dulcy* (1921), *To the Ladies* (1922), the amusing 'expressionist' *Beggar on Horseback* (1924) and *Hunter's Moon* (1958). His greatest individual success was *Green Pastures* (1930), adapted from Negro stories of the Deity and a Negro heaven, which won the Pulitzer Prize.
▷P T Nolan, *Marc Connelly* (1969)

CONNOLLY, Cyril Vernon
(1903–74)

English author and journalist. Educated at Eton and Oxford, he contributed to the *New Statesman* and other periodicals and wrote regularly for *The Sunday Times*. He was founder/editor of *Horizon* (1939–50) and briefly literary editor of *The Observer*. His only novel was *The Rock Pool* (1936). Among his works are *Enemies of Promise* (1938), which included a look at the prevailing literary scene and an autobiograpical fragment, *The Unquiet Grave* (1944), miscellaneous aphorisms and reflections, and various collections of essays. Inclined to sloth and prey to fitful depressions, his potential was greater than his achievement.

CONON (also QUESNES) DE BETHUNE
(d.1220)

Northern French trouvere poet. He was an important historical figure in his own right; born into the royal house of Flanders, he became one of the leaders of the Fourth Crusade. He was hugely influential in the literary development of northern France, being one of the first poets writing in the dialect of the area to gain popular acceptance elsewhere. His retort to the French queen when she mocked his northern French is famous: *Encore noe soit ma parole françoise/Si la puet on bien entendre en françois* (roughly: 'If you understand it/Then it's French enough for me').

CONRAD, Joseph, originally Jozef Teodor Konrad Nalecz Korzeniowski
(1857–1924)

Polish-born British novelist, born in Berdichev, in the Polish Ukraine, now in the USSR. His father was a revolutionary of literary gifts—he translated **Victor Hugo**'s *Les Travailleurs de la mer*—who was exiled to Vologda in 1862. In 1878 Joseph joined an English merchant ship and was naturalized in 1884 when he gained his certificate as a master. In the 10 years that followed, he sailed between Singapore and Borneo, and this gave him an unrivalled background of mysterious creeks and jungle for the tales to follow. There was also an interlude in the Belgian Congo which provided exotic colour for his *Heart of Darkness*, one of his three finest novellas, the others being *Youth* and *Typhoon*. In 1896 he married and settled at Ashford in Kent, where he lived in seclusion for the rest of his days. Conrad's first novel was *Almayer's Folly* (1894), and then followed *An Outcast of the Islands* (1896), *The Nigger of the Narcissus* (1897), *Lord Jim* (1900), *Nostromo* (1904), *The Secret Agent* (1907) and *Under Western Eyes* (1911), before *Chance* (1914) made him famous. It was only then that *Lord Jim* was recognized as a masterpiece. Perhaps the short story was his true medium—*Tales of Unrest* (1898), *Youth* (1902) and *Twixt Land and Sea* (1912). His semi-autobiographical *The Mirror and the Sea* and his *Personal Record* testify to his high artistic aims. He also wrote *Victory* (1919), but his later works, *The Arrow of Gold* (1919) and *The Rescue* (1920), owed their popularity largely to his earlier work.
▷J Baines, *Joseph Conrad: a critical biography* (1960)

CONROY, Frank
(1936–)

American novelist and autobiographer. He was born in New York City, and educated there and at Haverford College, from which he graduated in 1958. His first book was *Stop-Time* (1965), a dreamlike memoir of his own adolescence: its exploration of the boundaries of fiction and non-fiction won the admiration of **Norman Mailer**, the most vocal exponent of the 'non-fiction novel' and Mailer's imprimatur helped foster Conroy's career. He has not been a prolific writer, however. A collection of stories, *Midair*, appeared in 1985, and a novel, *Body & Soul*, in 1993. Currently director of the Writers' Workshop at the University of Iowa, Conroy previously taught at George Mason and Brandeis Universities, and at the Massachusetts Institute of Technology (MIT).

CONSCIENCE, Hendrik
(1812–83)

Flemish novelist, born in Antwerp. From 1866 he was director of the Wiertz Museum. His *Phantazy* (1837), a fine collection of tales, and his most popular romance, *De Leeuw van Vlaenderen* (1838, 'The Lion of Flanders'), earned him a place as the father of the Flemish novel. His series of pictures of Flemish life, beginning with *Hoe man schilder wordt*

(1843, 'How to become a Painter'), carried his name over Europe.

▷F Joster, *Hendrik Conscience* (1917)

CONSTABLE, Henry
(1562–1613)

English poet, the son of Sir Robert Constable of Newark. At 16 he entered St John's College, Cambridge, turned Catholic, and went to Paris. He was pensioned by King Henri IV, and seems to have been employed in confidential missions to England and Scotland. In 1592 he published his *Diana*, a collection of 23 sonnets; a second edition in 1594 containing 76, some by his friend, Sir **Philip Sidney**, and other poets. His other poems included a set of *Spiritual Sonnets*, first published in 1815.

▷G A Wickes, *Henry Constable: poet and courtier* (1954)

CONSTANT DE REBECQUE, Henri Benjamin (Benjamin Constant)
(1767–1830)

French author and politician, born of French Huguenot ancestry in Lausanne. Educated at Oxford, Erlangen and Edinburgh, he settled in Paris in 1795 as a publicist. He entered the Tribunate in 1799, but was banished from France in 1802 for denouncing the despotic acts of Napoleon. After travelling in Germany and Italy with **Madame de Staël**, he settled at Göttingen. On Napoleon's fall in 1814 he returned to Paris; during the Hundred Days became one of Napoleon's councillors, though previously he had styled Napoleon a Genghis Khan; and after the second restoration of the Bourbons wrote and spoke in favour of constitutional freedom. He was returned to the Chamber of Deputies in 1819, and became the leader of the liberal Opposition. He wrote *De la religion* (5 vols, 1824–31); but more important is a remarkable psychological novel, *Adolphe* (1816), about a passionate love affair which ends in tragedy. His correspondence appeared in 1844, his *Oeuvres politiques* ('Political Works') in 1875, his Letters to Madame Récamier and his family in 1882–8, and his *Journal intime* ('Personal Diary') in 1895. *Cahier rouge* (1907, 'Red Notebook') contains a vivid account of his youth.

▷P L Leon, *Benjamin Constant* (1930)

CONSTANTIN-WEYER, Maurice
(1881–1961)

French novelist, memoirist and biographer, who settled for a time in Canada. One of his 46 books became a success: *Un Homme se penche sur son passé* (1928, Eng trans *A Man Scans his Past*, 1929), achieved considerable popularity in France and in the USA. This was an account of his Canadian wanderings and his establishment of a horse and cattle ranch in Manitoba (1912). He wrote plays and many film scripts, and *A Man Scans his Past* was made into a Franco–German movie in 1958; but his work is now forgotten.

CONWAY, Hugh, pseud of Frederick John Fargus
(1847–85)

English novelist, born in Bristol, where he was an auctioneer in succession to his father. He took his writing name from the school frigate *Conway*, where he was a student for a time, but was not allowed to fulfil his ambition of joining the navy. He wrote clever newspaper verse and tales, but his greatest success was the melodramatic *Called Back* (1883), also popular as a play. Other works include *A Life's Idyll and other Poems* (1879), and the novels *Dark Days* (1884), *A Family Affair* (1885) and *Living or Dead* (1886).

▷'A Sketch of the Author's Life', included in *Called Back* (1885)

COOK, David
(1940–)

English novelist and television scriptwriter, born in Preston, Lancashire. His first novel, *Albert's Memorial*, appeared in 1972, since when Cook has acquired a reputation as the author of sympathetic and sensitive studies of vulnerable, decent people, written in delicate, flexible prose. His best-known work is *Walter* (1978), a thoughtful novel about a mentally impaired northerner. The film version was commissioned by and shown on the first evening's broadcasting of Channel Four Television in 1982. *Winter Doves* (1979) is a sequel to *Walter*.

COOK, Eliza
(1818–89)

English poet, daughter of a London tradesman. She contributed to magazines from an early age, and issued volumes of poetry in 1838, 1864 and 1865. She wrote *Eliza Cook's Journal* (1849–54), much of it republished as *Jottings from my Journal* (1860).

COOKE, or COOK, Ebenezer
(c.1667–c.1732)

American poet and satirist, he was one of the first observers of the colonial scene from an explicitly American point of view. He is believed to have been born in London and to have visited Maryland in the mid-1690s and later, before settling finally in Dorchester County sometime after 1710. He worked as a receiver-general and land-agent, and was later an attorney. His most important work is *The Sot-Weed Factor* (1708), a title later

appropriated by the novelist **John Barth**. Cooke's raucous couplets about a British tobacco merchant and his first contact with colonial 'civilization' were full of bombast, deflationary wit and some bile. The later *Sotweed Redivivus* (1730) was more conventional and didactic. Nothing is known about Cooke after 1731, when his compilation *The Maryland Muse* was published.
▷E H Cohen, *Ebenezer Cooke: The Sot-Weed Canon* (1975)

COOK-LYNN, Elizabeth
(1930–)
American writer, born in Fort Thompson, South Dakota. A member of the Crow Creek Sioux tribe and brought up on the reservation, Cook-Lynn's work focuses on the northern plains landscape and culture of the Lakota/Dakota people of North and South Dakota. She has published to date two collections of poetry—*Then Badger Said This* (1983) and *Seek the House of Relatives* (1985); the prose collection *The Power of Horses and Other Stories* (1990) and, most recently, the novel *From the River's Edge* (1991). She is also the founding editor (1985–) of the Native American literary magazine, *Wicazo-Sa Review*.

COOKSON, Catherine Ann
(1906–)
English popular novelist, born in Tyne Dock, County Durham. Her fiction is set in the north-east of England and is replete with tragedy, exploitation and romance. The author of more than 40 books, including the Mallen trilogy and the Tilly Trotter series, she is a favourite among habituées of the public library. She was made a DBE in 1993 for her charitable services in the north-east.
▷*Our Kate* (1969)

COOLIDGE, Susan, pseud of Sarah Chauncy Woolsey
(1835–1905)
American children's writer and literary critic, born in Cleveland, Ohio. She wrote the *Katy* books (*What Katy Did*, 1872, et seq) and other stories for girls, in an easy natural style, free from contemporary sentimentality.
▷Biographical sketch by 'EDWG' in *Last Verses* (1906)

COOMARASWAMY, Ananda
(1877–1947)
Ceylon-born Indian author and scholar. He was a leader of the 20th-century cultural revival in India, especially in the field of art.
▷R Livingston, *The Traditional Theory of Literature* (1962)

COONEY, Ray(mond)
(1932–)
English dramatist, director and producer, born in London. He made his debut as an actor in *Song of Norway* (1946), and appeared in several stage comedies and farces in the 1950s and 1960s. Best known as an author and director, his own first play, a farce, *One for the Pot*, appeared in 1961, and was followed by many others, including *Chase Me Comrade* (1964), *Move Over, Mrs Markham* (1969), *Two Into One* (1981), *Run for your Wife* (1983) and *Wife Begins at Forty* (1986). In 1983 he created the Theatre of Comedy, based at the Shaftesbury Theatre, London.

COOPER, Edmund
(1926–82)
English science-fiction novelist and short-story writer, born in Marple, Cheshire. From his first novel, published in the USA as *Deadly Image* and in the UK as *The Uncertain Midnight* (1958), until his final book, *A World of Difference* (1980, a collection of stories), Cooper was respected as a leading stylist of science fiction. Several of his works consider the form of a post nuclear world as a dark age through which society may have to pass before a new and perhaps more morally responsible civilization evolves.

COOPER, Giles Stannus
(1918–66)
Irish playwright and actor, born in Carrickmines, County Dublin. Although Cooper wrote several stage plays, his sensitivity to the voice and the use of sound resulted in his becoming an exceptional author for radio. His themes of the shortcomings of society, woven into largely naturalistic plays, caught the tenor of the times. *Mathry Beacon* (1956) and *Unman, Wittering and Zigo* (1958) are considered to be his best work. He died after a fall from a moving train near Surbiton, Surrey. In 1978, the annual Giles Cooper Awards for best radio scripts was inaugurated by the BBC and Methuen publishers.

COOPER, James Fenimore
(1789–1851)
American novelist, born in Burlington, New Jersey. His father, a wealthy Quaker and Federalist member of Congress, moved to Cooperstown, New York, then in a wild frontier region of great natural beauty. Cooper entered Yale College in 1803, but was expelled during his third year for a prank. In 1806 he shipped as a common sailor, and in 1808 entered the navy as midshipman. He rose to the rank of lieutenant, but in 1811 resigned his commission and married Susan, a sister of Bishop De Lancey of New York,

and settled down as a country gentleman. His first novel, *Precaution* (1819), was a failure; and the 32 which followed it were of uneven quality. The best were the stories of the sea and of Red Indians—*The Spy* (1821), *The Pilot* (1823), *The Last of the Mohicans* (1826), *The Prairie* (1826), *The Red Rover* (1827), *The Bravo* (1831), *The Pathfinder* (1840), *The Deerslayer* (1841), *The Two Admirals* (1842), *Wing-and-Wing* (1842) and *Satanstoe* (1845). His other writings include a scholarly *Naval History of the United States* (1839), and *Lives of Distinguished American Naval Officers* (1846). After visiting England and France, he was American consul at Lyons (1826–9), and then travelled in Switzerland and Italy till 1831. His later years were much disturbed by literary and newspaper controversies and litigation.
▷S Railton, *Cooper: a study of his life and imagination* (1978)

COOPER, Jilly
(1937–)

English novelist and author of miscellaneous and humorous non-fiction, born in Hornchurch, Essex. Since the appearance of her first book, *How To Stay Married*, in 1969, she has been hugely prolific, specializing initially in cocktail-and-horsey social humour, such as *Jolly Super* (1971) and *Men and Super Men* (1972). Following a series of romantic novels, including *Emily* (1975) and *Prudence* (1978), Cooper published *Riders* (1985), her first huge bestseller, a sensational tale of sex, party-life and horses, dashing young men and highly-charged women. Other similarly raunchy and popular entertainments followed, entitled *Rivals* (1988), *Polo* (1991) and *The Man Who Made Husbands Jealous* (1993).

COOPER, Susan Mary
(1935–)

English writer, born in Burnham, Buckinghamshire. A former journalist for *The Sunday Times* (1956–63), she is best known for her award-winning children's fantasy series *The Dark is Rising*, published in five volumes between 1965 and 1977. Each of the novels in the series focuses on the struggle between the forces of good and evil, personified as Light and Dark. Other works include the realistic wartime novel *Dawn of Fear* (US 1970, UK 1972) and (for adults) the novel *Mandrake* (1964). She is the recipient of the Boston *Globe-Horn* Book Award (1973) and the Newbery Medal (1976).

COOPER, Thomas
(1805–92)

English Chartist and poet, born in Leicester. Apprenticed to a shoemaker at Gainsbor-

ough, he taught himself Latin, Greek, Hebrew and French, and at 23 turned schoolmaster and Methodist preacher. He became leader of the Leicester Chartists in 1841, and got two years for sedition in Stafford jail. Here he wrote *The Purgatory of Suicides*, a poem in the Spenserian stanza, and *Wise Saws and Modern Instances* (both 1845). He published two novels, *Alderman Ralph* (1853) and *The Family Feud* (1854), and in 1855 became a Christian lecturer.
▷R J Conklin, *Thomas Cooper the Chartist, 1805–1892* (1935)

COOPER, William, pseud of Harry Summerfield Hoff
(1910–)

English satirical novelist, born in Crewe. After a spell as a schoolmaster in Leicester, he joined the civil service and during the late 1950s became Personnel Consultant to the Atomic Energy Research Authority. His fifth book, *Scenes from Provincial Life* (1950), tracing the early career of the lower middle-class anti-hero Joe Lunn, had an enormous impact and in retrospect is considered one of the most important of the 'angry' novels depicting provincial life in post-war Britain. Lunn reappears in *Scenes from Metropolitan Life* (written during the 1950s but not published until 1982), *Scenes From Married Life* (1961) and *Scenes from Later Life* (1983).

COORNHERT, Dirck Volkertz
(1522–90)

Dutch poet, translator (**Cicero**, **Seneca**) and dramatist, born in Amsterdam, who was also an engraver and theologian. Both in his poetry and his theology he strongly opposed the cruelties of Calvinism.
▷R M Jones, *Spiritual Reformers of the 16th and 17th Centuries* (1914)

COOVER, Robert Lowell
(1932–)

American novelist, short-story writer and playwright, born in Iowa and educated at the universities of Indiana and Chicago. His first novel was *The Origin of the Brunists* (1966), a claustrophobic and overheated fable about the emergence of a chiliastic religious sect around a mining accident; it won Coover the **William Faulkner** Award. His interest in the construction of mythical and fictive systems developed with *The Universal Baseball Association Inc., J. Henry Waugh, Prop.* (1968). Coover's next novel exploded controversially: a phantasmagorical account of the execution of Julius and Ethel Rosenberg, *The Public Burning* (1977) received considerable publicity for its use of Richard Nixon as a (realistically) scatological

narrator. Despite the fuss, the novel was a failure. Coover's best book remains his vivid collection of short stories, *Pricksongs and Descants* (1969), and in particular 'The Magic Poker', which rewrites *The Tempest* as a fable about the imagination. In the eighties and after, he has turned to elegant, reflexive forms which draw on literary pornography (*Spanking the Maid*, 1981) and baroque extensions of popular iconography (*Pinocchio in Venice*, 1991). Some of his plays were published in *A Theological Position* (1972).
▷J Cope, *Robert Coover's Fictions* (1986)

COPE, Wendy
(1945–)
English poet, born in Erith, Kent and educated at Oxford University. After 15 years as a primary-school teacher in London, she became a freelance writer. Cope has a talent for parody and for light-hearted demolitions of men; these gifts unite in her versions of male authors such as **Ted Hughes** or **Philip Larkin**. She is a little less cruel to **T S Eliot** in 'Limericks on The Wasteland'. The titles *Making Cocoa for Kingsley Amis* (1986) and *Men and their Boring Arguments* (1988) are fair indications of her approach. She has less tonal subtlety than **Stevie Smith** but more boisterous fun.

COPIĆ, Branko
(1915–)
Bosnian novelist, story writer and poet, born in Hasani. He was a Tito partisan. Copić is one of the most popular of Yugoslav writers since World War II. In his well-known novels dealing with the takeover of peasant land by communists in the Bosnian district of Bosanska Krajina, he managed to achieve—despite his declared 'commitment'—a remarkable degree of objectivity. His comic peasant character Nikoletina Bursaca—first introduced in *Dozivljaji Nikoletina Bursaca* (1956)—became a national folk hero. He has been Yugoslavia's leading children's writer, but his work has not yet attracted a translator.

COPPARD, A(lfred) E(dgar)
(1878–1957)
English short-story writer and poet, born in Folkestone. His schooling ceased when he was nine, and after being an office boy, then an accountant, he became a professional writer in 1919. In 1921 he published *Adam and Eve and Pinch Me*, and soon became celebrated for his tales of country life and character. His prose is remarkable for its detailed observation and poetic quality. Other volumes of stories include *The Black Dog* (1923), *The Field of Mustard* (1926) and *Lucy in Her Pink Jacket* (1954). His *Collected Poems* appeared in 1928.
▷*It's Me, O Lord!* (1957); J Schwartz, *The Writings of A.E. Coppard* (1931)

COPPÉE, François
(1842–1908)
French poet, born in Paris. For three years a war-office clerk, he soon turned to poetry, and with *Le Reliquaire* (1866, 'The Reliquary') and *Les Intimités* (1867, 'Intimacies') gained the front rank of the 'Parnassiens'. Later volumes of poetry were *Les Humbles* (1872), *Le Cahier Rouge* (1874, 'The Red Notebook'), *Olivier* (1876, his one long poem), *Les Récits et les Élégies* (1878, 'Stories and Elegies') and *Contes en vers* ('Stories in Verse'). His earliest dramatic poem, *Le Passant* (1869, 'The Wayfarer'), owed much to Sarah Bernhardt, and was followed by *Deux Douleurs* (1870, 'Two Sadnesses'), *L'Abandonnée* ('The Abandoned Woman'), *Le Luthier de Crémone* (1876, 'The Lute Maker from Cremona'), *La Guerre de Cent Ans* ('The Hundred Years War'), *Madame de Maintenon* (1881), *Severo Torelli* (1883), *Les Jacobites* (1885), *Le Pater* (1890), *Pour la couronne* (1895, 'For the Crown'). He won fame in yet another field with his *Contes en prose* ('Prose Tales'), *Vingt Contes nouveaux* ('Twenty New Tales'), and *Contes rapides* ('Brief Tales'). He wrote a novel about religious conversion, *La Bonne Souffrance* (1898, 'The Healthy Pain'), after he became a Catholic.
▷L Le Meur, *La vie et l'oeuvre de François Coppée* (1932)

CORBET, or CORBETT, Richard
(1582–1635)
English poet and prelate, the son of a gardener in Ewell, Surrey. He was educated at Westminster School then passed to Oxford, and in 1620 was made Dean of Christ Church. In 1624 he was consecrated Bishop of Oxford, and in 1632 translated to Norwich. His *Certaine Elegant Poems* (1647) reflects the jovial temper of the man. His longest piece is *Iter Boreale*, a holiday tour of four students; the best and best known is the *Faeries' Farewell*. His other volume of poems, *Poetica Stromata* (1648), was also published posthumously.
▷J E V Crofts, *A life of Bishop Corbett* (1924)

CORBIÈRE, Tristan, pseud of Édouard Joachim
(1845–75)
French poet, born in Coat-Congar, Finistère. Corbière—often bracketed with **Laforgue**— is a poet of great importance and influence. He was largely unknown until **Verlaine** brought him to the attention of the public.

His collection *Amours Jaunes* (1873, 'Yellow Loves') was an acknowledged influence upon **T S Eliot**. His bitter early work reflected the landscape of Brittany, and represented a powerful reaction against the excesses of romanticism. His later, ironic, poetry—which reads as if it had been written at least 50 years after its time—has been unduly neglected in France, but not elsewhere. There are good translations in *Selections from Les Amours Jaunes* (1954).
▷F C Burch, *Tristan Corbière* (1970)

CORELLI, Marie, pseud of **Mary Mackay** (1855–1924)
English popular romantic novelist, born in London, the illegitimate child of Charles Mackay, a journalist, and Ellen Mills, a widow whom he later married as his second wife. She was educated by governesses and trained as a pianist, but though accomplished her métier was writing, to which she devoted herself from 1885. *A Romance of Two Worlds* (1886) marked the beginning of an unprecedented career as a bestseller. A sentimental self-righteous moralist, lacking self-criticism or a sense of the absurd, she was the writer that critics loved to hate. Later in a prolific career she refused reviewers access to her latest books, but her aficionados included Gladstone and **Oscar Wilde** and her readership was immense. Her novels include *Thelma* (1887), *Barabbas* (1893), *God's Good Man* (1904), *The Devil's Motor* (1910), *Eyes of the Sea* (1917) and *The Secret Power* (1921).
▷E Bigland, *Marie Corelli, the woman and the legend* (1953)

CORINNA
(fl.c.500BC)
Greek poet of Tanagra in Boeotia. Her poems, which survive in little beyond substantial fragments of two long pieces, are lyrical narratives derived from Boeotian legends. The titles of others are known, and include *The Return of Orion, Iolaus* and *Seven against Thebes*. The two extant poems, written in short, octosyllabic lines and five- or six-line stanzas, describe a singing contest between the mountain gods of Cithaeron and Helicon, and the marriages of the daughters of Asopus. According to tradition, Corinna taught **Pindar** in his youth and later competed against him in poetic contests.

CORKERY, Daniel
(1878–1964)
Irish cultural leader, born in Cork. Educated at University College, Cork, he was Professor of English there from 1931 to 1947. He published a collection of short stories, *A Munster Twilight* (1917), depicting ethnic and class division in Irish life, and a novel, *The Threshold of Quiet* (1917). He made a great attack on the literary historians who saw Ireland in terms of the 18th-century 'Big House', in his *The Hidden Ireland* (1925). He profoundly influenced new Irish writers such as **Frank O'Connor** and **Sean O'Faolain** and his love of the Irish language was the basis of his literary evangelism, as revealed in his *The Fortunes of the Irish Language* (1954). He also wrote *Synge and Anglo-Irish Literature* (1931) and several plays. He was elected to the Irish Senate in 1951.

CORMAN, Cid
(1924–)
American poet and editor, best known for his editorship of the **Pound**-influenced magazine *Origin*, which was amongst the earliest to publish the work of **Robert Creeley**, **Charles Olson** and others. He is a very prolific poet, author of over 70 collections in various styles (eg Beat, 'Japanese', 'projectionist'), none of which has yet engaged the attention of critics.
▷'Cid Corman Issue' of *Madrona* (Seattle, December 1975)

CORNEILLE, Pierre
(1606–84)
French dramatist, born in Rouen, where he tried to obtain a barrister's practice. In 1629 he removed to Paris, where his comedy *Mélite* (1629, Eng trans *Melite*, 1776), already performed at Rouen, proved highly successful. It was followed by *Clitandre* (1630), *La Veuve* (1634, 'The Widow'), *La Galerie du Palais* (1632, 'The Palace Gallery'), *La Suivante* (1633, 'The Lady's Maid') and *La Place Royale* (1633). In these early pieces intricate and extravagant plots are handled with ingenuity, but the writer's poetic genius flashes out only in occasional verses. For a time Corneille was one of Richelieu's 'five poets', engaged to compose plays on lines laid down by the cardinal; among the pieces thus produced were *Les Tuileries* (1635), *L'Aveugle de Smyrne* (1638, 'The Blind Man of Smyrna') and *La Grande Pastorale* (1639, 'The Great Pastoral'). Corneille, however, was too independent to retain Richelieu's favour. *Médée* (1635, 'Medea') showed a marked advance on his earlier works; and in 1636 *Le Cid* (Eng trans *The Cid*, 1637) took Paris by storm. Richelieu ordered his literary retainers to write it down; but adverse criticism was powerless against the general enthusiasm. *Horace* (1640, Eng trans *Horatius*, 1656), founded on the story of the Horatii, and *Cinna* (Eng trans *Cinna's Conspiracy*, 1713), appeared in 1640; *Polyeucte* (Eng trans *Polyeuctes*, 1655), a noble tragedy, in 1642; and *La Mort de Pompée* (Eng trans *Pompey the Great*, 1664) in 1643. *Le Menteur* (1643, Eng

trans *The Mistaken Beau; or, The Liar,* 1685) entitles Corneille to be called the father of French comedy as well as of French tragedy. *Théodore* was brought out in 1645, and *Rodogune* (Eng trans 1765) in 1646. Between 1647—when he was made an academician—and 1653 Corneille produced *Héraclius* (1646 or 1647, Eng trans *Heraclius, Emperor of the East,* 1664), *Don Sanche d'Aragon* (1649), *Andromède* (1649), *Nicomède* (1651, Eng trans *Nicomede,* 1671), and *Pertharite* (1651). These pieces, of which the last was damned, show a decline in dramatic and poetic power; and Corneille occupied himself with a verse translation of Thomas à Kempis's *Imitatio Christi, L'Imitation de Jésus-Christ* (1651). He returned to the stage in 1659 with *Œdipe,* which was followed by *La Toison d'or* (1660, 'The Golden Fleece'), *Sertorius* (1662), *Sophonisbe* (1663), *Othon* (1669), *Agésilas* (1666), *Attila* (1667) and *Tite et Bérénice* (1670). In 1671 he joined **Molière** and Quinault in writing the opera *Psyché.* His last works were *Pulchérie* (1672) and *Suréna* (1674, Eng trans *Surenas,* 1969). After his marriage in 1640 he lived habitually in Rouen until 1662, when he settled in Paris. During his later years his popularity waned before that of **Racine**, whose cause was espoused by **Nicolas Boileau** and the king. A master of the Alexandrine verse form, he concerned himself with moral and mental conflict rather than physical action.
▷P J Yarrow, *Corneille* (1963)

CORNEILLE, Thomas
(1625–1709)
French playwright, brother of **Pierre Corneille**, born in Rouen. He was a dramatist of merit, his tragedies—*Camma* (1661), *Laodice* (1668), *Pyrrhus* (1690), *Bérénice* (1657), *Timocrate* (1656), *Ariane* (1672), *Bradamante* (1696), and others—being in general superior to his comedies. He also wrote a verse translation of **Ovid**'s *Metamorphoses.*
▷D Collins, *Thomas Corneille, protean dramatist* (1968)

CORNFORD, Frances Crofts
(1886–1960)
English poet who lived most of her life in Cambridge. A grand-daughter of Charles Darwin, she wrote delicate poems of an intensely personal nature, often about favourite landscapes or minute incidents with companions. Her work has been much neglected, possibly because it can seem sentimental, but she is often capable of the sublime expression of emotional states. Her *Collected Poems* appeared in 1956.

CORRAZINI, Sergio
(1886–1907)
Italian 'crepuscular' poet, usually bracketed with the more gifted **Gozzano**. His poems,

influenced by **Laforgue**, are similarly bitter, sad and witty. He died of tuberculosis.
▷F Donini, *Vita e poesia de Sergio Corrazini* (1949)

CORRÊA GARÇÃO, Pedro Antonio
(1724–72)
Portuguese neo-classical poet, who was born in Lisbon. He became the leading member of the Arcádia Lusitana group (founded 1756), which aimed to free Portuguese poetry from foreign influences and restore the purity of the language. Under the name Córidon Erimanteu, he wrote many essays on his art. His master was **Horace**. He died in prison, for reasons which are not entirely clear.
▷T Braga, *A arcádia lusitana* (1898)

CORREIA, Raimundo
(1860–1911)
Brazilian poet, influenced by the French Parnassian poets and praised by the great **Machado de Assis**, who recognized in his poetry anguished yearnings after more than just the usual perfection of form. He was both subtle, as distinct from the facility of **Bilac**, and intense.

CORRIS, Peter
(1942–)
Australian writer of adventure novels, born in Stawell, Victoria. Although trained as a historian, and sometime literary editor of the defunct weekly *National Times,* his early addiction to the American 'hard-boiled' school of thrillers led to writing pastiches of **Raymond Chandler**. In *Cliff Hardy* (*The Dying Trade,* 1980, et seq) he created an antipodean Philip Marlowe and, like Marlowe and Chandler, both character and author matured over the years. Corris has created other pivotal characters, the most imaginative of whom is Richard Browning, a failed Australian actor who, upon his death, is found to have left a series of tape recordings of his adventures. Recent titles are *Browning PI* (1992) and *Browning Battles On* (1993), which takes the hero to an army training course in World War II and to an encounter with actor Peter Finch. The Browning titles are characterized by historicity—the last two titles each have six pages of textual notes.

CORSO, Gregory Nunzio
(1930–)
American poet, born in New York City. He had a difficult and violent childhood, and spent three years in jail for attempted robbery in his teens. He became friendly with **Allen Ginsberg**, and is associated with the Beat Poets in both style and content, although his rage against the 'hung-up' state of US society

is tempered with a sardonic, irreverent humour. His first poems appeared in *The Vestal Lady of Brattle* (1955), and he has published many subsequent volumes, including *Gasoline* (1958) and *Elegiac Feelings American* (1970). Later works like *Ankh* (1971) and *Earth Egg* (1974) reflect a fascination with Egypt and Eastern religion. Other books include a novel, *The American Express* (1961).

CORTADA, Joan
(1805–68)

Catalan novelist who wrote romantic historical novels modelled on those of Sir **Walter Scott**.
▷ *Hispanic Review*, XIII (1945)

CORTÁZAR, Julio
(1914–84)

Argentinian/French writer, born in Brussels. He grew up in Argentina, where he was educated. From 1935 to 1945 he taught in secondary schools in several small towns and in Mendoza, Argentina. From 1945 to 1951 he was a translator for publishers, then moved to Paris where he lived until his death, writing and freelancing for Unesco. He is one of the most widely recognized Spanish–American writers outside the Spanish-speaking world, owing this particularly to the filming of *Hopscotch* (*Rayuela*, 1963, Eng trans 1966), and of a short story, 'Blow-Up' (from *Blow-Up and Other Stories*, 1968), by the Italian director Michelangelo Antonioni. Others of his novels which have been translated include *Los premios* (1960, Eng trans *The Winners*, 1965) and *62: modelo para armar* (1968, Eng trans *62: A Model Kit*, 1972).
▷ S Boldy, *The Novels of Cortázar* (1980)

CORVO, Baron *see* ROLFE, Frederick William

CORY, William Johnson
(1823–92)

English poet, born in Torrington, Devon. Educated at Eton and King's College, Cambridge, he was assistant-master at Eton from 1845 to 1872, when he inherited an estate, assumed the name of Cory, and moved to London. He was author of a book of anonymously published poems, *Ionica, Poems* (1858, enlarged 1891), and wrote the 'Eton Boating Song' in 1865. His *Letters and Journals* were published in 1897.
▷ F C Mackenzie, *William Cory, a biography* (1950)

COSBUC, Gheoghe
(1866–1918)

Romanian poet and translator, born in Cosbuc. He was the son of the village priest.

He edited a Bucharest periodical with **Ion Caragiale** and others, and later became one of the most influential of all 19th-century Romanian editors. He in no way anticipated modernism, but was a popular (although intellectual) peasant poet who regarded the village as the proper foundation of national life.

ĆOSIĆ, Dobrica
(1921–)

Serbian novelist and political activist, born in Velika Drenova. He was active as a partisan during World War II, a period recounted in his first novel *Daleko je sunce* (1951, Eng trans *Far Away in the Sun*, 1963). His second novel *Koreni* (1954, 'Roots') examined Serbia's slow independence from the Ottoman Empire, while the three-volume *Deobe* (1961–3, 'Partitions') returned to the period of World War II. After the war, Ćosić served as a communist representative in the Yugoslav parliament, but in 1968 he was expelled from the central committee of the Serbian League of Communists. In the years that followed, he wrote his major work, the four-volume *Vreme smrti* (1972–9), which was published in an English-language abridgement as *A Time of Death, Reach to Eternity* and *South to Destiny* (1978–81) and then in full as *This Land, This Time* (1983). A controversial figure, he explores his nation's history with vivid directness.

COSTA, Cláudio Manuel da
(1729–89)

Brazilian poet, born in the Minas Gerais district. His suicide over a complex political issue—he had implicated others in an anti-Portuguese conspiracy—cut short a poetic career which had, ironically, been closely based on Portuguese models. Thus he was an 'Arcadian' poet who took a pseudonym (Glauceste Satúrnio) for his highly artificial pastoral poetry. He had wanted to break with his 'European' style, but was never able to do so decisively. However, he remains one of the two great *mineiro* lyrical poets, the other, **Alvarenga**, falling short of him.

COSTA I LLOBERA, Miguel
(1854–1922)

Catalan (Mallorcan) poet, priest and writer, one of the major figures in the earlier history of the Catalan revival. After travel in Italy and the acquirement of a classical style he won (1902) the title of *mestre en gai saber* ('master troubadour') for his excellence. His poetry, although finely made and technically influential, is somewhat artificial. He was translated into several European languages by other priests, too serene in their faith to discern the disturbing elements in human nature as portrayed in his work.

COSTER, Charles de
(1827–79)

Belgian storyteller, born in Munich. He studied at Brussels. His most famous work, the prose epic *La Légende et les Aventures Héroiques, Joyeuse et Glorieuses d'Ulenspiegel* (1866, Eng trans *The Legend of the Glorious Adventures of Tyl Ulenspiegel*, 1918), took 10 years to write.
▷H Liebrecht, *La vie et le rêve de Charles de Coster* (1927)

COTTIN, Sophie, née Risteau
(1770–1807)

French writer. At 17 she married a Parisian banker, who left her a childless widow at 20. For comfort she turned to writing, wrote verses and a lengthy history, and romantic fiction. She had already written *Claire d'Albe* (1799) and *Mathilde* (1805) when, in 1806, she wrote her most successful work, *Élisabeth, ou les exilés de Sibérie*, ('Elisabeth, or the Siberian Exiles').
▷L C Sykes, *Madame Cottin* (1949)

COTTON, Charles
(1630–87)

English writer, born at his father's estate of Beresford in Staffordshire. His father was a warm friend of **Ben Jonson**, Selden, **John Donne** and other illustrious men. The boy travelled on the Continent, and early wrote verses which were circulated privately. In 1656 he married his cousin Isabella, half-sister of the regicide John Hutchinson (1615–64). Though a sincere loyalist, he seems to have lived securely enough under the Commonwealth, and the decay of his father's estate was due mainly to unprosperous lawsuits. In 1664 he issued anonymously his burlesque poem, *Scarronides, or the First Book of Virgil Travestie*, added to in later editions in grossness as well as in bulk. Later works are his *Voyage to Ireland in Burlesque* (1670), *Burlesque upon Burlesque* (1675), *Planter's Manual* (1675), and a treatise on fly-fishing contributed in 1676 to the fifth edition of Walton's *Compleat Angler*. He also published a masterly translation of **Montaigne**'s *Essays* (1685).
▷E R Miner, *The Cavalier Mode from Honson to Cotton* (1973)

COTTRELL, Dorothy
(1902–57)

Australian-born writer of popular fiction and short stories, born in Picton, New South Wales. Crippled by polio at the age of five she was subsequently confined to a wheelchair. Her early years were spent on the Queensland station of relatives where, in 1922, she married an American employed there. Her first novel, *The Singing Gold*, an unsophisticated tale set in rural Queensland, was serialized in the US *Ladies Home Journal* before publication in 1928. This enabled the Cottrells to move to the USA, where despite her severe handicap she lived an active life and travelled extensively. She was much in demand as a journalist and short-story writer, and her work was published regularly in the *Saturday Evening Post*. A mystery novel, *The Silent Reefs* (1953), was set in her beloved Caribbean and later filmed. Although championed by Dame **Mary Gilmore** she was much criticized by Australian feminist writers for moving to the USA and becoming a lucrative author, though which was the greater offence is not clear.

COUCH, Sir Arthur Quiller
(1863–1944)

English writer, born in Bodmin, in Cornwall. He was educated at Clifton College and Trinity College, Oxford, where he was a lecturer in classics (1886–7). After some years of literary work in London and in Cornwall, where he lived from 1891, he became Professor of English Literature at Cambridge (1912). He edited the *Oxford Book of English Verse* (1900) and other anthologies, and published volumes of essays, criticism, poems, and parodies, among them *From a Cornish Window* (1906), *On the Art of Writing* (1916), *Studies in Literature* and *On the Art of Reading* (1920). He is also remembered for a series of humorous novels set in a Cornish background, written under the pseudonym 'Q'.
▷B Willey, *The Q Tradition* (1946)

COUPER, John Mill
(1914–)

Australian poet, born in Dundee, Scotland. His four published volumes are *East of Living* (1957), which includes an extended section on the drowning of the crew of Flinders's ship *The Investigator*, *The Book of Bligh* (1969), dealing with the *Bounty* mutiny and its aftermath, *In from the Sea* (1974) and *The Lee Shore* (1979). His preoccupation with seafaring themes suggests his sense of isolation in his adopted land.

COUPERUS, Louis
(1863–1923)

Dutch poet and novelist, born in The Hague. He was largely brought up in Batavia, in the Dutch East Indies, and lived in Italy. His naturalistic first novel, *Eline Vere* (1889, Eng trans 1892), was a success, and he went on to write several more, including novels set in the Dutch East Indies, and a powerful, fatalistic tetralogy of life in the Hague, *Dr Adriaan* (1901–4, Eng trans *The Books of the Small Souls*, 1914).

▷ W J Simons, *Louis Couperus* (1963)

COURAGE, James Francis
(1903–63)

New Zealand writer, born in Christchurch, who lived in London from his mid-twenties and wrote a number of books, usually with a theme of obsessive love. His first novel, *One House*, was published in 1933, but the second, *The Fifth Child*, set in New Zealand, did not appear until 1948. In *The Young Have Secrets* (1954) the author revisits, in the guise of an 18-year-old, the Christchurch of his youth. He returned to England for the setting of his last two novels, *A Way of Love* (1959), a homosexual love story, and *The Visit to Penmorten* (1961). **Charles Brasch** collected a number of his shorter pieces in *Such Separate Creatures: Stories* (1973).

COURTELINE, Georges, pseud of **Georges Moinaux**
(1860–1929)

French dramatist, born in Tours. A humorous journalist who turned to the stage, he wrote satirical comedies, many of them one-acters, including *Boubouroche* (1893), *Un Client sérieux* (1897, 'A Serious Client') and *Le Commissaire est bon enfant* (1900, 'The Commissioner is Good Natured'). He also published novels, such as *Le Train de 8ʰ47* (1888, 'The 8:47 Train', dramatized 1909) and *Messieurs les Ronds-de-cuir* (1893, 'The Pen Pushers').

▷ P Bournecque, *Le théâtre de Georges Courteline* (1969)

COURTHOPE, William John
(1842–1917)

English poet and critic, born in South Malling vicarage, near Lewes. He was educated at Harrow School and Corpus Christi College and New College, Oxford, where he was Professor of Poetry (1895–1901). In 1892–1907 he was first civil service commissioner. Among his critical works are *Addison* (1883), *Pope* (1889) and *History of English Poetry* (6 vols, 1895–1909). He also published some charming verse in *Paradise of Birds* (1870) and *The Country Town* (1920), and a satire on women's rights, *Ludibria Lunae* (1869).

▷ J W Mackail, *William J Courthope, 1842–1917* (1919)

COUTO, Rui Ribeiro
(1898–1963)

Brazilian novelist and poet. A leading member of the group which promoted Brazilian Modernism, his poetry has been respected without being much discussed. He wrote many competent novels. Titles include *O jardin das Confidêcias* (1921, 'The Burden of Confidences').

COUVREUR, Jessie, née **Huybers**
(1848–97)

Australian novelist and short-story writer, born in Highgate, London, of Dutch–French stock. She arrived with her family in Hobart, Tasmania in the early 1850s. She married a gambler and womanizer, Charles Fraser, but in 1883 instituted divorce proceedings. She returned to Europe where she married Auguste Couvreur, member of the Belgian parliament (1864–84) and journalist. On her husband's death (1894), she took over as Belgian correspondent for the London *Times*. Her first and best-known novel, *Uncle Piper of Piper's Hill* (1889), was followed by *In Her Earliest Youth* (1890), *The Penance of Portia James* (1891) and *Not Counting the Cost* (1895). *A Fiery Ordeal* (1897) drew more on her marital experiences. Unlike many of her Australian contemporaries, Couvreur wrote not of the land but of the city, families and social divisions. Distinctly English in style, her works give a vivid picture of Australian middle-class life in the latter half of the 19th century.

COUZYN, Jeni
(1942–)

South African-born Canadian poet. She was educated at the University of Natal, taught in Rhodesia and London, and has been a full-time writer since 1968. She took Canadian citizenship in 1975. Her first volume, *Flying* (1970), described her South African background, and documented the psychological impact of exile on everyday perceptions and relationships. *Monkeys' Wedding* (1972, rev edn 1978) was much less oblique and by no means as successful. *Christmas in Africa* (1975), *House of Changes* (1978) and *The Happiness Bird* (1978) turn again to South Africa for much of their imagery, but also include poems which develop a consciousness coloured by science fiction and technological fantasy. With exceptionally balanced irony, Couzyn explores female sexuality as if it were an alien excrescence, but in her most assured collection, *A Time to be Born* (1981), she has come to terms with the world and her own identity within it, a situation reflected in her selection of work for *The Bloodaxe Book of Contemporary Women Poets* (1984). In that same year an expanded edition of her fine selected poems, *Life By Drowning* (originally published 1983), also appeared.

COVERDALE, Miles
(1488–1568)

English Protestant reformer and biblical scholar, born in Yorkshire. He studied at Cambridge, was ordained priest at Norwich in 1514, and joined the Augustinian Friars at Cambridge, where he was converted to Protestantism. He lived abroad from 1528 to 1534 to escape persecution; and in 1535 published in Zürich the first translation of the whole Bible into English, with a dedication to Henry VIII. The Prayer Book retains the Psalms of this translation, and many of the finest phrases in the Authorized Version of 1611 are directly due to Coverdale. In 1538 he was sent by Thomas Cromwell to Paris to superintend another English edition of the Scriptures. Francis I had granted a licence, but during the printing an edict was issued prohibiting the work. Many of the sheets were burned, but the presses and types were hastily carried over to London. Grafton and Whitchurch, the noted printers of that day, were thus enabled to bring out in 1539, under Coverdale's superintendence, the 'Great Bible', which was presented to Henry VIII by Cromwell. The second 'Great Bible', known also as 'Cranmer's Bible' (1540), was also edited by Coverdale, who on Cromwell's fall found it expedient to leave England. While abroad he married and acted as Lutheran pastor in Rhenish Bavaria. In March 1548 he returned to England, was well received through Cranmer's influence, and in 1551 was made bishop of Exeter. On Mary I's accession he was deprived of his see, but was allowed to leave the country, at the earnest intercession of the King of Denmark, whose chaplain, Dr Macchabaeus (MacAlpine), was Coverdale's brother-in-law. Returning to England in 1559, he did not resume his bishopric, but in 1564 he was collated by Grindal to the living of St Magnus, near London Bridge, from which he resigned from growing Puritan scruples about the liturgy in 1566.
▷ J F Mozley, *Coverdale and His Bibles* (1953)

COWARD, Sir Noël Pierce
(1899–1973)

English actor, dramatist, and composer of light music, born in Teddington. At the age of 14 he appeared in *Peter Pan*, and thereafter in other plays, including many of his own. His first play, *I'll Leave It to You* (1920), was followed by many successes, including *The Vortex* (1924), *Hay Fever* (1925), *Private Lives* (1930), *Blithe Spirit* (1941), *This Happy Breed* (1943) and *Nude With Violin* (1956), all showing his strong satiric humour and his unique gift for witty dialogue. He wrote the music for, among others, his operetta *Bitter Sweet* (1929) and his play *Cavalcade* (1931),

and for a series of revues, including *Words and Music* (1932), with its 'Mad Dogs and Englishmen', *This Year of Grace* (1928) and *Sigh No More* (1945). He produced several films based on his own scripts, including *In Which We Serve* (1942), *Blithe Spirit* (1945) and *Brief Encounter* (1945). He published two autobiographies, *Present Indicative* (1937) and *Future Indefinite* (1954).
▷ S Morley, *A Talent to Amuse* (1969)

COWLEY, Abraham
(1618–67)

English poet, born in London, the seventh and posthumous child of a stationer. Attracted to poetry by **Spenser**'s *Faerie Queen*, he wrote excellent verses at 10, and at 15 published five poems. From Westminster School he proceeded in 1637 to Trinity College, Cambridge, and while there wrote, among many other pieces, a large portion of his epic the *Davideis*, its hero David, which was published with a reprint of his first book, *The Mistress*, and a number of other poems, in 1656. During the Civil War he was ejected from Cambridge (1644) but studied at Oxford for another two years. In 1646 he accompanied or followed the queen to Paris, was sent on Royalist missions, and carried on her correspondence in cipher with the king. He returned to England in 1654 and in 1655 was arrested, released on £1000 bail, and took the Oxford MD (1657). On Oliver Cromwell's death he returned to Paris, but went home to England at the Restoration, and received a comfortable provision.
▷ J G Taaffe, *Abraham Cowley* (1972)

COWLEY, Hannah
(1743–1809)

English playwright and poet, one of the first exponents of the comedy of manners. The daughter of a Devonshire bookseller, her first play, *The Runaway* (1776), was written in a fortnight, and produced by David Garrick at Drury Lane. Before retiring to Devon in 1801, she rapidly produced 13 works for the stage, the most successful being *The Belle's Strategem* (1780), which was frequently revived, notably by Henry Irving in 1881, with Ellen Terry as Letitia. She also wrote long narrative verses (1780–94) and, under the pseudonym Anna Matilda, carried on a sentimental, poetic correspondence in the *World*.

COWLEY, Malcolm
(1898–1989)

American writer, critic and editor, born in Belsano, Pennsylvania. His father was a doctor, which enabled him to attend Harvard, though he had to struggle to make a living as a neophyte writer in New York and

Paris. The experience of hardship, however, proved useful when he came to write *Exile's Return* (1934), about the illustrious group of American writers who convened in Paris after World War I. He returned to the theme with *A Second Flowering: Works and Days of the Lost Generation* (1973), and *The Dream of the Golden Mountains: Remembering the 1930s* (1980). He also published a volume of poetry, *Blue Juniata* (1929), and several volumes of essays. Long associated with *The New Republic* as literary editor (1929–44), and responsible for recognizing the talent of **John Cheever**, he is credited with resuscitating the career of **William Faulkner** by editing a Viking Portable selection of his work (1949).
▷ *Think Back on Us* (1967)

COWPER, Richard, originally **John Middleton-Murry**
(1926–)
English science-fiction novelist, born in Bridport, Dorset, son of the critic **John Middleton-Murry**. Although he has written some novels under the name of Colin Middleton-Murry, it is as Richard Cowper that he is most widely known. His first novel, confidently entitled *Breakthrough* (1967), led to many highly-regarded books, of which *The Road to Corlay* (1978) is perhaps the most acclaimed. Set in the future, it imagines a Britain governed by a totalitarian church, against which the Cult of the White Bird, led by a young man called Thomas, represents the only concerted opposition. This premise allows Cowper to consider serious political and moral themes within the context of a fast-paced narrative.

COWPER, William
(1731–1800)
English poet, son of the rector of Great Berkhamstead, Hertfordshire. He was educated at Westminster School, where Warren Hastings and the poet **Charles Churchill** were contemporaries. In 1752 he took chambers in the Middle Temple and was called to the Bar in 1754. He made no attempt to practise, but showed signs of mental instability. In 1763 he tried to commit suicide when he was offered the sinecure job of a clerkship in the House of Lords, involving a formal examination. Cured temporarily from his breakdown, he was received into the household of a retired evangelical clergyman, Morley Unwin, who with his wife Mary contrived to make the poet's stay at Huntingdon happy. On the death of Mr Unwin his widow removed with her children to Olney, in Buckinghamshire, which was henceforth to be associated with the name of Cowper. Unfortunately the curate of Olney, John Newton, was precisely the person to undo the work of tranquillizing the sick man. His gloomy piety, imposed on the poet, eventually caused a recurrence of his malady (1773), but the fruit of their association was the *Olney Hymns* (1779), to which Cowper contributed some hymns which are still favourites. In 1779 Newton accepted a charge in London and his absence was at once reflected in a restoration of the poet's spirits. Mrs Unwin suggested to him the writing of a series of moral satires which were published in 1782 (*Poems*) along with some occasional pieces which show the lighter side of his talent. Further to engage him in literary activity, Lady Austen now appeared on the scene (1781) as the occupant of Newton's vicarage. It is not known why her friendship with the poet was interrupted two years later, but *The Task*, published in 1785, came from her suggestion. Cowper's cousin, Lady Hesketh, took her place as literary director (1786), but Cowper seems to have exhausted himself as a creative poet and now turned only to translations—of **Homer**, which was not successful (1791), **Milton**'s Latin poems and some French and Italian translations. His genius, however, was still apparent in the short or occasional piece: 'On Receiving My Mother's Picture', 'To Mary' and 'Yardley Oak' (1791). Out of the darkest period, after Mrs Unwin's death in 1796, comes the wonderful, if tragic, 'Castaway'. The lighter side of Cowper's genius—the comic ballad 'John Gilpin', 'Table Talk', and the burlesque opening of *The Task*, a long poem on rural themes—should not be overlooked, but he is generally regarded as the poet of the evangelical revival and as the precursor of **Wordsworth** as a poet of Nature.
▷ Lord David Cecil, *The Stricken Deer* (1933)

COXE, Louis O(sborne)
(1918–)
American poet and critic, born in Manchester, New Hampshire, and educated at Princeton. His first book, *The Sea Faring and Other Poems*, was published in 1947. A major volume, *The Last Hero and Other Poems*, appeared in 1965. Among Coxe's other works are *Billy Budd* (1951), a three-act play based upon the novel of the same name by **Herman Melville** (written in conjunction with a university friend, Robert Chapman), and a highly-praised critical work on **Chaucer** (1963).

COZZENS, James Gould
(1903–78)
American writer, born in Chicago. He published his first novel, *Confusion* (1924), while a student at Harvard at the age of 19. He fought with the American air force in World War II, and on his release from service wrote the Pulitzer Prize-winning *Guard of Honour* (1948). Among his other works are *S.S. San*

Pedro (1931), *Ask Me Tomorrow* (1940), *The Just and the Unjust* (1942), *By Love Possessed* (1958) and *Children and Others* (1965).
▷M Bruccoli, *Cozzens: a new acquist of true experience* (1979) and *Cozzens: a life apart* (1983)

CRABBE, George
(1754–1832)
English poet, born in Aldeburgh on the Suffolk Coast, son of a 'salt-master' and warehousekeeper. His father's violence was offset by his mother's piety. Two of his three brothers perished at sea. His schooling was irregular, but he managed to pick up enough surgery in a nine month's course in London to enable him to set up poorly as a surgeon in Aldeburgh. This was not his chosen career, for he had already published *Inebriety, a Poem* in 1775 and *The Candidate*. He ventured into the literary world in London in 1780, but lived in poverty, unrelieved by appeals to various patrons of letters, until a favourable answer from **Edmund Burke** changed the course of his life. As the guest of Burke at Beaconsfield, he met the noted men of the day, published *The Library* (1781), and patronage flowed in. He was ordained in 1782 and the next year was established in the Duke of Rutland's seat at Belvoir with the prospect of various livings to follow his chaplaincy there. After his marriage to Sarah Elmy (1783) he spent happy years in charges in Suffolk (1792–1805); returned to Muston in Leicestershire; and finally settled in Trowbridge, Wiltshire. In 1783 *The Village*, a harshly realistic poem about village life sponsored by Burke and **Dr Johnson**, brought him fame. Twenty-four years passed before *The Parish Register* (1807) revealed his gifts as a narrative poet. He followed this with *The Borough* (1810), a collection of 24 tales in letter-form (which were later to form the basis of Benjamin Britten's opera, *Peter Grimes*). *Tales* followed in 1812, showing no decline in his powers of narrative and character-drawing. *Tales of the Hall* (1819) concluded this remarkable output of narrative genius. Crabbe's manner suited all tastes—he is still read because of his veracity and his masterly genre painting of humble and middle-class life. His strict moralism—the miseries of the poor are due to sin and insobriety—seems strange to the modern reader, but the grim stories of madness as in 'Sir Eustace Grey' (*Parish Register*) and the comic wooing in 'The Frank Courtship' (*Tales*), show his craft at its best.
▷T E Krebbel, *Life of George Crabbe* (1972)

CRACE, Jim (James)
(1946–)
English novelist and journalist, born in London, whose austere, literary prose has

brought him considerable acclaim. His first novel, *Continent*, appeared in 1986, followed two years later by *Gift of Stones*. Both look at the nature of narrative and story-telling, mythology, history and change. In the latter book, these themes are interwoven through a love story. The ironically entitled *Arcadia* (1992) presents a disturbing vision of the modern city.

CRADDOCK, Charles Egbert, pseud of Mary Noailles Murfree
(1850–1922)
American writer, born in Murfreesboro, Tennessee. She published short stories in the *Atlantic Monthly* from 1878, published as *In the Tennessee Mountains* (1884), and thereafter became a prolific novelist of mountain backwoods life.
▷E Parks, *Charles Egbert Craddock* (1941)

CRAIK, Dinah Maria, née Mulock
(1826–87)
English novelist, born in Stoke-upon-Trent. Settling in London at 20, she published *The Ogilvies* (1849), *Olive* (1850), *The Head of the Family* (1851) and *Agatha's Husband* (1853). Her best-known novel was *John Halifax, Gentleman* (1857). Her short stories were collected as *Avillion* (1853), and *Collected Poems* appeared in 1881. She also wrote essays, children's stories, and fairy tales. In 1865 she married George Lillie Craik, nephew of George Lillie Craik, a partner in the publishing house of Macmillan, and was assigned the benefits of a Civil List pension awarded in 1864 to less well-off authors.

CRANE, (Harold) Hart
(1899–1932)
American poet, born in Garrettsville, Ohio. He had little formal education and resisted attempts to place him in the business world, but worked as an advertising copywriter in New York before he found a patron who gave him the wherewithal to travel and devote himself to poetry. An alcoholic and homosexual, given to troughs of shame and remorse, he placed a heavy burden on his friends' tolerance and wallets. Nevertheless he managed to publish two volumes—*White Buildings* (1926) and the long, symbolic *The Bridge* (1930)—variously hailed as masterpieces and unintelligible. Crane is now recognized as one of America's major poets, having much in common with **Walt Whitman**. Returning to America from Mexico, where he had attempted unsuccessfully to write an epic poem on Montezuma, he drowned himself by leaping from a steamboat into the Caribbean.
▷J Unterecker, *Voyager: a life of Crane* (1969)

CRANE, Nathalia, pseud of Clara Ruth Abarbanel
(1913–)

American poet. A mysterious one-off in American literature, she published her first collection of verse, *The Janitor's Boy* (1924) at the age of 11; it was widely thought to have been written by an adult. Later works evoked the same surreal blend of simplicity and precocious understanding: certainly there were no more elements of doggerel than in the jog-trot, hymn-book rhythms of **Emily Dickinson**, who by the time Crane was publishing, was enshrined as a major American poet. Crane also wrote a visionary poem of the Children's Crusade, called *The Sunken Garden* (1926).

CRANE, Stephen
(1871–1900)

American writer and war correspondent, born in New Jersey. He worked as a journalist in New York before publishing his first novel, *Maggie: A Girl of the Streets* (1893). His reputation, however, rests on *The Red Badge of Courage* (1895), which relates vividly the experiences of a soldier in the American Civil War. (The surreal verse of *The Black Riders* dates from the same year.) He had no personal experience of the war but *The Red Badge of Courage* was received with acclaim, in particular for its psychological realism. He never repeated its success but was lionized by literary London (befriended by **Joseph Conrad** and meeting **H G Wells**) before succumbing to tuberculosis in Baden Baden.
▷R W Stallman, *Crane: a biography* (1968)

CRAPSEY, Adelaide
(1878–1914)

American poet of advanced leanings and entirely posthumous reputation. She was born in Brooklyn, New York, the daughter of an eccentrically brilliant clergyman. Educated at Vassar College and in Rome (where she investigated classical archaeology), she spent the remainder of her brief life as a teacher in a girls' school. Almost all of her work was written on her deathbed, using metrical forms resembling **Ezra Pound**'s neo-classical and quasi-oriental experiments, but which were developed parallel to his and were not influenced by them. A collection of *Verse* (1915) and an ambitious but unfinished *Analysis of English Metrics* (1918) are the only publications of this remarkable figure.

CRASHAW, Richard
(c.1613–49)

English religious poet, born in London, the only son of the Puritan poet and clergyman William Crashaw (1572–1626). From Charterhouse he proceeded in 1631 to Pembroke Hall, Cambridge, and c.1636 became a fellow of Peterhouse College. In 1634 he published a volume of Latin poems, *Epigrammatum Sacrocorum Liber* (2nd edn 1670), in which occurs the famous line on the miracle at Cana: '*Nymphas pudica Deum vidit et erubuit*' (the modest water saw its God and blushed). His Catholic leanings prevented him from receiving Anglican orders, and in 1643 he lost his fellowship for refusing to take the Covenant. He went to Paris and embraced Catholicism, and in 1646 published his *Steps to the Temple*, republished at Paris in 1652, under the title *Carmen Deo Nostro*, with 12 vignette engravings designed by Crashaw. Soon afterwards he was introduced by John Cowley to Queen Henrietta Maria, who recommended him at Rome; and in April 1649 he became a sub-canon at Loretto, but died four months afterwards.
▷M Praz, *Richard Crashaw* (1945)

CRATINUS
(c.484–c.419 BC)

Greek comic poet. Next to Eupolis and **Aristophanes**, he best represents the Old Attic comedy. He limited the number of actors to three, and was the first to add to comedy the interest of biting personal attack; even Pericles did not escape his pen. Of his 21 comedies, nine of which obtained the first public prize, on one occasion beating Aristophanes' *Nephelai* ('Clouds'), only some fragments are extant.

CRAWFORD, F(rancis) Marion
(1854–1909)

American novelist, born at Bagni di Lucca, Italy. After an extensive education in the USA and Europe and working as a journalist in India, he became a bestselling writer with the exotic *Mr Isaacs, A Tale of Modern India* (1882); thereafter he spent most of his life in Italy, where many of his more than 40 romantic and historical novels are set. Italian aristocratic society provided the subject-matter for the 'Saracinesca' series: *Saracinesca* (1887), *Sant' Ilario* (1889), *Don Orsino* (1892) and *Corleone* (1897). Meanwhile, in *The Novel: What It Is* (1893) Crawford set out his creed as a romantic novelist, who wrote to entertain rather than to improve his readers. His books are certainly not bereft of ideas, but despite his immense contemporary popularity, only his ghost stories, such as 'The Upper Berth' (1885) and 'The Screaming Skull' (1908) are widely read now.
▷J Pilkington Jr, *Francis Marion Crawford* (1964)

CRAWFORD, Isabella Vallancy
(1850–87)

Irish-born Canadian poet and short-story writer. An emigrant to Canada West from Dublin in 1858, Vallancy Crawford was one of 13 children of whom only three survived infancy. Earnings from her writing became the only source of support for her mother and herself after her father's death. She produced a range of periodical literature, including many short stories of which a number of selections have been published. However, it is her poetry that has earned her critical recognition, although only one volume, *Old Spookses' Pass, Malcolm's Katie and Other Poems* (1884), was published during her lifetime. In her poems she imbues the Canadian landscape with a mythic significance, imaging the forces of good, evil and love in a symbolic language specific to her Canadian pioneer experience; she was described by Northrop Frye as having 'the most remarkable mythopoeic imagination in Canadian poetry'. A revival of critical interest in her poetry during the 1970s—principally inspired by **James Reaney**'s admiration for her work—culminated in the important Crawford Symposium of 1977 (collected papers published in Ottawa, 1979).

CREASEY, John
(1908–73)

English crime and espionage writer, who used no less than 25 pseudonyms (male and female), of which J J Marric was perhaps the best known. Born in Southfields, Surrey, he was educated in London, and wrote full-time from 1935, two years after the first Department Z thriller was published. An astonishingly prolific writer, Creasey's better-known series characters were Inspector Roger West, the Hon Richard Rollison ('The Toff') and the former jewel thief John Mannering (better known as 'The Baron'). The Marric novels (1955, 1976, posthumous) all concern Commander George Gideon of Scotland Yard, and bear his name in their titles. With more than 550 novels to his credit, Creasey's work was variable in quality but was usually tightly plotted, with a skilful use of secondary narrative, and rarely muddied by abstract thought. His total sale of books is something around 70 million worldwide. Creasey stood for parliament as a Liberal candidate in 1950, and four times as a member of the All Party Alliance, which he had founded in 1967.
▷ R E Briney and J Creasey, 'A John Creasey Bibliography', in *Armchair Detective* (October 1968)

CRÉBILLON, Claude Prosper Jolyot de
(1707–77)

French novelist, younger son of **Prosper Jolyot de Crébillon**, born in Paris. After writing a number of slight pieces for the stage, he acquired great popularity as an author of elegant but licentious stories with satirical undertones aimed at the fashionable society in which he moved. In 1740 he married an Englishwoman called Lady Stafford. The indecency of his *Le Sopha, conte moral* ('The Sofa—a moral tale') having offended Madame de Pompadour, he was banished from Paris for five years, but on his return in 1755 was appointed in succession to his father as official literary censor, despite his reputation.
▷ P P Brooks, *The Novel of Worldliness* (1969)

CRÉBILLON, Prosper Jolyot de
(1674–1762)

French dramatist, born in Dijon. He studied in Paris for the law. His tragedy of *Idoménée* was successfully produced in 1703. It was followed by *Atrée et Thyeste* (1707), *Électre* (1709), and *Rhadamiste et Zénobie* (1711), his masterpiece. After writing several other pieces, Crébillon fell into neglect and produced nothing for over 20 years. He was then pushed forward as a dramatic rival to **Voltaire** by Madame de Pompadour, elected to the Academy, awarded a pension of 1000 francs, and appointed royal censor and a royal librarian. His *Catilina* was brought out with great success in 1748. Among his other works were *Xerxès*, *Sémiramis* (1717), *Pyrrhus*, and *Le Triumvirat*. His son was the novelist **Claude Prosper Jolyot de Crébillon**.
▷ P Le Clerc, *Voltaire and Crébillon Père* (1973)

CREEKMORE, Hubert
(1907–66)

American poet and novelist, whose work was deeply influenced by his Southern upbringing: raised in Mississippi, he had a powerful awareness of the social forces at work there, and the strong pressure of the past. His main achievement is a novel, *The Chain in the Heart* (1953), which is one of the best accounts (by a white author) of Afro-American life. He had a great interest in world literature, prompted partly by a search for the underlying mythologies and experiences that bind apparently disparate cultures.

CREELEY, Robert
(1926–)

American poet, born in Arlington, Massachusetts. Appointed to the faculty at Black Mountain College in North Carolina, he was linked with the Black Mountain school of

poets. In the mid-1950s he moved to California, where he mixed with prominent Beat writers like **Jack Kerouac** and **Allen Ginsberg**. His poems, characterized by dense syntax and abrupt endings, have appeared in numerous collections including *If You* (1956), *The Whip* (1957), *For You: Poems 1950–60* (1962), *St Martin's* (1971) and *The Collected Poems of Robert Creeley, 1945–75* (1982). He has written one novel, *The Island* (1963); other prose appears in *The Collected Prose of Robert Creeley: A Story* (1984).
▷ M Novik, *Robert Creeley, an inventory* (1973)

CRESSWELL, (Walter) D'Arcy
(1896–1960)
Expatriate New Zealand poet and writer of eccentric and archaic tastes, whose verse reflects his predilection for earlier times. Born in Christchurch, his first collections were published in London as *Poems (1921–1927)* (1928) and *Poems 1924–1931* (1932), but the best of his poetry is perhaps *Lyttelton Harbour* (1936). *The Letters of D'Arcy Cresswell* (1971) and *Dear Lady Ginger: An Exchange of Letters between Lady Ottoline Morrell and D'Arcy Cresswell* (1983) were edited by **Helen Shaw** and cast an explanatory light on his affectations.
▷ *The Poet's Progress* (1930); *Present Without Leave* (1939)

CRETIN, Guillaume
(d.1525)
French poet, born in Paris. Between Coustellier's edition of the poems in 1723 and the modern *Oeuvres Poétiques* (1932, ed Kathleen Chesney), Cretin's work received scant attention. A leader of the school of *Rhetoriqueurs* Cretin gave his name to the vogue of 'Cretinism'—the art of saying nothing in the most complicated of measures. Derided as one aspect of medievalism's last stand, Cretin's work has only recently been looked at afresh. The final decade of his life was the most productive, bringing him several royal prizes for 'ballades' and 'chants-royeaux'. A mysterious affair of mutual court animosity clouded the end of his life.

CREWS, Harry Eugene
(1935–)
American novelist, born in Georgia and temperamentally of the South, writing in a grotesque style marked by bizarre humour. His first novel, *The Gospel Singer* (1968), was followed by a succession of novels, including *The Hawk Is Dying* (1973), *The Gypsy's Curse* (1974), *A Feast of Snakes* (1976) and *All We Need of Hell* (1987). Crews has also written vivid journalism, much of it concerned with

the vagaries of life below the Mason–Dixon line. A compilation of his *Esquire* columns was published as *Blood and Grits* (1979).
▷ *A Childhood: The Biography of a Place* (1978)

CRISTOFER, Michael, originally Michael Procaccino
(1945–)
American playwright and actor, born in New Jersey. His most familiar plays are *Black Angel* (1976), *The Shadow Box* (1977, Pulitzer Prize) and *The Lady and the Clarinet* (1980), all of which portray people at the point of emotional crisis. The first deals with three terminally ill patients and their responses as life slips away from them, while the second examines the life of a former Nazi officer in hiding many years after World War II. *The Lady and the Clarinet* is a more humorous piece, a vivacious look at the hopes and fears in the love-life of an American career woman.

CRNJANSKI, Milos
(1893–)
Serbian poet, novelist and dramatist, born in Csongrád, Hungary. He was forced to fight for the Austro–Hungarian army in World War I, and his experiences turned him into a militantly right-wing pacifist; his views might be compared to those of the English novelist **Henry Williamson**. He stayed out of Yugoslavia until 1965, when he was able to return to Belgrade as a revered national figure. His bold lyrical poetry much influenced Serbs, and his long novel *Seobe* (1929–62, 'The Migrations') has been much admired as a masterful account of the 18th-century Serbs in Vojvodina, and one of the most significant Yugoslav novels of the 20th century. His critical study of the sonnets of **Shakespeare** is famous.
▷ A Kadic, *Contemporary Serbian Literature* (1964); T Eekman, *Thirty Years of Yugoslav Literature 1945–1975* (1978)

CROCE, Benedetto
(1866–1952)
Italian critic and philosopher who, though he wrote nothing creative, had an enormous influence on Italian and even on European literature. He has been compared to **Montaigne** in his capacity as an educator. His impact in Britain was felt through the historian and philosopher R G Collingwood. His notions that history is the story of liberty and that liberty is the highest value—rather than his Hegelian idealism—have proved exemplary, even if he has angered those both to the left and the right of him.
▷ C Sprigge, *Benedetto Croce, Man and Thinker* (1952)

CROCKETT, Samuel Rutherford
(1860–1914)

Scottish popular novelist, born in Little Duchrae, Kirkcudbright, of tenant-farming stock. Paying his way by journalism and travelling tutorships, he attended Edinburgh University and New College, Edinburgh. Becoming a Free Church minister in Penicuik, he wrote sardonic congregational sketches, of which 24, collected as *The Stickit Minister* (1893), brought immediate fame; this was consolidated in 1894 by *The Raiders*, *The Lilac Sunbonnet* (a seemingly innocent love story which ridiculed narrow religious sects) and two novellas. Resigning the ministry in favour of full-time writing in 1895, he wrote a variety of books, from tales of Covenanting and medieval Scotland, to European historical romances and (often sensational) stories of mining, industrialism and Edinburgh slums. His posthumous works include one detective and one theological science-fiction novel.
▷I M Donaldson, *Life and Work of Samuel Rutherford Crockett* (1989)

CROFTS, Freeman Wills
(1879–1957)

Irish author of detective fiction, born in Dublin. He abandoned a career as Chief Assistant Engineer on the Belfast and Northern Counties Railway in 1929 in order to concentrate on his writing and, later, moved to England. Crofts wrote 35 novels, of which 24 feature the doggedly methodical, unassuming, courteous and wry Inspector (later Superintendent) French of Scotland Yard. He made his first appearance in *Inspector French's Greatest Case* (1925), a tale of diamonds stolen from a Hatton Garden safe, beside which lies a dead body. Other notable French novels include *The Starvel Tragedy* (1927) and *The Hog's Back Mystery* (1933), books which also capture the atmosphere of London, from raffish criminal haunts, offices and shops to commonplace suburban streets and domestic interiors.

CROKER, John Wilson
(1780–1857)

Irish politician and essayist, born in Galway, the son of the surveyor-general of Irish customs. Educated at Trinity College, Dublin, in 1800 he entered Lincoln's Inn, and in 1802 was called to the Irish Bar. Two satires on the Irish stage (*On the Present State of the Irish Stage*, 1804) and on Dublin society (*Intercepted Letters from Canton*, 1804) proved brilliant hits; so did his *Sketch of Ireland Past and Present* (1807), a pamphlet advocating Catholic emancipation. Elected MP for Downpatrick in 1807, in 1809 he helped

to found the *Quarterly Review*, to which he contributed 260 articles. He was rewarded with the lucrative secretaryship of the Admiralty (1809–30) for his warm defence of Frederick, Duke of York in the case of Mary Anne Clarke. After 1832, he refused to re-enter parliament and would not even take office under Peel, his old friend (1834). He fell out with Peel over the repeal of the Corn Laws (1846). Among the 17 works that he wrote or edited were his *Stories for Children from English History* (1817), which suggested the *Tales of a Grandfather*; the *Suffolk Papers* (1823); his edition of **James Boswell**'s *Life of Johnson* (1831); and *Essays on the Early French Revolution* (1857). He is better remembered for his attack on **Keats**, and **Thomas Macaulay**'s attack on him (Macaulay 'detested him more than cold boiled veal'); and as the originator of the term Conservative, a founder of the Athenaeum Club, and the 'Rigby' of **Benjamin Disraeli**'s *Coningsby*.
▷M Brightfield, *John Wilson Croker* (1940)

CROKER, Thomas Crofton
(1798–1854)

Irish antiquary and folklorist, born in Cork. From 1818 to 1859 he was a clerk at the Admiralty. As a boy of 14 he had begun to collect songs and legends of the Irish peasantry and in 1818 he sent **Thomas Moore** nearly 40 old Irish melodies. In 1825 he published anonymously his *Fairy Legends and Traditions of the South of Ireland*, a work which charmed Sir **Walter Scott** and was translated into German by the brothers **Grimm** (1826). A second series followed in 1827. Of nearly 20 more works the best were *Researches in the South of Ireland* (1824), *Legends of the Lakes* (1829), *The Adventures of Barney Mahoney* (1832) and *Popular Songs of Ireland* (1839).

CROLY, George
(1780–1860)

Irish poet, romance-writer, biographer and Anglican preacher, born in Dublin. Educated at Trinity College, he took orders in 1804, and went to London in 1810, in 1835 becoming rector of St Stephen's, Walbrook. From 1817 he published some 40 works, the best-known of which is the weird romance of *Salathiel* (1829), based on the legend of the Wandering Jew. Other titles include the tragedy *Cataline* (1822), the satirical *May Fair* (1827), and a romance of the French revolution, *Marston* (1846).
▷R Herring, *A Few Personal Recollections* (1861)

CROMMELYNCK, Fernand
(1888–1970)

Major Belgian playwright and novelist, born in Paris of a French mother and a Belgian

father. His first real success was *Le Cocu magnifique* (1921, Eng trans *The Magnificent Cuckold*, 1966), which was produced in Paris by Lugné-Poë. In it a husband, based on the character of Kitely in **Ben Jonson**'s *Every Man in his Humour*, seeks to be certain that he has cause for jealousy, and thus reveals his perversity. This was followed by the profound farce *Tripes d'or* (1930, 'Golden Tripes'), a study of greed so powerful that it has shocked even the dramatist's admirers. After 1934 Crommelynck suddenly ceased to be productive, confining himself to a mystery novel and to a few film-scripts. But he had left an ineradicable mark on the theatre with six explosive and entirely original plays.
▷D Grossvogel, *20th Century French Drama* (1961)

CROMPTON, Richmal, original surname Lamburn
(1890–1969)

English writer, and author of the *Just William* books, born in Bury, Lancashire. She was educated in Lancashire and Derby and at Royal Holloway College, London. An honours graduate in classics (1914), she taught for some years, but was struck down with poliomyelitis in 1923. She published 50 adult titles thereafter but she is best known for her 38 short-story collections (and one novel, *Just William's Luck*) about the perpetual schoolboy, the 11-year-old William Brown. Children loved the judicious deliberation with which William's incursions and imitations are described in their reduction of ordered adult life to chaos.

CRONEGK, Johann Friedrich Reichsherr von
(1730–57)

German poet, verse dramatist and editor of his own periodical, *Der Freund*, born in Ansbach into the family of a Prussian general. He died young, of smallpox. His classical tragedies, written in Alexandrines, were influenced by **Edward Young** and by French models, and played a small but decisive part in the development of German drama. He was a close friend of **Gellert**.
▷W Gensel, *Cronegk* (1894, in German)

CRONIN, A(rchibald) J(oseph)
(1896–1981)

Scottish novelist, born in Cardross, Dunbartonshire. He graduated in medicine at Glasgow in 1919, but in 1930 abandoned his practice as a result of a breakdown in his health, and turned to literature. He had an immediate success with his brooding and melodramatic autobiographical novel *Hatter's Castle* (1931). Subsequent works include

The Citadel (1937), *The Keys of the Kingdom* (1941), *Beyond this Place* (1953), *Crusader's Tomb* (1956) and *A Song of Sixpence* (1964). The medical stories in his Scottish novels formed the basis of the popular radio and television series *Dr Finlay's Casebook* in the 1960s, and again in 1993. Towards the end of his life he lived largely in the USA and Switzerland.
▷*Adventures in Two Worlds* (1952)

CRONIN, Bernard
(1884–1968)

English-born Australian writer and journalist, born in Ealing, Middlesex. He wrote about 30 light novels under various pseudonyms, and some one-act plays, mainly for radio. The novels, based on his earlier experiences as a station-hand in Victoria and Tasmania, include *The Coastlanders* (1918), *Salvage* (1923) and *The Sow's Ear* (1933). In 1920 he founded the 'Derelicts' Club for indigent authors and artists, which later became the Society of Australian Authors.

CROSS, Zora
(1890–1964)

Australian novelist and poet, born in Brisbane. Experiencing a series of affairs and an unconsummated marriage, she wrote frank poems about sexuality, physical love and motherhood which were published as *A Song of Mother Love* (1916), *Songs of Love and Life* (1917) and *The Lilt of Life* (1918). She settled into a *de facto* relationship with editor **David McKee Wright**, by whom she had two daughters and, after his sudden death in 1928, she supported her family by journalism and acting. Her novels, little regarded now, include *Daughters of the Seven-Mile* (1924) and, much later, *This Hectic Age* (1944), in which a girl from the bush adjusts to the pace of life in Sydney. Her poetry, though, shows a true gift, as in *Elegy on an Australian Schoolboy*, published in 1921, on the death of her younger brother in World War I.

CROTHERS, Rachel
(1878–1958)

American playwright, born in Bloomington, Illinois. A feminist, in 1910 she published *A Man's World*, an attack upon moral double standards, the heroine of which proclaims herself 'a natural woman because I am a free one'; at the time this was considered an extremely important work. *Ourselves* (1913) looked at the problem of prostitution. Crothers succeeded where many playwrights fail, managing to combine polemic with box-office success, although she increasingly veered towards lighter work, as in *As Husbands Go*

(1932), which contrasts English and American marriages; and while *When Ladies Meet* (1932) recalls her earlier, sharper tone, it is also outwardly a comedy.

▷L C Gottlieb, *Rachel Crothers* (1979)

CROUSE, Russel
(1893–1966)

American playwright, producer and journalist, born in New York. He is best remembered for a series of collaborations with Howard Lindsay (1889–1968), including *Life With Father* (1939) and *Life With Mother* (1948), both adapted from books by **Clarence Day**, and the comedies *The Great Sebastians* (1956) and *Tall Story* (1959). Their most important work was *State of the Union* (1945), a political satire about a presidential candidate which won the Pulitzer Prize for Drama in 1946. He also wrote a number of musical shows with other collaborators, and some non-fiction.

CRUICKSHANK, Helen Burness
(1886–1975)

Scottish poet, born in Hillside, Angus. Educated at Montrose Academy, in 1903 she joined the Civil Service in London. After her return to Edinburgh in 1912 her home became a centre for Scottish writers. She contributed poems to **Hugh MacDiarmid**'s *Scottish Chapbook* and *Northern Numbers* and the two became friends. She was secretary to Scottish PEN between 1927 and 1934, and a teacher and confidante to writers such as **Lewis Grassic Gibbon**. Her poems were first published in 1934 in *Up the Noran Water* and five more collections appeared in 1954, 1968, 1971, 1976 and 1978. She wrote both in English and a dialect Scots that drew on her Angus heritage. Her work is marked by an economy of language and variety of forms, including prose-poetry and blank verse. In 1971 she was awarded an Honorary MA from Edinburgh University for her contributions to Scottish literature. **Hugh MacDiarmid** complimented her in a radio tribute as a 'catalyst' to the Scottish Renaissance.

CRUZ, Ramón de la
(1731–94)

Spanish dramatist, born in Madrid, where he spent his life. Although he began very much in the traditional neo-classicist mould, translating works by **Racine** and **Voltaire**, and even *Hamlet*, he broke with this tradition by turning to the popular portrayal of life in Madrid as encapsulated in the 'sainete', a short play or farce. He had also composed many 'zarzuelas' (light operas) and adapted a play by **Molière**. However, he believed that drama consisted of imitating life, and wrote colourful pieces doing just that. His 'sainetes' (of which he wrote over 400) were published in 10 volumes (1786–91). They originated a strong tradition, of which **Carlos Arniches** was to become the main inheritor.

CRUZ, Sor Juana Inés de la
(1648–95)

Mexican feminist, poet and playwright, born in San Miguel Nepantle, Amecameca, not far from Mexico City. A woman of legendary beauty, she has affinities with **Christine de Pisan**. Like Christine, she became celebrated for her scholarship at an early age, and was invited by the wife of the Viceroy of Mexico to live at the court. At the age of 19 disgust, probably prompted by shock at the ways of men (she may have had a love affair) and by the frivolity of court life, led her to enter the Carmelite Order. But the artificial rigour of this life, too, revolted her, and she returned to court. A year later she joined the Hieronymite convent (in which she remained), in Mexico City, on account (she declared) of her 'total lack of matrimonial ambition' and of her wish to 'live alone, in order to have no interruption to my freedom and my study'. When instructed by a bishop, an officer of the Inquisition, to give up learning as 'unbefitting to a woman' she issued the stately *Respuesta* (1691), the *Response*, a key document in the history of feminism. With consummate irony, she pointed out that she wrote secular poetry and drama only because, as a woman, she was incapable of religious devotion—and that merely artistic heresy was not punishable by the Pope. Her own sardonic, parodic, highly erotic, and mystical poetry, especially the 'Primero sueño' ('First Dream'), is individualistic and 'modern'. Her poems about male stupidity, in particular 'Rendonillas' ('Verses'), have hardly been forgiven, and have not been translated ('Stupid men, who accuse/women unreasonably/without seeing that you are the cause/of that very thing you blame ...'). In one of her plays she demonstrates that her Catholicism was but skin-deep: she explains the Aztec rite of eating the Corn God as a Satanic parody of the Communion. With Christine, **Sappho**, **Laura Riding** and **Emily Dickinson**, she is amongst the greatest and least understood of all writers. She sold all her books, scientific equipment and musical instruments, in order to care for the poor, and died of the plague while ministering to them.

▷A Reyes, *The Position of America* (1950); E A Chávez, *Sor Juana de la Cruz* (1970)

CRUZ E SOUSA, João da
(1861–98)

Brazilian poet, born in Destêrro (now Florianópolis), a son of slaves. It was the slave-owner who, noticing his unusual abilities, sent him to school. But, understandably, Cruz e Sousa could never transcend his sense of inferiority at being black. He spent a desperate life: his wife went mad and two of his children died in childhood. He was first influenced by **Baudelaire** and by **Anthero de Quental**, but essentially remained a disciple of **Olavo Bilac**, the Brazilian poet he admired most of all, possibly to his detriment (for he was more intrinsically gifted). He has been ranked with **Mallarmé**, but criticism has, in general, been rather more cautious.

ČSIKY, Gregor
(1842–91)

Hungarian dramatist, born in Pankota, Vilagos. A Professor of Theology at Temesvar seminary, he published some tales from religious history ('Photographs from Life'), and in 1875 a comedy, *Jaslot* ('The Oracle'), which was a success. Other plays followed, including comedies like *Mirkány Kariar* and *Anna* (1883), and tragedies—*Janus* (1877), *A Mágusz* (1878, 'The Magician') and *Theodora*. He also translated **Sophocles**, **Plautus** and **Molière** into Hungarian, as well as several English plays. *Az Ellenallhatatlan* ('The Irresistible'), which won a prize from the Hungarian Academy, typifies his talent for a direct, fresh approach to his subject.
▷G Hefedus, *Čsiky Gregor* (1953)

ČSOKONAI VITÉZ, Mihály
(1773–1805)

Hungarian poet, born in Debrecen, Hungary. He was Professor of Poetry at the university there until his way of life lost him the post. His fame persists, however, chiefly through his lyrics, which are based on old Hungarian folksongs. Among his works are the drama *Tempefoi* (1793), the poems *Magyar-Musa* (1797) and *Dorottya* (1804), a mock-heroic poem.
▷V Julow, *Čsokonai Vitéz Mihály* (1975)

CSOKOR, Franz Theodor
(1885–1965)

Austrian playwright who began writing in the expressionist vein, but had his popular successes in the traditional realm, with such plays as *3 November 1918* (1936), a cleverly rendered spectacle of the final dissolution of the Habsburg army. He continued to produce well-made plays until within a few years of his death.

CUADRA, José de la
(1903–41)

Ecuardorean novelist, poet and story writer, born in Guayaquil. After making his mark with early poems and stories, and qualifying

as a lawyer, de la Cuadra became a member, with **Aguilera Malta**, **Gil Gilbert**, and others, of the epoch-making, left-wing Grupo de Guayaquil, whose motto was 'Reality and nothing more than reality'. He became a university teacher, held posts in the provincial government of the Guayas, and shortly before his premature death was appointed a magistrate. His most famous work is a novel, *Los Sangurismos* (1934, 'The Sangurismos'), a brilliantly violent book; but the best Ecuadorean opinion has it that his finest work lies in the short stories he wrote from the collection *Horno* (1932, 'Furnace') onwards. However, the bitter novel he left unfinished, *Los monos enloquecidos* (1951, 'The Maddened Monkeys'), contains some of his best work.
▷A Flores, *The Literature of Spanish America* (1966–9)

CUADRA, Pablo Antonio, known as PAC
(1912–)

Nicaraguan poet, born in Managua, but brought up in his parents' native city of Granada (Nicaragua), for long Nicaragua's most distinguished man of letters. He was among the leading members of the Vanguardia movement, and was associated with its first manifesto (1931). His first collection, *Poemas nicaragüense* (1934, 'Nicaraguan Poems'), published in Santiago de Chile, was, according to a critic, 'the first book in the vernacular in central America'. He welcomed the Sandanista revolution, but was quick to denounce its excesses, and for a time went to live in Austin, Texas. His poetry was translated by **Thomas Merton**: *El jaguar y la luna* (1959, Eng trans *The Jaguar and the Moon*, 1974). Other works include *Cantos de Cifar y del Mar Dulce* (1971, Eng trans *Songs of Cifar and the Sweet Sea*, 1979) and selected translations in *the Birth of the Sun* (1987).
▷T Merton, *Emblems of a Season of Fury* (1963)

CUEVA, Juan de la
(c.1550–1610)

Spanish poet and dramatist, born in Seville. He wrote a number of rather undistinguished poems, but is regarded as an important figure in the development of Spanish drama. He is known especially for his use of new metrical forms, and for his introduction of historical material and overtly political themes into the drama.
▷R F Glenn, *Juan de la Cueva* (1973)

CULLEN, Countee
(1903–46)

American Black poet, born in New York. A leader of the so-called Harlem Renaissance,

he began his literary career with *Color* (1925), a book of poems in which classical models such as the sonnet are used with considerable effect. He published several subsequent volumes of verse, and a novel *One Way to Heaven* (1932), and collaborated with **Arna Bontemps** in the play *St Louis Woman* (1946).
▷ M Perry, *A bio-bibliography* (1971)

CUMBERLAND, Richard
(1732–1811)

English playwright, born in the lodge of Trinity College, Cambridge, maternal grandson of Dr Richard Bentley. From Bury St Edmunds and Westminster School he went to Trinity College, Cambridge, and was a fellow at 20. Becoming private secretary to Lord Halifax in 1761, he gave up his intention of taking orders. He was secretary to the board of trade from 1776 to 1782. Thereafter he retired to Tunbridge Wells, where he wrote farces, tragedies, comedies, pamphlets, essays and two novels, *Arundel* (1789) and *Henry* (1795). Of his sentimental comedies the best are *The Brothers* (1769), *The West Indian* (1771), *The Fashionable Lover* (1772), *The Jew* (1794) and *The Wheel of Fortune* (1795). He was caricatured by **Richard Brinsley Sheridan** in *The Critic* as Sir Fretful Plagiary.
▷ S T Williams, *Richard Cumberland* (1917)

CUMMINGS, E(dward) E(stlin), self-styled as e e cummings
(1894–1962)

American writer and painter, born in Cambridge, Massachusetts. Educated at Harvard, he is celebrated for his verse characterized by typographical tricks and eccentric punctuations, signed 'e e cummings', starting with his first volume *Tulips and Chimneys* (1924). His best-known prose work, *The Enormous Room* (1922), describes his wartime internment—brought about by an error by the authorities—in France. He also wrote a travel diary, a morality play, *Santa Claus* (1946), and a collection of six 'non-lectures' delivered at Harvard entitled *i* (1953). He studied art in Paris, and a collection of his drawings and paintings was published in 1931.
▷ N Friedman, *The Growth of a Writer* (1964)

CUMMINS, Maria Susanna
(1827–66)

American writer, born in Salem, Massachusetts. Her first novel, *The Lamplighter* (1854), was a moralistic fable about a Boston orphan and won considerable success. Cummins also contributed to *Atlantic Monthly*.

CUNHA, Euclydes da
(1866–1909)

Brazilian writer, born in Rio de Janeiro province. His coverage, as a journalist, of the Canudos rebellion (1896), resulted in the exuberantly written classic *Os Sertões* (1902, Eng abridged trans *Rebellion in the Backlands*, 1944). The book has become essential reading, because da Cunha was able to write with deep sympathy of the backland rebels (*sertanejos*), mestizo cowboys, who held the Brazilian troops at bay at Canudos for the best part of a year. They were led by a religious fanatic, Antônio Conselheiro (Antonio the Counsellor), into whom da Cunha, in his incidental criticism of the government of President Barros, showed remarkable insight. This was all the more extraordinary because he was himself the intellectual victim of Spencerian misconceptions about 'backward' peoples. No book, even by **Gilberto Freyre**, has been more influential in Brazil or Latin America. The author, a man in whom there was 'more than a touch of the pathologic', and who, with **Machado de Assis**, is Brazil's greatest writer of the modern era, was shot down in the street at Santa Cruz, by an enraged army officer.
▷ P Putnam, *Marvellous Journey* (1948)

CUNNINGHAM, Allan
(1784–1842)

Scottish poet and writer, born in the parish of Dalswinton, Dumfriesshire. His father was neighbour of **Robert Burns** at Ellisland and Allan, as a boy, was present at the poet's funeral. At 10 he was apprenticed to a stonemason, but he continued to pore over songs and stories. His first publications were his sham-antique verse and prose contributions to Cromek's *Remains of Nithsdale and Galloway Song* (1810). He already knew **James Hogg**, and through him he made the acquaintance of Sir **Walter Scott**, with whom 'Honest Allan' was always a great favourite. He moved to London, and became one of the best-known writers for the *London Magazine*, as well as manager of Francis Chantrey's sculpture studio (1815–41). Among his works were *Traditional Tales of the English and Scottish Peasantry* (1822), *Songs of Scotland, Ancient and Modern* (1825), *Lives of the most Eminent British Painters, Sculptors, and Architects* (6 vols, 1829–33), and *Life of Wilkie* (3 vols, 1843).
▷ D Hogg, *The Life of Allan Cunningham* (1875)

CUNNINGHAM, E V see FAST, Howard Melvin

CUNNINGHAM, James Vincent
(1911–85)

American poet, critic and academic. His poetry was influenced by that of **Yvor Winters**, and, unusually, he eventually became more highly thought of, as a poet, than his avowed master. He wrote witty, intellectual, incisive and always interesting—if somewhat cold—poetry, and his *Collected Poems and Epigrams* (1971) is a much respected volume. *Collected Essays* appeared in 1977.

▷ E B Hungerford, *Poets in Progress* (1962)

CUNNINGHAME GRAHAM, Robert Bontine
(1852–1936)

Scottish writer and politician, the grandson of the songwriter Robert Cunninghame Graham, born in London. He was educated at Harrow and from 1869 was chiefly engaged in ranching in the Argentine, until he succeeded to the family estates in 1883. In 1879 he married a Chilean poet, Gabriela de la Belmondiere. He was Liberal MP for North-West Lanarkshire (1886–92) and was imprisoned with John Burns, the socialist leader, for 'illegal assembly' in Trafalgar Square during a mass unemployment demonstration in 1887. He was the first President of the Scottish Labour Party in 1888. He travelled extensively in Spain and Morocco (1893–8), where an incident described in his *Mogreb-El-Acksa* (1898) inspired **George Bernard Shaw**'s *Captain Brassbound's Conversion*. He wrote a large number of travel books, but is best known for his highly individual, flamboyant essays and short stories, notably the much-anthologized 'Beattock for Moffat', collections of which are entitled *Success* (1902), *Faith* (1909), *Hope* (1910), *Charity* (1912) and *Scottish Stories* (1914). He was elected the first President of the National Party of Scotland in 1928, and of the Scottish National Party in 1934. **Joseph Conrad** and **William Henry Hudson** were among his close literary friends. He died in Argentina, where he was known as 'Don Roberto'.

▷ A F Tschiffely, *Don Roberto: Tornado Cavalier* (1937)

CUREL, François de
(1854–1928)

French dramatist, born in Metz into a family of aristocrats which had taken to industry. His first plays were presented at the Théâtre Libre, where they became critically celebrated. However the public never really took to anything of his except the now-forgotten comedy *L'Âme en folle* (1919, 'Soul in Folly'). Yet, a curious and enigmatic case, he remains admired. What seemed strained to contemporary critics in such plays as *La Figurante* (1896, 'The Stand-In')—commissioned by Bernhardt, who appeared in it—has seemed daring and proto-modernistic to later commentators. He has been called a 'dramatist's dramatist'. His strength lay in

analysis of strange psychological states; but he disturbed some critics' susceptibility to mysticism. His last and perhaps his most interesting play, *Orage mystique* (1927, 'Mystic Storm'), actually attempts to communicate with the dead. His very early *Les fossiles* ('The Fossils') is translated in *Contemporary European Plays I* (1931, ed Benfield Pressey).

▷ E Braunstein, *François de Curel et le théâtre d'idées* (1962)

CURNOW, (Thomas) Allen Munro
(1911–)

New Zealand poet and critic, born in Timaru, Canterbury, whose preoccupation with New Zealand's past and its quest for national identity is central to all his writing. His first verse was published as *Valley of Decision: Poems* (1933). *Sailing or Drowning* (1943) includes the poem 'Landfall in Unknown Seas', a commission from the Department of Internal Affairs to mark the 300th anniversary of Tasman's discovery of New Zealand; it was set to music by New Zealand composer Douglas Lilburn. Key collections are *Poems: Jack without Magic* (1946) and *At Dead Low Water and Sonnets* (1949). Major contributions were his editing of the anthology *A Book of New Zealand Verse 1923–45* (1945, rev edn 1951) and of the *Penguin Book of New Zealand Verse* (1960). His *Collected Poems 1933–1973* was published in 1974 and *Selected Poems, 1940–1989* in 1990. He has also written verse satire under the penname 'Whim-Wham', and four verse plays, including *The Axe: A Verse Tragedy* (1949), which in allegorical form treats of the introduction of Christianity to Polynesia.

CURROS ENRÍQUEZ, Manuel
(1851–1908)

Major Spanish poet, the political conscience of his people, writing in Galician. He was born in Celanova, Orense. He is counted as the equal in his literature to **Rosalía de Castro** and **Eduardo Pondal**. His lively and anti-clerical, liberal-minded poetry caused him to go into exile to Cuba, where he died. His most famous poem is the long *O Divino saitete* (1888, 'The Divine Bait'), about a journey he took to Rome with a friend.

CURTIS, George William
(1824–92)

American writer, born in Providence, Rhode Island. After four years in Europe (1846–50) he joined the staff of the New York *Tribune*, and was one of the editors of *Putnam's Monthly* from 1852 to 1869. He began the 'Editor's Easy Chair' papers in *Harper's Monthly* in

1853, and became principal leader-writer for *Harper's Weekly* on its establishment in 1857. A novel, *Trumps* (1862), and most of his books appeared first in these journals.

▷W Payne, *Leading American Essayists* (1910)

CURTIS, Jean Louis, pseud of Louis Lafitte
(1917–)

French novelist who wrote in traditional modes, entirely ignoring the *nouveau roman*. Initially an English teacher, he was a wartime pilot. His greatest success was his substantial, sympathetic but acid portrait of a town in occupied south-west France, *Les Forêts de la nuit* (1947, Eng trans *The Forests of the Night*, 1950). He continued to write sharp analyses of life in post-war Paris, of which *Gibier de Potence* (1949, Eng trans *Lucifer's Dream*, 1952), was filmed by Roger Richebé in 1951, with the legendary Arletty as one of the stars.

CURTIS, Tony
(1946–)

Welsh poet, born in Carmarthen and educated at University College, Swansea, and Goddard College, Vermont. He has published four collections of verse, a collection of prose-poems and short stories, two volumes of critical essays, and has edited several anthologies. A senior lecturer in English at the Polytechnic of Wales, he was Chair of The Welsh Academy from 1984 to 1987. In 1984 he won first prize in the National Poetry Competition.

CURWOOD, James Oliver
(1878–1927)

American writer, born in Owosso, Michigan. He was the author of popular novels of outdoor life, such as *The Courage of Captain Plum* (1908), *The Grizzly King* (1917) and *The Alaskan* (1923).

▷ *Son of the Forests, an autobiography* (1930)

CUSACK, (Ellen) Dymphna
(1902–81)

Australian author, born in Wyalong, New South Wales. Educated at Sydney University, she trained as a teacher. The first of her 12 novels, *Jungfrau*, was published in 1936 and dealt frankly, for its time, with sexual issues. This was followed in 1939 by *Pioneers on Parade*, written jointly with **Miles Franklin**. Illness forced her to retire from teaching in 1944, but in 1948 she won the (Sydney) *Daily Telegraph* novel competition with *Come In Spinner*, written in collaboration with **Florence James**; its outspoken handling of adultery and abortion delayed its publication until

1951. The story of the intertwined lives of a group of women in wartime Sydney, and the effects of the absence of their menfolk and the presence of American servicemen, it was an immediate success, but the full text was not published until 1988. Cusack wrote nine other novels and eight plays, which illustrate her preoccupation with social and political disadvantage. They have been translated into over 30 languages, and her plays have been broadcast by the BBC and the ABC. She edited and introduced *Caddie, the Story of a Barmaid* (1953, filmed 1976).

CYNDDELW BRYDYDD MAWR
(fl.1155–1200)

Welsh court poet, the most important of the 12th century. He wrote boldly and in demanding techniques, and had undergone a training so arduous that it would make a modern poet abandon his craft in desperation. His poetry is particularly notable for its vivid and brutal descriptions of battles.

▷J Lloyd-Jones, *The Court Poets of the Welsh Princes* (1848)

CYRANO DE BERGERAC, Savinien
(1619–55)

French writer and dramatist, born in Paris. As a soldier, in his youth he fought more than a thousand duels, mostly on account of his monstrously large nose. His works, often crude, but full of invention, vigour, and wit, include a comedy, *Le Pédant joué* (1654, 'The Pedant Outwitted') and the satirical science fantasy *Histoire comique des états de la lune et du soleil* (Eng trans *Voyages to the Moon and the Sun*, 1923). He was the subject of **Edmond Rostand**'s play, *Cyrano de Bergerac* (1897).

▷E Harth, *Cyrano de Bergerac and the politics of modernity* (1970)

CZECHOWICZ, Józef
(1903–39)

Polish poet who was born in Lublin—and died there as a result of a Nazi bomb. He was a leading poet in the inter-war *Awangarda* (Vanguard) movement. In his complex poetry ruralism and a strong affinity to folklore clashed with urban sophistication, often with surprising and powerful results. In his 'catastrophism' he influenced **Czeslaw Milosz**.

CZEPKO VON REIGERSFELD, Daniel
(1605–60)

German Lutheran poet, who spent much of his life in imperial service (and was ennobled for it). He was deeply influenced by **Jakob Böhme** and by his own friend the mystic

Abraham von Frankenberg. His poetry, most of which was not actually published until 1930—but which was known to and imitated by **Angelus Silesius**—used that of **Opitz** as its model, but is appealingly simple and sincere.

His mystical *Sextenta Monodisticha Sapienta* (1647) is his greatest achievement.

▷ W Milch, *Daniel von Czepko* (1924, in German); R Pascal, *German Literature in the 16th and 17th Centuries* (1968)

D

DABIT, Eugène
(1898–1936)

French novelist, born in Paris, son of a labourer. He left school early and did menial jobs without thought of becoming a writer. After war service, during which he read avidly, he studied writing, and published his first, most famous novel, *L'Hôtel du Nord* (1929), based on his observations of the goings-on in a 'hotel' (really a doss-house) which his parents ran in the 1920s. Translated under the same title in 1931, it won the Prix de Roman Populiste, and in 1938 was turned into the classic movie by Marcel Carné, with a script by **Jacques Prévert**. For once the film did justice to the book. A critic wrote that 'it neither smudges nor varnishes its reality. It gives you a barefaced, simple truth'. It still possesses this stark quality, and is a classic of fiction as well as of the screen. In France there is now a revival of interest in Dabit's work, which includes more novels, and a diary. He died of typhoid while touring Soviet Russia in the company of **André Gide**.

DABYDEEN, David
(1956–)

Guyanian-born British poet, novelist and historian, who emigrated to England in 1969, and whose books have established him as a leading interpreter of the black experience. His first volume of poems, *Slave Song* (1984), is a vivid and lyrical evocation of slavery on Guyanese sugar plantations, while a novel, *The Intended* (1991), examines a young boy attempting to make sense of his Guyanese heritage while growing up in a London slum. *Hogarth's Blacks: Images of Blacks in Eighteenth Century English Painting* (1985) is a provocative and invigorating account of English perceptions of other races.

DACH, Simon
(1605–59)

German lyrical poet and playwright, born in Memel. He and other quiet poets formed what became known as Der Königsberger Dichterschule ('the Königsberg School', c.1625–1650), to whose meetings **Martin Opitz**, the chief influence on the circle, was a visitor. Some of Dach's hymns became famous.
▷J Julian, *A Dictionary of Hymnology* (1892)

DADIÉ, Bernard
(1916–)

Ivory Coast Francophone novelist, poet and playwright. He served the government of Senegal, and set up a theatre there; then he returned to his own country to become Minister of Culture. His novel *Climbié* (1956, Eng trans 1971) is about an African whose acceptance of white rule turns into hatred for it. But his plays, although untranslated, remain his most outstanding work, especially *Monsieur Thôgó-gnini* (1970), a wild **Jarry**-like farce, and *Iles de tempète* (1973, 'Stormy Islands'), perhaps the finest of all works dealing with the slave Toussaint L'Ouverture, who became ruler of Haiti.
▷A C Brench, *Writing in French from Senegal to Cameroon* (1967)

DAFYDD AP GWILYM
(c.1315–c.1370)

Welsh poet and bard, born near Aberystwyth, often hailed as the greatest of Welsh poets. Of noble birth, he was well educated and obviously well read—he introduced many elements of the European mainstream into Welsh verse and, by virtue of the quality of his poetry, brought Welsh verse into the European mainstream. A poet in the wandering bard tradition, he was a lover of nature and natural things, and seems to have spent much of his time roaming the countryside; his verse is set in forests and peopled with birds and animals as well as the usual star-crossed lovers. He is sometimes credited with having invented the *cywydd* form of verse, and he was certainly responsible for its becoming the dominant form in Welsh verse after his time.
▷R Loomis (ed), *Dafydd ap Gwilym: The Poems, Translation and Commentary* (1982); T Parry, *History of Welsh Literature* (1955)

DAFYDD NANMOR
(fl.1460–80)

Welsh poet and bard of the school known as *Beirdd yr Uchelwyr* ('Poets of the Gentry'), writing in their favoured forms, the *awdl* and *cywydd*. He idolized the civilized aspects of life (not natural beauty, as was the norm in Welsh bardic poets) and social values. His poems tend to be inspired by people and their doings and are set firmly in the social world.

DAGERMAN, Stig
(1923–54)

Swedish novelist, poet and dramatist who, like his great compatriot **Karin Maria Boye**, killed himself at the height of his powers. He is still much read, and rightly treated as a major European writer. He was one of the leading members of the *fyrtiota-listerna*, the 'Forties Group', which included the poet **Erik Lindegren**. *Ormen* (1945, 'The Snake') was one of the most powerful first novels to appear in the 20th century: its theme—fear, modern angst—is precisely that which in the end he could not resist; his suicide, like **Cesare Pavese**'s in Italy, became legendary amongst his countrymen. He was influenced by **Kafka**, but not damagingly so, and also (more significantly) by the Norwegian novelist **Tarjei Vesaas**. Perhaps his best work is seen in the story collection *Nattens lekar* (1947, Eng trans *The Games of Night*, 1960), where humour modifies terror. Other work in English includes *Bränt Barn* (1948, Eng trans *A Burnt Child*, 1950).
▷A Gustafson, *A History of Swedish Literature* (1961)

DAGLARCA, Fazil Hüsnü
(1914–)

Turkish poet, born in Istanbul, and regarded, upon the death of **Hikmet**, as his successor in stature. He was an army officer from 1935 until 1950, when he retired with the rank of captain. After that he ran a famous bookshop in Istanbul (1959–72). He was a prolific writer, producing 60 collections of verse by 1980. His first book, issued on the day he became a career officer, and containing conventional verse, was called *Havaya cizilen dünya* (1935, 'A World Sketched on Air'). Since that time he has experimented in every possible genre of poetry (including that of the patriotic epic, the comic, the juvenile and the erotic), but has never been attached to any particular school: like **Whitman**, he 'contains multitudes'. He has always been a militant socialist realist, and often used the window of his bookshop as a notice-board, to the discomfort of most Turkish governments. His most engaging work is the 'neo-mystical' cycle *Mevlana'da olmak* (1958, 'Voyage—Alive in Mevlana') on the great Sufi master (and poet) **Jalal ad-din Rumi**. His poems have been translated (not always well) in *Our Vietnam War* (1967), *Songs of Algeria* (1961), *Selected Poems* (1969) and *The Bird and I* (1980).
▷Y N Nayir, *Daglarca: Critical Approaches, Interviews, Selected Poems* (1974)

D'AGUIAR, Fred(eric)
(1960–)

Guyanese poet, born in London and brought up in Guyana. Already he is established as one of the leading poets of his generation. D'Aguiar has compared writing poems with the childhood game of chasing fireflies and trying to catch on to them before their lights fade or dart away. *Mama Dot* (1985) and *Airy Hall* (1989) were both concept collections, containing many Mama Dot ... and Airy Hall ... titles. The first reflected the poet's Guyanese upbringing, whereas the second collection was coloured by his work as a psychiatric nurse in England. He edited the black section of Paladin's *The New British Poetry* anthology (1988).

DAHL, Roald
(1916–90)

British children's author, short-story writer, playwright and versifier, born in Llandaff, Glamorgan, of Norwegian parentage. His first stories were based on his wartime experiences in the RAF and were collected in *Over to You* (1946). Subsequent collections achieved enormous popularity and include *Someone Like You* (1954), *Kiss, Kiss* (1960) and *Switch Bitch* (1974). Plot was paramount to Dahl and when he began to run short of good ones he turned to writing books for children. He is among the most popular children's authors of all time but many parents, teachers and librarians disapprove of his anarchic rudeness and violence. *Charlie and the Chocolate Factory* (1964) is his best-known book and was successfully filmed. Others include *James and the Giant Peach* (1961), *The Enormous Crocodile* (1978), *The BFG* (1982), *Matilda* (1988) and *Esio Trot* (1990). *The Minpins* and *The Vicar of Nibbleswick* were published posthumously in 1991. He also wrote the screenplays for *You Only Live Twice* (1967) and *Chitty Chitty Bang Bang* (1968), and a number of his stories were adapted for television as *Tales of the Unexpected*.
▷ *Boy* (1984); *Going Solo* (1986)

DAHLBERG, Edward
(1900–77)

American novelist, poet and critic, born in Boston; at the age of 26, he settled in Europe. There, he wrote his first and semi-autobiographical novel, *Bottom Dogs* (1929), describing a depressing slum childhood. A later work, *Those Who Perish* (1934), deals with the effect of Nazi doctrine upon Jewish Americans. Dahlberg's writing also encompassed essays on contemporary society and literature, collected under such titles as *The Flea of Sodom* (1950) and *Alms for Oblivion* (1964). His poetry includes the collection *Cipango's Hinder Door* (1965).
▷ *Because I was Flesh* (1964)

DAHLGREN, Karl Fredrik
(1791–1844)
Swedish poet and humorist, born at Stensbruk in Ostergötland. He studied at Uppsala, and from 1815 was a preacher at Stockholm. His works—novels, tales, poems, dramas—fill five volumes (1847–52).

DAILEY, Janet
(1944–)
American writer of romantic and popular fiction. Born on a farm in Iowa, Dailey worked as her husband's secretary until she was 30. Since then she has produced books at the rate of a dozen a year, claiming that '150 pagers' take her 9 days, and '350 pagers' between 30 and 45 days. A strict writing schedule, the assignment of research to her husband Bill, and the publication of a fanzine *Janet Dailey Newsletter* have helped to maintain her prodigious output and success. She has written a novel for every state in the US (the Americana series) and also found time to compose lyrics for Country and Western songs. At its best, as in the Calder series which began with *This Calder Sky* (1981), Dailey's world is a blockbustering evocation of American grit.

DA LENTINO, Giacomo
(13th century)
Italian lyric poet at the court of Frederick II. He was born in Lentino, near Syracuse. **Dante** thought of him as the foremost Sicilian poet (see *Purgatorio*, XXIV, 55–60), but his substantial work does not survive in Sicilian, since scribes (insensitively) modernized it. Inheriting the traditions of *fin'amor* ('courtly love') from the troubadours, Da Lentino saw its concepts as grown hollow from overuse, and sought to revivify it. His development of the sonnet was his greatest technical achievement.
▷E Langley (ed), *The Poetry of Giacomo Da Lentino* (1915)

DALEY, Victor James William Patrick
(1858–1905)
Irish-born journalist and lyric poet, born in Navan, County Meath, who settled in Australia at the age of 20; he had intended to go to Adelaide but by mistake landed in Sydney. Daley wrote as 'Creeve Roe' and was considered one of the 'Celtic Twilight' school, but received high praise from John Archibald of the *Bulletin*, which printed much of his work. The only book published before his early death from tuberculosis was *At Dawn and Dusk* (c.1898), which gave its name to a bohemian club where Daley mingled with such writers as **Henry Lawson** and **Norman Lindsay**. After his death appeared *Poems* (1908), *Wine and Roses* with a memoir by A G Stephens (1911) and, later, a selection of his radical verse, *Creeve Roe* (1947).

DALIN, Olof von
(1708–63)
Swedish poet, essayist and historian, born in Vinberg. The son of a minister, he became a tutor to the aristocracy and later, between 1751 and 1756, to the future King Gustav III. He was the most influential literary figure of the Swedish Enlightenment, compiling a monumental history of Sweden (1747–62). He also published a personal newspaper, *Then swänska Argus* (1732–4), in the tradition of **Joseph Addison**'s and **Richard Steele**'s *Tatler* and *Spectator*; influenced by **Jonathan Swift**, it achieved enormous influence and popularity and is regarded as the foundation stone of modern Swedish prose. Among his other works were a verse tragedy, *Brynilda* (1738), and a brilliant prose allegory, *Sagan om hästan* (1740, 'The Story of the Horse'), which is his finest imaginative work.
▷K J Warburg, *Olof Dalin* (1884)

DALLAS, Ruth
(1919–)
New Zealand poet and writer for children, born in Invercargill. Her first collection of verse, *Country Road and Other Poems, 1947–52* (1953), indicated both her direction and her style—the simple unaffected observation of nature. It was followed by *The Turning Wheel* (1961) and *Day Book: Poems of a Year* (1966). Her *Collected Poems* was published in 1987. Her style lends itself admirably to her writing for younger readers, which includes the quartet *The Children in the Bush* (1971), *The Wild Boy in the Bush* (1971), *The Big Flood in the Bush* (1972) and *Holiday Time in the Bush* (1983), set around a single-parent family in the author's own Southland (the southern part of South Island) in the 1890s.

DALLEY, John Bede
(1876–1935)
Australian journalist and writer, born in Rose Bay, Sydney. Retiring from the legal profession after falling from a horse, he began writing for the *Bulletin* where, by 1911, he was chief leader writer and a contributor of verse and short stories. Satirical novels of upper-class Sydney life followed; the best known was *Max Flambard* (1928), but in the same year he also published *No Armour* and, in 1930, *Only the Morning*.

DALY, (John) Augustin
(1838–99)
American dramatist and manager, born in Plymouth, North Carolina. After a career as

a drama critic, he went into management, opening the Fifth Avenue Theatre, New York, in 1869, and his own theatre, Daly's, in 1879, with the company of which he visited London in 1884. In 1893 he opened the London Daly's with Ada Rehan in *The Taming of the Shrew*. He wrote and adapted nearly a hundred plays, of which the best was *Horizon* (1871), though the most popular were melodramas such as *Under the Gaslight* and *Leah the Forsaken*. He was chosen by **Tennyson** to adapt *The Foresters* for the stage in 1891.
▷M Felheim, *The Theatre of Augustin Daly* (1956)

DAM, Niels Albert
(1880–1972)

Danish novelist and story writer, born near Århus, Jutland. He had been writing for some 50 years before he received his due recognition. His books, slightly reminiscent of **Simenon**, and most of them dealing with crime, culminated in the novel *Morfars By* (1956, 'Grandfather's Town'), which presents the fantastic and timeless mythology of a small parish. Danes hailed him as a major modernist writer when he published his stories in *Mid moder og hendres sonner* (1969, 'My Mother and her Sons'): they were, a critic suggested, 'violent metaphysical bids to escape his sense of absolute fatedness'.

DAMPIER, William
(1652–1715)

English naval trader, travel writer and pirate, born near Yeovil. He is reputed to have been on the voyage during which Alexander Selkirk, the model for Robinson Crusoe, was sent—by his own request—into arid exile on the island of Juan Fernández. His own accounts of what he found on his travels are exhaustive and true to life. *A New Voyage Round the World* (1697) contains one of the first pieces of writing about Australia, including an unflattering assessment of its aboriginal inhabitants: 'the Hodmadods of Monomatapa, though a nasty People, yet for wealth are Gentlemen to these'. The voyage upon which that book was based had been in 1688, aboard the *Cygnet*. In 1699 he again explored the west coast of Australia, and published his findings in *A Voyage to New Holland* (1703–9).

DANA, Richard Henry, Sr
(1787–1879)

American poet and prose writer, born in Cambridge, Massachusetts. He was educated at Harvard, and admitted to the Bar at Boston in 1811. In 1818 he became associate editor of the *North American Review*, to which he contributed. His *Dying Raven* (1821), *The Buccaneer* (1827) and some others of his poems were warmly praised by critics, but his best work was in criticism.

DANA, Richard Henry, Jr
(1815–82)

American author and lawyer son of **Richard Henry Dana**. While a student at Harvard, he shipped as a common sailor, and made a voyage round Cape Horn to California and back, which he described in *Two Years before the Mast* (1840). After graduating in 1837 he was admitted to the Massachusetts Bar in 1840, and was especially distinguished in maritime law. Among his works are *The Seaman's Friend* (1841) and *To Cuba and Back* (1859). He also edited Wheaton's *International Law*, and was a prominent free-soiler and Republican.
▷R Gale, *Dana* (1969)

DANCOURT, Florent Carton
(1661–1725)

French dramatist, actor and court favourite. He became devout in his old age, which he spent in retirement in the country. He excelled in depicting the stupidity of the peasantry and the follies of the bourgeoisie. His best-known comedy is *Le Chevalier à la mode* (1687, 'The Fashionable Knight').
▷J LeMaître, *Le Théâtre de Dancourt* (1882)

DANE, Clemence, pseud of **Winifred Ashton**
(1888–1965)

English novelist and playwright, born in Blackheath, London. Her novels included *Regiment of Women* (1917), *Legend* (1919), *Broome Stages* (1931) and *The Flower Girls* (1954), the last two dealing with theatrical families. Many of her plays achieved long runs, including *A Bill of Divorcement* (1921); the ingenious reconstruction of the poet's life in *Will Shakespeare* (1921); the stark tragedy of *Granite* (1926); *Call Home the Heart* (1927); and *Wild Decembers* (1932), about the **Brontës**.

DANIEL, Arnaut
(fl.late 12th century)

Provençal poet, born at the Castle of Rebeyrac, in Périgord, of poor but noble parents. He became a member of the court of Richard C'ur de Lion and was esteemed one of the best of the troubadours, particularly for his treatment of the theme of love. He introduced the sestina, the pattern of which was later adapted by **Dante** and **Petrarch**.
▷E Pound, in *Literary Essays* (1954)

DANIEL, Samuel
(1562–1619)

English poet, the son of a music-master, born near Taunton. He entered Magdalen Hall, Oxford, in 1597, but left it without a degree. He was sometime tutor at Wilton to William Herbert, son of the Earl of Pembroke, afterwards at Skipton to Anne Clifford, daughter of the Earl of Cumberland. In 1604 he was appointed to read new plays; in 1607 became one of the queen's grooms of the privy chamber, and from 1615 to 1618 had charge of a company of young players at Bristol. He then retired to a farm which he possessed at Beckington, in Somerset. Daniel was highly commended by his contemporaries, although **Ben Jonson** described him as 'a good honest man...but no poet'. **Coleridge**, **Charles Lamb** and **William Hazlitt** all praised him. His works include sonnets, epistles, masques and dramas; but his chief production was a poem in eight books, *A History of the Civil Wars between York and Lancaster*. His *Defence of Ryme* (1602) is in admirable prose.
▷C Seronsy, *Samuel Daniel* (1967)

D'ANNUNZIO, Gabriele
(1863–1938)

Italian writer, adventurer and political leader, born in Pescara. He began as a journalist on the *Tribuna* in Rome, but made his name as a poet with several volumes of poetry, starting in 1879 with *Primo vere*. During the 1890s he wrote 'Romances of the Rose', a trilogy of novels with **Nietzsche**an heroes, *Il Piacere* (1889, Eng trans *The Child of Pleasure*, 1898), *L'Innocente* (1892, Eng trans *The Intruder*, 1898) and *Il Trionfo della morte* (1894, Eng trans *The Triumph of Death*, 1896). *Le Vergini delle rocce* (1896, Eng trans *The Maidens of the Rocks*, 1898) is one of a 'Lily' trilogy; *Il Fuoco* (1900, Eng trans *The Flame of Life*, 1900) is the first of a 'Pomegranate' series. Elected a parliamentary deputy (1897–1900), he became notorious for his passionate affair with the actress Eleonora Duse, for whom he wrote several plays, including *La Città morta* (1898, Eng trans *The Dead City*, 1900), *La Gioconda* (1899, Eng trans *Gioconda*, 1901), *Francesca da Rimini* (1901, Eng trans 1902) and *La figlia di Jorio* (1904, Eng trans *The Daughter of Jorio*, 1907). *Le Martyre de St Sébastien* (1911) is a mystery play set to music by Debussy. Grace, voluptuousness and affection characterize this apostle of a new Renaissance. An enthusiastic patriot, he urged Italian entry into World War I, and served as a soldier, sailor and finally airman. In 1916 he lost an eye in combat in the air, and in 1918 carried out a sensational aerial reconnaissance over Vienna. In 1919 he seized and held Fiume, despite the Allies, and ruled as dictator until he was removed by the Italian government (1920). He became a strong supporter of the Fascist Party under Mussolini.
▷P Julian, *D'Annunzio* (1973)

DANTAS, Julio
(1876–1962)

Portuguese dramatist, poet and short-story writer, born in Lagos. In his light lyrical poems and stories he displayed considerable talent, but his heavier work, such as historical dramas, attempted under the influence of the Norwegian and French schools, was less successful. His *A ceia dos cardeais* (1902) was translated by H A Saintsbury as *The Cardinal's Collation* (1927).
▷J Dias Cancho, *Julio Dantas* (1922)

DANTE, in full Dante Alighieri
(1265–1321)

Italian poet, born in Florence, a lawyer's son of the noble Guelf family. He was baptized Durante, afterwards abbreviated to Dante. According to his *La Vita Nuova* (c.1292, Eng trans *The New Life*, 1861), he first set eyes on his lifelong love, Beatrice Portinari (c.1265–90), at the age of nine in 1274. There is no evidence that she returned his passion; she was married at an early age to one Simone de' Bardi, but neither this nor the poet's own subsequent marriage interfered with his pure and Platonic devotion to her, which intensified after her death. The story of his boyish but unquenchable passion is told with exquisite pathos in *Vita Nuova*. Shortly after, Dante married Gemma Donati, daughter of a powerful Guelf family. In 1289 he fought at Campaldino, where Florence defeated the Ghibellines, and was at the capitulation of Caprona. He was registered in one of the city guilds—that of the Apothecaries—being entered as 'Dante d'Aldighieri, *Poeta*'. In 1300, after filling minor public offices, and possibly going on some embassies abroad, he became one of the six priors of Florence, but for only two months. It was towards the 'White Guelfs', or more moderate section, that his sympathies tended. As prior, he procured the banishment of the heads and leaders of the rival factions, showing characteristic sternness and impartiality to Guelf and Ghibelline, White and Black, alike. In 1301, in alarm at the threatened interference of Charles of Valois, he was sent on an embassy to Rome to Pope Boniface VIII. He never returned from that embassy, nor did he ever again set foot in his native city. Charles espoused the side of the *Neri* or Blacks, and their victory was complete. He was banished from Florence in 1309 and sentenced to death in absentia. From then on he led a wandering life, first in Verona, in Tuscany, in the Lunigiano, near Urbino, and then Verona again. He eventually settled in Ravenna (1318),

where for the most part he remained until his death. He was buried with much pomp at Ravenna, where he still lies, restored in 1865 to the original sarcophagus. Dante had seven children, six sons and one daughter, Beatrice, a nun at Ravenna; but his family became extinct in the 16th century. His most celebrated work is the *Divina Commedia* (Eng trans *Divine Comedy*, 1847), begun around 1307, his spiritual testament, narrating a journey through Hell and Purgatory, guided by **Virgil**, and finally to Paradise, guided by Beatrice. It gives an encyclopedic view of the highest culture and knowledge of the age, all expressed in the most exquisite poetry. The *Divina Commedia* may be said to have made the Italian language, which was before so rude and unformed that Dante himself hesitated to employ it on such a theme, and is said to have begun his poem in Latin. The next most important work is the fragment called the *Convivio*, or *Banquet*, which takes the form of a commentary on some of the author's *canzoni*, or short poems, of which there are only three, though the work, if completed, would have contained 14. The *De Monarchia* (in Latin) expounds Dante's theory of the divinely intended government of the world by a universal pope. Another unfinished work, *De Vulgari Eloquentia*, discusses the origin of language, the divisions of languages, and the dialects of Italian in particular. *Canzoniere* is a collection of short poems, *canzoni*, sonnets, etc; and, finally, there are a dozen epistles addressed mainly to leading statesmen or rulers. There are also some *Eclogues* and other minor works, as well as several of doubtful authenticity.
▷E Auerbach, *Dante, Poet of the Secular World* (1961); W Anderson, *Dante the Maker* (1980)

DANZIGER, Paula
(1944–)
American writer of fiction for children, a teacher before she turned to fiction. *The Cat Ate My Gymsuit* (1974) began a succession of knowing but light-hearted novels aimed at early adolescents. Titles such as *Can You Sue Your Parents For Malpractice?* (1979) and *The Divorce Express* (1982) hint at the contradictory combination of earnestness and offbeat humour which typify her work—and, as these characteristics are so common in adolescents, explain its success.

DA PONTE, Lorenzo, originally **Emanuele Conegliano**
(1749–1838)
Italian poet, born in Ceneda near Venice of Jewish parents. He was converted to Roman Catholicism and became Professor of Rhetoric at Treviso until political and domestic

troubles drove him to Vienna, where as a poet to the Court Opera he wrote the libretti for Mozart's operas *The Marriage of Figaro* (1786), *Don Giovanni* (1787) and *Così fan Tutte* (1790). In London he taught Italian and sold boots; in 1805 he moved to New York, where he sold liquor, tobacco and groceries and ended up as Professor of Italian literature at Columbia College from 1825.

DARÍO, Rubén, pseud of **Felix Rubén García Sarmiento**
(1867–1916)
Nicaraguan poet. He lived a wandering life as a journalist, full of amours and diplomatic appointments, and died of pneumonia. He inaugurated the Spanish American modernist movement with his major works, *Azul* (1888) and *Prosas Profanas* (1896, Eng trans *Prosas Profanas and Other Poems*, 1922), showing Greek and French (Parnassian and Symbolist) influence, which gave new vitality to Spanish poetry.
▷C D Watland, *Poet-Errant: a Biography of Darío* (1965)

DARK, Eleanor, née **O'Reilly**
(1901–)
Australian novelist, daughter of **Dowell O' Reilly**, born and educated in Sydney. Employed briefly as a stenographer, she married a general practitioner in 1922 and a year later moved to Katoomba in the Blue Mountains. Her earliest writings, short stories and verse, were contributed from 1921 to various magazines, mostly under the pseudonym 'Patricia O'Rane' or 'P. O'R'. *Slow Dawning*, her first novel, was completed in 1923 but she had to wait until 1932 to see it published. Her other novels include *Prelude to Christopher* (1934), *The Little Company* (1945), *Lantana Lane* (1959) and the trilogy, *The Timeless Land* (1941), *Storm of Time* (1948) and *No Barrier* (1953), which charts the early years of European settlement of New South Wales. A writer of ideas, and a committed socialist and feminist, she was awarded the Australian Literature Society's Gold Medal in 1934 and 1936, and in 1978 received the Australian Society of Women Writers' Alice Award.
▷H Anderson, *A Handlist of Books* (1954)

DARLEY, George
(1795–1846)
Irish poet and mathematician, born in Dublin. Educated at Trinity College, Dublin, from c.1822 he lived in London, and worked on the staff of the *London Magazine*. He published a volume of verse, *The Errors of Ecstasie* (1822) and a collection of prose stories, *Labours of Idleness* (1826). He also wrote a

pastoral drama, *Sylvia* (1827) and the unfinished poem *Nepenthe* (1835). He wrote essays on dramatic criticism, and also published mathematical textbooks.
▷A Leventhal, *George Darley, 1795–1846* (1950)

DARUSMONT, Frances *see* WRIGHT, Frances

DARWALL, Mary, née Whateley
(1738–1825)
English poet, born at Beoley, Worcestershire, daughter of a gentleman farmer, and scantily educated. From 1760 she kept house for her brother in Walsall, then married the vicar of Walsall (1766), with whom she ran a printing press. After his death in 1794 she moved to Wales. Her *Original Poems on Several Occasions* (1764), published with help from the poet **William Shenstone**, shows her accomplished in a range of styles, from graceful lyrics and pastoral and meditative poetry to lively satirical verse, often self-mocking, sometimes briskly feminist.
▷A Messenger, in *Bulletin of Research in the Humanities* (1986)

DARWISH, Mahmud
(1942–)
Palestinian poet, whose stark writing voices the desperation and alienation of the Palestinian people. He was born in the village of al-Birweh, near the Carmel mountains, which was erased from the Israeli map, but which Darwish successfully brought to the world's notice: 'I am a native of the Carmel,/A mountain which the evening melts down into kisses'. The author of 11 volumes of poetry and three of prose, he has won the Lotus Prize (1969), the Mediterranean Prize (1980) and the Lenin Prize (1982). One of the foremost representatives of the angry new voice of the Arab world, his outstanding collections in translation are *Victims of a Map* (1984) and *Sand and Other Poems* (1986).

DAS, Kamala
(1934–)
Indian (Malayalam) poet and novelist. She writes her poetry in English and most of her prose in her own language (eg *My Story*, 1976, translated by herself—one of the most important Indian autobiographies ever written). Kamala Das is generally regarded as the best of all Indian poets now writing in English; her novel, *Alphabet of Lust* (1977), is also a very remarkable work from an Indian woman who has been much criticized by members of her own sex in her own country for 'departing from traditional norms'. Her

poetry is sensuous, deeply felt and technically very finely accomplished.
▷D Kohli, *Kamala Das* (1975)

DASS, Petter
(1647–1707)
Norwegian poet and pastor, linked to the people and nature of Northern Norway, where he achieved heroic stature and became a figure of legend. Dass's songs and poems were spread orally and in manuscript form and had a tremendous common appeal. His poetry is characterized by an ornamental Baroque style, but more typically a Renaissance interest in the concrete, especially the relationship between people and their environment. His best-known work, *Nordlands Trompet* (1739, Eng trans *The Trumpet of Nordland*, 1954), is full of humour and love for his people and shows an intimate knowledge of the northernmost areas of Norway.
▷H Midbøe, *Petter Dass* (1947)

D'AUBIGNÉ, Théodore Agrippa
(1552–1630)
French soldier and scholar, born near Pons in Saintonge. Of noble family, but poor, he distinguished himself as a soldier in 1567 in the Huguenot cause, and was appointed vice-admiral of Guienne and Brittany by King Henri IV. His severe and inflexible character frequently embroiled him with the court; and after Henri's assassination (1610) he withdrew to a life of literary activity in Geneva, leaving a worthless son, Constant. His *Histoire universelle, 1550–1601* (1616–20, 'World History') was burned in France by the common hangman. His biting satire is shown in his *Aventures du baron de Foenestée* (1617) and in his *Confession catholique du Sieur de Sancy* (1660, 'The Catholic Confessions of the Sieur de Sancy'). His grand-daughter was Madame de Maintenon.

DÄUBLER, Theodor
(1876–1934)
German poet, born in Trieste. Only a few of his shorter poems are read now, but he is still deservedly studied in universities. An unhappy man, and always a wanderer, he was a misfit in the army and subsequently felt himself to be one elsewhere. His vast 30 000-line epic *Das Nordlicht* (1912, rev edn 1922, 'The Northern Lights'), is based on an all but inaccessible mystical system involving the earth's wish to join the sun. But this has passages of beauty, and he wrote a handful of expressionistic poems of higher quality.

DAUDET, Alphonse
(1840–97)

French writer, born in Nîmes. After being educated at the Lyons Lycée he became an usher at Alais; but, when only 17, he set out for Paris with his older brother, Ernest (1837–1921), who became a journalist and novelist of some mark, and both obtained appointments as clerk or private secretary in the office of the Duke of Morny. Alphonse's poem *Les Amoureuses* (1858, 'The Lovers') was followed by theatrical pieces (written partly in collaboration), *La Dernière Idole* (1862, 'The Last Idol'), *L'Oeillet blanc* (1865, 'The White Carnation'), *Le Frère aîné* (1868, 'The Elder Brother'), *Le Sacrifice* (1869) and particularly *L'Arlésienne* (1872, 'A Woman from Arles', with music by Bizet). His best-known work is his series of sketches and short stories of Provençal life, originally written for *Le Figaro*, especially *Lettres de mon moulin* (collected 1869, 'Letters from my Mill'), *Robert Helmont* (1874), *Contes du lundi* (1873, 'Monday Stories') and the charming extravaganza of *Tartarin de Tarascon* (1872), continued in *Tartarin sur les Alpes* (1885) and *Port Tarascon* (1890). *Le petit chose* (1868, 'Young What's His Name') is full of pathos and of reminiscences of his own early struggles. He also published long naturalistic novels, on the social conditions of the day, such as *Fromont jeune et Risler aîné* (1874, 'Fromont Junior and Risler Senior'), *Jacks* (1876), *Le Nabab* (1877, 'The Nabob') and *Numa Roumestan* (1881). In *L'Évangéliste* (1883) the Salvation Army was introduced; *Sapho* (1884) is a tale of the infatuation of a young man for a courtesan; and in *L'Immortel* (1888, 'The Immortal One') all the author's powers of ridicule are turned against the Académie française. His wife, Julia Allard Daudet (1845–1940), also published poetry.
▷ R H Sherard, *Alphonse Daudet* (1894)

DAUDET, Léon
(1867–1942)

French writer and political activist, son of **Alphonse Daudet**. He studied medicine but turned to journalism, and in 1899 helped to found the right-wing royalist newspaper *Action française*, of which he became editor in 1908. He sat in the Chamber of Deputies from 1919 to 1924. In 1925 his son was assassinated and subsequently he spent some time in Belgium as a political exile. He wrote several novels, but is best remembered for his numerous memoirs and critical works, especially *Le Stupide XIXe siècle* (1922, 'The Stupid 19th Century').
▷ J Marque, *Léon Daudet* (1971)

DAUTHENDEY, Max
(1867–1918)

German poet, philosopher, dramatist and novelist, a frustrated painter and a solitary and wandering man, born in Würzburg. His works run to nine volumes. Some have said that his poetry is so exotic as not to be poetry; but, although his elaborate theories of life and art are forgotten, it still has a few champions, who point to its 'orgiastic' qualities.
▷ H G Wendt, *Max Dauthendey: Poet-Philosopher* (1936)

DAUMAL, René
(1908–44)

French poet and essayist, born in Boulzicourt, Ardennes. At the age of 20 he became co-founder (with Roger Gilbert-Lecomte and the Czech painter Joseph Sima) of the group and magazine *Le Grand Jeu* ('The Great Game'). The move necessitated a formal break with the surrealists, with whom, however, he retained a similarity of attitude towards art. Both *Contre-ciel* (1936, 'Counter-heaven'), a collection of poetry, and *La grande beuverie* (1939, 'The Great Binge'), a fantasy, display Daumal's interest in the unconscious and its untapped potential; so too does his enthusiasm for the work of the Armenian mystic **Gurdjieff**, who had settled in France in the 1920s. Suffering from tuberculosis, he refused treatment, allowing himself to die—in the interest, or so it was claimed, of 'self-exploration'. His poems were collected by his wife and published as *Poésie noire, poésie blanche* in 1954.

D'AVENANT, Sir William
(1606–68)

English poet and playwright, born in Oxford, the son of an inn-keeper. His father kept the Crown, a tavern at which **Shakespeare** used to stop on the way between London and Stratford, thereby giving rise to the rumour that D'Avenant was Shakespeare's illegitimate son. At the age of 12 he wrote an 'Ode in Remembrance of Master Shakespeare', not printed, however, until 1638. After a short period of study at Lincoln College, Oxford, he became page to Frances, Duchess of Richmond; next he joined the household of the aged poet, **Fulke Greville**, Lord Brooke. In 1628 he turned to writing for the stage. During the next 10 years he produced many plays, including *The Cruel Brother* (1630) and *The Wits* (1636). In 1638, at the request of the queen, Henrietta Maria, he was appointed poet laureate in succession to **Ben Jonson**. About the same time he lost his nose through an illness, a calamity which exposed him to public ridicule. Later he became manager of Drury Lane Theatre. During the Civil War he was knighted by King Charles I for his gallantry at the siege of Gloucester (1643). In 1650 he was imprisoned in the Tower for two years, where he completed his epic, *Gondibert* (1651). He is considered to have been the founder of English opera with his *Siege of Rhodes* (1656), and opened a theatre, the Cockpit, in Drury Lane in 1658.

▷A Harbege, *Sir William D'Avenant, 1606–1668* (1935)

DAVENPORT, Guy (Mattison, Jr)
(1927–)

American writer of fiction and literary criticism, whose works often seem to fall between the two categories, being concerned with real or historical people and written in a deliberately naive and uncontrived prose. *Tatlin!* (1974) is a short-story collection headed by a tale about the Russian Constructivist; Leonardo appears in *Da Vinci's Bicycle* (1979); other historical characters include **Kafka** and **Pound**, about whom Davenport has also written a critical study (1983). In *Eclogues* (1981), his most distinctive volume, Davenport reintroduces Adriaan van Hovendaal from *Tatlin!* and explores his coming to terms with the non-Constructivist, non-absurd world of everyday reality; in doing so he creates a utopian vision derived from Fourier's concept of Harmony in which art plays the purest and most fundamental part. Davenport has translated **Archilochos of Paros**, **Sappho** and other classical writers and written an indexed guide to the *Iliad* and *Odyssey* (1967).

DAVICO, Oskar
(1909–)

Serbian poet and fiction writer, a teacher by profession, who was in 1932 sentenced to five years in prison for his communism. In 1941 he was interned in Italy for the same reasons, but escaped in the following year to join Tito. He made his reputation in 1929 with a set of prose poems much in the style of the French surrealists, whom he had met and studied in Paris. Later, as a result of his sufferings in the war, his poetry matured, and he wrote a powerful, if somewhat over-**Joyce**an novel, *Pesma* (1952, Eng trans *The Poem*, 1959), about the division between the intellectual and the active attitude to World War II.

DAVIDSON, Donald
(1893–1968)

American poet, critic and academic, a leading member of the Fugitive Group of poets which included **Ransom** and **Allen Tate**. He was born in Campbellsville, Tennessee. He was influential on the extreme conservative side (whereas **Robert Penn Warren** represented the liberal wing) of the so-called 'Southern Agrarian' programme advocated by this group in the manifesto *I'll Take My Stand* (1930). His poetry, taut and well-made but seldom linguistically inspired, was not as widely read as that of his colleagues.

DAVIDSON, John
(1857–1909)

Scottish poet, novelist and dramatist, born in Barrhead, Renfrewshire, the son of an Evangelical minister. Educated at the Highlander's Academy, Greenock, where he became a pupil-teacher (1872–6), and Edinburgh University, he became an itinerant teacher in Scotland. He had started to write in 1885 (four verse dramas and a couple of novels), and in 1889 moved to London where, among other works, he wrote *Fleet Street Eclogues* (1893) and *Ballads and Songs* (1894). **T S Eliot** later acknowledged a debt to the urban imagery and colloquialism of 'Thirty Bob a Week'. He wrote prolifically in the last years of his life, including a series of blank-verse *Testaments*, several other verse dramas, short stories and prose sketches. He eventually committed suicide by drowning himself at Penzance.

▷J Townsend, *Davidson, poet of Armageddon* (1961)

DAVIDSON, Lionel
(1922–)

English crime and espionage writer. Born in Hull, he served in Royal Navy submarines during the war and then worked as a magazine journalist until 1959. A highly original writer who has managed to avoid a formulaic approach, his first novel, *The Night of Wenceslas* (1960), was a superior spy thriller set in Czechoslovakia and was much praised for its settings, even though Davidson had never been there. Its successor was more exotic still, in all but the straightforwardness of narrative; *The Rose of Tibet* (1962) was hailed as 'pure' adventure. Later novels, such as *A Long Way to Shiloh* (1966, published in the USA as *The Menorah Men*) and *Smith's Gazelle* (1971), introduced an element of philosophical, almost mystical, quest; *Making Good Again* (1968) and *The Sun Chemist* (1976) explore aspects of modern Jewish life and politics, centring on the Holocaust. Davidson has also written juvenile fiction under the pseudonym David Line.

DAVIE, Donald Alfred
(1922–)

English poet, born in Barnsley and, after wartime naval service, educated at Cambridge. His first book was *Purity of Diction in English*

Verse (1952), a critical study that retrospectively reads like a manifesto for his own clear, rational prosody and thought and was taken as such by the Movement poets. His first important collection was *Brides of Reason* (1955), influenced by English Augustan poetry, morally robust and hostile to the excesses of **Dylan Thomas**; the only modernist poet to whom he claimed allegiance was **Pound**, on whom he later wrote *Poet as Sculptor* (1964) and *Pound* (1975). Though Davie was drawn to Pound's ear, it was sometimes suggested that he was attracted to his ultra-conservative politics. In 1964, he became Professor of English and then Pro-Vice-Chancellor at the new University of Essex (1964–8), presiding over a stormy outbreak of student radicalism; *Essex Poems* (1969) documents his pessimistic reactions. Similar upheavals awaited him in the USA, at Stanford University (1968–78), and later at Vanderbilt University in Nashville. *The Shires* (1974) and *In the Stopping Train* (1977) were his finest achievement to date, autobiographical but disciplined. His collections include *The Battered Wife* (1985).
▷ G Dekker, *Donald Davie and the Responsibilities of Literature* (1984)

DAVIES, Hubert Henry
(1876–1917)

English playwright, born in Woodley, Cheshire. He was a journalist in San Francisco, returned to England in 1901, and disappeared in 1917. His plays included *Cousin Kate* (1903) and *The Mollusc* (1907).

DAVIES, Idris
(1905–53)

Welsh poet, born in Rhymney, Gwent. He left school at 14 to become a miner in the pit where his father worked. He later took a correspondence course and went on to study at Loughborough College and Nottingham University, qualifying as a teacher. He published three volumes of verse, his work fired with anger and indignation at the social injustices that he had witnessed. From 1932 to 1951 he worked as a school-teacher, in the East of London and (after World War II) in Rhymney Valley.
▷ I Jenkyns, *Idris Davies* (1972)

DAVIES, Sir John
(1569–1626)

English poet and statesman, born in Tisbury, Wiltshire. Educated at Winchester School, Queen's College, Oxford, and the Middle Temple, he was called to the Bar in 1595. Entering politics, he was returned to parliament for Corfe Castle and after the death of Elizabeth found favour with James I, who

sent him to Ireland as solicitor-general. Three years later he was made Irish attorney-general and knighted. In Ireland he supported severe repressive measures and took part in the plantation of Ulster. He returned to the English parliament in 1614, representing Newcastle-under-Lyme, and practised as king's serjeant in England. He had been nominated chief justice a month before his death of apoplexy. In 1622 he collected in one volume his three chief poems—*Orchestra, or a Poeme of Dancing* (1596); *Nosce Te Ipsum* (1599), a long didactic piece on the soul's immortality; and *Hymns to Astraea* (1599), a collection of clever acrostics on the name Elizabeth Regina.
▷ M Seeman, *Sir John Davies, sein Leben und seine Werke* (1813)

DAVIES, Rhys
(1901–78)

Welsh novelist and short-story writer, born in the Rhondda Valley. After attending Porth County School he worked in offices and shops in London, soon establishing a reputation with his short stories and his first novel, *The Withered Root* (1927), which, typically, sets puritanical religion against the urges of sexuality. Of his 17 novels the most popular was *The Black Venus* (1944), dealing with the conflict between traditional practices and Anglicizing modernity in a Welsh village. Described as 'a Welsh Chekhov', he was particularly distinguished and prolific as a short-story writer, describing in an objective but ironic, humorous and poetic manner the lives of ordinary Welsh people, often women. Other stories are set in Europe and England; his collections include *Boy with a Trumpet* (1949) and *The Chosen One* (1967).
▷ R L Mégroz, *Rhys Davies: A Critical Sketch* (1932)

DAVIES, (William) Robertson
(1913–)

Canadian novelist, playwright, essayist and critic, born in Thamesville, Ontario. Educated in Canada and Balliol College, Oxford, he has taught, acted (he was Sir William Tyrone Guthrie's literary assistant) and been a journalist, was Editor of the *Examiner* (Peterborough, Ontario) from 1942 to 1963 and a professor of English at the University of Toronto (1960–81). His first novel was *Tempest-Tost* (1951), the first of 'The Salterton Trilogy', but he is best known for 'The Deptford Trilogy'—*Fifth Business* (1970), *The Manticore* (1972) and *World of Wonders* (1975). This work evolved from his earlier books set in Salterton, an imagined Ontario city, patently Kingston, which is dominated by its old families, Anglican Church, military school, university, and belief in the virtues of

England and the English. He is now a writer of international repute; *What's Bred in the Bone* (1985) was shortlisted for the Booker Prize.

DAVIES, William Henry
(1871–1940)

English poet, born in Newport, Monmouthshire, the son of a publican. Emigrating to the USA at the age of 22, he lived partly as a tramp and partly as a casual workman until the loss of a leg whilst 'jumping' a train caused him to return to England, where he began to write and lived the life of a tramp and pedlar in order to raise sufficient money to have his poems printed by a jobbing printer. A copy of this first work, *A Soul's Destroyer*, came into the hands of **George Bernard Shaw**, who arranged for its regular publication in 1907. The success of this book was consolidated by *The Autobiography of a Super-tramp* (1908). He continued to publish volumes of poems and lyrics, gathered in the *Collected Poems* (1943), two novels, and the prose *Adventures of Johnny Walker, Tramp* (1926). He continued his autobiography with *Beggars* (1909), *The True Traveller* (1912), *A Poet's Pilgrimage* (1918), *Later Days* (1925), and the posthumously published *Young Emma* (1980).
▷L Hocley, *W H Davies* (1971)

DAVIN, Dan
(1913–90)

New Zealand novelist and short-story writer, born in Otago. He was educated at Otago and Oxford universities, served in several units, including Intelligence GHQ, during World War II, then went into publishing. His novels, which fall firmly within the realist tradition, include *Cliffs of Fall* (1945), *The Sullen Bell* (1956) and *Brides of Price* (1972). The first and last are set in his homeland; *The Sullen Bell* examines the condition of the expatriate New Zealander. *Crete* (1953), part of the New Zealand Official War History, is an understated, at times quietly poetic, account of the battle for control of that island.

DAVIS, Harold Lenoir
(1896–1960)

American novelist, poet and cattle-herder, born in Douglas County, Oregon. He is remembered for his vividly debunking novel *Honey in the Horn* (1935), about Oregon pioneers, which won a Pulitzer Prize. His later work dealt in an enlightened and knowledgeable manner with the great outdoors. *Team Bells Woke Me* (1953) collected expertly constructed stories.

DAVIS, Jack Leonard
(1918–)

Australian author, born in north-western Western Australia, one of the most respected aboriginal writers. He published a book of verse, *The First-Born*, in 1970 and was then for some years joint editor of an aboriginal journal *Identity*. A second volume, *Jagardoo: Poems from Aboriginal Australia*, appeared in 1978 and was followed by the plays *The Dreamers* (1982) and *Kullark* (1979), which both treat of the problems of aborigines in contemporary white society. In 1993 he published the verse collection *Black Life*.

DAVIS, Owen
(1874–1956)

American playwright, born in Maine. He graduated from Harvard University in 1893, and began his writing career by attempting serious verse tragedy for the stage. He turned to a more profitable career producing popular melodramas, literally by the hundreds, which are now largely forgotten. He returned to serious drama as well, and was awarded the Pulitzer Prize for Drama for *Icebound* in 1923. He also adapted novels for the stage, including **F Scott Fitzgerald**'s *The Great Gatsby* (1926) and **Edith Wharton**'s *Ethan Frome* (1936), and wrote an autobiography, *I'd Like To Do It Again* (1931).

DAVIS, Rebecca (Blaine) Harding
(1831–1910)

American novelist, who lived for most of her life in Philadelphia, and was one of the pioneers of realistic fiction. Such books as *Margaret Howth* (1862) are marred by the moral tone then obligatory, but their real purpose is proto-naturalistic: to explore the underbelly of urban life. *Waiting for the Verdict* (1868) shocked many by its affirmative treatment of Blacks. 'Come right down here with me,' she told her readers, 'here into the thickest of the fog and mud and effluvia'.

DAVIS, Richard Harding
(1863–1916)

American novelist, newspaper correspondent and dramatist, the son of **Rebecca Harding Davis**, born in Philadelphia. He was known as 'the Beau Brummell of the Press', and was a dashing dandy and an often unscrupulous correspondent; but, although essentially superficial, he was also a master storyteller, whose fiction can still be read with pleasure: *Van Bibber* (1892), sketches about a New York socialite, and, above all, the novel *Soldiers of Fortune* (1897), are modelled on the formula established by **Anthony Hope** in *The Prisoner of Zenda*, and worthy of it.

DAVISON, Frank Dalby, properly **Frederick Douglas**
(1893–1970)

Australian novelist and short-story writer, born in Hawthorn, Melbourne, whose reputation was established in three different genres. Firstly, his novels of considerable empathy with wild animals, in *Man-Shy: A Story of Men and Cattle* (1931), where the heroine is a heifer who escapes from a round-up and at the end becomes matriarch of a herd of wild cattle, and *Dusty* (1946), in which a kelpie-dingo crossbreed, after living and working with man, succumbs in time to its primitive instincts. Secondly, his short stories and especially *The Wells of Beersheba* (1933), an epic of the Australian Light Horse in Palestine during World War I. Lastly, his massive novel *The White Thorntree* (1968), which took Davison 22 years to write; in four sections he describes the search for sexual happiness and the frustrations of a family in middle-class Sydney.

DAVISON, Peter
(1928–)

American poet, born in New York. He is a publisher by profession. His poetry is precise and well crafted, 'even' and 'gem-like'; the long poem *Dark Houses* (1971) elaborates on his father, whose presence is recaptured in Davison's autobiography, *Half-Remembered* (1973).
▷ *Praying Wrong: New and Selected Poems 1957–1984* (1984); G Rotella, *Three Contemporary Poets of New England* (1983)

DAWE, Bruce
(1930–)

Australian poet and short-story writer, born in Geelong, Victoria. Dawe's writings show an unwilling acceptance of the fact that life is short, brutal and, to a large extent, pointless. Despite this, they are shot through with a wry acceptance of fate; the laconic forms of Australian speech bring to life the human tragi-comedy of which he writes. His best stories were collected in *Over Here, Harv!* (1983). His verse has won many awards, and includes *Beyond the Subdivisions* (1968), *Condolences of the Season* (1971) and *Sometimes Gladness: Collected Poems 1954–1978*, of which a new edition taking the poems up to 1982 was published in 1983. Dawe received the **Patrick White** Literary Award in 1980.

DAWE, (William) Carlton Lanyon
(1865–1935)

Australian-born British writer of popular novels of adventure and romance. He published three early volumes of verse, *Sydonia and Other Poems* (1885), later incorporated in *Love and the World and Other Poems* (1886) and *Sketches in Verse* (1889), and a novelette *Zantha: and the Old Piano* (1886) before moving to London in the early 1880s. There he wrote *The Golden Lake; or the Marvellous History of a Journey through the Great Lone Land of Australia* (1891) and *Mount Desolation* (1892), followed by over 70 novels, many with Australian settings. He was an accomplished story-teller and his novels offered good entertainment to the users of the circulating libraries of the period; they included society romances and crime mysteries such as *The Mandarin* (1899), *The Grand Duke: a Novel* (1905), *The Plotters of Peking* (1907), *The Crackswoman* (1914) and *The Woman with Yellow Eyes* (1917). From 1931, with *Leathermouth* he began a series of tales featuring the extraordinary Colonel Leathermouth, ending with *Live Cartridge* (1937).

DAWSON, Jennifer
(1931–)

English novelist. Educated at St Anne's College, Oxford, she subsequently worked in publishing, education, and as a social worker in a psychiatric hospital, an experience which—the latter part at least—significantly influenced her first novel, *The Ha-Ha* (1961). A novel of madness, it has been much admired for its vivid reconstruction of schizophrenia and for its grasp of the social implications of schizophrenic perceptions and language. Subsequent novels, *Fowler's Snare* (1962), *The Cold Country* (1965), *Strawberry Boy* (1976) and *A Field of Scarlet Poppies* (1979), have explored similar ideas, but without the crispness of delivery found in some of Dawson's short stories, collected in *Hospital Wedding* (1978).

DAY, Clarence
(1874–1935)

American humorist, whose *Life With Father* (1935) was a popular success; its successor *Life With Mother* (1936) was posthumous. As a play (1939) the former, a fairly conventional but capable portrait of a naively angry man, set records. Day wrote for the *New Yorker* for many years, and helped to set its famous tone.

DAY, Dorothy
(1897–1980)

American writer and radical social reformer, born in Brooklyn, New York. A life-long socialist, she worked in the New York slums as a probationary nurse. Converted to Catholicism in 1927, she co-founded the monthly

Catholic Worker in 1933, drawing on her earlier experience as a reporter on Marxist publications like *Call* and *The Masses*. Under the influence of the French itinerant priest Peter Maurin (1877–1949), she founded the Catholic Worker Movement, whose Depression work was described in her *House of Hospitality* (1939). A pacifist and a fervent supporter of farm-worker unionization in the 1960s, she helped turn her church's attention to peace and justice issues. Other works include the autobiographical novel *The Eleventh Virgin* (1924) and *On Pilgrimage: the Sixties* (1972).
▷ *The Long Loneliness* (1952)

DAY, John
(1574–?1640)

English Jacobean dramatist, born in Norfolk. He studied at Caius College, Cambridge, and is mentioned in Henslowe's *Diary* in 1598 as an active playwright, and collaborated freely with **Henry Chettle**, **Thomas Dekker**, and others. His works, privately printed by Arthur Henry Bullen in 1881, include a graceful comedy, *Humour Out of Breath*, and *The Parliament of Bees*, an allegorical masque.

DAY, Thomas
(1748–89)

English writer and barrister, born in London. Educated at Charterhouse and Corpus Christi College, Oxford, he formed a close friendship with Richard Lovell Edgeworth. In 1765 he entered the Middle Temple, in 1775 was called to the Bar, but never practised. A disciple of **Rousseau**, he brought up an orphan and a foundling, one of whom, he presumed, would become his wife. That scheme miscarried; and he proposed first to Honora and next to Elizabeth Sneyd. She sent him to France to acquire French graces but on his return she laughed at him. Finally in 1778 he married an appreciative heiress, Esther Milnes, and spent 11 happy years with her, farming on philanthropic and costly principles in Essex and Surrey, until he was killed by a fall from a colt he was breaking in. He wrote a long children's tale, *The History of Sandford and Merton* (3 vols, 1783–9), a didactic novel in which the poor but virtuous Harry Sandford is a constant example to the rich, spoiled, but essentially good Tommy Merton. He wrote another moral tale, *The History of Little Jack* (1788), and a long poem, *The Dying Negro* (1773).
▷ M Sadler, *Thomas Day, an English disciple of Rousseau* (1928)

DAY-LEWIS, Cecil
(1904–72)

Irish poet, critic and detective-story writer, born in Ballintubbert, County Leix. He was educated at Sherborne School and Wadham College, Oxford, and published his first verse in 1925, *Beechen Vigil and Other Poems*. He made his name as a lyric poet with *Transitional Poems* (1929), and during the 1930s, with **W H Auden** and **Stephen Spender**, became associated with left-wing causes, and also wrote literary criticism in *A Hope for Poetry* (1934). He became a member of the Communist Party, which he renounced in 1939. During World War II he worked in the Ministry of Information, and then published *Poetry for You* (1944) and his major critical work, *The Poetic Image* (1947). He became Professor of Poetry at Oxford (1951–6) and at Harvard (1964–5), and published his last critical work, *The Poetic Impulse* (1965). He made notable translations of **Virgil** and St Valery, and was appointed poet laureate in 1968. Under the pseudonym of 'Nicholas Blake' he wrote a score of sophisticated detective novels. His autobiography, *The Buried Day*, was published in 1960. *The Poems of C. Day Lewis 1925–72* appeared in 1977.
▷ S Day-Lewis, *Cecil Day-Lewis: a biography* (1990)

DAZAI Osamu
(1909–48)

Japanese writer, born into a wealthy family from Tsugaru. He went to Tokyo to study, and started writing there, embracing the Japanese naturalist aesthetic and producing a string of deeply introspective, delicate novels. He also became involved with the underground left, joining the (proscribed) Communist Party, though he was forced, publicly, to renounce his Marxism and quit the party after being arrested by the Kempeito (secret police). This experience and that of the war left him deeply scarred, eventually leading to his suicide, but is not reflected in much of his writing, perhaps because of the political pressure put on him by the fascist regime. *The Setting Sun* and *No Longer Human* are, however, both about Japan's loss of the war, which affected him deeply, and are both available in translation.

DEAMER, (Mary Elizabeth Kathleen) Dulcie
(1890–1972)

New Zealand journalist, poet, playwright and novelist, born in Christchurch. In 1907, at 17, she won a short-story competition run by the Australian magazine *Lone Hand*. This was collected, with other stories, in *In the Beginning: Six Studies of the Stone Age* (1909, reprinted, with illustrations by **Norman Lindsay** as *As It Was in the Beginning*, 1929). Dulcie Deamer then joined a theatrical touring company, married the business manager and, when her husband died, sent their six children home to New Zealand to be brought up by her mother. She toured China, Burma and India with another company and then settled in Sydney in the early 1920s. Her poems and novels dealt mainly with mythology and with classical times; an early book of verse, *Messalina* (1932), contained portraits of classical and historic women. Another collection of poems was *The Silver Branch* (1948). Her novels include *The Suttee of Safa: A Hindoo Romance* (1913), *The Street of the Gazelle* (1922) and *The Devil's Saint* (1924). One of her plays, *Easter*, a morality play, was included in *Best Australian One-Act Plays* (1937). Known in the Sydney of the 1920s and 1930s as the 'Queen of Bohemia', her frenetic and heterosexual lifestyle has caused her to be shunned by some modern feminist commentators, but she did much to encourage literate women of her time.

DE AMICIS, Edmondo
(1846–1908)

Italian novelist and journalist. He became famous for his *La vita militare* (1868, 'The Military Life'), sketches recalling his service against the Austrian tyrant. But his enduring book, still to be found in most Italian bookshops and schools, is *Cuore* (1886, Eng trans *Heart: A School Boy's Journal*, 1895), a sentimental, philistine, almost **Kipling**esque, but none the less appealing and not quite unrealistic novel of academic life.

DEANE, John F
(1943–)

Irish poet, fiction writer and publisher, born on the Gaelic-speaking Achill Island. He resigned as a teacher to found and develop a National Poetry Society, Eigse Eireann/Poetry Ireland, in 1978; in 1985 he founded *The Dedalus Press*. In *The Stylized City* (1991), his seventh collection of poems, he developed a spiritual and meditative quality that has pervaded all his subsequent work. A prolific and enthusiastic interpreter of the work of other authors, through the Dedalus Press he has introduced illuminating editions of the work of, among others, the Romanian **Marin Sorescu** and Swedish poet **Tomas Tranströmer**. His fictions, *Free Range* (1994), are gentle unravellings of vulnerable 'souls' earthed in bitter, wracked bodies. His contribution to Irish literature is that of a generous, contemplative writer rather than a controversial one, though as a publisher he has certainly broken new ground.

DEANE, Seamus
(1940–)

Irish poet, critic and anthologist, born in Derry. Educated in Belfast and at Cambridge,

he became a Fulbright lecturer at Berkeley (1966–8) before returning to Ireland to become Professor of Modern English and American Literature at University College Dublin; in 1971 he became co-director of the Field Day Theatre Company, a post he held until 1993. His three-volume *Field Day Anthology of Irish Writing* was published in 1991. Of his own work, *Gradual Wars* (1972) was one of the first poetry collections to address the political unrest in Ireland since the late 1960s. Five subsequent collections and several volumes of essays, including the important *Heroic Styles: The Tradition of an Idea* (1985), made him spokesman for a questioning attitude that was often glibly dismissed as 'revisionist'. His critical analysis and declared 'desire to locate the Irish experience' in a European context make him a cultural commentator of singular importance.

DE BEAUVOIR, Simone
(1908–86)

French novelist, feminist, autobiographer and essayist, born in Paris and educated at the Sorbonne, where she later lectured. She will undoubtedly be remembered chiefly for the enormous impact made by her famous book *Le Deuxième Sexe* (1949, Eng trans *The Second Sex*, 1953), which despite its alleged shortcomings as a feminist tract, remains authoritative for its intelligence and the sheer weight of its case. It inspired many women to salutary writings and actions and has caused many of them to refer to its author as 'the mother of us all'. She was also a notable novelist (in particular in *Les Mandarins*, 1954, Eng trans *The Mandarins*, 1956) and a supreme autobiographer, as in *Memoires d'une jeune fille rangée* (1954, Eng trans *Memoirs of a Dutiful Daughter*, 1959). She was the lifelong companion of **Jean-Paul Sartre**.

▷R D Cottrell, *Simone de Beauvoir* (1975)

DEBELYANOV, Dimcho
(1887–1916)

Bulgarian poet, the leading Symbolist of his time, who was killed fighting in Greece. He wrote in the tradition of **Hristo Botev**, but infused his poetry (of which there is comparatively little) with the spirit of the French symbolists. Like Hungary's **Ady**, he brought to the literature of his language the right foreign influence just when it was needed, but without violating it. His haunting work, which has not been translated, finds mystical significance in the relations between all phenomena—a significance alluded to in **Baudelaire**'s famous sonnet beginning 'Nature is a living temple ... '.

▷C Manning and R Smal-Stocki, *The History of Modern Bulgarian Literature* (1960)

DE BOISSIÈRE, Ralph Anthony Charles
(1907–)

Trinidadian-born Australian novelist, born and educated in Port-of-Spain. Having worked as a clerk in commerce, he moved to Australia in 1947, taking citizenship there in 1970. His writing career has been intermittent and his output slow. *Crown Jewel* (1952) is a realistic portrait of working-class activity in pre-war Trinidad, while *Rum and Coca-Cola* (1956) covers the war years, when thousands of US servicemen arrived on the island, and replaces the social and political emphasis of its predecessor with a more psychological approach. *No Saddles for Kangaroos* (1964) is set in de Boissière's adoptive country and is much less perceptive. He also wrote the music for his own play, *Calypso Isle* (1955).

DE CAMP, L(yon) Sprague
(1907–)

American science-fiction and fantasy writer, born in New York City. His first book was a textbook on patents. He was one of the stable of writers associated with **John W Campbell** and *Astounding Science Fiction* magazine, and became an equally valued contributor to its sister publication *Unknown*, turning his attention to fantasy in the process. Notable titles include *Lest Darkness Fall* (1941), a time-travel story set in 6th-century Rome, and *The Wheels of If* (1948), an alternate world story. Both of these subjects were united in his *Incomplete Enchanter* sequence, written with Fletcher Pratt, one of a number of such collaborators, including his wife, Catherine A Crook. *Rogue Queen* (1951) is the most highly regarded novel in his *Viagens Interplanetarisas* sequence, which began in 1949. He also wrote a large number of fantasy and sword and sorcery adventure novels, and biographies of **H P Lovecraft** and Robert E Howard, whose *Conan the Barbarian* series he continued.

DECHEPARE, Bernard
(fl.mid 16th century)

Basque priest who wrote the first known book in the language, *Linguae Vasconum primitiae* ('Primitive Basque Language'), printed in 1545.
▷R Gallop, *A Book of the Basques* (1930); L Michelena, *Historia de la literatura vasca* (1960)

DEEPING, (George) Warwick
(1877–1950)

English novelist, born in Southend. He qualified as a doctor, but devoted himself to writing. It was not until after World War I, in which he served, that he gained recognition as an author with his bestseller, *Sorrell and Son* (1925), which was later filmed. Other novels include *Old Pybus* (1928) and *Roper's Row* (1929). In his stories, all sentimental, good breeding is represented as the cardinal virtue.

DE FILIPPO, Eduardo
(1900–92)

Italian dramatist, theatre director and actor. He was born in Naples and grew up in the theatre, acting with a family troupe. He formed the Teatro Umoristico with his brother and sister (1931–44), before founding Il Teatro di Eduardo in 1945, by which time he had already written or adapted more than 25 plays. *Natale in casa Cupiello* (1931, rev edn 1942) was revived in London in 1982 as *Ducking Out*. Unlike the work of his fellow-countrymen **Luigi Pirandello** and **Dario Fo**, there is nothing stylized about de Filippo's drama and as a result its understated approach often does not translate easily. *Questi fantasmi!* (1946) was staged as *Too Many Ghosts* in Oxford in the late fifties (subsequently published as *Oh, These Ghosts*, 1971), and *Filumena Marturano* (1946) has enjoyed English-language success as *The Best House in Naples* (1956, USA) and *Filumena* (1977, UK). De Filippo uses Neapolitan dialect as a personal, almost private, language of expression and though his use of farce is internationally recognizable, some of his most telling speech simply does not translate.
▷M Mignone, *Eduardo de Filippo* (1984)

DEFOE, Daniel
(1660–1731)

English author and adventurer, born in Stoke Newington, London, the son of a butcher. He appears to have travelled widely on the Continent before setting up in the hosiery trade in London in 1683. He took part in Monmouth's rebellion and joined William III's army in 1688. Up to 1704 he strenuously supported the king's party and earned William's favour with his satirical poem *The True-born Englishman* (1701), an attack on xenophobic prejudice. In Queen Anne's reign he ran into trouble with his famous satire *The Shortest Way with the Dissenters* (1702), the irony of which at first deceived the High Church party, but which eventually cost him a ruinous fine, the pillory and imprisonment during the Queen's pleasure. In Newgate prison he managed to continue his pamphleteering on such questions as 'occasional conformity' and wrote a mock-pindaric *Hymn to the Pillory*. In 1704, after his release, he founded a newspaper, *The Review*, which is of importance in the history of journalism. Appearing thrice weekly up to 1713, it aimed

at being an organ of commercial interests, but also expressed opinions on political and domestic topics, thus initiating the modern lead article. The 'Scandal Club', one of its features, anticipates the *Tatler* and *Spectator*. As well as writing *The Review* single-handed, he wrote, among much pamphleteering, the astonishingly vivid ghost story *The Apparition of One Mrs Veal*, allegedly, like so many of his fictions, a true account of an actual happening. After 1704 his political conduct becomes highly equivocal. He undertook various secret commissions for the Tory minister Harley, including dubious dealings with the Scottish commissioners for Union in 1706–7. On Harley's fall in 1708 he supported Nottingham's ministry and he again changed his coat on the return of Harley in 1710. On the accession of the House of Hanover in 1714 he tried to justify his career as a double-agent in his *Appeal to Honour and Justice* (1715). He now turned to the writing of fiction which was all passed off as actual history. In 1719–20, at the age of nearly 60, he published his best-known work, *Robinson Crusoe*. Among the other six fictions—the *Journal of the Plague Year* (1722) seems to have had a source in an actual diary—the most vivid is *Moll Flanders* (1722), which is still one of the best tales of low life. He did not repeat this triumph in *Roxana* (1724). *Memoirs of a Cavalier* and the brilliant (but uneven) *Captain Singleton* (both in 1720), along with *Captain Jack* (1722), make up an extraordinary outpouring of creative writing in these few years. He continued to write with unabated vigour, including a three-volume travel book (*Tour through the Whole Island of Great Britain*, 1724–7), *The Great Law of Subordination Considered* (1724), *The Complete English Tradesman* (1726), *Plan of the English Commerce* (1728) and *Augusta Triumphans, or the Way to make London the Most Flourishing City in the Universe* (1728). A writer of astonishing versatility, and the founder of British journalism, he published more than 250 works. He was buried in Bunhill Fields, Islington.
▷ B Fitzgerald, *Defoe, a History of Conflict* (1954); P Rogers, *Defoe: the critical heritage* (1972)

DE FOREST, J(ohn) W(illiam)
(1826–1906)

American novelist and historian. He was born in Humphreysville (now Seymour), Connecticut, and after elementary education lived abroad, in Syria, Italy and France, returning to the USA in 1856 to make his way as a writer. Among his early books were travelogues of his European years, but his first significant work was the notably unromantic *History of the Indians of Connecticut from the Earliest Known Period to 1850* (1851), which debunked prevailing myths. His first published novel was *Seacliff* (1859), a mystery which may have had an impact on **Henry James**. Further literary effort was prevented by the outbreak of the Civil War, in which De Forest served as an officer. He sent battlefield sketches to *Harper's Monthly*, many of which were gathered in the posthumous *A Volunteer's Adventures* (1946). His main fictional achievement came with *Miss Ravenel's Conversion from Secession to Loyalty* (1867) which, despite its romantic trappings, is nonetheless notably clinical and clear-sighted. After the war, De Forest worked for a time in the Freedmen's Bureau in South Carolina. *Kate Beaumont* (1872) and *Honest John Vane* (1875) are the best of his remaining novels; others are melodramatic and formulaic.
▷ J F Light, *J W De Forest* (1965)

DE GROEN, Alma Margaret
(1941–)

New Zealand playwright, born in Foxton, Manawatu, but resident in Australia. Her first play, *The Sweatproof Boy*, was published in 1969, followed by *The Joss Adams Show* (1970) and *The After-Life of Arthur Cravan* (1972). Her best-known play was *Going Home* (1977), centred on a group of expatriate Australians coming to terms with an alien way of life. *Chidley* (1977) deals with the Victorian eccentric and would-be sex reformer William Chidley, and her later work includes *The Rivers of China* (1985).

DEHMEL, Richard
(1863–1920)

German poet, born in Wendisch-Hermsdorf, Brandenburg, a forester's son. He worked for an insurance company, then served on the front line in World War I, where he was awarded the Iron Cross. He wrote intellectual verse showing the influence of **Nietzsche**, and in which he practised rigorous self-discipline, although he does succumb to the temptation of an over-rhetorical didacticism. His best-known collection is *Weib und Welt* (1896, 'Woman and World').
▷ E Ludwig, *Richard Dehmel* (1913)

DEIGHTON, Len (Leonard Cyril)
(1929–)

English thriller writer, born in London. He became, variously, an art student, a railway plate-layer and a BOAC steward. His first novel, *The Ipcress File* (1962), was written when he was 33 and became a bestseller, as have almost all his books. Flip, entertaining and exciting, along with **John Le Carré**, **Graham Greene** and **Eric Ambler** he has been responsible for taking the spy novel out of the genre ghetto into mainstream literature. Notable titles are *Funeral in Berlin* (1965), *Only When I Larf* (1968) and the *Game, Set and Match* trilogy: *Berlin Game* (1984), *Mexico Set* (1985) and *London Match* (1986). It was followed by another trilogy, *Spy Hook* (1988), *Spy Line* (1989) and *Spy Sinker* (1990). He also writes cookery books.

DEKEN, Aagje ('Agatha')
(1741–1804)

Dutch novelist, born in the northern Netherlands, best known for her friendship with **Elisabeth Wolff-Bekker**. Deken grew up in an orphanage in Amsterdam and became a domestic servant. Her friendship with Wolff led to a literary collaboration which resulted most successfully in *Sara Burgerhart* (1782), an edifyingly didactic novel, written in the epistolary style of **Richardson**'s *Clarissa*. Deken and Wolff settled at Trevoux in France, returning to the Hague in 1798. Wolff's last poem, *To A Friend*, articulated the wish that she might die before Deken. She did; but only by a few weeks.

DEKKER, Eduard Douwes, pseud
Multatuli
(1820–87)

Dutch government official and writer, born in Amsterdam. He served for many years in the Dutch civil service in Java, and in his novel *Max Havelaar* (1860), and in many bitter satires, he protested against the abuses of the Dutch colonial system.
▷G Bron, *Multatuli* (1958)

DEKKER, Thomas
(c.1570–?1632)

English dramatist and pamphleteer, born in London. Around 1598 he was employed by Philip Henslowe to write plays, and in 1600 published two comedies, *The Shoemaker's Holiday, or the Gentle Craft*, and *The Pleasant Comedy of Old Fortunatus*. His next play (with **John Marston**) was *Satiromastix* (1602), which held up to ridicule **Ben Jonson**, who had castigated Dekker in *The Poetaster* (1601). In 1603 he published a pamphlet, *The Wonderful Year*, which gives a heartrending account of the plague. To the same date belongs the tract, *The Bachelor's Banquet*, in which he describes with gusto the ills of henpecked husbands. His most powerful writing is seen in *The Honest Whore* (Part I, written with **Thomas Middleton**, in 1604; Part II, which was his own work, was written in 1605, and appeared in 1630). In 1607 he published three plays written in conjunction with **John Webster**, the *Famous History of Sir Thomas Wyat*, *Westward Ho!* and *Northward Ho!*.

The pamphlet *Bellman of London* (1608) gives a lively account of London vagabonds; and he pursued the subject in *Lanthorn and Candlelight* (1608). In *The Gull's Hornbook* (1609) the life of a town gallant is racily depicted. He also published a devotional work, *Fowre Birds of Noahs Ark* (1609). The excellent comedy, *The Roaring Girl* (1611), was written partly in collaboration with Middleton. From 1613 to 1616 he was mostly in prison for debt. With **Philip Massinger** he composed the *Virgin Martyr* (1622). *The Sun's Darling*, licensed in 1624, but not printed until 1656, was written in conjunction with **John Ford**. A powerful tragedy, *The Witch of Edmonton* (1623), was written with Ford and **William Rowley**. In 1637, he republished his *Lanthorn and Candlelight* as *English Villainies*. He was also the author of masques and entertainments.
▷G R Price, *Thomas Dekker* (1969)

DELAFIELD, E M, pseud of **Edmée Elizabeth Monica Dashwood**, née **de la Pasture**
(1890–1943)

English novelist, born in Llandogo, Monmouth. She began work as a nurse during World War I, and then became a civil servant, and served as a magistrate. She married in 1921, and was the prolific author of novels which took a mildly but affectionately satirical look at the mores of genteel provincial life. Her best-known works are the series which began with *Diary of a Provincial Lady* (1930). It ran to several more 'Provincial Lady' volumes, and was successfully adapted as a film.
▷*A Note By the Way* (1933)

DE LA MARE, Walter
(1873–1956)

English poet and novelist, born in Charlton in Kent, of Huguenot descent. Educated at St Paul's Choir School, he went to work for the Standard Oil Company in 1890, and wrote in his spare time. He retired on a state pension in 1908 to take up full-time writing. The promise of his first book of verse, *Songs of Childhood* (1902, by 'Walter Ramal'), his prose romance *Henry Brocken* (1904), his children's story *The Three Mulla Mulgars* (1910) and his novel of the occult *The Return* (1910) was fulfilled in his volumes of poetry *The Listeners* (1912), *Peacock Pie* (1913) and *The Veil* (1921), in the fantastic novel *Memoirs of a Midget* (1921), and in books of short stories such as *On the Edge* (1930). Romanticist and musician in words, De la Mare has delighted children and grown-up readers alike by the delicate enchantments and humour of his *Märchen* world. In 1953, he published a new volume of lyrics, *O Lovely England*. He was buried in St Paul's

Cathedral. A *Complete Poems* was issued in 1969.

▷ L Clark, *Walter de la Mare* (1960)

DELANEY, Shelagh
(1939–)

English playwright and screenwriter, born in Salford, Lancashire. Having left school at 16, Delaney completed her first and still best-known play a year later. *A Taste of Honey*, produced in London in 1958, is the story of a young white girl's abrasive home life and her pregnancy following a casual affair with a black sailor. It was immediately seen as part of a young, 'angry' movement dealing realistically with working-class, provincial life, and which included the playwrights **John Osborne** and **Arnold Wesker**. None of Delaney's more recent writing has achieved equal critical acclaim or notoriety. Among her later work is the screenplay for *Dancing with a Stranger* (1985), a film depicting the fraught life of Ruth Ellis, who murdered her lover and became the last woman to be hanged in England.

DELANO, Alonzo
(c.1802–1874)

American humorist and historian, born in Aurora in New York State. His most valuable collection of sketches, about the California of the prospectors, is *Life on the Plains and Among the Diggings* (1954).

DELANY, Samuel Ray
(1942–)

American science-fiction writer and literary theorist, born in New York City. He has held a number of academic posts. He was married to the poet **Marilyn Hacker** (1961–80), and used her poems in some of his novels. He is the most boldly experimental of science-fiction writers, and his early books are imaginative twists on genre themes. They reflect his growing fascination with language and the nature of the fiction-making process itself, notably in *Babel-17* (1966), *The Einstein Intersection* (1967) and *Nova* (1968). The massive, self-referential *Dhalgren* (1975) divided his admirers. Other important works include *Triton* (1976), the short stories in *Driftglass* (1971), *Tales of Neveryon* (1979) and several critical works on the language of science fiction.

▷ *The Making of Light on Water* (1988)

DE LA ROCHE, Mazo
(1885–1961)

Canadian novelist, born in Newmarket, Ontario. She wrote *Jalna* (1927), the first of a series of novels about the Whiteoak family.

Whiteoaks (1929) was dramatized with considerable success. Her autobiography, *Ringing the Changes*, was published in 1957.

▷ G Hendrik, *Mazo de la Roche* (1970)

DELAVIGNE, Jean François Casimir
(1793–1843)

French dramatist, satirist and lyricist, born in Le Havre. He became popular through his *Messéniennes* (1818, 'Messenians'), satires upon the Restoration. *Les Vêpres siciliennes* (1819, 'Sicilian Vespers'), a tragic piece, was followed by *L'École des vieillards* (1820, 'The School of Old People') and *Les Comédiens* (1821, 'The Actors'), *Louis XI*, (partly based on *Quentin Durward*, 1833) and *La Fille du Cid* (1839, 'The Daughter of El Cid').

▷ F Vaucheux, *Casimir Delavigne* (1893)

DELDERFIELD, R(onald) F(rederick)
(1912–72)

English playwright, journalist and novelist, born in London. A hugely prolific and popular author, he wrote a variety of plays between 1944 and 1962, and several historical novels. He is best remembered, however, for his epic romantic novels set in England, such as *There Was A Fair Maid Dwelling* (1960, published in the USA as *Diana*), in which a Cockney falls in love with a wealthy beauty. *God Is An Englishman* (1970) and *To Serve Them All My Days* (1972) are similarly well-plotted, well-paced novels with a vivid sense of time and place.

▷ *For My Own Amusement* (1968); *Overture For Beginners* (1970)

DELEDDA, Grazia
(1875–1936)

Italian writer and winner of the Nobel Prize for literature. She moved to Rome after her marriage in 1900, but her work in the next 20 years focused on peasant stories of her native Sardinia. They won her a considerable reputation for the lyricism and intensity of novels like *Cenere* (1904, 'Ashes'), *L'edera* (1908, 'Ivy'), *Marianna Sirca* (1915) and *La madre* (1920, 'The Mother'). Her later books left the Sardinian setting, but were similar in style. The posthumous *Cosima* (1937) is autobiographical. She won the 1926 Nobel Prize for literature.

▷ N Zoja, *Grazia Deledda, saggio critica* (1939)

DELIBES, Miguel
(1920–)

Spanish novelist, journalist, critic and hunter of small animals. He was born in Valladolid, where he was intimately involved with the newspaper *El Norte de castilla*. He found much favour with the public with such humorous books as *Diario de un cazador* (1955, 'Diary of a Hunter'); but his finest novel is often considered to be his third: *El camino* (1950, Eng trans *The Path*, 1961), narrated by a boy who does not want to go to school in the city. There are two views of the immensely prolific Delibes: that he has wasted his gifts by superficial experimentation and that he is a major writer awaiting recognition by critics. What is not in doubt is his skill.

▷ J Daiz, *Miguel Delibes* (1971)

DELILLE, Jacques
(1738–1813)

French poet, born near Aigues-Perse in Auvergne. His verse translation of **Virgil**'s *Georgics* (1769) was very popular, and was praised by **Voltaire**. After holding a canonry at Moissac, he was presented by the Comte d'Artois with the abbacy of Saint-Severin. *Les Jardins* (1782, 'The Gardens'), a didactic poem, was generally accepted as his masterpiece. The Revolution compelled Delille to leave France. He travelled in Switzerland and Germany, then in London spent 18 months translating *Paradise Lost*. After his return to France in 1802 he produced a translation of Virgil's *Aeneid* (1804), and volumes of verse in *L'Imagination* (1806), *Les Trois Règnes de la nature* (1809, 'The Three Reigns of Nature') and *La Conversation* (1812). During his life he was regarded by his countrymen as the greatest French poet of the day, and was even declared the equal of Virgil and **Homer**; but his fame was short-lived.

▷ E Guitton, *Jacques Delille, 1738–1813* (1974)

DeLILLO, Don
(1936–)

American novelist, born in New York City and educated at Fordham University in the Bronx. His characteristic concerns are the paranoia and obsessive sub-cultural codes entailed by existence within very large, suprahuman systems. DeLillo's first book, *Americana* (1971), is a road narrative of the sort associated with early **Thomas Pynchon** and the Beats. *End Zone* (1972) is an American football novel with an allegoric–linguistic undercurrent contrasting verbal and actual performance. *Great Jones Street* (1973) concerns a self-probing drop-out rock-star, Bucky Wunderlick. In the ambitious *Ratner's Star* (1976), a novel about the creation of fictions, DeLillo attempts a synthesis of **Lewis Carroll**, **Laurence Sterne** and science fiction. Subsequent works, *Players* (1977), *Running Dog* (1978) and *The Names* (1982), were less ambitious, but *White Noise* (1985) was a comic masterpiece centred on a mid-west professor of Hitler Studies whose family is affected by an environmental catastrophe that mirrors the toxic effects of fear and angst. Two later novels have explored aspects of fame and infamy. In *Libra* (1988) he probed the psyches of Lee Harvey Oswald and Jack Ruby. In *Mao II* (1991) the syntax is uninflected, Warholian, devoid of conventional 'meaning', and captures the narrow self-definitions of a media-haunted society.

DeLISSER, H(erbert) G(eorge)
(1878–1944)

Jamaican novelist, born in Falmouth, Jamaica. From 1904 to 1942 he was editor of the *Daily Gleaner* newspaper. His political conservatism is reflected in his novels, which are very much escapist entertainment, though accurate about racial tensions in Jamaica. His best-known, and most lasting, novel is *Jane's Career* (1914), originally published as *Jane: A Story of Jamaica* (1913). A pioneering work in Caribbean fiction, it chronicles the adventures of a young countrywoman who persistently manoeuvres her way up the social scale. Often reprinted also is *The White Witch of Rosehall* (1929), a historical pot-boiler.

▷ F Birbalsingh, 'The Novels of H. G. DeLisser', in *Passion & Exile: Essays in Caribbean Literature* (1988)

DELIUS, Anthony
(1916–)

South African poet, novelist and dramatist. He co-founded and became editor of the newspaper the *Saturday Post* (later the *Evening Post*); he was also parliamentary correspondent of the *Cape Times*. He has carried on the tradition early established in South Africa, before they all left for Europe, by **William Plomer**, **Roy Campbell** and **Laurens van der Post** (the latter two became members of the right only long afterwards). Delius's satire of accepted attitudes, a critic has said, 'acts like a paint-stripper'. *Black South-Easter* (1966), on the other hand, a symbolic voyage around the Cape on a windy night, could be considered to be the most sonorous long poem produced in its country since World War II. *Border* (1976) is a novel.

DELL, Ethel Mary
(1881–1939)

English novelist, born in Streatham. As a writer of light romantic novels she enjoyed a tremendous vogue in the years between the wars. Her books include her enormously successful first novel, *The Way of an Eagle* (1912), *The Lamp in the Desert* (1919), *The Black Knight* (1926) and *Sown Among Thorns* (1939).

DELL, Floyd
(1887–1969)

American novelist, playwright and social critic. He was born in Barry, Illinois, and educated there and in Davenport, Iowa, where he worked in journalism. After four years at the Chicago *Evening Post*, latterly (1911–13) as editor, he moved to New York. Increasingly interested in liberal and left-wing ideas, he became managing editor of *The Masses* (1914–17) but was arraigned under sedition laws for pacifist articles; the journal was relaunched as *The Liberator* (1918–20) with Dell as associate editor. His most important novel was his first, *The Moon-Calf* (1920). The young writer-hero Felix Fay, a version of Dell himself, also appears in a sequel, *The Briary-Bush* (1921). However, Dell's best and most revealing books are *Intellectual Vagabondage* (1926), billed as an 'apology' for the intelligentsia, and his autobiography *Homecoming* (1933). He published no more books after the mid-30s, but continued to work as an editor for the New Deal's Works Progress Administration in Washington, DC.

▷*Homecoming* (1933); J E Hart, *Floyd Dell* (1971)

DELLA CASA, Giovanni
(1503–56)

Florentine poet, diplomat, moralist and divine, born (probably) in Mugello. He ended his ecclesiastical career as Secretary of State to the Vatican. His troubled, sexually anxious lyrics, distinguished by daring technical innovations, were praised by **Tasso**, and were amongst the finest of his century. His *Galateo ovvero de' costumi* (1558, Eng trans *Galateo, of Good Manners and Behaviour*, 1576, modern edn 1914) is a remarkable and subtle exercise in human pragmatics.

▷*Publications of the Modern Language Association*, 41 (1926)

DELLA VALLE, Federico
(c.1560–c.1628)

Italian dramatist and poet, born near Asti in Piedmont. He was an embittered court laureate who worked for Spaniards, and who came to an almost gnostic view of existence. He wrote his four tragedies while at the court in Turin. They were rediscovered by **Croce**, who saw in them the spirit of the Baroque entering into Rennaissance humanism. Two, *Judit* and *Ester*, are from biblical subjects; *La reina di Scozia* is about Mary, Queen of Scots. They abound in pathos and psychological subtleties, and glow with their author's love of God, despite his view of existence as a living hell.

▷B Croce, *Nuovo saggi sulla letteratura italiana del Seicento* (1931)

DELONEY, Thomas
(c.1550–1600)

English balladist and writer of fiction. Nothing is known of his birthplace or education, although his works suggest familiarity with Latin and French. A London silk-weaver, he wrote a number of ballads, but is best known for his stories in pamphlet form, such as *Jack of Newbury*, *Thomas of Reading* and *Gentle Craft* which, with their lively dialogue and characterization, are seen as a forerunner of the novel proper.

▷R Howarth, *Two Elizabethan Writers of Fiction: Thomas Nashe and Thomas Deloney* (1956)

DELORIA, Ella
(1889–1971)

American linguist, ethnologist and novelist. Born at White Swan on the Standing Rock Sioux reservation in South Dakota, Deloria grew up in a family where traditional Dakota (Sioux) culture merged with Episcopal Protestantism. A graduate of Columbia University, she worked for several years in collaboration with the anthropologist, Franz Boas, gathering material on the Dakota language and culture she was passionate to preserve. These researches led to the publication of *Dakota Texts* (1932), a bilingual collection of traditional stories, *Dakota Grammar* (1941) and *Speaking of Indians* (1944), a description of Dakota culture written for the popular market. Her novel, *Waterlily*, written in the 1940s but unpublished until 1988, is set in the 19th century before White impingement on Dakota culture; more than simply an ethnographic record, it vividly dramatizes the everyday life of the Dakotas from the often-overlooked perspective of the women of the tribe. Deloria also compiled a Dakota–English dictionary and translated several oral narratives and autobiographies.

DEL RAY, Lester, pseud of **Filipe San Juan Mario Silvio Enrico Alvarez-del Ray**
(1915–93)

American science-fiction writer and editor, born in Clydesdale, Minnesota. He spent two years in college, then was a sheet metal worker before becoming a literary agent. He published his first science-fiction story in 1938 and went on to become a major figure in the mainstream of the genre. His writing is notable for its craftsmanship in plotting and thematic ingenuity. His most important science-fiction novels are *Police Your Planet* (1956, as 'Erik Van Rhin') and *The Eleventh Commandment* (1962). Almost half of his novels were written for children. He used several pseudonymns, including 'Philip St John' and 'Kenneth Wright'. He was science-fiction editor at Ballantine Books (1977–91) and encouraged many new writers.

DELVIG, Anton Antonovitch, Baron von
(1798–1831)

Russian poet, born in Moscow. He studied with **Alexander Pushkin** at the Tsarskoé Sélo school and became Keeper of the public library at St Petersburg. From 1825 to 1831 he published the miscellany *Severnye tsvety* ('Flowers from the North').
▷L Koehler, *Anton Antonovitch Delvig: a Classicist in the time of Romanticism* (1970)

DE MARCHI, Emilio
(1851–1901)

Italian novelist, born in Milan. Before he began to write, De Marchi was a teacher who read and imbibed **Manzoni**, as well as **Scott** and **Gogol**. Short stories were followed by the novels *Il capello del prete* (1888, 'The Priest's Hat') and *Dimitrio Pianelli* (1890, Eng trans 1905, 1977), the latter containing a memorable description of the boredom and horror of office work for a sensitive individual. Stylistically he is exemplarily plain. His later work is not quite as good.
▷S Pacifici, *The Modern Italian Novel from Manzoni to Svevo* (1967)

DE MENA, Juan
(1411–56)

Spanish poet and prose writer. Born in Cordoba, he was orphaned very young, educated in Salamanca and Florence, and came to be considered one of the most highly cultured men of his epoch. He was married, possibly twice, but had no children, and held a series of royal appointments under Juan II with the protection of Alvaro de Luna. Along with his close friend the **Marques de Santillana**, he developed the verse form called *arte mayor*, the first polished vernacular poetic form in Spanish. His most renowned work is the *Laberinto de la fortuna* (1444), also known as *Las trescientas*, but he is also remembered for *La coronación* (1438, published 1499), a laud to his friend the Marques; the *Iliada romanzada* (1442), a translation of the famous epic; and his lyric and cancioneril poetry.
▷M R Lida de Malkiel, *Juan de Mena, poeta del prerenacimiento español* (1950)

DE MORGAN, William Frend
(1839–1917)

English Pre-Raphaelite ceramic artist and novelist, son of the mathematician and logician Augustus De Morgan, born in London. He studied art at the Academy Schools, and started as a designer of tiles and stained glass, but became interested in pottery, and in 1871 established a kiln in Chelsea, where he turned out glazed ware in beautiful blues and greens. These won much praise in artistic circles but made little money. In 1905 he abandoned pottery and, at the age of 65, he began writing novels in a whimsical **Dickens**ian manner, like *Joseph Vance* (1906), *Alice-for-Short* (1907) and *Somehow Good* (1908). His wife, Evelyn Pickering (1855–1919), whom he married in 1887, was a Pre-Raphaelite painter, and completed his last two unfinished novels after his death, *The Old Madhouse* (1919) and *The Old Man's Youth* (1921).
▷F Seymour, *A Post Victorian Realist* (1920)

DENEVI, Marco
(1922–)

Argentinian novelist and playwright, reclusive but prize-winning and prolific. He was born in Sáenz Peña, the son of an Italian immigrant. Until 1954 Denevi worked in a bank. An avid reader of **Wilkie Collins**, he wrote the novel *Rosaura a las diez* (1954, 'Rosaura at Ten O'Clock'), which deals with the mysterious murder, apparently by a timid picture-restorer, of his young girl bride. This was filmed, televised, dramatized, and became a bestseller (but was not translated into English). *Ceremonia secreta* (1960, Eng trans *Secret Ceremony*, 1961), also won prestigious prizes, as have successive novels and plays. It remains surprising that this very able writer, not unlike his compatriot **Cortázar**, is not better known in English-speaking countries.
▷D A Yates, 'Prologue' to *Secret Ceremony* (1961)

DENHAM, Sir John
(1615–69)

Irish poet, born in Dublin, the only son of an Irish judge of English birth. He was educated in London and at Trinity College, Oxford. He studied law at Lincoln's Inn, and was called to the Bar in 1639. At the outbreak of the Civil War he was high-sheriff of Surrey, and immediately joined the king. He fell into Sir William Waller's hands on the capture of Farnham Castle, and was sent as a prisoner to London, but he was soon freed and went to Oxford. In 1641 he produced *The Sophy*, a historical tragedy of the Turkish court which was performed to great applause at Blackfriars; and in 1642 he published a long poem, *Cooper's Hill*, a topographical description of the scenery around Egham, which **Pope** imitated in his *Windsor Forest*. In 1648, being discovered in the performance of secret services for Charles I, he fled to Holland and France. In 1650 he collected money for the young king Charles II from the Scots resident

in Poland, and several times visited England on secret service. At the Restoration he was appointed surveyor-general of works, and in 1661 created a Knight of the Bath. He was a better poet than architect, but he had Christopher Wren as his deputy. He was buried in Poet's Corner in Westminster Abbey.
▷ B O'Hehir, *Harmony from discords: a life of Sir John Denham* (1968)

DENNERY, Adolphe Philippe
(1811–99)
French playwright, born in Paris. He was clerk to a notary, but from 1831 produced 133 dramas, vaudevilles and plays, the most successful being *Marie Jeanne* (1845). He also wrote the libretti for Gounod's *Le Tribut de Zamora* (1881) and Massenet's *Le Cid* (1885). He was the creator of the Norman watering-place, Cabourg.

DENNIS, C(larence Michael) J(ames)
(1876–1938)
Australian poet and journalist, born in Auburn, South Australia. After some experience of journalism in Adelaide he moved to Melbourne and lived by contributing light verse to many periodicals, including the Sydney *Bulletin*. His poems were collected as *Backblock Ballads and Other Verses* (1915); some featured the larrikin Bill and reappeared as *The Songs of a Sentimental Bloke* in 1915. They were immediately popular and were repeated in *The Moods of Ginger Mick* (1916). The two books were reprinted many times and the 'Trench' pocket editions were the favoured reading of Australian troops during World War I. Within the next five years Dennis published as many books, each of them in his individual style of prose-poetry which captured the vernacular working-class speech of the cities. The fashion passed; in 1922 Dennis returned to journalism and was for some time 'Staff Poet' on the Melbourne *Age*, contributing a daily column over the next 16 years.

DENNIS, John
(1657–1734)
English critic and playwright, born in London. He was educated at Harrow and Caius College, Cambridge. After a tour through France and Italy, he took his place among the wits and men of fashion, and produced biting criticism to support the Whigs. He wrote nine plays, but had little success with them, including a satire, *A Plot and No Plot* (1697), and *Rinaldo and Armida* (1699). **Pope**'s *Essay on Criticism* (1711) contained a contemptuous allusion to another play,

Appius and Virginia (1709), answered by Dennis the next month in *Reflections Critical and Satirical*, which triggered a long feud. Among his critical works are *The Grounds of Criticism in Poetry* (1704) and *An Essay on the Genius and Writings of Shakespeare* (1712).
▷ H G Paul, *John Dennis, his life and criticism* (1911)

DENNIS, Nigel Forbes
(1912–89)
English novelist and playwright, best known for his second book, *Cards of Identity* (1955), in which he comically satirizes the infringements of modern society upon the individual by means of a relatively conventional country-house plot. Born in Bletchingley, Surrey, Dennis was educated in Rhodesia and Germany. In 1935 and 1936 he was Secretary of the National Board of Review of Motion Pictures in the USA, later working as Assistant Editor on *New Republic* (1937–8), and as book reviewer on *Time* (1940–59), before returning to Britain as joint Editor of *Encounter* (1967–70) and book reviewer on the *Sunday Telegraph* (1961–82). His first novel was *Boys and Girls Come Out to Play* (1949), his third and last, was *A House in Order* (1966), which again concerns the preservation of identity under constraint. Dennis also wrote several plays, including an adaptation (1956) of *Cards of Identity* and *August for the People* (1961).

DE PISAN, Christine
(1361–c.1430)
French lyrical and didactic poet, critic, military theorist, biographer and feminist, born in Venice, daughter of the physician to Charles V of France. Beautiful, gifted and learned, she was at 15 happily married to Étienne de Castel, a royal secretary; but he died when she was 25, and, with two or three children to support, she became the first woman of substance to earn a living by writing. In a pedantic age, she had, alone, to defend her sex from the dominating, and misogynistic, Aristotelian ethos which was expressed in many major works, but not least in the *Roman de la Rose* of **Jean de Meung**, which she savagely attacked, thus initiating the first *Querelle* in French literature: the *Querelle des femmes* ('Women's Quarterly'). She wrote some of the most breathtaking love poetry in any language, including the *ballade* whose refrain is 'Vostre douceur me meine dure guerre' ('Thought of your sweetness wreaks havoc in me')—'a personal note is occasionally sounded', commented a professor, but there are hundreds of such lines in her poetry.

The most profound of her many long works is the 23 000-line octosyllabic *Livre la mutation de fortune* ('Book of the Mutations of Fortune'), an ironic allegory which employs erudite patriarchal techniques to undermine patriarchy. Some of her works were translated by **Caxton** (eg *The Book of Faytes of Arms and of Chivalrye*, modern edn, 1932). The revival of interest in her from a feminist viewpoint is now well under way. In the last years of her life she retired, with her daughter, to a convent.

▷A Kemp-Welch, *Of Six Medieval Women* (1903)

DE QUINCEY, Thomas
(1785–1859)

English critic and essayist, born in Manchester, the son of a merchant. He was educated at Manchester Grammar School, where he proved an apt pupil. In 1802 he ran away from school and wandered in Wales, and then to London, where he lived with a young prostitute called Ann. (He described this episode in his *Confessions of an English Opium-eater*, 1822.) Reclaimed from this wandering he spent a short time at Worcester College, Oxford. It was here that he became addicted to opium. A visit to his mother in Bath brought him into contact with **Coleridge**, then resident in Bristol, and through him with **Robert Southey** and **Wordsworth**. When these poets settled at the Lakes, De Quincey visited them there and, after a brief sojourn in London (which enabled him to make the acquaintance of **Charles Lamb**, **William Hazlitt** and others of the 'Cockney' school), he went to stay in Grasmere in 1809. In 1816 he married Margaret Simpson, by whom he had three daughters and five sons, two of the latter distinguishing themselves as soldiers. De Quincey now set up as an author. Except for *The Logic of Political Economy* (1841) and an unsuccessful novel, his whole literary output, including the *Confessions*, consisted of magazine articles. The *Confessions* appeared as a serial in *The London Magazine*, 1821, and at once made him famous. Visits to London varied his existence at the Lakes, but in 1828 the lure of the Edinburgh literary scene drew him to the northern capital, where he lived and worked till his death in 1859. For 20 years he lent distinction to *Blackwood's Magazine*, *Tait's Magazine* and, occasionally, *The Quarterly*, with articles like *Murder Considered as one of the Fine Arts* (1827), *Lake Reminiscences* (1834–40), the fantasies *Suspiria De Profundis* (1845) and *Levana and Our Ladies of Sorrows* (1845), and the 'Dream Fugue' at the end of *The English Mail-Coach*, and *Vision of Sudden Death* (1849).

▷H S David, *Thomas De Quincey* (1964); J S Lyon, *Thomas De Quincey* (1969)

DERÈME, Tristan, pseud of Phillippe Huc
(1889–1941)

French poet of the *fantaisiste* school. His works include *La Verdure dorée* (1922, incorporating eight previous collections of poems, 'The Gilded Foliage'), and *L'Enlèvement sans clair de lune* (1924, 'Kidnapping without Moonlight').

▷H Martineau, *Tristan Derème* (1927)

DERLETH, August
(1909–71)

Prolific ('a dazzling fount of energy') American novelist, biographer and poet, born in Sauk City (the Sac Prairie of his fiction), Wisconsin. In some years he produced over 20 titles, some of them near to pulp: 'I enjoy myself and thank God nobody takes me seriously,' he once exclaimed. Modelling himself on **Balzac**, he set out to write, more soberly, the history of his native city in his Sac Prairie saga, of which he published many volumes. *In Re: Sherlock Holmes: Adventures of Solar Pons* (1944), and its successors, introduce an enjoyable reincarnation of the famous detective.

DE ROBERTO, Federico
(1861–1927)

Italian novelist, journalist and critic, born in Naples. A friend to **Boito** and **Giacosa**, he began as a member of the Scapigliatura movement ('the shirtless ones', rooted in Milan and Turin, who advocated a vague bohemianism but also challenged the too-soft romantic assumptions of their time), but then turned for inspiration to **Verga**, whom he took as the model for his stories. His greatest work is the long novel *I Vicerè* (1894, Eng trans *The Viceroys*, 1962), which traces the history of a family, the Uzedas (descendants of Spanish viceroys), against the background of the Risorgimento. For many years this novel lay in the shadow of the then great Verga, but modern criticism rightly sees it as a masterpiece, and one of the paramount novels of its century. It lies firmly behind the achievement of **Lampedusa**.

▷S Pacifici, *The Modern Italian Novel from Manzoni to Svevo* (1967)

DE ROO, Anne
(1931–)

New Zealand writer for children. Her diverse output includes historical novels such as *Traveller* (1979) and *Because of Rosie* (1980) and tales of adventure, as in her first book *The Gold Dog* (1969), *Moa Valley* (1969) and *Scrub Fire* (1977). Other titles are *Boy and the Sea Beast* (1971), *Cinnamon and Nutmeg* (1972), *Mick's Country Cousins* (1974), and two related books, *Jackie Nobody* (1983) and *The Bat's Nest* (1986).

DÉROULÈDE, Paul
(1846–1914)

French politician and poet, born in Paris. A fervid nationalist, and the author of patriotic verses, his writings called for revenge on Germany, and he was active in the campaign against Dreyfus. In 1900 he was exiled for 10 years for sedition, but returned in 1905.

▷ 'H Galli' (ed), *Paul Déroulède raconté par lui-même* (1900)

DEROZIO, Henry Louis Vivian
(1809–31)

Eurasian poet and patriot, born in Calcutta. At 19 he had published two books of poems and was lecturing on English history and literature at the Hindu College, Calcutta. In the next four years he had translated de Maupertuis, lectured on philosophy, written a critique on Kant and edited four journals. He became involved in local politics, and instigated so much freethinking and social rebelliousness that he was dismissed from the College a few months before he died. Much of his verse is imitatively ornamental, but some of his sonnets put him among the lesser Romantics.

▷ E W Madge, *Henry Derozio, the Eurasian poet and reformer* (1965)

D'ERRICO, Ezio
(1892–1973)

Italian novelist, painter, thriller-writer and dramatist, born in Agrigento. He is now somewhat neglected. His avant-garde play *La foresta* (1959, 'The Forest') is a memorable contribution to the literature of terror, in this case that of the technological nightmare created by people who try to compensate for their lack of wisdom by creating over-sophisticated pseudo-scientific schemes.

DERY, Tibor
(1894–1977)

Hungarian novelist, playwright and short-story writer, born in Budapest. A Communist between the wars, he became disillusioned after Hungary was reduced to being a satellite state of the USSR. His best work, *Niki: The Story of a Dog* (1956), is set in and around Budapest just before the 1956 uprising; a sentimental but effective novel, it brought international acclaim for its author. Sentenced to nine years' imprisonment after the crushing of the 1956 revolt, he was eventually 'rehabilitated'. Notable among his later works are *The Portuguese Princess* (1967), a short-story collection, and *The Man With One Ear*

(1975), a cheerfully defiant novel about a libidinous old lecher.

DERZHAVIN, Gavril Romanovich
(1743–1816)

Russian poet, born in Kazan. In 1762 he entered the army as a private, but rose to officer rank, was transferred to the civil service, and later to governorships. In 1791 he became Secretary of State, in 1800 Imperial Treasurer, and in 1802 Minister of Justice. He published a wide-ranging variety of original and imaginative lyric poetry on many subjects, both personal and public, and is considered one of Russia's greatest poets.

▷ A V Zapadov, *Gavril Romanovich Derzhavin* (1958)

DESAI, Anita, née Mazumdar
(1937–)

Indian novelist, born in Mussoorie, Uttar Pradesh, the daughter of a Bengali father and a German mother. She was educated at Delhi University, and her works include novels for adults and children and short stories. *Clear Light of Day* (1980) and *In Custody* (1980) were both shortlisted for the Booker Prize and *The Village by the Sea* won the *Guardian* Award for children's fiction in 1982. In 1988 she published *Baumgartner's Bombay*, the grim story of a German expatriate adrift in India.

DESANI, Govindas Vishnoodas
(1909–)

African-born American novelist, born in Nairobi, Kenya. He went to Britain in 1926 and from 1928 was a correspondent for the *Times of India*, Reuters, and Associated Press. In the late 1930s he was a lecturer on antiquities for Bombay Baroda and Central India Railway and later lectured in England before becoming a broadcaster during World War II. From 1952 to 1966, pursuing a dual interest in yoga and meditation, he visited Buddhist and Hindu monasteries. Throughout the 1960s he filed a provocative column with the *Illustrated Weekly for India*. He has been an American citizen since 1979. His prose-poem *Hali* (1950) and some uncollected stories notwithstanding, his claim to posterity is dependent on *All About H. Hatterr* (1948). It reprinted the week after publication, then was neglected for several decades before being resurrected as a modern classic and placed on a pedestal alongside **James Joyce** and **Flann O'Brien**.

DE SAN PEDRO, Diego
(?1437–?1498)

Spanish prose writer. The *alcaide* of the castle of Peñafiel in Castilla in the middle of the

15th century, he is the most important of the writers of the courtly-love narrative genre known as the *novela sentimental*. He wrote *Tratado de amores de Arnalte e Lucenda*, an early courtly love narrative; poems for the *cancioneros*, *Las siete angustias de Nuestra Señora* (?1534); and *La pasión trovada* (1496, 'The Poetic Passion'). His most important work, and the best example of *novela sentimental* in Spanish, is *Cárcel de amor* ('Prison of Love'), published in 1499. This complex work begins as an allegorical novel, becomes an epistolary love story, and ends as a treatise on the goodness of women; it is one of the crowning achievements of 15th-century Spanish prose.

▷ K Whinnom, *Diego de San Pedro* (1974)

DESBORDES-VALMORE, Marceline
(1786–1859)

French poet, born in Douai. She was admired by **Paul Verlaine**, who identified a musicality in her verse akin to his own, and is considered a significant early exponent of *vers libre*. From childhood she pursued a theatrical career, appearing in her hometown and in Brussels, and eventually at the Opéra-Comique in Paris. She gave up singing around 1803, and began to devote herself seriously to poetry. Her main themes are domestic, as the titles of her collections show—*Contes et scenes de la vie de famille* ('Tales and Scenes of Family Life') and *Petits Flamands* ('Flemish Children'), for example—with much reference to romantic love and children. She also wrote one short novel, *Domenica*, published in 1885 within a collection of verse entitled *Scènes Intimes* ('Private Scenes'), and based on her experiences of life and art in bohemian circles.

DESCHAMPS, Eustache, called Morel
(c.1345–c.1406)

French poet, born in Vertus in Champagne. He was brought up by Machaut, who may have been his uncle and who probably taught him his craft. A soldier, a magistrate, a court favourite and a traveller in Italy and Hungary, he held important posts in Champagne, but after his patron, Charles V, died, his possessions were ravaged by the English. He composed 1175 lyrics, besides *Le Miroir de mariage* ('The Mirror of Marriage'), a long poem satirizing women, two dramatic works, and several poems in the then current fashion, deploring the miseries of the Hundred Years War.

▷ A Sarradin, *Eustache Des Champs. Sa vie et ses oeuvres* (1879)

DESMARETS, Jean, Sieur de Saint-Sorlen
(1596–1676)

French writer. A protégé of Richelieu, he was the author of many volumes of poetry and critical works, notably *Comparaison de la langue et la poésie française avec la grecque et la latine* (1670, 'Comparison of French Language and Poetry with Greek and Latin'). His play *Les Visionnaires* (1637) was a great success, and he also wrote two verse epics and a novel on biblical and classical themes. He was the first Chancellor and co-founder of the Académie française, and a protagonist in the ancients versus moderns controversy.

DESMASURES, Louis
(1515–74)

French dramatist and translator, born in Tournai. He became converted to protestantism in 1550, and finally had to leave France in 1562. He translated **Virgil**'s *Aenead*, but is most famous for his trilogy of plays on David (1563), which are important as very early examples of French proto-tragedy, and as propaganda for Desmasures's cause.

DESNICA, Vladen
(1905–67)

Dalmatian novelist, story writer, dramatist, essayist and translator (writing in Croatian), born in Zadar. Desnica, a lawyer until he became a full-time writer, wrote essays and did translations before World War I; only in the last 15 years of his life did he become prominent. His reputation rests on two novels and a handful of stories, of which the novel *Proljéca Ivana Galeba* (1957, rev edn 1960, 'The Springs of Ivan Galeb') is paramount. This story of a man confined to a hospital bed, piecing his past life together as he hovers between life and death—but denied emotion in the process—is one of the outstanding psychological studies in Croatian literature. Its failure to find a translator has puzzled many critics. It is a static, yet extreme book: the over-cerebral nature of Galeb's ponderings points desperately to a need for emotion and goodwill in a world into whose nature Desnica saw only too clearly, and which, only about a quarter of a century after his death, collapsed into violent and malign chaos.

▷ M Vaupotić, *Contemporary Croatian Literature* (1966)

DESNOS, Robert
(1900–45)

French poet, novelist and cinema critic, born in Paris, and deported by the Nazis to con-

DES PÉRIERS, Bonaventure

centration camps for the part he had played in the resistance to them: he died, weakened by starvation, of typhus at the notorious Terezin camp in Czechoslovakia. He was one of the most formidable and substantial of all the Surrealist poets, although much of his work has a deceptively playful surface. He is particularly famous for his poems for children, and for his writings on the cinema, which were collected in *Cinéma* (1966). The claim that he was a major poet of the 20th century is not a light one, but requires better investigation than it has so far had outside France. He has been attacked for abandoning Surrealism in favour of 'moralization' in his later work; but that attack has been challenged on the grounds that it misunderstands the profundity of his irony (which is, however, fully acknowledged in the earlier, more oneiric work). **André Breton** himself said of him that he had 'gone further than any of us into the unknown'. His works in translation include *22 Poems* (1971) and *The Voice* (1972).
▷M A Caws, *The Poetry of Dada and Surrealism* (1970)

DES PÉRIERS, Bonaventure
(c.1500–1544)
French writer, born in Autun. He was a member of the court of men of letters assembled by **Margaret of Angoulême**. In a dialogue, *Cymbalum mundi* (1537), under the pretence of attacking the superstitions of the ancients, he satirized the religious beliefs of his own day. The book raised a storm of indignation, against which Margaret was powerless to shield him; and rather than fall into the hands of his persecutors he is said to have killed himself. His *Nouvelles Récréations et joyeux devis* (1558, 'Novel Recreations and Delightful Talks') consists of 129 short stories, both comic and romantic. Des Périers has often been attributed with the chief authorship of Margaret's *Heptameron*.
▷J Nodier, *Bonaventures Des Périers* (1867)

DESPORTES, Philippe
(1546–1606)
French poet, born in Chartres, who was Henri III's court poet before succeeding **Ronsard**, with whom he had been associated, as 'prince of poets'. Opinions about him are divided: on the one hand he is said to have debased and enfeebled the style established by the Pléiade (Ronsard and six others) by 'prettifying' imitations from the Italians; on the other he is praised for his fluency and mastery of versification. The consensus is that he pleased a superficial public, but lacked learning or substance. His great enemy was the infinitely more gifted **François de Malherbe**.
▷G Brereton, *An Introduction to the French Poets* (1956)

DESSÌ, Guiseppe
(1909–77)
Italian novelist, born near Cagliare, in Sardinia. His first novel, *San Silvano* (1939), was influenced by **Joyce** and **Proust**. His best-known work, *Paese d'ombre* (1972, Eng trans *The Forests of Norbio*, 1975), is historical, and traces the life story of a man who lived from the time of the Risorgimento until the first part of the 20th century. Dessì was trying to do for Sardinia what **De Roberto** and **Lampedusa** had done for Sicily, and in large part he succeeded, although his book has not been regarded as of that quality. *Il disertore* (1961, Eng trans *The Deserter*, 1962), is an ironic novel about a coward and deserter who is accidentally decorated for bravery. Despite the translations of his work, Dessi has not yet received due credit, outside Italy, for his achievement.

DESTOUCHES, Philippe, originally Néricault
(1680–1754)
French playwright, born in Tours. He wrote 17 comedies, initially in the manner, but without the talent, of **Molière**. They include *Le Philosophe marié* (1727, 'The Married Philosopher') and *Le Glorieux* (1732, 'The Boaster'), his masterpiece. He spent six years in England as a diplomat from 1717 to 1723, and adapted **Addison**'s play *The Drummer* as *Le Tambour nocturne* (1733).
▷J Hankiss, *Destouches, l'homme et l'oeuvre* (1918)

DE TABLEY, Lord (John Byrne Leicester Warren)
(1835–95)
English poet and dramatist, born in Cheshire. He never achieved popularity, but became briefly well-known at his death. His verse, interesting for its anticipation of the decadent, fin de siècle style, was uninspired ('Time goes, old girl, time goes') and mostly imitative of **Tennyson**; but there are a few melancholy lyrics containing precise natural descriptions.
▷*Collected Poems* (1903); G B Taplin, *The Life, Works and Literary Reputation of Lord de Tabley* (1946)

DEUTSCH, Babette
(1895–1982)
American poet, novelist and critic, born in New York City. She published *Banners*, her first collection of poems, in 1919, the title

piece celebrating the initial achievements of the Russian Revolution. Russia became a special interest for her. She translated **Alexander Blok**'s *The Twelve* with a Russian scholar she later married, and continued to translate from both Russian and German. Her *Epistle to Prometheus* (1931) is an ambitious, book-length poetic interpretation of human history. Her collected poems appeared in 1969. Her work is noted for its perceptive preoccupation with love, war and desolation, and the historical place and fate of women. Among Deutsch's novels is *A Brittle Heaven* (1926), an autobiographical tale of a writing mother, while her criticism includes the highly regarded *Poetry in Our Time* (1952).

▷J Gould, *American Women Poets* (1980)

DEVAL, Jacques, pseud of Jacques Boularan
(1894–1972)

French boulevard playwright and novelist, best known for *Tovarich* (1933, 'Comrade'). A clever and witty comedy based on the theme of aristocrats forced into service—in this case White Russians in Paris—it ran, in the adaptation by **Robert Emmet Sherwood** (1936), for more than a year on Broadway and in London, and in more than 200 other cities. Deval, who served in the US army during World War II, wrote many other successful, superficial plays. One of his novels, the spy romance *Marie Galante* (1931), was presented on the stage in 1934 with music by Kurt Weill; it appeared as an American movie, featuring Spencer Tracy, in the same year.

DEVANEY, James Martin, journalistic pseud Fabian
(1890–1976)

Australian poet, short-story writer and journalist, born in Sandhurst (later Bendigo), Victoria, who spent much of his early life travelling the country, writing and teaching on outback stations. His love of the 'bush' and an observant eye enabled him to contribute nature notes for over 20 years to a Brisbane newspaper. His lyric poetry was first collected in *Fabian* (1923). Five collections followed, from which he selected *Poems*, published in 1950. He wrote some novels, including *The Currency Lass: A Tale of the Convict Days* (1927) and *Washdirt* (1946), a tale of the gold-rush days in his native Bendigo. Devaney cared for the poet **John Shaw Neilson** in Neilson's last years, wrote his biography, *Shaw Neilson* (1944), and edited a collection of Neilson's unpublished verse in 1946.

DEVANNEY, Jean
(1894–1962)

New Zealand-born novelist, born in Ferntown, South Island, who moved to Australia in 1929. Before leaving New Zealand she had published a book of short stories and four novels, one of which, *The Butcher Shop* (1926), had the distinction of being banned in Australia, New Zealand *and* Nazi Germany. Like many with her radical social beliefs, she visited the Soviet Union in the 1930s, but her continual challenging of authority caused her to be expelled from the Communist Party. However, her proletarian sympathies, as in *Sugar Heaven* (1936), the story of industrial action in the Queensland canefields (later translated into Russian), never faltered.

▷ *Points of Departure*, ed C Ferrier (1986)

DE VERE, Aubrey Thomas
(1814–1902)

Irish poet, born in Curragh Chase, County Limerick, the son of Sir Aubrey De Vere (1788–1846). Educated at Trinity College, Dublin, he became a friend of **Newman**, **Wordsworth** and **Tennyson**. In addition to many volumes of poems he published poetical dramas on Alexander the Great (1874) and Becket (1876), *Essays on Poetry* (2 vols, 1887), and works on Irish ecclesiastical politics and literary criticism.

DEVLIN, Denis
(1908–59)

Irish poet, born in Greenock, Scotland, and educated in Dublin, Munich and Paris; he served as a diplomat for much of his life. A skilled translator, his own work did not get its deserved respect and attention until the publication of *Collected Poems* (1964) and the more comprehensive *Collected Poems of Denis Devlin* (1989). His assimilation of Christian iconography into cosmopolitan settings has given him an important place in European verse-making.

DE VRIES, Peter
(1910–)

American novelist, born in Chicago of Dutch immigrant parents. He was educated at Dutch Reformed Calvinist schools but rebelled against their puritanism. He was the editor of a community newspaper in Chicago before working as a vending-machine operator, toffee-apple salesman, radio actor, furniture mover, lecturer to women's clubs, and associate editor of *Poetry*. In 1943 he lured **James Thurber** to Chicago to give a benefit lecture for *Poetry* and Thurber subsequently encouraged him to write for the *New Yorker*. This he did, later joining the editorial staff, and latterly restricting his contribution to captions for cartoons. A satirist in his mentor's mould, he plays with words like **S J Perelman** and is an inveterate (and inventive) punster and epigrammatist. He has written more than 20 novels, though none has eclipsed the reception of his first, *The Tunnel of Love* (1954).

DEYSSEL, Lodewijk van, pseud of Karel Joan Lodewijk Alberdinck Thijm
(1864–1952)

Dutch novelist, editor and critic, born in Amsterdam. His advocation of **Zola** led him to write the naturalistic novel *Een liefde* (1887, 'A Life'). Later he turned against naturalism and wrote an influential polemic against it (1891). He wrote essentially mystical prose poetry, and became Holland's most important critic, surveying virtually the whole of the lowlands culture in the 11 volumes of his *Verzamelde opstellen* (1922–3).
▷H G M Prick, *Lodewijk van Deyssel* (1964, in Dutch)

DE ZAYAS Y SOTOMAYOR, Mariá
(1590–?1660)

Spanish poet, novelist and playwright. Born in Madrid but brought up in Naples, she was one of the most dynamic and imaginative women writers of her time. One of the strongest defenders of women's rights of the century, she has been cited in modern times as one of the most effective pre-modern feminists. Though she was greatly praised in her day as a poet by such writers as **Lope Félix de Vega Carpio** and Castillo Solórzano, she is most famous for her short stories, which draw on the traditions of the Spanish picaresque novel, the pastoral novel and the work of **Boccaccio**. Her two most important books are *Novelas amorosas y ejemplares* (1637, 'Exemplary and Amorous Novels', published in Zaragoza, where she lived for a large part of her life), and *Desengaños amorosos, parte segunda del sarao y entretenimientos honestos* (1647, 'Disenchantments of Love, the Second Part of the Party and Entertainment'). It is not clear when she died, and she may have spent the last years of her life in reclusion in a convent.

DHONDY, Farrukh
(1944–)

English novelist, television editor and writer for children, born in Poona, India. Since his first collection of stories for children, *Come To Mecca* (1978), he has proven his versatility by working in a variety of media in different roles. *The Siege of Babylon* (1978) was a children's novel about a botched robbery, but since then he has increasingly written for an older audience. *Bombay Duck* (1990), his first

novel for adults, set in London, Edinburgh, Delhi and Bombay, was a rich mixture of old myths and new. As a commissioning editor for Channel 4 television, he has played a central role in encouraging writing talent from, in particular, Britain's black and Asian communities.

DHU AL-NUN AYYBUB
(1908–)

Leading Iraqi novelist, a professor of physics and chemistry, whose *Duktur Ibrahim* (1939, 'Doctor Ibrahim') analyses a Western intellectual to devastating effect; *Wa ala al-dunya al-salam* (1972, 'Farewell to the World') depicts struggles in his own country in the preceding decade. He was in exile in Vienna between 1954 and 1958 for political reasons, and wrote about this in a number of short stories, which were well thought of.

DIAMOND, I A L, originally Itek Dommnici
(1920–88)

Romanian-born American screenwriter. An immigrant to America in 1929, he graduated from Columbia University in New York and displayed sufficient promise to secure a contract as a junior writer at Paramount Studios (1941–3). He first received screen credit as the writer of the minor musical thriller *Murder In The Blue Room* (1944). His subsequent work comprised a string of generally undistinguished broad comedies and musicals before he embarked on a 25-year collaboration with the writer-director Billy Wilder (1906–) on *Love In The Afternoon* (1957). Together, they created witty, incisive classics of contemporary American cinema, including the uproarious farce *Some Like It Hot* (1959), bittersweet romantic comedies such as *The Apartment* (1960) and *Avanti!* (1972), and such cynical explorations of modern morality as *Kiss Me Stupid* (1964) and *The Fortune Cookie* (1966). He received the Writer's Guild Laurel Award in 1979 and collaborated a final time with Wilder on *Buddy, Buddy* (1981).

DIAPER, William
(1685–1717)

English poet, born in Bridgwater, Somerset, of a poor family. After graduating from Balliol College, Oxford, he entered the church and held various country curacies but was never ordained priest, remaining poverty-stricken despite efforts by **Swift** to help him. He published translations of classical authors, and pastoral verse: *Nereides: or, Sea-Eclogues* (1712, with mermen instead of shepherds), and *Dryades* (1712). Delicate observation of the natural world enlivens their conscious classicism. His *Brent* (posthumously published, 1727) anticipates **George Crabbe** in its anti-pastoral realism and satirical bite.

▷ *Complete Works*, ed with life and critical introduction by D Broughton (1951)

DIAZ DEL CASTILLO, Bernal
(?1492–1584)

Spanish historian, one of the more colourful of the *cronistas* of the Spanish conquest, who began as a soldier in the army of the conquistador Cortés in the attack on the Aztecs. Noted for its combination of character and anecdote, his *Historia Verdadera de la Conquista de la Nueva España* (abridged Eng trans *The Discovery and Conquest of Mexico*, 1956) gives a more human view of the conquest than other official histories. One of the main goals of his work was to correct the errors of earlier historians. His down-to-earth style is almost gossipy, full of digressions, stories, and repetitions reminiscent of the *novelas de caballería* and the epic romances.

DICK, Philip K(indred)
(1928–82)

American writer of science fiction, born in Chicago, Illinois. Educated at Berkeley High School, he worked as a record store manager and as a radio announcer. His career had two distinct phases; the first, from 1952 to 1955, remarkable for a profusion of short stories, the second, starting in 1962, notable for a torrent of novels. Despite a penchant for modish titles—*Do Androids Dream of Electric Sheep?* (1968) and *Galactic Pot-Healer* (1969), the story of a master-potter who has never thrown his own pots—he was not so much interested in technological gimickry and space-age jargon as in his characters. A spare and humorous writer, he received the Hugo Award in 1963.

DICKENS, Charles John Huffam
(1812–70)

English author, born in Landport, then a little suburb of Portsmouth. His father was John Dickens, a clerk in the navy pay office, and at that time attached to Portsmouth dockyard. In 1814 he was transferred to London, and in 1816 to Chatham, where, already a great reader, he got some schooling. In 1821 the family fell into trouble; reforms in the Admiralty made his father redundant and they had to leave Chatham, and moved to London, where they took a small house in Camden Town. But the father was soon arrested for debt in 1824 and sent to the Marshalsea prison with his whole family, apart from Charles, who was sent to work in a blacking factory at Hungerford Market, where, with half a dozen rough boys, he labelled the blacking bottles. Not only were his

days passed in this wretched work, but the child was left entirely to himself at night, when he had four miles to walk to his lonely bedroom in lodgings in Camden Town. On Sundays he visited his parents in the prison. On his father's release they all went back to Camden Town, and the boy was sent again to school, an academy in the Hampstead Road, for three or four years, after which he worked for a solicitor as an office boy (1827). Meantime, however, his father had obtained a post as reporter for the *Morning Herald*, and Charles decided also to attempt the profession of journalist. He taught himself shorthand; and he visited the British Museum daily to supplement some of the shortcomings of his reading. In 1828 he became a reporter of debates at the House of Commons for the *Morning Chronicle*, but at that time he was only interested in being an actor. It was not until 1835 that he succeeded in getting permanent employment on the staff of a London paper as a reporter and in this capacity he was sent around the country. Meanwhile in December 1833, the *Monthly Magazine* published a sketch 'Dinner at Poplar Walk', under the pen-name 'Boz' (the nickname of his younger brother, Augustus Moses). Other papers followed, but produced nothing for the contributor except the gratification of seeing them in print. He soon made an arrangement to contribute papers and sketches regularly to the *Evening Chronicle*, continuing to act as reporter for the *Morning Chronicle*, and getting his salary increased. The *Sketches by Boz* were collected and published early in 1836, the author receiving £150 for the copyright; he later bought it back for 11 times that amount. In the last week of March of that year appeared the first number of the *Pickwick Papers*; three days afterwards he married Catherine, the daughter of his friend George Hogarth, Editor of the *Evening Chronicle*. She bore him seven sons and three daughters between 1837 and 1852, three of whom predeceased him; in 1858 husband and wife separated. Success having definitely come his way, Dickens for the rest of his life allowed himself scant respite. In fulfilment of publishers' engagements he produced *Oliver Twist* (1837–9), which appeared in *Bentley's Miscellany*, and which Dickens edited for a time, *Nicholas Nickleby* (1838–9), *Master Humphrey's Clock*, a serial miscellany which resolved itself into the two stories, *The Old Curiosity Shop* (1840–1) and *Barnaby Rudge* (1841). From then on a great part of Dickens's life was spent abroad; especially notable were his visits to America in 1842 and 1867–8, his stay in Genoa in 1844–5 and in Lausanne in 1846, and his summers spent in Boulogne in 1853, 1854, and 1856. Meanwhile there came from his pen an incessant stream:

American Notes (1842), Martin Chuzzlewit (1843), The Christmas Tales—A Christmas Carol, The Chimes, The Cricket on the Hearth, The Battle of Life, The Haunted Man and The Ghost's Bargain (1843, 1846 and 1848); Pictures from Italy (1845), Dombey and Son (1846–8), David Copperfield (1849–50), Bleak House (1852–3), A Child's History of England (1854), Hard Times (1854), Little Dorrit (1855–7), A Tale of Two Cities (1859), The Uncommercial Traveller (1861), the Christmas numbers in Household Words and All the Year Round, Great Expectations (1860–1), Our Mutual Friend (1864–5) and The Mystery of Edwin Drood (1870, unfinished). To this long roll must be added public readings (1858–70), both in Britain and in America, private theatricals, speeches, innumerable letters, pamphlets, plays, the running of a popular magazine—first (1850) called Household Words and then (1859) All the Year Round. The scale of his achievement seems all but unrepeatable in the history of English fiction. He is the most widely known English writer after **Shakespeare**, and no other novelist has managed to find both popular success and critical respect on such a lavish scale. The breadth, perception and sympathy of his writing, his abiding concern with social deprivation and injustice, his ability to conjure up memorable characters in a few paragraphs (many of which have found an almost independent, semi-mythical status in the broader cultural consciousness), and the comic genius which permeates even his most serious works, have all ensured that he continues to find a receptive audience, both for the books themselves and in film and stage adaptations of his work. He died suddenly at Gadshill, near Rochester (the place he had coveted as a boy, and purchased in 1856), and was buried in Westminster Abbey.

▷J Butt and K Tillotson, Dickens at Work (1957); J Carey, The Violent Effigy (1973); P Ackroyd, Dickens (1990)

DICKENS, Monica Enid
(1915–92)

English novelist and author of non-fiction, born in London and a great-grand-daughter of **Charles Dickens**. After a disrupted education and her presentation at court as a débutante, she produced a series of semi-autobiographical novels. These include One Pair of Feet (1942), deriving from her nursing training in the early years of World War II, and My Turn to Make the Tea (1951), from her days as a junior reporter on a local newspaper. She developed in her writing a compassion for human problems such as alcoholism, the subject of The Heart of London (1961), and child abuse, which she examined in Kate and Emma (1964). For 20 years she was a popular columnist for Women's Own magazine.

▷An Open Book (1978)

DICKEY, James Lafayette
(1923–)

American poet and novelist. Born in Georgia, he was alleged to be President Jimmy Carter's favourite writer of verse, sharing with him an intense concern for the fragile harmony of nature and human enterprise. This is the substance of much of his verse from the first collection Into the Stone (1960), Drowning with Others (1962, republished in part as The Owl King, 1977) and Helmets (1964). Dickey's wider fame depends on his one novel, Deliverance (1972), a **Hemingway**esque rite of passage set against the damming and flooding of a wild valley. It was successfully filmed by John Boorman. Later poetry collections emphasized Dickey's deep narrative urge: The Zodiac (1976), The Strength of Fields (1977), whose title poem was written for Carter's inauguration, the remarkable Head-Deep in Strange Sounds: Free Flight Improvisations from the UnEnglish (1979) and Falling, May Day Sermon and Other Poems (1981). Dickey's poems have been collected in three volumes: Poems, 1957–1967 (1967), The Achievement of James Dickey (1968) and The Central Motion: Poems 1968–1979 (1983). The Self-Interviews (1970) are just that.

▷B Weigl and T R Hummer (eds), The Imagination as Glory (1984)

DICKINSON, Emily Elizabeth
(1830–86)

American poet, born in Amherst, Massachusetts, the daughter of an autocratic lawyer who became a Congressman. She was educated at Amherst Academy and Mount Holyoke Female Seminary in South Hadley. She spent her whole life in the family home at Amherst. A mystic by inclination, she withdrew herself at 23 from most social contacts and lived an intensely secluded life, writing in secret over a thousand poems. All but one or two of these remained unpublished until after her death, when her sister Lavinia brought out three volumes between 1891 and 1896 which were acclaimed as the work of a poetic genius. Further collections appeared, as The Single Hound (1914) and Bolts of Melody (1945). Her lyrics, intensely personal and often spiritual, show great originality both in thought and in form, and have had considerable influence on modern poetry.

▷C G Wolf, Emily Dickinson: a biography (1986)

DICKINSON, Goldsworthy Lowes
(1862–1932)

English academic, essayist and poet, born in London and educated at King's College, Cambridge, of which he became a fellow in 1887. He taught classics and political science, among other subjects, writing books on these topics and on international peace (he played a part in the founding of the League of Nations); his *The Greek View of Life* (1896) was a popular introduction to Ancient Greece. According to **W H Auden**, Dickinson had 'little talent' for poetry, a view borne out by *Poems* (1896) and other volumes. More successful were his *Letters from John Chinaman* (1901), a critique of Western ways, written in poetic prose and the fantasy *The Magic Flute* (1920). His autobiography, published in 1973, deals frankly with his homosexuality.
▷ E M Forster, *Goldsworthy Lowes Dickinson* (1934)

DICKINSON, Peter Malcolm de Brissac
(1927–)

African-born British writer of detective fiction and other novels, born in Livingstone, Zambia. Educated at Eton College and Cambridge, he writes with the same solid Englishness demonstrated by his series detective Superintendent James Pibble, who appeared in Dickinson's first detective novel *Skin Deep* (1968, published in the USA as *The Glass-Sided Ants' Nest*), and five others. His best novel is perhaps *The Poison Oracle* (1974), which deals with environmental menace within the context of a murder mystery. Between 1952 and 1969, Dickinson was an assistant editor at *Punch*, and his prose style occasionally evinces the heavy-handed polysyllabic irony the magazine once favoured. At his best, though, he is an intelligent literary technician with a gift for subtle, multi-faceted plotting.

DICKMANN, Max
(1908–)

Argentinian novelist and translator (**Dos Passos, Faulkner**), born in Buenos Aires. 'The most tenacious upholder of socially conscious realism in 20th-century Argentinian literature', he had his greatest success with *Madre América* (1935), a novel in the style of Dos Passos; but it was not translated. He was a member, with **Arlt**, of the Boedo group of writers who favoured proletarian fiction in the Scandinavian manner, in contrast to the Florida group of **Borges** who favoured verse and European literature in general. His work attracted less and less critical attention, and he exiled himself to the mountains, publishing nothing after 1968; more recently critics have started to point out what a 'widespread impact' his fiction in fact had, and it is now being re-read and re-appraised for its bitterness and honesty.
▷ N Lindstrom, *Jewish Issues in Argentine Literature from Gerchunoff to Szichman* (1989)

DIDEROT, Denis
(1713–84)

French writer, born in Langres in Champagne, the son of a master cutler. Trained by the Jesuits at home and in Paris, he refused to become either a lawyer or a physician, and was thrown upon his own resources, and worked as tutor and bookseller's hack (1734–44). In 1743 he married a young seamstress, who contrived to bring about a temporary reconciliation between father and son; but the marriage was not happy, and he had many love affairs. His *Pensées philosophiques* (1796, Eng trans *Philosophical Thoughts*, 1916) was burned by the parlement of Paris in 1746, and in 1749 he was imprisoned for his *Lettre sur les aveugles* (1749, Eng trans *An Essay on Blindness*, 1750). In 1748 he had published his first novel, *Les Bijoux indiscrets* (Eng trans *The Indiscreet Toys*, 1749). The bookseller Le Breton now invited him to edit an expanded translation of Ephraim Chambers's *Cyclopaedia* (1727) with d'Alembert. In Diderot's hands the character of the work was transformed. He enlisted nearly all the important French writers of the time as contributors, and, in place of a compendium of useful information, produced a work of propaganda for the *philosophe* party. For some 20 years he retained his post in spite of dangers and drawbacks. The sale of *Encyclopédie* was again and again prohibited, and its editor ran a constant risk of imprisonment or exile. D'Alembert abandoned him in despair in 1758. But his marvellous energy, his varied knowledge, and his faculty of rallying his fellow workers, enabled him to carry his vast undertaking to a successful conclusion. The first volume of the *Encyclopédie, ou Dictionnaire Raisonné des Sciences, des Arts et des Métiers* ('Encyclopaedia, or Critical Dictionary of Sciences, Arts and Trades') appeared in 1751; the 35th and last in 1776. In his later years he was rescued from financial difficulties by Catherine the Great of Russia, to whom in 1773 he paid a five-month visit. He died of apoplexy. One of the most prolific and versatile of writers, he was a novelist and a dramatist, a satirist, a philosopher, a critic of pictures and books, and a brilliant letter writer. His works also include *Pensées sur l'interprétation de la Nature* (1753, 'Thoughts on the Interpretation of Nature'), and two novels: *La Religieuse* (1796, Eng trans *The Nun*, 1797), an exposure of convent life; and

the **Laurence Sterne**-like *Jacques le Fataliste et son Maître* (1796, Eng trans *James the Fatalist and his Master*, 1797). In *Le Neveu de Rameau* (1821, Eng trans *Rameau's Nephew*, 1897), an imaginary conversation between the author and a parasite, the follies of society are laid bare with sardonic humour and piercing insight. His plays were somewhat unsuccessful examples of melodrama, the best efforts being two short pieces: *La Pièce et le prologue* (1820, 'The Play and the Prologue') and *Est-il bon? Est-il méchant?* (1784, 'Is He Good? Is He Bad?', not produced until 1913). His letters to Sophie Volland form the most interesting section of his voluminous correspondence. As a critic he stood far in advance of his contemporaries, and anticipated the Romanticists. His *Salons* (not published until 1957–67, in 4 vols), remarks on pictures exhibited, are the earliest example of modern aesthetic criticism.
▷L G Crocker, *The Embattled Philosopher: a biography of Diderot* (1954, rev edn 1966); other works by Crocker; P France, *Diderot* (1974)

DIDION, Joan
(1934–)

American writer, born in Sacramento, California. She was educated at the University of California at Berkeley (1952–6) and married the writer **John Gregory Dunne** in 1964. From 1956 to 1963 she was associate feature editor of *Vogue* in New York and has worked and written for the *Saturday Evening Post*, *Esquire*, and *National Review*. Her columns were published as *Slouching Towards Bethlehem* (1968) and *The White Album* (1979). Her novels portray contemporary social tensions in a laconic style that has aroused much admiration. *Run River* (1963) was her first novel, but she is best known for *A Book of Common Prayer* (1977), set in a banana republic devoid of history, and *Democracy* (1984), about the long and amorous affair between a politician's wife and Jack Lovett, a man who embodies everything her ambitious husband is not.
▷B Morton, *The Princess in the Consulate: the novels of Joan Didion* (1980)

DIGBY, Kenelm Henry
(1800–80)

English writer, born in Ireland, the youngest son of the Dean of Clonfert. Educated at Trinity College, Cambridge, he published a survey of medieval customs, *The Broad Stone of Honour* (1822), with additional volumes in 1828–9 and 1877, which was influential in the 19th-century cult of medievalism. Converted to Roman Catholicism, he published *Mores Catholici* (1831–42) and other works, including poetry.

▷K G Huston, *Sir Kenelm Digby: a checklist* (1969)

DIKTONIUS, Elmer
(1896–1961)

Finland–Swedish modernist poet, born into a Swedish-speaking family in Helsinki at a time when Finland was still part of the Russian tsar's realm. In the Civil War following Finnish independence in 1917, he sided with the Finnish Red militia. His social and political passion was linked to his broad view of life: his intentions to become a composer thwarted, he turned away from music to the written word as an instrument of expression. He was bilingual, and wrote poetry as well as prose in both Swedish and Finnish. His first collection of poems and aphorisms, *Min dikt* (1921, 'My poetry'), showed the influence of **Nietzsche** and of **Edith Södergran**, the figurehead of Finland–Swedish modernism. The powerful and daring stanzas of his programmatic poem *Jaguaren* ('The Jaguar'), in the collection *Hårda Sånger* (1922, 'Hard Songs'), demonstrates with a tremendous energy his desire to break with the literary norms and lifestyle of the past. The collection *Stark men mörk* (1930, 'Strong but Dark') marks the end of this period: in his later poems revolutionary idealism gave way to a more peaceful emphasis, on nature and the 'small things' in life. Sadly, Diktonius's creative power was lost prematurely: he spent the last few years of his life in a mental hospital.
▷G C Schoolfield, *Elmer Diktonius* (1985)

DILLARD, Annie
(1945–)

American essayist, poet and fiction writer, born in Pittsburgh, Pennsylvania, and educated at Hollins College, where she received both her BA and MA. She has worked as a contributing editor at *Harpers* magazine and as an adjunct professor at Wesleyan University, and has contributed to such diverse publications as *Atlantic Monthly* and *Sports Illustrated*. Her work often concentrates on the search for the spiritual in the natural environment, and in 1974 she won a Pulitzer Prize for her collection of essays entitled *Pilgrim at Tinker Creek*. She has won a number of other awards, including a Washington Governor's Award in 1978 and a Guggenheim Foundation Grant (1984–5).
▷C Rainwater and W Scheick (eds), *Contemporary American Women Writers: Narrative Strategies* (1985)

DILLON, George
(1906–68)

American poet, translator and editor (of *Poetry*, 1937–50), born in Jacksonville, Florida. With the mellifluous collection *The*

Flowering Stone (1931) he won a Pulitzer Prize; but thereafter he concentrated, for the most part, on translation: eg his rendering of *Flowers of Evil*, by **Baudelaire**, with **Edna St Vincent Millay**, published in 1936, and his well thought of *Three Plays* (1961) of **Jean Racine**.

DIMT, C *see* **BUSTA, Christine**

DINESEN, Isak *see* **BLIXEN, Karen, Baroness**

DING LING, pseud of **Jiang Bingzhi**
(1904–86)
Chinese novelist and short-story writer, born in Linli County, Hunan Province. A radical feminist, her father died when she was three and her mother flouted tradition by enrolling in school and becoming a teacher. Jiang was educated at Beijing University, where she attended left-wing classes and started publishing stories of rebelliousness against traditional society, such as *The Diary of Miss Sophia* (1928), which dealt candidly with questions of female psychology and sexual desires, *Birth of an Individual* (1929), and *A Woman* (1930). She joined the League of Left-Wing Writers in 1930 and became editor of its official journal. She joined the Communist Party in 1932, and after a spell of imprisonment, escaped to the communist base at Yenan, where she became a star attraction for Western journalists. Her outspoken comments on male chauvinism and discrimination at Yenan led to her being disciplined by the party leaders, until her novel, *The Sun Shines over the Sanggan River* (1948), about land-reform, restored her to favour. In 1958, however, she was 'purged', and sent to raise chickens in the Heilongjiang reclamation area known as the Great Northern Wilderness (Beidahuang). She was imprisoned (1970–5) during the Cultural Revolution, but rehabilitated by the party in 1979, and published a novel based on her experiences in the Great Northern Wilderness, *Comrade Du Wanxiang* (1979).

DINGELSTEDT, Franz von
(1814–81)
German poet and novelist, born in Halsdorf, near Marburg. He began writing as a journalist and satirical novelist and poet with radical views, and published the novels *Die neuen Argonauten* (1839, 'The New Argonauts') and *Unter der Erde* (1840, 'Under the Earth'), but then converted to establishment views. He was royal librarian at Württemberg from 1843 to 1850, and director of the court theatres at Munich, Weimar and Vienna. He

wrote stories, novels and plays, but is best remembered for his work as director of these theatres.
▷M Sauerlandt, *Franz von Dingelstedt* (1854); and other works by Sauerlandt

DINIS, Julio, pseud of **Joaquim Guilherme Gomes Coelho**
(1839–71)
Portuguese novelist, a lecturer in medicine, who was born and died—of tuberculosis—in Oporto. Often ignored as dull and guilty of idealizing the rural people in whose lives he was most interested, certain critics still find him a 'demure chronicler of quiet scenes' with 'an originality which so often eludes those who most furiously pursue it', and even as having a 'touch of Jane Austen'. However, the chief influences upon him were **Dickens**, **Thackeray** and **Balzac**. Certainly such novels as *Uma Familia Inglesa* (1868, 'An English Family'), while in certain respects over-optimistic about human nature, are punctuated with shrewd psychological insight and uncanny anticipations of the technique of interior monologue.
▷A F G Bell, *Portuguese Literature* (1922)

DINIZ DA CRUZ E SILVA, Antonio
(1731–99)
Portuguese poet, born in Lisbon. He took a law degree at the University of Coimbra in 1753, and became a founder member of the *Arcadia Lusitana*, a society dedicated to the revival of national poetry. He wrote the epic poem, *O Hyssope* (1774), and *Odes Pindaricas* (published posthumously in 1801), lyrics which earned him the title of the 'Portuguese Pindar'. His later life was spent in Brazil.

DIOGENES LAERTIUS
(3rd century)
Greek writer, whose *Lives of the Greek Philosophers*, in 10 books, gives a second-hand account of the principal Greek thinkers, but provides much information not otherwise available, as well as extracts from the work of writers which has not survived in other forms.

DIONYSIUS OF HALICARNASSUS
(1st century BC)
Greek critic, historian and rhetorician. From 30 BC he lived and worked in Rome. He wrote, in Greek, *Rōmaïkē Archaeologia*, a history of Rome down to 264 BC, a mine of information about the constitution, religion, history, laws and private life of the Romans. Of its 20 books, only the first nine are complete. He also wrote a number of valuable critical treat-

ises on literature and rhetoric, particularly *On the Arrangement of Words*.

▷ S F Bonner, *The Literary Treatises of Dionysius* (1939)

DIOP, Birago
(1906–90)

Francophone Senegalese veterinary surgeon who went into the diplomatic service, but then returned to care for animals. He was both a poet and a story writer, and in the last capacity became the greatest transcriber from the *griots* (oral storytellers) of his continent. His narrator was the Wolof, Amadou Koumba, a real *griot*; a selection of his incomparable and profound animal tales is translated in *Tales of Amadou Koumba* (1966).

DI PRIMA, Diane
(1934–)

American poet, playwright and novelist. Born in New York City and educated in Pennsylvania, between 1961 and 1963 she co-edited the poetry journal *Floating Bear* with LeRoi Jones (later known as **Amiri Baraka**), continuing as sole editor until 1969. With her first husband Alan Marlowe, she founded the New York Poets Theatre in 1961, the year of her second poetry collection, *The Monster*. Di Prima writes in many voices, the exotic and marvellous in her first book, *This Kind of Bird Flies Backward* (1958) and in *The New Handbook of Heaven* (1963); the directly personal in *Poems for Freddie* (1966, reprinted as *Freddie Poems*, 1974); the socially committed in *Revolutionary Letters* (1968). Since 1973, di Prima has worked on the *Loba* cycle, a self-defining work-in-progress that examines aspects of femininity in a physical, emotional and mythic way. Related works include *Brass Furnace Going Out: Song, After an Abortion* (1975). Her novel, *Memoirs of a Beatnik* (1969), is a comic performance.

DISCH, Thomas Michael
(1940–)

American science-fiction writer and poet, born in Des Moines, Iowa. His first novel, *The Genocides*, appeared in 1965, but he earned a reputation as a writer of serious intent and disturbingly dark vision with *Camp Concentration* (1968), a political allegory set in a near-future USA, but reflecting the repression of anti-war protests of the day. That dark, pessimistic vision is also evident in *Mankind Under the Leash* (1966) and in several volumes of stories, the most important of which is *Getting Into Death* (1973, rev edn 1976). The novel *On Wings of Song* (1979) is more optimistic in tone. He has also written mainstream and horror novels, stories for children, and several volumes of poetry, including *The Right Way to Figure Plumbing* (1971), *Burn This* (1982) and *Dark Verses and Light* (1991).

DISRAELI, Benjamin, 1st Earl of Beaconsfield
(1804–81)

British novelist and statesman, born in London. He was the eldest son of the Jewish writer **Isaac D'Israeli**, but his father, after a quarrel with his synagogue, had him baptized in 1817. He was educated at a private school in Walthamstow, and was articled as a solicitor. His first novel, *Vivian Grey* (1826), in which he imbued the youthful hero with much of his own arrogant demeanour and quick wit, was a great success. Elected to parliament in 1837, he became the head of the radical 'Young England' group of Tory MPs. As Chancellor of the Exchequer, he was responsible for the passage of the Reform Bill through parliament in 1867, and was twice prime minister at periods of great political ferment at home and abroad. As a writer, he is an important Victorian novelist, and followed his early success with a satirical work, *The Voyage of Captain Popanilla* (1827), and a society novel, *The Young Duke* (1831). He continued to write while establishing his parliamentary career, producing a string of novels which included *Contarini Fleming* (1832), *Alroy* (1833), *Ixion in Heaven* (1833), *The Infernal Marriage* (1834), *Henrietta Temple* (1837) and *Venetia* (1837), a novel about **Shelley** and **Byron**. His best-known and most politically influential novels are the 'state of the nation' trilogy of the 1840s, *Coningsby, or, The New Generation* (1844), *Sybil, or The Two Nations* (1845) and *Tancred, or The New Crusade* (1847). His periods of office inevitably slowed down his writing, but he went on to publish two more novels, *Lothair* (1870) and *Endymion* (1880), and left another, *Falconet*, unfinished at his death. He claimed that 'works are my life', and neatly symbolized that claim by taking the title 1st Earl of Beaconsfield on his elevation to the peerage in 1876, having originally invented it in his first novel.

▷ W Meynell, *Benjamin Disraeli: An Unconventional Biography* (1927); A Maorois, *The Life of Disraeli* (1928); M Komroff, *Disraeli* (1963)

D'ISRAELI, Isaac
(1776–1848)

English writer, born in Enfield, the son of a Jewish merchant of Italian descent, and father of **Benjamin Disraeli**. In 1801 he became a British subject. Although he had wished to be a creative writer, and published one or two novels, his *forte* was in literary illustrations of persons and history, as in his

Curiosities of Literature (1791–1834), *Calamities of Authors* (1812) and a commentary on Charles I (1831). **Byron** was an admirer of his work.
▷J Ogden, *Isaac D'Israeli* (1969)

DITLEVSEN, Tove
(1918–76)
Danish poet, novelist and short-story writer, whose autobiographical *Gift* (1971) was a shockingly frank portrayal of the author's sexual and marital problems and her drug addiction; the Danish word '*gift*' for 'married' also means 'toxin' or 'poison'. The same concerns are also explored in *Vilhelms Vaerelse* (1973, 'Vilhelm's Place'), which exposes a catastrophic marriage to the cold light one associates with Swedish film director Ingmar Bergman. Ditlevsen grew up in a working-class district of Copenhagen and came to attention with *Pigesind* (1939, 'A Young Girl's Mind'), a sequence of frank and probing lyrics which she continued a decade and a half later with *Kvinesind* (1955, 'A Woman's Mind'). Though often unsettling in their directness, her works retain an essential warmth and humanity, and a great sense of place.
▷ *Tove Ditlevsen om sig selv* (1975)

DIXON, Richard Watson
(1833–1900)
English poet, born in Islington. He studied at King Edward's School, Birmingham, Pembroke College, Oxford, and became a canon of Carlisle in 1874 and vicar of Warkworth in 1883. A member of the Pre-Raphaelite circle with Edward Burne-Jones and **William Morris**, and a teacher and supporter of **Gerard Manley Hopkins**, he wrote seven volumes of poetry and a *History of the Church of England* (6 vols, 1877–1902).
▷A Sambrook, *A Poet Hidden* (1962)

DIXON, Thomas
(1864–1946)
American novelist, born in North Carolina, but best known for his novels about the Reconstruction era, in which he expounded extreme and often violent segregationist views. Though he wrote more than 20 novels, the most celebrated is *The Clansman* (1905), part two of a trilogy begun with *The Leopard's Spots* (1902) and concluded with *The Traitor* (1907). Dixon dramatized it himself, but it received its widest dissemination (not necessarily in a context Dixon could have approved) as the basis of the Ku Klux Klan scenes in D W Griffiths's classic motion picture *The Birth of a Nation* (1914). Dixon himself experimented with film-making, attracted by its propagandist potential.

DJALSKI, Ksaver Sandor, pseud of **Ljubo Bratić**
(1854–1935)
Croatian novelist and story writer, born in Gredice. He was a prolific realist, much underrated outside his own country. An ardent nationalist, deeply influenced by **Balzac** and—less usually—by **Turgenev**, he moved, in his chronicles of the Croatian society (of all levels) of the end of the 19th century, from a bleak but refined pessimism to a mysticism which has seldom been well understood or appreciated. There is a translation of one of his stories in the *Slavonic and East European Review* (XVIII, 25, 1939), but otherwise his fine and subtle fiction cannot be as widely read as it deserves. He was an uneven writer, but at his best, as in the tales of *Pod starim krovovima* (1886, 'Under Old Roofs'), he was worthy to stand beside even **Senoa**.

DJORDIJIĆ, Ignjac
(1675–1737)
Dalmatian Jesuit (latterly Benedictine) poet, who is important as the last true representative of what is known as 'Dalmatian' or 'Dubrovnik' or 'Ragusan' (Dubrovnik was formerly called Ragusa) literature. This had grown up almost entirely because of Italian influences; but, while the 14th-century men knew Italian, the women did not—and so the men began to write in their own vernacular in order to impress the women. Djordijić wrote original religious poetry, much of which is also about love, just at the time when his literature went into decline owing to the opening up of Atlantic trade and the decline in the prosperity of Dubrovnik.

DJURHUUS, Jens H O
(1881–1948)
Faroese poet, whose *Yrkingar* (1914, 'Poems'), is the first individual collection to be published in Faroese. The poems have been said to be 'worthy, gloomy and tedious'.

DOBELL, Sydney Thompson
(1824–74)
English poet, born in Cranbrook, Kent. He worked with his father as a wine merchant in London and Cheltenham, but lived for some time in the Scottish Highlands and abroad, and became a passionate advocate of oppressed nationalities. His dramatic poem, *The Roman* (1850), was written in sympathy with Italian aspirations for unity, and he also wrote sonnets on the Crimean War (1855) and *England in Time of War* (1856). His chief works were in the style of the so-called Spasmodic School, caricatured by **William**

Aytoun, appearing under the pseudonym Sydney Yendys.

▷E Jolly (ed), *Life and Letters of Sydney Thompson Dobell* (1878)

DÖBLIN, Alfred
(1878–1957)

German novelist, born in Stettin. He grew up in Berlin, studied medicine at Berlin and Freiburg, and practised as a doctor and psychiatrist in Berlin from 1911. He published stories in the revolutionary expressionist journal *Der Sturm*, and a collection in 1913. He liked to work on a broad scale, however, as in the epic novels *Die drei Sprünge des Wang-Lun* (1915, 'The Three Leaps of Wan Lung'), an account of a failed rebellion set in 18th-century China, the satirical fantasy *Wadzek's Kampf mit der Dampfturbine* (1918, 'Wadzek's Fight with the Steam Machine'), *Wallenstein* (1920), and the futuristic *Berge Meere und Giganten* (1924, Eng trans *Giganten*, 1932). His masterpiece is *Berlin Alexanderplatz* (1929, Eng trans *Alexanderplatz Berlin*, 1931), the story of a hapless reformed criminal named Franz Biberkopf in the dark underworld of Weimar Germany. It is a modernist classic, and was influenced by the example of **James Joyce**. His socialist sympathies and Jewish background forced him to leave Germany for France in 1933, and he became a French citizen in 1936. He continued to write ambitious works in which the individual is in contention with huge and often deterministic social and historical forces, as in the novels *Pardon wird nicht gegeben* (1935, Eng trans *Men Without Mercy*, 1937) and the *Amazonas-Trilogie* (1937–47, 'The Amazon Trilogy'), as well as the later trilogy *November 1918* (1948–50). He fled to the USA in 1940, escaping through the Iberian peninsula in a hazardous journey described in *Shicksalreise* (1949, 'Fateful Journey'). He converted to the Roman Catholic faith in 1941, and returned to Germany in 1945, where he was a co-founder of the Academy of Science and Literature in 1949. He moved to France in 1951, but his last years were afflicted by illness, and he died in a nursing home in Baden-Württemberg. His last novel was *Hamlet oder Die lange Nacht nimmt ein Ende* (1956, 'Hamlet, or the Long Night is Ended').

DOBRACZYNSKI, Jan
(1910–)

Polish novelist and literary critic. He is a Catholic who writes novels on religious themes, notably in *Wybrańcy gwiazd* and *Listy Nikodema* (1948–52, Eng trans *The Letters of Nicodemus*, 1958). Critics not of the Catholic faith have tended to ignore him.

DOBSON, Henry Austin
(1840–1921)

English poet, born in Plymouth. He was educated at Beaumaris, Coventry, and Strasbourg as a civil engineer like his father, but from 1856 to 1901 was a board of trade clerk. His earliest poems, published in 1868 in *St Paul's Magazine*, were followed by *Vignettes in Rhyme* (1873), *Proverbs in Porcelain* (1877), *At the Sign of the Lyre* (1885), *The Story of Rosina* (1895) and *Collected Poems* (1897, rev edns 1902, 1909, 1913). Often in rondeau, ballade or villanelle form, these poems are marked by rare perfection. In prose he published monographs of **Henry Fielding** (1883), **Richard Steele**, Thomas Bewick (and his pupils), **Horace Walpole**, Hogarth, **Oliver Goldsmith**, **Fanny Burney** and **Samuel Richardson** (1902); and *Eighteenth Century Vignettes* (1892–6), *Four Frenchwomen* and other collections of graceful and erudite essays.

DOBSON, Rosemary de Brissac
(1920–87)

Australian poet, born in Sydney, granddaughter of **Austin Dobson**. She worked for some years with the Australian publishing firm Angus & Robertson and married Alec Bolton, then its London editor. Her poems reflect her love of antiquity and a keen, painterly, eye, and her fascination with manuscripts and fine printing, as seen in 'The Missal'. Her first collection was *In a Convex Mirror* (1944); her second, *The Ship of Ice*, won an award in 1948. Later books were *Child with a Cockatoo* (1955) and *Cock Crow* (1965); selections of her verse were published in 1973 and 1980. She edited the feminist anthology *Sister Poets* (1979), in which year she received the **Robert Frost** Prize; in 1984 she won the **Patrick White** Literary Award.

DOCTOROW, E(dgar) L(awrence)
(1931–)

American novelist, born in New York City. He was educated at Bronx High School of Science, Kenyon College and Columbia University. From 1960 to 1964 he was editor of the New American Library and has held teaching posts in several colleges and universities. His first novel was *Welcome to Hard Times* (1961), followed by *Big as Life* (1966) and *The Book of Daniel* (1971), based on the story of the Rosenbergs, who were executed for spying. *Ragtime* (1975) is generally regarded as his tour de force, in which he recreates the atmosphere of the Ragtime era with wit, accuracy and appealing nostalgia. It was filmed in 1981. Later books include *Loon Lake* (1980) and *The World's Fair* (1986).

DODERER, Heimito von
(1896–1966)

Austrian 'monumental' novelist, born near Vienna. More unequivocally unhappy about the collapse of the Habsburg empire than **Joseph Roth** or **Robert Musil**, and less subtle than either, he became a fervent Nazi, welcomed the Anschluss, and fought in World War II, as he had in World War I (when he was a prisoner in Siberia). One of his key themes he expressed in the word *Menschwerdung*, 'becoming human', a notion he invented during his Nazi period. In his fiction he continually looked back to the old Austria of the Habsburgs, a period he regarded as historically superior. His claim to fame lies solely in his *Die Strudlhofstiege* (1951, 'The Strudlhof Steps') and *Die Dämonen* (1956, Eng trans, *The Demons*, 1961). The earlier novel is a shorter 'prelude' to the ambitious longer *Die Dämonen*. There are two views of these long, intricately constructed, and sometimes ponderously humorous examinations of Viennese life: that they are relatively neglected masterpieces, and that they have been overrated. They are almost excessively influenced by **Musil**, **Proust** and, above all, by his friend the Austrian writer and painter **Alfred Paris von Gütersloh**. The critical tendency now seems to be veering towards the latter view; but a minority of readers remain devoted to him.

DODGE, Mary Elizabeth, née Mapes
(1831–1905)

American writer, born in New York. She married William Dodge, a lawyer, in 1851, and after his death in 1858 turned to writing books for children, notably *Hans Brinker; or, The Silver Skates* (1865), which became a children's classic. From 1873 she was the editor of *St Nicholas Magazine*.

DODSLEY, Robert
(1703–64)

English playwright, born in Mansfield, Nottinghamshire. He was apprenticed to a stocking weaver, but, probably ill-treated, ran away and became a footman. He spent his spare time reading, and in 1732 published *A Muse in Livery*. His *Toy Shop*, a dramatic piece, was through **Pope**'s influence acted at Covent Garden in 1735 with great success. With his profits, and £100 from Pope, he set up as bookseller, but still continued to write bright plays, including *The King and the Miller of Mansfield* (1737), *The Blind Beggar of Bethnal Green* (1741) and *Rex et Pontifex* (1745), which were collected as *Trifles* (1745). In 1738 he bought *London* from the yet unknown **Dr Johnson** for 10 guineas. Other famous authors for whom he published included Pope, **Edward Young**, Akenside and **Oliver Goldsmith**, and he founded the *Annual Register* with **Edmund Burke** in 1759. With a tragedy, *Cleone* (1758), acted at Covent Garden with extraordinary success, he closed his career as a dramatist. He is chiefly remembered for his *Select Collection of Old Plays* (12 vols, 1744–5) and his *Poems by Several Hands* (3 vols, 1748; 6 vols, 1758).

DOMETT, Alfred
(1811–87)

English-born New Zealand politician, journalist and poet, born in London. He was a friend of **Robert Browning**, who eulogized him in 'Waring'. Praised by **Tennyson**, his work was among the first to use New Zealand scenery and Maori myths, evoked in typically **Wordsworth**ian verse. In *Ranolf and Amohia: A South-Sea Day-Dream* (1872, rev edn 1883) he uses the classic devices of shipwreck, unrequited love and alienation, but the delicate detail is crushed beneath his political and philosophical digressions. He also published *Flotsam and Jetsam* (1877). An early settler in Nelson and its MP from 1855, he was involved in moves toward self-government and became premier of New Zealand briefly in 1862–3 during the Land Wars.
▷ *The Diary of Alfred Domett, 1872–1885* (1953)

DOMINGEZ DE MARGO, Hernando
(c.1602–1656)

Colombian poet, born in Bogotá. He was a Jesuit in Lima, but is thought to have left the order towards the end of his life, in order to become a priest in Guatavita. His claim to fame is his *Gongorist* epic *Poema heroico de San Ignacio Loyola* (1666), in which he ignores the famous asceticism in favour of an interest in South American matters.

DONALDSON, Stephen
(1947–)

American fantasy writer and short-story writer, born in Cleveland, Ohio, who endured countless rejections from publishers before his first book was finally accepted. Thereafter he became increasingly popular with each volume of the six-novel series *The Chronicles of Thomas Covenant* (1977–83), in which the titular character, who suffers from leprosy, is called on to save the Land, a utopian fantasy world, from the forces of evil. *The Mirror of Her Dreams* (1986) and its sequel *A Man Rides Through* (1988) are similar in theme to the Covenant chronicles, telling of a protagonist transported from our world—in this case, modern-day New York—to a fantastic realm which requires saving.

DONLEAVY, J(ames) P(atrick)

(1926–)

American-born Irish author, born in Brooklyn, New York, of Irish parents. After serving in the American navy during World War II, he studied microbiology at Trinity College, Dublin, and became a friend of **Brendan Behan**. While living on a farm in Wicklow he began painting, then wrote his first novel, *The Ginger Man*, published in 1955. Picaresque, bawdy, presenting an apparently totally irrational hero, it was hailed as a comic masterpiece. The novels, plays and stories that followed are on the same theme, that of his own 'dreams and inner desires', and have been described as paler versions of *The Ginger Man*. He became an Irish citizen in 1967 and among his other works are *A Singular Man* (1963), *Meet My Maker, The Mad Molecule* (short stories, 1964), *The Beastly Beatitudes of Balthazar B* (1968), written as a play in 1981, *The Onion Eaters* (1971), *A Fairy Tale of New York* (1973, a novel written from the play of 1960), *The Destinies of Darcy Dancer, Gentleman* (1971), *Schultz* (1980) and *Are you Listening, Rabbi Low?* (1987).

DONN, Robb

(1714–78)

Scottish poet, from Strathmore in Sutherland, where he quickly developed a reputation for his spontaneously composed Gaelic verse. He was illiterate, and spoke a very broad dialect of Gaelic, so the fact that a considerable quantity of his poetry has survived is a testament to his poetic gifts. He composed verse in the traditional Gaelic forms—he made love songs, praise songs, elegies and satires—and was renowned for his wit, achieving considerable standing in north Highland Gaelic society.
▷I Grimble, *The World of Robb Donn* (1979)

DONNAY, Maurice

(1859–1945)

French dramatist, born in Paris. His brittle *fin-de-siècle* comedy *Amants* (1895, 'Lovers') achieved considerable popularity, as did *Lysistrata* (1893), an adaptation of **Aristophanes**. Later successes in that vein included *La douloureuse* (1897, 'The Sad Woman') and *L'autre danger* (1902, 'The Other Danger'). His more serious works engaged with social problems, and were felt to be daring at that time in dealing with subjects like the marriage between Jew and gentile in *Le retour de Jérusalem* (1903, 'The Return from Jerusalem').
▷P Bathille, *Maurice Donnay. Son oeuvre* (1931)

DONNE, John

(?1572–1631)

English poet, born in London, the son of a prosperous ironmonger, but connected through his mother with Sir Thomas More. Though a Catholic, he was admitted to Hart Hall, Oxford, and later graduated at Cambridge, where his friendship with Sir Henry Wotton began. He decided to take up law and entered Lincoln's Inn in 1592. After taking part in the 2nd Earl of Essex's two expeditions to Cadiz in 1597 and the Azores in 1598 (reflected in his poems 'The Storm' and 'The Calm'), he became (1598) secretary to Sir Thomas Egerton, Keeper of the Great Seal, whose justice he celebrated in his fourth satire. His daring pieces and brilliant personality pointed to a career as notable as that of his great contemporary Francis Bacon, but his secret marriage to Egerton's niece, Anne More, caused him to be dismissed and thrown into prison. Having turned Protestant, he lived at Mitcham in Surrey, but still sought favour at the Court with an eye to employment. The work he undertook under the direction of Thomas (later Bishop) Morton was a religious polemic against the Catholics. He had already written his passionate and erotic poems, *Songs and Sonnets*, his six *Satires*, and his *Elegies*, but published no verse until 1611, when his *Anniversarie* appeared, a commemorative poem for Elizabeth Drury, daughter of his benefactor, Sir Robert Drury, whose house in the Strand offered hospitality to the poet when in London. A second *Anniversarie* followed, really a 'meditatio mortis' displaying his metaphysical genius at its best. His religious temper is seen in more lyrical form in the *Divine Poems*, some of which certainly date from before 1607. These, like most of his verse, were published posthumously but his pieces circulated widely among learned and aristocratic friends. How difficult his journey to the Anglican faith was may be judged from the satirical 'Progresse of the Soule' (1601). This ugly unfinished poem is antiheretical, but also sceptical in a disturbing way. Donne's hesitation over some 10 years to take orders is variously explained as due to a Hamlet-like indecision, or to a sense of unworthiness because of his profligate youth, or to his still having an eye on civil employment. He now courted the distinguished ladies of the time, in verse letters of laboured but ingenious compliment, among them Mrs Herbert and the Countess of Bedford. More injurious to his name was a splendid piece for the marriage of the king's favourite, Robert Carr, to the divorced Countess of Essex: a scandalous poem for a scandalous wedding. In Funeral poems, of which the first and second *Anniversaries* are the most brilliant, he also paid

court to the great. His prose works of this period include *Pseudo-Martyr* (1610), which is an acute polemic against the Jesuits. More interesting is his *Biothanatos*, which discussed the question of suicide, towards which, as he says in his preface, 'I have often...a sickly inclination'. He decides that suicide is permissible in certain cases, a conclusion at variance with that affirmed in his third *Satire*, but confirmed in a letter to his friend Sir Henry Wotton. King James VI and I encouraged him to go into the Church (1614), and promoted him, after several charges, to the deanship of St Paul's in 1621 when he relinquished his readership at Lincoln's Inn. Several of his sermons are still extant. In this middle period of his life he accompanied his patron, Sir Robert Drury, to France and Spain. In 1619 and 1620 he was in Germany, where he preached one of his noblest sermons before the exiled Queen Elizabeth of Bohemia, King James's daughter. Donne's creative years fall into three periods: from 1590 to 1601, a time of action, marked by passion and cynicism; from his marriage to his ordination in 1614, a period of anguished meditation and flattery of the great; and the period of his ministry, which includes two sonnet sequences, *La Corona* and *Holy Sonnets*, the latter containing (no. xvii) an anguished tribute to his wife, who died in 1617. Also of this period are the fine 'Hymne to God, the Father', 'To God My God, in my Sicknesse', and 'The Author's Last Going into Germany'.
▷R C Bald, *John Donne: a life* (1920); J B Leishman, *The Monarch of Wit* (1951)

DONNELLY, Ignatius
(1831–1901)
American politician and writer, born in Philadelphia. After qualifying for the Bar in 1852, he moved to Minnesota in 1856, later becoming Radical Republican Congressman (1863–9). He became identified with reform, editing the *Anti-Monopolist* and later the *Representative*, and was for several years President of the State Farmers' Alliance in Minnesota, a forerunner of the Populist party. As a prophet of reform his most enduring legacy is a horrific novel, *Caesar's Column* (1891), predicting tyranny and oppression. His powerful imagination and realism on the pitfalls ahead of reform were tarnished by his anti-semitism for which US Populism as a whole has been somewhat unjustly blamed. His *Atlantis, The Antediluvian World* (1882) was a highly popular development of the idea of a former continent drowned under the Atlantic Ocean. His *The Great Cryptogram* (1888) sought to prove Francis Bacon had

written the plays usually attributed to **Shakespeare** and had hidden ciphered messages in the plays declaring his authorship.
▷M Ridge, *Ignatius Donnelly: portrait of a politician* (1962)

DONOSO, (Yanez) José
(1928–)
Chilean novelist, born in Santiago. He attended the University of Chile and spent two years at Princeton on a Doherty Foundation Fellowship (1949–51). In his time a longshoreman, teacher, editor and journalist, with his first collection of short stories he won Chile's Municipal Prize in 1951, and in 1962 received the **William Faulkner** Foundation Prize for Chile, for his novel *Coronación* (1957, Eng trans *Coronation*, 1965). His work reflects urban life and its complications, madness, opulence and decay, and several novels have been translated into English: *El obsceno pájaro de la noche* (1970, Eng trans *The Obscene Bird of Night*, 1973); *Tres novelitas burguesas* (1973, Eng trans *Sacred Families*, 1977 (US); 1978 (UK)); and *Casa do Campo* (1978, Eng trans *A House in the Country*, 1984).
▷A C Polar, *Donoso: la destruccion de un mundo* (1975)

DOOLITTLE, Hilda, known as **H D**
(1886–1961)
American imagist poet, born in Bethlehem, Pennsylvania, the daughter of a professor of Astronomy. She was educated at Gordon School, the Friends' Central School in Philadelphia, and Bryn Mawr College (1904–6). She lived in London from 1911 and married **Richard Aldington** in 1913. After their divorce in 1937, she settled near Lake Geneva. Her many volumes of poetry include *Sea Garden* (1916), *The Walls do not Fall* (1944), *Flowering of the Rod* (1946) and *Helen in Egypt* (1961). She also wrote several novels, notably *Palimpsest* (1926), *Hedylus* (1928), *Bid Me to Live* (1960) and *Tribute to Freud* (1965).
▷*The Gift* (1982)

DORN, Ed(ward Merton)
(1929–)
American poet, born in Illinois. He studied with **Charles Olson** at Black Mountain College, but has tended to write in a more relaxed, idiomatic style that is often more reminiscent of the rhythms of prose typical of **Hemingway**. His multi-part *Gunslinger* (1968–75) is a brilliant amalgam of narrative, pure sound and theory, skating over a bewildering range of subjects with a jokey self-confidence

that is far removed from the interior 'confessional' mode that still dominated American verse at the time. A *Collected Poems* was published in 1982, bringing together the best of his other work. *What I See in the Maximus Poems* (1960) was a perceptive study of Olson's work, and there are reminiscences of Black Mountain in *Views* (1980).

▷D Wesling, *Internal Resistances: The Poetry of Ed Dorn* (1985)

DORST, Tankred
(1925–)

German dramatist, born in Sonnenberg in Thuringia. He is an experimental playwright, who has done much work for marionettes. Influenced by **Brecht** and **Kafka**, he was successful with *Die Kurve* (1960, Eng trans *The Curve*, in *The New Theatre of Europe 3*, 1968), an Absurdist drama which plays brilliantly, and *Freiheit für Clemens* (1962, Eng trans *Freedom for Clemens*, in *Postwar German Theatre*, 1967, ed G E Wellworth), about a prisoner who does not desire release.

DOS PASSOS, John Roderigo
(1896–1970)

American novelist, playwright, travel writer and poet, born in Chicago. The grandson of a Portuguese immigrant, he was educated at Choate and Harvard. In 1916 he went to Spain to study architecture but was caught up in World War I and served in the US Medical Corps. Thereafter he lived in the USA but travelled widely on journalistic assignments. In middle age he led a simple life on Cape Cod and later he and his wife moved to his father's farm at Spence's Point, Virginia, where he had spent summers as a boy. He had a precocious start as an author, publishing *One Man's Initiation* in 1917 when he was 21. The fiercely anti-war *Three Soldiers* (1921) confirmed his talent and in *Manhattan Transfer* (1925) his confidence and ambition grew, its rapid narrative transitions and collectivist approach foreshadowing the monumental *U.S.A.* trilogy: *The 42nd Parallel* (1930), *1919* (1932) and *The Big Money* (1936). A digressive, dynamic epic, it consists of a mishmash of newsreel footage, snatches of popular songs, brief but vivid sketches of public figures and prose-poetry. He also wrote three plays. An anti-capitalist, Dos Passos wrote a second trilogy, *District of Columbia* (1939–49; 1952), less radical in its criticism of the free-enterprise system. His later work continued the trend towards conservatism. *The Best Times* (1966), his last book, was a reminiscence of his boyhood and early manhood.

▷V S Carr, *Dos Passos: a life* (1984)

DOSTOYEVSKY, Fyodor Mikhailovich
(1821–81)

Russian novelist, born in Moscow, the second son of a physician's seven children. His mother died in 1837 and his father was murdered by his serfs a little over two years later. After leaving a private boarding school in Moscow he studied from 1838 to 1843 at the Military Engineering College at St Petersburg, graduating with officer's rank. His first published short story was 'Bednye Lyudi' (1846, Eng trans 'Poor Folk', 1887), which gained him immediate recognition. In 1849 he was arrested and sentenced to death for participating in the socialist 'Petrashevsky circle', but was reprieved and sent to Siberia, where he was confined in a convict prison at Omsk until 1854. From this experience grew *Zapiski iz myortvovo doma* (1861–2, Eng trans *Buried Alive; or, Ten Years of Penal Servitude in Siberia*, 1881). In 1861 he began the review *Vremya* ('Truth') with his brother Mikhail and he spent the next two years travelling abroad, which confirmed his anti-European outlook. In 1864 he published *Zapiski iz podpol'ya* (Eng trans *Notes from Underground*, 1918), whose estranged, frustrated hero prefigures the central characters of later works. At about this time he met Mlle Suslova, the model for many of his heroines, and succumbed to the gaming tables. He fell heavily into debt but was rescued by Anna Grigoryevna Smitkina, whom he married in 1867. They lived abroad for several years but he returned to Russia in 1871 as editor of *Grazhdanin*, to which he contributed his 'Author's Diary'. Like **Dickens**, Dostoyevsky was both horrified and fascinated by the Industrial Revolution, and his fiction is dark with suffering caused by poverty and appalling living conditions, crime and the exploitation of children. He is second only to **Tolstoy**. His novels—*Prestupleniye i nakazaniye* (1867, Eng trans *Crime and Punishment*, 1886), *Idiot* (1869, Eng trans *The Idiot*, 1887), *Besy* (1872, Eng trans *The Possessed*, 1913) and *Brat'ya Karamazovy* (1880, Eng trans *The Brothers Karamazov*, 1912)—were and are profoundly influential, and their impact on **Robert Louis Stevenson**'s *Dr Jekyll and Mr Hyde* (1886), among many others, is conspicuous.

▷J Frank, *Dostoevsky: I—The Seeds of Revolt, 1821–1848*; *Dostoevsky: II—The Years of Ordeal* (1976–83)

DOUGHTY, Charles Montagu
(1843–1926)

English travel writer and poet, born at Theberton Hall in Suffolk, the son of a clergyman, and educated at Caius College, Cambridge. Out of two years' travel and hardship in Arabia (1875–7) slowly grew his masterpiece of philological virtuosity, *Travels in Arabia Deserta* (1888), written in austere, didactic prose. He also wrote epic poems and plays, including *The Dawn in Britain* (1906) and *Mansoul* (1923).

▷ D Hogarth, *The Life of Charles M Doughty* (1928)

DOUGLAS, Lord Alfred Bruce
(1870–1945)

English poet, son of the 8th Marquis of Queensberry. He wrote a number of brilliant sonnets, collected in *In Excelsis* (1924) and *Sonnets and Lyrics* (1935). He is remembered for his association with **Oscar Wilde**, to which his father objected, thereby provoking Wilde to bring the ill-advised libel action which led to his own arrest and imprisonment. He wrote two books on Oscar Wilde, and *The Autobiography of Douglas* (1929).

▷ R C Cooke, *Bosie: the story of Lord Alfred Douglas* (1963)

DOUGLAS, Gavin
(1798–1843)

Scottish poet and prelate, born at Tantallon Castle, East Lothian, the third son of Archibald, 5th Earl of Angus. Educated at St Andrews and possibly Paris for the priesthood, from 1501 to 1514 he was Dean or Provost of the Collegiate Church of St Giles, Edinburgh. After the Battle of Flodden (1513), Douglas's nephew, the 6th Earl of Angus, married the widowed queen, Margaret Tudor. Through her influence Douglas obtained the bishopric of Dunkeld (1515), but was imprisoned under an old statute for receiving bulls from the pope and was not consecrated until more than a year later. On the fall of Angus in 1521, the bishop fled to England to seek the aid of Henry VIII, but died suddenly of the plague in London. His works include *The Palice of Honour*, presumably written in 1501, an allegory of the life of the virtuous man, and a magnificent translation of **Virgil**'s *Aeneid*, with prologues, finished about 1513, the first version of a Latin poet published in English. He may also have written *King Hart*, an allegory about the control exercised by the heart in human personality and behaviour.

DOUGLAS, George *see* BROWN, George Douglas

DOUGLAS, Keith Castellain
(1920–44)

English poet, perhaps the only one from the World War II era to approach the critical eminence of **Rupert Brooke** or **Wilfred Owen** from that of World War I. Born in Kent, he began publishing verse in magazines during his teens, but it was the encouragement of his tutor **Edmund Blunden** at Merton College, Oxford, that helped shape his distinctively clear-sighted approach. In 1943, Blunden arranged for the publication of a slim *Selected Poems*, using verses sent back from the Western Desert, where Douglas was serving with a tank regiment; it was the only book Douglas saw published in his lifetime. On 6 June 1944, following the D-Day landings in Normandy, he was killed by a shell fragment. It was his faintly surreal and bluntly un-optimistic memoir of the fighting in the Western Desert, *Alamein to Zem Zem* (1946), that began to establish a posthumous reputation which only became secure two decades after his death when **Ted Hughes**, an admirer, introduced an important selection. The *Complete Poems* appeared in 1979, edited by Desmond Graham.

DOUGLAS, Lloyd C(assel)
(1877–1951)

American Congregationalist minister, born in Indiana, who wrote world-wide bestsellers of immense readability and almost, according to every serious literary critic, incredible psychological bathos. He did not turn to fiction until he was past 50, when he wrote *Magnificent Obsession* (1929), about a Christian eye-surgeon, later immortalized in Douglas Sirk's deliberately high kitsch movie, starring Rock Hudson. Many have agreed with the famous judgement of an *Atlantic Review* critic, who spoke of his 'spiritual fascism'; others see him as 'harmless', and put him in the tradition of **Harold Bell Wright**. *The Robe* (1942) and *The Big Fisherman* (1948) are historical novels set in scriptural times; both were phenomenally successful.

DOUGLAS, (George) Norman
(1868–1952)

Scottish novelist and essayist, born in Tilquhillie, Deeside. His mother was part-German and he was educated at Uppingham School and at Karlsruhe, and joined the Foreign Office in 1894. He served in St Petersburg before settling in Capri in 1896, where his circle embraced **Compton Mackenzie**, **Ouida** and **D H Lawrence**. His first book, *Unprofessional Tales* (1901), was co-authored with his wife and published under the pseudonym 'Normyx', but *Siren Land* (1911) first attracted critical attention. An account of his travels in southern Italy, it is an exotic collage of anecdote, philosophy and myth. *Old Calabria* (1915) garnished his reputation and is a minor classic. Other travel books are *Fountains in the Sun* (1912), *Alone* (1921) and *Together* (1923). Of his novels, the most famous is *South Wind* (1917). Set in Nepenthe (Capri) among a floating population of expatriates, it is an unapologetic celebration of hedonism to which its author was a happy convert. *Looking Back* (1933) is an unusual autobiography, in which he recalls his life and his friends by taking up their calling cards and describing them one by one, at length or tersely, depending on his mood.

▷ R D Lindeman, *Norman Douglas* (1965)

DOUGLAS-HOME, William
(1912–92)

Scottish playwright, born in Edinburgh, and educated at Eton and Oxford. He was the author of a number of plays, principally light-hearted comedies, the best-known of which are *Now Barabbas* (1947), *The Chiltern Hundreds* (1947), *The Thistle and the Rose* (1949) and *The Reluctant Debutante* (1955).

▷ *Half-Term Report: an autobiography* (1954); *Mr. Home, pronounced Hume* (1979)

DOUGLASS, Frederick
(1817–95)

American writer, born into slavery in Maryland. He escaped to Massachusetts in 1838, where he was employed as a lecturer by anti-slavery societies, and wrote his most famous book, the autobiographical *Narrative of the Life of Frederick Douglass* (1845). He travelled to England and Ireland, but returned to America to buy his freedom, thus banishing his fear of recapture, and set up a campaigning anti-slavery newspaper, *North Star*. He was actively involved in political life, and held a number of appointments after the Civil War. In addition to a revised version of his *Narrative* (1892), he wrote two more autobiographical books, *My Bondage and My Freedom* (1855) and *The Life and Times of Frederick Douglass* (1881).

DOVE, Rita Francis
(1952–)

American poet, born in Akron, Ohio. She is Professor of English at the University of Virginia. Her first book was *Ten Poems* (1977). *The Yellow House On The Corner* (1980) contained a sequence of poems told from the point of view of negro slaves, and historical figures have recurred throughout her work. She was awarded the Pulitzer Prize for Poetry in 1987 for *Thomas and Beulah* (1986), in which she re-created the lives of her grandparents from courtship to death. Other collections include *Museum* (1983), *The Other Side of the House* (1988) and *Grace Notes* (1989). *Fifth Sunday* (1985) is a collection of short stories.

DOWLING, Basil Cairns
(1910–)

New Zealand poet, born in Southbridge, Christchurch, whose verse shows a lyricism and a romantic response to his natural surroundings. His early work was published by **Allen Curnow**'s Caxton Press in *A Day's Journey* (1941), *Signs and Wonders* (1944) and *Canterbury and Other Poems* (1949), evoking the pastoral qualities of his own South Island. After a break, *Hatherley, Recollective Lyrics* was published in 1968, followed by *A Little Gallery of Characters* (1971), *Bedlam* (1972) and *The Unreturning Native* (1973).

DOWSON, Ernest Christopher
(1867–1900)

English poet. Born in London and brought up largely in France, he studied at Oxford, then helped his fairly unbusinesslike father in managing the unwelcome inheritance of a dry dock in Limehouse, but spent more time in literary activity. His friends at the time included **Lionel Johnson**, **Arthur Symons**, **Oscar Wilde** and **Yeats**. From 1894 writing became his livelihood. His *Verses* appeared in 1896 and *Decorations* in 1899; he also published stories, a verse play and translations, and collaborated on two novels, but despite all this work he was usually short of money. He was for years in love with the young daughter of a Polish restaurateur, but she turned him down and married the waiter. From 1895 Dowson lived mostly in France, but returned to London in 1899 and died of tuberculosis at the age of 32. His poems, on which the influence of **Verlaine** and the 'decadents' is marked, are notable for finely judged vowel sounds and metre. The two best known, 'Vitae summa brevis' (1896) and 'Cynara' (1891), have contributed several stock phrases to English: 'days of wine and roses', 'gone with the wind' and 'I have been faithful to thee, Cynara! in my fashion'.

▷ *Letters* (1967, D Flower and H Maas eds); M Longaker, *Ernest Dowson* (1944, rev edn 1968)

DOYLE, Sir Arthur Conan
(1859–1930)

Scottish writer of detective stories and historical romances, nephew of the caricaturist Richard Doyle. Born of Irish parentage in Edinburgh, he was educated at Stonyhurst and in Germany, and studied medicine at Edinburgh. Initial poverty as a young practitioner in Southsea and as an oculist in London coaxed him into authorship. His debut was a story in *Chambers Journal* (1879), and his first book introduced that prototype of the modern detective in fiction, the super-observant, deductive Sherlock Holmes, his good-natured doctor friend Dr John Watson, and the whole apparatus of detection mythology associated with Baker Street. *The Adventures of Sherlock Holmes* were serialized in the *Strand Magazine* (1891–3). They were so popular that when Conan Doyle, tired of his popular creation, tried to kill off his hero on a cliff, he was compelled in 1903 to revive him. The serials were published as books with the titles *The Sign of Four* (1890), *The Hound of the Baskervilles* (1902), etc. Conan Doyle, however, set greater stock by his historical romances, *Micah Clarke* (1887), *The White Company* (1890), *Brigadier Gerard* (1896) and *Sir Nigel* (1906), which have more literary merit, and are underrated. A keen boxer himself, *Rodney Stone* (1896) is one of his best novels. *The Lost World* (1912) and *The Poison Belt* (1913) are essays into the pseudo-scientifically fantastic. He served as a physician in the 2nd Boer War (1899–1902), and his pamphlet, *The War in South Africa* (1902), correcting enemy propaganda and justifying Britain's action, earned him a knighthood (1902). He used his detective powers to some effect outside fiction in attempting to show that the criminal cases of the Parsee Birmingham lawyer, Edaljee (1903), and alleged murderer Oscar Slater (1909) were instances of mistaken identity. He also wrote on spiritualism, to which he became a convert in later life.

▷H Pearson, *Conan Doyle: His Life and Art* (1943); O D Edwards, *The Quest for Sherlock Holmes* (1982)

DOYLE, Charles
(1928–)

New Zealand poet, primarily of the city and the suburbs, but responsive to natural surroundings as in his 'Starlings and History'. *A Splinter of Glass* (1956) was followed by *The Night Shift: Poems on Aspects of Love* (1957) in which he was joined by **James Keir Baxter**, **Colin Johnson** and **Kendrick Smithyman**. Other work was collected in *Distances* (1963, poems of exile), *Messages for Herod* (1965) and *A Sense of Place: Poems* (1965). He edited an important anthology, *Recent Poetry in New Zealand* (1965), which presented 'work in progress' of 13 of his contemporaries including Baxter, Johnson and the newcomer **C K Stead**. He has also written criticism and studies of **R A K Mason** (1970) and James Keir Baxter (1976).

DOYLE, Sir Francis Hastings Charles, 2nd Bart
(1810–88)

English poet, born in Nunappleton near Tadcaster. Educated at Eton and Christ Church, Oxford, he was called to the Bar, held offices in the customs, and from 1867 to 1877 was Professor of Poetry at Oxford in succession to **Matthew Arnold**. He published his two series of Oxford lectures in 1869 and 1877. His verse collections of 1834 (enlarged 1840) and 1866, are unmemorable save for

such ballads of British military fortitude as 'The Loss of the *Birkenhead*' and 'The Private of the Buffs'.

▷ *Reminiscences and Opinions* (1886)

DOYLE, Roddy
(1958–)

Irish novelist, born in Dublin. For 14 years he worked as a teacher (of geography and English) in a community school in Kilbarrack, a deprived area in north Dublin—the 'Barrytown' of his novels. An early novel, *Your Granny's a Hunger Striker* (1982), took an irreverent approach to the issue of 'ghetto politics'. *The Commitments* (1988), *The Snapper* (1990) and *The Van* (1991) spoke for communities denied a media voice, their comic style acting as a vehicle for Doyle's clear understanding of the plight of the deprived. The Booker Prize-winning *Paddy Clarke Ha Ha Ha* (1993), narrated through the sense and senses of a 10-year-old boy, similarly exhibits the inherent tragedy that underlines all comedy. A 'failed dramatist' in his own estimation, Doyle has inherited by popular acclaim the status of **O'Casey** and **Brendan Behan** in his native city.

DRABBLE, Margaret
(1939–)

English novelist, born in Sheffield. Her elder sister is the novelist **A S Byatt**. The family was bookish; her father was a barrister, then a circuit judge, and, in retirement, a novelist. Her mother was an English teacher. She was educated at the Mount School, York (the Quaker boarding school where her mother taught), and Newnham College, Cambridge. She married the actor Clive Swift, acted for a short time herself, then turned to writing. Divorced from her first husband in 1972 (after having three children), she married the biographer **Michael Holroyd** in 1982. Often mirroring her own life, her novels concentrate on the concerns of intelligent, often frustrated middle-class women. *A Summer Bird-Cage* (1963), *The Garrick Year* (1964), *The Millstone* (1965), *Jersualem the Golden* (1967), *The Needle's Eye* (1972), *The Ice Age* (1977), *The Middle Ground* (1980) and the trilogy comprising *The Radiant Way* (1987), *A Natural Curiosity* (1989) and *The Gates of Ivory* (1991) are among her titles. She was the editor of the 5th edition of the *Oxford Companion to English Literature*, and has written a biography of **Arnold Bennett** (1974).

▷V G Myer, *Margaret Drabble: Puritanism and Permissiveness* (1974)

DRACHMANN, Holger Henrik Herholdt
(1846–1908)

Danish writer and artist, born in Copenhagen of a German family. A visit to London inspired him to revolutionary solidarity with the working class, particularly the exiled Communards, but his early poetry is mainly lyrical and subjective. Later volumes such as *Sange ved havet* (1877, 'Seaside Verses') and *Ranker og roser* (1879, 'Vines and Roses') are less conventional in form and feeling and anticipate important elements of Danish modernism. His novel *Derovre fra graensen* (1877, 'Over the Border') is nationalistic and somewhat conventional, anticipating **Jonas Lie**'s stories of respectable middle-class families. Drachmann was also an accomplished sea painter.

▷ J Ursin, *Holger Drachmann. Liv og vaerker* (1953)

DRAGÚN, Osvaldo
(1929–)

Argentinian playwright, considered by many to be the best of his generation. With no formal training, Dragún helped develop the 'New Realism' School of Argentine plays. Influenced by **Brecht**, **O'Neill** and **Valle-Inclán**, his works have won world-wide praise. Using a combination of political activism, humour, the absurd, and fantasy, his plays have progressed from portrayals of urban exploitation (*Historias para ser contadas*, 1956, 'Stories to be Told', *El Jardin del infierno*, 1959, 'Garden of Hell') to the sentimental (the sainete *Amoretta*, 'Little Love') and sublime (*Heroica de Buenos Aires*, 1966, 'Epic of Buenos Aires'). A motive force behind the Teatro Abierto festival in Buenos Aires, which stages 21 plays in 7 days, he has also lived and worked in Cuba (1961–3) and Spain (1967–72).

DRAKE-BROCKMAN, Henrietta
(1901–68)

Australian novelist and playwright, born in Perth, whose travels in the outback influenced much of her writing. Her novels, *Blue North* (1934) and *Sheba Lane* (1936), are set around the pearling town of Broome in the state's far north-west, and *The Wicked and the Fair* (1957) is based on the wreck of the Dutch ship *Batavia* on that coast in 1629. A collection of short stories, *Sydney or the Bush*, was published in 1948. Her first play was *The Man from the Bush* (1934) and four more were collected as *Men Without Wives, and Other Plays* (1955). The impact of Australia's harsh environment on character, and the theme of sacrifice, runs through much of her work, which often has a heavily romantic flavour.

DRAYTON, Michael
(1563–1631)

English poet, born in Hartshill near Atherstone, Warwickshire. He became a page in a wealthy household and spent the rest of his life in the households of patrons. His earliest work was *The Harmony of the Church* (1591), a metrical rendering of scriptural passages, which gave offence to the authorities, and was condemned to be destroyed. In 1593 he published a volume of eclogues, *Idea, the Shepherd's Garland*, which afterwards underwent considerable revision, and the first of his 'historical legends' in verse, *Piers Gaveston*. His first important poem, *Mortimeriados* (1596), recast in 1603 as *The Barons' Wars*, has some fine passages. *England's Heroical Epistles* (1597) has more polish and is more even than many of Drayton's other works. *Poems, Lyric and Pastoral* (c.1606) contains some of his most familiar poems, including the *Ballad of Agincourt* and *Fair Stood the Wind for France*. The first 18 'songs' or books of Drayton's greatest work, *Polyolbion*, were published in 1613, with annotation by John Selden, and the complete poem, the product of vast learning and the labour of years, appeared in 1622. In it he aimed at giving 'a chorographical description of all the tracts, rivers, mountains, forests, and other parts of Great Britain'. In 1619 he collected in one volume all the poems (except *Polyolbion*) which he wished to preserve. In 1627 he published a new volume of miscellaneous poems, among them the whimsical and delightful *Nymphisdia, the Court of Fairy*, a triumph of ingenious fancy. His last work, *The Muses' Elysium* (1630), contains some pastoral poems of finished elegance. His only surviving play is *The First Part of Sir John Oldcastle* (1600). He was buried in Westminster Abbey.

▷ J A Berthelot, *Michael Drayton* (1967)

DRDA, Jan
(1915–70)

Czech dramatist and novelist, born in Pribram. He began as a fine storyteller, but degenerated into an official communist writer, so that his reputation amongst many people depended entirely on his earliest work, and on a collection of stories he wrote about resistance to the Nazis—but published before the Stalinist takeover.

DREISER, Theodore Herman Albert
(1871–1945)

American novelist, born in Terre Haute, Indiana. The eleventh and penultimate child of a poor Catholic German immigrant father, he was brought up on the breadline and left home at 15 for Chicago. He did odd jobs before becoming a highly successful journalist and wrote *Sister Carrie* (1900), a powerful and frank treatment of a young working girl's climb towards worldly success. The publisher, fearful of accusations of obscenity, was diffident in its promotion and it flopped commercially. Dreiser next wrote *Jennie Gerhardt* (1911) on a similar theme, which established him as a novelist. There followed the first parts of a trilogy about Frank Cowperwood, a power-hungry business tycoon: *The Financier* (1912), *The Titan* (1914) and *The Stoic* (published posthumously in 1947). *The Genius* was published in 1915 and 10 years later came *An American Tragedy* (1925), based on a real-life murder case, which, despite reservations about its author's leaden prose, has survived as a classic. His best works have been admired by **Saul Bellow** and other notable writers.

▷R Lingeman, *Dreiser: At the Gates of the City, 1871–1907* (1986), and subsequent volumes

DREWE, Robert
(1943–)

Australian journalist and novelist, born in Melbourne. Sometime literary editor of the national newspaper, the *Australian*, he has twice won the Walkley Award for journalism. His first novel, *The Savage Crows* (1976), concerned George Robinson, the early 19th-century Protector of the Aborigines. Another novel followed and then two collections of short stories, *The Body Surfers* (1983) and *The Bay of Contented Men* (1989), which portray and parody the hedonistic Australian beach culture.

DREZEN, Youenn
(1899–)

Breton poet, dramatist, translator and novelist, whose books have become classics in their minority language; he began as a journalist. He has translated Greek tragedies and English and Spanish classics into Breton. *Chant à l'Ouest* is an epic poem about the Celts; however, his acknowledged masterpiece, written before he devoted himself to the theatre, is the novel *Notre-Dame des Carmélites* (1941). His chief aim has been to elevate Breton literature.

DRIEU LA ROCHELLE, Pierre
(1893–1945)

French novelist and political essayist, whose literary reputation has only recovered very slowly from his association with fascism and from his advocacy of collaboration during the Vichy period. Drieu fought with the French army during World War I—an experience recounted in *La comédie de Charleroi* (1934)—and became convinced that modern France was irretrievably decadent. This led him to flirt with Surréalisme and then with Third Period Communism before he discovered his intellectual niche on the far right.

His novel *Gilles* (1939) gives intermittent hints of his political convictions and these were not fully revealed or understood until his *Journal secret* was posthumously published in 1961. Having declared himself in support of collaborationism, Drieu was appointed editor of an important journal of literature and ideas, the *Nouvelle Revue Française*, a post he held until 1943. Following the Liberation, he took his own life, and his name was the target of dismissive obloquy until the early sixties when it became possible to see beyond his wartime derelictions and understand the complexities of his ideas and seriousness of his intellectual wanderings.

▷R Soucy, *Fascist Intellectual* (1979)

DRINKWATER, John
(1882–1937)

English poet, dramatist, and critic, born in Leytonstone. He was an insurance clerk who had already published several volumes of poems when he achieved an immediate theatrical success with his play *Abraham Lincoln* (1918), which he followed with *Mary Stuart*, *Oliver Cromwell* (both published in 1921), *Robert E. Lee* (1923) and a comedy, *Bird in Hand* (1927). His first volume of poems appeared in 1903, and he also wrote critical studies of **William Morris**, **Algernon Charles Swinburne** and **Byron**, and of lyric poetry. He was one of the founders of the Pilgrim Players and became manager of the Birmingham Repertory Theatre. He published two volumes of an unfinished autobiography, *Inheritance* (1931) and *Discovery* (1932).

▷G Matthews, *John Drinkwater: a lecture* (1925)

DRIVER, C(harles) J(onathan)
(1939–)

South African-born British novelist, he was educated at the University of Cape Town and later at Trinity College, Oxford, having had his South African passport revoked. His political activity in the Cape (he served as President of the desegregationist National Union of South African Students in 1963–4) forms the background to his first novel, *Elegy for a Revolutionary* (1969), whose themes are made more subtle and universal in the much stronger *Send War in Our Time, O Lord* (1970), a significant exploration of the white liberal dilemma. His later works, *Death of Fathers* (1972) and *A Messiah of the Last Days* (1974), maintain an interest in political activity within confined groups (an English public school, an anarchist collective); perhaps because he *has* worked as a teacher, the former is more convincingly portrayed. Driver has also published short fiction and some verse, including *I Live Here Now* (1979), which further documents his reactions to English society.

DRIZIC, Marin
(1520–67)

Dalmatian (Ragusan) dramatist, born in Ragusa (Dubrovnik). His comedies, such as *Dundo Maroje* (1550), about a miser, are similar in type to those of **Plautus**, were immensely popular in their own time, and have been successfully played since. He was one of the most influential of all those who played a part in the Serbo–Croatian literature which developed alongside that of Renaissance Italy.

DROST, Aarnout
(1810–34)

Dutch novelist and theologian, born in Amsterdam. The romantic historical novel for which he is best known is *Hermingard van de Eikenterpen* (1832). His short stories were collected in *Schetsen en verhalen* (1835–6).

DROSTE-HÜLSHOFF, Annette Elisabeth, Baroness von
(1797–1848)

German poet, born in Westphalia. Commonly regarded as Germany's greatest woman writer, she led a retired life and from 1818 to 1820 wrote intense devotional verses, eventually published as *Geistliche Jahre* in 1851. She wrote in a more restrained and classical style than that of most of her contemporaries, especially in her ballads and lyrics, though her long narrative poems, notably *Das Hospiz auf dem Grossen Sankt Bernard* (1838, 'The Hospice on the Great Saint Bernard') and *Die Schlacht im Loener Bruch* ('The Battle in the Loener Marsh'), were influenced by **Byron**. She also wrote a novella, *Die Judenbuche* (1841, 'The Jew's Beech-tree').
▷C Heselhaus, *Annette von Droste-Hülshoff. Werk und Lebel* (1971)

DROZ, Antoine Gustave
(1832–95)

French novelist, born in Paris. He was grandson of Jean Pierre Droz (1746–1823), an engraver of medals. He had devoted himself to art until he had his first and greatest success with *Monsieur, Madame, et Bébé* (1866, Eng trans *Papa, Mamma and Baby*, 1887). Later came *Entre nous* (1867, 'Between Ourselves'), *Les Étangs* (1876, 'The Ponds'), *L'Enfant* (1885, 'The Child'), and others.

DRUMMOND, William, of Hawthornden
(1585–1649)

Scottish poet, born in Hawthornden, near Roslin, Midlothian, the son of a courtier to King James VI and I. He was educated at the High School of Edinburgh, graduated MA at Edinburgh in 1605, studied law at Bourges and Paris, and on his father's death in 1610 became Laird of Hawthornden. Devoting his life to poetry and mechanical experiments, he was on the point of marrying Euphemia Cunningham of Barns when she died on the eve of their wedding (1615). He took a mistress, by whom he had three children, and married Elizabeth Logan of Restalrig in 1630. He had to subscribe to the National Covenant of 1638 but witnessed its triumph with a sinking heart that not even the most sarcastic verses could relieve. His death was hastened by grief for Charles I's execution. Drummond enjoyed the friendship of **Ben Jonson** who paid him a memorable visit in 1618–19, and Drummond's *Notes* of their talk form a charming chapter of literary history. His chief works are the pastoral lament *Tears on the Death of Moeliades* (ie Prince Henry, 1613); *Poems, Amorous, Funereall, Divine, Pastorall in Sonnets, Songs, Sextains, Madrigals* (1614); *Forth Feasting* (1617); and *Flowers of Sion* (1623). In prose he wrote *A Cypress Grove* (1630) and a *History of the Five Jameses*. He also wrote a *History of Scotland 1423–1524*, posthumously published in 1655.
▷F R Fogle, *A Critical Study of William Drummond of Hawthornden* (1952)

DRUMMOND DE ANDRADE *see* ANDRADE, DRUMMOND DE

DRUON, Maurice, pseud of Maurice Kessel
(1918–)

French novelist, whose reputation lies somewhat uneasily between the popular and the sub-critical. He has been in the Académie française since 1966. *Les Grandes familles* (1948–51, Eng trans *The Curtain Falls*, 1959), on the theme of a declining family, won the Prix **Goncourt**. After this he embarked on a series of historical novels, most of which have been translated; these are worthy popular literature on the grand scale, but have attracted little serious critical attention.

DRURY, Allen Stuart
(1918–)

Patriotic American novelist and journalist, born in Houston, Texas. Drury worked as Washington correspondent for the *New York Times* and *Readers Digest* before publishing his melodramatic novel *Advise and Consent* (1959), which was based on his experience of political intrigue. It won a Pulitzer Prize in 1960 and was made into a film, directed by Otto Preminger (1962). In 1971 he published a photographic encomium to the Nixon administration, calling the new president a 'decent man' surrounded by equally 'decent and worthy men'.

DRUTEN, John van
(1901–57)

English-born American playwright, born in London. He became famous with the production of his play *Young Woodley* in 1928, which was first produced in the USA after falling foul of the British censor. After several years and considerable success, he was granted American citizenship in 1944. *The Voice of the Turtle*, his most successful play with an American setting, was produced in 1943 and his adaptation of sketches by **Christopher Isherwood**, *I Am A Camera*, in 1951.
▷ *The Way to the Present* (1938).

DRYDEN, John
(1631–1700)

English poet, born at the vicarage of Aldwinkle All Saints, Northamptonshire, where his maternal grandfather was rector. He was educated at Westminster School under Richard Busby and at Trinity College, Cambridge, where he stayed until 1657. Going up to London in that year he attached himself to his cousin Sir Gilbert Pickering, Cromwell's chamberlain, in the hope of employment, which he might well have expected since on both sides his people were parliamentarians. His *Heroic Stanzas*, in quatrains, on the death of Cromwell (1658), was soon followed by his *Astrea Redux* (1660), celebrating the Restoration in heroic couplets, which was to be his staple measure even in the plays which soon poured from his pen for the amusement of 'a venal court'. The first of these 'heroic' verse plays to take the public taste was *The Indian Emperor* (1665), dealing with the conquest of Mexico by Cortes and his love for the emperor's daughter, and the last was *Aurungzebe* (1676). In 1663 he married Lady Elizabeth Howard, eldest daughter of the Earl of Berkshire. In 1667 he published *Annus Mirabilis, The Year of Wonders, 1666*, which established his reputation, and he was appointed poet laureate in 1668 following Sir **William D'Avenant**, and historiographer royal in 1670. Meanwhile he was turning out a series of comedies for the stage, including *The Rival Ladies* (1664, in rhymed verse), and culminating with *Marriage-à-la-Mode* (1673). He used blank verse for *All for Love* (1678), his best play and not unworthy to be placed beside **Shakespeare**'s *Antony and Cleopatra*. His adaptation of another of Shakespeare's plays, *Troilus and Cressida*, the following year, was by comparison a failure. Adaptation was a means of keeping up with the demands of the theatre on his service; he had already adapted *The Tempest* in 1670; **Milton**'s *Paradise Lost* (as *The State of Innocence*,

1677); and **Thomas Corneille**'s *The Mock Astrologer* (1668). He wrote a series of important critical essays as prefaces to his plays, including his charming *Essay of Dramatic Poesy* (1668), and the *Defence of the Epilogue* (to that popular play *The Conquest of Granada*, 1670). In 1680 he began a series of satirical and didactic poems, starting with the most famous, *Absalom and Achitophel* (1681), and followed by *The Medal* (1682) and *MacFlecknoe* (1684), written some years before, which did much to turn the tide against the Whigs. To this era also belong the didactic poem *Religico Laici* (1682), which argues the case for Anglicanism, and the much finer *The Hind and the Panther*, marking his conversion to Rome in 1685. A place in the Customs (1683) was his reward for his political labours. At the Revolution of 1688 he lost the poet laureateship and took to translation as a means of living. Of these his fine translation of **Virgil** was most profitable, that of **Juvenal** and **Persius** was prefaced by a *Discourse Concerning the Origin and Progress of Satire*, which had all his old ease and urbanity. His final work, published in 1699, was *Fables, Ancient and Modern* which, with its paraphrases of **Chaucer**, **Ovid** and **Boccaccio**, has delighted generations of readers. These works are only the most outstanding of a lifetime's industry. Dryden is transitional between the metaphysical poets of the school of **John Donne** and the neo-classic reaction which he did so much to create.
▷ C Ward, *A Life of John Dryden* (1961); G Wasermann, *John Dryden* (1964)

dsh *see* HOUEDARD, Dom Sylvester

DU BARTAS, Guilliaume de Salluste
(1544–90)

French poet from Gascony, effusive and thus eccentric-seeming to his contemporaries. Feeling divinely inspired (he has been compared to **Claudel**), he told the story of creation in *La Semaine* (1578), an enormously learned poem studded with marvellous images but as a whole quite unreadable. This was put into a crabbed, metaphysical English by **Joshua Sylvester**, who received nothing but obscurity for his immense pains. Yet du Bartas, who was famous throughout Europe in his times, is a rewarding poet in patches, 'a barbarous curiosity ... [his] is the only verse which ... provides anything approaching a counterpart to the prose of Rabelais'.

DUBILLARD, Roland
(1923–)

French story writer and playwright (and actor under the name of Grégoire), who writes Absurdist plays in a deceptively realistic, conventional style (not unlike the *One-Way Pendulum* of **N F Simpson**; but sometimes his inconsequential dialogue recalls that of **Pinter**). His best-known play is *Le Maison d'os* (1962, 'The House of Bones'), an allegory about death. The title of his essay *Méditation sur la difficulté d'être en bronze* (1972, 'Meditation on the Difficulty of Being in Bronze'), is characteristic.

▷J Guichardnaud, *Modern French Theatre* (1967)

DUBOIS, W(illiam) E(dward) B(urghardt)
(1868–1963)

American Black writer and editor, born in Great Barrington, Massachusetts. He studied at Fisk University, Tennessee, and at Harvard, where his doctoral thesis was on the suppression of the African slave trade. He was Professor of Economics and History at Atlanta University (1897–1910). He was co-founder of the National Association for the Advancement of Coloured People (1909), and edited its magazine, *Crisis* (1910–34), but later disassociated himself from the Association, finding it too conservative. He wrote a number of important works on slavery and the colour problem, including *The Souls of Black Folk* (1903), *John Brown* (1909), *The Negro* (1915), *Black Reconstruction* (1935) and *Colour and Democracy* (1945). He also wrote novels, including *The Dark Princess* (1928) and *Worlds of Color* (1961). A passionate advocate of radical Black action and an early supporter of the suffragette movement—which he tried to link with the struggle for black rights—he joined the Communist Party in 1961, and moved to Ghana at the age of 91, where he became a naturalized citizen just before he died.

▷*Autobiography* (1968)

DU CAMP, Maxime
(1822–94)

French poet, novelist and journalist, born in Paris. He travelled in the East, including a trip to the Near East with **Flaubert**. He wrote books on Paris and was a founder of the *Revue de Paris* (1851). His other writings include *Souvenirs littéraires* (1882–3, 'Literary Recollections'), and several novels.

DUCASSE, Isidore Lucien, pseud Comte de Lautréamont
(1846–70)

French writer of fantasy—a major influence on the Surrealist movement. Born in Montevideo, Uruguay, the son of a consular officer, he returned to France for his education, studying at both Pau and Tarbes. In 1868, the first instalment of his sensational masterpiece

Les Chants de Maldoror was published under a pseudonym borrowed from the title of a novel by **Eugène Sue**; it seems, however, that the printer refused to distribute the pamphlets, either because he was shocked by their contents or because he had not been paid. *Les Chants de Maldoror* first appeared in Belgium and Switzerland, where the author believed he would find a more sympathetic audience for his 'poetry of revolt'. Violent and perverse in the extreme, *Les Chants de Maldoror* transcends the human realm altogether, combining systematic blasphemy and sexual obscenity with a lyrical and hallucinatory cast of language that exercised an enormous influence on later writers like **André Breton** and **Alfred Jarry**. Shortly before his premature death, Ducasse published a volume of prose *Poèmes* (1870, under his own name) which, though less well known, confirm his wayward genius.

▷P Zweig, *Lautréamont: The Violent Narcissus* (1972)

DUCIĆ, Jovan
(1871–1943)

Serbian poet and critic, born in Trebijne. He left for the USA in 1941, and died in Gary, Indiana. He was always much influenced by the example of the French Parnassian and Symbolist poets whom he met as a young man in Paris. *Plave legende* (1908, 'Blue Legends') was an immensely popular collection of exquisite if somewhat artificial prose poems. He had initially followed in the footsteps of **Vojislav Ilić**, a lesser poet but a potent influence; he was the leading poet in the *Moderna* movement in Serbian poetry. He never really gave up his 'decadent' view of 'art for art's sake', and has been much criticized for it; but he remains the Serbian decadent poet par excellence, and not least for his fine technique.

DUCIS, Jean François
(1733–1816)

French poet and playwright, born in Versailles. His own tragedies are regarded as mediocre and he is best known for his adaptations of **Shakespeare** for the French stage, which he completed from earlier French versions, since he knew no English. They did help popularize Shakespeare in France, despite wild inaccuracies, and such liberties as allowing Othello to discover his mistake and spare Desdemona.

▷C Kueln, *Verben Ducis in seinen Bezegung zu Shakespeare* (1875)

DUCK, Stephen
(1705–56)

English ploughman-poet and scholar, born in Charlton in Wiltshire of humble parents. A self-educated farm-labourer, his verses came to the attention of Queen Caroline, who awarded him a pension and made him a Yeoman of the Guard in 1733. He published *Poems on Several Occasions* in 1736. He took holy orders in 1746 and was made rector of Byfleet in 1752, but committed suicide by drowning.

▷ R Davis, *Stephen Duck, the Thresher Poet* (1926)

DUCKWORTH, Marilyn Rose
(1935–)

New Zealand novelist, born in Otahuhu, Auckland, sister of **Fleur Adcock**. She was an early protégée of Hutchinson's pioneering 'New Authors' imprint with *A Gap in the Spectrum* (1959, 1985). Three others followed: *The Matchbox House* (1960), *A Barbarous Tongue* (1963) and *Over the Fence is Out* (1969). There was then a 15-year break before *Disorderly Conduct* (1984), with a background of the New Zealand rugby riots of 1981, and four more novels: *Married Alive* (1985), *Rest for the Wicked* (1986), *Pulling Faces* (1987) and *A Message from Harpo* (1989). Her themes are predominantly feminist, focusing on the manner in which her heroines cope with challenge.

DUDEK, Louis
(1918–)

Leading Canadian poet, born in Montreal, who has been both an academic and a publisher (Contact Press, DC Books). He has been called 'Canada's most important—that is to say consequential—modern voice'. At first deeply influenced by the Imagist movement and its poets (in particular **Pound**), he later made one of the most notable efforts to liberate Canadian poetry from its British influences. Most celebrated, after his earlier lyric poetry, are his long poems, such as *En Mexico* (1958), in which 'Pound is both hero and villain'. His *Collected Poetry* appeared in 1971; *Infinite Worlds* (1988) is the 'quasi-definitive' edition, edited by Robin Blaser.

▷ F Davey, *Louis Dudek and Raymond Souster* (1980)

DUDINTSEV, Vladimir
(1918–)

Russian novelist, born in Kupyansk, in the province of Kharkov. He is famous for only one book: *Ne khlebom yedinym* (1956, Eng trans *Not By Bread Alone*, 1957), the story of an inventor whose liveliness is stultified by bureaucrats and careerists. It became well known when subjected to attack by Soviet culture-clerks; it is not well written, but is full of energy.

DUFFY, Carol Ann
(1955–)

Scottish poet, born in Glasgow, considered one of the leading woman poets of her generation. It has been said of her that she writes love-poems 'as if she were the first one to do so'. Much influenced by the dramatic monologues of **Robert Browning**, but also—though not too obviously—by **Laura Riding**, she is striking in her use of a kind of toughened and good-natured whimsicality in her verse. Her collections include *Standing Female Nude* (1985) and *The Other Country* (1990). In 1993 she won the Whitbread Award for poetry for her collection *Mean Time*.

▷ *Bête Noir*, 6 (1989)

DUFFY, Maureen Patricia
(1933–)

English novelist, poet and dramatist, born in Worthing, Sussex. After attending university in London and five years' employment as a schoolteacher, she published her first novel in 1962, *That's How It Was*, which deals with the relationship between a mother and her illegitimate daughter. One of her most notable novels, *The Microcosm* (1966), looks at lesbian life through the eyes of three women. She has written novels set in the past, the present day, and the future, blending realism and fantasy, her subjects ranging from sexual and social themes to animal rights and the moral issues resulting from scientific progress. Her characters are often at the margins of society, hungry for affection. Her critical work includes *The Erotic World of Faery* (1972), a **Freud**ian analysis of English literature, and *The Passionate Shepherdess: Aphra Behn 1640–1689* (1977), an excellent study.

▷ J Rule, *Lesbian Images* (1975)

DU FRESNE, Yvonne
(1929–)

New Zealand novelist and short-story writer, born in Takaka of Danish Huguenot descent, the influence of which comes through in her novels, *The Book of Ester* (1982), in which the central character searches for her roots, and *Frédérique* (1987). Her short stories, in *Farvel* (1980) and *The Growing of Astrid Westergaard* (1985) show a Danish girl growing up in a New Zealand farming community, reliving the past history of her ancestors in her play.

DUGAN, Alan
(1923–)

American poet, born in Brooklyn, New York City. He was educated at Queen's College in New York, and served in World War II. In 1971 he became staff member for poetry at the Fine Arts Work Center in Provincetown, Massachusetts. His first book of poems was privately printed, and was followed by *Poems* (1961), which won him the Pulitzer Prize for Poetry in 1962. Subsequent works include *Poems 2* (1963), *Sequence* (1976), *Poems 6* (1989), as well as a *Collected Poems* (1969) and *New and Collected Poems* (1983). His terse, rather bleak poems are alleviated by an understated humour, and are directly rooted in experience.

DUGGAN, Alfred
(1903–64)

English historical novelist and biographer, writing for young people. Born in Buenos Aires, Argentina, he published *Knight With Armour*, his first novel, in 1950. While continuing to write fiction, he extended his range to biography in such books as *Thomas Beckett of Canterbury* (1952) and *Julius Caesar: A Great Life* (1955), both of which were praised for the clarity with which they presented social, moral and political issues. Duggan also wrote a series of *Look at ...* books, including *Look at Castles* (1960) and *Look at Churches* (1961). *Growing Up in the Thirteenth Century* (1962) describes the possible experience of young people in a feudal society.

DUGGAN, Eileen
(1894–1972)

New Zealand poet whose first verse, *Poems*, appeared in 1922. A collection of the same title in 1937 had an effusive introduction by **Walter de la Mare** and, like her next two books, *New Zealand Poems* (1940) and *More Poems* (1951), was published in London where her writing was identified with the Georgian school. She also wrote a collection of verse for children, *New Zealand Bird Songs* (1929).

DUGGAN, Maurice
(1922–74)

New Zealand writer, born in Auckland, who wrote excellently crafted short stories which employ melancholy motifs of movement, transition and loss. *Immanuel's Land* (1956) was followed by further titles in 1965 and 1970 and *Collected Stories* (ed **C K Stead**, 1981). Similar in mood is his work for children, as in his classic fantasy *Falter Tom and the Water Boy* (1958) and *The Fabulous McFanes* (1974).

DU GUILLET, Pernette
(?1520–1545)

French poet. Born in Lyons to a noble family, she was a well-educated woman, familiar with several European and Classical languages. She was married to the poet **Maurice Scève**

in 1536, and proved a considerable inspiration to his work. She died when she was only 25, probably as a result of an outbreak of plague, and the manuscripts of her poems were discovered after her death. Scève entrusted Antoine du Moulin with their publication, and *Rymes de gentile et vertueuse Dame D Pernette du Guillet* appeared in 1545. The collection was augmented for a second edition in 1552. Du Guillet's poetry, consisting of epigrams, songs and elegies, combines a marked originality with a rigorous technical control, and its content clearly reflects her erudition.

DUHAMEL, Georges
(1884–1966)

French novelist and poet. He originally studied medicine and worked as an army surgeon in World War I. This provided the background for *La Vie des martyrs* (1917, 'Life of the Martyrs') and *Civilisation* (1918, awarded the Prix **Goncourt**). Many of his 50 volumes of vigorous, skilful writing have been translated. They include *Salavin* (1920–32), *Le Notaire du Havre* (1913, Eng trans *News from Le Havre*, 1934), the first of the 10 parts of *Chronique des Pasquier* (1933–44, Eng trans *The Pasquier Chronicles*, 1937–45) and *Positions Françaises: Chronique de l'année 1939* (1940, Eng trans *Why France Fights*, 1940). He edited *Mercure de France*.
▷ *Light on My Days*, translation of two volumes of autobiography (1948)

DULEY, Margaret
(1894–1968)

Canadian novelist, born in Newfoundland. Duley had to curtail drama studies in London because of World War I and on her return to Canada became an active suffragette. She wrote for money and her novels—*The Eyes of the Gull* (1936), *Cold Pastoral* (1939), *Highway to Valour* (1941)—are mainly about female experience in harsh Newfoundland settings.
▷ A Feder, *Margaret Duley: Newfoundland Novelist* (1983)

DUMAS, Alexandre, in full, Alexandre Dumas Davy de la Pailleterie, known as 'Dumas père'
(1802–70)

French novelist and playwright, born in Villers-Cotterets, the son of General Alexandre Davy-Dumas and Marie Labouret, daughter of a tavern keeper and small landowner. After an idle youth, he went to Paris in 1823 and obtained a clerkship in the bureau of the Duc d'Orléans and spent some years writing. A volume of short stories and a couple of farces, however, were his only production when, at

27, he became famous for his *Henri III* (1829), performed at the Théâtre Français, which revolutionized historical drama. In 1831 he did the same for domestic tragedy with *Antony*, failed in verse with *Charles VII chez ses grands vassaux* ('Charles VII visits his Great Vassals'), and scored a tremendous success with *Richard Darlington*. In 1832 he carried the romantic 'history' to its culmination in *La Tour de Nesle* (in collaboration with Gaillardet). In that same year he fell ill with cholera, went to Switzerland to recuperate, and wrote for the *Revue des Deux Mondes* the first of his famous and delightful *Impressions de voyage* ('Travelling Impressions'). He was a prodigious worker, who would, after months of writing, refresh himself with a round of travel, and he always published his experiences, as in *En Suisse* (1833–7, Eng trans *Adventures in Switzerland*, 1960), *Le Midi de la France* (1840), and *Le Caucase* (1859, Eng trans *Adventures in Caucasia*, 1962). But it was as a storyteller that he gained enduring success. He worked with about 90 collaborators in all and disagreed violently with some of them. He borrowed indiscriminately, and brought to his borrowings his own immense and radiant personality. Still, it is undeniable that his thefts were many and flagrant. Edward Trelawny's *Adventures of a Younger Son*, for instance, appears in his collected works, and it is said that he was with difficulty restrained from signing a book of the *Iliad* which someone else had turned into prose. He decided to put the history of France into novels, and his earliest attempt was *Isabelle de Bavière* (1836, Eng trans *Isabel of Bavaria*, 1846). It was followed by *La Salle d'Armes* (1838, Eng trans *Pauline*, 1844), *Acté* (1839, Eng trans 1904), *Othon l'archer* (1840, Eng trans *Othon the Archer*, 1860)—and others all on different lines. Then he turned again to the historical vein in *Le Chevalier d'Harmenthal* (1843, Eng trans *The Château d'Harmental*, 1856) and *Ascanio* (1843, Eng trans *Francis I*, 1849). In the following decade he wrote outstandingly. In 1844, with a number of digressions into new provinces such as *Cécile* (Eng trans *Cecile*, 1904), *Fernande* (Eng trans 1904), *Amaury* (Eng trans 1854), *Le Comte de Monte-Cristo* (Eng trans *The Count of Monte Cristo*, 1846), there appeared *Les Trois Mousquetaires* (Eng trans *The Three Musketeers*, 1846). In 1845, *Vingt ans après* (Eng trans *Twenty Years After*, 1846), *La Fille du régent* (Eng trans *The Regent's Daughter*, 1847), and *La Reine Margot* (Eng trans *Margaret de Navarre*, 1845); in 1846, *La Guerre des femmes* (Eng trans *Nanot*, 1847), *Le Chevalier de Maison-Rouge* (Eng trans *Marie Antoinette*, 1846), *Le Bâtard de Mauléon* (Eng trans *The Bastard of Mauleon*, 1849),

La Dame de Monsoreau (Eng trans *Chicot the Jester*, 1857), and *Les Mémoires d'un médecin* (Eng trans *Memoirs of a Physician*, 1847); in 1848, *Les Quarante-cinq* (Eng trans *The Forty-Five Guardsmen*, 1848) and the beginnings of *Le Vicomte de Bragelonne* (Eng trans *The Vicomte de Bragalonne*, 1857) which was finished in 1850; and in 1849, *Le Collier de la reine* (Eng trans *The Queen's Necklace*, 1855). The next two years witnessed productions as varied as *La Tulipe noire* (1850, Eng trans *Rosa; or, The Black Tulip*, 1854) and *Le Trou de l'enfer* (1850–1, Eng trans *The Mouth of Hell*, 1906), and *La Femme au collier de velours* (1851, Eng trans *The Woman with the Velvet Necklace*, 1894). The historical masterpiece *Olympe de Clèves* (Eng trans *Olympe de Cleves*, 1894) came in 1852; between that year and 1854 he wrote the 10 delightful volumes of *Mes Mémoires* (Eng trans *My Memoirs*, 1907–9), with *Ange Pitou* (1853, Eng trans 1907) and *La Comtesse de Charny* (1855, Eng trans *The Countess of Charny*, 1858). Other achievements in the romance of French history were *Ingénue* (1854, Eng trans *Ingenue*, 1855), *Les Compagnons de Jéhu* (1857, Eng trans *Roland of Montreval*, 1860), *Les Louves de Machecoul* (1859, Eng trans *The Laste Vendee*, 1894) and *Les Blancs et les bleus* (1867–8, Eng trans *The Polish Spy*, 1869), with which the sequence ended. The list is incomplete, and reference can only be made in passing to the rest of his work during this period, such as drama (the great historical novels were also dramatized—the *Mousquetaires* cycle supplied at least three plays—as also were *Monte-Cristo* and others), history, *causerie*, journalism, etc. Dumas took a conspicuous part in the July Days; in 1837 he received the red ribbon; in 1842 he married Mlle Ida Ferrier, from whom he promptly separated. In 1855 he went for two years into exile at Brussels; from 1860 to 1864 he was helping Garibaldi in Italy, and conducting and writing a journal, and in 1886 he produced the last but one of his plays. By this time the end was near; he sank under his work. He had gone through a series of fortunes, and he left Paris for the last time with only a couple of napoleons in his pocket. He went to his son's villa in Dieppe, and stayed there until his death.

▷F H Gribble, *Dumas, Father and Son* (1930); R Todd, *The Laughing Mulatto* (1939)

DUMAS, Alexandre, known as **'Dumas fils'** (1824–95)

French writer, illegitimate son of **Alexandre Dumas**, born in Paris when his father was only 22 years old. He was soon legitimized, and at 16, after a course of training at the Institution Goubaux and the Collège Bourbon, he left school for the world of letters and

the society to which his father, then almost at his peak, belonged. He was basically respectable, however, and having sown some wild oats settled down to serious work. He started in fiction and succeeded and went on to drama. He took to theorizing about art, morals, politics, and even religion, and was successful. His novels—from *La Dame aux camélias* (1848, Eng trans *The Lady with the Camelias*, 1856) to *L'Affaire Clémenceau* (1864, Eng trans *Wife Murder; or, The Clémenceau Tragedy*, 1866)—are all readable, and the former was a great success in dramatic form (1852). His essays, speeches, letters, and prefaces generally are brilliant. Of his 16 plays, *Le Demi-Monde* (1855, Eng trans *Le Demi-Monde*, 1921), *Le Fils naturel* (1856, Eng trans 1879), *Les Idées de Mme Aubray* (1867, Eng trans 1965), *Une Visite de noces* (1871, 'A Wedding Party'), *Monsieur Alphonse* (1873, Eng trans 1874) and *Denise* (1885, Eng trans 1885) are masterpieces. Other famous dramas in which he had a share are *Le Supplice d'une femme* (1865, 'The Torture of a Woman'), whose chaotic original is due to Émile de Girardin; *Héloïse Paranquet* (1866), in collaboration with Durantin; and *Les Danicheff* (1876, Eng trans 1876). He may have assisted **George Sand** in preparing several of her works for the stage, and he completed and produced his father's *Joseph Balsamo* (1878).
▷ F H Gribble, *Dumas, Father and Son* (1930)

DU MAURIER, Dame Daphne
(1907–89)

English novelist and short-story writer, daughter of the actor-manager Sir Gerald Du Maurier. She wrote a number of highly successful period romances and adventure stories, many of which were inspired by Cornwall, where she lived, including *Jamaica Inn* (1936), *Rebecca* (1938), *Frenchman's Creek* (1942) and *My Cousin Rachel* (1951), several of which have been filmed. Her short story, 'The Birds' (published in *The Apple Tree*, 1952), became a classic Hitchcock movie. Later books included *The Flight of the Falcon* (1965), *The House on the Strand* (1969), *The Winding Stair*, a study of Francis Bacon (1976), *The Rendezvous and other Stories* (1980), and a volume of memoirs, *Vanishing Cornwall* (1967).
▷ *Growing Pains: The Shaping of a Writer* (1977, published in the USA as *Myself When Young*); M Forster, *Daphne du Maurier* (1993)

DU MAURIER, George Louis Palmella Busson
(1834–96)

French-born British artist, cartoonist and novelist, born in Paris. He was the grandson of émigrés who had originally fled to England at the Revolution; in 1851 he went to London himself and studied chemistry, but returned to Paris to study art there and in Antwerp and Düsseldorf. Back in England he made his name as an illustrator, with new editions of **William Makepeace Thackeray**'s *Esmond* and his ballads, **John Foxe**'s *Book of Martyrs*, and stories in periodicals like *Once A Week* and the *Cornhill Magazine*. Finally he joined the staff of *Punch* (1864–96), where he became best known as a gentle satirist of middle- and upper-class society (some of his illustrations were collected as *English Society at Home*, 1880). He also wrote and illustrated three novels, *Peter Ibbetson* (1891), *The Martian* (1897), and the phenomenally successful *Trilby* (1894), the story of a young singer under the mesmeric influence of another musician, Svengali.
▷ D Whiteley, *George du Maurier: his life and work* (1948)

DUNBAR, Paul Laurence
(1872–1906)

American poet, born in Dayton, Ohio, the son of escaped Negro slaves. He gained a reputation with *Lyrics of Lowly Life* (1896), many of which were in dialect. He published several other volumes of verse, and four novels. His *Complete Poems* appeared in 1913.
▷ A Gayle Jr, *Oak and Ivy: a biography of Dunbar* (1971)

DUNBAR, William
(c.1460–c.1520)

Scottish poet, probably born in East Lothian. He seems to have studied at St Andrews University from 1475 to 1479. He became a Franciscan novice, and diligently visited every significant town in England. He preached at Canterbury but later left the order. He appears next to have been secretary to some of James IV's numerous embassies to foreign courts. In 1500 he obtained a pension from the king, and the following year visited England, probably with the ambassadors sent to arrange the king's marriage to Margaret Tudor, daughter of Henry VII. Early in 1503, before the queen's arrival, he composed in honour of the event his most famous poem, *The Thrissil and the Rois*, perhaps the happiest political allegory in English literature. It now seems that he lived chiefly about court, writing poems and sustaining himself with the vain hope of Church preferment. In 1508 Walter Chepman printed seven of his poems—the earliest specimen of Scottish typography. He visited the north of Scotland in May 1511, in the train of Queen Margaret, and his name disappears altogether after the Battle of Flodden (1513). He was certainly dead by 1530. He reached his highest level in his satires, *The Twa Marriit Wemen and the Wedo* and *The Dance of the Sevin Deadly Synnis*. His *Lament for the Makaris* is a masterpiece of pathos.

▷ J Baxter, *William Dunbar, a biographical study* (1952)

DUNCAN, Robert Edward, originally Edward Howard Duncan
(1919–)

American poet, born in Oakland, California. He was adopted by Theosophists in 1920 and named Robert Edward Symmes. Educated at the University of California, he was editor of *Experimental Review* (1938–40) and *Phoenix and Berkeley Miscellany* (1948–9). Aligned with the 'Black Mountain' poets, and influenced by **George Barker** and **Ezra Pound**, he wrote in a style that emphasized natural forms and processes. His collections include *Heavenly City, Earthly City* (1947), *The Opening of the Field* (1960), *Roots and Branches* (1964) and *The Years as Catches* (1966). His 1944 essay, 'The Homosexual in Society', is an important document in the development of gay cultural politics.

▷ *The Truth and Life of Myth: an essential autobiography* (1968)

DUNCAN, Sara Jeanette (Janet)
(1861–1922)

Canadian novelist, columnist and travel writer, born in Ontario. When she joined the *Toronto Globe* in 1886 she became the first woman to work in the editorial department of a Canadian newspaper. Using the pseudonym Garth Grafton she wrote columns for other newspapers. In 1888 she undertook a round-the-world trip with a friend, Lily Lewis, which resulted in her first full-length book, *Round the World by Ourselves* (1890). After her marriage to Everard Cotes, a museum curator in Calcutta, she spent the next 25 years in India. Her fiction, whether specifically about India, as in *The Simple Adventures of a Memsahib* (1893), or about generally paternalistic habits of mind, as in *The Imperialist* (1904), a book about small-town life in Ontario, contains acute observation of colonial attitudes.

▷ M Fowler, *Redney: The Life of Sarah Jeanette Duncan* (1983)

DUNLAP, William
(1766–1839)

American playwright, born in Perth Amboy, New Jersey. Initially a painter, who was commissioned to make portraits of George and Martha Washington, he was the first American to make the theatre his only profession, and as a dramatist and manager he dominated the American stage in the 20 years from 1790 to 1810. Following *The Father; or, American Shandyism* (1789), a comedy of manners, he wrote almost 70 plays, many of them very quickly, several being adaptations of foreign dramas. Among his more successful plays, *André* (1798), based upon an incident during the American War of Independence, is considered the first tragedy to be wholly derived from American history. Dunlap was an innovative but only intermittently successful manager, and in 1805 he was declared bankrupt. Six years later he left the theatre and returned to his previous career as an artist. He is also the author of such books as *A History of the Rise and Progress of the Arts of Design in the United States* (1834).

▷ O Coad, *William Dunlap* (1917)

DUNN, Douglas Eaglesham
(1942–)

Scottish poet, born in Inchinnan, Renfrewshire. He was educated at Renfrew High and Camphill schools, Paisley, before attending the Scottish School of Librarianship and Hull University, where he was employed in the library simultaneously with **Philip Larkin**, who became a friend and mentor. His first collection of poems, *Terry Street* (1969), articulates contempt and warmth in almost equal measure for the working-class suburb of Hull where he was then living. The two subsequent collections—*The Happier Life* (1972) and *Love or Nothing* (1974)—rather disappointed readers who had been drawn to *Terry Street* by its bleak humour and tacky glamour. In *Barbarians* (1979), however, he echoed and extended that first collection, and has subsequently demonstrated that he is one of Britain's finest contemporary poets, technically accomplished and artistically ambitious. He returned to Scotland in 1984. *Elegies* (1985), his sixth collection, is his best-known. Written on the death of his first wife, it is a moving valediction, emotionally raw but tightly controlled. It won the Whitbread Prize. *Secret Villages*, a collection of stories, was published in 1985, and his *Selected Poems: 1964–1983* in 1986. A new collection of poems, *Northlight*, appeared in 1988, and another, *Dante's Drum-kit*, in 1993. He edited *Scotland: An Anthology* (1991) and *The Faber Book of Twentieth Century Scottish Verse* (1992). He has been Professor of English at St Andrews University since 1991.

DUNN, Max
(1895–1963)

Irish-born journalist and poet, born in Dublin, who settled in Australia in the early 1920s after serving in World War I. He published a number of books of verse between *Random Elements* (1943) and *The Mirror and the Rose* (1954), and a collection of his translations from the Chinese was issued as *The City of Wide Streets* in 1952.

DUNN, Nell (Mary)
(1936–)

English novelist and playwright, born in London and educated at a convent school. She is known principally for her early, vivid, terse, documentary-style accounts of working-class life, set mainly in the south-London areas of Battersea and Clapham. Her first book was a collection of short stories, *Up The Junction* (1965), but her best-known work is probably the screenplay *Poor Cow* (1967, with Ken Loach), in which the heroine Joy, a young mother, takes jobs as a barmaid, model and factory-worker while her unloved husband languishes in prison. A play, *Steaming* (1981), looks at the lives of a group of women who meet regularly at a women's Turkish bath, and follows their campaign to prevent its closure.

DUNNE, Finley Peter
(1867–1936)

American humorist, born in Chicago. He worked as a journalist there, and was editor of *Chicago Journal* (1897–1900). With his creation of the Chicago Irish philosopher-bartender 'Mr Dooley' he became from 1900 the exponent of American–Irish humorous satire on current personages and events, in *Mr Dooley in Peace and War* (1898) and many other books.
▷ E J Bander, *Mr Dooley and Mr Dunne: The Literary Life of a Chicago Catholic* (1981)

DUNNE, John Gregory
(1932–)

American novelist, movie writer and journalist, born in Connecticut. He is the husband of novelist **Joan Didion**, with whom he has collaborated on several screenplays. His crime novels, *True Confessions* (1977) and *Dutch Shea Jr* (1982), are marked by a particularly strong moral sense, shaped by Irish Catholicism, which is perhaps most clearly seen in the Dunne–Didion film version of *True Confessions* (1981), in which Robert de Niro starred as a priest. The same concerns re-emerge in later books like *The Red, White and Blue* (1986) and the much acclaimed *Harp* (1989). Like his wife, Dunne is an acute observer of the Californian scene, but he brings an east-coast detachment to his accounts of Hollywood (*The Studio*, 1969), and the gambling industry (*Vegas*, 1974).
▷ *Quintana and Friends* (1978)

DUNNETT, Dorothy, née Halliday
(1923–)

Scottish novelist, born in Dunfermline and educated at James Gillespie's High School for Girls in Edinburgh. She began her career with the Civil Service as a Press Secretary in Edinburgh. A recognized portrait painter since 1950, she has exhibited at the Royal Academy and is a member of the Scottish Society of Women Artists. She has used her maiden name for a series of detective novels, starting with *Dolly and the Singing Bird* (1968), but her best-known works comprise a series of historical novels, including *Game of Kings* (1961) and *Checkmate* (1975). Featuring the fictional Scottish mercenary Francis Crawford of Lymond, these novels continue the Scottish tradition of historical romance. In 1986 she embarked upon a second historical series, this time featuring the house of Charetty and Niccoló.

DUNSANY, Edward John Moreton Drax Plunkett, 18th Baron
(1878–1957)

Irish novelist, poet and playwright, born in London. Educated at Eton and Sandhurst, he succeeded to the title in 1899, served in the 2nd Boer War with the Coldstream Guards, and thereafter settled in Ireland at Dunsany Castle in County Meath. In World War I he was an officer of the Inniskilling Fusiliers. By World War II, he was Byron Professor of English Literature in Athens, and was associated with the Irish revival led by **Yeats** and **Lady Gregory**. His literary works are highly poetic and imaginative. They began in 1905 with the mythological novel *The Gods of Pegana*, with illustrations by his frequent collaborator, S H Sime. His 'Jorkens' stories, beginning with *The Travel Tales of Mr Joseph Jorkens* (1931) were popular, while *The King of Elfland's Daughter* (1924) is his best-known work of fantasy. At W B Yeats's invitation he wrote many plays for the Abbey Theatre, including *The Glittering Gate* (1909) and *The Laughter of the Gods* (1919). These, and other works for theatre, enjoyed considerable popularity in both Britain and the USA. His verse is contained in *Fifty Poems* (1930) and *Mirage Water* (1939). He also wrote an autobiographical series: *Patches of Sunlight* (1938), *While the Sirens Slept* (1944), *The Sirens Wake* (1945) and *To Awaken Pegasus* (1949).
▷ M Amory, *Lord Dunsany* (1972)

DUNSTAN, (John) Keith
(1925–)

Australian journalist and writer, born in Melbourne. His satirical articles on the Australian way of life and its players have been collected into such books as *Wowsers* (1968), *Knockers* (1972) and *Sports* (1973). *Ratbags* (1979) brings together a notorious bilker of taxi-drivers, a state premier, a world-famous pianist and a self-made prince in a cross-section of Australia's eccentrics. Dunstan was President of the Bicycle Institute of Victoria between 1974 and 1978.

DUPONT, Pierre
(1821–70)

French popular poet and songwriter, born in Lyons, the son of a blacksmith. He moved to Paris, and enjoyed popular success as the writer of patriotic songs. He wrote knowledgeably about peasant life in books such as *Le chant des ouvriers* (1848, 'The Workmen's Song').

DURACK, Dame Mary
(1913–)

Australian author, born into a pioneering Western Australian family in Adelaide. *Kings in Grass Castles* (1959) is the saga of the Durack family from 19th-century Ireland to the time of Patsy Durack, one of Australia's greatest landowners, who died in 1898. *Sons in the Saddle* (1983) brings the story up to modern times. Other historical works include *The Rock and the Sand* (1969) and the play *Swan River Saga* (1975). She has also written a number of books for children, some with illustrations by her younger sister, Elizabeth Durack (1916–). Her libretto for the opera *Dalgerie*, with music by Australian composer James Penberthy, is based on her own novel *Keep Him My Country* (1955) and was produced at the Sydney Opera House in 1973.

DURAN, Augustín
(1793–1862)

Spanish poet and critic. He compiled a collection of literature in the Spanish ballad tradition, *Romancero general* (1828–32), and the critical work *Discurso sobre . . . la decadencia del teatro antiguo* (1828, 'Discourses on . . . the decline of classical theatre').

DURAS, Marguerite, pseud of Marguerite Donnadieu
(1914–)

French novelist, born in Indo-China. She studied law and political science at the Sorbonne in Paris. During World War II she took part in the Resistance at great risk to herself as a Jewess. She is considered one of the great European writers of the 20th century. Her books include the semi-autobiographical *La Douleur* (1985, Eng trans 1986) and *L'Amant* (1984, Eng trans *The Lover*, 1985, Prix **Goncourt**), novels like *Un Barrage contre le Pacifique* (1950, Eng trans *The Sea Wall*, 1952 (US); 1953 (UK)), *Le Vice-Consul* (1966, Eng trans *The Vice Consul*, 1968) and *Détruire, dit-elle* (1969, Eng trans *Destroy, She Said*, 1970), film scripts like *Hiroshima Mon Amour* (1960, 'Hiroshima My Love'), and a number of plays, including *La Musica* (1965, Eng trans *The Music*, 1966).
▷ A Cismaru, *Duras* (1971)

DURBRIDGE, Francis Henry
(1912–)

English crime novelist and playwright, born in Hull and educated at Birmingham University. He has on occasion conceded authorial credits to his fictional detective Paul Temple, who figured in a long and popular drama series on radio (and later, less successfully, on television). Temple's Watson was his wife Steve, who brought fragrant charm and unerring social antennae to their cases, which were firmly rooted in a professional middle-class milieu. The first of the Temple stories was 'novelized' from radio scripts as *Send for Paul Temple* (1938), and the character was still active in the 1970s.

DURCAN, Paul
(1944–)

Irish poet, born in Dublin; he graduated from University College Cork in 1973 in History and Archaeology. His poems, which have won the **Patrick Kavanagh** Award for Poetry (1974) and the Whitbread Poetry Prize (1990), are direct statements of commitment to a relentless humanist standpoint. The obliquity of some references in *O Westport in the Light of Asia Minor* (1975) eased into a more confessional, conversational style in *Teresa's Bar* (1976) and *Jesus and Angela* (1988), while a more meditative and reflective tone is present in the autobiographical *Daddy, Daddy* (1990) and the politically-informed *A Snail in my Prime* (1993). The loose long line structure he assimilated from the American Beats and the Russian Modernists often conceals the craft and passion that is the emotional trademark of all his work.

DURCYCH, Jaroslav
(1886–1962)

Czech novelist and poet, a doctor by profession, who was born in Hradec Králové and died in Prague. He was a conservative

Catholic, but one of liberal sympathies, always a spokesman for the proletariat; his drama and poetry failed, but his massive, fantastic and powerful historical novel *Bloudeni* (1929, Eng trans *The Descent of the Idols*, 1935) is the finest of all fiction about the Thirty Years War and the enigmatic Wallenstein. His untranslated *Rekviem* (1930, 'Requiem') continues the story.

D'URFÉ, Honoré
(1567–1625)

French novelist, born in Marseilles. He fought in the religious wars of France and later settled in Savoy. His great work *Astrée* (1607–27), a pastoral romance, though now not much read in its entirety for pleasure, is of crucial importance in the history of the French novel. Drawing on the examples of **Montemayor** and **Guarini**, he provided his grateful 17th-century readers with a model for courtship and conversation. The work was completed by his secretary, Baro, after his death.
▷ O C Revre, *Honoré d'Urfé* (1910); M Seymour-Smith, *Introduction to Fifty European Novels* (1979)

D'URFREY, Thomas
(1653–1723)

English dramatist and songwriter, born in Exeter of Huguenot ancestry. He was a nephew of **Honoré d'Urfé**, author of the famous romance of *Astrée*. He soon became a prolific playwright, his comedies especially being popular. Among these were *The Fond Husband* (1676), *Madame Fickle* (1677) and *Sir Burnaby Whig* (1681). In 1683 he published his *New Collection of Songs and Poems*, which was followed by a long series of songs, collected as *Wit and Mirth, or Pills to Purge Melancholy* (6 vols, 1719–20). Meanwhile he had written some plays, which were criticized as being immoral by Jeremy Collier. His fortunes declined as his comedies ceased to please.
▷ R S Forsyte, *A Study of the Plays* (1916)

DURRELL, Lawrence George
(1912–90)

English novelist, poet, travel writer and playwright, born in Julundur, India. He lived in India until he was 10, when his family moved back to England. He took numerous odd jobs—in night clubs, as an estate agent and in the Jamaica police—and once said he had been driven to writing 'by sheer ineptitude'. He convinced his family that life would be more congenial in a warmer climate and they moved to Corfu until the outbreak of World War II. He moved to France in 1957 but travelled widely as a journalist and in the service of the Foreign Office. His first novel was *Pied Piper of Lovers* (1935) and his second, *Panic Spring*, appeared two years later under the pseudonym Charles Norden, so woeful were the sales of its predecessor. He made his name with the 'Alexandria Quartet'—*Justine* (1957), *Balthazar* (1958), *Mountolive* (1958) and *Clea* (1960)—a complex, interlocking series set in Egypt, remarkable for its sensuous language, intrigue and devious plotting, the nature of modern love being its central topic. He followed this with a two-novel sequence, *Tunc* (1968) and *Nunquam* (1970). The *Avignon Quincunx*—*Monsieur* (1974), *Livia* (1978), *Constance* (1982), *Sebastian* (1983) and *Quinx* (1985)—is also conceived on a grand and elaborate scale. His generous output includes travel books, *Prospero's Cell* (1945) and *Bitter Lemons* (1957), verse (*Collected Poems, 1931–1974*), comic sketches, criticism, plays and a children's novel, *White Eagles Over Serbia* (1957). His long friendship with **Henry Miller** is recorded in their correspondence published in 1988. His brother, the naturalist Gerald Durrell, has written several popular books about his experiences, including the bestselling memoir, *My Family and Other Animals* (1956), in which he described his family's time in Corfu as like living 'in one of the more flamboyant and slapstick comic operas'.
▷ J Unterecker, *Lawrence Durrell* (1964)

DÜRRENMATT, Friedrich
(1921–90)

Swiss author, born in Konolfingen, Bern, the son of a pastor; he studied there and at Zürich and turned from painting to writing. The theme which recurs in all his work is that life is a calamity which has to be accepted for what it is but without surrender. His novels include the detective story *Der Richter und sein Henker* (1952, Eng trans *The Judge and his Hangman*, 1954), *Der Verdacht* (1953, Eng trans *The Quarry*, 1961 (US); 1962 (UK)), *Die Panne* (1956, Eng trans *A Dangerous Game*, 1960), and his plays *Romulus der Grosse* (1949, Eng trans *Romulus*, 1961) and *Die Ehe des Herrn Mississippi* (1952, Eng trans *The Marriage of Mississippi*, 1958), which established his international reputation. *Ein Engel kommt nach Babylon* (1953, Eng trans *An Angel Comes to Babylon*, 1962) is a parable in which an angel brings chaos instead of happiness, and *Der Besuch einer alten Dame* (1956, Eng trans *The Visit*, 1958) describes the return of an old lady to her native village to revenge herself on a seducer. Other plays include *Die Physiker* (1962, Eng trans *The Physicists*, 1963), *Play Strindberg: Totentanz nach August Strindberg* (1969, Eng trans *Play Strindberg: The Dance of Death*, 1972), *Porträt eines Planeten* (1970, Eng trans *Portrait of a Planet*, 1973), and a novel, *Der Sturz* ('The Fall'), published in 1971.

▷M B Peppard, *Dürrenmatt* (1969)

DUTT, Michael Madhu Sudan

(1824–73)

Indian poet, born in Sagandari, Bengal. He absorbed European culture, became a Christian and wrote poetry and drama in English and Bengali, such as the plays *Sarmishtha* (1858), *Padmavati* (1859), and the blank verse epics *Tillotama* (1860) and *Meghanad-Badha* (1861).

▷H M Das Gupta, *Studies in Western Influence on 19th Century Bengali Poetry* (1935)

DUTT, Toru

(1856–77)

Indian poet who wrote in English. She died at 21, her promise almost wholly unfulfilled. She had a gift for retelling Hindu tales in English verse. Her poems are collected in *A Sheaf Gleaned from a French Field* (1976) and *Ancient Ballads and Legends of Hindustan* (1882).

▷H Das, *Life and Letters of Toru Dutt* (1921)

DUTTON, Geoffrey Piers Henry

(1922–)

Australian poet, novelist, critic and editor, born in Kapunda, South Australia. After service during World War II he travelled overland back to Australia and became engaged in publishing. His verse collections include *Night Flight and Sunrise* (1944), the prize-winning *Antipodes in Shoes* (1958) and *A Body of Words* (1977). Other work includes his novels *The Mortal and the Marble* (1950), *Tamara* (1970) and *Queen Emma of the South Seas* (1976), based on the real life of a Samoan–American woman who founded a trading empire in the South Pacific. He has also written critical studies of **Patrick White** (1961) and **Walt Whitman** (1961), three historical biographies of pioneering Australians, as well as art appreciation, short stories (*The Wedge-Tailed Eagle*, 1980), and books for children. His work as a scholarly and enthusiastic editor has produced the acclaimed *The Literature of Australia* (1964, rev edn 1976) and representative anthologies of Australian verse.

DUUN, Olav

(1876–1939)

Norwegian novelist, born in Tosnes. He worked as a farmer and fisherman before training as a teacher, and the experience gave him a profound feeling for the lives of rural Norwegians. Between the wars he became an important exponent of the new 'national language', *Landsmål* (later known as *Nynorsk*

or New Norwegian), for which he was twice shortlisted for the Nobel Prize, but which has thwarted international translation and recognition of his work. Immensely prolific, his major fictional achievement is the massive six-volume *Juvikfolke* (1918–23, 'The People of Juvik'), which asserts human indomitability in the face of large-scale natural forces.

▷A Overland, *Olav Dunn* (1955)

DWYER, James Francis

(1874–1952)

Australian novelist, born in Camden Park, New South Wales, who began his writing career while in prison on a forgery charge by sending pieces to a weekly magazine. On release he started in journalism, but in 1906 left for London and New York, where his short stories found a ready outlet in *Collier's* and *Harper's Bazaar*. He wrote 10 adventure novels beginning with *The White Waterfall* (1912). In search of material he travelled to Europe, North Africa and Asia, and settled in Pau, France. He escaped back to the USA after the German invasion but returned to Pau in 1945.

▷*Leg Irons on Wings* (1949)

DYER, Sir Edward

(c.1545–1607)

English poet and diplomat, born in Sharpham Park, Somerset. He studied at Balliol College or Broadgates Hall, Oxford, and became a courtier. He was a friend of Sir **Fulke Greville** and Sir **Philip Sidney**; the latter wrote a song in praise of their friendship, while Dyer commemorated Sidney's death in a moving elegy. Only half a dozen of his poems have survived, of which the best known is 'My Mind to Me a Kingdom is'.

▷R M Sargent, *At the Court of Queen Elizabeth: the life and hymns of Sir Edward Dyer* (1935)

DYER, George

(1755–1841)

English writer, **Charles Lamb**'s friend, born in London. From Christ's Hospital he went to Emmanuel College, Cambridge, taking his BA in 1778. In 1792 he settled in Clifford's Inn, London, and, with 'poems' and a vast mass of hack work, produced the *History of the University of Cambridge* (1814) and *Privileges of the University of Cambridge* (1824). He contributed 'all that was original' to Valpy's classics (141 vols, 1809–31), and became totally blind soon after his life's work was done.

▷*The Poet's Fate* (1797)

DYER, John
(1699–1757)

Welsh poet and painter, born in Llanfynydd parish, Dyfed. Educated at Westminster School, he abandoned law for art, and in 1725 published his most successful work, *Grongar Hill*, notable for its warmth of feeling, simplicity and exquisite descriptions of landscape. The poem, which advocates a 'quiet in the soul', was inspired by the scenery of the valley of the river Towy in Carmarthenshire, and was written while he was an itinerant painter. In 1750 he published *The Ruins of Rome*, and was ordained the following year. Thereafter he held various livings in Leicestershire and Lincolnshire. His longest work, *The Fleece* (1757), a didactic poem, is praised by **Wordsworth** in a sonnet.

▷ 'The Poems of John Dyer' and 'The Life of John Dyer' in Dr S Johnson, *The Lives of the English Poets* (1779–81)

DYGASINSKI, Tomasz Adolf
(1839–1902)

Polish novelist who began writing late in life. He has affinities with **Kipling**, who eventually influenced him, and with **Zola**. His novels, none of which has been translated into English, are concerned with the humanly pessimistic implications of Darwinism, in which he believed.

DYGAT, Stanislaw
(1914–78)

Polish novelist, born in Warsaw. He spent most of World War II in a Nazi camp. His novels, of which *Podróz* (1958, 'Journey') is perhaps the most celebrated, are humorous and ironical in a typically Polish manner.

DYK, Viktor
(1877–1931)

Czech political poet, playwright and novelist, born in Psovska, near Melnik. Imprisoned by the Austrians, he became National Democratic MP in the new Czech parliament in 1919. His poetry began as one of protest tinged with nihilism, but ended with an acceptance of death. He wrote epics, historical plays and some less distinguished prose. He ended as a leading right-wing opponent to the regime.

DYSON, Edward
(1865–1931)

Australian writer, mainly of short stories, born in Morrison, Ballarat, Victoria. He is best known for his classic tale 'A Golden Shanty' in which Chinese fossickers keep returning to take bricks from a goldfields pub, the puzzled proprietor of which finally discovers that the bricks are made of gold-bearing clay. Dyson's stories appeared as *Below and On Top* (1898), *Fact'ry 'Ands* (1906) and *Benno and Some of the Push* (1911); he also published two novels which are merely a sequence of episodes in similar vein. A collection of his verse, *Rhymes from the Mines and Other Lines*, appeared in 1896, and the best of his stories were selected and introduced by **Norman Lindsay** as *The Golden Shanty: Short Stories* in 1963.

E

EARLE, John
(c.1601–1665)

English prelate, born in York. In 1641 he became tutor to Charles II, then Prince of Wales, and also served him as chaplain during his exile in France. He became Bishop of Worcester (1662), and of Salisbury (1663). In 1628 he published anonymously *Microcosmographie*, a set of witty character sketches and epigrammatic essays.

EASTLAKE, William
(1917–)

American novelist, born in New York City. His service in World War II provided him with the material for his best-known novel, the fantasy *Castle Keep* (1965), about a handful of American soldiers in a 10th-century castle in whose defence they die; this was filmed in 1969 by Sydney Pollack. Eastlake has also written many short stories, and the novel *Bronco People* (1958), set in New Mexico.

EBERHART, Richard Ghormley
(1904–)

American poet, born in Minnesota, and the author of almost 30 collections. Among the most notable are *A Bravery of Earth* (1930), *Reading the Spirit* (1936), *The Quarry* (1960) and *Fields of Grace* (1972). His *Selected Poems 1930–1965* won a Pulitzer Prize in 1966, and *Collected Poems 1930–1976* a National Book Award in 1977. A traditional, lyrical, reflective writer, deliberating upon the natural world and the cycles of life and death, Eberhart's writing has been acclaimed as being in the romantic tradition of **Blake**, **Wordsworth** and **Whitman**. He is considered to be one of the most important of 20th-century American poets. Since 1972, he has been Honorary President of the Poetry Society of America.

EBERS, Georg Moritz
(1837–98)

German Egyptologist and novelist, born in Berlin. Lecturer (1865) and professor (1868) at Jena, he visited the East in 1869, and from 1870 to 1889 was Professor of Egyptology at Leipzig. He discovered and published (1875) the celebrated hieratic medical *Papyrus Ebers*, and wrote on biblical sites in Goshen, Sinai and Egypt. He is best known as the author of numerous historical novels based on ancient Egypt.
▷H R A Gosche, *Georg Ebers der Forscher und Dichter* (1887)

EBERT, Karl Egon
(1801–82)

Bohemian poet, born in Prague. His poems include the national epic *Vlasta* (1829).

EBNER-ESCHENBACH, Marie, née von Dubsky
(1830–1916)

Austrian dramatist and writer of novellas. She was born at Castle Zdislawitz in Moravia, into the nobility, into which she also married. Somewhat stagestruck, she failed with her first writing ventures, which were in the form of drama; but her regional *novellen*, starting with her first success, *Ein Spätgwborener* (1874), much influenced by **Turgenev**, were amongst the most skilful and well observed of their time. The best of her tales include *Das Gemeindekind* (1887, Eng trans *The Child of the Parish*, 1887) and *Unsühnbar* (1890, Eng trans *Beyond Atonement*, 1892).

EÇA DE QUEIROS, José Maria de
(1845–1900)

Major Portuguese novelist, a towering figure in his country's fiction, who is still much neglected—and persistently underrated, in the European terms in which he should be considered. He was born in Lisbon, and died in a bitter Parisian exile. Although essentially a 19th-century figure, Eça established realism in the Portuguese novel. His point of departure was **Zola**, but he soon developed his own direction, which was more akin to that of his true master, **Flaubert**: to analyse what was humanly wrong with the society of his own country. His profound self-study, as the sadomasochistic writer Ega, in one of his masterpieces, *Os Maias* (1888, Eng trans *The Maias*, 1965), which has incest as its main theme, has in particular not had its due. However, no one has questioned that he is Portugal's finest prose stylist. *O Crime do Padre Amero* (1876, Eng trans *The Sin of Father Amaro*, 1962) depicts clerical 'immorality' in a bourgeois setting; *O primo Basilio* (1878, Eng trans *Cousin Basilio*, 1958) is a variation on the theme of Flaubert's *Madame Bovary.* Eça's *Cartas de Inglaterra* (1903, Eng trans *Letters from England,* 1970), provides an invaluable outsider's view of Victorian England.

▷M Seymour-Smith, *Introduction to Fifty European Novels* (1979)

ECHEGARAY Y EIZAGUIRRE, José
(1833–1916)

Spanish dramatist, born of Basque descent in Madrid, and joint winner of the Nobel Prize for literature in 1904. He taught mathematics, held portfolios in various ministries (1868–74), then won literary fame by many plays in prose and verse. His plays are usually on simple themes, but with elaborate plot twists and rhetorical passages, and some incorporate social comment, as in his masterpiece, *El gran Galeoto* (1881, 'The Great Galeoto'). He returned to politics as Minister of Finance (1905), and to science as Professor of Physics, Madrid University (1905).

▷J Mathias, *Echegaray* (1970)

ECHERUO, Michael Joseph Chukwudalo
(1937–)

Nigerian poet, born in Umunumo and educated at Port Harcourt, Ibadan, and Cornell University, New York. An expert on **Joyce Cary**, about whom he has written two critical monographs (1973, 1979), Echeruo is himself very much concerned with the cultural confrontation of Europe and Africa. This is the substance of his main collection, *Mortality* (1968), which documents aspects of his experience as an African in the USA. *Distanced* (1975) is a more philosophical but also more lyrical collection. Echeruo's academic career progressed from the University of Nigeria, Nsukka (1961–74) to the University of Ibadan (1974–80); since 1981 he has been Vice-Chancellor of Imo State University at Owerri.

▷ *Poets, Prophets and Professors* (1977)

ECHEVERRIA, Estaban
(1805–51)

Argentinian poet, novelist, essayist, socialist and critic, born in Buenos Aires. From 1826 until 1830 he lived in Paris, where he absorbed the essence of European romanticism, which he later introduced to his country. He died in exile because of his opposition to the terrible dictator General Juan Manuel de Rosas. The novela *El matadero* (1871, Eng trans *The Slaughter House,* 1959), written in about 1840, is one of the earliest of the great Latin-American anti-dictator documents; here the country is shown as an abattoir run by insane butchers. He is Argentina's key romantic poet; part of his famous poem 'La cautiva'

('The Captive') is translated in the *Penguin Book of Latin American Verse* (1971, ed E Curacciolo-Trejo).

ECKERMANN, Johann Peter
(1792–1854)

German author, born in Winsen in Hanover. He studied at Göttingen. The publication of his *Beiträge zur Poesie* (1823, 'Contributions on Poetry') led to his move to Weimar, where he assisted **Goethe** in preparing the final edition of his works. He achieved fame by his *Gespräche mit Goethe in den letzten Jahren seines Lebens, 1823–32* (1836–48, Eng trans of part as *Conversations with Goethe,* 1839).

▷E Hitschman, *Johann Peter Eckermann, eine psychoanalytische-biographische Studie* (1933)

ECKHART, Johannes, known as **Meister Eckhart**
(c.1260–1327)

German Dominican mystic, born in Hochheim in Thuringia, of a noble family. One of the most famous teachers of his time, he was eventually prosecuted for heresy, but died before the matter had been settled. His works—seldom in authentic texts—are difficult to interpret, and have been variously understood. Like **Böhme**, he was rediscovered by 19th-century romantic thinkers who were ignorant of theological history. Orthodox scholarship now likes to claim him as an eccentric descendant of Aristotle, Aquinas and the schoolmen; but it seems that, despite his denials to the Pope, he was a sound heretic. He was certainly a pantheist, and to some extent (though less than Böhme), one of a gnostic temper. His influence is to be found in Kant, Hegel and in German romantic poetry. The poets, however, though ignorant of his theology, could be claimed to have understood the essence of his thinking better than the scholars. He wrote in both Latin and the German vernacular.

▷J M Clark (ed), *The Great German Mystics* (1949); *Meister Eckhart: An Introduction* (1957, with translations); F E Copleston, *A History of Philosophy,* vol iii (1953)

ECO, Umberto
(1932–)

Italian novelist and semiotician, born in Alessandria in Piedmont. A student of philosophy at Turin University, he was awarded a doctorate for his thesis on St Thomas Aquinas. He taught at Turin (1956–67), and was appointed Professor of Semiotics (the study of signs in all realms of culture) at the University of Bologna in 1971. Imbued with a 'taste and passion' for the Middle Ages, he undertook a prolonged study of the commentary of Beatus of Liébana, an 8th-century saint, on the Book of Revelation and of 11th-century illuminations, all of which bore fruit in *The Name of the Rose* (1980). A suspense story set in a medieval monastery, centring on the criminal investigation of Brother William of Baskerville, an English Franciscan, it is indebted to **Arthur Conan Doyle**'s Sherlock Holmes stories, despite having been described as 'a completely semiotic book'. It was an international bestseller and was successfully translated to celluloid in a film of the same name directed by Jean-Jaques Arnaud. *Foucault's Pendulum*, his second novel, was published in 1989.

EDEN, Dorothy
(1912–82)
New Zealand writer of suspense and historical novels, the best known of which is probably *Bride by Candlelight* (1954). Early books, such as her first, *Singing Shadows* (1940), had a New Zealand setting. A move to London in the 1950s inspired contemporary themes such as Nazi Europe in *The Shadow Wife* (1968), and a spy plot in *Waiting for Willa* (1970). Her Gothic romances, mainly Victorian in period, ranged from England and Ireland to South Africa and to the China of the Boxer Rebellion. With her fortieth and last book, *An Important Family* (1982), she returned to her home province of Canterbury.

EDGAR, David
(1948–)
English dramatist, born in Birmingham. He studied drama at Manchester University before becoming a journalist in Bradford, and wrote several plays for touring fringe theatre companies before deciding to write for the stage full time. *Destiny* (1976), a large-scale play looking at the roots of fascism in British society, was produced by the Royal Shakespeare Company. His eight-hour adaptation of **Dickens**'s *The Life and Adventures of Nicholas Nickleby* for the RSC (1980) brought his work to a massive audience. *Maydays* (1983), the first contemporary play to be presented by the RSC at the Barbican Theatre in London, was similarly ambitious. *Entertaining Strangers* (1985), which is set in mid-19th-century Dorchester, counterpoints the commercial ambitions of the owner of a brewery with the fury of a fundamentalist preacher, against the backdrop of industrialization and a cholera epidemic. Other works include *The Shape of the Table* (1990), which charts the negotiations between a communist government and the forces acting against it in the autumn of 1989, a television documentary *Civil War* (1991), a radio play *A Movie Starring Me* (1991), and several adaptations, including *The Strange Case of Dr Jekyll and Mr Hyde* (1991).

EDGELL, Zee
(1940–)
Belizean novelist. Educated at the University of the West Indies, she worked as a journalist in Jamaica before travelling abroad. She has held posts in education and public service at home and abroad and spent a year in Somalia working for UNICEF. Her commitment to feminist issues is evident in her novels, which emphasize the resourcefulness of women in the face of difficult situations. In *Beka Lamb* (1982), for example, the adolescent heroine, who has grown up in Belize, a matriarchal society influenced by the Catholic Church and beset by political tensions, works hard to overcome her faults. In *In Times Like These* (1991), the central character returning to Belize with her illegitimate twins shows moral courage in confronting the complex web of personal relationships and political intrigue.

EDGEWORTH, Maria
(1767–1849)
Irish novelist, eldest daughter of the inventor and educationist Richard Lovell Edgeworth, born in Blackbourton, Oxfordshire. After being educated in England, she returned to Edgeworthstown in County Longford, Ireland in 1772 to act as her father's assistant and governess to his many other children. With her father, and to illustrate his educational ideas, she published *Letters to Literary Ladies* (1795), *The Parent's Assistant* (1796) and *Practical Education* (1798). In 1800 she published her first novel, *Castle Rackrent*, which was an immediate success, followed by *Belinda* in 1801. She was praised by Sir **Walter Scott** and was lionized on a visit to London and the Continent, where she turned down a proposal of marriage from the Swedish Count Edelcrantz for the sake of her father. The next of her 'social novels' of Irish life was *The Absentee* (1809), followed by *Ormond* (1817). All her works were written under the influence of her father, which may have inhibited her natural story-telling talent. After her father's death (1817) she did little more writing apart from a late novel, *Helen* (1834), but devoted herself to looking after the family property, and 'good works'. She is also remembered for children's stories.
▷P H Newby, *Maria Edgeworth* (1950)

EDMOND, Lauris
(1924–)
New Zealand poet and novelist, born in Dannevirke. Her first verse, *In Middle Air*, was published in 1975. Her second collection, *The Pear Tree* (1977), was written after the

death of her daughter; death and transience are major themes in her work, as in *Seasons and Creatures* (1986) and *Summer near the Arctic Circle* (1988). *Selected Poems* appeared in 1984, as did her only novel to date, *High Country Weather. Hot October, an Autobiographical Story* was published in 1989. She has compiled *Women at War*, which draws on written memoirs and oral history, edited the letters of New Zealand poet **A R D Fairburn**, and written some unpublished plays.

EDSCHMID, Kasimir, pseud of **Eduard Schmid**
(1890–1966)

German expressionist prose writer, author of short stories, novels and influential essays, born in Darmstadt. He was one of the earliest spokesmen for Expressionism (he remains its most coherent expositor) and in his own prose aimed, initially, for effects both shocking, vitalist and ecstatic. *Die achatnen Kugeln* (1920, 'The Agate Balls'), is an ironic *Bildungsroman* on the theme of a rich heiress's education through living amongst beggars and whores. Later, after celebrating **Byron**'s incestuous feelings in *Lord Byron* (1929, Eng trans 1930), he became more darkly satirical. His later work, after he had been forbidden by the Nazis to publish, is more straightforward. His Diary, *Tagebuch 1958–1960* (1960) is an illuminating work.

EDWARDS, Amelia Ann Blandford
(1831–92)

English novelist and Egyptologist, born in London. She was the author of *My Brother's Wife* (1855), *Debenham's Vow* (1869), *Lord Brackenbury* (1880), and other romantic novels. She was founder of the Egyptian Exploration Fund, and contributed papers on Egyptology to the principal European and American journals, and wrote *A Thousand Miles up the Nile* (1877) and *Pharaohs, Fellahs, and Explorers* (1891).
▷ K S MacQuoid, *Amelia Blandford Edwards* (1897)

EDWARDS, Hugh
(1878–1952)

English novelist, born in Gibraltar of a naval family. He was in army service in India and Africa until he was invalided out before World War I. He wrote five novels, one of which is a minor classic, often reprinted: *All Night at Mr Stanyhurst's* (1933), a historical novel which conceals a tale within a tale; 'its rapport with the late eighteenth century is uncanny', wrote a critic, 'every word counts, the final effect is hauntingly poetic'. It was greatly admired by **Graham Greene**.

EDWARDS BELLO, Joaquín
(1887–1968)

Chilean novelist and essayist, born in Valparaíso, a descendant of **Andrés Bello**. Edwards Bello was, in his first phase, one of Chile's foremost naturalist novelists, writing under the direct influence of **Zola** (he had been educated in Europe). His savage *El inútil* (1910, 'The Useless One'), about the downfall of a Chilean in Paris, obliged him to leave Chile. Later, in *El roto* (1920, 'The Debauchee'), his chief work, he set his horrendous tale of the 'lower depths' in Chile itself, and included statistics of alcoholism and tuberculosis in Santiago. But he was not a subtle writer, nor one of much psychological penetration.

EEDEN, Frederik Willem van
(1860–1932)

Dutch novelist, dramatist, translator, poet and critic, born in Haarlem. He was a pioneering psychiatrist who had studied under Charcot in Paris, and who later became aware of **Freud**. He translated much of **Tagore**'s work, was more widely read in foreign literatures than any of his contemporaries, and probably holds more appeal for the modern reader than almost all of them. During his life he founded two communes, and was a friend to **Upton Sinclair**. He was one of the leading members of De Nieuwe Gids, 'The Men of the Eighties', the Dutch group which swept away the cobwebs of literary conventions which had outstayed their usefulness. His two chief works are the novels *De kleine Johannes* (1887–1906, Eng trans *Little Johannes*, 1895) and *Van de koele meren des doods* (1900, Eng trans *The Deeps of Deliverance*, 1902). The first, tracing the development of a boy's soul, foreshadows his own conversion to Roman Catholicism (1922); the second, his finest work of all, is a case-study based on one of his own patients, a woman who sank into drug addiction and prostitution, but was cured by religious understanding. His drama was popular in its time.

EEKHOUD, Georges
(1854–1927)

Belgian poet, novelist and translator (of **Webster** and **Marlowe**), born in Antwerp. At first associated with the socialistic group Jeune Belgique, Eekhoud broke decisively away from it in 1893, when he felt that it was adopting as its ideal a 'Parnassian' cult of objectivity. Taking **Zola** as his inspiration he began to write naturalistic novels in which, however, he expressed a genuine love and respect for criminals and outcasts. Despite some tiresome fin de siècle affectations, his fiction remains interesting and readable, but

it is now neglected. In *Escal-Vigor* (1899, Eng trans *Strange Love*, 1933) he deals boldly (for that time) with his homosexuality; *La Nouvelle Carthage* (1888, Eng trans *The New Carthage*, 1917) memorably castigates 'urban progress' as carried out by hypocritical or misguided bureaucrats. The posthumous *Le Terroir incarné* (1928, 'The Terror Incarnate'), one of his most impressive and powerful works, is the most concise expression of his zestful and indignant philosophy—and it makes clear why he broke away from Jeune Belgique.
▷G Turquet-Milnes, *Some Modern Belgian Writers* (1916)

EGAN, Pierce
(1772–1849)
English sporting writer, born in London. A London journalist, he was the author of many works, including *Boxiana; or Sketches of Antient and Modern Pugilism* (1812–13). He achieved fame with his description of the life of a 'man about town', *Life in London*, published in serial form in 1820 and as a book in 1821, with coloured illustrations by the brothers Cruikshank. In 1824 he launched a weekly sporting journal *Pierce Egan's Life in London*, incorporated into *Sporting Life* in 1859. His son, 'Pierce the Younger' (1814–80), was also a journalist and writer, and published dozens of 'cheap' novels.
▷J Reid, *Bucks and Bruisers: Pierce Egan and Regency England* (1971)

EGERTON, Sarah, née Fyge, later Field
(1670–1723)
English poet, born in London, daughter of a well-born physician. She left home in disgrace after publishing a lively feminist polemic, *The Female Advocate* (1686), and married an attorney who died early. Her second marriage to the Rev Thomas Egerton, a widower of 50, was unhappy. She wrote conventional elegies on **Dryden** (1700), but her more original *Poems on Several Occasions* (1703) contains passionate accounts of her loves, marriages and sufferings, and spirited satire against tyrannical husbands and female prudes.
▷*The Female Advocate* in *Satires on Women*, (1976, ed F Nussbaum); J Medoff, in *Tulsa Studies in Women's Literature*, 1 (1982)

EGGE, Peter Andreas
(1869–1959)
Norwegian novelist, born in Trondheim. Of humble peasant stock and too poor to pursue his education, he was discovered by **Knut Hamsun**, who arranged for the publication of his first novel, *Common People* (1891). His first real success was with *The Heart* (1917), which is a serious and penetrating study of marriage between two dissimilar personalities, and *Hansine Solstad* (1926), a delicate, sympathetic description of a woman wrongfully accused of theft in her youth, whose supposed crime dogs her through life. Egge also wrote plays in which he followed **Ibsen** in creating drama from defects of character.
▷C M Woel, *Peter Egge* (1929)

EGGLESTON, Edward
(1837–1902)
American writer and pastor, born in Vevay, Indiana. He was a Methodist minister in Minnesota, and editor of journals like *Little Corporal*, *National Sunday School Teacher* and *Hearth and Home*. He also wrote several classic novels, among them *The Hoosier Schoolmaster* (1871), which was based on his brother's experience as a small-town teacher, *The Circuit Rider* (1874), on his own as an itinerant minister, and *The Graysons* (1888), in which Abraham Lincoln was a central character.
▷W P Randel, *Eggleston, author of 'The Hoosier Schoolmaster'* (1946)

EGLITIS, Anslavs
(1906–)
Latvian poet and prolific writer of fiction, in exile in America, whose work has not been much translated—with the exception of the well-regarded story 'The Best Seller', in *Texas Quarterly* (Autumn 1960).

EGUREN, José María
(1874–1942)
Peruvian poet and translator (**Wilde**, **Baudelaire**), born in Lima, the natural predecessor to **César Vallejo**. He was also a painter. It was his country childhood that enriched his imagination. He offered discerning Peruvian readers a quiet and modest alternative to the 'trumpet solos' of the publicist **Chocano**, and gradually the best critics, including José Carlos Mariátegui and **González Prada**, recognized his genius as one of remarkable originality. There are translations of his poetry in the *Penguin Book of Latin American verse* (1971, ed E Curacciolo-Trejo) and in *Latin-American Poetry* (1942).
▷J C Mariátegui, *Siete ensayos* (1952); I Goldburg, *Studies in Spanish-American Literature* (1920)

EHRENBURG, or ERENBURG, Ilya Grigorievich
(1891–1967)
Russian writer, born in Moscow. In 1908 he was imprisoned for revolutionary activities, but escaped to Paris, where he worked as a journalist until 1917, when he returned to

EHRENSTEIN, Alfred

Russia, but went back to Paris as a correspondent. Among his best works are *The Extraordinary Adventures of Julio Jurenito* (1921), a satire on the aftermath of World War I, *The Fall of Paris* (1941) and *The Storm* (1947), both novels about World War II, and *The Thaw* (1954), a novel about the period of de-Stalinization. He published his memoirs *People, Years, Life* in six volumes from 1960 to 1966.

EHRENSTEIN, Alfred
(1886–1950)

Austrian poet and story writer, born in Vienna of Jewish descent. After studying philosophy, he became a prolific writer of fiction, essays and of the expressionist poetry for which he is now best remembered. His political ideas were revolutionary, and he left Germany in 1932 and died in New York. Most of his poetry of protest, as has been said, 'seems thin today', but a few notable exceptions still crop up in anthologies.
▷C Middleton and M Hamburger (eds), *Modern German Poetry 1910–1969* (1962)

EICH, Gunter
(1907–72)

German poet and writer of *hörspielen* (radio plays)—this has become a highly developed art in his country, and he was one of the pre-Nazi pioneers of it—who was born in Lebus on the Oder. He was married to **Ilse Aichinger**. He was associated with the literary circle Gruppe '47, and his poetry, amongst the most notable produced by his generation, was influential in the early post-Nazi days for its relentless examination of the Nazi past; however, by mood and habit he was a mystical poet maintaining the tradition of **Angelus Silesius**. His most famous and successful radio play was *Träume* (1950, 'Dreams'). In English translation are *Journeys* (1968) and *Selected Poems* (1971).
▷*Encounter 30*, 3 (1963)

EICHENDORFF, Joseph, Freiherr von
(1788–1857)

German poet, novelist and critic, born near Ratibor, into a noble family. He studied law and became a government official. He is regarded as one of the most important Romantic lyricists writing in German, and his poems were set by a number of composers, including Schumann and Mendelssohn. They reveal his profound veneration for the divine gifts of natural beauty. His novels include the idyllic *Aus dem Leben eines Taugenichts* (1826, Eng trans *Memoirs of a Good-for-Nothing*) and *Das Marmorbild* (1826, 'The Marble Statue').

▷L R Radner, *Eichendorff: the spiritual geometer* (1970)

EKELÖF, (Bengt) Gunnar
(1907–68)

Swedish poet. A leader of the post-war modernists, he is considered one of the most significant Swedish poets of this century. Much influenced by the French Symbolists, he published his first book of poetry, *Sent på jorden* ('Late Arrival on Earth'), in 1932, followed by *Dedikation* (1934, 'Dedication'), *Sorgen och stjärnan* (1936, 'Sorrow and the Star') and *Färjesång* (1941, 'Ferry Song'). *En Mölnaelegi* (1960), which is concerned with the nature of time, was translated into English (*A Mölna Elegy*, 1979), as were his *Selected poems* (1966) and *Guide to the Underworld* (1967).
▷S Karlsson and A Liffman, *En bok om Gunnar Ekelöf* (1956)

EKELUND, Vilhelm
(1880–1949)

Swedish poet and essayist. A Symbolist and early modernist, his works include poetry such as *Stella Maris* (1906), and volumes of essays inspired by **Nietzsche**, including *Classical Ideal* (1909).
▷S Ahlstrom, *Vilhelm Ekelund* (1940)

EKMAN, Kerstin
(1933–)

Swedish novelist. Born in Risinge, Östergötland, she worked as a teacher and in the film industry before emerging as a successful writer of thrillers. Her tetralogy tracing feminine patterns of civilization within the framework of a Swedish railway town, *Häxringarna* (1974, 'The Witches' Circles'), *Springkällan* (1976, 'The Spring'), *Änglahuset* (1979, 'House of Angels') and *En stad av ljus* (1983, 'City of Light'), established her as one of Sweden's leading contemporary novelists, its carefully researched realist elements mingling with mythical and symbolic dimensions which become particularly prominent in the final volume. *Rövarna i Skuleskogen* (1988, 'The Robbers in the Skule Forest') is a vivid and far-reaching critique of civilization, while *Händelser vid vatten* (1993, 'Events by Water') explores issues of culture and memory in an isolated community in the north of Sweden. She was elected a member of the Swedish Academy in 1978, but the failure of the Academy to express its support for **Salman Rushdie** following the death sentence placed on him by Iranian fundamentalists persuaded her to leave it in 1989.
▷M Schottenius, *Den kvinnliga hemligheten. En studie i Kerstin Ekmans berättarkonst* (1992)

EKWENSI, Cyprian Odiatu Duaka
(1921–)

Nigerian novelist. After attending college in Ibadan and in Ghana, he trained as a pharmacist in London and lectured on the subject in Lagos for 10 years before moving into broadcasting as head of features. He was later director of the Nigerian Ministry of Information and Head of Information Services at Enugu. His first novel was *People of the City* (1954, rev edn 1963), a powerful account of the problems of urbanization in Africa, a theme he returned to in *Jagua Nana* (1961), the story of a Lagos prostitute. In *Burning Grass* (1962), the nomadic life of Fulani herders becomes a wider symbol of social conditions in post-colonial Africa, as does the big game hunt in *Beautiful Feathers* (1963). In *Iska* (1966) and *Survive the Peace* (1976) he tackles the corruption and tribalist violence of modern Nigerian politics, culminating in the latter book, with its ironic title, set in the aftermath of the Biafran civil war. He has also written children's books.
▷ E Emenyona, *Cyprian Ekwensi* (1974)

ELIN, Pelin, pseud of Dimitur Ivanov
(1877–1949)

Bulgaria's greatest story writer, and an editor and children's author, born in Baylovo. He wrote little in the last 25 years of his life, but remained active in literary circles. In his many writings he depicted the peasantry (*shopi*) of the country around Sofia, where he lived, with a loving detachment and always with a large dose of psychological realism. He was less artificial than any of his contemporaries, and his rural tales are still read and loved; his collected work was published in Bulgaria in 1958–9 and took up 10 volumes. He also wrote plays. He had the approval of the communist government, but did not like socialist realism, and declared that the emotions of men, and not machines, should determine literature. One of his stories is contained in *The Peach Thief and Other Bulgarian Stories* (1968).
▷ C Manning and R Smal-Stocki, *The History of Modern Bulgarian Literature* (1960)

ELIOT, George, pseud of Mary Ann or Marian Evans
(1819–80)

English novelist, born on Arbury Farm in Astley. In her father, Robert Evans, a Warwickshire land agent, a man of strong character, were seen many of the traits transferred by his daughter to Adam Bede and Caleb Garth. She lost her mother, whom she loved devotedly, in 1836, and soon afterwards took entire charge of the household. Masters came from Coventry to teach her German, Italian and music—of the last she was passionately fond throughout her life. She was also an immense reader. In 1841 her father moved to Coventry, and there she met Charles Bray, a writer on the philosophy of necessity from the phrenological standpoint, and his brother-in-law, Charles Hennell, who had published in 1838 a rationalistic *Inquiry concerning the Origin of Christianity*. Under their influence she rejected her earlier evangelical Christianity. In 1844 she took on the laborious task of translating Strauss's *Leben Jesu* (published in 1846). After her father's death in 1849 she travelled on the Continent with Mr and Mrs Bray; returning to England in 1850 she began to write for the *Westminster Review*. She became assistant editor in 1851, and the centre of a literary circle, two of whose members were Herbert Spencer and George Henry Lewes. She translated Feuerbach's *Essence of Christianity* (1854), the only book that bore her real name. Gradually her intimacy with Lewes grew, and in 1854 she formed a liaison with him which lasted until his death in 1878. In July 1854 she went abroad with him, staying three months in Weimar, where he was preparing for his *Life of Goethe*. After a longer stay in Berlin, they returned and lived first in Dover, then in East Sheen, then in Richmond. In 1856 she attempted her first story, 'The Sad Fortunes of the Rev. Amos Barton', the beginning of the *Scenes of Clerical Life*. It came out in *Blackwood's Magazine* in 1857, and at once showed that a new author of great power had risen. 'Mr Gilfil's Love Story' and 'Janet's Repentance' followed quickly. Her first novel, *Adam Bede* (1859), had an enormous success. *The Mill on the Floss* (1860), *Silas Marner* (1861), *Romola* (1863) and *Felix Holt* (1866) appeared next in succession. Her first poem, *The Spanish Gypsy* (1868), was followed next year by *Agatha, The Legend of Jubal* and *Armgart*; and in 1871–2 appeared *Middlemarch*, generally considered her greatest work. After that came *Daniel Deronda* (1876), her last great novel. After the death of Lewes, she was coaxed to write *Impressions of Theophrastus Such* (1879), a volume of somewhat miscellaneous essays. She fell in love again with a banker 20 years her junior, John Walter Cross (died 1924), a friend of long standing whom she married in May 1880. She died a few months later, and was buried in Highgate Cemetery, in the grave next to that of Lewes. As a novelist, George Eliot will probably always stand among the greatest of the English realist school; her pictures of farmers, tradesmen, and the lower middle-class, generally of the Midlands, are hardly surpassed in English literature.
▷ G S Haight, *George Eliot* (1968); F R Leavis, *The Great Tradition* (1948)

ELIOT, T(homas) S(tearns)
(1888–1965)

American-born British poet, critic and dramatist, and winner of the Nobel Prize for literature, born in St Louis, Missouri. After four years at Harvard (1906–10, where the chief influence upon his development was that of Irving Babbitt with his 'selective' humanism and his resistance to modern trends) he spent a year in Paris, attending lectures and improving his command of the French language. He returned to Harvard to study philosophy for three years. He had distinguished teachers, such as Josiah Royce and **George Santayana**, and, for a time, Bertrand Russell. A travelling scholarship from Harvard took him to Merton College, Oxford, for a year, where he worked on a doctoral dissertation on F H Bradley, and read **Plato** and Aristotle under H H Joachim. Persuaded by **Ezra Pound**, to whom he had shown his poems, he remained in England where he lived from then on (1911), taking up naturalization in 1927. After teaching for a term in High Wycombe, and for a year at Highgate Junior School, he worked for eight years in Lloyds Bank before becoming a director of the publishing firm of Faber. The enthusiastic support of Pound led to the publication of Eliot's first volume of verse, *Prufrock and Other Observations* (1917). He was introduced by Bertrand Russell into the Bloomsbury Circle, where the quality of his work was immediately recognized. His next two small volumes, *Ara vos prec* (1920) and the more important *The Waste Land* (1922), were published by Leonard and **Virginia Woolf** at the Hogarth Press. *The Hollow Men*, which followed in 1925, gave more excuse for regarding Eliot at that point as a cynical defeatist. *The Waste Land* had appeared in the first number of *The Criterion*, a quarterly review which Eliot edited from 1923 to 1939. *The Criterion* aimed at impartiality in presenting opposed political philosophies and is indispensable for a study of ideas, political and religious, between the wars, as well as for the literary developments, both here and abroad during that period. In 1927, the year in which he became a British subject, Eliot was baptized and confirmed, having been raised as a Unitarian. The publication of a volume of essays *For Lancelot Andrewes* (1928) gave his first public statement of his adherence to the Anglo-Catholic movement within the Church of England. *Ash Wednesday* (1930) is the first fruit of this new sacramental attitude. The religious plays *The Rock* (1934) and *Murder in the Cathedral* (1935) which followed sealed his reputation as the poet who had revived the verse play in the interests of Catholic devotion. His later dramas, *The Cocktail Party* (1950), *The Family Reunion* (1939), *The Confidential Clerk*

(1954) and *The Elder Statesman* (1958), were to aim at being West End successes rather than sacred plays in church precincts, but Catholic doctrine inspired all these plays, sometimes to the embarrassment of critics and audience alike. Before this incursion into the theatre world he produced his greatest work, *Four Quartets* (1944), which, despite its obscurity, is one of the greatest philosophical poems in the language. The most rewarding is probably the last, *Little Gidding*. Eliot's critical work consists of literary criticism, such as *The Sacred Wood* (1920, on Jacobean dramatists), the admirable *Homage to Dryden* (1924), *The Use of Poetry and the Use of Criticism* (1933), *Elizabethan Essays* (1934) and *On Poetry and Poets* (1957). When writing or lecturing on literature generally he could be very provocative, as in his *Modern Education and the Classics* (1934), where he said that the Classics were to be studied not for their own sake but as a buttress for the Faith; and in *After Strange Gods* (1934), where he tries to stretch some great writers on the Procrustean bed of 'Christian Sensibility'. In social criticisms, as in *The Idea of a Christian Society* (1939) and *Notes Towards the Definition of Culture*, he is hierarchal and undemocratic. The new poetry, as announced by Ezra Pound, **T E Hulme** and Eliot, was to be related to modern life and expressed in modern idiom, preferably in free verse. Rhetoric and romantic clichés were to be avoided. In his late essay 'Milton II', in *On Poetry and Poets*, he confessed that he and his friends had insisted over much on these ideas and this was a sort of recantation for his abuse of **Milton**. But critics today have no doubt of the salutary effect of their crusade and of Eliot's poetry as having justified it. In 1948 he was awarded the Nobel Prize for literature.
▷M Grant, *T S Eliot: the critical heritage* (2 vols, 1982); P Ackroyd, *Eliot: a life* (1984)

ELISABETH, QUEEN OF ROMANIA
see **CARMEN SYLVA**

ELISIO, Filento, 'Arcadian' pseud of **Padre Manuel do Nascimento**
(1734–1819)

Portuguese poet and translator, born in Lisbon. Nascimento got his 'Arcadian' name from the future Marquesa de Alorna, poet, to whom he had taught Latin. But he was a member of the opposing, neo-classical group (a *dissidente*): the Grupo da Ribeira das Naus. He is almost as famous for his escape from the Inquisition (1777–8), on the fall of his protector Pombal. He had been accused of atheism for not believing in the literal truth of the Flood. He was prolific (some 750 000 lines in a long lifetime), and highly artificial (**Horace** was his main model), but exceedingly influential upon his successors, mostly on account of what he showed could be done with Portuguese in poetic forms.

▷C Olavo, *O vida amargurada de F. Elisio* (1944)

ELISSAMBURU, Jean-Baptiste
(1828–91)

Basque lyric poet, regarded as a worthy contemporary of **Indalecio Bizcarrondo**.
▷R Gallop, *A Book of the Basques* (1930); L Michelena, *Historia de la literatura vasca* (1960)

ELKIN, Stanley Lawrence
(1930–)

American author and academic, born in Brooklyn, New York. He was educated at the University of Illinois, where he took a PhD. While his stories in *Criers and Kibitzers, Kibitzers and Criers* (1966) have their champions, and *The Living End* (1979)—three stories about heaven and hell—is his most widely read book, he is pre-eminently a novelist. *Boswell* (1964), about a professional wrestler obsessed with death and greatness, marked his debut and was followed by *A Bad Man* (1967), *The Dick Gibson Show* (1971) and *The Franchiser* (1976), all fixated with modern America. *George Mills* (1982) and *The Magic Kingdom* (1985) are set, respectively, in Sultanic Turkey and contemporary St Louis.
▷P Bailey, *Reading Stanley Elkin* (1985)

ELLIOTT, George Paul
(1918–80)

American novelist, story writer and poet, born in Knightstown, Indiana. He was a professor at Syracuse University for most of his life. His poetry is lyrical and straightforward. The most impressive of his novels was *David Knudsen* (1962), about the son of one of the scientists who invented the bomb used at Hiroshima: he has to rid himself of his 'radiation sickness', which stands for his aggressive scientism. Stories were collected in *Among the Dangs* (1962) and *An Hour of Last Things* (1969).

ELLIOTT, Sumner Locke
(1917–1991)

Australian novelist and playwright, born in Sydney. His mother, Sumner Locke (1881–1917), who died soon after his birth, wrote popular stories of 'selection' life (on government-allocated land). Elliott became an actor and wrote several plays, of which *Rusty Bugles* (1948) achieved great success and some notoriety when its realistic army language was heavily censored. By that time he had left for the USA, where he settled, becoming a US citizen in 1955. He was in demand as a scriptwriter for NBC and CBS television and his play *Buy Me Blue Ribbons* was produced on Broadway in 1951. His semi-autobiographical novel *Careful, He Might Hear You* (1963) deals with the traumatic experiences of his own childhood and the battle for his custody. It was translated into many languages and became a successful film in 1983. *Water under the Bridge* (1977) is a complex and untidy novel set in inner Sydney, from the opening of Sydney Harbour Bridge in 1932 to the early 1950s.

ELLIS, Alice Thomas, pseud of Anna Margaret Haycraft
(1932–)

English novelist, born in Liverpool and brought up in Wales. She studied at Liverpool School of Art, and was a postulant at a convent in Liverpool, but married in 1956. Her novels include *The Sin Eater* (1977), a bitterly sharp comedy of manners involving English, Irish and Welsh characters of differing religious faiths. Subsequent novels are similarly satirical, sometimes dark, and reveal a sympathy for religious belief and the nuances of love and loathing. In *The Other Side of the Fire* (1983) several women confront a variety of emotional catharses. *The Clothes in the Wardrobe* (1987), *The Skeleton in the Cupboard* (1988) and *The Fly in the Ointment* (1989), comprise a trilogy about contemporary life.

ELLIS, Edward Sylvester
(1840–1916)

American novelist and historian, born in Geneva, Ohio. He was amongst the most successful—under various pseudonyms—of the 'dime novelists': *Seth Jones* (1860), Number 8 of Beadle's Dime Novels, a frontier tale about a man who disguises himself as a hunter, sold almost half a million copies. An inaccurate history of the United States which he wrote sold all over the country.

ELLIS, George
(1753–1815)

British satirist and poet, born in Grenada, West Indies, the son of a planter. He won early popularity with his *Poetical Tales by Sir Gregory Gander* (1778), and contributed satires on Pitt and others to the Whig *Rolliad*, though later he was co-founder with George Canning of the Tory *Anti-Jacobin*. A friend of Sir **Walter Scott**, he edited *Specimens of Early English Poets* (1790) and *Specimens of Early English Romances in Metre* (1805).

ELLISON, Harlan Jay
(1934–)

American science-fiction writer, essayist, critic and editor, born in Cleveland, Ohio.

His outspoken, pugnacious attitudes and willingness to tackle taboo subjects like sex and drugs have made him a controversial figure in science-fiction circles. His best work has been in short-story form, and significant collections include *I Have No Mouth, and I Must Scream* (1967, rev edn 1983), *The Beast That Shouted Love at the Heart of the World* (1969, rev edn 1984), *Deathbird Stories* (1975), and the massive retrospective *The Essential Ellison* (1987). He is an acerbic critic of film and television, and an influential editor, notably in the ground-breaking *Dangerous Visions* anthologies (1967, 1972). He has written several novels, screenplays, and television scripts.
▷ *All the Lies That Are My Life* (1989)

ELLISON, Ralph Waldo
(1914–94)

American novelist, born in Oklahoma City, Oklahoma. Bookish as well as musical, he studied music at Tuskagee Institute and served during World War II in the US Merchant Marine. He met **Richard Wright** in 1937, through whom he became aware of social and racial injustice, and who encouraged him to write. His early work appeared in *New Challenge* magazine. *Invisible Man* (1952), his only completed novel, is the quest of a nameless black man, travelling from South to North, in search of a personal and racial identity. Allusive but highly original and ingenious, it had a seminal influence on other black writers and won the National Book Award. He was Albert Schweitzer Professor in the Humanities at New York University (1970–9). He published two books of essays, *Shadow and the Act* (1964) and *Going to the Territory* (1986), but the long-awaited second novel never appeared.
▷ R Dietze, *Ellison: the genesis of an artist* (1982)

ELLMANN, Richard
(1918–87)

American biographer and academic, born in Detroit, Michigan. He graduated from Yale University and after the war he lived in Dublin for a year, where he wrote his first book, *Yeats; the Man and the Mask* (1948). Some 10 years later came his masterful biography of **James Joyce**, now accepted as one of the pinnacles of 20th-century biography, as much for its elegant composition as its astute judgement and erudition. A professor at Northwestern University, Illinois, until 1968, he moved to Oxford in 1970 as Goldsmiths' Professor of English Literature, where he remained till his death. His biography of **Oscar Wilde** (1987), a 20-year labour of love, was published posthumously to universal acclaim. Selected essays were published under the title, *a long the riverrun* in 1988.
▷ *Literary Biography: inaugural lecture* (pamphlet, 1971)

ELMSLIE, Kenward Gray
(1929–)

American poet, playwright and librettist, born in New York. His verse has something of the surrealized illogic of **John Ashbery** and other 'New York School' writers, but in collections like *The Champ* (1968), *Circus Nerves* (1971) and, in particular, *Tropicalism* (1975), he is closer to the lushly musical imagery of **Wallace Stevens**. He has also acknowledged the impact of the great American songwriters on his work. Elmslie received the **Frank O'Hara** Award in 1971. He has adapted works by figures as disparate as **Henry James** and **Truman Capote** for the stage. His only novel is *The Orchid Stories* (1973). He wrote librettos for *Miss Julie* (1965), *Lizzie Bordern* (1965) and others.

ELSKAMP, Max
(1862–1931)

Major Belgian poet and engraver, described by a critic as being of 'agonised sensibility', born in Antwerp, which he seldom left. His high stature is recognized in Belgium, but not yet elsewhere. He was carefully read, valued and assimilated by **Apollinaire** and **Verhaeren**, but can still be dismissed by English critics as a 'pious dilettante', a lesser **Verlaine**. A responsible innovator, he was uninterested in fame, and only published his poems in a trade edition when he was approaching 40. His accompanying engravings are as important to the poems as are those of **Thomas Hardy** to his earlier poems. He is, essentially, a religious poet—his contemplation shot through and through with erotic longing—over-prolific, puzzling, but authentically devout and completely original. The poems of his last years are his most fascinating (eg in *Aegri Somnia*, 1924, 'A Sick Man's Dreams') and suggestive. A reliable collected edition of his poems was published in 1967.

ELSSCHOT, Willem, pseud of Alfons de Ridder
(1882–1960)

Belgian (Flemish) novelist and gifted and graceful minor poet, born in Antwerp, who began, with *Villa des Roses* (1913)—a novel about life in a Paris pension—in the naturalist style of **Zola**. After a period of silence he changed his style drastically, to become a major whimsical satirist and parodist. He was better known in Holland, where his work was rediscovered by the Forum group in the early 1930s, than in his native Belgium. Three of his best novels have been translated as *Three Novels* (1963): *Lijmen* (1924, *Soft Soap*), *Het been* (1938, *The Leg*) and *Het dwaalicht* (1946, *Will O' the Wisp*). These, together with *Kaas* (1933, 'Cheese'), have in them more than a touch of the genius of that great Uruguayan dissector of urban anguish **Juan Carlos Onetti**. As the director of an advertising agency, Elsschot put his own experiences of mendacious publicity to brilliant use. He is particularly noted for his realistic and witty approach to all kinds of literary pretension—but this attitude has cost him the neglect of all but the most discerning critics.

▷F Smits, *Willem Elsschot* (1952, in Dutch)

ÉLUARD, Paul, pseud of Eugène-Emile Paul Grindel
(1895–1952)

Major French poet, born in Saint-Denis. Éluard was from almost the beginning of his career as a poet a leading member of **André Breton**'s Surrealist group, and was also involved with the Dada movement. But he developed into France's leading 20th-century love poet. His chief Surrealist poetry is in *Les Dessous d'une vie ou la pyramide humaine* (1926, 'The Underbelly of Life or the Human Pyramid'); this contains many 'automatic' and dream poems. Throughout World War II, in the course of which he had to hide in a mental hospital and pretend to be one of the patients, Éluard was in the Resistance; after it he was a member of the Communist Party. His poetry changed, to become more direct and idiomatic; it was much concerned with his second wife Nusch, and with her tragic death. Much of the earlier poetry had similarly been concerned with his first wife Gala, whom he lost to the Surrealist Salvador Dali. English translations include: *Thorns of Thunder* (1936); *Selected Writings* (1951); *Last Love Poems* (1980).

▷P Nugent, *Paul Éluard* (1974)

ELYTIS, Odysseus, pseud of Odysseus Alepoudelis
(1911–)

Greek poet and winner of the Nobel Prize for literature, born in Heraklion, Crete. Educated at Athens University and at the Sorbonne, Paris, he has worked in broadcasting and as a critic of art and literature. His pseudonym is said to combine the three most prevalent themes in his work: Greece, hope and freedom. He was deeply influenced by the surrealists, both French and Greek, and his career as a poet began in the 1930s. His early poems exude a love of Greece, sun and life, but after war experience in Albania a natural *joie de vivre* is set against violence and the imminence of death. His greatest achievement is *To axion esti* (1959, Eng trans

The Axion Esti, 1974), a long, optimistic poem which took 14 years to write. In 1979 he was awarded the Nobel Prize for literature.

▷I Ivask, *Elytis: analogies of light* (1980)

EMBIRIKOS, Andreas
(1901–75)

Greek poet and novelist, born in Braila, in Romania, but resident for most of his life in France and England. He burst on to the Greek literary scene in 1935 with *Ipsikaminos* ('Furnace'), a collection of poetry that baffled and offended contemporary critics; a citation from the French Surrealist André Breton on its front page served to locate the work in a genre then unknown in Greece. His next two collections, the titles of which translate as 'The Vibrations of the Necktie' and 'The Appearance of Angels in a Steam Engine', were in the same vein, but were published only in literary journals. Embirikos then turned to prose, anticipating the 'automatic writing' of **Kerouac** and the American 'Beat' writers, and developing a style that mixed formal Greek *Katharevousa* and clichés culled from magazines and newspapers. In his later career he discovered **Freud** and moved away from the unbridled Surrealism of his earlier works: *Endochora* ('Hinterland'), a novel published in 1945, saw him coming to terms with Freud's acceptance of sexual instinct, and his next two books, *Argo* and *Zemphyra*, displayed an unbridled eroticism that had them censored.

EMECHETA, (Florence Onye) Buchi
(1944–)

British novelist, born near Lagos, Nigeria. She was educated at the Methodist Girls' High School, Lagos, and the University of London, and has worked as a teacher, librarian and social worker. She moved to England with her student husband in 1962 and has since lived in London with her five children. Writing of marriage as a battle of the sexes, her novels are powerful social documents, graphic in their depiction of man's inhumanity to woman (she separated from her husband). Relevant titles are *In the Ditch* (1972) and *Second-Class Citizen* (1974), which were later published together as *Adah's Story* (1983), *The Bride Price* (1976), *The Slave Girl* (1977), *The Joys of Motherhood* (1979), *Double Yoke* (1982) and *The Rape of Shavi* (1983). *Gwendolen* (1989) focuses on the cultural isolation of a young Caribbean immigrant. She has also written children's stories and television plays.

▷*Head Above Water* (1986)

EMERSON, Ralph Waldo
(1803–82)

American poet and essayist, born in Boston of a long line of ministers. He graduated at

Harvard in 1821, and after teaching at different places, became in 1829 pastor of the Second Church (Unitarian) in Boston, and married his first wife, Ellen Louisa Tucker (d.1832). In that year he preached views on the Lord's Supper which were disapproved of by the majority of his congregation; this led him finally to resign his pulpit. In 1833 he went to Europe, and visited **Thomas Carlyle** at Craigenputtock, next year beginning that 38 years' correspondence which shows the two men with all their characteristics, different as optimist and pessimist, yet with many profound sympathies. In 1834 he moved to Concord and the following year married his second wife, Lydia (Lidian) Jackson (1802–92). In 1836 he published a prose rhapsody entitled *Nature*, which, like his earlier poems, was read by few, and understood by fewer still, but which contains the germs of many of his later essays and poems. It was followed by 'The American Scholar', an oration delivered at Harvard University. These two publications, the first in the series of his collected works, strike the keynote of his philosophical, poetical and moral teachings. The 'address before the Divinity Class, Cambridge, 1838', which follows them, defined his position in, or out of, the church in which he had been a minister. A plea for the individual consciousness (as against all historical creeds, bibles, churches) for the soul of each man as the supreme judge in spiritual matters, it produced a great sensation, especially among the Unitarians, and much controversy followed in which Emerson took no part. In 1849 he revisited England to lecture on *Representative Men* (published in 1850). His *English Traits* appeared in 1856, *The Conduct of Life* in 1860, *Society and Solitude* in 1870, *Letters and Social Aims* in 1876. The idealist or transcendentalist in philosophy, the rationalist in religion, the bold advocate of spiritual independence, of intuition as a divine guidance, of instinct as a heaven-born impulse, of individualism in its fullest extent, making each life a kind of theocratic egoism—this is the Emerson of his larger utterances. For him nature was a sphinx, covered with hieroglyphics, for which the spirit of man is to find the key.
▷G W Allen, *Emerson: a biography* (1981)

EMINESCU, Mikhail
(1850–89)

Romanian poet, born in Ipoteşti. He studied at Czernowitz, Vienna and Berlin, and worked as a librarian, then editor, but eventually suffered a mental collapse in 1883 which left him with recurring bouts of madness until his death. He wrote lyric verse which was widely read and translated after his death. His works were collected in four volumes in 1939; his masterpiece is generally felt to be the long poem *Luceafărul* (1883).
▷G Calinescu, *Mikhail Eminescu* (1965)

EMPSON, Sir William
(1906–84)

English poet and critic, born in Howden, Yorkshire. He was educated at Winchester and Magdalene College, Cambridge, where he studied mathematics and literature. His first work of criticism was his university dissertation, published as *Seven Types of Ambiguity* (1930). From 1931 to 1934 he was Professor of English Literature in Tokyo, and at Peking (1937–9 and 1947–53), having been in the meantime with the BBC's Far Eastern Service. In 1953 he became Professor of English Literature at Sheffield University. His other critical works included *The Structure of Complex Words* (1951) and *Milton's God* (1961). *Collected Poems*, noted for wit, concentration and complexity of thought, was published in 1955.
▷R Gill, *William Empson, the man and his world* (1974)

ENCINA, or ENZINA, Juan de la
(c.1469–c.1534)

Spanish dramatist and poet, born near Salamanca. He was successively secretary to the first Duke of Alva, musical director in Pope Leo X's chapel at Rome, and prior of León in Spain. Besides his *Cancionero* (1496, 'Songbook'), he wrote in 1521 a poetical account of his pilgrimage to Jerusalem. His fame rests on 14 dramatic poems, 7 of which were the first secular poems to be dramatized in Spain (1492).
▷J R Andrews, *Juan Del Encina* (1959)

ENCKELL, Raabe
(1903–74)

Leading Finland–Swedish poet, dramatist, critic, essayist and painter, born in Tammela. He was an enthusiastic, even rather naive, supporter of every kind of modernism in his early years; but his finely crafted work is more highly technically accomplished than significant for its content. He is a versatile showman, capable of great charm. He has been called a 'humanist never unaware of the fragility of his emotional and aesthetic world'.
▷L Ekelund, *Raabe Enckell* (1974, in Swedish)

ENDO Shusako
(1923–)

Japanese novelist and short-story writer, born in Tokyo. After his parents divorced, he and his mother converted to Roman Catholicism. He graduated in French literature from Keio University, then studied for several years in Lyons. He has gained wide recognition in the West and, although he is considered by some Japanese to be un-Japanese, has won many literary awards. In 1981 he was elected to the Nihon Geijutsuin, the Japanese Arts Academy. His books include *Silence* (1966), *The Sea and Poison* (1972), *Wonderful Fool* (1974), *Volcano* (1978), *When I Whistle* (1979) and *Stained Glass Elegies* (1984). Inveterately a moralist, he is often labelled 'the Japanese Graham Greene'.

ENGEL, Johann Jakob
(1741–1802)

German writer, born in Parchim. He intended to follow his father as a Lutheran pastor, but instead became a teacher. He wrote a number of plays, mainly in the comic manner of **Gotthold Lessing**, but is best known for the novel *Herr Lorenz Stark* (1795), and popular philosophical books, including the four-volume *Der Philosoph für die Welt* (1775–1803, 'The World's Philosopher').
▷C Schroeder, *Johann Jakob Engel* (1897)

ENGEL, Marian
(1933–85)

Canadian novelist, born in Toronto and educated at McMaster University and McGill University. She worked as a teacher in Canada and the USA and lived for a time in London and Cyprus. Her first novel, *No Clouds of Glory*, was published in 1968. She chaired the Writers' Union of Canada in 1973–4, and won a Governor General's Award for *Bear* in 1976; her most famous novel, it explores the complex relationship between a woman and a bear, intertwining myth and reality. Her last book, *The Tattooed Woman*, was published posthumously.
▷G Gibson, *Eleven Canadian Novelists* (1973)

ENGLE, Paul Hamilton
(1908–91)

American poet, novelist and critic, born in Cedar Rapids, Iowa. Among his collections of poetry are *Worn Earth* (1932) and *American Song* (1951), while his novels include *Always the Land* (1941) and *An Old-Fashioned Christmas* (1964). Although his writing is formal, elegant and accessible, he is best remembered as a penetrating critic and an inspirational teacher. His courses in literature and writing at the University of Iowa gave confidence to many aspiring authors.

ENGLISH, Isobel
(1925–)

English novelist and short-story writer, born in London. Although she has written comparatively few books, she was quickly established as a considered, sensitive chronicler of middle-class manners and anxieties. Her first novel, *The Key That Rusts* (1954), records a doomed love affair between the narrator's married step-brother and another woman; *Every Eye* (1956) follows a woman's journey across Europe, as she relives various past experiences. Later novels, including *Four Voices* (1961), and a collection, *Life After All and Other Stories* (1973), use a similar technique of observed and interior narrative.

ENGLISH, Thomas Dunn
(1819–1902)

American physician, lawyer and ballad-writer whose memory survives in his poem 'Ben Bolt'. This was a popular song during the Civil War, but gained worldwide prominence when **George Du Maurier** introduced it in *Trilby*. He was also the author of more than 50 now-forgotten plays.

ENNIUS, Quintus
(c.239–169 BC)

Roman poet, born in Rudiae in Calabria, and probably of Greek extraction. He is said to have served in the wars, and returned from Sardinia to Rome with Cato the Elder. Here he taught Greek, gained the friendship of Scipio Africanus, and attained the rank of Roman citizen. He introduced the Greek hexameter into Latin, using it in his *Annals*, which became the model for Latin epic poetry. His style, though rough, is striking. In addition, he wrote satires, didactic verse, epigrams and numerous plays. Only fragments of his works survive.
▷O Skutsch, *The Annals of Quintus Ennius* (1953)

ENQUIST, Per Olov
(1934–)

Swedish playwright and novelist. His best-known work for the theatre is a collection of three plays published in 1981 under the collective title *Triptych*, comprising *Lesbian Night* (about **August Strindberg** and his wife), *To Phaedra* and *The Life of the Slow-Worms* (about **Hans Christian Andersen**). His major novel is *The Legionaries* (1968), a controversial documentary about the expulsion of Baltic refugees to Russia from Sweden after World War II.
▷A Landsmanis, *De misstolkade legionarerna* (1970)

ENRIGHT, D(ennis) J(oseph)
(1920–)

English poet, critic and literary journalist, he was born in Leamington, Warwickshire, and educated at Downing College, Cambridge, and the University of Alexandria, where he taught English (1947–50) and published his first collection of verse, *Season Ticket* (1948). His academic career continued east of Suez with appointments in Japan, Thailand and Singapore, interspersed with periods in Birmingham and Berlin. He was Honorary Professor of English at the University of Warwick from 1975 to 1980. University life figures in the novel *Academic Year* (1955), but Enright seems to have remained aloof from intellectual fashion and academic politics, carving out his own humanistic course. A *Collected Poems* appeared in 1981, suggesting a sensibility influenced by the 'Movement' poets of the fifties (**Larkin**, **Amis**, **Tom Gunn**), but more expansive and continental. Enright is the editor of *The Oxford Book of Death* (1983), a valuable anthology that wholly avoids morbidity.
▷ *Memoirs of a Mendicant Professor* (1969)

ENRÍQUEZ GÓMEZ, Antonio, properly Enríquez de Paz
(1602–c.1662)

Spanish playwright and poet, born in Segovia, the son of a baptized Portuguese Jew. In 1636 he fled to France to escape the Inquisition, and became major-domo to Louis XIII. He wrote comedies, a mystic poem, an epic, *El sansón nazareno* (1656) and a picturesque satirical novel in both prose and verse, *El siglo pitagórico* (1644, 'The Pythagorean Century'). Later he professed the Jewish faith, and in 1660 his effigy was burned at a Seville auto-da-fé.

ENZENSBERGER, Hans Magnus
(1929–)

German poet, born in Kaufbeuren and educated at Nuremberg, Freiburg and Hamburg. He saw service with the militia towards the end of World War II and worked as an editor for the Suddeutsche Rundfunk at the end of the fifties, the period when his first significant poetry was published in *verteidigung der wölfe* (1957). He lived for a period in Norway (1961–6), but has since lived in Germany, first in Berlin and later in Munich. The first English translations of his work were made by **Michael Hamburger** and appeared in 1966. Owing something to **Georg Trakl**, **Gottfried Benn** and, above all, **Brecht**, Enzensberger has developed a radical, international and epic style which attained its most distinctive expression in the long-form poem *Der Untergang der Titanic* (1978, translated by the poet as *The Sinking of the Titanic*, 1980), which opposes the reifications of industrial society with the blind forces of nature and instinct. *Die Gedichte* (1983, 'Poems') was published by Suhrkamp, Frankfurt, for whom he has acted as editor since 1960. Enzensberger has translated a wide range of British, American, Scandinavian, Latin-American and Russian literature, and like **Günter Grass**, has been a commentator on European unification.
▷ R Grimm, *Über Enzensberger* (1984)

EÖTVÖS, József, Baron
(1813–71)

Hungarian author and statesman, born in Budapest. He became an advocate in 1833, but soon devoting himself to literature, published a work on prison reform, and the novels, *A Karthausi* (1838–41, 'The Carthusian'), *A Falu Jegyzöje* (1845, Eng trans *The Village Notary*, 1850) and others. In the revolution of 1848 he was Minister of Public Instruction, holding this post again under Andrássy in 1867–71 after three years of exile.
▷ D Jones, *Five Hungarian Writers* (1966)

'EPHELIA'
(fl.1679)

The unidentified author of *Female Poems on Several Occasions* (1679), born in London, by her own account, to well-connected parents who died young. Her poems show the frank eroticism typical of Restoration love-songs. Among others published under her name is a political broadside, *Advice to his Grace* (1681), warning the Duke of Monmouth against 'mad ambition'. Attempts to identify her as the daughter of the poet **Katherine Philips** have not been substantiated, and it remains possible that 'Ephelia' was the pseudonym of a group of male poets.
▷ *Poems by Ephelia*, ed with critical essay by M E Mulvihill (1993); G Greer, et al (eds), *Kissing the Rod* (1988)

EPICHARMUS
(c.540–450 BC)

Greek poet, born in Cos or Syracuse, who wrote 35 or more comedies performed in Syracuse. Only fragments of his works survive.
▷ L Berk, *Epicharmus* (1964)

EPIMENIDES
(6th century)

Semi-legendary Cretan poet and priest, traditionally credited with a *Theogony*.
▷ H Demoulin, *Epimenides de Crète* (1901)

ERASMUS, Desiderius
(c.1466–1536)

Dutch humanist and scholar, one of the most influential Renaissance figures, born in Rotterdam. Educated by the Brethren of the Common Life at Deventer, he joined an Augustine monastery at Steyn near Gouda in 1487, and was ordained a priest in 1492. But he was already reacting against scholasticism and was drawn to the Humanists. He studied and taught in Paris, and later in most of the cultural centres in Europe, including Oxford (1499) and Cambridge (1509–14), where he was Professor of Divinity and of Greek. He travelled widely, writing, teaching and meeting Europe's foremost intellectuals (including John Colet and Thomas More, while in England), and was the very model of a cultivated and dedicated scholar. He published many popular, sometimes didactic, works like *Adagia* (1500, Eng trans *Proverbs or Adages*, 1569), *Enchiridion Militis Christiani* (1503, Eng trans *Manual of a Christian Knight*, 1533), and the famous *Encomium Moriae* (1511, Eng trans *In Praise of Folly*, 1549). He also published scholarly editions of classical authors and the Church Fathers, and edited the Greek New Testament (1516). He became strongly critical of the pedantries and abuses of the Catholic Church and his *Colloquia familiaria* (1518, Eng trans *The Colloquies*, 1965) helped prepare the way for Martin Luther and the Reformation; but he also came to oppose the dogmatic theology of the Reformers and specifically attacked Luther in *De Libero Arbitrio* (1523, Eng trans *Discourse on the Freedom of the Will*, 1961). Despite these controversies he enjoyed great fame and respect in his last years, which he spent in Basle. The story of his father's life forms the theme of **Charles Reade**'s *The Cloister and the Hearth*.
▷J M Sowards, *Desiderius Erasmus* (1975)

ERBA, Luciano
(1922–)

Italian poet. His brief political education was conducted in the anti-fascist cells of wartime Milan, his native city, after which he was forced to flee to Switzerland in 1944. He taught in France before returning to Milan; he has subsequently held academic positions in Bari, Trieste, Bologna, Padua and Verona, as well as in the USA. A member of the 'Fourth Generation', he rejected literalism and a committed stance in favour of a highly condensed style that infuses everyday experience with epiphanic significance, but which is nonetheless broadly pessimistic and consciously disillusioned. Erba has not been highly prolific, and has not gained wide appreciation in the English-speaking world, though a significant selection of his work

appeared in *The New Italian Poetry* (1981, ed L R Smith). His most important volumes are *Il bel paese* (1956, 'The Beautiful Land'), *Il male minor* (1960) and *Il nastro de Moebius* (1980, 'The Moebius Strip'), for which he won the Viareggio Prize. He is an expert on **Cyrano de Bergerac** and, along with other French authors, has translated him into Italian.

ERBEN, Karel Jaromir
(1811–70)

Czech poet and Slavonic folklorist, born in Miletin. In 1851 Erben became archivist of the city of Prague. His ballad collection *Kytice* (1853, 'The Garland') is deservedly regarded as one of Europe's greatest transformations of popular ballad material into sophisticated literary form. The 12 ballads, with their emphasis on the grim and irrational elements in folk belief are, as critics have frequently pointed out, far from being mere 'echoes'. *101 Slavonic Fairy-Stories and Tales in their Original Tongues* (1864) and *Popular Czech Songs and Rimes* (1862–4) preserve some of his work in English translation.

ERCILLA Y ZÚÑIGA, Alonso de
(1553–c.1595)

Spanish poet, born in Bermeo on the Bay of Biscay. He entered the service of Philip II, and accompanied him in 1554 to England on the occasion of his marriage to Queen Mary I. Shortly after, he joined the expedition against the Araucanians in Chile whose amazing heroism inspired his monumental epic poem, *La Araucana* (1569–89, Eng trans 1945). An unfounded suspicion of his complicity in an insurrection nearly led to his execution. Fearing for his life, he returned to Spain, but Philip treated him with indifference so he made a tour through Europe, and for some time was chamberlain to the Emperor Rudolf II. In 1580 he returned to Madrid, where he lived in poverty till his death.
▷J T Medina, *Vida de Ercilla* (1948)

ERCKMANN-CHATRIAN
(1822–99)

The compound name of two French writers—Lorrainers both, Émile Erckmann (1822–99), born in Phalsbourg, and Alexandre Chatrian (1826–90), born in Abreschwiller. Their literary partnership dates from 1848, but they had little success until the publication of *L'Illustre Docteur Mathéus* (1859, Eng trans *The Illustrious Dr Mathéus*, 1872). *Le Fou Yégof* (1862, Eng trans *The Great Invasion of 1813–14; or, After Leipzig*, 1870) is one of a series of novels, to which also belong *Histoire d'un conscrit de 1813* (1864, Eng trans *The Conscript: A Tale of the French War of 1813*, 1865), *Waterloo* (1865, Eng trans 1865) and

Le Blocus (1867, Eng trans *The Blockade*, 1869). Well-known plays by them are *Le Juif polonais* (1869, Eng trans *The Polish Jew*, 1871), *L'Ami Fritz* (1864, Eng trans *Friend Fritz*, 1873), *Les Rantzau* (1882, Eng trans *The Rantzaus*, 1882) and *La Guerre* (1872, Eng trans *War*, 1872). After the annexation of Alsace-Lorraine to Germany, a strong anti-German feeling was shown in several of their books—the best of these is *L'Histoire du plébiscite* (1872, Eng trans *The Story of the Plébiscite*, 1872). They had quarrelled over money just before Chatrian died.

ERDMAN, Nikolai Robertovich
(1902–70)

Russian playwright, born in Moscow, where he became involved in political cabaret at an early age. His first play, *Mandat* (Eng trans *The Mandate*, 1975), achieved great popularity when produced by Meyerhold in 1925. This ideological farce satirized the bourgeoisie who were trying desperately to adapt to communism. It was followed by another satire, *Samoubiytsa* (1928, Eng trans *The Suicide*, 1979). Among its many targets was the Soviet system, so it is not surprising that Stalin banned it during rehearsals in 1932, ending the theatrical career of 'our new Gogol', as **Gorky** called him. It seems that he may have been exiled to Siberia for writing political fables, but he later found work as a film scenarist.
▷M Hoover, 'Nikolai Erdman: A Soviet Dramatist Rediscovered', in *Russian Literature Triquarterly*, no 2 (Winter 1972)

ERDRICH, Louise
(1954–)

American novelist, short-story writer and poet, who grew up in North Dakota of mixed Chippewa, French and German descent. Her work is centrally concerned with themes of cultural identity (usually seen from a female perspective), and much of it is set in her native state. Her first books were *Jacklight* (1984), a collection of poems, and the lyrical, multi-narrator novel, *Love Medicine* (1984), which traces the history of two Native American families across three generations. The later novels *Beet Queen* (1986), *Tracks* (1988) and *The Bingo Palace* (1994) continue the story of these families and their white neighbours back to the early 1900s. Erdrich has since published another poetry collection, *Baptism of Desire* (1989), and *The Crown of Columbus* (1991), a fictional exploration of the continuing impact of Columbus's voyage on Native American culture (written with her husband Michael Dorris).

ERENBURG, Ilya
(1891–1967)

Russian novelist and journalist, famous for his reportage of World War II, born in Kiev.

A versatile writer, a born survivor, he was susceptible to many currents of thought, from Roman Catholic mysticism to communism. He lived in Paris, returned to Russia after the advent of communism, went back into exile, returned again to Russia for the war, acted as an apologist for Stalin—and was finally a leader in the Thaw, from which he took the name of his novel *Ottepel* (1954, Eng trans *The Thaw*, 1955). The best of his prolific fiction is the early *Neobychayne pokhozdeniya Khulio Khuretino* (1922, Eng trans *The Extraordinary Adventures of Julio Jurentino*, 1930), in which he satirized the contemporary world.
▷V Alexandrova, *History of Soviet Literature* (1963)

ERI, Vincent Serei
(1936–)

Papua New Guinean novelist, author of the first significant novel from that country. He was born in Moveave and educated by Catholic missionaries and at the University of Papua New Guinea, Port Moresby. He has held various government offices both at home and in Australia. Eri's novel *The Crocodile* (1970) describes the period of colonialism and concerns the opposition of traditional values with modernity. The crocodile itself is a totem of power, magic, and both fertility and death, and the novel concludes ambiguously, its central character precariously balanced between worlds.

ERINNA
(4th century BC)

Greek poet (mistakenly believed in antiquity to have lived in the 7th century), born on the island of Telos. Though she died at the age of only 19, she won fame for her epic, *The Distaff*, on the joys of childhood. Only four lines of this and a handful of epigrams survive of her work.
▷C Latte, *Erinna* (1953)

ERNST, Paul
(1866–1933)

German author of short stories, novels, drama and poetry, born in Elbingerode. Ernst once carried great weight in his literature, but his stock has fallen in favour of other writers. He began as a naturalist and Marxist, but ended up as a grand old man of Nazi letters for his (not unusual) misinterpretation of the 'superman' of **Nietzsche** as a Hitler-like being. He now reads as an over-solemn, ponderous writer; but at one time his vast epics and what he called his 'meta-tragedies' were popular and respected. However, some of his hundreds of short tales (usually grouped within a framing story) are spoken of as classics in the genre; they are quite unpretentious, and do not partake of any of the grandiosity of what he believed was his chief work.

ERSKINE, John
(1879–1951)

American novelist, born in New York City and educated to PhD level at Columbia University, where he later taught. He also taught at Amherst College and pursued his musical interests as a pianist for the New York Philharmonic. He wrote over 45 books, the best-known of which is the satirical *The Private Life of Helen of Troy* (1925), which became a bestseller. In addition to his early novels, which often retold famous legends in humorous ways, he wrote four autobiographical books, each concentrating on a different aspect of his life, and was a well-known critic and semi-biographical novelist.

ERTEL, Aleksandr Ivanovich
(1855–1908)

Russian novelist, born in Voronezh, who is prized in particular for his novel *Gardeniny, ikh dvornya, priverzhentsy i vragi* (1888, 'The Gardenins, Their House, Adherents and Enemies'), which was praised by **Tolstoy**, under whose influence it was, in part, written. He had perhaps a deeper and more realistic approach to Russia's peasant problems than any of his contemporaries, was a master of dialogue, and may well not be the merely 'minor writer' he has been considered by critics. He was regarded as the spokesman for the 'populist intelligentsia', but later became interested in religion.

ERTZ, Susan, pseud of Mrs Ronald McCrindle
(c.1894–1985)

American novelist, born in Walton-on-Thames. She was the author of many popular novels including *Madame Claire* (1922) and *The Prodigal Heart* (1950).

ERVINE, St John Greer
(1883–1971)

Irish playwright and author, born in Belfast. In 1900 he emigrated to London, where he wrote novels and plays. From 1915 to 1916 he was manager of the Abbey Theatre, Dublin, where his first plays, *Mixed Marriage* (1911) and *Jane Clegg* (1914), were produced. After World War I, in which he served with the Dublin Fusiliers and lost a leg, he won a high reputation as a drama critic, working on *The Observer* and the *Morning Post*, and for the BBC (1932). His most successful plays are perhaps *Anthony and Anna* (1926), *The First Mrs Fraser* (1929) and *Robert's Wife* (1937); other publications include seven novels and several biographies.
▷*Some Impressions of My Elders* (1922)

ESPINA, Antonio
(b.1894)

Spanish novelist, biographer, poet and essayist, born in Madrid. Espina's novels, the better known of which is *Luna de copas* (1929, 'Moon of Hearts'), were much influenced by the literary theories of **Ortega y Gasset**, and have often been compared to the fiction of **Jarnés** and **Arderíus** (with the latter of whom he founded a left-wing review, *Nuevo España*). He has written lively biographies, and his best book is reckoned to be *Luis Candeles, el bandido de Madrid* (1929, Eng trans in *Great Spanish Short Stories*, 1932). He is generally reckoned to have 'spread his talents in too many directions', but his book on **Ganivet** (1942) is regarded as one of the best on this enigmatic character. He also wrote on **Quevedo** and **Cervantes**. An anti-Francoist, he spent 10 years in prison (1937–46), then went to Mexico, and was finally allowed to return to Spain in 1955.

ESPINEL, Vicente de
(1551–1624)

Spanish writer, born in Ronda. He served as a soldier in France and Italy, meeting with some of the adventures related in his *Relaciones de la vida del Escudero Márcos de Obregón* (1618, Eng trans *The History of the Life of the Squire Marcos de Obregon*, 1816), a book largely drawn upon by **Lesage** for his *Gil Blas*. After his return to Spain he took holy orders. He also published a volume of poems (1591) and a translation of the *Ars Poetica* of **Horace**. He was, if not the inventor, the improver of the 10-line stanza, and is credited with adding the fifth string to the guitar.
▷G Haley, *Vicente Espinel e Marcos de Obregon* (1959)

ESPINOSA, Pedro de
(1578–1650)

Spanish poet, born in Antequera, a centre for artists and poets. Initially he wrote love poetry, mainly inspired, it is said, by the poet Cristobalina Fernández de Alarcón. Disillusioned at his failure to win her, Espinosa retired to a hermitage. He became a priest and entered the service of an Andalusian grandee. He continued writing poetry, both secular and religious, such as 'Soledad de Pedro de Jesús' ('Solitude of Pedro de Jesús'), often describing nature with scientific precision, but he is chiefly remembered for his anthology of contemporary poetry, *Las Flores de Poetas Ilustres* (1605, 'The Flowers of Famous Poets'), with more than 200 compositions mainly by Andalusian poets. This book is often regarded as the beginning of the baroque period in Spanish poetry.

ESPRONCEDA, José de
(1808–42)

Spanish poet and revolutionary, born in Almendralejo in Estremadura. He travelled widely in Europe, partly to escape persecution for his liberalism, and partly in pursuit of Teresa Marcha, who is commemorated in his unfinished poem *El Diablo mundo* (1841, 'The Devil of the World'). He wrote romantic poems in the **Byron**ic manner, and is considered by some the greatest lyricist of his time.

▷J Casalduero, *Espronceda* (1961)

ESQUIROS, Henri Alphonse
(1814–76)

French poet and politician, born in Paris. He published poems and romances. For his *Évangile du peuple* (1840, 'The People's Gospel'), a democratic commentary on the life of Jesus, he was fined and imprisoned; this inspired his *Chants d'un prisonnier* (1841, 'A Prisoner's Songs'). His *Vierges folles* ('Foolish Virgins'), *Vierges martyres* ('Virgin Martyrs') and *Vierges sages* (1841–2, 'Wise Virgins') showed more of his socialistic sympathies. After the revolution he became a member of the Legislative Assembly, but the *coup d'état* of 1851 drove him to England, where he gathered the materials for his *L'Angleterre et la vie anglaise* (1860–9, Eng trans *The English at Home*, 1861), *Cornwall and its Coasts* (1865, written in English) and *Religious Life in England* (1867, written in English). In 1870 he was administrator of Bouches-du-Rhône, and was sent to the National Assembly (1871) and the Senate (1875).

ESSON, Louis
(1879–1943)

Australian playwright, born in Edinburgh, and considered the first to create a corpus of native Australian plays. Influenced by the nationalistic atmosphere of Dublin's Abbey Theatre, in 1922 he joined with **Vance Palmer** in establishing the Pioneer Players in Melbourne, where his 'bush' plays were regularly performed. Collections of his plays include *The Time is Not Yet Ripe* (1912) and *Dead Timber and Other Plays* (1920). Later works were edited by his widow as *The Southern Cross and Other Plays* (1946) and *The Woman Tamer* (1976). Two collections of verse were *Bells and Bees* (1910) and *Red Gums* (1912). Other writings were collected after his death into an anthology, *Ballads of Old Bohemia* (1980). Esson was perhaps at his best in his short plays such as *Dead Timber*

(1911), *The Drover* (1919) and *Andenagora* (1937).

ESSOP, Ahmed
(1931–)

Indian novelist, living in South Africa. As a young man he wrote verse under the name Ahmed Yousuf. He took his degree at the university in Pretoria and has taught at senior school level in Johannesburg, where his first two novels were published. *The Visitation* (1980) is concerned with double selves and with the hypocrisy that sustains respectable society. *The Emperor* (1984) is more forcefully satirical though ultimately less satisfying, and Essop's best work is probably to be found among the stories in *The Hajji* (1978), which are finely judged studies of human vanity and pretensions.

ESTANG, Luc, pseud of Lucien Bastard
(1911–91)

French Catholic novelist, critic and literary editor (of the magazine *La Croix*, 1940–55). He began as a poet; his main province (although he continued to publish verse) soon became the practice of fiction in the passionate and rebellious tradition established by **Georges Bernanos**, upon whom he wrote illuminatingly. He is best known outside France for his powerful novel *Le Bonheur et le salut* (1961, Eng trans *The Better Song*, 1961), the story of a man weighed down with guilt.

ESTAUNIÉ, Édouard
(1862–1942)

French novelist, whose work is now somewhat overlooked by readers, born in Dijon and educated by Jesuits. He thought himself neglected, and certainly his sales were small; but he was always, and still is, held in high estimation by discerning critics. In reaction to his pious and strict education, he first became a 'perplexed positivist' (as critics called him), and wrote in the naturalist style of **Zola**. *L'Empreinte* (1895, 'The Imprint') is one of the most quietly deadly of all indictments of Jesuit teachers as they were in his childhood. Gradually and doubtingly he returned to his old faith, in subtle and grave novels which were certainly read and digested by such writers as **François Mauriac**. Although his novels were put into other languages, he has yet to find an English translator.

ESZTERHAS, Joe
(1944–)

Hungarian-born American screenwriter. A former journalist, his first filmed screenplay was for the trade union drama *F.I.S.T.* (1978)

and his work has tended to alternate between explorations of political and social issues, such as white supremacy in *Betrayed* (1988) and Nazism in *The Music Box* (1989), and more overtly commercial entertainment like *Jagged Edge* (1985) and *Sliver* (1993), which blend murder, sexual shenanigans and a shoal of red herrings before moving towards an often predictable surprise revelation in the film's final reel. Among the highest-paid screenwriters in Hollywood, he was rumoured to have received $3 million for writing the controversial adult thriller *Basic Instinct* (1992).

ETCHAHOUNIA, Pierre Topet d'
(1786–1862)

Major Basque poet, born in Etchahounia in the French Basque provinces. He is famous for having cursed his father for forbidding him to marry a poor girl: 'God curse Gaztelondo Topet and all those who fall in love with poor girls!' is now proverbial. He beat up the rich (and allegedly unfaithful) woman whom he did marry, killed a man for sleeping with her (although he had not done so), was refused permission to live at home, and spent much of his life as a beggar and travelling bard. His trenchant poetry, free from ecclesiastic and pious cant, often questioning the existence of God, is the best there is in the Basque language. It survives only because it is easily memorable: his family burned it on a bonfire as soon as he died. It was collected in *Le Poète Pierre Topet, dit Etchahun, et ses ouevres* (1946). **Chamisso** told his story most memorably.

ETHEREGE, Sir George
(?1635–1691)

A Restoration dramatist, he was born probably in Maidenhead. Secretary to the ambassador at Constantinople from 1668 to 1670 or 1671, he married a wealthy widow, and in 1685 was sent to be resident at the Imperial court at Ratisbon. He varied the monotony of this banishment with coursing, drinking, play, flirtation with actresses and correspondence with **Thomas Middleton**, **Dryden** and Betterton. He seems to have died in Paris. In English literature he is founder of the comedy of intrigue. He sought his inspiration in **Molière**, and out of him grew the legitimate comedy of manners and the dramatic triumphs of **Richard Brinsley Sheridan** and **Oliver Goldsmith**. His three plays are *The Comical Revenge or, Love in a Tub* (1664); *She Would if She Could* (1668); and *The Man of Mode or, Sir Fopling Flutter* (1676)—all highly popular in their day.
▷D Underwood, *Etherege and the 17th-century Comedy of Manners* (1957)

ÉTTIENE, Frank
(1936–)

Haitian writer, who wrote the first novel in Creole, *Disaffection* (1975): 'a dead end in itself, perhaps, but a very important one', wrote a critic. It was greatly influenced by **Jacques Roumain**, founder of the Haitian Communist Party, whose final novel had abounded in Creolisms.

EUCKEN, Rudolph Christoph
(1846–1926)

German writer, born in Aurich, Ostfriesland, winner of the Nobel Prize for literature. He was educated at the University of Göttingen, where he studied philosophy, and worked firstly as a schoolteacher, and later as a professor at the universities of Basle and Jena. His family were Lutheran, but he developed as a freethinker and idealist. His numerous books were all philosophical works, the most influential of which was *Der Sinn und Wert des Lebens* (1908, Eng trans *The Meaning and Value of Life*, 1916), but he was awarded the Nobel Prize for literature in recognition of his 'earnest search for truth' and 'idealistic philosophy of life'.

EURINGER, Richard
(1891–1953)

German novelist and writer on flying, born in Augsberg, whose books influenced other writers on flying, particularly **Gerd Gaiser**. A pilot in World War I, he became an ardent Nazi and a 'Reichscultursenator'. But such novels as *Fliegerschule 4* (1929, 'Flying School 4') were efficient, authentic and well thought out.

EURIPIDES
(484 or 480–406 BC)

Greek dramatist, regarded, with **Aeschylus** and **Sophocles**, as one of the three great tragedians. He brought a new style to tragedy and the treatment of traditional mythology. Of about 80 of his dramas whose titles are known, 18 survive complete. He won the tragic prize only five times, and he died at the court of Archelaus, King of Macedonia. He did not take much part in public life; in politics he was moderate, approving of a democracy, but not of demagogues. The names and probable order of his surviving plays are: *Alcestis* (438 BC, Eng trans 1930), *Medea* (431 BC, Eng trans 1959), *Hippolytus* (428 BC, Eng trans 1959), *Andromache* (425 BC, Eng trans 1957), *Hecuba* (424 BC, Eng trans 1959), *Supplices* (423 BC, Eng trans 1957), *Heraclidae* (416 BC, Eng trans *Heracles*, 1959), *Troades* (415 BC, Eng trans *The Women of Troy*, 1954), *Helena* (412 BC, Eng trans 1951), *Phoenissae* (410 BC, Eng trans *The Phoenician Women*,

1959), *Orestes* (408 BC, Eng trans 1959); the *Bacchae* (405 BC, Eng trans 1954) and *Iphigenia Aulidensis* (405 BC, Eng trans *Iphigenia in Aulis*, 1959) were put on the Athenian stage only after the author's death; and it is uncertain to what period belonged the *Ion* (Eng trans 1937), *Heracles Furens* (Eng trans *The Madness of Heracles*, 1969), *Iphigenia Taurica* (Eng trans *Iphigenia in Tauris*, 1953), *Electra* (Eng trans 1950), and *Cyclops* (Eng trans 1957), whilst it is doubtful whether the *Rhesus* (Eng trans 1959) is genuine. He is notable for highlighting unusual opinions and portraying socially marginal characters. Sophocles, who deemed him 'the most tragic of poets', also commented that while he himself showed people as they ought to be, Euripides portrayed them as they are. Fascinated by the dark side of human nature and the conflicts this engenders, and believing that passion is often at the root of tragedy, Euripides's skill as a playwright is of the highest order; he can construct plots which are exciting beyond anything attempted by his predecessors, and he has an unerring instinct for 'situation'. But in his desire to get on to the situation as rapidly as possible, he substitutes a bald prologue for a proper exposition, and instead of working out the dénouement, makes a *deus ex machina* cut the knot of the situation. To the same end he sacrifices consistency in character. His popularity increased after his death; his plays were revived more frequently than those of **Aeschylus** or **Sophocles** and the number that have survived is greater than both of theirs put together.

EUSDEN, Laurence
(1688–1730)

English poet, born in Spofforth. He became poet laureate in 1718, but not on account of his poetic genius, merely because he had celebrated the marriage (1717) of the Duke of Newcastle (who was responsible for nominations for the position). He wrote little of value, was lampooned by **Pope**, who placed him in the realms of dullness in *The Dunciad*, and died rector of Coningsby, Lincolnshire.

EVANS, Augusta, later Augusta Wilson
(1835–1909)

American novelist, born in Columbus, Georgia, who from 1868, the date of her marriage, wrote under her married name of Wilson. *St Elmo* (1866) attracted more ridicule than praise, but this story of the prudish Edna Earle's 'taming' of the supposedly **Byron**ic St Elmo, written with much pretentious erudition, became a bestseller. It offers good example of how 'unwholesome and eminently forgettable trash' can sweep a nation—but only for a short time.
▷W P Fidler, *August Evans* (1951)

EVANS, Caradoc, pseud of David Evans
(1878–1945)

Welsh short-story writer and novelist, born in Llanfihangel-ar-Arth, Dyfed. He spent much of his childhood at Rhydlewis, but left home in 1893, working as a shop assistant in Carmarthen, Barry, Cardiff and finally London. While in London, he attended evening classes and eventually found employment as a journalist in 1906. His collections of short stories, *My People* (1915), *Capel Sion* (1916) and *My Neighbours* (1919), savagely exposed the hypocrisies, lust and greed of the Chapel-going people of his native West Wales. His play, *Taffy* (1923), was in similar vein and in his own time he was vilified by the Welsh as a traitor for his assaults on many cherished aspects of the Welsh way of life, from Nonconformity and the Eisteddfod to the integrity and intelligence of the common people.
▷T L Williams, *Caradoc Evans* (1970)

EVANS, Donald
(1884–1921)

American poet, who had a small influence upon **Wallace Stevens**. Evans was a Greenwich Village decadent, well known in his lifetime, who tried to write in the tradition of **Fargue**, and who killed himself. His poetry is now virtually forgotten. His final collection was entitled, characteristically, *Ironics* (1919). He had, a contemporary said, 'a genius for exquisite masks of cynicism', 'in graceful defiance of society'. It has been asserted that he also influenced **E E Cummings**.

EVANS, George Essex
(1863–1909)

Australian poet. Born in London, he went to Australia in 1881 and settled in Queensland. After teaching in country areas he turned to journalism and wrote on agricultural matters. His first book was a long narrative poem, *The Repentance of Magdalene Despar* (1891). It was followed by *Loraine and Other Verses* (1898), *The Secret Key and Other Verses* (1906) and *Queen of the North* (1909). At his best and strongest when writing of the Australian countryside which he came to love, he also wrote ceremonial verse such as 'An Ode for Commonwealth Day', 'An Australian Symphony' and a sentimental favourite, 'The Women of the West'. *The Collected Verse of George Essex Evans* was published in 1928.

EVANS, Matilda Jane, pseud Maud Jeanne Franc
(1827–86)

English-born Australian novelist and writer of moral tales for children under her pseudonym. Born in Peckham Park, Surrey, she emigrated to Australia in 1852, opening a school and later becoming a deaconess in the Baptist Church. She wrote many novels and short stories, all with a high moral tone and aimed primarily at adolescents. Her first novel was *Marian: Or, The Light of Someone's Home* (1861), which was followed by 14 more, including *Vermont Vale: Or, Home Pictures in Australia* (1866) and *Minnie's Mission: An Australian Temperance Tale* (1869). They were popular for many years as Sunday School prizes.

EVANS, Theophilus
(1693–1767)

Welsh historian, born in Newcastle Emlyn. He was an Anglican priest. The style of his histories and sermons is bold and assertive; *A History of Modern Enthusiasm* (1752, rev edn 1757), in English, is a striking example of his contempt for Methodism, which he believed was, if secretly, a Romish sect. His marvellous history of Wales, *Drych y Prif Oesoedd* (1740) is often regarded as a work of epic proportions, abounding in striking metaphors.

EVELYN, John
(1620–1706)

English diarist and author, born of wealthy parentage in Wotton, near Dorking. He was brought up in Lewes (1625–37), then entered Balliol College, Oxford, and in 1640 the Middle Temple. He witnessed Strafford's trial and execution, and in November 1642 joined the king's army for three days. The Covenant being pressed on him, he travelled for four years on the Continent. In Paris in 1647 he married the ambassador's daughter, Mary Browne (1635–1709), and in 1652 settled at Sayes Court, Deptford. He spent a lot of time at court after the Restoration and acted on public committees and from 1685 to 1687 was one of the commissioners of the privy seal. From 1695 to 1703 he was treasurer of Greenwich Hospital and was a prominent fellow of the Royal Society. In 1694 he removed to his brother's at Wotton. Evelyn, as active and intelligent as he was honest and God-fearing, was yet neither sage nor hero. He was always active in Church affairs and was especially prominent in the rebuilding of St Paul's Cathedral. He dealt with a multitude of subjects. Of his three dozen works the chief are *Fumifiguim, or the Inconvenience of the Air and Smoke of London dissipated* (1661); *Sculptura, or the Art of Engraving on Copper* (1662); *Sylva, or a Discourse of Forest-trees* (1664); and the delightful *Diary* (discovered in an old clothes-basket at Wotton in 1817), covering the years 1641–1706 and containing vivid portraits of his contemporaries.
▷ B Saunders, *Evelyn and His Times* (1970)

EVERSON, William
(1912–)

American poet, born in Sacramento, California. A religious, contemplative man, he was for 18 years a Roman Catholic monk in a Dominican order, and produced several collections of poetry under the name of Brother Antoninus. These include *The Crooked Lines of God: Poems 1949–1954* (1959) and *The Last Crusade* (1969). Other volumes, under the name of Everson, include *X War Elegies* (1943) and *The Veritable Years: Poems 1949–1966* (1978). In both guises, as Everson and Brother Antoninus, the poet deliberates in sometimes confessional, sometimes sensual, verse upon man's search for moral and spiritual values in an uncertain, violent world.

EWALD, Johannes
(1743–81)

Danish Romantic poet and dramatist, born in Copenhagen, and writer of the Danish national anthem. At the age of 15 he ran away from home to fight in the Seven Years War (1756–63), then turned his attention to writing. He was one of the first Danish poets to use national legends and myths as material, as in his biblical drama *Adam og Eva* (1769), the historical drama *Rolf Krage* (1770) and the lyrical drama *Balders Död* (1773). He also wrote an operetta, *Fiskerne* (1779, 'The Fishermen'), which contains the song 'King Kristian stood by the lofty mast', which is now the Danish national anthem.
▷ L Labe, *Johannes Ewald* (1943)

EWART, Gavin Buchanan
(1916–)

Scottish poet, educated at Cambridge, who worked as an advertising copywriter for nearly 20 years. His main poetic model was the lean-limbed style of **Auden**. His first collection of verse appeared when he was just 23, but he only fully found his stride with the distinctive *Londoners* (1964) and the tellingly titled *Throwaway Lines* (1966). He uses the rhythms and recurrent obsessions of demotic forms—limericks in particular—to create a heavily stressed and usually rhymed verse that is robustly Anglo-Saxon. Many of the poems are sexual or scatological, mixing obscenity with lightly-worn learning and often revealing a depth of feeling under their nonsensical skittishness. Perhaps the most distinctive and individual collection is *Or Where a Young Penguin Lies Screaming* (1977). A *Collected Ewart* appeared in 1980, as did *The Penguin Book of Light Verse*, which he edited with obvious relish. He has continued to produce 'little ones'.

EWERS, J(ohn) K(eith)
(1904–78)

Australian writer of fiction, history and literary criticism, born in Subiaco, Perth. His first novel was *Money Street* (1933), followed by *Fire on the Wind* (1935) based on his family's experiences in a bushfire. He wrote for children in *Tales from the Dead Heart* (1944) and *Written in Sand* (1947), retellings of aboriginal myths. *With the Sun on My Back* (1953) was a prize-winning account of his travels in northern Australia, and he wrote one of the first studies of Australian literature in *Creative Writing in Australia* (1945). His *I Came Naked*, poetic reflections on life, was produced in a limited edition in 1976.

EWING, Julianna Horatia, née Gatty
(1841–85)

English writer for children, daughter of Margaret Gatty (1809–73), also a children's writer. Born in Ecclesfield, Yorkshire, she soon began to compose nursery plays, which are said to have suggested to her mother the starting of *Aunt Judy's Magazine* (1866), which she later edited, publishing in it many of her charming stories, such as *Jackanapes*. Her numerous books included *A Flat Iron for a Farthing* (1870), *Lab-lie-by-the-Fire* (1873) and *Daddy Darwin's Dovecot* (1881). Her *The Brownies and Other Tales* (1870) provided the name by which the junior section of the Girl Guide movement is known.
▷ G Avery, *Mrs Ewing* (1961)

EYVINDUR, known as Skáldaspillir (The Plagiarist), properly Eyvindur Jónsson
(d.c.990)

Norwegian court poet of the Viking Age. Born of a noble family, he was a devoted follower of King Haakon I, 'the Good' of Norway, whom he eulogized in his *Hákonarmál*. He later wrote a eulogy in praise of Earl Haakon of Norway (*Haleygjatal*), and an *Íslendingadrápa* about Icelanders.

F

FABRE, Ferdinand
(1830–98)

French novelist, born in Bédarieux. He was educated for the priesthood, but took to writing novels instead, in which he created vivid portrayals of country priests. He wrote *L'abbé Tigrane, candidat à la papauté* (1873, Eng trans *The abbé Tigrane. Candidate for the papal chair*, 1876) and other stories of rustic life in Cévennes.

FABRE D'ÉGLANTINE, Philippe François Nazaire
(1750–94)

French dramatist, poet, and revolutionist, born in Carcassonne. He wrote *Le Philinte de Molière* (1790), a sequel to Molière's *Le Misanthrope*. A member of the National Convention, he devised some of the new names of months for the Revolutionary Calendar, but, having fallen out of favour with Robespierre, was eventually guillotined.
▷L Jacob, *Fabre d'Églantine, chef des Fripons* (1946)

FADEYEV, Aleksandr Aleksandrovich, pseud **Bulgya**
(1901–56)

Russian novelist of the socialist realism school. He was deeply influenced by **Tolstoy**, and wrote *Razgrom* (1926, Eng trans *The Rout*, 1926), set in the Russian civil war, and *Molodaya gvardiya* (1945, Eng trans *The Young Guard*, 1962), portraying Russian resistance against the Germans in World War II. As general-secretary of the Soviet Writers' Union (1946–55) he mercilessly exposed any literary 'deviationism' from the party line but became a target himself and, compelled to revise the last-named work (1951), took to drink and finally shot himself.
▷V M Ozerov, *Aleksandr Aleksandrovich Fadeyev* (1960)

FAGUNDES VARELA, Luis Nicolau
(1841–75)

Brazilian poet, a typically romantic and Bohemian figure in whose work all the main trends of romanticism may be found. He never entirely escaped from the European models which had initially inspired him, but his elegies for his wife and son ('Cântico do Calvario') are moving and deservedly famous. His most interesting and enduring work was written in collaboration with his sister: *Anchieta ou o Evangelho das Selvas*, a long religious poem.
▷A Soares-Amora, *Grandes Poetas Românticos do Brasil* (1949)

FAGUNWA, Daniel O
(c.1910–1963)

Nigerian writer in Yoruba. A chief, he died in a boating accident. When the Anglophone novels of **Amos Tutuola** became famous worldwide, many Nigerians felt that Tutuola owed too large a debt to the former's four Yoruba novels, which were popular in Nigeria, but, naturally enough, unknown elsewhere. **Wole Soyinka**'s *Hunter's Saga* (1968) is an adaptation from Fagunwa's 1939 novel of the same title (in Yoruba). His books, of which the first, *Forest of a Thousand Demons* (1938), was translated in 1968, began a remarkable literary account of the Yoruba cosmogony.

FAINLIGHT, Ruth Esther
(1931–)

American poet, she was educated in England and in 1959 married the novelist **Alan Sillitoe**, with whom she has occasionally collaborated. Most of her work is premised on a refusal to subordinate 'life', with its compromises and hesitations, to 'art'; she refuses to deal in absolutes, calling on fairy tales and popular mythology to demonstrate the merits of adaptation without compromise. This approach lies behind her first completely individual volume, *Cages* (1966), and the aptly titled *To See the Matter Clearly* (1968). Fainlight seems to have gone through periods of quiet re-assessment and even abnegation at the start of successive decades, but returned to impressive form with *The Region's Violence* and *Twenty One Poems* (both 1973) and *Climates* and *Fifteen to Infinity* (both 1983). In the latter pair, her perceptiveness is strikingly heightened and a strong-lined metre reinforces her growing philosophical resonance. She has published one collection of short stories, *Daylife and Nightlife* (1971).

FAIRBAIRNS, Zoë Ann
(1948–)

English novelist, journalist and pamphleteer, who has written on the Campaign for Nuclear

Disarmament, women's issues, and the consequences of bad housing. Her concern for the state of contemporary society is also the central theme of her fiction. *Live as Family* (1968) and *Down: an Exploration* (1969), both deal with the individual's relationships with class and the community. *Stand We at Last* (1983) is perhaps her most important novel, a family saga spanning the years from the mid-19th century to the present day, and written from a feminist perspective. *Closing* (1987) returns to the modern era to look at the life of women in what the author considers an exploitative society.

FAIRBURN, A(rthur) R(ex) D(ugard)
(1904–57)

New Zealand poet and artist, born in Auckland. An extrovert lyricist, he was a commanding figure from the 1930s to the 1950s. His early verse was published as *He Shall Not Rise* (1930), followed by *Dominion* (1938), a long poem showing the effects of the Depression and the influence of **T S Eliot**; it was later included in *Three Poems* (1952). His *Poems 1929–1941* (1943) was reissued with other short material as *Strange Rendezvous* (1952). His *Collected Poems* came out in 1966. He was poetry editor of the *Year Book of the Arts in New Zealand* (1945–51). His prose was noted for its satire, hiding a strong vein of national pride, as in *We New Zealanders: An Informal Essay* (1944). A posthumous selection was issued in 1967 as *The Women Problem and Other Prose*.
▷ *The Letters of A R D Fairburn* (1981)

FAIRFAX, James Griffyth
(1886–1976)

Australian lyric poet and journalist, born in Sydney and descended from John Fairfax of Warwick (1804–77), founder of the *Sydney Morning Herald*. James Fairfax's first collection was *The Gates of Sleep and Other Poems* (1906). Other books of verse include *The Troubled Pool* (1911), *The Horns of Taurus* (1912) and *The Temple of Janus: a Sonnet Sequence* (1917). He served with the Australian forces in the Middle East in World War I, of which his impressions are recorded in *Mesopotamia: Sonnets and Lyrics at Home and Abroad, 1914–1919* (1919). After the war he entered the British parliament for Norwich Town (1924–9). His cousin, John Fitzgerald Fairfax, served in World War II and was a war correspondent in the South Pacific (1944–6). He published a number of books: a life of his distinguished ancestor *The Story of John Fairfax* (1941), elegant essays in *Run o' Waters* (1948) and some fine lyric verse in *A Drift of Leaves* (1952).

FAIZ, Faiz Ahmed
(1905–90)

Pakistani poet, who to some extent became the 'national poet' of his newly created country. But he was a communist (he received the Lenin Prize in 1962) who incurred the wrath of its governments: they put him in prison for plotting to overthrow them, which in some sense he had (although the charges were probably trumped up). He wrote some verse in Punjabi because he was in favour of fuller recognition of the minority languages of Pakistan. He wrote much dreary Marxist verse, but possessed qualities which put him far above the usual proponents of such material: he was a master of technique in his main language, Urdu, and was a remarkable love poet. *Poems by Faiz* (1971) is bilingual.

FALCÃO, Cristóvão
(1515–53)

Portuguese poet, born in Pertalegre. He led an adventurous life, which apparently included imprisonment for an affair he had, aged 14, with the 12-year-old Maria Brandão—for which she was sent to a convent. It has, however, been suggested on the one hand that Falcão did not exist, and on the other (and more plausibly) that his friend **Bernardim Ribeiro** invented him in the poem *Trofas de Crisfal* (1554), published as by Falcão. However, the consensus now is that Falcão is to be 'regarded as an inspired imitator of Ribeiro whom he never personally knew'. *Trofas* is a 900-line eclogue of great distinction, containing 'passionate *saudade* and sentimental grief ... mystic visions ... simplicity ... love of Nature'.
▷ A Bell, *Portuguese Literature* (1922)

FALCONER, William
(1732–69)

Scottish poet and seaman, born in Edinburgh. A barber's son, he went to sea, and was soon shipwrecked off Greece, this voyage forming the subject of his long poem, *The Shipwreck* (1762). He then entered the royal navy, being appointed purser on the frigate *Aurora* in 1769, which foundered with all hands near Capetown. His *Demagogue* (1764) is a satire on Wilkes and Marlborough, and he was also author of the *Universal Marine Dictionary* (1769).

FALK, Johann Daniel
(1768–1826)

German writer and philanthropist, born in Danzig (Gdansk, Poland). He founded the 'company of friends in need' for helping destitute children, and established the Falk Institute at Weimar. Of his writings the best known are his satirical works like *Der Mensch* (1795, 'The Man'), and a study on **Goethe**.

FALKEBERGET, Johann Petter, originally Lillebakken
(1879–1967)

Norwegian novelist, born in Nordre-Rugel. A miner from the age of eight, and the son of a miner, he wrote realistic novels of working-class life in his area. His first novel was *Svarte Fjelde* (1907, 'Black Mountains'). He also wrote *Den fjerde nattevakt* (1923, 'The Fourth Night-Watch'), and two trilogies, *Christianus Sextus* (1927–35) and *Nattens brød* (1940–59, 'Night's Bread').

FALLADA, Hans, pseud of Rudolf Ditzen
(1893–1947)

German writer, born in Greifswald. He achieved international fame with his novel of German social problems, *Kleiner Mann, Was Nun?* (1932, Eng trans *Little Man, What Now?*, 1969) in which a devoted young couple struggle against the hardship of rampant inflation and unemployment. *Wolf unter Wölfen* (1937, Eng trans *Wolf Among Wolves*, 1938) is a tragic novel of post-World War I Germany. Several important works appeared posthumously, including *Der Trinker* (1950, Eng trans *The Drinker*, 1952).
▷H Schulder, *Hans Fallada, humanist and social critic* (1970)

FALLON, Padraic
(1905–74)

Irish poet, born in Athenry, County Galway. He worked for 40 years as a customs official, before retiring to England where he died. Neglected for most of his lifetime, the posthumous publication of his *Collected Poems* (1990) established him as a remarkable chronicler of an aesthetic and religious fusion, in which the central dilemma is: 'much is man and/not enough'. His quiet, authoritative tone is allied to a craftsmanship that gives his poems a universal integrity much stronger than their Catholic themes might at first suggest.
▷D Davie, in D Dunn (ed), *Two Decades of Irish Writing* (1975)

FALLON, Peter
(1951–)

Irish poet and publisher, born in Germany and educated in Dublin. In 1970 he founded The Gallery Press, one of the most important Irish publishers of the latter part of the 20th century. His early work, *The First Affair* (1974), was prompted by the pop-orientated metropolitanism prevalent at the time. However, in 1982 he went to live on a farm in County Meath, and subsequent collections, *Winter Work* (1983), *The News and Weather* (1987) and *Eye to Eye* (1992), demonstrate a sensitive and evocative understanding of rural values and pieties. Such work bears complimentary comparison with that of **Patrick Kavanagh**, while the selected poems *News of the World* (1994), for example, show him still utilizing the breath line and minimalist techniques of such admired American writers as **Charles Olson** and **Gary Snyder**.

FALUDY, Gyorgy
(1913–)

Hungarian poet and translator, who left Hungary after 1956 and settled in Canada. He translated **Villon** into Hungarian, wrote graceful and skilled lyrics, and a well-regarded autobiography, *My Happy Days in Hell* (1962).

FANGEN, Ronald
(1895–1946)

Norwegian novelist and dramatist, born in Kragero. He made an immediate sensation with a strident expressionistic play, but established himself more enduringly with such novels as *Duel* (1932, Eng trans 1934). His earlier work is humanistic, but he later became a member of the Oxford Movement, and turned to a somewhat simplistic Christianity. His *En lysets engel* (1945, Eng trans *Both are My Cousins*, 1949) is a memorable novel about a quisling. He was killed in an air crash.

FANSHAWE, Sir Richard
(1608–66)

English poet and translator, born in Ware. He fought on the Royalist side, and became an MP on the accession of Charles II. He was the first to translate the *Lusiads* of **Camoens** (1655). His original poetry is of little account. His wife Ann's *Memoirs* (complete edition 1829) is a fulsome tribute, with some of his letters.
▷*Annual Bulletin of the Modern Humanist Research Association*, xlii (1938)

FANTHORPE, U(rsula) A(skham)
(1929–)

English poet, educated at Oxford and the University of London Institute of Education, where she obtained a teacher's diploma. Since the mid-70s, though, she has worked as an admissions clerk in a Bristol hospital. Her characteristic style, already evident in *Side Effects* (1978), her first collection, is discreetly gossipy, and there is a touch of **Betjeman** or possibly **Larkin** in her ironically polite evasions. In writing of the natural or the wider human scene, she is quizzical, but still capable of genuine wonder. Later volumes are *Four Dogs* (1980), *Standing To* (1982) and *Voices Off* (1984). A major selection appeared in 1986.

FARGUE, Léon-Paul
(1876–1947)

French poet, anecdotist and literary journalist, born in Paris, and paramount interpreter of that city's streets, bars and railway stations (he was known as the 'the Paris stroller'). In his quiet way, Fargue, a much respected major-minor poet, sought and achieved perfection in his melancholy aspiration to recapture an irretrievable past. In that way, if in no other, he resembles **Marcel Proust**. He began in the Symbolist manner, but soon developed his own method, which was to reproduce as exactly as he could the nuances of his own superb conversation. He was a close friend to, and in many ways is the poetic counterpart of, the composer Erik Satie. Some of the best of his enchanting journalism is collected in *Lantern Magique* (1942, Eng trans *Magic Lantern*, 1946). His major work was contained in long prose-poems: essentially, in their precise cadences, they are poems: these express his unique belief that 'poetry is the only dream that one must not dream', and his desire to discover the universe within his beloved Paris. Many exquisite shorter poems are to be found in translated anthologies of French verse.
▷ L R Schub, *Léon-Paul Fargue* (1973)

FARIA, Otavio de
(1908–)

Brazilian novelist who set out to create a **Balzac**ian picture, a 'Tragedia Burguesa' ('Bourgeois Tragedy'), but from an individualistic viewpoint, of the middle classes of his country. Perhaps somewhat neglected by translators and critics alike, the vast patchwork of this cycle has been consistently interesting, well observed and intelligent.

FARIA Y SOUSA, Manuel de
(1590–1649)

Portuguese poet, born near Pombeiro. He went to Madrid c.1613, and from 1631 to 1634 was secretary to the Spanish embassy in Rome. He wrote on Portuguese history and on **Camoens**, and left approximately 200 Portuguese sonnets, 12 eclogues, and three treatises on poetry.

FARJEON, Eleanor
(1881–1965)

English writer, born in Hampstead. She led a richly imaginative fantasy life as a child, described in her autobiographical *A Nursery in the Nineties* (1935). She wrote fantasies and children's stories, beginning with her successful first novel, *Martin Pippin in the Apple Orchard* (1916), and collaborated with her brother Herbert in *Kings and Queens* (1932) and the play *The Glass Slipper* (1944). There is an annual Eleanor Farjeon Award for outstanding service to children's literature.
▷ D Blakelock, *Eleanor, a portrait* (1966)

FARMER, Philip José
(1918–)

American science-fiction and fantasy writer, born in Indiana. A fan from an early age, he began writing comparatively late, and published his first novel in 1952. He is an idiosyncratic figure in the genre hierarchy, and his work is marked by an unusually frank treatment of sexuality, often in tandem with other biological themes. The defining characteristics of his later work are its zany humour and his penchant for creating overarching literary structures which draw not only on his own works but also on the inventions and characters of other writers. His best-known works are the *Riverworld* series (from 1965), and the less well-defined aggregation of stories sometimes known as the 'Wold Newton' series, which postulates the creation of a small group of mutant supermen, manifest as fictional characters like Tarzan and Doc Savage.

FARNOL, John Jeffery
(1878–1952)

English author, born in Aston. He lived from 1902 to 1910 in the USA as a scene painter. His first successful novel was *The Broad Highway* (1910), and he went on to establish a reputation for romantic adventure stories in a period setting, such as *The Amateur Gentleman* (1913), *The Geste of Duke Jocelyn* (1919) and *Peregrine's Progress* (1922).
▷ E French, *Jeffrey Farnol* (1964)

FARQUHAR, George
(c.1677–1707)

Irish playwright, born in Londonderry, possibly in 1677 (but he is said to have fought at the Boyne). Educated at Trinity College, Dublin, he became an actor in a Dublin theatre, but proved an indifferent performer. The accidental wounding of a fellow actor so shocked him that he quitted the boards, and shortly after received a commission in a regiment stationed in Ireland. His first comedy, *Love and a Bottle* (1698), proved a success. His *Constant Couple* (1700) met with an enthusiastic reception, and he wrote a sequel, *Sir Harry Wildair* (1701). In 1703 he produced *The Inconstant*, founded on **John Fletcher**'s *Wild Goose Chase*. Having married in the same year, he fell into pecuniary difficulties, and died in poverty. During his last illness he wrote the best of his plays, *The Beaux' Stratagem* (1707), and died while its wit and invention were making the town roar with delight. *The Recruiting Officer* had been produced with success in 1706. Farquhar is one of the best of the comic dramatists, and has on the whole more variety and character than any of his compeers.

▷ E Rothenstein, *George Farquhar* (1967)

FARRAR, Frederic William
(1831–1903)

English clergyman and writer, born in Bombay. He was ordained in 1854, taught at Harrow, became Headmaster of Marlborough (1871–6), Honorary Chaplain to Queen Victoria (1869–73), and later became a chaplain-in-ordinary. He was made a canon of Westminster and Rector of St Margaret's in 1876, Archdeacon of Westminster in 1883, Chaplain to the House of Commons in 1890, and Dean of Canterbury in 1895. His theological writings were many, but he is chiefly remembered for the bestseller *Eric, or Little by Little* (1858), one of several school stories that he wrote.

▷ *My Object in Life* (1883)

FARRELL, J(ames) G(ordon)
(1935–79)

English novelist, born in Liverpool. His early works, such as *The Lung* (1965), were realistic novels set in the present day. He found his proper metier, however, in the historical novel. *Troubles* (1970) is set in Ireland after World War I, and has obvious analogies to the current disturbances. *The Siege of Krishnapur* (1973), set in Hindustan in 1857, won him the Booker Prize, while *The Singapore Grip* (1978) is about the Japanese capture of Malaysia in World War II. Together these novels display his major theme—the slow, at times painful, at others absurd, decline of the British Empire. Farrell drowned in a fishing accident in Ireland.

FARRELL, James T(homas)
(1904–79)

American novelist, short-story writer, critic and essayist, born in Chicago. He paid for his own education at the University of Chicago (1925–9) and lived in Paris in the early 1930s. A lapsed Catholic and a naturalist in the mould of **Émile Zola**, he owes most to the style of **Sherwood Anderson**. His first novel was *Young Lonigan* (1932), which began the *Studs Lonigan* trilogy of life on Chicago's South side, realistically and graphically expressed. The other volumes were *The Young Manhood of Studs Lonigan* (1934) and

Judgement Day (1935). An accomplished study of defeat (the hero dies aged 29), it was a landmark in American fiction. This was followed by a five-novel sequence centred on Danny O'Neill (1936–53), and another trilogy, on Bernard Clare (1946–52). He published more than 50 novels in all.

▷ A M Wald, *Farrell: the revolutionary socialist years* (1978)

FARRÈRE, Claude, pseud of Frédéric Charles Pierre Édouard Bargone
(1876–1957)

French novelist, born in Lyons. He was a naval officer (1899–1919) who turned to writing. He made his name with novels of the exotic and tales of travel and adventure. Works include *Fumée d'opium* (1904, 'Smoking Opium') and *Les condamnés à mort* (1920, 'Those Condemned to Death').

▷ M Revon, *Claude Farrère* (1924, in French)

FARROKHZAD, Forugh
(1935–67)

Iranian poet, major in her context, born in Tehran. She began writing classical poetry at 14, was unhappily married at 16, and soon lost her child to the custody of her brutal husband in a travesty of a divorce case. She was killed in a car accident. Her first two collections (both 1955) were both entitled *Asir* ('The Captive'): the second caused a scandal, since she confessed to sensual feelings for a man, not admitted by women in her country except in private. But the discerning recognized a new and bright talent. She wrote in a subtle and well-cadenced free verse, and is cherished as a major modernist poet.

▷ E W Fernea and B Q Bezirgan, *Middle Eastern Muslim Women Speak* (1977)

FARSON, James Negley
(1890–1960)

American author, born in Plainfield, New Jersey. He trained as a civil engineer but moved to England and went from there to Russia, where he had an export business and where he witnessed the 1917 revolution. From then on he led an adventurous life as airman, sailor and journalist, which is reflected in his varied works. These include *Sailing Across Europe* (1926), *Seeing Red* (1930), *Bomber's Moon* (1941) and *A Mirror for Narcissus* (1957).

▷ *The Way of a Transgressor* (1935)

FARWELL, George
(1911–76)

English-born Australian writer, radio broadcaster and actor, born in Bath. Settling in Australia in 1936 he wrote of the country, which he travelled extensively, in *Land of Mirage* (1950) and *Vanishing Australians*

(1961), and in his biographies of Ned Kelly, Edward Ogilvie and Charles Sturt. A selection of his writings was published as *Farwell Country* (1977).

▷ *Rejoice in Freedom* (1976)

FAST, Howard Melvin

(1914–92)

Immensely prolific American novelist, playwright and political commentator; he also wrote crime fiction under the pseudonym E V Cunningham. Born in New York City, Fast came of age in the radical 1930s and was drawn into its prevailing left-wing atmosphere, expressing his solidarity in a sequence of historical novels, *The Unvanquished* (1942), *Citizen Tom Paine* (1943) and *Freedom Road* (1944), whose contemporary relevance was transparently obvious. His allegiance to Popular Front communism eventually led to his being imprisoned for 'contempt of Congress' in 1947, and to his blacklisting by Hollywood, but he later recanted in a much-quoted account of writers' dealings with the Party, called *The Naked God* (1957); *Being Red* (1990) was written in a more indulgent political climate and one in which the American Left was firmly established in the academic curriculum. His best-known book is *Spartacus* (1951); it was initially published privately, and owed its success to the absence of preachy ideological speeches, and to a powerful Hollywood adaptation. With slightly ironic timing, Fast was awarded the Stalin Peace Prize in 1953.

FAULKNER, William

(1897–1962)

American novelist and winner of the Nobel Prize for literature, born near Oxford, Mississippi. His school career was undistinguished and he was rejected by the US army when America entered World War I, but he became a pilot in the Canadian Flying Corps. Later he attended Mississippi University and did odd jobs. While working in New Orleans he met **Sherwood Anderson**, who offered to recommend his first novel, *Soldier's Pay* (1926), to a publisher on condition that he did not have to read it. Other novels followed but their sales were unremarkable. In 1929, the year of his marriage, he took a job as a coal-heaver and while on night-work at a local power station is said to have written *As I Lay Dying* (1930) in just six weeks, working between midnight and 4am. *Sanctuary* (1931) was intended as a pot-boiler and was more successful commercially, but it had a profound impact on **Jean-Paul Sartre** and **Albert Camus**. However, it is novels like *The Sound and the Fury* (1929), *Light in August* (1932), *Absalom, Absalom!* (1936), *The Hamlet* (1940) and *Intruder in the Dust* (1948) that account

for his high reputation. In *Sartoris* (1929) he first describes the decline of the Compson and Sartoris families, indicative of the Old South, and the rise of the nouveau riche Snopeses, who dominate the later trilogy *The Hamlet* (1940), *The Town* (1957) and *The Mansion* (1959). Like most of the earlier books, these are set in and around Jefferson in the imaginary Yoknapatawpha County. A rare deviation is *A Fable* (1954), a reworking of Christ's Passion, set on the Western Front which, though ambitious, is accounted a noble failure. The tone of the novels is invariably sombre and elegiac but the prose sings like lyric poetry and Faulkner is revered as one of the modern masters of the novel. He was awarded the 1949 Nobel Prize for literature.

▷ J Blotner, *Faulkner: a biography* (2 vols, 1974)

FAUSET, Jessie Redmon

(1882–1961)

Black American novelist, born in New Jersey. She was the first Black woman to become a member of Phi Beta Kappa. She was associated with **William Dubois** and became a co-editor of his magazine *Crisis*. Her four novels all deal with problems of race; the best is probably *The Chinaberry Tree* (1931), whose oblique theme is the necessity for Black women not to try to become White; but its predecessor, *Plum Bun* (1929), which contrasts two sisters, one of whom tries to pass as White in Greenwich Village while the other accepts her heritage in Harlem, runs it a close second. She has more recently been accused of an illiberal, defeatist attitude; but her work undoubtedly served its cause well.

FAVART, Charles Simon

(1710–92)

French dramatist, born in Paris, the son of a pastrycook. He began writing comic opera, and the success of his first production, *Deux Jumelles* (1734), obtained for him financial backing which enabled him to continue with this genre. He married in 1745 Marie Justine Benoîte Duronceray (1727–72), a talented actress of the Opéra-Comique with whom he pioneered a new realism in costume. At the end of 1745 the Opéra-Comique, which he was directing, was obliged to close, and the Favarts went to Flanders with a company of actors attached to Marshal de Saxe, who made an unscrupulous attempt to procure Mme Favart as his mistress. When she fled from him he took out *lettres de cachet* against her husband, who had to remain in hiding until 1750, when the marshal's death put an end to the persecution, and Favart was able to return to Paris and write more comic operas. Among the best out of more than a hundred

are *Les amours de Bastien et Bastienne* (co-written with his wife, 1753, 'The Loves of Bastien and Bastienne'), *Ninette à la cour* (1755, 'Ninette at Court') and *Les Trois Sultanes* (1776, 'The Three Sultans' Wives').
▷ E Maddelen, *Goldoni e Favart* (1889)

FAY, András
(1786–1864)
Hungarian poet, playwright and novelist. He lived in Budapest, and was a pioneer of the social novel. He also wrote a set of fables in the manner of **Aesop** which achieved great success.

FAZEKAS, Mihály
(1766–1828)
Hungarian poet, a botanist by profession, born in Debrecan. His poems were of great simplicity, influencing and anticipating **Petöfi**. His peasant epic in hexameters, *Lüdas Matyi* (written in 1804, published in 1815), is his most famous work, and was successfully filmed in Hungary (by Kálmán Nádasdy and L Radony) in 1950.

FEARING, Kenneth Flexner
(1902–61)
American poet and novelist, born in Oak Park, Illinois, and educated at Wisconsin University. He published his first collection, *Angel Arms*, in 1929. Subsequent volumes include *Dead Reckoning: A Book of Poetry* (1938); *Stranger at Coney Island and Other Poems* (1949) and *New and Selected Poems* (1956). Fearing's writing reflects his belief that an increasingly mechanized society results in an erosion of human compassion and decency. His novels, which include *The Big Clock* (1946), are considered less important than his poetry.

FEDERMAN, Raymond
(1928–)
French-born American novelist and saxophonist. He was born in Paris and emigrated to the USA in 1947, where he spent three years as a jazz musician and took citizenship in 1953. He took a degree at Columbia University and a doctorate at UCLA. After teaching at Santa Barbara, he switched coasts and since 1968 has been based at the State University of New York, Buffalo. His first full-length fiction, *Double or Nothing* (1971), is an autobiographical *Bildungsroman* marked by the authorial digressions and revisions which also dominate *Take It or Leave It* (1976), a title that reflects Federman's capricious approach. His bilingual *The Voice in the Closet* (1979) considered the Holocaust, introducing as characters both the novelist himself and his transcultural idol

Beckett, on whose work Federman wrote persuasively in *Journey to Chaos* (1965). *The Twofold Vibration* (1982) is a hybrid of Beckett and science fiction; Federman asked that it be considered 'exploratory' rather than 'experimental' fiction, but the latter tag has stuck unmercifully. *Smiles on Washington Square* (1985) demonstrates the phrase's redundancy.
▷ J Klinkowitz, in *Literary Disruptions* (2nd edn 1980)

FEDIN, Konstantine
(1892–1977)
Russian novelist, story writer and critic, born in Saratov. Fedin ended up as a toady of the Stalinist establishment, a persecutor of 'subversive' writers; but he had been a gifted writer, who in 1921 had left the Communist Party under the influence of the Serapion Brothers, that group of independent spirits who wished to keep art clear of politics. His first and certainly best novel, *Goroda i gody* (1924, Eng trans *Cities and Years*, 1962), reflected his experience of internment in Germany throughout World War I: it deals with the problem of maintaining individual integrity in revolutionary struggle. By the 1930s, however, Fedin had chosen the route of what Trotsky called the 'fellow traveller': the writer who is not of the Party but essentially with its aims. His last truly independent book was an autobiography much concerned with **Gorky**, whom he had known: *Gorki sredi nas* (1943–4, 'Gorky Amongst Us'). For this he was officially reprimanded. His massive trilogy, *Pervye radosti*, *Neobyknovennoye* and *Kostyor* (1945–62, Eng trans *Early Joys*, 1948, *No Ordinary Summer*, 1950 and *The Conflagration*, 1968), although facile, is as good as obligatory socialist-realist fiction can be, and offers indispensable information about Russia between 1910 and World War II.
▷ J Blum, *Konstantine Fedin* (1967)

FEIBLEMAN, Peter S
(1930–)
American novelist and dramatist, born in New York but brought up in New Orleans. For eight years he worked as an actor in Spain and elsewhere; he had studied drama at the Carnegie Institute. He is best known for his first novel, *A Place Without Twilight* (1958), about a New Orleans Black girl whose skin is 'twilight'. He dramatized this for Broadway in 1961. Later novels have not met with such a good reception.

FEIKEMAN, Feike *see* MANFRED, Frederick

FEINSTEIN, Elaine
(1930–)

English novelist, poet, critic and translator, born in Bootle, Lancashire, and educated at Cambridge. During the 1960s she was a lecturer in English literature at Essex University. *The Circle* (1970), her first novel, deals with a woman's simultaneous craving for emotional independence and her desire to be insulated by marriage. Subsequent books have also examined the female experience, *The Amberstone Exit* (1972), for example, confronting the trauma of birth and motherhood. *The Survivors* (1982), on the other hand, derives partly from the history of her own family, and looks at the fate of early 20th-century Jewish refugees from Russia. Feinstein has also translated several Russian women poets and written an authoritative biography of **Marina Tsvetayeva**, *A Captive Lion* (1987).

FEITH, Rhijnvis
(1753–1824)

Dutch poet, born in Zwolle. He became mayor there in 1780. He wrote some sentimental love novels, and the lyrical *Oden en Gedichten* (1796–1810, 'Odes and Poems'). Of his tragedies, the best known are *Thirza* (1784), *Johanna Gray* (1791), and *Ines de Castro* (1793). He published a collection of criticism, *Brieven* (1784–94, 'Letters').

FELINSKI, Alojzy
(1771–1820)

Polish poet and playwright who wrote in the style of the French neo-classicists: his *Barbara* (1813, staged in Warsaw in 1817), which created a sensation, is especially admired for the 13-syllable metre of its lines, and is still regarded as a great drama.

FELIPE, León, pseud of León Felipe Camino
(1884–1968)

Spanish poet and translator (of **Whitman**), born in Tábora, Zamora. He was originally a pharmacist, but took to a wandering life in his early middle age. His virulent and highly colloquial denunciations of Franco led some critics to suppose that his poetry was essentially one of declamation; this proved a premature judgement, for his *Obras completas* (1963, 'Complete Works') revealed him to be a poet no more or less declamatory than his master, Whitman—and sometimes as subtle. He has been described by a conservative critic as 'too blunt in his directness'; but one of different persuasion, while conceding his occasional 'prosiness', and convinced by his almost biblical humaneness rather than by his theoretical politics, asked, 'can one be too blunt?' His style was wholly original in its Spanish context, and his subtleties and ironies were not always appreciated by critics who saw him as a necessarily crude red.
▷ *TriQuarterly*, 16 (1970)

FÉNELON, François de Salignac de la Mothe
(1651–1715)

French prelate and writer, born in the château de Fénelon in Périgord. At 20 he entered the seminary of St Sulpice in Paris, and was ordained in 1675. After some time spent in parochial duties, he became director of an institution for women converts to the Catholic faith in 1678. Here he wrote *Traité de l'éducation des filles* (1678, Eng trans *The Education of Young Gentlewomen*, 1699), urging a more liberal education for women, and criticizing the coercion of Huguenot converts. At the revocation of the Edict of Nantes (1685) he was sent to preach among the Protestants of Poitou. From 1689 to 1699 he was tutor to Louis XIV's grandson, the young Duke of Burgundy, and as such he wrote the *Fables* (first collected in parallel translation as *Twenty-Seven Tales and Fables, French and English*, 1729), *Dialogues des Morts anciens et modernes* (1713, with augmented posthumous editions, Eng trans *Fables and Dialogues of the Dead*, 1723), *Abrégé des vies des anciens Philosophes* (pub 1726, Eng trans *The Lives and Most Remarkable Maxims of the Antient Philosophers*, [sic] 1726), and *Les Aventures de Télémaque* (1699, Eng trans *The Adventures of Telemachus*, 1699). He had been presented by the king to the abbey of St Valéry (1694) and to the archbishopric of Cambrai (1695). He had formed in 1687 the acquaintance of the celebrated quietist mystic, Madame Guyon, and, convinced of the unfairness of the outcry against her, he advised her to submit her book to Jacques Bossuet, who condemned it. Fénelon acquiesced, but refused to join in any personal condemnation. Fénelon composed his own *Explication des maximes des saints sur la vie intérieure* (1697, Eng trans *The Maxims of the Saints Explained*, 1698) in defence of certain of Madame Guyon's doctrines. A fierce controversy ensued, and in the end the pope condemned the *Maximes des saints*. Fénelon's *Télémaque* was considered by the king a disguised satire upon his court and from then on Fénelon was strictly restrained within his diocese. From this date he lived almost exclusively for his flock, but in the revived Jansenistic dispute he engaged earnestly on the side of orthodoxy. His works are voluminous, and on a variety of subjects.
▷ P Janet, *Fénelon, une biographie* (1892)

FENOGLIO, Beppe
(1922–63)

Italian story writer, born in Alpa, to working-class parents. He left much unpublished at his early death, and this has proved hard to edit. He fought for 18 months with the partisans in the latter part of World War II, and his chronicle of it provided him with the material for his first book, *I ventitrè giorni della città di Alba* (1951, 'The 23 Days of the City of Alba'). It is written in a startling and not always effective mixture of dialect, regular Italian, and even English. His best-known and most vivid book is *Il partigiano Johnny* (1968, 'Johnny the Partisan').

FENTON, James
(1949–)

English poet, born in Lincoln. A highly thought of, intellectual poet, who has deliberately set himself apart from the mainstream, Fenton publishes little. He is mainly a political and satirical rather than a 'personal' poet, who makes a virtue out of reticence. He wrote some sharply satirical poems in collaboration with John Fuller, in *Partingtime Hall* (1987); his own main collections are *Terminal Moraine* (1972) and *The Memory of War and Children in Exile: Poems 1968–83* (1983).

FERBER, Edna
(1887–1968)

American writer, born in Kalamazoo, Michigan. She was the author of numerous novels and short stories, including *Dawn O'Hara* (1911), *Gigolo* (1922), *So Big* (1924, Pulitzer Prize), *Cimarron* (1929) and *Saratoga Trunk* (1941). She is probably best remembered as the writer of *Show Boat* (1926), which inspired the musical play of that name. She also wrote plays with **George Kaufman**, such as *Dinner at Eight* (1932) and *Stage Door* (1936).
▷J G Gilbert, *Edna Ferber: a biography* (1978)

FERGUSON, Sir Samuel
(1810–86)

Irish poet and Celtic scholar, born in Belfast. Called to the Irish Bar in 1838, he was appointed in 1867 the first Deputy Keeper of Irish Records. As President of the Royal Irish Academy he gave a powerful impetus to the study of early Irish art. His spirited poems were published as *Lays of the Western Gael* (1865), *Congal* (1872), *Poems* (1880) and *The Forging of the Anchor* (1883). His edition of the *Leabhar Breac* appeared in 1876; his *Ogham Inscriptions* in 1887.
▷A Dearing, *Sir Samuel Ferguson, Poet and Antiquarian* (1931)

FERGUSSON, Robert
(1750–74)

Scottish poet, born in Edinburgh, the son of a solicitor's clerk. He was educated at the High School of Edinburgh and of Dundee, and at St Andrews University, where he excelled. He was employed in the commissary office in Edinburgh, contributing poems to Ruddiman's *Weekly Magazine* from 1771, which gained him local fame. His company was much sought and convivial excesses permanently injured his health. Following an awakening of religious interest, inspired by a meeting with the minister John Brown, he fell into deep depression, and was reduced to insanity by a fall downstairs. He died in a public asylum. He was a major influence on and inspiration to **Robert Burns**, who placed a headstone on his grave in 1789. He left 33 poems in Scots, and 50 poems in English. Essentially an Edinburgh poet, his most famous poem is *Auld Reekie* (1773), tracing a day in the life of the city. Other major and well-known poems are *Elegy on the Death of Scots Music*, *The Daft Days* (his first published poem), *Hallow Fair*, *To the Tron Kirk Bell*, *Leith Races* and the satirical *The Rising of the Session*.
▷A Law, *Robert Fergusson and the Edinburgh of his Time* (1974)

FERLINGHETTI, Lawrence
(1919–)

American poet and publisher, born in Yonkers, New York. He studied at the University of North Carolina, Columbia University, and the Sorbonne, and served in the US Naval Reserve (1941–5). He worked for *Time* magazine in New York, then moved to San Francisco in 1951, where he became a prime mover in the so-called 'San Francisco Renaissance'. He was co-founder of the City Lights Bookstore, which acted as a meeting place, cultural forum and publishing house for radical poets. His own work made a major contribution to Beat poetry and beyond, beginning with *Pictures of the Gone World* (1955) and *A Coney Island of the Mind* (1958). He has published over 40 books of poetry, including *Endless Life: The Selected Poems* (1981), two novels, and a number of plays.
▷N Cherkassky, *Ferlinghetti: A Biography* (1979)

FERMOR, Patrick Michael Leigh
(1915–)

English travel writer of English and Irish descent. Expelled from King's School, Canterbury, he set out in 1933 on a leisurely walk from Rotterdam to Constantinople. *A Time of Gifts* (1977) recounted the journey as far as Hungary; *Between the Woods and the Water*

(1986) took it to its terminus. Both have been praised for their incisive grasp of the mood of pre-war Europe, and few doubted the veracity of his account despite its being more than 40 years in gestation. Later he spent an adventurous war in Albania, Greece and Crete where, disguised as a shepherd, he lived for two years organizing the Resistance and the capture and evacuation of the German commander, General Kreipe. Among his other books are *The Traveller's Tree*, about the West Indies, which won the Heinemann Foundation Prize in 1950; *Mani* (1958), which was awarded the Duff Cooper Memorial Prize; and *Three Letters from the Andes* (1991), vivid accounts of a journey in the early 1970s.

▷ *A Time to Keep Silent* (1953)

FERNANDEZ, Lucas
(1474–1542)

Spanish dramatist, born in Salamanca. His *Farsas i églogas al modo y estilo pastoril y catellano* ('Religious Plays and Pastoral Poems') consists of three secular plays, three religious plays, and a pastoral sung dialogue—he was a musician, and taught music in Salamanca. One of these plays depicts the conversion of Dionysius the Areopagite to Christianity, and is the first of its kind.

FERNANDEZ, Pablo
(1930–)

Cuban poet, who returned to Cuba after the Castro Revolution, but then fell foul of the regime. After his first collected edition (1962), his poetry became more concentrated and self-critical. Two of his poems are translated in the *Penguin Book of Latin American Verse* (1971, ed E Curacciolo-Trejo).

FERNANDEZ FLOREZ, Wenceslao
(1885–1964)

Spanish novelist and essayist, born in La Coruña. A lifelong Franco supporter, his view of life was harsh, bitter and yet sentimental. His great success was *Las siete columnas* (1926, Eng trans *The Seven Pillars*, 1934). His work is not now so much heeded, although in its time it was much appreciated.

FERNÁNDEZ DE LIZARDI, José Joaquin
(1776–1827)

Mexican novelist and journalist, known as 'El Pensador Mexicano' ('The Mexican Thinker'), after a periodical he founded and edited. He wrote the first Latin-American novel proper, the enlightened and picaresque *El Periquillo Sarniento* (1816), an attack on the manners and morals of his time which has been underestimated outside Mexico.

▷ J R Spell, *The Life and Works of José Fernández de Lizardi* (1931)

FERNÁNDEZ MORENO, Baldomero
(1886–1950)

Argentinian poet, born in Buenos Aires into a Spanish family. A doctor by profession, he lived in Spain during most of the 1890s. His poetry, more Spanish than Argentinian in inspiration, has often been compared to that of **Antonio Machado**. The best of his poetry, which set out to please no one, least of all himself, has a distinguished melancholy, not unlike that of **Hardy** or **Housman**: 'There is nothing to compare with this moment/Of the morning, uncertain and solitary/When your bedsheet is your shroud …'.

▷ E Carilla, *Genio y figura de Baldomero Fernández Moreno* (1973)

FERNANDEZ RETEMAR, Roberto
(1930–)

Cuban poet, editor and critic, born in Havana. He has played an active role in Cuba's literature after the Revolution. His first collection, *Elegía como un himno* ('Elegy Like a Hymn') appeared in 1950. Since then he has won many prizes. Two poems are translated in the *Penguin Book of Latin American Verse* (1971, ed E Curacciolo-Trejo).

FERRARI, Paolo
(1822–89)

Italian dramatist, born in Modena. He wrote many excellent comedies, including *Goldoni* (1852) and *Parini e la satira* (1857, 'Parini and the Lampoon'). In 1860 he became Professor of History at Modena, and afterwards at Milan.

▷ N de Belli, *Il Teatro di Paolo Ferrari* (1922)

FERRÉ, Rosario
(1940–)

Puerto Rican poet and narrator, one of the most expressive in Spanish America. Part of an important emerging group of Puerto Rican authors, she was born in Ponce, and studied at Wellesley, Manhattanville College, receiving her PhD from the University of Maryland in 1986. She founded and edited the influential literary journal *Zona de Carga y Descarga* (1972–5). A regular contributor to newspapers, Ferré also writes short stories, poetry, essays and translations.

FERREIRA, Antonio
(1528–69)

Portuguese poet, born in Lisbon. He studied law at Coimbra, and became a judge in Lisbon, where he spent his life. A contemplative man who had little time for the popular Iberian subjects of war and

commerce, he turned to classical models for his inspiration, and introduced a classical style into Portuguese verse and drama, earning the title 'The Portuguese Horace'. His best-known work is the two-act historical tragedy on classical lines, *Inês de Castro* (1587).
▷A Roig, *Antonio Ferreira, études sur sa vie et son oeuvre* (1970)

FERREIRA DE CASTRO, José Maria
(1898–1974)
Portuguese novelist, born in Oliveira de Azeméis. He emigrated to Brazil when he was 13 years old, and worked on a rubber plantation and then as a journalist. He achieved success with *Emigrantes* (1928, Eng trans *Emigrants*, 1962), and then won international acclaim for *A selva* (1930, Eng trans *Jungle*, 1935), a searing indictment of conditions on the rubber plantations. A later novel, *A Lã e a Neve* (1947, 'Wool and Snow'), examines, in his usual harsh style, the relationship between the shepherds of Covilhã and the voracious textile operatives who then exploited them. *A Missão* (1954, Eng trans *The Mission*, 1961) contains three short novels.
▷A Gabral, *Ferreira de Castro* (1940, in Portuguese)

FERRIER, Susan Edmonstone
(1782–1854)
Scottish novelist, born in Edinburgh, the tenth child of a lawyer who became principal clerk to the Court of Session with Sir **Walter Scott**. With the death of her mother in 1797 she took over the running of the house, and looked after her father until his death in 1829. Her first work, *Marriage* (1818), a novel of provincial social manners, was followed by *The Inheritance* (1824) and *Destiny* (1831), a Highland romance. She enjoyed a close friendship with Scott, who was for a time credited by some with the authorship of her books. Following the publication of these works she was converted to evangelical Christianity, and became a member of the Free Church, concentrating on charitable works rather than on writing. Towards the end of her life she lived in relative seclusion, her eyesight failing badly.
▷A Grant, *Susan Ferrier of Edinburgh* (1957)

FET, Afanásy, pseud of Afanásy Shenshin
(1820–92)
Russian romantic poet, born on an estate in the Orlov district, of a German mother and a Russian father. Fet was the poet through whose works many Russian children were introduced to poetry. He is often described as 'illegitimate' because his parents' foreign marriage was not recognized in Russia: ('Foeth', transformed to 'Fet', was his mother's

name). He was not quite the great poet he has often been made out to be, but one very melodious about 'nature and love', and valuable for his expression of the essentially unexamined theme of anxiety about being alive. His early life was unhappy: he was rejected by his muse 'Yelena', who then killed herself. But he made a rich marriage in 1856, and seemed to prosper, even though he was proscribed by radicals for his reactionary views (in fact the product of naivety rather than thought). He translated **Horace**, **Goethe** and **Schopenhauer** (whose attitudes much affected him), became depressed, tried to kill himself, and suddenly died. His reputation grew after his death, and his influence on such more important poets as **Blok**, was decisive— his historical, as distinct from his intrinsic, importance is thus major. There are English translations in the *Penguin Book of Russian Verse* (1965, ed Dimitry Obolensky).

FEUCHTWANGER, Lion
(1884–1958)
German writer, born in Munich. He won a European reputation with the 18th-century historical novel *Jud Süss* (1925), presenting an elaborately detailed picture of the lives, sufferings and weaknesses of central European Jewry, and the 14th-century tale *Die hässliche Herzogin* (1923), which as *The Ugly Duchess* (1927) was a great success in Britain. During World War I he was interned in Tunis. His thinly disguised satire on Hitler's Munich putsch, *Erfolg* (1930, 'Success'), earned him the hatred of the Nazis. In 1933 he fled to France, where in 1940 he was interned by the German army, but escaped to the USA. He also wrote numerous dramas, and collaborated with **Bertolt Brecht** in a translation of **Christopher Marlowe**'s *Edward II*. His later works included detailed part-biographies of Goya (1952) and **Rousseau** (1954).
▷L Boettche and P G Krohn, *Lion Feuchtwanger* (1960)

FEUILLET, Octave
(1821–90)
French novelist, born in Saint Lô. He was one of **Dumas**'s literary assistants. From 1848 he published in the *Revue des deux mondes* a series collected in *Scènes et proverbes* and *Scènes et comédies* (1853–6). He wrote many popular novels and plays, including the sentimental novel *Roman d'un jeune homme pauvre* (1858, Eng trans *The Romance of a Poor Young Man*, 1859), which remains his most famous work.
▷A Greuwe, *Die Literatur den Krinolin* (1974)

FÉVAL, Paul Henri Corentin
(1817–87)

French novelist, born in Rennes. His many novels include *Les Mystères de Londres* (1844, 'The Mysteries of London') and *Le Bossu* (1858, 'The Hunchback'); some of his novels had an extraordinary success when dramatized.

▷A Delaigue, *Un homme des lettres* (1898)

FEYDEAU, Ernest Aimé
(1821–73)

French novelist. He was a stockbroker and an archaeologist, and achieved a notorious success with his novel *Fanny* (1858). His stories depict the worst features of society in the time of the Empire. *Sylvie* (1861) is a novel of more than ordinary power.

FEYDEAU, Georges Léon Jules Marie
(1862–1921)

French dramatist, the son of **Ernest Aimé Feydeau** and a prostitute. His name is synonymous with French bedroom farce. He wrote his first play, *Le Tailleur pour Dames* (1886, Eng trans *A Gown for his Mistress*, 1969), when he was 24 and subsequently maintained a prolific output. His characters are Parisian bourgeois couples seeking diversion from each other; his farces, therefore, rely on the twin themes of adultery and the chase. Among his plays are such enduring (and rather endearing) classics as *Le Dindon* (1896, Eng trans *Paying the Piper*, 1972), *La Dame de chez Maxim* (1899, 'The Lady from Maxim's'), *L'Hôtel du libre Échange* (1899, Eng trans *Hotel Paradiso*, 1957) and *Une Puce à l'oreille* (1907), produced as *A Flea in Her Ear* (trans by **John Mortimer**) at the National Theatre in 1965.

▷A Shenkan, *Georges Feydeau* (1972)

FIACC, Padraic, real name Joseph O'Connor
(1924–)

Irish poet, born in Belfast; he was brought up and educated in New York, but returned to the city of his birth in 1946. His first collection, *By the Black Stream* (1969), announced a Republican voice couched in transatlantic idiom. His important and sadly prophetic *The Wearing of the Black: An Anthology of Contemporary Ulster Poetry* (1974) was largely neglected. Subsequent collections of his own work, *Nights in the Bad Place* (1977) and *Missa Terribilis* (1986), have a tragically valedictory and somewhat bitter tone. However, *The Selected Padraic Fiacc* (1979) gives a fuller picture, of a humanist at odds with his surroundings, understanding, but helpless in the face of, the escalating violence he sees around him.

FIBIGER, Mathilde
(1830–72)

Danish novelist. Born in Copenhagen, she worked as a governess. Her fame rests on her first novel, *12 Breve til Clara Raphael* (1851, '12 Letters to Clara Raphael'): boldly asserting feminine integrity and independence on the basis of Romanticism, liberalism and religious convictions, the novel provoked a major controversy but subsequently became a seminal text for the women's movement in Denmark. Her second novel, *En Skizze efter det virkelige Liv* (1852, 'Sketch from Real Life'), was an attempt to appease her readership, but *Minona* (1854), defending the role of feminine eroticism, was attacked as being immoral. Finding it increasingly hard to support herself as a writer, she became Denmark's first woman telegraphist (1863).

▷T Andersen and L Busk-Jensen, *Mathilde Fibiger—Clara Raphael. Kvindekamp og kvindebevidsthed i Danmark 1830–1870* (1979)

FICKE, Arthur (Davison)
(1883–1945)

American poet and critic, born in Iowa. He is now best-remembered for a brief but enduring encounter with **Edna St Vincent Millay**, and for his involvement in the 'Spectra' hoax. This was a rather earnest protest (his accomplice was the poet Witter Bynner) against the Imagists and Vorticists. Ficke was blusteringly anti-modernist. He liked Japanese art and wrote two books about it. *Sonnets of a Portrait Painter* (1914) was his main collection of poetry.

FIDLER, Kathleen
(1899–1980)

English author of books for children, born in Coalville, Leicestershire. Her first volume, *The Borrowed Garden*, appeared in 1944. Her most popular novels, however, proved to be those about the chirpy Brydon family, whose adventures feature in 17 books, from *The Brydons at Smuggler's Creek* (1946) to *The Brydons Go Canoeing* (1963). She is also the creator of the Dean family, whose exploits fill nine books, from *The Deans Move In* (1953) to *The Deans' Dutch Adventure* (1982). Her other books include *Stories From Scottish Heritage* (3 vols, 1951) and the *True Tales of ...* series, collections of historical stories from various regions of Britain. In 1982 the annual Kathleen Fidler Award was instituted for new novel-writing for children of 8 to 11 years old.

FIEDLER, Leslie A(aron)
(1917–92)

Controversial American literary critic, whose essay 'Come Back to the Raft Again, Huck

Honey!', reprinted in *An End to Innocence* (1955), adumbrated his belief that US literature had been dominated by suppressed homoerotic agenda. This notion was taken further in his most important critical work, the hugely influential and still debated *Love and Death in the American Novel* (1960). The argument was less assured in *The Stranger in Shakespeare* (1972), in which the commonplace perception that the plays are haunted by women, blacks and Jews was pushed to absurd lengths. A charismatic teacher at the State University of New York in Buffalo, Fiedler attempted to share his students' lifestyle and values; one of the pitfalls, a conviction for marijuana possession, was documented in *Being Busted* (1970). His novels—*The Second Stone* (1963), *Back to China* (1965) and *The Messengers Will Come No More* (1974)—were less compelling than his short fiction; the best of the collections are *The Last Jew in America* (1966) and *Nude Croquet* (1969). Other critical works include *No! In Thunder* (1960), a typically forceful discussion of classical American literature and *What Was Literature?* (1982), the latter suggesting a diminution of his powers.

FIELD, Eugene
(1850–95)

American writer, born in St Louis, Missouri. He became a journalist at 23, and from 1883 was a columnist with the *Chicago Morning News*, achieving a reputation as humorist and poet with his column 'Sharps and Flats'. He wrote the well-known nursery lullaby 'Wynken, Blynken, and Nod' and the sentimental 'Little Boy Blue', and published several books of children's verse.
▷S Thompson, *The Life of Eugene Field* (1927); and other works by Thompson

FIELD, Nathan
(1587–c.1620)

English actor and dramatist, born in London. He was educated at St Paul's school and in 1600 became one of the children of the Queen's Chapel. He was one of the comedians of the Queen's Revels (1604–13) and various other troupes. As a playwright he collaborated with **Francis Beaumont** and **John Fletcher**, and with **Philip Massinger** in the latter's *The Fatal Dowry* (c.1618, published 1632) and wrote two comedies, *A Woman is a Weathercocke* (1612) and *Amends for Ladies* (1618).
▷R F Brinkley, *Nathaniel Field, actor-playwright* (1928)

FIELDING, Henry
(1707–54)

English novelist, born at Sharpham Park, near Glastonbury in Somerset, the son of an army lieutenant and a judge's daughter, and brother of **Sarah Fielding**. He was educated privately, then at Eton. He fell in love with a young heiress at Lyme Regis, attempted to abduct her and was bound over to keep the peace. He went to London and in 1728 published a satirical poem, *The Masquerade*, and a comedy, *Love in Several Masques*. Thereafter he studied at the University of Leiden (1728–9), before returning to London, and in the space of eight years he wrote 25 dramatic pieces: light comedies, adaptations of **Molière**, farces, ballad operas, burlesques (including *Tom Thumb*), and a series of satires attacking Sir Robert Walpole and his government. This last prompted the introduction of the Theatrical Licensing Act of 1737 and effectively ended Fielding's career as a playwright and as a theatre manager (he had formed his own company, and was running the Little Theatre, Haymarket). He now turned to the law and was admitted as a student at the Middle Temple; he was called to the Bar in 1740, but did not shine on the circuit on account of disabling gout. While still a student he turned to journalism and became editor of *The Champion* (1739–41). Incensed by the publication of **Samuel Richardson**'s prudish *Pamela* in 1740, he ridiculed it in a pseudonymous parody, *An Apology for the Life of Mrs Shamela Andrews* (1741). In 1742 came *The Adventures of Joseph Andrews and his Friend, Mr Abraham Adams*. Three volumes of *Miscellanies* (including *The Life of Jonathan Wild the Great*) followed in 1743. *The History of Tom Jones, a Foundling* was probably begun in the summer of 1746 and was completed towards the end of 1748. In the interim he caused a scandal by marrying Mary Daniel, the maid of his first wife, Charlotte Craddock (d.1744). He was made a justice of the peace for Westminster and Middlesex in 1748 and campaigned vigorously against legal corruption, and helped his half-brother, Sir John Fielding (1721–80) to found the Bow Street Runners as an embryo detective force. In 1749 *The History of Tom Jones, a Foundling* was published to public acclaim, though its reception by some literary luminaries was unenthusiastic. **Samuel Johnson** called it vicious and there were those who held it responsible for two earth tremors that shook London shortly after its publication. But it endures as one of the great comic and picaresque novels in the English language, and **Coleridge** thought the plot one of the three most perfect ever planned. He followed it with *Amelia* in 1751. In 1752 he was heavily involved with *The Covent Garden Journal*, which contains some of his most acerbic satire. During his last years, however, illness overtook him. He was still ardent in his fight against corruption but at

the age of 45 he could not move without the help of crutches. He died in Lisbon where he had gone in search of better health.
▷F H Dudden, *Henry Fielding* (2 vols, 1952); I P Watt, *The Rise of the Novel* (1957)

FIELDING, Sarah
(1710–68)

English novelist and translator, born in East Stour, Dorset, sister of **Henry Fielding**. Her most popular novel was *The Adventures of David Simple in Search of a Faithful Friend* (1744), a romance dealing with four young people, rejected by their families and society, in which the author's sympathy is clearly with the young women struggling to make an independent and respectable living. A sequel, *Familiar Letters Between the Principal Characters in David Simple*, appeared in 1747, together with a second edition of the first book. They are ambitious, progressive works and to these two volumes **Henry Fielding** contributed prefaces. A friend of **Samuel Richardson**, she wrote the first study of his *Clarissa* in 1749. She published several other works, including a translation of **Xenophon**'s *Memorabilia and Apologia* in 1762.

FIERSTEIN, Harvey Forbes
(1954–)

American playwright and actor, born in Brooklyn, New York. An art student at the Pratt Institute, he entered showbusiness as a female impersonator in gay nightclubs. A gravelly-voiced, overweight figure at this time, he made his dramatic debut as an asthmatic lesbian cleaning-woman in the Andy Warhol play *Pork* (1971) and appeared frequently in off-Broadway productions before writing his own plays, such as *In Search Of The Cobra Jewels* (1973), *Freaky Pussy* (1975) and *Flatbush Tosca* (1975), a transvestite version of the opera. In 1976 he wrote and acted in *The International Stud*, the first of three bittersweet, semi-autobiographical plays covering the life of sardonic, incurably romantic New York drag queen Arnold Beckoff and his search for respect, a loving boyfriend and domestic bliss. Premiered on Broadway as *Torch Song Trilogy* (1982), it won Tony awards for Best Play and Best Actor; Fierstein also wrote and starred in the film adaptation (1988). He won a further Tony for the book of the long-running Broadway musical *La Cage Aux Folles* (1983) and has also written the plays *Spookhouse* (1984), *Safe Sex* (1987) and *Legs Diamond* (1989).

FIGUEROA, John Joseph Maria
(1927–)

Jamaican poet, born in Kingston, Jamaica, and educated at Holy Cross College, Worcester, Massachusetts. He was a distinguished

educator, latterly with the Open University, and edited *Caribbean Voices* (1971). His poetry is notable for its sensuous treatment of the Caribbean landscape, broad cross-cultural references, and a Christian religious sensibility. **Derek Walcott** best described the distinctive quality of his verse: 'more than Roman Catholic in themes, positively Roman in manner'. *Ignoring Hurts* (1976) and *The Chase* (1992) both include poems from his earlier collections, *Blue Mountain Peak* (1943) and *Love Leaps Here* (1962).

FIKRET, Tevfik
(1857–1915)

Turkish poet, born in Istanbul. Learned in French language and literature, he became editor of the magazine *Servet-i Funan*, which was so vital in opening up the European traditions to Turkish writers. He was the principal writer of the Edebiyat-i Cedide, or New Literature movement—opposed to a recalcitrant Sultan (well and angrily punished by Fikret in his poetry), and to stultification—which had grown from the earlier Tanzimat (Transformation) movement. He helped to adapt the sonnet to Turkish poetry, and experimented with many European forms. Essentially, he carried on and perfected the work started by **Abdüllhak Hamid Tarhan**, and was notable for the way in which his poetry remained essentially Turkish in character even while making use of Western models.
▷T S Halman, *Modern Turkish Literature* (1980)

FILICAIA, Vincenzo da
(1642–1707)

Italian lyric poet, born in Florence. He studied there and at Pisa, and held a post under the Grand-Duke of Tuscany. He is remembered for his patriotic sonnets, and his ode on the liberation of Vienna from the Turks (1684).
▷G Caponi, *Filicaia e son opere* (1901)

FINCH, Robert
(1900–)

Canadian poet, born in Freeport, Long Island, New York and educated at the University of Toronto. He has worked as a lecturer of French, a writer-in-residence, and a painter (with exhibitions in New York and Paris). He twice received a Governor General's Award (1947 and 1962). His work, at times satirical, frequently employs complex imagery: the poems in his collection *Acis in Oxford* (1961), for example, were inspired by Handel's oratorio *Acis and Galatea*, and the collection *Dover Beach Revisited and Other*

Poems (1966) takes its inspiration from **Matthew Arnold**'s poem and the events of World War II.

FINDLATER, Jane
(1866–1946)

Scottish novelist, born in Lochearnhead, Perthshire, daughter of a Free Church minister, and sister of **Mary Findlater**. She had a great success with her first novel, *The Green Graves of Balgowrie* (1896), an 18th-century fiction based on family papers. It was followed by *A Daughter of Strife* (1897), *Rachel* (1899), *The Story of a Mother* (1902) and *The Ladder to the Stars* (1906). In collaboration with her sister she wrote the novel *Crossriggs* (1908) and other works.

▷E MacKenzie, *The Findlater Sisters* (1964)

FINDLATER, Mary
(1865–1963)

Scottish novelist, born in Lochearnhead, Perthshire, daughter of a Free Church minister, and sister of **Jane Findlater**. She wrote several novels of her own, including *Betty Musgrave* (1899) and *The Rose of Joy* (1903), a volume of *Songs and Sonnets* (1895), and collaborated with her sister on the novel *Crossriggs* (1908) and other works.

▷E Mackenzie, *The Findlater Sisters* (1964)

FINDLEY, Timothy
(1930–)

Canadian playwright and novelist, born in Toronto and educated at St Andrew's College and Jarvis Collegiate as well as at the Royal Conservatory of Music, and the Central School for Speech and Drama in London. He worked as an actor and a Hollywood scriptwriter before turning to full-time writing in 1962. He chaired the Writers' Union of Canada in 1977–8 and has received over 10 special awards, including a Governor General's Award (1977). He is best known for his novel *The Wars* (1977), an account of a Canadian officer in World War II whose experiences lead him to treason and suspected madness.

▷Timothy Findley issue of *Canadian Literature* (Winter 1981)

FINE, Anne
(1947–)

English novelist, born in Leicester and educated at Warwick University. Primarily a writer for children and teenagers, she started with such titles as *The Summer-House Loon* (1978), but made her reputation with *Goggle Eyes* (1989, published in the USA as *My War with Goggle Eyes*), a moving but witty account of a young girl coming to terms with her divorced mother's new boyfriend. This won the Carnegie Medal, as did *Flower Babies* (1993), while *Madame Doubtfire* (1987, published in the USA as *Alias Madame Doubtfire*, 1988) was turned into a successful Hollywood movie in 1994. A two-edged writer, whose characters often combine wisdom with a faint degree of malice, Fine has also written a disturbing and powerful adult novel about obsessive love, *The Killjoy* (1986).

FINEMAN, Irving
(1893–)

Popular American Jewish novelist, an engineer by profession, who wrote the fictionalized biography of Henrietta Szold, founder of Hadassah. *Ruth* (1949) was a version of the Bible story, while *Jacob* (1941) was autobiographical. *Fig Tree Madonna* (1951) was a successful play.

FINLAY, Ian Hamilton
(1925–)

Scottish artist, poet and writer, born in the Bahamas to Scottish parents who returned to their native country when he was a child. He spent a brief period at Glasgow School of Art before World War II. In the 1950s he began his career as a writer, and became increasingly concerned with the formal qualities of individual words; his writings of the early 1960s played a leading part in the foundation of the 'concrete poetry' movement. Since then the major theme of his art has been the relationship between words and images. In 1966 he moved, with his wife, to a farmhouse near Dunsyre in the Pentland Hills, later named 'Little Sparta', and began to transform the grounds into an original modern conception of a classical garden, with sculptures and stone inscriptions carefully placed within the landscape. Like his prints, posters and other works, these are produced in collaboration with a number of skilled craftsmen. He also designed the garden at Stockwood Park, Luton, another monument to classical culture.

FINLAYSON, Rod(erick David)
(1904–92)

New Zealand writer and one-time champion rifle shot, born in Devonport, Auckland, whose short stories are in the 'tale-teller' mode rather than the sketches of character or place of earlier writers; he depicts a realistic Maori rather than a 'noble savage'. His collections include the first, *Brown Man's Burden* (1938, rev edn 1973), and *Sweet Beulah Land* (1942). His novels are *Tidal Creek* (1948) and *The Schooner comes to Atia* (1952). *Other Lovers* (1976) includes the novellas 'Frankie and Lena' and 'Jim and Miri'. He also wrote a historical novel for younger readers, *The*

Springing Fern (1965), and published a study of **D'Arcy Cresswell** in 1972.

FIRBANK, (Arthur Annesley) Ronald
(1886–1926)

English novelist, born in London, the son of a wealthy company director. Educated at Uppingham and Cambridge, where he was converted to Roman Catholicism, in 1909 he left university without taking a degree and travelled extensively in Spain, Italy, the Middle East and North Africa. Sunstroke as a child left him delicate and although he acquired friends he was by nature solitary, invariably unaccompanied on his frequent visits to the theatre. A homosexual, he cultivated eccentricity such as the palm tree in his apartment which he employed a gardener to water twice a day. His novels (written on piles of blue postcards) are slight but innovative and anticipate **Evelyn Waugh**, **Anthony Powell**, **Ivy Compton-Burnett** and others. In 1905 he published a volume containing two short stories, *Odette d'Antrevernes*, and several novels followed, among them *Vainglory* (1915), *Valmouth* (1919) and *Prancing Nigger* (1924), inspired by a visit to Haiti. None made much of an impact though the **Sitwell**s championed him. His last complete work before his premature death from a disease of the lungs, *Concerning the Eccentricities of Cardinal Pirelli* (1926), is quintessential Firbank, the dialogue witty and inconsequential, the hero meeting his end while in ardent pursuit of a choir boy.
▷M Berkowitz, *Ronald Firbank* (1970)

FIRDAUSI, or FERD(A)USI, pseud of Abu-'l Kasim Mansur
(c.935–c.1020)

Persian poet, born near Tús in Khorasan. When he was about 60 he spent some years at the court of Mahmud of Ghazni, where he wrote his masterpiece the *Shah Náma* ('Book of Kings'). When this was finished in 1008, the poet, receiving 60 000 silver dirhams instead of the promised 60 000 gold dinars, fled from Ghazni, leaving behind him a scathing satire on the sultan. Mahmud at length sent the 60 000 gold dinars to Firdausi at Tus, just as his remains were being carried to the grave. The *Shah Nama*, based on actual events from the annals of Persia, is for the most part composed of mythological and fanciful incidents. He also wrote a number of shorter pieces, kasidas and ghazals. His *Yusuf u Zulaykha* is based on the story of Joseph and Potiphar's wife.
▷H T Anklescriz, *Firdausi* (1934)

FIRENZUOLA, Agnolo
(1493–1548)

Italian author, born in Florence. He became Abbot of Prato, where he wrote the rather worldly tales in *Ragionamenti* (1525), and paraphrased the *Metamorphoses* of **Apuleius**. He was absolved of his vows in 1526 and spent 11 years in silence, but returned to writing in the last decade of his life, including religious works.

FISCHART, Johann
(c.1545–1590)

German satirist, whose **Rabelais**ian works lash with inexhaustible humour the corruptions of the clergy, the astrological fancies and other follies of the time. *Flöhhatz, Weibertratz* (1573) is outrageously comic and original. Essentially different are *Das glückhafft Schiff von Zürich* (in verse, 1576, 'The Lucky Ship of Zurich') and his spiritual songs.
▷A Hauffer, *Fischart* (1921)

FISHER, Roy
(1930–)

English poet and jazz pianist, born in Handsworth, Birmingham, and educated at the University of Birmingham. In 1982, Fisher left the Department of American Studies, University of Keele, where he had taught for 10 years, in order to write full-time. His verse combines a clear-eyed registration of detail with an almost improvisational freedom of voice. This was evident as early as his first volume *City* (1961), the subsequent *Ten Interiors with Various Figures* (1966) and *The Memorial Fountain* (1967) and the striking *Nineteen Poems and an Interview* (1975), which is a valuable source regarding his artistic priorities. *The Thing About Joe Sullivan* (1978) is a remarkable, unified sequence. A collected *Poems 1955–1980* appeared in 1980. Fisher has also written a number of unusual prose poems, including *Metamorphoses* (1970) and *The Cut Pages* (1971).
▷D Davie, in *Thomas Hardy and British Poetry* (1972)

FISHER, Vardis Alvero
(1895–1968)

American novelist, born in Annis, Idaho, into a Mormon family. Many of his novels are set in his own region. Best known is the autobiographical tetralogy about Vridar Hunter: *Tragic Life* (1932), *Passions Spin the Plot* (1934), *We Are Betrayed* (1935) and *No Villain Need Be* (1936). Chiefly interesting here is the section in the last novel dealing with Fisher's experiences as a teacher of English at the Mormon University of Utah. *The Testament of Man* (1943–60) is even more ambitious, and contains 12 novels. *Children of God* (1939), about the early Mormons, won him the Harper Prize Novel Award. Fisher's fiction is always interesting, although sometimes badly accomplished, and his relative critical neglect is not altogether deserved; however, it may not be unconnected with the rather hysterical anti-communism of his later years, and with his grandiose claims for his *Testament of Man* series.

▷ *Time* (12 August, 1946)

FISHTA, Gjergi
(1871–1940)

The best-known Albanian writer of the interwar period. He was a Franciscan friar who, almost alone and unaided, ushered a native modern literature into Albania. He was educator, politician, editor, translator, playwright, poet, novelist. The intrinsic value of his work, judged by international standards, is not more than highly competent and vigorous, and he ended, owing to his Catholic conservatism, as a member of the extreme right. Thus his direct influence has been felt mostly by Albanian writers in exile.

FITCH, (William) Clyde
(1865–1909)

American dramatist, born in Elmira, New York, whose first play, the melodrama *Beau Brummell* (1890), became a vehicle for the popular and dashing actor, Richard Mansfield. During the following 20 years, Fitch went on to write over 60 Broadway plays. The earliest, such as *Nathan Hale* (1899), were based upon incidents in American history, but by far the most popular were his later society melodramas. These were well-plotted and often gently satirized the self-styled New York aristocracy. They include *The Girl with the Green Eyes* (1902) and *The Woman in the Case* (1909). Many of his plays were conceived with specific star actors in mind and were written extremely quickly, *The Truth* (1906) supposedly written in a gondola on the Grand Canal in Venice.

FITZBALL, Edward, originally Ball
(1792–1873)

English popular dramatist. He won outstanding popularity in the 1820s for his countless fantastically staged and highly intricate melodramas. He looted his material where he chose and took wild liberties with originals, such as his *The Flying Dutchman* (1827), derived from John Howison's haunting story, *The Pilot*, from **James Fenimore Cooper**'s *The Red Rover* (1829) and **Edward Bulwer-Lytton**'s *Paul Clifford* (1835). His *Jonathan Bradford* (1833), based on a famous murder case, ran for 260 nights at the Surrey Theatre. He wrote a vivid autobiography, *Thirty-Five Years of a Dramatic Author's Life* (1859), which is an invaluable source for 19th-century English theatre history.

FITZGERALD, Edward
(1809–83)

English scholar and poet, born near Woodbridge, Suffolk, the translator of **Omar Khayyám**. A country gentleman by birth and inclination, he was educated at King Edward VI School in Bury St Edmunds and Trinity College, Cambridge, where he developed close literary friendships with **Thackeray**, **Thomas Carlyle** and **Tennyson** (who dedicated his poem *Tiresias* to him). He had a brief and unsuccessful marriage, wrote poetry, and in 1851 published *Euphranor: A Dialogue on Youth* (a comment on English education), followed by a book of aphorisms, *Polonius: A Collection of Wise Saws and Modern Instances* (1852). After studying Spanish privately, he published blank-verse translations of six plays by **Calderón de la Barca** in 1853. An interest in Persian poetry led him to publish, anonymously, a translation of *Salámán and Absál*, an allegory by Kami (1856). In 1859 he published, anonymously at first, his free poetic translation of quatrains from the *Rubáiyát of Omar Khayyám* (4th rev edn, 1879). He also translated **Aeschylus** and **Sophocles**, and two more plays by Calderón, and left a host of delightful letters, edited and published after his death.

▷ J Richardson, *Edward Fitzgerald* (1960)

FITZGERALD, F Scott (Francis Scott Key)
(1896–1940)

American novelist, born in St Paul, Minnesota. He was educated at Newman School, New Jersey, and Princeton, where one of his contemporaries was **Edmund Wilson**. He enlisted in the US army in World War I but never left America. He married **Zelda Fitzgerald**, and in 1920 published his first novel, *This Side of Paradise*, based on his experience at Princeton. He captured the spirit of the 1920s ('The Jazz Age'), especially in *The Great Gatsby* (1925), his best-known book. Other novels include *The Beautiful and the Damned* (1922) and *Tender is the Night* (1934). His short stories were equally notable, published in *Flappers and Philosophers* (1920), *Tales of the Jazz Age* (1922), *All the Sad Young Men* (1926) and *Taps at Reveille* (1936). He lived the strenuous life of a playboy in Europe and America, during which time his wife grew increasingly mentally unstable. He described his own problems—and those of his generation—in an influential essay, 'The Crack Up' (1935). Himself driven by debts and alcoholism, Fitzgerald wrote short stories for popular journals, notably the *Saturday Evening Post*; in the same spirit he went to Hollywood in 1937 as a scriptwriter, where he wrote a final, unfinished novel about a Hollywood producer, *The Last Tycoon* (1941).

▷A Mizener, *The Far Side of Paradise* (1951, rev edn 1965); M Bruccoli, *Some Sort of Epic Grandeur: a biography of Fitzgerald* (1981)

FITZGERALD, Penelope Mary
(1916–)

English novelist and biographer, born in Lincoln and educated at Oxford. Her biographies include *Edward Burne-Jones* (1975) and *Charlotte Mew and her Friends* (1984). The vivid evocation of period, place and character for which her biographies are noted also distinguishes her elegant, intricately-constructed fiction. *The Bookshop* (1978) conjures up the enclosed world of a small Suffolk community, with all its rivalries and in-fighting, while *Offshore* (1979), which won the Booker Prize, deals with a group of people living on barges on the River Thames. This is a novel born of salutory experience: Penelope Fitzgerald had herself, with her family, lived on a Thames barge, which sank. *The Gate of Angels* (1990) is a love story set in Cambridge in 1912.

FITZGERALD, R(obert) D(avid)
(1902–87)

Australian poet, born in Hunters Hill, Sydney, nephew of the poet John Le Gay Brereton (1871–1933). Trained as a surveyor, he spent five years in Fiji and returned to Australia to take up a position in government service. His first published poems were privately printed in *The Greater Apollo: Seven Metaphysical Songs* (1927), followed by *To Meet the Sun* (1929). A further collection, *Moonlight Acre*, appeared in 1938. His *Essay on Memory*, a long philosophical poem, appeared in 1938 and won the *Sydney Morning Herald* Sesquicentenary Prize in that year. An extensive historical narrative poem *Between Two Tides* was published in 1952, and a collection of his prose appeared in 1976 as *Of Places and Poetry*.

FITZGERALD, Zelda, née Sayre
(1900–48)

American novelist and painter, born in Montgomery, Alabama; she married **F Scott Fitzgerald**. She published a poor novel, *Save Me the Waltz* (1932), which has been occasionally somewhat over-valued by critics who believe that her husband scotched her talent. However, other prose fragments are of interest, as are many of her paintings.

▷N Milford, *The Life of Zelda Fitzgerald* (1970)

FITZMAURICE, George
(1877–1963)

Irish playwright, born in County Kerry. He drew on the life and language of his mother's farming family for his hard-hitting rural comedies, but also wrote powerful poetic folk drama which remained unappreciated until after his death. His best-known work, *The Country Dressmaker* (1907), was a huge success at the Abbey Theatre in Dublin under **Yeats**'s regime. A combination of critical incomprehension and the playwright's retiring nature allowed his work to be almost forgotten until a series of revivals at the Abbey in the 1970s, and the republishing of his works in *The Plays of George Fitzmaurice* (1970).

FLANNER, Janet
(1892–1978)

American literary journalist and novelist, born in Indianapolis. She was Paris correspondent of the *New Yorker* under the name Genêt. A leading member of the eventually influential coterie of (mostly) homosexual women (they included **Natalie Barney**, **Mina Loy** and **Djuna Barnes**) who lived in Paris between the wars, Flanner's 'Letters from Paris' to the *New Yorker* still provide the most articulate guide to all but their sexual affairs. They were edited as *Paris Letters* (1966–71) in two volumes. Her now neglected feminist novel, *The Cubical City* (1926), about Paris, attacks sexual puritanism and stuffiness.

▷I Drutman (ed), *Janet Flanner's World: Uncollected Writings, 1932–1975* (1979); S Weinstock, *Women of the Left Bank* (1986)

FLAUBERT, Gustave
(1821–80)

French novelist, born in Rouen, the son of a doctor. He studied law reluctantly at Paris, where his friendship with **Victor Hugo**, **Maxime du Camp**, and the poet **Louise Colet**, his lover from 1846 to 1854, stimulated his already apparent talent for writing. When barely past his student days he was afflicted by an obscure form of nervous disease, which may have been to some extent responsible for the morbidity and pessimism which characterized his work from the very beginning. These traits, together with a violent hatred and contempt for bourgeois society, are revealed in his first masterpiece, *Madame Bovary* (1857, Eng trans 1881), a painful but powerful tragedy of an unhappy bourgeois wife who seeks solace in dreams of ideal love, and squalid affairs. The book achieved a *succès de scandale* after it had been condemned as immoral and its author prosecuted, albeit unsuccessfully, but it has held its place among the classics. His second work, *Salammbô* (1862,

Eng trans 1886), dealt with the struggle between Rome and Carthage and is rather overweighted with archaeological detail. *L'Éducation sentimentale* (1869, Eng trans *Sentimental Education*, 1896) was less effective, but in 1874 appeared the splendid *La Tentation de St Antoine* (Eng trans *The Temptation of St Anthony*, 1895), the masterpiece of its kind. *Trois contes* (1877, Eng trans *Stories*, 1903) reveals his mastery of the short story and foreshadows **Guy de Maupassant**, whom he influenced. After his death appeared *Bouvard et Pécuchet* (1881, Eng trans *Bouvard and Pecuchet*, 1896), which had not received his final revision. His correspondence with **George Sand** was published in 1884. He brought a new awareness of form, structure and aesthetic detachment to the novel.
▷ E Starkie, *Flaubert: the making of the novelist* (1967)

FLECKER, James Elroy
(1884–1915)

English poet, born in Lewisham. Educated at Uppingham, he studied Oriental languages at Trinity College, Cambridge, then entered the consular service. He was posted first to Constantinople and then to Beirut. He wrote two posthumously published verse dramas, *Hassan* (staged 1923) and *Don Juan* (1925), and published several volumes of rich verse, *The Bridge of Fire* (1907), *The Golden Journey to Samarkand* (1913) and *Old Ships* (1915). His *Collected Poems* appeared in 1947.
▷ G E Hodgson, *James Elroy Flecker* (1925)

FLECKNOE, Richard
(c.1600–c.1678)

Irish poet, and probably a priest. After travelling (1640–50) in Europe, Asia, Africa and Brazil, he went to London, where he took part in the wars of the wits, wrote five plays, and published *Short Discourse on the English Stage* (1664), which provoked **Dryden** to caricature him as 'MacFlecknoe' in his satire on **Thomas Shadwell**, and inspired a good-humoured lampoon by **Andrew Marvell**.

FLEISCHMAN, (Albert) Sid(ney)
(1920–)

American children's author, and writer of westerns and TV scripts, born in Brooklyn. In his teens he worked as a night-club magician, before becoming a journalist. He is preoccupied with frontier-life in the decades of westward expansion, and many of his books are given a historical setting, backed-up by meticulous but lightly-worn research. They tell tall stories about strange characters. *Chancy and the Grand Rascal* (1966) is typical. Fleischman has been called the 'American Leon Garfield' and, as with **Leon Garfield**,

the finer points of his work are more often appreciated by adults than by children.

FLEMING, Ian Lancaster
(1908–64)

English novelist, born in London, brother of **Peter Fleming**. Educated at Eton and Sandhurst, he studied languages at Munich and Geneva universities, worked as a foreign correspondent with Reuters in Moscow (1929–33), and then as a banker and stockbroker (1933–9). During World War II he was a senior naval intelligence officer, and was then the foreign manager of *The Sunday Times* (1945–59). His varied career gave him the background for a series of 12 novels and seven short stories featuring Commander James Bond, the archetypal, suave British secret service agent 007, starting with *Casino Royale* (1953) and including *From Russia with Love* (1957), *Dr No* (1958), *Goldfinger* (1959), *Thunderball* (1961) and *The Man with the Golden Gun* (1965). They sold millions of copies world-wide, and have been turned into highly successful films.
▷ J Pearson, *The Life of Ian Fleming* (1966)

FLEMING, Margaret
(1803–11)

Scottish child author, born in Kirkcaldy, Fife. She was distantly related to Sir **Walter Scott**, who referred to her as 'Pet Marjorie', and she was the theme of an exquisite essay by Dr **John Brown**. She wrote poems and a three-volume diary.

FLEMING, May Agnes
(1840–80)

Canadian writer of romantic fiction, born in Portland, New Brunswick. She was Canada's first bestselling novelist and, writing three novels a year, earned an annual income of $15 000. She began publishing under a pseudonym, Cousin May Carlton, but after her wedding in 1865 (the result of a whirlwind romance) she used her married name. Her romantic fantasies about teachers, seamstresses and other poor women achieving prosperity in propitious marriages went against the grain of her own life. She left her alcoholic husband and, when she died at an early age of Bright's disease, he found that she had excluded him from her will.

FLEMING, Paul
(1609–40)

German lyric poet, born in Hartenstein. The first German to use the sonnet form, he is best known for his lyrical and religious poetry in *Geistliche und weltliche Poemata* (1642, 'Spiritual and Worldly Poems'). His love poems, inspired by Elsabe Niehus, are

unusually sincere and direct in feeling and expression for their time.
▷H Pyritz, *Paul Fleming deutsch Liebeslyrik* (1943)

FLEMING, (Robert) Peter
(1907–71)

English travel writer and journalist, born in London, the brother of **Ian Fleming**. Educated at Eton and Christ Church, Oxford, he took a stop-gap job in the Economic Advisory Council before being appointed assistant literary editor of *The Spectator*. In 1932 he read an advert in *The Times* for members to make up an expedition to explore rivers in Central Brazil and ascertain the fate of Colonel Percy Fawcett who had disappeared without trace in 1925. It provided the colourful copy which surfaced in *Brazilian Adventure* (1933), a landmark in travel literature and an immediate bestseller. In a similar vein are *One's Company* (1934) and *News From Tartary* (1936), an account of 'an undeservedly successful attempt' to travel overland from Peking to Kashmir.
▷D Hart-Davis, *Peter Fleming, a biography* (1986)

FLEMING, W(illiam) M(ontgomerie)
(1874–1961)

Australian parliamentarian and children's author, born in Avon Plains, Victoria. At 27 he became the youngest member of the NSW legislative assembly, and was a member of the Australian federal parliament (1913–22). Many of his short stories and poems appeared in the *Bulletin* and *Sydney Morning Herald*, and were collected as *Bunyip Says So* (1923) and *The Hunted Piccaninnies* (1927), based on aboriginal animal folk tales. His only adult novel, *Broad Acres* (1939), became a radio serial the following year.

FLETCHER, Giles
(?1588–1623)

English poet, brother of **Phineas Fletcher**, and cousin of **John Fletcher**. He was educated at Westminster School and Trinity College, Cambridge. A classical scholar, he became reader in Greek language at Cambridge, and in 1619 became rector of Alderton in Suffolk. His chief work is his long **Spenser**ian allegorical poem *Christ's Victory and Triumph* (1610).

FLETCHER, Giles, the Elder
(1546–1611)

English poet, politician and diplomat, who came to the attention of Queen Elizabeth's ministers after a successful political career and was sent on overseas missions to Germany and Russia. The second of these trips was later to lead to his book *Of the Russe Commonwealth* (1591), one of the first pieces of travel writing in English. He also produced a volume of poetry, *Licia* (1593). He was head of a literary family—his sons **Giles** and **Phineas Fletcher** were both poets, and his nephew was **John Fletcher**, the playwright.

FLETCHER, John
(1579–1625)

English dramatist, closely associated with **Francis Beaumont**, born in Rye, Sussex, the third son of that dean of Peterborough who disturbed the last moments of Mary, Queen of Scots. He came of a literary family, being the nephew of **Giles Fletcher**, the elder and cousin of the **Spenser**ian poets **Giles** and **Phineas Fletcher**. All that we know of him, apart from his work for the theatre, is that he entered Benet (now Corpus) College, Cambridge, and that he died of the plague in 1625. The problem of disentangling his own plays from those on which he collaborated with Beaumont, **Philip Massinger**, **William Rowley** and **Shakespeare**, is very difficult but three or four certainly of his own devising are outstanding and the collaboration with Beaumont yielded some memorable plays. The best of his own plays are *The Faithful Shepherdess*, which ranks as a pastoral with **Ben Jonson**'s *Sad Shepherd* and **Milton**'s *Comus; The Humorous Lieutenant*, acted in 1619, and *Rule a Wife and Have a Wife* (1624), on the favourite theme of conjugal mastery. Of the 10 or so plays on which he collaborated with Beaumont the best known are *The Knight of the Burning Pestle* (attributed mainly or possibly solely to Beaumont), *Philaster* (1610), a romantic comedy, *A King and No King* (1611) and *The Maid's Tragedy* (1611), generally accounted their best work. Collaboration with Shakespeare probably resulted in *Two Noble Kinsmen*, a melodramatic version of **Chaucer**'s *Knight's Tale*, and *Henry VIII* (or insertions therein). A vein of tender poetry in Fletcher and his relaxed type of versification are useful evidence in disentangling his various collaborations.

FLETCHER, John Gould
(1886–1950)

American poet and essayist, born in Little Rock, Arkansas. He followed the Imagists while living in London and Paris (1908–33), but later turned to American subjects and became a leading spirit of the Southern Agrarian movement, contributing to *I'll Take My Stand* (1930). He won the Pulitzer Prize in 1939 for his *Selected Poems*. *South Star* (1941) contains a verse history of his native state. He published his autobiographical *Life is my Song* in 1937.
▷E B Stephens, *John Gould Fletcher* (1967)

FLETCHER, Phineas
(1582–1650)

English poet, brother of **Giles Fletcher**, cousin of **John Fletcher**, and son of **Giles Fletcher, the Elder**, Queen Elizabeth's minister in Germany and Russia, and an occasional poet. He was educated at Eton and Cambridge, and in 1621 became rector of Hilgay in Norfolk. His *Purple Island, or the Isle of Man* (1633), contains an elaborate description of the human body viewed as an island, the bones being its foundations, and the veins its rivers.

FLINT, Frank Stewart
(1885–1960)

English poet and translator, born in London. A civil servant in the Ministry of Labour, he made important contributions to the Imagist movement in *Cadences* (1915). His poetry in *In the Net of Stars* (1909) and *Otherworld* (1920) is more lyrical and romantic. A brilliant linguist, he also produced many translations.

FLODOARD OF RHEIMS
(c.893–966)

French annalist and divine, he was Canon of Rheims, which had become a major centre of learning during the Carolingian Empire, and taught there in the library. Flodoard's annals, which cover the years 919–66, are an important historical source for information on western Europe in the period, and are particularly vivid in their account of the Norse invasions of the Northern French coasts.

FLORENCE of WORCESTER
(fl.1100)

English chronicler. A monk at the abbey of Worcester, he was the first in a series of English monastic historians in the 12th and 13th centuries, the greatest of whom was William of Malmesbury. Florence's Latin *Chronicle* is an important historical source for late Saxon and early Norman England, and drew heavily on the *Anglo-Saxon Chronicle*, a version of which was kept at Worcester.

FLORIT, Eugenio
(1903–)

Cuban poet and critic, born in Madrid of a Spanish father and a Cuban mother, but who spent most of his life as a teacher in the USA. His poetry, in the manner of his mentor **Jiménez**, was admired by **Alfonso Reyes**. He has made valuable comment on the work of **Neruda**, **Lorca** and many other Spanish poets. His *Obras Completas* ('Complete Works') were published in three volumes, 1982–5.
▷M D Servodedio, *The Quest for Harmony: The Dialectics of Communication in the Poetry of Eugenio Florit* (1979)

FO, Dario
(1926–)

Italian dramatist and actor, born in San Giano, Lombardy. He began his career as a stage designer and author of comic monologues, and from 1959 to 1968 ran a small theatre company in Milan with his wife, the actress Franca Rame. His reputation as a comic author was established before the abolition of stage censorship in 1962 allowed him to align himself openly with the political left in plays attacking government corruption and bureaucracy. His international fame rests primarily upon *Morte accidentale di un anarchico* (1970, Eng trans *Accidental Death of an Anarchist*, 1979), in which a political prisoner falls from a window while in police custody, and the frenetic *Non si paya, no si paya* (1974, Eng trans *Can't Pay, Won't Pay*, 1981), a protest against taxation which achieved popularity in Britain during the heated debate over the Poll Tax. Both use traditional techniques of farce in order to propound a socialist point of view.
▷P Puppa, *Il Teatro di Fo* (1978); Tony Mitchell, *Dario Fo* (1984)

FOGAZZARO, Antonio
(1842–1911)

One of Italy's leading novelists of the 19th century, born in Vicenza. A music lover, he was tutored by a poet, and his first works were poetic—but they were unsuccessful. His first novel, rather in the style of English 'sensation' fiction, and indebted to **Wilkie Collins**, was *Malombra* (1881, Eng trans *The Woman*, 1907), and is still quite as readable and interesting as the best of that genre. But his masterpiece appeared in 1888: *Piccolo mondo antico* (Eng trans *The Patriot*, 1906), tells the story of a Venetian of the first part of the 19th century, contrasting him with his wife: his Christian faith is great, but he is weak, her faith is weak, but she possesses an iron will. This is one of the great novels of its time, second only to **Manzoni**'s *I promessi sposi*. None of Fogazzaro's other novels matches this, but all contain remarkable passages. He was a faithful son of his Church, which repaid him by putting most of his work on the forbidden list.
▷T Gallerati-Scott, *The Life of Antonio Fogazzaro* (1922, reprinted 1972)

FOIX, J V
(1893–1987)

Catalan Surrealist or 'superrealist', and, simultaneously, traditionalist, who ended up as the grand old man of Catalan letters. He had long been a Catalan nationalist. He ran his family's pastrycook business, but kept this strictly separate from his literary activities.

The consistently humorous nature of his enterprises has eluded most of his foreign critics. Most of his work is ostensibly based on an early poetic diary he wrote between 1911 and 1920—but some of this was actually written after 1920. Much of *Gertrudis* (1927), poetic fragments to a destructive but creative female figure invented by Foix, is highly traditional in form, although modernist in content. *Sol i de dol* (1936, 'Alone and In Mourning'), a collection of sonnets, is similarly strict and classical in form. He ended by being called 'the Master of Sarri ', the place of his birth. His project was, essentially, to rediscover the past by seeking out the future; he is a difficult writer, but has been found to be a rewarding one.

FOLLAIN, Jean
(1903–71)

French poet, born in a village near Canisy. A lawyer, he was appointed judge in 1951. He was killed in a car accident. His poetry, in which he often seeks the universal in the re-creation of his own Norman childhood, has debts to **Fargue** and, above all, to **Guillevic**. He received many prizes, and is particularly well translated and explicated in *Contemporary French Poetry* (1965).

FOLLETT, Ken(neth Martin)
(1949–)

English crime and adventure novelist, whose bankability reached staggering heights in the early 1990s. Follett, though, imbibed socialism with his free school milk in Cardiff and has donated enormous sums to the Labour Party (for whom his second wife, Barbara, works as an image consultant). He has claimed that his politics are at least subliminally detectable in adventure stories like *Storm Island* (1978, published in the USA as *Eye of the Needle*), *The Key to Rebecca* (1980) and *The Man from St. Petersburg* (1982), each of which contains a mild revisionist subtext. For a writer in this genre, Follett is notably enlightened in his treatment of women characters, who are given purposeful, strong parts and are rarely treated as victims or comforters.

FOLZ, Hans
(c.1450–before 1515)

German Meistersinger, born in Worms. He settled in Nürnberg as a barber-surgeon, and became prominent as an advocate of the extension of Meistergesang by the use of new 'Töne', of which he himself provided 27. His obscene songs are particularly notable.

FONTANE, Theodor
(1819–98)

German poet and novelist, born in Neuruppin. He worked in the family chemist's business until in 1849 he turned to literature in Berlin. Periods of residence in Britain between 1855 and 1859 as a newspaper correspondent led to ballads such as *Archibald Douglas* and *Die Brücke am Tay* ('The Tay Bridge'), and other British-flavoured pieces. He was a war correspondent in 1866 and 1870–1, and became the secretary of the Prussian Royal Academy of Arts. He wrote his first novel, *Vor dem Sturm* (1878, 'Before the Storm'), at the age of 56; it is considered by many to be his best. It is set against the events of the Franco–Prussian war in 1812–13, but he turned to the subject of the position of women in German society in *L'Adultera* (1882, Eng trans *The Woman Taken in Adultery*, 1979) and *Effi Briest* (1895, Eng trans 1967), among others. His appraisal of social mores extended into the realms of politics and power in *Die Poggenpuhls* (1896, Eng trans *The Poggenpuhl Family*, 1979) and *Der Stechlin* (1898, 'Stechlin'). His novels influenced **Thomas Mann**.
▷A R Robinson, *Fontane: an introduction to the man and his work* (1976)

FONTANES, Louis, Marquis de
(1757–1821)

French writer and politician, born in Niort. In 1777 he went to Paris, where he acquired a reputation for his melancholy, introspective poems, among which are *Le Cri de mon coeur* (1778, 'The Cry of my Heart'), *Le Verger* (1788, 'The Orchard'), a metrical translation of **Pope**'s *Essay on Man* (1783), and an imitation of **Thomas Gray**'s *Elegy*. He supported the Revolution, but later criticized it, and was the prime founder of the *Mercure de France* in 1799. In 1804 he was made President of the Corps Législatif. In 1810 he entered the senate, and was raised to the peerage by Louis XVIII.
▷A Wilson, *Fontanes. Un essai biographique* (1929)

FONTENELLE, Bernard le Bovier de
(1657–1757)

French author, born in Rouen. A nephew of **Corneille**, he began his literary career in Paris. In the great quarrel of Moderns versus Ancients, he sided with the Moderns, assailing the Greeks and their French imitators, and receiving in return the satiric shafts of **Boileau**, **Racine**, **Rousseau** and **La Bruyère**. After the failure on the stage of his *Aspar*, he produced an imitation of **Lucian**, *Nouveaux Dialogues des morts* (1682, Eng trans *New*

Dialogues of the Dead, 1683), and the 'precious' *Lettres Diverses de Monsieur le Chevalier d'Her...* (1687, Eng trans *Letters of Gallantry from Monsieur le Chevalier d'Her...*, 1687). In 1697 he was made secretary to the Académie des Sciences, of which he later was president. He died in Paris in his hundredth year. He had attempted almost every form of literature—idylls, satires, dialogues, critical essays, histories and tragedies. His *Entretiens sur la pluralité des mondes* (1686, Eng trans *A Discourse on the Plurality of Worlds*, 1687) and *Histoire des oracles* (1686, Eng trans *The History of the Oracles*, 1688), are considered his best works.

FONVIZIN, or FON-VIZIN, Denis Ivanovich
(1745–92)

Russian dramatist, born in Moscow. He wrote in the tradition of **Molière** and **Holberg** (whom he had translated), but in a thoroughly and successfully Russian style. His masterpiece is *Nedorosl* (1782, Eng trans *The Minor*, in *Masterpieces of the Russian Drama*, ed G Z Patrick and G R Noyes, 1933). He wrote many indignant political works, reminiscent of **Voltaire**. In his last years he could not speak properly, owing to the effects of a stroke. Another play by him, *The Choice of a Tutor*, is translated in *Five Russian Plays* (1916, ed C E Beechofer).
▷ H Rogger, *National Consciousness in Eighteenth Century Russia* (1960)

FOOTE, Samuel
(1720–77)

English wit, playwright and actor, born in Truro. His brilliant mimicry of prominent people led to legal proceedings being taken against him on several occasions. His plays, which include *Taste* (1752) and *The Minor* (1760), were mainly political satire, and have not stood the test of time.
▷ M M Belden, *The Dramatic Works of Samuel Foote* (1929)

FOOTE, Shelby
(1916–)

American novelist and historian, born in Greenville, Mississippi. His second novel, *Follow Me Down* (1950), which gives a multiple view of a violent murder, established his name. *Shiloh* (1952) is a historical novel, dealing with the Civil War. Foote is now even better known for his detailed history, *The Civil War: A Narrative* (1958–74), than for his novels.
▷ *Mississippi Quarterly* (October, 1971)

FORBES, (Joan) Rosita
(1893–1967)

English writer and traveller, born in Swinderby, Lincolnshire. Having visited almost every country in the world and particularly Arabia and North Africa, she used her experiences as the raw material for exciting travel books, including *The Secret of the Sahara-Kufara* (1922), *From Red Sea to Blue Nile* (1928), *The Prodigious Caribbean* (1940), *Appointment in the Sun* (1949) and *Islands in the Sun* (1950).
▷ *Gypsy in the Sun* (1967)

FORD, Ford Madox, originally Ford Hermann Hueffer
(1873–1939)

English novelist, editor and poet, born in Merton, Surrey, the son of Francis Hueffer, the music critic of *The Times* and grandson, on his mother's side, of the Pre-Raphaelite painter Ford Madox Brown. Brought up in pre-Raphaelite circles, he published his first book when he was only 18, a fairy story entitled *The Brown Owl* (1891), and a novel, *The Shifting of the Fire*, appeared the following year. In 1894 he eloped with and married Elsie Martindale, presaging a life of emotional upheaval. He met **Joseph Conrad** in 1898 and they co-authored various works including *The Inheritors* (1901) and *Romance* (1903). He founded the *English Review* in 1908, which he edited for 15 months and in which he published **Thomas Hardy**, **H G Wells**, **D H Lawrence** and **Wyndham Lewis** among others. In 1924, while living in Paris, he was founder-editor of the *Transatlantic Review*, which gave space to **James Joyce**, **Ezra Pound**, **Gertrude Stein** and the young **Ernest Hemingway**. He wrote almost 80 books in a hectic career but is best remembered for three novels: *The Fifth Queen* (1906), *The Good Soldier* (1915) and *Parade's End*, the title he gave to what is often known as the Tietjens war tetralogy: *Some Do Not* (1924), *No More Parades* (1925), *A Man Could Stand Up* (1926) and *Last Post* (1928).
▷ A Mizener, *The Saddest Story* (1972)

FORD, Jesse Hill, Jr
(1928–)

American novelist and short-story writer. Born in Troy, Alabama, he worked in public relations and technical journalism before his first novel, *Mountains of Gilead* (1961), was published. *The Liberation of Lord Byron Jones* (1965) is the story of a black funeral parlour owner who is 'set free' from the contradictions of his colour and from an unfaithful wife when he is murdered by her white policeman lover. The novel's success was fostered by a Hollywood film. The *Feast of Saint Barnabas* (1969) also deals with racial violence and is perhaps more clearly imagined and executed, reflecting the virtues of Ford's fine short stories, which were collected as *Fishes, Birds, and Sons of Men* (1967). He has also written a play, *The Conversion of Buster Drumwright* (1964), which was adapted as a musical two decades later.

FORD, John
(c.1586–c.1640)

English dramatist, born in Ilsington, Devon. He studied for a year at Oxford and entered the Middle Temple in 1602. He was expelled for debt but readmitted. He was greatly influenced by **Robert Burton**, whose *Anatomy of Melancholy* (1621) turned Ford's dramatic gifts towards stage presentation of the melancholy, the unnatural and the horrible in *The Lover's Melancholy* (1629), *'Tis Pity She's a Whore* (1633), *The Lady's Trial* (1639), etc. He also wrote a masterful chronicle play, *Perkin Warbeck* (1634). Ford often collaborated with **Thomas Dekker**, **William Rowley** and **John Webster**.
▷D Anderson, *John Ford* (1972)

FORD, Richard
(1796–1858)

English travel writer, born in Winchester. After studying at Trinity College, Oxford, he was called to the Bar, but never practised. He spent the years 1830–4 in riding tours in Spain, and wrote the popular and characterful *Handbook for Travellers in Spain* (1845), followed by *Gatherings from Spain* (1846). He introduced the British public to the works of Velazquez.
▷B Ford, *Richard Ford en Sevilla* (1963)

FORD, Richard
(1944–)

American novelist, born in Jackson, Mississippi. He graduated from the University of California, Berkeley, with an MA in 1970, and taught English at Williams College, Massachusetts, and Princeton University. His first novel was *A Piece of My Heart* (1976), followed by *The Ultimate Good Luck* (1981). Both subjected their respective protagonists to a journey of internal discovery. His best novel is *The Sportswriter* (1986), in which he creates a memorable character in the wary Frank Bascombe. A harsh, uncompassionate realist, Bascombe has renounced fiction for sports writing, which teaches him that 'there are no transcendent themes in life'. *Rock Springs* (1987) is a collection of stories, while *Wildlife* (1990) is a short novel about the disintegration of a family. He edited the *Granta Book of the American Short Story* (1991).

FORESTER, C(ecil) S(cott)
(1899–1966)

British writer, born in Cairo. He studied medicine, but turned to writing full-time after the success of his first novel, *Payment Deferred* (1926). He also wrote *The African Queen* (1935, which was made into a successful film), *The General* (1936) and *The Ship* (1943). He is best known for his creation of Horatio Hornblower, a British naval officer in the Napoleonic era whose career he chronicled in a series of popular novels, starting with *The Happy Return* (1937) and *Ship of the Line* (1938, James Tait Black Memorial Prize). He also wrote biographical and travel books and collaborated with C E Bechofer Roberts on a play about Nurse Edith Cavell.
▷C Parkinson, *The Life and Times of Hornblower* (1970)

FORSSELL, Lars
(1928–)

Swedish poet, essayist and playwright. He has been well known throughout Scandinavia since the early 1950s. His poetry is continuously experimental, sometimes fashionable and superficial, but at others, as in *F C Tietjens* (1954), an exercise in **Pessoa**n ingenuity, more profound and self-searching. His play *Krönigen* (1956) was translated as *The Coronation* in 1963; he has translated **Pound** and **T S Eliot** into Swedish.

FORSTER, E(dward) M(organ)
(1879–1970)

English novelist and critic, born in London. He was educated at Tonbridge School, where he was miserable, and King's College, Cambridge, where he revelled in the 'Bloomsbury circle' of G E Moore, G M Trevelyan and **Lowes Dickinson**, whose biography he wrote in 1934, and with whom he founded the *Independent Review* in 1903. In his novels he examined with subtle insight the pre-1914 English middle-class ethos and its custodians the civil service, the church and the public schools. An indictment of the latter is embodied in *The Longest Journey* (1907), and a period in Italy provided the background for *Where Angels Fear to Tread* (1905) and *A Room with a View* (1908). *Howards End* (1910) was written after he had been tutor in Nassenheide (1905). But it is in his masterpiece, *A Passage to India* (1924), that he puts English values and Indian susceptibilities under his finest scrutiny. The spiritual tensions of two clashing civilizations are resolved in the strange symbolism of the Malabar Cave. He was awarded the James Tait Black Memorial and Femina Vie Heureuse prizes for the latter in 1925. His Indian experiences as secretary to the Maharajah of Dewas Senior (1921) he described in *The Hill of Devi* (1953). Collections of short stories include *The Celestial Omnibus* (1914) and *The Eternal Moment* (1928); collections of essays, *Abinger Harvest* (1936) and *Two Cheers for Democracy* (1951). His Cambridge Clark lectures,

Aspects of the Novel (1927), expressed his literary aesthetics as firmly opposed to Aristotle. He was elected a fellow of King's College, Cambridge in 1946. *Marianne Thornton* (1958) is a domestic biography. In 1951 he collaborated with Eric Crozier on the libretto of Britten's opera, *Billy Budd*. His novel *Maurice* (written 1913–14), on the theme of homosexuality, was published posthumously in 1971.
▷J Beer, *The Achievement of E M Forster* (1962); N Beauman, *Morgan: a biography of E. M. Forster* (1993)

FORSTER, Margaret
(1938–)

English novelist, biographer and critic, born in Carlisle and educated at Oxford. Her early novels include the topical *Georgy Girl* (1965), depicting the emotional and sexual freedoms and dangers suddenly confronting young women in a liberated decade. In her later novels, each with a strong sense of character and social context, she has looked at the problems of middle-aged married women (*Marital Rites*, 1981), and adolescent children (*Private Papers*, 1986). Her biographies include a sympathetic *Elizabeth Barrett Browning* (1988), while its companion novel, *Lady's Maid* (1990), speculates intriguingly upon the life of Browning's maid, Wilson. In 1993 she published an excellent and authoritative biography, *Daphne du Maurier*.

FORSYTH, Frederick
(1938–)

English author of suspense thrillers, born in Ashford, Kent. Educated at Tonbridge School, Kent, he served in the Royal Air Force and later became a journalist. His reputation rests on three taut thrillers, *The Day of the Jackal* (1971), *The Odessa File* (1972) and *The Dogs of War* (1974), meticulously researched, precisely plotted nail-biters.

FORT, Paul
(1872–1960)

French poet, born in Reims. He settled in Paris, where in 1890 he founded the 'Théâtre des Arts' to present a wide range of European drama and recitals of Symbolist poetry. He is best known for his popular *Ballades françaises* (1st vol 1897, 'French Ballads'), which eventually numbered 17 volumes, and in which he brought poetry closer to the rhythms of everyday speech. He also wrote several plays, founded and edited the literary magazine *Vers et Prose* (1905–14), and wrote *Histoire de la poésie française depuis 1850* (1927, 'History of French Poetry since 1850').
▷A Lowell, *Six French Poets* (1915)

FORTIGUERRA, Niccolo
(1674–1735)

Italian poet and prelate. He was bishop and papal chamberlain to Clement XI, and is remembered for his satirical epic, *Il Ricciardetto* (1738).

FOSCOLO, Ugo
(1778–1827)

Italian author, born in Zante. He was educated at Spalato (Split) and Venice. His bitter disappointment when Venice was ceded to Austria found vent in the *Lettere di Jacopo Ortis* (1802, Eng trans *Letters of Ortis*, 1818). Believing that France was destined to liberate Italy, he served in the French armies, but, no longer fooled by Napoleon's intentions, he returned to Milan, and published in 1807 his best poem, *I Sepolcri* (1807, Eng trans *The Sepulchres*, 1820). He translated **Laurence Sterne**'s *Sentimental Journey*, and wrote two tragedies, *Ajace* and *Ricciarda*. In 1809 he was for a few months Professor of Eloquence in Pavia. After 1814, when the Austrians entered Milan, he finally sought refuge in London. There he published his *Saggi sul Petrarca* (1847, 'Essays on Petrarch'), *Discorso sul testo del Decamerone* (1828, 'Discourse on the text of the *Decameron*'), *Discorso sul testo di Dante* (1825, 'Discourse on the text of Dante'), and various papers in the *Quarterly Review* and *Edinburgh Review*. His last years were embittered by poverty and neglect, and he left a long poem, *Le Grazie* (1848, 'The Graces'), incomplete on his death.
▷L Fabiani, *Ugo Foscolo* (1972)

FOSTER, David
(1944–)

Australian writer, born in Sydney, he studied as a scientist and worked in the USA before devoting himself to writing. His work is overlaid with a pseudo-scientific vocabulary which hides a quirky sense of humour and fantasy. In *Moonlite* (1981) he relates a patriarchal society on a Scottish isle to an allegory of the colonization of Australia. *The Empathy Experiment* with D K Lyell (1977) is 'straight' sci-fi, and *The Adventures of Christian Rosy Cross* (1986) is a parable, or parody, of the Rosicrucian faith as portrayed by its hero the Comte de Rosencreutz. *Testostero: A Comic Novel* (1987) is a laboured reworking of **Carlo Goldoni**'s comedy 'The Venetian Twin'.

FOUQUÉ, Friedrich Heinrich Karl, Baron de la Motte
(1777–1843)

German writer and soldier, of Huguenot ancestry. He served as a Prussian cavalry officer in 1794 and 1813. The interval between these campaigns was devoted to literary pursuits, and the rest of his life was spent in Paris and on his estate at Nennhausen, and after 1830 in Halle. He published a long series of romances, based on Norse legend and old French poetry, his masterpiece being the fairy-tale *Undine* (1811).

FOWLES, John Robert
(1926–)

English novelist, born in Leigh-on-Sea. Educated at Bedford School, Edinburgh University and New College, Oxford, where he studied French, he served in the Royal Marines (1945–6). Thereafter he taught in schools in France, and in Greece (1951–2) and London. An allusive and richly descriptive writer, his first novel was *The Collector* (1963), still perhaps his most sensational, in which he probes the reasons why a young man of one class 'collected', incarcerated and dissected the girl, from another class, whom he thought he loved. *The Magus* (1965, rev edn 1977) is the book which made his name. Drawing on his own experience, it is set in the 1960s on a remote Greek island. It is a disturbing and much-imitated yarn about an English school-teacher, his bizarre experiences, and his involvement with a master trickster. *The French Lieutenant's Woman* (1969), however, exceeded it in popularity, in large part due to the film version with Meryl Streep in the title role. Later books—*Daniel Martin* (1977), *Mantissa* (1982) and *A Maggot* (1985)—suffered a critical backlash but underlined his willingness to experiment, as well as the fecundity of his imagination. He also published a collection of short stories, *The Ebony Tower* (1974). An essay on the significance of nature in his work, originally written in 1979, was re-issued as *The Tree* (1992), and was followed by *Tessera* (1993), which he describes as 'a piece of juvenilia'.

FOX, Paula
(1923–)

American writer of fiction for children and adults, born in New York. Fox's children's books concern characters who remain confused and ill-at-ease for longer than is usual in juvenile fiction. *The Slave Dancer* (1973) is her most powerful narrative story. Set in 1840, it tells the nightmarish tale of a boy being kidnapped into slavery in New Orleans. In similar vein, the earlier *How Many Miles to Babylon* (1967) is the story of a small black boy who is seized by older children. Fox's adult novels tend to be less dramatic, concerned with suburban domestic themes. *Desperate Characters* (1970) was turned into a movie by **Frank D Gilroy**.

FOX, William Price
(1926–)

American humorist and short-story writer, born in Illinois. He remains best known for *Southern Fried* (1962), a collection of stories set in South Carolina, where he grew up. The book has achieved the status of a classic of American humour. Despite significant endorsements for his later fiction—*Dixiana Moon* (1981) was praised by **Kurt Vonnegut** and **John D Macdonald**—Fox has not enjoyed wide critical acclaim. His stories, which usually involve petty crime, are told in a conventional style, refreshingly free of subtext and complexity.

FOXE, John
(1516–87)

English martyrologist, born in Boston in Lincolnshire. At 16 he entered Brasenose College, Oxford, and was fellow of Magdalen 1538–45. During the reign of Mary I he lived on the Continent, where he met Knox, Grindal and Whittingham. On Elizabeth's accession he received a pension and a prebend of Salisbury (1563), but lived chiefly in London and was debarred from further preferment because of his objection to wearing the surplice. He published numerous controversial treatises and sermons, as well as an apocalyptic Latin mystery play called *Christus Triumphans* (1556). His best-known work is his *History of the Acts and Monuments of the Church*, popularly known as *Foxe's Book of Martyrs*, the first part of which was published in Latin at Strasbourg in 1554 (Eng trans 1563). Written in vivid English prose, it is a history of the English Protestant martyrs from the 14th century to his own day.

FRAME, Janet Paterson
(1924–)

New Zealand novelist and short-story writer, born in Dunedin. She was educated at Otago University Teachers Training College. Her first book was a collection of short stories, *The Lagoon: Stories* (1952), which she followed five years later with a novel, *Owls Do Cry*. Having spent much time in psychiatric hospitals after severe mental breakdowns, her novels walk a tight-rope between danger and safety, where the looming threat of disorder attracts those it frightens. Honoured in her homeland but only belatedly receiving international recognition, key books are *Scented Gardens for the Blind* (1963), *A State of Siege* (1966), *Intensive Care* (1970) and *Living in the Maniototo* (1979). *The Adaptable Man*, first published in 1965, was reprinted in 1993. Her short stories were collected in *The Reservoir and Other Stories* (1966) and in *You Are Now*

Entering the Human Heart (1983). *The Carpathians* was published in 1988. Some early verse is collected in *The Pocket Mirror* (1967). The background to her work is implicit in three volumes of autobiography, *To the Island* (1983), *An Angel at my Table* (1984) and *The Envoy from Mirror City* (1985).

FRAME, Ronald
(1953–)

Scottish novelist and short-story writer, born in Glasgow. Educated there and at Oxford, he has been powerfully dedicated to overturning the rugged proletarianism which has dominated writing from and about his native city. His earliest novel, *Winter Journey* (1984), won the first **Betty Trask** Award, a prize given to the best 'romantic fiction' of the year. This rather misleadingly pigeonholed Frame, whose work was subsequently felt to be rather too bourgeois and perfumed for 1980s tastes. However, in the collections *A Long Weekend With Marcel Proust* (1986) and *A Woman of Judah* (1988) and the novel *Sandmouth People* (1987) he established a strongly distinctive vision—arguably derived from **Dickens**—in which personality is artifice and coincidence dominates. Despite their odd, 'period' dressing, *Penelope's Hat* (1989) and *Bluette* (1990) were convincingly postmodern. In 1988, his play *Paris* won the **Samuel Beckett** Prize. Later novels have been less successful, but there are signs of a new direction and a less textured prose style.

FRANC, Maud Jeanne *see* EVANS, Matilda Jane

FRANCE, Anatole, pseud of Anatole François Thibault
(1844–1924)

French writer and winner of the Nobel Prize for literature, born the son of a Parisian bookseller. He began his literary career as a publisher's reader, 'blurb' writer and critic, and published his first volume of stories, *Jocaste et le chat maigre* ('Jocasta and the Thin Cat'), in 1879 and then his first novel, *Le Crime de Sylvestre Bonnard* (1881). He had married in 1877 after being appointed Keeper at the Senate Library, a position he was to lose in 1891 because of a literary quarrel with Leconte de Lisle. Under the literary patronage of Madame de Caillavet, whose love affair with him brought about his divorce (1893), he poured out a number of graceful, lively novels, critical studies and the like, such as the Parnassian *Le Livre de mon ami* (1885, 'My Friend's Book'), a picture of childhood happiness, which stands in strong contrast to the later satirical, solipsistic and sceptical works such as *Les Opinions de Jérôme Coignard* (1893). Another remarkable collection

of short stories was published under the title *Balthasar* (1889), and his vast classical knowledge found expression in *Thaïs* (1890). The Dreyfus case (1896) stirred him into politics as an opponent of church and state and champion of internationalism. His *Île des pingouins* (1908, 'Isle of Penguins'), in which the evolution of mankind is satirically treated, was followed by *Les Dieux ont soif* (1912, 'The Gods are Thirsty'), a fable about the Terror, and *La révolte des anges* (1914, 'The Angels' Revolt'), a satire on Christianity and theology. He was awarded the Nobel Prize for literature in 1921.
▷ R Virtanen, *Anatole France* (1968); J Roujon, *La vie et les opinions d'Anatole France* (1925)

FRANCIS, Dick (Richard Stanley)
(1920–)

English jockey and author, born in Surrey, a highly successful example of a top-class sportsman who became a writer on his own subject. He turned professional at the age of 28, and was on the point of winning the 1956 Grand National when his horse Devon Loch collapsed 50 yards from the winning post. He retired the following year and became a racing correspondent with the *Daily Express*. He also began writing popular thrillers with a racing background which won him the Golden Dagger Award of the American Crime Writers' Association in 1980. He has written over 30 novels since publishing his autobiography.
▷ *The Sport of Queens* (1957 and subsequent revisions)

FRANCO, Veronica
(1546–91)

Italian poet and 'courtesan', a woman who had learned much about men, and was not uncritical of them. She was born and died in Venice, and had her portrait painted by Tintoretto. Her poetry, while ostensibly **Petrarch**an, is notably erotic and abounds in the unusual. Her *terza Rima* (1575) was edited in 1912. She has not yet been sufficiently studied for her original qualities.

FRANK, Anne
(1929–45)

German Jewish concentration-camp victim, born in Frankfurt-am-Main. She fled from the Nazis to Holland in 1933 with her family, and after the Nazi occupation of Holland hid with her family and four others in a sealed-off office back-room in Amsterdam from 1942 until they were betrayed in August 1944. She died in Belsen concentration camp. The lively, moving diary she kept during her concealment was published as *Het Achterhuis*

(1947, Eng trans *The Diary of Anne Frank*, 1952), was dramatized in 1958, filmed in 1959, and Anne Frank became a symbol of suffering under the Nazis. Her name was given to villages and schools for refugee children throughout western Europe.
▷E Schnabel, *The Footsteps of Anne Frank* (1959)

FRANK, Bruno
(1887–1945)

German author, born in Stuttgart. He wrote historical novels, such as *Die Fürstin* (1915, 'The Princess'), *Aus vielen Jahren* (1937, 'From Many Years') and *Die Tochter* (1943, 'The Daughter'), in a style reminiscent of **Thomas Mann**. His lyric poetry is also noteworthy. Of Jewish descent, he fled the Nazi regime and went to Beverly Hills in California. His *Der Reisepass* (1937, 'The Travel Pass') was directed against National Socialism.

FRANK, Leonhard
(1882–1961)

German poet and novelist, born in Würzburg. His novel *Die Räuberbande* (1914, 'The Gang of Robbers') describes the adventures of a gang of roguish boys. He fought in World War I and conceived a horror of war which led to his strongly pacifist *Der Mensch ist gut* (1917, 'Man is Good'). *Die Ursache* (1915, 'The Cause') attacked the repressive educational system in Germany, while *Der Bürger* (1924, 'The Citizen') is about the deadening effect of bourgeois society on the spirit. His *Karl und Anna* (1928), also a war story, was successfully turned into a play. He left Germany and went to live in Hollywood, where he wrote several books, including *Von drei Millionen drei* (1932, 'From Three Million and Three'), and the autobiographical novel *Links wo das Herz ist* (1952, 'On the Left, Where the Heart Is').
▷C French and H Jobs, *Leonhard Frank: 1882–1961* (1962)

FRANK, Waldo David
(1889–1967)

American novelist and journalist, born in Long Branch, New Jersey. He co-edited *The Seven Arts* (1916–17) and later wrote novels and other works coloured by mysticism and expressionism, including *City Block* (1922), *The Unwelcome Man* (1917), *The Rediscovery of America* (1929) and the play *New Year's Eve* (1939).
▷P J Carter, *Waldo Frank* (1867)

FRANKAU, Gilbert
(1884–1953)

English novelist, born in London, father of **Pamela Frankau**. A son of Julia Frankau,

who wrote under the name of 'Frank Danby', writing came easily to him. His early works were great successes and he continued to write best-sellers, for he was, above everything, a professional writer, with a flair for anticipating popular taste. Of his many best-sellers, the following are notable: *One of Us* (1912), *Peter Jackson, Cigar Merchant* (1919), *Men, Maids and Mustard-Pots* (1923), *World without End* (1943).
▷*Gilbert Frankau's Self-Portrait: a novel of his own life* (1940)

FRANKAU, Pamela
(1908–67)

English novelist, daughter of **Gilbert Frankau**. In her early novels such as in *The Marriage of Harlequin* (1927), her first novel, she epitomized the era of the 'bright young things'. Like her father, a true professional, she outgrew this phase and her later novels were serious in intent. Typical are *The Willow Cabin* (1949) and *A Wreath for The Enemy* (1954). *The Offshore Light* (1952) was written under the pseudonym Eliot Naylor.
▷*I Find Four People* (1935)

FRANKL, Ludwig, Ritter von Hochwart
(1810–93)

Austrian poet of Jewish origin, Professor of Aesthetics at the Vienna Conservatory (1851). He established the first Jewish school in Jerusalem (1856). He wrote epics, ballads, satirical poems, many of which have been translated.
▷Biographical note in *Moderne Klassiker* (1852)

FRANKLIN, Benjamin
(1706–90)

American statesman and scientist, youngest son and 15th child of a family of 17, born in Boston, Massachusetts. He was apprenticed at 12 to his brother James, a printer, who started a newspaper, the *New England Courant*, in 1709. When James was imprisoned by the speaker of the Assembly for his outspoken criticism, Benjamin assumed the paper's management. The two brothers later fell out and Benjamin drifted to Philadelphia, where he secured work as a printer. During 1724–6 he worked for 18 months in London, before returning to Philadelphia to establish his own successful printing house, and in 1729 he purchased the *Pennsylvania Gazette*. A year later he married Deborah Read, by whom he had two children. He also had an illegitimate son, William. In 1732 he began *Poor Richard's Almanac*, which attained an unprecedented circulation. In 1736 Franklin was appointed Clerk of the Assembly, in 1737 Postmaster of

Philadelphia, and in 1754 Deputy Post-master-General for the Colonies, being elected and re-elected a member of the Assembly almost uninterruptedly until his first mission to England. In 1746 he began his renowned researches in electricity and most famously its relationship with lightning, which made him an FRS. In 1757 he was sent to England to insist upon the right of the province to tax the proprietors of land held under the Penn charter for the cost of defending it from the French and Native Americans. In 1764 he was again sent to England to contest the pretensions of parliament to tax the American colonies without representation. The differences, however, between the British government and the colonies became too grave to be reconciled by negotiation, and in 1775 Franklin returned to the USA, where he participated actively in the deliberations which resulted in the Declaration of Independence. To secure foreign assistance in the war Franklin was sent to Paris in 1776. His skill as a negotiator and his personal popularity, reinforced by the antipathy of French and English, favoured his mission, and on 6 February 1778, a treaty of alliance was signed, while munitions of war and money were sent from France. On 3 September 1783, his mission was crowned with success through Britain's recognition of the independence of the United States. Franklin was US minister in Paris till 1785, when he returned to Philadelphia, and was elected President of the state of Pennsylvania, a post to which he was twice re-elected. He was also a delegate to the convention which framed the constitution of the USA. In 1788 he retired from public life.
▷C van Doren, *Benjamin Franklin* (1939); R W Clark, *Benjamin Franklin: a biography* (1983)

FRANKLIN, (Stella Marian Sarah) Miles, pseud Brent of Bin Bin
(1879–1954)

Australian novelist, born in Talbingo, near Tamut, New South Wales. Known to her family as Stella, she was a fifth-generation Australian, her great-great-grandfather having been a convict in the First Fleet. She was the eldest of seven children and spent her first 10 years at a farm in the bush country, described in *Childhood at Brindabella* (1963). Later the family moved downmarket to a district fictionalized in *My Brilliant Career* (1901) as Possum Gully. Eventually they settled in a Sydney suburb. Having flirted with nursing she turned to journalism, became involved in the feminist movement, wrote *My Brilliant Career*, and emigrated in 1906 to the USA, where she worked as secretary to the Women's Trade Union League. Moving to England in 1915, despite a deep aversion to

war, she helped with the war effort, serving with the Scottish Women's Hospital at Ostrovo, in Macedonia. In 1932 she returned permanently to Australia, where the 'Brent of Bin' series, starting with *Up the Country* (1928), made the pseudonymous author the subject of much speculation. Her best work appeared under her own name, including the early autobiographical novels *All That Swagger* (1936) and *My Career Goes Bung* (1946), and a collection of essays on Australian literature, *Laughter, Not for a Cage* (1956). The annual Miles Franklin awards are now among Australia's most prestigious literary prizes. The popularity of her novels, and the filming of *My Brilliant Career*, have tended to obscure the considerable contribution which she made to the social and professional development of Australian women.
▷M F Barnard, *Miles Franklin* (1967)

FRANKO, Ivan
(1856–1916)

Ukrainian novelist, poet and scholar, born near Drogobych. **Shevchenko** apart, he was the leading writer of his time in the Ukraine. His fiction, of which there are good examples in *The Boa Constrictor and Other Stories* (1957), is influenced by **Zola**, but, its socialist tendencies apart, is richly observant of rural and urban customs. His poetry, not major but skilful and widely read, passed through all the modes of the time, from neo-Romantic to Symbolist. The poem *Moysey* (1905, Eng trans *Moses*, 1938), is said to be 'a jewel of Ukrainian literature'. There is a *Selected Poems* in translation (1948).
▷*Ukrainian Quarterly* (1945–60, passim)

FRANZOS, Karl Emil
(1848–1904)

Austrian novelist, born of Jewish parentage in Podolia on the Austro–Russian border. His themes and settings were taken from Galicia, the Bukovina, south Russia and Romania; his novels, which contain vivid pictures of life among Jews and peasants, include *Aus Halbasien* (1876, 'From Asia Minor'), *Die Juden von Barnow* (1877, 'The Jews of Barnow'), *Ein Kampf ums Recht* (1882, 'A Struggle over the Law') and *Der Pojaz* (1905, 'The Pojaz').

FRASER, George MacDonald
(1925–)

English historical novelist, who grew up in Carlisle and Glasgow. Trained as a journalist, he was Deputy Editor of the *Glasgow Herald* in 1968–9, but following the success of his first novel *Flashman* (1969) he left to become a full-time writer. In this and subsequent novels, starting with *Royal Flash* (1970),

Fraser turned the bully of **Fielding**'s *Tom Brown's Schooldays* into a representative figure of the English caste system and of imperial values, contrasting him in a parallel sequence of books with the more down-to-earth McCauslan. Flashman also appears as an old man in such otherwise unrelated books as *Mr American* (1980), though these too tend to be concerned with Britain's role in a changing world and the responsibilities of the ruling class. Fraser has written effectively for the screen, scripting the James Bond film *Octopussy* (1983) and a 1987 adaptation of the life of Casanova. His war experiences fuelled the surprisingly lyrical and elegiac *Quartered Safe Out Here* (1992).

FRASER, G(eorge) S(utherland)
(1915–80)

Scottish poet, literary critic and university teacher. He was born in Glasgow, but his family moved to Aberdeen and he was educated at St Andrews University. He came to prominence in 1941 when he wrote an introduction to *The White Horseman*, an anthology of prose and verse of the so-called 'New Apocalypse' movement, which emphasized turbulently romantic imagery over the quieter classicism and plain speech of a previous generation. It was, on the face of it, an unlikely affiliation for the quiet, almost schoolmasterly Fraser, and his own verse was less enthusiastically exotic; it is collected in *Poems of G S Fraser* (1981). Fraser spent many years abroad, mostly in Egypt and Eritrea, working as a staff writer for the Ministry of Information, and many of his most moving poems take the form of an exile's letters home. Perhaps his most significant book, however, is *The Modern Writer and His World* (1953, rev edn 1964), in which he argues that 'modernity' was a question of attitude rather than of historical period.
▷*A Stranger and Afraid: Autobiography of an Intellectual* (posthumous 1983)

FRAYN, Michael
(1933–)

English dramatist, journalist and humorist, born in London. A journalist by training, he has published a number of comic novels, among them *The Tin Men* (1965), and *Towards the End of the Morning* (1967), about the newspaper business. His stage plays include *Alphabetical Order* (1975), set in the library of a provincial newspaper; *Clouds* (1976), about two rival journalists in Cuba; *Noises Off* (1982), a frenetic farce about putting on a frenetic farce; and *Benefactors* (1984), a piece about middle-class mores. His finest play is *Make and Break* (1980), a satirical look at the lives of salesmen at a foreign trade fair. He also wrote the script for the

film *Clockwise* (1986), and is a translator of **Anton Chekhov**.

FRÉCHETTE, Louis Honoré
(1839–1908)

'Canadian laureate', born in Lévis, Quebec. He was called to the Bar, and elected to the Dominion parliament in 1874. He published prose works and plays, and his poems *Mes loisirs* (1863), *La voix d'un exil* (1867), which attacked Canadian politics, and others, were 'crowned' by the Académie française.
▷M Dugas, *Un romantique canadien* (1934)

FREDERIC, Harold
(1856–98)

American novelist, born in Utica, New York. After a poverty-stricken youth, he became a journalist and was in 1884 appointed European correspondent of the *New York Times*. He wrote *Seth's Brother's Wife* (1887), *The Return of the O'Mahony* (1892) and others, novels depicting his own background, but his best work is *The Damnation of Theron Ware* (1896), about the intellectual awakening of a young minister.
▷A Briggs, *The Novels of Harold Frederic* (1969)

FREDRO, Count Aleksander
(1793–1876)

Polish memoirist, poet and major comic dramatist (in brilliant verse), born in Suchorów. He fought in the Napoleonic wars, and then returned to farming on his estate. One notable work is the recreation of his Napoleonic years, *Trzy po trzy* (1877, 'Three On Three'), modelled on **Laurence Sterne**'s *Tristram Shandy*. His comedies were of very high quality until he was silenced by a spiteful review by an envious poetaster, whereupon, over-sensitively, he wrote more plays, but would not allow them to be performed. A few of them have been translated, for example, *Dami i huzary* (1825, Eng trans *Ladies and Hussars*, 1925).
▷J Krzyzanowski, *Polish Romantic Literature* (1930)

FREELING, Nicolas
(1927–)

English crime novelist, born in London, who worked throughout Europe as a cook. He is best known as the creator of the Dutch detective, Inspector Van der Valk. He first appeared in *Love in Amsterdam* (1962), and solved many cases over the subsequent decade until the author killed him off in *A Long Silence* (1972). Van der Valk considers crime as being not so much an aberration, but part of the natural fabric of life. This emerges most absorbingly in *Criminal Conversation* (1965), a case in which a banker accuses a neurologist of murder and in which the characters' personalities and motives are studied in depth. Although Van der Valk has been revived in the occasional short story, he has not been wholly resuscitated. Other policemen have taken his place, but Freeling remains justly famed for the earlier novels.

FREEMAN, John
(1880–1929)

English poet, born in London. He rose from clerk to become secretary and director of an insurance company (1927). His *Stone Trees* (1916) and other volumes of poetry made his reputation. He won the Hawthornden Prize with *Poems New and Old* in 1920 and wrote studies of *George Moore* (1922) and *Herman Melville* (1926).
▷G Freeman and Sir John Squires (eds), *John Freeman's Letters* (1936)

FREEMAN, Mary E Wilkins
(1852–1930)

American novelist and story writer, born in Randolph, Massachusetts. Her schooling was interrupted by poor health. In her youth she acted as secretary to the elder **Oliver Wendell Holmes**. Her 238 stories about New England life, not unlike those of Mrs **Gaskell** in *Cranford*, made an important contribution to American regional, or 'local colour', fiction. Paramount amongst these are the 24 tales in *A New England Nun* (1891). She was not so happy in the novel form, but in her late collection of tales *Edgewater People* (1918) she recaptured all her old skill and pathos.

FREILIGRATH, Ferdinand
(1810–76)

German poet and democrat, born in Detmold. He abandoned commerce for literature, but became a protagonist of German democracy and his writings became more and more political. He was obliged to seek refuge in Belgium and Britain for his *Glaubensbekenntnis* (1844, 'Confession of Beliefs'). He returned to Germany in 1848 and became leader of the Democratic party. He was again expelled after a trial for his poem *Die Toten an die Lebenden* (1848, 'The Dead and the Living'), and returned to London in 1851. He translated many English classics into German. He lived in Stuttgart from 1868, and published his *Neue Gedichte* ('New Poems') in 1870.
▷H Eulenberg, *Ferdinand Freiligrath* (1948)

FRENAUD, André
(1907–)

French poet, born in Burgundy, who became impelled to write when he found himself a German prisoner-of-war in 1940. His manner was much influenced by the surrealists, but he is essentially a poet in search of small joyful facts with which he can defeat his own guilty pessimism. His early work was often about the miseries of a France occupied by Nazis. *La Sainte face* (1948, 'The Holy face') and *Il n'y a pas de paradis* (1962, 'There is no Paradise') collected earlier poems. He is represented in the *Penguin Book of French Verse* (1975, ed A Hartley).

FRENCH, Alice, pseud Octave Thanet
(1850–1934)

American short-story writer and novelist. French was born in Massachusetts but lived mainly in Arkansas and Iowa, the states which form the backdrop for her 'local colour' fiction. She was a prolific contributor to national literary magazines and her short stories were, and still are, better regarded than her longer fiction. *Stories of a Western Town* (1893) contains work in her typical vein. French was interested in workers' rights, but advocated co-operatives rather than unions. She was a staunch defender, against editors' objections, of the Arkansan idioms used in her dialogue.

FRENCH, Marilyn
(1929–)

American novelist and feminist scholar, born in New York and educated at Hofstra College and Harvard University. Her first work of fiction was *The Women's Room* (1977), a massive bestseller which, with sympathy and balance, traces its heroine's development from 1950s housewife to emancipated 1970s woman. Her two subsequent novels, *The Bleeding Heart* (1980) and *Her Mother's Daughter* (1987), have brought a strong feminine philosophy to bear on the social and moral dilemmas of the late 20th century. She has examined the female role in literature and society in *Shakespeare's Division of Experience* (1981), *Beyond Power: On Women, Men, and Morals* (1985) and *The War Against Women* (1992).

FRENEAU, Philip Morin
(1752–1832)

American sailor and poet, born in New York. Having written satirical verse in the pre-revolutionary period, he commanded a privateer in the American War of Independence, was captured by the British, and wrote *The British Prison Ship* (1781). He also wrote a number of shorter poems, including 'The Indian Burying Ground' and 'The Wild Honeysuckle'.
▷P M Marsh, *Freneau: Poet and Journalist* (1967); and other works by Marsh

FRENSSEN, Gustav
(1863–1945)

German novelist, born a carpenter's son in Barlt in Holstein. He studied for the church but turned to writing and attracted attention by his *Jörn Uhl* (1901), a novel of peasant life. *Hilligenlei* (1906, 'Holy Land'), a life of Jesus Christ set in a Germanic background, aroused much controversy.
▷W Johnson, *Gustav Frenssen. Art und Ahnen* (1934)

FRÈRE, Maud
(1923–79)

Belgian novelist, born in Brussels. Her first stories were for children, in *Vacances secrètes* (1956, Eng trans *Secret Holiday*, 1957). She then graduated to psychological novels of some substance, including *Guido* (1965).
▷M Pierson-Piérard, *Maud Frère* (1960, in French)

FREUCHEN, Lorentz Peter
(1904–57)

Danish novelist, born in Nykobing. He was an expert on Inuit (Eskimo) life and a leading explorer of Greenland, where his adventurous but stylistically undistinguished novels, such as *Nordkaper* (1929, Eng trans *The Sea Tyrant*, 1932), are set.

FREUD, Sigmund
(1856–1939)

Austrian neurologist who founded psychoanalysis, born in Freiburg, Moravia. The fragment *On Nature* by **Goethe** was instrumental in converting him from legal to medical studies. Although, like **Jung**, he was not himself a creative writer, his influence upon modern literature (and art of all kinds) has been, like that of his one-time associate Jung—who broke away from him—profound and incalculable. He did not, as is so often asserted, 'discover' the unconscious mind; but he provided the first plausible model of the manner—not always as pleasant as the authorities of his time liked—in which it might work. There is hardly a major writer of the 20th century who has not been in some way touched by his theories, the chief one of which was the so-called Oedipus Complex, which propounded that a son is in unconscious conflict with his father for the possession of his mother (or, in a modified form, for his mother's love). His masterpiece is *Die Traumdeutung* (1900, 'The Interpretation of Dreams'). His collected works in translation were issued in 24 volumes between 1953 and 1964.
▷F H Hoffmann, *Freudianism and the Literary Mind* (1945)

FREYRE, Gilberto de Mello
(1900–87)

Brazilian writer and intellectual. He was educated in Rio de Janeiro and in Texas and New York City. After working as a journalist in his native city of Recife (1927–30), he moved to an academic career and came to prominence with a large-scale historical work, *Casa-grande & Senzala* (1933, Eng trans *The Masters and the Slaves*, 1946), which altered previous thinking about colonial Brazil and its relations with Europe. The book won him the Felippe d'Oliveira Award (1934), the first of many prestigious prizes and honorary doctorates. Freyre was hugely prolific, publishing more than 50 books. His poetry and fiction are not highly regarded, but his impact on Brazilian consciousness is immeasurable.
▷D de Melo Menezes, *Gilberto Freyre* (1944, in Spanish)

FREYTAG, Gustav
(1816–95)

German novelist and playwright, born in Kreuzburg in Silesia. From 1839 to 1847 he was *Privatdozent* of German at Breslau University. A deputy to the North German Diet, he attended the Prussian crown prince in the Franco-German campaign (1870). His comedies and other plays, such as *Die Valentine* (1846) and *Die Journalisten* (1853), proved brilliant successes, but his greatest achievement is *Soll und Haben* (1855, Eng trans *Debit and Credit*, 1858), a realistic novel of German commercial life. It was followed by *Die Verlorene Handschrift* (1864, Eng trans *The Lost Manuscript*, 1865), and the series (1872–81) called *Die Ahnen*, ('The Ancestors'). He set down his dramatic theories in *Technik des Dramas* (1863, 'Technique of Drama').
▷H Lindau, *Gustav Freytag* (1907)

FRIDEGÅRD, Jan
(1897–1968)

Swedish novelist, born in Uppland, one of the many working-class writers of the first half of the century. His *Lars Hård* (1935–6) was an outstanding and controversial work. Its eponymous hero is an asocial but thin-skinned cynic whose path leads through personal degradation to salvation brought about by love and religious understanding. Fridegård achieved considerable popularity with his historical novels; a number of his other works reflect his spiritualist beliefs.
▷E Schön, *Jan Fridegård, Proletärdiktaren och folkkulturen* (1978)

FRIED, Erich
(1921–90)

Austrian poet, novelist and translator (notably of **T S Eliot**, **Dylan Thomas** and

Shakespeare), who emigrated to London in 1938 and remained there for the rest of his life. He was born in Vienna, and his parents perished in the Holocaust. His earlier poetry was politically 'unengaged', fashionably modernistic in its techniques, and doggedly optimistic; but he later switched to a more purposeful poetry of engagement. He will probably be best remembered for his fine translations.

FRIEDMAN, Bruce Jay
(1930–)

American novelist. In *Stern* (1962) he mined the same territory as **Philip Roth**'s *Portnoy's Complaint*, creating a funny and often trenchant account of American–Jewish hang-ups. *A Mother's Kisses* (1964) is in very similar vein, but *The Dick* (1971) marked a change of pace and tone, as well as subject-matter, and is considerably underrated. His most recent novel is *Tokyo Woes* (1985). Friedman has also written short stories, collected in *Far from the City of Class* (1963) and *Let's Hear It for a Beautiful Guy* (1984).

FRIEL, Brian
(1929–)

Irish playwright and short-story writer, born in Omagh. His first play, *This Doubtful Paradise* (1959), was produced in Belfast. His first major success was *Philadelphia, Here I Come!* (1964), a play about emigration and the relationship between a man and his son. Friel's writing is poetic, sometimes ironic, always compassionate and poignant. He often concentrates upon the relation between people, language, custom and the land, these forming the principal theme of his most important plays, *Translations* (1980), and the enormously successful *Dancing at Lughnasa* (1990), both of which are set in County Donegal. The first looks at a group of English soldiers anglicizing Celtic placenames in order to make new maps in 1883, while the second, set in 1936, concentrates on the sad, isolated but resiliently optimistic lives of the five adult Mundy sisters. With actor Stephen Rea, Friel was a co-founder of the Field Day Theatre Company (1980). His short-story collections include *A Saucer of Larks* (1962) and *The Diviner: Brian Friel's Best Short Stories* (1983).
▷U Dantanus, *Brian Friel* (1988)

FRIEL, George
(1910–75)

Scottish novelist, born in Glasgow, where he lived and worked throughout his life. Educated at St Mungo's Academy and Glasgow University (the only one of seven children to go to university), he trained as a teacher at Jordanhill College, Glasgow. When war broke out he served in the RAOC and then returned to teaching, a profession he grew to loathe and distrust, although he always retained his concern for children. His experiences at the chalkface are at the heart of *Mr Alfred M.A.* (1972), which has been described as 'one of the great Scottish novels'. The story of the eponymous teacher's disillusionment and downfall, betrayed by one of his wretched girl pupils, it eloquently and ironically depicts a society and an education system in a state of disintegration, the result of a breakdown in communication. Other novels include *The Bank of Time* (1959), *The Boy Who Wanted Peace* (1964), *Grace and Miss Partridge* (1969) and *An Empty House* (1975).

FRIIS MOLLER, Kai
(1888–1960)

Danish minor poet, critic and, mainly, translator (**Kipling**, **Baudelaire**, and many others). He was born and died in Copenhagen. He is said to have been feared, as a literary journalist, for his sarcasm.

FRISCH, Max Rudolph
(1911–91)

Swiss novelist and playwright, born in Zürich. In 1933, forced by economic circumstances to abandon the study of German literature at Zürich University, he became a journalist. Later he trained as an architect, but not before publishing *Blätter aus dem Brotsack* (1940, Eng trans *Leaves from a Knapsack*, 1942), while serving with the Swiss frontier guard. In 1958 he became the first foreigner to be awarded the **Büchner** Prize of the German Academy for language and poetry. His bibliography is extensive but as a novelist he is chiefly known outside German-speaking Europe for the novels *Stiller* (1954, Eng trans *I'm Not Stiller*, 1958), and *Homo Faber* (1957, Eng trans 1959) and *Der Mensch erscheint im Holozän* (1979, Eng trans *Man in the Holocene*, 1980). He has had international success as a playwright after being a disciple of **Bertolt Brecht** in the 1940s, *Biedermann und die Brandstifter* (1953, Eng trans *The Fire Raisers*, 1962) and *Andorra* (1961, Eng trans 1962) having become modern stage classics.
▷U Weisstein, *Frisch* (1967)

FRISCHLIN, Phillipp Nikodemus
(1547–90)

German dramatist and humanist writer, born in Balingen. His life was made difficult by his ardent temperament and his sharply satirical tongue, and he died while trying to escape from a castle in which he had been imprisoned for telling the truth too scurrilously. A good Latinist, he wrote plays in that language; he

also translated five plays by **Aristophanes** into Latin. Only one surviving play is in German.
▷D F Strauss, *Nicodemus Frischlin* (1856, in German)

FRISHMAN, David
(1862–1922)

Hebrew writer of short fiction, poet, editor, translator (of **Goethe**, **Shakespeare**, **Tagore**, and many other eminent writers) and critic, born in Zguerzsh, near Łodz. Some of the stories of this brilliant and versatile scholar deal with ghetto life; his posthumous *Bimid-bar* (1923) is a series of tales based on episodes in the Pentateuch, and represent his genius at its most profound.
▷M Waxman, *A History of Jewish Literature* (1960)

FRÖDING, Gustav
(1860–1911)

Swedish poet, born in Alstern near Karlstad. He studied at Uppsala and became a schoolmaster and journalist, but suffered bouts of mental illness. He is considered the greatest Swedish lyric poet, often compared to **Robert Burns**, combining dialect and folksong and homespun philosophy in his portrayal of local characters, as in *Guitarr och dragharmonika* (1891, 'Guitar and Harmonica'), *Nya dikter* (1894, 'New Poems') and *Räggler å paschaser* (1896, 'Drops and Fragments'). The gentle humour of his earlier poems later turned to a tragic quest for the Holy Grail.
▷J Landquist, *Gustav Fröding, en biografi* (1956)

FROMENTIN, Eugène
(1820–76)

French novelist and painter, born in La Rochelle. Visits to Algeria and the Near East provided him with abundant material for his paintings, which betray the influence of Delacroix. His three travel books also provide vivid pictures of the Algerian scene. But he is best known as the author of *Dominique* (1862, Eng trans 1932), a nostalgic autobiographical novel, and *Les Maîtres d'autrefois* (1876, Eng trans *Masters of Past Time*, 1948), written during a tour of Belgian and Dutch art galleries, which contains some brilliant art criticism.
▷A R Evans, *The Literary Art of Eugène Fromentin* (1964)

FROST, Robert Lee
(1874–1963)

American lyric poet, 'the voice of New England', born in San Francisco, the son of a New England father and Scottish mother. He studied at Dartmouth College and Harvard, but did not graduate from either. Betweeen 1899 and 1912 he worked as a teacher, cobbler and poultry farmer. He spent the years 1912 to 1915 in Britain, where he made contact with **Edward Thomas** and **Ezra Pound** and was encouraged by **Rupert Brooke**, **Lascelles Abercrombie** and **Wilfrid Gibson**. Pound's review of *A Boy's Will* (1913) and *North of Boston* (1914) helped bring Frost an international reputation, and he returned to the USA in triumph after Britain became involved in World War I. He became Professor of English at Amherst (1916) and co-founded the Bread Loaf School of English at Middlebury College. He was Professor of Poetry at Harvard from 1939 to 1943 before returning to Amherst (1949–63). His verse, which was seen as quintessentially New England, aimed to capture the 'abstract vitality of our speech'. Though ostensibly pastoral, it was never narrowly regionalist and was marked by a tragic vein, often overlooked but memorably defined by **Lionel Trilling** at Frost's 85th birthday dinner when the critic controversially talked of Frost's 'terrifying' vision. He was awarded the Pulitzer Prize in 1924, 1931 and 1937, and received a US senate citation of honour in 1950. His standing with the American establishment was secured when he read 'The Gift Outright' at John F Kennedy's inauguration. A *Complete Poems* (to date) appeared in 1949; all the extant verse was collected and edited by Edward Connery Latham two decades later, following posthumous editions of the letters (1964) and the prose (1966). Poems such as 'The Death of the Hired Man', 'Stopping by Woods on a Snowy Evening' and 'Out, Out' are among the most anthologized in American literature.
▷W H Pritchard, *Frost: a literary life reconsidered* (1984)

FRUG, Simon Samuel
(1860–1916)

One of the earliest Yiddish poets, born in southern Russia. He helped to create a viable Jewish poetry, but his best work remains his earliest, written before 1888, in Russian.

FRUGONI, Carlo
(1692–1768)

Italian poet, born in Genoa, laureate at the courts of the Farnese and the Bourbons. He wrote an abundance of pleasant, skilful, empty verse, absurdly over-praised in its time, and now the object of a peculiar scorn. He himself suspected it of being of small worth. He was bitterly attacked by **Alfieri**, and one of his apologists called him 'the uncorrupted father of corrupted children'.

FRUGONI, Francesco
(c.1620–c.1686)

Italian Baroque poet and prose writer, born in Genoa, whose chief work is his series of 12 stories called *Del cane di Diogene* (1689), describing the barkings of a dog against all the peoples and customs, of all times, of whom Frugoni could think. This massive work has not yet had the attention it deserves, although **Croce** wrote about it, and Frugoni is often omitted from dictionaries in favour of his inferior namesake **Carlo Frugoni**.

FRY, Christopher Harris
(1907–)

English dramatist, born in Bristol, educated at Bedford Modern School. He combined being a schoolmaster with a love of the stage, which became a full-time occupation on his appointment as Director of Tunbridge Wells Repertory Players (1932–6). In 1940 he became Director of the Playhouse at Oxford, having in the meantime written two pageant-plays, *Thursday's Child* and *The Tower*, and also *The Boy with a Cart*, a charming rustic play on the subject of the Sussex saint, Cuthman. After service in the Non-Combatant Corps during World War II he began a series of outstanding plays in free verse, often with undertones of religion and mysticism, including *A Phoenix too Frequent* (1946), *The Lady's not for Burning* (1949), *Venus Observed* (1950), *A Sleep of Prisoners* (1951), *The Dark is Light Enough* (1954), *Curtmantle* (1962) and *A Yard of Sun* (1970). He has also produced highly successful translations of **Jean Anouilh** and **Jean Giraudoux**.
▷D Stanford, *Christopher Fry* (1954)

FUCHS, Daniel
(1909–93)

American novelist and short-story writer. He grew up in New York City and used his background to great effect in the sequence of novels known collectively as *The Williamsburg Trilogy*, first published in that form in 1972. It comprises *Summer in Williamsburg* (1934), *Homage to Blenholt* (1936) and *Low Company* (1937), which was unaccountably 'translated' as *Neptune Beach* on its publication in the UK (1937). The stories are bleak, though not without humour, and tap into the same transatlantic link that saw the French Existentialists find common cause with the work of **John Dos Passos** and with **Faulkner**'s 'potboiling' *Sanctuary*. In 1971 Fuchs returned to fiction with a satiric portrayal of California in *West of the Rockies*. His short stories were collected in *The Apathetic Bookie Joint* (1979).

FUCINI, Renato, pseud Neri Tanfucio
(1843–1921)

Italian writer, born in Monterotondo, near Pisa, the son of a country doctor. He studied agriculture and engineering in Pisa, and became city engineer in Florence. He had a bright wit which found outlet in dialect verse, published as *Cento Sonetti* (1872, 'A Hundred Sonnets'). When Florence ceased to be a capital city he lost his post and retired to the country. *Le veglie di Neri* (1884, 'The Vigils of Neri'), a collection of tales, is his best-known work. *All'aria aperta* (1897, 'In the Open') is reckoned the best modern collection of Italian humorous novellas. He also wrote books for children, and personal anecdotes.
▷ *Renato Fucini* (1943)

FUENTES, Carlos
(1928–)

Mexican novelist and playwright, born in Panama City. While very young he travelled extensively as his father changed diplomatic posts. Educated at the Colegio Frances Morelos, his graduate studies took him to the National University of Mexico and the Institut des Hautes Études Internationales in Geneva, which led to a career in international affairs. A secretary of the Mexican delegation to the International Labor Organization, he eventually became cultural attaché to the Mexican Embassy in Geneva (1950–2) and press secretary to the United Nations Information Centre, Mexico City. He served as the Mexican ambassador to France (1975–7), and has held a variety of teaching posts. An energetic cultural promoter, writer of articles and reviewer, he has published prolifically since his first collection of fantastic, myth-inspired short-stories, *Los dias enmascarados* ('The Masked Days') in 1954. Many of his novels have been published in English, among them *Terra nostra* (1975, Eng trans 1976 (US); 1977 (UK)), regarded as his masterpiece, the culmination and synthesis of his novel-writing practice and thought on the identity and destiny of Spain and Latin America.
▷D de Guzman, *Carlos Fuentes* (1972)

FUGARD, Athol
(1932–)

South African dramatist and theatre director, born in Middleburg, Cape Province, and educated at Port Elizabeth Technical College and Cape Town University. After leaving university in 1953 he worked as a seaman and journalist before becoming a stage manager and settling firmly into a theatrical career in 1959 as actor, director and playwright. Since 1965 he has been director of the Serpent Players in Port Elizabeth, and in 1972 co-founded the Space Experimental Theatre, Cape Town. His plays are set in contemporary South Africa, but his presentation of the bleakness and frustration of life for those especially on the fringes of society raises their political and social deprivation to the level of universal human tragedy. His work has met with official opposition; *Blood Knot* (1960), portraying two coloured brothers, one light- and one dark-skinned, was censored, and some of his work has only been published and produced abroad. His plays include *Boesman and Lena* (1969), *Statements After an Arrest under the Immorality Act* (1972), *Sizwe Banzi is Dead* (1973), *Dimetos* (1976) and *A Lesson from Aloes* (1979). He has also written film scripts and a novel, *Tsotsi* (1980). Fugard has become increasingly popular in Britain, and later plays, *Master Harold and the Boys* (1982), *The Road to Mecca* (1984) and *A Place with the Pigs* (1987), have been staged at the National Theatre. The latter play veers away from the South African themes of his earlier work, being inspired by a newspaper story about a Red Army deserter who hid in a pigsty for over 40 years.

FUKAO Sumako
(1893–1974)

Japanese poet, born into an old but declining samurai family in Hyogo. A close friend of **Akiko Yosano**, she was extremely open, by Japanese standards, to foreign influences, modelling herself at one point on **Colette**. Her verse, full of intense, personal, sometimes erotic themes, underwent a severe change of style after Japan's defeat in 1945, when she began to be motivated by social *angst*, and a despair at the state of the country. She never recovered her previous good spirits; though she lived to see Japan's rise to economic prosperity, her poetic response to this was to complain in verse about the cost in damage to the environment and the erosion of the rights of the individual.

FULDA, Ludwig
(1862–1932)

German playwright, born in Frankfurt am Main. He is less important for his plays— deriving from **Ibsen**, **Hauptmann** and others—than for the form of the fairy-play, which he developed in *Der Talisman* (1893), which is an adaptation of 'The Emperor's Clothes' by **Hans Christian Andersen**. He greatly influenced another much more substantial dramatist, **Yevgeny Shvarts**.

FULLER, Charles H, Jr
(1939–)

American playwright, born in Philadelphia, and noted for his sensitive, unbiased but unflinching exploration of relationships, especially those between blacks and whites, and between blacks and a white-dominated bureaucracy. Among his most successful plays are *The Brownsville Raid* (1976), based upon a true incident in 1906, in which an entire US Army regiment was honourably discharged after none of the 167 black soldiers admitted inciting a riot on Brownsville, Texas. The Pulitzer Prize-winning *A Soldier's Play* (1981) is also set in the army, this time in a barracks in Louisiana during World War II, and deals with the aftermath of the murder of an unpopular sergeant. Fuller is co-founder and co-director of the Philadelphia Arts Theater.

FULLER, Henry Blake
(1857–1929)

American poet, critic and novelist, born in Chicago. His work is now somewhat underrated. His first novel, published under the pseudonym of 'Stanton Page', was a romantic tale set in Italy; but his *The Cliff Dwellers* (1892) was the first true 'city novel' in American literature. **Edmund Wilson** thought him superior to **William Howells**. Certainly his naturalism, which was taken up by **Norris**, **Dreiser** and **Farrell**, was far more thoroughgoing than that of Howells. The title 'cliff dwellers' describes the denizens of skyscrapers, and the novel itself savagely depicts the ugly fruitlessness of the quest for wealth and wealth alone. The European romances with which he interspersed his serious books are far less good, but *On the Stairs* (1918), once again depicting squalid materialist struggles, and the posthumous *Not on the Screen* (1930), a satire on the film industry as well as a story of Chicago, are both excellent realistic novels. A minor poet himself, he helped make *Poetry Chicago*, for a time, the most important poetry magazine in the world.
▷C Van Vechten, *Henry Blake Fuller* (1929); C M Griffin, *Henry Blake Fuller: A Critical Biography* (1939)

FULLER, Roy Broadbent
(1912–91)

English poet and novelist, born in Oldham. He went to school in Blackpool, trained as a solicitor, and spent his professional career as a solicitor with building societies. His first collection of poetry, *Poems*, appeared in 1939 and was, he fully admitted, very strongly influenced by **W H Auden**. His experience of war in the Royal Navy (1941–5) prompted *The Middle of a War* (1942) and *A Lost Season* (1944). This saw the development of the note of characteristic self-criticism which was to become an integral part of his later poetry. His traditionalist attitude kept him apart from the strong current of neo-Romantic revival initiated by **Dylan Thomas** after the war, but his *Brutus's Orchard* (1957) and *Collected Poems* (1962) established him as a major poet, and his later works include *Buff* (1965), *Song Cycle from a Record Sleeve* (1972), *An Old War* (1974), *From the Joke Shop* (1975) and *Retreads* (1979). His novels show great skill in observation and intricacy of plot, and include *Second Curtain* (1953), *The Ruined Boys* (1959), *The Perfect Fool* (1963) and *The Carnal Island* (1970). He was Professor of Poetry at Oxford 1968–73, and *Owl and Artificers* (1971) is a stimulating and entertaining collection of his lectures. He also published the autobiographical *Souvenirs* (1980), *Vamp Till Ready* (1982), *The Strange and the Good* (1989) and *Spanner and Pen* (1991).

▷A E Austin, *Roy Fuller* (1979)

FULLERTON, Mary Eliza
(1868–1946)

Australian poet, novelist and journalist, born in Glenmaggie, Victoria, who wrote under various names. As 'Alpenstock' she contributed to contemporary journals. In her own name she published three books of verse and wrote a series of novels: *Two Women* (1923), *The People of the Timber* (1925) and *A Juno in the Bush* (1930). Encouraged by **Miles Franklin** she published two more collections of her verse under the pseudonym 'E' in the belief that it would not receive recognition under a female name. *Moles Do So Little with their Privacy* (1942) was followed by *The Wonder and the Apple* (1946).

FURPHY, Joseph
(1843–1912)

Australian writer, who described himself as 'half bushman and half bookworm'. Born in Yering, Yarra Valley, Victoria, of hard-working and well-read Irish emigrant parents, he worked as a farmer and a bullock-driver before moving to Shepparton, Victoria, in 1883. There he worked at the iron-foundry which had been established by his elder brother. This security enabled him to contribute, under the name 'Tom Collins', a series of articles to the *Bulletin* magazine, and to write a 1220-page manuscript, *Such is Life: Being Certain Extracts from the Diary of Tom Collins*. After much revision and abridgment, this novel was published in 1903. Some excised sections were published after his death as *Rigby's Romance* (1921, rev edn 1946) and *The Buln-Buln and the Brolga* (1948). His reputation, however, rests on his one major work with its credo 'Temper, democratic; bias, offensively Australian', which encapsulated his hard-working philosophy and marked a move away from the common romantic concept of Australia's pioneering days. *The Poems of Joseph Furphy* was published posthumously in 1916.

▷M Franklin, *Joseph Furphy* (1944)

FUSSENEGGER, Gertrud
(1912–)

Austrian novelist and poet, born in Pilsen. She has not attracted much critical attention, but *Die Brüder von Lasawa* (1948, 'The Brothers von Lasawa'), which is typical of her historical novels, is a vivid and worthy tale of the Thirty Years War.

FUTABATEI Shimei
(1864–1909)

Japanese novelist, born in Edo (Tokyo), and of enormous historical importance as he was the first writer of Japanese fiction to attempt to make the written word as intelligible as the spoken, in contrast to his predecessors and his near-contemporary **Izumi**, who wrote in a form of literary Japanese far removed from everyday speech. *Ukigumo* (1887, 'Drifting Clouds') broke new ground in being composed in the vernacular. Futabatei was also the first translator into Japanese of the works of **Gogol** and **Turgenev**, again employing vernacular language.

▷M G Ryan, *Japan's First Modern Novel* (1967)

G

GABORIAU, Émile
(1835–73)

French writer of detective fiction, born in Saujon in Charente-Inférieure. He is credited with inaugurating the *roman policier* in France. He had already contributed to some of the smaller Parisian papers, when he leapt to fame with *L'Affaire Lerouge* (1866), featuring his detective Lecoq. It was followed by *Le Dossier 113* (1867), *Monsieur Lecoq* (1869), *Les Esclaves de Paris* (1869, 'Slaves of Paris'), *La Corde au cou* (1873, 'Rope Around the Neck'), and several others.

GABRYELLA *see* ZMICHOWSKA, Narcyza

GACE BRULÉ
(b.c.1160)

French troubadour poet, in the Provençal tradition. Little is known of his life. His poems, almost 70 of which survive, deal, conventionally, with courtly love, but are distinguished from those of his contemporaries by a slightly more melancholic air than is found elsewhere.
▷H P Dyggve, *Gace Brulé, Trouvere Champenois* (1951)

GADDA, Carlo Emilio
(1893–1973)

Italian novelist from Milan, who worked throughout his active life as an engineer. In his early days he was associated with the group of writers who published in the Florentine avant-garde magazine *Solaria*—these included **Vittorini** and **Montale**. He had published many fragments of his first, and extraordinary novel, *Quer pasticciaccio brutto de via Merulana* (1957, Eng trans *That Awful Mess on the Via Merulana*, 1965), before the whole appeared. It is a unique novel in many ways: in its use of dialect, in its adaptation (almost beyond recognition) of techniques invented or employed by **Dos Passos**, **Joyce** and other modernists, and in its strange plot, which concerns a police officer's failure to solve a murder case. *La cognizione del dolore* (1963, rev edn 1970, Eng trans *Acquainted With Grief*, 1969) is set in a South America which is recognizably Italy; *Eros e Priapo (Da furore a cenere)* (1967, 'Eros and Priapus (From Frenzy to Ashes)') is a profound analysis of Italian fascism. When Gadda was charged with obscurity, he claimed the same of reality—and remains one of the most substantial and critically well explored of modernist writers.
▷R M Adams, *After Joyce: Studies in Fiction after Ulysses* (1977)

GADDIS, William
(1922–)

American novelist, born in New York City. He was educated at Harvard University, worked for the *New Yorker* (1946–7), lived and travelled abroad, and freelanced as a speech and filmscript writer from 1956 until the 1970s. He has written three novels: *The Recognitions* (1955), a densely allusive post-Christian epic about art, forgery, money and magic; *JR* (1976), about an 11-year-old ragged capitalist operating from pay phones and post-office money orders; and *Carpenter's Gothic* (1985), in which a Vietnam War veteran works as a media consultant for a fundamentalist preacher. An ambitious satirist, he is one of America's most prominent contemporary novelists. He won the National Book Award in 1976.
▷S Moore, *A Reader's Guide to William Gaddis's The Recognitions* (1982)

GÁDONYI, Géza
(1863–1922)

Hungarian novelist, poet and dramatist, born in Agárd, who lived a hermit-like existence in Eger. He owed his initial popularity to cheap but skilfully written and humorous crime books; but *Az én falum* (1898) was in a different class from all that had preceded it, being a vivid if socially uncontroversial portrait of rural life. Following this he wrote three historical novels, which are still read, including *A láthatatlan ember* (1902, Eng trans *Slave of the Huns*, 1969), about Attila's Huns. His work, unusually, became more interesting as he grew older and more mystical. *A bor* (1902) is a good stage comedy of village life.

GAINES, Ernest J(ames)
(1933–)

Black American novelist, whose powerful writing draws heavily on his childhood in rural Louisiana. His work might be characterized as post-**Faulkner**, written from the other side of the racial fence. His first novel, *Catherine Carmier* (1964), had something of the hysteria inherent in Faulkner's, and other white Southerners', approach to miscegenation. Gaines came to wider prominence with his third book, the remarkable *Autobiography of Miss Jane Pittman* (1971), which focused on a centenarian black woman whose life and troubles encapsulated the history of the Afro–American people since Emancipation. It was subsequently made into a successful film. In his most ambitious book, *A Gathering of Old Men* (1983), Gaines revived the multi-perspectival style favoured by Faulkner to tell the story of a violent stand-off between white racists and a black man accused of murdering a Cajun farmer.

GAISER, Gerd
(1908–76)
German novelist and painter, born in Ober-riexingen, Württemberg, who served as a fighter pilot throughout World War II. He has been accused by certain critics of continuing the fascist spirit under concealed forms; another view is that he merely remained extremely conservative, as well as critical of the Federal Republic and its 'economic miracle'. Sometimes, certainly, he sounds, in his archaic and heroic descriptions of dream-like trances of emotional elitism, like a late expressionist writer of Nazi persuasions. Of his novels, one in particular stands out: *Die sterbende Jagd* (1953, Eng trans *The Falling Leaf*, 1956). This describes the deterioration of morale in, and destruction of, a Nazi fighter squadron towards the end of World War II. This depiction of life in the air—although it owed something to another airforce writer, *Reichskultursenator* and Nazi Richard Euringer—had never been done before.
▷B Keith-Smith (ed), *Essays in Contemporary German Literature* (1966)

GALCZYNSKI, Konstanty
(1905–53)
Polish poet, born in Warsaw. He became well known when he started to contribute short poems to the magazine *Kwadryga*, and became a member of the literary group named after it. He was taken prisoner by the Nazis when they seized Poland, and set to forced labour—an experience that may have contributed to the heart attack from which he prematurely died. He could not satisfy the communists, and his efforts to please them, although embarrassing to him—even if possibly ironic—were not successful. His poetry at its best set out to please no one, rather the contrary, and he is one of Poland's most original talents, a writer of a uniquely grotesque and mocking poetry. Titles include

Zaczurowana dorozka (1948, 'The Enchanted Coach'). However, he remains little read, and hardly translated, outside Poland.
▷C Milosz, *The History of Polish Literature* (1969)

GALE, Norman
(1862–1942)
English minor poet, editor and memorable writer on the pleasure of cricket. He edited a very early selection (1901) from the poetry of **John Clare**, and was thus a (now forgotten) pioneer, with **Arthur Symons**, in the rehabilitation of this major poet. Gale's *Collected Poems* appeared in 1914.

GALE, Zona
(1874–1938)
American novelist, story writer and dramatist, born in Portage, Wisconsin. Her earliest, regional stories, and her first novel, *Romance Island* (1906), were marred by excessive sentimentality, but at the same time so acutely observed that it was evident that she was already a writer of unusual and delicate powers. She was scorned and disliked for her increasing pacifism and feminism; but, with the novel *Birth* (1918), in which she anticipated **Duhamel**'s *Salavin*, the iron finally entered her soul; she dramatized this in 1924 as *Mr Pitt*. Meanwhile, with *Miss Lulu Bett* (1920), appearing in the same year as (and artistically superior to) **Sinclair Lewis**'s *Main Street*, she became famous. Her dramatization of it won her a Pulitzer Prize (1921). Always mystical, she turned to **Gurdjieff** and to Orage, who was teaching the latter's ideas in New York; this strengthened her later work, such as the autobiographical *Portage, Wisconsin* (1928), the story collection *Yellow Gentians and Blue* (1927) and the novel *Papa le Fleur* (1933), now neglected and too hastily written off, giving it a new psychological accuracy and confidence. She became an avid supporter of La Follette's Progressive Party. The title of the biography of her by her fellow-Wisconsin author **August Derleth** is singularly appropriate: *Still, Small Voice* (1940).

GALLAGHER, Tess
(1932–)
American poet, born in Port Angeles, Washington, and educated in Seattle (where one of her teachers was **Theodore Roethke**) and in Iowa City. Her Irish ancestry was explored in her third collection, *Under Stars* (1978), which lacks the sheer force of its predecessor *Instructions to the Double* (1976). Her characteristic tone at this period was elegiac, but without undue sentimentality, and she favoured a strong, syllabic style that registers physical sensation and emotion vividly but

without sentimentality and may still have owed something to Roethke. *Portable Kisses* and *On Your Own* both appeared in 1978, the year that Gallagher—twice divorced—began living with the short-story writer **Raymond Carver**, whom she married shortly before his death. *Willingly* (1984) demonstrates her ability to create 'voices' which are rhetorically individual and far removed from the prevailing 'confessional' mode of the previous generation in American verse.

▷ Interview in *Ironwood* (October 1979)

GALLANT, Mavis
(1922–)

Canadian short-story writer and novelist, born in Montreal. Her father was English, her mother German–Russian–Breton, and she spent her childhood going from school to school, 17 in all, which made education 'virtually impossible'. Living entirely by writing, she contributes mainly to the *New Yorker* from her home in Paris. She has written two novels, *Green Water, Green Sky* (1959) and *A Fairly Good Time* (1970), several collections of short stories, and a diary of the 1968 street troubles in Paris.

GALLEGOS, Rómulo
(1884–1969)

Venezualan novelist, born in Caracas. In his country's first democratic elections (1948) Gallegos became President, but his liberalism displeased the military and certain powerful elements in the United States, and he was deposed within a few months. He lived in exile until 1958, when he was welcomed back as an honoured hero. He published a collection of stories in 1913, and in 1920 his first novel, *El último Solar* ('The Last of the Solars'), a lively and pessimistic account of corrupt politicians, failed idealism, and decadent artists. Then in 1929 he published his most famous novel, and the only one to have been translated; *Doña Bárbara* (Eng trans 1931). This is about a barbaric cattle rancher, Doña Bárbara, and her encroachments on the land of her neighbour. This made Gallegos so famous that the dictator, **Goméz**, bribed him with a senate seat—it would have meant death to refuse, so Gallegos accepted, but then used his health as an excuse not to attend sessions of the senate before, in 1931, fleeing Venezuela for a voluntary exile of four years, until Gomez died. He wrote more capable novels, but *Doña Bárbara* remains his greatest.

▷ L Dunham, *Rómulo Gallegos: vida y obra* (1957)

GALLICO, Paul William
(1897–1976)

American novelist and short-story writer, born in New York City. Having graduated from Columbia University, Gallico became a journalist before publishing his first novel, *The Adventures of Hiram Holliday*, in 1939. He is mainly remembered, however, for his shorter works, especially the hugely successful *The Snow Goose*, (1941). Set on the Essex marshes on the eve of Dunkirk, it is the poignant story of a young girl and a lonely, crippled man who care for an injured Canada Goose. Other popular Gallico stories which continue his theme of love and faith, include *The Small Miracle* (1951), and the popular Mrs Harris series, about a redoubtable London char-lady. In 1969 Gallico published *The Poseidon Adventure*, later turned into a successful film.

GALLUS, Gaius Cornelius
(c.70–26 BC)

Roman poet, born in Forum Julii (Fréjus) in Gaul. He lived in Rome and was a friend of **Virgil**. Appointed prefect of Egypt by Augustus, he was recalled and banished, and committed suicide. He was considered the founder of the Roman love elegy, from his four books of elegies upon his mistress 'Lycoris' (in reality the actress Cytheris). Only part of one line of his verse survives.

▷ J P Boucler, *Gaius Cornelius Gallus* (1966)

GALSWORTHY, John
(1867–1933)

English novelist, playwright and winner of the Nobel Prize for literature, born in Coombe, Surrey. Educated at Harrow and New College, Oxford, he was called to the Bar in 1890, but chose to travel and set up as a writer. He met **Joseph Conrad** and they became lifelong friends. He published his first book, a collection of short stories, *From the Four Winds*, in 1897, under the pseudonym John Sinjohn. In 1906 he had a success with his first play, *The Silver Box*, and in the same year published *The Man of Property*, the first in his celebrated *Forsyte Saga* series (the others were *In Chancery*, 1920, and *To Let*, 1921). In these novels is recorded a departed way of life, that of the affluent middle class which ruled England before World War I. The class is criticized on account of its possessiveness, but there is also nostalgia, for Galsworthy, as a man born into that class, could appreciate its virtues. This nostalgia deepens in what was collectively entitled *A Modern Comedy* (1929), which includes *The White Monkey* (1924), *The Silver Spoon* (1926) and *Swan Song* (1928). In this second cycle of the Saga the post-war generation is under scrutiny, but not without the author's appreciation of their plight in an age in which their world had crashed. Among his other novels are *The Island Pharisees* (1904), *The Country House* (1907), *Fraternity* (1909) and

The Patrician (1911). He was also a prolific playwright, and produced more than 30 plays for the London stage. They best illustrate his reforming zeal, and also his sentimentality. *Strife* (1909) shows employers and men locked in a four-month struggle, which ends through the death of the strike-leader's wife. *Justice* (1910) helped to achieve its object of humanizing the penal code. *The Skin Game* (1920) attempts to hold the scales between the aristocratic Mr Hillcrist and the rich parvenu Hornblower, but the latter is so vulgar that sympathies are tipped against him. Technically these plays are first-rate theatre but are marred, especially in the later ones, *A Bit o' Love* (1915) and *Loyalties* (1922), by the parsimony of the language in dialogue which did well enough in the novels but makes the plays appear rather bare. He won the Nobel Prize for literature in 1932.

▷D Holloway, *John Galsworthy* (1968)

GALT, John
(1779–1839)

Scottish novelist and Canadian pioneer, born in Irvine, Ayrshire, the son of a sea-captain. Educated at Greenock Grammar School, he became a junior clerk in a local merchant's firm in 1796. After contributing to local journals, he moved to London in 1804 and set up in business as a merchant. The venture was not a success, and from 1809 to 1811 he travelled for his health's sake in the Levant, where he met **Byron**. On his return he published *Letters from the Levant* and other accounts of his travels. He busied himself in various business posts, and wrote a number of school textbooks under the pseudonym 'Rev T Clark'. He then started to write novels for *Blackwood's Magazine*. *The Ayrshire Legatees* appeared in 1820, followed by *The Steam-Boat* in 1821. Its successor, *The Annals of the Parish* (1821), is his masterpiece, in which the description of events in the life of a parish minister throws interesting light on contemporary social history. He produced in quick succession *Sir Andrew Wylie* (1822), *The Provost* (1822) and *The Entail* (1823). His historical romances were less successful. He went to Canada in 1826, founded the town of Guelph, and played a prominent part in organizing immigration, but returned ruined in 1829, and produced a new novel, *Lawrie Todd* (1830), followed by *The Member* (1832), on corruption in politics. He also wrote a *Life of Byron* (1830) and an autobiography (1834). In his depiction of life in small towns and villages Galt has few rivals. He possesses rich humour, genuine pathos and a rare mastery of Scottish dialect.

▷I Gordon, *John Galt: a life of a writer* (1972)

GÁLVEZ, Manuel
(1887–1962)

Argentinian novelist and poet, born in Paraná into a Spanish family. Educated by Jesuits, he went to Buenos Aires and there founded a literary review and became an inspector of schools. His first books were pallid collections of *modernista* poetry. Like **Maurras**, he was deaf, and also like Maurras, he was politically reactionary—although his Catholicism was genuine, whereas the atheist Frenchman's was political. But he had begun as a socialist, was learned, interested in social issues, and never essentially illiberal—his main fault has been said to lie in his 'religious bigotry'. His master, too, was the liberal **Benito Pérez Galdós**, although his avowed ambition was to achieve for Argentinian society what **Balzac** achieved for French. In his prolific fiction he does not succeed in reconciling the various impulses that move him—naturalist zest, Catholic piety, authoritarian irritability, but he is always interesting. It is to be regretted that his inferior *Miercoles santo* (1930, Eng trans *Holy Wednesday*, 1934) should be available in English but that his tensest and finest novel, *El mal metafísico* (1917, 'Metaphysical Evil'), a psychological study of an unfortunate at odds with society, should not. He wrote a panoramic three-part novel about the war with Paraguay, and a life of Rosas.

GAMA, José Basilio da
(1740–95)

Brazilian poet, born in São José do Rio das Mortes in Minais Gerais province. He became a Jesuit novice, was expelled along with the rest of the Society in 1760, returned to Portugal, and there abandoned it. Pombal, virtual ruler of Portugal, suspected him of Jesuitry, and he therefore incorporated into the epic poem *O Uraguai!* (1769), on the Portuguese–Spanish war against the Native Americans, many attacks on the Jesuits. He was not able to be sincere in his expression, but it seems that his sympathy with the Native Americans was genuine, and that he deserves his reputation of being the first poet to introduce them into Brazilian poetry.

▷D M Driver, *The Indian in Brazilian Literature* (1942)

GAMBOA, Federico
(1864–1939)

Mexican novelist and dramatist, born in Mexico City. One of Mexico's leading naturalists, he began by translating from the French, and thus got to know the novels of **Zola** very well. His earlier fiction was crude and sensationalist, but it became subtler, and *Santa* (1903), 'Saint', although on the almost too well-worn naturalist theme of prostitution, deserved its status as Mexico's first bestseller. He went on to write several more novels and plays of the same type. He is now remembered as a good storyteller rather than as a precursor of the more important novelists of Mexico.

GANIVET, Angel
(1865–98)

Spanish essayist, novelist and thinker. He was almost equal in importance to, but not as well recognized outside his own country as, **Miguel Unamuno** (with whom he had an important and eventually published correspondence) in the formation of the 'Generation of '98'. Ganivet's was a divided personality: on the one hand strict and ethical, on the other adventurously promiscuous. Knowing that he had syphilitic paralysis, he drowned himself in the Dvina in Riga, where he was Spanish consul. His profoundly argued *Idearium español* (1897, Eng trans *Spain: An Interpretation*, 1946), analyses Spain as sick with *aboulia*—lack of will, chronic apathy, fixed ideology. (The term was coined by Unamuno, from whom Ganivet gained much of his inspiration.) His two semi-autobiographical novels, provocative and still neglected outside Spain, are *La conquista del reino de maya por el último conquistador español Pío Cid* (1897, 'The Conquest of Maya's Kingdom by the Last Spanish Conquistador Pío Cid'), and *Los trabajos del indefatigable creador Pío Cid* (1898, 'The Labours of the Indefatigable Creator Pío Cid'). He commented on **Ibsen** and other playwrights, and even wrote an Ibsenite play, *El escultor de su alma* (1904, 'The Sculptor of his Soul').
▷H Ramsden, *Angel Ganivet's 'Idearium español': A Critical Study* (1967)

GANN, Ernest K(ellogg)
(1910–)

American novelist, born in Nebraska, best known as the author of *The High and the Mighty* (1953, screenplay 1954), the story of passengers in a plane set to crash into the Pacific. An earlier novel, *Island in the Sky* (1944), had been about the survivors of a plane crash and, like the better-known book, was made into a film starring John Wayne. Gann's other novels include *Blaze of Noon* (1946) and *Band of Brothers* (1973). He has written the non-fiction *The Black Watch: America's Spy Pilots and their Planes* (1989).
▷*Fate is the Hunter* (1961); *A Hostage to Fortune* (1978)

GAOS, Vicente
(1919–)

Spanish poet and critic. Born in Valencia, he studied philosophy and literature at the University of Madrid, and has spent a substantial amount of time in North American universities teaching Spanish literature. His criticism includes *La poética de Campoamor* (1955, 'The Poetry of Campoamor'), an annotated version of Don Quijote (1967), and *Temas y problemas del la literatura española* (1979, 'Themes and Problems of Spanish Literature'). The 1940s and 50s were his most productive period as a poet: it was then that he wrote *Arcangel de mi noche* (1944), awarded the Adonais Prize, and *Profecia del recuerdo* (1956), considered to be his best collection. Together with **José Luis Hidalgo** and José Hierro, he was a member of the influential group of poets contributing to the poetry journal *Proel* in Santander.

GARBORG, Arne Evenson
(1851–1924)

Norwegian writer, born in Jaeren. He rejected his agricultural background and became a rural schoolmaster, working subsequently as a journalist and junior civil servant. The conflict precipitated his father's suicide. Garborg later lost his government post when he published *Mannfolk* (1886, 'Men'), in which he passionately argued that economic and social pressures drove respectable young Norwegians into the arms of prostitutes. He wrote a cycle of lyric poems, *Haugtussa* (1895, 'The Hill Innocent'), and a series of realistic novels, such as *Bondestudenter* (1883, 'Peasant Students'), *Fred* (1890, 'Peace') and *Traette Maend* (1891, 'Tired Men'). He was a leader in the movement to establish a new Norwegian literary language (*Landsmål*, 'country language') based on western country dialects (later called *Nynorsk*, 'New Norwegian'), and from 1877 edited the periodical *Fedraheimen*, which provided him with a mouthpiece for his lifelong attack on Lutheran theology.
▷R Thesen, *Arne Garborg og det norske folket* (1944)

GARCÍA GUTIÉRREZ, Antonio
(1813–84)

Spanish dramatist, born in Chiclana. He ran away from medical studies to become a soldier. His first success, *El trovador* (1836, 'The Troubadour'), provided Verdi with his opera *Il Trovatore* (1853). His romantic theatre, although there is some deliberately sensational trash in his 50 plays, was, at its best, as in *Juan Lorenzo* (1865), exceedingly skilful, written in a clever mixture of prose and verse, and with sure and unusually acute portrayals of women.
▷N B Adams, *The Romantic Drama of García Gutiérrez* (1922)

GARCÍA LORCA, Federico
(1898–1936)

Spanish poet and playwright, born in Fuente Vaqueros. He was assassinated on the orders of the Nationalist Civil Governor early in the Spanish Civil War at Granada. His gypsy songs, which include *Canciones* (1927, Eng trans 1976) and *Romancero Gitano* (1928 and 1935, Eng trans *Gypsy Ballads*, 1963), probably his best and most widely read poetry, reveal a classical control of imagery, rhythm and emotion. He is best known for his powerful dramatic tragedies, which deal with elemental themes in a striking fashion. The best of these plays are *Bodas de Sangre* (1933, Eng trans *Blood Wedding*, 1947), *Yerma* (1934, Eng trans 1947) and *La Casa de Bernarda Alba* (first performed in 1945, Eng trans *Bernarda Alba*, 1947). The elegiac poems in *Llanto por la meurta de Ignacio Sánchez Mejías* (1935, Eng trans *Lament for the Death of a Bullfighter and Other Poems*, 1937) have been seen as a foreshadowing of his own death.
▷I Gibson, *The Death of Lorca* (1973)

GARCÍA MÁRQUEZ, Gabriel
(1927–)

Colombian novelist, winner of the Nobel Prize for literature, born in Aracataca. Educated at a Jesuit school, he studied law and journalism at the National University of Colombia, Bogotá. He was a journalist from 1950 to 1965, when he devoted himself to writing. One of Latin America's most formative and formidable writers, celebrated for his craft as well as his rhetorical exuberance and fecund imagination, he is a master of 'magic realism', the practice of rendering possible events as if they were wonders and rendering impossible events as if they were commonplace. Spinning from one fantastic, hyperbolic happening to another, his fictions are carried along in a torrent of narrative. *Cien años de soledad* (1967, Eng trans *One Hundred Years of Solitude*, 1970) is the novel by which he is best known in the western world, a vast, referential 'total' novel charting the history of a family, a house, a town, from edenic, mythic genesis through the descent into history of war, politics, and economic exploitation to annihilation at a moment of apocalyptic revelation. It is one of the great novels of the 20th century. Many others have subsequently been translated, including *El otoño del patriarca* (1975, Eng trans *The Autumn of the Patriarch*, 1976), *Crónica de una muerte anunciada* (1981, Eng trans *Chronicle of a Death Foretold*, 1982) and *El amor en los tiempos del coléra* (1985, Eng trans *Love in the Time of Cholera*, 1988). He was awarded the Nobel Prize for literature in 1982.
▷V Llosa, *Gabriel García Márquez, historia de un deicidio* (1971)

GARCIA TERRÉS, Jaime
(1924–)

Minor Mexican poet and critic, who in his collections has adopted a style less indigenous than European. He has been perhaps better known outside Mexico for his left-wing affiliations than for his poetry. His chief volume is *Los reinos combatientes* (1961, 'The Combatant Kingdoms').

GARCILASO DE LA VEGA
(1503–36)

Spanish poet and soldier, born in Toledo. He fought bravely in the wars of Charles V, and died of a wound received near Fréjus. Although he was not a prolific writer, his work is carefully crafted and polished, and his language is impetuous but deeply musical. He introduced the **Petrarch**an sonnet into Spain, and wrote odes in imitation of **Virgil**.
▷D Castanian, *El Inca Garcilaso de la Vega* (1969)

GARDAM, Jane
(1928–)

English novelist and short-story writer, born in Coatham, Yorkshire, who worked as a journalist and editor. Many of her books consider the relation of people to the landscape, and to emotional change. Her novel *God on the Rocks* (1978) is set before World War II in a seaside town in northern England and depicts a young woman growing to maturity. It was shortlisted for the Booker Prize. *Crusoe's Daughter* (1985) surveys the life of Polly Flint in her lonely cottage by the sea from 1904 until the mid-1980s, and is partly a homage to **Defoe**'s *Robinson Crusoe*.

GARDNER, Erle Stanley
(1889–1970)

American crime novelist, born in Malden, Massachusetts. He was educated at Palo Alto High School, California, studied in law offices and was admitted to the Californian Bar, where he became an ingenious lawyer for the defence (1922–38). A hugely prolific writer, he dictated up to six or seven novels simultaneously to a team of secretaries and used a number of pseudonyms. His best-known creation is the lawyer-sleuth Perry Mason, hero of 82 courtroom dramas, who first appeared in *The Case of the Velvet Claws* (1933); subsequent titles used the 'Case of' formula. With a little help from Della Street, his faithful secretary, and private eye Paul Drake, Mason frequently defied the rulebook in his quest to clear his client's name. With the late Raymond Burr playing Perry Mason, the books enjoyed enhanced popularity when they were made into a long-running television series. He also wrote a series of detective novels featuring the District Attorney Doug Selby ('the DA').

▷ A Johnston, *The Case of Erle Stanley Gardner* (1947)

GARDNER, Isabella
(1915–81)

American poet, born in Newton, Massachusetts, who worked in the theatre and published nothing until after her third marriage in 1947. Her husband, whom she divorced 10 years later, encouraged her writing and her first collection, *Birthdays from the Ocean*, appeared in 1955. Other volumes include *The Looking Glass* (1961), *West of Childhood: Poems 1950–65* (1965) and *That Was Then: New and Selected Poems* (1980). The theme of this last book is death, often in tragic circumstances. Yet although her recurring subjects include the failure of love, an underlying resilience and optimism for life pervade the elegiac fabric of her writing. Much admired by **Sylvia Plath**, she was the recipient of the first **Walt Whitman** Citation of Merit in 1981.

▷ J Gould, *Modern American Women Poets* (1984)

GARDNER, John Champlin, Jr
(1933–82)

American novelist and literary theorist. In the 1970s, Gardner engaged in a number of public debates with **William Gass**, in which Gardner bore a standard for literary fiction as a repository for the thoughtful examination and restitution of social values; *On Moral Fiction* (1978) was the most complete statement of his position. This was already evident in his fiction, starting with *Resurrection* (1966), the hefty *Sunlight Dialogues* (1972), the pastoral *Nickel Mountain* (1973), and *October Light* (1976), which had a more sombre quality; nonetheless, 'light' and the idea of enlightenment were the dominant themes of his fiction. His stories were collected in *The King's Indian* (1974). Like his namesake, **John Edmund Gardner**, with whom he was occasionally (and hilariously) confused, he showed an interest in the mentality of evil; *Grendel* (1971) is a remarkable reworking of *Beowulf* from the monster's point of view. This also reflected his academic interest in early English literature, particularly **Chaucer** and the *Gawain* poet. He was killed in a motorcycle accident.

▷ G Morris, *A World of Order and Light: John Gardner's Fiction* (1984)

GARDNER, John Edmund
(1926–)

English crime and espionage novelist. He began with a series of books spoofing imitators of **Ian Fleming**'s James Bond—Gardner described his own series character Boysie Oakes as a 'counter-irritant'—and found himself invited by the Fleming estate to use the Bond name, in such titles as *Licence Renewed* (1981), *For Special Services* (1982) and *Role of Honour* (1984). Oakes had appeared as early as 1964 (within months of Fleming's death) in *The Liquidator*. Though primarily an entertainer, Gardner is deeply interested in the effects of crime: on the victims, on those that seek to protect them, and on the perpetrators. This is behind the Derek Torry books, which began with *A Complete State of Death* (1969, published in the USA as *The Stone Killer*, 1973), and it explains the impulse to bring back Sherlock Holmes's greatest adversary in *The Return of Moriarty* (1974) and *The Revenge of Moriarty* (1975). Unexpectedly, perhaps, Gardner's degree from Cambridge was in theology and for a period in the mid-50s he was in holy orders.

▷ *Spin the Bottle: The Autobiography of an Alcoholic* (1964)

GARFIELD, Leon
(1921–)

English novelist, born in Brighton, the author of adventure novels for children, most of which have 18th-century settings. His first, *Jack Holborn* (1964), was intended for adults but his publisher suggested it should be altered with a younger readership in mind. Its grim, exciting, convoluted narrative is fairly typical of Garfield's novels, the best of which are *Smith* (1967), *Black Jack* (1968) and *John Diamond* (1980), which won the Whitbread Award. A cycle of 12 short novels, *Garfield's Apprentices* (1976–8), skilfully evokes the lives of 18th-century London apprentices. He has successfully adapted **Shakespeare** stories for children and, with Edward Blishen, won the Carnegie Medal for *The God Beneath the Sea* (1970), a retelling of Greek mythology.

GARIOCH, Robert, pseud of **Robert Garioch Sutherland**
(1909–81)

Scottish poet, born in Edinburgh. Educated at the Royal High School, Edinburgh, and Edinburgh University, he spent most of his professional career as a teacher in Scotland and England. He made his literary debut in 1933 with the surrealistic verse play *The Masque of Edinburgh* (published in expanded form in 1954). His first publications, *Seventeen Poems for Sixpence* (1940), in which he collaborated with **Sorley MacLean**, and *Chuckies on the Cairn* (1949), were hand-printed. His later work included *Selected Poems* (1966), *The Big Music* (1971), *Dr Faust in Rose Street* (1973) and *Collected Poems* (1977). He favoured the Scots language, in which he wrote in various styles and moods, from the colloquial to the literary. He translated into Scots works as diverse as **Pindar**, **Hesiod**, **George Buchanan**'s Latin plays *Jeptha* and *Baptistes*, Anglo-Saxon elegies, and the poems of the 19th-century Italian dialect poet Giuseppe Giacchino Belli. His prose works included *Two Men and a Blanket* (1975), an account of his experience in prisoner-of-war camps during World War II. Garioch particularly acknowledged the influence of **Robert Fergusson** on his poetry, perhaps most clearly seen in his sonnet on Fergusson's grave, his *To Robert Fergusson* and *The Muir*.

GARLAND, (Hamilton) Hamlin
(1860–1940)

American writer, born in West Salem, Wisconsin. He often interrupted his schooling to help his father farm in Iowa, but in 1884 went to Boston to teach and finally to write. In short stories such as the collections *Main Travelled Roads* (1887) and *Prairie Folks* (1892), in verse and in novels, he vividly, often grimly, described the farmlife of the Midwest. *Rose of Dutcher's Coolly* (1895) was an important forerunner of the 1920s 'revolt from the village'. *A Daughter of the Middle Border* (1921), the sequel to his autobiographical novel *A Son of the Middle Border* (1917), won the Pulitzer Prize. *Crumbling Idols* (1894) was a collection of essays, setting out Garland's theories of 'veritism'.
▷J Holloway, *Hamlin Garland: a biography* (1960)

GARNER, Alan
(1934–)

English novelist, whose fantasy writing for young readers powerfully blends the mystical and the realistic. Born into a working-class family in Alderley Edge, near Manchester, he left to study classics at Oxford University, but returned to the area to write. Local history, myth and landscape feature strongly in his novels. His first, *The Weirdstone of Brisingamen* (1960), and its sequel, *The Moon of Gomrath* (1963), are ambitious adventure tales where the mythical past intrudes into the lives of two children, Colin and Susan. Garner's subsequent works are emotionally complex and mysterious. *The Owl Service* (1967) won both the Carnegie Medal and the Guardian Award, and *The Stone Book Quartet* (1976–8) is a vibrant celebration of family and heritage told through a day in the life of a child from each of four generations of the Garner family.
▷N Philip, *A Fine Anger. A Critical Introduction to the work of Alan Garner* (1981)

GARNER, Helen
(1942–)

Australian writer, born in Geelong, Victoria, who taught in Melbourne schools until being dismissed for answering frankly her pupils' questions on sex. Her adult fiction appeals strongly to adolescents, today's problems being examined in a clear-sighted and non-judgemental manner. *Monkey Grip* (1977) deals sympathetically with the subculture of drug addiction; it won the National Book Award in the same year and was filmed in 1981. Two novellas, *Honour* and *Other People's Children* (both 1980), handle lightly the interplay of adult characters with the legacy of the 'swinging sixties' in Australia. *The Children's Bach* (1984) is a highly regarded treatment of stress in middle-class suburban family life. *Postcards from Surfers* (1985) is a collection of short stories on disparate themes, but with a pervasive Australian atmosphere.

GARNETT, David
(1892–1981)

English novelist, son of **Edward Garnett**, born in Brighton. He studied botany at the Royal College of Science. His first book, *Lady into Fox* (1922), won both the Hawthornden and the James Tait Black Memorial Prize. *A Man in the Zoo* (1924) and *The Sailor's Return* (1925) were also successful, as were several other novels. Literary adviser to the Nonesuch Press (1923–32) and literary editor of the *New Statesman* (1932–4), he joined the RAF in 1939, and used his experience to write *War in the Air* (1941).
▷*The Golden Echo: memoirs 1892–1914* (1915)

GARNETT, Edward
(1868–1937)

English writer and critic, son of **Richard Garnett**. As a publisher's reader he fostered the careers of many literary figures, including **Joseph Conrad**, **John Galsworthy** and **D H Lawrence**. He was the author of the set of critical essays *Friday Nights* (1922). He also wrote plays, including *The Breaking Point* (1907) and *The Trial of Jeanne d'Arc* (1912). His wife, Constance, née Black (1862–1946), was a distinguished translator of Russian literature.
▷H E Bates, *Edward Garnett* (1950)

GARNETT, Eve
(20th century)

English children's author and illustrator, born in Worcestershire. She studied at the Royal Academy of Art and has combined life as an author with her work as a professional artist, which has included a commission for murals at Children's House, Bow, and an exhibition at the Tate in 1939. Her name as an author rests upon *The Family from One End Street* (1937, Carnegie Medal), one of the first attempts to present working-class family life sympathetically in children's fiction. This book and its sequel, *Further Adventures of the Family from One End Street* (1956), remain popular.
▷ *First Affections* (1982)

GARNETT, Richard
(1835–1906)

English writer and bibliographer, born in Lichfield. He was Keeper of printed books at the British Museum (1890–9), and author of verse, critical works and biographies, including *Shelley* (1862), *Carlyle* (1883) and *The Age of Dryden* (1895). His best-known original work is his collection of tales on pagan themes, *Twilight of the Gods* (1888). His son was **Edward Garnett**.
▷ H Cordier, *Le Docteur Richard Garnett* (1906)

GARNIER, Robert
(1534–90)

French poet and playwright, born in Maine. He was the most distinguished of the predecessors of **Corneille**. His *Oeuvres complètes* (2 vols, 1923, 1949, 'Complete Works') include eight masterly tragedies, of which perhaps the best are *Antigone* (1580) and *Les Juives* (1583, 'The Jewesses').
▷ M Mouflard, *Robert Garnier: 1545–1590* (1961)

GARRETT, George Palmer, Jr
(1929–)

American poet, novelist and author of screenplays, born in Orlando, Florida. His first publication was a collection of poetry, *The Reverend Ghost* (1957), but his best-known work is a novel, *Death of the Fox* (1971). This is not only a historical novel in which the central character is Sir Walter Raleigh, but a meditation on the historical process itself, and is considered by critics to be his finest work. Garrett is a prolific and wide-ranging author whose screenplay credits rather bizarrely include *Frankenstein Meets the Space Monster* (1966).

GARRIGUE, Jean
(1914–72)

American poet, born in Evansville, Indiana. His first volume, *The Ego and the Centaur*, appeared in 1947; other collections include *The Monument Rose* (1953) and *New and Selected Poems* (1967). Garrigue's love and travel poetry in particular have been acclaimed for their technical poise and richness of language. The exuberant, closely observed *A Water Walk by the Villa D'Este* (1959), is considered one of her finest books.
▷ M A Shea (ed), *Jean Garrigue* in *Twentieth Century Literature*, 29 (1983)

GARSHIN, Vsevolod Mikhailovich
(1855–88)

Russian author, born in Bachmut. He wrote short stories, greatly influenced by **Tolstoy**, but without his breadth, including *Krasnyĭ Tsvetok* (1883, 'The Red Flower'), which is set in a lunatic asylum, and *Signal* (1912, 'The Signal'). He served in the Turkish war, and was wounded and invalided home in 1878; his story about a wounded soldier, *Chetyre Dnya* (1877, Eng trans *Four Days*, 1912), was a huge success. His work is narrow but emotionally intense. A melancholic, he eventually committed suicide.
▷ N Byelyaev, *Garshin* (1938)

GARTH, Sir Samuel
(1661–1719)

English physician and poet, born in Bowland Forest, Yorkshire. He was physician in ordinary to George I, and physician-general to the army. A member of the Kit-Cat Club, he is remembered for his burlesque poem, 'The Dispensary' (1699), a satire on uncharitable apothecaries and physicians. 'Claremont' (1715) is a topographical poem in the manner of **Pope**'s 'Windsor Forest'. He also edited a composite translation of **Ovid**'s *Metamorphoses*, published in 1717.
▷ H W Cushing, *Dr Garth the Kit Kat poet, 1661–1718* (1906)

GASCAR, Pierre, pseud of **Pierre Fournier**
(1916–)

French novelist, born in Paris. He found himself imprisoned in a concentration camp in the Ukraine for almost the entire duration of World War II, and the novel he based on this experience, *Le Temps des Morts* ('The Time of the Dead'), won him the Prix **Goncourt** in 1953. The theme of man's potential for cruelty and inhumanity is continued in *Les Bêtes* ('The Beasts'), a collection of short stories published in 1953, and in *La Barre de Corail* (1958, 'The Coral Reef'). He is known particularly for *Le Fugitif* (1961, 'The Fugitive'), set in Germany after the war; other novels include *Les Chimères* (1969, 'The Chimeras'), *L'Arche* (1971), *Dans la forêt humaine* (1976, 'In the Human Forest'), *Le Règne végétal* (1981, 'Vegetable Kingdom') and *Le Fortin* (1983, 'The Fort').

GASCOIGNE, George
(c.1525–1577)

English poet and dramatist, born in Cardington in Bedfordshire. He studied at Trinity College, Cambridge, entered Gray's Inn, wrote poems, and sat in parliament for Bedford (1557–9), but was disinherited for his extravagance. He married **Nicholas Breton**'s widowed mother (to improve his finances), but, still persecuted by creditors, served in Holland under the Prince of Orange (1573–5). Surprised by a Spanish force and taken prisoner, he was detained for four months. He then settled in Walthamstow, where he collected and published his poems. He translated in prose and verse, from Greek, Latin and Italian. *The Complaynt of Phylomene*, a verse narrative in the style of **Ovid**, was begun in 1563. *The Supposes* is from the *I Suppositi* of **Ludovico Ariosto**; *Jocasta* (1566, with Francis Kinwelmersh), practically a translation from Dolce's *Giocasta* (based on the *Phoenissae* of **Euripides**), is the second tragedy in English blank verse; *The Glasse of Government* (1575) is an original comedy. *The Steele Glas* is the earliest blank-verse satire; and in the *Certayne Notes of Instruction on Making of Verse* (1575) there is the first considerable English essay on the subject. To this zealous experimenter English literature owes a deep debt, though much of his work is hopelessly tedious.
▷L T Prouty, *George Gascoigne, Elizabethan Courtier, Soldier and Poet* (1942)

GASCOYNE, David Emery
(1916–)

English poet, born in Harrow and educated at Regent Street Polytechnic, London. He became famous as England's 'only surrealist' at the age of 19. His poems, often dealing with violence, music and night, can be sometimes solipsistically neurotic yet at other times are very much concerned, at least when he was writing in the 30s, with European politics, as in *Roman Balcony* (1932) and *Man's Life is this Meat* (1936). His best work transcends the sloganizing or avant-garde and embraces existential fears of death and loneliness with unusual bravery. A provocative critic in his *Short Survey of Surrealism* (1936), he praises Dada ('a spit in the eye of the world'), Dali, and de Sade ('the first reasoned socialist') and contends that 'the surrealist attitude is totally in accord with … dialectical materialism'. *Poems 1937–42* (1942) and *Night Thoughts* (1956) turn away from Surrealism towards a calmer mood without abandoning much of his earlier substance.
▷M Rémy, *David Gascoyne, ou l'urgence de l'inexprimé* (1984)

GASKELL, Mrs Elizabeth Cleghorn, née Stevenson
(1810–65)

English novelist, born in Cheyne Row, Chelsea, London. Her father was in succession teacher, preacher, farmer, boarding-house keeper, writer and Keeper of the records to the Treasury. She was brought up by an aunt in Knutsford—the Cranford of her stories—and grew up well-adjusted and beautiful. She married in 1832 William Gaskell (1805–84), a Unitarian minister in Manchester. Here she studied working men and women, and made important contributions to what came to be known as the 'Condition of England' novel. In 1848 she published anonymously *Mary Barton*, followed by *The Moorland Cottage* (1850), *Cranford* (1853), *Ruth* (1853), *North and South* (1855), *Round the Sofa* (1859), *Right at Last* (1860), *Sylvia's Lovers* (1863), *Cousin Phillis* (1865) and *Wives and Daughters* (1865). As well as her novels she wrote *The Life of Charlotte Brontë* (1857).
▷M Allott, *Elizabeth Gaskell* (1960)

GASKIN, Catherine Majella Sinclair
(1929–)

Irish writer of historical romances, born in Dundalk. Gaskin grew up in Australia and was educated in Sydney. She published her first two novels, *This Other Eden* (1945) and *With Every Year* (1947), while still in her teens. *Sara Dane* (1955) was her first big success and became a television series. Her books are entertainments, which she thinks 'an honourable enough motive'.

GASS, William H(oward)
(1924–)

American novelist, born in Fargo, North Dakota. He was educated at Ohio Wesleyan University, Delaware, and Cornell University. A philosopher and literary critic, as well as novelist, he derives from and is allied with the *symbolistes*, New Critics and the structuralists. His aesthetic theories are set out in *Fictions and the Figures of Life* (1970) and in subsequent years he engaged in public debate with fellow novelist **John Gardner**, a defender of 'moral fiction'. His novels are *Omensetter's Luck* (1966), and *Willie Masters' Lonesome Wife* (1971), an essay-novella; Gass's stories are collected as *In the Heart of the Heart of the Country* (1968). His massive autobiographical novel, *The Tunnel*, has been in progress for more than 20 years.

▷A Saltzman, *The Fiction of William Gass: The Consolations of Language* (1986)

GATSOS, Nikos
(1915–)

Greek Surrealist poet, author of the celebrated *Amorgas* (1943), which contains the famous line, 'one lost elephant is always worth more than the quivering breasts of a girl'. It has been called the 'most substantial Surrealist poem ever to be written'. The best English translation is to be found in *Six Poets of Modern Greece* (1960).

GATTI, Armand
(1924–)

French playwright, greatly concerned with revolutionary politics. Born to a poor immigrant family, he was deported at the age of 17 to a labour camp in Germany. He later became active in the movement for the decentralization of the theatre in France, but was also concerned with international politics: *Un Homme seul* (1969, 'A Man Alone') is based on an incident in the Chinese civil war, and *La Naissance* ('The Birth') addresses the struggle for independence in Guatemala. Another of his major interests was the creative response of the individual to his or her environment, *Les treize soleils de la rue St-Blaise* ('The Thirteen Suns of St-Blaise Street') being the fruit of an interchange of ideas among members of an audience at the Théâtre de l'Est in Paris.

GATTO, Alfonso
(1909–76)

Italian poet from Salerno, usually classed along with **Quasimodo** and others as 'hermetic' (a term originally employed by the critic Francisco Flora to describe the 'closed' poetry of **Onofri**). His poetry became more open when, after he had served time in prison for his anti-fascist views, he joined the partisans and became a communist (until 1951). His most admired poetry is contained in his collection *La madre e la morte* (1960, 'Mother and Death'): lucid and more accessible than his earlier poetry, these poems are full of pathos and a sense of death. He was killed in a car accident. There are English translations in C L Golino, *Contemporary Italian Poetry* (1962)

GAUNT, Mary
(1861–1942)

Australian traveller and writer, born in Chiltern, Victoria, who later lived in England and Italy. She wrote a considerable number of novels, some set in Australia such as her first, *Dave's Sweetheart* (1894). *Kirkham's Find* (1897) was an early feminist novel; his find is 'pure gold'—the very independent Phoebe. *The Uncounted Cost* (1910) was banned by London circulating libraries because the fallen heroine did *not* pay the price. Other novels, *As the Whirlwind Passeth* (1923) and *Joan of the Pilchard* (1930), have historical backgrounds. Her books achieved wide sales and she indulged her love of sailing and travel; her travel books include *Alone in West Africa* (1912) and *A Woman in China* (1914).

GAUTIER, Théophile
(1811–72)

French poet and novelist, born in Tarbes. From painting he turned to literature, and became an extreme 'romanticist'. In 1830 he published his first long poem, *Albertus*, in 1832 the striking *Comédie de la mort* ('The Comedy of Death'). His poetry reached its height in *Émaux et camées* (1856, 'Enamels and Cameos'). In 1835 appeared his celebrated novel, *Mademoiselle de Maupin*, with its defiant preface. He wrote many other novels and masterly short stories—*Les Jeunes-France* (1833), *Fortunio* (1838), *Une Larme du diable* (1839, 'A Tear from the Devil'), *Militona* (1847), *La Peau de tigre* (1852, 'The Tiger's Skin'), *Jettatura* (1857), *Le Capitaine Fracasse* (1863), *La Belle Jenny* (1865, 'Beautiful Jenny'), *Spirite* (1866), and others. His theatrical criticisms were collected as *L'Histoire de l'art dramatique en France* (1859, 'A History of the Theatre in France'); his articles on the Salon form perhaps the best history of the French art of his day. *Caprices et zigzags* (1852, 'Whims and Zigzags'), *Constantinople* (1853, Eng trans *Constantinople of To-day*, 1854), *Voyage en Russie* (1867, Eng trans *A Winter in Russia*, 1874) and *Voyage en Espagne* (1850, Eng trans *Wanderings in Spain*, 1851) contain delightful travel sketches. Other works were an enlarged edition of his *Émaux et camées* (1872); *Les Grotesques* (1844), on 16th- and 17th-century writers; *Honoré de Balzac* (1858); *Ménagerie intime* (1869), a kind of informal autobiography; *Histoire du romantisme* (1872, 'A History of Romanticism'); and the posthumous works, *Portraits et souvenirs littéraires* (1875, 'Literary Portraits and Recollections') and *L'Orient* (1877). Most of his works were translated in 24 volumes by F C de Sumichrast and Agnes Lee (1900–3). His daughter Judith Gautier (1845–1917) wrote novels, plays, poems and translations.
▷R Grant, *Théophile Gautier* (1975)

GAVIN, Catherine
(1907–)

Scottish novelist, born in Aberdeen and educated at its university, where she lectured in history before working as a war correspondent and then journalist for *Time*. A writer of factually sound historical fiction, she often involves spying and romance in her stories. In the 1930s she twice stood as a Conservative candidate for Parliament, and in her writing shows a devoted fascination for great men, such as Admiral Jellicoe in *The Devil in Harbour* (1968) or Napoleon in *The French Fortune* (1991).

GAWAIN Poet, the
(fl.c.1380)

Anonymous English poet, presumed author of *Cleanness*, *Patience*, *Pearl* and—the Arthurian masterpiece after which he is named—*Sir Gawain and the Green Knight*. All four poems, written in the same north-of-England dialect, are found together in a manuscript dating from around 1200. Each of the shorter poems has an explicitly religious theme: *Cleanness* discusses spiritual purity with reference to several biblical episodes; *Patience* is the retold tale of Jonah and the whale; and *Pearl* is a dream-poem of the afterlife. *Gawain* itself is a richer, longer, less overtly didactic work: the story of one of King **Arthur**'s knights and a threatening stranger who comes to Camelot, it can be read as a straightforward adventure or as a quest for spiritual knowledge; either way it is one of the most remarkable works in the history of English poetry.

GAY, John
(1685–1732)

English poet, born in Barnstaple, Devon, into a prosperous Nonconformist family. Educated at Barnstaple Grammar School, he was apprenticed to a silk-mercer in London, but soon returned home and became a writer. In 1708 he published his first poem, *Wine*, and in 1711 a pamphlet on the *Present State of Wit*. Appointed secretary to the Duchess of Monmouth (1712), in 1713 he dedicated to **Pope** the georgic *Rural Sports*. In 1714 he published *The Fan* and *The Shepherd's Week*, and accompanied Lord Clarendon, envoy to Hanover, as secretary. When the duchess died he wrote a poem on the newly-arrived Princess of Wales. *What d'ye Call It?* (1715) was called 'a tragi-comi-pastoral farce'. *Trivia*, a clever picture of town life, came next; and later he bore the blame of *Three Hours after Marriage* (1717), a play which he had written with Pope and Arbuthnot. In 1720 he published his poems by subscription, clearing £1000; but this and some South Sea stock vanished in the crash of 1720. In 1724 he produced *The Captives*, a tragedy, and in 1727 the first series of his popular *Fables*. But his greatest success was *The Beggar's Opera* (1728), set to music by Pepusch, the outcome of a suggestion made by **Jonathan Swift** in 1716. Its popularity was extraordinary; it ran

62 nights, and by the 36th, Gay had netted over £700; immediately he started on a sequel, *Polly*, which was prohibited, but which in book form brought in £1200. After this he lived chiefly with the Duke and Duchess of Queensberry, the kindest of his many patrons. He wrote another opera, *Achilles* (produced posthumously in 1733). He was buried in Westminster Abbey.
▷P M Sparks, *John Gay* (1965)

GEE, Maggie
(1948–)

English novelist, born in Poole, Dorset. After graduating from Oxford, she was creative writing fellow at the University of East Anglia (1982). Her novels are vividly contemporary and reveal a profound concern for the political and environmental issues of our time. The earlier fiction is experimental and dark: *Dying, In Other Words* (1983) begins with the death of a woman who later becomes the apparent narrator. Both this and *The Burning Book* (1983) are powerful in postnuclear imagery. Although *Light Years* (1985) is apparently more optimistic, in that a disintegrating marriage is repaired, *Grace* (1988) returns to confront the nuclear issue in the accounts of an anti-nuclear campaigner and the detective shadowing her. *Where Are The Snows* (1991) considers obsessive love. In 1994 she published *Lost Children*, about family bonds and the price of secrecy.

GEE, Maurice Gough
(1931–)

New Zealand novelist, born in Whakatane and educated in Auckland. Between 1967 and 1976, the year of his fourth novel *Games of Choice*, he worked as a librarian, writing fiction in his spare time. Thereafter his work gained enormously in sophistication and resonance. *Plumb* (1978), *Meg* (1981) and *Sole Survivor* (1983) all concern the Plumbs, and are extremely perceptive about the tensions and contradictions of family life. Gee's understanding of children is evident in his juvenile writing—*The World Around the Corner* (1980), *The Halfmen of O* (1982), *The Priests of Ferris* (1984) and *Motherstone* (1985)—of which he is a major practitioner, and it carries over into his adult writing in *The Burning Boy* (1990), a haunting study of a brutally scarred youth and the woman who tries to bring him out of his emotional isolation.
▷D Hill, *Introducing Maurice Gee* (1981)

GEIBEL, Emmanuel von
(1815–84)

German poet, born in Lübeck. He studied at Bonn, and was tutor (1838–9) in Athens to the family of the Russian ambassador. He made many translations from the Greek, Spanish and Italian authors, and with **Paul Heyse** founded the Munich school of poetry, which emphasized harmony and form. He also wrote plays in classical form.

▷C L Leimbach, *Emmanuel von Geibel. Des Dichters Leben und Werke* (1877)

GEIJER, Erik Gustav
(1783–1877)

Swedish poet and historian, born in Ransäter in Värmland. He studied at Uppsala and was appointed Professor of History there in 1817. A founder of the Gothic Society and its journal, *Iduna*, in 1811, in which he published much of his best poetry, he had a profound influence on both literature and historiography in Sweden, promoting a Romantic aesthetic. His works included *Impressions of England* (1809–10, Eng trans 1932) and a *History of the Swedish People* (1832–6), both of which are included in *Samlade Skrifter* (13 vols, 1849–82). He was also the first to make a full Swedish translation of a **Shakespeare** play, *Macbeth* (1815).

▷S Stolpe, *Geijer. En essay* (1947)

GELBER, Jack
(1932–)

Controversial American playwright, whose powerful study of drug addiction, *The Connection* (1959), adopted and Americanized devices associated with **Brecht**. Early productions sustained the premise that the 'actors' were actual users, bribed to perform with real doses of heroin. The play also featured live on-stage jazz performances. Perhaps inevitably, nothing else of Gelber's has ever received as much attention. *The Apple* (1961) was thought to be rambling and wordy, a too self-consciously Americanized version of **Luigi Pirandello**'s *Sei personaggi in cerca d'autore*. The later *Square in the Eye* (1965) was quite simply too conventional, a straightforward proscenium piece about a would-be artist. *Rehearsal* (1976) was a partial return to a more experimental mode. Gelber has also written a novel, *On Ice* (1964), which usefully documents the kind of social and artistic context out of which he emerged.

GELLERT, Christian Fürchtegott
(1715–69)

German poet and moralist, born in Hainichen, Saxony. He was educated at Leipzig, and in 1751 became a professor there. He was a prolific writer of stories and fables, and two of his comedies, *Das Los in der Lotterie* (1746, 'The Lottery Ticket') and *Die kranke Frau* (1747, Eng trans *The Sick Wife*, 1928), were popular favourites. His moralistic novel

Leben der schwedischen Gräfin von G- (1747–8, Eng trans *The History of the Swedish Countess of Guildenstern*, 1757) shows the influence of **Samuel Richardson**.

▷L Spriegel, *Der Leipziger Goethe und Gellert* (1934)

GELLHORN, Martha Ellis
(1908–)

American journalist, travel writer and fiction writer. She was born in St Louis, Missouri, and educated at Bryn Mawr College. She became a foreign correspondent for *Collier's Weekly*, covering the Spanish Civil War, the invasion of Finland, and the European theatre in World War II. She almost certainly saw more violent action than her relentlessly macho first husband, **Hemingway**, her marriage to him neatly coinciding (1940–5) with the wider hostilities, and proving appropriately stormy. Her interest in human conflict remained undimmed and she continued to report on wars in Java (1946), Vietnam (1966), the Middle East (1967) and Central America (1983–5). Her earlier reportage was collected in *The Face of War* (1959). Her first novel, *What Mad Pursuit*, had appeared exactly 25 years earlier, followed by others— *A Stricken Field* (1940), *Liano* (1948) and *The Wine of Astonishment* (1948)—which suggested that her instincts were journalistic rather than strictly literary. For that reason, the short stories in *The Trouble I've Seen* (1936), *The Honeyed Peace* (1953), *Two by Two* (1958) and *The Weather in Africa* (1978) are much stronger, marked by acute observation, sympathy for the weak or oppressed and moral straightforwardness.

▷ *Travels with Myself and Another* (1979)

GELLIUS, Aulus
(c.123–c.165)

Latin author, born probably in Rome, where he practised law. He studied philosophy in Athens, and there began to collect the material for *Noctes Atticae* ('Attic Nights'), a collection of dinner-table conversations on literature, history, law, antiquities and miscellaneous subjects. The value of *Noctes Atticae* is chiefly in the numerous quotations it gives from Greek and Roman books which would otherwise be completely unknown.

GEMS, Pam (Iris Pamela)
(1925–)

English dramatist, born in Hampshire. Among her best-known plays are *Piaf* (1978) and *Camille* (1984), portraying women as victims in worlds ruled by men. Although she had written several radio, television scripts and stage plays before the mid-1970s, it was her *Dusa, Stas, Fish and Vi* which brought her widespread recognition when it was staged in London in 1975. A look at the lives of four contemporary women, it was a courageous piece of feminist drama. She also wrote *The Danton Affair* (1986), dealing with the conflict between Danton and Robespierre, and a musical stage adaptation of the 1930 film *The Blue Angel* (1991).

GENET, Jean
(1910–86)
French author, born in Paris. At the age of seven months his mother gave him to the Hospice des Enfants Assistés in Paris and two days later he went to foster parents. He showed a religious temperament as a child and served as an altar boy in the local church, but later turned to crime and spent many years in reformatories and prisons, in France and abroad, for theft, male prostitution, and other crimes. He began to write in 1942 in Fresnes prison where he was serving a life sentence after 10 convictions for theft. His first novel, *Notre-Dame des fleurs* (1944, Eng trans *Our Lady of the Flowers*, 1949), created a sensation. In it he first portrayed his world of homosexuals and criminals, evoking in a characteristically ceremonial and religious language his view of a universe of violence and betrayal, prison and inevitable death. Later novels include *Miracle de la rose* (1946, Eng trans *Miracle of the Rose*, 1965), *Pompes funèbres* (1947, Eng trans *Funeral Rites*, 1969) and *Querelle de Brest* (1947, Eng trans 1966). In 1948 he was granted a pardon by the President after a petition by French intellectuals. The book *Saint Genet* (1952, Eng trans 1963), by **Jean-Paul Sartre**, widened his fame among the French intelligentsia. Several plays, including *Les Bonnes* (1946, Eng trans *The Maids*, 1954), *Les Nègres* (1958, Eng trans *The Blacks*, 1960) and *Les Paravents* (1961, Eng trans *The Screens*, 1962), and poems such as *Les Condamnés à mort* (1942, 'Those Condemned to Death'), *Chants Secrets* (1947, 'Secret Songs') and *La Galère, la parade, un chant d'amour* (1947, 'The Galley-ship, the Parade, the Love Song'), share the criminal underworld setting and profoundly pessimistic outlook of the novels, expressed in ritualistic and mystical style. On release from prison he was associated with revolutionary movements in many countries. He wrote an autobiography, *Le Journal du voleur* (1949, Eng trans *Thief's Journal*, 1954).
▷ Jean-Paul Sartre, *Saint-Genet: actor and martyr* (1963)

GENLIS, Stéphanie Felicité Ducrest de St Aubin, Comtesse de
(1746–1830)
French writer, born in Champcéri near Autun. At the age of 16 she married the Comte de Genlis, and in 1770 was made lady-in-waiting to the Duchess of Chartres, to whose husband, Orléans 'Égalité', she became mistress. She wrote four volumes of short plays entitled *Théâtre d'education* (1779) for her charges, the royal children, including the future King Louis-Philippe, and nearly a hundred volumes of historical romances and 'improving' works. Her *Mémoires* (1825) contain interesting social comments on the period.
▷ J Hammond, *Keeper of Royal Secrets* (1913)

GEORGE, Stefan
(1868–1933)
German poet, born in Büdesheim near Bingen. He edited (1892–1919) *Blätter für die Kunst*, a journal devoted to the work of a group of advanced poets and writers to which he belonged, and wrote lyric verse in *Hymnen* (1890, 'Hymns'), *Der siebente Ring* (1907, 'The Seventh Ring') and *Der Stern des Bundes* (1914, 'The Federal Star'), which shows the influence of the French Symbolists and the English pre-Raphaelites. He also translated the works of **Baudelaire**, **Shakespeare** and **Dante**. His poems, dispensing with punctuation and capitals, are an expression of mood, conveying an impression rather than a meaning. In *Das neue Reich* (1928, 'The New Reich') he advocated a new German culture, not in accord with that of the Nazis.
▷ E K Bennett, *A Critical Study* (1954)

GERARD, Edwin Field, originally Gerhard
(1891–1965)
Australian poet of German extraction, born in Yunta, South Australia, who changed his name at the start of World War I and joined the Australian Imperial Force in 1915. He served at Gallipoli and later in the Middle East; his verses on war themes appeared in such periodicals as the *Bulletin* under the names 'Gerardy' or 'Trooper Gerardy'. These were published as *The Road to Palestine and Other Verses* (1918) and *Australian Light Horse Ballads and Rhymes* (1919). His later ballads, in a nostalgic 19th-century style, have not been published in book form.

GERCHUNOFF, Alberto
(1883–1950)
Argentinian novelist and journalist, born, of Russian Jewish parents, in Proskurov, Ukraine. In 1889 the family moved to Argentina under a scheme devised by Baron Hirsch, a Jewish philanthropist. But Gerchunoff's father was murdered by a drunkard, and he grew up as a 'peasant' in Rajil (Entre Rios), and then as a poor boy in Buenos Aires, doing all kinds of menial jobs. He became editor of

the leading newspaper *La Nación*. Of his many realist novels and collections of sketches, the most famous and important is *Los gauchos judios* (1910, Eng trans *The Jewish Gauchos of the Pampa*, 1955), a vivid picture of the immigrant Jews, based on his time in Rajil. He wrote books on **Heine** and Spinoza.
▷ *Hispanic American Historic Review* (34–5, 1955)

GERHARDIE, or GERHARDI, William Alexander
(1895–1977)
English novelist, born of English parents in St Petersburg, where he was educated. He served in the British Embassy at Petrograd (1917–18), later with the military mission in Siberia, before going to Worcester College, Oxford, where he wrote a lively study of **Anton Chekhov** (1923) and *Futility: A Novel on Russian Themes* (1922). In 1925 came *The Polyglots*, his most celebrated novel, described by **Anthony Powell** as 'outstanding... particularly in the rare gift of making child characters come alive'. Among his later novels only *Of Mortal Love* (1936), a love story blending humour, pathos and tenderness, and admired by **Edwin Muir** and others, stands comparison with his early fiction. *Memoirs of a Polyglot*, his autobiography, was published in 1931, a biographical history of *The Romanoffs* in 1940, and *God's Fifth Column*, an idiosyncratic account of the years 1890–1940, appeared posthumously in 1981.
▷ D Davies, *William Gerhardie: a life* (1990)

GERSHON, Karen, pseud of Karen Lowenthal
(1923–92)
German-born poet, who emigrated to Great Britain in 1938, and went to Israel in 1969. She wrote in English. Her poems first appeared in *Quarto* magazine, a broadsheet edited by **James Reeves**. Her first collection did not appear until 1966, when it attracted some notice for its moving descriptions of her plight as a refugee—her parents died in Hitler's camps.
▷ *Legacies and Encounters: Poems 1966–1971* (1972)

GERSHWIN, Ira *see* RYSKIND, Morrie

GERSTÄCKER, Friedrich
(1816–72)
German writer and traveller, born in Hamburg. He worked his way through the USA, South America, Polynesia and Australia, and wrote colourful adventure stories, collected in *Mississippi-Bilder* (1847, Eng trans *Western Waters*, 1864).
▷ *Gerstaecker's Travels* (1854)

GESSNER, Salomon
(1730–88)
Swiss pastoral poet, who also painted and engraved landscapes, born in Zürich, where he was a bookseller. *Daphnis* (1754), a sentimental bucolic, was followed two years later by a volume of *Idyllen* ('Idylls') and by *Inkel und Yariko* ('Inkel and Yariko'). His *Tod Abels* (1758, 'Abel's Death'), a type of idyllic heroic prose poem, had the greatest success. His landscape paintings are all in the conventional classic style, but his engravings are of real merit. In 1772 he published a second volume of *Idyllen* and a series of letters on landscape painting.
▷ R Zuerchner, *Salmon Gessner, 1730–1788* (1968)

GEZELLE, Guido
(1830–99)
Flemish poet, born in Bruges. Ordained in 1854, he was for 28 years a curé in Courtrai. He published many volumes of lyrical verse, wrote on philology and folklore, founded literary magazines, and is regarded as the founder of the West Flemish school; he inaugurated a revival in the use of Flemish as a literary language.
▷ K de Busschere, *Guido Gezelle* (1959)

GHELDERODE, Michel de, previously Adhemar Martens
(1898–1962)
Belgian dramatist, born in Ixelles. He studied art and music and these interests influenced his writing, as did Flemish folklore and history, in which he was steeped from childhood, the puppet theatre, Elizabethan drama, and Catholic tradition. Although Flemish, he spoke and wrote in French. Between 1927 and 1930 he wrote plays for the Flemish Popular Theatre, including *Barabbas* (1928, Eng trans 1960), which portrays the horror of Christ's last days, and *Pantagleize* (1929, Eng trans 1957), a tragic farce about an absurdly innocent poet. *Fastes d'Enfer* (1929, Eng trans *Chronicles of Hell*, 1960) is one of his grotesque and violent evocations of medieval Flanders, while *Les Aveugles* (1933, Eng trans *The Blind Men*, 1960) is a dramatization of Breughel's satirical painting. A recluse, Ghelderode became internationally famous after controversial productions of his cruel but poetic plays in Paris in the late 1940s.
▷ R Beyen, *Michel de Ghelderode ou la hantise du masque* (1971)

GHIL, René
(1892–1925)
French Symbolist poet, born in Tourcoing in the Flemish part of France. The all-pervading influence upon his verse was that of

Mallarmé, but he evolved his own 'scientific' conception of poetry, explained in *Traité du verbe* (1886, 'Treatise on the Word'), and illustrated it with *Légendes d'âmes et de sang* (1885, 'Legends of Soul and Blood'). He claimed that all words had their analogues in colours and in music. He had a few faithful adherents in his own time, but is now generally regarded as a worthy curiosity who tried but failed to give to poetry the status of a science.
▷ M Raymond, *From Baudelaire to Symbolism* (1950)

GHOSE, Manmohan
(1869–1924)
Indian Anglophone poet, a brother to the underrated mystic **Aurobindo Ghose**, born in Bhagalopore. He was educated in England, and lived there until he was 25. From 1902 until 1921 he was Professor of English at Presidency College, Delhi. He was a friend to **Stephen Phillips** and **Laurence Binyon**, and wrote pleasant Edwardian verse somewhat in the style of the latter, but without its distinction. Collections of his work include two volumes of *Selected Poems* (1969 and 1974).

GHOSE, Sri Aurobindo
(1872–1950)
Indian poet and mystic, almost always known as Aurobindo, who was the most distinguished of all Indians who wrote poetry in the English language. 'He is often', a critic aptly wrote, 'dismissed unread'. He was educated in England, was unjustly imprisoned by the British for 'terrorism', had a vision of Vishnu while incarcerated, went to Pondicherry, founded an *Ashram*, and lived there in meditation for the rest of his life. His enormous verse epic, *Savitri* (final version, 1954), of 24 000 lines, is now hardly read in Great Britain, and even his more modest, and less archaic, *Last Poems* (1952) is hardly known. Yet these last poems, even if they are not in fact 'like the best of 17th-century Metaphysical poetry' (as has been stated), are remarkable. He regarded his philosophy as an expression of original Vedanta, and he has been taken seriously by serious thinkers, though not of the West. His *Letters* (1949) contain stimulating statements about literature.
▷ S Radhakrishnan and C A Moore (eds), *A Source Book in Indian Philosophy* (1957)

GHOSE, Sudhin Nath
(1899–)
Indian Anglophone novelist who has lived in Europe and England. His pleasant, lightweight novels, such as *Cradle of the Clouds*

(1951), render an accurate picture of Calcutta and its surroundings.

GHOSE, Zulfikar
(1935–)
Indian-born American poet and novelist, born in Sialkot (now in Pakistan). He was educated at Keele University and became cricket correspondent of *The Observer* (1960–5), before moving to the USA. The verse in *The Loss of India* (1964) looks back affectionately at the past and peers uncertainly into the future, as does that of *Jets of Orange* (1967), although in the latter volume there is an increasing sense of detachment. His elegant, intellectual, deliberate and meditative style, and the richness of his experience of various cultures, gains even greater authority in such novels as *The Native* (1972), *The Beautiful Empire* (1975) and *A Different World* (1979). Together, these comprise *The Incredible Brazilian* trilogy, a magical realist history of Brazil seen through the eyes of a reincarnated character named Gregorio. Ghose's essays of literary criticism include *The Fiction of Reality* (1984).
▷ *Confessions of a Native-Alien* (1965)

GIACOMO, Salvator di
(1860–1934)
Neapolitan writer. He wrote novels and plays, and songs and lyrics in dialect. He was librarian in the National Library in Naples and also compiled several historical and bibliographical works.
▷ L Russo, *Salvator di Giacomo* (1921)

GIACOSA, Giuseppe
(1847–1906)
Italian dramatist, born in Colleretto-Parella, Piedmont. He was a successful practitioner of various types of play, ranging from historical dramas and comedies in verse to contemporary social problem pieces. Representative of the former are *Il Conte Rosso* (1880, 'Count Rosso') and *La Contessa di Challant* (1891, 'The Countess of Challant'). His social problem plays include *Resa a discrezione* (1888, 'The Surrender of Discretion'), *Tristi amori* (1887, 'Sad Loves'), *Diritti dell' anima* (1894, 'Rights of the Soul'), *Come le foglie* (1900, 'Like the Leaves') and *Il piu forte* (1904, 'The Strongest'). He was not a radical, but emphasized bourgeois ideals of decency, homely virtues and established institutions. Consequently, his plays are not performed in modern repertory, though *Come le foglie*, his best piece, dealing with the disintegration of a wealthy family, has been filmed. With Luigi Illica he also collaborated on the libretti for *La Bohème*, *Madame Butterfly* and *Tosca*.

GIARDINELLI, Mempo
(1947–)

A very influential Argentinian writer, he has written widely across such genres as the crime novel, experimental novel and poetry. He was born in Resistencia, in the province of Chaco, and because of the political situation in Argentina moved to Mexico in 1976, only returning to Argentina after the restoration of democratic government in the 1980s. His novels *El cielo con las manos* (1981, 'Touching the Sky With Your Hands') and *La revolución en bicicleta* (1980, 'The Revolution on Bicycle') are representative of the style of Post-Boom writers; his novel *Luna Caliente* (1989, 'Hot Moon') won the Premio Nacional de Novela in Mexico in 1983.

GIBBON, Lewis Grassic, pseud of James Leslie Mitchell
(1901–35)

Scottish novelist, born on the farm of Hillhead of Seggat, Auchterless, Aberdeenshire. His father was a farmer and he was educated at the local school before attending Mackie Academy, Stonehaven, which he left after a year to become a newspaper reporter. Stirred by the promise of the Russian Revolution he became a member of the Communist Party. In 1919 he moved to Glasgow where he was employed on the *Scottish Farmer*, but his career in journalism was curtailed when he was dismissed for fiddling expenses. He attempted suicide, returned home and decided to enlist. He spent three and a half years with the Royal Army Service Corps in Persia, India and Egypt. In 1923 he left the army but poverty drove him to join up again, this time in the Royal Air Force, where he served as a clerk until 1929. His first published book was *Hanno, or the Future of Exploration* (1928) and others followed rapidly: *Stained Radiance* (1930), *The Thirteenth Disciple* (1931), *Three Go Back* (1932) and *The Lost Trumpet* (1932). *Sunset Song*, his greatest achievement, was published in 1932, the first of his books to appear under his pseudonym. Written in less than two months it was published under his mother's name as the first in a projected trilogy of novels, *A Scots Quair*, on the life of a young girl called Chris Guthrie. The second volume, *Cloud Howe*, appeared in 1933 and the third part, *Grey Granite*, in 1934. An unfinished novel, *The Speak of the Mearns*, was published in 1982. He also wrote a biography of the Scottish explorer, Mungo Park (1934), and published *The Conquest of the Maya* (1934).
▷D Young, *Beyond the Sunset* (1973)

GIBBONS, Stella Dorothea
(1902–89)

English writer, born in London. She worked as a journalist and later began a series of successful novels. She also wrote poetry and short stories, but her reputation rests on *Cold Comfort Farm* (1933), a light-hearted satire on the melodramatic rural novels such as those written by **Mary Webb**, which won the Femina Vie Heureuse Prize, and established itself as a classic of parody.

GIBBS, Wolcott
(1902–58)

American short-story writer and critic, whose most effective device was the ironic squib. He was born in New York City and it is hard to imagine him anywhere else. For much of his career he was closely associated with the *New Yorker* as desk editor and drama critic, and the best of his work is definitive of the magazine's urbane wit and intelligence; his one play, *Season in the Sun* (1950), contains a lively portrait of *New Yorker* editor Harold Ross. Early pieces of writing were collected in *Bed of Neuroses* (1937), which anticipates **Woody Allen**, and which was partly reprinted in a late publication *More in Sorrow* (1958)— a book which summarized Gibbs's lofty tolerance of human frailties.

GIBRAN, or JIBRAN, Kahlil
(1883–1931)

Lebanese mystical writer, poet and artist, born in Bisharri in the Lebanese mountains, but resident, from 1912, in New York. Early on he discovered a spiritual affinity with **William Blake**, especially as expressed in his drawings, and later on with **Nietzsche**'s work. Among his earliest works is *al-Ajnihah al-mutakassirah* (1911, Eng trans *Broken Wings*, 1922), in which he liberated Arabic from its archaic, classical roots and replaced it with the language of nature, allegory, metaphor and symbolism. Best-known for *The Prophet* (1923), written in English, Gibran's books have sold more than 20 million copies worldwide, and his poetry has been translated into more than 20 languages. By writing his later works in English, notably *Jesus the Son of Man* (1928) and *The Garden of the Prophets* (1934), Gibran was assured of a much wider readership and of a place among the great thinkers and artists of his time.
▷M Naimy, *Kahlil Gibran: His Life and His Work* (1965)

GIBSON, Wilfrid Wilson
(1878–1962)

English poet and playwright, born in Hexham. He was educated privately, and from 1902 wrote numerous volumes of verse, starting with *Urlyn the Harper and Other Songs*, on the plight of ordinary people faced with industrial change. Later volumes included *The Island Stag* (1947). He also wrote plays, including *Daily Bread* (1910) and a collection of verse plays, *Within Four Walls* (1950). A realist, he was concerned with everyday matters, particularly industrial poverty.

▷J Gawsworth, *Ten Contemporaries* (1932)

GIBSON, William
(1914–)

American playwright, born in New York. He is best known for *The Miracle Worker* (1960), his play about **Helen Keller**, which began life as a TV script in 1957, and then became the much-watched film (1962), starring Anne Bancroft. Other work includes the two-hander, *Two For The See-saw* (1958), a romantic interlude between a lawyer and a girl suffering from ulcers, and *Golda* (1977), about the Israeli leader, Golda Meir. Gibson will also go on record for having thought up the title *The Butterfingers Angel, Mary and Joseph, Herod the Nut, and the Slaughter of 12 Hit Carols in a Pear Tree* (1975).

GIBSON, William Ford
(1948–)

American science-fiction writer, resident in Canada since 1968. His work is associated with the 'Cyberpunk' genre of contemporary science fiction, generally set in run-down, near-future urban locations where technology defines the environment but is not, as in traditional science fiction, the point of the story. His most successful books are the ground-breaking 'Neuromancer' trilogy, comprising *Neuromancer* (1984), *Count Zero* (1986) and *Mona Lisa Overdrive* (1988), in which the protagonist seeks escape from physical alienation in 'Cyberspace', an infinitely complex virtual reality construction. His other books include the short-story collection *Burning Chrome* (1986) and *Virtual Light* (1993).

GIDE, André Paul Guillaume
(1869–1951)

French novelist, writer, diarist, man of letters and winner of the Nobel Prize for literature, born in Paris. His father, who died when Gide was 11, was Professor of Law at the Sorbonne. An only, lonely child, Gide had an irregular upbringing and was educated in a Protestant secondary school in Paris, and privately. A devotee of literature and music, he embarked on his career by writing essays, then poetry, biography, fiction, drama, criticism, memoirs and translation. He wrote more than 50 books in all, and came to be regarded as the grand old man of French literature. By 1917 he had emerged as the prophet of French youth and his unorthodox views were the subject of much debate. Though he married his cousin in 1892, he was bisexual with a strong physical attraction towards men. His international reputation rests largely on his stylish novels in which there is a sharp conflict between the spiritual and the physical. Significant titles are *L'Immoraliste* (1902, Eng trans *The Immoralist*, 1930), *La Porte étroite* (1909, Eng trans *Strait is the Gate*, 1924), *Les Caves du Vatican* (1914, Eng trans *The Vatican Swindle*, 1925), *La Symphonie Pastorale* (1919, Eng trans *Two Symphonies*, 1931) and *Les Faux-monnayeurs* (1926, Eng trans *The Counterfeiters*, 1927, rev edn 1950, *The Coiners*). He was a founder of the magazine *La Nouvelle Revue Française*, and kept up a voluminous correspondence, as well as being a critic of French bureaucracy at home and in the African colonies. His *Journals*, covering the years from 1889 to 1949, are trenchant, witty and self-revealing, and an essential supplement to his autobiography, *Si le grain ne meurt* (1920–1, Eng trans *If It Die...*, 1935). In 1947 he was awarded the Nobel Prize for literature.

▷G D Painter, *Gide: a critical biography* (1968); R H S Crossman, in *The God That Failed* (1950)

GIJSEN, Marnix, pseud of **Jan-Albert Goris**
(1899–)

Belgian (Flemish) novelist, poet, dramatist and critic, a diplomat by profession, born in Antwerp. For long regarded as the most important living author in the Flemish-Dutch language, he has also written in English and French. He was at one time a delegate to the United Nations, and went on to even greater diplomatic placings; yet his mature writings show no signs of this dual career, and he has referred to himself as the 'Euro-American homunculus'. He retired in 1968. He first emerged as a poet, much influenced by the third phase of German Expressionism; his ironic, elegant fiction began to appear after World War II: *Het boek van Joachim van Babylon* (1947, Eng trans *The Book of Joachim of Babylon*, 1951) and *Klaaglied om Agnes* (1951, Eng trans *Lament for Agnes*, 1957) are the best known. In the first he presents the biblical Susanna as a modern wife; the second is an autobiographical story about the woman whom he loved in his youth. The most revealing book by this interesting and vital confessional writer, a Catholic who turned agnostic in revulsion at the intolerance of his church, is *De leejaren van Jan-Albert Goris* (1975, 'Jan-Albert Goris's Years of Apprenticeship').

▷R P Meijer, *Literature of the Low Countries* (1978); M Gijsen, *Belgian Letters* (1946)

GIL GILBERT, Enrique
(1912–73)

Ecuadorean story writer, novelist and poet, born in Guayaquil, and one of the famous Guayaquil Group. Always fiery, he left school when he quarrelled with his uncle, the headmaster, over his communism, which was to be lifelong. He was a close friend to **Aguilera Malta**. Throughout his life he suffered from persecution from various governments, and an event of 1970, when he was tortured, shortened his life. His manuscripts were burned in the streets and, later, one of his novels was destroyed by sadistic prison guards. He wrote six books of fiction, of which the most famous is *Nuestro Pan* (1941, Eng trans *Our Daily Bread*, 1943), a capable public service novel about the exploitation of rice workers.
▷ *Hispania* (February, 1940)

GIL POLO, Gaspar
(c.1535–1591)

Spanish poet, born in Valencia. He continued **Jorge de Montemayor**'s *Diana* in his *Diana enamorada* (1564, 'Diana in Love'), which was very popular throughout Europe, and was used by both **Cervantes** and **Shakespeare** as a basis for a plot. It marks a stage in the history of the novel.

GIL Y CARRASCO, Enrique
(1815–46)

Spanish poet and major novelist in the tradition of Sir **Walter Scott**, born in Villafranco del Bierzo, Léon. His *El señor de Bembibre* (1844) has been described both as 'the culminating work of the Romantic historical novel, beyond all question', and as 'the best historical novel in [Spanish] literature'. Well documented, it is still much read for its superb descriptions of Gil's native region, as well as for its well-told story of a frustrated love affair. Gil's poetry is seen at its best in his elegy (1842) for his close friend **Espronceda**. Unlike his romantic contemporaries, he excelled in the tender nature lyric ('La violeta', 1839, is one of his most famous poems). He died in Berlin of tuberculosis soon after accepting a diplomatic post there.
▷ D G Samuels, *Enrique Gil y Carrasco: A Study in Spanish Romanticism* (1939)

GILBERT, Kevin
(1933–93)

Australian activist and writer, born in Condoblin, New South Wales, who adopted the culture of his part-aboriginal mother. While serving a life-sentence for murder he learned to read and write, later becoming Australia's first 'aboriginal' playwright. He was paroled in 1971 and in that year his play *The Cherry Pickers* was produced. Two collections of his verse have been published, *End of Dreamtime* (1971) and *People are Legends* (1978).

GILBERT, William
(1804–89)

English novelist, born in Bishopstoke. He abandoned the East India Company's service for the study of surgery, and that in turn for literature. His 30 works, published from 1858 onwards, include the delightful *King George's Middy* (1869), a biography of Lucrezia Borgia, and several **Defoe**-like novels.
▷ *The Doctor of Beauweir: an autobiography* (2 vols, 1869)

GILBERT, Sir William Schwenck
(1836–1911)

English parodist and librettist of the 'Gilbert and Sullivan' light operas, born in London. He studied at King's College, London, and became a clerk in the privy-council office (1857–62). Called to the Bar in 1864, he failed to attract lucrative briefs and made his living from magazine contributions to *Punch* and *Fun*, for which he wrote much humorous verse under his boyhood nickname 'Bab', which was collected in 1869 as the *Bab Ballads*. He also wrote a Christmas burlesque, *Dulcemara, or The Little Duck and The Great Quack* (1866), and *The Palace of Truth* (1870), which both made a hit on the stage, followed by *Pygmalion and Galatea* (1871). But it is as the librettist of Sir Arthur Sullivan's (1842–1900) light operas that he is best remembered. Their famous partnership, begun in 1871, scored its first success with *Trial by Jury* under D'Oyly Carte's able management at the Royalty Theatre, London, in 1875. The same jibing, ludicrously topsy-turvy wit, beautifully accentuated by Sullivan's scores, pervaded the procession of light operas that followed, from *The Sorcerer* (1877), *HMS Pinafore* (1878) and *The Pirates of Penzance* (1879) to *The Gondoliers* (1889) and *The Grand Duke* (1896), which played first at the Opéra Comique and from 1881 in the newly-built Savoy Theatre. It was a carpet in the Savoy, considered too costly by the ever-argumentative Gilbert, that touched off a quarrel between him and Sullivan. They created only three more pieces before Sullivan's death and Edward German's efforts to fill the gap in *Fallen Fairies* (1909) proved unsuccessful.
▷ H Pearson, *Gilbert: his life and strife* (1957)

GILCHRIST, Ellen Louise
(1935–)

American short-story writer and novelist, born in Vicksburg, Mississippi. Her only debt to **Faulkner**, with whom she was (pointlessly)

compared, is that she renders her settings and characters with such unmediated presence as to seem almost possessed by them. Her first collection of stories, *In the Land of Dreamy Dreams* (1981), established her distinctive manner which depends almost entirely on dialogue, with very little linking narrative. *The Annunciation* (1983) was far more discursive, its characters and situations somewhat stereotyped, and suggested that Gilchrist's gift was for the shorter form. Later story collections include *Victory over Japan* (1984, National Book Award), *Drunk with Love* (1986) and *Light Can Be Both Wave and Particle* (1989). A second novel, *The Anna Papers*, also appeared in 1989; three fictions of intermediate length were collected in *I Cannot Get You Close Enough* (1990).
▷ *Falling Through Space* (1988)

GILDER, Richard Watson
(1844–1909)

American editor and poet, born in New Jersey, who was a maker of literary opinion in the last quarter of the 19th century. He was an editor of both *Scribners* and *Century* magazines. His verse, once highly regarded, and his opinions, for all their temporary influence, are now forgotten or abhorred—he once refused to receive **Robert Louis Stevenson** when he was passing through New York, because he had heard (untrue) rumours about his 'private life'. His sister Jeanette (1849–1916) took **Thomas Hardy** to account for obscenity.

GILL, Brendan
(1914–)

American novelist and book reviewer, born in Hartford, Connecticut, who worked for many years on the *New Yorker*, having joined it on graduation (1956) from Yale. He has a light touch, and such novels as his first, *The Trouble of One House* (1950), an unsentimental study of a dying woman, offered sophisticated *New Yorker* readers exactly what they desired. The comic *The Day the Money Stopped* (1957) was adapted by Gill and **Maxwell Anderson** as a successful Broadway play.

GILLETTE, William Hooker
(1853–1937)

American actor and playwright, his most famous role was Sherlock Holmes, in a stage adaptation written in collaboration with **Conan Doyle**. Gillette was born in Hartford, Connecticut, and polished his suave delivery at the Monroe School of Oratory, a branch of Boston University. His first major success

was *The Professor* (1881), which was mounted at Madison Square Garden, and contained the lineaments of his Holmes characterization. The later *Held by the Enemy* (1886) and *Secret Service* (1895) played a significant role in revising and reconciling northern attitudes to the Civil War. Gillette retired after World War I, but cornered the market in lucrative comebacks and revivals. The best of his dramas were collected and edited by Rosemary Cullen and Don Wilmeth (1983) and they stand up surprisingly well.
▷ D Cook, *Sherlock Holmes and Much More* (1970)

GILLIATT, Penelope
(1932–)

English film and theatre critic, novelist and screenwriter, born in London. She has written a handful of novels, including *The Cutting Edge* (1978), which describes the relationship between two brothers, and six collections of short stories, including *Splendid Lives* (1977), a sympathetic study of a fleet of eccentrics. She was nominated for an Oscar for her screenplay for *Sunday Bloody Sunday* (1971), a highly topical piece dealing with the triangular relationship between a middle-aged man and woman and their shared, younger male lover. Her profiles of film-makers, several of which appeared in the *New Yorker*, are considered among the best of their kind.

GILMAN, Caroline Howard
(1794–1888)

American editor, memoirist and poet, born in Massachusetts. She went with her husband, a New England Unitarian minister, to the South, where she wrote a number of accounts of their life there, including *Recollections of a Southern Matron* (1838). From 1832 she edited *The Rose Bud*, one of the first US weekly publications for juveniles. Her *The Poetry of Travelling in the United States* (1838) is remarkable for its reconciliatory attitude and its emphasis on the universally shared and superior (though she does not say so) morality of women.

GILMAN, Charlotte Anna, née Perkins
(1860–1935)

American feminist and writer, born in Hartford, Connecticut. Brought up by her mother, she was educated at Rhode Island School of Design. She married a painter, Charles Stetson, in 1884, but separated in 1888, divorcing in 1894. Moving to California, she published her first stories, most memorably 'The Yellow Wall-Paper' (1892) and a collection of poetry, *In This Our World* (1893). She lectured on women's issues, as well as wider social concerns, and in 1898 wrote *Women and*

Economics, now recognized as a feminist landmark. In 1902 she married her cousin George Gilman, a New York lawyer. She founded, edited and wrote for the journal *Forerunner* (1909–16). Her later works include *The Man-made World* (1911) and *His Religion and Hers* (1923). She commited suicide on being told that she was suffering from incurable cancer.

▷ *The Living of Charlotte Perkins Gilman: An Autobiography* (1935)

GILMORE, Dame Mary Jean
(1865–1962)

Australian poet and author, born in Cotta Walla, near Goulburn, New South Wales. She moved with her family to Wagga Wagga, New South Wales, at the age of 10. Her early teaching career in the mining town of Broken Hill gave her an abiding interest in the labour movement. She became the first woman member of the Australian Workers' Union and, in 1896, joined William Lane's Utopian 'New Australia' settlement in Paraguay, South America. There she met and married a shearer, William Gilmore, and they returned to Australia in 1902, to settle in Sydney from 1912 onwards. Her socialist sympathies were now harnessed to campaigning for the betterment of the sick and the helpless, through the women's column which she edited for over 20 years in the Sydney *Worker* newspaper, but also in her six volumes of poetry. *Marri'd and Other Verses* (1910) was followed by *The Passionate Heart* (1918), *The Wild Swans* (1930) and the radical *Battlefields* (1939). Selected verse was published in 1948 (rev edn 1969) and in her 89th year she published her last collection, the more tranquil *Fourteen Men* (1954). A further *Selected Poems* came out in 1963. Her reminiscences *Old Days: Old Ways* (1934) and *More Recollections* (1935) illustrate her lifelong efforts to preserve early Australian traditions and folklore. She was created DBE in 1937, and William Dobell's controversial portrait of her was unveiled on her 92nd birthday in 1957. A collection of tributes to Dame Mary was published in 1965, and an edition of her letters in 1980.

▷ W H Wilde, *Three Radicals* (1969)

GILROY, Frank D(aniel)
(1925–)

American playwright and writer of screenplays, born in the Bronx. Gilroy's first play, *Who'll Save the Plowboy* (1962), was about a soldier with doubts about the military life, and his second, the Pulitzer Prize-winning *The Subject was Roses* (1964), focused on the conflict between a returning soldier and his Irish–American family. Subsequent Broadway productions were failures and Gilroy has since concentrated on TV and the cinema. *Desperate Characters* (1971), his best screenplay, and directed by Gilroy for his own company, is a well-realized suburban drama based on **Paula Fox**'s novel, and set in New York's east side.

GINSBERG, Allen
(1926–)

American poet, born in Newark, New Jersey. Brought up in a Jewish community, his father was also a poet and his mother was a left-wing Russian emigrant. He was educated at Columbia University. A homosexual and drug experimentalist, he was born of the Beat movement and was friendly with **Jack Kerouac**, **William Burroughs** and others. *Howl and Other Poems* (1956), his first book, was a *succès de scandale*. The title poem was named by Kerouac because it seemed to him to release from some primal level of human consciousness 'the pent-up rage and frustrations of the inner being'. Whether this was so or not, it launched Ginsberg on a high profile career as public performer and icon of the counter-culture. Numerous collections have appeared including *Kaddish and Other Poems* (1961), *The Gates of Wrath: Rhymed Poems, 1948–52*, and *First Blues: Rags & Harmonium Songs 1971–74* (1975). Despite his initial anti-establishment stance, he has won honours and awards. His *Journals* were published in 1977.

▷ E Mottram, *Ginsberg in the 60s* (1972)

GINZBURG, Natalia
(1916–)

Italian author, born in Palermo into a liberal Jewish family who resisted the rise of fascism in the 1930s. Her first husband died in a Nazi prison, and she was forced to leave her home in Turin and live in a small town in the Abruzzi. Her first novel, *La strada che va in città* (1942), was written there and evokes a striking sense of an enclosing environment. Her spare, deceptively simple prose communicates the inarticulacy and emotional deprivation of her female protagonists. Domestic life remains her subject in her more light-hearted family memoir *Lessico famigliare* (1963), which won the Strega Prize, and in her later novels and plays which reveal how the break-up of the restrictive family unit has had little beneficial effect on the female condition.

▷ C S Bowe, 'The Narrative Strategy of Natalia Ginzburg', in *Modern Language Review*, 68 (1973)

GIONO, Jean
(1895–1970)

French novelist, born in Manosque, Provence, where many of his works are set. He fought in World War I and consequently became a pacifist; he was imprisoned for a time at the start of World War II as a result of this stance. The central character of his early works, such as the semi-auto-biographical *Jean le Bleu* (1933), is often a beneficent Nature, to which mere humans are secondary. His later novels, or chroniques, such as *Le Hussard sur le Toit* (1951), express a deepening distaste for the modern world, especially for the urban and the industrial.

GIOVANNI, Nikki, née Yolande Cornelia Giovanni, Jr
(1943–)

American poet, educated at Fisk University, an important location in the development of Black consciousness. Though her earlier work, *Black Judgement, Black Feeling, Black Talk* (both 1968) and *Poem of Angela Yvonne Davis* (1970), was closely associated with the radical and quasi-separatist mood of the 1960s, her later verse became more intro-spective and personal, more akin to the work of **June Jordan** and **Alice Walker**, with whom she conducted a significant debate, published as *A Poetic Equation* (1974). An encounter the year before with **James Baldwin**, *A Dialogue* (1973), was even more influential. Giovanni's more recent collections include the lyrical *Cotton Candy on a Rainy Day* (1978) and *Those Who Ride the Night Winds* (1983). Like Jordan, she has also written successfully for children.
▷*Gemini: An Extended Autobiographical Statement of My First Twenty-Five Years of Being a Black Poet* (1971)

GIPPIUS, or HIPPIUS, Zinaida Nikolayevna
(1869–1945)

Russian poet, novelist and critic (under the names of 'Anton the Extreme', and 'Comrade Herman'), born in Belev, Tula. After she went into exile (1919) she spelled her name 'Hip-pius', and she is sometimes known under it. She was married to **Merezkhovski**, who was more popular in his time, but who was infi-nitely less gifted. It took some time for Gip-pius's very high merits as a poet to become widely acknowledged, since in her capacity as a critic she poured deserved scorn on many now forgotten writers, who nevertheless bequeathed their hatred of her sharp and 'very partisan' pen to others. In fact, Gippius not only played a paramount part in freeing Russian poetry from a prosody it had outworn, but also was one of the best woman poets of the 20th century. She and her husband, weary of the Orthodox Church and its hypocrisy, founded a new mystical faith, a

compound of the ideas of **Dostoyevsky, Solo-viev**, and others. Yet with this apparently out-landish mysticism she combined an extreme wit and a mordant sensibility. She had wel-comed the February Revolution of 1917, but rejected the Bolsheviks on account of their godlessness. Her memoirs *Zhivye litsa* (1925, 'Living Faces') deserve to be read not as eccentric outpourings, but as sober proph-ecies of the fall of Stalinism; even more wis-dom may be gleaned from the English translation of selections from her diaries, *Between Paris and St Petersburg* (1975). But paramount are her pellucid love lyrics and her religious poetry. *Moy lunny drug* (1925, 'My Moonlight Friend') is the most evocative of all portraits of **Blok**. There are English translations of her work in *Selected Works of Zinaida Gippius* (1972) and *Intellect and Ideas in Action: Selected Correspondence* (1972).
▷O Maslenikov, *The Frenzied Poets: Andrey Biely and the Russian Symbolists* (1952); V Zlobin, *A Difficult Soul: Zinaida Gippius* (1980)

GIRALDI, Giambattista, surnamed Cynthius, Cinthio, Centeo, or Cinzio
(1504–73)

Italian writer, born in Ferrara. He was Pro-fessor of Natural Philosophy at Florence and then of *belles lettres*. Later, he held the chair of rhetoric at Pavia. He is the author of nine plays in imitation of **Seneca**, of which *Orbec-che* (1541) is regarded as the first modern tragedy on classical lines to be performed in Italy. His *Ecatommiti* (published in 1565) is a collection of tales that was translated into French and Spanish and gave **Shakespeare** his plots for *Measure for Measure* and *Othello*.
▷P R Horne, *The Tragedies of Giambattista Giraldi* (1962)

GIRARDIN, Delphine de, née Gay
(1804–55)

French writer, born in Aix-la-Chapelle, first wife of Émile de Girardin. A fashionable figure, graced by beauty, charm and wit, she was acclaimed by the outstanding literary men of the period. She contributed *feuilletons* to her husband's paper under the pseudonym of the Vicomte Charles de Launay, elegant sketches of society life, and wrote some poetry, plays and novels, of which *Le Lorg-non* (1831, 'The Eyeglasses') is the best.
▷L Séché, *Muses romantiques* (1910)

GIRAUD, Albert
(1860–1929)

Belgian poet, born in Louvain. He would now be almost unknown had Schönberg not set the lyrics of his *Pierrot Lunaire* (1884) to famous (and once notorious) music. Too artificially haughty to have been a major poet, Giraud's work was well-made and genuinely melancholy, but it is for its style and not its content that it is now read.

▷ R Frickx and M Joiret, *La Poésie française de 1880 à nos jours* (1976)

GIRAUDOUX, (Hippolyte) Jean
(1882–1944)

French writer, born in Bellac in Limousin. After a brilliant academic career and extensive travel, he joined the diplomatic service and became head of the French Ministry of Information during World War II, until his affiliations became suspect. As a poet and novelist, steeped in symbolism, much affected by psychoanalytic theories, he pioneered an Impressionistic technique in literature, exemplified particularly in *Provinciales* (1909), *Simon le Pathétique* (1918), and the reflection of his war experiences, *Retour d'Alsace, août 1914* (1916, 'Return from Alsace in August 1914'). His plays, for which he is chiefly remembered and in which he remains essentially a poet, are mainly fantasies based on Greek myths and biblical lore, satirically treated as commentary on modern life. They include *La Folle de Chaillot* (1945, Eng trans *The Madwoman of Chaillot*, 1949), *La Guerre de Troie n'aura pas Lieu* (1935) and *Pour Lucrèce* (1953). The last two were translated as *Tiger at the Gates* (1955) and *Duel of Angels* (1958) by **Christopher Fry**. He also wrote literary criticism, some short stories, and two film scripts.

▷ L LeSage, *Giraudoux: his life and works* (1959)

GIRONELLA, José María
(1917–92)

Spanish novelist from Girona, in Catalonia, who began as a poet and who tried to emulate **Benito Pérez Galdós**. He was a sturdy, digressive, documentary realist (but critics accused him of lack of impartial documentation), whose tetralogy *Los cipreses creen en Dios* (1953, Eng trans *The Cypresses Believe in God*, 1955), *Un milión de muertos* (1961, Eng trans *One Million Dead*, 1963), *Ha estallado las paz* (1966, Eng trans *Peace After War*, 1969) and *Condenados a vivir* (1971, 'Condemned to Live'), created much controversy owing to its partiality towards the repressive Franco regime (for which, as a young man who had just given up studying for the priesthood, he fought). He took a more liberal approach later in his career, and opposed censorship. But his view of the Civil War is no longer accepted as an adequate one. His account of his grave mental illness of the early

1950s is contained in the selection *Phantoms and Fugitives* (1964).

▷ R Schwartz, *José Maria Gironella* (1972); *Hispania*, 42 (1958)

GIRRI, Alberto
(1919–)

Argentinian poet and translator whose poetry is (notably) composed in European rather than in Latin-American styles. He may be called a 'hermetic' poet, but the general tendency of his work is obvious: its very restraint, elegant and ironic, calls attention to his passionate humanism. His distinguished poems speak for their themes rather than for themselves. There are English translations in the *Penguin Book of Latin American verse* (1971, ed E Curacciolo-Trejo).

GISSING, George Robert
(1857–1903)

English novelist, born in Wakefield, Yorkshire, the son of a pharmacist who imbued him with a love of literature. On his father's death Gissing was sent to boarding school, where he earned a scholarship to Owens College (now the University of Manchester). From there he won another scholarship to the University of London but before he could take it up he became enamoured of Marianne ('Nell') Harrison, thought to have been a prostitute, from whom he contracted venereal disease. Intent on transforming her into a seamstress, he stole from coat-pockets in his college, for which he was sentenced to a month's hard labour and expelled from college. He was packed off to America in disgrace, where he came close to starvation, but while in Chicago he wrote a melodramatic tale of English life which was bought by the *Chicago Tribune*. He subsisted by writing for a spell but he returned to England in 1877, met up again with Harrison in London and started his first novel, *Workers in the Dawn* (1880), which predicts disaster when two such people marry. Ignoring his own sound advice he married Nell in 1879. Doggedly productive, he fed the circulating libraries with three-decker novels which appeared with almost annual regularity: *The Unclassed* (1884), *Isabel Clarendon* (1886), *Demos* (1886), *Thyrza* (1887), *A Life's Morning* (1888) and *The Nether World* (1889), one of the most graphic accounts of Victorian poverty ever written. His industry, however, was not financially rewarding and the couple struggled until Nell died in 1888. Now better off, he travelled on the continent and turned his thoughts to more middle-class matters. The result was his finest fiction: *The Emancipated* (1890), *New Grub Street* (1891), a grim rebuke to all aspiring

authors, *Denzil Quarrier* and *Born in Exile* (both 1892), *The Odd Women* (1893), *In the Year of the Jubilee* (1894), *Eve's Ransom* and *Sleeping Fires* (both 1895), *The Paying Guest* (1896) and *The Whirlpool* (1897). Late in 1890 he met Edith Underwood, of a similar background to Nell, and they married in 1891. They had two sons and many rows and separated in 1897. His latter years were slightly more prosperous and happy than his earlier ones. In Paris in 1898 he met a Frenchwoman, Gabrielle Fleury, with whom he moved to the south of France for the sake of his lungs. He wrote several books in his final five years: a notable critical biography of **Dickens** (1898), a travel book, *By the Ionian Sea* (1900), and *The Private Papers of Henry Ryecroft* (1902), a spoof autobiography that was instantly successful. Few writers have stuck at their vocation with Gissing's single-mindedness. He lacked the sense of humour that made Dickens a favourite but he never shirked from depicting the unpalatable and few have caught so memorably the drudgery of day-to-day existence. His *Commonplace Book* was published in 1962 and *The Diary of George Gissing, Novelist* appeared in 1982.
▷ G Tindall, *The Born Exile* (1974)

GIUSTI, Giuseppe
(1809–50)

Italian poet and political satirist, born near Pistoia. In a brilliant series of elegantly crafted satirical poems he mercilessly denounced the enemies of Italy and the vices of the age. He was elected to the Tuscan chamber of deputies in 1848.
▷ S Horner, *The Tuscan Poet* (1928)

GJELLERUP, Karl Adolph
(1857–1919)

Danish novelist and theologian, born in Roholte, who rather unexpectedly received the 1917 Nobel Prize, which he shared with **Pontoppidan**. His work, influenced by Buddhist philosophy, has failed to last and, as he settled in Germany (1892), may be regarded as more German than Danish.
▷ P A Rosenberg, *Karl Gjellerup, Der Dichte und Denker* (1921–2)

GLANTZ, Margo
(1930–)

Mexican novelist and writer, born in Mexico City. She earned her doctorate in literature at the Sorbonne in Paris. Her interest lies in language and repression, and the role of women in subversion of patriarchy and of language itself. Her most famous work is *Las mil y una calorias* ('The Thousand and One Calories'), which is subtitled 'a dietetic novel'.

GLANVILLE, Brian Lester
(1931–)

English novelist and sportswriter, perhaps best known for his authoritative and intelligent soccer articles in *The Sunday Times*. Glanville published his first novel, *The Reluctant Dictator* (1952), when he was only 21, and has since continued to write underrated fiction, by no means exclusively with sporting backgrounds. Only in *The Dying of the Light* (1976), perhaps his most profound novel, does sport take on a symbolic character; even here, though, it is rendered with convincing detail. The most straightforward of the footballing novels, *The Rise of Gerry Logan* (1963), is probably his best-known book, but it gains much of its power from Glanville's ability to capture the coded language and gesture of distinct social groups, something he has also done to great effect in short-story collections like *The King of Hackney Marshes* (1965) and, with a Jewish central character, in the novel *A Second Home* (1965). Glanville's sports books for young readers have the same uncompromised and uncondescending manner as his adult writing.

GLAPTHORNE, Henry
(1610–c.1644)

English dramatist, born in Whittlesey. Between 1629 and 1643, he wrote a few poems and some plays, including *Albertus Wallenstein; Argalus and Parthenia*, a poetical dramatization of part of the *Arcadia*; *The Hollander* and *Wit in a Constable* (comedies); and *The Ladies Priviledge. The Lady Mother* was also attributed to him.
▷ Memoir by M H Shepherd in *Plays and Poems of Henry Glapthorne* (1874)

GLASGOW, Ellen Anderson Gholson
(1874–1945)

American novelist, born in Richmond, Virginia. She was best known for her stories of the South, including *The Descendant* (1897), *The Voice of the People* (1900), *Virginia* (1913), and *In This Our Life* (1941, Pulitzer Prize). *Barren Ground* (1925) is a more optimistic and progressivist narrative.
▷ L W Wagner, *Ellen Glasgow: beyond convention* (1982)

GLASKIN, Gerald Marcus
(1923–)

Australian writer of novels, short stories and non-fiction, born in Perth. After service in World War II he received attention for his novel *A World of Our Own* (1955) on the problems of ex-servicemen returning to civilian life. Many novels followed, including *A Lion in the Sun* (1960), and a book on

Australia's 'empty north', *The Land that Sleeps* (1961).

GLASPELL, Susan
(1882–1948)

American writer, born in Davenport, Iowa. She was the author of novels, including *Fidelity* (1915), *Brook Evans* (1928) and *The Fugitive's Return* (1929), also of plays, among them *Trifles* (1917) and *Alison's House* (1930), based on the life of **Emily Dickinson**, which won a Pulitzer Prize.

▷A Waterman, *Susan Glaspell* (1966)

GLASSCO, John
(1909–81)

Canadian poet, novelist, translator and editor, born in Montreal. Glassco has probably been most widely read in his capacity as author of the elegant pornographic classic variously known as *The English Governess* (1960), or *Under the Birch*, or *Harriet Marwood, Governess*, which he wrote as 'Miles Underwood', and which is written with great literary panache, humour and irony. But he was a gifted elegiac poet, a fine technician and author of a number of beautiful and deservedly prized poems such as 'Deserted Buildings Under Shefford Mountain'. He translated the *Journal* and the *Complete Poems* of **Hector de Saint-Denys Garneau**. His *Selected Poems* appeared in 1971. His completion of the novel *Under the Hill* by Aubrey Beardsley (1959) was regarded as a brilliant tour de force.

▷*Time* (2 December, 1974); *The Canadian* (21 February, 1976)

GLASSOP, Lawson
(1913–66)

Australian journalist and war correspondent, born in Lawson, Blue Mountains, New South Wales, whose reputation rests solely on his reportage-style novel *We Were the Rats* (1944), which described, in vivid and accurate soldiers' language, episodes of the North African war. It was banned in New South Wales until 1961 when an expurgated edition was published. A sequel, *The Rats in New Guinea* (1963), was less successful. Glassop also wrote a novel and a book for children.

GLATSTEIN, Jacob
(1896–1971)

Polish Yiddish poet and critic, born in Lublin; he emigrated to the USA just before World War I, and died in New York, where he had made his living as a leading Yiddish journalist. He travelled to Warsaw in 1909 to show his work to the master **Peretz**, who endorsed his promise. After he arrived in New York, at the age of 18, Glatstein felt discouraged, and started to write poetry in English. This short period turned out to be a useful one, for he came under the influence of **Tagore**, whose mysticism stayed with him. He then met a number of Yiddish poets, and, together with Nokhem Minkoff (1893–1958) and Aaron Glanz-Leyeles (1889–1966), he established the In Zikh movement—it derived its name from the Yiddish magazine, and meant 'within the self'. It was in part an expressionistic reaction against the dynamic, and more politically oriented, earlier group called Die Yunge ('The Young'). But Glatstein was never dogmatic, and he helped to introduce a carefully cadenced free verse into Yiddish poetry. His own poetry, vital, sharply ironic, true to his inner self, all of it with his personal signature etched into it, is paramount in the Yiddish (and Jewish) poetry of the 20th century. It is to be found in competent translation in *Poems* (1970) and *The Selected Poems of Jacob Glatstein* (1972). Two autobiographical volumes, about his return to Poland in the mid-1930s to see his dying mother, are outstanding: *Ven yash iz geforn* (1938, Eng trans *Homeward Bound*, 1969), and *Ven yash iz gekumen* (1940, Eng trans *Homecoming at Twilight*, 1962).

▷*Commentary* (January 1972); J R Hadda, *Yankev Glatstein* (1980)

GLAZAROVÁ, Jarmila, née Podivinská
(1901–)

Czech novelist, born in Malá Skála. A country doctor's wife, her early novels, already socialist in tone, dealt with the hard lives of the peoples of Moravia and Czech Silesia and, competently if not profoundly, with the problems of women. Later she became the communist government's cultural attaché to Moscow and a member of parliament. Little she wrote after 1948 has any literary value, although *Leningrad* (1950) won a State Prize.

GLEIG, George Robert
(1796–1888)

Scottish novelist and historian, born in Stirling, the son of the Bishop of Brechin. He studied at Glasgow and Balliol College, Oxford, joined the army, and served in the Peninsular War (1813) and in North America (1814). He took orders (1820), and became Chaplain-General of the army (1844) and Inspector-General of military schools (1846). He wrote *The Subaltern* (1825) and other novels, and books on military history and biographies of Wellington and Warren Hastings.

▷W Walker, *Life of George Robert Gleig* (1892)

GLEIM, Johann Wilhelm Ludwig
(1719–1803)

German poet, born in Ermsleben near Halberstadt. He held religious and political offices, and was the leader of the 'Anacreontic' school of lyric poets, celebrating the joys of wine, love and friendship, as in *Lieder* (1745, 'Songs') and *Lieder nach dem Anakreon* (1766, 'Anacreontic Songs'). His patriotic *Lieder eines Preussischen Grenadiers* (1758–78, 'Songs of a Prussian Grenadier') contributed to the war poetry of the age of Frederick II, the Great.

GLEN, Esther
(1881–1940)

New Zealand journalist and writer for children. Aware of the lack, she started writing a children's supplement for the family newspaper, the Christchurch *Sun*, and later for the *Press*. Her first novel for younger readers was *Six Little New Zealanders* (1917), followed by its sequel *Uncles Three at Kamahi* (1926). Although she only wrote four books—the others were *Twinkles on the Mountain* (1920) and *Robin of Maoriland* (1929)—her influence on New Zealand children's writing was considerable, and in 1945 the New Zealand Library Association established the annual Esther Glen Award for distinguished contributions to the genre.

GLEN, William
(1789–1826)

Scottish poet, born in Glasgow. He spent most of his life in the West Indies. His only volume of poems and songs, *Poems Chiefly Lyrical*, published posthumously in 1815, contains the popular Jacobite lament, 'Wae's me for Prince Charlie'.

GLOAG, Julian
(1930–)

English novelist. His first book, *Our Mother's House* (1963), revolving around a clandestinely buried parent, gained wider currency through a film adaptation starring Dirk Bogarde. Gloag's later books were less elegant and original but also more profound. *A Sentence of Life* (1966) is a curiously affirmative murder story, as is *A Woman of Character* (1973), which is notable for its attempt to convey distinctively female concerns. Other novels include *Sleeping Dogs Lie* (1980) and *Blood for Blood* (1985).

GLOVER, Denis James Matthews
(1912–80)

New Zealand poet, publisher and printer of fine books, born in Dunedin. His Caxton Press was established in 1933, and brought out prose and poems from the country's leading contemporary writers. After his return from naval service in World War II, recounted in his book of reminiscences *Hot Water Sailor* (1962), he immediately published **Allen Curnow**'s anthology *A Book of New Zealand Verse 1923–45* (1945), which made an immediate impact on New Zealand writers. His own verse first appeared in *Several Poems* (1936) and *Thirteen Poems* (1939), and is collected in *The Wind and the Sand: Poems 1934–44* (1945), *Enter without Knocking: Selected Poems* (1964, enlarged edn 1971), and *Selected Poems* (1981, with an introduction by Allen Curnow). His wartime experiences are further narrated in *D-Day* (1944).

GLÜCK, Louise Elisabeth
(1943–)

American poet, born and educated in New York. Though her first verses were obviously influenced by **Robert Lowell** and other male poets, she has developed a distinctively female perspective, most noticeably in her reworking of the story of King David's concubine Abishag the Shunamite in *The House on the Marshland* (1975). In the seventies she gradually modulated the staccato contractions of her debut collection *Firstborn* (1968) in favour of more varied and expressive rhythms that sometimes recall **Rilke** and even **Heinrich Heine**. Later collections include *Teh* (1976), *Descending Figure* (1980) and *Ararat* (1990).

GLYN, Elinor, née Sutherland
(1864–1943)

British popular novelist, born in Jersey, Channel Islands. She married in 1892. She began writing with *The Visits of Elizabeth* (1900), but found fame with *Three Weeks* (1907), a book which gained a reputation for being risqué. She kept her public enthralled with such books as *Man and Maid* (1922), *Did She?* (1934) and *The Third Eye* (1940). Nonsensical, faulty in construction and ungrammatical, her novels were nevertheless avidly read. She went to Hollywood (1922–7), where 'it' (her version of sex appeal) was glamorized on the screen.
▷ *Romance Adventure* (1936)

GODBER, John (Harry)
(1956–)

English playwright, born in Upton, Yorkshire. He studied at Bretton Hall College and Leeds University, and worked as a drama teacher, before becoming artistic director of the Hull Truck Theatre Company in 1984. His plays, which are mostly comedies, deal with working-class characters, usually in the contexts of sport, as in *Up 'n' Under* (1984), about Rugby League players, or entertainment, as in *Bouncers* (1984), which is set in a discotheque. *Teechers* (1987) draws on his experience of education. Godber believes strongly in physical theatre, but he also has the ability to convey deep emotion without sentimentality. He has written scripts for popular television programmes such as *Brookside*, as well as the series *The Ritz* (1987).

GODDEN, (Margaret) Rumer
(1907–)

English novelist, poet and children's author, born in Eastbourne, Sussex. She lived for many years in India, a country and culture which provide the backdrop to much of her fiction. Her third novel and first major success, *Black Narcissus* (1939), describes the struggles of nuns attempting to found a mission in the Himalaya region. Her first book for children was *The Dolls' House* (1947). She frequently writes from the point of view of a young person, most notably in *The Greengage Summer* (1958), a delicate story of love and deception set in the Champagne area of the Marne. Highly regarded for the atmospheric lucidity of her prose, Godden's most recent books include *Coromandel Sea Change* (1991), a love story set in southern India.
▷ *A Time to Dance, No Time to Weep* (1987); *A House with Four Rooms* (1989)

GODFREY, Dave
(1938–)

Canadian poet and writer of fiction, born in Toronto. Godfrey has played in a jazz band and worked in university English departments in Ghana and in Canada. His time spent in Africa resulted in *The New Ancestors* (1967), a fictional consideration of the background to the revolution of 1966. Not everyone felt the novel gave a fair picture of politics in Ghana, but it won a Governor General's Award. His earlier collection of short stories, *Death Goes Better with Coca-Cola* (1967), portrayed what Godfrey has described as 'a certain reticence in Canadian society'.
▷ G Gibson, *Eleven Canadian Novelists Interviewed* (1973)

GODWIN, Francis
(1562–1633)

English prelate and author, born in Hannington, Northamptonshire, the son of Bishop Thomas Godwin (1517–90). Educated at Oxford, he became rector of Sampford, Bishop of Llandaff (1601) and of Hereford (1617). His eight works include *A Catalogue of the Bishops of England* (1601), but he is best known for his science-fiction romance, *Man in the Moon or a Voyage Thither, by Domingo Gonsales* (1638), used as a source by Bishop John Wilkins, **Cyrano de Bergerac** and **Jonathan Swift**.

GODWIN, Gail
(1937–)

American novelist and dramatist, born in Alabama. Her first novel was *The Perfectionist* (1970), but her most famous and highly regarded has been *The Odd Woman* (1974), a well-made and suspenseful study of an introspective college instructor who, although intelligent and aware, cannot prevent herself from over-idealism in her affair with an over-cautious academic. *Dream Children* (1976) is a collection of her stories.
▷ A Z Mickelson, *Recent American Fiction by Women* (1979)

GODWIN, William
(1756–1836)

English political writer and novelist. Born at Wisbech, he passed his boyhood at Guestwick in Norfolk. After three years at Hindolveston day school, three more with a tutor at Norwich, and one as usher in his former school, in 1773 he entered Hoxton Presbyterian College; in 1778 he left it as pure a Sandemanian and Tory as he had gone in. But during a five years' ministry at Ware, Stowmarket and Beaconsfield, he turned Socinian and republican, and by 1787 was a 'complete unbeliever'. Meanwhile he had taken up writing. The French Revolution gave him an opening, and his *Enquiry Concerning Political Justice* (1793) brought him fame and a thousand guineas, and captivated **Coleridge**, **Wordsworth**, **Robert Southey**, and later and above all **Shelley**, who became his disciple, son-in-law and subsidizer. It was calmly subversive of everything (law and 'marriage, the worst of all laws'), but it deprecated violence, and was deemed caviare for the multitude, so its author escaped prosecution. His masterpiece, *The Adventures of Caleb Williams* (1794), was designed to give 'a general review of the modes of domestic and unrecorded despotism'; unlike most novels with a purpose, it is really a strong book. In 1797 he married Mary Wollstonecraft, who was pregnant by him; but she died soon after the baby was born. Four years later he married Mrs Clairmont, who had two children already, and a third was born of the marriage. So there were poor Fanny Imlay (1794–1816), who died by her own hand; **Mary Wollstonecraft Shelley** (née Godwin); Charles Clairmont; 'Claire' Clairmont (1797–

1879), the mother by **Byron** of Allegra; and William Godwin (1803–32). A bookselling business long involved Godwin in difficulties, and in 1833 he was glad to accept the sinecure post of yeoman-usher of the Exchequer. His tragedy, *Antonio* (1800), was hopelessly damned. The best of his later prose works are *The Enquirer* (1797) and *St Leon* (1799).
▷F K Brown, *The Life of William Godwin* (1926)

GOES, Albrecht
(1908–)
German poet and novelist, a Lutheran pastor's son, who himself became a pastor (until he resigned from his ministry in 1953 in order to devote his time to writing) and was a chaplain to the army in Russia during World War II. His graceful poetry is in the tradition of his fellow pastor and native of Württemberg, **Eduard Mörike**; but his finest work, praised by **Martin Buber**, is in the harrowing novel *Das Brandopfer* (1954, Eng trans *The Burnt Offering*, 1956), about the humane wife of a butcher who takes over his business when he is called up, and is instructed to supply meat to Jews, who gradually disappear. Goes is an art critic, and was known for many years as a mediator between East and West Germany, and as a broadcaster about Nazi crimes, which he insisted must not be forgotten.
▷E W Rollins and H Zohn (eds), *Men of Dialogue: Martin Buber and Albrecht Goes* (1969)

GOETHE, Johann Wolfgang von
(1749–1832)
German poet, dramatist, scientist and court official, born in Frankfurt-am-Main. He was educated privately and studied reluctantly for his father's profession, law, at Leipzig (1765–8), but a love affair with Käthchen Schönkopf inspired his first two plays, *Die Laune des Verliebten* (1767, 'The Lover's Feelings') and *Die Mitschuldigen* (1769, 'The Guilty Parties'), which was, however, not staged until 1787. After a protracted illness he continued his law studies at Strasbourg from 1770, where he came under the influence of **Johann Herder**, the pioneer of German Romanticism. He read **Oliver Goldsmith**'s *Vicar of Wakefield* and dabbled in alchemy, anatomy and the antiquities. Another love affair, with Friederike Brion, inspired 'Röslein auf der Heide' and several fine lyrics. In 1771 he qualified, returned to Frankfurt, became a newspaper critic and captured the thwarted spirit of German nationalism in that early masterpiece of *Sturm und Drang* drama, *Götz von Berlichingen mit der eisernen Hand* (1772, trans by Sir **Walter Scott** as *Goetz of Berlichingen with the Iron Hand*, 1799), which

in the person of the chivalrous robber-knight whose values had outlived his age, epitomized the man of genius at odds with society. *Faust* was begun, and Goethe followed up his first triumph with his self-revelatory cautionary novel, *Die Leiden des jungen Werthers* (1774, Eng trans *The Sorrows of Werther*, 1780), which mirrored his hopeless affair with Charlotte Buff, a friend's fiancée. Werther is made to solve the problem of clashing obligations by nobly and romantically committing suicide. Goethe himself, however, 'saved himself by flight'. *Clavigo* (1774), a Hamlet-like drama, followed in the same vein, based on **Beaumarchais'** *Mémoires*. Lili Schönemann inspired the love lyrics of 1775. In the autumn he surprisingly accepted the post of court-official and privy councillor (1776) to the young Duke of Weimar. He conscientiously carried out all his state duties, interested himself in a geological survey, and taken in hand, emotionally, by the young widow, Charlotte von Stein, exerted a steadying influence on the inexperienced duke. His 10-year relationship with Charlotte did little to help his development as a creative writer, valuable as his 'anchor' might have seemed to him psychologically. In 1782 he extended his scientific researches to comparative anatomy, discovered the intermaxillary bone in man (1784), and formulated a vertebral theory of the skull. In botany he developed a theory that the leaf represented the characteristic form of which all the other parts of a plant are variations, and made foolish attempts to refute Newton's theory of light. He wrote a novel on theatrical life, *Wilhelm Meisters Theatralische Sendung*, not discovered until 1910 (1911, Eng trans *Wilhelm Meister's Theatrical Mission*, 1913), which contains the enigmatic poetry of Mignon's songs, epitomizing the best in German romantic poetry, including the famous 'Nur wer die Sehnsucht kennt' ('Only He Who Knows Yearning'). His visits to Italy (1786–8 and 1790) cured him of his emotional dependence on Charlotte von Stein and contributed to a greater preoccupation with poetical form, as in the severely classical verse version of his drama, *Iphigenie* (1789, Eng trans *Iphigenia in Tauris*, 1793), and the more modern subjects *Egmont* (1788) and *Tasso Torquato* (1790, Eng trans 1980). His love for classical Italy, coupled with his passion for Christiane Vulpius, whom he married in 1806, found full expression in *Römische Elegien* (1782–9, Eng trans *Roman Elegies*, 1793). From 1794 dates his friendship with **Schiller**, with whom he conducted an interesting correspondence on aesthetics (1794–1805) and carried on a friendly contest in the writing of ballads which resulted on Schiller's part in *Die Glocke* and on Goethe's in the epic idyll *Hermann und*

Dorothea (1798, Eng trans 1801). They wrote against philistinism in the literary magazine *Horen*. Goethe's last great period saw the prototype of the favourite German literary composition, the *Bildungsroman* in *Wilhelm Meisters Lehrjahre* (1795, Eng trans *Wilhelm Meister's Apprenticeship* and *William Meister's Travels*, 1824–7), continued as *Wilhelm Meisters Wanderjahre* (1821). *Wilhelm Meister* became the idol of the German Romantics, of whom Goethe increasingly disapproved. He disliked their enthusiasm for the French Revolution, which he satirized in a number of works, including the epic poem *Reineke Fuchs* (1794, Eng trans *Reynard the Fox*, 1886), based on a medieval theme, and the drama *Die natürliche Tochter* (1803, 'The Natural Daughter'), and their disregard for style, which he attempted to correct by example in his novel *Die Wahlverwandtschaften* (1809, Eng trans *Elective Affinities*, 1960) and the collection of lyrics, inspired by Marianne von Willemer, *Westöstlicher Divan* (1819, 'Western-Eastern Divan'). But his masterpiece is his version of **Christopher Marlowe**'s drama of *Faust*, on which he worked for most of his life. Begun in 1775, its first part was published after much revision and Schiller's advice in 1808 (produced 1819, Eng trans *Faustus*, 1821), and the second part in 1832 (both parts trans 1838). The disillusioned scholar, Faust, deserts his 'ivory tower' to seek happiness in real life, makes a pact with Satan, who brings about the love-affair, seduction and death of Gretchen, an ordinary village girl, and subtly brings Faust by other such escapades to the brink of moral degradation. Part one is generally regarded as one of the classics of world literature. Goethe took little part in the political upheavals of his time. Yet Napoleon made a point of meeting him at the congress of Erfurt (1803), and Goethe in 1813 kept aloof from the *Befreiungskriege* ('Wars of Liberation'), having identified Napoleon with the salvation of European civilization. A towering influence on German literature, Goethe was buried near Schiller in the ducal vault at Weimar.
▷J P Eckermann, *Gespräche mit Goethe* (1836); G H Lewes, *The Life of Goethe* (1906)

GOGARTY, Oliver St John
(1878–1957)

Irish poet and memoir-writer, born in Dublin. Also a playwright, politician and surgeon, this polymath knew **James Joyce** and was the model for 'stately, plump Buck Mulligan' in *Ulysses*. He was a senator of the Irish Free State from its foundation in 1922 until 1939, in which year he moved to the USA. His garrulous, witty prose is at its best in *As I Was Going Down Sackville Street* (1937) and *Tumbling In The Hay* (1939). It is on these volumes, rather than the *Collected Poems* (1952), that his lessened reputation now rests.

GOGOL, Nikolai Vasilievich
(1809–52)

Russian novelist and dramatist, born in Sorochinstsi in Poltava. In 1829 he settled in St Petersburg, and in 1831–2 published his first major work, *Vechera na khutore bliz Dikanki* ('Evenings on a Farm near Dikanka'), followed by two collections of short stories, *Mirgorod* (1835, Eng trans 1928) and *Arabesques* (1835, Eng trans 1982) which contained some of his finest stories, like *Shinel'* ('The Overcoat'), *Nevsky Prospect*, and *Zapiski symashedshevo* ('The Diary of a Madman'), which introduce a nightmarish world of his fantastic imagination, exemplifying his irrational fears, frustrations and obsessions. In 1836 he brought out his play, *Revizor* (Eng trans *The Inspector-General*, 1892), the best of Russian comedies, a wild and boisterous satire exposing the corruption, ignorance and vanity of provincial officials. He left Russia for Italy in 1836, and in Rome wrote the first part of *Myortvye dushi* (1842, Eng trans *Dead Souls*, 1854), one of the great novels in world literature. It deals with an attempt by small landowners to swindle the government by the purchase of dead serfs whose names should have been struck off the register. His later work shows increasing obsession with his own sinfulness and he burnt many of his remaining manuscripts, including the second part of *Myortvye dushi*. He returned to Russia in 1846.
▷H Troyat, *Nikolai Gogol* (1971)

GOLD, Herbert
(1924–)

American novelist, born in Cleveland, Ohio, and educated at Columbia University and at the Sorbonne. Though rarely grouped with them and considered to be a more 'popular', journeyman writer, Gold shares with **Bellow** and **Malamud** a profound concern for the identity problems and cultural expectations of the Jewish American male. Perhaps his most important book is the autobiographical *My Last Two Thousand Years* (1972), which underlines how often he has mined painful personal experience for his novels; *Fathers* (1967) and *Family* (1981) are both subtitled 'a novel in the form of a memoir', recalling **Mailer**'s similar hybrids. Notable among his other novels are *The Prospect Before Us* (1954), *Salt* (1963), *Swiftie the Magician* (1974) and *He/She* (1980), which demonstrates his ability to render convincing female characters.

GOLD, Michael
(1893/4–1967)

American radical novelist, playwright and journalist, he was born Itzok Granich or Granitz—sometimes given as Irwin or Irving—in New York City. He spent a year at New York University and at Harvard, but claimed that his real education had taken place in the slums of the Lower East Side. An early play, *Down the Airshaft* (1916), attempted to capture this environment. He spent two years in Mexico, which sharpened his social conscience and converted him to communism. On his return, he began writing for the left-wing *Liberator*, for which his essay 'Towards Proletarian Art' (February 1921) became one of the defining texts of American proletarianism. In 1926 he co-founded *New Masses*, a descendant of *Liberator* and *Masses*, committed to the aggressive revolutionism of Stalin's 'Third Period'. His journalism was as violent as his politics were apocalyptic; he famously attacked **Hemingway**, whom he considered to be excessively detached from everyday reality, and the popular **Thornton Wilder**, whose work espoused what Gold dubbed 'The Gospel of the Genteel Christ'. Ironically, his own fiction was gentler and almost lyrical; the semi-autobiographical *Jews Without Money* (1930) is centred on an unexpectedly pastoral idyll in Central Park. Gold's sketches of US workers were collected in *120 Million* (1929) and his earlier essays for the *Daily Worker*, with whom he was to be a columnist until shortly before his death, appeared as *The Hollow Men* (1941). Gold's reputation has revived with a fresh interest in American proletarianism.
▷ J Pyros, *Michael Gold: Dean of American Proletarian Writers* (1979)

GOLDBERG, Leah
(1911–70)

Lithuanian poet, critic and university teacher, writing in Hebrew. She settled in Palestine from 1935, and became well known as the translator of classics such as **Tolstoy**'s *War and Peace* into Hebrew. She was one of the most prized of the lyrical poets of Israel, but little of her work has been translated.

GOLDFADEN, Avraham
(1840–1908)

The father of the modern Yiddish theatre, born in the Ukraine. He founded the first modern Yiddish theatre at Jassy, in Romania, in October 1876. Professional to his fingertips—actor, song-writer, producer, manager—he wrote some lively plays, including *The Witch* (1879). His plays are still produced in Hebrew in Israel, and his *Shulamit* (1880) was revived in New York in 1951.
▷ C Madison, *Yiddish Literature* (1968)

GOLDING, Louis
(1895–1958)

English novelist and essayist. His best-known work is *Magnolia Street* (1932), the story of a typical street in a provincial city whose inhabitants were Jews on one side, Gentiles on the other.
▷ *The World I Knew* (1940)

GOLDING, Sir William Gerald
(1911–93)

English novelist and winner of the Nobel Prize for literature, born in St Columb Minor, Cornwall. He was educated at Marlborough Grammar School and Brasenose College, Oxford, where—after first taking examinations in botany, zoology, chemistry and physics—he revolted against science and transferred to English literature, devoting himself to Anglo-Saxon. After five years at Oxford he published his first book, *Poems* (1934), a rarity which he later disowned. He spent the next five years working in small theatre companies, as an actor, director and writer, and in 1958 he adapted the short story 'Envoy Extraordinary' for the stage as *The Brass Butterfly*. He married in 1939 and spent the war years in the Royal Navy. From 1945 to 1961 he was a teacher of English and philosophy at Bishop Wordsworth's School, Salisbury, a career he detested. He gained international celebrity with *The Lord of the Flies* (1954), which has become a classroom classic. A chronicle of the increasingly tribal and primitive activities of a group of schoolboys shipwrecked on a desert island in the wake of a nuclear war, Golding said that it arose from his five years' war service, and 10 years of teaching small boys. *The Inheritors* (1955) was his second novel and in theme and tone it is the blood-brother of its predecessor, human malevolence surfacing through mobatrocity and in the arena of power. Next came *Pincher Martin* (1956), *Free Fall* (1959), *The Spire* (1964) and *The Pyramid* (1967). There was a gap of 12 years before *Darkness Visible* (1979), during which he wrote short stories, a film script and aborted novels. In later years he returned to his old productivity. With *Rites of Passage* (1980), the first of a trilogy about a 19th-century voyage from England to Australia, he won the Booker Prize. *Close Quarter* (1987) was its sequel and the trilogy closed with *Fire Down Below* (1989). His only other novel was *The Paper Men* (1984). In 1983 he was awarded the Nobel Prize for literature.
▷ M K Weeks and I Gregor, *William Golding: a critical study* (1967)

GOLDMAN, William
(1931–)

American novelist and author of film screen-plays, born in Chicago. Since his first novel, *The Temple of Gold* (1957), Goldman has written several books, including *Marathon Man* (1974) and *The Color of Light* (1984), the latter the story of Chubb Fuller and his attempts to be a responsible, honourable man in contemporary society. Goldman, though, is more widely known through his screen-plays, a form of which he is a modern master. *Marathon Man*, the terse, thrilling story of a Nazi who emerges from hiding to claim a cache of diamonds in New York, was mem-orably filmed to his own script in 1976. Other Goldman screenplays include *Butch Cassidy and the Sundance Kid* (1969), *All the Presi-dent's Men* (1976) and *A Bridge Too Far* (1977). He has also written one of the finest memoirs of the film business, *Adventures in the Skin Trade: A Personal View of Hollywood and Screenwriting* (1983).

GOLDONI, Carlo
(1707–93)

Italian dramatist, born in Venice. He studied for the law, but his heart was set on writing plays. A tragedy, *Belisario* (1732), proved a success; but he soon discovered that his forte was comedy, and he decided to write for the Italian comic stage. He spent several years in wandering over north Italy, until in 1740 he settled in his birthplace, where for 20 years he poured out comedy after comedy. He wrote no fewer than 250 plays in Italian, French and the Venetian dialect. He was greatly influenced by **Molière** and the *commedia dell' arte*, although many of his subjects are derived from direct observation of daily life. His best-known plays are *La locandiera* (1753, Eng trans *La Locandiera (The Mistress of the Inn)*, 1912), *I rusteghi* (1760, Eng trans *The Boors*, 1961), which provided the plot for *The School for Fathers* produced in London in 1946, and *Le baruffe chiozzote* (1762, Eng trans *The Squabbles of Chioggia*, 1914). In 1762 he undertook to write for the Italian theatre in Paris, and was attached to the French court until the revolution. He pub-lished his *Mémoires* in 1787 (Eng trans *Memoirs*, 1814).
▷H Taylor, *Goldoni: a biography* (1914)

GOLDSCHMIDT, Meïer Aron
(1819–87)

Danish journalist and novelist, born in Vor-dingborg of Jewish parentage. He founded a satirical periodical, *Corsaren*, in 1840. His best-known novels are *En Jøde* (1845, Eng trans *Bendixen the Jew*, 1852, and as *The Jew of Denmark*, 1952), and *Hjemløs* (1853, Eng trans *Homeless*, 1857). They are acutely psychological and relate characters to social pressures in a distinctively 'modern' way. He also wrote his autobiography (1877).
▷M Brøndstadt, *Meïer Godschmidt* (1965)

GOLDSMITH, Oliver
(?1730–1774)

Irish playwright, novelist and poet, born in Pallasmore, County Longford, Ireland, the son of the curate of Kilkenny West. Educated at local schools and Trinity College, Dublin, he was rejected for the church, and thereupon started for America, but got no farther than Cork. He was next equipped with £50 to study law in London: this disappeared at a Dublin gaming-table. In 1752 he went to Edinburgh to study medicine, and stayed there nearly two years, but was more noted for his social gifts than his professional acquirements. He drifted to Leiden, again lost at play what money he had, and finally set out to make the 'grand tour' on foot, living on his wits and as a flute-playing 'busker', returning penniless in 1756. For a time he practised as a poor physician in Southwark, then was proof-reader to **Richardson**, and next an usher in Dr Milner's 'classical academy' at Peckham. Ralph Griffiths of the *Monthly Review* retained him for a few months and in Feb-ruary 1758 appeared his first definite work, a translation of the Memoirs of Jean Marteilhe, a persecuted French Protestant. He next wrote an *Enquiry into the Present State of Polite Learning in Europe* (1759), which attracted some notice, and better days dawned for Goldsmith. He started and edited a weekly, *The Bee* (1759), and contributed to *The Busy Body* and *The Lady's Magazine*. Then came overtures from **Tobias Smollett** and **John Newbery** the bookseller. For Smol-lett's *British Magazine* he wrote some of his best essays; for Newbery's *Public Ledger* he wrote the *Chinese Letters* (1760–71; repub-lished as *The Citizen of the World*). In 1764 the 'Literary Club' was founded, and he was one of its nine original members. His anony-mous *History of England* was followed by *The Traveller*, a poem which gave him a foremost place among the poets of the day. *The Vicar of Wakefield* (1766) secured his reputation as a novelist. *The Good Natur'd Man*, a comedy (1768), was a moderate success. But he again escaped from enforced compilation of his-tories with his best poetical effort, *The Deserted Village* (1770). Three years after-wards he achieved high dramatic honours with *She Stoops to Conquer*. A year later he died of a fever. He was buried in the Temple Churchyard, and the club erected a monu-ment to him in Westminster Abbey. In the year of his death were published the unfinished rhymed sketches called *Retaliation*, and in 1776 *The Haunch of Venison*.

▷S Gwinn, *Oliver Goldsmith* (1935); G S Rousseau, *Oliver Goldsmith: the critical heritage* (1974)

GOLDSWORTHY, Peter
(1951–)

Australian writer, practitioner in medicine, and amateur of music, which activities all figure in his writing. He was born in Minlaton, South Australia. His short stories are published as *Archipelagoes* (1982), *Zooing* (1986) and *Bleak Rooms* (1988). *Little Deaths*, a novella and nine short stories, was published in 1993. In his first novel, *Maestro* (1989), a Middle European émigré music teacher lives above a down-at-heel hotel in Darwin. A teenage pupil fantasizes about his past, and eventually comes to terms with adult responsibilities. A second novel, *Honk if You are Jesus* (1992), is a sophisticated romp around bio-ethics, *in vitro* fertilization, and American 'god-botherers'. His verse has been published as *Readings from Ecclesiastes* (1982), which won the Commonwealth Poetry Prize, and *This Goes with This* (1988). *This Goes with That: Selected Poems* was published in 1991.

GOLL, Yvan
(1891–1950)

French–German poet, novelist and playwright. Born of Jewish parents in St Dié, Alsace-Lorraine and brought up bilingually, he distinguished himself as a European pacifist. To avoid conscription in Germany, he emigrated to Switzerland in 1914 where he started writing Expressionistic poetry. Disillusioned by the political inefficiency of Expressionism, he returned to France in 1919, where he was among the first to proclaim Surrealism as the poetic mode of the future. His life was overshadowed by exile and emigration, and his poetry haunted by images of homelessness and restless itineration. In his three *Livres de Jean sans Terre* (1936–9), he both celebrates and deplores his personal destiny, using a poetic self-mythicization. Goll's love poetry, mostly written with his wife Claire in the form of poetic dialogues (*Poèmes d'Amour*, 1925; *Poèmes de Jalousie*, 1926; *Poèmes de la Vie at de la Mort*, 1927), expresses his quest for a refuge in poetry, in love, or in the simple physical closeness of lovers. From 1939 to 1947 he lived in New York, then returned to Europe, and began his poetic masterpiece, *Traumkraut* (1951), a volume full of unforgettable images of life and love and death. He died of leukaemia.

▷P G Pouthier, *Yvan à Claire — Yvan an Claire — Yvan to Claire. Studien zur Thematik und Symbolik der 'Clairelyrik' Yvan Golls* (1988)

GOMBROWICZ, Witold
(1904–69)

Polish novelist, one of the major writers in his language this century. He was born in Maloszyce, studied law and economics in Warsaw and Paris, and spent most of his working life as a bank employee in Argentina, where he had gone on a visit on the eve of World War II. Beginning with the short stories in *Pamietnik z okresu dojrzewania* (1933, 'A Recollection of Adolescence'), his work is much concerned with patterns of sexual and psychological dependency, and it is clear from Gombrowicz's journal, published as *Dziennik, 1953–1966* (3 vols, 1957–66), that many of the complexes and inhibitions portrayed are his own. The slightly pathological tone of the early stories largely disappears in his best books, *Ferdydurke* (1937, Eng trans 1961) and *Pornografia* (1960, Eng trans 1966), which sustain a certain ironic distance from their vulnerable characters and claustrophobic situations. *Trans-Atlantyk* (1953) is a more conventional account of the Polish community in Argentina. A collected works, *Dziela zebrane* (11 vols 1969–77) began to appear in the year of his death; the strange *Opetani* (1973, Eng trans *Possessed, or The Secret of Myslotch*, 1980) was published posthumously.

▷E Thompson, *Gombrowicz* (1979)

GOMEZ DE AVELLANEDA Y ARTEAGA, Gertrudis
(1814–73)

Cuban Romantic poet, playwright, and novelist, important for her anti-slavery stance, for her erotic poetry, her prolific theatrical production, and for her early feminism. After being educated by her parents in Cuba, she travelled to Europe in the 1830s. In Spain she was widely praised for her work, and took part in some of the most important literary tertulias (organized literary conversations) of her day. She was nominated to enter the Spanish Royal Academy but was rejected because of her gender.

GÓMEZ DE LA SERNA, Ramón
(1888–1963)

Spanish novelist, biographer, aphorist, critic, humorist and dramatist, born in Madrid—he died in Buenos Aires, where he had fled to escape the barbarities of the 1939 dictatorship. Gómez is an odd man out in Spanish literature: often called 'the Spanish Chesterton', he was even more gifted, and certainly bolder. He is most famous for one of the least important, although always delightful, parts of his work: his invention of the *greguería* (1909), a pithy aphorism which seeks to rearrange petty reality so that it recovers its original lack of triviality, for example, 'Within her wristwatch the time was so tiny that she never had enough of it for anything'. *Some greguerías* (1944) is an English selection from about a score of volumes of these. His way of writing and characterizing people had much in common with that of **Ramón Valle-Inclán** (on whom he wrote a book, 1944): he used the gestures, physical peculiarities and behaviour of his subjects in order to define their essence. He famously achieved this task—always without malice—on behalf of **Wilde**, **George Bernard Shaw**, Goya, El Greco and many others. His fiction has been seriously underrated since his death: in *Rebeca!* (1936, 'Retreat'), he portrays himself in erotic search of a figment of his own invention; recognizing that reality is 'more productive', he marries a Jewish wife—Gómez himself did this. *Cinelandia* (1923, Eng trans *Movieland*, 1930), is one of the funniest novels ever written about the pretensions of Hollywood. The richest work of this now neglected writer is probably *Automoribundia* (1948, 'Auto-deathography'), one of his many auto-biographical works, all of which deal uninhibitedly—and with a candour that shocked his contemporaries—with his inner life.

▷ R Cardona, *Ramón: A Study of Gómez de la Serna and His Works* (1957)

GONÇALVES DIAS, António
(1823–64)

Brazilian poet, dramatist and translator, Brazil's paradigmatic romantic, born in Maranhão. He suffered the unfortunate fate of being drowned within sight of his native town, which contributed to his high reputation. He went to Coimbra to study law, but there became enamoured of poetry, in which he showed great technical skill. His intense patriotism, sympathy with both Native Americans and Blacks—he was himself of Native American and Negro as well as white blood, and could therefore identify with all three races—and ability for direct lyrical expression made him the Brazilian national poet *par excellence*. He was one of the first poets whose so-called 'Indianism' was genuine rather than merely exotic and decorative.

GONCHAROV, Ivan Alexandrovich
(1812–91)

Russian novelist, born in Simbirsk. He graduated from Moscow University (1834), and led an uneventful life in the civil service, punctuated by a trip of Japan, which he described in *Freget Pallada* (1858, Eng trans *The Frigate Pallas: Notes on a Journey*, 1965). He wrote three novels, the most important being *Oblomov* (1857, Eng trans 1915), one of the greatest and most typical works of Russian realism. Neither *Obyknovennaya istoriya* (1847, Eng trans *A Common Story*, 1894) nor *Obryv* (1870, Eng trans *The Precipice*, 1916) attains the same heights.

▷ V Sechkarov, *Ivan Goncharov: his life and works* (1974)

GONCOURT, Edmond de
(1822–96)
GONCOURT, Jules de
(1830–70)

French novelists, born in Nancy and Paris respectively. Primarily artists, in 1849 they travelled across France making watercolour sketches and taking notes of everything they saw. Their important work began when, after collaborating in studies of history and art, especially Japanese art, they turned to writing novels. Their subject was not the passions but the manners of the 19th century, combined with a sense of the enormous influence of environment and habit upon man. The first of their novels, *Les Hommes de Lettres* (1860, 'The Men of Letters'; new edn as *Charles Demailly*, 1868), was followed by *Soeur Philomène* (1861, Eng trans *Sister Philomène*, 1890), *Renée Mauperin* (1864, Eng trans 1864 (US); 1887 (UK)), *Germinie Lacerteux* (1865, Eng trans 1887), *Manette Salomon* (1867), and *Madame Gervaisais* (1869), their greatest novel. After Jules's death, Edmond published the extraordinarily popular *La Fille Élisa* (1878, Eng trans *Elisa*, 1959), *La Faustin* (1882, Eng trans 1902) and *Chérie* (1885, 'Darling'). The interesting *Idées et Sensations* (1866, 'Ideas and Sensations') had already revealed their morbid acuteness of sensation, and *La Maison d'un artiste* (1881, 'An Artist's House') had shown their love for *bric-à-brac*. In the *Lettres de Jules de Goncourt* (1885) and in the *Journal des Goncourt* (9 vols, 1888–96) they revealed their methods and their conception of fiction. Various translations have been made of the de Goncourts' journals and letters, including *The Journal of the De Goncourts* (1908); *Paris Under Siege, 1870–1871* (1969); and *Edmond and Jules de Goncourt, with letters and leaves from their journals* (1894). Edmond, in his will, founded the Académie Goncourt to foster fiction with the annual Prix Goncourt.

▷ R B Grant, *The Goncourt Brothers* (1972); A Billy, *La vie des Frères Goncourt* (1956)

GÓNGORA Y ARGOTE, Don Luis de
(1561–1627)

Spanish lyric poet, born in Córdoba. He studied law, but in 1606 took orders and became a prebendary of Córdoba, and eventually chaplain to Philip III. His earlier writings are elegant and stylish. His later works, consisting for the most part of longer poems, such as *Soledades* (Eng trans *The Solitudes*, 1931), *Polifemo* (Eng trans *Polyphemus and Galatea*, 1977) and *Piramo y Tisbe* ('Pyramus and Thisbe'), are written in an entirely novel style, which his followers designated the *stilo culto*. A major figure in his own day, he had fallen into disregard until the 20th century, but his reputation has been fully restored.

▷D W and V R Foster, *Góngora* (1973)

GONZAGA, Tomás António, pseud Dirceu
(1744–1809)

Portuguese poet, born in Oporto of an English mother and Brazilian father. He studied for the law, and was sent to Vila-Rica in 1782 where he met the 'Marilia' of his verses. He was exiled to Mozambique for his revolutionary activities. There he married a rich mulatta and became a leading citizen of Mozambique. His *Marilia de Dirceu* (1792) contains the best verses in the Arcadian tradition apart from **Manoel Bocage**, and they are considered masterpieces of the Mineiro school.

GONZÁLEZ, Angel
(1925–)

Spanish poet, born in Oviedo. He reached maturity at a time when Spanish poetry was at a low ebb: of the members of the great 'Generation of '27' **Lorca** had been murdered, and the rest were in exile (with the exception of **Aleixandre**, too ill to leave Spain)—of the next generation, **Hernandez**, too, had been killed. Spanish poetry was in a doldrums from which it has by no means yet recovered. Of the younger poets (rather hopefully called the 'Generation of '50'), González is one of the more outstanding and intelligent. As if in reaction to his rich heritage, he wrote deliberately prosaic poetry, saying in effect, 'there is no time for any rich indulgence now'. This was apparent in his first and best collection, *Áspero mundo* (1956, Eng trans *Harsh World*, 1977).

▷E A Llorach, *Angel González, poeta* (1969, in Spanish)

GONZÁLEZ DE ESLAVA, Fernán
(1534–c.1601)

Mexican playwright, born in Spain. He wrote 16 allegorical plays, or *coloquios*, which are of historical importance as demonstrating the sort of drama required by commissioning ecclesiastical authorities to commemorate various events.

GONZÁLEZ MARTÍNEZ, Enrique
(1871–1932)

Major Mexican poet, whose single sonnet, 'Tuércele el cuello al cisne' ('Let us twist this swan's neck'), signalled the end of the Latin-American *modernismo* movement. He was born in Guadalajara, and was by profession a physician, later a diplomat. Himself initially a *modernista* poet, he turned away from the exotic in his later poetry, which has been neglected in favour of his famous sonnet. There are two translations in the *Penguin Book of Latin American Verse* (1971, ed E Curacciolo-Trejo).

GONZÁLES PRADA, Manuel
(1848–1918)

Peruvian poet and social critic, born in Lima, and one of the most powerful influences upon Peru's greatest poet, **César Vallejo**, and also upon the founder of the Peruvian Socialist Party, José Carlos Mariátegui. He succeeded **Ricardo Palma** as Head of the National Library. He was among the first in Peru to emphasize the importance of the Native American, and thus also influenced **José María Arguedas**. He was a noted enemy of the Church and its hierarchy. His poetry, which is important, but much of which appeared posthumously because of his reluctance to publish it, stands somewhat apart from his political activity (with the exception of the anti-clerical *Miniscúlas*, 1901). His manner is *modernista*, but the content of his poems transcends this, reflecting both his extreme originality, his mastery of form, and his essential anarchism.

▷L A Sánchez, *Don Manuel* (1930, in Spanish)

GOODE, Arthur Russell *see* RUSSELL, Arthur

GOODGE, W(illiam) T(homas)
(1862–1909)

English-born Australian writer of humorous verse and tales, born in London. He arrived in Sydney aged 20 and for some years tramped the outback, a period which produced material for yarns and poems which later appeared in the *Bulletin* magazine. His tall tales of the 'Gimcrack Club' and of outback heroes were not collected in book form, but the best of his verse was published as *The Great Australian Adjective* (1965), the title of his most famous poem.

GOODMAN, Paul
(1911–72)

American sociological journalist, poet, fiction writer and libertarian psychoanalyst. He was born and educated in New York. He co-wrote *Communitas* (1947), an influential tract on urban utopics, with his elder brother Percival and developed his very American strain of social anarchism in a later book about *Gestalt*

Therapy (1951). In 1960 he published *Growing Up Absurd*, which argued that US society offered only meretricious consolations and no substantial goals to its youth. The book was an instant success and established Goodman as a beneficent father- (or perhaps uncle-) figure to the youthful subculture of the 1960s. A novel *The Empire City* (1959) gathered themes from both *Communitas* and *Growing Up Absurd*; though it has some features in common with **Tom Wolfe**'s *The Bonfire of the Vanities*, it fatally lacks the wit. Goodman was more comfortable with short fiction, producing three fine volumes: *The Facts of Life* (1945), *The Break-Up of Our Camp* (1949) and *A Visit to Niagara* (1961). His collected stories were published as *Adam and His Works* (1968). *Collected Poems* appeared posthumously in 1974.
▷K Widmer, *Paul Goodman* (1980)

GOODRICH, Frances *see* HACKETT, Albert

GOOGE, Barnabe
(1540–94)

English poet, born in Alvingham in Lincolnshire. He studied both at Cambridge and Oxford, travelled on the Continent, and became one of the gentlemen-pensioners of Queen Elizabeth. His best works are a series of eight *Eclogues, Epytaphes and Sonnets* (1563), which are one of the earliest examples of the pastoral form in English, and his *Cupido Conquered*.

GORBANEVSKAYA, Natalya Evgen'evna
(1936–)

Russian poet. She was born in Moscow and took her degree in Leningrad, having been expelled from Moscow University. A period of hospitalization as a result of acute vertigo attacks prefigured a more sinister committal in a state psychiatric hospital a decade later (1970–2), after she had engaged in anti-Soviet activities, including the founding of a *samizdat* journal and protest against the invasion of Czechoslovakia; the latter event was documented in her book *Polden'* (1970, published in the UK as *Red Square at Noon*, 1972). Shortly after her release she emigrated to France. Gorbanevskaya's work is known in the West through Daniel Weissbort's 1972 translation, which probably contained more of her poems than had been officially published in the Soviet Union up to that time. Her verse is highly musical and lexically playful, to a degree that renders 'translation' problematic. She also uses a rather personal and highly flexible symbolic system in which external states—cold, snow and ice—take on and shed significance with bewildering speed.

Since moving to France, she has edited a new journal, *Kontinent*.

GORDIMER, Nadine
(1923–)

South African novelist, winner of the Nobel Prize for literature, born in Springs, Transvaal. She was educated at a convent school, and at the University of the Witwatersrand, Johannesburg. One of the world's premier novelists in English, her work is rooted in South Africa, where she has continued to live. Her first book was a collecton of short stories, *Face to Face* (1949), followed by another collection, *The Soft Voice of the Serpent* (1952). In 1954 she married, as her second husband, Reinhold Cassirer, a Jewish refugee from Nazi Germany. The previous year she had published her first novel, *The Lying Days*, in which a white girl triumphs over the provincial narrowness and racial bigotry of her parents' mining village existence, though she too has to come to terms with the limitations of her social background. This recurrent theme dominated Gordimer's early books, such as *Occasion for Loving* (1963) and *The Late Bourgeois World* (1966). Apartheid, and her characters' reaction to it, is ever present in her fiction, most powerfully in *The Conservationist* (1974), joint winner of the Booker Prize. Other important titles are *A Guest of Honour* (1970), *Burger's Daughter* (1979), *July's People* (1981) and *A Sport of Nature* (1987), in which a self-possessed white girl is transformed into a political activist intent on returning Africa to the rule of the Africans. Much fêted, she has received many awards, including the Malaparte Prize from Italy, the **Nelly Sachs** Prize from Germany, the Scottish Arts Council's **Neil Gunn** Fellowship and the French international award, the Grand Aigle d'Or. She was awarded the 1991 Nobel Prize for literature.
▷R H Haugh, *Nadine Gordimer* (1974)

GORDON, Adam Lindsay
(1833–70)

Popular Australian poet, born in Fayal in the Azores where his mother's father had a plantation. He completed his education in England but vanished to Australia after a series of reckless adventures and had a brief career in the South Australian Mounted Police. He was a skilled horseman and established a livery stable in Victoria. There he received severe head injuries in a riding accident and then lost his money when the stable burned down. The subsequent death of his infant daughter precipitated a mental breakdown and his suicide. He is remembered for ballads that reflect his interest in horses: 'The Sick Stockrider', 'How We Beat the Favourite' and 'The Ride From the Wreck'. Much of his best work is collected in *Sea Spray and Smoke Drift* (1867, reissued 1876 with preface by **Marcus Clarke**) and *Bush Ballads and Galloping Rhymes* (1870). He is the only Australian poet honoured in the Poets' Corner of Westminster Abbey. His poem 'The Swimmer', with its undertones of suicide, was set as the last song in Elgar's *Sea Pictures*.

GORDON, Caroline
(1895–1981)

American novelist, born in Todd County, Kentucky and educated at Bethany College. She worked as a high school teacher and a reporter as well as a literary critic—her support for the New Criticism school of thought is reflected in her *How to Read a Novel* (1957). The agrarian Old South provides the backdrop for most of her novels: her first, *Penhally* (1931), set on a Kentucky plantation, was closely followed by *Alek Maury, Sportsman* (1934), and *None Shall Look Back* (1937), a fictionalized account of a confederate general's life. In 1947 she converted to Catholicism, which increasingly influenced her later work.
▷ Caroline Gordon issue of *Southern Quarterly* (Spring 1990)

GORDON, Giles Alexander Esme
(1940–)

British short-story writer, novelist and literary agent. He was born and educated in Edinburgh, and worked in publishing for a decade (1962–72), before becoming one of the most respected literary agents on the London scene. His first collection of short stories, *Pictures from an Exhibition*, appeared in 1970 and his first novel, *The Umbrella Man*, in 1971, and he continued to produce high-quality fiction throughout the seventies. Among his most ambitious works are *About a Marriage* (1972) and *100 Scenes from Married Life* (1976), both of which concern a couple whose ups and downs are presented in the manner of a British **Updike**. The essay *Book 2000: Some Likely Trends in Publishing* (1969) is mostly prescient, but his backing for the strand of 'experimental fiction' represented by the late **B S Johnson** has turned out to be one of his less successful bets. In 1993, he published a name-dropping but engaging volume of memoirs, *Aren't We Due a Royalty Statement?*

GORDON, Mary Catherine
(1949–)

American novelist, born in Long Island, New York, and educated at Barnard College and Syracuse University. She worked as a teacher in a community college and as a lecturer at Amherst College. Her work is strongly influenced by both her feminism and her Catholicism. Her first novel, *Final Payments* (1978), presents a protagonist who accepts the role of caring for her bedridden father, and finds herself both liberated and frightened by his death. Gordon has to date written four novels, two collections of short stories, and a book of essays, in addition to various uncollected fiction, and has twice received the Janet Kafka Prize (1979 and 1982).
▷ D Cooper-Clark (ed), *Interviews with Contemporary Novelists* (1986)

GORDON, Yehudah Leib
(1830–92)

Hebrew poet, novelist, translator (**Byron** and others) and essayist, born in Vilna, who wrote under his initials, YLB. He was the leading poet of the Haskalah movement ('the Enlightenment': the effort of Jews, in the late 18th and 19th centuries, to acquire European culture). He was the most popular Jewish poet of his time. His poetry on biblical themes influenced the entire course of Jewish poetry. He was imprisoned by the Russians, and contracted an illness from which he died prematurely.
▷ A B Rhine, *Leon Gordon* (1920)

GORDONE, Charles
(1926–)

American playwright, born in Cleveland and brought up in Indiana. He was the first black playwright to win a Pulitzer Prize, for *No Place To Be Somebody* (1969), subtitled 'A Black-Black Comedy', a play in three acts about a black criminal dealing in an underworld dominated by whites. As an actor Gordone starred in his own one-man miscellany, *Gordone Is Muthah* (1970), and has been active in support of the employment of black actors.

GORE, Catherine Grace Frances, née Moody
(1799–1861)

English novelist, born in East Retford, Nottinghamshire. She was a prolific and immensely popular writer of novels, mainly of fashionable life in the manner of the 'silver fork' school. They include *Mothers and Daughters* (1831), *Mrs Armytage* (1836) and *The Banker's Wife* (1843). She also wrote three plays, and short stories.

GORKY, Maxim, pseud of Aleksei Maksimovich Peshkov
(1868–1936)

Russian novelist, born in Nizhniy Novgorod. He was successively pedlar, scullery boy, gardener, dock hand, tramp and writer, a restless nomadic life he described brilliantly in his

autobiographical trilogy, *Detstvo* (1913–14, Eng trans *My Childhood*, 1915), *V lyudakh* (1915–16, Eng trans *In the World*, 1918) and *Moi universitety* (1922, Eng trans *My University Days*, 1923). He first achieved fame with his story *Chelkash* (1895), followed by others in a romantic vein, glorifying the unusual, with vividly drawn characters, mostly tramps and down-and-outs. *Foma Gordeyev* (1899, Eng trans 1902) marks his transition from romanticism to realism. In 1902 he produced his best-known play, *Na dne* (Eng trans *A Night's Lodging*, 1905; better known as *The Lower Depths*, 1912). Involved in strikes and imprisoned in 1905, he lived abroad until 1914 and then engaged in revolutionary propaganda. From 1922 to 1928 he lived abroad again on account of his health, but then returned, a whole-hearted supporter of the Soviet regime. He sponsored 'social realism' as the official school in Soviet literature and art.
▷ R Hare, *Maxim Gorky, romantic realist and conservative revolutionary* (1962); Dan Levin, *The Stormy Petrel: the life and work of Maxim Gorky* (1965)

GOROSTIZA, José
(1901–79)

Major Mexican poet, born in Villahermosa, Tabasco. Writing in the metaphysical tradition established by **Sor Juana Inés de la Cruz**, as well as in that of European poets such as **Valéry**, Gorostiza was the leading member of the group which published in the magazine *Contemporáneos* (1928–31), an avant-garde vehicle which reflected the nihilistic themes then being pursued in European, especially French, poetry. He has written comparatively little, but nonetheless has the reputation of being the most distinguished 'philosophical' poet of modern Mexico; often called a 'nihilist', it is more true to say that he explores reality from an initially nihilist point of view. His masterpiece, *Muerte sin fin* (1929, 'Death Without End'), 'the most important Mexican poem to appear up to that time', is a lyrical meditation on the question of God or Nothingness.

GÖRRES, Johann Joseph von
(1776–1848)

German writer, born in Koblenz. In 1812 Koblenz became the literary centre of the national movement. Denouncing absolutism with great vigour, he angered the Prussian government, and had to flee the country (1820). In 1827 he was made Professor of Literature at Munich, where he devoted himself to literature and controversial theology. His chief work was his *Christliche Mystik* (1842, 'Christian Mysticism').
▷ J N Sepp, *Görres* (1873)

GORTER, Herman
(1864–1927)

Dutch poet, born in Wormerveer, the son of a prominent journalist. He was an important figure in modern Dutch literature. His lushly **Keats**ian poem *Mei* (1889, 'May'), influenced by the Persephone of **Albert Verwey**, as well as by the work of **Willem Kloos** and Jacques Perk, was taken as a final model, by the so-called 'Men of the Eighties', of what the new poetry should be. In the next decade Gorter's poetry matured into something more refined and enigmatic: the strange, almost hermetic poems of this period—Verwey described them as 'sensitivist'—are included in *De school der poëzie* (1897, 'The School of Poetry'). These are his most interesting and rewarding work, and repay examination today. But the poet felt that the introspection involved in this type of composition was driving him into madness, and so became a student (and translator) of Spinoza, and, soon after that, a Marxist. But his epic *Pan* (1916), supposed to excite everyone into hurrying up the process of dialectical materialism, instead puzzled them: they found it as hermetic as ever. Gorter met Lenin and visited Russia, became disillusioned, and ended as an often illuminating but theory-bound critic, writing about poets such as **Shelley** and **Dante** from a Marxist perspective; on leaving the Communist Party in 1921 he became, perhaps prophetically, an early 'Eurocommunist'.

GOSSE, Sir Edmund William
(1849–1928)

English poet and critic, born in London, son of Philip Henry Gosse. He was educated privately, and became assistant librarian in the British Museum (1867–75), then translator to the Board of Trade (1875–1904) and finally librarian to the House of Lords (1904–14). He was an eminent man of letters in his day, and moved in influential circles; his personal friends included **Swinburne**, **Hardy**, **Stevenson** and **Henry James**. His reputation as a critic was damaged after attacks on his accuracy and scholarship by Churton Collins in 1885, an incident which troubled him throughout his life. He initially regarded himself as a poet, and published several works, including *On Viol and Flute* (1873) and *Collected Poems* (1911). His *Studies in the Literature of Northern Europe* (1879), and other critical works, first introduced **Ibsen** to English-speaking readers. He also wrote on **William Congreve** (1888), **John Donne** (1899), Jeremy Taylor (1904), Sir Thomas Browne (1905), **Algernon Charles Swinburne** (1917) and **François de Malherbe** (1920), although his special field was *Seventeenth-century Studies* (1883). He is best remembered for his masterpiece *Father and Son* (1907), a classic biographical study

of his relationship with his father which is also a reflection of their times and social milieu.
▷A Thwaite, *Edmund Gosse, a literary landscape* (1984)

GOSVAMI, Kisori Lal
(1865–1932)
Popular Hindi novelist, who wrote crude and sensationalist romances, but who had some small but definite interest in character, which lifted his works above the genre.

GOTLIEB, Phyllis
(1926–)
Canadian poet and science-fiction writer, born in Toronto. Gotlieb's poetry has been gathered in *The Works: Collected Poems* (1978). Her outstanding single collection was *Ordinary, Moving* (1969), which explored her Jewish childhood and background in a lively mosaic of telephone numbers, playground rhymes and the like. More recently she is known primarily for her science fiction. *Sunburst* (1964), still considered by many to be her best novel, is narrated by a 13-year-old who manages to triumph over a group of mutant children. Her trilogy about cats who possess the secrets of the past ended with *The Kingdom of the Cats* (1985) and featured a pair of crimson felines.

GOTTFRIED VON STRASSBURG
(fl.1200)
German poet. He wrote the masterly German version of the legend of *Tristan and Isolde*, based on the Anglo-Norman poem by **Thomas**. He is also noteworthy as an early exponent of literary criticism, having left appraisals of the work of poets of the period.
▷M S Bates, *Gottfried von Strassburg* (1971)

GOTTSCHALL, Rudolf von
(1823–1909)
German writer, born in Breslau. A keen Liberal, he produced two volumes of political verse (1842–3). From 1864 he lived in Leipzig and edited *Brockhaus'sche Blätter* and *Unsere Zeit*. He also wrote a comedy entitled *Pitt und Fox* (1854, 'Pitt and Fox'), tragedies and historical novels.
▷M Brasch, *Ein literarisches Portrait* (1893)

GOTTSCHED, Johann Christoph
(1700–66)
German writer, born in Judithenkirch near Königsberg. In 1730 he became Professor of Philosophy and Poetry at Leipzig, and in 1734 of Logic and Metaphysics. He laboured to improve his mother-tongue as a literary vehicle, and to reform the German drama by banishing buffoonery and raising the style and tone. He founded the Leipzig school of acting and criticism, introducing French classical principles. But he became pedantic and vain, and showed a petty jealousy of all literary authority save his own, opposing Bodmer and **Gotthold Lessing**. His drama, *Der Sterbende Cato* (1732, 'The Dying Cato'), notwithstanding its immense success, is sadly barren.
▷W Rieck, *Johann Christoph Gottsched* (1972)

GOTZ, Johann Nikolaus
(1721–81)
German poet and pastor from Worms, whose **Anacreon**tic poetry was written in close imitation of the more gifted **Johann Gleim** and **Johann Uz**.

GOUDGE, Elizabeth (de Beauchamp)
(1900–84)
English writer of fiction for adults and whimsically religious books for children. She was born in Wells, Somerset. After attending Reading University's Art Department she worked for several years as a teacher of design and handicrafts. Her first novel was *Island Magic* (1934) but she waited 10 years before producing the bestselling *Green Dolphin Country* (1944), a historical romance set in New Zealand. After that her popularity, especially in libraries, remained steady. *The Little White Horse* (1946), for children, won the Carnegie Medal.

GOULD, Alan
(1949–)
Australian poet, born in London of Icelandic descent, a heritage which is reflected in his verse. His first collection was *Icelandic Solitaries* (1978), and the prize-winning *Astral Sea* (1981) derives much from Icelandic sagas. *The Passing of the Hours* followed in 1984. *The Man who Stayed Below* (1984) is his first novel, a study of the doom-laden captain of a sailing clipper on the Melbourne–London run. *The Enduring Disguises* (1988) contains three novellas.

GOULD, Nat(haniel)
(1857–1919)
English journalist and novelist of 'The Turf', born in Manchester. After working on provincial and London newspapers, he visited Australia in 1884 and became racing editor of the Sydney *Referee*. For that paper he became a successful tipster under the name 'Verax', and also published two serials, the second of which, 'With the Tide', was later published as *The Double Event* (1891). Two years later this was dramatized by George Darrell and staged in Melbourne with 20 horses in the 'cast'. Through the great success

of this melodrama Gould's subsequent books became popular both in Australia and England. He returned to England in 1895 and from that time wrote over 130 novels, mainly thrillers of racing or other sporting plots, but also of the theatre, which was one of his delights. He wrote three volumes of auto-biography, *On and Off the Turf in Australia* (1895), *Town and Bush* (1896) and *The Magic of Sport; Mainly Autobiographical* (1909).

GOURMONT, Rémy de
(1858–1915)
French poet, novelist and critic, born in Bazo-ches-en-Houlme, Normandy. Having been dismissed from his post at the Bibliothèque Nationale Paris, because of an allegedy pro-German article in *Mercure de France*, of which he was a co-founder, he lived the life of a recluse. His creative work—poetry and novels in the Symbolist manner—is cerebral and stylistic, betraying a *fin de siècle* obsession with words as sound more than as sense. But his evaluative and critical work, which includes *Le Livre des masques* (1896–8, 'The Book of Masques') and *Promenades philosophiques* (1905–9, 'Philosophical Excursions'), is clear-sighted and individualistic, exhibiting scholarship and intellectual curiosity. His novels include *Sixtine* (1890) and *Un Cœur virginal* (1907, Eng trans, by **Aldous Huxley**, *A Virgin Heart*, 1921).
▷J de Gourmont, *Souvenirs de Rémy* (1924)

GOVER, Robert
(1929–)
American novelist, born in Philadelphia. A few of his books have appeared under the pseudonym of 'O Govi'; another, *Victor Versus Mort*, has appeared, undated, only in Portuguese. His best-known novel is his first: *One Hundred Dollar Misunderstanding* (1962), the first of a trilogy, which traces the relationship between a white man and a 13-year-old black prostitute. The sequels are *Here Goes Kitten* (1964) and *J C Saves* (1968). A writer who puts sex to the fore in all of his novels, he has been described by one critic as 'at times an accomplished satirist'.

GOVONI, Corrado
(1884–1965)
Italian poet and novelist, born in Tamara, Ferrara. He passed through the gamut of all the mainstream Italian movements: initially, a friend to Sergio Corrazzini, he wrote in the style of the 'twilight' poets, the Crepusculari; then he was an adherent of the Futurists; finally he associated himself with the group around the Florence magazine *La voce*. Like **Willem Elsschot** and **Thomas Hardy** he illus-trated much of his verse with sketches and

designs which were an integral part of them. He is particularly remembered for his pas-sionate lament for his son Aladino, who was murdered by Nazis in 1944, in his volume *Aladino: lamento su mio figlio morto* (1946, 'Aladino: Lament for My Dead Son'). Although a minor poet, he was greatly admired by **Eugenio Montale** and, latterly, by **Primo Levi**. There are English translations in C L Golino (ed), *Contemporary Italian Poetry* (1962).

GOWER, John
(c.1325–1408)
English poet, born into a wealthy family in Kent. He spent most of his life in London, and had contacts with the court in the service of Richard II and Henry IV. He was a per-sonal friend of **Chaucer**, and wrote *Speculum Meditantis*, in French verse, which was dis-covered at Cambridge only in 1898. Other works include the *Vox Clamantis*, elegiacs in Latin (1382–4), describing the rising under Wat Tyler; and the long poem entitled *Confessio Amantis*, written in English, perhaps in 1383. There are extant also 50 French ballads, written by Gower in his youth. The *Confessio Amantis* comprises a prologue and eight books, and largely consists of over a hundred stories taken from **Ovid**'s *Metamorphoses*, the *Gesta Romanorum*, and medieval histories of Troy. He was blind from about 1400.
▷J A Burrows, *Ricardian Poetry: Chaucer, Gower, Langland and the Gawain Poet* (1971)

GOYEN, (Charles) William
(1915–83)
American novelist and short-story writer from Texas, he is unmistakably 'Southern' in his instinct for slightly baroque situations, but is also rather more quietly philosophical and lyrical than most of those writers who are saddled with that label. *The Faces of Blood Kindred* (1960) is his only stereotypically 'Southern' book. His first novel, *The House of Breath* (1950), is incidentally reminiscent of **Truman Capote**'s precocious *Other Voices, Other Rooms*, which appeared two years earl-ier, but it signally failed to excite the public. Goyen's reputation has remained somewhat restricted. *The Fair Sister* (1963) is a rework-ing of a short story about a female evangelist. *Come the Restorer* (1974) is more broadly comic. Goyen's final work was the posthum-ous *Arcadio* (1984), a strange novel about a hermaphrodite. He also wrote plays, some of them based on his novels and stories.

GOYTISOLO, Juan
(1931–)
Spanish novelist and critic, born in Barce-lona. He was associated with progressive,

anti-Franco writers in his early career, when he co-founded the group 'Turia' with **Ana María Matute** and others. Then in 1957, unlike his brother **Luis Goytisolo**, he left Spain for Paris, where he worked for the publisher Gallimard. His early novels, such as *Juegos de manos* (1954, Eng trans *The Young Assassins*, 1959), were more or less straightforwardly realistic; later, influenced both by his ambisexuality and by the Arabic elements in Spanish literature, he became a determined and highly influential modernist and postmodernist, of international stature. His two best-known novels are *Reivindicación del conde Don Julian* (1970, Eng trans *Count Julian*, 1974), and *Juan sin tierra* (1976, Eng trans *John the Landless*, 1977), essentially a 'deconstruction' of the official history of Spain in the period 1939–64.
▷J Ortega, *Juan Goytisolo* (1972, in Spanish)

GOYTISOLO, Luis
(1937–)

Spanish novelist, born in Barcelona, the brother of the more internationally known and translated **Juan Goytisolo**. He is a publisher by profession, whose work has been somewhat unfairly overshadowed by that of his more ambitiously experimental brother. His best novels are *Recuento* (1973, 'Inventory') and *Los verdes de mayo hasta el mar* (1976, 'The Green of May to the Sea'), both of them explorations of the creative process.

GOZZANO, Guido
(1883–1916)

Italian poet, born near Turin, who, after 12 years of suffering, died of tuberculosis. He was among the first and most important of the poets styled by **Borgese** as Crepusculari (the others were Sergio Corazzini, **Marino Moretti**, Carlo Chiave, Carlo Vallini—to whom Borgese first applied the term—and Fausto Maria Martini): this quiet, anti-rhetorical, self-mocking 'twilight' poetry arose in the first instance as an inevitable reaction to the *Sturm und Drang* of **D'Annunzio** and his many bombastic followers. It also gave an approving nod in the direction of **Pascoli**. The mood can be found elsewhere, in such American poets as **Robinson** and **T S Eliot** (who was aware of Gozzano through Pound), and has persisted, both in Italian poetry and, again, elsewhere, as in **James Reeves**. The tone is that of the ill (perhaps wryly syphilitic), world-weary, cynical ex-dandy and aesthete. But while Gozzano is typical, he was also a major poet, and has been virtually endorsed as such since **Montale** catalogued his virtues. His most famous poem is 'Totò Merùmeni', certainly the original for Eliot's 'Prufrock'. His genius has in its quiet way

dominated the 20th century. There are English translations in *The Man I Pretend To Be* (1981, contains a translation of Montale's pioneer essay).

GOZZI, Count Carlo
(1720–1806)

Italian dramatist, born in Venice. He wrote *Tartana* (1757), a satirical poem against **Carlo Goldoni**; a very popular comedy, *Fiaba dell' amore delle tre Melarance* (1761, Eng trans *The Love of Three Oranges*, 1949); and several similar 'dramatic fairy-tales', the best-known, from **Schiller**'s translation of it, being *Turandot* (Eng trans *Turandot, Princess of China*, 1913). His brother, Count Gasparo (1713–86), edited two journals in Venice, and was press censor there. Among his works are *Il mondo morale* (1760, 'The Moral World') and *Lettere famigliari* (1755).
▷E Borghesani, *Carlo Gozzi e l'opera sua* (1904)

GRABBE, Christian Dietrich
(1801–36)

German dramatist, born in Detmold. He lived an irregular, highly neurotic life, and died of tuberculosis and alcoholism. A precursor of Realism, he wrote powerful tragedies on the lives of *Don Juan und Faust* (1822), *Kaiser Friedrich Barbarossa* (1829) and *Napoleon* (1831).
▷A Bergmann, *Christian Dietrich Grabbe* (1954, in German); and other works by Bergmann

GRACE, Patricia
(1937–)

New Zealand novelist and short-story writer, born in Wellington. She was one of the first published Maori writers, producing a collection of short stories, *Waiariki*, in 1975, followed by her novel *Mutuwhenua: The Moon Sleeps* (1978) on cultural conflicts in a mixed marriage. Next came *The Dream Sleepers and Other Stories* (1980), a further novel, *Potiki* (1986), with its emphatic Maori viewpoint of Paheka (white settler) standards, and *Electric City and Other Stories* (1987). She treats the Maori culture and community in realistic narrative and deals much with the significance of their extended family relationships.

GRACIAN, (y Morales) Baltasar
(1601–58)

Spanish philosopher and writer, born in Belmonte, Aragon. He entered the Jesuit order in 1619 and later became head of the College at Tarragona. His early works such as *El Héroe* (1637, Eng trans *The Hero*, 1652),

El Político (1640, 'The Politician'), *El Dis-
creto* (1646, Eng trans *The Compleat Gentleman*, 1729) and *Oráculo manual y arte de
prudencia* (1647, Eng trans *The Courtier's
Manual Oracle and the Art of Prudence*, 1685)
are all heavily didactic guides to life. He set
out his literary ideas on *conceptismo*, the art
of conceited writing, in *Agudeza y arte de
ingenio* (1642, 'Subtlety and the Art of
Genius'). He is best known, however, for his
three-part allegorical novel, *El Criticón*
(1651, 1653, 1657, 'The Critic'), in which civilization and society are portrayed through
the eyes of a savage.
▷A Coster, *Baltasar Gracian* (1958)

GRACQ, Julien, pseud of **Louis Poirier**
(1910–)
French novelist, critic and translator (of **Kleist**'s *Penthesilea*), who studied with the influential philosopher Alain, and went on to
become a history teacher. His fiction arises,
essentially, from his understanding of the
mythology of the Middle Ages. He learned
much from the surrealists and from their
precursors, such as **Lautréamont**, but his
methods do not resemble theirs, even though
Breton (upon whom he wrote a book, *André
Breton*, 1948) hailed him as a new white hope
on the appearance of his haunting first book,
Au Château d'Argol (1939, Eng trans *The
Castle of Argol*, 1951). His reputation was
made, however, with *Un Beau Ténebreux*
(1945, Eng trans *A Dark Stranger*, 1949),
about a young man who refuses the love of
an enigmatic woman. Gracq, an outspoken
critic of the literary establishment, declined
the Prix **Goncourt** awarded him for *La Rivage
des Syrtes* (1951, 'By the Shores of Syrtes'),
an exploration of the Grail Myth avowedly
reminiscent of the fiction of **Ernst Jünger**. His
masterpiece, *Un Balcon en forêt* (1958, Eng
trans *Balcony in the Forest*, 1959), draws on
his war experiences in the Ardennes. *La Pre-
squ'ile* (1970, 'The Peninsula'), contains three
stories set in the Middle Ages. His style is
unparalleled in modern times for its richness.

GRAF, Oscar Maria
(1894–1967)
German novelist and poet. He was born in
Berg in Bavaria, the son of the village baker,
but left home at 16 to become an anarchist.
Always an outspoken, bold and highly individualistic man, he feigned insanity in order
to escape service in World War I, since he
had been given an unreasonable order. When
the Nazis put his name on a list of recommended books, he wrote an open letter,
'Burn Me Too'; in 1938 he ended up in New
York, where he remained—but he could not
become a US citizen until 1958 because he
refused to sign the clause which would require

him to bear arms on behalf of US politicians.
He wrote many novels and stories, most of
them describing rural life and the threat of
totalitarianism; the most moving is *Bolwieser*
(1932, Eng trans *The Station Master*, 1933).
His poetry and his 'Utopian' novels are far
less successful. His masterpiece was first published in English, *The Life of My Mother*
(1940), and only later in German. Its title
defines it.
▷S K Johnson, *Oskar Maria Graf: The Critical Reception of His Prose Fiction* (1979)

GRAHAM, Harry
(1874–1936)
English writer of light verse, whose *Ruthless
Rhymes for Heartless Homes* (1909) was for
many decades one of the most popular collections. **Geoffrey Grigson** wrote of his acrid
verses: 'They are the ruthless vesicles of the
Galsworthy age, the nasty contradictions, in
effect, of the kind vesicles of A.A. Milne'.
Graham published *More Ruthless Rhymes* in
1930.

GRAHAM, W(illiam) S(ydney)
(1918–90)
British poet, born in Greenock. Graham had
a never-ending fascination with the fracture
and failure of communication. His prosody
was tough and highly rhythmic, drawing on
Anglo-Saxon and Celtic forms. Both his personality and literary output were affected by
medication given for psychological problems.
He spent most of his life outside Scotland,
largely in the far south-west of England. *The
Voyages of Alfred Wallis* (1948)—the title
relates to the naive painter—marked a significant maturation of his style; the adjectives
that had adorned his earlier volumes, *Cage
without Grievance* (1942) and *The Seven Journeys* (1944), fell away like autumn leaves.
Graham's great achievement was *The Night-
fishing* (1955), a long poem comparable with
MacDiarmid's 'On a Raised Beach', and
influenced by **Joyce** and **Marianne Moore**. He
then remained virtually silent for 15 years,
returning with *Malcolm Mooney's Land*
(1970), a further meditation on the relationship between language and reality; Graham
once asked, rhetorically, 'What is the Language Using Us For?'.
▷T Lopez, *The Poetry of W S Graham* (1989)

GRAHAME, James
(1765–1811)
Scottish poet, born in Glasgow. He studied
law at Glasgow University and was called to
the Bar, but was forced to give up his career
because of ill-health. He took Anglican
orders in 1809 and became a curate in Ship-
ton, Gloucestershire and later Sedgefield,

Durham. He wrote a dramatic poem, *Mary, Queen of Scots* (1801), but most of his poetry was evocative of the quiet Scottish countryside, particularly *The Sabbath* (1804) and *The Birds of Scotland* (1806), with an introduction that made it 'popular ornithology'. Christopher North (**John Wilson**) thought highly of him, but he was not rated by **Byron**.

▷Memoir in *The Sabbath* (1839, 9th edn)

GRAHAME, Kenneth
(1859–1932)

Scottish children's writer, born in Edinburgh, the son of an advocate. He was brought up in Inverary, Argyll, until 1864, and then by his grandmother in Cookham Dene, Berkshire. He was educated at St Edward's School, Oxford, and in 1876 entered the Bank of England as a gentleman clerk. He became its secretary in 1898 and retired for health reasons in 1908. His early work consisted of collected essays and country tales, *Pagan Papers* (1893), *The Golden Age* (1895) and *Dream Days* (1898), which revealed a remarkably subtle, delicate and humorous sympathy with the child mind. In 1908 he published his best-known work, *The Wind in the Willows*, originally written in the form of letters to his son Alastair, and repeatedly revised before publication. Despite its quaint and unforgettable riverside characters, Rat, Mole, Badger and Toad, it did not at first win acclaim, critics such as **Arthur Ransome** dismissing it as inferior to his previous work. Gradually, however, its popularity grew, and within a few years of Grahame's death it had become a children's classic.

▷P Green, *Kenneth Grahame* (1959)

GRAINGER, Dr James
(1721–66)

Scottish poet, born in Duns and educated in Edinburgh, where he took a degree in medicine. After an undistinguished career in the army, he returned to Edinburgh to practise medicine, and turned to writing to supplement his income, producing poems (largely paeans to nature, especially the Grampians), essays and a volume of combined critical works and medical musings, but meeting with little success. He is chiefly remembered for *Sugar Cane* (c.1760), a long poem describing his subsequent experiences as a plantationer in the West Indies.

GRANADA, Fray Luis de
(1504–88)

Spanish religious writer, born in Granada of humble origin and probably orphaned very young. Protected by the Count of Tendilla whom he served as a page, he joined the Dominican order and studied in Valladolid, where

he had the greatest theologians of the day as his teachers. He became a priest in Cordoba, where he flourished under Juan de Avila, the greatest theologian of his age. Later he fell into disfavour with Philip II through neutrality over his claim to the throne in Portugal. He wrote three books in prose, sacred works on prayer, meditation and moral guides: *El Libro de Meditacion y Oracion* (1552, 'The Book of Meditation and Prayer'), *Guía de Pecadores* (1556, 'Guide for Sinners') and *Introduccion del Símbolo de la Fé* (1582–5, 'Introduction to the Symbol of Faith'), in which he considers the natural beauties of creation and the excellence of Christianity. He was the most famous sacred orator of his day, and his sermons were used as models until the 18th century.

GRAND, Sarah, pseud of Frances Elizabeth Bellenden McFall, née Clarke
(1854–1943)

British novelist, born of English parentage in Donaghadee, Ireland. At the age of 16 she married an army doctor, D C McFall (d.1898). In 1923 and from 1925 to 1929 she was Mayoress of Bath. Her reputation rests on *The Heavenly Twins* (1893) and *The Beth Book* (1898), in which she skilfully handles sex problems. Her later works, including *The Winged Victory* (1916), are advocacies of feminine emancipation.

GRANT, Anne, née MacVicar
(1755–1838)

Scottish poet and essayist, born in Glasgow, the daughter of an army officer. She lived in North America as a child (1758–68). In 1779 she married the Rev James Grant, minister of Laggan. Left a widow in 1801, she turned to writing and published *Poems* (1803), *Letters from the Mountains* (1806), *Memoirs of an American Lady* (1808) and *Superstitions of the Highlanders* (1811). In 1810 she moved to Edinburgh, where she mixed in the best literary circles, and in 1825 received a pension of £50 through the influence of Sir **Walter Scott**.

GRANT, James
(1822–87)

Scottish novelist and historical author, born in Edinburgh. After a childhood in Newfoundland and military service, he published a long series of novels and histories, that were illustrative mainly of the achievements of Scottish arms abroad. Among his many works are *The Romance of War* (1845), his first novel; *Adventures of an Aide-de-Camp* (1848); *Bothwell* (1854); *Frank Hilton, or the Queen's Own* (1855); *British Battles on Land*

and Sea (1873); and a classic history of his native city, *Old and New Edinburgh* (1880).

GRANT, Robert
(1852–1940)

American novelist, born in Boston, and a member of its patrician class. A supposedly liberal judge (and in the matter of divorce he was so), he helped to send the communists Sacco and Vanzetti to execution for a crime which he knew they had not committed. He wrote mostly light romances and adventure stories, but *The Chippendales* (1909) was praised for the picture it gave of the frivolous, turn-of-the-century Boston.
▷ *Fourscore* (1934)

GRANVILLE-BARKER, Harley
(1877–1946)

English actor, playwright and producer, born in London. As an actor, he was distinguished by his appearance in **Shaw** plays—he played Marchbanks in *Candida* in 1900. In 1904 he became co-manager of the Court Theatre with Vedrenne, and there followed a four-year season that was a landmark in the history of the British theatre. First performances in England of plays by **Maeterlinck**, **Arthur Schnitzler**, **Gerhart Hauptmann**, **W B Yeats**, **John Galsworthy**, **John Masefield** and George Bernard Shaw were performed in circumstances that set new standards of acting and design. In 1907 he left the Court and continued his success with a series of **Shakespeare** plays at the Savoy. He retired from the stage in the early 1920s. Barker wrote several plays, including *The Marrying of Ann Leete* (1902), *The Voysey Inheritance* (1905), *Waste* (performed privately in 1907, publicly in 1936) and *The Madras House* (1910). With William Archer he devised a scheme for a national theatre. He was married first to Lillah McCarthy and then to Helen Huntington Gates, with whom he made the standard translations of plays by **Gregorio Martínez Sierra** and the **Álvarez Quintero** brothers. His prefaces to Shakespeare's plays (4 vols, 1927–45) are valuable for their original criticism and ideas on production.

GRASS, Günter Wilhelm
(1927–)

German novelist, born in Danzig (Gdansk, Poland). He was educated at Danzig Volksschule and Gymnasium. Having trained as a stonemason and sculptor, he attended the Academy of Art, Düsseldorf, and the State Academy of Fine Arts, Berlin. He served in World War II and was held as a prisoner-of-war. He has worked as a farm labourer, miner, apprentice stonecutter and jazz musician, and was a speech-writer for Willy Brandt when he was Mayor of West Berlin. *Die Blechtrommel* (1959, Eng trans *The Tin Drum*, 1962) was the first of the novels that have made him Germany's greatest living novelist. Ostensibly the autobiography of Oskar Matzerath, detained in a mental hospital for a murder he did not commit, it caused a furore in Germany because of its depiction of the Nazis. Intellectual and experimental in form, theme and language, his books consistently challenge the status quo and question our reading of the past. A prolific playwright, poet and essayist, he excels in fiction. Important books are *Katz und Maus* (1961, Eng trans *Cat and Mouse*, 1963), *Hundejahre* (1963, Eng trans *Dog Years*, 1965), *Örtlich betäubt* (1969, Eng trans *Local Anaesthetic*, 1970), *Der Butt* (1977, Eng trans *The Flounder*, 1978), *Das Treffen in Telgte* (1979, Eng trans *The Meeting at Telgte*, 1981), *Die Ratten* (1987, Eng trans *The Rats*, 1987) and *Unkenrufe* (1992, Eng trans *The Call of the Toad*, 1992). He has illustrated many of of his own book jackets.
▷ K Miles, *Günter Grass* (1975)

GRAU, Jacinto
(1877–1958)

Spanish playwright, born in Barcelona, who left Spain after Franco's victory to live in Buenos Aires. His powerful and profound plays never had the attention they deserved, but a substantial number of good critics have recognized him as a major writer. He was unpopular with those who had power in the Spanish theatre because of his consistent and sarcastically conducted struggle against commercialization—he was mostly produced outside Spain. His richly prophetic work is now being re-examined by the critics of his own country. He wrote, first, formal tragedies, but then moved to the form of farce, in which framework he presented tragic themes. His work has not yet been translated, but *El señor de Pygmalión* (1921, 'Mr Pygmalion'), was seen in Paris and Prague in the early 1920s; his plays are now gradually being revived. His greatest works are probably his last, *En el infierno se est án mudando* (1958, 'Moving Day in Hell') and—the best of all the modern plays on the Don Juan theme—*El burlador que no se burla* (1930, 'The Seducer Who Does Not Seduce').

GRAU, Shirley Ann
(1929–)

American novelist, born in New Orleans and educated at Tulane University; she taught creative writing at the University of New Orleans in 1966–7. Her short stories began appearing in magazines such as the *New Yorker* and *The Saturday Evening Post* as early as 1954. Her first book, *The Black*

Prince and Other Stories (1955), was highly acclaimed. In 1965 she won a Pulitzer Prize for her novel *The Keepers of the House*, which tells the story of a mixed race family whose members are related to the Klan. She has been termed a 'regional writer' because of her concerns with the South and race relations.

GRAVES, Alfred Perceval
(1846–1931)

Irish writer and educationist, born in Dublin. An inspector of schools in England, he wrote much Irish folk verse and songs, including 'Father O'Flynn', and an autobiography, *To Return to All That* (1930). A leader of the Celtic revival, he helped to found the Irish Literary Society in London.
▷ *To Return to All That* (1930)

GRAVES, Richard
(1715–1804)

English author, born in Mickleton. Educated at Pembroke College, Oxford, he became a fellow of All Souls, Oxford, in 1736, and also rector of Claverton, near Bath. Of his great output, only his novel *The Spiritual Quixote* (1772), a comic tilt at changing Methodist views which satirizes the evangelical preacher George Whitefield, is remembered. His other novels, though little read, contain well-observed portraits of the social conditions of his age.
▷ F Kilvert, *Richard Graves of Claverton* (1858)

GRAVES, Robert von Ranke
(1895–1985)

English poet, novelist, essayist and critic, born in London and educated at Charterhouse. He joined up in 1914 and his first poetry—*Over the Brazier* (1916), *Fairies and Fusiliers* (1917)—was published during the conflict. Poems by him also appeared in the popular anthology *Georgian Poetry*, but he did not discover his distinctive voice until 1924, when his war-shattered nerves had experienced the delights and disillusions of married love. A year later he met **Laura Riding** with whom he went into exile to Majorca on the proceeds of his autobiography, *Goodbye to All That* (1929), and a hack Life of T E Lawrence. He lived, travelled and collaborated with Riding until 1939, returned to England for World War II, but returned to settle permanently in Majorca with his second wife, Beryl Hodge, in 1946. His best poetry, written between about 1928 and 1943, is pellucid, tender and evocative, far closer to the Metaphysical Poets than the Victorians. Generally regarded as the best love poet of his generation, he has a broad-based bibliography. His historical novels, like *I, Claudius* (1934), *Claudius the God* (1934) and *The Golden Fleece* (1945), are confident and imaginative reconstructions. *The White Goddess* (1948) is his most significant non-fiction title, its credo being that real poets get their gift from the Muse. His interest in myth prompted *Greek Myths* (1955) and *Hebrew Myths* (1963).
▷ M Seymour-Smith, *Robert Graves' Life and Work* (1983)

GRAY, Alasdair James
(1934–)

Scottish novelist, painter and playwright, born in Glasgow. He was educated at Whitehill Secondary School and Glasgow School of Art. Painting was his first vocation and he came late to novel writing; *Lanark*, his first novel, was published in 1981. A gargantuan effort, it is a phantasmagoric exploration of modern city life related by Duncan Thaw, in which science fiction is counterbalanced by stark realism, the setting being a place called Unthank, palpably Glasgow. In *1982, Janine* (1984), the hero—if he can be called that—is a divorced, alcoholic, insomniac supervisor of security installations who is telling his story to the mirror in a dismal Borders' hotel. Like others of Gray's works it is erotically charged and very funny. *Unlikely Stories, Mostly* (1983), a collection of stories, demonstrated his versatility, and with *The Fall of Kelvin Walker* (1985), Gray showed that he was adept at social satire, the story being that of a Scotsman on the make in the media who gets his comeuppance. Wickedly inventive and typographically unconventional, his hallmark is a debunking of Received Pronunciation, a hilarious example of which is to be found in *Something Leather* (1990), typically described by the puckish author as 'the first British fiction since the *Canterbury Tales* to show such a wide social range in such embarrassing sexual detail'. Other books include *Old Negatives* (1989), a collection of poems, and *McGrotty and Ludmilla* (1990), 'the Aladdin story set in modern Whitehall'. *Poor Things*, a rich parody of Victorian thrillers, appeared in 1992.

GRAY, David
(1838–61)

Scottish poet, born in Merkland, near Kirkintilloch, Dunbartonshire, the son of a handloom weaver. He studied divinity at Glasgow University, but took to poetry and in 1860 moved to London with **Robert Buchanan**, although he died of consumption the following year. His only collection of poetry was *The Luggie and Other Poems*, published posthumously in 1874. Its title piece is a long

lyrical poem in praise of the stream near his birthplace, written in the manner of **James Thomson**'s *The Seasons* (1730). It also contained 'In the Shadows'.
▷A V Stuart, *David Gray, Poet of the Luggie* (1961)

GRAY, John Henry
(1866–1934)

English poet, born in London. Converted to Roman Catholicism in 1890, he was educated (after work as an apprentice metal turner) at London University and Scots College, Rome, being ordained as a priest in 1901. A member of the **Wilde** circle in the nineties, he befriended **Paul Verlaine**. His first poetry volume, *Silverpoints* (1893), contains translations of French contemporaries as well as original verse. *Poems* (1931) has moments comparable to **Gerard Manley Hopkins** but has otherwise much that is unadventurously pious or neo-Georgian. He edited editions of **Thomas Campion** and **John Suckling** in 1896.
▷Father Brocard Sewell (ed), *Two Friends: John Gray and André Raffalovitch: Essays Biographical and Critical* (1963)

GRAY, Oriel
(1921–)

Australian playwright for stage, television and radio, born in Sydney. She originally worked with the Sydney New Theatre, and her communist sympathies resulted in a series of plays based on exploitation and oppression. In 1955 *The Torrents* shared first prize in the Playwrights Advisory Board competition with **Ray Lawler**'s *Summer of the Seventeenth Doll*, but was not published until 1988. Two of her plays did achieve independent life: *Drive a Hard Bargain* (1960) and *The Golden Touch* (1965).
▷*Exit Left: Memoirs of a Scarlet Woman* (1985)

GRAY, Simon
(1936–)

English dramatist, director and novelist, born on Hayling Island. He has written novels and several television plays, but is best known as a stage dramatist. His first play, *Wise Child*, was produced in 1967. Subsequent plays include *Butley* (1971); *Otherwise Engaged* (1975); *The Rear Column* (1978); *Quartermaine's Terms* (1981); *The Common Pursuit* (1984); and *Melon* (1987). He was a lecturer in English Literature at Queen Mary College, London for 20 years, and many of his plays are set in the world of academics, publishers, or academics who publish. His best television play is *After Pilkington* (1987), a wry thriller set in Oxford. He has also published books about the process of staging a play, *An Unnatural Pursuit* (1985) and *How's That for Telling 'Em, Fat Lady?* (1988).

GRAY, Thomas
(1716–71)

English poet, born in London. His father, Philip Gray, was of so violent and jealous a temper that his wife, Dorothy Antrobus, was obliged to separate from him. It was mainly through her efforts that Gray was sent to Eton (1727) and afterwards to Peterhouse, Cambridge (1734). At Eton he met **Horace Walpole**, whom in 1739 he accompanied on the grand tour. They spent two and a half years in France and Italy, but quarrelled at Reggio and parted. Walpole afterwards returned to blame himself, and the breach was healed within three years. Gray returned to England in September 1741. In 1742 he wrote his *Ode on a Distant Prospect of Eton College*, and had begun the *Elegy Written in a Country Churchyard* in Stoke Poges, Buckinghamshire. In the winter he went back to Cambridge, took his bachelorship in civil law, and took up residence in Peterhouse. This was perhaps the happiest period of his life; he wrote letters and enjoyed the company of his friends. The *Ode on Eton College* was printed in 1747 and the *Elegy* was printed in February 1751. His mother died in 1753, and was buried at Stoke Poges, with an epitaph from her son's pen on her tombstone. In 1750 he began the *Pindaric Odes*; the *Progress of Poesy* was finished in 1754; *The Bard*, begun at the same time, in 1757. He moved to Pembroke College, where he spent the remainder of his life quietly in scholarly seclusion. His two Pindaric odes were printed in 1757, and put their author at the head of living English poets. The laureateship was offered to him in 1757, but he declined. From 1760 he devoted himself to early English poetry; later he made studies in Icelandic and Celtic verse, which bore fruit in his Eddaic poems, *The Fatal Sisters* and *The Descent of Odin*—genuine precursors of Romanticism. In 1768 he collected his poems in the first general edition, and accepted the professorship of history and modern languages at Cambridge. He was now comparatively rich, and enjoyed an enviable reputation. He was buried beside his mother at Stoke Poges.
▷R Cremer, *Thomas Gray, a biography* (1955)

GRAZZINI, Anton Francesco, 'Il Lasca'
(1503–84)

Italian author of comedies, poet and novelist, born in Florence. His nickname means 'The Roach'. His comedies give a lively picture of Florence, and his poetry was admired in its time for its humour and skill. His best work, in the tradition of **Boccaccio**, is his unfinished

Le cene (edited in 1882, 'The Suppers'), a series of tales within a frame. **D H Lawrence** translated one: *The Story of Doctor Manente* (1929).

▷R J Rodin, *Anton Francesco: Poet, Dramatist and Novelliere 1503–1584* (1970)

GREEN, Anna Katherine
(1846–1935)
American detective-story writer, born in Brooklyn. She began her writing career with well-turned and well received verse, no longer read today. Her father was a trial lawyer, and *The Leavenworth Case* (1878) was the first crime fiction to be written by a woman. The style of this well plotted and exciting novel— it was successfully dramatized, and she married one of the actors—now seems awkward, but is no worse than that of **Agatha Christie**; it was successfully reprinted in 1934. Green wrote more of the same, including *The Doctor, His Wife, and the Clock* (1895).

GREEN, Anne
(1899–1989)
American novelist and translator, born in Savannah, Georgia, and sister to one of France's most distinguished novelists and diarists, **Julien Green**; she translated some of his work into English. She described their early upbringing in a now underrated volume of reminiscences, *With Much Love* (1948). Her skilful and sardonic novels, also underrated—perhaps in part because of her brother's fame—include *The Selbys* (1930) and *The Old Lady* (1947).

GREEN, Henry, pseud of Henry Vincent Yorke
(1905–73)
English novelist, born in Tewkesbury, Gloucestershire, and brought up in his family home in the West Country. Educated at Eton and Oxford, he became managing director in his father's engineering company in Birmingham, but pursued a parallel career as a novelist. While still an undergraduate he published *Blindness* (1926), the story of a clever and artistic boy who, blinded in a senseless train accident, turns to writing with powers extraordinarily heightened by his affliction. A contemporary of **Anthony Powell** and **Evelyn Waugh**, his second novel, *Living* (1929), gave a unique insight into life on the factory floor in Birmingham. An elliptical writer and highly stylized, like **Ivy Compton-Burnett** he relies heavily on dialogue, plot being conspicuous by its absence. Partial to terse and sophisticated titles such as *Party Going* (1939), *Caught* (1943), *Loving* (1945), *Back* (1946), *Concluding* (1948), *Nothing* (1950)

and *Doting* (1952), his influence and reputation extended far beyond the literary cognoscenti, and his writing was much admired in Europe. *Pack My Bag: A Self Portrait* (1940) is autobiographical.

GREEN, Julien
(1900–)
French novelist, born of American parents in Paris. Educated partly in the USA, he was bilingual, and became a convert to Catholicism. He began a successful series of psychological studies in a melancholy vein, written in French but later translated, with *Mont-Cinère* (1925, Eng trans as *Avarice House*, 1927 (US); 1928 (UK)). His other works include *Adrienne Mesurat* (1927, Eng trans *The Closed Garden*, 1928), *Léviathan* (1929, Eng trans *The Dark Journey*, 1929), which won the Harper Prize Novel contest, and *Moïra* (1950, Eng trans *Moira*, 1951). For details of his life, see his *Journals* I, II and III (1938–46) from a continuing series (the first eight *Journals* were translated in two vols as *Journal 1928–66* in 1969; other translations of the *Journals* exist), and *Memories of Happy Days* (1942) and *Memories of Evil Days* (1976) (both written in English).
▷G S Burne, *Julien Green* (1972)

GREEN, Matthew
(1696–1737)
English poet. Brought up in a strict Dissenting family, he worked at the Custom House throughout his short career. *The Grotto*, a poem on Queen Caroline's grotto at Richmond, was printed in 1733; manuscripts of other poems were published posthumously by his friend Richard Glover, but only *The Spleen* (1737) won lasting acclaim. A light-hearted essay in octosyllabic verse commending simple rural life as a cure for melancholy, it is a witty and original variant of the Horatian 'retirement' genre made popular by **John Pomfret**.
▷H R Smith, in *Notes and Queries*, 199 (1954)

GREEN, Paul E(liot)
(1894–1981)
American playwright, born on a farm at Lillington, North Carolina. He grew up with an intimate knowledge of the conditions and experiences of black employees, and his early short plays, produced by the Carolina Playmakers, confront the problems of poor blacks and whites. His first full-length piece, *In Abraham's Bosom* (1926), produced in New York, portrays the attempt of an illiterate black man to found a school for black children; he is eventually lynched. This received a Pulitzer Prize. Later works include *The Field God*

(1927), dealing with religious intolerance, and *Johnny Johnson* (1936), a vigorous anti-war play with music by Kurt Weill. In 1937 Green wrote *The Lost Colony*, the first of a series of 15 dramas of American history designed to be performed in large open-air amphitheatres.
▷V S Kenny, *Paul Green* (1971)

GREEN, Roger (Gilbert) Lancelyn
(1918–)

English writer for children, actor, and biographer, born in Norwich. He is best known for his adaptations of classical and Old English stories, such as *King Arthur and his Knights of the Round Table* (1953) and *Heroes of Greece and Troy* (1960). Abridged and at times lacking in the gamey flavours of the originals, they are nonetheless skilfully retold, and have acted as invaluable introductions for several generations of schoolchildren. His biography of **C S Lewis** (1974; written with Walter Hooper) is one of several studies he has written on some of the most important names of modern children's literature.

GREENBERG, Uri Zvi
(1896–1981)

Hebrew poet, born in Galicia of a noted Hasidic family, who also, in his earlier life, wrote in Yiddish. He went to Palestine in 1924. His wrathful, nationalistic and sometimes wildly polemical poetry, much influenced by the Bible, has not been much translated. He believed in the establishment of a Jewish state on both sides of the Jordan, but is most famous for his poems—powerful lamentations—about the Holocaust.

GREENE, Asa
(1789–c.1837)

American humorist, bookseller and physician. As a novelist he revelled in burlesque narratives and delighted in comical titles. *The Life and Adventures of Dr. Dodimus Duckworth* (1833) is a mock-heroic biography of a fellow New Englander and *Travels in America, by George Fibbleton Esq., Ex-Barber to His Majesty the King of Great Britain* (1833) was a genial spoof on the recently-published travelling experiences of Mrs Trollope.

GREENE, (Henry) Graham
(1904–91)

English novelist, short-story writer, essayist, playwright and biographer, born in Berkhamsted. He was educated at Berkhamsted School where his father was headmaster, a factor which made his schooldays difficult. In *A Sort of Life* (1971), the first of two autobiographies (*Ways of Escape*, the second volume, appeared in 1980), he recounts how

he played Russian roulette and of how, aged 13, he tried to cut open his leg with a penknife. He went to Balliol College, Oxford, and while there published *Bubbling April* (1925), a collection of verse. He became a Roman Catholic in 1926 and took up journalism as a career with *The Times*. He married in 1927, but was later separated from his wife, although they never divorced. *The Man Within* (1925), like its two immediate successors—*The Name of Action* (1930), *Rumour at Nightfall* (1932)—made little impression and he subsequently disowned them though he later allowed the first to be included in the Collected Edition. *Stamboul Train* (1932) was his first fully successful novel. Like many of his subsequent novels it is sombrely romantic, fusing tragedy and comedy in a peculiar no-man's land that critics christened 'Greeneland'. *It's a Battlefield* (1934) and *England Made Me* (1935) are likewise 'entertainments', an almost derogatory epithet that Greene first fastened to *Stamboul Train*. A prolific writer, he wrote a great number of novels, stories, plays and biographies as well as film criticism. He was the film critic for *Night and Day*, and was partly responsible for its demise when the magazine was successfully sued after he had accused Twentieth Century Fox of 'procuring' Shirley Temple 'for immoral purposes'. His career as 'a Catholic novelist' began with *Brighton Rock* (1938), a thriller which asserts that human justice is inadequate and irrelevant to the real struggle against evil. A recurring theme in his work, this is explored in his other 'Catholic' novels—*The Power and the Glory* (1940), *The Heart of the Matter* (1948) and *The Quiet American* (1955)—whose unorthodoxy often led him into controversy with the church's hierarchy. Other notable novels include *The Third Man* (1950, filmed by Carol Reed), *The End of the Affair* (1951), *Our Man in Havana* (1958), *A Burnt-Out Case* (1961), *The Comedians* (1965), *Travels With My Aunt* (1969), *The Honorary Consul* (1973), *The Human Factor* (1978), *Doctor Fischer of Geneva* (1980), *Monsignor Quixote* (1982) and *The Captain and the Enemy* (1988). The multifarious settings reflect his wanderlust and his fascination with uncomfortable countries—Argentina, the Congo, Mexico, Vietnam—as well as his seeming disregard for his personal safety. He settled in a modest flat in Antibes in 1966, where he lived for the rest of his life. In 1982, he broke his relative seclusion by publishing an incendiary pamphlet, *J'Accuse*, which brought him into conflict with the local authorities in Nice. He also published travel books: *Journey Without Maps* (1936), *The Lawless Roads* (1939) and *In Search of a Character: Two African Journals* (1961). The *Collected Essays* appeared in 1969; the *Collected Stories* in 1972. His plays include *The*

Living Room (1953), *The Potting Shed* (1957) and *The Complaisant Lover* (1959). *A World of My Own—A Dream Diary* appeared in 1992. Few modern writers have his range and power, critical acclaim and popular success; he is cited often by his peers as the greatest novelist of his time, although there are dissenting voices from that judgement, including that of **Anthony Burgess**.
▷J A Atkins, *Graham Greene* (1957, rev edn 1966)

GREENE, Robert
(1558–92)

English dramatist, born in Norwich and educated at Cambridge. He wrote a stream of plays and romances. The latter are often tedious and insipid, but they abound in beautiful poetry. One of them, *Pandosto*, supplied **Shakespeare** with hints for the plot of *The Winter's Tale*. The most popular of his plays was *Friar Bacon and Friar Bungay*. As Greene helped to lay the foundations of the English drama, even his worst plays are valuable historically. After his death appeared the pamphlet entitled *The Repentance of Robert Greene, Master of Arts*, in which he lays bare the wickedness of his former life. His *Groat's Worth of Wit bought with a Million of Repentance* contains one of the few authentic contemporary allusions to Shakespeare.
▷W H Chapman, *William Shakespeare and Robert Greene: the evidence* (1912)

GREENWOOD, Walter
(1903–74)

English writer, born in Salford. His novel *Love on the Dole* (1933), inspired by his experiences of unemployment and depression in the early 1930s, made a considerable impact as a document of the times and was subsequently dramatized. He also wrote other novels with a social slant, and several plays.
▷*There Was a Time* (1967)

GREGORY, Horace
(1898–1982)

American poet, anthologist, translator (**Catullus**, **Ovid**) and critic, born in Milwaukee, Wisconsin. He was married to the poet Marie Zaturenska, with whom he wrote the estimable *A History of American Poetry 1900–1940* (1946). His poetry, a little flat and lacking in inspiration, but well-crafted and thoughtful, is in *Collected Poems* (1964) and *Another Look* (1976). He wrote useful critical works on **Dorothy Richardson** and **Amy Lowell**.
▷*Spirit of Time and Place: The Collected Essays* (1973); 'Gregory Issue' of *Modern Poetry Studies* (1973)

GREGORY, Isabella Augusta, Lady, née Persse
(1852–1932)

Irish playwright, born in Roxborough, County Galway. After her marriage in 1880 to Sir William Henry Gregory (1817–92), Governor of Ceylon (1872–7), she became an associate of **W B Yeats** in the foundation of the Abbey Theatre in Dublin, and the Irish players. For these she wrote or translated around 40 short plays, the best of which are *Spreading the News* (1904) and *The Rising of the Moon* (1907). She was a leading figure in the Irish literary revival of the period, and her home at Coole Park was a focus for that movement. She also wrote Irish legends in dialect, possessed a wide knowledge of Irish folklore which emerges in much of her work, and translated **Molière**.
▷A Saddlemayer, *In Defence of Lady Gregory* (1966)

GREIG, Maysie Coucher, properly Jennifer Greig Smith
(1901–71)

Australian journalist and writer of romantic fiction, born in Sydney. She moved to England in 1920, writing short stories and serials for London newspapers. Her first book, *Peggy of Beacon Hill* (1920), was later filmed, and was followed by nearly 200 novels. Until the 1950s she was one of the mainstays of the circulating libraries under her own name and as Jennifer Ames.

GRENFELL, Julian Henry Francis
(1888–1915)

English poet. Educated at Eton and Balliol College, Oxford, he was killed in World War I. He is remembered for his fine war poem 'Into Battle' which was published in *The Times* in 1915 and is much favoured by anthologists.
▷V Meynell, *Julian Grenfell* (1917)

GRESSET, Jean-Baptiste-Louis
(1709–77)

French poet and playwright, born in Amiens. He was the eldest of nine children, two of whom were to become nuns, and one of his first poems was inspired by the death of his sister Marguerite in an Augustine order, at the age of 15. Gresset joined the Jesuits when he was 17, becoming a teacher but also finding time to devote to his literary concerns. His poetry in the 1730s was marked by religious themes, sometimes treated satirically: *Ver-Vert* (1734) caused the Jesuits to send him to La Flèche for a penitential period. He was also the author of several plays, including a tragedy, *Édouard* (1740); a drama, *Sidney*, first performed in 1745; and a comedy, *Le*

Méchant (1747), which remained for some years in the repertoire of the Comédie-Française.

GREVILLE, Charles Cavendish Fulke
(1794–1865)

English diarist. He was educated at Eton and Christ Church, Oxford, and became private secretary to Earl Bathurst, and was clerk of the privy council (1821–59). His position gave him particular access for studying court and public life, which is reflected in his noted *The Greville Memoirs* (1875–87), and also in his *Letters* (1924) and *The Greville Diary* (1927).

GREVILLE, Sir Fulke, 1st Baron Brooke
(1554–1628)

English poet and courtier, born in Beauchamp Court, Warwickshire. He was educated at Shrewsbury and Jesus College, Cambridge. A friend of Sir **Philip Sidney** and a favourite of Queen Elizabeth, he held many important offices, including Secretary for Wales (1583–1628) and Chancellor of the Exchequer (1614–21). He was created baron in 1620. He wrote several didactic poems, over a hundred sonnets, and two tragedies, including *The Tragedy of Mustapha* (1609), printed in 1633. His best-remembered work is his *Life of the Renowned Sir Philip Sidney* (published 1652) with its vivid pictures of contemporary figures. He died a tragic death, murdered by an old retainer who thought himself cut out of his master's will.
▷R A Rebholz, *The Life of Fulke Greville* (1971)

GRÉVILLE, Henry, pseud of **Alice Durand**, née **Fleury**
(1842–1902)

French novelist, born in Paris. She accompanied her father to St Petersburg in 1857, and wrote Russian society novels.

GREVIN, Jacques
(1538–70)

French Renaissance poet and playwright, born in Clermont en Beauvaisis. He studied in Paris. His *Théâtre*, published in 1561, marks an important stage in the restoration of ancient tragic and comic forms to French drama, anticipating the Neo-Classical period. He also wrote some circumstantial dramas, including *Hymne à Monseigneur le Dauphin*, written for the occasion of his marriage to Mary Stuart on 24 April 1558. However, Grevin is better remembered for his poetry (which was admired by **Pierre de Ronsard** among others): *L'Olimpe* (1560) comprises love sonnets, satires, pastoral works and odes. Around 1562 he abandoned poetry in order to concentrate on medicine, but he died eight

years later, aged 32, after a period of service as physician to Marguerite de France, Duchess of Savoie, in Turin, leaving a wife and probably a daughter.

GREY, Francis William
(1860–1939)

English novelist, playwright and poet, born and educated in England. He moved to Ottawa to teach at the university there. He is best known for *The Cure of St Philippe: A Story of French–Canadian Politics* (1899) in which an intrusive, ironic Trollopian narrator tells in Victorian style the story of a parish in French Canada, involving small-town church and election business. The novel is one of the best of its kind. In comparison, his historical and religious plays are overly didactic, and his poetry in *Love Crucified and Other Sacred Verse* (1902) is undistinguished. He returned to Britain to live in Edinburgh for the last years of his life.

GREY, Zane
(1875–1939)

American novelist, born in Zanesville, Ohio. He began his working life as a dentist, but after a trip out west in 1904 turned out 'westerns' with machine-like regularity, totalling 54 novels and an overall sale estimated at more than 12 million copies. His best known, *Riders of the Purple Sage*, sold nearly two million copies. His hobby of big-game fishing off the coasts of Australia and New Zealand was utilized in such books as *Tales of Fishing* (1919). His success was due to the 'escapist' lure of his simple adventure plots and attractive, authentic settings.
▷C Jackson, *Zane Grey* (1973); J Kerr, *Man of the West* (1957)

GRIBOYEDOV, Aleksander Sergeyevich
(1795–1829)

Russian writer and diplomat, born in Moscow. He wrote *Góre ot Umá* (1824, Eng trans *The Misfortune of Being Clever*, 1914, also trans as *Góre ot Umá*, 1857), a comedy in rhymed iambics, which satirizes the contemporary Moscow society so aptly that it has provided household phrases for the Russian people. Involved in the Decembrist Revolt, he was, however, cleared, and in 1828 became Russian ambassador to Persia. He was killed in an anti-Russian demonstration at the embassy in Teheran.
▷V N Orlov, *Griboyedev* (1954); and other works by V N Orlov

GRIEG, (Johan) Nordahl Brun
(1902–43)

Norwegian poet and dramatist, born in Bergen. He studied at Oslo and Oxford, and

spent much of his youth travelling, mirrored in his volumes of early poetry such as *Rundt Kap det Gode Haab* (1922, 'Round the Cape of Good Hope') and *Norge i våre hjerter* (1925, 'Norway in our Hearts'). His novel, *Skibet gaar videre* (1924, 'The Ship Sails On'), crystallized his experiences on a voyage to Australia as an ordinary seaman and was the model for **Malcolm Lowry**'s *Ultramarine*. A committed anti-fascist, he wrote dramas about national freedom, as in *Vår aere og vår makt* (1935, 'Our Honour and Our Might') and *Nederlaget* (1937, 'Defeat', about the Paris Commune of 1871). During World War II he joined the Resistance, escaped to London, and broadcast his patriotic verses back to his homeland. His plane was shot down over Berlin in 1943.
▷F J Hallund, *Nordahl Grieg. En dikter og hans tid* (1962)

GRIER, Eldon Brockwill
(1917–)

Canadian poet, born in London. Grier began as a painter, working for a time in Mexico (the subject of some of his best poems) as Diego Rivera's plasterer. He married an artist, Sylvia Tait, in 1953, and taught at the Montreal Museum of Art. It was not until his mid-thirties, when he contracted tuberculosis, that he 'quite inexplicably' wrote his first poems. The work he has produced since then—*Selected Poems 1955–1970* (1971), *The Assassination of Colour* (1978)—shows the influence of his background in painting. He has been called, rather predictably, a 'verbal colourist'.

GRIERSON, Constantia, née Crawley
(c.1705–1732)

Irish poet, born in Graiguenamanagh, County Kilkenny, to poor country people. Mainly self-educated, she was already proficient in classical languages and Hebrew when she went to Dublin around 1721. In 1726 she married George Grierson, a bookseller, for whom she corrected editions of **Virgil**, **Terence** and **Tacitus**. **Swift** described her as 'a woman of uncommon learning' and commended her poems. She wrote learned philosophical poetry, but also had a talent for easy, natural expression in more personal verse.
▷*Poems by Eminent Ladies*, ed G Colman and B Thornton (1755); A C Elias, in *Swift Studies*, 2 (1987)

GRIFFIN, Gerald
(1803–40)

Irish novelist, born in Limerick. He wrote for local journals and went to London in 1823 to make a career in literature. He failed as a dramatist, but was more successful with collections of short stories of southern Irish life like *Holland Tide* (1826) and *Tales of the Munster Festivals* (1827). His novel, *The Collegians*, on which **Dion Boucicault**'s drama *Colleen Bawn* is founded, was published anonymously in 1829. In 1838 he burned his manuscripts and entered a monastery.
▷*The Dead March Past* (1940)

GRIFFITHS, Trevor
(1935–)

English dramatist, born in Manchester. His first plays, *The Wages of Thin* (1969) and *Occupations* (1970) were staged in his native Manchester. In 1973, *The Party* was staged by the National Theatre; set in May 1968, the play revolves around a discussion of left-wing politics, with Laurence Olivier, in his last stage role, playing the central character of John Tagg, an eloquent Glaswegian Trotskyist. *Comedians* (1975) is the story of a group of young apprentice comedians learning their craft under the guidance of an ageing comic. Other plays include *Real Dreams* (1986), a typically angry political piece, and *The Gulf Between Us* (1992), which tackles the issues of the Gulf War in the style of a dream play.

GRIGOROVICH, Dmitri
(1822–99)

Russian novelist, born in Simbirsk. He knew every Russian writer of account—he had been a student with **Dostoyevsky**—and his memoirs *Literaturnye vospominaniya* (1929) are a vital source book. His first narratives were written under the influence of the critic Belinski's 'natural school', and protested against social inequality. *Anton Goremyka* (1947) influenced **Turgenev** in its intimate portraiture of the Russian peasant. *The Cruel City* (1891) collects stories, while *Rybaki* (1853, Eng trans *The Fisherman*) was his best-known novel in English-speaking countries.

GRIGSON, Geoffrey Edward Harvey
(1905–85)

English poet, critic and editor, born in Pelynt, Cornwall. The founder of the influential magazine *New Verse* (1933–9), he published several volumes of precisely-observed and tersely expressed verse, gathered in *Collected Poems, 1924–62* (1963). A later *Collected Poems* included his subsequent work in the period 1963–82, and was followed by *Montaigne's Tree* (1984). He was an often outspoken literary critic; erudite, eclectic and idiosyncratic, his was a refreshing anti-establishment voice.
▷*The Crest on the Silver* (1950)

GRILLPARZER, Franz
(1791–1872)

Austrian dramatic poet, born in Vienna. He was in the imperial civil service from 1813 to 1856. He first attracted notice in 1817 with a tragedy, *Die Ahnfrau* ('The Ancestress'), followed by *Sappho* (1818, Eng trans 1820), *Das goldene Vlies* (1820, Eng trans *Medea*, 1879), *Des Meeres und der Liebe Wellen* (1831, Eng trans *Hero and Leander*, 1938), *Der Traum ein Leben* (1834, Eng trans *A Dream is Life*, 1946), and others. He wrote lyric poetry and one excellent prose novel, *Der arme Spielmann* (1848, 'The Poor Musician'), the only one of his works set in the Vienna of his own day.
▷ J Nadler, *Franz Grillparzer* (1952)

GRIMALD, Nicholas
(1519–62)

English poet and playwright, born of Genoese ancestry in Huntingdonshire. He studied at Christ's College, Cambridge, and became Ridley's chaplain, but recanted under Queen Mary I. He contributed 40 poems to Tottel's *Songes and Sonettes* (1557), known as *Tottel's Miscellany*, and translated **Virgil** and **Cicero**. He also wrote two Latin verse tragedies on religious subjects.
▷ L R Merrill, *The Life and Poems of Nicholas Grimald* (1925)

GRIMM, Jacob Ludwig Carl
(1785–1863)
GRIMM, Wilhelm Carl
(1786–1859)

German folklorists and philologists, born in Hanau in Hesse-Kassel. They both studied at Marburg. In 1808 Jacob became librarian to Jérôme Bonaparte, King of Westphalia, and published a work on the Meistersingers (1811). In 1812 the brothers published the first volume of the famous *Kinder und Hausmärchen* (*Grimm's Fairy Tales*, first translated as *German Popular Stories*, 1823)—a work which formed a foundation for the science of comparative folklore. The second volume followed in 1815; the third in 1822. In 1829 the two moved to Göttingen, where Jacob became professor and librarian, and Wilhelm under-librarian (professor 1835). They were among the seven professors dismissed in 1837 for protesting against taking the oath of allegiance to the King of Hanover. In 1841 the brothers received professorships in Berlin, where they commenced the compilation of the massive *Deutsches Wörterbuch* (1854–1961, 'German Dictionary'). As a philologist, Jacob Grimm published *Deutsche Grammatik* (1819, 'German Grammar'), perhaps the greatest philological work of the age. His *Deutsche Rechtsalterthümer* (1828, 'German Legal Antiquities') and *Deutsche Mythologie* (1835, Eng trans *Teutonic Mythology*, 1883–8) dealt with German usages in the Middle Ages and the old Teutonic superstitions. He also published *Geschichte der deutschen Sprache* (1848, 'History of the German Language') and *Reinhart Fuchs* (1834, 'Reynard the Fox'). He also formulated 'Grimm's Law' of sound changes, an elaboration of earlier findings by the Swedish philologist Ihre and the Danish scholar Rask, but an important contribution to the study of philology. Wilhelm's chief independent work was *Die deutsche Heldensage* (1829, 'The German Heroic Myth').
▷ H Gerstner, *Die Brüder Grimm* (1974)

GRIMMELSHAUSEN, Hans Jacob Christoffel von
(c.1622–1676)

German novelist, born in Gelnhausen in Hesse-Kassel. He served on the imperial side in the Thirty Years War (1618–48), led a wandering life, but ultimately settled down in Renchen near Kehl, where he became a senior civil servant of the town. In later life he produced a series of remarkable novels. His best works are on the model of the Spanish picaresque romances. The sufferings of the German peasantry at the hands of the lawless troopers who overran the country have never been more powerfully pictured than in *Der Abenteuerliche Simplicissimus Teutsch und Continuatio* (1669, Eng trans *Simplicissimus the Vagabond*, 1924). It was followed by *Trutz Simplex* (1669, Eng trans *Mother Courage*, 1965), *Der seltzame Springinsfeld* (1670, Eng trans *The Singular Life Story of the Heedless Hopalong*, 1981), *Das wunderbarliche Vogelnest* (1672, 'The Amazing Bird's Nest'), and others.
▷ K Negus, *Grimmelshausen* (1974)

GRINGOIRE, or GRINGORE, Pierre
(c.1475–1538)

French poet and dramatist, born in Caen. While taking the chief roles in a theatrical society he was active in the production of pantomime farces, and is one of the creators of the French political comedy. He attacked the enemies of Louis XII and thus found cover for his comments on the vices of the nobility, the clergy and even the pope himself. In later life he was a herald to the Duke of Lorraine, and wrote religious poetry. His works include the famous *Mystère de Monseigneur Saint Loys* (c.1524). Gringoire figures in **Victor Hugo**'s *Notre Dame*, and in a play by **Théodore Banville**.
▷ E Bardel, *Gringoire* (1925)

GRIPE, Maria
(1923–)
Swedish writer of novels for children and young adults, brought up in Örebro and educated at Stockholm University. The recipient of numerous national and international awards, among them the **Hans Christian Andersen** Medal in 1974, she has seen her books translated into more than 20 languages. The breakthrough came with her ninth novel, *Josefin* (1961), about a lonely young girl, struggling to cope with the puzzling and frightening world of the grown-ups around her; as in Gripe's five later novels about the young boy Elvis Karlsson (1972–9), events are told strictly from the child's point of view. These novels remained within the confines of realism, but in later books Gripe incorporates supernatural elements within a realistic frame, eg in the fairy-tale *Glasblåsarnas barn* (1964, 'The Glass-blower's Children'), and in *Tordyveln flyger i skymningen* (1978, 'The Chafer Flies at Dusk'), in which past and present, natural and supernatural are skilfully interwoven. In *Skuggan över stenbänken* (1982, 'The Shadow across the Stone Bench'), the first of a series of 'shadow' novels set at the turn of the century, she further develops this style, blending the realistic with elements of a classical horror story. She works in close conjunction with her illustrator husband, Harald Gripe.
▷G Fagerström, *Maria Gripe, hennes verk och hennes läsare* (1977)

GROSSI, Tommaso
(1791–1853)
Italian poet, born in Bellano on Lake Como. He studied law at Padua and practised at Milan. His first poem, *La Prineide* (1814, 'The Prineide'), was a battle poem in the Milanese dialect. There followed several historical romances, the most notable of which is *Marco Visconti* (1834, Eng trans 1836) and the epic poem for which he is best known, *I Lombardi alla prima crociata* (1826, 'The Lombards on their First Crusade'), which Verdi used for his opera *I Lombardi*.
▷E Flori, *Scorci e figure del romanticismo* (1938)

GROSSMAN, Edith (Howitt) Searle
(1863–1931)
New Zealand writer of four novels, all of a moralistic cast heightened by symbolism. Her first, *Angela: A Messenger*, was published in 1890, as Edith Searle, soon followed by *In Revolt* (1893). Its sequel appeared 14 years later—*The Knight of the Holy Ghost* (1907)—and then came the more prosaic *The Heart of the Bush* (1910), which pleaded for mutual understanding in marriage. She also wrote verse for the short-lived *Zealandia*. Despite the religious overtones of her work she was a militant feminist who preached, among other things, a more honest approach to sexual matters, and was one of the first female graduates from the then University of New Zealand.

GROSSMITH, George
(1847–1912)
English humorist, actor and writer, born in London. For several years he was a police court reporter on *The Times*. In 1870 he became a singer and entertainer, creating several leading roles in the premieres of comic operas by **Gilbert** and Sullivan. He published his *Reminiscences of a Clown* in 1888, and *Piano and I* in 1910. He is best remembered, though, for his collaboration with his brother Weedon Grossmith on *The Diary of a Nobody*, serialized first in *Punch* and published in book form in 1892. An imaginary journal of domestic life in Holloway, London, it records the life of the amiable, over-dignified and often ridiculous city clerk Mr Pooter, striving to better himself culturally and socially but who, unwittingly, becomes the butt of numerous jokes he fails to understand.
▷T Joseph, *George Grossmith* (1982)

GROTH, Klaus
(1819–99)
German poet, born in Heide in Holstein. A schoolteacher, in 1866 he became Professor of German Language and Literature at Kiel. His masterpiece, *Quickborn* (1852), is a series of poems in Low German (*Plattdeutsch*) dealing with life in Dithmarshen. Some of his work is in High German, and he published children's tales and short stories.
▷H Siercks, *Klaus Groth* (1899)

GRUFFYDD, William John
(1881–1954)
Welsh poet, scholar, editor (of *Y Llenor*) and critic, born in Bethel. He went to Oxford and read in Classics. Later he became a professor at the University of Cardiff. His poetry, neither profound nor major, but well crafted, was notably influenced by that of **Thomas Hardy**. His criticism and anthologies were influential.

GRYPHIUS, or GREIF, Andreas
(1616–64)
German lyric poet and dramatist, born in Glogau, Silesia. He travelled in Holland, France and Italy, studying medicine and astronomy, and returned to his native town. His early misfortunes led him to the 'all is vanity' theme of his lyrics, expressed in deep

gloom, collected under the title *Sonn-und-Feiertagssonette* (1639, 'Sonnets for Sundays and Holidays'). His dramas mainly concern martyrdom and include *Leo Armenius* (1650), *Catharina von Georgien* (1657) and *Papinianus* (1659). But he also wrote the charming pastoral, *Die geliebte Dornrose* (1660, Eng trans *The Beloved Hedgerose*, 1928), the comedies *Herr Peter Squentz* (1663, Eng trans *Absurda Comica, or Master Peter Squentz*, 1964), which resembles the Bottom scenes in **Shakespeare**'s *A Midsummer Night's Dream*, and *Horribilicribrifax* (1663), satirizing the Thirty Years War. He was indirectly influenced by Shakespeare and **Joost van den Vondel**.
▷ H Becker, *Andreas Greif, poet between epochs* (1973)

GUARESCHI, Giovanni
(1908–68)
Italian journalist and writer, born in Parma. He became editor of the Milan magazine *Bertoldo*. After World War II, in which he was a prisoner, he returned to Milan and journalism, but it was *Mondo piccolo 'Don Camillo'* (1950, Eng trans *The Little World of Don Camillo*, 1951) which brought him fame. These stories of the village priest and the communist mayor with their broad humour and rich humanity have been translated into many languages, and have been followed by *Mondo piccolo 'Don Camillo e il figliol prodigo'* (Eng trans *Don Camillo and the Prodigal Son*, 1952) and others. He illustrated his books with his own drawings.
▷ *Diario clandestino, 1943–1945* (1949)

GUARINI, Giovanni Battista
(1538–1612)
Italian poet, born in Ferrara. He was entrusted by Duke Alfonso II with diplomatic missions to the pope, the emperor, and was sent to Venice and Poland. His chief work was the famous pastoral play, *Il Pastor Fido* (1585, 'Fido the Shepherd'), really an imitation of **Torquato Tasso**'s *Aminta*.
▷ V Russi, *Battista Guarini ed il Pastor Fido* (1885)

GUERARD, Albert Joseph
(1914–)
American novelist and critic, born in Houston, Texas. He is better known as a critic (he has written influential books on **Conrad** and **Hardy**), and his novels may not yet have received their full critical due. He did intelligence work in France during World War II, and this forms the background for *Maquisard: A Christmas Tale* (1945). *Night Journey* (1950), a more substantial novel, was often compared by reviewers—and not inappropriately—to **George Orwell**'s *1984*. Set in a future Europe divided between the dictatorship of the East and the so-called Democracy of the West, it memorably tries to rescue, from the realistically presented chaos, a notion of idealistic socialism.

GUÉRIN, Charles
(1873–1907)
French Symbolist poet, born in Lunéville. He travelled in Germany and Italy and periodically stayed in Paris. His work is confined to a few collections, including *Le Cœur solitaire* (1898, 'The Lonely Heart') and *L'Éros funèbre* (1900, 'Eros in Mourning'). A later series, *L'Homme intérieur* (1906, 'The Inner Man'), echoed his late conversion to the Catholic faith.
▷ Joseph B Hanson, *Le Poète Charles Guérin* (1935)

GUÉRIN, Eugénie de
(1805–48)
French writer, born in the château of Le Cayla (Tarn), sister of **Georges Guérin**, to whom she was devoted. She is chiefly known for her *Journal* (1855), which is imbued with mysticism, but she also wrote poems and edited her brother's papers.

GUÉRIN, Georges Maurice de
(1810–39)
French poet, born in the château of Le Cayla (Tarn), brother of **Eugénie de Guérin**. He entered the community of Lamennais at Le Chesnay in Brittany. He followed his master in his estrangement from Rome, and, going like him to Paris (1833) to try journalism, became a teacher at the Collège Stanislas. He married a rich Creole lady in November 1838, and died of consumption. His *Reliquiae*, including the *Centaur* (a kind of prose poem), letters and poems, were published in 1860.
▷ V W Brooks, in *The Malady of the Ideal* (1913)

GUERRA, Tonino (Antonio)
(1920–)
Italian screenwriter, born in Sant' Arcangelo, Romagna. A poet and novelist, he first wrote for the cinema as a collaborator on the script for *Uomini E Lupi* (1956, 'Men and Wolves'). *L'Avventura* (1960, 'The Adventure') began a lengthy partnership with director Michelangelo Antonioni that resulted in a series of elliptical works seeking to convey a melancholic search for self-awareness and the futility of meaningful communication between men and women. Their most notable films together include *La Notte* (1961, 'The Night') and *Deserto Rosso* (1964, 'Red

Desert'). Declaring that his writing reveals a 'different face' for each of his collaborators, he has brought a poetic sensibility to a vast range of work that often laments the passing of an earlier age or the loss of a more traditional set of values. He has received Oscar nominations for his contribution to the screenplays for *Casanova '70* (1965), *Blow-Up* (1966) and *Amarcord* (1973). He has worked extensively with some of the most distinguished film-makers in contemporary European cinema, and a selection of his finest scripts would include *Cadaveri Eccellenti* (1976, 'Illustrious Corpses') for Francesco Rosi, *La Notte Di San Lorenzo* (1981, 'The Night of San Lorenzo') for the Taviani brothers, *Landscape In The Mist* (1988) for Theo Angelopoulos and *Stanno Tutti Bene* (1990, 'Everybody's Doing Fine') for Guiseppe Tornatore.

GUERRAZZI, Francesco Domenico
(1804–73)

Italian writer and politician, born in Leghorn. He had won a great reputation by his patriotic and political fictions when, on the Grand Duke of Tuscany's flight (1849), he was proclaimed dictator in spite of his disinclination for a republic. On the duke's restoration he was condemned to the galleys, but ultimately permitted to select Corsica as his place of banishment. Restored to liberty by later events, he sat in the parliament of Turin (1862–5). His chief works of fiction are *La Battaglia di Benevento* (1827, 'The Battle of Benevento'), *L'Assedio di Firenze* (1836, 'The Siege of Florence') and *Isabella Orsini* (1844).
▷P Miniati, *Francesco Domenico Guerrazzi* (1927)

GUEST, Barbara
(1920–)

American abstract poet, born in Wilmington, North Carolina, and educated at the University of California, Berkeley. She married (briefly) into the British aristocracy, but has otherwise pursued a career utterly removed from convention and only slightly reminiscent of Anglophile/phobe predecessors such as **Hilda Doolittle** ('HD'), about whom Guest wrote *Herself Defined: The Poet H.D. and her World* (1984). Her own verse is highly chromatic, drawing something from **Wallace Stevens** but often influenced by fine art rather than other poets. Titles like *The Location of Things* (1960) and *The Blue Stairs* (1968) confirm the Stevens connection, but later books are more vividly and personally observed; they include *Moscow Mansions* (1973), *The Countess from Minneapolis* (1976) and *The Türler Losses* (1979). Guest has written one novel, *Seeking Air* (1978).

GUEVARA, Antonio de
(1490–1545)

Spanish prelate and writer. A Dominican, he became Bishop of Mondoñedo and confessor of Charles V. He used in his book on Marcus Aurelius the exalted style which anticipated the euphuism of **John Lyly**. His *Epistolas familiares* (1541–3, Eng trans *The Familiar Epistles of Anthony de Guevara*, 1574) were also very popular in an English version.
▷E Grey, *Guevara, a forgotten author* (1973)

GUEVARA, Luis Vélez de
(1570–1644)

Spanish dramatist. He wrote many plays in the style of **Lope de Vega**. His novel *El Diablo cojuelo* (1641, 'The Limping Devil') was used as the model for **Alain Le Sage**'s *Diable boiteux*.
▷F E Spencer and R Schevil, *The Dramatic Works of Luiz Vélez de Guevara* (1937)

GUEVERA, Miguel de, Frey
(c.1578–1640)

Mexican Augustinian monk who included a famous sonnet, 'No me mueve, mi Dios, para querete' ('Do not move me, my God, to love thee'), in his papers; it was therefore attributed to him, but it has been shown that he did not write it.
▷C M Huff, *The Sonnet 'Ne me mueve, mi Dios': its Theme in Spanish Tradition* (1948)

GUILHEM IX, Duke of Aquitaine, Count of Poitou
(1071–1126)

The earliest known and perhaps the first of the Provençal troubadours, 'sworn enemy to all that is modest and sacrosanct', 'a vehement lover of women', and one of the most extraordinary figures in European literature—he has been found the more so, no doubt, because of the influence upon him of mystical Sufic poetry, which, with its gnostic overtones, is often not understood by modern critics. The establishment in his territory (richer than those of the King of France) of the proto-Catharist mystical order of Fontrvrault, offers the key to the understanding of a man who, on the one hand, sacrificed an army of 60 000 men in a pointless crusade (1101), and on the other perhaps 'invented' *amour courtois* ('courtly love') and who was, according to a contemporary, 'one of the most courtly men in the world'. He left 11 poems whose high quality no one has doubted: five are capably and amusingly obscene, one is an exercise, and the rest are exquisitely cryptic.
▷*Romanische Forschungen*, LXXIII (1961); R R Bezzola, *Les Origines de la littérature courtoise en occident* (1944–62)

GUILLÉN, Jorge
(1893–1984)

Spanish poet, born in Valladolid. The first edition of his important work *Cántico*, published in 1928, was a collection of 75 poems. By the edition of 1950, following his flight to the USA and his establishment in a teaching post at Wellesley, that number had risen to 334. *Cántico* consists of what the author terms 'pure poetry'—verse stripped of the prosaic, the explanatory or the merely functional. His other major work is *Homenaje* (1967, 'Homage'), which includes translations as well as original poems; the breadth and quality of the learning displayed confirmed his standing as a major poet. His critical works include the 1961 volume, published in English, *Language and Poetry*.

GUILLÉN, Nicolás
(1902–89)

Major Cuban poet, born in Camagüey. His poetry is famous for its relating of Negro to Latin-American themes: he was the first to recognize that the Black presence on his island was not merely exotic. He became Cuba's best-known poet, celebrated even by the illiterate. Much of his poetry is political, as was natural from a man who for many years was a leading member of the Communist Party of Cuba. He received a state funeral. There are two volumes of his poetry in translation: *Man-Making Words* (1972) and *The Great Zoo* (1972).
▷ L V Williams, *Self and Society in the Poetry of Nicolás Guillén* (1982)

GUILLEVIC, pseud of Eugène Guillevic
(1907–)

French poet from Carnac, in Brittany. His first small collection, *Requiem*, appeared in 1938. Although from the war years onwards a committed communist (and active in the resistance), Guillevic is above all a poet of objects and shapes: he wants to express 'things' ideas of themselves ... their philosophy of themselves in an alien world peopled by ... men'. Thus a kind of religious sense pervades his dialectical materialism, and creates a tension which has fascinated many translators. 'The reader', wrote one of his translators, 'is hypnotized out of himself to find himself.' Available in English translation are *Guillevic* (1968, 1969) and *Selected Poems* (1974).

GUILLOUX, Louis
(1899–1980)

French novelist, born in Brittany. His first publication, *Sang noir* (1935, Eng trans *Bitter Victory*, 1936), established his reputation as a philosophical novelist who was able to create rounded characters; set on his home territory, it is a study of an intellectual—reminiscent, in many respects, of Roquentin in **Sartre**'s subsequent work *La Nausée*—who is disgusted by his surroundings but apparently unable to act to improve his lot. *La Maison du peuple* (1937, 'The People's House') received praise for its portrayal of poverty, while *Jeu de patience* (1949, 'Game of Patience') is the portrayal of a small town and its life throughout the cataclysms of the first half of the century.
▷ V Brombert, *The Intellectual Hero* (1960)

GUIMARÃES, Afonso Henriquez da Costa
(1870–1921)

Brazilian poet, born in Ouro Prêto, in the province of Minas Gerais. He wrote under the name 'Alphonsus de Guimaraens'. He was influenced by the slightly earlier Brazilian poet **João Cruz e Sousa**, and his poetry is written in a distinctly Symbolist manner inherited from him. It is characteristically concerned with devoutly-held religious preoccupations, which often spill over into mysticism. He published a number of collections of poems in his lifetime, while others appeared posthumously. A *Complete Works* was published in Portuguese in 1960.

GUIMARAES, Bernardo
(1825–84)

Brazilian poet and novelist, born in Minas Gerais. He graduated in law, and worked, none too successfully, as a judge and schoolteacher, before moving to Rio de Janeiro and practising journalism (1858–61). He is best known for the novel *A escrava Isaura* (1875, 'Isaura the Slave Girl'), which at the time was a powerful anti-slavery tract, and has recently been made into a television soap opera. His progressive politics also found expression in *O ermitao de Muquem* (1866, 'The Hermit of Muquem'), the titular character of which is part-Indian. Guimaraes remains important in the development of a distinctly Brazilian school of novel-writing. His poems, too, have had an influence; his *Poesias completas* was published in 1959.

GUIMARÃES ROSA, João
(1908–69)

Brazilian novelist and story writer, one of the most important Latin-American writers of his century, born in Cordisburgo, Minas Gerais. He qualified and practised as a doctor, but became a diplomat in 1932. The chief area of his concern was that of **Euclydes da Cunha**: the backlands of Brazil, in the north of Minas Gerais. His greatest affinities are not with any other Brazilian writer but with the Peruvian **José María Arguedas**, who deeply admired him: both men tried to write in a 'native' form of their own European language—to revitalize its tired and 'civilized' complacency. *Sagarana* (1946 rev edn 1958, Eng trans 1966) collects nine 'parables of the sertão', some of them about animals, which often behave, a critic has said, 'in a markedly totemistic way' (eg an ass rescues his drunken master from drowning). His masterpiece is *Grande Sertáo: veredas* (1956, rev edn 1958), for which its translators chose the title *The Devil to Pay in the Backlands* (1968). This is a monologue by a bandit, Riobaldo, and tells a magical story of how the speaker entered into a bargain with the devil, and fell into homosexual love with Diadorim, an angel who finally turns out to be a woman, the daughter of the friend whose murder he has been trying to avenge. Of all the Brazilian novelists of such high calibre only the more accessible **Graciliano Ramos** has had similar power.

GUIMERÁ, Ángel
(1849–1924)
Catalan poet and dramatist, born in Santa Cruz, Tenerife. His work falls into three periods, of which the first and third—for the most part, historical plays—show the influence of the French Romantics. His middle period owes its preoccupation with contemporary life to **Ibsen**. He is regarded as the greatest Catalan dramatist. His most famous play is *Terra Baixa* (1896, 'Lowlands'), on which D'Albert based his opera *Tiefland*.
▷J Minack, *Guimerá* (1959)

GÜIRALDES, Ricardo
(1886–1927)
Argentinian novelist, poet and editor, born in Buenos Aires. Güiraldes is one of the most important figures in his country's literature. With the young **Borges**, and others, he founded the leading periodicals *Martin Fierro* and *Proa*. He lived between Buenos Aires and Paris (where he died prematurely, of Hodgkin's Disease), and was thus in touch with European influences. His masterpiece is *Don Segundo Sombra* (1926, Eng trans 1935), the story of a childhood on a gaucho ranch, whose triumph is its style: an elegant blend of literary Argentinian, much influenced by his friend **Larbaud**, and the vernacular. It is just the kind of book one might expect of a man who said, towards the end of his suffering, 'I aim to master myself and to enter the path that will conduct me to the goal of a better self'—he had become an adherent of Vedanta. In 1932 his record of his search, *El sendero* ('The Way'), was published.
▷G Previtali, *Ricardo Güiraldes and Don Segundo Sombra* (1963)

GUIRAUT DE BORNELH
(c.1165–1220)
Provençal troubadour, born in Excideuil, and the leading poet of Limousin-Périgord. Although the poetry of his contemporary **Bernard de Ventadorn** is nowadays usually preferred, it was Guiraut who was hailed as the master in his time, and who was later praised by **Dante**. Like Bernard, he was of humble origin. Fifty of his songs are extant.
▷H J Chaytor, *The Troubadours of Dante* (1902)

GUIRAUT RIQUIER
(c.1254–1292)
Provençal troubadour—the last major one—born near Narbonne of modest parentage. By his time the poetry of *amour courtois* ('courtly love'), or, more properly, *fin'amor*, had run its course. The last of his 89 extant poems are more religious than amorous.
▷J Anglade, *Le Troubadour Guiraut Riquier* (1905)

GUITRY, Sacha
(1885–1957)
French actor and dramatist, who was born in St Petersburg. He wrote nearly a hundred plays, mostly light comedies, many of which have been successfully performed in English. The son of the actor-manager Lucien Guitry (1860–1925), he first appeared on the stage in Russia with his father's company. His first appearance in Paris was in 1902, still under his father's management. He went to London in 1920 with *Nono*, a play written when he was 16. It starred the second of his five wives, the enchanting Yvonne Printemps. He also wrote and directed several delightful films, including *Le Roman d'un tricheur* (1936, 'The Tale of a Cheat') and *Les Perles de la couronne* (1937, 'The Pearls in the Crown').
▷J Harding, *Sacha Guitry, the last boulevardier* (1968)

GUITTONE D'AREZZO
(1230–94)
Italian poet and moralist, born near Arezzo. As a young man he wrote love poetry in the style of the Provençal troubadours; then in 1265 he became a monk, joining an order known as 'the merry friars' ('frati godenti') and the content (though hardly the style) of his work changed. He was persistently criticized by **Dante**, perhaps jealous of his fame and standing, as 'vulgar' and, no doubt, because Dante's own early style had been learned from that of Guittone. He left 50 *canzoni*, 251 sonnets, eight verse epistles, and some vital letters. A very few have preferred him to Dante. He was an esoteric master of the gnostic mysteries of *fin'amor*—the proper

name for 'courtly love'—and his apparent obscurities have hardly yet been elucidated. There are some able translations by Joseph Tusiani in *The Age of Dante: An Anthology of Early Italian Poetry* (1974).
▷V Moleta, *The Early Poetry of Guittone d'Arezzo* (1976)

GULLBERG, Hjalmar
(1898–1961)

Swedish poet and translator (**Sophocles, Aristophanes** and other classical writers), born in Målmo, the bastard son of a rich man; his mother left him to foster-parents. Rather like **Graves** in England, he was fully aware of but eschewed modernist techniques in favour of a generally ironic mode of expression in tight traditional forms. He had at his best an affinity with **San Juan de la Cruz**, whom he also translated. One of his most intense (and humorous) sequences is *Kärlek i tjugonde seklet* (1933, 'Love in the Twentieth Century'). He achieved a high position in his nation's regard, and this was enhanced when, after many years of silence, he published the famous *Dödsmask och lustgård* (1952, 'Death Mask and Paradise'). In the grip of a progressive and crippling paralytic illness, his last collection was *Ögon, läppar* (1959, 'Eyes, Lips'), mostly written in tribute to the woman who cared for him. His work is well represented in the volume translated by J Moffett: *'Gentlemen, Single, Refined,' and Selected Poems 1937–1959* (1979). This important poet has been seriously neglected outside Scandinavia, in part owing to postwar Swedish critics' too hasty dismissal of him as 'middlebrow'.
▷C Fehrman, *Hjalmar Gullberg* (1968)

GUMILEV, Nikolai Stepanovich
(1886–1921)

Russian poet, a leader of the Acmeist school which revolted against Symbolism. His exotic and vivid poems include *Kolchan* (1915, 'The Quiver'), with some fine verses of war and adventure, and *The Pyre* and *The Pillar of Fire*, which contain his best pieces. He also wrote criticism and translated French and English poetry. He was shot as a counter-revolutionary. His wife was the poet **Anna Akhmatova**.
▷L I Strekhobsky, *Craftsman of the Word* (1949)

GUNDULÍC, Ivan
(1589–1638)

Ragusan poet, the leading figure of the golden age of the Serbo–Croatian literature which flourished alongside that of the Italian Renaissance. His model was **Tasso**, whose *La Gerusalemme liberta* ('Jerusalem Liberated')

he always intended to translate, but did not. His two chief works, amongst many others, were the pastoral play *Dubravka* (published in 1837), and the epic poem *Osman* (published in 1826), part of which is missing. The latter, celebrating the victory of the Poles over the Turkish Sultan Osman—thus establishing a pan-Slavic Christianity—is said to be amongst the greatest works of its time in any language.

GUNN, Neil Miller
(1891–1973)

Scottish novelist, born in Dunbeath, Caithness, the son of a fisherman. Educated at the village school, and privately in Galloway, he passed the Civil Service examination in 1907, and moved to London. He was in the Civil Service until 1937, from 1911 as an officer of customs and excise in Inverness and elsewhere in Scotland. After writing a number of short stories, his first novel, *Grey Coast* (1926), was immediately acclaimed, and was followed by *The Lost Glen* (serialized in 1928) and the even more successful *Morning Tide* (1931). Other works include a historical novel on the Viking age, *Sun Circle* (1933), *Butcher's Broom* (1934), *Highland River* (1937, James Tait Black Memorial Prize), *Wild Geese Overhead* (1939), *The Silver Darlings* (1941), and the contrasting war-time novels *Young Art and Old Hector* (1942) and *The Green Isle of the Great Deep* (1944). Gunn was at his best when describing the ordinary life and background of a Highland fishing or crofting community, and when interpreting in simple prose the complex character of the Celt. His last novels were *The Well at the World's End* (1951), *Bloodhunt* (1952) and *The Other Landscape* (1954). *The Atom of Delight* (1956) is a philosophical autobiography.
▷F R Hart and J B Pick, *Neil M Gunn: a Highland life* (1981)

GUNN, Thom(son) William
(1929–)

English poet, born in Gravesend. He attended University College School, London, and, following national service, read English at Trinity College, Cambridge. His first collection, *Fighting Terms* (1954), labelled him a 'Movement' poet. He moved to the USA in 1954 where he has lived ever since. His second book, *The Sense of Movement* (1957), is overtly existentialist; his third, *My Sad Captains* (1961), is more contemplative. Subsequent volumes—*Touch* (1967), *Moly* (1971) and *Jack Straw's Castle* (1976)—were not universally well-received, but he is undoubtedly one of the major poets of the second half of the century. His *Selected Poems 1950–1975* were published in 1979, and *The Passages of Joy*, in which he writes frankly about his homosexuality, appeared in 1982. *The Man with Night Sweats* (1992) included a series of elegies on men who had died 'before their time' as a result of AIDS. *Collected Poems* was published in 1993.

▷ A Bold, *Thom Gunn and Ted Hughes* (1976)

GUNNARSSON, Gunnar
(1889–1975)

Icelandic novelist, born in Fljótsdalur, East Iceland, who wrote all his major works in Danish before re-writing them in Icelandic. At the age of 18 he went to Denmark to seek fame and fortune. His first novel, *Af Borgslægtens Historie* (1920, Eng trans *Guest the One-Eyed*, 1920), was the first Icelandic work to be turned into a feature film. A prolific writer, his acknowledged masterpiece was the autobiographical novel, *Kirken paa Bjerget* (5 vols, 1923–8, Eng trans *Ships in the Sky* and *The Night and the Dream*, 1938).

▷ E O Gelsted, *Gunnar Gunnarsson* (1926)

GUNTER, Archibald Clavering
(1847–1907)

English-born American novelist (and engineer, broker and chemist). *Mr Barnes of New York* (1887), published by himself when it was turned down by publishers, became an overnight bestseller. It is a ridiculous novel, presenting an American who is able to meet every possible eventuality—he is a crack shot, an expert lover, and even a skilled surgeon; but it remains compulsively readable, for Gunter had the storyteller's gift; it now reminds its readers not only of **James Thurber**'s Walter Mitty but also of **Upton Sinclair**'s Lanny Budd (Barnes is an international trouble-shooter). *Fresh the American* (1881) was a play about an American millionaire.

GÜNTHER, Johann Christian
(1695–1723)

German poet, born in Strugan in Silesia. He lived a somewhat dissolute life, and died in poverty, rejected by his family. His poetry has a surprising range, and is unusually direct in language and emotional expression for that period. He wrote love lyrics notable for their sensitivity and their lack of affectation, as well as satires, political poems, religious poems, student songs and drinking songs.

GUNTHER, John
(1901–70)

American author and journalist, born in Chicago. He was a foreign correspondent for the *Chicago Daily News* and for NBC. He established his reputation with the bestselling *Inside Europe* (1939), followed by a series of similar works, in which firsthand material is blended with documentary information to present penetrating social and political studies. Other books include the autobiographical *Death Be Not Proud* (1949) and *A Fragment of Autobiography* (1962).

GURDJIEFF, George
(c.1865–1949)

Armenian novelist and thinker, born in or near Kars. His *Beelzebub's Tales to His Grandson* (1949) circulated in manuscript during his lifetime, but was not published until after his death. A modern Christian gnostic, Gurdjieff synthesized an extraordinary and profound system—to which his novel is a non-literary and deliberately shocking guide—which influenced many writers, including **Kipling**, **Ouspensky**, **Mansfield**, **Aldous Huxley**, **Priestley** and many others.

▷ J Moore, *Gurdjieff* (1992)

GURNEY, Ivor
(1890–1937)

English composer and poet, born in Gloucester. He became a chorister in Gloucester Cathedral in 1900, and then a pupil of the organist, Sir Herbert Brewer. At the Royal College of Music he studied compositon under Stanford. On military service in France during World War I he was wounded and gassed and, after spending much time in hospital, published two collections of poems: *Severn and Somme* (1917) and *War's Embers* (1919). After the war he returned to the Royal College of Music to study with Vaughan Williams and in 1920 published his first songs, *5 Elizabethan Songs*, before returning to Gloucester. He suffered increasingly from depression, eventually entering a mental hospital from which he was transferred to a London hospital, where he died of tuberculosis. An instinctual writer of both music and poetry rather than a skilled craftsman, his songs are considered his most important work; he remained largely uninfluenced by the contemporary folk-song movement, looking rather to Elizabethan music and the German classics for inspiration.

GUSTAFSON, Ralph
(1909–)

Canadian poet, story writer and essayist, born in Lime Ridge, Québec, one of the most versatile of the Canadian poets of the older generation. **A J M Smith** has said of him that he has improved, and become more original, since he developed away from his early romanticism, through his love for **Hopkins** and **Donne**, and into his later and more subtly

allusive and elliptical style. His *Collected Poems* appeared in 1987 in two volumes.
▷W Keitner, *Ralph Gustafson* (1979)

GUSTAFSSON, Lars
(1936–)

Swedish novelist and philosopher, born in Västerås and educated in Uppsala. His doctoral thesis, *Språk och lögn* (1978, 'Language and Lies'), explored the problem of language as a barrier between experience and understanding, much influenced by Wittgenstein. He takes a mystical stance and is much drawn to arcane and gnostic systems. His major literary work is a series of novels under the general title of *Sprichorne i muren* (1971–83, 'Cracks in the Wall'). His collected verse was published in 1981; an English selection appeared 10 years earlier.

GÜTERSLOH, Albert Paris von, pseud of Albert Conrad Kiehtreiber
(1887–1973)

Austrian painter and novelist, born in Vienna, who was highly influential—in particular on the novelist **Heimito von Doderer**—as a practitioner of Expressionism. He worked as a stage designer for Max Reinhardt, but was also a professor of fine arts, until the Nazis forced him to work in a factory. The most extraordinary of his baroque novels, and one which is still studied and admired, is *Soone und Mond* (1962, 'Sun and Moon'), which is, simultaneously, a massive allegory of Austria as it tottered from grand empire to shabby and always menaced republic, and a 'huge gloss on the perennially puzzling parable of the Unjust Steward'. He started this major work as early as 1935. Gütersloh was certainly one of those few writers who rose above the generally moribund state of Austrian letters between the wars.

GUTHRIE, A(lfred) B(ertram)
(1901–91)

American novelist, born in Bedford, Indiana, but brought up in Montana. He went to live in Kentucky, and his first successful novel, *The Big Sky* (1947), is about a mountain man, of the 1840s, from that state. In his major novels, *The Big Sky*, *The Way West* (1949) and *These Thousand Hills* (1956), he tries to recreate the reality of the Frontier—a reality which had all too soon become, in the 20th century, the cheaply exploited myth of dime novels and low-budget westerns. He was probably less artistically successful than the other novelist, in a similar innovatory tradition, who emerged at about the same time, **Walter Van Tilburg Clark**; but Guthrie's achievement, despite stylistic lapses and a falling off in later novels, such as *Arfive*

(1971), has yet to be assessed. With Jack Sher, he wrote the screenplay for the classic movie *Shane* (1951).
▷T W Ford, *A B Guthrie, Jr* (1968)

GUTHRIE, Ramon
(1896–1973)

American poet, born in New York. Guthrie studied at the Sorbonne during the 1920s and became a professor of French in New Hampshire. His first significant collections appeared when Guthrie was already approaching old age—*Graffiti* (1959) and *Asbestos Phoenix* (1968)—and his most highly-regarded work was published just a few years before his death. *Maximum Security Ward* (1970) is about a sick old man summoning up all his powers of imagination, memory and wit to overcome a sense of desolation.

GUTIÉRREZ GONZÁLEZ, Gregorio
(1826–72)

Colombian poet, born in Ceja del Tambo, Antioquia, whose manners he celebrated in his famous bucolic poem *Memoria sobre el cultivo del maíz en Antioquia* (1868, 'Memories Concerning the Cultivation of Maize in Antioquia'). Gutiérrez González is a homely humorist who naturalizes his source, the *Georgics* of **Virgil**, in the interests of Antioquia's beauties and customs. The poem is still readable.

GUTIÉRREZ NÁJERA, Manuel
(1859–95)

Mexican poet and story writer, born in Mexico City. Educated in a French school, he was mainly influenced by French models, such as **Verlaine** and the symbolists. His versification has been praised as achieving the most pleasing qualities in Spanish for 'perhaps a century' before him. He drank heavily, was haunted by his ugliness, and yet was never able to express himself with real power—only with mellifluousness. His prose sketches are delicate but void of true meaning. He is reckoned to have been an important precursor of *modernismo*.
▷B G and J L Carpenter, *Manuel Gutiérrez Najera* (1966)

GUTZKOW, Karl Ferdinand
(1811–78)

German author, born in Berlin. He was influenced by the French Revolution of 1830, and for his *Wally die Zweiflerin* (1835, 'Doubting Wally') got three months' imprisonment as a champion of the 'Young Germany' movement. He next became a journalist, and in 1847 director of the Court Theatre at Dresden, having meanwhile written many dramas,

the most successful being *Richard Savage* (1839) and *Zopf und Schwert* (1844, 'Pigtail and Sword'). Among his romances is *Die Ritter vom Geiste* (1850–2, 'The Knights of the Spirit').
▷ E W Dubert, *Karl Gutzkow und seine Zeit* (1968)

GUZMAN, Martín Luis
(1887–1976)

Mexican novelist, editor and journalist, born in Chihuahua. With **Azuela**, Guzmán was the most important novelist of the revolution, all the events of which he recorded in his fiction. Originally a lawyer, he became a supporter of Madero, and then, after the latter's assassination, private secretary to Pancho Villa. Later, a revolutionary who could not abide revolutionaries, he abandoned Mexico for New York and Madrid—but finally returned in 1936. *El águila y la serpiente* (1928, Eng trans 'The Eagle and the Serpent', 1930), though not quite achieving the literary quality of the fiction of Azuela, became the most famous of all Mexican novels of the Revolution. Partly autobiographical, it tells of his own participation. *La sombra del caudillo* (1929, 'In the Shadow of the Leader'), his best novel, deals with the dominance of Obregón. His *Memorias de Pancho Villa* (1938–51, Eng trans *Memoirs of Pancho Villa*, 1965) is certainly a novel, but is told in the authentic voice of the illiterate caudillo.
▷ J S Brushwood, *Mexico in its Novel* (1970);

W M Langford, *The Mexican Novel Comes of Age* (1971)

GWYNN, Stephen Lucius
(1864–1950)

Irish biographer and literary historian, born in Dublin into a scholarly family, grandson of William Smith O'Brien. Educated in Dublin and at Brasenose College, Oxford, he became a schoolmaster and then a journalist in London (1896–1904). He moved into Irish nationalist politics as MP for Galway (1906–18), and later wrote a fine memoir of his leader, *John Redmond's Last Years* (1919). His wife became a Roman Catholic and their sons prominent Roman Catholic intellectuals. His literary output was prodigious, his *Masters of English Literature* (1904) proving one of the great best-sellers of all time. Perhaps his most remarkable work is *Experiences of a Literary Man* (1926), a great record of the meaning of life in the midst of literature.

GYP, pseud of the **Comtesse de Mirabeau de Martel**
(1849–1932)

French novelist, born in the château of Koëtsal in Brittany. She wrote a series of humorous novels, describing fashionable society, of which the best known are *Petit Bob* (1868, 'Little Bob') and *Mariage de Chiffon* (1894, 'Chiffon Marriage').
▷ *Sac à papier, correspondence with Trois Étoiles* (1886)

H

HAAVIKKO, Paavo
(1931–)

Finnish poet, fiction writer and playwright. He was born in Helsinki, the son of a prosperous businessman. His first job was in the property market, but he began publishing in his early twenties and was immediately hailed as one of the most significant Finnish poets to emerge since the war. His earlier work appeared in *Runot 1951–1961* (1962), which was superseded by another collection in 1974. A concern with Finnish independence runs through his work, sometimes cast in a rather dense and enigmatic form. His best-known work is a quasi-allegorical story, 'Lumeton Aika' ('Before the Snow'), about a future invasion and suppression of national identity. His plays include *Ratsumies* (1974, 'The Horseman'), which the composer Aulis Sallinen made into an opera, with a libretto by Haavikko. Like **T S Eliot**, he draws on contemporary realities—most often, business—to support mythic examinations of human motivation and progress. Haavikko's poetry was first translated into English by **Anselm Hollo** (1974).
▷ H Sihvo, *Soutu Bysanttiin* (1980)

HABIB of Isfahan, Mirza
(c.1854–1897)

Persian translator, born in Chahar Muhal. His chief achievement was a rather odd (but brilliant) one: he put into Persian the English *Adventures of Hajjii Baba of Isahan*, by James Morier, in 1906. This is said to have exercised considerable political influence.
▷ H Kamshad, *Modern Persian Prose Literature* (1966)

HABINGTON, William
(1605–54)

English poet, born in Hindlip, Worcestershire. His father, Thomas (1560–1647), an antiquary, was imprisoned, and his uncle, Edward (?1553–1586) executed, for complicity in Babington's plot. He was educated at St Omer and Paris, and married Lucy Herbert, daughter of the first Lord Powis. He immortalized her in his *Castara* (1634), a collection of metaphysical lyrics which are uneven in quality but contain some pieces of considerable charm. He also wrote *The*

Historie of Edward the Fourth (1640), and a play, *The Queen of Aragon* (1640).
▷ K Allott, introduction and commentary to *The Poems of William Habington* (1948)

HACKER, Marilyn
(1942–)

American poet and editor, born and educated in New York City. In 1961 she married the science-fiction writer **Samuel R Delany**, with whom she edited the little magazine *Quark* (1969–70); she has also been associated with *City Magazine* (1967–70), *Little Magazine* (1977–80) and, since 1980, *13th Moon*. Her early verse was privately printed, and her first commercially published volume was *Presentation Piece* (1970), in which she combines rich, metaphysical imagery and form with disturbingly direct and frank subject-matter, much concerned with death and sexual experimentation. Later collections—*Separations* (1976), *Assumptions* (1980) and *Taking Notice* (1980)—are not so powerful, though they are technically more polished. Hacker won a National Book Award in 1975.

HACKETT, Albert
(1900–)

American playwright and actor, born in New York. He wrote in collaboration with his wife, Frances Goodrich (1891–1984), and they are best remembered for their highly successful stage adaptation of *The Diary of Anne Frank* (1955), which won them a Pulitzer Prize in 1956. Their other stage works include *Western Union, Please* (1939) and *The Great Big Doorstep* (1942). They were also very successful screenwriters, and their many credits include such Hollywood favourites as *The Thin Man* (1934), *Easter Parade* (1948) and *Seven Brides for Seven Brothers* (1954).

HACKS, Peter
(1928–)

German dramatist, poet and critic, born in Breslau (Wrocław, now in Poland). He is often regarded as Germany's leading dramatist of the post-war era. Essentially a disciple of **Bertolt Brecht**, he left West for East Germany in 1955. From 1960 to 1963 he directed the Deutches Theater, but after that the communists actively discouraged his increasingly critical attitude towards them: they claimed

that he lacked a sense of reality. For a time he had to support himself by writing historical plays and translations of classics. Possibly the best of his many and diverse plays, which draw upon any precedent which happens to suit him (**Aristophanes**, Greek myth, **Shakespeare**), are *Moritz Tassow* (1961) and the comic and satirical tour de force about **Goethe** and Charlotte von Stein: *Ein Gespräch im hause Stein über den abwesenden Herrn von Goethe* (1976, 'A Conversation in the Stein Household about the Absent Mr Goethe').
▷J R Scheid, *'Enfant Terrible' of Contemporary East German Drama: Peter Hacks in his Role as Adaptor and Innovator* (1977).

HACOHEN, Shalom
(1772–1845)
Hebrew poet and dramatist, born in Poland. He was one of the earliest members of the Haskalah ('Enlightenment') movement: the 18th- and 19th-century Jews who sought to acquire European culture. He wrote successful verse plays while living in Germany and then in Austro-Hungary.
▷M Waxman, *A History of Jewish Literature* (1960)

HADEWIJCH
(mid-13th century)
Dutch mystic and poet. She wrote poetry and devotional prose in the tradition of St Bernard, and was one of the key mystics of her time. Nothing is known of her life. Some of her letters are translated in *Medieval Netherlands Religious Literature* (1965), by E Colledge.

HÁFIZ, pseud of Shams ed-Dín Muhammed
(d.c.1388)
Persian lyrical poet, born in Shíráz. From the charming sweetness of his poetry he was named by his contemporaries *Chagarlab*, or 'Sugar-lip'. His *ghazals* are all on sensuous subjects—wine, flowers, beautiful damsels—but they also possess an esoteric significance to the initiated, and his name is a household word throughout Iran. Háfiz, like nearly all the great poets of Persia, was of the sect of Súfi philosophers, the mystics of Islam. His tomb, two miles northeast of Shíráz, has been magnificently adorned by princes, and is visited by pilgrims from all parts of Iran.
▷G M Wickens, 'Hafez', in *Encyclopaedia of Islam* (1971, rev edn)

HAFIZ IBRAHIM
(1871–1932)
Egyptian poet and translator (of **Hugo**'s *Les Misérables*), called 'the poet of the Nile', born

on a Nile boat. He was Egypt's leading classical Arabic poet, famous for his skilled and sonorous obituaries, such as his well-known one for Queen Victoria. He is of mainly historical importance, not being much read for pleasure today.
▷*Middle Eastern Affairs* (1952)

HAFSTEIN, Hannes (Pétursson)
(1861–1922)
Icelandic politician and poet, born at Möðruvellir in the north of Iceland, the first Icelandic premier under Home Rule (1904–7, 1912–14). He studied at Reykjavík and Copenhagen University, where he became a brilliant lawyer. He returned to Iceland in 1887 a fervent nationalist with a growing reputation as a lyric poet, and became leader of the independence party in the campaign for Home Rule from Denmark. In his premiership he brought about large improvements in education, health care and commerce, and inaugurated a telephone and telegraph system. In his poetry he was one of the early proponents of realism in Icelandic literature.

HAGEDORN, Friedrich von
(1708–54)
German poet, born in Hamburg. In 1733 he became secretary to the 'English Court' trading company at Hamburg, and wrote satirical, narrative and 'society' verse, much of it dedicated to a cheerful, optimistic outlook on life. His fables were popular in his own day.
▷C J Schmid, *Biographie der Dichter* (1879)

HAGEDORN, Hermann
(1882–1964)
American biographer, editor and poet, born in New York. Much of his writing and editing was devoted to Theodore Roosevelt, whom he admired beyond idolatry. He also wrote a biography of Albert Schweitzer. His verse—which has not lasted—was conventional, somewhat in the mould of the more popular side of **Rudyard Kipling**.
▷*The Hyphenated Family* (1960)

HAGELSTANGE, Rudolf
(1912–84)
German religious poet and novelist, born in Nordhausen. Hagelstange began his career as a journalist before being conscripted in 1940. His *Venezianisches Credo* (1945), an eloquent sonnet sequence, had earlier been passed round secretly as an underground condemnation of Nazism. *Ballade vom verschütteten Leben* (1952, Eng trans *Ballad of the Buried Life*, 1962), about two German soldiers trapped in a shelter at the end of the war, has been acclaimed as one of the most

powerful long poems of the century. Other poetry is collected in *Gast der Elemente Zyklen und Nachdichtungen 1944–72* (1972, 'Guest of the Elements').

HAGGARD, Sir (Henry) Rider
(1856–1925)

English novelist, born in Bradenham Hall, Norfolk, the son of a lawyer. Educated at Ipswich grammar school, he went to Natal in 1875 as secretary to Sir Henry Bulwer, and next year accompanied Sir Theophilus Shepstone to the Transvaal. He returned in 1879 (finally in 1881) to England, married, and settled down to a literary life. His *Cetewayo and his White Neighbours* (1882) pleased the Cape politicians, but attracted no attention elsewhere. *King Solomon's Mines* (1885) made him famous, and was followed by *She* (1887), *Allan Quatermain* (1887), *Eric Bright-eyes* (1891), *The Pearl Maiden* (1903), *Ayesha: The Return of She* (1905) and many other stories. Other publications include *Rural England* (1902) and *The Days of My Life* (1926).
▷M Cohen, *Rider Haggard* (1960)

HAGGARD, William, pseud of Richard Henry Michael Clayton
(1907–)

English novelist, born in Croydon, Surrey. Employed by the Civil Service in London, he served with the Indian Army during World War II. One of the finest exponents of the spy and suspense novel, Haggard's most popular character is Colonel Charles Russell of the Security Executive, a high-level branch of British Intelligence, who features in over 20 novels after his first appearance in *Slow Burner* (1958). A stiff-upper-lipped patriot, he is an autocrat, motivated more by duty than principle, and intensely suspicious not only of left-wingers but also of all intellectuals. Other novels, such as *The Diplomatist* (1987), feature as hero the black Englishman, Willy Smith.

HAGIWARA Sakutaro
(1886–1942)

Japanese poet, born into a wealthy rural family living and farming on the Kanto plain. His work, however, is strongly associated with Tokyo and is fondly regarded by its citizens. He was the first Japanese poet to make extensive use of free verse. His two best collections of verse, *Tsuki ni Hoeru* (1917, Eng trans *Howling at the Moon*, 1978) and *Aoneko* (1923, 'Blue-Cat'), are full of introspective, quiet portraits of tiny, often very dark, aspects of life in Tokyo. He was an admirer of **Edgar Allan Poe**, and his verse reflects this in its themes and mood. His prose writings,

mainly deeply pretentious musings on literary theory, are incomprehensible.

HAHN-HAHN, Ida, Countess
(1805–80)

German novelist, born in Tressow in Mecklenburg-Schwerin. She wrote society novels influenced by the 'Young Germany' movement, before turning Catholic and founding a convent in Mainz (1854).
▷E I Schmid Juergens, *Ida Gräfin Hahn-Hahn* (1933)

HAICÉAD, Pádraigín
(1600–54)

Irish poet, born in Tipperary. He was a Dominican monk. He has been compared to **Céitinn** for his patriotism and eloquence. He played a part in the battle against Cromwell, but was obliged to flee to Louvain—where he had been ordained—when the latter prevailed.

HAILEY, Arthur
(1920–)

English-born Canadian popular novelist, born in Luton. He became a naturalized Canadian in 1947. He has written many bestselling blockbusters about disasters, several of which enjoyed a new lease of life when filmed. Indicative titles include *Hotel* (1965), *Airport* (1968) and *Wheels* (1971).

HALAS, Frantisek
(1901–49)

Usually regarded as the greatest of the 20th-century Czech poets, born in Brno. 'Halasism' was a term of opprobrium amongst the clerks in charge of Czech communist culture. He had welcomed the Stalinist takeover, but then died feeling betrayed (he referred to his 'whored up dreams'). He began as a proletarian poet, but soon, after a brief period during which he was a part of the Czech inter-war 'poetist' movement—an optimistic, playful affair, in defiance of the realities which threatened Czechoslovakia—adopted an extreme 'subjectivism'. The two individual poets who most influenced him were **Rilke** (himself eventually a Czech, though writing in German), and the father of Czech poetry, **Karel Mácha**. His most characteristic collection, *Staré zeny* (1935, Eng trans *Two Women*, 1947), expresses his anxiety and his view of the human predicament as something essentially tragic, which yet might be overcome by true hope. Poetry in translation includes: *Our Lady Bozena Nemcová* (1944) and *A Garland of Children's Verse* (1968).
▷A French, *The Poets of Prague* (1969)

HALDEMAN, Joe (Joseph William)
(1943–)

American science-fiction writer, born in Oklahoma City. He served as a combat engineer in the Vietnam War, and was severely wounded in action. His first novel, *War Year* (1972), was set in Vietnam, but his experiences there are also reflected in much of his science fiction, beginning with *The Forever War* (1974). *Mindbridge* (1976) was more experimental in form than in content. *All My Sins Remembered* (1977) is notable for its cogent portrait of a man attempting to create internal order from the chaos around him, while the *Worlds* trilogy (1981–92) treats a similar theme, albeit with a female protagonist and a more wide-ranging canvas. He has written a number of other novels and stories, but is not prolific.

HALE, Edward Everett
(1822–1909)

American essayist, biographer and fiction writer, born into a distinguished Boston family. After Harvard he became a journalist and Unitarian clergyman, finally becoming Chaplain to the US Senate. His philanthropical and political writings include *Letters on Irish Immigration* (1852); among his biographical works is *Franklin in France* (1887–8); and he wrote two fascinating volumes of autobiography, *A New England Boyhood* (1893) and *Memories of a Hundred Years* (1902). There is a strongly moralistic tone to his writing, particularly in his many works for children, but he could also be humorous, as in the story 'My Double and How He Undid Me' (1859). His varied fiction is now almost forgotten, apart from the famously patriotic 'The Man Without a Country' (1863), which many were convinced was a factual account.
▷J Holloway, *Edward Everett Hale: A Biography* (1956)

HALE, Nancy
(1908–90)

American novelist and critic, wife of the scholar Fredson Bowers, and grand-daughter of **Edward Everett Hale**. She was born in Boston. Her novels and stories are lively and amusing, but her chief work is *A New England Girlhood* (1958).

HALE, Sarah Josepha, née Buell
(1788–1879)

American writer, born in Newport, New Hampshire. In 1828 she became Editor of the *Ladies' Magazine*, Boston. She wrote a novel, *Northwood* (1827), and a book of *Poems for Our Children* (1830), which contained 'Mary had a Little Lamb'.
▷R Finley, *The Lady of Godey's* (1931)

HALÉVY, Léon
(1802–83)

French writer, brother of Jacques Halévy, born in Paris. He became Professor of Literature at the Polytechnic School. He wrote the introduction to Saint-Simon's *Opinions* (1825), also histories, poetry, fables, novels, dramatic poems, and translations of such works as *Macbeth* and *Clavigo*. His most important books are his *Résumé de l'histoire des juifs* (1827–8, 'Short History of the Jews'), *Poésies européennes* (1837, 'European Poetry'), and *La Grèce tragique* (1845–61, 'The Tragedy of Greece').

HALÉVY, Ludovic
(1834–1908)

French playwright and novelist, son of **Léon Halévy**, born in Paris. In 1861 he became secretary to the Corps Législatif. With **Henri Meilhac** he wrote libretti for the best-known operettas of Offenbach, and for Bizet's *Carmen*, and produced vaudevilles and comedies. His *Madame et Monsieur Cardinal* (1873) and *Les petites Cardinal* (1880) are delightful sketches of Parisian theatrical life. *L'Invasion* (1872) contained his personal recollections of the war. His charming *L'Abbé Constantin* (1882) was followed by *Criquette* (1883, Eng trans 1891), *Deux Mariages* (*Un mariage d'amour*, 1880, Eng trans *Marriage for Love*, 1890); and *Un grand mariage* (1883, 'A Grand Marriage'), *Princesse* (1884) and *Mariette* (1893).
▷*Carnets* (1935)

HALEY, Alex Palmer
(1921–92)

American novelist and biographer, born in Ithaca, New York state, and brought up in North Carolina. He worked as a coastguard for 20 years from 1939, turning to writing only with the publication in 1965 of *The Autobiography of Malcolm X*, Haley co-authoring the book after the assassination of the black activist. *Roots*, published in 1976, was a phenomenal success, being adapted for television and winning a Pulitzer Prize the following year. Beginning with the life of Kunta Kinte, an African who was enslaved and taken to America, this novel—or, to use Haley's preferred term for his realism, 'faction'—documented the history of black Americans; its essentially optimistic approach rendered it accessible to a large white audience.

HALIBURTON, Hugh, pseud of **James Logie Robertson**
(1846–1922)

Scottish poet, born in Milnathort, Kinross. He became a student-teacher in Haddington, East Lothian, and later studied at Edinburgh. He became the first English master at Edinburgh Ladies' College, later Mary Erskine's School (1876–1913). In the guise of a shepherd in the Ochil Hills, 'Hugh Haliburton', he published *Horace in Homespun: A Series of Scottish Pastorals* (1886) and *Ochil Idylls* (1891). He also wrote essays, and produced editions of several Scottish poets.

HALIBURTON, Thomas Chandler
(1796–1865)

Canadian writer and jurist, born in Windsor, Nova Scotia. He was called to the Bar in 1820, and became a member of the House of Assembly, chief justice of the common pleas (1828), and judge of the supreme court (1842). In 1856 he retired to England, and from 1859 to 1863 was Conservative MP for Launceston. He is best known as the creator of Sam Slick, a sort of American Sam Weller, in newspaper sketches collected between 1837 and 1840 as *The Clockmaker, or Sayings and Doings of Samuel Slick of Slickville*, continued as *The Attaché, or Sam Slick in England* (1843–4). Other works include *Traits of American Humour* (1843) and *Rule and Misrule of the English in America* (1850).
▷V Chittick, *Thomas Chandler Haliburton* (1924)

HALIDE EDIB, (Adivar)
(1884–1964)

Turkish novelist, dramatist and politician, born in Istanbul, and educated at the American College for Girls there. She published her first novel in 1909. In 1919 she became, together with her husband, a leading supporter of Kemal Attatürk—but later they had to go into exile on account of their opposition to his policies. During this period she wrote several books on Turkish affairs in English. Her novels are competent studies of educated women and their problems, and include *Atesten Gömlek* (1922, Eng trans *The Daughter of Smyrna*, 1938) and (in English) *The Clown and his Daughter* (1935).

HALIFAX, Charles Montagu, 1st Earl of
(1661–1715)

English statesman and poet, a nephew of the Parliamentary general, the Earl of Manchester, born in Horton, Northamptonshire. From Westminster he passed in 1679 to Trinity College, Cambridge. He held high political office, including Chancellor of the Exchequer and Prime Minister, and was responsible for setting up the Bank of England. His most notable poetical achievement was a parody on **Dryden**'s *The Hind and The Panther*, entitled *The Town and Country Mouse* (1687), of which he was joint author with **Matthew Prior**.

HALIKARNAS BALIKÇISI, pseud of **Cevat Sakir**
(1886–1973)

Turkish novelist, 'The Fisherman of Halicarnassus', born in Istanbul. He attended Oxford in the early years of the 20th century, and was later imprisoned for 'sedition'. An enterprising man, he was famous as a translator, journalist and a tourists' guide to the Aegean coast. His popular novels, such as *Deniz Gurbetçileri* (1969, 'Exiles of the Sea'), are based on his vast knowledge of the coast.

HALL, Basil
(1788–1844)

Scottish travel writer, born in Edinburgh. A naval officer (1802–23), he wrote popular works on Korea, Chile, Peru and Mexico and *Travels in North America* (1829). He also wrote novels and short stories. He died insane.
▷ *The Midshipman* (1862)

HALL, Donald (Andrew)
(1928–)

American poet and editor, born in New Haven, Connecticut. He was educated at Harvard and Oxford, and pursued an academic career alongside his writing and editing. In addition to editing many anthologies, he was poetry editor of *Paris Review* (1953–62). His highly crafted but sometimes rather academic poems made creative use of established forms. His first important book was *Exiles and Marriages* (1955). Other significant collections include *The Alligator Bride: Poems New and Selected* (1969), *Kicking the Leaves* (1978) and *The Twelve Seasons* (1983). The increasing expansiveness of his later work is most fully evident in the rural sequence *The One Day* (1988). His other works include books for children, literary criticism, and a prose memoir, *String Too Short to Be Saved* (1961), which he later adapted as the verse drama *The Bone Ring* (1987).

HALL, Oakley Maxwell
(1920–)

American writer of popular fiction for the mystery, crime and Western markets. For 20 years he was Director of Programs in Writing at the University of California (Irvine) and he has published a book on *The Art and Craft of Novel Writing* (1989). His recent fiction includes *Lullaby* (1982), *The Children of the Sun* (1983) and *Apaches* (1986). He also wrote the libretto for an opera based on **Wallace Stegner**'s *Angle of Repose*.

HALL, (Marguerite) Radclyffe
(1886–1943)

English writer, born in Bournemouth. She began as a lyric poet with several volumes of verse, some of which have become songs, but turned to novel writing in 1924 with *The Forge* and *The Unlit Lamp*. Her *Adam's Breed* (1926) won the Femina Vie Heureuse and the James Tait Black Memorial prizes, but her best-known book, *The Well of Loneliness* (1928), which embodies a sympathetic approach to female homosexuality, caused a prolonged furore and was banned in Britain for many years.
▷U V Troubridge, *The Life and Death of Radclyffe Hall* (1961)

HALL, Rodney
(1935–)

English-born Australian writer and critic, born in Solihull, Birmingham. He was poetry editor of the *Australian* (1967–78) and has published a number of books of verse, beginning with *Penniless till Doomsday* (1962). His *Selected Poems* appeared in 1975. Novels include *The Ship on the Coin* (1972) and *Just Relations* (1982), a hallucinatory tale of the small township 'Whitey's Falls', where most of the inhabitants are geriatric and inter-related. Hall's other contribution has been the editing of important anthologies: *Impulses in Australian Poetry* (1968, with **Thomas Shapcott**), *Australian Poetry* (1970) and *The Collins Book of Australian Poetry* (1981).

HALL, Roger Leighton
(1939–)

English-born New Zealand playwright, born in Woodford Wells, Essex. His *Glide Time* (1976), a satirical look at office life, was a success upon first production, as was *Middle-Age Spread* (1977), a tragi-comedy of mid-life crises which had a successful London West End season. He wrote the book for a musical, *Footrot Flats* (1983), based on the newspaper comic strip, and *The Hansard Show* (1986). Later essays in more serious vein were less successful, and *Conjugal Rites* (1990) signalled a return to domestic farce.

HALL, Willis
(1929–)

English dramatist, born in Leeds. His early work was written for radio; his first stage success was *The Long and the Short and the Tall* (1958), dealing with the members of a British military patrol lost in the Malayan jungle in 1942. Hall followed this with the short plays *Last Day in Dreamland* and *A Glimpse of the Sea* (both 1959), both set in a seaside resort. He has since collaborated extensively with **Keith Waterhouse**, notably on *Billy Liar* (1960), derived from the latter's novel about a north-country Walter Mitty, and on the farce, *Say Who You Are* (1965). *Saturday, Sunday, Monday* (1973) and *Filumena* (1973), based on plays by **Eduardo de Filippo**, were both enormous successes.

HALLE, Adam de la
(c.1235–1287)

French poet and composer, born in Arras, nicknamed 'le bossu d'Arras', 'the Hunch-back' (although he was not misshapen). He followed Robert II of Artois to Naples in 1283. He was the originator of French comic opera, with *Le Jeu de Robin et de Marion* ('A Play about Robin and Marion'), and the modern comedy of the half-autobiographical composition called *Le Jeu Adan ou de la feu-illée* ('A Play about Adam'). He also wrote poems in medieval verse forms.
▷T Nisard, *Adam de la Halle* (1867)

HALLECK, Fitz-Greene
(1790–1867)

American poet, born in Guilford, Connecticut. He became a clerk in New York, and in 1832 private secretary to John Jacob Astor; in 1849 he retired to Guilford on an annuity left him by Astor. He published numerous poems, including the long mock-**Byron**ic poem, *Fanny* (1819), a satire on the literature, fashions and politics of the time.
▷N F Adkins, *Fitz-Greene Halleck* (1930)

HALLGRÍMSSON, Jónas
(1807–45)

Icelandic lyric poet, born in Hraun in the north of Iceland, the most important innovator in modern Icelandic poetry. He attended the Latin School at Bessastaðir, where he read deeply in classical and Old Icelandic literature, and then studied law at Copenhagen University before turning to natural history and literature. As a student he and his friends founded the periodical *Fjölnir* (1835–47), which added inspiration to the independence movement led by Jón Sigurðsson. His poetry brilliantly combined fervent nationalism—as in 'Island' (1835), with which *Fjölnir* was launched—and intensely lyrical romanticism, and he is still the best loved of all Icelandic poets. His collected poems were first published in 1847; an English edition appeared in 1930.
▷T V Gislason, *Jónas Hallgrímsson* (1903)

HALLIWELL, David
(1936–)

English actor, director and playwright, born in Brighouse, Yorkshire. Halliwell has written many plays, but is best-known for his first, produced in the UK as *Little Malcolm and His Struggle Against the Eunuchs* (1965) and in the USA as *Hail Screwdyke* (1966). This anarchic piece captured the contemporary mood of antagonism against authority among many young people, particularly those in further education.

HALPER, Albert
(1904–)

American novelist and story writer, born in Chicago. A latter-day naturalist, with great sympathy for the working classes of whose bitter lives he wrote, Halper has been underrated by most literary critics. *The Golden Watch* (1953) is evocative of the pre-World War I years in Chicago. *This is Chicago* (1952) is an influential anthology of stories about the city. His autobiographical *Good-bye, Union Square* (1970), recalling his first big success, *Union Square* (1933), contains a wealth of significant detail. His style is not elegant, but it has drive and power.

HAMBURGER, Michael Peter Leopold
(1924–)

German-born poet and translator, he has lived since 1933 in the UK. He published his first ground-breaking translation of **Hölderlin** in 1943, while still a student. Hamburger served in the Royal Army Education Corps during the war, and after it became a university teacher in London and Reading. During the late sixties and seventies he held visiting professorships at a number of US campuses, having established an international reputation for his versions of poets, mostly but not exclusively German, who had hitherto been unknown or under-appreciated in English, such as **Georg Trakl**, **Günter Grass** and **Nelly Sachs**. Hamburger's own poetry combines sensuousness and intellectual force; his critical book *The Truth of Poetry* (1969) is indirectly revealing about the 'tensions' underlying his own work. The *Travelling* sequence (1972, 1975, 1976) and *Palinode* (1977) trace his artistic itinerary, confirming that the stylistic associations he has contracted with other poets are subordinated to his own vision. A *Collected Poems 1941–1983* was published in 1984, following an important essay collection on German literature, *A Proliferation of Prophets* (1983).
▷ *A Mug's Game: Intermittent Memoirs 1924–1954* (1973)

HAMEIRI, Avigdor, pseud of **Emil Feuerstein**
(1887–1970)

Hungarian Hebrew poet, translator (of **Stefan Zweig**, **Max Brod**, and others), editor, novelist and journalist, born in Bereg in the Carpathian section of Russia. He was the one Jewish writer to be influenced by, and to have affinities with, the 'father of Hungarian literary modernism', **Endre Ady**. He fought in World War I, and was taken prisoner by the Russians. He settled in Palestine in 1921, and eventually became the co-editor of the 'Jewish Hansard', the *Divrei Knesset*. His best-known work is *Hashigaon Hagadol* (1929, Eng trans *The Great Madness*, 1954), one of the most impressive and terrible novels written about World War I.
▷ M Waxman, *A History of Jewish Literature* (1960)

HAMILTON, Edmond
(1904–77)

American writer of science fiction, born in Ohio. Hamilton started writing in the 1920s, contributing to the pulp magazines under a range of pseudonyms. It was largely through Hamilton's work for *Weird Tales and Amazing Stories* that certain basic sci-fi concepts (galactic civilizations, cosmic radiation) took hold. His lasting fictional creation was the tritely-named Captain Future. Hamilton's wife, Leigh Brackett, also wrote science fiction.

HAMILTON, Patrick
(1904–62)

English novelist, born in Hassock, Sussex. His gift was the rendition of a particular brand of English middle-class existence, marked by reticence, fear and sublimated desire. *Craven House* (1926) was his first novel, but it was with *Rope* (1929) and *Gaslight* (both filmed by Alfred Hitchcock) that he became well known. Apart from *Hangover Square* (1940), his most substantial achievement was the 'Gorse' trilogy: *The West Pier* (1951), *Mr Stimpson and Mr Gorse* (1953) and *Unknown Assailant* (1955).
▷ S French, *Patrick Hamilton* (1994)

HAMILTON, William
(c.1665–1751)

Scottish poet, of Gilbertfield, near Glasgow, born in Ladyford, Ayrshire. An army officer like his father, he turned to writing and collecting verse. He was the friend and correspondent of **Allan Ramsay**, with whom he exchanged a series of *Familiar Epistles*. His most notable poem is the mock heroic *Last Dying Words of Bonny Heck*, about a greyhound. In 1772 he published an English translation of **Blind Harry**'s *Wallace*.

HAMILTON, William
(1704–54)

Scottish poet, born in Bangour, West Lothian. Educated at the High School of Edinburgh, and Edinburgh University, he contributed romantic songs and ballads to **Allan Ramsay**'s *Tea-table Miscellany* (1724). He joined in the Jacobite Rising of 1745, and on its collapse escaped to Rouen, but was permitted to return in 1749 and to succeed to the family estate of Bangour. The first collection of his poems was edited by Adam Smith in 1748. He is best known for his ballad, 'The Braes of Yarrow'.

HAMMERSTEIN, Oscar II
(1895–1960)

American librettist. He was the author of a large number of musical plays, often in collaboration with the composer Richard Rodgers (1902–79), of which the most popular were *Rose Marie* (1924), *Desert Song* (1926), *Music in the Air* (1932), *Oklahoma!* (1943), *Carmen Jones* (1943), *The King and I* (1951) and *The Sound of Music* (1959). He shared a Pulitzer Prize in 1950 with Rodgers and co-writer Joshua Logan (1908–88) for *South Pacific* (1949).

HAMMETT, (Samuel) Dashiell
(1894–1961)

American crime writer, born in St Mary's County, Maryland. He grew up in Philadelphia and Baltimore and left school at 14. He was a messenger boy, newsboy, clerk, time keeper, yardman, machine operator, and stevedore before joining the Pinkerton Detective Agency as an operator. World War I ruined his health, and interrupted his sleuthing but he took it up again on his discharge. He served his literary apprenticeship in magazines like *Black Mask*, writing stories as hard and multi-faceted as diamonds. His four best novels—*Red Harvest* (1929), *The Dain Curse* (1929), *The Maltese Falcon* (1930) and *The Glass Key* (1931)—made the scarred ex-detective a celebrity in Hollywood and New York, where he met **Lillian Hellman**, with whom he lived for the rest of his life; but he had already taken to the bottle and never equalled his first literary successes. *The Thin Man* (1934), written in a brief period of sobriety in **Nathanael West**'s mismanaged hotel, has an inflated reputation largely because it was made into a popular film, as were all of Hammett's novels. Drinking and gambling excessively, he made a living scriptwriting. He enlisted during World War II but was discharged with emphysema, but he continued to drink immoderately until 1948 when an attack of delirium tremens turned him to temperance. Politically a radical, he was anti-McCarthy and served a six-month jail sentence for his sympathies. A collection of short stories, *The Big Knockover and Other Stories* (1966), appeared posthumously. Original, unsentimental and an acute social observer, he is the father of the hard-boiled school of detective fiction.

▷D Johnson, *Dashiel Hammett: a life* (1983)

HAMMOND INNES, Ralph
(1913–)

English novelist, born in Horsham, Sussex. A former journalist, he published his first novel, *The Doppelganger*, in 1937. He has since written over 30 books and become established as one of the most prominent authors of adventure fiction. Mystery, suspense and romance play their part in his novels, in which the recurring theme is the struggle between man and nature, and the effect of man's actions upon the natural world. Possibly his most famous title is *The Mary Deare* (1956, published in the USA as *The Wreck of the Mary Deare*), dealing with a sea captain's struggle to save his ship after it runs aground on a treacherous reef in the English Channel. Not only has it become one of the most popular of sea stories, its comparatively slender plot gives scope for some of Hammond Innes's finest descriptive writing.

HAMP, Pierre, pseud of **Pierre Bourillon**
(1876–1962)

French author, born in Nice of humble parentage. He was in every sense a self-made and self-educated man, and brought to bear in his novels a realism bred of firsthand experience. Among his works are *Marée fraîche* (1908, 'Fresh-Caught Fish'), *Le Rail* (1912), *Les Métiers blessés* (1919, 'The Injured Trades'), *Le Lin* (1924, 'Flax') and *La Laine* (1931, 'Wool'), his novels of industrial life forming a cycle which he called *La Peine des hommes* ('The Suffering of Men').

HAMPOLE, Richard Rolle de
(c.1290–1349)

English hermit and poet, the 'Hermit of Hampole' (near Doncaster), born in Thornton in Yorkshire. He was sent to Oxford, but at 19 became a hermit. He wrote English lyrics and religious books in Latin and English, and translated and expounded the Psalms in prose. However, *The Pricke of Conscience (Stimulus Conscientiae)* is no longer thought to be by him.

▷F Comper, *The Life of Richard Rolle* (1928)

HAMPTON, Christopher
(1946–)

English dramatist, born in the Azores and educated at Oxford. His first play, *When Did You Last See My Mother?* (1964), led to his appointment as the Royal Court Theatre's first resident dramatist. The Court produced all his earlier plays, including *Total Eclipse* (1968), *The Philanthropist* (1970), *Savages* (1973), set in Brazil, and *Treats* (1976). His finest play is considered to be *Tales From Hollywood* (1982), but his most commercial success has been *Les Liaisons Dangereuses*, a penetrating study of sexual manners, morality and responsibility, adapted from the novel by **Pierre Laclos**, which was staged in 1985 and filmed in 1988. *White Chameleon* was staged at the National Theatre in 1991. He has made many adaptations and translations, including the serialization of Oswald Wynd's *The Ginger Tree* for television in 1989.

HAMSUN, Knut, pseud of **Knut Pedersen**
(1859–1952)

Norwegian novelist, winner of the Nobel Prize for literature, born in Lom in Gudbrandsdal. He had no formal education, and spent his boyhood with his uncle, a fisherman on the Lofoten Islands. He worked at various odd jobs, including shoemaking, coal-mining and teaching, and twice visited the USA (1882–4, 1886–8), where he worked as a streetcar attendant in Chicago and a farmhand in North Dakota. He sprang to fame with his novel *Sult* (1890, 'Hunger'), followed by *Mysterier* (1892, 'Mysteries') and the lyrical *Pan* (1894). His masterpiece is considered *Markens grøde* (1917, 'Growth of the Soil'), which was instrumental in his award of the 1920 Nobel Prize for literature. His last novel was the unfinished *Ringen slutlet* (1936, Eng trans *The Circle is Closed*, 1937), which reflected the emotional breakdown and therapeutic breakthrough of the 1920s. A recluse during the inter-war years, he lost popularity during World War II for his Nazi sympathies and support of the Quisling regime, for which he was imprisoned in 1948, but his reputation has been largely rehabilitated.
▷R Ferguson, *The Life of Knut Hamsun* (1987)

HAN SUYIN
(1917–)

Chinese-born English novelist, born Elizabeth Chow in Peking, the daughter of a Belgian mother and a Chinese railway engineer. She studied medicine at Yenching, Brussels and London, where after the death in the civil war of her husband, General Tang, she completed her studies. She then practised in Hong Kong which, with its undercurrents of pro-Western and anti-Western loyalties, Old China versus the New, White versus Yellow, provided the background for her first partly-autobiographical novel *A Many Splendoured Thing* (1952) which, in the love affair of an emancipated Chinese girl and an English journalist, symbolizes the political and ideological climate of the British colony. It was made into a film in 1955. In 1952 she married an English police officer in Singapore, where she practised in an anti-tuberculosis clinic. Her other novels include *Destination Chungking* (1953), *And the Rain my Drink* (1954), *The Mountain is Young* (1958) and *Four Faces* (1963). She also wrote a semi-autobiographical and historical trilogy, *The Crippled Tree* (1965), *A Mortal Flower* (1966) and *Birdless Summer* (1968), and two volumes of contemporary Chinese history, *The Morning Deluge* and *The Wind in the Tower* (1972).

HANDKE, Peter
(1942–)

Austrian dramatist and novelist. Trained as a lawyer, his plays are obscure and the subject of some controversy. His first play, *Publikumsbeschimpfung* (1966, Eng trans *Offending the Audience*, 1970), presents four people who speak randomly and insult the audience. The titles of his other plays are intriguing, such as *Das Mündel will Vormund sein* (1696, Eng trans *My Foot My Tutor*, 1971), *Der Ritt über den Bodensee* (1971, Eng trans *A Ride Across Lake Constance*, 1972), *Wünschloses Unglück* (1972, Eng trans *A Sorrow Beyond Dreams*, 1975 (US); 1976 (UK)) and *Kaspar* (1968, Eng trans *Kaspar*, 1969). His novels include *Die Angst des Tormanns beim Elfmeter* (1970, Eng trans *The Goalie's Anxiety at the Penalty Kick*, 1972 (US); 1977 (UK)) and *Die linkshändige Frau* (1976, Eng trans *The Left-Handed Woman*, 1978 (US); 1980 (UK)).
▷J Schlueter, *The Plays and Novels of Peter Handke* (1981)

HANKA, Václav
(1791–1861)

Czech scholar, poet and forger of medieval poetic manuscripts—apparently he committed his forgeries in order to enrich Czech culture. He succeeded in passing off his epics and lyrics, and they were duly praised by scholars as genuine; but eventually, in a cause célèbre of the 1880s, they were exposed. He was inspired by **Chatterton**, and was expert at his dubious job (in which he was aided by others).

HANKIN, St John
(1869–1909)

English dramatist, born in Southampton. After writing theatre criticism for various journals, and humorous sequels to well-known plays for *Punch*, success came with his second play, *The Return of the Prodigal* (1905), an inversion of the biblical parody in which a worthless son pesters his socially ambitious family for money. Other plays include *The Cassilis Engagement* (1907) and *The Last of the de Mullins* (1909), a drama of an unmarried mother who opens a hat shop. Later that year, Hankin committed suicide by drowning himself in a river in Wales. His plays have almost vanished from the repertoire, but his theatrical achievement was to bridge the gap between the wit of **Oscar Wilde** and the social polemic of **Bernard Shaw**.

HANLEY, James
(1901–85)

Irish novelist and short-story writer, born in Dublin. He grew up in Liverpool, and first went to sea in 1914, plunging himself into a period of hard work and licentious living. *Boy* (1931), one of his first novels, is the life of a young shipworker, with episodes clearly drawn from Hanley's own experiences. *The Furys* (1935) details the travails of the poor Fury family around the time of the General Strike. His short-story collections include *People are Curious* (1938). His gritty, unremitting realism, along with his frank treatment of sex, was capable of causing outrage in his day; now, however, much of his writing seems prolix and relatively artless.
▷ *Broken Water* (1937)

HANRAHAN, Barbara
(1939–)

Australian novelist and printmaker, born in Adelaide, whose novels have a particular ability to convey a sense of place and time. Her first book, *The Scent of Eucalyptus* (1973), is a memoir of her childhood, and was continued in *Kewpie Doll* (1984). Novels include the Gothic *The Albatross Muff* (1977) and *The Frangipani Gardens* (1980). Frequently using a younger female as observer of adult behaviour, she contrasts genteel attitudes with the seamier underside of society.

HANSBERRY, Lorraine Vivian
(1930–65)

American playwright, born in Chicago, educated at the University of Wisconsin and the first black woman to have a play produced on Broadway. This was *A Raisin in the Sun* (1959), a semi-autobiographical account of the emotional and racial problems faced by a black family attempting to move into a neighbourhood traditionally dominated by whites. It was enormously successful and became the basis for *Raisin*, a musical, in 1973. Other plays include *The Sign in Sidney Brustein's Window* (1964), about a community of mixed racial and religious background in Greenwich Village, New York.

HANSEN, Martin Alfred, pseud of Jens Alfred Martin Hansen
(1909–55)

Danish novelist. He came from farming stock, worked on the land and as a teacher, but after 1945 devoted himself to writing. His early novels deal with social problems in the 1930s (*Nu opgiver han*, 1935, 'Surrender'; *Kolonien*; 1937, 'The Colony'). He developed a more profound style in *Jonathans Rejse* (1941, 'Jonathan's Journey') and *Lykkelige Kristoffer* (1945, 'Lucky Christopher'), outwardly picaresque novels but in reality closely related to his work for the Danish underground press during the Occupation. With *Løgneren* (1950, 'The Liar'), a psychological novel intended first for broadcasting as a serial, he reached a wider public. In 1952 came his most original work, the metaphysical *Orm og Tyr* ('The Serpent and the Bull'). Other writings include *Torne-busken* (1946, 'The Thorn Bush', short stories).
▷ C M Woel, *Martin Alfred Hansen. Liv og digtning* (1959)

HANSFORD JOHNSON, Pamela
(1912–81)

English novelist, playwright and critic. Born in London to theatrical parents, her background provided what **Margaret Drabble** has called 'a peculiar vantage point for an unprejudiced insight into a wide range of behaviour'. She left school at 18, working in a bank and as a book reviewer. For a short time in the early 1930s she was engaged to be married to **Dylan Thomas**. Her first novel, *This Bed Thy Centre* (1935), was set in working-class south London, and her many subsequent novels, such as the tragi-comical *The Unspeakable Skipton* (1958), are observant of both the world of her youth, and of society in the sixties and seventies, and range from the comic to the morally insightful. Her critical works include writings on **Thomas Wolfe** and **Proust**. In 1950 she married the novelist **C P Snow** and they collaborated on many literary projects.
▷ I Linbdblad, *Pamela Hansford Johnson* (1982)

HANSSON, Ola
(1860–1925)

Swedish poet and novelist, born in Hönsinge. Having acquired a name with his naturalistic lyric poetry, he left Sweden for Germany in

1890 in the face of negative criticism and public apathy on the publication of his erotic volume, *Sensitiva amorosa* (1887). Thereafter he wrote mostly in German, much influenced by **Nietzsche**, concentrating on the kind of moral anarchism he sketched out in *Parias* (1890, 'Pariahs'). The verses in *Ung Ofegs visor* (1892, Eng trans *Young Ofeg's Ditties*, 1893) are cool and accomplished.

▷O Friesen, *Kylfverstenen, Af von Friesen och Hansson* (1909)

HARDING, Lee
(1937–)

Australian science-fiction writer and editor who also writes for adolescents, born in Colac, Victoria. His first novel, *The Displaced Person* (1979), won the Childrens' Book of the Year Award in 1980. He has written a number of science-fiction novels, and edited the anthologies *Beyond Tomorrow* (1975), *An Encounter with Science Fiction* (1976, with **Ursula Le Guin**) and *Rooms of Paradise* (1978).

HARDWICK, Elizabeth
(1916–)

American essayist, critic and novelist, born in Lexington, Kentucky. She established her literary reputation by writing essays for the *Partisan Review*. Her first novel, *The Ghostly Lover* (1945), describes the relationship between a white woman and her black servant during the era of racial segregation, while the second, *The Simple Truth* (1955), again scrutinizes prejudice and versions of the truth, this time within the legal system and the judiciary. Equally as important as her novels are her collections of essays, ranging across a wide variety of cultural and political issues, but with a keen sensitivity to moral values and human worth. They are collected in *A View of My Own* (1962), *Seduction and Betrayal: Women and Literature* (1974) and *Bartleby in Manhattan* (1983). She was also, in 1963, a founding editor of the *New York Review of Books*. For some time she was married to **Robert Lowell**.

▷D Pinckney, *Paris Review, Writers at Work*, 7th series (1986)

HARDY, Alexandre
(c.1570–c.1631)

French dramatist, born in Paris. His over 500 melodramatic pieces are largely lifted from Spanish authors, but he reduced the role of the chorus in French drama.

▷K Garsche, *Hardy als Barockdramatiker* (1971)

HARDY, Frank
(1917–)

Australian radical novelist and short-story writer, whose writings are filled with his burning anger at injustice and a love of the 'underdog'. He was born in Koroit, Victoria. His first book, *Power without Glory* (1950), immediately made his name. Thinly disguised as fiction, it tells of the less than legal activities of a Melbourne millionaire of the period, and resulted in a libel action which Hardy won. The story of the trial is told in *The Hard Way* (1961). Hardy's true strength is the short story, where his fondness for the larrikin character is evident; the best are collected in *It's Moments Like These* (1972) and *The Great Australian Lover* (1972). He also wrote a scathing account of a strike by aboriginal stockmen in *The Unlucky Australians* (1968).

HARDY, Thomas
(1840–1928)

English novelist, poet and dramatist, born in Upper Bockhampton, near Dorchester, the son of a stonemason. As a boy he learned to play the fiddle and was bookish. He was educated locally and at 16 was articled to an architect. At 22 he went to London to train as an architect, and returned home in 1867 to pursue his chosen profession, but he had already begun his first novel, *The Poor Man and the Lady*, which was never published. There is speculation that around this time he met and fell in love with Tryphena Sparks, to whom he was related. The nature of their relationship is unclear but in 1868 he was sent to St Juliot, Cornwall, where he met Emma Gifford, whom he married in 1874. By then he had published four novels—*Desperate Remedies* (1871), *Under the Greenwood Tree* (1872), *A Pair of Blue Eyes* (1873), and *Far From the Madding Crowd* (1874). The marriage was not idyllic but, ironically, when Emma died in 1912 Hardy was moved to write some of the most moving love poems in the language. A flood of novels continued to appear, vibrant, brooding descriptive passages providing the backdrop to potent tragicomedies. Among the most durable are *The Return of the Native* (1878), *The Mayor of Casterbridge* (1886) and *Tess of the D'Urbervilles* (1891). Though Hardy was held in high esteem, critics carped at his seemingly inbred pessimism, and both *Tess* and *Jude the Obscure* (1895) were attacked virulently; thereafter Hardy turned his attention to poetry which he had always regarded as superior to fiction. His first collection, *Wessex Poems*, appeared in 1898; his last, *Winter Words*, in 1928, the year of his death. After Emma's death he married Florence Dugdale and lived in Dorset, much visited by aficionados and the literati. *The Dynasts*, a gargantuan drama in blank verse, occupied him for many years and was published in three instalments between 1904 and 1908. A biography published initially in two parts in 1928 and 1930 is thought to have been largely dictated by Hardy to Florence though it appeared under her name.

▷ E Hardy, *Thomas Hardy, a critical biography* (1954); I Howe, *Thomas Hardy* (1968)

HARE, David
(1947–)

English dramatist, director and film-maker, born in Bexhill, and one of the finest playwrights of his generation. He graduated from Cambridge and was active in fringe theatre for many years, co-founding Portable Theatre in 1968 and Joint Stock in 1974. He succeeded **Christopher Hampton** as resident dramatist and literary manager of the Royal Court Theatre, London, 1967–71, and at Nottingham Playhouse in 1973. *Slag* was staged in 1970, *The Great Exhibition* in 1972, and *Knuckle* in 1974, but the best of his early works is *Teeth 'n' Smiles* (1975), a commentary on the state of modern Britain. His plays often have linked films, such as *Plenty* (1978), with the complementary television film *Licking Hitler* (1978), and *The Secret Rapture* (his major play to date) and the complementary political film *Paris by Night* (1989). His other television films are *Dreams of Leaving* (1980), and *Saigon... Year of the Cat* (1983). He wrote and directed his first feature film, *Wetherby*, in 1985.

HÄRING, Georg Wilhelm Heinrich, pseud **Willibald Alexis**
(1798–1871)

German writer, born in Breslau. He wrote the historical romance *Walladmor* (1823–4), professedly as by Sir **Walter Scott**, a fraud that led to its translation into several languages (into English, very freely, by **Thomas De Quincey**, 1824). It was followed by *Die Geächteten* (1825, 'The Outlaws'), *Schloss Avalon* (1827, 'Castle Avalon'), and books of travel, sketches and dramas.

▷ P K Richter, *Willibald Alexis, als Literatur und Theaterkritiken* (1931)

HARINGTON, Sir John
(1561–1612)

English courtier and writer, born in Kelston near Bath. From Cambridge he went to the court of his godmother, Queen Elizabeth. His wit brought him into much favour, which he endangered by the freedom of his satires. In 1599 he served under Essex in Ireland, and was knighted by him on the field, much to the queen's displeasure. To strengthen his amazing application to King James VI and I for the office of Chancellor and Archbishop of Ireland he composed in 1605 *A Short View of the State of Ireland*, an interesting and singularly modern essay. He is remembered as the metrical translator of **Ludovico Ariosto**'s *Orlando Furioso* (1591); his other writings include **Rabelais**ian pamphlets, epigrams, *The Metamorphosis of Ajax* (1596), containing the earliest design for a water closet, and a *Tract on the Succession to the Crown*.

▷ T Rich, *Harington and Ariosto* (1940)

HARJO, Joy
(1951–)

American poet, born in Tulsa, Oklahoma. Of mixed Creek, Cherokee and French descent, Harjo often draws on Native American history and mythology in her work. She has published four collections of poetry: *The Last Song* (1975), *What Moon Drove Me to This?* (1980), *She Had Some Horses* (1983), *Secrets from the Center of the World*, with Steven Strom (1989) and, most recently, *In Mad Love and War* (1990). A saxophone player, she often incorporates music in public readings of her poems.

HARLAND, Henry, also writing as **Sidney Luska**
(1861–1905)

American novelist and short-story writer, born in New York, not, as he claimed, in St Petersburg. After brief attendance at Harvard Divinity School and working as a clerk, he turned to writing sentimental melodramatic novels about Jewish immigrants to the USA, such as *My Uncle Florimund* (1888). Then, in 1890, he went to Britain and came under the influence of **Henry James**. Harland is best known for having founded, in 1894, the infamous quarterly *The Yellow Book*, which became one of the leading influences on turn-of-the-century tastes and aesthetics. His best-known fiction, *The Cardinal's Snuff Box* (1900), if anything looks backward to the 19th century rather than forward to the 20th; it is as light and skittish as the title suggests.

▷ K Beckson, *Henry Harland* (1978)

HARNESS, Charles L(eonard)
(1915–)

American science-fiction writer, born in Colorado City, Texas. He worked as a mineral economist for much of the 1940s before becoming a patent attorney. His small body of work, which began with *Flight Into Tomorrow* (1953, also known as *The Paradox Men*), has perhaps found a more appreciative audience amongst his peers (such as **Brian Aldiss** and **Michael Moorcock**) than with the reading public at large. *The Ring of Ritornel* (1968), like *Flight Into Tomorrow*, is set in a technocratic tyranny; *The Catalyst* (1980) in a world where bureaucracy has stifled invention. Harness uses these settings to examine, respectively, the rise and fall of civilizations, and the nature of creativity. His best work represents the genre at its most thoughtful, disciplined and inventive.

HARNICK, Sheldon *see* **ABBOTT, George Francis**

HARPUR, Charles
(1813–68)
Australian poet, born in Windsor, New South Wales, described as 'the grey forefather of Australian poetry'. Harpur made use of traditional, ornate 18th-century English verse patterns, with an overlay of pastoral Australian imagery, in an attempt to create an appropriate colonial style. The little of Harpur's verse that was published during his lifetime, at the expense of Harpur or his friends, is in *Thoughts, a Series of Sonnets* (1845), *The Tower of the Dream* (1865) and a few small pamphlets. His reputation as a poet was not helped by the first posthumous collection, *Poems* (1883), in which the editor excised Harpur's expressions of his personal radicalism and his strong sense of injustice not only for personal misfortunes but also for the social inequalities of 19th-century Australia. Although regularly featured in anthologies, it was only in 1984 that a reasonably complete edition of Harpur's verse, with critical material, was published as *The Poetical Works of Charles Harpur*.

HARRINGTON, (Edward) Michael
(1928–)
American social commentator, born in St Louis, Missouri. He is best known for his massive and strongly advocated study of poverty in the USA, *The Other America* (1962), the title of which coined a phrase that became part of the language and of political rhetoric. A new edition was deemed relevant in 1970, and in 1984, as Reaganomics began to bite, Harrington published a work with an even more pessimistic title, *The New American Poverty*. He remains a rare example of a social scientist who writes well, conveying passion without undue histrionics.
▷ *The Long Distance Runner* (1988)

HARRIS, Frank James Thomas
(1856–1931)
Irish writer and journalist, born, according to his autobiography, in Galway, but according to his own later statement, in Tenby. He ran away to New York at the age of 15,

became a bootblack, a labourer building Brooklyn Bridge, and a worker in a Chicago hotel, but in 1874 embarked upon the study of law at the University of Kansas. About 1876 he returned to England and entered the newspaper world. Perhaps the most colourful figure in contemporary journalistic circles, an incorrigible liar, a vociferous boaster, an unscrupulous adventurer and philanderer, with an obsession with sex which got his autobiography *My Life and Loves* (1923–7) banned for pornography, he nevertheless had a considerable impact on Fleet Street as Editor of the *Fortnightly Review*, *Saturday Review*, *Vanity Fair* and of the *Evening News*, which became under his aegis a pioneer in the new cult of provocative headlines and suggestive sensationalism. He is also remembered for his *Contemporary Portraits* (1915–30), a series of profiles, interesting but distorted by personal prejudice, as well as biographies of **Oscar Wilde** (1920) and **George Bernard Shaw** (1931), some novels, short stories and plays, and two original but not particularly scholarly works on **Shakespeare**.

HARRIS, Joel Chandler
(1848–1908)
American author, born in Eatonton, Georgia. He was in turn printer, lawyer and journalist on the staff of the Atlanta *Constitution* (1876–1900). His *Uncle Remus* (1880) made him internationally famous, at once to children and to students of folklore. Later works are *Nights with Uncle Remus* (1883), *Mingo, Daddy Jake, Aaron in the Wildwoods, Sister Jane, Tales of the Home Folks, Plantation Pageants, Minervy Ann* (1899), and a history of Georgia (1899).
▷ P M Cousins, *Joel Chandler Harris: A Biography* (1968)

HARRIS, (Theodore) Wilson
(1921–)
British novelist, born in New Amsterdam, British Guiana (now Guyana). He was educated at Queen's College, Georgetown and worked as a surveyor. In 1959 he moved to London. He is one of the pre-eminent Caribbean writers, his masterpiece being *The Guyana Quartet* (1960–3); starting with a poetic exploration, it evolves into a composite picture of Guyana, its various landscapes and racial communities. Later works include *The Waiting Room* (1967), *The Tree of Life* (1978) and *Carnival* (1985).

HARRISON, Harry (Henry Maxwell)
(1925–)
American science-fiction writer and editor, born in Connecticut. His original surname was Dempsey, but was changed by his father

as a child. He has travelled widely, and lived in a number of countries. He was an illustrator, mainly of comics, before turning to writing. Much of his most popular work is marked by a sharp sense of humour and a liking for pastiche, as in the multi-volume adventure sequence *The Stainless Steel Rat* (from 1957), featuring his memorable creation Slippery Jim DeGriz. His more serious achievements include *Make Room, Make Room* (1966), a fraught meditation on over-population, and the *Eden* trilogy (1984–8).

HARRISON, Jim (James Thomas)
(1937–)

American novelist, novella-writer and poet, born in Grayling, Michigan and educated at Michigan State University. He writes a rugged, outdoors fiction which has inevitably been compared with **Hemingway**. In fact Harrison has little of Hemingway's softness of touch and simple lyricism. But the early novels, especially *Wolf* (1971) and *Farmer* (1976), were promising. His recent detour into the realm of the novella, which began with *Legends of the Fall* (1979) and continued in 1991 with *The Woman Lit by Fireflies*, has resulted in a rather intense gloominess. His many volumes of poetry have not been much seen outside the USA.

HARRISON, Keith
(1932–)

Australian-born academic, poet and critic, born in Melbourne. His books include *Points in a Journey* (1966), *Songs from the Drifting House* (1972) and *A Town and Country Suite* (1980). He is now resident in North America.

HARRISON, Tony
(1937–)

English poet, whose background in working-class Leeds and subsequent education in the classics create a social tension which has proved his most fruitful theme. The desire to give a poetic voice to those who have historically lacked one informs much of his work, and he deliberately intrudes vernacular speech into traditional poetic forms. He has gained international recognition for his verse translations and adaptations for the theatre, notably of the York Mystery Plays and the Greek tragedies. He has also explored the possibilities of poetry on television with an effective broadcast of his poem *V* (1985), a denunciatory journey through modern British life.

HARROWER, Elizabeth
(1928–)

Australian novelist, born in Sydney, who lived in London during the 1950s. Her novels vary in place and time, but all emphasize the mutual dependence of the weak on the strong, of the female on the male, and all rely on the darker side of human relationships for their drive. The motifs of her first novel, *Down in the City* (1957), are repeated in *The Long Prospect* (1958) and *The Catherine Wheel* (1960). *The Watch Tower* (1966), undoubtedly the best of her writing to date, refines the tensions and conflicts of her earlier works. Harrower's novels are not Australian but international.

HARSANYI, Zsolt
(1887–1943)

Hungarian writer of skilled best-sellers based on the lives of various eminent people such as Liszt, Rubens and Galileo. Many, for example *The Lover of Life* (1942), were translated into English; they are not now much read.

HARSDÖRFFER, Georg Philipp
(1607–58)

German poet and translator (of Italian and Spanish pastorals), born in Nürnberg into a rich patrician Protestant family. His socially ingratiating and over-ornate work has led to his being described as a dilettante, and to a certain extent this is deserved; but more recent critics point to his intelligence and good-heartedness, and emphasize that his attempts to popularize culture were sincere.

HART, Moss
(1904–61)

American dramatist and director, born in the Bronx, New York. He began his career as office boy to the impressario Augustus Pitou, to whom he sold his first play, *The Beloved Bandit*, when still a teenager. His second, *Once in a Lifetime* (1930), was successfully produced after extensive re-writing by **George S Kaufman**. Although he continued to write on his own, his most successful work was always to be collaborative. With Kaufman he wrote several plays, the most popular being the wry comedies *Merrily We Roll Along* (1934), *You Can't Take It With You* (1936) and *The Man Who Came to Dinner* (1939), described by one critic as 'a merciless cartoon' of the critic Alexander Woollcott's 'bad manners, shameless egoism, boundless mischief, and widely assorted friendships'. Hart is also remembered for writing the sketches for the Irving Berlin revue, *As Thousands Cheer* (1933), and the book for the Kurt Weill/**Ira Gershwin** musical, *Lady in the Dark* (1941).
▷ *Act One: An Autobiography* (1959)

HARTE, (Francis) Bret(t)
(1836–1902)

American author, born in Albany, New York. He went to California in 1854, and became a compositor in San Francisco. Sketches of his experiences among the miners attracted much attention. He was secretary of the US Mint in San Francisco (1864–70) and during this period wrote some of his most famous poems, among them 'John Burns of Gettysburg' and 'The Society upon the Stanislau'. In 1868 he founded and edited the *Overland Monthly*, to which he contributed, among others, *The Luck of Roaring Camp* and *The Outcasts of Poker Flat* (both 1870). He was American consul at Krefeld (1878–80) and at Glasgow (1880–5), and then lived in London until his death.
▷R O'Connor, *Bret Harte, a biography* (1966)

HARTLEY, L(eslie) P(oles)
(1895–1972)

English writer, born near Peterborough. His early short stories, *Night Fears* (1924) and *The Killing Bottle* (1932), established his reputation as a master of the macabre. Later he transferred his **James**ian power of 'turning the screw' to psychological relationships and made a new success with such novels as his trilogy *The Shrimp and the Anemone* (1944), *The Sixth Heaven* (1946) and *Eustace and Hilda* (1947), and also *The Boat* (1950)— among his finest work—and *The Go-Between* (1953). Later novels include *A Perfect Woman* (1955), *The Hireling* (1957) and *My Sister's Keeper* (1970).
▷A Mulkeen, *Wild Thyme, Winter Lightning: the symbolic novels of L. P. Hartley* (1974)

HÄRTLING, Peter
(1933–)

German novelist and essayist, born in Chemnitz. For much of his writing life the inability to return to his roots has fuelled his fiction, which has been obsessed with the relationship between history and memory, particularly in the trilogy which culminated in *Das Familienfest oder Das Ende einer Geschichte* (1969, 'The Family Party, or the end of a Story'), in which a fictitious historian explores a fire from which he had escaped in his youth. Prior to the re-unification of Germany his work had become despairingly nihilistic. He has expressed strong views on children's literature and writes for children himself. With the playwright **Rolf Hochhuth**, Härtling has also edited the work of the cyclical novelist, Otto Flake.

HARTMANN VON AUE
(c.1170–1215)

German poet of the Middle High German period, who took part in the Crusade of 1197. The most popular of his narrative poems is *Der arme Heinrich* (c.1195, 'Poor Heinrich'), which, based on a Swabian tradition, is utilized in **Henry Longfellow**'s *Golden Legend*. *Erec* (c.1180–5) and *Iwein* (c.1200) are both drawn from the Arthurian cycle, and closely follow **Chrétien de Troyes**. In *Gregorius* (c.1188), he relates how worldly passion is expiated by religious faith. The songs are mainly love songs.

HARTNETT, Michael
(1941–)

Irish poet, born in Newcastle West, County Limerick. He is a prolific poet in both Gaelic and English, although in 1975, in response to political events in Ireland, he announced with *A Farewell to English* that he would no longer write poems in that language. At that stage his original work *Anatomy of A Cliché* (1968) and his 'transcreations' *Gypsy Ballads* (1973, from the Spanish) and *Tao: A Version of the Chinese Classic of the Sixth Century* (1971) had established him with a reputation for elegant experimentation. The next decade was mainly devoted to translations from other Gaelic writers, before he returned to writing original English poems with the two-volume *Collected Poems* (1984–5). These reinstated him as one of Ireland's most intense observers of implosive emotional politics. In 1990 he was awarded the American Ireland Literary Award, and in 1993 he published *Haicéad*, the first substantial translation of **Pádraigín Haicéad** (c.1600–1654).

HART-SMITH, William
(1911–90)

English-born Australian–New Zealand poet, born in Royal Tunbridge Wells, Kent. He went with his parents to New Zealand, and thereafter moved between Australia (serving with the Australian army in World War II) and New Zealand before returning to Auckland, where he died. He is considered an Australian poet as it was there that he discovered his talent and most of his significant work has been published, including his first, *Columbus Goes West* (1943). His work shows a sympathy with nature and primitive cultures, both aborigine and Maori, and has been likened favourably to the best of **D H Lawrence**'s verse. *Selected Poems 1936–84* (1985) brings together the finest of his work.

HARTZENBUSCH, Juan Eugenio
(1806–80)

Spanish dramatic poet, born in Madrid. He was director of the national library (1862), and wrote 69 plays in all, of which the medieval *Les amantes de Teruel* (1836, Eng trans *The Lovers of Teruel*, 1938) is the best. He translated **Schiller**, and wrote some poetic fables.

HARVEY, Gabriel
(c.1550–1630)

English poet, born in Saffron Walden, the son of a rope-maker. Educated at Christ Church, Cambridge, he became a fellow of Pembroke Hall. Although he was cantankerous and arrogant, he became **Edmund Spenser**'s friend. He published some satirical verses in 1579, and attacked both **Robert Greene** and **Thomas Nashe**. He claimed to be the father of the English hexameter.
▷W Schrickx, *Shakespeare's Early Contemporaries* (1956)

HARWOOD, Gwen, properly Gwendoline Nessie
(1920–)

Australian poet and librettist, born in Taringa, Brisbane. Originally a student and teacher of music, Harwood did not publish her first book of verse, *Poems*, until 1963. *Poems, Volume Two* followed in 1968, and then *Selected Poems* (1975) and *The Lion's Bride* (1981). During that period she wrote librettos for leading Australian composers: Larry Sitsky's operas *The Fall of the House of Usher* (1965), *Lenz* (1972) and *The Golem* (1979), as well as James Penberthy's *Choral Symphony* and Ian Cugley's *Sea Changes*. Much of her poetic work, appearing originally under a number of pseudonyms, is suffused with physical or emotional pain. Harwood has received the **Robert Frost** Award (1977) and the **Patrick White** Literary Award (1978). *Blessed City* was the Melbourne *Age* Book of the Year for 1990.

HARWOOD, Harold Marsh
(1874–1959)

English dramatist, born in Eccles, Lancashire. He served as an army physician during World War I, and married in 1918 Fryn Tennyson Jesse, the author with whom he collaborated on many light plays. He was best known for his political play, *The Grain of Mustard Seed* (1920). He managed the Ambassadors Theatre, London (1920–32).

HARWOOD, Lee
(1939–)

English poet, born in Leicester and educated at Queen Mary College, London. He worked at a variety of jobs while developing a poetic style which is fragmentary, surreal—he has translated and written about **Tristan Tzara**—

but also extremely direct and simply registered. It has become more so as the years have gone by, as seen in the verses in collections like *Title Illegible* (1965), *The Man With Blue Eyes* (1966) or *The Beautiful Atlas* (1969). *H.M.S. Little Fox* (1975) is a linked, romantic sequence; *Notes of a Post Office Clerk* (1976) documents a life in which straightforward communication is of the essence, but is also somewhat problematic. A selected poems, entitled *Crossing the Frozen River*, appeared in 1988.
▷A Kingsley Weatherhead, *The British Dissonance* (1983)

HASAYN, Taha
(1889–1973)

Major Egyptian novelist, story writer, critic and setter and keeper of standards, born in Maghagha. He was blind from early in his life. He obtained the first PhD to be granted in Egypt from the new University at Cairo, for his thesis (1915) on the Arabic poet **Ahmed ibn Abdullah Abul-Ala**. From 1950 until 1952 he was Minister of Education in the government of Mustafa al-Nahass (overthrown by General Neguib), a lapse that was soon forgiven in recognition of his work for education in his country. His autobiography, *Al-Ayyam* (1925–67, Eng trans *An Egyptian Childhood*, 1932, *The Stream of Days*, 1948, *A Passage to France*, 1976), is both a classic account of how the blind react to sound, and an important record of the progress (and regress) of an unhappy country. It helped, as a critic wrote, to mould 'the sensibilities of two generations'. The novel *Shjarat al-bus* (1944, 'The Tree of Misery'), and the stories collected in *Al-Muadhdhabun fi al-ard* (1949, 'The Sufferers on Earth') are the reflections of an essentially humane and liberal sensibility on a grotesquely unjust social system.
▷P Cacchia, *Taha Husayn: His Place in the Egyptian Literary Renaissance* (1956); D Semah, *Four Egyptian Literary Critics* (1974)

HAŠEK, Jaroslav
(1883–1923)

Czech novelist and short-story writer, born in Bohemia. A compulsive and accomplished hoaxer and practical joker who despised pomposity and authority, he is best known for the novel *Dobrý voják Svejk* (1912, Eng trans with two of its sequels as *The Good Soldier Schweyk*, 1930; complete version 1973), a brilliantly incisive satire on military life. The character of Schweyk, an irresponsible and undisciplined drunkard, liar, scrounger and Philistine, is widely thought to be at least partly autobiographical in inspiration. In 1915 he deserted the Austrian Army (Austria ruled Czechoslovakia at the time) and crossed over to the Russian side. Characteristically, however, he managed to make satirical attacks on both regimes.

▷C Parrott, *The Bad Bohemian: the life of Hašek* (1978)

HASENCLEVER, Walter
(1890–1940)

German dramatist and poet, born in Aachen. He wrote the lyrical poems *Der Jüngling* (1913, 'The Youngster') and *Tod und Auferstehung* (1916, 'Death and Resurrection'), and pioneered German Expressionism with his father–son drama *Der Sohn* (1914, 'The Son'). He later wrote a series of comedies, including *Ein besserer Herr* (1927, 'A Better Gentleman'), and film scripts. A pacifist, he committed suicide in a French internment camp.

▷P J Cremers, *Walter Hasenclever* (1922)

HASHIMOTO Osamu
(1948–)

Japanese novelist. Like **Haruki Murakami**, Hashimoto has achieved enormous success in Japan by breaking away from the accepted norms of realistic fiction, introducing a new and invigorating way of writing into Japanese fiction. In Hashimoto's case, it was the student underground movement of the 1970s and left-wing politics which gave rise to these fresh insights, his first novel, *Peach Bottom Girl* (Eng trans 1977), launching him to popular success, at least with a young audience. He is a wicked parodist, often turning Japanese cultural conventions on their head, but, perhaps because of this, has yet to gain a reputation outside Japan.

HASLUCK, Nicholas
(1942–)

Australian writer of short stories, novels and verse, born in Canberra. The former are collected in *The Hat on the Letter 'O'* (1978), the title story of which exemplifies Hasluck's quirky and sometimes enigmatic writing. His first novel, *Quarantine* (1978), is in the end inconclusive and unsatisfying, but *The Bellarmine Jug* (1984), despite its complex plot, won the Melbourne *Age* Fiction Award for that year. It casts back to the mutiny of the Dutch ship *Batavia* off the coast of Western Australia in 1629, and forward to the overthrow of Sukarno in Indonesia. *Offcuts: From a Legal Literary Life* (1993) is a collection of acute essays and articles reflecting his varied interests.

HAUCH, Johannes Carsten
(1790–1872)

Danish writer, born in Fredrikshald (Halden). He was lecturer in natural sciences at Sorø (1824–46), and in 1846 was appointed Professor of Northern Literature at Kiel. The Holstein revolution (1848) drove him to Copenhagen, where he became Professor of Aesthetics. He wrote historical tragedies, lyrical poems, tales and romances.

▷K Galster, *Carsten Hauchs Barndom og Ungdom/Manndom og Alddom* (1930, 1935)

HAUFF, Wilhelm
(1802–27)

German novelist, born in Stuttgart. He studied at Tübingen, was a tutor, then editor of a paper. His fairy tales and short stories are admirable for their simplicity and playful fancy—*Die Bettlerin vom Pont des Arts* (1826, Eng trans *The Beggar-Girl of the Pont-des-Arts*, 1844) and *Phantasien im Bremer Ratskeller* (1827, Eng trans *The Wine-Ghosts of Bremen*, 1889) in particular. *Lichtenstein* (1826, Eng trans 1846) is an imitation of Sir **Walter Scott**.

HAU'OFA, Ep'li
(1939–)

The first Tongan writer to achieve an international reputation, he was born in Papua New Guinea, educated in Fiji and Australia, and has since worked in both places as a teacher. Between 1978 and 1981 he served as deputy chamberlain to the King of Tonga, before returning to academic life. His literary reputation depends on *Tales of the Tikongs* (1983), a collection of wryly satirical short stories about life in the South Pacific. Hau'ofa has written about development issues and contributed a text to *Our Crowded Islands* (1977), a photographic survey of Fiji by Randy Thaman.

HAUPTMANN, Gerhart
(1862–1946)

German dramatist and novelist, winner of the Nobel Prize for literature, born in Obersalzbrunn, Silesia. He studied sculpture in Breslau and Rome before settling down in Berlin in 1885. His first play, *Vor Sonnenaufgang* (1889, Eng trans *Before Dawn*, 1909), introduced the new social drama of **Ibsen**, **Émile Zola** and **August Strindberg** to Germany, but Hauptmann alleviated the extreme naturalism with a note of compassion. *Einsame Menschen* (1891, Eng trans *Lonely Lives*, 1898), for example, in which a man is torn between his love for two women, a young girl student and his plain, self-effacing wife, portrays the wife, not the student, as the heroine. *Die Weber* (1892, Eng trans *The Weavers*, 1899) deals with the broader setting of the Silesian weavers' revolt

of 1844 and introduces a new theatrical phenomenon, the collective hero. *Florian Geyer* (1896, Eng trans 1894), a historical play, marks a transition to a strange mixture of fantasy and naturalism maintained in other such outstanding works as *Hanneles Himmelfahrt* (1893, Eng trans *Hannele*, 1894), *Die Versunkene Glocke* (1896, Eng trans *The Sunken Bell*, 1898), *Fuhrmann Herschel* (1898, Eng trans *Drayman Herschel*, 1913) and *Rose Bernd* (1903, Eng trans 1913). His later plays in a variety of styles offer no advance, although the comedies *Der Biberpelz* (1893, Eng trans *The Beaver Coat*, 1912) and *Der rote Hahn* (1901, Eng trans *The Conflagration*, 1913), were later adapted and revised by **Bertolt Brecht** to suit the East German communist censorship. His novels include *Der Narr im Christo: Emmanuel Quint* (1910, Eng trans *The Fool in Christ: Emmanuel Quint*, 1911) and *Atlantis* (1912, Eng trans 1912). He was awarded the Nobel Prize for literature in 1912.
▷C F W Behl, *Hauptmann: his life and work* (1958)

HAUSOFER, Albrecht
(1903–45)

German poet and dramatist who was shot as a member of the group which tried to assassinate Hitler. His plays on classical themes were disguised criticisms of the Hitler regime. His sonnets written in prison, *Moabiter Sonette* (1946, Eng trans *Moabit Sonnets*, 1978), are his most moving work.

HAVEL, Vaclav
(1936–)

Czech dramatist and statesman, born in Prague, where he was educated at the Academy of Dramatic Art. He began work as a stagehand at the Prague *Theater Na zábradlí* ('Theatre on the Balustrade'), becoming resident writer there from 1960 to 1969. His work includes *Zahradní slavnost* (1963, Eng trans *The Garden Party*, 1969), *Spiklenci* (1970, 'The Conspirators') and *Audience* (1976, Eng trans *Temptation*, 1976). Deemed subversive, he was frequently arrested, and in 1979 was imprisoned for four and a half years. He was again imprisoned in February 1989, but was released three months later. In December 1989, after the overthrow of the Czechoslovakian Communist Party, he was elected President by direct popular vote. He oversaw the peaceful division of Czechoslovakia into separate Czech and Slovak states in 1992, and retained political office in the new Czech state.
▷M Goetz-Stankiewicz, *The Silenced Theatre: Czech dramatists without a stage* (1979)

HAVLICEK BOROVSKY, Karel
(1821–56)

Czech poet, epigrammatist, satirist, editor and critic, born in Borová. One of his country's great anti-clerical liberals and patriots, he founded, in 1848, the first Czech daily newspaper; he fought the Austrian tyranny until, effectively, it murdered him: exiled to the Tyrol, he was released only when he was dying of tuberculosis. His posthumously published unfinished attack on the established Catholic Church and on the Austrian tryanny, *Krest sv Vladimira* (1876, Eng trans *The Conversion of St Vladimir*, 1930), is still stingingly exemplary.

HAWES, Stephen
(c.1475–1525)

English allegorical poet, born probably in Aldeburgh, Suffolk. He was attached to the court from 1502 as groom of the chamber to Henry VII. His chief work is the allegory, *The Passetyme of Pleasure* (1509), dedicated to the king. He also wrote *The Example of Virtue* (1504), *The Conversion of Swearers* (1509), an attack on blasphemy, and *A Joyful Meditation* (1509), a celebration of the coronation of Henry VIII.
▷W Murison, *Stephen Hawes* (1908)

HAWKER, Robert Stephen
(1803–75)

English poet, born in Plymouth. He was educated at Pembroke College, Oxford, and won the Newdigate Prize for poetry in 1827. In 1834 he became vicar of Morwenstow, on the Cornish coast, where he shared many of the superstitions of his people as to apparitions and the evil eye. His poetry includes *Tendrils* (1821), the Cornish ballads in *Records of the Western Shore* (1832–6), *Reeds Shaken with the Wind* (1843) and *The Quest of the Sangraal* (1864), the first part of a projected Arthurian epic. His best-known ballad is *The Song of the Western Men*, with its refrain 'And shall Trelawny die?', based on an old Cornish refrain. Twelve hours before his death he was admitted to the Roman Catholic Communion.
▷M F Burrows, *Robert Stephen Hawker* (1926)

HAWKES, John Clendennin Burne, Jr
(1925–)

American novelist and short-story writer, he writes disturbing plotless fictions in which sexual aberration, social and cultural devastation and violence are married in a cool and almost playful way. His first book was a novella, *Charivari* (1949), followed by *The Cannibal* (1949), a bleak story of post-war Germany, and a pair of short novels called

The Goose on the Grave, and *The Owl* (1954). His critical, if not commercial, breakthrough came with *The Lime Twig* (1961), which resembles a surreal version of *Brighton Rock*, and *Second Skin* (1964), a darkly exotic fantasy. Nothing written since has had quite the same power, though Hawkes has continued to write highly individual fictions, including *The Blood Oranges* (1971), *The Passion Artist* (1979), *Adventures in the Alaskan Skin Trade* (1985) and *Whistlejacket* (1988). The earlier short stories and novellas were collected in an aptly titled collection, *Lunar Landscapes* (1969).
▷P O'Donnell, *John Hawkes* (1982)

HAWKESWORTH, John
(c.1715–1773)

English author, born in London. In 1744 he succeeded **Dr Johnson** on the *Gentleman's Magazine*. In 1752 he started, with Johnson and others, *The Adventurer*, half of whose 140 numbers were from Hawkesworth's pen. He published a volume of fairy tales (1761), wrote a play, *Edgar and Emmeline* (1761), edited **Jonathan Swift**, and prepared the account of Captain Cook's first voyage, which formed volumes two and three of Hawkesworth's *Voyages* (3 vols, 1773).

HAWTHORNE, Julian
(1846–1934)

American novelist, born in Boston, the son of **Nathaniel Hawthorne**. His work, although fluently written, does not stand comparison with his father's; nor was it very successful. The 'Gothic' and Swedenborgian *Garth* (1877) is the most interesting of his novels. He also wrote the disappointing *Nathaniel Hawthorne and His Wife* (1884).

HAWTHORNE, Nathaniel
(1804–64)

American novelist and short-story writer, born in Salem, Massachusetts, the son of a merchant captain, who died when the boy was only four years old. He and his mother lived in straitened circumstances. At the age of 14 he went with her to a lonely farm in the woods of Raymond, Maine, and there became accustomed to solitude. He began his first novel at Bowdon College, graduating in 1825, but progress was slow. After his return to Salem he shut himself away for 12 years 'in a heavy seclusion', writing tales and verses. In 1828 he published anonymously his first novel, *Fanshawe*, which was unsuccessful. Continuing to contribute to annuals and magazines, he edited in 1836 a short-lived periodical. Meanwhile some of his short stories had gained such favourable notice from the London *Athenaeum* that in 1837 a volume of them, *Twice-told Tales*, was published. His genius, however, was not yet appreciated in his own country. In 1839 the historian George Bancroft, then collector of the port of Boston, appointed him weigher and gauger in the custom-house, a post he held until 1841. He then joined for a year the Brook Farm idyllic, semi-socialistic community near Boston. Meanwhile he wrote and published a series of simple stories for children from New England history: *Grandfather's Chair, Famous Old People* and *Liberty Tree* (1841). Moving to Concord, Massachusetts, he issued *Biographical Stories* (1842) for children, and brought out an enlarged edition of the *Twice-told Tales* (1842). He wrote sketches and studies for the *Democratic Review*, which formed the *Mosses from an Old Manse* (1846). The *Review* failed; and, as he lost all his savings at Brook Farm, he was forced to accept a place in the custom-house again—this time as surveyor in Salem. By the time his contract had finished he had completed (1850) *The Scarlet Letter*, still the best-known of his works. At Lenox, Massachusetts, he then entered upon a phase of remarkable productiveness, writing *The House of the Seven Gables* (1851), *Wonder Book* (1851), *The Snow Image* (1852) and *The Blithedale Romance* (1852), which drew upon the Brook Farm episode. He settled in Concord in 1852, and wrote a campaign biography of his old schoolfriend, President Franklin Pierce, and on Pierce's inauguration became consul at Liverpool (1853–7). He completed *Tanglewood Tales* in 1853, as a continuation of *Wonder Book*. A year and half spent in Rome and Florence, beginning in 1858, supplied him with the materials for *The Marble Faun* (1860), published in England as *Transformation*. Returning to Concord, he wrote for the *Atlantic Monthly* the brilliant papers on England collected as *Our Old Home* (1863). He began a new romance, based on the idea of an elixir of immortality, which remained unfinished at his death. With little faculty for poetry, Hawthorne had a singular command over the musical qualities of prose. Although exceptionally fitted for conveying subtleties of thought and fantasy, his style is invariably clear and strongly marked by common sense. Hawthorne was only gradually recognized in his own country.
▷H James, *Hawthorne* (1879); F Crews, *The Sins of the Fathers* (1966)

HAY, George Campbell, pseud **Deòrsa Caimbeul Hay**
(1915–84)

Scottish poet, born in Argyll, the son of **John Macdougall Hay**. He wrote poetry in English, Scots, and in Gaelic under the name Deòrsa Caimbeul Hay. Educated at Oxford,

he served in North Africa and the Middle East during World War II, an experience which left him a semi-invalid. The immediate post-war years were productive in poetic terms, however. Writing under the name Deòrsa Caimbeul Hay he published his first Gaelic collection, *Fuaran Slibh* in 1947. This was followed by *Wind on Loch Fyne* (1948), a volume of his English and Scots poems (the latter are rather fewer in number), and a second, more assured Gaelic collection, *O na Ceither Airdean* (1952). While his poetry is concerned with the landscape and people of Scotland, it is informed by a poetic and linguistic sensibility which lifts it beyond the parochial. His later work appeared alongside poets like **Sorley MacLean** in *Four Points of a Saltire* (1970) and **Derick Thompson** in *Nuabhàrdachd Ghàidlig* (1976). His incomplete long poem *Mochtàr is Dùghall*, written during the war, was published in 1982, and explores the poet's experiences of the Arab world.
▷ In *Four Points of a Saltire* (1970)

HAY, Gyula
(1900–75)

Hungarian playwright, born in Abony. He was involved with the Kun government, and lived in Germany and Russia (as a then card-carrying communist). When the communists came to power in Hungary they soon put him in prison—finally he went to live in exile in Switzerland. A leading dramatist in his country, and a serious one, his first success—some think it his best play—was *Isten, császár, paraszt* (1932, 'God, Emperor, Peasant'), staged by Max Reinhardt. It is about the confrontation between King Sigismund and Jan Huss. A later play deals with Atila. He was one of the most accomplished dramatists of the century in the technical sense. His *Geboren 1900* (1971, Eng trans *Born 1900*, 1982) is an invaluable and lively record.

HAY, Ian, pseud of Major-General John Hay Beith
(1876–1952)

Scottish novelist and dramatist, born in Manchester, the son of a cotton merchant. He was educated at Fettes College, Edinburgh and St John's College, Cambridge, and became a language master at his old school. He served in World War I, and was awarded the Military Cross. His light popular novels, *Pip* (1907), *A Safety Match* (1911) and *A Knight on Wheels* (1914), were followed by the war books *The First Hundred Thousand* (1915), *Carrying On* (1917) and *The Last Million* (1918). Many novels and comedies followed, the best known of the latter being *Tilly of Bloomsbury* (1919) and *Housemaster* (1936). He was director of public relations at the War Office (1938–41).

HAY, John Macdougall
(1881–1919)

Scottish novelist, born in Tarbert, Loch Fyne, in Argyll. He took an arts degree at Glasgow University and proceeded to teaching posts at Stornoway and then Ullapool. There he was crippled by rheumatic fever and left teaching to become a minister in the Church of Scotland. He returned to university in 1905 and graduated five years later, helping to support himself in the meantime with reviews for Glasgow and London magazines. At his second parish, Elderslie, near Paisley, he wrote and published his first and most successful novel, *Gillespie* (1914). A realistic novel in the tradition of **George Douglas Brown**'s *The House with the Green Shutters*, its protagonist is characterized by cunning and ambition with which he nearly ruins his town (based on Tarbert). The novel was highly praised by **Thomas Hardy** and by American critics. Hay's second novel, *Barnacles* (1916), and his poetry, *Their Dead Sons* (1918), were not as successful. His son is the poet **George Campbell Hay**.
▷ F R Hart, *The Scottish Novel* (1978)

HAY, William Gosse
(1875–1945)

Australian writer, born in Burnside, South Australia, whose mother was related to Sir **Edmund Gosse** and to William Gosse (1842–81), the English-born explorer who 'discovered' Ayers Rock. Hay's first novels, set in a fictionalized Australia, were *Stifled Laughter* (1901), *Herridge of Reality Swamp* (1907) and *Captain Quadring* (1912). His mother and sister were lost on a ship returning to England and Hay retreated to Tasmania, the setting for his last books, which were published between 1919 and 1937. His only other completed work was *An Australian Rip Van Winkle* (1921). His novels had a Gothic element, introduced, according to Hay, to 'raise Australian literature ... to her tragic and ballad-like history'; his use of historicity lifts his work above the melodrama of his contemporaries and ranks him with **Thomas Love Peacock** and Sir **Walter Scott**.

HAYASHI Fumiko
(1903–51)

Japanese writer, born into a family of itinerant gypsy-like peddlars. Hayashi's childhood was deeply unstable, and left her with an overwhelming desire for security, which turned her into a workaholic, and fostered a hedonism which led her into the Tokyo bohemian set of the 1930s. Her first book, *Horoki*, was closely drawn from her childhood experiences and those of Tokyo, and was hugely successful. It was the first of an enormous number of works (well over 200). Her best, and bleakest, is *Ukigumo* ('Drifting Cloud'), which was written in the aftermath of collapse and defeat in 1945 (she had been a war correspondent in China and South-East Asia for *Mainichi Shimbun* from 1937 to the end of the war), and is an extremely powerful tale of doomed love amid the superbly evoked ruins of a nation utterly destroyed.

HAYCOX, Ernest
(1899–1950)

American writer of Westerns, born in Portland, Oregon. Often made into films, his tales have some small sense of historical truth. Typical is *Starlight Rider* (1933).

HAYDEN, Robert E(arl)
(1913–80)

American poet, born in Detroit, Michigan, and brought up by foster parents. From 1936 to 1940 he worked as a researcher for the Federal Writers' Project. He published his first collection, *Heart-Shape in the Dust*, in 1940. His stature as one of the most important of modern American poets was confirmed in 1966 on the publication of *Selected Poems*. This reveals a profound and compassionate insight into the Afro–American experience, recorded in work of authoritative formal elegance, in which the historical and the personal appear fused in an original voice. Hayden became the first black poet to be invited to take up the prestigious office of Consultant in Poetry to the Library of Congress. His *Collected Poems* appeared posthumously in 1985.

HAYES, Alfred
(1911–85)

English-born American novelist, who was raised in New York. He also wrote plays, poems and screenplays (Rossellini's *Paisan*, 1946). His greatest successes were *The Girl on Via Flaminia* (1949), a love story, and the terse and, in a stylistic sense, **James**ian *In Love* (1953).

HAYKAL, Muhammad Husayn
(1888–1956)

Egyptian novelist, whose *Zaynab* (1913), written in France and published under a pseudonym, was the first truly realistic novel to be published in Egypt. A whole school of fiction developed from this, in certain ways making possible Egypt's first great writer of novels, **Naguib Mahfouz**.

HAYLEN, Leslie Clement
(1899–1977)

Australian politician, journalist and writer, born in Amungla, Canberra, whose novels

were originally serialized in *Australian Women's Weekly* and then on radio; the first of these was *The Game Darrells* (1933). Of his many plays, two were published; *Two Minutes' Silence* (1933) is an anti-war drama, later filmed, and *Blood on the Wattle* (1948) deals with the Eureka Stockade revolt of 1854.
▷ *Twenty Years' Hard Labour* (1969)

HAYLEY, William
(1745–1820)

English poet and writer, born in Chichester. He was a prolific writer and, although his work was held up to scorn by **Byron**, a popular one. His most ambitious works are *The Triumphs of Temper* (1781) and *The Triumphs of Music* (1804), while **Blake** illustrated his *Ballads founded on Anecdotes of Animals* (1805). He also wrote essays, plays, and biographies of **Milton**, Romney and his friend **Cowper**. Another friend, **Southey**, rather damningly suggested that 'everything about that man is good except his poetry'.
▷ W T Le Viness, *The Life and Work of William Hayley* (1945)

HAYNE, Paul Hamilton
(1830–86)

American poet, biographer and editor, born in Charleston, South Carolina, friend of **Henry Timrod** and member of the Russell's Bookstore Group of chivalric Southern writers. Hayne has been called the 'last literary cavalier'. Although his health was too frail to fight for the Confederates in the Civil War, his fervidly romantic martial poems achieved considerable renown. In Britain his admirers included **Swinburne** and **Tennyson**. *The Battle of Charleston Harbor* is his best-known poem. *Poems* (1855) and *Sonnets and Other Poems* (1857), both appearing before the Civil War, contain elegant and reflective nature verse.
▷ K H Becker, *Paul Hamilton Hayne: His Life and Letters* (1951)

HAYS, Mary
(1760–1843)

English essayist, novelist and polemicist, born in Southwark, London, the daughter of Rational Dissenters. In *Cursory Remarks* (1791), which appeared under the pseudonym of 'Eusebia', she proclaimed her support for a deity but denounced the practices of the established church. *Letters and Essays* (1793) discusses politics and feminism. *Memoirs of Emma Courtney* (1796) describes, in fictional form, a similar quest for knowledge and reason, yet the heroine is rejected by the man she loves and resorts to marrying a man for whom she has little feeling. Two years later, Hays published an anonymous *Appeal to the*

Men of Great Britain in Behalf of the Women, a robust tract calling for increased intellectual and financial independence for women.

HAYWOOD, Eliza, née Fowler
(c.1693–1756)

English novelist, born in London. After being deserted by her husband, she became an actress and wrote a number of scandalous society novels, in which the characters resembled living persons so closely, the names being thinly concealed by the use of asterisks, as to be libellous. **Pope** denounced her in *The Dunciad*. She issued the periodical *The Female Spectator* (1744–6) and *The Parrot* (1747). Her works include *Memoirs of a Certain Island adjacent to Utopia* (1725) and two 'straight' novels, *The History of Betsy Thoughtless* (1751) and *The History of Jemmy and Jenny Hessamy* (1753).

HAZAZ, Chaim
(1899–)

Hebrew novelist and dramatist, born in the Ukraine. He left Russia in 1917, and finally went to Palestine in 1931. His fiction deals mainly with Yemenite Jews, amongst whom he lived; the epic *Yaish* (1947–52), in particular, about a mystic, has been described as having 'almost classical status'. He wrote a vivid play on the subject of the 'false messiah', Sabbatai Tsevi, in 1950. Only *Mori Said* (1940) was translated (under that title, 1956).

HAZLITT, William
(1778–1830)

English essayist, born in Maidstone, Kent, the son of a Unitarian minister, who moved to Boston, Massachusetts, in 1783, and to Wem in Shropshire in 1787. At the age of 15 the boy was sent to Hackney College to study for the ministry, but had abandoned the notion when in 1796 he met **Coleridge**, and by him was encouraged to write *Principles of Human Action* (1805). Having tried portrait painting, he published in 1806 his *Free Thoughts on Public Affairs*, in 1807 his *Reply to Malthus*, and in 1812 he found employment in London on the *Morning Chronicle* and *Examiner*. From 1814 to 1830 he contributed to the *Edinburgh Review* and his *Round Table* essays and *Characters of Shakespeare's Plays* appeared in 1817. Between 1818 and 1821 he delivered at the Surrey Institute his lectures on *The English Poets, English Comic Writers*, and *Dramatic Literature of the Age of Elizabeth*. His marriage with Sarah Stoddart in 1808 proved a failure and they were divorced in Edinburgh in 1822. His essays in the *London Magazine* were later republished in his *Table Talk* (1821) and *Plain Speaker* (1826). A passion for Sarah Walker, the daughter of a tailor with whom he lodged, found expression in the frantic *Liber Amoris* (1823). In 1824 he married a charming widow with £300 a year, who travelled with him to Italy, but left him for ever on the return journey. His *Spirit of the Age, or Contemporary Portraits* appeared in 1825, and his *Life of Napoleon Bonaparte* between 1828 and 1830. His last years darkened by ill-health and money difficulties, he died with the words, 'Well, I've had a happy life'. He was a deadly controversialist, a master of epigram, invective and withering irony. His style ranges from lively gossip to glowing rhapsody; the best of his work is in his later collections of essays.
▷P Howe, *The Life of William Hazlitt* (1922); S Jones, *William Hazlitt* (1982)

HAZZARD, Shirley
(1931–)

Australian-born American novelist, born and educated in Sydney. Her first book, *The Evening of the Holiday*, was published in 1966. Between 1952 and 1962 she worked in New York at the United Nations, an organization she was to satirize in her second novel, *People in Glass Houses* (1967). She later published a factual exposé of the UN in *Defeat of an Ideal* (1973). Other novels are *The Bay of Noon* (1970) and *The Transit of Venus* (1980), which charts the turbulent emotional involvements of an Australian woman in sophisticated America; this book established her as a major contemporary writer. Many of her short stories have appeared in the *New Yorker* magazine; some are collected in *Cliffs of Fall* (1963).

H D *see* DOOLITTLE, Hilda

HEAD, Bessie
(1937–86)

South African-born Botswanian novelist. Born in Pietermaritzburg, she worked as an agricultural labourer in Botswana, of which she became a citizen. The central character of her first novel, *When Rain Clouds Gather* (1968), repeats her escape from apartheid to the relative, but still compromised, freedom of Botswana. Later books—*Maru* (1971), *A Question of Power* (1974) and *A Bewitched Crossroad* (1984)—document different aspects of the same basic situation, always concentrating on the fine line between heroism and self-reliance on the one hand, and abject cultural surrender on the other. *The Collector of Treasures* (1977) was a transcription of native folk tales.
▷C Heywood, *Aspects of South African Literature* (1976)

HEAD, Richard
(c.1637–1686)

English hack-writer, born in Ireland. He is best known as the author of part one of *The English Rogue* (1665–71), the other three parts being by the bookseller Francis Kirkman.

HEANEY, Seamus Justin
(1939–)

Irish poet and critic, born in Castledawson, County Derry, in Northern Ireland. Educated at St Columba's College, Londonderry, and Queen's College, Belfast, he lectured there (1966–72) before becoming a full-time writer. An Ulster Catholic, the violence in the North so disturbed him that he moved to the Republic in 1972, and taught at Caryfort College, Dublin, from 1975. He made his debut as a poet with *Eleven Poems* (1965). Redolent of the rural Ireland in which he grew up, his work seems nurtured by the landscape, lush, peaty and, to an extent, menacing. One of the greatest modern poets writing in English, he is regarded as a worthy successor to **W B Yeats**. Significant collections are *Death of a Naturalist* (1966), *Wintering Out* (1972), *North* (1975), *Bog Poems* (1975), *Stations* (1975), *Field Work* (1979), *Station Island* (1984) and *The Haw Lantern* (1987). *Selected Poems 1965–75* appeared in 1980, and *New Selected Poems 1966–87* in 1990. A new volume, *Seeing Things*, appeared in 1991, along with his first play, *The Cure at Troy*, a translation of **Sophocles**'s *Philoctetes* for the Field Day Theatre Company in Dublin. *Sweeney's Flight* (1992) is Heaney's version of the Irish odyssey of Mad Sweeney.

HEARN, (Patricio) Lafcadio Tessima Carlos
(1850–1904)

Irish–Greek novelist, journalist and travel writer, born in Greece. He was educated in France and England, and emigrated to the USA in 1869, where he set about a writing career. He was hampered by his partial blindness and a morbid sense of inferiority, and caused a scandal through his relationship with a mulatto woman. His writings of the period include the novel *Chita* (1889), set on the Gulf Coast of Louisiana, a volume of stories translated from **Gautier** (1882), the Negro-French proverbs collected in *Gombo Zhêbes* (1885), and many newspaper sketches of Creole life. In 1890 he travelled to Japan, where he settled, became a Japanese citizen, took the name Koizumi Yakumo, and wrote a series of books about Japanese life and manners.

▷P Murray, *A Fantastic Journey* (1993)

HEARNE, John
(1926–)

Canadian-born Jamaican novelist; he has also written thrillers as John Morris, in collaboration with Morris Cargill. After military service in the RAF, Hearne studied at Edinburgh University and took a postgraduate degree in London before working as a teacher and moving to Jamaica. His first novel, *Voices under the Window* (1955), was distinctive for its portrayal of a developing professional middle class in the West Indies and remains Hearne's most read work. Later books also focused on intellectuals, often politically motivated, as in *Stranger at The Gate* (1956) and *Autumn Equinox* (1959), but almost always perceived as belonging to white society by virtue of their social and cultural aspirations. Hearne stopped writing literary fiction for nearly two decades, concentrating on espionage stories which reminded many readers that James Bond's original stamping ground had been Jamaica (or 'Cayuna', in Hearne's books); however, in 1981 he returned to more serious work with *The Sure Salvation*, a powerful psychological allegory about the Atlantic slave trade.

HEATH, Roy A(ubrey) K(elvin)
(1926–)

Guyanese novelist, born in what was then called British Guiana. He moved to London in the late 1950s, working as a teacher before becoming a barrister in 1964. He has called himself 'a chronicler of Guyanese life in this century': *A Man Come Home* (1974) deals with the working class, while *From the Heat of the Day* (1979) is concerned with the middle-class Armstrong family. His works are realistic studies of the quotidian struggle for a better life, blended with folk myths of obeah, the local version of voodoo. Social cohesion and a rich physical life are to the fore in his work, at times to the detriment of individual characterization. More recent works, such as *The Shadow Bride* (1988), tend to be better balanced in this regard.

HEAVYSEGE, Charles
(1816–76)

English-born Canadian poet, novelist and dramatist, born in Huddersfield. He went to Canada in 1853, became a journalist in Montreal, and wrote competent fiction and drama. He wrote *Sonnets* (1855) and a narrative poem, *Saul: A Drama* (1857). He is well represented in **A J M Smith**'s *Oxford Book of Canadian Verse* (1960).

HEBBEL, Friedrich
(1813–63)

German dramatist, born in Wesselburen in Dithmarshen. He studied in Hamburg from

1835 and after stays in Heidelberg, Munich, Copenhagen, settled in Vienna (1846). His only contemporary play is *Maria Magdalena* (1842, Eng trans 1914), his favourite settings being of a legendary, historical or biblical character, as in *Herodes und Mariamne* (1849, Eng trans *Herod and Mariamne*, 1914) and his masterpiece, the *Nibelungen* trilogy (1855–60, Eng trans *The Nibelungs*, 1921). Hebbel constantly portrayed the inherent Hegelian conflict between individuality and humanity as a whole.
▷T Campbell, *The Life and Works of Friedrich Hebbel* (1919)

HEBEL, Johann Peter
(1760–1826)
German poet and storyteller in Alemannic (and sometimes in German), born in Basel. He was a priest who became a headmaster, and, ultimately, Prälat, the highest office in the Evangelical Church in Germany. His simple poetry was much loved by **Goethe**, **Rilke**, **Kafka** and many others, but was for long underestimated by critics. His standing in German literature has aptly been compared to that of **Burns** in British literature.
▷A Altwegg, *Johann Peter Hebel* (1935, in German)

HÉBERT, Anne
(1916–)
French–Canadian poet, novelist, playwright and story writer, born in Sainte-Catherine-de-Fossambault, near Québec. She is cousin to **Hector de Saint-Denys Garneau**, and he personally influenced her early poems. The harsh, bright, dry 'nun-like' poems of her first collection, *Les Songes en équilibre* (1942, 'Dreams in Equilibrium'), immediately attracted attention, and won a prize. Her extreme hardness of approach produced in **Edmund Wilson** 'a mortal chill'. She is highly praised in France, where one critic called her 'one of the greatest contemporary poets' in her language. Her play *Le Temps sauvage* (1963, 'The Savage Time'), about an over-possessive mother, was successful, as was her rather more conventional novel *Kamouraska* (1970, Eng trans 1973), based on a real-life case of murder.
▷*Selected Poems of Saint-Denys-Garneau and Anne Hébert* (1962); P Pagé, *Anne Hébert* (1965, in French)

HECHT, Anthony Evan
(1923–)
American poet, born in New York City. His first volume, *A Summoning of Stones*, appeared in 1954. Hecht's early verse was noted as being rather traditional, its style tending to the ornate, even courtly, but his

poetry gradually became increasingly austere, *The Hard Hours* (1967) representing the more ascetic seam of his writing. He subsequently returned to a greater complexity. *Millions of Strange Shadows* (1977) is perhaps his most representative collection, in which lyricism combines with technical mastery.

HECHT, Ben
(1894–1964)
American writer, born in New York. Starting as a journalist in Chicago, he wrote novels, plays and filmscripts. From 1946 he was dedicated to the Zionist cause and vilification of Britain as in *A Flag is Born* (1946). His plays include *The Front Page* (1928), and his screenplays include *Wuthering Heights* (1939), *Spellbound* (1945) and *Notorious* (1946).
▷*A Child of the Century* (1955)

HECKO, Frantisek
(1905–60)
Slovak novelist, born in Suchá nad Parnou. His *Cervené vino* (1948, 'Red Wine') was one of the best novels ever written about Slovak village life; but by the time of *Drevená dedina* (1951, 'The Wooden Village') he had fallen prey to socialist realism, and his sense of obligation destroyed the sharpness of his observation.

HEDENVIND-ERIKSSON, Gustav
(1880–1967)
Swedish novelist and short-story writer, born in Jämtland. An inspirational figure among the working-class writers of the first half of the century, he spent many years as a navvy. His writing often presents events in a wide historical perspective, as in, for example, *De förskingrades arv* (1926, 'The Inheritance of the Dispossessed'), which tells the story of the industrialization of northern Sweden. The figure of the navvy as an examplar of worker solidarity and as a free, migrating spirit is central in his books, as is the spirit of his home province. There is a strong element of myth and folktale in his writing, particularly in the short fiction of *Jämtländska sagor* (1941, 'Jämtland Tales').
▷Ö Lindberger, *Gustav Hedenvind-Eriksson* (1945)

HEIBERG, Gunnar Edvard Rode
(1857–1929)
Norwegian dramatist and director, born in Christiania (now Oslo). As artistic director of the Bergen Theatre, he staged the first performances of **Ibsen**'s *Vilbarden* (*The Wild Duck*) and *Rosmensholm*. His own first play, *Tante Ulrikke* (1884), was in the same socially aware vein. He wrote expressionist plays in

the radical and rational tradition of Norwegian literature, such as *Balkonen* (1894, 'The Balcony') and *Kjaerlighetens Tragedie* (1904, 'The Tragedy of Love').
▷ E Skavlan, *Gunnar Heiberg* (1950)

HEIBERG, Johan Ludvig
(1791–1860)
Danish playwright, son of Peter Andreas Heiberg, and the creator of vaudeville in Denmark. He wrote a series of enormously popular musical comedies, of which his masterpiece was *Nej!* (1836, 'No!'). His romantic play *Elverhøj* (1828, 'Hills of the Elves'), is considered a classic. He was married to the actress Johanne Luise Heiberg, and later became director of the Theatre Royal in Copenhagen (1849–56). He also wrote on philosophy and was significant as an interpreter of Hegel.
▷ M Borup, *Johan Ludvig Heiberg* (1947)

HEIDENSTAM, (Karl Gustav) Verner von
(1859–1940)
Swedish writer, winner of the Nobel Prize for literature, born in Olshammer. He lived in southern Europe and the Middle East (1876–87), and published his impressions in a volume of poetry, *Vallfart och Vandringsår* (1888, 'Pilgrimage and Years of Wandering') which, together with his programmatic work, *Renässans*, inspired a literary renaissance in Sweden and established him as the leader of the new romantic movement of the 1890s. He published several further volumes of poetry, including *Endymion* (1889), the epic *Hans Alienus* (1892), *Dikter* (1895, 'Poems'), and *Ett folk* (1897–8, 'One People'). In later years he turned to historical fiction, as in *Karolinerna* (1897–8, 'The Carlists') and *Folkungaträdet* (1905–7, 'The Tree of the Folkungs'). Though he was a friend of **Strindberg**, their relationship soured into bitter antagonism and rivalry. He was awarded the 1916 Nobel Prize for literature.
▷ H Kamras, *Den unge Heidenstam* (1942)

HEIJERMANS, Herman
(1864–1924)
Dutch dramatist and novelist, born in Rotterdam to a Jewish family. He first became well known as a newspaper columnist: after a false start in business, he began to contribute sketches of Dutch life to *Der Telegraaf*. He went on to become Holland's foremost dramatist, becoming internationally famous with *Op Hoop van Zegen* (1901, Eng trans *The Good Hope*, 1912), produced in 1900, a naturalistic sea drama which led to improvements in the fishing trade. This played in London with great success, with Ellen Terry in a

leading role. His novels, stories and one-acters were also very popular, since he had the capacity to create character within a short compass. The best-known Dutch playwright since **Vondel**, his like has not been seen again in modern Dutch theatre.
▷ S L Flaxman, *Herman Heijermans and his Dramas* (1954)

HEILBRUN, Carolyn, pseud **Amanda Cross**
(1926–)
American essayist and novelist, using her pseudonym for her fiction. Born in New Jersey, Heilbrun began her career as an academic at Columbia University, and served on the editorial board of *Signs*, a feminist journal. Her critical books include a study of *The Garnett Family* (1961) and *Reinventing Womanhood* (1979), a book about the androgynous. She describes her mannered detective novels featuring Kate Fansler, English professor and amateur sleuth, as social comedies in the mould of **Dorothy L Sayers**. Several of them, such as *The James Joyce Murder* (1967), have a literary theme. *Poetic Justice* (1970) is about **Auden**.
▷ M T Reddy, *Sisters in Crime: Feminism and the Crime Novel* (1988)

HEIN, Piet, pseud **Kumbel**
(1905–)
Danish poet, designer and inventor. His poems include several collections of aphoristic *Gruk* (10 vols, 1940–9, 'Grooks'). He defined the 'super-ellipse' (a special curve) and used it for architectural and design purposes; he also devised the 3D Soma Cube. From 1969 to 1976 he lived in Britain. His pseudonym is an Old Norse word for a gravestone.
▷ *Kumbelslyre* (1950)

HEINE, Heinrich
(1797–1856)
German poet and essayist, born of Jewish parents in Düsseldorf. At the age of 17 he was sent to Frankfurt to learn banking, and next tried trading on his own account in Hamburg, but soon failed. In 1819 he went to Bonn; there, and at Berlin and Göttingen, he studied law, taking his doctor's degree in 1825. But his mind was fixed on poetry. In Berlin in 1821 he published *Gedichte* ('Poems'), which was an immediate success. A second collection, *Lyrisches Intermezzo* ('Lyrical Intermezzo'), appeared in 1823. The first and second volumes of the prose *Reisebilder* ('Pictures of Travel') were published (1826–7) and *Das Buch der Lieder* (1827, rev edn 1844, Eng trans *Book of Songs*, 1856) created excitement throughout Germany. In 1825 he became a Christian to secure the

rights of German citizenship, but only alienated the esteem of his own people. His revolutionary opinions remained insuperable hindrances to his official employment in Germany. When his enthusiasm was roused by the July revolution in Paris, he went there in 1831, going into a voluntary exile from which he never returned. After 1825 he travelled in England and Italy; he worked on newspapers in Bavaria; and he wrote two more volumes of *Reisebilder* (1830–1, all four vols Eng trans *Pictures of Travel*, 1855). The July revolution seems to have awakened a seriousness in Heine. He turned from poetry to politics, and assumed the role of leader of the cosmopolitan democratic movement. One of his chief aims was to make the French and the Germans acquainted with one another's intellectual and artistic achievements. From this came the *Französische Zustände* (1833, Eng trans *French Affairs*, 1889), first printed in the *Allgemeine Zeitung*; *De l'Allemagne* (1835), the French version of *Die Romantische Schule* (1836, Eng trans *The Romantic School*, 1882); and *Philosophie und Literatur in Deutschland* ('Philosophy and Literature in Germany'), part of the miscellaneous writings entitled *Der Salon* (4 vols, 1835–40). His ambiguous attitude and his attack on Ludwig Börne brought down upon him the enmity of his revolutionary compatriots. On the eve of a duel, which his book on Börne, *Ludwig Börne: Eine Denkschrift* (1840, Eng trans *Ludwig Börne: Portrait of a Revolutionist, 1881*) ultimately cost him, he married Eugénie Mirat ('Mathilde', d.1883), a Paris *grisette*, with whom he had been living for seven years. From 1848 he was confined to bed by spinal paralysis. He lingered on in excruciating pain, borne with heroic patience. During these years he published *Neue Gedichte* (1844, revised 1851, Eng trans *New Poems*, 1910) and *Deutschland Ein Wintermärchen* (1844, Eng trans *Germany: A Winter's Tale*, 1944); a satirical poem, *Atta Troll: Ein Sommernachtstraum*, the 'swansong of romanticism' (1847, Eng trans *Atta Troll and Other Poems*, 1876); a collection of poems, *Romanzero* (1851, Eng trans *Romancero*, 1905); and three volumes of *Vermischte Schriften* (1854, 'Various Writings'). Many of his poems were set to music, most notably by Schubert and Schumann.

▷H Spencer, *Heinrich Heine* (1982)

HEINESEN, William
(1900–91)

Faroese novelist, short-story writer and poet, born in Tórshavn; he wrote in Danish and was a member of the Danish Academy. He made his debut with *Arktiske Elegier og andre Digte* (1921, 'Arctic Elegies and Other Poems'), in which the cycle of nature is the central theme. *Blaesende Gry* (1934, 'Windy Dawn'), his first novel, is a love story set against a period of declining traditions in Faroese society. In *Den sorte Gryde* (1949, 'The Black Pot') he satirized the boom period enjoyed by the Faroese fishing industry during the British wartime occupation. *De fortabte Spillemaend* ('The Lost Minstrels'), published a year later, is a piece of magical realism written long before that term became current; it is a paean to life and joy and a diatribe against ideology and mediocrity. Heinesen's sane and humane voice and his wonderful talents as a storyteller have made him one of the most significant Scandinavian writers of the century.

▷W Glyn Jones, *Faerø og kosmos. En indføring i William Heinesens forfatterskab* (1974)

HEINLEIN, Robert Anson
(1907–88)

American science-fiction writer, born in Missouri. He served as a naval officer, then studied physics, before turning to writing in 1939. Much of his early work falls into his 'Future History' scheme, although he largely abandoned it after 1950. He made the breakthrough into 'mainstream' publishing with a series of science-fiction stories for children, beginning with *Rocket Ship Galileo* (1947), and established himself as one of the two or three most important practitioners of the 'hard' science-fiction genre. The harsh, hectoring militarism of *Starship Troopers* (1959) caused great controversy. The oddly whimsical fantasy *Stranger in a Strange Land* (1961) is his best-known work, although not his most typical. His later science-fiction novels tended to become mired down in that same hectoring manner, to the detriment of the action. *The Moon Is A Harsh Mistress* (1966) is the best of them.

HEINRICH VON MELK
(12th century)

German poet about whom little is known. Two well-known Early Middle High German poems are attributed to him: *Von des tödes gehugde* and *Das Priesterleben*. The first is a sermon with a grim passage on the physical details of death; the second castigates the clergy for their sinfulness. Heinrich seems to have been a nobleman who sought seclusion at the Abbey of Melk in Lower Austria. He is associated with the very ascetic Cluniac Reform movement.

HEINRICH VON NEUSTADT
(12th century)

German poet, a physician, of whom little is known beyond the fact that he lived and practised in Vienna. He wrote the romance *Apollonius von Tyrland*, a vast poem in Middle

High German, based on a Latin poem and on Byzantine material, and a quite different allegorical devotional poem, *Von Göttes Kukunft* ('On The Coming of God'), which is concerned with the making of a perfect man.
▷M O'C Walshe, *Medieval German Literature* (1962)

HEINSE, Johann
(1746–1803)

German romance writer and poet, born in Thuringia. His verse was admired by **Goethe**, although its overt sensuality and lasciviousness shocked him. He wrote several novels in a similarly unrestrained vein, including *Ardinghello* (1787) and the partly autobiographical *Hildegard von Hohenthal* (1795–6).
▷R Terras, *Wilhelm Heinses Ästetik* (1972)

HEISSENBUTTEL, Helmut
(1921–)

German novelist, radio playwright, avant-garde poet and essayist, born in Rüstringen. Like **William Burroughs**, he produces 'collages', 'cut-ups' and other similarly arranged material. His poetry comes near to being 'concrete', without ever quite reaching that status. His most substantial work is the novel *Projekt Nr 1, D'Alemberts Ende* (1970, 'Project No 1, The End of D'Alembert'), a vastly complex 'cut-up'—statistics, stream-of-consciousness monologues, and other material—which questions the very existence of 'individuality'. He has been described as a 'neo-Dadaist'.
▷R A Burns, *Commitment, Language and Reality* (1975).

HEKTOROVIĆ, Petar
(1487–1572)

Dalmatian poet, born in Hvar. Educated in Italy, Hektorović wrote the most original Serbo–Croatian work of his time, a fishing eclogue, *Ribanje i ribarsko prigovaranie*, which he published in Venice in 1568. It contains folk-songs, and improves upon the artificiality of its Italian models.

HÉLINAND DE FROIDEMENT
(?1160–?1229)

French *trouvère*, Cistercian monk and scholar, born near Beauvais. Much of his work is lost, but *Vers de la mort* (1194–7, 'Poetry of Death') influenced the later form, the *danse macabre*. The form of the poem is known by his name, and was much imitated.

HELIODORUS
(fl.3rd and 4th century)

Greek romance writer and Sophist, born in Emesa in Syria. One of the earliest Greek novelists, he was the author of *Aethiopica*, which narrates in poetic prose, at times with almost epic beauty and simplicity, the loves of Theagenes and Chariclea.

HELLAAKOSKI, Aaro
(1893–1952)

Finnish poet, critic and geologist, born in Oulu. Regarded as a leading precursor of modernism, he first wrote ardent lyrics, but later came under the influence of French poetry, in particular that of **Apollinaire**: the result was an apocalyptic type of poetry, Nihilist, Cubist and Symbolist. His first important collection was *Jääpeili* (1928, 'Ice Mirror').
▷U Kupiainen, *Aaro Hellaakoski* (1953, in Finnish)

HELLENS, Franz, pseud of **Fredéric van Ermengem**
(1881–1972)

Belgian writer, born in Brussels. As a polemicist he was best known for proclaiming that the French-language writers of Belgium formed an integral part of French literature. This attitude, together with the review he founded with **André Salmon**—it appeared under many names, the best-known being *Le Disque vert* ('The Green Disc')—was exceedingly influential. He wrote over a hundred volumes in every genre, from poetry to quasi-Surrealist fiction. One commentator has shrewdly noted that his work 'is more respected than admired'; yet it is deeply interesting, and as a critic Hellens has no equal in modern Belgium. He knew everyone of importance, discovered **Michaux** and **Ghelderode**—and his work undoubtedly acted as an indispensable catalyst for those more creatively gifted.

HELLER, Joseph
(1923–)

American novelist, born in Brooklyn, New York. He served in the US army air force in World War II, drawing on the experience for his black comedy, *Catch 22*, based on the simple premise that a fighter-pilot who wants to be excused duty need only ask, but by asking proves that he is sane and fit to fly. After selling slowly for some years it became an international bestseller and a byword for war's absurdity. Heller returned to the theme with a play, *We Bombed in New Haven* (1968), and produced a sequel to *Catch 22, Closing Time*, in 1994. Later books—*Something Happened* (1974), *Good as Gold* (1979), *God Knows* (1984), a fictional monologue by the biblical King David, and *Picture This* (1988)—tended to receive churlish notices but are no less satiric, and the first is an existentialist masterpiece. During the later period his output was hampered by a neurological ailment, described in the autobiographical account below.

▷ *No Laughing Matter* (with Speed Vogel, 1986)

HELLMAN, Lillian Florence
(1907–84)

American playwright, born into a Jewish family in New Orleans. Educated at New York University and Columbia University, she worked for the New York *Herald Tribune* as a reviewer (1925–8) and for M-G-M in Hollywood as reader of plays (1927–32). She was married for a time to the dramatist **Arthur Kober**, but lived for many years with the detective writer **Dashiell Hammett**, who encouraged her writing. She had her first stage success with *The Children's Hour* (1934), which ran on Broadway for 86 weeks. This was followed by *Days to Come* (1936) and *The Little Foxes* (1939), which was later adapted into a film starring Bette Davis. During World War II she also wrote the anti-fascist plays *Watch on the Rhine* (1941, winner of the Critics Circle Award) and *The Searching Wind* (1944). When she came before the Un-American Activities committee in 1952 during the Joseph McCarthy era she coined the famous phrase 'I can't cut my conscience to fit this year's fashions'. This period was described in her *Scoundrel Time* (1976). Her other plays included *The Autumn Garden* (1951) and *Toys in the Attic* (1960). Her autobiographical works included *An Unfinished Woman* (1969) and *Pentimento* (1973). A left-wing activist, and sensitive to social injustice and personal suffering, her voice was one of the most persuasive in the modern American theatre. A mercurial woman, she nurtured her animosities, and sued for libel when **Mary McCarthy** said of her that 'every word she writes is a lie, including "and" and "the"', a reference to the misrepresentations in her memoir *Scoundrel Time*. But Hellman died before the case came to court.

▷ *An Unfinished Woman* (1969); *Pentimento* (1973); *Scoundrel Time* (1976)

HELPRIN, Mark
(1947–)

Jewish–American novelist, born in New York State. He was educated at Harvard and Oxford, and served for a time in the Israeli army. His first collection of stories, *A Dove of the East* (1975), was followed by a picaresque novel, *Refiner's Fire* (1977). The potent fusion of fantasy and realism in *Ellis Island and Other Stories* (1980) was recognizably an extension of an important Jewish tradition, and emerged in even more extravagant form in his massive novel *A Winter's Tale* (1983),

a burgeoning, inventive fable of urban life. All his books are strongly moralistic in intent.

HEMANS, Felicia Dorothea, née Browne
(1793–1835)

English poet, born in Liverpool, the daughter of a merchant. Between 1808 and 1812 she published three volumes of poems, and in 1812 married an Irishman, Captain Alfred Hemans. He deserted her in 1818, and she turned to writing for a living. She produced a large number of books of verse of all kinds, love lyrics, classical, mythological, sentimental, including *The Siege of Valencia* (1823) and *Records of Women* (1828). She is perhaps best remembered for the poem *Casabianca*, better known as 'The boy stood on the burning deck', and 'The stately homes of England'.

▷ H F Chorley, *Memories of Mrs Hemans* (1837)

HEMINGWAY, Ernest Millar
(1899–1961)

American novelist and short-story writer, winner of the Nobel Prize for literature, born in Oak Park, a respectable suburb of Chicago. His father was a doctor and a keen sportsman, an enthusiasm his son was to share though he also inherited a melancholic, self-destructive personality. He was educated at grammar school and the palatial Oak Park and River Forest Township High School, where he distinguished himself only in English. His mother wanted him to become a violinist but, modelling himself on **Ring Lardner**, he was determined to become a journalist and a writer. He got a job on the *Kansas City Star* as a cub reporter where he was paid 15 dollars a week and was given a copy of the style book which told him to write in the manner of the mature Hemingway. In April 1918 he resigned and joined the Red Cross, to be hurled into World War I as an ambulance driver on the Italian front, where he was badly wounded. Returning to America he began to write features for the Toronto *Star Weekly* in 1919 and married Hadley Richardson, the first of four wives, in 1921. That same year he went to Europe as a roving correspondent and covered several large conferences. In Paris he moved easily and conspicuously among other émigré artists and came into contact with **Gertrude Stein**, **Ezra Pound**, **James Joyce** and **F Scott Fitzgerald**. *A Moveable Feast* records this time, reliving the struggle he and his new wife had to make ends meet. *Three Stories and Ten Poems* was given a limited circulation in Paris in 1923 and in 1924 he published *In Our Time*, which met with critical approval in America a year later. *The Sun Also Rises* (1926) and a volume of short stories, *Men Without Women* (1927),

confirmed his reputation, and in 1928, divorced from Hadley and re-married to Pauline Pfeiffer, he moved to Key West in Florida. Disentangling fact from myth in the years that followed is not easy. Drinking, brawling, posturing, big-game hunting, deep-sea fishing and bull-fighting, all competed with writing. Nevertheless the body of work is impressive, if uneven. In 1929, he published *A Farewell to Arms*, and in 1932 the wildly overrated bull-fighting book, *Death in the Afternoon*. *Green Hills in Africa* tells of tension-filled big-game hunts. Perhaps his most popular book is *For Whom the Bell Tolls*, published in 1940, about the Civil War in Spain to which Hemingway went as a journalist. Significant later titles are *Across the River and Into the Trees* (1950) and *The Old Man and the Sea* (1952). He won the Pulitzer Prize in 1953 and the Nobel Prize for literature in 1954. He cheated death on more than one occasion and had the strange pleasure of reading his own obituary twice; however, he was given to numbing depressions and shot himself in Ketchum, Idaho, after having lived for years in Cuba.
▷S Donaldson, *By Force of Will* (1977); M Reynolds, *The Young Hemingway* (1986)

HÉMON, Louis
(1880–1913)

French novelist, born in Brest. He went to live in England, and then emigrated to Canada, where he was killed in a railway accident. His *Lizzie Blakeston* (1908) had passed without notice, but the posthumous *Maria Chapdelaine* (serial 1914, Eng trans, 1921) was a well-deserved success when published in book form in Montreal in 1916. It is a Canadian rather than a French classic, because it depicts, with lyrical and admiring fervour, the bleak lives of Canadians who live in the forests north of Montreal.

HEMON, Roparz
(1900–78)

Breton novelist, short-story writer, poet and academic. Born in Brest, he made efforts as a child and a young man to acquire the Breton language, although it was not used by his family, and wrote in Breton; he is considered one of the major literary figures of that language. He founded a Breton journal, *Gwalarn* ('North-west') in 1925, and shortly afterwards set about compiling, single-handedly, a comprehensive Breton dictionary. In 1944 he emigrated to Ireland, where he taught at the Institute for Advanced Studies, Dublin, and lived for the rest of his life. His novels include: *An Aotrou Bimbochet e Breizh* (1925, 'Monsieur Bimbochet in Brittany'); *Alanig an tri roue* (1950, 'Alan of the Three Kings'); and *Mari Vorgan* (1962). A collection of his short stories, *War ribl an hent* ('At the Roadside'),

was published in 1971, and some poetry, under the title *Barzhonegou*, in 1967.

HENDERSON, Hamish
(1919–)

Scottish folklorist, composer and poet, born in Blairgowrie, Perthshire. One of his early poetic works, 'Ninth Elegy for the Dead in Cyrenaica' (1948), won him the **Somerset Maugham** Award, but his considerable literary output has been overshadowed by his outstanding contributions to folk-song. Through his researches in the field for the School of Scottish Studies he was largely responsible for bringing great but unknown traditional singers, such as Jeannie Robertson, to the fore, thereby ensuring the survival of the Scots ballad tradition. Many of his own compositions—notably 'Freedom Come All Ye', 'Farewell to Sicily' and 'The John Maclean March'— have themselves become part of the traditional singer's repertoire. A selection of his writings, *Alias MacAlias*, appeared in 1992.
▷P Orr (ed), *The Poet Speaks* (1966)

HENEY, Helen
(1907–)

Australian writer, born in Sydney, who lived between the wars in Poland and worked in Europe for UNRRA and the Red Cross. Her novels deal mainly with the conflict of cultures, particularly of an individual in an alien group, as in *The Chinese Camellia* (1950) and *Dark Moon* (1953). She has published a biography of the Polish–Australian explorer Sir Paul Strzelecki (1961), *Australia's Founding Mothers* (1978), a study of women during the formative years of the colonies, and has edited *Dear Fanny: Women's Letters to and from New South Wales, 1788–1857* (1985).

HENLEY, Beth (Elizabeth)
(1952–)

American actress, dramatist and screenwriter, born in Jackson, Mississippi. Her first major success was *Crimes of the Heart* (1978), describing a poignant, often comic reunion of three sisters, whose self-reliance and combined emotional strength enables them to overcome the effects of violence and despondency. Staged by the Actors' Theatre of Louisville in 1979, it transferred to Broadway two years later and received a Pulitzer Prize. Several plays have followed, of which the most familiar is *The Miss Firecracker Contest* (1980), which incorporates Henley's recurring theme, that of family relationships in the American deep south.
▷K Betsko and R Koenig, *Interviews with Contemporary Women Playwrights* (1987)

HENLEY, William Ernest
(1849–1903)

English poet, playwright, critic and editor, born in Gloucester. Crippled by tuberculosis as a boy, he spent nearly two years in Edinburgh Infirmary (1873–5), where he wrote several of the poems in *A Book of Verses* (1888). In Edinburgh he became a close friend of **Robert Louis Stevenson**, with whom he collaborated in four plays, *Deacon Brodie* (1880), *Beau Austin* (1884), *Admiral Guinea* (1884) and *Macaire* (1885). Other volumes of his verse, with its unusual rhymes and esoteric words, followed: *The Song of the Sword* (1892), *Collected Poems* (1898), *For England's Sake* (1900), *Hawthorn and Lavender* (1901), *A Song of Speed* (1903) and *In Hospital* (1903), which contains his best-known poem, 'Invictus'. A pungent critic, he successfully edited the *Magazine of Art*, (1882–6) and the *Scots Observer* (1889), which became *The National Observer*. He was joint compiler of a dictionary of slang (1894–1904).
▷ J Flora, *W E Henley* (1970)

HENNINGSEN, Agnes
(1868–1962)

Danish novelist and playwright. Born on the island of Funen, she married twice and gave birth to four children. Her work, depicting women in a notable range of roles, focuses on their relations to men and to eroticism. While her novel *De spedalske* (1903, 'The Lepers') defines sexuality as fundamental to all human relations, her play *Elskerinden* (1906, 'The Mistress') exposes the implications of the conventional feminine role. *Kærlighedens Aarstider* (3 vols, 1927–30, 'Love's Seasons'), in which naturalism is fused with psychological realism, asserts the significance of women's eroticism, challenges the centrality of motherhood to women's lives and underlines the impact of self-realization through work. Her eight volumes of *Erindringer* (1941–55, 'Memoirs') have won considerable acclaim.
▷ B Wamberg, *Letsindighedens pris. En bog om Agnes Henningsen* (1983)

HENRI, Adrian Maurice
(1932–)

English poet, born in Birkenhead and saddled throughout his career with the 'Mersey Sound' tag. That was the title given to *Penguin Modern Poets 10* (1967), a hugely popular paperback compilation of his work (shared with **Roger McGough** and **Brian Patten**), which went through an unprecedented two revisions (1974, 1983), and has continued to sell well. Its success prompted him to try his luck as a performer, with the multi-media Liverpool Scene group (1968–

70); *Tonight at Noon* (1968) also belongs to this period. Henri is also a painter, whose canvases have the same immediacy and Pop imagery as his verse. Clearly influenced by the Black Mountain poets—**Charles Olson**, **Robert Creeley**, **Robert Duncan**—Henri also owes a less immediately obvious debt to the autobiographical approach and magpie linguistics of **MacDiarmid**. Significantly, his most substantial work is entitled simply *Autobiography* (1971), which is searchingly honest and unaffected. *The Best of Henri* (1975) collected the work of the sixties, but he refused to go down with the decade; *From the Loveless Motel* (1980) and *Penny Arcade* (1983) are collections of later material.
▷ J Raban, *The Society of the Poem* (1971)

HENRY, O, pseud of William Sydney Porter
(1862–1910)

American writer, master of the short story, born in Greenboro, North Carolina. Brought up during the depression in the South, he settled in Austin, Texas, where he became a bank-teller. In 1894 he 'borrowed' money from the bank to help his consumptive wife and to start a literary magazine, the *Rolling Stone*, but ran away at the height of the scandal. He returned, however, in 1897 to his wife's deathbed. He was found technically guilty of embezzlement, and spent three years in jail (1898–1901), where he adopted his pseudonym and began to write short stories. His second marriage came to nothing and he roamed about the New York back streets from 1902, where he found ample material for his tales. His first of many collections was *Cabbages and Kings* (1904). His use of coincidence and trick endings, his purple phraseology and caricature have been criticized, but nothing can detract from the technical brilliance and boldness of his comic writing.
▷ D Stuart, *O. Henry: a biography* (1986)

HENRYSON, Robert
(c.1425–c.1508)

Scottish poet. He is usually designated 'schoolmaster of Dunfermline', and was certainly a notary in 1478. His work is part of the tradition of the Scottish 'makars' (as shapers of literary artifice), and his best-known poem is the *Testament of Cresseid*, a kind of supplement to **Chaucer**'s poem on the same subject. Of his 14 extant poems, *Robene and Makyne* is the earliest Scottish specimen of pastoral poetry. His other works include a metrical version of 13 *Morall Fabels of Esope the Phrygian*, possibly his masterpiece.
▷ R L Kindrick, *Robert Henryson* (1979)

HENTY, George Alfred
(1832–1902)

English novelist and journalist, born in Trumpington. Educated at Westminster and Caius College, Cambridge, he became a special correspondent for the *Morning Advertiser* during the Crimean War and for the *Standard* in the Franco–Prussian War. He was best known, however, for his 80 historical adventure stories for boys, including *With Clive in India* (1884) and *With Moore at Corunna* (1898).
▷ G M Fenn, *G. A. Henty: The Story of an Active Life* (1907)

HEPPENSTALL, Rayner
(1911–81)

English novelist and critic, born in Huddersfield, Yorkshire, and who for many years was a producer for the BBC's Third Programme. He had a wide circle of artistic and literary friends, including **George Orwell**; but, although gifted, he was justifiably regarded as extremely eccentric. His first novel, *The Blaze of Noon* (1935), was followed by several more, including *The Connecting Door* (1962). Each is lucid, intriguing and casts a sceptical but sympathetic eye over human emotions and frailties. His final novel, *The Pier* (1986), is a murder story told by an elderly writer who lives in a small seaside town.
▷ *The Intellectual Part* (1963); *Portrait of the Artist as a Professional Man* (1969)

HERBERT, Sir A(lan) P(atrick)
(1890–1971)

English writer and politician. He was called to the Bar but never practised, having established himself in his twenties as a witty writer of verses, joining *Punch* in 1924. His first theatrical success with Nigel Playfair in the revue *Riverside Nights* (1926) was followed by a series of brilliant libretti for comic operas, including *Tantivy Towers* (1930), a version of Offenbach's *Helen* (1932), *Derby Day* (1932) and *Bless the Bride* (1947). He was also the author of several successful novels, notably *The Secret Battle* (1919), *The Water Gipsies* (1930) and *Holy Deadlock* (1934). In *What a Word* (1935) and many humorous articles he campaigned against jargon and officialese. From 1935 to 1950 he was Independent Member of Parliament for Oxford University, and introduced a marriage bill in the House of Commons that became law as the Matrimonial Causes Act 1938, and did much to improve divorce conditions.
▷ *My Life and Times* (1970); S Glasspool, *Sir A P Herbert: A Short Guide to his Literary Work* (1973)

HERBERT, Frank Patrick
(1920–86)

American science-fiction writer, born in Tacoma, Washington. He was a journalist before turning to full-time fiction writing. His first novel, *The Dragon in the Sea* (1956), is an acute psychological study set on a submarine, but his breakthrough came with his series of novels about the desert planet *Dune* (1965), one of the most complex and fully realized examples of an alternative world in science fiction. The five sequels were mixed in quality, but extended the premises and issues of the novel in considerable depth. Persistent themes of his work include the development of higher or artificial intelligence in human and non-human species, genetic engineering, ecology and overpopulation. Important titles include *The Green Brain* (1966), *The Santaroga Barrier* (1968) and *Hellstrom's Hive* (1973).

HERBERT, George
(1593–1633)

English metaphysical poet and clergyman, member of a distinguished Anglo–Welsh family, the son of Lady Magdalen Herbert (to whom **John Donne** addressed his *Holy Sonnets*) and brother of Lord Herbert of Cherbury. Educated at Westminster and Trinity College, Cambridge, he was elected a fellow there at the age of 22 in 1614, and Public Orator in 1619. He was MP for Montgomery in 1624–5. His connection with the court, and particularly the favour of King James VI and I, seemed to point to a worldly career, and his poems, 'Affliction' and 'The Collar', indicate the sharpness of the decision which finally directed him to the Church. In 1630, under the influence of Laud, he took orders and spent his few remaining years as the zealous parish priest of Bemerton in Wiltshire. Like his friend Nicholas Ferrar, but without Ferrar's mystical piety, he represents both in his life and works the counter-challenge of the Laudian party to the Puritans. The Church was Christ's comely bride to be decked with seemly ornament and 'The mean thy praise and glory is'. This twofold conception, along with his ideal of Christian humility and unwearying service, pervades all his writing, verse and prose alike. Practically all his religious lyrics are included in *The Temple, Sacred Poems and Private Ejaculations*, posthumously published in 1633. His chief prose work, *A Priest in the Temple*, containing guidance for the country parson, was published in his *Remains* (1652).
▷ J J D Faniell, *The Life of George Herbert of Bemerton* (1902); J B Leishman, *The Metaphysical Poets* (1934)

HERBERT, William, 3rd Earl of Pembroke
(1580–1630)

English poet. He was a patron of **Ben Jonson**, **Philip Massinger** and Inigo Jones, and a lord chamberlain of the court (1615–30). He became Chancellor of Oxford University in 1617 and had Pembroke College named after him. **Shakespeare**'s 'W H', the 'onlie begetter' of the *Sonnets* has been taken by some to refer to him.
▷T Tyler, *The Herbert-Fitton Theory of Shakespeare's Sonnets* (1898); R Holzapfel, *Shakespeare's Secret* (1961)

HERBERT, Xavier
(1901–84)

Australian novelist, born in Port Hedland, Western Australia, who, after much travel, settled in the Northern Territory. He is known mainly for his first novel and his last, *Capricornia* (1938) and *Poor Fellow My Country* (1975); the intervening years were spent drifting round Australia, a period which reinforced Herbert's sympathy with the situation and the treatment of Australia's aboriginals. This is strongly evoked in his writing, and especially in the sprawling *Poor Fellow My Country*. Longer than *War and Peace*, and the longest novel then published in Australia, it remains the lasting testament of a painstaking and poignant writer.

HERBERT, Zbigniew
(1924–)

Polish poet, born in Lvov and educated at the universities of Cracow, Toruń and Warsaw, where he studied economics, law and philosophy. He was a resistance fighter during World War II. His work takes a satiric but uncynical view of Stalinism, and often calls on a quietly heroic interpretation of biblical mythology. This is noticeable in *Struma świata* (1956, 'Harmony of Light') and *Hermes, pies i gwiazda* (1957, 'Hermes, A Dog and a Star'), and is the dominant tone in the first English translation (1968), edited by **Czeslaw Milosz** and Peter Dale Scott; thereafter the tone is less passive, more robustly argumentative in a way that sometimes recalls his English Metaphysical namesake, **George Herbert**. In *Pan Cogito* (1974, 'Mr Cogito') he adopts a Cartesian persona to examine his beliefs *vis-à-vis* history, and the style is stripped and rhythmic, almost discursive, but with no metaphoric entanglements. A collected poems, *Wiersze zebrane*, appeared in Warsaw in 1971, and an important English translation (made by John and Bogdana Carpenter) three years later. Herbert has also written plays and essays on art; some of the latter are reprinted in *Barbarzyrica w ogrodzie* (1962, 'Barbarian in the Garden').

HERBST, Josephine Frey
(1897–1969)

American novelist, born in Iowa, she was perhaps the best-known female exponent of US 'proletarian' fiction in the 1930s. Her fiction was closely observed (though sometimes too obsessively documentary) and showed a fine insight into the lives of working people. Her main achievement was a trilogy of novels written during the mid- to late-1930s, when Popular Front communism was being defined as 20th-century Americanism; it consists of *Pity Is Not Enough* (1933), *The Executioner* (1934), *Rope of Gold* (1939). Later works, such as *Satan's Sergeants* (1941) and *The Watcher with the Horn* (1955), were more discursive, but Herbst is still readable.

HERCULANO, Alexandre
(1810–66)

Portuguese historian and novelist, born in Lisbon. He was not only Portugal's apostle of liberal romanticism but also her first objective historian: less through his novels (such as *O Bobo*, 1843) than through his *História de Portugal* (1846–53) and cognate works, in which he took (for the first time) an objective approach—which brought down upon him the wrath of the obscurantist church. His influence on all his successors, especially on **Antonio Soares de Passos**, has therefore been salutary and wide.

HERDAL, Harald
(1900–)

Danish left-wing poet and novelist, born in Copenhagen into a slum. His love poetry is especially prized for its freedom from the socialist dogma which many critics have felt distorted his fiction; but the latter, naturalist in cast, has moments of power and authentic descriptions of working-class misery. Titles include *Digte 1929–49* (1949, 'Poems'). He also wrote a number of autobiographical works.

HERDER, Johann Gottfried
(1744–1803)

German critic and poet, born in Mohrungen in East Prussia. He studied at Königsberg, and there made the acquaintance of Kant and Hamann. In 1764 he became teacher in a school and assistant pastor in a church in Riga. Between 1766 and 1769 he wrote two works, in which he maintained that the truest poetry is the poetry of the people. In 1769 he met **Goethe** in Strasbourg. In 1770 he was appointed court preacher at Bückeburg, and in 1776 first preacher in Weimar. Herder's love for the songs of the people, for unsophisticated human nature, found expression in

an admirable collection of folksongs, *Stimmen der Völker in Liedern* (1778–9, 'Voices of the Peoples in Songs'), *Vom Geist der Ebraïschen Poesie* (1782–3, Eng trans *The Spirit of Hebrew Poetry*, 1833), a treatise on the influence of poetry on manners (1778), in oriental mythological tales, in parables and legends, in his version of the *Cid* (1805), and other works. The supreme importance of the historical method is fully recognized in these and a book on the origin of language (1772), and especially in his masterpiece, *Ideen zur Geschichte der Menschheit* (1784–91, Eng trans *Outlines of a Philosophy of the History of Man*, 1800), which is remarkable for its anticipations of evolutionary theories. He is best remembered for the influence he exerted on Goethe and the growing German Romanticism.
▷H Reisiger, *Johann Gottfried Herder* (1942)

HEREDIA, José María
(1803–39)

Cuban poet, born in Santiago de Cuba, cousin of the French poet **José María de Heredia**. He was exiled to the USA for anti-government activities in 1823. He is remembered mainly for his patriotic verse and for his ode to Niagara (1824), but the earlier 'En el teocalli de Cholula' ('In the Pyramid of Cholula') is a significant philosophical poem.
▷A Harms, *Heredia* (1975)

HEREDIA, José María de
(1842–1905)

French poet, born in Santiago de Cuba, cousin of the Cuban poet **José María Heredia**. He went at an early age to France, where he was educated. One of the Parnassians, he achieved a great reputation with a comparatively small output, his finest work being found in his sonnets, which appeared in the collection *Les Trophées* (1893).
▷C Utrera, *Heredia* (1939)

HERFORD, Oliver
(1863–1935)

American illustrator and humorist. Herford was born in Sheffield, England, but moved to America as a child. He was educated at Antioch College, Ohio, and at art schools in London and Paris. He produced over 50 books of frothy nonsense, mainly illustrated by his own drawings. These—with titles such as *Pen and Inklings* (1893), *Rubaiyat of a Persian Cat* (1904) and *A Little Book of Bores* (1906)—satisfied a contemporary hunger for undemanding entertainment but have little lasting worth, except for bibliophiles and anthologists with space to fill.

HERGESHEIMER, Joseph
(1880–1954)

American novelist and essayist, born in Philadelphia. He studied art, but made his name with *Mountain Blood* (1915), *The Three Black Pennys* (1917), *Tubal Cain* (1918), *Java Head* (1919), *The Bright Shawl* (1922), *The Foolscap Rose* (1934) and other romantic novels and short stories about early American life.
▷*The Presbyterian Child* (1924)

HERLIHY, James Leo
(1927–)

American novelist, short-story writer and playwright, born in Detroit. He was educated at Black Mountain College, an influential liberal arts school in North Carolina. He is best known for his novel *Midnight Cowboy* (1965), the story of a handsome but naive cowboy who forsakes his small-town life for the dark side of New York, where he forms an unlikely alliance with a crippled pickpocket. It was successfully filmed in 1967. His other novels include *All Fall Down* (1960), about the disintegration of a middle-class family, and *The Season of the Witch* (1971), in which he returned to the theme of a runaway drifter in New York, this time female. He also wrote a number of plays and two volumes of short stories.

HERMANS, Wilhelm Frederik
(1921–)

Leading contemporary Dutch novelist, critic, poet, editor, scientist and dramatist, born in Amsterdam. Until 1973 he was a professor of physical geography at Amsterdam. A somewhat self-conscious modernist, Hermans has set himself the task—reminiscent of the French atheist–existential movement—of trying to make sense of a world that seems devoid of meaning. If Hermans had a model, then this was certainly also a French one: the novelist **Louis-Ferdinand Céline**. His first novel, written after some attempts at poetry, was *Conserve* (1947), his best-known one *De tranen der acacia's* (1949, 'The Tears of the Acacias'), which is set in occupied Amsterdam. In *De god Dernkbar kamer van Damocles* (1956, Eng trans *The Dark Room of Damocles*, 1962) he attempted a more humanistic kind of novel.

HERMLIN, Stephen, pseud of Rudolf Leder
(1915–)

German poet and story writer, born in Chemnitz. He returned from exile to East Germany in 1947, and soon ran foul of the authorities for his Surrealist poems. He later turned to socialist realism in such collections as *Stalin* (1949).

HERMODSSON, Elisabet
(1927–)

Swedish writer, composer and artist. Born in Göteborg, she studied at the University of Stockholm as well as attending art school. Her work encompasses a range of media and genres, the volume *Dikt-ting* (1966, 'Poems Objects') conflating poetry and pictures. On the basis of humanist, Christian and subsequently feminist convictions she has formulated a far-reaching cultural critique to which environmental concerns are central, for example in the poems in *Mänskligt landskap, orättvist fördelat* (1968, 'Human Province, Unfairly Distributed'), in the essays in *Synvända* (1975, 'Sight Distortion'), and in the 'ecological oratorio' *Skapelse utlämnad* (1986, 'Creation Abandoned'). Her feminism first found expression in the 1970s, notably in *Disa Nilssons visor* (1974, 'Disa Nilsson's Songs'), a volume of poems set to music and illustrated by the author, and designed to offer an antithesis to the conventional image of woman presented in **Birger Sjöberg**'s popular *Fridas visor* of 1922.

▷ B I Bergsten, *'Förflytta berg till bokstäver': Utvecklingslinjer i Elisabet Hermodssons författarskap* (1989)

HERNÁNDEZ, José
(1834–86)

Argentinian poet, born near Buenos Aires. He founded the newspaper *Rio de la Plata* in 1869. He is known for his *gaucho* poetry of life on the pampas, where he had spent his early life among the cattlemen. His masterpiece is the epic *El gaucho Martín Fierro* (1872–9).

HERNÁNDEZ, Miguel
(1910–42)

Spanish poet and playwright, a goatherd's son, who was encouraged by **Juan Ramón Jiménez**, **Antonio Machado** and members of the Generation of '27 (**Lorca** and others) to publish his precise and *Gongorista* early poetry. Under the influence of **Neruda**, he became a communist, fought against Franco, and died in a prison hospital of cold, starvation and tuberculosis. His last poems, simple and direct, are of love and yearning for his little son, whom he had never seen. When his poems were first published, some of the best were omitted by the censors; now he has the reputation of yet another major poet-victim of 20th-century barbarism. His best work has been translated in *Songbook of Absences* (1972), and another selection is contained in *Miguel Hernández and Blas de Otero: Selected Poems* (1972). His poetry, sombre and rooted in the past, yet fully contemporary, is amongst the greatest and most

original produced by Spain in his century. Essentially, he was the youngest and last voice of the Generation of '27, since when Spanish poetry has floundered.

▷ G Nichols, *Miguel Hernández* (1978)

HERNÀNDEZ CATÁ, Alfonso
(1885–1940)

Cuban story writer, born of a Spanish father and a Cuban mother. He was at first a follower of **Benito Pérez Galdós**, who was his mentor. His sharp, laconic tales, much influenced by Pérez Galdós and **Maupassant**, were selected and introduced by **Barrios** in 1936. He died in a plane crash.

HERNTON, Calvin C(oolidge)
(1933–)

Black American poet and social researcher, he is almost certainly best known outside the USA for a slim but passionate essay on *Sex and Racism* (UK, 1969; the earlier US version appended *in America* to the title). Though essentially a work of sociology, it reflected much of what Hernton was doing in his verse. Born in Tennessee, his educational and professional life has been marked by a steady oscillation between north and south. His main poetic achievement is *The Coming of Chronos to the House of Nightsong* (1964), a powerful bluesy rap that is too subtly mediated to be stereotyped as 'angry'; nor is it exclusively about 'the Black experience' but resonates with mythic and philosophical concerns. Hernton published a major collection, *Medicine Man*, in 1976; some of the later work reflects his important but largely neglected work on the use of marijuana. Other non-poetic works include *White Papers for White Americans* (1966) and *Coming Together: Black Power, White Hatred and Sexual Hangups* (1971), a more obviously radicalized version of the *Sex and Racism* thesis.

▷ R Berke, *Bounds Out of Bounds* (1981)

HERODOTUS
(c.485–425 BC)

Greek historian, born in Halicarnassus, a Greek colony on the coast of Asia Minor. When the colonies were freed from the Persian yoke, he left his native town and travelled in Asia Minor, the Aegean islands, Greece, Macedonia, Thrace, the coasts of the Black Sea, Persia, Tyre, Egypt, and Cyrene. In 443 BC the colony of Thurii was founded by Athens on the Tarentine Gulf, and Herodotus joined it. From Thurii he visited Sicily and Lower Italy. On his travels, he collected historical, geographical, ethnological, mythological and archaeological material for his history which was designed to record not only the wars but the causes of the wars between

Greece and the barbarians. Beginning with the conquest of the Greek colonies in Asia Minor by the Lydian king Croesus, he gives a history of Lydia, and then passes to Persia, Babylon and Egypt. In books five to nine we have the history of the two Persian wars (494–478 BC). **Cicero** called him 'the father of history'.
▷A de Selincourt, *The World of Herodotus* (1962)

HERONDAS, or HERODAS
(3rd century BC)

Greek poet, a native of Cos or Miletus. His work *Mimiambi* ('Iambic Mimes'), pictures of Greek life in dialogue, comprising some 700 verses, was discovered on an Egyptian papyrus in 1891.
▷F Will, *Herondas* (1973)

HERRERA, Fernando de
(c.1534–1597)

Spanish lyric poet, born in Seville. He took holy orders and was known as 'El Divino'. Many of his love poems are remarkable for tender feeling, while his odes sometimes attain the grandeur of **Milton**. He wrote a prose history of the war in Cyprus (1572), and translated Stapleton's life of Sir Thomas More from Latin.
▷M G Randel, *The Historical Prose of Fernando de Herrera* (1971)

HERRERA Y REISSIG, Julio
(1875–1910)

Uruguayan *modernista* poet, born in Montevideo. Herrera's poetry was artificial and affected, but also perfect in its expression: he influenced the so-called ultraists—late purveyors of art-for-art's sake—and his work was eventually edited (final edition, 1958) by the leading ultraist, **Guillermo de la Torre**. He withdrew himself from society and lived in an attic—'Tower of the Panoramas'—in Montevideo until heart disease killed him. His vision of a perfect pastoral world unsullied by greed or commerce is moving, but he does not have the experience (he invented the disreputable life of a *poète maudit* for himself) to turn it into great, as distinct from undeniably exquisite, poetry.
▷B Gicovate, *Julio Herrera y Reissig and the Symbolists* (1957)

HERRICK, Robert
(1591–1674)

English poet, born in London, the son of a goldsmith. He was apprenticed to his uncle, also a goldsmith, but went to Trinity Hall, Cambridge, at the age of 22. After graduating in 1620 he took holy orders and was presented with a living in Devon (1629), of which he was deprived as a royalist in 1647. The following year he published *Hesperides: or the Works both Humane and Divine of Robert Herrick Esq*, with a separate section of religious verse entitled *Noble Numbers*. Despite *Noble Numbers* he is the most pagan of English poets, vying with his Latin models in the celebration of imagined mistresses—Julia, Anthea, Corinna, and others. He was at his best when describing rural rites as in *The Hock Cart* and *Twelfth Night*, and in lyrical gems such as 'Gather ye rosebuds while ye may' and 'Cherry Ripe'. Youth and love and the pagan fields were his themes at a time when the west country was devastated by the Civil War. He resumed his living in his Devon parish in 1662 after the Restoration.
▷M Chute, *Two Gentlemen: the lives of George Herbert and Robert Herrick* (1960); John Press, *Robert Herrick* (1961)

HERRICK, Robert Welch
(1868–1938)

American novelist. In his quiet and understated way, he restated the main components of the American myth: the opposition of self-reliant and morally encompassed individuals with 'society'. He viewed the USA from a somewhat privileged angle, growing up in Cambridge, Massachusetts and receiving his education at Harvard. He combined a literary career with faculty positions at MIT (1890–3) and Chicago University (1893–1923). His first book was a collection of stories, *Literary Love-Letters* (1897), followed by a novel, *The Man Who Wins* (also 1897), in which he considers the incompatability of altruistic vocation and the success ethic. Later books, including *The Web of Life* (1900), the bestselling *The Master of the Inn* (1908) and *The Healer* (1911), likewise focus on a young physician, but almost all of his protagonists confront similar dilemmas. *The Memoirs of an American Citizen* (1905), possibly Herrick's own favourite, was edited by the critic and historian Daniel Aaron in 1963. Despite Aaron's advocacy, Herrick's reputation has not revived. His writing career had virtually come to a halt when, in 1935, he was appointed secretary to the governor of the US Virgin Islands.
▷B Nevius, *Robert Herrick: The Development of a Novelist* (1962)

HERSEY, John Richard
(1914–93)

American author, born in Tientsin, China. He was educated at Yale, and was correspondent in the far east for the magazine *Time*. *Hiroshima* (1946), the first on-the-spot description of the effects of a nuclear explosion, took over an entire issue of the *New Yorker* on August 31 1946. His novels include *A Bell for Adano* (1944), which was dramatized and filmed, *The War Lover* (1959), *The Child Buyer* (1960), *Under the Eye of the Storm* (1967) and *The Walnut Door* (1977).

▷D Sanders, *John Hersey Revisited* (1990)

HERTZ, Henrik, originally **Heyman**
(1798–1870)

Danish poet, born in Copenhagen. He published a collection of rhymed satirical letters, *Gjengangerbreve* (1830, 'Letters of a Ghost'), and several dramas, including *Svend Dyrings Hus* (1837) and *Kong Renés Datter* (1845).

▷M Brondsted, *Henrik Hertzs Teater* (1946)

HERVIEU, Paul Ernest
(1857–1915)

French dramatist and novelist, born in Neuilly. His plays included *L'Énigme* (1901), *Le Dédale* (1903, 'The Labyrinth') and other powerful pieces, which usually took family problems as their subject-matter. He also wrote a successful drama about the Revolutionary period, *Théroigne de Méricourt* (1902), which was created for the famous actress Sarah Bernhardt.

▷P Gaultier, *Maîtres de la pensée française* (1921)

HERWEGH, Georg
(1817–75)

German revolutionary poet, born in Stuttgart. In 1836 he took up journalism, but in 1839, under threat of being court-martialled for insubordination during his military service, he fled to Switzerland. There he published *Gedichte eines Lebendigen* (1841, 'Poems from One Who is Alive'), establishing him as a revolutionary poet. He was well received in Germany, but his popularity came to an end when he led an invasion of Baden (1848), his behaviour earning him criticism from all sides, and he returned to Switzerland, publishing very little before his death.

▷V Fleury, *Le poète Georg Herwegh* (1911)

HERZEN, Alexander Ivanovich
(1812–70)

Russian political thinker and writer, born in Moscow, the illegitimate son of a nobleman. He was imprisoned in 1834 for his revolutionary socialism and exiled to the provinces. In 1847 he left Russia for Paris, and in 1851 settled in London, becoming a powerful propagandist through his novels and treatises, and by the smuggling into Russia of his journal *Kolokol* (1857–67, 'The Bell'). His memoirs were published in *Byloe i dumy*

(1861–7, Eng trans *My Past and Thoughts*, 1924–7), and are his most important writings.

▷Y M Steklov, *Aleksander Hertzen* (1920)

HESIOD
(c.8th century BC)

Greek poet, born in Ascra, at the foot of Mount Helicon, the son of a sea captain. One of the earliest known Greek poets, he is best known for two works, *Opera et dies* ('Works and Days') and *Theogonia* ('Theogony'). The *Opera et dies* is generally considered to consist of two originally distinct poems, one exalting honest labour and denouncing corrupt and unjust judges; the other containing advice as to the days, lucky or unlucky, for the farmer's work. The *Theogonia* teaches the origin of the universe out of Chaos and the history of the gods. Hesiod's poetry is didactic. *Opera et dies* gives an invaluable picture of the Greek village community in the 8th century BC, and the *Theogonia* is of importance to the comparative mythologist.

▷A R Burn, *The World of Hesiod* (1966)

HESSE, Hermann
(1877–1962)

German-born Swiss novelist and poet, winner of the Nobel Prize for literature, born in Calw in Württemberg. He was a bookseller and antiquarian in Basel from 1895 to 1902, and published his first novel, *Peter Camenzind*, in 1904 (Eng trans 1961). From then on he devoted himself to writing, living in Switzerland from 1911, becoming a naturalized citizen in 1923. *Rosshalde* (1914, Eng trans 1970) examines the problem of the artist. *Knulp* (1915, Eng trans 1971) is a tribute to vagabondage. *Demian* (1919, Eng trans 1971) is a psychoanalytic study of incest, while *Narziss und Goldmund* (1930, Eng trans *Death and the Lover*, 1932) portrays the two sides of man's nature by contrasting a monk and a voluptuary. *Steppenwolf* (1927, Eng trans 1929) mirrors the confusion of modern existence, and *Das Glasperlenspiel* (1943, Eng trans *Magister Ludi*, 1949) is a Utopian fantasy on the theme of withdrawal from the world. Hesse was awarded both the **Goethe** Prize and the Nobel Prize for literature in 1946. His poetry was collected in *Die Gedichte* in 1942 (a selection, Eng trans *Hours in the Garden and Other Poems*, 1979), and his letters, *Briefe*, appeared in 1951. *Beschwörungen* (1955, 'Affirmations'), confirmed that his powers were not diminished by age. Though he disclaimed any ruling purpose, the theme of his work might be stated as a musing on the difficulties put in the way of the individual in his efforts to build up an integrated, harmonious self. All this is expressed in sensitive and sensuous language rising to the majestic and visionary.

▷J Mileck, *Hesse: his life and art* (1978)

HETHERINGTON, John Aikman
(1907–75)

Australian journalist, war correspondent and biographer of major Australian figures including Field Marshal Sir Thomas Blamey (1954 and 1973), Dame Nellie Melba (1967) and **Norman Lindsay** (1973). He was born in Sandringham, Victoria. Collections of his biographical cameos include *Australians: Nine Profiles* (1960) and *Uncommon Men* (1965), while *Pillars of the Faith* (1966) portrays Victorian churchmen.

▷*The Morning was Shining* (1971)

HEWETT, Dorothy Coade
(1923–)

Australian writer of poems and plays, born in Wickepin, Western Australia, whose poetry is collected in *What about the People?* (1961, a collaboration with her third husband Merv Lilley), and four other volumes including *Journeys* (1982). Little of her prolific output of plays has been published, but *This Old Man Comes Rolling Home* (1976) and *The Man from Mukinupin* (1979) deserve notice. Her first novel, *Bobbin Up* (1959), received acclaim; its story of the political and sexual awakening of a group of factory girls stands in direct line of descent from feminist writings of the 1920s and 1930s. *The Toucher* (1993) tells of an elderly novelist and her relationship with a much younger man.

HEWLETT, Maurice Henry
(1861–1923)

English novelist, poet and essayist, born in London, the son of a civil servant. He was the Keeper of land revenue records (1896–1900), and made his name with his historical romance *The Forest Lovers* (1898). He wrote several more novels on historical themes, and a trilogy of novels featuring the invented scholar-gipsy John Maxwell Senhouse. He also wrote nature sketches and several volumes of poetry; the long poem *The Song of the Plow* (1916) is perhaps his best work.

▷L Binyon (ed), *The Letters of Maurice Hewlett. To Which is Added a Diary in Greece* (1926)

HEYER, Georgette
(1902–74)

English historical and detective novelist, born in London of partly South Slav descent. She studied at Westminster College, London, and after marriage in 1925 travelled in East Africa and Yugoslavia until 1929. By that time she had produced several well-researched historical novels from various periods, including *The Black Moth* (1921) and *Beauvallet* (1929). She risked fictional studies of real figures in crisis with books on William I, The Conqueror, Charles II, and the battle of Waterloo. However, it was not until *Regency Buck* (1935) and later novels that she really came into her own with the Regency period, on which she made herself an outstanding authority. *My Lord John* (1976), on Henry V's brother, was unfinished at her death. She also wrote modern comedy detective novels with dexterity, such as *Death in the Stocks* (1935) and *Behold, Here's Poison* (1936), and used detective and thriller plots with pace and irony in historical fiction such as *The Talisman Ring* (1936), *The Reluctant Widow* (1946) and *The Quiet Gentleman* (1951).

▷J A Hodge, *The Private World of Georgette Heyer* (1984)

HEYM, Georg
(1887–1912)

German poet, born in Hirschberg, Silesia, and educated at the universities of Würzburg, Jena and Berlin, where he first read law at his father's command before mutinously turning to the study of Chinese. His writing is an expression of his frustration with, and rebellion against, the restrictive conventions of Prussia's middle-class establishment. In his most famous poems he deliberately focuses on those who live on the periphery of society: suicides, murderers, the mentally deranged and the physically deformed. He shows himself fascinated by the elementary, impulsive power of the demonic and the grotesque which stands in such blatant contrast to the general predictability of society. Exploding from a violently disturbing imagery and a suggestive use of colours, Heym's poetry is full of apocalyptic visions of war, death, and human alienation. He died in an attempt to rescue a friend from drowning while ice-skating. The only volume of poetry published in his lifetime, *Der ewige Tag* (1911), was soon followed by the posthumous *Umbra Vitae* (1912) and *Dichtungen* (1922).

▷P Bridgwater, *The Poet as Hero and Clown. A Study of Heym and Lichtenstein* (1986)

HEYM, Stefan, originally Helmut Flieg
(1913–)

German novelist and journalist, born in Chemnitz, the son of a Jewish businessman. He fled Germany in 1937, and later served in the US army, taking part in the Normandy Landings of 1944, before settling in Munich when peace came. He moved to East Germany in 1953, since when much of his writing has been concerned with a critique of capitalism and an often ironic commentary on the deficiencies of the erstwhile Eastern bloc. *The Eyes of Reason* (1951, written in English), the tale of three Czech brothers, makes explicit Heym's support for the communist state. *Fünf Tage im Juni* (1974, 'Five Days in June') recounts the GDR workers' revolt of 1953 in a manner sharply at odds with the official version. He has recently been critical of the 'instant capitalism' which followed the fall of the Berlin Wall.

HEYSE, Paul Johann von
(1830–1914)

German writer and winner of the Nobel Prize for literature, born in Berlin. He settled in Munich in 1854. He excelled as a short-story teller, his short stories being marked by a graceful style, sly humour and frequent sensuality. These were collected in *Das Buch der Freundschaft* (1883–4, 'The Book of Friendship') and other volumes. He also wrote novels, plays and epic poems, and translations of Italian poets. He was awarded the 1910 Nobel Prize for literature.
▷ L Ferrari, *Paul Heyse und die literarische Strömungen seiner Zeit* (1939)

HEYWARD, DuBose
(1885–1940)

American novelist, poet and playwright, born in Charleston, South Carolina. His first book of poems, *Carolina Chansons* (1922), co-written with **Hervey Allen**, was followed by *Skylines and Horizons* (1924) and *Jasbo Brown* (1931). He is best known for *Porgy* (1925), a novel about black life in the waterfront district of Charleston, or rather for the dramatic adaptation he and his wife, Dorothy, made of it, which won a Pulitzer Prize on the stage in 1927 and was made into the opera *Porgy and Bess* by George Gershwin in 1935. His other novels include *Peter Ashley* (1932), a Civil War drama, and *Star Spangled Virgin* (1939), set in the Virgin Islands during the period of the New Deal.
▷ F Durham, *Du Bose Heyward: The Man Who Wrote 'Porgy'* (1954)

HEYWOOD, John
(c.1497–c.1580)

English epigrammatist, playwright and musician, born perhaps in London. After studying at Oxford, he was introduced at Court by Sir Thomas More, who was a distant cousin by marriage, and made himself, by his wit and his skill in singing and playing on the virginals, a favourite with Henry VIII and with Queen Mary I, to whom he had been music teacher in her youth. He was a devout Catholic, and after the accession of Elizabeth went to Belgium. He wrote several short plays or interludes, whose individual characters represent classes, such as the Pedlar, the Pardoner, and the like. They thus form a link between the old moralities and the modern drama. He is remembered above all, however, for his collections of proverbs and epigrams. His wearisome allegorical poem, *The Spider and the Flie*, contrasts Catholicism and Protestantism. He was the grandfather of **John Donne**.
▷ R C Johnson, *John Heywood* (1970)

HEYWOOD, Thomas
(c.1574–1641)

English dramatist, poet and actor, born in Lincolnshire, the son of a clergyman. He was educated at Cambridge, and was writing plays by 1596. In 1598 he was engaged by Philip Henslowe as an actor with the Lord Admiral's Men. Up to 1633 he had a large share in the composition of 220 plays. He was also the author of a historical poem, *Troja Britannica* (1609); an *Apology for Actors* (1612); *Nine Bookes of Various History concerning Women* (1624); a long poem, *The Hierarchie of the Blessed Angells* (1635); a volume of rhymed translations from **Lucian**, **Erasmus**, and **Ovid**; various pageants, tracts and treatises; and *The Life of Ambrosius Merlin* (1641). 24 of Heywood's plays have survived. The best is *A Woman Kilde with Kindnesse* (1607), a domestic tragedy; and with this may be coupled *The English Traveller* (1633). His work is usually distinguished by naturalness and simplicity. In the two parts of *The Fair Maid of the West* (1631), and in *Fortune by Land and Sea* (1655), partly written by **William Rowley**, he gives some spirited descriptions of sea fights. *The Rape of Lucrece* (1608) is chiefly notable for its songs; *Love's Maistresse* (1636) is fanciful and ingenious; and there is much tenderness in *A Challenge for Beautie* (1636). In *The Royall King and Loyall Subject* (1637) the doctrine of passive obedience to kingly authority is stressed.
▷ F S Boas, *Thomas Heywood* (1950)

HIBBERD, Jack
(1940–)

Australian playwright, born in Warracknabeal, Victoria. His prolific output tends often to short pieces with a satirical or abrasive tone, some of which are brought together in his *Three Popular Plays* (1976). Of his other plays, *Dimboola* (1969, published 1974) and *A Stretch of the Imagination* (1972, published 1973) are considered his best. His first novel, *Memoirs of an Old Bastard* (1989), is intended as the first of a trilogy.

HICHENS, Robert Smythe
(1864–1950)

English novelist. He studied music, but made his name as a novelist with books such as

445

The Green Carnation (1894), a novel about London society in the decadent manner, *The Garden of Allah* (1905), a desert romance set in North Africa, *The Call of the Blood* (1906), *The Paradine Case* (1933) and *That Which is Hidden* (1939).
▷ *Yesterday* (1947)

HICKS, Granville
(1901–82)

American literary critic and novelist. He was born in New Hampshire and came to prominence as a notably doctrinaire Marxist journalist on *New Masses*. His most important contribution to the critical debate in the 'proletarian' period of American literature was a book called *The Great Tradition* (1933), which marks out very different territory from that considered by **F R Leavis** under the same title. Hicks left the Communist Party in 1939 and turned on former comrades with the same ferocity he had once reserved for bourgeois individualists; *I Like America* (1938) was a significant pointer to this turning of his intellectual tide. He wrote several novels, but his other significant work is a closely observed memoir called *Small Town* (1946), which offers an unexpected insight into this complex and deceptive literary figure.

HIDALGO, Bartolomé
(1788–1822)

Uruguayan poet and playwright, born in Montevideo but of Argentinian parents. Although not a *gaucho* (roaming cowboy), Hidalgo was the first man to write recognizably *gauchesque* poetry. This popular 19th-century poetry, written in the dialect of the ranches, and using the cowboys' *cielito* rhythms (a four-line stanza), was in fact practised by sophisticated urban poets, either for political or satirical purposes. His octosyllabic *Diálogos* (1822, 'Dialogues') sold on the streets and cleared the way for **Lussich** and then for **José Hernandez** and his more serious *Martín Fierro*.

HIDALGO, José Luis
(1919–47)

Spanish poet and painter. Born in Torres, a village in Santander, he studied painting in Valencia and Madrid, and eventually became a talented artist. He was the leader of an important group of poets who contributed to the journal *Proel*, and to which **Vicente Gaos** and **José Hierro** also belonged. Though he only published three books of poetry in his lifetime, his work has received extensive critical attention. *Raiz* (1943, 'Roots') and *Los animales* (1944, 'The Animals') contain relatively simple poems dedicated to themes of nature and regeneration, while *Los muertos*

(1947, 'The Dead'), his most important work, reflects on ideas of death, silence and God.

HIDAYAT, Sadiq
(1903–51)

Persia's greatest writer of the 20th century, born in Teheran into a distinguished literary family. He studied in Paris in 1926, and then attempted, unsuccessfully, to train for dentistry and engineering. He was deeply versed in ancient Iranian lore, as also in foreign literatures. He translated the work of many leading European writers into his own language. He wrote short stories, parodies, novels, sketches, plays and collections of folk stories. Prodigiously gifted, he was unable to get his life into any kind of order, was an alcoholic and a drug addict, and finally gassed himself in despair in a Paris apartment. His masterpiece is the novel *Buf-i kur* (1936, Eng trans *The Blind Owl*, 1957), one of the dozen greatest works of the 20th century, in which the narrator investigates the subtle relationship between his external and his internal lives.
▷H Kamshad, *Modern Persian Prose Literature* (1966)

HIERRO, José
(1922–)

Spanish poet, born in Madrid, who grew up in Santander, where he started writing at 14. He collaborated in a magazine called *Proel*, where his first poetry was published. In post-World War II Spain there were two principal schools of poetry, known as the 'rooted' and the 'unrooted'. Hierro was regarded as the leading poet of the latter. Rather than conform to accepted views, these poets aimed to reflect their awareness of the reality and conflict around them. Hierro won the Adonais prize for 'Alegría' (1947, 'Joy') and a critics' prize for 'Cuanto Sé de Mí' (1957, 'How Much I Know of Myself'). Also well known are 'Tierra Sin Nosotros' (1947, 'Land without Us') and 'Libro de las Aluciones' (1964, 'Book of Illusions'), amongst others. Although known as a social poet, Hierro's poetry is really a medium for personal exploration; his style and language are colloquial, not formal.

HIGGINS, George V(incent)
(1939–)

American novelist, born in Brockton, Massachusetts. He was admitted to the Massachusetts Bar in 1967, but worked in newspapers before becoming a successful attorney. He has used his experience of low-life and his observation of criminals at close quarters to telling effect in a spate of acclaimed literary thrillers. *The Friends of*

Eddie Coyle (1972) was his first book and he has published many since, invariably told almost entirely in dialogue and using Boston as a backdrop. Titles include *Cogan's Trade* (1974), *Kennedy for the Defence* (1980), *Imposters* (1986), *Outlaws* (1987) and *Wonderful Years, Wonderful Years* (1988).
▷G Daldry, in *Watching the Detective* (1990)

HIGGINS, Jack, pseud of Harry Patterson
(1929–)
English thriller writer, born in Newcastle-upon-Tyne. He also writes as Martin Fallon, Hugh Marlowe and James Graham. He was educated at Roundhay School, Leeds, Beckett Park College for Teachers, and the London School of Economics. He was a teacher and college lecturer before becoming a bestselling author with the success of *The Eagle Has Landed* (1975), a tale of derring-do set during World War II in which the Germans plot to kidnap Winston Churchill.

HIGGINSON, Thomas Wentworth
(1823–1911)
American writer, born in Cambridge, Massachusetts. He was ordained to the ministry, from which he retired in 1858. Meanwhile he had been active in the anti-slavery agitation, and, with others, was indicted for the murder of a man killed during an attempt to rescue a fugitive slave, but escaped through a flaw in the indictment. In the Civil War he commanded the first regiment in the Union army raised from among former slaves. In 1880–1 he was a member of the Massachusetts legislature. His books include, as well as histories of the USA, *Outdoor Papers* (1863), *Army Life in a Black Regiment* (1870), *Oldport Days* (1873), *Common-Sense about Women* (1881), *Hints on Writing and Speech-making* (1887) and *Concerning All of Us* (1892).
▷H N Meyer, *The Colonel of the Black Regiment* (1967)

HIGHSMITH, Patricia
(1921–)
American thriller writer, born in Fort Worth, Texas. Her first novel, *Strangers on a Train* (1950), was filmed by Alfred Hitchcock. Her third, *The Talented Mr Ripley* (1955), was awarded the **Edgar Allan Poe** Scroll by the Mystery Writers of America. She creates a world which **Graham Greene** has characterized as claustrophobic and irrational, one 'we enter each time with a sense of personal danger'.
▷F Cavigalli, *Über Patricia Highsmith* (1986)

HIGUCHI Ichiyo
(1872–96)
Japanese writer whose short life is remarkable chiefly for *Takekurabe* (1896, 'Comparison of Stature'). A delicate, self-consciously artful love story, it showed great promise, especially in its use of language, but was her only substantial work of fiction. She also kept a literary journal, which was published posthumously, and a short work entitled *Nigorie* (1895, 'Muddy Stream').
▷R L Danly, *In the Shade of Spring Leaves: The life and writings of Higuchi Ichiyo, a Woman of Letters in Meiji Japan* (1982)

HIJUELOS, Oscar
(1951–)
American writer of Cuban extraction, born in New York. He grew up in a multi-ethnic neighbourhood, but retained close ties with his family's Cuban roots, which have emerged strongly in his three novels. His first book, *Our House in the Last World* (1984), revealed the influence of the Latin-American 'magic realists' on his work. He achieved a great success, and established his international reputation, with his epic, passionate, doom-laden account of the lives of two Cuban musicians in America, *The Mambo Kings Play Songs of Love* (1990), which was later filmed. A third novel, *The Fourteen Sisters of Emilio Montez O'Brien* (1993), is a colourful, sprawling, but intricately-woven story of a female-dominated Cuban–Irish family.

HIKMET, Nazim
(1902–63)
Turkish poet, dramatist and critic, born in Salonika (then Turkish, now Greek). His surname was Ran, but he did not use it. He is usually regarded as Turkey's greatest poet of the 20th century; certainly he is the only one to be really well known abroad. He was a Marxist who was sentenced, in 1938, to 25 years in jail for sedition—he was released under an amnesty in 1950, and soon fled abroad. He died in Moscow. In 1950 he and **Neruda** shared the dubious honour of receiving the Lenin Peace Prize. During the 1930s he revolutionized Turkish poetry by introducing free verse decisively into it (although he was not the first to use it). The chief influence upon him in this was **Mayakovsky**—it became popular, however, through the efforts of the Turkish poets, such as Ahmet Hasim, who imported it from France. One of his best-known poems is the epic *Seyh Bedreddin Destam* (1936, Eng trans *The Epic of Sheik Bedreddin*, 1977), dealing with the subject of a 15th-century rebel sheik. Hikmet's grandiosity (he wrote very prolifically, at enormous length, usually in 'stepped lines', and

without 'blotting a line') and his tendentious and slogan-saturated work has not made it easy for all readers to accept him as a major poet, and it seems to be agreed that he is a poet despite his communism rather than because of it. But he was inventive, and could reach great heights. The best translations of his poems are by **Taner Baybars**, in *Selected Poems* (1967); other volumes include *Poems* (1954), *The Moscow Symphony* (1970), *The Day Before Tomorrow* (1972) and *Things I Didn't Know I Loved* (1975).

HILDESHEIMER, Wolfgang
(1916–)

German painter, playwright, novelist and translator (**Shaw**, **Joyce**, **Djuna Barnes**), an associate of Gruppe '47, born in Hamburg into a Jewish family. He is an Israeli citizen. He was educated in England, and was in the British army in Palestine during World War II. He achieved fame with his collection of stories *Lieblose Legende* (1952, 'Loveless Legends'), satires on bourgeois capitalism in which he employed Surrealist techniques. He then became Germany's foremost proponent of the Theatre of the Absurd, with such plays as the three collected in *Spiele in denen es dunkel wird* (1958, 'Plays in Which Darkness Falls').
▷M Esslin, *The Theatre of the Absurd* (1969)

HILL, Aaron
(1685–1750)

English poet, dramatist and speculator, born in London. He wrote *Zaire* (1736) and *Mérope* (1749, adapted from **Voltaire**), and wrote the scenario for Handel's opera *Rinaldo* (1711). He was one of **Pope**'s victims in *The Dunciad*, and replied with *Progress of Wit* (1730). He left an epic poem, *Gideon* (1749), unfinished. He had a wide circle of literary friends, and launched the bi-weekly journal *The Plain Dealer* in 1724.
▷D Brewster, *Aaron Hill, poet, dramatist, projector* (1913)

HILL, Ernestine
(1900–72)

Australian writer and traveller, born in Rockhampton, Queensland, who, from the early 1930s, criss-crossed the continent many times. These journeys resulted in her first book, *The Great Australian Loneliness* (1937), in *Australia, Land of Contrasts* (1943) and in her important collection of Northern Territory myths, legends and characters, *The Territory* (1951). She wrote on the Murray River irrigation scheme, *Water into Gold* (1937) and *Kabbarli* (1973), a memoir of Daisy Bates, the white 'grandmother' of the aborigines. Her only novel was *My Love Must Wait* (1941), a bestselling life of circumnavigator Matthew Flinders.

HILL, Geoffrey William
(1932–)

English poet, born in Bromsgrove, Worcestershire. Educated at Keble College, Oxford, he made his career in academia. A deep, dark and densely allusive writer, brooding on death, sex and religion, his first collection of *Poems* was published by a small press in 1952. *For the Unfallen: Poems 1952–1958* (1959) marked his true emergence, since when he has become appreciated by the cognoscenti. His later collections, *Preghiere* (1964), *King Log* (1968), *Mercian Hymns* (1971), *Somewhere is Such a Kingdom: 1952–1971* (1975), *Tenebrae* (1978) and *The Mystery of the Charity of Charles Péguy* (1983), all won prestigious literary prizes. He has been a professor at Boston since 1988, and his other writings include a book of literary criticism, *The Enemy's Country* (1991).
▷V Sherry, *The Uncommon tongue: the poetry and criticism of Geoffrey Hill* (1987)

HILL, Susan Elizabeth
(1942–)

English novelist and radio dramatist, born in Scarborough, who published her first novel, *The Enclosure* (1961), while a student at London University. Her novels are strong in terms of character and atmosphere, particularly climate. A recurring theme, and one which permeates *The Albatross and other Stories* (1971) and *The Bird of Night* (1972), is a sense of malevolence, violence and despair, while *In the Springtime of the Year* (1974) vividly evokes the aftermath of bereavement, and the pain of memory and loneliness. After a long silence, she published *Air and Angels* in 1991, a love story set in India and Cambridge. *Mrs de Winter* (1993), a sequel to **Daphne du Maurier**'s *Rebecca*, is the most successful of a vogue for sequels, because, as **Anita Brookner** observed, the author 'gives us a Susan Hill novel'. A stage adaptation of *The Woman in Black* (1983), a musical chiller in which a ghost takes revenge for her child's death by murdering other children, has been a long-running success in London.

HILLERMAN, Tony
(1925–)

American mystery writer, born in Oklahoma, where he was brought up in the Native American community. He trained as an anthropologist before working as a journalist, and later taught journalism. He became Emeritus Professor of Journalism at the University of New Mexico, Albuquerque, in 1985. He is best known for his mystery novels, which are set in the Navajo and Hopi areas of New Mexico and Arizona; featuring two Navajo detectives, they draw on his knowledge of anthropology. A controversial writer, his works have aroused much debate and strong opposition from some Native American communities for their depiction of native religion and witchcraft. Titles include *Dance Hall of the Dead* (1973), *People of Darkness* (1980), *The Dark Wind* (1982), *The Ghostway* (1985), *The Thief of Time* (1988) and *Coyote Waits* (1990). He has also written essays and children's fiction.

HILLIARD, Noel Harvey
(1929–)

New Zealand novelist, born in Napier. He is the author of a tetralogy which began with *Maori Girl* (1960), the first contemporary novel to use a Maori as a central character, through *Power with Joy* (1965), to *Maori Woman* (1974) and *The Glory and the Dream* (1978). With the last, the cohesive design of the four books is shown; Maori and white settler cultures and conflicts are resolved in human relationships. A complementary novel, *A Night at Green River* (1969), stresses the same idealism in the renunciation of culture for social cohesion. His short stories are contained in *A Piece of Land* (1963), *Send Somebody Nice* (1976) and *Selected Stories* (1977).

HILLYER, Robert Silliman
(1895–1961)

American poet, teacher and critic, born in New Jersey. Hillyer was a highly conventional poet, against anything written by or after **T S Eliot**—whom, with **Pound**, he jealously, bitterly but not effectively attacked. *Poems for Music* (1947), however, a collection of what he considered to be his best lyrics, is an attractive and skilful volume in its old-fashioned way. He was also a skilled pasticheur of the 18th-century heroic couplet. He made a version of the Egyptian *Book of the Dead: Book of the Dead—The Coming Forth By Day* (1923), which is probably his most original work. He died embittered by the hostility he had aroused in opposing the award to Pound of the Bollingen Prize. As a neoclassicist he was neither as witty nor as effective as **A D Hope**, and is now virtually forgotten.

HILTON, James
(1900–54)

English novelist, born in Leigh, Lancashire. He quickly established himself as a writer, his first novel, *Catherine Herself*, being published in 1920. Many of his successful novels were filmed—*Knight without Armour* (1933), *Lost Horizon* (1933, awarded the Hawthornden Prize in 1934), *Goodbye Mr Chips* (1934) and *Random Harvest* (1941).
▷ *To You, Mr Chips* (1938)

HILTON, Walter
(d.1396)

English mystic and writer. An Augustinian canon of Thurgarton, Nottinghamshire, he was the author of *The Ladder of Perfection* and possibly *The Cloud of Unknowing*, two books important in the history of English prose.

HIMES, Chester Bomar
(1909–84)

American novelist, whose later successes with Harlem-based cop thrillers overshadowed his earlier work. Himes was born in Jefferson City, Missouri, and educated in Ohio. He spent nearly nine years in prison for armed robbery and after his release worked (1938–41) on a writers project as part of the New Deal's Works Progress Administration. His first novel was *If He Hollers Let Him Go* (1945), a tough-minded account of racial prejudice in the Californian shipyards and factories. *Cast the First Stone* (1952) exorcized his prison experiences, after which he emigrated to Europe. There, his tough detective stories were welcomed as serious existential fiction. The later, satirical *Pinktoes* (1961) spoofed the French taste for literary erotica. Many appeared in Maurice Duhamel's influential *Série Noir* at Gallimard. *For Love of Imabelle* (1957) was originally a story called 'La reine des pommes' and was republished (and subsequently filmed) as *A Rage in Harlem*. On its first appearance, it gained Himes the influential Grand Prix de Littérature Policière (1958). In subsequent Harlem books, Himes developed two black detectives, Grave Digger Johnson and Coffin Ed Jones, who live up to their soubriquets handsomely but are nonetheless intensely moral figures, battling against corruption.
▷ *The Quality of Hurt* (1972); S F Miliken, *Chester Himes: A Critical Appraisal* (1976)

HIND, Archie
(1924–)

Scottish novelist. Born and educated in Glasgow, he celebrated the city in his novel *The Dear Green Place* (1965), which juxtaposes the harsh reality of urban existence with a pastoral vision. Hind has not published any more novels, but has continued to work in community education projects in housing schemes and with young offenders.

HINDE, Thomas, pseud of **Sir Thomas Willes Chitty**
(1926–)

English novelist, born in Felixstowe, Suffolk. At various times, Hinde has worked as a teacher, a revenue rating officer and a personnel officer with Shell International. He published his first novel, *Mr. Nicholas*, in 1952 and has since published several others, of which *Games of Chance* (1965) is possibly his best. His works are well-crafted, well-paced, solid reads, with strongly-defined characters. Some critics compare his style to that of **Graham Greene**. In fact, Hinde once entered a competition in the *New Statesman*, to supply the first 150 words of a supposedly new Graham Greene novel. Hinde won, beating two entries sent pseudonymously by Greene himself.

HINES, (Melvyn) Barry
(1939–)

English novelist, born in Barnsley, Yorkshire. He worked for a time as a physical education teacher. His novels are all set in his native Yorkshire, and deal with working-class life across a wide spectrum of experience. He is best known for *A Kestrel for a Knave* (1974), also known as *Kes* following a successful film adaptation from his own screenplay, one of a number of collaborations with the film-maker Ken Loach. Its story about an undersized, emotionally isolated young boy's love for a pet falcon is told with craft and sensitivity. His other novels include *The Blinder* (1966), about a young footballer, *The Gamekeeper* (1975), and the industrial novel *The Price of Coal* (1979).

HINO Ashihei
(1907–60)

Japanese novelist, born in Fukuoka in the south of Japan. Initially an officer in the army, he was expelled for left-wing activities. He was, briefly, imprisoned but renounced Marx to become a patriotic, right-wing activist, rejoining the army as an enlisted soldier. He is best known for *Mugi to Heitai* (1938, 'Barley and Soldiers'), his account of his participation in the Japanese assault on Hsuchou. It paints a realistic, (but propagandistic) picture of the ordinary Japanese soldier fighting in Asia. He was officially proscribed after the war, being so closely identified with the pre-war regime, but continued to write prolifically. He laboured long and hard to produce *Kakumei Zengo* (1929), which he regarded as his life's work and is a huge, sprawling and very dull novel tracing Japan's collapse through the lives of a Fukuoka family. He committed suicide immediately after its publication, having completed his work and being unable to bear his disgust at Japan's abject humiliation.

HIPPIUS, Zinaida *see* **GIPPIUS, Zinaida**

HITA, ARCHPRIEST OF *see* **RUIZ, Juan**

HJARTARSON, Snorri
(1906–86)

Icelandic poet, born in Borgarfjöroður. He studied art in Copenhagen and Oslo, but soon turned to writing and published a novel written in Norwegian, *Höjt flyver ravnen* (1934, 'High Soars the Raven'). He returned to Iceland in 1936 to become one of the most influential poets of his day, combining traditional and modern poetry with musical and painterly images. He published only four volumes of poetry, including the innovative *Kvaeði* (1944, 'Poems') and the late *Haustrokkrið Y fir mer* (1979, 'The Autumn Mist Surrounds Me'), and was awarded the Nordic Council's Literary Award for 1981.
▷S Egilson, *Ljóðmaeli Sveinbjarner Egilssonar* (1952)

HLASCO, Marek
(1931–69)

Polish story writer, born in Warsaw. All his writings caused intense controversy—his first book was burned in the streets in many towns, by order of the priest—and he went into exile, or 'defected to the west' (1958). A melancholy man, seized by a black vision of the future, he killed himself in Wiesbaden. *Pierswsky krok w chmurach* (1956, Eng trans of the title story, 'A First Step into the Clouds', in *Introduction to Modern Polish Literature*, 1964, H Gillon and L Krzyzanowski eds) enraged the orthodox, both Communist and Catholic, but made him into an idol for the young. *Cmentarze* (1958, Eng trans *The Graveyard*, 1959) was a bitter account of the results of Stalinism. Ultimately, his prose bearing too-evident traces of the influence of **Hemingway**, he ran out of true imaginative material: invention gave way to absolute disgust. But at his best, as in *The Graveyard*, and in *Nastepny do raju* (1958, Eng trans *Next Stop—Paradise*, 1959), he was a writer of great moral power.
▷*Polish Review*, 4 (1961)

HLAVACEK, Karel
(1874–98)

Czech Symbolist poet and designer, born in Prague into a working-class family. The shortness of his writing career (he died of tuberculosis at 23) drew deserved attention to his, tragically, only partially realized gifts, and much influenced the course of Czech poetry. His poems—two small collections, *Pozde k ránu* (1896, 'Late Towards Morning')

and *Mstiva kantiléna* (1898, 'Vengeful Can-
tilena')—so far untranslated into English, are
self-consciously decadent, but also carry
within them genuine and moving intimations
of his doom. He has some affinities with the
English **Ernest Dowson** and with the Pole **Przybyszewski** who, like **Wilde** and **Huysmans**,
influenced him. The poet most closely associated with him, as 'decadent', is **Jiri Karasek ze
Lvovic**. Hlavacek revolted against everything:
youth, illness, social injustice, but in his melodic poetry there is far more than self-indulgence.

HO CHING-CHI
(1924–)
Chinese playwright and Communist Party
activist. His most famous work is the opera
Pai mao nii (1944, Eng trans *The White-
Haired Girl*, 1954), written in collaboration
with the academic Ting Yi, depicting the
struggle of the peasants against feudal
oppression and their eventual liberation
through communism. It was based on a traditional folk-tale, and became the model for
the doctrine of socialist realism as practised
in China.

HO, or HUO, Xuan Hu'o'ng
(fl.c.1780–c.1820)
Vietnamese poet, whose precise identity is
unknown—we know from her work that Ho
is her real family name, but Xuan Hu'o'ng is
a pseudonym. An educated, cultured woman,
she produced some of the most sensuous,
wittiest and most readable verse to come out
of Asia in the 19th century. Typically, a poem
by Ho will pretend to be about a harmless
domestic activity (weaving or making rice
cakes), which will make it seem innocent, but
there is a second level of meaning, usually
sex. She has been hailed as a proto-feminist,
as she argues in her verse that the sexes should
be more equal, and often comes out against
marriage, saying that love between men and
women should be freely given.

HOAGLAND, Edward Morley
(1932–)
American novelist, short-story writer and
naturalist. He and his prose style have been
likened to **Hemingway**, but he is much closer
in temperament to **Thoreau** or **Peter Matthiessen**. Hoagland similarly combines exact
observation of natural phenomena with an
astonishingly vivid turn of phrase and a firm,
unsentimental understanding of the 'politics'
of the natural world and mankind's treatment
of animals. This was dramatized in his circus
novel *Cat Man* (1956) and in *The Circle Home*
(1960), a successful novel about boxing. Like
Thoreau, Hoagland is not out of place in the

city; he grew up in New York and regards its
functioning as very little different from that
of the woods or the jungle and subject to
the same complex of emotions. *The Peacock's
Tail* (1965) is a vivid, latter-day attempt at a
proletarian novel. Hoagland's essays began
to appear in book form at the end of the
sixties. *The Courage of Turtles* (1971) is subtitled 'fifteen essays about compassion, pain
and love', and these are his abiding themes,
whether he is talking about animal communities, sex or childbirth. *Heart's Desire*
(1988) collects the best of his pieces.

HOBAN, Russell Conwell
(1925–)
American writer for children, later an adult
novelist, born in Lansdale, Pennsylvania.
Bedtime For Frances (1960) was the first of
several picture books about a young badger.
The Mouse and His Child (1967) was one of
his most successful works for children, but
two years later he moved to England and
made the switch to adult writing. Much of his
subsequent work, beginning with *The Lion of
Boaz-Jachin and Jachin-Boaz* (1973), has had
a fantasy or science-fictional strand to it. His
most acclaimed novel to date is *Riddley
Walker* (1980), a post-nuclear holocaust
novel written in a language which combines
scraps of English with lumpy neologisms.

HOCCLEVE, or OCCLEVE, Thomas
(c.1368–1426)
English poet. He spent his life as a clerk in
the privy seal office in London (1378–1425).
His chief work is a free but tedious version
of the *De Regimine Principum* of Aegidius
Romanus, in **Chaucer**'s seven-line stanza. He
also wrote *Ars Secondi Mori*; an autobiographical poem, *La Male Regla* (1406);
and *Regiment of Princes* (1412).
▷J Mitchell, *Thomas Hoccleve: a study* (1968)

HOCHHUTH, Rolf
(1931–)
German dramatist, born in Eschwege
Werran. He studied history and philosophy
at Munich and Heidelberg, and worked as an
editor before turning to documentary drama.
His main claim to fame is the controversial
subject-matter of his plays. *Der Stellvertreter*
(1963, Eng trans *The Representative*, 1963)
accused Pope Pius XII of not intervening to
stop the Nazi persecution of the Jews. It
caused a furore, as did the implication in his
second play, *Soldaten* (1967, Eng trans *Soldiers*, 1968), that Winston Churchill was
involved in the assassination of the Polish
war-time leader, General Sikorski. He also
wrote a novel, *Eine Liebe in Deutschland*

(1978, 'German Love Story'), about Nazi atrocities.

▷M E Ward, *Hochhuth* (1977)

HOCHWALDER, Fritz
(1911–)

Austrian dramatist, born in Vienna, who has written thoughtful plays, both comedies and tragedies, in essentially traditional modes. He dominated post-war Austrian theatre, even though he lived in Zürich, to which he had escaped from the Nazis in 1938. The chief early influence upon him was the expressionistic German playwright **Georg Kaiser**, whose friend he became. He has written several deserved successes, including the famous and much produced *Das heilige Experiment* (1943), a depiction of the last day (16 July 1767) of the Jesuit mission in Brazil, and the powerful *Der öffentliche Anklager* (1949), about Robespierre's successor Fouquier-Tinville, who sought out the 'enemy of the people' to guillotine him—only to discover that the culprit was himself.

▷H F Garten, *Modern German Drama* (1964)

HODDIS, Jakob von, pseud of Hans Davidsohn
(1884–1942)

German expressionist poet and co-founder of *Der neue Club* (June 1910). He published the famous 'first expressionist poem', 'Weltende' (Eng trans 'World's End', in *Twentieth-Century German Verse*, 1963, ed Patrick Bridgewater) in 1911; in the following year he became mentally ill and lived in a hospital until the Nazis removed him and had him murdered. He was a minor poet whose verse does, however, possess all the qualities of the first phase of Expressionism.

▷C Middleton and M Hamburger (eds), *Modern German Poetry 1910–1969* (1962)

HODGE, Merle
(1944–)

Trinidadian novelist. Educated at University College, London, she worked as a French lecturer at the University of West Indies, Jamaica, whilst completing a doctorate on French Caribbean literature. She spent four years in Grenada working with Malcolm Bishop, leader of the Socialist Revolution, but left when the US invaded in 1983. She now works as a writer and lecturer in Trinidad. Her novel, *Crick Crack, Monkey* (1970), sensitively explores the themes of cultural ambivalence, alienation and search for identity, through the experiences of the adolescent narrator, Tee.

HODGSON, Ralph
(1871–1962)

English poet, born in Yorkshire. He became a journalist in London and published three volumes of Georgian poems with the recurring theme of nature and England: *The Last Blackbird* (1907), *Eve* (1913) and *Poems* (1917), containing 'The Song of Honour', 'The Moor', 'The Journeyman', and the polemic against the destruction of animals for feminine vanity in 'To Deck a Woman'. He lectured in Japan (1924–38), and made his home in Ohio, USA. An anthology of his works appeared as *The Skylark and Other Poems* (1958). He was awarded the Order of the Rising Sun (1938) and the Queen's Gold Medal (1954). His *Collected Poems* appeared in 1961.

▷G B Saul, in *Withdraw in Gold: three portraits of genius* (1970)

HOEL, Sigurd
(1890–1960)

Norwegian novelist, playwright and journalist, born and brought up in Nord-Odal. He began by studying science, but won a competition for Nordic short novels with *Idioten* ('The Idiot') in 1918 and thereafter worked as a literary and theatrical critic. Following a collection of short novels *Veien vi går* (1922, 'The Way We walk'), Hoel's literary career began in earnest with *Syndere i sommersol* (1927, 'Sinners in the Summer Sun'). In this novel, a group of young intellectuals attempts to live out a free concept of life, but is forced to confess its inability to change society's conservative norms; a recurring theme in Hoel's novels is the way in which varying forms of patriarchal structure bring about deceit and faithlessness, wreaking social and psychological havoc. He emphasizes the significance of childhood and adolescent experiences on one's adult life. Despite the psychological determinism of novels such as *En dag i oktober* (1931, 'A Day in October') or *Fjorten dager før frostnettene* (1935, 'A Fortnight before the Frosty Nights'), they convey one positive message: an understanding of the psyche can have a liberating effect. His most successful novel was *Møte ved milepelen* (1947, 'Meeting with the Milestone'); this, like much of his other work, was influenced by the ideas of his close friend, Wilhelm Reich.

▷R Øystein, *Sigurd Hoel. Et nærbilde* (1991); L Sverre, *Sigurd Hoels Fiction. Cultural Criticism and Tragic Vision* (1984)

HOFFMAN, Alice
(1952–)

American novelist, born in New York City and educated at Adelphi University, New

York, and Stanford University. She is regarded by many as one of the leading writers of her generation. Her first novel, *Property Of* (1977), concerns a 17-year-old entranced by the leader of a street gang involved with violence and drugs. In much of her subsequent fiction, which also considers the search for identity in a turbulent world, realism is fused with fantasy so that the everyday events about which she writes attain an almost mythical importance. *White Horses* (1982) examines a young girl's obsession for an older brother, while the austere and haunting *At Risk* (1988) deals with the effect upon her family of a young woman suffering from AIDS.

HOFFMAN, Daniel
(1923–)

American poet and critic, born in New York. He has written influential books on poets as various as **Stephen Crane**, **Robert Graves** and **Ezra Pound**, but is best known for his essentially conservative but often modernistic and playful poetry, in such collections as *Broken Laws* (1971) and in *Hang-Gliding from Helicon: New and Selected Poems 1948–1988* (1988). He writes, he has said, 'to defy desolation'.
▷ *Poetry* (Chicago, May 1989)

HOFFMANN, August Heinrich, called 'Hoffmann von Fallersleben'
(1798–1874)

German poet and philologist, and composer of the German national anthem, born in Fallersleben in Lüneburg. He was Keeper of the university library of Breslau (1823–38), and Professor of German there (1830–42). A popular writer of light lyrics, he published *Lieder und Romanzen* ('Songs and Romances') in 1841; but the publication of his *Unpolitische Lieder* ('Apolitical Songs') in 1842 cost him his chair. In 1860 he became librarian to the Duke of Ratibor at Korvei, where he died. He is best known for his popular and patriotic *Volkslieder* (1842, 'Folk Songs'), including 'Alle Vögel sind schon da' and the song 'Deutschland, Deutschland über Alles' (1841), which became the German national anthem in 1922. He also published several works on philology and antiquities, including *Horae Belgicae* (1830–62, 'Belgian Hours').
▷ K H de Raaf, *Heinrich von Fallersleben* (1943)

HOFFMANN, Ernst Theodor Wilhelm, called 'Amadeus'
(1776–1822)

German writer, music critic and caricaturist, born in Königsberg. Trained as a lawyer, he had an unsettled career until 1816, when he attained a high position in the Supreme Court in Berlin. A remarkable essay on Mozart's *Don Giovanni*, the composition of an opera (*Undine*, 1816) and the direction of the Bamberg theatre for two months (1808), testify to his real interests. He was the archpriest of ultra-German romanticism. His wit bubbled over in irony, ridicule and sarcasm, and his imagination was inexhaustible, but utterly undisciplined, wild and fantastic. His shorter tales were mostly published in the collections *Fantasiestücke* (1814, 'Fantasies'), *Nachtstücke* (1817, 'Night-time Tales') and *Die Serapionsbrüder* (1819–21, Eng trans *The Serapion Brothers*, 1886–92). His longer works include *Elixiere des Teufels* (1816, Eng trans *The Devil's Elixirs*, 1824), *Seltsame Leiden eines Theaterdirektors* (1818, 'Strange Sufferings of a Theatre Director'), *Klein Zaches, genannt Zinnober* (1819, 'Little Sachs, called Cinnaber'), and the partly autobiographical *Lebensansichten des Katers Murr* (1821–2, 'Opinions of the Tomcat Murr'). Three of his stories provided the basis for Offenbach's opera, *Les Contes d'Hoffmann* (1880, Eng trans *Tales of Hoffmann*, 1881), and also for Delibes's *Coppelia*. As a composer his most important opera was *Undine*, a precursor of the scores of Weber and Wagner. He also composed vocal, chamber, orchestral and piano works. He was an influential writer on music, notably in his reviews of Beethoven's works.
▷ H D Daemmrich, *The Shattered Self* (1973)

HOFFMEISTER, Adolf
(1902–)

Czech dramatist, poet, essayist, cartoonist and painter. He was a minor figure, given to much experimental activity, but a vigorous one, who left valuable records of the avant-garde movement. He fled from his country when the Nazis took it over, but returned to become a diplomat (Czech ambassador to France) after the Communist takeover. *The Unwilling Tourist* (Eng trans 1942) is about Lidice and other matters pertaining to the Nazis.

HOFMANN, Gert
(1931–93)

German novelist and dramatist, born in Limbach in Saxony. For most of his life he taught literature in various universities. He was the German equivalent of the Austrian writer **Thomas Bernhard**, upon whose methods Hofmann frankly based his own. But his work is less humorous, and puts more emphasis on the guilty German past. His major novels are *Auf dem Turm* (1982, Eng trans *The Spectator at the Tower*, 1984) and, above all, *Der Blindensturz* (1985, Eng trans *The Parable of the*

Blind, 1986), in which the influence of the Argentinian writer **Ernest Sábato** is prominent.

▷*World Literature Today* (Spring, 1981, Summer, 1989)

HOFMANN VON HOFMANNSWALDAU, Christian
(1617–79)

German poet and translator (from Italian poetry), of noble birth, born in Breslau. A man of some substance in his native city, he became one of the leading disciples of **Martin Opitz**, and is renowned for his technical expertise. He has, however, been accused of lacking personal feeling, and being uninvolved in his themes, his bombastic style (establishing the so-called Second Silesian School) a matter of no more than skill.

HOFMANNSTHAL, Hugo von
(1874–1929)

Austrian poet and dramatist, born in Vienna into a banking family of Austro-Jewish-Italian origins. While still at school he attracted attention by his symbolic, neo-romantic poems or 'lyrical dramas' such as *Gestern* (1896, 'Yesterday'), *Der Tod des Tizian* (1901, Eng trans *The Death of Titian*, 1920) and *Leben* (1894, 'Life'), in which the transitory and elusive nature of life and its short-lived pleasures compel the quest for the world of the spirit. An emotional and intellectual crisis, a sudden awareness of the drying-up of his lyrical gifts, precipitated the *Ein Brief des Lord Chandos* (1901, 'A Letter from Lord Chandos'), an imaginary correspondence between Lord Bacon and a young Elizabethan nobleman, in which Hofmannsthal, in the guise of the latter, gives his reasons for abandoning poetry, his new hatred for abstract terms, his doubts of the possibility of successful communication. Thenceforth he devoted himself to drama, most of his works being based on that of other dramatists: *Electra* (1903), *Das gerettete Venedig* (1905, trans from **Otway**'s *Venice Preserved*), and the morality plays *Jedermann* (1911, Eng trans *The Salzburg Everyman*, 1930) and *Das Salzburger grosse Welttheater* (1922, 'The Great World Theatre of Salzburg', based on **Calderón de la Barca**'s *El gran teatro del mundo*). One of his major works is the comedy, *Der Schwierige* (1921, Eng trans *The Difficult Man*, 1963). Having renounced **Stefan George** and his circle, Hofmannsthal turned to the composer Richard Strauss, for whom he wrote the libretti for Richard Strauss's *Der Rosenkavalier* (1911, 'Knight of the Rose'), *Ariadne auf Naxos* (1912, 'Ariadne on Naxos'), *Die Frau ohne Schatten* (1919, 'The Woman without a Shadow') and others. With Strauss and Max Reinhardt, he was instrumental in founding the Salzburg Festival after World War I. His statue there was demolished by the Nazis in 1938.

HOGAN, Desmond
(1951–)

Irish novelist and short-story writer, born in County Galway. In 1976 Hogan published his first novel, *The Ikon Maker*, tracing the journey of a mother following her son from Dublin to England. Subsequent novels include *A Curious Street* (1984) and *A New Shirt* (1986). Like many others of his generation, Hogan refuses to sentimentalize Dublin, and in the latter novel especially, presents it as a city peopled by a bewildered and resentful social underclass, a place disfigured by raucous clubs and demeaned by heroin. His collection of stories, *Lebanon Lodge* (1988), again looks at the lives of outsiders and the disenchanted: Irish exiles in London; Irish–Americans in the mid-west, and travelling players. His is a tough, sometimes tragic, often ironic vision.

HOGAN, Linda
(1947–)

American writer, born in Denver, Colorado. Of Chickasaw descent, Hogan's work is often concerned with Native American culture, reflecting as well her continuing involvement with environmental issues. She has published six volumes of poetry—*Calling Myself Home* (1979), *Daughters, I Love You* (1981), *Eclipse* (1983), *Seeing Through the Sun* (1985), *Savings* (1988) and *The Book of Medicines* (1993)—and the short-story collections *That Horse* (1985), *The Big Woman* (1987) and *Red Clay* (1991). Her first novel, *Mean Spirit* (1990), is set in Oklahoma during the time of the Osage oil boom in the 1920s, and describes a series of brutal murders against a background of judicial corruption, aimed at disinheriting the Osages of their land and mineral rights. Hogan is also the co-editor of the anthology of women's short fiction, *The Stories We Hold Secret* (1986).

HOGG, James
(1770–1835)

Scottish poet and novelist, known as the 'Ettrick Shepherd', born on Ettrickhall Farm in the Ettrick Forest, Selkirkshire. As a boy he tended sheep and had only a spasmodic education. However, he inherited a rich store of oral ballads from his mother. In 1790 he became shepherd to William Laidlaw at Blackhouse in Selkirkshire, who encouraged him to write. On a visit to Edinburgh in 1801 to sell his employer's sheep, he had his *Scottish Pastorals, Poems, Songs, etc.*, printed, but

without success. He was fortunate, however, in making the acquaintance of Sir **Walter Scott**, then Sheriff of Selkirkshire, who published several of Hogg's mother's ballads in the second volume of his *Border Minstrelsy* (1803). With the proceeds of *The Mountain Bard* (1803) Hogg dabbled unsuccessfully in farming, but eventually settled in Edinburgh. Another volume of poems, *The Forest Minstrel* (1810), was unsuccessful, but *The Queen's Wake* (1813) gained him cordial recognition. A bequest of a farm at Altrive Lake (now Edinhope) from the Duchess of Buccleuch enabled him to marry in 1820 and to produce in rapid succession a number of works in both verse and prose. He ended his days a well-known figure in Edinburgh society, a regular contributor to *Blackwood's Magazine*, and was the 'Ettrick Shepherd' of **John Wilson**'s *Noctes Ambrosianae*. He described himself as 'the King of the Mountain and Fairy School'. His poems of the supernatural are at their best when he avoids Gothic elaboration and relies on the suggestive understatement of the ballad style, as in his 'Kilmeny' and 'The Witch of Fife'. 'The Aged Widow's Lament' shows the influence of the Scottish vernacular tradition. His debt to **Robert Burns** is apparent in 'The Author's Address to his Auld Dog Hector' and in the riotous 'Village of Balmaquhapple'. Of his prose works, the most remarkable is *Private Memoirs and Confessions of a Justified Sinner* (1824), a macabre novel which anticipates **Robert Louis Stevenson**'s *Dr Jekyll and Mr Hyde* with its haunting 'split personality' theme. In 1834 he published his *Domestic Manners and Private Life of Sir Walter Scott*, against the wishes of Scott's family.
▷A Strout, *James Hogg: a biography* (1946)

HOLAN, Vladimir
(1905–80)

Czech poet and translator, born in Prague. Initially a member of the 'Poetist' school, he became political when Czechoslovakia was handed over to the Nazis. Then the communists repudiated his socialist-realist verse as 'decadent' and he retreated into a long silence. When he re-emerged in the 1960s, and could publish what he had written in his period of enforced silence, it was as the leading poet of his time. A critic has written that although he was 'over-prolific' and 'frequently too influenced by Eliot', his work nevertheless 'conveys a sense of loneliness and gentleness which is as impressive as it is authentic'. There is an English translation in *Selected Poems* (1971).

HOLBERG, Ludvig, Baron
(1684–1754)

Norwegian writer, born in Bergen, and considered the founder of both Norwegian and Danish modern literature. He was educated in Copenhagen and wrote a book on the history of Europe (1711), then settled in Denmark after travelling widely in Europe, largely on foot (1714–16). He published various historical and legal works, and in 1717 was appointed Professor of Metaphysics at Copenhagen University, then of eloquence (1720), and history (1730). His career as a satirist began with a comic epic, *Peder Paars* (1719), followed by a series of more than 30 classic comedies for the newly-opened Danish theatre in Copenhagen (1722–7). Thereafter he concentrated on historical books, including biographies and histories of Denmark, the Church, and the Jews. After one more satirical classic, *Niels Klims underjordiske reise* (1741, 'Niels Klim's Subterranean Journey'), he wrote only reflective and philosophical works.
▷F J Billeskev Hansen, *Holberg* (1974)

HOLCROFT, M(ontague) H(arry)
(1902–93)

New Zealand writer, critic and historian, born in Rangiora, Canterbury. He was editor of the influential periodical *The Listener* from 1949 to 1967, from which he drew *The Eye of the Lizard* (1960) and *Graceless Islanders* (1970), both reissued as *A Voice in the Village: The Listener Editorials of M H Holcroft* (1989). He wrote three novels in the late 1920s, beginning with *Beyond the Breakers* (1928), and became a prolific essayist on literature and life. *The Deepening Stream* (1940) won first prize in the New Zealand Centenary literary competition, and was followed by *The Waiting Hills* (1943) and *Encircling Seas* (1946); these were collected as *Discovered Isles: A Trilogy* in 1950. Through his essays he exercised considerable influence on his successors. He wrote a study of **Ursula Bethell** (1975) and autobiographical works including *Dance of the Seasons* (1952), *Reluctant Editor: the 'Listener' Years, 1949–67* (1969) and *The Way of a Writer* (1984).

HOLCROFT, Thomas
(1745–1809)

English playwright and novelist, born in London, the son of a shoemaker. After three years as a Newmarket stable boy, then eight as a shoemaker, schoolmaster, and servant-secretary to Granville Sharp, in 1770 he became a strolling player. But settling in London (1778), where he became a friend of **William Godwin**, **Thomas Paine** and **Charles Lamb**, he took to writing. *Alwyn, or the Gentleman Comedian* (1780) was the first of four novels. He also wrote nearly 30 plays, mostly melodramas, of which *The Follies of a Day* (1784) and *The Road to Ruin* (1792) were the best. His eldest son, William (1773–89), robbed his father of £40 and having been found by him on an American-bound vessel, shot himself. An ardent democrat, in 1794 Holcroft was tried for high treason with Sir Thomas Masterman Hardy, John Horne Tooke and others and acquitted, but the adverse publicity reduced him to poverty and made him go abroad to Hamburg and Paris (1799 –1801). His entertaining Memoirs were continued by **William Hazlitt** (1816).

▷R Baine, *Thomas Holcroft and the Revolutionary Novel* (1965)

HÖLDERLIN, Johann Christian Friedrich
(1770–1843)

German poet, born in Lauffen on the Neckar. He studied theology at Tübingen, and philosophy with Schelling and Hegel under Fichte at Jena. With a growing enthusiasm for poetry, he developed an aversion to the 'snug parsonage' for which he was intended. As family tutor in Frankfurt-am-Main (1796–8) he found in the wife of his banker-employer, Susette Gontard (the 'Diotima' of his works), the feminine embodiment of all he venerated in Hellenism. His early poetry owed far too much to **Friedrich Klopstock** and to **Schiller**, who published Hölderlin's efforts in his literary magazines, but the inspiration provided by 'Diotima' helped him to discover his true poetical self. However the commercial philistinism, which Hölderlin roundly condemned in his philosophical novel, *Hyperion* (1797–9, Eng trans 1965), and the understandable jealousy of the banker, made his stay in Frankfurt-am-Main finally impossible. During a temporary refuge at Hamburg he wrote splendid fragments for a verse drama on the death of Empedocles, elegiac odes and the magnificent elegy 'Menon's Laments for Diotima', which examines the discrepancy between the actual and the ideally possible. For a short time he tutored in Switzerland (1801), but returned to his mother at Nuertingen where he wrote 'Brot und Wein' ('Bread and Wine') and 'Der Rhein' ('The Rhine'). In July 1802, after a spell of employment by the German consul at Bordeaux, he returned in an advanced state of schizophrenia, aggravated by the news of 'Diotima's' death. For a short time he enjoyed the sinecure of court librarian to the Landgrave of Hesse-Homburg, procured for him and paid by his friend von Sinclair. After a period in an asylum (1806–7) he lived out his life in the charge of a Tübingen carpenter. It was the admiration of **Rainer Rilke** and **Stefan George** which first established Hölderlin as one of Germany's greatest poets, 80 years after his death.

▷R Ungar, *Hölderlin's Major Poetry* (1975)

HOLLAND, Josiah Gilbert
(1819–81)

American editor and novelist, born in Belchertown, Massachusetts. He became assistant editor of the Springfield *Republican* and part proprietor in 1851. In 1870, with Roswell Smith and the Scribners, he founded *Scribner's Monthly*, which he edited, and in which appeared some of his novels, including *Arthur Bonnicastle* (1873), *The Story of Sevenoaks* (1875) and *Nicholas Minturn* (1876).

▷H H Peckham, *Josiah Gilbert and his Times* (1940)

HOLLAND, Sir Richard
(c.1415–c.1482)

Scottish poet and member of the Douglas faction at the court of James II and member of the Earl of Moray's household in the north of Scotland. The facts of his life are largely unknown, though it is suggested that he moved to Shetland following the fall of the Douglas family in 1455. His only extant work is *The Buke of the Howlat* (c.1448) which exists in manuscript form and was first published by the Bannatyne Club in 1823. An alliterative poem, it allegorically recounts the behaviour and unkind fate of an owl who dresses up in the feathers of other birds to improve his appearance, but becomes so obnoxiously vain that Nature restores him to his original ugliness with the lesson that owls are always owls and doves always doves. The story of the Douglas family fall is interpolated into the plot.

HOLLANDER, John
(1929–)

American poet and critic, born in New York City. Educated at Columbia and Indiana universities, he subsequently became a lecturer at Yale. His verse is formal, intricate and often demanding, but equally, his wit, lyricism and poignancy have earned him popularity as well as critical acclaim. His works include *Movie-Going* (1962), *The Night Mirror* (1971), *Tales Told of the Fathers* (1975) and *Spectral Emanations: New and Selected Poems* (1978). His critical works include *Rhyme's Reason* (1981), an important study of poetic structure.

HOLLAR, Constance
(1880–1945)

Jamaican poet, born in Port Royal and educated locally and at London University, where she was one of the first black women students. She worked for the Jamaica Poetry League and published a poetry anthology, *Songs of Empire* (1932). In spite of the pervasive influence of English Georgian verse on her own poems (*Flaming June*, 1941), her sensitive response to Jamaican landscape and wildlife and sharp descriptive phrasing gives her poetry an individual voice.

▷J E C McFarlane, *Literature in the Making* (1956); L W Brown, *West Indian Poetry* (1978)

HÖLLERER, Walter

(1922–)

German poet, born in Sulzbach-Rosenberg, the site of the Archives for Contemporary German Literature, founded by Höllerer in 1977. He has been assiduous in his promotion of young authors and from 1954 to 1967, in his capacity as an editor of one of Germany's foremost literary journals, *Akzente*, has helped to chart the direction of post-war German literature. He is a lyrical poet, but emotion is stripped to a minimum, with an emphasis on image and symbol, as in *Der andere Gast* (1952, 'The Other Guest'). His fiction, such as *Die Elephantenuhr* (1973, 'The Elephant Clock'), tends to be heady and theoretical.

HOLLINGSWORTH, Margaret

(1940–)

English-born Canadian playwright, born in London. She won a national drama competition at the age of 18 and had plays broadcast on television and staged in London. In 1974 she took Canadian citizenship. Her one-act stage and radio plays are economical explorations of the lives of night-shift workers, retired men, and women trapped in unrewarding relationships. Her characters often sustain a dual existence, where dreams and make-believe run in tandem with mundane reality. Different ways of using language, as a means of non-communication as well as communication, are explored in plays such as *Ever Loving* (1980) and *Mother Country* (1980).

HOLLO, Anselm Paul Alexis

(1934–)

Finnish-born American poet, his father was the distinguished translator J A Hollo. Hollo was educated in Helsinki, Cedar Rapids, Iowa, and at Tübingen University. From 1958 to 1966 he worked as a programme coordinator for the BBC in London. His first poems had been published in Finnish as early as 1956, but he quickly became a cheerfully puckish figure on the British experimental scene. One typical project was the Finnish translation of John Lennon's *A Spaniard in the Works* (1966); it appeared as *Hispanjalainen Jakovainaa* (1967). Hollo's own verse had a strong oral, almost improvisational, character that developed further after he transplanted to the USA in the later

sixties. His first important collection was *Maya: Works 1959–1969* (1970). Like many of his generation, Hollo was unsettled by the decade's crumbling promise; *Spring Cleaning Greens* (1973) was a selection from his notebooks, significantly followed by the untypically ironic *Surviving With America* (1974). The next major collection was *Sojourner Microcosms* (1979), which combined new and older verse. Hollo's impact as a translator has been considerable, his work including translations of **Allen Ginsberg**, **Paavo Haavikko** and **William Carlos Williams**.

HOLM, Ann

(1922–)

Swedish writer for children, best known in Britain for the war novel *I Am David* (1965). First published in Denmark in 1963 under the title *David*, this short book is the tale of a boy—necessarily wise beyond his years—who escapes from a concentration camp and travels across Europe to the safety of Denmark. Holm's other work available in English includes *The Sky Grew Red* (1991), in which two children, one Danish, one English, try to keep Denmark out of the Napoleonic Wars. Although these books are set in times of conflict and austerity, Holm's message is one of obdurate optimism. Appealing to the idealism of youth, her implicit message is that a younger generation can heal the social and emotional wounds inflicted by the old order.

HOLM, Gro

(1878–1949)

Norwegian novelist. Born in Odda, in Hardanger, she subsequently inherited a farm in the area and ran it for many years. She emerged as a novelist comparatively late in life, and her output was not extensive; her fame rests on her trilogy about the people of Løstøl: *Sut* (1932, 'Trouble'), *Odelsjord* (1933, 'Freehold Land') and *Kår* (1934, 'Conditions'). In a terse, uncompromising style, these novels, set in a small farming community in the west of Norway, highlight the harsh economic conditions that prevailed throughout the second half of the 19th century and that resulted in large-scale emigration, particularly to the USA. The first-person narrator, who is married to a farmer and becomes the mother of six daughters, contributes a crucial feminine perspective, fundamental to the trilogy's unobtrusive but poignant critique of male traditionalism.

▷A Hageberg, 'Mannsamfunn og kvinnekår i Gro Holms *Løstølsfolket*', in *Kvinner og bøker. Festskrift til Ellisiv Steen på hennes 70-årsdag 4. februar 1978* (1978)

HOLMES, (John) Clellon
(1926–88)

American novelist, and the first journalist to use the term 'Beat Generation' to describe the aesthetic of **Jack Kerouac**, **Allen Ginsberg** and their friends. Born in Holyoke, Massachusetts, he was educated at Columbia University, and at the New School for Social Research. *Go* (published in the UK as *The Beat Boys*, 1959), was a story of rootless searching through America that paved the way for *On the Road* (1957). Holmes had met Kerouac in 1948, and the encounter had reinforced his own sense of a new social and cultural movement. Press interest in the Beats' lifestyle inspired an editor at the *New York Times* to commission an article, which appeared on 16 November 1952 as 'This is the Beat Generation'; this one occasional work overshadowed his subsequent career. *The Horn* (1958), which has a jazz background, and the more personal *Get Home Free* (1967), never received the attention given the earlier books. A collection of essays, *Nothing More to Declare*, also appeared in 1967; a later volume, *Passionate Opinions*, appeared shortly before his death and contained significant revaluations of the Beat movement. Holmes's verse, also undervalued, was collected as *Death Drag* (1979).
▷J Tytell, *Naked Angels* (1976)

HOLMES, Oliver Wendell
(1809–94)

American physician and writer, born in Cambridge, Massachusetts. He graduated at Harvard College in 1829, and, giving up law for medicine, spent two years in the hospitals of Europe. From 1839 to 1840 he was Professor of Anatomy and Physiology at Dartmouth College, and in 1842 made the discovery that puerperal fever, which killed mothers and newborns in huge numbers, was contagious. From 1847 to 1882 he was Professor of Anatomy at Harvard. He began writing verse while an undergraduate, but 20 years passed with desultory efforts, before *The Autocrat of the Breakfast Table* (1857–8) made him famous by its fresh unconventional tone. This was followed by *The Professor at the Breakfast Table* (1858–9) and *The Poet at the Breakfast Table* (1872). *Elsie Venner* (1859–60) was the first of three novels, foreshadowing modern 'Freudian' fiction. He published several volumes of poetry, starting with *Songs in Many Keys* (1862). He also wrote *Our Hundred Days in Europe* (1887), an account of a visit made in 1886.
▷J T Morse (jr), *Life and Letters of Oliver Wendell Holmes* (1896); E P Hoyt, *The Improper Bostonian* (1979)

HOLROYD, Michael de Courcy Fraser
(1935–)

English biographer, born in London. He studied sciences at Eton, and literature at Maidenhead Public Library. His first book was *Hugh Kingsmill: a critical biography* (1964). His two-volume life of **Lytton Strachey**, *The Unknown Years* (1967) and *The Year of Achievement* (1968), is recognized as a landmark in biographical writing. He is the official biographer of **George Bernard Shaw**, with *The Search for Love* (1988), *The Pursuit of Power* (1989) and *The Lure of Fantasy* (1991). He is married to **Margaret Drabble**.
▷*Unreceived Opinions* (1973)

HOLSTEIN, Ludvig
(1864–1943)

Danish poet, born in Kallhave (Zealand). He is Denmark's leading nature poet of modern times, celebrated by some as a pantheistic philosopher, but by many more as the finest of all describers of the natural scene, especially that of Zealand. There are translations of a few poems in *Twentieth Century Scandinavian Poetry* (1950, ed M S Allwood).

HOLT, Kåre
(1917–)

Norwegian novelist and author for children, born in the Vestfold region on the Oslo Fjord. He began to write after World War II, during which he took part in the Resistance against the Nazi occupiers. He has written historical fiction, and novels about the modern labour movement. One of his outstanding works is his *Kapplopet* (1974, 'The Race'), dealing with the personality of the explorer Roald Amundsen.
▷P Larsen, *Holt* (1975, in Norwegian)

HOLT, Victoria, pseud of **Eleanor Alice Burford Hibbert**
(1906–93)

British writer of popular historical romances, she also published as Eleanor Burford, Philippa Carr, Kathleen Kellow and (by far her best known) Jean Plaidy. Privately educated, she published her first novel under her own name in 1941, introducing 'Jean Plaidy' shortly afterwards with *Together They Ride* (1943) and 'Victoria Holt' in 1960 with *Mistress of Mellyn*. The pattern of the novels remains unchanged, consisting of insubstantial love stories and power struggles erected on a modestly researched background of historical fact. Perhaps the best known of the early Plaidy books is *The Royal Road to Fotheringay* (1955), which dramatized the life of Mary, Queen of Scots. In the 1960s (as Plaidy again), she embarked on a series of dynastic romances or 'Sagas' which confirmed the general suspicion that, whatever the ostensible period of the stories, she essentially wrote about the upper upper English middle class that was beginning to lose its role as she grew up in the aftermath of World War I.

HOLTBY, Winifred
(1898–1935)

English novelist and feminist, born in Rudston, Yorkshire. She was educated at Oxford, and served in France with the WAAC. She was a prolific journalist, and was a director from 1926 of *Time and Tide*. She wrote a number of novels, including *The Crowded Street* (1924) and *The Land of Green Ginger* (1927), but is chiefly remembered for her last and most successful, *South Riding* (1935).
▷V Brittain, *Testament of Friendship* (1940)

HOLTEI, Karl von
(1798–1880)

German actor and dramatic poet, born in Breslau. He wrote musical plays, such as *Der alte Freiherr* (1825, 'The Old Baron') and *Lenore* (1829), as well as novels and the autobiographical *Vierzig Jahre* (8 vols, 1843–50, 'Forty Years').

HOLTHUSEN, Hans Egge
(1913–)

German critic and poet from Rendsburg, who was involved in anti-Nazi movements towards the end of World War II. His sound and useful criticism, in the Christian tradition of T S Eliot, has been more influential than his poetry, which, however, was much read in Germany at the end of the 1940s for its mellifluous, **Rilke**-like qualities—it has been described as possessing an 'apocalyptic sense of spiritual crisis'.
▷C Middleton and M Hamburger (eds), *Modern German Poetry 1910–1969* (1962)

HÖLTY, Ludwig Christoph Heinrich
(1748–76)

German poet, born in Mariensee, Hanover. He was a co-founder of the *Göttigen Hain*, a literary coterie dedicated to promoting the national spirit in German verse. Some of his poetry is based on the Minnesänger. His range is limited, but his early death from consumption prevented development of his promise.
▷T Oberlin-Kaiser, *Ludwig Christoph Heinrich Hölty* (1964)

HOLUB, Miroslav
(1923–)

Czech poet and scientist, born in Plzeň. He took a PhD in immunology and has had a distinguished career in medicine, doing much to popularize science through his editing of the magazine *Vesmir*. His verse is informed with analytical scepticism, wryly humorous but admirably concise and cutting. He has published several collections, many of which have been translated into English. His *Selected Poems* were published in 1967; recent collections include *Sagittal Section* (1980), *Naopak* (1982) and *Interferon čilio divadle* (1982, Eng trans together as *On the Contrary*, 1982). He published a collection of essays, *The Dimension of the Present Moment*, in 1990.
▷*Zit v New Yorku* (1969, Eng trans *To Live in New York*, 1969)

HOLZ, Arno
(1863–1929)

German author and critic, born in Rastenburg, East Prussia. He started by writing lyric poetry, but is best known for his criticism. *Die Kunst, ihr Wesen und ihre Gesetze* (1890–2, 'The Nature and Laws of Art') inaugurated the German Impressionist school. *Revolution der Lyrik* (1899, 'Revolution in Lyric') rejected all metrical devices, and *Phantasus* (1898–9) was written on this theory. *Papa Hamlet* (1899) and the drama *Familie Selicke* (1890, 'The Selicke Family'), both written in collaboration with Johannes Aschaf, are influenced by **Émile Zola**.
▷W Milch, *Arno Holz* (1933)

HOME, John
(1722–1808)

Scottish clergyman and dramatist, born in Leith, Edinburgh. He graduated at Edinburgh in 1742. Fighting on the government side in the 1745 Jacobite Rising, he was taken prisoner at Falkirk (1746), but made a daring escape from Doune Castle. The next year he became minister of Athelstaneford, where he wrote the tragedy *Agis* and, in 1754, *Douglas*, founded on a Scottish ballad. Each of these was rejected in London by David Garrick, but *Douglas*, produced in the Canongate Theatre, Edinburgh (1756), met with brilliant success, and evoked the often quoted and possibly apocryphal 'whaur's yer Wullie Shakespeare noo?' from an over-enthusiastic member of the audience. It also won great popularity in London, but it gave such offence to the Edinburgh Presbytery that Home resigned his ministry (1757). The success of *Douglas* induced Garrick to bring out *Agis*, and to accept Home's next play, *The Siege of Aquileia* (1760). His other works are

The Fatal Discovery (1769), *Alonzo* (1773), *Alfred* (1778), occasional poems and, in prose, *A History of the Rebellion of 1745* (1802). He married in 1770, and in 1779 settled in Edinburgh.

▷H Mackenzie, *An account of the life and feelings of John Home* (1822)

HOMER
(8th century BC)

Greek epic poet, to whom are attributed two distinct but complementary epics, the *Iliad* (telling of the fall of Troy) and the *Odyssey* (telling of the wanderings of Odysseus on his adventurous way back to Ithaca). Nothing is known about Homer for certain (indeed, some scholars think that no 'Homer' ever existed, or that two or more poets may have been involved). The Homer of tradition seems to have lived in Ionia, directly across the Aegean from mainland Greece, and four city-states have claims to have been his birthplace: the Ionian mainland cities of Smyrna, Colophon and Ephesus, and the island of Chios. His most likely date is the second half of the 8th century BC, with the later poem, the *Odyssey*, being written about 700 BC, half a millennium after the fall of the city of Troy to an invading Mycenaean host around 1200 BC. The method of composition of the epics is also in dispute. Some scholars believe that shorter lays by earlier anonymous poets were simply combined and amended by Homer, others believe that the amalgamation of these shorter works into the majestic structure of the two great epics was an act of individual and supreme literary genius. Homer's lifetime seems to have coincided with the introduction of writing into the Greek world, and he may have utilized this new technique and committed his verses to writing, or dictated them to others. The tradition that he was blind may have little basis in fact. From the time that the *Iliad* and *Odyssey* were put into their present form in the seventh century BC, they have been regarded as the outstanding epic poems of Western literature.

▷W J Woodhouse, *The Composition of Homer's Odyssey* (1930); M I Finley, *The World of Odysseus* (1954)

HONE, William
(1780–1842)

English writer and bookseller, born in Bath. At the age of 10 he became a London lawyer's clerk, and at 20 started a book and print shop, which, however, soon failed. He struggled to make a living by writing for various papers, then started the *Traveller* (1815), and the *Reformist's Register* (1817). In December 1817 he was acquitted in three separate trials for publishing works calculated to injure public morals and bring the Prayer Book into contempt, an historic landmark in the freedom of the press. Among his later satires, illustrated by Cruikshank, were *The Political House that Jack built* (1819), *The Man in the Moon* (1820), and *The Political Showman* (1821). His obscure antiquarian interests were reflected in *Apocryphal New Testament* (1820), *Every-day Book* (1826), *Table-book* (1827–8) and *Year-book* (1829). Nonetheless, he landed in a debtor's jail, from which his friends extricated him to start him in a coffee house— also a failure. In his last years, growing devout, he became a preacher.

▷E Rickword, *Radical Squibs and Loyal Ripostes* (1971)

HOOD, Hugh John Blagdon
(1928–)

Canadian short-story writer and novelist, born in Toronto, now living in Montreal. Hood first came to notice with the early story collection *Flying A Red Kite* (1963), and has continued to work in the short form, publishing three volumes of collected stories (1978, 1989, 1991). But since *The Swing In the Garden* (1975) he has been engaged on a major serial novel, *The New Age/Le Nouveau Siècle*, set to occupy him until the year 2000. Already more than 10 volumes of this **Balzac**ian panorama have appeared.

▷K Garebian, *Hugh Hood* (1983)

HOOD, Thomas
(1799–1845)

English poet and humorist, born in London. At the age of 13 he was placed in a merchant's counting-house in the City, but, his health failing, was sent in 1815 to Dundee, to his father's relations, where he wrote for local newspapers and magazines. In 1818 he returned to London, and in 1821 was appointed sub-editor of the *London Magazine*; here he found himself in daily companionship with such men as **Bryan Waller Procter**, John Cary, **Allan Cunningham**, **Thomas De Quincey**, **William Hazlitt** and **Charles Lamb**. It was, however, the intimacy with John Hamilton Reynolds, whose sister he married in 1825, that chiefly encouraged and trained Hood's poetic faculty. Between July 1821 and July 1823 he published in the magazine some of his finest poems— 'Lycus the Centaur', 'Two Peacocks of Bedfont' and 'Ode to Autumn'. But these, issued anonymously, failed to attract notice when in 1827 he produced them and others in book form. In 1825 he published (anonymously) a volume of *Odes and Addresses to Great People* which was an instant success. In the first series of *Whims and Oddities* (1826) he exhibited his graphic talent in those 'picture-puns' of which he seems to have been the inventor. A second series appeared in 1827, followed by *National*

Tales. In 1829 he edited *The Gem*, a remarkable little 'annual', in which his *Eugene Aram* appeared. He left London for Winchmore Hill in 1829, where he began the first of the *Comic Annuals* which he produced yearly and single-handedly from 1830 to 1839. In 1834 the failure of a publisher plunged Hood into serious difficulties; and in 1835 the family went for five years to Koblenz and Ostend. During these years, struggling against tuberculosis, he wrote *Up the Rhine* (1839). He returned to England in 1840. In 1841 he became editor of the *New Monthly Magazine*, and in 1844 started a periodical of his own, *Hood's Monthly Magazine*. Meantime in the Christmas number of *Punch* (1843) had appeared 'The Song of the Shirt', and in *Hood's Magazine* there followed the 'Haunted House', the 'Lay of the Labourer', and the 'Bridge of Sighs'. His only surviving son, Tom (1835–74), published poems and humorous novels, and in 1865 became editor of *Fun*.
▷J C Reid, *Thomas Hood* (1963)

HOOFT, Pieter Cornelisz
(1581–1647)

Major Dutch Renaissance poet and playwright, born in Amsterdam. By the age of 22 he had been able, by means of extensive travels, to see the achievements of the European Renaissance for himself, and he determined to make the Netherlands another centre of this. He was aloof from politics, and cultivated the spirit of detachment he had learned from **Montaigne**. His massive prose history of his country's Wars of Independence, *Nederlandsche Historien* (1703), is a classic modelled on the example of **Tacitus**. He reacted against Calvinism in his tragedies and in his fervent poetry, initially influenced by **Petrarch** and **Ronsard**, but entirely his own. His poetry appears in translation in *Batavian Anthology* (1824), and in Weevers' *Poetry of the Netherlands in Its European Context* (1960), which is also exemplary for its appraisal of him.

HOOK, Theodore Edward
(1788–1841)

English writer, son of James Hook, born in London. Educated at Harrow School, he achieved early fame as the author of 13 successful comic operas and melodramas (1805–11). He was well known as a maker of puns and as a practical joker—his greatest performance was the Berners Street Hoax (1809). In 1812 he was appointed accountant general of Mauritius. In 1817 he was dismissed after a large deficiency was discovered in the accounts, and was later imprisoned (1823–5). Meanwhile, in 1820, he had started the Tory journal *John Bull*. He wrote a number of short stories and fashionable novels, such as

Maxwell (1830), *Gilbert Gurney* (1936) and *Jack Brag* (1837).
▷M Brightfield, *Thomas Hook and his novels* (1928)

HOPE, A(lec) D(erwent)
(1907–)

Australian poet and critic, born in Cooma, New South Wales, the son of a Presbyterian minister. Most of his childhood was spent in New South Wales and Tasmania. He graduated from Sydney University and took up a scholarship at Oxford. He returned to Australia in 1931 and was a distinguished academic, teaching English at several Australian colleges, before retiring in 1972 to concentrate on poetry. Regarded by some critics as austere, intellectual and lacking any identifiable Australian experience, he is a richly allusive poet, pre-eminent among his contemporaries. Few awards have passed him by since the appearance of his first collection, *The Wandering Isles*, in 1955. Subsequent volumes include *Poems* (1960), *A D Hope* (1963), *Collected Poems 1930–1965* (1966, expanded edn 1972), *Selected Poems* (1973), *A Late Picking* (1975), *A Book of Answers* (1978), *The Drifting Continent* (1979), *Antechinus* (1981) and *The Tragical History of Dr Faustus* (1982). One of Australia's most respected poets, his verse has also been honoured internationally with such awards as the Levinson Prize (1968) and the **Robert Frost** Award (1976). Far from being the austere figure often portrayed, he talked entertainingly on literature as 'Anthony Inkwell' in a long-running 1940s radio programme from children.
▷L Kramer, *A. D. Hope* (1979)

HOPE, Anthony, pseud of Sir Anthony Hope Hawkins
(1863–1933)

English novelist, born in London, the son of a clergyman in Clapton. Educated at Balliol College, Oxford, he was called to the Bar in 1887. He wrote several plays and novels in his spare time, and made his name as writer with a collection of sketches, *The Dolly Dialogues* (1894). But he is chiefly remembered for his 'Ruritanian' romances, *The Prisoner of Zenda* (1894; dramatized 1896) and its sequel, *Rupert of Hentzau* (1898).
▷C Mallet, *Anthony Hope and His Books* (1935)

HOPE, Christopher
(1944–)

South African novelist, poet and non-fiction writer, now resident in England. He was educated at the Christian Brothers College in Pretoria but left South Africa in 1975. The comedy in his first novel, *A Separate Development* (1981), about a boy who cannot decide whether he is black or white, can be described literally as frightful. The book was banned in South Africa. He won a Whitbread Award in 1985 for *Kruger's Alp* (1984), and *Serenity House* (1992) was shortlisted for the Booker Prize. Hope's relish for **Kafka**esque situations comes through most strongly in two non-fiction books, *White Boy Running* (1988) and *Moscow, Moscow* (1990). The vision, bleak and instructive, avoids moralizing through its sense of the comic and ridiculous.

HOPE, Laurence, pseud of Adela Florence Nicolson, née Cory
(1865–1904)

English poet, born in Stoke Bishop, Gloucestershire. She lived in India and wrote poems, influenced by **Algernon Charles Swinburne** and coloured by the Orient, among them the *Indian Love Lyrics*, some of which are best known in their musical settings by Amy Woodford Finden.

HOPKINS, Gerard Manley
(1844–89)

English poet, born in Stratford, London, the son of a prosperous marine insurance agent. He was educated at Highgate School and Balliol College, Oxford, where he was a pupil of Jowett and **Walter Pater** and a disciple of Pusey, and met his lifelong friend **Robert Bridges**. The religious ferment of the times absorbed him and finally he followed **John Henry Newman** into the Roman Catholic Church in 1866. In 1868 he became a Jesuit novice, was ordained a priest in 1877, and taught at Stoneyhurst School (1882–4). In 1884 he was appointed to the chair of Greek at University College, Dublin. None of his poems was published in his lifetime, but his friend Bridges brought out a full edition in 1918. His first and most famous poem, 'The Wreck of the *Deutschland*' (1876) used what he called 'sprung rhythm', which gave an extraordinary freshness to his best-loved poetry, such as 'The Windhover' and 'Pied Beauty'. The *Letters to Robert Bridges, The Correspondence of Gerard Manley Hopkins and Richard Watson Dixon* (1935), and the *Notebooks* (1937), set forth his ideals for poetry, and gave explanations of his experiments in prosody.
▷A G Sulloway, *Gerard Manley Hopkins and the Victorian Temper* (1972)

HOPWOOD, Avery
(1882–1928)

American dramatist, born in Cleveland, Ohio. Hopwood was a popular playwright who achieved considerable success with his first play *Clothes* (1906), a farce built upon the tight spots a poor girl gets herself into by dressing like a rich one. Following this he had a string of 'hits'. *The Gold Diggers* (1909)—about grasping chorus-girls—has been much revamped by Hollywood, originally in the early musical *Gold Diggers of Broadway* (1929). Hopwood did not live to see this version. During the 1920s he became a heavy drinker and drowned himself in the Mediterranean. His name is remembered most for a famous whodunit *The Bat* (1920) and for the eponymous literature prizes administered by the University of Michigan.

HORA, Josef
(1891–1945)

Czech poet who claimed the mantle of **Karel Mácha**, Czechoslovakia's great romantic poet, and who was second only to **Frantisek Halas** amongst the poets of his generation. He began as a communist, but in 1929 became an ardent socialist. He spent the war years confined to his flat by severe illness, and died just as the conflict ended. His *Pracující den* (1920, 'The Working Day'), is one of the best, least doctrinaire, and warmest collections of so-called 'proletarian poetry' ever published. But in *Máchhovské variace* (1936, 'Variations on Mácha'), written when he had become more metaphysical, he surpasses even this volume. He translated the *Eugene Onegin* of **Pushkin**, who influenced him, and has ever since his death been an example and inspiration to the young.
▷A French, *The Poets of Prague* (1969)

HORACE, Quintus Horatius Flaccus
(65–8 BC)

Roman poet and satirist, born near Venusia in southern Italy. His father was a manumitted slave who, as collector of taxes or auctioneer, had saved enough money to buy a small estate. Horace was taken to Rome and taught by the best masters. At the age of about 18 he went to Athens to complete his education; and he was still there when the murder of **Caesar** (44 BC) rekindled civil war. The same year he joined Brutus, who visited Athens while levying troops. He was present as an officer at the battle of Philippi (42 BC), and joined in the flight that followed the Republican defeat, but found his way back to Italy. His property having been confiscated, he found employment in the civil service; but poverty, he said, drove him to make verses. His earliest were chiefly satires and lampoons; but some of his first lyrical pieces made him known to **Virgil**, who about 38 BC introduced him to Maecenas, minister of Augustus and a munificent patron of art and letters. To his liberality Horace owed release

from business and the gift of the farm among the Sabine Hills. From then on his springs and summers were generally spent in Rome, his autumns at the Sabine farm or a small villa at Tibur. As the unrivalled lyric poet of the time he was virtual poet laureate after the death of Virgil. The first book of *Satires*, 10 in number, appeared in 35 BC; a second volume of eight satires in 30 BC; and about the same time the small collection of lyrics known as the *Epodes*. In 23 BC he produced his greatest work, three books of *Odes*. To about the same date belong his *Epistles*. The remainder of his writings are the *Carmen Seculare*; a fourth book of *Odes*; and three more epistles, one of which, known as the *Ars Poetica*, perhaps left unfinished at his death, had a profound influence on literary criticism in the 17th and 18th centuries. Horace's lasting popularity comes chiefly from the *Odes*, in which he combines mastery of form with elegance of style. His subjects range from great matters of state to personal lyric, and he commands a variety of metre unequalled among ancient poets.
▷ G Showerman, *Horace and his Influence* (1922); G Wilson, *Horace* (1972)

HORGAN, Paul
(1903–)

American Roman Catholic poet, historian, critic, essayist and, chiefly, novelist, born in Buffalo, New York. His major work is the trilogy of novels consisting of *Things as They Are*, *Everything to Live For* and *The Thin Mountain Air* (1964–77), set in Philadelphia and New Mexico. For his history of the Rio Grande, *The Great River* (1954), he was awarded a Pulitzer Prize. Horgan's style is undistinguished, but his achievement has probably been underestimated by critics. He is an authority on Lincoln, Beethoven and Stravinsky, of whom he was a friend.

HORNE, Donald Richmond
(1921–)

Australian writer, born in New South Wales, one of Australia's most original and influential writers. The author of *The Lucky Country* (1964), he became associate Professor of Political Studies at the University of New South Wales. His other books have included *The Permit* (1965), *Money Made Us* (1976), *Death of The Lucky Country* (1976), *His Excellency's Pleasure* (1977), *Right Way, Don't Go Back* (1978), *In Search of Billy Hughes* (1979), *Time of Hope* (1980), *Winner Takes All* (1981), *The Great Museum* (1984), *Confessions of a New Boy* (1985), *A History of the Australian People* (1985), *The Public Culture* (1986) and *The Lucky Country We Visited* (1987).
▷ *The Education of Young Donald* (1968)

HORNE, Richard Henry 'Hengist'
(1803–84)

English writer. He was educated at Sandhurst, and served in the Mexican navy and did his share of fighting at Vera Cruz, San Juan Ulloa and elsewhere. Having survived yellow fever, sharks, broken ribs, shipwreck, mutiny and fire, he returned to England and took up writing. He was the author of the epic *Orion* (1843), which he published at the price of one farthing to show his contempt for a public that would not buy poetry. In 1852 he went to Australia as commissioner for crown lands, and became a person of consequence in Victoria and published *Australian Facts and Prospects* and *Australian Autobiography* (1859). He returned to England in 1869. Among his books are *A New Spirit of the Age* (1844), in which **Elizabeth Barrett Browning** helped him, and two tragedies, *Cosmo de' Medici* (1837) and *The Death of Marlowe* (1837).
▷ A Blainey, *The Farthing Poet: Richard Hengist Horn* (1968)

HORNER, Lance
(1903–70)
ONSTOTT, Kyle
(1887–1966)

American popular novelists, specializing in heavily prurient tales of sex, sadism and miscegenation on Southern plantations. Onstott, who was a highly successful dog breeder, only contributed to *Mandingo* (1957), which was the first of the 'Falconhurst' cycle that Horner continued on his own with *Drum* (1962) and many others (all of which included the name Falconhurst in their titles). Overwrought, politically incorrect and shapeless, the books nonetheless enjoyed considerable success and have remained in print long past their apparent sell-by date.

HORNUNG, Ernest William
(1866–1921)

English novelist, born in Middlesbrough. Brother-in-law of **Arthur Conan Doyle**, he was the creator of Raffles, the gentleman burglar, hero of *The Amateur Cracksman* (1899), *Mr Justice Raffles* (1909) and many other adventure stories.

HORTATZIS, Georgias
(fl.1590)

Cretan poet and tragedian, born in Rethymno, who was the leading voice of his island when it was under Venetian occupation. He is one of the great names in the history of the post-classical theatre of Greece. Hortatziz, contemporary to the great artist Domenico Theotokopoulos (El Greco), transformed what had been a local idiom into a true literary language. He must have gathered his great classical learning in Italy, probably from the University of Padua. It is known for certain that he wrote three dramatic works: *Erolfili* (tragedy), *Katzourbos* (comedy) and *Gyparis* (pastoral); there are English translations of these in J Mavrogordato, *Three Cretan Plays* (1929).

HORVÁTH, Ödön von
(1901–38)

Austro–Hungarian, German-speaking dramatist, born in Fiume (now Rijeka in Yugoslavia). After being banned by the Nazis in the 1930s, Horváth's plays remained neglected in Germany until the 1950s and were almost unknown in Britain until **Christopher Hampton** began translating them during the 1970s. *Ges Chichten aus dem Wiener Wald* (1931, Eng trans *Tales from the Vienna Woods*, 1977) presents a wry and resigned picture of lower middle-class life, while *Don Juan kommt aus dem Kreig* (1936, Eng trans *Don Juan Comes Back From The War*, 1978), portrays Don Juan as a disillusioned warrior. Throughout his writing, Horváth paints a critical picture of bourgeois greed and what he suggests is the herd-like stupidity of those seduced by economic or political lures. One day during his exile in Paris, he sheltered from a storm beneath a tree in the Champs Elysées. When a branch snapped and struck him on the head, he died instantly.

▷I Huish, *A Student's Guide to Horvath* (1980)

HOSPITAL, Janette Turner
(1942–)

Australian novelist and short-story writer, born in Melbourne then brought up in Queensland. Her debut, *The Ivory Swing*, won Canada's Seal First Novel Award in 1982. She spends part of each year in Canada, and has also lived in India, the USA and Britain. She is currently based in her native city, where she teaches at La Trobe University. Her nomadic existence has informed her work: the theme of being displaced, of belonging somewhere else, looms large in, for instance, both the metaphysical thriller *Borderlines* (1985) and the aptly-named short-story collection *Dislocations* (1986).

HOSTOVSKY, Egon
(1908–73)

Czech novelist, who spent much of his life in exile—after 1948 in the USA. Much influenced by **Graham Greene**, he wrote intelligent and exciting thriller-type novels, of which *Spiknuti* (1964, Eng trans *The Plot*, 1961) is an excellent example.

HOUDAR DE LA MOTTE, Antoine
(1672–1731)

French critic, poet and playwright, who, despite his blindness and paralysis, was a considerable literary personage in his day. He believed that poetry could be expressed in prose (it has been said that this was because he could not write poetry), and has been called dull and unimaginative. But in *Inèz de Castro* (1723), the most successful play of the 17th century in France, but not taken seriously today, he departed from his own theories. He was in essence a disciple of **Fontenelle**, and took the side of the moderns in the celebrated *Querelle* between ancients and moderns.

HOUEDARD, Dom Sylvester, known as dsh
(1924–92)

British poet, priest, Benedictine monk and scholar, born in Guernsey. He was the literary editor for the *New Testament Jerusalem Bible* (1967), and at his death was completing the late George Melhuish's *On Death and the Double Nature of Nothingness*. He instigated and contributed to the annual Interfaith conferences at the Samye Ling Monastery, Dumfriesshire, Scotland, and founded, with Bob Cobbing, *The Association of Little Presses* (1965). Under the lower case designation 'dsh' he published during the 1960s and 70s over 1 000 'typetracts'. *12 Nahuatl Dancepoems from the Cosmic Typewriter* (1969) combined his innovative manner of text design with the verbal vision of a 'song-drunk/bird'. *Begin Again: a book of reflections & reversals* (1975) contrasted the silent aspects of his monastic life in Prinknash Abbey, Gloucestershire, with his cosmopolitan usage of the 'multi-valued letter'. Notorious for his appearance in *The Times* (1967) advertisement for the legalization of cannabis ('vive voce the propots') and his attacks on anti-homosexual legislation throughout the 1980s ('advocate the gladguys'), he is justly famous for his work in both Concrete and Sound-Poetry.

▷S Bann (ed), *Concrete Poetry: An International Anthology* (1967)

HOUGH, Emerson
(1857–1923)

American novelist. Hough was born in Iowa and began his career by practising law in New Mexico. His early writing consisted of magazine articles on the outdoor life but not before his mid-forties, with the publication of *The Mississippi Bubble* (1902), could he go fully freelance. This book, like many others he produced, was a historical romance set in the

American West. He also wrote a popular series for boys and was energetic in journalistic support for Yellowstone National Park.

▷ L A Stone, *Emerson Hough: His Place in American Letters* (1925)

HOUGHTON, William Stanley
(1881–1913)

English dramatist and critic, born in Ashton-upon-Mersey. A disciple of **Ibsen**'s, he was a drama critic for *The Manchester Guardian* when his first play, *The Dear Departed*, was staged at the Gaiety Theatre in 1908. His plays focus on everyday Lancashire life. The best of his later works are *The Younger Generation* (1910) and his best-known play, *Hindle Wakes* (1912).

HOULT, Norah
(1898–1986)

Irish novelist. She first made her mark with the grimly naturalistic and feminist stories in *Poor Women* (1928), and followed this up with the impressive *Holy Ireland* (1935), a massive novel of Irish life. In *There Were No Windows* (1944), her last novel of real note, she told a story based on the last unhappy years of **Violet Hunt**, once companion to **Ford Madox Ford**. *Selected Stories* (1946) reprints most of her best tales. Now neglected as an author, at her best Hoult reached the level achieved by **Christina Stead** and **Henry Handel Richardson**, from whom she learned much in her youth. In such work as *Four Women Grow Up* (1940) she could be sentimental, although she was always readable and sensible; but in other books, such as *Time, Gentlemen, Time!* (1930), she was sharp and the very opposite of sentimental.

HOUSEHOLD, Geoffrey Edward West
(1900–88)

English novelist, whose inside knowledge of military intelligence and political power-broking fuels his simply but subtly crafted adventure stories. Household has suggested the influence of **Robert Louis Stevenson** and **Conrad**; readers may find links with **John Buchan** and **John Le Carré**. By far his best-known book was his second, *Rogue Male* (1939, published in the USA as *Man Hunt*, 1942), an atmospheric survivalist thriller set in the English West Country. Later books include *A Rough Shoot* (1951) and *The Courtesy of Death* (1967), but the pace curiously slackened when Household began to move his adventures to more exotic settings. However, he continued to write novels well into the 1980s. He also published several short-story collections, of which *The Salvation of Pisco Gabar* (1938, extended US edn 1940) stands out, and juvenile fiction, notably

The Terror of Villadonga (1936, revised for US and subsequent editions as *The Spanish Cave*, 1936).

▷ *Against the Wind* (1958)

HOUSMAN, A(lfred) E(dward)
(1859–1936)

English scholar and poet, born in Fockbury, Worcestershire, brother of **Laurence Housman**. Educated at Bromsgrove School, he won a scholarship to St John's College, Oxford, where he failed in Greats finals and entered the Patent Office. Nevertheless he became a distinguished classical scholar, and in 1892 he was appointed Professor of Latin at University College, London, and Professor of Latin at Cambridge from 1911. He published critical editions of **Manilius** (1903–30), **Juvenal** (1905) and **Lucan** (1926). He is known primarily by his poetry, notably *A Shropshire Lad* (1896), which grew to be immensely popular after an indifferent initial reception, *Last Poems* (1922), and *More Poems*, published posthumously in 1936. Eighteen more appeared in *Laurence Housman's Memoir* (1937), and his *Collected Poems* appeared in 1939. The lyrics in *A Shropshire Lad* are arranged roughly to form a cyclical poem in which an uprooted country lad recalls the innocence and pleasures but also, and more poignantly, the frustrations and local tragedies of a countryside which is only an imagined Shropshire and indeed hardly pastoral in the old sense at all.

▷ I Kilvert, *A. E. Housman* (1955)

HOUSMAN, Laurence
(1865–1959)

English novelist and dramatist, younger brother of **A E Housman**, born in Bromsgrove. He studied art at Lambeth and South Kensington, and attracted attention by his illustrations of **George Meredith**'s poem 'Jump-to-Glory Jane'. He is best known for his *Little Plays of St Francis* (1922) and his Victorian biographical 'chamber plays', notably *Angels and Ministers* (1921) and *Victoria Regina* (1937). His novels included *Trimblerigg* (1924), a satire on Lloyd George, and he also published books of verse, including *An Englishwoman's Loveletters* (1900). His autobiography, *The Unexpected Years* (1937), reveals a romantic Victorian figure, a Conservative radical who espoused pacificism and votes for women.

▷ *The Unexpected Years* (1937)

HOVEY, Richard
(1864–1900)

American poet and dramatist, born in Normal, Illinois. Hovey, in turn brilliant graduate of Dartmouth, converted Christian, dandy and precocious poet and actor, tried, after a visit to Europe at the beginning of the 1890s, to become the American **Oscar Wilde**. He eventually became a professor of English literature at Barnard College. His best-known poetry was written in collaboration with his friend the Canadian poet **Bliss Carman** in the three collections of *Songs of Vagabondia* (1891–1901); but none of his work has lasted. ▷A H MacDonald, *Richard Hovey, Man and Craftsman* (1956)

HOWARD, Edward
(d.1841)

English novelist, a navy lieutenant. On his retirement he wrote sea stories, including *Rattlin the Reefer* (1836) and *Outward Bound* (1838).

HOWARD, Elizabeth Jane
(1923–)

English novelist, born in London and briefly an actress and a model before turning to arts administration and then writing. Her first novel, *The Beautiful Visit* (1950), set during and after World War I, looks at a young woman's attempts to escape her repressive family and to travel and write. War also features in *After Julius* (1965), which deals with the effects of a man's death at Dunkirk on his widow and daughters several years later. Subsequent novels, such as *Something in Disguise* (1969), also look at various aspects of love and marriage. Others, such as the series about the Cazalet family of which *Confusion* (1993) is the most recent, are set in the earlier years of the 20th century, and have an equally strong sense of time and place.

HOWARD, Henry, Earl of Surrey
(c.1517–1547)

English poet, son of the Duke of Norfolk. The Howards were the most powerful Catholic family in England at the time of the English Reformation under Henry VIII, and Henry Howard had to keep a low profile to avoid being caught up in the intrigue surrounding the events of that time. After a successful career as a young aristocrat, he implicated himself in a plot to further his father's cause and was imprisoned in the Tower of London, where he wrote much of his best verse. Particularly notable is his translation of parts of **Virgil**'s *Aeneid*, which is the earliest surviving example of the use of blank verse in English. His other poetry, much of it of considerable merit, is widely anthologized and was first published in 1557 in the *Miscellany* of Richard Tottel and Nicholas Grimald.

HOWARD, Richard Joseph
(1929–)

Prolific American poet, dramatist and notable translator of modern French literature (both fiction and non-fiction), born in Cleveland, Ohio. His own early work was influenced by **Auden**. He likes to write clever dramatic monologues, as in 'November 1889' from *Findings* (1971), a poem spoken by **Browning**. 'Move Still, Still So', from a more recent collection, features one of **Lewis Carroll**'s child models, speaking from her psychiatrist's couch in 1925.

HOWARD, Sir Robert
(1626–98)

English Restoration dramatist, son of the 1st Earl of Berkshire. His plays include *The Committee* (1663) and the *Indian Queen* (1664), the latter assisted by his brother-in-law, **Dryden**. His brothers Edward and James were also dramatists. He abandoned the theatre in 1668. ▷H Oliver, *Sir Robert Howard* (1963)

HOWARD, Sydney Coe
(1891–1939)

American dramatist, born in Oakland, California. After serving in World War I, he became a journalist in New York. His first stage success came in 1924 with *They Knew What They Wanted*, about the fate of a middle-aged Italian and his bride in the grape-growing district of California. It won a Pulitzer Prize. Prolific both as an original dramatist and a translator, his other plays include *The Silver Cord* (1926), dealing with maternal possessiveness, and *Yellow Jack* (1934), written with Paul de Kruiff, rather worthily recounting the research into the identification of the cause of yellow fever. Although to many Howard's might not be an instantly familiar name, his talents as the author of the screenplay of **Margaret Mitchell**'s *Gone With The Wind* (1939) have engaged millions.

HOWATCH, Susan
(1940–)

English novelist, born in Leatherhead, Surrey. She had published six novels before achieving success in 1971 with *Penmarric*, a romantic saga about three generations of a Cornish family, owners of a tin mine, and dwellers in a grand house which stands atop a cliff. Such novels as *The Rich are Different* (1977) maintained her popularity with the same formula of glamour, romance and riches until, in 1979, a BBC television adaptation of *Penmarric* introduced her to a new readership and gave her career a second wind. Her later works include a series of novels, among them *Ultimate Prizes* (1989), about the present-day Church of England.

HOWE, E(dgar) W(atson)
(1853–1937)

American journalist and novelist. He was born in the Indianan back-country, near Treaty, and brought up in Missouri, where he worked as printer's devil on his father's newspaper, the *Union of States*, followed by printing jobs throughout the prairie states. In 1873 he became publisher of the *Globe* in Golden, Colorado, and later (1877) co-founded with his brother another *Globe* in Atchison, Texas, which he edited until 1910. His most significant book, *The Story of a Country Town* (1883), is a melodramatic but vivid tale of jealousy set in the Missouri badlands. None of his later fiction has the same concentrated quality, though there are fine moments in both *An Ante-Mortem Statement* and *The Confession of John Whitlock, Late Preacher of the Gospel* (both 1891). For nearly 35 years Howe concentrated on newspaper work, travel writing, and the stolidly philosophical aphorisms gathered in *Country Town Sayings* (1911), which gained him the title of 'The Sage of Potato Hill'. That year, he established *E W Howe's Monthly* in Atchison, editing it until four years before his death. Other volumes of sayings include *Notes for My Biographer*, *Preaching from the Audience*, *Sinner Sermons* (all 1926) and *The Indignations of E W Howe* (1933).
▷ *Plain People* (1929); C Pickett, *E W Howe: Country Town Philosopher* (1968)

HOWE, Julia, née Ward
(1819–1910)

American feminist, reformer and writer, born in New York, wife of Samuel Gridley Howe. A wealthy banker's daughter, she became a prominent suffragette and abolitionist, and founded the New England Woman Suffrage Association (1868) and the New England Women's Club (1868). She published several volumes of poetry, including *Passion Flowers* (1854) and *Words for the Hour* (1857), as well as travel books and a play. She also wrote the 'Battle Hymn of the Republic' (published in *Atlantic Monthly*, 1862), and edited *Woman's Journal* (1870–90). In 1908 she became the first woman to be elected to the American Academy of Arts and Letters.
▷ L Richards, *Julia Ward Howe* (1916)

HOWELLS, William Dean
(1837–1920)

American novelist and critic, born in Martin's Ferry, Ohio. He became a compositor in a printing office from 1856 to 1861 on the staff of the *Ohio State Journal*. Stimulated by the works of **Cervantes**, **Pope** and **Heinrich Heine**, he began to write poetry which was published in the *Atlantic Monthly* (1860–1), which he later edited (1871–81). His biography of Lincoln (1860) managed to procure for him the post of US consul in Venice (1861–5). His association with *Harper's Magazine* (1886–91) made him the King of critics in America, writing an *Easy Chair* column for *Harper's* from 1900 to 1920. The 'reticent realism' of his early novels, as in the slight *Their Wedding Journey* (1872), matured in depth of feeling in *The Lady of the Aroostook* (1879) and finally gave way to **Tolstoy**an humanitarian naturalism in his masterpiece, *The Rise of Silas Lapham* (1885), a study of a flawed self-made man, and *A Hazard of New Fortunes* (1890) about the founding of a new magazine. His theories of fiction, which influenced **Mark Twain**, **Henry James** and **Oliver Wendell Holmes**, were expounded in *Criticism and Fiction* (1891). He also wrote the autobiographical *Years of my Youth* (1915) and *Literary Friends* (1900).
▷ K S Lynn, *William Dean Howells: an American life* (1971)

HOWES, Barbara
(1914–)

American poet, born in New York, and (1947–65) wife to **William Jay Smith**. She is a formal lyrical poet, but forthright within the limitations she sets for herself. *A Private Signal* (1977) is a selection from all her poetry to the date of its publication. She has been influenced by **Emily Dickinson**, old French poetry, and by **Genevieve Taggard**.
▷ L Bogan, *Selected Criticism* (1955)

HOWES, Edith
(?1874–1954)

New Zealand writer for children, whose early titles, such as *The Sun's Babies* (1910) and *Fairy Rings* (1911), indicate her style. Although publishing for overseas markets, she introduced local elements in *Where Bell-Birds Chime* (1912) and *Maoriland Fairy Tales* (1913), and was immensely popular between the wars. A teacher of science and botany, she used her stories to pass on instruction, in *The Cradle Ship* (1916) on the facts of life, and in *The Singing Fish* (1921) on equality between the sexes. Her 'real-life' books such as *Silver Island: A New Zealand Story* (1928) and *Young Pioneers* (1934) demonstrate the survival value of a knowledge of nature.

HOWITT, William
(1792–1879)
HOWITT, Mary
(1799–1888)

English educational writers, both born of Quaker stock, though in later life Mary converted to the Roman Catholic Church. In collaboration they wrote many books of popular instruction, including a book of verse *The Book of the Seasons, or, The Calendar of Nature* (1831), *Ruined Abbeys of Great Britain* and their most successful work, *A Popular History of England* (1856–64). Their prolific output covered poetry, fiction, history and social and economic issues. Howitt spent some time in Australia with his two sons and subsequently wrote *Land, Labour and Gold: Or, Two Years in Victoria* (1855) and *The History of Discovery in Australia, Tasmania, and New Zealand* (1865). The former is considered one of the most accurate, yet engaging, portraits of the Australia of the goldrush era. His other books include *A Popular History of Priestcraft* (1833) and *Rural Life in England* (1838). Mary wrote a *Popular History of the United States*, translated **Hans Christian Andersen**'s *Improvisatore* and, in 1846, his fairy tales under the title *Wonderful Stories for Children*.

HOYLE, Sir Fred
(1915–)

English astronomer and science-fiction writer, born in Bingley, Yorkshire. He was Plumian Professor of Astronomy at Cambridge University until 1973, and an eminent espouser of the Solid State theory of the creation of the universe, which he advocated with passion in his non-fiction books, beginning with *The Nature of the Universe* (1950). He published his first novel, *The Black Cloud*, in 1957. His science fiction shows a curious disregard for scientific plausibility or accuracy, but gives free rein to his imagination, and allows him to create worlds less intractable to his political and scientific views than the real one. Most of his fiction was written in collaboration with his son, Geoffrey Hoyle (1942–).
▷ *The Small World of Fred Hoyle* (1986)

HRABAL, Bohumil
(1914–)

Czech prose writer, who did not begin to publish until he was almost 50. He first became controversial amongst Stalinist conservatives with his earliest work, in 1963; then again, amongst decent Czechs, when he gave public support to the Soviet puppet Husák (who had suppressed his writings). It soon became clear that his support was ironic, since he had unpublishable typescript material in circulation. His most famous work is still *Ostre sledované vlaky* (1965, Eng trans *Closely Watched Trains*, 1968), although this critical account of a young World War II hero is the most conventional of his books. He writes in the tradition of **Jaroslav Hašek**, but is far more deliberately sophisticated and literary. *Closely Watched Trains* became a famous movie. A further volume in English translation is *The Death of Mr Baltisberger* (1975).

HRISTOV, Kiril
(1875–1944)

Bulgarian poet, born in Stara Zagora. Although he lived most of his life in exile, he was a central figure in his country's emerging literature, as dramatist and story writer as well as poet. His lyrical poetry, of a classical kind, was uninhibited and technically well accomplished.
▷C Manning, and R Smal-Stocki, *The History of Modern Bulgarian Literature* (1960)

HROSTWITHA (also Roswita or Hroswita or Hroswitha)
(fl.10th century)

German playwright and Benedictine nun, of Gandersheim, near Göttingen. She is the author of six comedies in Latin (*Gallicanus, Dulcitus, Callimachus, Abraham, Pafnutius*, and *Sapientia*) which are closely modelled on the work of **Terence**, but are Christian in theme. As the first known plays by a woman, they are of great historical importance. Furthermore, the verse in which they are written is lively and witty; her works are ripe for a long-overdue revival.

HSU Chih-mo
(1895–1931)

Chinese poet, critic and academic, educated in Peking and Britain. On his return to China he took up a number of academic posts, eventually becoming professor of literature at Peking University, and founding the liberal 'Modern Review' group of poets and writers. Like **Wen I-to**, he was a formalist, stressing the importance of structure and technique in verse, often, his detractors would claim, at the expense of content. Some idea of the austere beauty of his work can be gleaned from *Poems*, posthumously published in translation in Peking. He was killed in an aeroplane crash at Tsinafu.

HUBBARD, L(afayette) Ron(ald)
(1911–86)

American Scientologist and science-fiction writer, born in Tilden, Nebraska, and the inspiration behind the Church of Scientology. From the age of 16 he travelled extensively in

the Far East before completing his education at Woodward Preparatory School and George Washington University. He became a professional writer of adventure stories, turning to science fiction in 1938, with such classics as *Slaves of Sleep* (1939), *Fear* (1940), *Final Blackout* (1940), *Death's Deputy* (1940) and *Typewriter in the Sky* (1940). He served in the US navy during World War II, and in 1950 published *Dianetics: The Modern Science of Mental Health*, which claimed to be pioneering in its exploration of the human mind and its detailed description of how the mind works. This was followed by *Science of Survival* (1951), which formed the basis of the Scientology philosophy which has made a significant impact on many American artists. The first Church of Scientology was founded by a group of adherents in Los Angeles in 1954; in 1955 Hubbard became the executive director of the Founding Church Washington. From 1959 to 1966 he made his base in East Grinstead in England, and resigned his position as executive director of the church in 1966. In 1982 he returned to science fiction with an epic bestseller, *Battlefield Earth: A Saga of the Year 3000*, followed by a 10-volume series under the composite title *Mission Earth* (1985–87).
▷R Miller, *Bare-Faced Messiah: the true story of L. Ron Hubbard* (1987)

HUBER, Therese
(1764–1829)
Prolific German novelist and journalist, born in Göttingen. Her father, C G Heyne, was a distinguished professor, but Huber herself had no formal education. She abandoned her first husband, Georg Foster, an explorer and travel writer, for her lover L F Huber. She obtained a divorce from Foster in 1793, a year before his death in Paris, where he had become painfully disillusioned with the realities of the French Revolution. Until his death, she published all her work under her second husband's name. Her novel *Die Familie Seldorf* (1795) is an early female *Bildungsroman*.

HUCH, Ricarda
(1864–1947)
German novelist, historian and feminist, born in Brunswick into a wealthy Protestant merchant family. She studied history at Zürich, taught at a girls' school there, travelled extensively in Italy, married (unhappily) twice, and finally settled in Munich in 1910. A neo-romantic, she rejected naturalism, and wrote novels including the semi-autobiographical *Erinnerungen von Ludolf Ursleu dem Jüngeren* (1893, 'Memoirs of Ludolf Ursleu the Younger') and *Aus der Triumphgasse* (1902, 'Out of Triumph Lane'), criticism including *Die Blütezeit, Ausbreitung und Verfall der Romantik* (1899–1902, 'The Blossoming, Spread and Decline of Romanticism'), and social and political works including *Der Grosse Krieg in Deutschland* (1912–14, 'The Great War in Germany'). She also wrote on religious themes, in *Luthers Glaube* (1915, 'Beliefs of Luther') and *Das Zeitalter der Glaubensspaltung* (1937, 'The Age of Schism'). The first woman to be admitted to the Prussian Academy of Literature in 1931, she resigned in 1933 over the expulsion of Jewish writers. She lived in Jena during World War II.
▷H Baumgarten, *Ricarda Huch* (1968)

HUCHEL, Peter
(1903–81)
German poet and editor, born in Berlin. He withdrew a planned collection of his already well regarded poetry in 1933 as a protest against the Nazi seizure of power. After World War II, in which he served and was taken prisoner on the Russian front, he became East Germany's most liberal and dignified man of letters, and courageous editor of the magazine *Sinn und Form*. Dismissed from this post as not sufficiently dedicated to socialist realism, he eventually (1971) emigrated to West Germany. He was a Symbolist poet in the tradition of **Wilhelm Lehmann** and **Oscar Loerke**, drawing his imagery from nature; but his awareness of his times and his disillusion with the policies of the East German government (whose early reforms he had welcomed) gradually penetrated into his verse; he ended as perhaps the most admired German poet of his generation.
▷J Flores, *Poetry in East Germany* (1971)

HUDSON, William Henry
(1841–1922)
American-born British author and naturalist, of Argentine extraction, born near Buenos Aires. He moved to England in 1869 and became a British subject in 1900. His early writings concerned the natural history of South America, but he is best known for his delightful account of his rambles in the New Forest in *Hampshire Days* (1903) and his romantic novel *Green Mansions* (1904). His ornithological works include *Birds in London* (1898), *Birds of La Plata* (1920), *The Book of a Naturalist* (1919), and *Rare, vanishing and lost British Birds* (1923). A bird sanctuary, containing Sir Jacob Epstein's 'Rima' sculpture, was erected to his memory in Hyde Park, London (1925).

HUERTA, Vicente García de la
(1730–87)
Spanish poet and critic, born in Zafra. He was head of the Royal Library in Madrid. His

famous tragedy of *Raquel* (1778) was based upon the story of Alfonso VIII's love for the beautiful Jewess, Rachel.

HUGH PRIMAS
(fl.1150)

French Latin poet, associated mainly with the town of Orléans. A satirist, like **Walter of Châtillon**, he often employed the Goliardic measure. We know from his often clever and amusing poetry that he was not of noble birth, and that he was dogged by money troubles all his life, but his habit of attacking in verse those on whom he relied for a living could scarcely have helped him. He is thought to have died in poverty in the hospice at Orleans.

HUGHES, David John
(1930–)

English novelist, born in Alton, Hampshire and educated at Oxford. He has worked widely as a magazine editor, documentary and feature-film writer, and film critic. His books include *A Feeling in the Air* (1957), *Memories of Dying* (1976) and *The Imperial German Dinner Service* (1983), demanding fictions revealing a fascination for interior reality and the historical process. Two of his best-known books, *The Pork Butcher* (1984) and *But for Bunter* (1985), consider this theme in markedly different ways. The first examines the German destruction of a French village in retaliation for the killing of a German soldier, while in the second, an elderly man purporting to have been the model for Billy Bunter, the Fat Owl of the Remove at Greyfriars School, presents his account of 20th-century British history. At each critical turn, Bunter himself is found to have played a crucial role.

HUGHES, Hatcher
(1883–1945)

American playwright, born in North Carolina. He was a professor of drama at Columbia University. His play *Hell Bent For Heaven*, a drama set in a mountain community in North Carolina, won the Pulitzer Prize for Drama in 1924. His other works include *Wake Up, Jonathan* (1921), co-authored with **Elmer Rice**, the comedy *Ruint* (1925), which returned to a mountain community setting, and *The Lord Blesses the Bishop* (1934).

HUGHES, John
(1677–1720)

English essayist, dramatist and poet, born in Marlborough, Wiltshire. Hughes worked as a clerk in the Ordnance Office and wrote for the *Tatler* and *Spectator*. **Joseph Addison** was

an admirer of the plays, the most striking being *The Siege of Damascus*. The play excited the author too. He died on its opening night.

HUGHES, (James Mercer) Langston
(1902–67)

American poet, short-story writer and dramatist, born in Joplin, Missouri, and educated at Lincoln University, Pennsylvannia. Throughout the 1920s he was a leading figure in the Black renaissance, but his influence was belatedly recognized. *Weary Blues* (1926) was his first of several collections of verse, culminating in *Selected Poems* (1959). His memorable character, 'Jesse B Simple', first made his entrance in racy newspaper sketches and thereafter in several volumes before the publication in 1957 of *The Best of Simple*. His lyrical verse, resonant of his vast knowledge of folk culture, jazz, the blues and colloquial speech, was highly popular and made him famous, but critics were slow to take him seriously. *The Big Sea* (1940) and *I Wonder as I Wander* (1956) are autobiographical.
▷M Meltzner, *Langston Hughes* (1968)

HUGHES, Monica
(1925–)

English-born children's author, born in Liverpool. She emigrated to Canada in 1952, where she has become especially known for her understanding depiction of adolescent characters and for her science fiction. The 'Isis' trilogy, her best-known work, typifies her narrative approach: visitors from one culture (planet) to another force re-evaluation; new perspectives on life are discovered; readers are instructed. As a didactic novelist she is considered very 'suitable'.

HUGHES, Richard Arthur Warren
(1900–76)

English novelist, born in Weybridge, Surrey, of Welsh descent. He was educated at Charterhouse and Oriel College, Oxford. He wrote poetry and plays from an early age, co-founded and directed the Portmadoc (Caernarvonshire) Players (1922–5), wrote a one-act play, *The Sister's Tragedy* (1922), and a volume of verse, *Gypsy Night and Other Poems*, in the same year, followed by *Confessio Juvenis* (1925). He travelled widely in Europe, America and the West Indies, and eventually settled in Wales. He is best known for *A High Wind in Jamaica* (1929, entitled *The Innocent Voyage* in the USA), a superior adventure yarn about a family of children captured by pirates while sailing to England. In *Hazard: A Sea Story* (1938) he also drew on his experience of the sea. Of his later work, *The Fox in the Attic* (1961), and *The Wooden*

Shepherdess (1973), the first of an unfinished series covering the period from World War I to the rise of the Nazis and their aftermath, were significant.

▷P Thomas, *Richard Hughes* (1973)

HUGHES, Shirley

(1919–)

English writer and illustrator for children, born in Lancashire. She began as an illustrator of other people's works, but by 1960 she was writing her own books for young children. *Lucy and Tom's Day*, produced in that year, was the first of six volumes about those two children. There followed a number of works about Alfie, a grubby but lovable chub, including *Alfie's Feet* (1982), the comic tale of the eponymous urchin's pedal appendages. Her other works, light and gleeful, but realistic, include *Here Comes Charlie Moon* (1980).

HUGHES, Ted (Edward James)

(1930–)

English poet, born in Mytholmroyd, a mill town in West Yorkshire. When he was seven his family moved to Mexborough, Yorkshire, where his parents opened a stationery and tobacco shop. At the local grammar school he began to write poetry—bloodcurdling verses about Zulus and cowboys. He won a scholarship to Pembroke College, Cambridge, where he opted for English literature, but switched to archaeology and anthropology, which was to have a profound effect on his poetry. After graduating he had a number of colourful jobs—zookeeper, gardener, nightwatchman—and occasionally published poems in university poetry magazines. He married the American writer **Sylvia Plath** in 1956 and they settled in Cambridge where Hughes taught while Plath studied. That same year he won an American poetry competition, judged by **W H Auden**, Sir **Stephen Spender** and **Marianne Moore**, with the poems that were to form *The Hawk in the Rain* (1957). For the next few years he lived in America where he taught and was supported by a Guggenheim Foundation grant. *Lupercal* (1960), his second collection, won the **Somerset Maugham** Award and the Hawthornden Prize. In 1963 Sylvia Plath committed suicide and for the next few years no new book of adult verse emerged, though he did complete books of prose and poetry for children. *Wodwo* (1967) was his next major work, and in 1970 came *Crow*, an evocation of a mythical, symbolic bird and witness to the history of man and his destruction. Among later volumes are *Cave Birds* (1975), *Season Songs* (1976), *Gaudete* (1977), *Moortown* (1979), *The Remains of Elmet* (1979), on which he collaborated with the photographer

Fay Godwin, and *Wolfwatching* (1989). Of his books for children, the most remarkable is *The Iron Man* (1968). Drawn magnetically towards the primitive, he is a writer at one with nature, mesmerized by its beauty but not blind to its cruelty and violence. Much acclaimed and imitated, he was appointed poet laureate in 1984, and published the collection *Rain-Charm for the Duchy and other Laureate Poems* in 1992.

▷T West, *Ted Hughes* (1985)

HUGHES, Thomas

(1822–96)

English reformer and novelist, born in Uffington, Berkshire. He was educated at Rugby and Oriel College, Oxford, was called to the Bar in 1848, and became a county court judge in 1882. He was Liberal MP (1865–74), was closely associated with the Christian Socialists, supported trade unionism, and helped to found the Working Men's College, of which he was principal from 1872 to 1883, and a model settlement in Tennessee, USA. He is primarily remembered as the author of the semi-autobiographical public school classic, *Tom Brown's Schooldays* (1856), based on his school experiences at Rugby under the headmastership of Dr Thomas Arnold. The sequel, *Tom Brown at Oxford* (1861), was less successful. He also wrote a number of biographies and social studies.

▷E C Mack and W H G Armytage, *Thomas Hughes* (1952)

HUGO, Richard

(1923–82)

American poet, born in Seattle where, for 12 years, he worked for the Boeing air company. He later became Professor of English at the University of Montana. His early poems were marked by a linguistic compression akin to **Emily Dickinson** (see the 6-line poem 'Somersby' in *The Lady in Kicking Horse Reservoir*, 1973), but later work, found in *31 Letters and 13 Dreams* (1977), became more sprawlingly confessional.

HUGO, Victor Marie

(1802–85)

French poet and author, and leader of the French Romantic movement, born in Besançon, the son of a general. He was educated in Paris at the Feuillantines, in Madrid, and at the École Polytechnique. At the age of 14 he produced a tragedy; and at 20, when he published his first set of *Odes et Ballades* (1822), he had been victor three times at the Floral Games of Toulouse. In 1823 he published *Han d'Islande* (Eng trans *Han of Iceland*, 1825), a wild romance of an impossible Iceland; and followed it with *Bug-Jargal*

(1824, Eng trans *The Slave King*, 1833), a second set of *Odes et ballades* (1826), and *Cromwell* (1827), a play whose preface set out Hugo's poetical creed. In 1828 his *Orientales* revealed him as a master of rhythms. In 1830 came *Hernani* (Eng trans 1830)—the first of those 'five-act lyrics' of which Hugo's drama is composed. In 1831 he produced one of his best-known novels, *Notre-Dame de Paris* (Eng trans *The Hunchback of Notre-Dame*, 1833), an outstanding historical romance, and *Les Feuilles d'automne* ('Autumn Leaves'), which includes some of his best poetry and his best play, *Marion Delorme* (Eng trans *The King's Edict*, 1872). *Le Roi s'amuse* (1832, Eng trans 1843), which was banned, is superbly written, and as Verdi's opera *Rigoletto* has become universally popular. *Lucrèce Borgia* (Eng trans *Lucretia Borgia*, 1847) and *Marie Tudor* followed in 1833. In 1834 came *Claude Gueux*, which is pure humanitarian sentimentalism, and the *Littérature et philosophie mêlées* ('Literature and Philosophy Combined'), a collection of his youthful writings in prose. In 1835 came *Angelo* (Eng trans *Angelo*, 1855), a third melodrama in prose, and the admirable *Chants du crépuscule* (Eng trans *Songs of Twilight*, 1836), and in 1836 the opera of *La Esmeralda*, by Dargomizhsky. In 1837 *Les Voix intérieures* ('Inner Voices') appeared, in which the poet's diction is held by some to have found its noblest expression, and in 1838 *Ruy Blas* (Eng trans 1860), after *Hernani* the most famous of his dramatic works. In 1840 *Les Rayons et les ombres* ('Sunlight and Shadows'), yet another collection of sonorous verse, appeared. He failed at the Théâtre Français in 1843 with the ponderous trilogy of *Les Burgraves*. During the 1840s he became involved with republican politics, and was elected to the Constituent Assembly in 1848. After the *coup d'état* he was exiled by Napoleon III, and went to Guernsey in the Channel Islands (1851–70) where he issued his satirical *Napoléon le petit* (1852, Eng trans *Napoleon the Little*, 1852). His next book of poetry, *Les Châtiments* (1853, 'The Punishments'), was followed by *Les Contemplations* (1856, 'Contemplations'), the best of his earlier poems, and perhaps his greatest poetic achievement, the *Légende des siècles* (1859, 'Legend of the Centuries'). His greatest novel, *Les Misérables* (Eng trans 1862), a panoramic piece of social history, appeared in 1862. This was followed by the extraordinary rhapsody called *William Shakespeare* (1864, Eng trans 1864), *Les Chansons des rues et des bois* (1865, 'Songs of the Street and the Forest'), the novel *Les Travailleurs de la mer* (Eng trans *Toilers of the Sea*, 1866), an idyll of passion, adventure and self-sacrifice, set in Guernsey (1866), and *L'Homme qui rit* (1869, Eng trans *By*

Order of the King, 1870), a piece of fiction meant to be historical. He returned from Guernsey to Paris in 1870, and stayed through the Commune, but then departed for Brussels, protesting publicly against the action of the Belgian government in respect of the beaten Communards, in consequence of which he was again expelled. In 1872 he published *L'Année terrible* ('The Terrible Year'), a series of poems about the war, and in 1874 his last romance in prose appeared, *Quatre-vingt-treize* (Eng trans *Ninety-Three*, 1874). In 1876 he was made a senator, and published the second part of the *Légende*. *L'Histoire d'un crime* (1877, 'The Story of a Crime') has been described as 'the apotheosis of the Special Correspondent', and *L'Art d'être grand-père* (1877, 'The Art of Being a Grandfather') contains much charming verse. His declining years produced *Le Pape* (1878, 'The Pope', a humanitarian, anticlerical, and above all theatrical, poem), more poetry in the form of *La Pitié suprême* (1879, 'The Greatest Pity'), *L'Âne* (1880, 'The Ass'), *Les Quatre Vents de l'esprit* (1881, 'The Four Winds of the Spirit'), and the play *Torquemada* (1882). He was buried in the Panthéon.

▷A Maurois, *Hugo and His World* (1966); H Peyre, *Hugo, Philosopher and Poet* (1980)

HUIDOBRO, Vicente
(1893–1948)

Chilean poet, publicist, critic, playwright, novelist and biographer, born in Santiago, and one of the most influential figures in Latin-American literature. Huidobro was a flamboyant man, who once stood for the presidency of Chile; but he was also a hugely gifted poet. He wrote in Spanish and in French. He and/or **Reverdy** (it has never been decided who preceded whom) invented the short-lived movement called creationism, which demanded that poems should grow as naturally as trees: 'Why do you sing of the rose, O poets?/Make it blossom in the poem.' Huidobro's critical thinking was first prompted by his response to the innovative side of the *modernismo* of **Darío**, and then to his reading of **Apollinaire** on cubism. It may well be that his 1916–17 visit to Spain, where he tried, 'caudillo-like', to promote cubism and creationism, was the decisive factor in the foundation of ultraism, or *ultraísmo* (1919), which eventually led to the seminal essay of **Ortega y Gasset**, *The Dehumanisation of Art*. Huidobro resolutely lived out his private life in public: when he met Ximena Amuntágui, a high school student, in 1925, he announced his passion, and intention to leave his wife and children, in the nation's leading newspaper. But by 1932 and his return to Chile, he was somehow respectable, despite having become a communist. His novels and biographies are all considerable works, but it is as a lyric poet that he will be remembered: in *Altazor* (written in 1919; published in 1931, definitive text, 1981, Eng trans 1988) and *Temblor de cielo* (1928, 'Quivering Sky'), both prose poems, he wrote what many agree are the most substantial experimental poems of the century. There are many translations: *Arctic Poems* (1974); *The Selected Poetry* (1981); *The Poet is a Little God* (1990).

▷H A Holmes, *Vicente Huidobro and Creationism* (1933); R de Costa, *Vicente Huidobro: The Careers of a Poet* (1984)

HULL, E(dith) M(aude)
(early 20th century)

English 'queen of desert romance', about whom very little is known. Her real name was Winstanley and, according to her travel book, *Camping in the Sahara* (1926), she visited Algeria when she was young. Although her life has not been conclusively documented, it is known that she married a gentleman pig-farmer in Derbyshire and wrote *The Sheikh* (1919), her first and enormously popular desert romance, while her husband was away during World War I. The story of an independent Englishwoman who refuses offers of marriage in order to travel, is captured and raped by a sheik, whom she then marries, it was transformed into film (1921) as a vehicle for Rudolph Valentino. Hull swept on to write *The Sons of the Sheikh* (1925) and *The Lion-Tamer* (1928), equally pulsating stories of exotic romance.

HULME, Keri Ann Ruhi
(1947–)

New Zealand writer of mixed Maori, Orkney and English descent, born in Otautahi, Christchurch. She achieved notice by winning the Booker Prize with her first novel, *The Bone People* (1983), a spell-binding mixing of Maori myth and Christian symbolism. After another novel, *Lost Possessions* (1985), she published a collection of short stories, *Te Kaihau: The Windeater* (1986). Some of her verse in Maori and English is collected in *The Silences Between* (1982).

HULME, T(homas) E(rnest)
(1883–1917)

English critic, poet and philosopher, born in Endon, Staffordshire. He was educated at Newcastle-under-Lyme High School, and was sent down from St John's College, Cambridge, for brawling. After a stay in Canada he taught in Brussels and developed an interest in philosophy. He joined **Ezra Pound**, **Wyndham Lewis** and Epstein as a champion of modern abstract art, of the poetic movement known as 'Imagism' (his own small number of surviving poems are in that style) and of the anti-liberal political writings of Georges Sorel, which he translated. Killed in action in France, he left a massive collection of notes, edited under the titles *Speculation* (1924) and *More Speculation* (1956), which expose philistinism and attack what he considered to be weak and outworn liberalism. Most of his poetry appeared in *The New Age* in 1912. He was described by **T S Eliot** as 'classical, reactionary and revolutionary'.

▷M Roberts, *T. E. Hulme* (1982)

HUME, Alexander
(c.1556–1609)

Scots poet, of whom little is known beyond his having been educated at St Andrews and having thereafter spent some time in France. He became a minister during the upheaval and turmoil caused by the Scottish Reformation, and his Scots poetry reflects this and Hume's own religious commitment in its preaching, sermonly tone. His best-known poem is 'Of the Day Estivall' ('Of the Summer Solstice'), in his collection *Hymnes, or Sacred Songs, wherein the richt use of poesie might be espied*, which was published in Edinburgh in 1599. There is, perhaps, a certain tension between the subtitle of the collection and its somewhat plodding content.

HUME, Fergus
(1859–1932)

English writer. Brought up in Dunedin, New Zealand, he was called to the New Zealand Bar and practised as a lawyer. He was a pioneer of the detective story in *The Mystery of a Hansom Cab* (1887), and returned to England in 1888, where he published around 140 other detective novels, including *The Bishop's Secret* (1900) and *The Caravan Mystery* (1926).

HUM-ISHU-MA *see* MOURNING DOVE

HUMPHREY, William
(1924–)

American novelist and short-story writer, born in Clarksville, Texas. After studying at Southern Methodist University and the University of Texas at Austin, he taught in New York State and elsewhere, then spent some years in Italy. *The Last Husband and Other Stories* (1953) draws on the life of communities in rural Texas, addressing such themes as adolescence, male pride, and adultery. These themes were developed in *Home from the Hill* (1958), his most successful novel. His insight into character and narrative gift was demonstrated in further novels, including *Hostages to Fortune* (1984), about a writer beset by tragedy. A remarkably vivid autobiography, *Farther Off from Heaven* (1977), reveals the roots in childhood of his fictional concerns.

▷J W Lee, *William Humphrey* (1967)

HUMPHREYS, Emyr Owen
(1919–)

Welsh novelist, poet and dramatist, born in Prestatyn, Clwyd, and educated at University College, Aberystwyth, where he read history, learned Welsh and became a nationalist. He has worked as a teacher and a BBC Wales drama producer. The author of 19 novels, he won the **Somerset Maugham** Award for *Hear and Forgive* (1952), and the Hawthornden Prize for *A Toy Epic* (1958). He has also published two collections of short stories and six volumes of verse. Some of his poems have been set to music by the composer Alun Hoddinott.

HUNEKER, James Gibbons
(1857–1921)

Influential American critic and essayist, born in Philadelphia. His writing career began with musical criticism, but he later wrote on drama, literature and art, always enthusiastically promoting the new, the exciting, and the European. Like his friend and follower **H L Mencken**, he opposed the drabness of American puritanism and portrayed the pursuit of the arts as 'a magnificent adventure'. His most popular book of essays, *Iconoclasts* (1905), dealt with dramatists such as **Ibsen** and **Shaw**. His fiction—the exotic stories of *Melomaniacs* (1902) and *Visionaries* (1905) and the sexually advanced novel *Painted Veils* (1920)—continues the work of his essays by other means, with the same relentless allusions to foreign writers, and discussion of artistic, particularly musical, concerns.

▷A T Schwab, *James Gibbons Huneker: Critic of the Seven Arts* (1963)

HUNT, E(verette) Howard
(1918–90)

American spy and detective novelist and political operative; as an adviser to Richard Nixon's re-election committee he became embroiled in the Watergate scandal in 1972. Conspiracy theorists also claim that Hunt appears on photographs of the notorious 'grassy knoll' on Dealey Plaza, Dallas, where John F Kennedy was ambushed in November 1963, and among the mysterious 'tramps' arrested subsequent to the assassination. Born in Hamburg, New York, he graduated from Brown University in 1940, and served with the Air Force (1943–6) after writing scripts for the hugely influential *March of Time* newsreels. He was recruited as a political officer after the war and saw diplomatic service in Paris, Vienna, Mexico, Tokyo and Montevideo; an impression of his career can be had from **Mailer**'s CIA novel *Harlot's Ghost* (1991). Hunt's first novel was called *Maelstrom* (1948), reissued seven years later as *Cruel is the Night*. Others included *Dark Encounter* (1950) and *The Judas Hour* (1951). He also used pseudonyms, writing as John Baxter, Robert Dietrich and David St John, and detective fiction as Gordon Davis. Following his release from prison in 1977, he resumed his writing career; his work provides a fascinating insight into the clandestine side of US politics from the end of World War II through the Bay of Pigs (in which he had a hand), to Vietnam and beyond.

▷*Undercover: Memoirs of an American Secret Agent* (1974)

HUNT, (James Henry) Leigh
(1784–1859)

English poet and essayist, born in Southgate, Middlesex, the son of an immigrant US preacher. Educated at Christ's Hospital, his first collection of poetry was privately printed as *Juvenilia* in 1801. With his brother, a printer, he edited, from 1808 to 1821, *The Examiner*, which became a focus of liberal opinion and so attracted leading men of letters, including **Byron**, **Thomas Moore**, **Shelley** and **Charles Lamb**. He was imprisoned with his brother for two years (1813–15) for a libel on the Prince Regent. *The Examiner*, however, was more a literary and social than a political forum. It introduced Shelley and **Keats** to the public—Keats' sonnet *On First Looking into Chapman's Homer* first appeared there in 1816, the year in which Hunt issued his own romance, *The Story of Rimini*. He founded and edited *The Indicator* (1819–21). In 1822 he joined Shelley in Italy with his wife and seven children to found a new quarterly, *The Liberal*. Shelley's tragic death by drowning that year forced Hunt to accept the hospitality of Lord Byron at his palace in Pisa. The association with Byron was unhappy and *The Liberal* (1822–3) was short-lived. After Byron's death in 1824, Hunt returned to England in 1825 to carry on a busy life of literary journalism, liberal politics and poetry. His house at Hampstead attracted all that was notable in the literary world, not without envy or ridicule, however, as **Dickens**' caricature of him as Harold Skimpole in *Bleak House* shows. His importance is less in his works, poetic or critical, than in his being one of those invaluable people who introduce authors to each other, but his *Examiner* is not to be dismissed, and his autobiography is a valuable picture of the times.

▷E Blunden, *Leigh Hunt* (1930)

HUNT, Violet
(1866–1942)

English novelist and biographer, born in Durham, the daughter of the painter Alfred William Hunt. Having trained as a painter, she turned to writing, her first novel, *The Maiden's Progress: A Novel in Disguise*, appearing in 1894. She was an outspoken supporter of women's suffrage and most of her 17 books, such as *Unkist, Unkind!* (1897) and *Tales of the Uneasy* (1911), deal frankly, for the time, with the psychological effects on women of sexual repression. *White Rose of Weary Leaf* (1908), in which human relationships are restricted by social conventions, is often judged to be her finest novel. Her memoirs include a rather unreliable book about the Pre-Raphaelite painters, *Those Flurried Years* (1926). Although she never married, Violet Hunt had several turbulent and well-publicized affairs, but in later life withdrew into virtual seclusion.
▷M and R Secor, *F.M.Ford and V. Hunt's 1917 Diary* (1983)

HUNTER, Evan, originally Salvatore A Lambino
(1926–)

American novelist, born in New York City. Writing under the name 'Ed McBain', he is renowned for his '87th Precinct' thrillers. He was educated in New York, served in the US navy and taught before concentrating on his career as a novelist. As Evan Hunter he is best known for *The Blackboard Jungle* (1954), about a young teacher in an inner-city high school confronted with recalcitrant students and sundry social problems. It was acclaimed for its realism and topicality.

HUNTER, Mollie
(1922–)

Scottish writer, born in Longniddry, East Lothian. Until 1960 she worked as a freelance journalist, but she is best known for her work in children's fiction, and has published 25 books of various types in this field, including fantasy and historical fiction. Her works include *Hi Johnny* (1963), *Haunted Mountain* (1972) and *A Stranger Came Ashore* (1975). She has been Writer-in-Residence at Dalhousie University in Halifax, Canada, and has lectured and written on writing for children. She has been the recipient of many major awards, including the Scottish Arts Council Literary Award (1972), the Carnegie Medal (1975) and the Arbuthnot Lectureship (1975).

HUNTER, Norman
(1899–)

English writer for children, born in London. He is best known as the begetter of Professor Branestawm, the archetypal crackpot genius, who made his debut in *The Incredible Adventures of Professor Branestawm* (1933). The professor, despite the hazardous nature of his many experiments, has enjoyed remarkable longevity; *Professor Branestawm's Crunchy Crockery* was published on the 50th anniversary of the original adventure. During a period of 21 years in South Africa Hunter produced no fiction, but his arrival back in the United Kingdom in 1970 brought a return to writing. Subsequent volumes include *Dust-up at the Royal Disco* (1975). He has also worked as a copywriter and a conjuror.

HUNTER, N(orman) C(harles)
(1908–71)

English playwright and novelist, born in Derbyshire. He served in the army before joining the BBC as a producer. He is best remembered for his play, *Waters of the Moon* (1951), in which several guests, stranded in a hotel by heavy snowfalls, are forced to come to a new understanding of each other. This and other plays, such as *A Touch of the Sun* (1958), are clearly influenced by **Chekhov**. His smoothly-structured, naturalistic dramas were increasingly criticized during the 1950s and 60s for their preoccupation with middle-class mores and their sentimentality, although with time they may come to be looked upon again more kindly.

HUON, Ronan
(1922–)

Breton poet who has always aimed at a minority audience, and who has written a scholarly Breton grammar. His poetry is modestly modernistic, and its reputation is high amongst readers of Breton.

HURSTON, Zora Neale
(c.1901–1960)

American black novelist, born in Eatonville, Florida. The nine secure years she spent there, described in *Dust Tracks on a Road* (1942), ended when her mother died and her father, a Baptist preacher and thrice mayor of the town, remarried. Her life from then on was 'a series of wanderings'—occasional work, interrupted education, working as a wardrobe assistant with a theatre troupe—until she enrolled as a full-time student at Baltimore's Morgan Academy. Moving to Washington DC she became a part-time student at Howard University and began to write. Influenced by her studies in cultural anthropology at Barnard College and Columbia University, she became a prominent figure in the Harlem Renaissance. A precursor of black women writers like **Alice Walker** and **Toni Morrison**, her novels include *Jonah's

Gourd Vine (1934), *Their Eyes Were Watching God* (1937), *Moses, Man of the Mountain* (1939) and *Seraph on the Suwanee* (1948). In the 1950s she withdrew from public life, and was distanced from many contemporaries by her controversial attack on the Supreme Court's ruling on school desegregation. She argued that pressure for integration denied the value of existing black institutions. Her last years were plagued by ill-health and she died in poverty.
▷ *Dust Tracks on a Road* (1942)

HURTADO DE MENDOZA, Diego de
(1503–75)

Spanish poet and historian, born in Granada; he was one of the great Renaissance humanists. As well as Spanish, he had mastery of Arabic, Hebrew, Greek and Latin. He was an important diplomat who was entrusted with the task of arranging marriages between Henry VIII and the Duchess of Milan, and Mary Tudor with Don Luis of Portugal (he failed in both instances). It was once widely believed that he wrote the picaresque *Lazarillo de Tormes*, and, although he probably did not, he was capable of it. His fine 'indecent' poem, *Fábula de cangrejo* ('Fable of the Crab'), deservedly enjoyed long and wide circulation, as did his *jocoso* (light verse) work. But his outstanding book is his account of the Morisco rebellion of 1568–70, *La guerra de Granada* (1627, 'The Granada War'), a biting history in the style of Sallust, which spares no one. Philip II expelled him from court in 1568.

HUTCHINSON, Pearse
(1927–)

Irish poet, writing in both Gaelic and English, born in Glasgow and educated in Dublin. He moved to Spain in the 1950s to teach English in Barcelona, but returned to Dublin in 1970. His four collections in Gaelic and nine in English reveal a consistent identification with the underdog, a championing of the deprived. *The Frost is All Over* (1975) opens with the words 'to kill a language is to kill a people', and this central theme led him to important translations from the fringe European languages of Galico–Portuguese and Catalan. His *Selected Poems* (1982) portray the depth of his beliefs and demand a reader's complicity with his insistence on compassion and understanding.

HUXLEY, Aldous Leonard
(1894–1963)

English novelist and essayist, son of the editor Leonard Huxley and brother of the biologist Sir Julian Sorell Huxley, born in Godalming, Surrey. He was educated at Eton and Balliol College, Oxford, where he read English, not biology as he intended, because of an eye disease, which compelled him to settle in the warmer climate of California (1937). Some **Shelley**an poetry, literary journalism and a volume of short stories *Limbo* (1920) were followed by *Crome Yellow* (1921) and *Antic Hay* (1923), satires on post-war Britain. *Those Barren Leaves* (1925) and *Point Counter Point* (1928) were written in Italy, where he associated with **D H Lawrence**, who appears as Mark Rampion in the last named. In 1932, in his most famous novel, *Brave New World*, Huxley warned of the dangers of moral anarchy in a scientific age, by depicting a repulsive Utopia, in which Platonic harmony is achieved by scientifically breeding and conditioning a society of human robots, for whom happiness is synonymous with subordination, a much more sinister prophecy than **George Orwell**'s *1984*, which still required thought control and police terror. Despite the wit and satire, Huxley was in deadly earnest, as his essay *Brave New World Revisited* (1959) shows. An alternative possibility, of bestial individualism in the degeneration of the survivors of an atomic war, is explored in *Ape and Essence* (1948). From such pessimism Huxley took refuge in the exploration of mysticism. *Eyeless in Gaza* (1936) and *After Many a Summer* (1939, James Tait Black Prize) pointed the way to *Time must have a Stop* (1944), in which he attempted to describe a person's state of mind at the moment of, and just after, death. *The Doors of Perception* (1954) and *Heaven and Hell* (1956) describe a controversial short-cut to mysticism, the drug mescalin which reduces the 'sublime' mystical state to a mere function of the adrenal glands. In contrast, the novelette *The Genius and the Goddess* (1955) reverts to the earlier Huxley, the problems posed by the discrepancy between an extraordinary intellect and a deficiency in other human endowments. *Island* (1962) is a more optimistic utopian novel. Huxley wrote numerous essays on related topics, beginning with *Proper Studies* (1927), biographies, and a famous study in sexual hysteria, *The Devils of Louden* (1952).
▷ S Bedford, *Aldous Huxley, a biography* (2 vols, 1973–4)

HUXLEY, Elspeth Josceline, née Grant
(1907–)

English novelist, born in Kenya. In 1931 she married Gervas Huxley (1894–1971), grandson of Thomas Henry Huxley, and has written many novels and essays on her native land, its history, and its problems. Her best-known novel is *The Flame Trees of Thika* (1959), which deals with her childhood, as do

The Mottled Lizard (1962) and *Death of an Aryan* (1986, also known as *The African Poison Murders*).
▷ *Love Among the Daughters* (1968)

HUYGENS, Constantjin
(1596–1687)

Dutch poet, statesman, composer and humanist, son of the scientist Christian Huygens, born in The Hague. The recipient of a rich and pious Calvinist education, he was one of the foremost linguists of his day, having seven languages at his command. He was also one of the best-known men of his time, and was knighted by Charles I (1622) and honoured by the French King (1632). He regarded his poems as 'cornflowers': they embellished, as he saw it, his religious and political work. He admired **John Donne** (19 of whose poems he translated) and **Giambattista Marino**, and his poetry is akin to that of both, being highly emotional but also 'metaphysical'—distinguished by its many conceits and daring play on words. He has been called 'the last of the true Renaissance virtuosi'. His play *Tryntje Cornelis* (1653) is surprisingly down-to-earth. It was for long thought that Huygens did damage to his poetry by regarding it so casually; but it is now becoming apparent that this gave it 'non-literary' qualities of great interest. There are English translations in: J Bowring and H S van Dijk (eds), *Batavian Anthology* (1824); F J Warnke, *European Metaphysical Poetry* (1961).
▷ A G H Bachrach, *Sir Constantine Huygens and Britain* (1962)

HUYSMANS, Joris Karl
(1848–1907)

French novelist of Dutch origin, born in Paris. From ultrarealism, as in his *Les Soeurs Vatard* (1879, 'The Vatard Sisters'), *À vau-l'eau* (1882, 'Downstream') and *À rebours* (1884, 'Against the Grain'), he changed over to a devil-worshipping mysticism as in *Là-Bas* (1891, 'Over There'), but returned to the Roman Church with *En Route* (1892). His *L'Art Moderne* (1882) is a superb study of Impressionist painting. The decadent, aesthetic hero of *À rebours* (1884) was much admired by **Oscar Wilde** and his circle, and established Huysmans as a leading light in the decadent movement of the period.
▷ R B Baldick, *The Life of J. K. Huysmans* (1955)

HYDE, Douglas
(1860–1949)

Irish poet, folklorist, academic and politician, born in Frenchpark, County Roscommon, where his father was the Protestant rector.

Ostensibly studying law at Trinity College Dublin, he published poems under the pseudonym 'An Craoibhin Aoibhinn' ('The Agreeable Little Branch'), which he also used in his subsequent translations from the Gaelic of folktales and poems. In 1892 he became president of the National Literary Society and a year later, the year of his marriage, held a similar position in the faction-ridden Gaelic League. In 1932 he was elected first President of the Republic of Ireland and held office until 1944. In literature his most important work was *Abhran Gradh Chuige Connacht* (1893, Eng trans *Love Songs of Connacht*, 1893), though it is arguable that his essay *The Necessity for De-Anglicising Ireland* (1892), a plea for cultural autonomy, has had greater influence on consequent cultural-political attitudes.
▷ *I Believed* (1950); D Daly, *The Young Douglas Hyde: The Dawn of Irish Revolution and Renaissance* (1974)

HYDE, Robin, pseud of Iris Guiver Wilkinson
(1906–39)

New Zealand journalist, poet, and novelist, born in South Africa of an Anglo–Indian father and Australian mother. In *Journalese* (1934) New Zealand society in the 1930s is viewed with acute perception. Her newspaper background is evident in her novels, which often blend fact and fiction as in *Passport to Hell* (1936) and in *Nor the Years Condemn* (1938) with the real-life anti-hero and misfit James Douglas Stark. Here, and in *Check to Your King* (1936), a novelized account of Baron Charles de Thierry (the French adventurer and eccentric who sought to establish himself as Sovereign Chief of New Zealand in the 1830s), she shows her empathy with the outcast and under-dog. The autobiographical *A Home in this World* (1937) describes the social pressures which drove her to drugs and eventual suicide. She wrote three collections of verse, *The Desolate Star* (1929), *The Conquerors* (1935) and *Persephone in Winter* (1937). She visited China in 1938, a time when she produced her best work in *Houses by the Sea, and Later Poems* (1952), which also includes backward glances at the innocence of her childhood.

HYNE, Charles John Cutcliffe Wright
(1865–1944)

English traveller and author, born in Bibury. He is remembered above all as the creator of the fictional character 'Captain Kettle' in several adventure stories.

HYRY, Antti
(1931–)
Finnish writer of stories and novels, born in Kuivaniemi. An experimentalist, he has cultivated a naively objective style which more recently has tended towards monotony.

HYSLOP, James
(1798–1827)
Scottish poet, born in Kirkconnel, Dumfriesshire. While a shepherd he wrote the poem 'The Cameronian's Dream' (1821).
▷ Biographical sketch in *The Poems of James Hyslop* (1887)

I

IAMBLICHUS
(2nd century)

Syrian–Greek author of a lost Greek romance, *Babyloniaca*.

IBÁÑEZ, Sara de
(1909–71)

Uruguayan poet, born in Chamberlain as Sara de Casadei, she married the poet Roberto Ibáñez in 1928. Her first collection, *Canto* (1940), had a prologue by **Neruda**, in which he praised her as 'great, exceptional and cruel'. Using strict forms, she wrote in a hermetic or Surrealist style; despite praise from many more than Neruda, eg **Carrera Andrade**, her work has been neglected in English-language surveys and anthologies.
▷D E Marting, *Women Writers of Latin America* (1987)

IBÁÑEZ, Vicente Blasco
(1867–1928)

Spanish novelist, born in Valencia. He dealt in realistic fashion with provincial life and social revolution. Notable works are *Sangre y Arena* (1908, Eng trans *Blood and Sand*, 1913), *La Barraca* (1899, Eng trans *The Cabin*, 1919) and *Los Cuatro Jinetes del Apocalipsis* (1916, Eng trans *The Four Horsemen of the Apocalypse*, 1918 (US); 1919 (UK)), which vividly portrays World War I and earned him world fame.
▷A Day, *Vicente Blasco Ibáñez* (1972)

IBARBOUROU, Juana de
(1892–1979)

Uruguayan poet, born in Melo, on the border with Brazil. She was one of the most distinguished 'wife and mother' poets of the 20th century, not unlike **Judith Wright**, but with more Latinate opportunity to express her passions (for the military man whom, as Juana Fernandéz, she married in 1914). Her poems became famous throughout Argentina and, indeed, Spanish America. She felt misunderstood, and declared: 'the adjective erotic attached itself to those poems like a fly on a pile of butcher's refuse'. But it was widely understood that no one had before published such erotic poetry in Spanish in modern times. She was named 'Juana of America' at a grand ceremony in Montevideo (1929), at which men, including poets such as **Alfonso Reyes**, broke down and wept with joy. But when she published more verse, in 1930, it went almost unnoticed, and by the end of her life she had become prone to depression and religious devotion. More of a phenomenon, perhaps, than a writer, her early verse does have the spontaneity of complete subjectivity within a patriotic and conventional context.
▷M J de Queiroz, *La poesia de Juana de Ibabourou* (1961)

IBN 'ARABI
(1165–1240)

Arab mystic poet. His writings present in obscure language a form of pantheism.
▷R Landau, *The Philosophy of Ibn 'Arabi* (1959)

IBRAHIM, Sonallah
(1935–)

Egyptian novelist, whose candid 1968 novel, translated as *The Smell of It* (1971), about a young man's sexual frustrations in Cairo, aroused interest because it was banned. As a critic wrote, with it the Egyptian novel could be considered to have 'come of age'.

IBSEN, Henrik
(1828–1906)

Norwegian dramatist, born in Skien, the founder of modern prose drama. The son of a wealthy merchant who went bankrupt, he worked as a chemist's assistant in Grimstad (1844–50), intending to study medicine, and wrote his first play there, *Catilina*, which was rejected. He got a job in journalism in Bergen, then was given a post as stage director and resident playwright at Ole Bull's Theatre, for which he wrote five conventional romantic dramas. In 1857 he was appointed director of the Norwegian Theatre in Christiania (Oslo), having just written his first play of significance, *Kongsemnerne* ('The Pretenders'), on a historical theme from Norway's past, in the manner of **Schiller**. In 1862 he wrote *Kjaerlighedens Komedie* ('Love's Comedy'), with its satirical theme of marriage as a millstone to idealism. The theatre went bankrupt the following year, and Ibsen went into voluntary exile for the next few years, to Rome, Dresden and Munich (1864–92), and it was there that he wrote the bulk of his dramas. The dramatic poem *Brand* appeared in 1865, and gave him his first major success, as well as the award of a government pension. The existentialist *Peer Gynt* followed in 1867, and a third historical drama, *Kejser og Galilaer* ('Emperor and Galilean') in 1873. He then turned to his plays of realism and social issues, which revolutionized European drama and on which his towering reputation rests: *Samfundets støtter* (1877, 'Pillars of Society'), *En dukkehjem* (1879, 'A Doll's House'), *Gengangere* (1881, 'Ghosts'), *En folkefiende* (1882, 'An Enemy of the People'), *Vildanden* (1884, 'The Wild Duck'), *Rosmersholm* (1886), *Fruen fra havet* (1888, 'The Lady from the Sea') and *Hedda Gabler* (1890). Thereafter he returned to Norway; his last plays are characterized by a strong emphasis on symbolism, with *Bygmester Solness* (1892, 'The Master Builder'), *Lille Eyolf* (1894, 'Little Eyolf'), *John Gabriel Borkman* (1896) and *Naar vi døde vaagner* (1899, 'When We Dead Awaken'). In 1900 he suffered a stroke which ended his literary career.

▷M Meyer, *Ibsen* (3 vols, 1967–71)

IBUSE Masuji
(1898–)

Japanese writer, born in Hiroshima into a wealthy family. He moved to Tokyo to study at Waseda University and settled there. He is a writer of rich, colourful and humorous novels of ordinary life, of which *Seikatsu no Tankyu* (1937, 'Making a Living') is the most popular in Japan. His reputation in the West, however, rests on his *Kuroi Ame* (1966, 'Black Rain'), an uncharacteristically dark work about the atomic bomb dropped on his home town.

IBYCUS
(fl.mid 6th century BC)

Greek poet from Rhegium in Italy. He lived at the court of Polycrates, tyrant of Samos, and wrote choral lyrics in Doric anticipating **Pindar**. Legend has it that he was slain by robbers near Corinth, and as he was dying he called upon a flock of cranes to avenge him. The cranes then hovered over the theatre at Corinth, and one of the murderers exclaimed, 'Behold the avengers of Ibycus!' This led to their conviction. The story is told in **Schiller**'s ballad.

▷M Noethiger, *Die Sprache des Stresichorus und des Ibycus* (1971)

ICAZA, Jorge
(1906–78)

Ecuadorean novelist, born in Quito. Icaza was his country's most important *indigenista* novelist, and, although his most important book, *Huasipungo* (1934, Eng trans *The Villagers*, 1964), one of the most brutal novels ever written, is not as subtle or profound in its depiction of Native Americans as are the novels of Icaza's Peruvian contemporary **José**

María Arguedas, it is epoch-making in its context. Icaza began as a playwright and denouncer of abuses. Then, with the collection of stories, *Barro de la sierra* (1933, 'Mountain Clay'), Icaza began his ruthless examination of the injustices of the *latifundio* system of great landed estates. *Huasipungo* (it means 'inherited land') is rather more an indictment of governmental injustice than a convincing portrait of Native Americans, but the frequent dismissal of it on account of its too 'brutal realism' can only raise questions about the critic's own attitude, for Icaza's protest, though exaggerated, is vivid and truthful enough to transcend political questions—whatever the stature of his artistry. *En las calles* (1935, 'In the Streets') *Huasipungo*'s successor, a satirical novel, is less effective. But later works, such as the scarifying picture of city life *El chulla Romero y Flores* (1958, 'The Upstart Romero y Flores') and the trilogy *Los atrapados* (1972, 'The Trapped'), continuing Icaza's almost uniquely brutalist exploration of racial prejudice, add to his achievement. The view that Icaza's 'totally black and bleak portrayal of human brutishness fails to convince' is, paradoxically, challenged by the same critic's concession that he 'moves us by his conviction'. Director of the National Library, he is still regarded by many as Ecuador's greatest novelist—but he is far surpassed in artistry by **Aguilera Malta**.

▷J R Spell, *Contemporary Spanish American Fiction* (1944)

IDRIESS, Ion Llewellyn
(1889–1979)

Australian author, born in Waverley, Sydney. After a wandering life as opal miner, rabbit exterminator and crocodile hunter, he served with the Australian Imperial Forces at Gallipoli and in the Near East. He then travelled widely throughout Australia and in the Pacific Islands, episodes that were to provide colour for his books, such as *Madman's Island* (1927), which was based on his own experiences while marooned. His first success was *Lasseter's Last Ride* (1931), the story of the search for a legendary lost gold reef. In the next 40 years Idriess wrote a book almost every year, of which the best known are *Flynn of the Inland* (1932), about Rev John Flynn, founder of Australia's Flying Doctor Service; *The Desert Column* (1932), based on his service with the Australian Light Horse during World War I; *The Cattle King* (1936); and *The Red Chief* (1953). His earlier experiences resulted in his being commissioned to write six 'survival' guides for the Australian Army during World War II.

▷ *The Silver City* (1957)

IDRIS, Yusuf
(1927–91)

Egypt's outstanding modern short-story writer, also a novelist and playwright, born in al-Bayrum in the Nile delta. He qualified as a doctor and became a medical inspector in 1951. He began publishing short fiction as a result of his urge to portray the poor of Cairo and the shocking conditions in which they lived. He was often imprisoned. Later he turned to journalism and to surrealistic fiction and drama. His most successful play is *Al-farafir* (1964, Eng trans *Flipflap and his Master*, 1977); but he is most valued for his stories, some of which may be found in *In the Eye of the Beholder: Tales from Egyptian Life* (1978) and in *The Cheapest Nights* (1978).
▷J Beyerl, *The Style of the Modern Arabic Short Story* (1971); M Mikhail, *Images of Arab Women* (1979)

IGLÉSIES, Ignasi
(1871–1928)

Catalan dramatist, known as the '*poeta dels humils*' ('poet of the humble'), born in San Andrés de Palomar. His plays, influenced by **Ibsen**, dealt almost exclusively with the cruel lot of working people, such as his own parents. Of these, *Els Vells* (1903, 'The Old People'), was perhaps the most affecting and well made. A critic has suggested that he is 'a first-rate topical dramatist, an acute social commentator' but consequently has little to offer 'except to his own age'.
▷R Tacis y Marca, *La literatura catalana moderna* (1937)

IGNATOW, David
(1914–)

American poet, born in Brooklyn, New York. After working at various jobs, including salesman and newspaper man, he turned to academia, and is now Professor Emeritus at York College, City University of New York. He published his first collection, *Poems*, in 1948. His recurring theme of the relation of man to his political and natural environment is expressed in lyrical, often brief poems in such works as *Facing the Tree: New Poems* (1975) and *Whisper to the Earth* (1981). His *New and Collected Poems 1970–1985* appeared in 1987. Ignatow writes from personal experience—so much so that some critics have observed that his poetry represents the transformation of autobiography into art.
▷ *The One in the Many* (1989)

IHIMAERA, Witi Tame
(1944–)

New Zealand author, born in Gisborne, who, with his collection of short stories *Pounamu, Pounamu* (1972), became the first published Maori writer in English. Other collections followed: *The New Net Goes Fishing* (1977) and *Dear Miss Mansfield: A Tribute to Kathleen Mansfield Beauchamp* (1989). In the first two, he alludes to the Paheka (white settler) fantasy *The Wizard of Oz* in his exploration of Maori identity. In his epic novel *The Matriarch* (1986) he attempts, through the life of his hero Te Kooti, to reconstruct world and New Zealand history in terms of Maori legend. With Don Long he edited *Into the World of Light* (1982), an important anthology of Maori writing. He was for some years a diplomat with the New Zealand Department of Foreign Affairs.

ILF, Ilya, pseud of Ilya Arnoldovich Faynzilberg
(1897–1937)
PETROV, Yevgeny, pseud of Yevgeny Petrov Katayev
(1903–42)

Russian satirists and comic writers. All their important writing was done in collaboration. Ilf was the son of a bank clerk, and was originally a graduate of an Odessa technical college. Petrov was the younger brother of **Valentin Katayev**, who first suggested the famous collaboration. Previous to this, both had worked as journalists on various papers, and Petrov had even been a policeman. Their account of a search for a chair in which diamonds are secreted, *Dvenadstat stulyev* (1928, Eng trans *Diamonds to Sit On*, 1930, *The Twelve Chairs*, 1961), has become a comic classic not only in Russian but also all over the world. The anti-hero, Ostap Bender, is one of the greatest—and most lovable—confidence-men in world literature. Through him the authors criticized the bureaucratic and other ridiculous aspects of the Soviet system as it was then being applied; but it reads as well today as it did then, because it mercilessly satirizes not just communism but every politician's 'plan for humanity'. Bender was murdered in *The Twelve Chairs*, but he proved so popular that he had to be resurrected in *Zolotoy telyonok* (1931, Eng trans *Little Golden Calf*, 1932, *The Golden Calf*, 1962), a less effective novel because here the two writers pursued a more obviously Marxist line—in the interval between the two books Soviet cultural policy had hardened. Thus, their third book, *Odnoetazhnaya Amerika* (1936, Eng trans *Little Golden America*, 1937), though an amusing satire, is far behind the first two. Ilf died in 1937, a victim of tuberculosis. Petrov was killed in World War II, while serving as a correspondent for *Pravda*. They wrote much else beside their three novels, mostly story-cycles, and this is collected in the five volumes of their *Sobraniye sochninenii* (1961, 'Collected Works').

ILIĆ, Vojislav
(1860–94)

Serbian poet and dramatist, born in Belgrade. His straightforwardly lyrical poetry was widely influential in a period when poetry was going through some artifice, resulting in much of what has been called 'versified prose'. His epic and narratives are less impressive.
▷M Pavic, *Vojislav Ilić* (1963, in Serbian)

ILLYÉS, Gyula
(1902–83)

Hungarian novelist, essayist, critic, memoirist, for long regarded as his country's finest poet. His main inspiration came from his peasant origins and from his long sojourn in Paris as a student, when he made friends with **André Malraux** and briefly flirted with Surrealism. His book *Puszták népe* (1936, Eng trans *People of the Puszta*, 1967), an account of the atrocious conditions on the manorial estate upon which he was born (the son of a mechanic), awakened the conscience of the Hungarian people to the semi-feudal conditions in which they lived. He became a member of parliament in 1945, but later defied the communist government, and was even for a time silenced by it—and 'investigated' by its 'cultural' secret police. The historical plays of his final years dealt in impressive fashion with the complex and unconquerable notion of freedom. His *Once Upon a Time: Forty Hungarian Folktales* was published in England in 1964; a *Selected Poems* appeared in English in 1971.
▷T Kabdebo and P Tabori, *Tribute to Gyula Illyés* (1968)

IMMERMANN, Karl Leberecht
(1796–1840)

German dramatist and novelist, born in Magdeburg. In 1817 he entered the public service of Prussia, and served in Münster, Magdeburg and Düsseldorf. His fame rests upon his tales (*Miscellen*, 1830) and the satirical novels *Die Epigonen* (1836, 'Those who Follow After') and *Münchhausen* (1839). He also wrote plays, poetry, and autobiographical works.
▷B V Wiese, *Karl Immermann* (1969)

INCHBALD, Elizabeth, née Simpson
(1753–1821)

English novelist, playwright and actress, born in Bury St Edmunds, the daughter of a farmer. She ran away to go on the stage and in 1772 married John Inchbald, an actor in London. She made her debut at Bristol as Cordelia. After the death of her husband in 1779 she appeared at Covent Garden, but from 1789 made her name as a playwright and author of 19 sentimental comedies, including *The Wedding Day* (1794) and *Lover's Vows* (1798), the play which the Bertram children are acting in a famous scene in **Austen**'s *Mansfield Park*. She also wrote the novels *A Simple Story* (1791) and *Nature and Art* (1796). She was editor of the 24-volume *The British Theatre* (1806–9).

INGAMELLS, Rex, properly Reginald Charles
(1913–55)

Australian poet, born in Ororoo, South Australia. He was founder of the nationalistic 'Jindyworobak Club', a frustrated attempt in the late 1930s to graft a characteristically 'Australian' school of poetry on to the dying trunk of colonist writing. It did not survive the impact of World War II and the flood of writing from the USA and other cultures. Ingamells compiled a 'history' of the movement, *Jindyworobak Review 1938–48*, and a survey of its writings *The Jindyworobaks* appeared in 1979. Ingamells's own verse first appeared in *Gumtops* (1935) and *Forgotten People* (1936), followed by four other books and the epic *The Great South Land* (1951). He edited an anthology for schools, *New Song in an Old Land: Australian Verse* (1944), and the best of his own work was published as *Selected Poems* in the same year.

INGE, William Motter
(1913–73)

American playwright and novelist, born in Independence, Kansas. He was educated at Kansas University and George Peabody College for Teachers, and taught and wrote art criticism for the St Louis *Star-Times*. Outside the mainstream of American theatre, he is nevertheless important for four plays—*Come Back, Little Sheba* (1950), *Picnic* (1953), *Bus Stop* (1955) and *The Dark at the Top of the Stairs* (first produced in 1947 and revised in 1957)—in which he transforms the lives of drab people living in drab surroundings into significant dramas of human experience. He was awarded the Pulitzer Prize in 1953.
▷R B Schuman, *William Inge* (1965)

INGELOW, Jean
(1820–97)

English poet and novelist, born in Boston, Lincolnshire. She wrote devotional poetry, lyrics and ballads, of which the short poem 'High Tide on the Coast of Lincolnshire 1571', published in *Poems* (1863), is her best. Other well-known poems include 'Divided' and 'A Story of Doom' (1867). Her tales for children include *Mopsa the Fairy* (1869), and her adult novels were *Off the Skelligs* (1872),

Fated to be Free (1875) and *Sarah de Beranger* (1879).

▷ *Some Recollections of Jean Ingelow* (1972)

INGEMANN, Bernhard Severin
(1789–1862)

Danish poet and novelist, born in Thorkildstrup in Falster. He is best known for his idealized romantic historical novels *Valdemar Sejer* (1826), *Kong Erik* (1833) and *Prins Otto af Danmark* (1835), and historical poems *Waldemar the Great* (1824), *Queen Margaret* (1836) and *Holger Danske* (1837). From 1822 he lectured at the Royal Academy of Sorø, near Copenhagen and was headmaster from 1842 to 1849.

▷ C Langballe, *Bernhard Severin Ingemann* (1949)

INGRAHAM, Joseph Holt
(1809–60)

American novelist and clergyman, born in Portland, Maine. He was for some time a sailor, and then taught languages at a college in Mississippi. He published some sensational romances, such as *Pirate of the Gulf* (1836) and *Scarlet Feather* (1845); but after he was ordained to the Episcopal priesthood (1852) he wrote religious romances such as *The Prince of the House of David* (1855).

INGRAHAM, Prentiss
(1843–1904)

American soldier of fortune and novelist, son of **Joseph Holt Ingraham**. He served in Mexico, Austria, Africa and Cuba before settling in New York and writing some 700 'dime novels', many with Buffalo Bill (William Cody) as the hero. He also wrote plays, short stories and poems.

INGRAM, Anne, Viscountess Irwin, née Howard
(c.1695–1764)

English poet, daughter of the Earl of Carlisle, she grew up at Castle Howard, Yorkshire. Her first husband Richard Ingram, Viscount Irwin, died in 1721; she was married again in 1737 to Col William Douglas (d.1748). She was appointed to the Princess of Wales's court, and was familiar with leading figures in literary circles, including **Pope**, **Lady Mary Wortley Montagu** and **Horace Walpole**. She published *Castle Howard* (1732), a descriptive poem, but is better known for *An Epistle to Mr Pope* (1736), a good-humoured retort to his misogynistic *Characters of Women*. Her lively letters recording her travels abroad, life in court and city, and reflections on literature remain mostly unprinted.

▷ R Lonsdale (ed), *Eighteenth-Century Women Poets* (1989)

INNES, Michael *see* STEWART, JIM

INNES, Ralph Hammond *see* HAMMOND INNES, Ralph

IONESCO, Eugène
(1912–94)

Romanian-born French playwright, educated at Bucharest and Paris, where he settled in 1940. He pioneered a new style of drama with his short surrealistic plays, including *La Cantatrice chauve* (1950, Eng trans *The Bald Soprano*, 1956), *La Leçon* (1951, Eng trans *The Lesson*, 1958), *Les Chaises* (1952, Eng trans *The Chairs*, 1957), *Amédée* (1954, Eng trans *Amedee*, 1955), *Victimes du devoir* (1953, Eng trans *Victims of Duty*, 1958), *Le Tableau* (1955, Eng trans *The Picture*, 1968) and *Rhinocéros* (1959, Eng trans *Rhinoceros*, 1960), based on the highly personal material of his dreams, hidden desires and inner conflicts, on the **Freud**ian assumption that humanity has a dream-world in common. His contempt for realism, the robot-like deficiencies of his characters, the suggestive irrationality of their outpourings, his paradoxical view that art is the attempt to communicate an incommunicable reality, have led to criticism by disciples of social realism. His later plays include *Jeux de Massacre* (1970, Eng trans *Wipe-Out Game*, 1971), *Macbett* (1972, Eng trans 1973) and *Voyages chez les Morts ou Thème et Variations* (1980, Eng trans *Journey Among the Dead*, 1983); among many essays and other writings, he wrote the novel *Le Solitaire* (1973, Eng trans *The Hermit*, 1974 (US); 1975 (UK)).

▷ R Hayman, *Ionesco* (1972); A Lewis, *Ionesco* (1972)

IRELAND, David
(1927–)

Australian novelist, born in Lakemba, Sydney, whose work combines elements of Surrealism, anarchy, nihilism and whimsy. His first book was *The Chantic Bird* (1968), followed by *The Unknown Industrial Prisoner* (1971). His most recent was *Bloodfather* (1987) which, in its hero's turning from printing to writing, suggests elements of autobiography. The slight *Archimedes and the Seagle* (1984), in which the narrator is Archimedes, a setter or 'dogperson', is perhaps the most accessible of his writing.

IRELAND, Kevin Jowsey
(1933–)

New Zealand poet, born in Auckland. His taut, traditional verse first appeared as *Face to Face* (1963), *Educating the Body* (1967) and *A Letter from Amsterdam* (1972). He sends up his own style in *Literary Cartoons* (1977) and marked his return home from many years in England and Ireland with *The Year of the Comet: Twenty-Six 1988 Sonnets* (1987) and *Tiberius at the Beehive* (1990).

IRIARTE Y OROPESA, Tomas de
(1750–91)

Spanish poet, writer of fables, born in Orotava, Tenerife. He was the author of *Fábulas Literarias* (1782), in which a number of animals are made to speak out against the author's literary enemies; he was also a translator of **Horace**. He loved music, and wrote a long poem on the subject, as well as a poetic tribute to Haydn.
▷R Cox, *Tomas de Iriarte* (1972)

IRVING, John Winslow
(1942–)

American novelist, born and educated in Exeter, New Hampshire, and subsequently at the universities of Pittsburgh, Vienna, New Hampshire and Iowa. His early novels, *Setting Free the Bears* (1969), *The Water-Method Man* (1972) and *The 158-Pound Marriage* (1974), established a quirky style marked by recurrent obsessions—Vienna, animals, wrestling, psychoanalysis, and bizarre relationships—but failed to achieve popular success. This changed with *The World According to Garp* (1978), a modern fairy tale about an illegitimate child, which swings between innocent affirmation and sexual violence and mutilation, and between great narrative simplicity and intertextual literariness. A huge success, it was made into a Hollywood film. This propelled Irving out of academic life into full-time fiction writing. *The Hotel New Hampshire* (1981) was also bought for the movies, but it read like a reworking of the earlier books. Its successor, *The Cider House Rules* (1985), though unmistakably from the same source, was more humane and socially engaged. In 1989 he published *A Prayer for Owen Meany*.
▷G Miller, *John Irving* (1982)

IRVING, Washington
(1783–1859)

American writer, born in New York, the son of a prosperous hardware merchant. He studied law, but on account of his delicate health was sent in 1804 to Europe. He visited Rome, Paris, the Netherlands and London, and in 1806 returned to New York, and was admitted to the Bar. His first publication was *Salmagundi* (1808), a series of satirical essays in semi-monthly sheet in imitation of the *Spectator*, which ran for 20 issues. His first characteristically boisterous work was *A History of New York, by Diedrich Knickerbocker* (1809), a good-natured burlesque upon the old Dutch settlers of Manhattan Island. He served as an officer in the 1812 war, wrote biographies of American naval heroes, became a friend of Sir **Walter Scott** and under the pseudonym 'Geoffrey Crayon' wrote *The Sketch Book* (1819–20), a miscellany, containing such items as 'Rip Van Winkle', 'The Legend of Sleepy Hollow' and 'Westminster Abbey', which have something of his sadness at the loss of his betrothed and his brothers' fortune. Another sketch book, *Bracebridge Hall* (1822), was followed after three years' travel in France and Germany by another miscellany, *Tales of a Traveller* (1824). His stay in Spain (1826–9) produced such studies as *The History of the Life and Voyages of Christopher Columbus* (1828), *A Chronicle of the Conquest of Granada* (1829) and *Voyages of the Companions of Columbus* (1831). After leaving Spain, he was for a short time secretary to the United States Legation in London. On his return to his native city (1832) he was welcomed enthusiastically, but the criticisms by **James Fenimore Cooper** and others that he had written only about Europe resulted in *A Tour on the Prairie* (1835) and *The Adventures of Captain Bonneville, USA* (1837). He reached the height of his career when he was appointed US ambassador to Spain (1842–6).
▷S T Williams, *The Life of Irving* (1935)

IRZYKOWSKI, Karol
(1873–1944)

Polish novelist and critic. He is most celebrated for his single novel, *Paluba* (1903), which may be translated as 'The Old Bitch', although it means much more than that in the book, which is a kind of search for the full meaning of the term. It is an account of 'life's bashful moments' and is often said to have anticipated **Freud**. But at least one critic believes this to be impossible (*The Interpretation of Dreams* was published in 1900). However, *Paluba* does anticipate **Proust** and many other modernist writers, and is one of the most startling novels in a literature of many startling novels. Irzykowski died of wounds he received in the Warsaw rising. That he is not internationally known, and more widely translated, has been described as 'scandalous'.
▷*Slavonic and East European Review*, 29 (1951)

ISAACS, Jorge
(1837–95)

Colombian novelist and poet, born in Cali in Antioquia to an English Jewish father and a Spanish mother. He is most famous for his novel *Maria* (1867, Eng trans 1890). A journalist and diplomat, Isaacs' chief work, regarded (perhaps a little facilely) as the finest

Latin-American romantic novel, is a story, set in the Cauca valley in Antioquia, of the love between a doomed foster-child and the son of the house. Its merits lie less in its story, however, than in the descriptions of the countryside. Isaacs, who took part in the civil war of 1876 on the liberal side, was mainly influenced by French models, and his *Poesias* (1864) suffer from his over-dependence on **Lamartine**. *María* is still widely read.

ISHERWOOD, Christopher William Bradshaw
(1904–86)

English-born American novelist, born in Disley, Cheshire. He was educated at Repton and Corpus Christi College, Cambridge, studied medicine at King's College, London (1928–9), but gave it up to teach English in Germany (1930–3). His first two novels were *All the Conspirators* (1928) and *The Memorial* (1932). His best-known works, *Mr Norris Changes Trains* (1935) and *Goodbye to Berlin* (1939), were based on his experiences in the decadence of post-slump, pre-Hitler Berlin. In collaboration with **W H Auden**, a school friend, he wrote three prose-verse plays with political overtones in which by expressionist technique, music hall parody and ample symbolism, the unsavoury social climate was forcefully exposed against idealist remedies: *The Dog beneath the Skin* (1935), *The Ascent of F6* (1937) and *On the Frontier* (1938). He travelled in China with Auden in 1938 and wrote *Journey to a War* (1939). In 1939 he emigrated to California to work as scriptwriter for Metro-Goldwyn-Mayer and in 1946 took American citizenship. He translated the Hindu epic poem, the *Bhagavad-Gita*, with Swami Prabhavananda (1944), who also collaborated in *Shan-Kara's Crest-Jewel of Discrimination* (1947) and *How to Know God; the Yogi Aphorisms of Patanjali* (1953). The Broadway hit *I am a Camera*, and the musical *Cabaret*, were based on his earlier Berlin stories, especially *Sally Bowles* (1937). He also translated **Baudelaire**'s *Intimate Journals* (1947). Later novels include *Prater Violet* (1945), *The World in the Evening* (1954) and *Meeting by the River* (1967). He has also written several autobiographical books, and the semi-autobiographical *Lions and Shadows* (1938).
▷ *Christopher and His Kind* (1963)

ISHIGURO, Kazuo
(1954–)

Japanese-born British novelist. Originally from Nagasaki, he settled in Britain and came to notice as a student on the influential creative-writing course at the University of East Anglia. After working as a community worker in Glasgow in the late 1970s (and,

more incidentally, as a grouse beater for the Queen Mother, an experience which may have fostered his later interest in the English ruling class), he published the delicate *A Pale View of Hill* (1982), which represented a highly personal approach to modern Japanese history and society. *An Artist of the Floating World* (1988) was much more mannered, and so too, in the most positive sense, was *Remains of the Day* (1989), which shifted the setting to England for the first time. An elegiac study of a vanishing class told through the eyes of a butler, it won Ishiguro the Booker Prize and has subsequently been filmed.

ISHIKAWA Takuboku
(1886–1912)

Japanese poet, born in Iwate in the northeast of Japan, into the family of a Zen priest. He worked as a teacher and an itinerant newspaper vendor before moving to Tokyo to follow his enthusiasm for poetry, becoming the most influential poet of his day, though not commercially successful. His ascetic, disciplined, Buddhist upbringing manifested itself in his maturity in a leftish, liberal cast of mind, and occasional flirtations with anarchism. He rejected the then predominant literary theory known as Japanese naturalism, being more interested in the ideas coming out of the turmoil following the Russian revolution of 1905, as can be seen in his collections *Ichiakuno una* (1910, 'Handful of Sand') and *Kuu beshiki* (1909, 'Poems to Eat'). After a life of poverty, he died of tuberculosis at the age of 26.
▷ Y Hijiya, *Ishikawa Takuboku* (1979)

ISLA, José Francisco de
(1703–81)

Spanish satirist, born in Vidanes, northwest Spain. After joining the Jesuits, for some years he lectured on philosophy and theology in Segovia, Santiago and Pamplona, and became famous as a preacher, but still more as a humorist and satirist by his writings, especially his novel of *Fray Gerundio* (1758–70, 'Friar Gerundio'). The *Cartas de Juan de la Encina* (1732, 'Juan de la Encina's Letters') are a good example of his style. A more characteristic one is the *Dia Grande de Navarra* ('The Great Day of Navarre'). What **Cervantes** had done with the sham chivalry and sentiment of the romances, Isla strove to do in *Fray Gerundio* with the vulgar buffooneries of the popular preachers, and especially the preaching friars of the day. It was well received by all except the friars, but the Inquisition stopped the publication of the book. In 1767 he shared the fate of the Jesuits in their expulsion from Spain, and went to Bologna. He translated **Alain Le Sage**'s *Gil Blas*, which he humorously claimed to have restored to its native language.

ISLAM, Kazi Nazrul
(1899–1976)

Bengali poet, hailed as the 'Rebel Poet of Bengal' and later as the 'National Poet of Bangladesh', born into extreme poverty in the West Bengali village of Churulia. He rose to fame in the 1920s as a poet and leader of the anti-British movement in India with his poem *The Rebel*, which brought him overnight fame. He published a bi-monthly radical magazine, *Dhumketu* ('The Comet') which was virulently revolutionary and anti-British in tone, and spent 40 days on hunger-strike in jail. In the 1930s he concentrated more on composing music and songs—over 4000 songs and lyrics in all— and made a huge name also as an actor and radio personality. In 1942 he contracted a brain disease that left him bereft of his faculties, including his speech; after Partition, which he had always opposed, he lived in penury until he was brought home in honour to the newly independent state of Bangladesh and installed as the national poet. A Muslim, he married a Hindu and was a lifelong advocate of Muslim–Hindu unity; he wrote more than 500 devotional Hindu songs.

ITAPARICA, Frei Manuel de Santa María
(1704–c.1770)

Brazilian Franciscan monk and minor poet, born in Bahia. He published his poems in Lisbon in 1769; the 'Descrição' ('Description') is a poem about the Brazilian landscape based on classical modes.

IVANISEVÍC, Drago
(1907–)

Croatian poet, translator, critic and dramatist, born in Trieste. After World War II he became drama director of the Croatian National Theatre. His poetry, his main sphere of activity, is modernistic, hermetic and owes its greatest debt to French Surrealism. Many believe that his finest collection is *Jubav*, which contains lyrics in the dialect of his home town in Dalmatia, Split.

IVANOV, Georgy
(1894–1958)

Russian poet and novelist from Kovno, who began as an associate of **Gumilev** and the Acmeist group of poets, of which he was but a minor member; he also owed much, and most fruitfully, to **Kuzmin**. Later, in exile in France, he produced more mature, chiselled, almost always 'chillingly pessimistic' poetry, and he came to be regarded as the major poet of the emigration. His prose includes the fascinating memoirs *Peterburgsiye zimy* (1928, 'Petersburg Winters').

IVANOV, Vsevolod Vyachislavovich
(1895–1963)

Russian fiction writer, born in Semipalatinsk in Siberia. He fought for both sides in the Russian Civil War, but latterly for the Reds. He was one of the foremost members of the Serapion Brothers, a 'fellow travelling' group which aims, with varying degrees of determination, to maintain the autonomy of art from politics. His realistic *Bronepoezd 14–69* (1922, Eng trans *Armoured Train 14–69*, 1933) made him known throughout Europe. Although his other large-scale treatments of the Revolution were widely taken to be approving, they were in fact just the opposite: Ivanov despised political activism. He was unable to pursue his true vein under Stalinism, and his writing declined into a highly competent sort of modern reportage. Some critics have extolled his vivid and well-made short stories. There is a version of his early autobiography translated under the title of *I Live a Queer Life* (1936).
▷E J Brown (ed), *Major Soviet Writers* (1973)

IVANOV, Vyacheslav Ivanovich
(1866–1949)

Russian poet and critic. He studied in Berlin and lived in Greece and Italy, where he was converted to Roman Catholicism. The publication of his first poems established him as a leading figure in the Symbolist movement, but his poetry was later enriched by a powerful strain of mysticism and his philological interests, and he wrote studies on the cult of Dionysus, on **Dostoyevsky**, **Byron** and **Nietzsche**.
▷C Tschoepel, *Vyacheslav Ivanov* (1968)

IWASZKIEWICZ, Jaroslaw
(1894–1980)

Polish poet, novelist, dramatist and storywriter, born in Kalnik (near Kiev). He was one of the founders of the important Warsaw Group, the Skamander. His poems published during the 1920s attracted much attention for their expressionist fervour and descriptions of nature. His fiction is equally vital: often autobiographical, it uses techniques not unlike those of **Dos Passos**. His collection of literary essays, *Lato w Nohant* (1936), was translated as *Summer at Nohant* (1942). A prolific writer, Iwaszkiewicz was one of the most important of the 20th century.

IZUMI Kyoka
(1873–1939)

Japanese writer, born into an artisan family in Kanazawa. He set out for Tokyo in his late teens to become a novelist. This he did, becoming the finest craftsman of the Japanese language then writing. His very traditional novels are written in a beautifully refined, highly literary form of Japanese which began increasingly to be seen as archaic as his career progressed. Despite the enormous elegance and grace of works such as *Uta Andon* (1911, 'Lantern Song'), he became an anachronism as literature assimilated a growing number of non-Japanese influences and saw the need to be accessible to its readership. His work now seems the product of a far earlier age.

J

JABAVI, Noni
(1920–)

South African Xhosa writer who married an Englishman. Her father D D T Jabavi was a famous scholar, who wrote *The Influence of English on Bantu Literature*, and was a Professor at Fort Hare University. Noni's *Drawn in Colour* (1960) describes a visit to her sister in Uganda, where she lived with her husband for a time; *The Ochre People* (1963) is about a return visit to her home. The quaint English of the latter has aroused controversy: some critics think it an obstacle, others that it is 'admirably supple'.

JABRA, Jabra Ibrahim
(1919–)

Palestinian novelist, short-story writer, poet, critic and translator, born in Bethlehem and educated in Jerusalem and Cambridge, England. Since 1948 he has worked as a cultural bureaucrat in Iraq. Fluent in English, he wrote one of his novels, *Hunters in a narrow street*, in English (1960), while his translation of part of Sir James Frazer's *Golden Bough* influenced a whole school of Arab poets. His other novels, however, have been written in Arabic. His masterpiece, *Al-Safina* (1969, 'The Ship'), features intellectual and cosmopolitan Arabs on a Mediterranean cruise ship. The complex issues raised by their debates and pessimistic outcome to their journey may remind some readers of **Thomas Mann**'s *Magic Mountain*. Also important is *Al-Bahth 'an Walid Masud* (1987, 'In search of Walid Masud'), in which the mysterious disappearance of a heroic freedom fighter furnishes a pretext for a presentation of the Palestinian predicament from multiple perspectives. All Jabra's writings make great play with myth and metaphor and are heavy with reference to both eastern and western culture. Almost certainly he is the most influential of critics writing in Arabic today.

JACCOTTET, Philippe
(1925–)

Swiss-born French poet and translator, who has consistently documented his own literary and imaginative processes in published notebooks, *Carnets/La Semaison 1954–67* (1963, 1971, published in the USA as *Seedtime*, 1977), and in such books as *L'entretien des muses: Chroniques de poésie* (1968). Educated in Lausanne, he worked as a translator there from 1946, before migrating to southern France in 1953, when he published his crucial second collection, *L'Effraie*. The poems are mostly rhymed and in conventional metres that consistently suggest a plain-speaking, unliterary manner. The work of the early sixties in *Airs* (1967) is formally more varied and adventurous, and also more distanced in tone, a tendency reinforced in later volumes. Gallimard published a substantial compilation as *Poésie 1946–1967* (1971), but it was not until 1974 that **Cid Corman** completed the first substantial English translations, which were issued as *Breathings*. Jaccottet's own translations have included works by **Thomas Mann**, **Homer**, **Robert Musil**, the complete works of **Hölderlin**, the mysterious **B Traven**'s *The Death Ship* (1967), and others. He has won several awards for his work in this field, notably the Voss Prize (1966).
▷A Clerval, *Philippe Jaccottet* (1976)

JACKSON, Helen Maria
(1830–85)

American novelist, poet and writer for children, born in Amherst, Massachusetts, where she went to school with **Emily Dickinson**. Jackson's own poetry was grossly overvalued by **Emerson**, who acclaimed her as 'America's greatest woman poet'. In fact it is her two prose works championing the Native American cause which have survived best: the polemical *A Century of Dishonor* (1881) and the sentimental but highly popular novel *Ramona* (1884). Even so, it is the connection with Emily Dickinson which has done most to keep Jackson's name alive. The novel *Mercy Philbrick's Choice* (1876) is generally considered to contain a fictional portrait of her Amherst schoolfriend.
▷R Odell, *A Life* (1939)

JACKSON, Shirley
(1919–65)

American writer, born in San Francisco. A masterly storyteller who wrote in the genre of the psychological Gothic, Jackson published several novels and numerous short stories, many written for the *New Yorker* and other magazines. Her collection *The Lottery* (1949) included two of her best stories: 'The Daemon

Lover', describing the desperate loneliness of a New York woman seduced by a super-naturally elusive lover, and the title story, a bleak allegorical tale in which a remote rural community enacts its annual harvest tra-dition of selecting a human sacrifice by lottery. Perhaps Jackson's most powerful novel is *The Haunting of Hill House* (1959), depicting a woman's psyche torn by madness, guilt and fear, and told within the con-ventions of a haunted-house story; the book was filmed in 1963 as *The Haunting*. Jackson managed always to describe the bizarre as if entirely natural and everyday, a prime exam-ple being *We Have Always Lived in the Castle* (1962). In contrast, she also wrote lighter, humorous sketches of domestic life, such as *Life Among the Savages* (1953) and *Raising Demons* (1957), and several stories for chil-dren.
▷J Oppenheimer, *Private Demons: the Life of Shirley Jackson* (1988)

JACOB, Max
(1876–1944)

French 'cubist' poet, clown, mystic, novelist, critic, professional astrologer, artist, visionary and monk (he converted himself to Roman Catholicism in 1915, and his 'godfather' in this process was Picasso), born in Quimper. He was *the* pivotal avant-garde figure of the 20th century. A Jew, he died in Drancy con-centration camp. Always on the vital edge of various avant-garde movements, in essence he belonged to none; but each owed a massive debt to his example. He knew everybody of note. His greatness is contained in his con-versation (some of it recorded in L Emié's untranslated *Dialogues avec Max Jacob*, 1956) and in his letters (*Lettres*, ed S J Collier, 1966, again untranslated) and in a single col-lection of prose-poems, *Le Cornet de dés* (1917, 'The Dice Cup'). But his many mystical works, in particular *L'Homme de cristal* (1946, 'The Crystal Man'), are also seminal within their area. Available in English trans-lation are *Drawings and Poems* (1951) and *The Dice Cup: Selected Prose Poems* (1980).
▷J M Schneider, *Clown at the Altar* (1978)

JACOB, Naomi Ellington
(1884–1964)

English actress, novelist, essayist and biogra-pher, born in Ripon, Yorkshire. Her first novel, *Jacob Ussher*, appeared in 1926, fol-lowing which the enormously industrious Jacob published almost 80 books, including two on her eightieth birthday. *The Beloved Physician* (1930) examines the fraught per-sonal and professional life of a female doctor. Her most successful novel, however, was *Four*

Generations (1934), the fourth of her seven-volume 'House of Gollantz' saga, a huge nar-rative embracing many characters and several countries and a heady concoction of romance and exoticism. She also produced books of womanly advice, such as *Me—in the Kitchen* (1935) and *Me—Thinking Things Over* (1964), which are not without charm, and in 1936 published a workmanlike biography of Marie Lloyd.
▷J Norbury, *Naomi Jacob* (1965)

JACOB, Violet, née Kennedy-Erskine
(1863–1946)

Scottish poet and novelist, born in Montrose, Angus, the daughter of the laird of Dun. She married Major Arthur Otway Jacob and lived for some years in India. Although she began her writing career as a historical novelist with *The Sheep-stealers* (1902), she is best known for poems in the Angus dialect, such as *Songs of Angus* (1915), *More Songs of Angus* (1918), *Bonnie Joan* (1922) and *The Northern Lights* (1927). Her partly autobiographical *Lairds of Dun* (1931) is a standard history of her native district.

JACOBI, Johann Georg
(1740–1814)

German poet and editor (of *Iris*, which prin-ted many of the first poems of **Goethe**), bro-ther to the philosopher Friedrich Heinrich Jacobi, born in Düsseldorf. He was a pro-fessor of philosophy at Halle and then at Frei-burg. His verse, though skilful, consists in the main of 'pseudo-Anacreontic trivialities'.

JACOBS, William Wymark
(1863–1943)

English short-story writer, born in Wapping, London. He was a post-office official (1883–99) and began writing humorous yarns of bargees and tars, most of which were illus-trated by Will Owen, such as *Many Cargoes* (1896), *The Skipper's Wooing* (1897) and *Deep Waters* (1919). He also wrote macabre tales, such as his best-known story, *The Mon-key's Paw* (1902).

JACOBSEN, Jens Peter
(1847–85)

Danish novelist, born in Thisted in Jutland. He studied science at Copenhagen, translated Charles Darwin and became, under the influence of Georg Brandes, the leader of the new Danish naturalistic movement. Having contracted tuberculosis in Italy, he published some beautiful poems and short stories such as 'Mogens' (1872), and also two psycho-logical novels, *Fru Marie Grubbe* (1876) and *Niels Lyhne* (1880). Half-realist, half-drea-mer, his deliberate impressionist style found many disciples, **Rainer Rilke** among them. Jacobsen's collected works were edited by Fredrik Nielsen in the early 1970s.

▷A Gustafson, in *Six Scandinavian Novelists* (1940)

JACOBSEN, Jorgen-Frantz
(1900–38)

Faroese novelist and essayist. He was a journalist in Copenhagen for a number of years, and there contracted the tuberculosis which killed him. His posthumous novel *Barbara* (1939, Eng trans 1948) has ensured his survival. It is about an Epicurian woman of the 18th-century Faroes—a legendary figure in fact—who married two priests and refused a third.

JACOBSON, Dan
(1929–)

South African-born British novelist, long resident in London. Jacobson is a highly regarded writer who has never quite received full recognition. Earlier novels such as *The Trap* (1955) and *A Dance in the Sun* (1956) dealt with South African problems; later Jacobson expanded his range, especially in his short stories (*Through the Wilderness*, 1977, is a selection), and became a writer of exquisitely observant and objective qualities, yet one with much compassion.

▷ *Midstream* (1966)

JACOBSON, Howard
(1942–)

English novelist and travel-writer, born in Manchester. He has taught English at Cambridge University and at Wolverhampton Polytechnic, the latter providing the setting for his first, comic novel, *Coming From Behind* (1983), describing the life of a lecturer, Sefton Goldberg, obsessed by thoughts of failure. Subsequent novels—*Peeping Tom* (1984) and *The Very Model of a Man* (1992)—are a similar deft blending of vibrant satire, eroticism and literary sophistication. His travel books include *In the Land of Oz* (1987), while *Roots Schmoots* (1993), an investigation into the heritage of Jewishness and what it means to be a Jew in contemporary society, continues in documentary terms one of the recurring themes of his fiction, that of personal identity in a modern, fast-moving world.

JAHHN, Hans Henny
(1894–1959)

German novelist and dramatist who, a lifelong pacifist, devoted himself not only to writing but also to musical composition and organ-building. He was born near Hamburg,

the son of a shipbuilder. He was out of Germany for much of his life, in Norway and Denmark, but he returned for his last nine years. When **Oscar Loerke** awarded him the **Kleist** Prize in 1920 for his violent and expressionistic drama *Pastor Ephraim Magnus* (1919) there was a storm of controversy. This play depicts an unhinged parson who enshrines the headless corpse of his brother, and tears out his own eyes in the wish to be crucified. Although Jahn gradually eschewed Expressionistic techniques in favour of more conventional presentation, his subject-matter remained similar. The essence of all his work, including his celebrated (but unfinished) trilogy of novels *Fluss ohne Ufer* (1949–61, Eng trans, first volume only, *The Ship*, 1961), is the conflict between perversity and sexual terror—the influence of **Freud** was decisive—and a quasi-religious wish for harmony. Jahn, who founded his own cultural organization, never quite achieved coherence, but he remains a fascinating and, above all, powerful writer.

JAHIER, Piero
(1884–1966)

Italian poet and translator (of **Julien Green**, **Graham Greene**, **Robert Louis Stevenson**, and many others) from Genoa, a writer somewhat apart from groups and movements. His father was a protestant minister who killed himself. A railway official by profession, Piero Jahier remained aloof from fascism (being carefully watched by Mussolini's secret policemen, as an independent socialist). He was associated with the magazine *La voce*, and eventually became its director. His satirical novel *Resultanze in merito alla vita e al carattere di Gino Bianchi* (1915, 'The Outcome Concerning the Life and Character of Gino Bianchi') remains one of the most scarifying attacks on the dehumanizing effects of bureaucracy ever written. His *Con me e con gli Alpini* (1919, 'With Me and the Alpini'), a mixture of prose and verse dealing with his service with the Alpine troops, was one of Italy's most popular books of World War II. His genius may most clearly be perceived in *Ragazzo* (1919, rev edn 1939, 'Boy'), an autobiography. He anticipated the 'hermeticism' of later poets such as **Ungaretti**, but, though he contributed to many periodicals, added little of substance to his output.

▷A Testa, *Piero Jahier* (1970, in Italian)

JAIMES FREYRE, Ricardo
(1868–1933)

Bolivian poet, historian and socialist, born in Tacna. Jaimes Freyre was one of the most important in the *modernista* movement. From 1916 until 1923, and then from 1927 until his death, he lived in Argentina—but he

remained a Bolivian at heart, and served as Minister of Education and Foreign Minister (1923–7) in his country's government. He founded the *Revista de Améérica* with the key figure of the *modernista* movement, **Rubén Darío**. He held eccentric theories about rhythm, but his own technique was unerring. His famous first collection, *Castalia bárbara* (1899, 'Pagan Fountain'), is incomparably his best. Influenced in particular by **Carducci**, as well as by Spanish models and the Nordic mythology which is its subject, it conveys an icy and prophetic vision of the future, especially in 'El Canto del mal', ('Song of Evil', Eng trans in M Seymour-Smith, *Macmillan Guide to Modern World Literature*, 1986). His second collection, *Los sueños son vida* (1917, 'Dreams are Life'), shows some decline in his powers.
▷E Carilla, *Ricardo Jaimes Freyre* (1962, in Spanish)

JAKOBSDÓTTIR, Svava
(1930–)
Icelandic short-story writer, novelist and playwright. Born in Neskaupstadður, she worked as a journalist and studied in the USA and England. She became active in the Icelandic women's movement in 1970, and from 1971 to 1979 she represented the Socialist Party in the Icelandic parliament. Her first collection of short stories, *12 konur* ('12 Women'), appeared in 1965, followed in 1967 by *Veizla undir grjótvegg* ('Party beneath a Stone Wall'). Her texts, highlighting the problems of alienation in modern society and, especially, the position of women in a patriarchal system, tend to open in an atmosphere of everyday realism which alarmingly assumes Surrealist and absurd proportions. The novel *Leigjandinn* (1969, 'The Lodger') is an allegory about oppression, the central female character representing a curtailment of freedom that is not only sexual but also political and military. *Gunnlaðar saga* (1987, 'The Story of Gunnlod') is a novel making extensive use of myth as a means of illuminating the present.
▷D Kristjánsdóttir, ' "Frihed og sikkerhed er dybest set modsætninger." Introduktion til Svava Jakobsdóttirs forfatterskab', in *Litteratur og samfund*, vol 33/34 (1981)

JAKSIC, Djura
(1832–78)
Serbian poet, dramatist and story writer, born in Srpska Crnja, Banat. He took part in the 1848 revolution, tried and failed to be a painter, and then settled down to the life of schoolmaster—and perfervid, hyperbolic romantic poet; in the latter he was unhappily half-successful. Only his lyrical poetry is now of value, but this—at its best—has its rightful place in the Serbian canon.

JALAL AD-DIN RUMI, Mohammed ibn Mohammed
(1207–73)
Persian lyric poet and mystic, born in Balkh. He settled at Iconium (Konya) in 1226 and founded a sect. He wrote a lot of exquisite lyrical poetry, including a long epic on the Sufi mystical doctrine, *Masnavi y ma' navi*.
▷A L Aristah, *Rumi, the Persian, the Sufi* (1974)

JAMES, Brian, pseud of John Tierney
(1892–1972)
Australian short-story writer and novelist, born in Eurunderee, New South Wales, whose father taught **Henry Lawson** in his 'bush' school. Himself a teacher, James writes of the educational system in his two novels, *The Advancement of Spencer Button* (1950) and *Hopeton High* (1963). His short stories, much influenced by Lawson, appeared in the *Bulletin* and were collected as *First Furrow* (1944), *Cookabuddy Bridge* (1954) and *The Bunyip of Barney's Elbow* (1956). The best were selected by **Norman Lindsay** as *The Big Burn and Other Stories* (1965).

JAMES, C(yril) L(ionel) R(obert)
(1901–89)
Trinidadian writer, lecturer, political activist and cricket enthusiast, born in Tunapuna, Trinidad. He won a scholarship to Queens Royal College. An autodidact and a useful cricketer, he was urged to leave Trinidad for England by Constantine O'Leary and it was there that *The Life of Captain Cipriani* was published in 1929 at O'Leary's expense. James repaid the kindness by acting as his mentor's amanuensis for his newspaper column and five books. James's aim was the freedom of the black races through Marxism and revolution. For his political activities he was deported from the USA, while in Trinidad his former pupil, Eric Williams, the prime minister, put him under house arrest. Perhaps his most influential book was *The Black Jacobins: Toussaint L'Ouverture and the San Domingo Revolution* (1938). He wrote only one novel, *Minty Alley* (1936), a study of the relationship between education and working-class West Indians. *Beyond the Boundary* (1963) is in part autobiographical: it is a fusion of anecdote, report, analysis and comment, in which sport and politics are harmoniously and ingeniously conjugated.
▷Autobiographical account in *Radical America* (1970)

JAMES, Florence
(1902–93)

New Zealand writer, born in Gisborne, who went to Australia as a child, began a career in music but later moved to art, and then read philosophy. At Sydney University she met **Dymphna Cusack** with whom she wrote *Come In Spinner*. In 1948 this long novel won first prize in a competition in the Sydney *Daily Telegraph* which promised publication, but the strict indecency laws of Australia at that time meant that it was only issued after much debate in a bowdlerized version, edited by James, in 1951. A committed Quaker, she spent time in London's Holloway Women's Prison in the 1960s for her activities with the Campaign for Nuclear Disarmament. A close friend and supporter of **Christina Stead**, she worked in London for the publishing firm of Constables and helped publish younger Australian writers such as **Kylie Tennant**. With Cusack she also wrote a children's book, *Four Winds and a Family* (1947).

JAMES, George Payne Rainsford
(1799–1860)

English novelist, born in London. Influenced by Sir **Walter Scott** he wrote over a hundred historical romances, such as *Richelieu* (1829), *Danley* (1830), *Henry Masterton* (1832), *Arabella Stuart* (1844) and *The Cavalier* (1859). His habit of opening his novels with two horsemen was parodied by **Thackeray** in *Barbazure*, where he is characterized as 'the solitary horseman'. He served as a British Consul in Europe and America for many years.
▷ S Ellis, *The Solitary Horseman* (1927)

JAMES, Henry
(1843–1916)

American novelist, brother of **William James**, born in New York, of Irish and Scottish stock. Until his father's death he was known as Henry James, junior; his father, Henry James (1811–82), was a well-known theological writer and lecturer, and an exponent of Swedenborg and Sandemanianism. After a roving youth in America and Europe (where he met **Ivan Turgenev** and **Gustave Flaubert**), and desultory law studies at Harvard, he began in 1865 to contribute brilliant literary reviews and short stories. His work as a novelist falls into three periods. To the first, in which he is mainly concerned with the 'international situation', the impact of American life on the older European civilization, belong *Roderick Hudson* (1875), *The American* (1877), *Daisy Miller* (1879), *Washington Square* (1880), *Portrait of a Lady* (1881), *Princess Casamassima* (1886), in which he probes the shadier aspects of European political life, and finally *The Bostonians* (1886). From 1876

he made his home in England, chiefly in London and in Rye, Sussex, where he struck up an oddly contrasted friendship with the brilliant pioneer of science fiction and self-conscious reformer of mankind, **H G Wells**, a friendship which lasted until the latter's savage attack on the Jamesian ethos in the novel *Boon* (1915). His second period, devoted to purely English subjects, comprises *The Tragic Muse* (1890), *The Spoils of Poynton* (1897), *What Maisie Knew* (1897) and *The Awkward Age* (1899). James reverts to Anglo-American attitudes in his last period, which includes *The Wings of a Dove* (1902), *The Ambassadors* (1903), possibly his masterpiece, *The Golden Bowl* (1904) and two unfinished novels. Collections of his characteristic 'long short stories' include *Terminations* (1895), *The Two Magics* (1898) and *The Altar of the Dead* (1909). James is the acknowledged master of the psychological novel, which has profoundly influenced the 20th-century literary scene. Plot is sacrificed in the interests of minute delineation of character. Many seemingly insignificant incidents, however, subtly contribute allegorically or metaphorically to the author's intentions. The outbreak of World War I brought out his pro-English sympathies. He became a British subject and shortly before his death was awarded the OM. He also wrote critical studies such as *French Poets and Novelists* (1878), and the essay 'On the Art of Fiction' (1884), travel sketches such as *The American Scene* (1906) and three volumes of memoirs, *A Small Boy and Others* (1913), *Notes of a Son and a Brother* (1914) and the unfinished *The Middle Years* (1917).
▷ F O Matthiessen, *Henry James: the major phase* (1944); L Edel, *Henry James* (5 vols, 1953–72)

JAMES, M(ontague) R(hodes)
(1862–1936)

English writer of ghost stories, born in Goodnestone, Kent. Educated at Eton and Cambridge, he had a distinguished career as an archaeologist, medievalist and palaeographer, becoming Provost of King's College and then of Eton, and publishing numerous scholarly works. *Ghost Stories of an Antiquary* (1904) was followed by three more collections, all demonstrating James's technique of establishing a comfortable, everyday, contemporary setting, and then gradually introducing supernatural horror; erudite scholarly details, often invented, add an air of veracity, and evil manifestations tend to be hinted at rather than explicitly described. Among his best stories are 'Oh, Whistle, and I'll Come to You, My Lad' (1904) set, typically, in East Anglia, and 'Casting the Runes' (1911).

▷M Cox, *M. R. James: An Informal Portrait* (1983)

JAMES, P(hyliss) D(orothy)
(1920–)

English thriller writer, born in Oxford, the eldest child of an official in the Inland Revenue. She was educated at Cambridge Girls' High School. Before World War II she worked in the theatre; during the war she was a Red Cross nurse, and also worked in the Ministry of Food. Later she was employed in hospital administration before working in the home office, first in the police department, where she was involved with the forensic science service, thereafter in the criminal law department. Since 1979 she has devoted herself to writing. *Cover Her Face*, published in 1962, was her first novel, a well-crafted, but slight detective story. She has written steadily since, many of her works featuring the superior detective who is also a minor poet, Commander Adam Dalgleish; these include *A Mind to Murder* (1963), *The Black Tower* (1975) and *Death of an Expert Witness* (1977). *A Taste for Death* (1986), a macabre, elegant and substantial story, enjoyed an international vogue and was followed by *Devices and Desires* (1989). *The Skull Beneath the Skin* (1982) featured a female private detective, Cordelia Gray. One of the new 'queens of crime', she was awarded the Crime Writers Association Diamond Dagger in 1987. She was made a life peer in 1991, and became Baroness James of Holland Park.

JAMES, William
(1842–1910)

American philosopher, elder brother of **Henry James**. William James was not a creative writer, but he exercised a vast influence both on politicians (who, like Mussolini, often misunderstood him) and on writers, such as his pupil **Gertrude Stein**, who remained ever grateful to him, and, not least, on his brother. A profound thinker with an occasionally fatal gift for popularization, he was a pioneer psychologist (influencing both branches of his subject, the behaviouristic and the introspective), who transformed the complex and obscurely expressed opinions of the philosopher Charles Sanders Pierce into the popular philosophy of pragmatism (Pierce thereupon referred to his own concept as 'pragmaticism'). James and **Bergson** were responsible for the formulation of the concept of 'stream of consciousness', a term which James himself coined. In his sympathetic *Varieties of Religious Experience* (1902) he showed himself to be a master of literary style, and simultaneously encouraged his readers, in an age of painful loss of faith, not to be afraid of religious and mystical experiences; the essence of pragmatism was that things were to be judged in terms of their useful function, hence beliefs are true if and because they work, not vice versa.
▷E de Bono (ed), *The Greatest Thinkers* (1976)

JAMESON, (Margaret) Storm
(1891–1986)

English novelist, born in Whitby. Her first success was *The Lovely Ship* (1927), which was followed by more than 30 books that maintained her reputation as storyteller and stylist. These include *The Voyage Home* (1930), *The Delicate Monster* (1937), *Cloudless May* (1943), *The Black Laurel* (1948), *The Hidden River* (1955), *A Cup of Tea for Mr Thorgill* (1957), *Last Score* (1961), *The Aristide Case* (1964), *The White Crow* (1968). She also wrote poems, essays, criticism and biography, and several volumes of autobiography, including *No Time Like the Present* (1933) and *Journey from the North* (1969).
▷*The Writer's Situation* (1950)

JAMI
(1414–92)

Persian poet, born in Jam in Khorasan. Among his poems were *Yūsuf o Zalīkhā* (Eng trans *The Book of Joseph and Zuleika* by A Rogers, 1892) and *Salámán u Absál* which was translated by **Edward Fitzgerald** as *Salamán and Absál: an Allegory* (1856). He also wrote prose works.
▷E Bertel, *Jami* (1949)

JAMMES, Francis
(1868–1938)

French writer, born in Tournay in the Pyrenees. He wrote poems of nature and religion, such as *De l'angélus de l'aube à l'angélus du soir* (1898, 'Between the Morning and the Evening Angelus Bells'), *Deuil des primevères* (1901, 'Primroses in Mourning'), *Triomphe de la vie* (1904, 'The Triumph of Life') and *Géorgiques Chrétiennes* (1911–12, 'Christian Georgics'), and prose romances such as *Le Roman du lièvre* (1903, 'The Romance of the Book').
▷R Mallet, *Francis Jammes* (1961)

JANIN, Jules Gabriel
(1804–74)

French critic and novelist, born in St Etienne. He turned to journalism in his youth, and his dramatic criticisms in the *Journal des Débats* made his reputation as an opponent of Romanticism and advocate of a Classical revival. His strange and at least half-serious story *L'Âne mort et la femme guillotinée*

(1829, 'The Dead Donkey and the Guillo-tined Woman') was followed by *Barnave* (1831), half-historical novel, half polemic against the Orléans family. He also compiled a *Histoire de la littérature dramatique* (1858, 'History of Dramatic Literature').

JANOWITZ, Tama
(1957–)

American novelist and short-story writer, born in San Francisco. She made her mark with the novel *American Dad* (1981), in which a psychiatrist is overawed by his father's physical and sexual prowess. *Slaves of New York* (1986), a short-story collection, deals with the garish gallery-goers, the low-lifes and no-lifes, of modern Manhattan. *A Cannibal in Manhattan* (1987) is a subtle, blackly humorous parable which refuses to engage in overt moralizing or political point-scoring. A writer who became trendy with young readers in the late 1980s, she has the talent and the lightness of touch to avoid that generic strait-jacket.

JANSSON, Tove
(1914–)

Finland–Swedish author and artist, whose Moomintroll books for children, starting with *The Magician's Hat* (1949) and illus-trated by herself, are as much appreciated by adults. Set in the fantastic yet real world of the Moomins, the books emphasize the secur-ity of family life. They have reached an inter-national audience and she has been the recipient of many literary prizes. In later years she has written a number of books such as *Sommarboken* (1972, 'The Summer Book') for adults.
▷W G Jones, *Tove Jansson* (1984)

JAPRISOT, Sébastien, anagrammatical pseud of Jean-Baptiste Rossi
(1931–)

French novelist, born in Marseilles, and edu-cated there and at the Sorbonne. He wrote his first novel, *Les mals partis* (1948), at the age of 17 and then translated **J D Salinger**'s *The Catcher in the Rye* into French. While working in advertising, he wrote two suc-cessful crime novels, *Piège pour Cendrillon* (1962, Eng trans *Trap for Cinderella*, 1962), for which he won the Grand Prix de la Lit-térature Policière, and *Compartiment tueurs* (1962, Eng trans *The Sleeping Car Murders*, 1962); a later work, *La dame dans l'auto avec des lunettes et un fusil* (1966, Eng trans *The Lady in the Car with Glasses and a Gun*, 1966) was awarded the Prix d'Honneur. For most of the next decade, Japrisot worked in the film industry as a scriptwriter, returning to fiction in 1978 with *L'Été meurtrier* (Eng

trans *One Deadly Summer*, 1978). All of his novels have been adapted for the screen. In 1986 he published *La passion des femmes* (Eng trans *Women in Evidence*, 1986) and in 1991 *Un long dimanche de fiançailles* (Eng trans *A Very Long Engagement*, 1993), a remarkable story about a young disabled woman's quest for the truth about her fiancé, killed in odd circumstances during World War I.

JARDIEL PONCELA, Enrique
(1901–52)

Spanish dramatist and novelist, born in Madrid. Wishing to revolutionize drama and the novel, he collapsed under the weight of his own ambition. He was a humorist who made early contributions to the Theatre of the Absurd, and whose innovations in the novel have not yet been taken seriously enough. His most substantial work is the novel *La 'tournée' de Dios* (1932, 'The Tour of God').
▷D D Mackay, *Enrique Jardiel Poncela* (1974)

JARNÉS, Benjamin
(1888–1949)

Spanish novelist, biographer and critic, born in Codo, Saragossa. He was in a seminary from 1898 until 1908. He left Spain for Mex-ico at Franco's victory, but the tyranny allowed him to return to Spain to die (in Madrid) when he was infirm and could offer no threat to it. He has been called, with some justice, 'the most notable novelist of the Gen-eration of 1927', which itself was mainly one of poets (such as **Lorca**, **Alberti** and **Cernuda**). His fiction questions the nature of reality, and mocks its readers' conventional expectations at every point. His work was suppressed by Franco's censors, but there is now a new interest in it. He wrote several quizzical bio-graphies, including one (the best) of **Stefan Zweig**.
▷J S Bernstein, *Benjamin Jarnés* (1971)

JARRELL, Randall
(1914–65)

American poet and critic, born in Nashville, Tennessee. He served in the air force in World War II. He loved teaching and eschewed pres-tigious universities for unfashionable girls' colleges in the south. A potent, passionate and compassionate writer, he published sev-eral collections including *Blood for a Stranger* (1942) and *The Lost World*, published posthumously in 1966. His *Complete Poems* appeared in 1969. An uncompromising critic and merciless reviewer of bad verse, he wrote one novel, *Pictures from an Institution* (1954), an early satirical campus novel. He committed suicide, possibly as a result of his war experience.

▷K Shapiro, *Randall Jarrell* (1967)

JARRY, Alfred
(1873–1907)

French writer, born in Laval, Mayenne. He was educated at Rennes. His play, *Ubu roi* (Eng trans 1951), an attack on bourgeois conventions, was first written when he was 15; later rewritten, it was produced in 1896. In a crude parody of *Macbeth*, Ubu, the hero, symbolizes the crassness of the bourgeoisie pushed to absurd lengths by the lust for power. He wrote two sequels, *Ubu enchaîné* (1900, Eng trans *Ubu Enslaved*, 1953) and *Ubu cocu* (not published until 1944, Eng trans *Ubu Cuckolded*, 1965), and a two-act musical version of *Ubu roi* for marionettes, *Ubu sur la butte* (1901), as well as short stories and poems and other plays. He invented a logic of the absurd, which he called *pataphysique*, and his work is considered a precursor of the Theatre of the Absurd. He died an alcoholic.

▷R Shattuck, *The Banquet Years: the arts in France, 1885–1919* (1959)

JASMIN, pseud of Jacques Boé
(1798–1864)

Provençal poet, born in Agen. A barber by profession, he wrote homely verses in his local Gascon dialect. Among his best pieces (collected in *Las Papillôtos*, 1835, French trans *Las Papillôtos*, 1860) are the mock-heroic *Charivari* (1825); *L'Abuglo de Castèl-Cuillé* (1835, Eng trans by **Longfellow**, *The Blind Girl of Castel-Cuillé*); *Françovneto* (1840); and *La Semaine d'un Fils* (1848, 'A Son's Week').

▷J Andrieu, *Jasmin et son oeuvre* (1881)

JASTRUN, Mieczyslaw, pseud of
Mieczyslaw Agatstein
(1903–)

Polish poet and translator who, although he contributed poems to the publications of the inter-war *Skamander* group, never really belonged to any of the main movements in Polish poetry. Of Jewish origin, he was in considerable danger throughout World War II, during which he was a member of the resistance. He is an elegiac poet, who has learned much from **Rilke** (from whom he has made translations) and from the French symbolists. He would have liked to be a meditative poet without commitment, but history assigned him another course. Poland's most intellectual poet, devoted above all to **Cyprian Norwid**, he has long enjoyed high respect. Three poems are included in **Czeslaw Milosz**'s *Post-War Polish Poetry* (1965).

JÁUREGUI, José Martínez de
(1583–1641)

Spanish poet, painter, critic and translator, born in Seville, who settled in Madrid and was (essentially) a representative of the movement now known as *culturanismo*—a cultivation of extreme classical artificiality. Yet Jáuregui, characteristically, had earlier censured *culturanismo* as being excessively artificial. Jáuregui translated the *Aminta* of **Tasso** (1607) and imitated **Ovid** in *Orfeo* (1624). He wrote some memorable poetry, in particular in his vigorous re-creation of the *Pharsalia* of **Lucan**, (1684), which for some is an improvement on the original. Two of his poems are translated in J M Cohen's *Penguin Book of Spanish Verse* (1965).

JAURÈS, Jean
(1859–1914)

French socialist leader and political writer from Castres, who was assassinated. His anti-Marxist socialist ideas, many of them gained through Lucien Herr, librarian at the École Normale, had a profound influence on such writers as Charles Péguy and **Roger Martin Du Gard**; the latter dealt with them (and with Jaurès's assassination) in his epic novel *Les Thibault*.

JEAN BODEL
(c.1165–1210)

French poet and playwright, from Arras. Even if he is not a great poet, his work contrasts favourably with much medieval lyric poetry in being down-to-earth, set in the society he obviously lived in with relish. He was, however, forced to withdraw from society when he contracted leprosy, and produced his best-known poetical work, the *Congés*, as a farewell to his friends. He is also the author of *Le Jeu de Saint Nicholas*, the first French miracle play. Typically, much of its action is set in a tavern.

JEAN LEMAIRE DE BELGES
(1473–c.1515)

French poet and historian, born either in Bavai (then known as Belges) or in Belgium (hence the epithet) and educated at the University of Paris. His poetry is ponderous and portentous, full of allusion and often on classical themes, yet he was one of the first poets to employ such material to explore the Renaissance theme of humanism. His best work is to be found in *La Concorde des deux langages* (1511), a poetical debate on the relative merits of French and Italian.

▷P Spack, *Jean le Maire de Belges* (1926)

JEAN PAUL, pseud of Johann Paul Friedrich Richter
(1763–1825)

German novelist and humorist, born in Wunsiedel in north Bavaria. In 1781 he was sent to Leipzig to study theology, but turned to literature. He got into debt, and in 1784 fled from Leipzig, to hide in the poverty-stricken home of his widowed mother at Hof. His first literary efforts were satires which no-one would publish, until in 1783 **Johann Voss** of Berlin gave him 40 louis d'or for *Grönländische Prozesse* (1784, 'The Greenland Law-suits'). The book was a failure, and for three years Jean Paul struggled on at home. In 1787 he began to teach, and during his nine years of tutorship produced the satirical *Auswahl aus des Teufels Papieren* (1789, 'Extracts from the Devil's Papers'); the beautiful idylls *Leben des vergnügten Schulmeisterleins Maria Wuz'* (1793, 'Life of the Cheery Little Schoolteacher, Mariz Wuz), *Quintus Fixlein* (1796; trans by **Thomas Carlyle** as *Life of Quintus Fixlein*, 1827), and the *Der Jubelsenior* (1797, 'The Chairman of Revels'); grand romances, such as *Die unsichtbare Loge* (1793, 'The Invisible Lodge'), *Das Kampanertal* (1797, Eng trans *The Campaner Thal*, 1864) on the immortality of the soul; and the prose idyll, *Jean Pauls biographische Belustigungen* (1797, 'Jean Paul's Prospective Autobiographies'). *Die unsichtbare Loge* was his first literary success; but *Hesperus* (1795, Eng trans 1865) made him famous. For a few years he was the object of extravagant idolatry on the part of the women of Germany. In 1801 he married and three years later settled at Bayreuth, living there until his death. The principal works of his married life were the romances *Titan* (1800–3, Eng trans 1868), which he himself considered his masterpiece and *Flegeljahre* (1804–5, Eng trans *Walt und Vult*, 1846), *Des Feldpredigers Schmelzle Reise nach Flätz* (1809, Eng trans by Carlyle *Schmeltzle's Journey to Flätz*, 1827) and *Dr Katzenbergers Badereise* (1809, 'Dr Katzenberger's Trip to the Spa'), the best of his satirico-humorous writings; the idyll *Leben Fibels* (1812, 'Fibel's Life'); the fragment of another grand romance, *Der Komet; oder, Nikolaus Marggaf* (1820–2, 'The Comet; or, Nicholas Marggaf'); reflections on literature (*Vorschule der Ästhetik*; improved edn 1812, Eng trans *Preparatory School of Aesthetics*, 1830); another series on education (*Levana*, 1807, Eng trans 1848), a book that ranks with **Rousseau**'s *Émile*; various patriotic writings (1808–12); and an unfinished autobiography, *Wahrheit ans Jean Pauls Leben* (1826–33, 'The Truth About Jean Paul's Life'). Jean Paul stands alone in German literature. All his great qualities of imagination and intellect were made subservient to his humour, which has the widest range, moving from the petty follies of individual men and the absurdities of social custom up to the paradoxes rooted in the universe.

JEFFERIES, (John) Richard
(1848–87)

English naturalist and novelist, born near Swindon, the son of a Wiltshire farmer. He started as a provincial journalist and became known by a letter to *The Times* (1872) on the Wiltshire labourers. His first real success, *The Gamekeeper at Home* (1878), was followed by other books on rural life, including *Wild Life in a Southern County* (1879), *Hodge and his Masters* (1880), *Wood Magic* (1881), the autobiographical *Bevis: The Story of a Boy* (1882), and his last and most successful novel, *Amaryllis at the Fair* (1887). *The Story of my Heart* (1883) is a strange autobiography of inner life; *After London, or Wild England* (1885), is a curious romance of the future.
▷P E Thomas, *Richard Jefferies: his life and work* (1972)

JEFFERS, (John) Robinson
(1887–1962)

American poet and dramatist, born in Pittsburgh, whose first collection, *Flagons and Apples*, appeared in 1912. His principal themes derive from biblical stories and Greek and Roman legend, and concern the corruption of moral values and the purpose of mankind in a dark and dangerous world; they first became apparent in *Tamar and Other Poems* (1924), the title poem being based upon the Old Testament story of the rape of Tamar. In this and other works Jeffers attempted to reclaim a psychological intensity in poetic expression. Other collections include *The Women at Point Sur* (1927), *Be Angry at the Sun* (1941) and *Hungerfield and Other Poems* (1954). He also wrote a version of *Medea* (1946).

JEFFREY, William
(1896–1946)

Scottish poet, born in Kirk o' Shotts, Lanarkshire, and educated at Glasgow and Edinburgh universities. Having served in France in World War I, where he was gassed, he became a journalist for the *Glasgow Evening Times* and then the *Glasgow Herald* as theatre critic before being first published in 1921 with *Prometheus Returns and other Poems*. Scottish influences on his work include the Makars as well as border ballads; images of his native land's scenery recur in his work, as in *The Lands of Lomond* (1926), *Mountain Songs* (1928) and *The Golden Stag* (1932), though he was also capable of the very different *Fantasia in an Industrial Town* (1933). He also derives heavily from **Blake**, **Tennyson** and, more latterly, **Yeats**.

▷A Scott (ed), *Selected Poems of William Jeffrey* (1951)

JELLICOE, (Patricia) Ann
(1927–)

English dramatist and theatre director, born in Middlesborough, and the author of two important plays, *The Sport of My Mad Mother* (1956) and *The Knack* (1961). The first is an Absurdist celebration of youth and captures the wishful anarchism among the younger generation of the time. *The Knack* is less obscure, and a more successful satire of sexual conventions and expectations. During the 1970s, Jellicoe moved to Devon and has since concentrated on writing plays for amateur community productions, many intended to be acted in a promenade fashion in the open air. Plays such as *The Tide* (1980) and *The Western Women* (1984) deal with historical events, demand large casts and are notable for revealing the crucial role played by women in local affairs.

JENKINS, (John) Robin
(1912–)

Scottish novelist, born in Cambuslang, Lanarkshire, and educated at Hamilton Academy and Glasgow University. At various times an English teacher in Scotland, Afghanistan, Spain and Borneo, he has set many of his stories in these countries. A prolific writer, his works begin with *So Gaily Sings the Lark* (1950), carry on to *Willie Hogg* (1993), and fall into three main groups: those set in Scotland; those set in 'Norania', his fictional Afghanistan; and those dealing with 'Kalewentan', a far eastern sultanate. Interested in exploring human beings' moral possibilities, in those of his works set outside Scotland, such as *Dust on the Paw* (1961), he looks at the paradoxes of society's values. In his Scottish novels he concentrates on Calvinism, often dealing with characters, as in *A Would-be Saint* (1978), who are so holy that the concept of 'good' must be re-examined. His best-known novels are *The Cone-Gatherers* (1955) and *Fergus Lamont* (1979).

▷F R Hart, *The Scottish Novel* (1985)

JENNINGS, Elizabeth
(1926–)

English poet, born in Boston, Lincolnshire. A student at Oxford, she became friends with several writers who went on to form the Movement. Her early work—1953 saw the publication of her first volume, *Poems*—was confident and rational, technically tight, and displayed the influence of the Movement ethos, although she was never formally allied to that group. A nervous breakdown at the start of the 1960s appeared to rid her poetry of its repressed edge, and subsequent volumes, such as *The Mind has Mountains* (1966), are concerned far more about the emotional and spiritual life. Latterly her work has become a serene evocation of her Catholicism; *Moments of Grace* (1980) is typical in this regard. Her *Collected Poems* were published in 1967 and 1986.

JENS, Walter
(1923–)

German novelist, critic (notably of **Euripides**) and radio playwright, born in Hamburg. A well-known theological and scriptural scholar, Jens was a member of the literary circle Gruppe '47. His **Kafka**esque novel *Der Blinde* (1951) was translated as *The Blind Man* in 1954.

JENSEN, Johannes Vilhelm
(1873–1950)

Danish novelist, essayist and poet, winner of the Nobel Prize for literature, born in Farsö, Jutland, one of 10, one of whom was **Thit Jensen**. His native land and its people are described in his *Himmerlandshistorier* (1898–1910), but many of his works, such as *The Forest* and *Madama d'Ora* (1904), are based on his extensive travels in the Far East and America. In *Den Lange Rejse* (1908–22, *The Long Journey*, 1922–4) the journey traced, however, is that of man through the ages, the three constituent novels being an expression of Jensen's Darwinism. His psychological study of Kristian II of Denmark, *Kongens Fald* (1933, 'The Fall of the King'), his short prose works, *Myter* (1904–44), 14 of which were translated into English as *The Waving Rye* (1959), and his lyric poetry (1901–41), all serve to vindicate his high place in modern Scandinavian literature. He was awarded the Nobel Prize for literature in 1944.

▷E O Gelsted, *Johannes Vilhelm Jensen* (1938)

JENSEN, Thit
(1876–1957)

Danish novelist and lecturer, born in Farsø on Jutland. One of 10 sisters and brothers—one of whom was **Johannes Jensen**—she published her first novel in 1903. Early works such as *Martyrium* (1905, 'Martyrdom') and *Ørkenvandring* (1907, 'Through the Desert') are pleas for women's equality in marriage. However, her later work deals with the conflict between the demand for equality and motherhood. While the central character in *Gerd* (1918) rejects conventional feminine roles in favour of a career, the renowned MP in the sequel, *Aphrodite fra Fuur* (1925, 'Aphrodite from Fuur'), experiences a sense of fragmentation that forces her back into a more traditional existence. The theme of motherhood was subsequently explored by Jensen in a number of historical novels. Her public lectures, most famously in favour of contraception, made her a highly controversial figure.

▷L Møller Jensen, *Roser og laurbær. Om grundstrukturen i Thit Jensens kvindepolitiske forfatterskab* (1978)

JENSEN, Wilhelm
(1837–1911)

German poet and novelist, born in Heiligenhafen in north-east Holstein. He studied medicine and history at a variety of universities, and his main works, such as *Vom römischen Reich deutscher Nation* (1882, 3 vols, 'The Roman Empire of the German Nation'), are concerned with German history. In 1888 he moved to Munich where he spent most of his life. His writing includes tragedies, songs, poetry, and novels such as *Flut und Ebbe* (1877, 'Ebb and Flow') and *Aus See und Sand* (1897, 'From Sea and Sand').

▷W Birchfield, *Wilhelm Jensen als Lyriker* (1913)

JEROME, Jerome K(lapka)
(1859–1927)

English humorous writer, novelist and playwright, born in Walsall, Staffordshire, and brought up in London. Successively a clerk, schoolmaster, reporter, actor and journalist, he became joint editor of *The Idler* in 1892 and started his own twopenny weekly, *To-Day*. His magnificently ridiculous *Three Men in a Boat* (1889), the account of a boat trip up the Thames from Kingston to Oxford, established itself as a humorous classic of the whimsical. Other books include *The Idle Thoughts of an Idle Fellow* (1889), *Three Men on the Bummel* (1900), *Paul Kelver* (1902), the morality play *The Passing of the Third Floor Back* (1907), and his autobiography, *My Life and Times* (1926).

▷A Moss, *Jerome K. Jerome: his life and work* (1929)

JERROLD, Douglas William
(1803–57)

English author, dramatist and wit, born in London, the son of Samuel Jerrold, actor and manager. In 1813 he joined the navy as a midshipman, but on the close of the war he started life anew as a printer's apprentice, and in 1819 was a compositor on the *Sunday Monitor* but rose to become its dramatic critic. In 1825 he was engaged to write plays

for the Coburg Theatre, and from 1829 for the Surrey Theatre. From 1841 he was one of the original contributors to the newly-launched *Punch* magazine, writing under the pseudonym 'Q', and edited the *Illuminated Magazine* (1843–4), *Douglas Jerrold's Shilling Magazine* (1845–48) and *Douglas Jerrold's Weekly Newspaper* (1846–8). In 1852 he became Editor of *Lloyd's Weekly Newspaper*. He wrote several novels, including *The Story of a Feather* (1844), and *Cakes and Ale* (1852, essays and tales), *Punch's Letters to his Son* (1843), *Punch's Complete Letter-writer* (1845), and *Mrs Caudle's Curtain Lectures* (1846), as well as several plays, including *Black-ey'd Susan* (1829), and the comedies *The Bride of Ludgate* (1831), *The Prisoner of Ludgate* (1831), *Time Works Wonders* (1845) and *The Catspaw* (1850). *Other Times* (1868) is a selection from his political writings in *Lloyd's*. His son William Blanchard Jerrold (1826–84), succeeded his father as Editor of *Lloyd's* and also wrote novels and plays.

▷W Jerrold, *Douglas Jerrold* (1914)

JESSE, Fryn (Friniwyd Tennyson)
(1888–1958)

English novelist, dramatist and editor of several volumes of the *Notable British Trials* series, born in Chiselhurst, Kent. A great-niece of **Tennyson**, she studied painting, but during World War I took up journalism and after it served on Herbert Hoover's Relief Commission for Europe. In 1918 she married H M Harwood, the dramatist, and with him collaborated in a number of light plays and a series of war-time letters, *London Front* (1940) and *While London Burns* (1942). But she is best known for her novels set in Cornwall, such as *The White Riband* (1921), *Tom Fool* (1926) and *Moonraker* (1927), as well as *The Lacquer Lady* (1929), set in Burma and regarded by many as her best novel, and *A Pin to See a Peepshow* (1934), based on the Thompson-Bywaters murder case. She also published collected poems, *The Happy Bride* (1920), and remarkable accounts of the trials of Madeleine Smith (1927), Timothy Evans and John Christie (1958).

▷ *Sabi Pas, or I Don't Know* (1935)

JEWETT, (Theodora) Sarah Orne
(1849–1909)

American novelist, born in South Berwick, Maine. She wrote a series of sketches, *Deephaven* (1877), and a more structured fiction, *The Country of the Pointed Firs* (1896), which developed her interest in the psychology of small, out of the way places and their inhabitants. She also wrote romantic novels and stories based on the provincial life of her state, such as *A Country Doctor* (1884) and *A White Heron* (1886), and a historical

novel, *The Tory Lover* (1901). She was the first President of Vassar College (1862–4).
▷F O Matthiessen, *Sarah Orne Jewett* (1929)

JEWSBURY, Geraldine (Endsor)
(1812–80)

English novelist, born in Measham, Derbyshire, the daughter of a businessman. From 1854 she lived in Chelsea, to be near her friend Jane Welsh Carlyle. She contributed articles and reviews to various journals, and wrote six novels, including *Zoë* (1845), *The Half Sisters* (1848), *Marion Withers* (1851) and *Right or Wrong* (1859). *A Selection from the Letters of Geraldine Jewsbury to Jane Carlyle* (1892) aroused controversy over the emotional nature of their relationship.
▷S Howe, *Geraldine Jewsbury* (1935)

JHABVALA, Ruth Prawer
(1927–)

British novelist, short-story and screenplay writer, born in Cologne, Germany, of Polish parents. Her parents emigrated to Britain in 1939. She graduated from Queen Mary College, London University, married a visiting Indian architect, and lived in Delhi (1951–75). Most of her fiction relates to India, taking the viewpoint of an outsider looking in. Significant novels include *To Whom She Will Marry* (1955), *Esmond in India* (1958), *The Householder* (1960), *A Backward Place* (1963) and *Heat and Dust* (1975), which won the Booker Prize. Her short stories have been collected in several volumes. In association with film makers James Ivory and Ismail Merchant, she has written several accomplished screenplays, among them *Shakespeare Wallah* (1965), *A Room with a View* (1986) and *Howard's End* (1992).

JIMÉNEZ, Juan Ramón
(1881–1958)

Spanish lyric poet, winner of the Nobel Prize for literature. He was born in Moguer, Huelva, which he made famous by his delightful story of the young poet and his donkey, *Platero y Yo* (1914, Eng trans *Platero and I*, 1956), one of the classics of modern Spanish literature. He abandoned his law studies and settled in Madrid. His early poetry, impressionistic and rich in evocative imagery and sound, echoed that of **Paul Verlaine**. *Almas de Violeta* (1900, 'Violet Souls'), *Arias Tristes* (1903, 'Sad Arias') and *Jardines lejanos* (1905, 'Far-off Gardens') belong to this period. With *El silencio de oro* (1922, 'The Silence of Gold') there came a mood of optimism and a zest for experimentation with styles and rhythms. In 1936 he left Spain because of the Civil War and settled in Florida. In his last period he emerges as a major

poet, treating the major themes of life in novel sounds, illusions and styles in a subtly spun *vers libre*. He was awarded the Nobel Prize for literature in 1956.
▷D Fogelquist, *Jiménez* (1976)

JIRÁSEK, Alois
(1851–1930)

Czech historical novelist and dramatist, born in Hronov. Throughout his life he taught history in a Prague secondary school. He is important because his nationalist novels still reflect, to a remarkable degree, the Czechs' own view of their oppressed past. His characterization is weak, but he regarded the Czech masses as his true subject. His collected works ran to 47 volumes.
▷K Nejedlý, *Alois Jirásek* (1952)

JOCHUMSSON, Matthías
(1835–1920)

Icelandic poet and clergyman, born at Skógar in Thorskafjörður, a farmer's son. After training as a merchant in Copenhagen, he became a Lutheran pastor (1865) at various places in Iceland. Best known as a lyric poet, he drew for his inspiration on the historic traditions of the sagas and on the dramatic natural scene. He composed the words of the choral anthem written for the millennial celebrations of 1874 (*Ó, Guð vors lands*—'God of our Land') which is now the national anthem. He was regarded as unofficial poet laureate. He also wrote plays, including a historical drama about Bishop Jón Arason (1900), and translated **Byron**, **Ibsen**, and **Shakespeare**'s major tragedies.
▷D Ostlund, *70th Birthday Essays* (1905)

JODELLE, Étienne
(1532–73)

French poet and dramatist. He was the only Parisian member of the Pléiade, and he wrote the first French tragedy, *Cléopatre captive* (1552, 'Cleopatra the Prisoner'), based on classical models. He also wrote two comedies, including *Eugène*.
▷E H Balmas, *Un poeta del Rinascimento francesca* (1962)

JOHANNES SECUNDUS, Jan Everts, or Everaerts
(1511–36)

Dutch poet, writing in Latin, born in The Hague. He studied law at Bourges, and was secretary to the Archbishop of Toledo, the Bishop of Utrecht, and the Emperor Charles V. His famous work is *Basia*.

JOHANNES VON SAAZ, also known as **Johannes von Tepl**
(c.1350–1415)

German author, born in Schüttwa. He wrote *Der Ackermann aus Böhmen* (c.1400, 'The Bohemian Peasant'), a classic piece of German prose in which the author, in the character of a peasant, reproaches Death for the loss of his wife, Margarete, before the heavenly Judge, but eventually accepts that God has ordained these events.

JOHN OF HOWDEN
(d.1274)

English Latin poet and canon of Howden. An important figure in his day in many ways, he followed a career in politics which led him to court, where he became clerk to Eleanor, queen to Henry III of England. He was also a gifted astronomer and astrologer. His poems are on religious themes and employ mystical imagery. They centre mainly on the Passion of Christ and that of Mary, and they represent a growing cult of mysticism and personal devotion within the late 13th-century church.

JOHNS, W(illiam) E(arl)
(1893–1968)

English aviator and writer, author of the 'Biggles' stories, born in Hertford. He served in the Norfolk Yeomanry and when commissioned in 1916, transferred to the Royal Flying Corps where he served wtih some distinction. He retired from the Royal Air Force in 1930, edited *Popular Flying* and *Flying* in the 1930s, and served in the Ministry of Information (1939–45). His wartime marriage broke up after 1918 and he lived for many years with a lady his publishers prevented him from marrying, considering that his status as a children's author forbade his divorce. His stories are rattling good flying yarns, with his World War I experiences almost bodily transferred to later periods. In World War I he had been captured and sentenced to be shot; the 'Biggles' series reflects unspoken anger at the expendability of airmen in bureaucratic thinking, while his World War II female pilot, 'Worrals', is savagely contemptuous of male self-satisfaction and hostility to acceptance of women as equals. He later tried his hand, less successfully, at space exploration stories.
▷P B Ellis and P Williams, *The Life of Captain W. E. Johns* (1981)

JOHNSON, B(ryan) S(tanley William)
(1933–73)

English experimental novelist, born in London and briefly lionized there for having brought a Continental playfulness to contemporary fiction. His first significant book, *Travelling People* (1963), is an exhaustive illustration of **James**ian 'point of view' in fiction, and is full of typographical and other estranging devices. *Albert Angelo* (1964) was relatively conventional up to a notorious intervention—'Fuck all this lying'—by the author himself. *Trawl* (1966) carried a Wittgensteinian conceit to extraordinary lengths by having holes cut in some pages: language-as-net. Johnson's most celebrated post-modernist device was his 'loose-leaf' novel *The Unfortunates* (1969), which consisted of 27 separate sections, all but the first and last of which could be read in any order the reader chose. After this, there was nowhere to go but back towards more conventional narrative; *House Mother Normal* (1971) and *Christy Malry's Own Double-Entry* (1973) are both disappointing, though the first reflects Johnson's obsessive interest in ageing, which resulted in the posthumously published *See the Old Lady Decently* (1975), a quasi-documentary account of his mother's death. Having prepared a collection of short stories with the ironic title *Aren't You Rather Young to be Writing Your Memoirs?* (1974), and despite respectful critical and commercial attention, Johnson hanged himself in a fit of recurrent depression.
▷A Burns and C Sugnet, *The Imagination on Trial* (1976)

JOHNSON, Colin *see* **MUDROOROO, Nyoongah**

JOHNSON, Denis
(1949–)

American novelist and poet, born in Munich and brought up in Tokyo, Manila and Washington, DC. His first novel, *Angels* (1983), is a skilfully carved slice of US low life; the book's latter section, a description of a young man's days on Death Row, is particularly well wrought. *Fiskadoro* (1985), a post-holocaust tale, is a detour in Johnson's development as a novelist, but *Resuscitation of a Hanged Man* (1991), the story of a sombre failed suicide turned private investigator, marks a return to the wit and gritty realism of his debut. His volumes of poetry include *Inner Weather* (1976); he won the **Robert Frost** Poetry Prize in 1983.

JOHNSON, Diane
(1934–)

American novelist, biographer and critic, Professor of English at the University of California. Johnson was born in Illinois and several of her novels look at Californian life from a mid-West point of view. *Burning* (1971) is an apocalyptic (and prophetic) portrait of life in Los Angeles. She has produced an authorized biography of **Dashiell Hammett**, was co-author (with Stanley Kubrick) of the screenplay for **Stephen King**'s *The Shining*, and has written, in *Lesser Lives* (1972), an account of the trials of **Thomas Love Peacock**'s daughter. *Terrorists and Novelists* (1982), a collection of reviews, is further testimony to her range and energy. *Natural Opium* (1993), a travel book written on the rebound from a messy divorce, was waspish and self-critical.

▷ J Todd, *Women Writers Talking* (1983)

JOHNSON, Dorothy M(arie)
(1905–84)

American novelist, born in Iowa. She grew up in Montana. The author of two classic western stories, 'The Man Who Shot Liberty Valance' and 'A Man Called Horse' (immortalized by Richard Harris, but not published until 1984 in *The Reel West* and *The Western Hall of Fame* respectively), she was a journalist, working as a magazine editor in New York for 15 years before returning to Montana and joining the staff of a local paper. She also wrote full-length novels. *Warriors For A Lost Nation* (1969) was a biography of Sitting Bull.

JOHNSON, Eyvind Olof Verner
(1900–76)

Swedish novelist and short-story writer, joint winner of the Nobel Prize for literature, born of working-class parents in the far north of Sweden. After a number of years in mainly manual occupations he spent most of the 1920s in Paris and Berlin. His four-part *Romanen om Olof* (1934–7, 'The Story of Olof') is the finest of the many working-class autobiographical novels written in Sweden in the 1930s. He was much involved in anti-Nazi causes, and produced a number of novels, especially the *Krilon* series (1941–3), castigating totalitarianism. The same humanitarian values are evident in his later historical novels, particularly *Strändernas svall* (1946, 'Return to Ithaca'), *Drömmar om rosor och eld* (1949, 'Dreams about Roses and Fire') and *Hans nådes tid* (1960, 'The Days of his Grace'). He shared the 1974 Nobel Prize for literature with his fellow Swede, **Harry Martinson**.

▷ G Orton, *Eyvind Johnson* (1972)

JOHNSON, James Weldon
(1871–1938)

American author, born in Jacksonville, Florida. He practised at the Bar there from 1897 to 1901, and in 1906 he was American consul at Puerto Cabello, Venezuela, and at Corinto, Nicaragua (1909–12). He was secretary of the National Association for the Advancement of Colored People (1916–30) and was awarded the Spingarn Medal (1925). His finest poetry is included in *God's Trombones* (1927). From 1930 he was Professor of Creative Literature at Fisk University. He wrote extensively on Black problems, and compiled collections of Black poetry.

▷ E D Levy, *James Weldon Johnson: Black Leader, Black Voice* (1973)

JOHNSON, Josephine Winslow
(1910–)

American novelist and poet. She won a Pulitzer Prize with her first novel *Now in November* (1934), a celebration of unmechanized farming life, a subject she knew intimately, having grown up on a farm. (Johnson's husband eventually became editor of *Farm Quarterly*.) Other novels, written in a distinctively quiet but stylish manner, have sombre themes. *Wildwood* (1946) is about a frustrated and lonely young girl growing up in the oppressive home of relatives, and the main character of *The Dark Traveller* (1963) is a schizophrenic.

JOHNSON, Linton Kwesi
(1952–)

Jamaican-born reggae poet and performer, he has lived in Britain since the age of nine. He studied sociology at London University and holds a creative writing fellowship at Warwick University. His verdict on British culture was most succinctly expressed in the title of a 1980 book and recording, *Inglan is a Bitch*. He writes powerful, committed verse which follows the cadences of Caribbean speech and the alternately pointed and hypnotically elongated rhythmic values of reggae and dub. His distinctive style was immediately evident in *Voices of the Living and the Dead* (1974) and he became part of a revived poetry/performance movement in Britain, adopted by Michael Horovitz's New Departures road show and latterly by the Anti-Nazi League in its crusade against British racism. His most powerful work is the sombre rumble of *Dread Beat an' Blood* (1975), which is almost as effective on the page as it is on the Virgin Records album that followed.

JOHNSON, Lionel Pigot
(1867–1902)

English poet and critic, born in Broadstairs, Kent, but brought up in Wales. The son of an army officer, he was educated at Winchester and New College, Oxford, where he distinguished himself by the excellence of his work. After graduating, he moved to London, surrounded himself with books, and made a living in literary journalism. He converted to Roman Catholicism in 1891—thus becoming one of the most notable converts of this era—and fell under the spell of the Celtic Twilight, as *Poems* (1895) and *Ireland and Other Poems* (1897) testify. His most famous and frequently anthologized poem, however, is *By the Statue of King Charles at Charing Cross*. A member of the Rhymers' Club, and a friend of **Oscar Wilde** and **W B Yeats**, he was influential in his day and, a percipient critic, did much to promote an appreciation of **Thomas Hardy**. But he was an immoderate drinker and often appears tipsy and ridiculous in anecdotes. He died as a result of a fall caused by the effects of alcohol.

▷A W Patrick, *Lionel Johnson: poète et critique* (1939)

JOHNSON, Louis
(1924–88)

New Zealand poet and critic, whose first work was collected as *Stanza and Scene: Poems* (1945). A poet of the city, and a leading member of the 'Wellington Group', he attracted attention with his next two books, both published in 1951: *The Sun Among the Ruins* and *Roughshod Among the Lilies*. After *Bread and a Pension: Selected Poems* (1954) he moved to Australia where he published *Selected Poems* (1972) and *Fires and Patterns* (1975). Returning to New Zealand, his later work was published as *Coming and Going: Poems* (1982) and *Winter Apples* (1984). *Last Poems* was published posthumously in 1990. He was active in support of his fellow poets, founding, and for many years editing, the *New Zealand Poetry Yearbook*. He also edited a quarterly, *Numbers*, and his Capricorn Press published much work by his contemporaries.

JOHNSON, Pamela Hansford *see*
HANSFORD JOHNSON, Pamela

JOHNSON, Pauline
(1861–1913)

Canadian poet, born on the Six Nations Reservation near Ontario. Her father was a Mohawk, while her English mother was related to **William Dean Howells**. Her earliest poems were published in magazine form in 1884, and her work was collected in several volumes, including *Canadian Born* (1903) and *Flint and Feather* (1912). From 1892 to 1909 she gave extensive public readings of her work, often dressed in Native American costume and using the name Tekahionwake. She also wrote short prose works, collected in *Legends of Vancouver* (1911) and other volumes.

▷B Keller, *Pauline* (1981)

JOHNSON, Samuel, known as **Dr Johnson**
(1709–84)

English writer, critic, lexicographer, and conversationalist, born in Lichfield, Staffordshire. The son of a bookseller, he read voraciously in his father's shop. Educated at Lichfield Grammar School and Pembroke College, Oxford, he left without taking a degree in 1731. He taught briefly at a school in Market Bosworth, and then moved to Birmingham where he did some writing. In 1735 he married a widow 20 years older than himself, Elizabeth ('Tetty') Porter, and they opened a school at Edial, near Lichfield, where one of the pupils was the future actor, David Garrick. The school failed, and in 1737, accompanied by the young Garrick, Johnson and his wife moved to London, where he finished writing a tragedy, *Irene* (not to be staged for 12 years), and earned a living writing parliamentary reports for *The Gentleman's Magazine*. In it he published (anonymously) his first poem, *London: A Poem in Imitation of the Third Satire of Juvenal* (1738). In 1744 he produced a topical and successful *Life* of his friend **Richard Savage**. Meanwhile he had been cataloguing the great library of Edward Harley, Earl of Oxford, and was able further to indulge his huge appetite for reading. In 1747 he issued a prospectus of a *Dictionary of the English Language*, which was to take him eight years to complete. During this time he published a long didactic poem, *The Vanity of Human Wishes* (1749), based on another of **Juvenal**'s satires. Garrick fulfilled a boyhood promise by producing his *Irene* at Drury Lane Theatre (1749), and Johnson himself wrote and edited, practically single-handedly, a bi-weekly periodical, *The Rambler*, which ran for 208 issues (1750–2), full of moral essays written (anonymously) by himself. In 1752 his wife died, plunging him into lasting depression. His great Dictionary appeared in 1755, which gave rise to a celebrated letter in which Johnson disdained an offer of patronage from Lord Chesterfield. Johnson was awarded an honorary degree at Oxford, but he had to continue literary hack-work to earn a living, contributing reviews for the *Literary Magazine*, and *The Idler* series of papers in *The Universal Chronicle* (1758–60). During this time his mother died, and in a week he wrote his moral fable, *Rasselas: The Prince of Abyssinia* (1759), to defray the funeral expenses. With the accession of George III in 1760, Johnson was granted a pension of £300 for life, which brought him financial security for the first time. In 1763 he met the young Scot, **James Boswell**, who would become his biographer, and with whom he would share a delightful tour of the Hebrides in 1773 (*A Journey to the Western Isles of Scotland*, 1775). In 1764

he founded the Literary Club with a circle of friends, including Joshua Reynolds, **Edmund Burke** and **Oliver Goldsmith**; later members were Boswell, Garrick and Charles James Fox. In 1765 he published his critical edition of **Shakespeare**'s plays (8 vols), with its classic Preface, and then set to work on his monumental *Lives of the Most Eminent English Poets* (10 vols, 1779–81). In that year his friend, the brewer Henry Thrale, died; his widow, Hester Thrale, who had looked after Johnson for many years, fell in love with an Italian musician, Gabriele Piozzi, and Johnson's wounded fury at their marriage in 1784 provoked a total estrangement. He died in dejection, and was buried in Westminster Abbey.
▷J Boswell, *Life of Johnson* (1791, 1799); J Wain, *Samuel Johnson* (1944)

JOHNSON, Uwe
(1934–84)

German novelist, born in Pomeranian Poland and educated in Rostock and Leipzig. He belongs to the first generation of writers to experience the post-war division of Germany as a normal fact of life rather than a novelty. He rarely wrote direct political commentary, preferring to concentrate on the moral and psychological implications of division; critics expecting—or demanding—a more realistically politicized approach were themselves deeply divided over his first published novel, *Mutmassungen über Jakob* (1959, Eng trans *Speculations about Jakob*, 1963), and it may be that lack of general understanding led him to a more straightforward narrative approach in later books. *Das dritte Buch über Achim* (1961, Eng trans *The Third Book about Achim*, 1967) is fascinating as a study of the East German attitude to sport, but Johnson's philosophical agenda are somewhat downplayed. *Zwei Ansichten* (1965, Eng trans *Two Views*, 1966) is a rather banal Cold War love story, but Johnson returned to form with the huge and hugely impressive *Jahrestage: Aus dem Leben den Gesine Cresspahl* (4 vols, 1970–83, Eng trans *Anniversaries: From the Life of Gesine Cresspahl*, 1975), in which he picks up the lives of characters from his first novel and projects them back into the Nazi years and forward into post-war exile, and represents a profound essay in historical memory. Johnson was awarded the **Raabe** Prize in 1975 and the **Thomas Mann** Prize in 1978.
▷M Boulby, *Uwe Johnson* (1974)

JOHNSTON, or JONSTON, Arthur
(1587–1641)

Scottish physician, poet and humanist, born in Caskieben, Aberdeenshire. He graduated MD at Padua in 1610, and visited many academic institutions. He practised medicine in France, and his fame as a Latin poet spread across Europe. In about 1625 he was appointed physician to King Charles I. His famous translation of the Psalms of David into Latin verse was published in Aberdeen in 1637. He edited the *Deliciae Poetarum Scotorum Hujus Aevi* (1637), an anthology of Latin poetry from Scotland, to which he also contributed notable poems. In 1637 he became Rector of King's College, Aberdeen.
▷J W L Adams, in *Scottish Poetry, a critical survey* (1955, ed J Kinsley)

JOHNSTON, (William) Denis
(1901–84)

Irish playwright, born in Dublin, the son of a Protestant liberal judge. Educated at St Andrew's School, Dublin, Merchiston Castle School, Edinburgh, Cambridge and Harvard, he joined the English (1925) and Northern Ireland (1926) bars. His impressionist play, *Shadowdance*, was rejected by Lady **Gregory** for the Abbey Theatre, then retitled *The Old Lady Says 'No'*, and became a major success at the Gate Theatre in 1929, followed by a further triumph with *The Moon on the Yellow River* (1931) and several others for the next three decades. His autobiographical *Nine Rivers from Jordan* (1953) recounted his experiences as a war correspondent. His *In Search of Swift* (1959) was an impressive argument for **Jonathan Swift**'s inability to marry Esther Johnson ('Stella') having been caused by an illegitimate half-sibling relationship. He wrote a later autobiographical work, *The Brazen Head* (1977). His daughter is the novelist **Jennifer Johnston**.
▷J Ronsley, *Denis Johnston, a retrospective* (1981)

JOHNSTON, George Benson
(1913–)

Canadian poet and translator of Old Norse sagas, born in Hamilton, Ontario, known for his solemn treatments of ridiculous subject-matter. Johnston is a fine exponent of traditional verse forms. His poems are witty and concise, and he is given to the creation of comic characters with names like Miss Knit. This, coupled with the fantastic element on display in *Ark Redivivus: Selected Poems* (1981), gives him the air of a Canadian **Lear**, as in 'And often at the droop of day/When evening grumbles in/The great dufuflu has his say/Above the braffic's din.'

JOHNSTON, George Henry
(1912–70)

Australian author and journalist, born in Malvern, Victoria. After studying commercial art, he worked as a journalist and during World War II as a war correspondent, when his syndicated dispatches from New Guinea, India and Burma, Italy and the North Atlantic were read world-wide. He wrote five books on his war experiences, published between 1941 and 1944, before returning to journalism. He worked in London as European editor of the Sydney *Sun*, then made a new home in the Greek islands with his wife and fellow-author, **Charmian Clift**, with whom he wrote three novels, and who described their life in the islands in short stories and essays. Johnston wrote a number of novels including *Monsoon* (1948), *The Cyprian Woman* (1955) and *Closer to the Sun*, which won the US Literary Guild Award in 1960. As well as short stories and plays, he achieved distinction with his semi-autobiographical trilogy *My Brother Jack* (1964), *Clean Straw for Nothing* (1969) and the unfinished *A Cartload of Clay* (1971).

JOHNSTON, Jennifer Prudence
(1930–)

Irish novelist, born in Dublin, the daughter of **Denis Johnston**, and educated at Trinity College, Dublin. In such works as *The Gates* (1973) Johnston monitors the class and religious divisions in contemporary Ireland, and the slow erosion of the Irish Protestant gentry. *How Many Miles to Babylon?* (1974), in which two childhood friends from either end of the social scale are plunged into World War I, is particularly notable for its atmospheric portrayal of life in the trenches. In *Shadows on Our Skin* (1977), Joe Logan, a Londonderry Catholic youth, dreams of becoming a poet, his schoolteacher becomes engaged to a British soldier, and Joe's brother returns from England to join the Provisional IRA. Subsequent novels, including *Fool's Sanctuary* (1987), deploy similar themes.

JÓKAI, Maurus or Mór
(1825–1904)

Hungarian novelist, born in Komáróm. He was an active partisan of the Hungarian struggle in 1848. As well as dramas, humorous essays and poems, he wrote many novels and romances, including *Török világ Magyarországon* (1852, 'The Turks in Hungary'), *Egy magyar nábob* (1853, Eng trans *An Hungarian Nabob*, 1898) and its continuation *Kárpáthy Zoltán* (1854), *Az uj földesur* (1862, Eng trans *The New Landlord*, 1868), *A fekete gyemántók* (1870, Eng trans *Black Diamonds*, 1896), *A jövő század regénye* (1873, 'Romance of the Coming Century'), *Egy ember a ki mindent tud* (1875, 'The Modern Midas'), *Az élet komédiásai* (1876, 'The Comedians of Life') and *A löcsei fehér asszony* (1884, 'The White Woman of Leutschau'). He was editor of several newspapers, and conspicuous as a Liberal parliamentarian.
▷M Nágy, *Jókai* (1968)

JOLLEY, (Monica) Elizabeth
(1923–)

English-born Australian author of novels, short fiction and plays, born in Birmingham. She settled in Western Australia in 1959 and in *Five Acre Virgin* (1976) collected some of her writing between those years. It received immediate critical praise and was followed by *The Travelling Entertainer* (1979), longer pieces from the same period. Her first novel was *Palomino* (1980). *The Newspaper of Claremont Street* (1981) is the story of a small-town gossip. *Mr Scobie's Riddle* won the Melbourne *Age* Book of the Year Award in 1982. In her later books *My Father's Moon* (1989) and *Cabin Fever* (1990) she returns to her earlier years in post-war England. This partly autobiographical trilogy was completed with the elegiac *The Georges' Wife* (1993). She has also written a number of plays, mostly for radio. With her translator Françoise Cartano she won the inaugural 1993 France–Australia Award for Literary Translation for her novel *The Sugar Mother* (1988, as *Tombe du Ciel*).

JØLSEN, Ragnhild
(1875–1908)

Norwegian novelist, who studied sculpture, but also trained as a telegraphist. She was attracted to a bohemian lifestyle, and her early death appears to have been the result of an overdose. Her texts, in which folklore and dreams are prominent elements, have been described as products of the tensions between a traditional way of life on the ancient family estate and the new values prevailing in the modern industrial communities. Most notably, the fin de siècle atmosphere of her texts is coloured by a sexual outspokenness which shocked her contemporaries. In *Rikka Gan* (1904), which exploits certain features of the Gothic novel, eroticism is seen to be linked with domination and death as the heroine becomes the mistress of the new owner of Gan to preserve the farm for her family. In *Fernanda Mona* (1905), which takes as its starting-point the same setting, there are conspicuous instances of perverted sexuality. *Hollases krønike* (1906, 'The Chronicles of Hollas'), about an agricultural community, combines the everyday with the supernatural.
▷J Garton, 'Ragnhild Jølsen', in *Norwegian Women's Writing 1850–1990* (1993)

JONES, David Michael
(1895–1974)

English poet and artist, born in Kent. His father was Welsh and though he only lived

briefly in Wales he identified himself strongly with the country. After art school he served in World War I and had an abiding interest in martial matters. He became a Roman Catholic in 1921. In 1922 he met Eric Gill, the beginning of a long association. His war experience is central to *In Parenthesis* (1937), the first of his two major literary works. *The Anathemata* (1952) is likewise personal but draws heavily on his religious influences. He published a series of fragments of another large religious work as *The Sleeping Lord* (1974), but never finished it. As an artist he is less well known but his paintings, water-colours, drawings and inscriptions have a lucidity that some of his literary work lacks.
▷K Raine, *David Jones, Solitary Perfectionist* (1974)

JONES, Ebenezer
(1820–60)

English poet, born in Islington, London. He was brought up a strict Calvinist and despite long hours as a clerk completed *Studies of Sensation and Event* (1843), which were admired by **Robert Browning** and **Dante Gabriel Rossetti**. In his *Land Monopoly* (1849) he anticipated the economic theory of Henry George by 30 years.
▷T Mardy Rees, *The Neglected Poet* (1909)

JONES, Henry Arthur
(1851–1929)

English dramatist, together with **Arthur Wing Pinero** the founder of the 'realist problem' drama in Britain, born in Grandborough, Buckinghamshire. He was in business until 1878, when *Only Round the Corner* was produced at Exeter. His first great hit was a melo-drama, *The Silver King* (1882). This was followed by *Saints and Sinners* (1884), *Rebellious Susan* (1894), *The Philistines* (1895), *The Liars* (1897), *The Manoeuvres of Jane* (1898), *Mrs Dane's Defence* (1900), *Mary Goes First* (1913) and other social comedies, many of which also engaged with serious social issues. He was a highly popular writer in his own day.
▷R A Cordell, *Jones and the Modern Drama* (1932)

JONES, James
(1921–77)

American novelist, born in Robinson, Illinois, the son of a dentist. Educated at the University of Hawaii, he served in the US army as a sergeant (1939–44), boxed as a welterweight in Golden Gloves tournaments, and was awarded a Purple Heart. His wartime experience in Hawaii led to *From Here to Eternity* (1951), a classic novel dealing with the period before Pearl Harbor, for which he received a National Book Award. Later work was disappointing, with the exception of *The Thin Red Line* (1962), which was a sequel.
▷F McShane, *Into Eternity—James Jones: the life of an American writer* (1985)

JONES, LeRoi *see* BARAKA, Amiri

JONES, Marion
(1934–)

Trinidadian novelist, one of the leading woman writers of her generation. *Pan Beat* (1973), her first novel, deals impressively with several middle-class marriages in Port of Spain. *J'Ouvert Morning* (1976) is about a Port of Spain family, the Grants; it has been described as 'soap-operaish' but also as a 'riveting document of a troubled society in a state of transition'.

JONES, Thomas Gwynn
(1871–1949)

Welsh poet, translator (**Ibsen**, **Goethe**'s *Faust*, and much else), scholar, critic, novelist and playwright, born in Gwyndy Uchaf, Betwsyn-rhos, Denbighshire. An industrious and learned man, who was almost entirely self-taught, he served his apprenticeship on various newspapers. His best-known novel is *John Homer* (1923). Poetry was his chief medium of expression, and he was amongst the most skilled Welsh technicians of his day, in a field in which technical accomplishment is very high. It has been declared that the psychology of his mythological poems is 'exquisitely exacting'.
▷W B Davies, *Thomas Gwynn Jones* (1970)

JONES, Erica, née Mann
(1942–)

American novelist and poet, she was born and educated in New York City, and taught college there for several years. Thrice married and divorced, she retains the name of her second husband. Approaching Jong's fiction by way of her verse helps confirm that her novels are more serious and sombre than their soft-core eroticism and mass-market appeal initially suggest. The wry and sardonic poems in *Fruits and Vegetables* (1971) and *Half-Lives* (1973) are superficially reminiscent of **Sylvia Plath** and they clearly establish Jong's Jewish background as an essential aspect of her literary personality. In 1973, she published the massively bestselling *Fear of Flying*, which was hailed as a sort of female *Portnoy's Complaint*. The novel introduced the angst-haunted Isadora Wing, and documents her search for the guilt-free 'zipless fuck' and for a degree of self-determination in her sexuality. Isadora returns in *How to Save Your Own Life* (1977) and in *Parachutes and Kisses* (1984), in which her eternal quest is renewed. In between, Jong wrote *Fanny, Being the True History of the Adventures of Fanny Hackabout-Jones* (1980), a clever, feminist send-up of 18th-century erotic novelists like **John Cleland**. Isadora also narrates *Any Woman's Blues* (1990).

JONKER, Ingrid
(1933–65)

South African poet (writing in Afrikaans), who drowned herself as a response to the cruelty of the Apartheid policy then practised by the South African government. Her poems are moving although perhaps not in themselves enduring protests against violence and evil. There is an English translation in *Selected Poems* (1968).

JONSON, Ben (Benjamin)
(1572–1637)

English dramatist, born in Westminster, probably of Border descent. He was educated at Westminster School under Camden, to whom he paid the tribute 'Camden most reverend head to whom I owe/All that I am in arts, all that I know'. After working for a while with his stepfather, a bricklayer, he volunteered for military service in Flanders before joining Henslowe's company of players. He killed a fellow player in a duel, became a Catholic in prison, but later recanted. His *Every Man in his Humour*, with **Shakespeare** in the cast, was performed at the Curtain in 1598 to be followed not so successfully by *Every Man Out of His Humour* in 1599. The equally tiresome *Cynthia's Revels*, largely allegorical, was succeeded by *The Poetaster*, which at least was salted by a personal attack on **Thomas Dekker** and **John Marston**. He now tried Roman tragedy, but his *Sejanus* (1603) and his later venture, *Catiline* (1611), are so larded with classical references as to be merely closet plays. If he was trying to show Shakespeare how to write a Roman tragedy he failed badly, but his larger intent of discarding romantic comedy and writing realistically (though his theory of 'humours' was hardly comparable with genuine realism) helped to produce his four masterpieces—*Volpone* (1606), *The Silent Woman* (1609), *The Alchemist* (1610) and *Bartholomew Fair* (1614). *Volpone* is an unpleasant satire on senile sensuality and greedy legacy hunters. *The Silent Woman* is farcical comedy involving a heartless hoax. **Dryden** praised it for its construction, but *The Alchemist* is better with its single plot and strict adherence to the unities. *Bartholomew Fair* has indeed all the fun of the fair, enlivened by his anti-Puritan prejudices, though the plot gets lost in the motley of eccentrics. After the much poorer *The Devil is an Ass* (1616), Jonson turned

or rather returned to the masque—he had collaborated with Inigo Jones in *The Masque of Blacknesse*, 1605—and produced a number of those glittering displays down to 1625 when James VI and I's death terminated his period of Court favour. His renewed attempt to attract theatre audiences left him in the angry mood of the ode 'Come leave the loathed stage' (1632). Only his unfinished pastoral play *The Sad Shepherd* survives of his declining years. Ben attracted the learned and courtly, to several of whom his superb verse letters are addressed. His lyric genius was second only to Shakespeare's. 'Drink to me only with thine Eyes' in *Volpone* (of all places) and 'Queen and Huntress chaste and fair' and 'Slow, slow fresh Fount' in the dreary stretches of *Cynthia's Revels* are but a few of these gemlike lyrics. His *Timber; or Discoveries*, printed in the folio of 1640, prove him a considerable critic with a bent towards the neoclassicism which **Cowley** and Dryden inaugurated.

▷ D Riggs, *Ben Jonson, a life* (1989)

JÓNSSON, Bólu-Hjálmar
(1796–1875)

Icelandic folk-poet, born in Eyjafjörður. A man of fierce pride and temper, he lived on a peasant croft and struggled with poverty all his life, making a meagre living from woodcarving. He was also one of the most eloquent and natural of poets; his verses, whether railing against the church and authority or revelling in marvellous poetic imagery, circulated orally all over the country, and were only collected and published after his death.

▷ Dð Gislason, in *Lögrétta 27* (1932)

JONSTON, Arthur *see* JOHNSTON, Arthur

JORDAN, June
(1936–)

American poet, essayist, political activist and writer for children. She was born in New York City, and educated at Barnard College and the University of Chicago. After working as assistant movie producer, she became a college teacher in Connecticut and New York; she was Professor of English at the State University of New York, Stony Brook, and is now Professor of African American Studies and Women's Studies at the University of California, Berkeley. Jordan's main literary model is **Orwell**. In 1973 she published *Poem: On Moral Leadership as a Political Dilemma*, her response to Watergate. *Things That I Do in the Dark* (1977) was a selection that for the first time made clear the extent to which her militancy was not so literal and dogmatic as to leave no room for a more oblique, metaphoric vision and a chancy, experimental prosody. In 1993 she published a volume of love poetry, *Haruko*, which touched on bisexuality and feelings of loss and was remarkable for its stoically maintained pessimism. Among Jordan's works for young people are *His Own Where*— (1971) and *Kimako's Story* (1981).

JORDAN, Neil
(1950–)

Irish film-maker and writer, born in Sligo. After reading history and literature at University College, Dublin, he worked at various jobs in London before returning home and helping to form the Irish Writers Co-operative (1974). His first collection of stories, *Night in Tunisia* (1976), earned the Guardian Fiction Prize and was followed by the acclaimed novels *The Past* (1980) and *The Dreams of the Beast* (1983). Interested in exploring cinema as a visual means of story-telling, he was given the opportunity to work as a script consultant on *Excalibur* (1981). He made his directorial debut with the thriller *Angel* (1982) and has boldly emphasized the fairy-tale and fantasy elements of such challenging works as *The Company of Wolves* (1984) and *Mona Lisa* (1986). He turned his hand to comedy with *High Spirits* (1988) and *We're No Angels* (1989), but returned to serious drama with *The Crying Game* (1992).

JÖRGENSEN, Johannes
(1866–1956)

Danish novelist and poet, born in Svendborg. He lived most of his life in Italy, in Assisi, where he became a Roman Catholic (1896), but returned to Svendborg, his birth-place, shortly before his death. He published several volumes of poetry, as well as biographies of St Francis of Assisi (1907), St Catherine of Siena (1915), and St Birgitta of Sweden (1941–3), and an autobiography, *Mit livs Legende* (Legend of my Life, 1916–28).
▷W G Jones, *Johannes Jörgensen* (1969)

JOSEPH, Jenny
(1932–)

English poet, born in Birmingham and educated at Oxford University. Variously a journalist, pub landlady, lecturer and language teacher, she was first published in the 1950s by **John Lehmann**. Her first volume, *The Unlooked-for Season*, appeared in 1960, followed by *Rose in the Afternoon* (1974), *The Thinking Heart* (1978), *Beyond Descartes* (1983) and *Collected Poems* (1992). Her poems' philosophical qualities recall **R S Thomas** and their sometimes plain diction **Philip Larkin**, but they are neither so introverted nor so depressive as his work. *Persephone* (1986), an innovative mixture of

narrative prose, drama, poetry and photo-story moving between Greek legend and modern analogues, won the James Tait Black Prize.

JOSEPH, M(ichael) K(ennedy)
(1914–81)

English-born New Zealand academic, novelist and poet, born in Chingford, Essex, who wrote one of the best novels to come out of World War II in *I'll Soldier No More* (1958), which deals with the war in the West and provides a grim picture of occupied Germany after 1945. It was followed by *A Pound of Saffron* (1962), a satire of power politics in Auckland University, and by two novels of a 'possible future' in *The Hole in the Zero* (1967) and *The Time of Achamoth* (1978). He returned to wartime again in *A Soldier's Tale* (1976) and there is a posthumously published historical novel *Kaspar's Journey* (1988). He wrote two collections of verse, *Imaginary Islands* (1950) and *The Living Countries* (1959); the best were collected in *Inscription on a Paper Dart: Selected Poems 1945–72* (1974), and he published a study of **Byron** in 1964.

JOSIKA, Baron Miklós von
(1794–1865)

Hungarian novelist, who introduced the historical novel into Hungarian literature, and is sometimes referred to as the Hungarian Sir **Walter Scott**, from his adherence to the romantic tradition of that writer. He was involved in the revolution of 1848, and had to live in exile in Brussels and Dresden. His best-known novel is his first, *Abafi* (1836).
▷F Szinneyi, *Josika Niklós* (1915)

JOSIPOVICI, Gabriel David
(1940–)

English novelist, dramatist and academic, born in Nice and educated in Cairo, Gloucestershire and Oxford. In 1963 he became a lecturer at Sussex University, and was appointed Professor of English in 1984. Josipovici's fiction and drama are often described as 'experimental', but the values expressed in his major critical work *The World and the Book* (1971) suggest that playfulness is in itself the moral function of fiction. Certainly, he is little interested in conventional narrative; **Beckett**, **Pinter**, and the *nouveau roman* would seem to be his main influences. *The Inventory* (1968) established his interest in things as active, but non-human, agents in plot, and in the idea of words-as-things. This became more overt in *Words* (1971), *Migrations* (1977) and in *The Air We Breathe* (1981), which marked a widening of his vision. Josipovici's short stories and plays were first collected in the punning *Mobius the Stripper* (1974). Of his later dramatic works the radio play *Vergil Dying* (broadcast 1979, published 1981) stands out as a remarkable feat of imagination. His other critical books include *The Lessons of Modernism* (1977) and a collection of occasional pieces, *The Mirror of Criticism* (1983).

JOTUNI, Maria
(1880–1943)

Finnish novelist, story-writer and dramatist, born in Kuopio. Her first and best work consists of realistic and humorous stories; they did not get much attention in their own time, but since then have been much admired. Her plays, unpretentious and well made, were more popular and successful.

JOUBERT, Joseph
(1754–1824)

French writer and moralist, born in Montignac in Périgord. He studied and taught at the college of Toulouse. He then went to Paris, and lived through all the fever of the Revolution. In 1809 he was nominated by Napoleon to the council of the new university. His friend **François Chateaubriand** edited a small volume from his papers, and Joubert found fame with his *Pensées* (1838, 'Thoughts'), which are in the best French tradition of **La Rochefoucauld**, Pascal, **La Bruyère** and Vauvenargues.
▷I Babbitt, *Masters of Modern French Criticism* (1912)

JOUHANDEAU, Marcel
(1888–1979)

French novelist and essayist, born in Guéret, near Limoges. A schoolteacher, the son of a butcher, he situated much of his fiction in 'Chaminadour', a version of his home town. *La Jeunesse de Théophile* (1921, 'The Early Life of Théophile'), *Monsieur Godeau Intime* (1926, 'Monsieur Godeau Intimately') and *Monsieur Godeau Marié* (1932, 'Monsieur Godeau Married') are all semi-autobiographical, while *Chaminadour* (3 vols, 1934–41) paints on a broader canvas. *Essai sur moi-même* (1946, 'Essay About Myself') continues the confessional in non-fictional form, although other volumes, such as *Confidences* (1954), deal more generally with life, treating especially of his religious views, which were summarized as 'mystique de l'enfer' ('the mystery of hell'), and stressed the continued reality of evil.

JOUVE, Pierre-Jean
(1887–1976)

French mystical poet, music critic (Mozart, Berg), translator (**Hölderlin**, **Shakespeare**) and novelist, born in Arras. He began his writing career as a poet under the auspices of the Unanimiste or Abbaye group (**Duhamel**, **Romains**, and others), but in 1928 boldly repudiated, in the preface to his collection *Noces* (1928, 'Nuptials'), all that he had written before 1925: he had experienced a 'conversion to spiritual values' (not to Catholicism, as some claimed), and thenceforth devoted himself to what he called 'the Nada theme … borrowed from mystical Spain … [Nada is] the right word for opening the essential door'. His poetry, as reminiscent of that of **Baudelaire** as it is of anyone, 'posits a world of seemingly irreconcilable contraries' which he 'seeks to harmonize'. Later decisive influences were those of **Freud** and (though the latter has been less noticed) **Jung**. His fiction is important but now somewhat neglected, in particular his first novel about a woman tormented by her erotic mysticism, *Paulina 1880* (1925, Eng trans 1973). In Britain he has elicited the particular admiration of **David Gascoyne**. Also available in translation is *An Idiom of Night* (selected poems, 1968).
▷M Callander, *The Poetry of Pierre-Jean Jouve* (1965)

JOUY, Victor Joseph Étienne de
(1764–1846)

French playwright, librettist and writer, born in Jouy near Versailles. Until 1797 he served as a soldier in India and at home. He wrote *L'Hermite de la Chaussée d'Antin* (1812–14, 'The Hermit of the Chaussée d'Antin') and other prose works, and a number of popular comedies, vaudevilles, comic operas and one tragedy, *Tippo-Saïb* (1813).

JOVINE, Francesco
(1902–50)

Italian novelist and story writer from Guardialfiera (Molise), Campobasso. He was by profession a school inspector. He had written a novel in the 1930s, but did not attract critical attention until he published *Signora Ava* (1942, Eng trans *Seeds in the Wind*, 1946), a historical novel about the aftermath of the Risorgimento (the title refers to a figure in a popular song). This was ignored at its publication, but interest in it developed after the end of World War II. Jovine joined the Resistance and then (1948) the communists. His most famous (just posthumous) novel was the partly autobiographical *Le terre del Sacramento* (1950, Eng trans *The Estate in Abruzzi*, 1952), set in southern Italy, against the background of Mussolini's march on Rome.
▷M Grillandi, *Francesco Jovine* (1971, in Italian)

JOYCE, James Augustine Aloysius
(1882–1941)

Irish writer, born in Dublin which, despite his long exile, provides the setting for most of his work. Educated by Jesuits at Clongowes Wood College and Belvedere College, he went to University College, Dublin. A linguist and voracious reader, he corresponded with **Ibsen**. Among other influences were **Dante**, **George Moore** and **W B Yeats**. Catholicism's bigotry distressed him and he went to Paris for a year (1902), living in poverty and writing poetry. His mother's death prompted his return to Ireland, when he stayed briefly in the Martello Tower which features in the early part of *Ulysses*; he then left Ireland with Nora Barnacle, who was to be his companion for the rest of his life. He taught English for a spell in Trieste, but had to scrounge to make ends meet. After a war spent mainly in Switzerland the couple settled in Paris. By now Joyce was the author of two books: *Chamber Music* (1907), a volume of poems, and *Dubliners* (1914), a collection of short stories that includes among other celebrated items, 'The Dead'. The stories were greeted enthusiastically, and Joyce was championed by **Ezra Pound**. The autobiographical *A Portrait of the Artist as a Young Man* appeared in instalments in *The Egoist* (1914–15). Petitioned by Yeats and Pound on his behalf, the Royal Literary Fund in 1915 made him a grant and shortly afterwards the civil list followed suit. But his health was failing, his eyesight deteriorating and he was deeply disturbed by his daughter's mental illness. In 1922 his seminal novel, *Ulysses*, was published in Paris on 2 February. It immediately provoked violent reactions, but the story of Leopold Bloom's day-long perambulation through Dublin is now regarded as epochal, a great leap forward for fiction. It was not published in the United Kingdom until 1936. Plagued by worsening glaucoma, Joyce supervised publication of *Finnegans Wake* in 1939. Much critical energy has been spent trying to analyse Joyce's work, but readers continue to delight in his word play, comedy and irrepressible power of invention.
▷R Ellman, *James Joyce* (1965)

JÓZSEF, Attila
(1905–37)

Hungarian poet, born in Budapest, his country's most distinguished poet after **Endre Ady**, and in certain important respects the latter's heir. József suffered from severe bi-polar mental illness, and ended his life by throwing himself in front of a train at Szársó. He is the poetic counterpart of the composer Bela Bartók, and should be as well known. He was of working-class origin, and began as a communist steeped in the poetry of Ady.

Then, breaking away from communism, he was successively influenced by **Villon**, Surrealism and folk poetry. His style and his rhythms are original in Hungarian poetry, and can hardly be captured in any other language. But John Bákti's *Selected Poems and Texts* (1973) is a notable attempt, with a useful introduction.

JUAN DE LA CRUZ, San, originally Juan de Yepes y Alvarez
(1542–91)

Spanish mystical poet, born in Fontiveros, Old Castille. He was canonized in 1726. In the English world he is known as St John of the Cross. A Carmelite, he joined the movement's reforming wing, and became the director of St Teresa's convent in Ávila. Persecuted by the orthodox members of his movement, he ended in banishment in a convent in Andalusia. His mystical poetry, influenced by **Garcilaso de la Vega**, describes the union of the soul with God after its spiritual and erotic journey through its 'dark night'. They were translated with some success by **Roy Campbell** (1960).
▷P Crisógono, *San Juan de la Cruz* (1929, in Spanish, translated 1958)

JUDAH BEN SAMUEL HA-LEVI
(c.1075–1141)

Spanish Hebrew poet and philosopher. A doctor by profession, he lived in various cities in Spain, including his birthplace, Tudela. His most famous prose work is *The Kuzari*, one of the greatest of medieval theological books; it is the only Jewish classic written in Platonic dialogue form. He set out for the Holy Land in the last years of his life, and travelled about the Middle East; but no one knows his exact fate. His philosophy was in itself an attack on the inadequacy of philosophy: God is known by his revelation, and his existence therefore requires no proof. Judah's poetry has become very well known, and some of it is even incorporated into the Jewish liturgy. He also wrote poems of love and friendship. Much of his work is in translation.
▷R Kayser, *The Life and Times of Jehudah Halevi* (1949)

JUHÁHZ, Ferenc
(1928–)

Hungarian poet from Bia, who, during the 1960s and 70s, achieved international status; since that time, however, Juháhz seems to have lost direction. At first an ambitious socialist realist, hungry for recognition, he broke away from this with *Óda a repüleshez* (1953, 'Ode to Fight'); later works, influenced by **Weöres** and by his reading of modernist foreign poets, did not 'liberate ... the Hungarian poetic imagination', as has foolishly been claimed, but did make bold experiments, and displayed remarkably inventive gifts. His chief poem, which he has not yet bettered, is 'A szarvassa változott királyfi' ('The Boy Changed into a Stag'), in the volume *A virágok hatalma* (1956, 'The Potency of Flowers'), in which he takes his inspiration from the music of his compatriot Béla Bartok. Later work has so far been of less account. There is an English translation in *Selected Poems* (1970).

JUHASZ, Gyula
(1883–1937)

Hungarian poet, who began as a member of the *Nyugat* group which originated with **Endre Ady**. Not unlike his Romanian counterpart **George Bacovia**, he 'slipped into the background', making his living as a teacher in small schools and dedicating himself to adoration of 'Anna', an actress said to have been 'undeserving'. His poetry is polished and melancholy, word perfect, and impressionistic. He was a supporter of the 1919 communist regime, and wrote some verse, his least distinguished, expressing his dreams of a just future. He killed himself in Szeged when his hopes for this future, and for himself, finally ran out.

▷J Reményi, *Hungarian Writers and Literature* (1964)

JULIANA, or JULIAN OF NORWICH, Dame
(1342–c.1416)

English mystical writer who, after an illness in 1373, experienced *A Shewing of God's Love* (Eng trans 1958). A modest and self-critical woman, an anchoress of little book-learning, she illuminated her visions of the Passion of Christ with a serenity that has made her seem highly convincing even to sceptics of her mystical experience. Her main work is the *Revelations of Divine Love*, of which the most accessible edition is that of 1966.

▷P Molinari, *Julian of Norwich* (1958)

JUNG, Johann Heinrich, pseud Jung Stilling
(1740–1817)

German mystic and writer. He was a schoolteacher before qualifying in medicine, then he became Professor of Political Economy at Marburg (1787–1804), then at Heidelberg, and wrote semi-mystical, pietistic romances and works on political economy, as well as a charming autobiography which began with *Heinrich Stillings Jugend* ('Heinrich Stilling's Youth'), and had grown to five volumes when

edited by **Goethe** (1777–1804). A sixth volume was published in 1817.

▷H Müller, *Jung Stilling* (1965)

JÜNGER, Ernst
(1895–)

German novelist, brother of the poet **Friedrich Georg Jünger**. He served in the German army in World War I, and his post-war fiction served to keep alive the spirit of Prussian militarism and, increasingly, the mystique of technological advance. Though initially an enthusiastic supporter, he was disappointed by the Nazis on their accession to power. Enlisting again, he served in France during World War II, where he became a major influence on the French right-wing. There has been considerable controversy about the intention of his novels, *Marmorklippen* (1939, 'On the Marble Cliffs') and *Heliopolis* (1949), both of which seem to extol deutero-fascist ideas, but which have also been interpreted as texts of resistance. Jünger himself complicated the issue by remaining silent on it, while continuing to write in a not dissimilar vein.

JÜNGER, Freidrich Georg
(1898–)

German poet, younger brother of **Ernst Jünger**; unlike the totalitarian idealist Ernst, he opposed Nazism quite unequivocally, and emigrated to Switzerland in 1937. The best of his somewhat classical poems is the anti-Nazi 'Der Mohn' (1934, Eng trans 'The Poppy', *Twentieth-Century German Verse*, 1963, ed Patrick Bridgewater), which was secretly circulated throughout Germany.

JUNQUEIRA FREIRE, Luis José
(1832–55)

Brazilian romantic poet who belongs to the third, 'subjectivist' phase of his country's poetry, which characterized the decade in the middle of which he died. It is his confusions rather than his conclusions which are interesting, and the title of his best-known collection is *Contradicções Poéticas* (1867, published with his complete poetry). For a time he was a Benedictine monk, but he withdrew before taking his final vows.

▷H Pires, *Junqueira Freire, sua vida, sua época, sua obra* (1929)

JUNQUEIRO, Ablio Manuel Guerra
(1850–1923)

Portuguese lyric poet and satirist, born in Freixo. He became a deputy in 1872, opposed the Braganzas (the ruling Portuguese dynasty) and was tried for *lèse majesté* in 1907. After the revolution, when a republic was established, he was minister to Switzerland

(1910). His poetry shows the influence of **Victor Hugo**, and is concerned with social and political reform, rather than more traditional subjects. His work was very popular in his own day, when he was seen as a champion of the people.

JUSSERAND, Jean (Adrien Antoine) Jules
(1855–1932)

French writer and diplomat, born in Lyons. He served in the French embassy in London from 1887 to 1890, and from 1902 to 1925 was ambassador to the USA. He wrote (in French and in English) on the English theatre, *Le Théâtre en Angleterre depuis la conquête jusqu'aux prédécesseurs immédiats de Shakespeare* (1878, 'The English Theatre from the Norman Conquest until Shakespeare's Immediate Predecessors'); a book on the early novel, *Le Roman au temps de Shakespeare* (1887, Eng trans *The English Novel in the Time of Shakespeare*, 1890); a literary history of the English people, *Histoire littéraire du peuple anglais* (1895–1909); and *Amerique jadis et maintenant* (1916, Eng trans *Americans of Past and Present Days*, 1916, Pulitzer Prize).

JUSTICE, Donald Rodney
(1925–)

American poet, born in Miami, Florida. He has taught at a number of universities. His poetry is notably well-made, and reveals a great formal concern with the nuances of language as well as emotion. His first book, *The*

Summer Anniversaries (1960), has been followed by a relatively small body of work, but each has served to increase his standing. He won the Pulitzer Prize for Poetry in 1980 for his *Selected Poems* (1979). Other volumes include *Night Light* (1967), *Departures* (1973), *The Sunset Maker* (1987), which also contains stories and a memoir, and the libretto *The Death of Lucifer* (1988).

JUVENAL, Decimus Junius Juvenalis
(c.55–c.140)

Roman lawyer and satirist, born in Aquinum in the Volscian country. Almost nothing is known of his life except that he lived in Rome, was poor and was a friend of **Martial**. His 16 brilliant verse satires of Roman life and society (c.100–c.128), written from the viewpoint of an angry Stoic moralist, range from savage attacks on the vices and the extravagance of the rich to portrayals of the precarious makeshift life of their hangers-on and the hardships of the poor. Society women came under his lash in the celebrated sixth satire, and his work takes occasional swipes at Jews and other foreigners. **Dryden**'s versions of five of Juvenal's satires are amongst the best of his works. **Dr Johnson** imitated two of the most famous in his *London* and *Vanity of Human Wishes*.
▷G Highet, *Juvenal the Satirist* (1954)

JUVONEN, Helvi
(1919–59)

Finnish poet, born in Iisalmi. Strongly influenced by both **Emily Dickinson** and **Marianne Moore**, she wrote original modernist poetry, distinguished by its use of animal and plant imagery.

K

KABAK, Abraham Abba
(1881–1944)

Hebrew novelist and critic, born in Smorgon, Russia, and died in Jerusalem. He wrote a famous life of Jesus. He was one of the most prolific writers of fiction of his generation. His major work was the medieval historical trilogy *Shlomoh Molkhoh* (1928–30, Eng trans of part of it, 1973): in this account of the martyred visionary Cabalist Solomon Molcho (c.1500–1532) his mastery became fully apparent. His earlier fiction, written in Russia, deals with the harsh lot of the Jew in alien surroundings.

KAFFKA, Margit
(1880–1918)

Hungary's first major feminist woman author, who was a friend to, and influenced by, **Endre Ady**. Her life and achievement were, like those of **Apollinaire**, cut short by the influenza epidemic which swept over Europe after World War I. She has become significant to Hungarian writers in recent years, but her stories—her best work—have yet to be translated.

KAFKA, Franz
(1883–1924)

Austrian novelist, born of German Jewish parents in Prague. He graduated in law from Prague, and although overwhelmed by a desire to write, found employment (1907–23) as an official in the accident prevention department of the government-sponsored Workers' Accident Insurance Institution. A hypersensitive, almost exclusively introspective person with an extraordinary attachment to his father, he eventually moved to Berlin to live with Dora Dymant in 1923, his only brief spell of happiness before succumbing to a lung disease. His short stories and essays, including, 'Der Heizer' (1913, 'The Boilerman'), 'Betrachtungen' (1913, 'Meditations') and 'Die Verwandlung' (1916, Eng trans 'The Transformation', 1933; better known as 'Metamorphosis'), were published in his lifetime, but he refused to do the same for his three unfinished novels, which, through his friend **Max Brod**, were published posthumously and translated by **Edwin** and **Willa Muir**. They are *Der Prozess* (1925, Eng trans *The Trial*, 1937), *Das Schloss* (1926, Eng trans *The Castle*, 1937) and *Amerika* (1927, Eng trans *America*, 1938). Literary critics have interpreted *Das Schloss* variously as a modern *Pilgrim's Progress* (but there is literally no progress), as a literary exercise in Kierkegaardian Existentialist theology, as an allegory of the Jew in a Gentile world, or psychoanalytically as a monstrous expression of Kafka's Oedipus complex, but his solipsism primarily portrays society as a pointless, schizophrenically irrational organization into which the bewildered but unshocked individual has strayed. Kafka has exerted a tremendous influence on Western literature, not least on such writers as **Albert Camus**, **Rex Warner** and **Samuel Beckett**. As *The Trial*, *Der Prozess* has been memorably filmed by Orson Welles (1962) and staged by **Steven Berkoff** (1970). A number of his other writings have been published posthumously, including *Briefe an meinem Vater* (1919, Eng trans *Letters to my Father*, 1954), *Briefe an Milena* (1952, Eng trans *Letters to Milena*, 1967) and *Briefe an Felice* (1967, Eng trans *Letters to Felice*, 1974), and his diary and other correspondence.
▷J P Stern, *The World of Kafka* (1980); A Thorlby, *Franz Kafka* (1972)

KAHN, Gustave
(1859–1936)

French Symbolist poet and essayist, self-proclaimed inventor of *vers libre*, born in Metz. Kahn was one of the first, along with **Laforgue**, to use the techniques of free verse, and was an influential theoretician of the new form of prosody, which he defended in a preface to *Premieres Poèmes* (1897), a republication of earlier work. Probably his most lasting impact was as co-founder of two important journals—*Le Symboliste* and *Vogue*. Later work appeared posthumously in *Poèmes 1921–1935* (1939).
▷J C Ireson, *L'Oeuvre poétique de Gustave Kahn* (1962)

KAILAS, Uuno, pseud of Frans Uuno Salonen
(1901–33)

Major Finnish poet, born in Heinola. He moved to Nice to try to cure himself of the tuberculosis which was the scourge of

Finland, but died there, still a young man. His health had been undermined when he took part in the doomed Aunus expedition in 1919, to support the independence of Russian Karelia. He introduced German expressionism to Finland with his volume of translations *Kaunis Saska* (1924). Finland's one authentic modern *poète maudit*, Kailas was manic for a whole year (1928–9, he had been misdiagnosed as schizophrenic). His style became increasingly classical as he drew nearer to death, and his last collection, *Sleep and Death* (1931), is his most powerful.

KAISER, Georg
(1878–1945)

Major German expressionistic dramatist, poet and novelist, born in Magdeburg. He wrote 78 plays, and was thus the most prolific, as he was the most influential and gifted, of the expressionist playwrights. He went into exile as soon as the Nazis took power. His own life itself had more than an 'expressionist tinge' (it included a six-month spell in jail for stealing and pawning a landlord's furniture: his defence—supposed to annoy the judges, which it did, as it now does some critics—was that he needed the money to maintain the high standards of his youth and his artistic requirement for luxuries and immunity from bourgeois pseudo-morality), and helps to explain the strident tone of his work, which lives on because the best of it transcended the expressionist movement. *Von Morgens bis Mitternacht* (1916, Eng trans *From Morn to Midnight*, 1920), originally produced by Max Reinhardt, features a non-character, The Bank Cashier, the deadness of whose inner life is exposed and revealed by presenting it in the form of fantasy: he mistakes the friendliness of a woman customer, embezzles money, has misadventures, and kills himself at midnight after a Salvation Army girl has betrayed him to the police. Other plays, such as *Gas I* and *Gas II* (1918–20) work in the same way. Later he wrote romantic dramas, and, finally, a *Hellenic Trilogy* (1948), which has been underrated. He wrote two libretti for Kurt Weill, and a now neglected novel, *Es ist genug* (1932, 'It is Enough'), about incest.

KALÉKO, Masche
(1912–)

German poet, born in Kladow who, from 1938, has lived in New York with her conductor/composer husband. She made her reputation in the 1930s, and was praised by **Thomas Mann** for her 'mocking, melodious voice', with its echo of **Heine**. Five of her poems are translated in *Twentieth-Century German Verse* (1963, ed Patrick Bridgewater).

KÁLIDÁSA
(fl.450)

India's greatest dramatist, he is best known through his drama *Sákuntala* (Eng trans 1853).
▷H H Wilson, *The Hindu Theatre* (1871)

KALLAS, Aino, née Krohn
(1878–1956)

Finnish story writer and 'prose balladeer', born in Viipuri parish; she married the diplomat Oskar Kallas in 1900, and lived with him in Estonia, whose history and customs she carefully studied. Her stories, a cross between poetry and raw, instinctive prose, deal with subjects, such as adultery, which were then 'forbidden to women'. She was fortunate in having a good and loyal translator in A Matson, who translated *Barbara von Tisenhusen* (1923, Eng trans 1925), and most of its successors. She lived in London for 12 years (1922–34) while her husband was ambassador; later she had to go into exile (1944–53) in Stockholm. Despite translations, outside Finland and Estonia she has not yet been accorded the recognition she deserves.

KALLOC'H, Yann Ber
(1888–1917)

French poet, a Breton nationalist who wrote in Breton; he was killed in World War I. He was the dominant figure in Breton literature, and has hardly been equalled except by **Tanguy Malmanche**. His richly audacious, bitter and melancholy poems were collected after his death, with a French translation: *A Genoux* (nd, 'Kneeling').

KALVOS, Andreas
(1792–1869)

Greek poet, born on Zakynthos six years before the great **Solomos**. The marriage of his aristocratic mother and humble father caused a scandal on the island, and his father abandoned his mother, taking the young Kalvos and his brother abroad. After a desultory education and peripatetic childhood, Kalvos settled in Florence, where he met the Italian poet **Ugo Foscolo**, becoming his secretary and following him into exile in Switzerland and then London. Kalvos's first writings were all in Italian; his Greek poems consist solely of two slim volumes, published simply as *Lyra* in 1824 and 1826. They contain some of the most powerful poems ever written in Greek, among them his muse on the death of **Byron** and an ode on his mother's death. Having flourished, like Solomos, during the Greek War of Independence, he retired from the fray to become a university professor in Corfu, and finally the headmaster of a girls' school in Louth in Lincolnshire, where he died.

KAMBARA Ariake
(1876–1952)

Japanese poet, from Tokyo. He began his writing career as a novelist, winning a minor literary prize in 1897 with *Daijihi*. Immediately after this he began to publish poetry which was strongly influenced by British Romantics such as **Byron**, **Keats** and **Shelley**. He also admired the French Symbolists, and advocated many of the tenets of their approach to verse composition, himself exerting a strong influence over his younger contemporaries over what turned out to be a short creative life—he gave up composition in 1908, after the publication of his seminal collection *Yumeishu*, to concentrate on criticism and editing.

KANE, Chiekh Hamidou
(1928–)

Francophone Senegalese novelist, born of a Muslim family. He differs from most other modern African writers in that his chief concern is with the conflict between Islam and European technological civilization. The partly autobiographical *L'aventure ambiguë* (1961, Eng trans *Ambiguous Adventure*, 1963) is, after the work of **Camera Laye**, probably the most substantial of its time. It tells the story of a man whose Koranic faith, and even his mysticism, is destroyed by his Parisian education; he himself chooses to die.
▷A C Brench, *The Novelists' Inheritance in French Africa* (1967); W Cartey, *Whispers from a Continent* (1969)

KANEKO Mitsuharu
(1895–)

Japanese poet, sadly unknown outside his homeland. He produced little of any lasting worth before the war (his experience of which, after an initial flirtation with extreme nationalism, turned him into something of a liberal pacifist, causing his work to be suppressed), but since then has been considered one of the leading lights of Japanese poetry.
▷H Hibbett (ed), *Contemporary Japanese Literature* (1975)

KANIN, Garson
(1912–)

American actor, novelist and playwright, born in New York. *Born Yesterday* (1946), set in Washington in World War II, is one of his most famous farces. The more serious *Smile of the World* (1949) traces the moral decline of an ambitious lawyer. *Hollywood* (1974) is an amusing and informative autobiography.

KANTARIS, Sylvia
(1936–)

English poet, born in Grindleford, Derbyshire. She spent 10 years in Australia, during which time she received a doctorate in French literature from the University of Queensland. She won the Poetry Magazine (Australia) Award in 1969 and her first volume of poetry, *Time and Motion* (1975), was published in Sydney. In 1974 she made her home in Cornwall, and in 1986 was appointed Cornwall's first 'Writer in the Community'. She has published two jointly authored collections (1983 and 1988) and a selected poems, *Dirty Washing* (1989). In her poetry, personal reflections on love and loss, comfort and despair, are imaged with warmth and wit, in a language that is described by herself as kaleidoscopic—'multifolate,/manifold with meaning'.

KARADŽIĆ, Vuk Stefanović
(1787–1864)

Serbian poet and philologist, born in Tršić. He published collections of national songs and tales, and evolved the simplified Cyrillic alphabet in order to produce literature in the vernacular, a reform which was resisted initially, especially by the Orthodox Church, but his orthography was officially adopted in 1868, having already been taken up by Serbian writers. He translated the New Testament into Serbian.
▷D Wilson, *The Life and Times of Vuk Stepanovic Karadžić* (1970)

KARAGATSIS, Michaelis, pen-name of Dimitri Rodopoulos
(1908–60)

Greek novelist and short-story writer. A prolific writer, he was hailed for his extreme realism and inventiveness of plot, and had already published four novels and two volumes of stories by 1940. His novels are concerned with a 'tragic eroticism', the characters being brought to disaster by an unquenchable erotic passion that masters them. In *Colonel Liapkin* (1933), as in *Junkermann* (1936), Karagatsis's most famous novel, the protagonists, both foreign men, come to Greece and initially prosper before being brought to ruin by their compulsive sexual desire; in *Chimera*, also published in 1936, it is a foreign woman who similarly courts disaster. Karagatsis's post-war attempts to construct a roman-fleuve around the character of Michaelis Roussis were less successful: in the event only the first three of the projected series were published. In his later years he again turned to 'erotic' writing, but after the publication of a short story, 'O Megalos Hypnos' ('The

Great Sleep'), in 1946, he received little further critical acclaim.

KARAMZIN, Nikolai Mikhailovich
(1766–1826)

Russian historian and novelist, born in Mikhailovka in Orenburg. Among his writings are *Pisma ruskovo putishestvenika* (1790–2, 'Letters of a Russian Traveller'), an account of his travels in western Europe, several novels, including *Bednaya Lisa* (1792, 'Poor Lisa') and *Natalia, boyarskaya doch* (1792, 'Natalia, the Boyar's Daughter'), and a great unfinished *Gosudarstvo rossúskovo* (1816–29, 'History of Russia') down to 1613. His influence on the literature of Russia and its development was considerable. He modernized the literary language by his introduction of western idioms and his writing as a whole reflected western thought.
▷H Nebel Jr, *Nikolai Mikhailovich Karamzin: a Russian sentimentalist* (1967)

KARAOSMANOGLU, Yakub Kadri
(1889–1974)

Turkish novelist, born in Cairo. He was a 'Young Turk', a prominent supporter of Mustafa Kemal, and served him as member of parliament and diplomat. He came to fame as a writer with his novels of the 1920s and 30s, dealing with corruption in high places and bad rural conditions. The most famous is *Yaban* (1932, 'Stranger'), an exposure of the poor conditions in the villages—this was translated into German (1934), but not into English. He was not a major novelist by international standards because he allowed his journalism to affect his style adversely, but all his fiction is highly efficient, humane and well plotted.

KARASEK ZE LVOVIC, Jiri, pseud of Josef Karasek
(1871–1951)

Czech poet, playwright and novelist. He was perhaps the leading Czech 'decadent', being influenced by **Wilde** and the earlier **Huysmans**. His works fill 19 volumes. He was an interesting writer, whose most powerful influence was the mystical Catholicism of the Middle Ages, of which he was a scholar. He was associated with **Neumann**, **Dyk**, and various other writers who had at different times been under the Austrian tyranny.
▷G Kahn, *Symbolistes et Décadents* (1912)

KARAVELOV, Lyuben
(1835–79)

Bulgarian story writer and revolutionary, born in Koprivshtsa. He lived most of his life abroad: in Russia, Serbia, Hungary and Romania, but died in his own country. He was influenced by *narodnik* thought in Russia, and, in particular, by **Gogol**. An ethnographer, he edited émigré revolutionary journals. His masterly stories created the prototype of the obstinate old Bulgarian peasant still known and appreciated in Bulgaria. He is a major figure in his literature, who just lived to see his aim, Bulgarian independence, realized.
▷C Manning and R Smal-Stocki, *The History of Modern Bulgarian Literature* (1960)

KARINTHY, Frigyes
(1887–1938)

Hungarian humorous writer and translator, who put some of **Jonathan Swift** into Hungarian. His best-known book is *Utázas a Kopony ám Körül* (1937, Eng trans *A Journey Round My Skull*, 1939), an extraordinary account of a brain operation he underwent, and which soon proved his undoing. He was a member of the *Nyugat* (*West*) group, whose essays in the absurd and paradoxical made him into his country's **Chesterton**.

KARLFELDT, Erik Axel
(1864–1931)

Swedish lyric poet, winner of the Nobel Prize for literature, born in Folkärna, Dalarna. He published several volumes of highly individual nature poetry reflecting the traditional language and customs of peasant life in his native province. In *Fridolins visor* (1898, 'Fridolin's Songs') he introduced a peasant character/persona who combined simplicity with deep learning; he reappeared in *Fridolins lustgård* (1901, 'Fridolin's Pleasure Garden'). Critics have not been kind to his poetry, but it proved enduringly popular with the public until it began to darken with oddly erotic volumes like *Flora och Bellona* (1918). He was secretary of the Swedish Academy from 1912. He was posthumously awarded the 1931 Nobel Prize for literature.
▷T Fogelquist, *Erik Axel Karlfeldt* (1941)

KARP, David
(1922–)

American author, born in New York of Russian–Jewish descent. He served in the American army, worked as a journalist, as a radio, TV and paperback writer, and emerged as a serious novelist with *One* (1953), an **Orwell**ian condemnation of totalitarianism. Other works include *The Day of the Monkey* (1955), on British colonialism, *All Honourable Men* (1956), *The Sleepwalkers* (1960) and *Last Believers* (1964).

KARPÍNSKI, Franciszek
(1741–1825)

Polish poet, born in Holosków. He was an impoverished aristocrat who never succeeded in obtaining a patron, but lived to a great age and was admired by those romantics who, like him, had no money with which to pay their respects. He is now generally seen as the leading lyrical poet of his age. His memoirs are a model of candour.

KARR, (Jean Baptiste) Alphonse
(1808–90)

French writer, born in Paris. His *Sous les tilleuls* (1832, 'Under the Linden Trees') by its originality and wit found its author an audience for a long series of novels, of which *Geneviève* (1838) is the best. In 1839 he became Editor of *Le Figaro*, and started the issue of the bitterly satirical *Les Guêpes* ('The Wasps'). His *Voyage autour de mon jardin* (1845, Eng trans *A Tour Around My Garden*, 1855) is his best-known book. He wrote his reminiscences, *Livre de bord* (4 vols, 1879–80, 'Logbook'). His daughter, Thérèse (1835–87), published tales and historical books.
▷L Bauthier, *Portraits du 19ième siècle* (1894)

KARYOTAKIS, Costas
(1896–1928)

Greek poet, born in Tripolis, who killed himself in Preveza. His death had a major effect on the development of Greek poetry— although not perhaps a profound one, or even one of a weight which his work, which has hardly worn well, can quite carry. But a manifestation fairly called 'Karyotakism', a literary fashion for nihilism, certainly pervaded Greek poetry for some years after his death. He was a minor civil servant who became disenchanted with everything, and who wrote well-accomplished and deeply sarcastic verses demonstrating that every effort on earth merely (for example) amuses 'the fire demons far beneath the ground ... and those who live on high'. Beyond this nihilism, there is little of interest in his work.

KASACK, Hermann
(1896–1966)

German novelist, dramatist and poet, a publisher by profession, born in Potsdam. He began as a strident expressionist poet, and always considered himself above all a poet, but his most discussed and possibly most successful work is the novel *Die Stadt hinter dem Strom* (1947, Eng trans *The City Beyond the River*, 1953), the haunting and **Kafka**esque tale of a 'dead zone' occupied by dead souls. This has been a little too confidently dismissed by certain more recent critics as 'now exposed' as relying on 'nineteenth-century values that are no longer adequate'. Such critics prefer the later novel, *Fälschungen* (1953, 'Falsifications').

KASCHNITZ, Marie Luise, pseud of **Marie Luise von Kaschnitz-Weinberg**
(1901–74)

German poet, story writer, critic and novelist, born in Karlsruhe into an old aristocratic family. Technically proficient, her poetry developed, and became increasingly rich in psychological content; her novels, in particular *Das Haus der Kindheit* (1956, 'The House of Childhood'), are equally telling. Although the writers who have helped to form her style and method include **Kafka** and **Beckett**, her work has often been too hastily written off as over-traditional; but she is likely to have a revival.

KASPROWICZ, Jan
(1860–1926)

Polish poet, dramatist and translator (eg of **Shakespeare**'s *Hamlet* and of plays by **Aeschylus** and **Euripides**), one of the leading members of the neo-romantic 'Young Poland' (Mloda Polska) movement which ran from the 1890s until the outbreak of World War I, and which was a reaction to the Positivism which preceded it. He was born in Szymborze into a poor peasant family. In his youth he was jailed by the Prussians for his pro-Polish activities. He was, like many Polish writers, essentially a mystic, with gnostic tendencies (he divided every aspect of the world into good and evil, and saw life as a battle-ground between them). Although he was learned and intelligent, his thought at times appears tawdry; but his best poetry is of a far higher order. Amongst his many poems, his *Hymny* (1921, 'Hymns'), written at the turn of the century, are the most important, since they combine his love of the landscape of his country with his understanding of Polish peasant songs, thus revealing what has been called his 'profoundly pagan interpretation of Christianity'. The effort of synthesis begun in the Hymns culminates in the posthumous *Mój świat* (1926, 'My World').

KASSÁK, Lajos
(1887–1967)

Hungarian poet, novelist, autobiographer and painter of working-class origins, born in a town that is today in the Czech Republic. Critics have not yet succeeded in sorting out his confusions. He began as a 'proletarian' writer, a travelling blacksmith, then became a pacifist, then a communist opposed to socialist realism. His best poetry is reminiscent of **Whitman**; but his most important work is his huge autobiography, *Egy ember élete* (1927–39, 'The Life of a Man').
▷*Modern Language Journal* (February 1951)

KÄSTNER, Erich
(1899–1974)

German writer, born in Dresden. He is best known for his books for children. His writing career, however, began with two volumes of verse, *Herz auf Taille* (1928, 'Heart on Waistline') and *Lärm im Spiegel* (1929, 'Noise in the Mirror'), both cleverly satirical. His novels include *Fabian: Die Geschichte eines Moralisten* (1931, Eng trans *Fabian: The Story of a Moralist*, 1932) and *Drei Männer im Schnee* (1934, Eng trans *Three Men in the Snow*, 1935). His delightful children's books, which include *Emil und die Detektive* (1928, Eng trans *Emil and the Detectives*, 1930), *Annaluise und Anton* (1929, Eng trans 1932) and *Das fliegende Klassenzimmer* (1933, Eng trans *The Flying Classroom*, 1934), gained him worldwide fame. Among his later writings is the autobiographical *Als ich ein kleiner Junge war* (1957, Eng trans *When I was a Little Boy*, 1959).
▷L Enderle, *Erich Kästner Bildbiographie* (1960)

KATAYEV, Valentin
(1897–)

Russian novelist and playwright, born in Odessa, the elder brother of Yevgeny Katayev (**Yevgeny Petrov**). A humorous and easy-going writer of the 'Odessa school'—of just such good-natured, easy-going character—Katayev came early under the influence of the (in Trotsky's phrase) 'fellow travelling' Serapion Brothers, although he did not join them. His best novel, the richly comic *Rastratchiki* (1926, Eng trans *The Embezzlers*, 1929), set against Stalin's New Economic Policy, tells of two drunks who go off with some money from a trust-fund for a good time. When cultural policy became sterner Katayev fell into line for a time: *Beleet parus odinoky* (1936, Eng trans *Lonely White Sail*, 1937) represented something of an escape for him; regarded by some as his best book, it deals with children, who were at that time allowed to be portrayed as naturally 'irresponsible' (ie not as hardline communists). Later he turned to highly original memoirs in which he combined fact, fiction and fun (often made of Soviet officialdom, but not in a way censors could put their finger on, although they reproved Katayev when they could). His stage comedies, the most famous of which is *Kvadratura kruga* (1918, Eng trans *Squaring the Circle*, 1934), offered excellent and intelligent entertainment.

KATONA, József
(1791–1830)

Hungarian playwright who wrote many now-forgotten historical dramas, including one,

Bánk Bán (1814, 'The Viceroy'), a Shakespearean drama set in 13th-century Hungary, which became a classic after his death. It was first performed in 1833, and was by mid-century regarded as the greatest of all Hungarian tragedies. It deals with a problem that beset Hungary until only recently: what attitude could be taken to an oppressive ruler? It was made into an opera by Ferencz Erkel in 1861.

KATZ, Steve
(1935–)

American author of disruptive 'novels' which confirm **Philip Roth**'s contention that the most important literary distinction is not between 'fiction' and 'non-fiction', but between the 'written' and 'unwritten' worlds. In Katz's second novel, *The Exagggerations of Peter Prince* (1968, the extra consonant is perfectly deliberate), he allows his ending to remain in what he has called the 'archive of the unwritten'. This is the underlying theme of *Stolen Stories* (1984), a much later collection of short pieces, and it emerges throughout his masterpiece *Wier and Pouce* (1984), a synoptic novel which uses the death of John F Kennedy as a symbol of betrayed hopes and dreams and then proposes that only by unfettered story-telling can we survive a world without valid dreams. His other works include *The Lestriad* (1962), which was published only in Italy, and *Moving Parts* (1977). Since the mid-70s, he has lived in Boulder, Colorado, where he teaches in the university English department.
▷J Klinkowitz, *The Life of Fiction* (1977)

KATZNELSON, Jehuda Loeb
(1847–1917)

Hebrew (and Russian) writer and scholar, born in Tchernigov, Russia. His renditions of ancient legends are outstanding, and the work he wrote on the origins of Jewish laws concerning hygiene is still consulted.

KAUFMAN, George S(imon)
(1889–1961)

American playwright, born in Pittsburgh. In collaboration with **Moss Hart** he wrote *You Can't Take it with You* (1939, Pulitzer Prize) and *The Man Who Came to Dinner* (1939). Other works include *The Solid Gold Cadillac* (with Howard Teichmann, 1953) and many musicals, some of which have been filmed.
▷S Meredith, *George S. Kaufman and his Friends* (1974), revised as *Kaufman and the Algonquin Round Table* (1977)

KAVAN, Anna
(1901–68)

English novelist and short-story writer, born in France to English parents. Originally called Helen Edmonds, she changed her name by deed poll; other attempts to erase her origin included a refusal to reveal her place of birth or her exact age. *Let Me Alone* (1930) was published under her married name, Helen Ferguson, although, confusingly, one of the characters is called Anna Kavan. She was a heroin addict for many years, and the alternation of numbness and pain which typifies that life is evident in *Ice* (1967), her best novel, a **Kafka**esque account of flight and fear in a frozen world where order has collapsed. *My Madness* (1990) contains the whole of *Ice*, as well as selections from her short stories and autobiographical writings.

KAVANAGH, Patrick Joseph
(1905–67)

Irish poet and novelist, born in County Monaghan. The son of a cobbler and smallholder he farmed before leaving for Dublin in 1939 to pursue a career as a writer and journalist. A caricature of the roistering Irish poet, perhaps his greatest achievement is *The Great Hunger* (1942), a long, angry and passionate poem which does not gloss the harsh reality of life for a frustrated Irish farmer and his sister. In *Tarry Flynn* (1948), an autobiographical novel, he depicts sensitively and convincingly the countryside where he was brought up. Kavanagh's unorthodox and virtually antisocial lifestyle in Dublin led to a savage anonymous profile (actually by another poet, Valentin Iremonger). In his libel action, *Kavanagh* v *The Leader* (1953), he was the victim of a brutal cross-examination by opposing counsel John A Costello, from which he never really recovered. Poems written in the last decade of his life when his health was failing are generally thought to be inferior, but the best are admirably direct, intelligently and wittily contemplating his sexual isolation and his attempts to overcome his academic stage-Irishness. *Collected Poems* was published in 1964, and the *Complete Poems* followed in 1972.

KAVANAGH, P(atrick) J(oseph)
(1931–)

English poet and novelist, born in Worthing, Sussex. Following the death of his first wife, Sally Phillips, in 1958, he wrote one of the 20th-century's most tender and inspiring autobiographies, *The Perfect Stranger* (1966). It was followed in 1990 with *Finding Connections*, another autobiography, tracing Kavanagh's Irish ancestors in Australia and elsewhere. A constant searching quality, fused by a devout Catholicism, informs his eight collections of poetry. *Collected Poems* (1987) gathers work from six of these and conveys an unfashionable pastoralism, given sustaining quality by Kavanagh's sure technique and his passionate involvement with his adopted Gloucestershire.

KAVERIN, Veniamin, pseud of Veniamin Zilber
(1902–)

Russian novelist, playwright and critic, born in Pskov, who studied under Boris Eikhenbaum and Yury Tynyanov, two of the critics whose 'formalism' made Russia's main contribution to critical theory in the 20th century, and who deeply influenced him. Formalism began as a reaction to Futurism, by tersely defining literature as 'the sum total of all stylistic devices employed in it', a slogan which could easily be accommodated by official Marxism; later it developed into something subtler, different and more independent of politics—and Kaverin to a certain extent anticipated this. He joined the 'fellow-travelling' but independent group of writers who called themselves the Serapion Brothers, and modelled himself on **Laurence Sterne**. His early and hilariously funny and deftly plotted novel about the Leningrad underworld, *Konets khazy* (1926, 'End of a Gang'), remains one of his best books; but *Khudozhnik neizvesten* (1931, Eng trans *The Unknown Artist*, 1947), about a character modelled on the restless poet **Viktor Khlebnikov**, represents the height of his achievement. Later he became involved with socialist realism, but then, in advance of the temporary Kruschev 'Thaw', began to publish more books of criticism again.
▷ D G P Piper, *Kaverin* (1970)

KAWABATA Yasunari
(1899–1972)

Japanese writer and winner of the Nobel Prize for literature, born in Osaka. He was educated at Tokyo University (1920–4), reading English and then Japanese literature. In 1922 he published some short stories, *Tales to hold in the Palm of your Hand*. His first novel, *Izu no odoriko* (Eng trans *The Izu Dancer*, 1955), was published in 1925. He experimented with various Western novel forms, but by the mid-1930s returned to traditional Japanese ones. Later novels, which are typically melancholy, include *Yukiguni* (1935–47, Eng trans *Snow Country*, 1957), *Sembazuru* (1949, Eng trans *Thousand Cranes*, 1959), *Kyoto* (1962) and *Yama no oto* (1949–54, Eng trans *The Sound of the Mountain*, 1971). He won the 1968 Nobel Prize for literature, the first Japanese writer to do so. He committed suicide.
▷ G B Peterson, *The Moon in the Water: on Tanizaki, Kawabata and Mishima* (1979)

KAYE, Louis, pseud of Noel Wilson Norman
(1901–81)

Australian writer, born in Claremont, Tasmania, whose short stories were eagerly sought by overseas magazines. He is best known for his novels which between them cover most aspects of Australian outback life, from sheep farming in *Tybal Men* (1931), through opal prospecting in *Tightened Belts* (1935), to stock droving in *Pathways of Free Men* (1935). Despite Kaye's youthful experiences in the Australian outback his stories show a tendency to adopt the style and language of the American 'western'.

KAYE, M(ary) M(argaret)
(1909–)

English novelist, born in Simla, India. A daughter of the Raj, she married into the army and subsequently travelled extensively with her husband. She is the author of several detective novels with exotic settings, written with a lively mixture of mystery and romance. *Death in Kenya* (1983) is a representative example. She is best known, however, for her bestselling historical romantic epics. *Trade Wind* (1963), set in 19th-century Zanzibar, is a story of the slave trade, while her two most famous books, *Shadow of the Moon* (1957) and *The Far Pavilions* (1978), are both set in 19th-century India.
▷ *The Sun in the Morning* (1990)

KAYE-SMITH, Sheila
(1887–1956)

English novelist, born in St Leonards, Sussex. She wrote novels mainly about fate and Sussex. In 1924 she married T P Fry, a clergyman and heir to a baronetcy, and in 1929 became a Roman Catholic. Her writings include *Sussex Gorse* (1916), *Tamarisk Town* (1919), *Joanna Godden* (1921) and *The End of the House of Alard* (1923). She was satirized by **Stella Gibbons** in *Cold Comfort Farm*.
▷ E T Hopkins, *Sheila Kaye-Smith and the Weald Country* (1925)

KAZAKOV, Yury
(1927–)

Russian story writer, born in Moscow. Writing in the tradition of **Bunin** and **Turgenev**, Kazakov has by some been regarded as old-fashioned and lacking in innovatory technique; but his quiet tales of the humble people of central Russia have been greatly prized, and may best be read in *Selected Short Stories* (1963), which has a valuable critical introduction by G Gibian, but which is in Russian.

KAZANTZAKIS, Nikos
(1883–1957)

Greek novelist, poet and dramatist, born in Heraklion, Crete. After studying law at Athens University, he spent some years travelling in Europe and Asia. He published his first novel *Toda Raba* in French in 1929 (Eng

trans 1964), but is best known for the novel *Vios kai Politeia tou Alexi Zorba* (1946, Eng trans *Zorba the Greek*, 1952) and the epic autobiographical narrative poem, *Odyseia* (1938, Eng trans *The Odyssey, a Modern Sequel*, 1958). He wrote several other novels, including *O Christos Xanastavronetai* (1954, Eng trans *Christ Recrucified*, 1954), *O Kapetan Michalis* (1953, Eng trans *Freedom or Death*, 1955) and *O Teleftaios Peirasmos* (1955, Eng trans *The Last Temptation of Christ*, 1960), and translated many literary classics into modern Greek. He spent his last decade living in Antibes, in France.
▷ P Bien, *Nicos Kazantzakis* (1968)

KAZINCZY, Ferenc
(1759–1831)

Hungarian writer, born in Érsemlyén. He published a radical journal, and was imprisoned for his membership of a Jacobin society. He was a leading figure in the Hungarian literary revival and a strong advocate of the reform of the language, and is often referred to as 'the father of Hungarian criticism'. He translated many European classics and wrote poetry, including the first sonnets in Hungarian; there are 22 volumes of his letters. He died of cholera.
▷ J Váczy, *Kazinczy Ferences Kora* (1915)

KEANE, Molly
(1904–)

Irish novelist, born in County Kildare into 'a rather serious Hunting and Fishing and Church-going family'. Her father originally came from a Somerset family and her mother, a poet, was the author of 'The Songs of the Glens of Antrim'. When young she wrote only to supplement her dress allowance, adopting the pseudonym M J Farrell. *The Knight of the Cheerful Countenance*, her first book, was written when she was 17. Between 1928 and 1952 she wrote 10 novels, including *The Rising Tide* (1937), *Two Days in Aragon* (1941) and *Loving Without Tears* (1951), drawing her material from the foibles of her own class. A spirited, impish writer, she also wrote plays, such as *Spring Meeting* (1938), *Ducks and Drakes* (1942), *Treasure Hunt* (1949) and *Dazzling Prospect* (1961). When her husband died at 36 she stopped writing for many years, but *Good Behaviour* (1981), shortlisted for the Booker Prize, led to the reprinting of many of her books and a revival of critical appreciation. *Loving and Giving* (1988) is a bleak comedy seen through the eyes of an eight-year-old girl who is a witness to the break-up of her parents' marriage and the desuetude of the family mansion.
▷ B O'Toole, in *Across a Roaring Hill: The Protestant Imagination in Modern Ireland* (1985, Gerald Dawe and Edna Longley, eds)

KEATS, Ezra Jack
(1916–83)

American illustrator and children's story-teller, born in Brooklyn. His early picture-books, for which he wrote his own text, mixed gouache and collage. In his final books the style was becoming increasingly impression-istic. He was interested in the emotional experience of young children, rather than in the purely narrative aspects of a story, and, as in *Apt. 13* (1971), was particularly good at focusing on the life of city children in high-rise apartments.

KEATS, John
(1795–1821)

English poet, born in London, the son of a livery-stable keeper. He went to school at Enfield. In 1811 he was apprenticed to a sur-geon at Edmonton, and later (1815–17) was a medical student in the London hospitals, but took to writing poetry. **Leigh Hunt**, his neighbour in Hampstead, introduced him to other young romantics, including **Shelley**, and published his first sonnets in *The Exam-iner* (1816). His first volume of poems (1817) combined 'Hymn to Pan' and the 'Bacchic procession' which anticipate the great odes to come. In 1818 he published the long mytho-logical poem *Endymion*. He returned from a walking tour in Scotland (1818), which exhausted him, to find the savage reviews of *Endymion* in *Blackwood's Magazine* and the *Quarterly*. To add to his troubles his younger brother Tom was dying of consumption, and his love affair with Fanny Brawne seems to have brought him more vexation than comfort. It was under these circumstances that he published the volume of 1820, *Lamia and Other Poems*, a landmark in English poetry. Except for the romantic poem 'Isa-bella or The Pot of Basil', a romance based on **Boccaccio**'s *Decameron*, and the first ver-sion of his epical poem, 'Hyperion', all the significant verse in this famous volume is the work of 1819, such as the two splendid romances 'The Eve of St Agnes' and 'Lamia', and the great odes—'On a Grecian Urn', 'To a Nightingale', 'To Autumn', 'On Mel-ancholy' and 'To Psyche'. In particular, 'The Eve of St Agnes' displays a wealth of sen-suous imagery almost unequalled in English poetry. In 'Lamia', the best told of the tales, he turns from stanza form to the couplet as used by **Dryden** in his romantic *Fables*. Keats's letters are regarded as equally impor-tant as his poems, and throw light on his poetical development no less than on his unhappy love affair with Fanny Brawne. It is clear that he was both attracted and repelled by the notion of the poet as teacher or prophet. Having prepared the 1820 volume for the press, Keats, now seriously ill with consumption, sailed for Italy in September 1820, reached Rome and died there attended only by his artist friend Joseph Severn. The house in which he died (26 Piazza di Spagna), at the foot of the Spanish steps, is now known as the Keats–Shelley house, a place of literary pilgrimage with an outstanding library of English romantic literature.
▷ R Gittings, *John Keats* (1968)

KEDRIN, Dmitry
(1908–45)

Russian poet, born in Bogodukhovo; he was murdered by unknown attackers. He is best known for his long poem *Zodche* (1938), tell-ing of Ivan the Terrible's cruelty to his archi-tects. His verse, simple and evocative of common suffering, became popular during World War II.

KEE, Robert
(1919–)

English broadcaster and writer. After reading history at Magdalen College, Oxford, he joined the RAF and was shot down over Hol-land, spending four years in a POW camp. His first novel, *A Crowd is Not Company* (1947), reflected this experience and won him the Atlantic Award for literature. Other nov-els include *The Impossible Shore* (1949) and *A Sign of the Times* (1955). As a print journal-ist, he worked for *Picture Post* (1948–51) and was a special correspondent for *The Observer* (1956–7) and *The Sunday Times* (1957–8). Joining the BBC, he worked on *Panorama* from 1958 to 1962. He was the recipient of the Richard Dimbleby BAFTA Award (1976); his other major television work includes the series *Ireland* (1981), co-founding the breakfast programme TV-am (1983), and *Seven Days* (1984–8). His non-fiction books include *The Green Flag* (1972), *Ireland: A His-tory* (1980) and *Trial and Error* (1986).

KEILLOR, Garrison
(1942–)

American humorous writer and radio per-former, born in Minnesota. He graduated from Minnesota University in 1966, already writing for the *New Yorker*. In 1974 he first hosted the live radio show 'A Prairie Home Companion', delivering a weekly monologue set in the quiet, fictional mid-western town of Lake Wobegon, 'where all the women are strong, all the men are good-looking, and all the children are above average'. When the show closed in 1987 he was celebrated for his wry, deliberate, hypnotic storytelling. Most of his written work appears first in the *New Yorker*. Described as 'the best humorous writer to have come out of America since Thurber', his books are *Happy to be Here*

(1981), *Lake Wobegon Days* (1985), *Leaving Home* (1987), *We Are Still Married* (1989), the novel *Radio Romance* (1991), and *The Book of Guys* (1993).

KELLER, David H
(1880–1966)

American physician and writer, born in Philadelphia. He made his notoriety from his series *Sexual Education* (1929), in a day when such matters were hardly discussed; but he is prized by a few science-fiction enthusiasts for the bizarre and effective plots of his speculative novels and stories. Two of these admirers, Moskowitz and Sykera, compiled *Life Everlasting*, a collection of his best tales (1948).

KELLER, Gottfried
(1819–90)

Swiss poet and novelist, born near Zürich. He studied landscape painting at Munich (1840–2), but turned to literature. From 1861 to 1876 he was state secretary of his native canton. His chief works are *Der grüne Heinrich* (1854, Eng trans *Green Henry*, 1960), *Die Leute von Seldwyla* (1856; which includes *A Village Romeo and Juliet*), *Sieben Legenden* (1872, Eng trans with the previous work as *Seven Legends* and *The People of Seldwyla*, 1929), *Züricher Novellen* (1878, 'Zurich stories') and *Martin Salander* (1886, Eng trans 1963). He excelled as a writer of short stories, and his powers of characterization and description and his sense of humour are best illustrated in his volumes of *Novellen*.
▷ J M Lindsay, *Gottfried Keller: his life and works* (1968)

KELLER, Helen Adams
(1880–1968)

American writer, born in Tuscumbia, Alabama. She became deaf and blind at 19 months, but, educated by Anne M Sullivan (Mrs Macy), she later learned to speak, graduated in 1904, and attained high distinction as a lecturer, writer and scholar.
▷ *The Story of My Life* (1902)

KELLEY, William Melvin
(1937–)

Black American novelist, whose books all begin with the letter D. He was brought up in the Bronx, but went on to Harvard, where he studied under **John Hawkes** and **Archibald MacLeish** and won the **Reed** Prize in 1960. His first novel, *A Different Drummer* (1963), was a fantasy about mass (and voluntary) black emigration from a southern state. *A Drop of Patience* (1965) took its title from *Othello* and much else from *Porgy and Bess*. The story of a blind jazz musician, it offers a powerful study of white attitudes to black creativity. *Dem* (1967) are the whites of America, viewed with hostility but little rancour. Kelley's experimental vein resurfaced in *Dunfords Travels Everywheres* (1970), an ambitious failure. His stories were collected in *Dancers on the Shore* (1965). Kelley has been important in registering the variety and internal hierarchies of 'the black experience' in the USA.

KELLGREN, Johan Henric
(1751–95)

Swedish poet and journalist, born in Floby. He was editor from 1780 of the journal *Stockholmsposten*, where he made a reputation as a satirist. He was librarian (1780) and later secretary and literary adviser to King Gustav III, with whom he collaborated on a tragedy, *Gustav Wasa* (1782), and became a member of the newly-founded Swedish Academy in 1786. As a poet he excelled in patriotic and lyrical verse, and, although a representative of the Enlightenment, was not unsympathetic to the new ideas of Romanticism. Ek and Sjöding edited a nine-volume collected works (1923–70).
▷ O Sylwan, *Johan Henric Kellgren* (1939)

KELLY, George Edward
(1887–1974)

American dramatist, born in Philadelphia, whose first successful play, *The Torchbearers* (1922), satirizes a young woman's plunge into near-amateur dramatics. Kelly came to prominence two years later with *The Show-Off*, a classic portrayal of a boaster. *Craig's Wife* (1925) is a more caustic look at female possessiveness within a loveless marriage, and won a Pulitzer Prize. Although ambitious and domineering women feature again in plays such as *Behold the Bridegroom* (1927) and *Maggie the Magnificent* (1929), none of Kelly's later plays was as well-received as his earlier work. This made him so disenchanted with the theatre that after 1931 he wrote only intermittently, his last play, *The Fatal Weakness* (1946), dealing again with a flawed marriage.

KELLY, Hugh
(1739–77)

Irish playwright, born in Killarney, County Kerry. With little formal education, he began as an apprentice staymaker before being inspired by the actors who frequented his father's pub to experience the London theatre. He went there in 1760, soon becoming a journalist, publishing his theatre criticism in a volume entitled *Thespis* (1766). His first comedy, *False Delicacy* (1768), was an overnight success despite its stock and uninspired nature and set him up as a rival to **Oliver Goldsmith**. However, after a number of other, less successful plays and work for the government as a newspaper hack, he tried a career in law which also failed. He took to drink in the 1770s and died shortly afterwards.

KELMAN, James
(1946–)

Scottish novelist, short-story writer and playwright, born in Glasgow, one of five brothers. His father was a frame maker and picture restorer. He left school at 15 to become an apprentice compositor, abandoning this two years later when his family decided to emigrate to America. However, he returned soon after and worked at various short-term jobs whose nature is clear to readers of his fiction: labouring, bus-conducting and stocking shelves in stores. For long periods he was unemployed, but he was a voracious reader and when his unemployment benefit was about to be cut he enrolled expediently at Strathclyde University. He left, nonetheless, in his third year, dissatisfied with the irrelevance of the philosophy course. In any case he was now determined to be a writer, and since 1983, with the publication of *Not Not While the Giro*, a collection of laconic stories, he has carved a niche as the spokesman for the disaffected, downtrodden and disenfranchised. Invariably, he is associated with the west of Scotland and the working class. He writes in the demotic voice and uses swear words liberally, but few deny his potency or authenticity. *The Busconductor Hines* (1984), a triumph of the mundane, confirmed his promise. *A Chancer*, the story of a small-time gambler, followed a year later. *Greyhound for Breakfast* (1987) evoked comparisons with **Chekhov** and **Beckett**, though the clipped style was quintessential Kelman. *A Disaffection*, his third novel, the story of a secondary-school teacher at odds with the system and society, found a wide audience through its shortlisting for the Booker Prize in 1989. Further stories were collected in *The Burn* (1991), and three plays are included in *Hardie and Baird & Other Plays* (1991). His fourth novel, *How late it was, how late* (1994), a witty and satirical exploration of blankfaced bureaucracy, was acknowledged by many critics to contain his best work to date.
▷I Bell, in *Planet* (1986–7)

KELTON, Elmer
(1926–)

American writer of Westerns, born in Texas. Kelton's father was a cowboy and his grandfather a ranch foreman. Kelton himself trained as a journalist and was associate editor of *West Texas Livestock Weekly* (1968–90). He maintained his two careers (agricultural journalist and writer of fiction) for over 30 years. He has won four Spur Awards, and *The Man Who Rode Midnight* (1987) won the Western Heritage Award. He has used several pen-names. *Sons of Texas* (1990) was published under the name Tom Early.

KEMAL, Namik
(1840–88)

Turkish dramatist, novelist, poet, critic and historian, born in Tekirdagi into an aristocratic family. He soon had to flee the country as a result of his membership of a revolutionary society. In London he and other patriots published the subversive paper *Hürriyet* (1868). When he returned to Istanbul his play *Vatan* (1872) caused riots, and he was sent to Famagusta in Cyprus, from which he continued his activities. He is important as one of the first writers to break out of the stultifying literary tradition.

KEMAL, Orhan, pseud of **Mehmet Resit Ogutcu**
(1914–70)

Turkish novelist, story writer and dramatist, mostly of the oppressed lower and criminal classes, popular and much read in his own country, but so far without a translator. He was too prolific, and thus careless; his style, though direct, was distinctly rough; but his understanding of the psychopathic mentality was without parallel in his country's realist literature, and deserves to be more widely known.

KEMAL, Yashar, pseud of **Yashar Kemal Gokçeli**
(1922/3–)

Turkish novelist, perhaps the best-known internationally, he has also gained widespread sympathy as a political activist, briefly interned by the Turkish authorities for his communist activities in Istanbul. His first novel, *Ince Memed* (1955, Eng trans *Memed, My Hawk*, 1961), won the Varlik Prize and established his international reputation. A sequel *Ince Memed II* (1969) is known in English as *They Burn the Thistles* (1973); a third, as yet untranslated volume appeared in 1984. Kemal's work is marked by a profound sympathy for the peasantry of southern Turkey, and it is his solidarity with them that radiates through his best novel, *Ortadirek* (1960, Eng trans *The Wind From the Plain*, 1963), which is the first part of a trilogy completed by *Yer Demir, Gök Bakir* (1963, Eng trans *Iron Earth, Copper Sky*, 1974) and *Ölmez Otu* (1969, Eng trans *The Undying Grass*, 1977). Much of his work has been translated into English by his wife, Thilda Kemal.

KEMELMAN, Harry
(1908–)

American novelist, whose 'Rabbi' books overturn the usual urban setting for detective (and Jewish) fiction and take place in a small Massachusetts town, similar to that in which Kemelman makes his home. He was born in Boston and went to Boston University and Harvard. His professional career has been divided between writing and business. His novels all concern Rabbi David Small, a younger, Judaic Father Brown; these titles all follow the formula of the first, *Friday the Rabbi Slept Late* (1964), which won an 'Edgar', the Mystery Writers of America **Edgar Allan Poe** Award. The week cycle was completed in 1978 with *Thursday the Rabbi Walked Out*. Short stories appeared in *The Nine Mile Walk* (1967).

KENDALL, (Thomas) Henry
(1839–82)

Australian pastoral and lyric poet, born in Milton, Ulladulla, New South Wales. After early years spent in the New South Wales countryside, he settled in Sydney and contributed verse to local newspapers and journals, first collected in *Poems and Songs* (1862). After his marriage in 1868 he moved to Melbourne where a second book, *Leaves from Australian Forests*, was published in 1869. Continuing problems with debt and alcohol led to separation from his family, but friends eventually restored him to health and in 1879 he won the International Exhibition poetry competition. The next year saw publication of his third and last collection, *Songs from the Mountains*. Renowned in his day for poems such as 'Bell Birds' and 'September in Australia', his patriotic and ceremonial verse shows that Kendall was a significant poet of the colonial period, reflected in the definitive *The Poetical Works of Henry Kendall* (1966).

KENEALLY, Thomas Michael
(1935–)

Australian novelist, born in Sydney, New South Wales. He studied for the priesthood and the law and served in the Australian Citizens' Military Forces. He has taught and lectured in drama. He would like, he has said, to disown his first two novels—*The Place at Whitton* (1964) and *The Fear* (1965). His third novel, *Bring Larks and Heroes* (1967), was 'an attempt to follow out an epic theme in terms of a young soldier's exile to Australia'. *Three Cheers for a Paraclete* (1968) and *The Survivor* (1969) were 'character' studies in the English tradition, but it was the publication of *The Chant of Jimmy Blacksmith* (1972), based on the slaughter of a white family by a hitherto docile Aboriginal employee, that

marked the beginning of his mature fiction. As gifted as he is prolific, he is a born storyteller whose sympathies lie with the oppressed and the outcast. His reputation grew steadily until he published *Schindler's Ark* (1982), which tells how a German industrialist helped over 1000 Jews survive the Nazis. It was a controversial winner of the Booker Prize because it blurred the boundary between fact and fiction. It was memorably filmed, as *Schindler's List*, in 1994. Recent books include *A Family Madness* (1985), *The Playmaker* (1987), *By the Line* (1989), *Flying Hero Class* (1991) and *Woman of the Inner Sea* (1992). His writings include political commentary and travel, but later novels have been criticized for apparent haste.
▷P Quartermaine, *Thomas Keneally* (1991)

KENNAWAY, James
(1928–68)

Scottish novelist, born in Auchterarder, Perthshire, into a quiet middle-class background, the son of a solicitor and a doctor. He went to public school at Glenalmond. He did national service before going to Trinity College, Oxford, after which he worked for a London publisher and began to write in earnest. He married in 1951, and *The Kennaway Papers* (1981), edited by his wife Susan, gives an insight into his mercurial character and their turbulent relationship. *Tunes of Glory* (1956) was his first novel and remains his best known. The author himself wrote the screenplay to the successful film starring Alec Guinness and John Mills in a class confrontation set in a military barracks in Scotland. *Household Ghosts* (1961) was equally powerful, and was made into a stage-play (1967) and a film (1969) under the title *Country Dance*. Later books of note are *The Bells of Shoreditch* (1967), *Some Gorgeous Accident* (1967) and the autobiographical *The Cost of Living Like This* (1969). *Silence*, a novel, was published posthumously in 1972.

KENNEDY, John Pendleton
(1795–1870)

American novelist and social commentator. He was born and educated in Baltimore, Maryland, and saw service in the war of 1812 against the British. He subsequently entered the Maryland legislature (1820–3), and was elected to Congress in Washington as a representative from Maryland, serving two terms (1838, 1840–4). His passage in politics was eased by a substantial legacy from his uncle. In 1852, President Fillmore appointed him Secretary of the Navy. Kennedy is remembered primarily for two books, *Swallow Barn* (1832), a satirical and episodic 'Sojourn in the Old Dominion', and the later *Horse-Shoe Robinson* (1835), a more structured romance

in the tradition of Sir **Walter Scott**. They were published under the pseudonym Mark Littleton. Here and in his two other fictional works, *Rob of the Bowl* (1838) and the **Swift**ian *Quodlibet* (1840), he seems to make a case for a modest balance of aristocratic values and democratic reform (*Quodlibet* is a devastating satire on Jeffersonism run amok). Kennedy's collected works were published in 10 volumes just after his death (1871–2) and included a life by Henry T Tuckerman.
▷ J V Ridgely, *John Pendleton Kennedy* (1966)

KENNEDY, Margaret Moore
(1896–1967)
English novelist, journalist and playwright, born in London, the daughter of a barrister. She was educated at Cheltenham College and Somerville College, Oxford. A historian by training, her first book was *A Century of Revolution* (1922). Thereafter she wrote novels, all of which gained a fair measure of success, particularly her second, *The Constant Nymph* (1924), and its sequel, *The Fool of the Family* (1930). She also wrote plays, notably *Escape Me Never* (1933).
▷ V Powell, *The Constant Novelist* (1983)

KENNEDY, William Joseph
(1928–)
American novelist and screenwriter, born in Albany, New York. Educated at Siena College, Loudonville, New York, he served in the US army (1950–2) before becoming a journalist and eventually a full-time writer. *The Ink Truck* (1969) is distinct from subsequent novels for it does not use the locale of his hometown as a backdrop. *Legs* (1975) is the first of the 'Albany' novels, a mixture of fact and fiction which retells the story of Legs Diamond, the notorious gangster. In *Billy Phelan's Greatest Game* (1978) Albany is as important as the two main characters, the gamester Billy Phelan and journalist Martin Daugherty. *Ironweed* (1983), his best-known novel, describes the homecoming of a fallen baseball star, now down-and-out, drunk and maudlin. Jack Nicholson made an accurate film portrayal and the book won a Pulitzer Prize. *Quinns's Book* was published in 1988.
▷ E C Reilly, *William Kennedy* (1991)

KENNEDY, X J, pseud of Joseph Charles Kennedy
(1929–)
American poet, born in Dover, New Jersey, and educated at Columbia University, New York, and the Sorbonne. After service in the US Navy, he taught at Michigan University (1956–62), where his poetic career began with the extraordinary *Nude Descending a Staircase* (1961), a brilliant collection which for sheer force of character he has not matched since. The following year Kennedy moved to the University of North Carolina (1962–3), and subsequently to Tufts University, Massachusetts, where he was promoted to Professor of English in 1973. Kennedy's reputation was consolidated by *Breaking and Entering* (1972), which was published in the UK, and by *Emily Dickinson in Southern California* (1974), a delightfully unlikely juxtaposition that manages to give a reasonable sense of the vividly metrical, simply rhymed approach which makes him such a successful poet for children. With the exception of the extraordinary *Hangover Mass* (1984) his later work has been disappointing, though a selection, *Cross Ties* (1985), reawakened interest in his work.

KENNELLY, Brendan
(1936–)
Irish poet, novelist and playwright. Born in Ballylongford, County Kerry, he has been Professor of Modern Literature at Trinity College, Dublin since the mid-1970s. A prolific author with over 30 poetry collections, five plays and two published novels to his credit he also edited the *Penguin Book of Irish Verse* (1970, 1986). The immediacy of language and accessibility of themes which is evident in his early work, *Collection One* (1966), is echoed nearly 30 years later in the fierce rhetoric of *Cromwell* (1983) and *Judas* (1991). These two works are vigorously pacifist, addressing intolerance and the subversion of language by politics.

KENNY, Maurice
(1929–)
American poet, born in Watertown, New York State, of Mohawk descent, whose work has influenced a whole generation of Native American poets. He has published over 18 collections of poetry and fiction, his poetry including *North: Poems of Home* (1979), *Kneading the Blood* (1981), *The Smell of Slaughter* (1982), *Is Summer This Bear* (1985) and *Greyhounding This America* (1986). His poems, written in a characteristic incantatory style, often celebrate the vitality of the earth and the natural world. *Blackrobe* (1982), a cycle of poems about the 17th-century Jesuit missionary priest Isaac Jogues, was nominated for a Pulitzer Prize, and *The Mama Poems* won an American Book Award in 1984. Recently, many of his poems have been collected in *Between Two Rivers: Poems 1956–1984* (1987). Kenny is a longtime resident of Brooklyn, co-edits the poetry journal *Contact/II*, and is the publisher of Strawberry

Press. *Rain and Other Fictions* was published in 1985.

KERNER, Andreas Justinus
(1786–1862)

German poet, born in Ludwigsburg in Württemberg. He became a physician at Wildbad, and settled finally in Weinsberg in 1818. He published several volumes of poetry between 1811 and 1852. He studied animal magnetism, believed in occultism, and wrote *Die Seherin von Prevorst* (1829, 'The Clairvoyant of Prevorst'), a study of a psychic case.
▷H Buttiker, *Justinus Kerner* (1952)

KEROUAC, Jack (John)
(1922–69)

American novelist, born in Lowell, Massachusetts. His parents, devout Roman Catholics, came from rural communities in the French-speaking part of Quebec, and French was spoken in the home. He did not begin to learn to speak English until he was six. His childhood was happy, but various disasters struck the stability of the family, including the death of an older brother and floods which destroyed his father's print shop and press. He was educated at Lowell High School before accepting a football scholarship at Columbia University, but he turned his back on both and spent the early years of World War II working as a grease monkey in Hartford before returning to Lowell, where he got a job as a sports journalist on the *Lowell Sun*. His major energies, however, were spent working on an autobiographical novel that was never published. In 1942 he went to Washington where he worked briefly on the construction of the Pentagon before joining the US merchant marines, subsequently enlisting in the US navy (1943). After only a month he was discharged and branded an 'indifferent character'. His life is frequently seen as a rebellion against authority but his various scrapes and outbreaks of outrageous behaviour were less the actions of a subversive than of a weak-willed conservative influenced by persuasive friends like **Allen Ginsberg**, **Gary Snyder** and Neal Cassady, whom Kerouac portrayed as Dean Moriarty in his most famous novel, *On the Road* (1957). He was identified as leader of the so-called 'Beat Generation', a label he came to regret and repudiate. *The Town and the City* (1950), his first novel, showed the scars of his reading of **Thomas Wolfe**. *On the Road* was his second. Loose, apparently structureless and episodic, it follows two friends as they weave their way across America. It has been much imitated (on film as well as in fiction) and made Kerouac a cult-hero. Later books—*The Dharma Bums* (1958), *Doctor Sax* (1959), *Big Sur* (1962)—were even more self-indulgent as he flirted with Zen Buddhism.
▷A Charters, *Jack Kerouac: a biography* (1973)

KESEY, Ken Elton
(1935–)

American author, born in La Junta, Colorado. Associated with the 'Beat' movement, he worked as a ward attendant in a mental hospital, an experience he used to telling effect in *One Flew Over the Cuckoo's Nest* (1963), narrated by an Indian named Chief Bromden whose father was the last chief of the tribe. Filmed in 1975 by Milos Forman it won five Oscars, including that for Best Film. *Sometimes a Great Notion* (1966) sank like lead and he relinquished 'literature' for 'life'. He served a prison sentence for marijuana possession and formed the 'Merry Pranksters', whose weird exploits are described at length in *The Electric Kool-Aid Acid Test* (1967) by **Tom Wolfe**. *Sailor Song* (1990) confirmed the underlying green values of *Demon Box* (1987), a collection of stories and pieces, and returned to something like the roistering fantasy of the earlier books.
▷S Tanner, *Ken Kesey* (1983)

KESSON, Jessie, originally Jessie Grant McDonald
(1915–)

Scottish novelist, short-story writer and playwright, born in Inverness. Not knowing who her father was, she soon moved to Elgin with her mother. Estranged from many of the family, mother and daughter lived meagrely on their own resources, becoming adept at evading the Cruelty Inspector and the rent man. In her teens, however, Jessie was sent to an orphanage in Skene, Aberdeenshire. Later she entered service, settling in 1934 on a farm with her husband Johnnie, a cottar. Although she managed eventually to devote herself to writing, she worked for many years as a cinema cleaner, artists' model and a social worker in London and Glasgow. *The White Bird Passes* (1958), *Glitter of Mica* (1963), *Another Time, Another Place* (1983) and *Where the Apple Ripens* (1985) recreate faithfully, and without sentimentality, her hard early years in a farming community.

KESTEN, Hermann
(1900–)

German-born American novelist, playwright, biographer (Copernicus, Ferdinand and Isabella of Spain,) and translator (**Julien Green**, **Jules Romains**), born in Nuremberg of Jewish parents. In 1932 he wrote his anti-Hitler novel *Der Scharlatan* ('The Charlatan'), which meant that he had to leave Germany the following year. He spent the war in America, and took American citizenship. Outstanding amongst his many books is *Die Zwillinge von Nürnburg* (1947, Eng trans *The Twins of Nuremberg*, 1946), a novel about inter-war Germany.

KEY, Francis Scott
(1780–1843)

American lawyer and poet, born in Maryland, author of *The Star-Spangled Banner*. During the British bombardment of Fort McHenry, Baltimore, in September, 1814, which he witnessed from a British man-of-war, he wrote a poem about the lone American flag seen flying over the fort as dawn broke. It was published as *The Defence of Fort McHenry*, and later set to a tune by the English composer, John Stafford Smith (*To Anacreon in Heaven*). In 1931 it was adopted as the American national anthem as *The Star-Spangled Banner*.

KEYES, Daniel
(1927–)

American science-fiction writer, born in New York City. He taught English at the University of Ohio, Athens, and was briefly an associate editor of the science-fiction magazine *Marvel Science Fiction* in 1951. His reputation rests on his novel *Flowers for Algernon* (1966), originally written as a short story in 1959. It is a moving account of a man whose intelligence is artificially increased to the level of genius, but with tragic consequences, and was successfully filmed as *Charly* (1968). He did not repeat the book's success with his second novel, *The Touch* (1968), about the psychological results of a nuclear accident.

KEYES, Frances Parkinson
(1885–1970)

American novelist, born at the University of Virginia. In 1904 she married Henry Wilder Keyes, Governor of New Hampshire (1917–19), and a senator (1919–37); she made use of her position to write *Letters From a Senator's Wife* (1924), and to travel widely. *The Old Gray Homestead* (1919), her first novel, was followed by dozens of successful works, her popularity proving to be enduring. She is now best known for the murder mystery *Dinner At Antoine's* (1948), set in New Orleans during the run-up to Mardi Gras.

KEYES, Sidney Arthur Kilworth
(1922–43)

English poet, born in Dartford, Kent, and educated at Tonbridge School and Oxford University, where he co-edited *Eight Oxford Poets* (1941), which included his own work.

His first book of poems, *The Iron Laurel*, was published in 1942, and his second, *The Cruel Solstice*, in 1944 (Hawthornden Prize), after his death in action in Libya. His *Collected Poems* appeared in 1945.
▷J Guenther, *Sidney Keyes: a biographical enquiry* (1967)

KHAN, Ismith
(1925–)

Trinidadian-born American novelist, born in Port of Spain. Although Khan's novels are about Trinidad, he did not publish them until he had put a distance between his native land and himself. His first, *The Jumbie Bird* (1961), is in part autobiographical, and centres on the Khan family and its Indian roots. Khan's unusual fiction offers an interesting and valuable contrast to that of the better known **V S Naipaul**.

KHANDEKAR, Vishnu Sakharam
(1898–1976)

Indian (Marathi) novelist who was able to support himself by his writing, although he also had to work in the Indian movie industry. He was left-wing in his views, but never failed to be objective. *White Clouds* (1940) deals with Gandhi's spinning people. *Yayati* (1959, Eng trans 1978) is his major novel, a searing attack on modern materialism, cast in the form of a retelling of a celebrated episode of the *Mahabharata*.

KHARMS, Daniil, pseud of **Daniil Yuvachov**
(1905–42)

Russian poet, dramatist and critic, born in St Petersburg. He was a member (with his friend **Nicolay Zabolotsky**) of the late avant-garde group which called itself OBERIU (acronym of the Russian for Association for Real Art) which gathered itself around the officially 'pure' children's writer **Samuel Marshak** in the hope of surviving the Stalinist onslaught against individuality in art. Kharms could be said to have invented the term 'The Theatre of the Absurd' with his play *Yelizaveta Bam* (1927). He died in a Stalinist prison.
▷G Gibian, *Russia's Lost Literature of the Absurd* (1974)

KHLEBNIKOV, Velimir, pseud of **Viktor Khlebnikov**
(1885–1922)

Major Russian poet and dramatist, born in Tundutovo, in the Astrakhan province, of an ornithologist father; he studied biology as a student, and this left its mark on his poetry. Whatever the final verdict on Khlebnikov's intrinsic achievement, he was one of the most original poets of the 20th century. As well as being an arch intellectual, he was certainly half-mad, and thus spent much of his time attempting to calculate an algorithm by which he could derive the cyclic laws of history; he was on the move for the whole of his short life, and finally died of malnutrition. But he was also a genuine visionary (in a way not wholly uncommon in Russia at that dangerous time), and it is in its visionary qualities that the true value of his extraordinary poetry lies. With **Mikhail Kuzmin**, **Vyacheslav Ivanov** and others he did 'hatch', as has been aptly said, the Russian Futurist movement (a year behind the birth of the Italian movement of the same name, but superior to it in quality), yet in essence he was a religious poet, expressing himself in terms of Slavic mythology and pagan folk epic. Like **Laura Riding**, he wanted to redefine every word in his language; to that end he (with others) devised *zaum*, a 'transrational' language which would lead to world peace (another concern of Riding's) and to heaven on earth. His numerological eccentricities are not irrelevant to his achievement, but they are not a part of it: he was capable of coherent (if always mystical) and inspired lyrics and longer poems, all of which are now continually being restudied and reassessed by readers and critics—to some of whom the nature of the madness behind them is once again relevant. There are English translations of his work in *Smoke Train: Selected Poetry and Prose* (1976).

KHODASEVICH, Vladislaw
(1886–1939)

Russian poet, translator (of Polish and Hebrew poetry) and critic, born in Moscow; he died in exile and in poverty in Paris. His father was Polish, his mother Jewish, and he was always fascinated by Jewish culture and history. **Nabokov**, whose very earliest literary efforts he encouraged, pointed to him as 'the greatest Russian poet of our time'—he knew he exaggerated, but was thus fruitfully able to attract attention to Khodasevich's achievement. A man who, had he not been a poet of such high quality, might have been called unduly sensitive, he was certain that he stood at the end of Russian culture, and in a sense he was right. A Platonist, disgusted by the world, he tried to retreat into himself and to write of the purity he had discovered within his own mind; after his exile to Paris, in which he was helped, painlessly, in 1922, by the good offices of his friend **Gorky**, he also tried to make a success of himself as an émigré poet. But he failed, and after 1928 relapsed into a virtual silence relieved only by some exquisite critical essays. He took after, and almost worshipped, **Pushkin**, hated Futurism and everything 'modern', but was nevertheless and despite himself eminently a poet of the modern sensibility. 'Ballata', (Eng trans 'Ballad'

in the *Penguin Book of Russian Verse*, 1965, ed Dimitry Obolensky), is typical in its invocation to poetry, and shows him at his greatest.

▷V Nabokov, *Strong Opinions* (1973); S Karlinsky and A Appel (eds), *The Bitter Air of Exile* (1977)

KHVYLOVY, Mikola, pseud of Mykola Fitilov
(1893–1933)

Ukrainian story writer, critic and poet, born in Trostyanets, a village in the Kharkov province. He was a keen supporter of the Soviet presence in his country, and was the organiser of the VAPLITE group of proletarian writers. But Stalin's stupidity and bullying drove him to resistance and then to suicide. He wrote satirical stories (his best work), strident poetry and some immature criticism. Stories are translated in *Stories from the Ukraine* (1960, ed W K Matthews).

KIANTO, Ilmari
(1874–1970)

Finnish novelist and (initially) poet, born in Pulkkila. He wrote two classic novels, *Punainan viiva* (1909, 'The Red Line'), and *Ryysyrannan Jooseppi* (1924, 'Ryysyranna's Joseph'), under the combined influences of **Zola** and **Strindberg**, but wholly Finnish in conception. They describe rural poverty with a vivid humour that makes them virtually unique in the literature.

KIELLAND, Alexander L(ange)
(1849–1906)

Norwegian novelist, born in Stavanger, where he became burgomaster in 1891, having withdrawn from literary life. A follower of Georg Brandes, he was an exponent of the realist school. His stylish novels of social satire included *Garman og Worse* (1880), *Skipper Worse* (1882) and *Tales of Two Countries* (1891). He also wrote plays and short stories. Despite intense lobbying by **Bjørnson** and **Jonas Lie**, he was not awarded a state literary pension; though he returned to writing later, disappointment drove him to reject the literary world.

▷J Lunde, *Alexander Lange Kielland* (1970)

KIELY, Benedict
(1919–)

Irish novelist, story writer and critic, born near Dromore, County Tyrone, and much influenced by **William Carleton**. He was a Jesuit novitiate, but was forced to abandon this vocation owing to severe illness. He has been adjudged more skilful in the short story than in the novel, although *The Cards of the Gambler* (1953) was successful. His stories, popular with readers of the *New Yorker*, have been said to 'weave a kind of tapestry around a scarcely satiric love of humanity'. They are collected in *A Journey to the Seven Streams* (1963), *A Ball of Malt and Madame Butterfly* (1973) and elsewhere.

▷ G Eckley, *Benedict Kiely* (1975)

KILLENS, John Oliver
(1916–87)

American novelist, born in Macon, Georgia, whose fictional work represents an episodic commentary on the lives and struggles of Afro-Americans. His experience as a soldier in racially segregated units during World War II led him to write *And Then We Heard the Thunder* (1962), one of the most powerful American war novels. It was Killens's second book; its predecessor, *Youngblood* (1954), is a part-sociological, part-symbolic story of racial prejudice, and advocates working-class solidarity rather than separatism as the most valid response to oppression. *'Sippi* (1967) is too obviously marked by the civil rights and Black Power rhetoric of the time, and despite Killens's ideological sophistication, is far less well argued than the essays in *Black Man's Burden* (1966). *The Cotillion* (1971) is at once more sophisticated in imaginative terms and a return to a plainer, folksier style. It was turned into an effective musical (1975) with music co-written by Smokey Robinson. His desire to understand the wider aspects of 'the black experience' led him to write *The Great Black Russian* (1988), a posthumously published novel about the mulatto **Pushkin**. Killens also wrote intelligent and unpatronizing children's books.

KILLIGREW, Anne
(1660–85)

English poet, born in London into a Royalist family connected with the Restoration theatre. She was appointed maid of honour to the Duchess of York, and painted portraits of the duke and duchess. Her *Poems* (1686), prefaced by the famous ode to her memory by **Dryden**, are mostly pious, melancholy and conventionally baroque in style. She died of smallpox.

▷ A Messenger, *His and Hers: Essays in Restoration and Eighteenth-Century Literature* (1986)

KILLIGREW, Thomas
(1612–83)

English dramatist, brother of Sir **William Killigrew**, page in the household of Charles I, and afterwards a companion of Charles II in exile and his groom of the bedchamber after

the Restoration. He published in 1664 nine indifferent plays, written, he claimed, in nine different cities. The most popular of them was *The Parson's Wedding*. He was for some time manager of the king's company, and obtained permission to give female parts to women. His son, Thomas Killigrew (1657–1719), wrote a theatrical comedy, *Chit Chat* (performed 1719).

▷ A Harbage, *Killigrew: Cavalier dramatist* (1930)

KILLIGREW, Sir William
(1606–95)

English dramatist, brother of **Thomas Killigrew**. He fought in the Civil War, and wrote a comedy, *Pandora*, and tragi-comedies, such as *Selindra*, *Ormasdes* and *The Siege of Urbin*.

KILMER, (Alfred) Joyce
(1886–1918)

American poet, saddled eternally with credit for writing 'Trees', a poem so over-quoted— 'I think that I will never see/A poem lovely as a tree'—and easily spoofed that it has blurred perceptions of his very real gifts. Kilmer published only three collections—*Summer of Love* (1911), the ubiquitous *Trees and Other Poems* (1914) and *Main Street* (1917)—before he was killed on the Western Front, where he was a volunteer; he was awarded a posthumous Croix de Guerre for gallantry. His wife Aline also wrote verse, notably *Candles That Burn* (1919).

KILPI, Volter
(1874–1939)

Finnish novelist, born in Kustavi. Much neglected owing to the highly individualistic style of the books he published in the last six years of his life, when he discovered his own voice, he is one of the most extraordinary writers of his period. His *Alastalon salissa* (1933, 'Alastolo's Hall'), is an often comic meditation on death, reminiscent of **Edgar Lee Masters** as well as of **Joyce**, with whose *Ulysses* it has been compared. *Kirkolle* (1937, 'On the Way to Church'), is a similar but more lyrical meditation, celebrating the moment at the expense of all else. Kilpi was deaf for most of his life, and this contributed to his hermetic style; but the posthumous *Gulliverin matka Fantomimian mantereelle* (1944, 'Gulliver's Journey to Fantomimia') achieves a new clarity.

▷ J Ahokas, *A History of Finnish Literature* (1973)

KILVERT, (Robert) Francis
(1840–79)

English clergyman and diarist. He was a curate at Clyro in Radnorshire and later vicar of

Bredwardine on the Wye. His *Diary (1870–79)*, giving a vivid picture of rural life in the Welsh marches, was discovered in 1937 and published in three volumes (1938–40).

▷F Grice, *Kilvert: priest and diarist* (1975)

KINCAID, Jamaica, originally **Elaine Potter Richardson**
(1949–)

American novelist and journalist, born in St John's, Antigua. Her novels include *At the Bottom of the River* (1983) and *Lucy* (1991), the latter being the sensitive tale of a young West Indian girl who, having fled to New York, grows ever more appreciative of, and eager to return to, her own land. The book is, in part, autobiographical: Kincaid herself has made the same journey, and is currently a staff writer for the *New Yorker*. She enjoys a certain cachet among a feminist audience, and has also written a non-fictional account of her home island, *A Small Place*.

KINCK, Hans Ernst
(1865–1926)

Norwegian novelist and dramatist, born in Øksfjord. His works illustrate his deep love of nature and his interest in the lives of peasants, and include *Sneskavlen brast* (1918–19) and *Driftekaren* (1908, 'The Drover'), a verse play. *Ungtfolk* (1893, Eng trans *A Young People*, 1929) introduced the problematic question of social betterment, taken up again in *Emigranter* (1904, 'Emigrants').

▷E Beyer, *Hans Ernst Kinck* (1956–65)

KING, Francis Henry
(1923–)

English novelist, critic and short-story writer, born in Adelboden, Switzerland, but who spent much of his childhood in India before the family returned to England. After graduating from Oxford, he worked for the British Council, travelling extensively, before retiring to write full-time in 1964. His novels include *The Dividing Stream* (1951), *The Widow* (1957), and the novellas in *Flights* (1973), sensitive fiction whose outward highly-wrought delicacy is sometimes deceptive, for his writing often plunges into the decadent and the bizarre, even horrific. *Act of Darkness* (1983), for instance, is a violent murder mystery set in India, while *Voices in an Empty Room* (1984) deals with the paranormal. He has also written travel books and a short study of **E M Forster** (1978).

KING, Grace Elizabeth
(1851–1932)

American author of local-colour fiction about New Orleans. Her stories first appeared in magazines such as *Harpers* and *Century Magazine*, and were then collected in three volumes—*Monsieur Motte* (1888), whose title story was King's first published work, *Tales of Time and Place* (1892) and *Balcony Stories* (1893). She wrote several historical novels on religious themes and one about the Reconstruction period in New Orleans, *The Pleasant Ways of St. Medard* (1916). She was also a stalwart of the Louisiana Historical Society.

KING, Henry
(1592–1669)

English poet, born in Worminghall, Buckinghamshire, and educated at Westminster School and Christ Church, Oxford. He entered the church, rising to Bishop of Chichester in 1641, and was a friend of **Jonson**, **Donne** and **Izaak Walton**. During the interregnum he was deprived of his bishopric, living in retirement from 1643 to 1660. He published sermons, elegies on Charles I, and a metrical paraphrase of the Psalms; his *Poems, Elegies, Paradoxes, and Sonnets* (1657) were published without authority. The poignant 'Exequy to his Matchless never to be forgotten Friend', written on the death of his young wife Anne in 1624, has secured his reputation as a minor but gifted Metaphysical poet.

▷*Poems*, ed with life and critical introduction by M Crum (1965)

KING, Stephen Edwin
(1947–)

American author of horror fiction, perhaps the most successful practitioner of the art since **Edgar Allan Poe**. He was born in Portland, Maine. His debut novel *Carrie* (1974)—the story of a socially and sexually repressed girl who uses the gift of psychokinesis to take revenge on her tormentors—was a bestseller, as have been most subsequent works, each book augmenting the already vast army of his followers. His short-story collections include *Skeleton Crew* (1985). In novels and stories alike, his most common theme is the irruption of the irrational, the supernatural, into the solid, semi-rural milieu of New England. Like *Carrie*, *The Shining* (1977) and *The Dead Zone* (1979) were successfully filmed. His status as a bestseller, and his popularity with young fans of horror, tend to obscure the fact that, as a storyteller, he is a consummate craftsman.

KING, William
(1663–1712)

English poet, born in London and educated at Westminster School and Christ Church, Oxford, where he took a law degree and became advocate in Doctors' Commons. In

Dialogues of the Dead (1699) he joined in the 'Battle of the Books' against Richard Bentley. Appointed judge in Ireland in 1701, later keeper of records at Dublin Castle, he spent more time writing humorous verse than on his duties. He returned to England in 1708 to live by his pen, publishing copiously: pamphlets, satires and burlesque poems, including *The Art of Cookery* (1708), an imitation of **Horace**. As **Samuel Johnson** remarked, his purpose was to be merry, and he succeeded.
▷Dr S Johnson, *Lives of the Most Eminent English Poets* (10 vols, 1779–81); G G Williams, in *Sewanee Review*, 35 (1927)

KINGO, Thomas Hansen
(1634–1703)

Danish poet and prelate, born in Slangerup, of Scottish descent. The greatest Baroque poet in Denmark's literary history, he was Bishop of Fyn from 1677. He wrote collections of hymns (*Aandeligt sjungekor*, 1674 and 1681, 'Spiritual Chorus'; and *Vinterparten*, 1689, 'The Winter Part') and much secular and religious poetry. His complete works were published in seven volumes between 1939 and 1975.
▷J Simonsen, *Thomas Kingo* (1970)

KINGSLEY, Charles
(1819–75)

English author, born at Holne vicarage, Dartmoor. In 1838 he entered Magdalene College, Cambridge, and took a classical first in 1842. As curate and then rector (1844) he spent the rest of his life at Eversley in Hampshire. His dramatic poem, *The Saint's Tragedy, or The True Story of Elizabeth of Hungary* (1848), was followed by *Alton Locke* (1850) and *Yeast* (1851), brilliant social novels which had enormous influence at the time. He had thrown himself into various schemes for the improvement of the working classes, and like F D Maurice was a 'Christian Socialist'. As 'Parson Lot' he published an immense number of articles on current topics, especially in the *Christian Socialist* and *Politics for the People*. *Hypatia* (1853) is a brilliant picture of early Christianity in conflict with Greek philosophy at Alexandria. *Westward Ho!* (1855) is a lifelike representation of Elizabethan England and the Spanish Main. *Two Years Ago* (1857) and *Hereward the Wake* (1866) were his later novels. In 1860 he was appointed Professor of Modern History at Cambridge; *The Roman and the Teuton* (1864) was based on his Cambridge lectures. In 1869 he resigned his professorship and was appointed canon of Chester. In 1869–70 he made a voyage to the West Indies, and on his return issued the charming account *At Last*. In 1873 he was appointed canon of Westminster and chaplain to Queen Victoria. The collected works of this combative, enthusiastic and sympathetic apostle of what was called (*not* by him) 'muscular Christianity' fill 28 volumes (1879–81), and include *Glaucus* (1855), *The Heroes* (1856), *The Water Babies* (1863), *Town Geology* (1872), *Prose Idylls* (1873) and *Health and Education* (1874).
▷S Chitty, *The Beast and the Monk* (1974)

KINGSLEY, Henry
(1830–76)

English novelist, brother of **Charles Kingsley**. He was educated at King's College School, London, and Worcester College, Oxford. From 1853 to 1858 he worked as a gold prospector in Australia, and on his return published a vigorous picture of colonial life in *Recollections of Geoffry Hamlyn* (1859). After this came *Ravenshoe* (1861), his masterpiece, followed by *Austin Elliot* (1863), and then *The Hillyars and the Burtons*, another novel of Australian life (1865). In 1869–70 he edited the *Edinburgh Daily Review*.
▷J S D Mellick, *The Passing Guest: a life of Henry Kingsley* (1983)

KINGSLEY, Mary St Leger *see* MALET, Lucas

KINGSLEY, Sidney, originally Sidney Kirschner
(1906–)

American dramatist, born in New York City and educated at Cornell University. He won a Pulitzer Prize with his first play, *Men in White* (1933), set in a hospital, which deals with a young intern's conflicting sense of duty and search for personal happiness. His second, extremely successful drama, *Dead End* (1935), is a realistic study suggesting that poverty is the seedbed of crime. His following two plays were both failures, but *The Patriots* (1943), a historical drama recounting the formative years of American democracy, and which served as a call for national unity during World War II, restored him to critical and popular acclaim. In his later plays, *Detective Story* (1949) and *Night Life* (1962), he returned to describing tough social conditions.

KINGSMILL, Hugh, originally Hugh Kingsmill Lunn
(1889–1949)

English biographer and anthologist, younger brother of Arnold Lunn and Brian Lunn. Educated at Harrow, Oxford and Dublin, he became a writer, initially winning odium for iconoclasm degenerating into idleness. But after the failure of his *Matthew Arnold* (1928), he recovered himself with the satirical fantasy *The Return of William Shakespeare* (1929), produced works of art in his *Frank Harris*

(1932) and his elegant essays *The Table of Truth* and *The Progress of a Biographer* (1949). He produced excellent anthologies, such as *Invective and Abuse* (1944), *Johnson Without Boswell* (1940) and *The Worst of Love* (1931), while with Hesketh Pearson he established a delightful art-form in conversational literary journeys such as *Skye High* (1937), *This Blessed Plot* (1942) and *Talking of Dick Whittington* (1947).

▷M Holroyd, *The Collected Hugh Kingsmill* (1964, rev edn 1971)

KINGSTON, Maxine Hong
(1940–)

Chinese–American novelist and autobiographer, born and educated in California. *The Woman Warrior* (1976) is an account of her coming to terms with the tension between two inimical cultures; though barely fictionalized, it also poses serious literary questions about narrative method and the relationship between fantasy and memory. *China Men* (1980) is in similar vein, but *Tripmaster Monkey* (1989) transfers the essential dilemmas and desires of the earlier books to a Sino–American man who considers himself to be an avatar of the sacred Monkey King.

KINGSTON, William Henry Giles
(1814–80)

English author, son of a merchant in Oporto, where he spent much of his youth. He wrote over 150 boys' adventure stories including such favourites as *Peter the Whaler* (1851) and *The Three Midshipmen* (1862).

▷M R Kingsford, *The Life, Work and Influence of William Kingston* (1947)

KINKEL, Gottfried
(1815–82)

German poet, born in Oberkassel near Bonn. He lectured at Bonn on theology, poetry and the history of art. Involved in the revolutionary movement of 1848, he was imprisoned in Spandau (1850), from where he escaped. He taught German in London until 1866, when he was appointed Professor of Archaeology and Art at Zürich. As a poet his fame rests upon *Otto der Schütz* (1846, 'Otto the Hunter'), *Der Grobschmied von Antwerpen* (1872, 'The Blacksmith of Antwerp'), *Tanagra* (1883, Eng trans *Tanagra: an idyll of Greece*, 1893), *Gedichte* (1843–68, 'Poems'), and a drama, *Nimrod* (1857). He also wrote a history of art (1845) and monographs on **Ferdinand Freiligrath** (1867) and Rubens (1874). His first wife, Johanna (1810–58), a distinguished musician, wrote a novel, *Hans Ibeles in London* (1860), and, with her husband, *Erzählungen* (1849, 'Tales'), a collection of tales.

KINNELL, Galway
(1927–)

American poet and translator. He was born in Providence, Rhode Island, and educated at Princeton University and the University of Rochester, and has taught at campuses throughout the USA. His early work was gathered as *First Poems, 1946–1954* (1970), establishing a direct, semi-'confessional' style, with a muscular edge. *The Avenue Bearing the Initial of Christ into the New World* (1974) collected work from 1946 to 1964, a pattern of dates that suggests again that Kinnell's reputation was as slow to build as his art was deliberate, undemonstrative and carefully crafted. The title poem uses Avenue C in New York as a focus for a study of human suffering. *The Book of Nightmares* (1971) covered similar ground in a single long poem. Later books include *The Last Hiding Places of Snow* (1980) and *The Fundamental Project of Technology* (1983). He has written one novel, *Black Light* (1966), and has published many translations, most significantly his versions of **François Villon** (1965, 1977, 1982). Kinnell won the Pulitzer Prize in 1983.

▷ *Walking Down the Stairs* (interviews, 1978)

KINOSHITA Junji
(1914–)

Japanese playwright, one of the first modern Japanese dramatists. His work varies between the two extremes of intellectual, issue-based theatre and popular, accessible plays. He is best known for *Yuzuru* (1949, 'Twilight Crane'), which is based on a folk tale and is a repertory classic in Japan, being an accessible and rewarding play. *Furu* (1947, 'Wandering'), on the other hand, about the Meiji Restoration in 1868 and the subsequent political upheavals, is a superbly crafted piece of historical theatre, being particularly strong in its depiction of the mental sufferings of the protagonists. His work at its weightiest, however, tends to sacrifice theatricality for analysis, and some of it is barely possible to stage.

KINSELLA, Thomas
(1928–)

Irish poet and translator (from the ancient Irish), born in Dublin. Although highly thought of in his native country, and described there as one of Ireland's 'most original and stimulating' practitioners, Kinsella's poetry has not yet been much read outside it. More indebted to the work of English and American poets (**Auden** in particular) than to that of his Irish predecessors, Kinsella's later poetry has moved in a **Jung**ian direction, being much concerned with the notion of 'individuation'. This has led some Irish critics to declare that he has 'brooded himself to pieces'; but others point to his establishment of 'reasonably authentic myth'.

▷ *Selected Poems 1956–1968* (1973); M Harmon, *The Poetry of Thomas Kinsella* (1974)

KINSELLA, W(illiam) P(atrick)
(1935–)

Canadian novelist and short-story writer, born in Edmonton. He worked in the retail business, as a restaurateur and taxi driver in Victoria, British Columbia, before joining the English faculty at the University of Calgary, Alberta (1978–83) following the publication of his first collection of stories. *Dance Me Outside* (1977) and the later *Born Indian* (1981) and *The Moccasin Telegraph* (1983) are all concerned with a young Indian boy and his rites of passage. Based on an earlier baseball story, Kinsella's first novel was *Shoeless Joe* (1982), a fable about the betrayal and restitution of innocence; its connections to *A Catcher in the Rye* and *The Great Gatsby* are confirmed when **J D Salinger** and the historical 1919 Chicago White Sox team appear as characters. The novel was subsequently made into the movie *Field of Dreams* (1989). Kinsella's later novel—*The Iowa Baseball Confederacy* (1986), and the stories in *The Further Adventures of Slugger McBatt* (1988)—are more conventional, but collections like *The Thrill of the Grass* (1984) and *The Fencepost Chronicles* (1986) continue the line of his earlier books.

KIPLING, Rudyard
(1865–1936)

English writer and winner of the Nobel Prize for literature, born in Bombay, the son of John Lockwood Kipling (1837–1911), Principal of the School of Art in Lahore. He was educated at the United Services College, Westward Ho!, in Devon, in England, but returned in 1880 to India, where he worked as a journalist on the Lahore *Civil and Military Gazette*. His mildly satirical verses *Departmental Ditties* (1886), and the short stories *Plain Tales from the Hills* (1888) and *Soldiers Three* (1889), won him a reputation in England. He returned in 1889 and settled in London, where *The Light that Failed* (1890), his first attempt at a full-length novel, was not altogether successful. In London he met Wolcott Balestier, the American author-publisher, with whom he collaborated in *The Naulakha* (1892), and whose sister Caroline he married (1892). A spell of residence in his wife's native state of Vermont ended abruptly in 1899 through incompatibility with in-laws and locals, and the remainder of Kipling's

career was spent in England. Meanwhile he had written the brilliantly successful *Barrack Room Ballads* (1892) and *The Seven Seas* (1896), both collections of verse, and further short stories published as *Many Inventions* (1893) and *The Day's Work* (1899). The two *Jungle Books* (1894–5) have won a place among the classic animal stories, and *Stalky and Co* (1899) presents semi-autobiographical but delightfully uninhibited episodes based on the author's schooldays. *Kim* appeared in 1901, and the children's classic *Just So Stories* in 1902. The verse collection *The Five Nations* (1903) included the highly successful 'Recessional', written for Queen Victoria's diamond jubilee in 1897. Later works include *Puck of Pook's Hill* (1906), *Rewards and Fairies* (1910), *Debits and Credits* (1926), and the autobiographical *Something of Myself* (1937). Kipling's real merit as a writer has tended to become obscured in recent years and he has been accused of imperialism and jingoism, but this ignores not only the great body of his work which was far removed from this sphere, but also his own criticisms and satire on some of the less admirable aspects of colonialism. He was awarded the Nobel Prize for literature in 1907.

▷ C Carrington, *Rudyard Kipling: his life and work* (1955)

KIPPHARDT, Heinar
(1922–)

German novelist and playwright, born in Heidersdorf, Silesia. A psychiatrist until 1951, he became famous overnight with his play *In der Sache J. Robert Oppenheimer* (1964, Eng trans *In the Matter of J. Robert Oppenheimer*, 1967), a chilling re-shaping of the moral case against the American Atomic Energy Commission. This is one of the most effectively **Brecht**ian plays since Brecht. In the novel *März* (1976, 'March') he turns back to his psychiatric experience.

KIRK, Hans
(1898–1962)

Danish novelist, born into a radical, atheistic doctor's family in North Jutland. He graduated in law from the University of Copenhagen in 1922, then worked at the Danish Embassy in Paris before becoming a journalist for a Danish provincial newspaper. A communist, he came to notice with his first novel *Fiskerne* (1928, 'The Fishermen'), a collective narrative that focuses on the relationship between social class and religion in a small fishing and farming community by the Limfjord. This and the subsequent connected works *Daglejerne* (1936, 'The Day-Labourers') and *De ny Tider* (1939, 'New Times'), about the rise of the industrial working

classes in Denmark, firmly established the collective novel as a popular and prestigious form in Danish literature of the 1930s.
▷C Jensen, *Folkelighed og utopi. Brydninger i Hans Kirks forfatterskab* (1981)

KIRKUP, James
(1923–)

English poet, born in South Shields, and the holder of academic posts, first at home (Leeds University, 1950–2), then, from the early 1960s, in Japan, where he became Professor of English Literature at Kyoto University. His collections include *A Correct Compassion* (1952) and *Zen Contemplations* (1978). As its title suggests, the latter—sparse, economical, unostentatious—shows the influence of Japan on his work. He has also published plays, fiction and a frank autobiography, *The Only Child* (1957).

KIRKWOOD, James
(1930–89)

American dramatist, novelist and actor, born in Los Angeles. He acted on both stage and in television, but is best known as a writer. His plays include an adaptation of *There Must Be A Pony* (1962), *UTBU (Unhealthy To Be Unpleasant)* (1965) and *PS. Your Cat is Dead* (1975, from his own novel). His other novels include *Good Times/Bad Times* (1966), *Some Kind of Hero* (1975) and *Hit Me With A Rainbow* (1980). He co-wrote the book (script) for the broadway smash-hit musical *A Chorus Line* (1975, with Nicholas Dante), for which they were awarded a Pulitzer Prize for Drama, with composer Marvin Hamlisch (1944–), lyricist Edward Kleban (1939–87) and director Michael Bennett (1943–).

KIRSANOV, Semyon
(1906–72)

Russian poet, born in Odessa. At first associated with and influenced by **Mayakovsky**, he later became a reluctant Stalinistic poet; however, he contributed vital satirical poems in the 1956 'Thaw'.

KIRSHON, Vladimir
(1902–38)

Russian dramatist, born in St Petersburg, who vanished and was then murdered in the Purges—despite the fact that his well-made plays were all 'politically correct'. *Khleb* (1930, Eng trans *Bread*, in *Six Soviet Plays*, ed E Lyons, 1934) is typical in its supposed demonstration that wealthy farmers ('kulaks') were villainous starvers of the common people. He also wrote many film scenarios.

KIŠ, Danilo
(1935–)

Yugoslavian novelist, born in Subotica, Vojdovina, in the extreme north of the province, near the Hungarian and Romanian borders. He was educated in Belgrade, and moved to France as a teacher of Serbo–Croat. His first novel, *Mansarda; Psalam 44* ('The Garret, Psalm XLIV'), appeared in 1962, but it was the strongly autobiographical *Bašta, pepeo* (1965) which, as *Garden, Ashes* (1976), established his reputation in the West. Its impact was reinforced by *Grobnica za Borisa Davidoviča* (1976, Eng trans *A Tomb for Boris Davidovich*, 1978), a collection of short stories about the Holocaust, a subject Kiš had already explored in the brilliant *Peščanik* (1972, Eng trans *Hourglass*, 1990). Though favourably received elsewhere, *A Tomb* was greeted with charges of plagiarism in Yugoslavia, to which Kiš responded vigorously in the satirical *Čas anatomije* (1978, 'The Anatomy Lesson'). Later works incude *Enciklopedija mrtvih* (1983, Eng trans *The Encyclopedia of the Dead*, 1987).

KISFALUDY, Karoly
(1788–1830)

Hungarian dramatist, brother of the poet Sandor Kisfaludy (1772–1844). He turned his back on his noble upbringing, and lived the life of a bohemian artist. He was the regenerator of the national drama, and became famous for his *A' Tatárok Magyar Országban* (1819, 'Tartars in Hungary'). His brother's poetry continued to reflect the noble family tradition.
▷F Szinnyei, *Kisfaludy Karoly* (1927)

KITAHARA Hakushu
(1885–1942)

Japanese poet and lyricist who achieved great popular success in his day, and is still widely read. Writing in all the traditional forms, *waka*, *haiku* and free verse, Kitahara was a highly accomplished wordsmith with a spare, elegant turn of phrase, and produced intensely personal verse, much of it with a rhythmical structure which made it ideal for use as song lyrics, which partly accounts for his popularity.

KITZBERG, August
(1856–1927)

Estonian playwright and story writer, born in Halliste, Pärnumaa. His plays about country life, sometimes using folklore material, have become classics of the Estonian theatre. The most famous is *Libahunt* (1911), on a werewolf theme.

KIVI, Aleksis, originally **Stenvall**
(1834–72)

Finnish playwright and novelist, born in Nur-mijärvi or Palojoki, the son of a poor tailor. He managed to gain a place at Helsinki University but did not graduate. He wrote in Finnish not Swedish, establishing the western dialect as the modern literary language of Finland, and is considered the father of the Finnish theatre and novel. He wrote the first Finnish novel, *Seitsemän veljestä* (1870, Eng trans *Seven Brothers*, 1929), and a collection of Finnish poems, *Kanervala* (1866). As a dramatist he wrote rural comedies like *Num-misuutarit* (1864, 'The Cobblers on the Heath'), and a tragedy, *Kullervo* (1864), based on one of the central figures in the national epic, the *Kalevala*.
▷V Tarkiainen, *Alexis Kivi* (1950)

KIVIMAA, Kaarlo Arvi
(1904–)

Finnish poet, critic, novelist and dramatist, born in Hartola. From 1949 he was Director of the Finnish National Theatre. Originally associated with the Torchbearer Group of the 1920s, his novels, poetry and drama all seek to promote 'Europeanism', as well as to express his melancholy appreciation of the beauties of his country.

KIZER, Carolyn Ashley
(1925–)

American poet, born in Spokane, Washington. She was educated at Columbia University and the University of Seattle, and founded the journal *Poetry Northwest* in Seattle. She worked briefly for the State Department as an adviser on Pakistan, and has taught at a number of universities. Her first collection, *Poems* (1959), was followed by *The Ungrateful Garden* (1961). Subsequent volumes include *Knock Upon Silence* (1965), *Midnight Was My Cry* (1971), *Mermaids in the Basement: Poems for Women* (1984) and *The Nearness of You: Poems for Men* (1986). She won the Pulitzer Prize for Poetry in 1985 for *Yin* (1984). Her translations from several languages, including Urdu and Chinese, are gathered in *Carrying Over* (1988).

KLABUND, pseud (meaning 'transformation') of **Alfred Henschke**
(1890–1928)

German poet, dramatist and novelist, born in Crossen on the Oder. He died young of tuberculosis, which had made him into an invalid for much of his life. His work was widely read in the years before his death, which was lamented by his friend **Gottfried Benn**. His plays were clever, his short novels readable; his poetry, which was wide in its range, went deeper, especially his sensual poems and his adaptations from the Chinese. Two of his historical novels were translated, *Pjotr* (1923, Eng trans *Peter the Czar*, 1925), and *Borgia* (1928, Eng trans 1929); but the finest, the posthumous *Rasputin* (1929), was not.
▷C Middleton and M Hamburger (eds), *Modern German Poetry 1910–1969* (1962)

KLEIN, A(braham) M(oses)
(1909–72)

Canadian editor, critic, essayist, translator of Hebrew and Yiddish writers, and accomplished author of prose and poetry, born in the Ukraine. He lived in Montreal from early infancy, graduating from McGill in 1930 and the Université de Montreal law school in 1933. He was a committed Zionist, of which the poetry of *The Second Scroll* (1951) is an important expression. He has been described as 'the first contributor of authentic Jewish poetry to the English language', and was an important influence on the younger generation of Jewish writers based in Montreal including **Irving Layton** and **Leonard Cohen**. *The Rocking Chair* (1948) won a Governor General's Award, and includes the much anthologized poem, 'Portrait of the Poet as Landscape'.

KLEIST, Ewald
(1715–59)

German poet, born in Zeblin, near Köslin, in Pomerania. A nobleman by birth, he studied at Königsberg University, then joined the Danish army in 1736. He left in 1740 and was commissioned in the Prussian army later that year. His poetry of the early 1740s is melancholic, reflecting his dislike of military life. In 1749 he published, to widespread acclaim, *Der Frühling* ('Spring'). A major by the beginning of the Seven Years War, he turned to patriotic verse during that campaign. One of his last works was the epic *Cissides und Paches* (1759), set in ancient Greece after the death of Alexander the Great. He died of wounds received during the battle of Kunersdorf.

KLEIST, Heinrich von
(1777–1811)

German dramatist and poet, born in Frankfurt an der Oder. His family had a long military tradition, but he left the army in 1799 to study, and soon devoted himself to literature. His work is marked by a sometimes anguished struggle to come to terms with his doubts over man's ability to shape his own fate and destiny amid the political and personal upheavals of the age. His best plays are still popular, notably *Prinz Friedrich von Homburg* (1811, Eng trans *The Prince of*

Homburg, 1959), and his finest tale is *Michael Kohlhaas* (1808–10). He committed suicide.

▷W Silz, *Heinrich von Kleist* (1961)

KLINGER, Friedrich Maximilian von
(1752–1831)

German playwright and novelist, born in Frankfurt-am-Main. He was an officer in the Russian army from 1780 to 1811, and curator of Dorpat University from 1803 to 1817. The 'Sturm und Drang' school was named after one of his tragedies, *Der Wirrwarr* ('Confusion'), published as *Sturm und Drang* (1776, literally 'Storm and Stress': the phrase was adopted as the label for a major school of 19th-century German writing). He wrote several other plays and some novels.

▷M Rieger, *Friedrich Maximilian Klinger* (3 vols, 1880–96)

KLITGAARD, Mogens
(1906–45)

Danish novelist, born into a lower middle-class family. One of the most innovative of the Danish social realists of the 1930s, he came to notice with his first novel *Der sidder en Mand i en Sporvogn* (1937, 'A Man Sits in a Tramcar'). It is an atmospheric, unromantic fiction about the social and psychological downfall of a Copenhagen shopkeeper, Lundegaard, whose business goes bust in the recession years. This and subsequent works such as the everyday novel *Elly Petersen* (1941) and the montage fiction *Den guddommelige Hverdag* (1942, 'The Divine Ordinary Day'), in which Klitgaard makes clever use of documentary clips from the media, reveal the author's main preoccupations: the big city and the little man or woman in crisis. Like his German contemporary **Hans Fallada**, Klitgaard focuses on the poorly paid white-collar worker, whose dangerous attraction to the authoritarian ideologies he highlights, occasionally counterpointing a utopian hint of social insight and group solidarity.

▷J Levy, 'Mogens Klitgaard', in *Dansk digtere i det 20. århundrede*, vol 2 (1981)

KLOOS, Willem
(1859–1938)

Dutch poet, translator (**Euripides**) and critic, the central figure—with his friend **Verwey**—in the 'Movement of the Eighties'. Fired by his understanding of **Keats** and **Shelley**, he successfully challenged the didactic course of Dutch poetry. He is most famous for his early sonnets, *Het Boek van Kind en God* (1888, 'The Book of the Child and God'); but in his later life he could not maintain his inspiration, and his verse became more academic and self-consciously beautiful. As a critic he set enduring standards for the poetry of his country.

▷K H de Raaf, *Willem Kloos, de mensch, de dichter, de criticus* (1934)

KLOPSTOCK, Friedrich Gottlieb
(1724–1803)

German poet, born in Quedlinburg. Inspired by **Virgil** and **Milton**, he began *Der Messias* ('The Messiah') as a student at Jena (1745), continued it at Leipzig (1748), and completed it in 1773. He settled in Hamburg in 1771 with a sinecure appointment, and pensions from Frederik V of Denmark (from 1751) and the Margrave of Baden. Regarded in his day as a great religious poet, he helped inaugurate the golden age of German literature. He wrote a number of plays, works on language, and a series of lyrical and highly accomplished odes.

▷G Kaiser, *Klopstock* (1962)

KLYUYEV, Nikolay
(1887–1937)

Russian poet from a family of educated peasants in the Olonets province who, although he sang praises of the Revolution (because he believed that it represented the fulfilment of God's mission to Russia), was murdered by it when they sent him to Siberia as a kulak (wealthy peasant). He was an 'Old Believer', a member of the 'Khlysty' ('God's People') sect, and he had a great influence not only upon the more sophisticated, but also more susceptible, **Blok**, but also on **Yesenin**. When he first went to Moscow he surprised everyone with his peasant dress and dedicated religiosity, taken as shameless hypocrisy by some, but as prophetic certainty by others. His early poetry, intensely folkloristic, filled with local colour, and pious, was very popular. He wandered around Russia, became disillusioned about the role of the Revolution, and was eventually arrested; **Gorky** interceded for him, but this gave him only a temporary reprieve. For long he was persona non grata in Soviet Russia, but now his important poetry is being reassessed. One of his most famous poems is his lament for Esenin's suicide, which is translated in *Poems* (1977), which has a useful and informative introduction.

▷L Trotsky, *Literature and Revolution* (1923); V Zavalashin, *Early Soviet Writers* (1958)

KNEALE, Nigel
(1922–)

Manx writer and dramatist, born on the Isle of Man. After working in a lawyer's office, he first gained attention with a collection of short stories, *Tomato Cain* (1949), which won the **Somerset Maugham** Award. After a spell at RADA he joined the drama department of the BBC in a general capacity and progressed to writing the serial *The Quatermass Experiment* (1953): an imaginative science-fiction drama, reflecting the paranoia of the day, its immense popularity led to *Quatermass II* (1955), *Quatermass and the Pit* (1959), *Quatermass* (1978) and three feature films. His early television adaptations also include *Curtain Down* (1952), *Wuthering Heights* (1953) and *1984* (1954). His film scripts include *The Abominable Snowman* (1957), *First Men in the Moon* (1964), *The Witches* (1966) and *Halloween III* (1983). His television plays include *The Year of the Sex Olympics* (1968), *Bam! Pow! Zap!* (1969), *Beasts* (1975) and *Kinvig* (1981).

KNIGHT, Damon Francis
(1922–)
American science-fiction writer, born in Oregon. He was a member of the New York fan group The Futurians, and wrote a history of their activities. He published his first story in 1941, but made his initial impact in the genre as a critic and reviewer. His own best fiction has been in the form of short stories, notably those which he wrote in the 1950s. His stories are collected in several volumes, including *Far Out* (1961), *Off Centre* (1965) and *Turning On* (1966). His novels have rarely achieved the same standard, but the best of them include *The People Maker* (1959) and *Why Do Birds* (1992). He was a significant editor of anthologies, notably the long-running *Orbit* series, and did much to create the institutional base of contemporary science fiction.

KNOWLES, James Sheridan
(1784–1862)
Irish dramatist, born in Cork, the son of a schoolmaster and a cousin of **Richard Brinsley Sheridan**. After serving in the militia he studied medicine at Aberdeen, but took to the stage. He did not achieve distinction and subsequently opened a school in Belfast and (1816–28) in Glasgow. His tragedy, *Caius Gracchus* (1815), was first performed in Belfast. *Virginius*, his most effective play, had been a success in Glasgow before William Macready produced it at Covent Garden in 1820. As well as *William Tell* (1825), his most successful plays were *The Hunchback* (1832), *The Wife* (1833) and *The Love Chase* (1837). He appeared with fair success in many of his own pieces. About 1844 he became a Baptist preacher, drew large audiences to Exeter Hall, and published two anti-Roman Catholic works.
▷ L H Meeks, *Sheridan Knowles and the theatre of his time* (1933)

KNOWLES, John
(1926–)
American novelist, born in Fairmont, West Virginia and educated at Yale University. He has been a reporter, an assistant editor of a magazine, and a writer-in-residence. In 1961 he won three special awards, including a **Rosenthal** Foundation Award and a **Faulkner** Foundation Award. His first novel, *A Separate Peace* (1959), remains his most famous; it tells the story of two boys at a boarding school in New England during World War II and their intense and ambivalent relationship. He is the author of eight other novels, including a sequel to his first entitled *Peace Breaks Out* (1981), which does not, however, live up to its predecessor.

KNOX, Edmund George Valpy, pseud Evoe
(1881–1971)
English humorous writer and parodist, brother of **Ronald Arbuthnott Knox**. He joined the staff of *Punch* in 1921 and became editor from 1932 to 1949, contributing articles under his pen-name. His best work was republished in book form and includes *Fiction as She is Wrote* (1923), *Quaint Specimens* (1925), *Folly Calling* (1932), and others.

KNOX, Ronald Arbuthnott
(1888–1957)
English theologian, writer and detective novelist, born in Birmingham, the son of an Anglican bishop and brother of **Edmund George Knox**. Educated at Eton and Balliol College, Oxford, he became a fellow and lecturer at Trinity College, Oxford, in 1910, but resigned in 1917 on his reception into the Church of Rome. He was Catholic chaplain at Oxford from 1926 to 1939. Author of numerous works of apologetics, his modern translation of the Bible, widely used by Roman Catholics, is specially noteworthy. His essays are distinguished by their satirical wit and trenchant criticism of some contemporary modes and manners. He published his autobiographical *A Spiritual Aeneid* in 1918. He also wrote several detective novels, such as *Still Dead* (1934).

KNUDSEN, Erik
(1922–)
Danish poet, born in Slagese, Zealand, who has taken a socialist and anti-American line which has much in common with such German writers as **Hans Magnus Enzensberger**. His poetry, beginning by expressing some interest in religion, has gradually eschewed this, in favour of an aggressive atheism and a belief in love as the only redeeming quality in

an otherwise doomed world. His mature style is reflected in his collection *Forsog på at gå* (1978, 'Attempts to Walk').

KNUDSEN, Jacob
(1858–1917)

Danish novelist, born in Redding, a South Jutland village. He studied theology, and became a schoolteacher, then a minister, and finally a lecturer. *Den gamle Praest* (1899, 'The Old Pastor') has the unusual theme of a pastor's exhortation to a parishioner to seek redemption from an act of murder, not through giving himself up to the law, but through killing himself. *Gjaering-Afklaring* (1902, 'Fermentation-Clarification') is largely autobiographical. Knudsen has been found to be an unattractive novelist, cold and repellent, but he is one of great interest because of the nature of his subjectivity.
▷C Roos, *Jacob Knudsen* (1954, in Danish)

KOBAYASHI Takiji
(1903–33)

Japanese novelist and political activist. Born on the northern island of Hokkaido, he went to Tokyo having become a convinced Marxist. He wrote two political novels: *Toseikatsusha* (1934, 'Party Worker') and *Kani Kosen* (1929, Eng trans *The Factory Ship and the Absentee Landlord*, 1933), which depicts the grim struggle for better conditions of a group of canning factory workers. At the height of the fascist regime's power, Kobayashi was arrested by the Kempeito (secret police) in Tokyo for subversive political activities and murdered by them.

KOBER, Arthur
(1900–74)

Polish-born American dramatist, writer of newspaper sketches and screenwriter, who was brought to New York from Poland as a child of four. Many of his dialect stories set in the Bronx were published by the *New Yorker*. His best-known play is *Having Wonderful Time* (1937, a comedy about people trying to improve themselves; it became the musical *Wish You Were Here*, 1952). He was for a time married to **Lillian Hellman**.

KOCH, C(hristopher) J(ohn)
(1932–)

Australian novelist, born in Hobart, Tasmania, which features in his first novel *Boys in the Island* (1958, rev edn 1974), concerned with growing up—sooner than one wants. Making much use of symbolism and imagery, it was followed by *Across the Sea Wall* (1965, rev edn 1982) which moves between India and Australia and, again,

describes the betrayal of innocence. Koch's exotic thriller *The Year of Living Dangerously* (1978) is set in a tense Indonesia just before the downfall of Sukarno in the 1960s. It became immensely popular through Peter Weir's adventure film in which symbol, in the shape of Javanese 'Wayang' puppets, once more punctuates the action. *Crossing the Gap: a Novelist's Essays* (1993) explores his experiences of Australia's Empire past and Asian future.

KOCH, Kenneth Jay
(1925–)

American poet and playwright. Though identified with the 'New York School', along with **Frank O'Hara** and **John Ashbery**, he was raised in Cincinnati and educated at Harvard. He taught at Rutgers University, New Jersey in the mid-1950s, and in 1962 joined the faculty at Columbia University. His long poem *The Burning Mystery of Anna in 1951* (1979) offers a picture of life in New York during that time. His first major work, however, was the surreal epic *Ko, or A Season on Earth* (1959), written in the same poetic form as **Byron**'s *Don Juan* and embodying the New York School's slightly cavalier approach to semantics. In 1973 he won the Frank O'Hara Prize, awarded in memory of his friend. Later collections include *The Art of Love* (1975) and *Days and Nights* (1982). *A Selected Poems* appeared in 1985. Koch has also written a considerable number of lyric plays, including *George Washington Crossing the Delaware* (1962) and *The Tinguely Machine Mystery, or The Love Suicides at Kaluka* (1965), both of which reflect some of the fine-art concerns of the New York poets. Koch has long been interested in teaching poetry to the young and to the terminally ill; he discusses the former in *Rose, Where Did You Get That Red?* (1973) and the latter in *I Never Told Anybody* (1977).
▷*John Ashbery and Kenneth Koch: A Conversation* (1965)

KOCH, Martin
(1882–1940)

Swedish novelist, born in Stockholm. Regarded as a seminal figure among the many working-class writers of the first half of the century, he was above all a moralist. In *Arbetare* (1912, 'Workers') he contrasts what he sees as the two extremes of working-class existence: the criminality of the lumpenproletariat and the morality of the organized socialist whose duty it is to lead the former out of its darkness. His finest work—for which he has been compared to **Dostoyevsky**—was *Guds vackra värld* (1916, 'God's Beautiful World'), in which he ultimately posits a vaguely Christian religiosity

KOCHANOWSKI, Jan

as an antidote to the condition of modern industrial man.

▷G D Hansson et al, *Martin Koch—tre studier* (1988)

KOCHANOWSKI, Jan
(1530–85)

Polish poet—the greatest Slavic writer of his time. Born in Sycyna, he served as a courtier, but withdrew from court life in 1570 and settled down to a farming life in Czarnolas. His earlier work had been done in both Latin and Polish, but his most important was the wholly Polish work that he did in his retired life. His famous and much valued *Piésni* (1586, Eng trans *Chants*, 1932), are the most Horatian of any truly original European writer's. His *Fraszki* (1584, 'Trifles'), brilliant epigrams, were unlike anything written in his language up to that date. The first tragedy in Polish, *Odpawa postow greckich*, (1578, Eng trans *The Dismissal of the Greek Envoys*, 1918), was modelled on **Seneca**, and surpassed him, although it has been called 'static'. It has been said that his influence proved as vital to Polish poetry as that of **Spenser** and **Shakespeare** to English. A selection is translated (badly) in *Poems* (1908).

▷J Langlade, *Kochanowski: L'Homme, le penseur, le poète lyrique* (1932)

KOCK, Charles Paul de
(1794–1871)

French novelist, born in Passy. He produced an enormously long series of novels about Parisian life, vivacious, piquant and very readable. They were highly popular at the time, and were widely read in England. *Georgette* (1820, Eng trans 1843), *Mon voisin Raymond* (1822, Eng trans *My Neighbour Raymond*, 1903) and *L'amant de la lune* (1847, 'The Lover of the Moon') were among the most popular.

▷T Trimm, *Paul de Kock* (1877)

KOESTLER, Arthur
(1905–83)

Hungarian-born British author and journalist, political refugee and prisoner, born in Budapest. He studied pure science at Vienna and, embracing the cause of Zionism as described in *Promise and Fulfilment* (1949), worked on a collective farm in Palestine (1926). However, his idealism gradually modified by his experiences, he became a political correspondent and later scientific editor for a German newspaper group. Dismissed as a communist, he travelled in Russia (1932–3), but became disillusioned, breaking with the party finally in 1938, as described in *The God that Failed* (1950). He reported the Spanish Civil War (1936–7) for the London *News*

Chronicle, was imprisoned under sentence of death by Franco, as retold in *Spanish Testament* (1938) and *Dialogue with Death* (1942), and again by the French (1940). He escaped from German-occupied France via the French Foreign Legion, and, after a short imprisonment in London, joined the Pioneer Corps. These experiences, described in *Scum of the Earth* (1941), provided the background of his first novel in English, *Arrival and Departure* (1943). The degeneration of revolutionary idealism in Roman times under Spartacus he portrayed in *The Gladiators* (1939), which was followed in 1940 by the striking modern equivalent, *Darkness at Noon*, Koestler's masterpiece and one of the great political novels of the century. Intelligent humanism and anti-communism provide the themes for such essays as *The Yogi and the Commissar* (1945), *The Trail of the Dinosaur* (1955), *Reflections on Hanging* (1956) and *The Sleepwalkers* (1959), on the theories, lives and struggles with religious orthodoxy of Copernicus, Kepler and Galileo. *The Act of Creation* (1964), *The Ghost in the Machine* (1967) and *The Case of the Midwife Toad* (1971) were among his later works; *Bricks to Babel* (1980) is a selection from his non-fiction writings. He and his wife committed suicide together when he became terminally ill.

▷I Hamilton, *Koestler: a biography* (1982)

KOLCSEY, Ferenc
(1790–1838)

Hungarian poet, critic and orator, born in Szödemeter. He is best known as author of the Hungarian national anthem, *Himnusz* (1823, Eng trans *Hymn*, 1947), but this was not his best or most vital work. He introduced the critical essay, as a form, into his language, and he made pioneer use of ballads and folklore in his poetry. He was second only to **Ferenc Kazinczy** in reforming the Hungarian language so that it could accommodate a new type of literature. For all his efforts for his country, his own more personal poetry is extremely pessimistic.

KOLIQUI, Ernest
(1903–75)

Albanian poet and storyteller. His stories of the northern highlands of Albania, never translated, have not been bettered stylistically in traditional literature; but he became embroiled with fascism and, after the war, fled to Rome.

KOLLÁR, Jan
(1793–1852)

Czech poet and Slavonic scholar, a Hungarian Slovak. He was Protestant pastor at

Pest (1813–49), and then Professor of Archaeology at Vienna. He was a proponent of a cultural Pan–Slavic union. He wrote a cycle of sonnets, which eventually rose to over 600 in number, and compiled an edition of Slovakian folk-songs.

▷A Mráz, *Jan Kollár Literarna študia* (1952)

KOLLONTAI, Alexandra Mikhaylovna
(1872–1952)

Russian feminist and revolutionary, the world's first female ambassador. Born in St Petersburg into an upper-class family, she rejected her privileged upbringing and became interested in socialism. Married to an army officer, she nevertheless joined the Russian Social Democratic Party, and for her revolutionary behaviour was exiled to Germany in 1908. In 1915 she travelled widely in the USA, begging the nation not to join World War I, and urging the acceptance of socialism. In 1917, following the Revolution, she returned to Russia, becoming commissar for public welfare. In this post she agitated for domestic and social reforms, including collective childcare and easier divorce proceedings. Although her private liaisons shocked the party, she was appointed minister to Norway (1923–5, 1927–30), Mexico (1926–7) and Sweden (1930–45), becoming ambassador in 1943. She played a vital part in negotiating the termination of the Soviet–Finnish war (1944). Her works, such as *The New Morality and the Working Class* (1918), and her collection of short stories, *Love of Worker Bees* (1923), aroused considerable controversy because of their open discussion of subjects like sexuality and women's place in society and the economy. Her autobiography, written in 1926, was not published in Russia.

KOLMAR, Gertrud
(1894–?1943)

German–Jewish poet, born in Berlin. A shy and modest loner, she was known among her contemporaries for her immense kindness. Working as a language teacher and interpreter, she was fluent in English, French, Russian and Hebrew. Later, she dedicated herself to the education of deaf-and-mute children. From 1928 she gradually withdrew from a public life, becoming a nurse to her ailing elderly parents. When most of her relatives left Germany in 1933, Kolmar stayed with her father. She is believed to have been murdered in Auschwitz; the exact date is unknown. Her poetry is of a highly individualistic kind and difficult to categorize. Using enchanting, often haunting, imagery, her work is infused with visionary melancholy, demanding protection for the vulnerable and innocent. In *Gedichte* (1917,

'Poems') she celebrates the vision of a simple female existence, while in *Preußische Wappen* (1934, 'Prussian Heraldry') she shows her fascination with historical figures.

▷K Krolow, 'Das lyrische Werk Gertrud Kolmars', in *Akzente 3* (1956)

KOLTSOV, Alexey
(1809–42)

Russian minor poet, self-taught, born in Voronezh. His imitations of folk-songs caused him to be compared to **Burns**, but **Tolstoy** believed that his genius was spoiled by getting into city company.

KØLTZOW, Liv
(1945–)

Norwegian novelist, born in Oslo, who studied at the University there. Her first novel, *Hvem bestemmer over Bjørg og Unni?* (1972, 'Who Decides What Happens to Bjørg and Unni?'), became an important text for 'second-wave' feminism, exploring as it does the social and political manipulation of women and the potential for achieving change. Her subsequent works are more markedly modernist, with fragmented narratives focusing uncertainties as to language and reality. *Historien om Eli* (1975, 'The Story of Eli') is a female *Entwicklungsroman*, the central character's shadowy identity strikingly conveyed by the language, while *Hvem har dit ansikt?* (1988, 'Who Has Your Face?') employs narrative experimentation, including the conflation of the narrator and the central character, to suggest the complexities of identity.

▷J Garton, 'The Personal is Political', in *Norwegian Women's Writing 1850–1990* (1993)

KONINGII, Abraham de
(1587–1619)

Dutch poet and dramatist, born in Belle in Flanders. He is often regarded as the most important precursor of **Vondel**. He was brought up in the *rederijker* (from the French *rhétoriqueur*) tradition, a name given to 'amateur poets' to read aloud in the Chambers of Rhetoric, but was not afraid to break out of it when he felt it would be effective.

KONOPNICKA, Maria
(1842–1910)

Polish story writer and poet, born in Suwalki. She was chiefly known as a poet, but, with a few notable exceptions, her poetry has not lasted, as it is spoiled by her excessive emotionalism and rather specious-sounding patriotism (for all that this was entirely sincere). The best of her poetry is translated in *Five Centuries of Polish Poetry* (1960). The greatest of her books was written for children: *O krasnoludkach i o sierotce Marysi* (1896, Eng trans *The Brownie Scouts*, 1947), a classic fairy-tale about a little girl and some dwarfs. But the best of her stories are of quite a different order: lacking her usual earnestness, they give incomparable shrewd and warm-hearted appraisals of women from the lower classes. They are still being published, and still being widely read. One, 'Still Life', appears in English translation in *Introduction to Modern Polish Literature* (1964, H Gillon and L Krzyzanowski eds).

▷M Kridl, *Survey of Polish Literature* (1911)

KONRAD VON WÜRZBURG
(1220–87)

German Middle High and epic burgher poet, born in Würzburg. He was supported by patrons of Basle, where he settled, and died. A well educated man, from a non-aristocratic family, he wrote all kinds of poems, from lyric to epic. A follower of **Gottfried von Strassburg**, author of *Tristan*, he also wrote shorter works, such as *Der Schwanritter*, a version of the Lohengrin legend. Highly influential, he is now better remembered for his versatility and mastery than for his originality.

▷A Moret, *Un Artist méconnu* (1932)

KONSTANTINOV, Aleko
(1863–97)

Bulgarian story writer and satirist who called himself 'the lucky one'—until his sharp and irreverent pen got him murdered. He was a senior lawyer until his innate integrity forced him into satirical humour instead. An inveterate traveller with a keen sense of the division in his country between East and West, he invented the most famous of all Bulgarian characters, Bay Ganyu (*Bay Ganyu*, 1895), a 'partisan thug' who travels about at home and abroad selling various articles. The name of Bay Ganyu is a by-word in Bulgaria, and Konstantinov himself the finest ironist his country ever produced.

▷C Manning and R Smal-Stocki, *The History of Modern Bulgarian Literature* (1960)

KONSTANTINOVÍC, Radomir
(1928–)

Serbian novelist and editor of literary journals, born in Subotica. He has modelled himself mainly upon **Beckett**—and is often compared to his compatriot and contemporary **Bulatovic**. *Exitus* (1960, Eng trans 1965) excited some interest outside Yugoslavia, but he has also been called pretentious and impenetrable.

▷*Slavonic and East European Review*, XI, 94 (1961)

KONWICKI, Tadeusz
(1926–)

Lithuanian-born dissident writer and filmmaker. After fighting with guerrilla forces in Lithuania against both German and Russian occupation in World War II he moved to Poland, where he has made his home. His book *Mala apokalipsa* (1979, Eng trans *A Minor Apocalypse*, 1983) was banned. In the 1950s, *Przy budowie* (1950, 'At the Construction Site') was a much prized novel about the party as an engineer of souls. He was denounced in 1968. His latest book, *Wschody i zachody kziezyca* (1982, Eng trans *Moonrise, Moonset*, 1988), is about the early struggles of the Solidarity movement. His films include *Salto* (1965) and *Ostatni dzień lata* (1958, 'The Last Day of the Summer').

▷J Wegner, *Konwicki* (1973)

KOONTZ, Dean R(ay)
(1945–)

American author of bestselling formula fiction (horror, science fiction, detection), the secrets of which he attempted to pass on in *Writing Popular Fiction* (1973) and *How To Write Best-Selling Fiction* (1981). He was born in Everett, Pennyslvania, and published his first novel, *Star Quest* (1968), at the age of 23. Since then he has published in excess of 50 novels, using at least three pseudonyms, of which 'Brian Coffey' is the most widely recognized. *The Demon Seed* (1973) was a huge bestseller and it conveniently illustrates how Koontz has managed to manipulate genre and sub-generic styles in such a way as to attract the uncommitted without alienating hard-core readers. A decade later, in *Phantoms* (1983), he attempted a wholesale mythology on a scale not seen since **H P Lovecraft**.

KOPIT, Arthur L(ee)
(1937–)

American dramatist, born in New York City, and educated at Harvard, where he began writing and directing his own plays. His best-known earlier works are Absurdist, disturbing farces. *Oh Dad, Poor Dad, Mamma's Hung You in the Closet and I'm Feelin' So Sad* (1960), a dark parody of the Oedipus story, is sub-titled 'a pseudo-classical tragi-farce in a bastard French tradition'. Kopit satirizes socially ambitious middle-class America in *The Day the Whores Came Out to Play Tennis* (1965). The more serious *Indians* (1968) is set in the Wild West and attacks America's treatment of its Native American population, while *Wings* (1978) follows the fortunes of a stroke victim. The more recent *End of the World* (1984), in which a millionaire commissions a play about nuclear weapons, returns to the world of macabre comedy.

KOPS, Bernard
(1926–)

English dramatist, born in London, who worked variously as a docker, salesman, chef and waiter before devoting himself to writing full-time. As with playwrights such as **Arnold Wesker**, who also sought to portray real, Jewish working-class life on the stage, Kops deals with social and economic issues and makes a plea for tolerance, and for the accrual of intellectual rather than monetary riches. Several critics, however, have accused Kops of political naivety and sentimentality. *The Hamlet of Stepney Green* (1957) is a mordantly comic variation on the Hamlet story, in which the Hamlet-character, attempting to come to terms with the world around him, promises to carry the spirit of revolution forward. *Enter Solly Gold* (1962), in which a confidence-trickster poses as a rabbi, is a more ruthless comedy exposing social and moral hypocrisy. His more recent plays have been less successful and include *Simon at Midnight* (1985).

KORAÏS, Adamantios
(1748–1833)

Greek educator and man of letters, born in Smyrna. By profession a physician, Koraïs moved to Paris in the years of the Revolution and wrote his marvellous and indispensable account in *Koray's Letters Written from Paris 1788–1792* (Eng trans 1898). He edited classical Greek documents, and also wrote the famous *Atakta* (1828–35), the first proper lexicon in modern Greek.

KORINFSKY, Apollon
(1868–1937)

Russian minor poet and translator (of **Coleridge**'s *The Ancient Mariner*). His contemplative lyrics found great favour just before the advent of modernism, but then he fell out of vogue.

KORNBLUTH, C(yril) M
(1923–58)

American science-fiction writer, born in New York City. He is most famous for *The Space Merchants* (1953), a futuristic satire on consumer capitalism, one of four novels he wrote in collaboration with **Frederik Pohl**. *The Syndic* (1953), a solo production, is set in a utopian New York ruled by the Mafia. *Not This August* (1955) is a more conventional science-fiction work, envisaging an America in the grip of the Soviet Union. Kornbluth was perhaps best suited to the short story; his most accomplished tales, such as 'The Little Black Bag', display a calm, almost quaint humanity which was a rarity in contemporary science fiction.

KÖRNER, Karl Theodor
(1791–1813)

German lyric poet, born in Dresden. He wrote plays and fiery patriotic songs such as *Leier und Schwert* (1814, 'Lyre and Sword'), which contained the *Schwert-Lied* ('Sword Song'), written shortly before his death in battle during the Napoleonic Wars, a patriotic end which served to inflate his literary reputation.
▷K Bergens, *Theodor Körner* (1912)

KORNILOV, Boris
(1907–39)

Russian poet, whose wild and alcoholic life ended when he was arrested by Stalin's secret police and murdered. He was briefly married to **Olga Berggolts**. High claims for his reflective poetry have been made by a few critics, and he was republished after the 1956 'Thaw'; but he has not yet attracted much critical attention.

KORNIYCHUK, Oleksandr
(1905–72)

Ukrainian dramatist, born in Khrystinovka. He was a socialist realist and a politician who held various high offices in Sovietized culture. He married the Polish author Wasilewska. His *Front* (1942, Eng trans *The Front*, in *Four Soviet Plays*, 1944), set on the Russo–German front, was the most sensational of his well-made, tendentious plays. For this he was hailed as a Soviet hero, and won the Stalin Prize. He wrote almost all his works in his native language, and they were translated into Russian for popular consumption. Another play available in English is *V stepyakh Ukrainy* (1942, Eng trans *Guerillas of the Ukrainian Steppes*, in *Four Soviet Plays*, 1944).

KOROLENKO, Vladimir
(1853–1921)

Russian novelist, born in Zhitomir. Returning from exile in Siberia (1879–85), he published his most famous story, *Son Makara* ('Makar's Dream'), and earned a reputation as a supporter of the underprivileged. He was involved in the Populist Movement, and opposed the Bolshevik Revolution in 1917. He is best known for his short stories, but left an important autobiography unfinished at his death.
▷M Comtet, *Vladimir Korolenko, 1853–1921: l'homme et l'oeuvre* (1975)

KOSINSKI, Jerzy Nikodem
(1933–91)

Polish-born American novelist, born in Łodz. Educated in political science at Łodz University, he taught there (1955–7) before emigrating to the USA in 1957. He wrote two

polemical books, *The Future is Ours, Comrade* (1960) and *No Third Path* (1926), under the pseudonym Joseph Novak. The trauma of war had rendered him (literally) speechless and his novels, particularly the quasi-autobiographical *The Painted Bird* (1965), set language at a considerable premium, espousing sexual experimentation and a radically existential morality as the basis of a brutal survivalism. Later works include *Steps* (1968), *Being There* (1971), *The Devil Tree* (1973), *Cockpit* (1975), *Blind Date* (1977), *Passion Play* (1979), *Pinball* (1982) and *The Hermit of 69th Street* (1988).
▷P R Lilly Jr, *Words in Search of Victims* (1988)

KOTSYUBYNSKY, Mykhaylo
(1864–1913)

Ukrainian novelist and short-story writer, born in Vinnitsa. After a rebellious youth he became, with the greatest reluctance, a government official. The best-known of all his fiction is the novel *Tini zabutkh predkiv* (1911, Eng trans *Shadows of Forgotten Ancestors*, 1979), based on legends of the Hutsul region, and a masterpiece by any standards— as the late date of its translation (which has an important introduction) suggests. Most prefer *Fata Morgana* (1903–10), a more straightforward novel about a Ukrainian village in ferment. A highly intelligent man, and a great writer by international standards, Kotsyubynsky developed from a comparatively crude populist realist into an almost fully-fledged modernist, learning from **Hamsun** and **Strindberg**. *Chrysalis* (1958) selects from his stories.
▷ *Ukrainian Review*, VII

KOTZEBUE, August Friedrich Ferdinand von
(1761–1819)

German dramatist, born in Weimar. He filled various offices in the service of Russia, and was a facile writer of plays, tales, satires, historical works, etc; he was stabbed to death by a Jena student, because he had ridiculed the *Burschenschaft* movement. Besides quarreling with **Goethe**, Kotzebue satirized the leaders of the Romantic school. Among his 200 lively but superficial dramas are *Menschenhass und Reue* (1788, Eng trans *The Stranger*, 1798), *Die Hussiten vor Naumburg* (1801, Eng trans *The Patriot Father*, 1830) and *Die beiden Klingsberge* (1799, Eng trans *Father and Son*, 1814).
▷H N Fairchild, *The Noble Savage* (1928)

KOTZWINKLE, William
(1938–)

American fantasy writer. He was born in Scranton, Pennsylvania, and educated in New Jersey and Pennsylvania. Early short stories were collected as *Elephant Bangs Train* (1971), but his first novel was *Hermes 3000* (1972). It was written in a rather formulaic science-fiction style which was formed into something far wittier and more penetrating in *Doctor Rat* (1976), his best book. *The Fan Man* (1974) was droll but lightweight and Kotzwinkle's fiction-writing began to take a back seat to screenwriting. He scripted the hugely successful *E.T.: The Extra-Terrestrial* for Steven Spielberg in 1982, and the following year 'novelized' *Superman III*. Like Spielberg, Kotzwinkle has an instinctive purchase on the dream-life of Americans.

KOVACIC, Ante
(1834–89)

Croatian novelist and radical polemicist who eventually, in part owing to his poverty, became insane. But he had been the best realistic novelist writing in his language. His finest novel, and one which ought to have been translated, was the semi-autobiographical *U registraturi* (1888, 'The Apprentice'), about a peasant boy who comes to town to serve a bad master. This combines his usual realism with elements of the picaresque and the grotesque.

KOVALEVSKAYA, Sofya Vasilyevna
(1850–91)

Russian mathematician and novelist, daughter of a Moscow artillery officer. Married to a brother of Alexander Kovalevsky, she made a distinguished name for herself throughout Europe as a mathematician. As a woman she found it impossible to obtain an academic post in Europe until finally she obtained a lectureship at Stockholm and then a professorship in 1889. She worked on Abelian integrals, partial differential equations and the form of Saturn's rings. She also made a name as a novelist, her works including *Vera Brantzova* (1895) and the novella *The Nihilist Girl* (1890), which reveal her lively gift as a storyteller. In 1878 she published her autobiography, *A Russian Childhood*.
▷A Rakhmanova, *Sofya Kovalevskaya* (1953)

KOZLOV, Ivan Ivanovich
(1779–1840)

Russian poet, born in St Petersburg. He translated **Byron** and **Thomas Moore**. He turned to poetry at the age of 42, after going blind at the age of 30. His romantic poems include *Chernets* (1824) and *Knyaginya Natalya Dolgarukiya* (1828).
▷G R V Barratt, *Ivan Kozlov* (1972)

KRAMER, Larry (Lawrence)
(1935–)

American novelist, playwright and author of film screenplays, born in Bridgeport, Connecticut. Kramer is a prominent spokesman for the American homosexual rights movement, although his novel *Faggots* (1978), an outspoken portrayal of promiscuous gay life in New York City, caused heated controversy both within and outside the movement. He is best known for his impassioned plays *The Normal Heart* (1985) and *The Destiny of Me* (1992), both of which address the issue of AIDS. The first piece, arguably a tract rather than a fully-fledged drama, has been produced in many countries and had an enormous impact, alerting many people to the seriousness of the disease and to how little progress had been made to combat it.

KRAMER, Theodor
(1897–1958)

Austrian minor poet who emigrated to England when the Nazis invaded his country. He wrote most of his best poetry while in his exile.

KRAMM, Joseph
(1908–)

American playwright and actor, born in South Philadelphia. He graduated from the University of Pennsylvania, and worked as a journalist for a time. He is chiefly remembered for his only successful play, *The Shrike* (1951), a drama about a man driven to attempt to commit suicide in order to be free of his insanely possessive wife. This won the Pulitzer Prize for Drama in 1952. His only other notable play is *Giants, Sons of Giants* (1962), in which the central character is another unhappy man.

KRANJCEVIĆ, Silvije Strahimir
(1865–1908)

Croatian poet, born in Senj. He reacted violently to Rome, where he was sent to study for the priesthood, and returned angrily to Zagreb; from 1893 until his death he taught, edited his periodical *Nada*, and changed the course of Croatian poetry by his example. There is controversy as to when he wrote his best poems: one school holds that this was before he was 35, but another finds his best in the late and deeply pessimistic collection *Pjesme* (1908, 'Poems').

KRASÍNSKI, Count Zygmunt
(1812–59)

Polish poet, dramatist and novelist, born in Paris. His father, General Wincenty, who married Ursula (née Princess Radziwill), fought in the Napoleonic Wars. The general educated his son well, and while he was studying law at Warsaw University he began to write fiction and verse. He was close to **Mickiewicz**, who deeply influenced him. The conflict in Krasiński stimulated by his father's eventual 'loyal' acceptance of Russian rule, and his own patriotic impulses forced him into writing works of a visionary nature—in them occurred the famous line, 'Murder will spread by electric current', incomprehensible to most of his contemporaries—which ultimately have less to do with Polish independence than with the nature of existence itself. This prominent tradition in Polish literature—that of a torn nation—was to culminate in the strange and rich works of **Micinsky, Witkiewisz** and, in an entirely different, less confused manner, in **Bruno Schulz**. In the play *Nieboska komedia* (1835, Eng trans *The Undivine Comedy*, 1924), really a gnostic vision, he resolved the conflict between his loyalty to his father's position and his belief in an independent Poland by envisaging a victory of the Polish people followed by their perishing in a grand realization that only Christ could save them. *Irydion* (1836, Eng trans *Iridion*, 1927), a more mature prose play, dealt, majestically, with the problem of how to avoid hatred in politics. After an unhappy affair he found a woman, Delphina Potocka, who understood him, and to her he dedicated *Przédświt* (1843, 'Pre-Dawn'), another visionary poem about the future of Poland or, perhaps, since he was so smothered by his father (who predeceased him by only one year, and who forced him to make an undesirable marriage to an heiress in 1843), of humanity itself. He remains one of the most puzzling and yet powerful—and hitherto hardly investigated—European writers of his age. The translations by Martha Walker Cook of 1875 should be ignored, since they are grossly inaccurate.

▷M M Gardner, *The Anonymous Poet of Poland: Zygmunt Krasinski* (1919); W Lenicki (ed), *Zygmunt Krasinski: Romantic Universalist* (1964)

KRASZEWSKI, Józef Ignacy
(1812–87)

Polish historical novelist and poet, born in Warsaw. He was one of the most prolific of all Polish authors, producing more than 300 works. His best-known novel is *Jermola: obrazki wiejskie* (1857, Eng trans *Jermola*, 1891), a tale of peasant life. In 1884 he was imprisoned at Magdeburg for treason.

KRAUS, Karl
(1874–1936)

Austrian critic and dramatist, and publisher and sole writer of the radical satirical magazine *Die Fackel* ('The Torch'), from 1899 to

1936. He was among the first to champion the work of the German playwright, **Frank Wedekind**. He himself wrote the apocalyptic and satirical plays, *Die letzten Tage der Menschheit* (1918, 'The Last Days of Mankind') and *Die Unüberwindlichen* (1928, 'The Unconquerable Ones'), both savage portraits of politics and social morality. He wrote several volumes of poetry, and a great deal of criticism.
▷F Filed, *The Last Days of Mankind, Karl Kraus and his Vienna* (1967)

KRETZER, Marx
(1854–1941)

German novelist, born in Posen (Poznań). Essentially a writer on social problems and working people, he has, on account of his naturalism, been called the German **Zola**. His books include *Die Betrogenen* (1882, 'The Duped', concerning poverty and prostitution), *Die Verkommenen* (1883, 'The Fallen'), *Meister Timpe* (1888) and *Das Gesicht Christi* (1897, 'The Face of Christ').

KREVE-MICKIEVICIUS, Vincas
(1882–1954)

Lithuanian poet, dramatist, playwright and essayist, who left Lithuania in 1944, after having been in hiding for four years (he had been Lithuanian Foreign Minister), and finally settled in America. He is usually known simply as 'Kreve'. He was an important figure in his country's literature, both for his stories (some are published in English translation as *The Herdsman and the Linden Tree*, 1964) and for his remarkable unfinished novel about the life of Christ, *Dangaus ir zemes sunus* (1907–63, 'Children of Heaven and Earth'). *Pagunda* (1950, Eng trans *The Temptation*, 1965) is about Stalinist duplicity and remains instructive. He wrote a few works in Russian and Polish.
▷*Essay in English*, in *Studio baltici* (1952)

KREYMBORG, Alfred
(1883–1966)

American minor poet, editor and critic, born in New York. His first collection of poems, the imagistic *Mushrooms* (1916), attracted some attention by its attempt to achieve simplicity and directness, but he was soon eclipsed by such figures as **Pound** and **Stevens**. In his magazine *The Glebe* (1913–15) he published **Joyce** and **Aldington**. He later edited *Broom* (1921–4).
▷*Troubadour* (1925)

KREZLA, Miroslav
(1893–1981)

Croatian dramatist, poet, novelist and, in his earlier days, attacker of the Catholic hierarchy, who dominated his literature. He served in the Austrian army, but then became a noted nationalist and communist (however, he did not join Tito in the war against Hitler); he attacked socialist realism as a mean and narrow creed. His greatest work is in drama, in particular his three-part play, in the **Ibsenite** tradition—it is untranslated—on the decline of a Croatian family, *The Glembays* (1930–2). His novel *Hravatski bog Mars* (1922, 'The Great God Mars') is a savage satire on the Austrian use of Croatian peasants as cannon fodder. *Povratak Filipa Latinovicza* (1930, Eng trans *The Return of Philip Latinovizc*, 1972) is about an artist trying to make sense of the chaos of World War II; *Na rubu pameti* (1938, Eng trans *On the Edge of Reason*, 1976) is a very powerful and ironic study of the disintegration of the life of a middle-aged lawyer owing to his sudden blurting out of the truth at a party. Krezla has been called, with justice, 'among the most neglected of the world's great writers'.
▷A Kadic, *Slavonic and East European Review*, 104 (1967)

KRIGE, Uys
(1910–87)

South African short-story writer, playwright, poet and journalist, born in the Cape Province and trained in law at Stellenbosch University. He lived in Spain between 1931 and the start of the Civil War. During World War II he was a war correspondent in Abyssinia and Egypt, and was then a POW in Italy (his escape is documented in *The Way Out: Italian Intermezzo*, 1946, rev edn 1955). His first book of Afrikaans stories, *Die Palmboom* ('The Palm Tree'), had appeared in 1940, but it was with his second, *The Dream and the Desert* (1953), that he became more widely known. The stories in it evoked a South African childhood with a dreamy irony that also emerges in his verse, for which he has stuck to Afrikaans. The most striking single collection is *Ballade van die Groot Begeer* (1960, 'Ballad of the Great Desiring'); a substantial collected poems appeared in 1985. Krige has also written a large number of original and adapted plays. Outstanding is *Die Twee Lampe* (1951, Eng trans *The Two Lamps*, 1964). A tale of generational conflict against a background of racialism and religious sectarianism (and in a swampy, treacherous setting), it struck a sizeable chord in the American South when it was translated.
▷C van Heymingen and J Berthoud, *Uys Krige* (1966)

KRISTENSEN, Tom
(1893–1974)

Danish novelist and poet, born in London to Danish parents and brought up in Copenhagen. He wrote under the shadow of World

War I and the ideological turmoil it caused. His debut collection of poetry, *Fribytterdrømme* (1920, 'Freebooter Dreams'), reveals an inclination for revolt, adventure and sensuality which is counterbalanced by the controlled form of the poems. This focus on anarchism, revolution and destruction was continued in the expressionist novel *Livets Arabesk* (1921, 'The Arabesque of Life'), but after a journey to China and Japan in 1922 Kristensen became increasingly critical of what he saw as his poetic and personal search for excitement. His self-scrutiny culminated in the semi-autobiographical novel *Hærværk* (1930, 'Vandalism'), which follows a downwardly mobile journalist and poet on a drinking odyssey through Copenhagen: the novel is a warning against soul-searching and ends on an open but sobering note. After *Hærværk*, Kristensen's poetic flow began to ebb, and he concentrated on a career as a newspaper critic and essayist.
▷J Andersen, *Dansende stjerne—en bog om Tom Kristensen* (1993)

KROENENBERGER, Louis
(1904–80)

American editor, novelist and critic, born in Ohio. He was for many years the drama critic of *Time*. His novels *The Grand Manner* (1929) and *The Grand Right and Left* (1952), owing a little to **Swinburne**'s *Lesbia Brandon*, satirize, respectively, politics and the wealthy; *A Month of Sundays* (1962) is set in a luxurious lunatic asylum. *No Whipping, No Gold Watches* (1970) is autobiographical.

KROETSCH, Robert
(1927–)

Canadian novelist and poet, born in Alberta. Kroetsch's work is set mainly in Alberta and the Northwestern territory. The early novel *But We Are Exiles* (1965) is about a crew struggling to steer their boat out of the Mackenzie river, and *The Words of My Roaring* (1966) takes a comic look at an Alberta election. *The Studhouse Man* (1969), which won a Governor General's Award, concerns the narrator's search for a mare across Alberta. *Alberta* (1968) is a work of non-fiction, published in the Travellers' Canada series. Kroetsch's poetry is best sampled in *The Stone Hammer Poems* (1973).

KROETZ, Franz Xaver
(1946–)

German playwright, born in Bavaria. He had little formal education and was unsuccessful in his ambition to become an actor. He joined the Communist Party in 1972, shortly after the production of his first play *Wildwechsel*.

The decision reflected his strong identification with the working class, but also, as in the touching *Stellerhof* (1972, Eng trans *Farmyard*, 1976) and its sequel *Geisterbahn* (1975, 'Horror Train'), with *lumpen* figures who fall outwith the scope of the competing political ideologies. This is also the subject of early pieces like *Heimarbeit* (1971, Eng trans *Homeworker*, 1974), which was the first of Kroetz's plays to be produced in the UK; *Wunschkonzert* (1973) made an impact at the 1974 Edinburgh Festival, translated as *Request Programme*. Kroetz left the Party in 1980; by that time he was, in the title of a surreal play from the following year, *Nicht Fisch nicht Fleisch* ('Neither Fish nor Flesh'), stranded between alienation and accommodation with the 'normalized' politics of the Cold War twilight. In 1982 he published a 'reader' of prose pieces and scripts which not so much clarified his position as confirmed his irresolution.
▷R W Blevins, *Franz Xaver Kroetz: The Emergence of a Political Playwright* (1983)

KROG, Helge
(1889–1962)

Norwegian left-wing dramatist, born in Christiania (now Oslo). He followed on from **Ibsen**, without adding anything important except for his absolute commitment to Marxism. Fulfilling a role not unlike that of **Shaw** in Britain, he wrote well-made, gripping plays, such as *Opbrudd* (1936, Eng trans *Break-up*, 1939), often demonstrating the superiority of women, in which he firmly believed.

KROLOW, Karl
(1915–)

German poet and translator (mainly of French and Spanish poetry), born in Hanover. In his first phase he wrote, essentially, in the tradition of **Oskar Loerke** and **Wilhelm Lehmann**; but at the same time he imported Surrealist techniques into German poetry. He had published a book during World War I, but became known just after it. In his second phase he inclined more towards an Absurdism influenced by **Hans Arp** and by modern linguistic theory; still later, he abandoned the surreal mode for a minimalist one. Many feel him to embody the mainstream of post-war German poetry. His works in English translation are *Leave Taking* (1968); *Poems Against Death* (1969).

KRÚDY, Gyula
(1878–1933)

Hungarian prose-poet, 'an isolated and enigmatic figure in modern Hungarian literature', who drank himself to an early death. He was

prolific, writing 60 novels and over 3000 stories. He has become more famous since his death, but his Sinbad (*Szindbád*) novels were always popular. Sinbad is, to all intents and purposes, a portrait of himself. Krúdy has been compared to **Marcel Proust**. His best-known novel is *A vörös postakocsi* (1912, Eng trans *The Crimson Coach*, 1967), which also deals with Sinbad.
▷J Reményi, *Hungarian Writers and Literature* (1964)

KRYLOV, Ivan Andreevich
(1768–1844)

Russian writer of fables, born in Moscow. He started writing from the age of 20. Secretary to a prince, and then aimless traveller through Russia, he obtained a government post in 1806, and, settling down, wrote nine collections of fables which appeared between 1809 and 1843. He also translated **Jean de la Fontaine**'s *Fables*.
▷N Stepanov, *Ivan Andreevich Krylov* (1973)

KUDDOUS, Ehsan Abdel
(20th century)

Egyptian realistic novelist, who began as a journalist. He is best known for his novel about the Suez affair of 1956, *Don't Shut Off the Sun*. His work has not been translated into English.

KUHLMANN, Quirinus
(1651–89)

German poet and mystic (or 'religious fanatic'), born in Breslau. Married three times, he unsuccessfully attempted to convert the Sultan of Turkey; he was burned at the stake (but for political rather than religious reasons) after preaching his **Böhme**- and Quaker-influenced notion of the Kingdom of God upon Earth. He was an erotico-religious poet of immense gifts and technical ability: criticism, while admiring of his qualities, has not yet come to terms with the nature of his mysticism. He was regarded as egocentric, but, as one critic has written, 'actually he was completely selfless in his earnestness and impelled by a sense of mission so profound and enduring as to amount to obsession'. But even this unusually generous judgement fails to lay emphasis on his sense of humour, reflected in some of his bizarre and complex titles. There are a few translations of his work in *The German Lyric of the Baroque in English Translation* (1962).
▷W Dietze, *Quirinus Kuhlmann, Ketzer und Poet* (1963)

KULISH, Mykola
(1892–1937)

Ukrainian dramatist, born in Kherson. He was murdered by Stalin in a concentration camp on the grounds of his 'nationalism'. His masterpiece is *Narodny Malakhiy* (1929, 'The People's Malakhiy'). His *Patetchyna sonata* (1943, Eng trans *Sonata Pathétique*, 1975, performed in 1931), about the ill effects of the Revolution, probably spelled his doom—its success in Russian cities, including Moscow, led to its being banned. Kulish was first arrested in 1934, but managed to survive for three years.

KUMIN, Maxine
(1925–)

American poet, novelist, and writer for children, born in Philadelphia and educated at Radcliffe. Her first novel, *Through Dooms of Love* (1965), describing the clash between a radical, college-educated girl and her pawnbroker father, was directly autobiographical. As a poet Kumin has been tagged 'Roberta Frost', but she is more than the Earth Mother poet this nickname implies. Although her work is autobiographical it is not confessional in the manner of her friend and collaborator, **Anne Sexton**. Recently, as in *Nurture* (1989), which focuses on threatened species, her work has become more passionately environmental.

KUMINIĆ, Evgenij
(1850–1904)

Croatian novelist, born in Berséc. His nationalistic novels, written under the influence of **Zola**, do not really transcend their message: that everything Hungarian in Croatian society was corrupt. But he was a vivid writer, particularly prized for his fictional account of his military life, *Pod puskom* (1889).

KUNDERA, Milan
(1929–)

Czechoslovakian-born French novelist, born in Brno, the son of a pianist. He was educated in Prague at Charles University and the Academy of Music and Dramatic Arts Film Faculty. He worked as a labourer and as a jazz musician before devoting himself to literature. For several years he was a professor at the Prague Institute for Advanced Cinematographic Studies. *Zert* (Eng trans, *The Joke*, 1969), his first novel, was published in 1967. After the Russian invasion in 1968 he lost his post and his books were proscribed. In 1975 he settled in France and took French citizenship. *Zert* and the stories in *Směšné lásky* (1970, Eng trans *Laughable Loves*, 1974) are his only books to have been published in his homeland; the publication in 1979 of *Kniha smíchu a zapomnění* (Eng trans *The Book of Laughter and Forgetting*, 1980 (US); 1982 (UK)) prompted the revocation

of his Czech citizenship. Once described as 'a healthy sceptic whose novels are all anti-something', in exile he has emerged as one of the major world writers of the late 20th century. Other novels are *Zivot de jinde* (1973, Eng trans *Life is Elsewhere*, 1974), *Valčik na rozloučenou* (1976, Eng trans *The Farewell Party*, 1976 (US); 1977 (UK)), *Nesnesitelná lehkost bytí* (1984, Eng trans *The Unbearable Lightness of Being*, 1984) and *Immortality* (1991). He also published a critical work, *Umění romanu* (1960, Eng trans *Art of the Novel*, 1988).
▷R Porter, *Kundera: a voice from Central Europe* (1981)

KUNERT, Günter
(1929–)

German poet, short-story writer and play-wright. Born in Berlin, he received his education in the East after the post-war division, but moved to West Germany in 1979, following his expulsion from the Communist Party as a result of his 'negative stance' on the socialist utopia. His first collection *Wegschilder und Mauerinschriften* (1950, 'Streetsigns and Graffiti') was a bleak meditation on the late war and the present 'peace'. The tone darkened further with *Unter diesem Himmel* (1955, 'Under These Skies') and *Erinnerungen an einen Planeten* (1963, 'Memories of a Planet'), which communicated his growing sense of isolation. In 1975, when he was writer-in-residence at Warwick University, he published the prose *Der andere Planet. Ansichten von Amerika* (1974, 'The Other Planet: Views from America'), whose title echoes the **Stefan George** poem used in Schönberg's Second String Quartet: '*Ich fühle Luft von anderen Planeten*' ('I feel an air from other planets blowing'). Kunert was inhaling mysterious airs from the West and his final split with the GDR authorities swiftly followed. His career as a 'free' writer has been largely undistinguished.
▷M Krüger, *Kunert Lesen* (1979)

KUNITZ, Stanley Jasspon
(1905–)

American poet, born in Worcester, Massachusetts and educated at Harvard University. A literature academic, he taught poetry at the New School for Social Research in New York City (1950–7) and Columbia University (from 1963). His first collection of verse was *Intellectual Things* (1930). *Selected Poems 1928–1958* was awarded a Pulitzer Prize in 1959. Subsequent books include *The Testing-Tree* (1971), *The Terrible Threshold: Selected Poems 1940–1970* (1974) and *Next-to-Last Things* (1985). He has also published literary reference books.

▷G Orr, *Stanley Kunitz: an introduction to the poetry* (1985)

KUO Mo-jo
(1892–1972)

Chinese poet, academic and revolutionary, born into a bourgeois Szechuan family, he became the leading light of revolutionary literature. Kuo studied medicine in Japan, starting his writing career whilst there by translating foreign classics into Chinese from Japanese sources. He returned to China to fight in the Civil War of 1925, as a result of which his work was banned by the nationalist *Kuomintang*. His early work—*Nü-shen* (1921, Eng trans *The Goddesses*, 1958) was his first collection of verse—is liberal-democratic in tone, but it became increasingly didactic and polemical as he embraced communism. His play *Chu-Yuan* (1942) is a reworking of a traditional piece about a hero-poet, now with a pro-communist message grafted on to it. In 1949, immediately after the revolution, his status as grand old man of revolutionary literature was confirmed by his being appointed president of the First All China Congress of Writers and Artists.

KUPRIN, Alexander
(1870–1938)

Russian novelist. He gave up the army for literature. As a teller of short tales he ranks next to **Anton Chekhov**, although his work is uneven in quality. Those translated include *Poedinok* ('The Duel'), *Reka zhizni* ('The River of Life'), *Slavyanskaya dusha* ('A Slav Soul'), *Granatovyi braskyet* ('The Bracelet of Garnets') and *Sasha*. He left Russia and settled in France after the Revolution of 1917, but returned to his homeland in 1937.
▷N Loker, *Alexander Kuprin* (1978)

KUREISHI, Hanif
(1954–)

English novelist, playwright and author of film screenplays, born in Bromley, Kent, and educated at King's College, London. He attracted considerable attention with *Outskirts* (1981), a play looking at the fate of two south-London white men who committed a savage racial attack. A recurring theme in Kureishi's work is that in the face of racial and cultural prejudice, much of which is deliberately maintained by a profiteering social class, it is almost impossible to sustain productive human relationships. In such film scripts as *My Beautiful Launderette* (1985) and more particularly *Sammy and Rosie Get Laid* (1987) and *London Kills Me* (1991) he vividly portrays British inner-city life as a cultural and moral wasteland. *The Buddha of*

Suburbia (1989) is a satirical novel about racial attitudes in south-east London.

KUSANO Shimpei
(1903–)

Japanese poet, arguably the greatest living, certainly one of the most accessible. He has achieved his enormous reputation within Japan by articulating a closeness to nature, which Japanese people like to think of as a national trait, and (a quality highly unusual in Japanese poetry) a sense of humour. This has also enabled him to acquire a reputation in the West, especially in the USA. There are English translations in *Frogs and Others*, translated by C Corman (1969).

KUSHNER, Tony
(1956–)

American playwright, born in New York City. He grew up in Lake Charles, Louisiana, and was educated at Columbia University and New York University. His plays are highly political in both content and intention, and are informed by an acute sense of historical awareness. *Yes, Yes, No, No* was produced in 1985, and was followed by several more before the appearance of his most important and controversial work to date, the two-part epic on the catastrophic effects of AIDS in New York, *Angels of America*, which won him the Pulitzer Prize for Drama in 1993. Its two parts, running to almost seven hours, are *Millenium Approaches* (1991) and *Perestroika* (1992).

KUTTNER, Henry
(1914–58)

American fantasy and science-fiction writer, born in Los Angeles. He began his writing career by contributing stories of occult fantasy to **H P Lovecraft**'s *Weird Tales* from 1936, and turned to science fiction in 1937. His stories were ingenious and often deftly humorous, a tendency which was enhanced by his marriage to the writer **C L Moore** in 1940. Much of their subsequent work was collaborative. He wrote, both by himself and with his wife, under various pseudonyms, the most important of which is 'Lewis Padgett'. He was a prolific writer, but a number of his/their stories are highly regarded. He was less successful in the novel format, but his best is *Fury* (1947). He enrolled with his wife in the University of California in 1950, after which they wrote a number of mystery stories, but very little science fiction.

KUZMIN, Mikhail
(1872–1936)

Major Russian poet, novelist, dramatist, composer and translator—still neglected (although not untranslated) outside his own country. He was born in Yaroslavl but grew up in St Petersburg. Kuzmin was an exceedingly complex, subtle-minded figure, who has not been understood by non-Russian critics. He was homosexual, and the Russians were then as intensely puritanical about homosexuality as any people in the world. Therefore, although, like so many Russians, he was essentially a mystic whose chief interests lay in Gnosticism and allied movements or schemes of thought, he was forced to pose as a decadent dandy, the **Oscar Wilde** of the North. He had another persona: as a follower of the 'Old Believers' sect—thus, he could own a waistcoat for every day of the year, and yet also act as a peasant. He was immensely erudite, and understood what he knew. After 1929 he was forbidden to publish, and only his death saved him from being murdered in the purges. He studied music under Rimsky-Korsakov, and wrote music for some of his own delicate plays. His fiction is lively and adept at dealing with homosexual (as well as heterosexual) relationships over the heads of Stalinist censors. *Krilya* (1906, Eng trans, with some poems and other prose, *Wings*, 1972) is a major novel on a homosexual theme, and caused a scandal when it appeared. His early poems consciously rejected Symbolism, and yet partook of it (thus the common association of him with the Symbolist movement is correct, yet also incorrect). He is seen at his greatest in his later poetry, which takes German Expressionism as a kind of springboard, but develops the expressionist procedures into something uniquely individual and moving. Central in Russian literature until 1929, then forgotten for too long, Kuzmin's work is now in the process of full reappraisal. There is an English translation of his work in *Selected Prose and Poetry* (1980).
▷ G Gibian and H W Tjalsma (eds), *Russian Modernism* (1976); *Slavonic Review* 34 (1975)

KYD, Thomas
(1558–94)

English dramatist, born in London. He was probably educated at Merchant Taylors' School, and was most likely brought up as a scrivener under his father. His tragedies early brought him a reputation, especially *The Spanish Tragedy* (c.1587). Kyd translated from the French (1594) a tedious tragedy on Pompey's daughter Cornelia, perhaps produced *Solyman and Perseda* (1592) and *Arden of Faversham*. He has been credited with a share in other plays, and probably wrote the lost original *Hamlet*. Between 1590 and 1593 he was in the service of an unknown lord. Imprisoned in 1593 on a charge of atheism (Unitarianism), which he tried to shift on to

Christopher Marlowe's shoulders, **Ben Jonson**'s 'sporting Kyd' died in poverty.

▷A Freeman, *Kyd: facts and problems* (1967)

KYRKLUND, Paul Wilhelm ('Willy')
(1921–)

Swedish novelist, story writer and dramatist, who was born and raised in Helsinki but later settled in Sweden. His *Twåsam* (1949, 'Twosome') showed that he was Sweden's most notable disciple of **Kafka**. A cool writer, he repels some by his creation of an ironic distance between his narrative and those he most pities.

L

LABÉ, or CHARLIEU, Louise
(c.1520–1566)

French poet, born in Parcieux, Ain. Educated in the Renaissance manner, she learned Latin and music, and was a skilled rider. In 1542 she fought, disguised as a knight, at the siege of Perpignan. In 1550 she married a wealthy rope manufacturer, Ennemond Perrin, at Lyons, and was then called 'la Belle Cordière' (the Lovely Ropemaker). In 1555 she published her *Oeuvres* ('Works'), which included 3 elegies and 23 sonnets in the **Petrarch**an manner. She also wrote a prose work, *Débat de Folie et d'Amour* (1555, 'Debate Between Folly and Love'), and was noted for her love affairs, which are reflected in her work.
▷F Zameron, *Louise Labé, sa vie et son oeuvre* (1945)

LABICHE, Eugène
(1815–88)

French playwright, born in Paris. He wrote one novel, *La Clef des Champs* (1838, 'Key of the Fields'), and was the author of over 150 skilfully observed and crafted comedies, farces and vaudevilles, which dominated the light theatre of his day in France. His *Frisette* (1846) was the original of **John Maddison Morton**'s *Cox and Box*, and his *Le Voyage de M. Perrichon* (1860) is a perennial favourite.
▷P Soupault, *Eugène Labiche, sa vie et son oeuvre* (1945)

LA BRUYÈRE, Jean de
(1645–96)

French writer, born in Paris. He was educated by the Oratorians, and was chosen to aid Jacques Bossuet in educating the Dauphin. For a time he was treasurer at Caen. He became tutor to the Duc de Bourbon, grandson of the great Condé, and received a pension from the Condés until his death. His *Caractères* (1688), which gained him a host of implacable enemies as well as an immense reputation, consists of two parts, the one a translation of Theophrastus, the other a collection of maxims, reflections and character portraits of men and women of the time. He found a powerful protector in the Duchesse de Bourbon, a daughter of Louis XIV. His *Dialogues sur le quiétisme* (1699, 'Dialogues on Quietism') were directed against **François Fénelon**. A writer rather than a thinker of any

real depth, his insight into character is shrewd rather than profound.
▷E Gosse, in *Three French Moralists* (1918)

LA CEPPÈDE, Jean de
(1550–1623)

French poet. Born in Marseilles or Aix, he grew up in Aix during a time of intense religious and political conflict, and began to write poetry at an early age. He studied law, becoming a *conseiller* in the Parlement of 1578 and rising to president of Aix's Chambre des Comptes in 1608. He benefited financially from his marriage to Madeleine de Brancas in 1585. A religious poet, he published his *Imitation des Psaumes de la Pénitence*, poems based on the psalms of David, together with *Douze Méditations* in 1594. However, he is best known for his *Théorèmes sur le sacré mystère de nostre redemption* ('Theorems on the Sacred Mystery of Our Redemption'), sonnets reputedly composed over a period of 30 years, and which were published in two volumes in 1613 and 1631 respectively. These poems draw on both Christian and secular sources in their treatment of religious conflict and the quest for harmony, in both the individual and society.

LA CHAUSSÉE, Pierre Claude Nivelle de
(1692–1754)

French playwright, born in Paris. He began writing plays after he was 40 and produced several of a sentimental nature which enjoyed great popularity. *La Comédie larmoyante* ('Tearful Comedy'), as his work was named by critics, had some influence on later writers, including **Voltaire**. Among his plays were *Le Préjugé à la mode* (1735, 'Fashionable Prejudice'), *Mélanide* (1741) and *L'École des mères* (1744, 'School for Mothers').
▷G Lanson, *Nivelle de la Chaussée et la comédie larmoyante* (1903)

LACLOS, Pierre Ambroise François Choderlos de
(1741–1803)

French novelist and politician, born in Amiens. Romantic and frustrated, he spent nearly all his life in the army but saw no active service until he was 60 and ended his career as a general. He is remembered by his one masterpiece, *Les Liaisons dangereuses* (1782,

Eng trans *Dangerous Connections*, 1784). This epistolary novel reveals the influence of **Rousseau** and **Samuel Richardson** and is a cynical, detached analysis of personal and sexual relationships, influenced by both Clauswitz and his own profound feminism. He also wrote *De l'éducation des femmes* (1785, 'On the Education of Women').
▷ R Vaillant, *Laclos par lui-même* (1953)

LA COUR, Paul
(1902–56)
Danish poet, born in Zealand. His poetry is outside the mainstream, but nevertheless thoroughly modernistic in spirit. He was at first predominantly a nature poet, in the tradition established by **Jensen**; but later, in his most vital work, *Fragmenter af en Dagbog* (1943, 'Fragments of a Diary'), a kind of pantheist. The influence of this book on modern Danish poetry has been decisive.
▷ P Schmidt, *Paul la Cour* (1971, in Danish)

LACRETELLE, Jacques de
(1888–1985)
French novelist, scion of a noble and literary family, born in its Burgundian château, who has failed to obtain his due outside France, despite his admission to the Académie Française in 1938. His friend **Marcel Proust** was the first decisive influence upon his versatile fiction, and his *La Vie inquiète de Jean Hermelin* (1920, 'The Restless Life of Jean Hermelin') was an immediate and deserved success. Then, with his oblique comment on the Dreyfus case, *Silbermann* (1922, Eng trans 1923), he started to write in the more 'classical' style of **André Gide**, who admired—and published—him. He followed the Silbermann theme in two more novels. *Le Bonifas* (1925, Eng trans *Marie Bonifas*, 1927), the moving tale of a rejected old maid, was in more realistic mode. *Les Haut Ponts* (1932–4, 'The Tall Bridges') was a short *roman-fleuve* about a family not unlike Lacretelle's own. His *Le Pour et le contre* (1946, 'For and Against'), an experiment in autobiography, was a failure on its publication, but will undoubtedly be reissued. *Les Vivants et leur ombre* (1977, 'The Living and Their Shadows') was a masterful and funny parody of the *nouveau roman* after its decline—it has often been taken as an actual attempt at a 'new novel', but Lacretelle's motives were clear. The work of this ceaselessly experimental and resourceful novelist is due for reappraisal.
▷ D Alden, *Jacques de Lacretelle: An Intellectual Itinerary* (1958)

LA FARGE, Christopher
(1897–1956)
American novelist, born in New York, son of John La Farge, architect, and brother of the novelist **Oliver**. He wrote a novel in verse, *Each to the Other* (1939), and *The Sudden Guest* (1946), which is in prose, a selfish woman's account of the damage done by a hurricane of 1944, during which she behaved with a total lack of consideration for others—the woman, here, represents America and its foreign policy.

LA FARGE, Oliver
(1901–63)
American anthropologist and novelist, who is reckoned to have been a more powerful writer than his by no means incapable brother **Christopher La Farge**. The vivid *Laughing Boy* (1929), like *The Enemy Gods* (1937), is about Navajo Native American life. The former won the Pulitzer Prize. He wrote many studies of Native Americans. *Raw Material* (1945) is autobiographical.
▷ D McNickle, *Indian Man* (1971)

LA FAYETTE, Marie Madeleine Pioche de Lavergne, Comtesse de
(1634–93)
French novelist and reformer of French romance-writing, born in Paris, daughter of the governor of Le Havre. She married the Comte de La Fayette in 1655, and in her 33rd year formed a liaison with **La Rochefoucauld** which lasted until his death in 1680. Down to her own death she still played a leading part at the French court, as was proved by her *Lettres inedites* (1880, 'Unabridged Letters'); prior to their publication it was believed that her last years were given to devotion. Her novels are *Zaïde* (1670, Eng trans *Zayde: A Spanish History*, 1678) and her masterpiece, *La Princesse de Clèves* (1678, Eng trans *The Princess of Cleves*, 1679), a study in conflict between love and marriage in the court-life of her day, which led to reaction against the long-winded romances of **Gautier Calprenède** and **Madeleine de Scudéry**.
▷ M J Durry, *Madame de la Fayette* (1962)

LA FONTAINE, Jean de
(1621–95)
French poet, born in Château-Thierry in Champagne. He assisted his father, a superintendent of woods and forests. He soon devoted himself to the study of the old writers and to verse writing. In 1654 he published a verse translation of the *Eunuchus* of **Terence**, and then went to Paris, where **Friedrich Fouqué** became his patron. His *Contes et nouvelles en vers* ('Stories and Tales in Verse') appeared in four volumes, 1665–74 and in an augmented edition in 1686, his *Fables choisies mises en vers* (Eng trans *Fables*, 1804) in three volumes 1668–9, augmented 1693, and his *Amours de Psyché et de Cupidon* (Eng trans

The Loves of Cupid and Psyche, 1744) in 1669. For nearly 20 years he was maintained in the household of Mme de la Sablière. In 1684 he presented an admirable *Discours en vers* ('An Oration in Verse' on his reception by the Academy. La Fontaine was a brilliant writer and his verse, especially as found in the *Contes* and *Fables*, is lively and original.
▷L Roche, *La vie de La Fontaine* (1913)

LAFORET DIAZ, Carmen
(1921–)

Spanish novelist and short-story writer. Born in the Canary Islands, she studied at Barcelona University and then moved to Madrid. She achieved instant fame in 1945 with her first novel *Nada* ('Nothing'), which portrays economic and psychological depression in the wake of civil war and is based on her own arrival in Barcelona in 1939. *La isla y los demonios* (1952, 'The island and the devils'), set in the Canaries, conjures up an equally unsettling picture of family life gently simmering with neurosis and sexual frustration. In 1956 she published an ambitious but less well-received novel based on her conversion to Catholicism in 1951, *La mujer nueva* ('The new woman'). She went on to write *La insolación* (1963, 'Sunstroke'), tracing 20 years of Nationalist rule in Spain.

LAFORGUE, Jules
(1860–87)

French poet. Born in Montevideo, Uruguay, and educated largely in Paris, he was brilliantly precocious. Up to the time of his marriage, he worked as reader to the Empress Augusta of Germany. His compressed poetic career was undertaken with a level of seriousness and dedication which belies Laforgue's reputation as a dilettante or *flâneur*. In the verse published in his lifetime—*Les Complaintes* (1885), *L'Imitation de Notre-Dame la Lune* (1886) and *Le Concile féerique* (1886)—there are only hints of the qualities that would make him such an important influence on later French poets and on the younger **T S Eliot**. The verse is stylish and witty, superbly reworking popular materials, and the Pierrot poems created a new cultural role for the *commedia* figure, as passive, nihilistic and androgynous; the same anti-heroic temperament is evident in the rewritten folk materials that make up *Moralités légendaries* (1887). However, it was the mere dozen poems in Laforgue's posthumous *Les Derniers Vers* (1890) that had such an impact, validating free verse (Laforgue had translated **Whitman**) and suggesting that poetry could be as abstract or impressionist as music or painting. A *Poésies complètes* appeared in 1894, but it was not until Pascal Pia's two-volume edition of 1979 that an authoritative

text was available. His influence on French literature is almost equal to that of **Rimbaud**.
▷M Collie, *Jules Laforgue* (1977)

LAGERKVIST, Pär Fabian
(1891–1974)

Swedish novelist, poet and playwright, winner of the 1951 Nobel Prize for literature. He studied at Uppsala and began his literary career first as a prose writer and then as an expressionist poet with *Ångest* (1916, 'Angst') and *Kaos* (1918, 'Chaos'), in which he emphasizes the catastrophe of war. Later, in the face of extremist creeds and slogans, he adopted a critical humanism with the (later dramatized) novel *Bödeln* (1933, 'The Hangman') and the novel *Dvärgen* (1944, 'The Dwarf'), which explored the problems of evil and human brutality. His novel *Barabbas* (1950) concerns the thief in whose place Christ was crucified. Man's search for God was also explored in the play *Mannen utan själ* (1936, 'The Man without a Soul'). An ideological play, *Låt människan leva* (1949, 'Let Man Live'), was a study of political terrorism in which Jesus Christ, Socrates, Bruno, Joan of Arc and an American negro appear as victims.
▷L Sjöberg, *Pär Lagerkvist* (1976)

LAGERLÖF, Selma Ottiliaa Lovisa
(1858–1940)

Swedish novelist, the first woman winner of the Nobel Prize for literature (1909), and the first woman member of the Swedish Academy (1914). She taught at Landskrona (1885–95), and first sprang to fame with her novel *Gösta Berlings saga* (1891, 'The Story of Gösta Berling'), based on the traditions and legends of her native Värmland, as were many of her later books, such as her trilogy on the Löwensköld family (1925–8, Eng trans *The Rings of the Lowenskolds*, 1931). She also wrote the children's classic *Nils Holgerssons underbara resa genom Sverige* (1906–7, 'The Wonderful Adventures of Nils'). Although a member of the neo-romantic generation of the 1890s, her work is characterized by a social and moral seriousness, as in *Antikrists Mirakler* (1897, 'The Miracles of Anti-Christ') and *Bannlyst* (1918, 'The Outcast').
▷V Edström, *Selma Lagerlöf* (1984)

LAGUNA, Andrés
(1499–1560)

Spanish satirist, born in Segovia, whose *El viaje de Turquía* ('Voyage to Turkey'), if it is his, circulated widely in manuscript (it was first published in 1905). He was a doctor, and is the most likely author of this lively satire—sometimes called a masterpiece—in dialogue form about a man who, captured by the

Turks, manages to pass himself off as a doctor. The work is notably influenced by **Erasmus**.

▷ M Bataillon, *Erasmo y España* (1966)

LA HARPE, Jean François de
(1739–1803)

French poet and critic, born in Paris. In 1763 he produced a successful tragedy, *Warwick*, followed by others. His best-known works are, however, his critical lectures *Lycée, ou Cours de littérature* (1799–1805, 'The Study of Literature'). His *Correspondance littéraire* (1801), by the bitterness of its criticisms, rekindled fierce controversies. He supported the revolution at first, but after five months' imprisonment (1794) became a firm supporter of church and crown.

▷ C A Sainte-Beuve, *Causeries de lundi* (1850–69)

LAMANTIA, Philip
(1927–)

American poet, who espouses an aesthetic of extreme Romanticism, influenced by religious experience and by drugs. Born in San Francisco, he received a rather cursory education and acquired a distinctive blend of hard-boiled street awareness and arcane knowledge. He was taken up by Parker Tyler, the leading US theorist of Surrealism, who published the 15-year-old Lamantia's first verses in *View* magazine (1942), later giving him a job as assistant editor. Lamantia's first collection, *Erotic Poems*, appeared in 1946, but there was a substantial gap between it and *Ekstasis* (1959), which contains some of his most distinctive poems. Lamantia destroyed most of his early poems, though they were resurrected for the compendious *Destroyed Works: Hypodermic Light, Mantic Notebook, Still Poems, Spansule* (1962). He was experimenting with hallucinogens as early as 1954, and reading *Touch of the Marvelous* (1966) is a little like experiencing one of the European Decadents re-scripted and shot on faulty stock by B-movie genius Roger Corman. *Selected Poems 1943–1966* (1967) confirmed the significance of his instinctive assault on academicism and the Puritan mythos of **T S Eliot** and **Frost**. Two years later, inclusion in *Penguin Modern Poets 13* (1969) opened him up to British readers. Later work is less compelling and more pedestrian, but there are excellent things in *Becoming Visible* (1981).

▷ P Tyler, introduction to *Touch of the Marvelous* (1966)

LAMARTINE, Alphonse Marie Louis de
(1790–1869)

French poet, statesman and historian, born in Mâcon. He was brought up on ultraroyalist principles, spent much of his youth in Italy, and on the fall of Napoleon entered the garde royale. His first volume of poems, probably his best known and most successful, the *Méditations*, was published in 1820. He was successively secretary of legation at Naples and *chargé d'affaires* at Florence. In 1829 he declined the post of foreign secretary in the Bourbon ministry of the Prince de Polignac, and with another series of poems, *Harmonies poétiques et religieuses* (1829, 'Poetical and Religious Harmonies'), achieved his unanimous election to the Academy. Lamartine, still a royalist, disapproved of the revolution of 1830. A tour to the East produced his *Souvenirs d'Orient* (1841, Eng trans *Recollections of a Pilgrimage to the Holy Land*, 1850). Recalled to France in 1833, he became deputy for Mâcon. Between 1834 and 1848 he published his poems, *Jocelyn* (1836, Eng trans 1837) and *La Chute d'un ange* (1838, 'The Fall of an Angel'), and the celebrated *Histoire des Girondins* (1846, Eng trans *History of the Girondins*, 1847–8). He did not support the Orléanist regime and he became a member of the Provisional Government (1848), and, as Minister of Foreign Affairs, its ruling spirit. In the presidential election of December 1848 he was defeated by Louis-Napoléon and when he came to power as Napoleon III Lamartine devoted himself to literature, publishing *Confidences* (1849 and 1851, Eng trans *Memoirs of My Youth*, 1849 and 1851), *Raphaël* (1849, Eng trans 1849) (both autobiographical), *Geneviève, Tailleur de pierres de St-Point* (1851, Eng trans *The Stonecutter of St Point*, 1851, a prose tale), and *Histoire de la restauration* (1850). He wrote on Joan of Arc, Cromwell, Madame de **Sévigné**, and others, and issued monthly *Entretiens familiers* ('Intimate Conversations').

▷ M F Guyard, *Alphonse de Lamartine* (1956)

LAMB, Charles
(1775–1834)

English essayist and poet, born in the Temple, London, where his father was a clerk to Samuel Salt, a wealthy bencher. Educated at Christ's Hospital (1782–9), where he formed a lasting friendship with **Coleridge**, he obtained a position in the South Sea House, but in 1792 was promoted to the India House, where he remained for more than 30 years. In 1792, also, Samuel Salt died, and with a legacy from him, his own salary, and whatever his elder sister Mary (1764–1847) could earn by needlework, the family retired to humble lodgings. In 1796 the terrible disaster occurred which was destined to mould the future life of Charles Lamb. The strain of insanity inherited from their mother began to show itself in Mary, and in an attack of mania she stabbed her invalid mother to death. Her brother's guardianship was accepted by the authorities and to this trust Lamb from that moment devoted his life. In the meantime he had fallen in love, but renounced all hope of marriage when the duty of tending his sister appeared to him paramount. Lamb's earliest poems (1795), first printed with Coleridge's in 1796–7, were prompted by this deep attachment. In 1798 Lamb and Charles Lloyd attempted a slight volume of their own (*Blank Verse*) and here for the first time Lamb's individuality made itself felt in 'Old Familiar Faces'. In 1797 he also published his little prose romance, *The Tale of Rosamund Gray and Old Blind Margaret*; and in 1801 *John Woodvil*—the fruit of that study of the dramatic poetry of the Elizabethan period, in whose revival he was to play so large a part. Meantime, Lamb and his sister were wandering from lodging to lodging, and in 1801 they moved to Lamb's old familiar neighbourhood, where they stayed for 16 years. Charles's experiments in literature had as yet brought him neither money nor reputation and so he wrote a farce, *Mr H* (1806), which failed. For **William Godwin**'s 'Juvenile Library', Charles and Mary wrote in 1807 their *Tales from Shakespeare*—Mary taking the comedies, Charles the tragedies. This was Lamb's first success. The brother and sister next composed jointly *Mrs Leicester's School* (1807) and *Poetry for Children* (1809). Charles also made a prose version of the *Adventures of Ulysses*, and a volume of selections from the Elizabethan dramatists showed him as one of the most subtle and original of critics. Three years later his unsigned articles in **Leigh Hunt**'s *Reflector* on Hogarth and the tragedies of **Shakespeare** proved him a prose writer of new and unique quality. In 1818 Lamb collected his scattered verse and prose in two volumes as the *Works of Charles Lamb*, and this paved the way for his being invited to join the staff of the new *London Magazine*. His first essay, in August 1820, 'Recollections of the old South Sea House', was signed 'Elia', the name of a foreigner who had been a fellow-clerk. The first collection of the *Essays of Elia* was published in 1823; *The Last Essays of Elia* appeared in 1833. In 1825 Lamb, who had been failing in health, resigned his post in the India House. The brother and sister were now free to wander and finally they moved to Edmonton. The absence of settled occupation had not brought Lamb the comfort he had looked for: the separation from his friends and the now almost continuous mental alienation of his sister left him companionless, and with the death of Coleridge in 1834 the chief attractions of his life were gone. In December of that year, he too died and was buried in

Edmonton churchyard. His sister survived him by nearly 13 years, and was buried by his side. Lamb's place in literature is unique and unchallengeable. He is familiar through his works, which are composed in the form of personal confidences; through his many friends, who have made known his every mood and trait; and through his letters, the most fascinating correspondence in the English language.
▷ E V Lucas, *Life of Charles Lamb* (2 vols, 1905, 1921)

LAMBERT, Eric
(1918–66)

English-born Australian author, born in Stamford, Lincolnshire, who went to Australia in his teens and served with Australian forces during World War II. Befriended by **Frank Hardy**, he turned to communism in the late 1940s and in 1951 published *The Twenty Thousand Thieves*, based on his own wartime experiences; the title derives from an epithet applied to the Allied division in North Africa. Lambert portrayed the soldier as a bronzed, courageous hero and his officer as a drink-befuddled buffoon, but the book was a popular success. He wrote over 15 novels of which some, such as *The Veterans* (1954), returned to the theme of war, but none repeated his first success. He went to London in 1955 and from there reported, for a Sydney newspaper, the Hungarian uprising of 1956, which alienated him from the Australian communists. He wrote two novels on the theme of the Eureka goldfield revolt of 1854, and *Kelly* (1964), based loosely on the life of the Australian outlaw Ned Kelly.

LAMDAN, Yitzchak
(1899–1954)

Hebrew poet, born in Mlinov, Ukraine. He went to Palestine in 1920. His most famous, and still much read, poem was *Masada* (1924): this is the name of the last fortress held by the Jews against the Romans, although the poem itself is about a *halutz* Jew returning to his homeland. Another famous, and more profound, poem, is 'For the Sunset', a kind of concealed dialogue between God and Jacob.
▷ L A Yudkin, *Isaac Lamdan* (1971)

LAMMING, George Eric
(1927–)

Barbadian novelist, born in Carrington Village. He was a teacher in Trinidad and in Venezuela before going to England in 1950, where he worked as a factory labourer and hosted a book programme for the BBC West Indian Service. His first novels, with their unfamiliar background and argot, received a lukewarm reception. Beginning with *In the*

Castle of My Skin (1953), he has explored the West Indian experience in a complex and highly textured way. Of his novels, *The Emigrants* (1954) is the saddest; *Season of Adventure* (1960) articulates his own dilemma as an artist; *Natives of My Person* (1972), with its archaic vocabulary and mythic roots, is perhaps his tour de force.

▷S P Paquet, *George Lamming* (1982)

LA MOTTE, Antoine Houdar de
(1672–1731)

French poet and playwright, born in Paris. He was translator of the *Iliad* into French verse (1714). Of his other writings, perhaps the best known is the play *Inès de Castro* (1723).

▷P Du Pont, *Antoine La Motte* (1898)

L'AMOUR, Louis
(1908–88)

American writer of crude, effective Wild West novels. Born in Jamestown, North Dakota, he grew up riding and hunting in the West, and earned his living in a variety of ways—prize-fighter, tugboat deckhand, lumberjack, gold prospector and deputy sheriff. His first novel about the Wild West, *Hondo* (1953), was an instant success, and he followed it with another 80 novels, including *Hopalong Cassidy and the Riders of High Rock* (1951), *High Lonesome* (1962), *Ride the Dark Trail* (1972) and *The Iron Marshall* (1979), of which several were made into successful films. In 1984 he was awarded the Presidential Medal of Freedom.

▷*Education of a Wandering Man* (1989)

LAMPEDUSA, Giuseppe Tomasi di
(1896–1957)

Italian novelist, born in Palermo, Sicily, son of the Duke of Parma and grandson of the Prince of Lampedusa. His family had once been rich but indolence, divided inheritance and apathy had reduced its circumstances. As a youth he was wild but he turned bookish and scholarly and, despite familial disapproval, buried himself in his library where he read voraciously and eclectically in several languages. His mother, born Beatrice Mastrogiovanni Tasca, was the dominant influence in his life and it was not until she died that he felt free to embark on the novel that is his memorial, his only book, *Il Gattopardo* (1958, Eng trans *The Leopard*, 1960). Set in Sicily in the latter half of the 19th century it is a historical novel, violent, decadent and nostalgic. It was rapturously received then vilified by the Italian literary establishment, including Moravia, but has subsequently come to be regarded as one of the greatest Italian novels of the 20th century.

▷A Vitello, *I Gattopardi di Donnafugato* (1963)

LAMPMAN, Archibald
(1861–99)

Canadian poet—one of the group known as the 'Confederation Poets'; he was born in Morpeth, Canada West and spent most of his life in and around Ottawa. His poetry is attuned to the music and mystery of a 'sweet sombre land'—a natural world that allows the mind and the soul space to grow. Although his poems regularly appeared in Canadian, American and British periodicals, only one volume of his work was published during his lifetime: *Among the Millet and Other Poems* (1888). However, **Duncan Campbell Scott**, friend, fellow poet and literary executor, edited and arranged the posthumous publication of Lampman's poetry, including *The Poems of Archibald Lampman* (1900) and *At the Long Sault and Other New Poems* (1943).

▷S Djwa, 'Lampman's Fleeting Vision', in *Canadian Literature*, 55 (1973); L R Early, in R Lecker, J David and E Quigley (eds), *Canadian Writers and Their Work: Poetry Series: Volume II* (1983)

LAMPO, Hubert
(1920–)

Belgian (Flemish) novelist, born in Antwerp. An eclectic writer, he has written realistic novels of a psychological cast, historical fantasies, occult works, and criticism. *Terugkeer naar Atlantis* (1953, 'Return to Atlantis') is perhaps his most substantial work. It deals with a man's search for a new reality: he can no longer believe that his father 'died' 30 years earlier, and so looks for him. *Hélène Defraye* (1945) is, on the other hand, a straightforwardly realistic novel.

LAMPRECHT, Pfaffe
(fl.1130)

German poet and priest, from Trier. He is principally remembered as the author of the Middle High German epic life of Alexander, *Alexanderlied* (c.1130), though he is by no means responsible for all the text which has survived to the present day, as it was edited, added to and changed by any number of subsequent individuals. He is thought to be the author of an ascetic introduction to the work which (though it is not altogether consistent with the rest of the poem) warns of the worthlessness and triviality of worldly things. The poem is of little value, except historically, as one of the earliest non-religious long works in German.

LANCASTER, G B, pseud of **Edith Joan Lyttleton**
(1873–1945)

Australasian author of novels and short stories. Of Scottish–Canadian descent, born in Clyne Vale, Tasmania, and reared on a sheep station outside Canterbury, New Zealand, she lived in London between 1909 and 1925. She was a prolific author, with hundreds of short stories and 13 novels to her credit. Her first novel was *Sons o' Men* (1904) and her last *Grand Parade* (1943), the story of the colonization of Nova Scotia. She travelled extensively in Europe and North America, and only three of her novels have an identifiably Australian origin, of which the most significant is *Pageant* (1933), the tale of a Tasmanian family in which she drew extensively upon her family history. In *Promenade* (1938) she returned to a New Zealand historical theme but she was always more popular in Britain than in either of her homelands, which saw her as an 'expatriate' writer.

LANDÍVAR, Rafael
(1713–93)

Guatemalan poet and Jesuit priest, born in Santiago de los Cabelleros. After the expulsion of the Jesuits from Spanish territory he went to Italy, where he wrote, in Latin hexameters, *Rusticatio Mexicana* (1781), a lively description of Mexico in the tradition of **Virgil**.

LANDOLFI, Tomasso
(1908–79)

Italian fiction writer, critic and translator, born in Pico. As a story writer (and distinguished translator from Russian, French and German literatures) he was described as a 'hermetic': one whose 'obscurity' came from his inability to express his hatred for fascism in literary form. But he went to prison in any case. His roots were in the pessimistic **Leopardi**, but he also sought inspiration from **Kafka**, **Proust** and the Sicilian **Pirandello**. He was best in shorter forms, but the long *La pietra lunare* (1939, 'The Moon Stone'), a novel about a creature half-goat, half-woman, significantly named Gurù, is one of the strangest books published in modern Italy. *La muta* (1964, Eng trans *The Mute*, 1971), is about a man who murders a beautiful mute in order that she may be spared the horror of speech. Many have seen *Cancroregina* (1950, Eng trans *Cancerqueen*, 1971) as his most powerful evocation of his concern with the irrelevance of words: the pilot of a spaceship records his thoughts and fears, knowing that they will never be read.

In *Le due zitelle* (1946, Eng trans *The Two Old Maids*, 1961) Landolfi posits a Roman Catholic monkey, who proves himself superior to the bourgeois world. Much more appreciated in the USA than in Great Britain, Landolfi's quasi-Surrealist vision has yet to be more fully recognized. He was an influence on the final work of **Italo Calvino**. He remained aloof from all literary movements and avoided publicity.
▷ *Modern Language Notes*, 89 (1974)

LANDON, Letitia Elizabeth
(1802–38)

English popular poet and novelist, born in London, who wrote under the initials 'L. E. L.'. Her work is more important as a guide to early 19th-century taste than in itself; her most popular novel was *Ethel Churchill* (1837). She killed herself accidentally when treating herself with prussic acid.
▷ H Ashton, *Letty Landon* (1951)

LANDOR, Walter Savage
(1775–1864)

English writer, born in Warwick, the son of a doctor. At 10 he was sent to Rugby, but was removed for insubordination; he was also sent down from Trinity College, Oxford, which he entered in 1793. Soon after publishing *Poems* in 1795 (which he soon withdrew), he quarrelled with his father, but was reconciled, and retired to South Wales on an allowance of £150 a year. The exotic *Gebir* (1798), a poem showing the influence of **Milton** and **Pindar**, was the occasion of his lifelong friendship with **Robert Southey**; but it was a failure. On his father's death in 1805 Landor had a considerable income, but much of it went in equipping volunteers to fight Napoleon in Spain (1808). Next year he purchased Llanthony Abbey in Monmouthshire, but soon quarrelled with neighbours and tenantry alike, and had ruin staring him in the face. In 1811 he married Julia Thuillier, but the marriage was not a success and in 1814 he left her in Jersey and crossed to France. Rejoined by his wife in Tours, he went in 1815 to Italy, where he remained in Como, Pisa and Florence until 1835, with the exception of a short visit to England. *Count Julian*, lacking in all the qualities of a successful tragedy, had appeared in 1812; and to this period belongs his best-known work, *Imaginary Conversations* (i and ii, 1824–9). A second quarrel with his wife in 1835 led to his return to Bath until 1858. During these years he wrote the *Examination of Shakespeare* (1834), *Pericles and Aspasia* (1836), *Pentameron* (1837), *Hellenics* (1847) and *Poemata et Inscriptiones* (1847). In 1858 an unhappy scandal (see his *Dry Sticks Fagoted by Landor*, 1858), which involved him in an action for libel, again drove him to Italy and he lived in Florence until his death.

▷R H Super, *Landor, a biography* (1954)

LANG, Andrew
(1844–1912)

Scottish writer, born in Selkirk, nephew of the scholar William Young Sellar. Educated at The Edinburgh Academy, St Andrews and Glasgow universities and Balliol College, Oxford, he was a fellow of Merton College, Oxford (1868–74), studying myth, ritual and totemism. He moved to London in 1875 to take up journalism, and became one of the most versatile writers of his day. He specialized in mythology, and took part in a celebrated controversy with Friedrich Max Müller over the interpretation of folk tales, arguing that folklore was the foundation of literary mythology. He wrote *Custom and Myth* (1884), *Myth, Ritual and Religion* (1887), *Modern Mythology* (1897) and *The Making of Religion* (1898). He wrote a *History of Scotland* (3 vols, 1899–1904) and a *History of English Literature* (1912), and published a number of fairy books which enjoyed great popularity. He also produced studies of many literary figures, including *Books and Bookmen* (1886) and *Letters to Dead Authors* (1886), a translation of **Homer**, and several volumes of verse.

▷R L Green, *Andrew Lang, a critical biography* (1946)

LANG, John George
(1816–64)

Australian novelist, journalist and lawyer, born in Sydney, who in his teens was an outstanding Latin scholar. He went to England in 1837, read law at Cambridge but was sent down for blasphemy and completed his studies at Middle Temple. He returned to Australia in 1841 and is credited with the anonymous, and incomplete, *Legends of Australia* (1842) and thus with being Australia's first native-born novelist. He left precipitately for India in 1842 and for three years practised law in Calcutta. In 1846 he established an English-language newspaper in Meerut, northern India, which serialized some of his nine novels, including *Too Clever by Half* and *Too Much Alike* (1853–4). He travelled in Europe and had many friends in London literary circles; he contributed stories to **Charles Dickens**'s magazines *All the Year Round* and *Household Words*. His most significant fiction was *Botany Bay; Or, True Tales of Early Australia* (1859).

LANGE, Antoni
(1861–1929)

Polish poet, dramatist, critic and writer of speculative fiction. His neglected poetry is unusual, as is his novel *W czwartym wymiarze* (1912, 'In the Fourth Dimension'), which is comparable with **H G Wells**. His most famous poem is called 'Rym', in which he learnedly analyses the nature and the techniques of poetry.

LANGE, Per
(1901–)

Danish poet, born in Rungsted. An erotic and mystical writer, he was a leading figure in the mid-1920s, when he tried to overcome the chaos of the period by writing in clear-cut classical forms. *Orfeus* (1932) is his most characteristic collection.

LANGGÄSSER, Elizabeth
(1899–1950)

German Roman Catholic novelist and poet, born in Alzey, Hesse, a victim of multiple sclerosis for the last 12 years of her life. Her poetry, in the tradition of **Wilhelm Lehmann**, combines a love of nature with a zealous Catholic mysticism. But her best-known work by far is the novel *Das unauslöschliche Sigel* (1947, 'The Indelible Seal'). This, in some ways reminiscent of **Bernanos**, tells of the struggle for the soul of a Jewish convert to Catholicism between God and Satan; it is cast in surreal, almost hysterical terms; but its power transcends its pious dogmatism.

LANGHORNE, John
(1735–79)

English poet, born in Winton, Kirkby Stephen. From 1766 he was rector of Blagdon, Somerset, and was a justice of the peace from 1772. He published several volumes of poetry, and his best-known poem is 'The Country Justice' (1774). He also published an Oriental tale of the kind then fashionable, and *Genius and Valour: a Scotch pastoral* (1764). With his brother, the Rev William Langhorne (1721–72), he translated **Plutarch**'s Lives (6 vols, 1770).

▷H MacDonald, in *Essays Presented to David Nichol Smith* (1945)

LANGLAND, or LANGLEY, William
(c.1332–c.1400)

English poet, born possibly in Ledbury in Herefordshire, thought to have been the illegitimate son of the rector of Shipton-under-Wychwood in Oxfordshire. Educated at the Benedictine school at Malvern, he became a clerk, but, having married early, could not take more than minor orders, and possibly earned a poor living in London from

1362 by singing in a chantry and by copying legal documents. In that year he began the composition of his famous *Vision of William concerning Piers the Plowman*. This has great defects as a work of art, but the moral earnestness and energy of the author (or authors as has been theorized) sometimes glow into really noble poetry brightened by vivid glimpses of the life of the poorer classes.

LANGLEY, Eve
(1908–74)

Australian novelist, born in Forbes, New South Wales, whose interest centres mainly on her personal quirks, such as wearing trousers before it became usual, always carrying a gun or sheath knife, and changing her name to 'Oscar Wilde'. She moved to New Zealand in 1932 and had a short and unhappy marriage although raising three children. Back in Sydney she threw herself into the literary milieu but later lived, and tragically died, as a recluse. She wrote a number of novels of which the best are *The Pea Pickers* (1942) and its sequel *The White Topee* (1954), in which the feminine 'hero' Steve plays out her own fantasies of virginal love which possibly mirror the sexual conflicts of her author.

LANIER, Sidney
(1842–81)

American poet, born in Macon, Georgia. He was a Confederate private in Virginia, an advocate in Macon, a flute player with the Peabody Orchestra, Baltimore, and lecturer in English literature at Johns Hopkins University (1879). Among his writings are a novel, *Tiger Lilies* (1867), critical studies such as *The Science of English Verse* (1880) and *The English Novel* (1883), as well as poetry. He believed in a scientific approach towards poetry-writing, breaking away from the traditional metrical techniques and making it more akin to musical composition, illustrated in later poems such as 'Corn' and 'The Symphony'.
▷A H Starke, *Sidney Lanier* (1933)

LAO She, originally Shu She-yu
(1899–1966)

Chinese poet, novelist and playwright, born into a poor family in Peking. He escaped poverty by means of his academic gifts, leaving China to teach at the University of London between 1924 and 1930. The poems which he produced in this period were liberal in tone and often humorous. Once he embraced communism in the 1930s, however, all traces of humour disappeared from his work. He is, perhaps, best remembered for *Lo-t'o Hiangtzu* (1937, Eng trans *Rickshaw Boy*, 1945), a novel detailing and condemning the exploitation of the urban poor by the rich.

LAPINE, James Elliot
(1949–)

American playwright and director, born in Mansfield, Ohio. He studied design at the California Institute of the Arts and drama at Yale Drama School. He came to notice with the play *Table Settings* (1980), followed by his staging of the Off-Broadway musical hit *March of the Falsettos* (1981, which was followed by *Falsettoland* in 1990) and *A Midsummer Night's Dream* (1982). He wrote *Sunday in the Park with George* (1984), with music and lyrics by **Stephen Sondheim**, for which he won a Pulitzer Prize in 1985. Further collaborations with Sondheim followed, including *Into The Woods* (1987).

LARBAUD, Valéry-Nicolas
(1881–1957)

French poet, essayist, critic, translator (of some of **James Joyce**, Sir Thomas Browne, **Whitman** and others), born in Vichy. Larbaud inherited a fortune, and spent it wisely—in travel and in shrewd furtherance of the cause of good writing. Particularly illuminating are his correspondences with **Gide** and **Fargue** (1948 and 1971 respectively). For the last part of his life he was a semi-invalid, the result of a stroke he had suffered in 1935. Most vital and influential of his own varied works were his *Journal de A O Barnabooth* (1913, Eng trans *A O Barnabooth, His Diary*, 1924) and the poems of this same young American, first published as *Poèmes par un riche amateur* (1908, Eng trans *Poems of a Multimillionaire*, 1955). Although these poems owe much in form to Whitman, they are original in a manner reminiscent of **Fernando Pessoa**, inasmuch as their author presents himself under a 'heteronym'. All his fiction is substantial, and his *Journal 1912–1935* (1955) is essential reading for those who require a complete knowledge of 20th-century French literature. His life (1950) was written by G Jean Aubry, French biographer of **Conrad**, but this has not yet been translated into English.
▷M Raymond, *From Baudelaire to Surrealism* (1950)

LARDNER, Ring (Ringgold Wilmer)
(1885–1933)

American short-story writer and journalist, born in Michigan. He was a successful sports writer and newspaper columnist in Chicago, St Louis and New York, and drew on that sporting background in his first collection of stories, *You Know Me Al: A Busher's Letters* (1916), set in the world of baseball. His racy

vernacular idioms and rather black, somewhat cynical humour mark him out as a distinctive voice. Story collections include *Gullible's Travels* (1917), *Treat 'Em Rough* (1918), *The Love Nest* (1926) and *First and Last* (1934). He also wrote one novel, *The Big Town* (1921), satirical verse, a satirical pseudo-autobiography, *The Story of a Wonder Man* (1927), and a musical comedy, *June Moon* (1929).
▷D Elder, *Ring Lardner* (1956)

LARIVEY, Pierre
(c.1550–1612)

French dramatist of Italian descent. As the introducer of Italian-style comedy to the French stage he foreshadowed **Molière** and **Jean Regnard**. His licentious *Comédies facétieuses* (2 vols, 1579, 1611, 'Facetious Comedies') were adaptations of existing Italian pieces.
▷L Morin, *Les trois Pierre de Larivey* (1937)

LARKIN, Philip Arthur
(1922–85)

English poet, librarian and jazz critic, born in Coventry, Warwickshire, where his father was city treasurer. He was educated at King Henry VIII School, Coventry, and at St John's College, Oxford. The Oxford of the time is evoked in his early novel, *Jill* (1946). After leaving Oxford, he took up librarianship and *A Girl in Winter* (1947), his only other novel, tells of a day in the life of a refugee librarian employed in a drab English provincial town. He eventually became librarian at the University of Hull in 1955. His early poems appeared in the anthology, *Poetry from Oxford in Wartime* (1944), and in a collection, *The North Ship* (1945). **W B Yeats**, **Thomas Hardy** and **Dylan Thomas** were then his presiding influences. He was friendly with **Kingsley Amis** who made the hero of his novel *Lucky Jim* (1954), Jim Dixon, share Larkin's antipathy towards Mozart. *XX Poems* was published in 1950 when he was in Belfast and marked the emergence of an individual 'voice'. Further collections appeared at measured intervals: *The Less Deceived* (1955), *The Whitsun Weddings* (1964) and *High Windows* (1974). *Collected Poems* was published posthumously in 1988 and became a bestseller. He also edited *The Oxford Book of Twentieth Century English Verse* (1937). The self he projected to the world from his fastness in Hull was of a xenophobic, reactionary old fogey, downcast and ill at ease in the modern world. But much of the time his tongue was firmly in his cheek and his poetry reveals a considerable talent for technique and a sure grasp of modern idiom. His articles on jazz were collected in *All What Jazz?* (1970), and his essays in *Required Writing* (1983).
▷A Motion, *Philip Larkin* (1993)

LA ROCHEFOUCAULD, François, 6th Duc de
(1613–80)

French writer, born in Paris. He devoted himself to the cause of the queen, Marie de Medici, in opposition to Richelieu, and became entangled in a series of love adventures and political intrigues, the result being that he was forced to live in exile from 1639 to 1642. About 1645 he formed a liaison wth Mme de Longueville. He then joined the Frondeurs and was wounded at the siege of Paris. In 1652, wounded again, he retired to the country. On Mazarin's death in 1661 he returned to the court of Louis XIV, and about the same time began a liaison with Mme de Sablé. A surreptitious edition of his *Mémoires*, written in retirement, was published in 1662, but as it gave wide offence he denied its authorship. His *Réflexions, ou sentences et maximes morales*, appeared in 1665. His last years were brightened by his liaison with Mme **de La Fayette**, which lasted until he died. For brevity, clearness and style the *Réflexions* could hardly be excelled. Their author was a remorseless analyst of man's character, and tracks out self-love in its most elusive forms and under its most cunning disguises.
▷W G Moore, *La Rochefoucauld* (1969)

LA ROCHEJAQUELEIN, Marie Louise Victoire
(1772–1857)

French writer, wife of the soldier Louis du Verger de Larochejaquelein. She published valuable *Mémoires* of the Napoleonic War (1815).

LARRA, Mariano José de
(1809–37)

Spanish poet, satirist and political writer, born in Madrid. As a journalist he was unequalled and he published two periodicals between 1828 and 1833, but it was as a satirist that he became well known. His stylistically masterly prose writings include *El Doncel de Don Enrique el Doliente* (1834, 'Don Enrique's Manservant'), a novel, *Macías* (1834), a play, and adaptations of French plays.
▷R B Moreno, *Mariano Larra* (1957)

LARRAMENDI, Padre Manuel de
(1690–1766)

Basque Jesuit humorist and scholar, who wrote in Castilian as well as Basque, born in Andoain, Guipúzoca. He is most famous for his Basque grammar, *Imposible vencido* (1729), and his *Diccionario trilingüe* (1736). He was amongst the first to assert that Basque was the original language of Spain (which is likely). He also liked to assert that it was one of the 75 languages which came into existence after the building of the Tower of Babel, and that it was spoken by God. He wrote a fascinating history, in Castilian, of his native province, which was not printed until long after his death (1882).

▷R Gallop, *A Book of the Basques* (1930); L Michelena, *Historia de la literatura vasca* (1960)

LARRETA, Enrique Rodríguez
(1875–1961)

Argentinian novelist, essayist, poet and playwright. Born in Buenos Aires, he received his doctorate in jurisprudence and social sciences. He travelled extensively in Europe, and from 1910 to 1918 was a diplomat for Argentina in France. He was best known as one of the 'Seis de la fama', the six most important writers in Latin America in the first decades of this century, though he was far from being that. His first novel, *Artemisa*, was published in 1896. Twelve years later he published his most important novel, *La gloria de don Ramiro* (1908, 'The Glory of don Ramiro'), which combines modern Spanish narration with highly polished archaic Spanish dialogue to create a highly interesting, 'modernist' effect. In addition to many other novels, he wrote two books of essays, several plays, and a book of 88 sonnets.

▷H Campanella, *Enrique Larreta, el hombre y el escritor* (1987)

LA SALE, or SALLE, Antoine de
(c.1398–1470)

French writer, born in Burgundy or Touraine. He lived at the courts of Provence and Flanders, and wrote *Chronique du petit Jehan de Saintré* (1456), may have written the ironic satire *Quinze joyes de mariage* (early 15th-century, Eng trans *The Fifteen Comforts of Matrimony*, 1682), and was the reputed author of *Cent nouvelles nouvelles* (1462, 'One Hundred New Tales', modelled loosely on **Boccaccio**'s *Decameron*).

▷A Bronavski, *Le petit Jehan de Saintré, une enigme littéraire* (1922)

LASKER-SCHÜLER, Else
(1869–1945)

German–Jewish poet, playwright and painter. Born in Elberfeld, Wuppertal, she was never much concerned with factual authenticity. 'I was born in Thebes, Egypt ... ' is how her own account of her life begins. Apart from her drama *Die Wupper* (1909) and the travelogue *Das Hebräerland* (1934), it is her poetry for which she is most renowned. Comprising numerous volumes of poetry from *Styx* (1902) to *Mein blaues Klavier* (1943, 'My Blue Piano'), it is marked by a completely unselfconscious mythicization of herself and her friends, climaxing in love/play poetry full of unbridled images of ardour, tenderness and passion; not without reason was she once called 'the snake charmer of love'. Conjuring up biblical or ancient oriental settings, she renames her friends and lovers, turning them into the legendary aristocracy of real and sometimes imaginary kingdoms. Her private poetic myth had its counterpart in her bohemian life style. A public assault by Nazis in 1933 made her flee to Switzerland before moving to Jerusalem in 1937.

▷S Bauschinger, *Else Lasker-Schüler. Ihr Werk und ihre Zeit* (1980)

LASKI, Marghanita
(1915–88)

English novelist and journalist, born in Manchester, niece of Harold Joseph Laski. Educated at Oxford, her first novel, *Love on the Supertax*, appeared in 1944. She wrote extensively for newspapers and reviews. Her later novels include *Little Boy Lost* (1949) and *The Victorian Chaise-longue* (1953). She also wrote a play, *The Offshore Island* (1959), as well as editing and writing various studies and critical works.

LA TAILLE, Jean de
(?1535–1608)

French dramatist and essayist, born in Bondaroy. He studied at the Collège de Boncourt in Paris before going to Orléans to study law, but once there his literary career quickly overtook his interest in the legal profession. He returned to Paris and by 1562 had published his masterpiece, *Saül le Furieux* ('Saul the Furious'), as well as *Le Negromant* ('The Necromancer') and *Les Corivaux. La Famine ou les Gabéonites* ('The Famine or the Gabeonites'), a sequel to *Saul*, appeared in 1573. He is also known for an important essay, *De la Tragédie*, on the renaissance of the classical unities in French drama. He is rarely considered without some reference to his younger brother Jacques, whose work Jean published after his death at the age of 20: this included two tragedies, *Alexandre* and *Daire* (Darius), and several poems, in both Latin and French.

LATINI, Brunetto
(c.1210–c.1295)

Florentine writer and statesman. A member of the Guelf party, he was exiled to France from 1260 to 1266, and there wrote the encyclopaedic *Li Livres dou Trésor*, a survey of extant learning written in French. His other works include the poems *Tesoretto* and *Farolello*, and a commentary on part of **Cicero**'s *De inventione.*

▷T Sundby, *Della vita e delle opera* (1884)

LATORRE, Mariano
(1886–1955)

Chilean story writer and novelist, born in Cobquecura, into a family which was originally Basque on his father's side and French on his mother's. A librarian and teacher, he became famous as an innovator who wrote incomparably about the topography of Chile, and was his country's master of *criollismo* (the equivalent of *costumbristo*, ie regionalism). He said that Nature 'had imposed its presence' in his works. His best stories are contained in *Sus mejores cuentos* (1962, 'His Best Stories'). He also wrote a novel, *Zurzulita* (1920), dealing with the clash between town and country. A critic has said that his chief virtue is his *afán* ('desperate anxiety').

▷H Castillo, *El criollismo en la novela chilena* (1962)

LA TOUR DU PIN, Patrice de
(1911–75)

French Catholic poet whose early work was hailed by conservative critics as the grand answer, by a young poet, to the shocking confusions of Surrealism. He was encouraged by **Jules Supervielle**. His work is grandiloquent, mystical, and, some say, 'rather colourless', but it remains respected amongst its readers, and is eminently and undoubtedly worthy of consideration within the Catholic tradition established by **Paul Claudel**. His *La Vie recluse en poésie* (1938) was translated as *The Dedicated Life in Poetry* (1948).

LATTIMORE, Richmond
(1906–84)

American poet, born in China, who had perhaps the highest reputation of his generation as a translator (**Pindar**, **Homer**, **Aristophanes**, **Euripides**, **Hesiod** and others). His translation of the *Iliad* is particularly prized. His own poetic gift, though less distinguished, nevertheless contributed to his skill as a translator; it is to be found in *Poems from Three Decades* (1972).

LAUBE, Heinrich
(1806–84)

German playwright and manager, born in Sprottau in Silesia. He was one of the leaders of the 'Young Germany' movement and editor of *Die elegante Welt* ('The Elegant World'), its literary organ. He was director of Vienna's Burgtheater (1850–67), and

among his writings are works on the theatre, on historical themes, novels such as *Das junge Europa* (1833–7, 'Young Europe'), *Die Karlsschüler* (1847, 'The Boys of the Karls-School'), a drama of the young **Schiller**, and a biography of **Franz Grillparzer**.

▷M Dürst, *Heinrich Laube* (1951)

LAUDER, Sir Thomas Dick
(1784–1848)

Scottish writer, born in Fountainhall, Midlothian. He served in the Cameron Highlanders and in 1808 married the heiress of Relugas in Morayshire. He succeeded to the baronetcy in 1820, and lived at the Grange, Edinburgh, from 1832 until his death. He was Secretary to the Board of Scottish Manufacturers (1839–48), and was a proponent of the establishment of technical and art schools. He wrote two romances, *Lochindhu* (1825) and *The Wolf of Badenoch* (1827), but his best works are *An Account of the Great Morayshire Floods* (1830) and the unfinished *Scottish Rivers*, which appeared in *Tait's Magazine* (1847–9). He also compiled *Highland Rambles and Legends to Shorten the Way* (1837) and *Legends and Tales of the Highlands* (1841).

LAURENCE, Margaret, originally Jean Margaret Wemyss
(1926–87)

Canadian novelist of Scots–Irish descent, born in the prairie town of Neepawa, Manitoba. Her first stories appeared in the high-school paper. Aged 18, she left home to study at United College (now Winnipeg University), from which she graduated in 1947, the same year she married John Laurence, a civil engineer. His job took them to England, Somaliland and, in 1952, to Ghana, where they spent five years. *A Tree for Poverty* (1954), a collection of translated Somali poetry and folk-tales, and the travel book *The Prophet's Camel Bell* (1963), came from her East African experience. *This Side Jordan* (1960), her first novel, was set in Ghana. She moved to England in 1962 and a year later a collection of stories, *The Tomorrow-Tamer*, set in West Africa, appeared. In Penn, Buckinghamshire, she wrote her famous Manawaka series based on her home town: *The Stone Angel* (1964), *A Jest of God* (1966), *The Fire-Dwellers* (1969), *A Bird in the House* (1970) and *The Diviners* (1974). One of Canada's most potent novelists, she received Governor General Awards in 1967 and 1975, and in 1972 was made a Companion of the Order of Canada.

▷W H New, *Margaret Laurence: the writer and her critics* (1977)

LAURENTS, Arthur
(1920–)

American writer of scripts for hit musicals, such as *West Side Story* (1957). His first success was *Home of the Brave* (1945), about racial prejudice. The finest of his screenplays was for *The Snake Pit* (1948).

LAUTRÉAMONT, Comte de *see* DUCASSE, Isidore Lucien

LAVANT, Christine, pseud of Christine Habernig, née Thornhauser
(1915–)

Austrian Roman Catholic poet, born in Gross-Eding. The daughter of a miner, and partially blind and deaf from birth, she was forced to earn a living from knitting; then she built up a deserved reputation as Austria's leading lyrical mystical poet, drawing on nature and her reading of **Rilke** to gain her haunting effects.

LA VARENDE, Jean-Balthazar Marie Mallard, Comte de
(1887–1959)

French novelist and biographer. Born in the Pays d'Ouche, Normandy, he manifested a lifelong attachment to his ancestral home, the Chateau de Bonneville-Chamblanc. His work reflects an intense interest in the lives of the aristocracy, coupled with a fervent belief in its right to power and privilege. He despised what he considered to be the decadence of the bourgeoisie and, through his fiction, sought to escape into the old order. Most of his prolific output of novels is set in the early 19th century, and he often uses his own forebears as heroes. He was awarded the Grand Prix du Roman of the Académie française in 1938, for *Le Centaure de Dieu* ('God's Centaur'). His biographies include *Guillaume le Bâtard, conquérant* (1946).

LAVATER, Johann Kaspar
(1741–1801)

Swiss physiognomist, theologian and poet, born in Zürich. In 1769 he took Protestant orders. He made himself known by a volume of poems, *Schweizerlieder* (1767, 'Swiss Songs'). His *Aussichten in die Ewigkeit* (1768–78, 'Prospects of Eternity') is characterized by religious enthusiasm and mysticism. He attempted to elevate physiognomy into a science in his *Physiognomische Fragmente* (1775–8, Eng trans *Essays on Physiognomy designed to promote the knowledge and the love of mankind*, 5 vols, 1789–98). While tending the wounded at the capture of Zürich by Masséna (September 1799) he received a wound, of which he later died.
▷T Hasler, *Johann Lavater* (1942)

LAVEDAN, Henri
(1859–1940)

French dramatist, born in Orléans, author of both comedies and 'problem plays'. His most famous play, was *Le Prince d'Aurec* (1892, Eng trans *The Prince d'Aurec*, in *Three Modern Plays from the French*, 1914), about a prince who borrows money from a Jewish baron who makes financial loans to anti-Semitic aristocrats in order to become their equal; the prince ends by deciding to live an honest life, which is dealt with in an inferior sequel, *Les Deux Noblesses* (1894, 'The Two Nobilities'). Pierre Fresnay directed a movie version of Lavedan's play *Le Duel* ('The Duel') in 1939, with himself, Yvonnes Printemps and Raimu in the leading parts.

LAVER, James
(1899–1975)

English writer and art critic, born in Liverpool. He won the Newdigate Prize for verse at Oxford in 1921, and later books of verse included *His Last Sebastian* (1922) and *Ladies' Mistakes* (1933). He was Assistant Keeper, later Keeper at the Victoria and Albert Museum from 1922 to 1959. He wrote several books of art criticism, including *French Painting and the 19th century* (1937) and *Fragonard* (1956), and made a substantial contribution to the history of English costume with such books as *Taste and Fashion* (1937), *Fashions and Fashion Plates* (1943) and *Children's Costume in the 19th Century* (1951).

LAVIN, Mary
(1912–)

Irish short-story writer and novelist, born in East Walpole, Massachusetts. Her parents returned to Ireland when she was nine and she has lived there ever since. 'Miss Holland', her first short story, was published in the *Dublin Magazine* where it was admired by Lord **Dunsany**, who encouraged her and later wrote an introduction to her first collection, *Tales from Bective Bridge* (1942), which was awarded the James Tait Black Memorial Prize. Notwithstanding two early novels— *The House in Clewe Street* (1945) and *Mary O'Grady* (1950)—she has concentrated on the short story. She has published many collections, and a *Collected Stories* appeared in 1971. Further collections are *A Memory and Other Stories* (1972), *The Shrine and Other Stories* (1977) and *A Family Likeness* (1985). Her laurels include the **Katherine Mansfield** Prize and the Gregory Medal, founded by **W B Yeats** to be 'the supreme award of the Irish nation'.
▷R Peterson, *Mary Lavin* (1978)

LAWLER, Ray
(1921–)

Australian playwright, born in Melbourne, who has also worked as an actor, producer and director. His first play was *Cradle of Thunder* (1952), but it was not until his tenth, *Summer of the Seventeenth Doll* (1955), that he attracted notice. This takes its title from the collection of fairground dolls which mark the 16 summers in which Roo and his mates have holidayed from their cane-cutting jobs in Queensland and gone south to their Melbourne girlfriends 'for the mating season'. *Kid Stakes* (1975) looks back to the beginning of these relationships, and *Other Times* (1976) to the period immediately after World War II. The three plays were collected as *The Doll Trilogy* in 1978. *The Piccadilly Bushman* (1961) looks at divided loyalties, and *The Man Who Shot the Albatross* (1972, not published) concerns William Bligh of the *Bounty* and his later career as Governor of New South Wales.

LAWRENCE, D(avid) H(erbert)
(1885–1930)

English novelist, poet and essayist, born in Eastwood, Nottinghamshire, the son of a miner. With tubercular tendencies, of which he eventually died, he became, through his mother's devotion, a schoolmaster and began to write, encouraged by the notice taken of his work by **Ford Madox Ford** and **Edward Garnett**. In 1911, after the success of his first novel, *The White Peacock*, he decided to live by writing. In 1912 he eloped with Frieda von Richthofen, a cousin of the German war ace Baron Mannfred von Richthofen and wife of Ernest Weekley, a professor at Nottingham University. They travelled in Germany, Austria and Italy from 1912 to 1913, and married in 1914 after her divorce. Lawrence had made his reputation with the semi-auto-biographical *Sons and Lovers* (1913). They returned to England at the outbreak of World War I and lived in an atmosphere of suspicion and persecution in a cottage in Cornwall. In 1915 he published *The Rainbow*, an exploration of marital and sexual relations, and was horrified to find himself prosecuted for obscenity. He left England in 1919, and after three years' residence in Italy, where he produced another exploration of sex and marriage, *Women in Love* (1921), he went to America, settling in Mexico until the progress of his disease drove him back to Italy where his last years were spent. His sensitive spirit was again shocked by his further prosecutions for obscenity over the private publication in Florence of *Lady Chatterley's Lover* in 1928 and over an exhibition of his paintings in London in 1929. *Lady Chatterley's Lover* was not published in the UK in unexpurgated

form until after a sensational obscenity trial in 1961. Opinion is still divided over Lawrence's worth as a writer but there can be no doubt about his effect on the younger intellectuals of his period. He challenged them by his attempt to interpret human emotion on a deeper level of consciousness than that handled by his contemporaries. This provoked either sharp criticism or an almost idolatrous respect. His descriptive passages are sometimes superb, but he had little humour, and this occasionally produced unintentionally comic effects. His finest writing occurs in his poems, where all but essentials have been pared away, but most of his novels have an enduring strength. His other major novels include *Aaron's Rod* (1922), *Kangaroo* (1923, reflecting a visit to Australia) and *The Plumed Serpent* (1926, set in Mexico). His collected poems were published in 1928, and his *Complete Poems* in 1957. A *Complete Plays* appeared in 1965; his other writings include vivid travel narratives, essays, works of literary criticism, including *Studies in Classic American Literature* (1923), and two studies of the unconscious.
▷K Sagar, *The Life of D H Lawrence* (1980)

LAWSON, Henry Hertzberg
(1867–1922)

Australian poet and short-story writer, born in New South Wales, the son of a Norwegian sailor and gold miner. His mother Louisa Lawson (1848–1920) was a strong personality who, in 1887, founded a radical journal, *The Republican*, and, in 1888, *Dawn*, a monthly magazine of strong feminist sympathies which began the movement for women's suffrage in New South Wales. From his mother and her friends Henry acquired the radical opinions which coloured his own writing. He travelled widely in Australia and New Zealand and contributed to the *Bulletin*, but his first collection, *Short Stories in Prose and Verse*, was published by Louisa in 1894. Lawson then prepared two substantial collections, of verse in *In the Days When the World Was Wide* (1896) and stories in *While the Billy Boils* (1896). Another collection of verse and two of prose followed. Lawson then moved with his wife and son to London, where he prepared for Blackwood's Magazine a collection of his earlier stories, published as *The Country I Come From* (1901), and worked on the tales which were to appear the same year as *Joe Wilson and His Mates*. Returning to Australia in 1902, Lawson separated from his wife. His later years were marred by ill health and alcoholism. During this period, and since his death, his tales and poems have appeared in numerous editions. A definitive seven-volume edition was edited by Colin Roderick (1967–72), including not only the verse and

stories, but also Lawson's letters and auto-biographical writings.
▷M Clark, *In Search of Lawson* (1978)

LAWSON, John Howard
(1894–1977)
American dramatist, born in New York City. He was a politically alert man, angered by the economic and social injustice he considered was blighting the USA. His first play, *Processional* (1925), is set during a coal-mining strike in West Virginia. He wrote seven more dramas before completing *Marching Song* (1937), another play in which the workers successfully rise up against a repressive management. In Hollywood as a screenwriter, Lawson was identified as a communist and summoned before the House Un-American Activities Committee as one of the 'Hollywood Ten'. He was convicted of contempt, served a one-year prison sentence and emerged effectively blacklisted. He wrote only one more play, *Parlor Magic* (1963).

LAXNESS, Halldór Kiljan, pseud of Halldór Guðjónsson
(1902–)
Icelandic novelist, born in Reykjavík, winner of the Nobel Prize for literature in 1955. Brought up on the farm of Laxnes, near Reykjavík, he travelled widely to seek experience. After World War I he steeped himself in Expressionism in Germany, Catholicism in a monastery in Luxembourg, and Surrealism in France, before going to Canada and the USA (1927–30), where he was converted to socialism. In his fiction he explored the reality of Iceland, past and present, and rejuvenated Icelandic prose, in a series of incomparable epic novels like *Salka Valka* (1931–2), *Sjálfstætt fólk* (1934–5, *Independent People*, 1945–6), *Heimsljós* (1937–40, *World Light*, 1969) and *Íslandsklukkan* (1943–9, 'Iceland's Bell'). After World War II he continued to turn out a stream of brilliantly executed novels on Icelandic life: *Atómstöðin* (1948, Eng trans *The Atom Station*, 1961), *Gerpla* (1952, Eng trans *The Happy Warriors*, 1958), *Brekkukotsannáll* (1957, Eng trans *The Fish Can Sing*, 1966), *Paradísarheimt* (1960, Eng trans *Paradise Reclaimed*, 1962) and *Kristnihald undir Jökli* (1968, Eng trans *Christianity at Glacier*, 1972). He has also written a number of plays, and adapted some of his own novels for the stage.
▷P Hallberg, *Laxness* (1971)

LAYAMON
(fl.early 13th century)
English poet and priest at Ernley (now Areley Regis), on the Severn near Bewdley. In c.1200 he wrote an alliterative verse chronicle, the *Brut*, a history of England which was an amplified imitation of **Robert Wace**'s *Brut d'Angleterre*. It is important in the history of English versification as the first poem written in Middle English, and contains the first English versions of the stories of **Arthur**, Lear, Cymbelene and others.
▷J S P Tetlock, *The Legendary History of Britain* (1950)

LAYE, Camera
(1928–80)
Major Francophone novelist, born in French Guinea of a Malinke family. Of his generation, Laye probably had more (deserved) attention paid to him by critics than any other African novelist. 'No other novelist', it has been written, 'approached him in artistry or in psychological insight'. But some accused him of a 'lack of commitment' to the Black struggle. He grew up away from the influence of colonialism; his father was a smith, a master of both metalwork and magic. Laye was sick and weak for the last years of his life; in 1965 he left his own country in disgust, for Senegal—President Touré had him condemned to death *in absentia*. His two masterpieces are his first two novels: the autobiographical *L'Enfant noir* (1953, Eng trans *The Dark Child*, 1954), and *Le Regard du roi* (1954, Eng trans *The Radiance of the King*, 1956). The first is based on his own enchanted childhood, the second is a profound allegory about a white man's search for a king he wished to serve. Later work, such as *Le Maître de la parole* (1978, 'The Wordmaster'), is powerful in parts but weaker as a whole.
▷A C Brench, *The Novelists' Inheritance in French Africa* (1967); W Cartey, *Whispers from a Continent* (1969)

LAYTON, Irving
(1912–)
Romanian-born Canadian poet, lecturer, critic and editor, educated at MacDonald College, Quebec and McGill, Montreal. The author of some 50 volumes of poetry, Layton proclaims: 'the poet must insist on a complex, imaginative awareness and remain the sworn enemy of all dogmas and dogmatists'. His famous rebuke of Canadian torpor, 'A dull people, without charm/or ideas', is deliberately provocative, reflecting his passionate belief in the poet's role as social discomforter. He received the Governor General's Award for *Collected Poems: A Red Carpet for the Sun* in 1959; a selected volume of poetry, *A Wild Peculiar Joy*, representing the work of more than 40 years, was published in 1982 (rev edn 1989).
▷E Mandel, *The Poetry of Irving Layton*

(1981); W Francis, *Irving Layton and His Work* (1985)

LAZARUS, Emma
(1849–87)

American poet and essayist, born in New York. She published striking volumes of poems and translations, including *Admetus and other poems* (1871), *Songs of a Semite* (1882) and *By the Waters of Babylon* (1887). She also wrote a prose romance, *Alide: An Episode of Goethe's Life* (1874), and a verse tragedy, *The Spagnaletto* (1876). A champion of oppressed Jewry, she is best known for her sonnet, 'The New Colossus' (1883), inscribed on the Statue of Liberty in New York harbour.
▷H E Jacob, *The World of Emma Lazarus* (1949)

LEACOCK, Stephen Butler
(1869–1944)

English-born Canadian humorist and economist, born in Swanmore, Hampshire. Educated at the University of Toronto, he became first a teacher, later a lecturer at McGill University, and in 1908 head of the economics department there. He wrote several books on his subject, including *Elements of Political Science* (1906), *Practical Political Economy* (1910) and *The Economic Prosperity of the British Empire* (1931). But it is as a humorist that he became widely known. Among his popular short stories, essays and parodies are *Literary Lapses* (1910), *Nonsense Novels* (1911), *Behind the Beyond* (1913), *Winsome Winnie* (1920) and *The Garden of Folly* (1924). He also wrote biographies of **Mark Twain** (1932) and **Dickens** (1933). *The Boy I Left Behind Me*, an autobiography, appeared in 1946.
▷D M Legate, *Stephen Leacock: a biography* (1970)

LEAR, Edward
(1812–88)

English artist, humorist and traveller, born in London. In 1832 he was engaged by the 13th Earl of Derby to make coloured drawings of the rare birds and animals in the menagerie at Knowsley Hall (Merseyside). Under the earl's patronage he travelled widely in Italy and Greece, making landscape sketches and oil paintings which he published in several travel books, including *Sketches of Rome* (1842) and *Illustrated Excursions in Italy* (1846). He became a friend of his patron's grandchildren, whom he entertained with nonsense limericks and other verse which he illustrated with his own sketches and first published (anonymously) as *A Book of Nonsense* in 1846. Later he published *Nonsense Songs, Stories, Botany, and Alphabets* (1870), *More Nonsense Rhymes* (1871) and *Laughable Lyrics* (1876). He spent most of his latter years in Italy.
▷S Chitty, *That Singular Person Called Lear* (1988)

LEAVIS, F(rank) R(aymond)
(1895–1978)

Influential English critic who taught at Cambridge University for the whole of his life. He first learned from **I A Richards**, but developed Richards's ideas about practical and close criticism into a kind of crusade against industrialization and 'mass culture'. His chief mentors were **D H Lawrence** and **Blake**. He was notoriously ill-mannered and paranoid in style, but had been badly treated at Cambridge, and had ample justification for his prickly attitudes. Few writers who came under his influence do not owe him something, but he is now less important as a polemicist—his battle against mass culture having been lost, and his other concerns having passed into the hands of the environmentalists—than as a gifted if somewhat narrow critic who extolled **Donne**, **Hopkins** and **T S Eliot**, at the expense of **Milton**, **Swinburne** and other exponents of what he took to be musical rhetoric. The oft-repeated judgement that he was 'the most important English-speaking critic of his time' is a debatable point—chiefly because of his unwillingness to see the virtues of those poets and novelists he disliked. His wife was **Q D Leavis**, also a noted critic.
▷M Bell, *F R Leavis* (1988)

LEAVIS, Q(ueenie) D(orothy)
(1906–81)

English literary critic. Born in London, she studied at Girton College, Cambridge, under **I A Richards**. Though her powerful sociological analysis of 19th-century fiction made a substantial impact on her husband **F R Leavis**, whom she married in 1929, she has only rarely (and posthumously) received full credit for it. This is partly due to the fact that, despite writing regularly for Leavis's journal *Scrutiny*, and continuing to publish perceptive essays and papers on literary subjects, she wrote only one book, *Fiction and the Reading Public* (1932). Though by no means a doctrinaire feminist, she had a particular interest in women's writing and wrote shrewdly about the **Brontë** sisters, **Jane Austen** and **Edith Wharton**. Some of her best essays were posthumously collected.

LEAVITT, David
(1961–)

American novelist and short-story writer, born in Pennsylvania. Brought up in Northern California, and educated at Yale, he then worked for a time in publishing in New York. His first collection of stories, *Family Dancing* (1984), demonstrated both his observant interest in emotional disturbances within middle-class American families, especially those caused by cancer and homosexuality, and his cool, sometimes dryly witty style. These themes were further explored in the novels *The Lost Language of Cranes* (1986), in which a family has to deal with the homosexuality of both father and son, and *Equal Affections* (1989), which explores the history and structure of a family deeply affected by the mother's cancer. Further stories appeared in *A Place I've Never Been* (1990).

LEBENSON, Micha Joseph
(1828–54)

Hebrew (Lithuanian) poet and brilliant translator from the German (**Schiller**'s *Virgil*), born in Vilna. His father was the great Haskalah ('Enlightenment') scholar Abraham Dov Lebenson (1794–1878). He also wrote historical epic poems.

LE CARRÉ, John, pseud of David John Moore Cornwell
(1931–)

English novelist, born in Poole, Dorset. He was educated at Sherborne School, Berne University, and, after military service in Austria, at Oxford. He taught French and German for two years at Eton before going into the British Foreign Service as second secretary in Bonn, and consul in Hamburg, from which post he resigned in 1964 to become a full-time writer. His novels present the unglamorous side of diplomacy and espionage, a world of boredom, squalor and shabby deceit in complete contrast to the popular spy fiction of **Ian Fleming**. His settings and characters have a compelling authenticity and he questions the morality of present-day diplomacy and traditional patriotic attitudes. His first published novel, *Call for The Dead* (1961), introduced his 'anti-hero' George Smiley, who appears in most of his stories. *A Murder of Quality* appeared in 1962, followed the next year by the very successful *The Spy Who Came In From The Cold*. After *The Looking-Glass War* (1965) and *A Small Town in Germany* (1968), a departure from his usual subject and style entitled *The Naive and Sentimental Lover* (1971) was not well received, and he returned to his former world with *Tinker, Tailor, Soldier, Spy* (1974), *The Honourable Schoolboy* (1977), *Smiley's People* (1980), *The Little Drummer Girl* (1983), *A Perfect Spy* (1986), *The Russia House* (1989) and *The Secret Pilgrim* (1992), in which Smiley takes his final bow. His most recent novel is *The Night Manager* (1993). Many of his novels have been successfully filmed or televised, although the presumed end of the Cold War may have removed his most fertile subject-matter.
▷ E Homberger, *John Le Carré* (1986)

LE CLÉZIO, J(ean)-M(arie) G(ustave)
(1940–)

French philosophical novelist of highly individual style. His work is dominated by tremendous mythological or elemental oppositions and can be seen to form a single, continuous cycle representing the novelist's quest for truth. His early life was markedly peripatetic. He was born in Nice, educated there and in Africa, spending a year at Bristol University in England (1958–9), and a further year in London (1960–1). After taking another degree in Aix-en-Provence, he went to Bangkok to teach at the Buddhist University (1966–7), moving on to Mexico and spending the years 1969 to 1973 living with the Embara Indians in Panama. He returned to the south of France in 1973. His first novel was *Le Procès-Verbal* (1963, Eng trans *The Interrogation*, 1964), followed by *La Fièvre* (1965, 'Fever'), *Le Déluge* (1966, Eng trans *The Flood*, 1967) and *Le Livre des fuites* (1969, Eng trans *The Book of Flights*, 1971), among others. Thereafter, English-language interest in his work declined, though he is still read and admired in France. Following the publication of *Désert* (1980), his best book for many years, he was awarded the French Academy's Prix **Morand**.
▷ J Waelti-Walters, *J-M G Le Clézio* (1977)

LECONTE DE LISLE, Charles Marie
(1818–94)

French poet, born in Réunion. After some years of travel he settled down to a literary life in Paris. He exercised a profound influence on all the younger poets, headed the school called *Parnassiens*, and succeeded to **Victor Hugo**'s chair at the Academy in 1886. His early poems appeared as *Poésies complètes* (1858). Other volumes are *Poèmes barbares* (1862) and *Poèmes tragiques* (1884); and he translated many classics. His verse is marked by regularity and faultlessness of form.
▷ P Flottes, *Leconte de Lisle* (1954)

LEE, (Nelle) Harper
(1926–)

American novelist, born in Alabama and educated at Alabama State University. Her only novel, *To Kill A Mockingbird* (1960), was an immediate success, and has subsequently enhanced its reputation as a modern classic. Narrated by Scout, a six-year-old white tomboy in the American south, it is centred on a trial at which Scout's father is the defence lawyer for a black man accused of raping a white woman. It won a Pulitzer Prize in 1961, and was made into a highly successful film (1962) starring Gregory Peck.

LEE, Harriet
(1757–1851)

English novelist, born in London. She wrote with her sister, **Sophia Lee**, *The Canterbury Tales*, one of which was dramatized by **Byron** and called *Werner, or, The Inheritance*. Her other novels included *Errors of Innocence* (1786), an epistolary novel, and *Clare Lennox* (1797).
▷D Punter, *The Literature of Terror* (1980); K Rogers, *Feminism in 18th century England* (1982)

LEE, John Alfred Alexander
(1891–1982)

New Zealand politician and novelist, born in Dunedin. He won the DCM in World War I in France, where he lost an arm. He was a Labour MP for many years and member of cabinet as under-secretary in the 1935 and 1938 governments, but his bitter ambition and his vindictiveness towards Prime Minister Savage hastened Savage's death and his own expulsion. He formed his own party in 1939 but lost his seat in 1943. His novels *Children of the Poor* (1934), *The Hunted* (1936) and *Civilian into Soldier* (1937) are partly autobiographical; all his serious fiction is powerful but crude socialist propaganda, written originally for serialization in his own magazine *John A Lee's Weekly*, though *The Politician* did not appear until 1987, after his death. He wrote *Socialism in New Zealand* (1938) with an introduction by Clement Attlee and published a number of accounts of his political life.
▷*The John A Lee Diaries, 1936–40* (1981)

LEE, Laurie
(1914–)

English poet and author, born in Slad, Gloucestershire. He was educated at the village school and in Stroud, Gloucestershire. He worked as a scriptwriter for documentary films during the 1940s and his travels in many parts of the world are the subject of much of his writing. A nature-poet of great simplicity, his works include *The Sun My Monument* (1944), *The Bloom of Candles* (1947) and *My Many-Coated Man* (1955). *A Rose For Winter* (1955) describes his travels in Spain, and his autobiographical books, *Cider With Rosie* (1959), *As I Walked Out One Midsummer Morning* (1969) and *I Can't Stay Long* (1975) are widely acclaimed for their evocation of a rural childhood, and of life in the many countries he has visited. *A Moment of War* (1991) takes up from the end of *As I Walked Out*, and recounts his experiences in Spain during the Civil War.

LEE, Nathaniel
(1649–92)

English dramatist. From Westminster he passed to Trinity College, Cambridge. He failed as an actor through nervousness (1672), produced nine or 10 tragedies between 1675 and 1682, and spent five years in Bedlam (1684–9). His best play is *The Rival Queens* (1677). He wrote with **Dryden** two plays, *Oedipus* and *The Duke of Guise*.

LEE, Sophia
(1750–1824)

English writer, sister of **Harriet Lee**. She enjoyed greater success as a dramatist than her sister, notably with her play *The Chapter of Accidents* (1780; the success of which enabled her to open a girls' school in Bath), and the verse tragedy *Almeyda, Queen of Grenada* (1796). Her historical novel *The Recess* (1783–5) was a success, and she also wrote a lengthy ballad, *The Hermit's Tale* (1787). Her epistolary novel *The Life of a Lover* (1804) has autobiographical elements.
▷D Punter, *The Literature of Terror* (1980); K Rogers, *Feminism in 18th century England* (1982)

LEE, Vernon, pseud of Violet Paget
(1856–1935)

English aesthetic philosopher, critic and novelist, born in Boulogne of English parentage. She travelled widely in her youth and settled in Florence. Studies of Italian and Renaissance art were followed by her philosophical study, *The Beautiful* (1913), one of the best expositions of the empathy theory of art. She also wrote two novels and a dramatic trilogy, *Satan the Waster* (1920), giving full rein to her pacifism.
▷P Gunn, *Vernon Lee: Violet Paget, 1856–1935* (1969)

LEEUW, Aart van der
(1876–1932)

Dutch poet and novelist, born in Delft. He is one of the more interesting of now almost completely neglected Dutch writers, having taken his inspiration from the English poet **Thomas Traherne**. The style of his novels—his best work—has been mistaken as 'romantic', but in fact he was a mystic trapped in a century inimical to his genius. He made his real mark late in his life, with the novels *Ik en mijn speelman* (1927, 'I and My Minstrel') and *De kleine Rudolf* (1930, 'Little Rudolf').

LE FANU, Joseph Sheridan
(1814–73)

Irish novelist and journalist, born in Dublin, a grand-nephew of **Richard Brinsley Sheridan**. Called to the Bar in 1839, he soon abandoned law for journalism. He began writing for the *Dublin University Magazine*, of which he became editor and proprietor (1869), and later bought three Dublin newspapers. His novels include *The House by the Churchyard* (1863), and the best-known of them, *Uncle Silas* (1864). His short stories are collected in *In a Glass Darkly* (1872), and he wrote 14 other works, remarkable for their preoccupation with the supernatural. His *Poems* were edited by **Alfred Perceval Graves** (1896). His reputation, which had fallen into neglect, was restored by the publication of *Madam Crowl's Ghost* (1923), edited by **M R James**, and he is again recognized as an important writer in the fields of mystery, suspense and the supernatural.
▷I Melada, *Sheridan Le Fanu* (1987)

LEFFLAND, Ella
(1931–)

American novelist and short-story writer. She was born and grew up on the West Coast, and the San Fransciso Bay area, in particular, forms the setting for much of her fiction. *Love out of Season* (1974) describes the hectic San Francisco scene of the 1960s from a woman's perspective. Some of her stories are collected in *Last Courtesies* (1980).

LE FORT, Gertrud von
(1876–1971)

German novelist and poet, born into an aristocratic, originally Huguenot, family in Minden. As a Protestant she wrote her most famous collection of poems, *Hymnen an die Kirche* (1924, Eng trans *Hymns to the Church*, 1937); then she became a Catholic, and wrote dedicated novels and poems of high competence in the interests of her new faith. Her *Die Letze am Schafort* (1931, Eng trans *The Song of the Scaffold*, 1953), formed the basis for Poulenc's well-known opera *Dialogues de Carmelites* (1956), which in turn inspired the film script by **Bernanos** on the same theme. Selected novellas are in *The Judgement of the Sea* (1962).
▷I O'Boyle, *Gertrude le Fort: An Introduction to her Prose* (1964)

LE FRANC, Marie
(1879–1964)

French (Breton) novelist who emigrated to Canada and there published her first novel, *Grand Louis l'Innocent* (1927), which had a great success. Her work deals with simple French Canadians, whose lyrical inner lives she sought to convey.
▷*Corymbe*, special number devoted to Marie Le Franc (1936, in French)

LE GALLIENNE, Richard
(1866–1947)

English writer, born of Guernsey ancestry in Liverpool. In 1891 he became a London journalist but later lived in New York. He published many volumes of prose and verse from 1887, when his first collection, *My Ladies Sonnets*, was published. He was an original member of the Rhymers Club with **Yeats**, **Wilde** and others. His style, that of the later 19th century, is old-fashioned, but his best books are *Quest of the Golden Girl* (1896), *The Romantic Nineties* (1926) and *From a Paris Garret* (1936).

LE GUIN, Ursula, née Kroeber
(1929–)

American science-fiction writer, born in Berkeley, California, the daughter of the anthropologist Alfred Louis Kroeber (1876–1960). She was educated at Radcliffe College and Columbia University. A prolific writer both for adults and children, she has demonstrated that it is possible to work in genre and be taken seriously as a writer. Much of her work focuses on subjective views of a universe incorporating numerous habitable worlds, each spawned by beings from the 'Hain'. Hain novels include *Rocannon's World* (1966), *Plant of Exile* (1966), *The Left Hand of Darkness* (1969) and *The Word for World is Forest* (1976). In a prodigious oeuvre for children, known as the 'Earthsea' trilogy—*A Wizard of Earthsea* (1968), *The Tombs of Atuan* (1971) and *The Farthest Shore* (1972)—she depicts a magical but threatening world where every village has its small-time sorcerer and the forces of evil are uncomfortably close. She continued this trilogy in an overtly feminist vein with *Tehanu* (1990).
▷E C Cogell, *Understanding Ursula K. Le Guin* (1990)

LEGUIZAMÓN, Martiniano
(1858–1935)

Argentinian novelist and dramatist, born in Rosario del Tala. One play, *Calandria*, 1895, reached the stage. The collection *Recuerdos de la tierra* (1896, 'Memories of the Land'), like his play, dealt with legends such as that of the gaucho outlaw Calandria, murdered by the police. He later more or less abandoned fiction, to become a historian.

LEHMANN, Geoffrey John
(1940–)

Australian poet, editor and taxation specialist, born in Sydney. After reading German

Literature at Sydney University he practised as a solicitor and then taught commercial law. His poetry has a strong sense of times past; whether dealing with the life of his father or of a Roman general, his clear verse gives shape and life to a loved image. His first book, *The Ilex Tree* (1965, with **Les Murray**) was followed by five others including *From an Australian Country Sequence* (1973) and *Nero's Poems* (1981). His *Selected Poems* was published in 1976. As editor he has produced *Comic Australian Verse* (1972), and with Robert Gray has co-edited *The Younger Australian Poets* (1983) and *Australian Poetry in the Twentieth Century* (1991). His legal and artistic *alter ego* has written a standard work on taxation law and *Australian Primitive Painters* (1977).

LEHMANN, (Rudolph) John Frederick
(1907–87)

English poet and writer, born in Bourne End, Buckinghamshire, son of Rudolph Chambers Lehmann. He was educated at Eton and Trinity College, Cambridge, and founded the periodical in book format, *New Writing* (1936–41). He was managing director of the Hogarth Press with Leonard and **Virginia Woolf** (1938–46), and ran his own firm, John Lehmann Ltd, with his sister, **Rosamond Lehmann**, as co-director from 1946 to 1953. In 1954 he inaugurated *The London Magazine*, which he edited until 1961. His first publications were volumes of poetry, including *A Garden Revisited* (1931) and *Forty Poems* (1942). He also wrote a novel, *Evil was Abroad* (1938), and studies of *Edith Sitwell* (1952), *Virginia Woolf and her World* (1975) and *Rupert Brooke* (1980). He wrote his autobiography in three volumes, *The Whispering Gallery* (1955), *I am my Brother* (1960) and *The Ample Proposition* (1966). His *Poems New and Selected* appeared in 1986.
▷ *In My Own Time* (3 vols, 1969)

LEHMANN, Rosamond Nina
(1901–90)

English novelist, daughter of Rudolph Chambers Lehmann and sister of Beatrix and **John Lehmann**, born in High Wycombe, Buckinghamshire. She was educated at Girton College, Cambridge, which provided the background for her first novel, *Dusty Answer* (1927). Her novels show a fine sensitive insight into character and her women especially are brilliantly drawn. Among her other books are *A Note in Music* (1930), *An Invitation to the Waltz* (1932) and its sequel *The Weather in the Streets* (1936), and *The Echoing Grove* (1953). Her last novel was *A Sea-Grape Tree* (1970). She also wrote a play, *No More Music* (1939), and a volume of short

stories, *The Gypsy's Baby* (1946). She produced the autobiographical *The Swan in the Evening* in 1967. She later developed a belief in spiritualism, and became President of the College of Psychic Studies.
▷ G Tindall, *Rosamond Lehmann: an appreciation* (1985)

LEHMANN, Wilhelm
(1882–1968)

German poet, critic and novelist, born in Venezuela (his father was a Lübeck merchant). His influence on the modernist poets who became his successors was wide and decisive (eg on **Eich**, **Krolow** and many others); yet his own procedures were not modernist but, as a critic has pointed out, traditional in the manner of **Robert Graves** or, in particular, **Robert Frost**. He was a prisoner-of-war in England during World War I. His early work consisted of novels and stories; he did not begin to publish poems until he was over 50. He initiated, under the influence of his close friend **Oscar Loerke**, and inspired by his reading of **Goethe**, a new kind of poetry: a pantheistic and Symbolist nature poetry in which everything is to be interpreted in the light of the 'Green God' which refers man back to the nature from which he has been estranged: 'God and the world appear only to the summons of mysteriously planned syllables'. His novels and stories, less memorable, have been described as 'rhapsodically idyllic'.
▷ C Middleton and M Hamburger (eds), *Modern German Poetry 1910–1969* (1962)

LEHTONEN, Joel
(1881–1934)

Finnish poet, translator (**Stendhal** and others) and novelist, born in Saaminki. His earlier, neo-romantic work, in verse and prose, shows the influence of **Nietzsche**; but with the novel *Putkinotko* (1919), his masterpiece, a Finnish counterpart to **Goncharov**'s *Oblomov*, he came into his own. The rest of his life was spent in a series of vain attempts to defeat depression through writing, each book of the greatest interest, but ultimately he killed himself in Huopalahti.

LEIBER, Fritz Reuter, Jr
(1910–92)

American fantasy and science-fiction writer, born in Chicago. He studied psychology and physiology at the University of Chicago, and worked as an editor and a teacher. His first story, 'Two Sought Adventure' (1939), launched his sophisticated and increasingly complex *Fafhrd and the Grey Mouser* heroic-fantasy series, characters he returned to throughout his career. Other important fantasy works include *Conjure Wife* (1953) and *Our Lady of Darkness* (1977). His science fiction has generally been seen as secondary to his work in fantasy, but he has made significant contributions to the genre, notably in the short story, but also with the novels *The Big Time* (1961) and *The Wanderer* (1964).

LEINO, Eino, pseud of Armas Eino Leopold Lönnbohm
(1878–1926)

Finnish poet and novelist. He published his first collection, *Maaliskuun lauluja* (1896, 'Spring Songs'), aged only 18. He developed the *Kalevala* metre into a distinctive, sombrely lyrical style of his own, best exemplified in the two volumes of *Helkavirsiä* (1903, 1916, 'Whitsongs'), the second of which is shadowed by his reaction to World War I. He also wrote novels, and made fine translations of **Dante**, **Racine**, **Corneille**, **Goethe** and **Schiller**.
▷P Saarikoski, *Eino 'Leino'* (1974)

LEIRIS, Michel
(1901–90)

French anthropologist, writer and poet, born in Paris. After an early involvement with the Surrealist movement (1925–9), he joined the trans-African Dakar–Djibouti expedition of 1931 to 1933. He returned to study and take up anthropology as a profession, and went on to travel widely in Africa and the Caribbean. His writings, many of them autobiographical, as in *L'Âge d'homme* (1939, Eng trans *Manhood*, 1966) and *La règle du jeu* (4 vols, 1948–76, 'The Rules of the Game'), are marked by a consuming interest in poetry, and he combined anthropology with a distinguished career as a literary and art critic. His major works include *L'Afrique Fantôme* (1934, 'Phantoms of Africa') and *Afrique Noire: la création plastique* (1967, Eng trans *African Art*, 1968).
▷M Nadeau, *Michel Leiris et la quadrature du cercle* (1963)

LEIVICK, Halper
(1882–1962)

Yiddish poet and dramatist from Minsk who was arrested in Russia, for revolutionary activities, in 1912. He managed to escape while he was being transported to Siberia; eventually (1913) he went to New York and settled there. For a long time his mystical, strident poetry had a large following amongst readers of Yiddish; now it is falling into neglect. He wrote some 20 plays, of which the most successful was *The Golem* (1925).

LELAND, Charles Godfrey, pseud Hans Breitmann
(1825–1903)

American author, born in Philadelphia. He graduated at Princeton in 1845, and afterwards studied at Heidelberg, Munich and Paris. He was admitted to the Philadelphia Bar in 1851, but turned to journalism. From 1869 he resided chiefly in England and Italy, and investigated the gypsies, a subject on which between 1873 and 1891 he published four valuable works. He is best known for his poems in 'Pennsylvania Dutch', the famous *Hans Breitmann Ballads* (1871; continued in 1895). Other similar volumes gained him great popularity during his lifetime. He also translated the works of **Heinrich Heine**.
▷ *Memoirs* (1893)

LELCHUK, Alan
(1938–)

American novelist, born in New York, educated at Columbia University there, and in London and at Stanford University, California. He was a member of the faculty and writer-in-residence for 15 years (1966–81) at Brandeis University, Massachusetts, and was associated with the literary journal *Modern Occasions*. Lelchuk's scandalous debut was the anarchic *American Mischief* (1973), a multifaceted novel about campus revolt, the relationship between liberalism and libertinism, and the questionable value of 'art' over 'life', whose complexities were overlooked in the furore over a scene in which **Mailer** (who sued) is assassinated in what was intended to be the most demeaning way imaginable. It was clear that Lelchuk was attempting to satirize the excesses of fellow-Jews like Mailer and **Philip Roth**, and similar themes emerged in his later books. *Shrinking: The Beginning of My Own Ending* (1978), his third novel, is a perceptive satire on the literary and psychic odysseys of the sixties, carried out as they were (Mailer and Roth again) in the full glare of media publicity. *Miriam at Thirty-Four* (1974) and *Miriam in Her Forties* (1985) tells the story of a gifted but unstable photographer who serves as a barometer of cultural obsessions and hang-ups.

LEM, Stanislaw
(1922–)

Polish science-fiction writer, born in Lwów. He completed his medical studies after World War II, and began to write fiction. He is widely regarded as one of the most significant literary voices working in the science-fiction genre, and his work is characterized by great seriousness of purpose balanced by brilliant black humour and cutting satire, and a resistance to any attempts to impose absolute systems of explanation on a fluid reality. His

major books include the 'Ijon Tichy' series of stories (from 1957) and the novel *Solaris* (1961). His other writings included **Borges**-like essays and imaginary reviews, and books of startling cosmological speculation.
▷ *Wysoki zamek* (1966)

LEMAÎTRE, François Élie Jules
(1853–1914)

French playwright and critic, born in Vennecy, Loiret. His articles, written first for the *Journal des débats*, were issued in book form as *Impressions de théâtre* (1888–98, 'Impressions of a Theatre-goer'), and those written for *Revue bleue* on modern French literature became *Les Contemporains* (1886–99, 'Our Contemporaries'). A masterly critic with a charming, lucid style, he also wrote *Rousseau* (1907), *Racine* (1908), *Fénelon* (1910) and *Chateaubriand* (1912). His plays and short stories are less distinguished.

LEMOINE, Sir James MacPherson
(1825–1912)

Canadian naturalist and writer, born in Quebec. He became superintendent of inland revenue at Quebec in 1858. He studied archaeology, ornithology and other sciences, wrote on Canadian history and was the first Canadian author to receive a knighthood.

LEMON, Mark
(1809–70)

English author and journalist, born in London. In 1835 he wrote a farce, followed by several melodramas, operettas, novels (the best of which is, perhaps, *Falkner Lyle*, 1866), children's stories, a *Jest Book* (1864) and essays. In 1841 he helped to establish *Punch*, becoming first joint editor (with **Henry Mayhew**), then sole editor from 1843.
▷ A A Adrian, *Mark Lemon: first editor of Punch* (1966)

LEMONNIER, Antoine Louis Camille
(1844–1913)

Belgian writer, writing in French, born in Ixelles near Brussels. He took up art criticism in 1863, and by his novels *Un Mâle* (1881, Eng trans *A Male*, 1917), *Happe-Chair* (1888) and other works, full of strong Flemish realism and mysticism, won fame as one of Belgium's leading prose writers. He wrote books on art, including *Gustave Courbet* (1878), *Alfred Stevens et son oeuvre* (1906, 'Alfred Stevens and his Work') and *L'École Belge de la peinture* (1906, 'The Belgian School of Painting').
▷ B M Woodridge, in *Le roman belge contemporain* (1930)

LENAU, Nikolaus, in full Nikolaus Niembsch von Strehlenau
(1802–50)

German poet, born in Czatad in Hungary. He studied law and medicine at Vienna. He suffered from extreme melancholy and in 1844 he became insane, dying in an asylum near Vienna. His poetic power is best shown in his short lyrics, collections of which appeared in 1832, 1838 and 1844. His longer pieces include *Faust* (1836), *Savonarola* (1837) and *Die Albigenser* (1842, 'The Albigensians').
▷ E Castle, *Nikolaus Lenau* (1902)

LENCLOS, Ninon de, pseud of Anne de Lenclos
(1620–1705)

French feminist and light poet, described by male literary historians as a 'courtesan', who was born and died in Paris. She founded a salon which favoured Jansenists, was a close friend to **Saint Evremond**, and could hold her own with **La Rochefoucauld** and the other thinkers and wits of her time.

L'ENGLE, Madeleine
(1918–)

American novelist, born in New York City and educated at Smith College, Northampton, Massachusetts and at the New School for Social Research in New York. A prolific writer for children, who also writes for adults, she imbues her work with explicitly Christian ideas and morals. Described by one critic as 'perilously near the sugary', and by another as 'one of the truly important writers of juvenile fiction in recent decades', her most popular titles include *A Wrinkle in Time* (1962, **Newbery** Medal) and *The Young Unicorns* (1968), both of which combine elements of fantasy with tough ethical concerns.

LENGYEL, Menyhért or Melchior
(1880–1957)

Hungarian dramatist who lived in America for much of his life. He scored many successes in the theatre: the most famous was *Taifun* (1909, Eng trans *Typhoon*, 1912), a romantic thriller about Japanese agents in Paris. He wrote the scenario for Bartók's ballet, *The Miraculous Mandarin*.

LENNEP, Jacob van
(1802–68)

Dutch writer and lawyer, born in Amsterdam. He achieved a great reputation for legal knowledge. His most popular works were comedies, such as *Het Dorp aan die Grenzen* (1831, 'The Village on the Frontier'). Of his novels, several, such as *De Roos van Dekama* (1836, Eng trans *The Rose of Dekama*, 1846)

and *De Pleegzoon* (1835, Eng trans *The Adopted Son*, 1847), have been translated.
▷T van Lennep, *Het Leven van Mr Jacob van Lennep* (1909)

LENNGREN, Anna Maria
(1754–1817)

Swedish poet and journalist. Born in Uppsala, she received a good education and became an accomplished translator from French and Latin. She joined the radical *Stockholms-Posten* as a journalist in 1780. She published—up to 1797 anonymously—elegant satires which renewed and invigorated Swedish journalism, and sharply observed, humorously realistic poems. The latter, superbly skilful in their handling of metre and rhyme and characterized by a simple and mercilessly precise language, convey vivid images of a broad range of contemporary life, and expose the ruling classes to an intrepid satire. A number of her poems were set to music and remain popular songs to this day.
▷'Från Smakens Tempel till Parnassen. Om Anna Maria Lenngren', in E Møller Jensen (ed), *Nordisk kvinnolitteraturhistoria*, vol I: *I Guds namn* (1993)

LENNOX, Charlotte, née Ramsay
(c.1729–1804)

British novelist and playwright, born in New York, whose early adventures inform the spirited character of her fictional heroines. Sent from New York, where her father was posted, to England when she was 15, she found herself unprovided for when her father died, and supported herself as an actress and writer. Her first novel, *The Life of Harriot Stuart* (1750), is a romantic adventure yarn, but her next and most famous work, *The Female Quixote* (1752), is a satirical romp through the life of Arabella, a young lady besotted with French romantic novels. She also wrote *Shakespeare Illustrated* (1753–4), an examination of the playwright's sources, translated many French works, and was much admired by **Samuel Johnson**, who cites her under Talent in his Dictionary.

LENORMAND, Henri René
(1882–1951)

French dramatist, born in Paris. He was the author of *Les Possédés* (1909, 'The Possessed'), *Le Mangeur de rêves* (1922, 'The Eater of Dreams'), a modern equivalent of *Oedipus Rex*, *L'Homme et ses fantômes* (1924, 'Man and his Phantoms'), and several other plays in which **Freud**'s theory of subconscious motivation is adapted to dramatic purposes. He discusses the aesthetics of his dramatic style in *Confessions d'un auteur dramatique* (1949, 'Confessions of a Playwright').
▷P Blanchart, *Le théâtre de Lenormand* (1947)

LENZ, Jakob Michael Reinhold
(1751–92)

German author, born in Livonia. He was one of the young authors who surrounded **Goethe** in Strasbourg. He first wrote two plays which were well received, *Der Hofmeister* (1774, 'The Steward') and *Die Soldaten* (1776, 'The Soldiers'). Like all the 'Sturm und Drang' poets he was a fervent admirer of **Shakespeare**, and this was expressed in his *Anmerkungen übers Theater* (1774, 'Remarks on the Theatre'). He was a gifted writer of lyrics, some of them being at first attributed to Goethe, and also wrote several novels, but of lesser quality. He suffered a mental breakdown while still young and died in poverty.

LENZ, Siegfried
(1926–)

German novelist and short-story writer, born and raised in the Masurian Lakes area of East Prussia. He studied philosophy and English literature, then worked for the newspaper *Die Welt* from 1948 before becoming a full-time writer three years later. His realist, socially committed novels display a tender, at times ponderous, concern for the individual in a dehumanizing age. *Stadtgespräch* (1963, 'Town Conversation') centres on a would-be self-sacrificing resistance leader; *Deutschstunde* (1968, 'German Lesson') analyses the relationship between a young hooligan and his policeman father; while in *Das Vorbild* (1973, 'The Example') three teachers fail to find decent role models for the young.

LEONARD, Elmore John
(1925–)

American thriller writer, born in New Orleans. He lived in Dallas, Oklahoma City and Memphis before his family settled in Detroit in 1935. During World War II he served in the US navy and afterwards studied English literature at Detroit University. Throughout the 1950s he worked in advertising as a copywriter but since 1967 he has concentrated on screenplays and novels, remarkable for their relentless pace and vivid dialogue. Regarded as the foremost crime writer in America, his books include *Unknown Man No. 89* (1977), *The Switch* (1978), *Gold Coast* (1980), *Stick* (1983), *La Brava* (1983), *Glitz* (1985) and *Touch* (1987).
▷D Geherin, *Elmore Leonard* (1989)

LÉONARD, Nicholas-Germain
(1744–93)

French minor poet and sentimental novelist, born in La Basse-Terre in Guadeloupe. His poetry, influenced by that of the then popular Swiss **Salomon Gessner**, and by the Latin poet **Tibullus**, reflects his over-sensitive temperament and the unhappiness caused to him by the failure of his first love. A diplomat, he was about to embark from France to serve in Guadeloupe when he died.

▷ W M Kerby, *The Life, Diplomatic Career and Literary Activity of Nicholas-Germaine Léonard* (1925)

LEONARD, Tom
(1944–)

Scottish poet, born in Glasgow, whose phoneticized dialect verse has been the despair of 'southron' readers and the more po-faced of his compatriots; in the 1973 *Poems*, he provided an RP 'translation' in parallel text for the benefit of the former. Like **Edwin Morgan**, whom he encountered at Glasgow University in the late sixties, he is a dedicated experimenter with poetic form, attempting everything from strict metres and forms to linguistic 'found objects', complex word association to snippets of conversation heard in bus queues. His first published collection was the slim *Six Glasgow Poems* (1969), followed by *A Priest Came On at Merkland Street* (1970), *Poems* (1973) and *Bunnit Husslin* (1975). The best of his early work was collected as *Intimate Voices: Writing 1965–83* (1984). He edited *Radical Renfrew: Poetry from the French Revolution to the First World War* (1990).

LEONOV, Leonid
(1899–)

Russian novelist and dramatist, born in Moscow, the most gifted writer in his country to accept and try to accommodate himself to the Stalinist regime. From the West his works, continually sniped at by orthodox critics in the Soviet Union, have been viewed as paradigmatic of the struggle between creative individualism and Marxist–Stalinist theory. In his early novella *Konets melkogo cheloveka* (1924, 'End of a Petty Man'), written while the atmosphere was comparatively free of interference, he prophesied his creative future, but reversed the roles of writer and scientist—a scientist is persuaded by a **Dostoyevsky**an double to destroy all his research. He was initially influenced by **Leskov** and **Gogol** in his use of *skaz*, highly individualized first-person narration. Gradually he took, almost reluctantly, the direction of realism, which, as things became more difficult, turned into half-observance of socialist realism. His important novels are *Barsuki* (1924, Eng trans *The Badgers*, 1947), *Vor* (1927, Eng trans *The Thief*, 1931), about a man who cannot accept the New Economic Policy, and *Russkiy les* (1953, Eng trans *The Russian Forest*, 1966),

in which he obliquely criticized the crazed and humanly wasteful policies of Stalin. His plays, well-made psychological thrillers, generally avoided the problems he faced as a novelist. The final verdict upon him is likely to be that he was a great writer lost to Stalinist dogma.

▷ E J Brown, *Russian Literature Since the Revolution* (1969)

LEOPARDI, Giacomo
(1798–1837)

Major Italian poet, born of poor but noble parentage in Recanati. At the age of 16 he had read all the Latin and Greek classics, could write French, Spanish, English and Hebrew, and wrote a commentary on Plotinus. After a short stay in Rome, he devoted himself to literature, but finding his home increasingly unbearable he began to travel and, an invalid, lived successively in Bologna, Florence, Milan and Pisa. In 1833 he accompanied his friend Ranieri to Naples, and there in constant bodily anguish and hopeless despondency he lived until his death. His pessimism was unquestionably the genuine expression of Leopardi's deepest nature as well as of his reasoned conviction. He was specially gifted as a writer of lyrics, which were collected under the title *I Canti* (1831, Eng trans *The Poems*, 1893) and are among the most beautiful in Italian literature. His prose works include the dialogues and essays classed as *Operette Morali* (1827, trans in a bilingual edn under original title, 1983), and his *Pensieri* (7 vols, 1898–1900, 'Thoughts') and letters.

▷ H H Whitfield, *Giacomo Leopardi* (1954)

LEOPOLD, Jan Hendrik
(1865–1925)

Dutch Symbolist poet, born in s' Hertogenbosch. He was an early member of the 'Men of the Eighties' group, comprising **Verwey** and others. Deaf and lonely, he turned, as so many Dutchmen did at that time, to Eastern mysticism—then to Persian poetry and to the philosophy of Spinoza. He adapted ancient Sufic poetry to his own ends, and wrote technically flawless lyrics in which there is expressed much beautiful despair. Available in English translation are *The Flute* (1949) and *The Valley of Irdin* (1957).

LE PAN, Douglas
(1914–93)

Canadian poet, novelist, professor and diplomat—'man of letters and man of affairs', born in Toronto and educated at the university there and at Oxford. His first collection, *The Wounded Prince* (1948), charts a perilous voyage 'into the dark interior'—of mind and heart—in the symbolic craft of a Canadian *coureur de bois* canoe. He received the Governor General's Award for his second volume of poetry, *The Net and the Sword* (1953), and again in 1964, for a novel, *The Deserter*. *Weathering It* (1987) collects the elegant work of 40 years.

▷S C Hamilton, 'European Emblem and Canadian Image', in *Mosaic III: 2* (1970); J M Kertzer, 'The Wounded Eye', in *Studies in Canadian Literature* (1981)

LEPROHON, Rosanna
(1829–79)

Canadian novelist, born in Montreal, the mother of 13 children and the author of several novels acclaimed as some of the truest portraits of 19th-century French–Canadian life. Five of these books were serialized in the *Literary Garland* between 1847 and 1851. Her three major titles are *The Manor House of de Villerai* (1860), *Antoinette de Mirecourt* (1864) and *Armand Durand* (1868). In all three she managed to communicate the French–Canadian viewpoint to an English–Canadian audience.

▷C Gerson, *Three Writers of Victorian Canada and their Works* (1983)

LE QUEUX, William Tufnell
(1864–1927)

English mystery and espionage writer, an immensely prolific author whose backlog of manuscripts was still appearing several years after his death. Born in London, he was educated by tutors there and in Italy; he also studied painting at the Louvre and was an accomplished artist. Le Queux worked as Foreign Editor of the *Globe* (1890–3) and thereafter as a freelance writer, sending back despatches from the First Balkan War in 1912. His overseas contacts added a gloss to the story (one he did much to encourage) that he was a spy himself and his claim to have an inside track on political intrigues in the Habsburg and Hohenzollern courts gained some credence in 1914 when the outbreak of war confirmed the gloomy prognostications of quasi-fictional propaganda like *The Invasion of 1910, with a Full Account of the Siege of London* (1906). Le Queux's novels had long been anti-German, and after the invasion of Belgium he readily turned his hand to atrocity stories. After the war, he emigrated to Switzerland, where he continued writing, publishing almost 200 books—novels, short-story collections and propaganda—in his lifetime, and several more from beyond the grave.

▷N St Barbe Sladen, *The Real Le Queux* (1938)

LERMONTOV, Mikhail Yurevich
(1814–41)

Russian poet, born of Scottish extraction (Learmont) in Moscow. He attended Moscow University for a short time and then the military cavalry school of St Petersburg, where he received a commission in the guards. A poem written in 1837 on the death of **Alexander Pushkin** caused his arrest and he was sent to the Caucasus. Reinstated, he was again banished following a duel with the son of the French ambassador. Another duel was the cause of his death in 1841. He wrote from an early age, but much of his work was not published until the last years of his short life and his fame was posthumous. The sublime scenery of the Caucasus inspired his best poetic pieces, such as 'The Novice', 'The Demon', 'Ismail Bey', and others. His novel, *Geroy nashevo vremeni* (1839, Eng trans *A Hero of Our Times*, 1854), is a masterpiece of prose writing. He wrote also a romantic verse play, *Maskarad* (1842, 'Masquerade').

▷J Garrard, *Mikhail Lermontov* (1982)

LERNER, Laurence
(1925–)

South African-born British poet, novelist and critic, born in Cape Town. After a distinguished academic career in South Africa and England, he became a professor at Vanderbilt University, Tennessee. Best known as a critic, he is generally regarded as a sound, traditional, even if not adventurous, poet. *Selected Poems* (1984) is representative.

LERNET-HOLENIA, Alexander
(1897–)

Austrian playwright, novelist and poet, born in Vienna of (on his father's side) Franco–Belgian stock. He fought as a cavalry officer on the Russian front in World War I. His experience of the collapse of the Habsburg Empire, as in the case of **Joseph Roth**, was catastrophic; but he took a different and more defiantly nostalgic approach. He has been accused of being 'facile', and certainly he wrote (excellent) detective stories and other 'entertainments'; but his best works are far from facile. He was first successful as a playwright, with such brilliant comedies as *Olla-potrida* (1926, 'Nasty Hotchpotch'), which have been noted for their theatricality. Of his many and diverse novels, *Mars im Widder* (1941, 'Mars in Aries'), is a fine oblique critique of the Nazis who had just taken over his country. He was also a critic and biographer.

LEROUX, Etienne, pseud of **Stephanus Petrus Daniel Le Roux**
(1922–)

South African novelist (writing in Afrikaans), author of the 'phantasmal' trilogy *Sewe Dae by die Silbersteins* (1962, Eng trans *Seven Days at the Silbersteins*, 1967), which was praised by **Graham Greene** and other critics but has not yet found a wide audience. It is a strange but eventually rewarding novel, constructed on **Jung**ian concepts, and pessimistically implying that 'individuality' in the strictly Jungian sense is impossible in the Western world. It was followed by more novels, including *18–44* (1967).

LE SAGE, Alain René
(1668–1747)

French novelist and dramatist, born in Sarzeau in Brittany. In 1692 he went to Paris to study law, but an early marriage drove him to seek his fortune in literature. The Abbé de Lionne, who had a good Spanish library, allowed Le Sage free access to it, with a pension of 600 livres. The first fruit was a volume (1700) containing two plays in imitation of Rojas and **Lope de Vega**. In 1702 *Le Point d'honneur* ('A Point of Honour'), from Rojas, failed on the stage. His next venture (1704) was a remake of Avellaneda's *Don Quixote*. In 1707 *Don César Ursin*, from **Calderón de la Barca**, was played with success at court, and *Crispin rival de son maître* ('Crispin, His Master's Rival') in the city; but more successful was the *Diable boiteux* ('The Devil with a Limp', largely based on **Luiz Vélez de Guevara**). In 1708 the Théâtre Français accepted his work but shelved one play and rejected another, which later became his famous *Turcaret*. In 1715 *Gil Blas* (vols 1 and 2) came out, followed between 1717 and 1721 by an attempt at an *Orlando*. In 1724 came volume three of *Gil Blas*; in 1726 a largely extended *Diable boiteux*; in 1732 *Guzman de Alfarache* and *Robert Chevalier de Beauchêne*; in 1734 *Estebanillo Gonzalez*; in 1735 vol four of *Gil Blas* and the *Journée des Parques* ('The Day of the Fates'); between 1736 and 1738 the *Bachelier de Salamanque*; in 1739 his plays, in two vols; in 1740 *La Valise trouvée* ('A Suitcase Discovered'), a volume of letters; and in 1743 the *Mélange amusant*, a collection of facetiae. The death of his son (1743), a promising actor, and his own increasing infirmities, made him abandon Paris and literary life, and retreat with his wife and daughter to Boulogne, where his second son held a canonry, and he lived there until his death in his 80th year. Le Sage's reputation as a dramatist and as a novelist rests in each case on one work: on *Turcaret* and *Gil Blas* respectively. Some critics deny originality to one who borrowed ideas, incidents and tales from others as Le Sage did, but he was the first to perceive the capabilities of the picaresque novel. His delightful style makes him the prince of raconteurs, and the final effect of his work is all his own.

▷ E Lintilhac, *Alain Le Sage* (1893)

LESKOV, Nicolai Semyonovich
(1831–95)

Russian novelist and short-story writer, born in Gorokhovo, Oryol province. His parents dying when he was 17, he had a picaresque career in the provinces before becoming, aged 30, a journalist in St Petersburg. *No Way Out* (1864) and *At Daggers Drawn* (1871) met with critical disparagement, being insufficiently innovative for the mood of the time. Despite the disdain of reviewers, his work slowly accumulated a faithful general readership, who responded to his wit, narrative power and vibrant use of common speech. His first major work was the short story 'Lady Macbeth of the Mtsensk District' (1865), which was first published in **Dostoyevsky**'s periodical *Epoch*. His volumes of short stories include *Details of Episcopal Life* (1880), while his most enduring longer fiction is the novel *Cathedral Folk* (1872).

LESLIE, Sir Shane (John Randolph)
(1885–1971)

Irish writer, born in Glaslough, County Monaghan, into a conservative Irish Protestant landed family. Educated at Eton, Paris University and King's College, Cambridge, he visited Russia in 1907 and became friendly with **Tolstoy**. He was converted to Roman Catholicism in 1908 and unsuccessfully contested Londonderry in the Irish Nationalist interest in 1910. He published poems of some quality and produced a brilliant analysis of the pre-war generation in *The End of a Chapter* (1916). Under the influence of **Henry Adams** he followed it with a startling attempt at Irish geopolitics, *The Celt and the World*, intended to attract the Anglophobe Irish–Americans to the Allied cause: it influenced the young **F Scott Fitzgerald** but was otherwise forgotten and never published in Britain. He wrote impressive novels based on his boyhood and youth, *Doomsland*, *The Oppidan* and *The Cantab*, and published some useful clerical biographies, investigated the relations of George IV and Mrs Fitzherbert (from whom he was descended), and wrote cautious memoirs, as well as some good short stories with faintly chilling supernatural themes.

LÉSMIAN, Boleslaw, pseud of **Boleslaw Lesman**
(1878–1937)

Polish poet and translator (of, in particular, **Poe**), born in Warsaw; he was educated in Kiev. He was cautious in what he published, producing only three collections in Polish in his lifetime. His earliest poetry was written in Russian. Known as 'the poets' poet', and a highly original one, he was mainly influenced in his thinking by **Bergson**. His poetry abounds in neologisms, called 'Lésmianisms' by critics in his lifetime. A cult figure, he was recognized as a major poet only after the end of World War II. To be understood, his poetry needs to be read in the context of Russian Symbolism from which he drew his initial inspiration. It is steeped in allusion to Polish folklore: 'Lésmian,' wrote a Polish critic, 'seemed to be outside the current literary fashion, a symbolist who would persist with his weird ... coinages and macabre ballads ... His originality is now undisputed.'

▷R H Stone, *Boleslaw Lésmian: The Poet and his Poetry* (1976)

LESSING, Doris May, née Tayler
(1919–)

Rhodesian writer, born in Kermanshah, Iran, the daughter of a British army captain. Her family moved to Salisbury in Southern Rhodesia (now Zimbabwe), which she left at the age of 14. She continued her own education while living on the family farm by reading in European and American literature, and started to write novels. She lived in Salisbury from 1937 to 1949, where she became involved in politics and helped to start a non-racialist left-wing party. She was married twice while living in Rhodesia (Lessing is her second husband's name). Her experiences of life in working-class London after her arrival in 1949 are described in *In Pursuit of the English* (1960). She joined the Communist Party briefly, and left it in 1956, in which year Rhodesia declared her a 'prohibited immigrant'. Her first published novel was *The Grass is Singing* (1950), a study of the sterility of white civilization in Africa. *This was the Old Chief's Country* (1951), a collection of short studies, continued this theme. In 1952 *Martha Quest* appeared, the first novel in her sequence *The Children of Violence* (completed in *A Proper Marriage*, 1954, *A Ripple from the Storm*, 1958, *Landlocked*, 1965, and *The Four-Gated City*, 1969). This sequence, to a certain extent autobiographical, explores through the life story of the heroine, Martha, contemporary social and psychological problems. The theme running through the whole sequence is the ideal city where there is no violence. The city is, however, unattainable, and political and personal catastrophe is seen as inevitable. Other novels include *The Golden Notebook* (1962) and *Briefing for a Descent into Hell* (1971), both studies of so-called 'mental breakdown' and return to normality, which question the conventional definitions of 'sanity' and 'insanity'. Other collections of short stories include *A Man and Two Women* (1963), *African Stories* (1964) and *The Story of a Non-marrying Man* (1972). Latterly, in *Canopus in Argos: Archives*, a quintet of novels, she has attempted science fiction but

her commitment to exploring political and social undercurrents in contemporary society has never wavered and can be seen to potent effect in *The Good Terrorist* (1985) and *The Fifth Child* (1988).

▷R Whittaker, *Doris Lessing* (1988)

LESSING, Gotthold Ephraim
(1729–81)

German writer, born in Kamenz in Saxony, the son of a pastor. In 1746 he started as a theological student at Leipzig. Soon he was writing plays in the French style; leaving Leipzig in debt, in Berlin he joined the unorthodox Mylius in publishing *Beiträge zur Historie des Theaters* (1750, 'Contributions to the History of the Theatre'), and independently wrote plays, translated and did literary hackwork. His chief means of support was the *Vossische Zeitung*, to which he contributed criticisms. In 1751 he went to Wittenberg, took his Master's degree, and produced a series of *Vindications* of unjustly maligned or forgotten writers, such as Cardan, Lemnius, and others. Back in Berlin, in *Ein Vademecum für Herrn S.G. Lange* (1754, 'A Handbook for Herr S.G. Lange') he displayed unrelenting hostility to pretentious ignorance and with Moses Mendelssohn he wrote an essay on *Pope, ein Metaphysiker* (1755). After writing a trio of comedies, in 1755 he produced his classic German tragedy *Miss Sara Sampson* (1755), based on English rather than French models. In 1758 he was assisting Mendelssohn and **Christoph Nicolai** with a new critical Berlin journal (*Briefe', die neueste Literatur betreffend*, 'Letters Concerning the Most Recent Literature'), in which he protested against the dictatorship of French taste, combated the inflated pedantry of the **Gottsched** school, and extolled **Shakespeare**. While secretary to the governor of Breslau he wrote his famous *Laokoon; oder, Über die Grenzen der Malerei und Poesie* (1766, Eng trans *Laocoon; or, The Limits of Poetry and Painting*, 1853), a critical treatise defining the limits of poetry and the plastic arts. The comedy *Minna von Barnhelm* (1767, Eng trans *The Disbanded Officer*, 1786) is the first German comedy on the grand scale. Appointed playwright to a new theatre in Hamburg in 1767, he wrote the *Hamburgische Dramaturgie* (1769), in which he finally overthrew the dictatorship of the French drama. The Hamburg theatre failed, and Lessing was soon in the thick of a controversy, this time with Klotz, a Halle professor, producing the *Briefe antiquarischen Inhalts* (1769, 'Letters on an Antiquarian Theme') and *Wie die Alten den Tod gebildet* (1769, 'How the Ancients Portrayed Death'). In 1769 the Duke of Brunswick appointed Lessing as Wolfenbüttel librarian; and he at once began to publish some of the

less-known treasures of the library in *Zur Geschichte und Literatur* (1773–81, 'On History and Literature'). In 1772 he wrote the great tragedy *Emilia Galotti*. Shortly before his marriage he spent eight months in Italy as companion to the young Prince Leopold of Brunswick. Between 1774 and 1778 he published the *Wolfenbüttelsche Fragmente eines Ungennanten* ('Anonymous Fragments from Wolfenbüttel'), a rationalist attack on orthodox Christianity from the pen of Reimarus which, universally attributed to Lessing, provoked a storm of refutations. The best of Lessing's counter-attacks were *Anti-Goeze* (1778) and the fine dramatic poem, *Nathan der Weise* (1779, Eng trans *Nathan the Wise*, 1868), one of the noblest pleas for toleration ever written. Later works were *Erziehung des Menschengeschlechts* (1780, 'Education of the Human Race') and *Ernst und Falk* (1778–81, Eng trans *Ernst and Falk*, 1854–72), five dialogues on freemasonry.
▷H B Garland, *Lessing, founder of modern German criticism* (1937)

LEVER, Charles James
(1806–72)

Irish novelist, born of English parentage in Dublin. He graduated from Trinity College, Dublin in 1827, and then went to Göttingen to study medicine. His most popular work, *Charles O'Malley* (1841), is a description of his own college life in Dublin. About 1829 he spent some time in the backwoods of Canada and North America, and related his experiences in *Arthur O'Leary* (1844) and *Con Cregan* (1849). He practised medicine in various Irish country towns, and in 1840 in Brussels. Returning to Dublin, he published *Jack Hinton* in 1843, and from 1842 to 1845 acted as editor of the *Dublin University Magazine*, and wrote further novels. In 1845 he again went to Brussels, Bonn, and Karlsruhe, where he published the *Knight of Gwynne* (1847), and to Florence, where he wrote *Roland Cashel* (1850). Then, completely changing his style, he wrote *The Daltons* (1852), followed by the *Fortunes of Glencore* (1857). He was appointed British vice-consul in Spezia in 1858, and continued to write, his work including *Luttrel of Arran* (1865) and three other novels in rapid succession, and some racy essays in *Blackwood's* by 'Cornelius O'-Dowd'. In 1867 he was promoted to the consulship in Trieste. Lever's work contained brilliant, rollicking sketches of a phase of Irish life which was passing away, though no doubt his caricatures created a false idea of Irish society and character.
▷E Donney, *Charles Lever: his life in his letters* (1906)

LEVERSON, Ada
(1865–1936)

English novelist and journalist, born in London. After being educated privately, she became a member of the circle which included **Max Beerbohm** and **Oscar Wilde**, whom she bravely supported during his trials in 1895. Wilde referred to her as 'The Sphinx'. Having published literary parodies in *Punch*, she contributed stories for *The Yellow Book* and, as 'Elaine', wrote over 100 columns for *The Referee*, in some of which she satirized other advice columnists. Her six novels, written between 1907 and 1916, include such titles as *Love's Shadow* (1908), *Tenterhooks* (1912) and *Love at Second Sight* (1916). Domestic stories of difficult marriages (not unlike her own to the gambler Ernest Leverson), they rely for their readability mainly on the author's wit.
▷J Speedie, *Wonderful Sphinx: The Biography of Ada Leverson* (1993)

LEVERTIN, Oscar
(1862–1906)

Swedish poet, critic and essayist. He was born in Stockholm, of a Jewish family, and studied at the University of Uppsala. From 1899 he was professor of literature at the University of Stockholm. His work focuses a conflict between emotion and reflection, with an early book of poetry such as *Legender och visor* (1891, 'Legends and Songs') employing an exuberant, complex language to convey a romanticism that includes a preoccupation with religion and the Middle Ages. His prose texts range from the brilliant pastiches of *Rococonoveller* (1899, 'Short Stories from the Rococo') to the evocative portrait essays in *Diktare och drömmare* (1898, 'Writers and Dreamers'). As a critic in the daily *Svenska Dagbladet* from 1897 he exerted a huge influence.
▷B Julén, *Hjärtats landsflykt. En Levertin-studie* (1961)

LEVERTOV, Denise
(1923–)

English-born American poet, born in Ilford, Essex, into a literary household; she was the daughter of a Welsh mother and a Russian Jewish father who became an Anglican clergyman. Educated privately, she emigrated to the USA in 1948. She was appointed poetry editor of *The Nation* in 1961. *The Double Image* (1946) was her first collection of verse and others have appeared steadily. A 'British Romantic with almost Victorian background', she has been outspoken on many issues (Vietnam, feminism, etc), and her poetry is similarly questioning. Her attachment to the 'Black Mountain' poets like **Charles Olson** and **William Carlos Williams** is palpable but her voice is distinctive. *With Eyes at the Back of Our Heads* (1959), *Relearning the Alphabet* (1970), *To Stay Alive* (1971) and *Footprints* (1972) particularly stand out.

▷L Wagner, *Denise Levertov* (1967)

LEVET, Henri-Jean-Marie
(1874–1906)

French poet and dandy, now almost forgotten, whose exotic *Cartes postales* (1900, 'Postcards') influenced **Larbaud** and **Fargue**, and are still worth reading for their quiet audacity and charm.

▷M Raymond, *From Baudelaire to Symbolism* (1950)

LEVI, Carlo
(1902–75)

Italian novelist, journalist and politician, born in Turin. He qualified as a doctor in 1923, but soon became immersed in literature and politics. He was imprisoned by the Fascists in 1935–6, then went into exile before returning to Italy to join the resistance. His most important novel, *Christ Stopped At Eboli* (1945), is set in the quasi-pagan, poverty-stricken deep south of his homeland. His non-fiction includes an examination of the Mafia and Sicily, *Words Are Stones* (1955), and a Russian travelogue, *The Future Has An Ancient Heart* (1956). He remained politically active throughout his life, and in 1963 was elected as a Communist senator.

LEVI, Primo
(1919–87)

Italian writer and chemist, born in Turin to Jewish parents. On completing his schooling he enrolled at Turin University to study chemistry for, as he wrote in *Il sistemo periodico* (1984, Eng trans *The Periodic Table*, 1984), he believed that 'the nobility of Man . . . lay in making himself the conqueror of matter'. During the war he fled into the mountains and formed a small guerrilla force; but he was betrayed and in December 1943 was arrested, turned over to the SS, and despatched to Auschwitz. He was one of the few to survive, partly because he contracted scarlet fever when the Germans evacuated the camp as the Russians approached. Those 10 months in Auschwitz haunted him for the rest of his life and may have prompted his suicide. His first book, *Se questo è un uomo* (Eng trans *If This Is a Man*, 1959), was completed soon after his return to Turin and was published in 1947. A graphic account of life in a concentration camp, it is written with a chemist's detached sensibility, making it all the more powerful. He continued to combine his career

as a chemist with that of a writer. His best-known book is *Il sistemo periodico*, a volume of memoirs and autobiographical reflections. One of the 20th century's most incisive commentators, his other titles include *La chiave a stella* (1978, Eng trans *The Wrench*, 1987), *Se non ora, quando?* (1982, Eng trans *If Not Now, When?*, 1985) and *Altrui mestiere* (1985, Eng trans *Other People's Trades*, 1985).

LEVIN, Ira
(1929–)

American novelist and playwright, born in New York City. *A Kiss Before Dying* (1953), a tightly plotted murder story, made his reputation and remains one of the most highly rated of post-war crime novels. His plays include *Deathtrap* (1978), but it is as a popular novelist that he is best known. The horror story *Rosemary's Baby* (1967), the science-fictional study of suburban alienation *The Stepford Wives* (1972), and the nutty Nazis novel *The Boys From Brazil* (1976) are among his most read works. All have been filmed. His best novel, however, is probably the lesser-known *This Perfect Day* (1970), in which his mastery of suspense is most expertly employed.

LEVIN, Meyer
(1905–81)

American novelist, known for his studies of Jewish life in Chicago, where he was born. His early experience as a journalist formed the backdrop to his first novel *Reporter* (1929). This was drawn a little too closely from life; a libel suit was threatened and the book had to be withdrawn. Levin went on to publish *Frankie and Johnny* (1930) and *Yehuda* (1931), about life in a Zionist commune in Palestine. In *The Golden Mountain* (1932) he retold some Hasidic folk-tales. *The Old Bunch* (1937), about immigrant children living in Chicago, was informed by personal experience.

▷*In Search* (1950)

LEVINE, Philip
(1928–)

American poet, born in Detroit. After graduating from the universities of Detroit and Iowa, he lectured at California State University at Fresno, and since 1981 has been Professor of English at Tufts University, Medford. Compassion and concern for the conditions of the working-class of both Detroit and southern California form the basis of much of his poetry, published in such collections as *Silent America: Vivas For Those Who Failed* (1965) and *5 Detroits* (1970). Subsequent volumes include *The Names of the Lost* (1976) and *One For the Rose* (1981).

A collection of *Selected Poems* appeared in 1984.

LEWALD, Fanny
(1811–89)

German novelist, born in Königsberg (now Kaliningrad). Jewish by birth, she became a Lutheran convert in 1828 to marry a young theologian, who died just before the wedding. In 1845 she met Adolf Stahr (1805–76), a Berlin critic, with whom she lived until he was free to marry in 1855. She was an enthusiastic champion of women's rights, which were aired in her early novels, *Clementine* (1842), *Jenny* (1843) and *Eine Lebensfrage* (1845, 'A Question About Life'). Her later works were family sagas, like *Von Geschlecht zu Geschlecht* (1863–5, 'From Generation to Generation') and *Die Familie Darner* (3 vols, 1887, 'The Darner Family'). She wrote records of travel in Italy (1847) and Great Britain (1852), and published an autobiography, *Meine Lebensgeschichte* (1861–3, 'The Story of my Life').

LEWES, G(eorge) H(enry)
(1817–78)

English writer, born in London, grandson of the comedian, Charles Lee Lewes (1740–1803), and companion and supporter of **George Eliot** from 1854. Educated at Greenwich and in Jersey and Brittany, he went to Germany for nearly two years in 1838, studying the life, language and literature of the country. On his return to London he started writing about anything and everything for the *Penny Encyclopaedia* and *Morning Chronicler*, later was a contributor to numerous journals, reviews and magazines, and was Editor of the *Leader* (1851–4), and of the *Fortnightly* (1865–6), which he himself founded. He was unhappily married, with a family, when he began his lifelong affair with **George Eliot**. His works include two novels, *Ranthorpe* (1847) and *Rose, Blanche and Violet* (1848), and 10 plays, but he is best known for his writings on biography, the theatre, and later the sciences. His most important work in that vein was his *Life and Works of Goethe* (1855).
▷A R Kaminsky, *George Henry Lewes as literary critic* (1968)

LEWIS, Alun
(1915–44)

Welsh soldier-poet and short-story writer, born in Cwmaman, near Aberdare. He was educated at Cowbridge School, the University College of Wales, Aberystwyth and at Manchester University. A lieutenant in the army, his first work, a volume of short stories about army life, was *The Last Inspection* (1942), followed by a volume of poetry, *Raiders' Dawn*, in the same year. He died of gunshot wounds at Chittagong during the Burma campaign. Another volumes of verse, ironically entitled *Ha! Ha! Among the Trumpets*, was published posthumously in 1945, followed by a collection of short stories and letters, *In the Green Tree* (1948).
▷A John, *Alun Lewis* (1970)

LEWIS, C(live) S(taples)
(1898–1963)

British novelist, literary scholar and religious writer, born in Belfast. He lost his Christianity while at school, won a scholarship to Oxford in 1916, but served in World War I before entering University College in 1918. His first book of poems, *Spirits in Bondage*, was published in that year. He became a fellow of Magdalen College in 1925, where he headed an informal group of writers known as 'The Inklings', which included **J R R Tolkein** and **Charles Williams**. He was appointed to the newly created Chair of Medieval and Renaissance English at Cambridge University in 1954. He was a distinguished teacher, and wrote a number of important scholarly works, including *The Allegory of Love* (1936), on medieval poetry, and *English Literature in the Sixteenth Century* (1954). He returned to Christianity in the period 1929–31 and won a wide popular audience during World War II for his broadcast talks (collected as *Mere Christianity*, 1952) and his books on religious subjects, notably *The Screwtape Letters* (1940), in which a senior devil instructs a junior on methods of winning souls away from the true path. His most important adult novels are the science-fiction trilogy *Out of the Silent Planet* (1938), *Perelandra* (1939) and *That Hideous Strength* (1945), in which the allegorical battle for the survival of mankind is set out in distinctly religious symbolism. His series of seven books for children, collectively known as *The Chronicles of Narnia*, which began with *The Lion, The Witch and The Wardrobe* (1950) and ended with *The Last Battle* (1956, Carnegie Medal), is similarly suffused with Christian allegory and ethics, and is among the most important writing for children of the century. His other works include two slight fantasy novels, *The Great Divorce* (1945) and *Till We Have Faces* (1956).
▷*Surprised By Joy* (1955); A N Wilson, *C. S. Lewis: A Biography* (1990)

LEWIS, Janet
(1899–)

American poet, novelist and author of children's books, born in Chicago. The first of her six collections of poetry, *The Indians in the Woods* (1922), established her as a poet preferring to look back with nostalgia to a time when man appeared to be more serene, and in greater harmony with nature. Her first historical novel, *The Invasion* (1932), depicts Native Americans acclimatizing themselves to the British presence during the early 1760s. It became the first of a series, each concerned with moral dilemmas and social convention. *The Trial of Soren Qvist* (1947) is set not in the USA, but in 17th-century Jutland. Lewis's major collection of verse, *Poems Old and New*, appeared in 1981.

LEWIS, M(atthew) G(regory)
(1775–1818)

English novelist, born in London. He was educated at Westminster School and Christ Church, Oxford, and in Germany, where he met **Goethe**. In 1794 he was an attaché to The Hague and it was there he wrote *Ambrosio, or the Monk* (1796), a Gothic novel now generally known as *The Monk*, which was influenced by his formative reading of tales of witchcraft and the supernatural, and **Ann Radcliffe**'s *Mysteries of Udolpho*, and which inspired his nickname 'Monk' Lewis. Many others in a similar vein followed, including a musical drama, *The Castle Spectre* (1798). He published several volumes of verse, but his best-known poem, 'Alonzo the Brave and the Fair Imogine', appeared in *The Monk*. Concerned about the treatment of the slaves on the estates he had inherited in the West Indies, he went there in 1817, but died of yellow fever on the way home. His *Journal of a West Indian Proprietor* was published in 1834.
▷ L F Peck, *A Life of Monk Lewis* (1961)

LEWIS, Saunders
(1893–1985)

Welsh dramatist, poet and nationalist, born in Cheshire. He studied English and French at Liverpool University, and in 1924 published a study of English influences on classical Welsh 18th-century poetry, *A School of Welsh Augustans*, having become lecturer in Welsh in University College, Swansea, in 1922. He was co-founder of the Welsh Nationalist Party (later Plaid Cymru) in 1925, and became its president in 1926. He became a Roman Catholic in 1932. Imprisoned in 1936 for a token act of arson against building materials for construction of an RAF bombing school at Penyberth, he was dismissed from Swansea and made his living by journalism, teaching and farming until his appointment as lecturer (later senior lecturer) in Welsh at University College, Cardiff, in 1952. He published many essays, 19 plays in Welsh and English, poems, novels, historical and literary criticism, chiefly in Welsh. He retired from public life in 1957, but continued publishing plays, his last being *Excelsior* (1980).
▷ P Davies, *Saunders Lewis* (1950)

LEWIS, (Harry) Sinclair
(1885–1951)

American novelist, winner of the Nobel Prize for literature, born in Sauk Center, Minnesota, the son of a doctor. Educated at Yale, he became a journalist and wrote several minor works before *Main Street* (1920), the first of a series of bestselling novels satirizing the arid materialism and intolerance of American small-town life. *Babbitt* (1922) still lends its title as a synonym for middle-class American philistinism. Other titles of this period are *Martin Arrowsmith* (1925), *Elmer Gantry* (1927) and *Dodsworth* (1929). From then on he tended to exonerate the ideologies and self-sufficiency he had previously pilloried; the shift of attitude did nothing to diminish his popularity. His later novels include *Cass Timberlane* (1945) and *Kingsblood Royal* (1947). He refused the Pulitzer Prize for *Arrowsmith*, but accepted the Nobel Prize for literature in 1930, being the first American writer to receive it.
▷ M Schorer, *Sinclair Lewis: an American life* (1961)

LEWIS, (Percy) Wyndham
(1882–1957)

English novelist, painter and critic, born in Amehurst, Nova Scotia. He was educated at Rugby School and the Slade School of Art. With **Ezra Pound** he instituted the Vorticist movement and founded *Blast* (1914–15), the magazine which expounded their theories. From 1916 to 1918 he served on the Western Front, as a bombardier, then as a war artist. In the early 1930s, his right-wing sympathies were out of vogue. He emigrated to Canada at the beginning of World War II, returning to London in 1945. In 1951 he went blind. His novels, *Tarr* (1918), *The Childermass* (1928), and *The Apes of God* (1930) are powerful, vivid satires reflecting his talent as a painter; other important novels are *The Revenge for Love* (1937) and *Self Condemned* (1954), which is partly autobiographical. *The Human Age* (1955), a trilogy which was conceived with *The Childermass* and continued with *Monstre Gai* and *Malign Fiesta* (both 1955), was modelled in part on **Dante** and **Milton**, and had a projected but never written fourth part. As a writer he has been ranked by some critics alongside **James Joyce**; as a painter, he was both the foremost experimentalist of his time in British art, and a portraitist of the highest calibre. Other writings include political and critical essays, short stories, and the

autobiographies *Blasting and Bombardiering* (1937) and *Rude Assignment* (1950).
▷ J Meyers, *The Enemy: a biography* (1980)

LEWISOHN, Ludwig
(1883–1955)

German-born American critic and novelist, he moved to the USA as an eight-year-old. Educated in Charleston, South Carolina, he became an academic, specializing in European (particularly German) literature and the reciprocal impact of Judaism and modern culture. His *The Spirit of Modern German Literature* (1916) is still an important source, as are his books about the Diaspora: *Israel* (1925), *The Answer: The Jew and the World* (1939), and the later *The American Jew* (1950). The best of his novels are *The Broken Snare* (1908), *Don Juan* (1923) and *The Case of Mr Crump* (1926). His last book was *In a Summer Season* (1955).
▷ *Up Stream* (1922); *Mid-Channel: An American Chronicle* (1929)

LEYDEN, John
(1775–1811)

Scottish poet and orientalist, born in Denholm, Roxburghshire, the son of a farmer. He studied medicine at Edinburgh University, and was licensed as a preacher in 1798. He wrote a book on European settlements in Africa (1799), helped Sir **Walter Scott** to gather materials for his *Border Minstrelsy*, and his translations and poems in the *Edinburgh Magazine* attracted attention. In 1803 he sailed for India as assistant surgeon at Madras, travelled widely in the East, acquired 34 languages, and translated the gospels into five of them. He accompanied Lord Minto as interpreter to Java, and died of fever at Batavia. His ballads have taken a higher place than his longer poems, especially *Scenes of Infancy* (1803). His dissertation on Indo–Chinese languages is also well known.
▷ J Reith, *John Leyden* (1923)

LEZAZA LIMA, José
(1910–76)

Cuban novelist and poet. In the 1930s he was one of Cuba's leading intellectuals. Brought up against a militaristic background, he early developed asthma, an illness which was to plague him throughout his life. First known as a poet and prose poet, Lezaza Lima's acknowledged masterpiece is his novel *Paradiso* (1966, Eng trans 1974), described by one critic as a 'Bildungsroman, and a poetic summation of all the themes of [Lezaza Lima's] poetry'. This is now required reading for all students of the Latin-American novel in its middle phase. So great was this author's stature in Cuba that when confronted with evidence of his negative sentiments about Castro's Cuba, he was left alone (although isolated).
▷ R S Minc (ed), *Latin-American Fiction Today* (1980)

LI PO
(c.700–762)

Chinese poet, born in the province of Szechwan. He led a dissipated life at the emperor's court and later was one of a wandering band calling themselves 'The Eight Immortals of the Wine Cup'. Regarded as the greatest poet of China, he wrote colourful verse of wine, women and nature. It is believed that he was drowned while attempting to kiss the moon's reflection. *Li T'ai-po Chüan-chi* ('The Complete Works') were published in 3 vols in 1977. Collections of Li Po's translated work have been published in 1922 and 1973.
▷ A Waley, *The Poetry and Career of Li Po* (1950)

LIBEDINSKY, Yury
(1898–1959)

Russian novelist and dramatist, born in Odessa. He is best remembered for *Nedelya* (1922, Eng trans *A Week*, 1923), the first fully 'proletarian novel'. Libedinsky was a slavish follower and even designer of official communist literature, but he was not entirely incapable, and eventually he got himself into trouble—if mainly through others' jealousy of him—with Stalin's cultural officials on charges of 'Trotskyism'. The 'characters' in *A Week* are formulaic Bolshevik types, not existing in reality; but they were very influential on later, and better, communist fiction, such as Fyodor Gladkov's *Cement* (1925, Eng trans 1929).

LICHTENBERG, Georg Christoph
(1742–99)

German aphorist, diarist, scientific writer and satirist. Born, the son of a pastor, in Oberramstadt, he was crippled in an accident in childhood. He early attracted attention by his brilliance at mathematics and science, which he studied at Göttingen University, where he became Professor of Physics. Lichtenberg, although a 'child of the Enlightenment', was essentially a deflationist of even its certainties. His ironic and exemplary writings are major, but, as has been said, they have suffered neglect because he never expressed himself in the major forms. **Goethe** called his work 'the most amazing divining rod: wherever he makes a joke, a problem is hidden'. He was Germany's **Swift**, but more akin to mysticism (he praised **Böhme**). Of the translations of his work, *The Lichtenberg Reader* (1959) is the best. His acute interpretations of the drawings of

Hogarth are translated as *Lichtenberg's Commentaries on Hogarth's Engravings* (1966).
▷J P Stern, *Lichtenberg* (1959)

LICHTENSTEIN, Alfred
(1889–1914)

German poet. He is remembered as an early expressionist whose 'Die Dämmerung' ('Dusk', Eng trans in *Twentieth-Century German Verse*, 1963, ed Patrick Bridgewater) was the second programmatically expressionist poem to appear in print, the first having been the 'World's End' of **Jakob von Hoddis**, upon which it is modelled. He was killed in action in World War I.
▷C Middleton and M Hamburger (eds), *Modern German Poetry 1910–1969* (1962)

LIDMAN, Sara
(1923–)

Swedish author, born in Missenträsk in the far north of the country. The area was the setting for her early novels such as *Tjärdalen* (1953, 'The Tar Still') and *Hjortronlandet* (1955, 'Cloudberry Land'). The support for the underdog visible in these novels became more overtly political in the 1960s after her experiences of South Africa, Kenya and Vietnam. In the highly-acclaimed series of novels beginning with *Din tjänare hör* (1977, 'Thy Servant Heareth'), she returns to her roots and takes as her theme the building of the railways of the north. She has experimented with documentary forms of writing and has also written plays.
▷J Mawby, in *Writers and Politics in Modern Scandinavia* (1978)

LIE, Jonas Lauritz Idemil
(1833–1908)

Major Norwegian novelist and poet, born in Eker near Drammen. He trained as a lawyer but abandoned law for literature; like Sir **Walter Scott**, he saw writing first and foremost as a means of paying off debt. His novels, which present realistic portayals of fisher-life in Norway, include *Den fremsynte* (1870, 'The Visionary'), *Lodsen og hans Hustru* (1874, 'Lodsen and his Wife'), *Livsslaven* (1883, 'One of Life's Slaves') and *Kommandørens Døtre* (1886, 'The Commander's Daughters'). He also wrote fairy-tales like *Trold* (1891–2, 'Trolls'), and some poetry and plays.
▷A Garborg, *Jonas Lie* (1925)

LIGNE, Charles Joseph, Prince de
(1735–1814)

Belgian soldier and writer, born in Brussels, son of an imperial field marshal whose seat was at Ligne near Tournai. In the Seven Years War (1756–63) he served at Kolin, Leuthen and Hochkirch, and in the Russo–Turkish war (1787–93) at the siege of Belgrade (1789). A skilful diplomatist, the favourite of Maria Theresa and Catherine the Great of Russia, and the friend of Frederick II, the Great, **Voltaire** and **Rousseau**, he wrote *Mélanges* (34 vol, 1795–1811), *Oeuvres posthumes* (1817, a collection of his work, published posthumously), a biography of Prince Eugène (1809), and *Lettres et Pensées* (1809, 'Letters and Thoughts').

LIHN, Enrique
(1929–88)

Chilean poet and story writer, born in Santiago, and regarded as the leading member of the so-called 'Generation of '50'. A decisive influence upon him was his meeting with the poet **Nicanor Parra** (upon whose work he wrote a book, 1952), and by 1963 with the small collection *La pieza oscura* (Eng trans, *The Dark Room and Other Poets*, 1978), he had established himself as a highly original poet, writing hauntingly and mystically about his feelings as a stranger in a world no longer familiar to him. *Agua de arroz* (1964, 'Rice Water'), contains stories of the same kind. Much has been translated: *The Endless Malice* (1969) and *If Poetry is to be Written Right* (1977). He died prematurely, of cancer.
▷*Dactylus*, 6 (1986)

LILIENCRON, Detlev von
(1844–1909)

German poet and novelist, born in Kiel. He fought in the Prussian army in 1866 and 1870. He went to America but returned to Holstein in 1882, where for a time he held a civil service post. He is best known for his lyrics, which are fresh, lively and musical. His first volume, *Adjutantenritte* ('The Adjutant's Rides'), appeared in 1883. Other volumes of verse were *Der Heidegänger* (1890, 'The Moors Walker'), *Neue Gedichte* (1893, 'New Poems') and *Gute Nacht* (1909, 'Good Night'). He also wrote novels and a humorous epic poem, *Poggfred* (1896). A selection of translations of his poems was published in 1914 as *Selected Poems*.
▷O J Bierbaum, *Detlev von Liliencron* (1892)

LILIEV, Nikolay, pseud of Nicolay Mihaylov
(1863–1960)

Bulgarian Symbolist poet, and gifted translator (for example, of **Shakespeare**), who was born in Stara Zagora and died in Sofia. He was educated in France, and helped to bring French literary influences to Bulgaria. His poetry, which owes much to **Paul Verlaine**, is musical and carefully wrought.

▷C Manning and R Smal-Stocki, *The History of Modern Bulgarian Literature* (1960)

LILLO, Baldomero
(1867–1923)

Chilean story writer, born in Lota. He was one of Chile's earliest social realists, and its first one of real account. His father, though middle-class, worked as an official in the mines, and his son thus knew the atrocious conditions in them at first hand—and better when he himself went to work for a mining company. He learnt to apply the methods of **Zola** to specifically Chilean affairs, and was a far more accomplished artist than **Blest Gana**. He achieves, a critic wrote, 'a heartrending power through physical descriptions of people distressed by oppression'. His best stories are in *Sub terra* (1904, 'Underground'); his most famous tale of all is 'La compuerto número 12', ('Hatch 12'), about a terrified child forced to work in a mine.

LILLO, George
(1693–1739)

English dramatist and jeweller, born in London of mixed Dutch and English Dissenting parentage. He wrote seven plays, including *The London Merchant, or the History of George Barnwell* (1731) and *Fatal Curiosity* (1736), both tragedies. His *Arden of Feversham*, which was published posthumously in 1759, is a weak version of the anonymous play of that title (1592). Among the first to put middle-class characters on the English stage, he had a considerable influence on European drama.
▷T Drucker, *The Plays* (1979)

LIMA, Jorge de
(1893–1953)

Brazilian Mulatto poet, novelist, translator (**Bernanos**, **Claudel**) and artist, born in União, Alagoas. Throughout his life he practised as a doctor, and, although he was an early adherent of (Brazilian) *Modernismo*, he is something of a law unto himself. He is sometimes regarded as Brazil's greatest poet of the century. In 1935 he became a Roman Catholic, and combined the earlier influence of Surrealism with that of **Claudel**. His best poetry, in *Essa negra Fuló* (1928, 'That Nigger Fuló'), and the remarkable *Invenção de Orfeu* (1952, 'The Invention of Orpheus'), is 'negrista', or Afro–Brazilian, and reaches somnambulatory heights above even those of **Bandeira**. His three novels, including *O anjo* (1934, 'The Angel'), are unjustly neglected. His poetry has been translated in *Anthology of Contemporary Latin-American Poetry* (1942, ed Dudley Fitts) and in *The Poem Itself* (1964, ed Stanley Burnshaw).

▷P Cavalcanti, *Vida e obra de Jorge de Lima* (1969, in Portuguese)

LINDAU, Paul
(1839–1919)

German writer, born in Magdeburg. He founded *Die Gegenwart* (1872, 'The Present') and *Nord und Süd* (1877, 'North and South'), and wrote books of travel and works of criticism. He is better known as a writer of plays and novels; the most successful of the former was perhaps *Maria und Magdalena* (1872, Eng trans 1874). The novels include *Herr und Frau Bewer* (1882), and *Berlin* (1886–7). His brother, Rudolf Lindau (1829–1910), wrote travel books and novels, and was an editor of *Revue des deux mondes* and *Journal des débats*.

LINDEGREN, Erik
(1910–58)

Swedish poet. Born in Luleå, he attended the University of Stockholm. His first major book of poetry, *Mannen utan väg* (1942, 'The Man without a Way'), gradually established him as a leading Swedish modernist, the 'exploded sonnets' with their Surrealist imagery conveying the urgency of humankind's desperate situation. The affinity between his poetry and music and pictorial art, including Swedish Surrealist painting, is apparent in his next collection, *Sviter* (1947, 'Suites'). The poems in *Vinteroffer* (1954, 'Winter Rites') draw on mythical and ritual patterns to assert the significance of art. An accomplished translator, he also wrote the libretto of the opera *Aniara* (1959), based on **Harry Martinson**'s epic poem about the space age.
▷R Lysell, *Erik Lindegrens imaginära universum* (1983)

LINDGREN, Astrid
(1907–)

Swedish children's novelist, born in Vimmerby. At 18 she had an illegitimate child who was raised by her parents; she portrayed them in *Samuel August från Seudstorp och Hanna: Hult* (1975). She established her reputation with *Pippi Långstrump* (1945, Eng trans *Pippi Longstocking*, 1954), and while she wrote at least 50 more books, including *Mästerdetektiven Blomkvist* (1946, Eng trans *Bill Bergson Master Detective*, 1951), none has eclipsed its popularity.
▷V Edström, *Astrid Lindgren* (1987)

LINDSAY, Sir David see LYNDSAY, David

LINDSAY, David
(1878–1945)

English novelist, born in Blackheath, London, where he spent his formative years.

Much of his childhood, however, was spent in Jedburgh with his father's relations. Intent on taking up a university scholarship, he had to abandon this avenue when his father deserted the family. Instead, he became an insurance broker, a career he pursued successfully for 20 years. After World War I he left the City and moved to Cornwall to fulfil his ambitions to be a full-time novelist. Over the next two decades he published five books. *A Voyage to Arcturus* (1920) is his most notable work. Often ghettoized as science fiction, it has been more accurately described by the critic Roderick Watson as 'an allegory of spiritual and philosophical search'. It was a powerful and original work, and **C S Lewis** was not alone in declaring it an influence. Subsequent books, including *The Haunted Woman* (1922) and *The Violet Apple*, published posthumously in 1976, demonstrate that there was depth to Lindsay's talent, though the reading public remained largely impervious to it.
▷J B Pick, C Wilson and E Visiak, *The Strange Genius of David Lindsay* (1970)

LINDSAY, Frederic
(1933–)

Scottish novelist and screen-writer, born in Glasgow. He was educated at Glasgow University, Jordanhill College, and Edinburgh University. He worked at the Mitchell Library, Glasgow (1950–4), then as a teacher (1961–6) and lecturer (1966–78), before becoming a full-time writer in 1979. His first book was a volume of poetry published in 1975, but he is best known as a novelist and screen writer. His first novel, *Brond* (1984), is a complex and multi-layered examination of the mysterious workings of the state intelligence machine; he later adapted this for television. *Jill Rips* (1987) also burrows into the world of political and business intrigue and corruption, through a powerful inversion of the Jack the Ripper story, in which male victims fall to a female killer in a fictionalized Glasgow. He published a third novel, *A Charm Against Drowning*, in 1988, and has also written for theatre and radio. Another powerful psychological thriller, *After the Stranger Came*, appeared in 1992.

LINDSAY, Harold Arthur
(1900–69)

Australian novelist and children's writer, born in Adelaide, who travelled widely through the continent and became expert on the aborigines' life in the Australian deserts. Between 1941 and 1946 he was instructor in survival techniques to soldiers in Australia and New Britain, Papua New Guinea, passing on to them the bushcraft he had learned on his travels; this he later published as *The Bushman's Handbook* (1948). After the war he broadcast on nature topics and contributed to newspapers and periodicals. He wrote five adult novels, including *The Red Bull* (1959), which drew on his earlier experiences of forestry, and a number of novels for younger readers, mainly in collaboration with the anthropologist Norman Tindale, including the award-winning *The First Walkabout* (1954) and *Aboriginal Australians* (1963).

LINDSAY, Jack
(1900–90)

Australian poet, novelist, historian and translator. Born in Melbourne, the eldest son of artist and writer **Norman Lindsay** and brother of **Philip Lindsay**, he later mixed with Sydney's bohemians and described the era vividly in *The Roaring Twenties* (1960). His first book of verse, *Fauns and Ladies* (1923), a mock-classical collection illustrated by his father, was published in Sydney. With a friend, he founded the Fanfrolico Press for which Lindsay translated many classics and his father contributed illustrations. He left for England in 1926 where the Press prospered, to be acclaimed by collectors of fine printing and 'curiosa'. During World War II he published more verse, *Second Front* (1944), and war novels such as *We Shall Return* (1942), on Dunkirk. Later verse included *Peace is Our Aim* (1950). He achieved international respect as an historian and, in the 1960s, produced impressive critical studies of artists such as Turner and Cézanne. Well-known for historical novels such as *Light in Italy* (1941), he also wrote novels of contemporary life, such as *Rising Tide* (1953). The three volumes of his autobiography, *Life Rarely Tells* (1958), *The Roaring Twenties* and *Fanfrolico and After* (1962), capture vividly the many-faceted interests of a Renaissance Man. *Blood Vote*, his novel of the World War I anti-conscription movement, set in Brisbane, was written in 1937, mislaid by the author, rediscovered and eventually published in 1987. From the late 1930s much of his writing was informed by a naive Marxist philosophy and coloured by events of the time, such as the Spanish Civil War and the Nazi–Soviet conflict.

LINDSAY, Joan, properly Lady Lindsay
(1896–1984)

Australian writer, born Joan à Beckett Weigall, who married Sir Daryl Lindsay of the prominent literary and artistic family. Born in Melbourne, she was trained in art but turned to writing; her earlier works, largely autobiographical, were *Time without Clocks* (1962), the 'timeless clockless summers' of her married years, and *Facts Soft and Hard* (1964). The haunting Victorian period piece

Picnic at Hanging Rock (1967) was inspired by a painting and became a successful film in 1975. The disappearance of three schoolgirls on a school outing allows Lindsay to explore a favourite theme of the relationship between actual and imagined time. The final chapter of the book was held back by the publishers and not issued until after Joan Lindsay's death, as *The Secret of Hanging Rock* (1987).

LINDSAY, (John) Maurice
(1918–)

Scottish poet, critic and editor, born in Glasgow. Educated at Glasgow Academy, he trained as a musician at the Scottish National Academy of Music. Between 1946 and 1960 he worked as drama and music critic for the *Bulletin*, Glasgow. After working with Border Television (1961–7), first as Programme Controller and latterly as Chief Interviewer, he became (1967) Director of the Scottish Civic Trust, and in 1983 Honorary Secretary General of Europa Nostra. His poems reflect his concern for worldly affairs: they are short, more statements than meditations. His major works are his critical treatments of **Robert Burns** and his *History of Scottish Literature* (1977). His own poetry was first published in *The Advancing Day* (1940) and the best of his work is brought together in *Collected Poems* (1979).

LINDSAY, Norman Alfred William
(1879–1969)

Australian artist and writer, born in Creswick, Victoria, whose diverse (and now dated) novels mostly portray aspects of a **Rabelais**ian Melbourne peopled by drunken but lovable artists and disapproving clergy. They include *A Curate in Bohemia* (1913), the rollicking *A Cautious Amorist* (1932), *Age of Consent* (1938) and *The Cousin from Fiji* (1945). Some of his novels were banned in Australia until the late 1950s. His children's book *The Magic Pudding* (1918) stars hero Bunyip Bluegum, a perennial favourite with adults too. A highly respected artist, he illustrated not only much of his own work but books by contemporaries including **Hugh McCrae**, **Kenneth Slessor** and **Douglas Stewart**. His sons were **Jack** and **Philip Lindsay**.

LINDSAY, Philip
(1906–58)

Australian historian, biographer, novelist and writer for films, third son of **Norman Lindsay** and brother of **Jack Lindsay**. After publishing an early collection of verse he followed Jack to England to pursue a journalistic career, and began a long series of picaresque novels with a tale of the buccaneer

Captain Henry Morgan in *Panama is Burning* (1932). The books that followed dealt with most periods of British history including *Gentleman Harry Retires* (1936), *Pudding Lane* (1940), *The Devil and King John* (1942) and his last, *Rusty Sword* (1946). A respected medievalist, he also wrote the lives of English kings Henry V (1934) and Richard III (1939), and of Australian batsman Don Bradman (1951).
▷ *I'd Live the Same Life Over* (1940)

LINDSAY OF PITSCOTTIE, Robert
(c.1500–c.1570)

Scottish writer and historian, and minor laird from the Cupar area of Fife. Little is known about his life, but he is the originator (and author of large parts of) the *History and Chronicles of Scotland* (c.1580), a highly readable and, largely, accurate source for the history of 16th-century Scotland. It is written very elegantly, with a dry wit, an example of which is his comment on the death of James II (killed by an exploding gun at the siege of Roxburgh): 'This Prince mair curieous nor became him or the maiestie of ane King, did stand neir hand by quhen the artaillezerie was dischargeand' (he stood too close when the artillery was firing).

LINDSAY, (Nicholas) Vachel
(1879–1931)

American poet, born in Springfield, Illinois. He studied painting in Chicago and New York, and from 1906 travelled America like a troubadour, trading and reciting his very popular ragtime rhymes for hospitality. His irrepressible spirits appear in *General Booth enters Into Heaven* (1913) and *The Congo* (1914). His later volumes of verse were less successful, and, suffering from extreme depression, he returned to Springfield and committed suicide.
▷ E Ruggles, *The West-Going Heart* (1959)

LINKLATER, Eric
(1899–1974)

Scottish novelist, born in Penarth, the son of a shipmaster. His paternal ancestors were Orcadian and he spent much of his childhood on the islands, returning there in later life. He was educated at the grammar school and university in Aberdeen, and served in World War I as a private in the Black Watch. In the mid-1920s he worked as a journalist on the *Times of India*, returning to Aberdeen as assistant to the Professor of English (1927–8). A commonwealth fellowship took him to the USA from 1928 to 1930, after which he had a varied career as a broadcaster and a prolific writer of novels, popular histories, books for children (*The Wind on the Moon* was awarded the Carnegie Medal in 1944), plays and memoirs. *Juan in America* (1931), a picaresque classic, is his most enduring novel. His other novels include *White Maa's Saga* (1929), *Poet's Pub* (1929), *Laxdale Hall* (1933), *Magnus Merriman* (1934), *Juan in China* (1937), *Private Angelo* (1946), *The House of Gair* (1953), *The Ultimate Viking* (1955) and *The Voyage of the Challenger* (1972). *The Man on My Back* (1941), *A Year of Space* (1953) and *Fanfare for a Tin Hat* (1970) are autobiographical.

▷ M Parnall, *Eric Linklater: a critical biography* (1984)

LINNA, Väinö
(1920–92)

Finnish novelist of working-class background. Born in Vrjala, he worked in a factory at Tampere before starting to write. His best-known works are *Tuntematen sotilas* (1954, Eng trans *The Unknown Soldier*, 1957), a controversial novel about the Russo–Finnish war, and his trilogy *Tä ällä Pohjantähden alla* (1959–62, 'Here Under the North Star'), about Finnish independence in 1918. He gave up fiction writing in the early 1960s.

▷ N Stormbom, *Väinö Linna* (1963)

LINS DO RÊGO, José
(1901–57)

Brazilian novelist, famous author of the 'Sugar Cane Cycle', born in Pilar, Paraíba. Son of a sugar-planter family, he was brought up in a privileged atmosphere. A chronic hypochondriac (thus learned in medicine), obsessive practical joker, elaborate public insulter of his friends, he is one of the few writers, besides the inefficient **Cervantes**, to have worked as a tax inspector. The first three (and best) books of the five-novel 'Sugar Cane Cycle' were translated in one volume as *Plantation Boy* (1966). The sociological viewpoint is generally enlightened and anti-racist, but has been criticized by Marxists as following that of Lins do Rêgo's friend, **Gilberto Freyre**: the tyrannical planters are shown as granting more freedom to their serfs than the new factory tyrants, *usinas*. Later Lins do Rêgo's novels were influenced by the one novelist of his generation superior to him, **Graciliano Ramos**; it has been suggested that the greatest and best-written of his novels, never distinguished by careful writing, is *Euridice* (1947), the story of a sex killer. Also notable are *Pureza* (1937, Eng trans, *Purity*, 1948), *Fogo morto* (1943, Eng trans, *Dead Fire*, 1944), and the 'backlands novel', recalling **da Cunha**, *Os cangaceiros* (1953, 'The Outlaws').

▷ H J Maxwell, *Lins do Rêgo's Sociological Novels* (1954)

LIN YÜTANG
(1895–1976)

Chinese author and philologist, born in Changchow, Amoy. He studied at Shanghai, Harvard and Leipzig, became Professor of English at Peking (1923–6), secretary of the Ministry of Foreign Affairs (1927), lived mainly in the USA from 1936, and was Chancellor of Singapore University (1954–5). He is best known for his numerous novels and essays on, and anthologies of, Chinese wisdom and culture, and as co-author of the official romanization plan for the Chinese alphabet.

▷ *My Country and My People* (1935)

LIPPARD, George
(1822–54)

American novelist, born in Pennsylvania. He gained a reputation as the author of arresting, occasionally lurid, novels about city life and its inherent immorality, which were intended to have a reforming effect on their readers. Titles most representative of his stance are *The Quaker City: or, The Monks of Monk Hall* (1844), which won widespread popularity both in the USA and abroad, and *New York: Its Upper Ten and Lower Million* (1854). Following in his wake came a genre of 'city novel writing'. He also wrote romantic historical fiction, such as *Blanche of Brandywine* (1846) and *Legends of Mexico* (1847).

LISPECTOR, Clarice
(1917–77)

Ukrainian-born Brazilian novelist, whose reputation has been slow to develop in the English-speaking world. She was trained in law in Rio de Janeiro and spent much of her adult life abroad; her husband was in the Brazilian diplomatic service. She has been hailed as the first major woman writer to emerge from Latin America, but her concerns are neither exclusively nor narrowly feminist. Her early fiction—*Perto do coracao salvagem* (1944) and *O lustre* (1949)—is still virtually unknown in the anglophone countries and even the more direct narrative of *A maçâ no escuro* (1961, Eng trans *The Apple in the Dark*, 1967) occasionally falls foul of untranslatable elements and rhythms in the original Portuguese. This is particularly true of *A paixão segundo G H* (1964, Eng trans *The Passion According to G H*, 1988). Her most popular book is *A hora da estréla* (1977, Eng trans *The Hour of the Star*, 1986), a winsome and slightly formulaic novel prepared for the press shortly before her death. Lispector also wrote short fiction, but is more effective in her longer evocations of developing consciousness.

LISSAUER, Ernst

(1882–1937)

German poet and dramatist, born in Berlin. Much of his writings had a strong nationalist flavour. *1813* (1913), a poem cycle, is a eulogy on the Prussian people in their fight to remove Napoleon from their land, as is the successful drama *Yorck* (1921) about the Prussian general. The poem *Hassgesang gegen England* (1914, 'Hate-Song against England') achieved tremendous popularity in wartime Germany with its well-known refrain 'Gott strafe England' ('God Punish England'). Other works include a play about **Goethe** called *Eckermann* (1921), poems on Bruckner, *Gloria Anton Bruckners* (1921), a critical work, *Von der Sendung des Dichters* (1922, 'The Vocation of a Poet'), and some volumes of verse.

LISTA Y ARAGON, Alberto

(1775–1848)

Spanish pre-Romantic poet, born in Seville. As a professor in Madrid he taught **Espronceda**. He was accused of teaching 'revolutionary ideas' by the authorities, and consequently co-founded the Free University of Madrid. He was associated, in the poetic 'School of Seville', with **Blanco White**. He adapted **Pope**'s *Dunciad*. But his own poetry was less important than his teaching, which was famous throughout Spain. As an *afrancesado* ('Frenchified Spaniard', ie, one who, like **Quintana** or **Meléndez Valdés**, believed that, after the Napoleonic armies entered Spain, Fernando VII should no longer reign), he was in exile in France between 1813 and 1817.
▷J C J Metford, *Alberto Lista and the Romantic Movement in Spain* (1940)

LITTLE, Jean

(1932–)

Canadian children's author, born in Taiwan. Little has been partially sighted from birth, has worked as a teacher of crippled children in Ontario, and her much-translated novels frequently feature a handicapped main character. *Mine For Keeps* (1961) was about a child suffering from cerebral palsy, and *From Anna* (1972) was about the wartime experiences of a partially-sighted German child living in Toronto. Her books are positive in tone, showing children working through difficult situations.

LITVINOFF, Emanuel

(1915–)

British novelist and short-story writer, perhaps best known for the collection *Journey Through a Small Planet* (1972). Born in London, and apprenticed to the garment trade, he served with the Royal West African Frontier Force during World War II. His main fictional concern, however, is the fate of Holocaust survivors; *The Lost Europeans* (1959) is a bleak portrayal of post-war reconstruction and the uneasy *rapprochement* between exiled Jews and gentile compatriots who remained in Germany during the Third Reich. In the thriller *Falls the Shadow* (1983) he treats the same subject-matter in a more open style. For *The Man Next Door* (1968) and in many of his stories, Litvinoff switches the scene to London, but the trilogy comprising *A Death Out of Season* (1973), *Blood on the Snow* (1975) and *The Face of Terror* (1978) is concerned with a generation of young Russian idealists whose hopes are fulfilled by the Bolshevik Revolution and then shattered by the Stalinist reaction. Director of the Contemporary Jewish Library in London since the late 1950s, he has also edited the *Penguin Book of Jewish Short Stories* (1979).

LIVELY, Penelope Margaret

(1933–)

English novelist and children's author, born in Cairo, Egypt. She read history at Oxford, and a preoccupation with the relationship between the present and the past, and a vivid sense of time and place, form the central thread of much of her writing. In her children's book *The Ghost of Thomas Kempe* (1973), a present-day family is haunted by a 17th-century sorcerer, while the heroine of *A Stitch in Time* (1976) finds strange links between herself and the child who, a hundred years previously, embroidered a sampler hanging in her family's home. The adult novel *Moon Tiger* (1987) chronicles the life of intellectual, independent historian Claudia Hampton, while in *Cleopatra's Sister* (1992), a palaeontologist and a young journalist meet when the aircraft on which they are travelling is hijacked and forced to land at Callimba, a fictitious state on the north African coast. Lively has also written *The Presence of the Past: An Introduction to Landscape History* (1976).

LIVESAY, Dorothy

(1909–)

Canadian poet, born in Winnipeg, Manitoba and educated at the University of Toronto, the Sorbonne and the University of British Columbia; she has been a social worker, journalist, documentary scriptwriter, lecturer and editor. She is a poet of intense emotional impact, for whom the political is always personal: she writes of her poetry as reflecting the pull 'between community and private identity that is characteristic of being a woman'. Winner of the Governor General's Award for *Day and Night* (1944) and *Poems For People*

(1947), at her best she is a poet of rare luminosity. The collected poems of *The Two Seasons* (1972), those selected for *The Self-Completing Tree* (1986) and the collection of essays, poems, letters and reminiscences, *Right Hand Left Hand* (1977), cover the range of her work.

▷ 'Livesay Special Issue' of *A Room of One's Own*, V: 1/2 (1979)

LIVIUS ANDRONICUS
(fl.3rd century BC)

Roman writer, known as 'the father of Roman dramatic and epic poetry', probably a Greek by birth, from Tarentum. He was taken prisoner at the Roman capture of the city and sold as a slave in Rome in 272 BC. He was afterwards freed by his master. He translated the *Odyssey* into Latin Saturnian verse, and wrote tragedies, comedies and hymns after Greek models. Only fragments are extant.

▷ S Mariotti, *Livio Andronico e la traduzione artistica* (1952)

LIVY, properly Titus Livius
(59 BC–17 AD)

Roman historian, born in Patavium (Padua), of a noble and wealthy family. He settled in Rome in about 29 BC and was admitted to the court of Augustus. He never flattered the emperor, but avowed his preference for a republic. He praised Brutus and Cassius, sympathized with Pompey, and stigmatized **Cicero**, as an accessory to the murder of **Caesar**, as having got from Mark Antony's bravoes only his deserts. Of the great Caesar himself he doubted whether he was more of a curse than a blessing to the commonwealth. Such friendship as they had for each other Livy and Augustus never lost. Livy died in his native Patavium. His history of Rome from her foundation to the death of Nero Claudius Drusus (9 BC) comprised 142 books, of which those from the 11th to the 20th, and from the 46th to the 142nd, have been lost. Of the 35 that remain, the 41st and 43rd are imperfect. The 'periochae', or summaries of the contents of each book, composed in the wane of Roman literature to catalogue names and events for rhetorical purposes, have all survived except those of books 136 and 137. But what has been spared is more than enough to confirm in modern days the judgement of antiquity which places Livy in the forefront of Latin writers. His impartiality is no less a note of his work than his veneration for the good, the generous, the heroic in man. For investigation of facts he did not go far afield. Accepting history as an art rather than a science, he was content to take his authorities as he found them, and where they differed was guided by taste or predilection.

The fame of his work comes chiefly from his vision of Rome as destined to greatness.

▷ P G Walsh, *Livy, his historical methods* (1961)

LIZARDI, Xabier de, pseud of José Maria Aguirre
(1896–1933)

Spanish–Basque poet, about whom very little is known except in the Basque provinces, where, however, he is widely regarded as having been the purest and most original lyrical poet of the 20th century.

▷ R A Gallop, *Book of the Basques* (1930)

LLEWELLYN, Richard, pseud of Richard Doyle Vivian Llewellyn Lloyd
(1907–83)

Welsh author, born in St David's, Pembrokeshire. He established himself, after service with the regular army and a short spell as a film director, as a bestselling novelist with *How Green was my Valley* (1939), a novel about a Welsh mining village. Later works include *None but the Lonely Heart* (1943), *The Flame of Hercules* (1957), *Up into the Singing Mountain* (1963), *Green, Green My Valley Now* (1975) and *I Stand On A Quiet Shore* (1982).

LLWDD, Morgan
(1619–59)

Welsh Puritan polemicist and poet, born in Cynfal Fawr. As a Puritan clergyman, he fought for the parliamentarians in the Civil War, and ended as the minister of Wrexham Parish Church. Three of his 11 works are in English; the rest are in Welsh. He was a wizard with words, a demagogue, and he believed in the imminent coming of Christ's Kingdom upon earth. His work is more interesting than much in the same tradition: he was well versed in esoteric lore, from the hermetic Books through astrology to the writings of **Jakob Böhme**, and he was a genuine mystic rather than a prophet. His fiery prose has been described as, at its best, 'unequalled in Welsh'.

▷ *Anglo-Welsh Review*, 23, 51 (1974)

LOBO, Francisco Rodrigues
(c.1580–1622)

Portuguese writer, born in Leiria. He wrote *Primavera* (1601, 'Spring') and other remarkable prose pastorals and verse. He was drowned in the Tagus. His lyrics are of great beauty and his work holds a valuable place in the literature of his country.

▷ R Jorge, *Francisco Lobo* (1920)

LOCHHEAD, Liz
(1947–)

Scottish poet and dramatist, born in Motherwell, Lanarkshire. After studying at Glasgow School of Art (1965–70), she worked as an art teacher at Bishopbriggs High School, Glasgow, before becoming a full-time writer in 1979. A frank and witty poet, with a nice line in irony, she has published several collections, including *Dreaming Frankenstein and Collected Poems* (1984), and *True Confessions and New Clichés* (1985), a collection of songs, monologues and performance pieces. Her most powerful work has been written for the stage, where she has profitably re-worked the staples of Scottish history in *Mary Queen of Scots Got Her Head Chopped Off* (1987), literary biography (**Mary Shelley** in *Blood and Ice*, 1982), popular culture in *The Big Picture* (1988), and horror fiction in a version of **Bram Stoker**'s *Dracula* (1985), which restored the serious intent of the original, all from a thoroughly modern perspective. She translated **Molière**'s *Tartuffe* (1985) into demotic Glaswegian, and has written for radio and television. She wrote the text for the epic music theatre production *Jock Tamson's Bairns* in Glasgow in 1990.

LOCKE, Elsie Violet
(1912–)

New Zealand historian and writer for children, born in Hamilton. Her first book was *The Runaway Settlers*, in which a mother flees her husband and with her large family settles in New Zealand. *The End of the Harbour* (1968) and *Journey under Warning* (1983) again deal with events in colonial New Zealand and *A Canoe in the Mist* (1984) features the eruption of Mt Tarawera in 1886. The autobiographical *Student at the Gates* appeared in 1981.

LOCKE, William John
(1863–1930)

English novelist, born in Demerara, British Guiana (Guyana). He was educated in Trinidad and at Cambridge. He taught between 1890 and 1897 at Clifton and Glenalmond. Disliking teaching, he then became secretary of the Royal Institute of British Architects until 1907. In 1895 appeared the first of a long series of novels and plays which with their charmingly written sentimental themes enjoyed a huge success during his life in both Britain and America. *The Morals of Marcus Ordeyne* (1905) and *The Beloved Vagabond* (1906) assured his reputation. Others of his popular romances included *Simon the Jester* (1910), *The Joyous Adventures of Aristide Pujol* (1912) and *The Wonderful Fear* (1916). His plays, some of which were dramatized versions of his novels, were produced with success on the London stage.

LOCKER-LAMPSON, Frederick
(1821–95)

English writer, born in London. He came of naval ancestry, and from government service passed to the Admiralty. He left government service in 1850. *London Lyrics* (1857) revealed him as a writer of bright and clever light verse dealing with society topics. Later collections of verse were *Lyra Elegantiarum* (1867) and *Patchwork* (1879). Among his influences was the work of **Winthrop Praed**.
▷A Lampson, *An Appendix to the Rowfant Library* (1900)

LOCKHART, John Gibson
(1794–1854)

Scottish biographer, novelist and critic, born in Cambusnethan, Lanarkshire, the son of a Church of Scotland minister. He spent his boyhood in Glasgow, where at 11 he went from the high school to the college. At the age of 13, with a Snell exhibition to Balliol College, he went up to Oxford. In 1813 he took a first in classics. Then, after a visit to the Continent to see **Goethe** in Weimar, he studied law at Edinburgh, and in 1816 was called to the Bar. While still at Oxford he had written the article 'Heraldry' for the *Edinburgh Encyclopaedia*, and translated **Schlegel**'s *Lectures on the History of Literature*. From 1817 he turned increasingly to writing, and with **John Wilson** ('Christopher North') became the chief mainstay of *Blackwood's Magazine*. There he exhibited the cruelty with which he savaged other writers and the caustic wit that made him the terror of his Whig opponents. In 1819 he published *Peter's Letters to His Kinsfolk* in three volumes, a clever skit on Edinburgh intellectual society. In 1820 he married Sophia, eldest daughter of Sir **Walter Scott**, and wrote four novels—*Valerius* (1821), *Adam Blair* (1822), *Reginald Dalton* (1823) and *Matthew Wald* (1824). *Ancient Spanish Ballads* appeared in 1823, biographies of **Robert Burns** and Napoleon in 1828 and 1829, and the memoirs, *The Life of Sir Walter Scott*, his masterpiece, in 1837–8 (7 vols). In 1825 he moved to London to become Editor until 1853 of the *Quarterly Review*. In 1843 he also became auditor of the Duchy of Cornwall. His closing years were clouded by illness and deep depression; by his only daughter and her husband, J R Hope-Scott, becoming Catholic; and by the loss of his wife in 1837, and of his two sons in 1831 and 1853. The elder was the 'Hugh Littlejohn' of Scott's *Tales of a Grandfather*; the younger, Walter, was in the army. Like Scott, Lockhart visited Italy in search of health, and he too came back to Abbotsford to die. He is buried in Dryburgh Abbey beside Scott.

▷A Lang, *Life and Letters of John Gibson Lockhart* (1896)

LOCKRIDGE, Ross
(1914–48)

American novelist, the author of just one title before taking his own life at the age of 34. Lockridge was born in Bloomington, Indiana, and had taught at Indiana University and Simmons College before publication of the ambitious *Raintree County* (1948). This told about events on a single day (4th July) but, unlike **Joyce**'s *Ulysses*, it was expansive in tone and owed more to the influence of **Thomas Wolfe**. The book was hailed as a triumph. Hollywood tried to turn it into another *Gone With The Wind*, starring Montgomery Clift and Elizabeth Taylor. The film's oblivion is deserved; the novel will enjoy recurrent waves of interest.

LODGE, David John
(1935–)

English novelist and critic, born in London. His earlier novels include the realistic light comedy *The Picturegoers* (1960). In *The British Museum is Falling Down* (1965) and *How Far Can You Go?* (1980), in which Roman Catholics wrestle with the moral problems of contemporary life, he introduces various forms of literary allusion and parody. This device is perfected in comedies such as *Small World* (1984), which echoes the form of an Arthurian Romance. It is a sequel to the highly amusing *Changing Places* (1975), in which Philip Swallow, a shy English academic, changes places with his sardonic American counterpart, Maurice Zapp. The 19th-century state-of-the-nation novel provides the literary model for *Nice Work* (1988), a comedy in which an industrialist and an academic shadow each other's working lives. Lodge's criticism includes *Language of Fiction* (1961) and *Working With Structuralism* (1981).

LODGE, Thomas
(c.1558–1625)

English dramatist, romance writer and poet, born in West Ham. From Merchant Taylors' School he went to Trinity College, Oxford, and from there in 1578 to Lincoln's Inn, but led a wild life. He published a *Defence of Poetry* anonymously in 1580, and an attack on abuses by moneylenders, *An Alarum against Usurers*, in 1584, along with his first romance, *The Delectable Historie of Forbonius and Priscilla*, followed by *Scillaes Metamorphosis* in 1589. About 1588 he took part in a buccaneering expedition to the

Canaries, and wrote another romance, *Rosalynde* (1590), his best-known work, which supplied **Shakespeare** with many of the chief incidents in *As You Like It*. He went on a second freebooting expedition to South America in 1591. He wrote many other works, including *The Wounds of the Civil War* (1594) and *A Looking-glass for London and England* (with **Robert Greene**, 1594). He turned Catholic and is believed to have taken a medical degree at Avignon (1600), and to have written a *History of the Plague* (1603). Among his remaining writings are *A Fig for Momus* (1595); translations of **Seneca** (1614) and Josephus (1602); *Life of William Longbeard* (1593); *Robin the Divell, Wits Miserie and Worlds Madness* (1596), and a collection of poems, *Phillis* (1593).

▷W D Roe, *Thomas Lodge* (1967)

LOERKE, Oscar
(1884–1941)

German poet, novelist, writer on music and critic, born in Jungau an der Wischel (now in Poland). A publisher (S Fischer Verlag), he held important cultural posts until effectively deprived of them by the Nazis, who suspected him—he called their regime 'Das Unheil' ('the mischief'), and lived in lonely estrangement in his last years. In his poetry, which decisively influenced the late flowering of his friend **Wilhelm Lehmann**, he developed expressionist techniques (strictness of form, 'uprooted' metaphors) in the interests of what has been called a 'cosmo-centric' *Naturlyrik*. His later poems, which took into account 'the mischief', are his most profound, and may well outlast those of the more modernistic successors whom he influenced. His remaining works were edited by **Hermann Kesten**.

▷C Middleton and M Hamburger (eds), *Modern German Poetry 1910–1969* (1962)

LOESSER, Frank Henry
(1910–69)

American lyricist, born in New York. His first work on Broadway came as lyricist on *The Illustrator's Show* (1936). One of the most important American songwriters for the stage and screen, he is best known for his brilliantly colloquial songs for *Guys and Dolls* (1950), a ground-breaking musical comedy based on the stories of **Damon Runyon**, which achieved massive success on stage, and later as a film (1955). He shared the Pulitzer Prize for Drama in 1962 with writer Abe Burrows (1910–85) for the hit musical comedy *How to Succeed in Business Without Really Trying* (1961).

LOFTING, Hugh John
(1886–1947)

English children's novelist, born in Maidenhead. The 'Dr Dolittle' books (1920–53), for which he is famous (despite slurs that they are racist and chauvinistic), had their origins in the trench warfare of World War I, of which he had first-hand experience. The idea of the doctor who learns animal languages came to him from his reflections on the part that horses were playing in the war. There were a dozen Doolittle books, which he also illustrated, and though he tired of his eponymous hero—on one occasion attempting to abandon him on the Moon—his popularity with readers kept him alive. Lofting was mainly resident in the USA from 1912.

LOFTS, Norah
(1904–83)

English novelist, born in Bury St Edmunds. The author, under her own name, of historical romances such as *The Brittle Glass* (1942), she also wrote thrillers, such as *Lady Living Alone* (1944), under the pseudonym Peter Curtis. The heroine of *The Brittle Glass*, the young daughter of a Norfolk trader, is a typical Lofts protagonist, an independent woman seeking self-determination in a patriarchal world. *Madselin* (1969) depicts the clash in medieval England between the conquering Normans and oppressed Saxons, as seen through the eyes of the titular character. *Crown of Aloes* (1974) is about Queen Isabella of Spain. Although at times stereotypically romantic, Lofts' novels also have a more realistic side and a contemporary resonance, given that their protagonists are often strong, resilient women who are left to pick up the pieces in a Europe laid waste by the violence of men.

LOGAN, John
(1748–88)

Scottish poet and clergyman, born in Soutra, Midlothian. He was educated at Musselburgh Grammar School and Edinburgh University, and was appointed minister of South Leith in 1773. He wrote a successful play, *Runnemede*, in 1784, and moved to London. He is mainly remembered for his plagiarism of several poems of his friend Michael Bruce, including 'Ode to the Cuckoo', which he included in his own volume of poetry (1781).
▷J Anderson, *A Life of John Logan* (1953)

LOGAN, John
(1923–87)

American poet, academic and editor of poetry journals, born in Red Oak, Iowa, and educated at Iowa University. Logan's critical reputation has always been high, but his sometimes difficult verse has prevented him from becoming a truly popular author. His first collection, *A Cycle for Mother Cabrini*, appeared in 1955. It was followed by *Ghosts*

of the Heart (1960), *The Zig-Zag Walk* (1969) and *Poem in Progress* (1974). His *Collected Poems* appeared in 1988. He published a volume of autobiographical fiction, *The House That Jack Built*, in 1974 (rev edn 1984).

LOGAN, Joshua *see* HAMMERSTEIN, Oscar II

LOGAU, Friedrich, Freiherr von, pseud Salomon von Golaw
(1604–55)

German epigrammatic poet, born in Brockuth into a noble family. His epigrams, his only known work, written under his pseudonym, combine worldly wisdom, devout Christianity, and sharp satire. He was forgotten until revived by **Gotthold Lessing** in 1759.
▷P Hempel, *Der Kunst Logau* (1967)

LOHENSTEIN, Daniel Caspar von
(1635–82)

German poet, dramatist, translator (**Gracian**, **Marino**) and novelist, born in Nimptsch in Silesia. The son of a tax-collector, and himself a busy lawyer and city functionary of Breslau, he rose above all this to become a major writer as tragedian and as novelist. His most substantial work is the unfinished novel *Grossmüthiger Feldherr Arminius* (1689), which a few critics have interpreted as an intended repository of all essential knowledge. It is a neglected and underestimated work.
▷*German Life and Letters, XXIV* (1971–2)

LO-JOHANSSON, Ivar
(1901–91)

Swedish novelist and short-story writer, born in Sörmland, a major figure among the working-class writers of the first half of the century. In his youth he worked and travelled throughout Europe and his first books are proletarian travel-narratives based on these experiences. He was a campaigning writer who, in novels such as *Godnatt, jord* (1933, 'Goodnight, Earth') and short stories such as *Statarna* (1936–7, 'The Statare'), highlighted the conditions of farmworkers and other oppressed groups in naturalistic detail. Many of his novels had an autobiographical basis, particularly the series introduced by the warm-hearted *Analfabeten* (1951, 'The Illiterate Man'). Beginning with *Passionerna: Älskog* (1968, 'The Passions: Love'), he produced seven volumes of stories focusing on the passions that afflict humanity; they contain some of the most powerful short fiction written in Swedish.
▷M Edström, *Äran, kärleken, klassen* (1976)

LOM, Iain, Gaelic name of **John MacDonald** (1624–1710)

Gaelic poet, descended from the MacDonald chiefs of Keppoch. He was involved in the clan feuds as a staunch Catholic and bitter enemy to the Covenanters of the clan Campbell. His verse was often political, as in works such as 'L'a Inbhir L'ochaidh', in which he glories in the Royalist victory over the Marquis of Argyll, Archibald Campbell. He composed elegies and public poems in honour of the MacDonald chiefs and also wrote in support of the Jacobite cause. His poetry is in the traditional form of classical poets and is remarkable for its consistent loyalty to clan and to king. Charles II appointed him poet laureate in Scotland at the time of the Restoration. A poet of public affairs to the end of his long life, he denounced William of Orange as a 'borrowed king' and wrote a satire of the 1707 Act of Union. A collection of his poems and songs, *Orain Iain Luim*, was published in 1964.

LOMONOSOV, Mikhail Vasilievich (1711–65)

Russian scientist and writer, born in Denisovka, near Archangel. The son of a fisherman, he ran away to Moscow in search of education, and later studied at St Petersburg and at Marburg in Germany under the philosopher Christian von Wolff. Turning to science, he became Professor of Chemistry at St Petersburg Academy of Sciences in 1745, and set up the first chemical laboratory in Russia there. In 1755 he founded Moscow University. Apart from his many works on science, he also wrote poetry on scientific and religious subjects. His writings include works on rhetoric (1748), grammar (1755) and Russian history (1766); his greatest contribution to Russian culture was his systematization of the grammar and orthography.
▷I Serman, *Poeticheskii stil' Lomonsova* (1966)

LONDON, Jack (John Griffith) (1876–1916)

American novelist, born in San Francisco. He was successively sailor, tramp and gold miner before he took to writing. He used his knowledge of the Klondyke in the highly successful *Call of the Wild* (1903) and *White Fang* (1907), both about a stoical sled-dog. He used his knowledge of the sea in *The Sea-Wolf* (1904) and *The Mutiny of the 'Elsinore'* (1914). As well as pure adventure tales, he also wrote the more serious political novel *The Iron Heel* (1907), and his autobiographical tale of alcoholism, *John Barleycorn* (1913).

▷R O'Connor, *Jack London: a biography* (1964)

LONGFELLOW, Henry Wadsworth (1807–82)

American poet, born in Portland, Maine. He graduated at Bowdoin College in Brunswick, Maine, where one of his classmates was **Nathaniel Hawthorne**. In 1826 the college trustees sent him to Europe to qualify for the chair of foreign languages, and he spent three years abroad (1826–9) before taking up the chair at Bowdoin (1829–35). He married in 1831, but his wife died in 1835. *Outre Mer*, an account of his first European tour, appeared in 1835; and *Hyperion*, which is a journal of the second, in 1839. In 1836, after another visit to Europe, when he met **Thomas Carlyle**, he became Professor of Modern Languages and Literature at Harvard, and held the chair for nearly 18 years. *Voices of the Night* (1839), his first book of verse, made a favourable impression, which was strengthened by *Ballads* (1841), which included 'The Skeleton in Armour', 'The Wreck of the Hesperus', 'The Village Blacksmith' and 'Excelsior'. *Poems on Slavery* appeared in 1842. He made a third visit to Europe in 1842, and the next year married his second wife, Frances Appleton, who died in a fire in 1861. *The Belfry of Bruges and other Poems* appeared in 1846. One of his most popular poems is *Evangeline* (1847), a tale (in hexameters) of the French exiles of Acadia. *The Golden Legend* (1851) is based on *Der arme Heinrich* of **Hartmann von Aue**. His most popular work, *Hiawatha* (1855), is based on the legends of the Redskins, using a metre borrowed from the Finnish epic, the *Kalevala*. *The Courtship of Miles Standish* (1858) is a story in hexameters of the early days of the Plymouth colony in Massachusetts. It was followed by *Tales of a Wayside Inn* (1863), which included 'Paul Revere's Ride', and an undistinguished translation of **Dante**'s *Divina Commedia* (1865–7). He paid a last visit to Europe in 1868–9. As a poet he was extremely popular during his lifetime and although his work lacks the depth of great poetry, his gift of simple, romantic story-telling in verse makes it still read widely with pleasure.
▷N Arvin, *Longfellow, his life and works* (1963)

LONGLEY, Michael (1939–)

Irish poet, born in Belfast. He graduated from Trinity College, Dublin in 1963, and worked as a schoolmaster until 1970, when he became Director for Literature and Traditional Arts of the Arts Council of Northern Ireland. His first collection, *No Continuing City: Poems 1963–1968* (1969), revealed an already mature talent and a compassionate, humane voice which emerged even more strongly in *An Exploded View: Poems 1968–1972* (1973). He is a scrupulous craftsman in both free and metric verse forms, and covers a wide range of subject-matter. He writes beautifully on nature, perceptively about human relationships, and with deep feeling on the Irish situation. Later books include *Poems 1963–1983* (1985) and *Gorse Fires* (1991). He edited **Louis MacNeice**'s *Selected Poems* (1988).

LONGUS
(?3rd century)

The author of the Greek pastoral romance *Daphnis and Chloe*. He was probably a native of Lesbos.

▷B P Reardon, *Les courants littéraires grecs* (1971)

LÖNNROT, Elias
(1802–84)

Finnish philologist and folklorist, born in Sammatti in Nyland. He studied medicine, and was district medical officer for 20 years in Kajana. As a result of his folklore researches, he was appointed Professor of Finnish at Helsingfors (now Helsinki) (1853–62). His major achievement was the collection of oral popular lays, which he organized into a long, connected epic poem of ancient life in the far north, the *Kalevala* (the shorter *Old Kalevala* in 1835, the longer version in 1849). Having standardized the national epic, he also compiled a great Finnish–Swedish dictionary (1866–80), which helped to establish a literary Finnish language.

▷W Wilson, *Folklore and Nationalism in Modern Finland* (1976)

LONSDALE, Frederick, originally Frederick Leonard
(1881–1954)

British playwright, born in Jersey, the son of a tobacconist. He was known for his witty and sophisticated society comedies, among them *The Last of Mrs Cheyney* (1925), *On Approval* (1927) and *Canaries Sometimes Sing* (1929). He collaborated in operettas, including *Maid of the Mountains* (1916).

▷F Donaldson, *Frederick Lonsdale* (1957)

LOOS, Anita
(?1893–1981)

American scriptwriter and novelist, born in California. Starting her literary career at the age of 10, when she wrote for her father's paper, she began writing film-scripts and silent-film subtitles for D W Griffith in 1912. Her comic masterpiece, *Gentlemen Prefer Blondes* (1925), with its naive, gold-digging heroine, Lorelei Lee, summed up the mood of the Roaring Twenties. It scored a huge success as novel, musical and movie, and she became one of Hollywood's most influential screenwriters, working with her second husband, director John Emerson. She also wrote stage-plays, including *Gigi* (1952), an adaptation of **Colette**'s novel, and two gossipy Hollywood memoirs, *A Girl Like I* (1966) and *Kiss Hollywood Goodbye* (1974). Doubt has been cast on her commonly accepted birthdate by her biographer, Gary Carey, who suggests she was born in 1888.

▷G Carey, *Anita Loos, A Biography* (1988)

LOOY, Jacobus van
(1855–1930)

Dutch story writer and painter, born in Haarlem. A typical Dutch impressionist, he recorded the dream-world of a child in his *Jacob* (1930).

LOPEZ, Vicente
(1815–1903)

Argentinian novelist and historian, born in Buenos Aires, the son of a famous statesman, Vicente Lopez y Planos. He wrote in the manner of Sir **Walter Scott**, achieving his finest novel with *La novia del hereje o La Inquisición de Lima* (1854, 'The Heretic's Fiancée, or the Lima Inquisition'), which forms a later part of the cult of the pirate introduced by **Byron**. His historical work is also important. His anger was always directed at fanatical and sadistic Roman Catholic inquisitors and torturers, and this type finds its fullest expression in the psychotic Father Andrés in *La novia*.

LÓPEZ VELARDE, Ramón
(1888–1921)

Major Mexican poet and impressionistic prose writer, born in Zacatecas. His supposedly patriotic poems to his country, although full of love for it, are also full of a subtle irony which, however, for the most part has not been perceived by critics. He was one of the greatest love poets of his age in any language, and perhaps the most ironic of all. He learned mainly from the early **Lugones**—whom he soon surpassed; from the *modernista* style fashionable when he began to write; and, above all, from **Jules Laforgue**. By 1910 he had found his own very distinctive voice: satirical, quiet, phenomenological, far ahead of his time. His posthumous prose sketches, most conveniently to be found in his complete poems, *Poesías completas* (1957) are also remarkable. His influence upon Latin-American poetry as a whole, as well as on Mexican, has been unobtrusive but absolute, and he did more, in fact, than even **González**

Martínez to bring poetry out of the *modernista* phase in which it was beginning to stultify.

▷A W Phillips, *Ramón López Velarde* (1962, in Spanish)

LOPEZ Y FUENTES, Gregorio
(1897–1966)

Mexican novelist and poet, born in Veracruz. His poems are of little account, being but pale imitations of **Darío**; but his fiction, particularly the novels *Tierra* (1933, 'Earth'), about the revolutionary leader Zapata, and *El indio* (1935, Eng trans *They That Reap*, 1937), is in a higher category, and the latter, although not 'the great Indianist classic' that it has been called, is a worthy indictment of the Mexican government's failure to protect the Native Americans and their way of life.

LORCA *see* GARCÍA LORCA

LORDE, Audre Geraldine
(1934–92)

American poet, born in New York of West Indian parents, she was proud to be black, feminist, lesbian *and* a mother of two children. From her earliest collection, *The First Cities* (1968), through to the later *Our Dead Behind Us* (1987), she singlemindedly explored themes of race and sex, using memories of her own childhood and the efforts of a light-skinned mother to 'beat me whiter every day'.

▷*Zami: A New Spelling of My Name* (1982)

LORRIS, Guillaume de
(fl.13th century)

French poet. He wrote, before 1260, the first part (c.4000 lines) of the *Roman de la Rose* (completed c.1280, Eng trans *The Romaunt of the Rose* by **Chaucer**, c.1370), which was later continued by **Jean de Meung**. Nothing certain is known of his life.

LOTI, Pierre, pseud of Louis Marie Julien Viaud
(1850–1923)

French naval officer and novelist, born in Rochefort. He entered the navy in 1869 and served in the east, retiring as captain in 1910, but was recalled to service in World War I. His voyages as a sailor and as a traveller provide the scenes for most of his writings, and from the native women of the South Sea Islands he gained his pseudonym Loti, 'Flower of the Pacific'. *Aziyadé* (1879), his first novel, was a series of pictures of life on the Bosphorus and it was followed by the very successful *Rarahu* (1880), published in 1882 as *Le Mariage de Loti* (Eng trans *Rarahu; or, The Marriage of Loti*, 1892). Semi-autobiographical, and set among the coral seas, this story of the love of an Englishman for a Tahitian girl immediately captured the imagination. Of his novels, the best known is *Pêcheur d'Islande* (1886, Eng trans *An Iceland Fisherman*, 1888), a descriptive study of Breton fisher life in Icelandic waters. Other works include *Le Roman d'un Spahi* (1881, Eng trans *The Romance of a Spahi*, 1890), *Mon Frère Yves* (1883, Eng trans *My Brother Yves*, 1884), *Madame Chrysanthème* (1887, Eng trans 1889) and *Vers Ispahan* (1904, 'Towards Ispahan').

LOUW, N P Van Wyck
(1906–70)

South African poet and radio dramatist (writing in Afrikaans), and his literature's leading practitioner until his death. He was and will remain important. Despite his prejudices about racial matters, he was not a member of the extreme right. He was influenced by **Nietzsche**, **Roland Holst** and Hendrik Marsman. *Raka* (1941, Eng trans 1941), a narrative poem on folkloric themes, is generally regarded as the best poem of its kind in Afrikaans. His most notable play is *Germanicus* (1956). There are English translations in the *Penguin Book of South African Verse* (1968, Jack Cope and Uys Krige eds).

LOUŸS, Pierre
(1870–1925)

French poet and novelist, born in Ghent. He moved to Paris, where in 1891 he founded a review called *Le Conque* to which **Mathurin Régnier**, **André Gide** and **Paul Valéry** were contributors. In this were printed his first poems, most of which later appeared in *Astarté* (1891). His lyrics, based on the Greek form which he so much admired, are masterpieces of style. Other volumes are *Poésies de Méléagre de Gédara* (1893), *Scènes de la vie des courtisanes de Lucien* (1894, 'Scenes from the Life of the Courtesans by Lucian') and *Les Chansons de Bilitis* (1894, Eng trans *The Songs of Bilitis*, 1928). In 1896 his novel *Aphrodite* (Eng trans 1906) was published with great success, and a psychological novel *La Femme et le pantin* (Eng trans *Woman and Puppet*, 1902) appeared in 1898.

▷C Farrere, *Mon Ami Pierre Louÿs* (1953)

LOVECRAFT, H(oward) P(hillips)
(1890–1937)

American science-fiction writer and poet, born in Providence, Rhode Island, where he lived all his life. Educated at local schools, he married the writer Sonia Greene in 1924 but they were divorced in 1929. A writer from

1908, he supported himself by ghost writing and as a revisionist. From 1923 he was a regular contributor to *Weird Tales*. His cult following can be traced to the 60 or so stories first published in that magazine and to what has posthumously come to be known as the 'Cthulhu Mythos', which holds that in the days before mankind the earth was inhabited by fish-like beings called the 'Old Ones' who worshipped the gelatinous Cthulhu. Not surprisingly Lovecraft had difficulty in accumulating readers but he gradually attracted a small but fanatical following in America and abroad, particularly France. In an area in which accepted literary criteria go by the board, Lovecraft was unique. Among his various collections are *The Shadow over Innsmouth* (1936), *The Outsider and Others* (1939), *Dreams and Fancies* (1962) and *Dagon and Other Macabre Tales* (1965), the posthumous volumes edited by August Derleth. His novellas included *The Case of Charles Dexter Ward* (1928), and *At the Mountains of Madness* (1931).
▷ A Derleth, *H P Lovecraft: A Memoir* (1945)

LØVEID, Cecilie
(1951–)

Norwegian poet, novelist and playwright. She grew up in Bergen, studied at art college, and had her first literary text published in 1969. Her work, which often employs a collage technique and transcends the conventional notions of genre, is heavily dependent on the effects of imagery and sound, the experimental language centring on the female body. The poetic novel *Most* (1972) focuses, like so many of her subsequent works, on a female-male relationship, while *Alltid skyer over Askøy* (1976, 'Always Clouds over Askøy') traces the changing experiences of several generations of women. The novel *Sug* (1979, Eng trans *Sea Swell*, 1986), with its kaleidoscopic composition and stylistic experimentation highlights a search for feminine identity which also becomes a search for language. Linguistic boldness is also characteristic of her radio drama *Måkespisere* (Eng trans *Seagull Eaters*, 1989), first performed in 1982 and winner of the Prix Italia the following year.
▷ J Garton, 'Cecilie Løveid', in *Norwegian Women's Writing 1850–1990* (1993)

LOVEIRA, Carlos
(1882–1928)

Cuban novelist and politician. He began writing when he became involved with the organization of the Cuban railway workers. His fiction is polemical but vivid and well observed. His best novel is *Juan Criollo* (1927), an undisguised critique of the independent Cuban governments.

LOVELACE, Earl
(1935–)

Trinidadian novelist, whose first novel, *While Gods Are Falling* (1965), gave one of the most vivid and memorable portraits of Port of Spain, in whose slums it is set. Its central character, Walter Castle, wants to escape from a place of such meaninglessness; Lovelace's second novel, *The Schoolmaster* (1968), is a bitter account of a place in Trinidad that might have been expected to yield 'meaning'. It was held by critics to mark an advance on the first novel, which, for all its power, was obviously influenced by **Alan Paton**. *The Dragon Can't Dance* (1979), again set in the slums, was even more vivid and accomplished, although its author's progressive message did not find universal agreement.

LOVELACE, Richard
(1618–57)

English cavalier poet, born in Woolwich, or perhaps in Holland, the eldest son of a Kentish knight. He was educated at Charterhouse and Gloucester Hall, Oxford. He found his way to court and went on the Scottish expedition in 1639. In 1642 he was imprisoned for presenting to the House of Commons a petition from the royalists of Kent 'for the restoring the king to his rights', and was released on bail. He spent his estate in the king's cause, assisted the French in 1646 to capture Dunkirk from the Spaniards, and was flung into jail on returning to England in 1648. In jail he revised his poems, including 'To Althea, from Prison', and in 1649 published his collection of poems, *Lucasta*. He was set free at the end of 1649. In 1659 his brother published a second collection of his poems, *Lucasta: Posthume Poems*.
▷ C S Ker, *Richard Lovelace* (1949)

LOVER, Samuel
(1797–1868)

Irish writer, artist and songwriter, born in Dublin. In 1818 he established himself there as a marine painter and miniaturist. One of the founders of the *Dublin University Magazine*, he published *Legends and Stories of Ireland* in 1831 with his own illustrations. In 1835 he moved to London, where he wrote two popular novels, *Rory O'More* (1836) and *Handy Andy* (1842). He helped **Dickens** found *Bentley's Miscellany* and in 1844 started an entertainment, called 'Irish Evenings', which was a hit both in England and the USA (1846–8) with songs like 'The Low-Backed Car' and 'Molly Bawn'.
▷ W B Samuel, *The Life of Samuel Lover* (1874)

LOWELL, Amy
(1874–1925)

American imagist poet, born into an extremely wealthy family in Brookline, Massachusetts, sister of Abbott Lowell and Percival Lowell. She travelled extensively with her parents in Europe, and bought the parental home, 'Sevenals', in 1903. She wrote volumes of *vers libre* which she named 'unrhymed cadence', starting with the conventional *A Dome of Many-coloured Glass* (1912) and *Sword Blades and Poppy Seeds* (1914). She also wrote polyphonic prose. Her other works include *Six French Poets* (1915), *Tendencies in Modern American Poetry* (1917) and a biography of **Keats** (1925).
▷ F C Flint, *Amy Lowell* (1969)

LOWELL, James Russell
(1819–91)

American poet, essayist and diplomat, born in Cambridge, Massachusetts, the son of a minister. He graduated from Harvard in 1838. In 1841–4 he published two volumes of poetry, in 1845 *Conversations on the Old Poets*; and in 1843 he helped to edit *The Pioneer*, with **Nathaniel Hawthorne**, **Edgar Allan Poe** and **John Whittier** for contributors. In 1846, at the outbreak of the war with Mexico, he wrote a satiric poem in the Yankee dialect denouncing the pro-slavery party and the conduct of the government, and out of this grew the *Biglow Papers* (1848). A great many serious poems were written about 1848, and formed a third volume. *A Fable for Critics* (1848) is a series of witty and dashing sketches of American authors. In 1851–2 he visited Europe. In 1855 he was appointed Professor of Modern Languages and Literature at Harvard and went to Europe to finish his studies. He also edited the *Atlantic Monthly* from 1857, and with Charles Eliot Norton the *North American Review* (1863–7). His prose writings—*Among my Books* (1870) and *My Study Windows* (1871)—are of a very high quality. The second series of *Biglow Papers* appeared during the Civil War, in 1867. Lowell was an ardent abolitionist, and from the first gave himself unreservedly to the cause of freedom. Though he had never been a politician he was appointed in 1877 US Minister to Spain, and was transferred in 1880 to Great Britain, where he remained until 1885.
▷ H E Scudder, *James Russell Lowell* (2 vols, 1901)

LOWELL, Robert Traill Spence, Jr
(1917–77)

American poet, born in Boston, Massachusetts, of a patrician New England family, the great-grand-nephew of **James Russell Lowell**. He attended St Mark's School, then Harvard, but left after two years to go to Kenyon College to study poetry, criticism and classics under **John Crowe Ransom** in what he called 'the heyday of the New Criticism'. He then attended Louisiana State University and afterwards worked briefly for a New York publisher. During World War II he was a conscientious objector and was imprisoned for six months (1944). In 1940 he married the writer **Jean Stafford** and became an ardent convert to Roman Catholicism. It was a fraught and violent liaison, Lowell being subject to periods of mental instability exacerbated by heavy drinking. His first collection was *Lands of Unlikeness* (1944), the first step towards what amounts, in the words of one critic, 'to his own exhaustive critical biography'. But it was not until the publication of his widely-acclaimed second volume, *Lord Weary's Castle* (1946), awarded the Pulitzer Prize in 1947, that he was accorded the status of a major poet. Divorced from Jean Stafford, he married the writer **Elizabeth Hardwick** but that union also faltered and he married in 1973 another writer, **Caroline Blackwood**. *Life Studies* (1959) was again intensely 'confessional', as were *For the Union Dead* (1964) and *Near the Ocean* (1967), in what was a highly productive period during which he also wrote many plays and translations. He had a high public profile during the Vietnam years, as can be gauged from *Notebook* (1968), but his personal life began to disintegrate. Rather than shrink from his problems he faced them directly in *The Dolphin* (1973), making public personal letters and anxieties, and inviting new notoriety. Latterly his poetry became increasingly obscure and monotonous, and *Day by Day* (1977), published shortly before he died, did not enhance his reputation.
▷ I Hamilton, *Robert Lowell: a biography* (1985)

LOWER, Lennie
(1903–47)

Australian humorous writer, born in Dubbo, New South Wales, who wrote for various Sydney journals before publishing *Here's Luck* in 1930. Through the success of this picaresque novel his work was in demand by national periodicals, and in turn brought forth a series of books from *Here's Another* (1932) to *Lennie Lower's Annual* (1941). Essentially a writer of his time, the **C J Dennis** of the 1930s, Lower's humour relied heavily on the male chauvinist vernacular of the period and on the author's atrocious punning. A selection, *The Best of Lennie Lower*, came out in 1963.

LOWRY, (Clarence) Malcolm
(1909–57)

English novelist, born in Cheshire. He was a rebel, wanderer, and chronic alcoholic. He

left public school to sign as a deck-hand on a ship bound for China, but returned to take a degree at St Catherine's College, Cambridge. He wrote about the voyage in his first novel, *Ultramarine* (1933), but completed only one more book in his lifetime, his masterpiece *Under the Volcano* (1947), a relentlessly confessional story about the last day of an alcoholic British consul. He lived in Mexico with his first wife, and in a squatter's shack in British Columbia with his second (1940–54), where he did his most productive writing. They returned to England, where he died 'by misadventure', choking in his sleep. Posthumous publications from his mass of writings include stories, poems, letters, and three novels, *Lunar Caustic* (1963), *Dark as the Grave Wherein my Friend is Laid* (1968) and *October Ferry to Gabriola* (1970).
▷D Day, *Malcolm Lowry* (1974); G Bowker, *Pursued by Furies* (1993)

LOY (Lowy), Mina
(1882–1966)

English playwright, poet, satirist and painter, born in London. After studying art during the early years of the century, she moved to Florence and composed a manifesto exhorting female artists to interpret Futurist ambitions from a feminist point of view. Becoming disenchanted with the movement, she wrote *The Pamperers*, an unpublished play violently attacking what she considered the Futurists' overwhelming male vanity. Moving to New York City in 1916, she married Arthur Cravan, an aspiring Dadaist, 'fugitive, forger and master of disguise', who abandoned her within months. Loy published modernist poetry in many small magazines and busied herself in a number of artistic ventures. In 1923 she published a collection, *Lunar Baedecker*, reissued, with more verses, as *Lunar Baedecker & Time-Tables* (1958). More pieces were collected posthumously as *The Last Lunar Baedecker* in 1982.
▷V M Kouidis, *Mina Loy* (1980)

LOZEAU, Albert
(1878–1924)

Elegant and gifted French–Canadian poet who became known as the 'poet of the closed-in life', owing to his confinement, from the age of 18, to his bed with a form of spinal paralysis. He is well represented in **A J M Smith**'s *Oxford Book of Canadian Verse* (1956).

LU HSUN, or LU HSIN
(1881–1936)

Chinese writer, born in Shaohsin in Chekiang, of a family of scholars. In 1909 he became Dean of Studies at the Shaohsin Middle School and later its principal. By 1913 he was Professor of Chinese Literature at the National Peking University and National Normal University for Women. In 1926 he went as professor to Amoy University and later was appointed Dean of the College of Arts and Letters at Sun Yat-Sen University, Canton. His career as an author began with a short story, *Diary of a Madman* (1918). In 1921 appeared *The True Story of Ah Q* (Eng trans 1941). Considered his most successful book, it has been translated into many languages. Between 1918 and 1925 he wrote 26 short stories and these appear in two volumes entitled *Cry* and *Hesitation*.
▷H Sung-k'ang, *Lu Hsun and the New Culture Movement in Modern China* (1957)

LUBRANO, Giacomo
(1619–93)

Italian Jesuit Baroque poet, born in Naples. A renowned preacher, he was a follower of **Marino**.

LUCAN (Marcus Annaeus Lucanus)
(39–65)

Roman poet, born in Corduba (Córdoba) in Spain, the nephew of the philosopher **Seneca, 'the Younger'**. He studied in Rome and in Athens, and became proficient in rhetoric and philosophy. He was recalled to Rome by the emperor Nero, who held him in high favour and made him quaestor and augur. In 60 he won the poetry competition in the first Neronia games. In 62 he published the first three books of his epic *Bellum Civile* (*Pharsalia*) on the civil war between Pompey and **Caesar**. Soon the emperor, perhaps jealous of Lucan's literary successes, forbade him to write poetry or plead in the courts. In 65 Lucan joined the conspiracy of Piso against Nero, but was betrayed and compelled to commit suicide. A precociously fluent writer in Silver Latin, the epic *Pharsalia* is all that has survived of his writing.
▷M P O Morford, *Lucan the Poet* (1967)

LUCAS, Edward Verrall
(1868–1938)

English essayist and biographer, born in Eltham, Kent. He became a bookseller's assistant, a reporter, contributor to and assistant editor of *Punch* and finally a publisher. He compiled anthologies, wrote novels (the best of which was *Over Bemerton's*, 1908), books of travel and about 30 volumes of essays in a light, charming vein. An authority on **Charles Lamb**, he wrote a Life of him in 1905.
▷*Reading, Writing and Remembering* (1932)

LUCAS, F(rank) L(awrence)
(1894–1967)

English critic and poet, born in Hipperholme, Yorkshire. A fellow of and former reader in English at King's College, Cambridge, he wrote many scholarly works of criticism, including *Seneca and Elizabethan Tragedy* (1922) and *Eight Victorian Poets* (1930). Among his volumes of poetry are *Time and Memory* (1929) and *Ariadne* (1932). His plays include *Land's End* (1938). He also wrote novels and popular translations of Greek drama and poetry.

LUCE, Clare Boothe *see* BOOTHE, Clare

LUCEBERT, pseud of Lubertys Jacobus Swaanswijk
(1924–)

Dutch poet, graphic artist and photographer from Amsterdam. Lucebert was the most radical member of the 'Experimentalist Group' of the 1950s, and was called by his colleagues 'Emperor of the Fifties'. He is an internationally known painter. His apparently nonsensical poems, full of word play, have been presented as having a world of their own. Later he turned more towards art.

LUCIAN
(c.117–c.180)

Greek satirist, rhetorician and writer, born in Samosata in Syria. Having learned Greek and studied rhetoric, he practised as an advocate in Antioch, and wrote and recited show speeches for a living, travelling through Asia Minor, Greece, Italy and Gaul. Having made a fortune and a name in this way, he settled in Athens, and there devoted himself to philosophy. There, too, he produced a new form of literature, the humorous dialogue. Lucian lived at a time when the old faiths, the old philosophy, the old literature, were all rapidly dissolving. Never was there a better target for satire and Lucian revelled in it. The absurdity of retaining the old deities without the old belief is brought out in such works as the *Deorum Dialogi* ('Dialogues of the Gods'), *Mortuorum Dialogi* ('Dialogues of the Dead') and *Charon*. Whether philosophy was more disgraced by the shallowness or the vices of those who now professed it, is discussed in his *Symposium, Halieus, Biōn Prasis, Drapetae* and others. The old literature had been displaced by novels or romances of adventure of the most fantastic kind, which Lucian parodies in his *Vera Historia* ('True History'). His style, which is notable for the purity of his Attic Greek, is straightforward and elegant.
▷J Bompaire, *Lucian écrivain* (1958)

LUCIE-SMITH, (John) Edward McKenzie
(1933–)

British poet, editor and writer on art and aesthetics. He was born in Kingston, Jamaica, educated at the King's School, Canterbury, and at Merton College, Oxford, where his first verses were published; his upbringing in the Caribbean forms the background to *A Tropical Childhood* (1961), vividly realized poems that somehow make a nonsense of his supposed loyalty to 'Group' values. He has admitted the influence of Victorian poets, **Robert Browning** foremost, on his longer, more dramatic forms, and *Confessions and Histories* (1964) confirms the extent of the debt. He became highly prolific, producing at least a volume a year until the mid-70s, when his poetic output faltered. His writing on the visual arts is intelligent, occasionally brilliant and thoroughly un-British. *Movements in Modern Art since 1945* (1969, published in the USA as *Late Modern*) has long been a stand-by for the educated amateur and has been regularly updated (1975, 1984). Among Lucie-Smith's many credits as editor are the Penguin books of *Elizabethan Verse* (1965) and of *Satirical Verse* (1967).

LUCILIUS, Gaius
(c.180–c.102 BC)

Roman satirist, born in Suessa Aurunca in Campania. He wrote 30 books of *Satires*, of which only fragments remain. These *saturae* (or medleys), written in hexameters, are on a mixture of miscellaneous subjects, everyday life, politics, literature, travel. Their occasionally mocking and critical tone gave the word 'satire' its modern meaning.
▷G C Fiske, *Lucilius and Horace* (1920)

LUCRETIUS (Titus Lucretius Carus)
(?94–?55 BC)

Roman poet and philosopher. His great work is his hexameter poem *De Rerum Natura* (Eng trans *On the Nature of Things*, 1937), in six books, in which he tried to popularize the philosophical theories of Democritus and Epicurus on the origin of the universe, with the special purpose of eradicating anything like religious belief, which he savagely denounces as the one great source of man's wickedness and misery. A calm and tranquil mind was his aim, the way to it being through a materialistic philosophy. His poem abounds in strikingly picturesque phrases, episodes of exquisite pathos and vivid description, rarely equalled in Latin poetry.
▷E E Sikes, *Lucretius* (1936)

LUDLOW, Fitzhugh
(1836–70)

American editor and writer, author of *The Hasheesh Eater* (1857), born in New York.

Ludlow possessed a versatile talent, working as a teacher and a lawyer in addition to his literary pursuits. His best-known book, plainly inspired by **De Quincey**, began as a magazine article entitled *Apocalypse of Hasheesh*. After publication of the expanded version he worked as a hack travel writer and reviewer. He had a collection of stories published in 1867, but narcotics were generally blamed for a muted end to his promising career.

LUDLUM, Robert
(1927–)

American writer of suspense fiction, whose understanding of history and politics in no way conflicts with narrative pace or popular taste. Following graduation from Wesleyan University, Connecticut, his first career was as an actor; he has been a full-time writer since 1969. Novels written under his own name—he has also written as Jonathan Ryder and Michael Shepherd—all follow the title formula of his first, *The Scarlatti Inheritance* (1971): typical examples include *The Matlock Paper* (1973), *The Chancellor Manuscript* (1977), *The Holcroft Covenant* (1978) and *The Parsifal Mosaic* (1982). Ludlum sees modern history in particular as a contrivance rather than a neutral record of reality and the appeal of his work lies in his exposition of how interest groups, by no means always political, construct their own versions of reality.

LUDWIG, originally **Emil Cohn**
(1881–1948)

German author, born in Breslau (Wrocław). He wrote some novels and plays, but made his name as a biographer of the intuitive school, with biographies of **Goethe**, Napoleon, Wilhelm II, Bismarck, Christ, Lincoln, and others, in which he assembled carefully researched sources in a manner more appropriate to fiction narrative. He lived in Switzerland, and became a Swiss citizen in 1932, but settled in the USA in 1940.

LUDWIG, Otto
(1813–65)

German novelist, playwright, critic (particularly of **Shakespeare**) and frustrated composer (he studied music with Mendelssohn and wrote a youthful opera), born in Eisfeld, Thuringia, to which he was, it has been suggested, attached 'with almost pathetic intensity'. He was of delicate constitution and led a secluded life. He was overdependent on various literary models and somewhat swaddled in theory (he was the principal advocate of the movement known as Poetic Realism, a term he coined, which tried to steer a course between realism and idealism in the interests

of a humane approach), but in his novel *Zwischen Himmel und Erde* (1856, rev edn 1862, Eng trans *Between Heaven and Earth*, 1911) he transcended his difficulties and disabilities to produce a genuinely tragic provincial tale: set within a 'frame', and therefore technically a *Novelle*, it portrays the family of a steeplejack. His plays are less successful, but made him famous.
▷G Brandes, *Main Currents in Nineteenth-Century Literature* (1901–5)

LUGONES, Leopoldo
(1874–1938)

Argentinian poet, novelist, critic, and (later) nationalistic fascist, born in Villa María del Rio Seco. When young he worked closely with **Rubén Darío**, and was, with **Jaimes Freyre**, one of the three most important of the *modernista* poets. He began as an anarchistic socialist and has some affinities with the Peruvian **José Santos Chocano**, having been an inveterate and over-rhetorical exhibitionist. Much of his best work, which transcends his glaring faults, is contained in his collection *Lunario sentimental* (1909, 'Sentimental Lunarium'), which imports French Symbolist and even Japanese procedures. He was very influential in Argentinian literature, both for his earlier importations from the European avant garde and then for his celebration of the Argentinian countryside. He had much political influence on the extreme right in his last years before he killed himself by taking cyanide. Some of his best poetry is translated in the *Penguin Book of Latin American verse* (1971, ed E Curacciolo-Trejo).
▷J L Borges and B Edelberg, *Leopoldo Lugones* (1955)

LUGOVSKY, Vladimir
(1901–57)

Russian poet, who fought for the Bolsheviks and who later worked with Eisenstein on the film *Ivan the Terrible* (1942–6). He was at first a Symbolist, then an Acmeist, then a Futurist, but finally became a Constructivist. Not a poet of great importance, but a pleasant and helpful man, he became popular towards the end of his life amongst those not unhappy with communist rule.

LUIS DE LEON, Fray
(?1528–1591)

Spanish writer, born in Belmonte, in Aragón, of an old Jewish family. By 1560 he had received a doctorate in theology from the University of Salamanca; a year later he began a long battle with the Dominican order by winning the Chair of St Thomas Aquinas from one of their protégés. On 27 March 1572 he was arrested by the Inquisition and jailed,

in part for his interpretation of the Hebrew tradition. He fought the accusation until 1576, when he was freed and totally absolved, and after spending many years in the reforms of his Augustinian order died in Madrigal. His life was marked by controversy and a firm belief in his own righteousness. His most important prose works are *De los nombres de Cristo* (1583, Eng trans *The Names of Christ*, 1955), *La perfecta casada* (1583, Eng trans *The Perfect Wife*, 1943), and a commentary on Job. Today, however, it is his polished and precise poetry, virtually unknown in his lifetime, which receives the most critical attention. The odes he wrote are among the most famous poetry in the Spanish language, combining the pure nature of **Horace** with the Christian elements of the poetry of **San Juan de la Cruz**. He was deeply influenced by classical models like **Virgil**, and closely followed **Garcilaso de la Vega**.
▷O Macrí, *Fray Luis de Leon: Poesías* (2nd edn, 1982)

LUNDKVIST, Artur
(1906–92)

Swedish poet, prose-writer, critic and translator, born in Skåne. He was a member of the Swedish Academy. Initially a primitivist much influenced by **Whitman** and **D H Lawrence**, and one of the earliest exponents of modernism in Sweden, he collaborated on and largely stimulated the pioneering anthology *fem unga* (1929, 'five young men'). His prose writings are of three main types: travel books; collages of poetry, prose poems, sketches and essays; and historical novels. He was above all an eclectic, who gathered his ideas world-wide, and the contents of his prodigious output (70 books) reflects his varied sources. He played a vital role in introducing contemporary international literature into Sweden, particularly that from the Anglo–American, French and Hispanic worlds.
▷C-E Nordberg, *Det skapande ögat. En färd genom Artur Lundkvists författarskap* (1981)

LURIE, Alison
(1926–)

American novelist, born in Chicago and educated at Radcliffe College, Massachusetts. Since 1968 she has taught at Cornell University, since 1976 as Professor of English, and academic life forms the backdrop to her first books, the ironically titled *Love and Friendship* (1962), *The Nowhere City* (1965) and *Foreign Affairs* (1984); the two latter novels also deal with cultural displacement, Easterners in the Far West in the first, an American in London in the second, which won Lurie the Pulitzer Prize. Her skill in using enclosed, even hermetic worlds to reflect the progress and problems of the wider culture

can be gauged in *Imaginary Friends* (1967), about a chiliastic cult, and in *The War Between the Tates* (1974), set against the background of the Vietnam War. *The Truth about Lorin Jones* (1988) is a more recent novel, but Lurie has increasingly turned to non-fictional commentary, brilliantly in *The Language of Clothes* (1981), often contentiously in *Don't Tell the Grown-ups: Children's Literature* (1990).

LURIE, Morris
(1938–)

Australian writer of Polish origin, born in Melbourne, whose early work is in the **Woody Allen**-Jewish vein of adolescent humour, as in *Flying Home* (1978), which captures the rootlessness of the diaspora. Collections of short stories, of 'factional' prose pieces, and three plays followed. He is perhaps at his best in short stories, such as his collection *Outrageous Behaviour* (1984). He has since published *Madness: A Novel* (1991), but his autobiography is perhaps his most involving work.
▷*A Whole Life* (1987)

LUSKA, Sidney *see* HARLAND, Henry

LUSSICH, Antonio de
(1848–1928)

Uruguayan poet, born in Montevideo, the son of an Austrian sailor. He was a friend of **José Hernandez**, author of *Martín Fierro*, and certainly influenced him. His gaucho poetry is remarkable for its extremely accurate use of dialect.

LUYKEN, Jan
(1649–1712)

Dutch poet, born in Amsterdam. The chief influence on his life and work (which included etchings), was the German mystic **Böhme**. Some of his best poetry is translated in *Coming After: An Anthology of Poetry from the Low Countries* (1948).

LUZI, Mario
(1914–)

Italian poet, translator and scholar, once classed with the 'hermetics', born in Florence. The 'hermeticism' of such poets as **Gatto** was in part a result of the necessity on the part of writers to veil their humane attitudes from the failed novelist Mussolini's culture-police; but it was also a bid to regain the purity of the word, and Luzi, while no fascist, was devoted to the latter, as his many essays in the magazines *Il Frontespizio* and *Letteratura* testify. A scholar and teacher of French literature, the chief initial influence upon him was that of **Mallarmé**. A difficult but eloquent and rewarding writer, of very great integrity, Luzi is often regarded as the most important poet of the generation immediately following that of **Montale**. English translation: *In the Dark Body of Metamorphosis* (1975).

LUZZATTO, Moses Chayim
(1707–47)

Hebrew poet, dramatist and mystic, born in Padua, Italy, who wrote on national themes. He wrote his first play while still a boy, but only fragments of it survive. His allegorical play *Migdal* (1927), influenced by **Tasso**, has been described as marking 'the culmination of a vast dramatic literature': his style, modelled on the Bible, dominated the Hebrew language for well over a century. His Psalter was condemned as sacrilegious, and destroyed; eventually he had to flee to Amsterdam to avoid persecution. In the latter part of his life he became a devotee of Cabalism, an important follower of Isaac Luria (1534–72), and wrote a 'Second Zohar'.
▷S Ginsburg, *The Life and Works of Moses Chayim Luzzatto* (1931)

LUZZATTO, Shmuel David
(1800–65)

Italian Hebrew poet and writer, who wrote in both Hebrew and Italian, born in Trieste. At the age of 14 he planned to act as the regenerator of his nation; in 1829 he became professor at the Rabbinical College at Padua, where he died. He is regarded as one of the great Jewish scholars.
▷N H Rosenbloom, *Luzzatto's Ethico-Psychological Interpretation of Judaism* (1965); S Morais, *Italian Hebrew Literature* (1926)

LYALL, Gavin Tudor
(1932–)

English thriller writer, born in Birmingham and educated there and at Pembroke College, Cambridge. Service in the peacetime Royal Air Force (1951–3) lent a strong interest in aviation to his work, most convincingly in his first novel, *The Wrong Side of the Sky* (1961) and its successor *The Most Dangerous Game* (1963). Before turning to full-time fiction writing, Lyall worked for *Picture Post*, the BBC, and *The Sunday Times*; he married the journalist Katharine Whitehorn in 1958. In *The Secret Servant* (1980) he introduced the military intelligence operative Harry Maxim, who reflects the quintessentially English character of Lyall's imagination and values; he also appears in *The Conduct of Major Maxim* (1982). Lyall's novels are strongly plotted and well researched, without extraneous detail or mere set-dressing.

LYBECK, Mikael
(1864–1925)

Finland–Swedish poet, dramatist and novelist, born in Nykarleby. The main theme of his fiction is his hatred of religious fanaticism, plenty of which was evident in his environment. His novels, greatly influenced by those of **Kielland**, but not to their disadvantage, reach a high degree of psychological penetrativeness.

LYDGATE, John
(c.1370–c.1451)

English monk and poet, born in Lydgate, near Newmarket. He became a Benedictine monk at Bury St Edmunds. He may have studied at Oxford and Cambridge. He travelled in France and perhaps Italy, and became prior of Hatfield Broadoak (Essex) in 1423. A court poet, he received a pension in 1439, but died in poverty. Lydgate's longer works are the *Troy Book*, the *Siege of Thebes* and the *Fall of Princes*. The *Siege of Thebes* is represented as a new Canterbury tale, and was based on a French verse romance. The versification is rough, and the poem dull and long-winded. The *Troy Book* was based on Colonna's Latin prose *Historia Trojana*, and the *Fall of Princes* on **Boccaccio**. Other works include the *Daunce of Machabre*, from the French, *Temple of Glas*, a copy of **Chaucer**'s *House of Fame*, and *London Lickpenny*, a vivid description of contemporary manners in London.
▷D Pearsall, *John Lydgate* (1970)

LYLY, John
(c.1554–1606)

English dramatist and novelist, 'the Euphuist', born in the Weald of Kent. He took his BA at Magdalen College, Oxford, in 1573, and studied also at Cambridge. William Cecil, Lord Burghley, gave him some post of trust in his household, and he became vice-master of the St Paul's choristers. Having in 1589 taken part in the Marprelate controversy, he was returned to parliament for Aylesbury and Appleby (1597–1601). His *Euphues*, a romance in two parts—*Euphues, The Anatomie of Wit* (1579) and *Euphues and his England* (1580)—was received with great applause. One peculiarity of his 'new English' is the constant employment of similes drawn from fabulous stories about the properties of animals, plants and minerals; another is the excessive indulgence in antithesis. His earliest comedy was *The Woman in the Moone*, produced in or before 1583. *Campaspe* and *Sapho and Phao* were published in 1584, *Endimion* in 1591, *Gallathea* and *Midas* in 1592, *Mother Bombie* in 1594, and *Love's Metamorphosis* in 1601. The delightful songs (of doubtful authorship) were first printed in the edition of 1632.

▷J D Wilson, *John Lyly* (1905)

LYNCH, Benito
(1885–1951)

Major Argentinian novelist, born in Buenos Aires. The subject of both his novels and his stories is gaucho (cowboy) life, but he does not flatter the gaucho, who, in his estimation, is dour and violent. He excelled in description, and the lack of translation of his work, especially of his great novel *El inglés de los guesos* (1924, 'The Englishman of the Bones'—'guesos' is the gaucho pronunciation of 'huesos', meaning bones), is a major literary scandal. This tells of a love affair between an English archaeologist and a simple girl; he ruins her, and she hangs herself. Lynch also excelled in his portrayals of women, whom he valued more than men. *El romance de un gaucho* (1933, 'The Romance of a Gaucho'), written entirely in gaucho slang, tells a similar story. After this Lynch abandoned the literary world.

LYNDSAY, or LINDSAY, Sir David of the Mount
(c.1486–1555)

Scottish poet, born probably at the Mount near Cupar, Fife, or at Garmylton (now Garleton), near Haddington, East Lothian. In 1512 he was appointed 'usher' of the newborn prince who became James V. In 1522 or earlier he married Janet Douglas, the king's seamstress. In 1524 (probably), during the regency of the Douglases, he lost or changed his place, but was restored to favour in 1529 when James V became king in his own right. In 1538 he appears to have been Lyon King-of-Arms. He went on embassies to the Netherlands, France, England and Denmark, and he (or another David Lyndsay) represented Cupar in the parliaments of 1540–6. For two centuries he was the poet of the Scottish people. His poems, often coarse, are full of humour, good sense and knowledge of the world, and were said to have done more for the Reformation in Scotland than all the sermons of Knox. The earliest and most poetic of his writings is the allegorical *The Dreme* (1528), followed by *The Complaynt of the King* (1529) and *The Testament and Complaynt of Our Soverane Lordis Papyngo* (1530). He wrote a satire on court life in *Ane Publict Confession of the Kingis Auld Hound Callit Bagsche* (1536). His most remarkable work was *Ane Satyre of the Thrie Estaitis*, a dramatic work first performed at Linlithgow in 1540, and revived with great success at the Edinburgh Festival; the most amusing was *The Historie of Squyer Meldrum*.

▷W Murison, *Sir David Lindsay* (1938)

LYTLE, Andrew
(1902–)

American novelist, editor and historian, born of a family prominent on both sides in Murfeesboro, in Tennessee. He was associated with the group of poets and writers who called themselves the Fugitives or Southern Agrarians (they included **Allen Tate**, **Ransom** and **Penn Warren**). He was a professor of history at various universities and edited the *Sewanee Review* (1961–73). He also practised as a farmer. It is generally conceded that his four novels have never received the critical attention they deserve. *The Long Night* (1936) is a tragedy of revenge set in the Civil War; *At the Moon's End* (1941) is historical; the powerful ghost story *A Name for Evil* (1947) is about a modern Southerner who cannot let go of his vision of the past and brings ruin to himself and to his family; *The Velvet Horn* (1957), regarded as his masterpiece, deals with a boy's rites of passage just after the Civil War. **Caroline Gordon**, for long the wife of Tate, and herself a major novelist, called this novel a 'landmark in American fiction'.

▷M E Bradford (ed), *The Achievement of Lytle* (1973)

M

MAARTENS, Maarten, pseud of **Jost Marius Willem van der Poorten Schwart** (1858–1915)

Dutch novelist, born in Amsterdam. He spent part of his boyhood in England, went to school in Germany, and studied and taught law at Utrecht University. He wrote powerful novels in English, including *The Sin of Joost Avelingh* (1889) and *God's Fool* (1893). His Letters were edited by his daughter (1930).

MAC AN BHAIRD, Eoghan Ruadh (c.1530–1610)

Irish (Gaelic) bard. He has been described as the 'professor in chief of poetry' for Red Hugh O'Donnell's battles against the English at the end of the 16th century. In 1603, however, Mac an Bhaird turned on O'Donnell, who had made peace and become Earl of Tyrconnell. Nonetheless, on the earl's death five years later Mac an Bhaird wrote the superb lamentation *A Bhean Fuair Faill ar an Bhfeart* ('O Woman That Has Found Opportunity at the Tomb'), famously if freely rendered by **James Clarence Mangan** (1803–69) as *O Woman of the Piercing Wail*. The themes of a ravaged country and a grieving nation are paramount in Mac an Bhaird's work. Some of the later poems ascribed to him by Professor Tomas O'Raghallaigh have been attributed by later scholars to others.
▷A de Blacam, *Gaelic Literature Surveyed* (1929; reprinted 1973)

MACAN T-SAOIR, Donnachadh Ban *see* **McINTYRE, Duncan Ban**

MacARTHUR, Charles (1895–1956)

American playwright, born in Pennsylvania. MacArthur was a heavy drinker and prankster. While working as a journalist in Chicago he managed to convince the Chief of Police that one **Henry Wadsworth Longfellow** had been wrongly charged with rape. During World War I he is said to have dropped empty whisky bottles over Berlin—friends suggested he might simply have leaned out of the plane and breathed over the city. He is best known for his collaborations with **Ben Hecht**: *The Front Page* (1928) for the stage, and *Barbary Coast* (1935) and *The Scoundrel* (1935) for

the silver screen, plus their enduring adaptation of *Wuthering Heights* (1939).

MACAULAY, Dame (Emilie) Rose (1881–1958)

English novelist and essayist, born in Rugby, Warwickshire, the daughter of a Cambridge University lecturer in classical literature. Educated at Oxford High School and Somerville College, Oxford, where she read history, her first novel was *Abbots Verney* (1906), followed by *Views and Vagabonds* (1912) and *The Lee Shore* (1920), winner of a £1000 publishers' prize. Her later novels include *Potterism* (1920), *Dangerous Ages* (1921, which won the Femina Vie Heureuse Prize), *Told by an Idiot* (1923), *Orphan Island* (1924), *Crewe Train* (1926), *Keeping Up Appearances* (1928), *They were Defeated* (1932), *I Would be a Private* (1937) and *And No Man's Wit* (1940). After World War II she wrote two further novels, *The World My Wilderness* (1950), and *The Towers of Trebizond* (1956), which won the James Tait Black Memorial Prize. Her travel books include *They Went to Portugal* (1946), *Fabled Shore* (1949) and *The Pleasure of Ruins* (1953).
▷C B Smith, *Rose Macaulay, a biography* (1972)

MACAULAY, Thomas Babington, 1st Baron Macaulay (1800–59)

English author, born in Rothley Temple, Leicestershire, son of Zachary Macaulay (1768–1838). In 1812 he was sent to a private school at Little Shelford near Cambridge, and moved in 1814 to Aspenden Hall in Hertfordshire, from where, an exceptionally precocious boy, he entered Trinity College, Cambridge, in 1818. He detested mathematics, but twice won the Chancellor's Medal for English verse, and obtained a prize for Latin declamation. In 1821 he carried off the Craven Prize, in 1822 took his BA, and in 1824 was elected to a fellowship. He was one of the most brilliant debaters in the Cambridge Union. Called to the Bar in 1826 he had no liking for his profession but literature had irresistible attractions for him. In 1823 he became a contributor to *Knight's Quarterly Magazine*, in which appeared some of his best verses—*Ivry*, *The Spanish Armada* and

Naseby. In 1825 he was discovered by Francis Jeffrey, and his famous article on **Milton** in the August number of the *Edinburgh Review* secured him a position in literature. For nearly 20 years he was one of the most prolific and popular of the writers on the *Edinburgh Review*. In 1830 he entered parliament for the pocket borough of Calne, and in 1834, mainly for the sake of his family, impoverished by his devotion to philanthropy, he accepted the office of legal adviser to the Supreme Council of India, with a salary of £10 000, and sailed for Bengal, returning to England in 1838. In 1839 he was elected member of parliament for Edinburgh, and entered Lord Melbourne's cabinet as secretary of war. The *Lays of Ancient Rome* (1842) won an immense popularity; so too did his collected *Essays* (3 vols, 1843). His connection with the *Edinburgh Review* ceased in 1845; he had by then begun his *History of England from the Accession of James II*. In 1846 he was re-elected for Edinburgh but was defeated at the general election of 1847. In 1852 he was again returned for Edinburgh and in 1856 he retired. The first two volumes of his *History* appeared in 1848, and at once attained greater popularity than any other purely historical work. The next two followed in 1855, and an unfinished fifth volume was published in 1861. In 1849 he was elected Lord Rector of Glasgow University. In 1857 he was raised to the peerage as Baron Macaulay of Rothley. He was buried in Westminster Abbey. Macaulay has been convicted of historical inaccuracy, of sacrificing truth for the sake of epigram, of allowing personal dislike and Whig bias to distort his views of men and incidents, but as a picturesque narrator he has no rival.
▷ J Millgate, *Macaulay* (1973)

MacBETH, George Mann
(1932–92)

Scottish poet and novelist, born in Shotts, Lanarkshire. He was educated at King Edward VII School in Sheffield and New College, Oxford, and was a producer of poetry programmes at the BBC (1955–76). He was associated with the informal coterie known as The Group (and was represented in *The Group Anthology*, 1963), and with performance poetry in the 1960s. He published 20 books of verse, some of it experimental in form and violent in matter, although his later work was more traditional in form. A *Collected Poems 1958–70* appeared in 1971, and was later updated as *Collected Poems 1958–82*. He also published children's books and 10 novels, the last of which was *The Testament of Spencer* (1992), which appeared shortly after his death.
▷ *A Child of the War* (1987)

MacCAIG, Norman Alexander
(1910–)

Scottish poet, born in Edinburgh, the son of a chemist. His mother was born in Scalpay, Harris, and, as he wrote in 'Return to Scalpay', 'Half my thought and half my blood is Scalpay'. A poet of town and country, his formative years were spent in Edinburgh; he was educated at the Royal High School and the university, where he read classics. He became a primary school teacher, for which his friend **Hugh MacDiarmid** pronounced he had 'a real vocation', and for nearly 40 years it engaged his daylight hours. His first two collections—*Far Cry* (1943) and *The Inward Eye* (1946)—tarred him as a member of the New Apocalypse school and the label stuck 'long after it was contravening the Trades Description Act'. He disowned these poems when *Collected Poems* was published in 1985. *Riding Lights* (1955) is the first evidence of the real MacCaig, lucid, direct and richly descriptive. His distinctive voice, witty and philosophical, is heard in numerous subsequent collections including *The Sinai Sort* (1957), *A Round of Applause* (1962), *Measures* (1965), *A Man In My Position* (1969), *The White Bird* (1973), *The Equal Skies* (1980), *A World of Difference* (1963) and *Voice-Over* (1988). He was the first fellow in creative writing at Edinburgh University (1967–9), and on retiring from schoolteaching he lectured in English studies at Stirling University (1970–9). The finest Scottish poet of his generation writing in English, he was awarded the Queen's Gold Medal for Poetry in 1986. A new edition of *Collected Poems* appeared in 1990.
▷ R Fulton, in *Contemporary Scottish Poetry* (1974)

MacCARTHY, Denis Florence
(1817–82)

Irish author, born in Dublin. He trained for the priesthood, but wrote poetry, much of it in a historical and patriotic vein. He also published highly-regarded translations of a number of plays by **Calderón de la Barca**, and published *Shelley's Early Life* (1872).

MAC CONMIDHE, Giolla Brigdhe Albanach
(c.1180–c.1260)

Irish court poet, born in County Tyrone. He was called 'Albanach' ('Scottish') because of his Scottish connections. He is most famous for his last poem, a lament for the King of Ulster, Brian O'Neill, who was killed at the Battle of Down in 1260. At a time when Bardic poets were almost too heavily restrained by both metrical and linguistic rules, Mac Conmidhe succeeded in leaving genuine poetry without breaking them.

▷A de Blácam, *Gaelic Poetry Surveyed* (1933)

MacCUARTA, Seamus Dall
(c.1650–1733)

Irish (Gaelic) poet, born in County Louth; he spent most of his life there and, later, in the midlands of Meath. His claim to literary fame is based on his use of '*tri rann agus amhran*', three verses in syllabic metre followed by one in song metre, the best-known example of which is the lyric *The Cuckoo's Return* (nd). This form was imported by MacCuarta from the south-east of Ulster and due to its structure has been compared to the contemporary English-language sonnet. He was revered in his lifetime, and his most famous poem, *Is Fada Me* (nd, 'Long Have I Been'), is evidence of a lovable if vulnerable man: 'I never repented as I should, but spent my life composing songs; but now that I am sick and weak, O God have mercy on Blind Jim'.

▷S Deane (ed), *Field Day Anthology of Irish Writing: Vol 1* (1991)

MacDERMOT, Thomas Henry ('Tom Redcam')
(1870–1933)

Jamaican poet and novelist, born in Clarendon of Irish parents. As journalist and editor of the *Jamaica Times* (1904–23) before retiring to England because of ill-health, he campaigned vigorously to encourage local writing, and was himself one of the fathers of modern West Indian literature. He was honoured as Jamaica's first poet laureate for his patriotic and descriptive verse, published posthumously in *Orange Valley and other poems* (1951). His novels, *Becka's Buckra Baby* (1903) and *One Brown Girl and — : A Jamaican Story* (1909), were clumsy but earnest attempts to illustrate the innate worth of humble black people.

▷W A Roberts, *Six Great Jamaicans* (1952); L W Brown, *West Indian Poetry* (1978); K Ramchand, *The West Indian Novel and its Background* (1983)

MacDIARMID, Hugh, pseud of Christopher Murray Grieve
(1892–1978)

Scottish poet, pioneer of the Scottish literary renaissance, born in Langholm, Dumfriesshire. Educated at Langholm Academy, he became a pupil-teacher at Broughton Higher Grade School in Edinburgh before turning to journalism. He served with the Royal Army Medical Corps in Greece and France during World War I, and was a munitions worker in World War II. After World War I he married

Peggy Skinner and settled as a journalist in Montrose, where he also became a town councillor (1922), and edited anthologies of contemporary Scottish writing, such as *Northern Numbers* (1920–2) and *The Scottish Chapbook* (1922–3), in which he published his own early poetry. Beginning with such outstanding early lyrical verse as *Sangschaw* (1925) and *Penny Wheep* (1926), he established himself as the leader of a vigorous Scottish Renaissance by *A Drunk Man Looks at the Thistle* (1926), full of political, metaphysical and nationalistic reflections on the Scottish predicament. In his later works, however, this master of polemic, or 'flyting', increasingly allowed his poetical genius to be overburdened by philosophical gleanings in the service of a customized form of communism. Nevertheless, items such as 'The Seamless Garment', 'Cattle Shaw' and 'At Lenin's Tomb' raise these later works to a very high level. Other works include *To Circumjack Cencrastus* (1930), the two *Hymns to Lenin* (1930; 1935), *Scots Unbound* (1932), *Stony Limits* (1934), *A Kist o' Whistles* (1947) and *In Memoriam James Joyce* (1955). His numerous essays such as *Albyn* (1927) and *The Islands of Scotland* (1939) suffer from the same intellectual scrapbook tendency. Founder-member of the Scottish National Party, and intermittently an active communist, he stood as a communist candidate in 1963. He dedicated his life to the regeneration of the Scottish literary language, repudiated by his fellow Scottish poet, **Edwin Muir**, in 1936. He succeeded brilliantly by employing a vocabulary drawn from all regions and periods, intellectualizing a previously parochial tradition. In 1931 he met his second wife, Valda Trevelin, and in 1933 he went into self-imposed exile on the island of Whalsay, in Shetland. After World War II he lived in a cottage at Brownsbank, near Biggar, Lanarkshire. His autobiography was published in *Lucky Poet* (1943) and *The Company I've Kept* (1966).

▷A Bold, *Hugh MacDiarmid: a biography* (1985)

MAC DOMHNAILL, Seán Clárach
(1691–1754)

Irish poet, the leading Jacobite writer, born in County Cork, who lived in Munster. Much of his poetry supports Bonny Prince Charlie (whom he does not, by tradition, directly name), but the best of it consists of *aisling*, or 'vision' poems.

▷R O Foghludha, *Seán Clárach* (1934, in Irish)

MacDONAGH, Donagh
(1912–68)

Irish dramatist, born in Dublin, the son of **Thomas MacDonagh**. Orphaned by his

father's execution in 1916 and the drowning of his mother in an attempt to plant the tricolour on an island in Dublin Bay in 1917, he was educated at Belvedere College and University College, Dublin, became a barrister in 1935 and was made a district justice in 1941. A hunchback, he won success as a writer of the exuberant *Happy as Larry* (1946), and other plays such as *God's Gentry* (1951, a study of tinker life) and *Step-in-the-Hollow* (1957). He was a highly acclaimed broadcaster, and edited with Lennox Robinson *The Oxford Book of Irish Verse* (1958), which drew criticism for its loose interpretation of Irishness. He published poems, *The Hungry Grass* (1947) and *A Warning to Conquerors* (1968), and a perceptive essay on his father, placing him in the context of the European intellectual death-wish in World War I.
▷Introduction to *The Oxford Book of Irish Verse* (1958)

MacDONAGH, Thomas
(1878–1916)

Irish poet, critic and nationalist, born to a schoolteaching family in Cloughjordan, County Tipperary. He went to Dublin, where he helped **Patrick Pearse** to found St Enda's College (1908), and published several volumes of delicate and sardonic poems, original works and translations from the Irish. In 1914 he founded the Irish Theatre with Joseph Plunkett and **Edward Martyn**. He was also an outstanding critic of English literature, and his aspirations for Irish literature derived from his deep love of English and his recognition of comparable possibilities, as may be seen by his *Literature in Ireland* (posthumous, 1916) and *Thomas Campion* (1913), and by his articles in the *Irish Review*. He took part in the Irish Volunteers, was very belatedly drawn into preparations for the Easter Rising of 1916, commanded at Jacob's Factory in the fighting, and was executed. The poet **James Stephens** impressively introduced his *Poetical Works* (1917) after his death, and **W B Yeats** wrote his epitaph in 'Easter 1916'.
▷A W and E Parks, *Thomas MacDonagh, the Man, the Patriot and the Writer* (1967)

MACDONALD, Alexander (Gaelic **Alasdair Mac Maighstir Alasdair**)
(c. 1695–c. 1770)

Scottish poet, born in Islandfinnan, where his father was minister, and educated in Glasgow. He was the foremost Gaelic literary figure of the 18th century, and his poems reflect the turbulent times in which he lived. He took part in the 1745 rebellion on the Jacobite side, and his best verse is inspired by the subsequent upheavals in and diminution of Gaelic culture. His masterwork is *Birlinn*

Chlann Raghnaill (c.1780), a long poem about the war galley of Clan Ranald, which laments the fate of Gaeldom after the '45. A translation of the poem by **Hugh MacDiarmid** was published in 1935.

MACDONALD, George
(1824–1905)

Scottish novelist, lecturer and poet, born in Huntly, Aberdeenshire, the son of a farmer. He was educated at King's College, Aberdeen, and Highbury Theological College. He became a Congregationalist pastor at Arundel, but his unorthodox views—especially his belief in purgatory, and in a place in heaven for everyone, even animals—caused conflict with his parishioners, and finally brought about his resignation. After the success of his first publication, the poem 'Within and Without' (1856), he turned to writing and lecturing, publishing the allegorical novel *Phantastes* (1858), which met with a cold reception. He followed this with a series of novels, including *David Elginbrod* (1863), *Robert Falconer* (1868) and *Lilith* (1895), confessing that he used his books as his pulpit. He is now best known for his children's books, among them *At the Back of the North Wind* (1871), *The Princess and the Goblin* (1872) and *The Princess and Curdie* (1888), but his adult works have enjoyed a revival, especially among evangelical Christians.
▷W Raeper, *George MacDonald* (1987)

MACDONALD, John *see* LOM, Iain

MACDONALD, John D(ann)
(1916–86)

American mystery writer, born in Pennsylvania. He served in the army during World War II and spent time in the East, the stimulus for his first published fiction, a short story, 'Interlude in India'. After the war he moved to Florida. His first mystery, *The Brass Cupcake*, was published in 1950. Since then his books have sold many millions of copies, the most popular being his stories of Travis McGee, all of which have a colour in their title, eg *The Deep Blue Goodbye* (1964), *The Lonely Silver Rain* (1985). Macdonald's efficient plotting has been much-admired. The chauvinist treatment of sex is par for the course in mystery writing of this period.

MacDONALD, Ross, pseud of **Kenneth Millar**
(1915–83)

American thriller writer, born in Los Gatos, California, of Canadian parentage, and raised in Ontario. He took a PhD at the University of Western Ontario, and became a college teacher. From the 1950s he lived in southern California. One of the finest writers in the genre, his Lew Archer series, a chip off **Raymond Chandler** and **Dashiell Hammett**'s block, is sustained by tough and witty dialogue and rare intelligence. His wife **Margaret Millar**'s novels are no less intelligent and literary. Immensely popular yet academically acceptable, many of his novels have been hijacked by Hollywood. Durable titles are *The Moving Target* (1949), *The Drowning Pool* (1950), *The Barbarous Coast* (1956), *The Galton Case* (1959), *The Underground Man* (1971) and *The Blue Hammer* (1976). He also wrote as John MacDonald and John Ross MacDonald.

▷J Speir, *Ross MacDonald* (1978)

MacEWEN, Gwendolyn
(1941–87)

Canadian poet and novelist, born in Toronto, where she was for many years a part-time children's librarian. Her first husband was the poet, **Milton Acorn**; her second a Greek singer, with whom she ran the Greek Horse, a Toronto coffee-house, during the 1970s. Her poetry is exuberant, direct and accessible. 'A Breakfast for Barbarians' begins: 'my friends, my sweet barbarians,/there is that hunger which is not for food'. She produced eight collections in all. In 1965 she received a Canada Council grant to research a historical novel in Egypt. The result was *King of Egypt, King of Dreams* (1971), an imaginative portrait of the eccentric pharaoh Akhnaton.

▷J Bartley, *Invocations: The Poetry & Prose of Gwendolyn MacEwen* (1983)

MAC GEARAILT, Gearóid, Earl of Desmond
(d.1398)

Irish poet, a Norman nobleman who had become assimilated into his adopted country. He is said to have written the earliest Gaelic love poem, beginning, 'Bad luck to him who speaks ill of women'. He wrote in the style of the French troubadour poets.

MacGILL, Patrick
(1890–1963)

Irish navvy, novelist and poet, born in the Glenties, County Donegal. Sold into servitude by his farming parents, he escaped to go to Scotland, working as a farm-labourer and a navvy. He wrote verses, hawked them round, attracted the attention of patrons and worked on the London *Daily Express* before being adopted as secretary by Canon John Dalton of Windsor. Eventually this resulted in his brilliant, naturalistic semi-autobiographical novel of migrant navvy life,

Children of the Dead End (1914), to be followed by a powerful feminist parallel narrative of the forcing of female Irish labour into prostitution, *The Rat-Pit* (1915). MacGill volunteered when war broke out, gave a kaleidoscopic account of the troops before embarkation (*The Amateur Army*, 1915), and followed it up well with *The Red Horizon* (1916) and *The Great Push* (1916), describing action in France in which he was wounded. He returned to Ireland as a theme with *Glenmornan* (1919), an anti-clerical but self-excoriating novel of his native parish, the comedy of economic adventures *Lanty Hanlon* (1922), the study of the impact of Sinn Féin, *Maureen* (1920), and a somewhat romanticized return to navvy-land, *Moleskin Joe* (1923), while *Black Bonar* (1928) looked at the self-made petty capitalist more savagely. MacGill married Margaret Gibbons (who published charming stories as Mrs Patrick MacGill), and went to the USA in 1930, where he declined into poverty and developed multiple sclerosis.

MACGILL-EAIN, Somhairle *see* MACLEAN, Sorley

MAC GIOLLA MEIDRE, Bryan *see* MERRIMAN, Bryan

MÁCHA, Karel Hynak
(1810–36)

Czech romantic (but also proto-existentialist) poet, still widely regarded as his country's greatest. His major and main work, the robber-romance epic *Máj* (1836, Eng trans *May*, 1932) introduced iambic verse into a language whose rhythm had hitherto been predominantly trochaic, and combined **Byron**ic with metaphysical and atheistic themes. Its opening lines are the best-known poetry in Czech. The poem is one of the first long works in any language to reject 'the order of the Universe and the absolute', and can carry the weight of this rejection. Mácha rejects both God and the power of love, favouring instead an eternity of loneliness. A son of a poor family, he lived a wandering bohemian life (much of it actually in Bohemia), then was forced to take a post in a lawyer's office. He died of cholera in the midst of plans to marry the mother—described as a 'shallow coquette'—of his son. His masterpiece was coldly received by the professors of his day—they detected 'irregularities'—but is now very widely studied. There is little on him in English.

▷*Slavonic and East European Review*, 15, 54 (1937)

MACHADO, Antonio
(1875–1939)

Spanish writer, born in Seville. His father was the eminent folklorist Machada y Alvarez. He wrote lyrics characterized by a nostalgic melancholy, among them *Soledades* (1903, 'Solitudes'), *Galerías y otros poemas* (1907, 'Galleries and Other Poems') and the more philosophical *Campos de Castilla* (1912, 'Fields of Castille'). His brother Manuel (1874–1947), also a poet, collaborated with him on several plays.

MACHADO DE ASSIS, Joaquim Maria
(1839–1908)

Brazilian novelist, born in Rio de Janiero. He was an epileptic, and a mulatto from a humble family background, but became a high-ranking official in the civil service. He was the co-founder of the Brazilian Academy of Letters in 1896, and its president from 1897. His novels dissect the minutiae of Brazilian upper-class life in dazzling, measured, highly discursive, and cunningly ambiguous prose. He also wrote several volumes of short stories. His principal novels are *Mémorias pósthumos de Brás Cubas* (1881, Eng trans *Epitaph of a Small Winner*, 1952), *Quincas Borba* (1891, Eng trans *Philosopher or Dog?*, 1954), *Dom Casmurro* (1900, Eng trans 1953) and *Esaú e Jacó* (1904, Eng trans *Esau and Jacob*, 1966). A complete edition of his works in Portuguese was issued in 1959.
▷H Caldwell, *Machado de Assis: the Brazilian master and his novels* (1970)

MACHAR, Josef Svatopluk
(1864–1942)

Czech poet, born in Kolin. A bank official in Vienna, he was the author of satirical and political verse, known for the trilogy *Confiteor* (1887, 'I Confess'), the verse romance *Magdalena* (1893), and the epic *Warriors of God* (1897). His 9-volume *Svědomim věků* (1902–26, 'The Conscience of the Age') is a pessimistic epic of humanity's progress, or lack of it. He became Inspector General of the Czechslovak Army in 1919, having been imprisoned by the Austrians during World War I.
▷V Martinek, *Josef Svatopluk Machar* (1948)

MACHEN, Arthur
(1863–1947)

Welsh-born English novelist, born in Carleon-on-Usk. Popular with readers, but never subjected to the critical appraisal he deserves, Machen wrote such famous books as *The Great God Pan* (1894) and *The Hill of Dreams* (1907). If referred to at all, these have been described as 'escapist', but in fact they depict an inner turmoil that is very far from escapist. *Things Far and Near* (1923) is an interesting volume of recollections. He wrote many well-executed tales of the uncanny, collected in the excellent *Tales of Horror and the Supernatural* (1964).

MACHIAVELLI, Niccolò
(1469–1527)

Italian statesman, writer and political philosopher. He was born in Florence, but nothing much is known of his early life. In 1498, Savonarola's regime in Florence was overthrown, and despite his lack of political experience Machiavelli was among those who rapidly rose to power in the new republic. His reports and correspondence demonstrate a shrewd appraisal of people and events and enabled him to try out ideas he was later to develop in his political works. When the republic was dissolved in 1512, Machiavelli was dismissed from his post (the reasons are unclear), and in 1513 suffered the further disaster of arrest on the charge of conspiracy against the new regime. He was tortured, and although soon released and pardoned, was obliged to withdraw from public life and devote himself to writing. To console himself, as he explained in a famous letter to his friend Francesco Vettori, he studied ancient history, pondered the lessons to be learned from his experiences in government service, and drafted 'a little book' on the subject. That was his masterpiece, *El principe* (not published until 1532, Eng trans *The Prince*, 1560). It was intended to be a handbook for rulers, advising them what to do and what to say to achieve political success, and its main theme is that rulers must always be prepared to do evil if they judge good will come of it. Machiavelli's admirers have praised him as a political realist, his critics (historically the more numerous and vocal) have denounced him as a dangerous cynic and amoralist. He dedicated the book to the Medici, hoping to secure their sympathetic attention, but he was never offered any further political offices and spent his last 15 years as a writer. He wrote a series of *Discorsi sulla prima deca di Tito Livio*, a full-scale analysis of republican government, completed in about 1518 and published in 1531 (Eng trans *Discourses on Livy*, 1636), a treatise *Dell'Arte della guerra* (1521, Eng trans *The Art of War*, 1562), *Mandragola* (Eng trans 1940), a comic play about a seduction (completed in about 1518), and several minor literary and historical works. He died among family and friends, and was buried in Santa Croce, Florence.
▷R Ridolfi, *The Life of Machiavelli* (1963)

MacINNES, Colin
(1914–79)

English novelist and essayist. He was the son of the novelist **Angela Thirkell**, who took him to Australia as a child. After completing his education there, he returned to Britain and served in the Intelligence Corps during the war, a discipline that taught him to see through surface detail to the reality underneath. MacInnes became a perceptive commentator for a variety of liberal newspapers and journals on the sub-cultures of the 1950s. *To the Victor the Spoils* (1950), his first novel, was a definitive account of social and cultural disenchantment. It was followed by the more sanguine *June in Her Spring* (1952) and *City of Spades* (1957), one of the first books by a white writer to examine the fate of Britain's Caribbean immigrants. In 1959 he published *Absolute Beginners*, a work of raw immediacy which has become a classic statement of a society poised on the brink of major change. *Mr Love and Justice* (1960) followed, together with collections of MacInnes's journalism. Another of the minority groups for whom he spoke was the homosexual community; *Loving Them Both* (1974) was an account of gay and bisexual relationships in the post-Wolfenden era.
▷T Gould, *Inside Outsider* (1984)

MACK, Amy Eleanor
(1876–1939)

Australian naturalist and writer for children, born in Port Adelaide, the younger sister of **Louise Mack**. She was editor of the women's page of the *Sydney Morning Herald* between 1907 and 1914, where some of her stories first appeared. Her 'bushland' tales for younger children were published in *A Bush Calendar* (1909) and *Bushland Stories for Children* (1910). Five other titles appeared up to 1914 and *The Wilderness* was published in 1922. Despite, perhaps, an unfashionable anthropomorphicism, her stories provide a solid background of natural history and are still popular.

MACK, (Marie) Louise Hamilton
(1874–1935)

Australian novelist, journalist and war correspondent, born in Hobart, Tasmania, sister of **Amy Mack**. Her first juvenile novel *The World is Round* appeared in 1896; the trilogy *Teens* (1897), *Girls Together* (1898) and the much later *Teens Triumphant* (1933), drew on her own school experiences. She moved to London in 1901 and wrote the popular *An Australian Girl in London* (1902); nine other adult novels include *The Red Rose of Summer* (1909) and *The Music Makers* (1914). She spent some years in Florence during which she edited the English-language *Italian Gazette* (1904–7). In 1914 she went to Belgium for the London *Daily Mail* and *Evening News* as the first woman war correspondent; her adventures were published in 1915 as *A Woman's Experiences in the Great War*.

MACKAY, Jessie
(1864–1938)

New Zealand poet of Scottish descent, born in Rakaia Gorge, Canterbury, and recognized as the first native-born poet of any merit. Her verse drew heavily on the vocabulary of Celtic and Scandinavian myth, but she was a liberal thinker and ardent feminist. She fought for the issues of the day, as in her 'Vigil, April 10, 1919' on the eve of a Prohibition referendum. Her first collections were *The Spirit of the Rangatira* (1889), *The Sitter on the Rail* (1891) and *From the Maori Sea* (1908); her last, *Vigil* (1935).
▷N F H McLeod, *A Voice on the Wind* (1955)

MACKAY, Robert, English name of Rob Donn MacAoidh
(1714–78)

Gaelic poet, born in Strathmore, Sutherland. He became a herdsman for the MacKay chief, Lord Reay. As an oral bard he became known as 'Rob Donn', describing rural life in his area and the disintegration of clan society on Strathnaver and Strathmore after the 1745 Jacobite Rising.

MACKAY, Shena
(1946–)

Scottish novelist and story writer. She published her first short novels (in one volume), *Dust Falls on Eugene Schlumberger [and] Toddler on the Run*, in 1964. In 1993 she published *Dunedin*, a novel along the lines of, and with much of the substance of, **Henry Handel Richardson**'s *The Fortunes of Richard Mahoney*. Her stories explore, with non-moralizing humour and knowing panache, the vagaries of human existence.

MacKAYE, Percy Wallace
(1875–1956)

American dramatist, born in New York City, whose first play, *The Canterbury Pilgrims* (1903), describes in blank verse the Wife of Bath's amorous stalking of **Chaucer**. He went on to write *Jeanne D'Arc* (1906), but his most successful play, *The Scarecrow* (1908), was an adaptation of *Feathertop*, a short story by **Nathaniel Hawthorne**. MacKaye also wrote hugely ambitious masques intended to be staged as public events, one of which, *St Louis* (1914), calls for 7 500 actors.

MACKELLAR, Dorothea
(1885–1968)

Australia's most often quoted poet, born in Sydney. Her fame rests solely on 'My Country', first published in the London *Spectator* in 1908. Later revised and included in her first collection *The Closed Door* (1911), its opening lines 'I Love a Sunburnt Country,/A Land of Sweeping Plains ...' evoke an emotional response from Australians the world over.

MACKENZIE, Sir (Edward Montague) Compton
(1883–1972)

English writer, born in West Hartlepool. Educated at St Paul's School and Magdalen College, Oxford, he studied for the English Bar but gave up his law studies in 1907 to work on his first play, *The Gentleman in Grey*. His first novel, *The Passionate Elopement*, was published in 1911. There followed his story of theatre life, *Carnival* (1912), which was a huge success, and the autobiographical *Sinister Street* (2 vols, 1913–14) and *Guy and Pauline* (1915). In World War I he served in the Dardanelles, and in 1917 became director of the Aegean Intelligence Service in Syria, described in his book on the Secret Service, *Extremes Meet* (1928). His considerable output included *Sylvia Scarlett* (1918), *Poor Relations* (1919), *Rich Relatives* (1921), *Vestal Fire* (1927), *The Four Winds of Love* (4 vols, 1937–45), *Aegean Memories* (1940), *Whisky Galore* (1947), *Eastern Epic, vol I* (1951) and *Rockets Galore* (1957). His monumental autobiography, *My Life and Times* (1963–71), came out in 10 *Octaves*.

MACKENZIE, Henry
(1745–1831)

Scottish writer, known as the 'Man of Feeling', born in Edinburgh, the son of a doctor. He was educated at Edinburgh University. He became a crown attorney in the Scottish Court of Exchequer (1765), and in 1804 Comptroller of Taxes. For more than half a century he was 'one of the most illustrious names connected with polite literature in Edinburgh', and a regular contributor to the *Scots Magazine and General Intelligencer*. His sentimental, but highly influential, novel, *The Man of Feeling*, was published in 1771, followed by *The Man of the World* in 1773, and *Julia de Roubigné* in 1777. He also wrote two tragedies, *The Spanish Father* (1773, but never performed), and *The Prince of Tunis* (1773). He was one of the founders of the Royal Society of Edinburgh (1783). He is also remembered for his recognition of **Robert Burns**, and as an early admirer of **Lessing** and of **Schiller**. His memoirs were published as *Anecdotes and Egotisms* (1927).

MACKENZIE, Seaforth, pseud of **Kenneth Ivo Mackenzie**
(1913–55)

Australian novelist and poet, born in Perth, whose importance was not fully recognized until long after his suicide by drowning. The first of his four novels, *The Young Desire It* (1937), remains one of the best of 20th-century accounts of the strains, homosexual and otherwise, of adolescence, and, although not as accomplished, is worthy to rank with the *Young Törless* of **Robert Musil**. Of his novels the best known is *Dead Men Rising* (1951), based on a mass break-out of Japanese prisoners-of-war from a New South Wales prison camp in 1944 which Mackenzie, as a drafted soldier, witnessed. His poems (*Selected Poems*, 1961, *The Poems of Kenneth Mackenzie*, 1972), published under his real name, are amongst the best written this century by an Australian: brilliant in natural technique, they are visionary and death-haunted.
▷ E Jones, *Kenneth Mackenzie* (1969)

MACKENZIE, Kenneth Ivo *see* MACKENZIE, Seaforth

MACKINTOSH, Elizabeth *see* TEY, Josephine

MACLAREN, Ian, pseud of **John Watson**
(1850–1907)

Scottish minister and writer, born in Manningtree, Essex. He was a Presbyterian minister in Liverpool from 1880 to 1895. His amazing success with his *Beside the Bonnie Brier Bush* (1894) gave rise to the name 'Kailyard School', and was followed by *Days of Auld Lang Syne* (1895) and others. He also wrote religious works, such as *Children of the Resurrection* (1912).
▷ W R Nicoll, *Ian MacLaren* (1908)

MacLAVERTY, Bernard
(1942–)

Irish short-story writer and novelist, born in Belfast. He was educated at Queen's University, and worked as a laboratory technician, then as a teacher in Edinburgh and on Islay. He has been a full-time writer since 1981. His best work is found in his humane, highly crafted, emotionally powerful short stories, collected in *Secrets* (1977), *A Time to Dance* (1982), and *The Great Profundo* (1987), followed by a 'Best of' selection in 1990. His first novel, *Lamb* (1980), reflected a persistent theme in his work, that of alienation and the difficulties of human contact, while *Cal* (1983) dealt more directly with guilt and the political turmoil of his native city. He has also written screenplays for both his novels, plays for radio and television, and children's books.

MACLEAN, Alistair
(1922–87)

Scottish author, born in Glasgow. He was educated at Inverness Royal Academy, Hillhead High School and Glasgow University. He served in the Royal Navy from 1941 to 1946. In 1954, while a school-teacher, he won a short-story competition held by the *Glasgow Herald*, contributing a tale of adventure at sea. At the suggestion of Collins, the publishers, he produced a full-length novel, *HMS Ulysses*, the next year, and this epic story of war-time bravery became an immediate bestseller. He followed it with *The Guns of Navarone* in 1957, and turned to full-time writing. He preferred the term 'adventure story' to 'novel' in describing his work. His settings are worldwide, including the China Seas (*South by Java Head*, 1958), Greenland (*Night Without End*, 1960), Florida (*Fear is the Key*, 1961), the Scottish islands (*When Eight Bells Toll*, 1966), a polar scientific station (*Ice Station Zebra*, 1963) and the Camargue (*Caravan to Vaccares*, 1970). As well as two secret service thrillers (written as Ian Stuart), *The Dark Crusader* (1961) and *The Satan Bug* (1962), he wrote a Western (*Breakheart Pass*, 1974) and biographies of T E Lawrence and Captain Cook. Other titles include *Where Eagles Dare* (1967), *Force Ten From Navarone* (1968) and *Athabasca* (1980). Most of his stories were made into highly successful films.

MacLEAN, Sorley, or MACGILL-EAIN, Somhairle
(1911–)

Gaelic poet, born on the island of Raasay, off Skye. He attended Raasay school and Portree High School on Skye before reading English at Edinburgh University (1929–33). He began to write while a student, and by the end of the 1930s was already an established figure on the Scottish literary scene. In 1940 he published *Seventeen Poems for Sixpence*, which he produced with **Robert Garioch**, and in 1943, after his recovery from wounds sustained during active service at El Alamein, came *Dàin do Eimhir* (*Poems to Eimhir*), which contained, among other shorter poems, many of his love lyrics addressed to the legendary Eimhir of the early Irish sagas. Influenced by the metaphysical poets as well as the ancient and later Celtic literature and traditional Gaelic song, he reinvigorated the Gaelic literary language and tradition, creating a medium capable of expressing contemporary intellectual challenge, much as his friend **Hugh MacDiarmid** was reinstating Scots as a serious literary language. A teacher and headmaster until his retirement in 1972, his major collection of poems, *Reothairt is Contraigh* ('Spring Tide and Neap Tide'),

appeared in 1977. His work has been translated and issued in bilingual editions, and has reached a wide and appreciative public all over the world. His *Collected Poems* appeared in 1991.
▷T McCaughey, in *The History of Scottish Literature* (vol 4, 1987, ed Cairns Craig)

MACLEISH, Archibald
(1892–)

American poet and librarian, born in Glencoe, Illinois. Educated at Yale and the Harvard Law School, he married Ada Hitchcock in 1916. After military service in France and his graduation from law school in 1919, he taught constitutional law briefly at Harvard College but moved to Europe in 1923 to concentrate on writing. His first book of poems, *The Happy Marriage*, was published a year later. His many works include *The Pot of Earth* (1925), *The Hamlet of A. MacLeish* (1928), and *Conquistador* (1932), winner of that year's Pulitzer Prize for poetry. For his *Collected Poems 1917–1952* he was awarded a second Pulitzer Prize as well as the Bollingen Prize and a National Book Award in 1953; and *J.B.*, a verse play, won both the Pulitzer Prize in drama and the Antoinette Perry Award for best play in 1959. He was Librarian of Congress (1939–44), Assistant Secretary of State (1944–5), co-founder of UNESCO, and Boylston Professor of Rhetoric and Oratory at Harvard University.
▷G Smith, *Archibald MacLeish* (1971)

MacLENNAN, (John) Hugh
(1907–)

Canadian novelist, born in Glace Bay, Nova Scotia—the setting of *Each Man's Son* (1951)—and educated at Dalhousie University, Oriel College, Oxford, and Princeton. While teaching classics in Montreal, he wrote *Barometer Rising* (1941), arguably the first important modern Canadian novel, at whose climax is the apocalyptic munition ship explosion which devastated Halifax, Nova Scotia, in 1917, and which MacLennan had experienced as a boy. Positively or not, it became a defining text in the development of a distinctive Canadian consciousness. *Two Solitudes* (1945) was equally successful at home, as were *The Precipice* (1948) and *The Watch That Ends the Night* (1959), both of which reflected his acute psychological grasp. *Voices in Time* (1980) looks forward to a bleak, post-nuclear future. His essays were collected as *The Other Side of Hugh MacLennan* (1978).
▷E Cameron, *Hugh MacLennan: A Writer's Life* (1981)

MACLEOD, Fiona *see* SHARP, William

MacLEOD, Mary

MacLEOD, Mary, English name of **Màiri nighean Alasdair Ruaidh**
(c.1615–1705)

Gaelic poet, born in Rodel on Harris. She first came to the MacLeod court at Dunvegan, on Skye, as a nurse and looked after several members of the family during her long life there. She depended upon the MacLeod court for favour and the leisure to write her songs, of which only 16 survive. One of these tells how she was sent away in disfavour and then later restored to Dunvegan by the new heir. Her songs and verses were composed in honour of the MacLeods and in honour of other great families such as the Mackenzies of Applecross. Her poetry, which praised the chiefs and their great generosity, is notable for its break from classical syllabic metres, being composed in the form of a freer, more spontaneous stress pattern.
▷J Carmichael Watson, *Gaelic Songs of Mary MacLeod* (1934)

MAC LIAMMÓIR, Míchéal (Michael Wilmore)
(1899–1978)

Irish actor, painter and writer, born in Cork. His family moved to London, and he became a child actor as Michael Darling in Herbert Beerbohm Tree's production of *Peter Pan*, with **Noël Coward** as Lost Boy. He studied art at the Slade School, becoming a distinguished painter and designer inspired by Beardsley, and also became a proficient multilinguist after residence abroad. With his lifelong friend Hilton Edwards, he founded the Gate Theatre Company in Dublin (1928), having toured Ireland with the **Shakespeare**an Company of Anew MacMaster. His company's work made the most of dramatic possibilities of Irish writing, drew in much European drama using his translations, adaptations, design and lighting, and offered classical material as bold in rethinking as anything in London or New York. He wrote distinguished fiction, plays and memoirs in Irish and in English, and in the 1960s his one-man shows crowned an outstanding international reputation. *The Importance of Being Oscar* (1960) magnificently realized the dramatic possibilities of **Wilde**'s life, while paying homage to his life-long beloved idol. *I Must Be Talking to My Friends* (1963, on Irish history and literature) and *Mostly About Yeats* (1970) were worthy successors. His most famous film appearance was as Iago in Orson Welles' *Othello* (1949, brilliantly described in his *Put Money in Thy Purse* 1954) and (for voice only) as the narrator in *Tom Jones* (1963).
▷*An Irish Actor Young and Old* (1977), and other autobiographical volumes

MacMHUIRRIC, Niall
(c.1637–1726)

Last of the Gaelic professional poets, whose livelihood it was to write elegies and encomiums for their patrons. He is known primarily for his two elegies composed for Allan MacDonald of Clanranaland, who died in 1715, one elegy classical and the other vernacular. His political or Jacobite poetry was written in the old style of formal bardic verse. In this he stands in contrast to the innovations of **John MacDonald** and **Mary MacLeod**. The family of MacMhuirric was the chief bardic family of Scotland. They were powerful landowners and flourished in the Highlands and Western Isles from the 13th to the 18th centuries. Niall and his predecessor Cathal MacMhuirric are two of the greatest members of the family and a selection of their work may be found in the *Red Book of Clanranaland*.
▷D Thompson, *An Introduction to Gaelic Poetry* (1974)

MacNAMARA, Brinsley, real name **John Weldon**
(1890–1963)

Irish novelist and dramatist, the son of a schoolmaster in the town of Delvin, County Westmeath in the midlands. In 1910 he joined the Abbey Players, touring with them in the USA. His novel *The Valley of the Squinting Windows* (1918) led to unprecedented scenes: the book, a satire on village life, was burned publicly in Delvin, the school was boycotted and his father was forced to leave the region (he later died prematurely in Dublin following an unresolved court case against the school's Catholic directors). His son divided his time between County Clare, where he wrote a series of novels including *The Clanking of Chains* (1920) and *The Various Lives of Marcus Igoe* (1929), and Dublin, where he produced plays for the Abbey Theatre. The most interesting of these is the grim *Look at the Heffernans* (1926). MacNamara became increasingly bitter and reactionary and in 1939 resigned as director of the national theatre following a production of **Sean O'Casey**'s 'vulgar and worthless plays' and in particular the 1935 production of *The Silver Tassie*. He died intestate in Dublin.
▷P O Farrell, *The Burning of Brinsley MacNamara* (1990)

MacNEICE, (Frederick) Louis
(1907–63)

Irish poet, born in Belfast, the son of a Church of Ireland clergyman who became a bishop. Educated at Marlborough and Merton College, Oxford, he became a lecturer in classics at Birmingham (1930–6) and in Greek

at Bedford College, University of London (1936–40). He was closely associated with the British left-wing poets of the 1930s, especially **W H Auden**, with whom he wrote *Letters from Iceland* (1937). His poetry often has a biting colloquial humour and, with his writing for radio, ranges over a vast area of contemporary experience, ideas and images. His volumes of poetry include *Blind Fireworks* (1929), *Autumn Journal* (1938), *Collected Poems* (1949), *Autumn Sequel* (1954), *Eighty-Five Poems* and *Solstices* (both 1961). He was the author of a pseudonymous novel, *Round about Way* (1932, as 'Louis Malone'), and several memorable verse plays for radio, notably *The Dark Tower* (published with other radio scripts in 1947), as well as translations of **Aeschylus** and of **Goethe**'s *Faust*. He also produced several volumes of literary criticism. A volume of autobiography, *The Strings Are False*, appeared posthumously in 1965, and his *Collected Poems* in 1966.
▷ *The Strings are False* (1965)

MACPHERSON, James
(1736–96)
Scottish poet, renowned as the 'translator' of the legendary Gaelic bard **Ossian**, born in Ruthven, Inverness-shire, a farmer's son. He was educated at King's College and Marischal College, Aberdeen, and studied for the ministry, but in 1756 became a village schoolmaster in Ruthven. In 1758 he published an epic poem, *The Highlander*, and two years later he published some fragments of Gaelic oral poetry, which he had collected and translated, as *Fragments of Ancient Poetry Collected in the Highlands of Scotland* (1870). In the introduction (by Hugh Blair) it was suggested that a great poetic epic relating to the legendary hero Fingal, as told by his son Ossian, was still extant. In 1760, Macpherson was commissioned by the Faculty of Advocates in Edinburgh to tour the Highlands in search of this material, which he published in 1762 as *Fingal: an Ancient Epic Poem in Six Books*, followed by *Temora, an Epic Poem, in Eight Books* (1763). They were received with huge acclaim, but a storm of controversy soon arose about their authenticity. Macpherson could not or would not produce any originals, and it appears that he used only about 15 genuine pieces of original verse which he altered and amended, and invented the rest to create an epic form for them. In 1763 he was appointed Surveyor-General of the Floridas, but soon returned to London and became a wealthy merchant with interests in the East India Company as agent to the Nabob of Arcot. He sat in parliament as MP for Camelford from 1780. He was buried, at his own request and expense, in Westminster Abbey.

MACPHERSON, Jay
(1931–)
English-born Canadian poet and academic. She made a reputation with *The Boatman* (1957, rev edn 1968), which contained subtle, gracefully metaphysical lyrics of an essentially literary nature, and with a core of fervent Christian feeling at its heart. Since that time she has written little, and *Welcoming Disaster* (1974), adddessed to her teddy bear, her 'glum chum', was not as well received.
▷ *Canadian Literature* (Winter, 1960)

MACPHERSON, Mary
(1821–98)
Scottish Gaelic poet, born on the Isle of Skye, who was a passionate advocate of Highland Land Reform. She was an interestingly uneven poet, the best of whose work transcends its polite intentions.

MACROBIUS, Ambrosius Theodosius
(5th century)
Roman writer and neo-Platonist philosopher, born probably in Africa. He wrote a commentary on **Cicero**'s *Somnium Scipionis*, and *Saturnalia*, a series of historical, mythological and critical dialogues in the manner of **Athenaeus**.

MADÁCH, Imre
(1823–64)
Hungarian dramatist and poet, born in Alsó-Sztregova. Regarded by some as the 'greatest philosophical poet of Hungary', his dramatic poem, *Az ember tragédiaja* (1861, Eng trans *The Tragedy of Man*, 1933), is the nearest work to *The Dynasts* of **Thomas Hardy** in world literature (Hardy did not know it, or Hungarian). It brought Madách into contention as one of the world's great playwrights of his century, but has not yet become well-enough known outside Hungary, for all the critical work that has been done upon it. Its protagonists are Adam, optimist, Lucifer, pragmatist and Eve, enigmatic cause of both Adam's fall and his redemption.
▷S Hevesy, *Introduction to the Tragedy of Man* (1935); J Gassner, *Master of the Drama* (1940)

MAERLANT, Jacob van
(c.1235–c.1300)
Flemish didactic poet. He was the author of verse translations of French and Latin originals, including the *Roman de Troie* (c.1264, 'The Tale of Troy') and de Beauvais' *Speculum Majus* (1284), as *Spiegel Historiael*, a history of the world.

MAETERLINCK, Count Maurice
(1862–1949)

Belgian dramatist and winner of the Nobel Prize for literature, born in Ghent. He studied law at Ghent University, but became a disciple of the Symbolist movement, and in 1889 produced his first volume of poetry, *Les Serres chaudes* ('The Greenhouses'). In the same year came his prose play, *La Princesse Maleine* (Eng trans *The Princess Maleine*, 1890), and in 1892 *Pelléas et Mélisande* (Eng trans *Pelleas and Melisande*, 1894), on which Debussy based his opera. Other plays include *Joyzelle* (1903, Eng trans 1906) and *Marie-Magdeleine* (1910, Eng trans *Mary Magdalene*, 1910). *La Vie des abeilles* (1901, Eng trans *The Life of the Bee*, 1901) is one of his many popular expositions of scientific subjects, and he also wrote several philosophical works. He was awarded the Nobel Prize for literature in 1911.
▷ B Knapp, *Maurice Maeterlinck* (1975)

MAFFEI, Francesco Scipione, Marchese di
(1675–1755)

Italian dramatist, born in Verona. He fought in the War of the Spanish Succession (1703–4) under his brother Alessandro, a field-marshal. A leading reformer of Italian drama, his tragedy *Merope* (1714, Eng trans 1740) ran through 70 editions, and the comedy *Le Ceremonie* (1728) was also successful. He also wrote scholarly works, including *Verona illustrata* (1731–2).
▷ G Silvestri, *Un europeo del Settecento* (1954)

MAGALHÃES, Domingos José Gonçalves de
(1811–82)

Brazilian romantic poet, a Rio doctor who published his first collection in 1832, then went to Europe—France and Italy—and met many representatives of the romantic movement. On his return to Brazil his style changed, and he founded a magazine in order to promote romanticism. His second collection, *Poéticos e Saudades* (1836), is usually considered to have inaugurated romanticism. He wrote verse plays and epics. His importance is more historical than intrinsic: even Brazil's 'first national play', *Antonio José* (1838), written by him, is dull.
▷ J A Castelo, *Gonçalves de Magalhães* (1946, in Portuguese)

MAGINN, William
(1794–1842)

Irish writer, born in Cork. He was educated in his father's private school and at Trinity College, Dublin, and took his LL D. He taught in Cork for 10 years, and in 1823 moved to London. He was a prolific contributor to *Blackwood's Magazine*, and the *Standard*, and was the joint founder of *Fraser's Magazine* (1830). A collection of his tales was edited by Eric Partridge (1933).
▷ R S Mackenzie (ed), *Miscellaneous Writings* (1855–7)

MAGRIS, Claudio
(1939–)

Italian writer, born in Trieste. He taught German at the University of Turin (1970–8), and now lectures at Trieste University. His writing includes non-fiction works on Austro-Hungarian culture and literature, and literary criticism, including a book on the writer **Joseph Roth**. His best-known work is *Danubio* (1986, Eng trans *Danube*, 1989), a compendious account of the great central European river which is part invention, part travelogue, and part cultural, historical and literary meditation. His cerebral, playful novels include *Illazioni su una sciabola* (1984, Eng trans *Inferences from a Sabre*, 1990) and *Altro mare* (1991, Eng trans *A Different Sea*, 1993).

MAHFOUZ, or MAHFUZ, Naguib
(1911–)

Egyptian novelist and winner of the Nobel Prize for literature, born in the al-Gamaliyya old quarter of Cairo, the setting for several of his works. The youngest son of a merchant, he graduated from King Fuad I (now Cairo) University in 1934 with a degree in philosophy. An avid reader of French, British, Russian, American and Arab writers, he especially admired the critical writings of ostracized fellow Egyptians such as **Taha Husayn**. He worked in university administration and then for the government's Ministry of Waqfs, or religious foundations, and in journalism. He started writing as a boy and by 1939 had already written three novels, one of which, *Kifah Tiba* (1944, 'The Struggle of Thebes'), drew a parallel between the Hyksos invasion of ancient Egypt and the pre-war British occupation of modern Egypt. He later began work on *Al-Thulathiya* (1956–7, 'The Cairo Trilogy'), a monumental, somewhat autobiographical work, described by **John Fowles** as revealing 'the struggles and convolutions of Egyptian society with a Balzacian breadth and degree of technical innovation unparalleled in any other writer of his time'. Nevertheless, it was overshadowed by the notoriety surrounding *Awlad Haratina* (1967, Eng trans *The Children of Gebelawi*, 1981), serialized in the magazine *al-Ahram*. An allegorical work which marks a departure from his previous style and shows his disillusionment with

religion, it depicts average Egyptians living the lives of Cain and Abel, Moses, Jesus and Muhammad, and portrays the decline of five communities towards futility and nihilism. It was banned throughout the Arab world, except in Lebanon. Becoming more interested in the plight of the individual, in *Al-Liss wa-l-Kilab* (1961, 'The Thief and the Dogs'), *Al-Shahhadh* (1965, 'The Beggar'), *Tharthara fawq al-Nil* (1966, 'Chit-Chat on the Nile') and *Miramar* (1967, Eng trans 1978) he explores the fate of members of different classes in Egyptian society after the Nasserite revolution, these works affirming his tragic vision of life and universalizing the experience of his characters. Described as 'a Dickens of the Cairo cafés' and the 'Balzac of Egypt', he won the Nobel Prize for literature in 1988. His work is still unavailable in many Middle Eastern countries on account of his outspoken support for President Sadat's Camp David peace treaty with Israel. At the heart of his profound fiction is his mystical Sufism.
▷S Somekh, *The Changing Rhythm: a study of Mahfuz's novels* (1973)

MAHON, Derek
(1941–)

Irish poet, born in Belfast. He was educated at Belfast Institute and Trinity College, Dublin, and taught before turning to journalism and other writing. He was associated with the 'Northern Poets' in Belfast in the 1960s, with **Seamus Heaney** and **Michael Longley**. A poet of place, drawn to squalid landscapes and desperate situations, his acknowledged influences are **Louis MacNeice** and **W H Auden**. *Twelve Poems* was published in 1965, since when there have been a number of others including *Night-Crossing* (1968), *The Snow Party* (1975), *The Hunt by Night* (1982), *A Kensington Notebook* (1984) and *Antarctica* (1985). *Poems 1962–1978* (1979) contained some revised versions of earlier works, and a new *Selected Poems* appeared in 1991.
▷Introduction to the *Penguin Book of Contemporary Irish Poetry* (1990)

MAHONY, Francis Sylvester, pseud Father Prout
(1804–66)

Irish priest and humorous writer, born in Cork. He became a Jesuit priest, but was expelled from the order for a late-night frolic and was ordained a priest at Lucca in 1832. He moved to London in 1834 and forsook his calling for journalism and poetry, and contributed to *Fraser's Magazine* and *Bentley's Miscellany*. He is remembered as author of the poems 'The Bells of Shandon' and 'The Lady of Lee'.
▷C Kent, memoir in *Works* (1881)

MAHY, Margaret
(1936–)

New Zealand writer of children's fiction, born in Whakatane, whose books are internationally recognized: *The Haunting* (1982) won the Carnegie Medal, as did *The Changeover: A Supernatural Romance* (1984). Her work ranges from texts for picture books, through short stories, to novels for younger readers and teenagers and, in *Aliens in the Family* (1986), to science fiction. Her younger tales are full of fantasy but in *The Tricksters* (1986) and the award-winning *Memory* (1987) she adopts contemporary settings and raises current concerns.

MAIDEN, Jennifer Margaret
(1949–)

Australian poet, born in Penrith, New South Wales, who has published a number of collections of prose and verse between *Tactics* (1974) and *For the Left Hand* which appeared as a special issue of *Poetry Australia* in 1981. Both *Mortal Details* (1971) and *The Warm Thing* (1983) contain verse and prose. She has also edited anthologies of verse and written plays.

MAILER, Norman Kingsley
(1923–)

American novelist, journalist and polemicist, born in Long Branch, New Jersey. He was brought up in Brooklyn and educated at Harvard. During World War II he served in the Pacific and his first novel *The Naked and the Dead* (1948) draws heavily upon his own experience. An anti-war blast and social satire, it was a remarkable work for one so young and it became a bestseller, establishing him as a leading novelist of his generation. He maintained his antagonism towards contemporary society and mores in *Barbary Shore* (1951) and *The Deer Park* (1955) but the writing of the period documents his gradual ideological transformation from liberal socialism through Trotskyism to a species of anarchistic libertarianism which he has characterized as left conservatism, and which involves an elaborate eschatology compounded of Judaistic mythology, existentialism, and private, **Hemingway**esque obsessions about courage, sex, cancer and death. A proponent of the 'New Journalism', and one who helped define that solipsistic genre, he has created a vast body of work, impressive for its energy and its self-obsession. *Advertisements for Myself* (1959), whose own blurb admitted that 'some of the pieces are mediocre', is generally regarded as one of his more successful books. As a polemicist, campaigner and protester he was prominent throughout the 1960s, publishing

An American Dream (1965), *Why Are We In Vietnam?* (1967) and *Armies of the Night* (1968), whose subject is the 1967 protest march on the Pentagon. It won a National Book Award and the Pulitzer Prize. Subsequent books include *Miami and the Siege of Chicago* (1969), *The Prisoner of Sex* (1971), *Marilyn* (a pictorial life of Marilyn Monroe, 1973), *The Executioner's Song* (1979), a fictionalized study of the execution of convicted killer Gary Gilmore, *Ancient Evenings* (1983), a gargantuan historical novel, and a thriller, *Tough Guys Don't Dance* (1984). His most recent novel is *Hamlet's Ghost* (1991), an account of the CIA from the end of World War II to the assassination of John F Kennedy. He has also been active as a screenwriter, film director and actor, with such works as *Maidstone* (1970) and *Tough Guys Don't Dance* (1987).
▷H Mills, *Mailer: a biography* (1982)

MAILLART, Ella Kini
(1903–)
Swiss travel writer, born in Geneva. She represented Switzerland in the 1924 Olympic Games in Paris in the single-handed sailing competition, captained the Swiss Ladies Hockey Team in 1931 and skied for her country from 1931 to 1934. In 1932 she crossed Russian Turkestan and wrote of her tribulations in both French and English. In 1934, working as a journalist for *Petit Parisien*, she went to Mongolia to report on the Japanese invasion and returned via Peking across Tibet and into Kashmir with **Peter Fleming**, described in *Oasis interdites* (1937, Eng trans *Forbidden Journey*, 1937). She worked and journeyed in Iran and Afghanistan, and then spent the war years living in an ashram in southern India under the tutelage of Sri Ramama. She was one of the first travellers into Nepal when it opened in 1949, and wrote *The Land of the Sherpas* (1955).

MAIS, Roger
(1905–55)
Jamaican novelist and dramatist, he worked as a journalist, civil servant and photographer. A supporter of the People's National Party and associate of Norman Manley in the 1930s and 40s, he was imprisoned for his anticolonial article, 'Now we know' (*Public Opinion*, 1944). Considered a pioneer of national literature, the themes of Mais's three major novels draw on his socio-political commitment to the working class and explore the inner life of the individual. *The Hills were Joyful Together* (1953) is a violent depiction of the sufferings of the inhabitants of a Kingston tenement yard, whilst *Brother Man* (1954) explores the practical difficulties of translating dreams of brotherhood to reality.

His final novel, *Black Lightning* (1955), set in rural Jamaica, concentrates on the complex relationship between the West Indian artist and his home community.

MAISTRE, Xavier, Comte de
(1763–1852)
French novelist, painter and soldier, born in Chambéry, brother of the political philosopher Joseph Marie, Comte de Maistre. Exiled after the French occupation of Savoy (1798), he joined the Russian army and became a general. He spent most of the rest of his life in Russia, publishing several appealing works, such as *Voyage autour de ma chambre* (1794, 'Journey around my Room'), describing a period of imprisonment he endured, and *Les Prisonniers du Caucase* (1825, 'The Prisoners of the Caucasus') and *La Jeune Sibérienne* (1825, 'The Young Siberian Woman').
▷A Berthier, *Xavier de Maistre* (1921)

MAJEROVA, Marie, pseud of Marie Tusarová
(1882–1967)
Czech novelist from Úvaly in the Kladno mining area, and a communist from the inception of the party in 1921. She spent some years amongst anarchists in Paris, in the course of a courageous and independent life; it was this experience, and her compassion—rather than her rather naive communism—that made her into a powerful novelist. She did not please the Stalinist dictators of her country. Of her novels only *Havírská balada* (1938, Eng trans *Ballad of a Miner*, 1960) has appeared in English.

MAJOR, Clarence
(1936–)
Black American poet and novelist, born in Atlanta, Georgia, and educated in Chicago, and at the New School for Social Research, New York. In an attempt to capture the reality of the Afro–American experience, he devised a surreal approach which can be obscure as well as powerful, but which is much concerned with the artificiality of accepted social and cultural norms. His most significant verse appeared in his second collection *Love Poems of a Black Man* (1965), though later books such as *Symptoms and Madness* (1971), *The Cotton Club* (1972), *The Syncopated Cakewalk* (1974) and *Some Observations of a Stranger at Zuni in the Latter Part of the Century* (1989) are no less effective. Major also edited the influential anthology *The New Black Poetry* (1969). His fiction includes the autobiographical *All-Night Visitors* (1969) and *No* (1973), which bears comparison with **Richard Wright's**

Black Boy. Major's concern for the linguistic aspects of the black experience in the USA resulted in a *Dictionary of Afro-American Slang* (1970, published in the UK as *Black Slang*, 1971).

MALAMUD, Bernard
(1914–86)

American novelist, born in Brooklyn, New York, and educated at Columbia University, New York. He taught at Oregon State University (1949–61) and Bennington College (1961–86). One of the leading writers of contemporary America and among the 'urban-Jewish' Americans, he was more influenced by mainstream American writers than those ghettoized by their creed. *The Natural* (1952), his first novel, which used baseball as an extended metaphor for life, took as its starting point the mythic aspects of professional sport, and followed the fading career of the once-promising big-hitter Roy Hobbs. With *The Assistant* (1957) the mood was darker but the critical reception was warm. *A New Life* (1961) marked a new departure, from the compressed urban environment to mountainous western America, where Seymour Levin arrives at a small college to teach and analyse happiness. *The Fixer* (1966), set in Tsarist Russia, was his bleakest and most potent book, streaked with self-deprecating humour. He wrote four more novels: *Pictures of Fidelman* (1969); *The Tenants* (1971); *Dubin's Lives* (1979); and *God's Grace* (1982), a prophetic, apocalyptic allegory. He was also an accomplished short-story writer and *The Stories of Bernard Malamud* was published in 1983. He won the National Book Award twice, in 1959 and 1967, and the Pulitzer Prize in 1967.
▷J Helterman, *Understanding Malamud* (1985)

MALAPARTE, Curzio, pseud of Kurt Erich Suckert
(1898–1957)

Italian novelist and playwright, born in Prato, near Florence, to German–Italian parents. A liking for extreme politics dogged his life: in the 1920s, his attraction towards Fascism did not stretch to obeying the dictates of the Duce; in 1933 he received a five-year prison sentence, later commuted. A restless individual, he was a journalist and film-maker as well as a writer of fiction. *Kaputt*, a portrayal of a war-ravaged Europe first published in 1944, verges on nihilism, and is regarded as his best work. A later novel, *La pelle* (1949, 'The Skin'), draws on his experiences of Naples in 1944.

MALET, Lucas, pseud of Mary St Leger Kingsley
(1852–1931)

English novelist, daughter of **Charles Kingsley**. In 1876 she married the Rev W Harrison, rector of Clovelly, and as 'Lucas Malet' completed her father's *Tutor's Story* (1916) and wrote powerful novels, including *Mrs Lorimer* (1882), *Colonel Enderby's Wife* (1885), *The Wages of Sin* (1890), *The Carissima* (1896) and *Sir Richard Calmady* (1901). She became a Roman Catholic in 1899.

MALGONKAR, Manohar Dattatray
(1913–)

Indian novelist and short-story writer. A professional big-game hunter in his early twenties, he worked for the Indian government before taking a commission in the army, where he reached the rank of lieutenant-colonel. Between 1953 and 1959, he ran his own mining concern and stood as independent parliamentary candidate. His fiction is brightly coloured and romantic, with an emphasis on narrative action rather than psychological profundity. His first novel was *Distant Drum* (1960), but it was with his first British-published book, *Combat of Shadows* (1962), that he rose to prominence, fulfilling an appetite for stories of the Raj. *The Princes* (1963) and *A Bend in the Ganges* (1964) are more profound. Later novels include *The Garland Keepers* (1980) and *Bandicoot Run* (1982). Malgonkar's short fiction has been collected in a number of volumes, most notably *A Toast in Warm Wine* (1974) and *Bombay Beware* (1975). His non-fiction includes Indian social history and a perceptive study (1978) of Gandhi's assassins.
▷J Y Dayananda, *Manohar Malgonkar* (1974)

MALHERBE, François de
(1555–1628)

French poet, born in Caen. He ingratiated himself with Henri IV, and received a pension. He was an industrious writer, producing odes, songs, epigrams, epistles, translations and criticisms. He founded a literary tradition—'Enfin Malherbe vint'—and led his countrymen to disdain the richly-coloured and full-sounding verses of **Pierre de Ronsard**, and to adopt a style clear, correct and refined, but cold and prosaic.
▷R Fromilhague, *La vie de Malherbe* (1954)

MALLARMÉ, Stéphane
(1842–98)

French Symbolist poet, born in Paris. He taught English in various schools in Paris and elsewhere and visited England on several occasions. He translated **Edgar Allan Poe**'s

'The Raven' as 'Le Corbeau' (1875). In prose and verse he was a leader of the Symbolist school, revelling in allegory, obscurity, bizarre works and constructions, *vers libre* and word-music. *L'Après-midi d'un faune* ('A Faun's Afternoon'), illustrated by Manet (1876), is his best-known poem and made the wilful obscurity of his style famous. His *Les Dieux antiques* (1880, 'The Ancient Gods'), *Poésies* (1899) and *Vers et prose* (1893) were other works admired by the 'decadents'. He planned a work called his *Grand Oeuvre* which would represent the attainment of a pure poetic essence in a distilled, concentrated language, but completed only fragments of it.

▷H Mondor, *La vie de Mallarmé* (2 vols, 1941)

MALLEA, Edourdo
(1903–82)

Major Argentinian novelist, essayist and editor, born in Bahia Blanca, son of a humane and self-sacrificing country doctor who greatly influenced him. He was a key figure in the literature of his country; from 1931 he was literary editor of the newspaper *La Nación*. His ambition in his fiction was always to explore the essence of Argentina: his own statement to Angel Flores in the latter's *Spanish American Literature: The Twentieth Century* (1992) is most eloquent of this. But he was an inveterate traveller, and his books drew intelligently from European models, including **Chekhov**, **William Blake**, **Unamuno** and **Pérez de Ayala**. All he wrote is of high value — some find him a greater writer than the more politically ambiguous **Borges**. But, like Borges, he has been attacked by Marxists, most particularly by **Viñas**. Important books of his that have been translated include *Historia de una passión argentina* (1937, Eng trans *History of an Argentine Passion*, 1983) and *Todo verdor perecer* (1941, Eng trans *All Green Shall Perish and Other Novels and Stories*, 1966).

▷J H Richard, *The Writings of Edourdo Mallea* (1959); H E Lewald, *Edourdo Mallea* (1977)

MALLET, David, originally Malloch
(c.1705–1765)

Scottish poet, born near Crieff, Perthshire, the son of a schoolmaster. After a period working as the janitor at Edinburgh High School (1717–18), he studied at the university. In 1720 he became a tutor, working from 1723 to 1731 in the family of the Duke of Montrose. Living mostly in London, he changed his name 'from Scots Malloch to English Mallet'. *William and Margaret* (1723), developed from the fragment of an old ballad, gained him a reputation as a poet, which he

enhanced by *The Excursion* (1728). He also tried his hand at play-writing. *Mustapha* had a brief success in 1739; *Eurydice* (1731) and *Elvira* (1763), both tragedies, were failures. *Alfred, a Masque* (1740), was written in conjunction with **James Thomson**, and one of its songs, 'Rule Britannia', was claimed by both.

MALLET-JORIS, Françoise, pseud of Françoise Lilar
(1930–)

Belgian-born French novelist, she was born in Antwerp, and educated in the USA and at the Sorbonne. Her first novel, *Le Rempart des Béguines* (1950), appeared in the US as *The Illusionist* (1952) and in the UK as *Into the Labyrinth* (1957). Until the 1980s she was routinely translated, the translations often miscasting her vivaciously individual feminism as a sober intellectual stance rather than as a more instinctive reaction to social conditioning. Affected by existentialism, she is deeply concerned with personal authenticity, a theme that emerges strongly in *Les Mensonges* (1956, Eng trans *House of Lies*, 1957) and *L'Empire Céleste* (1958, Eng trans *Café Céleste*, 1959), for which she was awarded the prestigious Prix Femina. The autobiographical *Lettre à moi-même* (1963, Eng trans *A Letter to Myself*, 1964) traces her conversion to Roman Catholicism. Her later work is more conventional in approach. For many years she worked in publishing and as a songwriter; in 1973, she was elected President of the Académie **Goncourt**.

▷M Détry, *Mallet-Joris* (1976)

MALLIN, Tom
(1927–77)

English novelist, born in West Bromwich in the Midlands. Orphaned at four, he was educated at boarding school, and at Birmingham School of Art, winning a scholarship to the Royal Academy. Military service (1945–7) took him to the Middle East, after which he worked as a cartoonist, sculpting in his spare time. His first novel was *Dodecahedron* (1970), a remarkable debut for a 43-year-old. He published three other novels, *Knut* (1971), *Erowina* (1972) and *Lobe* (1977), all of them playful rather than 'experimental' fantasies. A fifth, *Bedrok*, was published posthumously.

▷Interview with Alan Burns in *The Imagination on Trial* (1981)

MALLOCK, William Hurrell
(1849–1923)

English novelist, born in Devon. His single famous book is the novel *The New Republic* (1877, of which it is necessary to refer to the

1975 edition by John Lucas, since this identifies the characters). *The New Republic* anticipates the New Right in its fanatic hatred of liberalism; but it is not incapable satire. It is a roman à clef in which the author ridicules such figures as **Matthew Arnold**, **Walter Pater**, T H Huxley and others. Lucas comments: 'Mallock is often outrageous, frequently silly ... But he is always readable ...'. He also describes *In An Enchanted Island* (1889), about Cyprus, as 'one of the best travel books ever written'.

▷A B Adams, *The Novels of Mallock* (1934)

MALMANCHE, Tanguy
(1875–1953)

French playwright, writing in Breton, who was an important figure in his minority literature after the early death of **Yann Ber Kalloc'h**. Most of his plays were translated into French. His masterpiece was *Gurvan le chevalier étranger* (1923, 'Gurvan, the Strange Knight'), a character about whom he wrote more plays. He has been compared both to **Claudel** and to **Synge**.

MALMBERG, Bertil
(1889–1958)

Swedish poet. Born in Härnösand, he published his first book of poetry in 1908, focusing contemporary Swedish Symbolism. From 1917 to 1926 he lived in Germany. The poems in *Orfika* (1923, 'Orphica') are characterized by elaborate metric forms which convey a far-reaching aestheticism shot through with feelings of guilt. *Dikter vid gränsen* (1935, 'Poems on the Border') is imbued with a profound, often Spenglerian pessimism, its formal expression inspired by myths and archetypes. The plainer, toned-down poems of the 1940s, for example in *Under månens fallande båge* (1947, 'Beneath the Falling Arc of the Moon'), show him as a modernist. *Åke och hans värld* (1924, 'Åke and His World') is a perceptive prose account of the development of a child.

▷I Algulin, *Tradition och modernism. Bertil Malmbergs och Hjalmar Gullbergs lyriska förnyelse efter 1940–talets mitt* (1969)

MALORY, Sir Thomas
(d.1471)

English writer. **Caxton**'s preface to Malory's masterpiece, the *Morte d'Arthur*, states that Malory was a knight, that he finished his work in the ninth year of the reign of Edward IV (1469–70), and that he 'reduced' it from some French book. It is probable that he was the Sir Thomas Malory of Newbold Revel, Warwickshire, whose quarrels with a neighbouring priory and (probably) Lancastrian

politics brought him imprisonment. Of Caxton's black-letter folio only two copies now exist. An independent manuscript was discovered at Winchester in 1934. *Morte d'Arthur* is the best prose romance in English and was a happy attempt to give epic unity to the whole mass of French Arthurian romance. **Tennyson**, **Swinburne** and many others took their inspiration from Malory.

▷S Johnson, in *Lives of the Most Eminent English Poets* (10 vols, 1779–81)

MALOUF, David
(1934–)

Australian novelist, born in Brisbane. His father's family came to Australia in the 1880s from Lebanon and his mother's from London just before World War I. He was educated at Brisbane Grammar School and Queensland University, where he subsequently taught for two years. He went abroad for a decade and returned to Australia, tutoring at Sydney University before leaving for Italy. A full-time writer since 1978, an early project was the libretto for an opera of **Patrick White**'s *Voss*. Previously concentrating on poetry, his first novel was *Johnno* (1975) and in 1979 he was awarded the New South Wales Premier's Literary Award for *An Imaginary Life* (1978), which had been serialized in the *New Yorker*. Other works include the novella *Fly Away Peter* (1982) and the novels *Harland's Half Acre* (1984), *Great World* (1991) and *Remembering Babylon* (1993). *Antipodes*, a collection of stories, appeared in 1985, and some of his poetry in *Poems 1959–1979* (1992). His most recent operatic collaboration was with composer Michael Berkeley in *Baa Baa Black Sheep*, taken from **Kipling**'s autobiographical story of that title, and premiered in 1993.

▷P Neilsen, *Imagined Lives: a study of the novels of David Malouf* (1990)

MALRAUX, André
(1901–76)

French writer, born in Paris. He studied oriental languages and spent much time in China, where he worked for the Kuomintang and was active in the 1927 revolution. He also fought as a pilot with the Republican forces in the Spanish Civil War, and in World War II he escaped from a prisoner-of-war camp to join the French resistance movement. He was Minister of Information in de Gaulle's government (1945–6), minister delegate from 1958 and Minister of Cultural Affairs (1960–9). He is best known for his novels, which are a dramatic meditation on human destiny and are highly coloured by his personal experience of war, revolution and resistance to tyranny. Among them are *Les Conquérants* (1928, Eng trans *The Conquerors*, 1929), *La Condition humaine* (1933, Eng trans *Man's*

Fate, 1934, winner of the Prix **Goncourt**) and *L'Espoir* (1937, Eng trans *Man's Hope*, 1938). He also wrote *La Psychologie de l'art* (1947, Eng trans *The Psychology of Art*, 1949), *Les Voix du silence* (4 vols, 1951, Eng trans in 4 vols *The Voices of Silence*', 1953), and other books on art and museums.
▷C Malraux, *Le bruit de nos pas* (3 vols, 1965–9); A Madsen, *Malraux* (1979)

MAMELI, Goffredo
(1827–49)

Italian poet and patriot, born in Genoa. He was a volunteer in Garibaldi's forces and wrote his patriotic poem *Fratelli d'Italia* ('Brothers of Italy'), which was adopted as the Italian national anthem in 1946. He died in the defence of Rome against the French. His other poetry is undistinguished.
▷A Viviani, *Mameli* (1937)

MAMET, David
(1947–)

American dramatist, screenplay writer and film director, born in Chicago. He graduated from Goddard College in Vermont and studied acting in New York. His plays, such as *American Buffalo* (1975), *Glengarry Glen Ross* (1983) and *Speed-the-Plow* (1988), address the psychological and ethical issues that confront modern, urban society, its professional superstructure and near-criminal substructure. His other plays include *Sexual Perversity in Chicago*, and *Duck Variations* (both 1976); *Reunion*, and *The Water Engine* (both 1977); *A Life in the Theater* (1978); *Edmond* (1982); and *The Shawl* (1985). He has translated plays by **Anton Chekhov**, and his screenplays include a new adaptation of *The Postman Always Rings Twice* (1981), and *The Untouchables* (1987). He wrote and directed *House of Games* (1987), a look at seedy professional gambling, and, with Shel Silverstein, *Things Change* (1988). He published a book of essays, *Writing in Restaurants*, in 1986.
▷C W E Bigsby, *David Mamet* (1985)

MANCHESTER, William
(1922–)

American novelist, foreign correspondent and contemporary historian, born in Attleboro, Massachusetts. His magnum opus is *The Death of a President* (1967), written at the behest of the Kennedy family. A landmark in reportage, it received mixed reviews and sold in millions but has subsequently been superseded as new evidence on the assassination of President Kennedy has emerged. Manchester has also written biographies of, among others, General Douglas MacArthur (1978) and **Winston Churchill** (1984–8).
▷*Controversy* (1976)

MANDEL, Eli
(1922–)

Canadian poet and critic, born in Estevan, Saskatchewan. Mandel is a poet in the so-called 'mythopoeic' tradition recommended by the Episcopalian critic-priest Northrop Frye. It has been said of him that had 'Carl Jung written poetry, he might have written some of Mandel's poems'; the remark is helpful in pointing to the nature of Mandel's achievement, which has been described as a 'bellweather of changing poetic fashion'. His vision of the future is summed up in his well-known lines: 'Notice: there will be no further communication/lectures are all cancelled/all students are expelled/the reading of poetry is declared a public crime'.
▷*Dreaming Backwards: Selected Poems 1954–1981* (1981); *Waves*, 10, no. 4 (1982)

MANDELSTAM, Nadezhda Yaklovlevna,
née **Khazina**
(1899–1980)

Russian writer and memoirist. Born in Kiev, she studied art and, following travel in Europe, worked as a translator. In 1919 she met the poet **Osip Mandelstam** and became his companion. Her main works were memoirs of him, known in English as *Hope Against Hope* (1970) and *Hope Abandoned* (1972, Eng trans 1974). After Osip's death in 1938, she lived largely in poverty, making a scant living by giving English lessons.

MANDELSTAM, Osip
(1891–1938)

Russian poet, critic and translator, born in Warsaw. He grew up in Leningrad and attended Heidelberg University. His wife was **Nadezhda Mandelstam**. A classicist whose Russian 'sounds like Latin', he had a fierce love of Greek poetry. Three books of poems appeared during his lifetime: *Kamen* (1913, Eng trans *Stone*, 1981), *Tristia* (1922) and *Stikhotvoreniya* (1928, 'Poems'). *Sobraniye sochineniy* (1964–71, Eng trans *The Complete Poetry*, 1973) was published in 1973. Regarded by some as the greatest Russian poet of the century, his life after the revolution was filled with pessimism for the future of Russia. Arrested, exiled and rearrested, he died of a heart attack on his way to one of Stalin's camps.
▷N Struve, *Osip Mandelstam* (1982)

MANDER, (Mary) Jane
(1877–1949)

New Zealand novelist, who spent much of her writing life in England and the USA. One of the last of the 'colonial' writers, her early novels, beginning with *The Story of a New Zealand River* (1920) and *The Passionate*

Puritan (1921), glory in the building of a new liberal society in her homeland, but frustration with puritan sentiments drove her abroad. Her last New Zealand novel was *Allen Adair* (1925); *The Besieging City* (1926) is set in New York and *Pins and Pinnacles* (1928) in London.

MANDEVILLE, Bernard
(1670–1733)

Dutch-born British satirist, born in Dort in Holland. He took his MD at Leiden in 1691, and immediately settled in London in medical practice. He is known as the author of a short work in doggerel verse originally entitled *The Grumbling Hive* (1705), and finally *The Fable of the Bees* (1723). Writing in a vein of acute paradox, he affirms that 'private vices are public benefits', and that every species of virtue is basically some form of gross selfishness, more or less modified. The book was condemned by the grand jury of Middlesex, and was attacked by William Law the nonjuror, by Berkeley, Warburton, Hutcheson and others. Other works arguing for an improvement in the status of women are *The Virgin Unmasked* (1709), *Free Thoughts on Religion* (1720), and *A Modest Defence of Public Stews* (1724), on the condition of brothels.
▷ J M Robertson, *Pioneer Humanists* (1907)

MANDEVILLE, Jehan de, or Sir John
(14th century)

The name assigned to the unknown compiler of a famous book of travels, *The Voyage and Travels of Sir John Mandeville, Knight*, published apparently in 1366, and soon translated from the French into all European tongues. It may have been written by a physician, Jehan de Bourgogne, otherwise Jehan á la Barbe, who died in Liège in 1372, and who is said to have revealed on his death-bed his real name of Mandeville (or Maundevylle), explaining that he had had to flee from his native England for a homicide. Some scholars, however, attribute it to Jean d'Outremeuse, a Frenchman. 'Mandeville' claims to have travelled through Turkey, Persia, Syria, Arabia, North Africa and India, but much of the book is a compilation from various literary sources.
▷ J W Bennett, *The Rediscovery of Sir Jehan Mandeville* (1954)

MANE, Mordecia Zevi
(1860–87)

Russian Hebrew poet and essayist, born near Vilno. The son of a poor teacher, by the time of his premature death he had demonstrated his originality and independence of his contemporaries: his nature poetry, which has been compared, for the quality of 'fright' in it, to the music of Schubert, is among the most accomplished and distinguished in the history of Russian Jewish literature.
▷ M Waxman, *A History of Jewish Literature* (1960)

MANFRED, Frederick
(1912–)

American novelist, born near Doon, Iowa and educated at Calvin College, Michigan. He has worked as a salesman, a reporter, and a writer-in-residence, and has twice received a National Endowment for the Arts grant (1976 and 1983). He wrote under the name 'Feike Feikeman' until 1951. Manfred's subject-matter is the American midwest, and his work is characterized by epic and autobiographical elements. His first novel, *The Golden Bowl* (1944), concerns two generations of farmers; *Boy Almighty*, written a year later, is an account of life in a midwestern tuberculosis sanitarium. He has written over 20 novels, but has received little critical acclaim—perhaps due to the narrowly midwestern focus of his work.
▷ R C Wright, *Frederick Manfred* (1979)

MANGAN, James Clarence
(1803–49)

Irish poet, born in Dublin, the son of a grocer. His life was a tragedy of hapless love, poverty and intemperance. He worked as a lawyer's clerk, and later found employment in the library of Trinity College, Dublin. There is fine quality in his original verse. Although he knew no Irish, he published English versions of Irish poems in *The Poets and Poetry of Munster* (1849), notably 'My Dark Rosaleen', 'The Nameless One' and 'The Woman of Three Cows'. He also published translations from German poets in *Anthologia Germanica* (1845).
▷ D J O'Donaghue, *The Life and Writings of James Clarence Mangan* (1897)

MANGAN, (John Joseph) Sherry
(1904–61)

Radical American poet and journalist, he claimed to be a great nephew of the Irish poet **James Clarence Mangan**. Born in Lynn, Massachusetts, he graduated from Harvard in 1925 and in 1927 founded the fashionably lower-case *larus: The Celestial Visitor*, a short-lived little magazine in which he published his own verse and that of others. Gradually radicalized, he moved away from his own earlier aestheticism and collaborated on a poetry series 'Vanguard Verse' with his friend **John Wheelwright**. He also wrote international socialist propaganda under a number of Irish aliases, and was sent to Europe as a US delegate to the Fourth International.

His most important verse is collected in the volume *No Apology for Poetrie* (1934). For a period he maintained dual identities as a mainstream journalist and Trotskyist cadre, but in 1943 he was appointed *Life*'s head in Europe. Largely forgotten, he came to notice again with a revival of academic interest in the American far left that came, paradoxically, with the Reagan years.

▷A M Wald, *The Revolutionary Imagination* (1983)

MANIFOLD, John Streeter
(1915–85)

Australian poet and collector of folk-songs, born in Melbourne of a pioneering pastoral family. Educated at Cambridge University where he joined the Communist Party, he served during World War II with the British Intelligence Corps. His first collection was *Verses 1930–1933* (1933). On his return to Australia he published *Selected Poems* (1947) and *Nightmares and Sunhorses* (1961), but his interest in folk songs and ballads was evinced in *Bandicoot Ballads* (1953), followed by a number of books on folk music and verse. He is probably best known for editing the *Penguin Australian Song Book* (1964), but *Who Wrote the Ballads? Notes on Australian Folksong* (1964) is a scholarly appraisal of an important area in Australian literature. His academic interest in music is well demonstrated in two unjustly neglected earlier books, *Music in English Drama from Shakespeare to Purcell* and *Music of the Elizabethan Stage* (1964).

MANILIUS, Marcus
(fl.early 1st century)

Roman poet who wrote the *Astronomica*, a didactic poem on astrology, in five books, amounting to some 4500 lines. Nothing is known of his life except that he was working in the reigns of Augustus and Tiberius. His writing sometimes achieves eloquence but is often weighed down by the demands of technical and mathematical instruction. The poem is of some interest as the most substantial extant work by a contemporary of **Ovid**, but chiefly because it engaged half a lifetime's attention from **A E Housman**, the outstanding Latinist of the early 20th century, whose edition appeared in 1903–30.

MANKIEWICZ, Herman Jacob
(1897–1953)

American screenwriter, born in New York. A member of the United States Marine Corps, he later worked in Europe for the Red Cross Press Service, as Isadora Duncan's publicity manager and as Berlin correspondent for the *Chicago Tribune*. Returning to the USA in 1922, he was Assistant Drama Editor for the *New York Times* (1922–6) and wrote his first screenplay for *The Road To Mandalay* (1926). A prolific writer, he was also much in demand as a script doctor and in addition was the producer of a number of films, including the Marx Brothers comedies *Horse Feathers* (1932) and *Duck Soup* (1933). A member of the Algonquin Round Table set and a frequent contributor to the *New Yorker*, he was once dubbed 'The Central Park West Voltaire' and the move to Hollywood was widely seen as the prostituting of a fine, witty literary talent. His most significant contribution to the cinema came as the co-writer of Orson Welles' *Citizen Kane* (1941), for which he received an Oscar. Other credited screenplays include *The Royal Family of Broadway* (1930), *Dinner At Eight* (1933), *It's A Wonderful World* (1939) and *The Enchanted Cottage* (1946). His brother was the writer-director Joseph L Mankiewicz (1909–93).

MANKOWITZ, (Cyril) Wolf
(1924–)

English author, playwright and antique dealer, born in Bethnal Green, London. An authority on Wedgwood, he published *Wedgwood* (1953) and *The Portland Vase* (1953), and was an editor of *The Concise Encyclopedia of English Pottery and Porcelain* (1957). Other publications include the novels *Make Me an Offer* (1952) and *A Kid for Two Farthings* (1953), and a collection of short stories, *The Mendelman Fire* (1957). Among his plays is *The Bespoke Overcoat* (1954), and his films, *The Millionairess* (1960), *The Long, The Short, and the Tall* (1961), *Casino Royale* (1967) and *The Hebrew Lesson* (1972), as well as his documentary on Yiddish cinema, *Almonds and Raisins* (1984).

MANLEY, Mary de la Rivière
(c.1672–1724)

British writer, born in Jersey, the daughter of a future governor of Jersey. After her father's death (1688) she was lured into a bigamous marriage with her cousin, John Manley of Truro, MP, who soon deserted her. She went to England, where she had a success with the publication of her letters. In 1696 she wrote two plays, *The Lost Lover* and *The Royal Mischief*. She wrote gossipy chronicles disguised as fiction, especially the scandalous anti-Whig *The New Atalantis* (1709). In 1711 she succeeded **Jonathan Swift** as editor of *The Examiner*. She wrote a fictional account of her own early struggles in *The Adventures of Rivella* (1714). Her last work was *The Power of Love, in Seven Novels* (1720).

▷*Letters Written by Mrs Manley* (1696)

MANN, Heinrich
(1871–1950)

German novelist, brother of **Thomas Mann**, born in Lübeck. He began to be described as the German **Zola** for his ruthless exposure of pre-1914 German society in *Im Schlaraffenland* (1901, Eng trans *Berlin, the Land of Cockaigne*, 1925), and the trilogy describing the three classes of Kaiser Wilhelm II's empire, *Die Armen* (1917, 'The Poor'), *Der Untertan* (1918, 'The Subject') and *Der Kopf* (1929, 'The Head'). He is best known for the macabre, Expressionist novel, *Professor Unrat* (1904, 'Professor Nonsense'), describing the moral degradation of a once outwardly respectable schoolmaster, which was translated and filmed as *The Blue Angel* (1932). He lived in France (1933–40) and then escaped to the USA. Other works include *Die kleine Stadt* (1901, 'The Little Town'), set in a small Italian town, and a remarkable autobiography, *Ein Zeitalter wird besichtigt* (1945–6, 'Exposition of an Era'). His influence is noticeable on **Jakob Wasserman** and **Lion Feuchtwanger**.
▷R N Lina, *Heinrich Mann* (1967)

MANN, Leonard
(1895–1981)

Australian novelist and poet, born in Toorak, Melbourne. His service in France during World War I resulted in the powerful novel *Flesh in Armour* (1932), with its strong imagery of men and battles. Six more novels followed, of which the last, *Venus Half-Caste* (1963), was an early portrayal of mixed race conflict in Australia, and typified Mann's social realism. This was more muted in his verse, the first collection of which was *The Plumed Voice* (1938) followed by *The Delectable Mountains* (1944) and *Elegiac and Other Poems* (1957).

MANN, Thomas
(1875–1955)

German novelist and winner of the Nobel Prize for literature, brother of **Heinrich Mann**, born into a patrician family of merchants and senators of the Hanseatic city of Lübeck. His mother was a talented musician of mixed German and Portuguese West Indian blood. The opposition between a conservative business outlook and artistic inclinations, the clash between Nordic and Latin temperaments inherent in his own personality, and the Schopenhauerian doctrine of art being the self-abnegation of the will as the end product of decay, were to form his subject-matter. At the age of 19, without completing school, he settled with his mother in Munich, and after dabbling at the university, he joined his brother in Italy, where he wrote his early masterpiece, *Buddenbrooks: Verfall einer Familie* (1901, Eng trans *Buddenbrooks: The Decline of a Family*, 1924), the saga of a family like his own, tracing its decline through four generations, as business acumen gives way to artistic sensibilities. At the age of 25 he thus became a leading German writer. On his return to Munich he became reader for the satirical literary magazine, *Simplicissimus*, which published many of his early, remarkable short stories. The novelettes *Tonio Kröger* (1902, Eng trans 1928), *Tristan* (1903, Eng trans 1928) and *Der Tod in Venedig* (1912, Eng trans *Death in Venice*, 1925), all deal with the problem of the artist's salvation, positively in the case of the first, who resembles **Goethe**'s Werther, negatively in the last, in which a successful writer dies on the brink of perverted eroticism. World War I precipitated a quarrel between the two novelist brothers, Thomas's *Betrachtungen eines Unpolitischen* (1918, Eng trans *Reflections of a Nonpolitical Man*, 1983) revealing his militant German patriotism, already a feature of his essay on Frederick the Great (1915) and a distrust of political ideologies, including the radicalism of his brother. *Der Zauberberg* (1924, Eng trans *The Magic Mountain*, 1927) won him the Nobel Prize for literature in 1929. It was inspired by a visit to his wife at a sanatorium for consumptives in Davos in 1913 and tells the story of such a patient, Hans Castorp, with the sanatorium representing Europe in its moral and intellectual disintegration. The same year, Mann delivered a speech against the rising Nazis and exposed Italian fascism in *Mario und der Zauberer* (1930, Eng trans *Mario and the Magician*, 1930). He left Germany for Switzerland after 1933 and in 1936 delivered an address for **Freud**'s eightieth birthday. Both shared an enthusiasm for the biblical patriarch, Joseph, and Mann wrote a tetralogy of novels on his life, *Joseph und seine Brüder* (1933–43, Eng trans *Joseph and his Brothers*, 1934–44). He settled in the USA in 1936 and wrote a novel on a visit to Goethe by an old love, Charlotte Buff, *Lotte in Weimar* (1939, Eng trans 1940). His anti-Hitler broadcasts to Germany were collected under the titles *Achtung Europa!* (1938) and *Deutsche Hörer!* (1942, Eng trans *Listen Germany! Twenty-Five Messages to the German People over the BBC*, 1943; augmented edn of 55 messages, 1945). In 1947 he returned to Switzerland and was the only returning exile to be fêted by both West and East Germany. His greatest work, a modern version of the medieval legend, *Doktor Faustus* (1947, Eng trans *Doctor Faustus*, 1948), combines art and politics in the simultaneous treatment of the life and catastrophic end of a composer, Adrian Leverkühn, and German disintegration in two

world wars. His last, unfinished work, hailed as Germany's greatest comic novel, *Bekenntnisse des Hochstaplers Felix Krull* (1922; 1953, Eng trans *Confessions of Felix Krull, Confidence Man*, 1955), written with astonishing wit, irony and humour and without the tortuous stylistic complexities of the *Bildungsroman*, commended itself most to English translators. Essentially a 19th-century German conservative, whose cultural landmarks vanished in World War I, he was compelled towards a critique of the artistic. Ambivalently the artist and the bourgeois fearer of bohemianism, the unpolitical man with political duties, he was a brilliant storyteller in the classical German tradition, whose subject-matter was paradoxically the end of that tradition. Other later works include *Der Erwählte* (1951, Eng trans *The Holy Sinner*, 1951), *Die Betrogene* (1953, Eng trans *The Black Swan*, 1954) and *Last Essays* (1959), on **Schiller**, Goethe, **Nietzsche** and **Anton Chekhov**.
▷H Hatfield, *Thomas Mann* (1951)

MANNER, Eeva-Liisa
(1921–)
Finnish poet, dramatist and writer of fiction, born in Helsinki, and a leading figure in postwar modernism. Her earlier poetry was traditional, but later she turned to free verse and themes reminiscent of **T S Eliot**, and so began to attract attention.

MANNERKORPI, Juha
(1915–)
Finnish novelist, translator (**Sartre, Camus**) and poet, who was born in Ohio, USA, the son of a parson. He is a successful radio playwright in his own country. Although he is thought highly of for his terse, suggestive style, he has not produced any major work.

MANNIN, Ethel
(1900–84)
English novelist, travel and short-story writer, born in London, of Irish ancestry. Her early works include *Venetian Blinds* (1933), a novel set in working-class south London around World War I. She wrote over 40 novels, of which *Red Rose* (1941), based on the life of the anarchist Emma Goldman, most closely reflects her own concerns. Her commitment to the far left is evident in such works of non-fiction as *Women and the Revolution* (1938) and *Rebels' Ride* (1964). She travelled widely, and wrote several books on the Middle East (such as *A Lance For The Arabs*, 1963) as well as volumes on Germany, Burma and Japan.

MANNING, Olivia
(1908–80)
English novelist, born in Portsmouth, the daughter of a naval officer. Much of her youth was spent in Ireland and she had 'the usual Anglo-Irish sense of belonging to nowhere'. She trained at art school, and then went to London, and published her first novel, *The Wind Changes*, in 1937. She married in 1939 and went abroad with her husband, Reggie Smith, a British Council lecturer in Bucharest. Her experiences there formed the basis of her Balkan trilogy, comprising *The Great Fortune* (1960), *The Spoilt City* (1962) and *Friends and Heroes* (1965). As the Germans approached Athens, she and her husband evacuated to Egypt and ended up in Jerusalem. She returned to London in 1946, where she resided until her death. A prolific author, her publications include *Artist Among the Missing* (1949), *School for Love* (1951), *A Different Face* (1953), and her Levant Trilogy, comprising *The Danger Tree* (1977), *The Battle Lost and Won* (1978) and *The Sum of Things* (1980). The Balkan Trilogy and the Levant Trilogy form a single narrative entitled *Fortunes of War* which **Anthony Burgess** described as 'the finest fictional record of the war produced by a British writer'.
▷K Dick, *Friends and Friendship* (1974)

MANNYNG, Robert, also known as **Robert of Brunne**
(d.c.1338)
English chronicler and poet, born in Bourne in Lincolnshire. In 1288 he entered the nearby Gilbertine monastery of Sempringham. His chief work is *Handlynge Synne* (c.1303), a free and amplified translation into English rhyming couplets of the *Manuel des Pechiez* of William of Wadington. It is a landmark in the transition from early to later Middle English, and a colourful picture of contemporary life. He also composed a rhyming translation of **Robert Wace**'s *Brut d'Angleterre*, with a translation from French of a rhyming chronicle, *The Story of Ingeland*, by the Augustinian canon, Peter Langtoft.
▷R Crosby, *Robert Mannyng of Brunne: a new biography* (1942)

MANRIQUE, Jorge
(1440–79)
Spanish poet, born of a noble family in Paredes de la Nava. He is best remembered for his fine elegy on his father's death, *Coplas por la muerte de su padre* ('Verses for the Death of his Father'). He also wrote love-songs, satires and acrostic verses, and was killed in the Civil Wars of the period.

▷A Serraro de Hero, *Personalidad y destino de Jorge Manrique* (1966)

MANSFIELD, Katherine, pseud of Kathleen Mansfield Beauchamp
(1888–1923)

New Zealand short-story writer, born in Wellington, the daughter of a successful businessman. Educated at Queen's College, London, she returned to New Zealand for two years to study music, and left again for London in 1908, determined to pursue a literary career. She lived on the breadline and like a bohemian and met, married and left her first husband, George Bowden, in the space of three weeks. Finding herself pregnant (not by her husband) she was installed by her mother in a hotel in Bavaria, but she miscarried. The experience bore fruit in the stories collected in *In A German Pension* in 1911, most of which had previously appeared in *The New Age*. That same year she met **John Middleton Murry**, and thereafter her work began to surface in Murry's *Rhythm*. From 1912 the couple lived together (they did not marry until 1918), mingling with the literati, particularly **D H Lawrence**, who portrayed them as Gudrun and Gerald in *Women in Love*. In 1916, she and Murry founded the short-lived magazine *Signature*, but she began to suffer from tuberculosis which precipitated her premature death. Her first major work was *Prelude* (1917), a recreation of the New Zealand of her childhood. *Bliss, and other stories* (1920), containing the classic stories 'Je ne parle pas francais' and 'Prelude', confirmed her standing as an original and innovative writer, named in company with **Anton Chekhov** despite the backstabbing of her near-contemporary, **Virginia Woolf**. The only other collection published before her death at Fontainebleau was *The Garden Party, and other stories* (1922). Her other collections are *The Dove's Nest and Other Stories* (1923) and *Something Childish and Other Stories* (1924, published in the USA as *The Little Girl and Other Stories*, 1924). *The Letters of Katherine Mansfield*, edited by Murry, appeared in 1928 and *Katherine Mansfield's Letters to John Middleton Murry 1913–1922*, detailing the couple's stormy but tender relationship punctuated by lengthy separations, in 1951. **Vincent O'Sullivan** edited a selection, *Poems of Katherine Mansfield* (1988), and her work for the theatre was collected in *Katherine Mansfield: Dramatic Sketches* (1988).
▷A Alpers, *The Life of Katherine Mansfield* (1980)

MANTU, Saadat Hasan
(1912–55)

The leading Urdu short-story writer of his time. He was also a prolific translator. His stories, some of which are collected in *Black Milk* (1955), often led him into the law courts.

MANZONI, Alessandro
(1785–1873)

Italian novelist and poet, born in Milan of a noble family. He went to Paris from 1805 to 1807, published his first poems in 1806, married happily in 1810, and spent the next few years in writing sacred lyrics and a treatise on the religious basis of morality. But the work which gave him European fame is his historical novel, *I promessi sposi* (1827, Eng trans *The Betrothed Lovers*, 1828), a Milanese story of the 17th century, and the most notable novel in Italian literature. Despite his Catholic devoutness, he was a strong advocate of a united Italy, and became a senator of the kingdom in 1860.
▷A Colquhoun, *Manzoni and His Times* (1954)

MAO DUN, pseud of Shen Yanbing
(1896–1981)

Chinese writer, born in Wuzhen, Zhejiang Province. Educated at Beijing University, he became one of the foremost left-wing intellectuals and writers in China. In 1920 he was a founder-member of the Literary Research Society, and was Editor of the *Short Story Monthly* (1921–3). Moving to Shanghai, he taught a course of fiction at Shanghai College, and became editor of the Hankow National Daily. In 1926 he joined the Northern Expedition as a propagandist, but had to go underground in Shanghai as a communist activist. He wrote a trilogy of novellas, published as *Shih* (1930, 'Eclipse'), and a bestselling novel, *Ziye* (1932, 'Midnight'), about financial exploiters in the decadent Shanghai of the time. His other major works were *Hong* ('Rainbow'), and a collection of short stories in *Spring Silkworms*. In 1930 he helped to organize the influential League of Left-Wing Writers. After the communists came to power in 1949 he was China's first Minister of Culture (1949–65), and was founder-editor of the literary journal *People's Literature* (1949–53). During the Cultural Revolution he was kept under house arrest in Beijing (1966–78).
▷M Galik, *Mao Tun and Modern Chinese Literary Criticism* (1969)

MAP, or MAHAP or MAPES, Walter
(c.1137–1209)

Ecclesiastic and writer, sometimes said to have been a Welshman, probably a native of Herefordshire. Of noble stock, he studied at Paris, became a clerk to Henry II of England, went on a mission to Rome, and became canon of St Paul's and archdeacon of Oxford (1197). Although famous in his day as a writer and wit, the only work which can be attributed to him with certainty is the satirical miscellany *De Nugis Curialum* ('Of Courtier's Trifles') a collection of anecdotes and reflections, and tales gleaned from history, romance and gossip.

▷T Wright, *Latin Poems Commonly Attributed to Walter Map* (1879)

MAPU, Abraham
(1808–67)

Hebrew novelist, born in Slobodka-Kovna. A member of the Haskalah ('the Enlightenment', the 18th- and 19th-century Jews who sought to acquire European culture), and Cabalist, he was the author of the first truly original Hebrew novel. He was so learned at a young age that he earned the rare soubriquet of 'Illuy'—a 'phenomenon'. This was justified, for, after learning several European languages, he published *Ahavat Zion* (1853, Eng trans *Amnon, Prince and Peasant*, 1887; *The Days of Isaiah*, 1902), a historical novel of the times of Isaiah; this, although influenced by French romanticism, like his second great novel *Ashmat Shomron* (1865), is vivid and wholly free from didacticism. Because of Mapu's Cabalistic involvements, both novels—and a third somewhat undervalued one, set in contemporary times—carry profound hidden meanings, which have not yet, however, been openly discussed.

▷D Patterson, *Abraham Mapu* (1964)

MÁRAI, Sandor
(1900–)

Influential Hungarian novelist and essayist, born in Kassa. Upon the advent of communism in his country he left for exile in Italy. His *Egy polgár vallomásai* (1934, 'Confessions of a Bourgeois') is a key novel of its period. While, like **Thomas Mann**'s *Buddenbrooks*, it never sentimentalizes its subject, it finds within it no less dignity than any other kind of society. Márai felt that the most civilized values could be preserved by quiet defence of the existence of the bourgeoisie. An eclectic, he was influenced by writers as diverse as **Cocteau**, **Duhamel** and **Mallarmé**. His style became famous, and was much admired; but in later work, such as his journal, *Napló: 1957–1957* (1958) and his memoirs *Föld ... föld* (1972), his style became more precious.

MARAN, René
(1887–1960)

Caribbean-born African novelist, born in Martinique (but of Black parents from French Guinea). He wrote in French, and was perhaps the most influential of all the earlier writers of the modern African novel. Long before Colin Turnbull's *The Mountain People*

(1972) gave its famous description of the Ik of Uganda, Maran had shown imaginatively, in his masterpiece, *Batoula* (1921, translated in the following year), which won the Prix **Goncourt**, just how such a society could come into existence. This was also the first novel, as has been said, 'to portray Negroes as Negroes, and not as white men in blackface'. Maran wrote many more exotic and worthy books, but became disillusioned and could not repeat the success of his first. Ultimately he felt more concerned with Africa than with the Caribbean.

▷W Cartey, *Whispers from a Continent* (1969)

MARC, Ausias
(1397–1459)

Catalan poet, the last great medieval writer in the language and the first major one to use only Catalan. Marc is an example of a figure of undeniably high international stature being lost to the majority of readers through linguistic ignorance. All his 128 poems, divided into cycles (of love and death) are intensely individual, and amount to a passionate and profound examination of the concept of courtly love, of which he was critical, but which he tried to purify by stripping it of formalities and hyperbole, in order to concentrate upon the precise truth. He has been translated at least twice into Castilian, but not yet into English. His influence was wide, as much on Castilian as on later Catalan poetry.

▷A Terry, *Catalan Literature* (1972)

MARCABRU
(fl.1140)

Troubadour from Gascony, and one of the most influential. Details of his life are sketchy and have to be inferred from his songs, but he seems to have found employment in many royal houses, including that of Alfonso VII of Castile, by virtue of his great poetic and musical skill. His verse is usually about courtly love and contains highly complex language and inventive imagery. He lived a colourful life, and his memory and reputation were revered by subsequent troubadours. One version of his life story has it that he was eventually murdered by someone who objected to the way Marcabru had portrayed him in a song. There is no way of knowing whether this is true, but it is a tribute to the power of his work.

MARCEAU, Félicien, pseud of Albert Carette
(1913–92)

Belgian-born French writer. As Carette, Marceau served as a broadcaster in Brussels during World War II, and was sentenced to prison for it. He escaped and changed his name and nationality, becoming a successful and shrewd popular novelist and playwright. His first success was the satirical play *L'Oeuf* (1956, Eng trans *The Egg*, 1958), on the theme of society's hypocrisy. Among his many novels *Les Élans du Coeur* (1955, Eng trans *The Flutterings of the Heart*, 1957), an account of a provincial family in decline, is the most substantial. He was elected to the Académie française in 1975, amid protests during which he maintained that he had been cleared of actual Nazidom in 1962.

MARCEL, Gabriel Honoré
(1889–1973)

French existentialist philosopher and dramatist, born in Paris. He was a Red Cross Worker in World War I but made his living thereafter as a freelance writer, teacher, editor and critic. In 1929 he became a Catholic and came reluctantly to accept the label 'Christian Existentialist', partly in order to contrast his views with those of **Jean-Paul Sartre**. He emphasized the importance and possibility of 'communication' between individual people, as well as between themselves and God, but was suspicious of all philosophical abstractions and generalizations which misrepresented the freedom, uniqueness and particularity of human individuals. He was not himself a system-builder and his philosophical works tend to have a personal, meditative character, as in *Journal métaphysique* (1927, Eng trans *Metaphysical Journal*, 1952), *Être et avoir* (1935, Eng trans *Being and Having*, 1949), *Le Mystère de l'être* (1951, Eng trans *The Mystery of Being*, 1951), *Les Hommes contre l'humain* (1951, Eng trans *Men Against Humanity*, 1952) and *L'Homme problématique* (1955, Eng trans *Problematic Man*, 1967). His plays include *Un Homme de Dieu* (1925, 'A Man of God'), *Le Monde Cassé* (1933, 'The Broken World'), *Ariadne: Le Chemin de Crête* (1936, Eng trans *Ariadne*, 1952) and *La Dimension Florestan* (1956, 'The Florestan Dimension').
▷S Keen, *Gabriel Marcel* (1967)

MARCH, Auziàs
(1397–1459)

Catalan poet, born in Valencia. He was pioneer of the trend away from the lyricism of the troubadours towards a more metaphysical approach. Influenced by Italian models, he wrote chiefly on the themes of love and death.
▷A Pagès, *Auziàs March et ses prédécesseurs* (1912)

MARCH, William, pseud of W E M Campbell
(1893–1954)

American novelist and story writer, born in Mobile, Alabama. His best, and now perhaps neglected novel, is his last, *The Bad Seed* (1954), which was dramatized by **Maxwell Anderson** and played on Broadway with great success. The gripping and convincingly told story of a little girl who is a mass murderess, it is in essence a fable almost as persuasive as **William Golding**'s *Lord of the Flies*. When it was made into a movie the audience had to be assured, at the end, that it could not really be true. March also wrote *Company K* (1933) and *The Little Wife* (1935), a **Faulkner**esque novel, set in Mobile. His best stories are in *Some Like Them Short* (1939). His fiction is overdue for critical reappraisal.
▷A Cooke (ed), *A William March Omnibus* (1956, with an introduction)

MARCHWITZA, Hans
(1890–1965)

German novelist, born in Scharley in Silesia. An early member of the KPD, the communist party which was banned by the Nazis but then took power after World War II, Marchwitza's trilogy about miners, the first volume of which is *Die Kumiaks* (1934), became officially approved reading in the German Democratic Republic (the former East Germany). His work, however, has little artistic value. *Meine Jugend* (1947, 'My Youth') was an autobiographical novel.

MARDEKAR, B S
(1905–56)

Indian (Marathi) poet who was influenced by **T S Eliot**'s *Prufrock*, but who never found a worthy English translator.

MARECHAL, Leopoldo
(1900–70)

Argentinian novelist, poet, dramatist and essayist, born in Buenos Aires. Because he was one of the few writers to collaborate with Perón—and thus gain high official posts—he was for some time eschewed by critics; but the importance of his work, much of it experimental, is now more frequently canvassed. He is usually described today as of 'major significance'. He began as a socialist and an *ultraista* poet, but turned to the novel when he could no longer, as he maintained, 'translate his life experiences into poetry'. His poetry is not now much discussed (one of his most sonorous poems is translated in *An Anthology of Contemporary Latin-American Poetry*, 1942, ed Dudley Fitts). His major work, derived from **Joyce**'s *Ulysses* and based on **Dante**'s *Inferno*, is the novel *Adán Buenosayres* (1948). This records an imaginary journey undertaken by Marechal (Adam) around Buenos Aires, and ends in a confrontation with Christ. Later works include *Heptameron* (1965). The work of Marechal, owing to lack of translations, has not yet been tested in the light of world opinion—but of his importance in Argentinian literature there can be no doubt.

▷ *Papers on French, Luso-Brazilian, Spanish-American Relations* (1970)

MARECHERA, Dambudzo
(?1954–)

Zimbabwean novelist and short-story writer of strikingly original vision, whose work is set against anti-colonial struggle and internecine conflict. Little is known about his early life and career, but he attended the University of Rhodesia in Harare (from which he was sent down in 1974 for unspecified opposition activities) and, more briefly, New College, Oxford. His first published work was *The House of Hunger* (1978, Guardian Fiction Prize), a novella and group of short stories which portray the struggle for independence as a brutal Darwinian opposition of tribalist loyalties and antagonisms. This was followed in 1980 by a novel, *Black Sunlight*, in which a press-photographer (ironically named Christian) documents a hellish slough of terrorism and violence, his cool journalistic detachment gradually unravelling as the plot descends into horror. Despite being one of the most significant figures of the highly touted new African writing 'movement' of this period, Marechera suffered disproportionately during the inevitable backlash.

▷ D Caute, *The Espionage of the Saints* (1986)

MARGARET OF ANGOULÊME, also
known as **Margaret of Navarre**
(1492–1549)

Queen of Navarre, and one of the most brilliant women of her age. The sister of Francis I of France, she married first the Duke of Alençon (d.1525) and then, in 1527, Henry d'Albret (titular King of Navarre), to whom she bore Jeanne d'Albret, mother of Henri IV of France. Margaret had from her youth a strong interest in Renaissance learning, and was much influenced by **Erasmus** and the religious reformers of the Meaux circle, who looked to her for patronage and protection. Although she remained a Roman Catholic, she was also influenced by the writings of Luther, with which she had a certain sympathy. She encouraged agriculture, learning and the arts, and her court was the most intellectual in Europe. The patron of men of letters, including the heretical poet **Clément Marot**, she herself was a prolific writer. Her works included long devotional poems published as *Le Miroir de l'âme Pécheresse* (1531, 'The Mirror of a Sinner's Soul') and *Les Marguerites de la Marguerite des princesses* (1547, 'The Daisies of Princess Marguerite'), the

shorter *Chansons religieuses* ('Religious Songs'), dramas, and the secular poem *La Coche* ('The Coach'); her last works, written at the end of her life in some mental anguish, were found and published in 1895 as *Les Dernières poésies* ('The Last Poems'). Her most celebrated work was *Heptaméron*, a collection of stories on the theme of love, modelled upon the *Decameron* of **Boccaccio**.

▷ L Febvre, *Autour de L'Heptaméron* (1944)

MARGARET OF NAVARRE *see*
MARGARET OF ANGOULÊME

MARGUERITTE, Paul
(1860–1918)
MARGUERITTE, Victor
(1866–1942)

French novelists, born in Algeria. They wrote in collaboration or separately novels and histories, many dealing with the Franco–German war period, such as the series *Une Époque* (1898–1904).

▷ S Barreaux, *Paul et Victor Margueritte* (1909)

MARIE DE FRANCE
(fl.c.1160–90)

French poet, born in Normandy. She spent much of her life in England, where she wrote her *Lais* sometime before 1167 and her *Fables* sometime after 1170. She translated into French the *Tractatus de Purgatorio Sancti Patricii* (c.1190, 'St Patricius's Treatise on Purgatory') and her works contain many classical allusions. The *Lais*, her most important work, dedicated to 'a noble king', probably Henry II of England, comprises 14 romantic narratives in octosyllabic verse based on Celtic material. A landmark in French literature, they influenced a number of later writers.

▷ H Hoepffner, *Les lais de Marie de France* (1935)

MARINETTI, Emilio Filippo Tommaso
(1876–1944)

Italian writer, born in Alexandria, one of the founders of Futurism. He studied in Paris and Genoa, and published the original Futurist manifesto in *Figaro* in 1909. In his writings he glorified war, the machine age, speed and 'dynamism', and in 1919 he became a fascist. His publications include *Le Futurisme* (1911), *Teatro sintetico futurista* (1916, 'The Synthetic Futurist Theatre') and *Manifesti del Futurismo* (4 vols, 1920, 'Manifesto of Futurism'). He condemned all traditional forms of literature and art, and his ideas were applied to painting by Boccioni, Balla and others.

▷ W Vaccari, *Vita e tumulti di Filippo Tommaso Marinetti* (1959)

MARINKOVIĆ, Ranko
(1913–)

Croatian novelist, satirist, story writer and dramatist, born on the island of Vis. He had intimate connections with the Croatian National Theatre. He published his early short stories, still regarded as the genre in which he works most effectively, in Krleža's journal *Pecat*. His best-known and most discussed work is the novel *Kiklop* (1965, 'Cyclops'), an over-complex work that yet has vivid passages, is studded with knowing literary allusions, and is remarkable for its portrait of an individual caught up in and destroyed by the toils of the city (Zagreb just before World War II).
▷A Kadić, *From Croatian Renaissance to Yugoslav Socialism* (1969)

MARINO, or MARINI, Giambattista
(1569–1625)

Italian poet, born in Naples. He was ducal secretary at Turin, and wrote his best work, the *Adone* (1622), at the court of France. His principal gift lies in his ability to conjure up rich and evocative descriptions of nature and the external world, but he shows no great insight into the human heart. His florid hyperbole and overstrained imagery were copied by the Marinist school.
▷J V Mirollo, *The Poet of the Marvellous* (1963)

MARION, Frances, originally Frances Marion Owens
(1887–1973)

American screenwriter and novelist, born in San Francisco. A reporter with the *San Francisco Examiner*, she had worked as a commercial artist and model before arriving in Hollywood in 1913 as the protégé of director Lois Weber. A prolific screenwriter during the silent era, she was associated with actress Mary Pickford on such films as *Rebecca Of Sunnybrook Farm* (1918) and *Pollyanna* (1920). One of the first female war correspondents during the latter stages of World War I, she also directed such films as *Just Around The Corner* (1921) and *The Love Light* (1921). Adept at heart-tugging melodrama, hard-bitten adventure yarns and epic romances, she was also much praised for her skilled adaptations of *Stella Dallas* (1925), *The Scarlet Letter* (1926) and *The Wind* (1928). Surviving the transition to sound, she wrote star vehicles for the likes of Greta Garbo and Jean Harlow and received Academy Awards for *The Big House* (1930) and *The Champ* (1931). She retired from screenwriting in 1940 and subsequently wrote such novels as *Westward The Dream* (1948) and *The Powder Keg* (1954).
▷*Off With Their Heads!* (1972)

MARIVAUX, Pierre Carlet de Chamblain de
(1688–1763)

French playwright and novelist, born in Paris of a good Norman family. He published *L'Homère travesti* ('Homer Burlesqued'), a burlesque of the *Iliad*, in 1716, and from then on wrote several comedies, of which his best is *Le Jeu de l'amour et du hasard* (1730, Eng trans *Love in Livery*, 1907). His best-known novel, *La Vie de Marianne* (1731–41, Eng trans *The Life of Marianne*, 1736–42), was never finished; it is marked by an affected 'precious' style—'Marivaudage'. His numerous comedies are the work of a clever analyst rather than a dramatist. His other romances, *Pharsamon* (1737, Eng trans *Pharsamond*, 1950) and *Le Paysan parvenu* (1735–6, Eng trans *The Fortunate Villager*, 1765) are considerably inferior to *Marianne*.
▷E J H Greene, *Marivaux* (1965)

MARK, Jan(et) Marjorie
(1943–)

English author of children's books, born in Welwyn Garden City, Hertfordshire; she now lives in Norfolk, the setting of several of her quietly witty novels, including *Thunder and Lightnings* (1976) and *Handles* (1983). She has also written a science-fiction trilogy intended for older children, comprising *The Ennead* (1978), *Divide and Rule* (1979) and *Aquarius* (1982), a comparatively grim study of an exploitative society.

MARKFIELD, Wallace Arthur
(1926–)

American novelist and short-story writer, born in Brooklyn, New York, where he also attended college. Though squarely of the 'Jewish–American' school, his fiction is perhaps closer to **Woody Allen**'s prose than to **Philip Roth**'s, full of tongue-in-cheek literary allusions and cultural transvaluations. The best example comes in his first and best-known book, *To an Early Grave* (1964), which re-works Paddy Dignam's funeral in **Joyce**'s *Ulysses* in a way that also recalls **Bellow**'s *Seize the Day*. The association with Roth is stronger in *Teitelbaum's Widow* (1970), a funny-sad exploration of the Jewish Oedipus complex, but comparing Markfield's book to *Portnoy's Complaint* is not to suggest that it is derivative, merely to underline the extent to which he is conscious of the literary traditions in which he works. *You Could Live If They Let You* (1974) was taken to be a fictionalized biography of comedian Lenny Bruce; it examines the darker ramifications of Jewish humour. Markfield's stories were collected in 1977 with the modest title *Multiple Orgasms*.

▷Markfield issue of *Review of Contemporary Fiction* (1982)

MARKHAM, Edwin, originally **Charles Edward Anson Markham**
(1852–1940)

American poet, born in Oregon and educated in California. He is now remembered chiefly for 'The Man with the Hoe' (1899), a relatively tough-minded poem (inspired by the Millet painting) about the dignity and injustices of labour. It was an immediate success on its first publication in the San Francisco *Examiner* and Markham attempted to repeat the formula in later poems such as the similarly inspired 'The Sower', which was collected in *Lincoln and Other Poems* (1901). Outwardly he was a conventional schoolmaster-poet, dedicated to muscular-Christian virtues and to democracy. However, his inner life was clearly a great deal more complex; thrice married and twice divorced, he was driven by unappeasable desires and the nightmarish fear of his own dark side, which emerges in a late poem, 'The Ballad of the Gallows Bird'. His collected poems were published in 1950, prompting a revisionist approach to his life and career.
▷L Filler, *Edwin Markham: His Mystery and Its Significance* (1966)

MARKHANDEYA, Kamala, pseud of **Mrs Kamala Purinya Taylor**
(1924–)

Indian novelist writing in English, member of a noble family which served the princes of Madras. She married an Englishman and moved to England after an education in Mysore. Her novels have consistently gained in psychological depth. One of the best is *A Silence of Desire* (1960), about a man who is opposed to his wife's resort to a faith-healer.

MARKISCH, Peretz
(1895–1952)

Yiddish poet, novelist and dramatist, born in Polonoya; he turned from Russian to Yiddish in 1917. He left Russia in 1921, returned in 1926 to become the leading Soviet–Jewish writer, received the Order of Lenin in 1939, but was murdered by Stalin in the Jewish purges. His epic poem *Milkhome* (1928) was written in praise of Jewish heroism.
▷A Roback, *The Story of Yiddish Literature* (1940)

MARKOOSIE, pseud of **Markoosie Patsauq**
(1942–)

Canadian Inuit writer, born in Port Harrison, Quebec. Patsauq worked for several years as a pilot in the Northwest Territories, and in state and local government in Quebec. His novel *Harpoon of the Hunter* (1970), an atmospheric retelling of an Inuit legend about a young boy's initiation to manhood, was first serialized in an Inuit newsletter and later translated by himself; it was the first piece of Inuit fiction to be published in English.

MARLOWE, Christopher
(1564–93)

English dramatist, born in Canterbury, a shoemaker's son. From the King's School there he was sent to Benet (now Corpus Christi) College, Cambridge. He graduated BA in 1583 and MA in 1587. His *Tamburlaine the Great*, in two parts, was first printed in 1590, and probably produced in 1587. In spite of its bombast and violence it was infinitely superior to any tragedy that had yet appeared on the English stage. Earlier dramatists had used blank verse, but it had been stiff and ungainly, and Marlowe was the first to discover its strength and variety. *The Tragical History of Dr Faustus* was probably produced soon after *Tamburlaine*; the earliest edition is dated 1604. *Faustus* is rather a series of detached scenes than a finished drama and some of these scenes are evidently not by Marlowe. *The Jew of Malta*, produced after 1588 and first published in 1633, is a very uneven play. *Edward II*, produced about 1590, is the most mature of Marlowe's plays. It has not the magnificent poetry of *Faustus* and the first two acts of *The Jew of Malta*, but it is planned and executed with more firmness and solidity. *The Massacre at Paris*, the weakest of Marlowe's plays, has descended in a mutilated state. It was written after the assassination of Henri III of France (1589) and was probably one of the latest plays. *The Tragedy of Dido* (1594), left probably in a fragmentary state by Marlowe and finished by **Thomas Nashe**, is of slight value. Marlowe had doubtless a hand in the three parts of *Henry VI*, and probably in *Titus Andronicus*. A wild, shapeless tragedy, *Lust's Dominion* (1657) may have been adapted from one of Marlowe's lost plays. The unfinished poem, *Hero and Leander*, composed in heroic couplets, was first published in 1598; a second edition, with Chapman's continuation, followed the same year. Marlowe's translations of **Ovid**'s *Amores* and of the first book of **Lucan**'s *Pharsalia* add nothing to his fame. The pastoral ditty, 'Come, live with me and be my love', to which Sir Walter Raleigh wrote an Answer, was imitated, but not equalled, by **Robert Herrick**, **John Donne** and others. It was first printed in *The Passionate Pilgrim* (1599), without the fourth and sixth stanzas, with the author's name, 'C. Marlowe', written below. Another anthology, Allot's *England's Parnassus* (1600), preserves a fragment by Marlowe, beginning 'I walked along a stream for pureness rare'. Marlowe led an irregular life, mingled with the rabble, and was on the point of being arrested for disseminating atheistic opinions when he was fatally stabbed in a tavern brawl. In tragedy he prepared the way for **Shakespeare**, on whose early work his influence is firmly stamped.

▷F S Boas, *Christopher Marlowe* (1940); H Levin, *The Over-Reacher* (1954)

MARMION, Shackerley
(1603–39)

English dramatist, born in Aynho, Northamptonshire. He was educated at Wadham College, Oxford, squandered a fortune, and fought in the Low Countries. He was the author of an allegorical epic, *Cupid and Psyche* (1637), and three comedies, *Holland's Leaguer* (1632), *A Fine Companion* (1633) and *The Antiquary* (1635), generally regarded as his best play.

▷G E Bentley, *The Jacobean and Caroline Stage* (1956)

MARMOL, José Pedro Crisólogio
(1818–71)

Argentinian Romantic poet and novelist, born in Buenos Aires, who is most famous for his effective diatribes against the 19th-century proto-fascist dictator of Argentina, Juan Manuel de Rosas, who imprisoned him. He owed his main inspiration to **Byron**, and several of his narrative poems are direct imitations. His most important poetic work is *Cantos del peregrino* (1847, 'Songs of the Pilgrim'). His novel *Amalia* (1844, rev edn 1851), also an attack on Rosas, was one of the most important Latin-American Romantic novels. Mármol conterpoints, with subtle irony and skill, the romantic stuff of a conventional 'tragic affair' with the realistic horrors of the Rosas regime. Like Byron, he also wrote many lyrics. He was able to return to Buenos Aires with due honour after Rosas had been overthrown (1852).

▷*University of Colorado Studies*, 22, 2–3 (1935); M C Suárez-Murias, *La novela romántica en Hispanoamérica* (1963)

MARMONTEL, Jean François
(1723–99)

French author, born in Bort in the Limousin. He studied in a Jesuit college. Settling in Paris in 1745 on the advice of **Voltaire**, he wrote successful tragedies and operas, and in 1753 got a secretaryship at Versailles through Madame de Pompadour. In the official journal, *Le Mercure*, by then under his charge, he began his *Contes moraux* (1761, 'Moral Tales'). Elected to the Academy in 1763, he became its secretary in 1783, as well as royal historian of France. His most celebrated work was *Bélisaire* (1766, 'Belisarius'), a dull and wordy political romance, containing a chapter on toleration which excited furious hostility. His uncritical *Éléments de littérature* (1787) consists of his contributions to the *Encyclopédie* (35 vols, 1751–80), to which he was the main contributor on literature. His *Mémoires d'un père* (1804, Eng trans *Memoirs of Marmontel*, 1805) include portraits of many of his contemoraries.

▷S Lenel, *Jean François Marmontel* (1902)

MARNAU, Fred
(1918–)

Austrian poet and novelist, born in Bratislava. He lived in England, and his poems appeared in bilingual editions, all translated by E O Sigler; such collections of his long-lined and rhetorical poems as are contained in *The Wounds of the Apostles* (1944) attracted some favourable attention. Later he was read only in Austria.

MAROT, Clément
(c.1497–1544)

French poet, born in Cahors. He entered the service of **Margaret of Angoulême**, Queen of Navarre. He was wounded at the battle of Pavia in 1525, and soon after imprisoned on a charge of heresy, but liberated next spring. He made many enemies by his witty satires, and in 1535 fled first to the court of the Queen of Navarre, and later to that of the Duchess of Ferrara. He returned to Paris in 1536, and in 1538 began to translate the Psalms into French, which, when sung to secular airs, helped to make the new views fashionable; but accused of heresy by the Sorbonne, he had again to flee in 1543. He made his way to Geneva, where Calvin was devoting himself to the Reformation. Marot decided not to stay there because of this and went on to Turin. His poems consist of elegies, epistles, rondeaux, ballads, sonnets, madrigals, epigrams, nonsense verses and longer pieces; his special gift lay in badinage and graceful satire.

▷C A Mayer, *Marot* (1969)

MARQUAND, John P(hillips)
(1893–1960)

American novelist, born in Wilmingon, Delaware. He was educated at Newbury Port High School, Massachusetts, and Harvard University. He served with the military, was a war correspondent and wrote advertising copy. He started as a writer of popular stories for magazines, featuring the Japanese detective Mr Moto, and later gently satirized affluent middle-class American life in a vein

similar to **Sinclair Lewis**, whom he admired, in a series of notable novels. Key titles are *The Late George Apley* (1937), *Wickford Point* (1939) and *Point of No Return* (1949).
▷M Bell, *John P Marquand: an American life* (1979)

MÁRQUEZ, Gabriel García *see* GARCÍA MÁRQUEZ

MARQUIS, Don(ald Robert Perry)
(1878–1937)
American novelist, playwright and poet, born in Walnut, Illinois. His formal education was aborted at 15 and he worked at various jobs before studying art for a spell. He had a varied career as a journalist and wrote serious plays and poems, but he became a celebrity as a comic writer with *The Old Soak's History of the World* (1924). *archy and mehitabel* (1927) and *archys life of mehitabel* (1933) follow the fortunes of Archy the cockroach who cannot reach the typewriter's shift key (hence the lower case titles) and Mehitabel, an alley cat.
▷E Antony, *O Rare Don Marquis* (1962)

MARRIC, J J *see* CREASEY, John

MARRYAT, Florence
(1838–99)
English novelist, daughter of **Frederick Marryat**, born in Brighton. She was successively Mrs Ross Church and Mrs Lean, and from 1865 published about 80 novels, as well as a drama and many articles in periodicals. She edited *London Society* (1872–6).
▷E Showalter, *A Literature of their Own* (1977)

MARRYAT, Frederick
(1792–1848)
English naval officer and novelist, the son of an MP. In 1806 he sailed as midshipman under Lord Cochrane. After service in the West Indies, he had command of a sloop cruising off St Helena to guard against the escape of Napoleon. He also did good work in suppressing the Channel smugglers, and some hard fighting in Burmese rivers. On his return to England (1826) he was given the command of the *Ariadne* (1828). He resigned in 1830, and from then on led the life of a writer. He was the author of a series of novels on sea life of which the best known are *Frank Mildmay* (1829), *Peter Simple* (1833), *Jacob Faithful* (1834) and *Mr Midshipman Easy* (1834). In 1837 he set out for a tour through the USA, where he wrote *The Phantom Ship* (1839) and a drama, *The Ocean Waif*. He received £1200 for *Mr Midshipman Easy* and £1600 for his *Diary in America* (1839), but

was extravagant and unlucky in his money matters, and eventually was financially embarrassed. *Poor Jack, Masterman Ready, The Poacher* and *Percival Keene* appeared before he settled (1843) on his small farm of Langham, Norfolk, where he spent his days in farming and in writing stories for children, including the once very popular *Children of the New Forest* (1847).
▷O Warner, *Captain Marryat* (1953)

MARS-JONES, Adam
(1954–)
English novelist, short-story writer, editor and critic, born in London and educated at Cambridge. Mars-Jones's first book, *Lantern Lecture*, a volume of short stories, appeared in 1981. Two years later, he co-edited *Mae West is Dead: Recent Lesbian and Gay Fiction*, and in 1987, in collaboration with **Edmund White**, published a second book of stories, *The Darker Proof: Stories from a Crisis*. Much of this work examines the effect of AIDS upon those close to the victims of the disease, and arose from Mars-Jones's own experience as a 'buddy', a volunteer friend to a sufferer. His discursive, sympathetic style is evident once again in the novel *The Waters of Thirst* (1993).

MARSÉ, Juan
(1933–)
Spanish novelist, born Juan Fonseca in Barcelona; his mother died at his birth, and he was immediately adopted by the Marsé family. He published his first novel, *Encarrados con un solo juguete* ('Locked in with a Single Toy'), in 1961, by which time he was mixing with other emerging writers. An opponent of the Franco regime, he exiled himself to Paris, where he knew other exiles such as **Juan Goytisolo**. Later he went into the cinema business. He began to make a reputation as an ironic critic of society with *Ultimas tardes con Teresa* (1965, 'Last Evenings with Teresa'), a novel influenced by the techniques of **Ramón Valle-Inclán**, the extraordinary Catalan Josep Pla and, mainly, the Castilian **Luis Martín-Santos**, a psychiatrist who with his single completed novel changed the direction of Spanish fiction. Like Martín-Santos, Marsé flayed the submissiveness of post-Civil War Spanish society, by means of the technique Martín-Santos called 'dialectical realism'. In *Si te dicenque caí* (1973, Eng trans *The Fallen*, 1979), whose publication in Spain was delayed, Marsé even more robustly mocked the society around him. His other translated novel, *La muchacha de las bragas de oro* (1978, Eng trans *Golden Girl*, 1981), mercilessly burlesques the

memoirs of the half-repentant Falangist rector of Madrid University, Pedro Laín Entralgo.

MARSH, Dame (Edith) Ngaio
(1899–1982)

New Zealand detective novelist and theatre director, born in Christchurch. After a brief career on stage and as an interior decorator, she introduced her detective-hero Roderick Alleyn in *A Man Lay Dead* (1934), which was followed by 30 more stories ending with *Light Thickens* (1982). In theatre, she toured with the Wilkie company in **Shakespeare** during the early 1920s, and devoted much time to theatrical production in New Zealand in the 1940s and 1950s. She also wrote on art, theatre and crime fiction, as well as the libretto for a fantasy-opera *A Unicorn for Christmas* (1962) to music by New Zealand composer David Farquhar.
▷ *Black Beech and Honeydew* (1966, rev edn 1981)

MARSHAK, Samuel
(1887–1964)

Russian children's writer, poet and translator, born in Voronezh. Devoted to children, his voluminous work for them largely determined the official Bolshevik line; it was not nearly as poor as it might have been. **Nahzda Mandelstam** said of him, in her memoirs, 'he was a superb fisher of men, whether weak, susceptible ones or men of power': her husband suffered his first attack of angina pectoris while listening to Marshak expound 'the official line'. But, while a natural toady, Marshak possessed talents which lifted him above the wholly mediocre. His translations of the Sonnets of **Shakespeare**, and of other classics, are efficient—and he gave what help he could to those more gifted and less fortunate than himself. *V nachala zhinzi* (1960, 'At Life's Beginning') is his autobiography.

MARSHALL, (William) Alan
(1902–84)

Australian writer, born in Noorat, Victoria. Permanently crippled by polio at six, he went to business college and worked as an accountant before becoming a columnist for Melbourne newspapers. He travelled widely within Australia and also spent time in Asia, but it was his own story of childhood and struggle with handicap in *I Can Jump Puddles* (1955) that brought him to notice. He produced five collections of short stories between 1946 and 1975, as well as writings for children, on travel and Australian country life, and an evocation of aboriginal myths in *People of the Dreamtime* (1952). His anecdotal style thinly disguises the personal narrative,

and this best comes out in his collection *Hammers over the Anvil* (1975) where he throws away his observational manner and speaks in his own voice. *The Complete Short Stories* was published in 1977.

MARSHALL, Paule
(1929–)

American author, born in Brooklyn, New York City. Her parents emigrated from Barbados during World War I and she grew up in Brooklyn during the Depression. In 1948 she studied at Hunter College, New York City, but left prematurely because of illness. Later she graduated from Brooklyn College and worked for *Our World Magazine*. *Brown Girl, Brownstones* (1959), her first novel, is regarded as a classic of Black American literature, telling the story of the coming of age of Seling Boyce, the daughter of Barbadian immigrants living through the Depression and World War I. Later novels are *The Chosen Place* (1969), *The Timeless People* (1969) and *Praisesong for the Widow* (1983).

MARSON, Una
(1905–65)

Jamaican poet and playwright, educated at Hampton School. She trained as a social worker but was equally interested in journalism, founding and editing *The Cosmopolitan magazine*. She worked in England (1932–6), as secretary to the League of Coloured Peoples, then private secretary to Emperor Haile Selassie. She wrote the first play performed by black colonials in London (*At What a Price*, 1932). Back in Jamaica she was a dynamic figure in many fields: she founded the Save the Children Fund, the Readers' and Writers' Club, and a progressive paper, *Public Opinion*. Between 1930 and 1945 she published four books of verse, and during World War II she presented the BBC's influential 'Caribbean Voices' programme in London. By her use of jazz rhythms and Jamaican dialect in verse and her focus on issues of gender, race and identity, she pioneered a new movement in Jamaican writing in the 1940s.
▷ E Smilowitz, *Critical Issues in West Indian Literature* (1984)

MARSTON, John
(1576–1634)

English dramatist and satirist, born in Wardington, Oxfordshire, the son of a Shropshire lawyer and an Italian mother. He studied at Brasenose College, Oxford, and then studied law at the Middle Temple. Apart from *The Insatiate Countess* (which is of doubtful authorship), all his plays were published

between 1602 and 1607. He then gave up playwriting, took orders in 1609, and (1616–31) was a clergyman at Christchurch, Hampshire. His first work was *The Metamorphosis of Pygmalion's Image: and Certain Satires* (1598), a licentious poem which was condemned by Archbishop Whitgift. Another series of uncouth and obscure satires, *The Scourge of Villany*, appeared in the same year. He began to write for the theatre in 1599. Two gloomy and ill-constructed tragedies, *Antonio and Mellida* and *Antonio's Revenge*, were published in 1602; in them passages of striking power stand out above the general mediocrity. A comedy, *The Malcontent* (1604), more skilfully constructed, was dedicated to **Ben Jonson**, with whom he had many quarrels and reconciliations. *Eastward Ho* (1605), written in conjunction with **George Chapman** and Jonson, is far more genial than any comedy that Marston wrote single-handed. For some reflections on the Scots the authors were imprisoned (1604). Other plays include a comedy, *The Dutch Courtesan* (1605), *Parasitaster, or the Fawn* (1606), *Sophonisba* (1606, a tragedy) and *What You Will* (1607). The rich and graceful poetry scattered through his last play, *The Insatiate Countess* (1613), is unlike anything that occurs in Marston's undoubted works, and it may have been completed by another hand.
▷A F Caputi, *John Marston, Satirist* (1961)

MARSTON, John Westland
(1819–90)

English dramatic poet, father of **Philip Bourke Marston**, born in Boston, Lincolnshire. He gave up law for literature; and in 1842 his *Patrician's Daughter* was brought out at Drury Lane by the actor William Macready. It was the most successful of more than a dozen plays, all **Sheridan-Knowles**ian, and all forgotten. He wrote a novel (1860), a good book on *Our Recent Actors* (1888), and a mass of poetic criticism.

MARSTON, Philip Bourke
(1850–87)

English poet, son of **John Westland Marston**, born in London. He became blind at the age of three. He was grief-stricken at the death of his fiancée and then of his sisters, and his friends, **Oliver Madox Brown** and **Dante Gabriel Rossetti**. He is remembered for his friendship with Rossetti, **Walter Watts-Dunton** and **Swinburne** rather than for his sonnets and lyrics—although a few of these are exquisite. *Songtide, All in All* and *Wind Voices* were the three volumes of poetry he published between 1870 and 1883. A collection of his short stories was published posthumously in 1887.
▷C C Osborne, *Philip Bourke Marston* (1926)

MARTI, José
(1853–95)

Cuban poet and rebel. Born in Havana, the son of a Spanish settler, he was continually in trouble with the Spanish authorities for his views on independence; he was eventually killed by Spaniards on the military expedition of 1895: he had been proclaimed supreme leader just before his murder. But Marti was not just a simple patriot: he had one of the best minds of his time, and intellectually stood, as has been said, 'head and shoulders above his contemporaries'. His poetry is more direct in its expression of feelings than that of his contemporaries, and his prose contains many correct prophecies about race and integration.
▷I A Schulman, *Simbolo y color en la obra de José Marti* (1960)

MARTIAL (Marcus Valerius Martialis)
(c.40–c.104)

Roman poet and epigrammatist, born in Bilbilis in Spain. He went to Rome in AD64 and became a client of the influential Spanish house of the **Seneca**s, through which he found a patron in L Calpurnius Piso. The failure of the Pisonian plot to assassinate **Cicero** lost Martial his warmest friends—**Lucan** and Seneca. He courted imperial and senatorial patronage by his verses for particular events. When the Emperor Titus dedicated the Colosseum in AD80, Martial's epigrams in *Liber Spectaculorum* ('Book of Spectacles') brought him equestrian rank; his flattery of Domitian was gross and venal. The first 12 books of the *Epigrams* began to appear in 86. Advancing years having bereft him of Domitian and his friends of the palace, in a fit of homesickness he borrowed from his admirer, the younger **Pliny**, the means of returning to Bilbilis, where he spent the rest of his life. His best work is often his most scurrilous.
▷P Nixon, *Martial and the Modern Epigram* (1927)

MARTIN, C(atherine) E(dith) M(acauley)
(1847–1937)

Scottish-born Australian novelist and poet, born on the Isle of Skye, known now mainly for her early novel of the trials of a colonial woman and wife, *An Australian Girl*, originally published anonymously in 1890. Other novels were *The Silent Sea* (1892, as by Mrs Alick Macleod), *The Old Roof-Tree* (1906) and *The Incredible Journey* (1923), a sympathetic tale of two aboriginal women in search of a kidnapped child. Her serial work 'Bohemian Born' never appeared in book form. A book of verses, *The Explorers and Other Poems*, came out in 1874 under the initials M C.

MARTIN, Claire, née Montreuil
(1914–)

French–Canadian novelist and translator, born in Quebec, who began her career in radio. Her books are often about the duplicities of love and triangular relationships alive with deception. This is especially so in her early work: *Doux-amer* (1960, Eng trans *Best Man*, 1983) and *Quand j'aurai payé ton visage* (1962, Eng trans *The Legacy*, 1986). She won a Governor General's Award in 1967 for her two volumes of autobiography—*Dans un gant de fer* (1965) and *La Joue droite* (1966)—in which she described an oppressive childhood in a patriarchal household. These were translated as *In An Iron Glove* (1973) and *The Right Cheek* (1975). Her own translations into French have included books by **Robertson Davies** and **Margaret Laurence**.

MARTIN, David
(1915–)

Hungarian–German novelist and poet of Jewish descent, now settled in Australia. He began writing in London in the late 1930s and became known for his novel *Tiger Bay* (1946), later a popular film. His prolific output includes novels, eight collections of verse and many books for children. He explores the sensitivities of the displaced Jew in *Where a Man Belongs* (1969) and the theme of alienation emerges frequently in other books. *My Strange Friend*, a study in autobiography, was published in 1991.

MARTIN, Sir Theodore
(1816–1909)

Scottish writer and biographer, born in Edinburgh. The well-known series of poetic parodies collected as the *Bon Gaultier Ballads* (1855), written in conjunction with **Aytoun**, were followed by verse translations from **Goethe**, **Horace**, **Catullus**, **Dante** and **Heine**. He was requested by Queen Victoria to write the life of Prince Albert (5 vols, 1874–80), and he also wrote biographies of Aytoun (1867), Lord Lyndhurst (1883) and the Princess Alice (1885). His wife, Helen Faucit (1820–98), was a well-known actress, noted for her interpretations of **Shakespeare**'s heroines. The couple were frequent visitors to the royal household.

MARTIN, Violet Florence, pseud Martin Ross
(1862–1915)

Irish writer, born in County Galway. She is known chiefly for a series of novels written in collaboration with her cousin **Edith Somerville**, including *An Irish Cousin* (1889) and *Some Experiences of an Irish R.M.* (1908). She also wrote travel books about the Irish countryside, and two autobiographical works, *Some Irish Yesterdays* (1906) and *Strayaways* (1920).
▷M Collis, *Somerville and Ross* (1968)

MARTIN DU GARD, Roger
(1881–1958)

French novelist and winner of the Nobel Prize for literature, born in Neuilly-sur-Seine. After studying history, he qualified as an archivist before turning to writing, publishing his first novel, *Devenir* ('Becoming'), in 1909. In that same year the *Nouvelle Revue Française*, with which he had a long and fruitful association, was founded. After serving in World War I he lived as a recluse and devoted himself to writing in various forms, including novels, plays and memoirs. His novels include *Jean Barois* (1913), which deals, among other matters, with the Dreyfus affair, and *Vieille France* (1933, 'Old France'), a study of a less-than-idyllic rural life. He is best known, however, for his eight-novel series *Les Thibault* (1922–40) dealing with family life during the first decades of the 20th century. He was awarded the Nobel Prize for literature in 1937. The correspondence (1913–51) between him and **André Gide** was published in 1968.
▷D L Schak, *Martin du Gard* (1967)

MARTINEAU, Harriet
(1802–76)

English writer, sister of James Martineau, born in Norwich, the daughter of a textile manufacturer of Huguenot descent. In 1821 she wrote her first article for the (Unitarian) *Monthly Repository*, and then produced *Devotional Exercises for the Use of Young Persons* (1826), and short stories about machinery and wages. Her next book was *Addresses for the Use of Families* (1826). In 1829 the failure of the house in which she, her mother and sisters had placed their money obliged her to earn her living. In 1832 she became a successful author through writing tales based on economic or legal ideas, in *Illustrations of Political Economy*, followed by *Poor Laws and Paupers Illustrated* (1833–4), and settled in London. After a visit to the USA (1834–6) she published *Society in America* and a novel, *Deerbrook*, in 1839, followed by a second novel, *The Hour and the Man*, about Toussaint l'Ouverture. From 1839 to 1844 she was an invalid at Tynemouth but recovered through mesmerism (her subsequent belief in which alienated many friends), and made her home at Ambleside in 1845, the year of *Forest and Game-law Tales*. After visiting Egypt and Palestine she issued *Eastern Life* (1848). In 1851, in conjunction with H G Atkinson, she published *Letters on the Laws of Man's Social Nature* which was so agnostic that it gave much offence, and in 1853 she translated and condensed Comte's

Philosophie positive. She also wrote much for the daily and weekly press and the larger reviews. *An Autobiographical Memoir* was published posthumously in 1877. Her brother James Martineau (1805–1900) wrote many theological works, and also poems and hymns.

▷V Wheatley, *Life and Work of Harriet Martineau* (1957)

MARTÍNEZ, Luis A
(1869–1909)

Ecuadorian novelist, born in Ambato. He wrote about farming, and then became an enlightened Liberal Minister of Education. His novel *A la costa: costombres ecuatoriana* (1904, 'Ecuadorean Customs') is a well-written naturalist polemic in fictional form, attacking wealthy city idlers and praising the natural life of the honest farmer. It is as relevant to modern-day Ecuador as it was to the Ecuador of 1904.

MARTINEZ ESTRADA, Ezequiel
(1895–1964)

Argentinian writer. He started off as a post-office worker but later taught literature at universities in Argentina and Mexico, continuing in Cuba, where he went after Castro's revolution, while he prepared a biography of Jose Martí, the Cuban writer and nationalist. Although he wrote widely—articles, drama, essays, stories, poetry—he is best known as a poet and essayist, with an interest in philosophy, psychology and politics. His view of contemporary Argentina is pessimistic and even bitter; although he never abandoned his political involvement, his focus changed to Third World problems. Some of his poetry collections are: *Oro y Piedra* (1918, 'Gold and Stone'), *Nefelibal* (1922), *Argentina* (1927) and *Humoresca* (1929). His most successful stories were *Tres Cuentos Sin Amor* (1956, 'Three Stories without Love'), and he also wrote a play in verse entitled *Titeres de Pies Ligeros* (1929, 'Puppets on Light Feet').

MARTÍNEZ SIERRA, Gregorio
(1881–1947)

Spanish novelist and dramatist. A theatre manager and an original and creative producer as well as publisher, he was also a prolific writer. His plays *Canción de Cuna* (1917, Eng trans *The Cradle Song*, 1934), *El Reino de Dios* (1916, Eng trans *The Kingdom of God*, 1927) and *El Sueño de Una Noche de Agosto* (1918, Eng trans *The Romantic Young Lady*, 1929) were also popular in Britain and America. Much of his writing was done in collaboration with his wife Maria, whose feminist opinions find expression in some of the plays.

▷G Serrat, *Imager humana y literara de Gregorio Martínez Sierra* (1965)

MARTÍN GAITE, Carmen
(1925–)

Spanish novelist, one of the three most important female novelists in Spain in the latter half of the 20th century (the others are **Carmen Laforet** and **Ana Maria Matute**). Born in Salamanca, she received her doctorate from the University of Madrid, and has written scholarly works on the 18th century and literary criticism. She gained her reputation as a social realist writer and member of the Post-war Generation, but more recently has worked in psychological novels and the fantastic. Her main themes are the lives of women in society, communication, the isolation of the individual, and the deeper side of reality. She has won many literary honours, including the Premio Nadal (1959) and the Premio Nacional de Literatura (1979).

MARTÍN-SANTOS, Luis
(1924–64)

Spanish novelist, born in Larache, Morocco, who helped to revolutionize and make viable the form of the novel in his country during the Francoist period. He was a psychiatrist by profession (he directed the mental hospital at San Sebastian), whose first writings were technical—although in the light of his enormous achievement they are now interesting, especially his early work on the German philosopher Dilthey. He was killed in a car accident as fatal to Spanish literature as to himself. His only finished novel was the significantly titled *Tiempo de silencio* (1962, Eng trans *Time of Silence*, 1965—truthful imaginative exploration of reality was virtually silenced by Franco's censors), which deals with a man, Pedro, living in the sick and submissive society of Madrid in 1949, in which he cannot discover the sort of fulfilment he might naturally, as a human being, expect. This novel exposed the artistic disingenuousness of the attempts made by such pro-Francoist authors as **Gironella** to explain their hero to his liberal European critics. Its technique, which tries to reconcile subjectivity with objectivity in a manner much influenced by the psychology of Karl Jaspers, has been decisive in its effect on subsequent literature. All Martín-Santos's work is pervaded by his desire to understand and relieve mental illness, and this may ultimately prove to be even more important than his aesthetic innovations. His stories were collected in *Apólogos* (1970, 'Apologues'), and an attempt has been made to reconstruct his unfinished novel, *Tiempo de destrucción* (1975, 'Time of Destruction'), about a law student, which seems to have been even more pessimistic and savage in its criticism of post-Civil War society than his first.

▷ J C Mainer (ed), Introduction to *Tiempo de Destrucción* (1975)

MARTINSON, Harry Edmund
(1904–78)

Swedish poet and novelist, joint winner of the Nobel Prize for literature, born in Jäshög in Blekinge. After a harsh childhood as a parish orphan he went to sea as a stoker in 1919 and travelled worldwide in the following decade. He made his poetic debut in 1929 along with a number of young vitalist poets but soon found an individual and quickly acclaimed voice, particularly as a nature poet with such volumes as *Nomad* (1931) and *Natur* (1934); these established his reputation as a renewer of the poetic language. During the 1930s he was married to the writer **Moa Martinson**. He came increasingly to question whether or not man possessed sufficient ethical maturity to control his own technological inventions and this led to his masterpiece, the poetic space epic *Aniara* (1956), which deals with the evacuation by rocket of a radiation-damaged earth; it was set to music as an opera by Karl-Birger Blomdahl. His account of his childhood and youth in *Nässlorna blomma* (1935, 'Flowering Nettle') and *Vägen ut* (1936, 'The Way Out') is his moving contribution to the many working-class autobiographical novels of the Swedish 1930s. His tramp novel *Vägen till Klockrike* (1948, 'The Road to Klockrike') is a worthy addition to that genre. He shared the 1974 Nobel Prize for literature with the Swedish novelist **Eyvind Johnson**. A Harry Martinson Society was founded in 1984.

▷ I Holm, *Harry Martinson* (1960)

MARTINSON, Moa
(1890–1963)

Swedish novelist. Born near Norrköping to an unmarried mill-hand, she received only intermittent schooling, trained as a cold-buffet manageress, married early and gave birth to five sons. Having been widowed, she was subsequently married (1929–41) to the author **Harry Martinson**. Her political interests resulted in articles for the radical press; her first novel, *Kvinnor och äppelträd*, which uses the maternal body as its structuring principle, appeared in 1933 (Eng trans *Women and Apple Trees*, 1985). As the leading woman among the Swedish 'proletarian' writers of the 1930s, she enjoyed a huge success with her autobiographical trilogy, *Mor gifter sig* (1936, 'Mother Gets Married'), *Kyrkbröllop* (1938, 'Church Wedding') and *Kungens rosor* (1939, 'The King's Roses'). Quick-witted and sharp-tongued, she achieved a considerable reputation as a speaker; but her lasting popularity with the Swedish reading public rests on her knowledgeable yet suggestive narratives about working-class life.

▷ E Witt-Brattström, *Moa Martinson. Skrift och drift i trettiotalet* (1988)

MARTORELL, Joanot
(c.1413–1468)

Catalan prose writer. His *Tirant lo Blanc* (1490, Eng trans 1984) was described by **Cervantes** in *Don Quixote* as 'the best book of its kind in the world'; but, like the poetry of **Ausias Marc** (who married Martorell's sister), its greatness was for long forgotten through linguistic ignorance, despite the fact that Catalan is easy to read for those who know romance languages. When it appeared in English in 1984 a new and delighted audience discovered it. It thus joined the hitherto closed list of 'great medieval and Renaissance classics', as its translator hoped it would. Martorell left it unfinished, and it was completed and published by Martí Joan de Galba (whose contribution was probably very slight). Ostensibly a tale of chivalrous adventure, it owed much to the Catalan mystic Ramon Llull, and is unrivalled for its psychological penetration and its erotic realism. It anticipated much of what is now taken for 'modern' (eg the existence of the unconscious mind), and its calculated mixture of farce, fantasy, onslaught upon conventional morality and effortless recognition of the dangerous relationship between love and mystical insight, makes it read very like a new work.

MARTYN, Edward
(1859–1923)

Irish playwright, now best known for his friendship with **George Moore** and **W B Yeats**. He was born in County Galway. His reaction against the main movement in Irish theatre culminated in the founding of the Abbey Theatre. He was for four years the President of Sinn Fein. His plays, now somewhat underrated, were modelled upon those of **Ibsen**; *Romulus and Remus* (1916) is memorable for its savage and not inaccurate caricatures of Moore and Yeats. *Regina Eyre* (produced in 1919, not published), which was hissed when it was performed, is a courageous and interesting variation on the *Hamlet* theme, in which he reverses the gender of the characters. His dialogue was often inept, and had he had a collaborator he might have achieved much more.

▷ G Moore, *Hail and Farewell* (1911–14)

MARTYNOV, Leonid
(1905–)

Russian poet from Omsk, who graduated from the Futurist movement, and who at first wrote in the style of **Mayakovsky**. His best-known poem is the narrative *Lukomorye* (1945, 'Cove'), on the theme of never-never land, set, in his case, in a Siberia almost unknown to his contemporaries (unless they had been sent there). This effectively combines contemplative folklorism with the colloquial. Criticized by cultural officers of state, he reacted by composing a somewhat more conformist poetry which, after a long gap, brought him honours and recognition.

MARULIĆ, Marko
(1450–1524)

Dalmatian poet and classical scholar, born in Split, who achieved renown in Europe. Like the other writers of Dalmatia of his age and that following it, he studied in Italy (Padua) and based his practice on what he learned there. Much of what he wrote is in Latin, but his epic poems, on biblical themes, are in Serbo–Croat—the first literary writings in that language of known authorship.
▷ *Slavonic and East European Review*, XLI (1962)

MARVELL, Andrew
(1621–78)

English poet, born in Winestead rectory, south east Yorkshire, the son of a clergyman. He was educated at Hull Grammar School and Trinity College, Cambridge. He travelled (1642–6) in Holland, France, Italy and Spain. After a period as tutor to Lord Fairfax's daughter, when he wrote his pastoral and garden poems, he was appointed tutor to Cromwell's ward, William Dutton. In 1650 he wrote his *Horatian Ode upon Cromwell's Return from Ireland*, which also reflected the warmest sympathy for Charles I. In 1657 he became **Milton**'s assistant. In January 1659 he took his seat in parliament as member for Hull, for which he was returned again in 1660 and 1661. From 1663 to 1665 he accompanied Lord Carlisle as secretary to the embassy to Muscovy, Sweden and Denmark, but the rest of his life was devoted to his parliamentary duties, fighting against intolerance and arbitrary government. His republicanism was less the outcome of abstract theory than of experience. He accepted the Restoration while still admiring Cromwell. His writings show him willing to give Charles II a fair chance, but convinced eventually that the Stewarts must go. His last satires are a call to arms against monarchy. Though circulated in manuscript only, they were believed to endanger his life. He died due to the stubborn ignorance of his physician—a baseless rumour suggested poison. Marvell's works are divided by the Restoration into two very distinct groups. After 1660 he concentrated on politics, except when his friendship for Milton drew from him the lines prefixed to the second edition of *Paradise Lost*. In 1672–3 he wrote *The Rehearsal Transpros'd* against religious intolerance; and in 1677 his most important tract, the *Account of the Growth of Popery and Arbitrary Government*, was published anonymously. As a poet, Marvell belongs to the pre-Restoration period, although most of his poetry was not published until 1681 as *Miscellaneous Poetry*. A subsequent volume was entitled *Poems on Affairs of State* (1689–97).
▷ P Legouis, *Andrew Marvell, poète, puritain, patriote* (1928); J B Leishman, *The Art of Marvell's Poetry* (1966)

MASAMUNE Hakucho
(1879–1962)

Japanese writer. Born in the South of Honshu, Japan's main island, he gravitated towards Tokyo in early adulthood. Masamune, of all his contemporaries, was one of those most open to western influences—he read western literature, often expressed a desire to go abroad, embraced Christianity and even described himself as 'worshipping the West'. His novels, however, are still very Japanese in conception; like so many of his contemporaries, he was an exponent of Japanese naturalism, and his writing is introspective, realistic and full of minute descriptive detail, coming close at times to internal monologue.

MASAOKA Shiki
(1867–1902)

Japanese poet, from Ehime but living in Tokyo. Masaoke was the greatest poet of his day, working with the traditional poetic forms, especially *waka* and *haiku*, refining them and devising new ways of seeing them, to the extent that there is good reason to think of him as the originator of the modern haiku (as a concise, beautiful and above all self-sufficient expression of some idea or feeling). Some of his most beautiful and poignant verse was written in the final stages of his drawn-out and agonizing death from spinal tuberculosis. His famous poem *Drop of Ink* was composed when he was totally paralysed.
▷ 'Masaoka Shiki and Tanka Reform' in D Shively (ed), *Tradition and Modernisation in Japanese Culture* (1971)

MASEFIELD, John Edward
(1878–1967)

English poet and novelist, born in Ledbury, Herefordshire. Educated at the King's School, Warwickshire, and schooled for the merchant service, he served his apprenticeship on a windjammer and acquired that intimate knowledge of the sea which gives atmosphere and authenticity to his work. Ill-health drove him ashore, and after three years in New York he returned to England to become a writer in 1897, first making his mark as a journalist. His earliest poetical work, *Salt Water Ballads*, appeared in 1902; *Dauber* (1913) confirmed his reputation as a poet of the sea. *Nan* (1909) is a tragedy of merit. His finest narrative poem is *Reynard the Fox* (1919). Other works are *The Everlasting Mercy* (1911); *The Widow in the Bye-Street* (1912); *Shakespeare* (1911); *Gallipoli* (1916); and the novels *Sard Harker* (1924), *Odtaa* (1926) and *The Hawbucks* (1929). His plays are *The Trial of Jesus* (1925) and *The Coming of Christ* (1928). He became poet laureate in 1930. Later books included the sea-novels *Dead Ned* (1938) and *Live and Kicking Ned* (1939). His final work was *Grace before Ploughing* (1966).

▷ *So Long to Learn* (1952)

MASON, Alfred Edward Woodley
(1865–1948)

English novelist, born in Dulwich. He was educated at Oxford, became a successful actor, and subsequently combined writing with politics, as Liberal MP for Coventry (1906–10). His first published novel was *A Romance of Wastdale* (1895). The adventure novel *Four Feathers* (1902) captured the popular imagination and *The Broken Road* (1907) cemented his success. With *At the Villa Rose* (1910) he started writing detective novels and introduced his ingenious Inspector Hanaud. From then on he alternated historical adventure and detective fiction. Several of his books have been filmed.

▷ R L Green, *Alfred Mason: the adventures of a story-teller* (1952)

MASON, Bobbie Ann
(1940–)

American novelist and short-story writer, born in Mayfield, Kentucky. One of the much-hyped 'dirty realists' who came to prominence in the mid-1980s, she writes of ordinary Americans, often poor and rural, facing common problems: inter-generational strife; lack of understanding; lack of cash. Her short-story collections *Shiloh* (1982) and *Love Life* (1989) include her best work to date; the economy of her prose seems most suited to a short form. Her novels, *In Country* (1985) and *Spence + Lila* (1988), are also brief.

MASON, Bruce Edward George
(1921–82)

New Zealand playwright, born in Wellington, whose plays, beginning with *The Pohutukawa Tree* (1956, rev edn 1963), were widely produced; his *The End of the Golden Weather*

(1962, rev edn 1970) received over 500 performances in every New Zealand city. Later work was written for solo performance, often drawing on his previous writings. Four such plays were published as *Bruce Mason Solo* (1981). Three plays for television and a full-length stage play, *Blood of the Lamb* (1980), were produced after his death. His *New Zealand Drama: A Parade of Forms and a History* (1973) was written for school use but gives useful background on his plays.

MASON, F Van Wyck
(1901–78)

American popular novelist, born in Boston. He has written mysteries, adventure stories, books for juveniles and, perhaps most notably, historical novels, such as *Proud New Flags* (1951), about the navy in the American Civil War. *Cutlass Empire* (1949) is about the pirate Henry Morgan.

MASON, R(onald) A(rthur) K(ells)
(1905–71)

New Zealand poet, born in Auckland, who came to attention aged 19 with *The Beggar* (1924), which he paid to have published. Legend has it that, disappointed with the sales, he dumped the remaining copies in Waitemata harbour. *No New Thing: Poems, 1924–29* was published in 1934, *End of Day* followed in 1936 and *Recent Poems* (with work by **Allen Curnow**, **Denis Glover** and **A R D Fairburn**) in 1941. His work is collected in *This Dark Will Lighten: Selected Poems, 1923–41* (1941) and *Collected Poems* (1962, with an introduction by Curnow).

MASON, William
(1725–97)

English poet and clergyman. He was a friend of **Thomas Gray**, who had been attracted to him by his *Musaeus* (1747), a lament for **Pope** in imitation of **Milton**'s *Lycidas*. He published two poor tragedies, *Elfrida* and *Caractacus*; the *English Garden* (1772–82), a tedious poem in blank verse; and, as Gray's executor, the *Memoirs of Gray* in 1775. He became vicar of Aston, Yorkshire, in 1754, and canon of York in 1762.

▷ J W Draper, *William Mason* (1924)

MASSEY, Gerald
(1828–1907)

English mystic and poet, born near Tring. He became a Christian socialist, edited a journal, lectured, and between 1851 and 1869 published several volumes of poetry, including *Babe Christabel and other Poems* and *Craigcrook Castle*. He also wrote mystical and speculative theological or cosmogonic works, and claimed to have discovered a 'Secret Drama' in **Shakespeare**'s sonnets.

MASSIE, Allan
(1938–)

Scottish novelist, critic and journalist, born in Singapore and brought up in Aberdeenshire. Educated at Glenalmond and Cambridge, he taught in a private school before going to Italy, where he taught English as a foreign language. His first two novels—*Change and Decay In All Around I See* (1978) and *The Last Peacock* (1980)—placed him firmly in the camp of **Ronald Firbank** and **Evelyn Waugh**, but those who saw him as other than Scottish were off the mark. Although inclined to think in terms that transcend place, his sensibility is native. *The Death of Men* (1981) was a stylish thriller drawing on the kidnapping in Italy of Aldo Moro. In 1986 he turned again to Italy with *Augustus*, a historical novel purporting to be the long-lost memoirs of the maligned emperor. *Tiberius* (1990) and *Caesar* (1993) brilliantly perpetuated the conceit, drawing on his knowledge of the ancient world while convincingly filling in gaps with his imagination. *A Question of Loyalties* (1989), set in Vichy France, and *The Sins of the Father* (1991), in which the children of war criminals and victims attempt to cope with their parents' legacies, similarly demonstrate his unwillingness to allow history to remain the preserve solely of historians. In both there are no pat answers, only sympathy and a quest to interpret the past from an unconventional point of view. *These Enchanted Woods* (1993) makes comic play of the contrasting attitudes of an aggressive London speculator with the country society of rural Perthshire. As well as being a prolific novelist, Massie has written books on **Muriel Spark**, the Caesars and Lord **Byron**. He is also a respected reviewer and a columnist, with trenchant political views.

MASSINGER, Philip
(1583–1640)

English dramatist, born in Salisbury, the son of a retainer of the Earl of Pembroke. After leaving Oxford without a degree he became a playwright and was associated with Philip Henslowe, who died in 1616. In later years he wrote many plays on his own, but much of his work is mixed up with that of other men, particularly **John Fletcher**. He and Fletcher are buried in the same grave. Probably the earliest of Massinger's extant plays is *The Unnatural Combat*, a dreadful tragedy, printed in 1639. The first in order of publication is *The Virgin Martyr* (1622), partly written by **Thomas Dekker**. In 1623 was published *The Duke of Milan*, a fine tragedy, but too rhetorical. Other plays include *The Bondman* (1623),

The Roman Actor (1626), *The Great Duke of Florence* (1627) and *The Emperor of the East* (1631). **Nathan Field** joined Massinger in writing the fine tragedy *The Fatal Dowry*, printed in 1632. *The City Madam*, licensed in 1632, and *A New Way to Pay Old Debts*, printed in 1633, are Massinger's most masterly comedies—brilliant satirical studies, though without warmth or geniality. It is difficult to say how much Massinger was involved in the plays under the names of **Francis Beaumont** and Fletcher.
▷A Dunn, *Massinger: the man and the playwright* (1957)

MASTERS, Edgar Lee
(1869–1950)

American author, born in Garnett, Kansas. A successful lawyer in Chicago, he wrote poetry, and became famous with the satirical *Spoon River Anthology* (1915), a book of epitaphs in free verse about lives of people in Illinois. He published several more collections and some novels, and returned to his first success with *The New Spoon River* (1924), attacking the new style of urban life. *Across Spoon River* (1936) is an autobiography.
▷H W Masters, *Edgar Lee Masters: a biographical sketchbook* (1978)

MASTERS, John
(1914–1983)

British writer, born in Calcutta into a Raj family and going into the army, in India, from Sandhurst. After service during World War II in Asia, he took up full-time writing in 1948, turning out adventure stories, mainly for American magazines, and then producing a string of historical novels, many of them (including *Nightrunners of Bengal*, 1951) set in India. He also wrote extensively about World War I, producing a history, *Fourteen Eighteen* (1971), and a trilogy of novels, *Loss of Eden* (1979–80). His fiction tends to go for breadth of action rather than depth of vision, but can astonish the reader in doing so, and the nostalgia underlying much of his work is usually kept at a discreet distance.

MATAVULJ, Simõ
(1852–1906)

Serbian novelist, story writer and translator (of **Zola**, **Mérimée**, **Maupassant**), born in Belgrade. Much of his work was translated into French and Italian, but nothing into English. His semi-naturalistic depictions of the South Adriatic are anything but idealistic. He wrote six collections of stories and two novels, of which *Bakonja fra Brne* (1892) is a comic classic, set in a Catholic monastery. His true master was Maupassant.

MATHEWS, Aidan
(1956–)

Irish poet, fiction writer and playwright, born in Dublin. In 1976 he won the **Patrick Kavanagh** Award for Poetry, in 1978 the **Macaulay** Fellowship for Writing and in 1984 the Listowel Drama Award. An intellectual intensity informs his verse, particularly *Windfalls* (1977) and *Minding Ruth* (1983). His short-story collections *Adventures in a Bathyscope* (1988) and *Lipstick on the Host* (1992) and his novel *Muesli at Midnight* (1990) show an entertaining sense of the absurd, one which is almost overwhelmingly present in the surreal drama *The Diamond Body* (1985). A rejection of traditional political imperatives—as in the three-line *The Deanth of Irish* (1987): 'The tide gone out for good,/Thirty-one words for seaweed/whiten on the foreshore'—has gained him over the years a questionable reputation as 'Irish fabulist'.

MATHEWS, Harry Burchell
(1930–)

American writer of bizarre lexical fantasies. He was born in New York City and educated at Harvard and at the École Normale de Musique in Paris. In 1952 he moved to Europe, where his brand of highly literary fiction is more readily understood than in the US; he has lived there, mainly in France, ever since. He is a member of the hermetic Ouvroir de Littérature Potentielle (Oulipo). In 1960, he joined **John Ashbery**, **Kenneth Koch** and **James Schuyler** in founding the influential magazine *Locus Solus*, which was based in France. His fictional writing includes *The Conversions* (1962), *Tlooth* (1966) and his masterpiece, *The Sinking of the Odradek Stadium* (1971–5), originally published in the *Paris Review*, which concerns the correspondence between a librarian and his Thai wife. *Cigarettes* (1982) was a slighter work. Mathews's collected verse was published as *Armenian Papers* (1987).

MATHEWS, John Joseph
(1894–1979)

American writer, born in Pawhuska, Indian Territory (now Oklahoma). Of mixed Osage and French descent, Mathews studied sciences at the University of Oklahoma and Merton College, Oxford. His studies interrupted by World War I, he served for a time as a pilot in the US Air Service. After the war, he spent several years studying and working as a newspaper correspondent in Europe before returning to Pawhuska in 1929, where he began both to write and to take an active part in Osage tribal affairs, serving several years on the Tribal Council. His first important work, *Wah'Kon-Tah: the*

Osage and the White Man's Road, a non-fictional account of Osage life, was published in 1932. This was followed by *Sundown* (1934), a semi-autobiographical novel describing a young mixed-blood Osage's struggle to fit in with either White or Native American worlds, and *Talking to the Moon* (1945), a lyrical, **Thoreau**-like account of the 10 years he lived in solitude on a ranch in northeastern Oklahoma. His major work, on which he spent some 30 years, was the cultural history *The Osages: Children of the Middle Waters* (1961); based on a series of interviews Mathews conducted with tribal elders, it traces the history of the Osages from traditional accounts of the creation to the mid-20th century.
▷G Bailey, 'John Joseph Mathews', in M Liberty (ed), *American Indian Intellectuals* (1978)

MATKOVIĆ, Marijan
(1915–)

Croatian dramatist, born in Karlovac. He has written many radio plays. Essentially Matković is an innovative and inventive follower of Krleža. His trilogy *The Gods Also Suffer* (1959–61) is a mocking examination of the 'personality cult'.

MATOS, Antun Gustav
(1873–1914)

Croatian poet, story writer, essayist, critic and part-time cellist who deserted from the hated Austrian army in 1898, and fled to Paris. He acted as Croatian (and to an extent Serbian) literature's **Endre Ady**, if at a less intensive pitch: he brought French procedures into what became Yugoslavia. He was most important as a critic, although his poems, the product of his closing years, are well made.

MATOS GUERRA, Gregorio de
(1623–96)

Brazilian baroque poet, influenced by **Góngora** and **Quevedo**. He was the first to depict the evils of Brazilian society in satirical verse, his most lively work. His lyrics are indifferent.

MATTHIAS, John Edward
(1941–)

American poet. He grew up in Columbus, Ohio, attended university there and in California, and spent 1966–7 in London as a Fulbright Fellow. Since then, he has taught English at the University of Notre Dame, Indiana, where he became full professor in 1980. His first verse collection, *Other Poems* (1971), marked him out as a disciple of **John Berryman** but, since the period of his Fulbright Fellowship, he has been increasingly influenced by English life and landscape, particularly that of East Anglia, and his work is closely aligned to the mystical historicism of **David Jones** and **Geoffrey Hill**. More playful than either, he often constructs poems out of elaborate linguistic conceits and transpositions, as in 'Turns' and the remarkable 'Double Derivation, Association and Cliché: From the Great Tournament Roll of Westminster' (both 1975). Later collections include *Rostropovich at Aldeburgh* (1979) and *Bathory and Lermontov* (1980), in which he experiments with historical 'rhymes' and coincidences, and the magnificent *Northern Summer* (1984), his finest work. His most recent published verse evokes **Edward Thomas**, using leys and pilgrimage routes to create a poetry of great historical focus.

MATTHIESSEN, F(rancis) O(tto)
(1902–50)

American literary critic. He was born near Pasadena, California, and grew up in Illinois. Though from a wealthy background, he quickly espoused socialism (though originally it was intermingled with Christian ideals). He studied at Yale and Harvard, and spent a year as Rhodes Scholar at Oxford. His studies of **Henry James** (1944) and **T S Eliot** (1935, rev edn 1947) are direct and perceptive. Joining the faculty at Harvard, he supported civil liberties causes and trade unionism, arguing that individualism was the bane of American life and culture: this was the underlying thrust of his masterpiece, *American Renaissance* (1941), a panoramic study of the literary environment of **Nathaniel Hawthorne**, **Ralph Waldo Emerson**, **Walt Whitman** and **Herman Melville**, that galvanized a generation of American students. At the end of World War II, Matthiessen became involved in Henry Wallace's Progressive third party movement and was widely reviled from left and right for either closet communism or 'accommodationism'. His journal *From the Heart of Europe* (1948) suggested growing introspection; two years later, Matthiessen threw himself from a hotel room window. He bequeathed his inheritance to the struggling journal *Monthly Review*; his intellectual legacy is harder to calculate, but his ideas remain of consequence in American letters.
▷W Cain, *F O Matthiessen and the Politics of Criticism* (1988)

MATTHIESSEN, Peter
(1927–)

American novelist, travel writer, naturalist and explorer, born in New York City. He has made anthropological and natural history expeditions to Alaska, the Canadian Northwest Territories, Peru, New Guinea, Africa, Nicaragua and Nepal, out of which have come a number of eloquent ecological and natural history studies, which reflect the concerns of the cultish novel *At Play in the Fields of the Lord* (1965). He won the National Book Award with the bestselling *The Snow Leopard* (1978), one man's inner story of a mystical trek across the Tibetan plateau to the Crystal Mountain to catch a glimpse of the rarest and most beautiful of the great cats. Other novels include *Race Rock* (1954), *Partisans* (1955), the superb *Far Tortuga* (1975) and *Killing Mister Watson* (1990). In recent years, Matthiessen has taken up the cause of Native Americans; *In the Spirit of Crazy Horse* (1983), an account of a 1975 shoot-out with the FBI, was delayed by litigation.

MATTO DE TURNER, Clorinda
(1854–1909)

Peruvian novelist, poet, and playwright. One of the most important Latin-American female writers of the 19th century, she occasionally wrote under the pseudonym of 'Carlota Dumont'. She is claimed by some critics as an early feminist, though she is most famous for her *Aves sin nido* (1889, 'Birds Without a Nest'); the only Indianist novel of the 19th century, it has a Romantic plot, realist detail, a strong anti-clerical message, and displays elements of *criollismo* (narratives on popular customs and language). Her other major work was *Tradiciones cuzqueñas* (1884–6, 'Traditions of Cuzco'), a development of the uniquely Peruvian genre invented by **Ricardo Palma**.
▷A Tauro, *Clorinda Matto de Turner y la novela indigenista* (1976)

MATURIN, Charles Robert
(1782–1824)

Irish dramatist and novelist, born in Dublin. Educated at Trinity College, Dublin, he became a curate in Loughrea and Dublin. He made his name with a series of extravagant novels in macabre vein that rivalled those of **Ann Radcliffe**. These included *The Fatal Revenge* (1807), *Melmoth the Wanderer* (1820), which influenced **Honoré de Balzac**, and *The Albigenses* (1824). His tragedy, *Bertram*, had a success at Drury Lane in 1816; its successors, *Manuel* (1817) and *Fredolpho* (1819), were failures.
▷W Scholten, *Charles Robert Maturin: the terror novelist* (1933)

MATUTE, Ana María
(1926–)

Spanish novelist, born in Barcelona, one of those who decided to remain in Spain after the Civil War and to denounce injustice under the eyes of the censors. She came into prominence in the 1950s and 1960s as one of a

generation who had experienced the war as children: her best-known novel, the long *Los hijos muertos* (1958, Eng trans *The Lost Children*, 1965), examines just this problem in the objectivist manner then almost statutory in a Spain where little that was directly critical of the regime could appear. She has continued to explore these themes, of war and children, in a series of novels and stories upon which critical opinion is divided: one school holds that her work is, though worthy, poorly written and excessively rhetorical, the other that she is a major novelist.
▷M E W Jones, *The Literary World of Ana María Matute* (1970); J W Díaz, *Ana María Matute* (1971)

MAUGHAM, W(illiam) Somerset
(1874–1965)

British writer, a modern master of the short story, born in Paris, of Irish origin. He was educated at King's School, Canterbury, read philosophy and literature at Heidelberg and qualified as a surgeon at St Thomas's Hospital, London. Afflicted by a bad stammer, he turned to writing in his student days and a year's medical practice in the London slums gave him the material for his first novel, the lurid *Liza of Lambeth* (1897), and the magnificent autobiographical novel, *Of Human Bondage*, eventually published in 1915. Attempts to have his plays accepted having failed, he settled in Paris and with **Laurence Housman** revived a 19th-century annual, *The Venture* (1903–4). With the success of *Lady Frederick* (1907), four of his plays ran in London in 1908. In 1914 he served first with a Red Cross unit in France, then as a secret agent in Geneva and finally in Petrograd, attempting to prevent the outbreak of the Russian Revolution. *Ashenden* (1928) is based on these experiences. He travelled in the South Seas, visiting Tahiti, which inspired *The Moon and Sixpence* (1919), in which an Englishman, Strickland, leaves his wife and stockbroking to end his life in a leper's hut. Maugham spent two years in a Scottish tuberculosis sanatorium and this again finds expression in several short stories. He then visited the Far East, writing such plays as *East of Suez* (1922) and *Our Betters* (1923). In 1928 he settled in the South of France, where he wrote his astringent, satirical masterpiece, *Cakes and Ale* (1930). A British agent again in World War II, he fled from France in 1940 with only a suitcase, and lived until 1946 in the USA where he ventured into mysticism with *The Razor's Edge* (1945). But he is best known for his short stories, several of which were filmed under the titles *Quartet* (1949), *Trio* (1950) and *Encore* (1951). The best of them, 'Rain', was originally published in the collection *The Trembling of a Leaf*

(1921). His sparse, careful prose has sometimes unjustly been mistaken for superficiality. He refused to do more than tell a story; all else is propaganda, which seriously impairs a work of art. Other works include *Catalina* (1948), *The Complete Short Stories* (3 vols, 1951), *A Writer's Notebook* (1949) and essays on **Goethe**, **Anton Chekhov**, **Henry James** and **Katherine Mansfield** in *Points of View* (1958).
▷*Summing Up* (1938); *Strictly Personal* (1941); R Calder, *Willie: the life of Maugham* (1989)

MAUPASSANT, Guy de
(1850–93)

French novelist, born in the Norman château of Miromesnil. He was educated at Rouen and spent his life in Normandy. After a short spell as a soldier in the Franco–German war he became a government clerk, but encouraged by **Gustave Flaubert**, a friend of his mother's, he took to writing and mingled with **Émile Zola** and other disciples of Naturalism. His stories range from the short tale of one or two pages to the full-length novel. Free from sentimentality or idealism, they lay bare with minute and merciless observation the pretentiousness and vulgarity of the middle class of the period and the animal cunning and traditional meanness of the Norman peasant. His first success, *Boule de suif* (1880, 'Ball of Tallow'), exposes the hypocrisy, prudery and ingratitude of the bourgeois in the face of a heroic gesture by a woman of the streets, while *La Maison Tellier* (1881, Eng trans *The House of Madame Tellier and Other Stories*, 1959) tells with penetrating satire and humour the tale of an outing for the inmates of a provincial house of ill-repute. At the other end of the scale *Le Horla* (1887, Eng trans 1890) and *La Peur* (posthumous 1925, 'The Fear') describe madness and fear with a horrifying accuracy which foreshadows the insanity which beset de Maupassant in 1892 and finally precipitated his death. His short stories, the form in which he excelled, number nearly 300, and he wrote several full-length novels, including *Une Vie* (1883, Eng trans *A Woman's Life*, 1888) and *Bel-Ami* (1885, Eng trans *Bel-Ami*, 1891).
▷F Steegmuller, *Maupassant* (1950)

MAUPIN, Armistead
(1944–)

American novelist, born into a 'mossbacked' Republican family in Washington DC, and brought up mainly in North Carolina. Educated at the University of North Carolina, he served in Vietnam, where he later returned to build housing for the disabled, receivir Presidential Commendation for thi: Turning to journalism, he began to fictional column for the *San Francisco Chronicle*. This soon evolved into *Tales of the City* (1978) and five subsequent novels, a saga that focuses on the lovable homosexual Michael ('Mouse') Tolliver and his unconventional collection of friends as they each discover that the concept of family is broader than kin. Warm-hearted, witty and emotional, these stories gained huge popularity with straight and gay readers alike. A writer concerned with promoting tolerance, and a respected gay rights advocate, Maupin moved beyond this series in 1992 with the novel *Maybe the Moon*.

MAURIAC, François
(1885–1970)

French novelist and winner of the Nobel Prize for literature, born in Bordeaux of Roman Catholic parentage, and regarded as the leading novelist of that faith. He started as a poet, publishing his first volume of verse in 1909. In his novels, his treatment of the themes of temptation, sin and redemption, set in the brooding Bordeaux countryside, showed his art as cathartic, exploring the universal problems of sinful, yet aspiring, man. His principal novels, all translated into English, are *Le Baiser au Lépreux* (1922, Eng trans *The Kiss to the Leper*, 1923); *Génitrix* (1923, Eng trans 1930); *Thérèse Desqueyroux* (1927, Eng trans 1928; and *Le Noeud de Vipères* (1932, Eng trans *Vipers' Tangle*, 1933). Also important is his play *Asmodée* (1938, Eng trans 1939). He was awarded the 1952 Nobel Prize for literature.
▷M Alyn, *François Mauriac* (1960)

MAURICE, Furnley, properly Frank Leslie Thompson Wilmot
(1881–1942)

Australian poet, born in Collingwood, Melbourne. For the last 10 years of his life he was manager of the Melbourne University Press. He produced his early verse on a hand press; his first published work was *Eyes of Vigilance* (1920), which included his impassioned poem against war, 'To God, from the Warring Nations', which had originally appeared in 1916. He loved the country, but wrote of the town with the style and verve of the old bush poets. *Melbourne Odes* (1934) sings of city life in the 1930s depression years. His best work was edited by Percival Serle in *Poems by Furnley Maurice* (1944).

MAUROIS, André, pseud of Émile Herzog
(1885–1967)

French novelist and biographer, born in Elbeuf. He was one of a family of Jewish industrialists from Alsace who settled in Normandy after 1870. During World War I he was a liaison officer with the British army, and began his literary career with two books of shrewd and affectionate observation of British character, *Les Silences du Colonel Bramble* (1918, 'The Silences of Colonel Bramble') and *Les Discours du Docteur O'-Grady* (1920, 'The Speeches of Dr O'Grady'). His large output includes such distinguished biographies as his *Ariel* (1923), a biography of **Shelley**, *Disraeli* (1927), *Voltaire* (1935), *À la recherche de Marcel Proust* (1949, 'In Search of Marcel Proust'), and *La vie de Sir Alexander Fleming* (1959, Eng trans *The Life of Sir Alexander Fleming*, 1959). He also wrote several novels, fantasies, tales for children, and critical and philosophical essays.
▷J Suffel, *André Maurois* (1963)

MAURRAS, Charles
(1868–1952)

French minor poet and traitor, born in Martigues. A tragic figure, the deaf Maurras was for many years the leading voice in the ultra right-wing, anti-Semitic, royalist movement, Action Française. His chief claim to distinction lies in his forceful, classical and lucid style; but, for all his courage, his polemical arguments were highly emotional and prejudiced. His deafness meant that he understood little of how ordinary people lived, felt or thought. He collaborated with the Vichy government and was sentenced to life imprisonment in 1945. He is now little read, although the long introduction to *La Musique intérieure* (1925), a collection of artificial poems of little account, is moving in its loftily sad isolation from real experience.
▷M Mourre, *Charles Maurras* (1958); C H Sisson, *The Avoidance of Literature* (1986)

MAVILIS, Lorentsos
(1860–1912)

Greek poet, born in Corfu and educated on the island and then for 15 years at German universities, where he studied philosophy (particularly the work of **Schopenhauer**), Sanskrit and Indian religion. He returned to Corfu in 1893 and wrote the bulk of his slim poetic output over the next seven years. His sonnets are concerned with moral and human nobility, and he himself took part in the struggles against the Turks in Crete in 1896 and then in Epirus in the following year. He died on a battlefield outside Iannina in 1912, while he was serving as an officer in the Garibaldi Officer Corps.

MAVOR, Elizabeth Osborne
(1927–)

Scottish novelist and biographer, born in Glasgow and educated at Oxford. She has written four novels, of which the first, *Summer in the Greenhouse*, appeared in 1959. One of her recurring themes is of women attempting to come to terms with their emotions and hoping thereby to discover a sense of direction in a sometimes violently chaotic world. In *A Green Equinox* (1973) Hero Kinoull, during one short summer, suffers a series of traumatic experiences while trying to make sense of her complicated sexual life. Mavor's biographies include the intriguing *The Ladies of Llangollen: A Study in Romantic Friendship* (1971), dealing with the relationship between Lady Eleanor Butler and Sarah Ponsonby who, in 1778, shocked society by setting up a remote home together in Wales.

MAXTON, Hugh, pseud of W J McCormack
(1947–)

Irish poet and critic, born in County Wicklow. A lecturer in Modern Literature at Trinity College Dublin, he brought a new severity to analysis of Irish studies with two volumes of literary criticism, *Sheridan Le Fanu and Victorian Ireland* (1980) and *The Battle of the Books* (1987). As Hugh Maxton (after **Hugh MacDiarmid** and James Maxton), his challenging, sometimes cryptic verse fuses mid-European themes with modern Irish political and social concerns. *Jubilee for Renegades: Poems 1976–1980* (1982), *The Puzzle Tree Ascendant* (1988) and *New and Selected Poems: The Engraved Passion* (1991) show a remarkable willingness to experiment with form, and present a humane and liberating philosophy.

MAXWELL, William
(1908–)

American novelist, story writer and critic, born in Lincoln, Illinois. From 1936 he worked (eventually becoming fiction editor) for the *New Yorker* magazine, of whose values his readable and well-crafted novels might be called an enshrinement. Reacting against the protesting note to be found in the fiction of **Sherwood Anderson** and the early **Sinclair Lewis**, Maxwell found beauty and dignity in the midwestern middle-class: *They Come Like Swallows* (1937) tells of the way in which a mother's premature death affects an Illinois household, while *The Folded Leaf* (1945) is about two midwestern students who have to try to come to terms with what they are offered by their limited circumstances. Maxwell also wrote many short stories.

MAY, Thomas
(1595–1650)

English dramatist and historian, born in Sussex. He was educated at Sidney Sussex College, Cambridge, and became a member of Gray's Inn and a courtier. He wrote dramas, comedies, poems and translations of **Lucan**'s *Pharsalia* (1627), **Virgil**'s *Georgics* (1628) and **Martial** (1629). A Puritan, he was secretary and official historian to the Long Parliament, and produced a *History of the Parliament 1640–1643* (1647), and a *Breviary* (1650).
▷A G Chester, *Thomas May: man of letters* (1932)

MAYAKOVSKY, Vladimir Vladimirovich
(1894–1930)

Russian poet and playwright, born in Bagdadi (now Mayakovsky), Georgia. The son of an impoverished Russian nobleman, he was involved in the Social Democratic movement during his youth, but when he was imprisoned for 11 months he renounced politics for art. Writing was his first love, however, and in 1912 he wrote a poem that was published in the miscellany *Poshchochina obshchestvennomu vkusu* ('A Slap in the Face of Public Taste'). An enthusiastic supporter of the Revolution in 1917, both his play *Misteriya-Buff* (1918, Eng trans *Mystery-Bouffe*, 1968) and the long poem *150 000 000* (1919–20) are masterpieces of the period. But when the Civil War ended and the New Economy Policy was introduced in 1921, he found himself at odds with the new, conservative leaders. In response he wrote *Pro eto* (1923, 'About This'), poems pre-Revolution in sentiment, and satirical plays like *Klop* (1929, Eng trans *The Bedbug*, 1960) and *Banya* (1930, Eng trans *The Bath-House*, 1968), concerned with the betrayal of the Revolution by its self-appointed officials. His fame in the former Soviet Union is dependent on three works: *Vladimir Ilyich Lenin* (1924), *Khorosho!* (1927, 'Good!') and the unfinished *Vo ves golos* (1929–30, translated into Scots by **Edwin Morgan**, 1972). Towards the end of his life he was severely castigated by more orthodox Soviet writers and critics for his outspoken criticism of the bureaucracy and his unconventional opinions on art, and was even forced to abandon the Left Front for the Arts for the reactionary Russian Association of Proletarian Writers. But he was always regarded as an outsider, and this, together with an unstable personal life, undoubtedly contributed towards his suicide.
▷E Brown, *Mayakovsky: a poet in the revolution* (1973)

MAYHEW, Henry
(1812–87)

English author, born in London, and first joint editor of *Punch* with **Mark Lemon**. He ran away from Westminster School and collaborated with his brother Augustus (1826–75) in writing numerous successful novels

such as *The Good Genius that turns Everything to Gold* (1847) and *Whom to Marry* (1848). He also wrote on many subjects, his best-known work being the classic social survey, *London Labour and the London Poor* (1851–62). Another brother, Horace (1816–72), also collaborated with Henry and was a contributor to *Punch*.
▷ G S Jones, *Outcast London* (1971)

MAYKOV, Appolon
(1821–97)
Russian poet, born in Moscow into a noble family. His father was a painter and his mother was a writer. Conservative critics pronounced him the heir of **Pushkin** for his careful and chiselled poetry, but after his death he was rightly relegated to the role of skilful (and often tedious) minor poet. There are some translations of his work in John Pollen's *Russian Songs and Lyrics* (1917).

MAYNE, Jasper
(1604–72)
English playwright and poet, born in Hatherleigh, Devon. He is known as the author of two plays, *The City March* (1638) and *The Amorous War* (1648), both clearly influenced by **Ben Jonson**. The former is a satire set in London, portraying the duping of a rich uncle by an unscrupulous nephew, while the latter is a tragi-comedy dealing with love and infidelity. They are rumbustious pieces, but sprawling and cumbersome; they are forgotten now, and the more uncharitable might add that it is not without good reason. Mayne was also the author of a volume of verse, *To The Duke of York on Our Late Sea Flight* (1665).

MAYNE, Seymour
(1944–)
Canadian poet and broadcaster. Mayne was born in Montreal and in 1985 became Professor of English at Ottawa University. The titles of his collections—*Diaspora* (1977), *Abel and Cain* (1980) and *The Impossible Promised Land* (1981)—reflect the biblical and Jewish preoccupations of his verse. His work has been described as 'persistent'. He is certainly energetic and in addition to his writing and broadcasting has edited several magazines and founded two small presses.

MAZURANIĆ, Ivan
(1814–90)
Croatian poet and politician, born in Novi Vinodol. He completed the missing two cantos of the *Osman* of **Gundulić**. His epic *Smrt Smail-age Cengiœa* (1846, Eng trans *The Death of Smail Aga*, 1918) is often pointed to as the finest Croatian poem of its century. It

tells of the 1840 execution by ambush, at the hands of the Montenegrins, of a tax-collecting Turk, but is unusual in that it gives some dignity to the greedy tyrant. Mazuranić was governor of Croatia from 1873, and was also an educational reformer.
▷ *Slavonic and East European Review*, XLIV (1966)

McALMON, Robert
(1896–1956)
American writer, small-press publisher and literary socialite, long resident in Paris, a member of the 'lost generation' of **Gertrude Stein**. His own verse and prose are unimportant and characterized by what a critic called 'pathetic nihilism'; but his mediocre career and his autobiography, *Geniuses Together* (1938), are of genuine interest.
▷ R E Kroll, *Robert McAlmon: Expatriate Publisher and Writer* (1957)

McAULEY, James
(1917–76)
Australian poet, critic and writer, born in Lakemba, Sydney. He spent much time during and after World War II in Papua New Guinea, where he likened the destruction there of traditional social structures to the larger upheavals of the western world. His verse, unlike that of his contemporaries, is of a classical and visionary style, and was first collected in *Under Aldebaran* (1946). Never a copious writer, his second volume, *A Vision of Ceremony*, did not appear until 1956, followed by *Captain Quiros* (1964), an epic narrative of the 16th-century Portuguese explorer of Melanesia. Not sympathetic to modern fashions, in 1955 McAuley foisted on Max Harris, unsuspecting editor of a modernistic broadsheet *Angry Penguins*, the collected works of a fictitious dead poet, 'Ern Malley', thus hastening the demise of that periodical and starting a controversy which lasted for 40 years. McAuley founded the conservative literary and political journal *Quadrant* and edited it from its inception in 1956 to 1963. He also published some books of critical writing and compiled *A Map of Australian Verse: The Twentieth Century* (1975).

McBAIN, Ed *see* HUNTER, Evan

McCARTHY, Cormac
(1933–)
American novelist, born in Rhode Island but educated in Tennessee. He began publishing in the sixties and seventies. His first novels were Gothic and grotesque stories about life in the Southern backwoods. Early books such as *Child of God* (1974) lapsed into incredible

depths of depravity and violence. In more recent fiction, particularly with the epic *Blood Meridian* (1985), McCarthy has achieved a powerfully descriptive narrative style. *All the Pretty Horses* (1993), the first book in a projected trilogy, was universally greeted as his finest work.

McCARTHY, Justin
(1830–1912)

Irish politician, novelist and historian, born in Cork. He joined the staff of the *Northern Times*, Liverpool, in 1853, and in 1860 entered the reporters' gallery for the *Morning Star*, becoming its chief editor in 1864. He resigned in 1868, and devoted the next three years to a tour of the USA. Soon after his return he became connected with the *Daily News*, and contributed to the *London*, *Westminster* and *Fortnightly Reviews*. He entered parliament in 1879 for Longford. He is better known, however, as a novelist than as a politician. His novels include *Dear Lady Disdain* (1875) and *Miss Misanthrope* (1877). Other works include *A History of our Own Times* (7 vols, 1879–1905) and *The Four Georges and William IV* (4 vols, 1889–1901).
▷ *An Irishman's Story* (1904)

McCARTHY, Mary Thérèse
(1912–89)

American novelist and critic, born in Seattle, Washington, of mixed Catholic, Protestant and Jewish descent. She and her three younger brothers were orphaned as young children in 1918 and they were raised by grandparents, uncles and aunts. At the age of eight she won a state prize for an article entitled 'The Irish in American History'. She was educated at Forest Ridge Convent, Seattle, and Anne Wright Seminary, Tacoma, and graduated from Vassar College, New York in 1933. She married an actor, Harold Johnsrud, who died in a fire. She began to write book reviews for the *Nation* and the *New Republic* and was an editor for *Covici Friede* in 1936–7; from 1937 to 1948 she was an editor and theatre critic for the *Partisan Review*, during which period she wrote articles, stories and eventually novels. In 1938 she married the critic **Edmund Wilson**, but they divorced soon afterwards. In 1948 she married Bowden Bowater, whom she divorced in 1961 to marry James West, an information officer. Her voice has often been described as scathing, yet although she brought little emotional warmth to her work, she was a highly intelligent, observant novelist. Her best-known fiction is *The Company She Keeps* (1942), *The Groves of Academe* (1952) and *The Group* (1963), a bestseller about eight Vassar graduates and their sex lives. She also wrote documentary denunciations of US involvement in the Vietnam war,

in *Vietnam* (1967) and *Hanoi* (1968). Other works include *A Charmed Life* (1955), *Sights and Spectacles* (1956), the autobiographical *Memories of a Catholic Childhood* (1957) and *Cannibals and Missionaries* (1979).
▷ C Gerlderman, *Mary McCarthy* (1988)

McCLURE, James Howe
(1939–)

British crime novelist, born and educated in South Africa, on whose political and cultural situation he commented through the medium of the 'police procedural' and through the relationship of the white policeman Lieutenant Kramer and his Zulu assistant Sergeant Zondi. They first appeared in *The Steam Pig* (1971) and *The Caterpillar Cop* (1972), elegantly plotted thrillers revealing a journalist's eye for significant detail; McClure has worked for several newspapers in South Africa, and subbed for some years on the *Oxford Times* and *Oxford Mail* (1966–74). Other Kramer and Zondi novels include *The Gooseberry Fool* (1974) and *The Blood of an Englishman* (1980). McClure has also written 'ride-along' accounts of police activity in Liverpool (*Spike Island*, 1980) and San Diego (*Copworld*, 1985).

McCLURE, Michael Thomas
(1932–)

American poet, born in Marysville, Kansas, and educated there and in Arizona and California. He has taught at the California College of Arts and Crafts in Oakland since 1962. A highly prolific writer, much of his work reflects his interest in visual imagery, often of an apocalyptically violent nature and frequently combining historical characters, chiefly outlaws, in surreal juxtaposition. McClure's interest in Native American anthropology and in European post-Symbolist styles is reflected in the titles of his second and third volumes, *Peyote Poem* (1958) and *For Artaud* (1959), but it was with his fourth, the fiery *Hymns to St Geryon and Other Poems* (1959) that he emerged as an individual voice; it was the first of his collections to appear (1969) in the UK. The important prose *Meat Science Essays* (1963) appeared in Britain shorn of the notorious opening piece 'Phi Upsilon Kappa', a Lawrentian discourse on the word 'fuck'. McClure writes in a passionate upper-case telegraphese, a title like *Oh Christ God Love Cry of Love Stifled Furred Wall Smoking Burning* (1969) is representative. Later volumes are more conventionally lyrical and include *September Blackberries* (1974) and *Fragments of Perseus* (1978). McClure has also written experimental plays and appeared as an actor in two of **Norman Mailer**'s films.

McCONKEY, James Rodney
(1921–)

American novelist and academic, born in Ohio. McConkey taught at Cornell and his literary criticism includes *The Novels of E. M. Forster* (1957) and *Chekhov and our Age* (1985). Memory is a constant refrain in his fiction. *Crossroads* (1968) contains fragments of autobiography and in *The Tree House Confessions* (1979) a 50-year-old man dredges up memories of the past when visiting a treehouse built for his dead son. Memory is again at play in a recent title: *Kayo: the Authentic and Annotated Autobiographical Novel from Outer Space* (1987).

McCORD, David Thompson Watson
(1897–)

American writer of light verse. A graduate of Harvard, McCord was for a while editor of its *Alumni Bulletin*. *One At A Time* (1977) brings together work from five collections of children's and humorous verse. The earlier *Selected Poems* (1957) is amusingly annotated by McCord himself. In an extended career he has published books consistently at the rate of a volume a year since the mid-1920s. In addition to his own poetry, which displays good command of metre and rhyme, he will be remembered for *What Cheer*, an anthology of humorous verse which he edited in 1945.

McCORMACK, W J *see* MAXTON, Hugh

McCORMICK, Eric Hall
(1906–)

New Zealand cultural historian, born in Taihape. As biographer, editor and critic he contributed greatly to the recognition of New Zealand literature from 1940. He was secretary of, and later editor to, the National Historical Committee which commissioned publications to mark the centenary of European settlement in 1840. For this series he wrote *Letters and Art in New Zealand* (1940), the first critical conspectus of New Zealand writing. This was later expanded as *New Zealand Literature: A Survey* (1959). His other critical works include *Alexander Turnbull: His Life, His Circle, His Collections* (1974), on the wealthy merchant who left his library of 50 000 books to the nation; biographies of prominent New Zealand scholars, and studies of a New Zealand artist in *The Expatriate, a Study of Frances Hodgkins* (1954) and *Portrait of Frances Hodgkins* (1981). *The Inland Eye: a Sketch in Visual Autobiography* (1959) gives his personal and critical creed.

McCOY, Horace
(1897–1955)

American novelist and journalist, born in Tennessee, best-known as the author of *They Shoot Horses Don't They* (1935), his first novel. He had worked as a mechanic, salesman and taxi driver before joining the *Dallas Journal*, and publishing his first story, *Brass Buttons*, in 1927. Much of his early work was printed in detective magazines such as *Black Mask*. *No Pockets in a Shroud* (1937), about corruption beneath the surface of an apparently decent American town, *I Should Have Stayed Home* (1938), a portrait of degenerate Hollywood life, along with later books, confirmed McCoy's bleak outlook, as did the Sydney Pollack movie of *They Shoot Horses Don't They* (1969).

McCRACKEN, Esther Helen, née Armstrong
(1902–71)

English playwright and actress, born in Newcastle-upon-Tyne. From 1924 to 1937 she acted with the Newcastle Repertory Company. Her first play, *The Willing Spirit*, was produced in 1936, but it was with *Quiet Wedding* (1938) that her reputation was made as a writer of domestic comedy. Other successes were *Quiet Weekend* (1941) and *No Medals* (1944). Her first husband, Lt-Col Angus McCracken, died in action in 1943, and the following year she married Mungo Campbell.

McCRAE, George Gordon
(1833–1927)

Scottish-born Australian poet, born in Leith, Edinburgh, the eldest son of lawyer Andrew Murison McCrae, Writer to the Signet, and father of **Hugh McCrae**. He went with his mother the artist Georgiana Huntly McCrae to Australia in 1841 and developed an affection for the aborigines. He first published *Two Old Men's Tales of Love and War* (1865) and, two years later, *The Story of Balladeädro* and *Mämba, 'The Bright-Eyed'*, some of the earliest Australian poems on aboriginal themes. A selection of his varied verse was published in 1915 as *The Fleet and Convoy and Other Verses*.
▷H McCrae, *My Father and My Father's Friends* (1935)

McCRAE, Hugh Raymond
(1876–1958)

Australian artist and poet, born in Melbourne, son of **George McCrae**. He spent some time in New York and returned to make a precarious living by acting small parts in plays and films, and contributing sketches and verse to the *Bulletin*. He published much verse, often illustrated by his close friend **Norman Lindsay**. *Silvarum Libri* (1909) was reissued as *Satyrs and Sunlight* in 1911. The titles of his collections echo the world of **Norman Gale** and **Rupert Brooke**: *Colombine* (1920), *Idyllia* (1922), *Forests of Pan* (1944) and *Voice of the Forest* (1945). *The Best Poems of Hugh McCrae*, ed R G Howarth, appeared in 1961.

McCUAIG, Ronald
(1908–93)

Australian journalist and lyric poet, born in Newcastle, New South Wales. He was the writer of satirical verse for the *Bulletin* between the wars, which was privately published as *Vaudeville* (1938) and *The Wanton Goldfish* (1941), collected in *Quod Ronald McCuaig* (1946) and further cumulated in *The Ballad of Bloodthirsty Bessie* (1961). His style varied between crude cynicism and delicate 17th-century pastiches; examples of both are in *The Passionate Clerk: Selected Poems* (1992).

McCULLERS, (Lula) Carson, née Smith
(1917–67)

American novelist, born in Columbus, Georgia, where she was brought up and attended high school, graduating in 1933. Between 1934 and 1936 she went to classes at Columbia University, New York, and New York University. In 1937 she married Reeves McCullers, with whom she moved to Charlotte, North Carolina; in 1941 they moved to Greenwich Village and divorced, but were remarried in 1945, finally divorcing again in 1948. *The Heart is a Lonely Hunter*, her first book, about a deaf mute, appeared in 1940, distinguishing her immediately as a novelist of note. She wrote the best and the bulk of her work in a six-year spell through World War II. Along with **William Faulkner**, **Tennessee Williams** and **Truman Capote** she is credited with fashioning a type of fiction labelled by critics as Southern Gothic. Fusing, in her own words, 'anguish and farce', she peopled her work with grotesque characters who are expressionistic extensions of normal, universal human problems. *Reflections in a Golden Eye* appeared in 1941, followed by *The Member of the Wedding* (1946), *The Ballad of the Sad Cafe* (1951) and *Clock Without Hands*, a last ironic look at the South, in 1961.
▷V S Carr, *The Lonely Hunter* (1975)

McCULLEY, Johnston
(1883–1958)

American popular novelist, born in Ottawa, Illinois (not in Canada, as is sometimes supposed). He is known primarily for the creation of Zorro, a mysterious nemesis with a lightning sword-blade and the ability to vanish apparently at will. McCulley wrote more than 25 Zorro stories, beginning with *The Mask of Zorro* (1924)—masks feature with disconcerting prominence in his work—and continuing through highly successful radio and television series. The prose scarcely commands serious attention, but his main character is one of the great popular creations.

McCULLOUGH, Colleen
(1937–)

Australian novelist, born in Wellington, best known for the Cleary family's saga of sex, religion and disaster, *The Thorn Birds* (1977), later produced as a televison series. Her earlier book *Tim* (1974) was also filmed, as was *An Indecent Obsession* (1981). A delicate novella, *The Ladies of Missalonghi* (1987) showed that she is capable of some fine writing, and her latest books, a series of six novels set in Ancient Rome, demonstrate a concern for historical detail.

McCUTCHEON, George Barr
(1866–1928)

Prolific American novelist, born in Indiana. McCutcheon worked for a time on his hometown paper, the *Lafayette Chronicle*, but resigned as soon as his fiction became successful. He is still best-known for his two early books, *Graustark* (1901), set in an imaginary Balkan kingdom, à la *The Prisoner of Zenda*, and *Brewster's Millions* (1902), an account of the farcical consequences of suddenly inheriting a fortune. The second of these was turned into a British film in 1935, and there have been several remakes. McCutcheon's readers were hungry for more Balkan adventure and he obliged with two sequels and other novels in similar vein. His own favourite was his single realistic novel, *Mary Midthorne* (1911).

McDONALD, Nan(cy May)
(1921–74)

Australian poet, born in Eastwood, Sydney, who for much of her life was editor for the publishers Angus & Robertson. *Pacific Sea* (1947) won the inaugural Grace Leven Prize for Poetry. Other books were *The Lonely Fire* (1954) and *The Lighthouse and Other Poems* (1959). *Selected Poems* was published in 1969. Her stoic reflections on life and suffering seem to anticipate her early death from cancer.

McDONALD, Roger
(1941–)

Australian novelist and poet, born in Sydney. Following two books of verse, *Citizens of Mist* (1968) and *Airship* (1975), he turned to fiction with *1915* (1979), a highly successful retelling of the Gallipoli campaign which was later turned into an award-winning television series. His second novel, *Slipstream* (1982), is loosely based on the exploits of pioneer aviator Charles Kingsford Smith. His third, *Rough Wallaby* (1989), is a comedy of crooked doings on and off the racetrack. A work of non-fiction, *Shearer's Hotel* (1992), is based on the writer's experiences as camp cook for itinerant shearers in the outback and won the 'Banjo' Award for non-fiction in 1993. *Water Man* (1993) describes the grip of a long-dead water diviner on an outback town.

McEWAN, Ian Russell
(1948–)

English novelist and author of screenplays and short stories, born in Aldershot, Hampshire, and educated at the universities of Sussex and East Anglia. His first books, the short-story collections *First Love, Last Rites* (1975) and *In Between the Sheets* (1978), combine elegant writing with explicit sexual imagery and themes of obsession and perversion, and drew immediate critical controversy. The novel, *The Comfort of Strangers* (1981), while still macabre has a greater psychological depth. *The Child in Time* (1987) deals sympathetically with the emotional trauma experienced by a couple whose infant daughter is stolen and never discovered. His oratorio, *Or Shall We Die?* (1983), is an impassioned outcry against nuclear arms, while the screenplay for the film *The Ploughman's Lunch* (1983) bleakly and wittily satirizes the political atmosphere under Margaret Thatcher's Conservative government. Later novels include *The Innocent* (1990), a thriller set in Germany during the 1950s, and *Black Dogs* (1992).

McFARLANE, John Ebenezer Clare
(1894–1962)

Jamaican poet, born in Spanish Town and educated at Cornwall College. He joined the civil service, rising to the rank of Financial Secretary of Jamaica. He founded the Poetry League of Jamaica in 1923, became its second poet laureate, and edited the first anthology of Jamaican poetry, *Voices from Summerland* (1929). His taste and poetic style were romantic, as shown in his narrative poems, *Beatrice* (1918), *Daphne* (1931) and *The Magdalen* (1957), and shorter *Poems* (1924); but his most valuable contribution to West Indian literature was as patron and critic.

McFEE, William Morley Punshon
(1881–1966)

English-born American novelist and short-story writer. McFee's first book, *Letters from an Ocean Tramp* (1908), reflected his experience as a ship's engineer. Later he served with the British Navy in World War I, although by this time his home was in the USA. *Aliens* (1914) and *Casuals of the Sea* (1916), his first two novels, both focused on the experiences of British families during the war. Sometimes compared to **Conrad**, merely because so much of his fiction is set at sea, McFee's narrative voice, especially in the short stories (which feature Chief Engineer Spenlove, McFee's *alter ego*) is closer to **Somerset Maugham**.

McGAHERN, John
(1934–)

Irish novelist and short-story writer, born and educated in Dublin. His first novel was *The Barracks* (1963), a highly acclaimed study of a family, set in a provincial Irish police station. Its successor, *The Dark* (1965), was no less concentrated but it also signalled the beginning of a certain claustrophobia in McGahern's writing that persisted through the short-story collection *Nightlines* (1970) and a third novel, *The Leavetaking* (1974, rev edn 1984), and virtually exhausted itself in *The Pornographer* (1979), which explores the gap between the written and unwritten worlds, the fantasy of sex and the reality of death. McGahern had worked as a primary-school teacher in Dublin from 1963 to 1970, and held a research fellowship at the University of Reading for the final two years of that period. His work of the 1980s was—with the exception of the stories in *High Ground* (1985)—less successful than his first three books, but he returned to form with *Amongst Women* (1990), the story of an elderly IRA man, which was shortlisted for the Booker Prize.

McGEE, Thomas D'Arcy
(1825–68)

Irish-born Canadian writer and politician, born in Carlingford, County Louth. Educated at a Catholic 'hedge school', he was influenced by the mass movements of the Rev Theobald Mathew and Daniel O'Connell against drink and the Union. He became Editor of the Catholic *Boston Pilot* at the age of 19, wrote fiction and supported a variety of romantic causes, returning to Ireland in 1845 where he was identified with the Young Ireland *Nation*. After the abortive rebellion of 1848 he returned to the USA, where he argued for US annexation of Canada in his New York *Nation*. He lost Catholic support by sympathy for Mazzini's anti-Papal Roman Republic, and started the *American Celt* in Boston, publishing high-flown Romantic poems and *A History of the Irish settlers in North America* (1851). He moved to Montreal in 1857, founded the *New Era* newspaper, took Canadian citizenship and became an MP in 1858, and was Minister of Agriculture

(1864–8). He was a strong advocate of Canadian Confederation. He was assassinated in Ottawa for his opposition to a threatened Fenian invasion of Canada. His literary work as poet, publicist and political thinker improved as he aged; his published works included *A Popular History of Ireland* (1862–9) and *Poems* (1869).

▷I M Skelton, *The Life of Thomas McGee* (1925)

McGINLEY, Phyllis
(1905–78)

American (Roman Catholic) author of skilful light verse, born in Oregon. She was very widely read during her lifetime, during which she was praised by **W H Auden**; but her work has failed to last, not being quite of the order of that of **Harry Graham**, **Ogden Nash** and others of that calibre. Many of her verses appeared in the *New Yorker*. She also wrote successful and charming books for children.

McGONAGALL, William
(c.1825–1902)

Scottish poet and novelist, son of an immigrant Irish weaver. He spent some of his childhood on the island of South Ronaldsay in the Orkneys, settled with his family in Dundee at the age of 11, and became a hand-loom weaver with his father. In 1846 he married Jean King. He did some acting at Dundee's Royal Theatre, and in 1878 published his first collection of poems, including 'Railway Bridge of the Silvery Tay'. From then on he travelled in central Scotland, giving readings and selling his poetry in broadsheets. In Edinburgh he was lionized by the legal and student fraternity. He visited London in 1880 and New York in 1887. His poems are uniformly bad, but possess a disarming naivety and a calypso-like disregard for metre which remain entertaining. His *Poetic Gems* were published in 1890, and *More Poetic Gems* in 1962, followed by others.

McGOUGH, Roger
(1937–)

English poet, playwright and performer, born in Liverpool and associated for ever with the 'Mersey Sound', a title used for the hugely successful *Penguin Modern Poets 10* (1967, 1974, 1983), which he shared with **Adrian Henri** and **Brian Patten**. Educated at Hull University, he worked as a schoolteacher and art college lecturer; he enjoyed brief, bizarre pop success with the performing group Scaffold. McGough's characteristic stance is the lugubrious self-ironizing wit and runaway punning that John Lennon brought to Beatles interviews, with something of the same faintly adolescent desire to shock. Much more of a 'street' poet than either Henri or Patten, he uses the rhythms of speech in a curiously subversive way. This was evident in the novel-plus-poems *Frinck, A Life in the Day of, and Summer with Monika* (1967), and it saw service again in collections like *Gig* (1973), *In the Glassroom* (1976) and the superb *Waving at Trains* (1982). McGough has written many plays, often with music, and a number of funny children's books.

McGRATH, John Peter
(1935–)

English writer, director and film-maker, born in Birkenhead, Cheshire. Following National Service, he studied at St John's College, Oxford (1955–9), where his earliest plays were performed. Subsequently moving into television, he was one of the creators of the innovative police drama series *Z Cars* in 1962, and wrote such programmes as *Diary of A Nobody* (1966) before writing the film scripts *Billion Dollar Brain* (1967) and *The Bofors Gun* (1968). In 1971 he founded the 7:84 Theatre Company, which dedicated itself to the production of radical populist drama and took its name from the fact that 7 per cent of the population owned 84 per cent of the country's wealth. Artistic Director of 7:84 Scotland from 1973 to 1988, with his plays he attempted to illuminate Scottish historical struggles and explore issues vital to the current political agenda in the country. Notable works include *The Cheviot, The Stag and The Black, Black Oil* (1973), *The Game's A Bogey* (1974) and *Women in Power* (1983). As founder of Freeway Films in 1983 he has made such television drama as *Blood Red Roses* (1986) and *Border Warfare* (1988) and the film *The Dressmaker* (1988). His passionate and critical commitment to Scottish theatre is reflected in books like *The Bone Won't Break: On Theatre and Hope in Hard Times* (1990). Recent work, such as *Waiting for the Dolphins* (1991) and *The Wicked Old Man* (1992), has seen him question the changing validity of socialism in contemporary Europe.

▷A Bold, 'The Impact of 7:84', in *Modern Scottish Literature* (1983)

McGRATH, Patrick
(1950–)

English novelist and short-story writer, born in London; he grew up near Broadmoor Hospital, where his father was Medical Superintendent for many years. Perhaps partly as a result, his writing reveals a grim, Gothic imagination, in the tradition of **Edgar Allan Poe**, spiced with mordant comedy. His first collection of short stories, *Blood and Water and Other Tales*, appeared in 1989, as did his first, macabre novel *The Grotesque*, a gripping tale involving the tense relationship between a landowner and his butler. *Spider* (1990), and the excellent and compulsive *Dr Haggard's Disease* (1993), continue to exploit psychological horror in vivid, taut, elegant prose.

McGUANE, Thomas Francis, III
(1939–)

American novelist. He was born and educated in Michigan, which is the setting of his first comic novel, *The Sporting Club* (1968). Its guying of the **Hemingway** code is equally evident in a third novel, *Ninety-Two in the Shade* (1973), which deals with big-game fishing among the Florida Keys. McGuane scripted and directed a Hollywood version of the book, having already written a screenplay for another Michigan story, *The Bushwhacked Piano* (1970, 'novelized' 1971), and for the Marlon Brando vehicle, *The Missouri Breaks* (1976). In that year, he married (and divorced) the actress Margot Kidder. Subsequent novels have been less powerful; they include *Panama* (1978), *Nobody's Angel* (1982), *Something to Be Desired* (1984) and *Keep the Change* (1989). *An Outside Chance* (1980) is a collection of essays on sport and his collected stories are contained in *To Skin a Cat* (1986).

McGUCKIAN, Medbh, née McCaughan
(1950–)

Irish poet. Born in Belfast, she received a convent education there before studying English at Queen's University. She has been a school-teacher in Belfast since 1975 and was married two years later. Her first volume, *Single Ladies: Sixteen Poems*, appeared in 1980; it has a directness that she was later to reject in favour of the denser language of *The Flower Master* (1982) and, her most important work to date, *Venus and the Rain* (1984). Despite the obvious artifice and craft of her later work, its emotional range is increasingly simple and accessible.

McGUINNESS, Frank
(1956–)

Irish playwright, born in Buncrana, County Donegal; he moved to Dublin as a teacher in the mid-1980s. An early play, *The Factory Girls* (1982, rev edn 1988), gave evidence of his ambition to give voice to the misunderstood or the misrepresented. This was given most eloquent substance in his questioning of tribalism, enforced fidelities and personal loyalties in *Observe the Sons of Ulster Marching Towards the Somme* (1985). Its questioning of the traditional nationalist/loyalist divide was followed by the blistering anger against human waste of *Carthaginians* (1988), which debated the false evaluation of martyrdom that prevented dialogue in his native Ulster for much of the latter part of the 20th century.

McILVANNEY, William Angus
(1936–)

Scottish novelist and poet, born in Kilmarnock, Ayrshire, brother of sports writer Hugh McIlvanney. He was educated at Kilmarnock Academy and Glasgow University and taught from 1960 to 1975, when he took up writing full-time. His first novel was *Remedy is None* (1966), a paean to working-class values, in which a student avenges what he surmises is his mother's betrayal of his father. *A Gift from Nessus*, published two years later, developed the same theme as a travelling salesman chooses self-assertion over self-destruction. With *Docherty* (1975) McIlvanney extended his range without abandoning his roots, in the convincing story of the eponymous 'hard man', an Ayrshire miner, whose uncompromising life is seen through the eyes of his son. It won the Whitbread Award. *The Big Man* (1985) was set in similar territory and pitched Dan Scoular, a hero in his own locality, into a bare-knuckle fight where there is more at stake than money. Though he has been described by **Alan Bold** as 'a rhetorician occasionally overcome by his own verbosity', he has an enviable way with metaphor and simile and in the thrillers featuring the Glasgow detective Jack Laidlaw—*Laidlaw* (1977), *The Papers of Tony Veitch* (1983) and *Strange Loyalties* (1991)—comparisons with **Raymond Chandler** are not inappropriate. Volumes of poetry include *The Longships in Harbour* (1970) and *These Words* (1984). His short stories are collected in *Walking Wounded* (1989), and his essays and journalism in *Surviving the Shipwreck* (1991).

McINERNEY, Jay
(1955–)

American novelist, born in Hartford, Connecticut. His early posts included being a reader for Random House publishers, and working as one of the fabled fact-checkers on the *New Yorker* magazine. The latter occupation is the profession of the central character of his novel *Bright Lights, Big City* (1984), an acclaimed account of young New York professionals during the 1980s boom years. *Brightness Falls* (1992) is, as the title suggests, a companion piece or antidote to the earlier work, representing a move away from the frenzied trendies of *Bright Lights, Big City* into the real world where yuppies grow old and marriages crumble. His other works include *Ransom* (1985), being the titular character's experiences in contemporary Japan.

McINTYRE, Duncan Ban, English name of **Donnchadh Ban Macan t-Saoir**
(1724–1812)

Gaelic poet, and gamekeeper of Beinnodòrain, born in Glenorchy, Argyll. He worked as a forester, fought as a Hanoverian at Falkirk in 1746, and from 1799 to 1806 was one of the City Guard of Edinburgh. He composed a great deal of rich, celebratory nature poetry which, since he was illiterate, was written down by the minister's son at Killin and published in a collection of 1768. Some of it has been translated into English by **Hugh MacDiarmid** and **Iain Crichton-Smith**, including his long poem 'Moladh Beinn Dòbhrainn' ('The Praise of Ben Doran'). He also wrote formal occasional verse, love poems, satires and songs.

McKAY, Claude, originally **Festus Claudius**
(1889–1948)

American poet and novelist, and supposed instigator of the 'Harlem Renaissance' in Afro–American writing. McKay was born in Jamaica, where he served as a policeman—an experience recounted in *Constab Ballads* (1912)—before moving to the USA and a period of study at **Booker T Washington**'s Tuskegee Institute in Alabama. During the 1920s and the early 1930s he mostly lived abroad, working on a communist newspaper in London (1919–20), before returning to New York to co-edit the *Liberator* (1921–2). His fourth and most important poetry collection, *Harlem Shadows* (1922), asserted a kind of instinctualism at odds with his socialist principles. In 1922 he moved to the new Soviet Union for a year, living in France and Tangier for the next decade before returning to New Deal America. His most important fiction was written abroad: *Home to Harlem* (1928), *Banjo* (1929) and *Banana Bottom* (1933). McKay's fiction portrayed the Afro–American as a repository of essentially non-intellectual and explicitly sexual energies. It was a view that had a major impact on both black and white reactions to his race. His autobiography, *A Long Way from Home* (1937), predated his religious conversion, but the decision was clearly anticipated in his thinking during the mid-thirties.
▷W F Cooper, *Claude McKay: Rebel Sojourner in the Harlem Renaissance* (1987)

McKENNA, Stephen
(1888–1967)

English novelist, born in London. His sociopolitical novels of the rich upper crust, of which he was a member, are now virtually forgotten; but they were intelligent, if not penetrating, accounts of what he saw and understood in the course of a career in government posts. His only real success was *Sonia* (1917), a melodramatic but skilful chronicle of fashionable life in the first years of the 20th century. *While I Remember* (1921) is autobiographical.

McKIE, Ronald
(1909–91)

Australian journalist and writer, born in Toowoomba, Queensland, who worked in Singapore and China before serving with the Australian forces in World War II. He was a war correspondent in Burma and Italy, and after the war covered the Potsdam Conference and the trial of Norwegian traitor Vidkun Quisling. His war books include an account of the Japanese invasion of Singapore, *This Was Singapore* (1942), *Proud Echo* (1953) and *The Heroes* (1960), which describes the barbaric executions of prisoners-of-war in Singapore. He wrote other books on South-East Asia, and three novels; the award-winning *The Mango Tree* (1974), a tale of Australian childhood in the early years of this century which won the **Miles Franklin** Award, *The Crushing* (1977), a tragi-comedy of social pretensions in a small Queensland sugar town, and *Bitter Bread* (1978), a study of contrasting characters in the Depression years. *We Have no Dreaming* (1988) is an autobiographical journey which takes a sympathetic look at the Australian search for identity.

McLUHAN, (Herbert) Marshall
(1911–80)

Canadian writer, born in Edmonton. He studied English literature at the universities of Manitoba and Cambridge. In 1946 he became professor at St Michael's College, Toronto. In 1963, having directed two surveys into culture and communication media, he was appointed director of the University of Toronto's Centre for Culture and Technology. He held controversial views on the effect of the communication media on the development of civilization, claiming that it is the media *per se*, not the information and ideas which they disseminate, that influence society. He sees the invention of printing, with its emphasis on the eye rather than the ear, as the destroyer of a cohesive, interdependent society, since it encouraged man to be more introspective, individualistic and self-centred. His publications include *The Mechanical Bride* (1951), *The Gutenberg Galaxy* (1962), *Understanding Media* (1964), *The Medium is the Message* (with Q Fiore, 1967) and *Counter-Blast* (1970).
▷D Duffy, *Marshall McLuhan* (1969)

McMURTRY, Larry Jeff

(1936–)

American novelist, born in Wichita Falls, Texas, whose vision of his state's history has gone some considerable way towards establishing the generic Western as a serious contemporary form. He attended North Texas State College at Denton and then Rice University, Houston, where he later taught. In addition to academia, McMurtry has worked as a journalist and antiquarian bookseller, but Hollywood's interest in his work consolidated his reputation, often at the expense of his more strictly literary worth—*Horseman, Pass By* (1961) was successfully filmed (and re-issued, 1963) as *Hud*, and McMurtry wrote the screenplay for Peter Bogdanovich's prize-winning movie of his third novel, *The Last Picture Show* (1966). Later books also dealt with the opposition of freedom and rootedness, new and inherited values, and a kind of heroic resistance to circumstance. This was evident, among others, in *All My Friends are Going to be Strangers* (1972), the comic *Terms of Endearment* (1975), basis of a third successful film, and in *Cadillac Jack* (1982), but it was with *Lonesome Dove* (1985), the epic story of a quixotic cattle drive from Texas to Montana, that McMurtry staked his claim to greatness. Subsequent works include *Some Can Whistle* (1989), which some took to be a fragment of autobiography, and the disappointing *Buffalo Girls* (1990).
▷C D Peavy, *Larry McMurtry* (1977)

McNEILE, Herman Cyril *see* SAPPER

McNICKLE, D'Arcy

(1904–77)

American writer, born in St Ignatius, Montana, the son of an Irish–American father and Métis mother. A member of the Confederated Salish and Kutenai tribes, McNickle is known both as a historian and publicist of Native American issues and as an accomplished novelist and biographer. His early short fiction and first novel, *The Surrounded* (1936), were written while he worked as an editor in New York. Increasingly drawn to work for Native American causes, McNickle took up a post in the reformist Collier administration at the BIA, and later became programme director of the Center for American Indian History in the Newberry Library, Chicago. In his novels and short stories, McNickle presented an unromanticized view of the West and the harsh lives of those living on farms and reservations during the Depression. His many non-fiction works, such as *They Came Here First: The Epic of the American Indian* (1949) and *Indians and Other Americans: Two Ways of Life Meet* (1959), deal with Native American history

and contemporary issues. He also published a biography of **Oliver La Farge**, and a children's story, *Runner in the Sun: a Story of Indian Maize* (1954). *Wind From an Enemy Sky*, his second novel, was published posthumously in 1978.
▷D R Parker, *Singing an Indian Song: a Biography of D'Arcy McNickle* (1992)

McPHERSON, James Alan

(1943–)

American novelist, born in Georgia. He graduated from both Harvard Law School and the creative writing course at the University of Iowa, and became a professor of literature, first at the University of California in Santa Cruz, and then at the University of Virginia. He is primarily known as a writer of short stories set in the south, as in his best-known book, *Elbow Room* (1977), which won a Pulitzer Prize in 1978. His other fiction includes *Hue and Cry* (1969), *A World Unsuspected* (1987) and *The Prevailing South* (1988).

MEDWALL, Henry

(1462–c.1505)

English dramatist. He wrote *Fulgens and Lucres*, the earliest extant English secular play written before 1500. Little is known of his life, but he was a chaplain to Cardinal Morton, and held various livings. His only other extant work is a morality play, *Nature*, printed in 1530.
▷P Hogrefe, *The Thomas More Circle* (1959)

MEGGED, Aharon

(1920–)

Israeli novelist who was born in Poland but was taken to Palestine at the age of six. He has become one of the outstanding Hebrew novelists. His first book, a story collection, *Ruah Yamim* (1950, 'Spirit of the Sea'), deals with the people of the kibbutz in which he lived for so long, and with the stevedores of Haifa with whom he worked. *Ha-Hai Al Ha-Met* (1967, Eng trans *The Living and the Dead*—it should be 'on', not 'and'), one of the most revealing of Israeli novels, is about a young Israeli who discovers that a 'founding father' of the state was anything but the upright person his legend insists upon: Jason Rabinowicz, the young protagonist, refuses to sanctify his old hero, and therefore is being sued for breach of contract by his publishers—his trial is a lengthy one.

MEHREN, Stein

(1935–)

Norwegian poet and essayist, who has also written novels and plays. Intellectual and particularly interested in philosophy, Mehren is preoccupied with the relationship between language and reality, between time and memory. Both in his poems, where he describes modern society's violence and alienating mass-consumption, and in his tender love poems, Mehren is a master of the art of bringing out the music and the beauty of the language.

▷P T Andersen, *Stein Mehren—en logosdikter* (1982)

MEHRING, Walter
(1896–1981)

German Dadaist poet and playwright, born in Berlin. Mehring's early satirical songs, contained in *Geschichte, Lieder und Chansons des Walter Mehring* (1929, 'Stories, Songs and Chansons of Walter Mehring') were sung at Max Reinhardt's cabaret in Berlin. His play *Der Kaufmann von Berlin* (1929, 'The Merchant of Berlin') was too scandalous and was banned. He left Germany in 1933 and, after a period of internment in France, escaped to the USA and lived at Ascona. *No Road Back* (1944) was a collection of poems and *The Lost Library* (1951) an autobiography and individual view of modern culture.

MEHTA, Ved Parkash
(1934–)

Indian writer, born in Lahore. He was one of seven children of a Hindu doctor who was an officer in the Health Services of the Indian government. Blind from the age of eight, he went to the USA for his education when he was 15 and attended the Arkansas School for the Blind at Little Rock and Pomona College, before going to Oxford and Harvard universities. While at Pomona he published his first book, the autobiography *Face to Face* (1957). He has had a distinguished career as a journalist, contributing chiefly to the *New Yorker*. Employing amanuenses he has written biographies (*Mahatma Gandhi and His Apostles*, 1977), stories, essays and portraits of India. His enduring achievement, however, is *Continents of Exile*, an acclaimed series of autobiographical books: *Daddyji* (1972), *Mamaji* (1979), *Vedi* (1982), *The Ledge Between the Streams* (1984), *Sound-Shadows of the New World* (1986) and *The Stolen Light* (1989).

MEI SHENG
(d.140BC)

Chinese poet. He is often credited with the introduction of the five-character line. For this reason he is sometimes called the father of modern Chinese poetry.

▷E von Zach, *Die chinesische Anthologie* (1958)

MEILHAC, Henri
(1831–97)

French playwright, born in Paris. From 1855 he produced a long series of light comedies—some in conjunction with **Ludovic Halévy**, and, some, including *La Belle Hélène* (1865), well known through Offenbach's music. His masterpiece is *Frou-Frou* (1869). He also collaborated with Halévy and Gille respectively in the libretti of the operas *Carmen* (1875) and *Manon* (1884).

▷F Gaiffe, *Le rire et la scène française* (1932)

MEINHOLD, Johann Wilhelm
(1797–1851)

German pastor and poet, born on the island of Usedom. He was the Lutheran pastor there and at Krummin and Rehwinkel. He published poems and dramas, but is best known for his novels *Maria Schweidler, die Bernsteinhexe* (1838, Eng trans *Maria Schweidler, the Amber Witch*, 1844) and *Sidonie von Bork, die Klosterhexe* (1847, 'Sidonie von Bork, the Nunnery Witch').

MEIRELES, Cecília
(1901–64)

Major Brazilian Catholic poet, critic, and dramatist, born in Rio de Janeiro. She was well established as a poet from 1919, when she published her first collection; but she rejected everything she had written before *Viagem* (1939, 'Voyages'). An orphan, unhappily married, her convincing rejection of the consolations of 'ordinary' experience is in itself replete with experience. Her poetry, which crosses the metaphysical and the lyrical in a fluid, dream-like manner, has been described as second only, in her century, to that of **Laura Riding**. Two representative poems are translated in the *Penguin Book of Latin American Verse* (1971, ed E Curacciolo-Trejo).

▷'Critical study' by D Damosceno, in *Obra poética* (1967, in Portuguese)

MELEAGER
(c.140–c.70 BC)

Greek poet and epigrammatist, from Gadara, in Syria. He was the author of 128 exquisite short elegiac poems and epigrams included in his anthology *Stephanos* (Garland).

▷C Redinger, *Meleagros von Gadara* (1895)

MELÉNDEZ VALDÉS, Juan
(1754–1817)

Spanish poet, born near Badajoz. He became a professor of Classics at the University of Salamanca, fought for Napoleon in the War of Independence, and held political office in Madrid. Considered the greatest lyric poet of his time, he is known for his odes, ballads and romantic verses.

▷R Froldi, *Un poeta illuminista* (1967)

MELGAR, Mariano
(1791–1815)

Peruvian *mestizo* poet and translator (**Ovid**, **Virgil**), executed (shot) during the Battle of Umachiri, and therefore a national hero. He was born in Arequipa. He introduced new forms into the poetry, and had studied the Quechua language and its poetry. He was not a romantic, but was in every sense his country's leading precursor of the movement. His poetry was burned by priests owing to its erotic content; thus they ensured that it would circulate more widely.
▷ A T Azurra, *Melgar, precursor del romanticismo* (1966)

MELL, Max
(1882–1971)

Austrian playwright, novelist and poet, born in Marburg. He was overpraised by his friend **Hugo von Hofmannsthal**, which may have led to an artificially inflated reputation. But although wholly traditional and never profound, his stories achieved a high level of competence, and his verse plays were the subject of major productions in the conventional theatre. His message is a simple one of Christian piety in the medieval mode; his knowledge of Austrian folkways was deep.

MELO, Francisco Manuel de
(1608–66)

Portuguese writer, born in Lisbon. He had an arduous and hazardous life as soldier, political prisoner, and exile in Brazil, whence he returned in 1657. He wrote in both Spanish and Portuguese, and is better remembered for his critical works and his history of the Catalan wars than for his voluminous poetry.
▷ E Prestage, *Don Francisco Manuel de Melo* (1922)

MELVILL, Elizabeth
(c.1580–c.1630)

Scottish Presbyterian poet renowned for her piety. She was the daughter of Christina Boswell and Sir James Melvill of Halhill, a courtier and memoirist. On her marriage to John Colville of Culcross she became Lady Culcross and has been identified as the 'M.M.' (Mistress Melvill) credited on the title page for *Any Godlie Dreame, Complyit in Scottish Meter*, published in Edinburgh in 1603. This vehement but elegant Calvinist tract was popular enough to require regular reprinting up to the end of the 19th century. More recently Melvill's work has been included in feminist anthologies, such as *Kissing The Rod* (1988, ed G Greer et al).

MELVILLE, Herman
(1819–91)

American novelist, born in New York. He became a bank clerk but, in search of adventure, joined a whaling ship bound for the South Seas. He deserted at the Marquesas and spent some weeks with a savage tribe in the Typee valley, an episode which inspired his first book, *Typee* (1846). Having been taken off by an Australian whaler, he was jailed in Tahiti as a member of a mutinous crew, but escaped and spent some time on the island. This adventure was the basis of his second book, *Omoo* (1847). *Mardi* (1849) also dealt with the South Seas, but entered the realm of satire not too successfully, so that Melville returned to adventure fiction with *Redburn* (1849) and *White Jacket* (1850), in which he drew on his experiences as a seaman on the man-of-war which brought him home from Tahiti. In 1847 he had married, and after three years in New York he took a farm near Pittsfield, Massachusetts, where **Nathaniel Hawthorne** was his neighbour and friend. It was during this period that he wrote his masterpiece, *Moby-Dick* (1851), a novel of the whaling industry, whose extraordinary vigour and colour and whose philosophical and allegorical undertones reflecting on the nature of evil have given it a place among the classic sea stories. Later novels included *Pierre* (1852), in a symbolic vein which was not appreciated by his readers, and the satirical *Confidence Man* (1857). *Billy Budd* was published posthumously in 1924 and used as the subject of an opera by Benjamin Britten in 1950. Melville also wrote short stories, most notably 'Benito Cereno' and 'Bartleby the Scrivener', which were collected, with others, in *The Piazza Tales* (1856). Now regarded as one of America's greatest novelists, he was not so successful during his life, even *Moby-Dick* being unappreciated. After 1857, disillusioned and by then a New York customs official, he wrote only some poetry. Recognition did not come until some 30 years after his death.
▷ E H Miller, *Herman Melville* (1975); C Olson, *Call Me Ishmael* (1947)

MEMMI, Albert
(1920–)

French–Tunisian academic and novelist, born in Tunisia to a French–Jewish family; Arabic was his native language, but he was later naturalized as a French citizen, and he wrote in French. He was largely responsible for instituting Maghrebian studies in France, editing an *Anthologie des ecrivains maghrébins d'expression français* in 1964, and teaching at L'École Pratique des Hautes Études in Paris. He became well-known with his autobiographical novel *La Statue de Sel* (1953,

'Pillar of Salt'), which was prefaced by **Albert Camus**; his other novels, pursuing the theme of cultural dominance, include *Agar* (1953) and *Le Scorpion* (1969). Also an essayist, he published the two parts of *Portrait d'un juif* in 1962 and 1969, *L'Homme Dominé* in 1968 and *Juifs et Arabes* in 1975. He is ranked among the greatest and most influential of Maghrebian/French writers.

MENA, Juan de
(1411–56)
Spanish poet and intellectual, born in Córdoba and educated at Salamanca and Rome. His early poetry (*La coronación*, 1438, 'The Coronation') and prose works such as his carefully constructed *Omero romançado* (c.1442), a translation of the *Ilias latina*, already display the highly Latinate style and intellectual concerns which mark his later works, and which reached their culmination in his *El laberinto de Fortuna* (1444, 'The Labyrinth of Chance'), an allegorical poem which depicts three wheels representing the past, present and future. The purpose of the poem is clearly political, being an attempt to win the support of King John II for Alvaro de Luna against the Castilian nobility.
▷M R Lida de Malkiel, *Juan de Mena, poeta del prerrenacimiento español* (1950)

MENANDER
(c.343–c.291 BC)
Greek poet, and the greatest writer of Attic New Comedy, born in Athens. His comedies were more successful with cultured than with popular audiences; but Quintilian praised him, and **Terence** imitated him closely. He wrote more than a hundred comedies, but only a few fragments of his work were known until 1906, when Lefebvre discovered in Egypt a papyrus containing 1328 lines from four different plays. In 1957, however, the complete text of the comedy *Dyskolos* (Eng trans 1960) was brought to light in Geneva.
▷O Veh, *Beitrage zu Menander Protektor* (1955)

MENCETIĆ, Sisko
(1457–1527)
Ragusan poet, born in Ragusa (Dubrovnik). He was one of the earliest of the Serbo–Croat writers in the Dalmatian literature which modelled itself upon that of the Italian Renaissance. He wrote love lyrics in the style of **Petrarch**.

MENCKEN, H(enry) L(ouis)
(1880–1954)
American journalist, editor, critic and historian of language, born in Baltimore.

Mencken was a popular, readable, intelligent writer, whose great enemy throughout his life was what he called the boo-joy (bourgeois). He has been represented as a proto-fascist, but that is to miss his irony and deliberate desire to write for non-literary readers: his criticisms of democracy did not advocate dictatorship. He championed many writers, including **Dreiser** and **Sherwood Anderson**, and edited *The Smart Set* and the *American Mercury*. His *The American Language* (1919–48) is an authoritative and invaluable mine of information: *Prejudices* (1919–27) remains a readable and amusing collection of iconoclasm. He was not profound, but he was seldom foolish.

MENDELE, Mocher Seforim, pseud
(meaning 'Mendele the Bookseller', ie 'propagator of knowledge') of **Sholem Jacob Abramovitch**
(1835–1917)
Yiddish and Hebrew novelist, known as the grandfather of both modern branches of Jewish literature. With **Scholem Aleichem** and **Peretz** he may be said to have founded modern Yiddish literature. He worked all his life, from Odessa, to try to create a dignified Jewish life within Russia. His finest novel, in Yiddish, *Dos Wunshfingerl* (1889, 'The Wishing Ring'), has not been translated, but much else has, notably *Fishke, the Lame* (1869, translated in 1929 and again in 1960) and *Di Kliatche* (1873, *The Nag*, 1955). Mendele himself translated most of his Yiddish fiction into Hebrew, and thus influenced the fiction of the latter language. He also introduced the novel and the short novel into Yiddish.
▷M Waxman, *A History of Jewish Literature* (1947)

MENDÈS, Catulle
(1841–1909)
French writer, born in Bordeaux of Jewish parentage. A Parnassian, he founded the *Revue Fantaisiste* (1859), and later recorded the history of the movement in *La légende du Parnasse contemporain* (1884, 'The Legend of Le Parnasse contemporain'). He switched to Romanticism and wrote poems, novels, dramas and libretti as well as articles and criticism.
▷A Bertrand, *Catulle Mendès, une biographie critique* (1908)

MENDES, Murilo
(1902–)
Brazilian poet and diplomat, born in Minas province. He began as a Surrealist, but his later work, written under the influence of his conversion to Catholicism, has been com-

pared to that of the Spanish poet **Antonio Machado**.

MENDES PINTO, Fernao
(c.1510–1583)

Portuguese travel writer, author of the famous and (in the 17th century) very popular *Peregrinaçam da Fernam Pinto* (1614, Eng trans *The Voyages and Adventures of Ferdinand Mendes Pinto*, 1653, abridged 1894, adapted as *The Great Peregrination*, 1949). This book, for long regarded as almost pure fantasy, describes Pinto's astonishing life and travels to China, Japan, Africa and elsewhere (including, certainly, countries he did not visit). Its prophetic importance lay in part in Pinto's shrewd and ironic use of information about supposedly 'barbaric' peoples to show up the actual barbarity and greed of 'civilized' ones. There has long been controversy about the merits of the *Peregrination*, and **Congreve** referred to its author as 'a liar of the first magnitude'; but the consensus is now that he was a great anticipator of the modern form known as 'faction', fiction based on facts— and so far the finest practitioner of it. The text of this masterpiece was undoubtedly tampered with by its earliest editors, but its essence comes through.
▷M Collis, in *The Great Peregrination* (1949)

MENDOZA, Inigo Lopez de
(fl.1450)

Spanish statesman and poet, father of Pedro Gonzalez de Mendoza and great-grandfather of Diego Hurtado de Mendoza. He was created Marquis of Santillana by John II of Castile in 1445 for his services on the field. He was a wise statesman, a sturdy patriot, and an admired poet of **Petrarch**an sonnets, lyrics, allegories and didactic poems. He left an excellent account of the Provençal, Catalan and Valencian poets, and was an early folklorist and collector of popular proverbs.
▷J Rodriguez-Puertolas, *Fray Inigo de Mendoza y sus 'Coplas de Vita Christi'* (1968)

MENON, Vallatol Narayana
(1879–1958)

Indian (Malayalam) poet, with **Takazi** and **Basir** the best-known writer in his language. He created versions of the great classical texts, the *Ramayana* and the *Rig Veda*, in Malayalam. A Sanskrit scholar, he had a profound understanding of the difficult and complex Sanskrit poetics, and his own work—in the most Sanskritized of all the Indian languages—amply displays this. He was a nationalist poet, but his patriotism expressed itself in an abiding love for the ancient India: 'it was,' wrote a critic, 'his mission to make

the classical vision part of contemporary consciousness'. The direction in his poetry is of a movement from romanticism to realism.

MENZEL, Wolfgang
(1798–1873)

German critic and historian, born in Waldenburg in Silesia. He studied at Jena and Bonn, but from 1825 lived mainly in Stuttgart, where he made a reputation as an outspoken journalist and critic. He edited magazines, and wrote poems, novels, histories of German literature and poetry, a history of the world, literary criticism and polemics.

MERA, Juan León
(1832–94)

Ecuadorian novelist and poet. Born in Ambato, he lived under and supported the repressive theocrat García Moreno. Mera had a deeply religious background, and was to experience difficulty in combining traditional Catholicism with his Romantic style of writing. His most famous novel is *Cumandá, o un drama entre salvajes* (1871, 'Cumandá, or a Drama Among the Natives'), a novel which attempts to deconstruct European stereotypes of nature, indigenous peoples, and human existence. His Romantic poetry collected in *Melodías indígenas* (1868, 'Native Melodies') is not now considered as important as his collection of Ecuadorian popular poetry *Cantares del pueblo ecuatoriano* (1892).

MERCER, David
(1928–80)

English dramatist, born in Wakefield. After studying painting at King's College, Newcastle, he moved to Europe and began to write. His first television play, *Where the Difference Begins* (1961), signalled his interest in fusing the personal and the political in work that challenged the conventions of television drama. Further plays, like *A Climate of Fear* (1962), *A Suitable Case for Treatment* (1962) and *In Two Minds* (1967), explored his fascination with mental health, psychiatry and his struggle to reconcile a belief in socialism with the repression revealed during his stays in Eastern Europe. Winner of the 1965 *Evening Standard* Award for most promising playwright, his stage work includes *Ride A Cock Horse* (1965), *Flint* (1970) and *Cousin Vladimir* (1978). His film scripts include *Morgan* (1965) and *Providence* (1977). He continued to address issues of personal alienation and the class system in later television plays like *Huggy Bear* (1976), *The Ragazza* (1978) and *Rod of Iron* (1980).

MEREDITH, George
(1828–1909)

English novelist, born in Portsmouth, the grandson of a famous naval outfitter (the 'great Mel' of *Evan Harrington*). He was educated privately in Germany and was thus able to view the English class system with detachment. In London, after being articled to a solicitor, he turned to journalism and letters, his first venture appearing in *Chambers's Journal* in 1849, the year in which he married Mary Ellen Nicolls, a widowed daughter of **Thomas Love Peacock**. This disastrous marriage gave him an insight into relations between the sexes, which appear as largely in his work as his other great interest, natural selection as Nature's way of perfecting man. His works did not bring him much financial reward and he had to rely on his articles in *The Fortnightly* and his work as a reader in the publishing house of Chapman and Hall. His prose works started with a burlesque Oriental fantasy, *The Shaving of Shagpat* (1855), followed in 1859 by *The Ordeal of Richard Feverel*, which is based on parental tyranny and a false system of private education. He did not achieve general popularity as a novelist until the delightful *Diana of the Crossways* appeared in 1885. In the meantime he wrote less successful works, such as his two novels on the Italian revolt of 1848, *Sandra Belloni* (1864) and *Vittoria* (1866). Other popular works are *Evan Harrington* (1860), which throws light on Meredith's origins; *Harry Richmond* (1871); and best of all, *Beauchamp's Career* (1875), which poses the question of class and party and is well constructed and clearly written. This cannot be said of Meredith's later major novels, *The Egoist* (1879), a study of refined selfishness, and *The Amazing Marriage* (1895). These two powerful works are marred by the artificiality and forced wit which occurs in so much of his poetry. His first volume of verse (1851) is quite unremarkable, but *Poems and Lyrics of the Joy of Earth* (1883) displays his new cryptic manner and discusses the two master themes—the 'reading of earth' and the sex duel. His masterpiece on the latter theme had appeared in 1862 when he was influenced by the pre-Raphaelite poets and painters. This is *Modern Love*, a novelette in pseudo-sonnet sequence form in which the novelist in him plays powerfully on incompatibility of temper. His 'reading of earth' is expressed cryptically in the magnificent *Woods of Westermain*, intelligibly in *The Thrush in February* and thrillingly in *The Lark Ascending*. The volume called *A Reading of Life* (1901) adds little to the record. The modern revaluation of the Victorians has enhanced the fame of this very cerebral poet.

▷L Stevenson, *The Ordeal of Meredith* (1954)

MEREDITH, Gwen(yth Valmai)
(1907–)

Australian playwright and scriptwriter especially, for over 30 years, of radio plays and serials. She was born in Orange, New South Wales. She has written very successful 'serious' stage plays, but is best known for popular serial stories on Australian radio such as *The Lawsons*, an everyday story of farming folk (1943–9), and the marathon-running *Blue Hills*, which went on air four days a week continuously between 1949 and 1976. While touching on human relationships and public concerns, neither series broached the then current standards of permissiveness.

MEREDITH, William Morris
(1919–)

American poet, librettist and anthologist, born in New York City. Meredith published his first collection, *Love Letter from an Impossible Land*, in 1944. His subsequent volumes include *Earth Walk: New and Selected Poems* (1970) and *Partial Accounts: New and Selected Poems* (1987). His verse is often wistful, sometimes ironic, always highly crafted and polished; traditional in its sense of rhyme and metre, it is noted for its subtle and precise observation of thought and feeling.

▷G Rotella, *Three Contemporary Poets of New England* (1983)

MEREZHKOVSKI, Dmitri Sergeyevich
(1865–1941)

Russian novelist, critic and poet, born in St Petersburg. He wrote a historical trilogy *Khristos i Antikhrist* (1896–1905, 'Christ and Antichrist'), and books on **Tolstoy**, **Ibsen**, and **Nikolai Gogol**. He opposed the Revolution in 1917 and fled to Paris in 1919, where he continued to write historical novels, including one on Jesus (1932–3) and another on **Dante** (1939). His wife was **Zinaida Gippius**.

▷C Bedford, *Dmitri Sergeyevich Merezhkovski and the Silver Age* (1975)

MERI, Veijo
(1928–)

Finnish novelist, born in Viipuri; he is one of Finland's most outstanding writers. His themes are almost always those of war or childhood, which he contrasts. Behind all his work is the figure of **Gogol**, whose bitter humour he has carefully adapted to modern times. Many books by him have been translated into French, but none into English.

MERILUOTO, Aila
(1924–)

Finnish poet and translator (**Harry Martinson**), born in Pieksämäki. Her first collection of 1946, *Lasimaaulaus* ('Stained Glass Window'), was hailed as a major breakthrough in Finnish lyrical poetry; but with *Portaat* (1961, 'Staircase'), under the influence of **Rilke** (a powerful presence in Finnish poetry) she became more intellectual and the straightforward voice vanished. Poems are translated in *Twentieth Century Scandinavian Poetry* (1950).

MÉRIMÉE, Prosper
(1803–70)

French novelist, born in Paris, the son of a painter. He studied law, visited Spain in 1830, and held posts under the ministries of the navy, commerce and the interior. He was appointed inspector-general of historical remains in France in 1833, and became a senator in 1853. His last years were clouded by ill-health and melancholy, and the downfall of the Second Empire hastened his death. He wrote novels and short stories, archaeological and historical dissertations, and travel stories, all of which display exact learning, keen observation, real humour, and an exquisite style. Among his novels are *Colomba* (1841, Eng trans 1856), *Mateo Falcone* (1833), *Carmen* (1847, Eng trans 1878), *La Vénus d'Ille* (1837, Eng trans *The Venus of Ille*, 1887), *Lokis* (1870), *Arsène Guillot* (1852), *La Chambre bleue* (1866, 'The Blue Room') and *L'Abbé Aubain* (1846, Eng trans *The Abbé Aubain*, 1903). His letters include the famous *Lettres á une inconnue* (1873, 'Letters to an Unknown Woman'), the *Lettres à une autre inconnue* (1875, 'Letters to Another Unknown Woman') and the letters to the bibliographer Panizzi (1881). He also wrote some plays.
▷P Léon, *Mérimée et son temps* (1962)

MERRILL, James Ingram
(1926–)

American poet, novelist and playwright, born in New York City. His first publication, *Jim's Book: A Collection of Poems and Short Stories*, appeared in 1942. A volume of 30 years of poetry, *From the First Nine: Poems 1946–1976*, was published in 1982. Although Merrill has also published two plays and two novels, he is principally known as a poet and, specifically, as 'the ouija poet'. His interest in the spirit world and use of a ouija board apparently to converse with it is recorded in a huge epic poem in three parts, collected under the title of *The Changing Light at Sandover* (1982). The mystic quality of much of his verse, dealing with the themes of loss and

lost time, has resulted in comparisons with **Yeats**.

MERRILL, Stuart Fitzrandolph
(1863–1915)

American Symbolist poet, born in Hempstead, Long Island, New York. He was educated in Paris, where he lived from 1889. His French poems *Les gammes* (1895), *Les quatre saisons* (1900), and others developed the musical conception of poetry, and made full use of alliteration. *Une voix dans la Foule* (1909) espouses a strongly democratic sympathy which is unmistakably American.
▷M L Henry, *Stuart Merrill, sa vie, sa oeuvre* (1929)

MERRIMAN, Bryan, anglicized version of Bryan Mac Giolla Meidre
(1747–1805)

Irish–Gaelic poet, born in Ennistymon, County Clare, the son of a stonemason. He became a schoolteacher and small farmer in Feakle, later (1790) marrying and settling as a mathematics teacher in Limerick. His reputation depends on a stupendous 1000-line mock-heroic epic, traditional in its use of dream-vision, but satirical and feminist in content: *Cúirt an Mheáin Oidhche* (c.1786, Eng trans as *The Midnight Court* by **Frank O'Connor** in the *Penguin Book of Irish Verse*, 1970), which has been described as 'by far the most successful sustained effort in verse in modern Irish'. It is a wild (and woundingly gross) attack on Irish Catholic puritanism, greatly and influentially praised by O'Connor, the most successful of its many translators. Imagining its author's presence at a ferocious fairy inquisition against bachelors, it lampoons sexual mores, celibacy, the clergy and male chauvinism, and all in vigorously earthy and erotic language. The poem was banned in all English translations after Irish independence, but the Irish language itself was deemed incapable of corrupting influence. Liberal Irish intellectuals have established an annual Merriman Summer School, convening in August in Clare.

MERTON, Thomas
(1915–69)

American poet and devotionist, born in France of an English father and an American mother. From 1941 he was a Trappist monk in Kentucky. His best book is perhaps the one which made him famous: the spiritual autobiography *The Seven Storey Mountain* (1948). This became a bestseller and exercised some influence upon religious thinking. He later became interested in Zen Buddhism, and wrote some of the best popular books about it. As a poet he is respected as a minor practitioner in the tradition of **Traherne** and **Hopkins**. He was electrocuted in an accident.

MERWIN, W(illiam) S(tanley)
(1927–)

American poet and dramatist, born in New York City. He was educated at Princeton University, and was briefly a tutor to the son of **Robert Graves**, and later a translator, a playwright-in-residence, and poetry editor of *The Nation* (1962). His first book, *A Mask of Janus* (1952), was followed by a series of elegant, lyrical poems in books like *Dancing Bears* (1954) and *The Moving Target* (1967). His imagery took on a more surreal tinge with *The Lice* (1967), and subsequent books seemed more contemplative in tone, and more concerned with absence and silence. They include *Writings To an Unfinished Accompaniment* (1973) and *Selected Poems* (1988). His other works include several plays and translations; and *Regions of Memory* (1987), a collection of prose.
▷ *Unframed Originals: Recollections* (1982)

MESONERO ROMANOS, Ramón de
(1808–82)

Spanish *costumbristo* writer (local colourist, or regionalist), and editor, born in Madrid, who sometimes wrote under the pseudonym of 'El Curioso Parlante'. He was a paramount (and acknowledged) influence upon **Pérez Galdós**. His *Manual de Madrid* (1831) is full of extraordinary facts and figures about the city. He edited the weekly *Seminario pitoresco español* (1836–57), and published essays on Madrid customs and society. Writing nostalgically and in reaction to Romanticism, he defended traditional values, but in so charming and observant a way that he could not possibly be described as reactionary. He had a considerable influence, especially in disabusing Spanish readers of the prejudice that a contemporary novel could not achieve an audience. 'It was he', wrote one critic, 'more than any other contemporary writer, who opened the pages of [Spanish] literature to ordinary daily life'. His complete works, *Obras*, were published in eight volumes between 1924 and 1926.
▷ *Romanic Review*, XXI (1930)

METASTASIO, Pietro, originally Trapassi
(1698–1782)

Italian poet, born in Rome. A gift for versifying gained him a patron in Gravina, a lawyer, who educated him, and left him his fortune (1718). He gained his reputation by his masque, *The Garden of Hesperides* (1722), wrote the libretti for 27 operas, including Mozart's *Clemenza di Tito* (libretto Eng trans *The Clemency of Titus*, 1828), and became court poet at Vienna in 1729.
▷ C Burney, *Life and Letters of Metastasio* (1796)

MEUNG, Jean de, or Jean Clopinel
(c.1250–1305)

French poet and satirist. He flourished in Paris under Philip IV, 'the Fair'. He translated many books into French, and left a witty *Testament*. His great work is his lengthy continuation (18 000 lines) of the *Roman de la Rose* by **Guillaume de Lorris**, which substituted for tender allegorizing his own satirical pictures of actual life and an encyclopaedic discussion of every aspect of contemporary learning, which inspired many later authors to write in support of or in opposition to his views.

MEW, Charlotte Mary
(1869–1928)

British poet and short-story writer, whose reputation has been sustained by the critical support of those such as **Walter de la Mare** and **Thomas Hardy**, who predeceased her only briefly; the circumstances of Mew's suicide, following the death of her sister, has fostered a certain romantic cult around her. Born in London, she was essentially self-educated and her work largely concerned the problems of women in a society that provided few reliable terms of reference or role models for female individuality. Her most famous poem is 'The Farmer's Bride' (1915), a vigorous narrative about an emotionally restricted life. In the late 1970s, Mew was rediscovered by the feminist movement; her collected verse and prose, reissued by Virago Press, made a significant impact on a revisionist awareness of post-Victorian social and cultural attitudes.
▷ P Fitzgerald, *Charlotte Mew and her Friends* (1984)

MEYER, Conrad Ferdinand
(1825–98)

Swiss poet and novelist, born in Zürich. After a period during which he concentrated mainly on ballads and verse romances, he composed the epic poem *Huttens Letzte Tage* (1871, 'Hutten's Final Days') and a number of historical novels such as *Jürg Jenatsch* (1876) and *Der Heilige* (1880, 'The Saint'), in which he excels in subtle and intricate psychological situations and complex characters.
▷ H Mayne, *Conrad Ferdinand Meyer und sein Werk* (1925)

MEYNELL, Alice Christiana Gertrude, née
Thompson
(1847–1922)

English essayist and poet, born in Barnes,
London, the daughter of a scholar and a concert pianist, and sister of the battle-painter
Elizabeth Butler. She spent her childhood on
the Continent, and became a convert to Catholicism. Her volumes of essays include *The
Rhythm of Life* (1893), *The Colour of Life*
(1896) and *Hearts of Controversy* (1917). She
published several collections of her own
poems, starting in 1875 with *Preludes*, and
anthologies of **Coventry Patmore**, of lyric
poetry, and of poems for children. In 1877 she
married Wilfrid Meynell (1852–1948), author
and journalist, with whom she edited several
periodicals.
▷A K Tuell, *Mrs Meynell* (1925)

MEYRINK, Gustav
(1868–1932)

German writer, born in Vienna. He translated
Dickens and wrote satirical novels with a
strong element of the fantastic and grotesque.
Among the best known are *Der Golem* (1915,
'The Golem'), *Das grüne Gesicht* (1916, 'The
Green Face') and *Walpurgisnacht* (1917, 'The
Witches' Sabbath').

MHAC AN TSAOI, Máiri
(1922–)

Irish Gaelic poet, born in Dublin. She has
written and translated a remarkable and
singular oeuvre of 'feminist-orientated'
poems and verses in Gaelic. She has always
emphasized, as in *Cré na Mna Tí* (1958, 'The
Housewife's Credo') for example, that it is
essential to realize and utilize creativity
despite the dictates of domesticity: 'like
Scheherazade, you will *need* to write poetry
also'. Her sense of the present being interdependent on a richly cultivated past is most
in evidence in the invaluable English translations *A Heart Full of Thought* (1959).

MICHAËLIS, Karin
(1872–1950)

Danish novelist, short-story writer and
journalist, born in Randers. The novel *Barnet*
(1902, 'The Child') focuses on the theme of
childhood, but she was to become best known
for her explorations of female sexuality. *Den
farlige Alder* (1910, Eng trans *The Dangerous
Age*, 1912), which resulted in international
fame, is an epistolary and diary novel about
a menopausal woman, pinpointing the lies
and dissimulation which are part of the social
construction of the feminine role. Her extensive output includes the seven-volume series
for children about Bibi (1929–39) and two
autobiographical series, *Træt på godt og*

ondt (1924–30, 'The Tree of Good and Evil')
and *Vidunderlige Verden* (1948–50, 'Marvellous World').
▷S Fabricius, 'Karin Michaëlis', in *Danske
digtere i det 20. århundrede*, I, Torben Brostrøm and Mette Winge (eds) (1980)

MICHAUX, Henri
(1899–1984)

Belgian poet, autobiographer, mystic, astrologer and artist (his art is not negligible), first
discovered by **Franz Hellens** and then encouraged by **Jules Supervielle**. Born in Namur, he
lived mostly in Paris. His most easily accessible work, and the one for which he is best
known, is *Un Certain Plume* (1930, Eng trans,
in part, in the usefully bilingual *Selected Writings*, 1968): this describes a Chaplin-like figure whose crazy adventures resemble
surrealistic narratives. He was influenced by
the surrealists, but always remained his own
man. The most pervasive influence upon all
his writings was his 14th-century lowlands
compatriot, the mystic Jan van Ruysbroeck;
but he was also a humorist of nearly the calibre of **Max Jacob**, who also exercised a vital
effect upon him. Much of his writing is
unclassifiable, but his poetry, which often
resembles in presentation the 'cubist' poetry
of **Pierre Reverdy** and **Vicente Huidobro**, has
long been popular amongst French-speaking
readers. His autobiography, *Les Grandes
Epreuves et les innombrables petites* (1966,
Eng trans *The Major Ordeals of the Mind and
the Countless Minor Ones*, 1974), is a classic
little read outside France and Belgium; it
demonstrates his critical but generous awareness of almost all the major philosophical and
religious developments of the 20th century.
André Gide issued a little book on him (based
on the text of a lecture), *Découvrons Henri
Michaux* (1941, 'We Discover Henri Michaux'), which is a useful if incomplete introduction. Also available in translation is *Light
Through Darkness* (1964).
▷M Bowie, *Henri Michaux* (1973)

MICHENER, James
(1907–)

American novelist, born in New York. A teacher and book editor during World War II,
he turned to writing following his service in
the navy. *Tales of the South Pacific* (1947),
which won a Pulitzer Prize, was adapted by
Rodgers and Hammerstein into the musical
South Pacific (1949). Later novels in a prolific
and prodigiously successful career include
Hawaii (1959), *Space* (1982) and *Poland*
(1983). Although often lacking the light touch
or insightful detail, these daunting doorsteps
do impress by the sheer accumulation of
information. His non-fictional output
includes *The Bridge at Andau* (1956), an

account of the Hungarian uprising; *Iberia* (1968), on travelling through Spain; and *Presidential Lottery* (1969), a critique of the American political system.

MICIŃSKI, Tadeusz
(1873–1919)

Polish poet, novelist, playwright and philosopher, one of the most peculiar and strangely gifted in a peculiar and strangely gifted literature. He was killed fighting the Bolsheviks. Few critics have known what to say of him, for in many of his strange poems and novels he practised a sort of Slavonic gnosticism, full of out-of-the-way learning. He offered hope only of a very special sort: it depended on the kind of knowledge gnostics insist can be used to circumvent the devil, who is equated with earthly existence. There was an early collection of poems, an extraordinary play, *W mroku zlotego palacu czyll Bazylissa Teofanu* (1909, 'In the Night of the Golden Palace or the Empress of Teophan'), which centres around a demonic empress, and two novels on gnostic themes. There is considerable new interest in him in Poland.

MICKIEWICZ, Adam Bernard
(1798–1855)

Polish poet, born near Novogrodek in Lithuania (Minsk). He published his first poems in 1822, and as founder of a students' secret society was banished to Russia (1824–9); there he produced three epic poems, glowing with patriotism. After a journey through Germany, France and Italy his masterpiece, the epic *Pan Tadeusz* (Eng trans *Master Thaddeus*, 1885), appeared in 1834—a brilliant delineation of Lithuanian scenery, manners and beliefs. After teaching at Lausanne, he was appointed Slavonic Professor at Paris in 1840, but was deprived of the post in 1843 for political utterances. He went to Italy to organize the Polish legion, but in 1852 Louis Napoleon appointed him a librarian in the Paris Arsenal. He died in Constantinople, where the emperor had sent him to raise a Polish legion for service against Russia. His body, first buried at Montmorency in France, was in 1890 laid beside that of the solider and patriot Kosciuzko in Cracow Cathedral. Mickiewicz is the national poet of the Poles, and one of the greatest of all Slav poets.
▷K Pruszynski, *Adam Mickiewicz: the life story of the greatest Polish poet* (1950)

MICKLE, William Julius
(1735–88)

Scottish poet, the son of a minister, born in Langholm, Dumfriesshire. Educated at Edinburgh High School, he failed as a brewer, and turned author in London. In 1765 he published a poem, *The Concubine* (or *Syr Martyn*), and in 1771–5 his version rather than translation of the *Lusiad* of **Camoens**. In 1779 he went to Lisbon as secretary to Commodore Johnstone, but his last years were spent in London. His ballad of *Cumnor Hall* (which suggested *Kenilworth* to Sir **Walter Scott**) is poor poetry, but 'There's nae luck aboot the hoose' ensured his immortality, even if his authorship of it has been challenged.

MIDDLETON, (John) Christopher
(1926–)

English poet and translator, born in Truro, Cornwall and educated at Merton College, Oxford. After service in the Royal Air Force, he taught English at the University of Zurich and German at the University of London, before moving to the USA (1966) as Professor of Germanic languages and literature at the University of Texas, Austin. His verse has a deceptive, fleeting quality, which is captured in the title of an important volume of essays, *The Pursuit of the Kingfisher* (1983); his poems are intense, often visionary, in a way that combines English models with the simultaneously more playful (as in the Surrealists) and intellectual tenor of the Continental traditions. In 1963 with his appearance in *Penguin Modern Poets 4*, Middleton began to attract wider attention. *Nonsequences: Selfpoems* (1965) brought this earlier period to an end. With his move to America, the verse became less interiorized, and more limber. *The Fossil Fish* (1970) and *Briefcase History* (1972) were ultra-terse, and, like the collection *The Lonely Suppers of W V Balloon* (1975), signalled his interest in that most un-English of forms: prose poetry. Later collections include *Pataxanadu* (1977) and *III Poems* (1983). Middleton has translated many modern German writers, including **Robert Walser**, **Christa Wolf** and **Gert Hofmann**.

MIDDLETON, Osman Edward
(1925–)

New Zealand short-story writer, born in Christchurch, whose work first appeared in book form in *Short Stories* (1953) and then in *The Stone* (1959), *A Walk on the Beach* (1964) and *The Loners* (1972). *Selected Stories* appeared in 1975, and two novellas, *Confessions of an Ocelot, and, Not for a Seagull*, in 1979.

MIDDLETON, Stanley
(1919–)

English novelist, born and educated in Nottingham, where he also worked as a schoolmaster from 1947 to his retirement in 1981.

Middleton's critical highwater mark was the (shared) award of the Booker Prize for his fourteenth novel, *Holiday*, in 1974. His work has been criticized for being middle-class and too deeply rooted in the anti-experimental tradition of conventional British fiction. His works are, however, highly reflexive, usually concerned with the lives of artists or teachers; they often compress time disturbingly. The best of the books are *Harris's Requiem* (1960), *Terms of Reference* (1966), *Brazen Prison* (1971) and *In a Strange Land* (1979), which returns to Middleton's favourite subject of music. His career acquired new impetus in the 1980s, presumably as a result of his retirement from school-teaching, and he has continued to publish a steady novel per year into the early nineties, most notably *After a Fashion* (1987) and *Recovery* (1988).

MIDDLETON, Thomas
(c.1580–1627)

English dramatist, probably born in London, where his father was a bricklayer. He is first mentioned in Henslowe's *Diary* in 1602, when he was engaged with **Anthony Munday**, **Michael Drayton** and **John Webster** on a lost play, *Cæsar's Fall*. First on the list of his printed plays is *Blurt, Master Constable* (1602), a light, fanciful comedy. Two interesting tracts, *Father Hubbard's Tale* and *The Black Book*, exposing London rogues, were published in 1604, to which year belongs the first part of *The Honest Whore* (mainly written by **Thomas Dekker**, partly by Middleton). *The Phœnix* and *Michaelmas Term* (both 1607) are lively comedies; even more diverting is *A Trick to Catch the Old One* (1608); and *A Mad World, My Masters* (1608), from which **Aphra Behn** pilfered freely in *The City Heiress*, is singularly adroit. *The Roaring Girl* (1611; written with Dekker) idealizes the character of a noted cutpurse and virago. Middleton was repeatedly employed to write the Lord Mayor's pageant. *A Chaste Maid in Cheapside* was probably produced in 1613, as was *No Wit, No Help like a Woman's*. *A Fair Quarrel* (1617) and *The World Lost at Tennis* (1620) were written in conjunction with **William Rowley**, as were probably *More Dissemblers Besides Women* (?1622) and *The Mayor of Quinborough*. In 1620 Middleton was appointed city chronologer, and a MS Chronicle by him was extant in the 18th century. The delightful comedy, *The Old Law*, first published in 1656, is mainly the work of Rowley, with something by Middleton, all revised by **Philip Massinger**. In the three posthumously-published plays, *The Changeling*, *The Spanish Gypsy* and *Women Beware Women*, Middleton's genius is seen at its highest. Rowley had a share in the first two and probably in the third. A very curious and skilful play is *A Game at Chess*, acted in 1624. *The Widow*, published in 1652, was mainly by Middleton. *Anything for a Quiet Life* (c.1619) may have been revised by **James Shirley**. Middleton was concerned in the authorship of some of the plays included in the works of **Francis Beaumont** and **John Fletcher**.
▷ R H Barker, *Thomas Middleton* (1958)

MIHURA SANTOS, Miguel
(1905–77)

Spanish playwright, and painter and editor of humorous magazines, born in Madrid into a family of actors. His somewhat Absurdist plays, not unlike the *One Way Pendulum* of **N F Simpson**, mocked mankind's enslavement to machinery. *Tres sombreros de copa* (1932, rev edn 1952, Eng trans *Three Top Hats*, in *Modern Spanish Theatre*, 1968, M Benedikt and G E Wellwarth eds), is his best-known play, and was very popular in Franco's dreary Spain when it was reissued. A very highly skilled craftsman, Mihura lacked depth and substance.
▷ R Mackay, *Miguel Mihura* (1977)

MIHYAYLOVSKI, Stoyan
(1856–1927)

Bulgarian poet, critic and editor, who spent his life punishing injustice; he was less satirical and humorous than **Aleko Konstantinov**, and more vituperative. But he made vituperation an art. A brutal pessimist, he saw no compromise between anarchy and enslavement. He has been called 'Bulgaria's **Juvenal**'. Even his scathing *Kniga za balgarskiya* (1897, 'Book of the Bulgarian People', set, provocatively, in Turkey), his most famous book, has not been translated into English.
▷ C Manning and R Smal-Stocki, *The History of Modern Bulgarian Literature* (1960)

MIKSZÁTH, Kálmán
(1847–1910)

Hungarian novelist, born in Szklabonya. He was the editor of the periodical *A Hon*, owned by **Jókai**. At first he was influenced by this great historical novelist, but gradually evolved his own more realistic procedures, becoming a quirky romantic satirist of highly original qualities. He treated the decline of his own rural middle-class with sympathy but without reservation. *A jópalócok* (1882, Eng trans *The Good People of Palocz*, 1893) and *Különös házasság* (1900, Eng trans *A Strange Marriage*, 1964) are typical of his work.
▷ J Reményi, *Hungarian Writers and Literature* (1964)

MILES, Josephine Louise

(1911–85)

American poet and literary scholar. Born in Chicago she studied at the University of California, Los Angeles, and then at Berkeley, joining the faculty in 1940 (shortly after the publication of her first verse collection, *Lines of Intersection*), becoming full professor in 1952 and University Professor in 1973. Her poems are frequently concerned with the minutiae of academic life and with ideas, and are written with the deliberately awkward asymmetry of natural speech; *Prefabrications* (1955), *Civil Poems* (1966) and *Kinds of Affection* (1967) are typical. As the 1960s advanced, she was a tolerant but never passively uncritical observer of the radical student movement; *Fields of Learning* (1968) expressed a sense of quiet detachment from its attendant idolatries. In a major critical essay, *Poetry and Change: Donne, Milton, Wordsworth and the Equilibrium of the Present* (1974) and in *Working Out Ideas: Predication and Other Uses of Language* (1979), she re-examined poetry's intellectual role. Miles's *Collected Poems* (1983) provoked a belated and often apologetic reassessment of her contribution to American verse.

MILLAR, Margaret

(1915–)

American novelist and short-story writer, born in Kitchener, Canada and educated at the University of Toronto. She worked as a screenwriter for Warner Brothers and was the president of Mystery Writers of America in 1957–8. The *Los Angeles Times* voted her Woman of the Year in 1965. She is the author of over 20 novels and several short stories, mostly in the detective fiction genre—though she probes more deeply into the psychology of her characters than most crime writers. She wrote her first novel, *The Invisible Worm*, in 1941. *Beast in View* (1955) won her the Mystery Writers of America **Edgar Allan Poe** Award, as did *Banshee* nearly 30 years later, in 1983.

MILLAY, Edna St Vincent

(1892–1950)

American poet, born in Rockland, Maine. Her first poem was published when she was a student at Vassar College. Moving into Greenwich Village, then at its height as a meeting place for artists and writers, she published *A Few Figs from Thistles* (1920). In 1923 came *The Harp Weaver and Other Poems*, for which she was awarded a Pulitzer Prize. During her lifetime she was a feminist and though she was latterly dismissed as arrogant, egotistic and whimsical, the admiration of writers like **Maya Angelou** has caused her

to be re-evaluated and there has been renewed interest in her sonorous verse.
▷ N A Brittan, *Edna St Vincent Millay* (1967)

MILLER, Arthur

(1915–)

American playwright, born in New York City. He was educated at the University of Michigan but changed his mind about an intended career in journalism when he won a play-writing prize and worked for the Federal Theater project instead. His *Death of a Salesman* (1949) won the Pulitzer Prize and brought him international recognition, though *All My Sons* (1947) had already placed him in the front rank of American dramatists. *The Crucible* (1953) is probably, to date, his most lasting work, since its theme, the persecution of the Salem witches equated with contemporary political persecution, stands out of time. Other works include *A View from the Bridge* (1955), the film script of *The Misfits* (1960), *After the Fall* (1963), *Incident at Vichy* (1964), *The Creation of the World and Other Business* (1972) and *Playing for Time* (1981). His marriage to Marilyn Monroe, from whom he was divorced in 1961, and his brush with the authorities over early communist sympathies, brought him considerable publicity. Recent plays include *Danger: Memory!* (1987). During the 1980s, almost all of Miller's plays were given major British revivals and without doubt, Miller is now more popular in Britain than in America, where the apparent spurning of serious work by Broadway has made it difficult even for the voice of Miller to be heard.
▷ N Carson, *Arthur Miller* (1982)

MILLER, Henry Valentine

(1891–1980)

American writer, born in New York. His parents were German–Americans and he was brought up in Brooklyn. He rebelled against a conventional upbringing and a traditional career pattern, and after two months at the City College in 1909 took a job with a cement company. With money from his father which was intended to finance him through Cornell, he travelled in the south west and Alaska. When he returned home he went to work in his father's tailor shop but left after trying to unionize the workforce. In 1920 he became employment manager for the Western Union Telegraph Co.; in 1927 he ran a speakeasy in Greenwich Village. But in 1930 he moved to France for nine years during which time he published *Tropic of Cancer* (1934) and *Tropic of Capricorn* (1938), as well as *Black Spring* (1936). He returned to the USA in 1940 but travelled extensively both at home and abroad before settling in Big Sur, California.

He has been described as a folk hero, an ardent Bohemian whose life was his work. Though much of his fiction is auto-biographical and explicitly sexual, he re-garded his childhood as seminal: 'From five to ten were the most important years of my life; I lived in the street and acquired the typical American gangster spirit'. This undoubtedly helped him overcome many impecunious years and rebuffs from state cen-sors. (American editions of the *Tropics* were not published until 1961 and 1962 respec-tively.) In his time, however, he became one of the most read American authors, solipsistic, surrealistic and blackly comic, empathizing with the outcast: prostitutes, hobos and artists. Important books are *The Colossus of Maroussi* (1941), a dithyrambic travel book, *The Air-Conditioned Nightmare* (1945), a bleak essay on contemporary America, and *The Rosy Crucifixion* trilogy of novels: *Sexus* (1949), *Plexus* (1953) and *Nexus* (1960). A guru of the sexually liberated 1960s, he fell foul of feminist critics in the 1970s.
▷J Martin, *Always Merry and Bright: the life of Henry Miller* (1978)

MILLER, Hugh
(1802–56)

Scottish geologist and writer, born in Crom-arty. Having lost his father at sea at the age of five, he had a rebellious school career, and was apprenticed as a stonemason at the age of 16, a trade he followed for 17 years. He developed an interest in fossils, and he devoted the winter months to reading, writing and natural history. In 1829 he published *Poems Written in the Leisure Hours of a Journeyman Mason*, followed by *Scenes and Legends of the North of Scotland* (1835). He contributed to **John Mackay Wilson**'s *Tales of the Borders* (1834–40), and to *Chambers's Journal*. He married the daughter of an Inv-erness businessman and worked as a bank accountant for a time (1834–9), but when he became involved in the controversy that led to the Disruption of the Church of Scotland (1843) with a ferocious open *Letter to Lord Brougham* (1839) he was invited to Edinburgh to start the anti-patronage journal *The Witness*, and became the outstanding journal-ist of the Disruption. He wrote a series of geological articles in *The Witness*, later col-lected as *The Old Red Sandstone* (1841). In 1845 he wrote *First Impressions of England* (1847). His *My Schools and Schoolmasters* (1854) is the story of his youth. A pioneer of popular science books, he combated the Darwinian evolution theory with *Footprints of the Creator* (1850), *The Testimony of the Rocks* (1857) and *Sketchbook of Popular Geology* (published posthumously, 1859).

Worn out by illness and overwork, he shot himself.
▷P Bayne, *Hugh Miller* (2 vols, 1871)

MILLER, Jason
(1939–)

American playwright and actor, born in Long Island, New York. He was educated at the University of Scranton, Pennsylvania. His first important play was *Nobody Hears A Broken Drum* (1970), set during the American Civil War. His best-known work is *That Championship Season* (1972), a play which, in the course of a college reunion, unpeels the veneer of middle-America to reveal the greed and corruption lying beneath. It won him a Pulitzer Prize in 1973. He has pursued a par-allel career as an actor, and was nominated for an Oscar for his role in the film *The Exor-cist* (1973).

MILLER, Joaquin, pseud of Cincinnatus Heine Miller
(1839–1913)

American poet, born in Liberty, Indiana. He became a miner in California, and fought in the Indian wars. After practising law in Oregon, he edited a paper suppressed for showing Confederate sympathies. In 1866–70 he was a county judge in Oregon, and after a spell as a Washington journalist, in 1877 he settled in California as a fruitgrower. His poems include *Songs of the Sierras* (1871). He also wrote a successful play, *The Danites of the Sierras* (1877). He wrote his auto-biography in *My Life among the Modocs* (1873) and *My Own Story* (new ed 1891).
▷M M Marberry, *Splendid Poseur: Joaquin Miller, American Poet* (1953)

MILLER, Walter Michael
(1922–)

American science-fiction writer, born in Flor-ida. He flew combat missions in World War II, and converted to Catholicism in 1947. He wrote around 40 short stories, collected in *Conditionally Human* (1962) and *The View from the Stars* (1965), many of which have been influential in the development of the genre. He is best known for his only novel, *A Canticle for Leibowitz* (1960), originally pub-lished in parts in magazine form (1955–7). One of the few serious attempts to deal with religion in a science-fiction narrative, it spans a millennium, and sets the preserving religious impulse against the destructive scientific one in a post-holocaust human civ-ilization moving inexorably towards another catastrophe. He has reportedly been working on a sequel into the 1990s.

MILLER, William
(1810–72)

Scottish poet, born in Glasgow, known as the 'Laureate of the nursery'. He was a wood-turner by profession, having relinquished a medical career through ill-health. In 1863, urged on by his friends, he published a collection of poems which brought him some fame. Today, however, he is remembered only as the author of 'Wee Willie Winkie', one of his numerous dialect poems about children and childhood.

MILLETT, John
(1928–)

Australian poet who served in the Australian air force in Britain during World War II; his experiences resulted in *Tail Arse Charlie*, published in *Poetry Australia* in 1982, and later dramatized for radio. Earlier he had produced four collections ranging from the semi-autobiographical *Calendar Adam* (1971) to *West of the Cunderang* (1982), all characterized by vivid use of language and a keen sense of *locale*.

MILLIGAN, Spike (Terence Alan)
(1918–)

English humorist, born in Ahmadnagar, India. A singer and trumpeter before doing war service, he made his radio debut in *Opportunity Knocks* (1949) and, along with Peter Sellers, Harry Secombe and Michael Bentine, co-wrote and performed in *The Goon Show* (1951–9). His unique perspective on the world, allied to an irrepressible sense of the ridiculous and the surreal, has been expressed in all the artistic media and has left an indelible influence on British humour. On stage, he has appeared in *Treasure Island* (1961, 1973, 1974, 1975) and *The Bed-Sitting Room* (1963, 1967), which he also co-wrote. Aside from numerous television series and small roles in feature films, he has published a variety of children's books, poetry, autobiography and comic novels including *Puckoon* (1963), *Adolf Hitler, My Part in His Downfall* (1971), *The Looney: An Irish Fantasy* (1987), and the autobiographical volumes *Where Have All the Bullets Gone?* (1985) and *Peacework* (1991).

MILLIN, Sarah Gertrude
(1889–1968)

South African novelist, a candid racist whose novel *God's Stepchildren* (1924) was used by the Nazis as an anti-Semitic tract. She was capable and skilful, and because of her undoubted talents has been described as 'perhaps the most unpleasant woman writer of this century'. Wife of a judge, haunted by fear of miscegenation, she wrote 15 other well-executed novels.

MILLS, C(harles) Wright
(1916–62)

American sociologist and academic. He was born in Waco, Texas, and joined the faculty of Columbia University, New York City. His two main contributions to social understanding were *White Collar* (1951), a critical account of the 'new', post-war middle classes, and *The Power Elite* (1956), a darker and more pessimistic study of social control by the military, politicians and corporate money. *The Causes of World War Three* (1958) suggested the direction of Mills's thought and his subsequent impact on the New Left in the USA. However, his career was drastically foreshortened: after writing the highly prescient *Listen Yankee: The Revolution in Cuba* (1960), he died aged just 46.
▷ J Eldridge, *C Wright Mills* (1983)

MILMAN, Henry Hart
(1791–1868)

English poet and church historian, born in London, son of Sir Francis Milman (1746–1821), physician to George III. He was educated at Eton and Oxford, where he won the Newdigate Prize (1812). In 1816 he became vicar at Reading, from 1821 to 1831 Professor of Poetry at Oxford, and in 1849 Dean of St Paul's. His *Poems and dramatic works* (3 vols, 1839) are almost forgotten, except for a few hymns.

MILNE, A(lan) A(lexander)
(1882–1956)

English author, born in St John's Wood, London. He was educated at Westminster and Trinity College, Cambridge, where he edited the undergraduate magazine *Granta*. He joined the staff of *Punch* as assistant editor, and became well known for his light essays and his comedies, notably *Wurzel-Flummery* (1917), *Mr Pim Passes By* (1919) and *The Dover Road* (1922). In 1924 he achieved world fame with his book of children's verse, *When We were Very Young*, written for his own son, Christopher Robin. Further children's classics include the enchantingly whimsical *Winnie-the-Pooh* (1926), *Now We are Six* (1927) and *The House at Pooh Corner* (1928), memorably illustrated by E H Shepard. He wrote an autobiography, *It's Too Late Now* (1939).
▷ A Thwaite, *A. A. Milne* (1990)

MILNES, Richard Monckton, 1st Baron Houghton
(1809–85)

English politician and writer, born in London. His father, 'single-speech Milnes'

(1784–1858), declined the Chancellorship of the Exchequer and a peerage; his mother was a daughter of the fourth Lord Galway. At Cambridge he was a member of the Apostles Club with many future leading literary figures like **Tennyson** and **Thackeray**. He was MP for Pontefract from 1837 until he entered the House of Lords in 1863. A patron of young writers, he befriended **David Gray**, and was one of the first to recognize **Swinburne**'s genius, and secured the poet laureateship for Tennyson (1850). He was the 'Mr Vavasour' of **Disraeli**'s novel *Tancred*. A traveller, a philanthropist, and an unrivalled after-dinner speaker, he went up in a balloon and down in a diving-bell; he was the first publishing Englishman who gained access to the harems of the East; he championed oppressed nationalities, liberty of conscience, fugitive slaves, the rights of women; and carried a bill for establishing reformatories (1846). As well as his poetry—his collected *Poetical Works* appeared in 1876—and essays, he published *Life, Letters and Remains of Keats* (1848). ▷J Pope-Hennessey, *Monckton Milnes* (1950–2)

MILOSZ, Czeslaw
(1911–)

Polish poet, novelist and essayist, winner of the Nobel Prize for literature, born in Szetejnie, Lithuania. *Trzy zimy* (1936, 'Three Winters'), his second book of poems, had established a reputation for him by the time war broke out. In 1945, after having worked for Polish Radio and a variety of underground publications, he brought out *Ocalenie* ('Rescue'), a collection primarily of war poems. Not until 1980, in which year he won the Nobel Prize for literature, was another book of his published in Poland. He spent much of the intervening 35 years in exile, first in Paris, then in California. His prose works include the novel *Zdobycie wladzy* (1953, 'The Seizure of Power'). *Collected Poems 1931–1987* (1988) is a splendid summation of the career of Milosz, one of the greatest European poets of the century.

MILOSZ, Oscar-Vladislas de Lubisez
(1877–1939)

Lithuanian mystic, poet, novelist, philosopher, scientist and dramatist who wrote in French (his family, related to that of **Czeslaw Milosz**, moved to Paris when he was 11 years old). There are two views: that he was pretentious and crazy, and that he was one of the greatest poets of the 20th century. The truth lies in between: he was not pretentious, but his lush and complex work is hard to read and harder to understand—he could fairly be described as a substantial minor poet of

profound interest. After the Russian revolution he represented Lithuania as minister to France and the League of Nations. His poems are indeed almost impenetrable; but, as Marcel Raymond wrote, he sometimes sang 'as Rilke sang': an opulent integrity informs all his work, so that his reader immediately knows that his unique and erudite synthesis of music, Cabala, modern physics (he anticipated Einstein in the formulation of relativity), Swedenborg and other mystics is genuine. Available in English translation are *14 Poems* (1952) and the novel *Miguel Manera* (1919).

MILTON, John
(1608–74)

English poet, born in Bread Street, Cheapside, the son of a composer of some distinction. From St Paul's School he went up to Christ's College, Cambridge, where he spent seven not altogether blameless years, followed by six years of studious leisure at Horton which he regarded as preparation for his life's work as a poet. His apprentice work at Cambridge—apart from some poems of elegant Latin written there or at Horton—includes the splendid 'Nativity Ode', the brilliant epitaph on **Shakespeare** and 'At a Solemn Music'. The poems he wrote at Horton—*L'Allegro* and *Il Penseroso, Comus* and *Lycidas*—he also regarded as preparatory to the great poem or drama which was to be 'doctrinal and exemplary for a nation'. *Lycidas* (1637) is an excellent pastoral elegy, though it was censured for its outburst against the Laudian clergy by critics who were ignorant of the Renaissance pastoral convention. On this ominous note Milton concluded his formal education with a visit to Italy (1638–9). The fame of his Latin poems had preceded him and he was received in the academies with distinction. His Italian tour was interrupted by news of the imminent outbreak of Civil War in England. This event, into which he threw himself with revolutionary ardour, silenced his poetic outpourings for 20 years except for occasional sonnets, most of which were published in a volume of *Poems* in 1645. They range from civilities to friends to trumpet-blasts against his and the Commonwealth's detractors. Two stand out—the noble 'On His Blindness' and 'On the Late Massacre in Piedmont'. On his return to London in 1639 Milton undertook the education of his two nephews, but in 1641 he emerged as the polemical champion of the revolution in a series of pamphlets against episcopacy, including an *Apology for Smectymnuus* (1642). *Smectymnuus* was an attack on episcopacy by five Presbyterians. He was now launched on his second series of controversial pamphlets—the divorce pamphlets which were occasioned by the refusal of his 17-year-old bride, Mary Powell, daughter of a Royalist, whom he married in 1642, to return to him after a visit to her home. The first of these, *The Doctrine and Discipline of Divorce* (1643), involved him in three supplementary pamphlets against the opponents of his views on divorce, and these occasioned a threat of prosecution by a parliamentary committee dominated by the Presbyterians who were now to be reckoned his chief enemies after the episcopacy pamphlets. *Areopagitica, A Speech for the Liberty of Unlicensed Printing* (1644) was the famous vindication which is still quoted when the press is in danger. The contemporary *Tractate on Education*, a brilliant exposition of the Renaissance ideals of education, has much less appeal today. Meanwhile his wife returned to him in 1645 accompanied by her whole family as refugees after Naseby, and two years later, his father having left him enough to live on comfortably, he was able to give up schoolmastering. The execution of King Charles I launched him on his third public controversy, now addressed however to the conscience of Europe. As Latin secretary to the new council of state to which he was appointed immediately after his defence of the regicides (*The Tenure of Kings and Magistrates*, 1649), he became official apologist for the Commonwealth. As such he wrote *Eikonoklastes* and two *Defensiones*, the first, *Pro Populo Anglicano Defensio* (1650), addressed to the celebrated humanist Salmasius. The second, also in Latin, *Defensio Secunda* (1654), contains autobiographical matter and so supplements the personal matter in the *Apology for Smectymnuus*. Meanwhile, his wife having died in 1652, leaving three daughters, he married Catherine Woodcock, whose death two years later is the theme of his beautiful sonnet 'Methought I saw my late espoused Saint'. Although blind from 1652 onwards, he retained his Latin secretaryship until the Restoration (1660), which he roused himself to resist in a last despairing effort as pamphleteer. But the fire had gone out of him, and *The Readie and Easie Way*, which pointed to dictatorship, became the target of the Royalist wits. After the Restoration Milton went into hiding for a short period, and then after the Act of Oblivion (August 1660) he devoted himself wholly to poetry with the exception of his prose *De Doctrina Christiana* (which did not appear until 1823). He married his third wife, Elizabeth Minshull, in 1662 and spent his last days in what is now Bunhill Row. His wife survived him. The theme of *Paradise Lost* (completed 1665, published 1667) had been in Milton's mind since 1641. It was to be a sacred drama then; but when in 1658 his official duties were lightened so as

to allow him to write, he chose the epic form. The first three books reflect the triumph of the godly—so soon to be reversed; the last books, written in 1663, are tinged with despair. God's kingdom is not of this world. Man's intractable nature frustrates the planning of the wise. The heterodox theology of the poem which is made clear in his late *De Doctrina Christiana* did not trouble Protestant readers till modern critics examined it with hostile intent; at the same time they made him responsible for that 'dissociation of sensibility' in the language of poetry which had fatal effects on his 18th-century imitators. *Paradise Regained* (1671) ought to have appeased these critics, for its manner is quiet and grave, though not without grand rhetorical passages. The theme here is the triumph of reason over passion; Christ is more the elevated stoic than the redeemer. Resignation is the note of *Paradise Regained*, but *Samson Agonistes*, published along with it in 1671, shows the reviving spirit of rebellion, due no doubt to the rise of Whig opposition about 1670. The parallel of his own fortunes, both in the private and the public sphere, with those of Samson made Milton pour out his great spirit into this Greek play, which also became the libretto of Handel's oratorio. His last years were spent in sociable comfort in Cripplegate; he was buried next to his father in St Giles' Churchyard, Cripplegate.

▷ D Masson, *The Life of John Milton* (7 vols, 1859–80); W Parker, *John Milton* (2 vols, 1968)

MILUTINOVÍC SARAJLIJA, Sima
(1791–1847)

Serbian poet, dramatist, would-be folk-song collector (he lacked system) and historian, born in Sarajevo. He was a paradigmatically romantic poet who led a life of adventure. His poetry is fervently patriotic, but exceedingly confused. Perhaps his most significant role was as tutor to **Petar Petrovíc Njegos**, whose style he certainly influenced.

MIOMANDRE, Frances de, pseud of François Durand
(1880–1959)

French writer, born in Tours. His first book was a collection of verse, but he was best known as a novelist, and was awarded the Prix **Goncourt** for *Écrit sur l'eau* in 1908. Many of his books are set in Provence, and are characterized by detailed observation, picturesque description, and an elegant, rather old-fashioned prose style. *Direction Étoile* (1937) is one notable exception, a fantasy set on the Paris Métro. He also translated the work of a number of Spanish writers, including **Unamuno**, **Cervantes** and **Asturias**.

MIRA BAI
(c.1498–1546)

A *bhakti* poet and mystic, devoted to Krishna. She was born a Rajput princess, and was duly married to a prince before she was 20. However, even then she had already surrendered herself to Krishna and neglected her husband as a result. Mira Bai constantly had to fight against the traditional roles ascribed to women in society, the crisis coming on the death of her husband when her father-in-law insisted that she become a *sati*. She escaped to a community of bhakti devotees who supported her, eventually becoming a wandering ascetic attached to a temple in the holy city of Dwarka. Mira Bai's poetry reflects her deep love for Krishna, especially in her use of the romantic symbolism of the 'mystical marriage' between herself and her Lord. In common with other mystics Mira Bai often expresses her devotion in two contrasting ways. Firstly, in describing Krishna's beauty and the blissful experience of being in his presence; and secondly in expressing the deep pain of separation from Krishna. Mira Bai is unusual in that she cannot be placed in any particular category, her notion of Krishna encompassing both his mythological and the transcendent natures. As a result she is able to identify herself with him on the personal level and by seeing herself as being absorbed in him. Indeed, it is this that helps to explain her wide appeal.

MIRANDA, Francisco de Sá de
(1481–1558)

Portuguese poet, playwright and Renaissance humanist and moralist. He introduced the Italian style (he spent some years in Italy and Sicily in the 1520s) into his literature with his eclogue *Alexo*, of which he is one of the major exponents and formers. He helped prepare the way for **Camoens**, though was in no way his equal as a poet. He was at first a courtier; in 1532 he returned to his own estates, where he lived the life of a gentleman deeply and expressively displeased with the frivolity of all he saw about him. He wrote some poetry in Castilian, and, of all the poets of major historical importance, was perhaps the least skilled in technique; yet by sheer persistence and hard work he founded the new school which culminated in Camoens.
▷A F G Bell, *Portuguese Literature* (1922)

MIRBEAU, Octave
(1850–1917)

French dramatist, novelist, and journalist, born in Trevières (Calvados). A radical, he attracted attention by the violence of his writings. His play *Les Affaires sont les affaires* (1903, 'Business is Business') was adapted by Sidney Grundy (1905). Other works include *Le Jardin des supplices* (1898, Eng trans *Torture Garden*, 1931) and *Le Journal d'une femme de chambre* (1900, Eng trans *A Chambermaid's Diary*, 1934).
▷M Renan, *Octave Mirbeau* (1924)

MIRÓ, Gabriel
(1879–1930)

Spanish novelist, born in Alicante; he was and still is renowned for his sensuous and evocative style. A Spanish critic called him 'a hermit drunk with sensuality'. His novel about Christ, as seen through the eyes of his contemporaries, *Figuras de la Pasión del Señor* (1917, Eng trans *Figures of the Passion of our Lord*, 1925), was condemned by his fellow Roman Catholics but established his reputation with discerning critics. The first volume of his two-part novel *Nuestre padre San Daniel* (1921) has been translated (*Our Father San Daniel*, 1930); the second volume, *El obispo leproso* (1926, 'The Leprous Bishop'), has not. This work is an unequivocal masterpiece, set in the last two decades of the 19th century, and depicting a bishop who loves life, and so is rewarded with a horrible disease—but this, it is shown with great affirmative conviction, cannot eat into his heart. The Spanish Academy of Letters refused recognition of Miró owing to his liberalism; now he is revered in Spanish letters.

MIRO, Ricardo
(1883–1940)

The national poet of the small country of Panama, born in Panama City. He worked to free Panama from Colombian rule, and after independence was declared in 1903 devoted himself to literary journalism, editing the periodical *Nuevos Ritos* ('New Rites') and founding a newspaper. His poetry helped give Panama a sense of national identity, but it has never been seriously suggested that it exports well, and he is absent from most anthologies of Latin American verse.

MIRON, Gaston
(1928–)

French–Canadian poet, born in Saint-Agathe-des-Montes, Québec. In the 1950s and 1960s he became a legendary personality in Québec and Montreal, the author of long poems which he did not care if he published or not, and with a dramatically separatist stance. The best-known of these poems was 'La Vie agonique', ('The Anguished Life'). He reached the status of 'Miron le magnifique' with the publication of the collection *L'Homme rapaillé* (1970), a collection of 57 poems on the theme of 'the present impossibility of writing a book'. He has been called the 'single most influential figure in French–Canadian literature today'. Poems are translated in *The Poetry of French Canada in Translation*, edited by **John Glassco** and published in 1970.

▷ J Brault, *Miron le magnifique* (1966, in French)

MISHIMA Yukio, pseud of Hiraoka Kimitake (1925–70)

Japanese writer, born in Tokyo. He published his first story in 1944 at the age of 19. He attended Tokyo University before becoming a civil servant and embarking on a prolific writing career which, as well as 40 novels, produced poetry, essays and modern Kabuki and Nō drama. His first major work was *Kamen no Kokuhaku* (1949, Eng trans *Confessions of a Mask*, 1958) which dealt with his discovery of his own homosexuality and the ways in which he attempted to conceal it. After many other works, notably the novels *Kinkakuji* (1956, Eng trans *The Temple of the Golden Pavilion*, 1959) and *Utage no ato* (1960, Eng trans *After the Banquet*, 1963), he wrote his great tetralogy, *Hojo no umi* (1965–70, Eng trans *The Sea of Fertility*, 1972–4), which, with a central theme of reincarnation, spanned Japanese life and events in the 20th century. Passionately interested in the chivalrous traditions of Imperial Japan, he believed implicitly in the ideal of a heroic destiny, the pursuit of an absolute ideal of beauty, and the concept of a glorious and honourable death in battle. He became an expert in the martial arts of *karate* and *kendo*, and in 1968 founded the Shield Society, a group of a hundred youths dedicated to a revival of *Bushido*, the Samurai knightly code of honour. The most extreme expression of his elitist right-wing views was in an essay *Taiyo to tetsu* (1968, Eng trans *Sun and Steel*, 1970), and in the same year he committed suicide by performing *seppuku* after a carefully-staged token attempt to rouse the nation to a return to pre-war nationalist ideals. Among his other novels are *Ai no kawaki* (1950, Eng trans *Thirst for Love*, 1969), *Shiosai* (1954, Eng trans *The Sound of Waves*, 1956) and *Gogo no eilo* (1963, Eng trans *The Sailor Who Fell from Grace with the Sea*, 1965); his plays include *Sado koshaku fujin* (1965, Eng trans *Madame de Sade*, 1967) and *Waga tomo Hitler* (1968, 'My Friend Hitler').

▷ H S Stokes, *A Life of Mishima* (1974)

MISTRAL, Frédéric (1830–1914)

Provençal poet and winner of the Nobel Prize for literature, born in Maillane near Avignon. After studying law at Avignon, he went home to work on the land and write poetry. He helped to found the Provençal renaissance movement (Félibrige school). In 1859 his epic *Mirèio* (Eng trans 1890) gained him the poet's prize of the Académie française and the *Légion d'honneur*. He was awarded a Nobel Prize for literature in 1904. Other works are an epic, *Calendau* (1861), poems *Lis Isclo d'or* (1876), a tragedy *La Reino Jano* (1890), and a Provençal–French dictionary (1878–86).

▷ L Larguier, *Mistral* (1930, in French)

MISTRAL, Gabriela, pseud of Lucila Godoy de Alcayaga (1889–1957)

Chilean poet, diplomat and teacher, winner of the Nobel Prize for literature, born in Vicuña. As a teacher she won a poetry prize with her *Sonetos de la muerte* ('Sonnets of Death') at Santiago in 1915. She taught at Columbia University, Vassar and in Puerto Rico, and was formerly consul at Madrid and elsewhere. The cost of publication of her first book, *Desolación* (1922, 'Desolation'), was defrayed by the teachers of New York. Her work is inspired by religious sentiments and a romantic preoccupation with sorrow and death, infused with an intense lyricism. Her career as a teacher led her to write a great deal of work for children, notably the songs in *Ternura* (1924); much of her children's writing is translated in *Crickets and Frogs* (1972). She was awarded the Nobel Prize for literature in 1945.

▷ M Arce de Vázquez, *Gabriela Mistral: the poet and her work* (1964)

MISTRY, Rohinton (1952–)

Canadian novelist and short-story writer, born in Bombay. He emigrated to Toronto in 1975, working in a bank for a decade while establishing himself as a writer. He has twice won the Hart House Prize (1983, 1984), for his short stories, a collection of which, *Tales From Firozsha Baag* (1987), was his first book to be published. *Such A Long Journey* (1991), his first novel, is the tale of Gustad Noble, a Zoroastrian, and his family, set during the war which resulted in the birth of Bangla Desh. It was shortlisted for the Booker Prize.

MITCHELL, (Sibyl) Elyne Keith (1913–)

Australian writer, born in Melbourne, author of a popular children's series of novels about horses, beginning with *The Silver Brumby* (1958), followed by *Silver Brumby's Daughter* (1960) and others including *Snowy River Brumby* (1980). She also wrote *The Colt from Snowy River* (1979), a novel based on the film of **Banjo Paterson**'s poem *The Man from Snowy River* (1982), and two books on World

War I, *Light Horse: The Story of Australia's Mounted Troops* (1978) and *The Lighthorse Men* (1987). From her home on the western slopes of the Snowies she has also written *Australia's Alps* (1942) and *The Discoverers of the Snowy Mountains* (1985).

MITCHELL, Margaret
(1900–49)

American novelist, born in Atlanta, Georgia. She studied for a medical career, but turned to journalism. After her marriage to J R Marsh in 1925, she began the 10-year task of writing her only novel, *Gone with the Wind* (1936), which won the Pulitzer Prize, sold over 25 million copies, was translated into 30 languages and was the subject of a celebrated film in 1939.
▷A Edwards, *The Road to Tara* (1983)

MITCHISON, Naomi Mary Margaret, née Haldane
(1897–)

British writer, born in Edinburgh, the daughter of the physiologist J S Haldane. Educated at the Dragon School, Oxford, she won instant attention with her brilliant and personal evocations of Greece and Sparta in a series of novels such as *The Conquered* (1923), *When the Bough Breaks* (1924), *Cloud Cuckoo Land* (1925) and *Black Sparta* (1928). In 1931 came the erudite *Corn King and Spring Queen*, which brought to life the civilizations of ancient Egypt, Scythia and the Middle East. She has travelled widely, and in 1963 was made Tribal Adviser and Mother to the Bakgatla of Botswana. She has written more than 70 books, including her memoirs in *Small Talk* (1973), *All Change Here* (1975) and *You May Well Ask* (1979), among many other writings. She married the Labour MP Gilbert Richard Mitchison (1890–1970) in 1916. Since 1937 she has lived in Carradale in the Mull of Kintyre, Scotland.
▷J Benton, *A Century of Experiment* (1990)

MITFORD, Mary Russell
(1787–1855)

English novelist and dramatist, daughter of a spendthrift physician. At the age of 10 she won £20 000 in a lottery and went to school in Chelsea. As the family became more and more impoverished she had to write to earn money. Several plays were produced successfully but failed to keep the stage. Her gift was for charming sketches of country manners, scenery and character, which after appearing in magazines were collected as *Our Village* (5 vols, 1824–32). She received a civil list pension in 1837 which was increased on her father's death from subscriptions raised to pay his debts. In 1852 she published *Recollections of a Literary Life*.
▷V Watson, *Mary Russell Mitford* (1949)

MITFORD, Nancy Freeman
(1904–73)

English writer, daughter of the 2nd Baron Redesdale and sister of Unity Mitford. She established a reputation with her witty novels such as *Pursuit of Love* (1945) and *Love in a Cold Climate* (1949), followed by *The Blessing* (1951) and *Don't Tell Alfred* (1960). After the war she settled in France and wrote her major biographies *Madame de Pompadour* (1953), *Voltaire in Love* (1957), *The Sun King* (1966) and *Frederick the Great* (1970). As one of the essayists in *Noblesse Oblige*, edited by herself (1956), she helped to originate the famous 'U', or upper-class, and 'non-U' classification of linguistic usage and behaviour. Her sister Jessica (1917–) wrote *Hons and Rebels* (1960), an autobiography that told the story of the Mitfords' unconventional childhood.
▷S Hastings, *Nancy Mitford* (1985)

MITTELHOLZER, Edgar
(1909–65)

Guyanian novelist. Born and educated in Guyana, he worked as a customs official and journalist before serving in the Navy in World War II. Settling in London in 1945, he became a full-time writer in 1952 when he received a Guggenheim Fellowship. Of mixed race origins, his unhappy personal life led to psychological illness and his eventual suicide. He wrote 22 novels, mostly set in modern Guyana, plus his autobiography, *A Swarthy Boy* (1963). One of the pioneers of Caribbean literature, his first novel, *A Morning at the Office* (1950), was acclaimed for its realistic portrayal of racial tensions in city life. His trilogy, *Children of Kaywana*, portrays Guyana's unchronicled past. Although much of his later work is flawed by excessive violence, his earlier novels are distinguished by their narrative excitement, sense of place and array of fascinating characters.
▷M Gilkes, 'Pioneers', in *The West Indian Novel* (1981)

MIYOSHI Tatsuji
(1900–64)

Japanese poet, from Tokyo. He was highly influential in the middle years of the 20th century, being the centre of a number of literary circles, though his work—long poems in blank verse with elaborate imagery—is not now so highly esteemed. His chief importance lies perhaps in his editorship of a series of literary magazines, especially *Buntai*, which was the arena in which a number of up-and-coming writers of the 1930s cut their literary teeth.

▷D Keene (ed), *The Modern Japanese Prose Poem: An Anthology of Six Poets* (1980)

MLODÓZENIEC, Stanislaw
(1895–1959)

Polish poet prominent in the Futurist movement inspired by **Marinetti**, but more particularly a 'Polish primitivist'. He was born to peasant parents in Dobrocice. In his poetry he combined strident Futurist presentation with folkloristic themes—the latter of which are the more interesting and original. He went to London after the Russian takeover, but returned to Warsaw to die. He is well represented in *Five Centuries of Polish Poetry* (1960).

MO, Timothy
(1950–)

British novelist and journalist, born in Hong Kong of an English mother and a Cantonese father. He was educated at Oxford. Mo writes incisively but compassionately about cultural ambitions and the lack of comprehension between races. His first novel, *The Monkey King* (1978), concerns family and business affairs in Hong Kong and the Chinese mainland, while *Sour Sweet* (1982) looks at the precarious and sometimes comic fate of a family of Chinese immigrants to London, who open a restaurant and brush against the Chinese criminal fraternity. *An Insular Possession* (1986) is a more ambitious, longer work, set during the 19th-century opium wars between China and Britain, partly a novel of political intrigue, partly a comedy of manners. *The Redundancy of Courage* (1991) continues the more serious theme, charting the life of a hotel worker who becomes politically involved following the American invasion of East Timor in 1975.

MOBERG, (Carl Artur) Vilhelm
(1898–1973)

Swedish author, born in Algutsboda in Småland. He came from a family of crofters and enlisted soldiers and remained loyal to his background. His best-known work is the series of novels that deal with documentary accuracy with the 19th-century mass migration of Swedes to the USA: *Utvandrarna* (1949, Eng trans *The Emigrants*, 1951), *Invandrarna* (1952, Eng trans *Unto a Good Land*, 1957), *Nybyggarna* (1956, 'The Settlers') and *Sista brevet till Sverige* (1959, 'Last Letter to Sweden'). His unfinished *Min svenska historia 1–2* (1970–1, 'My Swedish History') looks at history from the viewpoint of the common people. He was a popular

dramatist and several of his novels, notably *The Emigrants*, have been filmed.

▷P Holmes, *Vilhelm Moberg* (1980)

MOCKEL, Albert
(1866–1945)

Belgian Symbolist poet, critic and editor, born in Ougrée. He founded *La Wallonie* (1886–93), the Symbolist review. Initially influenced by **Gorter**, he soon turned for inspiration to **Mallarmé** and to Mallarmé's French disciple **René Ghil**. His poetry is in a melodious free verse, much influenced by the Wagnerian notion of key motifs, and, as in *La Flamme immortelle* (1924, 'The Immortal Flame'), his major work, is schematic and impersonal. Today, he is much respected but not widely read.

MOE, Jørgen Engebretsen
(1813–82)

Norwegian folklorist and poet, Bishop of Christiansand (1875–81). With Peter Christian Asbjørnsen he collected and edited *Norwegian Folk Stories* (1841–4). He also published a book of Romantic verse (1850), and a children's classic, *I brønden og i kjærnet* (1851).

▷P C Asbjørnsen, *Mannen og livsverket* (1947)

MOGUEL Y URQUIZA, Juan Antonio
(1745–1804)

Basque novelist, born in Eibar, Guipúzoca. He achieved the remarkable feat of translating the *Pensées* of Blaise Pascal into Basque. His moralistic but nonetheless lively and acutely observed novel *Pero Abarca*, first published in Castilian in 1899 (in Basque in 1955), circulated widely in Basque manuscript in his lifetime. It was written in dialogue, and its protagonist, a street barber, Maisu Juan, became a legendary character.

▷R Gallop, *A Book of the Basques* (1930); L Michelena, *Historia de la literatura vasca* (1960)

MOIR, David Macbeth
(1798–1851)

Scottish physician and writer, born in Musselburgh, East Lothian, where he practised as a physician from 1817 until his death. Under his pen-name of Delta (δ) he contributed verses to *Blackwood's Magazine* (collected 1852), and is remembered for his humorous *The Life of Mansie Wauch, Tailor in Dalkeith* (1828).

▷Sir G Douglas, *The Blackwood Group* (1897)

MOLESWORTH, Mary Louisa, née Stewart (1839–1921)

Scottish novelist and writer of children's stories, born in Rotterdam. She spent her childhood in Manchester, Scotland and Switzerland. She began writing as a novelist under the pseudonym 'Ennis Graham', but she is best known as a writer of stories for children, such as *Carrots: Just a Little Boy* (1876), *The Cuckoo Clock* (1877), *The Tapestry Room* (1879), and the more realistic *Two Little Waifs* (1883).

▷R L Green, *Mrs Molesworth* (1961)

MOLIÈRE, stage name of Jean Baptiste Poquelin (1622–73)

French playwright, born in Paris, the son of a well-to-do upholsterer. He studied with the Jesuits at the Collège de Clermont, under the philosopher and scientist Pierre Gassendi. He may have been called to the Bar. His mother, who had some property, died when he was 10 years old, and thus when he came of age he received his share of her fortune. He declined to follow his father's business, hired a tennis court, and embarked on a theatrical venture (1643) with the Béjart family and others, under the title of L'Illustre Théâtre, which lasted for over three years in Paris. The company then proceeded to the provinces from Lyons to Rouen, and had sufficient success to keep going from 1646 to 1658. Prince François de Conti took it under his protection for a time; and when he took to Catholic Methodism, Molière obtained the patronage of the king's brother, Philippe d'Orléans, so that his troupe became the servants of Monsieur. He played before the king on 24 October 1658, and organized a regular theatre, first in the Petit Bourbon, then, on its demolition, in the Palais Royal. In the provinces Molière had acquired experience as a comic writer, mostly in the style of the old farces. But he had also written *L'Étourdi* (1655, Eng trans *The Blunderers*, 1762) and *Le Dépit amoureux* (1656, Eng trans *The Amorous Quarrel*, 1762). As a theatre manager he had to perform tragedy as well as comedy. **Corneille**'s *Nicomède*, with which he opened, was not a success; and though the other great tragedian of the day, **Racine**, was a personal friend of Molière's, their connection as manager and author was brief and unfortunate. But Molière soon realized his own immense resources as a comic writer. *Les Précieuses ridicules* (Eng trans *The Conceited Young Ladies*, 1762) was published in November 1659, and every year until his death he produced at least one of his comic masterpieces. In the spring of 1662 he married Armande Béjart, an actress in his own company, probably about 19, and the youngest member of the Béjart family, of which two other sisters, Madeleine and Geneviève, and one brother, Joseph, had been members of L'Illustre Théatre. It has been suggested that Madeleine Béjart and Molière were lovers, that Armande was Madeleine's daughter, even that Molière was the father of his own wife! It is also said that Armande was unfaithful to her husband. In August 1665 the king adopted Molière's troupe as his own servants. In 1667 symptoms of lung disease showed themselves. He died in his home in the rue de Richelieu the night after having acted as the *Malade* in the seventh performance of his last play, *Le Malade Imaginaire* (1673, Eng trans *Doctor Last in his Chariot*, 1769). He was generous and amiable; and there are insufficient grounds for the accusations of irreligion brought against him. The dates and titles of his other plays are: *Sganarelle* (1660, Eng trans *The Picture*, 1745); *Don Garcie de Navarre* (1661, Eng trans *Don Garcia of Navarre; or The Jealous Prince*, 1714); *L'Ecole des maris* (1661, Eng trans in parallel *The School for Husbands*, 1732), *Les Fâcheux* (1622, Eng trans *The Impertinents*, 1732), *L'Ecole des femmes* (1662, Eng trans *The School for Wives*, 1971); *La Critique de l'École des femmes* (1663, Eng trans in parallel *School for Wives criticis'd*, 1755), *Impromptu de Versailles* (1663, Eng trans in parallel *The Impromptu of Versailles*, 1755); *Le Mariage forcé* (1664, Eng trans *The Forced Marriage*, 1762), *La Princesse d'Élide* (1664, Eng trans *The Universal Passion*, 1737), *Tartuffe* (partially, 1664, Eng trans 1670); *Le Festin de Pierre [Don Juan]* (1665, Eng trans in parallel *Don John*, 1755), *L'Amour médecin* (1665, Eng trans *The Quacks*, 1705); *Le Misanthrope* (1666, Eng trans 1762), *Le médecin malgré lui* (1666, Eng trans *The Dumb Lady*, 1672), *Mélicerte* (1666, Eng trans 1755), *Le Sicilien* (1666, Eng trans *The Sicilian*, 1732); *Tartuffe* (1667, a revised version); *Amphitryon* (1668, Eng trans 1690), *George Dandin* (1668, Eng trans 1732), *L'Avare* (1668, Eng trans *The Miser*, 1672); *Monsieur de Pourceaugnac* (1669, Eng trans *The Cornish Squire*, 1734); *Les Amants magnifiques* (1670, Eng trans in parallel *The Magnificent Lovers*, 1755), *Le Bourgeois gentilhomme* (1671, Eng trans *The Citizen Turned Gentleman*, 1672); *Les Fourberies de Scapin* (1671, Eng trans *The Cheats of Scapin*, 1677); *La Comtesse d'Escarbagnas* (1671, 'The Countess of Escarbagnas') and *Les Femmes savantes* (1672, Eng trans *The Female Virtuosoes*, 1690). To this must be added part of *Psyché* (1671), in collaboration with **Philippe Quinault** and **Corneille**, two farces, a few court masques, and some miscellaneous poems.

▷J Palmer, *Molière* (1930)

MÖLLER, Poul Martin
(1794–1838)

Danish literary figure, born in Uldum. He graduated in theology at Copenhagen and later became a Professor of Philosophy, first in Oslo, and then in Copenhagen. His chief work, *En dansk Students Eventyr* ('Adventures of a Danish Student'), which he finished in 1824, but which was published posthumously, is a charming, light-hearted account of undergraduate life in Copenhagen. During a journey to China he wrote in verse nostalgically of his homeland. *Sceneri Rosenborg Slotshave* (1819–21, 'Scenes from the Garden at Rosenberg Castle') is a representative work, showing how he avoids the abstract and metaphysical, for his credo was 'all poetry that does not come from life is a lie'. He made the first Danish translation of *The Odyssey*, wrote philosophical essays and coined brilliant aphorisms.

▷F Nielson, *Om Poul Möller* (1961)

MOLNÁR, Ferenc
(1878–1952)

Hungarian novelist and dramatist, born in Budapest. He is best known for his novel *A Pál-utcai fiúk* (1907, 'The Paul Street Boys'), and his plays *The Devil* (1907), *Liliom* (1909, Eng trans 1944), which formed the basis of the musical comedy *Carousel* (1921 as a stage play; 1945 as a musical by Rodgers and **Hammerstein**; 1956 as a musical film), and *A zenélő angyal* (1930, Eng trans *Angel Making Music*, 1934), all of which have achieved success in English translation. He emigrated to the USA in 1940.

▷I Vécsei, *Molnár Ferenc* (1966)

MOMADAY, N(avarre) Scott, also known by the Kiowa name **Tsoai-talee**
(1934–)

Native American novelist and autobiographer, born in Oklahoma and raised on a reservation in the South West. He attended the University of New Mexico, Albuquerque, and Stanford University, California, where he returned as professor in 1972, having taught at other Californian campuses. Like **Ralph Ellison** in black writing, his reputation is based on one definitive text, the Pulitzer Prize-winning novel, *House Made of Dawn* (1968), which concerns the conflict between Native American and Anglo-Saxon culture. Its themes were already present in Momaday's collection of Kiowa tales, *The Journey of Tai-me* (1967, revised and commercially published as *The Way to Rainy Mountain*, 1969), and recur in his powerful memoir *The Names* (1976). However, it was not until 1989 that he wrote another full-length fiction; *The*

Ancient Child is about a half-Kiowa artist's rediscovery of his ethnic heritage.

▷A Velie, *Four American Indian Literary Masters* (1982)

MOMBERT, Alfred
(1872–1942)

German poet and contemplative who remained aloof from literary movements, but who in certain important respects anticipated Expressionism. In 1940 he was taken, as a Jew, into a concentration camp, but a friend secured his release; he died in Switzerland. Occasionally compared, perhaps over confidently, to **William Blake**, he erected a vast and unfortunately grandiose 'cosmic myth' to account for his feelings of union with nature and his belief in the transmigration of souls. But his poetry remains a quarry in which jewels may often be found. The massive mystical closet-play *Aeon* (1907–11), occasionally glowing in its authentic sense of the fulfilled inner life, is worthy if not quite a masterpiece. His late *Sfaira der Alte* (1936–42, 'Sfaira the Elder'), in which he is Sfaira the old poet, is a moving allegorical account of the struggle between himself and Nazism—he had refused to leave Germany—and is cast in a wholly pantheistic form.

MOMMSEN, Christian Matthias Theodor
(1817–1903)

German scholar and writer, born in Garding, Schleswig. He studied law in Kiel, and was briefly a newspaper editor before holding professorships at universities in Leipzig, Zurich, Breslau and Berlin. Although his writings were historical and scholarly rather than literary, their vivid and dramatic narratives brought him the Nobel Prize for literature in 1902. His most famous work was the multivolume *Romische Geschichte* (1854–85, Eng trans *History of Rome*, 1862–86), but he wrote a number of other historical works, and edited the *Corpus Inscriptionum Latinarum*, a collection of all Latin inscriptions then extant. His *Gesammelte Schriften* ('Collected Writings') were published in Berlin (1905–13).

▷V Klosterman, *Theodor Mommsen* (1958–80)

MONRO, Harold (Edward)
(1879–1932)

English poet and anthologist, born in Brussels. After graduating from Cambridge, he travelled abroad and was involved with various progressive communities before taking up the promotion of English poetry. He founded the influential *Poetry Review* in 1912 and

the Poetry Bookshop in London the following year. Generous to other poets, he published the Georgians and the Imagists; some of his own work is close to the former, including such popular pieces as the closely observed 'Milk for the Cat' (1914), but his best, least romantic and most original poems, mainly written in his later years, are bitter in tone, reflecting a loneliness related to his alcoholism and bisexuality. These include 'Strange Meetings' (1917), 'The One, Faithful ...' (1933) and 'Bitter Sanctuary' (1933). His *Collected Poems* (1933) were edited by his second wife, Alida.
▷J Grant, *Harold Monro and the Poetry Bookshop* (1967)

MONROE, Harriet
(1860–1936)

American poet and critic, born in Chicago. In 1912 she founded the magazine *Poetry*, which was influential in publicizing the work of **Vachel Lindsay**, **T S Eliot**, **Ezra Pound** and **Robert Frost**, among others. She wrote the 'Columbian Ode' for the Chicago World's Columbian Exposition (1892), celebrating the 400th anniversary of the west's 'discovery' of America. In 1917 she edited the influential free verse anthology, *The New Poetry*. Her own work was collected in *Chosen Poems* (1935).
▷*A Poet's Life* (1937)

MONSARRAT, Nicholas John Turney
(1910–79)

English novelist, born in Liverpool. He was educated at Winchester and at Trinity College, Cambridge, abandoned law for literature and wrote three quite successful novels, and a play, *The Visitors*, which reached the London stage. During the war he served in the navy, and out of his experiences emerged his bestselling novel *The Cruel Sea* (1951), which was filmed. *The Story of Esther Costello* (1953) repeated that success, followed by *The Tribe That Lost Its Head* (1956) and *The Pillow Fight* (1965). He settled in Ottawa, Canada, as director of the UK Information Office (1953–6) after holding a similar post in South Africa (1946–52).

MONTAGU, Lady Mary Wortley, née Pierrepont
(1689–1762)

English writer, born in London, the daughter of the Earl (later Duke) of Kingston. Mostly self-educated, she taught herself Latin and wrote poetry from childhood. In 1712 she eloped with Edward Wortley Montagu and lived in London, where she gained a reputation for wit and was on close terms with **Addison**, **Pope** and others. From 1716 to 1718 she lived in Constantinople while her husband was on embassy; the sparkling letters she wrote from Turkey were published posthumously (1763). On her return she was prominent in intellectual and court circles for 20 years, became a friend of the feminist Mary Astell, was involved in a bitter literary feud with Pope, wrote satirical verse, published political essays (1737–8) in support of Sir Robert Walpole, and campaigned successfully for the introduction of smallpox inoculation. In 1739 she travelled to Italy in vain pursuit of a young writer Francesco Algarotti with whom she had fallen in love, then stayed on the Continent until shortly before her death. As a poet and essayist she was versatile, witty and accomplished, but her letters, whether written for publication or as personal correspondence, are in a class apart for candour, intelligence, keen observation and vivid expression.
▷*Complete Letters*, ed R Halsband (1965–7); R Halsband, *The Life of Mary Wortley Montagu* (1956)

MONTAGUE, Charles Edward
(1867–1928)

English novelist and essayist, of Irish parentage. He was on the staff of *The Manchester Guardian* from 1890 to 1925. His numerous writings include the novels *A Hind Let Loose* (1910), *Rough Justice* (1926) and *Disenchantment* (1922), an account of his experiences as a soldier in World War I.

MONTAGUE, John
(1929–)

Irish poet, born in New York and educated in Dublin, at whose University College he graduated in History and English. He has received many awards, and is a popular reader of his own work to audiences in Ireland and in the USA. He has published some 30 volumes of verse, as well as a play, a novel, a critical work, and some stories. Critical response has been generous but often imprecise, coping, as it has to, with an unusually versatile and varied corpus of work, much influenced by such American poets as **William Carlos Williams**, and with, as has been remarked, some lack of direction. It is the impact of his whole work, rather than individual poems, which has impressed critics.
▷T D Redshaw (ed), *Hill Field: Poems and Memories for John Montague on his 60th Birthday* (1989)

MONTAIGNE, Michel Eyquem de
(1533–92)

French essayist, third son of the Seigneur de Montaigne, born at the Château de Montaigne in Périgord. As an experiment in

humanist upbringing, he spoke no language but Latin until he was six, and at the Collège de Guienne in Bordeaux he remained for seven years, boarding in the rooms of his famous teachers, George Buchanan and **Marc-Antoine de Muret**. He subsequently studied law; but from the age of 13 to 24 little is known of him, though it is certain that he was frequently in Paris, knew something of court life, and took his full share of its pleasures. He obtained a post in connection with the *parlement* of Bordeaux, and for 13 years was a city counsellor. He formed a close friendship with Étienne de la Boëtie (1530–63). He married (1565) Françoise de la Chassaigne, daughter of a fellow counsellor. A translation (1569) of the *Natural Theology* of a 15th-century professor at Toulouse was his first attempt at literature, and supplied the text for his *Apologie de Raymon Sebond* ('Apologia for Raymond Sebond'), in which he exhibited the full scope of his own sceptical philosophy. In 1571, as his two elder brothers had died, he succeeded to the family estate at Château de Montaigne, and there lived the life of a country gentleman, varied only by visits to Paris and a tour in Germany, Switzerland and Italy. There he began those *Essais* (1572–80 and 1588, Eng trans *Essays*, 1603) which were to give him a place among the foremost names in literary history. The record of his journey (1580–1), in French and Italian, was first published in 1774. Unanimously elected Mayor of Bordeaux (against his wishes), he performed his duties to the satisfaction of the citizens, and was re-elected. Despite the free expression of scepticism in his writings, he devoutly received the last offices of the church. From the very first, men like Pascal, differing completely from him in all the fundamental problems of life (as in his inconclusive philosophy, his easy moral opinions, his imperfect sense of duty), have acknowledged their debt to his fearless and all-questioning criticism, expressed mainly in haphazard remarks, seemingly inspired by the mere caprice of the moment, but showing the highest originality, the very broadest sympathies, and a nature capable of embracing and realizing the largest experience of life.
▷D M Frame, *Montaigne* (1965)

MONTALE, Eugenio
(1896–1981)

Italian poet, winner of the Nobel Prize for literature, born in Genoa. He worked as a journalist and critic, and was an early opponent of fascism. World War I and its aftermath left him with a deep pessimism, which permeates his writing. He was the leading poet of the modern Italian 'Hermetic' school, and his primary concern was with language and meaning. His works include *Ossi di Seppia* (1925, 'The Bones of Cuttlefish'), *Le occasioni* (1939, 'Opportunities'), *Finisterre* (1943, 'Finistère'), *La bufera e altro* (1956, 'The Storm and Other Things'), *Satura* (1962, Eng trans *Satura: Five Poems*, 1969) and *Xenia* (1966, Eng trans 1970). He was awarded the Nobel Prize for literature in 1975.
▷S Ramat, *Eugenio Montale* (1965)

MONTCHRESTIEN, Antoine de
(?1575–1621)

French playwright, economist and poet (probably originally named Mauchrestien). He was orphaned at an early age, but acquired a university education as companion to two brothers, Jacques and François Thézart, whose sister Suzanne he later married. He published an edition of five tragedies in 1601, including *L'Ecossaise ou le désastre* ('Mary Queen of Scots'), which was banned following diplomatic embarrassment over its treatment of Mary Stuart's death. He worked for many years in commerce, and wrote a *Traité de l'économie politique* (1615), calling for national economic reform. He was also Governor of Chatillon-sur-Loire for a time. His poetry includes *Susane ou la Chasteté*, published in 1601. He died fighting on the rebel side in the Huguenot revolt.
▷R Griffiths, *The Dramatic Technique of Antoine de Montchrestien* (1970)

MONTEIRO LOBATO, José Bento
(1882–1948)

Influential Brazilian essayist, satirist and children's writer, born in Taubaté, São Paulo. He created a still well known comic character, the backlands cowboy (*caboclo*) Jecá Tatú, in *Urepês* (1918) and subsequent books: it is a sympathetic but in no way uncritical portrait. In time Monteiro Lobato was jailed for his generally liberal ideas. He was also the author of much-loved children's books.

MONTEMAYOR, Jorge de
(c.1515–1561)

Spanish novelist and poet, born in Portugal. He was a musician and singer as well as a poet. He wrote the unfinished pastoral romance *Diana* (1559) in Castilian, which influenced Sir **Philip Sidney** and **Shakespeare**.
▷J B Auraille-Arce, *La novela pastoril española* (1959)

MONTESINO, Ambrosio
(c.1448–c.1512)

Spanish poet and religious writer. Montesino was a Franciscan monk, under the protection of Ferdinand and Isabella. He later rose to become the bishop of Cerdeña and his work was favoured by the powerful Cardinal Cisneros. Under the aegis of Cisneros, Montesino issued a deluxe edition of the *Vita Christi* of Landulfo of Saxony specially commissioned by the king and queen (1503). Two of his prose works, a breviary and meditations on Saint Augustine, remain unedited. However, it is for his poems that he is best known. These are preserved in the *Cancionero de Diversas Obras* (1508, 'Songbook of Diverse Works'), in which his compositions in honour of the birth of Christ stand out.

MONTESQUIEU, Charles de Secondat, Baron de la Brède et de
(1689–1755)

French philosopher and jurist, born at the Château La Brède near Bordeaux. He became counsellor of the *parlement* of Bordeaux in 1714, and its president in 1716. He discharged the duties of his office faithfully, but, until defective eyesight hindered him, by preference devoted himself to scientific researches. His first great literary success was the *Lettres persanes* (1721, 'Persian Letters'), containing a satirical description, put in the mouths of two Persian visitors to Paris, of French society. Weary of routine work, he sold his office in 1726 and settled in Paris. He travelled for three years to study political and social institutions, visiting, among other places, England, where he remained for two years (1729–31), mixing with its best society, frequenting the Houses of Parliament, studying the political writings of Locke, and analysing the English constitution. *Causes de la grandeur des Romains et de leur décadence* (1734, 'Causes of the Greatness and Decadence of the Romans') is perhaps the ablest of his works. His monumental *De l'esprit des lois* (1748, 'The Spirit of the Laws') was published anonymously and put on the Index, but passed through 22 editions in less than two years. By the spirit of laws he means their *raison d'être*, and the conditions determining their origin, development and forms; the discussion of the influence of climate was novel. The work, which held up the free English constitution to the admiration of Europe, had an immense influence. In 1748 he published *Lysimaque*, followed in 1750 by *Défense de l'esprit des lois*, a dialogue on despotism, *Arsace et Isménie* (Eng trans 1927), a romance, and an essay on taste (*Goût*) in the *Encyclopédie* (1751–80). A member of the Académie française from 1728, he died totally blind.
▷ J Starobinksi, *Montesquieu par lui-même* (1953)

MONTGOMERIE, Alexander
(c.1545–c.1611)

Scottish poet, probably born at Hessilhead Castle near Beith in Ayrshire. He was 'maister poet' to James VI and I. He was detained in a continental prison, and embittered by the failure of a lawsuit involving loss of a pension. Implicated in Barclay of Ladyland's Catholic plot, he was denounced as a traitor in 1597, and went into exile. His fame rests on the *Cherrie and the Slae*, published twice in 1597, and his love lyrics, especially 'To his Mistress'.
▷ R D S Jack, *Montgomerie* (1985)

MONTGOMERY, James
(1771–1854)

Scottish poet, born in Irvine, Ayrshire. The son of a Moravian pastor, he settled down, after various occupations, as a journalist in Sheffield, where in 1794 he started the *Sheffield Iris*, which he edited until 1825. In 1795 he was fined £20, and spent three months in York Castle for printing a 'seditious' ballad; in 1796 he was fined £30 and served six months for describing a riot. However, by 1832 he had become a moderate Conservative, and in 1835 accepted a pension of £150 from Peel. He died in Sheffield; his poems (4 vols, 1849) have been described as 'bland and deeply religious'.

MONTGOMERY, L(ucy) M(aud)
(1874–1942)

Canadian novelist, born in Clifton, Prince Edward Island. She qualified as a schoolteacher from Prince of Wales College, Charlottetown, and after studying at Dalhousie College, Halifax, Nova Scotia, she returned to Cavendish to care for her grandmother for 13 years. She published as her first book the phenomenally successful *Anne of Green Gables* (1908), the story of an orphan girl adopted in error for a boy by an elderly brother and sister. She followed it with several sequels, of which *Rilla of Ingleside* (1921) is an invaluable description of the impact of World War I on the island community. She married the Rev Ewan MacDonald in 1911, and moved to his manse at Leaskdale, Ontario. Her works are sometimes highly satirical; at her best she captures memorably the mysteries and terrors of early childhood, as in *Magic for Marigold* (1929), while her later works show qualities which recall **Guy de Maupassant**.
▷ H M Ridley, *The Story of Lucy Montgomery* (1956)

MONTGOMERY, Robert
(1807–55)

English preacher and poet, born in Bath, the illegitimate son of a clown. He studied at Lincoln College, Oxford; and from 1843, after some years in Glasgow, became minister of Percy Chapel, London. *The Omnipresence* of the Deity (1828) and Satan (1830) are remembered by **Thomas Macaulay**'s onslaught in the Edinburgh Review (April 1830).

MONTHERLANT, Henri Millon de
(1896–1972)

French novelist and playwright, born in Neuilly-sur-Seine. He was severely wounded in World War I, after which he travelled in Spain, Africa and Italy. A man of athletic interests, in his novels, as in his plays, he advocates the overcoming of the conflicts of life by vigorous action, disdaining the consolation of bourgeois sentiment. His novels, all showing his mastery of style, include the largely autobiographical La Relève du matin (1920, 'The Morning Relief'), Le Songe (1922, 'The Dream'), Les Bestiaires (1926, Eng trans The Bullfighters, 1927), Les Jeunes filles (1935–9, 'The Young Girls') and L'-Histoire d'amour de la rose de sable (1954, 'The Love Story of the Sandflower'). His plays include La Reine morte (1942, 'The Dead Queen'), Malatesta (1946), Don Juan (1958) and Le Cardinal d'Espagne (1960, 'The Cardinal of Spain').
▷H Perruchot, Henri de Montherlant (1959)

MONTI, Vincenzo
(1754–1828)

Italian poet, born in Alfonsine. He was professor at Pavia and official historian to Napoleon, although his political allegiances were apparently flexible, if his poems condemning the French Revolution, then welcoming the triumph of Napoleon, and finally celebrating his defeat, are anything to judge by. He wrote epics and tragedies on classical models and translated **Homer** from Latin and Italian versions rather than the original text.
▷D Chomenti Vasselli, Vincenzo Monti nel dramma dei suoi tempo (1968)

MOOCK, Armando
(1894–1942)

Important Chilean playwright, much of whose best work was seen in Buenos Aires. Mocosita (1929, 'The Youngster') and Rigoberto (1935) were both effective and highly popular comedies. His most serious play, however, had been the tragic (and autobiographical) Monsieur Ferdinand Pontiac (1922). In general, the lighter Moock's always finely made plays became, the more successful they were.

MOODIE, Susanna
(1803–85)

English novelist and poet, born in Bungay, Suffolk. After her marriage she reluctantly emigrated to Canada, where her husband took up farming with limited success. She began writing partly in order to contribute to the family income, publishing a collection of verse, Enthusiasm and Other Poems, in 1831. Her novels include Mark Hurdlestone and the Gold Worshipper (1853) and Flora Lyndsay (1854), sentimental light reading in which the women are strong and determined and the men weak. Her most popular non-fiction books, Roughing It in the Bush, or Life in Canada (1852) and Life in the Clearings Versus the Bush (1853), are loosely based upon her own experiences.

MOODY, William Vaughn
(1869–1910)

American dramatist and poet, born in Indiana. His plays are crucially important in the history of American theatre, because he was among the first to move from popular adaptations of French farce in order to deal realistically with wholly American subject-matter and themes. The Great Divide (1906, originally A Sabine Woman), uses the story of a woman's abduction from Massachusetts by a man from Arizona, their tempestuous association and eventual marriage, to reflect the cultural differences between a settled, inflexible society on the one hand and the wild spirit of the frontier on the other. Moody also wrote an incomplete trilogy in verse, and several volumes of poems of which Poems (1901), containing the much-anthologized 'Gloucester Moors', is perhaps the most representative.

MOON, Lorna, pseud of (Helen) Nora Wilson Low
(1886–1930)

Scottish short-story writer and novelist, born in Strichen, Aberdeenshire. Her father was a plasterer who worked mostly abroad. After an itinerant life he acquired the Temperance Hotel in Strichen, a haunt of commercial travellers. One, an American called Hebditch, who dealt in jewellery, married Lorna, and they left for America, where they had a child. Eventually she reached Hollywood, where she wrote scripts for Metro-Goldwyn-Mayer, who employed her on the screenplay for Mr. Wu, starring Lon Chaney, which was a huge success. A friend of **Frances Marion** and **Anita Loos**, she wrote for magazines in her spare time, contributing stories about Strichen, barely disguised as 'Pitouie'. Her first book, Doorways in Drumorty (1926), was a collection of stories; when it was published in Britain it was banned from the local library in Strichen, as was her novel Dark Star (1929). Wickedly and deftly puncturing her parents' social pretensions and the Nosey Parker proclivities of village life, she combined Gothic tragedy with black humour, sharpened no doubt by distance from her targets. When she died of consumption in Albuquerque, New Mexico, it made front-page news in America.

MOORCOCK, Michael
(1939–)

English novelist, whose work transcends the 'science fiction' and 'fantasy' categories into which it has often been shoe-horned. Born in Mitcham, Surrey, Moorcock became, at 17, editor of *Tarzan Adventures* and was a regular contributor to the *Sexton Blake Library*. From the mid-1960s onwards, he was editor, then publisher, of the influential SF series *New Worlds*, establishing a working routine that often required up to 15 000 words a day. He also wrote comic strips. Much of Moorcock's fiction has been organized in cycles. The 'Elric' novels began with *Stormbringer* in 1965. Perhaps his best-known sequence, starring the morally and sexually ambiguous 'Jerry Cornelius', started with *The Final Programme* (1968). Moorcock introduced 'Karl Glogauer' in *Behold the Man* (1969), a controversial re-working of the Crucifixion. A further enormous mythic cycle began with *The Eternal Champion* in 1970. Moorcock has also written in non-SF mode, but even here his work is notably open-ended. He wrote the sprawling, **Dickens**ian *Mother London* (1988) before embarking on a complex, emotionally demanding cycle, beginning with *Byzantium Endures* (1981), that will ultimately lead his anti-semitic anti-hero to the death camps.
▷M Moorcock, with C Greenland, *Michael Moorcock: Death is no Obstacle* (1991)

MOORE, Brian
(1921–)

Irish–Canadian novelist, born in Belfast. He served with the British Ministry of War Transport during the latter stages of World War II. After the war he worked for the United Nations in Europe before emigrating to Canada in 1948, where he became a journalist and adopted Canadian citizenship. He spent time in New York before moving to California. Though he has written thrillers under the pseudonym Michael Bryan, he is best known for novels like *The Feast of Lupercal* (1957), *The Luck of Ginger Coffey* (1960), *Catholics* (1972) and *The Temptation of Eileen Hughes* (1981). Particularly admired for his portrayal of women, he won the Author's Club First Novel Award with *The Lonely Passion of Judith Hearne* (1955), though it was not, strictly speaking, his first novel. *The Great Victorian Collection* (1975) was awarded the James Tait Black Memorial Prize, and both *The Doctor's Wife* (1976) and *Black Robe* (1985) were shortlisted for the Booker Prize.
▷H Dahlie, *Brian Moore* (1981)

MOORE, Charles Leonard
(1854–1923)

American poet from Philadelphia, whose verse was hailed in its time, but is now completely forgotten. He wrote the once celebrated 'Ode to America', sometimes still recited at Klu Klux Klan meetings.

MOORE, Edward
(1712–57)

English dramatist, born in Abingdon, Berkshire, the son of a dissenting minister. He was a draper in London who, to avoid going bankrupt, took to writing plays. The comedy *Gil Blas* (1751), based on **Le Sage**, and the prose tragedy *The Gamester* (1753), are his best-known productions. He also edited the weekly journal *The World* (1753–7).
▷J M Caskey, *The Life and Works of Edward Moore* (1927)

MOORE, George Augustus
(1852–1933)

Irish writer, born in Ballyglass, County Mayo. He was the son of a landed gentleman in southwest Ireland who was an MP and bred horses for racing. His youth was spent partly there and partly in London. He was educated at Oscott College, Birmingham, and intended for the army, but soon became an agnostic, abandoned a military career and lived a bohemian life in London until his father's death in 1870 left him free to become a dilettante artist and writer in Paris. After 10 years of this life, **Émile Zola**'s example revealed to him his true métier as a novelist of the realist school. His importance as a writer is that in the years of relative poverty in London, from 1880 to 1892, he introduced this type of fiction into England, with *A Modern Lover* (1883), *A Mummer's Wife* (1885) and others. *Esther Waters* (1894), the last of his novels in this vein, was regarded as rather offensive, but these novels of low life, drawn from Moore's own experience of racing touts and shabby lodgings, introduced the public to a wider world than the fashionable novel of the day. During the Boer War Moore sought exile in Ireland—such was his hatred of England's wars—and this had the double effect of arousing his interest, as in *Evelyn Innes* (1898) and *Sister Teresa* (1901), in love, theology and the arts, and encouraging his preoccupation with the texture of his prose which increasingly engaged his attention. The Irish scene also helped to turn his attention away from sordid realism as in *A Drama in Muslin* (1886), and the stories in *An Untilled Field* (1903). Moore returned to England early in the century and eventually occupied a flat in Ebury Street where he wrote dialogues, essays (*Conversations in Ebury Street*, 1924)

and confessions—a sure sign that he had exhausted his experience for novel writing. He had already written *Confessions of a Young Man* (1888), but then came *Memoirs of My Dead Life* (1906) and the belated and inferior *In Single Strictness* (1926). The most famous of his works of this sort is *Hail and Farewell* in three parts (1911–14), *Ave* (1911), *Salve* (1912) and *Vale* (1914). The malicious element in this trilogy, in which he wrote about his friends and his associates in setting up the Abbey Theatre in Dublin, particularly **W B Yeats**, does not detract from his claim to be one of the great memoirists. With this prose style now perfected, Moore turned in his last phase to romanticize history, beginning with the masterpiece *The Brook Kerith* (1916), which relates an apocryphal story of Paul and Christ among the Essenes. *Héloïse and Abelard* (1921) tells the famous love story with distinction and compassion. He also wrote the mythical *Aphrodite in Aulis* (1930).
▷J Hone, *The Life of George Moore* (1936)

MOORE, John
(1729–1802)

Scottish physician and writer, father of the soldier Sir John Moore. After studying medicine and practising in Glasgow, he travelled with the young Duke of Hamilton (1772–8), and then settled in London. His *View of Society in France, Switzerland, Germany and Italy* (1779–81) was well received, but it is for the novel *Zeluco* (1789), which suggested **Byron**'s *Childe Harold*, that he is best remembered today. His other novels are *Edward* (1796), and the epistolary *Mordaunt* (1800).
▷J M S Tompkins, *The Popular Novel in England* (1932)

MOORE, Marianne Craig
(1887–1972)

American poet, born in Kirkwood, Missouri, and educated at the Metzger Institute, Carlisle, Pennsylvania, Bryn Mawr College, and Carlisle Commercial College. She taught commercial studies there, tutored privately, and was a branch librarian in New York (1921–5). She contributed to the Imagist magazine, *The Egoist*, from 1915, and edited *The Dial* from 1926 until its demise in 1929. America's most popular female poet of the 20th century, she was acquainted with seminal modernists like **Ezra Pound** and **T S Eliot**, but New York was her milieu not Paris, and she associated with the Greenwich Village group including **William Carlos Williams** and **Wallace Stevens**. She was much liked and admired by contemporaries, even those—like Eliot—at odds with her artistic beliefs. Idiosyncratic, a consummate stylist and unmistakably modern, she has supplied a much-quoted definition of the creative ideal as 'imaginary gardens with real toads in them'. Her first publication was *Poems* (1921); *Selected Poems* appeared in 1935 and *The Complete Poems* in 1968. She published *Predilections*, a collection of essays, in 1955.
▷E P Sheehy and K A Lohf, *The Achievement of Moore, 1907–1957* (1958)

MOORE, Thomas
(1779–1852)

Irish poet, born in Dublin, the son of a Catholic grocer. He was educated at Whyte's School, Trinity College, Dublin, and the Middle Temple. His translation of **Anacreon** (1800) proved a great success, followed by *Poems* (1801) and, with his musical talent as a singer, procured him admission to the best society. In 1803, after being appointed registrar of the Admiralty Court in Bermuda, he arranged for a deputy and returned after a tour of the USA and Canada. In 1811 he married an actress, Bessy Dyke, and later settled in Wiltshire. Meanwhile he had published the earlier of the *Irish Melodies* (1807–34) and *The Twopenny Post-bag* (1812). In 1817 the long-expected *Lalla Rookh* appeared, for which Longmans paid him 3000 guineas; the *Irish Melodies* brought in £500 a year. Moore had 'a generous contempt for money', his Bermuda deputy embezzled £6000, and in 1819, to avoid arrest, he went to Italy and then to Paris. He returned in 1822 to Wiltshire, where he spent his last 30 years, during which he published *The Loves of the Angels* (1823), and a novel (*The Epicurean*, 1827), and wrote biographies of **Richard Brinsley Sheridan** and **Byron** and other works. In 1835 he received a pension of £300, but his last days were clouded by the loss of his two sons. In his lifetime his work was as popular as that of his friend, Byron. His poetry was light, airy, graceful, but soulless. He is best in his lyrics.
▷T de Vere White, *Tom Moore, the Irish Poet* (1977)

MOORE, Thomas Sturge
(1870–1944)

English poet, critic and wood-engraver, born in Hastings in Sussex, brother of the philosopher George Edward Moore. He is known as the author of polished verse of classical style, beginning with *The Vinedresser* (1899), verse dramas, works on Dürer and other artists, and as a distinguished designer of book-plates, including those of his friend **W B Yeats**. His *Collected Poems* appeared in four volumes between 1931 and 1933.
▷F C Gwynn, *Moore and the life of art* (1951)

MOORHOUSE, Frank
(1938–)

Australian fiction writer. He was born in Nowra, New South Wales, and educated at the University of Queensland, Brisbane, before beginning his career as a journalist on the Sydney *Telegraph*. It is not quite accurate to describe him either as a 'short-story writer' or as a 'novelist'—he writes what he himself has described as 'discontinuous narratives'. His first book, *Futility and Other Animals* (1969), had a flavour of **Saki**, but it was in later books, *The Americans, Baby* (1972), *The Electrical Experience* (1974), *Conference-ville* (1976) and *The Everlasting Secret Family* (1980), that he unfolded an increasingly dominant interest in sexual ambiguity and experiment. This played a surprisingly central role in his epic—and self-admittedly obsessed—study of the League of Nations, *Great Days* (1993), which in turn reintroduced a character who had appeared (in old age) in some sections of the earlier *Forty-Seventeen* (1987). Neither book is strictly a 'novel', but *Great Days* has a consistency of narrative line that Moorhouse had not attempted before and is much less impressive. He has also written a variety of screenplays.

MÓRA, Ferenc
(1879–1934)

Hungarian popular novelist, poet and story writer, born in Kiskunfélegyháza. He wrote about the Szeged region, where he lived and died, with intimate realism. *Aranykoporsó* (1933, Eng trans *The Gold Coffin*, 1964) is about the early days of Christianity; but his finest psychological study, about a schoolmaster, *Hannibal föltamasztasa* (1924), has not yet been translated. However, some of the sketches in which he excelled above all are in *Ének a búzmerzökröl* (1927), which was translated in 1931 as *Song of the Wheatfields*.

MORAES, Dom(inic Frank)
(1938–)

Indian–Anglican poet and journalist, born in Bombay and educated at Jesus College, Oxford. He has written numerous non-fiction books about India, including *Bombay* (1980); a Time-Life publication, *Mrs Gandhi* (1980); and a portrait of the cricketer *Sunil Gavaskar* (1987). However, there is little distinctively Indian about his poetry, which has been criticized for lack of cultural conviction. His first collection, *A Beginning* (1957), won a Hawthornden Prize, the first time one had been awarded to a non-Anglo-Saxon poet. Moraes broke nearly 20 years of poetic silence in 1983 with *Absences*.
▷E Lall, *The Poetry of Encounter: Three Indo-Anglican Poets* (1983)

MORAES VINCIUS, Mello de
(1913–)

Brazilian poet and dramatist, associated with the second phase of Brazilian Modernism. He was initially influenced by **Péguy** and French mysticism; this was succeeded by a more ironic and socially aware poetry, haunted by various notions of time. Some of his poetry appears in translation in the *Penguin Book of Latin American Verse* (1971, ed E Curacciolo-Trejo) and in John Nist's *Modern Brazilian Poetry* (1962).

MORAND, Paul
(1889–1975)

French diplomat and writer, born in Paris. In the French diplomatic service from 1912 to 1944, his early posts included the secretaryship of the French embassies in London (where he was also minister plenipotentiary in 1940), Rome and Madrid. In 1939 he was head of the French mission of economic warfare in England, in 1943 minister at Bucharest and in 1944 ambassador at Berne. He turned to writing in 1920, beginning with poetry, then publishing short stories and novels, with a background of cosmopolitan life in post war Europe. These include *Ouvert la nuit* (1922, 'Open All Night'), *Fermé la nuit* (1923, 'Closed at Night') and *Lewis et Irène* (1924). He also wrote travel books, studies of cities, and political and biographical works. Among his later works were *Vie de Maupassant* (1942, 'Life of Maupassant'), *Journal d'un attaché d'ambassade* (1948, 'Journal of a Diplomatic Attaché'), *Fouquet* (1961) and *Tais-toi* (1965, 'Be Quiet').
▷B Delvaille, *Paul Morand* (1966)

MORANTE, Elsa
(1916–85)

Italian novelist, poet and short-story writer, born and educated in Rome. Her first publication, a collection of short stories called *Il gioco segreto* (1941, 'Secret Jest'), coincided with her marriage to **Alberto Moravia**; they subsequently divorced. Her second book, *Menzogna e sortilegio* (1948, 'Lies and Riddles'), won the Viareggio Prize and was later published in the USA as *House of Liars* (1951). Its successor, *L'isola di Arturo* (1957, Eng trans *Arturo's Island*, 1959), was a lyrical-elegiac account of childhood and the violation of innocence. It won Morante the prestigious Strega Prize. Her greatest single achievement, however, was *La storia* (1974, Eng trans *History*, 1977), a large-scale, almost **Faulkner**ian narrative about the degeneracy of the Italian family under fascism. Though politically engaged and consistently espousing Morante's Christian-

Marxist principles, the novel never deteriorates into a tract. Morante's verse includes *Il mondo salvato dai ragazzini e altri poemi* (1968); she also translated **Katherine Mansfield** into Italian.

▷G Venturi, *Elsa Morante* (1977)

MORATA, Olympia
(1526–55)

Italian Humanist scholar and poet, daughter of the poet and scholar Pellegrino Morato. She gave public lectures when 15; but, having in 1548 married the German physician Andreas Grundler, she followed him to Germany, became a Protestant, and died penniless, leaving numerous Latin and Greek poems, a treatise on **Cicero**, dialogues and letters.

MORATIN, Leandro de
(1760–1828)

Spanish dramatist and poet, born in Madrid. He began as a designer of jewellery, and later held official and ecclesiastical positions. He wrote a number of successful comedies influenced by French ideas and especially by **Molière**, and translated *Hamlet*. He also wrote poetry, and a history of Spanish literature. His work is carefully crafted, and reflects his belief in reason and orderly morality. His acceptance of the post of librarian to Joseph Bonaparte resulted in his exile to Paris in 1814.

MORAVIA, Alberto, pseud of Alberto Pincherle
(1907–90)

Italian novelist and short-story writer, born in Rome of middle-class parents. He spent some years in a sanatorium as a result of a tubercular infection. Before the outbreak of World War II he travelled extensively and lived for a time in the USA when out of favour with the fascist government. His first novel, *Gli indifferenti* (1929, Eng trans *The Indifferent Ones*, 1932), which achieved popular success, contains many of the ingredients of his later novels and short stories. He analyses without compassion but without explicit moral judgement the members of decadent bourgeois society in Rome, portraying in a fatalistic way their preoccupation with sex and money, their apathy, their lack of communication, the total incapability of action of even the intellectuals who acknowledge the corruption but cannot break away from it. In *La romana* (1947, Eng trans *The Woman of Rome*, 1949) many of these themes remain but his canvas has broadened to include the corruption and socio-economic problems of the working class. In *Raconti romani* (1954, Eng trans *Roman Tales*, 1956) he turns his critical eye to the corruption of the lower

middle class. His works include *Agostino* (1944, Eng trans 1947), *L'amore coniugale* (1949, Eng trans *Conjugal Love*, 1951), *La ciociara* (1957, Eng trans *Two Women*, 1958), *L'attenzione* (1965, Eng trans *The Lie*, 1966), *La vita interiore* (1978, Eng trans *Time of Desecration*, 1980) and *L'uomo che guarda* (1985, Eng trans *The Voyeur*, 1986). His former wife is **Elsa Morante**.

▷K Longobardi, *Alberto Moravia* (1970)

MØRCH, Dea Trier
(1941–)

Danish novelist and artist. Having trained in graphics in Denmark, she continued her education at art colleges in Eastern Europe, and her first published books record her impressions of the Soviet Union and Poland. She made her breakthrough with *Vinterbørn* (1976, Eng trans *Winter's Child*, 1986), a collective novel set in a maternity ward at a Copenhagen hospital, and lovingly illustrated by the author. With the women's perspective predominating, the text depicts pregnancy and childbirth as radicalizing experiences, carrying with them the potential of an alternative community. The novel achieved considerable success in Denmark and abroad, and has also been made into a film. *Kastaniealleen* (1978, 'Chestnut Avenue') is a sensitive exploration of the relationships between an elderly couple and their grandchildren, while *Den indre by* (1980, 'The Inner City') highlights the problems of combining family life with an active political commitment, especially for women.

▷G Agger, 'Dea Trier Mørch', in T Broström and M Winge (eds), *Danske digtere i det 20. århundrede*, vol V (1982)

MORE, Hannah
(1745–1833)

English playwright and religious writer, born in Fishponds, near Bristol, daughter of a schoolteacher. She was educated at the boarding school in Bristol run by her elder sisters, where she wrote verses at an early age. She was engaged in 1767 to a Mr Turner, who failed to marry her for six years and eventually settled £200 a year on her and left her. In 1773 she published *The Search after Happiness*, a pastoral drama for schools, and then went to London in 1774, where she joined the 'Blue Stocking' coterie of Elizabeth Montagu and her friends. She wrote two tragedies for David Garrick: *Percy* (1777) and *The Fatal Secret* (1779). Led by her religious views to withdraw from society, she retired to Cowslip Green near Bristol, where she did much to improve the condition of the poor. She published *Sacred Dramas* (1782) and a collection of religious poems in *Bas Bleu* (1786), and an essay *Estimate on the Religion*

of the Fashionable World (1790). Her moral tracts for the poor, *Village Politics by Will Chip* (1793) and *Cheap Repository Tracts* (1795–8), led to the founding of the Religious Tracts Society. She also wrote a didactic novel, *Coelebs in Search of a Wife* (1809).
▷M G Jones, *The Life of Hannah More* (1952)

MORÉAS, Jean, originally **Yannis Papadiamantopoulos**
(1856–1910)
Greek-born French poet, born in Athens. He wrote first in Greek, then settled in Paris (1879) and became a leader of the Symbolist school, to which he gave its name in 1886. He gradually grew interested in a return to classical and traditional forms, however, and formed a new grouping under the name École Romane, dedicated to antiquity, by 1891. His works include *Les Syrtes* (1884), *Cantilènes* (1886, 'Ballads'), *Le Pèlerin passioné* (1891, 'The Passionate Pilgrim') and *Les Stances* (1905, 'Stanzas'), the masterpiece of his classical period.
▷R Niklaus, *Jean Moréas, poète lyrique* (1936)

MORETTI, Marino
(1885–1979)
Italian poet (one of the more important, with **Gozzano**, of the Crepusculari) and novelist, from Cesenatico. Moretti was unlucky never to have attracted an English translator: had he done so, it is likely that he would now be internationally regarded as a major writer. He was a lifelong friend to **Palazzeschi**, and at times influenced by him—but at others he seemed to go in an exactly opposite direction. He also knew the great Sienese novelist **Tozzi** well. He refused a prize awarded to him by the fascists, which had been designed to obtain his support; previously he had signed the anti-Fascist manifesto of **Benedetto Croce**. It was his early poetry, along with that of Carlo Chiave, which led **Borgese** to coin the term 'crepuscular'; yet, with the exception of Casnati, Edoardo Sanguinetti and a few other critics, this has been neglected. His early novel *Il sole de sabato* (1916, 'Saturday's Sunshine'), about a poor and afflicted woman who learns, convincingly, to love through her sufferings, was a popular success. He wrote many more powerful and varied novels, and then returned triumphantly to poetry. When he died he was Italy's most neglected great writer, and undoubtedly his time is yet to come.
▷S Pacifici, *The Modern Italian Novel from Capuana to Tozzi* (1973); F Casnati, *Marino Moretti* (1952, in Italian)

MORGAN, Charles Langbridge
(1894–1958)
English author, born in Kent, the son of a civil engineer. He served in Atlantic and China waters as a midshipman (1911–13), but finding it uncongenial, resigned. He rejoined the navy in 1914 and was later interned in Holland until 1917. On repatriation he went to Oxford University, where he published *The Gunroom* (1919) on his early experiences, and became a well-known personality. In 1921, on leaving Oxford, he joined the editorial staff of *The Times*, and was their principal drama critic from 1926 to 1939. Under the pen-name of 'Menander' he also wrote for the *Times Literary Supplement* critical essays called *Reflections in a Mirror*, which were later (1944–5) collected in two series. His novels and plays show high professional competence, but lack vividness and urgency. *Portrait in a Mirror* (1929), which won the Femina Vie Heureuse Prize in 1930, is his most satisfying novel. Later works show too much preoccupation with values of the heart to the detriment of narrative sweep, and his earnestness seems unduly solemn, pompous and vaguely sentimental. Nonetheless, *The Fountain* (1932) won the Hawthornden Prize and *The Voyage* (1940) won the James Tait Black Memorial Prize. His plays are *The Flashing Stream* (1938), *The River Line* (1952) and *The Burning Glass* (1953).
▷H C Duffin, *The Novels and Plays of Charles Morgan* (1959)

MORGAN, Edwin George
(1920–)
Scottish poet and critic, born in Glasgow. His education at Glasgow University was split by service in the Royal Army Medical Corps during World War II, an option he chose as a conscientious objector. He was appointed Assistant Lecturer in English at Glasgow University in 1947, and remained there until 1980, rising to titular Professor of English in 1975. He published his first volume of poems, *The Vision of Cathkin Braes*, and a translation of *Beowulf*, in 1952. His verse from the 1950s is introspective and rather gloomy, unlike his later work, which is marked by an apparently irrepressible (although never simply naive) optimism and a readiness to embrace change. By the time of *A Second Life* (1968), he had embraced his homosexuality, and given free rein to his willingness to be influenced by developments in American (both North and South) and European arts. His wide-ranging and often formally experimental work finds room for science fiction alongside a minute observation of reality. His work is defiantly non-parochial, but has remained rooted in Glasgow, where he has continued to live, playing a maverick role in the city's cultural

life. An incomplete *Collected Poems* was published in 1990, followed by a collection of his influential essays and critical writings, *Crossing The Border* (1990). A skilled translator, he collected his translations of various writers, such as **Pasternak**, **Pushkin** and **García Lorca**, in *Rites of Passage* (1976). His adaptation of **Edmond Rostand**'s *Cyrano de Bergerac* into demotic Glaswegian in 1992 was highly acclaimed.
▷R Fulton, *Contemporary Scottish Poetry* (1974)

MORGAN, (George) Frederick
(1922–)

American poet and literary journalist, born in New York City. Morgan was the founder and for many years editor of the prestigious and influential literary magazine, the *Hudson Review*, and did not publish his first collection, *A Book of Change*, until 1972, when he was 50. However, as one critic observed, he subsequently 'lost no time in catching up to his contemporaries'. His poetry is diverse both in form and subject-matter, although a recurring theme is the quest for personal values and the realization that death is daily more imminent. His *Poems: New and Selected* appeared in 1987.

MORGAN, Lady Sydney, née Owenson
(1783–1859)

Irish novelist, born in Dublin. Her father, a theatrical manager, got into financial difficulties and she supported the family, first as governess, next as author of sentimental poems and novels. In 1812 she married a surgeon, Thomas Charles Morgan (1783–1843), who was later knighted. Her works—lively novels, verse and travels—were bestsellers of their day, and include *St Clair* (1804), *The Wild Irish Girl* (1806), *O'Donnel* (1814), *Florence Macarthy* (1816), *The O'Briens and the O'Flahertys* (1827) and *Memoirs* (1862).

MORGENSTERN, Christian
(1871–1914)

German poet and philosopher. Morgenstern, first a disciple of **Arthur Schopenhauer**, then of **Nietzsche** and, finally, of the anthroposophy of **Rudolph Steiner**, wrote much 'serious poetry' but, despite the intrinsic interest of this, and the efforts of a few (on the whole old-fashioned) critics to rehabilitate it, could express himself to truest effect only in his world-famous 'nonsense poems'—the profoundest ever written in that genre. His most famous humorous poetry deals with the absurd characters Palmström and Herr von Korf (and others), and is contained in *Galgenlieder* (1905, 'Gallows Song'), *Palmström* (1910) and posthumous collections; but he

began in this vein, in 1895, with *In Phantas Schloss*, ('In Phanta's Castle'). He travelled in Norway, where he met **Ibsen**, whom, as well as **Strindberg** and **Hamsun**, he translated. His project, in which he succeeded, perhaps mainly because in comic form he could combine playfulness with religious (non-Christian) profundity, was to 'strip language of the bourgeois conventions in which we have taken refuge'. He died of tuberculosis. Works in English translation are: *The Gallows Songs* (1964); *The Gallows Songs: A Selection* (1966); *Gallowsongs* (1970).
▷E Hofacker, *Christian Morgenstern* (1978)

MORI Ogai (Rintaro)
(1862–1922)

Japanese writer, aristocrat, soldier, doctor and bureaucrat, and a towering figure in the history of the transformation of Japanese culture and society in the 20th century. Born into a samurai family in Shimane, Mori (whose given name was Rintaro) studied medicine, rising to become director of the Army Medical Corps and being influential in the introduction of western medicine. He started writing by translating European literature (one of the first to do so), then produced his own historical fiction in a style strongly influenced by the directness and accessibility of the Europeans (again, one of the first to do so). His style was to supplant traditional literary forms as practised by the likes of **Kyoka Izumi**. The best example of his fiction available in translation is *Incident at Sakai and Other Stories*.
▷R J Bowring, *Mori Ogai and the Modernisation of Japanese Culture* (1979)

MORICZ, Zsigmond
(1879–1942)

Hungarian novelist and dramatist, of peasant stock, whose plays laid the foundations of his country's modern theatre. Moricz was Hungary's leading naturalist, influenced by **Zola**, with whom he may fruitfully be compared. He is outstripped in importance in Hungarian literature only by **Endre Ady**, whose friend he became, and from whose poetry he took his original inspiration. He was the first prose writer to challenge the sentimentality of the peasant–landlord relationship, which it had suited the more conservative novelists to idealize—but Moricz saw his peasants with a clear eye, and thus anticipated such writers as **Roger Martin du Gard**, who were also to present country people as they really are. He did not spare his polite readers the full facts, erotic or otherwise, and was thus execrated. His most powerful novel is *Legy jó mindhalálig* (1920, Eng trans *Be Faithful unto Death*, 1962), about a child who struggles against the evil adult world. This is still well known and widely read in Hungary, and Moricz continues to be rightly revered there. He was a writer of international stature, each of whose works should automatically have been put into English. *A fáklya* (1917, Eng trans *The Torch*, 1931) is about an idealistic priest whose life is shattered by his parishioners.

▷ *American Slavic Review*, 4 (1945)

MORIER, James Justinian
(1780–1849)

English novelist, son of the consul at Smyrna. He turned to literature after a diplomatic career and wrote a number of travel books. His great merit is that inimitable picture of Persian life, *The Adventures of Hajji Baba of Ispahan* (1824), followed by the less brilliant *Hajji Baba in England* (1828).

MÖRIKE, Eduard
(1804–75)

German poet and novelist, born in Ludwigsburg. He entered the theological seminary at Tübingen in 1822 and became vicar of Kleversulzbach in 1834, retiring in 1843. He was weak, hypochondriacal, unhappily married and lazy, yet he produced a minor masterpiece in *Mozart auf der Reise nach Prag* (1856, 'Mozart on the Journey to Prague') and many poems of delicacy and beauty with something of the deceptive simplicity of **Heinrich Heine**. These were collectively published in 1838.

▷ M More, *Mörike: the man and the poet* (1957)

MORITZ, Karl Philipp
(1756–93)

German writer, born in Hameln. He was in turn hat-maker's apprentice, actor, teacher and professor. Self-educated, he travelled in England and Italy and wrote *Reisen eines Deutschen in England* (1783, 'Travels of a German in England'), and *Reisen eines Deutschen in Italien* (1792–3, 'Travels of a German in Italy'). His autobiographical novel, *Anton Reise* (1785–90), influenced **Goethe**. He was a precursor of the German Romantic movement, delved into the past, and wrote *Versuch einer deutschen Prosodie* (1786, 'Essay on German Prosody'), which he dedicated to Frederick II, the Great.

▷ W Rose, *From Goethe to Byron* (1924)

MORLEY, Christopher Darlington
(1890–1957)

American novelist and essayist, born in Haverford, Pennsylvania. He was a Rhodes scholar at Oxford, and joined the editorial staff of Doubleday's from 1913 to 1917 and later contributed to numerous periodicals such as *Ladies' Home Journal*, the New York *Evening Post* and the *Saturday Review of Literature*. His chief works, whimsical and urbane, included *Parnassus on Wheels* (1917), and a sequel *The Haunted Bookshop* (1919), *Thunder on the Left* (1925), *Swiss Family Manhattan* (1932), *Human Being* (1932), *Streamlines* (1937), *Kitty Foyle* (1939), *The Ironing Board* (1949) and a book of poems, *The Middle Kingdom* (1944).

▷ *John Mistletoe* (1931)

MORPURGO, Rahel
(1790–1871)

Hebrew poet, who was born in Trieste, and was thus a part of the great flowering of Jewish literature which took place in the 18th and early 19th centuries. With her boldly magnificent ode dedicated to the revolutions of 1848 she well deserves her title of first Hebrew modern poet. It has been said that no woman who hopes to make a mark in poetry can afford to neglect study of her achievement. English translations of her work can be found in *Collected Poems and Letters* (1890).

MORRIS, George Pope
(1802–64)

American journalist and poet, born in Philadelphia. In 1823 he founded the *New York Mirror* (editor 1824–42), and later edited the *Evening Mirror* and the *Home Journal* (1846–64), publishing **Edgar Allan Poe**'s 'The Raven' in the former. He published many poems, including the celebrated 'Woodman, Spare that Tree!', which appeared in *The Deserted Bride* (1838).

MORRIS, Sir Lewis
(1833–1907)

Welsh poet and barrister, born in Carmarthen, and educated at the town's Queen Elizabeth Grammar School, Sherborne, and Jesus College, Oxford. His main literary works were *Songs of Two Worlds* (3 vols, 1872–5), followed in 1876 by *The Epic of Hades* and more verse and drama, largely drawing on incidents in Welsh history and mythology. In the later stages of his career he campaigned for the fostering of higher education in Wales and the establishment of a National University. In 1895 he was made knight-bachelor and thereafter entertained fruitless hopes of becoming poet laureate.

▷ D Phillips, *Sir Lewis Morris* (1981)

MORRIS, Mervyn
(1937–)

Jamaican poet, born in Kingston, and educated at the University of the West Indies and Oxford (as a Rhodes scholar). He might be described as a minimalist poet, being the master of the brief but cogent comment. His words bear a heavy burden, not least of which is the desire to maintain a variousness of perspective. A generous and careful critic and the editor of many anthologies of Caribbean poetry, he has a particular interest in overcoming the difficulties in transcribing oral, performance-based poetry. His own poems first appeared in the early 1960s in Jamaican journals and newspapers; collections include *The Pond* (1973), *On Holy Week* (1976) and *Shadowboxing* (1979).

MORRIS, William
(1834–96)

English craftsman, poet and socialist, born in Walthamstow, near London, of middle-class parents. Educated at Marlborough School and Exeter College, Oxford, he studied for holy orders, but his friendship with members of the Pre-Raphaelite Brotherhood, particularly the painter Edward Burne-Jones, aroused a deep love of Gothic architecture, and they both renounced the church. He turned to the study of architecture under George Edmund Street, but on the advice of **Dante Gabriel Rossetti** became a professional painter (1857–62). In 1859 he married a model, Jane Burden, and moved into the Red House at Bexley Heath, which he designed and furnished with the architect Philip Webb; from the ideas expressed there he founded in 1861, with the help of his pre-Raphaelite associates, the firm of Morris, Marshall, Faulkner and Company, which would revolutionize the art of house decoration and furniture in England. His literary career began with a volume of poetry, *The Defence of Guinevere, and other Poems*, in 1858, followed by *The Life and Death of Jason* (1867), a long narrative poem in rhyming couplets and the three-volumed *The Earthly Paradise* (1868–70), a collection of 24 classical and medieval tales in a **Chaucer**ian mould. He developed a passionate interest in the heroic literature of Iceland, and worked with Eiríkur Magnússon on a series of saga translations. He visited Iceland twice, in 1871 and 1873, and was inspired to write *Three Northern Love Songs* (1875) and a four-volumed epic, *The Story of Sigurd the Volsung and the Fall of the Nibelungs* (1876), regarded as his greatest work. Also at this time he published a verse morality, *Love is Enough, or The Freeing of Pharamond* (1872), a translation of **Virgil**'s *Aeneid* (1875), and a translation of **Homer**'s *Odyssey* (1887). He founded a Society for the Protection of Ancient Buildings in 1877. His experience as a master-craftsman, and his devotion to the Gothic, persuaded him that the excellence of medieval arts and crafts sprang from the joy of free craftsmen, which

was destroyed by Victorian mass-production and capitalism. He joined the Social Democratic Federation in 1883; his Utopian ideals did much to develop the philosophy of socialism, and when the Social Democratic Federation suffered disruption in 1884 he led the seceders into a socialist League. His socialist zeal inspired two prose romances, *The Dream of John Ball* (1888) and *News from Nowhere* (1891). Further prose romances concentrated more on story-telling: *The House of the Wolfings* (1889), *The Roots of the Mountains* (1889) and *The Story of the Glittering Plain* (1891), all set in the far north. His last books were a book of verse (*Poems by the Way*, 1891), and further prose romances: *The Wood beyond the World* (1895), *The Well at the World's End* (1896), *The Water of the Wondrous Isles* and *The Story of the Sundering Flood* (both published posthumously in 1897). In 1890, in a further rejection of Victorian values, he founded a publishing house, the Kelmscott Press at Hammersmith, for which he designed clear typefaces and wide ornamental borders; it produced a stream of his own works and reprints of English classics.

▷J W Mackail, *William Morris* (1899); P Henderson, *Morris, His Art, Writings and Public Life* (1967)

MORRIS, Wright Marion
(1910–)

American novelist, short-story writer and photographer, born in Nebraska and educated in Chicago and California. Throughout his career, in both his fiction and his photographic images, Morris has striven to keep alive the myth of America as a culture of newness. His first novel, *My Uncle Dudley* (1942), recounts a comic expedition from West to East; his third, *The World in the Attic* (1949), more sombrely confronts the vexed question of America's cultural 'thinness' and has an appropriately **James**ian tinge. Morris was awarded the National Book Award for *The Field of Vision* (1956), but despite other prizes he has never shaken off his critical marginality. Later novels include *Fire Sermon* (1971) and *The Fork River Space Project* (1977). He has written many books combining text and pictures, including *The Inhabitants* (1946) and *God's Country and My People* (1968). His highly visual short stories were gathered in *Green Grass, Blue Sky, White House* (1970), *Real Losses, Imaginary Gains* (1976) and other volumes. He published three volumes of memoirs, *Will's Boy* (1981), *Solo* (1983) and *A Cloak of Light* (1985).

▷G B Crump, *The Novels of Wright Morris* (1978)

MORRIS-JONES, John
(1864–1929)

Welsh scholar, translator (**Heine, Omar Khayyám**) and poet, born in Trefor on Anglesey. At Oxford he read mathematics. As a scholar he worked with great (as well as pedantic) zeal in the interests of purity of the language. His single collection of poems, *Caniadau* (1907), once highly regarded, is for the most part too sentimental for modern taste; but his poetry was skilfully wrought; two examples are included in the *Penguin Book of Welsh Verse* (1967).
▷ *Poetry Wales*, 15, 3 (1979)

MORRISON, Arthur
(1863–1945)

English novelist, born in Poplar, Kent, the son of an engine fitter. He became clerk to the People's Palace in Mile End Road, then a journalist on the *National Observer*, for which he wrote a series of stories published as *Tales of Mean Streets* (1894). His reputation rests on his powerfully realistic novels of London life such as *A Child of the Jago* (1896) and *The Hole in the Wall* (1902). He also wrote detective stories featuring a private investigator, Martin Hewett.
▷ A Brome, *Four Realist Novelists* (1965)

MORRISON, Toni Chloe Anthony, née **Wofford**
(1931–)

American novelist, winner of the Nobel Prize for literature, born in Lorain, Ohio. She was educated at Howard University and Cornell University, and taught at Howard before moving to New York in 1965. She worked in publishing as senior editor at Random House before turning to fiction. Labelled as a black **James Joyce** or **William Faulkner**, she explores in rich vocabulary and cold-blooded detail the story of black Americans. *The Bluest Eye* (1970) focuses on the incestuous rape of an 11-year-old girl; *Sula* (1974) again confronts a generation gap, but between a grandmother and the eponymous scapegoat; *Song of Solomon* (1977) is a merciless study of genteel blacks. Her most recent novels, *Tar Baby* (1981), *Beloved* (1987) and *Jazz* (1992), formidable in their mastery of technique and courageous in their subject-matter, confirmed her as one of the most important novelists of her generation. She won a Pulitzer Prize in 1988 and the Nobel Prize for literature in 1993.

MORSZTYN, Count Jan Andrezej
(c.1613–1693)

Polish poet, translator (of **Corneille**'s *Le Cid*—a masterpiece) and courtier. Charged with high treason, in 1683, because of his close relations with the court of Louis XIV (he may have intrigued for a French king to the Polish throne), he fled to France. His master was the Italian Baroque poet **Marino**, and his poetry has some affinities with that of English metaphysical poets such as **Crashawe**. He excelled in compact forms, in elaborate and over-elaborate conceits, and in those violent and paradoxical comparisons which characterize Baroque poetry. His two collections were *Kanicula* (1647, 'The Dog Star') and *Lutnia* (1661, 'The Lute'). Some poems are well translated in *Five Centuries of Polish Poetry* (1960, B Singer and J Peterkiewicz eds). He was a fine writer of erotic (or so-called 'obscene') verse, much of it addressed to his Scottish wife, Catherine Gordon.

MORSZTYN, Zbigniew
(c.1620–c.1689)

Polish poet who, like his namesake **Count Jan Andrezej Morsztyn**, was a leading exponent of the then-prevalent Baroque school of poetry. The key to his poetry, however, lies in his belief in the 'heresy' of Arianism, or (as it is often now called) 'Polish Unitarianism': after the Jesuits succeeded in expelling the Arians from Racow in 1638 he chose exile in Prussia, and died in Königsberg. (Essentially, the Arians or Unitarians believed in the doctrines of Socinus, who rejected the Trinity in the interests of the unipersonality of God.) His *Emblemata*, in the tradition of erotic mysticism, are contained in *Muza domowa* ('The Homely Muse'), not properly edited until 1954. He owed much to **Kochanowski**.

MORTIMER, John Clifford
(1923–)

English dramatist, novelist and barrister, born in London. He was called to the Bar in 1948, participating in several celebrated civil cases, and is a constant defender of liberal values. His series of novels featuring Horace Rumpole, an amiable, late-middle-aged defence barrister and frequenter of Pomeroy's bar, has been adapted for television as *Rumpole of the Bailey*. His other novels, including *Paradise Postponed* (1985) and *Summer's Lease* (1988), are highly popular, evoking, often savagely, what Mortimer perceives as the moral decline of the English middle-class. His many plays and adaptations for the stage include *The Dock Brief* (1958), *The Wrong Side of the Park* (1960), *Two Stars for Comfort* (1962) and an autobiographical play, *A Voyage round My Father* (broadcast 1963, staged 1970), which was filmed for television in 1982 with Laurence Olivier as the father. An autobiographical volume, *Clinging to the Wreckage*, appeared in 1982. He has made notable translations, especially of **George Feydeau**, and several TV screenplays

including *Brideshead Revisited* (1981), from the novel by **Evelyn Waugh**, *The Ebony Tower* (1984), from the story by **John Fowles**, and his own *Paradise Postponed* (1986). He has been twice married; his first wife was **Penelope Mortimer**.
▷ J R Taylor, *Anger and After* (1962)

MORTIMER, Penelope Ruth
(1918–)
Welsh novelist, born in Rhyl, Flint, and educated at a variety of schools, and at University College, London. Her first novel, *Johanna* (1947), appeared under the name of Penelope Dimont (using her first husband's surname). Her other novels, many of which look at the female experience of life among the English professional classes, include *Daddy's Gone A-Hunting* (1958), *My Friend Says It's Bullet-Proof* (1967) and *The Handyman* (1983). Her most famous, *The Pumpkin Eater* (1962), describes a woman who imagines that pregnancy will give a direction to her life, but who is persuaded by her husband to have an abortion. She was married for more than 20 years to **John Mortimer**.
▷ *About Time Too* (1993)

MORTON, John Cameron Andrieu Bingham Michael
(1893–1979)
English author and journalist. After serving in World War I he took up writing and published many books of humour, fantasy and satire, as well as a number of historical works including several on the French Revolution. From 1924 to 1975 he contributed a regular humorous column, 'By the Way', to the *Daily Express* under the name of 'Beachcomber'.

MORTON, John Maddison
(1811–91)
English dramatist, son of **Thomas Morton**, born in Pangbourne. He became a prolific writer of farces (mostly from the French), but is best remembered as the author of *Cox and Box* (1847). The rise of burlesque was his ruin and he became a 'poor brother' of the Charterhouse.
▷ F Wilson, *An Epistolary Remonstrance* (1887)

MORTON, Thomas
(1764–1838)
English dramatist, father of **John Maddison Morton**, born in Durham. He abandoned Lincoln's Inn for play writing, and produced *Speed the Plough* (1798, with its invisible 'Mrs Grundy'), *The Blind Girl* (1801), *Town and Country* (1807), *School for Grown Children* (1826), and other popular plays.

MOSCHEROSCH, Johann Michael
(1601–69)
German satirical writer, poet, and translator (**Quevedo**), born in Willstädt, near Strasbourg. His *Gesichte* (1643) began with translations from Quevedo, but then continued with original work—witty and effective attacks on greed, extravagance and pretentiousness. Moscherosch was one of the chief anticipators of **Grimmelshausen**.

MOSCHUS
(fl.c.150BC)
Greek pastoral poet from Syracuse and follower of **Theocritus**, he wrote a handful of surviving short poems on the pleasures of country life and love. He is credited also with the *Europa*, a mini-epic (*epyllion*) in 166 hexameters describing the abduction of Europa by Zeus, disguised as a bull, and her voyage to Crete on his back. Moschus's style well exemplifies Alexandrian ideals for poetry: it is concise, elegant, polished and apt to concentrate on picturesque detail. **Shelley** translated two of his short poems, as well as part of the *Lament for Bion* (attributed to Moschus, but almost certainly not by him).

MOSEL, Tad George Ault, Jr
(1922–)
American dramatist, born in Steubenville, Ohio. He was educated at Amherst, Yale School of Drama, and Columbia University. His only significant success on the stage came with his dramatization of **James Agee**'s novel *A Death in the Family* as *All The Way Home* (1960), which won him a Pulitzer Prize in 1961. He also co-wrote a biography of the American actress Katherine Cornell, *Leading Lady* (1978).

MOSLEY, Nicholas (Lord Ravensdale)
(1923–)
English novelist and biographer, born in London and educated at Eton and Oxford. His earlier books, such as *Spaces of the Dark* (1951) and *Corruption* (1957), are realistic novels set during World War II. Those of his 'middle period' include *Accident* (1965), which became the basis of a memorable film, and those of his 'later period', the stylistically experimental and intellectually ambitious *Catastrophe Practice* series. This comprises five volumes, beginning with *Catastrophe Practice* in 1979, and ending with *Hopeful Monsters* (1990), and ranges back and forth across history and continents. His biographies include two definitive volumes about his father, *Rules of the Game: Sir Oswald and Lady Cynthia Mosley 1896–1933* (1982) and *Beyond the Pale: Sir Oswald Mosley and family 1933–1980* (1983).

MOSLEY, Walter
(1952–)

American novelist, born in Los Angeles. His debut, *Devil in a Blue Dress* (1990), won the **John Creasey** Award for the year's best first crime novel. It and its two sequels, *A Red Death* (1991) and *White Butterfly* (1992), are narrated by the black private investigator Easy Rawlins. Although firmly within the crime genre, the trilogy also functions as a fictionalized history of black Americans since World War II. Far from being the white knight of **Raymond Chandler**'s ideal, Rawlins is continually compromised by real life; like the rest of his community, he literally cannot afford to be noble.

MOSS, Howard
(1922–87)

American poet, playwright and critic, born in New York City. He published his first collection, *The Wound and the Weather*, in 1946. It was followed by several more, including *A Winter Come, a Summer Gone: Poems 1946–1960* (1960), volumes of meticulously structured, reflective verse. His most familiar play is his first, *The Folding Green* (1958), revised and republished in 1980 as *Two Plays: The Palace at 4am and The Folding Green*. Perhaps his most significant book, however, is a critical work, *The Magic Lantern of Marcel Proust* (1962), which does much to clarify the **Proust**ian literary puzzle.

MOTION, Andrew Peter
(1952–)

English poet, born in London. He was educated at University College, Oxford, and taught at the University of Hull, where he met **Philip Larkin**. His biography of the poet, *A Writer's Life*, appeared in 1993, and won the Whitbread Award. He has worked in publishing since 1982. His early books established his concern with narrative in poetry, albeit obliquely rendered, and drew on historical as well as highly personal subjects. *Secret Narratives* (1983) and *Natural Causes* (1987) continued in that vein, but *Love—A Life* (1991), a verse anatomy of a marriage, was more direct in its statements. His novels *The Pale Companion* (1989) and *Famous for the Creatures* (1991) trace the development of the would-be writer Francis Mayne. He has written critical studies of **Edward Thomas** (1980) and Larkin (1982), and co-edited the *Penguin Book of Contemporary British Poetry* (1982).

MOTLEY, Willard
(1912–65)

American novelist, born in Chicago—one of the first of America's most eloquent Black writers. He came from middle-class Chicago, but moved into the slums to discover what life was like there—the results were *Knock on Any Door* (1947) and *We Fished by Night* (1951), the most accomplished of his four **Zola**-like novels. The latter reveals punks and gangsters 'in the leer of the neon night', ruled over by corrupt politicians and police. His work is crude and flawed, but exceptionally powerful.
▷ *Studi Americani* (7, 1961, article in English)

MOTTRAM, Ralph Hale
(1883–1971)

English novelist, born in Norwich. He began his working life as a banker. **John Galsworthy** is the main influence in his work, as is clearly seen in his first book, *Spanish Farm* (1924), and its sequels, *Sixty-Four, Ninety-Four* (1925) and *The Crime at Vanderlynden* (1926), a trilogy of novels based on his experiences in France and Flanders during World War I.

MOURNING DOVE, or HUM-ISHU-MA,
English name **Christine Quintasket**
(1888–1936)

American writer. Born in a canoe on the Kootenai River in Idaho while her parents were making a ferry crossing, Mourning Dove was a member of the Colville Confederated Tribes of Eastern Washington and the first Native American woman to publish a novel: *Cogewea, the Half-Blood* (1927). Receiving little formal education, she worked for most of her life as a migrant farm labourer, travelling always with her typewriter on which she produced the stories she heard from the Okanogans with whom she lived and worked, and which formed the basis of her published collection, *Coyote Stories* (1933). Passionately concerned to record the threatened traditions and oral literature of her people, and encouraged by her friend and literary collaborator, Lucillus McWhorter, she also travelled and lectured to audiences in the east about Okanogan traditions. Her novel, *Cogewea*, describing the trials of a young mixed-blood woman ranch-hand, combines the plot of a frontier romance with descriptions of Okanogan culture and lively colloquial dialogue. Her autobiographical writings were recently collected and published as *Mourning Dove: a Salishan Autobiography* (1990, ed Jay Miller).
▷A P Fisher, *The Transformation of Tradition: a Study of Zitkala-Sa and Mourning Dove* (1979)

MOWATT, Anna Cora
(1819–70)

American playwright and actress, best known for her social comedy, *Fashion, or Life in New York* (1845). Mowatt was of refined birth and character, and her success was seized on as proof that a woman could succeed in the theatre without compromising her standards of moral behaviour. The play was a mild and somewhat confusing satire about the marriage plans of a rich couple's daughter. On the wave of its success she formed her own company and brought it to London.

MPHAHLELE, Es'kia, originally Ezekiel
(1919–)

African novelist, short-story writer and critic. He was born in Pretoria, and (after working in a hospital for the blind) took his degree at the University of South Africa there, before completing a doctorate in the USA. He was fiction editor of the influential South African journal *Drum* (1955–7), before moving to Nigeria and the English faculty at the University of Ibadan (1957–61). Thereafter, he worked throughout Africa and in the USA before returning to his native country (1979) as Professor of African Literature at the University of Witwatersrand. Mphahlele's first book was a collection of stories, *Man Must Live* (1947), but his main achievement was a novel, *The Wanderers* (1971), which offered a bleak picture of the intellectual and emotional impact of exile, and developed ideas he had sketched out in an autobiographical volume, *Down Second Avenue* (1959). Mphahlele's introduction to the Penguin *African Writing Today* (1967) and the essays that comprise *Voices in the Whirlwind* (1972) represent a major statement in the development of African literary consciousness.
▷N C Manganyi, *Exiles and Homecomings: A Biography of Es'kia Mphahlele* (1983)

MROZEK, Slawomir
(1930–)

Polish playwright and novelist, born in Borzecin and trained as an architect at Krakow. He worked as a cartoonist until, following the positive reception of his story collection *Slon* (1958, Eng trans *The Elephant*, 1962) and his play *Policja* (1963, Eng trans *The Policeman*, 1961) in the USA and Britain, he moved to the West (until 1972). Several of his plays were produced at the Edinburgh Festival in 1964 and struck a chord with their **Kafka**esque portrayal of totalitarian absurdities. Later plays such as *Tango* (1966, published in Polish in 1973), a powerful study of family politics, and *The Prophets* (1970, published in Polish as *Testarium*, 1973) were first seen in translation. Mrozek's prose has been less widely recognized outside his native country, but *The Ugupu Bird* (1968) was a valuable selection of pieces. In 1975, he again left Poland and is now based in Paris.

MUCHA, Jiří
(1915–)

Czech novelist, born in Prague. He was imprisoned on a trumped-up charge by the communist regime. *Problémy nadporcika Knapa* (1946, Eng trans *The Problems of Lieutenant Knap*, 1945), the Czech version of which appeared after the English, consists of stories which draw on his World War II experiences as a Free Czech soldier, as does the novel *Spálaňa setba* (1948, Eng trans *Scorched Crop*, 1950); *Studené slunce* (1968, Eng trans *Living and Partly Living*, 1967) is based on his persecution by the Czech Stalinists. His father was a famous Art Nouveau painter, of whom he wrote an entertaining memoir, *Alphonse Mucha* (1966, Eng trans 1966).

MUDIE, Ian
(1911–76)

Australian poet, born in Hawthorn, South Australia, identified with **Rex Ingamells**'s 'Jindyworobak' movement. His *Corroboree to the Sun* (1941) was followed by other volumes, including *The Kingfisher* in 1970. Poems such as 'They'll Tell You About Me' are so full of Australian folk references and *patois* that they require a glossary almost as long as the verse. Formerly editor-in-chief of the renowned (now defunct) Australian publishing house of Rigby, his best verse is collected in *Selected Poems 1934–1974* (1976), although *The Blue Crane* (1959) is perhaps the most personal of his work. He edited *Poets at War* (1944), which was the first appearance between covers of many of the succeeding generation of poets, and has also written two historical books, *Riverboats* (1961) and *The Heroic Journey of John McDouall Stuart* (1968).

MUDROOROO, Nyoongah, originally Colin Johnson
(1939–)

Australian novelist of part-aboriginal descent, now writing as 'Mudrooroo Narogin', born in Beverley, Western Australia. His partly autobiographical first novel *Wild Cat Falling* (1965) tells of a half-caste's experiences on release from prison. He has since reworked the theme in *Doin' Wildcat* (1988), the story of a film production of his earlier book. He returns to the problems of mixed blood in *Long Live Sandawara* (1979), which portrays the conflicting calls of aboriginal culture and urban living. He has also written on aboriginal history and collaborated in *Before the Invasion: Aboriginal Life to 1788* (1980). *The Song of Jacky and Selected Poems* appeared in 1986 and *Master of the Ghost Dreaming* in 1991. He received the Special Award in the NSW State Literary Awards

1993 in recognition of his contribution over many years to aboriginal literature.

MUHSUM, Erich
(1878–1934)

German poet, dramatist, satirist and anarchist, one of the first victims of the Nazis. He was a minor Expressionist, many of whose activities were devoted to revolutionary politics.

MUIR, Edwin
(1887–1959)

Scottish poet, born in Deerness on the Mainland of Orkney. The son of a crofter, he left the Orkneys at 14 when his family migrated to Glasgow, where he suffered the period of drab existence described in his *The Story and the Fable* (1940), revised as *An Autobiography* in 1954. He moved from job to job, but spent much time reading **Nietzsche**, **Shaw**, **Ibsen**, **Heine** and Blatchford, and became interested in left-wing politics. In 1919 he married the novelist Willa Anderson (**Willa Muir**), with whom he settled in London, and travelled on the Continent from 1921 to 1924, where the couple collaborated in translations of **Kafka** and **Feuchtwanger**. Back in Scotland in 1925 he published his first volume of verse (*First Poems*), and then returned to France where he wrote novels, notably *The Marionette* (1927). He spent most of the 1930s in Sussex and St Andrews. On the outbreak of World War II he joined the staff of the British Council, and in 1945 returned to Prague as first director of the British Institute there, which was closed after the communist coup of 1948. He then took over the British Institute in Rome until 1950, when he was appointed warden of the adult education college at Newbattle Abbey, Midlothian. After a year as Eliot Norton Professor of Poetry at Harvard (1955–6), he retired to Swaffham Prior near Cambridge. His verses appeared in eight slim volumes— *First Poems* (1925), *Chorus of the Newly Dead* (1926, omitted from *Collected Poems*), *Variations on a Time Theme* (1934), *Journeys and Places* (1937), *The Narrow Place* (1943), *The Voyage* (1946), *The Labyrinth* (1949), *New Poems* (1949–51) and finally *Collected Poems* (1952). Further poems appeared in *The Listener* and other periodicals later. Muir's critical work includes a controversial study of John Knox, *Scott and Scotland* (1936), *Essays on Literature and Society* (1949) and *Structure of the Novel* (1928). A new *Collected Poems* was issued in 1991.
▷ W Muir, *Belonging* (1968)

MUIR, Willa, née **Anderson**, pseud **Agnes Neill Scott**
(1890–1970)

Scottish novelist and translator, born in Montrose, Angus. She showed an early aptitude for languages as a child, speaking both her parents' Shetland dialect and English. Educated at St Andrews University, she taught classics and educational psychology in London until forced to resign when marrying the 'atheist' **Edwin Muir** in 1919. Despite her ill-health, brought on by poor medical treatment after the birth of their son Gavin in 1927, the Muirs punctuated their lives in Scotland with much travelling, and lived for short periods in Prague, Rome and the USA. They translated jointly (although often only Edwin was credited), and were influential in spreading the work of **Kafka** in the 1930s. Her essay *Women: An Enquiry* (1925) dealt with the demoralizing effects of Scottish small-town life, a subject she returned to in her novel *Imagined Corners* (1931). *Mrs Grundy in Scotland* (1936) examined the role of women in Scottish culture. She wrote a moving account of her long and creative partnership with Edwin Muir, *Belonging* (1968), and finished his project *Living With Ballads* (1965) after his death.

MUKHERJEE, Bharati
(1940–)

Indian-born American novelist, born in Calcutta. Mukherjee, who lived in Canada from 1966 until 1980 and became a Canadian citizen in 1971, has since taken up permanent residence in the USA. She now sees herself writing in the American immigrant tradition. Until her move Mukherjee's books were very much concerned with her homeland. *The Tiger's Daughter* (1972) was about a westernized Indian's return to her native country, a theme taken up in non-fiction form in *Darkness: Days and Nights in Calcutta* (1977), a book co-written with her husband, the writer Clark Blaise. Her most recent novel, *The Holder of the World* (1993), continues her stand against what she sees as the tightly-reined, miniaturist school of 'Indian' novels written in English.

MULDOON, Paul
(1951–)

Irish poet, born in Moy, County Armagh, in Northern Ireland. He was educated at Queen's University in Belfast, and worked as a radio and television producer (1973–86), then held a number of academic posts. He currently lectures at Princeton University. Early collections like *New Weather* (1973) and *Mules* (1977) revealed a precocious talent. His subsequent work built on auspicious beginnings in even more extravagant, witty and politically aware fashion in *Why Brownlee Left* (1986). His *Selected Poems 1968–1983* appeared in 1986.

MULGAN, Alan E(dward)
(1881–1961)

New Zealand writer and journalist, born in Katikati, author of *Maori and Paheka: A History of New Zealand* (1922, with A W Shrimpton), *The City of the Strait: Wellington and its Province: a Centennial History* (1939), *Literature and Authorship in New Zealand* (1943) and *Great Days in New Zealand Writing* (1962). He has also published verse, a novel and a collection of plays, travel and history.
▷ *The Making of a New Zealander* (1958)

MULGAN, John Alan Edward
(1911–45)

New Zealand writer, son of **Alan E Mulgan**. He wrote only one novel, the sprawling **Hemingway**-esque *Man Alone* (1939). Through the struggles of his war-veteran hero, Johnson, in the Depression years, he analyses and criticizes the structure of contemporary New Zealand society. The novel is important in New Zealand literature for spawning other books on the theme of the 'isolated man', alone either by virtue of his nature, race or environment. Mulgan took his own life.
▷ *Report on Experience* (1949, posthumous)

MULISCH, Harry Kurt Victor
(1927–)

Dutch novelist, born and educated in Haarlem. Mulisch grew up during World War II, which plays a major role in his work, centrally in *Het stenen bruidsbed* (1959, Eng trans *The Stone Bridal Bed*, 1962), whose subject-matter is similar to **Kurt Vonnegut**'s *Slaughterhouse Five* and which remains one of the few works by which Mulisch is known in the English-speaking world. During the 1960s, he devoted much of his time to political and cultural journalism, writing a collection of manifesto pieces, *Voer voor psychologen* (1961, 'Food for Shrinks') and a sympathetic study of the Provo libertarians, *Bericht aan de rattenkoniing* (1966, 'Briefing for King Rat'). *Twee vrouwen* (1975) was translated as *Two Women* in 1980; it differs sharply from **Alberto Moravia**'s book of the same name. A collected edition of Mulisch's stories appeared in 1977; *The Decorated Man* (1984) brought together a group of longer short stories. *De mythische formule* (1981, 'The Mythic Formula') is an important anthology of conversations.
▷ J H Caspers, N S Huisman and J G M Weck, *Mulisch* (1971)

MÜLLER, Heiner
(1929–)

German playwright, frequently dubbed 'the new Brecht'. He was born in Eppendorf, Saxony, worked as a bookseller and journalist, and at the Maxim Gorki Theatre in Berlin. His early works are dialectical variations on classical forms, including *Herakles 5* (1966) and *Philoktet* (1968, Eng trans *Philoctetes*, 1981); scenes from both reappear in *Zement* (1973, Eng trans *Cement*, 1979). After the political upheavals of 1968, Müller's drama took on a darker and more experimental tone, culminating in his versions of *Hamlet* (1977), *Die Hamletmaschine* (1978) and *Shakespeare Factory 2* (1980), which call for the overthrow of dramatic orthodoxy. Later productions strongly resemble the static tableaux and mixed-media presentations of the radical American director Robert Wilson, but even here the continuity with Müller's earlier **Brecht**ian phase is clearly discernible.
▷ D Calandra, *New German Dramatists* (1983)

MÜLLER, Wilhelm
(1794–1827)

German lyrical poet and translator (the *Faustus* of **Marlowe**), born, the son of a tailor, in Dessau. He is most famous as the author of the 20-poem-cycle set by Schubert, *Die schöne Müllerin*—of which the music is always taken to be considerably superior to the fluent but rather facile verse.
▷ P S Allen, *Wilhelm Müller and the German Volkslied* (1902)

MULTATULI, pseud of **Eduard Douwes Dekker**
(1820–87)

Dutch novelist and aphorist whose pseudonym means 'I have suffered greatly', born in Amsterdam. A difficult and rebellious youth with a righteous indignation against injustice and stuffiness, he made the reverse of progress in the Dutch Colonial Service. His masterpiece, the preposterous but magnificent *Max Havelaar* (1860, Eng trans 1966), presents himself as hero against his hypocritical, racist, smug superiors in the East Indies. For the rest of his debt-ridden life he sought and obtained notoriety, and paved the way for the 'Men of the Eighties', who finally broke with the old and decayed literary conventions. He was the liveliest prose writer in Dutch in his century. **D H Lawrence**, among others, responded positively to his rage and fervour.

MUMFORD, Lewis
(1895–1990)

American author, editor and critic, a lecturer on social problems, born in Flushing, Long Island. Influenced by the theories of Patrick Geddes, he wrote extensively on urban society and human progress; *The Culture of*

Cities (1938) and *The City in History* (1961) are perhaps the best known, but the earlier *Technics and Civilisation* (1934) was also influential. He wrote *The Story of Utopias* (1922), *The Brown Decades* (1931), *Faith for Living* (1940), *The Human Prospect* (1955), *The Myth of the Machine* (1967), *The Pentagon of Power* (1971) and other works, examining the prospects for meliorism.

▷ *My Works and Days: A Personal Chronicle* (1979)

MÜNCHHAUSEN, Karl Friedrich Hieronymus, Baron von
(1720–97)

German soldier, born in Bodenwerder, a member of an ancient Hanoverian house. He was the narrator of ridiculously exaggerated exploits, and served in Russian campaigns against the Turks. A collection of marvellous stories attributed to him was first published as *Vademecum für lustige Leute* (1781–3, 'A Handbook for Jolly Folk'); then, much expanded, in English as *Baron Münchhausen's Narrative of his Marvellous Travels and Campaigns in Russia* (1785) by Rudolf Erich Raspe. This version was then expanded again and translated into German by G A Bürger as *Wunderbare Reisen zu Wasser und zu Lande, Feldzüge und lustige Abenteuer des Freyherrn von Münchhausen* (1786, 'Amazing Travels on Water and Land, Campaigns and Amusing Adventures of Baron von Münchhausen'). The legend was again expanded by **Karl Immermann** in the 1830s, and **Walter Hasenclever** in the 1930s. *Münchhausen* is based partly on 16th-century German jokes, and is partly a satire on James Bruce and other travellers.

MUNDAY, Anthony
(1560–1633)

English poet and playwright, born in London. A stationer and actor, he wrote many poems and pamphlets (including one inveighing against theatrical performances) and plays, mostly in collaboration. Among those credited to him in whole or part are *John a Kent and John a Cumber*, *The Downfall* and *The Death of Robert, Earle of Huntington*. He reported on the activities of English Catholics in France and Italy, and was pageant writer for London.

▷ C Turman, *An Elizabethan Man of Letters* (1928)

MUNK, Kaj, born Kaj Harald Leininger Petersen
(1898–1944)

Danish playwright, priest and patriot, born in Maribo, Laaland. He studied theology at Copenhagen University, and as priest of a small parish in Jutland wrote heroic and religious plays that led the Danish dramatic revival in the 1930s. His first play was *En Idealist* (1928), followed by *Cant* (1931), *Henrik VIII* (1931), *Ordet* (1932, 'The Word') and *Han sidder ved smeltedigien* (1938, 'He Sits by the Melting-Pot'). Though he had initially admired the two fascist leaders, their aggressive expansionism and repressive methods changed his mind; during World War II he was one of the spiritual leaders of the Danish Resistance. In 1943 he wrote a patriotic drama, *Niels Ebbeson*; early in 1944 he was taken from his home by the Gestapo one night and was found murdered in a ditch near Silkeborg next morning.

▷ B N Broust, *Kaj Munk—liv og død* (1984)

MUNONYE, John Okechukwu
(1929–)

Nigerian novelist, born in Akokwa and educated at Onitsha and the University of Ibadan. After further training in London, he returned to Nigeria as an education officer. His fiction is largely concerned with the confrontation of Catholic Christianity and traditional Igbo culture. The bleak tragedy of *The Only Son* (1966) and *Obi* (1969) gradually gives way, in the last volume of the trilogy, *Bridge to a Wedding* (1978), to a more philosophically accommodating and affirmative stance, already represented in his fifth novel, *A Dancer of Fortune* (1974). He also portrayed the harrowing civil war in *A Wreath for Maidens* (1973), which is more journalistic than the others.

MUNRO, Alice
(1931–)

Canadian short-story writer and novelist, born in Wingham, Ontario, where she was brought up before attending the University of Western Ontario. She wrote short stories from an early age, waiting until she was 'ready' to write the great novel. Her only novel to date, *Lives of Girls and Women* (1971), accomplished though it is, cannot claim to be that. Her stories, however, published for many years without being collected, are recognized as among the finest of the day. They are invariably set in rural and semi-rural Ontario, the landscape of her childhood; she has published several collections, from *Dance of the Happy Shades* (1968)—winner of the Governor General's Award for Fiction—and *The Progress of Love* (1987) to *Friend of My Mouth* (1990) and *Something I've Been Meaning to Tell You* (1992).

▷ 'The Colonel's Hash Resettled', in J Metcalf, *The Narrative Voice* (1972)

MUNRO, Hector Hugh *see* **SAKI**

MUNRO, Neil
(1864–1930)

Scottish novelist and journalist, born in Inveraray, Argyll, the son of a farmer. He worked in a law office before taking up journalism in Glasgow, where he became Editor of the *Glasgow Evening News* (1918–27). He wrote romantic Celtic tales in *The Lost Pibroch* (1896) and *Gilian the Dreamer* (1899), and historical Highland novels in *John Splendid* (1898), *Doom Castle* (1901) and *The New Road* (1914). However, he is best known for his humorous tales about a Clyde puffer, published as *The Vital Spark* (1906) and collected as *Para Handy and Other Tales* (1931). His memoir, *Brave Days*, was published posthumously in 1931.
▷G Blake, introduction to *The Brave Days* (1931)

MUNSHI, Kanaiyalal Maniklal
(1887–1982)

Indian (Gujarati) novelist and historian, close friend to and critic of Gandhi; he served in the Indian government after independence. One of his best books is in English: *Gujarat and its Literature* (1935). His chief literary work lies in his highly competent and readable historical novels.

MUNTHE, Axel
(1857–1949)

Swedish physician and writer, born in Oskarshamn. He practised as a physician and psychiatrist in Paris and Rome, was Swedish court physician and retired to Capri, where he wrote his bestselling autobiography, *The Story of San Michele* (1929), which has gone through endless editions since its first publication.
▷A Andrén, *Boker om Axel Munthe* (1957)

MURAKAMI Haruki
(1949–)

Japanese novelist, born in Kobe and educated (in classics) at Waseda University. He started his career in writing by translating the works of modern American writers (**Raymond Chandler**, **Truman Capote** and **Richard Brautigan** amongst others) into Japanese, and his own highly original novels are remarkable for being more influenced by the Americans than by his Japanese predecessors—his work could not contrast more vividly with the naturalism of such writers as **Hakucho Masamune** or **Toson Shimazaki**. Wild, surreal, mystical and often extremely funny, he is now the bestselling author in Japan. Of his works available in English, *A Wild Sheep Chase* (1982) is one of the best, and is a sort of detective novel in which a psychic detective searches for a war criminal, a woman with beautiful ears, and a supernatural sheep with a star on its back.

MURASAKI Shikibu
(c.970–c.1015)

Japanese author, responsible for the *Genji Monogatari* (Eng trans *The Tale of Genji*, 1925–35). She was a member of the Fujiwara family, one of the most powerful aristocratic dynasties in Japan, but her real name is unknown: 'Shikibu Murasaki' is a later fictive construction. Genji was the first great work in Japanese; indeed, there are many who think it still the greatest piece of literature Japan has ever produced. Complex, delicate and often sublimely beautiful, it far outclasses anything produced elsewhere in its day. Like many other aristocratic ladies in late Heian Japan, Murasaki also wrote a *Nikki* ('Diary') which, apart from being beautifully constructed, contains valuable insights into court life of the period.
▷I I Morris, *The World of the Shining Prince* (1964)

MURDOCH, Dame Iris Jean
(1919–)

Irish novelist and philosopher. Born in Dublin of Anglo–Irish parents, she was educated at Badminton School, Bristol, and Oxford, where she was fellow and tutor in philosophy at St Anne's College from 1948 to 1963. She published a study of **Jean-Paul Sartre** (like her, both a novelist and a philosopher) in 1953 and two important but unfashionable philosophical works, much influenced by **Plato**, *The Fire and the Sun* (1977) and *The Sovereignty of the Good* (1970). These deal with the relationships between art and philosophy, and between love, freedom, knowledge and morality. She began writing novels as a hobby. *Under the Net* appeared in 1954, to be followed by more than 20 titles in the next 25 years, including such well-known works as *The Sandcastle* (1957), *The Bell* (1958), *A Severed Head* (1961), *An Unofficial Rose* (1962), *The Red and the Green* (1965), *The Nice and the Good* (1968), *The Black Prince* (1972), *The Sea, The Sea* (1978, winner of the Booker Prize), *Nuns and Soldiers* (1980), *The Good Apprentice* (1985), *The Book and the Brotherhood* (1987) and *The Message to the Planet* (1989). The popularity of the fiction derives largely from her narrative skill in controlling tangled and shifting patterns of relationships, the ironic or even startling circumstances in which the characters find themselves, and the pervasive blend of realism and symbolism. She has also written several plays, including *A Severed Head* (adapted with **J B Priestley** in 1963), *Servants* *and the Snow* (1970), *The Two Arrows* (1972) and *Art and Eros* (1980).

MURE, Sir William
(1594–1657)
Scottish poet, born in Rowallan, Ayrshire. A staunch Protestant and Royalist, he was wounded at Marston Moor (1644), but later led his regiment at Newcastle (1644). He wrote a long religious poem, *The True Crucifixe for True Catholikes* (1629), a fine version of the Psalms (1639), and some love and courtly poems. *The Cry of Blood and of a Broken Covenant* (1650) is a poem on behalf of the Covenanters' cause. He also translated parts of **Virgil**'s *Aeneid*.

MURENA, H A, pseud of Hector Alberto Alvarez
(1923–75)
Argentinian novelist, poet and critic, born in Buenos Aires. He made his first vivid impression on the reading public of Argentina—an enlightened and sophisticated one— as a pessimistic social essayist and leftist critic of leftists. His thesis was that Latin Americans suffered from guilt and insecurity because they had deliberately—out of a mixture of pride and stupidity—cut themselves off from European culture. Murena illustrated his thesis with discussions of the work of most of the great Argentinian writers, including **Arlt**, **Horacio Quiroga** and the man whose intellectual heir he was, **Estrada Martínez**. His criticism of **Borges** was the sharpest ever made. His great novel, *Las leycs de la noche* (1956, Eng trans *The Laws of the Night*, 1976), the central book of a trilogy, is reminiscent of both Arlt and **Sabato** in the extreme horror of its situations. It was Borges above all who commended his fiction to the public. His final novels, under the umbrella title of *El sueño de la razón* (he was able to publish four of a projected seven titles before his untimely death) are quite different, and are exclusively concerned with language and the parody of overvalued authors. Prophet of the end of life on earth, Murena wrote a play and many excellent and original stories; his was one of the most formidable and interesting minds of his country.
▷ *Seis novelistas argentinos de la nueva promocion* (1959)

MURET, Marc-Antoine de
(1526–85)
French humanist and poet, born in Muret near Limoges. He lectured on civil law and classics in France, but later fled on a charge of heresy to Italy, where he edited Latin authors and wrote orations, poems and commentaries.
▷ C Dejob, *Marc-Antoine Muret* (1881)

MURGER, Henri
(1822–61)
French writer, born in Paris. He began life as a notary's clerk, and, devoting his time to literature, led the life of privation and adventure described in his first and best novel, *Scènes de la vie de Bohème* (1845, Eng trans *The Bohemians of the Latin Quarter*, 1887), the basis of Puccini's opera, *La Bohème* (1896). During his later years he led a dissipated life and wrote slowly and fitfully. *Le Manchon de Francine* ('Francine's Muff') is one of the saddest short stories ever written. Other prose works are *La Vie de jeunesse* (1861, 'The Youthful Life') and *Le Pays Latin* (1861, 'Latin Country'). His poems, *Les Nuits d'hiver* (1862, Eng trans *Winter Nights*, 1923), are graceful and often deeply pathetic; several were translated by **Andrew Lang** in his *Lays of old France*.
▷ R Baldick, *The First Bohemian* (1961)

MURNER, Thomas
(1475–1537)
German Roman Catholic satirist, the most prominent of his time, born in Oberehnheim in Alsace. In 1490 he became a wandering Franciscan friar, but died as a priest in his native village. His first full-scale satire, in rhyming verse, *Die Narrenbeschwörung* (1512, 'Invocation of Fools'), is candidly, right down to its title, modelled on **Brant**. Later he excoriated Luther, whom at first he believed was on the Catholic side. A vain, difficult and quarrelsome man, he has been described as possessing an 'almost tragic genius'. But he was the only Roman Catholic—he had hoped to reform the fabric of the Church, without rocking its foundations—whose mastery of theological dispute equalled that of his opponents. Much attention has been devoted to him in Germany, but there is no good work on him in English. His understanding of the colloquial and his closeness to how the common people thought and felt gives his poetry an edge which has now been fully recognized.
▷ R Newald, *Probleme und Gestalten des deutschen Humanisimus* (1963)

MURPHY, Arthur
(1727–1805)
Irish actor and playwright, born in Clomquin, Roscommon. He was educated at St Omer. He worked as a clerk in Cork and then London from 1747 to 1751. From 1752 to 1774 he published the weekly *Gray's Inn Journal*, and so got to know **Dr Johnson**. By going on the stage he paid his debts, and entered Lincoln's Inn in 1757. In 1758 he produced *The Upholsterer*, a successful farce; in 1762 he was called to the Bar, but continued to write farces and adaptations for

the stage. His translation of **Tacitus** (1793) is excellent, unlike his *Essay on Johnson* (1792) and *Life of David Garrick* (2 vols, 1801).

▷ J P Murphy, *Arthur Murphy* (1946)

MURPHY, Richard
(1927–)

Irish poet, born in Galway, but brought up in Ceylon and educated at Oxford and the Sorbonne. In the 1960s he 'retired' to the Aran Islands, later living outside Dublin and dividing his time between Ireland and Sri Lanka. His training in the Classics lends authoritative skill to such long narrative poems as *The Cleggan Disaster* (in *Sailing to an Island*, 1963) and *The Battle of Aughrim* (1968), but sometimes distracts from the lyrical assurance of the shorter poems and ballads that are a major part of *New Selected Poems* (1989).

▷ M Harmon, *Richard Murphy: Poet of Two Traditions* (1979)

MURPHY, Thomas
(1935–)

Irish dramatist, born in Tuem, County Galway. He gained international repute following Joan Littlewood's London production of his *A Whistle in The Dark* (1961). In 1969 he returned to Dublin and joined the Abbey Theatre as director and author of the startlingly innovative *The Morning After Optimism* (1971). Since then *Famine* (1977), *The Gigli Concert* (1984) and *Bailegangaire* (1985) have established him as a great dramatic voice, speaking for the vulnerable and the oppressed, the vain yet emotionally imprisoned, and the aged made angry by both physical and spiritual decay. Much of his later work has come about through his creative collaboration with the Galway theatre company Druid, for whom he worked as Writer in Residence during the 1980s.

▷ F O'Toole, *The Politics of Magic: The Work and Times of Thomas Murphy* (1987)

MURRAY, Charles
(1864–1941)

Scottish poet, born in Alford, Aberdeenshire. He trained as an engineer and had a successful career in South Africa, where in 1917 he became Director of Defence. His poems were written in the Aberdeenshire dialect and admirably portrayed country life and character at the turn of the century. His first major collection, *Hamewith* (1900), was his best and most characteristic. A *Complete Poems* was published in 1979.

▷ C Christie, *Some Memories of Charles Murray* (1943)

MURRAY, Les (Leslie Allan)
(1938–)

Australian poet, critic and editor, born in Nabiac, New South Wales. His childhood and adolescence were spent on a dairy farm. He attended Sydney University but left in 1960 without taking a degree. He has worked as a translator but has long been a freelance writer, frequently contributing literary journalism to newspapers and magazines. His poetry, which has made him one of Australia's leading literary figures, is revered for its perceptive and pungent evocation of rural life. His verse includes *The Ilex Tree* (1965, with Geoffrey Lehmann), *The Weatherboard Cathedral* (1969), *Poems Against Economics* (1972), a verse-novel in 140 sonnets called the *Boys Who Stole the Funeral* (1980), and *The People's Otherworld* (1983), which won the Australian Literary Society's Gold Medal the following year. His *Selected Poems: the Vernacular Republic* was published in 1976 and revised as *The Vernacular Republic; Poems 1961–1981* (1982). In 1993 he received his fifth National Book Council poetry prize for *Translations from the Natural World* (1992), which also won the NSW State Literary Prize for Poetry and the Victorian Premier's Prize in the same year. His latest verse is *The Middle Sea: Book 1 of a Verse Novel in Progress*, published in the *Sydney Review* (1993). Murray compiled and edited the *New Oxford Book of Australian Verse* (1986).

▷ P Nelson, *Study Notes on the Poetry of Les A Murray* (1978)

MURRY, John Middleton
(1889–1957)

British writer and critic, born in Peckham. He wrote some poetry and many volumes of essays and criticism which had a strong influence on the young intellectuals of the 1920s. In 1911 he met **Katherine Mansfield**, whom he married in 1918, and introduced her work in *The Adelphi*, of which he was founder and editor from 1923 to 1948. He also produced posthumous selections from her letters and diaries, and a biography in 1932. He edited the *Athenaeum* (1919–21). He became a pacifist and was editor of *Peace News* from 1940 to 1946. Towards the end of his life he became interested in agriculture, and started a community farm in Norfolk. His major works include critical studies on *Keats and Shakespeare* (1925), his friend *D H Lawrence* (1931), *William Blake* (1933) and *Swift* (1954). He also wrote religious works, including *To The Unknown God* (1924) and *The Life of Jesus* (1926). He published his autobiography, *Between Two Worlds*, in 1935.

▷ F A Lea, *The Life of John Middleton Murry* (1959)

MUSAEUS
(5th–6th century)

Greek epic poet, author of *Hero and Leander*, which has been translated into many languages.
▷M H Jellinek, *Die Sage in der Dichtung* (1890)

MUSÄUS, Johann Karl August
(1735–87)

German writer, born in Jena. He studied theology there, and in 1770 became professor at the Weimar gymnasium. His first book (1760) was a parody of **Samuel Richardson**'s *Sir Charles Grandison, Der deutsche Grandison*; in 1778–9 he satirized **Johann Lavater** in *Physiognomische Reisen* (Eng trans *Physiognomical Travels*, 1800). But his fame rests on his German popular tales (*Volksmärchen der Deutschen*, 1782–6, Eng trans *Popular Tales of the Germans*, 1791), which claimed, falsely, to be a collection taken down from the lips of old people. Their chief note is artificial naivety, but they are a blend of satirical humour, quaint fancy and graceful writing.
▷A Richli, *Johann Musäus* (1957)

MUSCHG, Adolf
(1934–)

Swiss novelist and story writer, writing in German, born in Zollikon near Zürich (where he teaches literature at the university). His novels, such as *Abissers Grund* (1974, 'Abisser's Motive'), tend to satirize his countrymen and their middle-class habits.

MUSHANOKOJI Saneatsu
(b.1885)

Japanese novelist, playwright and critic, born into an aristocratic family. His early work was marked by a romantic liberalism—he was greatly influenced by **Tolstoy**, even going so far as to set up an 'ideal village' on the Tolstoyan model. As World War II loomed closer, however, he became increasingly right-wing, drifting off into despair and a remote isolation after the defeat in 1945.
▷T Arima, *The Failure of Freedom: A Portrait of Modern Japanese Intellectuals* (1969)

MUSIL, Robert
(1880–1942)

Austrian novelist, born in Klagenfurt. He was trained as a scientist (he invented a chromatometer) and as a philosopher. During World War I he was an officer and drew on his experience for *Die Verwirrungen des Zöglings Törless* (1906, Eng trans *Young Törless*, 1955), a terrifying, sadistic story of life inside a military academy. Memorable though it is, it is eclipsed by *Der Mann ohne Eigenschaften*

(1930–43, Eng trans *The Man Without Qualities*, 1953–60), his unfinished tour de force. Portraying a society on the brink of the abyss through the eyes of Ulrich, the man who has dispensed with conventional qualities, its narrative covers just one year, 1913–14. Plotless but dealing in interrelated facts, it is multi-layered. It is widely acknowledged as one of the great novels of the century despite the confusion of final drafts which the author did not have time to tidy up before his sudden death in Geneva.
▷K Dinklage, *Robert Musil. Leben, Werk, Wirkung* (1960)

MUSKETT, Netta
(1887–1963)

English romantic and historical novelist, who published her first book, *The Jade Spider*, in 1927, and who continued writing prolifically until the 1960s. Muskett was not a wholly conventional romantic novelist, for while her books reflect a strict morality, her heroines are not necessarily paragons of virtue. For example, in *Painted Heaven* (1934) a woman who lost her fiancé, brothers and parents during World War I, attempts to find new happiness by having an illegitimate child. The result, however, is not contentment but insecurity: a 'painted heaven'. Later, Muskett looked at the conflicting work and family lives of the emerging career-women of the late 1950s.

MUSSET, (Louis Charles) Alfred de
(1810–57)

French poet and dramatist, born in Paris. After tentative study first of the law, then of medicine, he found he had a talent for writing and at 18 published a translation of **Thomas De Quincey**'s *Confessions of an Opium Eater* (*L'anglais mangeur d'opium*, 1828). His first collection of poems, *Contes d'Espagne et d'Italie* (1830, 'Tales of Spain and Italy'), won the approval of **Victor Hugo** who accepted him into his *Cénacle*, the inner shrine of militant Romanticism. But Musset had no real desire to commit himself to any particular cult; indeed he had already begun to poke gentle fun at the movement, and had indicated that he wished to 'se déhugotiser'. His first excursion into drama, *La Nuit vénitienne* ('A Night in Venice'), failed at the Odéon in 1830, and from then on he conceived an 'armchair theatre' with plays intended for reading only. The first of these, *La Coupe et les lèvres* ('The Cup and the Lips') and *À quoi rêvent les jeunes filles* ('What do Young Girls Dream Of?'), together with the narrative poem *Namouna*, were published as *Spectacle dans un fauteuil* ('Armchair Theatre') in 1832, and next year the tragi-comedies *André del Sarto* and *Les Caprices de Marianne* (1851,

'The Whims of Marianne') appeared in the *Revue des deux mondes* ('Review of Two Worlds'). Also among his *Comédies et proverbes* (1840), as these pieces were called, are *Lorenzaccio* (1834), *On ne badine pas avec l'amour* (1836, Eng trans *No Trifling with Love*, 1890) and *Il ne faut jurer de rien* (1836, 'Never Take an Oath'). *Un Caprice*, published in 1837, and several of his other 'armchair' plays were staged successfully more than 10 years later, and thus reassured he wrote *On ne saurait penser à tout* (1849, 'You Can Never Think of Everything'), *Carmosine* (1850, Eng trans 1865) and *Bettine* (1851) for actual performance. In 1833 Musset had met **George Sand**, and there began the stormy love affair which coloured much of his work after that date. The pair set out to spend the winter together at Venice, but Musset became ill, Sand became capricious, and in April the poet returned alone, broken in health and sunk in depression. His *Nuits*, from *Nuit de mai* (1835, 'A Night in May') through *Nuit de décembre* (1835, 'A Night in December') and *Nuit d'août* (1836, 'A Night in August') to *Nuit d'octobre* (1837, 'A Night in October'), trace the emotional upheaval of his love for George Sand from despair to final resignation. His autobiographical poem *Confessions d'un enfant du siècle* (1835, Eng trans *The Confessions of a Child of the Century*, 1892) is a study of the prevalent attitude of mind—the *mal du siècle*—resulting from the aftermath of revolution and the unrest of the early years of the century. *L'Espoir en Dieu* (1838, 'Hoping in God'), an expression of the soul's longing for certainty, is perhaps not altogether convincing. In 1838 he was appointed Home Office librarian. He died of heart failure.

MUSSET, Paul de
(1804–80)

French novelist and man-of-letters, brother to the dramatist **Alfred de Musset**, whose affair with **George Sand** prompted Paul de Musset's *Luis et elle* (1859). This was a thinly disguised response to Sand's own *Elle et lui* (also 1859), which dealt with the breakdown in her relationship with Paul's brother. It is as the author of a minor classic of French children's literature, the 'conte' *Monsieur le Vent et Madame la Pluie* (1860), which has been much reprinted, that Paul de Musset's name survives.

MYERS, Frederic William Henry
(1843–1901)

English poet and essayist, brother of Ernest James Myers, the son of a clergyman. A classical scholar, and a school inspector from 1872 to 1900, he wrote poems (collected 1921), essays, a book on *Wordsworth* (1881) and *Human Personality and its Survival of Bodily Death* (1903). He was one of the founders of the Society for Psychical Research in 1882.

MYERS, L(eopold) H(amilton)
(1881–1944)

English novelist and dramatist, born in Cambridge. As a result of a legacy, he was financially able to devote himself to writing full-time from an early age. Although he produced a verse play, *Arvat*, in 1908, he is principally remembered now for *The Near and the Far* (1929), an ambitious tetralogy of novels set in 16th-century India. Myers believed contemporary society to be spiritually and morally impoverished, and in his writing used an idealized past of the Moghul Empire to emphasize by comparison the poverty of the present.

MYKLE, Agnar
(1915–)

Norwegian novelist and short-story writer, who enjoyed a certain scandalous vogue in Britain at the beginning of the 1960s, when his two most important novels, *Lasso rundt fru Luna* (1954) and *Sangen on den røde rubin* (1956), were translated into English, as *Lasso Round the Moon* (1960) and *The Song of the Red Ruby* (1961) respectively. He grew up in Trondheim, and the restrictions of his middle-class home became one of the obsessive themes of his writing, which consistently argued in favour of eliminating social and moral restraints. His first story collection, *Taustigen* (1948, 'The Rope Ladder'), appeared when he was 35; his first novel was *Tyven, tyven, skal du dete* (1951, Eng trans *The Hotel Room*, 1963). In 1957 he was tried for obscenity following the publication of *Sangen on den røde rubin* (1956); his acquittal and that of his publisher was a significant moment in liberating modern fiction from 19th-century standards. Having written the autobiographical story of Ask Burlefot, Mykle wrote very little more and was mostly silent in his later years.
▷P Houm, *Ask Burlefot og vi* (1957)

MYRVILIS, Stratis, pseud of Stratis Stamatopoulos
(1892–1969)

Greek novelist and short-story writer, born on Mytilene. He served in the Balkan Wars and in World War I. Both his first collection of short stories, *Kokines Histories* (1915, 'Red Stories'), and his first novel, *Zoë en Tapho* (1924, Eng trans *Life in the Tomb*, 1931, 1977), were published only on Mytilene; it was not until *Zoë en Tapho* was republished in Athens in 1930 that it came to the attention of reviewers and made his reputation. A classic war tale written as the journal of a sergeant in the trenches, it earned the author comparison with **Erich Maria Remarque**. His next novel, *Dhaskala me ta Chrysa Matia* (1933, Eng trans *The Schoolmistress with the Golden Eyes*, 1964), again drew on his war memories, telling the story of a young soldier's return to Mytilene after the war; his guilt at the death of his friend in the fighting is exacerbated when he realizes he is falling in love with his friend's young widow. Myrivilis then returned to writing short stories, revealing a surprisingly lyrical feel for nature in a collection published in 1935. His later work includes a novel, *Panaghia Ghorghona* (1949, Eng trans *The Mermaid Madonna*, 1959), and two more collections of short stories (1952 and 1959).

N

NABOKOV, Vladimir
(1899–1977)

Russian-born American novelist, born in St Petersburg. His family was wealthy and aristocratic and he was a precocious child. He attended St Petersburg's relatively progressive Tenishev School, where he was accused of 'not conforming' to his surroundings. In 1919, following the Bolshevik Revolution, his family became émigrés, and he and his brother went to Cambridge on a scholarship, where he studied Russian and French literature. When he graduated in 1922 he rejoined his family in Berlin, where his father was the victim of a senseless murder. He lived for more than 15 years in Berlin but admitted to never having mastered the language, though his first literary success was a translation of some of **Heinrich Heine**'s songs. From 1937 to 1940 he was in Paris, where he met **James Joyce**, and then emigrated to the USA where he took citizenship in 1945. He published his first novels in Berlin: *Mashenka* (1926, Eng trans *Mary*, 1971), *Korol, Dama, Valet* (1928, 'King, Queen, Knave'), *Zashita Luzhina* (1936, 'The Defense') and *Otchayanie* (1936, 'Despair'). In Paris he wrote *Soglodataï* (1938, 'The Eye') and *Priglashenie na kazn'* (1938, 'Invitation to a Beheading'). All were written in Russian, under the pseudonym V Sirin, the author himself later collaborating on English translations. In the USA he taught at Wellesley College and Cornell University, and earned distinction as a lepidopterist. Writing now in English he published many short stories and novels including *The Real Life of Sebastian Knight* (1941), *Bend Sinister* (1947), *Pale Fire* (1962) and *Ada* (1969). *Lolita* (1959) was a *succès de scandale* and brought his name before the general public, and allowed him to abandon teaching and devote himself full-time to writing. From 1959 he lived in Montreux in Switzerland. Among 20th-century novelists he is regarded for his linguistic ingenuity and dazzling intellect. **H G Wells** was his first love but his debt to **Jane Austen**, **Dickens**, **Robert Louis Stevenson** and others is acknowledged in *Lectures on Literature* (1980). He also translated **Alexander Pushkin**'s *Eugene Onegin* (1963).

▷A Field, *Vladimir Nabokov, the life and art* (1977)

NAEVIUS, Gnaeus
(c.264–c.201 BC)

Roman poet and dramatist, born probably in Campania. He served in the first Punic war (264–241 BC), and started producing his own plays in 235. A plebeian, for 30 years he satirized the Roman nobles in his plays, and was compelled to leave Rome, ultimately retiring to Utica in Africa. Fragments of an epic, *De Bello Punico* ('The Punic Wars'), are extant.
▷M Barchiesi, *Nevio epico* (1962)

NAGAI Kafu
(1879–1962)

Japanese writer, born into an aristocratic samurai family in western Japan, though he is strongly associated with Tokyo, where he lived most of his life, particularly amongst the geisha houses of the Shinbashi area. He was one of the first writers from Japan to travel extensively in the West and to open himself to western influences, being particularly affected by his experiences of French culture, and producing a new, more generally accessible kind of fiction writing. At the same time, he was deeply rooted in Japan's own traditions, and was very much saddened by the passing of the traditional way of life in old Edo (the old name of Tokyo)—one critic said that he 'closed his eyes to historical change'. His wistful nostalgia and graceful style are at their best in *Bokuto Kitan* (1936, Eng trans *A Strange Tale from East of the River*, 1965), a collection of stories set in the geisha houses and eating places of Tokyo's red light district.
▷E Scheidensticker, *Kafu, the Scribbler* (1965)

NAIDU, Sarojini, née Chattopadhyay
(1879–1949)

Indian feminist and poet, born in Hyderabad and educated at Madras, London and Cambridge. Known as the 'nightingale of India', she published three volumes of lyric verse: *The Golden Threshold* (1905), *The Bird of Time* (1912) and *The Broken Wing* (1915). She organized flood-relief in Hyderabad

(1908), and lectured and campaigned on feminism, particularly the abolition of purdah. Associated with Mahatma Gandhi, she was the first Indian woman to be President of the Indian National Congress, in 1925. She was imprisoned several times for civil disobedience incidents, and took part in the negotiations leading to independence. In 1947 she was appointed governor of United Provinces (now Uttar Pradesh).

▷P Sengupta, *Sarojini Naidu* (1966)

NAIPAUL, Shiva(dhar Srinavasa)
(1945–85)

West Indian novelist and prose writer, born in Port of Spain, Trinidad. The younger brother of **V S Naipaul**, he became noted as a writer of exceptional promise with the publication in 1970 of his first work, *Fireflies*, which won three awards. By then based in London, he augmented his success with his novel *The Chip-Chip Gatherers* (1973), which won the Whitbread Award for Fiction. He travelled widely in the USA, India and the Caribbean, and wrote an account of an African journey in *North of South* (1978). His last works—six articles and the start of a projected work on Australia—are gathered in the posthumously published *An Unfinished Journey* (1986).

NAIPAUL, V(idiadhar) S(urajprasad)
(1932–)

Trinidadian novelist. His brother **Shiva Naipaul** was also a gifted writer. Educated at Queen's Royal College, Port of Spain, he left the Caribbean for Oxford in 1950, where he took his degree. The editor of 'Caribbean Voices' for the BBC, he dabbled in journalism before his first novel, *The Mystic Masseur* (1957), was published. *Miguel Street* (1959) collected sketches depicting lower-class life in Trinidad through the eyes of a growing boy. The book which made his name was *A House for Mr Biswas* (1961), a spicy satire spanning three Trinidadian generations but focusing on its eponymous six-fingered sign-writer. Thereafter the Caribbean figured less prominently in his work, which grew steadily darker and more complex. *In a Free State* (1971) won the Booker Prize, and in 1979 he published *A Bend in the River*, a masterly re-creation of what it is like to live under an African dictatorship. As well as novels he has written several trenchant 'travel' books including *An Area of Darkness: An Experience of India* (1964) and *Among the Believers: An Islamic Journey* (1981). *Finding the Centre* (1984) is autobiographical.

▷S Kamra, *The Novels of V S Naipaul* (1990)

NAIRNE, Carolina, née Oliphant, Lady
(1766–1845)

Scottish song writer, born in Gask, Perthshire, the daughter of a Jacobite laird. In 1806 she married her second cousin, Major Nairne (1757–1830), who became Lord Nairne in 1824. She lived in Edinburgh, but travelled widely in Ireland and Europe after her husband's death. Collecting traditional airs, she wrote songs to them under the pseudonym 'Mrs Bogan of Bogan', which were published in *The Scottish Minstrel* (1821–4), and posthumously as *Lays from Strathearn*. They include the lament for Prince Charles Edward Stuart, 'Will ye no' come back again', 'The Land o' the Leal', 'Caller Herrin'', 'The Laird o' Cockpen', 'The Rowan Tree' and 'The Auld Hoose', as well as the martial setting for 'The Hundred Pipers'.

▷K Oliphant, *Jacobite Lairds of Gask* (1970)

NAKANO Shigeharu
(1902–)

Japanese poet and novelist. In his twenties and early thirties, Nakano produced a stream of Marxist poetry, until he was arrested as a subversive by the *Kempeito* (secret police). This experience turned him into a novelist. He was a leading light in the pre- and post-war Marxist underground, which was part of a continuous thread in Japanese culture, giving rise to the student underground movement of the 1970s. Nakano's writing, whilst not short on rhetoric, also displays great literary prowess.

NALÉ ROXLO, Conrado
(1898–1971)

Argentinian dramatist, story writer, novelist, children's writer, poet and humorist, of Uruguayan descent, born in Buenos Aires. He was a close friend to the great **Roberto Arlt**. His essays and stories were often signed 'Chamico'. His poetry, witty and unambitious, has been compared to that of **Heine**; he later turned to a playful, unserious Surrealism. Most highly thought of now, however, are his fantasy dramas, slightly influenced both by the plays of the *grottesco criollo* school—a kind of early Argentinian theatre of the absurd, or cruelty—and (technically) by the two popular playwrights 'Darthéz and Damel'. Most successful is his witty reworking of the Faust legend, *El pacto de Christina* (1945, 'Cristina's Pact'), in which a girl makes an agreement with the devil in return for the love of a man. His single novel, *Extraño accidente* (1960, 'Strange Accident'), has been commended for its 'audacity', and its 'strange quality and poetic depth'.

▷A Flores, *The Literature of Spanish America* (1966–7)

NALKOWSKA
(1884–1954)

Polish novelist and dramatist, born in Warsaw, the daughter of a famous geographer and his wife, who were enlightened enough to give her a sound education, and to be proud of her. She was initially associated with the so-called Positivist movement, which preceded that of the neo-romantic 'Young Poland' (Mloda Polska). Her first novel, *Kobiety* (1906, Eng trans *Women*, 1920), published when she was only 22, was well intentioned, but too closely reflected what she thought she ought, as a Positivist, to believe: however, its characterization bore sure signs that she was a woman of unusual genius, who did not pander to male notions of women. Eighteen years later she had matured beyond recognition; *Romans Teresy Hennert* (1924, 'Teresa Hennert's Affair') is a scathing account of the bourgeois attitude to 'illicit' love in Poland after World War II. She wrote at least three more excellent psychological novels, of which *Granica* (1935, 'The Boundary') is perhaps the finest. She is most famous, however, for *Medaliony* (1946, Eng trans of part of it in *Introduction to Modern Polish Literature*, 1964, H Gillon and L Krzyzanowski eds): as a member of the International Commission to Investigate Nazi Crimes, she had, early, to investigate torture and concentration camps in Poland, and in these sketches, amongst the most harrowing and ironic ever written on this subject, she reported her findings. 'Professor Spanner', about making soap from prisoners, is peculiarly memorable for its bland summaries of the good reasons advanced for this process.

NAMARA, Fernando
(1919–)

Portuguese poet, novelist and essayist, born near Coimbra. He was a country doctor until 1965 (when he decided to devote himself to writing), as his eloquent *Retalhos da vida de um medico* (1949, Eng trans *Mountain Doctor*, 1956) testifies. His realistic, psychologically penetrating and socially aware fiction includes *O trigo e o joio* (1954, Eng trans *The Fields of Fate*, 1970).

NAOGEORGUS, or NAOGEORG,
Thomas, Latin name of **Thomas Kirchmair**
(1511–63)

German dramatist, classicist, poet, translator (**Sophocles** into Latin) and Lutheran preacher, born in Straubing. His *Pammachius* (1538), in Latin like his other plays, is a swingeing attack on the pope and all things papist. So is the verse epic *Regnum papisticum* (1555). *Pammachius* was performed in Cambridge in 1545, by members of Christ's College. *Mercator* (1540) is a notable Jederman (Everyman) comedy, in which salvation is seen as gained by good works.
▷F Wiener, *Naogeorgus im England der Reformationszeit* (1907)

NARAYAN, Rasipuram Kirshnaswamy
(1906–)

Indian novelist, born in Madras, south India. He was educated there and at Maharaja's College in Mysore. His first novel, *Swami and Friends* (1935), and its successor *The Bachelor of Arts* (1937), are set in the enchanting fictional territory of 'Malgudi'. Other Malgudi novels are *The Dark Room* (1938), *The English Teacher* (1945)—a thinly veiled account of his own marriage and the event that most matured and shaped his character, the early death of his beloved wife—*Mr Sampath* (1949), *The Financial Expert* (1952), *The Man-Eater of Malgudi* (1961), *The Painter of Signs* (1977) and *The Tiger for Malgudi* (1983). His novel *The Guide* (1958) won him the National Prize of the Indian Literary Academy. He has also published stories, travel books, books for children and essays, as well as *My Days: A Memoir* (1974). The best Indian novelist of his generation, his publication in Britain was brought about by **Graham Greene**.
▷C Vander, *R. K. Narayan* (1986)

NASH, (Frederic) Ogden
(1902–71)

American writer of light verse, born in Rye, New York. Educated at Harvard, he tried various occupations—teaching, editing, selling bonds, copy writing—before devoting himself to verse. Taking outrageous liberties with the English language ('I would live all my life in nonchalance and insouciance/Were it not for making a living, which is rather a nouciance'), he soon became the most popular modern versifier, frequently to be seen in the *New Yorker*, whose sophisticated tone he helped establish. No subject, however odd, inconsequential or mundane was safe from his wit. Puns, parody and pastiche—as well as alliteration—were his stock in trade, which he used to amuse as well as shock. He published many collections, including *Free Wheeling* (1931), *Hard Lines* (1931), *Parents Keep Out: Elderly Poems for Youngerly Readers* (1951), *The Private Dining Room and Other New Verses* (1953) and *Boy is a Boy* (1960). *I Wouldn't Have Missed It: Selected Poems of Ogden Nash* was published in 1983.
▷L B Axford, *An Index to the Poems of Ogden Nash* (1972)

NASHE, Thomas
(1567–1601)

English dramatist and satirist, born in Lowestoft. He studied for seven years at St John's College, Cambridge, travelled in France and Italy, and then went to London to earn a precarious living by his pen. His first work was the *Anatomie of Absurditie* (1589), perhaps written at Cambridge. He plunged into the Martin Marprelate controversy, showing a talent for vituperation which he expressed in his works. *Pierce Penilesse, his Supplication to the Divell* (1592) began the series of attacks on the Harveys (Richard Harvey had criticized Nashe's preface to **Robert Greene**'s *Menaphon*), which culminated in *Have with you to Saffron Walden* (1596), against **Gabriel Harvey**, who had by then assailed Greene's memory in *Foure Letters*. In 1599 the controversy was suppressed by the Archbishop of Canterbury. Nashe's satirical masque *Summer's Last Will and Testament* (1592) contains the song 'Spring the sweet Spring is the year's pleasant king'. *The Unfortunate Traveller* (1594) is a picaresque tale, one of the earliest of its kind. After **Christopher Marlowe**'s death, Nashe prepared his unfinished tragedy *Dido* (1596) for the stage. His own play *The Isle of Dogs* (1597), now lost, drew such attention to abuses in the state that it was suppressed, the theatre closed, and the writer himself thrown into the Fleet prison. His last work was *Lenten Stuffe* (1599), a panegyric on the red herring trade at Yarmouth.
▷M Schaluch, *Antecedents of the English Novel* (1963)

NATHAN, Robert Gruntal
(1894–1985)

American poet and novelist, born in New York City, educated at Harvard, and seven times married. His masterpiece is *Peter Kindred* (1919), a highly personalized fiction which gives an unparalleled portrayal of a social class undergoing a period of enormous change. Its lilting, almost poetic style is reproduced in *The Puppet Master* (1923) and *The Woodcutter's House* (1927), both of which are greatly underappreciated. In *The Bishop's Wife* (1928) an angel poses as an archdeacon and falls for the bishop's wife; *There Is Another Heaven* (1929) puts a converted Jew into a Calvinist heaven; and *One More Spring* (1933) offers a coy way through the economic depression. Ironically, Nathan's verse is much less compelling than his poetic prose; collections of poetry include *The Cedar Box* (1929) and *Winter in April* (1958).

NATION, Terry (Terence)
(1930–)

English television scriptwriter and novelist. Nation came to prominence as the original scriptwriter for the long-running *Doctor Who* television science-fiction series, (1963 onwards), in which the benevolent title character used an old-fashioned police telephone box, 'the Tardis', to travel through time and space. Nation also created the daleks, the Doctor's most deadly foes. These herd-like robotic creatures, shaped like pepper-pots, barking 'I obey!' or 'Exterminate!', enjoyed huge popularity and appeared in such films, based on Nation scripts, as *The Daleks: Invasion Earth 2150* (1966). Nation is also the author of *Rebecca's World* (1975), a science-fiction story for young people, and the post-nuclear catastrophe television series, *The Survivors* (1976). He has also collaborated on other series.

NAU, John-Antoine, pseud of Antoine Torque
(1860–1918)

French writer, born in San Francisco of French parents. He was brought up in France from the age of three, after the death of his father. As a young man he worked for a time as a sailor, and continued to travel widely. His novels utilize a variety of colourful locations which reflect that experience, as in *Cristobal le poète* (1912), which is set in Algiers, and *Thérèse Donati* (1921), which evokes the landscape and people of Corsica. He published several volumes of poetry as well as novels, and has the historical distinction of being the first recipient of the Prix **Goncourt** for his novel *Force ennemie* in 1903.

NAVARRETE, Fray Manuel de
(1768–1809)

Minor Mexican poet and Franciscan, who kept his poetry a secret from his superiors. He read widely, especially in the English pre-romantic school of the *Night Thoughts* of **Edward Young**, which influenced him.

NAWAL EL SAADAWI
(20th century)

Prominent and militant Egyptian doctor and novelist, born in Kafr Tahla. As a doctor she became aware of women's social and economic problems, and in her first non-fictional work in Arabic, *Women and Sex* (1972), and in her stories in *Two Women in One* (1975, Eng trans 1985), she highlighted their plight. *God Dies by the Nile* (1974, Eng trans 1985), considered a 'metaphor for the Sadat regime', further reveals how class and oppression by landlords augments their misery. Her outspokenness resulted in her losing her post as Director of Health in Cairo. In her later works, such as *She Has No Place in Paradise* (1987) and *Death of His Excellency, the Ex-Minister* (1987), all published outside Egypt, she further illustrated the impotence of the political and religious system in overcoming the influences of imperialism and colonialism.

NAZOR, Vladimir
(1876–1949)

Croatian poet, born in Postire on the island of Brač. He wrote lyrics and ballads as well as epic poems and dramatic works in a style similar to the Symbolists. His works include *Slav Legends* (1900), *Lirika* (1910, 'Lyrics'), *Carmen Vitae*, an anthology (1922), and a diary of his experiences with the Yugoslav partisans in World War II.

NEAL, John
(1793–1876)

American editor, poet, novelist and critic, born in Falmouth in Maine, who sometimes signed himself 'Jehu O'Cataract'. After going into business and failing, he qualified as a lawyer, then became editor of the *Portico*, a literary monthly published by the chauvinistic Delphian Club, from Baltimore. His melodramatic novel *Keep Cool* (1817), about a man's guilt because he has killed someone in a duel, made him famous. He wrote many more novels, including *Logan, A Family History* (1822), about an (actual) Englishman who married the Queen of Native American tribe. Neal soon after went to England, where he acted as secretary to Jeremy Bentham. His finest novel was *Rachel Dyer* (1828), about a Salem witch. His meandering *Wandering Recollections of a Somewhat Busy Life* (1869) is an invaluable source book.

NECATIGIL, Behçet
(1916–)

Turkish poet, radio dramatist and translator (**Heine**, **Hamsun**, **Böll** and others), born in Istanbul. A teacher of literature in lycées by profession, he has German connections, and has compiled a *Who's Who* of Turkish literature. He is, paradoxically, an intellectual poet whose work was entirely devoted to the expression and explanation of the lives and feelings of 'ordinary' (non-intellectual) people; as such, he is one of Turkey's most interesting and original poets of his generation.

NECHUY, pseud of Ivan Levytsky
(1838–1918)

Ukrainian novelist in the tradition of **Zola** and the naturalists. His novels were forbidden in Russia but he published in Polish Galicia. Once regarded as one of the greatest of his country's writers, his work has by now somewhat faded.

NEDREAAS, Torborg
(1906–)

Norwegian novelist of Jewish extraction, born in Bergen. She turned to writing late in life, after World War II. A left-wing feminist, her books highlight social life and class struggle in Norwegian urban society. Especially powerful are *Musikk fra en blå brpnn* (1960, Eng trans *Music from a Blue Well*) and *Ved neste nymåne* (1971, Eng trans *At the Next New Moon*), about a girl called Herdis growing up in Bergen between the wars. Her best stories were collected in *Stoppested* (1953, 'Stopping Place').
▷H Eriksen, *Nedreaas* (1979)

NEGRI, Ada
(1870–1945)

Italian poet, born in Lodi. She became a teacher in a small primary school, and made her literary debut with *Fatalità* (1892, 'Destiny'), a derivative and idealistic collection of humanitarian poems. Her subsequent works, nine more volumes of verse and a number of prose works, refined the political, feminist and mystical basis of her work.
▷M Magni, *L'opera di Ada Negri e la su umanita* (1961)

NEIHARDT John G(neisau)
(1881–1973)

American short-story writer, novelist and poet, born in Illinois. He lived amongst the Omaha Indians for nearly 10 years and his five-part epic, published collectively as *A Cycle of the West* (1949), deals with a tribe of Plains Indians. The cycle opened with *The Song of Hugh Glass* in 1915. Previous books had included *The Lonesome Trail* (1907), a collection of short stories featuring pioneering heroes, and *The River and I* (1910), an account of a river trip on the Missouri.

NEILSON, John Shaw
(1872–1942)

Australian poet, born in Penola, South Australia, the son of a Scottish-born poet and bushworker. His first work was published in the Sydney weekly *Bulletin* by A G Stephens, who befriended and guided Neilson, and took much of his early work. His first published collection, *Heart of Spring*, came out in 1919, followed by *Ballad and Lyrical Poems* (1923) and *New Poems* (1927). Though Neilson was uneducated and weakened by a life of hard work (sheep shearer, roadmaker, farmer), his verse couples surprising delicacy, almost naivety, with delicate imagery. *Collected Poems* appeared in 1934; later verse was published after Nielson's death in *Unpublished Poems*

(1947) and *Witnesses of Spring* (1970). The definitive edition is *The Poems of Shaw Nielson*, ed A R Chisholm (1965, rev edn 1973).

NEKRASOV, Nikolai Alexeievich
(1821–78)

Russian lyrical poet of the Realistic school, born near Vinitza, Podolia. He worked as a journalist and critic, and made his name with poems depicting the social wrongs of the peasantry, such as his unfinished narrative epic, *Komu na Rusi zhit khorosho?* (1879, Eng trans *Who Can Be Happy and Free in Russia?*, 1917). His writings have been widely acknowledged as an important influence by successive generations of Russian writers.
▷M Peppard, *Nikolai Alexeyevich Nekrasov* (1967)

NELLIGAN, Emile
(1879–1941)

Canadian poet—a controversial member of the École litteraire de Montreal—who has been described as 'the first modern Canadian poet', and a Symbolist poet of great musical sensibility. Most of his poems were composed in the five years before his incarceration in various mental institutions from 1899 to the end of his life. His most famous poem, 'Le vaisseau d'or' (1899, 'The Ship of Gold'), has been seen as a premonition of this tragic loss of self, this 'death in life': 'What of my heart's lost fate, poor derelict?/—Founded, alas! in the black gulf of Dream!' His poems were collected and edited by his friend Louis Dantin and published under the title *Emile Nelligan et son oeuvre* in 1904, but the most comprehensive edition of his work was compiled by Luc Lacourciere in 1952 (*Poesies Completes, 1896–1899*); English translations were made available by P F Widdows, *Selected Poems* (1960) and F Cogswell, *The Complete Poems of Emile Nelligan* (1983).
▷P Wyzynski, *Emile Nelligan* (1976)

NEMCOVÁ, Bozena, née Panklová
(1820–62)

Czech novelist, born in Vienna, of an Austrian father, a coachman on an estate in Bohemia, and a Czech mother. She garnered her considerable wisdom from her old grandmother, whom she lovingly and memorably portrayed in *Babicka* (1855, Eng trans *Granny*, 1962), one of the great books of the 19th century. At 17 she married unhappily—her husband, an excise man much older than her, could not reconcile his duties to his Austrian masters with her habits of thinking for herself and writing, and they parted in 1850. Beautiful, sensitive, intense, Nemcová became (almost like **George Eliot** in England)

the subject of much vulgar gossip, since she chose to have many love affairs (which were as unhappy as her marriage had been). However, she also became the first truly eminent Czech women writer—*Granny* has gone through over 300 Czech editions since it first appeared, and through many more in other Slavonic languages. She wrote many more novels and stories, some of them folk- and fairy-tales. She died prematurely, while trying to collect an edition of her works, as a result of exhaustion and disappointment. Some of her fairy-tales are translated in *The Shepherd and the Dragon* (1930).

NEMEROV, Howard
(1920–)

American poet, novelist and playwright, born in New York City. He was based in England while serving with the Royal Canadian Air Force during World War II. He has written several novels, including *The Melodramatists* (1949), but has won greater acclaim as a poet. His relatively accessible verse, in which, as he has said, he 'writes of history from the point of view of the loser', includes *The Image and The Law* (1947) and *The Next Room of the Dream* (1962). His *Collected Poems* (1977) won the National Book Award.

NÉMETH, László
(1901–75)

Hungarian novelist, dramatist, critic and translator (of **Tolstoy**'s *Anna Karenina*, reckoned to be one of the greatest translations of the 20th century), born in Nagybánya (now Baia-Mare in Romania). A medical doctor by profession, he burst on the literary scene in 1925 with his now-famous story, published in Hungary's premier literary magazine *Nyugat*, 'Horváthné meghal' ('Mrs Horvath Dies'). He wrote dramas about Galileo (1954, Act IV translated in *The Plough and the Pen*, 1963) and Gandhi. However, his best work was done in the novel: in *Iszony* (1947, Eng trans *Revulsion*, 1965), about an unhappy marriage, and *Bün* (1936, Eng trans *Guilt*, 1966). His reputation, despite the 'subtly intellectual' anti-Semitism of which he has—not altogether convincingly—been accused, has steadily grown. For many years between the wars he ran and wrote the magazine *Tanu* ('Witness'), in which he argued for what is (correctly but misleadingly) described as the 'populist' view, that Hungary had the right to choose between Soviet communism and capitalism. A resourceful man, perhaps excessively intellectual, he is a undoubtedly one of the giants of modern Hungarian literature.
▷ *The Personalist*, XXXI (1950)

NENNIUS
(fl.769)

Welsh writer, reputedly author of the early Latin compilation known as the *Historia Britonum*, which purports to give an account of British history from the time of **Caesar** to towards the end of the 7th century. The book gives a mythical account of the origins of the Britons, and recounts the Roman occupation, the settlement of the Saxons and King Arthur's 12 victories. Although it contains fanciful material of doubtful historical significance, its real value lies in its preservation of material needed for the study of early Celtic literature in general, and the Arthurian Legend in particular.
▷J F Kenney, *Sources for the Early History of Ireland* (1929)

NEPOS, Cornelius
(c.99–c.24 BC)

Roman historian, a native of Pavia or Hostilia in northern Italy. He was the contemporary and close friend of **Cicero**, and **Catullus** dedicated his poems to him. His *De Viris Illustribus* ('Lives of Famous Men'), of which only some 25 (mainly Greek warriors and statesmen) survive, are written in a clear and straightforward style. He was the first to adopt the pairing of Greek and Roman soldiers and statesmen, a form later followed by **Plutarch**.

NERUDA, Jan
(1834–91)

Czech writer, born in Prague. He was brought up in poverty, an experience reflected in some of his work, notably *Povídky malostranské* (1878, Eng trans *Tales of the Little Quarter*, 1957), and became a teacher before switching to a career in journalism. He suffered from persistent ill-health. He was a disciple of Romanticism but developed into the foremost classical poet in modern Czech literature. He is also known for some excellent prose and drama.
▷M Novotný, *Zivot, Jana Nerudý* (4 vols, 1951–6)

NERUDA, Pablo, born Ricardo Eliecer Neftalí Reyes
(1904–73)

Chilean poet, winner of the Nobel Prize for literature, born in Parral in southern Chile, and educated at Santiago. He made his name with *Veinte poemas de amor y una canción desesperada* (1924, Eng trans *Twenty Love Poems and a Song of Despair*, 1969). From 1927 he held diplomatic posts in various East Asian and European countries (in Spain during the Civil War) and in Mexico from 1940. It was on his way back to Chile from Mexico in 1943 that he visited the Inca city of Macchu Picchu, which was the inspiration of one of his greatest poems. Once settled in Chile again he joined the Communist Party and was elected to the senate in 1945. When the party was outlawed in 1948 he left to travel in Russia and China, returning in 1952. He was awarded the Stalin Prize in 1953. He was the Chilean ambassador in Paris (1970–2). His works include *Residencia en la Tierra* (I, II and III, 1933, 1935, 1947, 'Residence on Earth'), *Alturas de Macchu Picchu* (1945, Eng trans *The Heights of Macchu Picchu*, 1966), which later became part of *Canto General* (published in Mexico, 1950, Eng trans in part as *Poems from Canto General*, 1966), and *Odas elementales* (1954, Eng trans *Elementary Odes*, 1961). In 1971 he was awarded the Nobel Prize for literature. Already ill with cancer, he died of a heart attack shortly after the military overthrew the democratic socialist President Allende.
▷E Rodriguez Moregul, *El viajero immovil* (1967)

NERVAL, Gérard de, properly Gérard Labrunie
(1808–55)

French writer, born in Paris. He was greatly influenced by reading his uncle's collection of occult books as a youth. He published at the age of 20 a translation of **Goethe**'s *Faust*, expanded as *Faust, et le Second Faust* (1840), which Berlioz drew on in his *La Damnation de Faust* (1846). Desultory work, a love affair, fits of restless travel, dissipation, gloom and insanity, and death by his own hand, sum up the story of his life. Nerval wrote admirably both in prose and verse. But his travels, criticism, plays and poems are less interesting than his fantastic short tales, the *Contes et facéties* (1852, 'Stories and Jests'), the semi-autobiographical series of *Filles du feu* (1854, Eng trans *Daughters of Fire*, 1923) and *La Bohème galante* (1855, 'Gallant Bohemian Life'). He is often seen as a precursor of both the Symbolist and Surrealist movements.
▷L Cellier, *Gérard de Nerval* (1956)

NERVO, Amado
(1870–1919)

Mexican modernist writer and poet, whose prolific output fills 30 volumes and includes poetry, novels, short stories, criticism, essays and drama. Born in Tepic and educated at a parochial school where he was taught by Catholic priests, his works are imbued with a quest for truth and beauty. His first creative period, as a writer deeply involved in the Latin-American Modernist movement, was heavily influenced by French Symbolist and Parnassian poets and by other Latin-American Modernist poets. Later he developed a mature style unrelated to any school or poetic movement. His most important themes involve the search for God, the meaning of existence, mysticism, and worldly love.

NESBIT, Edith
(1858–1924)

English writer, born in London, the daughter of an agricultural chemist who died when she was three. She was educated at a French convent, and began her literary career by writing poetry, having met the **Rossettis** and their friends. In 1880 she married the Fabian journalist Hubert Bland. To help with the family finances she turned to popular fiction and children's stories about the Bastaple family, including *The Story of the Treasure Seekers* (1899), *The Would-be-Goods* (1901), *Five Children and It* (1902), *The New Treasure Seekers* (1904), *The Railway Children* (1906) and *The Enchanted Castle* (1907). She also wrote other novels, and ghost stories. After her husband's death in 1914 she married an engineer, Terry Tucker, in 1917. Her last novel was *The Lark* (1922).
▷N Streatfeild, *Magic and Magician* (1958)

NESIN, Aziz
(1915–)

Turkish story writer, novelist, dramatist and satirist, born in Istanbul. He was jailed repeatedly for his left-wing views and satirical publications. *Istanbul Boy* (1977) is a selection in English translation from his autobiography. The scourge of the establishment, he has published over 80 books, mostly of stories.

NESTROY, Johann Nepomuk
(1801–62)

Austrian dramatist, born in Vienna. He began life as an operatic singer, turned playwright and was director of the Vienna Carl-Theater (1854–60). His 60-odd plays, which include *Der böse Geist lumpazivagabundus* (1833, 'The Wicked Ghost Lumpazivagabundus'), *Einen Jux will er sich machen* (1842, 'He Wants to Play Pranks'), *Der Undbedeu tende* (1846) and *Judith und Holofernes* (1849, 'Judith and Holofernes'), are mostly elaborate jibes at theatrical sentimentality characterized by a deft play on words, thoughts and afterthoughts. They revolutionized the Viennese theatre and influenced Wittgenstein.
▷M Preisner, *Johann Nepomuk Nestroy* (1968)

NESVADBA, Josef
(1926–)

Czech writer of science fiction (one of the very few to practise this genre in his country since

Čapek), born in Prague. By profession he is a psychiatrist. He has published many novels and story collections, including *Tarzanova smrt* (1958, 'The Death of Tarzan') and *Kongres o dusi* (1968, 'Congress on the Soul'). A story by him, 'The Planet Circe', appears in *New Writing in Czechoslovakia* (1969).

NEUMANN, Stanislav Kostka
(1875–1947)

Czech poet, novelist and critic, born in Prague into a wealthy family against which he rebelled. He was imprisoned by the Austrian tyrants for advocating independence. An anarchist who finally became a convinced communist, he wrote in a free verse which was for a long time very popular, although he is less widely read today. He was essentially superficial, but the vitalist poetry of his youth, with its open praise of sensuality and its contempt for aristocratic puritanism, was bold and well expressed. He is not unlike **Felipe**, but altogether lacks the Spaniard's subtlety and power of phrase.

NEWBERY, John
(1713–67)

English publisher and bookseller, born in Berkshire, a farmer's son. He settled about 1744 in London as a seller of books and patent medicines. He was the first to publish little books for children, and he was himself—perhaps with **Oliver Goldsmith**—part author of some of the best of them, notably *Goody Two-Shoes*. In 1758 he started the *Universal Chronicle*, or *Weekly Gazette*, in which the *Idler* appeared. In the *Public Ledger* (1760) appeared Goldsmith's *Citizen of the World*. Since 1922 the Newbery Medal has been awarded annually for the best American children's book.

NEWBOLT, Sir Henry John
(1862–1938)

English poet, born in Bilston, Staffordshire. He studied at Clifton School and Oxford, became a barrister, and published a novel *Taken from the Enemy* (1892), followed by *Mordred: A Tragedy* (1895). He is best known, however, for his sea songs—*Admirals All* (1897), which contained 'Drake's Drum', *The Island Race* (1898), *Songs of the Sea*, and others. In World War I he was controller of telecommunications and an official war historian, and published *The Naval History of the Great War* in 1920.

NEWBY, Eric
(1919–)

English travel writer, born in London. He worked briefly in advertising before joining a

Finnish four-masted bark in 1938, an adventure described in *The Last Grain Race* (1956). In 1942 he was captured off Sicily while trying to rejoin the submarine from which he had landed to attack a German airfield. For some years he worked in the rag trade, which he eagerly left to take *A Short Walk in the Hindu Kush* (1958). In 1963, after some years as a fashion buyer to a chain of department stores, he made a 1200-mile descent of the Ganges, described with typical aplomb and wit in *Slowly Down the Ganges* (1966). Later he became travel editor of *The Observer*. Other significant books are *The Big Red Train Ride* (1978), the story of a journey from Moscow to the Pacific on the Trans-Siberian Railway, *Love and War in the Apennines* (1971), his autobiography, *A Traveller's Life* (1982), and *Round Ireland in Low Gear* (1987), about a wet journey on mountain bikes.

NEWBY, P(ercy) H(oward)
(1918–)

English novelist and critic, born in Crowborough, Sussex, in the house once owned by Sir **Arthur Conan Doyle**. Newby taught English in Cairo for many years and in 1949 joined the BBC, becoming Controller of the Third Programme in 1958 and Director of Radio Programmes from 1973 to 1975. Several of his novels reflect his love of Egypt, and while he does not evade the violence of the world, the predominant tone is sympathetic and often touching, as his characters attempt to discover an ethical code by which to live. *Something to Answer For* (1968) won the first Booker Prize in 1969. His other novels include *Leaning in the Wind* (1986) and *Coming in with the Tide* (1991), the latter set in south Wales at the turn of the century, and examining the lives of an ambitious builder and freethinker, and the fiercely religious woman he loves.

NEWMAN, John Henry
(1801–90)

English autobiographer, poet and religious writer. Appointed Vicar of St Mary's, Oxford, he became celebrated as a preacher and leader of the Tractarian (or Oxford) Movement, but in the early 1840s found himself drawing closer to Roman Catholicism. Converted in 1845, he became a Catholic priest and established the Birmingham Oratory. He was frequently embroiled in controversy and wrote extensively on the theological questions of the day, but is famous chiefly for the *Apologia pro Vita Sua* (1864), in which he set out the history of his religious views and defended himself forcefully against the charge of untruthfulness levelled against him by **Charles Kingsley**. This unusual autobiography established him as one of the great stylists in the history of English prose. His poem 'The Dream of Gerontius' (1865), provided the text of Elgar's oratorio, and his hymn 'Lead, kindly light' illustrates his gift for a memorable turn of phrase. Made a cardinal in 1879, Newman avoided public display and remained in Birmingham serving his congregation for the remainder of his life.
▷M Trevor, *Newman's Journey* (1974)

NEXÖ, Martin Andersen
(1869–1954)

Danish novelist, born in a poor quarter of Copenhagen. He spent his boyhood in Bornholm near Nexö (from where he took his surname). From shoemaking and bricklaying he turned to books and teaching, and in 1906 won European fame with *Pelle Erobreren* (4 vols, 1906–10, Eng trans *Pelle the Conqueror*, 1915–17), describing poor life from within and the growth of the Labour movement. He spent considerable time abroad, an experience that fostered his sympathy for the working class; *Morten hin Røde* (1945–7, 'Morten the Red') is an uncharacteristically dull, three-volume sequence.
▷B Houmann, *Martin Anderson Nexö og hans samtid* (1981–2)

NEZVAL, Viteslav
(1900–58)

Czech poet, novelist and dramatist, one of the most important writers of his generation, born in Biskoupky. Dedicated to the communist cause (though never to socialist realism) throughout his earlier life, for a time in the late 1940s and early 1950s he conformed to the shallow demands of his Stalinist cultural masters; but he finally abandoned this stance to complete a body of dedicated and personal work. He began as a 'proletarian' poet in the style of his friend **Jiří Wolker**, but soon became the leading light in Karel Teige's 'Poetist' movement, which advocated 'pure poetry'. When this transformed itself into Surrealism, Nezval went along, but discovered his own individual voice in doing so, producing an extraordinary and prolific body of poetry and fiction. There is currently a dearth of good translations from the poetry of Nezval.
▷A French, *The Poets of Prague* (1969)

NGUGI wa Thiong'o, originally **James T Ngugi**
(1938–)

Kenyan novelist, who writes in English and Kikuyu. He was born in Kamiriithu, in the Kiambu District, and educated at University College, Kampala, Uganda, and at Leeds University. While in England, his first novel,

Weep Not, Child (1964), was published, followed by an earlier novel, *The River Between* (1965), which filled in more of the cultural and socio-political background to the so-called Mau Mau emergency. *A Grain of Wheat* (1967) contrasts the shallow optimism of the Uhuru celebration of Kenyan independence with the violence of Mau Mau. His fourth novel, *Petals of Blood* (1977), has a hectoring, neo-Maoist tone, and clearly cost Ngugi considerable effort to write. In 1977 he was imprisoned by the Kenyan authorities under the catch-all Public Security Act; his experience is recounted in *Detained: A Writer's Prison Diary* (1981). For his next book, known in English as *Devil on the Cross* (trans 1982), he reverted to Kikuyu; it was originally published as *Caitaani Mutharaba-ini* (1980) and it is clear that the incantatory style of the original is largely lost in the prosy discursive English version.
▷D Cook and M Okenimkpe, *Ngugi wa Thiong'o: An Exploration of His Writings* (1983)

NI TSAN, or NI ZAN
(1301–74)

Chinese landscape painter, calligrapher and poet, born in Wu-hsi (Kiangsu Province). Of the Four Great Masters of the Yuan period, he may not be the greatest, but he certainly is the purest. A passionate lover of culture and aesthetics, he nevertheless spent the last 20 years of his life travelling the lakes of the lower Yangtze river with no possessions. His solitary temperament, search for purity and an absolute spiritual certainty and technical discipline permeate his work. Instead of showing the typical development from early to mature, his work consists of a rational, austere and disembodied assemblage of expressive forms, almost reduced to signs, which constituted a radical departure from all previous traditions.

NICHOLS, Peter Richard
(1927–)

English dramatist, born in Bristol. Starting his career as an actor and schoolteacher, he wrote for television before turning to the stage with *A Day in the Death of Joe Egg* (1967), concerning the stress imposed upon a couple whose child is mentally handicapped. Later works include *Privates on Parade* (1977), a musical recalling Nichols's own days in an army concert party; *Passion Play* (1981), dealing with the effects of adultery, and *Poppy* (1983), a musical in pantomime form about the English opium trade wars with China, for which the music was written by Monty Norman. *A Piece of My Mind* (1987), about a disconsolate playwright, was widely seen as an autobiographical work by an under-rated dramatist who had already threatened to retire from the theatre.
▷*Feeling You're Behind* (1984)

NICHOLSON, Norman Cornthwaite
(1914–87)

English poet, whose verse has the craggy quality of his native Lake District, where he continued to live throughout his life and about which he wrote several prose accounts. To the obvious literary associations of the area, he added a new awareness of its modern industrial transformation and, in the 1980s, retrenchment. His first poems were published in a volume (1943) shared with **Keith Douglas** and J C Hall, but after 1954 and *The Pot Geranium* Nicholson effectively gave up poetry for a decade, returning to form only with *A Local Habitation* (1972), which established his reputation. Later collections, such as *Sea to the West* (1981) documented a changed landscape. A *Selected Poems 1940–1982* appeared a year later. His account of life in Millom, Cumberland, was published as *Wednesday Early Closing* (1975).
▷P Gardner, *Norman Nicholson* (1973)

NÍ CHUILLEANÁIN, Eilean
(1942–)

Irish poet, born in Cork. She was educated in Cork and then at Oxford, specializing in Renaissance English, and later became a lecturer at Trinity College Dublin. From *Acts and Monuments* (1972) through to *The Second Voyage* (1986) and in *The Magdalene Sermon* (1990) she lucidly doles out 'a spoonful of light on the cellar walls below' the male-orientated monopoly of Irish writing in the latter part of the 20th century. Though often judged oblique and difficult, her work is a necessary challenge to that accepted hegemony.

NICOL, Abioseh, originally **Davidson Sylvester Hector Willoughby Nicol**
(1924–)

Sierra Leonean short-story writer and poet, born in Freetown. He was educated in Sierra Leone, Nigeria and, following a period as a science teacher in Freetown, at Christ's College, Cambridge. He worked as a doctor in London in the early 1950s, and subsequently at the University Medical School, Ibadan, Nigeria. In later years he was Sierra Leone's High Commissioner in the UK and ambassador to other European countries. Nicol has also worked for the United Nations. He was encouraged to write by **Langston Hughes**, and the stories in *The Truly Married Woman* and *Two African Tales* (both 1965) are reminiscent of Hughes's more lyrical style. Public duties limited his literary output thereafter, but he has produced one volume of poetry (1967) and has written and edited a number of important studies on Third World and women's issues.

▷A Roscoe, *Mother is Gold* (1971)

NICOLAI, Christoph Friedrich
(1733–1811)

German author, bookseller and publisher, born in Berlin. A champion of the German Enlightenment, he soon distinguished himself by a series of critical letters (1756), contributed to many literary journals, and for many years edited the *Allgemeine deutsche Bibliothek* (106 vols, 1765–92, 'General Library of German Writing'). He wrote topographical works, satires, anecdotes of Frederick II, the Great, and an autobiography, recording strange apparitions and hallucinations.

NICOLAY, John George
(1832–1901)

Bavarian-born American journalist and historian, co-author of a 10-volume uncritical biography of President Lincoln, *Abraham Lincoln: A History* (1890). Nicolay was taken to America when he was six years old and grew up in Illinois. He entered journalism and in his mid-twenties was editor and proprietor of the Pittsfield Free Press. He sold the paper, became Secretary of State for Illinois and in 1860 was made Lincoln's private secretary. After the president's assassination he collaborated with his friend John Hay to produce a historical biography. The work was delayed by Nicolay's public appointments—he served as US Consul in Paris from 1865 to 1869 and, on his return, as Marshal of the Supreme Court—but the 10 volumes were finally completed in 1890.

NICOLE, Christopher
(1930–)

West Indian (Barbadian) novelist, author of more than 50 books, some published under such pseudonyms as 'Leslie Arlen' and 'Peter Grange'. His most favoured form is the historical novel, and his historical novels—for example, the 'Amyot' trilogy, (*Amyot's Cay*, 1964; *Blood Amyot*, 1964; *The Amyot Crime*, 1966)—are, like his thrillers, efficient. However, as a critic has said, echoing the consensus: 'Nicole's contribution is sometimes suggestive, but it is too superficial to fulfil its possibilities'.

NIELSEN, Morten
(1922–44)

Danish poet. In just two collections of poetry, *Krigere uden Vaaben* (1943, 'Warriors without Weapons') and *Etterladte Digte* (1945, 'Posthumous Poems'), he strikingly captures the mood in Denmark under the German occupation during World War II. On the one hand, his poems reflect the meaningless, moribund and provisional character of the war years; on the other hand, they express the heightened sense of intensity, the isolated moments of beauty and fulfilment. Nielsen was involved in the resistance against the Nazi occupation and died in a shooting accident when he was only 22. His 'letters to a friend', *Breve til en Ven*, were published in 1962.

▷T Bredsdorff, 'Morten Nielsen', in *Danske digtere i det 20. århundrede*, vol 3 (1981)

NIELSON, Niels Jorgen
(1902–45)

Danish psychological novelist, born near Sikeborg in central Jutland. The reputation of his grim novels set amongst the peasantry of his native region has steadily grown. His most successful novel was the love story *En Kvinde ved Baalet* (1933, 'A Woman by the Bonfire').

NIETZSCHE, Friedrich Wilhelm
(1844–1900)

German philosopher, scholar and writer, though really unclassifiable by conventional labels. He was born in Röcken, Saxony, son of a Lutheran pastor (who died in 1849), and proved himself a brilliant classical student at the school at Schulpforta and at the universities of Bonn and Leipzig. He was appointed Professor of Classical Philology at the University of Basel at the age of 24 and became a Swiss citizen, serving briefly as a medical orderly in 1870 in the Franco–Prussian war but returning to the university in poor health. His first book, *Die Geburt der Tragödie* (1872, Eng trans *The Birth of Tragedy*, 1909), with its celebrated comparison between 'Dionysian' and 'Apollonian' values, was dedicated to Richard Wagner, who had become a friend and whose operas he regarded as the true successors to Greek tragedy. But he broke violently with Wagner in 1876, nominally at least because he thought the Christian convictions expressed in *Parsifal* 'mere playacting' and political expediency. In 1878 he was forced to resign his university position after worsening bouts of his psychosomatic illnesses and he spent most of the next 10 years at various resorts in France, Italy and Switzerland writing and trying to recover his 'shattered health'. But in 1889 he had a complete mental and physical breakdown, a collapse that was probably syphilitic in origin, and he was nursed for the next 12 years first by his mother at Naumberg then by his sister Elizabeth at Weimar. He never recovered his sanity. In the 16 years from 1872 he had produced a stream of brilliant, unconventional works, often aphoristic or poetical in form, which have secured him an enormous, if sometimes cultish, influence in modern intellectual history. The best-known writings are: *Unzeitgemässe Betrachtungen* (1873–6, Eng trans *Thoughts Out of Season*, 1909), *Die Fröliche Wissenschaft* (1882, Eng trans *The Joyful Wisdom*, 1910), *Also Sprach Zarathustra* (1883–92, Eng trans *Thus Spake Zarathustra*, 1900), *Jenseits von Gut und Böse* (1886, Eng trans *Beyond Good and Evil*, 1907), *Zur Genealogie der Moral* (1887, Eng trans *A Genealogy of Morals*, 1897) and *Ecce Homo* (Eng trans 1911, his autobiography, completed in 1888 but withheld by his sister and not published until 1908). One cannot derive systematic 'theories' from these often highly-wrought literary works but the characteristic themes are: the vehement repudiation of Christian and liberal ethics, the detestation of democratic ideals, the celebration of the *Übermensch* (superman) who can create and impose his own law, the death of God, and the life-affirming 'will to power'. His reputation suffered when his views were taken up in a simple-minded and perverted form by the German Nazis, but he is now regarded as a major, though very individual, influence on many strands of 20th-century thought, including existentialism and psychoanalysis, and on figures as various as Jaspers, Heidegger, **Thomas Mann**, **W B Yeats**, Mannheim and Foucault.

NIEVO, Ippolito
(1831–61)

Italian novelist, poet and dramatist, born in Padua. Although little known in his lifetime, Nievo was very prolific, and wrote much prose and verse besides the work for which he is justly most celebrated today: the extraordinary, posthumous *Le confessioni d'un italiano* (1867, Eng trans *The Castle of Fratta*, 1957), known for many years as *Le confessioni di un ottuagenario* because its publisher changed its title. Nievo fought alongside Garibaldi in his 1859 campaign, but then perished in a shipwreck off Sicily. This patriotic presentation of the years which led up to the Risorgimento, presented in the guise of a diary written by a man whose life spanned the years 1775–1855, immediately became famous; later critics have seen in it remarkable anticipations of modernity, because Nievo boldly combines autobiography with historical narrative.
▷ *Italian Quarterly*, 2 (1958)

NIGEL DE LONGCHAMPS
(c.1130–c.1205)

English poet of Norman descent (he may have been related to William de Longchamps,

Chancellor under Richard I). Known as 'Wireker', he was a Benedictine monk of Christ Church, Canterbury, and was possibly born in Longchamps in Normandy. His *Speculum stultorum* (1179–80, Eng trans in *A Mirror for Fools*, 1961), is a satire on monastic orders, with its anti-hero Burnellus, an ass who is unhappy with the size of his tail (a reference to the materialistic ambitions entertained by most priests). Gifted with a good measure of originality, he also wrote a prose complaint against the clergy, and adapted 17 Mary-legends into graceful Latin verse.
▷ F J E Raby, *Secular Latin Poetry* (1957)

NIJHOFF, Martinus
(1894–1953)

Dutch poet, critic, dramatist, translator (of **André Gide**, **T S Eliot** and **Shakespeare**) and editor, a leading figure in his literature. He is usually compared to Eliot, and this is fair inasmuch as Eliot deeply influenced him, and he was, like Eliot again, decisive in the formation of his country's critical tastes. His later poetry, deriving from the 'sensitivism' of the pre-Marxist **Gorter**, but aware of modern European currents, seeks intelligently for meaning: typical is the long poem 'Awater' from his *Nieuwe gedichten* (1934, 'New Poems'), in which the central figure is the man he is trying to understand, the representative of modern society. Nijhoff stands at the opposite pole, in Dutch poetry, to the more powerful **Achterberg**: where the latter is subjective, he tries to be objective.

NIKITIN, Ivor Savvich
(1824–61)

Russian poet, born in Voronezh. His verse veered somewhat uncertainly between imitation of folk-poetry and social protest. The long *Kulak* (1857), a realistic narrative of peasant life, was his best-known and liked poem. He was at his most talented and original when writing melancholy nature lyrics.

NILAND, D'Arcy Francis
(1919–67)

Australian author, born in Glen Innes, New South Wales. After his early years working in the bush, he went to Sydney and in 1942 married the New Zealand writer **Ruth Park**, after which he settled down to writing. Between 1949 and 1952 he won many prizes for short stories and novels, and in 1955 achieved international fame with his novel *The Shiralee* (filmed 1957). This was followed by *Call Me When the Cross Turns Over* (1957), *Gold in the Streets* (1959) and perhaps his best novel, *Dead Men Running* (1969, later an ABC serial). Niland also wrote radio and television plays, and hundreds of short stories, some of which were published in four collections between 1961 and 1966. With Ruth Park he wrote the story of their early married life and writing careers in *The Drums Go Bang* (1956).

NILSSON PIRATEN, Fritiof
(1895–1972)

Swedish novelist and short-story writer, born in Skåne. He is a storyteller in the oral tradition, whose humour and fine style have won lasting popularity and more transient critical notice. The elements of disillusion and tragedy in his writing are apparent even in his first book, *Bombi Bitt och jag* (1932, 'Bombi Bitt and Me'), and these become more marked in his later work. The collection *Historier från Färs* (1940, 'Stories from Färs') contains some of his best writing.
▷ M von Platen, 'Piratens två världar', in *Biktare och bedragare* (1959)

NIMS, John Frederick
(1913–)

American poet, critic and translator (*St John of the Cross*, **Euripides**), born in Muskegon, Michigan. His poetry is well known for its clear-cut precision: a critic has compared it to 'carved, antique furniture, or to cut glass'. He writes in classical metres, and is openly Catholic; 'form,' he has unfashionably written, 'is what ... poems come into the world with, like plants and animals'. *A Local Habitation* (1985) is a collection of his essays on poetry.
▷ *Selected Poems* (1985); J Dickey, *Babel to Byzantium* (1968)

NIN, Anaïs
(1903–77)

American writer, born in Paris to parents of mixed Spanish–Cuban descent. She spent her childhood in Europe until, at the age of eleven, she left France to live in the USA. Ten years later, after her marriage to Hugh Guiler, a banker, she returned to Paris, where she studied psychoanalysis under Otto Rank, became acquainted with many well-known writers and artists and began to write herself. Her first novel, *House of Incest*, was published in 1936 and was followed by volumes of criticism, among them *The Novel of the Future* (1968), and a series of novels including *Winter of Artifice* (1939), *A Spy in the House of Love* (1954) and *Collages* (1964). She also published an early collection of short stories, *Under a Glass Bell* (1944). Ultimately, however, her reputation as an artist and seminal figure in the new feminism of the 1970s rests on her seven *Journals* (1966–83). Spanning the years 1931–74 they are an engrossing

record of an era and some of its most intriguing and avant garde players, as well as a passionate, explicit and candid account of one woman's voyage of self-discovery.
▷ N Scholar, *Anaïs Nin* (1984)

NISTOR, Der, pseud of Pinchas Pinie Kahonovitch
(1884–1950)

Yiddish novelist, born in Berdichev—yet another Jew murdered on Stalin's orders, in the 'hospital' of a forced labour camp. Der Nistor wrote in the Hasidic tradition, and was never (like his contemporary **David Bergelson**), a wholehearted communist. Hasidism, based in the gnostic Cabala, was mystical, ecstatic, inward-looking, and Der Nistor was essentially a Symbolist. He began with prose poems, then proceeded to his major novel cycle, *Di mishpokhe Mashber* (1939–48, 'The Family Mashber'), an ostensibly realistic novel which in fact is alive with hidden meanings in the learned Hasidic tradition. The pseudonym 'Der Nistor' means 'the occult one'. There is a translation of *Di mishpokhe Mashber* into German, and an English one is overdue.
▷ A Roback, *The Story of Yiddish Literature* (1940)

NIVEN, Frederick John
(1878–1944)

Scottish novelist, born in Chile of Scots parentage. Educated at Hutcheson's Grammar School, Glasgow, and Glasgow School of Art, he travelled widely in South America and worked as a journalist (1898–1914). After World War I he emigrated to Canada. He wrote more than 30 novels, mostly set in Glasgow or Canada, including *The Lost Cabin Mine* (1908), *The Justice of the Peace* (1914) and *The Staff at Simsons* (1937). His major work was a trilogy on Canadian settlement, comprising *The Flying Years*, *Mine Inheritance* and *The Transplanted* (1935–44). He also published an autobiography, *Coloured Spectacles* (1938).

NIVEN, Larry (Laurence Cott)
(1938–)

American science-fiction writer, born in Los Angeles. He studied mathematics at Washburn University in Kansas, and has established a reputation as one of the leading writers of 'hard' science fiction, with the emphasis on technological and scientific extrapolation. He published his first story in 1964, and it began the future history series he called *Tales of Known Space*, which includes his most important work, notably the novel *Ringworld* (1970). His commercially astute collaboration with Jerry Pournelle (1933–)

began with the highly readable space epic *The Mote in God's Eye* (1974), and they have written a number of subsequent adventures. Outstanding amongst his recent work are collaborative works (with Steven Barnes, 1952–), including *The Barsoom Project* (1988) and *Dreampark* (1991), about a huge technology development plant in the California desert, and incorporating ideas about virtual reality.

NJEGOS, Petar Petrovíc, originally Rade Tomov
(1813–51)

Montenegrin poet, born in Njegusi. He succeeded his uncle as Prince of Montenegro, which he ruled as Prince–Bishop from 1830, and so took his name from his birthplace. His extraordinary long philosophical poem, *Luca mikrokozma* (1845, Eng trans *The Rays of Microcosm*, 1953; another translation under the same title in *Harvard Slavonic Studies*, III, 1957), puts him in the forefront of the European poets of his time—and perhaps ahead of many of them. In terms of the creation of the world and Satan's revolt, it has never been adequately discussed, nor have its gnostic elements been fully analysed. The poetic drama *Gorski vjenac* (1847, Eng trans *The Mountain Wreath*, 1930), describes the struggles of the Montenegrins against the usurping Turks. Njegos looked to **Milton**, **Hugo** and others, but was a markedly original writer. He died of tuberculosis.
▷M Djilas, *Njegos, Poet, Prince, Bishop* (1966)

NOAILLES, Anna Elizabeth de Brancoven, Comtesse Mathieu de
(1876–1933)

French poet and novelist, born in Paris of Romanian and Greek descent and acclaimed as 'Princesse des lettres'. With her first book, a collection of sensual and musical poems, *Le Coeur innombrable* (1901, 'The Innumerable Heart'), written under the influence of **Francis Jammes**, she won the hearts of the French poetry-reading public. This verse has now dated, but the best of it is still worthy of attention. However, her last poems show her at her most original. A friend to **Barrès**, she was greatly disliked by some French critics, and has hardly had her posthumous due.
▷C Fournet, *Un Grande Poète française moderne: la Comtesse de Noailles* (1950)

NODIER, Charles
(1780–1844)

French writer, born in Besançan. He was persecuted for an anti-Napoleon pamphlet in 1803, and held a number of jobs, including editing a newspaper, before becoming a librarian in 1824 in Paris. His novels were widely known in his own day and he had a profound influence on the Romanticists of 1830, but only his short stories and fairy tales are remembered, such as *Les Vampires* (1820) and *Le Chien de Brisquet* (1844, 'The Dog of Brisquet').
▷J Richer, *Charles Nodier* (1962)

NOOT, Jonker Jan van der
(1539–59)

Dutch poet, born in Brecht. He led an adventurous life: as Sheriff of Antwerp he took part in an uprising in 1567, and was obliged to flee to London and thence to Germany and France. When he could return to Antwerp, it was as a poverty-stricken poet. He is regarded as the first truly Renaissance poet of his country, reflecting the influence of **Ronsard**. He was translated (via a French version) by **Edmund Spenser**.

NORDAU, Max Simon, originally Südfeld
(1849–1923)

Hungarian author and physician, born of Jewish descent in Budapest. He studied medicine and established himself as physician, first in Budapest (1878) and then in Paris (1886). He wrote several books of travel, but became known as the author of works on moral and social questions, including *Die conventionellen Lügen der Kulturmenschheit* (1883, Eng trans *Conventional Lies of Our Civilization*, 1884) and *Entartung* (1892, Eng trans *Degeneration*, 1895), and as a novelist. He was also an active Zionist leader in Europe.

NORDENFLYCHT, Hedvig Charlotta
(1718–63)

Swedish writer of poetry and prose. Born in Stockholm, she was well educated and became one of the first female Swedish authors able to make a living from her work. Her first book of poetry, *Den sörgande Turtur-Dufwan* ('The Mourning Turtle-dove'), was published in 1742, introducing a new subjectivity and a strongly feminine self-assertion. Between 1744 and 1750 she published four volumes of poetry, all under the title of *Qvinligit Tankespel* ('A Woman's Thoughts'). In 1753 she became one of the leading members of a new literary society in Stockholm (*Tankebyggarorden*, 'The Society of Thought Builders') and subsequently published works in conjunction with other members. Famous for the love poetry she wrote late in her life, she is also renowned as the author of a challenge to **Rousseau**'s misogynism, *Fruentimrets försvar* (1761, 'The Defence of Woman').

▷S G Hansson, *Satir och kvinnokamp i Hedvig Charlotta Nordenflychts diktning. Några konflikter, motståndare och anhängare* (1991)

NORDSTRÖM, Ludvig
(1882–1942)

Swedish novelist, short-story writer and Utopian, born in Härnösand. At his best in humorous, often satirical, stories of small-town life, he was less successful in such more ambitious works as the multi-volume novel *Petter Svensks historia* (1925–7, 'Peter Swede's Story'), in which he attempted to express his vision of a Utopia based on urbanization and technology. His books of social reportage such as *Lort-Sverige* (1938, 'Dirt-Sweden') prompted vigorous debate.
▷G Qvarnström, *Från Öbacka till Urbs* (1954)

NORMAN, Marsha
(1947–)

American dramatist and novelist, born in Louisville, Kentucky. She graduated from the University of Georgia and for two years worked with emotionally disturbed children. The heroine of *Getting Out* (1977), her first play to be produced, is a murderer represented as both Arlie and Arlene, a double character from whose dialogue the audience learns of her complex emotional background. Norman's best-known play is the Pulitzer Prize-winning *'night Mother* (1982), a much more naturalistic piece dealing with the relationship between a woman who is about to commit suicide and her mother. The mother and daughter theme is continued in *The Fortune Teller* (1987), a novel examining the ethics of abortion.
▷K Betsko and R Koenig, *Interviews With Contemporary Women Playwrights* (1987)

NORRIS, (Benjamin) Frank(lin)
(1870–1902)

American novelist, born in Chicago. He first studied art but later turned to journalism, and while a reporter for the San Francisco *Chronicle* (1895–6) was involved in the Jameson raid in South Africa. He was influenced by **Zola** and was one of the first American naturalist writers, his major novel being *McTeague* (1899), a story of lower-class life in San Francisco, which formed the basis for the classic movie *Greed* (1924). He also wrote the first two volumes of an unfinished 'epic of the wheat' trilogy, *The Octopus* (1901) and *The Pit* (1903). The essay *The Responsibilities of the Novelist* also appeared posthumously as did *Vandover and the Brute*, a novel whose manuscript was believed lost during the San Francisco earthquake and only published in 1914.
▷F Walker, *Frank Norris: a biography* (1932)

NORRIS, Kathleen, née Thompson
(1880–1966)

American novelist, born in San Francisco. She began writing stories and published her first novel, *Mother*, in 1911. After that she wrote many popular novels and short stories, including *Certain People of Importance* (1922) and *Over at the Crowleys* (1946).

NORTH, Christopher *see* WILSON, John

NORTH, Sterling
(1906–74)

American author, born in Wisconsin. His early work—poetry—appeared during the 1920s in publications like *The Dial* and *Harpers*. He worked in newspapers for several years, eventually becoming the literary editor of two New York papers. His most successful book, a bestseller, was the rural idyll *So Dear To My Heart* (1947), which became a Walt Disney film the following year. A comment on the film—'mainly appealing to well brought up children'—might be applied to North's work as a whole. In the 1950s and 60s he published wholesome, juvenile non-fiction, such as *Abe Lincoln, Log Cabin to White House* (1956).

NORTON, Andre (Alice Mary)
(1912–)

American science-fiction writer, born in Cleveland, Ohio. She adopted the male pseudonym when she began to write fiction for boys. *Sword In Sheath* (1949) is typical of her work for adolescents, being high on adventure and low on subtlety. Her best-known work for adults is the *Witch World* series, which, with its sword-and-sorcery trappings, is as much fantasy as science fiction. *Web of the Witch World* (1964) is a typical volume from the series. Although by no means an innovator in the field, she merits respect as a compassionate novelist who, at least in her adult work, provides an antidote to the mechanical, militaristic spirit of much male science fiction.

NORTON, Caroline Elizabeth Sarah, née Sheridan
(1808–77)

Irish writer and reformer, born in London, grand-daughter of **Richard Brinsley Sheridan**. In 1827 she married a dissolute barrister, the Hon George Chapple Norton (1800–75), and bore him three sons. She took up writing to support the family, and published a successful book of verse, *The Sorrows of Rosalie* (1829). In 1836 she separated from her husband, who brought an action of 'criminal conversation' (adultery) against Lord Melbourne, obtained custody of the children and tried to obtain the profit from her books. Her spirited pamphlets led to improvements in the legal status of women in relation to infant custody (1839) and marriage and divorce (1857). She married Sir William Stirling-Maxwell in 1877, but died soon afterwards. Her other books of verse included an attack on child labour in *Voice from the Factories* (1836), *The Dream* (1840) and *The Lady of Garaye* (1862), and she also published three novels. She was the model for **George Meredith**'s central character in his novel *Diana of the Crossways* (1885).

NORTON, Mary
(1903–92)

English children's novelist, born in Leighton Buzzard. Aiming to become an actress she joined the Old Vic Theatre Company in the 1920s, but marriage took her to Portugal, where she first began to write, and later to America. Returning to Britain in 1943, she published her first book two years later. But it was *The Borrowers* (1952), an enchanting story about tiny people living beneath the floorboards of a big house, which established her as one of the foremost children's writers of her generation, and which won the Carnegie Medal. There were four sequels, the last being *The Borrowers Avenged* (1982).

NORTON, Thomas
(1532–84)

English lawyer, MP, and poet, born in London. He was a successful lawyer and a zealous Protestant, married to a daughter of Thomas Cranmer. He translated Calvin's *Christianae Religionis Institutio* (1561). With **Thomas Sackville** he was joint author of the tragedy *Gorboduc*, which was performed before Queen Elizabeth in 1562, and has some claim to be considered the first proper English tragedy.

NORWID, Cyprian Kamil
(1821–83)

Polish author and painter, since 1901 regarded as Poland's greatest writer. After brief success as a poet in Warsaw in his youth, he had little recognition in his lifetime. He lived in New York for three years, and finally went to Paris (he was befriended there by Chopin), where he lived in poverty from 1855 until his death in a home for destitute Poles. He was ridiculed for his later poetry, which was anti-romantic and decidedly 'modern' in tone. He anticipated Symbolism, and introduced free verse into Polish poetry. His poems are highly intellectual, although they sometimes contain vernacular expressions; they demand much effort from the reader— once again, in a 'modernist' style. His revival came in 1901, and has continued ever since. His plays are of the closet variety, but are deeply interesting. Not all of his essays and other prose, which included stories, have been preserved. Little has been translated into English, but good examples of poems are to be found in *Five Centuries of Polish Poetry* (1960). It is generally conceded that Norwid is, because of his aloof irony, a difficult writer; but no non-Pole who has studied him in depth has come away without recognizing him as both unique and of very high international stature. To Poles he is now a—to some *the*— central literary figure.
▷ *Slavonic and East European Review*, 27 (1949)

NOSAACK, Hans Erich
(1901–77)

German fiction writer, poet, critic and dramatist, from Hamburg, praised by **Jean-Paul Sartre**. His leading work, and his most accessible, is the novel *Der Fall d'Arthez* (1968, Eng trans *The d'Arthez Case*, 1971), a subtle and even prophetic work set in a state in which 'authenticity' is a treasonable crime, and whose protagonists strive, in various ways, to achieve it.

NOUVEAU, Germain
(1851–1920)

French poet, born in Pourrières. **Aragon** unwisely pronounced him, after his death, to be the equal of **Rimbaud**, whom Nouveau had met in the course of squandering a small inheritance. Under the influence of **Verlaine**, he converted to Catholicism. His poetry was hardly known until the surrealists and Aragon re-discovered it, although he had known many writers, including Jean Richpin, **Bourget** and the great **Charles Cros**. After being shipped home from the Lebanon by the French consulate, and conducting a long affair with Valentine Renault, he suffered a five-month bout of 'religious mania' (alcoholism). His poetry consists for the most part of overblown rhetoric in the style of Rimbaud, but there are occasionally inspired passages, which, together with his exotic life, gave the surrealists plenty of reason to admire him.
▷ L Forestier, *Germain Nouveau* (1971, in French)

NOVAK, Helga, pseud of **Helga Maria Karlsdottir**
(1935–)

German poet, story-writer, and writer of radio plays, born in Berlin. She lived first in

East Germany, then (from 1961 to 1970) in Iceland, and since then in her native city. She could not publish until 1965, when her first collection of satirical poems, *Ballada von der reisenden Anna* ('Ballad of Wandering Anna') appeared. Her most characteristic work is the overtly feminist and, once more, satirical, *Eines Tages hat sich die Sprechpuppe nicht mehr ausziehen lassen* (1972, 'One Day the Talking Doll Refused to be Undressed'). Translations of her work are available in *German Women Writers of the Twentieth Century* (1978).

NOVAK, Vjenceslav
(1859–1905)

Croatian novelist, poet and dramatist, influenced by **Zola**, who wrote in a naturalistic style of the harsh poverty and squalor of life on the Adriatic coast. None of his books was translated into English.

NOVALIS, pseud of Friedrich von Hardenberg
(1772–1801)

German Romantic poet and novelist, born at Wiederstadt. He was called the 'Prophet of Romanticism'. At Weissenfels (1795) he fell in love with a beautiful girl, whose early death left a lasting impression upon him, and in whose memory he wrote the prose lyrics of *Hymnen an die Nacht* (1800, Eng trans *Hymns to the Night*, 1948). He also published *Geistliche Lieder* (1799, Eng trans *Devotional Songs*, 1910). He left two philosophical romances, both incomplete, *Heinrich von Ofterdingen* (1802) and *Die Lehrlinge zu Sais* (1802, 'The Apprentices at Sais'). He died of tuberculosis.
▷F Hiebel, *Novalis* (1972, in German)

NOVO, Salvador
(1904–74)

Mexican poet, critic, translator (**O'Neill**, **Synge**) and playwright, born in Mexico City, one of the leading members of the *Contemporáneos* group, including **Gorostiza** and **Jaime Torres Bodet**. A homosexual, his affairs became legendary; but this caused him surprisingly little trouble in a distinctly *macho* society—until he took up a highly reactionary political attitude, when, in 1968, he fervently applauded the massacre of the students by President Díaz Ordaz. But a critic wrote: 'the fact that his politics were reactionary, unlike his attitude towards sexuality, does not invalidate his work, it simply determines it'. As a homosexual poet, he is not in the class of **Cernuda**, **Penna** or **Cavafy**, but his elegant and often playful irony has a distinct charm.

▷A Mangāna-Esquival, *Salvador Novo* (1971, in Spanish)

NOWAK, Tadeusz
(1930–)

Polish poet, story writer and novelist, born into a peasant family in Sikorzyce (near Dabrowa Tarmowska). He was educated in Kracow. Like so many Polish poets, his poetry is based in folk traditions; some have described him as a 'peasant surrealist'. In the 1960s he apparently gave up writing verse, to concentrate on novels and stories.

NOWRA, Louis
(1950–)

Australian playwright and novelist, born in Melbourne. Of his plays the best known are *Inner Voices* (1977), in which the central figure is Ivan, an imprisoned claimant to the Russian throne, and *Inside the Island* (published 1981 with *The Precious Woman*). He has written two novels, *The Misery of Beauty* (1976) and *Palu* (1987); the last again deals with imprisonment, this time as a political sacrifice of the wife of a New Guinea president. Nowra's autobiographical play *Summer of the Aliens* was produced in 1993 with the author as narrator; *The Temple* (1993) explores in documentary style the excesses of Australia's corporate high-flyers before the stock-market crash of the late 1980s and *Radiance* (1993) concerns three aboriginal sisters who meet again at the funeral of their mother.

NOYES, Alfred
(1880–1958)

English poet, born in Staffordshire. He began writing verse as an undergraduate at Oxford, and on the strength of getting a volume published in his final year he left without taking a degree. This book, *The Loom of Years* (1902), which was praised by **George Meredith**, was followed by *The Flower of Old Japan* (1903) and *The Forest of Wild Thyme* (1905), both of which attracted some notice. Noyes now turned to the subject of some of his most successful work—the sea, and in particular the Elizabethan tradition. *Forty Singing Seamen* (1908) and the epic *Drake* (1908) were in this vein. Having married an American, he travelled in the USA and became Visiting Professor of Poetry at Princeton (1914–23). Between 1922 and 1930 appeared his trilogy *The Torchbearers*, praising men of science. He published literary essays in *Some Aspects of Modern Poetry* (1924), a defence of traditionalism. He also wrote plays, and studies of **William Morris** and **Voltaire**. He wrote an anecdotal memoir, *Two Worlds for Memory* (1953).

NU'AYMAH, Mikhail
(b.1889)

Prolific Lebanese writer. He was born in Biskinta, at the base of the snow-capped Sannine mountains, where the simple life of the inhabitants and majestic landscape inspired his literary works, and to which he returned after 25 years' absence. Between 1902 and 1932 Nu'aymah studied and lived in Palestine, Russia, the USA and France. In Russia, along with his religious studies, he immersed himself in the works of **Gogol** and **Chekhov**, and later in the USA in those of the Transcendentalists. As a result, and together with the literary group which included **Kahlil Gibran**, he revitalized the art of Arabic fiction and literary criticism. Most notable of his translated works are *Fathers and Sons* (1917), a drama set during Ottoman times; *The Book of Mirdad* (1948), encapsulating his Sufistic notions, and *Memoirs of a Vagrant Soul* (1952).

▷N Nuaymah, *Mikhail Nuaymah* (1978, in Arabic)

NÚÑEZ DE ARCE, Gaspar
(1834–1903)

Spanish poet, dramatist and statesman, born in Valladolid. He held office in the government in 1883 and 1888, and in 1894 received a national ovation at Toledo. As a lyric poet he may be styled the 'Spanish Tennyson', and among his poems are *Gritos del Combate* (1875, 'Cries of Battle'), *Última Lamentación de Lord Byron* (1879, 'Lord Byron's Last Lamentation'), *El vértigo* (1879, 'Vertigo'), *La Pesca* (1884, 'Fishing') and *La Maruja* (1886). His plays include *La Cuenta del Zapatero* (1859, 'The Countess of Zapatero') and *El Haz de Leña* (1872, 'The Bundle of Firewood').

▷J Romano, *Gaspar Núñez de Arce* (1944)

NUTTALL, Jeff
(1933–)

British poet and controversialist, probably still best known for his polemic *Bomb Culture* (1968), very much a tract for the times. During the late 1960s, he was much involved in the performance art, politics-as-spectacle movement; he founded the mixed-media People Show in 1967, published his verse *Journals* and appeared in *Penguin Modern Poets 12* the following year. His verse is as passionately committed as **Allen Ginsberg**'s but, unlike the American's, his style did not survive the apocalyptic temper of 1968, which *Bomb Culture* helped define in the UK. Later work has been rather tired; the best of his verse is in *Poems 1962–69* (1970). Nuttall has written some fiction, most notably *Oscar Christ and the Immaculate Conception* (1968) and the overlooked *The Patriarchs: An Early Summer Landscape* (1978).

NYE, Robert
(1939–)

English novelist, poet and journalist. He grew up in London and the Home Counties, and has been closely associated with both *The Scotsman* and *The Times* as a literary reviewer, to which he brings considerable intelligence and taste, and an infectious love of poetry. He began writing verse very early and published two volumes, *Juvenilia* (1961, 1963), before toughening up his style and switching his attention largely to prose fiction. A collected edition of his verse appeared in 1992. Nye's first novel was the rather **Joyce**an *Doubtfire* (1968). *Tales I Told My Mother* (1969) is elegantly intertextual. Nye discovered his métier with *Falstaff* (1976), a novel about the original of **Shakespeare**'s character; ever since he has concentrated on semi-mythic historical characters—*Merlin* (1978), *Faust* (1980), Ralegh in *The Voyage of the Destiny* (1982), *The Memoirs of Lord Byron* (1989), and the original of Barbe-Bleue in *The Life and Death of My Lord Gilles de Rais* (1990). He is an able playwright and a notably uncondescending writer for children, but remains, chiefly, a poet.

O

OATES, Joyce Carol
(1938–)

American writer, born in Millersport, New York. She was educated at Syracuse University and the University of Wisconsin. Married in 1961, she taught English at the University of Detroit (1961–7), then was appointed Professor of English at the University of Windsor in Ontario. A hugely prolific novelist, story writer and essayist, she published her first novel, *With Shuddering Fall*, in 1964. Splintered with violence and impressive in its social scope, her fiction challenges received ideas about the nature of human experience. *Them* (1969), her fourth novel, won a National Book Award. Later novels include *Marya: A Life* (1986) and *You Must Remember This* (1989). Her interest in pugilism emerged in *On Boxing* (1987), first published in the *Ontario Review*, with which she has long had a connection.

OBALDIA, René de
(1918–)

French avant-garde playwright, novelist and poet. He was born in Hong Kong, but moved to France with his mother at an early age, and attended the Lycée Condorcet in Paris. As a naturalized Frenchman he had to serve in World War II, and spent a long period in a concentration camp. Released in 1945, he published a volume of Surrealist poetry, *Midi*, in 1949, and became a regular contributor to many literary reviews, including *Le Mercure de France* and *Le Contemporain*. He published two prize-winning novels, *Fugue à Waterloo* (1955) and *Le Centenaire* (1960), but is better known for his plays: *Génousie* (1960), *Le Satyre de la villette* (1963) and *Du vent dans les branches de Sassafras* (1965). A further volume of his poetry, *Innocentines*, appeared in 1969.

OBENG, R E
(20th century)

African writer, author of the first novel proper in English, *Eighteenpence* (1943), by a native African (published at his own expense in Ilfracombe, England), and therefore of historical importance. Much influenced by the Bible and missionaries' comforting words, it is nonetheless a genuinely pioneering book.

OBEY, André
(1892–1975)

French dramatist and novelist, born in Douai, whose first success (he had previously collaborated with **Denys Amiel**) was with *Noë* (1931, Eng trans *Noah* in *Twenty Best European Plays on the American Stage*, 1963, ed John Gassner), well described as 'histrionic theatre-poetry'. It played with success in various capital cities. **Thornton Wilder** adapted his *Le Viol de Lucrèce* (1931) as *Lucrece* (1932). A playwright boldly presentational in his techniques, he did much for the theatre in his year (1946–7) as Director of the Comédie-Française. He had many other fashionable and skilful successes.

OBLIGADO, Rafael
(1851–1920)

Argentinian poet, born in Buenos Aires. He met **Darío** and, being wealthy, was able to act as host to all the important Argentinian writers of his time—and some others. He wrote only a single collection, *Poesías* (1885, revised and enlarged 1906). This is defiant of European modes, and tries to develop national themes in the style of **Echeverria**, the chief influence upon him; but he wrote nothing of the first rank.

O'BRIEN, Edna
(1932–)

Irish novelist, short-story writer and playwright, born in Tuamgraney, County Clare. Educated at the Convent of Mercy, Loughrea, and at the Pharmaceutical College of Dublin, she practised pharmacy briefly before becoming a writer. Her dominant themes are loneliness, guilt and loss, articulated in musical prose. 'My aim', she has written, 'is to write books that in some way celebrate life and do justice to my emotions'. Among her celebrated books are *The Country Girls* (1960), *The Lonely Girl* (1962), *Girls in Their Married Bliss* (1964), *August is a Wicked Month* (1965) and *A Pagan Place* (1970). *The Collected Edna O'Brien*, containing nine novels, was published in 1978, and she has also published several collections of short stories. Recent novels include a collection of *The Country Girls Trilogy* with an epilogue (1986), and *The High Road* (1988). She has also written a number of plays and screenplays, a book of verse, *On the Bone* (1989), and some non-fiction.

▷G Eckley, *Edna O'Brien* (1974)

O'BRIEN, (Michael) Fitz-James
(1828–62)

Irish–American writer, born in County Cork. He composed sentimental poems from an early age, including the once popular 'Loch Ina' (1845). After spending an inherited fortune in London, he arrived in New York in 1852, immediately becoming a figure in literary Bohemia. He had some success with plays, particularly *A Gentleman from Ireland* (1854), and wrote numerous poems, stories and articles. However, he is now remembered mainly for a few fantastic stories influenced by **Poe**, such as 'The Diamond Lens' (1858) and 'What Was It?' (1859); these display much imagination, employing to great effect convincing shifts from the mundane to the bizarre, and pseudo-scientific explanations. O'Brien died fighting for the Union in the Civil War.

▷F Wolle, *Fitz-James O'Brien: A Literary Bohemian of the Eighteen-Fifties* (1944)

O'BRIEN, Flann, pseud of Brian O'Nolan
(1911–66)

Irish writer, born in Strabane, County Tyrone, the third child in a family of 12. His father working in the Customs and Excise, his early life was peripatetic but the family settled for a spell in a large house near Tullamore where Irish was the common tongue. Later they moved to Dublin and it was here that his formal education began at the Christian Brothers' school, renowned for its rigidly basic and brutally applied methods of education. In 1927 the family moved to the seaside suburb of Blackrock, where he wrote his earliest and finest books. He attended Blackrock College and University College, Dublin, studying German, Irish and English, although much of his time was frittered away at billiards or in pubs. From 1933 to 1934 he was in Germany where there is speculation (but no proof) that he married a girl called Clara who died of consumption a month later. He returned to Dublin, finished his thesis, had it rejected (it was finally accepted in 1935) and founded *Blather*, whose six editions he wrote mainly himself. On Irish radio he gave talks on literature, completed his eccentric but brilliant novel *At Swim-Two-Birds* (published four years later in 1939) and joined the Irish Civil Service, which occupied him until his premature retirement in 1953.

The death of his father and the need to supplement his salary to support his kin led him reluctantly to submit *At Swim-Two-Birds* to publishers. Its acceptance by Collins owed much to **Graham Greene**'s enthusiasm and led to the birth of the Flann O'Brien pseudonym. A year later, in 1940, came the debut of 'Myles na Gopaleen', the pseudonym under which he contributed a column to the *Irish Times* for some 20 years, and which he regarded as not so much a *nom de plume* as a *nom de guerre*. His second novel *An Béal Bocht* was published in Irish in 1941 (*The Poor Mouth*, 1973); *The Third Policeman*, written and rejected in 1940, was published posthumously in 1967. He is best known as an idiosyncratic newspaper columnist, and various anthologies appeared after his death—*The Best of Myles* (1968), *The Various Lives of Keats and Chapman and the Brother* (1976) and *Myles From Dublin* (1985).

▷T O'Keeffe, *Myles* (1973)

O'BRIEN, Kate
(1897–1974)

Irish playwright and novelist, born in Limerick. She was educated at Laurel Hill Convent, Limerick, and University College, Dublin. At 30 she began a career in London as playwright and in 1931 she published her prize-winning *Without My Cloak*, followed by *Mary Lavelle* (1936), *Pray for the Wanderer* (1938), *The Land of Spices* (1941), *The Last of Summer* (1943), *That Lady* (1946) and *As Music and Splendour* (1958). A remarkable observer of life, she was injured by a profoundly unhappy marriage to the Dutch historian Gustaaf Johannes Renier, and her novels are best understood by appreciation of her consciousness of a lesbian sexual identity. Her work reflected deep knowledge of Ireland and Spain as may be seen from her *Farewell Spain* (1937) and *My Ireland* (1962).

▷*English Diaries and Journals* (1943)

O'BRIEN, Richard Barry
(1847–1918)

Irish nationalist historian and biographer, born in Kilrush, County Clare. He studied at Newman's ill-fated Catholic University of Dublin, after which he was called to the Irish (1874) and English (1875) bars without practising much. He was drawn into skilful and detailed historical writing in the cause of Irish home rule, producing many detailed works whose nationalist apologetics did not greatly weaken their considerable historical value. His masterpiece, *The Life of Charles Stewart Parnell* (1898), is one of the great political biographies of all time. He was founder, chairman and (from 1906) president of the Irish Literary Society in London from 1892 to 1911.

O'BRIEN, Tim (William Timothy)
(1948–)

American novelist. Born and raised in a Minnesota prairie town, he served as a soldier in Vietnam (1969–70). On his return he studied for his doctorate in political science at Harvard and became a reporter for the *Washington Post*. His war experiences, described in his acclaimed war memoir *If I Die in a Combat Zone* (1973), strongly influence his novels. In *Going After Cacciato* (1979), which won the US National Book Award, Vietnam is the setting for an exploration of the nature of fear and courage. In *The Nuclear Age* (1986) the instinct for survival is frustrated by the fear of war and death. A thought-provoking writer with a delicate touch, O'Brien has won widespread praise both for his literary talent and for his ability to articulate the experience of Vietnam War veterans. The combination of writer and ex-soldier is most evident in *The Things They Carried* (1990), a highly personal collection of war stories.

Ó BRUADAIR, Dáibhidh (David)
(?1625–1698)

Irish Gaelic poet, recording the destruction of his culture, born in Cork into a family of some substance. He was impressively educated, but the wars and proscriptions drove his FitzGerald patrons in Kerry into danger and exile, and the poet's later verses dramatically and lyrically convey his fall from places of patronage and honour to the status of farm labourer. His work, complex and resourceful, innovative as well as traditional, offers a bridge from the earlier, assured world of the Gaelic bards to the dark dispossession of the next century. The Irish Texts Society published a bilingual edition of his surviving poems, *Duanaire Dháibhidh Uí Bhruadair* (1913–17).

Ó CADHAIN, Máirtín, anglicized name Martin Kane
(1906–70)

Irish Gaelic short-story writer and novelist, born in Spiddal, Connemara, the Gaelic-speaking area of Galway in the west of Ireland, who worked for a time as a schoolteacher. He was actively involved in the IRA and interned during World War II. In 1969 he became Professor of Irish at Trinity College Dublin. The second of five collections of short-stories, *An Braon Broghach* (1948, Eng trans 'The Hare Lip', in *The Field Day Anthology of Irish Writing*, 1991), established him as a stern critic of accepted social conventions. The novel *Cré Na Cille* (1949, 'The Clay of the Churchyard') is a commentary by the dead beneath the earth on the perfidities of the politicians in the 'fledgling Free State' on the 'uppersoil'. An unrepentant advocate of revolution, Ó Cadhain had a strong influence on subsequent generations of writers, a role which has often detracted attention from the stylish, inventive originality of his writing. ▷ *Pápéir Bhána Pápéir Bhreaca* (1969); A Titley, *Máirtín Ó Cadhain* (1975)

OCAMPO, Silvina
(1906–)

Argentinian writer, born into a wealthy family in Buenos Aires. With her sister **Victoria Ocampo** she is one of the most important women writers and poets of the first half of the 20th century in Latin America. She and her husband **Adolfo Bioy Casares** held an influential literary tertulia (conversation group) which included writers and poets like **Jorge Luis Borges**, **Maria Luisa Bombal** and **Ezequiel Martinez Estrada**. She writes dramatic and amorous poetry, as well as collections of short stories and juvenile fiction. Her titles include *Sonetos del jardin* (1948, 'Garden Sonnets') and the short-story collection *Informe del cielo y del infierno* ('Report on Heaven and Earth'). She is also an accomplished painter.

OCAMPO, Victoria
(1891–1979)

Argentinian writer, born into a rich family in Buenos Aires, the sister of **Silvina Ocampo**. She is most highly regarded as the editor and motivational force behind one of Latin America's most important literary journals, *Sur*, which combined the mission of publishing new Latin-American writers (like **Jorge Luis Borges**) and translations of major North American and European writers. Born into a wealthy family, she lived in Paris and London as a child, and learned French, English and Italian. Her literary creations are extensive, including biography (*338171 T.E.*, 1942, a biography of **T S Eliot**), essays and criticism (*Testimonios* is a 10-volume collection of these), novels, and translations.

O'CASEY, Sean
(1884–1964)

Irish playwright, born in a poor part of Dublin. He picked up whatever education he could and worked as a labourer and for nationalist organizations before beginning his career as a dramatist. His early plays, dealing with low life in Dublin—*Shadow of a Gunman* (1923) and *Juno and the Paycock* (1924)—were written for the Abbey Theatre. Later he became more experimental and impressionistic. Other works include *The Plough and the Stars* (1926), *The Silver Tassie* (1929), *Cockadoodle Dandy* (1949) and *The Bishop's Bonfire* (1955). He also wrote essays, such as *The Flying Wasp* (1936). He was awarded the Hawthornden Prize in 1926. His autobiography, begun in 1939 with *I Knock at the Door*, continued through six volumes to *Sunset and Evening Star* (1954).

▷E O'Casey, *Sean* (1971)

O CONAIRE, Pádraic (Patrick Conroy)
(1883–1928)

Irish Gaelic writer, born in Galway and educated in Gaelic-speaking Rosmuc. He went to sea, and spent many years in the London civil service, which he left in 1913 having won prizes in 1904 and 1909 for stories in Gaelic. He won fame as a novelist, essayist, travel-writer and short-story writer of deceptive simplicity and fine construction, sometimes working in children's fiction, sometimes taking up themes of psychological complexity which worried the more puritanical elements in the Gaelic revival. His later years were spent in writing and teaching Irish, chiefly in Galway.

▷*An Crann Géagach* (1919)

O'CONNER, Elizabeth, properly Barbara McNamara
(1913–)

Australian writer, born in Dunedoo, New South Wales, who has published three novels dealing with aspects of rural life in northern Queensland: *The Irishman* (1960), *Find a Woman* (1963) and *Spirit Man* (1980). *The Irishman*, the experiences of teamster Paddy Doolan and his sons, won the **Miles Franklin** Award in 1960 and was filmed in 1978. Her two best-known works, though, are perhaps *Steak for Breakfast* (1958) and *A Second Helping* (1969), autobiographical accounts of her life on outback cattle stations, reminiscent of **Monica Dickens**'s best work.

O'CONNOR, Edwin
(1918–68)

American novelist, born in Rhode Island. By profession he was a radio announcer, writer and producer, which provided him with the material for *The Oracle* (1951), about a 'radio personality'. His most famous book, which was filmed, was *The Last Hurrah* (1956), about a crooked but warm-hearted Boston political boss; it was based on the career of the politician James M Curley. *The Edge of Sadness* (1961), a novel graver in tone, about a Roman Catholic priest, and also set in Boston, won the Pulitzer Prize.

O'CONNOR, (Mary) Flannery
(1925–64)

American novelist, born in Savannah, Georgia, whose environs she rarely left during her short life. She was educated at Peabody High School, Midgeville, Georgia, graduating in 1942. Thereafter she attended Georgia State College for Women and the University of Iowa. Brought up a Catholic and in the 'Christ-haunted' bible-belt of the Deep South, she homed in on Protestant fundamentalists who dominated the region. The characters in her work seem superficially similar to those photographed by Diane Arbus: grotesque, deformed, freakish. This to her, however, was reality, and her heightened depicton of it is unforgettable. *Wise Blood* (1952), the first of her two novels, is a bizarre tragi-comedy, and its theme of vocation is taken up again in her second, *The Violent Bear It Away* (1960). Regarded as one of the finest short-story writers of her generation, her work in that form can be found in *A Good Man Is Hard To Find and other stories* (1955, 'nine stories about original sin'), and *Everything That Rises Must Converge* (1965), affected by the pain she was suffering in the closing stages of chronic disseminated lupus. *The Habit of Being: Letters of Flannery O'Connor* was published in 1979.

▷L Getz, *Flannery O'Connor, her life and library* (1980)

O'CONNOR, Frank, pseud of Michael O'Donovan
(1903–66)

Irish writer, born in Cork. He was a member of the Irish Republican Army in his teens (1921–2), fought in the War of Independence and was imprisoned. He then worked as a railway clerk in Cork, and later a librarian in Wicklow, Cork and Dublin. Although he wrote plays and some excellent literary criticism—*Art of the Theatre* (1947), *The Modern Novel* (1956), *The Mirror in the Roadway* (1957)—his best medium was almost exclusively the short story. **W B Yeats** said of him that he was 'doing for Ireland what Chekhov did for Russia'. Representative titles include *Guests of the Nation* (1931), *Bones of Contention* (1936), *Crab Apple Jelly* (1944), *Travellers' Samples* (1956), *Domestic Relations* (1957) and *My Oedipus Complex* (1963). He also wrote two volumes of memoirs, *An Only Child* (1961) and *My Father's Son* (1969), several plays, translations of Irish verse, a novel, *Dutch Interior* (1940), the critical studies *The Lonely Voice* (1963) and *Shakespeare's Progress* (1960), and a biography of Michael Collins, *The Big Fellow* (1937).

Ó'DÁLAIGH, Donnchadh Mór
(1170–1244)

Irish poet; he was the greatest religious poet of medieval Ireland. He was described by the Four Masters (in *The Annals of the Kingdom of Ireland*, written by four monks, and completed in 1636) as a poet who never was and never would be surpassed. His most famous

poem, 'Sorrowful My Pilgrimage to Loch Dearg', was translated by **Sean O'Faolain** in *With the Gaels of Wexford* (1955).
▷L McKenna, *Don Dé* (1922)

Ó DÁLAIGH, Muireadhach Albanach
(c.1180–c.1250)

Irish poet, an outstanding character of his time. Muireadhach is perhaps the only poet who has killed a tax-collector (with an axe). Owing to this indiscretion, he had to flee his home in County Sligo, and ended in Scotland (hence 'Albanach'). His poem on the death of his (probably Scottish) wife, beginning 'I was robbed of my soul last night', is one of the most famous in Irish literature.
▷R Flower, *The Irish Tradition* (1947)

O'DELL, Scott
(1898–)

American novelist, born in Los Angeles, and educated at the University of Wisconsin, Stanford University, and the University of Rome. He was a film cameraman in the 1920s, a newspaperman and a book reviewer, and served in the US Air Force in World War II. He has three adult novels to his name but is best known for his children's books, especially *Island of the Blue Dolphins* (1960), which is based on the true story of a young girl left alone on an island for several years. He has won numerous awards, including the **Newbery** Medal (1961) and the **Hans Christian Andersen** International Medal (1972).

ODETS, Clifford
(1906–63)

American playwright and actor, born in Philadelphia. In 1931 he joined the Group Theatre, New York, under whose auspices his early plays were produced. The most important American playwright of the 1930s, his works are marked by a strong social conscience and grow largely from the conditions of the great depression of that time. They include *Waiting for Lefty*, *Awake and Sing* and *Till the Day I Die*, all produced in 1935, and *Golden Boy* (1937). He was responsible for a number of film scenarios, including *The General Died at Dawn*, *None but the Lonely Heart* (which he directed), *Deadline at Dawn* and *The Big Knife*.
▷M B Gibson, *Odets, American Playwright: the years from 1906 to 1940* (1981)

Ó DIREÁIN, Máirtín
(1910–88)

Irish Gaelic poet, born on the Aran Islands. He spent most of his life as a civil servant in Dublin. He published some of his own poems

during the 1940s and quickly became the leading Gaelic poet of his generation. *Dánta 1939–1979* (1980, 'Poems') established him as a writer for whom memory was of paramount importance in the elucidation of experience. In *Ómós do John Millington Synge* (nd, 'Homage to John Millington Synge') he wrote 'The book was always in your heart/You brought the words in it to Life'. This could equally be applied to his own supple encapsulation of a declining Gaelic oral culture which he dignified into a lasting literary one.
▷S Deane (ed), *Field Day Anthology of Irish Writing: Vol 3* (1991)

Ó DOMHNAILL, Maghnas
(d.1563)

Irish poet and politician, of the house of O'Donnell. He wrote love poems in the troubadour manner, as well as satires. His prose *Life* of the saint, Colum Cille, written in 1532, is his most famous single work.

O'DONNELL, Peadar (Peter)
(1893–1986)

Irish revolutionary and writer, born in Meenmore, County Donegal, the son of a small farmer. He reflected the vigorous agrarian traditions of his native Donegal and added to them a lifelong republicanism and socialism. First a teacher, then labour organizer, then guerrilla republican leader, he opposed the 1921 Anglo–Irish Treaty, was captured in Civil War fighting, and escaped after a 41-day hunger-strike. A vigorous publicist and editor of *An Phoblacht*, the official IRA newspaper, he gave (and then withdrew) qualified support for Eamon de Valera in 1932, left the IRA in 1934, fought for the Spanish Republic in 1936–7 and wrote extensively on his experiences: the novel *Storm* (1925) on the Anglo–Irish war, *The Gates Flew Open* (1934) on his imprisonment, *Salud!* (1937) on the Spanish Civil War, and *There Will Be Another Day* (1963) on his campaign against land annuities which led to the Anglo–Irish Economic War of the 1930s. His editorship of the literary monthly, *The Bell* (1946–54), was invaluable in furthering Irish writing. His finest work is *Islanders* (1927), but his last novel, *The Big Windows* (1955), is also evocative of his power in social depiction.

O'DOWD, Bernard Patrick
(1866–1953)

Australian poet and journalist, born in Beaufort, Victoria, who, while a lifelong radical and republican, managed to combine his militancy with a career in public service. He was Librarian to the Supreme Court in Melbourne for 16 years and then from 1913 a parliamentary draughtsman. In that role he edited several law books and latterly, as head of the department (1931–5), was responsible for major Victorian state legislation. Meanwhile he was writing for and publishing various radical periodicals and in 1903 published his first collection of verse, *Downward?*, which included his best-known poem, 'Australia'. There followed *The Silent Land* (1906), *Dominions of the Boundary* (1907) and *The Seven Deadly Sins* (1909). After *Alma Venus* (1921) he wrote very little; a collected edition of his verse was published in 1941.

O'DUFFY, Eimar Ultan
(1893–1935)

Irish satirical playwright and novelist, born in Dublin. Educated at Stonyhurst (Jesuit) College in Lancashire, at first he followed his father in studying dentistry at University College, Dublin, but embraced the new Irish revolutionary cultural nationalism under the influence of **Thomas MacDonagh** and Joseph Plunkett, who published and produced his first play, *The Walls of Athens*, and whose Irish Theatre also staged his *The Phoenix on the Roof* (1915). He broke with them on the Easter Rising of 1916 where, as an Irish volunteer loyal to John MacNeill, he was one of the couriers who tried to transmit the order countermanding it. His best play, *Bricriu's Feast* (1919), satirized neo-Gaelicism, and his first novel, *The Wasted Island* (1919, rev edn 1929), is a valuable source on the origins of the Rising. He was responsive to **James Joyce**'s *Ulysses*, and wrote many novels, of which the Butlerian fantasies *King Goshalk and the Birds, The Spacious Adventures of the Man in the Street* and *Asses in Clover* are the most noteworthy. Emigrating to England in 1925, he ultimately espoused the Social Credit philosophy of Major C H Douglas, his autobiographical *Life and Money* (1932) winning some success.

OE Kenzaburo
(1935–)

Japanese novelist, born in Shikoku and educated at Tokyo University, where he studied French literature. His earliest fiction, influenced by **Kobo Abe**, attempts to come to terms with the bleak cultural landscape of post-war Japan. His first three novels, beginning with *Shisha no Ogori* ('The Arrogance of the Dead'), were all published in 1958, but it was not until 1963 that Oe found an effective personal voice. In that year, he visited Hiroshima and witnessed the delivery of his son, who was born with a major skull abnormality. Thereafter, his writing became more personal and engaged, less dependent on second-hand Decadence, imported from France. *Kojinteki na taiken* (1964) was the first of his books to be published in English, as *A Personal Matter*

(1968). Perhaps his finest book followed in 1967; *Man'en gannen no futtuboru* (Eng trans *The Silent Cry*, 1974) concerns two brothers' search for their roots. It won Oe the **Tanizaki** Prize. Four of his short novels of the 1970s were collected in translation as *Teach Us to Outgrow Our Madness* (1977). In the 1980s he began to explore new principles of organization for his fiction, drawing on social anthropology and philosophy.

▷Y Hisaaki, *The Search for Authenticity in Modern Japanese Literature* (1978)

OEHLENSCHLÄGER, Adam Gottlob
(1779–1850)

Danish poet and playwright, born in Copenhagen. The founder of Danish Romanticism, and the greatest Danish poet of his day, he was much influenced by **Goethe** and the **Schlegel** brothers. He published his symbolic poem, *Goldhornene* ('The Golden Horns') in 1802 and a verse fantasy, *Aladdin*, in 1805. He wrote some 24 blank-verse historical tragedies, starting with *Hakon Jarl* (1807, 'Earl Hakon'), followed by *Baldur hin Gode* ('Baldur the Good') in 1808, *Palnetoke* (1809), *Correggio* (1909, written in German), and *Axel og Valborg* (1910). He later wrote a cycle of verse romances, *Helge* (1814), and *Nordens Guder* ('Gods of the North'), an epic ballad cycle based on the Norse mythology of the *Edda*. He was appointed Professor of Aesthetics at Copenhagen in 1810. In 1829 he was crowned 'king of the Scandinavian singers' by **Elaias Tegnér** at Lund, and in 1849 was publicly proclaimed as the national poet of Denmark.

▷V Andersen, *Adam Oehlenschläger* (1899–1900)

O'FAOLAIN, Julia
(1932–)

Irish novelist, born in London, daughter of **Sean O'Faolain**. A writer whose exuberant, multi-layered fiction combines aspects of the domestic novel with political, religious and historical concerns, her early work draws on her experience as a convent-educated Irish girl studying in Rome and Paris; her short-story collection, *Man in the Cellar* (1974), reveals a macabre side to her humour. Catholicism has played a strong role in her later work. *Women in the Wall* (1975) is an examination of the female role in medieval society, based around the setting-up of a convent, and the Booker-shortlisted *No Country for Young Men* (1980) puts Irish nationalism under the microscope. *The Obedient Wife* (1982) and *The Irish Signorina* (1984) explore the criss-cross of different cultures and divergent ways of life, while *The Judas Cloth* (1992) is the story of a young priest, set during the reign of Pope Pius IX.

O'FAOLAIN, Sean
(1900–91)

Irish writer, born in Dublin. He was educated at the National University of Ireland, and took his MA at Harvard. He lectured for a period (1929) at Boston College, then took a post as a teacher in Strawberry Hill, Middlesex and in 1933 returned to Ireland to teach. His first writing was in Gaelic, and he produced an edition of translations from Gaelic, *The Silver Branch*, in 1938. Before this, however, he had attracted attention with a novel, *A Nest of Simple Folk* (1933). He never quite repeated its success with later novels, and from then on wrote many biographies, including *Daniel O'Connell* (1938), *De Valera* (1939) and *The Great O'Neill* (1942), this last being a biography of the 2nd Earl of Tyrone. He edited the autobiography of Wolfe Tone (1937) and published one of his own, *Vive-moi!* (1964). His *Stories of Sean O'Faolain* (1958) cover 30 years of writing and progress from the lilting 'Irishry' of his youth to the deeper and wider artistry of his maturity. A later version was published as *Collected Stories* in 1981. His daughter is the novelist **Julia O'Faolain.**
▷P A Doyle, *Sean O'Faolain* (1968)

O'FLAHERTY, Liam
(1897–1984)

Irish writer, born on Inishmore in the Aran Islands. Educated at Rockwell College, Tipperary and University College, Dublin, he fought in the British army during World War I and later wandered in North America and Latin America. He returned to Ireland in 1921 and fought on the Republican side in the Irish Civil War. He went to London in 1922 to become a writer, and published his first novels, *Thy Neighbour's Wife* (1923) and *The Black Soul* (1924). *The Informer* (1926) won the James Tait Black Prize and was a popular success. Other books, reflecting the intensity of his feeling and style, include *Spring Sowing* (1926), *The Assassin* (1928), *The Puritan* (1932), *Famine* (1937) and *Land* (1946). He also wrote three volumes of autobiography, *Two Years* (1930), *I went to Russia* (1931) and *Shame the Devil* (1934).

OFTERDINGEN, Heinrich von
(12th–13th century)

One of the famous *Minnesinger* or lyric poets of Germany, who flourished between the years 1170 and 1250.

OGILVIE, William Henry
(1869–1963)

Scottish poet, born near Kelso, who, after having admired the verse of **Adam Lindsay Gordon**, went to Australia at the age of 20 to work in Queensland. A highly skilled horseman, he worked round the State droving, mustering and breaking horses, and became a friend of Henry 'Breaker' Morant. All the while he was contributing ballads under the name 'Glenrowan' to such periodicals as the *Bulletin*. In 1898 he published his best-known book, *Fair Girls and Gray Horses*, and three years later went back to Scotland, never to return. *Hearts of Gold and Other Verses* (1903) and a compilation, *The Australian and Other Verses* (1916), were published in Australia after he left, as was another collection, *Saddle for a Throne* (1952). His verse, though sometimes over-sentimental, is the equal of other 'Bush' poets and its romanticism a welcome change from the male-oriented rhymes of **Banjo Paterson** and **Henry Lawson**. After his return to Scotland he contributed to *Punch* and *Country Life* among others and was called by **Hugh MacDiarmid** 'The Grand Old Man of Borders Song'. He was well known for his hunting verse, the best of which is in *The Collected Sporting Verse of W H Ogilvie* (1932).
▷*My Life in the Open* (1910)

OGOT, Grace
(1930–)

Kenyan story writer, born in Central Nyanza Province. Trained as a midwife, she became a headmistress and a scriptwriter for the BBC. Her stories have a strong folkloric element and have appeared in many important magazines, such as *Black Orpheus*. One of her best known, 'Tekayo', is in *African Writing Today* (1967).

O'GRADY, Desmond
(1935–)

Irish poet, born in Limerick. He was a friend of **Ezra Pound**, and worked as a teacher in Rome, Cairo and Alexandria before retiring in the mid-1980s to Kinsale in the south of Ireland. Known since the publication of *The Dark Edge of Europe* (1967) as 'the Poet O'Grady', his appetite for the epic, the rhetorical and the 'grand' style made him a somewhat dangerous influence on succeeding generations of poets. However, *New and Selected Poems* (1978), together with his informed translations—*The Gododdin* (1977), *A Limerick Rake: Versions from the Irish* (1978) and *Ten Arab Poets* (1992)—and his consistent injection of 'linguistic glamour' into classical themes, make him an important figure in late 20th-century European literature.

Ó'GRIANNA, Séamus
(1891–1969)

Irish novelist and story writer, born in County Donegal. His **Maupassant**-like, but frequently sentimental, stories, of which there were many, were very popular, but have not attracted the attention of critics.

O'HARA, Frank
(1926–66)

American poet and art critic, born in Baltimore, Maryland. Since the publication of *A City Winter* (1952) his poetry collections were influenced by his life in New York, and are often based on autobiographical incidents. The posthumously published *Selected Poems* (1973) won a National Book Award, while *Art Chronicles* (1975) is a collection of his fine-art criticism; he was the Assistant Curator of the Museum of Modern Art, New York, when he died. His best work came when he engaged in light, conversational celebrations of his adopted city. Wilfully ephemeral, such pieces as 'Steps' ('How funny you are today New York ...') are now more valuable as records of a bygone era than as art in their own right.

O'HARA, John
(1905–70)

American novelist and short-story writer, born in Pottsville, Pennsylvania. In his fiction Pottsville becomes 'Gibbsville', the setting for *Appointment in Samarra* (1934). Its naturalistic, fatalistic account of the last three days in the life of Julian English made him almost overnight a success. O'Hara was notoriously irascible and hypersensitive. 'Brash as a young man', wrote **John Updike**, 'he became with success a slightly desperate braggart'. Two of his works—*Butterfield 8* (1935) and *Pal Joey* (1940)—became film and stage successes. His short stories are obsessed with class, social privilege and feminist issues.
▷ F Farr, *John O'Hara: a biography* (1973)

O'HARA, Mary, pseud of Mary O'Hara Alsop
(1885–1980)

American novelist and children's writer, best-known for her winsome trilogy about horses, *My Friend Flicka* (1941), *Thunderhead* (1943) and *The Green Grass of Wyoming* (1946), all written on her Wyoming ranch. The Hollywood version of the first of these books, and its sequel, became two of the most popular family films of the forties. She was also a composer of piano suites.

OHNET, George
(1848–1918)

French novelist, born in Paris. Under the general title of *Les Batailles de la vie* ('The Battles of Life'), he published a series of novels, some of which went beyond one hundred editions.

Ó'HUIGINN, Tadghh Dall
(1550–91)

Irish poet, 'the greatest master of the dán direach [the rules of Irish classical metres] that ever lived'. He was brother of a Catholic archbishop, and lived in County Sligo. The subject-matter of most of his poetry, however, was conventional: it consisted of odes to chieftains. But his two *aislings*, or vision-poems, are different and more powerful.
▷ E Knott, *The Bardic Poems of Tagdh Dall* (1922–6)

O'KEEFFE, John
(1747–1833)

Irish dramatist, born in Abbey Street, Dublin, of a Catholic family. He left Ireland to work as an actor, but later returned to work under Henry Mossop at the Theatre Royal, Smock Alley, Dublin, the first Restoration theatre in either England or Ireland. Some 77 'Dramas' are listed in his *Recollections* (2 vols, 1826). Prolific but pedantic, he dined off **Richard Brinsley Sheridan's** description of him as 'the first that turned the public taste from the dullness of sentiment ... towards the sprightly channel of comic humour'. Following the Royal Shakespeare Company's 1976 revival of his *Wild Oats* (1791) he gained a misplaced reputation as a composer-playwright; as the earlier *Tony Lumpkin in Town* (1774) shows, he was, rather, a skilful assimilator of other people's plots and sanitized versions of traditional Irish folksongs. Following an accident in 1780 he began to go blind; he received an annuity from Covent Garden in 1803, and in 1826 a pension from George IV.
▷ F M Link (ed), *The Plays of John O'Keeffe* (4 vols, 1981)

OKRI, Ben
(1959–)

Nigerian novelist, poet and short-story writer, born in Minna, now living in London. His first, precocious novel was *Flowers and Shadows* (1980), but it was not until 1987, and the publication of its successor, *Incidents at the Shrine*, that he achieved recognition in the form of the Commonwealth Writers' Prize for Africa. *Stars of the New Curfew* (1988), a volume of short stories, marked time, but his career began a new stage with his third novel, *The Famished Road* (1991), which won the Booker Prize; the sequel, *Songs of Enchantment*, followed in 1993.

Ó'LAOGHAIRE, Peadar
(1839–1920)

Irish Gaelic writer and translator (he made a disastrous attempt at *Don Quixote*), born in

West Cork. A canon, he adapted ancient stories and also wrote a famous novel, *Séadna* (1904) on the Faust theme. He was the first important modern writer to employ Irish as a medium, and with *Séadna* is said to have 'put all lovers of the Irish language in his debt': even though it is unsuccessful in psychological terms, it is nonetheless a 'kind of bible with revivalists ... three hundred pages of living language!'

OLBRACHT, Ivan, pseud of Kamil Zeman
(1882–1952)

Czech novelist and story writer, born in Semily. Like many Czech writers, he supported the Communist Party in the inter-war period; he became a politician after World War II. He was at first much influenced by **Maxim Gorky**; but his later main work, *Nikola Suhaj loupeznik* (1933, Eng trans *Nikola Suhav—Bandit*, 1954), the success of which he could never repeat, is far more original in its retelling of the story of a popular Robin Hood-like hero. It remains one of the peaks of Czech achievement in the novel. Some of his stories are translated in *The Bitter and the Sweet* (1967).

OLDHAM, John
(1653–83)

English satirical poet, born in Shipton-Moyne, Gloucestershire. Educated at Oxford, he became a teacher. His most enduring works are those written after the exposure of the Popish Plot. These include *A Satire Upon a Woman, Who By Her Falsehood and Scorn Was the Death of My Friend* (1678); *A Satire Against Virtue* (1679), and the four *Satires upon the Jesuits* (1681). A highly intelligent and ebullient character, Oldham wrote not only in his own boisterous, aggressive style, but also parodied that of others, including **Horace**. He died from smallpox.

OLES', Oleksander, pseud of Oleksander Kandybar
(1878–1944)

Eastern Ukrainian poet and verse dramatist, born in Verkhosuly, Sumy. His fervent poetry is still remembered. After Ukraine became part of Soviet Russia he lived abroad, and died in Prague. He has been called Ukrainia's leading exponent of neo-romanticism.

OLESHA, Yury
(1899–1960)

Russian novelist and playwright from Odessa, one of the most gifted of his generation. He 'disappeared' during the 1930s, owing to his inability to conform, and was only 'rehabilitated' towards the end of his life, when he had been reduced to but a pale shadow of his old self. He approved of the Revolution but could not reconcile himself to its 'collective' results, and so, in his finest novel, *Zavist* (1927, Eng trans *Envy*, 1936 and *The Wayward Comrade and the Commissar*, 1960), classic by any standards, he 'sent it up', but in such a manner that some comrade-critics believed he was supporting it. It tells of the conflict between an efficient sausage-manufacturer and an irresponsible anarchist. He puts forward the undoubtedly vigorous case for the sausage manufacturer with a poker-faced, mocking irony, reserving his fiercest criticism for the anarchist. The result is certainly 'ambiguous', but the ambiguity has less to do with politics than with individualism versus life-as-organized by politicians, and *Envy* is therefore of perennial interest. After this he was unable to take his own course, but, as a historian has written, 'the problems of technology and bureaucracy described in his works are as applicable to the West as ... to the Soviet Union. One can only regret the failure of history to permit Olesha a normal artistic development'. After his 'disgrace', he wrote a script for a film of *The Idiot*, by **Dostoyevsky**, and translated much Turkmenian literature into Russian. His *Tri tolstyaka* (1924, 'The Three Fat Fellows') is a superb novel for children.
▷G Struve, *Soviet Russian Literature 1917–1950* (1951)

OLIPHANT, Laurence
(1829–88)

English travel writer and mystic, born in Capetown of Scottish descent, son of the attorney-general there. His first work, *A Journey to Khatmandu* (1852), was followed by *The Russian Shores of the Black Sea* (1853). As secretary to James Bruce, 8th Earl of Elgin, he travelled to China in 1857–8, thus finding material for further books. In 1861, while acting as *chargé d'affaires* in Japan, he was severely wounded by assassins. From 1865 to 1868 he sat for the Stirling burghs. His satirical novel, *Piccadilly* (1870), was a book of exceptional promise, full of wit and delicate irony. He joined the religious community of Thomas Lake Harris in the USA, and later settled in Haifa in Palestine. His mystical views he published in 1886 in *Sympneumata* (written with his wife and advocating purity in one's sex life) and *Scientific Religion* (1888).
▷P Henderson, *Life of Oliphant* (1956)

OLIPHANT, Margaret, née Wilson
(1828–97)

Scottish novelist, born in Wallyford, Midlothian. When she was 10 years old her family moved to England. She took her name from her mother; little is known about her father,

Francis Wilson, except that he once 'took affadavits' in a Liverpool customs house. Precocious, she wrote a novel when she was 16, but her first published work was *Passages in the Life of Mrs Margaret Maitland* (1849), and two years later she began her lifelong connection with the Edinburgh publishers Blackwood and *Blackwood's Magazine*, culminating in a history of the firm, which was published posthumously (1897). In 1852 she married her cousin, Frances Oliphant, an artist, but she was widowed in 1859 and found herself £1000 in debt with an extended family to support and educate. Her output was astonishing and uneven, hardly surprising in an author who wrote almost a hundred novels, the best known of which are in the group known as *The Chronicles of Carlingford*, consisting of *The Rector and the Doctor's Family* (1863), *Salem Chapel* (1863), *The Perpetual Curate*, (1864), *Miss Majoribanks* (1866) and *Phoebe Junior* (1876), which have earned her the sobriquet, a 'feminist Trollope'. She wrote novels of Scottish life, including *The Minister's Wife* (1869), *Effie Ogilvie* (1886) and *Kirsteen* (1890). Other notable works include *Hester* (1883), *Lady Car* (1889), *The Railway Man and His Children* (1891) and *Sir Robert's Fortune* (1895). She was awarded a Civil List pension in 1868, but her industry was unabated and she produced a spate of biographies, literary histories, translations, travel books, tales of the supernatural, and an autobiography (1899).
▷A L Coghill, *The Life and Letters of Mrs Oliphant* (1899)

OLIVEIRA, Antônio Mariano de, known as Alberto de Oliveira
(1857–1937)

Brazilian poet who was left untouched by Brazilian *modernismo*. He was one of the main figures to react against romanticism, which he did by turning to the French Parnassian school. He was a superb technician, but had less to say than his contemporaries **Bilac** and **Correia**.

OLIVER, Mary Jane
(1935–)

American poet (not to be confused with the Spanish writer Maria Oliver). She was born in Ohio and educated at the state university, but has spent most of her adult life in Provincetown, Massachusetts. She was awarded a Pulitzer Prize in 1984 for *American Primitive* (1983) which, like all her work, contained modest reflections on the pastoral life. She has, especially since she moved to New England, been compared with **Robert Frost**. Any malevolence to be found in her poetry is seen as ultimately friendly and controllable.

OLMEDO, José Joaquín
(1780–1847)

Ecuadorean poet and translator (of the *Essay on Man* of **Alexander Pope**), born in Guayaquil. He combined romantic matter with classical form, and in this style wrote one of the most famous Latin-American poems, *La victoria de Junín: Canto a Bolívar*, an ode to Simon Bolívar, to whom he was close friend and aide. His poetry is not much read today.

OLSEN, Ernst Bruun
(1923–)

Danish dramatist, born in Nakskov. He was originally an actor and producer, whose *Teenagerlove* (1962), on the pop industry, was an immense success throughout Scandinavia.

OLSEN, Tillie
(1913–)

American novelist, critic and short-story writer, born in Omaha, Nebraska. She did not publish her first volume of stories, *Tell Me A Riddle*, until 1962, when she was almost 50. A novel, *Yonnondio: From the Thirties*, followed in 1974 and *Silences*, a collection of essays, four years later. Her writing draws upon her own working-class experiences and identifies poverty as being the root of individual despair and political oppression. In the title story of *Tell Me A Riddle*, an elderly working-class woman looks back over her life and blames the failure of her hopes upon the pressures of being a wife and mother, while in the novel, a young woman recounts her family's journey from country to city in a disastrous attempt to find economic salvation.
▷J and R Newton (eds), *Feminist Criticism and Social Change* (1985)

OLSON, Charles John
(1910–70)

American poet. He was born in Worcester, Massachusetts, and educated at Wesleyan University, Yale, and at Harvard, where the young literary radical began to feel uncomfortable in the liberal American studies programme. During World War II, he worked as a civil liberties activist, and in 1947 published *Call Me Ishmael*, ostensibly a study of **Melville**, but one which strongly emphasizes Olson's concern for ethnic minorities and for working-class solidarity. In 1950 he published an essay called 'Projective Verse' in the magazine *Poetry New York*, in which he drew on **Whitman** and **William Carlos Williams** to advocate a poetry governed by human speech and the rhythms of breath; as a means of indicating these, the tab button and space bar of the typewriter were to become major poetic tools. From 1951 to 1956, Olson directed

Black Mountain College near Asheville, North Carolina, and became nominal head of the 'Black Mountain poets' (**Robert Creeley**, **Ed Dorn** etc). His most important work was *The Maximus Poems*, which appeared in several volumes during his lifetime (1953–70), but were left unfinished at his death. The sequence resembles William Carlos Williams's *Paterson* in its dramatic and lyric centring, but in later volumes it took on more of the mythological concerns of **Pound**'s *The Cantos*; the sequence as a whole was edited by George Butterick in 1983. The first important critical response had been by Ed Dorn, who published *What I See in the Maximus Poems* in 1960. Olson's shorter verse was collected as *Archaeologist of Morning* in the year of his death; *The Complete Shorter Poems* appeared in 1985.
▷G Butterick, *A Guide to the Maximus Poems* (1978)

OLSON, Elder James
(1909–)

American poet, essayist and critic, born in Chicago. Olson's first collection, *Thing of Sorrow*, appeared in 1934; a major volume, *Plays and Poems: 1948–1958*, in 1958, and *Last Poems* in 1984. His verse is strictly formal, lyrical and immensely highly crafted, with the result that he is often regarded as rather unobtrusive, a writer whose poetry is not as robust as his criticism. Certainly *The Poetry of Dylan Thomas* (1954) was a pioneering and serious attempt to grapple with this poet's output, while *Theory of Comedy* (1968) represents an orthodox Aristotelean interpretation of the nature of comedy in drama.

O'MacCAISIDE, Tomas, real name **Thomas Cassidy**
(c.1710–c.1770)

Irish Gaelic poet, born in County Fermanagh. He entered the priesthood as an Augustinian friar but, as he explains in *Eachtra an Brathar Ultaigh* (nd, 'The Spoilt Priest'), was expelled due to an alleged association with a woman; in *An Cassideach Ban* (nd, 'Cassidy the White') he argues 'All I got was the edge of the rug'. He wandered around Ireland as an 'itinerant story-teller' and bard before joining the French army in the 1730s. He deserted, was taken by 'sgiobuirigh' (kidnappers) in Hamburg, but escaped (by 'a bird-like leap') from a third-floor window. He eventually returned to Ireland, and spent the remainder of his life there.
▷A de Blacam, *Gaelic Literature Surveyed* (1929; reprinted 1973)

Ó'MAOIL CHONAIRE, Flaithri
(1560–29)

Irish scholar, translator and priest, an expert on the work of **St Augustine**. His chief work is his adaptation of the anonymous Catalan allegorical novel *El desseoso* (1515), as *Desiderius* (1616, modern edn 1941). This is the chief devotional work in Irish of its century.

OMAR KHAYYÁM
(c.1048–c.1122)

Persian poet, mathematician and astronomer, born in Níshápūr. His father was a tent-maker, hence his surname. He was well educated, particularly in the sciences and philosophy, in his home town and in Balkh. Later he went to Samarkand where he completed a seminal work on algebra. Consequently he was invited by Seljuq sultan Malik-Sháh to make the necessary astronomical observations for the reform of the calendar, and collaborated on an observatory in Isfahan. When his patron died in 1092 he made a pilgrimage to Mecca, on his return from which he served at the court as an astrologer. In his own country and time he was known for his scientific achievements but in the English-speaking world he is indelibly associated with the collection of *robáiyát*, or quatrains, attributed to him. As a poet he had attracted little attention until **Edward Fitzgerald** translated and arranged the fugitive pieces into *The Rubáiyát of Omar Khayyám*, first published anonymously in 1859. Replete with memorable sayings, they have been translated into all the world's major languages and have influenced Western ideas about Persian poetry. Though some questioned their authorship, it has been established that at least 250 *robáīyát* were the work of Omar.
▷A Dashti, *In Search of Omar Khayyám* (1971)

ONDAATJE, (Philip) Michael
(1943–)

Canadian poet and novelist. He was born in Ceylon and emigrated to Canada in 1962, in the footsteps of his brother. Two decades later, he portrayed his aristocratic and eccentric relatives in the beguiling memoir, *Running in the Family* (1982), displaying the same touch of surrealism that had marked his early verse collections. The first was *The Dainty Monsters* (1967), followed by *The Man With Seven Toes* (1969) and the prize-winning sequence *The Collected Works of Billy the Kid: Left Handed Poems* (1970), which mixed documentary fact with fantasy, and involved elements of prose writing. In that same year, Ondaatje wrote a critical study of the lyricist and novelist **Leonard Cohen**, which clarified some of his own literary concerns. The collected poems of the 1960s and 70s appeared as *There's a Trick With a Knife I'm Learning to Do* (1979, published in the UK as *Rat Jelly and Other Poems*, 1980) but by this time he was turning increasingly to prose. *Coming Through Slaughter* (1976) was a dreamlike reconstruction of the life of the semi-mythical jazz cornetist Buddy Bolden. Later novels included the more conventional *In the Skin of a Lion* (1987) and the hauntingly lyrical *The English Patient* (1991), for which he shared the Booker Prize with **Barry Unsworth**. Ondaatje has directed several films and is editor of the *Faber Book of Canadian Short Stories* (1990).

O'NEACHTAIN, Seán
(c.1650–1729)

Irish Gaelic poet, born in County Roscommon, Connaught, in the west of Ireland. In 1690 he moved with his family to Dublin, where much of his subsequent life was spent combining writing poetry with a professional career as a schoolmaster in the midlands of County Meath. His work in prose and rhyme is singular in its use of bilingual and transcultural puns. In the autobiographical *Stuir Eamonn Ui Chleiri* (nd, 'The Story of Eamonn O'Cleary'), for example, '*bhui le Dia*' literally means 'thanks be to God', but it can also mean 'yellow with God'—the apostate writer is in fact giving thanks for a gift of butter. In a wooing poem to Una Ni Bhroin O'Neachtain tells her 'water will be your music while the otters and fish cleverly wrestle together'; suprisingly, she did become his wife. He died quietly, and content.
▷S Deane (ed), *The Field Day Anthology of Irish Writing: Vol 1* (1991)

O'NEILL, Alexandre
(1924–)

Portuguese poet, born in Lisbon. He was a founder of the first (1947) Surrealist group in Portugal: this provided a way for poets both to mock Salazar's steely dictatorship and simultaneously to steer clear of its philistine censors, who believed that such writers were insane and harmless purveyors of literal nonsense. He has perhaps been praised above his powers by some Portuguese critics—he has none of the profundity of **Sá-Carneiro** or **Fernando Pessoa**; but he provided humorous delight and salutary satirical abilities at a time when these were desperately needed.

O'NEILL, Eugene Gladstone
(1888–1953)

American playwright, winner of the Nobel Prize for literature, born in New York, the son of the actor James O'Neill (1847–1920).

After a fragmentary education and a year at Princeton, he took various clerical and journalistic jobs and signed on as a sailor on voyages to Australia, South Africa and elsewhere. Then he contracted tuberculosis and spent six months in a sanatorium, where he felt the urge to write plays, the first being *The Web* (1914). He joined the Provincetown Players in 1915, for whom *Beyond the Horizon* (1920; Pulitzer Prize) was written. This was followed, during the next two years, by *Exorcism* (1920), *Diff'rent* (1920), *The Emperor Jones* (1921), *Anna Christie* (1922; Pulitzer Prize) and *The Hairy Ape* (1922). *Desire Under the Elms*, his most mature play to date, appeared in 1924. He then began experimenting in new dramatic techniques; in *The Great God Brown* (1926) he used masks to emphasize the differing relationships between a man, his family and his soul. *Marco Millions* (1931) is a satire on tycoonery. *Strange Interlude* (1928; Pulitzer Prize), a marathon nine-acter, lasting five hours, uses asides, soliloquies and 'streams of consciousness'. In the same year he wrote *Lazarus Laughed*, a humanistic affirmation of his belief in the conquest of death. *Mourning Becomes Electra* (1931) is a re-statement of the Orestean tragedy in terms of biological and psychological cause and effect. *Ah, Wilderness*, a nostalgic comedy, appeared in 1933 and *Days Without End* in 1934. Then, for 12 years he released no more plays but worked on *The Iceman Cometh* (New York 1946, London 1958) and *A Moon for the Misbegotten* (1947). The former is a gargantuan, broken-backed, repetitive parable about the dangers of shattering illusions. It is impressive by its sheer weight and redeemed by O'-Neill's never-failing sense of the theatre. *Long Day's Journey into Night* (1957; Pulitzer Prize), probably his masterpiece, whose tragic Tyrone family is closely based on O'Neill's early life, *Hughie* (1964) and *A Touch of the Poet* (1957) were published posthumously. He was awarded the Nobel Prize for literature in 1936, the first American dramatist to be thus honoured.
▷L Sheaffer, *Eugene O'Neill: son and playwright* (1968); *Eugene O'Neill: son and artist* (1973)

ONERVA, L, pseud of Hilja Onerva Lehtinen
(1882–1972)

Finnish poet, novelist, biographer (of, notably, **Leino**) and translator (from French poetry), born in Helsinki. She was a leading figure in the earlier part of the century, and remained respected until her death.

ONETTI, Juan Carlos
(1909–94)

Uruguayan novelist and short-story writer, born in Montevideo. He left school early and, following a succession of menial jobs, became a full-time writer in 1939, when he began working for the magazine *Marcha*. That year saw the publication of his short novel *El Pozo* ('The Well'), now recognized as a masterpiece. He moved to Buenos Aires shortly after. His next novel, *Tierra de Nadie* (1941, 'No Man's Land'), was the first of his works to be set in a fictional fusion of Buenos Aires and Montevideo, and as such is an important landmark in the creation of a modern, urban Latin American literature. He returned to his homeland in 1954, but left 20 years later for Spain after having been imprisoned by the military government. His short-story collections include *Un Sueño Realizado y otros cuentos* (1951, 'A Dream Comes True and other stories'). He has been described as 'the greatest urban novelist of our century'.

ONO NO KOMACHI
(c.810–c.880)

Japanese poet, born, probably, in Kyoto in the classical period of Japanese literature. Like many of the other great figures of classical literature in Japan, she was a court poet, writing in a rarefied form of the vernacular—it was more common for men to write in a form of Chinese, which is why so much surviving classical Japanese literature is by women (see **Shikibu Murasaki**). She is known in Japan as one of the Six Poetic Geniuses, the supreme writer of the verse form *tanka*
▷H C McCullough, *Ise Monogatari. Tales of Ise: Lyrical Episodes from Tenth Century Japan* (1968)

ONOFRI, Arturo
(1885–1928)

Italian poet and critic, born in Rome. His later work was much influenced by his interest in the anthroposophy of **Rudolph Steiner**. He is a difficult but rewarding poet, whose work **Sanguineti** represents fully in his important anthology *Poesia italiana del Novocento* (1969–71, '20th-century Italian Poetry').

ONSTOTT, Kyle *see* HORNER, Lance

OODGEROO, Noonuccal Moongalba,
originally **Kath(leen Jean) Walker**
(1920–93)

Australian Aboriginal artist and writer, born in Brisbane, Queensland, and brought up with the Noonuccal tribe on Stradbroke Island, Queensland. From the age of 13 she worked in domestic service in Brisbane, gaining her education mainly from the libraries of her employers. She joined the Australian Women's Army Service during World War II, and afterwards became involved in aboriginal

activism. In 1964 she became the first aboriginal writer to be published, with her collection of poems *We are Going*, followed by *The Dawn is at Hand* (1966). With other works these were republished in 1970 as *My People, a Kath Walker Collection*. In 1972 she published a book of aboriginal stories, *Stradbroke Dreamtime*. She won a number of awards, including the **Mary Gilmore** Medal. She visited the USA on a Fulbright Scholarship from 1978 to 1979, lecturing on aboriginal rights, and was active on many aboriginal interest committees including the Aboriginal Arts Board. In 1985 she published *Quandamooka, the art of Kath Walker*. She also ran a Centre for Aboriginal Culture, for children of all races, on Stradbroke Island. Australian composer Malcolm Williamson has set some of her poems for choir and orchestra: *The Dawn is at Hand* was premiered in 1989. In 1988 she adopted the aboriginal name Oodgeroo of the tribe Noonuccal.

OOKA Shohei
(1909–)

Japanese diarist and novelist, famed in Japan for his vivid and chilling account of fighting and being captured by the Americans during World War II, and for his novel *Nobi* (1951, Eng trans *Fires on the Plain*, 1957), which has also achieved a reputation in the West. *Nobi* is similar in tone to **William Golding**'s *Lord of the Flies*, in that it details what happens when a society breaks down, but, unlike Golding's book, it is based on personal experience.

OPATOSHU, Josef, originally Josef Opatofski
(1887–1954)

Yiddish novelist, born in Mlava in Poland, and died in New York, where he had gone in 1907. Until **Isaac Bashevis Singer**, his were the most powerful historical novels in his language. Indeed, he introduced the form. His trilogy about life in 19th-century Poland, *In Poilishe velder*, is largely episodic, and is hardly a novel by Singer's standards, but is nonetheless vivid and masterful. *A tog in Regensburg* (1933, Eng trans *A Day in Regensburg* 1968), on Jewish life in 16th-century Germany, is more coherent as a single work. His complete works in Yiddish were published in 14 volumes in New York (1928–36).
▷C A Madison, *Yiddish Literature* (1968)

OPIE, Amelia
(1769–1853)

English novelist and poet, born in Norwich. Despite having espoused radical political and social opinions, marrying the painter John Opie and becoming a friend of **Mary Wollstonecraft Shelley**, Opie produced several sensational but sternly moralizing novels. These include *Father and Daughter* (1801), in which a girl's seduction results in her father's madness, and *Adeline Mowbray, or The Mother and Daughter* (1804), in which a woman lives bitterly to regret rejecting an opportunity to marry. Her final novel, *Madeline*, appeared in 1822. After the death of her husband, Opie became a Quaker, abandoned her writing and devoted much of her time to good works, including the Bible and Anti-Slavery Societies.

OPITZ, Martin, or OPITZ VON BOBERFELD
(1597–1639)

German poet, born in Bunzlau in Silesia. The founder of the Silesian school of poets, he wrote a plea for the purification of the German language in *Aristarchus sive de contemptu linguae Teutonicae* (1617, written in Latin) and other works. In 1620 he fled to Holland to escape war and the plague, but still fell victim to that terrible disease. His didactic poems are cold and formal and lacking in feeling. His works include translations from classical authors (**Sophocles** and **Seneca**), the Dutchmen Daniel Heinsius and Grotius, and from the Bible. He also wrote a prose translation of **Ottavio Rinuccini**'s *Daphne* (1627), which formed the basis of the first German opera in 1627.
▷ J Gellinek, *Martin Opitz* (1973)

OPPEN, George
(1908–84)

American poet and publisher, whose career was profoundly affected by radical politics (and by the McCarthyite backlash of the 1950s). In the early 1930s, he and his wife co-founded The Objectivist Press, which published some of the most advanced poetry of the time, and took its name from **Louis Zukofsky**'s 1932 anthology; it was in this vein that Oppen wrote his first collection, *Discrete Series* (1934), which was sparse, taciturn and imagistic. His literary career was interrupted at that point. Oppen became a factory hand and union organizer in Detroit, served as an infantryman in World War II and was indicted by the House Un-American Activities Committee in 1950; he avoided prison by moving to Mexico and did not return to the US until Senator Joe McCarthy's death in 1957. He also began to write again and a second volume, *The Materials*, appeared in 1962, followed by *This in Which* (1965) and the Pulitzer Prize-winning *Of Being Numerous* (1968). A *Collected Poems* was published in 1975.

OPPENHEIM, Edward Phillips
(1866–1946)

English novelist, born in London. He had his first book published in 1887 and went on to become a pioneer of the novel of espionage and diplomatic intrigue. Among his best are *Mr Grex of Monte Carlo* (1915), *Kingdom of the Blind* (1917), *The Great Impersonation* (1920) and *Envoy Extraordinary* (1937).
▷ R Standish, *The Prince of Story-Tellers* (1957)

Ó RATHAILLE, Aodhagán (Little Hugh O'Rahilly)
(1670–?1730)

Classical Irish Gaelic poet, born in Kerry on lands formerly ruled by the MacCarthy earls of Clancarty, whose memory he idolized as a descendant of their hereditary bards. His poetry embodies the great Jacobite lament for the overthrow of Catholic Gaelic Ireland, much of it realized in rich lyrical and elegant development of the *Aisling* (patriotic dreamvision). Although essentially oral, his Gaelic poems survived in part and were edited for the Irish Texts Society bilingually (1900, rev edn 1911). His death date is unknown, usual estimates being based on a poem avowedly written on his death-bed which shows not the slightest sign of diminution of powers of proficiency, intricacy, beauty or invective.
▷ P Ua Duinnin, introduction to *Collected Poetry* (1900–11)

ORCZY, Baroness (Emma Magdalena Rosalie Marie Josefa Barbara)
(1865–1947)

Hungarian-born British novelist and playwright, born in Tarnaörs, the daughter of a musician. *The Scarlet Pimpernel* (1905) was the first success in the Baroness's long writing career. It was followed by many popular adventure romances, including *The Elusive Pimpernel* (1908) and *Mam'zelle Guillotine* (1940), which never quite attained the success of her early work.
▷ *Links in the Chain of Life* (1947)

O'REILLY, Dowell Philip
(1865–1923)

Australian poet and writer, born in Sydney, who worked variously as a teacher and public servant, and was for four years a member of the NSW Legislative Assembly. He published little work; his verse included *Australian Poems* (1894) and *A Pedlar's Pack* (1888) but, disappointed by poor sales, he destroyed the remaining copies. There was a novel, *Tears and Triumph*, in 1913, and a collection of short stories, *Five Corners* in 1920. The best of his work was collected in 1924 as *The Prose and Verse of Dowell O'Reilly*. In 1927 his second wife, his cousin Mollie Miles, published his courtship letters to her in *Dowell O'Reilly from his Letters*. He was the father of **Eleanor Dark**.

Ó RÍORDÁIN, Seán
(1916–77)
Irish Gaelic poet. Born into the bilingual community of Ballyvorney, County Cork, he worked as a tax-inspector until his retirement in 1965. From 1967 his pungent column in *The Irish Times* became an important focus of debate within Gaelic-speaking circles. Published from the 1940s onwards, his five collections of poems are small and slim evidence of the major influence he had on three generations of writers. His powerful, minimal verses have proved difficult to translate and appear to greatest advantage in English in Sean Dunne's *Poets of Munster* (1985).

ORIXE *see* ORMAECHEA, Nicolás de

ORMAECHEA, Nicolás de
(1888–1961)
Basque poet who used the pseudonym 'Orixe'. He translated the novel *Lazarillo de Tormes*, and wrote a long account in verse of the Basque people, and their history, called *Euskaldunak* (1950). It is not a great poem, but is certainly indispensable for those who wish to understand the Basque people. He was a close friend to **Lizardi**, some of whose qualities he shared.
▷R Gallop, *A Book of the Basques* (1930); L Michelena, *Historia de la literatura vasca* (1960)

ORMOND, John
(1923–90)
Welsh poet and film-maker, born in Dunvant, near Swansea, and educated at University College, Swansea. After training as a journalist he joined BBC Wales in 1957 as a director and producer of documentary films, including studies of Welsh painters and writers such as Ceri Richards, **Dylan Thomas**, **Alun Lewis** and **R S Thomas**. He himself established a reputation as a fine Anglo–Welsh poet.
▷Autobiography in M Stephens, *Artists in Wales* (1973)

ORTEGA Y GASSET, José
(1883–1955)
Spanish critic, journalist and philosopher, born in Madrid, son of a well-known novelist. Although not himself a creative writer, he had an effect greater than **Unamuno** on his country's literary practice. He studied in Germany, and picked up proto-existentialist ideas from teachers such as Hermann Cohen. He came, prophetically, to believe that Spain's future lay in Europeanization; as a politician in the Cortes in the years immediately preceding the Civil War he made proposals which, had they been accepted, could have led to peace—the decrying of him as proto-fascist has no foundation. He left Spain between 1936 and 1946, and never lived there permanently again. Two of his seminal books are *Meditaciones del Quixote* (1914, Eng trans *Meditations on Quixote*, 1961) and *La dehumanización del arte* (1948, Eng trans *The Dehumanization of Art*, 1948). In these he brought a phenomenological attitude to bear upon literary problems, and anticipated every single modern critical concept, particularly those of structuralism and deconstruction. He early saw that critics are quite unable to eliminate subjectivity from their interpretations of texts, and made proposals to deal practically with this. His best-known work in *La rebelión de las masas* (1930, Eng trans *The Revolt of the Masses*, 1932), often mistakenly taken as a right-wing and élitist document, is a masterly analysis of the 20th-century situation, in which the masses have revolted against minorities. He corrected any possible ambiguities inherent in this book in his posthumous *El hombre y la gente* (1957, Eng trans *Man and People*, 1957). He has radically influenced the majority of Spanish writers of his time and after him.
▷J F Mora, *Ortega y Gasset* (1963); R McClintock, *Man and His Circumstances* (1971)

ORTESE, Anna-Maria
(1915–)
Italian novelist and journalist, born in Rome. Her work was praised by **Bontempelli** and **Vittorini**, who became her mentor. Her first publication (1937) was a collection of surrealistic stories. She is best known, however, for her mythic treatment of Italy's southern cities, *Il mare non bagna Napoli* (1953, Eng trans *The Bay is Not Naples*, 1955), which received the Viareggio Prize, and for *Poveri e semplici* (1967, 'Poor and Simple People'), set in Milan, which won the Strega Prize.

ORTIZ, Simon
(1941–)
American writer, born in Albuquerque, New Mexico. Ortiz grew up in Acoma in New Mexico, in a family deeply rooted in the Pueblo's religious and artistic traditions, and much of his work is concerned with the importance of cultural survival for Native American peoples, especially those of the Southwest where he has lived most of his life. His first major poetry collection, *Going for the Rain* (1976), was followed by *A Good Journey* (1977), containing poems rich in details of everyday life in Acoma. Ortiz's military

experiences during the Vietnam era informed the cycle of poems that comprise *From Sand Creek: Rising in This Heart Which is Our America* (1981); set in a Colorado veterans' hospital, the poems juxtapose descriptions of the 1864 massacre of Sand Creek with accounts of military atrocities in Vietnam. Ortiz has also written many short stories, included in *Howbah Indians* (1978) and *Fightin': New and Collected Stories* (1983). *Fight Back: For the Sake of the People, For the Sake of the Land* (1980) is a mixture of poems and essays depicting the lives of Pueblos, Navajos and Whites working in New Mexico's uranium industry, and stresses the need for interethnic recognition and respect. Ortiz has also written two books for children—*The People Shall Continue* (1977) and *Blue and Red* (1982). More recently, he has published *After and Before the Lightning* (1991), a collection of poems inspired by the starkly beautiful landscape and harshness of life in South Dakota where he lived for some years.
▷A Wiget, *Simon Ortiz* (1986)

ORTON, Joe, originally **John Kingsley**
(1933–67)

English dramatist, born in Leicester. After training as an actor, he turned to writing vivid, outrageous farces, beginning with *The Ruffian on the Stair* (1963) and *Entertaining Mr Sloan* (1964). Subsequent plays include *Loot* (1966), *The Erpingham Camp* (1966) and *What the Butler Saw* (1969). He was murdered by his lover, failed artist Kenneth Halliwell, who subsequently killed himself.
▷J Lahr, *Prick Up Your Ears* (1978)

ORWELL, George, pseud of **Eric Arthur Blair**
(1903–50)

English novelist and essayist, born in Motihari in Bengal. He was educated at Eton, served in Burma in the Indian Imperial Police from 1922 to 1927 (later recalled in 1935 in the novel *Burmese Days*), and then literally went *Down and Out in Paris and London* (1933), making an occasional living as tutor or bookshop assistant. In 1935 he became a small country shopkeeper, and published two novels, *A Clergyman's Daughter* (1935) and *Keep the Aspidistra Flying* (1936). *Coming Up for Air* (1939) is a plea for the small man against big business. He fought and was wounded in the Spanish Civil War and he developed his own brand of socialism in *The Road to Wigan Pier* (1937), *Homage to Catalonia* (1938) and *The Lion and the Unicorn* (1941). During World War II, he was war correspondent for the BBC and *The Observer*, and wrote for *Tribune*. His intellectual honesty motivated his biting satire of communist ideology in *Animal Farm* (1945), which was made into a cartoon film; and the terrifying prophecy for mankind in *Nineteen Eighty-Four* (1949), the triumph of the scientifically-perfected servile state, the extermination of political freedom by thought-control and an ideologically delimited basic language of *newspeak* in which 'thought crime is death'. Other penetrating collections of essays include *Inside the Whale* (1940) and *Shooting an Elephant* (1950); his *Collected Essays* appeared in four volumes in 1968.
▷B Crick, *Orwell: a life* (1979)

ORZESKOWA, Eliza
(1841–1910)

Polish realistic novelist, whose notable work is mostly associated with the area around Grodno, where she was born. She was one of the most educated women of her time, largely owing to her enlightened father's library. She was associated with the 'Positivist' movement—a reaction to the 'romanticism' which had led to the failed uprisings of 1863–4—and her huge fictional output deals with 'ordinary people'; but she gradually became more idealistic. As a whole, her work, which has been undervalued until recently, may be compared to that of **Balzac**: a huge 'Polish Comedy'. She dealt with women, Jews, and—adeptly—with political censors. Novels available in English include *Meir Ezofowicz* (1878, Eng trans *An Obscure Apostle*, 1898), *Argonauci* (1899, Eng trans *The Modern Argonauts*, 1901) and *Piesn Przerwana* (1896, Eng trans *The Interrupted Melody*, 1912). Her books remain eminently readable.

OSARAGI Jiro, pseud of **Koyohiko Nojiro**
(1897–1973)

Japanese novelist, living in Tokyo, who is principally remembered as the author of a long and very popular series of historical adventure novels featuring the anti-hero Kurama Tengu. A sort of Robin Hood figure with a gift for swordplay and an extremely gloomy outlook—possibly a result of Osaragi's wartime experiences in the army—Tengu travels medieval Japan righting wrongs but not feeling very good about it. *Kikyo* is available in translation as *The Homecoming*, *Tabiji* as *The Journey*. They are, by Japanese standards, rattling good reads.

OSBORNE, John James
(1929–)

Welsh playwright and actor, son of a commercial artist. He left Belmont College, Devon, at 16 and became a copywriter for trade journals. Hating it, he turned actor (1948) and by 1955 was playing leading roles in new plays at the Royal Court Theatre. There his fourth play, *Look Back in Anger*

(1956; filmed 1958), and *The Entertainer* (1957; filmed 1960), with Sir Laurence Olivier playing Archie Rice, established Osborne as the leading young exponent of British social drama. The 'hero' of the first, Jimmy Porter, the prototype 'Angry Young Man', as well as the pathetic, mediocre music hall joker Archie Rice, both echo the author's uncompromising hatred of outworn social and political institutions and attitudes. An earlier play, *Epitaph for George Dillon*, written in collaboration with Anthony Creighton and exploring the moral problems of the would-be literary genius, was also staged in 1957. Among other works are *Luther* (1960), *Inadmissible Evidence* (1965), *Time Present* and *The Hotel in Amsterdam* (1968), and the filmscript of *Tom Jones*, which won him an Oscar. He wrote his credo in *Declarations* (1957), and two volumes of autobiography, *A Better Class of Person* (1981) and *Almost a Gentleman* (1991).

▷ S Trussler, *The Plays of John Osborne* (1969)

OSBOURNE, Lloyd
(1868–1947)

American writer, born in San Francisco. He was the son of Fanny Osbourne (née Vandegrift, 1840–1914) and stepson of **Robert Louis Stevenson**. He collaborated with Stevenson on several books, including *The Wrong Box* (1889), *The Wrecker* (1892) and *The Ebb Tide* (1894). He became American vice-consul in Samoa, and published several books of his own including *An Intimate Portrait of RLS* (1925).

▷ *Memoirs of Vailima* (1902)

O'SHAUGHNESSY, Arthur William Edgar
(1844–81)

English poet, born in London. In 1861 he began work in the British Museum, moving to the natural history department in 1863. An associate of the Pre-Raphaelites, he published *An Epic of Women* (1870), *Lays of France* (1872), *Music and Moonlight* (1874) and *Songs of a Worker* (1881). His best-known poem is 'The Music-Makers'.

OSKISON, John Milton
(1874–1947)

American novelist, short-story writer, biographer and journalist, born in Vinita, Indian Territory (now Oklahoma). Of mixed Cherokee and White descent, Oskison's Native American background was largely unknown to his readership at the time. His many short stories, written at the turn of the century and published in popular magazines, and his novels of the 1920s and 30s—*Wild Harvest* (1925), *Black Jack Davy* (1926) and *Brothers Three* (1935)—are all set in Cherokee Indian Territory, but differ in their emphases and style: whereas the stories often concentrate on Native American characters and make use of regional dialect, the novels follow the genre of the frontier romance and portray the lives of White settlers. His best novel is generally thought to be his last, a semi-autobiographical story of three mixed-blood brothers, with its theme of spiritual renewal through closeness to the land. Oskison also wrote biographies of the Texas statesman Sam Houston and the Shawnee chief, Tecumseh.

▷ D F Littlefield, Jr and J W Parins, 'Short Fiction Writers of the Indian Territory', in *American Studies 23:1* (1982)

OSSIAN, or Oisín Mac Fhinn Mhic Cumhail Mhic Tréanmóir Uí Baoisne

Legendary Gaelic bard and warrior, the son of Finn (Fingal). After many years' service in the *Fianna*, or sworn band of heroes, he departed for *Tír na n-Óg*, the land of perpetual youth, with its queen, Niamh Chinn Óir, from whom he returned after 300 years to age catastrophically and, after extended acrimony, to be converted to Christianity by St Patrick. Oral ballads, lyrics and prose ascribed to him, and a disputation supposedly recorded between Patrick and himself, were circulated in Ireland and Scotland, but the texts are probably from the 2nd century. The *Ossian* of **James Macpherson** supposes a coherence and royal status lacking in the original, since after Ossian's departure his father Fionn and his followers were finally defeated by the actual King of Ireland (or Tara), Cairbre Lifeachar, son of the Fianna's former suzerain, Cormac Mac Airt. The Fionn of Ossianic folklore had the intellectual's moral ambiguity also found in contrasting Odysseus myths: Macpherson's Fingal was of impeachable but interesting probity.

OSTROVSKY, Alexander
(1823–85)

Russian dramatist, born in Moscow. He studied law, but joined the civil service. He became director of a school of drama in 1885 and was given the task of choosing the repertoire for the Moscow Imperial Theatres. His own dramas are mainly domestic in nature, although he also looked at the darker side of official life, and his later work included historical dramas, and a fairy tale, *Snegurochka* (1873, 'Snow Maiden'), which Rimsky-Korsakov later used as the basis for his opera. His best-known play is *The Storm* (1860; Eng trans 1899).

▷ M Hoover, *Alexander Ostrovsky* (1981)

Ó SÚILLEABHÁIN, Eoghan Ruadh (Red Owen O'Sullivan)

(1748–84)

Irish Gaelic poet, born in County Kerry. He symbolizes the last phase of native Irish vernacular poetry. He was variously a teacher in proscribed Catholic ('hedge') schools, an itinerant labourer, a sailor serving with Rodney in the West Indies, a British soldier, and at all times an insatiable lover. His work followed Irish patriotic poetic traditions, and obvious parallels exist with his contemporary **Robert Burns**; and **W B Yeats**'s 'Red Hanrahan' was based on him, as is 'Owen Mac-Carthy' in Thomas Flanagan's *The Year of the French* (1979).

▷ D Corkery, in *The Hidden Ireland* (1924)

O'SULLIVAN, Vincent

(1937–)

New Zealand poet and critic, who has also written novels and short stories. His first verse was *Our Burning Time* (1965), followed by *Revenants* (1969). A black humour is uppermost in the series of 'Butcher' poems: *Butcher & Co* (1977) and *The Butcher Papers* (1982), and a satiric edge in *Brother Jonathan, Brother Kafka* (1980) and *The Pilate Tapes* (1986). He has also written a novel, *Let the River Stand* (1993); his short-story collections include *Dandy Edison for Lunch and Other Stories* (1981) and *The Snow in Spain* (1990), while drama includes work for radio and television in *Ordinary Nights in Ward Ten* (1984) and a stage play *Shuriken* (1983), dealing with cultural conflicts in a camp for Japanese prisoners-of-war during World War II. He is perhaps best-known for his editing of the Oxford *Anthology of Twentieth-Century New Zealand Poetry* (1970, rev edns 1976, 1987).

OSWALD VON WOLKENSTEIN

(1377–1445)

Austrian (Tyrolese) poet, a Minnesinger. Of aristocratic birth, he led an exceedingly adventurous life—he escaped from his home at the age of 10, to follow the Austrian army into Prussia, and was later imprisoned, by a trap she set for him, in the dungeon of the woman he loved. Many have enjoyed his varied work because in it 'there is more zest than discrimination', and because of his 'strongly sensual and turbulent nature' (as critics have expressed it). His directness and liveliness made him one of the most gifted German poets of his age, as well as one of the most technically accomplished. He invigorated his courtly themes with folk-song elements, and was a talented composer, many of whose melodies have survived.

▷ *London Medieval Studies for F. Norman* (1965)

OTCENÁSEKK, Jan

(1924–)

Czech novelist, born in Prague. He had a success with *Romeo a tma* (1958, Eng trans *Romeo and Juliet and The Darkness*, 1960), a wartime tale of a man's love for a Jewish girl in Nazi-occupied Prague, but his earlier *Obcan Brych* (1955), an attempt to reconcile conscience and communism, was reckoned by most to have been an over-ambitious failure.

OTERO, Blas de

(1916–79)

Spanish poet, born in Bilbao, the leading member of the so-called Generation of '36, the inferior successor to those of '98 and '27. His poetry has aptly been described as moving from the influence of **Miguel Hernández** to that of **Léon Felipe**. His poetry was more effectively lyrical than that of his contemporaries, was carefully wrought, and much respected. Poems in English translation are *Twenty Poems* (1964) and *Miguel Hernández and Blas de Otero: Selected Poems* (1972).

OTHÓN, Manuel José

(1858–1906)

Mexican poet and playwright, born in San Luis Potosí. He reacted against *modernismo*, being too mature in outlook to fall for its sugariness. In his outstanding collection *Poemas rústicos 1890–1902* (1902) he expressed his pantheistic beliefs in a manner which Mexico had never seen and will never see again. Then, in *Idilio salvaje* (1905, Eng trans 'Wild Idyll' by **Samuel Beckett** in *Translations of Mexican Poetry*, 1959), he recorded, in seven sonnets, his love for a young girl, which are amongst the great love poems of the 20th century.

▷ B Dromundo, *Manuel José Othón: su vida y su obra* (1959)

OTTLEY, Reginald Leslie

(1909–)

English-born Australian writer for children, born in London. His first book, *By the Sandhills of Yamboorah* (1965), won a New York *Herald Tribune* prize in the following year. It was followed by *The Roan Colt of Yamboorah* (1966) and the trilogy was completed with *Rain Comes to Yamboorah* in 1967. Seven other books appeared between 1968 and 1974, and a book of short stories, *Brumbie Dust*, in 1969.

OTWAY, Thomas

(1652–85)

English dramatist, born in Trotton in Sussex. From Winchester he passed in 1669 to Christ

Church, Oxford. He left the university without a degree in 1672, failed utterly as an actor, but made a fair hit with his tragedy *Alcibiades* (1675). In it the actress Elizabeth Barry made her first appearance, and Otway is said to have fallen in love with her. In 1676 Betterton accepted his *Don Carlos*, a good tragedy in rhyme. In 1677 Otway translated **Racine**'s *Bérénice*, as well as **Molière**'s *Cheats of Scapin*. In 1678–9 he was in Flanders as a soldier; in the May of the former year appeared his coarse but diverting comedy, *Friendship in Fashion*. The year 1680 yielded two tragedies, *The Orphan* and *Caius Marius*, and his one important poem, *The Poet's Complaint of his Muse*; to 1681 belongs *The Soldier's Fortune*. His greatest work, *Venice Preserved, or a Plot Discovered* (1682), is a masterpiece of tragic passion. For a time he sinks out of sight, to reappear again in 1684 with *The Atheist*, a feeble comedy, and in February 1685 with *Windsor Castle*, a poem addressed to the new king, James VII and II. He died in poverty. In 1719 a badly edited tragedy, *Heroick Friendship*, was published as his.
▷ E Rothstein, *Restoration Tragedy* (1967)

OUIDA, pseud of **Marie Louise de la Ramée**
(1839–1908)
English popular novelist, born in Bury St Edmunds. Her mother was English, her father a French teacher. 'Ouida' was a childish mispronunciation of 'Louise'. Educated in Paris, she settled in London in 1857. Starting her career by contributing stories to magazines, in particular to *Bentley's Miscellany* (1859–60), her first success was *Held in Bondage* (1863), shortly followed by *Strathmore* (1865), another three-decker aimed at the circulating libraries. She was soon established as a writer of hot-house romances, often ridiculed for her opulent settings, preposterous heroes and improbable plots, as well as for her ignorance of male sports and occupations. But her narratives were powerful and readers responded to her emotional energy and until her popularity waned in the 1890s she was a bestseller. From 1860 she spent much time in Italy and in 1874 settled in Florence where she lived lavishly in a style recognizable from her novels. She wrote almost 50 books, mainly novels, such as *Under Two Flags* (1867), *Folle-Farine* (1871) which was praised by **Edward Bulwer-Lytton**, *Two Little Wooden Shoes* (1874), *A Village Commune* (1881) and *In Maremma* (1882)—but also animal stories, essays and tales for children. Latterly her royalties dried up. She fell into debt, moved to Lucca in 1894, and her last years in Viareggio were spent in destitution.
▷ E Bigland, *Ouida* (1950)

OUOLOGUEM, Yambo
(c.1930–)
Mali poet, novelist, author of school textbooks, of Dogon ancestry, who was well known for his angry early poem 'When Negro Teeth Speak'. His best-known novel is *De Devoir de violence* (1968, Eng trans *Bound to Violence*, 1971); the pornographic *Les Milles et une bibles du sexe* (1969, 'The Thousand and One Bibles of Sex') has yet to find a translator.

OUSMANE, Sembene
(1923–)
Senegalese Francophone novelist and maker of films. The son of a fisherman, a militant socialist, he has been one of the most persistent and best known of his country's writers. He is not, like **Kane** or **Laye**, an elegant stylist, but—as in his first book, *Le Docker noir* (1956, 'The Black Docker'), set in Marseilles in the later 1930s—gives it to his reader hot and strong, in the tradition of **Zola**. *Les Bouts de bois de Dieu* (1960, Eng trans *God's Bits of Wood*, 1970) is generally regarded as his finest book. It is centred on the great strike of African railwaymen on the Dakar–Niger line in 1947–8, and has much of the power of Zola at his best.
▷ A C Brench, *The Novelists' Inheritance in French Africa* (1967); W Cartey, *Whispers from a Continent* (1969)

OUSPENSKY, Peter
(1878–1947)
Unorthodox but highly influential Russian philosopher (in the **Soloviev** tradition, but with more lucidity), who became a student of **Gurdjieff** in 1914, and eventually broke off relations with him in order to teach his own version of Gurdjieff's doctrine in London and America. He wrote several works of fiction, including *Strange Life of Ivan Osokin* (1947). His *In Search of the Miraculous* (1949) has been one of the most widely read religious books of the post-war period. His theories about time are behind both the 'time plays' of **Priestley** and the *Four Quartets* of **T S Eliot**.
▷ M Nicoll, *Living Time* (1949)

ØVERLAND, Arnulf
(1889–1968)
Norwegian poet, born in Kristiansund. He wrote radical poetry in volumes such as *Brød og vin* (1919, 'Bread and Wine') and *Berget det Blå* (1937, 'The Blue Rock'). A committed anti-fascist and socialist, he wrote *Den røde front* (1937, 'The Red Front'), which contained the famous warning 'You must not sleep', and circulated Resistance poetry during the German occupation of Norway, for

which he was imprisoned in a concentration camp. His post-war verse was more philosophical in tone.

▷C Hambro, *Arnulf Øverland* (1984)

OVID (Publius Ovidius Naso)
(43 BC–?17 AD)

Roman poet, born in Sulmo (Solmona), in the Abruzzi, son of a well-to-do *eques*. He was trained for the law in Rome, but gave his whole energies to poetry. His first literary success was his collection of love poems, the *Amores* ('Loves'). Then came his *Heroides* ('Heroines'), imaginary love letters from ladies of the heroic days to their lords. The *Ars Amandi*, or *Ars Amatoria* ('The Art of Love'), a handbook of seduction, appeared about 1 BC, followed by the equally outrageous *Remedia Amoris* ('Cures for Love'). His second period of poetic activity opens with the *Metamorphoses*, a collection of mythological and near-magical tales in 15 books, and with the *Fasti* ('Calendar'), designed to be in 12, of which six only were completed. Midway in composition he was banished by Augustus (AD8), for some unknown reason, to Tomis (Constanza) on the Black Sea, where he died. On his way from Rome he began his third period with the elegies which he published in five books, the *Tristia* ('Sorrows'). Similar in tone and theme are the four books of the *Epistolae ex Ponto* ('Letters from the Black Sea'). His *Ibis*, written in imitation of **Callimachus**, and his *Halieutica* ('Fishing Matters'), a poem extant only in fragments, complete the list of his works. Ovid is the most voluminous of the Latin poets and master of the elegiac couplet. His style is light, elegant and varied.

▷H Fränkel, *Ovid, a Poet between Two Worlds* (1945)

OWEN, Daniel
(1836–95)

Welsh novelist, born in Mold in Flintshire. After a poverty-stricken childhood, during which his father and two of his brothers were drowned in a mining accident, he studied for the Calvinist ministry, but gave this up when he came to doubt his vocation. He wrote 'for the common man'. His major novel is *Rhys Lewis* (1885), a first-person work telling the life-story of a minister. It contains a 'gallery of the best-known characters in Welsh-language fiction', and has been called 'the greatest single step forward in the history of the Welsh-language novel'.

▷J G Jones, *The Novelist from Mold* (1976)

OWEN, Goronwy, pseud of Goronwy Ddu o Fôn
(1723–69)

Welsh poet, born on Anglesey. Brought up in the demanding Bardic tradition, he was ordained priest (1746) and served for a year, on Anglesey, before being 'obliged to leave'. In 1657 he sailed for America, where, after a life of disappointment (in the course of which he lost two wives) he turned, as the vicar of a parish in the heart of the Virginia tobacco country, to a careful drinking—it had once been prodigal. These lapses apart, he was, as he has been called, the 'first great poet of the Welsh middle class', in whose work 'Horace and Dafydd Nanmor mingle'.

▷S Lewis, *A School of Welsh Augustans* (1924)

OWEN, John
(c.1560–1622)

Welsh epigrammatist, born in Llanarmon, Pwllheli. Educated at Winchester, he became a jurist fellow at New College, Oxford, in 1584. He was later employed as a schoolmaster at Trelleck, Gwent, and in 1595 became headmaster of Warwick school. He published 10 books of *Epigrammata*, written in Latin, between 1606 and 1613. His epigrams were bestsellers in their day, and particularly popular on the Continent.

▷*Owen the Epigrammist* (1909)

OWEN, Wilfred
(1893–1918)

English poet, born in Plas Wilmot, near Oswestry, Shropshire, where his father worked on the railway. Educated at the Birkenhead Institute and at Shrewsbury Technical School, he worked as a pupil-teacher at Wyle Cop School while preparing for the matriculation exam for the University of London. But money was too short for him to be able to take up courses there. In 1913 he left England to teach English in Bordeaux at the Berlitz School of Languages. He was tutoring a private pupil in the Pyrenees when war was declared. He enlisted in 1915 and in 1917 suffered concussion and trench fever on the Somme. In the summer of that year he was sent to recuperate at Craiglockart War Hospital, near Edinburgh, where he introduced himself to **Siegfried Sassoon**, who suggested improvements to his poems and encouraged him. However, he was posted back to France near the end of the war where he won the MC, but was killed on the bank of the Oise-Sambre Canal, near Ors, just a week before the Armistice was signed. Only five of his poems were published while he was alive, most of them being published between the summer he arrived at Craiglockhart and the time of his death. His work was first collected in 1920 by Sassoon and reappeared in 1931 with a memoir by **Edmund Blunden**. *The Collected Poems* was published in 1963. His poetry is distinguished by its directness, realism and vivid imagery, and individual poems like 'Dulce et Decorum Est' and 'Anthem for doomed Youth' have shaped the attitude of many towards war.

▷D S R Welland, *Wilfred Owen* (1960)

OWENSON, Sydney, Lady Morgan
(1776–1859)

Irish novelist and woman-of-letters. In her, wrote a critic, 'were met all the contradictions that identified Irish conflicts and troubles'. Her third novel, *The Wild Irish Girl* (1806), made her famous; she married the surgeon Sir Charles Morgan in 1812. She fought all her life for reconciliation of all kinds. The best of her warm, interesting but stylistically undistinguished novels is *The O'Briens and the O'Flahertys* (1827).

▷L Stevenson, *The Wild Irish Girl* (1936); M Campbell, *Sydney Owenson* (1988)

OYONO, Ferdinand
(1929–)

Francophone Cameroon novelist, son of a devoutly Roman Catholic mother. He studied law in Paris, and became a diplomat. He was also an actor. The great strength of such satirical novels as *Une Vie de Boy* (1956, Eng trans *Houseboy*, 1966) lies in their good-tempered but accurate descriptions of life in the Cameroons under French rule.

▷*Black Orpheus*, 2 (1958)

OZ, Amos
(1939–)

Israeli Hebrew-language writer, born in Jerusalem. At the age of 14 he went to live in a kibbutz, where he taught in the school and became a writer of international stature. His works, which deal with historical and contemporary themes of guilt and persecution, include *Makom aber* (1966, Eng trans *Elsewhere, Perhaps*, 1973), *Har ha-etsah ha-raah* (1976, Eng trans *The Hill of Evil Counsel*, 1978), *Israel* (1983, Eng trans *In the Land of Israel*, 1983) and *Menuhah nekhonah* (1984, Eng trans *A Perfect Peace*, 1985). His work has been widely translated (a process in which he has collaborated) and he has won many awards. *Mikha'el sheli* (1972, Eng trans *My Michael*, 1972), described by the *New York Times* as 'a modern Israeli *Madame Bovary*', is the book by which he is best known. *Kufsah shehorah* (Eng trans *Black Box*, 1988) appeared in 1988.

OZICK, Cynthia
(1928–)

American novelist and short-story writer, born in New York City. Educated at New York University and Ohio State University, she has said she began her first novel, *Trust* (1966), an American writer and ended it six and a half years later a Jewish one. Powerfully and originally expressing the Jewish ethos, her slight but significant oeuvre includes *The Pagan Rabbit and Other Stories* (1971), *Bloodshed* (1976), *Levitation* (1982), *The Cannibal Galaxy* (1983) and *The Messiah of Stockholm* (1987).

▷J Lowin, *Cynthia Ozick* (1988)

P

PAGAZA, Joaquin
(1839–1918)

Mexican poet and translator (**Virgil**, **Horace**). A priest, he tried to describe Mexico's beauties in the style of Virgil. His careful poetry influenced the great **Othón**.

PAGE, P(atricia) K(athleen)
(1916–)

English-born Canadian poet, novelist and artist. An early novel, *The Sun and the Moon* (1944), was published under the name Judith Cape and as a painter Page works as P K Irwin. Her first collection of poems was *As Ten as Twenty* (1946), which showed the influence of British Thirties writing. As an assistant editor of the magazine *Preview* Page was instrumental in the development of a modernist school of poetry in Canada. After marrying the Chairman of the Canadian Film Board, who was then made a High Commissioner to Australia, Page travelled widely. Some critics have noticed her work becoming purer, more oracular—a result, it is suggested, of an interest in Sufism.

PAGE, Thomas Nelson
(1853–1922)

American novelist and diplomat, born in Hanover County, Virginia. He practised law in Richmond, wrote many stories, some in Negro dialect, the best of which were *Marse Chan* (1884) and *Ole Virginia* (1887). He became American Ambassador to Italy from 1913 to 1919.
▷H Holman, *The Literary Career of Page, 1884–1910* (1978)

PAGNOL, Marcel
(1895–1974)

French dramatist and film-script writer, born near Marseilles. His childhood in Provençe informs his best work, the play trilogy *Marius* (1929, filmed in 1931), *Fanny* (1931, filmed 1932) and *César* (1936, having been filmed two years earlier), each part being a comedy of Marseilles life. He first became widely known with the memoir *Topaze* (1928), a satirical study of bourgeois bad faith, which was filmed five years later by Louis Gasneur. Provençe and its warmth, both literal and human, is at the centre of *La Gloire de mon père* (1957) and his other memoirs. He became a member of the Académie française in 1946, the first film-maker to be so honoured.

PAINE, Albert Bigelow
(1861–1937)

American editor and biographer of **Mark Twain**. Paine began his working life as the employee of a photography supply firm in Kansas. He submitted some prose sketches to *Harpers Weekly* and when they were accepted set off for New York. He published a successful book for children, *The Arkansaw Bear* (1898) and New York's theatre area was named after his play *The Great White Way* (1901). But his later career was determined by the success of his biography of Thomas Nast (1904), following which Mark Twain immediately engaged him as his secretary and official biographer. In addition to the biography (1912), Paine edited Twain's speeches and correspondence.

PAINE, Tom
(1737–1809)

English radical politician and writer, born in Thetford, Norfolk. He left school when he was only 13 and, after trying out many jobs, and much study, became an excise officer. He began to try to organize labour, and published his first pamphlet in 1772: *The Case of the Officers of Excise*; as a result of it he was dismissed. Soon after this he met **Benjamin Franklin**. In America he became editor of the radical *Philadelphia Magazine*; in the War of Independence, he fought in Washington's army. In 1887 he returned to England, where he wrote his most famous and influential work, *The Rights of Man* (Part 1, 1790, Part 2, 1792), which was, initially, a reply to the *Reflections on the Revolution in France* of **Edmund Burke**. In 1792 he was indicted for treason, and fled to France (where *The Rights* had been instantly translated). He took part in French affairs, but was imprisoned by Robespierre when he spoke (and wrote) against the execution of the French king. His release, after two years of confinement, was secured by a friend. In prison he wrote what is in fact his most substantial work: *The Age of Reason* (1794–6), an attack on the Church and (less successfully) an advocation of deism. He died in America in poverty and neglect. Paine's influence lay not in his originality of thought but in his passion and directness, which, if only very occasionally, cut through the elegance and intricacy of Burke, and cause it to look a little disingenuous. His defences of democracy have always been extremely persuasive.

▷H Pearson, *Tom Paine, Friend of Mankind* (1937); R R Fennessey, *Burke, Paine and the Rights of Man* (1963)

PAKKALA, Teuvo, pseud of T O Frosterus
(1862–1925)

Finnish dramatist and novelist, born in Oulu, who is now remembered for his plays. His fiction, although well written, has dated.

PALACIO, Pablo
(1906–47)

Ecuadorean novelist, militant socialist, translator and philosopher, born in Loja. Palacio was forgotten by readers for a decade after his death, but then rediscovered by the critic Jorge Enrique Adoum. In his works, a critic wrote in 1981, the contemporary reader 'began to rediscover the incredible profundity and modernity of the forgotten ... author. In this work, sometimes hermetic, always taciturn and hallucinated, the attentive reader finds many contemporary anxieties and obsessions'. Described by one critic as 'a character in one of Arlt's works', the syphilitic and eventually mad Palacio anticipates, in his stories in *Un hombre muerte a putapiés* (1927, 'The Man Kicked to Death'), and in his novels *Débora* (1928) and *Vida de ahorcado* (1932, 'A Hanged Life'), every modernist technique. His collected works appeared in 1964.

▷J Ruffinelli, *Critica en Marcha* (1980)

PALAMAS, Kostis
(1859–1943)

One of the greatest modern Greek poets, and for 50 years the most influential critic in the country. Born in Patras, the son of a magistrate, he was orphaned at the age of seven and brought up by an uncle in Missolonghi. In 1875 he went to Athens to study, and began to have his poems published in journals, although his first collection, *Tatraghoudhia tis Patridos Mou* ('The Songs of My Country'), did not appear until 1886. In 1889 he won the first Philadelphian Poetry Prize with his hymn to Athena, and he won again with 'Ta Matia tis Psychis Mou' ('Eyes of My Soul') the following year. The title of this second poem is taken from a very famous line by **Solomos**, and some critics have found Palamas's obvious homage to the great Greek masters too derivative. *Asalenti Zoë*, a collection published in 1904 (Eng trans *Life Immutable*, 1919), is still reckoned to be his greatest, containing 'He Phinikia' ('The Palm

Tree'), one of the most famous poems in the language. Although he did not publish anything during the last 10 years of his life, his death while the country was under enemy occupation was seized upon as a potent symbol of resistance, and his funeral was attended by a huge crowd.

▷G Katsimbalis, *Bibliography of Kostis Palamas* (1975, lists more than 2 500 essays and articles written by the poet)

PALAZZESCHI, Aldo, pseud of Aldo Giurlani
(1885–1974)

Italian poet and major novelist, born in Florence. He began, with his close friend **Moretti**, as an actor, but abandoned this career when he issued (1905) a collection of verse, *I cavalli bianchi* ('White Horses'). This, a curious and interesting debut, mixed the traces of the influence of **D'Annunzio** with (more surely) those of the school of poets who had reacted against his decadent bombast, the Crepusculari (of which Moretti was a representative). For a short period (1909–14) he was associated with the Futurist movement of **Marinetti**, but he broke with it to take his own course, one unique in modern Italian letters. His chief novels are the fantastic *Il codice di Perelà* (1911, Eng trans *Perela, The Man of Smoke*, 1936), about a man actually made of smoke (and himself a reflection of Palazzeschi's own faintly homosexualized aestheticism—an early hero was **Oscar Wilde**); his majestically tragic masterpiece *Le sorelle Materassi* (1934, Eng trans *The Materassi Sisters*, 1953), apparently relatively conventional, but written in a subtle parody of regular 'realistic' prose; and *Roma* (1953, Eng trans *Rome*, 1965), a satire on 'good government'. Many of his poems, such as 'Rio Bo', are still much anthologized.

▷G Pullini, *Aldo Palazzeschi* (1965, in Italian); S Pacifici (ed), *From Verismo to Experimentalism* (1969)

PALÉS MATOS, Luis
(1898–1959)

White Puerto Rican, born in Guayama, who became his country's most distinguished negrophile modern poet. His father—like his mother, a poet and freethinker—was a rural teacher who earned a pittance; Palés's childhood was one of acute poverty. The best account of his life is given in his unfinished novel *Littoral* (published in his *Obras*, 1984, 'Works'). A melancholy man, quite lacking in literary ambition, he published only two collections in his lifetime, but his poems circulated widely in typescript. 'Palés,' wrote the editor of a critical edition of his works, 'is the indispensable initiator of Negritude in the Hispanic Antilles.' In his poetry, especially in the influential *Tuntún* (1937), he mixed Spanish with African words and phrases, sometimes neologisms, to give a 'Negro' effect.

PALEY, Grace, née Goodside
(1922–)

American short-story writer, born in New York City. She was educated at Hunter College, New York, and has taught in several US colleges. Her fiction has all been in the short-story form, usually set in New York, and often with Jewish settings and themes. Her sharp ear for convincingly realistic dialogue is evident in all her stories. Those in *Little Disturbances of Man* (1959) have a wider range of social settings than *Enormous Changes at the Last Minute* (1974), which are all set in the run-down world of inner-city slums, but they share a common wit, compassion, and characteristic tone of voice. Her support of the peace movement is evident in *Later the Same Day* (1985), as well as in the non-fiction *365 Reasons Not to Have Another War* (1989). Other writings include *Begin Again: New and Collected Poems* (1992), and an essay collection, *Long Walks and Intimate Talks* (1991).

PALGRAVE, Francis Turner
(1824–97)

English poet and critic, born in Great Yarmouth, eldest son of Sir Francis Palgrave. He became a scholar of Balliol College, Oxford, and fellow of Exeter College, was successively vice-principal of a training college, private secretary to George Leveson-Gower (Earl Granville), an official in the education department, and Professor of Poetry at Oxford (1886–95). His works include *Idylls and Songs* (1854), *Essays on Art* (1866), *Hymns* (1867), *Lyrical Poems* (1871), *Visions of England* (1881), and *Landscape in Poetry* (1897). He is best known as the editor of the *Golden Treasury of Lyrical Poetry* (1875); *Sonnets and Songs of Shakespeare* (1877); selections from **Robert Herrick** (1877) and **Keats** (1885); and *Treasury of Sacred Song* (1889).
▷R H Palgrave, in *Collected Works* (1919–22)

PALLISER, Charles
(1947–)

American novelist and academic, born near Boston, Massachusetts, but who has made his home in Scotland, where he teaches at Strathclyde University. His first novel, *The Quincunx* (1989), set in Regency London, has an extremely intricate plot involving John Huffam's quest to discover the truth about his family's past, in which wealth and murder play equal parts. The research and the writing took Palliser 12 years and the result is both

a substantial and lengthy work. His second novel, *The Sensationist* (1991), the story of a disastrous contemporary love affair, is considerably shorter, and was followed by *Betrayals* (1994), a novel of 10 independent chapters, which develops his interest in literary pastiche.

PALMA, Ricardo
(1883–1919)

Major Peruvian writer, who invented a new and unique genre, the *tradición*, and is in many ways still one of Peru's chief keepers of conscience—nor can Peru be fully understood without close acquaintance with his works. The *tradición* is based on some single fact or folk belief, and then expands upon it in a kind of essay-fiction of some thousand words. His *Tradicions peruanas* were collected in 1957, and a good selection from them was translated in 1945 as *The Knights of the Cape*. Palma was an ultra-critical lover of his country and its ways, and these ironic, racy, colloquial pieces, examples of very high art which read spontaneously, cover almost every aspect of its life—and often anticipate events which have taken place since his death. He was director of the National Library. His son, Clemente Palma (1872–1946), was himself an important writer—though somewhat neglected at present—whose *Cuentos malévolos* (1904, rev edn 1923, Eng trans *Malevolent Tales*, 1984) and *Historietas malignas* (1925, Eng trans *Malignant Tales*, 1988) are **Schopenhauer**ian *tours de force*. Ricardo Palma wrote much else besides the *tradiciones*, including vital books on Peruvian Spanish.
▷J M Oviedo, *Ricardo Palma* (1968, in Spanish); E M Aldrich, *The Modern Short Story in Peru* (1966)

PALMER, (Edward) Vance
(1885–1959)
PALMER, Nettie (Janet Gertrude)
(1885–1964)

Australian writers, born in Bundaberg, Queensland, and Bendigo, Victoria, respectively. They worked in most genres, including novels, short stories, plays, poetry, and social and literary criticism. Vance Palmer established the Pioneer Players in Melbourne in 1922, and many of his plays were performed by that group. His *Separate Lives* (1931), *Sea and Spinifex* (1934) and *Let the Birds Fly* (1955) typify his anecdotal sketches and stories; his first serious attempt at the novel came in *Cronulla* (1924) but his best-known is *The Passage* (1930), set in a Queensland fishing village which itself develops into one of the main characters in a study of inevitable change. Palmer's political concerns show strongly in his trilogy of a power-broking union man, Macy Donovan, in a small mining community based on the copper town of Mt Isa in north-west Queensland. *Golconda* (1948), *Seedtime* (1957) and *Big Fellow* (1959) chart Donovan's climb to political power. Nettie Palmer graduated from Melbourne University, travelled and studied in Europe, and married Vance Palmer in London in 1914, creating a partnership that for nearly 40 years dominated the literary left. She was a prolific writer for contemporary journals but little of her criticism has been collected except for the ground-breaking *Modern Australian Literature 1900–1923* (1924). Her major contribution to Australian literature was in the advocacy of other, especially women, writers. She was among the first to recognize the worth of **Henry Handel Richardson** and to promote such diverse authors as **Barbara Baynton**, **Shaw Nielson** and **Katharine Susannah Prichard**.

PALMOTIĆ, Junije
(1607–75)

Ragusan poet and dramatist, who took over Italian Renaissance themes and adapted them to Ragusan (Dalmatian) settings.

PALTOCK, Robert
(1697–1767)

English lawyer and writer, born in London. He took up law and practised as an attorney at Clement's Inn. He wrote the fantasy novel *The Life and Adventures of Peter Wilkins* (1751), in which the shipwrecked hero finds himself in a distant land where people can fly by means of a silky outer skin. Its authorship remained a mystery till 1835.

PALUDAN, Jacob
(1896–1975)

Danish novelist, son of a professor of Danish literature at the University of Copenhagen, trained as a pharmacist. From a conservative stand, Paludan criticizes the Americanization of traditional European and Danish values and equates the rise of industrial mass culture with the victory of mediocrity. Paludan's debut novel *De vestlige Veje* (1922, 'The Western Roads'), about a Danish emigrant's encounter with the USA, is a denunciation of the transatlantic capitalism epitomized by New York. A master of the large-scale social realist novel, Paludan first gained a wide readership with *Fugle omkring Fyret* (1925, 'Birds around the Lighthouse'), a vivid novel about a small fishing and farming community, Sandhavn, which the commercial and political establishment, governed by a blind belief in material progress, seeks to transform into a major sea port. His subsequent works *Markerne modnes* (1927, 'The Fields Ripen') and

Jørgen Stein (1932–3), his last major piece of fiction and a canonical text in Danish literature, are classic novels of social and individual development. In two large volumes the latter presents a panorama of Denmark's transformation from 1914 to 1933, with the emphasis on the breakdown of the traditional patriarchal culture.
▷H Oldenburg, *Jacob Paludan. Historien om et venskab* (1984)

PALUDAN-MÜLLER, Frederick
(1809–76)

Danish poet. He wrote poems, dramas and romances, including the verse novel *Danserinden* (1833, 'The Dancer'), but his fame rests on *Adam Homo* (1841–9), a humorous, satiric, didactic epic about the worldly sin and moral decline of a successful man.
▷S Møller Kristensen, *Digtning og livssyn* (1959)

PANDURO, Leif
(1923–77)

Danish novelist and television dramatist, born in Copenhagen; he practised as a dentist until 1965, when he became a full-time writer. He came to notice with the witty, youthful novel *Rend mig i traditionerne* (1958, 'Sod The Traditions'), which demonstrates a linguistic energy and ingenuity reminiscent of **Salinger**'s *The Catcher in the Rye*. It views adult life and its norms through the quizzical eyes of David, a boarding-school pupil whose legs suddenly begin to perform subversive acts such as kicking the headmaster's backside or running away from school. David is admitted to a mental hospital but eventually discharged. The novel questions the validity of a sharp distinction between mental 'illness' and 'normality' and this remained one of Panduro's main preoccupations, evident also in novels such as *Den gale mand* (1965, 'The Mad Man'), *Daniels anden verden* (1970, 'Daniel's Other World') and *Høfeber* (1975, 'Hayfever'). While hyperbole and caricature are indispensable ingredients in his novels, Panduro's television plays are more naturalistic. Plays such as *Et godt liv* (1970, 'A Good Life'), *Rundt om Selma* (1971, 'Around Selma'), *I Adams verden* (1973, 'In Adam's World') and *Louises hus* (1977, 'Louise's House') set new standards for Danish television drama and achieved outstanding audience ratings: they typically depict the existential fall and subsequent awakening of an upper middle-class hero, whose psychological predicaments and social environment would be recognizable to many viewers.
▷J C Jørgensen, *Leif Panduro. En biografi* (1987)

PANFYOROV, Fyodor
(1896–1960)

Russian novelist, whose socialist-realist work, particularly *Bruski* (1931–7, Eng trans of part, *And then the Harvest*, 1920–39), was at one time widely discussed. He was criticized by **Gorky** for his poor craftsmanship, and is by now almost forgotten. *Svoimi glazmi* (1942, Eng trans *With Their Own Eyes*, 1942) held appeal during World War II.

PANNIKAR, Sardar, K M
(1895–1963)

Indian (Malayalam) statesman and ambassador, known in India for his poetry and drama, and, especially, historical novels.

PANSHIN, Alexei
(1940–)

American science-fiction writer and critic, born in Ann Arbor, Michigan. His first novel, *Rite of Passage* (1968, Nebula Award Winner), remains his best-known work: set mainly on a generation starship, it is the account of the survival tests undergone by the vessel's adolescents. The Villiers trilogy, which began with *Star Well* (1968) and continued in *The Thumb* (1968) and *Masque World* (1969), is more playful and less successful. His later works have been written in collaboration with his wife, Cory Panshin. These include the heroic fantasy *Earth Magic* (1978) and the critical study *SF in Dimension: A Book of Explorations* (1968).

PANZINI, Alfredo
(1863–1939)

Italian novelist, born in Senigallia. Like **Barrès** in France at approximately the same time, his theme for much of his fiction was 'rootlessness' and the emptiness of modern existence. Very learned in the classics, with a fine if somewhat over-elaborate and 'super-literary' style, he well understood the state of spiritual emptiness, but tended to equate it with the natural roughness and disorderliness of life, so that his appeal is to the academic, not to the common man. Yet he was popular, and such books as *Il bacio di Lesbia* (1937, 'Lesbia's Kiss') were widely read. He was adored by, and adored, Mussolini. One of his better books, *Io cerco moglie* (1920), was translated as *Wanted, A Wife* (1922).
▷S Pacifici, *The Modern Italian Novel from Capuana to Tozzi* (1973)

PAPADIAMANTIS, Alexandros
(1851–1911)

Greek novelist and writer of more than 200 'genre' tales. Born on Skiathos, the son of a priest, he was himself a cantor, and unlike his contemporaries refused to switch from *Katharevousa*, the official Greek used in church services and for official announcements, to demotic Greek. Although he later lived in Athens, almost all of his stories are set on his native island, and hark back to a golden age unspoilt by 'progress'. Those published before 1900 established his reputation, but it is his remarkable story of the gulf between human and divine justice, *Fonissa*, published in 1903 (Eng trans *The Murderess*, 1983), that has survived best; its protagonist is a 60-year-old woman, Frangogiannou, who comes to the realization that a woman's life is one of slavery, in turn to parents, husband and children, and so conceives of the idea of killing little girls to spare them their fate.

PAPATSONIS, Takis
(1895–)

Greek poet, critic and translator (of **Claudel**, **Aragon** and others), born in Athens who, although he came to poetic maturity at the time of the suicide of **Karyotakis**, reacted differently from the majority of his contemporaries to that event: instead of nihilism, romantic despair and decadence, he chose to express his religious (Catholic) faith. He was a civil servant and an expert in banking. His first poems appeared during World War I, when he was scarcely out of his boyhood, and anticipated many modernistic procedures. But he kept to his own path. His poetry has been called 'almost Surrealist'. Neglected by some, he is highly prized by others as a too-little-heeded and original religious poet.

PARDO BAZÁN, Emilia, Condesa de
(1851–1921)

Spanish writer, born of an aristocratic Galician family. Her literary vocation was formed early, then developed when the family moved to Madrid. This gave her access to the literary circles of the capital and cultivated her interest in contemporary European thought and affairs; her interests ranged over Darwinism, feminism and science, Russian and French literature. Besides her novels, she produced over 500 short stories, articles, criticism, poems and travel literature, as well as giving lectures. She was strongly influenced by the French naturalist writers, and this can be seen in her first novel, *Pascual Lopez* (1879). Her best-known books in this genre are *Los Pazos de Ulloa* (1886, 'The Manors of Ulloa') and *La Madre Naturaleza* (1887, 'Mother Nature'), both set in the rural decadence of her native Galicia. Later novels such as *La Quimera* (1905, 'The Chimera') and *La Sirena Negra* (1908, 'The Black Mermaid') are unmistakably modernist in atmosphere and psychology. Latterly she came under the influence of *fin-de-siècle* spiritualism and adopted more idealistic values. She also published works on **Zola** and naturalism, the revolution in Russia, and modern French literature. She was the first Spanish woman of note to sustain a feminist campaign, and she ran a library for women, amongst many other feminist activities.

▷M Hemingway, *Emilia Pardo Bazán. The Making of a Novelist* (1983)

PARDO Y ALIAGA, Felipe
(1806–69)

Peruvian poet, humorist and dramatist. He was born in Lima, his father having been a Spanish official. In 1840 he founded a satirical review, *El Espejo de Mi Tierra* ('Mirror of my Land'), with his pamphlet of that title attacking the new republic. His plays, poetry and essays are mainly satirical. The 'grandfather of Peruvian drama' was **Manuel Ascensio Segura**, a more substantial figure, but the exchanges between Pardo and the latter, leader of the *creolist* school of writing, form an important part of Peruvian literary history.

PAREJA DIEZ-CANSECO, Alfredo
(1908–)

Major Ecuardorean novelist, born in Guayaquil. His first novel, *La casa de los locos* (1929, 'The House of Madmen'), a savage and youthful *roman à clef* on corrupt politicians, made a sensation and sold out in a few days. But his first mature novel was *El muelle* (1933, 'The Voluptuous'), written after he had returned from a period in the United States: it is set in New York and Guayaquil at the time of the depression, and, although it reflects the author's Marxism, contains vivid and accurate portraits of both big and small business gangsters. He contributed to the book of stories, *Los que se van* (1930), brought out by the famous Grupo de Guayaquil, of which he was a member. His greatest novel is *Hombres sin tiempo* (1941, 'Men Without Time'), written as a result of his prison experiences (he, together with many others, was thrown into jail, as an MP, by the dictator Arroyo del Rio). This is influenced by **Thomas Mann**, under whose tutelage Pareja became a liberal rather than a communist. Later he became what he ironically called a 'bourgeois', prospered in business, wrote a bestseller, and was able to move with his family to Mexico. In 1951 he founded the newspaper *El Sol*. A historian as well as a novelist, he remains untranslated into English.

PARETSKY, Sarah
(1947–)

American crime writer, born in Eudora, Kansas and educated at the University of Kansas and the University of Chicago, where she received an MBA and a PhD in history. She worked for a research firm and as a marketing manager for an insurance company, before becoming a full-time writer in 1986. That same year she co-founded Sisters in Crime, an organization devoted to promoting women crime writers. Her novels feature the feisty female detective V I Warshawski (played on screen by Kathleen Turner in 1992), who faces such diverse problems as toxic waste and anti-abortionists. From these situations Paretsky looks at the nature of relationships between women, and at the line between the personal and professional as experienced by her outwardly tough but essentially warm-hearted heroine. Her most recent works include *Burn Marks* (1990) and *Guardian Angel* (1992).

PARGETER, Edith, pseud Ellis Peters
(1913–)

English novelist from Shropshire, also a highly successful crime writer under her pseudonym. Pargeter, always a prolific writer, wrote a string of quietly successful detective novels, many featuring Inspector Felse (*Fallen into the Pit*, 1951, was the first of these). Real success, however, came when she was in her sixties when, reading about a historical incident in which the relics of St Winifred were moved to Shrewsbury Abbey, she hit upon the idea of Brother Cadfael, a medieval detective. *A Morbid Taste for Bones: A Mediaeval Whodunnit* (1977, as Ellis Peters) was an instant hit, and a series was born. By no means as literary as **Umberto Eco**'s comparable *The Name of the Rose*, the Cadfael books are, nevertheless, prime examples of the sort of quintessentially English detective fiction where there is no gore and anything too unpleasant is described from a discreet distance. The period setting, though a strong selling point, is incidental. Pargeter was awarded the Crime Writers' Association Diamond Dagger Award—its highest—in 1993.

PARINI, Giuseppe
(1729–99)

Italian poet, born near Milan. He became a priest in 1754, and was professor at the Palatine and Brera schools (1769–99). He made his name as a poet by the sequence of poems called collectively *Il Giorno* (1763–1803, 'The Day'), which satirized the daily round of a young nobleman.

▷G Petronio, *Parini, storia della critica* (1957)

PARK, Ruth
(?1923–)

New Zealand-born Australian writer, born near Hamilton, and educated at Auckland university. She went to Australia in 1942 and married the author **D'Arcy Niland**. Her first success was in 1947 with the novel *The Harp in the South*, which won a newspaper competition. This story of slum life in the Surry Hills district of Sydney has been translated into 10 languages and forms a trilogy with *Poor Man's Orange* (1949) and the retrospective *Missus* (1986). *Swords and Crowns and Rings* (1977) won the **Miles Franklin** Award for its sensitive tale of an outcast of society. She created the popular books based on an ABC children's series about *The Muddle-Headed Wombat* between 1962 and 1981, and has also written novels for adolescent readers, including two set in Victorian Sydney, *Come Danger, Come Darkness* (1978) and the haunting *Playing Beatie Bow* (1980, filmed 1987). The autobiographical *A Fence Round the Cuckoo* (1992) was awarded the Foundation for Australian Literature Studies Award. A second volume of autobiography was published in 1993 as *Fishing in the Styx*.

PARKER, Dorothy, née **Rothschild**
(1893–1967)

American wit, short-story writer and journalist, born in West End, New Jersey, daughter of a clothes salesman. Her mother died when she was five and her father re-married; Dorothy could barely contain her antipathy to her stepmother and refused to address her. Her formal education ended in 1908 at the age of 14, but she was a voracious reader and, having read **Thackeray** when she was 11, decided to make literature her life. In 1916 she sold some of her poetry to the editor of *Vogue*, and was given the job of writing captions for fashion photographs and drawings. She then became drama critic of *Vanity Fair* (1917–20), where she met **Robert Benchley** and **Robert Sherwood** and formed with them the nucleus of the legendary Algonquin Hotel Round Table luncheon group. Famed for her spontaneous wit and acerbic criticism, she was at her most trenchant in book reviews and stories in the early issues (1927–33) of the *New Yorker*, a magazine whose character she did much to form. Her work continued to appear in the magazine at irregular intervals until 1955. Her reviews were collected in *A Month of Saturdays* (1971). She also wrote for *Esquire* and published poems and sketches. Her poems are included in *Not So Deep as a Well* (1930) and *Enough Rope* (1926), which became a bestseller. Her short stories were collected in *Here Lies* (1936). She also collaborated on several film scripts, including *The Little Foxes* and *A Star Is Born*. Twice married (1917 and 1933), she took her surname from her first husband. Both marriages foundered, there was a string of lacerating

love affairs, abortive suicide attempts, abortions, debts and drinking bouts, and she died alone in a Manhattan apartment with Troy, her poodle, at her side.
▷J Keats, *You Might As Well Live* (1971)

PÁRMENO, pseud of **José López Pinillos**
(1875–1922)

Spanish sensationalist novelist and playwright, born in Seville. Pármeno is a character in **Manuel Rojas**'s novel *Celestina*, suggestive of virile candour. Influenced by **Zola**, his crudely naturalistic and excessively violent novels have a certain raw power; he was unlucky in not finding an English translator, for he was readable.

PARNELL, Thomas
(1679–1718)

Irish poet and clergyman, born in Dublin. He was educated at Trinity College, took holy orders in 1700, and received the archdeaconry of Clogher (1706), and the vicarage of Finglass (1716). He also owned property in Cheshire, and he lived much in London, where his wit brought him the friendship of Harley, **Jonathan Swift** and **Pope**. After his wife's death in 1711 he took to drink, and died while on his way to Ireland. The following year Pope published a selection of his poems, the best-known of which are 'The Hermit', 'The Nightpiece on Death' and 'Hymn to Contentment'. His *Complete Poems* were first published in 1985.
▷O Goldsmith, *The Life of Parnell* (1770)

PARNICKI, Teodor
(1908–)

Polish novelist, born in Berlin and brought up in Moscow—he did not settle in Poland until he was 60—whose work is so learned, complex and subtle that it lacks what a critic has called its 'deserved international reputation'. He is Poland's most distinguished modern historical novelist, and he applied advanced modernist techniques in his revival of this form. His earlier novels took a conventionally **Freud**ian approach; but he soon matured. His untranslated later novels are interesting because they candidly take into account the inevitable subjectivity of the historian. His chosen areas of research—Rome in decline, Poland in the 11th century—are usually more or less unexplored territory. Typical of his novels—he is prolific, and each book is massive—is *Inne zcie Kleopatry* (1969, 'The Other Life of Cleopatra').

PARRA, Nicanor
(1914–)

Chilean poet, born in San Fabián de Aliceo. After the death of **Pablo Neruda** he became

Chile's leading poet (or, as he prefers to be called, antipoet). But in 1937, in a Chile dominated by Surrealism, Neruda and **Huidobro**, his first collection, *Cancionero sin nombre* (1937, 'Lyrics Without Name'), went almost unnoticed. But his second collection, *Poemas y antipoemas* (1954), although badly received, met with praise from Neruda himself. Parra, now a professor of theoretical physics, had discovered his own voice, whose intention was to create 'a poetic atmosphere of dynamic disarray'. In terms of English-language poetry, Parra's expression 'anti-poet' may perhaps best be understood as 'anti-lyrical'. By the side of Neruda or Huidobro he is a minor poet, but he has been influential on the American Beat poets, and he has in Chile a school of disciples. In common with many other writers of his century, Parra sees the world as a brutal and senseless place—Neruda and Huidobro, on the contrary, are visionary poets, for all their political beliefs—but he does so in a uniquely playful, likeable manner. There are many translations: *Poems and Antipoems* (1967), *Antipoems: New and Selected* (1985), *Emergency Poems* (1972), *Sermons and Homilies of the Christ of Elqui* (1984). For his most enthusiastic critics, he is the latest in a line of great antipoets, who include **Catullus**, **Villon** and **Quevedo**.
▷V M Valenzuela, *Contemporary Latin American Writers* (1971)

PARRA, Teresa de la
(1895–1936)
Venezuelan novelist, born into a wealthy family on an estate near Caracas, but educated in Paris. She wrote two important and well observed fictional autobiographies, *Ifigenia* (1924) and the more famous *Las memorias de Mamá Blanca* (1929, Eng trans *Mama Blanca's Souvenirs*, 1959), a witty account of the Venezualan capital and the countryside around it, as seen through the eyes of a refined Paris lady.

PARRY, Robert Williams
(1884–1956)
Welsh poet, born in Daffryn Nantlle. He won the National Eisteddfod in 1910, and was thereafter regarded as one of the country's leading new poets. After the Penyberth scandal in 1936, when three prominent Welshmen (including **Saunders Lewis**) were unjustly sentenced at the Old Bailey, he began to write political satire. His sonnets of the 1930s are his most prized work; two of these are well translated in the *Penguin Book of Welsh Verse* (1967).
▷B L Jones, *Robert Williams Parry* (1972)

PARRY-WILLIAMS, Sir Thomas Herbert
(1887–1975)
Welsh poet, scholar and critic, born in Rhyd-ddu. He won both Chair and Crown at the National Eisteddfod in 1912 and 1915. He was for most of his working life Professor of Welsh at Aberystwyth. With his kinsman **Robert Williams Parry**, he is the acknowledged master of the sonnet in the Welsh language. His best poetry is evocative of Welsh landscape, which he sees as formative of human character. He was an influential scholar of Welsh poetry. He was knighted in 1958.
▷*Poetry Wales* (1974, issue devoted to his work)

PARUN, Vesna
(1922–)
Croatian poet, born on Zlarin. She made a mark with her first and incomparably finest collection, *Zore i vihori* (1947, 'Dawns and Gales'), which paid no attention to the tenets of socialist realism, and was immediately criticized by party hacks. Forced into silence, she eventually returned to her childhood Catholicism, and wrote a less convincing and urgent poetry. Some of the love poems in *Bila sam djecak* (1963, 'I Was a Boy') are memorable.

PASÇOAES, Joaquim Teixera de, pseud
of **Joaquim Pereira de Vasconcelos**
(1877–1952)
Portuguese poet, editor and mystical nationalist, who declared, 'I was born to live beyond life', and tried to prove it with his vision of an incarnate God created by man as a result of his struggle against evil. *Saudade* is the specifically Portuguese version of **Unamuno**'s *aboulia*: apathy, lack of will, torpor, frozen ideology. Pasçoaes' poetry, after false starts, tried to define this with increasing exactitude, and he is therefore known as the *saudosista* poet *par excellence*. Egoistic, he was also crucial in the development of modern Portuguese literature. His magazine *A Águia* ('The Eagle'), which he edited from 1912 until 1916, was the gathering point for all the most gifted members of Pasçoaes's generation. His poetry is more interesting than his confused philosophy suggests: the long *Regresso ao Paraiso* (1912, 'Return to Paradise') is one of the more curious poems of its century.

PASCOLI, Giovanni
(1855–1912)
Italian poet and writer, born in San Mauro di Romagna. He was Professor of Latin at Bologna from 1907. Much of his poetry, set in the background of his native Romagna, is

of a tragic nature; his volumes of verse include *Myricae* (1891), *In Or San Michele* (1903, 'For San Michele') and *Canti di Castelvecchio* (1903, 'Songs of Castelvecchio'). *Sotto il Velame* (1900, 'Beneath the Veil') and *La Mirabile Visione* (1902, 'Heavenly Vision') are critical studies of **Dante**'s *Commedia Divina*.
▷P Mazzamuto, *Pascoli* (1966)

PASEK, Jan Chryzostom
(c.1636–c.1701)

Polish diarist, born in Rawa. A squire, he led an adventurous life, fighting invaders of Poland, but also a quiet one, buying and selling, and running his farm on what were for those days enlightened principles. He had little tolerance for the law. His memoirs in diary form, *Pamietniki* (1836), of which there is a translation in French, is an incomparable mixture of complexity and simplicity, ranging from vivid semi-fictional portraits of soldiers to lists of a peasant's proper duties. Furthermore, the book has great linguistic importance.
▷J K Heck, *Jan Chryzostom Pasek* (1902)

PASOLINI, Pier Paolo
(1922–75)

Italian critic, poet, novelist, film director and screen-writer, born and educated in Bologna. Most of his childhood was spent in Casara della Delizia, in his mother's birthplace of Friuli. He became notorious in the 1950s, principally through the publication of the first two parts of a projected trilogy, *Ragazzi di vita* (1955, Eng trans *The Ragazzi*, 1968) and *Una vita violenta* (1959, Eng trans *A Violent Life*, 1968). Superficially works of protest, they exhibit a strong thematic continuity with his early youthful poetry, portraying the timeless innocence of Friuli. His later writings did not match those of his youth, and during the 1960s and 1970s he devoted himself to directing films, many based on literary sources: *Il Vangelo Secondo Matteo* (1964, 'The Gospel According to Saint Matthew'), *Il Decamerone* (1971, 'The Decameron') and *Salò, o, Le centoventi giornate di Sodoma* (1975, 'Salo: The 120 Days of Sodom'). He was murdered as the result of a homosexual encounter with a young criminal.
▷E Siciliano, *Pasolini* (1981, in Italian)

PASTERNAK, Boris Leonidovich
(1890–1960)

Russian lyric poet, novelist and translator of **Shakespeare**, born in Moscow. He was the son of Leonid Pasternak (1862–1945), painter and illustrator of **Tolstoy**'s works. He studied law at the university, then musical composition under Scriabin, abandoning both for philosophy at Marburg. A factory worker in the Urals during World War I, he was employed in the library of the education ministry in Moscow after the Revolution. His early collections of verse, written between 1912 and 1916, were published under the title *Poverkh bar'erov* (1917, Eng trans *Above the Barriers*, 1931), followed by *Sestra moya zhizn': Leto 1917 goda* (1922, Eng trans *Sister my Life: Summer 1917*, 1967) and *Temy i variatsii* (1923, 'Themes and Variations'). Under the influence of his friend **Vladimir Mayakovsky** he wrote the political poems *Devyat'sot pyaty god* (1927, 'The Year 1905'), on the Bolshevik uprising, and *Levtenant Schmidt* (1927, 'Lieutenant Schmidt'), on the *Potemkin* mutiny. *Spectorsky* (1931) and *Vtoroye rozhdeniye* (1932, 'Second Birth') are autobiographical. Among his outstanding short stories are the collection *Vozdushnye puti* (1933, 'Aerial Ways') and particularly *Detstvo Lyuvers* (1922, Eng trans *The Childhood of Luvers*, 1945), a delicate presentation of a girl's first impressions of womanhood, and *Provest'* (1934, Eng trans *The Last Summer*, 1959), in which Pasternak's imagery is at its freshest and most unexpected. The long years under Stalin turned Pasternak into the official translator into Russian of Shakespeare, **Paul Verlaine**, **Goethe** and **Heinrich von Kleist**, but he did compose incidental verse such as *Na rannikh poezdakh* (1936–44, 'In Early Trains'). With Khrushchev's misleading political 'thaw' Pasternak caused a political earthquake with his first novel, *Doktor Zhivago* (1957, Eng trans *Doctor Zhivago*, 1958), banned in the Soviet Union. A fragmentary, poet's novel, it describes with intense feeling the Russian revolution as it impinged upon one individual, who was both doctor and poet. Its strictures on the postrevolutionary events are those not of an anti-Marxist but of a communist who is disappointed that history has not conformed to his vision. Expelled by the Soviet Writers' Union, he had to take the unprecedented step of refusing the 1958 Nobel Prize for literature, and in a thoroughly self-critical letter to Khrushchev, echoed **Ovid** by his plea that exile would for him be the equivalent of death.
▷R Hingley, *Pasternak, a biography* (1983)

PATCHEN, Kenneth
(1911–72)

American poet, novelist and painter. He grew up in Ohio, and was educated at the Experimental College, University of Wisconsin, Madison, and at Commonwealth College, Mena, Arkansas. After working as an agricultural labourer and as a freelance writer, he briefly joined the editorial staff at New Directions in 1939, the year of *First Will and*

Testament, his second volume of verse. Patchen wrote in a characteristically straightforward, unmetaphorical style, using the language of speech in a dramatically direct way; *First Will* actually contained an oral playlet which anticipated his later radio play *The City Wears a Slouch Hat* (1942), one of the forgotten masterpieces of modern American writing. *Selected Poems* appeared in 1947; later volumes included *A Surprise for the Bagpipe Player* (1956), *Hurrah for Anything* (1957), which included poems and drawings, and *Doubleheader* and *Hallelujah Anyway* (both 1966). *The Collected Poems* was published in 1968. Patchen also wrote a number of novels, most notably *The Journal of Albion Moonlight* (1941) and *The Memoirs of a Shy Pornographer* (1945).
▷ L Smith, *Patchen* (1978)

PATEL, Ravji
(1939–68)

Indian (Gujarati) poet, who has achieved more than any of his contemporaries—in a context in which non-fiction prose has been paramount. He was influenced by many European models, particularly **Lorca**, and his poetry will undoubtedly gain the closer international attention it deserves. His *In Memory of Hushilah*, in which he uses the forms of the traditional *marahya* in order to mock it, was translated into English in *Poetry India* (II, 2). His employment of folk-rhythms and dialects to create a new and viable Gujarati poetry has been widely admired.

PATER, Walter Horatio
(1839–94)

English critic and essayist, born in London, the son of a doctor. He was educated at King's School, Canterbury, and Queen's College, Oxford, became a fellow of Brasenose College and from then on lived the life of a scholar. His *Studies in the History of the Renaissance* (1873) shows the influence of the pre-Raphaelites with whom he associated. His philosophic romance, *Marius the Epicurean* (1885), appealed to a wider audience. His *Imaginary Portraits* (1887) and *Appreciations* (1889), followed by *Plato and Platonism* (1893), established his position as a critic, but already people were beginning to talk of his influence as being unhealthy, in the sense that he advocated a cultivated hedonism. That his neo-Cyrenaism, as it might be called, involved strenuous self-discipline hardly occurred to his critics, who found in his style alone an enervating quality. His influence on Oxford, however, was profound. He died having left unfinished another romance, *Gaston de Latour* (1896).
▷ A C Benson, *Walter Pater* (1906)

PATERSON, Banjo (Andrew Barton)
(1864–1941)

Australian bush poet and balladeer, born at 'Narrambla', Orange, New South Wales, best known for his verse 'Waltzing Matilda', which he set to an old Scottish melody to become the 'unofficial' national anthem of Australia. Under the pseudonym 'The Banjo' (the name of a bush racehorse) he contributed verse to the Sydney periodical, the *Bulletin*. *Clancy of the Overflow* appeared there in 1889, and *The Man from Snowy River* the following year. By 1895 these verses and others had become so popular, and had been reprinted so widely, that they were collected as *The Man from Snowy River, and Other Verses*, the first of many such collections of his work. *Rio Grande's Last Race, and Other Verses* followed in 1902, and his popular bush character appeared in *Saltbush Bill JP, and Other Verses* in 1917. His first *Collected Verse* was published in 1923. He also wrote two novels and a collection of short stories, a book of verse for children, illustrated by **Norman Lindsay**, *The Animals Noah Forgot* (1933), and edited a pioneering collection of *Old Bush Songs* (1905).
▷ C Gemmler, *The Banjo of the Bush* (1966)

PATMORE, Coventry Kersey Dighton
(1823–96)

English poet, born in Woodford, Essex. An assistant librarian at the British Museum, he was associated with the Pre-Raphaelite brotherhood whose members were much taken with his verse. The epitome of Victorian values, a father to six children and a husband to three wives, his best work is *The Angel in the House* (4 vols, 1854), a poetic treatment of married love which delighted a generation devoid of cynicism. A rabid Tory who put England's decline down to 'the disenfranchisement (in 1867) of the upper and middle classes by the false English nobles and their Jew', his conversion to Roman Catholicism after the death of his first wife may well have been responsible for the plummet in his popularity. Later works include *The Unknown Eros* (1877) and *The Rod, The Root and the Flower* (1895), a collection of religious meditations.
▷ J C Reid, *The Mind and Art of Coventry Patmore* (1957)

PATON, Alan
(1903–88)

South African writer and educator, born in Pietermaritzburg. Educated at the University of Natal, he spent 10 years as a schoolteacher, first at a native school and later at Pietermaritzburg College. From 1935 to 1948

he was principal of the Diepkloof Reformatory for young offenders, where he became known for the success of his enlightened methods. From his deep concern with the racial problem in South Africa sprang the novel *Cry the Beloved Country* (1948). His other novels were *Too Late the Phalarope* (1953) and *Ah, But Your Land is Beautiful* (1981). He also wrote *Hope for South Africa* (1958), a political study written from the Liberal standpoint, *Debbie Go Home* (1961, short stories), *Instrument of Thy Peace* (1968), *Apartheid and the Archbishop* (1973), and his autobiography, *Towards the Mountain* (1981). He was national president of the South African Liberal Party from 1953 to 1960.
▷E Callan, *Alan Paton* (1968)

PATON WALSH, Jill (Gillian Honoinne Mary)
(1937–)
English children's author, born in London and educated at Oxford. She began writing when she left teaching to raise a family. Her first book was *Hengest's Tale* (1966), a rather dour historical novel set in the Dark Ages. This was followed by *The Dolphin Crossing* (1967), about two boys helping at Dunkirk, but both were significantly surpassed by *Fireweed* (1970), a novel set in the London Blitz. *Goldengrove* (1972) and its sequel *Unleaving* (1976), taking their titles from a **Gerard Manley Hopkins** poem, are considered her best work. She won the Whitbread Award for *The Emperor's Winding-Sheet* (1974), and the Smarties Prize for *Gaffer Samson's Luck* (1984). Recent works have consolidated her focus on adolescence rather than childhood. She has also written for adults.

PATSAUQ, Markoosie *see* MARKOOSIE

PATTEN, Brian
(1946–)
English poet and playwright, born in Liverpool and educated at Sefton Park Secondary, after which he worked as a reporter. With **Roger McGough** and **Adrian Henri** he shared the phenomenally successful *Penguin Modern Poets 10* (1967). Patten was, perhaps, the closest of the three to the earlier English tradition, and there are moments in the early poems, those gathered in *Walking Out: The Early Poems of Brian Patten* (1970), or in the fine sequence *Notes to the Hurrying Man* (1969), which align him with the 19th-century greats. However 'serious' he appears, relative to McGough, Patten is never academically sententious; the bizarrely titled *The Eminent Professors and the Nature of Poetry as Enacted Out By Members of the Poetry Seminar One*

Rainy Evening (1972) neatly captures his view of the literary world's pretensions. Later volumes include *The Unreliable Nightingale* (1973) and *Love Poems* (1981). In 1983, he joined McGough and Henri in an updated version of *The Mersey Sound*. He has written for the theatre and for children; *Gargling with Jelly* (1985) is a small masterpiece.

PATTEN, William Gilbert, pseud Burt L Standish
(1866–1945)
American novelist, born in Maine. He began as a writer of Westerns, using the name William West Wilder. But it was with the pseudonym Burt L Standish that he achieved huge commercial success with his stories for boys featuring an all-American lad from Yale named Frank Merriwell. The series included more than 200 titles and is said to have sold more than 10 million copies. *Mr. Frank Merriwell* (1941) was a curiously belated attempt to bring his priggish hero up against contemporary issues.

PATTERSON, H Orlando
(1926–)
Jamaican novelist and sociologist. He is the author of *Children of Sisyphus* (1965), probably the most vivid and authentic study ever made of the Rastafarian cult in fictional form—it has not yet had its due from critics. Besides important sociological studies, he has written further novels, of which *An Absence of Ruins* (1967) and *Die the Long Day* (1972), stand out.

PAULDING, James Kirke
(1778–1860)
American writer, born in Great Nine Partners (Putnam County), New York. He was a friend and associate of **Washington Irving** in *Salmagundi* (1807–8), and during the 1812 war published the *Diverting History of John Bull and Brother Jonathan*. In 1814 a more serious work, *The United States and England*, gained him an appointment on the Board of Naval Commissioners. He also wrote *The Dutchman's Fireside* (1831), *Westward Ho!* (1832), a *Life of Washington* (1835), and a defence of *Slavery in the United States* (1836). From 1838 to 1841 he was secretary of the navy.
▷A L Herold, *James Kirke Paulding: Versatile American* (1926)

PAULIN, Tom
(1949–)
British poet, born in Leeds but brought up in Belfast. He was educated at the universities of Hull and Oxford, and now lectures at Nottingham University. He is usually numbered

among the Ulster Poets, and much of his writing in both poetry and prose is directly concerned with the political and social realities of life in Northern Ireland. His urban poems are hard-hitting and often violent in their preoccupations, and make skilful use of vernacular idioms. His principal collections include *A State of Justice* (1977), *The Strange Museum* (1980) and *Selected Poems 1972–1990* (1993). *The Riot Act* (1985) and *Seize the Fire* (1990) are versions of classic Greek texts with distinct contemporary resonances. He has also published essay collections, notably *Ireland and the English Crisis* (1984) and *Minotaur: Poetry and the Nation State* (1992).

PAUSTOVSKY, Konstantin
(1892–1968)

Russian novelist and memoirist, born in Moscow and brought up in Kiev. His most famous work is his six-part autobiography, *Povest o zhini* (1945–64, Eng trans *The Story of a Life*, 1964; *Slow Approach of Thunder*, 1965; *In That Dawn*, 1967; *Years of Hope*, 1968; *Southern Adventure*, 1969; *The Restless Years*, 1974). In this work, with its memories of such men as **Babel** and **Bulgakov**, Paustovsky presented what is perhaps the most 'human face' of all loyal communists, that of a man who could not be corrupted by even the worst excesses of Stalinism. It was somewhat overrated in the West, and has hardly lasted. His fiction and plays are, by contrast, run-of-the-mill.
▷G Simmonds (ed), *Soviet Leaders* (1967)

PAVESE, Cesare
(1908–50)

Italian novelist, poet, critic and translator, born in Piedmont. He was brought up in Turin where he worked for Einaudi, the publisher. Among his translations, that of **Melville**'s *Moby-Dick* (1932) is regarded as a classic. A leader of the Italian post-war Neorealist school he was politically disillusioned and sexually neurotic and he committed suicide. His poetry is slight; his finest works are novels like *La casa in collina* (1949, Eng trans *The House on the Hill*, 1961) and *La luna e i falò* (1950, Eng trans *The Moon and the Bonfire*, 1952), which express precisely and categorically his abhorrence of war and fascism.
▷D Lajolo, *Absurd Vice: a biography of Pavese* (1983)

PAYN, James
(1830–98)

English novelist, born in Cheltenham. He was educated at Eton, Woolwich Academy, and

Trinity College, Cambridge. In 1853 he published a volume of *Poems*, from 1859 to 1874 was editor of *Chambers's Journal*, and from 1882 to 1896 edited the *Cornhill*. He wrote a hundred novels, such as *Lost Sir Massingberd* (1864), *By Proxy* (1878) and *The Luck of the Darrells* (1885).

PAYNE, John Howard
(1791–1852)

American actor and playwright, born in New York. He made his debut there in February 1809, and in 1813 appeared in London. For 30 years he had a successful career as an actor and author of plays, chiefly adaptations. His play *Clari* contains the song 'Home, Sweet Home', the music being by Sir Henry Bishop. Payne was appointed American consul in Tunis in 1841.
▷G Overmeyer, *America's First Hamlet* (1957)

PAYNO Y FLORES, Manuel
(1810–94)

Mexican novelist, whose popular serialized adventure stories were well written and gave vivid pictures of the society of his times. Best known is *El fistol del diablo* (1845–6, 'The Devil's Scarf Pin'). He could be compared to **Henty**, but his range was far less wide, and he wrote for adults.

PAYRO, Roberto J
(1867–1928)

Argentinian novelist, dramatist and socialist, born in Mercedes, Buenos Aires. He was markedly anti-German, and was imprisoned by the Germans for his criticisms of them while he was working in Belgium during World War I. As a novelist his strength lay in his humorous, shrewd, and compassionate portrayal of rural life in the Argentine. He was a ruthless and effective critic of corruption. His real mentor was **Peréz Galdós**, and all his best novels owe a debt to the Spaniard. The episodic *Pago chico* (1908), about political corruption in the provinces, is less substantial than the longer, often very funny, picaresque *El casamiento de Laucha* (1906, 'Laucha's Marriage'), in which a scoundrel prospers amongst his fellow frauds. His gaucho plays were popular in their time, and his urban novel *Divertidas aventuras del nieto de Juan Moreira* (1910, 'Diverse Adventures of Juan Moreira'), again about a rogue, survives in dramatizations. Three stories are translated in *Tales from the Argentine* (1930).

PAZ, Octavio
(1914–)

Mexican poet, winner of the Nobel Prize for literature, born in Mexico City. He attended the National University of Mexico, and fought on the Republican side in the Spanish Civil War. Diplomat (he was ambassador to India in the 1960s), essayist and editor, with strong metaphysical leanings, he is best known for his poetry. His long poem, *Piedra de sol* (1957, Eng trans *Sun Stone*, 1963), is one of the most remarkable of 10 volumes that have appeared. There is also a perceptive study of Mexican character and culture, *El laberinto de la soledad* (1950, rev edn 1959, Eng trans *The Labyrinth of Solitude*, 1962). *Postdata* (1970, Eng trans *The Other Mexico: Critique of the Pyramid*, 1972), written after the student massacre and other events in 1968, revises views he had held earlier. Thereafter he emigrated to Britain. He was awarded the 1990 Nobel Prize for literature.

▷I Ivask, *The Perpetual Present: the poetry and prose of Octavio Paz* (1973)

P'BITEK, Okot
(1931–82)

Ugandan poet, writing in English. He was born in Gulu, northern Uganda, and attended the Government Training College at Mbarara (1952–4), returning to his home township as a teacher of English and religious knowledge. His first publication was *Lak tar miyo Kinyero wi lobo?* (1953), written in the Acoli language. A gifted footballer, p'Bitek was a Ugandan international. He decided to remain in England following a soccer tour and studied law at the University College, Aberystwyth, and social anthropology at Oxford, a discipline he then rejected along with the Christianity of his upbringing. He returned to Uganda for a time in 1962 and began to research folk culture and oral literature. *Song of Lawino* (1966) and its 'response' *Song of Ocol* (1970) were originally written in Acoli but translated by the poet himself. He controversially steered the Ugandan national theatre in the direction of folk arts; he was dismissed from the Cultural Centre in Kampala, and thereafter spent much of the rest of his life working in universities abroad—in Zambia, Nigeria and the US—before returning to Makerere as Professor of Creative Writing; he died shortly thereafter. Other works include collections of Acoli songs and tales, *The Horn of My Love* (1974) and *Hare and Hornbill* (1978), and an important book of essays *Africa's Cultural Revolution* (1973).

▷G A Heron, *The Poetry of Okot p'Bitek* (1976)

PEACOCK, Thomas Love
(1785–1866)

English novelist and poet, born in Weymouth, the son of a London merchant. He was a friend of **Shelley**. He entered the service of the East India Company in 1819 after producing three satirical romances, *Headlong Hall* (1816), *Melincourt* (1817) and *Nightmare Abbey* (1818). *Crochet Castle* (1831) concluded this series of satires, and in 1860 *Gryll Grange* appeared. He also published two romances, *Maid Marian* (1822) and *The Misfortunes of Elphin* (1829). The framework of his satirical fictions is always the same—a company of humorists meet in a country house and display the sort of crotchets or prejudices which Peacock, the reasonable man, most disliked: morbid romance, the mechanical sort of political economy, the 'march of science' and transcendental philosophy. The poets of the Romantic school, **Wordsworth**, **Coleridge**, Shelley, **Byron** and **Robert Southey**, are caricatured along with the Edinburgh Reviewers, who offer the extra target of being Scots.

▷M van Doren, *Thomas Love Peacock* (1911)

PEACOCKE, Isabel Maude
(1881–1973)

New Zealand writer of novels for adults and children. From 1915, with *My Cousin Phil*, to *The Good Intentions of Angela* (1937) and *Lizbett Anne* (1939), she produced 25 stories for children, young and older. The later books were among the first of their kind to establish a 'sense of place' and to set her characters in recognizable surroundings—usually her home town of Auckland. Her adult novels, however, are a late flowering of the melodramatic and moralistic Victorian novel with an emphasis on the sanctity of marriage and the benefits of resisting temptation; in *Cinderella's Suitors* (1918) her heroine eventually throws away an inheritance upon marriage, only to find that she gets the money after all as a reward for her self-denial. Four other adult novels appeared before 1929; she then returned to adult fiction in the 1940s. Her last book, *Change Partners*, was published in 1955.

PEAKE, Mervyn Laurence
(1911–68)

English author and artist, born in south China, where his father was a missionary. He was educated at Tientsin Grammar School, Eltham College and the Royal Academy Schools. While living on Sark (1933–5) and thereafter teaching at the Westminster School of Art, his reputation as an artist grew. His first book was a children's story, *Captain Slaughterboard Drops Anchor* (1939), with his own illustrations. *The Craft of the Lead Pencil* (1946), a book on drawing, was published in the same year as his first novel, *Titus Groan*, the first part of a Gothic fantasy trilogy completed in *Gormenghast* (1950) and *Titus Alone*

(1959). Another novel, *Mr Pye*, appeared in 1953, and his only play, *The Wit to Woo*, in 1957. He published two volumes of verse, *Shapes and Sounds* (1941) and *The Glass-blowers* (1950), a ballad set during the blitz, *The Rhyme of the Flying Bomb*, the lighter sketches collected in *A Book of Nonsense* (1972). He illustrated several classics, notably *Treasure Island*, *The Hunting of the Snark* and *The Ancient Mariner*.

PEARCE, Philippa
(1920–)

English children's novelist and short-story writer, born in Great Shelford, Cambridgeshire. From 1945 she spent 13 years scriptwriting in the BBC's schools broadcasting department, then became an editor, first with Oxford University Press and later with André Deutsch. Her first novel, *Minnow On the Say* (1955), combines the excitement of a treasure-hunt with the relaxed, at times poetic, depiction of her home territory. Her second, *Tom's Midnight Garden* (1958), won the Carnegie Medal; a magical but credible story of time travel and nascent sexuality, it is among the most enduringly popular of post-war novels for children. Her other books include *A Dog So Small* (1962), set, again, just south of Cambridge, and *The Strange Sunflower* (1966), about a boy's dream trip to Sunflower Land.

PEARSE, Patrick Henry
(1879–1916)

Irish poet, polemicist, politician and insurrectionist, born in Dublin of an English father and Irish mother. In 1908 he founded St Endas, a school in which he promoted traditional Gaelic–Irish language and custom. He was a member of the Irish Volunteers and the more socialist-orientated Irish Republican Brotherhood. He led the Easter Rising of 1916 and was executed by the British in May of that year. Despite late 20th-century revisionism, he remains a totem for much Republican thinking in Ireland and an inspiration for the positive role of Irish heritage in education. His pamphlet *The Murder Machine* (1916), a selection of articles on Irish school practices, attacks accepted schoolroom tactics of teaching rather than educating, and presents a stimulating argument for change. His *Political Writings and Speeches* (1952) and *Poems* (1958) are evidence of his deeply felt political and social commitment: 'I speak, being full of vision/I speak to my people, and I speak in my people's name to the masters of my people ... Beware of the thing that is coming, beware of the risen people' ('The Rebel').
▷R D Edwards, *Patrick Pearse: The Triumph of Failure* (1977)

PECHAM, or PECKHAM, John
(d.1292)

English Latin poet and Archbishop of Canterbury. A priest of the Franciscan order, he issued a codified series of rules for the clergy at the Lambeth Council of 1281. Written in church Latin, they represent a complete prescription for the way a priest should live his life, touching on love, chastity, obedience, etc. His religious poetry also reflects his conservative theology, and stresses the mystical experience of the love of Christ.

PEDRAYO, Ramón Otero
(1888–1972)

Galician writer, a member of the group centred around the Galician magazine *Non, Us*. He wrote an important book about Galician culture, *Ensaio sobre a cultura galega* (1954, 'Essay on the Galician Culture'), which was published in Lisbon at the height of the Franco tryanny.

PEELE, George
(c.1558–1596)

English Elizabethan dramatist, born in London. He went up to Oxford in 1571, where he took his bachelor's degree in 1577 and his master's in 1579. By 1581 he had moved to London, where for 17 years he lived a roistering Bohemian life as actor, poet and playwright. He was one of those warned to repentance by **Henry Greene** in his *Groatsworth of Wit* (1592). *The Arraignment of Paris* (1584) is a dramatic pastoral containing ingenious flatteries of Queen Elizabeth. Other works include his *Farewell* to Sir John Norris on his expedition to Portugal (1589, eked out by *A Tale of Troy*), *Eclogue Gratulatory* (1589) to the Earl of Essex, *Polyhymnia* (1590), *Speeches* for the reception of Queen Elizabeth (1591), and *Honour of the Garter* (1593). The historical play of *Edward I* (1593) is marred by its slanders against Queen Eleanor. His play, *The Old Wives' Tale* (1595), probably gave **Milton** the subject for his *Comus*. *David and Bethsabe* was published in 1599.
▷P H Cliford, *George Peele* (1913)

PÉGUY, Charles Pierre
(1873–1914)

French nationalist, publisher, and neo-Catholic poet, born of peasant stock in Orléans. He was educated at the École Normale and the Sorbonne, after which he opened a bookshop. In 1900 he founded the *Cahiers de la quinzaine* in which were first published his own works as well as those of such writers as **Romain Rolland**. Deeply patriotic, he combined sincere Catholicism with socialism and his writings reflect his intense desire for justice and truth. His most important works include *Le Mystère de la charité de Jeanne d'Arc* (1910, 'The Mystery of Joan of Arc's Charity'), *Victor Marie, Comte Hugo* (1910, 'Victor Hugo'), *L'Argent* (1912, 'Money') and *La Tapisserie de Notre Dame* (1913, 'The Tapestry of Notre Dame'). He was killed in World War I.

▷ R Rolland, *Charles Péguy* (1944)

PEKKANEN, Toivo
(1902–57)

Major Finnish novelist, dramatist and poet, born in Kotka. Until he was almost 30 he worked as a blacksmith. He was the first important Finnish 'proletarian' writer, a genre already well established in Norway and Sweden. *Lapsuuteni* (1953, Eng trans *My Childhood*, 1966), a starkly objective autobiography, is an established classic. His great Kotka saga, consisting of many volumes, has divided critics, some of whom see it as political, while others regard it as having an almost esoteric depth. His style has been well described as one of 'earnest artlessness'; his best works of fiction await translation into English.

▷ K Kare, *Toivo Pekkanen* (1952, in Finnish)

PELLICER, Carlos
(1897–1976)

Mexican poet, born in Villahermosa in Tabasco. He is most famous for his sonnets, which he began writing very early in his life; but he also wrote many poems in a pellucid free verse. He was a member of the *Contemporáneos* group, which established modern poetry in Mexico. For himself he chose to follow the traditions laid down by **Othón** and **Ramón López Velarde**, the two quintessentially Mexican, and proto-modern, poets of the generation that preceded his. Throughout his life he remained committed both to the left-wing and to a Bolivarist ideal of a union of Latin America; he went to Europe in 1937 with other Mexicans, **Paz** amongst them, to give support to the Spanish Republic. But he firmly believed that such beliefs were, as he said, 'in agreement with Christian doctrine'. In his poetry—which is unusually optimistic for a modern Mexican—it has been claimed that 'he uses landscape in such a way that through it the words are expressed'.

▷ *Southern Review* (Spring 1965)

PELLICO, Silvio
(1789–1854)

Italian writer and patriot, born in Saluzzo in Piedmont. He spent four years in Lyons, and in Milan (1810) was French tutor at the military school. His tragedies of *Laodamia* and *Francesca da Rimini* (1815) made his name, and he translated **Byron**'s *Manfred*. In 1820 he was arrested and imprisoned for two years in Venice. He was then, on a charge of Carbonarism, condemned to death, but had his sentence commuted to 15 years' imprisonment in the Spielberg near Brünn, and was released in 1830. During this time he wrote two other dramas. He published an account of his imprisonment, *Le mie Prigioni* (1833, 'My Prisons'), and subsequently numerous tragedies, poems and a catechism on the duties of man.

▷ I Rineri, *Della vita e delle opera di Silvio Pellico* (1898–1901)

PEMBERTON, Sir Max
(1863–1950)

English writer, born in Birmingham. Educated at Merchant Taylors' School and Gonville and Caius College, Cambridge, he was editor of *Chums* (1892–3) and of *Cassell's Magazine* from 1896 to 1906. He produced a succession of historical romances including *Impregnable City* (1895), *Queen of the Jesters* (1897), *The Show Girl* (1909), *Captain Black* (1911) and *The Mad King Dies* (1928). He also wrote revues and plays. He founded the London School of Journalism, and in 1920 became a director of Northcliffe newspapers, two years later publishing a biography of Lord Northcliffe (Alfred Harmsworth).

PEMBROKE, Countess of, née Mary Sidney
(1561–1621)

English poet and patron of the arts, born at Tickenhall near Bewdley, Worcestershire. Educated at home, she learnt Latin, French, Italian and probably Greek. She went to court in 1575 and two years later married Henry Herbert, Earl of Pembroke, her elder by 30 years. This involved her in the administration of four country estates; at the same time she maintained a close literary collaboration with her brother Sir **Philip Sidney**, which produced, amongst others, translations of the *Psalms*. She also edited his *The Countess of Pembroke's Arcadia* (1593), and wrote elegies for him; preserving his memory after his early death became her overriding concern.

▷ M P Hannay, *Philip's Phoenix* (1990)

PENA, Luis Carlos Martins
(1815–48)

Brazilian writer of comedies, who was one of the chief pioneers of his country's theatre, being the first playwright to write on Brazilian themes. His 19 comedies were almost all successful; *O Juiz de Paz na Roca* (1838, 'Justice of the Peace of the Plantation') was the first of them. His most famous play is the tragic farce *O Noviço* (1845, 'The Novice').

PENDSE, Shripad Narayan
(1913–)

Indian (Marathi) novelist, an heir to and improver on the tradition of serious fiction established by **Hari Narayan Apte**. Pendse is noted for his human and humane depiction of female characters in a male-dominated society. *Garambicha Bapu* (1952) was translated as *Wild Bapu of Garambicha* in 1969.

PENNA, Sandro
(1906–77)

Italian poet from Perugia, whose poetry dealt mainly with homosexual love, and did so more boldly and openly than any other 20th-century poet's other than **Cavafy**'s. He is thus, with **Cernuda**, valued as one of the century's most important writers of this kind. His chief preoccupation was with boys, not always a popular predilection; but in his work celebration of their beauty seems innocent and, in any case, foredoomed. His candour is therefore of a unique brand, and the lyric record which he left of his questing life—much of it spent cruising in Rome, where he lived—is an instructive one. He was greatly influenced, like **Quasimodo**, by the simplicity of the Greek lyric poets, and by his friend, early model and great encourager, the Triestine **Umberto Saba**. The tension in his poetry between the natural, which he so desperately sought, and the forbidden, gives it a highly significant aura. In him homosexuality was emphatically not a matter of 'choice'. There are English translations in: C L Golino (ed), *Contemporary Italian Poetry* (1962).
▷*Books Abroad*, 47 (1973)

PENNANEN, Jarno
(1916–)

Finnish novelist, translator and critic, born in Tampere. Her highly charged psychological novels and stories usually deal with children or young people; she is unlucky not to have found a translator.

PEPYS, Samuel
(1633–1703)

English diarist and Admiralty official, son of a London tailor. He was educated at St Paul's School and Trinity Hall and Magdalene College, Cambridge. After the Civil War he lived poorly with his young wife, Elizabeth St Michel, whom he married in 1655, but after the Restoration, through the patronage of the Earl of Sandwich, his father's cousin, he rose rapidly in the naval service and became secretary to the Admiralty in 1672. He lost his office and was imprisoned on account of his alleged complicity in the Popish Plot (1679), but was reappointed in 1684 and in that same year became President of the Royal Society. At the Revolution (1688) he was again removed from office. The celebrated Diary, which ran from 1 January 1660 to 31 May 1669, the year his wife died and his eyesight failed him, is of extraordinary interest, both as the personal record (and confessions) of a man of abounding love of life, and for the vivid picture it gives of contemporary life, including naval administration and Court intrigue. The highlights are probably the accounts of the three disasters of the decade— the great plague (1665–6), the great fire of London (1666) and the sailing up the Thames by the Dutch fleet (1665–7). The veracity of the Diary has been accepted. It was apparently written in cipher (a kind of shorthand), in which form it remained at Magdalene College till 1825, when it was deciphered and edited.
▷A Bryant, *Pepys* (3 vols, 1933–8)

PERALTA BARNUEVO, Pedro de
(1664–1743)

Peruvian poet and historian, born in Lima. He taught mathematics at San Marcos University in Lima, and served as Rector there. His *Lima fundada* (1732), a verse epic of Pizarro, set the Inquisition on his trail for 'endangering the Faith'. He was a pioneer of the scientific method, some of whose investigations now look ludicrous—by no means all of his *Gongoriste* conceits in his poetry are effective—but he was a deeply serious man, astronomer, engineer, and sceptic, whose efforts have now been fully appreciated.

PERCIVAL, James Gates
(1795–1856)

American poet, born in Berlin, Connecticut. He graduated from Yale in 1815, studied botany and medicine, and became Professor of Chemistry at West Point in 1824 and of geology at Wisconsin in 1854. His poems *Prometheus* and *Clio* appeared between 1822 and 1827, and *The Dream of a Day* in 1843.
▷F Cogswell, *James Gates Percival and His Friends* (1902)

PERCY, Thomas
(1729–1811)

English antiquary, poet and churchman, author of *Percy's Reliques*, born in Bridgnorth, the son of a grocer. Educated at Bridgnorth Grammar School and Christ Church, Oxford, he became vicar of Easton Maudit in Northamptonshire (1753) and also rector of Wilby (1756). Later he was appointed chaplain to the Duke of Northumberland and George III, Dean of Carlisle (1778) and Bishop of Dromore (1782). As a man of letters his fame rests on his *Reliques of Ancient English Poetry* (1765), largely compiled from a 17th-century manuscript of medieval ballads and other material found in a house in Shifnal, Shropshire, and much 'restored' by him. Earlier he had published the first English version of a Chinese novel, *Hau Kiou Choaun* (1761, translated from the Portuguese), and *Miscellaneous Pieces translated from the Chinese* (1762). Prompted by the success of **James Macpherson**'s spurious Ossianic translations, he also published, anonymously, *Runic Poetry translated from the Icelandic language* (1763), a group of five poems actually translated from Latin versions. He later wrote a ballad of his own, *The Hermit of Warkworth* (1771).

PERCY, Walker
(1916–90)

American novelist, born in Birmingham, Alabama. He studied medicine, intending to make this his career, but had to abandon it when he contracted tuberculosis. His first novel, *The Moviegoer* (1961), won a National Book Award. A philosophical writer, his novels are firmly grounded in social observation seen from the standpoint of a liberal Catholic Southerner. *Love in the Ruins* (1971) was subtitled 'The Adventures of a Bad Catholic at a Time Near the End of the World'. He is the author of several novels, including *The Last Gentleman* (1966), *The Second Coming* (1980) and *The Thanatos Syndrome* (1987). He also wrote *Novel-Writing in an Apocalyptic Time* (1984).
▷L A Lawson and V A Kramer, *Conversations with Walker Percy* (1985)

PEREC, Georges
(1936–82)

French novelist, born in Paris. His first novel, *Les Choses* (1965), won the Prix Renaudot, and was eventually published in English, in 1990, as *Things: A Story of the Sixties*. *La Vie mode d'emploi* (1978) won the Prix Medicis, and in 1985 was voted Novel of the Decade by the Salon du Livre. Published in English as *Life; A User's Manual* (1987), it is a compendious and complicated tome, the most finely wrought work of a playful polymath. A man devoted to literary and linguistic puzzles, Perec also succeeded in writing a complete novel, *La Disparition* ('A Void'), without using the letter E. In conjunction with his burgeoning career as a writer, he worked, from 1962 until his death, as an archivist in a medical research library in Paris.

PEREDA, José Maria de
(1833–1906)

Spanish novelist, born in Polanco near Santander. His novels give a realistic picture of the people and scenery of the region where he was born and where much of his life was spent, an outstanding example being *Sotileza* (1885, 'Sublety'). Other novels are *Del tal palo tal astilla* (1880, 'Like Father, Like Son'), *Pedro Sanchez* (1883) and, perhaps his finest, *Peñas arriba* (1895, 'Up the Mountain'). He was called 'the modern Cervantes'.
▷R Gullon, *Vida de Pereda* (1944)

PERELMAN, S(ydney) J(oseph)
(1904–79)

American humorous writer, born in Brooklyn, New York City. Graduating from Brown University in 1925 he contributed to magazines until the publication of *Dawn Ginsbergh's Revenge* (1929), which had the nation in stitches and secured the author's fame. He went to Hollywood and wrote scripts for, among others, the Marx Brothers. Latterly his work found its way to the *New Yorker* (from 1931) before coming to rest between hard covers. His writing is remarkable for its linguistic dexterity and ingenuity; he took pot shots at modern sitting ducks and most sunk under a side-splitting fusillade, though somehow the entertainment and advertising industries survived. He is at his best in *Crazy Like a Fox* (1944), *Westward Ha! or, Around the World in 80 Clichés* (1948), *The Swiss Family Perelman* (1950) and *The Road to Miltown, or, Under the Spreading Atrophy* (1957). *The Most of S J Perelman* was published in 1958.
▷D Herrmann, *S J Perelman: A Life* (1986)

PÉRET, Benjamin
(1899–1959)

French poet and short-story writer, born in Rézé. A member of the Dadaists and subsequently the Surrealists, he remained faithful throughout his career to the central figure of the latter group, **André Breton**, and to such methods as automatic writing. The best of his work was collected in *Main Forte* (1946) and *Feu Central* (1947). He fought in the Spanish Civil War, and later, following the fall of France, left his homeland, along with Breton, for Mexico. In 1949 he founded the Union Ouvrière Internationale (International Workers' Union), and once listed his hobby as 'insulting priests'.

PERETZ, Isaac Leib
(1851–1915)

Polish–Yiddish writer who was born in Zamoszcz. He spent his entire life in Poland. His first stories were in Polish, then he took to Hebrew; in 1888 he published his first story in Yiddish, and soon became the central literary figure in that language. Although quintessentially Jewish, he brought a deep understanding of Russian and European literatures into his fiction. He was an aggressive, courageous, Hasidic Messianist who argued against the doctrine of 'assimilation', and got himself banned from practising as a lawyer by the Tsarist authorities for it. The painter Chagall, amongst many others, was influenced by him. He wrote popular lyric poetry, realistic tales, and some lively plays. There are many volumes of English translations, including *My Memoirs* (1965) and *The Three Canopies* (1968).

▷C A Madison, *Yiddish Literature* (1968)

PÉREZ DE AYALA, Ramón
(1881–1962)

Spanish novelist, poet and critic, born in Oviedo. He first attracted attention with his poetry when *La paz del sendero* ('The Peace of the Path') was published in 1904. A sequel volume appeared in 1916 under the title *El sendero innumerable* ('The Innumerable Path'). As a novelist he combines realism with beauty, best shown in the philosophical *Belarmino y Apolonio* (1921). Other novels include the humorous and satirical *Troteras y Danzaderas* (1913), the anti-Jesuit *A.M.D.G.* (1910), and perhaps his best, *Tigre Juan* (1924) which, with *El Curandero de su honra* (1926, 'The Saviour of his Honour'), appeared in English as *Tiger Juan* (1933). Among his works of criticism are *Máscaras* (1917, 'Masks') and *Política y Toros* (1918, 'Politics and Bulls'). He was ambassador to London from 1931 to 1936.

▷F Agustin, *Ramón Pérez de Ayala, su vida e su obras* (1927)

PÉREZ GALDÓS, Benito
(1843–1920)

Spanish novelist, born in Las Palmas, Canary Islands. He moved to Madrid as a student in 1861, and supported his family by writing. He was a prolific novelist and dramatist, and also wrote journalism, travel diaries, criticism, and memoirs. He divided his novels, which are largely naturalistic in style, into categories in the manner of **Balzac**, the principle two being the novels of contemporary Spanish life and the 46-volume historical series he called 'Episodios nacionales'. He is an acute, psychologically percipient observer of life, and has been considered the greatest Spanish novelist after **Cervantes**. His best book is the novel *Fortunata y Jacinta* (1886–7, Eng trans *Fortunata and Jacinta*, 1986).

▷B J Dendle, *Galdós: the mature thought* (1980)

PERI ROSSI, Cristina
(1941–)

Uruguayan militant, iconoclastic, feminist short-story and novel writer, poet, and journalist. Her work is among the best experimental fiction written by a Latin-American writer, and tests the limits of genre, language and form. Her main interests lie in shifting literature, society, and gender roles, and both her poetry and her prose employ humour and irony to illustrate the disintegration of outdated modes of social interaction. Among her awards are the **Benito Pérez Galdós** Prize for *La rebelión de los niños* (1976, 'The Children's Rebellion') and the Ciudad de Palma Prize for *Linguistica General* (1979). She has lived in exile in Barcelona since 1972.

PÉRIER, Odilon Jean
(1900–28)

Belgian poet, playwright and novelist, born in Brussels. Unique in the literature, Périer's language is quite different from that of his contemporaries: unornamented, without affectation, and apparently uninfluenced by any ideas of his time. *Notre Mère la ville* (1922, 'Our Mother the Town') celebrates Brussels. He wrote a play and a novel called *Le Passage des Anges* (1926, 'The Crossing of Angels'). He died of a heart ailment. His finest work is usually said to be *Le Citadin*, a poem in classical alexandrines about Brussels; but in fact his work, although unusual, is not of major calibre.

PERRAULT, Charles
(1628–1703)

French writer, born in Paris. He studied law, and from 1654 to 1664 had an easy life working for his brother, the receiver-general of Paris. In 1663 he became a secretary or assistant to Colbert. His poem, *Le Siècle de Louis le Grand* (1687, 'The Century of Louis XIV'), and **Nicolas Boileau**'s outspoken criticisms of it, opened up the dispute about the relative merits of the ancients and moderns. To the modern cause Perrault contributed his poor *Parallèle des anciens et des modernes* (1688–96, 'Comparison of the Ancients and the Moderns'), and his *Hommes illustres qui ont paru en France pendant ce siècle* (1696–1700, 'Great Men Who Emerged in France this Century'). His *Mémoires* appeared in 1769. All his writings would have been forgotten but for his eight inimitable fairy tales, the *Histoires ou Contes du temps passé* (1697, Eng trans *Perrault's Popular Tales*, 1888), including 'Belle au bois dormant' ('The Sleeping Beauty'), 'Le Petit chaperon rouge' ('Red Riding Hood') and 'La Barbe-Bleue' ('Bluebeard').

▷M Soriano, *Les contes de Perrault* (1968)

PERRY, Grace
(1927–)

Australian poet and paediatrician, publisher and cattle-breeder, born in Sydney. Her medical experience is reflected in much of her verse, from the early *Red Scarf* (1963) to the verse-diary which gives the title to *Journal of a Surgeon's Wife and Other Poems* (1976), the chronicle of a doctor's wife in early colonial Australia. Her strong feeling of place emerges in *Black Swans at Berrima* (1972) and *Berrima Winter* (1974), set around her historic home town in New South Wales. Much of her work is published from the South Head Press, which she established in 1964, the year in which she founded the quarterly journal *Poetry Australia*.

PERS, Ciro de
(1599–1663)

Italian poet and dramatist (*L'umilià esaltata o vero Ester regina*, 1664), born in Castello di Pers in Friuli. He was friendly with and influenced by the Marinist, **Achillini**. He went to Malta on a diplomatic mission (1627–9), but, unfortunate with his erotic undertakings, became a Knight of Malta and withdrew into seclusion. The two main themes of his notable poetry, Marinist in style, were the misery of human existence and the ecstatically melancholy tension achieved by meditation.
▷B Croce, *Lirici marinisti* (1910)

PERSIUS (Aulus Persius Flaccus)
(34–62)

Roman satirist, born of a distinguished equestrian family in Volaterrae in Etruria. He was educated in Rome, where he came under Stoic influence. He wrote fastidiously and sparingly, leaving at his death only six admirable satires, the whole not exceeding 650 hexameter lines. These were published by his friend Cornutus after his death. **Dryden** and others have translated them into verse.
▷E V Marmorale, *Persio* (1956)

PERZYNSKI, Wlodzimierz
(1878–1930)

Polish dramatist and writer of fiction, born in Opaczno. His ironic plays, revealing middle-class values by means of skilful dialogue, are frequently said to have been underrated—none appears to have been translated into English. They have been compared to those of **Shaw**. His fiction, however, has dated.

PESADO, José Joaquin
(1801–61)

Minor Mexican poet, whose ornate pre-romantic poems tried to incorporate the past of the Mexican Native Americans in a Spanish traditional style.

PESSHANA, Camilo
(1867–1926)

Portuguese Symbolist poet, born in Coimbra. He lived for many years in Macao, where he died. Like Arthur Waley in England, Pesshana translated Chinese poetry into his own language—unlike Waley, he hardly knew Chinese. But the effect was similar. His carefully wrought poetry, among the best written in Portugal before that of **Pessoa**, most of it collected in *Clepsidra* (1920), had a strong influence on **Sá-Carneiro** and on Pessoa himself.

PESSOA, Fernando António Nogueira
(1888–1935)

Portuguese poet, born in Lisbon and educated in South Africa. He studied briefly at Lisbon University and worked as a commercial translator. In 1915, he founded the journal *Orfeu*. After 1914, he created four distinct 'heteronyms', each one stylistically distinct and to some extent antagonistic. There was the Symbolist 'Fernando Pessoa', the pastoral 'Alberto Caeiro', the Futurist 'Álvaro de Campos', and the elegant classicist 'Ricardo Reis'. In addition, Pessoa created many other partial heteronyms, identities proliferating towards the point where there was a new author for each and every poem. His/their complete works were published from 1952, and an English translation was prepared by Jonathan Griffin in four volumes (1974); three volumes of *English Poems* had already appeared in 1921. It has been unconvincingly suggested that, far from being a conscious literary strategy, Pessoa's heteronymity was a symptom of multiple personality disorder, and there is in his work an awkward, unresolved balance between hectic self-probing and obsessiveness on the one hand, classicist escapism on the other. But, although he did live on the edge of sanity, this is a deliberately staged conflict. His is one of the essential literary careers of the Modernist movement.
▷G Monteiro (ed), *The Man Who Never Was* (1982)

PETER DAMIEN (or DAMIANI), St
(c.1006–1076)

Italian poet, theologian and moralist. His theological writings are amongst the most severe arguments for the monastic way of life to be found anywhere: he views all love between humans as essentially evil, even within marriage, and he cites homosexuality as evidence of demonic possession. He was initially a friend of Pope Gregory VII, but later condemned him in verse. His own works were not universally popular within the church—Pope Leo IX condemned him for his cruelty. His religious poetry reflects his stern theology.

PETERKIEWICZ, Jerzy
(1916–)

Polish novelist, poet, playwright, critic and translator, long resident in the United Kingdom. His earlier and most interesting work is in Polish, his later in English. The Polish work, mostly poetry, is expressionistic. His English novels (eg *The Knotted Cord*, 1953) were catastrophic visions of nightmare futures and pasts running concurrently. Later he settled into a more predictable Roman Catholicism, and as a critic he has veered towards the Catholic right.

PETERKIN, Julia
(1880–1961)

American novelist, born in South Carolina. The wife of a plantation manager, she became known as the leading depictor of (and spokeswoman for) the region's Gullah Blacks. *Scarlet Sister Mary* (1928), which won a Pulitzer Prize, was dramatized, with white actors (such as Ethel Barrymore) in blackface. *Black April* (1927) was also a major novel. It is likely that criticism has not yet caught up with her achievement.

PETERS, Ellis *see* PARGETER, Edith

PETERSEN, Nis
(1897–1943)

Danish poet and novelist, cousin of **Kaj Munk**, born in South Jutland. He rebelled against a strict upbringing and became a journalist, casual labourer and vagabond until he became famous for his novel of Rome in the time of Marcus Aurelius, *Sandalmagernes Gade* (1931, Eng trans *The Street of the Sandal-makers*, 1932). His later poetry is highly considered; his verse appeared in a collected edition in 1949. His adult life was haunted by alcoholism and spiritual crises.
▷J Andersen, *Nis Petersen* (1957)

PETERSON, Ralph
(1921–)

Australian scriptwriter for radio, television and film, born in Adelaide. He has written for comedians Dick Bentley, Tony Hancock and Benny Hill, and attracted attention with his play *The Square Ring*, filmed by Ealing Studios with Jack Warner, Kay Kendall and Sid James; Peterson turned this into a novel in 1954. Since returning to Australia he has written a number of award-winning plays and television serials, a novel *Greater the Truth* (1956) concerning the conflicting claims on a journalist's conscience, and a play based on the defection of a diplomat, *The Third Secretary* (1972).

PETÖFI, Sandor
(1823–49)

Hungarian poet, born in Kiskörös. He was successively actor, soldier and literary hack, but by 1844 had made his name as a poet. In 1848 he threw himself into the revolutionary cause, writing numerous war songs. He fell in battle at Segesvár. His poetry broke completely with the old pedantic style, and, full of national feeling, began a new epoch in Hungarian literature. He also wrote a novel called *A hóhér kötele* (1846, 'The Hangman's Rope'), and translated **Shakespeare**'s *Coriolanus*.
▷L Havatny, *Igy élt Petöfi* (5 vols, 1955–7)

PETRARCH, Francesco Petrarca
(1304–74)

Italian poet and scholar. One of the earliest and greatest of modern lyric poets, he was the son of a Florentine notary, who, exiled (1302) along with **Dante**, settled in Arezzo, where Francesco was born. In 1312 his father went to Avignon, then the seat of the papal court; and there and in Bologna the boy devoted himself with enthusiasm to the study of the classics. After his father's death Petrarch returned to Avignon (1326). Being without means, he became a churchman, though perhaps never a priest, and lived on the small benefices conferred by his many patrons. It was at this period (1327) that he first saw Laura (possibly Laure de Noves, married in 1325 to Hugo de Sade; she died, the mother of 11 children, in 1348). She inspired him with a passion which has become proverbial for its constancy and purity. Now began also his friendship with the powerful Roman family of the Colonnas. As the fame of Petrarch's learning and genius grew, his position became one of unprecedented influence. His presence at their courts was competed for by the most powerful sovereigns of the day. He travelled repeatedly in France, Germany and Flanders, searching for MSS. In Liège he found two new orations of **Cicero**, in Verona a collection of his letters, in Florence an unknown portion of Quintilian. Invited by the senate of Rome on Easter Sunday, 1341, he ascended the capitol clad in the robes of his friend and admirer, King Robert of Naples, and there, after delivering an oration, he was crowned poet laureate. In 1353, after the death of Laura and his friend Cardinal Colonna, he left Avignon and his country house at Vaucluse for ever, disgusted with the corruption of the papal court. His remaining years were passed in various towns of northern Italy. Petrarch may be considered as the earliest of the great

humanists of the Renaissance. He himself chiefly founded his claim to fame on his epic poem *Africa* (Eng trans 1977), the hero of which is Scipio Africanus, and his historical work in prose, *De Viris Illustribus* ('On Famous Men'), a series of biographies of classical celebrities. Other Latin works are the eclogues and epistles in verse; and in prose the dialogues, *Secretum meum* ('My Secret'), the treatises *De Otio Religiosorum* (a work about the tranquillity of the monastic life) and *De Vita Solitaria* (Eng trans *The Life of Solitude*, 1924), and his letters—he was in constant correspondence with **Boccaccio**. It is as a poet that his fame has lasted for over five centuries. His title deeds to fame are in his *Canzoniere* (Eng trans *Sonnets and Stanzas*, 1879), in the Italian sonnets, madrigals, and songs, almost all inspired by his unrequited passion for Laura. The *Opera Omnia* ('Complete Works') appeared at Basel in 1544. His Italian lyrics were published in 1470, and have since gone through innumerable editions.
▷T Bergin, *Petrarch* (1970)

PETRESCU, Camil
(1894–1957)
Romanian novelist, playwright and poet who was well known in the inter-war period as a journalist, literary editor and theatre director. His remarkable genius collapsed in his last years, as a result of his attempt to become a socialist realist and to write a long novel reflecting the Marxist view of Romanian national history. He failed to complete it, and what he left of it is of no value. His greatest novel is *Patul lui Procust* (1933, 'Procrustian Bed'), which reflects the fruitful influence of the phenomenological philosopher Husserl, upon whom he had written a book. Here he anticipated many of the techniques to be employed by **Jean-Paul Sartre**. Also remarkable is the slightly earlier novel *Ultima noapte de dragoste, initia noapte de razboi* (1930, 'The Last Night of Love, the First Night of War').

PETRESCU, Cezar
(1892–1961)
Romanian popular novelist who also wrote for children. (He was not a relative of his namesake **Camil Petrescu**.) It has been said that, despite the lack of depth of his characters, his novels 'present the most complete tableau of Romanian life in the first half of [the 20th] century'. One, *Intunecare* (1927), has been translated as *Gathering Clouds* (1957). He has also been compared, with some aptness, to **Anthony Trollope**.

PETRONIUS ARBITER
(1st century)
Latin satirical writer, and author of the *Satyricon* ('Tales of Satyrs'). He is usually supposed to be the voluptuary Gaius Petronius, whom **Tacitus** calls 'arbiter elegantiae' at the court of Nero. He was governor of Bithynia for a time. The *Satyricon* is a long satirical romance in prose and verse, of which only parts of the 15th and 16th books, in a fragmentary state, are still extant. The work depicts with wit, humour and realism the licentious life in southern Italy of the moneyed class. The favour Petronius enjoyed as aider and abettor of Nero and his entourage in every form of sensual indulgence aroused the jealousy of another confidant, Tigellinus, who procured his disgrace and banishment. Ordered to commit suicide, he opened his veins.
▷H Rankin, *Petronius the Artist* (1971)

PETROV, Yevgeny *see* ILF, Ilya and PETROV, Yevgeny

PETRY, Ann
(1911–)
American novelist and short-story writer, born in Old Saybrook, Connecticut and educated at the University of Connecticut. She moved to New York in 1938 and worked as a reporter for *Amsterdam News* and *People's Voice*. She published her first short story, 'On Saturday the Siren Sounds at Noon', in 1943, after studying creative writing at Columbia University. Social realism characterizes her work: her first novel, *The Street* (1947), is an account of slum life and domestic unrest which ends in a tragic death, while *The Narrows* (1951) focuses on an inter-racial marriage, and again has a tragic outcome. Petry was the first black woman writer to sell over a million copies of a book.
▷M Pryse and H J Spillers (eds), *Conjuring: Black Women, Fiction, and Literary Tradition* (1985)

PÉTURSSON, Hallgrímur
(1614–74)
Icelandic poet, pastor and hymn-writer, the greatest devotional poet in Icelandic literature, who struggled with poverty all his life and died afflicted with leprosy. Born in the north of Iceland, he ran away to Denmark to become a blacksmith's apprentice, but was put to school in Copenhagen by an Icelandic patron, the future bishop Brynjólfur Sveinsson, who recognized his unusual abilities. He was entrusted with the task of rehabilitating the Icelandic survivors of a Moorish pirate raid on Iceland by 'Turks' (1627), whose captives had been sold as slaves and were now in Copenhagen after being ransomed. He fell in love with one of them, a 38-year-old Icelandic woman known as Turkish-Gydda. They married in Iceland, where Hallgrímur worked as a labourer before becoming pastor of the

church at Saurbær in the west of Iceland (1651). Here he wrote his masterpiece, *Passion Hymns* (1666), a cycle of 50 meditations on the Crucifixion. One of the hymns, *Allt eins og blómstrið eina* ('Just as the one true flower') is still sung at funerals in Iceland. The new cathedral in Reykjavík, Hallgrímskirkja, is named after him.

▷M Jónsson, *Hallgrímur Pétersson* (2 vols, 1947)

PEYREFITTE, Roger
(1907–)

French novelist. He wrote one serious novel, *Les Amitiés particulières* (1945, Eng trans *Special Friendships*, 1950), about homosexuality in a school, and then devoted himself to amusing, sophisticated but often irresponsible entertainments and exposés, such as *Les Clés de Saint Pierre* (1955, 'The Keys of St Peter'), which won him a bad reputation with critics and many readers. His penchant was for collecting embarrassing facts, which he then made even more ridiculous than they actually were.

PEZOA VÉLIZ, Carlos
(1879–1908)

Chilean poet, born in Santiago. He died prematurely from injuries received in the 1906 Valparaiso earthquake. His poetry—published posthumously as *Alma chilena* (1912, 'Chilean Soul'), is simple and unpretentious, and is now receiving the attention it has always deserved. There is an excellent anthology of his prose and poetry, *Antologia* (1957), with a useful introduction (in Spanish) by N Guzmán.

PHAEDRUS, Gaius Julius
(c.15 BC–c.50 AD)

Translator and adaptor of **Aesop**'s fables into Latin verse. Born in Macedonia, he was taken to Rome at an early age and became the freedman of Augustus or Tiberius. Under Tiberius he published the first two books of his fables, but his biting though veiled allusions to the tyranny of the emperor and his minister Sejanus caused him to be accused and condemned—his punishment is unknown. On the death of Sejanus he published his third book. The fourth and fifth books belong to his last years. He was more than a reproducer of Aesop; he invented fables of his own and also borrowed from other sources.

PHILIPPE, Charles-Louis
(1874–1909)

French novelist, born in Cérilly who, ill from early youth, died young of a syphilitic infection. He is best known for his naturalistic but softened, near-sentimental portraits of a prostitute and her pimp, *Bubu de Montparnasse* (1901, Eng trans 1932), but this is not quite typical of his work as a whole, which has attracted considerable critical interest since his death. His predominantly oral and highly complex style is original and has been influential (eg on **Larbaud**, but perhaps, too, on **Céline**). Such 'populiste' authors as **Eugène Dabit** also drew upon him for inspiration and example. In his unfinished novel *Charles Blanchard* (1913) he was experimenting in a rural setting. His *Le Père Perdrix* (1903) is available in English translation as *A Simple Story* (1924). 'Philippe', a critic has written, 'achieved that marvellous art which results from the reportage of the innocent eye and the humble heart'.

PHILIPS, Ambrose
(?1674–1749)

English poet, born in Shrewsbury. He was educated at St John's College, Cambridge, and became a fellow there. A friend of **Joseph Addison** and **Richard Steele**, he did hack work for Tonson, and gained a reputation by the *Winter-piece* in the *Tatler* and six Pastorals in Tonson's *Miscellany* (1709). These were praised in the *Guardian* at **Pope**'s expense, and Pope's jealousy started a bitter feud. He was dubbed 'Namby Pamby' by either **Henry Carey** or **Jonathan Swift** for the oversentimentality of some of his poetry. Of his plays only *The Distrest Mother* (1712), based on **Racine**'s *Andromaque*, found favour with his contemporaries. He was MP for Armagh, secretary to the Archbishop of Armagh, purse-bearer to the Irish Lord Chancellor, and registrar of the Prerogative Court.

▷Dr S Johnson, *Lives of the Most Eminent English Poets* (10 vols, 1779–81)

PHILIPS, John
(1676–1709)

English poet, born in Bampton, Oxfordshire. He was the son of the Archdeacon of Shropshire, and was educated at Winchester and Christ Church, Oxford. He wrote three very popular poems: *The Splendid Shilling* (1701), a **Milton**ic burlesque; *Blenheim* (1705), a Tory celebration of Marlborough's great victory; and *Cyder* (1708), an imitation of **Virgil**'s *Georgics*. He has a monument in Westminster Abbey.

▷Dr S Johnson, *Lives of the Most Eminent English Poets* (10 vols, 1779–81)

PHILIPS, Katherine, née **Fowler**, pseud 'Orinda'
(1631–64)

English poet, born in London, the daughter of a merchant. Called 'the matchless Orinda', at 16 she married James Philips of

Cardigan Priory. She is the first English woman poet to have her work published (it included an address to the Welsh poet **Henry Vaughan**). She received a dedication from Jeremy Taylor (*Discourse on the Nature, Offices and Measures of Friendship*, 1659). She ran a literary salon, described in the *Letter of Orinda to Poliarchus* (1705). She translated **Corneille**'s *Pompée*, which was performed in Dublin in 1663, and the greater part of his *Horace*. Her poems, surreptitiously printed in 1663, were issued in 1667. She died of smallpox on a visit to London.
▷P W Souers, *The Matchless Orinda* (1931)

PHILLIPS, Caryl
(1958–)

British novelist and author of non-fiction, born in St Kitts, West Indies. Brought up in England, he was educated at Oxford. His first novel, *The Final Passage* (1985), looks closely and often ironically at the West Indian experience of Britain. *A State of Independence* (1986), on the other hand, is a sympathetic study of a British West Indian who, after 20 years' absence from the Caribbean, returns on the eve of independence, only to discover that he has become an outsider. A writer noted for creating narrative in an episodic, fragmented, sometimes epistolary style, his powerfully haunting novel *Crossing the River* (1993) follows the lives, in different countries and different centuries, of two brothers and a sister sold into slavery.

PHILLIPS, David Graham
(1867–1911)

American feminist novelist and journalist, born in Madison, Indiana. He played a part in the 'muckraker' movement of reform-minded journalism in the early 20th century. He also wrote powerfully in several novels in favour of the emancipation of women, notably in *The Plum Tree* (1905) and *Susan Lennox: Her Fall and Rise* (1917), and was ultimately assassinated by a lunatic who regarded his efforts in this direction as contributory to female moral depravity. Despite the identification of his name with his attacks on political servitude to capitalist interests, it is for his devoted service to the cause of women's rights that he deserves best to be remembered.
▷L Filler, *Voice of Democracy* (1978)

PHILLIPS, Jayne Anne
(1952–)

American novelist and short-story writer, born in Buckhannon, West Virginia. She first became known in the UK as part of the 'dirty realism' school of American writers. If, however, that general label is at best an inexact description, in Phillips' case it is wholly inappropriate. While her work is based in a recognizable real world, it is also—as shown by her short-story collection *Black Tickets* (1979)—impressionistic, fanciful, and at times a touch precious. *Machine Dreams* (1984), her only novel to date, is easily her most accomplished and engaging work. The story of two generations of an American middle-class family who grow up to lose their illusions and see their dreams die, it is acted out against a background of social dislocation and the Vietnam War. Her other publications include the short-story collection *Fast Lanes* (1984).

PHILLIPS, John
(1631–1706)

English writer, brother of Edward Phillips, nephew of **Milton**. He was educated by his uncle, and replied to Salmasius's attack on him, and acted as his secretary. His *Satyr against Hypocrites* (1655) was a bitter attack on Puritanism, and *Speculum Crape Gownorum* (1682) on the High Churchmen.

PHILLIPS, Stephen
(1864–1915)

English dramatist and poet, born near Oxford and related to **Wordsworth** on his mother's side. He went to school at Oundle and then studied for the Civil Service but chose in preference to become an actor and a tutor. He published several volumes of poetry and, in 1898, won a 1000-guinea prize put up by a literary weekly. Four years later his verse play *Paolo and Francesca* became a stupendous hit at St James's Theatre and the critics hailed him as the new **Sophocles**, the new **Shakespeare**. The acclaim went to his head, the royalties were squandered, his marriage failed, the critics deserted him and friends tried in vain to take him in hand. His days ended in privation.

PHILLPOTTS, Eden
(1862–1960)

English novelist, dramatist and poet, born in Mount Aboo, India. He studied for the stage in London, but turned to literature instead (1893), and made his name by realistic novels chiefly dealing with Devonshire, such as *Lying Prophets* (1896), *Children of the Mist* (1898) and *Widecombe Fair* (1913). Of his plays, *The Farmer's Wife* (1917: staged 1924) and *Yellow Sands* (1926), which he wrote with his daughter Adelaide, were perhaps the most successful. He wrote more than 250 books in all, and collaborated with **Arnold Bennett** and **Jerome K Jerome** on plays.
▷*From the Angle of 88* (1951)

PHIPSON, Joan
(1912–)

Australian writer of fiction for children, born in Warrawee, New South Wales, whose first novel, *Good Luck to the Rider* (1953), won the Children's Book of the Year Award, as did the later *The Family Conspiracy* (1962). Her books range over a variety of themes, from fantasy to adventure, and from a historical re-creation *Bass and Billy Martin* (1972) to contemporary themes of the environment and urban life.

PICARD, Louis-Benoit
(1769–1828)

French dramatist and actor-manager, born in Paris. He wrote 85 plays, of which most were comedies. One, *Le conteur* (1793, 'The Story-teller'), remained in the repertory of the Comédie Française for 40 years; and many felt that he was the best painter of society since **Molière**. His work was meticulously crafted, and often shrewdly observant of contemporary manners.
▷W Staaks, *The Theatre of Louis-Benoit Picard* (1952)

PICCHIA, Paulo Menotti de
(1892–1976)

Brazilian poet. He was associated with Brazilian Modernism, but, before that, had become well known for his *Juca Mulato* poems, expressing (and anticipating) the 'back-to-primitive-roots' aspect of Modernism.

PICHETTE, Henri
(1924–)

French verse-dramatist, half-American by birth, whose oddly Surrealist–Classical plays were much heeded when they were given expensive productions in Paris. Characteristic is *Nucléa* (1952), written in alexandrines, about the struggle between good and evil.
▷L Pronko, *Théâtre d'avant garde* (1963, in French)

PICKEN, Ebenezer
(1769–1816)

Scottish poet, born in Paisley, the son of a silk weaver. He was educated at Glasgow University, and was a teacher in Edinburgh. He published several volumes of Scots poems, including satires, descriptive verses and songs; his principal works were *Poems and Epistles* (1788), and *Miscellaneous Poems and Songs* (1813). He also published an important *Pocket Dictionary of the Scottish Dialect* (1818).

PICKTHALL, Marjorie
(1883–1922)

English poet, short-story writer and novelist, born in Gunnersby. She emigrated with her family to Toronto in 1889, but returned to England after her mother's death in 1912, where she lived until 1920, briefly residing in Canada for the last two years of her life. She is best known as a poet of visionary lyrics, a reputation based on two major collections of poetry published during her lifetime—*The Drift of Pinions* (1913) and *The Lamp of Poor Souls* (1916)—but she was also the author of over 200 short stories, and a number of novels for adults and children. Her poetry presents a gentle imagery of natural beauty, tinted with the sadness of a vague sense of loss.

PIERCY, Marge
(1936–)

American novelist and poet, born in Detroit, Michigan. She was educated at the University of Michigan, and has taught in a number of colleges. Her writing stems from strongly held political and feminist standpoints. Novels like *Going Down Fast* (1969), *Small Changes* (1973) and *Vida* (1980) are revealing documents of the emerging feminist consciousness of the 1960s and 1970s. *Woman On the Edge of Time* (1976) was a science-fiction narrative which contrasted a future utopia with the economic, environmental and gender abuses of contemporary America. Later novels include *Gone to Soldiers* (1987), set during World War II. Her poetry has utilized vernacular language and speech rhythms to good effect.

PIEYRE DE MANDIARGUES, André Paul Édouard
(1909–91)

French novelist and poet, fondly remembered in the UK for the novel that provided the singer Marianne Faithfull with her one convincing film role, *Girl on a Motorcycle*. Pieyre de Mandiargues's ninth work of fiction, *La Motocyclette* (1963, published in the USA as *The Motorcycle*, 1966, in the UK as *The Girl on the Motorcycle*, 1966), was a work of highbrow erotica. As in all the other books, it presupposes that extremes of sensation yield moral or at least psychological insights. *Le Lis de Mer* (1956, Eng trans *The Girl Beneath the Lion*, 1958) is subtler but less dramatically compelling, and his other novels and short stories too often suggest formulaic wish-fulfilment. His verse has a sensuous quality that is reminiscent of the great French cabaret singers, but with a strong infusion of Surrealist imagery, and his admiration for the *trompe l'oeil* painter Arcimboldo—*Arcimboldo le Merveilleux* (1977, Eng trans *Arcimboldo the Marvellous*, 1978)—suggests a

sidelight on his characteristic technique. He has also translated into French works by **Yeats**, **Octavio Paz** and **Yukio Mishima**.
▷D Bond, *The Fiction of André Pieyre de Mandiargues* (1982)

PILKINGTON, Laetitia, née Van Lewen
(c.1706–1750)

Irish writer, born in Dublin, daughter of an obstetrician. She was an intimate friend of **Swift** and wrote verse from an early age. In 1725 she married a minor writer, Matthew Pilkington, who deserted her. She followed him to London but he divorced her in 1738 on grounds of adultery. Jailed for debt in 1742, she later supported herself by bookselling. Her vivacious *Memoirs* (1748–54) give a candid, racy account of her life and adventures, with revealing anecdotes of **Swift**, **Pope** and other authors. They include her poems: usually light-hearted or satirical, she can also write with dignity and feeling about personal misfortune.
▷ *Memoirs*, ed I Barry (1928); V Woolf, *The Common Reader* (1925)

PILLECIJN, Filip de
(1891–1962)

Belgian (Flemish) fiction writer. He worked in the Ministry of Education in the Belgian government under the Nazi occupation, and as a result served five years in prison for collaboration. His defence was that he had been serving Flemish interests. He wrote strange and brooding novels, combining decadence with neo-romantic elements (not altogether unlike **Gracq**): *Blauwbaard* (1931, 'Bluebeard'), in which there is a sort of gloating over the murders, is typical. His bitter experiences in World War II, and the price he paid, humanized him, and his later work was more generous in spirit. *Anvaard het leven* (1956, 'Taking Life As It Is'), for example, is a more straightforwardly realistic novel, both moving and well observed.

PILNYAK, Boris, pseud of Boris Andreyevich Vogau
(1894–1937)

Russian author, whose work was highly popular in the 1920s. He wrote novels and short stories including *Golý gok* (1922, Eng trans *The Naked Year*, 1929) and *Volga vpalaet b kaspinskoe more* (1930, Eng trans *The Volga Flows Down to the Caspian Sea*, 1932). His main theme was the effect of the Revolution on the middle classes in Russia. Despite efforts to please the ruling hierarchy, as in the anti-American novel *O-Key* (1932), his writings met with disapproval and he was arrested, charged with spying for Japan, and executed.

▷P Jensen, *Nature as Code: the achievement of Boris Pilnyak* (1979)

PILON, Jean-Guy
(1930–)

French–Canadian poet and editor, born in Saint-Polycarp, Quebec. His poetry, well represented in **A J M Smith**'s *Oxford Book of Canadian Verse* (1960), is well-wrought, cosmopolitan and optimistic. He has also written a novel, *Solange* (1965).

PILCHER, Rosamunde
(1924–)

English novelist, born in Lelant, Cornwall. She worked in the Women's Royal Naval Service but, from the age of 18 when her first story was published in *Woman and Home* magazine, pursued another career as a writer, at first publishing under the pseudonym Jane Fraser. The romance *A Secret To Tell* (1955) was the first book to appear under her own name, but three decades passed before that name became more widely known with the publication of the bestselling *The Shell Seekers* (1987). A romance of a bittersweet nature, it is the story of an artist's daughter who, finding that a painting of her father's is worth a small fortune, suddenly has the financial power to become independent—to the possible detriment of her family. The success of *The Shell Seekers* was followed in 1989 by *September*.

PINDAR, Greek Pindaros
(c.518–c.438BC)

Greek lyric poet, born of an old and illustrious family in Cynoscephalae near Thebes, the capital of Boeotia. He began his career as a composer of choral odes at 20 with a song of victory still extant (*Pyth. X*, written 498 BC). He soon reached the highest rank in his profession, and composed odes for a wide range of people—for the tyrants of Syracuse and Macedon, as well as for the free cities of Greece. In his poems he gives advice and reproof as well as praise to his patrons. He wrote hymns to the gods, paeans, dithyrambs, odes for processions, mimic dancing songs, convivial songs, dirges, and odes in praise of princes. Of all these poems only fragments are extant, but his *Epinikia* ('Triumphal Odes') can be read in their entirety. They are divided into four books, celebrating the victories won in the Olympian, Pythian, Nemean and Isthmian games. They show the intense admiration of the Greeks for bodily prowess and beauty; such gifts come from the gods and are sacred. The groundwork of Pindar's poems consists of those legends which form the Greek religious literature, and

his protest against myths dishonouring to the gods shows his pious nature.
▷C M Bowra, *Pindar* (1964)

PIÑERA, Virgilio
(1912–79)

Cuban playwright, novelist, story writer and poet, born in Matanzas province, son of a surveyor; he was the most important and influential dramatist of his generation. He came to Havana at the age of 28. From 1946 until 1958, just before the advent of the Castro regime, he lived in Argentina, where, among other things, he helped translate **Witold Gombrovich**'s *Ferdiduke* into Spanish. His semi-autobiographical play *Aire frio* (1959, 'Cold Air') is one of his best known; he was most influenced by **Eugene O'Neill** and by **Ionesco**. He was very active in the theatre as a director. He was homosexual, and when the authorities began to persecute homosexuals (1971), he fell from state favour, although he was allowed to continue with his activities as a translator. He died a neglected figure, of whom there were few obituaries, but his importance is now re-emerging.
▷S Bueno, *Historia de la literatura cubana* (1963); S Menton, *Prose Fiction of the Cuban Revolution* (1975)

PINERO, Sir Arthur Wing
(1855–1934)

English playwright, born in London. He studied law, but in 1874 made his debut on the stage in Edinburgh, and in 1875 joined the Lyceum company. His first play, *£200 a Year*, appeared in 1877, followed by a series of comedies. In 1893, with *The Second Mrs Tanqueray*, generally reckoned his best, he began a period of realistic tragedies which were received with enthusiastic acclamation and made him the most successful playwright of his day, although his popularity declined sharply with the rise of a new kind of theatre. He was the author of some 50 plays which included *The Squire* (1881), *The Magistrate* (1885), *Dandy Dick* (1887) and *The Profligate* (1889) from his earlier works, and from his later *The Gay Lord Quex* (1899), *His House in Order* (1906) and *Mid-Channel* (1909).
▷C Hamilton, *The Social Plays of Arthur Wing Pinero* (4 vols, 1917–22)

PINGET, Robert
(1919–)

Swiss (French) playwright, novelist and collaborator with **Samuel Beckett** (who translated some of his plays into English); he was born in Geneva. One of his chief works is the novel, later dramatized as *Lettre morte* (1960, Eng trans in *Plays*, 1965–7), *Le Fiston* (1959, Eng trans *No Answer*, 1961). Pinget's fiction

has affinities with Beckett's, but, as is often noted, also with the world as conceived in the writings of **Henri Michaux**. While his novels, of which *L'Inquisitoire* (1962, 'The Inquisitorial'), is outstanding, resemble *nouveaux romans* in presentation, they in fact contain 'a Balzacian multiplicity of characters'.
▷V Mercier, *The New Novel: From Queneau to Pinget* (1971)

PINILLOS, Manuel
(1914–)

Spanish poet and editor (of *Ambito*, 1951–62), born in Saragossa. Out of the mainstream, he has published quiet, meditative poetry influenced less by his compatriots than by **Hölderlin** and **Rilke**.

PINSKI, David
(1872–1959)

Yiddish novelist, essayist and, primarily, playwright, born in Mohilev in the Ukraine; he lived in Europe and, from 1899, in New York; he went to Israel late in his life, in 1950. Most of his plays were translated and adapted for British and American performances. He was most influenced by **Ibsen**, but wrote plays in almost every form: comedy, allegory, biblical, realistic. He had international stature. Best known of his plays are *Di Familie Tsvi* (1905, 'The Tsvi family or The Last Jew'), and the satirical masterpiece *Der Oytser* (1906, 'The Treasure'). He was an active socialist and Zionist, and wrote many vital essays on the Yiddish drama and its future (unhappily unfulfilled).
▷C A Madison, *Yiddish Literature* (1968)

PINTER, Harold
(1930–)

English dramatist, the son of a London East End tailor of Portuguese–Jewish ancestry (da Pinta). He became a repertory actor and wrote poetry and later plays. His first London production was trounced by the critics unused to his highly personal dramatic idiom. A superb verbal acrobat, he exposes and utilizes the illogical and inconsequential in everyday talk, not to illustrate some general idea (as does **Eugène Ionesco**), but to induce an atmosphere of menace in *The Birthday Party* (1957), or of claustrophobic isolation in *The Caretaker* (1958; filmed 1963). His TV play *The Lover* (1963) won the Italia Prize. Other plays include *The Collection* (TV 1961; stage 1962), *The Dwarfs* (radio 1960; stage 1963), and *The Homecoming* (1965). His filmscripts include *The Servant* (1963) and *The Pumpkin Eaters* (1964). Later plays include *No Man's Land* (1975), and *Betrayal* (1978), the story of an adulterous relationship told in reverse chronological order. He did not produce another full-length play until *Party Time* (1991). Three short pieces, under the title *Other Voices*, were shown at the National Theatre in 1982. The subsequent plays, *One for the Road* (1984) and *Mountain Language* (1988), both about 25 minutes in length, show that while he has lost none of his ability to create quickly an atmosphere of threat, his subject-matter is now explicitly political, *Mountain Language* being a play set in a prison camp in which the guards brutalize the inmates and their visiting relatives, while *A New World Order* (1990) also has a menacing political theme. More recent filmscripts include *The French Lieutenant's Woman* (1981), from the novel by **John Fowles**. He was married first (1956–80) to the actress Vivien Merchant (1929–83); in 1980 he married the writer and biographer Lady Antonia Fraser. In 1991 he helped launch a campaign against the celebration of Columbus's 'discovery' of America.

PINTO, Fernão Mendez
(c.1510–1583)

Portuguese adventurer and writer, born near Coimbra. At the age of 27 he made his way to India, and remained for 21 years in southeast Asia, leading a life of adventure, fighting pirates, trading and going on special missions to Japan or elsewhere. He returned in 1558, and wrote an extravagant account of his adventures, *Peregrinaçao* (1614, Eng trans *The Voyages and Adventures of Fernand Mendez Pinto*, 1653).

PIONTEK, Heinz
(1925–)

German poet, critic, novelist and translator, a more lyrical and intelligible poet—who was initially influenced by **Oskar Loerke** and **Wilhelm Lehmann**—than most of his contemporaries. He has translated **John Keats** well. Some critics have accused his later poetry of being versatile to the point of facility, but this is by no means a majority opinion. His criticism is incisive and to the point.

PIOVENE, Guido
(1907–75)

Italian novelist, travel writer, journalist and critic, from a noble family of Vicenza. A novelist directly in the French moralistic tradition, and in Italy in that of **Fogazzaro**, he veered from an extreme youthful fascism (inherited from his father) to a humane Marxism—a process which he examines, with wit and candour, in the essays of *La coda di paglia* (1962, 'The Coward'). His first, epistolary, novel, *Lettere di una novizia* (1941, Eng trans

Confession of a Novice, 1951), which was successfully filmed, and which made his name, was a Pirandellian exploration of the difference between reality and illusion. But his two more mature novels, *Le furie* (1963, 'The Furies') and *Le stelle fredde* (1970, 'The Cold Stars'), were his greatest achievements. Both are fantastic works, largely autobiographical, only classifiable as 'essay novels', but interspersed with dreams and (for example) a visit from **Dostoyevsky** from the spirit-world for a conversation with the author. He has been criticized for brittleness and tediousness, and Italian opinion is still divided as to his ultimate worth.

▷G Catalano, *Piovene* (1967, in Italian)

PIRANDELLO, Luigi
(1867–1936)

Italian dramatist, novelist and short-story writer, winner of the Nobel Prize for literature, born in Girgenti (Agrigento), Sicily. He studied philology at Rome and Bonn, becoming a lecturer in literature at Rome (1897–1922). After writing powerful and realistic novels and short stories, including *Il Fu Mattia Pascal* (1904, rev edn 1921, Eng trans *The Late Mattia Pascal*, 1923) and *Si Gira* (1916, Eng trans *Shoot!*, 1926), he turned to the theatre and quickly established his own extraordinary genre. Among his plays are *Sei personaggi in cerca d'autore* (1921, Eng trans *Six Characters in Search of an Author*, 1922), *Enrico IV* (1922, Eng trans *Henry IV*, 1922) and *Come Tu Mi Vuoi* (1930, Eng trans *As You Desire Me*, 1931). In 1925 he established a theatre of his own in Rome, the Teatro d'Arte, and his company took his plays all over Europe. Many of his later plays have been filmed. In 1934 he was awarded the Nobel Prize for literature.

▷D Vittorini, *Luigi Pirandello* (1937)

PIRES, José Cardoso
(1925–)

Portuguese novelist, dramatist and critic, born in Pêso de Régua. He criticized the Salazar regime in various oblique ways, as in *Dinossaure excelerntissime* (1972, 'Imperial Highness, Dinosaurus I'). His most serious work is *O hósepede de Job* (1963, 'Job's Guest'), about a rural father and son trying to deal with forces they cannot control—and is thus an allegory of modern Portugal.

PIRON, Alexis
(1689–1773)

French poet, playwright and wit, born in Dijon. He wrote farces for fairground theates, and eventually graduated to the legitimate stage, writing both tragedies and comedies. His works include the comic opera *Endriaque*

(1723) and a variety of plays, of which the extravagant satire *La métromanie* (1738) is the best known. Piron described himself as 'nothing, not even an Academician'.
▷P Chaponnière, *Piron* (1910)

PISEMSKY, Alexey
(1820–81)
Russian realist novelist and playwright, born in Kostromo province. He wrote two masterpieces, and a fine play: *Tyufyak* (1850, Eng trans *The Simpleton*, 1960), *Tysyacha dush* (1858, Eng trans *A Thousand Souls*, 1959), and the drama *Gorkaya sudbina* (1859, Eng trans *A Bitter Fate*, 1933), a peasant tragedy. Sceptical, sardonic, sarcastic, he was persistently underrated outside Russia (in which, however, he was always attacked by radicals and communist critics), until Ivy Litvinov translated his two major novels.
▷I D Ivanov, *Pisemsky* (1898, in Russian); M Slonim, *Modern Russian Literature* (1953)

PITTER, Ruth
(1897–1992)
English poet, born in Ilford, Essex, the daughter of a schoolmaster. She wrote verse from a very early age and later was encouraged by **Hilaire Belloc**. Her writing belongs to no particular school and for inspiration she has drawn mainly upon the beauty of natural things and her Christian faith. In 1955 she was awarded the Queen's Gold Medal for Poetry, having already won the Hawthornden Prize in 1936 with *A Trophy of Arms*. Other volumes include *First and Second Poems* (1927), *A Mad Lady's Garland* (1934), *Urania* (1951), *The Ermine* (1953), *Still by Choice* (1966) and *End of Drought* (1975). A *Collected Poems* appeared in 1990.
▷A Russell, *Homage to a Poet* (1969)

PIXÉRÉCOURT, René Charles Guilbert de
(1773–1844)
French dramatist, born in Nancy. Known as 'the father of melodrama', he wrote 111 plays. He had initial difficulties, but following the successful comedy *Les Petits Auvergnats* (1797, 'The Little Citizens of the Auvergne'), did not look back. He wrote all sorts of plays, but his Gothic melodramas, such as his dramatization of the *Mysteries of Udolpho of Mrs Radcliffe* (1797), did more than the plays of any other single writer to provide the standard fare of the 19th-century playgoer. A master-craftsman, he ably defended his own procedures. He was, wrote a modern French critic, 'superior to his work'.
▷M W Disher, *Blood and Thunder* (1949)

PIZARNIK, Alejandra
(1936–72)
Argentinian poet, whose work is characterized by mystery, surrealism, and a dreamy quality, which attempt to make reality greater than it is in normal life. She lived in Argentina and France, where she contributed to a number of literary magazines. Important themes in her work are death, the loss of innocence, nostalgia, and longing. Her works include *El deseo de la palabra* (1975, 'Desire of the Word') and *El Infierno musical* (1971, 'The Musical Hell'). She is considered one of the foremost Latin-American female poets of the 20th century.

PLAIDY, Jean *see* **HOLT, Victoria**

PLANCHÉ, James Robinson
(1796–1880)
English playwright, antiquary and herald, born in London of Huguenot ancestry. He was a prolific writer of burlesque and extravaganzas, such as *Amoroso, King of Little Britain* (1818), *Success; or, a Hit if you like it* (1825) and *High, Low, Jack and the Game* (1833). His best-known work is *The Vampyre; or the Bride of the Isles* (1820). He wrote the libretto for Weber's *Oberon*, and other operas. As a heraldic scholar he wrote *History of British Costumes* (1834) and other works. He was appointed Somerset Herald in 1866.
▷H Granville-Barker, *Exit Planché—enter Gilbert* (1932)

PLANTE, David Robert
(1940–)
American novelist, resident for much of his career in London. He grew up in Providence, Rhode Island, which became the basis of his later trilogy, *The Francoeur Family* (collected 1984). He was educated at Boston College and at the University of Louvain in Belgium. He taught at the English School in Rome and at schools in Massachusetts, then moved to the UK. Before receiving a measure of public and commercial recognition with the first of the autobiographical 'Francoeur' novels, *The Family* (1978), Plante had published five rather hermetic novels, which work almost musical variations on delicately registered patterns of sexual and familial relationship. Despite a darkening of tone that foreshadows the erotic violence of later books, these early novels represent different approaches to the same basic literary and philosophical issues. The 'Francoeur' novels continued with *The Country* (1981) and *The Woods* (1982). Later novels, *The Foreigner* (1984) and *The Catholic* (1985), are more extreme in their dissection of sexual identity and are as aggressively

overt as the early books were reticent and veiled.

PLATANOV, Andrey, formerly **Andrey Klimentov**

(1896–1951)

Russian short-story writer, dramatist, and poet. Platanov, who was born in Voronezh, was consistently underrated in his lifetime, both inside and—more shamefully—outside his own country. Only in the last decade has his work been re-examined and reappraised. He was an electrical engineer by training, but his first writings appeared in 1917 and 1918, while he was fighting with the Bolsheviks. He remained in his profession until 1927, when he decided to dedicate his life to writing. His work became interesting and invaluable as soon as he lost his youthful enthusiasm for the Revolution, and saw the results of 'total organization from above'. His *Chevengur* (Eng trans 1978) was not even published until 1972, and then in an incomplete text (the English version is complete); nor is he mentioned in official histories. He was at heart, like **Leo Tolstoy**, a constructive anarchist, and this caused his work to be proscribed after 1931. When a few years later his work reappeared, he had stripped it of its satirical tendencies; World War II gave him an opportunity to publish patriotic (but never poor) tales, and he regained some of his former popularity. It has now been recognized that all of his later writings are exceedingly subtle reactions to his circumstances, and nowhere more than in his style, which, the most advanced of all variations of *skaz* (idiomatic writing), combines parody of Soviet mediaspeak with inimitable rustic wisdom.
▷M Jordon, *Andrey Platanov* (1973)

PLATEN, August von, in full **Karl Georg August Maximilian Graf von Platen-Hallermünde**

(1796–1835)

German poet, born in Ansbach. He illadvisedly joined the Bavarian army, but royal patronage secured him indefinite leave and he studied widely at Würzburg and Erlangen. A perfectionist, he frequently wrote in metrically complex foreign forms, such as the Persian ghazal (*Ghaselen*, 1821 and 1824) and the **Petrarch**an sonnet; one of his greatest achievements was the *Sonette aus Venedig* (1825, Eng trans *Sonnets from Venice*, 1923), which combine a sense of beauty and of *Weltschmerz* ('world-weariness'). He also wrote ballads, such as 'Der Pilgrim vor St Just' (1820), plays (including satires on Romanticism), and diaries, which reveal the torments caused by his homosexuality. His feelings of isolation led to self-exile in Italy (where his disastrous life ended at Syracuse), and infused his poetry with its characteristic pessimism.
▷P Bumm, *August Graf von Platen: Eine Biographie* (1990)

PLATER, Alan Frederick

(1935–)

English dramatist, born in Jarrow-on-Tyne. Trained as an architect, his writing was first published in *Punch* (1958) and, since 1960, he has built up an enormous body of work, both originals and adaptations, reflecting his working-class origins, political beliefs and interest in jazz. A regular writer for *Z Cars* (1963–5), his many television plays include *Ted's Cathedral* (1964), *Close the Coalhouse Door* (1968) and *The Land of Green Ginger* (1974). He is also responsible for such literate and skilled screen translations as *The Good Companions* (1980), *Fortunes of War* (1987) and *A Very British Coup* (1988). Equally prolific in other media, he has contributed to *The Guardian*, and written film scripts like *The Virgin and the Gypsy* (1969) and *Priest of Love* (1980), as well as such novels as *Misterioso* (1987) and *The Beiderbecke Affair* (1985), from his television series of the same title. He received a BAFTA Writer's Award in 1989.
▷J R Taylor, *The Second Wave* (1971)

PLATH, Sylvia

(1932–63)

American poet, born in Boston, Massachusetts, the daughter of a German-born Professor of Biology and a school-teacher. Educated at Bradford High School and Smith College, where she suffered from deep depression and attempted suicide, she won a Fulbright Fellowship to Newnham College, Cambridge, in 1956, where she studied English and met and married **Ted Hughes**. After a spell of teaching in the USA they settled in England, first in London and then in Devon, but separated in 1962; a year later Sylvia committed suicide. She wrote poetry from early childhood; her first volume, *A Winter Ship* (1960), was published anonymously, but she put her name to her second volume, *The Colossus* (1960). After the birth of her second child she wrote a radio play, *Three Women* (1962), set in a maternity home. Often termed a 'confessional' poet because of the inclusion in her work of personal details about her own life and the influence of poets such as **Robert Lowell**, her earlier, highly controlled poetry gave way to an almost visionary expression and intensity, reaching its culmination in the last few days before her death. This late poetry was published posthumously in *Ariel* (1965), *Crossing the Water* (1971) and *Winter Trees* (1972). Her only novel, *The Bell Jar* (1963), about her student collapse, was published just before her death, under the

pseudonym Victoria Lucas. *Collected Poems*, edited by Ted Hughes, was published in 1982.
▷ A Stevenson, *Bitter Fame* (1989)

PLATO
(c.428–c.348 BC)

Greek philosopher, indisputably one of the most important of all Western philosophers, and so enormously influential that A N Whitehead was able to characterize the subsequent history of Western philosophy as a series of 'footnotes to Plato'. He was the pupil (or at least the associate) of Socrates and the teacher of Aristotle. Plato was probably born in Athens, of a distinguished family, but little is known of his early life. Any youthful political ambitions must have withered when his friend and mentor, Socrates, was condemned to death in 399 BC by the restored democracy in Athens. Plato immortalized the story of Socrates' trial and last days in three of his dialogues: the *Apologia*, the *Crito* and the *Phaedo*, where his profound affection and respect for Socrates come through vividly. After the execution he and other disciples of Socrates took temporary refuge at Megara with the philosopher Euclides, and he then travelled widely in Greece, Egypt, the Greek cities in southern Italy (where he no doubt encountered Pythagoreans) and Sicily (where he made friends with Dion, brother-in-law of Dionysius I, the ruler of Syracuse). He returned to Athens in c.387 BC to found the Academy, which became a famous centre for philosophical, mathematical and scientific study, and over which he presided for the rest of his life. He visited Sicily again in 367 BC, at Dion's request, to try and train Dionysius II to become a philosopher–statesman, but despite a second visit in 361–60, which placed him in some personal danger, the attempt failed completely. His corpus of writings consists of some 30 philosophical dialogues and a series of *Letters*, of which the Seventh is the most important (biographically and philosophically) and only the Seventh and Eighth are likely to be genuine. The dialogues are conventionally divided into three groups— early, middle and late—though the exact relative chronology of individual dialogues is a vexed and probably insoluble problem of scholarship. The early, 'Socratic' dialogues have Socrates as the principal character, usually portrayed interrogating his interlocutors about the definition of different moral virtues (piety in the *Euthyphro*, courage in the *Laches*, and so on); their initially confident assertions are shown to be confused and contradictory and all parties end up sharing Socrates' professed perplexity. The middle dialogues show the character 'Socrates' expressing more positive, systematic views, which are taken to be Plato's own. This group

includes the most dramatic and literary of the dialogues, the *Symposium*, *Gorgias*, *Phaedo*, and *Republic*, and presents such famous Platonic doctrines as the theory of knowledge as recollection, the immortality of the soul, the tripartite division of the soul, and above all the theory of forms (or 'ideas') which contrasts the transient, material world of 'particulars' (objects merely of perception, opinion and belief) with the timeless, unchanging world of universals or forms (the true objects of knowledge). The *Republic* also describes Plato's celebrated political utopia, ruled by philosopher-kings who have mastered the discipline of 'dialectic' and studied the hierarchy of the forms, including its apex, the form of the Good. The details of this visionary state—the rigid class structure of workers, soldiers and rulers, the education of the rulers (both men and women), their communism of property and family, their totalitarian powers—have been variously idealized, attacked, misinterpreted and imitated in subsequent political theory and literature, but the *Republic* remains one of the most compelling and influential works in the history of philosophy. The third group of 'late' dialogues is generally less literary in form and represents a series of sustained and highly sophisticated criticisms of the metaphysical and logical assumptions of Plato's doctrines of the middle period. *Parmenides*, *Theaetetus* and *Sophist* in particular have attracted the interest of contemporary analytical philosophers and contain some of Plato's most demanding and original work. Taken as a whole, his philosophy has had a pervasive and incalculable influence on almost every period and tradition, rivalled only by that of his greatest pupil Aristotle, which was its principal competitor for much of the Hellenistic period, the Middle Ages and the Renaissance.
▷ R M Hare, *Plato* (1982)

PLAUTUS, Titus Maccius, or Maccus
(c.250–184 BC)

Roman writer of comedies, born in Sarsina in Umbria. It is probable that he went to Rome while still young, and there learned his mastery of the most idiomatic Latin. In Rome he found employment in connection with the stage, and saved enough money to enable him to leave Rome and start in business on his own account in foreign trade. His plays show close familiarity with seafaring life and adventure, and an intimate knowledge of all the details of buying and selling and bookkeeping. He failed, however, in business, and returned to Rome in such poverty that he had to earn his livelihood in the service of a baker by turning a handmill. While thus employed he wrote three plays which he sold to the

managers of the public games. The money for these enabled him to leave the mill, and he spent the rest of his life in Rome. Probably he began to write about 224 BC, and, until his death, he continued to produce comedies. His plays appear to have been left in the hands of the actors, who probably interpolated and omitted passages to suit them for the stage, and some of the prologues may have been written after his death. About 130 plays were attributed to him in the time of Aulus Gellius, who believed most of them to be the work of earlier dramatists revised and improved by Plautus. Roman critics considered most of them spurious. **Marcus Terentius Varro** limited the genuine comedies to 21; and these so-called 'Varronian comedies' are those which are now extant, the *Vidularia* ('The Rucksack Play') being fragmentary. Plautus borrowed his plots to a large extent from the New Attic Comedy, which dealt with social life to the exclusion of politics.
▷K McLeish, *Roman Comedy* (1976)

PLESHCHEYEV, Alexey
(1825–93)

Russian poet and translator (**Heine**), who was sentenced to execution along with **Dostoyevsky** as a revolutionary, and, like him, reprieved and sent to Siberia. His verse is rather insipid, and today not much read.

PLIEVIER, Theodor
(1892–1955)

German novelist, of working-class birth, born in Berlin. He fled Nazi Germany in 1933 and returned to Berlin in 1945, where he published *Stalingrad*, the first in a trilogy of grippingly realistic war novels, for which he is best-known. This and its sequels, *Moskau* (1952) and *Berlin* (1954), were best-sellers.
▷H Wilde, *Theodor Plievier* (1965)

PLINY, Gaius Plinius Secundus, known as 'the Elder'
(23–79)

Roman writer on natural history. He came of a wealthy north Italian family owning estates at Novum Comum (Como), where he was born. He was educated in Rome, and when about 23 entered the army and served in Germany. He became colonel of a cavalry regiment, and a comrade of the future emperor Titus, and wrote a treatise on the throwing of missiles from horseback and compiled a history of the Germanic wars. He also made a series of scientific tours in the region between the Ems, Elbe and Weser, and the sources of the Danube. Returning to Rome in 52, he studied for the Bar, but withdrew to Como and devoted himself to reading and authorship. Apparently for the guidance of

his nephew, he wrote his *Studiosus*, a treatise defining the culture necessary for the orator, and the grammatical work, *Dubius Sermo*. By Nero he was appointed procurator in Spain, and through his brother-in-law's death (71) he became guardian of his sister's son, **Pliny the Younger**, whom he adopted. Vespasian, whose son Titus he had known in Germany, was now emperor, and became a close friend; but court favour did not wean him from study, and he brought down to his own time the history of Rome by Aufidius Bassus. A model student, amid metropolitan distraction he worked assiduously, and by lifelong application filled the 102 volumes of manuscript which, after using them for his universal encyclopaedia in 37 volumes, *Naturalis Historia* (77), he bequeathed to his nephew. In 79 he was in command of the Roman fleet stationed off Misenum when the great eruption of Vesuvius was at its height. Eager to witness the phenomenon as closely as possible, he landed at Stabiae (*Castellamare*), but had not gone far before he succumbed to the stifling vapours rolling down the hill. His *Naturalis Historia* alone of his many writings survives. Under that title the ancients classified everything of natural or non-artificial origin. Pliny adds digressions on human inventions and institutions, devoting two books to a history of fine art, and dedicates the whole to Titus. His observations, made at second-hand, show no discrimination between the true and the false, between the probable and the marvellous, and his style is inartistic, sometimes obscure. But he supplies information on an immense variety of subjects about which, but for him, we should have remained in the dark.
▷H N Wethered, *The Mind of the Ancient World* (1937)

PLINY, Gaius Plinius Caecilius Secundus, known as 'the Younger'
(c.62–c.113)

Roman writer and orator, born in Novum Comum, the nephew and adopted son of **Pliny** 'the Elder'. He wrote a Greek tragedy in his 14th year, and made such progress under Quintilian that he became noted as one of the most accomplished men of his time. His proficiency as an orator enabled him at 18 to plead in the Forum, and brought him much practice. He served as military tribune in Syria, and was *quaestor Caesaris*, then praetor, and afterwards consul in AD100, in which year he wrote his laboured panegyric of Trajan. In 103 and 105 he was in Bithynia and, among other offices, held that of curator of the Tiber, chiefly for the prevention of floods. He married twice; his second wife, Calpurnia, is fondly referred to in one of his most charming letters for the many gifts and accomplishments with which she sweetened his rather invalid life. It is to his 10 volumes of letters that Pliny owes his assured place in literature, giving an intimate picture of the upper class in the 1st century; above all, it is from his correspondence with Trajan that we get our clearest knowledge of how even the most enlightened Romans regarded the then obscure sect of the Christians and their 'depraved and extravagant superstition'.

▷A M Guillemin, *Pliné et la vie littéraire de son temps* (1929)

PLISNIER, Charles
(1896–1952)

Belgian fiction writer and poet, born in Hainaut, who began as a militant communist and ended as a mystical Christian; but who managed to effect the transformation in a significant and convincing manner. His *Faux passeportes* (1937, Eng trans *Memoirs of a Secret Revolutionary*, 1938), five connected stories which deal with mystical militants deceived by Stalinism and bureaucracy, won the Prix **Goncourt**. His roman-fleuve *Meutres* (1939–44, 'Murders'), powerful despite its tediousness—unfortunately a much noted flaw—analyses bourgeois bad faith in the light of individual sincerity and the quest for purity. Plisnier's most profound and original novel, however, is *Beauté des laides* (1952, 'The Beauty of Ugly Women').

PLOMER, William Charles Franklin
(1903–73)

British writer, born in Pietersburg, Transvaal. He was educated at Rugby, was a farmer and trader in South Africa before becoming an author, and also lived for a while in Greece and Japan. With **Roy Campbell** he ran a South African literary review, and in World War II he served at the Admiralty. His works include the novels *Turbott Wolfe* (1926), *Sado* (1931) and *Ali the Lion* (1936); collections of short stories *I Speak of Africa* (1928) and *Paper Houses* (1929); and *Collected Poems* (1960). He edited the diaries of **Francis Kilvert** and the poems of **Herman Melville**, and wrote the librettos for several of Benjamin Britten's operas, including *Gloriana*. He also wrote the autobiographical *Double Lives* (1943).

▷W Doyle, *William Plomer* (1969)

PLUNKETT, James, originally James Plunkett Kelly
(1920–)

Irish novelist and short-story writer, born in Dublin. He is best known for the novel *Strumpet City* (1969) and its sequel *Farewell Companions* (1977). The first deals with Ireland from 1907 to 1914; the latter spans from the Easter Rising of 1916 to the end of World War II. *Strumpet City* is more successful in evoking Dublin life in the years leading up to World War I; *Farewell Companions*, perhaps because of its greater timescale and array of characters, is less able to depict individual lives—instead, the cityscape and history itself might be regarded as the central characters. *The Circus Animals* (1990) picks up where *Farewell Companions* leaves off, being set in what the author sees as the poverty, both material and spiritual, of post-World War II Dublin.

PLUTARCH, Greek **Ploutarchos**
(c.46–c.120)

Greek historian, biographer and philosopher, born in Chaeronea in Boeotia. He was in Athens in 66, studying science and rhetoric. He paid more than one visit to Rome—once representing his native town—and gave public lectures in philosophy. After travels in Greece, Asia Minor and Egypt, he settled in Chaeronea. His extant writings comprise his historical works, and those that are grouped under the general head of *Opera Moralia* ('Moral Works'). To the former belong his *Vitae* ('Lives')—the work by which he is best known. These contain a gallery of 50 portraits of the great characters of the age preceding his own. They are mostly arranged in pairs, a Greek and Roman soldier or statesman with some resemblance between their respective careers being chosen for the subject of each. Plutarch's biographies are of value particularly for the view they offer of ancient history as it was understood in antiquity. The author adheres throughout to his professed purpose—portraiture of character; he lists the most famous actions or events which distinguish the career of each subject of his biography, often using them as the basis of moral reflection. His other surviving writings, the *Moralia*, are a collection of short treatises and dialogues on religion, philosophy, science and education. Though not a profound thinker, Plutarch occupies an important place in literary history. He was much read in the Renaissance, and the translation of the *Vitae* by Sir Thomas North (1579) was the major source for **Shakespeare**'s Roman plays.

PO-CHÜ-I
(772–846)

Chinese poet under the T'ang dynasty, born in Honan, of which he became governor in 831. He was so esteemed as a lyric poet that his poems were collected by imperial order and engraved on stone tablets.

▷A Waley, *The Life and Times of Po-Chu-I* (1949)

POE, Edgar Allan
(1809–49)

American poet and story writer, born in Boston, Massachusetts. After being orphaned in his third year, he was adopted by John Allan (1780–1834), a wealthy and childless merchant in Richmond, Virginia. From 1815 to 1820 the family lived in England, and the boy went to school in Stoke Newington. The year 1826 was spent at the University of Virginia; but, offended by his dissipation and gambling debts, his patron moved him to the counting-room, from where he ran away to Boston. He published *Tamerlane and other Poems* (1827), enlisted in the US army that year, and rose to be sergeant-major in 1829. He then procured his discharge and after a year's delay his admission to West Point Military Academy (1830), but the following March he was dismissed for deliberate neglect of duty. Now he was thrown on his own resources. A third edition of his *Poems* (1831) contained 'Israfel', his earliest poem of value, and 'To Helen'. In Baltimore he won a prize in 1833 for his story 'A MS. found in a Bottle'. From then on he lived with his aunt, Mrs Clemm, and wrote for the *Saturday Visitor*. His connection with the *Southern Literary Messenger* began with his tale *Berenice* in 1835 and he went to Richmond as its assistant editor (1835–7). In 1836 he married his cousin Virginia. He left Richmond in 1837, and after a year or less in New York, of which the chief result was *The Narrative of Arthur Gordon Pym*, in 1838 he established himself in Philadelphia. Here he published *Tales of the Grotesque* and *Arabesque* (1840), was connected with Burton's *Gentleman's Magazine* (1839), and for a year (1842–3) edited *Graham's Magazine*. He won another short-story competition in 1843 with 'The Gold Bug'. In 1844 he moved to New York, and in *The Evening Mirror* (1845) published 'The Raven', which won immediate fame. In 1847 his wife died. 'The Bells', 'The Domain of Arnheim', the wild 'prose poem' *Eureka* (1848) and a few minor pieces belong to the brief remainder of his life. He attempted suicide in November 1848, and had an attack of *delirium tremens* in June 1849. Recovering, he spent over two months in Richmond, lecturing there and at Norfolk. He became engaged to a lady of means, and in September went to wind up his affairs in the north. In October he was found in a wretched condition in Baltimore, and died in the hospital. Weird, wild, fantastic, dwelling by choice on the horrible, Poe's genius was nevertheless great and genuine. His short stories show great originality, and from some of them, such as 'The Murders in the Rue Morgue', Poe emerges as a pioneer of the modern detective story. The chief charm of his poems is exquisite melody.

▷ W Bittner, *Poe: a biography* (1962); D Hoffman, *Poe Poe Poe Poe Poe Poe Poe* (1972)

POGODIN, Nikolay, pseud of Nikolay Fedorovich Stukalov
(1900–62)

Soviet dramatist, born in the Don province. A socialist realist with humour and humanity, Pogodin's popular plays were on such themes as the Five-Year Plan and Lenin; he was also an exceedingly able craftsman, expert in creating gripping crowd scenes. His most famous play is undoubtedly *Kremlyovsky kuranti* (1940, Eng trans in *Soviet Scene: Six Plays of Russian Life*, 1946), the second of his Lenin trilogy.
▷ V Komissarzhecsky, *Moscow Theatres* (1959)

POHL, Frederik
(1919–)

American science-fiction writer, born in Brooklyn, New York. In 1938 he became a founder-member of a group of left-wing science-fiction writers known as the Futurists, which included **Isaac Asimov** and others. He served in the air force in World War II, worked as a literary agent, and edited various science-fiction magazines (1953–69). He describes his own multifarious books as 'cautionary literature', seeing science fiction as a kind of alarm signal. Of his vast output of novels, stories and anthologies, *The Space Merchants* (1953) and *Gladiator-at-Law* (1955), both written with C M Kornbluth, exemplify his social concern and strength as a storyteller.
▷ *The Way the Future Was* (1978)

POKAGON, Simon
(1830–99)

American writer, dubbed in his day the 'Indian Longfellow', and the author of the first major novel published by a Native American. The son of the Potawotomi chief Leopold who had ceded the area on which Chicago was eventually built to the Whites, Pokagon spent much of his life trying to get compensation on behalf of his people for the loss of this land, eventually winning $104 000 from the US government. He personally distributed his pamphlet, *The Red Man's Rebuke* (later published as *The Red Man's Greeting*), printed entirely on birchbark and describing his people's land claim, at the World's Fair in Chicago in 1893, at which exhibition his people were unrepresented. Pokagon's major work, the novel *Queen of the Woods*, was published posthumously in 1899. Beginning as a woodland idyll, the novel doggedly traces the destruction of a Native American couple and their children by external forces, ending with a bleak apocalyptic vision of the destructive power of alcohol.

▷D H Dickason, 'Chief Simon Pokagon: "The Indian Longfellow" ', in *Indiana Magazine of History*, 57 (1961)

POLACEK, Karel
(1892–1944)

Czech satirical novelist, who wrote particularly of the first republic. A Jew, he was murdered by the Nazis during their occupation of his country.

POLIAKOFF, Stephen
(1952–)

English dramatist. He achieved recognition with the plays *Hitting Town* and *City Sugar* (both 1975), both looking at the plight of urban young in a Britain of concrete shopping arcades and consumerism. Several plays followed on the same theme, but *Breaking the Silence* (1984), set in the aftermath of the Russian Revolution, is his finest work to date. *Coming Into Land* (1987) follows the fortunes of a Polish refugee as she tries to enter Britain. Other stage plays include *Strawberry Fields* (1977), *Shout Across the River* (1978) and *Sienna Red* (1992). His television plays include *Caught on a Train* (1980). He made his debut as a film director with *Hidden City* (1987), and both wrote and directed *Close My Eyes* (1991), based on *Hitting Town*.

POLITIS, Kosmas, pen-name of Paris Taveloudis
(1888–1974)

Greek novelist, born on Poros. He came late to prominence, and was over 40 when his first novel, *Lemonodhasos* ('Lemon Grove'), was published in 1930. *Eroica* (1938) is widely regarded as his best work; the novel is a nostalgic portrayal of youthful life on Poros. Politis himself was largely educated in Smyrna, later the scene of terrible suffering during the war with Turkey, and in his last novel, *Stou Chatzifrangou* (1963, 'At Chatzifrangos'), he describes a quarter of the town before the tragedy. His other books include *Gyri* (1946), set in the Patras district of that name.

POLIZIANO, Angelo
(1454–94)

Italian poet and humanist, often called Politian. A tutor in the household of Lorenzo d'Medici, he was the foremost Latinist of his time. But he is most famous for his poetry in the vernacular, particularly for the *Stanze*, in ottava rima, about the victory in tournament of the brother of Lorenzo Giuliano, and for *Orfeo*, the first dramatic treatment, in the form of a 'sacred representation', of a non-Christian subject. Poliziano's poetic gifts are rated very highly, and it has been said that he conveys 'a fragile vision of love and death … with Botticelian poignancy'. There is an English translation of *Orfeo* in: *Romanic Review*, 20 (1929); of *Stanze* in: *Delos*, 4 (1970).

▷ *Romanic Review*, 44 (1953)

POMFRET, John
(1667–1702)

English poet, born in Luton and educated at Bedford Grammar School and Queens' College, Cambridge. He was rector of Maulden, Bedfordshire (1695–1702). He published several poetical works, and his *Miscellany Poems on Several Occasions* (1702) were frequently reprinted, but *The Choice* (1700) eclipsed all the rest in popularity. Modelled on **Horace**'s Sat. II.6, it recommends a country life of 'pleasure, ease, and plenty' with no wife but a 'fair creature' nearby for company: this preference is said to have cost him promotion in the church.

▷Dr S Johnson, *The Lives of the English Poets* (1779—81)

POMPÉIA, Raul D'Avila
(1863–95)

Brazilian novelist and poet, born in Rio de Janeiro. A depressive (he killed himself) influenced by **Nietzsche**, Pompéia's chief claim to fame lies in his incomparable novel of school life, *O Ateneu* (1888, 'The Academy'), worthy to rank with **Musil**'s *Young Törless*. It is the story of a megalomaniac headmaster and of a boy's awakening into manhood, told with lucid irony and sensitivity. It is remarkable that this novel has not yet been translated. His other prose, and his poetry, has attracted much recent interest.

PONCE DE LEÓN, Luis
(1527–91)

Spanish monk, scholar and poet, born in Granada. In 1544 he entered the Augustinian order, and became Professor of Theology at Salamanca in 1561. From 1572 to 1576 he was imprisoned by the Inquisition for his translation and interpretation of the *Song of Solomon*; but shortly before his death he became general of his order. His poetical remains, published in 1631, comprise translations from **Virgil**, **Horace** and the *Psalms*; his few original poems are lyrical masterpieces.

▷W Carlos Williams, *In the American Grain* (1925)

PONDAL, Eduardo
(1835–1917)

Spanish poet (a doctor by profession), who wrote both in Galician and in Castilian. With

Rosalía de Castro and Manuel Curros Enríquez he was the leader of the Galician revival of his time; he was regarded as the romantic, Celtic voice of the movement. His sonorous, pessimistic poetry is still studied and admired.

PONGE, Francis
(1899–1987)

French poet—a title he has repudiated—and essayist, born in Montpellier. A committed communist from 1936 until after World War II, and perhaps always a dialectical materialist, he began publishing in 1926, but was virtually unknown until the mid-1940s, except to a few discerning critics such as Jean Paulhan. Of all the many avant-garde poets of France Ponge was the most sheerly phenomenological with regard to language: his project throughout his writings was to make language 'an object of scientific enquiry'. He therefore became one of the heroes of the structuralist magazine *Tel Quel*, edited by Philippe Sollers, who wrote on him (1963). He is a cerebral poet, or, rather, prose-poet (he wants to abolish the distinction), deliberately eschewing the lyricism of emotion except as an object of enquiry. His own enquiry, however, is witty, punning and frequently ironic. He invests the mundane objects he describes with great poignancy, thus mocking his own rejection of 'anthropocentric bias'. He was devoted to **Malherbe**, and wrote about him. His most accessible work is the long meditation on soap, *Le Savon* (1967, Eng trans *Soap*, 1969), actually written during the war when soap was a scarce commodity. His most characteristic work is to be found in the prose-poems of *Proêmes* (1948). He became a grand old man of French letters in his last years.

PONIATOWSKA, Elena
(1933–)

French-born Mexican writer, born in Paris. Her father was Polish and her mother was Mexican, and the family emigrated to Mexico when she was 10 years old. She is a fiercely original writer whose works include journalism (she is one of the most respected interviewers in Mexico), testimonial literature, short stories, novels (notably *Hasta no verte, Jesus mio*, 1969, 'Until I See You, dear Jesus') and literary criticism. Her most famous work is the collage *La noceh de Tlatelolco* (1971, Eng trans *Massacre in Mexico*, 1975). One of her main areas of interest is re-creating the modes of speech of the Mexican popular classes. She is a contributor to several of the best newspapers in Mexico.

PONTANO, Giovanni
(1429–1503)

Italian poet and scholar, born in Cerreto in Umbria. He served the Aragonese court at Naples, but ended his life in obscurity after having negotiated the surrender of the kingdom to France (1495), for which he was pardoned. He was, **Poliziano** apart, the foremost Latinist of his time, and founded an important tradition as the force behind the Neapolitan Academy. He wrote on all the vital subjects of his times, from morals and manners to astrology and philology, and his *Eclogues* (Eng trans 1957) and idylls were regarded highly by those who came after him. ▷E Percopo, *Vita do Giovanni Pontano* (1938)

PONTOPPIDAN, Henrik
(1857–1944)

Danish novelist and joint winner of the Nobel Prize for literature, born in Fredericia, the son of a pastor. He trained as an engineer but turned to writing. Among his novels were *Det forjaettede land* (1891–5, Eng trans *Land of Promise*, 1896), the transparently autobiographical *Lykke-Per* (1898–1904, 'Lucky Per'), the story of a young engineer's conflict with his spiritual father, and *De dødes rige* (1912–16, 'The Realm of the Dead'). He shared the Nobel Prize for literature in 1917 with his fellow Danish novelist, **Karl Gjellerup**. ▷K Ahnlund, *Henrik Pontoppidan* (1956)

POOLE, John
(1786–1872)

English playwright, of whom little is known, other than that his first piece, *Hamlet Travestie* (1811), helped usher in a 19th-century vogue for parodies of well-known contemporary and classical plays. A later comedy, *Paul Pry* (1825), was a huge success, partly because it provided a plum leading role for an actor-manager. It was much revived during and beyond Poole's own lifetime, although apparently frequently adjusted to suit the star of the moment.

POOT, Hubert Kornemiszoon
(1689–1733)

Dutch poet, born in Abtwoude into a family of peasants. He had some affinities with an English poet of a later age, **John Clare**, in that he began with an exaggerated respect for his contemporaries, almost all of whom were his considerable inferiors. His finest poetry, in the main consisting of nature lyrics, has the unmistakable mark of a major writer.

POPA, Vasko

(1922–)

Serbian Yugoslav, born in Grebenac and educated largely abroad, where he studied French literature and language. He served as a partisan during World War II, subsequently working as a publisher in Belgrade. His first collection, *Kora* (1953, 'Bark'), is derivative of French models and gives only intermittent signs of the folk-influenced originality of later collections. Perhaps his most important statement is the densely mythological *Sporendo nebo* (1968, 'Secondary Heaven'), which uses an elaborate 7 x 7 structure and evokes weighty philosophical agenda. An important stage in his reception abroad was Anne Pennington's translation for the Penguin Modern Poets series (1969); she also translated the later *Uspravna zemlja* (1972, as *Earth Erect*, 1973), and a substantial *Collected Poems* (1978), which documents Popa's rediscovery of native elements and the troubled history of his country.

POPE, Alexander

(1688–1744)

English poet, born in London. His father was a linen merchant who retired soon after his son was born, and the family moved to Binfield in Windsor Forest when Alexander was an infant. He was educated erratically at Catholic schools but was largely self-taught, which left gaps in his knowledge of literature. At the age of three he suffered his first serious illness and at 12 he was crippled by a tubercular infection of the spine which accounted for his stunted growth (4ft 6in). He began writing at an early age; 'Ode to Solitude' was completed in the same year as his illness. Reading and writing feverishly, he got to know members of the literati—William Walsh, Henry Cromwell, and Sir William Trumball—who acted as mentors, critics and encouragers. He wrote *The Pastorals* while a teenager and they were eventually published by Jacob Tonson in 1709. Metrically adept, they are remembered for his mastery of technique rather than their poetry. But already he had moved on and was working on the seminal work *An Essay on Criticism* (1711), whose couplets caused a stir. *The Rape of the Lock* followed in 1712 and confirmed him as a poetic force. A mock epic, this exquisite work can be enjoyed throughout as a true epic diminished to contemporary proportions. With *Windsor Forest* (1713) his popularity was further enhanced and he became a favourite in London where he was now living. **Joseph Addison** and **Jonathan Swift** were among his acquaintances and he became a member of the Scriblerus Club. His persistent ambition was to translate **Homer**, and the first instalment of the *Iliad* appeared in 1715; when

completed in 1720 its genius was immediately acknowledged though it bore flimsy resemblance to the original. During this time he also issued his *Works* (1717), a pot-pourri of odes, epistles, elegies and a translation of **Chaucer**'s *The House of Fame*. He also met and befriended Lady **Mary Wortley Montagu**, a friendship which foundered after they quarrelled in 1723. Pope contemptuously dismissed her in a few lines in his *Imitations of Homer*. With the success of the *Iliad*, Pope was financially secure and was regarded as the senior figure of English letters, much sought after and revered. He bought a villa in Twickenham and lived there until his death. In 1726 he completed the *Odyssey*, following the failure of his edition of **Shakespeare** (1725) which Lewis Theobald criticized for its slip-shoddiness and poor scholarship. Pope got his revenge in *The Dunciad* (1728), a mock-heroic satire, published anonymously, whose butt is 'Dulness' in general and, in particular, all the authors whom he wanted to hold up to ridicule. It is not, however, confined to personal animus, and literary vices are likewise exposed and scorned. With Swift, **John Gay**, Lord Oxford, Arbuthnot and Bolingbroke he arranged the publication of a *Miscellany* of which three volumes appeared between 1727 and 1728. Pope's contributions included *An Epistle to Dr Arbuthnot* (published separately in 1735) and *Martinus Scriblerus peri Bathous: or The Art of Sinking in Poetry*, a satirical invective that insulted various poetasters. That and *The Dunciad* prompted a tiresome literary feud which dragged on interminably. In 1733–4 he published his *Essay on Man* and wrote *Moral Essays* (1731–5). His last years were engaged in organizing his correspondence for publication, but while this marked a new development in English literature he tinkered too much with the originals and their value as social documents was impaired. Since his death his reputation has waxed, waned and waxed again. His technical brilliance has never been in doubt, but he lacked the surface warmth that endears lesser poets to the reading public. Nor was he an attractive figure, either in manner or physique. Much of this may have been due to inconsistent health, but without his abrasive side English satire would be the poorer, for he was the sharpest and most innovative of its practitioners.

▷M Mack, *Alexander Pope, a life* (1985)

PORTA, Carlo

(1776–1821)

Italian poet, born in Milan. Writing in the dialect of Milan, he showed his insight into human character in narrative poems which are satirical and grimly realistic. These include *La Nomina del Capellan* (1819, 'The

Selection of the Chaplain') and *Disgrazzi de Giovannin Bongee* (1812, 'The Misadventures of Giovannino Bongeri').
▷H Auréas, *Carlo Porta* (1959)

PORTA, Giovanni Battista della
(1543–1615)

Italian physicist and philosopher. He wrote on physiognomy, natural magic, the steam pump, the properties of lenses, and gardening, besides several comedies.

PORTER, Anna Maria
(1780–1832)

English novelist, born in Durham, younger sister of **Jane Porter** and Robert Ker Porter. Her novel *The Hungarian Brothers* (1807), about the French Revolution, was highly successful and achieved numerous editions. She wrote several other novels, and also ballads and poems.
▷G Curia, introduction to *Walsh Colville* (1974)

PORTER, Eleanor, née Hodgman
(1868–1920)

American novelist, born in Littleton, New Hampshire. She studied music at the New England Conservatory. She married in 1892. Her first novels included *Cross Currents* (1907) and *Miss Billy* (1911). In 1913 *Pollyanna* appeared; this was an immediate success and has retained its popularity ever since. A sequel, about the 'glad child', *Pollyanna Grows Up*, was published in 1915, and two volumes of short stories, *The Tangled Threads* and *Across the Years*, appeared posthumously in 1924.

PORTER, Gene(va), née Stratton
(1868–1924)

American novelist, born on a farm in Wabash County, Indiana. She married Charles D Porter in 1886, and as Gene Stratton Porter attained great popularity with *A Girl of the Limberlost* (1909) and other stories full of sentiment and nature study.
▷J P Meehan, *The Lady of the Limberlost* (1928)

PORTER, Hal
(1911–84)

Australian novelist, playwright and poet. He reacted strongly to the prevailing provincialism and realism of Australian literature in his youth, writing elegantly fanciful fictions and richly imagistic poetry. His best-known works are *The Tilted Cross* (1961), *The Right Thing* (1971) and, perhaps his best book, the autobiographical *Watcher on the Cast Iron*

Balcony (1964). *Selected Stories* appeared in 1971.

PORTER, Jane
(1776–1850)

English writer, born in Durham, sister of **Anna Maria Porter** and Robert Ker Porter, and daughter of an army surgeon. She made a great reputation in 1803 by her high-flown romance, *Thaddeus of Warsaw*, and had even more success in 1810 with *The Scottish Chiefs*, although her stage tragedy *Switzerland* (1819) was a failure. Other books were *The Pastors' Fireside* (1815), *Duke Christian of Lüneburg* (1824), *Tales Round a Winter's Hearth* (with her sister Anna Maria, 1824) and *The Field of Forty Footsteps* (1828). *Sir Edward Seaward's Shipwreck* (1831), a clever fiction, edited by her, was almost certainly written by her eldest brother, Dr William Ogilvie Porter (1774–1850).
▷*These Were the Muses* (1924)

PORTER, Katherine Anne Maria Veronica Callista Russell
(1890–1980)

American writer, born in Indian Creek, Texas. Brought up by a grandmother near Kyle, Texas, she ran away and got married at 16, but divorced at 19. She worked as a reporter and actress, moved to Greenwich Village, and went to Mexico (1920–2) and took up Mexican causes. She had started writing at a very early age, but allowed nothing to be published until 1928, with her first collection of stories, *Flowering Judas*. Later, in Paris, she married a consular official (divorced 1938), and wrote her first novel, *Hacienda* (1934). Back in the USA she married for a third time, a professor of English, but divorced four years later. Three short novels, published as *Pale Horse, Pale Rider* (1939), were a success. *Ship of Fools* (1962), a huge allegorical novel analysing the German state of mind in the 1930s was almost universally regarded as a failure. A volume of essays, *The Days before*, appeared in 1952. *Collected Short Stories* (1965) won a Pulitzer Prize.
▷R B West, *Katherine Anne Porter* (1963)

PORTER, Peter
(1929–)

Australian poet and critic, born in Brisbane. He has lived in England since 1951, though he frequently visits Australia. He has worked as a bookseller, journalist, clerk and advertising copywriter. A difficult, clever and allusive poet, his several collections include *Words Without Music* (1968), *A Porter Folio* (1969), *The Last of England* (1970) and *The Cost of Seriousness* (1978). His *Collected Poems* (1983) confirmed him as a gifted aphorist.

He has published two excellent volumes of translation from the Latin, *Epigrams by Martial* (1971) and *After Martial* (1972), demonstrating that affection for the classics which is displayed in his poem 'On First Looking Into Chapman's *Hesiod*' (1975).
▷ R Garfit, in *British Poetry since 1960* (1972, M Schmidt and G Lindop eds)

PÔRTO ALEGRE, Manuel José de Araújo
(1806–79)
Brazilian poet and romantic critic, who collaborated with **Magalhães** in his polemic magazine *Niterói-Revista Brasiliense*. But Pôrto Alegre's own verse is so disciplined as to be regarded by most critics as classical.

PORTO-RICHE, Georges de
(1849–1930)
French dramatist, born in Bordeaux. After an early success with *La Chance de Françoise* (1889, 'Françoise's Luck'), he wrote several successful psychological plays which investigated the relationships between men and women in love (known as 'théâtre d'amour), including *L'Amoureuse* (1891, 'The Woman in Love'), *Le Vieil Homme* (1911, 'The Old Man') and *Le Marchand d'Estampes* (1917, 'The Print Seller').

POSEY, Alexander
(1873–1908)
American poet. Born near Eufala, Creek Nation Territory (now Oklahoma), the son of a Creek mother and Scots–Irish father, Posey began to write and publish poetry at university. He was appointed to several public positions in the Creek Nation, and worked between times on his farm. It was as Editor of the Eufala *Indian Journal* from 1902 (during the turbulent period following the Dawes Act allotment legislation) that Posey made his literary mark with his series of humorous topical sketches, written in the form of letters by the imaginary Creek front-porch philosopher, Fux Fixico. Posey died in a drowning accident. His poems were collected and published posthumously by his wife, Minnie Harris, in 1910.
▷ D F Littlefield, *Alexander Posey: Creek Poet, Journalist and Humorist* (1992)

POSTOLI, Foquion
(1887–1927)
Albanian writer of the 1912 'liberation' period. He wrote competent patriotic novels—the best known was *Lulja e kujtimit* (1924, 'In Defence of the Homeland')—none of which was translated.

POTGIETER, Everhardus Johannes
(1808–75)
Dutch poet and critic, born in Zwolle. An anti-romantic, he co-founded the important magazine *De Gids* in 1837. His satirical prose against the complacency of his age was salutary; but his poetry, exquisite and finely wrought, has now dated. He had a vital influence upon Dutch literature.
▷ T Weevers, *Goethe and Holland* (1949)

POTOK, Chaim (Herman Harold)
(1929–)
American novelist, born and educated in New York City, where he studied at Yeshiva University and the Jewish Theological Seminary. He was ordained as a rabbi in 1954. After teaching in seminaries, he became scholar-in-residence at Har Zion Temple in Philadelphia (1959–63) and, later, special projects editor at the Jewish Publication Society, for whom he wrote a 14-pamphlet series on *Jewish Ethics* (1964–9). In view of Potok's highly committed exploration of Judaism in modern America, it may be as well to re-label 'Jewish-American' novelists like **Philip Roth** and **Bernard Malamud** as 'post-Jewish'. His novels explore the problems of Orthodox and Hasidic communities within an aggressively secular society, but they are, if anything, more directly concerned with conflicts *within* Judaism than between Jews and WASPs. *The Chosen* (1967) charts the growing friendship between a young progressive scholar and the son of a highly traditional Hasid. In 1972 Potok published the controversial *My Name Is Asher Lev* in which the hero abandons his religious calling to become a painter, shocking his community with a work called 'Brooklyn Crucifixion'. Later works include *The Book of Lights* (1982) and *Davita's Harp* (1985); in 1990, Potok revived his troubled artist-hero in *The Gift of Asher Lev. Wanderings* (1978) is a scholarly but personal history of the Jews.

POTTER, (Helen) Beatrix
(1866–1943)
English author and illustrator of books for children, born in Kensington, London, into a wealthy family. The atmosphere at home was oppressively quiet and Beatrix, supervised by nurses and educated by governesses, grew up a lonely town child longing for the country. She taught herself to draw and paint, and while still quite young did serious natural history studies of fungi with the intention of making a book of watercolours. She turned to sketching pet animals dressed as human beings to amuse younger children. The original version of *The Tale of Peter Rabbit* was enclosed with a letter to her ex-governess's

child in 1893 and later published at her own expense, with fuller illustrations, in 1900, as was *The Tailor of Gloucester* (1902). When Frederick Warne took over publication in 1903 she had her first popular success with *The Tale of Squirrel Nutkin* (1903). In an appreciative, if gently satirical, review **Graham Greene** considered *The Roly-Poly Pudding* (1908, later changed to *The Tale of Samuel Whiskers*), to be her masterpiece. Miss Potter was not amused. In 1913, eight years after she had moved to a farm at Sawrey, near Lake Windermere (where six of her books are set), she married William Heelis, a Lake District solicitor. Thereafter she devoted herself almost entirely to farming and the new National Trust. *Johnny Town-Mouse* (1918) was her last book in the familiar style. She devised an elaborate cryptic diary whose code was broken by Leslie Linder and published as *The Journal of Beatrix Potter 1881–1897* (1966). She was the outstanding writer and artist of picture-story books of her time, and Peter the Rabbit, Jemima Puddle-Duck, Mrs Tiggy-Winkle, Benjamin Bunny and the rest have become classics of children's literature.

POTTER, Dennis Christopher George
(1935–94)

English dramatist, born in Forest of Dean. Although he wrote for the stage (*Sufficient Carbohydrate*, 1984), he was primarily a television dramatist. Following *Vote, Vote, Vote for Nigel Barton* (1965), he wrote over 25 television plays and series. *Son of Man* (1969) was the first television screenplay that depicted Christ as a man who struggled as much with his own doubts as with those opposed to his teaching. Other controversial plays include *Brimstone and Treacle* (1978), *The Singing Detective* (1986) and *Blackeyes* (1989). He was also technically innovative: *Pennies from Heaven* (1978) required the actors to mime to popular songs of the 1920s and 30s that intercut the action; *Blue Remembered Hills* (1979), a memory play, required the adult actors to impersonate children, but his technical freshness seemed a little worn in *Lipstick On Your Collar* (1993), another television drama in which music plays a central role. His novel *Ticket to Ride* (1986) was later adapted as the film *Secret Friends* (1992). He was the undisputed master of the serious television play, which he might well have been said to have invented and made his own.

POUND, Ezra Loomis
(1885–1972)

American poet and critic, born in Hailey, Idaho. Brought up in Wyncote, near Philadelphia, he graduated at Pennsylvania University in 1906, became an instructor in Wabash College in Crawfordsville, Indiana, but after four months left for Europe, travelling widely in Spain, Italy and Provence. He published his first collection of poems, *A Lume Spento* (1908), in Venice. In London later that year he met **Ford Madox Ford**, **James Joyce** and **Wyndham Lewis**, and published *Personae* and *Exultations* in 1909, followed by a book of critical essays, *The Spirit of Romance*, in 1910. He was co-editor of *Blast* (1914–15), the magazine of the short-lived 'Vorticist' movement, and London editor of the Chicago *Little Review* (1917–19), and in 1920 became Paris correspondent for *The Dial*. From 1924 he made his home in Italy. He became involved with fascist ideas and stirred up much resentment by antidemocracy broadcasts in the early stages of the war. In 1945 he was escorted back to the USA and indicted for treason. The trial did not proceed, however, as he was adjudged insane, and placed in an asylum. Three years later, a distinguished jury of his peers controversially awarded him the Bollingen Prize for *The Pisan Cantos*. In 1958 he was certified sane and released, and returned to Italy. In addition to his poetry he wrote books on literature, music, art and economics, and translated much from Italian, French, Chinese and Japanese. As a poet, of the Imagist school at the outset of his career, he was a thorough-going experimenter, deploying much curious and often spurious learning in his illustrative imagery and in the development of his themes. **T S Eliot** regarded him as the motivating force behind 'modern' poetry, the poet who created a climate in which English and American poets could understand and appreciate each other; *The Waste Land* bore a tribute to *il miglior fabbro*. *Homage to Sextus Propertius* (1919) and *Hugh Selwyn Mauberley* (1920) are among his most important early poems. His *Cantos*, a loosely-knit series of poems, appeared first in 1917, continuing in many instalments, via *The Pisan Cantos* to *Thrones: Cantos 96–109* (1959). It was intended as a vast, self-glossing purview of world culture but degenerated into an anti-Semitic rant on Poundian obsessions like usury and the redundancy of democracy; in anguish, the poet himself wrote 'the damned stuff will not cohere'. His work in the classics and Chinese poetry are discernible in their form. Apart from his life work in poetry, significant collections are *Translations of Ezra Pound* (1933) and *Literary Essays* (1954).

▷N Stock, *The Life of Ezra Pound* (1970, rev edn 1982); H Kenner, *The Pound Era* (1971)

POURRAT, Henri
(1887–1959)

French novelist, born in Ambert in the Auvergne, where most of his work is set. His most famous books are the series of four novels under the title *Les Vaillances: farces et aventures de Gaspard des Montagnes* (1922–31), in which the daily life and customs of the Auvergne form a backdrop to a 19th-century tragedy, based on a story handed down in local tales, and narrated, in deference to the oral tradition, by a story-teller. He was dubbed 'France's Grimm' for his *Le Trésor des contes* (1948, Eng trans *A Treasury of French Tales*, 1953), which were also based on the folklore and peasant tales of the Auvergne. He was awarded the Prix **Goncourt** in 1941.

POWELL, Anthony Dymoke
(1905–)

English novelist, born in London, the son of an army officer. He was educated at Eton and Balliol College, Oxford, where he met several other young writers, including **Evelyn Waugh** and **Graham Greene**. He worked in publishing and journalism before World War II, and by 1936 had published four satirical novels, among them *Afternoon Men* (1931), *Venusberg* (1932) and *What's Become of Waring?* (1939). After the war he returned to book-reviewing, wrote a biography of John Aubrey (1948), and began the series of novels he called *A Dance to the Music of Time*—12 volumes, beginning with *A Question of Upbringing* (1951), covering 50 years of British upper middle-class life and attitudes. The light, witty, satirical tone of the pre-war novels developed, in *The Music of Time*, into an intricate and disciplined interweaving of personal relationships, ironic, humorous, and with extraordinary scope and depth of vision. He has won the James Tait Black Prize and W H Smith Literary Award. Since the completion of the cycle with *Hearing Secret Harmonies* (1975), he has published a four-volume autobiography, *To Keep the Ball Rolling* (1976–82), and two novels, *O, How the Wheel Becomes It!* (1983) and *The Fisher King* (1986), and two volumes of criticism, *Miscellaneous Verdicts* (1990) and *Under Review* (1992).
▷B Bergonzi, *Anthony Powell* (1962)

POWERS, J(ames) E(arl)
(1917–)

American novelist and short-story writer, born in Jacksonville, Illinois and educated at Northwestern University. He has worked as an editor, a lecturer and a writer-in-residence. His special awards include an American Academy Grant (1948), a Guggenheim Fellowship (1948), three Rockefeller Fellowships, and a National Book Award in 1963 for his first novel *Morte d'Urban* (1962), which relates the tale of an initially moral priest who becomes perverted by the capitalists who surround him. Powers began publishing short stories in the 1940s, and his subject-matter has remained constant from that time: he writes primarily about the midwest, race relations, and Catholicism.
▷J F Hagopian, *J F Powers* (1968)

POWNALL, David
(1938–)

British playwright and novelist. He was born in Liverpool, and educated at Long Wandsworth College, Hampshire, and at Keele University. He worked in the personnel department of Ford at Dagenham, and for Anglo-American in Zambia, where his first play, *As We Lie*, was produced in 1969. He has been resident writer with theatre groups in Lancaster and London, and was founder (1975) of the Paines Plough Theatre. His first novels, *The Raining Tree War* (1974) and *African Horse* (1975), draw on an African background, satirizing the tribalism and superstition of political conflict, and the economic and cultural repercussions of colonial rule. *Light on a Honeycomb* (1978) is a remarkable portrait of an English community for the insane, using it as a symbol for wider social malaise. *Beloved Latitudes* (1981) is more inward. Pownall's careful balance of violence and humour, redemption and despair, has been likened to **Evelyn Waugh**.

POWYS, John Cowper
(1872–1963)

English novelist, poet and essayist, born in Shirley, Derbyshire, where his father was vicar; his mother was descended from **John Donne** and **William Cowper**; his brothers were **T F** and **Llewelyn Powys**. He was brought up in the Dorset-Somerset countryside and though he spent much of his later life in America, his formative years greatly influenced his work. Educated at Sherborne and Corpus Christi College, Cambridge, he taught and lectured before becoming a prolific author. Of some 50 books, his best known are his novels, particularly *Wolf Solent* (1929), *A Glastonbury Romance* (1932), gargantuan in scale, in which the myths surrounding the ancient abbey have a supernatural effect on the citizens of the town, *Weymouth Sands* (1934), *Maiden Castle* (1936) and *Owen Glendower* (1940). His reputation is the subject of much argument, but his standing is probably that of a cult author, rather than a widely recognized one.
▷H P Collins, *John Cowper Powys, Old Earthman* (1966)

POWYS, Llewelyn
(1884–1939)

English essayist and novelist, brother of **John Powys** and **T F Powys**, born in Dorchester.

He suffered from recurrent tuberculosis which caused him to spend some years in Switzerland and in Kenya, and from which he died. From 1920 to 1925 he was a journalist in New York. His work include *Ebony and Ivory* (1922), *Apples be Ripe* (1930) and the biographical *Confessions of Two Brothers* (with his brother John, 1916), *Skin for Skin* (1925) and *The Verdict of Bridlegoose* (1926).
▷R H Ward, *The Powys Brothers* (1935)

POWYS, T(heodore) F(rancis)
(1875–1953)

English novelist and short-story writer, brother of **John** and **Llewelyn Powys**, born in Shirley, Derbyshire. He lived in seclusion and wrote original and eccentric novels of which the best known is *Mr Weston's Good Wine* (1927). Other works are *Mr Tasker's Gods* (1925), *Captain Patch* (1935) and *Goat Green* (1937).
▷H Coombes, *T. F. Powys* (1960)

PRAED, Rosa
(1851–1935)

Australian novelist, born in Bromelton, Logan River, Queensland, best known as a writer of romantic fiction under the name of Mrs Campbell Praed. The privations of her early married life on outback Queensland stations resulted in *An Australian Heroine* (1880) and *The Romance of a Station* (1889). In 1875 she left with her husband for London where she became a popular novelist and the 'Queen' of circulating libraries, mixing in literary circles which included **Oscar Wilde**. During the next 40 years she produced almost as many novels, many with an Australian setting. *Policy and Passion* (1881) dealt, as did many of the others, with the disillusion which marriage brings. She questioned the permanency of marriage in *The Bond of Wedlock* (1887), which created controversy as a play. The failure of her marriage, and the death of her four children in tragic circumstances, turned her to aspects of spiritualism and she set up house with a 'medium', Nancy Harward (1899–1927), producing a number of occult books.

PRAED, Winthrop Mackworth
(1802–39)

English poet, born in London. He was educated at Eton (where he founded the 'Etonian') and at Trinity College, Cambridge, where he twice won the Chancellor's Medal. Called to the Bar in 1829 he went on to become an MP and junior minister. A promising parliamentary career was cut short by consumption. His light, society verse, such as 'Good Night to the Season' and 'The Letter of Advice', has been likened to **Thomas Hood**

in comic vein, but the comparison flatters Praed. Yet, although he has been described rather dismissively as a 'clever punster', he nevertheless influenced several 19th-century poets, notably **Frederick Locker-Lampson**.
▷D Hudson, *A Poet in Parliament* (1939)

PRATCHETT, Terry
(1948–)

English fantasy writer, born in Beaconsfield, Buckinghamshire. He worked as a journalist, and later as a publicity officer, before becoming a full-time writer in 1987. His first book was a fantasy for children, *The Carpet People* (1971, rev edn 1992). Later books for children include the *Book of the Nomes* sequence (from 1989) and *Only You Can Save Mankind* (1992). *The Dark Side of the Sun* (1976) and *Strata* (1981) were parodies of science fiction, but his popular success was secured by the *Discworld* sequence of comic fantasy novels, which began with *The Colour of Magic* (1983).

PRATI, Giovanni
(1815–84)

Italian lyric and narrative poet, born near Trento. Court poet to the House of Savoy, he became a deputy to the Italian parliament (1862) and a senator (1876). His lyrics, which fill several volumes, include *Canti lirici* (1843, 'Lyrical Songs'), and *Canti del popolo* (1843, 'Songs of the People'). He enjoyed a popular success with the romantic poem *Edmenegarda* (1841), but later turned to a simpler form of expression.
▷P L Mannucci, *Giovanni Prati* (1934)

PRATOLINI, Vasco
(1913–89)

Italian novelist, born in Florence, usually classed as 'neorealist'. Neorealism was first defined by the critic Arnaldo Bocelli in 1930 as a sort of neo-naturalism. But it did not reach its zenith until after World War II, when Italian authors became free to write as they wished—and then it was much influenced by the busy Italian film industry. Pratolini, who came from a working-class background, was in 1936 a young fascist interested in literature, and contributing eagerly to a fascist periodical, when he met **Elio Vittorini**; the latter helped him to shed the fascism, and encouraged him to write. He made his name with the partly autobiographical *Il quartiere* (1945, Eng trans *A Tale of Santa Croce*, 1952), a skilfully written panorama of life in this Florence district in the 1930s. *Cronache di povere amanti* (1947, Eng trans *A Tale of Poor Lovers*, 1949), his masterpiece, presents a rich canvas—there are more than 50 characters—of working-class Florentine life from the rise of fascism. After the trilogy *Una storia italiana* (*Metello*, 1955, Eng trans 1968; *Lo scialo*, 1960, 'Waste'; *Allegoria e derisione*, 1966, 'Allegory and Derision'), Pratolini wrote little more. He has been criticized for his Marxism (and his popularity in the then Soviet Union), but acclaimed for his human warmth and emphasis on individual aspiration.

▷F Rosengarten, *Vasco Pratolini: The Development of a Social Novelist* (1965)

PRATT, E(dwin) J(ohn)
(1882–1964)

Canadian poet, born in Western Bay, Newfoundland. He spent his early years in small fishing villages and taught in remote island communities, then after gaining his PhD in theology from the University of Toronto (1917) joined the English department there (1920) and edited the *Canadian Poetry Magazine* from 1936 to 1942. He won Governor General's Awards for *The Fable of the Goats and Other Poems* (1932), *Brebeuf and His Brethren* (1940) and *Towards the Last Spike* (1952). *The Collected Poems of E. J. Pratt* (1958) has been described as charting the Canadian movement from a colonial to a national literature, and he is particularly renowned for narrative poetry that explores the growth of a national sense of time and space within the wider context of the world.

▷S Djwa, *E. J. Pratt: The Evolutionary Vision* (1974); Frank Davey, 'Apostle of Corporate Man' and 'Rationalist Technician', in *Canadian Literature* (43, 1970 and 61, 1974)

PREDA, Marin
(1922–)

Romanian novelist and story writer, widely thought of as the outstanding living writer of his country. Being of peasant origin, he steered a cunning and sometimes funny line between criticism of the communist regime and appearing to approve of it. Many of his colleagues hated him, especially for serving as a vice-president of the Writers' Union. His chief work is *Morometii* (1955–67), the first part of which was translated as *The Moromites* (1957). In this book his chief character, Ilie Moromete, is a philosophical peasant who delights in leading everyone up the garden path, and is in certain respects a representation of his creator, who has never seriously sought for anyone's approval.

PREMCHAND, pseud of **Dhanpat Rai Srivastav**
(1880–1936)

The leading Indian writer of fiction in Hindi, still unsurpassed for the picture he gives of North Indian life, born in Benares. Until 1914 he wrote mainly in Urdu; but after that he devoted himself to establishing Urdu forms, stories and novels, in Hindi. He was a follower of Gandhi, and gave up his teaching post in 1921 as a protest against British policies. He wrote more than 300 tales, as well as novels. Much is available in English, including the selection *The World of Premchand* (1969), his greatest novel, *Godan* (1935, Eng trans *The Gift of a Cow*, 1968) and *A Premchand Reader* (1962).

PRERADOVIĆ, Paula von, married name **Molten**
(1887–1951)

Austrian Roman Catholic poet, who was arrested in 1944 for her involvement with the anti-Nazi resistance. She wrote the words of the Austrian National anthem. Her well-respected and accomplished poetry, much of it devotional, was influenced by that of **Rainer Maria Rilke**.

PRESSBURGER, Emeric (Imre)
(1902–88)

Hungarian screenwriter, born in Miskolc. Educated at Prague and Stuttgart, he worked as a journalist in Hungary and Germany before entering the film industry. Resident in Britain from 1935, he worked on a number of projects for Sir Alexander Korda before writing the fast-moving thriller *The Spy In Black* (1939) for director Michael Powell. They subsequently formed The Archers, one of the most innovative production units in the history of British cinema. As film-makers their work embraced the notion of film as a medium to express grand emotions, poetry, fantasy and sensuality rather than the earth-bound social realism that had often characterized British cinema of the period. Among their most distinctive films are *The Life And Death Of Colonel Blimp* (1943), *A Matter Of Life And Death* (1946), *Black Narcissus* (1947) and *The Red Shoes* (1948). The partnership was dissolved in 1957. Working alone Pressburger had directed *Twice Upon A Time* (1953). He subsequently wrote a number of short stories and novels, one of which was adapted into the film *Behold A Pale Horse* (1964); he re-united with Powell as the writer of the children's film *The Boy Who Turned Yellow* (1972).

PREVELAKIS, Pandelis
(1909–)

Cretan novelist, born in Rethymno, and a pupil and imitator of the great **Kazantzakis**, although much more polished in style. A student of aesthetics and art, Prevelakis made a startling debut in 1938 with *To Chronico* *mias politeias* (Eng trans *The Tale of a Town*, 1978), a love story set against the backdrop of an anonymous town in silent decay. However, critical opinion is that his best books were written after World War II. *Pantermi Crete* ('Wretched Crete'), published in 1945, was a chronicle of the uprising of 1866, and his three-volume masterpiece *O Cretikos* (1948–50, 'The Cretan') traced events from this uprising until 1910. He himself said his intention was 'to express the whole soul of the Greek people at one point of its history'.

PRÉVERT, Jacques
(1900–77)

French poet and screenwriter, born in Neuilly-sur-Seine. A shop-worker, he turned to writing after his military service and worked for *L'Argus De La Presse* and the publicity agency Damour. A member of the Surrealist movement before being expelled for irreverence, he first made his name as the author of humorous, anarchic 'song poems' about street life in Paris, collected in *Paroles* (1946, Eng trans in part *Paroles: Selections*, 1958) and *Spectacle* (1951). Active as a writer and performer with the agit-prop theatre group Octobre, he wrote the screenplay for their film *L'Affaire Est Dans Le Sac* (1932, 'It's in the Bag') and subsequently pursued a career as a screenwriter, achieving his greatest renown during a 10-year collaboration with director Marcel Carné. Together they made such atmospheric classics of fatalistic pre-war French cinema as *Quai Des Brumes* (1938, 'Port of Mists') and *Le Jour Se Lève* (1939, 'Daybreak'), as well as their masterpiece, *Les Enfants du Paradis* (1944, Eng trans 1968). In later years he collaborated with his brother, the director Pierre Prévert (1906–88), on short, animated films for children, and worked extensively for French television between 1961 and 1968.
▷J Queval, *Jacques Prévert* (1955)

PRÉVOST, Abbé (Antoine François Prévost d'Exiles)
(1697–1763)

French novelist, born in Artois. Educated by the Jesuits, at 16 he enlisted in the army, but soon returned to the Jesuits, and had almost joined the order when he was again tempted to the soldier's life. In 1720, following an unhappy love affair, he joined the Benedictines of St Maur, and spent the next seven years in religious duties and in study. But about 1727 he fled for six years, first to London, where he started to write *Histoire de Cleveland*, and then to Holland (1729–31). He issued volumes 1–4 of *Mémoires d'un homme de qualité* (Eng trans *Memoirs of a Man of Quality*, 1938) in 1728 and volumes 5–6 in

1731, *Manon Lescaut* (Eng trans 1738) forming volume 8. He employed himself in additional novels—*Le Philosophe anglais; ou, Histoire de Monsieur Cleveland, fils naturel de Cromwell* (1731–9, Eng trans *The Life and Adventures of Mr Cleveland*, 1734) and *Le Doyen de Killerine* (1735–40, Eng trans *The Dean of Coleraine*, 1742–3)—and in translations. In London again after another affair he started *Le Pour et contre* (1733–40, 'Arguments For and Against'), a periodical review of life and letters, modelled on the *Spectator*. In France by 1735, he was appointed honorary chaplain to the Prince de Conti, and compiled over a hundred volumes more. He died suddenly at Chantilly. Prévost's reputation stands securely on *Manon Lescaut*. It remains fresh, charming and perennial, from its perfect simplicity, the stamp of reality and truth throughout, and a style so flowing and natural that the reader forgets it altogether in the interest of the story.
▷J Sgard, *Prévost, romancier* (1968)

PRÉVOST, Eugène Marcel
(1862–1941)

French novelist, born in Paris. A civil engineer, he worked in a tobacco factory until 1891. From the age of 25 he wrote in his leisure hours. Of his clever novels and plays many have been translated, including *Cousine Laura* (1890, Eng trans *Cousin Laura*, 1913), *Frédérique* (1900, Eng trans 1901) and *Léa* (1900, Eng trans *Léa, a Sequel to Frédérique*, 1902).

PRICE, Reynolds
(1933–)

American novelist, born in Macon, North Carolina and educated at Duke University and Oxford. He has been a professor of English in a number of universities and in 1976 chaired the National Endowment for the Arts Literature Advisory Panel. He has received numerous awards, including a Guggenheim Fellowship (1964) and a National Book Critics Award (1987). His first novel, *A Long and Happy Life* (1962), introduces the Mustian family who appear in several of his later books. He writes of rural life in North Carolina, but his work has become increasingly more abstract, with mythic elements featuring implicitly or explicitly. *Kate Vaiden* (1986) is his most critically acclaimed novel to date.

PRICHARD, Katharine Susannah
(1883–1969)

Australian writer, born in Levuka, on Ovalau, where her father was Editor of the *Fiji Times*. She started work on a Melbourne

newspaper, for which she made a trip to London in 1908. Four years later she returned to journalism in London. In 1915 her first novel, *The Pioneers*, won the 'colonial' section of a publisher's competition and was filmed in Australia the following year. In 1916 she returned to Australia, married Captain Hugo Throssell VC and in the next 50 years produced 12 novels, many poems, plays and short stories, and an autobiography, *Child of the Hurricane* (1963). In 1920 she had become a founding member of the Australian Communist Party, and her socialist convictions coloured much of her subsequent work, especially her powerful trilogy set in the West Australian goldfields, *The Roaring Nineties* (1946), *Golden Miles* (1948) and *Winged Seeds* (1950). Her last novel, *Subtle Flame* (1967), was a study in the conflicts facing a newspaper editor. Her son, Ric Prichard Throssell, wrote the play *For Valour* (1960, published 1976), a study of the economic and personal decline of a returned war hero, closely modelled on his father, and a biography of his mother, *Wild Weeds and Wind Flowers* (1975).
▷H D Brochmann, *Katharine Susannah Prichard* (1967)

PRIESTLEY, J(ohn) B(oynton)
(1894–1984)

English novelist, playwright and critic, born in Bradford. He was educated there and at Trinity Hall, Cambridge. He had already made a reputation by critical writings such as *The English Comic Characters* (1925), *The English Novel* (1927), *English Humour* (1928), and books on **George Meredith** (1926) and **Thomas Love Peacock** (1927) in 'The English Men of Letters' series when the geniality of his novel *The Good Companions* (1929) gained him a wide popularity. It was followed by other humorous novels, though not all of equal merit, including *Angel Pavement* (1930), *Let the People Sing* (1939), *Jenny Villiers* (1947) and *The Magicians* (1954). His reputation as a dramatist was established by *Dangerous Corner* (1932), *Time and the Conways* (1937), and other plays on space-time themes, as well as popular comedies such as *Laburnum Grove* (1933), and his psychological mystery, *An Inspector Calls* (1947). Best known as a writer of novels, Priestley was also master of the essay form. He was an astute, original and controversial commentator on contemporary society—*Journey Down the Rainbow* (1955), written with his wife Jacquetta Hawkes the archaeologist, was a jovial indictment of American life; in serious vein, his collected essays, *Thoughts in the Wilderness* (1957), deal with both present and future social problems.
▷J Braine, *J. B. Priestley* (1978)

PRIETO, Jenaro
(1889–1946)

Chilean novelist, author of *El socio* (1928, Eng trans, *The Partner*), 1931), a novel worthy of **Pirandello**, in which a man invents a business partner and is then, after he 'commits suicide', hunted as his murderer.

PRIJAM, Amitra
(1919–)

Indian (Punjabi) poet, well known throughout the Indian sub-continent for her mellifluous and reconciliatory poetry.

PRINCE, F(rank) T(empleton)
(1912–)

South African-born British poet, educated at Balliol College, Oxford, and at Princeton University. He served in the Intelligence Corps during World War II, subsequently joining Southampton University, where he taught English until 1974; he later held other academic posts in Britain and overseas, including a period of three years as Professor of English at the University of the West Indies. His elegant, traditionally rhymed and metred verse first appeared in book form in 1938 with the fine *Poems*. 'Soldiers Bathing' from the 1954 volume of that name is his best-known work and one of the finest to have emerged out of World War II. The best of the earlier work was collected as *The Doors of Stone* (1963). Later volumes include *Drypoints of the Hasidim* (1975), *Afterword on Rupert Brooke* (1976) and the magnificent *Yüan Chên Variations* (1981), the latter postdating a *Collected Poems*, which appeared in 1979. Prince has also been a significant scholar of **Milton** and of **Shakespeare**'s verse.
▷A Nigam, *F T Prince: A Study of His Poetry* (1983)

PRINGLE, Thomas
(1789–1834)

Scottish writer, born in Blakelaw, Roxburghshire, the son of a farmer. He was educated at Kelso Grammar School and Edinburgh University, and in 1811 became an archivist in the Register Office. In 1817 he started the *Edinburgh Monthly Magazine*, later *Blackwood's Magazine*. In 1820 he emigrated to Cape Colony, and for three years was government librarian at Cape Town. He started a Whig paper, but it was suppressed by the governor. Returning to London in 1826 he became Secretary of the Anti-Slavery Society. He wrote *African Sketches* (1834), and published two collections of poems and lyrics, *The Autumnal Collection* (1817), and *Ephemerides* (1828).
▷W Hay, *Thomas Pringle* (1912)

PRIOR, Matthew
(1664–1721)

English poet and diplomat, born in Wimborne, Dorset, the son of a joiner. Under the patronage of Lord Dorset he was sent to Westminster School, and from there with a scholarship from the Duchess of Somerset to St John's College, Cambridge. He was first employed as secretary to the ambassador to The Hague. In Queen Anne's time he turned Tory, and was instrumental in bringing about the treaty of Utrecht (1713), for which dubious service he was imprisoned for two years (1715–17) after the queen's death. His Tory friends recouped his fortunes by subscribing handsomely to a folio edition of his works (1719). He also received a gift of £4000 from Lord Harley to purchase Down Hall in Essex. Prior was a master of neat, colloquial and epigrammatic verse. His first work, a collaboration with Charles Montagu (Lord **Halifax**), was *The Hind and the Panther Transvers' to the story of the Country and the City Mouse* (1687), a witty satire on **Dryden**'s *Hind and the Panther*. His long poem, *Alma or The Progress of the Mind* (1718), was composed in prison. The long soliloquy in couplet form, *Solomon on the Vanity of the World*, is definitely tedious. His political verse, with the exception of his brilliant burlesque of **Nicolas Boileau**'s *Épître au roi* (*An English Ballad on the Taking of Namur*), is now of historical interest only. He is best known as the poet of light occasional verse—mock-lyrics such as *A Better Answer (to Chloe Jealous)*, or charming addresses to noble children (*A Letter to the Lady Margaret Cavendish when a Child*), and, in serious vein, *Lines Written in the Beginning of Mézeray's History of France*, a favourite with Sir **Walter Scott**. His wittiest trifle is *The Secretary*, but *Jinny the Just* is also popular. He was buried in Poets' Corner in Westminster Abbey.
▷F Bickley, *Matthew Prior* (1914)

PRISHVIN, Mikhail
(1873–1974)

Russian novelist and naturalist, born near Yelets. He was expelled from his school for rudeness to a teacher, who happened to be **Vasily Rozanov**. Arrested for Marxist activities during 1897–9, he first qualified as an agronomist. His first book, *V krayu nepuganykh* (1905, 'In the Country Where the Birds Show No Fear'), records his impressions of a Russian countryside unspoiled by human beings. Being a nature writer, he was relatively safe from Stalin's censors, and could enjoy the reputation he deserved. *Kalendar prirody* (1937, Eng trans *The Lake and the Woods*, 1952, *Nature's Diary*, 1958) and *Zhan-shen* (1933, Eng trans *Jen Sheng:*

The Root of Life, 1936) are his most representative works in translation.
▷M Slonim, *Soviet Russian Literature: Writers and Problems 1917–1977* (1977)

PRITCHETT, Sir V(ictor) S(awdon)
(1900–)

English writer and critic, born in Ipswich. He was educated at Alleyn's School, Dulwich, and Dulwich College. After working in the leather trade he became a newspaper correspondent in France, Morocco and Spain, and in 1929 published his first novel, *Claire Drummer*. His style is witty and idiosyncratic, his themes satirical, and he is particularly interested in the 'puritan' character with its fanaticism and guilt, which he portrays with increasing humour in his novels *Nothing Like Leather* (1935), *Dead Man Leading* (1937) and *Mr Beluncle* (1951). A highly-regarded literary critic, he travelled and lectured widely, especially in the USA. Among his critical works are *The Living Novel* (1946), *Books in General* (1953), and a biography of **Honoré de Balzac** (1973), and he is the author of many volumes of short stories, a form in which he excels, and two autobiographical books, *A Cab at the Door* (1968) and *Midnight Oil* (1973). *The Complete Essays* was published in 1991.

PROCTER, Adelaide Ann, pseud Mary Berwick
(1825–64)

English poet, born in London, daughter of **Bryan Waller Procter**. In 1851 she turned Roman Catholic. By her *Legends and Lyrics* (1858–60), some of which were written for *Household Words*, she won poetical renown. Her poems included 'The Lost Chord', which was set to music by Sir Arthur Sullivan.
▷J Janku, *Adelaide Ann Procter: ihr Leven und ihre Werke* (1912)

PROCTER, Bryan Waller, pseud Barry Cornwall
(1787–1874)

English poet, born in Leeds. After studying at Harrow with **Byron** and Peel he became a solicitor, went to London and in 1815 began to contribute poetry to the *Literary Gazette*. In 1823 he married Anne Benson Skepper (1799–1888). He had meanwhile published poems and produced a tragedy at Covent Garden, *Mirandola*, whose success was largely due to the acting of Macready and Kemble. He was called to the Bar in 1831, and from 1832 to 1861 was a metropolitan commissioner of lunacy. His works comprise *Dramatic Scenes* (1819), *Marcian Colonna* (1820), *The Flood of Thessaly* (1823) and

English Songs (1832), besides memoirs of Kean (1835) and **Charles Lamb** (1866).
▷R W Armour, *Barry Cornwall* (1935)

PROKOSCH, Frederic
(1908–89)

American novelist and poet. Born in Wisconsin, he attended Yale and King's College, London. His best-known novel is *The Asiatics* (1935), whose settings reflect Prokosch's travels; during World War II, he was the US cultural attaché in Stockholm. His novels about the war include *The Skies of Europe* (1941) and *The Conspirators* (1943). In later years, he wrote fiction based on the lives of great Europeans, Beatrice Cenci in *A Tale for Midnight* (1955) and a rather uncertain **Byron** in *The Missolonghi Manuscript* (1968). His most effective volume of poetry was *The Assassins* (1936). *Chosen Poems* (1947) gathers the best of them. A few years before his death he published *Voices* (1983), a powerful literary memoir.

PROPERTIUS, Sextus
(c.48–c.15 BC)

Roman elegiac poet, born probably in Asisium (Assisi) in Umbria. He had a portion of his patrimony confiscated after Philippi by the Triumvirs (41 BC), to reward their veterans, but he retained sufficient funds to proceed to Rome for education, and became a poet. He won the favour of Maecenas, to whom he dedicated a book of his poems, and even ingratiated himself with Augustus, whose achievements he duly celebrated. But the central figure of his inspiration was his mistress Cynthia. Propertius left Rome apparently only once, on a visit to Athens. Of his poems only the first book, devoted to Cynthia, was published during his lifetime.
▷G Luck, *The Latin Love Elegy* (1969)

PROUST, Marcel
(1871–1922)

French novelist, born in Auteuil, Paris. A semi-invalid all his life, he was cosseted by his mother, and her death in 1905, when he was 34 years old, robbed him of any desire to continue his 'social butterfly' existence. Instead he withdrew from society, immured himself in a sound-proof flat and gave himself over entirely to introspection. Delving into the self below the levels of superficial consciousness, he set himself the task of transforming into art the realities of experience as known to the inner emotional life. Despite the seemingly dilettante approach to life prior to his start on his novel, *A la recherche du temps perdu* (1913–27, 13 vols, trans by Scott Moncrieff as *Remembrance of Things Past*,

1922–31), it is evident from the various volumes which make up this title that no detail ever escaped his amazingly observant eye, and he subjected experience to searching analysis to divine in it beauties and complexities that escape the superficial response of ordinary intelligence. Thinking about the philosophy of Henri Bergson on the subconscious, his distinctions between the various aspects of time, and insistence on the truths perceived by involuntary memory, Proust evolved a mode of communication by image, evocation and analogy for displaying his characters—not as a realist would see them, superficially, from the outside, but in terms of their concealed emotional life, evolving on a plane that has nothing to do with temporal limitations. *À la recherche* started off with *Du côté de chez Swann* (1913, Eng trans *Swann's Way*, 1922), and, after a delay caused by the war, *À l'ombre des jeunes filles en fleur* (1919, Eng trans *Within a Budding Grove*, 1924), which won the Prix **Goncourt** in 1919. *Le Côté de Guermantes* (1920–1, 2 vols, Eng trans *The Guermantes' Way*, 1925) and *Sodome et Gomorrhe* (1922, 3 vols, Eng trans *The Cities of the Plain*, 1927) followed. These achieved an international reputation for Proust and an eager public awaited the posthumously published titles, *La Prisonnière* (1923, Eng trans *The Captive*, 1929), *Albertine disparue* (1925, Eng trans *The Sweet Cheat Gone*, 1930), and *Le Temps retrouvé* (1927, Eng trans *Time Regained*, 1931), each in two volumes. Apart from his masterpieces, there was also posthumous publication of an early novel, *Jean Santeuil* (1952, Eng trans 1955) and a book of critical credo, *Contre Sainte-Beuve* (1954, Eng trans *By Way of Sainte-Beuve*, 1958). A new English translation of his masterwork by **D J Enright** appeared under the title *In Search of Lost Time* in 1992.
▷G D Painter, *Proust: a biography* (2 vols, 1959–65)

PROUX, Prosper
(1811–75)

Breton poet, who made an influential anthology of Goliardic poetry, and who wrote 'hearty and often bawdy' poems, which are still read.

PROYSEN, Alf
(1914–70)

Norwegian novelist, short-story writer and balladist, born in Hedmark. His most famous creation internationally is Mrs Pepperpot, the central character of a number of short-story collections (such as *Little Old Mrs Pepperpot*, 1959). Despite being miniscule, she overcomes astonishing adversity, and is emblematic of the author's populist socialism. In his own country, Proysen's celebrity was more broadly based; he first achieved widespread popularity in 1948–9 with the publication of three satirical ballad collections (including *Musavisa*, 1949). His only novel, *Trost i Toklampa* (1950, 'Thrush in the Ceiling Light'), satirizes the idiocies of rural life, and contributed greatly to his status as the country's most popular writer since World War II.

PRUDENTIUS, Marcus Aurelius Clemens
(348–c.410)

Latin Christian poet, born in the north of Spain. He practised as a pleader, acted as civil and criminal judge, and afterwards received high office at the imperial court. A Christian all his life, he devoted himself in his later years to the composition of religious poetry. Of his poems the chief are *Cathemerinon Liber*, a series of 12 hymns (trans 1845); *Peristephanon*, 14 lyrical poems in honour of martyrs; *Apotheosis*, a defence of the Trinity; *Hamartigeneia*, on the origin of evil; *Psychomachia* (Eng trans *War of the Soul*, 1743), on the Christian Graces; and *Contra Symmachum*, against the heathen gods; and *Diptychon*, on scriptural incidents. He is the best of the early Christian verse-makers.
▷T R Glover, *Life and Letters in the 4th Century* (1901)

PRUS, Boleslaw, pseud of Aleksander Glowacki
(1847–1912)

Polish novelist, born in Hrubieszów. He belonged to the period of realism in literature which followed the unsuccessful revolt against Russian domination in 1863–4. His novels and short stories are written as social novels, mainly about common people, and include *Omyłka* ('The Blunder'), *Lalka* (1887, 'The Doll'), considered to be his masterpiece, a vivid and sympathetic picture of Warsaw, and *Emancypantki* (1893, 'Emancipated Women').
▷S Malkowski, *Boleslaw Prus* (1964)

PRYS-JONES, Arthur Glyn
(1888–1987)

Welsh poet, born in Denbigh and educated at Llandovery College and Jesus College, Oxford. A teacher by profession, he edited the first anthology of Anglo–Welsh poetry, *Welsh Poets* (1917), and published six volumes of his own, including *Poems of Wales* (1923), *Green Places* (1948), *High Heritage* (1969) and *Valedictory Verses* (1978). The doyen of Anglo–Welsh writers, he was President of the Welsh Academy from 1970 until his death.

PRZYBOS, Julian
(1901–70)

Polish poet and poetic theoretician, born of a poor peasant family in Gwóznica. He was the influential leader (in Cracow) of the poetry movement known as the First Vanguard—'rationalistic and constructivist'—and as such he opposed both the Second Vanguard and the *Skamander* group. **Czeslaw Milosz** (originally a Second Vanguard, or 'Catastrophist' poet) has written that although his 'obsession with a poetry controlled by the will sometimes leads him to the very edge of the ridiculous ... he is recognized as one of those who contributed most to the transformation of modern Polish verse'. He insisted that poets must avoid direct expression of the feelings but create their emotional equivalent in their images. There are elements of Futurism in his earlier work. Two poems are translated in *Post-War Polish Poetry* (1965, ed Milosz).

PRZYBYSZEWSKI, Stanislaw
(1868–1927)

Polish novelist, dramatist and critic, born in Lojewo. He was educated in Germany, and lived from 1898 in Cracow, where he became Editor of *Life* and a leader of the new literary 'Young Poland' movement. His work, reflecting his 'naturalist' ideas, included *Homo Sapiens* (1901), *Matka* (1903) and the drama *Śnieg* (1903, Eng trans *Snow*, 1920).
▷S Halsztynski, *Stanislaw Przybyszewski* (1958)

PSYCHARIS, Iannis
(1854–1929)

Novelist and poet of Chiot origin, but born in Odessa and educated in Constantinople. At the age of 15 he left for Paris and Germany, eventually settling in Paris in 1885, where he taught modern Greek at the École des Hautes Études, and where he lived for the rest of his life. He was the principal catalyst for the shift in Greek poetry from the use of the archaic *Katharevousa* to demotic Greek. His book on why this change was necessary, *To Taxidhi Mou* (1888, 'My Journey'), was immediately adopted as a handbook by many Greek poets. He also attempted to introduce the 'psychological' novel into Greek literature, with works such as *Zoë ki'Agapi sti Monaxia* (1904, 'Life and Love in Solitude') and *Ta Dheo Adherfia* (1911, 'The Two Brothers'); these did not receive a warm critical reception. However, his largely autobiographical *T'Oneiro tou Gianniris* (1897, 'The Dream of Gianniris'), a lyrical depiction of some of his years as a soldier, added greatly to his reputation.

PÜCKLER-MUSKAU, Hermann, Fürst von
(1785–1871)

German travel writer, patron of the arts, dandy, personality and poet (although his early collection has been called an 'indiscretion'). He owned extensive estates at Muskau, where he was born, and at Branitz, where he died. His travel books, including *Briefe eines Verstorbene* (1830–2, Eng trans *Tour in Germany, Holland and England 1826–1828*, 1832), were written in the style of **Sterne**.
▷E H Butler, *The Tempestuous Prince* (1929)

PUIG, Manuel
(1932–90)

Argentinian novelist, born in General Villegas. A gifted writer who wrote in both Spanish and English, he has been labelled with the 'magical realist' tag for his stylistic diversity and playful imagination. He came to attention with *La traición de Rita Hayworth* (1968, Eng trans *Betrayed by Rita Hayworth*, 1971), which made an ironic contrast of the 'gaucho' myth with a contemporary Argentine culture dominated by Hollywood and television, which Puig loved. *Boquitas pintadas* (1969, Eng trans *Heartbreak Tango*, 1973) was followed by a detective novel, *The Buenos Aires Affair* (1973). His biggest success was *El beso de la mujer araña* (1976, Eng trans *Kiss of the Spider Woman*, 1979). The story of the relationship which develops between two unlikely prisoners, it has been adapted for film and stage. The posthumous *Tropical Night Falling* appeared in 1992.

PUJMANOVÁ, Marie, née Hennerová
(1893–1958)

Czech novelist and poet, born in Prague. She took a conventionally Marxist view, but her trilogy of Czech life from before until after World War II, tracing the fortunes and misfortunes of two families, one working- one middle-class, effectively evokes the atmosphere of Czechoslovakia in those years, in particular the Nazi occupation.

PULCI, Luigi
(1432–84)

Italian poet, born in Padua. A protégé of Cosimo de Medici, he wrote *Il Morgante Maggiore* (1481, 'Morgante the Giant'), a burlesque epic, one of the most valuable specimens of the early Tuscan dialect. He also produced a comic novel and several humorous sonnets.
▷A Gianni, *Pulci uno e due* (1967)

PURCHAS, Samuel
(1577–1626)

English compiler of travel books, born in Thaxted in Essex. He studied at St John's College, Cambridge, and became vicar of Eastwood in 1604, and in 1614 rector of St Martin's, Ludgate. He assisted Hakluyt in his later years. His own great works were *Purchas his Pilgrimage, or Relations of the World in all Ages* (1613) and *Hakluytus Posthumus, or Purchas his Pilgrimes* (1625), based on the papers of Hakluyt and archives of the East India company. Another work is *Purchas his Pilgrim: Microcosmus, or the History of Man* (1619).

PURDY, Al
(1918–)

Canadian poet, born in Wooler, Ontario; his lack of academic qualifications or involvement is unusual among Canadian poets. The winner of Governor General's Awards for *The Cariboo Horses* (1965) and *Collected Poems* (1986), he is the author of more than 30 volumes of poetry, in which 'an engaging conversational fluency is almost always present'. Purdy's is a poetry that gives Canadian history a landscape and a presence: 'The carving is laid aside/in beginning darkness/at the end of hunger/after a while wind/blows down the tent and snow/begins to cover him/After 600 years/the ivory thought/is still warm' ('Lament for the Dorsets', in *Wild Grape Wine*, 1968).
▷T Marshall, *Harsh and Lovely Land* (1979)

PURDY, James Otis
(1923–)

American satirical novelist and short-story writer, much concerned with socially and sexually marginal characters and groups. He was born in Ohio, educated in Chicago and Mexico, and worked for some time as a translator and college lecturer. Early stories were privately published with the help of friends, as *Don't Call Me by My Right Name* and *63: Dream Palace* (both 1956), and Purdy has been only slowly and rather grudgingly accepted by the US literary establishment. He has acknowledged the assistance of **Edith Sitwell** in securing a sympathetic readership. His first novel was *Malcolm* (1959), subsequently dramatized by **Edward Albee**. Like its successor, *The Nephew* (1960), it deals with a quest for information about a missing character; together they serve as a prologue to Purdy's lifelong interest in outsiders. The 'hero' of *Cabot Wright Begins* (1964) is a rapist; later books, particularly *Eustace Chisholm and the Works* (1967), have dealt with homoeroticism. The writing is vivid and vernacular and often realistically oblique in dealing with

extremes of consciousness. Three novels about a disintegrating American family (1970–81) were collected as *Sleepers in Moon-Crowned Valleys* (1981). *Narrow Rooms* (1978) was strongly touted as a gay classic in the making. Purdy's verse has appeared in two volumes, *The Running Sun* (1971) and *Sunshine Is an Only Child* (1973).
▷ S D Adams, *James Purdy* (1976)

PUSHKIN, Alexander Sergevich
(1799–1837)

Russian poet, born in Moscow. His lineage was illustrious, and he attended the Lyceum at Tsarkoe Selo, in the environs of St Petersburg, where his talent for poetry first emerged. In 1817 he entered government service, but because of his liberalism was exiled in 1820 to the south. In 1824 he was dismissed and confined to his estate near Pskov, and did not return to Moscow until after the accession of Nicholas I. He married Natalia Goncharova in 1832, whose beauty attracted Baron Georges D'Anthès, a French royalist in the Russian service. Pushkin challenged him to a duel and was killed. Regarded as Russia's greatest poet, his first success was the romantic poem *Ruslan i Lyudmilla* (1820, 'Ruslan and Ludmilla'), followed by *Kavkazki plennik* (1822, 'The Prisoner of the Caucasus'), *Bakhchisarai fontan* (1826, 'Fountain of Bakhchisarai'), *Tzigani* (1827), and his masterpiece, *Evgeny Onegin* (1828, Eng trans *Eugene Onegin*, 1881), a sophisticated novel in verse that was much imitated but never rivalled. Prolific for one whose life was so short, he also wrote lyric poems, essays, the blank verse historical drama *Boris Godunov* (1825, Eng trans 1899), and, in 1830, the four 'Little Tragedies': *Motsart i Sal'eri* (Eng trans *Mozart and Salieri*, 1899), *Skupoy rytsar* (Eng trans *The Covetous Knight*, 1939), *Kamenny gost* (Eng trans *The Statue Guest*, 1899), and *Pir vo vremya chumy* (Eng trans *The Feast During the Plague*, 1946). His chilling novella of avarice and deceit, *Pikovaya dama* (1834, Eng trans *The Queen of Spades*, 1858), is one of his greatest works, its supernatural realism typifying much Russian fiction of the 19th century. He is to Russian literature what **Shakespeare** is to English.
▷ B Tomashevsky, *Alexander Pushkin* (1956–61); W Vickers, *Pushkin* (1970)

PUZO, Mario
(1920–)

American novelist, born in New York City. Educated at Columbia University, he served in the US air force during World War II and worked for 20 years as an administrative assistant in government offices at home and overseas. His first novel was *The Dark Arena* (1955), but his breakthrough came with his novel about the Mafia, *The Godfather* (1969), the epic story of Don Corleone and his extended 'family' of Sicilian immigrants who impose their will by brutal force and terror. It became a bestseller, and was filmed by Francis Coppola in 1972 with Marlon Brando playing Corleone.

PYE, Henry James
(1745–1813)

English poet, born in London. He studied at Magdalen College, Oxford. He held a commission in the Berkshire militia, in 1784 became MP for that county, and in 1790 succeeded Thomas Warton as poet laureate. In 1792 he was appointed a London police magistrate. The works of 'poetical Pye' number nearly 20, and include *Alfred: an Epic* (1801), with numerous birthday and New-Year odes, all extremely loyal and extremely dull.

PYLE, Howard
(1853–1911)

American illustrator and writer. In 1876 *Scribners Magazine* accepted some of Pyle's sketches while he was still helping in his father's leather business and on the strength of this success he moved to New York. Returning to Wilmington a few years later, he began to write children's books and a growing reputation for line-and-wash depictions of colonial life led to the opening of his own art school in 1900. His children's publications indulged a liking for medieval lore and legend, and included versions of Robin Hood and King Arthur.

PYM, Barbara Mary Crampton
(1913–80)

English novelist, born in Shropshire. She was educated at St Hilda's College, Oxford, and later worked at the International African Institute in London. Her fiction is deliberately confined within narrow bounds, characteristically exploring the tragi-comic lives of frustrated middle-class spinsters in a delicate, understated fashion. She published three novels in the 1950s, the best of which is *A Glass of Blessings* (1958), then lapsed into obscurity until, partly through the support of **Philip Larkin**, her *Quartet in Autumn* appeared in 1977. *The Sweet Dove Died* (1979) was the last book published in her lifetime, but four more novels, *A Few Green Leaves* (1980), *An Unsuitable Attachment* (1982), *Crampton Hodnet* (1985) and *An Academic Question* (1986), appeared posthumously.

PYNCHON, Thomas
(1937–)

American novelist, born in Glen Cove, New York, and educated at Cornell University. Seen by some as wilfully obscure, by others as a swashbuckling experimentalist, his sprawling, loquacious novels are ingenious, fabulous structures in which the normal conventions of the novel have been largely abandoned. Studiously avoiding public forums, he is obsessively studied and mined for autobiographical and more arcane references, of which there is no shortage. *V* (1963), a loose, episodic book, influenced by the Beats and by Pynchon's developing use of paranoia as a structural device, centres on a mysterious female principle at work in modern history. Subsequent publications include *The Crying of Lot 49* (1966) and *Gravity's Rainbow* (1973), concerning Tyrone Slothrop, lost in a surreal labyrinth but imbued with the wherewithal—in his reproductive organ—to predict exactly the sites of V-2 explosions in London. *Vineland* (1990) appeared to return to an earlier, more free-wheeling and satirical style and received mixed reviews, particularly in the UK. *Slow Learner* (1984) collected early stories and included a disarmingly straightforward introduction.

▷T H Schaub, *Pynchon: the voice of ambiguity* (1981)

Q

QUARLES, Francis
(1592–1644)

English poet, born in the manor house of Stewards near Romford, Essex, the son of the surveyor-general of victualling for the navy. He studied at Christ's College, Cambridge, and at Lincoln's Inn, and was successively cup-bearer to the princess Elizabeth (Queen of Bohemia) when she went to marry Elector Frederick V in Germany (1613), secretary to Archbishop Ussher (c.1629), and chronologer to the City of London (1639). He married in 1618 a wife who bore him 18 children and prefixed a touching memoir to his *Solomon's Recantation* (1645). Quarles was a royalist and churchman who suffered in the cause by having his books and manuscripts destroyed. He wrote abundantly in prose and verse. His *Emblems* (1635), in spite of many imperfections, occasionally shows a flash of poetic fire, and is his best-known work, although *Hieroglyphikes of the Life of Man* (1638) was also a popular success. Other poetical works include *A Feast of Wormes* (1620), *Argalus and Parthenia* (1629), *Divine Poems* (1630), *The Historie of Samson* (1631) and *Divine Fancies* (1632). The prose includes a book of aphorisms (*Enchyridion*, 1640) and *The Profest Royalist* (1645).
▷J Horder, *Francis Quarles* (1953)

QUASIMODO, Salvatore
(1901–68)

Italian poet, winner of the Nobel Prize for literature, born in Syracuse, Sicily. A student of engineering, he became a travelling inspector for the Italian state power board before taking up a career in literature and music. A professor of Literature at the Conservatory of Music in Milan, he wrote several volumes of spirited poetry. These reflect above all his deep interest in the fate of Italy, and his language is made particularly striking by the use simultaneously of both Christian and mythological allusions. He won the Nobel Prize for literature in 1959. His works include *Ed è Subito Sera* (1942, 'And Suddenly It Is Evening'), *La Vita non è sogno* (1949, 'Life is Not a Dream') and *La Terra impareggiabile* (1958, 'The Matchless Earth'). A collection of translated works was published as *Selected Poems* (1965).
▷P Mazzamutto, *Salvatore Quasimodo* (1967)

QUEEN, Ellery, pseud of Frederick Dannay
(1905–82)
LEE, Manfred B
(1905–71)

American writers of crime fiction, cousins, both born in Brooklyn, New York City. As businessmen they entered for a detective-story competition, and won with *The Roman Hat Mystery* (1929). From then on they concentrated on detective fiction, using Ellery Queen both as pseudonym and as the name of their detective. Others of their very popular stories are *The French Powder Mystery* (1930), *The Greek Coffin Mystery* (1932), *The Tragedy of X* (1940), *Double, Double* (1950) and *The Glass Village* (1954). They also wrote under the pseudonym Barnaby Ross, featuring the detective Drury Lane. In 1941 they founded *Ellery Queen's Mystery Magazine*.
▷F M Nevins Jnr, *Royal Bloodline: Ellery Queen, Author and Detective* (1974)

QUEIROS, Raquel de
(1910–)

Major Brazilian novelist, critic and translator, born in Forteleza, the daughter of a planter. Her early novels, written before 1940, are all remarkably mature for so young an author. In *O Quinze* (1930, 'The Year Fifteen') she outdid—even though it inspired her—the *Cane Trash* of Almeida. She rebelled against the patriarchal system she had seen in her youth, became involved with the left wing, and was unable to write as she wished under the dictator Vargas. Her masterpiece is *As Três Marias* (1939, Eng trans, *The Three Marias*, 1939), tracing the lives of three girls after they leave a convent school—in particular that of Maria Guta, who aborts her child rather than have it grow up in a world which would destroy it.
▷F P Ellison, *Brazil's New Novel* (1954)

QUENEAU, Raymond
(1903–76)

French novelist, poet and painter. He was born in Le Havre and educated at the Sorbonne. From 1938, he worked on *Encyclopédie de la Pléiade* and became its director for two decades (1955–75). His novels included *Le Chiendent* (1933, Eng trans *The Bark Tree*, 1968), a witty reworking of Descartes, the untranslatable, punning verse

novel *Chêne et chien* (1937), *Pierrot Mon Ami* (1942, Eng trans *Pierrot*, 1950) and *Zazie dans le métro* (1959, Eng trans *Zazie*, 1960). Queneau was a founder member of OuLiPo, the hermetic Ouvroir de Littérature Potentielle, a philosophy related to the 'Pataphysical 'science of imaginary solutions'; see *La littérature potentielle* (1973). Perhaps Queneau's most famous book is the *Exercices de style* (1947, Eng trans *Exercises in Style*, 1958) which gives a multiplicity of versions of exactly the same literary 'opening'. His verse was published in *Cent mille milliards de poèmes* (1961, Eng trans *One Hundred Million Million Poems*, 1983); an English edition of his poetry appeared in 1970. He also wrote as 'Sally Mara' and published 'her' *Oeuvres complètes* in 1962.
▷R Cobb, *Queneau* (1976)

QUENTAL, Anthero de
(1842–91)

Portuguese poet, born in Ponta Delgada in the Azores. He studied at Lisbon and Coimbra, publishing his first collection of sonnets in 1861 and his *Odes Modernas* in 1865. He followed the latter with a pamphlet, *Good Sense and Good Taste*, which exposed the view that poetry depends upon richness and vitality of ideas rather than upon technical skill with words. He lived in Paris and America from 1866 to 1871, and on his return to Portugal became a leading socialist until, after a severe nervous illness, he committed suicide.
▷J B Carreira, *Anthero de Quental* (1948)

QUENTIN, Dorothy, properly Madeleine Batten
(1911–)

New Zealand writer of romantic fiction who, in 30 years, wrote an average of two novels a year. From *Brave Enterprise* (1939) to *Goldenhaze* (1969), her 59 books are mainly set in a New Zealand which, whether urban or rural, she portrays as an ideal society in a sub-American utopia—clean, bright, efficient and open, with her characters imposed on this backdrop. Only occasionally, as in *Lugano Love Story* (1960), does the scene move to England or Europe. Her books were published in London and written for her large international readership.

QUESNES DE BETHUNE *see* CONON DE BETHUNE

QUEVEDO Y VILLEGAS, Francisco Gómez de
(1580–1645)

Spanish writer, born in Madrid. His father was secretary to the queen, and his mother a lady-in-waiting. He left the University of Alcalá with a reputation for varied scholarship. The fatal result of a duel drove him in 1611 to the court of the Duke of Ossuna, Viceroy of Sicily, who made him his right-hand man, and, when promoted to the viceroyalty of Naples, chose him for Minister of Finance. Quevedo was involved in Ossuna's fall in 1619, and put in prison, but allowed to retire to the Sierra Morena. He returned to Madrid in 1623 and was one of the favourites at the court of Philip IV. In his *Política de Dios* (1626, 'Politics of God') he appealed to the king to be a king, not in name only, but in fact; in 1628 he followed up this attack on government by favourites with an apologue, *Discorso de todos los diablos, o Infierno enmendado* ('Discourse on the Devil's Death; or, Hell Reformed'). He remained, however, on friendly terms with Olivares and accepted the honorary title of royal secretary. In 1639 a memorial in verse to the king, imploring him to look to the miserable condition of his kingdom, was one day placed in Philip's napkin. Quevedo was denounced as the author, arrested and imprisoned in a convent at Leon, where he was struck down by an illness, from which he never recovered. In 1643 Olivares fell from power, and Quevedo was free to return to Madrid. He died two years later. Quevedo was one of the most prolific Spanish poets, but his verses were all written for his friends or for himself, and, except those in the *Flores* of Espinosa (1605), the few pieces published in his lifetime were printed without his consent. His poetry is therefore largely of an occasional character. About a dozen of his short pieces are extant, but of his comedies almost nothing is known. His prose is even more varied than his verse. His first book (1620) was a biography of St Thomas de Villanueva, and his last one of St Paul (1644), and most of his prose is devotional. Of his political works the *Política de Dios* is the main one. His brilliant picaresque novel, the *Historia de la Vida del Buscón Pablos* (1626, Eng trans *The Life and Adventures of Buscon the Witty Spaniard*, 1657), or, as it was called after his death, the *Gran Tacaño*, at once took its place beside Enrique Moreno Baez's *Guzmán de Alfarache*. His five *Sueños* (Eng trans *Visions*, 1640) were printed in 1627; to obtain a licence they were barbarously mutilated.
▷O H Green, *Courtly Love in Quevedo* (1952)

QUINAULT, Philippe
(1635–88)

French playwright, born in Paris. He studied law, then began to write tragi-comedy in the 1650s, having gained some knowledge of high society—the usual setting for the genre—by working as a valet and gentleman-companion

QUINET, Edgar

to members of the aristocracy. He presents love intrigues, using traditional devices such as disguise and double identity. Among his works are *Les coups de l'amour et de la fortune* ('The winds of love and chance'), first performed in 1655, *Le fantôme amoureux* (1656, 'The Amorous Ghost') and *Le mariage de Cambyse* (1659, 'The Marriage of Cambyse'). He is also known for his collaboration with the composer Lulli, for whose operas he provided several libretti. He gave up writing plays in 1686 because of the Church's condemnation of the theatre, and assumed an extreme piety for two years prior to his death.

QUINET, Edgar
(1803–75)

French writer and politician, born in Bourg. He studied at Strasbourg, Geneva, Paris and Heidelberg. The remarkable introduction to his translation of **Johann Herder**'s *Philosophy of History* (1825) won him the friendship of Cousin and Michelet; a government mission to Greece produced *La Grèce moderne* (1830, 'Modern Greece'). *Ahasvérus* (1833), a kind of spiritual imitation of the ancient mysteries, was followed by the less successful poems, 'Napoléon' (1836) and 'Prométhée' (1838); in his *Examen de la vie de Jésus* (1838, 'Investigation of the Life of Jesus') he argued that Strauss was too analytic, and that religion is the very substance of humanity. Appointed Professor of Foreign Literature at Lyons in 1839, he began the lectures which formed his brilliant *Du génie des religions* (1842, 'On the Genius of Religions'); then once recalled to the Collège de France in Paris, he joined Michelet in attacking the Jesuits. His lectures caused so much excitement that the government suppressed them in 1846. At the revolution Quinet took his place on the barricades, and in the National Assembly voted with the extreme left. After the *coup d'état* of 1851 he was exiled to Brussels, from where in 1857 he emigrated to Switzerland. At Brussels he produced *Les Esclaves* (1853, 'The Slaves'), and in Switzerland *Merlin l'Enchanteur* (1860, 'Merlin the Wizard'). Other works were *La Révolution religieuse au XIXᵉ siècle* (1857, 'The Religious Revolution of the 19th Century'), *Histoire de mes idées* (1858, 'History of My Ideas'), *Histoire de la campagne de 1815* (1862, 'History of the Campaign of 1815') and *La Révolution* (1865). After the downfall of Napoleon III he returned to Paris, and during the siege strove to keep patriotism alive. He sat in the National Assemblies at Bordeaux and Versailles, and aroused great enthusiasm by his speeches. His last books were *La Création* (1870), *La République* (1872), *L'Esprit nouveau* (1874, 'The Spirit of the New'), and *Le Livre de l'exilé* (1875, 'The Book of Exile').

▷ A Vales, *Edgar Quinet, sa vie et son oeuvre* (1935)

QUINTANA, Manuel José
(1772–1857)

Spanish poet and advocate, born in Madrid, where his house became a resort of advanced liberals. Besides his classic *Vidas de los Españoles célèbres* (1807–34), he published tragedies and poetry written in a classical style, the best of which are his odes, ardently patriotic yet restrained. On the restoration of Ferdinand VII he was imprisoned (1814–20); but he recanted, and by 1833 had become tutor to Queen Isabella. He was crowned national poet in 1855.
▷ J V Selma, *Ideario de Manuel José Quintana* (1961)

QUINTASKET, Christine see MOURNING DOVE

QUIROGA, Elena
(1919–)

Spanish novelist, born in Santander. She began with a regional novel, *Viento del norte* (1950, 'North Wind'), set in Galicia, but later tried to extend her range. Her most successful novel is reckoned to be *Algo pasa en el calle* (1954, 'Something is Happening in the Street'), which was influenced by **Camilo José Cela**, and is more dramatic than the rest of her work. She is respected but has not yet attracted much critical following—or many translators.

QUIROGA, Horacio
(1878–1937)

Major Uruguayan story writer and (initially) poet, one of the greatest of his generation in Latin America. He was born in Salto. His life was a chapter of horrible accidents out of which he drew his always desperate inspiration to create a new genre: the mature horror story crossed with the animal fable. Influenced by **Lugones**, **Poe** and **Chocano**, he published a collection of *modernista* poems. Quiroga's father shot himself (probably), and so did his first wife and two of his children. He himself shot and killed a friend by accident at the turn of the century, and had to flee to Buenos Aires. He was a manic-depressive, subject to strange states of anxiety, tension, agitated depression and hypomania—all of which he tried to relieve through drink. He became a cotton planter in the Chaco region of Argentina, and no writer has evoked this uncanny wilderness with more accuracy. One critic has called him 'in the last analysis maladjusted'; but another claims that he 'succeeded in releasing himself from his own death-wish', and is therefore 'one of our century's greatest depictors of the extreme situation'. He is not always seen at his best in the English-language collections *Stories of the Jungle* (1922; 1923; 1940), but his work has now generated enormous new interest, both in Spain and elsewhere. He had something of the ability of **Carrasquilla** to see men in animals, and vice versa, but in his tales morbidity is taken to its last extreme. When he learned that he had cancer he shot himself.

▷N Jitrik, *Horacio Quiroga* (1967, in Spanish)

R

RAABE, Wilhelm, pseud **Jakob Corvinus**
(1831–1910)

German novelist, born in Eschershausen in Brunswick. He was a bookseller and student before turning to writing. Reacting against 19th-century progress and materialism, he wrote novels which were often grim, tragic and pessimistic although often alleviated by humour. They include *Der Hungerpastor* (1864, Eng trans *The Hunger-Pastor*, 1885), *Des Reiches Krone* (1870, 'Crown of the Realm') and *Meister Autor* (1871, 'Master Author').
▷H Pongs, *Wilhelm Raabe* (1958)

RABAN, Jonathan
(1942–)

English travel writer and novelist, born in Norfolk. He lectured at the University College of Wales and the University of East Anglia, and his earliest books were works of criticism, including *The Technique of Modern Fiction* (1968) and *The Society of the Poem* (1971). He wrote a study of cities in *Soft City* (1974), and turned to travel writing with *Arabia Through the Looking Glass* (1979), which established him as an important figure in the genre. His vivid style combines the colour of traditional travel narrative with a novelist's eye for telling detail and a social scientist's interest in the historical and sociological context of his experiences. Subsequent travel narratives include *Old Glory* (1981), an account of a voyage down the Mississippi, *Coasting* (1986), and *Hunting Mister Heartbreak* (1991), in which he followed the immigrant trail to America, where he now lives (Seattle). He published a novel, *Foreign Land* (1985), and edited the *Oxford Book of the Sea* (1992). *God, Man and Mrs Thatcher* (1989) is a political polemic.

RABE, David William
(1940–)

American dramatist, born in Iowa, whose preoccupation with modern American history and the Vietnam War, into which Rabe was drafted, pervades his writing. His 'Vietnam trilogy' begins with his first play, *The Basic Training of Pavlo Hummel*, and continues with *Sticks and Bones* (both 1971) and *The Orphan* (1973). In the first, a teenage soldier is killed after an altercation with another; in the second, a blinded serviceman returns home to the US, while the third is a loose modern reworking of **Aeschylus**'s *Oresteia*. However, the tautly written *Streamers* (1976) is considered his best work. Set in an army barracks in Virginia, the piece suggests that war is a natural condition of mankind. Less successful was *Hurlyburly* (1984), a satire set in Hollywood.

RABEARIVELO, Jean-Joseph
(1901–37)

Malagasy (Francophone) poet, the founder of his country's literature; he killed himself when French officials, whose relentlessness had already driven him to drugs, refused to allow him to visit France, where he had hoped to study. He never knew French perfectly but, by a mixture of luck and genius, managed to construct a poetic French which reflected the heart of Malagasy experience. He made use of popular ballad forms of Madagascar, especially the 'hain-teny' (traditional love poetry), to write hauntingly tropical poems evocative of the excited melancholy which was native to him. In English translation is *24 Poems* (1962).

RABELAIS, François
(?1494–?1553)

French satirist, said to have been born at a farmhouse near Chinon, or possibly in the town of Chinon, where his father was an advocate. At nine he was sent to the Benedictine abbey of Seuilly, and from there to the Franciscan house of La Baumette near Angers. He became a novice of the Franciscan order, and entered the monastery of Fontenay le Comte, where he had access to a large library, learned Greek, Hebrew and Arabic, and studied all the Latin and old French authors within his reach, as well as medicine, astronomy, botany and mathematics. In Fontenay he found a friend, André Tiraqueau, a lawyer and scholar; his patron, the Bishop of Maillezais, lived close by and he corresponded with Budaeus. But Franciscan jealousy of the old learning was transformed into jealousy of the new. His books were taken from him and he conceived a loathing for the convent, and fled to a Benedictine house near Orléans. Perhaps through

his friend the bishop, he obtained the pope's permission (1524) to pass from the Franciscan to the Benedictine order. He stayed with the bishop for at least three years. After studying medicine at Montpellier he left in 1532 and became a physician in the hospital. Lyons was then a great intellectual centre. There he began the famous series of books by which he will for ever be remembered. In 1532 there appeared at Lyons fair a popular book, *The Great and Inestimable Chronicles of the Grand and Enormous Giant Gargantua*. It was almost certainly not by Rabelais, but to this book he wrote, in the same year, a sequel, *Pantagruel*, in which serious ideas are set forth side by side with overwhelming nonsense. In 1534 he supplied a first book of his own, a new *Gargantua*, fuller of sense and wisdom than *Pantagruel*. Both books (published under the name of Alcofribas Nasier, an anagram of François Rabelais and translated by Sir **Thomas Urquart**, 1653) had a prodigious success. Meanwhile he had begun his almanacs or *Prognostication Pantagruéline* (Eng trans *Pantagruel's Prognostication*, 1660), which he continued for a number of years; few of them survive. In 1533 he accompanied Jean du Bellay, Bishop of Paris, to Rome; in 1536 he was in Italy again with du Bellay, the latter then a cardinal. There he amused himself with collecting plants and curiosities—to him France owes the melon, artichoke and carnation. He also received permission to go into any Benedictine house which would receive him, and was enabled to hold ecclesiastical offices and to practise medicine. From 1537 (when he took his doctorate) to 1538 he taught at Montpellier. From 1540 to 1543 he was in the service of the cardinal's brother, Guillaume du Bellay, sometimes in Turin (where Guillaume was governor), sometimes in France. Guillaume died in 1543, in which year Rabelais was appointed one of the *maîtres des requêtes*. In 1546 he published his third book, this time under his own name. The Sorbonne condemned it—as it had done its predecessors—and Rabelais fled to Metz, where he practised medicine. In 1547 Francis I died; Henri II sent the French cardinals to Rome; and du Bellay summoned Rabelais there as his physician (1548). In Rome until 1549, he thereafter stayed near Paris; he received two livings from the cardinal in 1551–2, and resigned them two years later. A 'partial edition' of a fourth book had appeared in 1548, the complete book in January 1552–3 (to be banned by the theologians); and a professed fifth book, *L'Isle sonante* ('The Sweet-Sounding Island'), perhaps founded on scraps and notes by Rabelais, in 1562. The riotous licence of his mirth has made Rabelais as many enemies as his wisdom has made him friends, yet his works remain the most astonishing treasury of wit, wisdom, commonsense and satire that the world has ever seen.
▷M A Screech, *Rabelais* (1979)

RABEMANANJARA, Jean-Jacques
(1913–)

Malagasy poet, dramatist and statesman, born in Tamatave. He was a follower and friend of his country's greatest writer, **Rabéarivalo**. The latter was driven to death by French bureaucrats, and Rabemananjara was imprisoned by the French, but he later became a Minister of National Development in the first free government of Madagascar (1960). His poetry is modelled on that of **Senghor** and **Claudel**. His plays, particularly *Les dieux malagaches* (1947, 'The Malagasy Gods'), are more original. His later work embraces a dazzling kind of post-*négritude*.

RACINE, Jean
(1639–99)

French dramatist and poet, born in La Ferté-Milon, the son of a solicitor. He was sent to the college of Beauvais, from where he went to Port Royal in 1655. He studied hard, and discovered a faculty for verse-making and a liking for romance that perturbed his teachers. At 19, when he went to study philosophy at the Collège d'Harcourt, he appears to some extent to have exchanged the severity of his Jansenist upbringing for libertinism and the life of letters. He wrote an ode, *La Nymphe de la Seine* (1660, 'The Nymph of the River Seine'), on the marriage of Louis XIV, finished one piece and began another for the theatre, made the acquaintance of **Jean de la Fontaine**, **Jean Chapelain** and other men of letters, and assisted a cousin who was a secretary to the Duc de Luynes. In 1661 he went to Uzès in Languedoc, hoping in vain to get a benefice from his uncle, the vicar-general of the diocese. Having returned to Paris, he obtained in 1664 a gift from the king for a congratulatory ode. Another ode, titled *La Renommée aux muses* ('The Muses' Reputation'), gained him the lifelong friendship of **Nicolas Boileau**; and now began the famous friendship of 'the four'—Boileau, La Fontaine, **Molière** and Racine. His earliest play, *La Thébaïde ou Les Frères ennemis* (1664, Eng trans *The Fatal Legacy*, 1723), was acted by Molière's company at the Palais Royal. His second, *Alexandre le grand* (1665, Eng trans *Alexander the Great*, 1714), was after its sixth performance played by the rival actors at the Hotel de Bourgogne, which led to a rupture with Molière. Racine showed himself as hostile to **Corneille**. Stung by one of **Nicole**'s *Lettres visionnaires* (1666, 'Visionary Letters') condemning in accordance with Port

Royal ethics the romancer or dramatist as an *empoisonneur public* ('poisoner of the people'), he published a clever letter to the author, full of indecent personal remarks. During the following 10 years Racine produced his greatest works—*Andromaque* (1667, Eng trans *Andromache*, 1675); *Les Plaideurs* (1668, Eng trans *The Litigants*, 1715), satirizing lawyers; *Britannicus* (1669, Eng trans 1714); *Bajazet* (1672, Eng trans *The Sultaness*, 1717); *Mithridate* (1673, Eng trans *Mithridates*, 1926), produced almost at the moment of his admission to the Academy; *Iphigénie* (1675, Eng trans *Achilles; or, Iphigenia in Aulis*, 1700), a masterpiece of pathos; *Phèdre et Hippolyte* (1677, Eng trans *Phaedre and Hippolytus*, 1756), a marvellous representation of human agony; and *Bérénice* (1670, Eng trans *Titus and Berenice*, 1701). Then the *troupe du roi* introduced a rival *Phèdre*, by Jacques Pradon, which was supported by a powerful party. Whether from mortification or from alleged conversion, Racine retired from dramatic work, made his peace with Port Royal, married in June 1677, and settled down to 20 years of domestic happiness. His wife brought him money (as well as two sons and five daughters); and he had found ample profit in the drama, besides enjoying an annual *gratification* that grew to 2000 livres, at least one benefice, and, from 1677, jointly with Boileau, the office of royal historian. In 1689 he wrote *Esther* (Eng trans 1715) for Madame de Maintenon's schoolgirls at Saint-Cyr; *Athalie* (Eng trans *Athaliah*, 1722) followed in 1691. Four *cantiques spirituels* and an admirable *Histoire abrégée de Port-Royal* (1742, 'Brief History of Port-Royal') make up Racine's literary work. In his later years he somehow lost the favour of the king. In France Racine is regarded as the greatest of all masters of tragic pathos; this estimate is not inflated. He took the conventional French tragedy from the stronger hands of Corneille, and added to it all the grace of which it was capable, perfecting exquisitely its versification, and harmoniously subordinating the whole action to the central idea of the one dominant passion.
▷L Goldman, *Racine* (1973)

RADCLIFFE, Ann, née Ward
(1764–1823)

English romantic novelist, born in London. At 23 she married William Radcliffe, a graduate of Oxford and student of law, who became proprietor and editor of the weekly *English Chronicle*. In 1789 she published the first of her Gothic romances, *The Castles of Athlin and Dunbayne*; then followed *A Sicilian Romance* (1790), *The Romance of the Forest* (1791), *The Mysteries of Udolpho* (1794) and *The Italian* (1797). She travelled much, and her journal shows how keen an eye she had for natural scenery and ruins. A sixth romance, *Gaston de Blondeville*, with a metrical tale, 'St Alban's Abbey', and a short Life, was published in 1826. Her reputation among her contemporaries was considerable. She was praised by Sir **Walter Scott**, and influenced writers such as **Byron**, **Shelley** and **Charlotte Brontë**. Her particular brand of writing found many imitators, most of them unfortunately inferior to herself, and prompted **Jane Austen**'s satire *Northanger Abbey*.
▷C F MacIntyre, *Ann Radcliffe in Relation to her Time* (1920)

RADICEVÍC, Branko
(1824–53)

Serbian romantic poet, born in Slavonski Brod. He studied law and medicine in Vienna, but most of his short life was devoted to his lyrical poetry, which became very popular. These poems were important because they were the first in the language to jettison 'poetical' decoration and to partake of natural speech. He was much affected by folk poetry and popular erotic song. He has been described as the 'founder of romantic Serbian poetry'.

RADIGUET, Raymond
(1903–23)

French novelist and poet, born in Saint-Maur. He is best known for two stories, *Le Diable au Corps* (1923, 'The Devil in the Flesh') and *Le Bal du Comte d'Orgel* (1924, 'The Count of Orgel's Ball'). Acclaimed as the 'Rimbaud of the novel', his writing is as austerely controlled as his personal behaviour was erratic and unpredictable. The nature of love is his dominant theme, comparable in his fiction to the high moral conception of love in the tragedies of **Racine**.
▷C R Goesch, *Raymond Radiguet* (1955)

RADNÓTI, Miklós
(1909–44)

Jewish Hungarian poet and translator, murdered (and thus immortalized) by the Nazis while on a forced march. He recorded his difficult childhood in the moving *Ikrek hava* (1939, Eng trans *The Month of Gemini*, 1979). His beginnings as a poet were uncertain and influenced by all kinds of French literary extremes. However, by the time that he published the collection *Jakalj csak, halalriélt* (1936, 'Man Condemned to Death, Just Keep Walking'—an uncanny anticipation of his own murder), it is clear that he was even then trying to reconcile himself to what he already seemed to know would be his fate. This inspired him to his best poetry—redolent of

humanity, and love for his wife—which is contained in the posthumous *Tajtékos ég* (1946, Eng trans *The Clouded Sky*, 1972).
▷*Slavonic Review* (June 1965)

RADUASKAS, Henrikas
(1910–70)
Lithuanian poet whose mature later work, written in exile in America, attracted the attention of **Randall Jarrell**. He has been compared to **Osip Mandelstam**, and is often seen by Lithuanians as their finest poet yet. Some of his poems are translated in *The Green Oak: Selected Lithuanian Poetry* (1962).

RAHBEK, Knud Lyne
(1760–1830)
Danish poet, critic and editor, born in Copenhagen. He became Professor of Aesthetics at Copenhagen University, and edited several literary journals, notably *Den Danske Tilskuer* (the Danish *Spectator*). As well as poetry, he wrote many plays, songs and works on drama.
▷A E Jensen, *Rahbek og Danske Digtere* (1960)

RAICKOVÍC, Stefan
(1928–)
Serbian poet, translator (of **Shakespeare**) and editor, born in Nesresnica. He is a lyrical poet, some of whose work appears in translation in *New Writing in Yugoslavia* (1970, ed B Johnson).

RAIFTERI, Antoine, real name Anthony Raftery
(c.1784–1835)
Irish (Gaelic) poet, born in Lios Ard, County Mayo. At nine he was blinded by smallpox, and he later became a 'wandering bard'— 'with eyes that have no light/With gentleness that has no misery', as he wrote in *Mise Raifteri An File* (nd, 'I Am Raftery the Poet'). Such poems as *Cill Liadan* (nd, 'Killeaden', or 'County Mayo') and the tender love poem to a local beauty *Maire Ni Eidhin* (nd, 'Mary Hynes') were largely part of an oral tradition until Lady Gregory and **Douglas Hyde** collected many of them in *Love Songs of Connacht* (1893; reprinted 1903, 1979). His informed use of rhyme and speech rhythms has led to much of his work being denigrated as 'mere song'. The warm and passionate humanity pervading all his preserved work demands and deserves recognition as some of the finest poetry ever written.
▷Lady Gregory, *Poets and Dreamers* (1903)

RAIMBAUT, Count of Orange
(c.1150–1173)
Provençal Troubadour who inherited the lands of Orange from his mother, Tiburge. Many stories were told about his exploits and early death, and one of the four women Troubadour poets, Beatrice, Countess of Die, is supposed to have addressed love poems to him. He began by writing in the difficult and deliberately esoteric *trobar clus* style, but was persuaded by his friends, who included **Guiraut de Bornelh**, to make it simpler and more straightforward.
▷W Pattison (ed), *The Life and Works of the Troubadour Raimbaut de'Orange* (1952)

RAIMUND, Ferdinand, pseud of Ferdinand Raimann
(1790–1836)
Austrian dramatist, born in Vienna. After serving an apprenticeship to a confectioner, he became a highly successful comic actor, although his aspiration to play the great tragic parts failed. As a playwright he was a leading exponent of the Viennese *Volksstück*, the play written in local dialect; it came to take two distinct forms, the *Zauberstück* (magic farce), set in a fairyworld, and the more plebeian *Lokalstück*. Raimund was a master of the first type of play. His most famous work is *Der Verschwender* (1833, Eng trans *The Spendthrift*, 1949), about the wastrel Julius von Flottwell who is saved by his servant Valentin (a part played by the author), because he is under the protection of a fairy. Some of this still excellent and much studied play is in verse. Raimund—who suffered, like so many of the great humorists, from depression—was bitten by a dog, and, thinking he had contracted rabies, shot himself while on his way to Vienna to consult a doctor.
▷J Michalski, *Ferdinand Raimund* (1968)

RAINE, Craig Anthony
(1944–)
English poet, born in Bishop Auckland, County Durham. Educated at Oxford, he lectured in several colleges. He became poetry editor at Faber and Faber in 1981, but later returned to Oxford. His first collection, *The Onion, Memory* (1978), established a characteristic method of attempting to 'see' familiar things in new and unusual ways, which he developed in even greater depth in the 'alien' viewpoint adopted in *A Martian Sends A Postcard Home* (1979). His work is ingenious, highly wrought and rich in linguistic invention. Later collections include *A Journey to Greece* (1979) and *Rich* (1984), which revealed a greater maturity and directness, and included a prose memoir of his

childhood, 'A Silver Plate'. *1953* (1990) was a version of **Racine**'s drama *Andromaque*.

RAINE, Kathleen Jessie
(1908–)

English poet and critic, educated at Girton College, Cambridge, where she was subsequently a research fellow. Her first volume of verse was *Stone and Flower: Poems 1935–43* (1943), which was inspired by a paramystical appreciation of nature. This has grown somewhat more intellectual but also more hermetically mystical over the years; Raine shows a profound understanding of the symbolic imagination, and has written persuasively about **Blake**, **Yeats**, **Hopkins** and **David Jones**. In more recent years, she has been markedly supportive of the work of Cecil Collins, a visionary painter in the Blake and Palmer tradition; essays include *Cecil Collins: Painter of Paradise* (1979) and a notable appreciation in *The Inner Journey of the Poet* (1982), an essay collection that usefully summarized her basic aesthetic stance. She has been prolific both as critic and poet; later volumes of verse include *The Hollow Hill* (1965), *The Oval Portrait* (1977) and *The Oracle in the Heart* (1980). A *Collected Poems* appeared in 1981.
▷ R J Mills, *Kathleen Raine* (1967)

RAINIS, Janis, pseud of Janis Plieksans
(1865–1929)

Latvian poet, dramatist and politician, who was born in Tadenava, and was for a time in exile owing to his campaigns against the Tsarist Russians. His wife, the poet known as Aspazija, was with him in Switzerland from 1906 until 1920 (the year of Latvian independence). His dignified, German-influenced style made him an illustrious name in his time, and he is still taught in schools. Some of his verse is in *Tricolor Sun* (ed W K Matthews, 1936), and one of his plays, *Speleju, dancoju* (1919) was translated in 1924 as *The Sons of Jacob*.
▷ V Kalve, *Latvian Literature* (1954)

RAJAGOPALACHARI, Chakrovati
(1879–1972)

Tamil (and Anglophone) Indian writer and politician who was associated with Gandhi, served as Nehru's deputy, and who eventually, in despair at Congress Party policies, founded the Swatantra Party. His chief work in English is his translation of the Tamil version of the great classical text, the *Ramayana*. He also wrote for children. A selection of his tales is available in *The Fatal Cart* (1946).

RAKIC, Milan
(1876–1938)

Serbian poet, a diplomat by profession, whose output is small but is much prized for its delicacy and precision (he was a perfectionist), somewhat in the style of the French Parnassians. A few of his poems are translated in Janko Lavrin's *An Anthology of Modern Yugoslav Poetry* (1963).

RAMLER, Karl Wilhelm
(1725–98)

German poet and translator (**Horace**), born in Kilberg. Like **Cowley**, he was taken seriously—as a 'master of form'—in his own day, even by **Goethe**, but is now seen as devoid of originality, and hardly has even Cowley's reputation as a minor poet; but, though unread now, he was a skilled craftsman.

RAMOS, Graciliano
(1892–1953)

Major Brazilian novelist, born in Quebrangulo, Alagoas, the son of a corrupt local judge and an unstable mother. If anyone can be considered to be the heir of the incomparable **Machado de Assis**, then it must be Ramos, who wrote the best prose of his generation. As a not very convinced communist, he was imprisoned by President Vargas in a concentration camp (1936), and his experiences there (recorded in his scarifying *Memórias do Cárcere*, 1953, 'Memories of Imprisonment') led to his early death. He was a realistic and, most essentially, a psychologically penetrating novelist of great power. He took a while to discover himself: his first novel, *Caetés* (1933), the name of a tribe which was known to have practised cannibalism, does not display his full subtlety and power, because its thesis, that everyone acts only from selfishness, is rather too glibly adhered to. But its successor, *São Bernardo* (1934, Eng trans, *Saint Bernard*, 1940), about a guilty plant owner, is a great novel by any standards. *Angústia* (1936, Eng trans *Anguish*, 1940), another masterpiece, is probably the most lucid and moving study of a sex killer written in the 20th century: the crime is attributed to a backlander's inability to function as a human being in a malevolent city. *Vidas sêcas* (1938, Eng trans *Barren Lives*, 1965) abandons the stream-of-consciousness method of its predecessor: it is the third-person narrative account of a backlander driven, finally, to the city, and to defeat. Ramos's collected works appeared in Brazil in 1961–2.
▷ B M Woodbridge, *Graciliano Ramos* (1954)

RAMSAY, Allan
(c.1685–1758)

Scottish poet, born in Leadhills, Lanarkshire. His father was manager of Lord Hopetoun's mines there, and his mother, Alice Bower, was the daughter of a Derbyshire mining expert. In 1704 he was apprenticed for five years to a wigmaker in Edinburgh. By 1718 he had become known as a poet, having issued several short humorous satires printed as broadsides. He had also written (1716–18) two additional cantos to the old Scots poem of *Christ's Kirk on the Green*, cheerful pictures of rustic life and broad humour. Ramsay then started business as bookseller, later adding a circulating library (1725), apparently the first in Britain. 'Honest Allan's' career was eminently prosperous, although the theatre he built in Edinburgh at his own expense (1736) was soon closed down by the magistrates. In 1740 he built himself a quaint house (the 'goose-pie') on the Castle Hill, where he spent his last years in retirement. He was buried in Greyfriars' Churchyard. Among his works are *Tartana, or the Plaid* (1718), *Poems* (collected edition published by subscription in 1721, by which it is said he realized 400 guineas—other editions in 1720, 1727, 1728), *Fables and Tales* (1722), *Fair Assembly* (1723), *Health, a Poem* (1724), *The Monk and the Miller's Wife* (1724), *The Tea-table Miscellany*, a collection of songs (4 vols, 1724–37), *The Evergreen* (1724), *The Gentle Shepherd, a Pastoral Comedy* (1725)—his best and most popular work, and *Thirty Fables* (1730).

RAMUZ, Charles-Ferdinand
(1878–1947)

Swiss writer, born in Cully near Lausanne. He wrote in French, mainly about life in his native canton of Vaud. His first book, *Le Petit Village* ('The Little Village'), appeared in 1903, and from then on he wrote prolifically. His pure prose style and fine descriptive power won him wide admiration and repute, his European popularity being somewhat tempered in Britain, though he has been translated into English—*Beauté sur la terre* (1927, Eng trans *Beauty on Earth*, 1929) and *Présence de la mort* (1922, Eng trans *The Triumph of Death*, 1946). Other writings include *Jean Luc persécuté* (1909, 'Jean Luc Persecuted') and *Besoin de grandeur* (1937, 'Need for Grandeur'). He wrote the narration for Stravinsky's *A Soldier's Tale*.
▷G Guisan, *Charles-Ferdinand Ramuz* (1967)

RAND, Ayn
(1905–82)

American conservative theorist and writer of propagandist fiction. She was born and educated in pre-revolutionary Russia but was brought to the USA as a child and seems to have overdosed rapidly on American individualism. Her Objectivist 'philosophy' was premised on enlightened selfishness and rejected altruistic welfarism in favour of aggressive self-reliance. Her four novels were little more than vehicles for these ideas. The best-known is perhaps *The Fountainhead* (1943), which was filmed starring Gary Cooper; others are *We, the Living* (1936), *Anthem* (1938) and *Atlas Shrugged* (1957). For anyone unable to absorb too much of her heated intellectual melodrama, there were briefer, cooler essays: *For the New Intellectual* (1961) and *The Romantic Manifesto* (1969). There was a strong revival of interest in Rand's work during the Reagan presidency, but this has rapidly faded.

RANDALL, James Ryder
(1839–1908)

American poet, born in Baltimore. He was first a teacher, then a journalist. His lyrics, which in the Civil War gave powerful aid to the Southern cause, include 'Maryland, My Maryland' (1861), 'Stonewall Jackson' and 'There's life in the old land yet'. A collected *Poems* appeared posthumously in 1910.

RANDOLPH, Thomas
(1605–35)

English poet and dramatist, born in Newnham near Daventry. He studied at Westminster School and Trinity College, Cambridge, where he was elected a fellow, and soon began to write, gaining the friendship of **Ben Jonson** and leading a boisterous life. He left a number of bright, fanciful poems, and six plays: *Aristippus, or the Jovial Philosopher* (1631); *The Conceited Peddler* (1631); *The Jealous Lovers* (1632); *The Muses' Looking-glass* (1632); *Amyntas, or the Impossible Dowry* (1635); and *Hey for Honesty* (1651).
▷S A and D R Tannenbaum, *Thomas Randolph* (1947)

RANSOM, John Crowe
(1888–1974)

American poet and critic, born in Tennessee. His family were Methodists and he was educated locally and at Oxford. He co-founded a little magazine called *The Fugitive* which, though short-lived (1922–5), established a pattern for the revival of post-bellum Southern literature—formal, classical, agrarian—and lent its name to a significant movement in American literature. He had a long association with Kenyon College (1937–58) and was formative in the founding of the *Kenyon Review*, which beat a drum for the New Criticism. His poetry came early in his career. *Poems About God* (1919), *Chills and Fever* (1924) and *Two Gentlemen in Bonds*

(1927) illustrate his aptitude as a balladist and elegist. Critical books include *God Without Thunder* (1930) and *The New Criticism* (1941).

▷T H Parsons, *John Crowe Ransom* (1969)

RANSOME, Arthur Mitchell
(1884–1967)

English journalist and writer of children's books, born in Leeds. His father was a history professor, and he was educated at Rugby where he was a poor scholar and—by virtue of bad eyesight—inept at games. He worked as an office boy in a publishing house before graduating to ghost-writing, reviewing and writing short stories, meanwhile living a bohemian existence. He became a reporter on the *Daily News* and, in 1919, for the *Manchester Guardian*. He was widely travelled and, having learned Russian in 1913, was sent to cover the Revolution, a welcome relief from his stormy relationship with his first wife. They divorced in 1924 and he married Trotsky's secretary, Evgenia Shelepin, with whom he fled from Russia, staying for a while in Estonia before settling in the Lake District. He had been a published author for a quarter of a century before the appearance of *Swallows and Amazons* (1930), the first of 12 perennially popular novels featuring two families of adventurous but responsible children, the Blacketts and the Walkers, who spend their school holidays revelling in the open air, free from the cramping attention of adults. Of his numerous other books, *Old Peter's Russian Tales* (1916) is worthy of note. *The Autobiography of Arthur Ransome* (1976) is interesting but unrevealing.

▷A B Shelley, *Arthur Ransome* (1960)

RAO, Raja
(1909–)

Indian novelist and short-story writer, born into the Brahmin caste in the south of the country. *Kanthapura* (1938), a novel, and the short-story collection *The Cow of the Barricades* (1947) both deal with the Indian independence movement, which he supported. His best-known work in English—and probably his best altogether—is *The Serpent and the Rope* (1960), a semi-autobiographical novel about an Indian's coming of age in France. His later, less acclaimed, novels include *The Policeman and the Rose* (1977).

RAPHAEL, Frederic Michael
(1931–)

American novelist, educated and resident in the UK. After Charterhouse School, he studied at St John's College, Oxford, an experience reflected in *The Glittering Prizes* (1976),

an autobiographical *roman à clef* which later set new standards as a television drama. Raphael's first novel was *Obbligato* (1956), about a singer; his third book was *The Limits of Love* (1960), the story of a deracinated Jew coming to terms with the lack of an informing system of belief. Raphael is a liberal agnostic, but—as in *The Glittering Prizes*—is strongly aware of how corrosive un-belief can be. *The Graduate Wife* and *The Trouble With England* (both 1962) are effective satires with a firm psychological grasp; *Richard's Things* (1973) is bolder and more abrasive. In the 1970s, Raphael seemed concerned to dramatize aspects of his own creative dilemma, but always without sentimentality and with impressive honesty. *Heaven and Earth* (1985) handled big themes without portentousness. Raphael's gift for dialogue lent itself to drama; he has written extensively for stage, screen and television, including scripts for **Hardy**'s *Far From the Madding Crowd* (1967) and **Iris Murdoch**'s *The Severed Head* (1970). Critically underpraised, he is a writer of significant intelligence; his judgements of others can be seen, for example, in *Cracks in the Ice: Views and Reviews* (1979).

RASHI, abbreviation of Rabbi Shelomoh Izhaqi, otherwise Solomon Ben Isaac
(1040–1105)

French Hebrew poet, who was born in Troyes, where he founded a Talmudic academy. His influence on Jewish thinking cannot be overestimated, for his commentaries on the Bible were read by all educated Jews throughout the Middle Ages, and beyond. Although difficult to read and understand now, his poetry is distinguished by its simplicity and its powerful devotional feeling.

▷H Hailperin, *Rashi and the Christian Scholars* (1963)

RASMUSSEN, Halfdan
(1915–)

Danish poet. He was born in Copenhagen, to a working-class family, and passed much of his early life in poverty. During World War II his first book of verse, *Soldat eller menske* (1941, 'Soldier or Man'), became an important rallying text for the Danish Resistance. The dark tone persisted after the war with *Korte skygger* (1946, 'Foreshortened Shadows') and other volumes, but increasingly he held up childhood and 'primitive' societies as alternatives to the compromised and over-intellectualized West; the war in Vietnam provided a particularly strong focus for these feelings. Rasmussen has written many volumes of verse for children—'børnerim' —of which perhaps the best is *Hokus Pokus* (1969, Eng trans *Hocus Pocus*, 1973). These have given him a broad and lasting appeal in Denmark.

▷ E Clausen, *Hilsen til Halfdan* (1983)

RASPUTIN, Valentin Grigorevich
(1937–)

Russo–Siberian novelist and a leading figure in the 'village' movement. He was born in Ust'-Uda, in the lakeland north of Irkutsk, where he attended university and still lives. His first novel, *Kray vozle samovo neba* (1966, 'The Land that Borders Heaven'), established him as a powerful voice in a new trans-Ural consciousness, in which young Siberian writers set themselves apart from the literary world of the cities, affirming localism over urban values, Asiatic rather than European themes and ideas. The first of his books to be translated into English was *Zhivi i pomni* (1975), which appeared as *Live and Remember* in 1978; but in 1981 the earlier *Den'gi dlya Marii* (1968, Eng trans *Money for Maria*, 1968) and *Posledny srok* (1976, Eng trans *Borrowed Time*, 1976) were collected under the general rubric *Two Village Tales*. Rasputin has written slowly and patiently, and is not prolific; however, his work significantly anticipates the de-Sovietization of Russia.

RASTELL, John
(1475–1536)

English printer, lawyer and dramatist, born in Coventry. He was called to the Bar and in 1510 set up his own printing press. Married to the sister of Sir Thomas More, he printed More's *Life of Pico*, a grammar by Linacre, the only copy of **Henry Medwall**'s play *Fulgens and Lucres*, and many law books. Himself a dramatist, his plays, printed on his own press, include *Nature of the Four Elements* (1519), *Of Gentylness and Nobylyte . . .* (c.1527) and *Calisto and Meleboea* (c.1527). An ingenious deviser of pageants, he presented several of them at court. His expedition to found a settlement in the 'New Found Lands' in 1517 came to nothing through mutiny on his ship.

▷ A W Reed, *Early Tudor Drama* (1926)

RATHERIUS (RATHER) OF LIEGE
(c.887–974)

Cleric and writer, born in Liège. Ratherius became Bishop of Verona three times, losing the position repeatedly after political intrigue. He was a hugely influential man of letters in 10th-century Europe—his *Praeloquia* (collections of sermons and other writings) were to be found in every centre of learning in Christendom. His writings, often illustrated with autobiographical anecdotes, argue that believers should go out and do battle with evil, and that a strict monastic regime is the best means of preparing for this. He also complains ceaselessly about the corruption, sloth and uxoriousness of the clergy. This did little to increase his popularity and made him an easier target for those who would intrigue against him.

RATOSH, Yonathan
(1908–)

Hebrew poet, born in Russia, but who went to Palestine early, and who wrote his unique and sonorous poetry in a special dialect, a mixture of Hebrew and the extinct language Ugaritic. The 'Canaanite' group, of whom he was one, wished to embrace a semitic state, and regarded the diaspora as an 'inconsequential period in Jewish history'. The notion of a semitic state has not been popular in Israel, and for this reason many readers have been cut off from an exceedingly original and powerful poet, and author of some of the most erotic poetry of the 20th century. Titles include *Yuhud* (1952).

RATTIGAN, Sir Terence Mervyn
(1911–77)

English playwright, born in London. Educated at Harrow and Oxford, he scored a considerable success with his comedy *French Without Tears* (1936). After that, most of his works, with the possible exception of *Adventure Story* (1949), a play about Alexander the Great, were internationally acclaimed; they reveal not only a wide range of imagination but a deepening psychological knowledge. Best known are *The Winslow Boy* (1946), based on the Archer Shee case, *The Browning Version* (1948), *The Deep Blue Sea* (1952), *Separate Tables* (1954) and *Ross* (1960), a fictional treatment of T E Lawrence. He was responsible for several successful films made from his own and other works.

RATUSHINSKAYA, Irina
(1954–)

Russian poet and literary *cause célèbre*. Ratushinskaya was achieving a reputation as a skilled poet with a concern for social issues in Moscow when, in the 1970s, she began to get into trouble with the Soviet authorities who found her work distasteful. She was eventually sentenced to seven years' internal exile for anti-Soviet activities. Her cause was, however, taken up in the West, where she found fame and a market for her verse. *No I'm Not Afraid* (1986) was, for a poetry book, very successful, and was followed by further volumes, notably *Dance with a Shadow* (1992). On her release from prison camp she went to live in the West, and has since published two volumes of autobiography: *Grey is the Colour of Hope* (1989) and *In the Beginning* (1991).

RAU, Santha Rama
(1923–)
Indian writer, who was educated in England and married an Englishman. Her father was an ambassador. She has written autobiographical works, and one novel, *Remember the House* (1956), influenced by **E M Forster**, whose *Passage to India* she successfully dramatized (1960).

RAVEN, Simon Arthur Noël
(1927–)
English novelist and playwright, born in London and educated at Charterhouse School and King's College, Cambridge. He began to write after a period in the army. His fictional output is mostly concentrated in two large cycles: *Alms for Oblivion* (1964–75) consisted of 10 novels, beginning with *The Rich Pay Late* and ending (appropriately) with *The Survivors*. A later sequence, entitled *The First-Born of Egypt*, was commenced in 1984 with *Morning Star* and is also largely concerned with the foibles and moral hubris of the upper classes. Of the novels that stand outwith the two cycles, *Doctors Wear Scarlet* (1960) and *The Roses of Picardie* (1980), are outstanding. Raven wrote screenplays for the James Bond film *On Her Majesty's Secret Service* (1969) and the bleak hostile school story, *Unman, Wittering and Zigo* (1971). He has adapted a large number of books for television, by **Aldous Huxley** and **W Somerset Maugham**, among others.

RAVENSCROFT, Edward
(1644–1704)
English lawyer turned playwright, born in London into the family of a lawyer. He abandoned law after the enormous success of his farce, *The Citizen Turn'd Gentleman* (1672) to concentrate on writing for the stage, achieving further successes with *Scaramouch, The London Cuckolds* and his last play, *The Anatomist* (all published posthumously). His work is bawdy, often downright crude, and very funny, but if his reputation has declined since his own day, it is due in large part to the prevalence of more censorious attitudes in public life rather than to a lack of sophistication in his work. Ravenscroft drew on a remarkably eclectic set of European influences, from **Molière** to *commedia dell'arte*, and is the first successful and consistent *farceur* in the history of the British stage.

RAWLINGS, Marjorie
(1896–1953)
American novelist, born in Washington DC and educated at the University of Wisconsin,

Madison. She worked as a journalist, an editor, and a syndicated verse writer before devoting herself to full-time creative writing in 1928. She was awarded the **O Henry** Award in 1933 for her short story 'Gal Young Un'. She published her first novel, *South Moon Under*, in the same year but is best remembered for her Pulitzer Prize-winning novel *The Yearling* (1938), later filmed, which centres on a young boy's attachment to his pet fawn. Her autobiographical work *Cross Creek* (1942) heightened her reputation as a 'regionalist' writer.
▷ E Silverthorne, *Marjorie Kinnan Rawlings: Sojourner at Cross Creek* (1988)

RAYHANI, Amin
(1876–1940)
Lebanese Arabic poet, who initiated the modern Arabic prose poem. Some of his work was written in English.
▷ A J Arberry (ed and translator), *Modern Arabic Poetry* (1950)

RAYNOUARD, François Juste Marie
(1761–1836)
French poet and philologist, born in Brignoles in Provence. A prosperous Paris advocate, in 1791 he entered the legislative assembly. Later he joined the Girondins, and was imprisoned. His poems and tragedies were successful, and in 1807 he was elected to the Academy, of which he became permanent secretary in 1817. He was elected to the imperial legislative body in 1806 and 1811. After 1816 he wrote on the Provençal language and literature, notably his *Lexique Roman* (1838–44).

REA, Domenico
(1921–)
Italian novelist and story writer, born near Naples, the legend of whose merry exoticism he seeks to challenge in such harsh tales of poverty as *Quel che vide Cummeo* (1955, 'What Cummeo Saw'). *Una vampata di rossore* (1959, Eng trans *A Blush of Shame*, 1963) is his most substantial work.
▷ L Russo, *I narratore* (1968)

READ, Sir Herbert Edward
(1893–1968)
English art historian, critic and poet, born near Kirby Moorside, Yorkshire. Educated in Halifax and at Leeds University, he became Assistant Keeper at the Victoria and Albert Museum in London (1922–31) and Professor of Fine Art at Edinburgh University (1931–3); he was Editor of the *Burlington Magazine* (1933–9), and held academic posts at Cambridge, Liverpool, London, and Harvard universities. As an art critic he revived interest

in the 19th-century Romantic movement, and championed modern art movements in Britain. His broad interests extended to industrial design, and his *Art and Industry* (1936) was seminal in the development of this new discipline. He was director of the first major British design consultancy, the Design Research Unit. As a poet he wrote *Naked Warriors* (1919, based on his war experiences), and published his *Collected Poems* in 1946. His other publications include *English Prose Style* (1928), *The Meaning of Art* (1931), *Form in Modern Poetry* (1932), *Art Now* (1933), *Art and Society* (1936), *The Philosophy of Modern Art* (1952), and the autobiographical *Annals of Innocence and Experience* (1940). His son is the writer **Piers Paul Read**.

▷H Treece, *Herbert Read* (1944)

READ, Piers Paul
(1941–)

English novelist and author of non-fiction, born in Beaconsfield, Buckinghamshire. The son of the poet and art critic Sir **Herbert Read**, he was educated at a Roman Catholic school, and published his first novel, *Game in Heaven With Tussy Marx*, in 1966. He has since become established as a mainstream storyteller, a realist whose work sympathetically deliberates moral and ethical issues. *A Married Man* (1979) is a representative work. His non-fiction books extend this interest, although rather more sensationally. *Alive! The Story of the Andes Survivors* (1974) is an account of the aftermath of an air crash in remote mountains, during which a group of athletes cannibalized fellow passengers in order to survive. *The Train Robbers* (1978) follows the prison lives and domestic intrigues of those who robbed a London–Glasgow mail train in 1963.

READE, Charles
(1814–84)

English novelist and playwright, born in Ipsden House, Oxfordshire, the youngest of eleven. After five harrowing years at Iffley, and six under two milder private tutors, in 1831 he gained a scholarship at Magdalen College, Oxford, and in 1835, having taken third-class honours, was duly elected to a lay fellowship. Next year he entered Lincoln's Inn, and in 1843 was called to the Bar, but never practised. In 1850 he first tried to write for the stage, producing about 13 dramas. Through one of these dramas he formed a platonic friendship with Mrs Seymour, a warmhearted actress, who from 1854 until her death (1879) kept house for him. His life after 1852 is a succession of plays by which he lost money, and novels that won profit and fame. These novels illustrate social injustice

and cruelty in one form or another, and his writing is realistic and vivid. They include *Peg Woffington* (1852), *Hard Cash* (1863), *Foul Play* (1869, with **Dion Boucicault**), *A Terrible Temptation* (1871) and *A Woman-hater* (1877). His masterpiece was his long, historical novel of the 15th century, *The Cloister and the Hearth* (1861).

▷M Elvin, *Charles Reade* (1931)

READING, Peter
(1946–)

English poet, born in Liverpool. He has worked as a lecturer and as a weighbridge operator. Influenced by **e e cummings**, and much given to pastiche, Reading's most characteristic poem is *C* (1984), a 'poem of 100 proses', supposedly assembled by a terminally-ill cancer patient. In other poems Reading mixes newsprint with his own inventions, in a rather uncertain manner, and takes a high risk with the reader with ironic and occasionally disturbing strategies. There is no lyrical element in his prolific verse, even in *The Essential Reading* (1986), which has been edited by Alan Jenkins.

REANEY, James
(1926–)

Canadian playwright and poet, born in South Easthope, Ontario, and educated at the University of Toronto. He won Governor General's Awards for Poetry (1950, 1959 and 1962) and Drama (1963). The founding editor of *Alphabet*, an active member of theatre groups in London and Winnipeg, a university lecturer and a critic, he perceives himself to be 'a teacher first' and observes of his work: 'I want to tell the story of the people I live with in Southwestern Ontario'. The poetic libretto of *Twelve Letters to a Small Town* (1962) and the dramatic trilogy of *The Donnellys* (performed on a cross-Canada tour in 1975), in particular, demonstrate the success of his endeavour.

RÈBORA, Clemente
(1885–1957)

Italian poet from Milan, whose first collection, *Frammente lirici* ('Lyrical Fragments'), was published in 1913. Soon afterwards he was badly wounded while on military service; he then became interested in **Leo Tolstoy**, translating his *Happy Ever After*, and devoted himself to care of the poor, living amongst them. In 1931 he entered a religious order, the Rosminian Fathers of Domodossala, and was ordained as a priest in 1936. He had a profound influence on his friend **Carlo Betocchi**. In his final poems, in *I canti d'infermità* (1956, 'Songs of Illness'), he 'identified poetry with liturgy', 'verse had become a concrete means of expressing his love for God and his fellow man'. Because this poetry is not merely pious, but rather fully aware of the difficulties of human existence, it is still frequently anthologized and gratefully read. There are English translations in M Marchione (ed), *Twentieth-Century Italian Poetry* (1974).

REBREANU, Liviu
(1885–1944)

Romanian novelist who, with **Duiliu Zam-firescu**, developed fiction in his country. He had a wide education (in Germany and Hungary as well as in Romania). His *Ion* (1920) was an almost epic account of Transylvanian peasant life. This he followed with the poignant *Padurea spînzuratilor* (1922, Eng trans *The Forest of the Damned*, 1930), which is worthy to be ranked with **Arnold Zweig**'s *Sergeant Grischa* as an indictment of injustice, but which never gained its deserved reputation. It is dedicated to the memory of his brother Emil, judicially murdered by the Austrians on the Romanian front in 1917. *Rascoala* (1933, Eng trans *The Uprising*, 1964) is a sequel to *Ion*, a violent and moving realization of the peasant uprising of 1907.

RECHY, John Francisco
(1934–)

American novelist, born and educated in El Paso, Texas. He gained instant fame—or notoriety—with his first novel, *City of Night* (1963), a frank and unsentimental study of homosexuality in the American city. To a degree, his later fiction has been a reworking of this first book, but by no means in a negative sense. For Rechy, the gay world is morally hermetic, a freemasonry governed by rules and conventions which are the opposite, or 'night', aspect of those that apply in straight society. The almost biblical associations of the title *City of Night* (which also echoes **James Thompson**'s 'The City of Dreadful Night') is sustained in Rechy's second book *Numbers* (1967). In *This Day's Death* (1970) it appears that Rechy is debunking the **Hemingway** myth. Other novels include *Rushes* (1979) and *Marilyn's Daughter* (1988). Rechy's defiant anti-revisionism—and underlying biblical symbolism—is well represented in *The Sexual Outlaw* (1978), an account of three days in the 'sexual underground'.

REDCAM, Tom, pseud of **Thomas Macdermot**
(1870–1933)

West Indian poet and novelist. He has been called, and there have been few to demur, 'the unpromising colonial father of West Indian

poetry', and his work is now seldom read or referred to.

REDGROVE, Peter William
(1932–)

English poet and novelist, born in Kingston, Surrey. He was educated at Queen's College, Cambridge, worked as a scientific journalist, taught at Falmouth School of Art (1966–83), and has held a number of poet-in-residence positions. He was a founder member of The Group in the 1950s, and published his first collection, *The Collector*, in 1960. His poetry is rich in both its linguistic density and visual imagery, and he has shown a persistent fascination with dreams and the unconscious, a subject he addressed in the study *The Black Goddess and the Sixth Sense* (1987). He has published numerous collections of poems, including *The Moon Disposes: Poems 1954–1987* (1987, enlarged 1989). His other writings include seven novels, plays, stories, and some non-fiction, including *The Wise Wound* (1978), a study of the fertility cycle, co-written with his wife, Penelope Shuttle.

REDI, Francesco
(1626–97)

Italian physician and poet, born in Arezzo. He studied at Florence and Pisa, and became physician to the dukes of Tuscany. He wrote a book on animal parasites and proved by a series of experiments that maggots cannot form on meat which has been covered. His best-known poem is the dithyrambic celebration of Bacchus and the wines of Tuscany, *Bacco In Toscana* (1685). He also wrote love sonnets on the **Petrarch**an model, and more earthy poems.
▷G Imbert, *Francesco Redi, l'uomo* (1975)

REDON, Odilon
(1840–1916)

French painter and lithographer, born in Bordeaux, usually regarded as a forerunner of Surrealism because of his use of dream images in his work. He made many charcoal drawings and lithographs of extraordinary imaginative power, but after 1900 he painted, especially in pastel, pictures of flowers and portraits in intense colour. He was also a brilliant writer; his diaries (1867–1915) were published as *A soi-même* ('To Himself') in 1922, and his *Lettres* in 1923.

REED, Bill
(1939–)

Australian playwright and novelist, born in Perth. His published plays range from *Burke's Company* (1969), on the tragic last days of the Burke and Wills expedition in 1861 and its aftermath, to *Truganini* (1977), a sequence of plays which contains *King Billy's Bones* and deals with the treatment of aborigines in colonial Australia. His later novels include the Gothic horror of *Stigmata* (1980), which won the Australian Natives' Association Literary Award for that year, and a fantasy on Sydney's underworld, *Crooks* (1984).

REED, Henry
(1914–)

English poet and dramatist. He was born in Birmingham and educated at the university there. After a period in the Army and at the Foreign Office, he made his living as a freelance writer and journalist. He established a reputation with his plays for radio, particularly those concerning the mannishly modernist composer Hilda Tablet (who was probably modelled on Ethel Smyth, among others). *The Private Life of Hilda Tablet* (1945) has been broadcast several times. Reed's reputation as a poet rests not so much on his own volume, *A Map of Verona* (1947), but on a single poem, 'Chard Whitlow', which is a brilliant satire of **T S Eliot**'s ponderously philosophical 'Burnt Norton' in *Four Quartets*. It is a rare example of a parody that is almost better than the original.

REED, Ishmael Scott
(1938–)

American novelist, poet and publisher. Born in Chattanooga, Tennessee, he grew up and was educated in Buffalo, New York. After graduation, he wrote for *Empire Star Weekly* before founding his own magazine, the *East Village Other*, which was dedicated to experimental writing. In 1967, Reed published his first novel, *The Freelance Pallbearers*, which was controversial for its sarcastic treatment of black politics. In his next and best novel, *Yellow Back Radio Broke Down* (1969), Reed introduced the concept of Hoodoo, a compression of racial and cultural mythologies represented by the person of Loop Garoo; Reed's best-known poem began 'I am a cowboy in the boat of Ra'. Later novels, such as *The Last Days of Louisiana Red* (1974), *Flight to Canada* (1976) and *Reckless Eyeballing* (1986), whose title echoed the indictment of a lynch victim, are more direct in their examination of the Afro–American condition, and less confident in their linguistic and typographical radicalism. Reed's poetry appeared in *Conjure* (1972), a collection of pieces from the sixties, in *Chattanooga* (1973) and in *New and Collected Poetry* (1988).

REED, Talbot Baines
(1852–93)

English author of books for boys, born in London, the son of Sir Charles Reed (1819–

81), chairman of the London School Board. He became head of his father's firm of typefounders, and wrote books on the history of printing (such as *History of the Old English Letter-foundries* (1887). His robust, moral, but entertaining school stories first appeared in the *Boy's Own Paper*. They include *The Fifth Form at St Dominic's* (1881), *The Master of the Shell* (1887) and *Cockhouse at Fellsgarth* (1891).

REES, Leslie
(1905–)

Australian playwright and author, born in Perth. A drama critic in London during the 1930s, he then became national radio drama editor for the Australian Broadcasting Corporation until 1966. He wrote the standard *History of Australian Drama* (1973–8) and has edited a number of anthologies, including *Australian Radio Plays* (1946). His own *Sub-Editor's Room* (1937) later became the first play to appear on Australian television, and he worked with **Ruth Park** on the dramatization of her *The Harp in the South* (1949). He has written much for children, including adventure tales such as *Panic in the Cattle Country* (1974), and, for younger readers, tales of animal wildlife in *The Story of Shy the Platypus* (1944). With his wife Coralie Clarke he wrote books of Australian travel such as *Spinifex Walkabout* (1953) and *People of the Big Sky Country* (1970).
▷ *Hold Fast to Dreams* (1982)

REES, Rosemary
(1876–1963)

New Zealand writer of popular fiction, whose first book was *April's Sowing* (1924). Some 20 books followed, of which *Wild, Wild Heart* (1928), *Home's Where the Heart Is* (1935) and *Love is a Lonely Land* (1958) may be taken as typical. She also wrote the popular *New Zealand Holiday* (1933) which, however, portrayed her country as a comfortable middle-class paradise—even in the 1930s. Superficially 'moral', her plots pose no severe problems for the characters, and social issues are neatly evaded.

REESE, Lizette Woodworth
(1856–1935)

American poet and schoolteacher, born in Maryland. *A Branch of May* (1887), Reese's first collection, was welcomed for its eschewal of Victorian sentimentality in favour of a spare, aphoristic style which some have seen as the first step, in the USA, towards modern Symbolism. But although one of Reese's sonnets—'Tears'—achieved enormous popularity and was much anthologized, she was not a Movement poet, preferring to ply a craft

REEVE, Clara

of private passion whilst holding down a job as high-school teacher for her entire working life. In her last years she published two volumes of autobiography.
▷ *A Victorian Village* (1929); *The York Road* (1931)

REEVE, Clara
(1729–1807)

English novelist of the 'Gothic' school, born in Ipswich, the daughter of the rector of Freston. She translated **John Barclay**'s *Argenis* (1772), and wrote *The Champion of Virtue, a Gothic Story* (1777), renamed *The Old English Baron*, which was avowedly an imitation of **Horace Walpole**'s *The Castle of Otranto*. Her other novels were *The Two Mentors* (1783), *The Exiles* (1788), *The School for Widows* (1791), *Memoirs of Sir Roger de Clarendon* (1793), and *Destination* (1799). She also wrote a critical account of *The Progress of Romance* (1785).
▷ Sir Walter Scott, memoir in *Old English Baron* (1823)

REEVES, James, pseud of John Morris Reeves
(1909–78)

English poet, critic, anthologist and children's writer, born in Finchley, London. He is best known as a writer (of poetry and fiction) for children, but as a poet he gradually built up a high reputation: **Edwin Muir** made the comment that 'perfection rarely draws attention to itself'; another critic described him as a 'uniquely English crepuscular poet in the psychological tradition of Gozzano'. *The Idiom of the People* (1958), an edition of the folksongs originally collected by Cecil Sharpe, stimulated many writers, including **Anthony Burgess**. With **Martin Seymour-Smith** he wrote, among other books, *Inside Poetry* (1968), an influential book of practical criticism.
▷ *Collected Poems* (1977)

REEVES, William Pember
(1857–1932)

New Zealand politician, historian, anthologist and poet, born in Lyttleton, Canterbury, and best known for his long poem 'A Colonist in his Garden', which was included in his *New Zealand and Other Poems* (1898). He published *The Passing of the Forest* privately in 1925; with George Phipps Williams he published two collections of light verse, and with J Ward *The Book of Canterbury Rhymes* (1866, rev edn 1883), a significant early anthology of New Zealand colonial verse. He was a member of cabinet from 1891 to 1896, but in 1896 left politics, moving to London as Agent-General for New Zealand,

and in 1905 becoming New Zealand's first High Commissioner. During this time he wrote a number of books on his homeland, of which *The Long White Cloud: Ao Tea Roa* (1898, rev edn 1924) includes many incisive yet affectionate portraits of contemporary personalities.
▷ K Sinclair, *William Pember Reeves: New Zealand Fabian* (1965)

REGINALD OF CANTERBURY
(fl.1080)

French poet from Poitou, who spent most of his life as a monk at the abbey of St Augustine in Canterbury. His best-known work is *Vita Sancti Malchi*, a lengthy verse biography of the hermit St Malchus.

REGNARD, Jean François
(1655–1709)

French comic dramatist, born in Paris, the son of a rich shopkeeper. He found himself at the age of 20 the master of a considerable fortune, and set out on his travels. In his autobiographical romance, *La Provençale* ('A Woman from Provence'), he tells of his and his Provençal mistress's capture and sale as slaves by Algerian corsairs, their bondage in Constantinople, and their ransom. After wanderings as far as Lapland, he found his vocation in the success of *Le Divorce* at the Théâtre-Italien in 1688. *Le Joueur* (1696, 'The Gambler'), a hit at the Théâtre-Français, was followed by *Le Distrait* (1697, 'The Absent-minded Man'), *Le Retour imprévu* (1700, 'The Unexpected Return'), *Les Folies amoureuses* (1704, 'Follies of Love'), and his masterpiece, *Le Légataire universel* (1708, Eng trans *The Sole Heir*, 1912).
▷ A Caleme, *Jean François Regnard, sa vie et son oeuvre* (1960)

RÉGNIER, Henri François Joseph de
(1864–1936)

French Symbolist poet, novelist and critic, born in Honfleur. He studied law in Paris, and then turned to letters. His *Poèmes anciens et romanesques* (1890, 'Ancient Poems and Romances') revealed him as a Symbolist, though later he returned to more traditional versification. In both poetry and prose his style and mood were admirably suited to evocation of the past, and expressive of a melancholy disillusionment induced by the passage of time. Poetical works include *La Sandale ailée* (1906, 'The Winged Sandal'), *Vestigia flammae* (1921, 'Traces of the Flame') and *Flamma tenax* (1928, 'The Steadfast Flame'). His novels were mainly concerned with France and Italy in the 17th and 18th centuries. Two of these are *La Double Maît-resse* (1900, 'The Double Mistress') and *Le Bon Plaisir* (1902, 'One's Pleasure').

▷E Buenzod, *Henri Régnier* (1966)

RÉGNIER, Mathurin
(1573–1613)

French satirist, born in Chartres. After taking orders he grew up dissipated and idle, obtained a canonry at Chartres, and enjoyed the favour of Henri IV. His whole work hardly exceeds 7000 lines—16 satires, three epistles, five elegies, and some odes, songs and epigrams, yet it places him high among French poets. He is best at satires, admirably polished, but vigorous and original and giving a lively picture of the Paris of his day.

▷J Vieney, *Mathurin Régnier* (1896)

RÉGNIER, Paule
(1888–1950)

French Catholic novelist and diarist, whose remarkable achievement is now in danger of being forgotten. An illness in infancy left her hunchbacked and crippled. She was extremely sensitive and religious, and turned to literature for solace as a young woman. After an unhappy love affair with a writer (Paul Drouot) who was killed in World War II, she became a poor recluse, struggled with her doubts, and eventually killed herself. She wrote two masterpieces, one a private *Journal* (1951), kept until the night before she died. Her novel *L'Abbaye d'Evolayne* (1933, 'The Abbey of Evolayne'), about a woman who became a nun but could not keep her vows, and killed herself in front of her monk-husband, is one of the most powerful of its time.

REID, Forrest
(1875–1947)

Irish novelist and croquet player. He was born in Belfast, where he lived for most of his life. After an uncongenial job in a tea company, he belatedly became a Cambridge student (1905). His fiction expresses his obsession with boyhood, which he ascribed to 'arrested development'. *The Garden God* (1905) deals, typically, with ideal boyhood friendship, while *Apostate* (1926) nostalgically describes his own childhood. The Tom Barber trilogy—*Uncle Stephen* (1931), *The Retreat* (1936) and *Young Tom* (1944)—atmospherically relates the perceptions of an imaginative young boy, together with dream-like supernatural events that seem at times profound, at others whimsical. Reid's spiritual appreciation of the Ulster landscape and his love of animals are omnipresent in all these lucid and lyrical works.

▷B Taylor, *The Green Avenue* (1980)

REID, Thomas Mayne
(1818–83)

Irish writer of boys' stories, born in Bally-roney, County Down. In 1840 he emigrated to New Orleans, settled as a journalist in Philadelphia (1843), and served in the US army during the Mexican war (1847), where he was severely wounded. Returning to Britain in 1849, he settled down to a literary life in London. His vigorous style and hairbreadth escapes delighted his readers. Among his books, many of which were popular in translation in Poland and Russia, were *The Rifle Rangers* (1850), *Scalp Hunters* (1851), *Boy Hunters* (1853), *War Trail* (1857), *Boy Tar* (1859) and *Headless Horseman* (1866). He went back to New York in 1867 and founded the *Onward Magazine*, but returned to England in 1870.

▷J Steele, *Captain Mayne Reid* (1977)

REID, Victor Stafford
(1913–)

West Indian novelist, born and educated in Jamaica. His early novels, *New Day* (1949) and *The Leopard* (1958), were innovative in many ways, particularly in their use of language. The latter, set in Kenya, is a book to be considered alongside such as **Achebe**'s *Things Fall Apart*. But Reid, although he has written for children, and a few adult stories, has, disappointingly, not followed them up.

REINMAR VON ZWETER
(c.1200–c.1255)

German poet and Minnesinger, born into a noble family in the Rhineland but living the life of a wandering minstrel, mainly in the southern German areas, especially in and around Vienna. His Middle High German verse is moral in tone, highly rhetorical and deeply conservative, preaching the value of a well-ordered society. Some 300 poems, many with music, survive.

REIZEN, Abraham
(1875–1953)

Lithuanian Yiddish poet and story writer, born in Kojdanov; he emigrated to the USA in 1908. He achieved great popularity with his tales and simple songs, many of which were set to music. The periodical, *Di Europe-ishe Literatur*, which he edited from 1919, was important for the translations it carried of European books into Yiddish. By 1924 his works took up 12 volumes.

REJ, Mikolaj
(1505–69)

'The father of Polish literature' (though this title has been challenged on the grounds that he came at the end of the Polish medieval tradition), born in Zorawno, a squire. At the age of about 40 he turned from Lutheranism to Calvinism. Poet and polemicist, a stern moralist, 'he wrote as he spoke'. Although learned in theological dispute, and widely read, he had little formal education (some schooling in Skalmierz and Cracow), and thus offers an incomparable guide to the vernacular of his time. He wrote didactic plays, verse, and homilies. Like many Poles of his time, he composed enormous epic poems. His main importance lies in his profound influence on the Polish literary language through his use of vernacular. His most famous work is *Zywot Czlowieka Poczciwego* ('Life of a Noble Man', 1568 in *Zwierzyniec*, 'The Speculum'), a 'faithful mirror of the life of an average nobleman in Poland', a sort of later Polish equivalent of **Castiglione**'s *The Courtier*.

REMARQUE, Erich Maria
(1898–1970)

German novelist, born in Osnabrück. He served in World War I, and published his famous war novel, *Im Westen nichts Neues* (1929, Eng trans *All Quiet on the Western Front*, 1929). He lived in Switzerland from 1929 to 1939, and published *Der Weg zurück* (1931, Eng trans *The Road Back*, 1931). In 1939 he emigrated to the USA, and became a naturalized citizen. There he wrote *Flotsam* (English and German language versions, 1941), *Arc de Triomphe* (1946, Eng trans *Arch of Triumph*, 1946), *Der schwarze Obelisk* (1956, Eng trans *The Black Obelisk*, 1957) and *Die Nacht von Lissabon* (1962, Eng trans *The Night in Lisbon*, 1964).
▷W K Pfeiler, *War and the German Mind* (1941)

REMÉNYIK, Sándor
(1890–1942)

Hungarian (Transylvanian) poet and editor, born in Kolozsvár, the chief city of Transylvania. He was in the peculiar position of being a Hungarian who was handed over to Romanian rule (1920). Two of his poems are translated into English in *Modern Magyar Lyrics* (1934, ed W Kirkconnell).

REMINGTON, Frederic Sackrider
(1861–1909)

American artist and author, known primarily for his action scenes of the American West, derived from first-hand experience as a ranchhand. Remington wrote his books—*Pony Tracks* (1895), *Crooked Trails* (1898), *The Way of An Indian* (1906) to name a few—as vehicles for his painting. His big break came when he was asked to do the drawings for Theodore Roosevelt's *Ranch Life and the*

Hunting Trail (1888). This led to other commissions. In total he illustrated more than 70 books, 17 of them his own. Remington also edited the correspondence of **Owen Wister**, author of *The Virginian*.
▷H McCracken, *Frederic Remington—Artist of the Old West* (1947); B M Vorpahl, *Frederic Remington and the West* (1978)

REMIZOV, Alexei Mikhailovich
(1877–1957)

Russian writer, born in Moscow. He lived in St Petersburg, but left Russia at the Revolution, going first to Berlin and finally settling in Paris. His writing is full of national pride and a deep love of old Russian traditions and folklore; it contains realism, fantasy and humour. His main works are the novels, *Prud* ('The Pond'), *Chacy* ('The Clock'), *Pyataya yazva* ('Fifth Pestilence') and *Krestovye syostri* ('Sisters of the Cross'), legends, plays and short stories.

RÉMUSAT, Charles François Marie, Comte de
(1797–1875)

French aristocrat, born in Paris, son of the Comte de Rémusat (1762–1823), who was chamberlain to Napoleon. Early on he developed liberal ideas, and took to journalism. He signed the journalists' protest which brought about the July Revolution (1830), was elected deputy for Toulouse, in 1836 became under-secretary of state for the interior and in 1840 Minister of the Interior. Exiled after the *coup d'état* of 1848, he devoted himself to literary and philosophical studies, until, in 1871, Thiers called him to the portfolio of foreign affairs, which he retained until 1873. Among his writings are *Essais de philosophie* (1842, 'Essays in Philosophy'); *L'Angleterre au XVIIIᵉ siècle* (1856, 'Eighteenth-century England'); studies on *St Anselm* (1853), *Bacon* (1857), *Channing* (1857), *John Wesley* (1870) and *Lord Herbert of Cherbury* (1874); *Histoire de la philosophie en Angleterre de Bacon à Locke* (1875, 'History of English Philosophy from Bacon to Locke'); and two philosophical dramas, *Abélard* (1877) and *La Saint Barthélemy* (1878, 'Saint Bartholomew's Day').

RENARD, Jules
(1864–1910)

French novelist, playwright, diarist and socialist (he was a friend of Jean Jaurès, the French socialist leader, and Léon Blum, the future socialist prime minister, and he was the conscientious socialist mayor of his old home town of Chitry-les-Mines from 1904 until his death). He is best known for his semi-autobiographical novel *Poil de Carotte* (1894,

Eng trans 1967), about the war between a mad mother and the son she loathes. This deserves its classic stature, as does *L'Ecornifleur* (1892, Eng trans *The Sponger*, 1957), which has been misunderstood because it is as acidly critical of the 'artistic' as of the 'bourgeois' temperament. His animal pieces *Histoires naturelles* (1894, Eng trans *Natural Histories*, 1966) have been called 'dated' but are not found so by those who understand animals. Renard combined the natural suspiciousness of the countryman with the sophistication of an urban littérateur who could co-found the *Mercure de France*: as his most important work, *Journal* (1925–7, Eng trans of selections, 1964), demonstrates, he was an exceedingly complex and honest man. The manuscript of the journal was destroyed—but even the poor text we have of it shows that Renard will endure as a major, and self-questioning, writer.

RENART, Jean
(fl.early 13th century)

French writer, who treats the themes of courtly love and military heroism. The references to historical figures and events in the works now attributed to him suggest that he lived in the late 12th and early 13th centuries. Almost nothing is known about his life, but Franklin Sweetser deduces an aristocratic lineage from Renart's apparent familiarity with court circles. The fact that Renart signed only one manuscript in full (that of *Le Lai de L'Ombre*) has led to some difficulty in identifying his works, but he is now believed to be the author of the courtly romances *L'Escoufle, Guillaume de Dole, ou Le Roman de la Rose* ('Guillaume de Dole, or The Romance of the Rose'), and the shorter *Le Lai de L'Ombre* ('The Poem of the Shadow'). P H Beekman also ascribes to him the poems *De Renart et de Piaudoue* ('The Story of Renart and Piaudoue') and *De plait Renart de Dammartin contre Vairon son roncin* ('The Trial of Renart against his Horse').

RENAULT, Mary, pseud of Mary Challans
(1905–83)

British historical novelist, born in London. She worked in medicine before turning to writing serious novels about war and hospitals, the best of which is *The Charioteer* (1953). She found her greatest success with her eminently readable adventure novels set in ancient Greece, including a trilogy about Alexander and several retellings of the Greek myths. Best known amongst these are *The Mask of Apollo* (1966), a spy-thriller starring an extrovert actor, and *The King Must Die* (1958), a retelling, with modern psychological insights, of the story of Theseus.

▷D Sweetman, *Mary Renault: A Biography* (1993)

RENDELL, Ruth Barbara, also writes as Barbara Vine
(1930–)

English novelist, born in London. She is established as one of Britain's finest authors of detective fiction, of which the most popular are her 'Wexford' books. Rendell's first novel, *From Doon With Death* (1964), introduces Chief-Inspector Reginald Wexford, a compassionate, humane man serving with the Kingsmarkham CID in southern England. Wexford's cases take place within a domestic, often middle-class and apparently comfortable world. In the twelfth Wexford novel, *Kissing the Gunner's Daughter* (1992), the discovery of three bodies leads him into a mire of greed, fear and obsession. These preoccupations find a darker home in the much more psychologically macabre novels Rendell writes under the name of Barbara Vine, of which *King Solomon's Carpet* (1991) is representative.

RENÉE, properly Renée Gertrude Taylor
(1929–)

New Zealand playwright, born in Napier. A strong feminist, she has been involved in drama workshops as writer and director since the mid-1960s. Her *Setting the Table* was broadcast, then produced on stage in 1981. Her first success on the professional stage was *Wednesday to Come* (1984); this became the central play of a trilogy, with *Jeannie Once* coming out in 1990 and *Pass It On* in 1986. The feminist theme is carried on in *What Did You Do in the War, Mummy?* (1982) and *Asking for It* (1983).

RENN, Ludwig, pseud of Arnold Friedrich von Golssenau
(1889–1979)

German novelist, one of the greatest chroniclers of World War I. His style in his early and greatest book, *Krieg* (1928, Eng trans *War*, 1929), was influenced by the explorer Sven Hedin. This pungent and still underrated account has long been known as inimitably superior to **Remarque**'s more facile *All Quiet on the Western Front*. Later work, especially after he turned to communism, is less important, but some of the novels repay closer investigation.

▷W K Pfeiler, *War and the German Mind* (1941)

RESTIF (or Rétif) DE LA BRETONNE, Nicolas Edme
(1734–1806)

French writer, born in Sacy, Yonne. His many voluminous and licentious novels, such as *Le Pied de Fanchette* (1769, 'Fauchette's Foot') and *Le Paysan perverti* (1775, 'The Corrupted Peasant'), give a vividly truthful picture of 18th-century French life, and entitle him to be considered as a forerunner of Realism. He described his own not unsullied life in the 16-volume *Monsieur Nicolas* (1794–7, Eng trans 1930). He also wrote on social reform.

▷C R Dawes, *Rétif de la Bretonne* (1946)

REUTER, Christian
(1655–after 1710)

German dramatist and novelist, born in Kütten in Saxony. He first attracted attention when, while a student in Leipzig, he pilloried his landlady (of the Red Lion) and her son in two comedies—Frau Muller sued him and eventually got him sent down, but is still laughed at as the hilariously vulgar Frau Schlampampe. Her son, Eustachius, was Schelmuffsky in the mock travel book *Schlemuffskys Curiose unde sehr gefärlich Reisbesreibung* (1796, Eng trans *Schlemuffsky's Curiosity*, 1962).

REUTER, Fritz
(1810–74)

German humorist, born in Stavenhagen in Mecklenburg-Schwerin. He studied law at Rostock and Jena. In 1833 he was condemned to death, as with other Jena students he had indulged in wild talk about the Fatherland, but his sentence was commuted to 30 years' imprisonment. Released in 1840, with his career spoilt and his health ruined, he tried to resume his legal studies, learned farming, and taught pupils. His rough *Plattdeutsch* (Low German) verse setting of the jokes and merry tales of the countryside, *Läuschen un Rimels* (1853, 'Anecdotes and Rhymes'), became at once a great favourite, and another humorous poem, *Reis' nah Belligen* (1855, 'The Trip to Belgium'), was equally successful, followed by a second volume of *Läuschen un Rimels* (1858) and the tragic poem *Kein Hüsung* (1858, 'No Home'). The rest of his best works, except the poem *Hanne Nüte* (1860), were all written in Low German prose. *Ut de Franzosentid* (1860, Eng trans *The Year '13*, 1873), *Ut mine Festungstid* (1862, 'During my Imprisonment') and *Ut mine Stromtid* (1862–4, 'During my Apprenticeship') made him famous throughout Germany. He lived in Eisenach from 1863 until his death.

▷K Batt, *Fritz Reuter, Leven und Werk* (1967)

REVERDY, Pierre
(1899–1960)

French poet and critic who, together with the Chilean poet **Vicente Huidobro**, invented the concept of 'creationism'. Reverdy, who was born in Narbonne, the son of a vine-grower ruined by the disaster of 1907, at first wanted to be an artist, and throughout his life was associated with painters (including Gris, Picasso and Braque, who illustrated his last posthumous collections of prose-poems). Creationism demanded that a poem be autonomous: that it should not imitate nature, but create in its own right. From this Reverdy, in constant touch with **Apollinaire** and the painters whom Matisse had in 1908 mockingly called cubist (Picasso, Braque), developed a poetry which came to be known as itself 'cubist': essentially what this meant was that Reverdy, as he said of Picasso, 'called upon himself to learn everything afresh'. The resulting poetry, profoundly religious, but by a man who was distressed by his inability to understand God, seems disjointed and, initially, unrewarding; but the integrity and deliberateness of the poet, as he painfully tries to re-create the world in images, grow on the reader. Available in English translation is *Poems* (1968).

▷R Greene, *The Poetic Theory of Pierre Reverdy* (1967)

REVIUS, Jacobus
(1586–1658)

Dutch poet, born in Deventer. A Calvinist parson, his devotional sonnets have been held to be amongst the best poetry ever produced by a Dutchman. His poetry is interesting to modern minds less for its author's convictions than for his concealed doubts. He helped in the translation of the Dutch Bible. There is a useful account of his work in *European Metaphysical Poetry* (1961) by F J Warnke, which includes some translations into English.

REVUELTAS, José
(1914–76)

Major novelist, playwright, essayist and political activist, born in Durango. He is regarded, with **Rulfo** and **Yañez**, as one of the founding fathers of modern Mexican fiction. In his youth he went to prison many times for organizing strikes, and his first novel, *Los muras de agun* (1941, 'The Walls of Water'), was about the penal colony at Isla Marias. Expelled from the Mexican Communist Party, he continued to work—as an anti-Stalinist—for Marxist ideals. His best-known novel outside Mexico is *El luto humano* (1943, Eng trans *The Stone Knife*, 1947), about three families who survive a failed strike at an irrigation system. His best novel is considered to be *Los errores* (1964, 'The Errors'), which embodies his criticisms of the failure of the Mexican Communist Party to live up to its ideals.

▷M R Frankenthaler, *José Revueltas: El solitario solidario* (1978)

REXROTH, Kenneth
(1905–82)

American poet, critic and father figure to the Beat Generation. Born in South Bend, Indiana, he was largely self-educated. He worked as a manual labourer during the 1920s and became a prominent figure in the libertarian movement on the West Coast during the 1930s. He was a conscientious objector during World War II, serving as a hospital orderly in San Francisco; during this time he published his first book of verse, *In What Hour?* (1940). Other volumes include *The Signature of All Things* (1950), the quest-poem *The Dragon and the Unicorn* (1952) and *In Defense of the Earth* (1956). *Collected Shorter Poems* appeared in 1967, and a volume of longer works a year later. The best of his critical writing was published in *The Rexroth Reader* (1972).
▷M Gibson, *Kenneth Rexroth* (1982)

REYBAUD, Louis
(1799–1879)

French journalist and politician, born in Marseilles. He travelled in the Levant and India and, returning to Paris in 1829, wrote for the Radical papers and edited a history of the French expedition to Egypt (1830–6). His *Réformateurs ou Socialistes modernes* (1840–3, 'Reformers, or Modern Socialists') popularized the word 'socialism'.

REYES, Alfonso
(1889–1959)

Major Mexican poet, critic, essayist, diarist and man of letters, born in Monterrey. By profession he was a diplomat, his country's ambassador to Argentina and Brazil. He was universally respected, as a creator in his own right and as a keeper of standards, and very widely influential. His poetry reflected his reading of **Góngora** and of other European poets, such as **Mallarmé** (upon whom he wrote an essential book, *Mallarmé de nosotros*, 1938, 'Mallarmé Between Ourselves'). His *Diario 1911–1930* (1960) is crucial reading for an understanding of Mexican literature in the period it covers. He spent many years in Spain, and became one of the world's leading authorities on the Golden Age of Spanish literature. *Selected Essays* (1964) is a good introductory selection. Two other important books of his about Mexico have been translated: *The Position of America* (1950) and *Mexico in a Nutshell* (1964).
▷B B Aponte, *Alfonso Reyes and Spain* (1972)

REYLES, Carlos
(1868–1938)

Major Uruguayan novelist, born in Montevideo. With **Horacio Quiroga** and **Onetti**, Reyles is the leading prose writer of his country. His first phase, after he had inherited a fortune (of which he quickly but 'disinterestedly' relieved himself) and gone to live in Spain, was wholly naturalist: his first efforts, already powerful, but flawed by theory, were based on the prescriptions of **Zola**. But he had also learned from the psychologically subtler **Pérez Galdós**, and his later fiction became more original. His atypical *El embrujo de Sevilla* (1922, Eng trans *Castanets*, 1929) is often cited as his finest novel, but, although an excellent evocation of Andalusia, this neglects his *El terruño* (1916, 'The Soil'), his most exact portrayal of a type who had turned up in his fiction from the start: the failed **Nietzsche**an intellectual, who is contrasted with Reyles's most vital creation, the practical woman Mamagela. This is the novel most favoured by Uruguay's most outstanding critic and her modern keeper of conscience, **Mario Benedetti**.
▷M Benedetti, *Literatura uruguaya siglo XX* (1969); L A Menagra, *Carlos Reyes* (1957) (both in Spanish)

REYMONT, Władysław Stanisław
(1867–1925)

Polish novelist, winner of the Nobel Prize for literature, born in Kobiele Wielke, near Radon, the son of a village organist. He held a variety of jobs—wandering actor, tailor, novice monk. His first novel, *The Promised Land* (1899, Eng trans 1928), was about urban life in the industrial town of Łodz, but his masterpiece is a study of rural life, *The Peasants* (1902–9, Eng trans 1924–5), a tetralogy which was instrumental in his being awarded the Nobel Prize for literature in 1924. Other books are *The Comédienne* (1896, Eng trans 1920), and a historical trilogy, *The Year 1794* (1914–19).
▷L Budnecki, *Wladyslaw Stanislaw Reymont* (1953)

REZÁC, Václav, pseud of Václav Vonavka
(1901–56)

Czech novelist, born in Prague. His early novels were more interesting than his later ones, which were socialist realist and consequently lost power and psychological conviction.

REZNIKOFF, Charles
(1894–1976)

American poet and historian. His central subject was the lives of Jews in modern America, which forms the substance of the autobiographical, blunt and often violent *Family*

Chronicle (1969). The best of Reznikoff's verse appeared in *Inscriptions*, published a decade earlier in 1959, and working essentially the same territory. *Holocaust* (1975) contained rather discursive lyrics on the extermination of his people in Europe. His projected four-volume *Testimony*, a history of the American Diaspora, never got past the first volume (1965) and the eve of World War I. In his poetry he subscribed to Objectivism, stripping his lyrics of the inessential; this occasionally led to prosiness, as in *By the Waters of Manhattan* (1962) and the edited volume *By the Well of Living and Seeing* (1974), which appeared shortly before his death.

RHIGAS, Konstantinos
(1760–98)

Greek poet, born in Velestino. He organized the anti-Turkish revolutionary movement in Vienna, but was betrayed and shot. He is mainly remembered as a patriotic hero, but was also the author of many patriotic songs and poems, and translated works of European literature into Greek.

RHYS, Jean, pseud of Gwen Williams
(1894–1979)

British novelist, born in the West Indies. Her father was a Welsh doctor, her mother a Creole. Educated at a convent in Roseau, Dominica, she moved to England in 1910 to train at the Royal Academy of Dramatic Art, but her father's death after only one term obliged her to join a touring theatre company. At the end of World War I she married a Dutch poet, Max Hamer, and went to live on the Continent, spending many years in Paris where she met writers and artists, including **Ernest Hemingway**, **James Joyce** and **Ford Madox Ford** (the last-named in particular encouraged her writing). In 1927 she published *The Left Bank and Other Stories*, set mostly in Paris or in the West Indies of her childhood. Four novels followed, *Quartet* (originally published as *Postures*, 1928), *After Leaving Mr Mackenzie* (1930), *Voyage in the Dark* (1934) and *Good Morning Midnight* (1939); her heroines were women attempting to live without regular financial support, adrift in European cities between the worlds of wealth and poverty. After nearly 30 years she published in 1966 what was to become her best-known novel, *Wide Sargasso Sea*, based on the character of Rochester's mad wife in **Charlotte Brontë**'s *Jane Eyre*. Further short stories followed in *Tigers are Better Looking* (1968) and *Sleep It Off, Lady* (1976); an autobiography, *Smile Please*, was published posthumously in 1979.
▷P Wolfe, *Jean Rhys* (1980)

RIBAS, Oscar
(1909–)

Lusophone Angolan novelist, poet and essayist, a major figure in African literature. Born in Luanda of mixed parentage, he was blind from 1930. He is the world's leading authority on his own people, the Kimbundu, whose folk beliefs and religion he has studied through his stories, enthnographic writings and poetry.

RIBEIRO, Aquilino
(1885–1963)

Portuguese novelist, story writer and essayist who, from the beginning until the end of his career, opposed hypocrisy, corruption and tyranny. He was born in Carregal da Tabosa. When his novel *Quando os Lobos uivam* (1958, Eng trans *Where the Wolves Howl*, 1963) appeared, the police arrested him, but, horrified by the protests from abroad, hastily released him. However, the book was never available in shops. It deals with a peasants' revolt against a government afforestation scheme and the salutary revenge of a father against petty clerks for the unjust imprisonment of his son. His first book was the story collection *Jardim das Tormentas* (1913, 'Garden of Torments'). His language is so rich in the vernacular that a special glossary was compiled as a guide to it. He has been called modern Portugal's 'most rewarding writer to the outsider precisely because he is the most Portuguese'.

RIBEIRO, Bernardim
(1482–1552)

Portuguese novelist and poet of whose life little is certainly known. He is supposed, on good evidence, to have died mad—driven thus by a fatal passion—in a Lisbon hospital. It is likely that he was a 'converted' Jew, although there in no trace of more than a formal Christianity in any of his work. His main poetry consists of six eclogues. His most famous work is the plotless novel known (from its first three words) as *Menina e moça* (1554, second and augmented edition, by another hand, 1557, 'The Young Girl'). It is episodic and its text is unsatisfactory, but it is one of the most feminist of all 16th-century novels; it is a 'gentle tale of love and languishment' in which the vital Portuguese concept of *saudade* originates. *Menina e moça* emphasizes, as **Freud** was later to emphasize, that there is inherent in the sexual urge some impossibility of complete fulfilment.
▷A F G Bell, *Portuguese Literature* (1922)

RICARDO, Cassiano
(1895–1976)

Brazilian poet. He was an adherent of Brazil's Modernist movement who became associated with the 'Green-Yellow' fascist movement of Plinio Salgado, since he felt that this best fitted Brazilian aspirations. He later revised his opinions.

RICE, Elmer, originally Elmer Reizenstein
(1892–1967)

American dramatist, born Elmer Reizenstein in New York. He studied law and turned to writing plays. His prolific output includes *The Adding Machine* (1923), *Street Scene* (1929), which won a Pulitzer Prize, *The Left Bank* (1931), *Two on an Island* (1940) and *Cue for Passion* (1958).
▷ *Minority Report* (1963)

RICE, James
(1843–82)

English novelist, born in Northampton. He studied at Queen's College, Cambridge, drifted from law into literature, and was proprietor and editor of *Once a Week* (1868–72). From 1872 he was involved in writing novels with Sir **Walter Besant**, beginning with the successful *Ready-Money Mortiboy* (1872).
▷ J Rice, *The Autobiography of Sir Walter Besant* (1902, ed S S Sprigge)

RICH, Adrienne Cecile
(1929–)

American poet, born in Baltimore, Maryland, and educated at Radcliffe College, Cambridge, Massachusetts. Her first volume of verse, *A Change of World* (1951), was published while she was still an undergraduate, but it foreshadowed her emergence as the most forceful American woman poet since **Elizabeth Bishop** and **Sylvia Plath**. Later collections include *Snapshots of a Daughter-in-Law* (1963) and *The Will to Change* (1971). The latter took her up to the point of her husband's suicide. Thereafter, Rich began to align herself more directly with the women's movement, often dating poems as if they documented stopovers on a campaign trail. Her prose became almost as influential as her verse. *Of Woman Born* (1976) is a ruggedly unsentimental account of maternity. *On Lies, Secrets, and Silence* (1979) collected the best of her occasional prose. In *Blood, Bread, and Poetry* (1986) she aligned herself with radical lesbianism, defined in a broad non-sexual way that embraces the entire cathexis that binds woman to woman. Later verse appeared as *The Dream of a Common Language* (1978) and *A Wild Patience Has Taken Me This Far* (1981), which established her lineage from **Emily Dickinson**. *The Fact of a Doorframe* (1984) collected her poetry from 1950.
▷ M Díaz-Diocaretz, *The Transforming Power of Language* (1984)

RICH, Barnabe
(c.1540–1617)

English soldier and romance writer, born in Essex. Under the patronage of Sir Christopher Hatton he served as a soldier in France, the Low Countries and Ireland. He was the author of exaggerated tales in *The Strange and Wonderful Adventures of Don Simonides* (1581) and *The Adventures of Brusanus, Prince of Hungaria* (1592). His *Apolonius and Silla* (contained in *Riche, his Farewell to the Militarie Profession*, 1581) was used by **Shakespeare** as a source for the plot of *Twelfth Night*. He was also a prolific pamphleteer on military matters, and on Ireland.

RICHARDS, Alun
(1929–)

Welsh novelist, short-story writer and playwright, born in Pontypridd, Glamorgan. He was educated at the Monmouthshire Training College, Caerleon, and at University College, Swansea. He has published six novels, including *The Elephant You Gave Me* (1963), *A Woman of Experience* (1969) and *Barque Whisper* (1979), and two collections of short stories (*Dai Country*, 1973, and *The Former Miss Merthyr Tydfil*, 1976), often drawing on his varied experiences working as a probation officer, a sailor and a teacher. Besides editing several short-story anthologies, he has written a book about Welsh rugby, and many plays and adaptations for television, notably *The Onedin Line*.
▷ Autobiography in M Stephens, *Artists in Wales* (1971)

RICHARDS, Frank, properly Charles Hamilton
(1875–1961)

English children's writer, author of the 'Tom Merry', 'Billy Bunter' and other school-story series. He wrote for boys' papers, and particularly for *The Gem* (1906–39) and *The Magnet* (1908–40). After World War II he published school stories in book and play form, and his *Autobiography* (1952).
▷ M Cadogan, *The Man Behind Chums* (1985)

RICHARDS, Ivor Armstrong
(1893–1979)

English scholar and literary critic, and initiator of the so-called 'New Criticism' movement. Professor at Cambridge (1922–9), with Charles Key Ogden he developed the idea of Basic English, and in 1924 published the influential *Principles of Literary Criticism*, followed by *Science and Poetry* (1825) and *Practical Criticism* (1929). In 1939 he left Cambridge for Harvard, where he was professor (1939–63). There he taught **William**

Empson, became a friend of **Robert Lowell**, and began himself to write poetry, publishing, among other collections, *Goodbye Earth and other poems* (1958), *The Screens* (1960) and *New and Selected Poems* (1978).
▷I P Schiller, *I A Richards's Theory of Literature* (1969)

RICHARDSON, Dorothy M(iller)
(1873–1957)

English novelist, born in Abingdon, Berkshire. After her mother's suicide in 1895 she moved to London and worked as a teacher, a clerk, and a dentist's assistant. She became a Fabian, and had an affair with **H G Wells** which led to a miscarriage and a near-collapse in 1907. Later (1917) she married a painter, Alan Odle. She started her writing career with works about the Quakers and George Fox (1914). Her first novel, *Painted Roofs* (1915), was the first of a 12-volume sequence entitled *Pilgrimage*, culminating with *Clear Horizon* (1935) and *Dimple Hill* (1938). She was the first exponent of the 'stream of consciousness' style later made famous by **Virginia Woolf**.
▷C R Blake, *Dorothy Richardson* (1960)

RICHARDSON, H(enry) H(andel), pseud of **Ethel Florence Lindesay Robertson**
(1870–1946)

Australian novelist and short-story writer, born in Fitzroy, Melbourne, the daughter of an Irish immigrant doctor, who claimed descent, through her grandfather, from the ancient Irish Earls of Lindesay. After an unhappy childhood in which her father died insane, she travelled widely with her mother and younger sister and studied music with distinction at Leipzig Conservatorium, graduating with honours in 1892. She married a fellow-student, John George Robertson, and they moved to London. Her first novel, *Maurice Guest*, was published there in 1908, under her masculine-sounding pseudonym, followed by *The Getting of Wisdom* in 1910. He major work was the trilogy *The Fortunes of Richard Mahoney*; the first book, *Australia Felix* (1917), was followed in 1925 by *The Way Home*. This sold so poorly that the final book, *Ultima Thule*, was initially privately published at her husband's expense, but the three were re-published together in 1930. In *Maurice Guest* and in her later novel *The Young Cosima* (1939), a study of the interwoven lives of Liszt, Wagner and Wagner's second wife Cosima von Bülow, her deep musical sympathies are evident. She wrote some short stories, and a rather imaginative 'autobiography', *Myself when Young* (posthumous, 1948).
▷N Palmer, *Henry Handel Richardson: a Study* (1950); V Buckley, *Henry Handel Richardson* (1970)

RICHARDSON, Jack Carter
(1935–)

American dramatist and novelist, born in New York. His first play, *The Prodigal* (1960), was an impressive re-interpretation of the Orestes–Agamemnon myth in terms of a struggle between idealism and pragmatism. His next play, *Gallows Humor* (1961), was a biting but intelligent satire on capital punishment. The rest of Richardson's career has lacked focus. The autobiographical *Memoir of a Gambler* (1979) is diagnostic.

RICHARDSON, Samuel
(1689–1761)

English novelist, born in Derbyshire, where his father, a London joiner, had apparently taken refuge after the Monmouth rebellion. He may have gone to Merchant Taylor's School. He was apprenticed to a printer, married his master's daughter, and set up in business for himself in Salisbury Court, where in the heyday of his fame (and in much enlarged premises) he received **Dr Johnson**, **Edward Young** and the blue stockings. He was represented as the model parent and champion of women, but his three daughters seem to have had a repressed upbringing. In a letter he says that as a boy he wrote love letters for a group of young women, and this may have been the origin of his epistolary novels. In 1741 he published *Letters Written to and for Particular Friends*, generally referred to as *Familiar Letters*, which gave advice on 'how to think and act justly and prudently in the common concerns of human life'. *Pamela* (1740), his first novel, is also 'a series of familiar letters now first published in order to cultivate the Principles of Virtue and Religion', and this was the aim of all his works; but the virtue taught was of the prudential sort and the manners mean and bourgeois. After holding out for conditions against her brutal employer, Pamela, in the sequel, plays the Lady Bountiful and mingles easily in genteel life. In his second novel, *Clarissa, Or the History of a Young Lady*, Richardson depicts the high life, of which he confessed he knew little. Clarissa Harlowe in the toils of Lovelace is the main theme, but parental repression is also to be corrected. With all her charm Clarissa is too much the victim of her pride for her tragedy to be truly moving, and Lovelace is too ambiguous a character to be credible. Nevertheless, the seven volumes issued in 1748 made Richardson famous, and he was flattered by society as he took the cure at Tunbridge Wells or was visited at his fine new house, Northend. He corresponded with several society women. Fine ladies and gentlemen such as Lady **Mary Wortley Montagu**, **Horace**

Walpole and Lord Chesterfield might 'hesitate dislike', but the middle classes were enthusiastic. Richardson's third novel, *Sir Charles Grandison* (1754), designed to portray the perfect gentleman, turns on the question of divided love. Not only English blue-stockings but Continental writers raved about Richardson's novels. **Denis Diderot**'s eulogy in *Le Journal étranger*, though extravagant, is sincere—his *La Religieuse* is modelled on Richardson—and **Rousseau**'s *La Nouvelle Héloïse* confesses his discipleship. Apart from its technical advantages and disadvantages, the epistolary method was a means to suggest authenticity at a time when mere fiction was frowned upon. Thus Richardson called himself the editor, not author, of his works. He was also a redoubtable correspondent.
▷A Dobson, *Samuel Richardson* (1902); I Watt, *The Rise of the Novel* (1957)

RICHEPIN, Jean
(1849–1926)

French poet, playwright and novelist, born in Medeah, Algeria. Before the appearance of his first romance in 1872 he had been *franc-tireur*, sailor and actor. His revolutionary book of poems, *La Chanson des Gueux* (1876, 'The Beggars' Song') led to a fine and his imprisonment.
▷A Zevcas, *Les Procès littéraires au XIXième siècle* (1924)

RICHLER, Mordecai
(1931–)

Canadian novelist, born in Montreal. He grew up in a Jewish working-class neighbourhood and attended Baron Byng high school and Sir George Williams College. He travelled in Europe, but returned to Canada in 1952, working for the Canadian Broadcasting Corporation before moving to England in 1959, since when he has been a professional writer. His first novel, *The Acrobats* (1954), was derivative of **Ernest Hemingway** and subsequently disowned. In 1955 he published *Son of a Smaller Hero*, about a young man endeavouring to escape the Jewish ghetto and North American society in general. It was the first of several books for which he was accused of anti-semitism. It was followed by *A Choice of Enemies* (1957), but his break-through came with *The Apprenticeship of Duddy Kravitz* (1959), about an endearing shyster. Subsequent novels—*St Urbain's Horseman* (1971), *The Incomparable Auk* (1963) and *Cocksure* (1968)—have enhanced his reputation as one of Canada's richest novelists, a bawdy humorist and vitriolic satirist.
▷V Ramraj, *Mordecai Richler* (1983)

RICHTER, Conrad Michael
(1890–1968)

American novelist and short-story writer, born in Pine Grove, Pennsylvania. After various menial jobs—farm work, clerking, and journalism—he moved to New Mexico, and the landscape of the South West made a profound impact on him. His best-known novel, *The Sea of Grass* (1937), concerns a cattle baron. The three novels that followed—*The Trees* (1940), *The Fields* (1946) and *The Town* (1950)—comprise a frontier trilogy published in collected form as *The Awakening Land* (1966). Other novels include *Always Young and Fair* (1947), *The Light in the Forest* (1953) and *The Waters of Kronos* (1960), a dream-like elegy for a vanished America that reflects Richter's occasional sententiousness; *The Mountain on the Desert* (1955) is a leaden spiritual odyssey.
▷E Gaston, *Conrad Richter* (1965)

RICHTER, Hans Werner
(1908–)

German novelist, born in Bansin, Usedom, a Baltic island. After service in World War II, during which he was taken prisoner, Richter helped to found the literary circle Gruppe '47. His worthy fiction has been described by most critics as 'formless' and having only documentary value, but may not have had its due as humane, highly informative prose. His *Die Geschlagenen* (1949), describing the Nazis' brutal behaviour in Italy, was twice translated, as *The Odds Against Us* (1950) and *Beyond Defeat* (1961).

RICHTER, Johann Paul Friedrich *see* JEAN PAUL

RICKWORD, Edgell
(1898–1982)

English poet and critic, born in Colchester and educated at Oxford University. The youngest of the trench poets in World War I, he was influenced originally by **Siegfried Sassoon** but came to find his own voice, which involved erotic and satirical lyrics as well as Symbolist poetry. He was first published in 1921 with *Behind the Eyes*; his later collected editions of poetry (1947, 1970, 1976) found gradual favour. A socialist from boyhood, he joined the Communist Party in 1934, edited the influential *Left Review*, joined the International Union of Revolutionary Writers and became known for unbending Far-Left orthodoxy; he left the communists, however, in the large exodus of 1956.
▷C Hobday, *Edgell Rickword: A Poet at War* (1989)

RIDGE, John Rollin, Native American name **Yellow Bird**
(1827–67)

American writer and poet. Born in Georgia, the son of a well-to-do Cherokee father and White mother, Ridge was early caught up in the violent and tragic history of his people in the mid-19th century. His grandfather, the Cherokee leader Major Ridge, having been a leading advocate for the tribe's removal to Indian Territory, the family were ever after targets for the opposing faction, and when Ridge was 12 his father was assassinated in front of him. Beset by enemies throughout his life, Ridge killed a man in a dispute in his late teens, and fled to Missouri where he tried to raise funds for a fair trial; but, his finances poor, he was soon lured by the gold rush to move to California, where he stayed the rest of his life. Meeting no luck as a prospector, Ridge turned to journalism and became a regular contributor of poems and sketches to the new literary magazine, the San Francisco *Pioneer*. His most famous work, however, was the *Life and Adventures of Joaquín Murieta* (1854), a bloodthirsty, romanticized account of the life of the Mexican bandit which established Murieta's status as a folk hero, and the first major piece of fiction published by a Native American. Ridge's collected poems were published posthumously in 1868.
▷ J W Parrins, *John Rollin Ridge: His Life and Works* (1991)

RIDGE, William Pett
(1857–1930)

English writer, born in Chatham, Kent. He was educated at the Birkbeck Institution, and worked as a civil servant for several years before turning to a career in journalism and novel-writing. He was a prolific writer, and published over 60 books in all. He is best known as an exponent of cockney humour, in works like *A Clever Wife* (1895) and *Mord Em'ly* (1898).

RIDING, Laura, née **Reichenfeld** (later **Laura Riding Gottschalk**, then, after 1941, **Laura (Riding) Jackson**)
(1901–91)

American poet, critic, story writer, novelist and polemicist. Daughter of an Austrian immigrant, she took some courses at Cornell University (and married Louis Gottschalk, a history instructor there). Her first collection of poetry, *The Close Chaplet*, appeared in England, under the imprint of the Hogarth Press, run by Leonard and **Virginia Woolf**. She was the lover (1926–9) and then the literary associate (1929–39) of **Robert Graves**, with whom she lived in Mallorca, London

and Rennes. In 1941 she married Schuyler Jackson, a minor poet and farmer, with whom she wrote a long (unpublished) study of language. It is generally agreed that her poetry is superior to her prose, which became increasingly convoluted and denunciatory of those whom she regarded as her enemies (chiefly, and notoriously, Graves himself). Her poetry is quite unlike any other poetry of this century: based, rhythmically, on a very surely-handled four-accent line, it seeks unabashedly to examine the reasons for human existence, and to establish human obligations. It has attracted the attention of many, including Graves, **Auden**, **Larkin**, **Robert Fitzgerald**, **Robert Nye**, but has never received satisfactory critical exegesis. *First Awakenings* (1992), edited by her friend Nye and assistants, adds considerably to the canon.
▷ Riding's introduction to *Collected Poems* (1938); J P Wexler, *Laura Riding's Pursuit of Truth* (1979)

RIFBJERG, Klaus
(1931–)

Danish novelist and poet, born in Copenhagen. He studied at the universities of Princeton and Copenhagen and worked as an assistant film director before becoming a full-time writer. From 1984 to 1991 he was literary director of Denmark's dominant publishing house, *Gyldendal*. Widely viewed as the modern Danish author par excellence, he has published more than 100 titles since his debut in 1956 with *Under vejr med mig selv* ('Under the Weather With Myself'), a provocatively 'premature' autobiography in poetic form. It heralded the modernistic movement in Danish poetry and was followed in 1960 by *Konfrontation* ('Confrontation'), a landmark collection of poetry exhibiting Rifbjerg's linguistic wizardry and gargantuan appetite for modern life. His almost sensual relationship to the writing process has also resulted in a string of novels. The first one, *Den kroniske uskyld* (1958, 'The Chronic Innocence'), is a highly entertaining account of two young men's disastrous sexual debuts and displays one of Rifbjerg's main preoccupations: the dangers connected with the transition from childhood to adulthood. Rifbjerg's later novels include *Anna (jeg) Anna* (1969, Eng trans *Anna (I) Anna*, 1982), in which his talent for portraying women reaches a peak, *De hellige aber* (1981, Eng trans *Witness to the Future*, 1987), about two boys who are transported forward in time, from 1941 to 1981, and *Engel* (1987, 'Angel'). Rifbjerg has been awarded numerous literary prizes.
▷ T Brostrøm, *Klaus Rifbjerg. En digter i tiden, I & II* (1991)

RIGGS, (Rolla) Lynn
(1899–1954)

American dramatist and poet, born in Clare-more, Cherokee Nation (now Oklahoma). Of Cherokee descent, Riggs never identified himself as a Native American writer and little of his work deals directly with Native American life. He is best known as the author of *Green Grow the Lilacs* (1930), the play upon which the musical *Oklahoma!* was based. In plays such as *Big Lake* (1927) and *The Cherokee Night* (1936), Riggs depicts his characters and situations with a brooding sense of tragedy and fatalism. The latter, the only one of his plays to centre on Native American characters, describes problems of cultural disintegration among the Cherokees over several generations in Indian Territory/Oklahoma. Though he made his career as a dramatist, Riggs also wrote imagist-style poetry, which he collected and published as *The Iron Dish* (1930).

RILEY, James Whitcomb
(1849–1916)

American poet, known as the 'Hoosier poet', born in Greenfield, Indiana. He made his name contributing homely dialect poems to the *Indianapolis Journal* (1877–85). He published several volumes, and is also known for his poems about children, including 'Little Orfant Annie' and 'The Raggedy Man', written as Benjamin F Johnson. Earlier in his career he had been fired from a newspaper job after forging a poem allegedly by **Edgar Allan Poe**.
▷P Revell, *James Whitcomb Riley* (1970)

RILEY, Joan
(1958–)

Jamaican novelist, working and writing in Britain, whose books explore the problems faced by different generations of West Indian immigrant women. *The Unbelonging* (1985) is about an 11-year-old girl brought to Britain to be re-united with her father. *Waiting in the Twilight* (1987) contains a retrospective view of immigrant life in the Britain of the 1950s and 1960s, while *Romance* (1988) features the archetypal presence of so much Caribbean writing—the charismatic grandmother.

RILKE, Rainer Maria
(1875–1926)

Austrian lyric poet, born in Prague. He deserted a military academy to study art history in Prague, Munich and Berlin. The spiritual melancholy of his early verse turns into a mystical quest for the deity in such works as *Vom lieben Gott und Anderes* (1900, Eng trans *Stories of God*, 1931) and *Das Stun-denbuch* (1905, Eng trans *Poems from the Book of Hours*, 1941), written after two journeys to Russia (1899–1900), where he met **Tolstoy** and was deeply influenced by Russian pietism. In 1901 he married Klara Westhoff, a pupil of Rodin, whose secretary Rilke became in Paris, publishing *Auguste Rodin* (1903, Eng trans 1919). Mysticism was abandoned for the aesthetic ideal in *Neue Gedichte* (1907, 1908, 'New Poems'). *Die Aufzeichnungen des Malte Laurids Brigge* (1910, Eng trans *Journal of My Other Self*, 1930) portrays the anxious loneliness of an imaginary poet; a key text of existentialism, it prefigured such works as **Sartre**'s *La Nausée*. In 1923 he wrote two masterpieces, *Die Sonnette an Orpheus* (Eng trans *Sonnets to Orpheus*, 1936) and *Duineser Elegien* (Eng trans *Duino Elegies*, 1939), in which he exalts the poet as the mediator between crude nature and pure form. One of the most important figures in modern European literature, his work greatly extended the range of expression and subtlety of the German language.
▷J F Hendry, *The Sacred Threshold* (1983)

RIMBAUD, (Jean Nicolas) Arthur
(1854–91)

French poet, born in Charleville, Ardennes, the son of an army captain and his stern, disciplinarian wife. After a brilliant academic career at the Collège de Charleville, he published in 1870 his first book of poems, and the same year ran away to Paris, the first stage in his life of wandering. He soon returned to Charleville, where he wrote, while leading a life of leisure, drinking and bawdy conversation, *Le Bateau ivre* (1871, Eng trans *The Drunken Boat*, 1952), which, with its verbal eccentricities, daring imagery and evocative language, is perhaps his most popular work. Soon after its publication in August 1871, **Paul Verlaine** invited Rimbaud to Paris, where they began a homosexual affair. In Brussels in July 1873 Rimbaud threatened to terminate the friendship, and was shot at and wounded by Verlaine, who was imprisoned for attempted murder. The relationship had, however, given Rimbaud some measure of stability, and from its height, the summer of 1872, date many of *Les Illuminations* (1886, Eng trans 1973), the work which most clearly states his poetic doctrine. These prose and verse poems show Rimbaud as a precursor of Symbolism, with his use of childhood, dream and mystical images to express dissatisfaction with the material world and a longing for the spiritual. In 1873 he published the prose volume *Une Saison en enfer* (Eng trans *A Season in Hell*, 1939), which symbolized his struggle to break with his past—his 'enfer' (hell); he was bitterly disappointed at its cold reception by the literary critics, burned all his

manuscripts, and at the age of 19 turned his back on literature. Then began years of varied and colourful wandering in Europe and the East—in Germany, Sweden, Aden, Cyprus and Harar, as soldier, trader, explorer and gun-runner. During these years, in 1886, Verlaine published *Les Illuminations* as by the 'late Arthur Rimbaud', but the author ignored, rather than was ignorant of, the sensation they caused and the reputation they were making for him. In April 1891, troubled by a leg infection, he left Harar and sailed to Marseilles, where his leg was amputated, and where he died.
▷E Starkie, *Rimbaud* (1961)

RINEHART, Mary
(1876–1958)
American novelist, born in Allegheny, Pennsylvania and educated at the Pittsburgh Training School for Nurses. She began by writing mysteries in order to supplement her family's income. Early success prompted her to continue writing, and she eventually, in addition to her lucrative mysteries, produced plays, popular romances, and factual articles, many of which were based on her own life experiences. She adapted her first novel, *The Circular Staircase* (1908), into a successful play, *The Bat* (1920). Her most enduring heroine was 'Tish', who was introduced in 1910 in stories for *The Saturday Evening Post* and later featured in several novels.

RINGELNATZ, Joachim, pseud of **Hans Böttischer**
(1883–1934)
German poet, of sharp intelligence and satirical capacity, who had been a sailor and had knocked around doing odd jobs. However, during World War I he commanded a minesweeper. His irreverent poetry is still eminently readable. He was most successful as a reciter of his own verses in cabaret.
▷C Middleton and M Hamburger (eds), *Modern German Poetry 1910–1969* (1962)

RINGWOOD, Gwen Pharis
(1910–84)
Canadian playwright. Ringwood grew up in Alberta and attended universities in Montana and North Carolina. Her plays, which number more than 60 and include musicals, show the influence of both **Synge** and **Lorca**. The best known, *Still Stands the House* (1939), is about a time of depression and drought on the prairie. She built up a solid reputation in Canadian theatre. A *Collected Plays* was published two years before her death.

RINUCCINI, Ottavio
(1562–1621)
Italian poet. He wrote *Dafne* (1594), the first Italian melodrama, based on the earlier Greek work.
▷E Li Gotti, *Restauri trecenteschi* (1947)

RIOU, Jakez
(1899–1937)
Breton story writer, perhaps the leading practitioner of this genre in his language in the 1930s.

RISCO, Vecente
(1874–1963)
Spanish novelist, poet and scholar, born in Orense. He wrote in Castilian mainly but wrote poetry in Galician, and was a notable leader of the Galician revival. *La puerta de paja* (1953, 'The Straw Door') was a didactic novel written with a semi-modernist technique; but it is Risco's Galician poetry that is chiefly remembered nowadays.

RISKIN, Robert
(1897–1955)
American playwright and screenwriter, born in New York City. After serving in the United States Navy during World War I, he worked as a freelance writer and later enjoyed success as a Broadway playwright, creating a number of smart, sophisticated comedies, including *She Couldn't Say No* (1926) and *Bless You Sister* (1927, with J Meehan). A screenwriter from 1931, he was under contract to Columbia, where he worked in collaboration with director Frank Capra on a succession of sparkling popular comedies that often celebrated the idealism of the common man as he triumphed over the cynicism of his corrupt masters. Winner of an Academy Award for *It Happened One Night* (1934), he received further nominations for *Lady For A Day* (1933), *Mr Deeds Goes To Town* (1936) and *You Can't Take It With You* (1938), and adapted **James Hilton**'s *Lost Horizon* (1937) for the screen. Also a producer, he created the Overseas Motion Picture Bureau in 1942. Ill health forced his early retirement, but his body of work was honoured with the Laurel Award from the Writer's Guild of America in 1954.

RIST, Johannes von
(1607–67)
German poet and dramatist, a Protestant pastor, born in Otensen near Hamburg. The leading disciple of **Opitz**, he wrote many plays, most of which have now disappeared; he is most outstanding, however, as a religious poet and many of his 600 hymns survive to the present day. He was attacked

for writing vigorous secular poetry, but gave this up. His best poetry is in the style of Opitz, but heavier.
▷ J Julian, *Dictionary of Hymnology* (1907)

RITCHIE, Anne Isabella Thackeray, Lady
(1837–1919)
English writer, daughter of **Thackeray**, born in London. A close companion of her father, and well acquainted with his friends of literary and artistic note, she contributed valuable personal reminiscences to an 1898–9 edition of his works, and also wrote memoirs of their contemporaries, such as **Tennyson** and **John Ruskin**. Her novels include *The Village on the Cliff* (1867), *Old Kensington* (1873) and *Mrs Dymond* (1885).

RITSOS, Iannis
(1909–90)
Hugely influential left-wing Greek poet, dogged by family tragedy and constant oppression by a right-wing Greek government. Born into a wealthy Athenian family, he was still a boy when they were financially ruined and both his father and sister went insane. He joined the Communist Party in 1934, and worked as a lawyer's clerk, actor and dancer before being thrust into the limelight with his third collection of poems, *Epitaphios*, in 1936: his lament of a mother over her dead son, killed in a demonstration of out-of-work tobacco workers, was promptly banned by the ruling Metaxas dictatorship. Politically active during the German occupation, Ritsos was exiled from the mainland after it, and lived until 1952 on a succession of islands, including Lemnos. His books remained banned until 1954. Following the coup d'état and establishment of the junta in 1967, the poet found himself exiled again, this time to Samos, and his books were once again banned, until 1972. He was twice nominated for the Nobel Prize for literature. Many of his works were made into anthems by the musician Mikis Theodorakis, and are still powerful songs of protest for Greece's dissaffected youth.

RITTER, Erika
(1948–)
Canadian playwright and stand-up comic, born in Saskatchewan. Ritter writes comedies which set independent and intelligent women at logger-heads with the urban world. She is not a 'soap-boxing' playwright and this, coupled with her authentic feel for comedy, has helped bring success at the box-office, as with *Automatic Pilot* (1980), which concerned the autobiographical routine of a female comic. *Ritter In Residence* (1987), like *Urban Scrawl* (1984), showed that she could communicate her shrewd angle on life in essay form as well as on the stage.

RIVAROL, Antoine
(1753–1801)
French writer, born in Bagnols in Languedoc. He went to Paris in 1780 where he adopted the aristocratic form 'Comte de', and worked his way into fashionable society, where he found much material for his sarcastic writings, and in 1788 set the whole city laughing at the sarcasms in his *Petit Almanach de nos grands hommes* ('Little Almanac of Our Great Men'). Emigrating in 1792, and supported by royalist pensions, he wrote pamphlets in Brussels, London, Hamburg and Berlin.
▷ A Le Breton, *Antoine Rivarol* (1896)

RIVAS, Angel de Saavedra *see* SAAVEDRA, Angel

RIVAS, Manuel Linares
(1867–1938)
Spanish playwright, now remembered chiefly for one drama, very popular in its time: *La garra* (1914, 'The Claw'), about a man destroyed by reactionaries because he sought a divorce.

RIVAUDAUD, André de
(c.1540–1580)
French dramatist, translator (of Epictetus) and poet, born in Poitou. His biblical play *Aman* (1556) has been called the 'first humanist religious tragedy', inasmuch as it conformed to classical rules. A Protestant, he attacked **Ronsard** for 'paganism'.
▷ R Lebègue, *Le Théâtre religieux en France* (1929)

RIVERA, José Eustacio
(1889–1928)
The most important Colombian novelist before **Gabriel García Márquez**, Rivera was also a poet, teacher, and lawyer. His adventurous life took him on travels throughout Colombia: to the oil fields as an inspector and to the jungle around the Orinoco and Río Negro basins as a member of a boundaries commission. He was also a member of the National Congress. His most important work is *La Vorágine* (1924, 'The Vortex'), a pessimistic view of man's inherently violent nature and a stunning presentation of the world of the jungle. This novel marks a complete rupturing of the idealized Romantic view of nature, and deeply affected later writers like **Mario Vargas Llosa** and **Miguel Angel Asturias**. An example of his Parnassian poetry is *Tierra de Promisión* (1921, 'The Promised Land').
▷ L A Sánchez, *José Eustacio Rivera* (1957)

RIVIÈRE, Jacques
(1886–1925)

French writer and critic, born in Bordeaux. In 1919 he became the first editor of the *Nouvelle Revue Française*, as such playing a prominent part in the cultural life of post-war France. His writings include novels, essays and a justification of the Christian conception of God, *À la trace de Dieu* (1925, 'Following God').

▷R Beaulieu, *Jacques Rivière* (1955)

RIZAL, José
(1861–96)

Filipino patriot and writer, born in Calamba, Luzon. He studied medicine at Madrid, and on his return to the Philippines published a political novel, *Noli me tangere* (1886, 'Do not touch me'), whose anti-Spanish tone led to his exile. He practised in Hong Kong, where he wrote *El Filibusterismo* (1891), a continuation of his first novel. Returning to the Philippines, he arrived just when an anti-Spanish revolt was erupting; he was accused of instigating it, and was shot.

▷A Coates, *Rizal: Philippine Nationalist and Martyr* (1968)

ROA BASTOS, Augusto
(1917–)

Major Paraguayan novelist—the greatest his country has produced—and poet. He was born in Asunción (Paraguay), although he now lives in Toulouse. His father, often misleadingly described as a worker on a sugar plantation, was in fact a cultured man, who had taken minor orders—a once successful importer, he was forced into bankruptcy by unfair competition. As a boy of 15, Roa Bastos was made to fight in the 'despicable' Chaco War against Bolivia. He was exiled to Buenos Aires after supporting the losing side in the 1947 civil war. A man of wide culture (he spent some years in Europe, part of them in Great Britain), his interesting poetry, initially neo-*gongorista*, has been somewhat neglected. He has long been a pacificist, and thus regarded by many patriotic critics as an incurable eccentric. But both *Hijo de hombre* (1959, Eng trans *Son of Man*, 1988) and *Yo el Supremo* (1974, Eng trans *I the Supreme*, 1988) have been hailed almost everywhere as great novels. Of the first, which traces the unhappy history of his country by means of episodes related by a narrator, **Marío Benedetti** wrote that with it Roa Bastos 'placed himself firmly in the pantheon of great writers'. *I the Supreme*, about the legendary (mad, but shrewd and learned) 19th-century dictator of Paraguay, Dr Francia, is perhaps the 'dictator novel' of all 'dictator novels'. **Carlos**

Fuentes called it 'one of the milestones of the Latin-American novel', and **John Updike** felt that its 'deliberate prodigiousness ... intimidated criticism'.

▷D W Foster, *The Myth of Paraguay in the Fiction of Roa Bastos* (1969); D W Foster, *Augusto Roa Bastos* (1978)

ROBBE-GRILLET, Alain
(1922–)

French novelist, born in Brest. Educated in Paris, he worked for some time as an agronomist and then in a publishing house. His first novel, *Les Gommes* (1953, Eng trans *The Erasers*, 1964), aroused much controversy and with the appearance of his later ones (*Dans le labyrinthe*, 1959, Eng trans *In the Labyrinth*, 1960, etc), he emerged as a leader of the *Nouveau Roman* ('new novel') group. He uses an unorthodox narrative structure and concentrates on external reality, believing this to be the only one. He has also written film scenarios, eg, *L'Année dernière à Marienbad* (1961, Eng trans in novel form and filmed as *Last Year at Marienbad*, 1962) and essays, *Pour un nouveau roman* (1963, Eng trans *Towards a New Novel*, 1965). Other publications include the novel *Projet pour une révolution à New York* (1970, 'Project for a Revolution in New York'), *La Belle Captive* (written with René Magritte, the painter, 1976; adapted as a screenplay, 1983, 'The Beautiful Prisoner'), *Djinn* (1981, Eng trans 1982) and *Angélique ou l'enchantement* (1984, 'Angelique; or, The Enchantment').

▷J Fletcher, *Alain Robbe-Grillet* (1983)

ROBBINS, Harold
(1916–)

American bestseller novelist, born of unknown parentage in the Hell's Kitchen area of Manhattan, New York City. At 15 he dropped out of George Washington high school, left his foster parents and eventually became an inventory clerk in a grocery store. During the Depression he showed entrepreneurial flair by buying up crops and selling options to canning companies and the canning contracts to wholesale grocers. He was a millionaire by the time he was 20, but speculation in sugar before the outbreak of World War II relieved him of his fortune. He became interested in writing in 1949. Drawing on his knowledge of street life, high finance and Hollywood, he produced a string of earthy bestsellers: *Never Love a Stranger* (1948), *The Dream Merchants* (1949), *A Stone for Danny Fisher* (1952), *79 Park Avenue* (1955) and *The Carpetbaggers* (1961), which together sold six million copies throughout the 1960s.

ROBBINS, Tom (Thomas Eugene)

(1936–)

American comic novelist, born in Blowing Rock, North Carolina. After working as a journalist and broadcaster, he published his first novel, *Another Roadside Attraction* (1971), in which Christ's mummified body, discovered in the Vatican cellars, becomes an advertising draw for a freeway hot-dog stand. In *Even Cowgirls Get the Blues* (1976) Robbins portrays the ultimate hitch-hiker, Cissy Hankshaw, to dramatize his curious view of a female-dominated America. *Still Life With Woodpecker* (1980) and *Jitterbug Perfume* (1984) both showed some signs of strain. Though often unthinkingly described as a '60s writer', Robbins's work is largely concerned with the long hangover left after the Great Society and Woodstock. It is an essentially pessimistic vision.

▷M Siegel, *Tom Robbins* (1980)

ROBERTS, Sir Charles George Douglas

(1860–1943)

Canadian writer and naturalist, born in Douglas, New Brunswick. A graduate of Fredericton, he was professor in King's College, Nova Scotia (1885–95), and settled in New York as an editor, joining the Canadian army at the onset of World War I. An outstanding lyric poet, he wrote *Orion and Other Poems* (1880), *In Divers Tones* (1887), and other verse, a history of Canada, *Canada in Flanders* (1918), and nature studies, in which he particularly excelled, including *The Feet of the Furtive* (1912) and *Eyes of the Wilderness* (1933).

▷W J Keith, *Sir Charles Roberts* (1969)

ROBERTS, Elizabeth Madox

(1881–1941)

American novelist and poet, born in Perrysville, Kentucky. Opinions are still divided as to her merits, but she was regarded in her day as a major novelist. Some have seen her as over-poetic and over-diffuse—as 'indeterminate'; others as transcending regionalism. Her works include *The Time of Man* (1926), about Kentucky hill-dwellers, *My Heart and my Flesh* (1927), a study of a family in decline, and *The Great Meadow* (1930), a historical novel about the settlement of Kentucky by emigrants from Virginia. Criticism has yet to assess her.

▷H M Campbell and R E Foster, *Elizabeth Madox Roberts: American Novelist* (1956)

ROBERTS, Kate

(1891–1985)

Welsh novelist and short-story writer, born in Rhosgadfan, near Caernarfon, Gwynedd. She was educated at the University College of North Wales, Bangor. Sometimes described as 'the Welsh Chekhov', she is generally regarded as the most distinguished prose writer in Welsh this century. She was a teacher of Welsh at Ystalyfera (1915–17) and Aberdare (1917–28), and later (with her husband Morris T Williams) bought Gwasg Gee, the publishers of the newspaper *Baner ac Amserau Cymru* (later *Y Faner*), and settled in Denbigh.

▷B Jones, *Kate Roberts* (1969)

ROBERTS, Keith

(1935–)

English author of science-fiction novels and short stories, born in Kettering, Northamptonshire. Considered one of the finest stylists of the genre, Roberts's works include *Pavanne* (1968) and *The Chalk Giants* (1975). *Molly Zero* (1980) is set 200 years hence, in a Britain governed by martial law. Molly Zero, destined to become one of the elite caste, rebels and in doing so confronts unexpected political and moral questions. Another version of future-Britain, this time a disintegrating country seen from the point of view of a resentful lavatory attendant, is the subject of the title story of *The Lordly Ones* (1986). Another story, 'The Checkout', features Anita, a modern-day witch and a familiar Roberts character.

ROBERTS, Kenneth Lewis

(1885–1957)

American novelist, essayist and dowsing expert, born in Kennebunk, Maine. After graduating from Cornell, he worked as a journalist from 1909 till 1928. He is considered one of the best historical novelists the USA has produced. *Arundel* (1930) was the first in a projected cycle presenting the history of Maine. It told the story of Benedict Arnold's expedition against Quebec and was based on careful research into journals and related papers. The series was never completed but there were two sequels, *Rabble in Arms* (1933) and *Captain Caution* (1934). Other historical novels include *Northwest Passage* (1937) and *Oliver Wiswell* (1940), about the American Revolution from the viewpoint of a loyal colonial soldier.

ROBERTS, W(alter) Adolphe

(1886–1962)

Jamaican poet and novelist, born in Kingston, son of a wealthy silk merchant. Educated privately, he was a journalist on the Jamaican *Daily Gleaner*, then in the USA from 1904, finally returning to Jamaica in 1949. His verse, *Pierrot Wounded and other poems* (1919) and *Pan and Peacocks* (1928), is graceful and accomplished in the English aesthetic tradition, but the last four of his many novels, *Royal Street* (1944), *Brave Mardi Gras* (1946) and *Creole Dusk* (1948), set in Louisiana, and *The Single Star* (1949), set in Cuba, reflect a more realistic interest in Creole culture and West Indian independence.

ROBERTSON, Angus
(1870–1948)

Scottish Gaelic poet and novelist, born on the Isle of Skye. He wrote one historical novel and many songs; his use of language has been described as 'grotesquely overloaded', but at its best was evocative both of Skye and of the injustices suffered by a Gaelic society. His essays on Celtic themes, *The Children of the Fore-World* (1933), contain his finest work.

ROBERTSON, Elizabeth Arnot
(1903–61)

English novelist, now virtually forgotten, who scored a success with her first novel, *Cullum* (1938). She was best known for her film-criticism. Her most widely-read novel was *Four Frightened People* (1931).

ROBERTSON, Thomas William
(1829–71)

English dramatist, brother of Madge Kendal, born in Newark-on-Trent, of an old acting family. Going to London in 1848, he was an actor, prompter and stage manager, wrote unsuccessful plays, contributed to newspapers and magazines, and translated French plays. His first notable success as a dramatist was with *David Garrick* (1864) and *Society* (1865), and his next comedy, *Ours* (1866), established his fame. *Caste* (1867), *Play* (1868), *School* (1869), *M.P.* (1870)—all performed by the Bancrofts at the Prince of Wales Theatre—and also *Home* (1869) and *Dreams* (1869) were all equally successful.
▷I E Pemberton, *Life and Work of Thomas William Robertson* (1893)

ROBINSON, Edwin Arlington
(1869–1935)

American poet, born in Head Tide, Maine. He was brought up in the town of Gardiner, Maine, which provided the background for 'Tilbury Town', the fictional New England village setting of his best poetry. He was educated at Harvard, and went to New York to find work. He made a name with an early collection of poetry, *The Children of the Night* (1897), followed by *Captain Craig* (1902), *The Town down the River* (1910), *The Man against the Sky*, which confirmed his reputation, and *King Jasper* (1935), his last work. Poems such as 'Miniver Cheevy' and 'Richard Cory' are now recognized as American classics, and are much anthologized. He was three times a Pulitzer Prize-winner, for his *Collected Poems* (1922), *The Man Who Died Twice* (1925) and *Tristram* (1927), one of his several modern renditions of Arthurian legends.
▷H Hagedorn, *Edwin Arlington Robinson* (1938)

ROBINSON, Henry Crabb
(1775–1867)

English journalist and diarist. He was articled to a Colchester attorney (1790–5), then travelled in Germany where he met **Goethe** and **Schiller**, and studied at Jena University. He joined *The Times* in 1807 as a foreign correspondent, and covered the Peninsular War as a war correspondent (1808–9)—the first of his kind. He worked as a barrister from 1813 to 1828. He knew and corresponded with many of the major literary figures of the day (**Coleridge**, **Wordsworth**, **Charles Lamb**, **William Blake**, etc), who all figure in his voluminous diaries, correspondence and reminiscences. He was one of the founders of London University (1828) and the Athenaeum Club in London.
▷E Morley, *Life and Times of Henry Crabb Robinson* (1935)

ROBINSON, Kim Stanley
(1952–)

American science-fiction writer, born in California. He published a small number of stories and an academic study of the novels of **Philip K Dick** prior to his first novel, *The Wild Shore* (1984), a sophisticated post-disaster novel set in California. *The Gold Coast* (1988) and *Pacific Edge* (1990) form a thematic trilogy with that book. He began a second major trilogy about the colonization of Mars with *Red Mars* (1992) and *Green Mars* (1993), which is intended to range over a vast 200-year timespan, encompassing the social, political and environmental issues raised on his lucidly imagined planet. He has written several other science-fiction works, including *Icehenge* (1984) and *A Short Sharp Shock* (1990).

ROBINSON, (Esmé Stuart) Lennox
(1886–1958)

Irish dramatist, born in Douglas, County Cork. His first play, *The Clancy Game*, was produced in 1908 at the Abbey Theatre, Dublin, where he was appointed manager in 1910 and then director from 1923 to 1956. Other plays include *The Cross Roads* (1909), *The Dreamers* (1915) and *The White-Headed Boy* (1920). He also compiled volumes of Irish verse, including the Irish *Golden Treasury* (1925), and edited Lady **Gregory**'s *Journals*

(1946). His autobiographical works were *Three Homes* (1938) and *Curtain Up* (1941).
▷F O'Connor, *My Father's Son* (1969)

ROBINSON, Mary ('Perdita'), née Darby
(1758–1800)

English poet and novelist, born in Bristol, daughter of a merchant and educated at schools in Bristol and London. Her adventures and tribulations started with marriage at 16; at 17 she was imprisoned for debt with her husband and infant daughter, and published her first poems; turned actress in 1776, she was mistress of the Prince of Wales, later George IV, who deserted her in 1780. Saved from destitution by an annuity secured by Charles James Fox, she travelled to France with her lover, Col Banastre Tarleton, but from 1783 was lamed by partial paralysis. Left by Tarleton in 1792 she struggled to support her family by writing. She associated with radical intellectuals, and her poems were highly admired by **Coleridge**. Her prolific output included satirical verse, love-sonnets (*Sappho and Phaon*, 1796), a long poem on the French Revolution, *Lyrical Tales* (1800), showing affinities with the nascent Romantic movement, two plays, and several novels of sentiment and Gothic romance, including the bestselling *Vancenza* (1792).
▷*Memoirs* (1801), ed J F Molloy (1930); M Steen, *The Lost One* (1937); R D Bass, *The Green Dragoon: the lives of Banastre Tarleton and Mary Robinson* (1957)

ROBINSON, Marilynne
(1943–)

American novelist and essayist, born in Sandpoint, Idaho and educated at Brown University and the University of Washington. Her first novel, *Housekeeping* (1980), was later filmed and has been hailed as a feminist classic; this lyrical novel focuses on the different life choices of two previously inseparable sisters. Robinson's work has been strongly influenced by the American Transcendentalists. In 1989 she published her first non-fiction book, *Mother Country: Britain, The Nuclear State, and Nuclear Pollution*. In 1982 she received both the **Hemingway** Foundation Award and the American Academy **Rosenthal** Foundation Award.
▷E A Meese, *Crossing the Double Cross: The Practice of Feminist Criticism* (1986)

ROBINSON, Roland
(1912–92)

Irish-born Australian poet and mythologist, born in County Clare. An admirer of the verse of English nature poet **Edward Thomas**, his love of the Australian bush often shows a similar turn-of-century ripeness. Considered the best among **Rex Ingamells**'s 'Jindyworobak' movement, Robinson's variety of output effectively distinguished him from others of that school, even in his first book *Beyond the Grass-Tree Spears* (1944). *Tumult of the Swans* (1953) won him the Grace Leven Prize in that year. A sparse collection of his verse was published in 1971 as *Selected Poems* and a further selection was edited, under the same title, in 1983. His keen interest in aboriginal life and lore was reflected in five books, from *Legend and Dreaming* (1952) to *Aboriginal Myths and Legends* (1966).
▷*The Drift of Things* (1973); *The Shift of Sands* (1976); *A Letter to Joan* (1978)

ROCHE, Denis
(1937–)

French avant-garde novelist, born in Paris. He served on the editorial board of the influential avant-garde magazine *Tel Quel* (1963–73). He studied dentistry. His verse and prose is in effect a complex questioning of its own right to exist: its readers—of whom there have not been so many—do not 'read' but study it. Roche wishes, however, 'to lay bare the world of excrement, sexuality and death': *Louve basse* (1976, 'Low She-Wolf') is a series of 13 texts; *Notre antéfixe* (1978) is a series not of words but of photographs of the author and his lover in 40 different poses in various hotel rooms, and is described as a novel.

ROCHEFORT, Christiane
(1917–)

French novelist, born in Paris. No novel by her has made the same impact as her first, *Le Repos du guerrier* (1958, Eng trans *Warrior's Rest*, 1959). This well-written and ironically told story of a girl's submission to a sadistic alcoholic contained much scabrous detail, and won the Prix de la Nouvelle Vague.

ROCHESTER, John Wilmot, Earl of
(1647–80)

English courtier and poet, born in Ditchley, Oxfordshire. He was educated at Burford school and Wadham College, Oxford. He travelled in France and Italy, and then returned to court, where his good looks and lively wit made him a prominent figure. In 1665 he showed conspicuous courage against the Dutch. He is said to have been a patron of the actress Elizabeth Barry, and of several poets. In 1667 he married a wealthy heiress, Elizabeth Malet, and plunged into a life of debauchery, yet wrote excellent letters, satires (particularly 'A Satyr against Mankind', 1675), and bacchanalian and amatory songs and verses. Finally he was moved to repentance by Bishop Burnet. Among the best of his poems are imitations of **Horace** and **Nicolas Boileau**, *Verses to Lord Mulgrave*, and *Verses upon Nothing*.

▷V de Sola Pinto, *Rochester, Portrait of a Restoration Poet* (1935)

ROD, Édouard
(1857–1910)

Swiss writer, born in Nyon in Vaud. He studied at Lausanne, Bonn and Berlin, was professor at Geneva, and settled in Paris. Among his 30 works are *La Chute de Miss Topsy* (1882, 'Miss Topsy's Fall'), *La Course à la mort* (1885, 'The Race to Death'), *Le Sens de la vie* (1889, 'The Sense of Life'), *Le Dernier Refuge* (1896, 'The Last Refuge') and *Les Unis* (1909, 'The United').

▷C Delhorbe, *Édouard Rod* (1938)

RODARI, Gianni
(1920–)

Italian children's writer and journalist, born in Omegna (Novara). He established himself with the boys' novel *Le avventure di Cipollino* (1950, 'The Adventure of Cipollino'), which he followed up with many more psychologically convincing yarns.

RODE, Helge
(1870–1937)

Danish dramatist, poet and essayist, born in Copenhagen. He was a dominant force in literature for much of his life, chiefly as a religious thinker. A mystic and early symbolist under the influence of **Maeterlinck**, he was at his best in such dreamy verse dramas as *Kampene i Stefan Borgs Hjem* (1900, 'The Battles in the Home of Stefan Borg').

RODENBACH, Georges
(1855–98)

Belgian poet and novelist, born in Tournai. His mature poetry, turning away from **Hugo**, emulated **Mallarmé** in its Symbolist procedures—but it is not unoriginal for all that, and has not been studied outside French-speaking countries as much as it deserves. It amounts to a remarkable, dreamy, moving evocation of the mysterious region of Flanders. *Bruges-la-Morte* (1892, 'Bruges: Dead City'), a novel, has a similar effect.

▷P Maes, *Georges Rodenbach (1855–98)* (1952, in French)

RODENBERRY, Gene
(1921–91)

American scriptwriter, producer and director, born in Texas. He was a pilot before turning to writing, and has worked mainly in television. He has earned lasting fame within science-fiction circles (and beyond) as the creator of the popular *Star Trek* series which, after a slow beginning when first screened in 1966–8, has built up a huge following in television, book and film formats. He was unable to repeat the success with several subsequent ventures in the science-fiction and horror field, but participated in the creation of *Star Trek: The Next Generation* (from 1987).

RODGERS, Richard *see* HAMMERSTEIN, Oscar II

RODGERS, W(illiam) R(obert)
(1909–69)

Irish poet and broadcaster. Born in Belfast, he was ordained as a Presbyterian minister in 1935 and served in Loughall, Co. Armagh, from 1935 to 1946. The following year he resigned and settled in London, where he made many contributions to the BBC. *Awake! And Other Poems* (1941), *Europa and the Bull* (1952) and the posthumous *Collected Poems* (1971) provide but small evidence of his work. His contagious respect for the craft of writing led to many unfinished and unpublished pieces, including the commissioned but uncompleted *The Character of Ireland* (with **Louis MacNeice**). In his largely unpublished Epilogue to this piece he wrote 'Here I come, always in at the tail-end,/A good man for a funeral or a wake:/Patient in graveyards, used to thinking long/and walking short'.

▷D Davin, *Closing Times* (1975; reprinted 1985)

RODÓ, José Enrique
(1872–1917)

Uruguayan essayist, born in Montevideo, author of the seminal *Ariel* (1900, Eng trans 1922), an immensely influential essay pleading for spiritual values to be upheld in the coming age of materialism (represented by Caliban). His attack on the United States as the materialistic state *par excellence* was prophetic. He was the foremost prose writer of the modernist movement in Latin America. His chief work, however, was his profound treatise on work and fulfilment, *Los motivos de Proteo* (1914, Eng trans *The Motives of Proteus*, 1928).

RODOREDA, Mercè
(1909–83)

Catalan writer, born in Barcelona. Beginning her career as a writer soon after the proclamation of the Spanish Republic, Rodoreda published prolifically between 1932 and 1937: five novels, plus numerous short stories in literary magazines, established her as a rising star of Catalan literature. With the end of the Spanish Civil War, however, and the suppression of the Catalan language, her books were banned and she fled to France to live in exile. Unable to write during this time, she published her first book for 20 years in 1957 (*Vint-i-dos Contes*, 'Twenty-two Stories'), followed in 1962 by her masterpiece, *La Plaça del Diamant* ('Diamond Plaza'), a stream-of-consciousness novel depicting the psychic and material horrors of the Civil War through the experiences of an ordinary Catalan woman. *Carrer de les Camèlies* ('Camellia Street'), a novel set in war-torn Barcelona in the 1940s and 50s, was published in 1966 and *La Meva Cristina i Altres Contes* ('My Christina and Other Stories') in 1967. Rodoreda returned to Spain in 1979, after Franco's death. Her books have been translated into many languages.

RODRIGUEZ, Claudio
(1934–)

Spanish poet, considered one of Spain's leading poets, his main themes being love and nature. He believes that love, in the universal sense, is poetry, and that everything in the universe should be celebrated, even suffering and death; that poetry should be cathartic and take us back to our roots so that we can view the world with innocence. His language, therefore, is brief and intense to reflect these beliefs. That his freshness and enthusiasm can still be seen in *Casi una Leyenda* (1991, 'Almost a Legend') as much as in his first book, *Don de la Ebriedad* (1953, 'Gift of Drunkenness'), speaks much for his conviction.

RODRÍGUEZ GALVAN, Ignacio
(1816–42)

Mexican poet and dramatist, born in Fizayuca. A rebel, his poetry is mostly spoilt by ultra-romantic grandiloquence. His verse plays were on colonial themes. He is not much read now, but remained important to late 19th-century critics.

ROE, Edward Rayson
(1838–88)

American clergyman and novelist, born in New Windsor, New York. He became chaplain in the volunteer service (1862–5), and afterwards pastor of a Presbyterian church in Highland Falls. The Chicago fire of 1871 furnished him with the subject of his first novel, *Barriers Burned Away* (1872), whose success led him to resign his pastorate in 1874. His other moralistic best sellers included *A Knight of the Nineteenth Century* (1877).

ROETHKE, Theodore
(1908–63)

American poet. He was born in Saginaw, Michigan, where his father grew and sold flowers, a setting that figures in many of the poems in *The Lost Son* (1948), his second and breakthrough collection. He was educated at Michigan University and Harvard and was Professor of English at Washington University from 1948. It was not until the publication of *The Waking* (1953) and the award of a Pulitzer Prize that he became widely known. He suffered from melancholia and in his work was occasionally self-indulgent; however, he wrote with a powerful rhythmic music that often yielded visionary effects. **Robert Lowell** and others of the 'Confessional' poets were influenced by him. *Words for the Wind* (1958) is a selection from his first four books; the *Collected Poems* appeared posthumously in 1968.

▷ J Parini, *Theodore Roethke: an American romantic* (1979)

ROF CARBELLO, Juan
(1905–)

Spanish doctor and psychoanalyst, born in Lugo, whose ideas have been highly influential in modern Spain. He is an immensely eclectic practitioner, as influenced by **Jung** and Binswanger (from whom the Scottish psychiatrist R D Laing culled his ideas) as by **Freud**. In his *Entre el silencio y la palabra* (1960, 'Between Silence and the Word'), he examines the thinking of Kierkegaard, **Rilke** and others. This book profoundly influenced the fiction of Rof Carbello's fellow psychiatrist **Martín-Santos**.

ROGERS, Samuel
(1763–1855)

English poet, born in Stoke-Newington. He entered his father's bank, in 1784 was taken into partnership, and in 1793 became head of the firm. In 1781 he contributed essays to the *Gentleman's Magazine*, next year wrote a comic opera, and in 1786 published *An Ode to Superstition*. In 1792 appeared *The Pleasures of Memory*, on which his poetical fame was chiefly based. There followed *An Epistle to a Friend* (Richard Sharp, 1798), the fragmentary *Voyage of Columbus* (1812), *Jacqueline* (1814, bound up with **Byron**'s *Lara*), and the inimitable *Italy* (1822–8). The last, in blank verse, proved a monetary failure; but the loss was recouped by the splendid edition of it and his earlier poems, brought out at a cost of £15000 (1830–4), with 114 illustrations by Turner and Stothard. In 1803, with £5000 a year, he retired from the bank as a sleeping partner, and settled down to bachelor life and an art collection which sold at his death for £50000. He was quietly generous to **Thomas Moore**, as well as to some unknown writers. But despite the kindest heart he had so unkind a tongue that 'melodious Rogers' is better remembered today

by a number of ill-natured sayings than by his poetry.
▷P W Claydon, *Samuel Rogers* (1889)

ROGERS, Will
(1879–1935)
American actor, rancher and humorist, born in Native American territory in what is now Oklahoma. His wisecracks became legendary, and led to his writing of a syndicated news column from 1926; he also appeared in many movies—whose directors allowed him to ad-lib at pleasure. *Will Rogers' Political Follies* (1929) illustrates his homely liberalism and cracker-barrel philosophy. *The Autobiography of Will Rogers* (1949) was compiled by Donald Day from all his writings and sayings. He was killed in an air accident.
▷H Croy, *Our Will Rogers* (1953)

ROHMER, Sax, pseud of Arthur Sarsfield Ward
(1886–1959)
English author of mystery stories, born in Birmingham. Interested in things Egyptian, he found literary fame with his sinister, sardonic, oriental criminal genius villain, Fu Manchu, whose doings were told in many spine-chilling tales, including *Dr Fu Manchu* (1913), *The Yellow Claw* (1915), *Moon of Madness* (1927) and *Re-enter Fu Manchu* (1957).

ROIDIS, Emmanuel
(1836–1904)
Greek short-story writer and critic, born in Syros but brought up in Genoa. He was educated abroad also, before returning to Athens in 1863. He achieved scandalous success when his first book *He Papissa Ioanna* (1866, Eng trans *Pope Joan*, 1888, abridged versions 1900, 1954) was condemned by the church, and provoked rioting in Athens. His style of ironic rationalism found few champions, but the series of short stories he wrote about his childhood on Syros received a warm critical reception. His own career as a critic included the discovery of **Iannis Psycharis**, and *Ta Idola* (1893, 'The Idols'), a linguistic study firmly in favour of demotic Greek—but written in the formal *Katharevousa*.

ROJAS, Fernando de
(c.1465–1541)
Spanish novelist of Jewish descent, born in Puebla de Montalbán. He wrote most (Acts I–XXI) of one of the most influential dialogue-novels in all European literature: *La Celestina, La Tragi-comedia de Calisto y Melibea* (1502). This sardonic and mock-moral tale of how a young gentleman makes use of a bawd (Celestina) to seduce a woman of prestigious family presents many problems, textual and otherwise. In all probability the whole text is by Rojas, and in it he was obliquely referring to the enforced conversion of the Spanish Jews. It was first translated by J Mabbe in 1631; there is a version in Penguin Classics by J M Cohen (1964), with an introduction.
▷M R L Malkiel, *Two Spanish Masterpieces* (1961)

ROJAS, Manuel
(1896–1973)
Chilean novelist and short-story writer; he was born in Buenos Aires, but returned to Chile early in life. Probably the best Latin-American realist writer, his work has been described as social realism or picaresque realism. His predominant themes include the effects of the urban environment on the human spirit, the accidental connections between people, and his own life—much of his work is at least partly autobiographical. His major work is *Hijo de ladrón* (1951), an attack on life in the city and social determinism, employing and adapting techniques like interior monologue to describe cruel and happy turns of fate, friendship and family ties.
▷D Cortés, *La narrativa anarquista de Manuel Rojas* (1986)

ROJAS ZORILLA, Francisco
(1607–48)
Spanish playwright, born in Toledo. One of the best Golden Age dramatists, he is usually thought to belong to the school of **Calderón de la Barca**, with whom he collaborated, but certain of his themes were unusual for the time and peculiar to him. Chief among these was honour, often shown as tested when duty conflicts with emotion. For example, in *El Caín de Cataluña* ('Cain of Catalonia') a father has to choose between condemning his son or evading justice. Rojas's best-known drama is *Del Rey Abajo, Ninguno* ('None Lower than the King'), where the protagonist mistakes the thief for the king and cannot avenge his honour. Exact dates for his works are difficult to ascertain, but most were published between 1640 and 1645.

ROLAND HOLST, Adriaan
(1888–1976)
Dutch poet and editor, born in Amsterdam. His highly, sometimes even excessively, romantic poetry is the Dutch equivalent of that of **W B Yeats**, who greatly influenced him. He studied at Oxford, and became interested in Celtic mythology. His poetry seemed incongruous in its context, but he came to be

universally respected, and in his old age won all the prizes his country could offer.

ROLAND HOLST-VAN DE SCHALK, Henriette
(1869–1952)

Dutch poet, whose progress was not unlike that of the Belgian **Charles Plisnier**, inasmuch as she progressed from communism to Christianity. She followed **Gorter**, the first influence on her fervid poetry, into communism, which she repudiated with the advent of Stalin. She was a leading feminist, and she wrote many useful biographies of people who interested her, among them **Leo Tolstoy**. But her rather careless although always burningly sincere poetry has not worn well.

ROLFE, Frederick William, styled Baron Corvo
(1860–1913)

English novelist and essayist, born in London. A convert to Roman Catholicism, his life was shattered by his rejection from the novitiate for the Roman priesthood at the Scots College in Rome; but it prompted his most famous work, *Hadrian VII* (1904), in which a comparable and obviously self-modelled 'spoiled priest' is unexpectedly chosen for the papacy, institutes various reforms and is ultimately martyred. He contributed to the *Yellow Book* in the 1890s with *Stories Toto Told Me* (afterwards republished in book form, 1895) and is also remembered for *Chronicles of the House of Borgia* and the posthumous *The Desire and Pursuit of the Whole*, published in 1934. Other novels are *Don Tarquino* (1905), and the posthumously published *Nicholas Crabbe* (1958) and *Don Renato* (1963).
▷A J A Symons, *In Quest of Corvo* (1934)

ROLLAND, Romain
(1866–1944)

French musicologist and author, winner of the Nobel Prize for literature, born in Clamecy, Nièvre. He studied in Paris and at the French School in Rome, and in 1895 gained his doctorate of letters with a thesis on early opera, *L'Histoire de l'opéra en Europe avant Lulli et Scarlatti* ('A History of Opera in Europe before Lulli and Scarlatti'). A number of dramatic works written at this time won comparatively little success. In 1910 he became Professor of the History of Music at the Sorbonne, and in the same year published *Beethoven*, the first of many biographical works including biographies of Michelangelo (1906), Handel (1910), **Tolstoy** (1911) and Gandhi (1924). His 10-volume novel cycle *Jean-Christophe*, the hero of which is a musician, was written between 1904 and

1912, and in 1915 he was awarded the Nobel Prize for literature. During World War I he aroused unpopularity by promulgating his pacifist and internationalist ideals in his writings, which were published in 1915 as *Au dessus de la mêlée* ('Above the Fray'). He lived in Switzerland until 1938, completing another novel cycle, *L'Âme enchantée* (1922–33, 'The Enchanted Spirit'), a series of plays upon the French Revolution, and a further study of Beethoven, as well as numerous pieces of music criticism. On his return to France he became a mouthpiece of the opposition to fascism and the Nazis, and his later works contain much political and social writing.
▷S Zweig, *Romain Rolland* (1929)

ROLLE OF HAMPOLE, Richard
(c.1290–1349)

English hermit, mystic and poet, born in Thornton in Yorkshire. He studied at Oxford, but at 19 became a hermit, first at Dalton and then at Hampole, near Doncaster. He wrote lyrics, meditations and religious works in Latin and English, and translated and expounded the Psalms in prose.
▷F Cooper, *Life of Richard Rolle* (1928)

ROLLENHAGEN, Georg
(1542–1609)

German dramatist and poet, born in Bernau. After some years as a schoolmaster, he became pastor at Magdeburg (1573). His *Froschmeuseler* (1595) is an adaptation of the pseudo-**Homeric** *Batrachomyomachy*, the battle between frogs and the mice. This is a clumsy but telling and well-observed satire on the society of his time. His son Gabriel (1583–1619) was also a well-known writer of plays and an emblem book.

ROLLI, Paolo Antonio
(1687–1765)

Italian poet, editor and librettist (for Handel and Bononcini), born in Rome. In 1716 he moved to England, at the invitation of the Earl of Pembroke: there he acted as a vital link between his own and English culture. **Goethe** in particular admired his poetry, which was based on classical models such as **Virgil**. He became tutor to the children of the Prince of Wales, who later became George II. His most famous work is his monumental translation of **Milton**'s *Paradise Lost*.
▷G E Dorris, *Paolo Rolli and the Italian Circle in London 1714–1744* (1967)

ROLLS, Eric C
(1923–)

Australian poet and naturalist, born in Grenfell, New South Wales. His verse ranges from experiences of farming life in *Sheaf Tosser* (1967), through *The Green Mosaic* (1977), with recollections of tropical New Guinea, to *Miss Strawberry Verses* (1978), a collection for younger readers. His non-fiction also expresses his love of nature: *They All Ran Wild* (1969) examines the impact on Australia of the importation of the rabbit in the 19th century, and *A Million Wild Acres* (1981), a loving study of a small forest, was the Melbourne *Age* Book of the Year choice. Partly autobiographical works are *The River* (1974) and *Celebration of the Senses* (1984).

RÖLVAAG, Ole Edvart, originally Ole Pedersen
(1876–1931)

Norwegian-born American writer. Born in a small fishing community in northern Norway, Rölvaag took the name of a cove near his birthplace when he settled in America. An avid reader from childhood, the first book he read was *The Last of the Mohicans* in Norwegian, and the seeming promise of the New World led him to abandon the life of a fisherman at 20 and take up the offer of a ticket from his uncle in South Dakota. His journey and early experiences as an immigrant were described in *Amerika-Breve* (1912, 'Letters from America'). Unsuited to the harshness of life as a prairie farmer, however, Rölvaag enrolled in a local school to improve his English, went from there to university and eventually took up a teaching career at St Olaf College in Minnesota. He published six novels, all dealing with the Norwegian immigrant experience and published in Norwegian in the US. His masterwork was *Giants in the Earth*, a grimly realistic, tragic story of the personal and psychological costs of pioneer life. Published initially in Norwegian in two parts—*I De Dage* (1924, 'In Those Days') and *Riket Grundlaegges* (1925, 'Founding the Kingdom')—the two volumes were combined for the English translation in 1927, which brought Rölvaag to a greater audience, although his importance in the literature of the American West has yet to be fully recognized.
▷P Reigstad, *Rölvaag, his life and art* (1972)

ROMAINS, Jules, pseud of Louis Farigoule
(1885–1972)

French writer, born in Saint-Julien Chapteuil. After graduating in both science and literature at the École Normale Supérieure, he taught in various lycées. In 1908 his poems, *La Vie unanime* ('The Unanimous Life'), established his name and, along with his *Manuel de déification* (1910, 'A Treatise on Deification'), the Unanimist school. He remained prominent in French literature, and from 1936 to 1941 was President of the International PEN Club. His works include the books of poems *Odes et prières* (1913, 'Odes and Prayers'), *Chants des dix années 1914–1924* (1928, 'Songs of the Ten Years 1914–24') and *L'Homme blanc* (1937, 'The White Man'), the dramas *L'Armée dans la ville* (1911, 'The Army in the Town') and *Knock, ou le triomphe de la médecine* (1923, Eng trans *Doctor Knock*, 1925), his most successful play, the novels *Mort de quelqu'un* (1910, Eng trans *The Death of a Nobody*, 1914) and *Les Copains* (1913, 'The Friends'), and the great cycle *Les Hommes de bonne volonté* in 27 volumes (1932–46, partial Eng trans in 18 vols as *Men of Good Will*, 1933–40), covering the early 20th-century era of French life. He published his autobiographical *Souvenirs et confidences d'un écrivain* ('Memories and Confidences of a Writer') in 1958.
▷M Berry, *Jules Romains* (1960, in French)

ROMERO, José Rubén
(1890–1952)

Mexican novelist, born in Contija de la Paz, who wrote one of Mexico's true picaresque novels of modern times, *La vida inútil de Pito Pérez* (1938, Eng trans *The Futile Life of Pito Pérez*, 1967), a neglected masterpiece, and the key to 'the philosophical complexities' of its author's country. He joined the *Maderistas* in 1911, and had to flee the country in 1914. He was Mexico's ambassador to Cuba from 1939 until 1945, when he retired. Sketches are collected and translated in *Notes of a Villager* (1988).

RONSARD, Pierre de
(1524–85)

French poet, born in the Château de la Possonnière in Vendôme. He served the dauphin and the Duc d'Orléans as a page, and accompanied James V with his bride, Mary of Lorraine (Guise), to Scotland, where he stayed three years. Becoming partially deaf, he abandoned arms for letters, and studied under the great humanist Jean Daurat, at first with his future fellow member of the Pléiade, Jean Antoine de Baïf, at the house of his father the scholar and diplomat Lazare de Baïf, and later at the Collège de Coqueret, where du Bellay and Rémy Belleau joined them. His seven years of study resulted first in the *Odes* (1550), which excited violent opposition from the older national school. In 1552 appeared his *Amours* ('Love Poems'), a collection of **Petrarch**an sonnets, followed by his *Bocage* (1554, 'Grove'), his *Hymnes* (1555), the conclusion of his *Amours* (1556), and the first collected edition of his poetry (1560). He subsequently wrote two bitter

reflections on the political and economic state of the country, *Discours des misères de ce temps* (1560–9, 'Discourse on the Miseries of Our Times') and *Remonstrance au peuple de France* (1563, 'Address to the People of France'), and in 1572, following the massacre of St Bartholomew, *La Franciade* ('The Hymn of France'), an unfinished epic. Charles IX, like his predecessors, heaped favours on the poet, who, despite recurrent illness, spent his later years in comfort at the abbey of Croix-Val in Vendôme. The most important poet of 16th-century France, Ronsard was the chief exemplar of the doctrines of the Pléiade, which aimed at raising the status of French as a literary language and ousting the formal classicism inherited from the middle ages. Despite the great success of Ronsard's poems in his lifetime, the classicists regained the upper hand after his death, and his fame suffered an eclipse until the 19th century, when the Romantic movement brought recognition of his true worth.
▷G Cohen, *Ronsard, sa vie et son oeuvre* (1924)

ROS, Uilleam *see* ROSS, William

ROSCOE, William
(1753–1831)
English historian, born in Liverpool. In 1769 he was articled to an attorney, and began to practise in 1774. In 1777 he published a poem, *Mount Pleasant*, and in 1787 *The Wrongs of Africa*, a protest against the slave trade. But it was his *Life of Lorenzo de' Medici* (1796) that established his literary reputation. His second great book, *Life of Leo X* (1805), like the former, was translated into German, French and Italian. He had retired from business in 1796, but in 1799 became partner in a Liverpool bank, which involved him in pecuniary embarrassment (1816–20). He also wrote poems, of which the best known is the children's classic, *The Butterfly's Ball and the Grasshopper's feast* (1807); he wrote an edition of **Pope**, and a monograph on Monandrian plants.
▷Sir C S Jones, *The Life of William Roscoe* (1931)

ROSEGGER, Peter, known until 1894 as P K (Petri Kettenfeier)
(1843–1918)
Austrian poet and novelist, born of peasant parents near Krieglach, Styria. In 1870 he published *Zither und Hackbrett* ('Zither and Chopping-board'), a volume of poems in his native dialect, and followed this with autobiographical works such as *Waldheimat* (1897, 'Home in the Woods') and *Mein Him-melreich* (1901, 'My Heavenly Kingdom'), and novels, including *Die Schriften des Wald-schulmeisters* (1875, 'Writings of a Woodland Schoolmaster'), *Der Gottsucher* (1883, 'The Searcher After God') and *Jakob der Letzte* (1888, 'Jacob the Last'), vividly portraying his native district and its people.

ROSEN, Michael Wayne
(1946–)
English writer and performer, chiefly for children, born in Harrow, London. His ebullient delivery and accessible verse have made him a favourite with children in both performance and print, as well as leading to his frequent appearance on radio shows about books, such as *Treasure Islands* on BBC Radio 4. His humorous, quirky collections include *Quick Let's Get Out of Here* (1983), *Don't Put Mustard in the Custard* (1984) and *We're Going On A Bear Hunt* (1989). He has received several prizes for his poetry, including the Signal Poetry Award (1982) and the Smarties Award (1989).

ROSENBERG, Isaac
(1890–1918)
English poet and artist, born in Bristol, the son of Jewish émigrés from Russia. Educated at council schools in the east end of London, he was apprenticed as an engraver before studying art at Slade School. He kept poor health and went to South Africa in 1914 but returned to England the following year, enlisted in the army and was killed in action in France. He published his first collection, *Night and Day*, in 1912, and *Youth* in 1915 before the posthumous appearance of *Poems* in 1922, a selection edited by **Gordon Bottomley** and introduced by **Laurence Binyon**. Though revered by the cognoscenti, his reputation languished until the appearance in 1937 of his *Collected Works* (newly edited in 1979). His comparatively poor upbringing, highly charged vocabulary and bluntly realistic attitude to the war mark him out from other war poets.

ROSENFELD, Isaac
(1918–56)
American critic and writer of fiction. Rosenfeld was a contemporary, and at one time rival, of **Saul Bellow**. His novel *Passage From Home* (1946), set in his native Chicago, was one of the first Jewish-American novels about adolescence. It promised much, but Rosenfeld was undisciplined and dissipated his talents in literary journalism, collected in *An Age of Enormity* (1962). Having called his generation 'moral undergroundlings', he died of a heart attack, aged 38, while living in squalor in a Chicago basement.

ROSENFELD, Morris
(1862–1923)

American poet, born in Poland and heavily influenced by an Orthodox Jewish upbringing. He was sent to London when he was 20 years old to learn tailoring and four years later emigrated to the USA, where he worked in the New York ghetto. His poems, which were printed in Yiddish newspapers, gave voice to the tribulations of his fellow sweatshop workers. *Songs from the Ghetto* (1898), a translated collection, was followed 10 years later by the three-volume *Works of Morris Rosenfeld*.

ROSENTHAL, Jack Morris
(1931–)

English dramatist, born in Manchester. Educated at Sheffield University, he joined the promotions department of Granada television in 1956 and made his professional writing debut with over 150 episodes of *Coronation Street* (1961–9). A contributor to the influential satirical programme *That Was The Week That Was* (1963), he created the series *The Lovers!* (1970). A prolific writer of individual plays dramatizing real-life stories, wartime nostalgia and Jewish domestic issues, his warmly humorous television work includes *The Evacuees* (1975), *Barmitzvah Boy* (1976), *Spend, Spend, Spend* (1977), *And A Nightingale Sang* (1989) and *London's Burning* (1986), which spawned the long-running series. His film scripts include *Lucky Star* (1980) and *Yentl* (1983) in collaboration with Barbra Streisand, whilst stage work includes *Smash!* (1981) and *Our Gracie* (1983). He is married to the actress Maureen Lipman.

ROSHWALD, Mordecai Marcelli
(1921–)

American author, born in Drohobycz, Poland, and educated at the Hebrew University of Jerusalem. Roshwald's first book, *The Education of Man* (1954), was published in Hebrew. Outside of academia—Roshwald worked for many years at the University of Minnesota—he is best known as the author of the futuristic novel *Level Seven* (1959), set in an underground bunker during a nuclear showdown.

ROSNY
joint pseud of the brothers
Boëx, Joseph Henri
(1856–1940)
Boëx, Séraphin Justin François
(1859–1948)

French novelists, born in Brussels. Their vast output of social novels, naturalistic in character, includes *L'Immolation* (1887, 'The Sacrifice') and *L'Impérieuse Bonté* (1905, 'Pressing Kindness'), signed jointly, and after 1908, when they separated, the older Rosny's *L'Appel au bonheur* (1919, 'The Appeal to Happiness') and *La Vie amoureuse de Balzac* (1930, 'Balzac's Love Life'), and *La Courtisane passionée* (1925, 'The Passionate Prostitute') and *La Pantine* (1929, 'The Puppet') by the younger Rosny.
▷M C Poinsou, *Joseph Henri Böex* (1907)

ROSS, William, also known as ROS, Uilleam
(1762–90)

Gaelic poet, born in Broadford, Skye and educated at Forres, Morayshire. In his youth he became proficient in the Gaelic dialects of the Western Highlands and in playing a number of different instruments. He was soon acknowledged for his great range of pastoral and descriptive verse, which also showed considerable spirit and humour. After only a few years' employment as parish schoolmaster of Gairloch, however, he died, probably of tuberculosis, but possibly of unrequited love for a woman called Marion Ross, who is described in his *Praise of the Highland Maid*. Two volumes of his work were posthumously published: *Orain Ghae'lach* (1830) and *An dara clobhualadh* (1834).

ROSSETTI, Christina Georgina
(1830–94)

English poet, born in London, daughter of **Gabriele Rossetti** and sister of **Dante Gabriel Rossetti**. Educated at home, she was to have been a governess but she retired through ill-health which may originally have been feigned or psychosomatic. She was precocious poetically; her grandfather printed a pamphlet by her before she was in her teens. She was engaged to James Collinson, the painter, but this was broken off when he returned to the Catholic faith, Christina being a devout High Anglican. Her first lyrics, including 'An End' and 'Dream Lane', were published in the first issue of *The Germ* (1850) under the pseudonym Ellen Alleyne. *Goblin Market*, her first and best-known collection, was published in 1862, and in 1866 came *The Prince's Progress. Sing Song: A Nursery Rhyme Book*, illustrated by Arthur Hughes, appeared in 1872. By the 1880s recurrent bouts of illness had made her an invalid, but she still continued to write, later works including *A Pageant and Other Poems* (1881), *Time Flies: A Reading Diary* (1895), and *The Face of the Deep: A Devotional Commentary on the Apocalypse* (1892). Technically a virtuoso, she ranged far emotionally and imaginatively.

▷E W Thomas, *Christina Georgina Rossetti* (1931)

ROSSETTI, Dante Gabriel, in full **Gabriel Charles Dante Rossetti**
(1828–82)

English poet, painter and translator, son of **Gabriele Rossetti** and brother of **Christina** and William Rossetti, born in London. His father was Gabriele Pasquale Giuseppe Rossetti, a Neapolitan political refugee; his mother was Frances Mary Lavinia Polidori Rossetti, daughter of Gaetano Polidori and sister of Lord **Byron**'s physician, Dr John Polidori. The household was artistic and more Italian than English. He was educated at King's College School and attended Cary's Art Academy, having shown early his inclination towards poetry and art. There was a short spell at the Antique School of the Royal Academy before he persuaded Ford Madox Brown to tutor him, but this was short-lived. With Holman Hunt and Millais he formed the Pre-Raphaelite Brotherhood. Throughout the 1840s his poetry and painting prospered, and he completed on canvas 'The Girlhood of Mary Virgin', 'How They Met Themselves' and 'Ecce Ancilla Domini', symbolic, historical, overpowering. Like Christina, several of his poems—'The Blessed Damozel' and 'My Sister's Sleep'—had appeared in *The Germ* in 1850, the year he met Elizabeth Siddal (or Siddall), whom he married in 1860 after a fraught and prolonged courtship. Already an invalid, she died in 1862 from a surfeit of laudanum. He met **John Ruskin** in 1854 and two years later **William Morris**, whom he manifestly influenced. His wife's death, however, affected him deeply and his work took on the taint of morbidity. (He exhumed her body to retrieve manuscripts left by her side.) *The Early Italian Poets* was published in 1861, translations from 60 poets such as **Dante** and **Guido Cavalcanti**. *Poems* appeared in 1870, drawing on those he had interred with his wife, but though he replied robustly to **Robert Buchanan**'s attack on him in 'The Fleshly School of Poetry' with 'The Stealthy School of Criticism', he fell into a depression and attempted suicide in 1872. Nevertheless, *Ballads and Sonnets* with the sonnet sequence 'The House of Life' and 'The King's Tragedy' appeared in 1881. At odds with Victorian morality, his work is lush, erotic and medieval, romantic in spirit, and of abiding interest and fascination.
▷C Davies, *Dante Gabriel Rossetti* (1925)

ROSSETTI, Gabriele
(1783–1854)

Italian poet and writer, father of **Christina Rossetti**, **Dante Gabriel Rossetti** and the critic William Michael Rossetti, and sometime curator of ancient bronzes in the Museum of Bronzes at Naples. He was a member of the provisional government set up by Murat in Rome (1813). After the restoration of Ferdinand I to Naples, he joined the Carbonari secret society and greeted the constitution demanded by the patriots in 1820 in a famous ode. On the overthrow of the constitution he went to London (1824), where he became Professor of Italian at the new University of London. Besides writing poetry he was a close student of **Dante**, whose *Inferno* he maintained was chiefly political and anti-papal.
▷R D Williams, *The Rossetti Family* (1932)

ROSSNER, Judith Perelman
(1935–)

American novelist, born and educated in New York City. Her first book, *To the Precipice* (1966), established her interest in women who are no longer willing or able to accept the overdetermining pressures of society, but who are not allowed simply to choose their destinies. This was handled with heavier irony in *Nine Months in the Life of an Old Maid* (1969) and in the rather better *Any Minute I Can Split* (1972), but had its definitive statement in *Looking for Mr Goodbar* (1975), an unforgiving and ruthless exploration of female sexuality and sexual stereotyping; it was mangled by Hollywood, its psychological and psycho-social insights reduced to prurient and voyeuristic sentimentalism. Later works have included *Attachments* (1977) and *August* (1983).

ROSSO, Renzo
(1926–)

Italian novelist, born in Trieste, and originally a student of philosophy at its university. He then studied the violin. His chief work is the novel *La dura spina* (1963, Eng trans *The Hard Thorn*, 1966), a subtle novel about a pianist whose powers of interpretation are becoming eroded by his unintentionally cruel womanizing.

ROSTAND, Edmond
(1868–1918)

French poet and dramatist, born in Marseilles. He published *Les Musardises* ('Dawdlings'), a volume of verse, in 1890 but rose to fame with *Cyrano de Bergerac* (1897, Eng trans 1898; also trans by **Anthony Burgess** for the film by Jean Paul Rappeneau, 1992), *L'Aiglon* (1900, Eng trans 1900), *Chantecler* (1910, Eng trans 1910), and other plays in verse which eschewed the prevailing moods of Naturalism and Expressionism in favour of a lighter, more vivacious popular style.
▷R Gérard, *Edmond Rostand* (1935)

ROSTEN, Leo Calvin
(1908–)

American anthologist, novelist and social scientist, born in Łodz, Poland. *The Education of H*y*m*a*n K*a*p*l*a*n* (1937), a comic tale set in a night school for adult immigrants to the United States, first established his reputation as a gentle humorist. His best-known book is probably *The Joys of Yiddish* (1968); following its success, he has written a number of popular anthologies of humour, many of them dealing largely with Jewish wit. These include *O Kaplan!, My Kaplan* (1976). Some of his works were originally published under the pseudonym Leonard Q Ross; using the same name minus the Q he has also written stage plays.

ROTH, Henry
(1906–)

American novelist. He was born in Tysmenica in the Austro–Hungarian Empire, arriving in the USA as a baby. His childhood is fictionalized in *Call It Sleep* (1934), one of the classics of 20th-century American literature. It dramatizes David Schearl's awakening consciousness against the background of New York City. Though 'authentic', it is by no means a sociological documentary, and is marked by a hallucinatory inwardness which is influenced by **Joyce**. During the Depression Roth worked for the New Deal Works Progress Administration and as a teacher, later making his living as a mental hospital assistant, duck farmer and machine toolist. *Shifting Landscape*, a collection of occasional pieces, was published in 1987. He took many years to complete his long-projected second novel, the first volume of which, *Mercy Of A Rude Stream*, appeared in 1994.
▷ *Nature's First Green* (1979)

ROTH, Joseph
(1894–1939)

Austrian novelist, short-story writer and critic, brought up on the eastern frontiers of the Austro–Hungarian Empire. His father was Austrian, his mother a Russian Jew. He had a miserable life. His father left his mother before he was born, the war disrupted his education, his wife went mad, and he survived by doing menial jobs and journalism until the 1930s when, exiled in Paris, he became an alcoholic and died destitute. A prolific writer, his major themes were not dissimilar to those of **Robert Musil**. His concern for those brought up in the Austro–Hungarian Empire, however, was linked with that of the Jewish diaspora. Narratively conventional, he was a versatile and readable writer, still underrated though more of his work has been translated in recent years. Key works are *Hiob: Roman eines einfachen Mannes* (1930, Eng trans *Job: The Story of a Simple Man*, 1931), *Radetzkymarsch* (1932, Eng trans *The Radetzky March*, 1934), *Beichte eines Mörders* (1936, Eng trans *Confessions of a Murderer*, 1938), *Hotel Savoy* (1924), *Tarabas* (1934, Eng trans 1935) and *Die Kapuzinergruft* (1938, 'Grave of the Capucins').
▷ *Juden auf der Wanderschaft* (1926, 'Wandering Jews')

ROTH, Philip Milton
(1933–)

American novelist, born in Newark, New Jersey. He attended Bucknell University as an undergraduate and received a master's degree from Chicago University where he taught (1956–8). His upbringing was Jewish, conventional and lower middle-class; he did not begin to fight the 'taboos that had filtered down to me' until he was in his late teens. An uncompromising, tough-minded writer, his portraits of Jews adept at scheming and compromise have frequently irritated rabbis and Jewish organizations. Daring to talk about abortion, masturbation and other sexual matters has led him into conflict with conservatives who have sought to restrict access to his books. His first book was *Goodbye Columbus* (1959), a collection of short stories, each obsessed with confrontations between Jews of radically different persuasions and temperaments. Two accomplished novels succeeded these—*Letting Go* (1962) and *When She Was Good* (1967) —before publication of his 'masturbation' masterpiece, *Portnoy's Complaint* (1969), made him notorious. The success of the monotone confession of Alexander Portnoy to his psychiatrist lies in the fascination of the narrator's 'voice'. Roth's prolific career has taken many turns; much more than a one-joke writer, he is constantly exploring the relationship 'between the written and the unwritten world', a distinction he finds more useful than that between imagination and reality, or art and life. Nathaniel Zuckerman, a writer, is the central presence in the trilogy of novels—*The Ghost Writer* (1979), *Zuckerman Unbound* (1981) and *The Anatomy Lesson* (1983)—and its epilogue, *The Prague Orgy* (1985), collected in *Zuckerman Bound* (1985). *The Counterlife* appeared in 1987 and the autobiographical *Patrimony* (which bore the teasing subtitle 'A True Story') in 1991. In 1993 he published the novel *Operation Shylock*. He is married to the actress Claire Bloom.
▷ *The Facts: A Novelist's Autobiography* (1988)

ROTROU, Jean de
(1609–50)

French playwright, born in Dreux. He went to Paris, qualified as a lawyer, and turned to writing plays, as well as becoming one of the five poets who worked into dramatic form the ideas of Richelieu. His first pieces were in the Spanish romantic style. Next followed a classical period, culminating in three masterpieces, *Saint-Genest* (1646), a tragedy of Christian martyrdom, *Don Bernard de Cabrère* (1648) and *Venceslas* (1647). He died of the plague. Thirty-five of his plays are still extant.
▷ H Chandon, *La vie de Rotrou* (1884)

ROUGET DE LISLE, Claude Joseph
(1760–1836)

French soldier, born in Lons-le-Saunier. He wrote and composed the French national anthem *La Marseillaise* (originally *Chant de guerre pour l'armée du Rhin*, 'War Song for the Army on the Rhine') when stationed in 1792 as captain of engineers at Strasbourg. Wounded at Quiberon (1795), he left the army, and published in 1796 a volume of *Essais en vers et en prose* ('Essays in Prose and Verse'). The *Marseillaise* was made known in Paris by troops from Marseilles.
▷ M Henry-Rosier, *Rouget de Lisle* (1937)

ROUMAIN, Jacques
(1907–44)

The leading figure in Haitian literature. Of an elite mulatto family, he was a poet, diplomat, essayist, editor and politician (he founded the Haitian Communist Party in 1934). His magazine *Revue Indigène* educated Haitian intellectuals. His best novel is his last: *Gouvenours de la rosée* (1944, Eng trans *Masters of the Dew*, 1947).

ROUMANILLE, Joseph
(1818–91)

French writer, born in Saint-Rémy, Bouches-du-Rhône. He taught at Avignon, his pupils including **Frédéric Mistral**. In 1847 he published *Li Margarideto*, a book of his own poems, in 1852 a volume of Provençal poems, and later many volumes of verse and prose in Provençal dialect. With Mistral and others he founded the 'Soci dou Félibrige' for the revival of Provençal literature.
▷ E Ripert, *Joseph Roumainille* (1948)

ROUSSEAU, Jean Baptiste
(1671–1741)

French poet, born in Paris, the son of a shoemaker. He wrote for the theatre, and composed lampoons on the literary frequenters of the Café Laurent which started feuds leading to recriminations, lawsuits and a sentence of banishment (1712). Thereafter he lived abroad, in Switzerland, Vienna (with Prince Eugene) and Brussels. His sacred odes and *cantates* are splendidly elaborate, frigid and artificial; his epigrams are bright, vigorous and unerring in their aim.

ROUSSEAU, Jean Jacques
(1712–78)

French political philosopher, educationist and author, born in Geneva. His mother died at his birth, and he had little early family life and no formal education. In 1728 he ran away to Italy and Savoy, where he lived with Baronne Louise de Warens (1700–62) and was baptized a Catholic, and after an itinerant existence for a few years eventually became her lover and general factotum (1733–41). In 1741 he was supplanted, and moved to Paris where he began to thrive, making a living from secretarial work and music copying. There he began a lifelong association with an illiterate maidservant at his inn, Thérèse le Vasseur; by her he had five children, all of whom he consigned to foundling hospitals, despite his later proclamations about the innocence of childhood. He composed an operetta, *Les Muses Galantes* (1745, 'The Gallant Muses'), which led to correspondence with **Voltaire** and acquaintance with **Diderot**, and through that came to contribute articles on music and political economy to the *Encyclopédie*. In 1750 he made his name with a prize essay, *Discours sur les sciences et les arts* (Eng trans *A Discourse on the Arts and Sciences*, 1752), which argued that civilization had corrupted our natural goodness and decreased our freedom; and in 1752 he triumphed with a second operetta, *Le Devin du village* (Eng trans *The Cunning Man*, 1766). He was now a celebrity, and in 1754 wrote *Discours sur l'origine et les fondements de l'inégalité parmi les hommes* ('Discourse on the Origin and Causes of Inequality Among Men'), in which he attacked private property and argued that man's perfect nature was corrupted by society. He travelled restlessly first to Geneva, where he was much influenced by Calvinism, back to Paris and then to Luxembourg in 1757, and in 1758 published his *Lettre à d'Alembert sur les spectacles* (Eng trans *A Letter to M. d'Alembert*, 1759), in which he argued against the establishment of a theatre in Geneva on Puritan grounds. In 1762 he published his masterpiece, *Du contrat social* (Eng trans *A Treatise on the Social Compact*, 1764), which begins with the ringing paradox, 'Man is born free; and everywhere he is in chains'. It postulated a social contract in which every individual surrenders his rights totally to the collective 'general will', which is the sole source of legitimate sovereignty and by definition represents the common good; the aberrant can then, in the sinister phrase, 'be forced to be free' in their own interests. His text, with its slogan 'Liberté, Égalité, Fraternité' ('Liberty, Equality, Fraternity'), became the bible of the French Revolution and of progressive movements in general, though clearly the main thesis was vulnerable to totalitarian perversions. Also in 1762 he published in novel form *Émile, ou de l'éducation* (Eng trans *Emilius and Sophia; or, A New System of Education*, 1762–3), a simple romance of a child reared apart from other children as an experiment; it greatly influenced educationists like Pestalozzi and Froebel, but so outraged the political and religious establishment that he had to flee to Switzerland. He moved to England in 1766 at the invitation of David Hume and went to live at Wootton Hall near Ashbourne in Derbyshire (1766–7), where he began writing his *Les Confessions* (Eng trans *Confessions*, 1783–91), a remarkably frank if somewhat narcissistic volume of self-revelations. He became seriously unstable at about this time, quarrelled with his English friends (particularly Hume), and fled back to France in 1767 with a full-blown persecution complex. In Paris from 1770 to 1778 he completed *Les Confessions* (published 1782–9), wrote a justification of his past actions (*Rousseau, juge de Jean Jacques*, 1780, 'Rousseau, Judge of Jean-Jacques') and *Rêveries du promeneur solitaire* (1782, Eng trans *The Reveries of a Solitary*, 1927), and eked out a living as a music copyist again. He declined further, became seriously insane, and died in Ermenonville. In 1794 his remains were placed alongside Voltaire's in the Panthéon in Paris. By the time of his death he had became very much a spokesman for Romanticism in Britain and Europe.

ROUSSEL, Raymond
(1887–1933)

French fabulist. He was born in Paris to a stockbroker father and an eccentrically artistic mother. He dabbled in verse when very young and wrote his first novel, *La Doublure*, at the precocious age of 10. In 1910 he published his most important work, *Impressions d'Afrique* (Eng trans *Impressions of Africa*, 1965), a surreal fantasy about parts of the continent he had never actually visited. The book is full of non-sequiturs, quasi-documentary asides and sheer invention. It made a considerable impact on such American writers as **John Ashbery** and **Harry Mathews**, who named their experimental journal after a later book of Roussel's; *Locus Solus* was published in part in 1918, but only appeared in its entirety in 1963. Roussel was a homosexual whose heavy addiction to barbiturates is reflected in the astonishing pace and arrhythmia of his prose. In 1933, following a long build-up in which he wrote testaments and letters of farewell, he committed suicide.
▷ M Foucault, *Death and the Labyrinth: The World of Raymond Roussel* (1966)

ROUSSIN, André
(1911–)

French boulevard playwright and theatre director, born in Marseilles. He co-founded the Rideau Gris Company in his native city. He won popular acclaim for his clever if ultimately frivolous farces, such as *La Petite Hutte* (1947). This, his most famous, was adapted by **Nancy Mitford**: as *The Little Hut* (1948) it delighted London and New York audiences.

ROWBOTHAM, David
(1924–)

Australian poet, born in Toowoomba, Queensland, who worked for the Brisbane *Courier-Mail* as literary and drama critic and later as literary editor before publishing *Ploughman and Poet* (1954). This was followed by a number of books including *All the Room* in 1964, in which year he was awarded the Grace Leven Prize. Three more books preceded *Selected Poems* (1975) and *Maydays* (1980). His rather spare style has gained him a reputation abroad in literary circles.

ROWE, Elizabeth, née Singer
(1674–1737)

English poet, born in Ilchester, Somerset, daughter of a dissenting minister. She was educated at boarding school, began writing early and had poems published in magazines from 1691. Her friends included the Countess of Winchilsea, **Matthew Prior**, and Isaac Watts. In 1710 she married a scholar, Thomas Rowe, and moved to London, but after his early death in 1715 she retired in grief to Somerset where she occupied herself with charitable works and writing. Her prose epistles on moral and religious themes, *Friendship in Death* and *Letters Moral and Entertaining* (1728–32), cast in the form of sentimental romance, were admired by **Dr Johnson** and **Samuel Richardson** and remained popular until the 19th century in England and America. Her poems also were highly esteemed for their piety, tender feeling, purity of sentiment and lyrical grace.
▷ *The Poetry of Elizabeth Singer Rowe*, ed with introduction by M F Marshall (1987); H F Stecher, *Elizabeth Singer Rowe, the Poetess of Frome* (1973)

ROWE, Nicholas
(1674–1718)

English poet and dramatist, born in Little Barford, Bedfordshire. He was educated at

Westminster, was called to the Bar, but from 1692 devoted himself to literature. Between 1700 and 1715 he produced eight plays of which three were popular—*Tamerlane* (1702), *The Fair Penitent* (1703) and *The Tragedy of Jane Shore* (1714), followed by *The Tragedy of Lady Jane Grey* (1715). Lothario in *The Fair Penitent* was the prototype of Lovelace in **Samuel Richardson**'s *Clarissa* and the name is still the synonym for a fashionable rake. Rowe translated **Lucan**'s *Pharsalia* and his edition of **Shakespeare** (1709–10) at least contributed to the popularity of his author. Rowe was under-secretary to the Duke of Queensberry from 1709 to 1711; in 1715 he was appointed poet laureate and a surveyor of customs to the port of London; the Prince of Wales made him clerk of his council, and Lord Chancellor Parker appointed him clerk of presentations in chancery.

▷Dr Johnson, *Lives of the Most Eminent English Poets* (10 vols, 1779–81)

ROWLEY, William
(c.1585–c.1642)

English actor and playwright. Little is known about him, except that he collaborated with **Thomas Dekker**, **Thomas Middleton**, **John Heywood**, **John Webster**, **Philip Massinger** and **John Ford**. Four plays published with his name are extant: *A New Wonder, a Woman Never Vext* (1632); *All's Lost by Lust*, a tragedy (1633); *A Match at Midnight* (1633); and *A Shoemaker, a Gentleman* (1638).

▷C W Stock, *William Rowley* (1910)

ROWSON, Susanna Haswell
(c.1762–1824)

American dramatist, novelist, poet, essayist and actress. Born in Portsmouth, England, she moved to the USA as a child, returned to England in 1777, and went back to America in 1793. Considered by many to be America's first professional novelist, she published seven sometimes sensational novels, including *Charlotte Temple, A Tale of Truth* (1791 in the UK, 1794 in the USA), a seduction tale modelled upon **Richardson**'s *Clarissa*. It sold badly in Britain but became a huge bestseller in America. For the stage she wrote a series of social comedies, including *The Female Patriot* (1794) and *Americans in England* (1796). Keenly interested in education for women, she wrote several tracts and essays on the subject, and in 1797 left the Boston theatre where she had been acting in order to found a boarding school for girls.

▷P Barker, *Susanna Rowson* (1986)

ROY, Gabrielle
(1907–83)

French–Canadian novelist, born in Manitoba, later resident in Quebec. Roy's first novel, *Bonheur d'occasion* (1945), translated as *The Tin Flute* (1947), was the first French–Canadian work to be awarded the Prix Femina. It was a realistic and compassionate novel about a slum family and a young woman's role in a society dominated by religion and the church. Subsequent novels drew on her prairie childhood and were marked by a strong and straightforward narrative style.

▷*La Détresse et l'enchantment* (1984), Eng trans *Enchantment and Sorrow* (1987); M Genuist, *La création romanesque chez Gabrielle Roy* (1966)

ROY, Jules
(1907–)

French air force officer (until 1953) and admirer of **Alfred de Vigny** and **Antoine de Saint-Exupéry**, who scored a popular success with his *La Vallé heureuse* (1946, 'The Happy Valley'), a semi-novel about his wartime air service. He began as a poet and essayist, and also wrote plays. His *Le Navigateur* (1954, Eng trans *The Navigator*, 1955) was a readable straight novel.

ROY, Namba, originally Nathan Roy Atkins
(1910–61)

Jamaican novelist. He was educated in Kingston but grew up among descendants of Maroons (escaped slaves) in Cockpit Country, where surviving African traditions of craftsmanship and oral narrative were formative influences. He joined the merchant navy in 1939, was invalided out in 1944, and settled in England with his English wife. He earned repute as a wood-carver and wrote two novels: *Black Albino* (1961), an imaginative re-creation of life in an 18th-century Maroon community, and *No Black Sparrows* (1989, posthumous), a realistic story about working-class struggles in 1930s Jamaica.

ROYDE-SMITH, Naomi
(c.1880–1964)

Welsh novelist, dramatist and biographer. In the early 1920s she held a literary salon with Rose Macauley, but never reached the latter's eminence. However, her many novels, although tending to the sentimental, were well constructed and well written. Her biography of the actress Sarah Siddons, *The Private Life of Mrs Siddons*, was published in 1933. She was married to the well-known **Shakespearean** actor Ernest Milton.

ROZANOV, Vasili Vasilievich
(1856–1919)

Russian writer, thinker and critic, born in Vetluga, Kostroma. He became a teacher in

provincial schools. His literary studies include that of **Fyodor Dostoyevsky**'s *Grand Inquisitor*, which, published in 1894, first brought him into prominence. Though a Christian, in his prolific writings he criticized from a **Nietzsche**an standpoint the contemporary standards in morals, religion, education, and particularly the too-strict attitude towards sex, which was for him the very soul of man. Much of his work is highly introspective, and his literary reputation is firmly based on the two books of fragments and essays *Uyedinyonnoe* (1912, Eng trans *Solitaria*, 1927) and *Opavshie listya* (1913; 1915, Eng trans *Fallen Leaves*, 1929).
▷M G Kurdyumov, *Vasili Vasilievich Rozanov* (1929)

ROZDHESTVENTSKY, Robert
(1932–)

Russian poet, born in the Arday region. He writes on topical themes, always with **Mayakovsky** in mind as an exemplar, in a light and easily assimilable style. He has travelled a great deal, and this is reflected in his lively, if not particularly profound, work.

ROZOV, Victor
(1913–)

Russian playwright, born in Yaroslavl. He was at first an actor, but, wounded early in the fight against the Nazis, turned to drama. His most famous play was *Vechno zhivye* (1956, Eng trans *Alive Forever*, in *Contemporary Russian Drama*, ed F D Reeve, 1968), upon which the film *The Cranes Are Flying* (1957) was based. His plays are light in the best possible way, with skilful characterization.

RÓZEWICZ, Tadeusz
(1921–)

Polish poet (regarded as an 'anti-poet') and story writer, born in Radomsko, whose view of life, stemming from his traumatic war experiences in the resistance to the Nazis, resembles that of **Samuel Beckett**. He acquired a huge following when he published his first poems immediately after World War II. These reflected his disenchantment with the idea of the relevance of 'beautiful poetry' to life as it really is in the 20th century. Later he took to writing rather more conventional plays of the absurd, most of which were translated (eg *Gone Out*, 1969). His reputation became a little dented when he published works 'warped by party propaganda', and he was attacked by communists and Catholics alike; but he abandoned this stance after 1956, and remains important for his initial impact on the Polish literary scene with his first collection, *Niepokóv* (1945, 'Anxiety').

Later plays include *Biale malzeństwo* (1975, Eng trans *Mariage Blanc*, 1983) and *Teatr niekonsekwencji* (1979, 'The Inconstant Theatre').
▷H Vogler, *Rósewicz* [sic] (1976)

RUBENS, Bernice Ruth
(1928–)

Welsh novelist and playwright, born and educated in Wales. She trained as a teacher and was an English mistress at a boys' school in Birmingham before working for the United Nations as a documentary film-maker. Her first novel was *Set on Edge* (1960), followed by *Madame Sousatzka* (1962, subsequently filmed), *Mate in Three* (1965) and *The Elected Member* (1969, published in the USA as *Chosen People*), for which she was awarded the Booker Prize. These were more overtly Jewish in subject-matter than subsequent books, but they clearly marked out Rubens's interest in familial guilt and the psychic damage caused by withdrawn or compromised love. In later books Rubens showed an interest in marginal social and sexual types, the 'cold and chosen ones'. Later novels include *A Five Year Sentence* (1978) and *Mr Wakefield's Crusade* (1985); there is some sense that in the later eighties and early nineties she has, like **Graham Greene** and, arguably, **Iris Murdoch**, interspersed more serious novels with lighter 'entertainments'. However, *A Solitary Grief* (1991) found her at the top of her powers, being a work of genuine profundity.

RUCCELLAI, Giovanni
(1475–1525)

Italian poet, a nephew of Lorenzo de Medici. He lived in Rome and took orders. His works include the blank verse *Le Api* ('The Bees'), an instructive poem based on book four of **Virgil**'s *Georgics*. He also wrote early Italian tragedies, such as *Rosamunda* (1515) and *Oreste* (1525).
▷A Marpicati, *Saggi critica* (1934)

RÜCKERT, Friedrich
(1788–1866)

German poet and scholar, born in Schweinfurt. He studied law, philology and philosophy at Würzburg, and during the Napoleonic wars stirred up German patriotism with his *Deutsche Gedichte* (1814, 'German Poems'). After the wars he studied oriental languages, of which he became professor at Erlangen (1826–41) and Berlin (1841–8), and recast in German verse many famous books of countries of the orient. His original work includes the lyrical *Liebesfrühling* (1923, 'The Springtime of Love'), the reflective poems *Die Weisheit des Brahmanen* (1836–9, 'The Wisdom of the Brahmans'), and the personal *Kindertotenlieder* ('Songs of the Deaths of Children'), posthumously published in 1872 and set to music by Mahler in 1902.

▷H Prang, *Friedrich Rückert* (1963)

RUDD, Steele, properly **Arthur Hoey Davis** (1868–1935)

Australian humorous writer, born in Drayton, Darling Downs, Queensland. Davis, a clerk in the public service, started by writing articles on rowing under the name Steele Rudd. His famous creations Dad and Dave began life in the Sydney *Bulletin* in 1895, in a series of humorous articles on 'selection' life (on crown land allocated for tenant cultivation), which appeared in book form as *On Our Selection* in 1899, followed by *Our New Selection* (1903). The popularity of the series led to his dismissal from the public service and to his starting *Steele Rudd's Magazine* in 1904. The chronicles of the Rudd family were covered in 10 books and extended to the stage and to both silent and sound films, but the formula lost its attraction and developed into farce, losing its earlier relevance to pioneering life and to Davis's own family experiences.

RUDNICKI, Adolf (1912–90)

Polish novelist, story writer and essayist, often called the 'Jeremiah of the Warsaw ghetto'. His first novel, *Szcury* (1931, 'The Rats'), with its downtrodden 'little man' protagonist, was one of the best examples of Polish inter-war **Kafka**-influenced books. After World War II he emerged as Poland's leading chronicler of the plight of the Jews, deeply sarcastic and deliberately 'rough', yet compassionate beneath this surface. There are two selections of stories in translation: *Ascent to Heaven* (1951) and *The Dead and Living Sea* (1957).

RUDOLF VON EMS (c.1200–c.1254)

German poet and knight from Hohenems (Ems) near Bregenz in what is now Austria. His Middle High German poetry owes stylistic and formal debts to his acknowledged mentor **Gottfried von Strassburg**, though he later disavowed Gottfried in favour of a more 'worldly' style. He wrote prolifically, and on a huge range of subject-matter: Romance (*Der Gute Gerhard*), religious epic (*Josapahat und Barlaam*) and history (*Alexander*). His last, most ambitious project was a history of the world (*Weltchronik*). Though this only gets as far as the Hebrew kings, it is still some 30 000 lines long. Rudolf died in Italy, in the service of the German King Konrad IV, defending Konrad's interests against the papacy.

RUEDA, Lope de (c.1510–1565)

Spanish dramatist, born in Seville. He became manager of a group of strolling players. A pioneer of Spanish drama, he wrote comedies in the Italian style, short humorous pastoral dialogues, known as *pasos*, a form developed by **Cervantes**, and 10 burlesques.

▷D V Otero, *Lope de Rueda* (1960)

RUFFINI, Giovanni Domenico (1807–81)

Italian writer, born in Genoa. In 1833 he joined Young Italy, and in 1836 had to flee to England. From 1875 he lived in Taggia in the Riviera. He wrote *Lorenzo Benoni: Passages in the Life of an Italian* (1853), *Dr Antonio* (1855), *Vincenzo* (1863), and other novels in English, and the libretto for Donizetti's *Don Pasquale* (1843).

▷A Linaker, *Giovanni Ruffini* (1882)

RUIBAL, (Argibay) José (1925–)

Spanish playwright and co-leader of the Underground Drama movement. He was born in Galicia, near Ponteverda, but lived in Latin America, mostly Uruguay and the Argentine, during his twenties and thirties. His early dramas were collected as *Los mendigos y seis peizas de caféteatro* (1969, title piece translated as *The Beggars*, 1969). The book was banned by the fascist government in Spain and was subsequently reissued under the more anodyne title *El mono piadoso* (1969). Ruibal's reputation established itself first in the USA, where he taught in the early 1970s at the University of New York, Albany, and the University of Minnesota, Minneapolis. His play *La máquina de pedir* (1970) was published in the US as *The Begging Machine* in 1975 in a special issue of the journal *Modern International Drama*; in 1971, his most important play *El hombre y la mosca* (published in Spanish, 1977) was produced in upstate New York as *The Man and the Fly*. It is densely symbolic, drawing on **Góngora y Argote**, Dalian Surrealism, **Kafka** and the **Čapek** brothers, and represents the most devastating of the Underground Dramatists' attacks on the Franco regime.

▷G E Wellwarth, *Spanish Underground Drama* (1972)

RUIZ, Juan (?1283–?1350)

Spanish writer, Archpriest of Hita, of whose life nothing certain is recorded—even his

name Juan Ruiz may be an invention; his *Libro de Buen Amor* ('Book of Good Love') is—along with *El Cid*—the most important long medieval Spanish poem. According to it, he was born at Alcalá de Henares, educated at Toledo, was a popular author of songs (some of which are in the book), and was archpriest of the village of Hita near Alcalá. But none of this may be true. The *Libro*, a masterwork by any standards, and a readable one, owes much to **Ovid**, to Goliardic poetry (poetry in Latin written by wandering scholars), to Latin secular drama and to the budding popular tradition as exemplified in its lyrics. Its subject is 'good love', as the title states—but it is an ironic and ambiguous work and no two scholars have ever agreed what exactly this 'good love' is; the author needed to cover his tracks, since he was producing a work in an esoteric tradition of very late courtly love (although this has been disputed). It incorporates the comic and morality tale, the sermon, the mock-autobiography and the fable. There is also much evidence of Islamic influence (perhaps absorbed from the author's alleged education in Toledo). **Chaucer** knew of it, and was influenced by it. The most scholarly edition of it was published in 1974.
▷M R L de Malkiel, *Two Spanish Masterpieces: the 'Book of Good Love' and 'The Celestina'* (1962)

RUIZ DE ALARCÓN Y MENDOZA, Juan
(1581–1639)

Spanish dramatist, born of a Spanish family in Mexico City. He studied at the University of Salamanca and probably practised law for a short time in Seville, where he took part in the literary life of the city. He returned to Mexico where he tried unsuccessfully to teach, then went back once more to Spain, where he tried to enter court life and was taunted by his contemporaries **Lope de Vega**, **Tirso de Molina** and **Quevedo** for his pretensions. He produced over 20 works, the main feature of which is their high moral tone: usually the good and just, if ordinary, man defeats the cheat and liar. His most famous play is probably *La Verdad Sospechosa* ('The Suspicious Truth'), and most of his plays deal with a moral point, eg *Las Paredes Oyen* ('Walls Have Ears') denounces gossip. Always held back by his physical defects (he was hunchbacked and knock-kneed), he envied Lope de Vega's popularity. His acute sense of inferiority (physical as well as worldly) may explain his recourse to moral rectitude. His work, however, is of high quality with sharply drawn characters and profound analysis of moral questions.
▷W Poesse, *Alarcón* (1972)

RUKEYSER, Muriel
(1913–80)

American poet, biographer, and translator, born and educated in New York. From the end of World War II until 1960 she was Vice-President of the House of Photography; technical and scientific ideas and processes play an important role in her verse. Her first collection, *Theory of Flight* (1935), reflects this most directly. In later volumes she develops a terse, imagistic style, stripped of rhetorical artifice and false emotion; collections include *Beast in View* (1944) and *Body of Waking* (1958). An important selection appeared as *Waterlily Fire* in 1962, and a full-scale *Collected Poems* two years before her death. Rukeyser also wrote biographies of Willard Gibbs (1942), Wendell Wilkie (1957) and Thomas Hariot (1971), reflecting her political interests. She also translated **Octavio Paz** and **Gunnar Ekelöf**.
▷L Kertesz, *The Poetic Vision of Muriel Rukeyser* (1980)

RULE, Jane Vincent
(1931–)

Canadian novelist and short-story writer, born in Plainfield, New Jersey, and educated in California and London. Her first novel was *Desert of the Heart* (1964), a bold study of two women tentatively approaching a lesbian relationship. Later books, such as *This is Not for You* (1970) and *Against the Season* (1971), explore similar territory, though in the latter book the range of characters is widened considerably. In *The Young in One Another's Arms* (1977) and *Contact with the World* (1980) homosexuality is used more broadly and metaphorically as an index of the estrangement felt by artists in an essentially philistine world. Typically, Rule uses a multiple narrative perspective. In 1975, she published the important study *Lesbian Images*, followed a decade later by *A Hot-Eyed Moderate* (1985), which includes essays on earlier lesbian writers such as **Marguerite Radclyffe Hall** and **Vita Sackville-West**. Her short stories are collected in *Themes for Diverse Instruments* (1975), *Outlander* (1981), a volume that also includes non-fiction, and *Inland Passage* (1985).

RULFO, Juan
(1918–)

Mexican novelist and short-story writer, born in Sayula, Jalisco. Much of his writing is based on his early life in the provinces, where his once-wealthy family were forced to flee following the loss of their fortune in the revolution. His early stories were collected in *El Llano en Llamas* (1953, *The Burning Plain*, 1956). The novel *Pedro Páramo* (1955, Eng trans 1959) is his most important work; taking as its central character an insecure and isolated man, it uses techniques such as interior monologues, along with the voices of dead peasants that linger on the air in their equally dead village, to construct a panorama of Mexican life in the early part of this century.

RUMENS, Carol
(1944–)

English poet, novelist and critic, born in London. A main theme of her poetry has been to try to give a response to the universal suffering of the 20th century: she has written, 'I believe that all the forces of the imagination should be employed to speak of their suffering'. But her love poems are also well regarded, and it has been said that she possesses 'an ability to touch the nerves underlying the domestic and the personal'. Her novel is *Plato Park* (1987), and she wrote a well-received study of **Jean Rhys** (1985).
▷ *Selected Poems* (1987)

RUNEBERG, Johan Ludvig
(1804–77)

Finnish poet, born in Jakobstaed (Pietarsaari). Writing in Swedish, his style was much influenced by his studies of Finnish folk-poetry, and he is considered the greatest poet of the national-Romantic school. He taught at Helsinki (1830–7), and at Porvoo (1837–57). He wrote several volumes of lyric verse, but his major works were *Elgskyttaråe* ('The Elk Shooters', 1832), a Norse epic, *Kung Fjalar* (1844, Eng trans *King Fjalar*, 1904), and his collection of patriotic ballads, *Fänrik Ståls Sägner* (1848–60, 'Tales of Ensign Stål', 2 vols), about Finland's war of independence (1808–9). It begins with 'Vårt land' ('Our land'), which has become the Finnish national anthem. He wrote epic poetry, notably *Hanna* (1836) and *Julquällen* (1841, 'Christmas Eve'), some plays, and edited for the Lutheran Church of Finland a Psalm Book which contained some 60 pieces of his own.
▷ T Wretö, *Johan Ludvig Runeberg* (1980)

RUNYON, (Alfred) Damon
(1884–1946)

American author and journalist, born in Manhattan, Kansas. After service in the Spanish–American war (1898) he turned to journalism and sports reporting for the *New York American* from 1911, and then feature writing with syndicated columns *Both Barrels* (1918–36) and *The Brighter Side*, from 1937. His first books were volumes of verse, *Tents*

of Trouble (1911) and *Rhymes of the Firing Line* (1912), but it was his short stories, written in a characteristic racy style, using the present tense, with liberal use of American slang and jargon, and depicting life in underworld New York and on Broadway, which won for him his great popularity. One collection, *Guys and Dolls* (1932), was adapted for a musical revue (1950). Other books include *Blue Plate Special* (1934) and *Take it Easy* (1939), and the play, with Howard Lindsay, *A Slight Case of Murder* (1935). From 1941 he worked as a film producer.
▷ T Clark, *The World of Runyon* (1978)

RUSHDIE, (Ahmed) Salman
(1947–)

British novelist, born in Bombay. His family moved to Pakistan when he was 17. He was educated at the Cathedral School, Bombay, then at Rugby in England where he experienced 'minor persecutions and racist attacks which felt major at the time'. He emigrated to Britain in 1965 and graduated from King's College, Cambridge in 1968. He worked as an actor and an advertising copywriter before becoming a full-time writer. Writing in the tradition of **James Joyce**, **Günter Grass** and the South American 'magic realists', he published his first novel, *Grimus*, in 1975, a muddled fable which sold poorly. With *Midnight's Children* (1981), a tour de force poised at the moment when India achieves independence, he emerged as a major international writer, inventive, imaginative and an intoxicating storyteller. It was awarded the Booker Prize. *Shame* (1983), a trenchant satire and a revisionist history of Pakistan and its leaders, was similarly conceived on a grand scale and was acclaimed another virtuoso performance. In *The Satanic Verses* (1988) he turned his attention towards Islam, in his familiar hyperbolic mode. The book was banned in India in 1988, and in 1989 Iran's Ayatollah Khomeini declared it blasphemous and issued a 'fatwa', or order of death, against him. Demonstrations followed and copies of the book were burned in Bradford along with effigies of the author, who was forced into hiding under police protection. Despite having to live in hiding since, he has published *Haroun and the Sea of Stories* (1990), a children's book, and a book of essays, *Imaginary Homelands* (1991). His public appearances are infrequent, and are usually part of his continuing attempt to have the fatwa revoked.

RUSKIN, John
(1819–1900)

English author and art critic, the son of a prosperous wine merchant in London.

Private tutoring took the place of schooling so that when he went up to Christ Church, Oxford in 1836, he was lacking in experience of the world. At Oxford he won the Newdigate Prize for poetry, and fancied himself as a poet until shortly after graduating, when he met Turner and discovered that his immediate task was to rescue the great painter from obscurity and neglect. *Modern Painters* (1843) was the result of this championship, which may well have embarrassed the painter. This work developed through another four volumes (1846–60) into a spiritual history of Europe with comments on every phase of morals and taste. For his task he had the advantage of frequent visits to the Continent with his parents. His marriage in 1848 to Euphemia (Effie) Chalmers Gray, who afterwards became Millais' wife, was legally annulled about the time he began his crusade on behalf of a new set of obscure or vilified painters, the pre-Raphaelite brotherhood, with which Millais was associated. *Modern Painters* and the offshoots of that great work, *The Seven Lamps of Architecture* (1848) and *The Stones of Venice* (1851–3), with its great chapter three 'On the nature of the Gothic', made him the critic of the day and something more than that, for the moral and social criticism in those works raised him into a moral guide or prophet, even though he had rejected the religious upbringing of his childhood. Following on the publication of the completed *Modern Painters* in 1860 he transferred his interest in art to the social question which had been implicit in much pre-Raphaelite painting. **Thomas Carlyle**'s attacks on utilitarianism no doubt helped, but Ruskin's resentment of the social injustice and squalor resulting from unbridled capitalism led him to a sort of Christian communism, for which he was denigrated. *Unto This Last* (1862), a protest against the law of supply and demand, was discontinued after four essays in *Cornhill Magazine* by **William Makepeace Thackeray** (1860). The contemptuous rejection of his social economics in this work, and in *Munera Pulveris* (1872), which was stopped after six essays in *Fraser's Magazine* (1862–3), was almost mortal to Ruskin. In *Sesame and Lilies* (1864–9), addressed to privileged young ladies, admonishing them on their duties, he likened his temper to that of Dean **Jonathan Swift**. In 1869 Oxford made him its first Slade Professor of Fine Art. He settled at Coniston, in the Lake District, and his incomparable vitality showed in the publication of various Slade lectures, but more memorably in *Fors Clavigera*, a series of papers addressed 'To the Workmen and Labourers of Great Britain' (1871–84), in which his social philosophy is fully discussed. Meanwhile he began to spend his fortune on such individual enterprises as the St George's Guild, a non-profit-making shop in Paddington Street, in which members gave a tithe of their fortunes, the John Ruskin school at Camberwell, and the Whitelands College at Chelsea. His last regret was that he had not, like St Francis, denuded himself of all wealth. In 1878, in failing health, he resigned the Slade professorship, but he returned to it briefly in 1883–4. In his last work, his unfinished autobiography *Praeterita*, also published in numbers (1886–8), he reminisced quietly, all passion spent save for a final jab at the railways which disturbed rural beauty. His last years were spent at Brantwood, Coniston, his solitude being consoled by the affection of his cousin Mrs Arthur Severn and her family. His influence was profound and enduring.
▷T J Wise and J P Smart, *A Life of John Ruskin* (1893)

RUSS, Joanna
(1937–)
American science-fiction writer, born in New York City. She has been Professor of English at the University of Washington since 1977. She published her first story in 1959. Her early work was more conventional in genre terms, but the novel *Picnic on Paradise* (1968), later incorporated in *Alyx* (1976), introduced the female adventurer to centre stage, and revised genre expectations in the process. Her most important novel is *The Female Man* (1975), a complex feminist study which postulates four alternate lives for its female protagonist, before bringing them together on the utopian female planet Whileaway. Her stories are collected in several volumes, and she has also written fantasy and juvenile novels, and criticism.

RUSSELL, Arthur, properly Arthur Russell Goode
(1889–1971)
Australian writer of adventure stories for children, born in Wedderburn, Victoria. His first book, *Dream Island: an Australian Story* (1926), was followed by perhaps his best-known, *Ginger for Pluck* (1926). Other titles include *The Sky Pirates* (1947) and *Mason's Circus* (1947). Set against a realistic Australian background, often on the south coast of Victoria, his stories mix standard elements such as hidden caves, smuggling, treasure and last-minute rescue, often with the aid of a wireless. Radio was one of Goode's subjects; he was for some years technical editor of a weekly magazine for Melbourne listeners, and edited a collection *Twenty-Six Radio Stories* (1931) as well as *Twenty-Six South Sea Stories* (1936).

RUSSELL, Bertrand Arthur William, 3rd Earl Russell

(1872–1970)

Welsh philosopher, mathematician, prolific author, winner of the Nobel Prize for literature, and controversial public figure throughout his long and extraordinarily active life. He was born in Trelleck, Gwent; his parents died when he was very young and he was brought up by his grandmother, the widow of Lord John Russell, the Liberal Prime Minister and 1st Earl. He was educated privately and at Trinity College, Cambridge, where he took first-class honours in mathematics and philosophy. He graduated in 1894, was briefly British Embassy attaché in Paris, and became a fellow of Trinity in 1895, shortly after his marriage to Alys Pearsall Smith. A visit to Berlin led to his first book, *German Social Democracy* (1896), and he was thus launched on an amazingly long, wide-ranging and fertile intellectual career. His most original contributions to mathematical logic and philosophy are generally agreed to belong to the period before World War I, as expounded for example in *The Principles of Mathematics* (1903), which argues that the whole of mathematics could be derived from logic, and the monumental *Principia Mathematica* (with Alfred North Whitehead, 1910–13), which worked out this programme in a fully developed formal system and stands as a landmark in the history of logic and mathematics. Russell's famous 'theory of types' and his 'theory of descriptions' belong to this same period. Wittgenstein came to Cambridge to be his student from 1912 to 1913 and began the work that led to the *Tractatus Logico-philosophicus* (1922), for the English version of which Russell wrote an introduction. He wrote his first genuinely popular work in 1912, *The Problems of Philosophy*, which can still be read as a brilliantly stimulating introduction to the subject. Politics became his dominant concern during World War I and his active pacifism caused the loss of his Trinity fellowship in 1916 and his imprisonment in 1918, during the course of which he wrote his *Introduction to Mathematical Philosophy* (1919). He had now to make a living by lecturing and journalism, and became a celebrated controversialist. He visited the Soviet Union, where he met Lenin, Trotsky and **Gorky**, which sobered his early enthusiasm for communism and led to the critical *Theory and Practice of Bolshevism* (1919). He also taught in Peking from 1920 to 1921. In 1921 he married his second wife, Dora Black, and with her founded (in 1927) and ran a progressive school near Petersfield; he set out his educational views in *On Education* (1926) and *Education and the Social Order* (1932). In 1931 he succeeded his elder brother, John, 2nd Earl Russell, as 3rd Earl Russell. His second divorce (1934) and marriage to Patricia Spence (1936) helped to make controversial his book *Marriage and Morals* (1932); and his lectureship at City College, New York, was terminated in 1940 after complaints that he was an 'enemy of religion and morality', though he later won substantial damages for wrongful dismissal. The rise of fascism led him to renounce his pacifism in 1939; his fellowship at Trinity was restored in 1944, and he returned to England after the war to be honoured with an OM, and to give the first BBC Reith Lectures in 1949. He was awarded the Nobel Prize for literature in 1950. He had meanwhile continued publishing important philosophical work, mainly on epistemology, in such books as *The Analysis of Mind* (1921), *An Enquiry into Meaning and Truth* (1940) and *Human Knowledge: Its Scope and Limits* (1948), and in 1945 published the bestselling *History of Western Philosophy*. He also published a stream of popular and provocative works on social, moral and religious questions, some of the more celebrated essays later being collected in *Why I am not a Christian* (1957). After 1949 he became increasingly preoccupied with the cause of nuclear disarmament, taking a leading role in CND and later the Committee of 100, and engaging in a remarkable correspondence with various world leaders. In 1961 he was again imprisoned, with his fourth and final wife, Edith Finch, for his part in a sit-down demonstration in Whitehall. His last years were spent in North Wales, and he retained to the end his lucidity, independence of mind and humour. The last major publications were his three volumes of *Autobiography* (1967–9).

RUSSELL, Eric Frank

(1905–78)

English science-fiction writer, born in Camberley, Surrey. He was the first writer from the UK to publish stories on a regular basis in US science-fiction magazines. The ingenious, often ironic short story was his most productive form. Much of his work was influenced by the outlandish pseudo-philosophical ideas of the American writer Charles Fort. His stories are collected in several volumes, including *Men, Martians and Machines* (1955), a collection of adventures featuring interplanetary explorers, which prefigures **Gene Rodenberry**'s *Star Trek* scenario, and *The Best of Eric Frank Russell* (1978). His novels, which include *Sinister Barrier* (1943, rev edn 1948) and *Sentinels From Space* (1953), are less satisfactory.

RUSSELL, George William, pseud **AE** or **A.E.**
(1867–1935)
Irish poet, painter, writer and economist, born in Lurgan, County Armagh. In 1877 the family went to Dublin, where at the Metropolitan School of Art Russell met **W B Yeats**, and, already something of a mystic, through him became interested in theosophy. This led him to give up painting, except as a hobby. Having worked first in a brewery, then as a draper's clerk, he published his first book in 1894, *Homeward: Songs by the Way*, and from then on became a recognized figure in the Irish literary renaissance. He was Editor of the *Irish Homestead* from 1906 to 1923, when it amalgamated with the *Irish Statesman*, and as editor of the latter from 1923 to 1930 he aimed at expressing balanced Irish opinion of the 1920s, although he held nationalistic sympathies. His writings include books on economics, *The Candle of Vision* (1918), which is an expression of his religious philosophy, books of essays, many volumes of verse, all expressing his mysticism, among them *The Divine Vision* (1903) and *Midsummer Eve* (1928), and a play, *Deirdre* (1907).
▷D Figgis, *A Study of a Man and a Nation* (1916)

RUSSELL, Willy (William)
(1947–)
English playwright, born in Whiston, Cheshire, who became a teacher after several years of working in industry. He is one of the most frequently performed of contemporary British dramatists, perhaps best known for the enormously popular *Educating Rita* (1979), in which a bubbly, working-class hairdresser embarks on an Open University English Literature course taught by a weary, middle-class lecturer. Combining poignant and mildly abrasive social comment with broad, sentimental humour, this is probably his most representative work. The musical *Blood Brothers* (1983) continues the formula, this time in the form of the story of two brothers who were separated at birth and brought up in different social classes. In the play *Shirley Valentine* (1986), a Liverpudlian housewife attempts to transform herself by impulsively deciding to become an independent woman.

RUTEBEUF
(c.1230–1286)
French trouvère, Champenois in origin but Parisian by adoption. He was the author of the semi-liturgical drama *Miracle de Théophile* (c.1260, a prototype of the Faust story), the *Dit de L'Herberie* ('The Tale of the Herb Market'), a monologue by a quack doctor, full of comic charlatanesque rhetoric, and also several typical stories.
▷L Chédat, *Rutebeuf* (1909)

RUTHERFORD, Mark *see* **WHITE, William Hale**

RUZZANTE, real name **Angelo Beolco**
(1502–42)
Italian dramatist and actor, born in Padua. He became famous under his stage name of 'Ruzzante'. He believed that the artist should shun grand effects in favour of the simple truths of peasant life, and most of his plays were comedies and dramas of rural life.
▷C Grabler, *Ruzzante* (1953)

RYDBERG, Abraham Viktor
(1828–95)
Swedish writer and scholar, born in Jönköping. After a hard childhood and early struggles to gain an education he worked as a journalist on the liberal newspaper *Götebergs Handels - och Sjöfartstidning* (1855–76), and was professor at Stockholm (1884–95). He wrote historical novels, including *Fribytaren på Östersjön* (1857, 'Freebooter in the Baltic'), *Singoalla* (1857), *Den siste atenaren* (1859, 'The Last Athenian') and *Vapensmeden* (1891, 'The Armourer'), and several volumes of Bible criticism. The leading cultural figure of his day, he also wrote works on philosophy, philology and aesthetics, translated **Goethe**'s *Faust*, and published a mythological study, *Undersökningar i germanisk mytologi* (1886–9).
▷K Warburg, *Viktor Rydberg* (1900)

RYLSKY, Maksym
(1895–1964)
Ukrainian poet and translator (**Pushkin**), born in Kiev. His father, a well-known intellectual, was of Polish descent. Forced to accommodate to Stalinism, he managed nevertheless to express his own voice—and often, indeed, overstepped the socialist-realist mark; later, with the 'Thaw', he regained something of his early power. Regarded by some as the master of his language and the greatest Ukrainian poet of the mid-20th century, he has not yet, unfortunately, been translated into English.

RYSKIND, Morrie
(1895–1985)
American lyricist and sketch writer, born in New York and educated at Columbia University. He wrote sketches for *The 49ers* (1922) and *Merry Go Round* (1927), and co-wrote *Animal Crackers* (1928) with **George Kaufman**. He worked with Kaufman again

on *Strike Up The Band* (1930) and *Of Thee I Sing* (1931). The latter brought him a Pulitzer Prize for Drama in 1932, shared with Kaufman and lyricist Ira Gershwin (1896–1983), a collaboration which also produced *Let 'Em Eat Cake* (1933). His other work includes screenplays, and a number of less successful musicals.

S

SAAR, Ferdinand von
(1833–1906)

Austrian dramatist, erotic poet, and, most successfully, writer of novellas, born in Vienna. He retired from a military life in order to devote himself to literature, and for many years lived in straitened circumstances. He was ultimately successful, but, at 70, fell victim to a painful cancer, and shot himself.

SAAVEDRA, Angel de, Duque de Rivas
(1791–1865)

Spanish poet, playwright, and politician, born in Córdoba. He was in exile from 1823 until 1834, when he inherited his title. Later he became a conservative prime minister. Now much of his work seems dated, but he has historical importance because for Spain he was the apotheosis of romanticism, and his play *Don Álvaro o la fuerza del sino* (1835, 'Don Alvaro or the Force of Destiny') was considered to be the Spanish equivalent of **Hugo**'s *Ernani*: 'not a single topic of romanticism is absent' from it, remarked a critic. Now it is remembered as having supplied the original for Verdi's opera *La forza del destino*. His poems were sonorous and influential, many of them being ballads in the style of Sir **Walter Scott**.
▷G Boussagol, *Angel de Saavedra, Duc de Rivas* (1926)

SABA, Umberto, pseud of Umberto Poli
(1883–1957)

Major Italian Jewish poet from Trieste. He kept himself intact from Italian literary politics—as ferocious and partisan as in any country in the world—and wrote as he wished, eventually reaching a peak of almost unprecedented eminence. The collection to which he added throughout his life, *Canzionieri*, is a 'massive lyric autobiography', 'a type of Odyssey of man in our times'. Thus a series of lyrics became an epic, and one of the most celebrated and loved long poems of our times.
▷J Cary, *Three Modern Italian Poets* (1969)

SABAHADDIN, Ali
(1909–48)

Turkish story writer and novelist, described by some as the best short-story writer of his time. He was born in Gümülcine in Thrace, and murdered also in Thrace—at Kirklarei—by Turkish policemen posing as peasants; this was during the presidency of Inönü. He wrote, in his shorter fiction, of the lives of Anatolian peasants, and as such was the chief pioneer of socialist realism in the mid-1930s. His finest novel is a portrait of an Anatolian town, *Kuyucakh Yusuf* (1937). His complete works, published in 1965–6, take up seven volumes. He is one of the very few writers whose gifts transcended his submission to socialist realism, driven by not only his genius but also by the truly terrible conditions prevailing in the Anatolia of his day.

SABATINI, Rafael
(1875–1950)

Italian-born novelist, born of Italian and British parentage in Jesi. Writing in English, he first made his name as an author of historical romances with *The Tavern Knight* (1904), which he followed after he settled in England in 1905 with many other such tales, including *The Sea Hawk* (1915), *Scaramouche* (1921) and *Captain Blood* (1922), historical biographies, and a study of *Torquemada* (1913).

SÁBATO, Ernesto
(1911–)

Major Argentinian novelist and essayist, born in Rojas, a village in the province of Buenos Aires, into an Italian family. He married a woman of Russian–Jewish origin, and has had to defend himself from almost every faction in what he has called his 'ill-fated' country: from anti-Semites, Peronists such as **Marechal**, Nazis (who abounded in Argentinia) and hardline Marxists (he was himself a communist until 1934). He became a professor of theoretical physics, but was dismissed in 1944 (when Peron was already in virtual control) for having been critical of Perónism. It is not insignificant that Sábato's cat is called **Freud** or that his dog is called **Jung**, nor that he is 'very unhappy' with himself, believing that he disrupts the lives of those around him—for this is the natural ambience of a man in whose non-fiction, fiction abounds, and vice versa. But, as has been claimed, he is primarily a novelist of the inner life, and readers with a capacity for introspection are at home with him in his three monumental novels: *El túnel* (1950, Eng trans, *The Outsider*, 1950, *The Tunnel*, 1988),

Sobré héroes y tumbas (1961, Eng trans, *On Heroes and Tombs*, 1981), and *Abaddón el exterminador* (1974, Eng trans *The Angel of Darkness*, 1991). These phantasmagorias, or 'gnostic eschatologies', written in tribute to 'the powers of the unconscious', are of enormous, although always fruitful, complexity, and have been described as 'the fullest presentation of Jungian ideas in modern fiction'; but they are eminently readable. His humane non-fiction, which includes a series of dialogues with **Borges**, is seminal, and forms a guide to Argentinian and Latin-American problems.

▷H D Oberhelman, *Ernesto Sábato* (1970)

SÁ-CARNEIRO, Mário de
(1890–1916)

Portuguese poet, story writer (*Céu em fogo*, 1915, 'Sky on Fire') and critic, whose poetry is amongst the best—with that of **Pesshana**—written in the early 20th century in Portugal. He was born in Lisbon and died by poison in Paris. He was a close friend to, and deeply influenced, **Pessoa**, Portugal's greatest poet since **Camoens**. Sá Carneiro was a genuine *poète maudit*, hugely gifted, and with some affinities to **Rimbaud**. At its worst his work is flatly decadent; at its best it is inspired and has not yet gained the recognition it deserves outside Portugal (where his genius is well recognized).

▷D Wohl, *Realidade e idealidade na lirica de Mário de Sá-Carneiro* (1968, in Portuguese, revised from the original German edition of 1960)

SACCHETTI, Franco
(c.1330–1400)

Italian novelist, born in Florence. He held several diplomatic offices. He wrote *Trecento Novelle* ('Three Hundred Stories') in the style of **Boccaccio**, first printed in 1724, of which 10 are translated in **William Roscoe**'s *Italian Novelists* (1825). He also published poetry and burlesques.

▷L Caretti, *Saggio sul Sacchetti* (1951)

SACHER-MASOCH, Leopold von
(1836–95)

Austrian lawyer and writer, born in Lemberg. He wrote many short stories and novels, including *Der Don Juan von Kolomea* (1866), depicting the life of small-town Polish Jews. The term 'masochism' has been coined to describe the form of eroticism detailed in his later works.

SACHS, Hans
(1494–1576)

German poet and dramatist, born in Nuremberg, the son of a tailor. He was bred a shoemaker, and early learnt verse-making from a weaver. On finishing his apprenticeship in 1511 he travelled through Germany, practising his craft in various cities, and frequenting the schools of the *Meistersinger*. On his return to Nuremberg in 1516 he started up business as a shoemaker, becoming a master of his guild in the following year. Sachs' literary career, which resulted in the tremendous output of more than 6300 pieces, falls into two periods. In the first he celebrated the Reformation and sang Luther's praises in an allegorical tale entitled *Die Wittenbergisch Nachtigall* (1523, 'The Nightingale of Wittenberg'), while his poetical fly-sheets, numbering about 200, considerably furthered the Protestant cause. In his second period his poetry deals more with common life and manners, and is distinguished by its vigorous language, good sense, homely morality and fresh humour. His best works are *Schwänke* ('Merry Tales'); serious tales; allegorical and spiritual songs; and Lenten dramas. He was the central character in Wagner's opera *Die Meistersinger von Nürnberg* (1886, 'The Master Singers of Nuremberg').

▷H von Wendler, *Hans Sachs* (1933)

SACHS, Nelly Leonie
(1891–1970)

German-born Swedish poet and playwright, joint winner of the Nobel Prize for literature, born in Berlin of a wealthy Jewish family. Between the wars she published a book of stories, *Tales and Legends* (1921), and several volumes of lyrical poetry. With the rise of Nazi power she studied Jewish religious and mystical literature, and in 1940 escaped to Sweden through the intercession of the Swedish royal family and **Selma Lagerlöf**. After World War II she wrote plays and poetry about the anguish of the Jewish people. She was awarded the 1966 Nobel Prize for literature, jointly with the Israeli novelist **Shmuel Yosef Agnon**.

▷W A Berendon, *Nelly Sachs zu Ehren* (1966)

SACKLER, Howard
(1929–82)

American playwright, director and actor, born in New York and educated at Brooklyn College. He is chiefly remembered for the success of his play *The Great White Hope* (1968), based on the career of the black American prizefighter Jack Johnson, which was a Broadway hit, and won him a Pulitzer Prize in 1969. His other works include a volume of poems, *Want My Shepherd* (1954) and a quartet of one-act plays, gathered together as *A Few Enquiries* (1970).

SACKVILLE, Charles, 6th Earl of Dorset
(1638–1706)

English courtier and poet. He succeeded to the earldom in 1677, having two years before been made Earl of Middlesex. He was returned by East Grinstead to the first parliament of Charles II, and became an especial favourite of the king, and notorious for his boisterous and indecorous frolics. He served under the Duke of York (James II) at sea, but could not endure his tyranny as king and ardently supported the cause of William III. His later years were honoured by his generous patronage of **Matthew Prior**, **William Wycherley** and **Dryden**. He wrote lyrics (such as 'To all you Ladies now at Land') and satirical pieces.
▷B Harris, *Charles Sackville* (1940)

SACKVILLE, Thomas, 1st Earl of Dorset
(1536–1608)

English poet and statesman, born in Buckhurst in Sussex, the only son of Sir Richard Sackville, Chancellor of the Exchequer. He studied law at Hart Hall, Oxford, and St John's College, Cambridge, and entered the Inner Temple and became a barrister. In 1555 he married, and in 1558 was in parliament. With **Thomas Norton** he produced the blank-verse tragedy of *Ferrex and Porrex* (later called *Gorboduc*) which in 1560–1 was acted before Queen Elizabeth, Sackville's second cousin. This work, after the style of **Seneca**, is claimed to be the earliest tragedy in English. He also wrote the verses *Induction* and *Buckingham's Complaint* for *A Mirror for Magistrates* (1563). His prodigality brought Sackville into disgrace, but he was later restored to political favour. It was he who announced Queen Elizabeth's death sentence to Mary, Queen of Scots in 1586. In 1599 he was made lord high treasurer, and in 1604 Earl of Dorset.
▷P Bacquet, *Un contemporain de Elisabeth I* (1966)

SACKVILLE-WEST, Vita Victoria Mary
(1892–1962)

English poet and novelist, born in Knole House, Kent, daughter of the 3rd Baron Sackville. Educated privately, she started writing novels and plays as a child. In 1913 she married the diplomat Harold Nicolson, and their marriage survived despite Nicolson's homosexuality and her own lesbian affair with Violet Trefusis. Her first published works were a collection of poems, *Poems of West and East* (1917), and a novel, *Heritage* (1919). In her *Orchard and Vineyard* (1921) and her long poem *The Land*, which won the 1927 Hawthornden Prize, her close sympathy with the life of the soil of her native county is expressed. Her prose works include the novels *The Edwardians* (1930), *All Passion Spent* (1931) and *No Signposts in the Sea* (1961), an account of her family in *Knole and the Sackvilles* (1947), and studies of **Andrew Marvell** and Joan of Arc. *Passenger to Teheran* (1926) records her years in Persia with her husband. A passionate gardener at Sissinghurst, Kent, her married home, she wrote a weekly gardening column for *The Observer* for many years. She was the model for **Virginia Woolf**'s *Orlando*.
▷M Steven, *Vita Sackville West: a critical biography* (1973)

SADE, Donatien Alphonse François, Comte de, (known as **Marquis**)
(1740–1814)

French writer, born in Paris. An army officer in the Seven Years War (1756–63), in 1772 he was condemned to death at Aix for his cruelty and unnatural sexual practices. He made his escape, but was afterwards imprisoned at Vincennes and in the Bastille, where he wrote works of sexual fantasy and perversion, including *Les 120 Journées de Sodome* (1784, Eng trans *The 120 Days of Sodom*, 1954), *Justine; ou, Les Malheurs de la vertu* (1791, Eng trans *Justine; or, the Misfortunes of Virtue*, 1954), *La Philosophie dans le boudoir* (1793, Eng trans *The Bedroom Philosophers*, 1965), *Juliette* (1798, Eng trans 1968) and *Les Crimes de l'amour* (1800, Eng trans, in part, as *Quartet*, 1963). He died in a mental asylum at Charenton. The word 'sadism', derived from his name, is used to describe the type of sexual activities which he practised.
▷J Lély, *La vie de Sade* (1952–7)

SADEH, Pinchas
(1929–)

Israeli novelist, who 'sees life as a parable' and is somewhat out of the mainstream of his country's literature. His first novel was translated as *Life is a Parable* (1966); later work is quaintly experimental (in one book none of the characters knows any of the others) and more secure.

SÁDI, SAADI, or SA'ADI, the assumed name of **Sheikh Muslih Addin**
(c.1184–?1292)

Persian poet, highly regarded in his native land. He was a descendant of 'Alī, Muhammad's son-in-law. He studied at Baghdad, travelled much, and near Jerusalem was taken prisoner by the Crusaders, but was ransomed by a merchant of Aleppo, who gave him his daughter in marriage. The catalogue of his works comprises 22 different kinds of writings in prose and verse, in Arabic and Persian, of which odes and dirges form the predominant part. The most celebrated of his works, however, is the *Gulistan* ('Rose Garden'), a kind of moral work in prose and verse, intermixed with stories, maxims, philosophical sentences, puns and the like. Next comes the *Bostan* ('Orchard Garden'), written in verse, and more religious than the *Gulistan*. Third comes the *Pend-Nameh* ('Book of Instructions').

▷H Massé, *Essai sur le poète Sádi* (1919)

SADLEIR, Michael
(1888–1957)

English author and publisher, born in Oxford, a son of Sir Michael Ernest Sadler, and great-grand-nephew of Michael Thomas Sadler; he took an older form of the name to avoid confusion. Educated at Rugby and Oxford, he joined the publishing firm of Constable, becoming a director in 1920. As well as numerous bibliographical works—he was Sandars reader in bibliography at Cambridge in 1937—he published novels, including *Hyssop* (1915), *These Foolish Things* (1937) and *Fanny by Gaslight* (1940), and biographies, of which *Michael Ernest Sadler: a memoir by his son* (1949) and *Anthony Trollope* (1927) are noteworthy.

SADOVEANU, Mihail
(1880–1961)

Romanian novelist, born in Pascani, Moldavia. At its best, in his stories, his style was simple and unaffected, and his story-telling powers were masterly. A prolific writer, his most famous tale is *Baltagul* (1930, Eng trans *The Hatchet*, 1964), about a woman who hunts down her husband's killers. His genius for evoking the Romanian rural scene has not been matched. *Povestiri din razboi* (1906, Eng trans *Tales of War*, 1962) shows him at his best, but *Mitrea Cocor* (1949, Eng trans 1953) is a tedious essay in socialist realism, and shows his powers greatly diminished.

▷J Steinberg, *Introduction to Rumanian Literature* (1966)

SAGAN, Françoise, pseud of Françoise Quoirez
(1935–)

French novelist, born in Cajarc in the Lot region, and educated at a convent in Paris and private schools. At the age of 18 she wrote, in only four weeks, the bestselling *Bonjour tristesse* (1954, Eng trans 1955; filmed 1958), followed by *Un Certain Sourire* (1956, Eng trans *A Certain Smile*, 1956; filmed 1958), both remarkably direct testaments of wealthy adolescence, written with the economy of a remarkable literary style. Irony creeps into her third, *Dans un mois, dans un an* (1957, Eng trans *Those Without*

Shadows, 1957), but moral consciousness takes over in her later novels, such as *Aimez-vous Brahms...* (1959, Eng trans 1960; filmed 1961 as *Goodbye Again*) and *La Chamade* (1966, Eng trans 1966). A ballet to which she gave the central idea, *Le Rendez-vous manqué* ('The Missed Rendezvous'), enjoyed a temporary *succès de scandale* in Paris and London in 1958. Her later works, including several plays, such as *Château en Suède* (1960, 'Castle in Sweden'), *Les Violons, parfois...* (1961, 'Sometimes, Violins...') and *Un Piano dans l'herbe* (1970, 'A Piano on the Grass'), and novels such as *L'Echarde* (1966, 'The Splinter'), *Le lit défait* (1977, Eng trans *The Unmade Bed*, 1978), *La Femme Fardée* (1981, Eng trans *The Painted Lady*, 1983) and *Un orage immobile* (1983, Eng trans *The Still Storm*, 1984) have had a mixed critical reception.

▷G Hourdin, *Le cas de Françoise Sagan* (1958)

SAHGAL, Nayantara
(1927–)

Anglophone Indian novelist, eloquent opponent and niece to Nehru, born in Allahabad. Her *A Situation in New Delhi* (1977) fascinatingly explored, with an insider's knowledge, the dangers inherent in the power-gap left on her uncle's death. *The Day in Shadow* (1971) is an acute feminist account of modern India.

SAID FAIK
(1906–54)

Major Turkish story writer and poet, born in the Anatolian town of Adapazari. The family house he lived in became, after his death, a museum. In an unmatched colloquial Turkish he wrote of the common people of Istanbul; especially those who lived on the periphery of society. They include, in particular, fishermen, vagabonds and tramps. It used to be asserted by professors that his style was 'unpolished'; but it has since become apparent that he could only capture the very essence of those whose lives he portrays (often he speaks in their own persons) by defying literary conventions. *A Dot on the Man* (1979) is a selection from his tales, most of which, however, still await a translator.

SAINT AMANT, Antoine Girard de
(1594–1661)

French poet, born in Rouen. An early exponent of French burlesque poetry, as in *Rome ridicule* (1649), he also wrote the mock heroic *Albion* (1643), the biblical epic, *Moyse sauvé* (1653, 'Moses Saved'), and an ode, *A la solitude* ('To Solitude').

▷J Legmy, *Le poète Saint Amant* (1965)

SAINT-DENYS GARNEAU, Hector de
(1912–43)

French–Canadian poet (and painter), born in
Montreal, who initiated the modern movement in French–Canadian poetry with his
collection *Regards et jeux dans l'espace* (1937,
'Gazes and Games in Space'). In it he made
the 'first free and unashamed use of free verse
rhythms and techniques'. He suffered from a
heart ailment, and wrote virtually all his
poetry between 1935 and 1938. His *Poésies
complètes* appeared in 1949. His cousin was
the equally gifted **Anne Hébert**, also (as a
child) an invalid. It is towards these two, suggests **A J M Smith** in his *Oxford Book of
Canadian Poetry* (1960), that we must turn
for a sense of the 'spiritual' in Canadian
poetry. His *Journal* (1954, Eng trans 1962) is
valued highly for its awareness of Canadian
problems and for its lucid expression of its
author's anguish.
▷J Glassco (translator), *Complete Poems*
(1985); E Kushner, *Saint-Denys-Garneau*
(1967)

**SAINT-ÉVREMOND, Charles Marguetel
de Saint Denis, Seigneur de**
(1610–1703)

French writer and wit, born in St Denis le
Guast near Coutances. He fought at Rocroi,
Freiburg and Nördlingen, was steadily loyal
throughout the Fronde, but in 1661 fled by
way of Holland to England on the discovery
of his witty and sarcastic letter to Créqui on
the Peace of the Pyrenees. He was warmly
received by Charles II, and in London he
spent almost all the rest of his days, delighting
the world with his wit. His satire, *La Comédie
des académistes* (1644, 'The Comedy of the
Academy'), is masterly, and his letters to and
from **Ninon de Lenclos** charming.
▷M Willmotte, *Saint-Évremond, critique littéraire* (1921)

SAINT-EXUPÉRY, Antoine de
(1900–44)

French novelist and airman, born in Lyons.
He became a commercial airline pilot and
wartime reconnaissance pilot. His philosophy
of 'heroic action' based on the framework of
his experiences as a pilot is expressed in his
sensitive and imaginative *Courrier sud* (1929,
'Southbound Mail'), *Vol de nuit* (1931, Eng
trans *Night Flight*, 1932), *Terre des Hommes*
(1939, Eng trans *Wind, Sand and Stars*, 1939)
and *Pilote de guerre* (1942, Eng trans *Flight
to Arras*, 1942); but his most popular work is
Le Petit Prince (1943, Eng trans *The Little
Prince*, 1944), a touching allegorical story of
a little boy from another planet who befriends
a pilot stranded in the desert. Saint-Exupéry

was declared missing after a flight in World
War II.
▷C Cate, *Saint-Exupéry, his life and times*
(1971)

SAINT-GELAIS, Mellin de
(?1487/?1490–1558)

French poet, born in Angoulême, and either
the son or nephew of Octavien de St-Gelais,
poet, and bishop of that town. Mellin was
brought up in the bishop's palace and was
later educated at the Collège de Poitiers,
where he studied law. He then spent some
time in Italy, at the universities of Bologna
and Padua, ostensibly completing his legal
studies, but actually preoccupied by poetry:
he flourished under the great Italian poets
of the day, among them **Petrarch**. He later
became a steward to François I, and is
believed to have acted for a time as chaplain
to the Dauphin, taking holy orders at some
point after 1518. His *Sanglais oeuvres de luy*
('Saint-Gelais's Works'), a poetry collection,
was first published in Lyons in 1547. **Pierre
de Ronsard** was among his admirers.

SAINT-JOHN PERSE, pseud of **Marie René
Auguste Alexis Saint-Léger Léger**
(1887–1975)

French poet and diplomat, winner of the
Nobel Prize for literature, born in St Léger
des Feuilles, an island near Guadeloupe. He
studied at Bordeaux, and after many adventures in New Guinea and a voyage in a skiff
along the China coast he entered the French
foreign ministry in 1904. He became sec-
retary-general in 1933, was dismissed in 1940
and fled to the USA, where he became an
adviser to Roosevelt on French affairs. The
Vichy government burnt his writings and
deprived him of French citizenship, but it was
restored in 1945. Although Symbolism was
an influence on his earliest verse, he had soon
superceded that school and all others. His
blank verse utilizes an exotic vocabulary of
little-used words and is at times opaque, at
times vertiginously vivid. The best known of
his earlier works, which include *Éloges* (1910,
'Eulogies') and *Amitiés du prince* (1924, 'The
Prince's Friendships'), is the long poem *Ana-
base* (1924; Eng trans *Anabasis* by **T S Eliot**,
1930). Later works include *Exil* (1942,
'Exile'), *Pluies* (1944, 'Rain'), *Amers* (1957,
Eng trans *Seamarks*, 1958) and *Chroniques*
(1960, Eng trans 1961). He was awarded the
Nobel Prize for literature in 1960.
▷J Champier, *Saint-John Perse* (1962)

**SAINT PIERRE, Jacques Henri Bernardin
de**
(1737–1814)

French author, born in Le Havre. After a
voyage to Martinique he served for some time

in the army engineers, but quarrelled with his chiefs and was dismissed, and next year was sent to Malta, with the same result. He was greatly influenced by the writings of **Rousseau**, and he made public employment impossible by the innumerable utopian criticisms with which he deluged the ministers. With dreams of a new state to be founded on the shores of the Aral Sea, he travelled to Russia, and returned in dejection to Warsaw. He abandoned a government expedition to Madagascar at the Île de France (Mauritius), to spend there almost three years of melancholy and observation. His *Voyage à l'Île de France* (1778, 'Journey to the Isle of France') gave a distinctly new element to literature in its close portrayal of nature. His *Études de la nature* (3 vols, 1784, 'Studies of Nature') showed the strong influence of Rousseau. A fourth volume (1788) contained the popular *Paul et Virginie* (Eng trans *Paul and Mary*, 1789), the story of the love between two young people, untainted by civilization, in the natural surroundings of Mauritius. His next works were *Voeux d'un solitaire* (1789, 'A Hermit's Vows') and the novel, *La Chaumière indienne* (1791, 'The Indian Cottage'). His *Harmonies de la nature* (1796) was a pale repetition of the *Études*. Napoleon heaped favours upon him, and he lived comfortably for the rest of his days.

SAINT-POL-ROUX, pseud of **Pierre-Paul Roux**
(1861–1940)

French poet, dramatist and essayist, born near Marseilles and often called 'Le Magnifique'. From 1898 he lived in some seclusion in a Breton manor. Some of his life's work was destroyed after a Nazi soldier had drunkenly entered his house in order to rape his daughter; he started shooting, murdered the housekeeper, and eventually caused the old poet to die of shock. Saint-Pol-Roux began his career promisingly, as a leading disciple of **Mallarmé**; he then became a self-styled 'ideorealist', seeking to magnify reality. The surrealists championed him as one of their chief precursors, but this did not satisfy him, and he continued to produce massive dramas and poems: always interesting and inventive, preposterous, unheeding of fashion. Many of them were published after his death. Yet he wrote the libretto for Gustave Charpentier's popular *Louise* (1900), although it is usually wrongly attributed to the composer.

SAINT-RÉAL, César Vichard, Abbé de
(1631–92)

French historian, born in Chambéry. He visited London, and in 1679 returned to his birthplace as historiographer to the Duke of Savoy. He wrote *Dom Carlos* (1672) and *La Conjuration que les Espagnols formèrent en 1618 contre Venise* (1674, 'The Spanish Conspiracy Against Venice in 1618'), early examples of the serious French historical novel.

SAINTE-BEUVE, Charles Augustin
(1804–69)

French writer, the greatest literary critic of his time, born in Boulogne-sur-Mer. His father was a commissioner of taxes who died three months before the birth of his son, leaving his wife in straitened circumstances. He attended school in Boulogne, then went to the Collège Charlemagne in Paris, and next (1824–7) took a course of medical study. One of his teachers at the Collège Charlemagne founded a literary and political paper called the *Globe*, and to it, along with Jouffroy, **Charles Rémusat**, Ampère and **Prosper Mérimée**, Sainte-Beuve became a contributor. For three years he wrote the short articles collected posthumously as *Premiers Lundis* (1874–5, 'First Mondays'). In 1827 a review praising the *Odes et Ballades* of **Victor Hugo** led to the closest relations between the poet and his critic, which lasted until broken in 1834 by Sainte-Beuve's affair with Madame Hugo. For a time he was a zealous advocate of the Romantic movement. In 1828 he published *Tableau de la poésie française au seizième siècle* ('Survey of 16th-Century French Poetry'), and in 1829 and 1830 *Vie et Poésies de Joseph Delorme* ('Life and Poems of Joseph Delorme') and *Les Consolations*, poems full of morbid feeling. In 1829 in the *Revue de Paris* he began the *Causeries* ('Chats', longer critical articles) on French literature. After the Revolution of July 1830 he again wrote for the *Globe*, now in the hands of the Saint-Simoniens, but he soon fell out with his new colleagues and for the next three years he was on the staff of the *National*, the organ of extreme republicanism. From 1830 to 1836 he became a sympathetic listener of Lamennais, but with the ultra-democratic opinions of Lamennais after his breach with Rome he had no sympathy. His single novel, *Volupté* (1835, 'Voluptuousness'), belongs to this period. In 1837 he lectured on the history of Port Royal at Lausanne, and in book form these lectures contain some of his finest work. In Lausanne he produced his last volume of poetry, *Pensées d'août* (1839, 'Thoughts of August'). A journey to Italy closes the first period of his life. In 1840 he was appointed Keeper of the Mazarin Library. During the next eight years he wrote mainly for the *Revue des deux mondes*. The political confusions of 1848 led him to become Professor of French Literature at Liège, where he lectured on *Chateaubriand et son groupe littéraire* (pub 1851, 'Chateaubriand and his Literary Set'). In 1849 he returned to Paris, and began to

write for the *Constitutionnel*, producing an article on some literary subject, to appear on the Monday of every week. In 1861 these *Causeries du lundi* were transferred to the *Moniteur*, in 1867 back to the *Constitutionnel*, and finally in 1869 to the *Temps*. In 1854, on his appointment by the emperor as Professor of Latin poetry at the Collège de France, the students refused to listen to his lectures, and he was forced to resign the office. The undelivered lectures contained his critical estimate of **Virgil**. Nominated a senator in 1865, he regained popularity by his spirited speeches in favour of that liberty of thought which the government was doing its utmost to suppress. It was his special instruction that he should be buried without religious ceremony. It is by the amount and variety of his work, and the ranges of qualities it displays, that Sainte-Beuve holds such a place among literary critics. He published many other literary works, including *Critiques et portraits littéraires* (1836–9, 'Literary Portraits and Critical Essays'), *Portraits de femmes* (1844, 'Portraits of Women'), and, posthumously, *M. de Talleyrand* (1870) and *Souvenirs et indiscrétions* (1872, 'Recollections and Indiscretions').
▷A Billy, *Sainte-Beuve et son temps* (1952)

SAINTINE, or **BONIFACE**, **Joseph Xavier**
(1798–1865)

French writer. He was the author of many plays, poems and tales, the best known being the sentimental *Picciola* (1836, Eng trans *Picciola, or Captivity Captive*, 1837).

SAKI, pseud of **Hector Hugh Munro**
(1870–1916)

British novelist and short-story writer, born in Burma, the son of a police inspector. Educated in England at Bedford Grammar School, he returned to Burma and joined the police force in 1893, but went to London in 1896 and took up writing for *The Westminster Gazette*, and from 1902 as the Balkans correspondent for *The Morning Post*. He settled in London again in 1908. He is best known for his short stories, humorous and macabre, which are highly individual, full of eccentric wit and unconventional situations. Collections of his stories are *Reginald* (1904), *The Chronicles of Clovis* (1911), *Beasts and Superbeasts* (1914) and the posthumously published *The Toys of Peace* (1919) and *The Square Egg* (1924). His novels *The Unbearable Bassington* (1912) and *When William Came* (1913) show his gifts as a social satirist of his contemporary upper-class Edwardian world. He was killed on the Western front during World War I.
▷E M Munro, *The Square Egg* (1924)

SAKUTARO Hagiwara
(1886–1942)

The greatest of modern Japanese poets, well translated in both Graeme Wilson's selection, *Face at the Bottom of the World* (1969), and (closer to the original) *Howling to the Moon* (1978), from the collection *Tsuki ni hoeru* (1917). He was the first substantial Japanese poet to employ the colloquial, and the result was startling: all new styles, as he rightly if immodestly claimed, stemmed from *Howling to the Moon*. He has been compared to **Baudelaire** and to **Lorca**, and it is true that he was much influenced by European poetry; but he forced himself to keep his poetry quintessentially Japanese yet new; there have been few to match him in his success. As a man he was often close to madness, always neurotic (he believed that consummation of a marriage ought to take place under 'the watchful eye of the bridegroom's mother'), drank to excess, and yet is, as a critic has written, 'in certain respects ... the subtlest poet of the century'.

SALA, George Augustus Henry
(1828–96)

English journalist and novelist, born in London of Italian ancestry. He studied art and drew book illustrations, but in 1851 became a contributor to *Household Words*, and later contributed to the *Welcome Guest*, *Temple Bar* (which he founded and edited 1860–6), the *Illustrated London News* and *Cornhill*. As a special correspondent of *The Daily Telegraph* he was in the USA during the Civil War, in Italy with Garibaldi, in France in 1870–1, in Russia in 1876, and in Australia in 1885. *Twice Round the Clock* (1859) is a social satire, and he also wrote novels such as *The Strange Adventures of Captain Dangerous* (1863) and *Quite Alone* (1864), many books of travel, and the autobiographical *Life and Adventures* (1895).

SALACROU, Armand
(1899–1990)

French dramatist, born in Rouen and brought up in Le Havre who, although hailed in many countries as one of the century's important playwrights, never had a real success in London or New York. This has puzzled many theatre critics, one of whom wrote: 'Salacrou's philosophy as well as his dramaturgy are in the mainstream of popular contemporary theatre'. He was also a remarkable stage technician. He was first encouraged, as a young socialist on the edge of the Surrealist and Dada groups, by **Tristan Tzara**. He made a fortune in advertising, but abandoned this for the theatre. He wrote all kinds of plays: boulevard farces, spectacle plays, dramas and

'problem plays'. A thoughtful and in no way superficial dramatist, his real concern was with what could replace true morality in the absence of a universal religious faith. His masterpiece may well be *L'Inconnue d'Arras*, (1935, 'The Unknown Woman of Arras'), a technically brilliant play about a man's re-living of his entire life in the second before he kills himself, which is frankly indebted to the *Der Vertraagde Film* ('Slow-Film') of the great Flemish writer **Herman Teirlinck**. Sal-acrou early said that he wanted to be 'compromised with his generation', and he always managed to disconcert critics.
▷J Guichardnaud, *Modern French Theatre* (1961)

SALDA, Frantisek Xaver
(1867–1937)

The leading Czech critic of all time, and a poet and novelist; he was born in Liberec. His own creative work is not usually more than indifferent, although well executed; but his criticism, essentially creative, taught his com-patriots to view their own literature against its European background. His masterpiece in this respect is *Duse a dilo* (1913, 'Spirit and Work'). It has often been remarked that a volume of selected criticism is overdue for translation into English.
▷R Wellek, *Essays on Czech Literature* (1963)

SALINAS, Pedro
(1891–1951)

Spanish poet, playwright and critic, who was born in Madrid and died in Boston in exile from Franco. He was in many senses the chief mentor to many of the Generation of '27, which included his pupil **Cernuda**, and was not only an acute critic and teacher but also a major love poet. His aim was to purge his language of rhetoric. The earlier poetry is playful, but the later is sombre. He translated *El Cid* into good modern Spanish verse. His works in English include *Lost Angels* (1938), *Truth of Two* (1940) and *To Live in Pronouns* (1974).

SALINGER, J(erome) D(avid)
(1919–)

American novelist and short-story writer, born in New York. His father was a Jewish cheese importer, his mother Scots. Brought up 'an affluent big-city boy', he attended schools in Manhattan, but instead of going to high school in 1932 he transferred to Mac-Burney's, a private institution which he left after a year. Two years later his father enrolled him at Valley Forge Military Acad-emy, 'Pencey Prep' of *The Catcher in the Rye*

(1951). He left school at 17, provided a danc-ing-partner for wealthy spinsters on a cruise liner, dabbled in writing, and went to Austria to retrace his father's footsteps. At 19 he enrolled at Ursinus College, Collegeville, Pennsylvania, where he lasted a semester before going to Columbia University where his performance was 'below average'. His constant ambition was to become a writer and after service as an infantryman in World War II he graduated from popular magazines to the *New Yorker*. *The Catcher in the Rye*, his first and enduringly popular novel (which sells 250 000 copies annually), made him the guru of disaffected youth. Its hero, Holden Caulfield, plays hooky from his Pennsylvania boarding-school and goes to New York, where he tries in vain to lose his virginity. Written in a slick and slangy first-person nar-rative, disrespectful to adults and authority, it provoked a hostile response from some critics who objected to the forthright language, iconoclasm and élitism. This did not prevent it becoming a college set text and a perennial bestseller. It was succeeded by four works about the Glasses—*Nine Stories* (1953, pub-lished in Britain as *For Esmé—With Love and Squalor, and Other Stories*), which included 'A Perfect Day for Bananafish', and con-tained the suicide of the brilliant Seymour Glass, who is the presiding genius of the fam-ily; *Franny and Zooey* (1961); *Raise High the Roof Beam, Carpenters* and *Seymour: an Introduction* (both 1963). Twice married and divorced, Salinger lives in rural reclusion in New Hampshire, apparently still writing and cultivating Zen philosophy.
▷I Hamilton, *In Search of J. D. Salinger* (1988)

SALKEY, Andrew
(1928–)

Panamanian playwright, poet and fiction writer, born in Colon. He graduated from the University of London in 1955 and spent the next 20 years working in London: he is par-ticularly respected for his pioneering work as a broadcaster and playwright for the BBC and as a teacher, mentor and founding mem-ber of the Caribbean Artists' Movement. He has written much children's fiction, centred in the Caribbean, and a number of adult novels, of which *A Quality of Violence* (1959) was the first, as well as a number of short stories based on the legendary Afro–Caribbean figure of Anancy, eg *Anancy's Score* (1973) and *Anancy Traveller* (1989). His poetry includes *In the Hills Where Her Dreams Live* (1979), which received the Sri Chimnoy Poetry Prize and Casa de las Amer-icas Poetry Prize. A symposium was held at the Commonwealth Institute in London in 1992 to celebrate the humour, compassion and Caribbean focus of his untiring and influential work.

SALMON, André
(1881–1969)

French poet, editor, novelist and art critic, born in Paris. Although only a minor figure, he was a playful and graceful poet, knew everyone of account (including many Belgian writers), and was closely associated with **Guillaume Apollinaire**, **Max Jacob**, **Franz Hellens** and the painters Braque and Picasso. *Souvenir sans fin* (1955–6, 'Endless Memories'), his autobiography, is a mine of intelligent information—and essential reading for those who wish to understand the modern period in French literature. His aim in poetry was 'to restore emotion to the impersonal'.
▷M Raymond, *From Baudelaire to Surrealism* (1950)

SALTEN, Felix, pseud of Siegmund Salzmann
(1869–1945)

Hungarian-born Austrian novelist and essayist, born in Budapest. He is known especially for his animal stories, particularly *Bambi* (1929) which, in translation and filmed by Walt Disney (1941), achieved great popularity in America and Britain. He also wrote *Florian* (1934, Eng trans *Florian: An Emperor's Horse*, 1934) and *Bambis Kinder* (1940, Eng trans *Bambi's Children*, 1940).

SALTYKOV, Michail Evgrafovich, pseud N Shchedrin
(1826–89)

Russian writer and satirist, born in Tver. He was exiled (1848–56) because of a satirical story called 'Contradictions' (1847), but later became a provincial vice-governor of Ryazen (1858–60) and Tver (1860–4). He edited with **Nikolai Nekrasov** the radical *Otechestvennye zapiski* ('Notes of the Fatherland'), and of his many books, *Gospoda Golovlevy* (1876, Eng trans *The Golloviev Family*, 1916) and *Skazki* (pub 1939, Eng trans *Fables*, 1931) are among those translated.
▷K Samine, *Saltykov-Schetchédrine* (1955)

SALVERSON, Laura Goodman
(1890–1970)

Canadian novelist, born in Winnipeg to poor Icelandic immigrants who moved to Minnesota when Salverson was 10. She married a railwayman in 1913 and led an itinerant life in the Canadian west. Not surprisingly, much of her work is about immigrant displacement. Her first novel, *The Viking Heart* (1923), concerned the mass immigration of one and a half thousand Icelanders to Canada in 1875.

The Dark Weaver (1937), a Governor General's Award winner, was strongly pacifist and feminist in tone. She could also write romantically, as in *Black Lace* (1938), a novel about piracy and dark intrigue in the reign of Louis XIV.

SAMAIN, Albert Victor
(1858–1900)

French poet, born in Lille. He was a clerk in the Prefecture of the Seine. His Symbolist poetry, though not original in subject, is delicate, fresh and musical, and was well received in his lifetime. Among his collections of verse are *Au jardin de l'infante* (1893, 'In the Infanta's Garden'), *Aux flancs de la vase* (1898, 'On the Sides of the Vase') and *Le Chariot d'or* ('The Chariot of Gold'), published posthumously.

SANCHEZ, Florencio
(1875–1910)

Uruguayan playwright and journalist. Born in Montevideo, he had no formal education, but became one of the most important and influential Latin-American playwrights of this century. His plays and sainetes (light one-act comedies), the first of which were performed in 1902, were deeply influenced by **Henrik Ibsen**, **Luigi Pirandello**, Roberto Bracco, **Bjørnstjerne Bjørnson**, and **Guiseppe Giacosa**. The period from 1903 to 1905 was his most productive, when he wrote *M'hijo el dotor* (1903, 'My Son the Doctor'), his most famous *La gringa* (1904), and *Baranca abajo* (1905, 'Downhill'). His favoured themes are the corruption caused by money and power, the effect of social problems on the individual, and the clash between the old and the new. *Moneda falsa* ('Counterfeit Money') is his one play in lunfardo, the dialect of Buenos Aires.

SANCHEZ, Thomas
(1944–)

American novelist, born in California. He was educated at San Francisco State University, and taught there for two years from 1967 to 1969, then spent some time in Europe. He became actively involved in political agitation on behalf of Native American causes on his return, and finished his first and best-known novel, *Rabbit Boss* (1973). It traces the disintegration of the Washo tribe and their ancient way of life through the story of a family across four generations. His later titles are *Zoot Suit Murders* (1978) and *Mile Zero* (1989).

SANCHEZ DE BADAJOZ, Garci
(c.1460–c.1526)

Spanish poet. According to tradition, he went mad from love (for whom, the legend does not say). He did, however, enjoy fame in his time as an erotic poet. His poems bear such titles as 'Lamentaciones de Amor', 'Infierno de Amor', and his parody 'Liciones de Job' ('Lessons of Job') was banned by the Inquisition, as he followed the fashion for adapting prayers to 'misas a lo profano' (masses to the profane), using erotic language. Probably his most successful poem was one entitled 'Sueño' ('Dream'), where the poet relates a vision of his own burial and the birds lament that he died of love.

SANCHEZ FERLIOSO, Rafael
(1927–)

Spanish novelist, whose *El jarama* (1956, Eng trans *The One Day of the Week*, 1962) received much attention at the time of its publication. It is an account of a Sunday outing, during which nothing happens except that someone is drowned; one critic called it 'one of the most boring works in the history of the novel ... no doubt intentionally', while a few others acclaimed it as a brilliant tour de force.

SAND, George, pseud of Amandine Aurore Lucie Dupin, Baronne Dudevant
(1804–76)

French novelist, born in Paris, the illegitimate daughter of Marshal de Saxe. Her father died when she was very young, and she lived principally at Nohant in Berri with her grandmother, Madame Dupin, on whose death she inherited the property. At the age of 18 she married Casimir, Baron Dudevant, and had two children, but after nine years left him and went to Paris with her children to make her living by literature in the Bohemian society of the period (1831). For the best part of 20 years her life was spent in the company and partly under the influence of various distinguished men. She scandalized bourgeois society with her unconventional ways and her love affairs. Her first lover was **Jules Sandeau**, from whose surname she took her pseudonym, and with whom she wrote a novel, *Rose et Blanche* (1831, 'Rose and Blanche'). She was always interested in poets and artists, including **Prosper Mérimée**, **Alfred de Musset**, with whom she travelled in Italy, and Chopin, who was her lover for 10 years. In the second decade her attention shifted to philosophers and politicians, such as Lamennais, the socialist Pierre Leroux, and the republican Michel de Bourges. After 1848 she settled down as the quiet 'châtelaine of Nohant', where she spent the rest of her life in outstanding literary activity, varied by travel. Her work can be divided into four periods. When she first went to Paris, her candidly erotic novels—*Indiana* (1832, Eng trans 1850), *Valentine* (1832, Eng trans 1900), *Lélia*

(1833, Eng trans 1978) and *Jacques* (1834, Eng trans 1847)—shared in the Romantic extravagance of the time, and declared themselves against marriage. In the next period her philosophical and political teachers inspired the socialistic rhapsodies of *Spiridion* (1838, Eng trans 1842), *Consuelo* (1842–4, Eng trans 1846), *Comtesse de Rudolstadt* (1843–5, Eng trans *The Countess of Rudolstadt*, 1847) and *Le Meunier d'Angibault* (1845, Eng trans *The Miller of Angibault*, 1847). Between the two periods came the fine novel *Mauprat* (1837, Eng trans 1847). Then she began to turn towards the studies of rustic life—*La Mare au diable* (1846, Eng trans *The Haunted Marsh*, 1848), *François le Champi* (1847–8, Eng trans *Francis the Waif*, 1889) and *La Petite Fadette* (1849, Eng trans *Little Fadette*, 1850), which are, by modern standards, her best works. The fourth period comprises the miscellaneous works of her last 20 years—some of them, such as *Les Beaux Messieurs de Bois-Doré* (1858, Eng trans *The Gallant Lords of Bois-Doré*, 1890), *Le Marquis de Villemer* (1860–1, Eng trans *The Marquis of Villemer*, 1871) and *Mlle la Quintinie* (1863), of high merit. Her complete works (over 100 vols), besides novels and plays, include the autobiographical *Histoire de ma vie* (1855, 'The Story of My Life'), *Elle et lui* (on her relations with de Musset, 1859, Eng trans *He and She*, 1900), and delightful letters, published after her death.
▷M Louise Pailleron, *George Sand* (2 vols, 1938–43)

SANDBURG, Carl
(1878–1967)

American poet, born in Galesburg, Illinois, of Swedish stock. After trying various jobs, fighting in the Spanish–American war and studying at Lombard College, he became a journalist in Chicago and started to write for *Poetry*. His verse, realistic and robust but often also delicately sensitive, reflects industrial America. Among his volumes of poetry are *Chicago Poems* (1915), *Corn Huskers* (1918), *Smoke and Steel* (1920), *Slabs of the Sunburnt West* (1922) and *Good Morning, America* (1928). His *Complete Poems* gained him the Pulitzer Prize in 1950. Interested in American folksongs and ballads, he published a collection in *The American Songbag* (1927). He also wrote a vast *Life of Abraham Lincoln* (1926–39).
▷Gay Wilson Allen, *Carl Sandburg* (1972)

SANDEAU, Jules Léonard Sylvian Julien
(1811–83)

French author, born in Aubusson. He went to Paris to study law, but soon devoted himself to letters. He co-wrote *Rose et Blanche* (1831, 'Rose and Blanche') with **George Sand**.

His first independent novel was *Madame de Sommerville* (1834) and his first success was *Marianna* (1840). His books give an accurate picture of the social conflicts of the France of his day, and he was master of the *roman de moeurs*. He became Keeper of the Mazarin Library in 1853, and librarian at St Cloud in 1859.

▷M Silver, *Sandeau, l'homme et la vie* (1937)

SANDEL, Cora, pseud of **Sara Fabricius**
(1880–1974)

Norwegian author and painter, born in Oslo and brought up in Tromsø in northern Norway. She lived as a painter in Paris from 1906 until 1921 and published her first novel, *Rosina*, in 1922. In many of her novels she condemns small-town and middle-class mores; another important theme in her work is the difficulty experienced by women in achieving artistic self-realization. Her poignant and subtly ironic manner of narration conveys great psychological insight and a profound knowledge of human nature. Following *Rosina*, her writing career began in earnest with the 'Alberte' trilogy (*Alberte* (1926), *Alberte og Friheten* (1936, 'Alberte and Freedom') and *Bare Alberte* (1939, 'Just Alberte'), in which she describes a woman's experiences of power and powerlessness. In the short novel collection *Vårt vanskelige liv* (1960, 'Our Difficult Life') Sandel addresses women's longing for acknowledgement and self-determination, while a further collection, *Barnet som elsket veier* (1973, 'The Child who loved Roads'), reflects her empathy with a child's view of the world. Although her protagonists belong to the perpetually powerless, they revolt unremittingly against their oppressive environment by means of obstinacy and fantasy, and sublime optimism pervades all her writing.

▷A H Lervik, *Menneske og miljø i Cora Sandels diktning* (1977)

SANDEMOSE, Aksel
(1899–1965)

Danish–Norwegian novelist, born into a working-class family in North Jutland. One of the most innovative, idiosyncratic and prolific Scandinavian authors of the 20th century, he experienced a resounding breakthrough with the modernist novel, *En flyktning krysser sitt spor* (1933, 'A Fugitive Crosses his own Track'), in which he immortalized the parochial and oppressive town of 'Jante', a fictitious version of his Danish birthplace Nykøbing Mors. The search for an antidote to the narrow-mindedness and ethnocentricity epitomized by 'Jante' drew Sandemose to consider the lives of North American immigrants, which he depicted in a trilogy of novels, *Ross Dane* (1928), *En*

sjømann går i land (1931, 'A Sailor Goes Ashore'), *September* (1939), and also in his debut collection of short stories, *Fortællinger fra Labrador* (1923, 'Stories from Labrador'). In 1930 he had himself become something of an immigrant, when he left Denmark for Norway, his mother's native country, and began to write in Norwegian. He then spent four years during World War II in exile in Sweden, where in 1944 he published another notable novel, *Det gångna är en dröm* ('The Past is a Dream'), a document fiction about a murder mystery. After the war, he returned to Norway.

▷E Haavardsholm, *Mannen fra Jante. Et Portrett av Aksel Sandemose* (1988)

SANDOZ, Mari Susette
(1896/1901–1966)

American novelist and popular historian, born in Nebraska to Swiss immigrants. Her biography of her father, *Old Jules* (1935), a frontier farmer who thought writers and artists 'the maggots of society', was rejected 13 times before being finally published. Her next book, *Slogum House* (1937), was a historical novel, but her best writing is to be found in closely researched books of non-fiction. *Crazy Horse* (1942) tells the life of the Sioux chief.

SANGUINETI, Edourdo
(1930–)

Italian critic (chiefly), poet and novelist, born in Genoa. He was reckoned to be the leader of the Italian avant garde in its revolt of the 1960s, and his anthologies of poetry, which have a genuine air of authority, have been particularly influential—and useful to non-Italian students of Italian poetry. His creative work is more an illustration of his complex critical method than interesting in its own right; but his mind is fascinating, and has fascinated a generation of often puzzled readers.

SANNAZARO, Jacopo
(c.1458–1530)

Italian poet, born in Naples. He sought favour at the court there. His *Arcadia* (1485), a pastoral medley of prose and verse which drew on the example of **Boccaccio**, is full of beauty and won him considerable fame. He also wrote Latin elegies, and religious works.

▷A Altamure, *Jacopo Sannazaro* (1951)

SANSOM, Clive
(1910–81)

English poet, anthologist and speech therapist, who moved to Tasmania at the age of 40. His verse includes *In the Midst of Death* (1940) and *The Unfailing Spring* (1943). The title poem of *The Witnesses and Other Poems* (1956) was a prize-winner in the 1951 Festival of Britain poetry competition. In Australia he published *The Cathedral* (1958), *Dorset Village* (1962) and *Return to Magic* (1969), which look back to his English heritage and religious faith. He also wrote a novel and a verse play, and compiled the two anthologies for which he is best known, *The English Heart* (1945) and *The World of Poetry* (1959).

SANSOM, William
(1912–76)

English short-story writer and novelist, whose work is marked by a strong balance of outward and internal realities. He lived in London and during the war served with the Volunteer Fire Brigade, an experience which inspired many of the stories in *Fireman Flower* (1944), perhaps his most distinctive collection. After the war he wrote *The Body* (1949), a powerful study of a fragmented personality. Thereafter, though he wrote prolifically, his skill seemed progressively less focused; his travel writing was, however, vividly done.
▷P Michel-Michot, *William Sansom: A Critical Assessment* (1971)

SANTAYANA, George
(1863–1952)

Spanish philosopher, poet and novelist, born in Madrid, and educated from 1872 in the USA. He taught at Harvard from 1889 and was professor there from 1907 to 1912, but always retained his Spanish citizenship and returned to Europe in 1912. He spent much time in England but settled in Rome in 1924 and passed his last years as the guest of a convent of nuns there. Santayana is always regarded as a very literary philosopher, and a fine stylist. He was a poet (*Sonnets and Other Verses*, 1894), a successful novelist (*The Last Puritan*, 1935) and a cultivated literary critic, aesthetician and essayist. His main philosophical works are: *The Sense of Beauty* (1896), *The Life of Reason* (1905–6), *Scepticism and Animal Faith* (1923), which is itself an introduction to the comprehensive four-volume work *Realms of Being* (1927–40), and *Platonism and the Spiritual Life* (1927). He also wrote a three-volume autobiography, *Persons and Places* (1944–53).
▷W E Arnett, *George Santayana* (1968)

SANTÍC, Aleksa
(1868–1924)

Serbian poet and nationalist, born in Mostar. At first he followed in the footsteps of **Illic**, but he later turned to his native folk-song for inspiration. His 'The Fields of Misery' has been translated in *Slavonic and East European Review* (XXIX, 73, 1951).

SANTILLANA, Iñigo López de Mendoza, Marqués de
(1398–1458)

Spanish scholar, soldier and poet, born in Carrión de los Condes. He led expeditions against the Moors in Spain, but is best known as a patron of the arts. Influenced by the poetry of **Dante** and **Petrarch**, he introduced their style and methods into Spanish literature. His shorter poems, especially his *serranillas* (pastoral songs), are among his best work, and he was the first Spanish poet to write sonnets. His principal prose work, *Proemio e carta a condestable de Portugal* (1449, 'Proem and Letter to the Constable of Portugal'), is a discourse on European literature of his day.
▷J Delgado, *Iñigo de Santillana* (1968)

SAPPER, pseud of **Herman Cyril McNeile**
(1888–1937)

English novelist and short-story writer, remembered chiefly for the invention of Bull-dog—originally Bull-Dog—Drummond, a laddish sprig of Edwardian England. Born in Bodmin, Cornwall, McNeile was educated at Cheltenham and at the Royal Military Academy at Woolwich. He joined the Royal Engineers as a regular in 1907 and was promoted to Captain on the eve of World War I; he won the Military Cross and rose to Lieutenant Colonel before his retirement. He published five collections of short stories during the war; his first novel, *Mufti*, appeared in 1919. and a year later he introduced Drummond in an eponymous novel bearing the tellingly Hannay-ish subtitle *The Adventures of a Demobilized Officer Who Found Peace Dull*. That is essentially the formula for the Drummond books, of which there were seven between 1920 and Sapper's death. The best is unquestionably *The Female of the Species* (1928, published in the USA as *Bulldog Drummond Meets ...*, 1943), in which the hero rescues his wife from kidnap by Sapper's stock gang of low-rent, unEnglish thugs. The social and political attitudes are far more extreme than in **John Buchan**'s books and there is a blimpishness that Buchan usually avoids. There is, however, no mistaking the vigour of the storytelling. Though now little read, Sapper has a significant place in British popular culture.

SAPPHO
(b.c.612 BC)

Greek lyric poet, born on the island of Lesbos. She went into exile about 596 BC from Mytilene to Sicily, but after some years

returned to Mytilene. She married Cercylas, and had a daughter, Cleis. She seems to have been the centre of a circle of women and girls, probably her pupils. Tradition represents her as homosexual because of the love and admiration she expresses in some of her poems addressed to girls. The greatest woman poet of antiquity, she wrote lyrics unsurpassed for depth of feeling, passion and grace. Only two of her odes are extant in full, but many fragments have survived. It is from her that 'lesbian' has acquired its modern meaning and the four-line sapphic stanza (used in Latin by **Catullus** and **Horace**) its name.
▷C M Bowra, *Greek Lyric Poetry* (1961)

SARDOU, Victorien
(1831–1908)

French dramatist, born in Paris. His first efforts were failures, but through his marriage to the actress Brécourt, who nursed him when he was sick, he became acquainted with Déjazet, for whom he wrote successfully *Monsieur Garat* (1860) and *Les Prés Saint-Gervais* (1860, Eng trans *The Meadows of Saint-Gervais*, 1871). Soon he had amassed a fortune and had become the most successful European playwright of his day, and his popularity was immense in the USA. Pieces like *Les Pattes du monde* (1860, 'The World's Legs'), *Nos intimes* (1861, Eng trans *Our Friends*, 1879), *La Famille Benoîton* (1865, 'The Benoîton Family'), *Divorçons* (1880, 'Let's Get Divorced'), *Odette* (1882) and *Marquise* (1889) are fair samples of his work. For Sarah Bernhardt he wrote *Fédora* (1883, Eng trans 1883), *La Tosca* (1887, Eng trans *Tosca*, 1900), etc, and with Moreau *Madame Sans-Gene* (1893); for Irving *Robespierre* (1899, Eng trans as a novel, 1899) and *Dante* (1903, Eng trans 1903). He attempted the higher historical play in *La Patrie!* (1869, Eng trans 1915). Today his plays appear over-technical and over-theatrical, and the plot and characters shallow and rather obvious.
▷J A Hunt, *Sardou and the Sardou Plays* (1913)

SARDUY, Severo
(1937–)

Cuban novelist and poet, considered one of the foremost Post-Boom writers in Latin America and the most famous young Cuban writer of the late 20th century. His experimental novels *De donde son los cantantes* (1967, 'From Cuba With a Song') and *Cobra* demonstrate the striking stylistic and thematic innovations for which he has been widely praised. He has also published essays, literary criticism, and two books of poetry. Living in France during the 1960s, he was on the staff of the influential journal *Tel Quel*.

SARGESON, Frank (Norris Frank Davey)
(1903–82)

New Zealand short-story writer and novelist, born in Hamilton. Through his easy use of colloquial idioms and speech patterns, he is regarded as the founder of modern New Zealand writing. He qualified as a lawyer but did not practise. In 1926 he went to Europe but returned to New Zealand two years later. He worked briefly as a market gardener, milkman, pantryman and freelance journalist, but his main energy was devoted to writing novels and short stories. He made his name with collections of short stories like *Conversations with My Uncle* (1936), *A Man and His Wife* (1940) and *That Summer and Other Stories* (1946), satirizing the provincial attitudes of his surroundings. A novel, *I Saw in My Dream* (1949), included the earlier *When the Wind Blows* of 1945. His *Collected Stories, 1935–1963* came out in 1964 and an expanded edition, as *The Stories of Frank Sargeson*, in 1973. Other novels include *Memoirs of a Peon* (1965) and *Joy of the Worm* (1969). He wrote three works of autobiography, *Once is Enough* (1973), *More than Enough* (1975) and *Never Enough!* (1977). These were collected in one volume as *Sargeson* in 1981.
▷B Benson, introduction to *The Collected Stories of Frank Sargeson* (1964)

SARKIA, Kaarlo
(1902–45)

Finnish poet and translator (**Baudelaire**, 'The Bateau Ivre' of **Rimbaud**—a famous tour de force in the literature), born in Kiikka. He helped to bring the influence of French poetry into Finnish. Like so many Finns, he suffered from tuberculosis, and his life was considerably shortened by it. His poetry is more technically brilliant and assured than significant in content.
▷E Tompuri, *Voice from Finland* (1947)

SARMENT, Jean, pseud of Jean Bellemère
(1897–1976)

French dramatist, poet, novelist and actor, known for such successful plays as *Le Pêcheur d'ombres* (1921, Eng trans *Fishing for Shadows*, 1940) and *Les Plus Beaux Yeux du monde* (1925, 'The Most Beautiful Eyes in the World'). The best of his proficient, bittersweet plays, influenced by **Musset** and the psychology of **Freud**, tend to be the earlier ones. He acted, with Michel Simon, in the 1934 movie **Marcel Pagnol** made of one of his own best plays: *Léopold le Bien-Aimé* (1927, 'Leopold the Well-Disposed').

SARMIENTO, Domingo Faustino
(1811–88)

Argentinian politician, educator and writer, born in San Juan, who became president of his country and wrote the most important essay of his day—*Civilización y Barbarie: La vida de Juan Facundo* (1848, 'Civilization and Barbarism: The Life of Juan Facundo'), better known simply as *Facundo*. After being arrested and condemned to death by the dictator Rosas, he fled to Chile, where he worked as a journalist and teacher. Much of his life was spent travelling the world to study educational reform. His *Facundo* is a combination of essay, novel and political treatise on the peoples of Argentina.

SAROYAN, William
(1908–81)
American playwright and novelist, born in Fresno, California. His first work, *The Daring Young Man on the Flying Trapeze* (1934), a volume of short stories, offered a hallucinatory but also strikingly sympathetic view of Depression America and was a great critical success; it was followed by a number of highly original novels and plays. *The Time of Your Life* (1939), a play, was awarded the Pulitzer Prize. Among later works are the autobiographical *My Name is Aram* (1940), *The Bicycle Rider in Beverley Hills* (1952), *The Human Comedy* (1943, a novel), *Days of Life and Death* and *Escape to the Moon* (1971), *Places Where I've Done Time* (1973), and the autobiographical *Obituaries* (1979).
▷ *Short Drive, Sweet Chariot* (1966)

SARRAUTE, Nathalie, née Tcherniak
(1920–)
Russian-born French writer, who was born in Ivanovno-Voznesenk. Her parents settled in France when she was a child. She was educated at the Lycée Fénelon and the Sorbonne, graduating in arts and law. She spent a year at Oxford (1922–3) doing graduate studies, and then studied sociology in Berlin, before establishing a law practice in Paris (1922–39). Her first book was a collection of sketches on bourgeois life, *Tropismes* (1939, Eng trans *Tropisms*, 1934), in which she rejected traditional plot development and characterization to describe a world between the real and the imaginary. She developed her theories further in her later novels: *Portrait d'un Inconnu* (1948, Eng trans *Portrait of a Man Unknown*, 1958), *Martereau* (1953, Eng trans 1959), *Le Planétarium* (1959, Eng trans 1960), *Les Fruits d'or* (1963, Eng trans *The Golden Fruits*, 1964), *Entre la vie et la mort* (1968, Eng trans *Between Life and Death*, 1969) and *Vous les entendez?* (1972, Eng trans *Do You Hear Them?*, 1973). She has also written plays, *Le Silence, suivi de Le Mensonge* (1967, Eng trans *Silence, and The Lie*, 1969), *Isma* (1970, Eng trans *Izzuma*, 1980) and *Elle*

est là (1978, Eng trans *It Is There*, 1980), and collections of essays.
▷ G R Besser, *Nathalie Sarraute* (1979)

SARRUF, Yaqub
(1852–1927)
Lebanese writer, who established himself in Egypt. His main task, as he saw it, was to popularize science; but he also wrote some popular historical fiction.

SARTON, (Eleanor) May
(1912–)
American poet and novelist, born in Wondelgem, Belgium, who emigrated with her family to the USA at the age of four, and became a naturalized citizen in 1924. Her first book, the poetry volume *Encounter in April* (1937), was followed by six more, including *Collected Poems* (1974). *The Silence Now*, a volume of new and uncollected early poems, appeared in 1989. Interspersed with these are novels such as *The Single Hound* (1938), dealing with a young English poet; *The Birth of a Grandfather* (1957), sympathetically examining the issue of growing older; and *Mrs. Stevens Hears the Mermaids Singing* (1965), looking at lesbian experience.

SARTRE, Jean-Paul
(1905–80)
French philosopher, dramatist and novelist, born in Paris. He studied at the Sorbonne with **Simone de Beauvoir** and taught philosophy at Le Havre, Paris and Berlin (1934–5). He joined the French army in 1939, was a prisoner of war in Germany (1941), and after his release became an active member of the Resistance in Paris. In 1945 he emerged as the leading light of the left-wing, left-bank intellectual life of Paris, but he eventually broke with the communists. In 1946, with Simone de Beauvoir, he founded and edited the avant-garde monthly *Les Temps modernes* ('Modern Times'). A disciple of Heidegger, he developed his own characteristic Existentialist doctrines, derived from an early anarchistic tendency, which found full expression in his autobiographical novel *La Nausée* (1938, Eng trans *Nausea*, 1949) and in *Le Mur* (1938, Eng trans *The Wall and Other Stories*, 1949), a collection of short stories. The Nazi occupation provided the grim background to such plays as *Les Mouches* (1943, Eng trans *The Flies*, 1946), a modern version of the Orestes theme, and *Huis clos* (1944, Eng trans *In Camera*, 1946; also known as *No Exit* and *No Way Out*). *Les Mains sales* (1948, Eng trans *Crime Passionnel*, 1949, under which title it was filmed) movingly portrayed the tragic consequences of a choice to join an extremist party. He

became the most prominent exponent of Atheistic Existentialism. His doctrines are outlined in *L'Existentialisme est un humanisme* (1946, Eng trans *Existentialism and Humanism*, 1948) and fully worked out in *L'Être et le néant* (1943, Eng trans *Being and Nothingness*, 1956). Other notable works include the three novels which comprise *Les Chemins de la liberté* ('Paths of Freedom'), *L'Âge de raison* (1945, Eng trans *The Age of Reason*, 1947), *Le Sursis* (1945, Eng trans *The Reprieve*, 1947) and *La Mort dans l'âme* (1949, Eng trans *Iron in the Soul*, 1950); the play *Les Séquestrés d'Altona* (1959, Eng trans *Loser Wins*, 1960); and a study of **Gustave Flaubert**, *L'Idiot de la famille* (1971, Eng trans *The Family Idiot*, 1982). In 1964 he was awarded, but declined to accept, the Nobel Prize for literature. In the late 1960s he became closely involved in opposition to American policies in Vietnam, and expressed support for student rebellion in 1968. His autobiography, *Les Mots* (Eng trans *The Words*, 1964), appeared in 1963.
▷ A C Solal, *Sartre* (1988)

SASSOON, Siegfried Louvain
(1886–1967)

English poet and novelist, born in Kent. His experiences in World War I formed in him a hatred of war, fiercely expressed in his *The Old Huntsman* (1917), *Counter-Attack* (1918) and *Satirical Poems* (1926). A semi-fictitious autobiography, *The Complete Memoirs of George Sherston* (1937), started with *Memoirs of a Fox-Hunting Man* (1928; Hawthornden Prize 1929), and continued in *Memoirs of an Infantry Officer* (1930) and *Sherston's Progress* (1936). Truly autobiographical are *The Old Century* (1938), *The Weald of Youth* (1942) and *Siegfried's Journey 1916–20* (1945). He also wrote an influential biography of **George Meredith** (1948). His later poems, including those in *Vigils* (1935) and *Sequences* (1956), are predominantly spiritual in tone, and he became a Roman Catholic in 1957. His *Collected Poems* appeared in 1961.

SASTRE, Alfonso
(1926–)

Spanish playwright, essayist, novelist and story writer who helped, under severe difficulties from the censorship, to found the Grupo de Teatro Popular Realista. Born in Madrid, he writes realistic 'problem' plays, but in many different modes; he has expressed his indebtedness to **Arthur Miller** and to **Sartre**. But the essence of his theatre, influenced by European models as it is, may ultimately be traced to Spanish dramatists. Together with **Buero Vallejo** he dominated the Spanish theatre in the difficult years of the Franco dictatorship. His plays are explicitly critical of society, and few of them could be performed. His *Escuadra hacia la muerte* (1953, Eng trans *The Condemned Squad*, 1964), in which an obviously Franco-style officer is murdered by his men, was closed after three performances, but this merely enhanced his reputation as an underground writer. He later wrote in a form he described as that of the 'complex tragedy', in which he admits the pervasive influence of **Valle-Inclán** (in particular), **Brecht**, and **Beckett**. *Ana Kleiber* (1952), a technically brilliant study of the anti-feministic character of fascism, is perhaps the most powerful of all his plays. English translations of five plays may be found in *The Modern Spanish Stage* (1970, ed Marion Holt), *Masterpieces of the Modern Spanish Theatre* (1967, M Benedikt and G E Wellwarth eds), *The New Theatre of Europe* (1962), *International Drama* (1968) and *The New Wave Spanish Drama* (1970, G E Wellwarth). He is perhaps the most gifted and incisive of all living playwrights.
▷ F Anderson, *Alfonso Sastre* (1971)

SATCHELL, William
(1860–1942)

English-born New Zealand author, born in London. He wrote four novels of an agnostic-philosophical cast, deploying romantic themes against a setting of nature and myth. After *The Land of the Lost* (1902), *The Toll of the Bush* (1905), *The Elixir of Life* (1907) and *The Greenstone Door* (1914), the author produced nothing more.
▷ P Wilson, *The Maorilander* (1961, rev edn 1968)

SAVAGE, Richard
(?1697–1743)

English poet, claimed to be the illegitimate child of Richard Savage, fourth and last Earl Rivers, and the Countess of Macclesfield. In the dedication to his comedy *Love in a Veil* (1718) he asserted the parentage, but in Curll's *Poetical Register* (1719) the story is for the first time fully given. **Aaron Hill** befriended him, and in 1724 published in *The Plain Dealer* an outline of his story which brought subscribers for his *Miscellanies* (1726). In 1727 he killed a gentleman in a tavern brawl, and narrowly escaped the gallows. His attacks upon his alleged mother (now Mrs Brett) became louder and more bitter in his poem *The Bastard* (1728). *The Wanderer* (1729) was dedicated to Lord Tyrconnel, nephew of Mrs Brett, who had befriended him. Savage led a dissipated life and the queen's pension (1732) of £50 for a birthday ode was squandered in a week's debauchery. On Queen Caroline's death (1737) **Pope** tried to help him, but after about a year he went to Bristol, was jailed for debt, and died there. He wrote a comedy, *Love in a Veil* (1718), and *The Tragedy of Sir Thomas Overbury* (1723), and at least one notable poem, *The Wanderer* (1729). He owes his reputation mainly to **Samuel Johnson**, who wrote what is perhaps the most perfect Life in English literature, though it was later discredited.

▷ S V Makover, *Richard Savage: a mystery in biography* (1909)

SAVERY, Henry
(1791–1842)

English-born Australian author, born near Bristol, where his father was a prominent banker. Savery is generally considered to be the first Australian novelist. A bankrupt, he was convicted of forgery and sentenced to death. This was commuted to transportation for life and he arrived at Hobart Town in 1825. His wife Eliza followed him, was rescued from a shipwreck, and arrived in 1828 to find her husband back in prison for debt; she left Hobart never to return. Meanwhile Henry was writing from prison for the local newspaper as 'Simon Stukeley'. His essays were published in 1829 and immediately became the subject of a libel suit. Eventually he secured his release and then, possibly with a view to his rehabilitation in society, published his autobiographical 'novel' *Quintus Servinton: A Tale Founded upon Incidents of Real Occurrence* (1830–1, 3 vols). Falling into debt once more, he returned in 1840 to the notorious Port Stanley prison where he died two years later. His reputation rests more on his primacy than on the quality of his writing, but he undoubtedly influenced **Henry Kingsley** and possibly **William Hay**.

SAVILLE, (Leonard) Malcolm
(1901–82)

English author, born in Hastings, Sussex. Saville wrote over 80 books, the vast majority for young people, beginning with *Mystery at Witchend* in 1943. This book introduced the characters who became known as The Lone Pine Club, and who reappeared in *Seven White Gates* (1944), and in almost 20 subsequent volumes. Other Saville characters include the secret agent Marston Baines, who featured in several books, such as *Marston, Master Spy* (1978), and who appealed to older boys, while the 'Susan and Bill' series, beginning with *Susan, Bill and the Ivy-Clad Oak* (1954), was designed for younger readers. Saville also wrote adult books on gardening, travel and various aspects of the south of England.

SAYERS, Dorothy L(eigh)
(1893–1957)

English detective-story writer, born in Oxford. Educated at the Godolphin School,

Salisbury, and Somerville College, Oxford (she took a first in modern languages), she taught for a year and then worked in an advertising agency until 1931. In 1924 she had an illegitimate son, and in 1926 married Captain Oswald Fleming. Her novels are distinguished by taste and style. Beginning with *Whose Body?* (1923) and *Clouds of Witness* (1926), she told the adventures of her hero Lord Peter Wimsey in various accurately observed milieux—such as advertising in *Murder Must Advertise* (1933) or campanology in *The Nine Tailors* (1934). Her other stories included *Strong Poison* (1930), *Gaudy Night* (1935), *Busman's Honeymoon* (1937) and *In the Teeth of the Evidence* (1939). She earned a reputation as a leading Christian apologist with two successful plays, *The Zeal of Thy House* (1937) and *The Devil to Pay* (1939), a series for broadcasting (*The Man Born to be King*, 1943) and a closely reasoned essay (*The Mind of the Maker*, 1941). A translation of **Dante**'s *Inferno* appeared in 1949 and of *Purgatorio* in 1955. *Paradiso* was left unfinished at her death.

▷ F Wolcher, *Der literarische Mord* (1953); B Reynolds, *Dorothy L. Sayers, Her Life and Soul* (1993)

SAYLES, John Thomas
(1950–)

American screenwriter, novelist, actor and film-maker, born in Schenectady, New York. A dedicated sportsman, he worked at a number of jobs after his graduation from Williams College, before winning **O Henry** awards for the short stories *I-80 Nebraska, M.490–M.205* (1975) and *Breed* (1977). His novels *Pride Of The Bimbos* (1975) and *Union Dues* (1979) earned extensive praise for their wit, irony and his ear for dialect. As a screenwriter he brought a knowing humour and inventiveness to such projects as *Piranha* (1978) and *The Howling* (1980). He made his directorial debut with *The Return Of The Secaucus Seven* (1979), an examination of the sense of disillusionment that infects a reunion of 1960s college radicals, which received an Oscar nomination for Best Original Screenplay. As a writer-director, he has been committed to exploring a radical political and social agenda whilst giving voice to characters marginalized within the mainstream film arena. His most accomplished films include *Lianna* (1982), *Matewan* (1987), *City Of Hope* (1991) and *Passion Fish* (1992), for which he received a further Oscar nomination. An occasional playwright and actor, he returned to novel writing with *Los Gusanos* (1991), an epic account of Cuban exiles in Miami.

SAYONOV, Vissarion
(1903–)

Russian descriptive minor poet, born in Siberia. A socialist realist, he excels in laconic observation of nature. There are a few translations of his work in *Modern Russian Poetry* (1966, V Markov and M Sparks eds).

SCANLAN, Nelle M(argaret), properly **Ellen Margaret**
(1882–1968)

New Zealand journalist, foreign correspondent, social commentator and, later, author of light novels and of the bestselling *Pencarrow* tetralogy. She was born in Picton. Her first book, *Primrose Hill* (1931), was a social comedy set in London, where she moved from Washington, DC, in 1923, as were others such as *The Marriage of Nicholas Cotter* (1936). By that time she had published *Pencarrow* (1932), the first of her 'New Zealand' quartet, followed by *Tides of Youth* (1933), *Winds of Heaven* (1934) and *Kelly Pencarrow* (1939). The four books make up a dynastic saga of a 'typical' New Zealand pioneering family through the evolution of that country's society.
▷ *Road to Pencarrow* (1963)

SCARFE, Francis
(1911–86)

English poet, born in South Shields, Durham and educated at the universities of Durham, Cambridge and Paris. A lecturer in French at Glasgow University Scarfe's more permanent home was Oxford. Coming to prominence in the 1930s, he combines lyrical passion like **Dylan Thomas**'s, surrealism akin to **David Gascoyne**'s, and an apocalyptic phrase-making and balladry comparable to **Auden**'s. Never finding an original poetic voice, he nevertheless made the combination his own. His best work is found in *Inscapes* (1940) and *Poems and Ballads* (1942). His critical prose includes *Auden and After* (1942) and *The Art of Paul Valéry* (1954).

SCARRON, Paul
(1610–60)

French writer, born in Paris, the son of a lawyer. He became an *abbé*, and gave himself up to pleasure. About 1634 he paid a long visit to Italy, and in 1638 began to suffer from a malady which ultimately left him paralysed. He obtained a prebend in Mans (1643), tried physicians in vain, and, giving up all hope of remedy, returned to Paris in 1646 to depend upon letters for a living. From this time he began to pour forth endless sonnets, madrigals, songs, epistles and satires. In 1644 he published *Typhon, ou la giganto-machie* (Eng trans *Typhon: or the Wars of the Gods and the Giants*, 1704); and made a still greater hit with his metrical comedy, *Jodelet, ou le maître valet* (1645, 'Jodelet; or, the Master-Butler'), followed by *Les Trois Dorothées* (1648, 'The Three Dorothies') and *Les Boutades du Capitaine Matamore* (1647, 'The Jests of Captain Matamore'), the plots taken from the Spanish. In 1648 appeared his *Virgile travesti* (part one, 'Virgil Burlesqued') and the popular comedy, *L'Héritier ridicule* (1653, 'The Ridiculous Heir'). One of the bitterest satires against Mazarin which he wrote for the *Fronde* probably lost him his pensions. The burlesque predominates in most of his writing, but it is as the creator of the realistic novel that he will always be remembered. *Le Romant comique* (1651–7, Eng trans *The Comical Romance*, 1665) was a reaction against the euphuistic and interminable novels of **Madeleine de Scudéry** and **Honoré d'Urfé**. The work of **Alain Le Sage**, **Daniel Defoe**, **Henry Fielding** and **Tobias Smollett** owes much to him. In 1652 he married Françoise d'Aubigné, afterwards Madame de Maintenon, who brought a hitherto unknown decorum into his household and writings.
▷ E Magne, *Scarron et son milieu* (1923)

SCARRY, Richard McClure
(1919–)

American illustrator and writer of children's books, born in Boston. He was educated at Boston Museum School of Fine Arts and served in the US army in the Mediterranean and North Africa. Didactic, detailed and scatty, his output is prolific and he is hugely popular with children tolerant of his formulaic approach. Indicative titles are *What Do People Do All Day?* (1968) and *Hop Aboard, Here We Go!* (1972).

SCÈVE, Maurice
(1510–64)

French Renaissance poet, born in Lyons. He was a leader of the *école lyonnaise*, which paved the way for the *Pléiade*, a group of poets which gathered around **Ronsard**. His most important poem is *Délie, object de plus hautte vertu* (1544, 'Delia, Object of the Highest Virtue'), on the subject of love. Other works include *La Saulsaye* (1547), and a didactic poem on the history of mankind, *Microcosme* (1563).
▷ V C Saulnier, *Maurice Scève* (1948)

SCHADE, Jens August
(1903–78)

Danish novelist and poet, born in Skive, Jutland. The major theme of his writing has been defined as 'the coincidental unity between everyday life and cosmic Eros'. The chief influences upon him were, from his own country, **Claussen**, and from Great Britain, **D H Lawrence**. The title of the novel *Mennesker modes og sod Musik opstaar i Hjwetet* (1944, 'People Meet and Sweet Music Fills the Heart') is characteristic.

SCHAEFER, Jack Warner
(1907–)
American short-story writer and novelist, born in Cleveland, Ohio. He was educated at Columbia University, and worked as a journalist, teacher and editor. His perennial subject was the American West, but he transcends the limitations of the 'western' genre in both psychological depth and literary merit, and is its most distinguished fictional chronicler. His first novel, *Shane* (1949), remains his best known, but his other works include the lengthy novel *Monte Walsh* (1965), a realistic if rambling account of cowboy life, and a number of short stories and novellas, gathered together in *Collected Stories* (1966) and *The Short Novels* (1967). A critical edition of *Shane* was published in 1984.

SCHAEFFER, Albrecht
(1885–1950)
German poet, novelist and essayist from Elbing. He was a young member of the circle of **Stefan George**—upon whom he wrote an illuminating essay in his *Dichter und Dichtung* (1923, 'Poets and Poetry'); to some extent he always suffered from the heaviness of thought associated with that master. He left Germany for America in 1939, and died in the year of his return home. He published much religious poetry and a *Bildungsroman* in the style of **Goethe**: *Helianth* (1920–1, shortened 1929). He believed that the world had been created by the Spirit, whose medium was himself and other selected poets.

SCHAEFFER, Susan F(romberg)
(1941–)
American novelist, poet and short-story writer, born in Brooklyn, New York. She received her PhD from the University of Chicago in 1966, and has since combined her academic with her writing career, currently working as a professor of English at Brooklyn College. Her novels, of which *The Madness of a Seduced Woman* (1983) is the best known, combine some of the trappings of romance, suitably updated, with a feminist sensibility. The latter, as is shown in *Buffalo Afternoon* (1989), is often extended to empathize with men: in this novel she deals with a young soldier's experience of Vietnam, and the traumatic aftermath of the war there. *The Injured Party* (1986) is a melioristic account of domestic life, in which a woman and her husband are reconciled after the death of the wife's ex-fiancé.

SCHAPER, Edzard
(1908–)
German novelist, essayist, dramatist and radio playwright, born in Ostrovo, Posen. He settled in Estonia in 1930, but was driven out by the Nazis and the Soviets (both of whom sentenced him to death *in absentia*, for his liberal journalism). After much travelling he eventually settled in Cologne in the early 1950s. A much respected and thoughtful Christian novelist (he moved from the Greek Orthodox Church to Catholicism in 1951), he has written both historical and contemporary novels. Two collections of stories have been translated: *Sterne über der Grenze* (1950, Eng trans *Star Over the Frontier*, 1961) and *Das Tier* (1928, Eng trans *The Dancing Bear*, 1961).
▷W Grenzmann, *Dichtung und Glaube* (1960)

SCHAUKAL, Richard
(1874–1942)
Austrian Symbolist poet, born in Brünn. He was in the Austrian civil service, and like **Hugo von Hofmannsthal** turned away from the decadence of the declining Austrian Empire to seek perfection in lyrical expression of poetic dreams in *Gedichte* (1893, 'Poems'), *Tage und Träume* (1899, 'Days and Dreams'), *Sehnsucht* (1900, 'Yearning'), and the posthumous collection *Spätlese* (1943, 'Late Harvest').

SCHEFFEL, Joseph Viktor von
(1826–86)
German poet and novelist, born in Karlsruhe. He studied law at Heidelberg, Munich and Berlin, but in 1852 went to Italy to write. His best book is *Der Trompeter von Säckingen* (1854, 'The Säckingen Trumpeter'), a romantic and humorous tale in verse. His other best-known books are the historical novel *Ekkehard* (1855), and the Lieder and student songs of *Gaudeamus* (1868).
▷J Proelss, *Scheffels Leben und Dichten* (1887)

SCHÉHADÉ, Georges
(1910–89)
Lebanese poet and dramatist. Born in Alexandria, he lived for long periods in Beirut, but made frequent visits to France. Two plays, *Monsieur Bob'le* (1952) and *La Soirée des proverbes* (1954, 'The Evening of Proverbs'), preceded *Histoire de Vasco* (1956), which won Schéhadé international fame in spite of an initially mixed critical reception, the enthusiasts praising its subtle and gentle satire while

the sceptics reduced its tragedy to pathos, rejecting its poetry and humour. *Vasco* received particular acclaim in Britain, where the play was first performed at the 1960 Edinburgh Festival by the Oxford Theatre Group. His poetry collections include *Poésies I, II and III* (1938, 1948, 1949), and *Anthologie du vers unique* (1977). Schéhadé's is a significant voice in the established tradition of French anti-war literature.

▷R Baldick, Introduction to *Theatre of War* (1967)

SCHENKKAN, Robert Frederic
(1953–)

American playwright and actor, born in Chapel Hill, North Carolina. He graduated in Theatre Arts from the University of Texas in 1975, and studied acting at Cornell University. His first play was *Final Passages*, originally produced as *Derelict in Buffalo* (1982), followed by the one-act plays *Intermission* and *Lunchbreak* (both 1982). His most successful work to date, *The Kentucky Cycle* (1991–2), won him a Pulitzer Prize for Drama in 1991. His other plays include *The Survivalist* (1983) and *Tall Tales* (1988).

SCHERFIG, Hans
(1905–79)

Danish novelist, born into a liberal and affluent printer's family in Copenhagen. A simultaneously venemous and warm-hearted satirist who exposes the vices of the class-based society, his most notable novel is *Det forsømte Foraar* (1940, Eng trans *Stolen Spring*, 1986), a classic in Danish literature, about pupils crippled by an authoritarian education system and the subsequent poisoning of a hated Latin teacher, Mr Blomme. The hallmarks of Scherfig's bestseller novels are their unconventional crime plots and their ironic, pseudo-objective narration, which imitates conventional modes of speaking or writing. Masterful examples are *Den forsvundne Fuldmægtig* (1938, Eng trans *The Missing Bureaucrat*, 1988), about a civil servant in crisis who eventually finds peace in prison, and *Frydenholm* (1962), an extensive, semi-documentary novel about Denmark under German occupation during World War II, with particular focus on the unlawful arrest and internment of the members of the Danish Communist Party in 1943. Scherfig had joined the Communist Party in 1932 and remained a stalwart communist through Stalinism and the emergence of the New Left right up to his death.

▷C E Bay (ed), *Hans Scherfig 1905–1979* (1989)

SCHICKELE, René
(1883–1940)

German Alsatian writer, born in Oberehnheim. His father was German, and his mother French. A journalist by profession, he wrote poems, plays and novels, including the trilogy of realist novels *Das Erbe am Rhein* (1925–31, 'The Inheritance on the Rhine'), and the poetry collections *Weiss und Rot* (1911, 'White and Red') and *Die Leibewache* (1914, 'The Bodyguard'). He was a pacifist, and argued in his writings for cultural unity in Europe.

SCHILLER, Johann Christoph Friedrich von
(1759–1805)

German dramatist, poet and historian, born in Marbach on the Neckar. His father was an army surgeon in the service of the Duke of Württemberg. He was educated at the grammar school in Ludwigsburg, and was intended for the church, but at the age of 13, at the personal request of the duke, was obliged to attend the latter's military academy, studying the law instead of theology, but finally qualified as a surgeon (1780) and was posted to a regiment in Stuttgart. Although outwardly conforming well, he found an outlet for his true feelings in the reading and eventually writing of *Sturm und Drang* verse and plays. His first play, *Die Räuber* (1781, Eng trans *The Robbers*, 1792), published at his own expense, was, on account of its seemingly anarchical and revolutionary appeal, an instant success when it reached the stage at Mannheim the following year. Schiller played truant from his regiment to attend the performance, was arrested but, forbidden to write anything but medical works in the future, fled and, in hiding at Bauerbach, finished the plays *Die Verschwörung des Fiesko zu Genua* (1783, Eng trans *Fiesco; or, The Genoese Conspiracy*, 1796) and *Kabale und Liebe* (1783, Eng trans *Cabal and Love*, 1795). For a few months he was dramatist to the Mannheim theatre. He next issued a theatrical journal, *Die rheinische Thalia*, begun in 1784, in which were first printed most of his play *Don Carlos* (1787, Eng trans 1798), many of his best poems, and the stories *Verbrecher aus verlorener Ehre* (1786, Eng trans *The Dishonoured Irreclaimable*, 1826) and *Der Geisterseher* (1787–9, Eng trans *The Ghost-Seer, or Apparitionist*, 1795). In 1785 he went by invitation to Leipzig and in Dresden, where **Karl Theodor Körner** was living, he found rest from emotional excitement and financial worries. Here he finished *Don Carlos*, written in blank verse, not prose, his first mature play, though it suffers artistically from excessive length and lack of unity. Amongst the finest fruits of his

discussions with Körner and his circle are the poems *An die Freude* (c.1788, 'Ode to Joy'), later magnificently set to music by Beethoven in his choral symphony, and *Die Künstler* (1858, 'The Artist'). After two years in Dresden and an unhappy love affair he went to Weimar, where he studied Kant, met his future wife, Charlotte von Lengefeld, and began his history of the revolt of the Netherlands. In 1788 he was appointed Honorary Professor of History at Jena, and married, but his health broke down through overwork from writing a history of the Thirty Years War, *Geschichte des dreissigjährigen Krieges* (1793, Eng trans *The History of the Thirty Years' War in Germany*, 1799), the letters on aesthetic education, *Briefe über die ästhetische Erziehung des Menschen* (1795, Eng trans *Upon the Aesthetic Culture of Man*, 1845), and the famous *Über naive und sentimentalische Dichtung* (1795–6, Eng trans *On Simple and Sentimental Poetry*, 1884), in which he distinguishes ancient from modern poetry by their different approaches to nature. His short-lived literary magazine, *Die Horen* (1795–7), was followed by the celebrated *Xenien* (1797, 'Epigrams'), a collection of satirical epigrams against philistinism and mediocrity in the arts, in which the new friendship between **Goethe** and Schiller found mutual expression. This inspired the great ballads (1797–8), *Der Taucher* ('The Diver'), *Der Ring des Polykrates* ('The Ring of Polycrates'), *Die Kraniche des Ibykus* ('The Cranes of Ibycus'), the famous *Lied von der Glocke* (completed in 1799, 'Song of the Bell') and, under the influence of **Shakespeare**, the dramatic trilogy, *Wallenstein* (1796–9, trans by **Samuel Taylor Coleridge**, 1800), comprising *Wallensteins Lager*, *Die Piccolomini*, and *Wallensteins Tod*, the greatest historical drama in the German language. This was followed by *Maria Stuart* (1800; Eng trans *Mary Stuart*, 1801; also trans by **Stephen Spender**, 1957), a remarkable psychological study of the two queens, Elizabeth and Mary, Queen of Scots, in which the latter by her death gains a moral victory. Schiller the historian is here at odds with Schiller the dramatist. Again, in *Die Jungfrau von Orleans* (1801, Eng trans *The Maid of Orleans*, 1835), Joan of Arc dies on the battlefield and is resurrected. *Die Braut von Messina* (1803, Eng trans *The Bride of Messina*, 1837) portrays the relentless feud between two hostile brothers, and the half-legend of *Wilhelm Tell* (1804, Eng trans *William Tell*, 1825) is made by Schiller a dramatic manifesto for political freedom. There is a fragment of *Demetrius* (1804–5; published 1859), his unfinished work. He was ennobled in 1802 and fell ill in 1804.
▷W Witte, *J C F Schiller* (1949)

SCHIMPER, Carl Friedrich
(1803–67)

German naturalist and poet, a pioneer in modern plant morphology. He was notable for his work on phyllotaxis, and in geology for his theory of prehistoric alternating hot and cold periods. Despite his talents, he failed to secure any academic post. Many of his scientific ideas were published as poems; several hundred are known.

SCHLAF, Johannes
(1862–1941)

German novelist and dramatist, born in Querfurt. He studied at Berlin and with **Arno Holz** wrote *Papa Hamlet* (1889), a volume of short stories, *Die Familie Selicke* (1890, 'The Selicke Family'), a social drama, *Peter Boies Freite* (1902, 'Peter Boie's Wooing'), and others.
▷S Bergen, *Johannes Schlaf* (1941)

SCHLEGEL, August Wilhelm von
(1767–1845)

German writer and pioneer of the German Romantic movement, brother of **Friedrich von Schlegel**, born in Hanover. He studied theology at Göttingen, but soon turned to literature. In 1795 he settled in Jena, and in 1796 married a widow, Caroline Böhmer (1763–1809), who separated from him in 1803 and married Friedrich Schelling. In 1798 he became Professor of Literature and Fine Art at Jena, and founded with his brother the literary journal *Das Athenäum*. In 1801–4 he lectured at Berlin. Most of the next 14 years he spent in the house of **Madame de Staël** at Coppet, though he lectured on *Vorlesungen über schöne Literatur und Kunst* (3 vols, 1810, Eng trans *Dramatic Art and Literature*, 1815) at Vienna in 1808, and was secretary to the Crown Prince of Sweden (1813–14). From 1818 till his death he was Professor of Literature at Bonn. He translated 17 plays of **Shakespeare**, and also translated works by **Dante**, **Calderón de la Barca**, **Cervantes** and **Camoens**, and edited the *Bhagavad-Gita* and the *Ramayana*.

SCHLEGEL, (Karl Wilhelm) Friedrich von
(1772–1829)

German writer and critic, and pioneer of the German Romantic movement, brother of **August Wilhelm von Schlegel**, born in Hanover. He was educated at Göttingen and Leipzig, in 1798 he eloped with Dorothea (1763–1839), the daughter of Moses Mendelssohn and wife of a Jewish merchant, Simon Veit, and mother of Philipp Veit the religious painter, and next year utilized his experiences in a notorious romance, *Lucinde* (1799). He then joined his brother at Jena,

and with him wrote and edited the journal *Das Athenäum*, in the interests of Romanticism. *Charakteristiken und Kritiken* (1801, 'Characterizations and Criticisms') contains some of both brothers' best writing. He studied oriental languages at Paris (1802–4), and in 1808 he published a pioneering work on Sanskrit and Indo–European linguistics, *Über die Sprache und Weisheit der Indier* (1808, 'On the Language and Wisdom of the Indians'). In 1808 he became a Roman Catholic, and joined the Austrian foreign service; it was he who penned the Austrian proclamations against Napoleon in 1809. His best-known books are two series of lectures: *Philosophie der Geschichte* (1829, Eng trans *The Philosophy of History*, 1835) and *Friedrich Schlegels Geschichte der alten und neuen Literatur* (1815, Eng trans *Lectures on the History of Literature*, 1818). There are also English versions of his *Philosophie des Lebens* (1828, *The Philosophy of Life*, 1847) and *Über die neuere Geschichte* (1811, *A Course of Lectures on Modern History*, 1849).
▷E Behler, *Friedrich von Schlegel* (1966)

SCHLEGEL, Johann Elias
(1718–49)

German dramatist and literary theorist, uncle of **August Wilhelm** and **Friedrich von Schlegel**, born in Meissen and educated at Leipzig University. The author of at least 14 plays, such as the tragedies *Canut* (1746) and *Hekuba* (1736) and the comedies *Der Geheimnisvolle* (1747) and *Die stumme Schönheit* (1747), Schlegel is better known for his criticism. In *Vergleichung Shakespears und Andreas Gryphs* (1741) he is the first of his countrymen to interpret **Shakespeare** sympathetically; in *Abhandlung von der Nachahmung* (1742–5) he qualifies the idea of Art as imitation of Life by stressing the selective and intensifying power of the medium involved.
▷E M Wilkinson, *Johann Elias Schlegel: A German Pioneer in Aesthetics* (1945)

SCHMIDT, Augusto Frederico
(1906–65)

Brazilian poet and publisher. He began as a *modernista* poet, but gradually abandoned this style for a simpler, more mystical type of poetry. As a publisher he issued works by **Ramos** and other leading writers. A few of his poems are translated in the *Penguin Book of Latin American Verse* (1971, ed E Curacciolo-Trejo).
▷J Nist, *The Modernist Movement in Brazil* (1967)

SCHNABEL, Johann Gottfried
(1692–after 1750)

German novelist and physician, born in Sandersdorf near Bitterfield. He published under the pseudonym of 'Gisander'. He served as a surgeon in the War of the Spanish Succession, and then practised in Hamburg and Stolberg. Of all the many novels which tried to emulate **Defoe**'s *Robinson Crusoe*, Schnabel's *Die Insel Felsenberg* (1731–43) was by far the most original and successful—it is still read with pleasure today. In many ways it epitomizes, although in German terms, just those individualistic and religious concerns which Defoe himself brought to British attention.
▷F Brüggemann, *Utopie und Robinsonade* (1914)

SCHNACK, Anton
(1892–1974)

German poet, story writer and novelist, born in Rieneck. His elder brother Friedrich (1888–1973) was a well-known popular writer. His delicate novels and stories, as well as his early expressionist verse, found favour with discerning readers.

SCHNEIDER, Rolf
(1932–)

German dramatist and story-writer, born in what was Karl–Marx Stadt. He lived and worked in the former East Germany, both as an editor (of *Aufbau*) and as a radio playwright. His most notable play is a semi-documentary on the trials at Nuremberg: *Prozess in Nürnberg* (1967). Some of his stories may be read in *Brücken und Gitter* (1965, Eng trans *Bridges and Bars*, 1967).

SCHNEUR, Zalman, originally Zalman Zalkind
(1886–1959)

Hebrew and Yiddish poet and novelist, born in Sklov, Russia, into a noted Hasidic family; he died in the USA, whence he had escaped from Germany during World War I. His attitude is well summed up by the affectionate description of him as one who followed 'the style of the big I'; his friend and mentor **Bialik** said of him that he 'assailed the universe'. His earlier poetry is in Yiddish, but he discovered his own voice in his Hebrew poetry. Many readers turned to his 'Noah Pandre' stories—in *Noah Pandre* (1908, Eng trans 1936) and in *Song of the Dnieper* (1945)—as an antidote to the notion of the servile Jew in Russia: in these a butcher's son shows the despots and racists what a Jewish fist can do. His **Whitman**esque poetry is not subtle, but is often overwhelmingly powerful.

SCHNITZLER, Arthur
(1862–1931)

Austrian dramatist and novelist of Jewish origin, born in Vienna. He practised as a physician in Vienna from 1885 before he turned

playwright. His highly psychological, often strongly erotic short plays and novels, executed with great technical skill, frequently underline some social problem, mostly against the familiar easy-going Viennese background. *Anatol* (1893, Eng trans 1911) and *Reigen* (1900, Eng trans *Hands Around*, 1920; better known as *La Ronde*, the title of a 1959 translation) are cycles of one-act plays linked with one another by the overlapping of one of the characters until the chain is completed by a character of the last meeting one from the first. Other notable works include *Der grüne Kakadu* (1899, Eng trans *The Green Cockatoo*, 1913), *Liebelei* (1895, Eng trans *Light-o'-Love*, 1912), *Der Weg ins Freie* (1908, Eng trans *The Road to the Open*, 1923), *Professor Bernhardi* (1912, Eng trans 1913), on anti-Semitism, and *Flucht in die Finsternis* (1931, Eng trans *Flight into Darkness*, 1931).
▷ B von Brentano, *Arthur Schnitzler* (1965)

SCHNURRE, Wolfdietrich
(1920–)

German story writer, satirist, poet, novelist and (notably) writer of *horspielen* (radio plays), born in Frankfurt am Main. He was one of the founders of the literary circle Gruppe '47, but soon resigned from it. Grotesque and tender by turns, his often memorable, and almost always laconic, work may have been neglected because of its extreme pungency and irony. He is represented in **Hamburger** and **Middleton**'s *Modern German Poetry* (1962).

SCHÖNHERR, Karl
(1867–1943)

Austrian folk dramatist, story writer and poet, born in Axams in the Tyrol. He practised as a doctor in Vienna until 1905, when he gave up medicine for literature. He is remembered chiefly for his drama. He began under the influence of **Anzengruber** and, to a smaller extent, **Werfel**. His comedies and tragedies of Tyrolese peasant life subsequently became more solid and original. Many of his plays, such as *Glaube und Heimat* (1910, 'Faith and Fireside'), are historical. *Der Weibsteufel* (1914, 'The Female Devil') is a skilfully written and powerful sex tragedy of naturalistic proportions about a woman who has her feeble husband murdered by a young hunter, whom she thereafter destroys. Schönherr wrote many more plays, some patriotic, some city comedies, and a gripping religious mystery about Judas: *Passionspiel* (1933). He was not commercially successful in the theatre in the latter half of his career.

SCHOPENHAUER, Arthur
(1788–1860)

German philosopher and essayist, born in Danzig. A radical philosopher of pessimism, besides being one of the very few philosophers who was also a great stylist, he had unbounded influence upon a host of writers, including **Friedrich Nietzsche**, **André Gide**, **Thomas Hardy**, **Thomas Mann**, the composer Richard Wagner (who exercised such an influence on French literature), and countless others. Popularly taken to have been an excessively unpleasant and vindictive man (as presented by, for example, **Bertrand Russell**), the truth is more complex—he bequeathed all he had to the relief of human suffering. Schopenhauer's beautifully and eloquently expressed tone, that life is not worth living unless the nature of what he called the Will is contemplated, chimed in exactly with both his era's loss of faith, and with its turning towards Indian religion (he drew much inspiration from the *Upanishads*). His mother Johanna Schopenhauer was herself a novelist of note, and an associate of **Goethe**. Schopenhauer also, by his insistence upon the fact that only self-denial and withdrawal from materialist aspirations can bring peace—in his terms surrender to the universal Will as distinct from the individual will—influenced many more modern thinkers, from **Rudolph Steiner** through **Buber** to **Jung**. For many he presented the only possible solution to the problem of the existence of evil in the world. The only consolation, for Schopenhauer, lies in *Mitleid*, compassion. His picture of suffering in the world, despite his insistence that his work had been dictated to him by a religious entity whose existence he denied, remains one of the most powerful of all.
▷ R Taylor (ed), *The Will to Live: Selected Writings* (1962); A S Zimmern, *Arthur Schopenhauer: His Life and Philosophy* (1932)

SCHORER, Mark
(1908–77)

American novelist, critic and biographer, born in Sauk City, Wisconsin and educated at the state university. He went on to teach at Dartmouth, Harvard, and Berkeley. His third novel, *The Wars of Love* (1953), won critical acclaim for its skilful portrayal of the complex and tragic relationships linking a one-female and three-male foursome through childhood to middle age. His short stories, collected in *The State of Mind* (1956), often concern retrospection and ambivalent nostalgia for early youth. He is best known, however, for his criticism, which includes famous essays on *Lady Chatterley's Lover* and *Wuthering Heights*, available in the collection *The World We Imagine* (1968).

SCHRADER, Paul
(1946–)
American film-maker, born in Grand Rapids, Michigan. Raised in a strict Calvinist household, he did not see his first film until in his late teens, but soon became a voracious viewer and incisive critic, whose influential writing includes *Transcendental Style In Film: Ozu, Bresson and Dreyer* (1972). A student of film at UCLA, he entered the film industry as a screenwriter, collaborating to memorable effect with director Martin Scorsese on a series of films that portrayed the hell-on-earth of contemporary urban existence, the brutality of traditional masculine values and the possibility of redemption. Their films together include *Taxi Driver* (1976), *Raging Bull* (1980) and *The Last Temptation Of Christ* (1988). He made his directorial debut with *Blue Collar* (1978), a gritty exposé of union corruption, and has also worked as a writer-director on a diverse range of films dominated by a strong visual sensibility and an emotional coldness. His work includes *American Gigolo* (1980), an examination of redemption through love, *Mishima* (1985), a stylized dramatization of the life and work of the Japanese writer, and *Light Sleeper* (1992), a convincing portrait of mid-life anxiety and the desire for change.

SCHREINER, Olive
(1855–1920)
South African author and feminist, born in Wittebergen Mission Station, Cape of Good Hope, the daughter of a German Methodist missionary and an English mother. She grew up largely self-educated and at the age of 15 became a governess to a Boer family near the Karoo desert. She lived in England (1881–9), where her novel, *The Story of an African Farm* (1883), the first sustained, imaginative work to come from Africa, was published under the pseudonym Ralph Iron. She had a fiery, rebellious temperament and a lifelong hatred of her mother; in her later works the creative artist gave way to the passionate propagandist for women's rights, pro-Boer loyalty and pacificism. These include the allegorical *Dreams* (1891) and *Dream Life and Real Life* (1893), the polemical *Trooper Peter Halket* (1897), a sociological study, *Woman and Labour* (1911), and her last novel *From Man to Man* (1926). In 1894 she married S P Cronwright, who took her name, wrote a biography of her (1924) and edited her letters (1926).
▷S C Cronwright-Schreiner, *The Life of Olive Schreiner* (1924)

SCHUBART, Christian Friedrich Daniel
(1739–91)
German poet, born in Obersontheim in Swabia. He wrote satirical and religious poems. He was imprisoned at Hohenasperg (1777–87) by the Duke of Württemberg, whom he had offended by an epigram. He is largely remembered for his influence on **Schiller**.
▷K M Klos, *Christian Schubart* (1908)

SCHULBERG, Budd Wilson
(1914–)
American novelist and screenwriter, born in New York City. He moved to California as a child, and was brought up in Hollywood, which became the satirically treated subject of his novel *What Makes Sammy Run?* (1941). His best-known work is the film *On the Waterfront* (1954), a hard-hitting, realist exposé of corruption on the New York docks which he turned into the novel *Waterfront* in 1955. *The Harder They Fall* (1947), about corruption in boxing, and *Everything That Moves* (1980), about the connection between gangsters and the unions, treated similar themes. *The Disenchanted* (1950) traced the decline of a writer based on **F Scott Fitzgerald**, while *Sanctuary V* (1969) entered the seamy world of Latin-American politics. His stories were collected in *Some Faces in the Crowd* (1950).
▷ *Moving Pictures: Memories of a Hollywood Prince* (1981)

SCHULZ, Bruno
(1892–1942)
Polish writer of magical short stories. He grew up in the predominantly Jewish town of Drohobycz, taught art at the local school, and was murdered there by a Wehrmacht officer during the occupation. He published only two books in his lifetime, both of which have enjoyed considerable success in English. *Sklepy cynamonowe* (1934, published in the UK as *The Street of Crocodiles*, in the USA as *Cinnamon Shops and Other Stories*, 1963) is a collection full of magical transformations and cabbalistic connections, centred on the experience of one Joseph N, who is clearly a projection of Schulz himself. A later book, *Sanatorium pod klepsydra* (1937, Eng trans *Sanatorium Under the Sign of the Hourglass*, 1978), shows Schulz bringing his unique vision to bear on wider social and philosophical questions. He was clearly still a writer of immense promise when he died.
▷E Baur, *Die Prose von Schulz* (1975)

SCHUYLER, James Marcus
(1923–91)
American poet, novelist, playwright and art critic, born in Chicago, whose poetry unflinchingly confronts the modern middle-class environment. Collections such as *Salute* (1960) and *The Home Book: Prose and Poems*

1951–1970 (1977) look in almost obsessive detail at the minutiae of daily life. His first novel, *A Nest of Ninnies* (1969), written with **John Ashbery** who, like him, was associated with the New York school of poets, is an almost plotless attack upon what the authors consider to be the vacuousness of much middle-class life. A similar theme pervades his next novel, *What's for Dinner?* (1978), almost a third of which is set in a hospital ward for alcoholics. He won the Pulitzer Prize for Poetry in 1981 for *The Morning of the Poet* (1980). His play, *Unpacking a Trunk* (1965), written with **Kenward Elmslie**, shows a group of people describing the objects they have retrieved from a trunk.

SCHWARTZ, Delmore
(1913–66)

American poet, story writer and critic, born in Brooklyn, New York City. He was educated at New York University and made a startling debut as a poet while still a student. Writing lyrics, fiction, drama and criticism, he was associated with the *Partisan Review* group of writers as editor (1943–55), and editor of *The New Republic* (1955–7). A profound ironist, in 1960 he became one of the youngest winners of the Bollingen Prize. His collections of verse include *In Dreams Begin Responsibilities* (1938), *Shenandoah* (1941), *Vaudeville for a Princess* (1950) and *Summer Knowledge* (1959). His stories are collected in *The World is a Wedding* (1948) and *Successful Love* (1961). **Saul Bellow** memorably portrayed him in *Humboldt's Gift* (1975).
▷J Atlas, *Delmore Schwartz: the life of an American poet* (1977)

SCHWOB, Marcel
(1867–1905)

French critic, novelist, dramatist, story writer, scholar (of English, German, classical and Indian literatures, and of the criminal *argot* of **François Villon**). He was born in Chaville, of Jewish parents. He anticipated many modern notions, such as that of 'biography as a mode of fiction'; his poetic *Le Livre de Monelle* (1894, Eng trans *The Book of Monelle*, 1929), based on his friendship with a prostitute, is a remarkable book by any standards. He had wide influence, especially on **Valéry** and **Jarry**.

SCIASCIA, Leonardo
(1921–89)

Sicilian novelist, born in Racalmuto. Taking Sicily for the focus of his work, his themes embrace its society past and present which he saw as exemplifying the political, social and spiritual tensions to be found on the wider stage of Europe. A teacher and politician, he first published *Favole della dittatura* (1950, 'Fables of Dictatorship'). *Le parrocchie di Regalpetra* (1956, Eng trans *Salt in the Wound*, 1969) pointed the way ahead for his fiction and subsequent works developed his early themes. *Candido* (1977) was published in English in 1977 and in the 1980s his novels, several of which were re-translated, reached a wider English-speaking audience. These include *Il consiglio d'Egitto* (1963, Eng trans *The Council of Egypt*, 1966) and *A ciascuno il suo* (1968, Eng trans *A Man's Blessing*, 1968 (US); 1969 (UK)).
▷G Jackson, *Sciascia: a thematic and structural study* (1981)

SCOTT, Alexander
(c.1515–1584)

Scottish lyrical poet of the school of **Dunbar**. Little is known of his early life, except that he became musician and organist at the Augustinian priory of Inchmahome, in the Firth of Forth, in 1548. He had associations with the court of Mary, Queen of Scots, and in 1565 was a canon of Inchaffray in Perthshire. He bought an estate in Fife in 1567 and became a wealthy landowner. He wrote 36 short poems, either courtly love lyrics or poems offering moral advice. He is considered to be the last of the Scottish 'Makars' (15th/16th-century poets).
▷A K Scott (ed), *Poems* (1953)

SCOTT, Duncan Campbell
(1862–1947)

Canadian poet, short-story writer, literary editor and critic (known in particular for his editions of **Archibald Lampman**'s poetry and his contributions to the Toronto *Globe* column, 'At the Mermaid Inn'). He was born in Ottawa and spent much of his life as an emissary of the Canadian Department of Indian Affairs. *The Magic House* and *Labour and the Angel* were published in 1893 and 1898 respectively, but it is his third volume of poetry, *New World Lyrics* (1905), that includes many of the 'Indian poems' for which he is best known. This preoccupation with the unsettling and often tragic interaction of indigenous and settler cultures also figures prominently in subsequent volumes, and the collected *Poems of Duncan Campbell Scott* (1926).

SCOTT, Evelyn, originally Elsie Dunn
(1893–1963)

American poet and novelist, born in Tennessee. She changed her name in 1913, aged 20, having run away to Brazil with a married university Dean. After several years of hardship in South America she returned to the USA and began her career as a writer with a volume of poetry, *Precipitations* (1920), in the Imagist vein. *The Wave* (1929), a popular novel about the Civil War composed as a montage of letters, newspaper reports, army records and poetic narrative, brought her greater notice. **William Faulkner**, whom she admired, judged her pretty good 'for a woman'.

SCOTT, F(rancis) R(eginald)
(1899–1985)

Canadian poet and critic, born in Quebec. As a witty and graceful poet, both satirical and otherwise, Scott was only a moderate practitioner, but he made Canadian readers aware of **T S Eliot** and **Pound**, was an active socialist, and compiled one or two influential anthologies. Some of his best poetry is collected in *The Eye of the Needle* (1957).
▷D Pacey, *Ten Canadian Poets* (1958)

SCOTT, Gabriel
(1874–1958)

Norwegian writer of novels, short stories, poetry and drama, strongly linked to the nature and people of the south coast of Norway. As a young author he won a name as a writer of children's books, but he is now remembered best for his novel *Kilden* (1918, 'The Source'), about the life and thoughts of the mild and loving fisherman Markus. As in all his novels, Scott here advocates a mystic and pantheistic form of Christianity, based on an individualistic closeness to nature and God, and asks critical questions about the kind of fundamentalist free-church movement he saw around him.

SCOTT, John
(1730–83)

English poet and essayist, best known for his celebration of village life in *Amwell* (1776). Born in Bermondsey, the son of a Quaker linen draper, his first verses were published in *The Gentleman's Magazine*. He was acquainted with **Johnson** and the philosophical Scot, **James Beattie**.

SCOTT, Mary
(1888–1979)

New Zealand writer of light novels and the *Barbara* series (1936–54) of rural sketches which drew upon her two decades of contributions to a regional newspaper. Born in Bay of Islands, she was among the first writers consistently to use a New Zealand setting for her novels, which became very popular overseas, especially in Europe. Her first novel, *Breakfast for Six*, did not appear until 1953, and was followed by others whose titles convey the remote, homely, rural 'backblocks' life on which they are based, from *Dinner*

Doesn't Matter (1957), *Tea and Biscuits* (1961) and *Turkey at Twelve* (1968), which describes a backblocks Christmas, to her last novel *Board but No Breakfast* (1978). Between 1960 and 1965, with **Joyce West**, she wrote five crime novels, again using local settings, beginning with *Fatal Lady* and including *The Mangrove Murder* (1963) and *No Red Herrings* (1964). She also wrote a more serious novel, *The Unwritten Book* (1957), evoking the grim side of rural life and drawing upon her own experiences.
▷*Days That Have Been* (1966)

SCOTT, Michael
(1789–1835)

Scottish author, born in Cowlairs, Glasgow, the son of a merchant. Educated at Glasgow High School and University (1801–5), he went to seek his fortune in Jamaica. He spent a few years in the West Indies, but in 1822 settled in Glasgow. His vivid, amusing stories, *Tom Cringle's Log* (1829–33) and *The Cruise of the Midge* (1834–5), first appeared serially in *Blackwood's Magazine*.
▷Sir G Douglas, *The Blackwood Group* (1897)

SCOTT, Paul Mark
(1920–78)

English novelist, born in London. He served in the British army (1940–3), and in the Indian army, in India and Malaya (1943–6). The first of his 12 novels was *Johnnie Sahib* (1952), but his great achievement is *The Raj Quartet* (*The Jewel in the Crown*, 1966; *The Day of the Scorpion*, 1968; *The Towers of Silence*, 1971; *A Division of Spoils*, 1975). Set in the years 1939–47, the overlapping novels give a vivid portrait of India at the demise of the Raj. Critical acclaim came late for the author, encouraged by a popular television adaptation of the books. *Staying On* (1977), which can be seen as a coda to the *Quartet*, was awarded the Booker Prize.

SCOTT, Sarah, née Robinson
(1723–95)

English novelist, born into a well-connected family and sister of the 'bluestocking' Elizabeth Montagu, she was educated at home in Kent. She travelled widely in England, was married briefly and unhappily (1751–3) to the Prince of Wales's tutor, then lived with her friend Lady Barbara Montagu in a female community near Bath teaching poor children (1754–65). Most of her six novels are conventional tales of moral sentiment, but *A Description of Millennium Hall* (1762), her most popular work, is interesting as one of the first female Utopias; narrated through a series of personal stories, it portrays life in a caring community of women as an appealing alternative to marriage.

▷W M Crittenden, *The Life and Writings of Mrs. Sarah Scott—Novelist* (1932); E R Napier, in *British Novelists, 1660–1800*, ed M Battestin, *Dictionary of Literary Biography*, 39 (1985)

SCOTT, Tom
(1918–)

Scottish poet, born in Partick, Glasgow; as a 'mature student' he graduated from Edinburgh University in the 1950s. With encouragement from **T S Eliot** he translated poems by **François Villon** into Scots (*Seeven Poems o Maister Francis Villon*, 1953). *An Ode til New Jerusalem* (1956), *The Ship and Ither Poems* (1963) and the biographic narrative *Brand the Builder* (1975) established him as a 'maister' in the language. In English, his near epic *The Tree* (1977) and the angry humanist poem *The Dirty Business* (1986) were further evidence of his skill as polemicist and poet. *The Collected Shorter Poems* (1993) assured his status as a major figure in 20th-century Scottish writing.

SCOTT, Sir Walter
(1771–1832)

Scottish novelist and poet, born in Edinburgh, son of a Writer to the Signet and of Anne Rutherford, a daughter of the Professor of Medicine at the university. When young he contracted polio in his right leg, which lamed him for life, and was sent to his grandfather's farm at Sandyknowe to recuperate, thus coming to know the Border country which figures often in his work. Neither at the High School, Edinburgh, nor at Edinburgh University did he show much promise. His real education came from people and from books—**Fielding** and **Smollett**, **Walpole**'s *Castle of Otranto*, **Spenser** and **Ariosto** and, above all, **Percy**'s *Reliques* and German ballad poetry. He did better in his father's office as a law clerk, and became an advocate in 1792. His first publication consisted of rhymed versions of ballads by Bürger in 1796. The following year he was an ardent volunteer in the yeomanry, and on one of his 'raids' he met at Gilsland spa Charlotte Charpentier, daughter of a French émigré, whom he married in Carlisle on Christmas Eve, 1797. Two years later he was made Sheriff-Depute of Selkirkshire. The ballad meanwhile absorbed all his literary interest. *Glenfinlas* and *The Eve of St John* were followed by a translation of **Goethe**'s *Göetz von Berlichingen*. His skill as a writer of ballads led to the publication by James Ballantyne, a printer in Kelso, of Scott's first major work, *The Border Minstrelsy* (vols 1 and 2, 1802; vol 3, 1803). The *Lay of the Last Minstrel*

(1805) made him the most popular author of the day. The other romances which followed—*Marmion* (1808) and *The Lady of the Lake* (1810)— enhanced his fame, but the lukewarm reception of *Rokeby* (1811), *Lord of the Isles* (1815) and *Harold the Dauntless* (1817) warned him that he should turn his attention away from the ballad form and concentrate on writing novels. In 1811 he built his country seat, Abbotsford, near Galashiels, in the Borders. The business troubles that overshadowed his later career began when he set up a publishing firm with James Ballantyne and his brother John in the Canongate in Edinburgh. All went well at first, but along with expanding business came expanding ambitions, and when Archibald Constable with his London connections entered the scene, Scott lost all control over the financial side of the vast programme of publication, much of it hack work, on which he now embarked; hence the bankruptcy in the middle of his great career as a novelist (1826). The Waverley novels fall into three groups—first, from *Waverley* (1814) to *The Bride of Lammermoor* (1819) and *A Legend of Montrose* (1819); next, from *Ivanhoe* (1820) to *The Talisman* (1825), the year before his bankruptcy; *Woodstock* (1826) opens the last period, which closes with *Castle Dangerous* and *Count Robert of Paris* (1832), in the year of his death. The first period established the historical novel based, in Scott's case, on religious dissension and the clash of races English and Scottish, Highland and Lowland, his aim being to illustrate manners but also to soften animosities. In *Guy Mannering* (1815) his great humorous characters first appear, and are found in *Old Mortality* (1816) and *The Heart of Midlothian* (1818). His Scottish vein exhausted, he turned to England in the middle ages in *Ivanhoe*. With *The Monastery* and *The Abbot* (1820) he moved to Reformation times, where he showed a respect for what was venerable in the ancient church, a mood which might have been predicted from his harshness to the Covenanters in *Old Mortality*. This group of works is distinguished by its portrait gallery of queens and princes. The highlights in his last period are the not entirely successful *Woodstock* (1826), and *The Fair Maid of Perth* (1828), where again the ballad motif appears. He worked best on a traditional or ballad theme, as in *Proud Maisie*, but Highland themes, as in *Pibroch of Donuil Dhu* (1816), equally proved his lyric powers. He was also writing other works for the publishers, much of which was simply hack work—the editions of **Dryden** (1808), of **Swift** (1814), and the *Life of Napoleon* (9 vols, 1827). However, the *Tales of a Grandfather* (1828–30) keeps its charm, and his three letters 'from Malachi

Malagrowther' (1826) are remembered for their patriotic assertion of Scottish interests. A national figure, he helped to supervise the celebration for George IV's visit to Edinburgh in 1822. His last years were plagued by illness, and in 1831–2 he toured the Mediterranean in a government frigate. He died at Abbotsford soon after his return, and was buried in the ruins of Dryburgh Abbey. Publication of a definitive edition of the *Waverley Novels* was begun in 1993 by Edinburgh University Press. The project is scheduled to take 10 years to complete, and the texts will incorporate a mass of textual corrections, and undo the substitution and excisions of his original editors.

▷J G Lockhart, *Memoirs of the Life of Sir Walter Scott, Bart* (10 vols, 1839); Sir Herbert Grierson, *The Life of Sir Walter Scott* (1938)

SCOTT, William Bell
(1811–90)

Scottish painter and poet, born in Edinburgh, brother of the painter David Scott and son of an engraver. While training as an engraver he also began to write poetry and had verses published for the first time in 1831. He exhibited paintings at the Royal Scottish Academy from 1834. He moved to London in 1837 and in the following year his first volume of poetry was published. He married in 1839, began exhibiting at the Royal Academy from 1842 and, in 1843, became Master of the Government School of Design in Newcastle. His major paintings were of scenes of Northumberland history which were exhibited in London and Newcastle prior to their installation (1861) at Wallington Hall, Northumberland. He moved back to London in 1864 and, in 1875, published *Poems* dedicated to his friends **Dante Gabriel Rossetti**, **William Morris** and **Swinburne**. His *Autobiographical Notes* were published posthumously in 1892.

SCOTT, Winfield Townley
(1910–68)

American poet and editor (*Providence Journal*), born in Haverhill, Massachusetts. A good craftsman, Scott worked in the tradition of **Robinson** and **Frost**, writing mostly of his native New England. His *Collected Poems* appeared in 1962.

SCRIBE, Augustin Eugène
(1791–1861)

French dramatist, born in Paris. After 1816 his productions became so popular that he established a type of theatre workshop in which numerous *collaborateurs* worked under his supervision, turning out plays by 'mass-production' methods. The best known are *Le Verre d'eau* (1840, Eng trans *A Glass of Water*, 1851), *Adrienne Lecouvreur* (1848, Eng trans 1883) and *Bataille des dames* (1851, Eng trans *The Ladies' Battle!*, 1851). Scribe also wrote novels and composed the libretti for 60 operas, including *Masaniello* (1842, Eng trans 1843), *Fra Diavolo* (1842, Eng trans 1857), *Robert le Diable* (1841, Eng trans *Robert the Devil*, 1842), *Les Huguenots* (1842, Eng trans *The Huguenots*, 1842) and *Le Prophète* (1847, Eng trans *The Prophet*, 1850).

▷E Legouý, *Augustin Scribe* (1874)

SCUDÉRY, Georges de
(1601–67)

French writer, born in Le Havre, brother of **Madeleine de Scudéry**. After a brief military career he wrote a number of plays which achieved some success. In 1637 his *Observations sur le Cid* led to a controversy with **Pierre Corneille**. He later wrote novels and had a small share in his sister's works, which first appeared under his name.

▷C Clare, *Un Matamore des lettres* (1929)

SCUDÉRY, Madeleine de
(1608–1701)

French novelist, born in Le Havre, sister of **Georges de Scudéry**. Left an orphan at six, she went to Paris in 1639 and with her brother was accepted into the literary society of Mme de Rambouillet's salon. From 1644 to 1647 she was in Marseilles with her brother. She had begun her literary career with the romance *Ibrahim ou l'illustre Bassa* (1641, Eng trans *Ibrahim; or, The Illustrious Bassa*, 1652), but her most famous work was the ten-volume *Artamène, ou le Grand Cyrus* (1649–59, Eng trans *Artamenes, or the Grand Cyrus*, 1653–5), written with her brother, followed by *Clélie* (10 vols, 1654–60, Eng trans *Clelia*, 1656–61). These highly artificial and ill-constructed pieces, full of pointless dialogue, were popular at the court because of their sketches of and skits on public personages. Her last novel was *Mathilde d'Anguilon* (1667). She was satirized by **Molière** in *Les précieuses ridicules* (1659, 'The Conceited Young Ladies').

▷C Aragonnès, *Madeleine de Scudéry, Reine du tendre* (1934)

SEAGER, Allen
(1906–68)

American novelist, autobiographer and critic, born in Michigan. He wrote several competent novels, and, more notably, a book of memoirs, *A Frieze of Girls* (1964), in which he tells of his youth in Michigan and his experiences at Oxford as a Rhodes Scholar. He wrote an early biography of **Theodore Roethke**, *The Glass House* (1968).

SEAMAN, Sir Owen
(1861–1936)

English writer. He was educated at Shrewsbury and Clare College, Cambridge, became Professor of Literature at Newcastle (1890), and was editor of *Punch* (1906–32). His parodies and verses on society which include *Paulopostprandials* (1833), *In Cap and Bells* (1889) and *From the Home Front* (1918), were very popular.

SEBASTIAN, Mihai
(1907–45)

Romanian dramatist and novelist, born in Braila, who was killed prematurely in a traffic accident. The Romanian theatre has not yet produced a dramatist of the calibre of **Caragiale**, but many pointed to Sebastian's *Ultima ora* (1945, 'The Last Hour') as one of the best comedies written since his time.

SEDAINE, Michel-Jean
(1719–97)

French poet and playwright, born in Paris. Self-educated, and a stonemason by trade, he went on to forge a prolific and varied literary career. He began by writing poetry, publishing *Poésies fugitives* ('Fleeting Poems') in 1752; the collection was considered in the main mediocre, although 'L'Épitre a mon habit' ('Letter to My Garment') was admired. Also a librettist for the opéra-comique, he enjoyed particular success with *Le Diable à quatre ou la Double Métamorphose* (1756 'The Four-part Devil'), written in collaboration with the composer Duni. Sedaine launched his career as a dramatist by providing short comic pieces for performance at the fairs of Paris; he also wrote three plays based on the fables of **La Fontaine**, *Blaise le savetier* (1759, 'Blaise the Cobbler'), *L'Huitre et les plaideurs* (1759, 'The Oyster and the Litigants') and *Le Jardinier et son seigneur* (1761, 'The Gardener and his Master'), and went on to write for Italian theatre. His *Le philosophe sans le savoir* (1765, 'The Philosopher who did not know it') is considered a masterpiece of the then-emergent *drame bourgeois*, and was much admired by **Diderot**.

SEDGWICK, Catharine Maria
(1789–1867)

American novelist and poet, born in Stockbridge, Massachusetts. She was the author of *A New England Tale* (1822), considered to be an early example of fiction addressed primarily to a female audience, and she went on to become noted for her depiction of the simple domestic virtues. Her novels are valuable historical records of American social customs, and are deceptively satirical. *A New England Tale* was intended as an attack on Calvinism and *Hope Leslie* (1927), by common consent her best book, was based upon careful research into Puritan documents. She was active in the Unitarian church and, despite the domestic settings for so much of her fiction, a staunch defender of women's right to lead a single life—a position which she argued at length in *Married or Single* (1857).

SEDLEY, Sir Charles
(1639–1701)

English courtier and poet, born probably in London. He was notorious at court for both debauchery and wit. He became an MP in 1668. He is remembered less for his plays— *The Mulberry Garden, Antony and Cleopatra, Bellamira*—than for a few songs and *vers de société*.
▷V de Sola Pinta, *Sir Charles Sedley* (1927)

SEEDORFF PEDERSEN, Hans Hartvig Otto
(1896–1971)

Danish poet, born in Århus. He gained the same kind of popularity in Denmark as **Humbert Wolfe** did in England, for his mellifluousness and superficial charm, but he was more 'Bacchic' in his inspiration. Critics believed him to be shallow, and his verse is not now much read.

SEEGER, Alan
(1888–1916)

American poet, born in New York City. Educated at Harvard, he left the USA to settle in Paris. When war was declared in Europe in 1914, he enlisted in the French Foreign Legion and fought courageously before being killed at the Battle of the Somme. His collection, *Poems*, was published later the same year. Although unjustly neglected in favour of the English war poets, Seeger is remembered for the much-anthologized poem, 'I Have A Rendezvous With Death'.

SEFERIADES, George *see* SEFERIS

SEFERIS, George, pen-name of George Seferiadis
(1900–71)

Greek poet and diplomat, who in 1963 became the first Greek winner of the Nobel Prize for Literature. He was born in Smyrna, the son of a university professor; in 1914 his family moved to Athens, where his father became Professor of International Law at the University. Seferis studied law in Paris and London and spent the rest of his life as a diplomat, serving as the Greek Ambassador to London from 1957–62. His first collection

of poetry, *Strophe* ('Turning Point'), published in 1931, was an immediate sensation: it defined the voice of a new generation, signalling a move away from the depression and narcissism that had been so fashionable. The extent of Seferis's debt to modernists such as **Pound** and **Eliot** became clear in his second collection, *Mythistorima* (1935, 'Myth History'), which contained some of the first free-verse poems in the language. His later collections include *Hemerologhia Katastromatos* ('Log Books') *I*, *II* and *III* (1940, 1944 and 1965). He was also a noted translator and worked on versions of **Valery**, Eliot, **Yeats** and Pound.
▷K K Katsimbalis, *Vivliografia* (1961)

SÉGALEN, Victor
(1878–1919)

French prose-poet, novelist and sinologist, a French Naval Officer by profession. He was born in Brest, and vanished under mysterious circumstances during an expedition to the forest of Hoelgoat. His best-known work, which certainly influenced **Claudel**, **Gide** and **Jouve** (who edited it with a preface in 1955), was the prose-poetry of *Stèles* (1912, rev edn 1914, Eng trans *Stelae*, selection, 1969; *Steles*, complete, 1987). These unique poems have been described as a 'reading' of Chinese civilization made at a time 'when it seemed to be coming to an end', and eventually became the subject of a cult. In some ways Ségalen (his first 'e' is sometimes accented, sometimes not) anticipated the work of the anthropologist Claude Lévi-Strauss.

SEGHERS, Anna, pseud of Netty Radványi, née Anna Reiling
(1900–83)

German novelist from Mainz, daughter of a Jewish antique-dealer. Her communist faith dominated her work, and led her ultimately to become a willing purveyor of socialist realism. Her later novels of the 1930s resembled her first, *Aufstand der Fischer von St Barbara* (1928, Eng trans *The Revolt of the Fishermen*, 1930), in essential content: revolution lends meaning and solidarity to hopeless and helpless individual lives. Seghers fled from Hitler in 1933 to France and Mexico, where she wrote the vastly successful (in part through the movie made by Fred Zinnermann) *Das siebte Kreuz* (1942, Eng trans *The Seventh Cross*, 1942), her best novel, and a powerful indictment of the cruelties of the Nazi regime. Her later novels, written in East Germany, are documents more or less completely convinced of the rightness of the new rulers.

SEGURA, Manuel Ascensio
(1805–71)

Peruvian dramatist, born in Lima. He wrote 14 plays, of which *La saya y el manto* (1841), satirical of politicians and their mistresses, is probably the best remembered. He very successfully redid *La Celestina* in Creole form in *Ña Catita* (1845, rev edn 1856). He played an important part in the development of Peruvian theatre.
▷I H Delgado, *Manuel Ascensio Segura y el teatro peruano* (1939)

SEIDEL, Ina
(1885–1974)

German novelist, biographer and poet from Halle an der Saale. She was a capable lyrical and narrative poet, but her chief work was done in fiction: in particular in her *Das Labyrinth* (1921, Eng trans *The Labyrinth*, 1932), an internally directed study of the inscrutable 18th-century naturalist and travel writer Georg Forster, and in *Das Wunschkind* (1930, Eng trans *The Wish Child*, 1935), an account of the Napoleonic Wars and the loss, to the reconciliatory central character, a courageous widow, of her son. This last, although in many respects dated, has acquired the status of something of a classic, especially amongst older readers.

SEIFERT, Jaroslav
(1901–86)

Czech poet, winner of the Nobel Prize for literature, brought up in a poor family in a working-class suburb of Prague. His first collection was *Město v slzáck* (1921, 'City of Tears') in which he looked back in anger at the human waste of World War I, urging a working-class revolution. In 1923 he moved to and fell under the spell of Paris and translated **Guillaume Apollinaire**. His second collection was *Samá láska* (1923, 'All Love') in which his private experience is to the fore. He was expelled from the Communist Party in 1929 and joined the Social Democrats. After Munich (1938) and the Nazi occupation his patriotism emerged in *Přílba Llíny* (1945, 'A Helmet of Earth'), in which he identifies himself with the people's grief. Most memorable are the poems which evoke the four days in May 1945 when the citizens of Prague rose against the tatters of the Nazi forces. He edited *Práce*, a trade union paper, but he was too much his own man to enjoy the trust of the Communist Party. New work was shunned and *Morový sloup* (1977, Eng trans *The Prague Column*, 1979) had to be published abroad. He was awarded the Nobel Prize for literature in 1984.

SELBY, Hubert, Jr
(1928–)

American novelist and short-story writer, born in Brooklyn, New York. He enlisted in the US Merchant Marines in 1944, but was hospitalized two years later with tuberculosis. In all, he spent nearly five years as a patient, subsequently working at a number of jobs until the publication of his controversial bestseller, *Last Exit to Brooklyn* (1964), a set of connected stories. It is a bleak, pitiless account of an urban hell, mired in violence, sexually brutalized, dependent on anodynes like alcohol and dope. In concentrating on his **Swift**ian satire and references to **Dante** and **Poe**, and on the obscenity trials which followed the book's publication, commentators often ignore Selby's concern with the effects of unemployment, strike-breaking and overcrowding. In his next book, *The Room* (1971), Selby delves painfully into the brutal fantasies and obsessions of a man in confinement. Few novels have ever concentrated so unforgivingly on a corrupt consciousness. *The Demon* (1976) concerns a sexual obsessive, while *Requiem for a Dream* (1978) suggests that 'acceptable' sops like television and food serve exactly the same psychic function as hard drugs. Selby's stories have been collected as *Song of the Silent Snow* (1986).
▷'Hubert Selby issue', *Review of Contemporary Literature* (1981)

SELLASIE, Sahle
(1936–)

Ethiopian (Chaha) author of the first book in Chaha, *Shinega's Village: Scenes of Ethiopian Life* (1964), which was translated in 1970. His fascinating detective story, *The Afersata* (1969), is in English.

SELVON, Sam
(1923–94)

Trinidadian novelist and playwright. Born and educated in Trinidad, he served in the Navy in World War II and worked as a journalist before moving to London in 1950. He became a full-time writer in 1954 and settled in Canada in 1978. He introduced a form of modified dialect in his novels in which narration of standard English is interspersed with dialogue in dialect. Novels with a Trinidadian setting, notably *A Brighter Sun* (1952), centre on the positive aspects of creolization. His trilogy: *The Lonely Londoners* (1956), *Moses Ascending* (1975), *Moses Migrating* (1983), follows the changing fortunes of Moses from the initial hardships of emigrant life in Britain. Combining mixed dialect with folk and calypso tradition, Selvon produced comedy ranging from slapstick to biting satire.

SEMPILL, Francis
(c.1616–1682)

Scottish poet, born at the ancestral home of Beltrees in Renfrewshire. Little is known of his life. He studied law, probably in Europe, and was appointed Sheriff-Depute of Renfrewshire in 1677. He was the son of **Robert Sempill** (?1595–?1665), who is well known for his poem 'The life and death of Habbie Simpson, the Piper of Kilbarchan'. Francis shared his father's gift for vernacular poetry and wrote 'The Banishment of Poverty by James Duke of Albany', in which he recounts being pursued by merciless poverty until he takes refuge in the debtor's sanctuary at the Abbey of Holyrood. His authorship is tentatively ascribed to numerous other pieces, including the poems 'Blythesome Wedding' and 'Maggie Lauder', though it is suggested that he may only have re-worked them from earlier sources. He worked in the traditional form of the *Christis Kirk* stanza which was used largely to create comic caricatures of peasant customs and rites.
▷J Paterson (ed), *The Sempill Ballads* (1849)

SEMPILL, Robert
(?1595–?1665)

Scottish poet, from the hamlet of Beltrees, Renfrewshire. A supporter of the Reformers, he spent some time in Paris, but left after the St Bartholomew's Day Massacre, and spent most of the rest of his life in Edinburgh. He was probably employed in some military capacity (he was present at the sieges of Leith and of Edinburgh), and there is evidence that he was at one point employed at court. He revived the methods of the Scottish 'Makars', started a trend for poetry in the vernacular, and invented the six-line stanza later christened the 'Standard Habbie'. He wrote *Habbie Simson, The Blythesome Bridal* and, possibly, *Maggie Lauder*. His father, Sir James Sempill (1566–1625), also wrote a number of poems, including the anti-Catholic *The Packman's Pater Noster* (1669). His son was **Francis Sempill**.
▷J Paterson (ed), *The Sempill Ballads* (1849)

SENANCOUR, Étienne Pivert de
(1770–1846)

French author, born in Paris. After nine years in Switzerland he returned to Paris about 1798. His fame rests on three books; *Rêveries sur la nature primitive de l'homme* (1799, 'Musings on the Primitive Nature of Man'), *Obermann* (1804) and *Libres Méditations d'-un solitaire inconnu* (1819, 'Free Meditations of a Solitary Unknown'). The influence of **Goethe**'s *Werther* (1774) is persistent in his work. Senancour, neglected in his day, was

appreciated by **George Sand**, **Charles Sainte-Beuve** and **Matthew Arnold**.
▷J Merlant, *Étienne Senancour* (1907)

SENARENS, Luis Philip
(c.1863–1939)
American 'dime novelist', born in Brooklyn, New York City. He wrote more than 1 500 books, mostly very short, under a variety of pseudonyms such as 'Noname' and 'Police Captain Howard'. His best-known work is *Frank Reade* and its successors.

SENDAK, Maurice Bernard
(1928–)
American illustrator and writer of children's books, born in Brooklyn, New York, to a family of indigent Polish immigrants. Sickly (he was often quarantined) and bookish, he attended Lafayette High School, but formal education did not appeal to him and he thrived on a diet of comics, movies and his father's Jewish folk tales. Working as a window-dresser, he encountered classic illustrators in a toy store and was subsequently introduced to and commissioned by a publisher to illustrate *The Wonderful Farm* (1951) by Marcel Aymé. For *A Hole Is To Dig* (1952) he produced humorous, unsentimental drawings and in 1956 came *Kenny's Window*, the first book he both illustrated and wrote. But it was *Where the Wild Things Are* (1963) that made him internationally famous. Exploring the fantasy world of mischievous Max in whose room grows a forest inhabited by scary monsters, it fascinated children and perturbed parents. It won the Carnegie Medal and sold hugely. After this acknowledged classic he produced another, *In The Night Kitchen* (1970). Latterly he has collaborated on operas as well as continuing to produce the distinctive, disturbing and daring books—*Outside Over There* (1981), *Nutcracker* (1981) and *Dear Mili* (1988)—that have made him the premier practitioner of his métier.

SENDER, Ramón J
(1902–82)
Spanish novelist, born in Alcolea de Cinca, Huesca. He fought in the war against Morocco (1922–4), then worked for left-wing journals such as *La Libertad* ('Freedom'). After the Spanish Civil War he eventually settled in the United States, teaching Spanish literature. His experiences informed his early fiction: *Iman* (1929) deals with an ordinary soldier's experiences of the Moroccan war, while *Contraataque* (1938, 'Counter-attack') is about the civil war. His more mature works, while retaining the compassion evident in his earlier writing, display deeper psychological insight and originality. *Requiem por un campesino espanol* (1960, 'Requiem for a Spanish Peasant') is a later take on the upheaval caused by the civil war, while *El lugar del hombre* (1939, 'The Place of Man') examines the effect on a community of the return of a poor labourer presumed to have been murdered by two villagers 15 years previously.

SENECA, Lucius Annaeus, called 'the Younger'
(c.4 BC–c.65 AD)
Roman Stoic philosopher, statesman and tragedian, born in Cordova, Spain, the son of Seneca the Elder. He was educated in rhetoric and philosophy for a career in politics and law, which he began in Rome in 31. But in 41 he was banished to Corsica by the Emperor Claudius on a charge of adultery with the emperor's niece Julia Livilla, sister of Caligula; he spent eight years there in study and wrote the three treatises called *Consolationes*. He was recalled to Rome in 49 through the influence of Agrippina the younger, 3rd wife of Claudius and sister of Julia and became tutor to her son, the future Emperor Nero. He enjoyed considerable political influence for a while and was made consul by Nero in 57. But his moral influence waned, and though he tried to withdraw progressively from public life to devote himself to philosophy he lost favour with Nero, was denounced as a party to the conspiracy of Piso, and was ordered to commit suicide, which he did with composure and dignity. He was an eclectic Stoic, a moralist rather than a theorist, and a stylist much imitated by later essayists. His writings include: *De Ira* ('On Anger'), *De Clementia* ('On Mercy'), *De Beneficiis* ('On Generosity'), *Epistolae morales ad Lucilium* ('Moral Letters to Lucilius') and the *Apocolocyntosis divi Claudii* (literally, 'The Pumpkinification of the Divine Claudius', a scathing satire); he also wrote a number of verse tragedies which were influential in Elizabethan drama in England.
▷A L Motto, *Seneca* (1973)

SENGHOR, Léopold Sédar
(1906–)
Senegalese politician and poet. Educated in Dakar and at the Sorbonne in Paris, he taught classics in France from 1935, where he became involved with literary figures and wrote poetry advocating the concept of 'negritude' to glorify African civilization and values. After World War II he sat in the French National Assembly (1946–58) and was a leader of the Senegalese independence movement. After independence in 1960, as leader of the Senegalese Progressive Union (UPS), he became the new nation's first president. In 1976 he reconstituted the UPS as the

Senegalese Socialist Party (PS) and gradually the one-party political system which he had created became more pluralist, although the PS remained the dominant force. Senghor was consistently re-elected until his retirement in 1980, his successor being Abdou Diouf.
▷A Guibert, *Léopold Sédar Senghor* (1961)

SENOA, August
(1838–81)

Croatian poet, dramatist, critic and novelist. His work in the theatre is important because he helped to free this from German influences, but his own best work is in his historical novels. Towards the end of his life he seemed to the younger men to be too conservative, but later his work was reappraised and collected in 20 volumes (1931–5).

SERAFIMOVICH, Alexsandr, pseud of Alexsandr Serafimovich Popov
(1863–1949)

Russian novelist and story writer. The son of a Cossack officer, he was born in Nizhne-Jumoyarskaya in the Don region. Serafimovich was always a champion of the under-privileged, although he did not become a communist until 1919; his populist tales, which he began publishing as a young man, forced him into exile from 1887 until 1890. The title story of *Peski*, 'Sand', (Eng trans *Sand and Other Stories*, 1957) elicited the admiration of **Leo Tolstoy**. Serafimovich's most famous work, which earned him the dubious sobriquet of 'co-founder of Soviet literature', is his least good; it is the 'proletarian' novel *Zhelezny potok* (1924, Eng trans *The Iron Flood*, 1935) which is capable in its attempt to blend folk and even surrealistic idiom with socialist realism, but which fails because the author has set out to destroy individuality in the interests of the Stalinist 'mass'. Serafimovich influenced **Sholokhov**, and, like him, dried up in later life.
▷E J Brown, *Russian Literature Since the Revolution* (1969)

SERAFINO AQUILANO DE' CIMINELLI
(1466–1500)

Italian poet, musician and courtier, born in Aquila in the Abruzzi. He first gained a reputation by his skilled adaptations of the lyrics of **Petrarch** for singing to the lute. He was a brilliant reciter and singer of his own verse, and his poems were translated or adapted by Sir **Thomas Wyatt** and many other English and European poets. He was more popular than any other Italian poet at the time of his death. Posterity has seen him as artificial, just as the scholar Pietro Bembo viewed him in his own time.

SERAO, Matilde
(1856–1927)

Italian novelist and journalist, born in Patras in Greece, the daughter of a Greek father and a Neapolitan political refugee. She graduated as a teacher in Naples, worked in a telegraph office, and started writing articles for newspapers (1876–8). Her first novel of Neapolitan life was *Cuore Infermo* (1881), after which she joined the Rome newspaper *Capitan Fracassa*. She had a huge success with her next romantic novel, *Fantasia* (1882), followed by *Conquista di Roma* (1886, 'Conquest of Rome'), *Riccardo Joanna* (1887), *All' Erta Sentinella* (1889) and *Il Paese di Cuccagna* (1891).
▷A Barti, *Serao* (1965)

SERGEYEV-TSENSKY, Sergey
(1875–1958)

Russian novelist, born in Tambov province. From a Dostoyevskian passion for morbid characterization, as in *Tundra* (1902, 'The Tundra'), he developed greater simplicity of style and social sense in the massive 10-volume novel sequence, *Preobrazhenye zapiski* (1914–40, 'Transfiguration'), which won him the Stalin Prize in 1942.
▷A V Pryenkov, *Sergeyev Tsensky* (1963)

SERLING, Rod
(1924–75)

American science-fiction writer and television playwright, born in Syracuse, New York. A combat paratrooper during World War II, he attended Antioch College and began writing radio scripts before securing a radio staff job in Cincinnati. He first wrote for television in 1951 and won the first of six Emmy Awards for *Patterns* (1955). His other plays include *Requiem for a Heavyweight* (1956) and *The Comedian* (1957). He created, wrote and hosted the popular anthology series *The Twilight Zone* (1959–64), which often reflected his interest in the individual's struggle against social and political pressures, while also showing his mastery of the surprise, twist-in-the-tail ending. If the *Twilight Zone* scripts now seem creaking and hackneyed, it is partly because their ideas have been so often imitated. Sterling created, hosted and occasionally wrote the similar series *Night Gallery* (1970–3) and frequently narrated documentaries on scientific and nature subjects. The author of over 200 television plays, his few film scripts include *Seven Days in May* (1964).

SERRAILLIER, Ian Lucien
(1912–)

English author of children's fiction, non-fiction and poetry, best known for *The Silver Sword*, which, since its publication in 1956, has acquired the status of a modern children's classic. Set in World War II, it is the account of a Polish family divided by the Nazis, and of the children's attempts to escape to safety and become reunited with their family. They do so, and the book ends on an upbeat note at a newly-founded international children's village in Switzerland. Serraillier's widest influence has probably been as editor of Heinemann Educational Books' New Windmill Series. His other adventure novels include *There's No Escape* (1950) and *The Cave of Death* (1965).

SERVICE, Robert William
(1874–1958)

English-born Canadian poet, born in Preston. He went to Canada, travelled as a reporter for the *Toronto Star*, served as ambulance driver in World War I and wrote popular ballads, most notably 'The Shooting of Dangerous Dan McGrew', which appeared in *Songs of a Sourdough* (1907), and those in *Rhymes of a Rolling Stone* (1912). The alliterative urge persisted in *Ballads of a Bohemian* (1920), *Rhymes of a Rebel* (1952) and the late *Carols of a Codger* (1954). He also wrote novels, of which *The House of Fear* (1927) is the most accomplished.
▷ *Ploughman of the Moon* (1945); *Harper of Heaven* (1948)

SETH, Vikram
(1952–)

Indian poet, novelist and travel writer, born in Calcutta and educated at universities in England, the USA and China. His first poetry collection, *Mappings* (1980), was followed by *The Humble Administrator's Garden* (1985) and *All You Who Sleep Tonight* (1990). His travel book, *From Heaven Lake: Travels Through Sinkiang and Tibet*, appeared in 1983. His first novel, *The Golden Gate* (1986), although written in verse, describes the lives of the contemporary Californian professional classes. His following novel was even more ambitious. At over 1300 pages, *A Suitable Boy* (1993) is one of the longest single-volume novels in English. Set in immediate post-independence India, it is a love story which encompasses a vast number of characters and attempts a complete portrait of Indian social, political and cultural life.

SETON, Anya
(1916–)

American historical novelist, born into an east coast middle-class family but fascinated by British (especially English) history. A Seton novel—the best-known include *Dragonwyck* (1944), *Foxfire* (1951), *Katherine* (1954) and *Avalon* (1965)—is typically written

with a great deal of earnest enthusiasm for the period in which it is set, be it Plantagenet England, Arthurian Cornwall or an 18th-century plantation. Historical accuracy is not the real aim, however, and Seton is more concerned with the emotional interactions between the characters (typically a shy but soon-to-blossom virgin and a rough but handsome older man). Their physical qualities are described minutely (and constantly). The packaging in which the books are sold tends to reflect these concerns admirably, placing them firmly in the low-to-middlebrow range of the women's market.

SETON, Ernest Thompson, pseud of **Ernest Seton Thompson**
(1860–1946)

English-born Canadian writer and illustrator of nature books. He was born in South Shields, County Durham, but early became a naturalized Canadian. He founded the Boy Scouts of America. His books on animals were instructive and popular. Among the best known are *Biography of a Silver Fox* (1909) and his autobiography, *The Trail of an Artist-Naturalist* (1940).

SETTLE, Elkanah
(1648–1724)

English dramatist, born in Dunstable. He went from Oxford to London to make a living by his pen. In 1671 he had a success with his bombastic tragedy of *Cambyses*. To annoy **Dryden**, the Earl of Rochester arranged for Settle's *Empress of Morocco* to be played at Whitehall by the court lords and ladies. In reply to Settle's attack in *Absalom Senior* (1682), Dryden scourged 'Doeg' with his scorn in the second part of *Absalom and Achitophel*, and Settle replied in *Reflections on several of Mr Dryden's Plays* (1687). He adapted *A Midsummer Night's Dream* as *The Fairy Queen* in 1692, with music by Henry Purcell. He was made poet of the City of London in 1691, and contributed pageants until 1708. He wrote short comic pieces known as 'drolls', of which only one, *The Siege of Troy* (1707), survives. He is remembered more through Dryden's scurrilous portrait than his own work.
▷ F C Brown, *The Life and Work of Elkanah Settle* (1910)

SEUSS, Dr, pseud of **Theodor Seuss Geisel**
(1904–91)

American author and illustrator of a profusion of children's books, born in Springfield, Massachusetts. Though his animals have been described as 'boneless wonders', there is no denying his ingenuity, particularly in early books like *And to Think that I Saw it*

on *Mulberry Street* (1937) and *The 500 Hats of Bartholemew Cubbins* (1938). He wrote the screenplay for the animated cartoon *Gerald McBoing Boing* (1950), which won several awards. In 1957 he began to write and draw a series of 'Beginner Books', intended to help teach reading, for Random House, starting with *The Cat in the Hat* (1958) and *Yertle the Turtle* (1958). By 1970, 30 million copies had been sold in America and Seuss had become synonymous with learning to read. He also wrote a bestselling book for adults, *You're Only Old Once!* (1986).
▷M Stoffler, *Dr Seuss From Then to Now* (1986)

SÉVIGNÉ, Madame de, née Marie de Rabutin-Chantal
(1626–96)

French letter writer, born in Paris. She was orphaned at an early age and was carefully brought up by an uncle, the Abbé de Coulanges, at the Abbaye de Livry in Brittany. She married the dissolute Marquis Henri de Sévigné in 1644, but he was killed in a duel in 1651. From then on, in the most brilliant court in the world, her thoughts were centred on her children, Françoise Marguerite (b.1646) and Charles (b.1648). On the marriage of the former to the Comte de Grignan in 1669, she began the series of letters to her daughter which grew sadder as friend after friend passed away. She died of smallpox, after nursing her daughter through a long illness. Madame de Sévigné's 25 years of letters reveal the inner history of the time of Louis XIV in wonderful detail, but the most interesting thing in the whole 1600 (one-third letters to her from others) remains herself.
▷J Aldis, *Madame de Sevigné* (1907)

SEWARD, Anna
(1747–1809)

English poet, known as the 'Swan of Lichfield', born in Eyam Rectory, Derbyshire. She lived from the age of 10 at Lichfield, where her father, himself a poet, became a canon. He died in 1790, but she continued to live on in the bishop's palace, and wrote romantic poetry. Her 'Elegy on Captain Cook' (1780) was commended by **Dr Johnson**. She bequeathed all her poems to Sir **Walter Scott**, who published them in 1810 (*Poetical Works*).
▷J Pearson, *The Swan of Lichfield* (1956)

SEWELL, Anna
(1820–78)

English novelist, born in Yarmouth. She was an invalid for most of her life. Her only book, *Black Beauty, The Autobiography of a Horse* (1877), a work for children which was written as a plea for the more humane treatment of animals, is perhaps the most famous fictional work about horses.
▷M Bayly, *The Life and Letters of Mrs Sewell* (1881)

SEXTON, Anne, née Harvey
(1928–74)

American poet, born in Newton, Massachusetts. A confessional poet in the mould of her teacher, **Robert Lowell**, and her friend, **Sylvia Plath**, with whom she is often bracketed, she writes frankly about her personal experiences, including a nervous breakdown. In 1948 she married Alfred Sexton and had two daughters. She taught at Boston University (1969–71) and Colgate (1971–2). *To Bedlam and Part Way Back* (1962) was her first collection of poetry; others are *All My Pretty Ones* (1962), *Live or Die* (1966), *Love Poems* (1969), *Transformations* (1971), *The Book of Folly* (1972), *The Death Notebooks* (1974), *The Awful Rowing Towards God* (1975), and the posthumously published *45 Mercy Street* (1976). The *Complete Poems* were published in 1981, seven years after she committed suicide.
▷D W Middlebrook, *Anne Sexton: A Biography* (1990)

SEYMOUR, A(rthur) J(ames)
(1914–89)

Guyanese poet and critic. He thought of himself primarily as a love poet and the sensuousness of his verse can be sampled in the 70th birthday tribute *A J Seymour at 70* (1984, ed Ian McDonald). Much of Seymour's poetry was printed privately and a Collected Poems is overdue. He compiled the *Dictionary of Guyanese Folklore* (1975) and the *Dictionary of Guyanese Biography* (1984).

SEYMOUR-SMITH, Martin
(1928–)

English poet, literary historian (*Guide to Modern World Literature*, 1986), biographer (**Graves**, **Kipling**, **Hardy**) and humorist (*How To Bluff Your Way in Literature*, 1966, rev edn 1971), born in London. Seymour-Smith's poems (eg *Reminiscences of Norma*, 1971), alternating uneasily between the 'embarrassingly over-passionate' and the bitterly or humorously cynical, are not at all in the mainstream, and have understandably, despite the admiration of a very few (Graves, **Sisson**, Nye, **Reeves**—all, however, his personal friends), been passed over as irrelevant to the needs of a properly flourishing literature. As a critic he is useful and very widely read in foreign literatures, but unreliable and often, it has been felt, wilfully non-conformist: in the words of Sisson, his work 'induces some hostility as well as gratitude' because 'it results in the rough handling of some reputations which many not un-influential persons think deserve more respect'. *Wilderness* (1994) collects later poems.

▷C H Sisson, *The Avoidance of Literature* (1978)

SHAARA, Michael Joseph, Jr
(1929–88)

American novelist, born in Jersey City, New Jersey. He graduated from Rutgers University, and served as a paratrooper before taking up an academic career as Professor of English at Florida State University, Tallahassee. That military background is a recurring theme in his fiction, which began with *The Broken Place* (1968). His most successful book was his second novel, *The Killer Angels* (1974), which recreated the battle of Gettysburg from the perspective of a group of officers in the Southern forces, and won the Pulitzer Prize for Fiction that year. His later novels were *The Herald* (1981) and *Soldier Boy* (1982).

SHADBOLT, Maurice Francis Richard
(1932–)

New Zealand biographer, novelist and short-story writer, born in Auckland. Some of his earlier work in *The New Zealanders* (1959) and *Summer Fires and Winter Country* (1963) was later used in *Strangers and Journeys* (1972), a rambling novel of contrasted families through two generations. His first novel was *Among the Cinders* (1965), followed by *The Presence of Music: Three Novellas* (1967). The best of his early work is in *This Summer's Dolphin* (1969), *An Ear of the Dragon* (1971) and *Figures in Light: Selected Stories* (1978). He has a keen sense of history as shown in his novels *A Touch of Clay* (1974) and *Season of the Jew* (1986) and, less seriously, in *The Lovelock Version* (1980), a light-hearted reworking of New Zealand history. Nonfiction includes a re-examination of the ANZAC myth in *Voices of Gallipoli* (1988).

SHADWELL, Thomas
(c.1642–1692)

English dramatist, born at Broomhill House, Brandon. He made a hit with the first of his 13 comedies, *The Sullen Lovers* (1668). He also wrote three tragedies. **Dryden**, grossly assailed by him in the *Medal of John Bayes*, heaped deathless ridicule upon him in *MacFlecknoe* ('Shadwell never deviates into sense'), and as 'Og' in the second part of *Absalom and Achitopel*. His works exhibit talent and comic force. He succeeded Dryden as poet laureate in 1689.

▷M W Alssid, *Thomas Shadwell* (1967)

SHAFFER, Peter Levin
(1926–)

English dramatist, born in Liverpool. His plays are variations on the themes of genius and mediocrity, faith and reason, and the question of whether God, if he exists, is benevolent or not. These ideas form the intellectual core of *The Royal Hunt of the Sun* (1964), *Equus* (1973) and *Amadeus* (1979). His first play was *Five Finger Exercise* (1958), followed by the comedies *The Private Ear* and *The Public Eye* (1962). *Yonadab* (1985), a story of incest and envy set in the Jerusalem of 1000 BC, was not well-received, but *Lettice and Lovage* (1987), a comedy, proved a great success. Other plays include *Black Comedy* (1965), *White Lies* (1967) and *The Battle of Shrivings* (1970). His twin brother, Anthony, also writes plays; his works include the successful thriller *Sleuth* (1970).

SHAFTESBURY, Anthony Ashley Cooper, 3rd Earl of
(1671–1713)

English moral philosopher, politician and essayist, the grandson of Anthony Ashley Cooper, 1st Earl of Shaftesbury, born in London. John Locke supervised his early education and he then attended Winchester College. He entered parliament in 1695 and sat as a Whig for Poole until 1698, succeeding as 3rd Earl in 1699 and regularly attending the House of Lords until ill-health forced him to abandon an active political life in 1702. He moved to Naples in 1711 and died there. He wrote stylish (if to a modern taste, overwrought) essays on a wide range of philosophical and cultural topics, and these are collected in three volumes under the title *Characteristicks of Men, Manners, Opinions, Times* (1711). He is usually regarded as one of the principal English deists, and he argued (both against orthodox Christianity and against Hobbes) that we possess a natural 'moral sense' and natural affections directed to the good of the species and in harmony with the larger cosmic order. He gained more favourable attention abroad, perhaps, than at home, and Leibniz, **Voltaire**, **Denis Diderot** and **Gotthold Lessing** were among those attracted by his work.

▷R L Brett, *The Third Earl of Shaftesbury* (1951)

SHAKESPEARE, William
(1564–1616)

English playwright, poet, actor, also joint-manager of a London acting company and part-owner of one of its theatres, born in Stratford-upon-Avon in Warwickshire, the eldest son of John Shakespeare, glover and wool dealer. By long-established tradition, his birthday is celebrated on 23 April, St George's Day. The register of Holy Trinity Church, Stratford, records that he was christened there on 26 April 1564. He lived for 52 years, partly in Stratford and partly in London, and died at his home in Stratford on 23 April 1616. Two days later, he was buried in the church in which he had been christened. His life turned on its Stratford–London axis: Stratford, where he grew up, where his parents, his wife and his children lived; London, where he made the theatre career that brought him fame and fortune, and from which he withdrew while still pre-eminent. His life can be divided into three consecutive periods. The first period, spent wholly in Stratford, included boyhood and education, early marriage and the birth of his three children. The second period began when, still a very young man, he left Stratford to work in London as an actor and playwright. It lasted for 25 years, in the course of which he became a permanent and leading member of a great acting company. For that company he then wrote plays that gave it a commanding place in the London theatre. With his principal colleagues, he was responsible for the day-to-day business management and artistic direction of the company, receiving a share of its profits in return and becoming part-owner of one of the two theatres in which it was based. On top of all that, he acted for many years, performing in his own plays and in those of other dramatists whose work was in his company's repertory. Throughout this period he had lodgings in London and he used most of his very considerable income to increase the security and status of his family in their Stratford home, spending time with them between theatre seasons. The beginning of the third period of his life was marked by his carefully-planned and gradual withdrawal from his heavy commitments in the theatre. Then, when he was in his late forties and possessed of ample means, he left London to live full time in Stratford, where he spent the remainder of his days. There is no documentary proof that he was educated at Stratford Grammar School, but the numerous classical allusions in his plays and poems were drawn from the Latin and Greek poets, dramatists, philosophers and historians closely studied by Elizabethan grammar school pupils; and John Shakespeare's civic status entitled him to send his son to Stratford's excellent school free of charge. In the winter of 1582–3, at the age of 18, he married Anne Hathaway, a farmer's daughter who lived in Shottery, near Stratford. She was 26, and pregnant by him. Having no income of their own, they lived with the elder Shakespeares. Less than six months after their wedding, their first child,

Susanna, was baptized in Stratford church. Early in 1585, Anne gave birth to twins: Hamnet, their only (and short-lived) son, and Judith, their second daughter. With a wife and three children to maintain, and still dependent on his father, Shakespeare decided to try his luck in the London theatre. Stratford was a regular touring venue for the London acting companies, and three troupes were playing there from 1583 to 1588. He must have begun to work in the theatre soon after the twins were born. There is evidence that he had written several very successful plays in 1592. The theatre impresario Philip Henslowe recorded in his diary that 'Harey the vj' played to packed houses at the Rose Theatre between March and June 1592. Clearly, he was referring to *Henry VI*; but whether to one part of that play or to all three is not plain. In the September of that year, **Robert Greene** wrote a pamphlet, *Greene's Groatsworth of Wit, Bought with a Million of Repentance*, which included a ranting and envious attack on 'an upstart crow', a 'Shake-scene'. The pun on Shakespeare's name was obvious, but Greene identified his target even more precisely by parodying a line from *Henry VI* Part 3. The three parts of *Henry VI* were not the only successes of these first seven years. He wrote two other histories (*King John* and *Richard III*); three comedies (*The Comedy of Errors, The Taming of the Shrew, The Two Gentlemen of Verona*); and a revenge-tragedy (*Titus Andronicus*). By 1592 he had tried out each of the then most popular forms of drama and made his own distinctive contributions to them. Theatre-going London was well aware that a new star had risen, its light shining as brightly as any then burning—even **Christopher Marlowe**'s. In June 1592 the theatres were closed by an outbreak of the plague and they were not allowed to re-open until the summer of 1594. While the London stages were silent, Shakespeare wrote two long narrative poems: *Venus and Adonis* (published 18 April 1593) and *The Rape of Lucrece* (published 9 May 1594). Both were dedicated to the 3rd Earl of Southampton; but no reliable information about his connection with that young patron of the arts has been discovered. In the literary and courtly circles in which they were read, the poems were highly praised for their eloquent treatment of classical subjects. The sonnets were probably in private circulation by 1598. Though they were not published until 1609, it is generally held that they were written between 1592 and 1598. The order in which he composed these 154 poems is not known; and nobody has succeeded in arranging them to tell a coherent 'story'. The temptation to read them as autobiography has been—and still is—strong, and many attempts have been made to identify the mysterious people—'young man', 'dark lady', 'rival poet'—who appear in them. Sonnet sequences were in vogue, and Shakespeare's own added considerably to his contemporary reputation. Later generations have ranked many of the individual sonnets in the collection among the world's finest poems. The language in which they treat recurrent themes—love's ecstasy and despair, implacable time, lust and its shames, separation, betrayal, fame and death—echoes that of the plays. When the theatres re-opened, Shakespeare joined the newly-formed Lord Chamberlain's Men as a 'sharer'. It was the turning point in his career. In the first years as an actor he had been a 'hired man', working for a wage. From now on, he was entitled to a share of the company's profits. Previously, too, he had been a freelance playwright and, though his work had found a ready market, he had little security. The founder of the Chamberlain's Men, James Burbage, and the other sharers, knew what they were about when they brought him into their company. They already had some of the best actors. For example, Richard Burbage, James's son, was considered to be as good a tragic and heroic actor as the great Edward Alleyn of the Admiral's Men; and Will Kempe was a very popular comic. It was with those two fellow sharers that Shakespeare, on behalf of the Chamberlain's Men, received the queen's payment for the company's performances at court during the Christmas festivities of 1594–5. By securing the exclusive services of the best playwright in London, the Chamberlain's Men were justifiably confident that they would outdo all their rivals. It is clear that Shakespeare wrote the following plays for his company between 1594 and 1598: *The Merchant of Venice, A Midsummer Night's Dream, The Merry Wives of Windsor, Much Ado About Nothing, As You Like It, Richard II, Henry IV* Parts 1 and 2 and *Romeo and Juliet*. The prodigious output of five comedies, three histories and one tragedy took the London theatre world by storm. The language and the characters of the plays captured people's imagination and entered their daily conversation: 'dull as a Justice Shallow' was a term used by a letter writer of the day; and a contemporary dramatist noted rather sourly that playgoers were talking 'pure Juliet and Romeo'. The material rewards of these triumphs enabled Shakespeare to meet the heavy expenses incurred when his father was awarded a grant of arms in October 1596. Henceforth, John Shakespeare was entitled to the style of 'Gentleman', an honour that would descend in due course to his eldest son. That style, and the heraldic display that went with it, was prized in an age of rigid social distinction; for the Shakespeares it was also

a tangible sign that the family had regained—surpassed, indeed—its former status in Stratford. Ironically, the award of honour was received little more than two months after Shakespeare's only son, Hamnet, died, aged eleven. Given the dynastic ambition common in that age and evident in Shakespeare's conduct of his worldly affairs, it was a heavy blow. Of his personal grief we have no record. The welfare of his wife and his daughters was now his main family preoccupation. In 1597 he bought New Place, a large and imposing mansion in Stratford, close by the Guild Chapel and the grammar school and a few minutes' walk from his parents' house. He spent freely on improvements to the house and garden before Anne, Susanna and Judith moved into their new home. At about this time, trouble with the owner of the site on which Burbage's playhouse (called the Theatre) stood, forced the Chamberlain's Men to move. They dismantled the Theatre and used much of its material to build a new playhouse—the Globe—on Bankside, south of the Thames. It was a bold and successful venture. Sited in the heart of London's pleasureland—dicing-houses, bear-gardens, brothels and theatres—the Globe was the finest playhouse of them all, bigger and better equipped than any of its rivals. Its huge stage, with 'cellarage' below and balcony above, provided the space and permitted the rapidity and continuity of action which the dramas of the day demanded and which Shakespeare most notably exploited in the plays he wrote for performance there. He followed the brilliant success of *Henry V* (the Globe's opener) with *Julius Caesar, Twelfth Night, Hamlet* and *Othello*. In all, he had now written 14 plays which were the exclusive property of the Chamberlain's Men, and nine before he joined them. Nor did his current successes lead to the neglect of his earlier plays. Unwilling to allow popular plays to 'fust unused', the company rang the changes on its play stock and often revived former works. Takings at the Globe far exceeded those at the Theatre. The accession of King James VI and I in 1603 brought the company new and very great benefits. He immediately conferred his own royal patronage on Shakespeare and his fellow sharers. They became the King's Men—'His Majesty's Servants'—and were granted a patent. James thought it good to see them often. Court performances had always been a prestigious and lucrative addition to their ordinary programme. They had played for Queen Elizabeth on average three times a year. Between 1603 and 1614, the King's Men averaged 13 royal command shows a year and got for each twice as much as Queen Elizabeth had paid. The darker tone of the plays that Shakespeare wrote in the early years of James

I's reign has led to speculation that it reflected some kind of personal and spiritual crisis. But nothing that is known about him amounts to a feasible 'explanation' of why he wrote a succession of 'problem plays' (or 'dark comedies') and tragedies between 1603 and 1608–9: *All's Well*, *Measure for Measure*, *King Lear*, *Macbeth*, *Antony and Cleopatra*, *Timon of Athens*, *Coriolanus* and *Troilus and Cressida*. Great popular successes at the Globe, these plays were also received with acclaim at court and when performed for wealthy and socially exclusive audiences in private halls and in the lawyers' Inns of Court. It was audiences of this kind who were now flocking to the so-called 'private theatres'. The term is misleading. Like the 'public playhouses', they were commercial enterprises. They charged much more for admission and attracted fashionable patrons willing to pay to sit in comfort, protected from the elements. Because they were roofed over, these theatres were artificially lit. Stage illusion of a kind not possible in the public theatres was an integral part of their more sophisticated entertainments. In 1608 Shakespeare's company decided to beat the opposition by joining it. The King's Men took over the most successful of the private theatres—the Blackfriars—using it for their winter seasons and performing at the Globe in the summer. They now got the best of both worlds and prospered exceedingly. Shakespeare, who had bought a share in the Blackfriars Theatre, immediately began to write plays that could be performed with equal success on two very different stages. He solved the technical problems with increasing sureness: *Pericles*, *Cymbeline*, *The Winter's Tale* and *The Tempest*. Those plays were enthusiastically received at the Blackfriars, at the Globe and at Court; and they have all held the stage to this day. Collectively known now as the 'Last Plays', they were the results of Shakespeare's characteristic urge to experiment with and make a distinctive contribution to developments in the art and craft of drama. Tragi-comedy was then all the rage and he wanted to find his own way of writing it. Meanwhile, there were signs that he was preparing to return to Stratford, where there was much to demand his attention. His parents were now dead and he was the head of the family, a position he took seriously. He had long been investing in land and tithes in and around the town. In 1607, Susanna had married a respected physician, Dr John Hall. Their daughter Elizabeth, Shakespeare's first grandchild, was born in 1608. Soon after writing *The Tempest*, he freed himself of his major commitment to his company by bringing forward **John Fletcher** to take over as the King's Men's chief dramatist. Shakespeare—whose own still very popular plays were company property, to be staged whenever the sharers wished—could now spend more time in Stratford. By 1612 he had completed his withdrawal, leaving management in the safe hands of his 'fellows'. In a legal document that he signed while visiting London in that year, he identified himself in these terms: 'William Shakespeare of Stratford-on-Avon in the County of Warwick, gentleman of the age of 48 years'. Even so he did not quite abandon his writing. In 1613, with John Fletcher's collaboration, he wrote *Henry VIII*. In the same year, he helped Fletcher by contributing several scenes and most of one act to *The Two Noble Kinsmen*. Shakespeare died on 23 April 1616. The nature of his fatal illness is not known, but the male Shakespeares of his generation were not long-lived. Of John Shakespeare's four sons, he was the last to go. He had made provision in his will to keep the bulk of his estate intact, entailed for the benefit of his descendants. His intentions were soon thwarted. His direct line of descent ended when his grand-daughter died childless in 1670. In 1623, his monument was erected in Holy Trinity Church. A few months later, John Hemminge and Henry Condell—two of his friends and principal colleagues in the King's Men—published his collected plays in the First Folio. But for them much of his work would have been lost; and all subsequent editions of his plays have been based on the text they so diligently and lovingly established. Attempts have been made at various times to ascribe his work to other writers, but no convincing evidence of that argument has yet prevailed.

▷ E K Chambers, *A Study of Facts and Problems* (1930); S Schoenbaum, *Shakespeare's Lives* (1938); E M Tillyard, *The Elizabethan World Picture* (1943)

SHAMIR, Moshe

(1921–)

Hebrew novelist and dramatist, born in Safed, Israel, and therefore a Sabra Jew. From 1941 until 1947 he was a member of the kibbutz Mishmar. He is a 'Palmach novelist'—that is to say, one of those who fought in the striking arm of the Haganah defence forces. His novel *Melech Basar Vedam* (1954, Eng trans *The King of Flesh and Blood*, 1958), set in Hasmonean times, deals with the question of whether Israel should be a moral or a political power. *Kivsath Harash* (1957, Eng trans *David's Stranger*, 1964) is also a historical novel, about King David.

SHANGE, Ntozake, pseud of **Paulette Williams**

(1948–)

Black American playwright, poet and novelist, she adopted her new name in 1971, after leaving the University of Southern California. Five years later, her remarkable 'choreopoem' *for colored girls who have considered suicide/when the rainbow is enuf* (1976) was produced on Broadway, a benchmark in the articulation of black feminist consciousness in America. The piece uses female personae, identified by colour, to articulate aspects of black American history. Later works have been less startling in impact. Other plays include *A Photograph: A Study of Cruelty* (1977) and *Spell #7: A Geechee Quick Magic Trance Manual* (1979). She has also written novels—*Sassafrass, Cypress & Indigo* (1976, rev edn 1982), *Betsey Brown* (1985)— and poetry, most notably *A Daughter's Geography* (1983).

SHAPCOTT, Thomas William
(1935–)

Australian poet, editor and critic, born in Ipswich, Queensland. From *Time on Fire* (1961), for which he received the Grace Leven Prize, he has been acknowledged as one of Australia's best-known poets, not least for his involvement in the politics of writing through the Australia Council's Literature Board and the 'New Australian Poetry' movement of the 1960s–70s. For the latter, with **Rodney Hall** he edited the anthology *New Impulses in Australian Poetry* (1968) and *Australian Poetry Now* (1970). Of his own work both *A Taste for Salt Water* (1967) and *Inwards to the Sun* (1969) won the Myer Award for Poetry. His *Selected Poems* was published in 1978.

SHAPIRO, Karl Jay
(1913–)

American poet and critic, born in Baltimore, Maryland. He was educated at the University of Virginia, Charlottesville, and then clerked in a family business before completing his studies at Johns Hopkins University, Baltimore. During the interim he published his first collection of verse, *Poems* (1935). However, his first major book was written while he was in military service during World War II. *V-Letter and Other Poems* (1944) won him the Pulitzer Prize; it was followed by *Essay on Rime* (1945) and the superb *Trial of a Poet* (1947). Work of this period was strictly rhymed and formally structured. Later, Shapiro grew interested in free verse and prose poetry, drawing on the unconscious as an inspiration. The major work in this style is *The Bourgeois Poet* (1964). Shapiro was influential as a critic. Early books were concerned with prosody; later, in *Beyond Criticism* (1953, rev edn as *A Primer for Poets*, 1965), he widened his range considerably. He has written one novel, *Edsel* (1971), a campus story; it reflects his own academic career in Indiana, Nebraska, Illinois and California. Shapiro is significant for his rejection of the

Europeanism of **T S Eliot** and **Pound** in favour of a robust Americanism; his models were **Whitman**, **William Carlos Williams** and **Randall Jarrell**, on whom he wrote an influential study (1967).
▷ J Reino, *Karl Shapiro* (1981)

SHARP, Alan
(1934–)

Scottish novelist and film-maker, born near Dundee and raised in Greenock. He left school at 14 and worked in the shipyards as an apprentice joiner. Following National Service in the army, his occupations ranged from labourer to assisting a private detective, before he began to write for BBC radio and television and completed a widely praised autobiographical novel, *A Green Tree in Gedde* (1964), which evoked his working-class background. He followed this with *The Wind Shifts* (1967) and then embarked upon a career as a screenwriter in Hollywood. Able to invest traditional genres such as the western and the thriller with trenchant resonances of issues in contemporary American life, his filmed screenplays include *The Hired Hand* (1971), *Ulzana's Raid* (1972), *Night Moves* (1975) and *The Osterman Weekend* (1983). More recently he has turned to direction with the film *Little Treasure* (1985).

SHARP, William, pseud Fiona Macleod
(1855–1905)

Scottish writer, born in Paisley, and educated at Glasgow University. After some time in Australia he settled in London (1879), working as a journalist and editor. Throughout his life he travelled widely. He published a collection of poetry, *Earth's Voices*, in 1884. He wrote books on contemporary English, French and German poets, but is chiefly remembered as the author of the remarkable series of Celtic—or neo-Celtic—tales and romances by 'Fiona Macleod'—a pseudonym he systematically refused to acknowledge. They include *Pharais* (1894), *The Mountain Lovers* (1895), *The Sin-Eater* (1895) and *The Immortal Hour* (1900).
▷ *William Sharp, a Memoir by Mrs Sharp* (1912)

SHARPE, Tom (Thomas)
(1928–)

English satirical novelist, born in London. He began his authorial career as a playwright in South Africa between 1951 and 1961, after which he returned to England. His first novel, *Riotous Assembly* (1971), ridicules corruption in a small South African town. He is more widely known, however, for his lampooning of the English academic establishment in *Porterhouse Blue* (1974), about the attempts of the fictional Porterhouse College, Cambridge, to resist modernization, and in *Wilt* (1976) and *Vintage Stuff* (1982). Henry Wilt, a lecturer at a college of further education, and the hero of the second book, reappears in two later novels. British bureaucracy and planning regulations are ruthlessly satirized in *Blott on the Landscape* (1975). Although Sharpe's humour is often vulgar, his satire is well aimed.

SHAW, Charles, pseud Bant Singer
(1900–55)

Australian writer, born in Melbourne, best known for his novel *Heaven Knows, Mr Allison* (1952), which had international success as a Hollywood film. Under the name Bant Singer he also wrote *You're Wrong Delaney* (1953) and two sequels in the 'hard-boiled' **Chandler** school of thriller fiction. In Australian style he wrote some short stories and a late flowering of the bush-ballad in *The Warrrumbungle Mare* (1943).

SHAW, George Bernard
(1856–1950)

Irish dramatist, essayist, critic, vegetarian and pamphleteer, winner of the Nobel Prize for literature, born of Irish Protestant parents in Dublin. His mother was a singing teacher in Dublin and later in London, and from her he inherited strength of character and the great love and knowledge of music so influential in his life and work. After short and unhappy periods at various schools, in 1871 he entered a firm of land-agents, disliked office routine, and left Ireland for good to follow his mother and sister Lucy, a musical-comedy actress, to London. His literary life had already begun in 1875 with a letter to the press (one of his favourite means of expression), shrewdly analysing the effect on individuals of sudden conversion by the American evangelists, Moody and Sankey. In London his early years were a long period of struggle and impoverishment, and of the five novels he wrote between 1879 and 1883, the best of which are probably *Love Among the Artists* and *Cashel Byron's Profession*, all were rejected by the more reputable publishers. An encounter (1882) with Henry George and the reading of Karl Marx turned his thoughts towards socialism, and while any direct propagation of it is absent from his plays, his faith in it and a 'kindly dislike' (if not dread) of capitalist society form the backbone of all his work. Political and economic understanding stood him in good stead as a local government councillor in St Pancras (1897–1903) and also on the executive committee of the small but influential Fabian Society, to which he devoted himself selflessly for many years (1884–1911) and for which he edited *Fabian Essays* (1889) and wrote many well-known socialist tracts. Journalism provided another lively platform for him, and it was as 'Corno di Bassetto', music critic for the new *Star* newspaper (1888–90), that he made his first indelible impact on the intellectual and social consciousness of his time. In this and in his later music criticism for *The World* (1890–4) and, above all, in his dramatic criticism for **Frank Harris**'s *Saturday Review* (1895–8), he was making his name. To this period also belong *The Quintessence of Ibsenism* (1891) and *The Perfect Wagnerite* (1898), tributes to fellow 'artist-philosophers' who, together with **John Bunyan**, **Dickens**, **Samuel Butler** and Mozart, he acknowledged had influence on his work. The rest of Shaw's life, especially after his marriage (1898) to the Irish heiress Charlotte Payne-Townshend, is mainly the history of his plays. His first, *Widowers' Houses*, was begun in 1885 in collaboration with his friend William Archer, but was finished independently in 1892 as the result of the challenge he felt to produce the newer drama of ideas he had been advocating. Into the earliest plays, which also include *Mrs Warren's Profession* (1898), *Arms and the Man* (pub 1898) and *Candida* (1897, one of the first in a long series of remarkable female portrayals), comes already the favourite Shavian theme of conversion—from dead system and outworn morality towards a more creatively vital approach to life—and this is further developed in *Three Plays for Puritans*: *The Devil's Disciple* (pub 1897), *Caesar and Cleopatra* (1901) and *Captain Brassbound's Conversion* (1900). His long correspondence with the famous Lyceum actress, Ellen Terry, was also at its peak during these years. At last Shaw was becoming more widely known, first of all in the USA and on the Continent, and then, with the important advent of the playwright-producer-actor, **Harley Granville-Barker**, in England itself, especially after the epoch-making Vedrenne-Barker Court Theatre season of 1904–7. This had been preceded by one of Shaw's greatest philosophical comedies, *Man and Superman* (1902), in which, in quest of a purer religious approach to life, Shaw advocated through his Don Juan the importance of man's unceasing creative evolutionary urge for world-improvement. Other notable plays from the early part of the century are *John Bull's Other Island* (1904), *Major Barbara* (1905), *The Doctor's Dilemma* (1906), and two uniquely Shavian discussion plays, *Getting Married* (1908) and *Misalliance* (1910). They further display Shaw's increasing control of his medium and the wide range of his subject-matter (from politics and state-craft to family life, prostitution and vaccination). Before the Joint Committee on

Stage Censorship of 1909 he proudly proclaimed himself as 'immoralist and heretic', and insisted on the civilized necessity for toleration and complete freedom of thought. Just before World War I came two of his most delightful plays; *Androcles and the Lion* (1912), a 'religious pantomime', and *Pygmalion* (1913), an 'anti-romantic' comedy of phonetics (adapted as a highly successful musical play, *My Fair Lady* in 1956, filmed in 1964). During the war, though he later toured the front at official invitation, he created controversy and recrimination with his fearless and provocative *Common Sense About the War* (1914). After the war followed three of his greatest dramas in near succession: *Heartbreak House* (1919), an attempt to analyse in an English **Chekhov**ian social environment the causes of present moral and political discontents; *Back to Methuselah* (1921), five plays in one, in which Shaw conducted a not altogether successful dramatic excursion from the Garden of Eden to 'As Far as Thought Can Reach'; and *Saint Joan* (1923), in which Shaw's essentially religious nature, his genius for characterization (above all of saintly yet very human women), and his powers of dramatic argument are most abundantly revealed. In 1925 Shaw was awarded the Nobel Prize for literature, but donated the money to inaugurate the Anglo–Swedish Literary Foundation. In 1931 he visited Russia, and during the 1930s made other long tours, including a world one with his wife in 1932, during which he gave a memorable address on political economy in the Metropolitan Opera House, New York. Greater perhaps than any of the plays written during the last years of his life are the two prose works: *The Intelligent Woman's Guide to Socialism and Capitalism* (1928), one of the most lucid introductions to its subjects, and *The Black Girl in Search of God* (1932), a modern *Pilgrim's Progress*. The later plays, except for *The Apple Cart* (1929), have scarcely received adequate public stage presentation but they continue to preach the stern yet invigorating Shavian morality of individual responsibility, self-discipline, heroic effort without thought of reward or 'atonement', and the utmost integrity. Plays such as *Too True to Be Good* (1932) and *The Simpleton of the Unexpected Isles* (1934) also show signs of sounding a newer and even more experimental dramatic note altogether. His *Collected Plays*, with their important Prefaces, was issued in seven volumes (1970–4).
▷M Holroyd, *George Bernard Shaw* (3 vols, 1989–91)

SHAW, Helen
(1913–85)

New Zealand poet and short-story writer, an early contributor to the periodical *New Zealand New Writing*. Her stories were first published in *The Orange Tree and Other Stories* (1957) and later in *The Gipsies and Other Stories* (1978). Verse includes her first volume, *Out of the Dark* (1968), *This is My Sorrow: As from Heloise to Abelard* (1981) and her last *Time Told from a Tower* (1985). She also edited a collection of **D'Arcy Cresswell**'s letters in 1983.

SHAW, Irwin
(1913–84)

American popular novelist, born in Brooklyn, who first became known with his *The Young Lions* (1948), about two American soldiers. *The Troubled Air* (1951), his best novel, dramatically analysed the situation in American radio caused by the anti-communist witch-hunting of the time. *Rich man, Poor Man* (1970), although skilful, more represented a soap-opera than a serious novel, and was made into one for television.

SHECKLEY, Robert
(1928–)

American science-fiction writer, born in New York City. He began publishing in 1952, and quickly gained a deserved reputation for witty, ingenious and highly crafted short stories, which still stand among the best the genre has to offer. His work grew more satiric and speculative in the 1960s, as exemplified in the novels *The Status Civilisation* (1960), set on a prison planet where accepted norms are reversed, and *Mindswap* (1966), in which an Earthman finds himself literally trading minds with a Martian, to unbridled satiric effect. His later works lack the sure sense of purpose of his earlier stories, although *The Alchemical Marriage of Alastair Crompton* (1978) is a strong exception, perhaps because it originated in an earlier short story. An incomplete *Collected Short Stories* appeared in five volumes in 1991.

SHEED, Wilfrid John Joseph
(1930–)

American novelist, born in London. He went to live in the USA aged 10, but returned to England to complete his education at Lincoln College, Oxford. From 1957 to 1966, he worked on *Jubilee* magazine in New York, later writing for *Commonweal* and *Esquire*. His first novel was *A Middle Class Education* (1960), a satirical attack on British public schools and universities. *The Hack* (1963) concerned a freelance theological journalist, whose career moves and ostensible principles work at some remove from each other. Later novels include *Office Politics* (1966), *People Will Always be Kind* (1973) and *Transatlantic Blues* (1978), but Sheed's most memorable work remains the 'short novel and long story' *The Blacking Factory, and Pennsylvania Gothic* (1968), which draws together his interest in the media, in guilt and acceptance, and in the damage inflicted by an uncaring upbringing. The essays in *Three Mobs: Labor, Church and Mafia* (1974) reflect some of his obsessions.

▷ *Frank and Maisie: A Memoir With Parents* (1985)

SHEFFIELD, John, 1st Duke of Buckingham and Normanby
(1648–1721)

English political leader and poet. He succeeded his father as third Earl of Mulgrave in 1658, served in both navy and army, and was lord chamberlain to James II and a cabinet councillor under William III, who in 1694 made him Marquis of Normanby. Queen Anne made him Duke of (the county of) Buckingham (1703); but for his opposition to Godolphin and Marlborough he was deprived of the Seal (1705). After 1710, under the Tories, he was Lord Steward and Lord President till the death of Anne, when he lost all power, and intrigued for the restoration of the Stuarts. Patron of **Dryden** and friend of **Pope**, he wrote two tragedies, a metrical *Essay on Satire*, an *Essay on Poetry*, and other works.

▷ J H Wilson, *The Court Wits of the Restoration* (1948)

SHELDON, Charles Monroe
(1857–1946)

American Congregationalist and novelist, born in New York. After studying theology he became pastor of a church in Topeka, Kansas. *In His Steps* (1896) tells the story of a minister, Rev Henry Maxwell, and his congregation, who become spurred into basing their every action on what Jesus would do in the same circumstances. The synopsis might not set a modern editor's eyes alight, but it became a fly-away success. Translated into more than 20 languages, and selling over six million copies, it was the biggest bestseller of its era. Little else Sheldon published, apart from his autobiography, is remembered. In his sixties he became editor of the *Christian Herald*.

▷ C M Sheldon, *His Life and Story* (1925)

SHELDON, Edward Brewster
(1886–1946)

American playwright, born in Chicago and educated at Harvard. He became most widely known as the author of *Romance* (1913), in which an elderly bishop tells the cautionary story of his youthful love for an opera singer in an attempt to prevent his grandson from marrying an actress. This rather far-fetched fable established Sheldon as a successful commercial author. He also wrote such plays as *Salvation Nell* (1908), *The High Road* (1912) and *The Garden of Paradise* (1914), the latter adapted from **Hans Christian Andersen**'s *The Little Mermaid*. Since his heyday, however, Sheldon's plays have slipped from the repertoire.

SHELDON, Sidney
(1917–)

American novelist and playwright, born in New York City. His early work includes the 1950 screenplay for *Annie Get Your Gun*, but he has since become far better known as a bestselling novelist. A Sheldon blockbuster is typically an amalgam of money, glamour, crime and grimy secrets. In *The Other Side of Midnight* (1974) a beautiful actress has to stand trial for murder; its less successful sequel, *Memories of Midnight*, was published in 1990. His other novels include *The Master of the Game* (1982) and *The Sands of Time* (1988); many have been made into TV miniseries. Sheldon himself was the creator of two TV series, *Hart to Hart* and *I Dream of Jeannie*, which he produced and directed.

SHELLEY, Mary Wollstonecraft, née Godwin
(1797–1851)

English writer, the daughter of **William Godwin** and Mary Wollstonecraft Godwin. In 1814 she eloped with **Percy Bysshe Shelley**. and married him as his second wife in 1816. They lived abroad throughout their married life. Her first and most impressive novel was *Frankenstein or, The Modern Prometheus* (1818), her second *Valperga* (1823). After her husband's death in 1822 she returned from Italy to England with their son in 1823. Her husband's father, in granting her an allowance, insisted on the suppression of the volume of Shelley's *Posthumous Poems* edited by her. *The Last Man* (1826), a romance of the ruin of human society by pestilence, fails to attain sublimity. In *Lodore* (1835) the story is told of Shelley's alienation from his first wife. Her last novel, *Falkner* appeared in 1837. Of her occasional pieces of verse the most remarkable is 'The Choice'. Her *Journal of a Six Weeks' Tour* (partly by Shelley) tells of the excursion to Switzerland in 1814; *Rambles in Germany and Italy* (1844) describes tours of 1840–3; her *Tales* were published in 1890. Two unpublished mythological dramas, *Proserpine* and *Midas*, were edited and published in 1922.

▷ E Bigland, *Mary Shelley* (1959)

SHELLEY, Percy Bysshe
(1792–1822)

English poet, born in Field Place, near Horsham in Sussex. He was educated at Syon House Academy and Eton, where he acquired the sobriquet 'Mad Shelley' for his independent spirit and was later dubbed 'Eton Atheist'. While at Eton he published *Zastrozzi* (1810), a Gothic novel. That year, with his sister Elizabeth, he produced *Original Poetry by Victor and Cazire*, and the following year another Gothic romance, *St Irvine, or, The Rosicrucian*. He attended University College, Oxford, where he read radical authors like **William Godwin** and **Paine**, and dressed and behaved in an eccentric and provocative manner. In 1811, he produced a pamphlet, co-authored with Thomas Jefferson Hogg, called *The Necessity of Atheism*, a formative declaration. Both authors were expelled. That and Shelley's elopement to Scotland with 16-year-old Harriet Westbrook caused a rift between him and his family that was never repaired. Shelley would not recant, and relinquished his right to his inheritance. He lived itinerantly for the next three years; in York, in the Lake District where only **Robert Southey** was at home, in Dublin where he advocated the repeal of the Union and Catholic emancipation, and at Lynmouth in Devon where he set up a commune of 'like spirits'. *Queen Mab* (1813) was the poetic fruit of this time but it made little impact. In London he met, befriended, subsidized and fell out with Godwin, and was close to **Thomas Love Peacock**. Despite having two children, his marriage to Harriet failed and he fell in love with Mary, the 16-year-old daughter of Godwin and Mary Wollstonecraft. Predictably they eloped, making up a *ménage à trois* with Mary's half-sister, Jane 'Claire' Clairmont. The three travelled on the continent where Shelley wrote an unfinished novella, *The Assassins* (1814), collaborated on a journal, and published *The History of a Six Weeks' Tour* (1817). Shelley returned to London, to face financial problems, and Mary gave birth to a daughter who died prematurely. The couple took a house near Windsor Great Park and he wrote *Alastor* (1816), its publication coinciding with the birth of his beloved son, William. 1816 was a traumatic year. He spent time with **Byron** at Lake Geneva, Harriet Westbrook drowned herself, and Shelley immediately married Mary. His reputation was growing. He met **Keats** and **William Hazlitt** and, having moved to Marlow in 1817, he wrote *An Address to the People on the Death of Princess Charlotte*, a fine political pamphlet. He published *The Revolt of Islam* in 1818, the year he finally left England for Italy where he was to spend the rest of his life. In Este he wrote *Julian and Maddalo* (1818), which explores his relationship with Byron, and in 1819 came the major part of *Prometheus Unbound*, his masterpiece. William's death in Rome devastated him and he moved to Tuscany, finally settling in Pisa. From the middle of 1819 to summer 1820 came an extraordinary burst of creative energy resulting in the completion of the fourth part of *Prometheus*, *The Masque of Anarchy* (1819, inspired by the Peterloo massacre), 'The Ode to the West Wind', 'To Liberty' and 'To Naples', the *Letter to Maria Gisborne* (1820) and *The Witch of Atlas*. His son Percy was born in November 1819. Still to come was *A Philosophical View of Reform* (1820), *Essay on the Devil* (1821), poems, *The Defence of Poetry* (1821) and *Swellfoot the Tyrant* (1820), a burlesque. *Adonais* (1821), an elegy and meditation on death, was inspired by the death of Keats. *Epipsychidion* (1821) was the fruit of a platonic affair with a beautiful Italian heiress locked away in a convent. Byron came to Pisa in 1821, where a bohemian group gathered. Roused by the Greek war of independence, Shelley wrote *Hellas* (1822), a verse drama. It was to be his last work. The *ménage* moved to Lerici. Mary had a miscarriage and Claire was distraught at the death of her daughter, Allegra, whom she had had by Byron. Returning from a visit to Byron and **Leigh Hunt** at Livorno in August 1822 in the schooner 'Ariel', Shelley, Edward Williams and an English boatboy were drowned when they were surprised by a sudden squall. Shelley's body was cremated at Viareggio. As much a political activist as a poet, Shelley's adventurous life and unconventional behaviour have tended to overshadow his poetry. He was revolutionary in both spheres of life, turning away from **Coleridge**'s German Romanticism and reaffirming Mediterranean values: an inspirational polemicist and a poet of genius. His *Letters* in two volumes appeared in 1964.
▷T J Hogg, *The Life of Shelley* (1858)

SHEN KUA
(1030–93)

Chinese administrator, engineer and scientist, born in Hangchow. He made significant contributions to such diverse fields as astronomy, cartography, medicine, hydraulics and fortification. As director of the astronomical bureau from 1072 he improved methods of computation and the design of several observational devices; in 1075 he constructed a series of relief maps of China's northern frontier area, and designed fortifications as defences against nomadic invaders. He surveyed and improved the Grand Canal over a distance of some 150 miles, using stone-filled gabions, wooden piles and long bundles of reeds to strengthen the banks and close gaps. In 1082 he was forced by intrigue to resign from his government posts, and occupied his last years in the writing of *Brush Talks from Dream Brook*, a remarkable compilation of about 600 observations which has become one of the most important sources of information on early science and technology.

SHENSTONE, William
(1714–63)

English poet, born near Halesowen, Worcestershire. He studied at Solihull Grammar School and Pembroke College, Oxford. In 1735 he inherited the estate of the Leasowes, and spent most of his income on 'landship gardening' to turn it into a show garden. In 1737 he published his best-known poem, 'The Schoolmistress' (revised in 1742) which, written in imitation of **Edmund Spenser**, foreshadowed **Thomas Gray**'s *Elegy*. He published *The Judgement of Hercules* in 1741. His *Pastoral Ballad* (1755) was commended by Gray and **Samuel Johnson**.
▷ A R Humphreys, *William Shenstone* (1937)

SHEPARD, Sam, originally Samuel Shepard Rogers
(1943–)

American dramatist and actor, born in Illinois. He moved to New York City and worked in the avant-garde theatre of the 1960s with one-acters. His first plays, *Cowboy* and *The Rock Garden*, were written in 1964 and produced by Theater Genesis in New York, followed by *Dog* and *Rocking Chair* (both 1965) at La Mama. *The Tooth of Crime*, a rock drama, was staged at the Royal Court Theatre, London, in 1974, followed by *The Curse of the Starving Class*, at the New York Shakespeare Festival, in 1976. He won the Pulitzer Prize with his 1978 play, *Buried Child*. He was resident playwright at the Magic Theater, San Francisco, for several years, and two of his plays were first staged there, *True West* (1979) and *Fool For Love* (1983). *A Lie of the Mind* (1985) was very successful in America. Few living American playwrights have such sensitivity for landscape and time as Shepard, and few can produce such economic theatrical intensity. He also appeared in films, and has written screenplays, including *Paris, Texas* (1984), a tale of drifting and homecoming.
▷ R Mottram, *Inner Landscapes* (1984)

SHEPHERD, Nan
(1893–1981)

Scottish novelist and critic, raised in Aberdeen, where she graduated from university in 1915. She worked until 1956 as a lecturer at Aberdeen College of Education and was a friend and correspondent of **Neil Gunn**. Her three novels, *The Quarry Wood* (1928), *The Weatherhouse* (1930) and *A Pass in the Grampians* (1933), all deal with aspects of a young woman's development in north-east Scotland. In these works she is concerned to show the way women are societized to make compromises which do not allow them to fulfil their potential. Her creative work has been largely ignored by critics. As well as writing novels she was also involved in academic research. Her last book was a non-fiction study of the mountains, *The Living Mountain* (1977).

SHERIDAN, Frances, née Chamberlaine
(1724–66)

Irish novelist and playwright, born in Dublin, daughter of an archdeacon. Educated by her brothers because of her father's disapproval of education for women, she wrote a romantic novel, *Eugenia and Adelaide*, at 15. She married the actor-manager Thomas Sheridan in 1747; they moved to London in 1754, then for reasons of health and economy to France in 1764. At **Samuel Richardson**'s urging she wrote a second novel, *Memoirs of Miss Sidney Biddulph* (1761, sequel 1767); its conservative morality and pathos, enlivened by humour and psychological realism, made it a popular success. Her son **Richard Brinsley Sheridan** borrowed incidents from it for *The School for Scandal*. She had two comedies staged by Garrick in 1763, and her intelligent, entertaining oriental tale *The History of Nourjahad* (1767) was admired and often reprinted.
▷ R L Mack, (ed), *Oriental Tales* (1992); A Lefanu (her daughter), *Memoirs of the Life and Writings of Mrs Frances Sheridan* (1824); M A Doody, in *British Novelists, 1660–1800*, ed M Battestin, *Dictionary of Literary Biography* 39 (1985)

SHERIDAN, Richard Brinsley
(1751–1816)

Irish dramatist, born in Dublin. He was grandson of **Jonathan Swift**'s friend, Thomas Sheridan, (1687–1738), and son of Thomas Sheridan (1719–88), a teacher of elocution, actor and author of a *Life of Swift*; his mother was the novelist and playwright **Frances Sheridan**. Richard Sheridan was educated at Harrow, and after leaving school, with a school-friend named Halhed wrote a three-act farce called *Jupiter* and tried a verse translation of the *Epistles of Aristoenetus*. After a romantic courtship, Richard married Elizabeth Linley in 1773. The young couple settled in London to a life much beyond their means. Sheridan now made more serious efforts at dramatic composition. On 17 January 1775 *The Rivals* was produced at Covent Garden, and after a slight alteration in the cast met with universal approval. In the same

year appeared a poor farce called *St Patrick's Day* and also *The Duenna*. In 1776 Sheridan, with the aid of Linley and another friend, bought half the patent of Drury Lane Theatre for £35 000 from Garrick, and in 1778 the remaining share for £45 000. His first production was a purified edition of Sir **John Vanbrugh**'s *Relapse*, under the title of *A Trip to Scarborough*. *The Critic* (1779), teeming with sparkling wit, was Sheridan's last dramatic effort, with the exception of a poor tragedy, *Pizarro*. On the dissolution of parliament in 1780 Sheridan was elected for Stafford, and he concentrated thereafter on his distinguished Parliamentary career until he was defeated in 1812. In 1792 his first wife died, and three years later he married Esther Ogle, the silly and extravagant daughter of the Dean of Winchester, who survived him. The affairs of the theatre had gone badly. The old building had to be closed as unfit to hold large audiences, and a new one, opened in 1794, was burned in 1809. This last calamity put the finishing touch to Sheridan's pecuniary difficulties, which had long been serious. He died in great poverty, but was given a magnificent funeral in Westminster Abbey.
▷ L Gibbs, *Sheridan* (1947)

SHERRIFF, R(obert) C(edric)
(1896–1975)

English playwright, novelist and scriptwriter, born in Kingston-upon-Thames. He achieved an international reputation with his first play, *Journey's End* (1929), based on his experiences in the trenches during World War I. His other plays include *St Helena* (1934), on the last years of the exiled Napoleon, and *The White Carnation* (1953), a ghost story. He also wrote several novels. He became a scriptwriter in Hollywood, and wrote the scripts for films like *The Invisible Man* (1933), *Goodbye Mr Chips* (1936), *The Four Feathers* (1938), *Lady Hamilton* (1941) and *The Dambusters* (1955).

SHERWOOD, Mary Martha, née Butt
(1775–1851)

English writer of children's books, daughter of a chaplain to George II, born in Stanford, Worcestershire. In 1803 she married Henry Sherwood and went to India with him (1805–66). Her 77 works include *Little Henry and his Bearer* (1815), and the long-popular *History of the Fairchild Family* (1818–47).
▷ N G Royde Smith, *The State of Mind of Mary Sherwood* (1946)

SHERWOOD, Robert Emmet
(1896–1955)

American playwright and author, born in New Rochelle, New York. He wrote his first play, *Barnum Was Right*, while at Harvard, and after service in World War I he became Editor of *Life* (1924–8), and a member of **Dorothy Parker**'s celebrated Algonquin Round Table. He won four Pulitzer Prizes, the first three for drama—*Idiot's Delight*, (1936), *Abe Lincoln in Illinois* (1939) and *There Shall be No Night* (1941)—and the last (1949) for his biographical *Roosevelt and Hopkins* (1949).

SHEVCHENKO, Taras
(1814–61)

Ukrainian poet and prose writer, born a serf in Kirilovka (Kiev). He showed an early interest in writing and drawing, and was taken up by a literary circle in St Petersburg, who bought his freedom in 1838. His early poems included Romantic ballads, love songs and historical subjects. He became professor at Kiev (1845), and founded an organization for radical social reforms. He was exiled to central Asia for 10 years, but was eventually freed in 1857, although kept under surveillance. He is remembered as the creator of a new Ukrainian literary language.
▷ W K Matthews, *Taras Sevchenko* (1951)

SHIGA Naoya
(1883–1971)

Japanese writer of short stories and one novel. He produced his best work during the turmoil of the run-up to the Sino–Japanese War and the rise of fascism, when he flirted, dangerously, with non-Japanese doctrines such as socialism and Christianity. He looked to the West for inspiration, but his novel *Anya Koro* (1926, Eng trans *A Dark Night's Passing*, 1976), is a distinctly Japanese and naturalist work of the kind known as *watakushi shosetsu* (I-novel). It is an internal monologue, set during a train journey, presented in a cold, sparse, unemotional (yet compelling) style.

SHILLABER, Benjamin Penhallow
(1814–90)

American humorist. He founded and edited *The Carpet Bag* (1851–3) and was the author of *The Life and Sayings of Mrs Partington* (1854), which used a popular invented character (credited for creating her lies elsewhere) as a basis for contemporary comment and satire.

SHIMAZAKI Toson
(1872–1943)

Japanese writer from Nagano in the west of Japan. Like most of his contemporaries, he espoused the literary doctrine known as Japanese naturalism, but took it a step further, writing a number of *watakushi shomei*

('I-novels'), closely narrated works in which little actually happens, the important thing being the narrator's states of mind and emotions. *Ie* (1910, 'Home') is a prime example of this esoteric, intricate, and distinctly Japanese form of writing. *Yokae mae* (1929–36, 'Before the Dawn') is an analysis of the hopes, fears and expectations of the peasantry at the time of the Meiji Restoration of 1868 seen through the eyes of a character closely modelled on Shimazaki's father. He was also a poet—his 1897 collection *Wakanashu* ('Seedlings') was an instant success, but its romantic, impressionistic verse veers between the sickly sweet and the hopelessly unfocused.

SHIRLEY, James
(1596–1666)
English late-Elizabethan dramatist, born in London. From Merchant Taylors' he passed in 1612 to St John's, Oxford, but migrated to Catharine Hall, Cambridge. He took orders, and held a living at St Albans. Turning Catholic, he taught (1623–4) in the grammar school there, but soon went to London and became a playwright. The suppression of stage plays in 1642 ended his livelihood, and he took to teaching again. The Restoration revived his plays, but brought him no better fortunes. His death was a result of the Great Fire of London. **Francis Beaumont** and **John Fletcher** and **Ben Jonson** were his models, but he has little of the grand Elizabethan manner. Most of his plays are tragi-comedies. His chief works are *Eccho* (1618), a poem on the Narcissus subject; comedies, *The Witty Fair One* (1628); *The Wedding* (1628); *The Grateful Servant* (1629); *The Example* (1634); *The Opportunity* (1634); *The Lady of Pleasure*, most brilliant of his comedies (1635); tragedies, *The Cardinal*, to the author himself 'the best of his flock' (1641); *The Traytor* (1631), a great drama. As a masque writer he is second only to Jonson; among his best masques are *The Triumph of Peace* (1633) and *The Contention of Ajax and Ulysses* (1659, including 'the glories of our blood and state').
▷A H Mason, *James Shirley* (1915)

SHLONSKY, Avraham
(1900–73)
Hebrew poet, born in Russia, who was educated in Palestine, and then returned to Russia. Only in 1921 did he come to Palestine permanently. He was a Marxist, and he wrote much of his political poetry under the influence of **Mayakovsky**, whose power and individualism he possessed. He is the sort of poet who, a critic has written, as we read him 'we feel he is the best'. His greatest poems are his more personal ones. With Eliezir Steinman he started an important magazine, *Kethubim*,

in 1925. He translated **Pushkin** and **Shakespeare**, and founded the Worker's Library. The best poems in English translation are to be found in Abraham Birman's *Anthology of Modern Hebrew Poetry* (1968).
▷M Waxman, *A History of Jewish Literature* (1947)

SHOLEM ALEICHEM, or Sholom, or Shalom, pseud of Solomon J Rabinowitz
(1859–1916)
Russian–Jewish author, born in Pereyaslev in the Ukraine, the son of Russian–Jewish shopkeepers. He spent much of his youth in and around the neighbouring town of Voronkov, which was to feature as Krasilevke, the setting of many of his stories. After working for some years as a rabbi, he devoted himself to writing and Yiddish culture, contributing to the Hebrew magazine *Hamelitz* and the first Yiddish newspaper, established in 1883. In 1893 he moved to Kiev, but the pogroms of 1905 drove him to the USA, where he attempted to establish himself as a playwright for the Yiddish theatre, which was flourishing in New York at the time. He travelled widely, giving readings of his work in many European cities, and from 1908 to 1914 spent most of his time in Italy to improve his health. He returned to settle in New York in 1914. His short stories and plays portray Jewish life in Russia in the late 19th century with vividness, humour and sympathy, and were first widely introduced to a non-Jewish public in 1943 in Maurice Samuel's *The World of Sholom Aleichem*; nearly all his work has been translated into English, including *Jewish Children* (Eng trans 1920), *Stories and Satires* (Eng trans 1959) and *Old Country Tales* (Eng trans 1966). The popular musical *Fiddler on the Roof* is based on his stories.

SHOLOKHOV, Mikhail Alexandrovich
(1905–84)
Russian novelist and winner of the Nobel Prize for literature, born in Kruzhilin. He was educated at schools in Moscow, Boguchar and Veshenskaya. From 1920 to 1922 he served in the army, after which he had multifarious occupations: teacher, clerk, tax inspector, labourer, playwright, actor and journalist. During World War II he was a war correspondent. His literary career began with some 30 short stories written between 1923 and 1927. Most focus on the merciless sociopolitical struggle within Don Cossack families and villages during the civil war and early years of Soviet rule. Uneven in quality, they nevertheless demonstrate a rapid development from a sedulous ape into an original craftsman. His masterpiece is *Tikhy Don* (4 vols, 1928–40, rev edn 1953, Eng trans in 2 vols: *And Quiet Flows the Don* and *The Don*

Flows Home to the Sea, 1934–40). Set in the years 1912–22, it is a monument to the Don Cossacks, offering a panoramic view of their life in time of peace and during the turbulent years of war and revolution. The characterization is splendid and the dialogue earthy. Since 1928 his authorship of the novel has been questioned on the grounds that he was too young and had previously shown no indication that he could write such an epic work, but the evidence to support these allegations is thin. *Podnyataya tselina* (1932–60, Eng trans in 2 vols: *Virgin Soil Upturned* and *Harvest on the Don*, 1935–60) is much inferior, attributable to his toeing of the official line, alcoholism and decline of his creative powers. He received the Stalin Prize in 1941 and the 1965 Nobel Prize for literature.
▷ I G Lezhnev, *Mikhail Sholokhov* (1948)

SHORT, Luke
(1908–75)
American writer of Westerns. Without literary merit, but with simple and bold plots, they sold phenomenally well.

SHORTHOUSE, Joseph Henry
(1834–1903)
English novelist, born in Birmingham. He became a chemical manufacturer. In 1881 his romance, *John Inglesant*, revealed a subtle and sympathetic insight into old-world phases of the spiritual mind. It was followed by *The Little Schoolmaster Mark* (1883–4), *Sir Percival* (1886), *A Teacher of the Violin* (1888), *The Countess Eve* (1888) and *Blanche, Lady Falaise* (1891).

SHUSHKIN, Vasily
(1929–74)
Russian writer of fiction and film-scripts, born in Siberia. He was killed in a car crash just after achieving extraordinary success with his novel about a repentant thief, *Kalina krasnaya* (1973, Eng trans *Snowball Berry Red*, 1979), and then with the film he made of it with himself in the leading role. There is much about him in the translation of his most famous work, which contains other stories.

SHUTE, Nevil, pseud of **Nevil Shute Norway**
(1899–1960)
English novelist, born in Ealing. He served in World War I and immediately afterwards began an aeronautical career. He was chief calculator of the Airship Guarantee Company during the construction of the airship R100, and he flew the Atlantic twice in her. He founded Airspeed Ltd, aircraft constructors, and became its managing director. He emigrated to Australia after World War II. His novels include *The Pied Piper* (1942),

Most Secret (1945), *The Chequerboard* (1947), *No Highway* (1948), *A Town Like Alice* (1949), *Round the Bend* (1951), *Requiem for a Wren* (1955), *Beyond the Black Stump* (1956) and *On The Beach* (1957), about an atomic war catastrophe. His success was largely due to his brisk style and his ability to make technical language and procedure understandable to a lay public.
▷ *Slide Rule* (1954)

SHVARTS, Yevgeny
(1896–1958)
Russian (Jewish) playwright (and novelist and storyteller), for adults and children, born in Kazan. His knowledge of the theatre was gained from his acting experience. He was only moderately well known until after his death, when his reputation suddenly and dramatically rose. His humorous attacks on the Stalinist system—he hardly made a secret of his witty scorn for it—did not escape the attention of the censors, for some of his plays were banned; but for some reason the really important ones, such as *Ten* (1940), *The Shadow* and *Drakon* (1943, Eng trans *The Dragon* in *Three Soviet Plays*, 1966), were not. He wrote for puppets and for live casts. In an age of deceit, treachery and craven foolishness, Shvarts was an exception: an honourable, witty and decent man, he left exactly that mark with his work. His usual method was to adapt a fairy tale, in the style established by **Ludwig Fulda**, and then pillory his Stalinist or Nazi victim. He owed much of his theatrical success to the efforts of N P Akimov, the director of Leningrad's Comic Theatre, who persisted in putting on his plays during his lifetime and then revived them in the 1960s after his death. He has been called 'the only Soviet playwright of status'.

SIDNEY, Sir Philip
(1554–86)
English poet and patron, born in Penshurst Place, Kent. The eldest son of Sir Henry Sidney (Lord Deputy of Ireland), he was educated at Shrewsbury School and Christ Church, Oxford. He may also have been enrolled at Cambridge. From 1572 to 1575 he travelled in France, Germany, Austria and Italy, where he spent a year studying history and ethics, and was painted by Veronese. Returning to England he did not rise politically as anticipated and waited until 1585 for his appointment as governor of Flushing, having been knighted in 1582. Much of his life was reposeful and conducive to composition. None of his work was published in his lifetime. The revised *Arcadia* was published in 1590 in three books, and again in an augmented edition in 1593. *Astrophel and Stella* appeared first, in 1591, with a corrupt text

in a pirated edition, then in the authorized version. *A Defence of Poetry* was published in 1595. The *Arcadia* was probably written while he was lodging with his sister, **Mary, Countess of Pembroke**. It is probable that Penelope Devereux, whose father approved of Sidney and wished him to marry his daughter, is the 'Stella' of the sonnets. However, she married Baron Robert Rich, and Sidney, in 1583, married Frances, daughter of Sir Francis Walsingham. Throughout this time he bestowed patronage on a number of poets as dedications in various works testify, the most notable being that in **Edmund Spenser**'s *The Shepheardes Calendar* in 1579. He spent his last years in the Netherlands, where he successfully plotted an attack on the town of Axel. In September of the same year he led an attack on a Spanish convoy transporting arms to Zutphen, was shot in the thigh and died from the infection. He was buried in St Paul's Cathedral, much loved by contemporary poets and alluded to with affection and respect by **W B Yeats**, **John Ruskin** and others.

▷M Wilson, *Sir Philip Sidney* (1931)

SIDONIUS APOLLINARIS, Gaius Sollius
(c.430–c.483)

Gallo-Roman poet and prelate, born in Lugdunum (Lyons) of a prominent Christian family. He held high civil offices in Rome, and in 472 became Bishop of Clermont-Ferrand in the Auvergne. His letters are modelled on **Pliny**'s; his poems comprise panegyrics on three emperors, and two poems celebrating a marriage. He was canonized as St Sidonius Apollinaris.

▷C E Stevens, *Sidonius and his Age* (1973)

SIENKIEWICZ, Henryk
(1846–1916)

Polish novelist, winner of the Nobel Prize for literature, born near Luków. He lived in the USA from 1876 to 1878, and after a hunting expedition in East Africa (1892) wrote the children's story *W pustyni i w puszczy* (1911, Eng trans *In Desert and Wilderness*, 1912). Most of his works, however, are strongly realistic; many have been translated, among them the trilogy, *Ogniem i mieczem* (1884, Eng trans *With Fire and Sword*, 1890), *Potop* (1886, Eng trans *The Deluge*, 1892) and *Pan Wolodyjowski* (1887–8, Eng trans *Pan Michael*, 1895); also *Rodzina Polanieckich* (1894, Eng trans *Children of the Soil*, 1895) and *Quo Vadis?* (1896, Eng trans 1896). He was awarded the Nobel Prize for literature in 1905.

▷M Gardner, *The Novels of Henryk Sienkiewicz* (1926)

SIGAL, Clancy
(1926–)

American novelist and journalist, resident in the UK since 1957. He was born in Chicago and educated in California. He worked in the union movement, as a story analyst in Hollywood, and as a literary agent. His involvement in the anti-war and civil rights movement led to his removal to Britain. His reputation is based almost entirely on two documentary novels, *Weekend in Dinlock* (1960), an **Orwell**ian study of a small mining village in the Midlands, and the 'report, memoir', *Going Away* (1962), which examines his responses to the country of his birth. A third novel, *Zone of the Interior* (1976), reflected Sigal's interest in radical therapeutic philosophies, but the author was perhaps too close (though not necessarily sympathetic) to the subject to maintain the precise reserve of the earlier books. Since the 1970s, Sigal has continued to write trenchant, often provocative journalism.

SIGOURNEY, Lydia Howard Huntley
(1791–1865)

American poet and essayist, born in Norwich, Connecticut. She began publishing her work anonymously because her husband, a wealthy businessman, feared his reputation would be damaged if it was known that his wife was a writer, especially one supporting such causes as that of the Native Americans. *Traits of the Aborigines of America* (1822) records Native American legend in blank verse. Native American themes recur in *Pocahontas and Other Poems* (1841). Since the early 1830s, as a result of her husband's business collapsing, Sigourney was publishing under her own name. She was also successful: the appearance of *Poems* in 1834 resulted in her being acclaimed as a 'female Milton'. Later books include *Pleasant Memories of Pleasant Lands* (1842), an entertaining record of her travels.

▷G S Haight, *Lydia Sigourney* (1930)

SIGUR-ĐARDÓTTIR, Fríða Á
(1940–)

Icelandic short-story writer and novelist. Born in Hesteyri, in the west of Iceland, she worked as a librarian before concentrating on writing. The short stories in her first book, *Þetta er ekkert alvarlegt* (1980, 'This Isn't Serious'), focus on marital relationships, while her novel *Sólin og skugginn* (1981, 'The Sun and the Shadow') explores feminine powerlessness. *Við gluggann* (1984, 'By the Window') is a book of short stories in which her earlier realism becomes marginalized by a style dependent on metaphor and stream of consciousness. Her novel *Meðan nóttin líður* (1990, 'While the Night is Passing') confronts a modern career woman with memories of six generations of women, all of them less independent than she is but enjoying an affinity with their families and their world that she lacks. The novel won the 1992 Nordic Council Literature Prize.

▷S Hilmarsdóttir, 'Fríða Á. Sigurdardóttir', in *Norsk Litterær Årbok* (1992)

SIGUR-ÐARDÓTTIR, Jakobína
(1918–)

Icelandic short-story writer and novelist. Born in the west of Iceland into a working-class family, she subsequently ran a farm with her husband in the north of the country. She writes a realist prose that is at once accessible and innovative, her critique of contemporary Iceland focusing on the swift transition from a traditional way of life to a modern, industrial economy dependent on foreign capital. She published a children's book in 1959, and her first collection of short stories, *Púnktur á skökkum stað* ('Full Stop in the Wrong Place'), in 1964. *Dægurvísa* (1965, 'Twenty-four Hour Tune') introduced the collective novel into Icelandic literature; and the novel *Snaran* (1968, 'The Noose'), written as one long address to a respondent who never replies, strikingly pinpoints the loss of identity brought about by the presence in Iceland this century of politically and economically powerful foreigners, notably Americans.

▷E Skyum Nielsen (ed), 'Indledning', *Tale i røret—moderne islandsk prosa* (1981)

SIGURJÓNSSON, Jóhann
(1880–1919)

Icelandic dramatist and poet, pioneer of Icelandic theatre and the first Icelandic writer in modern times to achieve international recognition. Born in Laxamýri in the north of Iceland, he studied veterinary science in Copenhagen but turned to literature instead. He wrote simultaneously in Danish and Icelandic in order to gain a wider audience, and used Icelandic folk-tale motifs for his most successful plays: *Fjalla-Eyvindur* in 1911 (Eng trans *Eyvind of the Mountains*), which was made into a film as *Berg Eyvind och hans hustru* (1917) by the Swedish director Victor Sjöström, and *Galdra-Loftur* in 1914 (Eng trans *The Wish*, 1967). His other plays were *Dr Rung* (1908), *Bónden á Hrauni* (1908, 'The Farmer at Hraun') and *Løgneren* (1917, 'The Liar'), based on a theme from *Njál's Saga*. He also wrote lyric poetry of touching sensitivity.

▷H Toldberg, *Jóhann Sigurjónsson* (1965)

SIKELIANOS, Angelos
(1884–1951)

Greek nature poet, born on Leucas in the Ionian islands. The publication of his *Prologos Sti Zoë* ('Prologue To Life') between 1915 and 1917 instigated a period of Greek mysticism. His work was brought to a wider public with the publication of *Panaghia* (1917), about the death of the dancer Isadora Duncan—his sister Penelope was married to the dancer's brother Raymond. Sikelianos also married an American, Eva Palmer, and with her help he attempted in 1927 to set up a Delphic University dedicated to 'intellectual independence, spiritual redemption and unity beyond the fragmented self'. Together they devised the first Delphic Festival, to promote this university, which resulted in the first staging of ancient Greek tragedy in its home since antiquity, but which was a spectacular financial disaster. Sikelianos turned to writing tragedies, and achieved a respectable critical success with *Sybil* (1940, 'The Sybil').

SILIUS ITALICUS, Tiberius Catius Asconius
(25–101)

Latin poet and politician. He became a prominent orator in the Roman courts, was consul in 68, and then proconsul in Asia (77). He lived thereafter in retirement on his rich estates near Naples, and became a patron of literature and the arts. Having contracted an incurable disease, he starved himself to death. He was the author of the longest surviving Latin poem, *Punica*, an epic in 17 books on the 2nd Punic War.

▷H M Butler, *Post Augustan Poets* (1926)

SILKIN, Jon
(1930–)

English poet, born into a Jewish family in London. He was educated at Dulwich College, and has been editor of the literary magazine *Stand* since 1952 (with a short break in 1957–60). A deeply committed poet, his work can be linguistically and semantically obscure, but his best writing has a powerfully direct, discursive appeal. *The Peaceable Kingdom* (1954) was his first substantial collection. Other important volumes include *Nature With Man* (1965), *The Little Time-Keeper* (1976) and *Autobiographical Stanzas* (1984). He has compiled a number of anthologies, and written a study of the poetry of World War I, *Out of Battle* (1972, rev edn 1987). *Selected Poems* appeared in 1980, and was revised in 1988.

SILKO, Leslie Marmon
(1948–)

American writer, born in Albuquerque, New Mexico. Of mixed Laguna, Mexican and White descent, Silko was brought up on the Laguna Pueblo reservation in New Mexico, and the Laguna cultural traditions and Southwestern desert landscape are central to her work. The poems in *Laguna Woman* (1974), her first publication, display the richly sensuous imagery combined with humour and naturalistic dialogue that characterize her work. Her novel *Ceremony* (1977) describes the spiritual and cultural reconstruction of a young Pueblo war veteran, fighting the destructive power of witchery over his people, while in the autobiographical *Storyteller* (1981), Silko blends personal family history and photography with stories and poems drawing on Laguna oral tradition and contemporary life. Through the publication of *Ceremony*, Silko began a correspondence with the poet **James Wright**, and their letters were published in 1985 as *The Delicacy and Strength of Lace*. The novel *Almanac of the Dead* (1992), published with poetic irony in the year of the Columbus quincentennial, is a dark, millennium-end account of the Native American peoples retaking of their ancestral lands in the face of an Anglo–American society in moral, psychological and ecological collapse.

▷P Seyersted, *Leslie Marmon Silko* (1980)

SILLANPÄÄ, Frans Eemil
(1888–1964)

Finnish novelist, winner of the Nobel Prize for literature, born in Hämeenkyrö. Of humble peasant stock, he became the foremost Finnish writer of his time and his work always reflected his origins. His major works were *Hurskas kurjuus* (1919, 'Meek Heritage'), a novel about the Finnish civil war, and *Nuorena nukkunut* (1931, Eng trans *The Maid Silja*, 1931), about the collapse of traditional values in Finland, and *Ihmiset suviyössä* (1934, 'People in the Summer Night'). He was awarded the 1939 Nobel Prize for literature. In old age he became a much loved radio broadcaster.

▷A Laurila, *F. E. Sillanpään Romaantaide* (1979)

SILLITOE, Alan
(1928–)

English novelist, born in Nottingham. He left school to work in a factory at 14, and served as a wireless operator in the RAF (1946–9). He lived in France and Spain (1952–8), and began writing while convalescing from tuberculosis. He scored a major success with his first novel, *Saturday Night and Sunday Morning* (1958), with its energetic young antihero, Arthur Seaton. The stories in *The Loneliness of the Long Distance Runner* (1959) were equally acclaimed. The outsider struggling in a brutal society is a recurring theme in his subsequent, more overtly political novels and stories, and the best of them echo the Midlands setting and gritty realism of his earlier books. They include *Key to the Door* (1962),

The Widower's Son (1977) and *Lost Loves* (1991). He has written several volumes of poems, plays and children's books. He married **Ruth Fainlight** in 1959.

SILONE, Ignazio, originally Secondo Tranquilli
(1900–78)

Born in the Abruzzi, the son of a tenant-farmer, he was inspired to political and literary activity by the corruption of local officialdom exacerbated by the ascendant fascist regime of the 1920s. His early novels, *Fontamara* (1933), *Pane e Vino* (1937) and *Il seme sotto la neve* (1941), mirror his strength of feeling for the peasant farmer, his growing disenchantment with party politics, and his personal integrity. All three were originally published in Switzerland where the author was in exile until 1944. On returning to Italy, his international reputation as a writer and left-wing intellectual was assured by novels which turned their attention from fascist corruption to communist betrayals, by his journalism, and by his autobiographical work, *Uscita di sicurezza* (1965).

SILVA, Antonio José da
(1705–39)

Portuguese playwright and Offenbachian librettist, born in Rio de Janeiro. He studied law at Coimbra, and was burnt with wife and mother by the Inquisition at Lisbon as a relapsed Jew.

▷T Braga, *O Poete Judeu e a Inquisição* (1901)

SILVA, José Asunción
(1865–95)

Colombian poet and novelist, born in Bogotá, son of the regional writer Ricardo Silva. Silva went to France and came under the influence of **Verlaine** and the French cult for **Poe**. He returned to Colombia, was desperately unhappy, and, persecuted by creditors, shot himself. At his least original he was simply an imitative decadent, but in his few outstanding poems, such as the famous 'Nocturno', written in memory of his beloved sister, who died in 1891, he achieved technical originality and a high degree of modernity. He is still much read, and his fictional autobiography, *De sobremesa* (1887–96, 'Sitting at Table After Eating'), re-written after he had lost the first manuscript at sea, is a key book.

▷A Miramón, *José Asunción Silva* (1957, in Spanish)

SILVERBERG, Robert
(1935–)

American science-fiction writer, born in New York City. He began writing science fiction while studying at Columbia University, and went through a high-pressure apprenticeship supplying magazine fodder at an incredible rate and under a welter of pseudonyms. He moved away from the stock conventions of the genre with the more stylistically and thematically experimental novel *Thorns* (1967), the beginning of a period of astonishingly intense and sustained creativity which included *Tower of Glass* (1970) and *The Stochastic Man* (1975). After a four-year break, he returned with the whimsical fantasy *Lord Valentine's Castle* (1980). His subsequent work, while polished and inventive, has been less high-powered, and has included historical novels as well as science fiction.

SIMAK, Clifford Donald
(1904–88)

American science-fiction writer, born in Milville, Wisconsin, of an immigrant Czech father and an American mother. During the Depression he entered journalism in Michigan and then joined the Minneapolis *Star*, to which he contributed a weekly science column for the rest of his life. He started publishing science-fiction stories in 1931; his major work was the story sequence *The City* (1952), a chronicle in which dogs and robots take over a world abandoned by men. *Way Station* (1962) and *All Flesh is Grass* (1965) are more subtle.

SIMENON, Georges Joseph Christian
(1903–89)

Belgian-born French novelist, born in Liège. At 16 he began work as a journalist on the *Gazette de Liège*. He moved to Paris in 1922 and became a prolific writer of popular fiction, writing under a plethora of pseudonyms. He also wrote serious psychological novels, much-admired but neglected in favour of almost a hundred short, economical novels featuring Jules Maigret, the pipe-smoking, persistent detective. His prototype is popularly supposed to have been the French detective Marcel Guillaume, though Simenon said he could not remember where the inspiration for him came from. A 'Commissaire Maigret' appeared in three of the *romans populaires* that Simenon produced but he bears little resemblance to the character now known the world over, partly through films and television adaptations. The first two in the series were published in 1931: *M. Gallet décède* (Eng trans *The Death of Monsieur Gallet*, 1932) and *Le Pendu de Saint-Pholien* (Eng trans *The Crime of Inspector Maigret*, 1933). Like **Arthur Conan Doyle** with Sherlock Holmes, Simenon often tried to shake off his sleuth but he reappeared at least once a year until the 1970s, when he finally put the cover on his typewriter. In *Les Mémoires de Maigret* (1960, Eng trans *Maigret's Memoirs*, 1963), in which Maigret is ostensibly the author, he describes his childhood and career, and with laboured humour displays slight resentment at the liberties taken by his creator. Simenon published more than 500 novels and innumerable short stories but told the *New Yorker*, 'I have no imagination; I take everything from life'. Autobiographical writings include *Quand j'étais vieux* (1970, Eng trans *When I Was Old*, 1971) and *Mémoires Intimes* (1981, Eng trans *Intimate Memoirs*, 1984).
▷ B de Fallois, *Georges Simenon* (1961, in French)

SIMIC, Charles
(1938–)

Yugoslavian-born American poet, born in Belgrade. He emigrated to the USA in 1954, and became a naturalized American citizen in 1971. He was educated at the University of Chicago and New York University, and worked as a proofreader before taking up an academic career. He has published around 20 books of terse but richly imagistic poems, and was awarded the Pulitzer Prize for Poetry in 1990 for his collection of 'prose poems' *The World Doesn't End* (1989). His other books include *Dismantling the Silence* (1971), the book-length poem *White* (1972, rev edn 1980), and the collections *Weather Forecast for Utopia and Vicinity: Poems 1967–1982* (1983) and *Selected Poems 1963–1983* (1983).

SIMMONS, James
(1933–)

Irish poet, born in Derry. He was the founding editor of the literary magazine *The Honest Ulsterman* (1968), lectured at the New University of Coleraine, and in the 1980s became co-administrator of The Poets' House, a cultural conference centre in Islandmagee. A prolific writer, his poems, ballads and lyrics 'give tongue' to a Protestant/Loyalist tradition that is significant in his thinking. The romanticism of his early work, *Energy to Burn* (1971), gave way to autobiographical detail in *West Strand Visions* (1974), but both styles and themes later came together, in the bitter-sweet *Judy Garland and the Cold War* (1976). He is an important voice in Irish letters.

SIMMS, William Gilmore
(1806–70)

American novelist, born in Charleston. He edited the *City Gazette* in Charleston and published *Lyrical and other Poems* (1827), *The Vision of Cortes* (1829), *The Tricolour* (1830), *Atalantis* (1832). Perhaps his best book, *The Yemassee* (1835), is a sympathetic

account of Native Americans, a subject he returned to in the short stories that make up *The Wigwam and the Cabin* (1845–6) and *The Cassique of Kiawah* (1859); *The Partisan* (1835) and its semi-sequel *Katharine Walton* (1851) are both powerful. Despite his liberal sympathies, he was an apologist for slavery and the South.
▷E W Parks, *William Gilmore Simms as Literary Critic* (1962)

SIMON, Claude Eugène Henri
(1913–)
French novelist, winner of the Nobel Prize for literature, born in Tananarive, Madagascar. He was educated at Collège Stanislas, Paris, and briefly at Oxford and Cambridge universities, and studied painting before serving in the French cavalry. In World War II he joined the Resistance in Perpignan. Some align him with practitioners of the *nouveau roman* but he owes more to **Proust**, **Joseph Conrad**, **James Joyce** and **Faulkner** than his contemporary, **Camus**. The absence of story, time and punctuation is his hallmark, his style rich, sensuous and complex. *Le Vent* (1957, Eng trans *The Wind*, 1959) and *La Route des Flandres* (1960, Eng trans *The Flanders Road*, 1962) are his most important novels, both eloquently expressing his innate pessimism. In 1985 he was awarded the Nobel Prize for literature.
▷R Jean, *La littérature et le réel* (1965)

SIMON, (Marvin) Neil
(1927–)
American dramatist, born in New York and educated at New York University, the only living American playwright to have had a Broadway theatre named after him. He began by writing gags for radio and television personalities, and had a New York hit with his first comedy, *Come Blow Your Horn* (1961). His plays include the musical farce *Little Me* (1962); *Barefoot in the Park* (1963); *The Odd Couple* (1965); the musical, *Sweet Charity*, and *The Star-Spangled Girl* (1966); *Plaza Suite*; and the musical *Promises, Promises* (1968). *The Gingerbread Lady*, a play about alcoholism, was not as enthusiastically received, but he persevered with serious themes, as in *The Prisoner of Second Avenue* (1972) and *The Sunshine Boys* (1972). Moving from New York to California he made another hit with *California Suite* (1976). *Chapter Two* opened in 1977, and in 1979, his fourth musical, *They're Playing Our Song*, gave him yet another hit. Later he produced a semi-autobiographical trilogy: *Brighton Beach Memoirs* (1983), *Biloxi Blues* (1984) and *Broadway Bound* (1986).
▷R Johnson, *Neil Simon* (1983)

SIMONIDES OF CEOS
(556–468 BC)
Greek lyric poet, born on the island of Ceos. He travelled extensively, and lived many years in Athens. When Persia invaded Greece he devoted his powers to celebrating the heroes and the battles of that struggle in elegies, epigrams, odes and dirges. He won poetical contests 56 times, and beat **Aeschylus** in a contest with an elegy on the heroes who fell at Marathon in 490 BC. A handful of epigrams in the Greek Anthology are all that survive of his work.
▷B Gentili, *Simonide* (1959)

SIMONIDES, Simon
(1558–1629)
Polish poet, born in Lvov. He was famous for his Latin verse, but is now remembered for his *Sielanki* ('Idylls', 1614, Eng translations of some in *Specimens of Polish Poetry*, 1914), modelled on **Theocritus**, and written in Polish. He is often, but wrongly, called Szymonowicz.

SIMONOV, Konstantin Mikhailovich
(1915–79)
Russian writer, born in Petrograd (St Petersburg). He worked as a metal-cutter as a teenager, studied as an evening student, and became a journalist. He was a war correspondent in Mongolia (1934–8), and much of his best writing came out of his experiences in World War II, including his novel about the defence of Stalingrad, *Dni i nochi* (1945, Eng trans *Days and Nights*, 1945). He achieved a considerable reputation by his historical poem about Alexander Nevski, his poems of World War II, and the play *Russkye liudi* (1943, Eng trans *The Russians*, 1944). He was awarded the Stalin Prize three times.
▷L Lazarev, *Dramaturgiye Konstantin Simonov* (1952)

SIMPSON, Helen de Guerry
(1897–1940)
Australian-born British writer, born in Sydney. Her early books included verse, a play, and a collection of fairy stories. The first to attract notice was *Boomerang* (1932), which despite its title had little Australian content, and *Under Capricorn* (1937), a story of Sydney in the early 1800s, filmed by Hitchcock in 1949 with Ingrid Bergman and Michael Wilding. Nine further novels followed, including another historical novel *Saraband for Dead Lovers* (1935) which was also filmed, and three in collaboration with **Clemence Dane**. *The Woman on the Beast* (1933) comprises three novellas including the

futuristic tale of an end-of-20th-century Australia. Other writings include historical biographies, *The Spanish Marriage* (1933) and *Henry VIII* (1934), and a study of the English traveller Mary Kingsley, *A Woman among Wild Men* (1938). She was killed in a London air raid.

SIMPSON, Louis Aston Marantz
(1923–)

American poet, novelist and critic, born in Jamaica, but who emigrated to the USA in 1940. His first collection, *The Arrivistes: Poems 1940–49*, was published in Paris in 1949. Later volumes include *Good News of Death and Other Poems* (1955); *Searching for the Ox* (1976), *At the End of the Open Road* (1963, Pulitzer Prize) and *The Best Hour of the Night* (1983). Much of his poetry has undertones of myth and legend and is noted for its elegant construction. Simpson has also published critical studies of **James Hogg**, **Ezra Pound** and **T S Eliot**, and two important critical works, *An Introduction to Poetry* (1967) and *A Revolution in Taste: Studies of Dylan Thomas, Allen Ginsberg, Sylvia Plath and Robert Lowell* (1978). A novel, *Riverside Drive*, appeared in 1965.

SIMPSON, N(orman) F(rederick)
(1919–)

English playwright, born and educated in London, whose unquantifiable style of surreal comedy and verbal improvization is in the haphazard tradition of **Carroll**, **Lear** and Monty Python. His first play, *A Resounding Tinkle* (1957), was staged at the Royal Court after winning a prize in a competition organized by *The Observer*, and inspired Kenneth Tynan to call him 'the most gifted comic writer the English stage has discovered since the war'. *One Way Pendulum* (1959), which he described as 'an evening of high drung and slarrit', and *The Cresta Run* (1965) established him as an important atonal voice in British theatre. He has written extensively for the stage and television, and has produced one novel, *Harry Bleachbaker* (1976).

SINCLAIR, May
(?1865–1946)

English novelist, born in Rock Ferry, Cheshire. She was educated at Cheltenham College, was an advocate of women's suffrage, and took an interest in psychoanalysis, which is revealed in some of her 24 novels. They include *The Divine Fire* (1904), *The Creators* (1910), *The Three Sisters* (1914) and *The Dark Night* (1924). Her novels *Mary Olivier* (1919) and *The Life and Death of Harriett Frean* (1922) reveal her adoption of the 'stream-of-consciousness' method; *Mary*

Olivier contains clear autobiographical echoes. She also wrote books on philosophical idealism.
▷H D Zegge, *May Sinclair* (1976)

SINCLAIR, Upton Beall
(1878–1968)

American novelist and social reformer, born in Baltimore, Maryland. He horrified the world with his exposure of meat-packing conditions in Chicago in his novel *The Jungle* (1906), which resulted in the passing of a Pure Food and Drug Bill by Congress ('I aimed at the public's heart, and by accident I hit it in the stomach'). Later novels such as *Metropolis* (1908), *King Coal* (1917), *Oil!* (1927) and *Boston* (1928) were increasingly moulded by his socialist beliefs. He was for many years prominent in Californian politics and attempted to found a communistic colony in Englewood, New Jersey (1907). He also wrote a monumental 11-volume series about Lanny Budd, starting with *World's End* (1940) and including *Dragon's Teeth* (1942), which won the Pulitzer Prize. He wrote autobiographical works (1932, 1962) and *A World to Win* (1946).
▷L Harris, *Upton Sinclair: American Rebel* (1975)

SINGER, Esther (Mrs Kreitman)
(1892–)

Polish Yiddish novelist, born in Radzymin, sister of **Isaac Bashevis** and **Israel Joshua Singer**. Her *Der sheydim tants* was published in Warsaw in 1936 and translated 10 years later as *Deborah*.

SINGER, Isaac Bashevis
(1904–91)

Polish-born American Yiddish writer, winner of the Nobel Prize for literature, born in Radzymin, the son of a rabbi, brother of **Esther** and **Israel Joshua Singer**. He was educated at the Tachkemoni Rabbinical Seminary in Warsaw (1920–2), and worked for 10 years as a proof-reader and translator. He emigrated to the USA in 1935, where he joined his brother, as a journalist for the *Jewish Daily Forward*. A firm believer in story-telling rather than commentary by the author, he set his novels and short stories among the Jews of Poland, Germany and America, combining a deep psychological insight with dramatic and visual impact. Considered by many to be the last and greatest Yiddish writer, he was awarded the Nobel Prize for literature in 1978. His novels include *The Family Moskat* (1950), *Satan in Goray* (1955), *The Magician of Lublin* (1960), *The Manor* (1967), *The Estate* (1970) and *Enemies: A Love Story* (1972). Among his short stories are *Gimpel*

the Fool and Other Stories (1957), *The Spinoza of Market Street* (1961), *The Séance* (1968), *A Friend of Kafka* (1970) and *A Crown of Feathers* (1973). He also wrote one play, *Schlemiel the First* (1974), and many stories for children. He wrote his autobiography, *In My Father's Court*, in 1966.
▷C Sinclair, *The Brothers Singer* (1987)

SINGER, Israel Joshua
(1893–1944)
Polish-born American Yiddish writer, born in Bilgorai, the son of a rabbi, brother of **Esther** and **Isaac Bashevis Singer**. He studied at the Rabbinical Yeshivah School in Warsaw, and after World War I became a journalist in Kiev. He became foreign correspondent in Warsaw for the New York *Jewish Daily Forward*, for which he continued to write after emigrating to the USA in 1933. His novels have been widely translated, and include *The Sinner* (*Yoshe Kalt*, 1933), *The Brothers Ashkenazi* (1936), *The River Breaks Up* (1938) and *East of Eden* (1939).
▷C Sinclair, *The Brothers Singer* (1987)

SINGH, Bhai Vir
(1872–1957)
Indian (Punjabi), poet who made the creation of a modern Punjabi literature his life's task. Best remembered today are his lyrical poems, which have been translated into English, if in a rather old-fashioned style, in *Nargas: Songs of a Sikh* (1924). He wrote a verse epic, and also a massive fictional trilogy about the history of Sikhs, which is essential reading for those who want to understand its subject, but is not, unfortunately, a readable work.

SINGH, Kushwant
(1915–90)
Pakistani novelist and major historian of the Sikhs, born in Hadali. His masterpiece is the searing *Train to Pakistan* (1956), certainly the most distinguished and graphic work on the subject of the partition of India; it tells of a Sikh–Muslim conflict in a border town.

SINGH, Nanak
(1897–)
Indian (Punjabi) novelist, author of the important *Ik miyan do talwar* (1961, Eng trans *Two Swords in a Single Scabbard*, 1961). It harks back to a past in which a section of the Sikhs calling themselves the Ghadar Party formed alliances with their traditional enemies in the interests of getting rid of the British. Those wishing to learn the history of India and of the 'Sikh problem' have always been obliged to read this imaginative account.

SINYAVSKY, Andrey
(1925–)
Russian novelist, critic and story writer from Moscow, who became a cause célèbre when, in 1966, with a lesser writer, Yuri Daniel, he was tried and sentenced (to seven years in prison), for publishing books abroad (he had used the name Abram Tertz) that were alleged to be 'slanderous to the Soviet Union'. After his release Sinyavsky went to Paris and became a teacher at the Sorbonne. His notoriety apart, Sinyavsky is and was an important Russian writer, a man who, through his writings, had graduated from a sincere Marxism to a position that has very aptly been defined as being closely akin to that of **Martin Buber**. His most substantial work, the novel *Lyubimov* (1965, Eng trans *The Makepiece Experiment*, 1965), is a profound piece of symbolism which transforms the particular Stalinist terror into one involving the world. His *Chto sotsialicheskiy realizm* (1960, Eng trans *On Socialist Realism*, 1967) says everything about that literary experiment which needs to be said. His art is seen at its most subtle and compelling in *Fantasticheskiye povesti* (1961, Eng trans *Fantastic Stories*, 1963), and in the aphorisms of *Golos iz khora* (1973, Eng trans *A Voice from the Chorus*, 1976). Sinyavsky is the direct descendant of the writers who, in the 1920s, called themselves the Serapion Brothers, and through them has roots in **Gogol** and **Dostoyevsky**.
▷R Lourie, *Letters to the Future* (1975)

SISSMAN, L E
(1928–76)
American poet, born in Detroit, Michigan. By profession he was an advertising executive. He had written poetry as a young man, but gave it up when he failed to find a publisher; then, at 35, started again. In 1964 he began to have his odd, highly original poems published in the *New Yorker*. His first collection was *Dying: An Introduction* (1968). He soon established himself as a much discussed poet who 'compartmentalized his careers': an 'autobiographical poet who treated illness and death with perspective, detachment'. The themes of illness and death became predominant in Sissman's poetry because in 1965 he was diagnosed as having Hodgkin's Disease, which killed him within 11 years. *Hello, Darkness: The Collected Poems* (1978) included much work that he had not published, and sealed his reputation as a courageous man who had left a body of poetry that made sense of his predicament.
▷D Hoffman (ed), *Harvard Guide to Contemporary American Writing* (1979)

SISSON, C(harles) H(ubert)
(1914–)

English poet, born in Bristol. He was educated at Bristol University and in Berlin, Freiburg and Paris. He served in the British Army Intelligence Corps in India (1942–5), and had risen to a high rank in the civil service on his retirement in 1973. He wrote a critical account of it in *The Spirit of British Administration* (1959). His tightly controlled and original poetry has grown more complex and ambiguous with passing volumes, and is somewhat pessimistic in tone, although never despairing. Important collections include *In the Trojan Ditch: Collected Poems and Translations* (1974) and *Collected Poems 1943–1983* (1984), and the later volumes *God Bless Karl Marx!* (1987), *16 Sonnets* (1990) and *Antidotes* (1991). He has also written two novels, several volumes of essays, and translations.
▷ *On the Look Out: A Partial Autobiography* (1989)

SITWELL, Dame Edith Louisa
(1887–1964)

English poet, born in Scarborough, Yorkshire, daughter of an eccentric, Sir George Sitwell, and sister of **Osbert** and **Sacheverell Sitwell**. She had an unhappy, lonely and frustrated childhood in the family home in Renishaw Hall, Derbyshire, until her governess introduced her to music and literature, in particular the poetry of **Swinburne** and the Symbolists. She first attracted notice by her editorship of an anthology of new poetry entitled *Wheels* (1916–21). This was a new type of poetry which repudiated the flaccid quietism of Georgian verse, but her shock tactics were not fully displayed till *Façade* appeared in 1923, with William Walton's music, and was given a stormy public reading in London. It was followed by *Bucolic Comedies* (1923), which is for the most part in the same fantastic vein, but the elegiac romantic style begins to appear and this vein is fully exploited in *The Sleeping Beauty* (1924), and finally worked out in the amazing *Elegy for Dead Fashion* (1926). The short poems of this romantic period, 'Colonel Fantock', 'Daphne', 'The Strawberry' and above all 'The Little Ghost who died for Love' are probably the most beautiful things she ever wrote. At the close of this period she suddenly flamed into indignation over the evil in society—in *Gold Coast Customs* (1929), expressing the horror underlying civilization. In the 1930s she turned to prose work. During World War II she denounced with great vehemence the cruelty of man in the prophetic utterance of *Street Songs* (1942), *Green Song* (1944) and *The Song of the Cold* (1945). She set out to refresh the exhausted rhythms of traditional poetry by introducing the rhythms of jazz and other dance music, and also by free association in expression and the transference of the bodily senses with the result that sense was sacrificed to the evocation of states of feeling. She abandoned this style in her later verse but there is a certain lack of control in her poems on the age of the atom bomb—*The Shadow of Cain* (1947) and *The Canticle of the Rose* (1949). Other works include *The English Eccentrics* (1933), *Victoria of England* (1936), *Fanfare of Elizabeth* (1946), *The Outcasts* (verse; 1962) and *The Queens and the Hive* (1962). Her autobiography, *Taken Care Of*, was published posthumously in 1965.
▷ V Glendinning, *A Lion among the Unicorns* (1981)

SITWELL, Sir (Francis) Osbert
(1892–1969)

English author, born in London, brother of **Edith** and **Sacheverell Sitwell**. He was educated at Eton, and his youth was spent mainly at the family home at Renishaw Hall, Derbyshire with occasional visits to Scarborough, which figures a good deal in his own satiric work, as a symbol of Victorian decrepitude. He served in the Brigade of Guards in World War I, and in 1916 was invalided home. This provided him with the leisure to set up as a satirist of war and the types which ingloriously prosper at home. Many of his satirical poems were published in the *Nation* and collected in *Argonaut and Juggernaut* (1919) and *Out of the Flame* (1923). After the war he narrowed his literary acquaintance to his sister and brother, **Ezra Pound**, **T S Eliot** and **Wyndham Lewis**. The object of the group was the regeneration of arts and letters, and in this pursuit the Sitwells acquired notoriety, Sir Osbert not least by his novel *Before the Bombardment* (1927), which anatomized the grandees of Scarborough and by implication the social orders in general. Neither this nor his other novel, *Miracle on Sinai* (1933), was successful, and his forte was always the short story, especially those, like the collection *Dumb Animal* (1930), where his delicacy of observation and natural compassion are more in evidence than his satire. The paternalism of the aristocracy is expressed in *England Reclaimed, a Book of Eclogues* (1927). His collected works show the contrast between his mordant satire and human kindliness—the satiric sharpness of *Triple Fugue* (1924) with the humanity of the stories in *Dumb Animal* parallels the resentment of the early verse with the acceptance of rural manners in the *Eclogues*. His aristocratic disposition took the form of travel in the grand manner in the 1930s. He had published *Discursions on Travel, Art and Life* in 1925, but then *Winters of Content* (1932) displayed mature descriptive powers. *Brighton* (1935, in collaboration with Margaret Barton) anticipated the vogue of 18th- and early 19th-century architecture. At the close of the 1930s *Escape with Me*, describing a journey to China, proved his most charming book of travel. All these elements contributed to the great autobiography he was planning. The first volume of *Left Hand: Right Hand* appeared in 1944, to be followed by *The Scarlet Tree* (1946), *Great Morning* (1947) and *Laughter in the Next Room* (1948). *Noble Essences* (1950) completed this work. Other collections of essays and stories include *Penny Foolish* (1935), *Sing High, Sing Low* (1944), *Alive-Alive Oh* (1947) and *Pound Wise* (1963).

▷ J Lehman, *A Nest of Tigers* (1968)

SITWELL, Sacheverell
(1897–1988)

English poet, essayist and biographer, the less flamboyant brother of **Osbert** and **Edith Sitwell**. His poetry was capable and interesting, but has never captured the imagination of readers, and is now hardly read, even though Michael Roberts included it in the most influential of all modern anthologies, *The Faber Book of Modern Verse* (1936). He is now best remembered for his mannered but lively travel books and eccentric cultural commentaries, such as *Monks, Nuns and Monasteries* (1965) and *Spanish Baroque Art* (1924). His reminiscences attracted some attention, but he was the least gifted of his remarkable family.

▷ J Lehmann, *A Nest of Tigers* (1968)

SJÖBERG, Birger
(1885–1929)

Swedish poet and novelist. Born in Vänersborg, he embarked on a career as a journalist. His first collection of poetry, *Fridas bok* (1922, 'Frida's Book'), centres on a young shop-assistant's relationship with his beloved in an idyllic Swedish town, the stylistic versatility opening up for parody and irony. Set to music by the poet, who was an accomplished performer, a number of these poems have become popular songs. The novel *Kvartetten som sprängdes* (1924, 'The Quartet That Was Broken Up') shows a **Dicken**sian breadth in its depiction of contemporary society, the many-faceted style imbued with a rich sense of humour. The modernist poems in *Kriser och kransar* (1926, 'Crises and Wreaths') rely on a wealth of imagery and boldly disjointed rhythms to convey a fragmented, anguished perspective on humankind.

▷ E H Olafson, *Fridas visor och folkets visor. Om parodi hos Birger Sjöberg (1985)*

SKALBE, Karlis
(1876–1945)

Latvian poet and teller of folk tales, born in Vecpiebalga canton. He is renowned for his pure language, which comes across in W K Matthews's translations of his poetry: *Tricolour Sun* (1936) and *Pussy's Water Mill* (1952). He died in exile in Stockholm.

SKALLAGRÍMSSON, Egil(I)
(c.910–990)

Icelandic poet and warrior, born on the farm of Borg in Iceland. His father had emigrated to Iceland after falling foul of King Harald Fine-Hair of Norway, and Egil became a professional Viking and court-poet. He fought in the service of King Athelstan of England at the battle of Brunanburh (937), fell out with King Erik Blood-Axe Haraldsson of Norway, but visited him when he was king in the city of York in 948; there he only escaped execution by composing a eulogy in Erik's honour, the *Höfuðlausn* ('Head Ransom'). In 960 he lost two young sons, and composed the greatest lament in Old Icelandic poetry, *Sonatorrek* ('On the Loss of Sons'). His other major verse-sequence was *Arinbjarnarkviða* ('The Lay of Arinbjörn'), a eulogy to his friend and protector, Arinbjörn. Egil is the eponymous hero of the Icelandic *Egils saga*, probably written by his descendant, **Snorri Sturluson**, which also contains more than 40 occasional verses ascribed to him.

▷ H Palsson and P Edwards, introduction to *Egil's Saga* (1976)

SKARMETA, Antonio
(1940–)

The most outstanding Chilean writer of the later 20th century, Skarmeta is a leading figure in the Post-Boom in Latin America. His novels *Soñe que la nieve ardía* (1975, Eng trans *I Dreamt the Snow was Burning*, 1985) and *La insurrección* (1982, Eng trans *The Insurrection*, 1983) deal with personal involvement in political struggles, while *Ardiente paciencia* (1985, Eng trans *Burning Patience*, 1987) is a humorous commentary on language, fame and love. Skarmeta also writes short stories, screenplays and literary criticism, and has been a visiting professor at various North American universities.

SKELTON, John
(c.1460–1529)

English satirical poet, born in Norfolk. He studied at both Oxford and Cambridge, and was created 'poet laureate' by both. Later he was tutor to Prince Henry (the future Henry VIII), took holy orders in 1498, and became rector of Diss in 1502, but seems to have been suspended in 1511 for having a concubine or

wife. He had produced some translations and elegies in 1489, but began to write satirical vernacular poetry, overflowing with grotesque words and images and unrestrained joviality, as in *The Bowge of Courte, Colyn Cloute* and *Why come ye nat to Courte*. Of these, the first is an allegorical poem; the second an unsparing attack on the corruptions of the church; and the last a sustained invective against Wolsey, for which Skelton had to take sanctuary at Westminster, although *The Garlande of Laurell* (1523) is dedicated to him. Other important works include *The Boke of Phyllyp Sparowe*, a eulogy, and the boisterous *The Tunnyng of Elynour Rummynge*.
▷C J Lloyd, *John Skelton* (1938)

SKELTON, Robin
(1925–)

English-born poet and academic, born in Yorkshire but mainly resident in Canada. The founder member of the Peterloo group of poets and painters, he has held several university posts, notably at the University of Victoria, where he was for a long time editor of the influential 'Malahat Review'. He also edited the important anthologies *Poetry of the Thirties* (1964) and *Poetry of the Forties* (1968). In the seventies he published a trilogy of books about the poetic craft: *The Practice of Poetry* (1971), *The Poet's Calling* (1975) and *Poetic Truth* (1978). His own poems are influenced by **David Gascoyne**, whose work he has edited.

SKENDO, Lumo, pseud of **Mid'hat Frasheri**
(1880–1949)

Albanian story writer and critic, scion of a famous literary family. He resisted fascist rule during World War II, but was driven out of Albania by Hoxha. Nothing has been translated, but his history of Albanian literature (1909) and his tales are still occasionally read.

SKRAM, (Bertha) Amalie, née **Alver**
(1847–1905)

Norwegian feminist novelist, born in Bergen, whose commercial life was the main setting for her work. After divorcing her first husband in 1878, she worked as a critic and short-story writer. In 1884 she married Erik Skram, a Danish writer, and following this wrote a collection of novels in which she explored women's issues, and sex in particular. Her best-known works include *Constance Ring* (1885, Eng trans 1988), the tetralogy *Hellemyrsfolket* (1887–98, 'The People at Hellemyr'), and *Foraadt* (1892, Eng trans *Betrayed*, 1987). She was divorced from Skram in 1900, and thereafter never recovered her mental health, ironically reflecting the plight she had fictionalized in *Professor Hieronimus* (1895, Eng trans 1899) and *På St Jørgen* (1895, 'At St Jørgen's').
▷I Engelstad, *Amalie Skram* (1978)

SKVORECKÝ, Josef
(1924–)

Czechoslovakian-born Canadian poet, born in Náchod, who since 1975 has lived in exile in the West, latterly in Toronto. Educated at Prague University, he fell foul of the communist authorities in 1958 with his first novel *Zbabělci* (Eng trans *The Cowards*, 1970). Later attacks on totalitarianism, such as *Smutek poručika Boruwky* (1966, Eng trans *The Mournful Demeanour of Lt Borucha*, 1973) and *Lvíče* (1969, Eng trans *Miss Silver's Past*, 1974) were less overt, but no less powerful. His best-known book, however, is *Bassaxofon* (1967, Eng trans *The Bass Saxophone*, 1977), which recalls the liberating power of jazz in the communist bloc. It is widely acknowledged that Skvorecký's fiction has been less powerful since his move to the West. *Příběh inženýra lidských duší* (1977, Eng trans *The Engineer of Human Souls*, 1984), a phrase associated with Stalin, seems for the first time discursive and polemical. Now a professor of English and film studies in Toronto, Skvorecký continues to write persuasively about movie making and jazz.

SLATER, Francis Carey
(1876–1959)

South African poet, born near Grahamstown. He was a bank manager until, in 1930, he resigned to devote himself to his writing. His greatest achievement, in a verse that seldom really catches fire, even though it is sometimes on the verge of it—in part owing to its author's very conscientiousness—is to give some expression to the feelings of the Xhosa peoples in 'Dark Folk' (1935), a sequence contained in his *Collected Poems* (1957).

SLAUERHOFF, Jan Jacob
(1898–1936)

Major Dutch poet, novelist and translator, regarded as Holland's great 'poète maudit', born in Leeuwarden. He was by profession a ship's doctor. His first collection, *Archipel* (1923, 'Archipelago'), immediately revealed his grand mastery of technique. With *Schuim en asch* (1930, 'Scum and Ashes') he reaches the high point of his inspiration. *Het verboden rijk* (1932, 'The Forbidden Empire') is a novel combining the life of **Camoens** with his own life. Slauerhoff has not yet gained the reputation he deserves outside Holland as a major poet by international standards.

SLAUGHTER, Frank G(ill), pseud C V Terry
(1908–)

American physician and novelist, his fiction almost always has a medical background; perhaps because his family name had unfortunate connotations in surgical circles, he also used a pseudonym. Slaughter qualified MD in 1930, wrote a number of technical books on surgery and psychosomatic medicine and then began to write novels. These include *Spencer Brade MD* (1942), *Air Surgeon* (1943), *In a Dark Garden* (1946), *The Stubborn Heart* (1950), *The Healer* (1955) and *Sword and Scalpel* (1957). They are detailed and authentic but never rely simply on technical infilling to support their plots, which are usually sound and satisfyingly rounded out.

SLAVEYKOV, Petko
(1827–95)

Bulgarian poet, diarist and nationalist, who dedicated his life to creating a Bulgarian tradition free of Turkish, Greek and Catholic influences. He became known as 'Grandpa Slavekov', and was a co-founder of the Democratic Party.
▷C Manning and R Smal-Stocki, *The History of Modern Bulgarian Literature* (1960)

SLAVEYKOV, Pencho
(1866–1912)

Bulgarian poet, son of **Petko Slaveykov**—and more distinguished as a literary genius, if not as a patriot. He differed from his father, too, in looking to the wider context of Europe. He was the most notable Bulgarian follower of **Nietzsche**. As a result of an accident in youth he was a lifelong cripple, and saw himself as Bulgaria's crippled 'overman'. His shorter and more lyrical poems are his best, since his longer philosophical ones are ponderous, and now read poorly. There are English translations of his work in V Pinto, *Bulgarian Prose and Verse* (1957).
▷C Manning and R Smal-Stocki, *The History of Modern Bulgarian Literature* (1960)

SLESINGER, Tess
(1900–45)

American novelist, she died before realizing her full potential, which was considerable. She grew up in New York City and became associated with the *Menorah Journal* crowd, about whom she wrote in her one completed novel, *The Unpossessed* (1934). It examines the tension between public and private values and the pressures imposed by marriage. This was also the subtext of a posthumous collection, *On Hearing That Her Second Husband Has Taken His First Lover* (1948). Slesinger went to work in Hollywood and, like **F Scott Fitzgerald**, left a novel about the movie industry unfinished at the time of her death.

SLESSOR, Kenneth Adolf
(1901–71)

Australian poet and journalist, born in Orange, New South Wales. He worked as reporter and columnist on various Sydney and Melbourne newspapers until he joined *Smith's Weekly* in 1927, later becoming editor-in-chief until 1939. He was appointed an official war correspondent and covered the Battle of Britain and then followed the Australian Imperial Forces through the Near East and North Africa, and on to New Guinea. Slessor had contributed many poems to various periodicals; in 1924 he published *Thief of the Moon*, and in 1926 *Earth-Visitors*. *Darlinghurst Nights and Morning Glories* (1933) celebrates 'The Cross', the bohemian district of Sydney. The title poem in his last collection *Five Bells* (1939) was written for a friend who fell overboard from a Sydney ferry. Although essentially a *bon-viveur* he loved the raffish atmosphere of his city, and his feeling for a romanticized past is shown in his *Five Visions of Captain Cook* (1931). His verse was collected in *One Hundred Poems: 1919–1939* (1944, reissued as *Poems*, 1957) and the best of his prose in *Bread and Wine* (1970). He edited *Australian Poetry* (1945) and co-edited *The Penguin Book of Australian Verse* (1958, rev edn 1961).
▷D Stewart, *A Man of Sydney—An Appreciation of Kenneth Slessor* (1977)

SLONIMSKI, Antoni
(1895–1970)

Polish poet, novelist and dramatist, a leader of the original *Skamander* movement, who escaped from Poland in the aftermath of the Nazi invasion and for many years lived in England. Like his *Skamander* colleagues, Slonimski was conservative but at the same time determinedly modernist—not to say ironic—in spirit, and his poetry has been much valued for its relatively simple statements of humane values. As a playwright he was often compared to **George Bernard Shaw**, as a novelist to **H G Wells**. The best selection from his poetry in translation is in **Czeslaw Milosz**'s *Post-War Polish Poetry* (1965).

SLOWACKI, Juliuz
(1809–49)

Polish poet and dramatist, born in Krzemuniec. He lived mostly abroad, and died in Paris. At first influenced by **Bryon**, he later became a mystic, and his last and best poems reflect this change. His letters, in *Auhelli* (1838, Eng trans 1930) and elsewhere, are remarkable. His collected works have been

translated into French. His greatest, unfinished, poem, *Król Duch*, which has the doctrine of metempsychosis as one of its themes, has been claimed as a masterpiece.
▷M Kridl, *The Lyric Poems of Juliusz Slowacki* (1958)

SLUTSKY, Boris
(1919–)

Russian poet from Slavyansk who is mainly distinguished because, without actually offending the authorities, he decisively rejected the mechanical rhetoric of the official Soviet bards. His first collection did not appear until he was almost 40. His famous 'Bog' (Eng trans, 'God', 1974), really about Stalin as monster, was an important piece of *samizdat*.
▷R M Gulland, *Soviet Russian Poets* (1961)

SMART, Christopher
(1722–71)

English poet, born in Shipbourne near Tonbridge. He studied at Pembroke College, Cambridge, and was elected a fellow in 1745. Improvidence, wit and a secret marriage upset his academic career and he settled to a precarious living in London. He died insane. **Samuel Johnson** assisted him in his monthly *Universal Visitor*. Smart's works include sacred poems, epigrams, birthday odes and occasional poems; the *Hilliad* (1753), a satire on a quack doctor; and several translations from the Bible and the classics. His most celebrated work is *A Song to David* (1763). His remarkable *Jubilate Agro* was not published until 1939, but has helped to confirm his modern reputation as an original poetic voice.

SMART, Elizabeth
(1913–86)

Canadian novelist and poet, born in Ottawa. Her long relationship with the poet **George Barker**, by whom she had four children while he was married to another woman, is fictionalized in her condensed and poetic novel *By Grand Central Station I Sat Down and Wept* (1945). She had moved to England in 1943; apart from one two-year spell back in Canada, she remained there until her death, working in copywriting and journalism. The publication in 1977 of *A Bonus* (poetry) and *The Assumption of the Rogues and Rascals* (prose) revived interest in her; *Eleven Poems* followed five years later, in 1983. Her journals are available in two volumes: *Necessary Secrets* (1986) and *Early Writings* (1987).
▷R Sullivan, *By Heart* (1991)

SMILEY, Jane
(1949–)

American novelist, born in Los Angeles and brought up in Saint Louis. She graduated from the University of Iowa with a PhD in creative writing and went on to hold teaching positions both there and at Iowa State University, where she is Distinguished Professor. Her first novel, *At Paradise Gate* (1981), was followed by the short stories and novellas gathered in *The Age of Grief* (1988) and *Ordinary Love and Good Will* (1989). Her most ambitious work to date is the novel *A Thousand Acres* (1991), a remarkable re-working of the *King Lear* story, set in a contemporary farming community in Iowa, which was awarded the Pulitzer Prize in 1992.

SMITH, A J M
(1902–80)

Canadian poet, anthologist and critic, born in Montreal. He was associated with **F R Scott**, and edited the influential *Oxford Book of Canadian Verse* (1960). He was for many years a teacher at the University of Michigan. His own poetry—of which he published little—was graceful, well crafted, sometimes stately, and mainly influenced by that of **W B Yeats**. He was regarded as the leader of 'academic poetry', and as being somewhat passionless—but this was his intention. His best work is in *Poems: New and Collected* (1967).
▷G Woodcock, *Odysseus Ever Returning* (1970)

SMITH, Alexander
(1830–67)

Scottish poet and essayist, born in Kilmarnock, Ayrshire, the son of a lace-pattern designer. He himself became a pattern designer in Glasgow and Paisley, though he was not particularly gifted in this, and was more interested in his own poetry, sending occasional pieces to the *Glasgow Citizen*. His *Life Drama* (1851) was highly successful at first but was satirized by **Aytoun** in *Firmilian, a Spasmodic Tragedy* (1854), and the adjective 'spasmodic' has stuck to Smith's poetry ever since. In 1854 he was appointed Secretary to Edinburgh University, and the following year produced *Sonnets on the War* with **Sydney Dobell**, his brother poet of the 'Spasmodic' school. *City Poems* (1857) and *Edwin of Deira* (1861) were followed by essays, collected under the title *Dreamthorp* (1863), novels, and *A Summer in Skye* (1865), an enthusiastic and vivid evocation of the island.
▷T Brisbane, *The Early Years of Alexander Smith* (1969)

SMITH, Charlotte, née Turner
(1749–1806)

English poet and novelist, born in London into a land-owning family. Her mother died

when she was three and she was educated at school in Kensington, but was married at 15 to the spendthrift son of a wealthy West Indian merchant. Her *Elegiac Sonnets* (1784) were written while he was in prison for debt. Financial difficulties and marital problems dogged her life; she separated from her husband in 1788 and relied on writing to support her large family, publishing, among other works, 10 novels in as many years (1788–98). All were cast in the popular sentimental mode, but in *Emmeline* (1788) she combined sentiment with Gothic elements and social comedy, while *Desmond* (1792) reflects the hopes of the French Revolution she then held. *The Emigrants. A Poem* (1793) voices her disillusionment. The melancholy that suffuses her poetry made it influential in establishing the sonnet as a vehicle for romantic feeling.
▷K Ravin, in *Eighteenth-Century British Poets*, pt 2, ed J Sitter, *Dictionary of Literary Biography* 109 (1991); C L Fry, *Charlotte Smith, Popular Novelist* (1980)

SMITH, Cordwainer, pseud of **Paul Myron Anthony Linebarger**
(1913–66)
American science-fiction writer, born in Milwaukee, Wisconsin. He spent much of his childhood in Europe, Japan and China. He served as a military adviser in Korea and Malaya, and was an expert in 'brainwashing' techniques and psychological warfare. Most of his science fiction (including his first story, 'War No 81-Q', written when he was only 15) falls within an overarching structure known as 'The Instrumentality of Mankind', an invented far-future universe which was never completed. The fragments are powerfully and romantically conceived, and reflect his ideological standpoint as a political right-winger and committed High Anglican. The main collections under this heading include *You Will Never Be The Same* (1963), *Under Old Earth* (1970) and his best book, *Norstrilia* (1975). He also wrote a Chinese fable, *The Ocean War* (1937), and three non science-fiction novels.

SMITH, Dodie, pseud (until 1935) **C L Anthony**
(1896–1990)
English playwright, novelist and theatre producer. She started as an actress but took up a business career. Her first play, *Autumn Crocus* (1930), was an instant success and enabled her to devote all her time to writing. Other plays include *Dear Octopus* (1938), *Letter from Paris* (adapted from *The Reverberator* by **Henry James**, 1952) and *I Capture the Castle* (adapted from her own novel, 1952).

Other works include the highly popular children's book *The Hundred and One Dalmations* (1956).
▷*Look Back with Love* (1974); *Look Back with Mixed Feelings* (1977); *Look Back with Astonishment* (1979); *Look Back with Gratitude* (1985)

SMITH, E(dward) E(lmer) 'Doc'
(1890–1965)
American science-fiction writer, born in Sheboygan, Wisconsin. He had a PhD in food chemistry, the source of his writing nickname. He was an immensely popular creator of science-fiction space adventure stories in the 'pulp' magazine era before World War II, and is widely regarded as the progenitor of 'space opera'. His work was reprinted in paperback and has been a consistent bestseller. Colourful, racy and exciting, it plays fast and loose with both probability and literary rectitude. His best-known works are the multi-volume sequences *Skylark* (begun 1928) and *Lensman* (begun 1948). The later *Family d'Alembert* series (begun 1964) appeared posthumously, and was completed by other writers.

SMITH, Horace or **Horatio** *see* **SMITH, James**

SMITH, Iain Crichton, Gaelic **Blain Mac A'Ghobhainn**
(1928–)
Scottish poet and novelist, born on the Isle of Lewis. He was educated at the Nicolson Institute, Stornoway, and Aberdeen University. His career as a writer ran in tandem with that of a teacher in Clydebank, Dumbarton and Oban (retired 1977). Bilingual in Gaelic and English, he is an ambidextrous writer, rooted in the native culture but sensible to the wider audience that English admits. His first collection of poems, *The Long River*, appeared in 1955. Five years later came *Burn is Aran*, stories and poems in Gaelic which were highly praised. Since then he has been prolific and, while his output is of varied quality, at his best he is one of the modern masters of Scottish literature. *Consider the Lilies* (1968) is undoubtedly his best-known work. Focusing on the plight of an old woman evicted from her croft and betrayed by the Church (Smith is no lover of the Free Church), it is a powerful indictment of the Clearances and the harsh reality of Highland life. *My Last Duchess* (1971) and *An End to Autumn* (1978) are similarly beautiful but bleak, although it would be wrong to imply that the sensibility behind them is humourless. Particularly since the publication of *Murdo and Other Stories* (1981) there is evidence of a writer hell-bent on mischief, the absurd side of his nature triumphing over

a tendency towards introspection. In his poetry, however, Calvinism and the Isle of Lewis fuse to generate love and hate in almost equal measure, producing in the best poems a dramatic grandeur and awesome tension. *Selected Poems* was published in 1982, and *Collected Poems* in 1992. He has been the recipient of many prizes.
▷A Bold, 'The Parish and the Island', in *Modern Scottish Literature* (1983)

SMITH, James
(1775–1839)
SMITH, Horatio Horace
(1779–1849)

English authors of *The Rejected Addresses.* They were educated at Chigwell, Essex. James succeeded his father as solicitor to the Board of Ordnance; Horace made a fortune as a stockbroker. Both wrote for magazines. When a prize was advertised for an address to be spoken at the opening of the new Drury Lane Theatre in 1812, the brothers produced a series of supposed 'Rejected Addresses', James furnishing imitations of **Wordsworth**, **Robert Southey** and **Coleridge**; Horace those of Sir **Walter Scott**, **Byron**, **Matthew** ('Monk') **Lewis** and **Moore**. James also wrote for the comic actor Charles Mathews and Horace wrote the *Tin Trumpet* (1836) and more than a score of novels. Of Horace's *Poems* (1846) the best known is the 'Ode to an Egyptian Mummy'.

SMITH, Lillian Eugenia
(1897–1966)

American novelist, editor and educator, born in Jasper, Florida. As a young woman she travelled and taught, and in 1925 became manager of a camp for girls at Laurel Falls, Georgia, a post she maintained until 1949, and where she introduced several of her own progressive teaching programmes in the arts. During the 1930s she founded a small magazine, publishing women and black writers, and in 1944 published her first novel, *Strange Fruit*, a tragic, interracial love story. Her anger against racial conflict and segregation is also evident in several of her subsequent books, including *Killers of the Dream* (1949, rev edn 1961) and *Now Is The Time* (1955). In 1964 she published *Our Faces, Our Words*, an impassioned examination of the American non-violent civil rights movement.
▷F Clay and L Blackwell, *Lillian Smith* (1971)

SMITH, Logan Pearsall
(1865–1946)

American-born British writer, born in Mill-ville, New Jersey, a member of a Philadelphia Quaker family. Educated at Harvard and Oxford, he settled in England and took British nationality in 1913. He produced critical editions of various authors, and *Milton and His Modern Critics* (1941), but is best remembered for his delightful essays, collected in *All Trivia* (1933) and *Reperusals and Recollections* (1936), and for his short stories, and his love of adverbs.

SMITH, Martin Cruz
(1942–)

American novelist, born in Reading, Pennsylvania, best known for his cold-war thriller, *Gorky Park* (1981), which was turned into a successful Hollywood film. A sequel, *Polar Star*, followed in 1990. Of part Hopi descent, Smith has also written two novels dealing with aspects of Southwestern history and culture: *Nightwing* (1977), a gruesome supernatural thriller in which plague-carrying bats terrorize the Navajo and Hopi reservations, and *Stallion Gate* (1986), describing the atomic testing at Los Alamos in the 1940s from the point of view of a young Pueblo GI posted as Oppenheimer's driver. His fantasy *The Indians Won* (1970) describes an alternative present-day US run by Native Americans, who have succeeded in defeating US forces in the 19th century. Smith has also written mystery novels under the pen-names Nick Carter and Simon Quinn.

SMITH, Pauline
(1882–1959)

South African novelist, born in Oudtshorn, Cape. Her output, two story collections and one novel, *The Beadle* (1926), is small but very distinguished, and attracted the admiration and friendship of **Arnold Bennett**. Her stories of Afrikaaner life, in particular 'The Pain' (1925), are evocative, accurate and moving.
▷G Haresnape, *Pauline Smith* (1970)

SMITH, Seba ('Major Jack Downing')
(1792–1869)

American humorist. Having failed, after graduation from Bowdoin, as a straight journalist and newspaperman, Smith adopted a pen-name and began to compose a series of highly successful letters poking fun at the administration of the day. They were printed all across the country and when collected as *Letters of J. Downing, Major, Downingville Militia* (1834), the book required 10 editions. Besides political satire, Smith published *Way Down East* (1854), containing affectionate portraits of Yankee life. His wife, Elizabeth Oakes Smith, was a well-known editor and columnist.

SMITH, Stevie, pseud of **Florence Margaret Smith**
(1902–71)

English poet and novelist, born in Hull. At the age of three she moved with her family to the house in the London suburb of Palmer's Green where she was to live with her aunt for most of her life. She attended the local High School and the North London Collegiate School for Girls before working for the Newnes publishing company. In 1935 she took a collection of her poems to a publisher, who rejected them and advised her to try a novel. This she did, and the result was *Novel on Yellow Paper*, published in 1936, a largely autobiographical monologue in an amusing conversational style, which proved a success and was followed in 1938 by *Over the Frontier*, in similar style. *The Holiday* (1949) was again to a great extent autobiographical but had a more conventional structure and told the story of a doomed love affair. Meanwhile her reputation as a poet was becoming established. *A Good Time Was Had By All* was published in 1937, the poetry light and child-like in tone, with chatty amusing language and short verses. She developed a more serious tone, with stronger themes, moving towards the concepts and language of Christianity. Loneliness is often her theme, as in *Not Waving but Drowning* (1957), and she is considered to be a comic writer, but one who talks of serious matters in an amusing tone. Her work also includes *Mother, What is Man?* (1942), *Harold's Leap* (1950), *Selected Poems* (1962), *The Frog Prince* (1966) and *Scorpion* (1972). She wrote many reviews and critical articles, and produced a volume of the line-drawings that often accompanied her poems, entitled *Some Are More Human Than Others* (1958). Her *Collected Poems* appeared in 1975.
▷K Dick, *Ivy and Stevie* (1971)

SMITH, Sydney Goodsir
(1915–75)

New Zealand-born Scottish poet, born in Wellington, son of Sir Sydney Alfred Smith. He moved to Edinburgh in 1928 when his father was appointed Regius Professor of Forensic Medicine there. He studied at Edinburgh University and Oriel College, Oxford, and with such works as *Skail Wind* (1941), *The Devil's Waltz* (1946), *Under the Eildon Tree* (1948, a great modern love poem), *Orpheus and Eurydice* (1955), *So Late into the Night* (1952) and *Figs and Thistles* (1959), established a reputation as the best modern Lallans (lowland Scots) poet after **Hugh MacDiarmid**. He published a loving description of Edinburgh in *Kynd Kittock's Land* in 1965. His first play, *The Wallace*, was commissioned for the Edinburgh Festival of 1960.

He also wrote a comic novel, *Carotid Cornucopius* (1947). His *Collected Poems 1941–75* appeared in 1975.
▷H MacDiarmid, *Sydney Goodsir Smith* (1963)

SMITH, Sydney
(1771–1845)

English clergyman, essayist and wit, born in Woodford, Essex. He was educated at Winchester and New College, Oxford, of which he became a fellow. He was ordained (1794) and served at Netheravon near Amesbury, and Edinburgh. In 1802, with Francis Jeffrey, Francis Horner and Lord Brougham, he started the *Edinburgh Review*. He next lived six years in London, and soon made his mark as a preacher, a lecturer at the Royal Institution on moral philosophy (1804–6), and a brilliant talker; but in 1809 was 'transferred' to the living of Foston in Yorkshire. In 1828 Lord Lyndhurst presented him to a prebend of Bristol, and next year enabled him to exchange Foston for Combe-Florey rectory, Somerset. In 1831 Charles Grey, 2nd Earl Grey appointed him a canon of St Paul's. His writings include 65 articles, collected in 1839 from the *Edinburgh Review*; *Peter Plymley's Letters* (1807–8) in favour of Catholic emancipation; *Three Letters on the Ecclesiastical Commission* (1837–9); and other letters and pamphlets on the ballot, American repudiation, the game laws, prison abuses, etc. Chiefly remembered as the creator of 'Mrs Partington', he was a kindly, sensible humorist who stands immeasurably above **Theodore Hook**, if a good way below **Charles Lamb**.
▷H Pearson, *The Smith of Smiths* (1940)

SMITH, Thorne
(1893–1934)

American novelist, born in Maryland. His early work was published in the navy's paper *Broadside*, and this encouraged him to bring out his first novel *Biltmore Oswald* (1918). His period of success began in 1926 with the publication of Topper, a fantastically plotted novel which was made into a film starring Cary Grant (replaced by a dog in the sequel) in the 1930s, and a TV series in the 50s. *Turnabout* (1931), one of Smith's most inventive books, describing a suburban couple who switch bodies but not personalities, is a good example of the author's fetching whackiness.

SMITH, Vivian
(1933–)

Australian lyric poet, born in Hobart, Tasmania, the seascapes and landscapes of which influenced his first collection, *The Other Meaning* (1956). *An Island South* (1967), *Familiar Places* (1978) and the prize-winning *Tide*

Country (1982) comprise a small but powerful corpus of verse in a traditional style. He has also edited the letters of **Vance Palmer** and his wife (1977), which provide fascinating glimpses of Australian literary circles of the day, and critical studies of *Vance and Nettie Palmer* (1975) and *The Poetry of Robert Lowell* (1974).

SMITH, Wilbur Addison
(1933–)

South African novelist, born in Zambia. A traditional, bestselling author, he writes yarns of stiff, upright machismo. He became a full-time writer in 1964; his subsequent success as an adventure novelist has enabled him to finance expeditions in Africa and Alaska among other places; these have, in turn, helped his research. *When the Lion Feeds* (1964) is a tale of gold prospectors in Africa; *Eagle In The Sky* (1974) has as its central characters a jet pilot and his Israeli girlfriend; and *The Eye of the Tiger* (1975) is about a seaborne treasure hunt which leads first to jealous competition, then to zealous violence.

SMITH, William Jay
(1918–)

American poet, author for children, translator and critic, born in Winnfield, Louisiana, who published his first collection, *Poems*, in 1947. Subsequent volumes include *Poems 1947–1957* (1957) and *The Tin Can and Other Poems* (1966). Smith's themes and verseforms are many and varied, and while this has left critics struggling almost in vain to classify his poetry, many have admiringly likened the effect, particularly of reading *The Tin Can*, to that of watching a splendid literary variety show.

SMITHER, Elizabeth Edwina
(1941–)

New Zealand poet and novelist, born in New Plymouth. Her taut elliptical verse, owing nothing to other schools of New Zealand writing, first appeared as *Here Come the Clouds: Poems* (1975), and she acknowledged an early influence in the collection *You're Very Seductive, William Carlos Williams* (1978). This was followed in 1979 by *Little Poems* (1979) and six further books before *A Pattern of Marching* (1989). She turned to prose with her historical novel *First Blood* (1983), describing the impact on a new colony of its first murder, and a later novel *Brotherlove, Sister-love* (1986). She has also written for children.

SMITHYMAN, (William) Kendrick
(1922–)

New Zealand critic and poet, born in Te Kopura, North Auckland, the first of his generation to be influenced by American writing. His first collection was *Seven Sonnets* (1946), but he produced little after *The Blind Mountain* (1950) until *Earthquake Weather* (1972) and *The Seal in the Dolphin Pool* (1974), followed by three further collections and then *Selected Poems* in 1989. He has written a good deal of criticism, and his *A Way of Saying* (1965) looks at the development of New Zealand poetry. He has also edited two early novels of **William Satchell** and the short stories of **Greville Texidor**.

SMOLENSKIN, Peretz
(1842–85)

Russian Jewish novelist and political activist and editor (of the celebrated periodical *Ha-Schachar*, 'The Dawn', which he founded). He was born in Monastyrshchina, Russia. Known mainly as the leader of the National Jewish Progressive Movement, as the opponent of the notion of 'assimilation'—which he regarded as a negative result of the Haskalah ('Enlightenment')—and as the author of learned and influential treatises in favour of a Jewish national identity, he was also a gifted novelist, and never more so than in his last book, *Kevurat Chamor* (1875–6, 'The Burial of an Ass').
▷R Brainin, *Peretz Smolenskin* (1896); C H Freudlich, *Peretz Smolenskin, Life and Thought* (1965)

SMOLLETT, Tobias George
(1721–71)

Scottish novelist, born on the farm of Dalquharn in the Vale of Leven, Dunbartonshire, grandson of Sir James Smollett. He was educated at Dumbarton Grammar School and Glasgow University, where he took a degree in medicine. He moved to London in 1740 to find a producer for his tragedy, *The Regicide* (1749), but, disappointed in his quest, sailed as surgeon's mate in the expedition to Carthagena against the Spanish in 1741. Three years later he settled in London, practising as a surgeon, but literature in the form of novel-writing was his real interest. His first efforts were successes—*Roderick Random* (1748) and *Peregrine Pickle* (1751). The former is modelled on Le Sage's *Gil Blas*, and as well as describing episodes in the life of the unprincipled hero, it made use of Smollett's experiences in the Carthagena expedition. *Peregrine Pickle* pursues the hero's adventures in love and war throughout Europe. *Ferdinand, Count Fathom* (1753) is the story of another heartless villain, whom

an easy repentance saves from the gallows. **Cervantes** was now his model—he translated *Don Quixote* in 1755—but his imitation of the master, *Sir Launcelote Greaves* (1762), is crude work. In 1753 he settled in Chelsea, editing the new *Critical Review*—which led to his imprisonment for libel in 1760—and writing his *History of England* (3 vols, 1757–8). Ordered abroad for his health, he visited France and Italy and saw little that pleased him. His caustic record, *Travels in France and Italy* (1766), earned for him **Sterne**'s nickname of 'Smelfungus'. His next publication was a coarse satire on public affairs, *The Adventures of an Atom* (1769). In 1771 he wrote *Humphrey Clinker* (1771), which is much more kindly in tone and is still a favourite, in the form of a series of letters from and to members of a party touring round England and 'North Britain'. He spent the last years of his life abroad, and died in Livorno, Italy.
▷L Melville, *The Life and Letters of Tobias Smollett* (1976)

SNODGRASS, W(illiam) D(eWitt)
(1926–)

American poet and critic, born in Pennsylvania and educated at Iowa University. His first collection, *Heart's Needle* (1959, Pulitzer Prize), records the breakdown of his marriage, his divorce and separation from his daughter. Some of his later verse, written in traditional, elegant forms, is also autobiographical but occasionally less bitter. Among his subsequent volumes are *Gallows Songs of Christian Morgenstern* (1967) and *After Experience: Poems and Translations* (1968), which includes translations from **Rilke**, and *Six Minnesinger Songs* (1983). He has lectured widely and written extensively on literary theory, some of his critical writing being collected in *In Radical Pursuit* (1975).

SNOILSKY, Count Carl
(1841–1903)

Swedish minor poet with grandiose ambitions, born in Stockholm. Author of graceful verses, a diplomat until he was involved in a divorce, he aspired to become Sweden's national poet, but alienated the liberals who had once been his readers with his latter-day conservatism. His literary achievement and style have been gratefully compared to those of the English poet **Anthony Thwaite**.

SNOW, C(harles) P(ercy), 1st Baron
(1905–80)

English novelist and physicist, born in Leicester. He was educated at Alderman Newton's School, and then studied science at Leicester University College, and Christ's College, Cambridge, and became a fellow of Christ's College (1930–50) and a tutor there (1935–45). During World War II he was chief of scientific personnel for the Ministry of Labour, and was a Civil Service commissioner from 1945 to 1960. As a writer he started with a detective story, *Death Under Sail* (1932), followed by *The Search* (1934), set in the corridors of science and power. This heralded his major sequence of novels, under the general title *Strangers and Brothers*, starting with a novel of that name in 1940. The continuity is maintained by means of the character Lewis Eliot, through whose eyes the dilemmas of the age are focused. It was followed after the war by *The Light and the Dark* (1947) and *Time of Hope* (1949). *The Masters* (1951) stages the conflict aroused by the election of a new master in a Cambridge college. *The New Men* (1954) poses the dilemma of the scientists in the face of the potentials of nuclear fission. Other volumes are *Home-comings* (1956), *The Conscience of the Rich* (1958), *The Affair* (1960), *Corridors of Power* (1964) and *The Sleep of Reason* (1968). Several have been adapted for theatre and television. Though the chief characters of his cycle are rather supine, being manipulated to exhibit the expressed problems, mostly of power and prestige, in all their facets, his work shows a keen appreciation of moral issues in a science-dominated epoch. His controversial *Two Cultures* (Rede lecture, 1959) discussed the dichotomy between science and literature and his belief in closer contact between them. Created a life peer in 1964, he was made Parliamentary Secretary at the Ministry of Technology (1964–6), and Lord Rector of St Andrews University (1961–4). In 1950 he married the novelist, **Pamela Hansford Johnson**.
▷J Thale, *C. P. Snow* (1964)

SNYDER, Gary
(1930–)

American poet, born in San Francisco. He was educated at the University of California. Originally associated with the Beat poets and portrayed as Japhy Ryder in **Jack Kerouac**'s *The Dharma Bums* (1958), he identified from the outset with the natural world and the values of simple living and hard physical work, making his way as a lumberjack and forestry warden. His writing is informed by an interest in Asian religious practices and literary traditions. This is already evident in *Myths and Texts* (1960) and *The Back Country* (1968) and reaches a climax in the **Whit-man**esque *Axe Handles* (1984). *Turtle Island* (1974) was awarded a Pulitzer Prize. *Earth House Hold* (1969) was a founding text of the ecology movement.
▷B Almon, *Gary Snyder* (1979)

SOARES DE PASSOS, António de
(1826–69)

Portuguese poet, a disciple of the romantic historian, poet and novelist Alexandre Herculano, who was born in Oporto. His poetry was skilful and sonorous but he has since been seen as over-sentimental and over-opulent; he had a large following in his time.

SÖDERBERG, Hjalmar
(1869–1941)

Swedish novelist and playwright, known as 'the **Anatole France** of Sweden'. He wrote several collections of witty short stories, such as *Historietter* (1898, Eng trans *Selected Short Stories*, 1935), and novels of upper middle-class life in Stockholm like *Förvillelser* (1895, 'Aberrations'), *Martin Bircks ungdom* (1901, Eng trans *Martin Birck's Youth*, 1930) and *Doktor Glas* (1905, Eng trans 1963). His plays included *Gertrud* (1905). In the last period of his life, he gave up fiction and turned to religious scholarship, obsessively researching the historicity of the New Testament.
▷B Bergman, *Hjalmar Söderberg* (1951)

SÖDERGRAN, Edith
(1892–1923)

Finland–Swedish Expressionist poet, the daughter of a peasant who worked in Alfred Nobel's factory. Her family moved to the Karelia peninsula, where the landscape and contact with the people had a profound effect. Following an unhappy love affair, she published *Dikter* (1916, 'Poems'). This was followed by *Septemberlyran* (1918, 'September Lyre') and *Rosenaltaret* (1919, 'The Rose Altar') and the ironically titled *Fremtidens skugga* (1920, 'The Shadow of the Future'), each of which attested to a growing sense of the poet as a prophetic, almost magical figure. Though she died when barely past 30, Södergran now exerts considerable influence on younger Swedish poets, who value her passionate, almost visionary imagery and a robust metre that occasionally suggests the works of **Emily Dickinson**.
▷L de Freyes, *Edith Södergran* (1970); G S Schoolfield, *Edith Södergran* (1984)

SOFFICI, Ardengo
(1879–1964)

Italian poet and painter, born near Florence. He was in Paris in the decade before World War I, and met **Max Jacob**, **Apollinaire** and Picasso; he came back to broadcast his new ideas in the review *Leonardo*, and became a ferocious adherent of the Futurism of **Marinetti**. He embraced fascism with enthusiasm, but survived to take a part in later literary-political activity. His poetry is still read and studied.

SOFRONOV, Anatoli
(1911–)

Russian playwright and editor (of a mass circulation magazine, *Ogonyok*), whose work pleased Communist Party officials. His agreeable *Million za ulybku* (1955) was seen, as the film *A Million for a Smile*, in London in 1967.
▷P Yershov, *Comedy in the Soviet Theatre* (1956)

SOLDATI, Mario
(1906–88)

Italian novelist and film-director from Turin. As a young man he went to the USA, whose mores he analysed in *America, primo amore* (1935, 'America, First Love'). He made a memorable film (1941) of the novel *Picolo mondo antico* by **Fogazzaro**. Educated by Jesuits, he attacked their hypocrisy in the sardonic and scarifying novel *L'amico gesuita* (1943, 'The Jesuit Friend'); *Salmace* (1955, Eng trans *The Confession*, 1958) contains short stories mocking sexual pretensions and various aspects of the Italian male fantasy of *virilità*. He returned to the theme of Catholic education in *La busta arancione* (1966, Eng trans *The Orange Envelope*, 1969).
▷D Heiney, *America in Modern Italian Literature* (1966)

SOLIS Y RIBADENEYRA, Antonio de
(1610–86)

Spanish author. He was private secretary to Philip IV and historiographer of the Indies. He wrote poems and dramas, and *Historia de la Conquista de Mexico* (1684).
▷L Arocene, *Antonio de Solis y Ribadeneyra* (1963)

SOLOGUB, Fedor, pseud of Fedor Kuzmich Teternikov
(1863–1927)

Russian novelist, born in St Petersburg. He was brought up by a wealthy family, and worked as a schoolmaster for 25 years before concentrating on writing from 1907, the year in which he published his best-known book, *Myelki byes* (1907, Eng trans *The Little Demon*, 1916). He also wrote a trilogy of symbolic novels, *Tvorimaya legenda* (1908–12, Eng trans *The Created Legend*, 1916), and many short stories, fables, fairy tales and poems.
▷S Rubinovitz, *Sologub's Literary Children* (1980)

SOLOMOS, Dionysios
(1798–1857)

The greatest of modern Greek poets, described by **Goethe** as 'the Byron of the East'. He was born on Zakynthos—his father was a rich nobleman on the island and controlled its tobacco monopoly—but studied at the university in Cremona and tutored in Italian at the University of Padua from 1815. He wrote his first poems there, in Italian, but returned to Zakynthos in 1818. He was embraced by the Society of Friends, a secret organization supporting Greek independence and a popular uprising against the Turks, and thereafter wrote all his poems in Greek. In 1823 he published *Hymnus is tis Eleftherian* (Eng trans *Hymn to Liberty*, 1957), a series of 158 quatrains personifying liberty as rising from the bones of all Greek heroes who had died in her defence; set to music by Mazaro in 1863, it became the national anthem of Greece. However, he is perhaps most famous for the hymn on the death of **Byron** which he wrote in 1824. He moved to Corfu in 1828, and lived there until his death.

SOLON
(640 or 638–559 BC)

Athenian lawgiver, a merchant and a poet. Archon in 594 (or 591), in a time of economic distress, he was appointed to reform the constitution. He set free all people who had been enslaved for debt (Seisachtheia), reformed the currency, and admitted a fourth class (Thetes) to the Ecclesia, so that they elected the magistrates, and to the Heliaea, so that they judged them. Thus he laid the foundations for the Athenian democracy; but he was a moderate and kept many privileges of the wealthy. After 10 years' voluntary exile, he returned (580) and, in a poem, stirred up the Athenians to capture 'lovely Salamis' (c.569). He died soon after the usurpation of Pisistratus, the story of his connection with Croesus being legendary.
▷I Linforth, *Solon the Athenian* (1919)

SOLOUKHIN, Vladimir
(1924–)

Russian fiction writer, poet, journalist and critic, born in the village of Alepino in Central Russia. He was, like **Shushkin** and others, a member of the 'village school' of writers. This group sought to circumvent the political demands of Party hacks by exercising their wish to 'return to Nature'. In his poetry, the least important part of his output, Soloukhin has been compared to **Yevtushenko**, although he is far less flashy. One of his most suggestive works is *Chornye doski* (1969, Eng trans *Searching for Icons*, 1971), in which he tells the story of how his boy-scouting activities led to his passionate regard for ancient Russian culture.

SOLOVIEV, Vladimir
(1853–1900)

Russian philosopher, theologian and poet, born in Moscow, son of the historian Sergei Mikhailovitch Soloviev. He proposed a universal Christianity which would unite the Catholic and Orthodox churches, and attempted a synthesis of religious philosophy with science. His main works were *The Crisis of Western Philosophy* (1875), *The Philosophical Principles of Integral Knowledge* (1877), *Russia and the Universal Church* (1889) and *The Justificaion of the Good* (1898).

SOLZHENITSYN, Aleksandr Isayevich
(1918–)

Russian writer and winner of the Nobel Prize for literature, born in Kislovodsk. He was brought up in Rostov where he graduated in mathematics and physics in 1941. After distinguished service with the Red Army in World War II, he was imprisoned (1945–53) for unfavourable comment on Stalin's conduct of the war. Rehabilitated in 1956, his first novel, *Odin den' Ivana Denisovicha*, (1962, Eng trans *One Day in the Life of Ivan Denisovich*, 1963), set in a prison camp, was acclaimed both in Khrushchev's Russia and the West, but his denunciation in 1967 of the strict censorship in Russia led to the banning of his later novels, *Rakovy Korpus* (1968, Eng trans, 2 vols, *The Cancer Ward*, 1968–9) and *V Kruge pervom* (1968, Eng trans *The First Circle*, 1968). They are semi-autobiographical, as he himself has suffered from cancer, and expose corruption in Russian society while defending socialism. He was expelled from the Soviet Writers' Union in 1969, and was awarded the Nobel Prize for literature in 1970. After some trouble with the authorities, he accepted it. His novel, *Avgust chetyrnadtsatovo* (1971, Eng trans *August, 1914*, 1972), the first part of a projected trilogy about the emergence of modern Russia, was published in the West in 1971, and *Arkhipelag Gulag* (3 vols, 1973–6, Eng trans *The Gulag Archipelago 1918–56*, 1974–8), a factual account of the Stalinist terror, between 1973 and 1975. In 1974 he was deported to West Germany. He later settled in the USA, but in 1994 returned to Russia. His memoirs, *Bodalsya telyonok s dubom* (1975), were published in translation (1980) as *The Oak and the Calf. Avjust chetyrnadtsatovo* was later much revised as 'Knot 1' of a projected mammoth account of the Russian Revolution, *Krasnoe Koleso* (1990, 'The Red Wheel'). He published *Kak Nam Obustroit' Rossiyu?* (Eng trans *Rebuilding Russia*, 1991) in 1990.
▷M Scammell, *Alexander Solzhenitsyn* (1984)

SOMERVILLE, Edith (Anna Oenone)
(1858–1949)

Irish novelist, born in Corfu, the daughter of an army officer and cousin of **Violet Martin**

('Martin Ross', 1862–1915). As a baby she returned to the family home of Drishane in Skibbereen, County Cork. Educated at Alexandra College, Dublin, she studied painting in London, Düsseldorf and Paris, and became a magazine illustrator. She met her cousin, Violet Martin, in 1886, with whom she began a lasting literary partnership as 'Somerville and Ross'. Starting with *An Irish Cousin* (1889), they completed 14 works together, including *The Real Charlotte* (1894) and *Some Experiences of an Irish RM* (1899), the success of which led to two sequels, *Further Expenses...* (1908) and *In Mr Knox's Country* (1915). After Violet's death in 1915, Edith continued to write as 'Somerville and Ross', producing *Irish Memoirs* (1917) and *The Big House at Inver* (1925). A forceful character, she became the first woman Master of Foxhounds in 1903, and was Master of the West Carberry pack from 1912 to 1919. She was also a founder-member of the Irish Academy of Letters (1933).
▷V Powell, *The Irish Cousins* (1970)

SOMERVILLE, William
(1675–1742)

English poet, born in Wolseley in Staffordshire. Educated at Winchester School and New College, Oxford (where he became a fellow), he was the squire of Edstone, Warwickshire. He wrote *The Chase* (1735), a long poem in praise of hunting. He also wrote *Field Sports* (1742), a poem on hawking, and *Hobbinol* (1740), a burlesque on rural May Day games.
▷E Sanford, *A Life of William Somerville* (1819)

SØNDERBY, Knud
(1909–66)

Danish novelist, born in the provincial town of Esbjerg and brought up in Copenhagen, which also forms the main location of his novels. His first novel, *Midt i en Jazztid* (1931, 'In the Middle of a Jazz Age'), focuses on a young law student, Peter Hasvig, torn between two women and the contrasting social spheres they represent; it reflects the influence of psychoanalytical ideas, and skilfully and unconventionally captures the 'modernity' of the inter-war years. His subsequent novel *To Mennesker mødes* (1932, 'Two People Meet') is a continued investigation of the fatal attraction across social barriers. Distinctive for his **Freud**ian criticism of the burden of culture, Sønderby's perspective becomes more universal in *En Kvinde er overflødig* (1936, 'A Woman is Superfluous'), about the generation gap in a close family, and in *De kolde Flammer* (1940, 'The Cold Flames'), a love story set in Greenland.

▷P Bager, *Fylde og tomhed. Om Knud Sønderbys forfatterskab* (1984)

SONDHEIM, Stephen Joshua
(1930–)

American composer and lyricist. As a young man he studied lyric-writing with **Oscar Hammerstein II**, and wrote incidental music for *Girls of Summer* (1956), before writing the lyrics for Bernstein's West Side Story (1957). The first shows for which he wrote both the music *and* the lyrics—still rather unusual in musicals—were *A Funny Thing Happened on the Way to the Forum* (1962) and *Anyone Can Whistle* (1964). *Company* (1970), about married life in New York, was followed, among others, by *Follies* (1971), *A Little Night Music* (1973) and *Merrily We Roll Along* (1981). He won a Pulitzer Prize in 1985 with **James Lapine** for *Sunday in the Park with George* (1984).

SONTAG, Susan
(1933–)

American critic, born in New York City. Though she emerged first as an experimental fiction writer, author of *The Benefactor* (1963) and *Death Kit* (1967), her main impact has been as a critic. She was formerly married to the **Freud**ian intellectual Philip Rieff and absorbed significant concerns from him. Her influential books include *Against Interpretation* (1966), *Styles of Radical Will* (1969), *On Photography* (1976) and *Illness as Metaphor* (1978), a study of the mythology of cancer (Sontag was later a sufferer herself), which she revised (1989) to take account of AIDS, another disease whose social and imaginative construction presents an intellectual challenge. Hugely well-read and polymathic, she is a major commentator, not just on the American scene.

SOPHOCLES
(c.496–405 BC)

Athenian tragedian, one of the great figures of Greek drama, born in Colonus, an Athenian suburb. He had to forgo his ambitions for the stage on account of a weak voice. He wrote well over a hundred plays (including conventional satyr plays of which only the *Ichneutae* ('Trackers') survives), as well as seven major plays, still extant, all written after his victory over **Aeschylus** in a dramatic contest in 468 BC. He won first prize at the Great Dionysia 18 times. The problem of burial is prominent in both the *Ajax* and *Antigone* (possibly c.441 BC), in the first as an Olympian directive that hatred should not pursue a noble adversary beyond the grave, in the second as a clash between a sister's duty to

bury a dead traitor brother and obedience to the law imposed by the state. Aeschylus, **Euripides** and Sophocles each wrote versions of *Electra*, the gruesome matricide by Orestes in revenge for his father's death at the hands of his mother's paramour. The great Sophoclean masterpiece, however, is *Oedipus Tyrannus* (c.430 BC), on which Aristotle based his aesthetic theory of drama in the *Poetics* and from which **Freud** derived the name and function of the 'Oedipus complex'. King Oedipus proclaims sentence on the unknown murderer of his predecessor, Laius, whose presence is thought to be the cause of a plague at Thebes. By a gradual unfolding of incidents, he learns that he himself was the assassin and that his wife Jocasta is also his mother. He blinds himself and goes into exile, and Jocasta commits suicide. The dramatic characteristics are the gradual reversal in fortune of an estimable, conventionally 'moral' person, through some untoward discovery in personal relationships, but also linked to some seemingly minor defect in character, in Oedipus' case, pride. This combination of a minor defect with the external cruel machinations of *ate*, or personal destiny abetted by the gods, constitutes, according to Aristotle, the famous 'tragic flaw' which arouses the tragic emotions of pity and fear in the spectator and allows their purgation in a harmless manner. This is in sharp contrast to Aeschylean tragedy, which is essentially static. There is no development in the plot; the hero is doomed from the beginning. The *Trachiniae* (c.420 BC, 'Women of Trachis') explores the ruinous love of Heracles and Deianira. The *Philoctetes* (produced in 409 BC) and *Oedipus Coloneus* (produced 401 BC) would hardly be called tragic, except for the grave circumstances which attend the achievement of glory.
▷C M Bowra, *Sophocles's Imagination* (1944)

SORDELLO, or SORDEL
(c.1200–c.1270)

Italian poet, Provençal troubadour, born in Goito near Mantua, into a noble family, and most famous as the subject of an impenetrable poem by **Robert Browning**. Little is known of him save that he was a wanderer who carried off women, including wives—and that he had a fine scorn for political and, surprisingly, moral corruption. **Dante** saw him as an exemplary guide for negligent princes in the *Purgatorio*. He left 42 poems in the Provençal language, all of high quality, and is by far the most important of the Italian-born troubadours. Most often quoted is his *planh* (lament) on the death of Lord Blacatz.

SOREL, Charles, Sieur de Souvigny
(1602–74)

French picaresque novelist, satirist, critic and moralist. A perceptive, ingenious and evasive man, he mostly parodied other writers, as in *Le Berger extravagant* (1627), where he mocks the sentimental romance of the *Astrée* of **Honoré d'Urfé**. But in his exceedingly popular *Histoire comique de francion* (1622–33) he is not only a mocker and ridiculer but also a realist of a very high order: this book gives one of the most vivid of all descriptions of early 17th-century French life, particularly low life. The two chief influences upon him were **Rabelais** and **Cervantes**; he in turn may have influenced **Molière**; certainly he affected the course of the French novel. In *Le Roman bourgeois* of Furetière he is characterized as Charosselles.

SØRENSEN, Villy
(1929–)

Danish short-story writer, philosopher and political thinker, born in Copenhagen, who studied at the universities of Copenhagen and Freiburg. A self-taught scholar of formidable learning, he made his literary debut in 1953 with a pioneering collection of stories, *Sære historier* (1953, Eng trans *Strange Stories*, 1956), followed by *Ufarlige historier* (1955, Eng trans *Harmless Tales*, 1991) and *Formynderfortællinger* (1964, Eng trans *Tutelary Tales*, 1988). Sørensen's stories are absurd and ambiguous, simple and subtle, reminiscent of **Hans Christian Andersen** as well as **Franz Kafka**. With the Cold War as their context but only vaguely defined in space and time, they question the validity of a rigid split between us and them, good and evil, reason and emotion. Sørensen's work, whether fiction or philosophy, can be seen as a continuous endeavour to define a political, philosophical and moral middle ground based upon the nature of man. In the 1980s and 1990s Sørensen has presented enlightening re-interpretations of great mythological traditions: *Ragnarok* (1982, Eng trans *The Downfall of the Gods*, 1989) about the Norse mythology; *Apollons Oprør* (1989, 'The Revolt of Apollo') about the Greek mythology; and *Jesus og Kristus* (1992, 'Jesus and Christ') about the Christian tradition. He has been awarded many prizes, most notably the Swedish Academy's Nordic Literature Prize in 1986.
▷J B Jensen, *Litterær arkæologi* (1978)

SORESCU, Marin
(1936–)

Romanian poet, born in Bulzesti, whose verse, distinguished by its black humour and cynicism, became very well known and much discussed in Romania after the publication of his first collection in 1964.

SORGE, Reinhard Johannes
(1892–1916)

German dramatist, born in Berlin, who was killed on the Somme. His (now almost comically) violent play *Der Bettler* (1912, 'The Beggar'), published before, but unproduced until after, his death, was the first Expressionist play; of little intrinsic interest, it showed the influence of **Nietzsche**, and suited the year 1917, when it was produced. After writing it he became a Roman Catholic, and wrote various religious dramas which have failed to withstand the test of time. But in the history of the German theatre he remains a quite important figure.
▷R H Thomas, *Expressionism in German Life, Literature and the Stage 1919–1924* (1939)

SORLEY, Charles Hamilton
(1895–1915)

Scottish poet, born in Aberdeen, where his father was Professor of Moral Philosophy. Educated at King's College Choir School, in 1908 he won a scholarship to Marlborough College where, impressed by the rolling Wiltshire countryside, he started to write poetry. Just before the outbreak of World War I, and prior to taking his place at University College, Cambridge, he visited Germany, which coloured ambivalently his attitude to the events that followed. One of the first to enlist, he believed in the war as a necessary evil, as his poems show. In 1915 he went with his battalion to France, where he was killed by a sniper at the Battle of Loos. *Marlborough and Other Poems* was published in 1916, thanks to his family, and his best and probably unfinished work is unsentimental, direct and free from cant. *The Collected Poems of Charles Hamilton Sorley* was edited in 1985.

SORRENTINO, Gilbert
(1929–)

American poet, novelist and short-story writer, born and educated in Brooklyn, New York. He did manual work for several years before editing the experimental literary magazine *Neon*, and working for Grove Press. His first novel was *The Sky Changes* (1966), an ingenious set of variations on traditional quest fiction. His next books, *Steelwork* (1970) and *The Imaginative Qualities of Actual Things* (1971), are plotless, literary and very cool. *Splendide-Hôtel* (1973) is a quasi-fictional study of the poet's role which uses the (not quite standard) alphabet and references to **Rimbaud** as structural devices. Sorrentino's wider reputation was secured,

unusually, by the publication of a nostalgic short story, 'The Moon in Its Flight', in *New American Review* (no.13, 1971). Sorrentino's subsequent fiction has tended to sustain the concerns of the earlier books, but often lacks their excitement. The best of his verse is in *Corrosive Sublimate* (1971) and *A Dozen Oranges* (1976).
▷G Sorrentino issue, *Review of Contemporary Fiction* (Autumn 1981)

SOSEKI Natsume, pseud of Natsume Kinnosuke
(1867–1916)

Major Japanese novelist and poet, born in Tokyo. Soseki was the most translated of the Japanese writers of his generation (which included the equally gifted **Toson**, not translated until later). He has influenced some important English writers, notably **Francis King**. He was himself influenced by **Zola** and naturalism, but brought a humour and considerable psychological subtlety to his work which most of his contemporaries lacked. His last novels, in particular *Kokoro* (1914, Eng trans 1956, another as *Heart*, 1957), are his finest—and so acute in their analysis of character and their investigations of sexual ambiguity that English readers find it hard to credit their early date. Other major novels include *Botchan* (1906, Eng trans *Young Master*, 1918, 1922), *Kusamakura* (1906, Eng trans as *Pillow of Grass*, 1927, as *Unhuman Tour*, also 1927, as *The Three-Cornered World*, 1965) and *Mon* (1910, Eng trans *The Gate*, 1971).
▷*Monumenta Nipponica*, XIV, 1958–9, XIX (1964)

SOSYURA, Volodymyr
(1898–1965)

Ukrainian poet, born in Debaltesvo in the Donets Basin. A popular poet who tried—unsuccessfully—to keep to the tenets of socialist realism, he was valued for the fervent lyricism of his work, which made few intellectual demands but spoke directly to the heart. Some of his verse is translated in *Poems of Ukraine* (1939, ed W Kirkconnell).

SOTO DE ROJAS, Pedro
(1584–1638)

Spanish poet and priest, born in Granada. He was one of the leading followers, at the Spanish court, of the more important **Góngora**, who became a friend. Soto de Rojas was Canon of San Salvador, and the most distinguished poet of the group which flourished in Granada. His *culterano* garden poem *Paraíso cerrado para muchos, jardinas abiertos para pocos* (1652—poetry was often not published in book form until after its author's death at this time), with its Góngorista title 'Paradise Shut to the Many, Gardens Open to the Few', has been deservedly compared to the 'garden' poetry of **Andrew Marvell**. His works were edited in 1950.

▷A G Morell, *Pedro Soto de Rojas* (1948, in Spanish)

SOUMAGNE, Henri, pseud of Henri Wagner
(1891–1951)

Belgian playwright, born into a Catholic family in Brussels. His deliberately blasphemous plays shocked audiences all over Europe, but particularly in his own country. His most famous play was *L'Autre Messie* (1923, 'The Other Messiah'), a presentation of a boxing match, before a group of Warsaw Jews in a bar, the result of which is supposed to settle the question of the existence of God (which has been doubted on the grounds that one of the antagonists has failed to discover a firm-breasted woman). Soumagne was a very capable theatrical craftsman who later turned to competent crime novels. He was accused of anti-Semitism, but the charge has been debated.

SOUSÂNDRADE, Joaquim de Sousa
(1833–1902)

Brazilian poet, re-discovered in the 1960s. His most important poem was *O Guesa errante* ('The Wandering Guesa'), of which only parts survive. It is about Guesa, a Colombian Native American who wanders the world before he is sacrificed to the gods. Sousândrade lived in New York for a while, and in this poem there is a section called 'The Inferno of Wall Street', written in English and in Portuguese. It is eccentric, but its attack on capitalism anticipates many more modern poets. His works were collected in 1964.

SOUSTER, Raymond
(1921–)

Canadian poet, novelist (pseud Raymond Holmes, and John Holmes), and editor. He was by profession the securities custodian of the Canadian Imperial Bank of Commerce. He is a leading representative of the second generation of those poets who reacted against the British influence upon Canadian poetry— the first one having included **F R Scott**. He attempts, as **George Woodcock** has pointed out, a poetry of 'direct experience', so that those used to embellishments such as metre or even rhythm, as well as metaphors, are often disappointed. But his short lyrics are widely admired and read. His *Collected Poems 1940–88* (1980–9) take up six volumes.

▷*Tamarack Review* (Winter 1965)

SOUTAR, William
(1898–1943)

Scottish poet, born in Perth, the son of a joiner. Educated at Perth Academy, he was conscripted into the Royal Navy (1916–19), where he contracted a form of spondylitis (ossification of the vertebrae), which was to confine him to bed for the last 13 years of his life. After demobilization he studied first medicine and then English at Edinburgh, returning to Perth in 1923. As an undergraduate he published his first volume of verse, anonymously, in *Gleanings by an Undergraduate* (1923), followed by *Conflict* (1931). In 1933 he published his first volume of verse in Scots, *Seeds in the Wind*, for children. This was followed by his *Poems in Scots* (1935) and *Riddles in Scots* (1937), which gave him a permanent place in the Scottish literary revival. The best examples of his work in English are *In the Time of Tyrants* (1939) and the collection *The Expectant Silence* (1944). His remarkable *Diaries of a Dying Man*, published in 1954, mark him out as an exceptional diarist. His *Collected Poems* appeared in 1948.

▷A Scott, *Still Life* (1958)

SOUTHALL, Ivan Francis
(1921–)

Australian author, born in Melbourne, who has written prolifically for children, including the escapist adventure series featuring airman Simon Black which began with *Meet Simon Black* (1950). His later books turned more to the contemporary concerns of modern youth and have won many awards. They include *Ash Road* (1966) and *The Long Night Watch* (1986). *Let the Balloon Go* (1968) was filmed in 1975. His war experiences, for which he received the DFC, and his interest in flying have resulted in a history of 461 Squadron, Royal Australian Air Force, *They Shall not Pass Unseen* (1956), and biographies of air hero Keith Truscott and aviation pioneer Lawrence Hargrave.

SOUTHERN, Terry
(1924–)

American novelist, born in Texas. He was educated at universities in Dallas, Chicago, Evanston and Paris. His free-wheeling, semi-parodic, irreverent and highly scatalogical style earned him a cult following in the 1960s and early 1970s, but he has written only sporadically since then. His first novel was *Flash and Filigree* (1958), followed by *Candy* (1958, USA 1964), which was first published in Paris to evade US obscenity laws. *The Magic Christian* (1960) was a bizarre satire about an immensely rich practical joker, and was followed by *Lollipop* (1962) then *Blue Movie*

(1970), an often hilarious novel about the making of a pornographic film. The stories in *Red-Dirt Marijuana* (1967) are more wide-ranging in their concerns. He has written journalism and a number of screenplays, including *Easy Rider* (1969).

SOUTHERNE, Thomas
(1660–1746)

Irish dramatist, born in Oxmantown, County Dublin. From Trinity College, Dublin, he passed to the Middle Temple, London, and in 1682 began his career with a compliment to the Duke of York in *The Loyal Brother*. **Dryden** wrote the prologue and epilogue, and Southerne finished Dryden's *Cleomenes* (1692). He served a short time under the Duke of Berwick and, at his request, wrote the *Spartan Dame*. His best plays were *The Fatal Marriage* (1694) and *Oroonoko* (before 1696), based on **Aphra Behn**.
▷J W Dodds, *Thomas Southerne, Dramatist* (1933)

SOUTHEY, Robert
(1774–1843)

English poet and writer, born in Bristol, the son of a linen draper. After his father's death an uncle sent him to Westminster School, but he was expelled in 1792 for his Jacobin sympathies and for denouncing whipping in the school magazine. He went on to Balliol College, Oxford. He met **Coleridge** in Bristol in 1794 and they planned to form a 'pantisocracy' or communist society but this fell through. They wrote a topical drama together, *The Fall of Robespierre* (1794), and Southey published an early volume of *Poems* (1795) and an epic poem, *Joan of Arc* (1795). Also in 1795 he married Edith Fricker, whose elder sister Sara married Coleridge. He made two trips to Lisbon (1795 and 1800), and then, after studying law, settled at Great Hall, Keswick (where Coleridge and his wife and sister-in-law were already); and there he remained. He had only £160 a year from his school friend Charles Wynn on which to live, until the government gave him a similar amount in 1807. By this time his political views had mellowed and Southey had become something of a Tory. He became poet laureate in 1813, and Peel raised his pension by £300 in 1835. He had joined the *Quarterly Review* in 1809 and remained a contributor under William Gifford and **John Lockhart**. Essentially a family man, he sustained a great shock when his wife died insane in 1838; and, though he married Caroline Anne Bowles, the poet, in 1839, she became little more than a nurse for his last years of life. His literary output was prodigious, and many of his short poems are familiar, such as 'Holly Tree', 'After Blenheim', 'The Scholar', 'Inchcape

Rock', 'Old Woman of Berkeley' and 'God's judgement on a wicked Bishop'. His other works include *The Curse of Kehama* (1810), *Roderick* (1814); biographies of *Nelson* (1813), *Wesley* (1820) and *Bunyan* (1830), *A Vision of Judgment* (1821), *Book of the Church* (1824), *Colloquies on Society* (1829), *Naval History* (1833–40), and *The Doctor* (1834–47), a miscellany, in which appears the nursery classic, *The Three Bears*. He also published a *Journal of a Tour of Scotland in 1819* (1929).
▷J Simmons, *Robert Southey* (1945)

SOUTHWELL, Robert
(?1561–1595)

English poet and Jesuit martyr, born in Horsham, Norwich. He was educated at Douai and Rome, and entered into the Society of Jesus in 1578. He was appointed prefect of the English College, was ordained priest in 1584, and two years later, arriving in England with Henry Garnet, was first sheltered by Lord Vaux, and next became chaplain to the Countess of Arundel, when he wrote his *Consolation for Catholics* and most of his poems. In 1592 he was betrayed, tortured and thrown into the Tower, and finally he was hanged and quartered at Tyburn for high treason. He was beatified in 1929. His longest poem is *Saint Peter's Complaint*; his most famous, *The Burning Babe*.

SOUTHWORTH, E(mma) D(orothy) E(liza) N(evitte)
(1819–99)

American novelist, born in Washington DC. She became a teacher and published *Retribution*, her first novel, in serial form in a Boston magazine in 1849. Over her writing career she wrote more than 40 novels, many of them being serialized before appearing as bound volumes. Mostly domestic melodramas supporting the social and moral conventions of the time, with titles such as *The Missing Bride* (1853) and *The Maiden Widow* (1870), they became enormously popular. *The Hidden Hand* (1859) is perhaps the most outspoken in that its heroine is unusually independent and determined to succeed on her own terms in a man's world.

SOUZA, Madame de, née Adelaïde Marie Emilie Filleul
(1761–1836)

French novelist, born in the Norman château of Longpré. She married the Comte de Flahaut (1727–93). At the outbreak of the French Revolution (1789) she found refuge with her only son in Germany and England, and there learned of her husband's execution at Arras. She turned to writing, and her first book was the delightful *Adèle de Sénange*

(1794). In 1802 she married the Marquis de Souza-Botelho (1758–1825), Portuguese minister in Paris. Later novels include *Émilie et Alphonse* (1799) and *Charles et Marie* (1801).

SOVA, Antonin
(1864–1928)

Czech poet and novelist, born in Pacov, Bohemia. As a poet he was amongst the three or four most influential of his generation. At first an impressionist writing in the shadow of French poets, he later developed his own brand of subjective and melancholy Symbolism. His personal poems, occasioned by his unhappy married life, were always much better than his more immediately popular 'Utopian' poetry. His novels, such as the autobiographical *Vypravy chudých* (1903, 'The Campaigns of the Poor'), are long-winded but never uninteresting.

SŁOWACKI, Juljusz
(1809–49)

Polish poet, born in Krzemieniec. He settled in Paris in 1831. He belonged to the Romantic school, the influence of **Byron**, among others, being perceptible in his work, which includes the historical drama *Marja Stuart* (1830, 'Mary Stuart'), the dramatized legend *Balladyna* (1834, Eng trans 1938), *Lilla Weneda* (1840), perhaps the most famous Polish tragedy, and *Mazeppa* (1839, Eng trans 1930). His letters to his mother from exile are regarded as classic models of Polish prose.

SOYA, Carl Erik Martin
(1896–1981)

Danish playwright and fiction writer, born in Copenhagen. He found recognition late. His candid novel about the problems and realities of puberty, *Sytten* (1953–4, Eng trans *Seventeen*, 1969), shocked many of his older compatriots; *Min Farmors Hus* (1943, Eng trans *Farmor's House*, 1964), another novel, is regarded as a Danish classic of childhood. His drama, influenced by **Freud**, **Pirandello** and **Abell**, is less serious or successful, but has been sporadically popular in Denmark.
▷N M Wamberg, *Soya* (1966, in Danish)

SOYINKA, Wole, pseud of **Akinwande Oluwole Soyinka**
(1934–)

Nigerian dramatist, poet and novelist, and winner of the Nobel Prize for literature. Born in Western Nigeria, he was educated in Abeokuta and Ibadan before moving to England to do research at Leeds University and study the contemporary theatre. He was for a while attached to the Royal Court Theatre as a play-reader, and it was there that his first play, *The Inventor*, was given a performance

in 1957, his verse-tragedy, *The Swamp Dwellers*, being produced by students in London the following year. He returned to Ibadan in 1959, and productions of *The Swamp Dwellers*, and a contrasting joyously ribald comedy *The Lion and the Jewel*, immediately established him in the forefront of Nigerian literature. In 1960 he founded the Masks amateur theatre company, and four years later, the professional Orisun Repertory. These companies played an essential part in Soyinka's building up of a new Nigerian drama, in English but using the words, music, dance and pantomime of the traditional festivals. His plays, like all his writing, are deeply concerned with the tension between the old and the new in modern Africa; history opposes tradition, and while there is value in many of the old ways, he condemns an uncritical clinging to the past. The richness of his language ranges from high-flown biblical English to the slang of the Lagos slums. His first poems were published while he was still an Ibadan undergraduate, but his first major collection, *Idanre and Other Poems* (1967), turned from his earlier humorous verse to more sombre themes; *A Shuttle in the Crypt* (1972) appeared after his release in 1969 from two years' political detention, and was as powerfully expressive of his ordeal as his play of 1970, *Madmen and Specialists*. His first novel, *The Interpreters* (1970), has been called the first really modern African novel. His other works include the plays *The Trials of Brother Jero* (1961) and *Kongi's Harvest* (1964), the novel *Season of Anomy* (1973), and the mostly prose 'prison notes', *The Man Died* (1973). He is presently Professor of Comparative Literature and head of the department of dramatic arts at Ife University. He was awarded the Nobel Prize for literature in 1986.

SPARK, Dame Muriel Sarah, née Camberg
(1918–)

Scottish novelist, short-story writer, biographer and poet, born in Edinburgh, the daughter of a Jewish engineer. She was educated in Edinburgh at James Gillespie's School for Girls (the model for Marcia Blaine School in *The Prime of Miss Jean Brodie*) where she was 'the school's Poet and Dreamer', and Heriot-Watt College (now University). After her marriage in 1938 she spent a few years in Central Africa. She came back to England in 1944 when her marriage broke down, and worked in the Political Intelligence Department of the Foreign Office, and stayed on in London after the war to become General Secretary of the Poetry Society and Editor of *Poetry Review* (1947–9). Since then she has devoted herself to writing, from the early

1960s living mainly in New York and Italy. She became a Catholic in 1954, an event of central importance to her life and work. Her early books include biographical studies of **Wordsworth** (1950) and **Emily Brontë** (1953), but she also published a collection of poems, *The Fanfarlo and Other Poems* (1952). She is pre-eminently a novelist and short-story writer. *The Comforters* (1957) was hailed by **Evelyn Waugh** as 'brilliantly original and fascinating' and her reputation grew steadily. She continued with *Memento Mori* (1959), *The Ballad of Peckham Rye* (1960), and *The Bachelors* (1961), but it was only with the publication of her sixth novel, *The Prime of Miss Jean Brodie* (1961), an eerie portrait of a school-teacher with advanced ideas and her influence over her 'crème de la crème' pupils, that she achieved popular success. Her many novels, which are invariably slim, elegant and imbued with bizarre elements, include *The Girls of Slender Means* (1963), set in a Kensington hostel, *The Abbess of Crewe* (1974), an allegorical fantasy set in an abbey but with parallels to the Watergate scandal, and *A Far Cry from Kensington* (1988), an evocative, comic but sinister portrayal of London in the 1950s. Her stories were collected in 1967 and 1985, and the first volume of her autobiography, *Curriculum Vitae*, was published in 1992. In 1993 she was created DBE.
▷ A Bold, *Muriel Spark* (1990)

SPEAR, Charles
(1910–)
New Zealand poet whose only collection, *Twopence Coloured* (1951), contains a collection of mannered, polished verse in a style reminiscent of the early 1900s, drawing heavily on a scholarly and well-read mind yet deeply concerned with contemporary life. It was well written of him that 'literature *is* life'.

SPEE, Friedrich von
(1591–1635)
German mystical poet and humane writer, born in Donauworth. He was a Jesuit priest. His *Guldenes Tugendbuch* (1649, written in 1632) is a collection of religious exercises in the tradition of Loyola; but *Cautio criminalis* (1631) is the most eloquent attack on the persecution of witches of his time, and was extremely influential, especially after it had been translated into German (1649). As a poet he initiated a new type of non-**Opitz**ian poetry, expressing his passion for Christ in **Petrarch**an, pastoral terms.
▷ W Kosch, *Friedrich von Spee* (1921, in German)

SPEIGHT, Johnny
(1920–)
English comic writer, born in London. A milkman, insurance salesman and member of a jazz band, he began writing after World War II for such comic stars as Frankie Howerd, Arthur Haynes and Morecambe and Wise. He made his mark on television with the play *The Compartment* (1962), and the creation of the loud-mouthed, working-class bigot Alf Garnett in the controversial assault on sacred cows like religion and royalty, *Till Death Do Us Part* (1964–74). The series earned him Screenwriters' Guild Awards in 1966, 1967 and 1968, and the character was revived for *In Sickness and In Health* (1985–). His other television series include *Spooner's Patch* (1979–82) and *The Nineteenth Hole* (1989–). His publications include *It Stands to Reason* (1973), *The Thoughts of Chairman Alf* (1973), and his autobiography, *For Richer, For Poorer* (1991).

SPENCE, Catherine Helen
(1825–1910)
Scottish-born Australian writer and feminist, born near Melrose. She arrived in Adelaide in 1839 with her parents, with the ambition to be 'a teacher first and a great writer afterwards'. While working as a governess she wrote the first novel of Australian life by a woman, published anonymously in London in 1854 as *Clare Morrison: a Tale of South Australia during the Gold Fever*. Her second novel, also anonymous, was *Tender and True: a Colonial Tale* (1856). Under her own name she wrote *Mr Hogarth's Will* (1865) and *The Author's Daughter* (1868). Both of these had previously been serialized in Adelaide newspapers, as was *Gathered In* in 1881, though not published in book form until 1977; her last novel, *Handfasted*, was not published until 1984. A concern with social problems led her into the public arena, and she made lecture tours of Britain and the USA. In *A Plea for Pure Democracy* (1861) she pressed for Proportional Representation, formed the Effective Voting League of South Australia, and stood for the Federal Convention in 1897, thereby becoming Australia's first woman candidate. *Catherine Helen Spence: an Autobiography* was unfinished at her death; it was completed anonymously in London by Jeanne Young in 1910.
▷ J Young, *Catherine Helen Spence: a Study and an Appreciation* (1937)

SPENCER, Bernard
(1909–63)
English poet, of 'the just after Auden generation', born in Madras. A diffident, ironic, mocking man (the qualities seeped into his work), he suffered from depression, which pervades his elegant, original poetry somewhat in the manner that it pervades that of **Bacovia**. An employee of the British Council

for much of his life, he edited, with **Lawrence Durrell** and Robin Fedden, the wartime Middle East publication *Personal Landscape*. In his lifetime he published three small collections. He died mysteriously while suffering from fever, depression and confusion. His friend Durrell summed up the consensus when he declared that the best of his work would last.

▷ *Collected Poems* (1981)

SPENCER, Elizabeth
(1921–)

American novelist, born in Mississippi. She was initially influenced by **Donald Davidson**, who had been one of the most fiercely conservative of the Fugitive Group. Her early fiction is mostly set in her native Mississippi, and derives from that of **Eudora Welty** and **Faulkner**. But in *The Voice at the Back Door* (1956) she discovered her own procedures, and this story of the corruption of a decent lawyer in pursuit of the 'art of the possible' is reckoned to be her most powerful novel. *The Snare* (1972) is set in New Orleans, and, characteristically of this author, depicts a woman who discovers herself by settling for less than she had originally demanded. She is also an accomplished story writer, as seen in *The Stories of Elizabeth Spencer* (1981).

▷ L D Rubin, *A Bibliographical Guide to the Study of Southern Literature* (1969)

SPENDER, Sir Stephen
(1909–)

English poet and critic, son of the journalist and biographer Edward Harold Spender (1864–1926), born in London. Educated at University College, Oxford, in the 1930s he was one of the 'modern poets', left-wing in outlook, who set themselves the task of recharging the impulses of poetry both in style and subject-matter. In his thought he is essentially a liberal, despite his earlier flirtings with communism. He translated **Schiller**, **Ernst Toller**, **Rainer Rilke** and **Federico García Lorca**, among others, besides writing much penetrating literary criticism. From his beginnings in 1930 with the novella *Twenty Poems* to *Engaged in Writing* (1957), he relived his experiences in his work. *Poems from Spain* (1939) links up with his service in the Spanish Civil War. In World War II he served as a fireman in the London blitz, and volumes of poems, *Runes and Visions* (1941), *Poems of Dedication* (1941) and *The Edge of Darkness* (1949), continue his self-analysis. Alongside these are critical evaluations such as *The Destructive Element* (1936), *Life and the Poet* (1942), *The Creative Element* (1944), and his first autobiography, *World within World* (1951). From 1939 to 1941 he was co-editor, with **Cyril Connolly**, of the brilliant

monthly, *Horizon*, and from 1953 to 1967 was co-editor of *Encounter*. He was Professor of English at University College, London (1970–7). His later work includes *The Struggle of the Modern* (1963), *The Year of the Young Rebels* (1969), *The Thirties and After* (1978) and *Chinese Journal* (with David Hockney, 1982). *Collected Poems 1928–85* was published in 1985, and his *Journals (1939–83)* in 1987. In 1991, he compiled the volume *Character Studies*, with proceeds from sales going to AIDS patients.

▷ H David, *Stephen Spender* (1993)

SPENSER, Edmund
(c.1552–99)

English poet, born in London, the son of a gentleman tradesman who was connected with the Spencers of Althorp. He was educated at Merchant Taylors' School and Pembroke Hall, Cambridge. His early writings, partly written at Cambridge, include translations of the *Visions* of **Petrarch** and some sonnets of **Joachim Du Bellay**. Shortly after leaving Cambridge (1576) he obtained a place in the Earl of Leicester's household and this led to a friendship with Sir **Philip Sidney** and the Areopagus, a society of wits. His first original work, *The Shepheard's Calender* (1579), dedicated to Sydney, heralded the age of Elizabethan poetry and no doubt assisted in his career as a courtier. In 1580 he was appointed secretary to Lord Grey de Wilton, lord deputy in Ireland, whose assignment was to crush Irish rebellion, and Spenser was involved in this. His reward for his work as one of the 'undertakers' for the settlement of Munster was Kilcolman Castle in the county of Cork, where he settled in 1586 and where he hoped to have leisure to write his *Faerie Queene* and other courtly works, written with an eye to the court no less than as a brilliant presentation of the art and thought of the Renaissance. In 1589 he visited London in company with Sir Walter Raleigh, who had seen the first three books of *The Faerie Queene* at Kilcolman and now carried him off to lay them at Queen Elizabeth's feet. Published in 1590, they were an immediate success, but a previous misdemeanour, the attack in *Mother Hubberd's Tale* on the proposed match between Elizabeth and the Duc d'Alençon, was not forgotten and the poet returned to Ireland in 1591 a disappointed man; he later published his wry reflections on his visit in *Colin Clout's Come Home Again* (1595). *Complaints*, published in 1591, contains, beside his early work, the brilliantly coloured but enigmatic *Muiopotmos; Mother Hubberd's Tale*, to which was now added a bitter satire on Court favour; *The Early Tears of the Muses*, which lamented the lack of

patronage; and his pastoral elegy for Sir Philip Sydney which is so frigid as to make us question their friendship. In 1594 he married again, celebrating his wooing of Elizabeth Boyle in the sonnet sequence *Amoretti* and his wedding in the supreme marriage poem *Epithalamion*. He revisited London in 1596, with three more books of *The Faerie Queene*, which were published along with the *Four Hymns*. This was a year of uncommon activity. Under the roof of Lord Essex he wrote *Prothalamion*, and his prose *View of the Present State of Ireland*, which, taken with the fifth book of *The Faerie Queene*, is probably the first explicit statement of the imperialism which is now discredited. In 1598 the Irish rose in rebellion and Kilcolman Castle was burned, but the Spensers escaped to Cork and from there to safety in London. He died the following year and was buried in Westminster Abbey.
▷ A C Judson, *The Life of Spenser* (1945)

SPEYER, Leonora
(1872–1956)

American poet, whose *Fiddler's Farewell* (1926) won a Pulitzer Prize and fulfilled the promise of her earlier collection *A Canopic Jar* (1921). At their best Speyer's poems speak with wit and perception about the female condition, but *Naked Heel* (1931) marked a withdrawal into a constrained formalism and halted her growing reputation. Her work has not, as yet, benefited from reappraisal.

SPIELHAGEN, Friedrich
(1829–1911)

German novelist, born in Magdeburg. He was an advocate of scientific objectivity in the novel, and wrote from an overly didactic perspective of middle-class liberalism and social justice. As well as poems, plays, books of travel, his works include *Durch Nacht zum Licht* (1861, 'Through the Night to the Light'), *Die von Hohenstein* (1863, 'The von Hohensteins'), *In Reih und Glied* (1866, 'In Rank and File') and *Susi* (1895). He also worked as an actor.
▷ E Mensch, *Er lebt noch immer* (1929)

SPILLANE, Mickey (Frank Morrison)
(1918–)

American mystery and detective novelist, born in Brooklyn, New York City. The author of almost 30 books, Spillane is a leading exponent of the sensational school of detective fiction, one critic describing his novels as having 'lurid action, lurid characters, lurid plot, lurid finish'. His first book, *I, the Jury* (1947), introduced Mike Hammer, his most famous character, a hard-drinking, hard-fighting, womanizing private investigator. Hammer punches his way with enormous relish through several books, including *Vengeance is Mine!* (1950) and *The Body Lovers* (1967). Spillane treats sex pruriently, and women as well as men become the objects of Hammer's insatiable violence.
▷ B Docherty, *American Crime Fiction* (1988)

SPINRAD, Norman Richard
(1940–)

American science-fiction writer, born in New York City. He began to publish fairly conventional science-fiction adventure stories in 1963, but by the time of *The Men in the Jungle* (1967) and *Bug Jack Baron* (1969), he had become identified with the 'new wave' movement which coalesced around the magazine *New Worlds*. Their priority was the exploration of inner rather than outer space by genre means, as well as a greater literary sophistication. *The Iron Dream* (1972) imagined an alternative world in which Adolf Hitler propagated his hateful ideas as a writer of fiction. *The Void Captain's Tale* (1983) and *Child of Fortune* (1985) are arguably his best science-fiction works. *Little Heroes* (1987) and *Russian Spring* (1991) are near-future dystopian nightmares. He has written a number of other novels, several short-story collections, and essays on science fiction and writing.

SPITTELER, Karl Friedrich Georg
(1845–1924)

Swiss poet and novelist, winner of the Nobel Prize for literature, born in Liestal (Basel). He studied law and theology at Basel, Zürich and Heidelberg, was a tutor in Russia, teacher and journalist in Switzerland, and retired to Lucerne in 1892. *Der Olympische Frühling* (1900–3, 'The Olympic Spring') is a great mythological epic, but perhaps his most mature work is *Prometheus der Dulder* (1924, 'Prometheus the Sufferer'). As well as poetry he wrote tales, (*Konrad der Leutnant*, 'Conrad the Lieutenant'), and others; essays (*Lachende Wahrheiten*, 'Laughing Truths'), and reminiscences. He was awarded the Nobel Prize for literature in 1919.
▷ J Frankel, *Karl Friedrich Spitteler* (1945)

SPONDE, Jean de
(1557–95)

French poet, humanist and translator (of **Homer**, Aristotle), whose predominantly metaphysical poems were rediscovered (by **Marcel Arland**), or at least revaluated in the 20th century; they were little published in his lifetime, and the first collection of them appeared in 1949. He is now taken as an apt representative of French baroque poetry.

SPRAGUE DE CAMP, L *see* **DE CAMP, L Sprague**

SPRING, Howard
(1889–1965)

Welsh novelist, born in Cardiff. From errand boy he became a newspaper reporter and literary critic and established himself as a writer with his bestselling *Oh Absalom* (1938), renamed *My Son, My Son*. Other novels include *Fame is the Spur* (1940), *Dunkerleys* (1946), *These Lovers Fled Away* (1955) and *Time and the Hour* (1957), as well as three autobiographical works (1939, 1942 and 1946).

SQUIRE, Sir John Collings
(1884–1958)

English author, born in Plymouth. He was educated at Blundell's and St John's College, Cambridge, and was literary editor of *The New Statesman* and founder editor of *The London Mercury* (1919–34). His work is composed of light verse and parody, as in *Steps to Parnassus* (1913) and *Tricks of the Trade* (1917); in anthologies he favoured minor poets. His writings also include criticisms and short stories. His *Collected Poems*, edited by **John Betjeman**, appeared in 1959.

ŠRÁMEK, Frána
(1877–1952)

Czech story writer, novelist, poet and dramatist, born in Sobotka. He was an impressionist, known chiefly for his novel *Telo* (1919, 'The Body'), about a young girl and her erotic and other experiences. His play *Léto* (1915, 'Summer'), was successfully produced. He was a close friend to **S K Neumann**. An honest and lyrical anarchist, he was highly influential in the period between the wars, when Czechoslovakia tasted its first independence, but lost himself in his later work when he tried to go outside his limitations. His collected works, published at the end of his life, take up 10 volumes.
▷J Knap, *Frána Šrámek* (1937, in Czech)

SREMEC, Stevan
(1855–1906)

Serbian novelist and story writer, born in Senta. He fought against the Turks in 1876–7. His comic novels and stories became classics, but never found a translator. Essentially they were shrewd but kindly, seeking their inspiration chiefly in **Gogol**.
▷A Barac, *A History of Yugoslav Literature* (1955)

SSU-MA HSIANG-JU
(d.117 BC)

Chinese poet, born in Ch'engtu, Suzechuan province. He wrote the *Tzu Hse Fu*, a series of poems describing and denouncing the pleasures of the hunt, which hold an important place in Chinese literary history.
▷Y Hervouet, *Un poète de cour sous les han* (1964)

STAAL, Marguerite Jeanne, Baronne de
(1684–1750)

French writer of memoirs, born in Paris, the daughter of a poor Parisian painter, Cordier, whose name she dropped for that of her mother, Delaunay. Her devotion to the interests of her employer, the Duchess of Maine, brought her two years in the Bastille, where she had a love affair with the Chevalier de Menil. In 1735 she married the Baron Staal. Her *Mémoires* (1755, Eng trans 1892) describe the world of the regency with intellect, observation and a subtle irony, and are written in a clear, firm and individual style. Her *Œuvres complètes* appeared in 1821.

STACPOOLE, Henry de Vere
(1863–1951)

Irish physician and writer, born in Kingstown (Dun Laoghaire), the son of a Presbyterian minister. Educated at Malvern College and St George's and St Mary's Hospitals in London, he made several voyages as a ship's doctor. He was the author of over 50 popular novels, including *The Blue Lagoon* (1909), *The Pearl Fishers* (1915) and *Green Coral* (1935). He wrote his autobiography in *Men and Mice* (1942 and 1945).

STADLER, Ernst
(1892–1914)

German poet, the most intelligent, stable and perhaps most gifted of all the expressionist poets who arose in Germany just before World War I, in which he quickly perished. He was a Rhodes Scholar at Oxford (1906–8). He was born in Alsace. Ironically, he had been involved, with **René Schickele**, in trying to cement Franco–German relations, and with Schikele had founded the magazine *Der Stürm*. He was influenced in his poetry above all by **Stefan George** and **Whitman**. Only one volume was published in his lifetime—it was immature, but *Der Aufbruch* (1915, 'The Uprising') is one of the most important collections of its time. In subsequent works, he had begun to form his own inimitable, visionary style. He was a coherent and sensible critic, and of him most of all, of all the German writers who died in World War I, it may be said that he would have gone on to become a towering figure. His loss was equal to that in Great Britain of **Wilfred Owen** and **Ivor Gurney**.

STAËL, Anne Louise Germaine Necker, Madame de (Baronness of Staël-Holstein)
(1766–1817)

French writer, born in Paris, the only child of the financier and statesman, Jacques Necker. In her girlhood she wrote romantic comedies, tragedies, novels, essays and *Lettres sur Rousseau* (1789). She married in 1786 the Baron Eric Magnus of Staël-Holstein (1742–1802), the bankrupt Swedish ambassador in Paris. She bore him two sons (1790 and 1792) and a daughter (1797), but the marriage was unhappy and she had many affairs, most notably with the writer **Constant de Rebecque**. Her vast enthusiasms and the passionate intensity of her affections created an irresistible personality. Her brilliant *salon* became the centre of political discussion, but with the Revolution and her father's fall she felt compelled to leave Paris for Coppet, by Lake Geneva, in 1792. From Coppet she went to England, where at Mickleham in Surrey she was surrounded by Talleyrand and others of the French *émigrés*. She joined her husband at Coppet in May 1793, and published her *Réflexions sur le procès de la reine* ('Reflections on the Queen's Trial') in the vain hope of saving Marie Antoinette. In 1795 she returned to Paris, where her husband had re-established himself as ambassador. She prepared for a political role by her *Réflexions sur la paix intérieure* (1795, 'Reflections on Civil Peace'), but was advised to return to Coppet. Her *Influence des passions* appeared in 1796. Napoleon allowed her to return to Paris in 1797, but received her friendly advances with such studied coldness that admiration soon turned to hatred. In 1800 she published her famous *Littérature et ses rapports avec les institutions sociales* (Eng trans *The Influence of Literature upon Society*, 1812). Returning to Paris in 1802, she published the novel *Delphine* (Eng trans 1903). At length her friendship with disaffected men like Moreau and Bernadotte, and the appearance of Necker's *Dernières vues* ('Last Views'), exhausted the patience of Napoleon, and in the autumn of 1803 she received orders to keep 40 leagues from Paris. Her husband had died, and in December 1803 she set out with her children for Weimar, where she dazzled the court, and met **Schiller** and **Goethe**. In Berlin she made the acquaintance of **August von Schlegel**. She next went to Vienna, but learned of her father's death and returned to Coppet, writing the touching eulogy, *Du caractère de M. Necker* (1818, Eng trans *Memoirs of the Private Life of My Father*, 1818). Then she set out for Italy with Schlegel, Wilhelm von Humboldt, and Bonstetten, but in 1805 returned to Coppet, where once again a brilliant circle assembled, to write *Corinne* (1807, Eng trans 1807), a romance which at once brought her European fame. She visited Germany at the end of 1807, and began to turn for consolation to religion—she was a Protestant. Her famous *De l'Allemagne* (Eng trans *Germany*, 1813) was finished in 1810, passed by the censor, and partly printed, when the whole impression was seized and destroyed, and she herself was ordered from Paris to Coppet. The work was published by John Murray in London in 1813. But her exile had now become a bitter reality; she found herself surrounded by spies. She escaped secretly to Berne, and from there made her way to St Petersburg, Stockholm and (1813) London. In England admiration reached its climax on the publication of *De l'Allemagne*, the most finished of all her works. It revealed Germany to the French and made Romanticism—she was the first to use the word—acceptable to the Latin peoples. Louis XVIII welcomed her to Paris in 1814, and the two million francs which Necker had left in the Treasury was honourably paid to her. The return of Napoleon drove her from Paris, and she spent the winter in Italy for the sake of the health of Albert de Rocca, an Italian officer in the French service, whom she had married secretly in 1816. She returned to Paris, where she died. Her surviving son and daughter published her unfinished *Considérations sur la Révolution française* (1818, Eng trans *Considerations on the Principal Events of the French Revolution*, 1818), considered her masterpiece by **Charles Sainte-Beuve**, the *Dix Années d'exil* (1821, Eng trans *Ten Years' Exile*, 1821), and her complete works (1820–1).
▷G Andrews, *Madame de Staël* (1964)

STAFF, Leopold
(1878–1957)

Polish poet, whose work has remained respected by his successors—many of whom turned to him for help. Originally he was associated with the pre-World War I movement, 'Young Poland', which brought Polish poetry into the 20th century; of later movements, he had most in common with, and most influence upon, the relatively conservative *Skamander* group. His own later poetry is exemplary in its simplicity and humanness. He could be compared to **Jaroslav Seifert** in Czechoslovakia, but was more gifted. There are English translations of his work in *An Empty Room* (1983)

STAFFORD, Jean
(1915–79)

American short-story writer and novelist, born in Covina, California. Her father had an unsuccessful career as a writer of westerns under the pseudonyms Jack Wonder and Ben Delight. Educated at Colorado University, she won a travelling scholarship to Heidelberg, Germany, in 1936. Returning to the USA she met literary establishment figures **Randall Jarrell**, and **Robert Lowell**, whom she married against his family's wishes in 1940. She worked on the *Southern Review* and taught at Flushing College. *Boston Adventure*, her first novel, was published in 1944 to great praise; *The Mountain Lion*, her second, appeared in 1947. But her stormy marriage to Lowell collapsed and she was admitted to psycho-alcoholic clinics. Divorced from Lowell in 1948, she married Oliver Jensen, an editor on *Life*, in 1950. In 1952 *The Catherine Wheel* was published. She was divorced for a second time in 1955 and later married the writer A J Liebling. She taught throughout the 1960s and published diverse books: short stories, children's books and interviews with the mother of Lee Harvey Oswald, *A Mother in History* (1966). She was one of America's most admired short-story writers, and her *Collected Stories* appeared in 1969, winning a Pulitzer Prize.

STAFFORD, William Edgar
(1914–)

American poet and lecturer, born in Hutchinson, Kansas, whose verse has won him many awards. His first collection, *West of Your City*, appeared in 1960, and a major volume, *Roving Across Fields: A Conversation and Uncollected Poems 1942–1982*, in 1983. Stafford is a poet of the western landscape, of rivers and mountains and the natural world. Several critics claim that in attempting to discover an ethical system by which man might live in harmony with himself and his environment, Stafford is reaffirming the original and central values of the American way of life. Among his other books is *Down in My Heart* (1947), which records Stafford's experiences as a conscientious objector during World War II.

▷ *You Must Revise Your Life* (1986); Donald Hall (ed), *Writing the Australian Crawl: Views on the Writer's Vocation* (1978)

STAGNELIUS, Erik Johan
(1793–1823)

Swedish Romantic poet, son of the Bishop of Kalmar. After graduating at Uppsala he became an unsalaried civil servant in Stockholm. He led a solitary life, and suffered ill-health which was exacerbated by alcohol and laudanum. After his death, of unknown causes, his works were collected and published (1824–6). His considerable output, all written within a decade, comprises epics, like *Vladimir den store* (1817, 'Vladimir the

Great'), plays like *Martyrerna* ('The Martyrs') and *Bacchanterna* (1822, 'The Bacchanalians'), but it is above all his lyric poetry, much of it found in *Liljan i Saron* (1821, 'Lilies of Sharon'), which captures the essence of his genius. He was constantly torn between idealism and erotic sensualism. The object of his desire often centred on Amanda—whether she was a factual character is uncertain and perhaps unimportant for in his poems she became a vision of all that is desirable in woman. Influenced by his reading of **Plato**, Schelling, theosophy, gnosticism and Romantic contemporaries, he gradually accepted the view of two warring factions in the universe: God versus the Devil, spiritual versus temporal; in the beginning the soul (*Anima*), Christ and the angels inhabited the perfect world but were tempted by an evil angel (*Achamot*) and plunged into an earthly existence under Demiurgen. Man's spirit is captive but can reach out to its divine origins in dreams, memories, poetry, beauty, nature and, above all, faith in Christ's redeeming sacrifice. Stagnelius contrasts dream and reality in a series of poems like *Endymion*, *Narcissus* and *Till Natten* ('Ode to Night'). In other poems themes from nature symbolize the soul's longing for heaven, as in *Floden*—'The River'—and *Flyttfåglarna*—'Migrant Birds'. Stagnelius employs a variety of verse forms with consummate skill. His poetry has an in-built tension between eroticism and spiritualism and is imbued with nature symbolism and imagery couched in the most melodic language in Swedish literature. Little-known in his lifetime, he became posthumously the most influential of Swedish Romantics on succeeding generations.

▷D Andreae, *Erik Stagnelius* (1919)

STAMPA, Gaspara
(c.1523–1554)

Italian poet, born in Padua. Her substantial *Rime* (1554), published after her death by her sister, tell the story of her love (in Venice) for the Count Collitano do Collato, who betrayed her. She was certainly the finest Italian woman poet of the Renaissance, and superior to many of the men. The poems, **Petrarch**an in style, but often subtly mocking male pretensions, are opulent, passionate and challenging to the prevailing ideas of the time. Since their rediscovery in the last century, by romantic critics, they have been much reinterpreted—and she has justly been compared, although she did not share all her predilections, with **Sappho**.

▷J Tusiani (ed and translator), *Italian Poets of the Renaissance* (1971); *Modern Language Notes*, 90 (1975)

STANDISH, Burt L *see* **PATTEN, William Gilbert**

STANKOVIĆ, Borisav
(1876–1927)
Serbian story writer, novelist and dramatist, born in Vranje. By profession he was a civil servant. His story collection *Iz starog jevandjelja* (1899, 'From the Old Gospel') established him as the finest chronicler of his native region, with its Eastern-influenced traditions and its 'backwardness', of which he saw both sides. His most famous work is the novel *Nečista krv* (1911, Eng trans *Sophka*, 1932), which describes the decline of a once great commercial family, but whose main theme is its careful account of a woman who marries a young boy. He is still widely read.

STAPLEDON, (William) Olaf
(1886–1950)
English science-fiction writer and social philosopher. He was born and raised in Wallasey, Cheshire, educated at Balliol College, Oxford, and took a doctorate at Liverpool University. During World War I, he served with the Friends' Ambulance Unit, and much of his writing, fictional and otherwise, is merely a vehicle for ideas about pacifism and social meliorism. Stapledon worked as a teacher, headmaster, shipping clerk with the Merseyside-based Holt Co, and as a Workers' Educational Association lecturer. His first novel, *Last and First Men* (1930), was 'a story of the near and far future', expressing his conviction that human survival depended on disarmament, the maintenance of peace and the rational management of social ills. It was followed by *Last Men in London* (1932) and by the underrated *Odd John* (1935) and *Starmaker* (1937). With **Norman Mailer** and the composer Shostakovitch, Stapledon spoke at the communist-fronted Waldorf Peace Conference in New York in 1946. A more discursive version of his philosophy can be found in *A Modern Theory of Ethics* (1929), which anticipated much of his better-known later work.
▷L A Fiedler, *Olaf Stapledon: A Man Divided* (1988)

STARING, Antonie Christiaan Wynand
(1747–1840)
Dutch poet, born in Gendringen who, living in an age of mostly florid rhetoric, provided a new example. His poetry was at first in the sentimental style of his age; then, under the influence of **Feith** and **Huygens**, he started to write in a new, terse manner. He wrote both narrative poems and a few starkly observed nature lyrics. **Potgieter** wrote illuminatingly

about him in his *Kritische Studien* (1875, 'Critical Studies').

STARK, Dame Freya Madeline
(1893–1993)
English writer and traveller, born in Paris. She spent her childhood in England and Italy, and attended Bedford College, London University, under the tutelage of W P Ker, Professor of Literature. She was a nurse on the Italian front during World War I, and afterwards studied Arabic at the School of Oriental and African Studies, London University, and was invited to Baghdad by the Prime Minister. There she worked on the *Baghdad Times*, followed the crusader routes and mapped the Valley of the Assassins in Luristan, described in *Valley of the Assassins* (1934). During World War II she worked for the Ministry of Information in Aden and Cairo, and was personal assistant to Lady Wavell, describing her experiences in *West is East* (1945). She travelled extensively, financed by her writings, in Europe, Asia and the Middle East. She produced more than 30 titles, including *The Southern Gates of Arabia* (1938), *Traveller's Prelude* (1950), *Beyond Euphrates* (1951), *The Coast of Incense* (1953), *Dust in the Lion's Paw* (1961) and *The Journey's Echo* (1963).

STATIUS, Publius Papinius
(c.45–96)
Roman poet, born in Naples, the son of a school-teacher. He won a poetry prize in Naples, and went to Rome, where he flourished as a court poet and a brilliant improviser in the favour of Domitian until 94, when he retired to Naples. His major work was the *Thebaïs*, an epic in 12 books on the struggle between the brothers Eteocles and Polynices of Thebes. Of another epic, the *Achilleïs*, only a fragment remains. His *Silvae*, or occasional verses, have freshness and vigour.
▷H E Butler, *Post Augustan Poetry* (1909)

STEAD, Christina Ellen
(1902–83)
Australian novelist, born in Rockdale, Sydney, the daughter of David George Stead, a leading English naturalist and writer. She trained as a teacher, but in 1928 left Australia for Europe, where she lived in London and Paris, working as a secretary in a Paris bank (1930–5). She went to live in Spain but left at the outbreak of war and, with her banker husband, settled in the USA. From 1943 to 1944 she was an instructor at the Workshop in the Novel at New York University, and in 1943 became a senior writer for M-G-M in Hollywood. *The Salzburg Tales*, her first collection of stories, was published in 1934, but

it was *Seven Poor Men of Sydney* (1934) which attracted attention, with its interweaving of dissimilar but casually connected lives. Her own experience was used to good effect in *House of All Nations* (1938), a critical look at the world of big finance, and her auto-biographical novel, *The Man Who Loved Children* (1940), describes suffocating family life under an egoistical father. Her later novels of suburban American and European life were less successful. In all she published 11 novels, including *A Little Tea, A Little Chat* (1948), *The People with the Dogs* (1952), *Cotter's England* (1956) and *Miss Herbert (The Suburban Wife)* (1976). The author of several novellas and the contributor of many short stories to the *New Yorker*, she left the USA in 1947 and settled in England, but finally returned to her homeland in 1974, in which year she was the first winner of the **Patrick White** Literary Award. *I'm Dying Laughing*, a novel begun in the 1940s and ridiculing American Hollywood radicals, was published posthumously in 1986.

▷ R G Geering, *Christina Stead* (1969)

STEAD, C(hristian) K(arlson)
(1932–)

New Zealand poet, critic and novelist, probably still better known for his pioneering study of literary modernism, *The New Poetic: Yeats to Eliot* (1964), than for his verse. He was born and educated in Auckland, where he returned as Professor of English in 1969. His poetry appeared in book form relatively late; *Whether the Will is Free* (1964) gathered work from the mid-50s onwards. It was followed by a novel, *Smith's Dream* (1971), and further verse collections: *Crossing the Bar* (1972), *Quesada* (1975) and *Walking Westward* (1979). The last of these introduced her interest in 'Open Form', which draws on some aspects of American Objectivism in an attempt to make the poem experiential rather than iconic, following the internal logic of the events described. In 1984 Stead published a second novel, *All Visitors Ashore*, which explores the psychology of living and writing on the opposite side of the globe from Europe.

STEDMAN, Edmund Clarence
(1833–1908)

American poet, critic and financier, born in Hartford, Connecticut. He studied at Yale, was war correspondent of the *New York World* (1861–3), and then became a New York stockbroker and banker. He published *Poems* (1860), *Victorian Poets* (1875), *Edgar Allan Poe* (1880), *Poets of America* (1886), *Nature of Poetry* (1892), *Victorian Anthology* (1896), and other works. He also co-edited an important *Library of American Literature*, issued in 11 volumes between 1888 and 1890, which was a significant taste-maker and may have affected early modernist writers.

STEELE, Sir Richard
(1672–1729)

Irish essayist, dramatist and politician, born in Dublin. He was educated at Charterhouse, where **Joseph Addison** was a contemporary, and Merton College, Oxford, after which he entered the army as a cadet in the Life Guards. Reacting against military life, he wrote *The Christian Hero* (1701), to show that the gentlemanly virtues can be practised only on a Christian basis. He next wrote three comedies, *The Funeral, or Grief à la mode* (1702), *The Tender Husband* (1703) and *The Lying Lover* (1704). In 1706 he became gentleman waiter to Prince George of Denmark, and in 1707 Robert Harley (Earl of Oxford) appointed him gazetteer. Steele's first venture in periodical literature, *The Tatler*, ran from 1709 to 1711 and was published on Tuesdays, Thursdays and Saturdays to suit the outgoing post-coaches. Its predecessor was **Daniel Defoe**'s *Review*, and like the *Review* included items of current news, but after No. 83 it concentrated on social and moral essays, with occasional articles on literature, usually written by Addison who had joined forces with Steele on issue No. 18. The chief fare, however, was social comedy, which covered the affectations and vices of society. These were exposed by humorous satire, with the aim of putting the Christian at ease in society. Christianity was to become fashionable and to this end—for formal preaching was unpalatable—a wealth of concrete social situations and types was created, including coffee-house politicians, 'pretty fellows', pedants and bores at every level of society. The coffee houses and chocolate houses provided most of these types, but society women and the family were the theme of many of the articles, for Steele's plea in *The Christian Hero* for a more chivalrous attitude to women implied the correction of female frivolity in high places and the insistence on the family as the source of genuine happiness. Steele is perhaps at his best in scenes of domestic felicity (cf Nos 95, 104 and 150), and these contain the intrusion of bourgeois sentiment and morality which was to be the mark of the age, in contrast to the aristocratic ethos of the Restoration. The beginnings of the domestic novel are here, not only in the relations between the pseudonymous editor, Isaac Bickerstaff, and his half-sister Jennie, but in numerous conversation pieces and in the social context provided by the Trumpet Club, forerunner of the more famous Spectator Club which Steele first outlined in No. 2 of that periodical, though Addison wrote most

of the articles. In 1713 Steele entered parliament, but was expelled the following year on account of a pamphlet, *The Crisis*, written in favour of the house of Hanover, a cause to which his periodical *The Englishman* was also devoted. He was rewarded on the succession of George I with the appointment of supervisor of Drury Lane theatre, and a knighthood followed. In 1718 a difference on constitutional procedure led to an estrangement from Addison, who was in the ministry, and loss of his office. In 1722 financial troubles made him retire to Wales, where he lived until his death. His letters to his wife ('dearest Prue'), whom he married in 1707, attest the sincerity of his sermons on married love.
▷R P Bond, *The Tatler* (1972)

STEELE, Wilbur Daniel
(1886–1970)

American short-story writer, novelist and playwright, born in North Carolina. Sometimes derided as a middle-brow writer, his short fiction, most often set in either Carolina or New England, is ingeniously plotted. *How Beautiful with Shoes*, dramatized in association with Anthony Brown in 1935, is the story of a southern beauty kidnapped by a maniac. She persuades her abductor that she is Mary, he is Jesus, and so she is his mother. He goes to sleep at her feet and is captured. *The Best Short Stories of Wilbur Daniel Steele* (1946) drew from four earlier collections.

STEEN, Marguerite
(1894–1975)

English writer, born in Liverpool, who began as a dancer and actress before writing a succession of quite popular, capably written, but essentially superficial novels such as *Gilt Cage* (1927). She wrote a life of William Nicolson (1943), whose companion she had been. Her most successful novel was *The Sun is my Undoing* (1941). Her work is now largely forgotten.

STEFÁNSSON, Davið
(1895–1964)

Icelandic poet, born in Fagriskógur, Eyjafjörður. Educated in Akureyri and Reykjavík, he worked as a librarian in Akureyri (1925–52). He became the most popular Romantic poet of his time with a series of volumes of lyrical poetry, starting with *Svartar fjaðrir* (1919, 'Black Feathers') and including *Kveðjur* (1924, 'Greetings'), *Í byggðum* (1933, 'In Human Habitations') and *Aðnorðran* (1936, 'From the North'). He also wrote a historical novel, *Sólon Islandus* (2 vols, 1940), and a successful play, *Gullna Hliðið* (1941, 'The Golden Gate').

▷E Heage, introduction to *The Golden Gate* (1967)

STEFANYK, Vasyl
(1871–1936)

Ukrainian poet and story writer, born in the small village of Rusiv. He is generally taken to have been Ukraine's greatest short-story writer, but the Soviets discouraged praise of him because of what they considered to be his lack of political commitment. His outstanding collection is *Kaminny khrest* (1900, Eng trans *The Stone Cross*, 1971). His style is laconic, often making use of local dialect, and his tales rarely exceed a few pages in length.
▷D S Struk, *A Study of Vasyl Stefanyk* (1973)

STEGNER, Wallace Earle
(1909–93)

American novelist and short-story writer. He was born in Lake Mills, Iowa, and educated there, in Utah and California. He worked on various campuses around the country, publishing his first novel, *Remembering Laughter* (1937), while teaching in Wisconsin. His fiction is largely concerned with life in the rural Mid-West and he has written various non-fiction accounts of American life and landscape; the best known is *Wolf Willow* (1962). Other novels include *On a Darkling Plain* (1940), *The Big Rock Candy Mountain* (1943), *Second Growth* (1947) and *A Shooting Star* (1961). The best of the short stories are in *The Women on the Wall* (1950). Stegner returned to form in the 1970s and won the Pulitzer Prize for *Angle of Repose* (1971).
▷F G and M G Robinson, *Wallace Stegner* (1977)

STEIN, Gertrude
(1874–1946)

American writer, born in Allegheny, Pennsylvania. She spent her early years in Vienna, Paris and San Francisco, and then studied psychology at Radcliffe College under William James, and medicine at Johns Hopkins University, but settled in Paris, where she was absorbed into the world of experimental art and letters. She sometimes attempted to apply the theories of abstract painting to her own writing, which led to a magnified reputation for obscurity and meaningless repetition. From 1907 she shared an apartment with a close friend from San Francisco, Alice B Toklas. Her influence on contemporary artists—particularly Picasso—is probably less than she imagined, though her collection of pictures was representative of the best of its era. Her first book, *Three Lives* (1908), reveals a sensitive ear for speech rhythms, and by far the larger part of her work is immediately comprehensible. The prose of *Tender Buttons* (1914) is repetitive, canonic and extremely musical. *The Making of Americans* (1925) is a vast, virtually unreadable family saga. She took a more ironic stance in the playfully titled *The Autobiography of Alice B. Toklas* (1933) and *Everybody's Autobiography* (1937). *Four Saints in Three Acts* (1934) and *The Mother Of Us All* (1947) were operas with music by Virgil Thomson. She stayed in Germany in the village of Chloz during World War II, and afterwards wrote *Wars I Have Seen* (1945) and the novel, *Brewsie and Willie* (1946), about the liberation by American soldiers.

▷J Hobhouse, *Everybody Who Was Anybody: a biography of Gertrude Stein* (1975)

STEINARR, Steinn, pseud of Aðalsteinn Kristmundsson
(1908–58)

Icelandic poet, born in Nauteyrarhreppur, north Iceland. A pioneer of Modernist poetry in Iceland, he moved to Reykjavík and joined the Communist Party as a young man. He wrote poetry of tremendous skill and sensibility which became progressively more abstract and metaphysical. His chief works were *Rauður loginn brann* (1934, 'The Red Flame Burned'), *Spor í sandi* (1940, 'Tracks in the Sand'), *Ferð án fyrirheits* (1942, 'Journey without Promise'), and his final masterpiece, *Tíminn og vatnið* (1948, 'Time and Water').

STEINBECK, John Ernest
(1902–68)

American novelist, winner of the Nobel Prize for literature, born in Salinas, California. He studied marine biology at Stanford University and worked as an agricultural labourer and semi-skilled technician, writing steadily. *Tortilla Flat* (1935), his first novel of repute, is a faithful picture of the shifting *paisanos* of California, foreshadowing the solidarity which characterizes his major work, *The Grapes of Wrath* (1939), a study of the poor in the face of disaster and threatened disintegration. His journalistic grasp of significant detail and pictorial essence make this book a powerful plea for consideration of human values and common justice. It led to much-needed reform, and won for Steinbeck the 1940 Pulitzer Prize. His other works include *In Dubious Battle* (1935), *Of Mice and Men* (1937), *The Moon is Down* (1942), *East of Eden* (1952) and *Winter of our Discontent* (1961), as well as the light-hearted and humorous *Cannery Row* (1945), *The Wayward Bus* (1942) and *The Short Reign of Pippin IV* (1957). He won the Nobel Prize for literature in 1962, a testament to his currently undervalued liberal humanism and generous solidarities.

▷E Steinbeck and R Wallsten (eds), *John Steinbeck: A Life in Letters* (1975); J Parini, *John Steinbeck: A Biography* (1994)

STEINER, Rudolph
(1861–1925)

German thinker who created the movement called Anthroposophy ('wisdom about man'). This, initially inferred from his understanding of the ideas of **Goethe**, but also drawing upon Eastern religions, particularly Indian, is based upon what Steiner called 'supersensible perception'. Anthroposophists believe that human consciousness is in a process of continual evolution. Anthroposophy has been greatly, and on the whole ignorantly, ridiculed. But although some of its precepts—such as reincarnation—are hard for many Western minds to grasp, and it is certainly hard to follow Steiner's own complex and ill-written expositions, it has also been very successfully influential in the realms of music, education (there are many Steiner schools in Great Britain, the USA and other countries) and farming. More to the point here, it has had a subtle effect on 20th-century literature. Not all the writers who have been influenced by it, or by aspects of it, have admitted to it, but two who did are the Russian **Andrei Bely** and the Italian **Arturo Onofri**; both of these, in particular Bely, were influential in their own right. It has many Gnostic features in common with the ideas of **Gurdjieff** and Ouspensky; **Jung** was not unsympathetic to it.

▷*Knowledge of the Higher Worlds* (1923)

STENDHAL, pseud of Henri Marie Beyle
(1783–1842)

French novelist, born in Grenoble, where he was educated at the École Centrale. During a Bohemian youth he wrote for the theatre but his plays are poorly constructed and stiff. A cousin offered him a post in the Ministry of War, and from 1800 he followed Napoleon's campaigns in Italy, Germany, Russia and Austria. Between wars he spent his time in Paris drawing-rooms and theatres. When Napoleon fell he retired to Italy, adopted his pseudonym, and began to write books on Italian painting (*Histoire de la Peinture en Italie*, 1817), on Haydn and Mozart, and travels in Italy (*Rome, Naples et Florence en 1817*, Eng trans *Rome, Naples and Florence*, 1818), as well as copious journalism. In 1821 the Austrian police expelled him from the country, and on his return to Paris he completed his book *De l'Amour* (1822, Eng trans *On Love*, 1928). After the 1830 revolution he was appointed Consul at Trieste and Civitavecchia, but his health deteriorated and he returned to Paris where he started a biography of Napoleon. His recognized masterpieces, *Le Rouge et le Noir* (1830, Eng trans

Red and Black, 1900; better known as *Scarlet and Black*, the title of a 1938 translation), and *La Chartreuse de Parme* (1839, Eng trans 1895), were published in 1830 and 1839 respectively. The first follows the rise and decline of Julien Sorel, a provincial youth in the France of the Restoration who can be relied on to make a drama out of a crisis. The second details the fortunes of Fabrice del Dongo at an insignificant Italian court during the same period. Though seminal French novels of the 19th century, neither received great understanding during his lifetime. Among his other novels are *Armance* (1822, Eng trans 1895) and *L'Abbesse de Castro* (1839, 'The Abbess of Castro'). *Lucien Leuwen* (1894, Eng trans 1951) and *Lamiel* (1889, Eng trans 1951), both unfinished, were published posthumously. Autobiographical volumes include his *Journal* (1888, selections translated as *Private Diaries*, 1955), *La Vie de Henri Brulard* (1890, Eng trans *The Life of Henry Brulard*, 1925) and *Souvenirs d'égotisme* (1892, Eng trans *Memoirs of an Egotist*, 1949).

STEPHANSSON, Stephan G, originally **Stefán Guðmundarson**
(1853–1927)

Icelandic-born Canadian poet, born in Kirkjuhóll in Skagafjörður. He emigrated with his family to North America in 1873, and worked as a railroad labourer and farmhand in Wisconsin before settling in Markerville, Alberta, as a farmer in 1889. There he raised a large family, took a prominent part in local affairs, and in the evenings composed several volumes of poetry in Icelandic, including *Úti á viðavangi* (1894, 'Out in the Open'), *Á ferð og flugi* (1900, 'En route'), and his major work, *Andvökur* (6 vols, 1909–38, 'Wakeful Nights'). A lifelong socialist, he expressed his horror of war in a controversial volume, *Vígslóði* (1920, 'The War Trail'). Recognized as one of the finest of Icelandic poets, his works also give a vivid picture of landscapes and conditions in western Canada.
▷ S Nordal, *Stephan Stephansson* (1959)

STEPHENS, James
(1882–1950)

Irish poet, born in Dublin. Sent to an orphanage as a child, he found work as a solicitor's clerk. His first published work was a volume of poems, *Insurrections* (1909), followed by his first novel, *The Charwoman's Daughter* (1912). *The Crock of Gold* (1912), a prose fantasy, made him famous, and turned him into a full-time writer. His later volumes were *Songs from the Clay* (1914), *The Demi-Gods* (1914), *Reincarnation* (1917) and *Deirdre* (1923). He moved to London in 1924. His

Collected Poems was first published in 1926, and revised in 1954.
▷ H Pyle, *James Stephens, writings and an account of his life* (1968)

STEPHENS, Meic
(1938–)

Welsh poet and editor, born in Treforest, near Pontypridd, Glamorgan and educated at the universities of Wales and Rennes. He founded *Poetry Wales* in 1965; his poetry collections include *Exiles All* (1973). He compiled and edited *The Oxford Companion to the Literature of Wales* in both Welsh and English (1986), edited the second edition of the *Oxford Illustrated Literary Guide to Great Britain and Ireland* (1992), and is co-editor of the *Writers of Wales* series (1970–), which comprises of 80 volumes. He was literature director of the Welsh Arts Council from 1967 to 1990.

STERLING, George
(1869–1926)

American poet, said to be the 'original' for the character of Russ Brissenden in **Jack London**'s *Martin Eden*. Sterling was a noted Bohemian. Born in New York he went out to the West Coast where the arch-stylist **Ambrose Bierce** took him under his wing. Sterling's poems, which he always submitted firstly to Bierce, for the master's approval, were exotic and rhythmical. Collections include *A Wine of Wizardry* (1909) and *The House of Orchids* (1911). Like his fictional counterpart, Sterling committed suicide.

STERLING, John
(1806–44)

Scottish writer, born at Kames Castle on the Island of Bute. Educated at Glasgow University and Trinity College, Cambridge, he turned to writing, and in 1828 bought the literary magazine, *The Athenaeum*, which he edited. He published numerous essays and long poems, and a novel, *Arthur Coningsby* (1833). He is best known as the subject of **Thomas Carlyle**'s *Life of John Sterling* (1851).

STERN, Gladys
(1890–1973)

English novelist, born in London, who was educated at English, German and Swiss schools and the Royal Academy of Dramatic Art. Brought up in the Jewish faith, she converted to Roman Catholicism after World War II. In 1914, at the outbreak of World War I, she published her first novel, *Pantomime*, although she is remembered now for her series of five semi-autobiographical novels tracing the fortunes of the Rakonitz family. The first, *Tents of Israel*, appeared in 1924, and the last, *The Young Matriarch*, 18 years later in 1942. The most memorable character, Toni, is a determined woman with a fierce sense of family tradition and independence, who builds a successful business empire which she refuses to relinquish for marriage, something she sees as ephemeral. Of her five-volume series of autobiography (1941–56), most notable are *All In Good Time* (1954) and *The Way it Worked Out* (1956).

STERN, Richard Gustave
(1928–)

American novelist and short-story writer, born in New York, long-time Professor of English at Chicago University. Stern's fiction is told in a spare, uninvolved fashion. His short stories *are* short, his novels concise. The most memorable of his books remains the first: *Golk* (1960) featured a comic adult character who sits, eats and sleeps in front of the TV. Stern has enjoyed various encounters with other writers. His correspondence with **Flannery O'Connor** appears in *The Habit of Being*, her collected letters, and *Stitch* (1965) resulted from a meeting with **Ezra Pound**.

STERNE, Laurence
(1713–68)

Irish novelist, born in Clonmel, County Tipperary, the son of an impoverished infantry ensign who died when the boy was two. His early youth was a struggle. In 1724 he was sent to Halifax Grammar School in Yorkshire and, seven years later, to Jesus College, Cambridge. In 1738 he was ordained, and appointed to the living of Sutton-on-the-Forest and made a prebendary of York, where his great-grandfather had been archbishop. In 1758 his marriage failed and his wife was committed to a lunatic asylum. In 1759 he wrote *The History of a Good Warm Watchcoat* (not published until after his death), and also the first two volumes of *The Life and Opinions of Tristram Shandy*, first published in York, but published anew in London in 1760. The public welcomed it; and in April **Robert Dodsley** brought out a second edition. This was followed by *Sermons* of the 'Rev. Mr Yorick'. In 1761, vols III and IV of *Tristram* came out, Sterne having meanwhile moved to Coxwold, thenceforward his infrequent home. Between 1761 and 1767 the rest of *Tristram* appeared; Sterne, whose health was now failing, was spending much of his time in France and Italy. *A Sentimental Journey through France and Italy* appeared in 1768; and the author died in London of pleurisy. Few writers have displayed such mastery over every form of humour both in situation and in character, a humour at times coming near to that of his acknowledged master **Cervantes**.

Yet the wild eccentricity of his manner and arrangement—a deliberate and usually successful bid for laughter—was also the convenient cloak for what some, such as **Oliver Goldsmith**, might call a singularly slipshod literary style. His indecencies, less gross than those of **Jonathan Swift** or **François Rabelais**, are all too prurient. He was unscrupulous in his borrowings. His pathos too often takes the form of overstrained sentimentalism. Yet this very sentimentalism was also his strength. For Sterne's great contribution to the development of the novel was to widen its scope and loosen its structure; and in his hands it became the channel for the utterance of the writer's own sentiments. His *Letters from Yorick to Eliza* (1775–9) contained his correspondence with a young married woman to whom he was devoted.
▷W C Cross, *Life and Times of Laurence Sterne* (1909–25)

STERNHEIM, Carl
(1878–1942)

German playwright and novelist, born in Leipzig. He was enjoying huge popularity during the 1920s, only to have his aggressive, cynical, debunking plays prohibited when the Nazis came to power. Sternheim excelled at satire, poking fun at the bourgeoisie in such plays as *Die Hose* (1911, 'The Knickers'), in which a woman loses her knickers in an embarrassing situation. The 'indelicacy' of the play caused a minor sensation when it was first produced. Other plays include *Burger Schippel* (1913), a caustic farce about a lowly plumber, who becomes a member of a bourgeois singing group and accumulates bourgeois ideals in the process.

STEVENS, Wallace
(1879–1955)

American poet, born in Reading, Pennsylvania. His father, of Dutch descent, was a lawyer for the Reading Hardware Company and wrote poetry. His education began at private schools, then schools attached to Lutheran churches and later Reading Boys' High School. He enrolled at Harvard (1897–1900) and afterwards went to New York where he started out in journalism but was neither successful nor happy. He entered New York Law School in 1901 and at the age of 28 began working for various law firms, ultimately becoming a diligent executive with an insurance company in Hartford, Connecticut. Poetry was a spare-time activity, and his first collection, *Harmonium*, was not published until 1923. His poetic career falls into three phases: 1898–1900, 1907–24 and 1928–55. Most of his early work, both poems and short stories, was published in *The Harvard Advocate*. In 1907 he began composing poems for Elsie Moll, his future wife. It was from the late 1920s to the middle 1950s, however, that he published the work that has established him as one of the century's great poets: *Ideas of Order* (1936), *The Man With the Blue Guitar* (1937), *Parts of a World* (1942), *Transport to Summer* (1947) and *The Auroras of Autumn* (1950). *Collected Poems* was published in 1954. Critics invariably point out the great influence of the French Symbolist movement, but he drew from many sources and his poems range over an extraordinary variety of subjects. His constant theme was the exploration of aesthetic experience as the key to fundamental reality.

▷G Lensing, *Wallace Stevens: a poet's growth* (1986)

STEVENSON, Anne Katherine
(1933–)

English poet, critic and biographer, born in Cambridge. She was educated in the USA, where she lived for several years, resulting in a volume of poetry, *Living in America* (1965). Returning to Britain, she published her second collection, *Reversals* (1969). Other volumes include *Travelling Behind Glass* (1974), *Enough of Green* (1977) and *Selected Poems* (1987). Her poetry is personal, elegiac, emotionally honest, and reflects the sense of the landscape of wherever she happens to be living at the time of writing, be it the Sierra Nevada (*Reversals*) or the north-east coast of Scotland (*Enough of Green*). Her authorized biography of **Sylvia Plath**, *Bitter Fame*, was published in 1989.

STEVENSON, Robert Louis Balfour
(1850–94)

Scottish author, born in Edinburgh, grandson of the engineer Robert Stevenson and son of Thomas Stevenson, engineer to the Board of Northern Lighthouses. A constant invalid in childhood, he was educated at The Edinburgh Academy (1861–3) before his ill-health forced the family to travel abroad. He studied engineering at Edinburgh University for a session (1867) with a view to the family calling, but transferred to law, becoming an advocate in 1875. His true inclination, however, was for writing. He collaborated in four mediocre plays, but for the next few years he travelled, mainly in France. His *Inland Voyage* (1878) describes a canoe tour in Belgium and northern France, and his *Travels with a Donkey in the Cevennes* describes a tour undertaken in the same year. In 1876 he was at Fontainebleau (which he made the subject of travel sketches), and it was at the neighbouring Grez that he met Fanny Osbourne, née Vandegrift (1840–1914), an

American separated from her husband. He followed her to America and they married in 1880, after her divorce. His return to Europe with his wife and stepson Lloyd Osbourne marked the beginning of a struggle against tuberculosis which his natural gaiety as a writer conceals. His wife and stepson have described their makeshift homes—Davos, Pitlochry and elsewhere—yet despite difficult circumstances he was 'making himself' as a writer not only of travel sketches but also of essays and short stories which found their way into magazines. *Thrawn Janet*, a story in the vernacular, appeared in *Cornhill Magazine* (1881), although an earlier tale, *An Old Song*, appeared in 1877 and was then lost until it was located and republished in 1982. *The Merry Men* was published serially in 1882, the same year as *The New Arabian Nights*. *Treasure Island*, the perfect romantic thriller, brought him fame in 1883 and his most successful adventure story, *Kidnapped*, appeared in 1886. *Catriona* (1893), introducing the love element, was also very popular. *The Master of Ballantrae* (1889) is a study in evil of a sort not uncommon in Scottish fiction, but also includes the wildest adventures. *The Strange Case of Dr Jekyll and Mr Hyde* (1886) is not a romance, but it further illustrates Stevenson's metaphysical interest in evil. *The Black Arrow* (1888) is of a rather lower quality, but *Weir of Hermiston* (published posthumously in 1896), though unfinished, is acclaimed by some as his masterpiece, its scope larger, and the issues involved more serious. *St Ives*, which was also left unfinished, was completed by Sir **Arthur Quiller Couch** in 1897. Stevenson's work as an essayist is seen at its best in *Virginibus Puerisque* (1881) and *Familiar Studies of Men and Books* (1882). *A Child's Garden of Verses* (1885) is not poetry in the adult sense, but it is one of the best recollections of childhood in verse. *Underwoods* (1887) illustrates his predilection for preaching in prose or verse; here the poetry is of the good talker rather than the singer, and the tone is usually nostalgic. Only occasionally, as in *The Woodman*, does he touch on metaphysical problems, but vernacular poems such as *A Lowden Sabbath Morn* subtly describe the Calvinism he had renounced but which intrigued him to the end. In 1889 Stevenson settled in Samoa and there with his devoted wife and stepson he spent the last five years of his life on his estate of Vailima, which gives its name to the incomparable series of letters, written to his friend Sidney Colvin. His experiences in the South Seas gave rise to two important long stories, 'The Beach of Falesá' (1893) and 'The Ebb-Tide' (1894), both of which indict European colonialism.

▷J C Furnas, *Voyage to Windward* (1950)

STEVENSON, William
(d.1575)

English scholar. He entered Christ's College, Cambridge, in 1546, and became a fellow; he is known to have staged plays there. He was probably the author of the earliest surviving English comedy, *Gammer Gurton's Needle* (1553), sometimes attributed to John Still or John Bridges.
▷F P Wilson, *English Drama, 1485–1585* (1969)

STEWART, Douglas Alexander
(1913–85)

New Zealand-born Australian author, born in Eltham, Taranaki, and educated at the Victoria University College. For 40 years he was at the forefront of Australian writing, first as assistant and then, from 1940 to 1961, as editor of the 'Red Page' in the *Bulletin* magazine. Stewart then became literary editor for the old-established Australian publishing house of Angus & Robertson, a position which he held until his retirement in 1971. His early books of lyric verse—*Green Lions* (1936) and *The White Cry* (1939)—evoke his homeland; his first Australian verse was in *The Dosser in Springtime* (1946) in which he began to use ballad form, later put to dramatic effect in a sequence on the infamous Scottish Massacre at *Glencoe* (1947). His verse drama *Fire in the Snow* (1939), on Scott's ill-fated Antarctic expedition, is a classic of radio drama. *Back of Beyond* (1954) and *The Birdsville Track* (1955) re-create his visual impressions of the life of the rugged interior. His last verse was in *Rutherford* (1962), the title poem addressed to his compatriot the New Zealand atomic scientist. *Selected Poems* was published in 1963 (rev edn 1973) and *Collected Poems 1936–1967* in 1967. He edited a number of anthologies including *Modern Australian Verse* (1964) and, with Nancy Keesing, two collections of bush ballads (1955–7). Biographies include *Norman Lindsay, a Personal Memoir* (1975) and *A Man of Sydney, an Appreciation of Kenneth Slessor* (1977).
▷ *Springtime in Taranaki* (1983); J McAuley, in *The Literature of Australia* (1964, ed G Dalton)

STEWART, George R(ippey)
(1895–1980)

American novelist, biographer and historian of the American West. Stewart's *Names on the Land* (1945) is the standard work on American place-names. His study of the westward overland route, *The California Trail* (1962), is a good example of his skill as a popularizer of history and scholarly information. His fiction is orthodox in style. *Doctor's Oral* (1939) tells the nerve-racking story of a graduate having to undergo an oral exam. *Storm* (1941) is a novelistic treatment of a weather system's journey across the States from the West coast to the East. Stewart held academic posts at Columbia, Michigan and Berkeley, and wrote a biography of **Bret Harte** (1931).

STEWART, Harold
(1916–)

Australian poet and orientalist, born in Drummoyne, Sydney, latterly resident in Japan. His first poems in *Phoenix Wings: Poems 1940–46* (1948) and *Orpheus and Other Poems* (1956) showed the considerable influence of Buddhist and Taoist culture. He has published two popular collections of translations of Japanese *haiku*, *A Net of Fireflies* (1960) and *A Chime of Windbells* (1969), but *By the Old Walls of Kyoto: A Yearly Cycle of Landscape Poems* (1979) is a more ambitious essay which, in a long narrative sequence, melds Japanese and western poetical traditions, illuminated by Stewart's own scholarly commentary.

STEWART, J(ohn) I(nnes) M(ackintosh), pseud Michael Innes
(1906–)

Scottish novelist and critic, born in Edinburgh. Educated at Edinburgh Academy and Oriel College, Oxford, he subsequently lectured at Leeds University, the University of Adelaide and Queen's University, Belfast. From 1969 to 1973 he was Reader in English Literature, Oxford University. The novels written under his own name are largely set in an academic and artistic milieu among the middle and upper classes. A prolific writer, he is best known in this vein for the so-called 'Pattullo' sequence, located in the sequestered world of the dons. *A Use of Riches* (1957) and *The Last Tresilians* (1963) are generally regarded as his most important works. As Michael Innes he has made an important contribution to the thriller genre. His range is remarkably wide, from intricate, locked-room type murders to large-scale crime intrigues. In his detectives, John Appleby, the gentleman turned policeman, and the formidable Inspector Cadover, he has created two memorable characters. Notable titles include *Hamlet, Revenge!* (1937), *Lament for a Makar* (1938) and *What Happened at Hazelwood?* (1946). He has also written works on **Kipling**, **Hardy**, **Joyce** and **Conrad**.

STEWART, Mary (Florence Elinor, Lady)
(1916–)

English romantic novelist, born in County Durham, and for several years a lecturer in English at Durham University. A popular and prolific novelist, she began writing her exotic love stories when complications during her first pregnancy left her unable to have children, and achieved instant success with *Madam, Will You Talk?* (1954) and such titles as *Nine Coaches Waiting* (1958) and *This Rough Magic* (1964). In the seventies she published a trilogy about Merlin, which began with *The Crystal Cave* (1970); she has also written several books for children, including *A Walk in Wolf Wood* (1980).

STICKNEY, (Joseph) Trumbull
(1874–1904)

American poet, born in Geneva. He spent his childhood in Europe. He was a brilliant scholar who, with **William Vaughn Moody**, tried to resuscitate verse drama in a manner which (the fragments he left suggest) anticipated later developments. His lyrical poetry is better accomplished and more sincerely felt than that of the majority of his contemporaries, but he did not live long enough to fulfil his promise, and high claims made for him by **James Reeves** and Séan Haldane are hardly justified. He died prematurely as a result of a brain tumour.
▷ S Haldane and J Reeves (eds), *Homage to Stickney* (1968); S Haldane, *The Fright of Time: Stickney* (1970); A B Whittle (ed), *The Poems* (1973)

STIERNHIELM, Georg, originally Olofsson
(1598–1672)

Swedish poet and linguist, known as the 'father of Swedish poetry'. He was elevated to the peerage with the name of Stiernhielm in 1631, and held various government appointments, including councillor of war (1663) and director of the college of antiquities (1667). He was the first Swedish poet to write in hexameters, in *Hercules* (1658), an epic allegorical poem about a young man at the crossroads of life. He helped to reform and purify the Swedish language by studying Old Norse literature and incorporating the old vocabulary into modern Swedish.
▷ B Swartling, *Georg Stiernhielm* (1909)

STIFTER, Adalbert
(1805–68)

Austrian novelist and painter, born in Oberplan, Bohemia. He studied at Vienna, and as private tutor to various aristocratic families had several unhappy love affairs. Deeply disturbed by the Revolution of 1848, he settled in Linz and became an official in the Ministry of Education. Unhappiness and illness terminated in suicide. His humanism, his love of traditional values and his belief in the greatness of life pervade the *Bildungsroman, Der Nachsommer* (1857, 'The Indian Summer'),

Witiko (1865–7), a heroic tale set in 12th-century Bohemia, and the short stories *Der Condor* (1840, Eng trans *The Condor*, 1946). He was also a considerable painter of city views. He wrote two collections of stories, *Studien* (1844–50, augmented 1855) and *Bunte Steine* (1853, Eng trans *Rock Crystal*, 1945).
▷ A Blackett, *Adalbert Stifter, a critical study* (1948)

STIRLING, William Alexander, 1st Earl of
(c.1567–1640)

Scottish poet and courtier, born in Alva, Clackmannanshire. A tutor of young noblemen, in 1613 he was attached to the household of Prince Charles (Charles I). He had already published a collection of songs and madrigals in *Aurora* (1604); in 1614 he published part one of his huge poem *Doomesday*, (part two, 1637). He received in 1621 the grant of 'Nova Scotia'—a vast tract in North America soon rendered valueless by French expansion. In 1631 he was made sole printer of King James VI and I's version of the Psalms. From 1626 until his death he was Secretary of State for Scotland. He was created Viscount (1630) and Earl of Stirling (1633), also Earl of Dovan (1639), but he died insolvent in London. His tragedies include *Darius* (1603), *Croesus* (1604), *The Alexandrean Tragedy* (1605) and *Julius Caesar* (1607).
▷ T H McGrail, *Sir William Alexander Stirling* (1940)

STIVENS, Dal(las George)
(1911–)

Australian writer, painter and amateur naturalist, born in Blayney, New South Wales, primarily known for his short stories which appeared in many anthologies and in eight collected volumes, of which the most representative is *Selected Stories 1936–1968* (1969). Stivens's love of the 'tall story' shows in *The Demon Bowler and other Cricket Stories* (1979). Five diverse novels include *A Horse of Air* (1970), an account of a dreamlike expedition into the central Australian desert in search of the mythical Night Parrot. Stivens received the **Patrick White** Literary Award in 1981.

STOCKTON, Frank R (Francis Richard)
(1834–1902)

American humorist and engraver, born in Philadelphia. He became assistant editor of *St Nicholas*, and first attracted notice by his stories for children. He is best known as author of *Rudder Grange* (1879). Later works include *The Lady, or the Tiger?* (1884), a teasing fairy tale still left unresolved in a sequel,

Mrs Cliff's Yacht (1896); *The Great Stone of Sardis* (1897) and *The Girl at Cobhurst* (1898).

▷M J Griffin, *Frank R Stockton: A Critical Biography* (1939)

STODDARD, Charles
(1843–1909)

American poet and travel writer, born in Rochester, New York. Because he attended college at Oakland he is often referred to as a Californian author. His travel book *South-Sea Idyls* (1873) became popular in Great Britain as well as in America, and influenced **Robert Louis Stevenson**, his friend, as well as starting a craze for Polynesia. His *Poems* (1867) were edited by **Bret Harte**. *A Troubled Heart* (1885) is the touching story of his conversion to Roman Catholicism. He was close to **Mark Twain**, and acted as his assistant.

STODDARD, Richard Henry
(1825–1903)

American poet and critic, born in Hingham, Massachusetts. He wrote literary reviews for New York periodicals from 1860. His poems include *Songs in Summer* (1857), *The Book of the East* (1867) and *Lion's Cub* (1891). *Under the Evening Lamp* (1893) and *Recollections* (1903) contain literary studies. His wife, Elizabeth Drew, née Barstow (1823–1902), was a novelist and poet.

STOKER, Bram, properly Abraham
(1847–1912)

Irish writer, born in Dublin. He was educated at Trinity College, Dublin, and studied law and science. He entered the civil service, but turned to literature, and partnered Henry Irving in running the Lyceum Theatre in London from 1878 to 1905. He wrote *Personal Reminiscences of Henry Irving* (1906). He is best remembered for the classic vampire story *Dracula* (1897), but wrote a number of other novels dealing with futuristic and occult themes, including *The Jewel of the Seven Stars* (1903), *The Lady of the Shroud* (1909) and *The Lair of the White Worm* (1911). *Dracula* has often been filmed, but usually with little accurate reference to the book.

STOLBERG, Christian, Count of
(1748–1821)

German poet, born in Hamburg. He was one of the Göttingen poet band and was in the public service of Holstein (1777–1800). Besides writing poems, he translated **Sophocles**.

▷E Schmidt, *Christian Stolberg* (1893)

STOLBERG, Friedrich Leopold, Count of
(1750–1819)

German poet, brother of **Christian Stolberg**. He was also a member of the Göttingen school, and was in the Danish service (1789–1800). Then turning Catholic, he published a history of Christianity. He produced poems, dramas and translations from the Greek.

ST OMER, Garth
(1931–)

West Indian novelist, born in Castries, St Lucia, who excels in reproducing the *patois* of his native island. His grim novel *J-, Black Bam and Marauders* (1972), set in St Lucia, impressed critics by its 'odour of decay'.

STONE, Irving, originally Irving Tennenbaum
(1903–89)

American popular novelist and playwright, born in San Francisco. He took his stepfather's name when his parents divorced and his mother remarried. He studied political science at the University of California at Berkeley, and worked as a saxophonist in a dance band. He wrote 25 books in all and is sometimes credited with having created the non-fiction novel. *Lust for Life* (1934), based on the life of Van Gogh, became a bestseller and did much to enhance the Dutch painter's reputation in the USA. *The Agony and the Ecstasy* (1961) fictionalizes the life of Michelangelo. He also wrote *Love Is Eternal* (1954), about Abraham Lincoln's wife; *Passions of the Mind* (1971), about **Sigmund Freud**; *The Origin* (1980), about Charles Darwin, and *Depths of Glory* (1985), about Camille Pissarro.

STONE, Louis, originally William Lewis Stone
(1871–1935)

English-born Australian novelist, born in Leicestershire, who migrated to Brisbane with his family in 1884. He is known mainly for his first book, *Jonah* (1911), which became a popular television series in 1982. He was one of the first to write of the town rather than the bush; his hero is the leader of a Sydney street gang who, through the help of Ma Yabsley, becomes a shopowner but fails to find fulfilment. His other novel, *Betty Wayside*, was serialized in 1914 but appeared the next year only in bowdlerized form; the passions of a lady pianist were not considered appropriate for the bookshops of the day.

STONE, Robert Anthony
(1937–)

American novelist, born in Brooklyn. *Dog Soldiers* (1974) has been Stone's most successful book to date. It tells of a Vietnam veteran involving his wife in heroin smuggling. Stone and Judith Rascoe turned it into a screenplay, filmed in the USA as *Who'll Stop The Rain?* (1978). *A Flag for Sunrise* (1982), set in a Latin-American country during a revolution, is a vehicle for political and philosophical views.

STOPPARD, Tom, originally Thomas Straussler
(1937–)

British dramatist, born in Zlin, Czechoslovakia. He went to England in 1946 from India, his mother having married a British army officer after being widowed in Singapore during World War II. The family settled in Bristol, and after attending schools in Nottingham and Yorkshire, Stoppard became a journalist in Bristol. In 1960 after his first play, *A Walk on the Water*, he went to London as a freelance journalist and theatre critic and wrote radio plays including *Albert's Bridge* (1967), *The Dissolution of Dominic Boot* and *M is for Moon Among Other Things* (both 1964). He made his name in 1967 with *Rosencrantz and Guildenstern are Dead* at the Edinburgh Festival, which then transferred to the National Theatre, having won the *Evening Standard* Award. Built around the two 'attendant lords' in **Shakespeare**'s *Hamlet*, the play hilariously examines the meaninglessness of life and questions the possibility of free will. His aim is a 'perfect marriage between the play of ideas and farce': *Jumpers*, commissioned in 1972 by the National Theatre, is a farcical satire of logical positivism, and *Travesties* (1974), written for the Royal Shakespeare Company, has **James Joyce**, Lenin and the Dadaist painter Tristan Zara, who all happened to be living in Zürich during World War I, working together on an amateur production of **Oscar Wilde**'s *The Importance of Being Earnest*. His other plays include *The Real Inspector Hound* (1968), *Dirty Linen* (1976), *Professional Foul* (1977, written for television and inspired by Amnesty International's Prisoner of Conscience Year), *Night and Day* (1978), *On the Razzle* (1981) and *The Real Thing* (1982). In 1977 he collaborated with André Previn on a 'play for actors and orchestra', *Every Good Boy Deserves Favour*, performed with the London Symphony Orchestra. He has also written a novel, *Lord Malaquist and Mr Moon* (1966), short stories, screenplays and film scripts, including *The Russian House* and *Billy Bathgate*. He was married for 20 years (until 1992) to Miriam Stoppard (1937–), a doctor and broadcaster specializing in child care and health.
▷M Billington, *Stoppard the Playwright* (1987)

STOREY, David Malcolm
(1933–)

English dramatist and novelist, born in Wakefield. An art student and professional Rugby League player, he made a hit with his novel, *This Sporting Life* (1960). His later novels include *Pasmore* (1972), *Saville* (1976) and *Present Times* (1984). His first play, *The Restoration of Arnold Middleton*, was staged at the Royal Court Theatre, London, in 1966. *In Celebration* (1969) was followed by *The Contractor* (1969), and *Home* (1970), a piece for four elderly characters who, it transpires, are the inmates of an asylum. *The Changing Room* (1971) deals with a rugby football team. Subsequent plays include *Cromwell* and *The Farm* (both 1973), and *Life Class* (1974), based on his experiences as an art student. *Mother's Day* (1976) and *Sisters* (1978) were premièred in Manchester, while *Early Days* (1980) and *The March on Russia* (1989) and *Stages* (1992) were put on at the National Theatre. He published a collection of poems, *Storey's Lives*, in 1992.
▷J R Taylor, *David Storey* (1974)

STORM, Theodor Woldsen
(1817–88)

German poet and story writer, born in Husum in Schleswig-Holstein. He was a magistrate and judge (1864–80), and had a wide circle of literary acquaintants and correspondents. His early writings are lyric poems, culminating in the cycle *Tiefe Schatten* (1865, 'Deep Shadows'), but he is remembered for his tales, characterized by a vivid, often eerie descriptive power.
▷G Storm, *Theodor Storm* (1912)

STORNI, Alfonsina
(1892–1938)

Argentinian feminist and poet, born in Switzerland. Starting young as an actress with a travelling theatrical company, she later became a teacher and journalist. Her poetry is largely concerned with love and sexual passion. Her books include *La inquietud del rosal* (1916, 'The Solicitude of the Rosebush'), *El dulce daño* (1918, 'Sweet Injury'), *Ocre* (1925, 'Ochre') and *Mascarillo y trébol* (1938). She committed suicide on discovering that she was suffering from cancer. An edition of her verse appeared in 1961.

STORY, William Wetmore
(1819–95)

American poet and sculptor, born in Salem, Massachusetts, son of Joseph Story. He practised law in Boston, but in 1856 settled in Rome and devoted himself to poetry and sculpture. His writings include *Poems*

(1847,1856,1886), *Roba di Roma* (1862), *Castle of St Angelo* (1877), *He and She* (1883), *Fiametta* (1885), *Excursions* (1891) and *A Poet's Portfolio* (1894).
▷H James, *William Wetmore Story and His Friends* (1903)

STOUT, Rex Todhunter
(1886–1975)
American detective-story writer, born in Noblesville, Indiana. Before becoming a writer he invented a school banking system that was installed in 400 cities throughout the USA. His great creation is Nero Wolfe, the phenomenally fat private eye who with the help of his confidential assistant, Archie Goodwin, got to the bottom of numerous mysteries, among them *The League of Frightened Men* (1935), *Black Orchids* (1942) and *A Family Affair* (1975).
▷J McAleer, *Rex Stout: a biography* (1977)

STOW, (Julian) Randolph
(1935–)
Australian novelist, poet and librettist. He was born in Geraldton, Western Australia, worked as an anthropologist in Australia and Papua New Guinea—which provided the background to *Visitants* (1979)—and subsequently taught at the universities of Adelaide, Leeds (UK) and Western Australia. His first novel was *A Haunted Land* (1956), followed by *The Bystander* (1957), which suggested his developing interest in the **Jung**ian unconscious and in visionary 'madness'. *Tourmaline* (1963) was an Australian version of **T S Eliot**'s *The Waste Land*. Perhaps his best novel is *The Merry-Go-Round in the Sea* (1965), which links such visions into recent history by contrasting the bitter 'experience' of a former POW with his innocent young cousin. In 1968 and 1969, while living in England, Stow wrote libretti for two music-theatre works by the composer Peter Maxwell Davies: *Eight Songs for a Mad King* and *Miss Donnithorne's Maggot*. Later novels include *The Girl Green as Elderflower* (1980) and *The Suburbs of Hell* (1984). *Midnite* (1967) is a notable book for children; Stow's verse is collected in *A Counterfeit Silence* (1969).
▷R Willbanks, *Randolph Stow* (1978)

STOWE, Harriet Elizabeth, née Beecher
(1811–96)
American novelist, daughter of Lyman Beecher, born in Litchfield, Connecticut. She was brought up with puritanical strictness and joined her sister Catherine Beecher at her Connecticut Female Seminary at Hartford in 1824. In 1836 she married the Rev Calvin Ellis Stowe, a theological professor at Lane

Seminary, with whom she settled at Brunswick, Maine in 1850. She contributed sketches of southern life to *Western Monthly Magazine*, and won a short-story competition with *A New England Sketch* (1834). She became famous for her *Uncle Tom's Cabin* (1852), prompted by the passing of the Fugitive Slave Law, which immediately focused anti-slavery sentiment in the North. Her second anti-slavery novel, *Dred* (1856), had a record sale in Britain, largely thanks to a review by **George Eliot**, but she lost her popularity with *Lady Byron Vindicated* (1870), although the charges made against **Byron** in the book were later proven. She wrote a host of other books, fiction, biography and children's books. Her best books deal with New England life, such as *The Minister's Wooing* (1859) and *Old Town Folks* (1869).
▷F Wilson, *Crusader in Crinoline* (1941)

STRACHEY, (Giles) Lytton
(1880–1932)
English biographer, born in London, the son of an Indian civil engineer and soldier. Educated at Leamington College and Liverpool University, where he read history, and Trinity College, Cambridge, he was a book reviewer for the *Spectator* (1904–14). He began his writing career as a critic with *Landmarks in French Literature* (1912), which shows clearly his affinities with **Charles Sainte-Beuve** and his francophile sympathies. He was a conscientious objector during World War I. *Eminent Victorians* (1918) was a literary bombshell, constituting, as it did, a vigorous, impertinent challenge to Victorian smug self-assurance. The irony, the mordant wit, the ruthless pinpointing of foible that was his method of evoking character, demolished stuffed legendary figures, and this book was a turning-point in the art of biography. After him, mere accumulation of facts (the product of conscientious hacks) could no longer be the accepted thing. Through Strachey, biography had become a literary genre. He followed up his success with *Queen Victoria* (1921), *Books and Characters, French and English* (1922), *Elizabeth and Essex: A Tragic History* (1928), *Portraits and Miniatures* (1931) and *Characters and Commentaries* (1933).
▷M Holroyd, *Lytton Strachey* (2 vols, 1967–8)

STRAMM, August
(1874–1915)
German poet and dramatist, born in Münster. He was by far the most radical, not to say strident, of the Expressionist group, and has even been called a 'Futurist'. He was killed on the Russian front while serving as a captain in the army. He was a leading contributor to the Expressionist magazine *Der Sturm*. His hectic

Schreidramen, 'scream-plays', less lasting and successful than his ceaselessly experimental war poetry, but important in the development of the European theatre, were in the 'telegraphic' style which he made his own. His terse poetry, equally staccato, but composed with great care, is still effective and moving. His play *Erwachen* (1915, 'Awakening') is translated in *Seven Expressionist Plays* (1968).
▷C Middleton and M Hamburger (eds), *Modern German Poetry 1910–1969* (1962)

STRAND, Mark
(1934–)

Canadian-born American poet and translator (of **Borges**'s *Texas*), born in Summerside, Prince Edward Island; he moved to America at the age of four. His spare verses are clearly mainly inspired from his reading of **Samuel Beckett**—who, however, as one of Strand's critics has declared, 'is of course the master' (of 'withholding information'). In his ambitious long poem 'The Untelling' Strand has, characteristically, written, 'Although I have tried to return, I have always/ended here, where I am now'. He was the United States Poet Laureate 1990–1.
▷*Selected Poems* (1980); D Kirby, *Mark Strand and the Poet's Place in Contemporary Culture* (1990)

STRAPAROLA, Giovan Francesco
(d.c.1557)

Italian novelist, born in Caravaggio. Between 1550 and 1554 he published *Piacevoli notti* (Eng trans *The Nights of Straparola*, 1894), a collection of 74 stories set on the island of Murano, in the style of the *Decameron*. Although relatively unsophisticated, they were popular throughout the 16th century.
▷G Boscardi, *Le Novelle di Giovan Francesco Straparola* (1952)

STRASHIMIROV, Anton
(1872–1937)

Bulgarian novelist and playwright. His work has often been characterized as somewhat spoiled by 'unruly' elements, or too 'rough' in style; but his unconventionality, and his tormented prose, are now due for reappraisal as more proto-expressionist than marred by academic improprieties. He has not been liked by all Bulgarians because he openly espoused the Macedonian cause, and even entered politics (1911) to do so. His most famous play is *Vampir* (1902, 'Vampire'). *Tvorchestvo i khivot* (1930, 'Creativity and Life') is one of the most interesting and informative of all Bulgarian biographies.
▷C Manning and R Smal-Stocki, *The History of Modern Bulgarian Literature* (1960)

STREATFEILD, (Mary) Noel
(1895–1986)

English children's author, born in Amberley, Sussex. She rebelled against her strict upbringing in a Victorian clergyman's family, becoming an actress and novelist and, with the massive success of her first children's book, *Ballet Shoes* (1936), established herself as the long-standing doyenne of children's writers. She followed this delightful backstage story of strong-willed child performers with further 'career' novels such as *Tennis Shoes* (1937), *The Painted Garden* (1949) and *White Boots* (1951). Perhaps her finest book, *The Circus is Coming* (1938), won the Carnegie Medal. Although the later work never surpassed her first successes, she continued to write popular and accomplished novels with sparky, believable characters.

STREUVELS, Stjin, pseud of Frank Lateur
(1871–1969)

Belgian (Flemish) novelist from Heule. He began as the baker for his village, but after 15 years took to writing, depicting the Flemish peasantry, it has been said, 'with the plastic power of a Breughel'. One of his novels, *Langs de wegen* (1902), was translated at the behest of **Ford Madox Ford**, as *Old Jan* (1936). **Willem Elsschot** also admired him, and under his real name of Alfons de Ridder wrote a book on him (1908). Streuvels' greatest novel, of major proportions, is the haunting and hallucinatory *Het leven en de dood in den ast* (1926, 'Life and Death in den ast'), in which two men have to keep a fire going in a chickory-drying house while a tramp dies.
▷A Denedts, *Stijn Streuvels* (1955)

STRIBLING, T(heodore) S(igismund)
(1881–1965)

American novelist, born in Clifton, Tennessee. Despite recent positive revaluation by Southern critics, Stribling is still an underestimated and neglected novelist, even though he gave inspiration to **Faulkner**. Like Faulkner, in his early life he wrote (for money and to attain freedom from wage-slavery) 'morally uplifting' tales for Sunday School readers, and pulp fiction. Although he never evolved a distinguished style—he could be pretentious—it is hard to see how he could have told his masterpiece, the trilogy consisting of *The Forge* (1931), *The Store* (1932) and *Unfinished Cathedral* (1934), the middle novel of which won him a Pulitzer Prize, other than in the way he did. This, which remains one of the most finely observed accounts of the ante-bellum South, tells the story of the rise of Miltaides Vaiden from poor man to rich landowner.

▷W Eckley, *Stribling* (1975)

STRINDBERG, (Johan) August
(1849–1912)

Swedish dramatist and novelist, born in Stockholm, considered the greatest writer of modern Sweden. After uncompleted studies at Uppsala University, he returned to Stockholm and worked as a private tutor, actor, journalist and librarian while attempting to begin his career as an author. He had a turbulent personal life, including three unsuccessful marriages and periods of severe persecution mania. He had a propensity for involvement in cultural and personal feuds and lived abroad for long periods, mainly in France and Italy. His first major play was *Mäster Olof* (1872), a historical drama—a genre he was to return to prolifically in the years around 1900 with, for instance, *Gustav Vasa* and *Erik XIV* (both 1899). His breakthrough came with a satirical novel about the art circles of Stockholm, *Röda rummet* (1879, 'The Red Room'), which created an uproar, but is regarded as marking both the arrival of the modern realistic novel in Sweden and that of the naturalist movement. His later naturalist novel *Hemsöborna* (1887, 'The People of Hemsö'), his sunniest work, has become a popular classic. Two collections of short stories, *Giftas I* and *II* (1884–6, 'Married'), put forward his ideas on marriage, women and emancipation. A small incident in the first volume led to his trial on a charge of blasphemy, of which he was acquitted. He then published a bitter autobiography, *Tjänstekvinnans son* (1886, 'The Son of a Servant'), to be followed by *Le Plaidoyer d'un fou* (1888, 'Confessions of a Fool'). The battle between the sexes is at the centre of the three major plays that follow: *Fadren* (1887, 'The Father'), *Fröken Julie* (1888, 'Miss Julie') and *Fordringsägare* (1889, 'The Creditors'). In the 1890s he turned for a time to experiments with the occult and pseudo-science, suffered a spiritual crisis verging on madness, and underwent a conversion with elements of Swedenborgian mysticism, all of which he described in his autobiographical *Inferno* (1897), and which is given dramatic expression in the trilogy *Till Damaskus* (1898–1904, 'To Damascus'). His efforts to find a dramatic means of expressing inner reality in those and later plays, like *Ett drömspel* (1902, 'A Dream Play'), make him a forerunner of expressionism and a major influence on modern theatre.

▷G Brandell, *Strindberg, ett författerliv* (1987); E Sprigge, *The Strange Life of Strindberg* (1949)

STRITTMATTER, Erwin
(1912–)

German novelist and dramatist, born in Spremburg. Initially a communist, he deserted from the Nazi army and later held high offices in East Germany. He then became a journalist. His play *Katzgraben* (1954), a rural comedy in verse, received high praise from, and was produced by, **Bertolt Brecht**. His novels are dutifully socialist realist, but somewhat redeemed from this by their humour and rustic comedy.

STRODE, William
(1602–45)

English poet and clergyman, born in Plympton. He was educated at Westminster School and Christ Church, Oxford, where he became canon and public orator. He is best known for his elegies and lyric verse, which were rediscovered by Bertram Dobell in 1907, and for his tragi-comedy, *The Floating Island*, performed by the students of Christ Church before Charles I in 1636.

STRONG, Leonard Alfred George
(1896–1958)

English novelist and poet, born in Plymouth. He was educated at Brighton College and Wadham College, Oxford. He took up school teaching until he established a reputation as a lyric poet with *Dublin Days* (1921), *The Lowery Road* (1923), and other volumes. He also wrote novels, including *Dewer Rides* (1929), a macabre novel set in Dartmoor, and *Deliverance* (1955). His collection of short stories, *Travellers*, won the James Tait Black Memorial Prize in 1945.

▷*Green Memory* (1961)

STRUG, Andrzej, pseud of Tadeusz Galecki
(1871–1937)

Polish novelist. He was exiled to Archangel by the Tsarist Russians, whom he opposed. Always a socialist, he took part in the 1905–6 revolution; he had previously supported Pilsudski, but soon joined the opposition to him after the latter's 1926 coup. But his novels transcend the political, even though they depict the dark side of capitalism, and deal for the most part with 'the underground people'. His novels have not yet been translated into English; *Jutro* (1909, 'Tomorrow'), from his earlier period, and the stories in *Klucz otchlani* (1929, 'The Key to the Precipice'), are amongst the most notable.

STRUGATSKY, Boris Natanovitch
(1931–)
STRUGATSKY, Arkady Natanovitch
(1925–91)

Russian science-fiction writers, born in the Soviet Union. As brothers they began to collaborate on science-fiction writing in the early 1950s. Their early works formed a generally optimistic future history on an interplanetary scale, but a change of tone crept in with books like *Trudno byt' bogom* (1964, Eng trans *Hard To be a God*, 1973), which were more ambiguous in their view of utopian political solutions. They began to draw on folklore and fable as well as science fiction, while their growing political and ideological disillusion is evident in invented worlds which reflect the bureaucratic disasters of their homeland, as in *Skazha o troike* (1968, Eng trans *Tale of the Troika*, 1972) or *Piknik na obochine* (1972, Eng trans *Roadside Picnic*, 1977). Subsequent works like *Za milliard let do kontsa sveta* (1976–7, Eng trans *Definitely Maybe: A Manuscript Discovered under Unusual Circumstances*, 1978) and the later *Grad obrechennyi* (1989, 'The Doomed City') were even bleaker in their vision.

STRUTHER, Jan, pseud of Mrs Joyce Anstruther Placzek
(1901–53)

English writer, born in London. Her most successful creation was Mrs Miniver, whose activities, first narrated in articles to *The Times*, became the subject of one of the best films of World War II.

STUART, Donald
(1913–83)

Australian writer, born in Cottesloe, Perth. He was the author of 'outback' novels, mainly set in the north-west of Western Australia, the first of which was *Yandy* (1950). *The Driven* (1961) tells of a long cattle drive and the developing relationships of the drover boss and his aboriginal and white companions. A semi-autobiographical series of six books, *The Conjuror's Years*, began in 1974 with *Prince of My Country* and concluded with *I Think I'll Live* (1981). His *Morning Star, Evening Star: Tales of Outback Australia* (1973) are unaffected yarns of the hardships and rewards, and the interaction of blacks and whites, in this harsh corner of the country.

STUART, Francis
(1902–)

Irish novelist, poet and dramatist, born in Queensland, Australia, of Irish parents. He was imprisoned on the Republican side during the Irish Civil War in the 1920s. During the next decade and a half he made a prolific start to his writing career, producing 10 novels, a collection of poems, two plays, *Things to Love For: Notes For an Autobiography* (1934) and the ever-useful pamphlet *Racing for Pleasure and Profit in Ireland and Elsewhere* (1937). He spent the duration of World War II in Berlin, from where he broadcasted to the neutral Republic of Ireland. Following post-war imprisonment as a collaborator, he published a series of passionately felt 'epiphanies from a ghetto', among them *The Pillar of Cloud* (1948), *Redemption* (1949) and *Victors and Vanquished* (1958). The searingly autobiographical *Black List, Section H* was published in 1972, followed by *Memorial* in 1973. A series of novels produced in the 1980s examines the uneasy relationship of virtue to the victimized, and is explicated most clearly in his essay *The Abandoned Snail Shell* (1987). ▷ G Elborn, *Francis Stuart: A Life* (1990)

STUART, Jesse Hilton
(1907–84)

American novelist, short-story writer and poet, born in Kentucky. Stuart, who worked as a farmer, newspaper editor and schoolteacher, began his writing career with short stories and gradually built them up into novel-length narratives. He held on to the short-story writer's technique of beginning *in medias res* and has been called the 'Grandma Moses' of the American novel, because of the primitive qualities of his characterization and plots. *Taps for Private Tussie* (1943) was a bestseller. The lasting legacy of Stuart's prolific career will not be one of his titles, but his placing of the Appalachians and the oral style of the region's characters on the literary map.

STUART, Ruth McEnery
(1849–1917)

American novelist and short-story writer, born in Louisiana and specializing in accurate rendering of Southern dialects. Most of her books were written after she had left the South to live in New York. Her biggest success was with *Sonny* (1896), the story of a poor white, but in other books she demonstrated an acute knowledge of Creoles and Negroes. She is considered better at short narratives than long fiction and *A Golden Wedding and Other Tales* (1893) is a good example of her short-story technique.

STUB, Ambrosius Christofferson
(1705–58)

Danish poet, born in Gummerup. A serious lyrical poet, he became buffoon-poet (drinking-songs, moralizing pieces) to wealthy men, received no recognition in his lifetime,

and died a pauper. His serious poetry, unpublished until some years after his death, has been compared to that of **Robert Herrick**.
▷H Brix, *Ambrosius Stub* (1960, in Danish)

STUCKENBERG, Viggo
(1863–1905)

Danish poet, born in Copenhagen. He was an important figure in the lyrical revival of the 1890s. His works include *Fagre Ord* (1895) and *Flyvende Sommer* (1898).

STURGEON, Theodore, pseud of **Edward Hamilton**
(1918–85)

American science-fiction writer, born in Staten Island, New York. He published his first stories while at sea as a teenager, and his first science fiction in 1939. Most of his work falls into the period 1946–61, with long fallow years on either side. He revealed a willingness to explore areas usually shunned in genre circles, particularly sexuality, and his best works have a satisfying sense of discovery, and a marvellous exuberance in the writing. He wrote many short stories, which have been collected in numerous editions, and several novels. His best-known work is *More Than Human* (1953), three linked novellas in which a half-dozen 'freaks' find themselves empowered through the force of their combined minds. His other works include a western, *The Rare Breed* (1966), and historical and detective fiction.

STURGES, Preston, originally **Edmund Preston Biden**
(1898–1959)

American screenwriter and film director, born in Chicago. Reared by his mother in a bohemian lifestyle that propelled him through Europe and America, he worked in the cosmetics industry, developing a 'kiss-proof' lipstick, before making his mark as a Broadway dramatist with the play *The Guinea Pig* (1929). In Hollywood from 1930, he became renowned for the speed and richness of his screenwriting talent, notably on *The Power And The Glory* (1933) and *The Good Fairy* (1935). He won an Oscar for the screenplay of the political satire *The Great McGinty* (1940), which also marked his directorial debut, and over the next five years created a succession of sharp social comedies that combined sophisticated wit with lowbrow slapstick. His most fondly-recalled work includes *The Lady Eve* (1941), *Sullivan's Travels* (1942) and *The Miracle of Morgan's Creek* (1944). Later films, however, failed to recapture the dizzy creativity of the war years. He received a posthumous Laurel Award for

Achievement in 1974 from the Writer's Guild Of America.

STURLUSON, Snorri
(1179–1241)

Icelandic historian, poet and chieftain, the outstanding writer of medieval Scandinavia. He was born at Hvammur in western Iceland and fostered at Oddi, the home of the powerful chieftain, Jón Loptsson. He amassed wealth and property, including the estate of Borg (former home of his ancestor, the saga hero **Egil Skallagrímsson**) and Reykholt, where he lived much of his life, and rapidly rose to prominence in national life, becoming law-speaker (president) of the Althing (parliament) for the first time in 1215. It was a time of great civil unrest in Iceland (the so-called Sturlung Age), with warring factions in the Icelandic republic jockeying for power, aided and abetted by King Haakon IV Haakonsson ('the Old') of Norway. Eventually, Snorri was assassinated at the king's behest at his home at Reykholt. As an author, Snorri Sturluson towers over his contemporaries. He wrote *Heimskringla*, a monumental prose history of the kings of Norway down to the year 1177, and compiled a prose account of Norse mythology in his *Prose* (or *Younger*) *Edda*, which is also a handbook of poesy illustrated with his own poetry. He is also believed to have written *Egils saga*, a prose biographical history of his ancestor, Egill Skallagrimsson.
▷M Ciklamin, *Snorri Sturluson* (1978)

STYRON, William
(1925–)

American novelist, born in Newport News, Virginia. His first novel, *Lie Down in Darkness*, appeared in 1951. *Set This House on Fire* (1960) portrayed Americans in Europe after the war and was hugely successful in France. Concerned with oppression in its myriad forms he has tackled the black–white question in *The Confessions of Nat Turner* (1967) and the fate of Holocaust survivors in *Sophie's Choice* (1979). *The Long March* (1953) was a taut novella about army life, and *This Quiet Dust* (1982) a miscellany of pieces.
▷*Darkness Visible: A Memoir of Madness* (1990)

SU TUNG-P'O, pseud of SU SHIH
(1036–1101)

Chinese painter, calligrapher, poet, philosopher and politician from Meishan, Sichuan province. Of peasant origins, his family had only recently moved into the mandarinate. Su Tung-p'o's father as well as his own son were literati, collectively known as

'the three Su'. Su Tung-p'o is almost unanimously referred to as one of the most prominent men of his time, a 'universal genius'. Excelling in all the fields of a literati, he epitomized the cultural ideal of 11th-century Chinese humanism. In addition, his checkered political career ranged from Prime Ministership to exile. A great part of Chinese aesthetics, now being taken for granted, derives from his writings and his formulation of *wen jen hua* (literati painting). According to him, the spiritual process of pictorial creation had to be the fruit of the identification of the painter with the object of his painting: 'To paint the bamboo, it is necessary to have it entirely within yourself'. Thus, he also saw the forms born out of the brush as revealing the state of mind of the painter, another concept which only appeared in the West during the latter half of the 19th century.
▷L Yutang, *The Gay Genius* (1947)

SUBERCASEAUX, Benjamin
(1902–73)

Chilean novelist, essayist and dramatist, born in Santiago. Subercaseaux studied in France, like **Jung**, under the psychiatrist Pierre Janet, to whose pioneer work so many of the French surrealists were devoted. After studying and rejecting Roman Catholicism in Rome, he joined the Waldenses, a heretical sect that renounced violence. His masterpiece, one still shamefully neglected outside Latin America, is the novel *Jemmy Button* (1950, Eng trans 1955). Based on a historical event, that of Robert Fitzroy's taking to England of four Tierro de Fuegian natives in order to expose them to 'Christian instruction', it contrasts the 'civilized' with the 'natural' world, and explores the strange and introspective character of Fitzroy. His play, *Pasión y epopeya de Halcón Kigero* (1957), is about an Araucanian chief. In his last years he devoted himself to anthropological studies.
▷A T Rioseco, *Breve historia de la literatura chilena* (1956)

SUCKLING, Sir John
(1609–41)

English poet and playwright, born in Norfolk. The archetypal Cavalier, he appeared more concerned with the dress of his troops, on which he spent prodigious sums, than with their military ability. He fought for King Charles I in the unsuccessful war against the Scots in 1639, and later fled abroad, where he may have committed suicide. His four plays include the tragedy *Aglaura* (1637), which was revised and republished as a comedy the following year. It is on his poetry, however, that his reputation rests. The posthumously published *Fragmenta Aurea* (1646) was reprinted in 1648 and 1659;

it contains what is probably his most famous work, 'Why So Pale and Wan, Fond Lover?' He is credited by John Aubrey with having invented 'the game of Cribbidge' [sic].

SUDERMANN, Hermann
(1857–1928)

German dramatist and novelist, born in Matzicken, East Prussia. He wrote a succession of skilful, if superficial, realist plays, *Die Ehre* (1889, 'Honour'), *Sodoms Ende* (1891, 'The Fall of Sodom'), *Heimat* (1893, Eng trans *Magda*, 1896), and others, and equally successful novels, including *Frau Sorge* (1887, Eng trans *Dame Care*, 1891), *Der Katzensteg* (1890, Eng trans *Regine*, 1894) and *Es war* (1894, Eng trans *The Undying Past*, 1906).
▷I Leux, *Hermann Sudermann* (1931)

SUE, (Marie Joseph) Eugène
(1804–57)

French novelist, born in Paris. He served as a surgeon in Spain (1823) and at Navarino Bay (1827) and wrote a vast number of **Byron**ic novels, many of which were dramatized, idealizing the poor to the point of melodramatic absurdity, but nevertheless highly successful at the time. They had a profound influence on **Victor Hugo**, whose *Les Misérables* has much in common with Sue's *Les Mystères de Paris* (1843). Other novels include *Le Juif errant* (1845, 'The Wandering Jew'), *Les Sept Péchés capitaux* (1849, 'The Seven Deadly Sins') and *Les Mystères du peuple* (1849, 'Mysteries of the People'), the last condemned as immoral and seditious. A republican deputy, he was driven into exile in 1851.
▷E de Mirecourt, *Eugène Sue* (1855)

SUERIO, Daniel
(1931–)

Spanish novelist, story writer and journalist, born in the province of La Coruña. Almost alone amongst contemporary Spanish novelists, he writes in the direct tradition of **Pío Baroja**. His realistic novels such as *Estos son sus hermanos* (1965, 'These Are Your Brothers'), about the brutal aftermath of the Civil War, are more successful than his experimental ones, such as the science-fiction *Corte de corteza* (1969, 'Brain Transplant').

SUETONIUS, Gaius Suetonius Tranquillus
(c.69–c.140)

Roman biographer and antiquarian. He was for a time a member of the Imperial service (119–c.122) and secretary to the Emperor Hadrian. His best-known work is his *Lives of the Caesars* (from Julius to Domitian). There survive also short biographies of **Virgil** and other Roman poets. In addition, Suetonius wrote numerous lost historical and miscellaneous works (in Greek as well as Latin). The *Caesares* (Eng trans *The Twelve Caesars* by **Robert Graves**, 1957) are an important historical source (though not always dependable without corroboration) and benefit from his access to the Imperial archives and his contact with eye-witnesses. His style (like his general approach) is brisk and straightforward, but he evidently enjoyed the numerous scandalous anecdotes he recorded.

SUCKOW, Ruth
(1892–1960)

American story writer and novelist, born in Hawarden, Iowa. When she started to publish, in the 1920s, Ruth Sukow was regarded as a major talent; since then she has fallen into near-oblivion. She was, however, a good if not profound regional writer, whose work (it has been generally agreed) suffered when she decided to move from the form of the story to that of the novel. The long and successful *The Folks* (1934) is readable, but is essentially a series of vignettes rather than a novel proper. But at least *Iowa Interiors* (1926) and *Children and Older People* (1931), collections of stories, are worthy of preservation for their honest realism.
▷M Omracanin, *Sukow: A Critical Study of Her Fiction* (1972)

SUITS, Gustav
(1883–1956)

Estonian poet and scholar, major in the context of his literature, born in Vônnu. When the Soviets annexed Estonia for the second time, in 1944, he fled to Sweden, where he was made a member of the Nobel Institute. He was too fastidious to produce the poetry of which he was capable, but the poetry he did write had a delicacy and craftsmanship which meant that it inspired others. His criticism of Estonian literature was crucial—he was a major keeper of standards. *Tuli ja tuul* (1950, Eng trans *Flames on the Wind*, 1953) shows him at his always slightly artificial best.
▷ *American Slavic and East European Review*, IX (1955)

SUKENICK, Ronald
(1932–)

American novelist of markedly experimental disposition (though he obstinately refuses the label). He was born in Brooklyn, New York and educated at Cornell and Brandeis universities, returning to the latter as a lecturer. He has taught at campuses throughout New York and in California. His first 'novel' *Up* (1968) is a reflexive anti-narrative about the difficulties of writing fiction; its successor *Out*

(1973)—not to be confused with a similarly disposed work of that name by **Christine Brooke-Rose**—moves the ostensible setting to the West Coast. In *98.6* (1975) and *Long Talking Bad Conditions Blues* (1979) he attempts to engage with a wider reality; however, the essence of Sukenick's work is to be found in the closed forms of his two short-story collections, *The Death of the Novel and Other Stories* (1969), which includes putatively unedited taped conversations, and *The Endless Short Story* (1986). His aesthetic is most cogently formulated, however, in an earlier study of **Wallace Stevens** called *Musing the Obscure* (1967), in which he examines the poet's desire to create self-contained and autotelic language-worlds.

SUKHOVO-KOBYLIN, Aleksandr
(1817–1903)

Russian dramatist, born in Voskresensk, near Moscow. He wrote only three plays, but these are recognized as masterpieces. A friend of **Gogol**, he was in 1850 tried for the murder of his mistress, and, although he was finally acquitted, the case dragged on for seven years. His first play, *Svadba Krechinskogo* (1855, Eng trans with his other two plays in *The Trilogy of Aleksandr Sukhovo-Kobylin*, 1969), was a comedy. *The Case* and *The Death of Tarelkin* are savage satires on Tsarist idiocy, bureaucracy and tyranny—and were banned until revived by Meyerhold, when they became a regular part of Soviet repertory. Harold B Segal's introduction to his translation of the *Trilogy* is exemplary as criticism and biography. Sukhovo-Kobylin's work has been described as a 'mounting diatribe of gorge', and certainly he is the Gogol of the theatre.

SULLY-PRUDHOMME, René François Armand
(1839–1907)

French poet and winner of the first Nobel Prize for literature, born in Paris. He studied science and developed an interest in philosophy which underlies most of his poetical works. His early *Stances et poèmes* (1865, 'Stanzas and Poems') was praised by **Charles Sainte-Beuve**. Later volumes, *Les Épreuves* (1866, 'Proofs'), *Croquis italiens* (1872, 'Sketches of Italy'), *Les Solitudes* (1869), *Impressions de la guerre* (1872, 'Impressions of War'), *Les Destins* (1872, 'Destinies'), *Les Vaines Tendresses* (1875, 'Hollow Tendernesses'), *La France* (1879) and *La Révolte des fleurs* (1874, 'The Flowers' Revolution'), confirmed his fame as a poet. His didactic poems *La Justice* (1878) and *Le Bonheur* (1888, 'Happiness') are masterpieces of subtlety. Other works are a metrical translation of book one of **Lucretius** (new edn 1886); in

prose, *L'Expression dans les beaux arts* (1883, 'Expression in the Fine Arts'), *Réflexions sur l'art des vers* (1892, 'Reflections on Poetic Art'), *Testament poétique* (1901, 'Poetic Testament') and *La Vraie Religion selon Pascal* (1905, 'The True Religion According to Pascal'). His *Oeuvres complètes* ('Complete Works') appeared between 1883 and 1908. He was awarded the Nobel Prize for literature in 1901.
▷P Flottes, *Sully-Prudhomme* (1930)

SUMARAKOV, Aleksandr
(1718–77)
Russian dramatist and poet, born in Finland. With the actor Volkov he established Russia's first permanent theatre, in St Petersburg; he provided most of its repertoire in the form of pseudo-classical tragedies in the French tradition, which (according to one critic) 'lacked taste and permanence'. He adapted *Hamlet*—with a 'respectable and happy ending'.
▷A Berkov, *Aleksandr Sumarakov* (1949, in Russian)

SUMMERS, Essie, properly **Ethel Snelson Flett**
(1912–)
New Zealand journalist and writer of popular romances, born in Christchurch. Her first book, *New Zealand Inheritance*, was published in 1957 but she had been a contributor to New Zealand and British periodicals since the mid-1930s. In over 50 novels she rarely strayed far from a set formula hinging on family history and faithfulness, as in *Bride in Flight* (1964) and *Heir to Windrush Hill* (1966). Her last book was *High-Country Governess* (1987).
▷ *The Essie Summers Story* (1974)

SUNDBERG, Kjell
(1934–78)
Swedish novelist and dramatist in the existentialist tradition—in certain ways a latter-day Swedish counterpart to Norway's **Stig Dagerman**—born in Östersund. He mercilessly satirized Sweden's Utopian pretentions in his *Den förvirrade medborgaren* (1967, 'The Confused Citizen'); this vein is continued in *Ja må han leva Häng dig om du kan* (1970, 'Many Happy Returns, Or Hang Yourself if You Can'). But Sundberg failed to develop his gifts beyond satire, and critical claims for him made in his lifetime proved to have been exaggerated.

SUNDMAN, Per Olof
(1922–92)
Swedish novelist and short-story writer, born in Vaxhom outside Stockholm. He was an elected member of the Swedish Academy, and politically active as a representative in parliament for the liberal Centre Party. His narratives—whether pure fiction, as in the short-story collection *Jägarna* (1957, 'The Hunters') or part documentary as in the novel *Expeditionen* (1962, 'The Expedition')—typically involve a limited number of characters who set out on a search or mission; his seemingly simple and straightforward prose, free from psychologizing and moralizing, blends the style of the Icelandic sagas with a touch of the detective story. His masterpiece is the documentary novel *Ingenjör Andrées luftfärd* (1967, 'The Flight of the Eagle'), adapted to film by the distinguished Swedish director Jan Troell in 1982, a detailed account of an ill-fated balloon-trip to the North Pole in 1897.
▷L G Warme, *Per Olof Sundman: Writer of the North* (1984)

SUPERVIELLE, Jules
(1884–1960)
Uruguayan-born French writer, born in Montevideo. He wrote many volumes of poems (including the notable *Poèmes de la France malheureuse*, 1939–41, 'Poems of Unfortunate France'), novels, tales (*L'Enfant de la haute mer*, 1931, 'The Child from the High Seas'; *L'Arche de Noè*, 1938, 'Noah's Ark'), plays (*La Belle au bois*, 1932, 'Beauty in the Woods'; *Shéhérazade*, 1949), and the libretto for *Bolivar*, an opera with music by Milhaud (1950).
▷J A Hiddleton, *L'univers de Supervielle* (1965)

SURREY, Henry Howard, Earl of
(c.1517–1547)
English courtier and poet, eldest son of Thomas Howard (who in 1524 succeeded as third Duke of Norfolk). He commanded troops in France but is now better remembered as a poet than a soldier, having helped to introduce the sonnet to England and being a pioneer of blank verse. He made a number of enemies in high places, however, and in 1547 was charged with high treason, on very flimsy evidence, found guilty and executed. Most of his work was first published in 1557, and collected in 1815–16.
▷E Casady, *Henry Howard, Earl of Surrey* (1938)

SURTEES, R(obert) S(mith)
(1805–64)
English journalist and novelist, born in Durham, where he was educated. He practised as a lawyer and later became a Justice of the Peace and High Sheriff of Durham County. He started the *New Sporting Magazine* in 1831 where he introduced John

Jorrocks, a sporting Cockney, in whom there is an appealing blend of the vulgar and the absurd. Later Jorrocks's adventures were contained in the highly popular *Jorrock's Jaunts and Jollities* (1838) and in *Hillingdon Hall* (1845). Their influence on **Dickens'** *Pickwick Papers* is conspicuous. His other great character, Mr Soapy Sponge, appears in *Mr Sponge's Sporting Tour* (1853), by which time he was combining his passion for sport with his literary work.

▷F Watson, *Robert Smith Surtees, a critical study* (1933)

SUSANN, Jacqueline
(?1926–1974)

American popular novelist, born in Philadelphia. After a moderately successful career as an actress she turned to writing, her first novel, *Valley of the Dolls* (1968), becoming an immediate bestseller. *The Love Machine*, published the following year, enjoyed the same success. She made no literary claims for her work but admitted to writing to provide her readers with an escape from their daily lives into the more sensational world of show business, where ruthless ambition leads to frustration and unhappiness.

SUTCLIFF, Rosemary
(1920–92)

English writer of sophisticated historical fiction, mostly for younger readers. She was born at West Clanden, Surrey, and trained at Bideford School of Art. Her gifts as a miniaturist are also evident in her prose, which is sharply detailed and coloured. Her first novel was *The Armourer's House* (1951), but she received greatest praise for *The Eagle of the Ninth* (1954), a story of the Romans in Britain, and for *The Lantern Bearers* (1959). Their vividness was enhanced by line drawings from C Walter Hodges (later illustrators included Charles Keeping and Shirley Felts). Though seriously affected by osteoarthritis, Sutcliff continued to write into the 1980s.

▷M Meek, *Rosemary Sutcliff* (1962)

SUTRO, Alfred
(1863–1933)

English dramatist, born in London. He gave up a successful business, translated **Maeterlinck**, and from 1900 wrote a series of successful plays—*The Foolish Virgins* (1904), *The Walls of Jericho* (1906), *John Glayde's Honour* (1907), *The Perplexed Husband* (1913), and others.

SUTTNER, Bertha, Freifrau von
(1843–1914)

Czech (Austro–Hungarian) novelist of Bohemian descent, daughter of an imperial general, Count Kinsky. She married Baron von Suttner, an engineer, in 1876. In 1915 she won a Nobel Prize, not for Literature, but for Peace (she founded an Austrian pacifist organization)—Alfred Nobel himself had been persuaded to set up his fund by her example. Her novel *Die Waffen nieder* (1889, Eng trans *Lay Down Your Arms, the Autobiography of Martha von Tilling*, 1892) shocked her readers by its pacifism.

▷E Key, *Florence Nightingale und Bertha von Suttner* (1919)

SVENSSON, Jon Stefán
(1857–1944)

Icelandic writer and churchman, born at Möðruvellir. Educated in France, he became a Jesuit scholar and taught at a Catholic school in Denmark. During convalescence in Holland from a severe illness (1911–12) he began to write a series of children's books about a boy called Nonni growing up in the north of Iceland, which made him a bestselling author. The *Nonni* books, originally written in German, have been translated into many languages.

▷H Hannesson, *Nonni Attrægur* (1937)

SVEVO, Italo, pseud of Ettore Schmitz
(1861–1928)

Italian novelist of German–Jewish descent, born in Trieste. Educated primarily in Bavaria, he wrote in Italian, but had to work as a French and German correspondence clerk in a Trieste bank. In 1892 he wrote and published privately his first novel, *Una Vita* (Eng trans, *A Life*, 1963), whose autobiographical hero felt ill at ease in the commercial world. It was followed in 1898 by *Senilità* (Eng trans *As a Man Grows Older*, 1932). Both fell flat largely through Svevo's ineptitude as a publisher, and in dejection he gave up writing and resolved to concentrate on business. His luck changed in 1906 when he went to a teacher of English then living in Trieste, **James Joyce**, who bolstered his confidence and promoted *La coscienza di Zeno* (Eng trans *The Confessions of Zeno*, 1930). Through Joyce a translation was published in Paris and Svevo soon won recognition in France and the rest of Europe, but he died soon afterwards in a car accident. He wrote a fourth novel, *La novella del buon vecchio e della bella fanciulla* (1929, Eng trans *The Nice Old Man and the Pretty Girl*, 1930), and a fifth, *Il vecchione* (pub 1967, Eng trans *The Grand Old Man*, 1968), was incomplete on his death. Critic Renato Poggioli wrote that 'For a cultivated Italian it is very easy to understand, but almost impossible to appreciate, the Italian of Svevo, perhaps the least literary and even the least literate, certainly the least polished Italian ever used by a man of letters in our

time.' To **V S Pritchett** he was 'the first of the psychological novelists to be beatified by a spirit of humility'.
▷P N Furbank, *Italo Svevo, man and writer* (1966)

SWADOS, Harvey
(1920–72)

American novelist and short-story writer. He was raised in Buffalo, New York, and educated at the University of Michigan. He was a college lecturer before publishing his first novel, *Out Went the Candle* (1955), a vivid portrayal of an American family dominated by business values; this was also the background to *The Will* (1963), which looks at the divisive impact of inherited wealth. His left-liberal stance was even more evident in his stories of auto-workers, *On the Line* (1957). In *Standing Fast* (1970), published not long before his death, Swados wrote with then unfashionable nostalgia about the Old Left; his own politicization was traced in *A Radical's America* (1962), one of the most direct and intelligent books of its kind to be written by an American and notably free of sentimentality. Other novels include *False Coin* (1959), *Nights in the Gardens of Brooklyn* (1960), *A Story for Teddy* (1965) and the posthumous *Celebration* (1975).

SWAN, Annie S(hepherd)
(1859–1943)

Scottish novelist, born near Coldingham, Berwickshire, and brought up in Edinburgh and at Gorebridge, Midlothian. In 1883 she married a schoolmaster (later doctor), James Burnett Smith, and from 1896 they lived in England; she returned to Scotland in 1927 after her husband's death. She published her first novel, *Ups and Downs*, in 1878, and made her name with a Border romance, *Aldersyde* (1883), followed by *Carlowie* (1884), *A Divided House* (1885) and *The Gates of Eden* (1887). From then on she published a large number of light romantic novels, and stories for women's magazines like *The Woman at Home*. She published her autobiography, *My Life*, in 1934.

SWENSON, May
(1919–89)

American poet, born in Logan, Utah, the daughter of Swedish Mormons. She later moved to New York City, where she began publishing poems in periodicals and anthologies. Her first collection, *A Cage of Spines*, appeared in 1958 and was followed by six more, including *To Mix With Time* (1963), which meditates upon travelling and the passing years; *Iconographs* (1970), a book of sometimes difficult concrete poetry, and

In Other Words: New Poems (1987), which includes the long poem, *Banyan*, a metaphorical reflection upon the world and its ways, narrated by an ape. She has also written an avant-garde play, *The Floor* (1966), and poetry for children in *Poems to Solve* (1966) and *More Poems to Solve* (1971).
▷S Gilbert and S Gubar, *Shakespeare's Sisters: Feminist Essays on Women Poets* (1979)

SWIFT, Graham
(1949–)

English novelist and short-story writer, born in London and educated at Cambridge and York universities. His writing is frequently preoccupied with history, memory, guilt and the natural world. His first novels, *The Sweet Shop Owner* (1980) and *Shuttlecock* (1981), were critically well received, but international acclaim arrived on publication of his third, the hugely successful *Waterland* (1983). Partly a social and natural history, partly a fictitious history of his family as remembered and imagined by Tom Crick, a teacher, this work is considered by some as one of the most important novels of its time. *Out of This World* (1988) looks at the relationship between a father and daughter, while *Ever After* (1992) records the life of Bill Unwin, a meditative academic.

SWIFT, Jonathan
(1667–1745)

Anglo–Irish poet, satirist and clergyman, born in Dublin, the son of English parents. He was educated at Kilkenny Grammar School and Trinity College, Dublin, where he obtained his degree only by 'special grace' in 1685. Family connections helped him to embark on a career as secretary to the renowned diplomat, Sir **William Temple**, then resident at Moor Park, Farnham. He supported his patron on the side of the Ancients in the 'Querelle des Anciens et des Modernes' which had spread to Britain from France. Swift's contribution was the mock-epic *Battle of the Books* which was published along with the much more powerful satire on religious dissension, *A Tale of a Tub*, in 1704. At Moor Park he first met Esther Johnson (1681–1728), then a child of eight, who from then on as pupil and lover or friend was to play an important role in his life and to survive for posterity in Swift's verse tributes and the *Journal to Stella* (1710–13), but it is uncertain if he ever married her. When Swift was presented to the living of Laracor near Dublin, 'Stella' accompanied him. In 1708, during one of his numerous visits to London, he met Esther Vanhomrigh (1690–1723), who insisted on being near him in Ireland with unhappy consequences to herself. She is the Vanessa of Swift's too clever poem *Cadenus* *and Vanessa*, a tribute to the lady but also a manoeuvre of disengagement. His visits to London were largely political, but he also visited the great in the literary and aristocratic circles. For the first time the literary world met on equal terms with statesmen. Having been introduced to the political world by Temple, he supported the Whigs, but, his first care being the English Church, he gradually veered to the Tory party. The friendship of Harley, later Earl of Oxford, assisted the change which was decisively made in 1710 when Harley returned to power. His *Four Last Years of the Queen Anne* described the ferment of intrigue and pamphleteering during that period. The chief aims of the Tory party were to make the Establishment secure and to bring the war with France to a close. The latter object was powerfully aided by his *On the Conduct of the Allies* (1713), one of the greatest pieces of pamphleteering. The death of Queen Anne in 1714 disappointed all the hopes of Swift and his friends of the Scriblerus Club, founded in 1713. Swift accepted his 'exile' to the Deanery of St Patrick's Cathedral, Dublin, and from then on, except for two visits in 1726 and 1727, correspondence alone kept him in touch with London. Despite his loathing for Ireland he threw himself into a strenuous campaign for Irish liberties, denied by the Whig government. The *Drapier's Letters* is the most famous of these activities, which were concerned with England's restrictions on Irish trade, particularly the exclusion of Irish wool and cattle. This campaign, and his charitable efforts for Dublin's poor, greatly enhanced his reputation. On his first visit to London after the Tory debacle of 1714 he published the world-famous satire *Gulliver's Travels* (1726). In 1729 he published his ironical *A Modest Proposal*. His poems in light verse now range from the diverting *The Grand Question Debated* (1729) to the *Verses on His Own Death* (1731), which, with its mixture of pathos and humour, ranks with the great satirical poems in the lighter manner. He himself considered his *On Poetry; a Rhapsody* (1733) to be his best verse satire. The ironical *Directions to Servants* and *A Complete Collection of Genteel and Ingenious Conversation* followed in 1731. The satire in the first part of *Gulliver's Travels* is directed at political parties and religious dissension. The second part can be equally enjoyed for the ingenious adventures and the detailed verisimilitude which is part of the manner. But there is deepening misanthropy culminating in the king's description of mankind as 'the most pernicious race of little odious vermin that Nature ever suffered to crawl upon the surface of the earth'. The third part, a satire on inventors, is good fun though less plausible. The

last part, in the country of the Houyhnhnms, a race of horses governed only by reason, is a savage attack on man which points to the author's final mental collapse. Politics apart, Swift's influence, like that of the 'Scriblerus Club' generally and **Pope** in particular, was directed powerfully against the vogue of deistic science and modern invention and in favour of orthodoxy and good manners.
▷I Ehrenpreis, *Jonathan Swift: the man, his works, the age* (2 vols, 1962–7)

SWINBURNE, Algernon Charles
(1837–1909)

English poet and critic, born in London, the eldest son of Admiral Charles Swinburne and Lady Jane Ashburnham. He was educated partly in France and at Eton (where he was savagely beaten and bullied) and Balliol College, Oxford, but left without taking a degree. He travelled on the Continent, where he came under the spell of **Victor Hugo**. He visited **Walter Savage Landor** in Florence (1864), and on his return became associated with **Dante Gabriel Rossetti** and **William Morris**. After a breakdown due to intemperate living, he submitted to the care of his friend **Theodore Watts-Dunton**, in whose house, No. 2, The Pines, he continued to live in semi-seclusion for the rest of his life. His first publication, the two plays *The Queen Mother* and *Rosamond* (1860), attracted little attention, but *Atalanta in Calydon* (1865), a drama in the Greek form but modern in its spirit of revolt against religious acquiescence in the will of Heaven, proved a success. He returned to Greek myth with his noble lyric drama *Erectheus* (1876). It was, however, the first of the series of *Poems and Ballads* (1866) which took the public by storm. The exciting rhythms of 'Hesperia', 'Itylus', 'The Garden of Proserpine' and 'The Triumph of Time' were intoxicating to English ears, but the uninhibited tone of certain passages affronted English puritanism. The second series of *Poems and Ballads* (1878) found it hard to maintain the excitement and the third series (1889) witnessed his waning vogue in this kind. Meanwhile he found scope for his detestation of kings and priests in the struggle for Italian liberty. *Songs before Sunrise* (1871) best expresses his fervent republicanism. He had been working on a trilogy of Mary, Queen of Scots since before 1865, when his *Chastelard* appeared. The second play of the series, *Bothwell, a Tragedy*, appeared in 1874 and *Mary Stuart* completed the trilogy in 1881. The year following, *Tristram of Lyonesse*, an Arthurian romance in rhymed couplets, achieved a real success and must be considered among the best of Victorian dealings with the medieval cycle. He had resented **Tennyson**'s moralistic treatment of

the theme in *The Idylls of the King. Tristram* is intense and passionate and has some great descriptive passages. When he returned to medieval romance in *A Tale of Balen* (1896), there was obvious lack of power. Swinburne represented the last phase of the Romantic movement. His absorption in romantic themes which he treated with a wealth of rhetoric and an excess of neologisms and archaisms has caused his reputation to diminish, but he made a genuine and lasting contribution to the poetic scene. His novel, *Love's Cross Currents* (1877), published under the pseudonym Mrs H Manners, is a curiosity, but his critical works, above all his work on **Shakespeare** and his contemporaries, are stimulating. His *Essays and Studies* (1875) and *Studies in Prose and Poetry* (1894) are his chief contribution to criticism.
▷G Lafourcade, *Algernon Swinburne* (1932)

SWINNERTON, Frank Arthur
(1884–1982)

English novelist and critic, born in London. Between 1906 and 1926 he was a reader employed by the publishers Chatto and Windus. He himself wrote over 40 novels, beginning with *The Merry Heart* (1909). *Nocturne* (1917) and *Young Felix* (1923) helped establish him as a perceptive observer of atmosphere and character. His activities as publisher's reader, as a literary critic for *The Observer*, and independent author of a score of critical works, brought him into contact with an enormous number of authors, including **Aldous Huxley**, **Lytton Strachey** and **H G Wells**, and put him at the centre of literary London for several decades.

SYLVESTER, Joshua
(1563–1618)

English minor metaphysical poet and translator, born in Kent. He is now chiefly remembered for his translation of the *Divine Days and Weeks* (1605) of **Du Bartas**, which had an extensive influence throughout the 17th century, although few have professed to understand what most of it (or the original) meant. A secretary in the service of the Merchant Adventurers, he died in Holland.
▷ *The Complete Works* (1880, reprinted 1967)

SYMMACHUS, Quintus Aurelius
(c.340–c.402)

Roman orator. He became prefect of Rome in 384 and consul in 391 under the emperor Theodosius I. He was devoted to paganism, and showed the highest nobility of character in his resistance to Christianity. His extant writings consist of letters, three panegyrics on Valentinian I and Gratian, and a *Relatio* ('Report') addressed to Valentinian II in 384, urging the restoration of the Altar of Victory.
▷T R Glover, *Life and Literature in the Fourth Century* (1941)

SYMONDS, John Addington
(1840–93)

English author, born in Bristol. He was educated at Harrow School and Balliol College, Oxford, where he won the Newdigate Prize for poetry, and was elected a fellow of Magdalen College in 1862. His *Introduction to the Study of Dante* (1872) was followed by *Studies of the Greek Poets* (1873–6), his great *Renaissance in Italy* (6 vols, 1875–86), and *Shakespeare's Predecessors in the English Drama* (1884). He also wrote sketches of travel in Italy and elsewhere and monographs on **Shelley**, Sir **Philip Sidney** and **Ben Jonson**. He translated the *Sonnets of Michelangelo and Campanella* (1878), Benvenuto Cellini's autobiography, and 12th-century students' Latin songs (1884). He wrote a *Life of Michelangelo* (1892), some verse, and an account of his residence (for health reasons) in Davos (1892).
▷P Grosskurth, *Symonds* (1964)

SYMONS, Alphonse James Albert
(1900–41)

English bibliophile and biographer, born in London, the brother of **Julian Symons**. His greatest success was *The Quest for Corvo* (1934), an extraordinary biography of the writer and novelist **Frederick Rolfe**, Baron Corvo. He was active in founding the First Edition Club and the Wine and Food Society, and worked for years on a bibliography of the 1890s writers. He published brief lives of the explorers H M Stanley and Emin Pasha and also wrote some brilliant impressionistic chapters of a biography of **Oscar Wilde** which, like many other projects, he left uncompleted.

SYMONS, Arthur William
(1865–1945)

Welsh critic and poet, born of Cornish stock in Wales. He did much to familiarize the British with the literature of France and Italy. He translated **Gabriele D'Annunzio** (1902) and **Baudelaire** (1925). He wrote a number of volumes of lyrics in the Decadent manner of the period, including *Days and Nights* (1889) and *London Nights* (1895), and critical works on *The Symbolist Movement in Literature* (1899) and *The Romantic Movement in English Poetry* (1909).
▷R Lhombreaud, *Arthur Symons* (1963)

SYMONS, Julian Gustave
(1912–)

English crime novelist, historian, critic and biographer, born in London, the brother of **Alphonse Symons**. Recognized for many years as a master of crime fiction, he published his first novel, *The Immaterial Murder Case*, in 1945. This was followed by almost 30 novels and volumes of short stories. *The End of Solomon Grundy* (1964) and *The Players and the Game* (1972), show him using the crime novel as a means of reflecting and commenting upon the hypocrisies and moral laxity of contemporary society. Elsewhere, as in *The Man Who Lost His Wife* (1970), Symons uses satire to make similar points. His *Bloody Murder*, a history of the genre from the detective story to the crime novel, first appeared in 1972 and has been updated several times. It is an indispensible guide to crime fiction.

SYNGE, John Millington
(1871–1909)

Irish dramatist, born near Dublin. He studied at Trinity College, Dublin, and then studied music in Germany before spending several years in Paris on literary pursuits until, on the advice of **W B Yeats**, he settled among the people of the Aran Islands (1899–1902), who provided the material for his plays *In the Shadow of the Glen* (1903), *Riders to the Sea* (1904), *The Well of the Saints* (1905), and his humorous masterpiece *The Playboy of the Western World* (1907) followed by *The Tinker's Wedding* (1909). He published *Poems and Translations* (1909), and completed his last play, *Deirdre of the Sorrows* (1910), while dying from Hodgkin's Disease. He had a profound influence on the next generation of Irish playwrights and was a director of the Abbey Theatre from 1904.

▷ H H Green and E M Stephens, *J. M. Synge* (1959)

SZABÓ, Lörinc
(1900–57)

Hungarian poet and translator (of English, French and Russian poetry), born in Miskolc. He came into early prominence as one of the European-oriented Nyugat group around **Babits**, with whom (together with **Tóth**) he produced a complete and authoritative translation of **Baudelaire**'s *Fleurs du Mal* (1923). His confusions became apparent in the inter-war period, when he passed through phases of anarchism, vitalism and, during World War II, admiration for the Nazis. His last works mainly consist of tortured sonnets, many of them erotic, in a few of which he impressively resolved the extremes between which he lived.

SZERB, Antal
(1901–45)

Hungarian Jewish novelist, critic and essayist, who was persecuted throughout his life for his race, being first barred from holding university posts by the Horthy regime, and then murdered by Nazis. His response, now recognized as profound, was to become his country's finest critic after **Mihály Babits**, and to write some of the most interesting of its fiction. He wrote histories of Hungarian and of world literature, and some extraordinary fiction, including *A Pendragon-legenda* (1934, Eng trans *The Pendragon Legend*, 1963), a fantastic detective thriller based on Rosicrucian intrigue.

SZYMONOWICZ, Simon *see* SIMONIDES, Simon

T

TABB, Father John Bannister
(1845–1909)

American Roman Catholic priest and poet. He served on the Confederate side in the Civil War, as a blockade runner, was converted and ordained, and then became suddenly famous with *Poems* (1894). His poetry is well-crafted, in classical, tight forms; although a few compared it with that of the 17th-century English metaphysicals, it was in fact very conventional in content, and is no longer highly regarded.
▷F A Litz, *Father Tabb: A Study of His Life and Works* (1950)

TACITUS, Publius or Gaius Cornelius
(c.55–after 115)

Roman historian. He studied rhetoric in Rome, rose to eminence as a pleader at the Roman Bar, and in 77 married the daughter of Agricola, the conqueror of Britain. In 88 he was praetor. Next year he left Rome for Germany, and did not return till 93. He was an eye-witness to Domitian's reign of terror, and we have his own testimony as to the relief wrought by the accession of Nerva and Trajan. Under Nerva he became *consul suffectus* in 97. The high reputation he enjoyed is attested by the eulogistic mention of him in **Pliny**'s letters of which there are 11 addressed to him. Tacitus's earliest surviving work is the *Dialogus de oratoribus*, a dialogue on oratory. This was followed by the *De vita Iulii Agricolæ*, a biography of his father-in-law, Agricola, and the *Germania*, a monograph of great value on the ethnography of Germany. Fourth in order comes the *Historiae*, or the history of the empire from the accession of Galba in AD 68 to the assassination of Domitian in 96. Tacitus is at his strongest here, and his material was drawn from contemporary experience. His last and outstanding work, the *Annales*, is a history of the Julian line from Tiberius to Nero (AD 14 to 68); of probably 18 books only eight have come down to us entire, four are fragmentary, and the others lost. His style is vigorous but often epigrammatic to the point of obscurity. He aimed at impartiality, but is often carried away by his scorn for tyrants like Tiberius.
▷ *The Annals of Imperial Rome* (Eng trans M Grant, 1956)

TADIJANOVÍC, Dragutin
(1905–)

Croatian poet and translator, born near Slavonski Brod. Under Tito he was director of the Institute for Croatian Literature, in Zagreb. He is a controversial poet, because his deceptively simple poems seem to some to be so close to prose as hardly to be poetry. But he is widely admired and read. His poems have a kind of mystical quality, or, as one critic has put it, 'primitive authenticity', which make them hard to refute. He remains untranslated.

TAGGARD, Genevieve
(1894–1948)

American poet, editor, teacher, biographer and critic, born in Waitsburg, Washington State, and reared in Hawaii. She taught at Sarah Lawrence, and influenced a number of writers, such as **Barbara Howes**. Her biography of **Emily Dickinson** (1930) was one of the first serious treatments of the subject. She founded and edited *The Measure, A Journal of Verse* (1920–6). Her own poetry, metaphysical in style, but ardent in its radicalism, has had few readers since her death. A characteristic collection is *Slow Music* (1946).

TAGORE, Sir Rabindranath
(1861–1941)

Indian poet and philosopher, winner of the Nobel Prize for literature, born in Calcutta, the son of a wealthy Hindu religious reformer, Debendranath Tagore (1817–1905). He studied law in England (1878–80) and for 17 years managed his family estates at Shileida, where he collected the legends and tales he later used in his work. His first book was a volume of poetry, *A Poet's Tale*, when he was 17 (1878), followed by a novel, *Karuna*, and a drama, *The Tragedy of Rudachandra*. In 1901 he founded near Bolpur the Santiniketan, a communal school to blend Eastern and Western philosophical and educational systems, which developed into Visva-Bharati University. He received the Nobel Prize for literature in 1913, the first Asiatic to do so, and was knighted in 1915—an honour which he resigned in 1919 as a protest against British policy in the Punjab. He was openly critical of Mahatma Gandhi's non-cooperation as well as of the Government attitude

in Bengal. His major works include *Binodini* (1902, Eng trans 1964, the first truly modern novel by an Indian writer), *The Crescent Moon* (1913, poems about childhood), *Gitanjali* (1912, Eng trans *Song Offerings*, 1912, a volume of spiritual verse), *Chitra* (1914, his first and finest play), *The Religion of Man* (1931) and *Farewell My Friend* (1940). He also wrote *My Reminiscences* (1917), and *My Boyhood Days* (1940).
▷K R Kripklami, *Rabindranath Tagore* (1962)

TAINE, John, pseud of Eric Temple Bell
(1883–1960)
British–American science-fiction writer, born in Aberdeen. He moved at the age of 19 to the USA, where he eventually became an academic mathematician. His first book, *Before the Dawn* (1934), about dinosaurs (in whom he maintained a lifelong interest), was published under his own name—the rest, more than a score, appeared under his pseudonym. Again under his own name, he published a number of successful popular books on mathematics, of which the still read *Men of Mathematics* (1937) was the best known. His science fiction was agreeable, well written, and quite popular in its day.

TAKAMURA Kotaro
(1883–1956)
Japanese poet and sculptor. The son of a sculptor, Takamura went to France after his formal education to study art, and there conceived a great admiration for the European way of life, particularly its individualism. He returned to Japan in 1909 to work as a sculptor, but started writing poetry instead. The most important influence on his work was Chieko, a painter, who became his wife and with whom, unable to put his individualistic ideas into practice in Japan, he lived an isolated, decadent existence in Tokyo until her descent into madness and eventual death in 1938. Their life together and his subsequent despair are documented in his verse. His writing is enormously eclectic in its influences, innovative and beautifully crafted. Of all the poets writing at the time, he is perhaps the most accessible to Western readers, and yet his voice remains distinctively Japanese. In English translation is *Chieko and Other Poems of Takamura Kotaro* (1980).

TAKAZI, pseud (the name of the place of his birth) of Sivasankara Pillai
(1914–)
Indian (Malayalam) novelist, and author of the famous *Chemmeen* (1956, Eng trans *Prawns*, 1962), a romance with a prawn-fishing setting. Other novels, influenced by **Zola**, deal with such delicate subjects as the 'untouchables' *The Scavenger's Son* (1947, Eng trans 1967); *Step on the Ladder* (1964–5, Eng trans 1966) deals with the Keralian past.

TALESE, Gay
(1932–)
American journalist, born in Ocean City, New Jersey. **Tom Wolfe**, generally regarded as the pioneer of 'new journalism', has recognized Talese as its true inventor. A reporter for the *New York Times* (1955–65), he wrote his first non-fiction 'short stories' for *Esquire* magazine, beginning in 1963. His new style reached maturity in his bestselling nonfiction 'novels', *The Kingdom and the Power* (1969), about the *New York Times*, and *Honor Thy Father* (1971), about the Mafia. He has been described as 'a reporter who can write and a writer who can report'.

TALEV, Dimitur
(1898–1966)
Bulgarian historical novelist who was born in Macedonia. In the years of socialist realism he was Bulgaria's leading writer of fiction; but his work far transcends this category—and, indeed, implicitly criticizes it. His *Prespanskite kambani* (1954, 'The Bells of Prespa'), the third part of a massive tetralogy dealing with Macedonian history by tracing the fortunes of a single family, is one of his most impressive works.
▷C Manning and R Smal-Stocki, *The History of Modern Bulgarian Literature* (1960)

TALIESIN
(late 6th century)
Ancient British court poet and subsequently mythical figure of supernatural powers. He is mentioned along with **Aneirin** by Nennius in his *Historia Britonum* (c.800) as a great poet of the Old North, but while his only certain association is with King Urien Rheged, which places him in what is now Cumbria, he would seem to have been a visitor, possibly from the p-Celtic kingdom of Strathclyde. The eight poems firmly ascribed to him, amidst many which are either doubtful or spurious in the much later *Book of Taliesin*, are poems in praise of Rheged and his son Owain. These, which seem authentic, describe battles against the Picts as well as the Angles from the east, which puts Taliesin firmly enough as a frontier bard of the Strathclyde as well as Cumbrian region. Although later Welsh opinion credited him with coming from Powys, he clearly thought of Urien as his patron. He also spoke warmly of the king and his son's courage in battle, and provided the basis for their place among leaders of the Brythonic resistance to the Anglo-Saxon invaders and

Pictish predators. He acquired an extraordinary identity of his own in legend, which attributed to him a supernatural birth, vast odysseys of travel, and a collegiality with Myrddin (Merlin). This Welsh tradition may go back to the 9th or 10th century. If all of the work ascribed to him is authentic, he is not only the product of multiple successive births but is alive and will survive us all. Authenticity limits him to the western Scottish borders, and to a poet of dignity, fidelity, patriotism and human affection.

▷J Morris Jones, *Taliesin* (1918)

TAMÁSI, Áron
(1897–1966)

Hungarian novelist and dramatist, born in Farkaslaka (now in Romania). From 1923 until 1926 he was in the USA. His chief interest throughout his life was in his Transylvanian (Szekler) background. Most of his books deal with the Szekler people in a straightforward and unbiased manner. His 'Abel' trilogy (1932–4), about a young forester who emigrates, was more successful in its first book—translated as *Abel Alone* (1966)—than at its end. Later, a liberal disillusioned with theoretical politics, he turned to an almost mythological interpretation of Szekler people, reaching his peak with *Szülöföldem* (1939, 'My Birthplace').

TAMAYO Y BAUS, Manuel
(1829–98)

Spanish playwright, born into an acting family, whose work was popular in its time. He is now remembered by some for his tragedy in the manner of **Alfieri**, *Virginia* (1853), but by more for his one truly original play, *Un drama nuevo* (1867, Eng trans *A New Drama*, 1916), which is set in **Shakespeare**'s England, and employs a play-within-play technique. A rabid conservative, disappointed with the failure of his last play, he gave up writing for the stage in 1870 and became Director of the National Academy.

TAMMASAARE, A H, pseud of **Anton Hansen**
(1878–1940)

Estonian novelist and playwright, the counterpart in fiction to **Marie Under** in poetry. Like Under, he was associated with the 1917 expressionist movement named after an Estonian mythical bird, 'Siuru', but, the most important Estonian novelist of his century, he transcended all movements. He translated **George Bernard Shaw**, and was influenced by him, by **Knut Hamsun** and, above all, by **Dostoyevsky**. His five-volume

masterpiece, the epic *Tode ja oigus* ('Truth and Justice'), about Estonian peasant life in the transitional period at the end of the 19th century and the beginning of the 20th, has so far been translated only into French and German.

▷A Mägi, *Estonian Literature* (1968)

TAMMUZ, Binyamin
(1919–)

Hebrew novelist and literary editor, born in the Ukraine. His work, well respected in Israel, has not yet been translated. He was a member of the extremist but highly influential 'Canaanite circle' around the poet **Ratosh**: the Jew of Israel, it is asserted by many Israeli critics, has no connection with the Jew of the diaspora—the diaspora was just an 'inconsequential period in Jewish history'. Tammuz wrote with these convictions, and, as in *Yaakob* (1971, 'Jacob'), in the tradition of Jewish reproof. He is therefore hard for outsiders to understand; but his tales of characters in flight from themselves are compelling, vivid and psychologically astute.

TAM'SI, Tchicaya U
(1931–88)

Congolese poet, novelist and playwright, born at Npili in what was then the French colony of Moyen Congo and is now the Congolese Republic. He was educated in French Lycées in Orléans and Paris from the age of 15, after his father was elected a deputy to the French National Assembly, and lived in Paris for most of the rest of his life. He published several volumes of Surrealist poetry, notably *Le Mauvais Sang* (1955, 'Bad Blood'), *Le Ventre* (1964, 'The Stomach') and *Feu de Brousse* (1964, 'Bush Fire'); his best-known poems are in *Epitomé* (1962), which records the events surrounding the imprisonment and murder of Patrice Lumumba. The best of his poems were translated into English by Gerald Moore in *Selected Poems* (1970).

TANIZAKI Jun'ichiro
(1886–1965)

Japanese novelist and playwright. He was born and educated in Tokyo, where he studied Japanese literature at the Imperial University. After the earthquake of 1923, he removed to Kyoto-Osaka, which was to be the setting of his greatest work, *Sasameyuki* (1948, Eng trans *The Makioka Sisters*, 1957). Tanizaki's aestheticism greatly influenced the younger **Yukio Mishima**, but takes a gentler form in his own work. It was, indeed, too gentle for pre-war Japanese critics and fellow-

writers, who demanded a more aggressive approach reflecting contemporary realities. From his first work onwards, Tanizaki was concerned with the transformative power of the imagination; *Shisei* (1910, 'Tattoo') is a story about a girl whose personality is changed by bodily decoration. His other great work was *Tade kuu mushi* (1929, Eng trans *Some Prefer Nettles*, 1955), a story that underlined his cultural nationalism. His works were still being translated in the 1980s: *Bushuko hiwa* (1935) and *Yoshino kuzu* (1937) appeared together in 1982 as *The Secret History of the Lord of Musashi* and *Arrowroot* respectively. Tanizaki wrote a number of plays, literary essays and translations.
▷ *Setsugoan yawa* (posthumous, 1968); G B Petersen, *The Moon in the Water* (1979)

TANNAHILL, Robert
(1774–1810)

Scottish poet and songwriter, born in Paisley, the son of a handloom weaver. He composed many of his best songs to the music of his shuttle. He helped to found a **Burns** Club in 1803 for which he composed songs set on traditional airs. His *Poems and Songs* (1807) proved popular, the best known being 'Gloomy Winter's noo awa', 'Jessie the Flower o' Dunblane', 'The Braes o' Gleniffer', 'Loudon's Bonnie Woods and Braes' and 'The Wood o' Craigielea'. But after a publisher declined a revised edition he drowned himself in a canal near Paisley.

TANNHÄUSER, Der
(c.1210–c.1270)

German poet and Minnesinger, probably from Bavaria. He was court poet to the ruler of Austria, and is thought (because of what he says in his poetry) to have travelled a great deal, including taking part in one of the crusades. This is the source of the body of legend (as in Wagner's opera) which has grown up around the historical figure. His literary significance lies in his breaking away from the rigid conventions of previous Minnesang. His verse contains humour, irony and even parody, as well as great sensuality in erotic passages. Several of his songs survive with melodies.

TANSILLO, Luigi
(1510–68)

Prolific Italian courtier poet, born in Venosa. He served the Viceroy of Spain in Naples, Don Pedro di Toledo. His most valued work lies in his **Petrarch**an sonnets and in his long *Le lagrime di San Pietro* (1585, 'The Tears of St Peter'). His quaint *La balia* (1566, Eng trans *The Nurse*, 1800) is a plea to mothers to breastfeed their children themselves.

TARDIEU, Jean
(1903–)

French dramatist, translator (of, amongst others, **Hölderlin**) and poet, now well recognized as an important precursor of the Theatre of the Absurd. He began as poet, and his name was often associated with that of **Ponge** as an experimenter with language. He started writing plays in 1947; his short chamber plays, as he termed them, are often mentioned as resembling those of **Ionesco** and **Genet**, but more often he anticipated or influenced those writers. In one of the plays, *Une Voix Sans Personne* (1956, 'A Voice Without Anyone'), there are no characters. His humour has been compared to that of the composer Erik Satie. Available in English translation is *The Underground Lovers and Other Experimental Plays* (1968).

TARKINGTON, (Newton) Booth
(1869–1946)

American author, born in Indianapolis. Many of his novels have an Indiana setting, but he is best known as the author of *Monsieur Beaucaire* (1900) and his 'Penrod' books—*Penrod* (1914) and *Seventeen* (1916). His other works include a trilogy, *Growth* (1927), including *The Magnificent Ambersons* (1918), which won the Pulitzer Prize and was made into a successful film by Orson Welles, *Alice Adams* (1921, Pulitzer Prize), and a book of reminiscences, *The World does Move* (1928).
▷ A D Dickinson, *Booth Tarkington* (1926)

TÁSAROV-RODINIOV, Aleksandre Ignatiyevich
(1885–1938)

Russian novelist, born in Astrakhan. His novel *Shokolad* (1922, Eng trans *Chocolate*, 1932) prophesied the Stalin 1938 crackdown in which he himself perished. *Linyov* (1924), later called *Trava i krov* ('Grass and Blood'), attacks Lenin. The author was a man who had worked keenly for the communists, but changed his mind. He was 'rehabilitated' comparatively early.

TASSO, Bernardo
(1493–1569)

Italian poet, born in Venice of an illustrious family of Bergamo. After suffering poverty and exile owing to the outlawry by Charles V (1547) of his patron, the Duke of Salerno, he took service with the Duke of Mantua. His romantic epic *Amadigi di Gaula* (1560), an epic on the Amadis of Gaul, is a melodious imitation of **Ludovico Ariosto**'s manner, but exaggerated in sentiment. He began another epic, *Iloridante*, which was finished by his son

Torquato Tasso (1587), and wrote numerous lyrics (1560).

▷E Williamson, *Bernardo Tasso* (1951)

TASSO, Torquato
(1544–95)

Italian poet, son of **Bernardo Tasso**, born in Sorrento. He shared his exiled father's wandering life, but in 1560 he was sent to study law and philosophy at Padua, where he published his first work, a romantic poem, *Rinaldo* (1562, Eng trans 1792). In the service of Cardinal Luigi d'Este he was introduced to the court of the Duke of Ferrara; and there, encouraged by the sisters of the duke, he began his great epic poem and masterpiece, *Gerusalemme Liberata* (1580, Eng trans *Godfrey of Bouillon: The Recovery of Jerusalem*, 1600), an idealized story of the First Crusade. In 1571 he accompanied Cardinal d'Este to France, and on his return to Italy in 1572 became attached to the service of Duke Alfonso at Ferrara. For the court theatre he wrote his beautiful pastoral play, *Aminta* (1573, Eng trans 1591). Tasso completed his great epic in 1575, and submitted it before publication to the critics of the day. Their fault-finding and Tasso's replies are recorded in his correspondence and in his *Apologia*. In 1576 he showed the first signs of mental disorder; he became suspicious and melancholy, and obsessed with fears of assassination. He was confined at Ferrara, but escaped, and eventually made his way to Naples, Rome and Turin, where he was welcomed by the Duke of Savoy. Returning to Ferrara in 1579 he met with a cold reception, and, wounded by some real or imagined slight, broke into furious invectives against the duke, his courtiers, and all the world. He was confined at Ferrara by order of the duke as insane, not, as is often alleged, for his love for the Princess Leonora, a story on which **Byron** based his *Lament of Tasso*. In his seven years' confinement he wrote many noble verses and philosophical dialogues and a vigorous defence of his *Gerusalemme Liberata*, published without his leave and with many errors. The cruel contrast between his fate and the growing fame of his great poem had excited popular interest, and in July 1586 he was freed on the intercession of Prince Vincenzo Gonzaga. He followed his new patron to Mantua, where he wrote his only tragedy, *Il Re Torrismondo* (1586, 'King Torrismondo'). Broken in health and spirits, he began again his restless wanderings, spending, however, most of these later years in Rome and Naples, helped and protected by many kind friends and patrons. He busied himself in rewriting his great epic, according to the modifications proposed by his numerous critics. The result, a poor semblance of his

masterpiece, was published as *Gerusalemme Conquistata* (1593, 'Jerusalem Conquered'). Summoned to Rome by Pope Clement VIII to be crowned on the Capitol as poet laureate, he took ill on arrival and died in the monastery of Sant' Onofrio on the Janiculum.

▷A Solerti, *Vita di Tasso* (3 vols, 1895)

TASSONI, Allessandro
(1565–1635)

Italian poet and critic, born in Modena into a noble family. He was resolutely anti-Spanish throughout his life, and wrote tracts against the Spaniards. His most famous work is the mock epic *La secchia rapita* (1622, Eng trans *The Rape of the Bucket*, 1825), describing a war between Bologna and Modena over a bucket. For those who can read it in context it is still often funny.

▷V G Rossi, *Tassoni* (1931, in Italian)

TATARKA, Dominic
(1913–)

Slovak novelist and translator (from the French), born in Drienové. He wrote conventional and then socialist-realist novels of little interest; but *Farská republika* (1948, 'The Parsons' Republic'), written before he began to pretend to conform to state requirements, is an important account of Slovakia under the Nazis, and of a man's efforts to escape its spiritual oppressiveness. *Démon šuhlasu* (1963, 'The Demon of Compliance'), a short work, announced his complete break with socialist realism, and for a long time after 1968 he could not publish in his own country.

▷A J Liehm, *The Politics of Culture* (1970)

TATE, (John Orley) Allen
(1899–1979)

American poet, born in Winchester. He made an abortive start in a business career before entering academe, and became a professor first at Princeton and later at Minnesota University. He was Editor of the influential *Sewanee Review* (1944–5). A metaphysical poet in thrall to **T S Eliot**, his writing career was diverse and encompassed many books, including biographies of Thomas Stonewall Jackson (1928) and Jefferson Davies (1929). Collections of verse include *Mr Pope and Other Poems* (1928), *Poems 1928–31* (1932), *The Mediterranean and Other Poems* (1936) and *Winter Sea* (1945). He converted to Catholicism in 1950. He won the Bollingen Prize in 1956. He was married to the novelist **Caroline Gordon** for 35 years; they divorced in 1959.

▷G Hemphill, *Allen Tate* (1964)

TATE, James

(1943–)

American poet, story writer (*Hottentot Ossu-ary*, 1974) and (in collaboration) novelist, born in Kansas City, Missouri. By profession he is an academic, but his prolific poetry (nearly 30 volumes) mixes all kinds of non-academic American traditions, crossing the styles of **Berryman**, **Mark Twain**, Surrealism in the style of **Mark Strand**, and Bob Dylan; he even, in the words of one of his admirers, 'hangs up his shingle' (in *Absences: New Poems*, 1972) 'as a nihilist': in these poems he feared 'not the void' but said 'exactly what was expected of' him. Later, in love poems, unexpected subtleties are found: 'Rub-berducky that part of woman/that has to be going to the store/... sexual eggs, I touch you': it has been explained that for Tate 'woman' is not 'a woman'. *Lucky Darryl* (1977) is a novel, written with Bill Knott. There is as yet a dearth of critical exegesis.

TATE, Nahum

(1652–1715)

Irish poet and dramatist, born in Dublin. He studied at Trinity College there and saw his first play staged in London in 1678. With **Dr Johnson**'s approval, he wrote a number of 'improved' versions of **Shakespeare**'s trag-edies, substituting happy endings to suit the popular taste. With **Dryden**'s help he wrote a second part to the poet's *Absalom and Achitophel* (1682) and with Nicholas Brady com-piled a metrical version of the psalms. 'While Shepherds watched their Flocks by Night' is attributed to him, and he wrote the libretto of Purcell's *Dido and Aeneas* (1689). He suc-ceeded **Thomas Shadwell** as poet laureate in 1692. His best-known work is *Panacea or a Poem on Tea* (1700).
▷H F S Thomas, *The Life and Times of Nahum Tate* (1934)

TATHAM, John

(b.1610)

English dramatist and poet, who flourished between about 1632 and 1664. At a young age he had some success with the pastoral *Love Crowns the End* (1632) before seeing military service in the English Civil War under Lord Carnarvon. Between 1657 and 1664 he wrote London's city pageants, which were generally called *London's Triumph(s)* or *London's Glory*. He also wrote verse, often echoing **Abraham Cowley**. His plays show a hatred of strangers, especially the Scots: thus his crude 1652 offering was entitled *The Scots Figgaries, or a Knot of Knaves*. He fades from historical view after about 1664.

TAUNAY, Alfred d'Escagnolle, Vicomte de

(1843–99)

Brazilian novelist of French descent. His *Memórias* (1948), which were published long after his death, are invaluable. Initially he wrote under pseudonyms ('Silvio Dinarte', 'Heitor Malgheiro'), and some early books were first published in French. He took part in the Mato Grosso Expedition. His mas-terpiece is the novel *Innocência* (1872, rev edn 1884, Eng trans *Innocence*, 1945), which com-bines beautifully observed regionalism with deep sympathy for the native population.
▷P Serpa, *Vicomte de Taunay* (1952, in Por-tuguese)

TAYAMA Katai

(1872–1930)

Japanese writer, born into a wealthy, upper middle-class family, and sent abroad (to Eng-land) to study. He is credited with inventing the *watakushi shosetsu* (I-novel), the most extreme product of Japanese naturalism, the dominant literary movement in the first half of the 20th century, in which realism is achieved by concentrating solely upon the internal workings of the narrator's mind. *Futon* (1907) is his best and best-known work, and is typical of his style. Nothing very much happens in it, except for the narrator losing his girlfriend; it is, instead, a long, intricately described account of his feelings and states of mind. *Inaka Kyoshi* (1909, 'The Country Teacher') is constructed along similar lines.

TAYLOR, (James) Bayard

(1825–78)

American travel-writer and poet, born in Chester county, Pennsylvania. Apprenticed to a printer, he wrote a volume of poems (1844), visited Europe, published *Views Afoot* (1846), and obtained a post on the *New York Tribune*. As its correspondent he made exten-sive travels in California and Mexico, up the Nile, in Asia Minor and Syria, across Asia to India, China and Japan, which he recorded in a great number of travel books which he later published. In 1862–3 he was secretary of legation at St Petersburg and in 1878 became ambassador at Berlin, where he died.
▷R C Bently, *Bayard Taylor, laureate of the Gilded Age* (1936)

TAYLOR, Edward

(c.1644–1729)

American Puritan poet, born near Coventry, England. His poems were not published until 1937, when they were fulsomely received by critics specializing in the sombre colonial period. Early in life he emigrated to Boston and went to Harvard. After graduation he became pastor of Westfield, a position he held for the rest of his life. He was married twice and had 13 children. On Taylor's death, a grandson, Ezra Stiles, deposited an unopened package of the poems in the library at Yale. The 1937 publication and a more comprehensive edition of Poems in 1960 have led to Taylor taking his place as foremost Puritan poet, and the only American of his period worthy to be compared with **George Herbert** or **Richard Crashaw**.

▷N S Grabo, *Edward Taylor* (1962)

TAYLOR, Elizabeth, born Elizabeth Coles
(1912–75)

English novelist, born in Reading, Berkshire. The daughter of an insurance inspector, she was educated locally at the Abbey School and worked as a governess and librarian. She married John Taylor, the director of a sweet factory, when she was 24, and wrote her first novel, *At Mrs Lippincote's* (1945), while her husband was in the Royal Air Force. This was followed by such novels as *Palladian* (1946), *A Wreath of Roses* (1949), *A Game of Hide-and-Seek* (1951), *Angel* (1957), *The Wedding Group* (1968), *Mrs Palfrey at the Claremont* (1971) and *Blaming*, published posthumously in 1976. Her hallmark is quiet, shrewd observation of middle-class life in the south-east of England, reminiscent of **Jane Austen** with whom she is quite often compared. Like her, her life was more domestic than literary. Her stories, collected in four volumes (1954–72), are no less admired than her novels.

▷R Liddell, *Ivy and Elizabeth* (1966)

TAYLOR, Sir Henry
(1800–86)

English poet, born in Bishop in Durham, the son of a gentleman farmer. He was an administrator in the colonial office (1824–72). He wrote four tragedies, *Isaac Comnenus* (1827), a remarkable study in character, *Philip van Artefelde* (1834), *Edwin the Fair* (1842) and *St Clement's Eve* (1862). A romantic comedy, *The Virgin Widow* (1850), was afterwards entitled *A Sicilian Summer*. In 1845 he published a volume of lyrical poetry, and in 1847 *The Eve of the Conquest*. His prose included *The Statesman* (1836) and an *Autobiography* (1885).

▷J B Bilderbeck, *Sir Henry Taylor and his Drama of Philip van Artevelde* (1877)

TAYLOR, Henry Splawn
(1942–)

American poet, born in Loudoun County, Virginia. He is Professor of Literature at the American University in Washington, DC. His first book of poems was *The Horse Show at Midnight* (1966), followed by *Breakings* (1971), *An Afternoon of Pocket Billiards* (1974) and *Desperado* (1979). He was awarded the Pulitzer Prize for Poetry in 1986 for his collection *The Flying Change* (1985). His other works include translations and anthologies.

TAYLOR, John
(1580–1653)

English poet and pamphleteer, known as the 'Water-poet', born in Gloucester. He became a Thames waterman, but, pressed into the navy, served at the siege of Cadiz (1625). At the outbreak of the Civil War (1642) he kept a public house in Oxford, but gave it up for another in London, and there wrote his own doggerel poems, full of natural humour and low wit. The chief event of his life was his journey on foot from London to Edinburgh (1618), described in his *Penniless Pilgrimage* (1618); similar books were his *Travels in Germanie* (1617) and *The Praise of Hempseed* (1618), a story of a voyage in a brown paper boat from London to Queensborough.

▷W Thorp, *John Taylor* (1922)

TAYLOR, Mildred D
(1943–)

American novelist, born in Jackson, Mississippi. Educated at Toledo University, she has worked as an English and history teacher with the Peace Corps in Ethiopia, and as a Peace Corps recruiter. An unusually powerful historical novelist for children, she focuses mainly on the era of the 1930s–1950s and the inequalities and oppression then faced by American blacks. A vivid writer who deals honestly with uncomfortable situations and ethics, her most notable fiction is the series that begins with *Song of the Trees* (1975), in which life is viewed through the courageous eyes of Cassie Logan, a highly intelligent black girl who cannot always make sense of the warped ways of her world.

TAYLOR, Peter Hillsman
(1917–)

American short-story writer, novelist, and playwright, born in Trenton, Tennessee and educated in Nashville, Memphis, and Kenyon College, Ohio. Concerned with the smaller crises and collisions of urban middle-class life in the southern states of America, primarily Tennessee, his vision is an alloy of sentiment and irony. He writes about what he knows and the areas where he grew up in Memphis, St Louis and Nashville. Representative stories are 'The Scoutmaster', 'The Old Forest', 'The Death of a Kinsman' and 'A Long Fourth'. *The Collected Stories of Peter Taylor* was published in 1969. His sole novel, *A Summons to Memphis* (1987), is a quiet but powerful tale of family tension and resentment; it won the Pulitzer Prize.

TAYLOR, Robert Lewis
(1912–)
American journalist, biographer and writer of fiction, born in Illinois, whose career began as a reporter on the *St. Louis Post*. Taylor's many years of writing profiles for the *New Yorker* led to full-length biographies, including *W. C. Fields: His Follies and Fortunes* (1949) and *Winston Churchill: An Informal Study in Greatness* (1958). His best work, however, is to be found in his picaresque fiction, especially the Pulitzer Prize-winning *The Travels of Jamie McPheeter* (1958), about a teenage boy travelling to California in the Gold Rush.

TAYLOR, Tom
(1817–80)
Scottish dramatist and editor, born in Sunderland. He studied at Glasgow and Trinity College, Cambridge, and was elected a fellow. Professor of English for two years at University College, London, and called to the Bar in 1845, he was secretary to the Board of Health (1850–72), and then to the Local Government Act Office. From 1846 he wrote or adapted over a hundred pieces for the stage, among them *Still Waters Run Deep* (1855), *Our American Cousin*, (1858), *The Ticket of Leave Man* (1863) and *'Twixt Axe and Crown*. He edited the autobiographies of Benjamin Haydon and Charles Robert Leslie, completed the latter's *Life and Times of Reynolds*, translated *Ballads and Songs of Brittany* (1865), and in 1874 became Editor of *Punch*. He was *The Times* art critic, and appeared as a witness for **John Ruskin** in the libel action brought against him by Whistler in 1878.

TCHERNIKOWSKI, Saul
(1875–1943)
Hebrew poet and master-translator, who was born in Mikhailovka in the Crimea, and did not learn Hebrew until he was seven years old. He was a doctor by profession, and practised as one in Russia and in Palestine (from 1930). He differs from most of his contemporaries in that he was not a conspicuously nationalistic or even religious poet: his work brought into Hebrew poetry a new, and secular note. He was in his youth a noted philanderer, and wrote lushly, candidly and beautifully of his continual state of ongoing and optimistic eroticism. His translations of the *Iliad*, *Odyssey*, *Gilgamesh* and the Finnish epic *Kalevala* are unmatched. Good translations into English are to be found in such anthologies as Birman's *Modern Hebrew*

Poetry (1947), and in J Klausner's *Saul Tchernikowski: Poet of Revolt* (1965).
▷M Waxman, *A History of Jewish Literature* (1947)

TEASDALE, Sara
(1884–1933)
American poet, born in St Louis, Missouri and educated at the Mary Institute and Hosmer Hall. The first person to receive a Pulitzer Prize for poetry (for her collection *Love Songs*, 1917), Teasdale initially earned a reputation as a writer of 'feminine' love poetry. However, much of her poetry is in fact based on her own sheltered early life and unhappy marriage, and expresses the conflicting needs for independence and freedom, love and security. She wrote nine collections of poetry, two of which were published after her death, a suspected suicide.
▷C B Schoen, *Sara Teasdale* (1986)

TEBALDEO, Antonio
(1463–1537)
Italian poet, born in Ferrara, who was at one time secretary to Lucrezia Borgia. He enjoyed the patronage of Pope Leo X in Rome, but then suffered after the sack of 1527, spending the rest of his life in poverty. When a cousin issued a collection of his poetry without his permission in 1499, it immediately became popular. But since the vogue for him faded, his poems have been regarded as somewhat feeble imitations of **Petrarch**.

TEGNÉR, Elaias
(1782–1846)
Swedish poet and churchman, born in Kyrkerud in Värmland, the son of a pastor. Educated at Lund, he was appointed lecturer there in 1802. His stirring *Krigssång för Landtvärnet* (1808, 'War-song for the Militia of Scania') made his name as a poet, and *Svea* (1811) made him famous. He was appointed Professor of Greek at Lund (1812–26), and Bishop of Växjö (1824). His best-known works include *Sång till Solen* (1817, 'Song to the Sun'), *Epilog vid magisterpromotionen i Lund 1820* (1820, 'Degree Day at Lund'), his religious idyll *Nattvardsbarn* (1820, 'The Communion Children'), *Axel*, a narrative romance of the days of King Karl XII (1822), and his masterpiece, *Frithjof's Saga* (1825). He also had a keen interest in education.
▷A Werin, *Elaias Tegnér* (1934)

TEIRLINCK, Herman
(1879–1967)
Major Belgian (Flemish) novelist, playwright and critic, born in Brussels, the son of Isidoor Teirlinck, himself a noted writer and Flemish nationalist. Eventually Herman was chosen

by the King of Belgium (Albert) to advise him on cultural and scientific matters, and then by King Baudouin to help him with the problems posed by the coexistence of Flemish and French in Belgium. From early on in his literary career he was as much read in Holland as in his own country, partly perhaps because he had taken his initial inspiration from the Dutchman Lodewijk van Deyssel. He started an epistolary novel with **Karel van de Woestijne**, but they did not complete it. His fictional masterpiece came late in his productive life: *Zelfportret op het Galgemaal* (1956, Eng trans *The Man in the Mirror*, 1963), in which a greedy and sensual old banker—a masterly portrait of the type—addresses himself in the second person. Teirlinck was also an important playwright, whose *De vertraagde film* (1922, 'Slow-Film') inspired *L'Inconnue d'Arras* (1935) of **Armand Salacrou**. Many find his plays superior to those of one who undoubtedly influenced him, **Maurice Maeterlinck**. The expressionistic and allegorical *De Man zonder lif* (1925, 'The Man without a Body'), certainly improves upon, whilst it frankly employs the form of, Maeterlinck's *L'Oiseau bleu* (1908), as well as drawing upon the methods of **Pirandello**. His experiments with theatre groups were important and influential, as were his essays on theatre. He was much loved and respected in Dutch and Flemish literary circles.

▷ T O van de Wal, *Herman Teirlinck* (1965, in Flemish); S Lilar, *The Belgian Theatre Since 1890* (1962)

TEMPLE, Sir William
(1628–99)

English diplomatist and essay writer, born in London. He studied at Emmanuel College, Cambridge. After a successful diplomatic career, during which he helped to cement the Triple Alliance between England, Holland and Sweden against France, and suggested the scheme of a reformed privy council of 30, he decided to concentrate on a literary life and established a considerable reputation as an essayist. His works include *Miscellanea* (1679, 1692) and the famous essay 'Upon the Ancient and Modern Learning'.

▷ C Marburg, *Sir William Temple* (1929)

TENCIN, Claudine Alexandrine Guérin de
(1681–1749)

French writer and courtesan, born in Grenoble. She entered the religious life, but in 1714 moved to Paris, where her wit and beauty attracted a crowd of lovers, among them the regent and Cardinal Dubois. She had much political influence, enriched herself, and helped the fortunes of her brother, Cardinal Pierre Guérin de Tencin (1680–1758). But her importance died with the regent and the cardinal in 1723. In 1726 she was imprisoned for a short time in the Bastille, after one of her lovers had shot himself in her house. Her later life was more decorous, and her *salon* one of the most popular in Paris. **Bernard le Fontenelle** was one of her oldest lovers; d'Alembert one of her children. Her romances include *Mémoires du Comte de Comminges* (1735, 'Memoirs of the Count of Comminges'), *Le Siège de Calais* (1739, 'The Siege of Calais') and *Les Malheurs de l'amour* (1747, 'Misfortunes of Love').

TENNANT, Emma Christina
(1937–)

British novelist, born in London and brought up in Scotland. Her first novel was published under the name 'Catherine Aydy' in 1964. Her fiction has shown a willingness to deal in imaginative and unconventional fashion with themes drawn from genre models, including fantasy, the supernatural, science fiction and detection, as in the apocalyptic *The Time of the Crack* (1973), in which a strange faultline threatens London, or *Hotel de Dream* (1976), in which dream and reality merge. Gothic strains are evident in *The Bad Sister* (1978), arguably her best book, and *Wild Nights* (1980). She draws directly on literary predecessors in *Two Women in London: The Strange Case of Ms Jeykll and Mrs Hyde* (1989) and *Faustine* (1992), while *Sisters and Strangers: A Moral Tale* (1990) is a fable in which Adam and Eve have survived until the present. She writes from a feminist perspective, and founded and edited the radical literary magazine *Bananas* (1975–9).

TENNANT, Kylie
(1912–88)

Australian author, born in Manly, New South Wales, whose novels demonstrate enduring faith in the essential Australian character, which she portrays with affection, sympathy and humour. Her earliest books, from *Tiburon* (1935) to the award-winning *The Battlers* (1941), describe the 1930s Depression as experienced in both city and outback. She spent a week in gaol in search of authenticity for *Tell Morning This* (1978), which pictures the seamy underside of Sydney in wartime; it was originally published in a censored version in 1953 as *The Joyful Condemned*. Her last book, *Tantavallon* (1983), is a surreal story which effectively combines the tragic and comic strands pre-eminent in her writing.

TENNANT, William
(1784–1848)

Scottish poet and scholar, born in Anstruther, Fife. He studied at St Andrews University, and in 1812 published a mock-heroic poem *Anster Fair*, which was the first attempt to naturalize the Italian *ottava rima*. He was a teacher from 1816 at Lasswade, from 1819 at Dollar Academy, and from 1835 Professor of Oriental Languages at St Andrews. His *Synopsis of Chaldaic and Syriac Grammar* (1840) became a standard authority. Other poems were the *Thane of Fife* (1822) and *Papistry Stormed* (1827); dramas were *Cardinal Beaton* (1823) and *John Baliol* (1825).

TENNYSON, Alfred, 1st Baron Tennyson
(1809–92)

English poet, born in Somersby rectory, Lincolnshire, the fourth son of the rector. His elder brothers, Frederick and Charles, also wrote poetry. He was educated at Louth Grammar School, and in 1827 went to Trinity College, Cambridge, where he became a member of an ardent group of young men, including Arthur Hallam, whose early death was to be mourned in that great elegiac poem *In Memoriam* (1850). His early ventures in verse, *Poems Chiefly Lyrical* (1830) and *Poems* (1833), were understandably slighted by the critics as being too sentimental. But the critics ought to have detected the great poet in the first version of 'The Lady of Shallott', 'Oenone', 'The Lotus-eaters' and other poems in the 1833 volume. Nine years of revising these poems and adding fresh material resulted in the volume of *Poems* of 1842, which established his fame. He had been engaged since 1833 in writing the series of loosely connected lyrics or elegies which as *In Memoriam* crowned his fame in 1850, the year he succeeded **Wordsworth** as poet laureate and the year of his marriage to Emily Sarah Sellwood. In 1853 he settled in a house on the Isle of Wight, 'Farringford', and in 1868 built 'Aldworth' in Sussex as a summer home. He was flattered by the homage of the entire nation from Queen Victoria downwards, such was his popularity. With his wife he made short tours but rarely left England. The volume of 1842 and *In Memoriam* contain some of the most finished artistry in English poetry, in which the mood of the poem is perfectly reflected in rhythm and language. After 1850 he devoted himself to the fashionable verse novelette—*Maud; a Monodrama* (1855), *Enoch Arden* (1864) and *Locksley Hall Sixty Years After* (1886). The public, however, was waiting for what was to be the crowning triumph. The first instalment of *Idylls of the King* (1859) seemed to the Victorians to be just that, but in *Geraint and Enid* and *Lancelot and Elaine* and throughout the whole series (completed in 1885) Victorian morality imposed on the old chivalric matter stifles the poetry except in the descriptive passages. In the 1870s he attempted drama. Henry Irving gave *Becket* a considerable run,

but *Harold*, *Queen Mary* and others were not successful. He had a late flowering in his seventies when he wrote the perfect poem *To Virgil*, *Tiresias*, and the powerful *Rizpah*, but the conflict between science and the Faith, discussed optimistically in *In Memoriam*, now becomes an obsession. *The Princess* (1847) gave him a chance to make a social comment, but the subject of woman's education is treated in serio-comic fashion, which is trying, and the image of John Bull he projects in the poem is offensive to modern taste. His last poem was a 16-line lyric written in 1889 while crossing from Lymington to the Isle of Wight, *Crossing the Bar*.
▷ T R Lousbury, *The Life and Times of Alfred Lord Tennyson, 1809–1850* (1862); Hallam Tennyson, *Alfred Lord Tennyson, a memoir* (1897)

TENNYSON TURNER, Charles
(1808–79)

English poet, born in Somersby, an elder brother of **Alfred Tennyson**. He graduated from Trinity College, Cambridge, in 1832, and was for many years vicar of Grasby, Lincolnshire. He took the name Turner under the will of a great-uncle. As well as collaborating with his brother in *Poems by Two Brothers* (1827), he wrote 341 sonnets (collected, with introductory essay by Spedding, 1880).
▷ H Nicholson, *Tennyson's Two Brothers* (1947)

TERENCE (Publius Terentius Afer)
(c.195–159 BC)

Roman comedy writer, born in Carthage. He became the slave of the Roman senator P Terentius Lucanus, who brought him to Rome, educated him, and set him free. His first play was the *Andria* (166 BC, 'The Girl from Andros'); its success introduced Terence to the most refined society of Rome. His chief patrons were Laelius and Scipio Æmilianus, the younger. After spending some years in Rome he went to Greece. Six of his comedies are still extant: *Andria* (166 BC), *Eunuchus* (161 BC), *Heauton Timoroumenos* (163 BC, 'Self-Tormentor'), *Phormio* (161 BC), *Hecyra* (165 BC, 'Mother-in-Law') and *Adelphi* (160 BC, 'Brothers'). His plays, Greek in origin and Greek in scene, were mostly based on **Menander**. His excellence lies in the fact that he wrote in singularly pure and perfect Latin. Many of his conventions and plot constructions were later used by **Molière**, **Richard Brinsley Sheridan**, and others.
▷ J Strauss, *Terence and Menander* (1955)

TERESA DE JESÚS, Santa
(1515–82)

Spanish Carmelite mystic and writer, born of a noble family in Ávila, Old Castile. In 1533 she entered a Carmelite convent there. About 1555 her religious exercises reached an extraordinary pitch of asceticism; she experienced ecstasies, and the fame of her sanctity spread widely. In 1562, with papal permission, she founded the Convent of St Joseph to re-establish the ancient Carmelite rule, with additional observances, later extending her reforms, which were adopted by many convents within her lifetime. Although she wrote some poetry, she is remembered mainly for her prose works, primarily her autobiography, *Libro de la vida* (1562) and *Las moradas* (1577, 'The Interior Castle'), in which she discusses her spiritual experiences by comparing the soul to a castle which contains many secret chambers, and her *Libro de las fundaciones* (1610, 'The Book of Foundations'), in which she describes her struggle to found various convents, but which is also a detailed and revealing chronicle of her tempestuous times. She stresses the physical aspects of her experiences and uses erotic imagery to convey a sense of spiritual rapture, but her most endearing feature is undoubtedly her distinctive prose style, which effectively captures the rhythm and intimacy of the spoken language, showing a disregard for conventional syntax and frequently losing its train of thought in mid-sentence. She was canonized in 1622.

▷ H Hatzfeld, *Estudios literarios sobre mistica española* (1968); E A Peers, *The Complete Works of Saint Teresa of Jesus* (1982)

TERHUNE, Mary Virginia
(1830–1922)

American author of more than two dozen highly popular romantic novels. Terhune began writing as Marion Harland and published her first novel, *Alone*, in 1854. She married a clergyman and moved to a parsonage at Newark, New Jersey, which later became the home of her son, Albert Payson Terhune, author of a series of novels about dogs. In middle life Mary Terhune became more noted for her books on etiquette and home economics than for her fiction. At the turn of the century few kitchens in the US lacked a copy of her *American Cookbook* (1896).

TERKEL, Studs (Louis)
(1912–)

American writer and oral historian, born in New York City. He grew up and went to Law School in Chicago. He has acted in radio soap operas, been a disc jockey, a radio commentator and a television host, and has travelled worldwide conducting interviews with the famous and the anonymous. Described by J K Galbraith as 'a national resource', his publications include *Giants of Jazz* (1957), *Division Street: America* (1967), *Hard Times*

(1970), *Working* (1974), about the Depression, *American Dreams: Lost and Found* (1980), and *The Good War: An Oral History of World War Two* (1984), for which he was awarded the Pulitzer Prize .

▷ *Talking to Myself* (1977)

TERSON, Peter, pseud of Peter Patterson
(1932–)

English dramatist, born in Newcastle, who worked as a teacher before his first play, *A Night to Make Angels Weep*, was produced at the Victoria Theatre, Stoke-on-Trent, in 1964. For 18 months he was resident dramatist with the theatre and has subsequently had over 20 plays staged there. He has also had a long association with the National Youth Theatre, for which he wrote *Zigger-Zagger* (1967), a large-scale play about fanatical football fans, and such works as *The Apprentices* (1968), *Good Lads at Heart* (1971) and *Geordie's March* (1979). Terson returned to the adult theatre and his native north-east with *Strippers* (1984), a study of women living in an area of increasing unemployment, who are forced to take jobs stripping in pubs and clubs to support their families.

TERZAKIS, Angelos
(1907–79)

Greek novelist, short-story writer and essayist. Initially influenced by the Symbolists, he found fame with a series of historical novels, notable for their intense realism. The first of these was *He Menexedhenia Politeia* (1937, 'The Violet City'), his third book. *He Prinkipessa Ysabeau* ('Princess Ysabeau'), widely regarded as his masterpiece, was published in 1946: it was set in the Peloponnese in the 13th century, and spawned a host of imitators. Terzakis won an equal reputation as an essayist, especially for his confessional works *Dhichos Theo* (1953, 'Without God') and *Mystiki Zoë* (1957, 'Mystic Life').

TEXIDOR, Greville, originally Margaret Foster
(1902–64)

English-born Australasian writer who, as a teenager after World War I, posed for Augustus John, Mark Gertler and others of that coterie. In 1929 she married Manuel Texidor, a Catalan industrialist, and later married a refugee from Nazi Germany, with whom she emigrated to New Zealand. Welcomed into Auckland's literary circle, Greville began writing and became a close friend of refugee writer **Anna Kavan**; their work was published in *New Zealand Writing*. Greville's short stories and verse appeared in England in 1943 and in Australia in 1944, when the periodical *Angry Penguins* printed her translations of 12 poems by **Lorca**. It also accepted *These Dark Glasses*, but this was not to be published until 1949. She later moved to Australia and then to the Costa Brava, but in 1962 she returned to Sydney, where she committed suicide. A collection of stories *In Fifteen Minutes you can say a Lot*, with an introduction by **Kendrick Smithyman**, was published in 1987.

TEY, Josephine, pseud of Elizabeth Mackintosh
(1897–1952)

Scottish crime and mystery writer, who also produced 'straight' fiction under the name of 'Gordion Daviot'. She grew up in Inverness and trained as a PE teacher. Her main invention, police inspector Alan Grant, tended to prefer cerebral rather than physical exercise. The most extreme instance of this—and probably the most notorious—is *The Daughter of Time* (1952), a re-opening of the file on Richard III's alleged murder of the little princes in the Tower of London; Grant conducts this masterpiece of retrospective investigation from his hospital bed. Grant was introduced in Tey's first novel, *The Man in the Queue* (1929, published in the USA as *Killer in the Crowd*, 1954), for which she used the Daviot pseudonym. *Miss Pym Disposes* (1946) and *The Franchise Affair* (1948) were non-Grant mysteries, as was the popular *Brat Farrar* (1949, published in the USA as *Come and Kill Me*, 1951); it dealt with double and demonic 'twins' and unconsciously revealed her essential Scottishness. This also emerged in her plays *Queen of Scots* (1934) and *Leith Sands* (1946), and in an impressive biography of Claverhouse (1937).
▷S Roy, *Josephine Tey* (1980)

THACKERAY, William Makepeace
(1811–63)

English novelist, born in Calcutta, where his father was in the service of the East India Company. His father died in 1816 and his mother remarried, so young Thackeray was sent home. He went to Charterhouse (1822) and Trinity College, Cambridge (1829), but left without taking a degree. His first venture in print was a parody of **Tennyson**'s prize poem *Timbuctoo*. After dissipating much of his patrimony in travelling abroad, he decided to improve his fortune by journalism, though art equally attracted him. A four-year stay in Paris as an art student came to a close through lack of funds in 1836. He had now married Isabella Shawe (1836), but financial worry, due to the bankruptcy of his stepfather, finally made him decide to earn a living in journalism, and he returned to London. He contributed regularly to *The Times*, the *New Monthly* and *Fraser's Magazine*. Domestic trouble now engulfed him. The birth of his third daughter affected Mrs Thackeray's mind, the home was broken up and the children sent to their grandmother in Paris. His first publications, starting with *The Paris Sketchbook* (1840), and written under various pseudonyms (Wagstaff, Titmarsh, Fitz-Boodle, Yellowplush, Snob, etc) were a comparative failure although they included *The Yellowplush Papers*, *The Great Hoggarty Diamond* and *The Luck of Barry Lyndon*, all contributed to *Fraser's Magazine* (1841–4). It was his work on *Punch* from 1842 onwards which attracted attention by exploiting the view of society as seen by the butler ('Jeames' Diary') and the theme of English snobbery. The great novels that were to follow—*Vanity Fair* (1847–8), *Pendennis* (1848–50), *Henry Esmond* (1852) and *The Newcomes* (1853–5), all monthly serials—established his fame. *Vanity Fair* is the first novel to give a view of London society with its mingling of rich parvenus and decadent upper class, through both of which the social climber, Becky Sharp, threads her way. The great historical novel, *Henry Esmond*, shows Thackeray's consuming love of the 18th century. Its sequel, *The Virginians* (1857–9), is not considered a success. *The Newcomes* shows a young love at the mercy of scheming relatives and mean-spirited rival suitors. Thackeray retired from *Punch* in 1854 and became the Editor of the *Cornhill Magazine*, where much of his later work appeared—ballads, novels, and so on, now largely unreadable. He also undertook lecturing tours at home and in America, the fruit of which, apart from *The Virginians*, was *The English Humorists of the 18th century* (1853) and *The Four Georges* (1860).
▷G N Ray, *William Makepeace Thackeray* (2 vols, 1955–8)

THARAUD, Jérôme
(1874–1953)
THARAUD, Jean
(1877–1952)

French writers, born in Saint-Junien, Limoges, and generally referred to as 'Les Frères Tharaud' in the manner of the Brothers **Goncourt**. They travelled together, and collaborated in a series of novels and essays characterized by a direct and unpretentious style which was more reportorial than novelistic, and revealed an interest in reflecting topical events. *Dingley, l'illustre écrivain*, set during the Boer War, won the Prix Goncourt in 1906; *La Fête arabe* (1911) dealt with the French colonization of North Africa, while *Un royaume de Dieu* (1921) and other novels focused on Jewish life in central Europe, where Jérôme taught at the University of Budapest. Jérôme was elected to the Académie Française in 1940, and Jean in 1946.

THAXTER, Celia
(1835–94)

American poet, born in New Hampshire, the daughter of a lighthouse-keeper who later became proprietor of a hotel much frequented by literary worthies, such as **Lowell**, **Whittier** and **Thoreau**. It was through such connections that Thaxter made lifelong friends of the publisher James T Fields, and his wife Annie, an association which opened the door to her publication in the *Atlantic* and then other national magazines. In her collections—*Poems* (1872) and *Drift-Weed* (1879)—children's and adult verse is mixed together, as are the influences of **Longfellow** and **Bryant**.

THELEMIS, George
(1900–76)

Greek poet, born in Samos. A teacher, he regarded poetry as a 'method of self-knowledge'; at least one English student of modern Greek poetry has called him 'different, original … misunderstood … more rewarding than **Ritsos** or **Elytis**'. He wrote one of the most revealing books on the poet **Cavafy**.
▷L Politis, *A History of Modern Greek Literature* (1973)

THEOCRITUS
(c.310–250 BC)

Greek pastoral poet, born probably in Syracuse, Sicily. He was brought up on the island of Cos, but lived for a time at the court of Ptolemy III, Philadelphus in Alexandria, returning later to Cos. The authenticity of some of his 30 extant bucolic poems has been disputed. They fall into three classes—half-epic, mimic and idyllic. Probably the half-epic poems were the earliest. He wrote a series of poems dealing with heroic legend, especially that of Heracles. His famous 15th Idyll, *Syracusii* ('The Ladies of Syracuse'), said to be copied from Sophron, describes delightfully the visit of a Syracusan lady and her friend, both living in Alexandria, to the festival of Adonis. Theocritus raised the rude pastoral poetry of the Doric race in Sicily into a new and perfect form of literature. His short poems dealing with pastoral subjects, and representing a single scene, came to be called Idylls (*eidullia*). He combined realism with romanticism, and every touch is natural. **Virgil** imitates him closely in his *Eclogues*; **Tennyson** was deeply influenced by him, as were the pastoral poets of the Renaissance.
▷A S F Gow, *Theocritus* (1952)

THEOGNIS
(fl.544–541 BC)

Greek elegiac poet, a Dorian noble of Megara on the Isthmus of Corinth. During the confusion which followed the overthrow of the tyrant Theagenes, he was driven from Megara, and visited Euboea and Sicily. Under his name survive 1389 elegiac verses, social, political and gnomic, but perhaps only some of them are his.
▷C M Bowra, *Early Greek Elegists* (1938)

THEOTOKAS, George
(1905–66)

Greek novelist. Born into a wealthy family in Constantinople, he studied in Athens, Paris and London, before returning to Greece. His essay *Elefthero Prefma* ('Free Spirit') was published in 1929 and served as a manifesto for his generation of novelists. His first three novels were not, however, so successful, and it was only with the publication of *Leonis* in 1940 that his reputation was secured; set in the Constantinople of Theotokas's childhood, it tells the story of a man's physical and spiritual growth. After World War II Theotokas turned to the theatre and to travel writing, completing *Asthenis Ke Hodhipori* (1964, 'Sick Persons and Travellers') about the Greco–German War; his later travel books include accounts of his journeys to America and the Middle East.

THEROUX, Paul Edward
(1941–)

American writer, born in Medford, Massachusetts. His literary output reflects his footloose life. *Waldo* (1969), his first novel, was followed by fictions that drew on his experience of three years in Africa. He subsequently taught at Singapore University, a sojourn that produced a collection of short stories, *Sinning with Annie* (1976), and a novel, *Saint Jack* (1973). Others, for example *The Family Arsenal* (1976), *Doctor Slaughter* (1984), which made an unfortunate transition to celluloid, and *The London Embassy* (1982), have been based in London where he lived part of the year. His novels are urbane and paradoxical, sometimes bleak and frequently funny; *Millroy the Magician* (1993) was a quantum step, concentrating themes and ideas that have surfaced throughout his career. The same can be said of his extended rail journeys, recounted in *The Great Railway Bazaar: By Train Through Asia* (1975), and *The Old Patagonian Express: By Train Through the Americas* (1979), in which Theroux emerges as a crusty loner, an intelligent observer with the tolerance of a misanthrope.

THESIGER, Wilfred
(1910–)

English traveller, born in Ethiopia (then Abyssinia), where his father was British Minister in charge of the Legation at Addis Ababa. He remained there till he was nine, when he transferred to Eton. Later he went to Oxford where he acquired—in the boxing ring—his prominent dog-leg nose. Described by Douglas Newbold, his Provincial Governor in the Sudan Service, as 'a misfit owing to excess of virtues and not because of any vices—a brave, awkward, attractive creature', he has won the Gold Medal of the Royal Geographical Society, shot 70 lions in the Sudan, ridden 115 miles on a camel in 24 hours, fought with the Special Air Service (SAS) in North Africa and written a classic of travel literature, *Arabian Sands* (1959). Drawn spiritually to remote parts of the globe—Arabia, Abyssinia, Kenya, Kurdistan, Nuristan, the White Nile and the Marshes of Iraq—he has spent much of his life among nomadic tribesmen with whom he instinctively empathizes. Described by **Eric Newby** as 'the last of the great explorers', he also wrote *The Marsh Arabs* (1964), *Desert, Marsh, Mountain* (1979) and *Visions of a Nomad* (1987). *The Life of My Choice*, his autobiography, was published in 1987.

THESPIS
(6th century BC)

Greek poet from Icaria, the reputed founder of Greek drama. He is said to have won the first prize for tragedy at a festival in Athens in c.534 BC. According to Aristotle, he used single actors to deliver speeches, in addition to the traditional chorus.
▷A W Pichard-Cambridge, *Thespis* (1962)

THEURIET, André
(1833–1907)

French poet and novelist, born in Marly-le-Roi, Seine-et-Oise. In 1857 he received a post under the finance minister. His collections of verse include *Le Chemin des bois* (1867, 'The Way through the Woods'), the so-called epic *Les Paysans de l'Argonne, 1792* (1871, 'The Peasants of Argonne, 1792') and *Le Bleu et le Noir* (1872, 'The Blue and the Black'). He is best known for his novels *Le Mariage de Gérard* (1875, Eng trans *Gerard's Marriage*, 1877), *Raymonde* (1877, Eng trans 1878) and *Sauvageonne* (1880, 'The Little Savage Girl').

THIBAUT (THEOBALD) IV
(1201–53)

French trouvère poet, Count of Champagne and Brie, and King of Navarre. He was more successful as a poet than as a ruler and soldier, though the chief virtues of his verse are its wide range of style and subject-matter—he is the author of pastoral and courtly poems, crusade songs, and religious works—and the fact that so much of it has survived. It is said that he was the lover of Blanche de Castile, Regent of France (he is even said to have poisoned her husband, the king), and that Blanche was the inspiration for many of his songs. This may not be true, but it shows, perhaps, his unpopularity at the time.

THIELE, Colin Milton
(1920–)

Australian writer of children's books, radio drama and poetry, born in Eudunda, South Australia. He is an educationist by profession, and much of his work has been directed to this end. His books for younger readers have been recognized by numerous awards and commendations: *The Sun on the Stubble* (1961), *Blue Fin* (1969, filmed 1978), *The Fire in the Stone* (1973, winner of the **Edgar Allan Poe** Award) and *Storm Boy* (1963, filmed 1976). Some writing evokes his home state of South Australia, for example the adult novel *Labourers in the Vineyard* (1970), set in the wine-growing district of the Barossa Valley.

THIRKELL, Angela Margaret, née **Mackail**
(1891–1961)

English novelist, daughter of John William Mackail, grand-daughter of Sir Edward Burne-Jones, and cousin of **Rudyard Kipling**. She wrote more than 30 novels set in 'Barsetshire', dealing with the descendants of characters from **Trollope**'s Barsetshire novels, including *Coronation Summer* (1937) and *Growing Up* (1943). Her son was the novelist **Colin MacInnes**.
▷M Strickland, *Angela Thirkell* (1972)

THIRY, Marcel
(1897–1977)

Belgian poet and novelist, born in Charleroi. His most famous work was his earliest: *Toi qui pâlis au nom de Vancouver* (1924, 'You Who Turn Pale at the Name of Vancouver'), based on his experiences as a soldier in World War I. His writing is interesting but haunted by a kind of grandiloquence which he seems unable to escape, and which threatens to engulf him in the commonplace. The main influence upon him has been **Apollinaire**.

THOMAS
(fl.12th century)

Anglo–Norman poet. He was author of the earliest extant text (c.1155–1170) of the legend of Tristan and Iseult, a fragment of 3144 lines covering the final episodes including the death of the lovers. Though he has greater pretensions to a literary style, Thomas lacks the impressive primitive simplicity of Béroul, author of the slightly later and fuller of the two early versions, both of which appear to be based on an earlier poem now lost. He is sometimes confused with **Thomas the Rhymer**.

▷M D Legge, *Anglo Norman Literature* (1963)

THOMAS, Audrey
(1935–)

Canadian short-story writer and novelist, born in Binghamton, New York and educated at Smith College, St Andrews University and the University of British Columbia. She lived in Ghana, England, and the USA before settling in Canada, where she works as a Visiting Professor at Concordia University in Montreal. She won the Atlantic Firsts Award in 1965 and has received numerous Canadian Council and Senior Arts grants. Novels include *Mrs Blood* (1970), *Songs My Mother Taught Me* (1973) and *Real Mothers* (1981). Shorter fiction, however, remains her forte, as seen in her early collection of stories, *Ten Green Bottles* (1967) and *Two in the Bush and Other Stories* (1981). Her work has been described as semi-autobiographical.

▷A Thomas issue of *Room of One's Own*, vol 10, no 3–4 (1985–6)

THOMAS, Brandon
(1849–1914)

English actor and playwright, born in Liverpool. He first appeared as a comedy actor in 1879, and wrote a number of successful light plays, one of which, *Charley's Aunt* (1892), has retained enormous popularity.

THOMAS, D(onald) M(itchell)
(1935–)

English poet and novelist, born in Cornwall. He was educated in England and Australia, and graduated from New College, Oxford, in 1958. He learned Russian while on National Service, and has published numerous translations. His early writings were poems which ranged across science fiction, erotica, and evocations of his native Cornwall, all represented in *Selected Poems* (1983). Later poems became, like those in *The Puberty Tree: New and Selected Poems* (1992), more directly autobiographical. His first novel was *The Flute Player* (1979), followed by *Birthstone* (1980), but his most successful has been the powerful, semi-fantastic meditation on **Freud**ian psychology, *The White Hotel* (1981). His other fiction includes the five 'improvisations' on Cold War themes which make up the *Russian Nights* sequence (1983–9), *Flying in to Love* (1992) and *Pictures at an Exhibition* (1993).

▷*Memories and Hallucinations* (1988)

THOMAS, Dylan Marlais
(1914–53)

Welsh poet, born in Swansea, the son of a schoolmaster. He worked for a time as a reporter on the *South Wales Evening Post* and established himself with the publication of *Eighteen Poems* in 1934. He married Caitlin Macnamara in 1936, with whom he was to have a stormy marriage, and published *Twenty-Five Poems* the same year. His other works include *The Map of Love* (1939), *Portrait of the Artist as a Young Dog* (1940), *The World I Breathe* (1940), *Deaths and Entrances* (1946) and a scenario, *The Doctor and the Devils* (1966). *Collected Poems, 1934–52*, was published in 1952 and he then turned to larger dramatic works. From 1944 he worked intermittently on a radio script about a Welsh seaside village—in its first form it was called *Quite Early One Morning*, but Thomas expanded it into *Under Milk Wood* (published 1954). Until then his work had been praised by critics, among them **Edith Sitwell**, for his striking rhythms, his original imagery and his technical ingenuities, but he could in no sense have been called a popular writer. *Under Milk Wood* was immediately comprehensible, **Rabelais**ianly funny, with moments of lyric tenderness and fresh yet recognizable similes, it presented most of the non-intellectual English concepts of Welsh thought and behaviour. It had a second success as a stage play, and inspired a jazz suite by Stan Tracey (1965). In 1955 *Adventures in the Skin Trade*, an unfinished novel, was published, and a collection of stories and essays, *A Prospect of the Sea*. An authoritative edition of his *Poems* appeared in 1971. He died of alcoholic abuse on a lecture tour of the USA.

▷C Fitzgibbon, *Dylan Thomas* (1965)

THOMAS, (Philip) Edward
(1878–1917)

English poet and nature writer, born in London of Welsh parents. He was educated at St Paul's School and Lincoln College, Oxford, where he got married. He became a hack writer of reviews, critical studies and topographical works. Not until 1914, encouraged by **Robert Frost**, did he realize his potential as a poet, writing most of his poetry during active service in World War I. *Six Poems* was published in 1916. He died in action at Arras (April 1917) before the publication of *Poems* (1917), under the pseudonym 'Edward Eastaway'. His impressive poetry, though rooted in the English tradition of nature poetry, broke with the Georgian tradition in its lack of rhetoric and formality and in its emphasis on the austerity of Nature and solitariness of man. He also wrote a novel, *The Happy-Go-Lucky Morgans* (1913), and several books about the English countryside.

▷W Cooke, *Edward Thomas, a critical biography* (1930)

THOMAS, Leslie John
(1931–)

English novelist and travel writer, born in Newport, Monmouthshire. The son of a sailor lost at sea in 1943, he described his boyhood life in an orphanage in *This Time Next Week* (1964). His first novel, *The Virgin Soldiers*, published two years later, is a bawdy comedy deriving from his experiences as a national serviceman in Malaya, and became a bestseller, establishing its author as one of the most popular of modern story-tellers. His writing is unaffected, atmospheric, truthful, funny and often poignant. His many other novels include *Onward Virgin Soldiers* (1971), *Tropic of Ruislip* (1974), *The Dearest and the Best* (1984) and *The Loves and Journeys of Revolving Jones* (1991). *Dangerous by Moonlight* (1993) follows the adventures of the hapless London police constable first encountered in *Dangerous Davies* (1976).

THOMAS, R(onald) S(tuart)
(1913–)

Welsh poet and priest, born in Cardiff. Educated at the University College of North Wales, Bangor, he trained for the church at St Michael's College, Llandaff. He was ordained deacon in 1936 and priest in 1937. He was rector of Manafon (1942–54), vicar of Eglwysach (1954–67) and vicar of St Hywyn, Aberdaron (1967–78). He published his first, deceptively simple volume of poetry, *The Stones of the Field*, in 1946, followed by *An Acre of Land* (1952) and *The Minister* (1953). He only came to attention outside Wales with the publication of *Song at the Year's Turning* (1955). His later volumes, such as *Poetry for Supper* (1958), *The Bread of Truth* (1963), *Laboratories of the Spirit* (1976) and *Between Here and Now* (1981), deal with pastoral themes and the nature of God, coupled with an intense love of Wales and its people, evoked by his use of nature imagery. His other works include *Later Poems, 1972–1982* (1983), *Experimenting with an Amen* (1986) and *Counterpoint* (1990).
▷R George Thomas, *R. S. Thomas* (1964)

THOMAS, William
(1832–78)

Welsh poet, born in Ynysddu, Monmouthshire. Originally a land surveyor, he was ordained into the rather Calvinistic Methodist ministry in 1859, by which time he had preached a number of sermons. His attempts to write poetry in English were a failure but the philosophical poem *The Storm*, 9 000 lines long, has been acknowledged the finest Welsh poem of the century. He also edited the Welsh poetry column in a number of periodicals. Collections of his work were published in 1854, 1867 and 1871 before a complete edition of the poems in Welsh, *Gweithiau Islwyn*, appeared in 1897.

THOMAS OF HAILES, or HALES
(fl.1250)

English friar and author of religious poetry. His *Luue Ron*, ('Love Runes'—a translation of *Amatoria Carmina*) compare human love to the divine, unfavourably, arguing that the sweetest love of all is the love of Christ. Thomas is eclectic in his sources: he makes use of biblical and classical references, and also of references to popular literature.

THOMAS THE RHYMER, or THOMAS RYMOUR OF ERCELDOUNE
(c.1220–c.1297)

Scottish seer and poet. He lived at Erceldoune (now Earlston, Berwickshire), and in 1286 is said to have predicted the death of Alexander III and the Battle of Bannockburn, thus becoming known as 'True Thomas'. Boece calls him Thomas Learmont. Legend relates that he was carried off to Elfland, and after three years allowed to revisit the earth, but ultimately returned to his mistress, the fairy queen. In a charter of Petrus de Haga of Bemersyde c.1260–1270 the Rhymer appears as a witness; and in another of 1294 Thomas of Erceldoune, 'son and heir of Thomas Rymour of Erceldoune', conveys lands to the hospice of Soutra. The Rhymer's 'prophecies' were collected and published in 1603. Sir **Walter Scott** believed him to be the author of the poem of *Sir Tristrem*, which was founded on a 12th-century French poem by another Thomas, a poet of genius, almost certainly an Englishman.
▷H M Flasdieck, *Tom der Reimer* (1934)

THOMPSON, E V (Ernest Victor)
(1931–)

English writer of historical and romantic fiction, especially well-known for the bestselling 'Retallick' saga. He was born in London, spent nine years in the navy, worked as an investigator for BOAC and was Chief Security Officer of the Department of Civil Aviation in (the then) Rhodesia. On his return to England in the seventies he settled in Cornwall, where much of his fiction is set, and won the Best Historical Novelist Award with *Chase The Wind* (1977). Since then his 'supreme readability' has ensured constant sales and success. He has also written a number of West Country guide books.

THOMPSON, Flora (Jane), née Timms
(1876–1947)

English social historian, born in Juniper Hill, Oxfordshire. She left school at 14 to work in the local post office. She married young and with her postmaster husband settled in Bournemouth, writing mass-market fiction to help support her increasing family. In her sixties she published the semi-autobiographical trilogy combined as *Lark Rise to Candleford* (1945), its three parts, *Lark Rise* (1939), *Over to Candleford* (1941) and *Candleford Green* (1943), having appeared separately. It is an outstanding feat of observation and memory, showing the erosion of rural society before modern industrialism.
▷M Lane, *Flora Thompson* (1976)

THOMPSON, Francis
(1859–1907)

English poet, born in Preston, Lancashire. He was brought up in the Catholic faith and studied for the priesthood at Ushaw College. By temperament unsuited for this, he turned to medicine at Owens College, Manchester, but failed to graduate. He moved to London, where extreme poverty and ill-health drove him to become an opium addict. From this he was rescued by Wilfrid and **Alice Meynell**, to whom he had sent some poems for the magazine *Merry England*. His health was restored at the monastery of Storrington Priory in Sussex, where he wrote several poems, including the well-known *Hound of Heaven*. From then on the Meynells looked after him until his death from tuberculosis. His works include *Poems* (1893), *Sister Songs* (1895, written for the Meynell girls) and *New Poems* (1897). His notable *Essay on Shelley* (1909) appeared posthumously, as did his *Life of St Ignatius Loyola* (1909). His poems, mainly religious in theme, are rich in imagery and poetic vision.
▷E Meynell, *Francis Thompson* (1913)

THOMPSON, Hunter S(tockton)
(1939–)

American journalist, author, editor and small game hunter, born in Louisville, Kentucky. An adherent of the 'new journalism', he eshews objectivity, his search for a story taking him into 'the middle of whatever I'm writing about'. This has led to bizarre incidents and idiosyncratic reportage, marked by intemperate language and behaviour. He was the first reporter to infiltrate the Hell's Angels and rode with them for a year, an experience which led to his being savagely beaten up and a book, *Hell's Angels: A Strange and Terrible Saga* (1966). The acme of the anti-establishment, he styled his unique brand of journalism 'Gonzo', awarded himself a doctorate and produced a stream of books as outspoken as they were outrageous, including *Fear and Loathing in Las Vegas* (1972), *Fear and Loathing on the Campaign Trail* (1972), *The Great Shark Hunt* (1972), *The Curse of Lono* (1977) and *Generation of Swine* (1988). Much of his work appeared originally in magazines, particularly *Scanlan's*, *Rolling Stone* and the *National Observer*, and at the end of the 1980s he contributed a weekly column to the *San Francisco Examiner*.

THOMPSON, James (Jim)
(1844–1901)

American novelist and editor, who also wrote poetry, born in Indiana. His historical novel, *Alice of Old Vincennes* (1900), based on George Rogers Clark's famous 1779 expedition, was a popular success. He wrote *Hoosier Mosaics* (1875), a series of sketches in dialect.

THOMSON, Derick, Gaelic Ruaraidh MacThómais
(1921–)

Scottish poet, born in Stornoway, Isle of Lewis. He was educated at the Nicolson Institute in Stornoway, and at the universities of Aberdeen, Cambridge and North Wales. He served in the Royal Air Force during World War II. He taught at the universities of Edinburgh, Aberdeen and Glasgow, where he became Professor of Celtic in 1963. In 1952 he founded, and remains the editor of, the Gaelic language quarterly *Gairm*, and helped set up the Gaelic Books Council in 1968. He has written important critical works on Gaelic poetry, notably *An Introduction to Gaelic Poetry* (1974, rev 1989), compiled a *New English-Gaelic Dictionary* (1981), and edited *The Companion to Gaelic Scotland* (1983). His own poetry constitutes one of the most significant bodies of modern Gaelic verse; much of it is collected, in both Gaelic and his own English versions, in *Creachadh na Clàrsaich* (*Plundering the Harp—Collected Poems 1940–1980*, 1982). His poetry tends to focus on his ambivalent relationship with the Outer Hebrides, and on his sometimes impatient sense of nationalism, but, like that of **Sorley MacLean**, continually finds universal truths emerging from the particular. A new collection, *Smeur an doch ais* ('The Bramble of Hope'), appeared in 1991.

THOMSON, James, occasional pseud 'B V'
(1834–82)

Scottish poet, born in Port Glasgow, the son of a merchant seaman. He was educated in the Royal Caledonian Asylum orphanage and trained as an army schoolmaster at the

Royal Military Asylum, Chelsea, but was dismissed from army service for alcoholism in 1862. A friend of Charles Bradlaugh, editor and owner of the *National Reformer*, between 1862 and 1875 he contributed many of his sombre, sonorous poems to the paper, including *The City of Dreadful Night* (1874), his greatest work. He became a lawyer's clerk in 1862, went into business (1864–9), went to the USA as a mining agent (1872–3), was war correspondent in Spain with the Carlists (1873), and from 1875 onwards depended largely on contributions to a tobacconists' trade monthly. Ill-health and melancholia drove him to narcotics and stimulants. *The City of Dreadful Night and other Poems* (1880) was followed by *Vane's Story* (1881), *Essays and Phantasies* (1881), *A Voice from the Nile* (1884), *Shelley, a Poem* (1885) and *Biographical and Critical Studies* (1896). His pseudonym B V, Bysshe Vanolis, was partly from **Shelley**'s second name, partly from an anagram of Novalis. The poet **Tom Leonard** published a remarkable biographical meditation on his life and work, *Places of the Mind*, in 1993.
▷I Waller, *James Thomson (BV)* (1950); T Leonard, *James B.V. Thomson* (1993)

THOMSON, James
(1700–48)

Scottish poet, born in Ednam, Roxburghshire. He was educated at Jedburgh School and studied at Edinburgh University for the ministry, but he abandoned his studies and went to seek his fortune as a writer in London. He published *Winter* (1726), a short poem in blank verse, *Summer* (1727), *Spring*, (1728), and *Autumn*, which appeared with the other three under the collective title *The Seasons* (1730). It was substantially revised in 1744, and became a source-book for much later bird poetry. In 1729 his *Sophonisba* was produced. His other tragedies were *Agamemnon* (1738), *Edward and Eleonora* (1739), *Tancred and Sigismunda* (1745) and *Coriolanus* (1748). The poem *Liberty* (1735–6) was inspired by the Grand Tour which he undertook as tutor to Charles Talbot's son in 1731, and was dedicated to the Prince of Wales, who awarded him a pension. 'A Poem sacred to the Memory of Isaac Newton' (1727) and 'Britannia' (1729), which criticized Walpole's foreign policy, secured him further patronage and the sinecure of Surveyor-General of the Leeward Isles (1744). *Alfred, a Masque* (1740) contains the song 'Rule Britannia', also claimed by **David Mallet**. The **Spenser**ian *The Castle of Indolence* (1748) is considered his masterpiece.
▷J Grant, *James Thomson* (1957)

THOOR, Jesse, pseud of Peter Karl Höfler
(1905–52)

Austrian poet, who went into exile—he became a silversmith in London—on the advent of Hitler. He was originally a communist. He was born in Berlin, but died at Lienz in his native Austria, of a heart ailment, while on a visit. Aloof from movements, still a trifle neglected (though well appreciated by those who know his work), he produced poems of great religious power, in his *Die Sonnete und Lieder* (1956, 'Sonnets and Songs'). He is regarded as one of the greatest sonneteers in the German language since **Andreas Gryphius**. His collected works were edited in German by **Michael Hamburger** (1965), who translated some of the poems in his (and **Christopher Middleton**'s) *Modern German Poetry* (1962).

THORARENSEN, Bjarni Vigfússon
(1786–1841)

Icelandic romantic poet and jurist, born in Brautarholt and brought up at Hlíðarendi. A precociously brilliant student, he went to Copenhagen University at the age of 15 to study law. After government service in Denmark, he was appointed a deputy justice in Reykjavík (1811), and justice of the supreme court (1817). In 1833 he was appointed governor of North and East Iceland. As a lyric poet he celebrated Icelandic nature and nationalism, using the metres of classical heroic poetry; one of his poems, *Eldgamla Ísafold* ('Ancient Iceland'), was regarded as an unofficial national anthem, set to the music of *God Save the Queen*.
▷Þ Gíslason, *Bjarni Thorarensen* (1932)

THOREAU, Henry David
(1817–62)

American essayist and poet, the 'hermit of Walden', born of Jersey stock in Concord, Massachusetts. He graduated from Harvard in 1837, became a teacher in Concord, and lectured. He soon gave up teaching, and joined his father in making lead pencils, but about 1839 began his walks and studies of nature as the serious occupation of his life. In 1839 he made the voyage described in his *Week on the Concord and Merrimack Rivers* (1849). Thoreau made the acquaintance of **Ralph Waldo Emerson**, and between 1841 and 1843 and in 1847 was a member of his household. In 1845 he built himself a shanty in the woods by Walden Pond, where he lived from 1845 to 1847 and wrote much of the *Week*, his essay on **Thomas Carlyle**, and the American classic, *Walden, or Life in the Woods* (1854). After the Walden episode he supported himself by whitewashing, gardening, fence building and land surveying. He also lectured now and then, and wrote for magazines. He made three trips to the Maine woods in 1846, 1853 and 1857, described in papers collected after his death (1864). In 1850 he made a trip to Canada, which produced *A Yankee in Canada* (1866). In 1835 he began to keep a daily journal of his walks and observations, from whose 30 volumes were published *Early Spring in Massachusetts* (1881), *Summer* (1884) and *Winter* (1887). Other publications are *Excursions in Field and Forest*, with memoir by Emerson (1863), *Cape Cod* (1865), *Letters to Various Persons*, with nine poems (1865), *Familiar Letters* (1894) and *Poems of Nature* (1896), and a celebrated essay, *Civil Disobedience* (1849), provoked by his opposition to the Mexican War.

▷ R D Richardson Jnr, *Thoreau: a life of the mind* (1986)

THORLÁKSSON, Jón
(1744–1819)

Icelandic poet and scholar, born in Selárdalur, the son of a parson. He himself became a parson, but was twice defrocked for illegal carnal intercourse. He was eventually rehabilitated and lived in penury in a country parish at Bægisá. He was a prolific writer of poetry and occasional verse, but his most important work was as a translator into Icelandic of **Pope**'s *Essay on Man* (1798), **Milton**'s *Paradise Lost* (1828) and **Friedrich Klopstock**'s *Messiah* (published 1834–8).

▷ R Beck, *Jón Thorláksson* (1957)

THORODDSEN, Jón, originally Thórðarson
(1818–68)

Icelandic novelist and poet, born in Reykhólar. Regarded as the father of the modern Icelandic novel, he studied law at Copenhagen and wrote drinking songs in the style of **Carl Bellmann**. He was an avid reader of Sir **Walter Scott**, and used him as a model for his first book, *Piltur og stúlka* (1850, 'Boy and Girl'), the earliest proper novel produced in Iceland. In 1850 he returned to Iceland and was appointed a district magistrate on the island of Flatey. In addition to a sheaf of lyrics, he also wrote an unfinished sequel to his first novel, *Maður og kona* ('Man and Woman', published posthumously in 1876).

▷ S J Þorsteinsson, *Thoroddsen og skaldsogur hans* (1943)

THORSTEINSSON, Steingrímur (Bjarnason)
(1831–1913)

Icelandic poet and scholar, born in Arnarstapi on Snæfellsnes. He studied classical philology and modern European literature at Copenhagen (1851–63), and worked in Copenhagen (1863–72), where he wrote patriotic poetry in support of Jón Sigurðsson's independence movement. He returned to Iceland as teacher, later headmaster, at the Latin School in Reykjavík (1872–1913). His major importance was to enrich Icelandic native culture through his fine translations of all the modern European poets, as well as *King Lear*, *The Arabian Nights*, *Robinson Crusoe*, and **Hans Christian Andersen**.

▷ H Petursson, *Steingrimur Thorsteinsson, lif og hanslist* (1964)

THORUP, Kirsten
(1942–)

Danish novelist, poet and writer of short stories and plays for television. Born in Gelsted, on Funen, she published her first book of poetry in 1967, evolving a modernist aesthetics which reflects the alienation and fragmentation of contemporary life. The poetic texts in *Love from Trieste* (1969, Eng trans 1980) and *I dag er det Daisy* (1971, 'It's Daisy Today') show the influence of the thinking of R D Laing, while the highly successful novel *Baby* (1973, Eng trans 1980) is an exploration of individual powerlessness in a context in which cause and effect, and thus a coherent pattern of meaning, are non-existent. She has subsequently enjoyed great success as a realist novelist, notably with *Lille Jonna* (1977, 'Little Jonna') and *Den lange sommer* (1979, 'The Long Summer'). A prolific writer of television drama, she based *Else Kant* (1978) on two novels by **Amalie Skram**.

▷ M-L Paludan, 'Kirsten Thorup', in T Brostrøm and M Winge (eds), *Danske digtere i det 20. århundrede*, vol V (1982)

THUBRON, Colin Gerald Dryden
(1939–)

English novelist and travel writer, born in London, a descendant of **John Dryden**. Thubron abandoned a career in publishing in order to travel, mainly in Asia and northern Africa, and the vivid accounts of his journeys have made him one of the most highly respected of travel writers. His best-known titles include *Among the Russians* (1983) and *Behind the Wall* (1987), an intriguing insight into modern China, in which personal day-to-day lives are set against the political and economic context. Among his novels are *A Cruel Madness* (1984), a study of instability, and *Falling* (1989), a poignant story of love and loss.

THUCYDIDES
(c.460–c.400 BC)

Greek historian of the Peloponnesian war, born near Athens. He suffered in the Athenian plague (c.430) but recovered. He commanded an Athenian squadron of seven ships at Thasos (424), when he failed to relieve Amphipolis; condemned as a traitor, he retired to his Thracian estates. He lived in exile for 20 years (possibly visiting Sicily), writing his eight-book *De Bello Peloponnesiaco*, and probably returned to Athens in 404. He did not live long enough to bring his history down to the end of the war (his account ends in 411 BC). Much of his matter is based on the speeches of leading politicians (reconstructed largely on the testimony of witnesses). He aimed at a lucid and unbiased narrative, and an almost scientific analysis of the reasons for the defeat of Athens. His work is of outstanding importance, both for the detailed information it gives about one of the great conflicts (of ideas as well as of interests) in antiquity and as a model of careful research. The *Hellenica* of **Xenophon** was written to carry Thucydides' narrative down to the end of the war in 404 BC.

▷ *The Peloponnesian War* (Eng trans Rex Warner, 1954)

THURBER, James Grover
(1894–1961)

American humorist and cartoonist, born in Columbus, Ohio. When he was six years old, one of his brothers shot him with an arrow and he lost the sight of his left eye; towards the end of his life, he gradually lost the sight in his good eye. He attended schools in Columbus and went to Ohio State University where, as he stated modestly in his fragmentary autobiography, *My Life and Hard Times* (1933), he passed all his courses save botany. In the early 1920s he reported for various papers in America and Europe but in February 1927 **E B White** introduced him to Harold Ross, Editor of the *New Yorker*, and he was instantly appointed its managing editor. It was not a job to which he was suited and he drifted into writing, before leaving the staff altogether. But he contributed regularly, humorous essays at first, then the inimitable sketches of dogs, barking seals and marital discord. His drawings first appeared in *Is Sex Necessary?* (1929) which he co-authored with White. A plethora of books followed, often combining humorous essays with characteristic doodles, including *The Owl in the Attic and Other Perplexities* (1931), *The Seal in the Bedroom and Other Predicaments* (1932), *The Middle-Aged Man on the Flying Trapeze* (1935), *Men, Women and Dogs* (1943) and *The Wonderful O* (1957). He was also a dramatist and appeared as himself in a brief run of *A Thurber Carnival* in 1960, and wrote a number of notable short stories, of which *The Secret Life of Walter Mitty*, filmed with Danny Kaye (1946), is best known. *The Years With Ross* (1959) is an anecdotal memoir recounting his experience of the unpredictable *New Yorker* editor.

▷ B Bernstein, *James Thurber, a biography* (1975)

THWAITE, Anthony Simon
(1930–)

English poet, born in Chester and educated at Kingswood School, Bath, and Christ Church, Oxford. He was literary editor of *The Listener* (1962–5) and *The New Statesman* (1968–72), and co-editor of *Encounter* (1973–85). He became poetry editor at Secker and Warburg in 1986. He edited **Philip Larkin**'s *Collected Poems* (1988) and *Letters* (1992). He has published a number of volumes, the most important of which are the Larkin-esque *The Owl in the Trees* (1963); *New Confessions* (1974), which is based on St Augustine and made use of the monologue form; and the lyrics in *Victorian Voices* (1980). His work has been collected in *Poems 1953–88* (1989), and is too varied to permit easy categorization.

THWAITES, F(rederick) J(oseph)
(1908–79)

Australian writer of popular and sentimental novels, born in Balmain, Sydney. Possibly Australia's bestselling author in the inter-war period, he published many of the books himself, starting with his first novel *The Broken Melody* (1930). Typical titles (and locales) are *Fever* (1939), *Whispers in Tahiti* (1940) and *Shadows over Rangoon* (1941). *The Broken Melody* was reprinted steadily between the wars, and in its description of the corrupting effects of cocaine addiction, and its impact on family life, was in advance of its time.

TIBULLUS, Albius
(c.50–19 BC)

Roman elegiac poet, perhaps born in Gabii. He acquired the friendship of the poet-statesman, M Valerius Messalla, and joined his staff, when Augustus commissioned him (30 BC) to crush a revolt in Aquitania. While he distinguished himself in the campaign, he disliked a soldier's life as much as he enjoyed Roman society. When he started with Messalla on a mission to Asia, he became ill on the voyage, and turned back at Corcyra. His sentimental elegiac love poems to his mistresses persuaded Quintilian to place Tibullus at the head of Roman elegiac poets.

▷ G Luck, *The Latin Love Elegy* (1969)

TICKELL, Thomas
(1686–1740)

English poet, born at Bridekirk, Carlisle. He was a fellow of Queen's College, Oxford

(1710–26). His complimentary verses on *Rosamond* (1709) gained him the favour, and his own virtues the friendship, of **Joseph Addison**, who, on becoming in 1717 secretary of state, made him his under-secretary; from 1725 he was secretary to the lords justices of Ireland. He was skilful in occasional poetry, and was favourably reviewed in the *Spectator*. His translation of book one of the *Iliad* appeared in 1715, about the same time as **Pope**'s. Pope professed to believe it the work of Addison himself, designed to eclipse his own version, and wrote the famous satire on Atticus. But though Addison corrected it, the translation was doubtless by Tickell. His longest poem is *Kensington Gardens*; his most popular, *Colin and Lucy*; his finest, the exquisite elegy prefixed to his edition of Addison's Works (1721).
▷R E Tickell, *Thomas Tickell and 18th Century Poetry* (1931)

TIECK, Johann Ludwig
(1773–1853)

German critic and poet of the Romantic school, born in Berlin. He lived the life of a writer, in Berlin, Dresden and near Frankfurt an der Oder. After two or three immature romances, he produced a new line in clever dramatized versions (*Märchendramen*) of *Der gestiefelte Kater* (1797, 'Puss in Boots'), *Ritter Blaubart* (1797, 'Blue Beard'), and others. He followed up this first success by the satire *Anti-Faust, oder Geschichte eines dummen Teufels* (1801, 'Anti-Faust, or the Story of a Dim Devil'), the horror story *Der Runenberg* (1804, 'The Rune Mountain'), and *Phantasus* (1812–17), a collection of traditional lore in story and drama. Besides supervising the completion of **August von Schlegel**'s translation of **Shakespeare**, he edited the doubtful plays and wrote a series of essays (*Shakespeares Vorschule*, 1823–9, 'Shakespeare's Preparatory School'). He translated *Don Quixote* in 1799–1804. He holds an honourable place among Germany's dramatic and literary critics, because of his *Dramaturgische Blätter* (2nd edn 1852, 'Dramaturgical Pages') and *Kritische Schriften* (1848, 'Critical Writings').
▷E H Zeydel, *Ludwig Tieck, the German Romanticist* (1935)

TIEN HAN
(1898–1968)

Chinese playwright, from Hunan province. Much of his work strikes the western reader as little more than propagandizing—his plays *Uei yu* (1931, 'Flood') and *Lu-kou-chi'iao* (1933, 'Drought') are vehicles for conveying strongly pro-communist messages. There is more literary merit in *Cha-fei-tien chih yeh* (1922, 'A Night in the Café') and *Huo hu chih yeh* (1921, 'The Night the Tiger Escaped') in that, although the political content is unmistakable, some attempt has been made to draw real characters and construct plotlines which do more than provide an opportunity for the downtrodden peasantry to arise and overthrow the evil oppressor.

TIKHONOV, Nikolay
(1896–1971)

Russian poet, born in St Petersburg. He began under the influence of **Gumilev** and the Serapion Brothers, and wrote an independent and affirmative poetry which had much in common with that of the Futurists; but, never strikingly original, he gradually submitted himself to officialdom, and his powers faded. However, he called upon his head the wrath of Zhdanov for his 'dissidence'. All his best poems were written in the 1920s.
▷G Struve, *Russian Literature Under Lenin and Stalin 1917–1953* (1971)

TIKKANEN, Märta
(1935–)

Finland–Swedish novelist and poet. Born in Helsinki, she completed a degree and then worked as a journalist. Her first novel, *nu imorron* (1970, 'now tomorrow'), uses stylistic experimentation to convey the situation of an over-worked wife and mother, while *Män kan inte våldtas* (1975, Eng trans *Manrape*, 1978), her first major success, is a realist account of a woman who takes revenge on the man who has raped her by raping him. The poems in *Århundradets kärlekssaga* (1978, Eng trans *Love Story of the Century*, 1984) depict the experience of a family in which the husband and father is an alcoholic. One of her other novels, *Rödluvan* (1986, 'Little Red Riding Hood'), employs mythical patterns to draw into focus a marital relationship.
▷M Mazzarella, 'Märta Tikkanen (1935–). Passion eller jämlikhet?', *Från Fredrika Runeberg till Märta Tikkanen. Frihet och beroende i finlandssvensk kvinnolitteratur* (1985)

TIMON OF PHLIUS
(c.325–c.235 BC)

Greek philosopher and poet from the northern Peloponnese. He was Pyrrho's leading disciple and his biographer, and an enthusiastic exponent of the theories of scepticism. After a period as an itinerant lecturer he retired to Athens where he was a leading member of the local intelligentsia and a versatile author. He wrote satyr-plays, comedies, tragedies, epic poems and a famous series of *Silloi*, satirical mock-heroic poems which parody and insult most earlier Greek philosophers, who are seen as doctrinaire, pretentious and generally aberrant predecessors of the Pyrrhonian enlightenment. Only brief fragments of his work have survived.

TIMROD, Henry
(1828–67)

American poet and critic, 'The Laureate of the Confederacy', born in Charleston, South Carolina, whose classically orientated, severe but fervently felt work is still anthologized for its importance in the development of American poetry. He published only one collection in his lifetime, *Poems* (1860), but the posthumous *Complete Poems* (1899) adds many more. He suffered from tuberculosis, which was aggravated by what he called the 'beggary, starvation, death, bitter grief, utter want of hope' which eventuated when the city of Columbia, where he had worked for a newspaper, was captured and burned in 1865. He is famous for his 'Katie' poems (to the woman he married), and for his elegies for the confederate dead, including the famous 'Ode': 'Sleep sweetly in your humble graves,/Sleep, martyrs of a fallen cause;/Though yet no marble column craves/The pilgrim here to pause'.
▷ E W Parks (ed), *The Essays of Henry Timrod* (1942, with an important introduction); Henry T Thompson, *Henry Timrod* (1928)

TING LING
(1907–)

Chinese writer, and *habitué* of literary circles in the run-up to the revolution. Her reputation rests solely on her masterly revolutionary document *T'ai-yang chao tsai Sung-kan-ho shang* (1948, Eng trans *The Sun Shines over the Sangkan River*, 1953), which was written when she had been sent into the country for political re-education. Ostensibly a novel (though large sections of it are obviously closer to *reportage*), it documents the overthrow of the feudal system and the effects of land reform on the peasantry. It won her the Stalin Prize in 1949, though she later fell out of favour with the communist authorities because of her maverick ways and a number of politically imprudent political statements.

TIPTREE, James, pseud of Alice Hastings Bradley Sheldon
(1915–87)

American science-fiction writer, born in Chicago. She spent much of her childhood in Africa and India (her mother was a geographer and travel writer), worked for the US Government until 1955, then trained as a psychologist. She published her first story as 'Alice Sheldon' in 1946, but began to write science fiction as James Tiptree in 1967, and was widely assumed to be a man until her

'exposure' in 1977. Her psychologically complex, death-haunted fiction is found at its best in the short story form, the most important of which are collected in *Ten Thousand Light Years From Home* (1973), *Star Songs of an Old Primate* (1978) and *Crown of Stars* (1988). Two important novellas, 'The Girl Who Was Plugged In' (1973) and 'Houston, Houston, Do Your Read' (1977), were issued together in 1989. *Up The Walls of the World* (1978) is the best of her four longer works, two of which are made up of interlinked stories.

TIRSO DE MOLINA, pseud of Gabriel Téllez
(c.1571–1648)

Spanish playwright, born in Madrid. He was prior of the monastery of Soria. Lacking his great contemporary **Lope de Vega**'s lyrical gifts, he wrote *Comedias* (5 vols, 1627–36), partly Interludes, and *Autos Sacramentales* (originally about 300), excelling in the portrayal of character, particularly of spirited women, and in his treatment of the Don Juan legend in his masterpiece, *El burlador de Sevilla* (1634, Eng trans *The Trickster of Seville*, 1959).
▷ K Vosler, *Lecciones sobre Zirso* (1965)

TODI, Jacopone da
(c.1230–1306)

Italian religious poet, born in Todi in the duchy of Spoleto. He practised as an advocate, was converted to an ascetic life in 1268 and became a Franciscan lay brother in 1278. He was imprisoned (1298–1303) for satirizing Pope Boniface VIII. To him is ascribed the authorship of the *Stabat Mater* and other Latin hymns. He also wrote *Laude* ('Hymns of Praise'), which became important in the development of Italian drama.

TODOROV, Petko
(1879–1916)

Bulgarian dramatist and writer of prose idylls, a friend and disciple of **Pencho Slaveykov**. His style, though a little artificial by today's standards, brought a new combination of sophistication and folkloristic elements into the literature.
▷ C Manning and R Smal-Stocki, *The History of Modern Bulgarian Literature* (1960)

TOLENTINO DE ALMEIDA, Nicolau
(1741–1811)

Portuguese poet who became rich by dint of cultivating the powers that were, but continued to feign poverty in his verse until his death: his satire could be repressed by 'the gift of a pheasant'. However, his poetry 'sheds a gentle light on the manners of the time', and his satire is interesting, especially because in it he appeared ironically to adopt the very position he wished to attack.

▷A Bell, *Portuguese Literature* (1922)

TOLKIEN, J(ohn) R(onald) R(euel)
(1892–1973)

South African-born philologist and author, born in Bloemfontein. Educated at King Edward VI School, Birmingham, and Merton College, Oxford, he became Professor of Anglo-Saxon there (1925–45), and of English Language and Literature (1945–59). His scholarly publications include an edition of *Sir Gawain and the Green Knight* (1925), and studies on **Chaucer** (1934) and *Beowulf* (1937). His interest in language and saga and his fascination for the land of Faerie prompted him to write tales of a world of his own invention peopled by strange beings with their own carefully constructed language and mythology. These include *The Hobbit* (1937), a fascinating tale of the perilous journey of Bilbo Baggins and the dwarfs to recover treasure from the sly dragon Smaug, and the more complex sequel, *The Lord of the Rings* (3 vols, 1954–5), in which Bilbo's nephew, Frodo, sets out to destroy a powerful but dangerous ring in Mordor, the land of darkness and evil. Later works include *The Adventure of Tom Bombadil* (1962), *Smith of Wootton Major* (1967) and *The Silmarillion* (posthumous, 1977).

▷C R Stimpson, *J. R. R. Tolkien* (1970)

TOLLENS, Hendrik
(1780–1856)

Dutch poet, born in Rotterdam. He was author of the Dutch national hymn (until the 20th century), *Wien Neerlandsch Bloed*. He also wrote comedies and a tragedy, romances and ballads.

▷G D J Schotch, *Tollens e zijn tid* (1860)

TOLLER, Ernst
(1893–1939)

German–Jewish poet and playwright, born in Samotschin. A political activist, he was imprisoned in Germany as a socialist revolutionary (1919–24). He was elected to the Bavarian diet in 1924, was banished by the Nazis in 1933 and went to the USA, where he committed suicide in New York in 1939. His expressionist plays include *Masse Mensch* (1921, Eng trans *Masses and Man*, 1923), *Die Maschinenstürmer* (1922, Eng trans *The Machine-Wreckers*, 1923), and others. He also wrote poetry and the autobiographical *Eine Jugend in Deutschland* (1933, Eng trans *I Was a German ...*, 1934).

TOLLET, Elizabeth
(1694–1754)

English poet, well educated by her father, Commissioner of the Navy, and a friend of Isaac Newton to whom she addressed one of her poems. She lived with her father in the Tower of London in her early years, later at Stratford and West Ham. Her *Poems on Several Occasions* (anonymous, 1724) show her well read and accomplished in both Latin and English verse. Her tonal range is wide, encompassing philosophical reflection, devout religious feeling, epigrammatic wit and light-hearted satire. The volume includes imaginary epistles by historical women, such as Anne Boleyn and Mary, Queen of Scots; 'Hypatia' pleads eloquently for the education and intellectual development of women.

▷D B Wyrick, in *Eighteenth-Century British Poets*, pt 1, ed J Sitter, *Dictionary of Literary Biography*, 95 (1990)

TOLSON, Melvin
(1900–66)

American poet, known for his stylistic mishmash of the formal and informal. Tolson was born in Missouri, was taught at Langston University and later became mayor of the town. He was a black American who tried to relate his Negro inheritance to the European traditions of his country. As such Tolson was somewhat overlooked by the wave of interest in more radical black writing during the 1960s and 70s, despite the fact that his last book, *Harlem Gallery* (1965), was the first volume in a projected epic about black history.

TOLSTOY, Count Alexey Konstantinovich
(1817–75)

Russian dramatist, lyrical poet and novelist, born in St Petersburg, distantly related to **Leo Tolstoy**. He wrote a historical trilogy in verse (1867, Eng trans *The Death of Ivan the Terrible*, 1869), *Tsar Fyodor Ioannovich* (1868, Eng trans 1874) and *Tsar Boris* (1870), but only the first work was staged in his lifetime. His other works include nonsense verse and a historical novel, *Prince Serebrenni* (1863, Eng trans 1874).

▷M Dalton, *Alexey Konstantinovich Tolstoy* (1972)

TOLSTOY, Count Alexey Nikolayevich
(1882–1945)

Russian writer, born in Nikolayevsk, Samara, distantly related to **Leo Tolstoy**. He joined the White Army after the 1917 Revolution, which he portrayed vividly in *Khozhdenie po mukam* (1920, Eng trans *Darkness and Dawn*, 1935), was an émigré in Paris (1919–23) but returned to Russia as an honoured man of letters. Other novels include *Khromoǐ barin* (1912, Eng trans *The Lame Prince*, 1912).

▷Y Krestinsky, *Alexey Nicolayevich Tolstoy* (1960)

TOLSTOY, Count Leo Nikolayevich
(1828–1910)

Russian writer, aesthetic philosopher, moralist and mystic, born on the family estate of Yasnaya Polyana in Tula province. He was educated privately and at Kazan University, where he read law and oriental languages but did not graduate. He led a dissolute life in town, played the gentleman farmer, and finally, in 1851, accompanied his elder brother Nikolay to the Caucasus, where he joined an artillery regiment and there began his literary career. *Istoria vcherashchnevo dnya* (1851, 'Accounts of Yesterday') was followed by the autobiographical trilogy, *Detstvo* (1852), *Otrochestvo* (1854) and *Yunost'* (1856, collective Eng trans *Childhood, Boyhood, Youth*, 1886). Commissioned at the outbreak of the Crimean War (1854), he commanded a battery during the defence of Sebastopol (1854–5). After the war, the horrors of which inspired *Sevastopolskiye rasskazy* (1855–6, Eng trans *Sebastopol*, 1887), he left the army, was fêted by the literary circle in St Petersburg (1856), travelled abroad, visiting Britain, and in 1862 married Sophie Andreyevna Behrs who bore him 13 children. He settled on his Volga estate and combined the duties of a progressive landlord with the six years' literary toil which produced *Vonya i mir* (1863–9, Eng trans *War and Peace*, 1866), by many considered the greatest novel ever written. This is at the same time a domestic tale, depicting the fortunes of two notable families, the Rostovs and the Bolkonskis, and a national epic of Russia's struggle, defeat and victory over Napoleon. The proud, shy, duty-conscious Prince Andrew and the direct, friendly, pleasure-loving but introspective, morally questing Pierre reflect the dualism in Tolstoy's own character. On his vivid description of military life Tolstoy mounts his conception of history, which demotes 'great men' to mere creatures of circumstance and ascribes victory in battle to the confused chance events which make up the unpredictable fortunes of war. In Pierre's association with freemasonry, Tolstoy expressed his criticism of the established autocratic order. His second great work, *Anna Karenina* (1874–6, Eng trans 1886), carries with it the seeds of Tolstoy's personal crisis between the claims of the creative novelist and the moralizing, 'committed' propagator of his own ethical code, which culminated in *Ispoved'* (1884, Eng trans *A Confession*, 1885) and the dialectical pamphlets and stories such as *A. Smert' Ivana Ilicha* (1886, Eng trans *(The Death of) Ivan Ilyitch*, 1887), *Kreytserova sonata* (1889, Eng trans *The Kreutzer Sonata*,

1890) and *V chom moya vera?* (1884, Eng trans *My Religion*, 1885). Christianity is purged of its mysticism and transformed into a severe asceticism based on the doctrine of non-resistance to evil. *Tsarstvo Bozhye vnutri vas* (2 vols, 1893–4, Eng trans *The Kingdom of God Is within You*, 1894), *Khozyain i rabotnik* (1894, Eng trans *Master and Man*, 1895), the play *Plody prosveshcheniya* (1889, Eng trans *The Fruits of Enlightenment*, 1891) and *Voskreseniye* (1899, Eng trans *Resurrection*, 1899) strayed so far from orthodoxy that the Holy Synod excommunicated him (1901), and he denounced the worship of Jesus as blasphemy. In *Chto takoye iskusstvo?* (1898, Eng trans *What is Art?*, 1898) he argued that only simple works, such as the parables of the Bible, constitute great art. Everything sophisticated, stylized and detailed, such as his own great novels, he condemned as worthless. He handed over his fortune to his wife and lived poorly as a peasant under her roof. Domestic quarrels made him leave home clandestinely one October night, accompanied only by a daughter and his personal physician. He caught a chill and died in a siding of Astapovo railway station, refusing to see his waiting wife to the last. His doctrines founded a sect and Yasnaya Polyana became a place of pilgrimage. Mahatma Gandhi, who had corresponded with him, adopted the doctrine of nonresistance. But he is best known as the consummate master of the 'psychological' novel. **Boris Pasternak**'s father, Leonid, illustrated Tolstoy's works.
▷A Maude, *The Life of Tolstoy* (1910); I Berlin, *The Hedgehog and the Fox* (1953)

TOMLINSON, Charles
(1927–)

English poet and erstwhile critic, born in Stoke-on-Trent. His melancholy and accomplished work, much of it sensitively descriptive of landscape, has failed to gain a wide audience, but is greatly admired in certain quarters. He has been said, by a generally hostile critic, to have 'renounced experience as a poetic source', but to possess a 'hidden acknowledgement' of 'vivid humanity'. He claims to create a 'moral landscape' through 'images' of a 'certain mental climate', and his attempts to achieve this have much intelligence, discernment and appreciation of foreign poetries, to which he is unusually sensitive.
▷ *Poems: a Selection* (1964); *The Flood* (1981)

TOMLINSON, Henry Major
(1873–1958)

English author, born in London. He worked in a shipping office in his native docklands before becoming a journalist, and his love of the sea is reflected in books like *The Sea and the Jungle* (1912), *Tidemarks* (1924) and other travel books, as well as novels such as *Waiting for Daylight* (1922) and his two best-known works, *Gallions Reach* (1927) and *All Our Yesterdays* (1930), an anti-war novel about World War I. He also wrote several other novels, the autobiographical reminiscences in *A Mingled Yarn* (1953), and a biography of **Norman Douglas** (1931).

TOOLE, John Kennedy
(1937–69)

American novelist, born in New Orleans. He was educated at Tulane and Columbia universities, and committed suicide without publishing anything in his lifetime. Eleven years after his death, his mother persuaded the novelist **Walker Percy** to read a manuscript he had left. *A Confederacy of Dunces*, a sprawling, blackly comic social satire set in his native New Orleans, was published in 1980, and won a Pulitzer prize and considerable attention. A second brief novel, *The Neon Bible* (1989), is an elegiac evocation of a rural Southern childhood.

TOOMER, Jean, originally Nathan Eugene Toomer
(1894–1967)

American writer of verse and poetic fiction. He grew up in Washington, DC, where his grandfather had been an influential black politician. Toomer showed no particular academic aptitude and became a physical training instructor; he also did manual work. His one major book was *Cane* (1923), an uncategorizable anthology of prose and verse segments which offers a haunting collage of black life in America. Perhaps partly because of his complex racial background, Toomer refused to align himself with the quasi-nationalism of the 'Harlem Renaissance'. His instincts were already metaphysical, as can be seen from the long poem 'Blue Meridian', a passionate **Whitman**esque vision of a racially and socially harmonized America. Like most of his work after *Cane*, it only became widely known after his death, largely through Darwin Turner's edited collection of Toomer's writings, *The Wayward and the Seeking* (1980); the *Collected Poems* appeared as late as 1988. In 1924 Toomer went to study with **Gurdjieff** at Fontainebleau, and later founded Gurdjieff centres in the USA. He largely stopped writing after the 1940s, and *Cane* stands out as his only substantial achievement. Its status as a great American masterpiece is now firmly established.
▷ N Y McKay, *Jean Toomer, Artist: A Study of his Literary Life and Work* (1984)

TOPELIUS, Zacharias Sakari (Zachris)
(1818–98)

Finnish novelist and scholar, born in Unsikaarlepyy. He studied at Helsinki, and became Editor of the *Helsingfors Tidningar* newspaper (1842–78). He was appointed Professor of Finnish history at Helsinki (1854–78) and rector (1875–8). Writing in Swedish, he is regarded as the father of the Finnish historical novel, with stories of life in the 17th and 18th centuries, published as *Fältskärns berättelser* (1853–67, Eng trans *The Surgeon's Stories*, 1883–4). He also published five volumes of lyrical poetry, and wrote several plays.
▷ V Vasenius, *Zacharias Topelius* (6 vols, 1912–56)

TÖPFFER, Rodolphe
(1799–1846)

Swiss cartoonist and writer, born in Geneva. In 1825 he founded a boarding-school (which he ran for the rest of his life), and in 1832 became Professor of Rhetoric at Geneva Academy. He was the author of the humorous short story 'La Bibliothèque de mon oncle' (1832, 'My Uncle's Library'), published in *Nouvelles genevoises* (1841, 'Stories of Geneva'), and *Rosa et Gertrude* (1846), amongst others. His drawings were equally felicitous, especially in his *Voyages en zig-zag* (1843–53, 'Zig-zag Journeys').

TORGA, Miguel, pseud of Alfredo Rocha
(1907–90)

Portuguese poet, dramatist, novelist, essayist and diarist. He was for many years a doctor in Coimbra, and was one of the most widely read and prolific writers of modern Portugal. He was several times nominated for the Nobel Prize. He kept a diary incorporating his poems and essays, and published it at intervals from 1941 onwards. By far his most popular book was *Bichos* (1940, Eng trans *Farruscio the Blackbird*, 1951), a series of animal–human fables which he followed up with others. *Vindima* (1945) is a harrowing novel about the failure of a vineyard on a Douro estate. A pessimistic writer and in his poetry an atheist, he also wrote plays. The publication of each instalment of his diaries was a literary event.

TORRE, Guillermo de
(1900–)

Spanish minor poet, critic, scholar, editor and translator, born in Madrid. An associate of the Chilean poet **Vicente Huidobro**, he was one of the leaders of the so-called *ultraísmo* movement—this propounded an expressionist theory very close to Huidobro's creationism, and was deeply influenced by cubism.

He remained an ardent defender of the avant garde, translated the poems of **Max Jacob** into Spanish, and was one of the early editors of **García Lorca**.

TORRES BODET, Jaime
(1902–74)

Mexican poet, editor and novelist, a member of the *Contemporáneos* group, born in Mexico City. He was by profession a diplomat and at one time served as Minister of Education. He progressed from a too prolific poet in a variety of styles, through Surrealism, to a final Hermeticism. His novels, all experimental and somewhat insubstantial, seem mostly to have been influenced by **Unamuno**; of these, *Margarita de niebla* (1927, 'Margaret the Cloud'), is typical.
▷ *Selected Poems* (1964, bilingual)

TORRES NAHARRO, Bartolomé
(?1485–?1520)

Major Spanish dramatist and poet, born in La Torre de Miguel Sesmero, Badajoz, but who wrote most of his plays in Italy. Little is known of his life, except that he was a priest who probably turned soldier. He was a member of the large Spanish colony in Rome, which he may have come to via imprisonment by Moorish pirates. His most famous play is *Ymenea* (?1516), derived from *La Celestina* by **Fernando de Rojas**; it develops the tradition of Latin comedies by **Plautus** and **Terence**. *Soldadesca* (1517) is a vigorous satire on the brutality and corruption of military life in Italy, characterized—as are most of his other plays—by a candid obscenity, which caused his work to be placed on the Index for a time.
▷ J E Gillet, *Tores Naharro and the Drama of the Renaissance*, vol 4 of Gillet's edition of some of Torres's works (1943–61)

TÓTH, Árpád
(1886–1928)

Hungarian poet, translator (**Keats**, **Flaubert**, **Wilde**, **Shelley**) and man of letters, born in Debrecen. He supported Bela Kun's brief Hungarian Soviet Republic in 1919 with an excited but hardly seriously Marxist poem, 'Hz ν Isten' (1919, 'The New God'), for which he was ever after subtly persecuted. He was a close friend to **Babits**, and is one of the leading representatives of the Nyugat generation. Like so many of his compatriots he was deeply influenced by **Ady** and by French poetry, and (with Babits and **Szabó**) translated **Baudelaire**. Lonely, poor and ill (he died of tuberculosis), Tóth graduated to a melancholy grandeur in his last exquisite poems of longing for a different life and for more real experience. Babits edited his works after his death.

▷ J Reményi, *Hungarian Writers and Literature* (1964)

TOULET, Paul-Jean
(1867–1920)

French poet and novelist, born in Pau. His early work reflects his Parisian life as dandy and self-conscious decadent, but it was never superficial, and deepened as he grew older and poorer and more serious. The Fantaisiste group of minor poets (c.1910–12) was formed around his example, and that of **Laforgue**, and this left its mark upon **Apollinaire**. Toulet wrote some interesting fiction, but it is as a minor poet that he is really important. His poems, all in *Contrerimes* (1920, 'Counterrhymes'), some of them written or revised when he was debilitated by alcohol and opium, are almost paradigmatically 'decadent'; but they are delicate and elegant, and the underlying despair—of ever being able to love or be loved—is genuine.

TOURGÉE, Albion W(inegar)
(1838–1905)

American novelist and carpetbagger, born in Ohio. Tourgée left university to join the Union Army in the Civil War. He led a successful protest against army food but was seriously wounded in action. The wheel of a gun carriage struck him in the back and he was temporarily paralysed from the waist down. After the war he moved to North Carolina and became involved in the politics of Reconstruction. His romantically plotted but realistically presented novels reflect Tourgée's strong Republican viewpoint. *Bricks Without Straw* (1880) shows a New England teacher in the South sympathizing with blacks, and *Hot Plowshares* (1883), set during Reconstruction, was one of the first books to talk about miscegenation.

TOURNEUR, Cyril
(c.1575–1626)

English dramatist. Little is known of his life. In 1600 he published his *Transformed Metamorphosis* (discovered in 1872), a satirical poem; and in 1609 a *Funeral Poem* on Sir Francis Vere. In 1613 he wrote an *Elegy* on Prince Henry. His fame rests on two plays, *The Revenger's Tragedy* (printed in 1607), which some critics believed was written by **Thomas Middleton** or **John Webster**, and the inferior *The Atheist's Tragedy*, printed in 1611.
▷ P B Murray, *A Study of Cyril Tourneur* (1964)

TOURNIER, Michel
(1924–)

French novelist and broadcaster, born in Paris. His critical acclaim has consistently outweighed his sales, although his works are more accessible than those of his more experimental peers. *Vendredi, ou les limbes du Pacifique* (1967, Eng trans *Friday, or the Other Island*, 1969) retells the Robinson Crusoe story from the point of view of the white sailor's 'inferior' assistant. *Le Roi des Aulnes* (1970, Eng trans *The Erl King*, 1972) won the Prix **Goncourt**, while his play *Le Fétichiste* (1974, 'The Fetishist') won the Grand Prix du Roman from the Académie française.

TOURTEL, Mary
(1874–1948)

English writer and illustrator, born in Canterbury and educated at Canterbury Art School. She began her career in the 1890s but found lasting fame with her 'Rupert the Bear' cartoon strip in the *Daily Express* between 1920 and 1935, after which time Rupert was carried on by others. About 50 Rupert books were published. Her hero was usually accompanied in his adventures by such characters as Bill Badger, Algy Pug and Podgy Pig; sometimes we see a pair of magic flying boots or an encounter with smugglers; other occasions involve simply a pleasant trip to the seaside. Unlike the work of **A A Milne** or **Beatrix Potter**, Tourtel's Rupert has insufficient wit or irony to please many older readers.
▷G Perry, *Rupert, A Bear's Life* (1985)

TOWNE, Robert Burton
(c.1935–)

American screenwriter, born in Los Angeles. A student of English and philosophy at Pomona State College, he later studied acting, served in the United States Army and worked as a commercial fisherman before writing the screenplay of *The Last Woman On Earth* (1960) for film producer Roger Corman. A contributor to such television series as *The Man From UNCLE* (1964–8) and a consultant on *Bonnie And Clyde* (1967), he gained almost legendary renown as a film industry 'script doctor' whose skills could transform the most unpromising material into something filmable and even memorable. He has made uncredited contributions to such screenplays as *The Godfather* (1972), *Marathon Man* (1976) and *Frantic* (1988). As a credited screenwriter, he received the Oscar for *Chinatown* (1974) and further nominations for *The Last Detail* (1973) and *Shampoo* (1975). His best work has focused on isolated individuals bemused by an uncertain and even unwelcoming wider world. He made his directorial debut with *Personal Best* (1982), a sensitive account of a lesbian relationship; he continues to rescue stricken scripts, although his disgust at the final version of his screenplay for *Greystoke* (1984)

led him to relinquish his on-screen credit to P H Vazak: the name of his recently deceased Hungarian sheepdog.

TOWNSEND, Sue
(1945–)

English humorist, novelist and playwright, born in Leicester. She is best known for *The Secret Diary of Adrian Mole Aged 13¾* (1982) and *The Growing Pains of Adrian Mole* (1984). Witty and perceptive works, they are written in the form of a diary from the point of a view of an intellectually ambitious adolescent boy living in the Midlands, who copes with a precarious family life and emotional problems and fantasies (mostly involving the beautiful teenager Pandora Braithwaite). His adventures continue in three further books, including *Adrian Mole: The Wilderness Years* (1993), in which Mole, aged 23¾, battles on in a perplexing world. Of her plays, *The Great Celestial Cow* (1984) looks at the cultural problems of Asian women in Leicester, while her bestselling novel, *The Queen and I* (1992), imagines the demise of the British Royal family.

TOWNSHEND, Aurelian
(c.1583–c.1643)

English poet, about whom few biographical details are known. He was brought up, and possibly born, in Norfolk. He entered the service of Sir Robert Cecil, with whom he travelled extensively in Europe, and left upon Cecil's death in 1612. He wrote lyrics and poetry, a handful of which survives, and later collaborated with the architect and artist Inigo Jones on two spectacular court masques, *Albion's Triumph* and *Tempe Restored*.

TOYNBEE, (Theodore) Philip
(1916–81)

English novelist and journalist, born in Oxford, a son of the historian Arnold Toynbee, and educated at Christ Church, Oxford. He was a journalist on *The Observer* for several years and published his first novel, *The Savage Days*, in 1937. He became highly regarded as an experimental novelist, his most structurally innovative works being the *Pantaloon* sequence, a semi-autobiographical series of four books, written in verse. The first, *Pantaloon, or The Valediction*, appeared in 1961, and the second, *The Fifth Day of the Valediction of Pantaloon*, in 1964. *The Sixth Day ... and The Seventh Day ...* followed in 1966 and 1968. Many literary critics were perplexed by the books, although several poets acclaimed them. Toynbee also wrote and edited non-fiction work, of which *The Distant Drum: Reflections on the Spanish Civil*

War (1976), on which he worked with his father, is the finest.

TOZZI, Federigo
(1883–1920)

Italian fiction writer (and, initially, poet) and dramatist, from Siena—one of Italy's greatest writers of his century, although critics were slow to catch up with this fact. **Moravia**, in a scarcely challenged judgement, believed him to be the 'fourth' Italian writer, after **Manzoni**, **Svevo** and **Verga**. Tozzi had a disturbed childhood: his mother was epileptic and died young, and he was at constant odds with his brutal father, an innkeeper; he was expelled from many schools. The events of his unhappy life—cut short by pneumonia— are of the utmost importance in his work, for in the latter he cultivated a gnostic, humorous stoicism which resembled that of **Kafka** and anticipated a mid-century attitude. During 1907, when he left home, and 1908, he worked for the railways. Then he returned to Siena, where he tried to manage two farms. Throughout the rest of his life he struggled against adversity, meanwhile writing his masterpieces: the stories in *Bestie* (1917, 'Animals') and *L'Amore* (1920, 'Love'), and the novels *Tre croci* (1920, Eng trans *Three Crosses*, 1921), *Il podere* (1921, 'The Farm') and *Ricordi di un impiegato* (1920, Eng trans *Journal of a Clerk*, 1964). He had, a critic has noted, an 'abrasive genius', well adapted to triumph over the too-soft Italian admiration for *bello estilo*, smooth, elegant style. **Borgese** praised him, and saw his worth, but it was left to the post-fascist critics to recognize his greatness. The insufficiency of translations of Tozzi—many of whose works were published posthumously—into English is one of the enduring scandals of modern letters. His complete works were published in Italian, in four volumes (1961–70), by Vallechi of Florence in *Opere*.
▷S Pacifici, *From Verismo to Experimentalism* (1969), *The Italian Novel from Capuana to Tozzi* (1973); *Italian Quarterly*, 14 (1971); F Ulivi, *Federigo Tozzi* (1962, in Italian)

TRABA, Marta
(1930–84)

Argentinian novelist and short-story writer, who also has written extensively on art history. She graduated from the Universidad Nacional in Argentina with a doctorate in literature in 1950, but has spent most of her life in other countries, most notably Colombia. She won the Casa de las Americas Prize in 1966 for her novel *Las ceremonias del verano* ('Ceremonies of Summer'). In the forefront of new Latin-American feminist writing, her most widely acclaimed novels are *Conversación al sur* (1981, 'Conversation of the South') and *En cualquier lugar* (1984, 'Anywhere'). One of her main themes is the difference between the utterable and the unutterable, the said and the understood.

TRAHERNE, Thomas
(c.1636–1674)

English poet, born in Hereford, the son of a shoemaker. He studied at Brasenose College, Oxford, became rector of Credenhill (1657) and in 1667 became chaplain to the Lord Keeper of the great seal, Sir Orlando Bridgeman. He wrote the anti-Catholic *Roman Forgeries* (1673), and *Christian Ethicks*, published after his death in 1675. His major work, *Centuries of Religious Meditations* in prose, was first published in 1908. He also wrote poetry, which was not published until 1903. A late discovery, *Poems of Felicity*, was published in 1910. His work is full of the strikingly original imagery of the mystic, yet a mystic who as a 'Christian Epicurean' was prepared to give *Thanksgiving for the Body*.
▷K W Salter, *Thomas Traherne* (1964)

TRAKL, Georg
(1887–1914)

Austrian poet, born and educated in Salzburg. He trained and worked as a pharmacist, and his verse—only one volume of which, *Gedichte* (1913, 'Poems'), was published in his lifetime—has an internal balance and precision that suggests every word has been weighed and gauged with almost scientific exactness. Though he has something in common with the French Symbolists, the only poet he closely resembles is **Friedrich Hölderlin**; he clearly also identifies with the *tabula rasa* consciousness of Kaspar Hauser and, in *Sebastian im Traum* (posthumous, 1915), with the martyred saint. The pre-war poems are registered in dark, brooding colours and aural tonalities and with a dense inwardness which displaces conventional semantics. Trakl's first and best English translator was **Michael Hamburger** (1952); since then, he has been tackled by **James Wright** and **Robert Bly** and, notably, by **Christopher Middleton**.
▷F M Sharp, *The Poet's Madness: A Reading of Trakl* (1981)

TRANSTRÖMER, Tomas
(1931–)

Swedish poet and psychologist, born in Stockholm. He graduated there in 1956, since when he has worked as a psychologist, including a spell at Roxtuna institution for young offenders. His first collection of poems, *17 dikter* (1954, '17 Poems'), characterized by a visionary reality couched in precise pictures, aroused attention and he has since become a leading poet of the post-war era. Refusing to be hustled by his activist colleagues demanding political 'commitment', he chose to ponder 'the great mystery of existence'. His poems consider the contrast between man's spiritual and mental existence, his need for solitude and yet social contact; and how history lives on in the present. These tensions are reflected in his poetic style which skilfully juxtaposes movement and stasis, muted language and striking images. His metaphors are often inspired by music, travel and nature. His 10 collections of poems have been translated into English either in part or *in toto* by Robin Fulton in *Three Swedish Poets* (1970), *Selected Poems* (1974) and *Collected Poems* (1987).

▷K Espmark, *Resans Formler* (1983)

TRANTER, John Ernest
(1943–)

Australian poet, editor and critic, born in Cooma, New South Wales. As editor of 'little magazines' such as *Leatherjacket* and *Transit*, he has been a constant proponent of modernism in poetry, as his own work shows. His first book, *Parallax*, was published as the June 1970 edition of *Poetry Australia*. Four later books were followed by *100 Sonnets* (1977), *Selected Poems* (1982) and *Under Berlin—New Poems 1988* (1988). He edited the anthologies *Preface to the 70s* for *Poetry Australia*, *The New Australian Poetry* (1979) and *Tin Wash Dish: Poems from Today's Australians* (1989), and co-edited *The Penguin Book of Modern Australian Poetry* (1991).

TRANTER, Nigel,
(1909–)

Scottish novelist and historian, born in Glasgow. Educated at George Heriot's School in Edinburgh, he trained as an accountant before becoming a full-time writer in 1936. His output has been prodigious, numbering well over a hundred books. His best known novels are those on historical themes, most notably the trilogy on the life of Robert the Bruce, *The Steps to the Empty Throne* (1969), *The Path of the Hero King* (1970) and *The Price of the King's Peace* (1971). His non-fiction works include significant studies of Scottish castles and fortified houses. A writer whose talent lies in careful historical research rather than stylistic graces, in *Nigel Tranter's Scotland* (1981) he gave an account of his life-long fascination with rural Scotland's history, heritage, and public affairs.

TRASK, Betty (Margaret Elizabeth)
(1895–1983)

English light romantic novelist, who lived reclusively in Frome, Somerset. She is best known today for her bequest, in 1983, of about £400 000 in order to create an annual award for novels of a non-experimental nature (the first winner of which was **Ronald Frame**). She herself published the first of more than 50 novels, *Cotton Glove Country*, in 1928, and continued writing until the late 1950s. Her books tend towards the heart-throb genre, with such florid titles as *Desire Me Not* (1935) and *Thunder Rose* (1952); her characters are decent, middle-class people and her recurring theme is the eventual triumph of true love. After her death, it was noted in *The Times* that although her novels dwelt upon love, there had sadly never been any reported romance in her own life.

TRAVEN, B, pseud of **Berick Traven Torsvan**, originally **Albert Otto Max Feige**, also known as **Ret Marut**
(1890–1969)

Polish-born German novelist of working-class stock, born in Swiebodzin, a Polish town since subsumed into Germany. His first stories emerged in Germany in 1925 as *Die Baumwollpflücker* (Eng trans *The Cotton-pickers*, 1956) and it is thought he was active as a communist there at the end of World War I. *Das Totenschiff* (1932, Eng trans *The Death Ship*, 1934), an anti-capitalist tale of a seaman caught up in a plan by shipowners to sink the Yorikke and cash in on the insurance, was highly popular. In the mid-1920s he went to Mexico and from there, in German, came 12 novels and short stories, the most famous being *Der Schatz der Sierra Madre* (1927, Eng trans *The Treasure of the Sierre Madre*, 1934, and filmed by John Huston in 1947).

▷W Wyatt, *The Man who was Traven* (1980)

TRAVERS, Ben (Benjamin)
(1886–1980)

English dramatist and novelist, born in Hendon. He was educated at Charterhouse, served in the RAF in both World Wars and was awarded the Air Force Cross (1920). A master of light farce, he wrote to suit the highly individual comic talents of Ralph Lynn, Robertson Hare and Tom Walls in such pieces as *A Cuckoo in the Nest* (1925), *Rookery Nook* (1926), *Thark* (1927) and *Plunder* (1928), which played in the Aldwych Theatre, London for many years. His last work was a comedy, *The Bed Before Yesterday* (1976).

TREASE, Geoffrey
(1909–)

English novelist and historian, born in Nottingham and educated at Oxford. A prolific author, Trease has turned his hand to many kinds of writing—history of the popular, romantic sort featuring cavaliers and castles, and novels. He is best known, however, as a children's author, and has written almost 90 books for younger readers, the first being *Bows Against the Barons* (1934), set during the Wars of the Roses. Almost all feature historical settings, and the majority take place in England. *The Popinjay Mystery* (1973) is a rip-roaring thriller about **Samuel Pepys**; *Aunt Augusta's Elephant* (1969) is a charming Edwardian tale. His books are strong on narrative drive and sense of place, and adapt extremely well for radio—many of his readers came to him in the 1950s and 60s via the BBC, though he is less in vogue now.

TREECE, Henry
(1911–66)

English novelist, poet and essayist, born in the West Midlands. His early creative years were devoted to poetry, which he financed by working as an English teacher. In 1938 he became the founder, with J F Hendry, of the 'New Apocalypse', a romantic literary movement of evanescent influence. His first novel, *The Dark Island* (1952), was written for adults, and centres on the struggle of the Welsh chieftain Caractacus against the Romans. He is now best known as a historical novelist for children. His books of that type, most of which have a child as the witness of the action, include *Viking's Dawn* (1955) and *The Dream-Time* (1967, about a Stone Age boy).

TREMAIN, Rose
(1943–)

English novelist, dramatist, historian and short-story writer, born in London and educated at the Sorbonne and East Anglia University. Her first books appeared only in the USA: *The Fight for Freedom for Women* (1973) surveys the suffragette movement in Britain and the US, while her life of Stalin (1975) makes a special study of his upbringing in order to analyse his adult actions. Her first novel, *Sadler's Birthday*, was published in 1976. Others include *The Swimming Pool Season* (1985), and her best-known, *Restoration* (1989), which looks at the reign of Charles II in order to study contemporary Britain. Her books are cerebral, stimulating, and often bleak. She has also written for the stage and radio, *Temporary Shelter* being published in *Best Radio Plays of 1984*.

TREMBLAY, Michel
(1942–)

French–Canadian dramatist, born in Montreal. His best-known play, *Les Belles Soeurs* (1968), originally produced in Montreal, is a broad and sometimes vulgar comedy written in *joual*, partly-Quebecois dialect and partly an anarchic mix of French, English and all kinds of slang. As *The Sisters-in-Law* it has played in many other countries, and as *The Guid Sisters* it has enjoyed great popularity in Scotland. His plays frequently dwell on sexual repression and its imaginative release: examples are *La Duchesse de Langeais* (1969), a monologue by an ageing drag artist, and *Sacrée Sandra (Sandra/Manon)* (1977), a play about sexual identity. Among his later plays, *Le Vrai Monde?* (1987, 'The Real World?') considers the problems of the writer confronting his own family and emotional heritage.

TRENCH, Frederick Herbert
(1865–1923)

Irish poet, dramatist and producer, born in Avoncore, County Cork. Educated at Haileybury and Keble College, Oxford, he wrote volumes of verse such as *Deirdre Wed* (1900) and *New Poems* (1907); his best-known poem is the dramatic metaphysical enquiry 'Apollo and the Seaman' (1907). He was artistic director of the Haymarket Theatre (1909–11), but his own efforts at writing for the stage met with little success.

TRESSELL, Robert
(1870–1911)

Irish novelist, born into a middle-class Dublin family. Having emigrated to South Africa, he returned and settled in England after his wife's death. There he became involved in left-wing politics and worked as a housepainter, both activities feeding into his great novel, *The Ragged Trousered Philanthropist*, an amusing and moving exposé of the moral turpitude and corruption at the heart of the Edwardian social system. Publishers were understandably wary of this 1 700-page manuscript, and at one point Tressell consigned it to the fire. It was eventually published after his death: in an abridged version in 1914, and in full in 1955.

TREVOR, William (William Trevor Cox)
(1928–)

Irish short-story writer, novelist and playwright, born in Mitchelstown, County Cork. Educated at St Columba's College and Trinity College, Dublin, he taught history and art, sculpted and wrote advertising copy before devoting himself to literature. His first book was a novel, *A Standard of Behaviour* (1958), but though he has published 10 subsequently, including *Mrs Eckdorff in O'Neill's Hotel* (1969), *The Children of Dynmouth* (1976) and *Nights at the Alexandra* (1987), he is by inclination a short-story writer. He has lived in England for much of his life, but Ireland is the source of his inspiration. A superlative storyteller, his collections include *The Day We Got Drunk on Cake* (1967), *The Ballroom of Romance* (1972), *Angels at the Ritz* (1975), *The News from Ireland* (1986) and *Family Sins* (1990). *The Stories of William Trevor* appeared in 1983. He has also written a number of plays and screenplays.

▷ G Schirmer, *William Trevor* (1990)

TRIANA, José
(1931–)

Cuban dramatist, who began to write under the influence of Cuba's leading playwright of the 1950s, **Virgilio Piñera**, and the European contemporary masters to whom he had turned for his models. His most celebrated play is *La noche de los asesinos* (1965), produced successfully in New York and in London as *The Criminals*. Drawing on *The Maids* of **Jean Genet** and *Les Enfants Terribles* of **Jean Cocteau**, it depicts the antics of three murderous, or perhaps just fantasizing, adolescents.

TRIFONOV, Yuri
(1925–81)

Russian novelist and dramatist, one of the most outstanding to have emerged since World War II. Born into a high-ranking family, his father was one of the Old Bolsheviks who had joined the Communist Party before the Revolution but who disappeared in one of Stalin's purges. Trifonov was never a dissident himself but achieved the delicate balancing act of maintaining both his membership of the Writers' Union and the respect of his more outspoken colleagues. He wrote two plays, *The House on the Embankment* (1980), depicting the privileges of the Soviet ruling class, and *Exchange*, a satirical tragicomedy about the difficulties of the Moscow housing market for ordinary citizens, which was produced in Britain in 1989. At his death, he was completing *Disappearance*, a novel portraying the effects of the purges and World War II upon Russia.

TRILLING, Lionel
(1905–75)

American critic and academic. He was born in New York City and educated there at Columbia University, where he returned as an instructor in 1932, three years after his marriage to fellow-critic Diana (Rubin) Trilling. He was admitted to the professoriat in 1948,

a year after publishing his only novel, *The Middle of the Journey* (1947), a quasi-allegorical but psychologically sophisticated account of political fellow-travelling and its aftermath. Trilling's first critical work was a study of **Matthew Arnold** (1939), still considered a definitive study of the moral imagination, as was its successor, on **E M Forster** (1943). His most important contributions to the recovery of liberalism in the post-war years and its synthesis with psychoanalytic ideas were *The Liberal Imagination* (1950), *The Opposing Self* (1955) and, in particular, *Freud and the Crisis of Our Culture* (1956, rev edn *Beyond Culture*, 1965). In that last year, he was appointed to the Woodberry chair of literature and criticism at Columbia University, which he held until 1970. His interest thereafter focused very largely on Romanticism; he published *Sincerity and Authenticity* in 1972. After his death, Diana Trilling supervised a 12-volume *Complete Works* (1978–80); she also compiled a volume of his short stories, *Of This Time, Of That Place* (1979).

▷ M Krupnick, *Lionel Trilling and the Fate of Cultural Criticism* (1986)

TRIPATHI, Govardhanram
(1855–1955)

Indian (Gujarati) novelist, author of the massive realist novel *Sarasvaticandra* (1887–1901), said to be as yet unbettered in the language.

TRIPP, John
(1927–86)

Welsh poet, born in Bargoed, Glamorgan, and brought up, a farrier's son, in Whitchurch, Cardiff. After working as a journalist in London, he returned to Wales in 1969 and worked as a free-lance writer for the rest of his life. He published six volumes of poetry, his principal subjects being the history of Wales and the present condition of its people.

TRISTAN L'HERMITE, pseud of **François l'Hermite**
(c.1601–1655)

French poet and playwright, the chief of those who prepared the way for the perfectly executed classical French drama of **Racine**. His most famous play, a tragedy, is *La Mariane* (1637), presented, as most of his plays were, at the Marais Theatre in Paris. He was a gambler who led an unhappy and difficult life, some of which he recounts in his racy autobiographical novel, *Le Page disgracié* (1643, 'The Disgraced Page').

▷ H C Lancaster, *A History of French Dramatic Literature in the XVIIth Century* (1932)

TROLLOPE, Anthony
(1815–82)

English novelist, born in London. His father was an unsuccessful lawyer and barrister and consequently his school days at Harrow and Winchester were miserable. Later, when the family's financial circumstances were at their lowest, they moved to Belgium where his father died. His mother, **Frances Trollope**, a woman of enviable energy, maintained the family by her prolific writing. In 1834 Trollope became a junior clerk in the General Post Office in London where he marked time, professionally speaking, until he was transferred to Ireland in 1841. He left the Civil Service in 1867, an important but idiosyncratic official whose achievements included the introduction in Great Britain of the pillar-box for letters. A year later he stood unsuccessfully for parliament, and from 1867 to 1870 he edited the *St Paul's Magazine*, in which several of his books were serialized. His first novel, *The Macdermots of Ballycloran*, did not appear until 1847, and his second, *The Kellys and the O'Kellys* (1848), shared its lack of success. With *The Warden* (1855), the first of the Barchester novels, came an inkling of Trollope's genius. It is the story of the struggle over Harding's Hospital, and introduced into English fiction some of its most durable and memorable characters— Mr Harding, who recurs constantly throughout the Barchester series, Archdeacon Grantly, and Bishop Proudie who, with his redoubtable wife, dominates *Barchester Towers* (1857). The rest of the series are: *Doctor Thorne* (1858), *Framley Parsonage* (1861), *The Small House at Allington* (1864), and *The Last Chronicle of Barset* (1867). Interconnected by character and unified by their West Country setting in the imaginary town of Barset, the novels are distinguished by their quiet comedy, slow pace and piquant detail. The series format appealed to Trollope's industry and he embarked on a second, more ambitious sequence—known collectively as the 'Palliser' novels, after Plantagenet Palliser, who features in each—with the publication in 1864 of *Can You Forgive Her?* Its sequel was *Phineas Finn* (1869), and others in the series are *The Eustace Diamonds* (1873), *Phineas Redux* (1876), *The Prime Minister* (1876) and *The Duke's Children* (1880). Regarding himself more as a craftsman than an artist, Trollope claims to have begun work every morning at 5.30 and to have generally completed his planned quota of literary work before he dressed for breakfast. His output was consequently prodigious and comprises 47 novels, travel books, biographies of **Thackeray**, **Cicero** and Lord Palmerston, plays, short stories and literary sketches. His two renowned series apart, other novels worthy of note include *The Three Clerks* (1857), *The Bertrams* (1859), *Orley Farm* (1862), *The Vicar of Bullhampton* (1870), *The Way We Live Now* (1875) and *Doctor Wortle's School* (1881). Periodically he falls from fashion but is currently enjoying a resurgence. His *Autobiography* (1883) is an antidote to more romantic accounts of the literary life.
▷ A O J Cockshut, *Anthony Trollope* (1955)

TROLLOPE, Frances, née Milton
(1780–1863)

English novelist, born in Stapleton near Bristol, the mother of **Anthony Trollope**. In 1809 she married Thomas Anthony Trollope (1774–1835), a failed barrister and fellow of New College, Oxford. In 1827 he fell into dire financial difficulties, which were not relieved by moving to Cincinnati, Ohio, in 1827. During her three years in the USA, Mrs Trollope amassed the material for her *Domestic Manners of the Americans* (1832), a critical and witty book much resented in America. Left a widow in 1835, she travelled widely on the Continent, writing articles and fiction for her livelihood, and eventually settled in Florence (1843), where she lived until her death. Of her novels, the most successful were *The Vicar of Wrexhill* (1837) and *The Widow Barnaby* (1839), with its sequel, *The Widow Married* (1840). In all she wrote 115 volumes, now mostly forgotten.
▷ U Pope-Hennessy, *Three English Women in America* (1929)

TROTZIG, Birgitta
(1929–)

Swedish modernist writer. Born in Gothenburg, she lived in France from 1954 to 1969, becoming a Roman Catholic in 1955. Consistently asserting the integrity of art, she is a major critic of Swedish materialism and secularization. Her texts confront their readers with a world of suffering and degradation in which a total empathy becomes the prerequisite for bridging the gap to others and thus to God. In an early novel such as *De utsatta* (1957, 'The Exposed'), the priest becomes a Christ-figure as well as a helpless human being, while in *Dykungens dotter* (1985, 'The Marsh King's Daughter') elements of fairy-tale and myth focus the fall and the significance of grace. She has published several volumes of prose fragments and essays, including *Ett landskap* (1959, 'A Landscape') and *Jaget och världen* (1977, 'The I and the World').
▷ U Olsson, *I det lysande mörkret. En läsning av Birgitta Trotzigs De utsatta* (1988)

TROYAT, Henri, pseud of **Lev Tarasov**
(1911–)
Russian-born French writer, a prolific producer of novels, novel-cycles, and biographies of Russian writers. Both his individual novels, such as *L'Araigné* (1938, winner of the Prix **Goncourt**), and four of the cycles—for instance, the five-volume *La Lumière des Justes* (1959–63)—paint a panoramic picture of Russian life from the mid-19th century. Now best known in the Anglophone world as a biographer, his studies in that field include works on **Pushkin** (1946, Eng trans 1950), **Tolstoy** (1965, Eng trans 1967) and **Chekhov** (1984, Eng trans 1986). He was elected to the Académie française in 1959.

TRUJILLO, Bernardo Arias
(1904–39)
Colombian novelist, born in Antioquia, whose 'tragically early death', wrote the historian of the Spanish–American novel Kessel Schwartz, 'prevented him from becoming one of the great Colombian novelists'. He wrote one novel, *Risaralda* (1936), set in Portobello on the Risaralda river; it is one of the very few Negro novels of Spanish America, unique for its time, and, although written in an over-grandiloquent style, remains a singular achievement.
▷G R Coulthard, *Race and Colour in Caribbean Literature* (1962)

TRUMBULL, John
(1750–1831)
American lawyer and poet, born in Watertown, Connecticut, first cousin of Jonathan Trumbull. He practised law in Boston, New Haven and Hartford, and became a judge of the Connecticut supreme court (1809–13). He wrote a satire on educational methods, *The Progress of Dullness* (1772–3), and a satire on British blunders in the American War of Independence, *McFingal* (1775–82), in imitation of **Samuel Butler**'s *Hudibras*.
▷A Cowie, *John Trumbull, Connecticut Wit* (1936)

TSAO YU, pseud of **Wan Chia-Pao**
(1905–)
Chinese playwright, usually described as 'modern China's first great' one, born in Chien-Kiang, Hupei. He started out as an actor, and made a famous appearance as Nora in **Ibsen**'s *Doll's House*. The play which made him famous was *Lei Yü* (1934, Eng trans *Thunderstorm*, in *Three Famous Chinese Plays*, 1946): an accomplished piece of drama, it was Western in style, but its characters remained Chinese. The most potent influence upon it was **Eugene O'Neill**.
▷F Bowers, *Theatre in the East* (1956)

TSO CH'IU MING
(c.6th century BC)
Chinese author, mentioned by Confucius in his *Analects*. He wrote the *Tso Chuan*, a commentary on the *Ch'un Ch'iu*, one of the five classics. Scholars also ascribe to him the *Kuo Yü*, and these two works comprise the most important historical sources of the period. The simplicity of his style served as a model to later writers.

TSUBOUCHI Shoyo
(1859–1935)
Japanese literary theorist and critic, born in Mino. An academic at Tokyo University, he produced, in 1886, his seminal *Shoetsu Shinzui* ('The Essentials of the Novel'). It was widely taken up and became a manifesto for Japanese naturalism, the dominant form of novel and story writing in Japan for the next 70 years. It holds, simply, that the writer should concentrate on what he knows, not speculate or indulge in fantasy, and that what is important is not what happens but how characters respond to what happens. The novels the theory gave rise to (those of **Shimazaki**, **Tanizaki**, **Natsume** and **Shiga**, amongst many others) are minutely described and closely narrated; in their most extreme form they become internal monologues.

TSUSHIMA Yuko
(1947–)
Japanese writer and novelist, born in Tokyo. The daughter of **Osamu Dazai**, Tsushima is a prolific and popular writer of short stories, one of the first of a generation of Japanese women writers to achieve a degree of popular success whilst writing about what might broadly be termed 'women's issues'. She has also written novels: *Choji* (1978, Eng trans *Child of Fortune*, 1983) is the tale of a divorcee who finds herself pregnant in a society where there is considerable stigma attached to unmarried motherhood.

TSVETAYEVA, Marina
(1892–1941)
Major Russian poet, dramatist and memoirist, usually regarded as of similar status to **Akhmatova**. Her pallid, romantic early poetry was technically well accomplished and gained her a high reputation; but now receives little attention. Her husband fought against the Bolsheviks (for her, Satan), and much of the poetry of her middle period—in particular *Lebediny stan* (1917–22, 'The Swans' Encampment')—is anti-Bolshevik in spirit. She also wrote a number of historical verse plays. **Pasternak**, in writing of her *Versty* (1922, 'Versts'), spoke of the 'intense lyrical power of her poetic form'. She emigrated in

1922, and became, in Paris, a symbol of Russia-in-exile. Her memoirs of such writers as **Blok**, **Voloshin** and **Kuzmin** are illuminating, although somewhat nervously self-centred. She proved too individualistic to be able to remain in Paris, returned to Russia in 1939, and hanged herself. Her poetry has been outstandingly well translated by **Elaine Feinstein**.

▷ E Feinstein, *A Captive Lion* (1987)

TU FU
(712–70)

Greatest Chinese poet of the T'ang Dynasty and one of the foremost lyricists in the language. He was born in Hsiang-yang, and spent much of his youth travelling, during which time he soaked up impressions of his country's sharply juxtaposed cultural riches and social ills. He was largely unsuccessful in his attempts to gain a position in the imperial service, gaining only temporary appointments. He saw his own situation reflected in the corruption, cynicism and waste of a dynasty which had lost its burnish of optimism and moral uprightness. 'The Ballad of Beautiful Women' is a famous example of his passionate good-heartedness; other poems like 'The Newlyweds' Parting' and 'The Chariots' Song' reflect the violent uncertainties of life at the time, but they are also beautifully crafted and full of memorable imagery. In his later years, Tu Fu was supported financially by an old friend, who enabled him to travel once more, in greater comfort than he had experienced in his youth. The best English-language source for Tu Fu is still Florence Ayscough's two-volume *The Autobiography of a Chinese Poet* (1929); a definitive edition of the complete works appeared in Peking in 1979.

▷ W Hung, *Tu Fu, China's Greatest Poet* (1952)

TUCCI, Niccolò
(1908–)

Italian-born American novelist, playwright, columnist and contributor to the *New Yorker*. His novels include *Before My Time* (1962) and *Unfinished Funeral* (1964). His short fiction can be found in *The Rain Came Last and Other Stories* (1990).

TUCHOLSKY, Kurt
(1890–1935)

German satirist, dramatist, novelist, pacifist and left-wing cabaret poet—in the tradition of **Ringelnatz** but more specifically political—who killed himself in Switzerland after the Nazis had burned his books and taken away his nationality. His chansons are still sung,

and are still enjoyable for the Berlin atmosphere which they so colourfully evoke. English translations (selections): H Zohn (ed), *The World is a Comedy* (1957); H Zohn and K F Ross, *What If?—Satirical Writings* (1967)

TUCKERMAN, Frederick Goddard
(1821–73)

American poet, one of the most important of his century, born in Boston. He qualified and briefly practised law, but spent the last 25 years of his life as a recluse in Greenfield, Massachusetts, making notes of eclipses and studying local fauna. Like **Hopkins** in England, with whom he has some affinities, he was scarcely known in his own lifetime, although his single collection, *Poems* (1860), was highly regarded by **Tennyson**. After his death his work, much of which consists of irregular sonnets (one of them speaks of the 'spermal odor of the barberry flower'—highly repulsive, like his metrical unconventionalities, to his more regular compatriots), went into oblivion, but was revised in 1831 by **Witter Bynner** with the *Sonnets of Frederick Goddard Tuckerman* (1931). His ode 'The Cricket', not published until 1950, and then in a bad text, is justifiably regarded as a key poem in American literature: occasioned by his wife's death in childbirth, it deals with his mystical refusal to interpret nature 'for the benefit of his readers' ('Then Cricket, sing thy song! or answer mine!/Thine whispers blame, but mine has naught but praises.').

▷ N Scott Momaday (ed), *The Complete Poems* (1965); S A Golden, *Tuckerman* (1966)

TUDUR ALED
(c.1465–c.1525)

Welsh poet, born in Denbighshire. Like **Dafydd ap Gwilym** and **Dafydd Nanmor**, he was amongst the greatest of the school of poets known as the *Beirdd yr Uchelwyr* (poets of the gentry). He was a master of the *awdl* and the *cywydd*, many of which survive. He was the last great Welsh poet; during his lifetime, Welsh literature and culture was beginning its great deterioration, as English began to supplant the native language.

TULSĪDĀS
(1532–1623)

Indian Hindi devotional poet, born in Eastern India. Traditionally believed to have lived for 120 years, the time allotted to a sinless human being, he wrote more than a dozen works. His best-known is *Rāmacaritamānas* ('The Holy Lake of Rāma's Deeds'), an immensely popular Eastern Hindi version of the *Rāmāyana* epic, which he began in 1574. His *bhakti* or devotional approach, concern for moral conduct, and idea of salvation through Rāma incarnated as absolute knowledge and love, suggest a Nestorian Christian influence on his work.

▷W D P Will, *The Holy Lake of the Acts of Ram* (1953)

TUNSTRÖM, Göran
(1937–)

Swedish author, born in Sunne, Värmland. His first work, *Inringning* ('Encircling'), appeared in 1958, since when he has published poems, plays, travel books (he and his wife, the painter Lena Cronquist, are intrepid travellers) and several long novels. His novels have an inventive plot borne by a rich tapestry of vivid, eccentric characters, but the underlying message is that we need more human love and kindness in our lives. Recurring themes are a search for identity, lost childhood and, inter-connected, father-and-son relationships. His own father, a clergyman whom he dearly loved, died when he was 12 and his world fell apart. In his fiction he recaptures his childhood and tries to come to terms with his loss. He also looks at human responsibility and betrayal in both provincial and international settings. His most popular novels to date are the prize-winning *Juloratoriet* (1982, 'The Christmas Oratorio') and *Tjuven* (1986, 'The Thief').

TUPPER, Martin Farquhar
(1810–89)

English writer, born in Marylebone. He studied at Charterhouse and at Christ Church, Oxford. He was called to the Bar (1835), but soon turned to writing. Of his 40 works, only *Proverbial Philosophy* (1838–67), a series of moralizing commonplaces in free verse, achieved huge worldwide popularity. He also published several novels and plays, and an autobiography, none of which are now read.

TURBERVILE, George
(c.1540–c.1610)

English poet, and secretary to Sir **Thomas Randolph**, born in Whitchurch, Dorset. He was educated at Winchester and New College, Oxford. He wrote epigrams, songs, sonnets, *The Booke of Falconrie* (1575), *The Noble Art of Venerie* (1576), and translated **Ovid**, the Italian poets and others. He was a pioneer in the use of blank verse.

TURGENEV, Ivan Sergeevich
(1818–83)

Russian novelist, born in the province of Orel. The child of landed gentry, he had an unsatisfactory childhood through the cruelty of his mother, whose great inherited wealth made her a petty tyrant in the home. After graduating from St Petersburg University he broke away by going to study philosophy in Berlin and there mingled with the radical thinkers of the day. He became firm friends with **Alexander Herzen**. He returned to Russia in 1841 to enter the civil service, but in 1843 abandoned this to take up literature. His mother strongly disapproved and his infatuation for a singer, Paulina Garcia (Mme Viardot), also displeased her. She stopped his allowance and until her death in 1850, when he came into his inheritance, he had to support himself by his writings. He began with verse, *Parasha* (1843), showing the influence of **Alexander Pushkin**, but soon recognized prose as his medium and in 1847 produced *Khor i Khalynich* ('Khor and Khalynich'), his first sketch of peasant life, which appeared again in *Zapiski okhotnika* (1852, Eng trans *Russian Life in the Interior*, 1855). This book, sympathetic studies of the peasantry, made his reputation, but earned governmental displeasure, as it was interpreted as an attack on serfdom. A notice praising **Nikolai Gogol** on his death in 1852 exacerbated the ill-feeling and resulted in a two years' banishment to his country estates. After his exile he spent much time in Europe, writing nostalgically of life in Russia. *Rudin* (Eng trans *Dmitri Roudine*, 1873) appeared in 1856, *Dvoryanskoye gnezdo* (Eng trans *A Nest of Gentlefolk*, 1869) in 1859, *Nakanune* (Eng trans *On the Eve*, 1871) in 1860, all faithful descriptions of Russian liberalism, with its attendant weaknesses and limitations. In his greatest novel, *Ottsy i dety* (1862, Eng trans *Fathers and Sons,* 1867), he portrayed the new generation with its reliance on the practical and materialistic, its faith in science and lack of respect for tradition and authority, in short the Nihilists. But the hero, Bazarov, pleased neither the revolutionaries who thought the portrait a libel nor the reactionaries who thought it a glorification of iconoclasm. Turgenev's popularity slumped in Russia but rose abroad, particularly in Britain, where the book was recognized as a major contribution to literature. Successive novels were *Dym* (1867, Eng trans *Smoke*, 1868) and *Nov'* (1877, Eng trans *Virgin Soil*, 1877). He returned to the short story, producing powerful pieces like *Stepnoy Korol' Lir* (1870, Eng trans *A Lear of the Steppes*, 1874) and tales of the supernatural to which his increasing melancholy drew him.

▷L Schapiro, *Turgenev, his life and times* (1978)

TURNER, Ethel Mary
(1870–1958)

English-born Australian novelist and children's author, born in Balby, Yorkshire. Her father, Bennett George Burwell, died before she was two, and for her writing she took her step-father's surname. She moved to Australia at the age of nine. With her sister Lilian she started *Iris*, a magazine for schoolgirls, for which Ethel wrote the children's page, later doing the same for the *Illustrated Sydney News* and the *Bulletin*. Her first book, *Seven Little Australians* (1894), is now a classic of Australian literature. It has been in print ever since publication, was filmed as early as 1939 and has been adapted for British and Australian television and as a stage musical. A sequel, *The Family at Misrule*, came out in 1895 and there followed a steady stream of juvenile books, short stories and verse. Her daughter Jean Curlewis (1899–1930) edited the children's column in the Sydney *Daily Telegraph*, wrote a number of books for older children including *The Ship that Never Set Sail* (1921) and collaborated with her mother on such books as *The Sunshine Family: a Book of Nonsense for Girls and Boys* (1923).

TURNER, George
(1916–)

Australian novelist, science-fiction writer and critic, born in Melbourne. *A Young Man of Talent* came out in 1959, and was followed by *A Stranger and Afraid* (1961), the first of five books loosely centred on the fictional town of Treelake. The second 'Treelake' title was *The Cupboard Under the Stairs* (1962), a powerful story of a mental hospital patient and his return to the world. It shared the **Miles Franklin** Award in 1962. In science fiction he has written a trilogy, *Beloved Son* (1978), *Vaneglory* (1981) and *Yesterday's Men* (1982), which, especially in using character and location to provide continuity, often mirrors the 'Treelake' tetralogy. *The Sea and the Summer* (1987) pictures the civilization in a 21st-century Melbourne after devastating *tsunamis* or tidal waves.
▷ *In the Heart or in the Head* (1984)

TURNER, Walter James Redfern
(1884–1946)

Australian-born British poet and critic, born in Melbourne. He left Australia in 1907 and served in World War I, during which his first and best collection of verse, *The Hunter and Other Poems* (1916), was published. The patron Edward Marsh included a number of Walter's poems in *Georgian Poetry 1916–17* (1917), as a result of which he was accepted into London literary circles. Later verse included *The Dark Fire* (1918) and *The Landscape of Cytherea* (1923). After the war he was sometime Literary Editor of the *Daily Herald*, drama critic of the *London Mercury* and music critic of the *New Statesman*. He became Literary Editor of the *Spectator* in 1942. His other books of verse, mainly on the

metaphysical concept of love, include *Marigold* (1926), *Pursuit of Psyche* (1931) and *Fossils of a Future Time* (1946). He wrote nearly 20 plays, though only two were both published and performed. An accomplished amateur musician, he wrote a number of serious studies, including *Beethoven: the Search for Reality* (1927) and *Mozart: the Man and His Work* (1937). He will perhaps be remembered best as the creator and General Editor of the Collins' series 'Britain in Pictures' (1941–6).
▷ W McKenna, *W J Turner: Poet and Music Critic* (1990)

TUTUOLA, Amos
(1920–)

Nigerian novelist, born in Abeokuta. He was educated at a Salvation Army school and later taught at Lagos High School. *The Palm-Wine Drinkard* (1952), his most popular book, written in a musical pidgin, deals with its hero's adventures among the 'Deads'—the spirits of the departed.
▷ G Collins, *Amos Tutuola* (1969)

TUWHARE, Hone
(1922–)

New Zealand Maori poet, a major figure who uses the strength of Maori oral tradition and the passions of working-class roots to drive home his political message. His first book, *No Ordinary Sun* (1964, rev edn 1977), became instantly popular, and was followed by *Come Rain Hail* (1970) and *Sapwood and Milk* (1973). *Selected Poems* was published in 1980, *Mihi: Collected Poems* in 1987, and *Deep River Talk: Collected Poems* in 1993.

TWAIN, Mark, pseud of Samuel Langhorne Clemens
(1835–1910)

American writer, born in Florida, Missouri. A printer first (1847–55), and later a Mississippi river-boat pilot (1857–61), he adopted his pen-name from a well-known call of the man sounding the river in shallow places ('mark twain' meaning 'by the mark two fathoms'). In 1861 he went to Carson City, Nevada, as secretary to his brother, who was in the service of the governor, and while there tried goldmining without success. He next edited for two years the Virginia City *Territorial Enterprise* and in 1864 moved to San Francisco as a reporter. His first success was *The Celebrated Jumping Frog of Calaveras County* (1865), published as a book with other sketches in 1867. In 1867 he visited France, Italy and Palestine, gathering material for his *Innocents Abroad* (1869), which established his reputation as a humorist. Later he was editor of a newspaper in Buffalo, where he married the wealthy Olivia Langdon. Later

he moved to Hartford, Connecticut, and joined a publishing firm which failed, but largely recouped his losses by lecturing and writing. *Roughing It* (1872) is a humorous account of his Nevada experiences, while *The Gilded Age* (1873), written with **Charles Dudley Warner**, a novel which was later dramatized, exposes the readjustment period after the Civil War. His two greatest masterpieces, *Tom Sawyer* (1876) and *Huckleberry Finn* (1884), drawn from his own boyhood experiences, are firmly established among the world's classics; other favourites are *A Tramp Abroad* (1880) and *A Connecticut Yankee in King Arthur's Court* (1889). Mark Twain pokes fun at entrenched institutions and traditions, but his 'debunking' is mostly without malice and his satire is free from bitterness, except in later work, such as *The Tragedy of Pudd'nhead Wilson* (1894), when fate had been unkind to him. In places his subject-matter is inclined to date, but his best work is not only classic humorous writing but a graphic picture of the 19th-century American scene.
▷J Kaplan, *Mark Twain, a biography* (1966); E Emerson, *The Authentic Twain, a biography of Clemens* (1984)

TWARDOWSKI, Samuel ze Skrzpny
(c.1600–1661)

Polish Baroque poet, born on the Lutynia River in western Poland. Educated by Jesuits, he acquired the nickname of the 'Polish Virgil' on account of his narrative poems. He wrote an opera, *Daphnis* (1638), and a pastoral romance called *Nadobna Pasqualina* (1655), which he claimed was based on an unknown Spanish original. This complex poem, whose intended symbolic meaning has never been fully ascertained, presents a woman defeating Venus and causing Cupid's suicide.

TYARD, or THIARD, Pontus de
(1521–1605)

French poet, born in Bissy-sur-Fleys (Saône-et-Loire). He belonged to the group of Lyons poets who took **Petrarch** for their master. Influenced, however, by the work of **Pierre de Ronsard**, his verse bridges the gap between the Petrarchan style and that of the Pléiade poets. Volumes of poetry include *Erreurs amoureuses* (1549–55, 'Mistakes in Love'), *Le Livre des vers lyriques* (1555, 'Book of Lyrical Verses') and *Œuvres poétiques* (1573, 'Poetic Works'). He was Bishop of Châlon-sur-Saône (1578–94) and wrote also theological and philosophical works, including *Discours philosophiques* (1587).
▷K M Hall, *Pontus de Tyard and his Discours philosophiques* (1963)

TYCHNA, Pavel
(1891–1967)

Ukrainian Symbolist poet and translator (mainly from Russian poetry), born in Pisky. Tychna is usually regarded as the greatest of 20th-century Ukrainian poets. *Sonyashni klyarnety* (1918, 'The Clarinets of the Sun') is one of the outstanding first collections in world literature, and has its place alongside the *Heraldos Negros* of **Vallejo**. Like **Blok**, he saw the Revolution of 1917 in religious, even cosmic, terms. Later he adopted socialist realism, was awarded state prizes, and lost all his gifts but his technique and rhetorical effectiveness. The original Tychna has much in common with the Hungarian **Ady**.

TYLER, Anne
(1941–)

American novelist and short-story writer, born in Minneapolis, Minnesota, and raised in Raleigh, North Carolina. She graduated from Duke University at 19, where she twice won the Anne Flexner Award for creative writing, and has been a Russian bibliographer and assistant to the librarian, McGill University Law Library. Writing mainly of life in Baltimore or in Southern small towns, and concerned with the themes of loneliness, isolation and human interactions, she has had a productive career since her debut in 1964 with *If Morning Ever Comes*. Significant subsequent titles include *Morgan's Passing* (1980), *Dinner at the Homesick Restaurant* (1982) and *The Accidental Tourist* (1985).
▷A Petty, *Understanding Anne Tyler* (1990)

TYLER, Royall
(1757–1826)

American dramatist and novelist, born in Boston and educated at Harvard. He enjoyed a long legal career in which he became Chief Justice of the Supreme Court of Vermont and, from 1811 to 1814, Professor of Jurisprudence at the University of Vermont. His claim to fame as a dramatist is based almost exclusively upon his first play, *The Contrast* (1787), a light satire in the style of **Sheridan**'s *The School for Scandal*, and the first comedy written by a native American author to be produced. It was enormously popular, but Tyler failed to match this success. He wrote satires and even a comic opera, farce and a sacred verse drama, but to no avail. His later work did not even find a producer. His best-known novel is *The Algerine Captive* (1797).

TYNAN, Katharine
(1861–1931)

Irish poet and novelist, born in Clondalkin, County Dublin. She was a friend of Parnell, the **Meynell**s and the **Rossetti**s and a leading

author of the Celtic literary revival. She married in 1893 H A Hinkson, who was a resident magistrate in County Mayo from 1914 to 1919. Her journalism established her reputation, but she also wrote some 18 volumes of tender, gentle verse, over a hundred novels, including *Oh! What a Plague is Love* (1896), *She Walks in Beauty* (1899) and *The House in the Forest* (1928), and around 40 other books, including five autobiographical works, the last of which was *Memoires* (1924). Her *Collected Poems* appeared in 1930.
▷ M G Rose, *Katharine Tynan* (1974)

TYNNI, Aarlo
(1913–)
Finnish poet and translator, born in Kolppana, Inkeri, and a forerunner of the post-World War II Finnish poetic modernism. Her own well-made poetry could be compared to that of the Australian **Judith Wright**, but she is perhaps best known for her invaluable anthology of translations from foreign poets of all ages and nations, *Tuhat laulujen vuotta* (1957, 'Songs of a Thousand Years').

TYRTAEUS
(fl.c.685–668 BC)
Greek elegiac poet, probably born in Sparta. His warsongs inspired the Spartans during the second Messenian War (650–630 BC).
▷ C M Bowra, *Early Greek Elegists* (1938)

TYUTCHEV, Fyodor Ivanovich
(1803–73)
Russian lyric poet, born in Ovstug, Oryol, of a noble landowning family. He spent 20 years abroad in the diplomatic service and then worked in the censorship department. His first collection of poems appeared in 1854 and was hailed with enthusiasm. A metaphysical romantic, he reached full recognition with the advent of Symbolism. The tragic love poems of his later period are outstanding in Russian literature.
▷ D D Yazykov, *Fyodor Ivanovich Tyutchev* (1904)

TZARA, Tristan
(1896–1963)
Romanian poet, born in Bucharest, one of the founders of Dadaism and later a Surrealist. The products of his involvement with Dadaism—revolutionary at the time, almost unreadable now—include *Vingt-cinq Poèmes* (1918, '25 Poems') and *Sept Manifestes Dada* (1924, 'Seven Dadaist Manifestos'). A resident of Paris from 1920, he contributed to the Dadaist journal *Litterature*, was an active participant in the movement's 'happenings' (which often degenerated into bunfights), and was responsible for some splendidly splenetic assaults on the bourgeois order. He became a card-carrying Surrealist in 1929, producing *L'homme Approximatif* two years later, but never recaptured the anarchic vitality of his early years.

U

UA BROLCHÁN, Máel Isu
(c.1000–1086)

Irish poet and monk, called 'the doyen and chief sage of all Ireland'. A few well-known religious poems, which can be found in *Early Irish Lyrics* (1956), have been attributed to him.

UDALL, or UVEDALE, Nicholas
(1504–56)

English dramatist, born in Hampshire. He was educated at Winchester and Corpus Christi College, Oxford, and became headmaster of Eton c.1534. He published a selection from **Terence**, *Flowers of Latin Speaking*, for his pupils, who soon learnt of his predilection for corporal punishment. His dismissal in 1541 for indecent offences did not affect his standing at the court. Edward VI appointed him prebendary of Windsor, and despite his great enthusiasm for the Reformation, he survived the reign of Queen Mary I without disfavour. He translated **Erasmus**, selections from the Great Bible and Latin commentaries on the later, but is chiefly remembered as the author of the comedy, *Ralph Roister Doister*, written c.1553 but not published until 1567, which, inspired by his favourite classical writers, **Plautus** and Terence, was to influence later English writers of comedies.
▷C M Saxby, in *Representative English Dramatists* (1903)

UHLAND, Johannn Ludwig
(1787–1862)

German lyric poet, the leader of the 'Swabian School', born in Tübingen, where he studied law. He published poems from an early age and gradually added to his *Gedichte* (1815, 'Poems'), which contain such popular songs as 'Der gute Kamerad' ('The Good Comrade'). He also wrote a number of admirable literary essays. He was a Liberal deputy for Tübingen at the assemblies of Württemberg (1819) and Frankfurt (1848).
▷G Schwarz, *Johann Uhland* (1964)

UHRY, Alfred Fox
(1936–)

American playwright, born in Atlanta, Georgia. He graduated from Brown University in 1958. He wrote lyrics for a number of musicals, including *The Robber Bridegroom* (1975), and also wrote for television. He scored a major success with his first serious stage drama, *Driving Miss Daisy* (1987), a lightweight but warm-hearted account of the relationship between an aristocratic Southern matron and her black chauffeur. It won him a Pulitzer Prize in 1988, and was successfully filmed in 1989.

UJEVÍC, Tin
(1891–1955)

Croatian poet, prose-poet, translator and critic, born in Vrgorac. He was well known from his youth, both as a promising poet, a political agitator and (later), for being, in the words of a critic, 'solitary, egocentric, disorderly and alcoholic'. Disapproval of Ujevíc's inexcusable lifestyle harmed appreciation of his extraordinary poetry for many years, but critics are now learning to read him more constructively, and to understand that his abundant criticism, much influenced by his Indian studies, may be more profound than chaotic: far from 'having no consistent view of literature', it has been suggested that he learned from Indian aesthetics that this is impossible. It is unfortunate that he should have lacked a translator, for such visionary work as is contained in, for example, *Ojadjeno Zvono* (1933, 'The Aggrieved Bell'), would have been—and still may be—influential in European poetry. Many of his critical insights into Yugoslav and French poetry are invaluable. As it stands he is one of the great untranslated poets of the 20th century.

UKRAINKA, pseud of Larysa Kosach-Kvitka
(1871–1913)

Ukrainian revolutionary poet and dramatist, born in Novohrad Volynsky. She died young of tuberculosis. She was a fine rhetorical poet, fervent and sincere, but her language and her attitudes have now dated. Her best work is in drama.
▷P Cundy, *Spirit of Flame* (1950)

ULFELDT, Leonora Christine
(1621–98)

Danish author, and daughter of the Danish king Christian IV. She was engaged at the age of 10 to Corfitz Ulfeldt, a nobleman who subsequently fell out with King Fredrik III and had to leave the country with his family.

In 1663 Leonora Christine was arrested and interned in the Blue Tower at Copenhagen Castle where she spent 22 years. While imprisoned, she wrote an autobiography in French. More importantly, she began her remarkable *Jammers Minde* ('Misery Remembered') which, although written in Danish, was not published until the mid-19th century. An attempt to gain a perspective on her situation, the text presents her experiences in terms of a biblical drama which encompasses strikingly realistic accounts of prison conditions and her fellow prisoners. Stylistically highly accomplished, the work testifies to her exceptional resilience as well as her profound religious conviction.
▷'Troskab, lidelse og lidenskab. Om Leonora Christine Ulfeldt', in E Møller Jensen (ed), *Nordisk kvindelitteraturhistorie*, vol I, (1993)

ULRICH VON LICHTENSTEIN
(c.1200–c.1275)
Middle High Austrian Minnesinger (Minnesang was the formal love poetry of the chivalric age), born of a noble family. He became Marshal of his native Styria. He assembled his work, deriving and developing from such poets as **Walther von der Vogelweide**, as *Frauendienst*, a collection of love lyrics framed by a connecting first-person tale in verse (about 4000 lines in itself). He was almost the last German-language poet to be devoted to the older notion of courtly love. Opinions differ as to his achievement, and of the degree of his truthfulness—but his account of how he served a mistress and a wife by standards of old-style *amour courtois* is fascinating.
▷O Sayce, *The Poets of the Minnesang* (1967)

UNAMUNO, Miguel de
(1864–1936)
Spanish philosopher and author, born in Bilbao, of Basque parentage. He was Professor of Greek at Salamanca from 1892. He wrote mystic philosophy, historical studies, brilliant essays, books on travel, and austere poetry. Among his most important works are *Vida de Don Quijote y Sancho* (1905, Eng trans *The Life of Don Quixote and Sancho*, 1927), his novel *Niebla* (1914, Eng trans *Mist*, 1928), *Del sentimiento trágico de la vida* (1913, Eng trans *The Tragic Sense of Life in Men and in Peoples*, 1926) and a volume of religious poetry, *El Cristo de Velázquez* (1920, Eng trans *The Christ of Velasquez*, 1951). From 1924 to 1930 he was exiled as a Republican to the island of Fuerteventura, and reinstated at Salamanca on the founding of the republic in 1931. Always a rebel and an individualist though with the deepest faith in and interest of his country at heart, he was soon at variance with the socialist regime. The Civil War for him was a nationalist struggle and he denounced foreign interference.
▷A Barea, *Miguel de Unamuno* (1952)

UNDER, Marie
(1883–1977)
Estonian poet, considered by many as the greatest in her language, who has been compared to **Rilke** and even to **Goethe**. She was the leading poet in the expressionistic and Futurist 'Siuru' Group (named after a fabulous bird in Estonian mythology), which in 1917 ushered in the most colourful and exciting period in this Finno–Ugric literature. Her work developed from a delicately impressionistic love poetry to one of magnificent visionary power: one of the great woman poets of the century in international terms, her work only awaits adequate translation for it to be so recognized. Translations of her poetry are in W K Matthews (ed), *Anthology of Modern Estonian Poetry* (1953).
▷A Mägi, *Estonian Literature* (1968)

UNDERHILL, Evelyn
(1875–1941)
English poet and mystic, born in Wolverhampton. She was educated at King's College, London. In 1907 she married Herbert Stuart Moore, a barrister, and in 1921 became lecturer on the philosophy of religion at Manchester College, Oxford. A friend and disciple of Hügel, she found her way intellectually from agnosticism to Christianity, wrote numerous books on mysticism, including *The Life of the Spirit* (1922), volumes of verse, and four novels. Her *Mysticism* (1911) became a standard work.

UNDSET, Sigrid
(1882–1949)
Norwegian novelist and winner of the Nobel Prize for literature, born in Kalundborg, in Denmark. The daughter of a noted Norwegian archaeologist, she inherited an interest in medieval Norway. From 1899 she worked in an office, and the problems facing young contemporary women formed the basis of her early novels, including *Jenny* (1911). Her masterpiece, *Kristin Lavransdatter* (3 vols, 1920–2), which tells a graphic story of love and religion in 14th-century Norway, was followed by *Olav Audunssön* (4 vols, 1925–7), *Gymadenia* (1929) and *Den trofaste hustru* (1936, Eng trans *The Faithful Spouse*, 1937). She became a Roman Catholic in 1924, after which her work deepened in religious intensity. She was awarded the Nobel Prize for literature in 1928. During World War II she

was exiled in the USA, an outspoken opponent of Nazism.
▷M Brunsdale, *Sigrid Undset* (1988)

UNGARETTI, Giuseppe
(1888–1970)

Italian poet, born in Alexandria. He first visited Italy when he was 26; soon afterwards he joined the army and fought on the Austrian front. From 1912 to 1914 he lived in Paris where he met **Guillaume Apollinaire**. His first collection, *Il porto sepolto* ('The Buried Harbour'), was published in 1916 with a preface by Mussolini, and immediately gained him admission to the ranks of the great Italian poets of the 20th century. Largely defying translation, he is less well known than **Eugenio Montale** or **Salvatore Quasimodo**, but among his distinguished collections is *Vita d'un uomo* (7 vols, 1942–61, 'Life of a Man'), which includes *Il dolore* (1947, 'Grief'). He studied in Paris, and was Professor of Italian Literature at São Paulo, Brazil (1936–42) and at Rome (1942–58). He is the author of 'hermetic' poems characterized by their symbolism, compressed imagery and modern verse structure.
▷P Piccioni, *Vita di un poeta* (1970)

UNRUH, Fritz von
(1885–1970)

German playwright and novelist, born in Koblenz. He served in World War I as a cavalry officer. He was an ardent pacifist, and the ideal of a new humanity underlies all his Expressionist works, particularly the novel *Opfergang* (1916, Eng trans *The Way of Sacrifice*, 1928), and the two parts of an unfinished dramatic trilogy, *Ein Geschlecht* (1916, 'A Species') and *Platz* (1920, 'Place'). He left Germany in 1932 and went to the USA, where he wrote several works, including *Der nie Verlor* (1948, Eng trans *The End is not Yet*, 1948) and *Die jüngste Nacht* (1948, 'The Youngest Night'). He returned to Germany in 1952.
▷A Kronacher, *Fritz von Unruh* (1946)

UNSWORTH, Barry (Foster)
(1930–)

English novelist, born in Durham; he was the first of his family not to go down the mines. Educated at Stockton Grammar School and Manchester University, he has travelled widely and held a variety of teaching posts, including some time at the University of Istanbul. His first novel, *The Partnership* (1966), was followed by four more before *Pascali's Island* (1980), which was shortlisted for the Booker Prize, and later filmed. His books often reflect on historical themes, and

are set in locations which mirror his own wanderings, notably Turkey, Greece, and Italy, the setting for *Stone Virgin* (1985). His major work is the novel *Sacred Hunger* (1992), an epic account of the 18th-century Atlantic slave trade, which was jointly awarded the Booker Prize, alongside **Michael Ondaatje**.

UNTERMEYER, Louis
(1886–1977)

American anthologist, critic, poet and (most lastingly of all) parodist (*Collected Parodies*, 1926). He was best known, however, for his anthologies, particularly for *Modern American Poetry* (1919) which, although mocked by such as **Cummings** ('mr u will not be missed/who as an anthologist/sold the many on the few/not excluding'), ran into many editions, and educated mid-market readers into an acceptance of modernism. He also compiled a useful set of brief biographies, *Makers of the Modern World* (1955).

UPDIKE, John Hoyer
(1932–)

American novelist, poet and critic, born in Shillington, Pennsylvania. He studied at Harvard and the Ruskin School of Drawing and Fine Art in Oxford (1954–5), then returned to New York and served for two years on the staff of the *New Yorker* (1955–7), the beginning of a long and fruitful relationship with the magazine to which he has contributed short stories, poems and book reviews. His first book was a collection of verse, *The Carpentered Hen and Other Tame Creatures* (1958), but his status as one of the world's major writers is due largely to his fiction. Beginning with *The Poorhouse Fair* (1959), he has published many novels and many collections of short stories. Sophisticated, linguistically supple, fluent and inventive, his beat is middle-class America, his concerns those that have dominated the 20th century: sex, marriage, adultery, divorce, religion, materialism. Among his best-known books are, *The Centaur* (1963), the Rabbit tetralogy—*Rabbit, Run* (1960), *Rabbit Redux* (1971), *Rabbit is Rich* (1981) and *Rabbit at Rest* (1990)—spanning 40 years in the life of a car salesman, *Couples* (1968), *The Coup* (1978) and *The Witches of Eastwick* (1984). More recent novels are *Memoirs of the Ford Administration* (1993) and *Brazil* (1994). *A Month of Sundays* (1975), *Roger's Version* (1986) and *S.* (1988) collectively represent a reworking of **Hawthorne**'s *The Scarlet Letter*. *Self-Consciousness*, a memoir consisting of six chapters concerning his hometown, his suffering from psoriasis, his stuttering, his thoughts on the Vietnam War, his paternal ancestors, and his attitude towards his religion, was published in 1989.

▷R Detweiler, *John Updike* (1972, rev edn 1984)

UPFIELD, Arthur W(illiam)
(1888–1964)

English-born Australian writer of detective fiction, almost all of it featuring the specialized skills of the half-Aboriginal Inspector Napoleon Bonaparte. Upfield grew up in Hampshire and trained as a surveyor and land agent before emigrating to the Antipodes in 1911. He lived in England again briefly after military service in World War I, but returned to Australia, working at a variety of jobs before turning to writing. His first novel, *The House of Cain*, appeared in 1928, but it was with *The Barrakee Mystery* the following year (published in the USA as *The Lure of the Bush*, 1965) that he made his mark. The novel introduced 'Bony' as a man poised between races and intellectual standpoints: blue-eyed, polished, university-educated, but also profoundly in touch with the tiny clues afforded the investigative detective by the natural environment. Upfield wrote 29 Bonaparte mysteries; an unfinished 30th was completed and published posthumously. The best of them are *Death of a Swagman* (1945), *An Author Bites the Dust* (1948), which takes good-natured revenge on the literary mafia, and *Bony and the Black Virgin* (1959). The later plots tend to plod a little, but they do also document a significant sea-change in Australian attitudes to Aboriginal and mixed-race people, to women and to culture.
▷J Hawke, *Follow My Dust! A Biography of Arthur Upfield* (1957)

UPWARD, Edward Falaise
(1903–)

English novelist, born in Romford, Essex, who met his contemporary, the future novelist **Christopher Isherwood**, while at school. They became lifelong friends. During the 1930s, Upward joined the Communist Party, and several of his books reflect his political hopes and fears. *Journey to the Border* (1938) is an account of a private tutor who becomes a political radical. When Upward began to doubt his commitment, he retreated for 20 years into literary silence, pondering Party dogma and political theory. He emerged in 1962 to publish *In the Thirties*. *The Rotten Elements* followed in 1969, and *No Home but the Struggle* in 1977. Together, they comprise *The Spiral Ascent* trilogy, a semi-autobiographical work charting the life and political times of Alan Sebrill, schoolteacher and Marxist.

URIS, Leon M(arcus)
(1924–)

American popular author, born in Baltimore. He dropped out of high school and joined the

Marine Corps, taking part in battles in the Pacific. *Battle Cry* (1956) uses the experience to telling effect. *Exodus* (1958) remains the book by which he is best known. Depicting the early years of the state of Israel, it was made into a highly successful film though it was not commended by the critics. *QBVII* (1970) concerns a libel trial over a former Nazi war criminal. *The Haj* was published in 1984.

URMUZ, or HURMUZ, pseud of D Demetrescu-Buzău
(1883–1923)

Romanian experimental writer who anticipated such Dadaists as his compatriot **Tristan Tzara**. His work is of little interest except from a historical viewpoint—the 'absurd' being an allegedly Romanian phenomenon (eg **Ionesco**).

URQUHART, Fred
(1912–)

Scottish short-story writer and novelist, born in Edinburgh, the son of a chauffeur. He grew up in Fife, Perth and Wigtown, leaving school at 15 and then working as bookseller's assistant and labourer. He published his first novel, *Time Will Knit*, in 1938. He has published 11 collections of his short stories, many initially broadcast by the BBC, and has edited nine anthologies of short stories. His other novels to date are *The Ferret Was Abraham's Daughter* (1949), *Jezebel's Dust* (1951) and *Palace of Green Days* (1979, the first of a projected series). He has been publisher's reader, and literary editor of *Tribune*. His outstanding achievement is his quite exceptional ability to convey narrative plots through the eyes of female characters, initially in the Scotland of his childhood and adolescence and more recently using ghost stories, historical fiction and other forms.
▷C Affleck, 'Fred Urquhart', in *Dictionary of Literary Biography*, Vol 139 (1994)

URQUHART, Sir Thomas
(c.1611–1660)

Scottish author, born in Cromarty, the son of a land-owner. He studied at King's College, Aberdeen, and travelled in France, Spain and Italy. On his return he took up arms against the Covenanting party in the north but was defeated and forced to flee to England. Becoming attached to the court, he was knighted in 1641. The same year he published his *Epigrams: Divine and Moral*. On succeeding his father in 1642 he returned north. In Cromarty, though much troubled by his creditors, he produced his *Trissotetras; or a most exquisite Table for Resolving Triangles, etc* (1645), a study of trigonometry based on

Napier's invention of logarithms. In 1649 his library was seized and sold. He again took up arms in the royal cause, and was present at the battle at Worcester (1651), where he lost most of his MSS. In London, through Cromwell's influence, he was allowed considerable liberty, and in 1652 he published his *Pantochronochanon* (1652), an exact account of the Urquhart family, in which they are traced back to Adam. He also published *Ekskubalauron* (1652), better known as *The Discoverie of a most Exquisite Jewel*, an attack on the Scottish clergy which contains a ribald account of James Crichton (the 'Admirable Crichton'), but is chiefly a work praising the Scots nation. In 1653 he issued his *Introduction to the Universal Language* and the first two books of that English classic, his brilliant translation of *Rabelais*. The third was not issued till after his death. He is said to have died abroad, in a fit of mirth on hearing of the Restoration. His learning was vast, his scholarship defective.

▷J Willcock, *Sir Thomas Urquhart of Cromartie* (1895)

USAKLIGIL, Halit Ziya
(1866–1945)

Turkish novelist, 'the towering figure in Turkish fiction at the start of the twentieth century', often called the 'Turkish Alphonse Daudet'. His most famous novels were *Mai ve Siyah* (1897, 'The Blue and the Black'), still one of the most moving novels about a writer's struggle for existence and recognition, and *Ask-i Memnu* (1900, 'Forbidden Love'), a love story set in Istanbul high society. He was a bold and lucid stylist, who prepared the way for later realists.

USIGLI, Rodolfo
(1905–)

Mexican dramatist, poet and theatre director, born in Mexico City of an Italian father and a Polish mother. He was Mexico's most important dramatist, his position being analogous to that in the United Kingdom of **Shaw** (who greatly admired his *Corona de Sombra*, 1943, Eng trans *Crown of Shadows*, 1946). He was always highly critical of the Mexican government, and not all his plays have been published or performed. The most original of his many plays is the Pirandellian *El gesticulador* (1937, 'The Gesticulator'), a masterful satirical analysis of Mexico's proneness to lying and the creation of false myths: a mad retired professor impersonates a revolutionary, and dies at the hands of his assassin.

▷E Anderson-Imbert, *Spanish-American Literature: A History* (1963)

USK, Thomas
(d.1388)

English poet, born in London and attached to a clerical order of some kind, judging by the theological knowledge he displays. He became secretary to John de Northampton, the democratic and Wycliffite mayor of London who, after his term, was charged with a number of crimes in office. Usk betrayed his master to save himself, but was later executed after mishandling intrigues at Court. His poem 'The Testament of Love' is a poor and uninventive imitation of **Chaucer** on **Boethius**: while in prison the narrator is visited and inspired by a beautiful lady called 'Love'. **C S Lewis** found the poem 'more interesting than beautiful'.

USLAR PIETRI, Arturo
(1906–)

Venezuelan historical novelist and story writer, born in Caracas. Originally a professor of economics, he has held government posts, and has taught at Columbia University in the USA. He is generally regarded as the leading historical novelist of modern Latin America. His two most important novels are *Las lanzas coloradas* (1931, Eng trans *The Red Lances*, 1963) and *El camino de El Dorado* (1947, 'The Road to El Dorado'). The first is a history of colonial Venezuela, dealing with Bolívar and with creoles and Spaniards. The second is the fictional biography of the tyrant Lope de Aguirre, worthy to be compared with the novel on the same subject by **Ramón Sender**. A much later success was *La visita en el tiempo* (1990), about the enigmatic figure of Don Juan de Austria. Uslar Pietri has been called a 'leading exponent of magic realism', but his writing, although lyrical, is more straightforward, and possibly less subtle, than that of **García Márquez** or **Roa Bastos**.

▷A Flores, *The Literature of Spanish America* (1966–9)

USPENSKI, Gleb Ivanovich
(c.1840–1902)

Russian author, born in Tula. He wrote novels of peasant life, such as *Vlact' zemli* (1882, 'Power of the Soil'), notable for their realism in contrast to the prevalent romantic conception of the agricultural worker. He died insane.

▷N Prutskov, *Gleb Ivanovich Uspenski* (1972)

USTINOV, Sir Peter Alexander
(1921–)

British actor and dramatist, born in London. The son of White Russian parents, Ustinov first appeared on the stage in 1938, and had established himself as an accomplished artist both in revues and legitimate drama by 1942, when four years' army service interrupted his career. His subsequent work for films as actor, writer and producer, and in broadcasting as a satirical comedian, has enhanced his reputation. He is a prolific playwright, and his works— most successful amongst which are *The Love of Four Colonels* (1951) and *Romanoff and Juliet* (1956)—are marked by a serious approach to human problems, often presented with an acute sense of comedy and a mastery of unconventional stagecraft. Among his other plays are *Photo Finish* (1962), *The Unknown Soldier and his Wife* (1967) and *Overheard* (1981). His other works include an autobiography, *Dear Me* (1977), the two novellas collected as *The Disinformer* (1989), and *The Old Man and Mr. Smith* (1990).

UTTLEY, Alison
(1884–1976)

English author of children's stories, born on a farm in Derbyshire. She was widowed in 1930 and turned to writing to support herself and her young son. *The Country Child* (1931) was followed by a flood of books, mainly for children, which revealed her great love for and knowledge of the countryside and country lore. Many of her books were in the **Beatrix Potter** tradition, featuring much-loved characters such as Grey Rabbit and Sam Pig.

▷ E Saintsbury, *The World of Alison Uttley* (1980)

UZ, Johann Peter
(1720–96)

German minor poet, born in Ansbach. A lawyer by profession, he helped to translate **Anacreon**, and wrote frivolous if skilful verse in the Anacreontic style; but his best poems, somewhat resembing those of **Klopstock**, were deeper in intention, seeking to fuse Christianity with a superficial hedonism.

V

VAA, Aslaug
(1889–1965)

Norwegian poet and dramatist, born in Telemark, and educated in literature and art history at universities in Paris and Berlin. Best known for her dialect-coloured poetry, distinguished by a strong feeling for nature and traditional life, she seeks fundamental values, often in contrast to the negative aspects of modern life. She made her debut with the poetry collection *Nord i leitet* (1934, 'In the Northern Horizon'), but her best-known work is the collection *Skjenkersveinens visur* (1954, 'The Innkeeper's Songs').
▷L Maehle, 'Det lydde eit bod—Om Aslaug Vaa og diktinga hennar', in *Frå bygda til verda* (1967)

VAFOPOULOS, George
(1903–)

Greek poet, born in the northern city of Thessaloniki and representative of a 'northern' school of writers. He started to publish poems in 1921, but achieved fame a decade later with his first collection, *Rhodhina tou Mytilene* ('Roses of Mytilene'), which displayed an unfashionable Neo-Classical approach, and the influence of **Costas Karyotakis**. After World War II Vafopoulos's poetry changed in tone, becoming more stark and cold, in collections such as *To Dhapedho* (1951, 'The Floor'). Unlike most Greek poets he often writes in the formal *Katharevousa*, and his poems have an ecclesiastical dignity to them.

VAICIULAITIS, Antanas
(1906–)

Lithuanian novelist and story writer, the leading prose writer of his generation. He went into exile to the USA. His reputation rests on his novel *Valentina* (1936), a subtle study of a girl who cannot decide whether to choose the man she loves or the one to whom she is indebted. But his folk-like tales written since then have their own unique delicacy and depth. He wrote (in English) *An Outline History of Lithuanian Literature* (1942).
▷R Silbajoris, *Perfection in Exile: Fourteen Contemporary Lithuanian Writers* (1970)

VAILLAND, Roger
(1907–65)

French novelist, born in Paris. His picaresque bohemian life was reflected in many of his works, among them *La Loi* (1957, Eng trans *The Law*, 1958), which was awarded the Prix **Goncourt**. The debut novel which made his name, however—*Drole de jeu* (1945, Eng trans *Playing With Fire*, 1948)—had as its subject a more serious matter, the French resistance, in which he had fought. A member of the Communist Party from 1952 to 1956, he also wrote plays and essays, such as his study of Choderlos de Laclos (1953).

VAIZGANTAS, pseud of Juozas Tumas
(1869–1933)

Lithuanian novelist and critic, born in Svedasai parish. A priest, educated in Latvia, he returned from abroad to devote himself to the cause of an independent Lithuania. His voluminous and worthy works, which fill 10 volumes, are not of literary importance, but they inspired many more gifted writers.

VAJDA, János
(1827–99)

Hungarian poet, editor and critic—by profession an actor and journalist—born in Pest (not then joined to Buda). Little heed was taken of Vajda in his own time, although he attracted attention as a critic; but he has now been elevated to major status, second only to **Ady**, whom in certain respects he anticipated. He was a close friend to **Petőfi**, to whom he was by no means inferior. It is in his anguished poems to his elusive 'Gina' that he anticipates Ady. Some of his poetry is indifferently translated in *The Magyar Muse* (1933, ed W Kirkconnell) and in *Hungarian Poems and Fables* (1877). His mind was altogether subtler than that of **Jokai** or his more thoroughgoingly romantic contemporaries, and he had to wait for Ady and others to understand and appreciate his 'self-tormenting pessimism'.
▷A Komlós, *Vajda János* (1954, in Hungarian)

VALA, Katri, pseud of Alice Wadenström
(1901–44)

Finnish poet, the leading woman poet of the semi-modernist Tulenkantajat ('Torchbearers') Group, and yet another Finnish victim of the scourge of tuberculosis. She was among the first to write in free verse. She died in exile in Sweden.

VALAORITÍS, Aristotelís
(1824–79)

Greek poet of the so-called 'Heptanesian' school, born in Leucas, but educated in Italy and France. In 1848 he returned to the Ionian islands and became involved in local politics. His second collection, *Elegies*, published in 1857, gained him attention; his lyricism seemed to have more in common with the French Romantics than with his Greek contemporaries, but his subject-matter was the Greek War of Independence, and poems like 'Samuel' and 'He Fyghi' ('The Flight') became songs of resistance. In the last 10 years of his life he gave up politics, retired to the island of Madouri, and dedicated himself to writing, but he never again achieved the popular acclaim of his earlier career.

VALAORITIS, Nanos
(1921–)

Greek poet, born in Lausanne, the great-grandson of the famous 19th-century poet **Aristotelís Valaoritis**. He has lived in London, Paris and Athens. He was friendly with **Bernard Spencer** and also with **Lawrence Durrell**, whom he helped to prepare a volume of translations from **Seferis** into English. His playful Surrealist poetry has a cosmopolitan following.

VALDELOMAR, Abraham
(1888–1918)

Peruvian fiction-writer, editor, critic and poet, born in Ica. He was one of the first *mestizos* to write fiction in Peru. He began as a crude imitator of **D'Annunzio**, but then turned away from romantic decadence to realism with his fictionalized biography of Doña Francisca Zubuiaga (wife of the celebrated General Agustin Gamarra), *La Mariscala* (1915). His best work is in the short story collections: *El Cabellero Caremelo* (1918) and *Los hijos del sol* (1921, 'Sons of the Sun'). The latter contained memorable stories of the Inca period.
▷ C A Cabellero, *Vida y obra de Abraham Valdelomar* (1964); E A Aldrich, *The Modern Short Story in Peru* (1966)

VALDÉS, Armando Palacio
(1853–1938)

Spanish novelist, born in Entralgo in Asturias. Some of his psychological and naturalistic novels were *Marta y María* (1886, Eng trans *The Marquis of Peñalta*, 1886), *Maximina* (1887, Eng trans 1888), *La Hermana San Sulpicio* (1889, Eng trans *Sister Saint Sulpice*, 1890), *La Espuma* (1890, Eng trans *Froth*, 1891) and *El Maestrante* (1893, Eng trans *The Grandee*, 1894).

VALDIVIELSO, José de
(1560–1638)

Spanish poet, dramatist and priest, born in Toledo. He was a close friend to **Lope de Vega**. His baroque essays in 'folk poetry' were studied by **Lorca**. He excelled in the ubiquitous Spanish form known as the *auto sacremental*: a one-act allegorical play, played at Corpus Christi, dealing with the Eucharist, which developed into all kinds of allegories, and finally degenerated into vulgar farce.
▷ B W Wardropper, *Introducción al teatro religioso del Siglo de Oro* (1967)

VALENTE, José Angel
(1929–)

Spanish poet and translator, born in Orense. He has lived abroad for much of his life, and lectured at Oxford in the 1950s on Spanish literature. He has been called a 'minimalist' poet because he aims at 'the maximum of expression with the minimum of verbal construction'. There are two literal translations of his dignified, intimate poems in J M Cohen's *Penguin Book of Spanish Verse* (1960).

VALENZUELA, Luisa
(1938–)

Argentinian writer and journalist, born in Buenos Aires. She has written seven novels and three collections of stories, and is considered among the most important women writers of Latin America. She moved to the USA in 1979, as a result of the political situation in Argentina, but since the reestablishment of democracy, has returned to Argentina. Most of her work is highly experimental, including such techniques as linguistic distortion, shifting points of view and use of metaphor to communicate an ironic view of gender relations. Titles include the short-story collection *Cabio de armas* (1975, 'Other Weapons'), the narrative collection *El gato eficaz* (1972, 'Cat-o-Nine-Deaths') and *Cola de lagartija* (1983, 'The Lizard's Tail'). She has won several awards, including Fulbright and Guggenheim fellowships.

VALERA, Don Juan
(1824–1905)

Spanish novelist and critic, born in Cabra in Córdoba. He held diplomatic posts in Europe and the USA, and was a deputy, Minister of Commerce, Minister of Public Instruction and councillor of state senator. His literary studies, *Estudios criticos* (1864), and essays, *Cuentos y Diálogos* (1882) made his reputation but his fame depends on his romances, *Pepita Jiménez* (1874, Eng trans 1891), *Las ilusiones del Doctor Faustino* (1876, 'The Illusions of Dr Faustus'), *El comendador*

Mendoza (1877, Eng trans *Commander Mendoza*, 1893), *Doña Luz* (1878, Eng trans 1892) and *La buena fama* (1895, 'The Good Reputation'). He was also a noted translator of **Goethe**'s *Faust* and other classics.

▷A Z Romera, *Don Valera y Alcala Galiano* (1966)

VALÉRY, Paul Ambroise
(1871–1945)

French poet and writer, born in Cette. He settled in Paris in 1892, and after publishing some remarkable verse in the style of **Stéphane Mallarmé**, he relapsed into a 20 years' silence, taken up with mathematics and philosophical speculations. He emerged in 1917 with a new poetic outlook and technique in *La Jeune Parque* (1917, 'The Young Fate'), a poem full of difficult symbolism. This was followed by a significant collection, *Charmes* (1922), containing 'Le Cimetière marin' (Eng trans *The Graveyard by the Sea*, 1946), 'L'Ébauche d'un serpent' ('The Outline of a Snake'), 'Au platane' ('In the Plane Tree'), and others, noted for the poetic shorthand, the compression and conciseness of his imagery and ideas. His prose works include *Soirèe avec M Teste* (1895, Eng trans *An Evening with Mr Teste*, 1925), and several aesthetic studies, such as the dialogue *Eupalinos ou l'architecte* (1924, Eng trans *Eupalinos; or, the Architect*, 1932), in which architecture and music are compared, and *L'Âme et la danse* (1924, Eng trans *Dance and the Soul*, 1951). A late, short play, *Le Solitaire* ('The Solitary Man'), foreshadows **Samuel Beckett**.

▷F Scarfe, *The Art of Paul Valéry* (1954)

VALLE Y CAVIEDES, Juan del
(c.1652–c.1697)

Peruvian poet and dramatist, born in Porcuna, Andalusia, but taken to Peru when still a small child. A disciple of **Quevedo**, he wrote mystical poetry, lyrics and, above all, satires. His work did not see public light, at least in bulk, until 1873, and only then by courtesy of the great **Ricardo Palma**. His best poetry attacks the medical profession with both wit and point.

▷D R Reedy, *The Poetic Art of Juan del Valle Caviedes* (1964)

VALLE-INCLÁN, Ramón María del
(1869–1936)

Spanish novelist, dramatist and poet, born in Puebla de Caramiñal. Among his works are four *Sonatas* on the seasons (1902–7), written in fine prose in the form of novels, a graphic but erroneous history *La guerra carlista* (1908, 'The Carlist War'), and the masterly *Águila de blasón* (1907, 'The Eagle of Honour') and *Romance de Lobos* (1908, Eng trans

Wolves! Wolves!, 1957), set in a vivid medieval background. Many of his novels and plays are collected in *Esperpentos*, and among several comedies is his *Cara de Plata* (1923, 'Silver Face').

▷A Zacharias, *Ramón del Valle-Inclán, an appraisal* (1968)

VALLÈS, Jules
(1832–85)

French writer, born in Le Puy-en-Velay of poor peasants. His fiction, his revolutionary attitude and his bitter manner make him into one of the more important precursors of **Céline**. He was imprisoned and later exiled for his part in the Paris Commune (1871). His works fill eight volumes; outstanding is his trilogy *Jacques Vingtras* (1879–86). He has been said to have hated the rich too extravagantly; this common but not universal judgement perhaps misses his sense of irony and burning hatred of injustice. His books and journalism, in particular his volume about his years of exile in London, *La Rue à Londres* (1883), are racy, vivid, observant and readable.

VALLEJO, César Abraham
(1892–1938)

Peruvian poet, novelist and playwright, born in Santiago de Chuco into a poor family of mixed Spanish and Peruvian Indian descent. He took a law degree and studied medicine in Lima, and held various jobs, including teaching posts. He was imprisoned in 1920–1 for political reasons, and moved to Europe in 1923, living mainly in France and Spain until his death. His first book of poems, *Los heraldos negros* (1919, 'The Dark Messengers'), announced an immensely powerful talent, but only one more volume appeared in his lifetime, *Trilce* (1922, Eng trans *Trilce*, 1973). The great *Poemas humanos* (1939) and *España, aparta de mé este cáliz* (1940, *Spain, Take Thou this Cup from Me*) were both posthumous, and are included in English translation in *The Complete Posthumous Poems* (1978). He also wrote some indifferent novels and several volumes of non-fiction, but his reputation rests on his poetry. English selections are *Neruda and Vallejo: Selected Poems* (1971) and *Selected Poems* (1976). A *Poesia completa* appeared in Spanish in 1978.

VALVERDE, José Maria
(1926–)

Spanish poet and critic, born in Valcia de Alcántara. A dry and intellectual but religious poet, Valverde began as a member of a group calling itself 'Juventud Creadora': he, and his friends, were searching for a means to circumvent the ferocious and philistine censorship imposed by the Franco dictatorship. He gradually became more open and emotional, largely as a result of his study of the great Peruvian **Vallejo**. He spent some time away from Spain, but then returned to Barcelona to teach.

VANBRUGH, Sir John
(1664–1726)

English playwright and baroque architect, born in London, the son of a tradesman and grandson of a Protestant refugee merchant from Ghent. He was educated in France, commissioned into Lord Huntingdon's regiment and suffered imprisonment in the Bastille as a suspected spy (1690–2). A staunch Whig, he became a leading spirit in society life and scored a success with his first comedy, *The Relapse* (1696), followed, again with success, by *The Provok'd Wife* (1697). *The Confederacy* (1705) was put on in the Haymarket, where **William Congreve** and Vanbrugh joined together as theatre managers. His *The Provok'd Husband* was left unfinished, and was completed by Colley Cibber (1728). A natural playwright of the uninhibited Restoration comedy of manners period, he also achieved success as architect of Castle Howard (1702) and in 1705 was commissioned to design Blenheim Palace at Woodstock. The immense baroque structure aroused the ridicule of **Jonathan Swift** and **Pope**, and the Duchess of Marlborough disliked the plans and was so appalled at its enormous cost that she long refused to pay Vanbrugh. He was made comptroller of royal works in 1714, and was Clarencieux king-of-arms (1705–25).
▷L Whistler, *Sir John Vanbrugh* (1938)

VANCE, Jack (John Holbrook)
(1916–)

American science-fiction and fantasy writer, born in San Francisco. His early stories were published in pulp magazines, but he signalled the emergence of a more mature talent with the science fantasy collection *The Dying Earth* (1950), set in a far future world dominated by magic, to which he returned in several later books. The creation of vividly evoked imaginary planets which began with *Big Planet* (1952) became the second principle stream of his fiction, and has produced some of his most significant work, including *The Dragon Masters* (1963) and *Showboat World* (1978). He wrote a number of sequence novels in both fantasy and science-fiction forms, including *Planet of Adventure* (from 1968) and *Cadwal Chronicles* (from 1987). He has also written mystery novels.

VANCURA, Vladislav
(1891–1942)

Czech novelist, murdered by a Nazi firing-squad as one of the reprisals for the death of Heydrich. He was originally a doctor, but devoted himself early to literature. A supporter of the communists, he was an experimental novelist who brought both vernacular and archaic elements into his language. *Pekar Jan Marhoul* (1924, 'The Baker Jan Marhoul') is a portrait of an ideal communist, in which Vancura used expressionistic techniques; only the adventure novel *Konec stárych casu* (1934) was translated into English, as *The End of Old Times* (1965). He has been mentioned as an influence on **Milan Kundera**.

VANDERHAEGE, Guy Clarence
(1951–)

Canadian short-story writer and novelist, born in Esterhazy, Saskatchewan, currently a professor of English at the University of Ottawa. He won a Governor General's Prize for fiction with his first collection of stories, *Man Descending* (1982). This was followed by another collection, *The Trouble with Heroes* (1983), *My Present Age* (1984), a novel about loneliness, and the acclaimed *Homesick* (1989). A writer of dry humour and effortless prose, Vanderhaege has contributed to several British periodicals and won the Geoffrey Faber Memorial Prize in 1987. A third collection of stories, *Things As They Are?*, appeared in 1992.

VANDERLOO, Jos
(1925–)

Belgian (Flemish) novelist, born in Zonhoven. His work draws on **Kafka** and other, Flemish, predecessors. *Het Gevaar* (1960, 'The Danger') is characteristic in its depiction of injustice and menace—ostensibly a fantasy, it is in fact closely realistic: three men who have received fatal medical treatment are refused the chance to enter into the 'normal' world.

VAN DER POST, Sir Laurens (Jan)
(1906–)

South African soldier, explorer, writer and philosopher. He served with distinction in World War II in Ethiopia, the Western Desert, Syria and the far east, where he was captured by the Japanese. On his release he joined Mountbatten's staff in Java. He has since worked for the British government on a variety of missions in Africa, and with the Kalahari Bushmen of southern Africa. A sensitive writer of lyrical insight, his books include *The Lost World of the Kalahari* (1958), *The Heart of the Hunter* (1961), *The*

Seed and the Sower (1963, filmed as *Merry Christmas, Mr Lawrence*, 1983), *The Hunter and the Whale* (1967), *A Story Like the Wind* (1972), *A Far Off Place* (1974), *A Mantis Carol* (1975), *Jung and the Story of Our Time* (1976) and *Yet Being Someone Other* (1982).
▷F Carpenter, *Laurens van der Post* (1969)

VAN DOREN, Carl Clinton
(1885–1950)

American critic and biographer, brother of **Mark Albert Van Doren**, born in Hope, Illinois. He studied at the state university and at Columbia, where he lectured in English literature (1911–30). He was literary editor of the *Nation* (1919–22), of the *Century Magazine* (1922–5) and of the *Cambridge History of American Literature* (1917–21). He was also a distinguished biographer of **Thomas Love Peacock** (1911), **James Branch Cabell** (1925), **Jonathan Swift** (1930), **Sinclair Lewis** (1933) and **Benjamin Franklin** (1938, Pulitzer Prize, 1939). He was on the management committee of the *Dictionary of American Biography* (1926–36). He edited Franklin's *Letters and Papers* (1947); his critical studies include *The American Novel* (1921) and, with his brother, *American and British Literature since 1890* (1925). He also wrote *The Ninth Wave* (1926), a novel, and his autobiography, *Three Worlds* (1936).

VAN DOREN, Mark Albert
(1894–1972)

American poet and critic, brother of **Carl Clinton van Doren**, born in Hope, Illinois. He studied at the state university and at Columbia, where he taught from 1920 and became Professor of English in 1942. He served in the army during World War I, followed his brother to the editorship of the *Nation* (1924–8) and was awarded the Pulitzer Prize (1940) for his *Collected Poems* (1939), chosen from such volumes of verse as *Spring Thunder* (1924) and *Now the Sky* (1928). Later volumes include *The Mayfield Deer* (1941), *The Country Year* (1946), *New Poems* (1948) and *Spring Birth* (1953). He collaborated with Carl in *American and British Literature since 1890* (1925), edited the *Oxford Book of American Prose*, wrote critical studies of **Henry Thoreau** (1916), **Dryden** (1920), **Shakespeare** (1939) and **Nathaniel Hawthorne** (1949), and the novels *Transients* (1935) and *Windless Cabins* (1940). Further collections of poetry were published in 1963, 1964 and 1967.

VAN DRUTEN, John William
(1901–57)

American playwright of Dutch extraction, born in London. He is remembered mainly for *I am a Camera*, his stage adaptation of **Christopher Isherwood**'s Berlin stories, produced in New York in 1951 and London in 1954. He had, however, come to prominence almost 30 years previously with *Young Woodley* (1925), a wry, sentimental piece about growing up. He became the successful author of a string of domestic light comedies, including *After All* (1929), *There's Always Juliet* (1931) and *The Distaff Side* (1933), in which Sybil Thorndike gave an acclaimed performance as the imperious mother. *Bell, Book and Candle* (1950), another comedy, but this time about witchcraft, provided an amiable vehicle for Rex Harrison.

VAN DUYN, Mona Jane
(1921–)

American poet, born in Waterloo, Iowa. She was educated at the University of North Iowa and the University of Iowa, and taught English at a number of universities, including the University of Louisville, Kentucky, and Washington University, St Louis. Her first collection, *Valentines in the Wide World* (1959), was followed by a small but admirable body of skilfully crafted and insightful poems in *A Time of Bees* (1964), *To See, To Take* (1970), *Bedtime Stories* (1972), *Merciful Disguises* (1973) and *Letters from a Father* (1982). A gap of eight years passed before her next volume, *Near Changes* (1990); it won her the Pulitzer Prize for Poetry in 1991.

VAN DYKE, Henry
(1852–1933)

American clergyman and writer, born in Germantown, Pennsylvania. He studied theology at Princeton and Berlin and was a prominent pastor of the Brick Presbyterian Church, New York (1883–99). He was Professor of English literature at Princeton (1899–1923) and, under Woodrow Wilson, American minister to the Netherlands (1913–16). He was awarded the Legion of Honour for his services as naval chaplain in World War I. His many writings include poems, essays and short stories, mostly on religious themes, such as the Christmas tale *The Story of the other Wise Man* (1896), *The Ruling Passion* (1901), *The Blue Flower* (1902), *The Unknown Quantity* (1912) and *Collected Poems* (1911).

VAN LERBERGHE, Charles
(1861–1907)

Belgian poet, born in Ghent into a wealthy family, who early allied himself to the French Symbolists. His poetry evoked, according to one critic, 'the mysterious Eve who gradually takes possession of a world of dreamlike fluidity'.

VAN OSTAIJEN, Paul
(1896–1928)

Belgian (Flemish) poet, critic and editor (of the magazine *Avontuur*), born in Antwerp. He died young from tuberculosis. He was Flanders' pioneer of Modernism, particularly of Expressionism, Dada and literary Cubism; and he had intimate contacts with the leading proponents of the first two of these movements while he was in Germany just after World War I. The most powerful influence upon his poetry, **August von Stramm**, had, however, been killed in the war. Neither his somewhat strident, but thoughtful and verbally exciting poetry, nor his criticism, received much attention until the 1950s, when Dutch and Belgian Flemish poets took him up as an important precursor. He was also an art critic of note.
▷E Schoonhaven, *Paul van Ostaijen* (1951, in French)

VAN SCHENDEL, Arthur
(1874–1946)

Major Dutch novelist, born in Batavia in present-day Indonesia, but who lived in Italy for many years. His masterpieces, among a number of well-crafted and deeply interesting novels, are *Het fregatschip Johanna Maria* (1930, Eng trans *The Johanna Maria*, 1935), about a man who, having sailed with his ship all his life, is cheated by death of his wish to own her, and *De waterman* (1933, Eng trans *The Waterman*, 1963), a similar but more extended chronicle. Van Schendel's novels give a marvellously compact and authentic portrait of Dutchmen of various types, but in addition are distinguished by a fruitful and poetic inquisitiveness about the nature of fate.

VAN VECHTEN, Carl
(1880–1964)

American novelist, photographer and critic. He was born in Cedar Rapids, Iowa, which he portrays in his third novel, *The Tattooed Countess* (1924), and took his degree at the University of Chicago. His early career was spent as a composer and music and drama reviewer in New York. He published three collections of critical essays, the prescient *Music after the Great War* (1915), *Music and Bad Manners* (1916) and, best of all, *Interpreters and Interpretations* (1917); each showed off his bright, witty intelligence. Arguably his most widely-known book today is *Tiger in the House* (1920), an unsentimental study of domestic cats; one perfectly innocent picture of a kitten cleaning its hindquarters was thought to be 'indecent', sparking off a brief but ludicrous furore. Van Vechten's first novel was *Peter Whiffle, His Life and Works* (1922), the imaginary memoirs of a dilettante. By far his best and most perceptive book is *Nigger Heaven* (1926), a hectic but often thoughtful story about life in Harlem; though Van Vechten was white, he made a significant impact on the literature of the 'Harlem Renaissance'. His desire to make visible the previously invisible comes through in the portrait photography which made him a star in the 1930s; a selection was published as *Portraits* in 1978.
▷E Lueders, *Carl Van Vechten* (1965)

VAN VOGT, A(lfred) E(lton)
(1912–)

American science-fiction writer, born in Manitoba, Canada. He moved to the USA in 1944, by which time he was an established writer. Fascinated by systematic methods of mental and physical development, however eccentric, he converted to Dianetics in 1950, and wrote little in the ensuing decade, but still has a prolific output to his name. He is best known as a writer of elaborate and highly speculative 'space operas', working on huge and complex canvases which fall neatly into genre expectations, but also attempt to push beyond them in metaphysical reach. His best-known works are *Slan* (1946, rev edn 1951), *The Weapon Shops of Ishar* (1951) and its sequel *The Weapon Makers* (1946), and the *Null-A* sequence of novels (from 1948).
▷ *Reflections of A E Van Vogt* (1975)

VAPTSAROV, Nikolai
(1909–42)

Bulgarian poet, sometimes described as Bulgaria's **Mayakovsky**, who was executed by the Nazis, and who therefore left a legend behind him. He was a committed communist, but his poems to his wife written during his last hours are, not surprisingly, more personal and moving than his other works.

VARGAS LLOSA, Mario
(1936–)

Peruvian novelist, born in Arequipa. After studying law and literature in Peru, he spent many years abroad as a student in Paris and Madrid, building up a reputation as a writer, eventually returning to Lima shortly before the restoration of democratic government in Peru in 1980. *La ciudad y los perros* (Eng trans *The Time of the Hero*, 1966 (US); 1967 (UK)), his first novel, published in 1962, is a powerful social satire and so outraged the authorities that a thousand copies were publicly burned. In 1965 came *La casa verde* (Eng trans *The Green House*, 1968 (US); 1969 (UK)), a novel that brings to life the teeming society of Peru in the days of the rubber boom. Subsequent novels are *Conversación en la catedral* (1969,

Eng trans *Conversation in the Cathedral*, 1975 (US)) and *Pantaléon y las visitadoras* (1973, Eng trans *Captain Pantoja and the Special Service*, 1978 (US and UK)). *La tia Julia y el escribidor* (1977, Eng trans *Aunt Julia and the Scriptwriter*, 1982 (US); 1983 (UK)), his masterpiece, is an energetic, inventive comedy which was made into a television series in Colombia. He has also written *La guerra del fin del mundo* (1981, Eng trans *The War of the End of the World*, 1984) and *La Historia de Alejandro Mayta* (1984, Eng trans *The Real Life of Alejandro Mayta*, 1986). *La orgía perpetua* (1975, 'The Perpetual Orgy') is an expression of his obsession with **Flaubert**'s *Madame Bovary*. A proponent of 'magic realism', he began on the extreme left, but has gravitated towards the right; he was defeated in his bid for the presidency of Peru—fortunately, many believe, for his considerable future as a writer.
▷C Rossman and A W Friedman (eds), *Mario Vargas Llosa* (1978)

VARNALIS, Kostis
(1883–1974)

Greek poet, a Cretan contemporary of **Sikelianos** and **Kazantzakis**. His early work, heavily influenced by the French Symbolists, was not well received. He studied literature at Athens and from 1908 worked as a teacher there. In 1919 he won a state scholarship to Paris, where he embraced dialectical materialism and Marxist ideology. The first book he wrote on his return, *To Fos Pou Kai* (1922, 'The Light That Burns'), as well as its successor, *Sklabi Poliorkimeni* (1927, 'The Enslaved Beseiged'), reflected these interests. In later years he turned to prose, publishing *He Aleethini Apologia tou Sokrati* (1931, Eng trans *The True Apology of Socrates*, 1955) and *To Heemerologia tis Penelopis* (1946, Eng trans *The Journal of Penelope*), which were influential on a generation of Marxist Greek poets.

VARNHAGEN VON ENSE, Karl August
(1785–1858)

German writer and diplomat, born in Düsseldorf. In 1809 he joined the Austrian army and was wounded at the battle of Wagram. In 1813 he went over to the Russian service, and was sent to Paris as an adjutant. Here he was called to the Prussian diplomatic service, and accompanied Hardenberg to the Congress of Vienna (1814) and to Paris, becoming next resident minister at Karlsruhe (till 1819). In 1814 he married Rahel Levin, who presided over a glittering literary salon in Berlin. He wrote lives of **Goethe** (1823), Marshal Keith (1844), General von Bülow (1853),

and others; *Biographische Denkmäler* (1824–30, 'Biographical Monuments') and *Denkwürdigkeiten* (1843–59, 'Things Worth Remembering'). His Correspondence and Diaries fill 22 volumes (1860–70), and are now considered his most valuable legacy.
▷C Misch, *Varnhagen in Beruf und Politik* (1925)

VARRO, Marcus Terentius
(116–27 BC)

Roman scholar and author, born in Reate. He studied at Athens, saw service under Pompey, and in the Civil War was legate in Spain. He awaited the result of Pharsalus with **Cicero** and Cato at Dyrrachium, and was kindly treated by the conqueror, who appointed him librarian. Under the second triumvirate Mark Antony plundered his villa, burned his books, and placed his name on the list of the proscribed. But he was soon exempted, and Augustus restored his property. His prose writings embraced oratory, history, jurisprudence, grammar, philosophy, geography and husbandry. The chief were *Saturae Menippeae* ('Menippean Satires'), *Antiquitates Rerum Humanarum et Divinarum* ('Antiquities in Matters Human and Divine'), *De Lingua Latina* ('On the Latin Language') and *De Re Rusticae* ('Country Affairs'). His *Disciplinarum Libri IX* was an encyclopaedia of the liberal arts; his *Imagines*, or *Hebdomades*, a series of 700 Greek and Roman biographies.
▷J Collart, *Varron grammairien latin* (1954)

VARRO, Publius Terentius
(c.82–37 BC)

Roman poet, called Atacinus from his birth in the valley of the Atax in Narbonensian Gaul. He wrote satires and an epic poem on Caesar's Gallic wars, called *Bellum Sequanicum*. His *Argonautica* was an adaptation of **Apollonius Rhodius** and his erotic elegies pleased **Propertius**.

VARTHEMA, Ludovico de
(c.1465–c.1510)

Italian traveller and writer, born in Bologna. He was the first European and Christian recorded to have entered, and left alive, the Islamic City of Mecca. He made a six-year journey through Arabia, Persia, India and on across the Pacific to the Spice Islands (1502–7). He published an account of his travels in *Itinerario de Lodovico de Varthema Bolognese* (1510).

VAS, Istvan
(1910–92)

Hungarian poet and essayist, whose graceful minor poems were written in the rational tradition established by **Mihály Babits** in his *Nyugat* magazine.

VASCONCELOS, Carolina Michaëlis De
(1851–1925)

Portuguese scholar and writer, born in Berlin. She studied and wrote on romance philology and literature. An honorary professor of Hamburg University, she lived, after her marriage in 1876, in Oporto, where she did much scholarly research on the Portuguese language, its literature, and especially its folk literature. Most noteworthy is her edition of the late 13th- or early 14th-century *Cancioneiro da Ajuda* ('Book of Songs of Help'). Other writings include *Notas Vicentinas* (1912, 'Vincentian Notes'), an edition of the poetry of **Francisco Sá de Miranda**, and essays, studies and correspondence with other Portuguese scholars.

VASCONCELOS, Jorge Ferreira de
(c.1515–c.1585)

Portuguese author of closet comedies (really novels in dialogue—they were not for theatrical production) and romance-writer. His Arthurian romance is less important than his three 'plays', *Eufrosina* (1555), *Ulissipo* (1618) and *Aulegrafia* (1619). The first of these, partly deriving, but very different, from the *Celestina* of the Spanish **Fernando de Rojas**, is his masterpiece. It is chiefly important for the incomparable picture it gives of Portugal, but also for its discussion of love, considered from a Platonic point of view, and its vivid characterization.
▷A F G Bell, *Portuguese Literature* (1922)

VASILEV, Pavlo
(1910–37)

Russian poet, born in Kazakhstan. A belated member of the peasant movement, he had vast energies and abilities, but seldom fulfilled them. His best poems are in various anthologies, including one in the *Penguin Book of Russian Verse* (1965, ed Dimitry Obolensky). He perished in the Purges through, as **Ehrenburg** put it, 'drinking and chattering too much'.

VASSILIKOS, Vasilis
(1933–)

Greek novelist, short-story writer and filmmaker. He was born in the northern Greek town of Kavala, and began his career as a reporter on the weekly magazine *Tachydromos* and also worked as the director of documentary films. He came to prominence with the publication of a trilogy of protest novels in the early 1960s: *To Fyllo*, *To Pighadhi* and *To Angeliasma* (Eng trans *The Leaf*, *The Well*, *The Message*, 1964). In 1966 he published *Z* (Eng trans, 1968), later made into a hugely popular film. The novel told the story of the murder of the socialist folk hero Lambrakis and was promptly banned by the right-wing government. His other novels include *Photographs* (1973), written, like most of his works, in a difficult style, using stream of consciousness narrative in the manner of **Joyce**.

VAUGHAN, Henry
(1622–95)

Welsh religious poet, born in Newton-by-Usk, Llansantfraed, Powys, twin brother of the alchemist Thomas Vaughan (1622–66). He was called the self-styled 'Silurist' as a native of south Wales, the land of the ancient tribe of Silures. He entered Jesus College, Oxford in 1638, and in 1646 published *Poems, with the tenth Satyre of Juvenal Englished*. He took his MD, and practised as a physician first in Brecon and then in Newton-by-Usk. The collection of poems entitled *Olor Iscanus* was published by his twin brother, without authority, in 1651. In 1650 he printed his *Silex Scintillans* ('Sparkling Flint'), a notable volume of mystical and religious poems, enlarged in 1655. In 1652 he published *The Mount of Olives*, devotions in prose, and the *Flores Solitudinis* ('Flowers of Solitude'), also in prose. *Thalia Rediviva: the Pastimes and Diversions of a Country Muse*, a collection of elegies, translations and religious pieces, was also published without authority (1678) by a friend.
▷R A Dunn, *The Mystical Poetry of Henry Vaughan* (1962)

VAUGHAN, William
(1577–1641)

Welsh poet and colonizer, born in south Wales. He graduated at Jesus College, Oxford (1597), and bought an interest in Newfoundland, where he sent out settlers in 1617. He wrote an allegory, *The Golden Fleece* (1626), and other works.

VAUTHIER, Jean
(1910–)

French avant-garde playwright and essayist, born in Liège. At first a journalist and illustrator, he took to the theatre late. But Gérard Philippe and Jean-Louis Barrault subsequently appeared in his plays, which have been successful. Barrault's production of his near-monodrama *Le Personnage combattant* (1956, 'The Character Against Himself') made him famous. This memorably depicts an old popular writer vainly trying to return to his youthful integrity—finally he is killed by a homosexual hotel servant. Mainly influenced by **Antonin Artaud**, but also by **Michel de Ghelderode**, Vauthier is a dramatist of great power and unconventionality, whose deeply religious *Les Prodiges* (1958), about a man who finds solace after being left by his evil lover, is probably his best play.

▷L Pronko, *Avant-Garde* (1962)

VAUX, Lord Thomas
(1516–56)

English poet, born at Harvonden and educated at Cambridge University. In 1523 he succeeded to his father's barony, and as a very young man he attended Cardinal Wolsey on diplomatic missions. Belonging to the court culture of Henry VIII and Edward VI, he emulated Sir **Thomas Wyatt** and **Surrey** in his verse. Some of his short, melancholy love lyrics were included in *Tottel's Miscellany* (1557) and then in Puttenham's *Art of English Poesie* (1589). His best work (from the mere 15 poems known to be his) is probably seen in the medieval love allegory *The Assault of Cupid* and *The Aged Lover Renounceth Love*, on bodily deterioration.

VAZOV, Ivan
(1850–1921)

Bulgarian national poet, born in Sopot. He wrote a collection of poems and songs under the title *Pod igoto* (1894, Eng trans *Under the Yoke*, 1896), and other novels. He was twice exiled from his native land for his nationalist sympathies, but became Minister of Education in 1897.

▷N S Derjavin, *Ivan Vazov* (1950)

VEGA, Lope de, in full Lope Félix de Vega Carpio
(1562–1635)

Spanish dramatist and poet, born in Madrid. Orphaned at an early age, he was a student and graduate of Alcalá. He served in the Portuguese campaign of 1580, and in the Spanish Armada (1588). He became secretary to the Duke of Alva, Marquis of Malpica, and Marquis of Sarria. A favourite with the ladies, he had many love affairs, was twice married, and fathered at least six children, three of them illegitimate, was banished from Madrid because of a quarrel, and lived two years in Valencia. He took orders in 1614, and became an officer of the Inquisition. He died poor, for his large income from his dramas and other sources was all but wholly devoted to charity and church. The mere list of Lope's works presents a picture of unparalleled intellectual activity. His first work of any length was a poem, the *Angelica*, written at sea in 1588, but not printed till 1602. The *Arcadia*, the story, in a pompous, pastoral setting, of the prenuptial vagaries of the Duke of Alva, was written before the duke's marriage, July 1590, but it was kept back till 1598. The *Dragoneta*, celebrating the death of Drake, appeared the same year, and was Lope's first publication under his name. But it was as a ballad-writer that he made his mark. The more notable of his miscellaneous works are the *Rimas* (1604); *Peregrino en su Patria* (1604, Eng trans *The Pilgrim of Casteele*, 1621), a romance; *Jerusalém Conquistada* (1609), an epic; *Pastores de Belén* (1612), a religious pastoral; *Filomena* (1621) and *Circe* (1624), miscellanies in the style of **Cervantes**; *Corona Trágica* (1627, 'Tragic Crown'), an epic on Mary, Queen of Scots; *Laurel de Apolo* (1630); *Rimas de Tomé de Burguillos* (1634), a collection of lighter verse, with the *Gatomaquia* (pub 1807), a mock-heroic. *Dorotea* (1632), in the form a prose drama, is obviously the story of his own early love adventures. Lope was a master of easy, flowing, musical, graceful verse. Though he had written plays, he did not become a writer for the stage until after 1588. He gave the public what it wanted—excitement pure and simple. Lope's plays may be roughly divided into the historical or quasi-historical and those that deal with everyday life. Of the latter the most characteristic are the 'cloak and sword plays'. The *Noche de San Juan* ('The Night of St John'), one of his very last plays; the *Maestro de Danzar*, one of his first; and the *Azero de Madrid*, the source clearly of **Molière**'s *Médecin malgré lui*, are excellent examples. Other plays include *Perro del hortelano* (Eng trans *The Gardener's Dog*, 1936), *Desprecio agradecido* ('Welcomed Contempt'), *Esclava de su Galán* ('Slave of her Gallant'), *Premio del bien hablar* ('The Talking Prize'); and *Alcalde de Zalamea*, a bold vigorous outline which **Calderón de la Barca** improved upon. The number of Lope's plays seems to have been 1500, exclusive of 400 *autos*. Of these the very names of all but between 600 and 700 have been lost, and often nothing but the name survives. There are about 440 plays and 40 *autos* in print or MS.

▷F C Hayes, *Lope de Vega Carpio* (1967)

VEGA, Ventura de la
(1807–65)

Argentinian–Spanish dramatist, poet, librettist and director of Madrid's national theatre. He left Argentina at the age of 11. His poetry is of little account, but he was a skilful playwright whose verse comedy *El hombre de mundo* (1845, 'The Man of the World') anticipated **Benavente**.

VEGETIUS (Flavius Vegetius Renatus)
(4th century)

Roman military writer under the emperor Theodosius I the Great. After AD 375 he produced the *Epitome Institutionum Rei Militaris* on classic legionary operations, mainly extracted from other authors, which during the Middle Ages was a supreme authority on warfare.
▷T R Phillips, *A Collection of Military Classics* (1941)

VELDEKE, Hendrik van (Heinrich von)
(c.1140–c.1205)

Dutch or German poet and knight from the Rhineland. His first work was a biography of St Servatius, which is written in a form of Low German very close to Dutch, and which seems to have been his native language. He is best known, however, for his *Eneit*, a reworking of a French Romance based on parts of **Virgil**'s *Aeneid*. It is in High German, though there are traces of the Dutch influence in it. An epilogue to the poem tells how it was stolen from him, half-finished, in Strasbourg, and returned to him nine years later in Thuringia. It contains fantastical imagery and shows considerable powers of poetic invention.

VELEZ DE GUEVARA, Luis
(1579–1644)

Spanish novelist and playwright. He graduated from the University of Osuna, joined the army and went to Italy. Later he settled in Madrid in the service of Conde Saldana, practising law but also writing. By 1608 he was an established author. His best-known works are *El Diablo Cojuelo* (1641, 'The Devil on Two Sticks'), a 'costumbrista' novel of contemporary manners, and his historical drama *Reinar Después de Morir* (1652, 'To Reign after Death'), about the life of Inés de Castro. He also collaborated with **Calderón de la Barca** and **Rojas Zorilla**. His style is satirical and baroque with a tendency to the unexpected and spectacular (supernatural and miraculous scenes in strange landscapes and dreamlike atmospheres). Despite his fame, Velez de Guevara was constantly plagued by money troubles which he unsuccessfully tried to relieve by four marriages.

VENANTIUS FORTUNATUS
(c.530–600)

Christian Latin poet, born near Treviso in northern Italy and educated at Ravenna. While there he became blind, but later regained his sight, and in 565 he left Italy for Gaul in order to give thanks for his recovery to St Martin of Tours at his shrine. He stayed in Gaul for the rest of his life, eventually becoming Bishop of Poitiers, and was later canonized. Venantius was a voluminous poet, producing 11 books of occasional verse on his life and travels, reminiscences of his friends and memorable meals, hymns (the best-known is 'Vexilla regis prodeunt') and an epic poem on the life of St Martin.
▷H Waddell, *Mediaeval Latin Lyrics* (1929)

VENEZIS, Elias, pen-name of Elias Mellos
(1904–73)

Greek novelist, born in the Turkish town of Ayvalik, opposite Mytilene. In 1922 he was conscripted by the Turks into the compulsory work corps in the interior. The experience furnished his first novel, *Number 31328* (1931), a realistic account of his captivity which was an immediate success. His other novels include *Ghalini* (1939, 'Calm'), an account of the plight of Aeolian people forced to return to Greece, and *Aeolixi Ghi* (1943, Eng trans *Aeolia* 1949), an evocative recreation of his childhood. In later works he moved away from personal experiences, and his reputation went into serious decline, with one critic identifying 'a literary feebleness and an exhaustion of the lyric impulse'.

VERDAGUER, Mosen Jacinto
(1845–1902)

Catalan poet, born in Folgarolas. He became a priest with a vast popular following. He wrote *L'Atlántida* (1877) and *Lo Canigó* (1886), two epic poems of great beauty, and on the first of these Manuel de Falla based his choral work *Atlántida*. His *Idilis y Cants Místichs* (1870, 'Mystical Idylls and Songs'), also set to music, have become part of the music of the Catalan Church.

VERDE, José Joaquim Cesário
(1855–86)

Portuguese poet, who was born and died, prematurely, in Lisbon. His poetry did not become widely known until a friend posthumously edited it, in a volume published a year after his death: *O Livra de Casário Verde* (1887). He had the gift of clarity in an age of overblown rhetoric, and in certain respects anticipated the later fascination with the city which was the hallmark of the early work of **Verhaeren**. He is one of those, like his compatriot **Sá-Carneiro**, who might have developed into a major poet.
▷J Serrão, *Cesário Verde* (1961, in Portuguese)

VERE, Edward de, 17th Earl of Oxford
(1550–1604)

English court poet, a cousin of Sir Francis Vere and Sir Horace Vere. He was an Italianate Englishman, violent and a spendthrift, but one of the best of the Elizabethan courtier-poets. Of his lyrics, published in various collections, 'What cunning can expresse' is perhaps the best.

VERGA, Giovanni
(1840–1922)

Italian novelist, born in Catania in Sicily. He wrote numerous violent short stories describing the hopeless, miserable life of Sicilian peasantry, including *La vita dei campi* (1880, Eng trans *Under the Shadow of Etna*, 1896) and *Cavalleria rusticana* (1884, Eng trans *Cavallera Rusticana and Other Tales of Sicilian Life*, 1893), which was made into an opera by Mascagni. The same **Zola**esque theme prevails in his novels, *I Malavoglia* (1881, Eng trans *The House by the Medlar Tree*, 1890), *Mastro Don Gesualdo* (1888, Eng trans *Master Don Gesualdo*, 1893), and others. **D H Lawrence** translated some of his works, including his *Novelle rusticane* (1882, Eng trans *Little Novels of Sicily*, 1925).
▷L Russo, *Giovanni Verga* (1947)

VERHAEREN, Emile
(1855–1916)

Belgian poet, born in St Armand near Termonde. He studied law, but turned to literature, writing in French. His poetry hovers between powerful sensuality, as in *Les Flamandes* (1883, 'The Flemish Women'), and the harrowing despair of *Les Débâcles* (1888), the affirmation of the life force and the revulsion against modern industrial conditions. His best work is possibly *La Multiple Splendeur* (1906). He died in a train accident.
▷M Sadleir, *Things Past* (1944)

VERISSIMO, Erico
(1905–)

Brazilian novelist, critic and travel writer, born in Porto Alegre. Of all modern Brazilian novelists, he has been most cosmopolitan and influenced by such fashionable American writers as **Hemingway**. There is some argument, owing to his extreme conservatism, as to whether he is essentially a popular or a serious novelist. His best-known novel is *Caminhos Cruzados* (1935, Eng trans *Crossroads*, 1943), a work owing much to *The Bridge of San Luis Rey*, by **Thornton Wilder**. His best novel, though, is undoubtedly the uncharacteristic *Noite* (1940, Eng trans *Night*, 1956), about an unknown and alienated stranger.

VERLAINE, Paul
(1844–96)

French poet, born in Metz. He was educated at the Lycée Condorcet and entered the civil service. Already an aspiring poet, he mixed with the leading Parnassian poets and writers in the cafés and salons. Under their battle cry 'Art for art's sake', against the formless sentimentalizing of the Romantic school, he gained recognition by contributing articles and poems to their avant garde literary magazines, especially the short-lived *Le Parnasse contemporain*. The youthful morbidity of his first volume of poems, *Poèmes saturniens* (1866, 'Saturnine Poems'), was criticized by **Charles Sainte-Beuve** as trying vainly to outdo **Baudelaire**. The evocation of a past age, the 18th century, provided the theme of his second work, *Fêtes galantes* (1869, Eng trans *Gallant Parties*, 1912), by many considered his finest poetical achievement. His love for the 16-year-old Mathilde Mauté during an engagement prolonged by the doubts of the girl's father was expressed in *La Bonne Chanson* (1870, 'The Pretty Song'). During the Franco–Prussian war Verlaine did guard duty in Paris and then served as press-officer for the Communards. The birth of a son did nothing to heal the incompatibilities of his married life, from which he escaped (1872) on travels in Flanders, Belgium and England in a homosexual affair with the fledgling poet **Arthur Rimbaud**, 10 years his junior. Their friendship ended in Brussels in 1873, when Verlaine, drunk and desolate at Rimbaud's intention to leave him, shot him in the wrist. Verlaine's overpowering remorse made it psychologically impossible for Rimbaud to leave, so he staged an incident in the street and had Verlaine arrested. He did not foresee that the police, searching for a motive, would suspect immorality. Verlaine was convicted and sentenced to two years' hard labour, and his past associations with the Communards disqualified him from any intercession by the French ambassador. *Romances sans paroles* (1874, Eng trans *Romances Without Words*, 1921) were written in Mons prison, where he studied **Shakespeare** in the original, and after his wife had left him, he turned Catholic (1874). He unsuccessfully attempted to enter a monastery on release, taught French at Stickney, Lincolnshire, and St Aloysius' College, Bournemouth (1875), where he completed his second masterpiece *Sagesse* (1880, 'Wisdom'), full of the spirit of penitence and self-confession that appeared again in *Parallèlement* (1889, 'In Parallel'). In 1877 he returned to France to teach English at the Collège of Notre Dame at Rethel. There he adopted a favourite pupil, Lucien Létinois, for whom he acquired a farm at Coulommes and whose death from typhus (1883) occasioned *Amour* (1888, 'Love'). *Poètes maudits* (1884, 'Accursed Poets'), comprising critical studies, was followed by short stories such as *Le Poteau* (1886, 'The Stake'), sacred and profane verse *Liturgies intimes* (1892, 'Intimate Liturgies') and *Élégies* (1893). Verlaine is the consummate master of a poetry

which sacrificed all for sound, in which the commonplace expressions take on a magic freshness. He lived during his last years in Parisian garret poverty, relieved by frequent spells in hospitals and finally by a grand lecture tour in Belgium, Holland and England (1893), the last sponsored in part by William Rothenstein, who drew several portraits of him.
▷C Morire, *Paul Verlaine, poète maudit* (1947)

VERMEYLEN, August
(1872–1945)

Belgian (Flemish) novelist, art historian, critic and statesman, born in Brussels. A Roman Catholic until he lost his faith, he was educated in Germany and Austria. He was a member of the Flemish literary society called 'De Distel' ('The Thistle'). He was one of the leading figures in the revival of Flemish literature which took place in Belgium at the end of the 19th century, and which was marked by the publication of the periodical *Van Nu en Straks*, which he co-founded. His most famous and best work is *De Wanderlende Jood* (1906, 'The Wandering Jew'), more of an allegory than a novel; its purpose is the promotion of an atheist humanism. He was a socialist politician in his last 20 years, and refused—notably—to join the Nazis when they promised a revival of Flemish literature at the expense of French.
▷R Roemens, *Het werk van Prof. Dr. August Vermeylen* (1953)

VERNE, Jules
(1828–1905)

French novelist, born in Nantes. He studied law, and from 1848 wrote opera libretti until in 1863, with the publication of *Cinq Semaines en ballon* (Eng trans *Five Weeks in a Balloon*, 1870), he struck a new vein in fiction—exaggerating and often anticipating the possibilities of science and describing adventures carried out by means of scientific inventions in exotic places, like submarines and space travel. He greatly influenced the early science fiction of **H G Wells**. His best-known books, all of which have been translated, are *Voyage au centre de la terre* (1864, Eng trans *A Journey to the Centre of the Earth*, 1872), *De la Terre á la Lune* (1865, Eng trans *From the Earth to the Moon*, 1873), *Vingt mille lieues sous les mers* (1869, Eng trans *Twenty Thousand Leagues Under the Sea*, 1873) and *Le Tour du monde en quatre-vingts jours* (1873, Eng trans *Around the World in Eighty Days*, 1874). Film versions of the last two achieved an astonishing popularity.
▷M L Allotte de la Frye, *Jules Verne* (1955)

VERRÍSIMO, Érico
(1905–75)

Brazilian popular novelist and travel writer, born in Cruz Alta, in the gaucho state of Rio Grande do Sul. Verrísimo's fiction, somewhat self-consciously influenced by English models such as **Aldous Huxley** and **Ernest Hemingway**, is uneven and often superficial, and his modernism has been found by most critics to be ersatz. But it is readable and seriously intended, and he has been much translated. The success of *Olhai os Lírios do Campo* (1938, Eng trans *Consider the Lilies of the Field*, 1947), an urban novel about a man torn between selfishness and love, was deserved. But his outstanding novel was the pessimistic and driven *Noite* (1940, Eng trans *Night*, 1964), in which the unnamed protagonist is an amnesiac. Verrísimo held lecturing posts in the United States, and wrote books for children.

VERWEY, Albert
(1865–1937)

Dutch poet, critic, dramatist, translator (of **Dante**) and scholar, from Amsterdam. A major figure in his literature, Verwey was one of the founders, with his friend and mentor **Kloos**, of the magazine of the 'Men of the Eighties', *De Nieuwe Gids* ('The New Guide'). This individualistic movement rescued Dutch literature from 'the dead weight of the past' by throwing off old clichés and rhetoric; its chief inspirers were the English poets **Shelley** and **Keats**. His *Persephone en andeare gedichten* (1885, 'Persephone and Other Poems') embodied these ideals. But then, like many Dutch poets, he came under the influence of Spinoza, and rejected sensuality (much advanced by the 'Eightiers') in favour of a pantheism based on Spinoza's philosophy; later still he became associated with the circle of **Stefan George** in Germany. Eventually he became a primarily philosophical poet, and as such lost some of his appeal. He is now remembered mainly as a critic who wrote some distinguished but not crucial poetry.
▷R P Meijer, *Literature of the Low Countries* (1971)

VERY, Jones
(1813–80)

American mystic and poet, born in Salem in Massachusetts and educated at the Harvard Divinity School. He lived quietly in Salem with his sisters, writing sonnets and prose pieces of intense religious inspiration. These were published in *Essays and Poems* (1839). So intense was his personality that he was briefly committed to a lunatic asylum; his friend **Emerson** defended him.
▷E Gittleman, *Jones Very, the effective years, 1833–40* (1967)

VESAAS, Tarjei
(1897–1970)

Norwegian novelist and lyric poet, from Telemark. A writer of symbolic and allegorical works, he was the most important novelist using *Landsmål* ('country language', renamed *Nynorsk*, 'New Norwegian') after World War II. His first novel was *Die svarte hestane* (1928, 'The Black Horses'). His best-known books are *Fuglane* (1957, Eng trans *The Birds*, 1968) and *Is-slottet* (1963, 'The Ice Castle'). He published his autobiography, *Båten om kvelden* ('Boat in the Evening') in 1968 but his mature style emerged in *Kimen* (1940, Eng trans *The Seed*, 1964).
▷R Skrede, *Tarjei Vesaas* (1964)

VESTDIJK, Simon
(1898–1971)

Major Dutch novelist, poet and critic from Harlingen, who wrote, his compatriots declared, 'faster than God can read'. During World War II he was imprisoned for a year by the Nazi occupiers. He is best remembered for his eight-novel roman-fleuve about Anton Wachter, but he wrote many other novels, chief amongst which was his own favourite, *De koperin tuin* (1950, Eng trans *The Garden Where the Brass Band Played*, 1965), in which a tragic love is played out against a musical background. His historical novels, and those based on Greek mythology, were amongst his most popular. He received most of the prizes available to Dutch authors, and was once put forward as the Netherlands' candidate for the Nobel Prize for literature, which he might worthily have won. He wrote much music and literary criticism, including a book about **Albert Verwey**.

VESTLY, Anne-Cath(arina)
(1920–)

Norwegian author of children's books. From her first stories about *Ole Aleksander Filibom-bom-bom* (from 1953 onwards), she has displayed a unique ability to find a language children will understand. Similarly full of warmth, solidarity and humour is her series about *Mormor og de åtte ungene* ('Grandma and the eight children', from 1957) and *Knerten* (from 1962). In her last two series, about the girls *Aurora* (from 1966) and *Guro* (from 1975), we meet families where the sex roles are reversed, expressing Vestly's wish for children both to learn something from reading her books and to question their environment.

VIAN, Boris
(1920–59)

French playwright, novelist and poet, born in Ville d'Avray. A Bohemian with a bad heart, he dabbled in many things—acting, jazz, engineering, anarchism, pornography—and excelled in fiction. A tragi-comic writer, he won a cult following for such novels as *L'Écume des jours* (1947, Eng trans *Froth on the Daydream*, 1967) and *L'Arrache-coeur* (1953, Eng trans *Heartsnatcher*, 1968).
▷D Noakes, *Boris Vian* (1964)

VIANA, Javier de
(1871–1925)

Uruguayan story writer, dramatist and novelist, born in Montevideo. Beginning under the influence of **Zola** and naturalism, Viana was amongst the first to write realistically of the too often sentimentalized gaucho, the cowboy. Critics did and do upbraid Viana for his brutality, but the extent of this—for example in his collection *Campo* (1896, 'The Open Spaces')—has been exaggerated. The melodrama of the novel *La gaucha* (1899) is relieved by some fine writing. Viana's later works, written as he became an alcoholic, remain popular, but are not as well observed as the earlier, especially the stories in his finest volume, *Gurí* (1901), in which he developed his technique to its peak.
▷J F Garganigo, *Javier de Viana* (1972)

VIAU, Théophile de
(1590–1626)

French poet, born in Clairac. He wrote the tragedy *Pyramé et Thisbé* (1621) and love poetry distinguished by its naturalness. He was condemned to the stake (1623) for the impiety and obscenity of the poems he contributed to *Le Parnasse satyrique*, but his sentence was commuted to exile for life.
▷F Lachevre, *Le procès de Théophile de Viau* (1909)

VIAUD, Louis Marie Julien *see* LOTI, Pierre

VICENTE, Gil
(c.1470–c.1537)

Portuguese dramatist, born in Lisbon, considered the father of Portuguese drama. He wrote 44 plays, 16 in Portuguese, 11 in Spanish and 17 using both languages. His early plays were religious, but gradually social criticism was added. His farces *Inês Pereira, Juiz da Beira* and the three *Autos das barcas* (*Inferno, Purgatório* and *Glória*, collective Eng trans *The Ship of Hell*, 1929) are his best. He displays great psychological insight, superb lyricism and a predominantly comical spirit.
▷L Keats, *The Court Theatre of Gil Vicente* (1962)

VIDA, Marco Girolamo, the 'Christian Virgil'
(c.1480–1566)

Italian Latin poet, born in Cremona. He was made Bishop of Alba in 1532. He wrote Latin orations and dialogues, a religious epic, *Christias* (1535), *De Arte Poetica* (1537, 'On the Art of Poetry'), and poems on silk-culture and chess (1527).
▷M P de Cesare, *Vida's Christiad and the Vergilian Epic* (1964)

VIDAL, Gore (Eugene Luther, Jr)
(1925–)

American novelist, essayist and polemicist, born at the United States Military Academy in West Point, New York, where his father was an aeronautics instructor. Much of his childhood was spent in Washington under the influence of his scholarly, witty and blind grandfather, Senator Thomas Gore. He was educated at Phillips Exeter Academy, where he began to write an (unfinished) novel about Mussolini. But he was a mediocre student and in 1943, instead of going to Harvard, joined the United States Army Reserve Corps, which gave him the material for his first novel, *Williwaw* (1946), published to some acclaim when he was just 19. However his second novel, *In a Yellow Wood* (1947), was slated and his third, *The City and the Pillar* (1948), a clinical and unsentimental account of a young man coming to terms with his homosexuality, precipitated a decline in his career. His next five novels, among them *Dark Green, Bright Red* (1950), *A Search for the King* (1950) and *The Judgment of Paris* (1952), also had a lukewarm reception. After a period as a TV commentator he returned to the novel in 1964 with *Julian*, his first major book, which purports to be the emperor Julian's autobiographical memoir and journal, followed by a trilogy of books dealing with affairs of state—*Washington, DC* (1967), *Burr* (1973) and *1876* (1976). His taste for camp extravagance reached its apotheosis in the 'apocalyptic' *Myra Breckenridge* (1968) and *Myron* (1974), 'Myra's comeback'. Since then his historical fiction has been dominant. Even his tour de force, *Creation* (1981), was overshadowed by *Lincoln* (1984), an engrossing, meticulously researched, insightful portrait of America's 16th President. In *Empire* (1987), set at the beginning of the American Empire, his fascination with power (he ran for congress in 1960) was again to the fore, and also in 1987 he published *Armageddon: Essays 1983–1987*, 'random pieces' that reflect his ambivalent obsession with what he has called, with characteristic hauteur, 'the land of the dull and the home of the literal'.

VIDRIĆ, Vladimir
(1875–1909)

Croatian poet, born in Zagreb. He combined decadence with an elegant lyricism, and his few poems are prized for their technical perfection and their evocative versions of Greek myths.

VIEBIG, Clara, pseud of Clara Viebig Cohn
(1860–1952)

German novelist, born in Trier. Now neglected, Viebig began as a follower of **Zola**. The background of her fiction is the menacing landscape of her native Eifel. *Das schlafende Heer* (1904, Eng trans *The Sleeping Army*, 1929) depicts Polish peasants under the Germans. Her most famous novel, telling the story of the life of a servant girl, was *Das tägliche Brot* (1900, Eng trans *Our Daily Bread*, 1908).
▷C Scheuffler, *Clara Viebig* (1926)

VIELÉ-GRIFFIN, Francis
(1864–1937)

American-born French Symbolist poet, the son of the American general Egbert Louis Vielé (1825–1902), born in Norfolk, Virginia. He made his home in Touraine, France, and became a leading exponent of *vers libre*. His poems collected under the titles *Cueille d'avril* (1886, 'April Harvest'), *Poèmes et Poésies* (1895, 'Poems and Verses'), *Sapho* (1911), and *La Sagesse d'Ulysse* (1925, 'The Wisdom of Ulysses'), are of high lyrical quality, tending towards musical impressionism, and embody a serene outlook on life. His brother, Herman Knickerbocker Vielé (1856–1908), was a painter and novelist.
▷J de Cours, *Francis Vielé-Griffin* (1970)

VIERECK, Peter
(1916–)

American poet and 'liberal conservative', son of George Sylvester Viereck, an originally German novelist and essayist well known in his day; he was born in New York. His first collection, *Terror and Decorum* (1948), won a Pulitzer Prize, and gained him wide attention, both hostile and otherwise. Wild and exuberant, these poems attempted to deal with his war experiences with a gleeful lyricism described by **William Carlos Williams** as 'sensitive, distinguished in feeling'. Later poetry, though copious, has foundered on Viereck's tendency to oversell himself and his modest technical gifts, and on his rhymes, which have been called 'ludicrous' (for example: 'Barrack/Weimaric/Pyrrhic/Wreck/Viereck'). His *New and Selected Poems 1932–1967* appeared in 1967. *Conservatism Revisited* (1949) is one of many similar studies.
▷M Henault, *Peter Viereck* (1969)

VIGNY, Alfred Victor, Comte de
(1797–1863)

French romantic writer, born in Loches, Indre-et-Loire. He served in the Royal Guards (1814–28), retiring with a captaincy. His experiences provided the material for *Servitude et grandeur militaires* (1835, Eng trans *Military Servitude and Grandeur*, 1919), a candid commentary on the boredom and irresponsibility, yet desire for devotion and self-sacrifice, induced by peace-time soldiering. He married an Englishwoman, Lydia Bunbury (1828). He had already published anonymously a volume of verse (1822) followed by *Eloa* (1824), the fallen angel condemned for self-pity, and *Poèmes antiques et modernes* (1826, 'Ancient and Modern Poems'; expanded edn 1829), which includes his grand poetic conception of Moses as the hopelessly overburdened servant of God. His life, marred by domestic unhappiness and his failure to enter parliament (1848–9), was that of a congenital misfit who bears his loneliness with dignity. This is reflected in his work, especially in that masterpiece of romantic drama, *Chatterton* (1835, Eng trans 1847), written for his love, the actress Marie Dorval, as well as in *Stello* (1832), which describes the tragic fates of the young poets, **Thomas Chatterton**, Gilbert and **Chénier**, and is concluded in the posthumously published sequel *Daphné* (1912). These exemplify Vigny's pessimism, and his exaltation of the poet as a godlike outsider whose knowledge is yet necessary for society. Other notable works include the historical novel *Cinq-Mars* (1826, Eng trans 1847), the plays *Le More de Venise* (1829, based on **Shakespeare**'s *Othello*) and *La Maréchale d'Ancre* (1831, 'The Wife of the Marshal of Ancre'), the philosophical poems glorifying social order and discipline, *Les Destinées* (post 1864), and the biographical notes, *Journal* (1867).
▷A Whitridge, *Alfred Vigny* (1933)

VIITA, Lauri Arvi
(1916–65)

Finnish novelist and poet, born in Pirkkala. His death in a car accident at the age of only 48 was a major loss to Finnish literature. His early vitalist poems in his initial collection *Concreter* (1947) made a strong impression. His novel *Moraine* (1950) was a study of urban life set during the bitter Finnish Civil War.

VIK, Bjørg
(1935–)

Norwegian short-story writer, playwright and novelist. She grew up in Oslo and began her career as a journalist, publishing her first volume of short stories in 1963. Elegant and complex, her short stories focus the situation of the middle-class housewife trapped by family duties and the demands of materialism. The texts in *Kvinneakvariet* (1972, Eng trans *An Aquarium of Women*, 1987), depicting women of different ages at times of crisis, reflect her involvement with 'second-wave' feminism, as does her successful play *To akter for fem kvinner* (1974, 'Two Acts for Five Women'). A leading figure in Norwegian literary life, she has also published a semi-autobiographical novel, *Små nøkler store rom* (1988, 'Small Keys Large Rooms').
▷J Garton, 'Bjørg Vik', in *Norwegian Women's Writing 1850–1990* (1993)

VILDE, Edouard
(1865–1933)

Estonian realist novelist and dramatist, one of the first considerable figures in the modern literature of his country. He ended as a fierce and anti-modernist conservative—yet, after a youthful period which he spent in journalism and purveying light popular fiction, he had contributed to the modernist movement. His (incomplete) collected works ran to 33 volumes, but nothing was translated into English. *Mäeküla piimamees* (1916, 'The Dairyman of Mäelüka') is often mentioned as his best novel.
▷A Mägi, *Estonian Literature* (1968)

VILDRAC, Charles, pseud of Charles Messager
(1882–1971)

French poet, critic, children's writer and dramatist. He was one of the founders of *L'Abbaye*, or unanimist, group (**Duhamel**, Vildrac's brother-in-law, **Romains** and others). His collection *Livre d'Amour* (1910, Eng trans *A Book of Love*) charmingly, and in a minor key, expresses the ideals of the group. He is best known, however, for his plays, and in particular for the successful seaport drama *Le Paquebot Tenacity* (1919, Eng trans *The Steamship Tenacity*, 1921), which was produced by Jacques Coupeau's Vieux Colombier.

VILHJÁLMSSON, Thor
(1925–)

Icelandic novelist and critic, born in Edinburgh, Scotland, but brought up in Reykjavík. He is the foremost Icelandic author writing in the existentialist tradition (he was in Paris just after World War II). Early stories are collected in *Andlit i spegli dropans* (1957, Eng trans *Faces Reflected in a Drop*, 1966). His novels are concerned with such themes as European culture, nuclear warfare, and with the unnatural speed of life in the modern world.

VILJANEN, Lauri Sakari
(1900–)

Finnish poet, translator (of European poetry), critic and academic, born in Kaarina. He was a leading associate of the semi-modernist Tulenkantajat ('Torchbearers') Group of the 1920s. He sought in many ways to be a counterpart in literature to Sibelius in music, and even dedicated a book to the composer's memory. Viljanen eventually came to be regarded by many younger Finns as 'dictatorial' and dated in his literary approach.
▷ E Tompuri, *Voice from Finland* (1947)

VILLAESPESA, Francisco
(1877–1936)

Spanish poet, novelist and dramatist, once widely read but now almost forgotten. He followed in the footsteps of **Rubén Darío**, but his poetry was too facile and vulgar to last. However, for a short time **Juan Ramón Jiménez** and **Antonio Machado** admired him as an authentic Spanish *modernista* poet in Darío's style.

VILLAURRUTIA, Xavier
(1903–50)

Mexican poet and dramatist, born in Mexico City. His uncle, the *modernista* poet Jésus Valenzuela, a founder of the magazine the *Revista Moderna* (1898–1911), had a decisive influence. **Paz** said of him: 'I discovered that his good manners hid an irritable temperament, and that the epigrams he fired off served to defend an insecure and anguished being, a victim of paralysis of will and depression'— of what the Spanish had called *abulia*. His early poetry was *modernista* in style, showing the influence of his reading of **Jammes** and other French poets, and above all of Mexico's greatest poet after **Sor Juana Inés de la Cruz**, **Ramón López Velarde**, of whose work he became a leading critic. With **Jaime Torres Bodet** and **Novo** he founded the influential magazine *La Falange* (1922–3), and with the latter the even more important *Ulisis* (c.1924), which preceded *Contemporáneos*, Villaurrutia becoming a leading member of those involved in the magazine. But when *Contemporáneos* collapsed under the onslaught of a more conventional and 'nationalist' poetic, Villaurrutia suffered, and stated to his audience: 'I suffer because I cannot please you'. He moved, with **Alfonso Reyes**, Mexico's keeper of conscience, into the realm of avant-garde theatrical activity: he translated plays by **Pirandello** and others, and contributed his own *En qué piensas?* (1938). Later he wrote *La Hiedra* (1941, 'Ivy'), an ironically commercial play, which was a success, and earned him many enemies amongst his former colleagues. But his poetry is the most important part of his work, and it is likely that he will be considered, with Reyes, as the most substantial of Mexico's 20th-century poets. It has been stated that he killed himself; in fact he died of a heart attack.
▷ E L Moretta, *The Poetic Achievement of Xavier Villaurutia* (1971)

VILLAVERDE, Cirilio
(1812–94)

Cuban novelist, born in Pinar del Rio, who was harrassed by the Spanish authorities for his identification with the cause of Cuban independence. He was forced to spend many years in the USA. He published the first part of his major novel, *Cecilia Valdés* (1839–1882, Eng trans 1962), at the age of 27, but could not complete it until he was 67. Its eponymous heroine is a beautiful mulatto, and the book has great importance in the history of the depiction of the racial problem in Cuba— it has a plain anti-slavery thesis. It is also, despite its sensationalist plot, of literary value, containing incomparably vivid descriptions of Cuban 19th-century life, and is worthy of Villaverde's avowed models, Sir **Walter Scott**, **Balzac** and **Manzoni**. He wrote other fiction, and two of his novellas deal with incestuous relationships (which also feature in *Cecilia Valdés*). He died in New York.
▷ G Coulthard, *Race and Colour in Caribbean Literature* (1962)

VILLIERS, George, 2nd Duke of Buckingham
(1628–87)

English playwright and politician, brought up in the household of Charles I. Villiers had an early introduction to the vicissitudes of the political life: his father was assassinated in the year of his birth. His marriage to Maria Fairfax in September 1657 cemented his alliance with one of the leading parliamentarian families, and allowed him to reclaim the bulk of the estates which, as a royalist, he had forfeited; **Cowley** celebrated the wedding in a poem addressed to the bridegroom. Villiers ended up by squandering his vast fortune, and in his latter years was roundly reviled as a debauchee. His personal excesses apart, he is best remembered for the witty play *The Rehearsal* (1671), an attack on the pomposity of heroic drama, and, it is thought, on **Dryden** in particular.

VILLIERS DE L'ISLE ADAM, Auguste, Comte de
(1838–89)

French writer, pioneer of the Symbolist movement, born in St Brieuc. He was a Breton count who claimed descent from the

Knights of Malta. He dedicated his *Premières Poésies* (1856–8, 'First Poetic Works') to **de Vigny**, but developed into a considerable stylist in prose. His famous short stories, *Contes cruels* (1883, 'Cruel Stories') and *Nouveaux Contes cruels* (1888, 'New Cruel Stories'), are after the manner of **Edgar Allan Poe**. Hegelian idealism and Wagnerian Romanticism inspire his highly didactic novels and plays. The former include *Isis* (1862) on the Ideal and *L'Ève future* (1886, 'Eve of the Future'), a satire on the materialism of modern science. The latter include his masterpiece, *Axel* (1885). A pronounced Catholic aristocrat, he lived for a while with the monks of Solesmes.
▷H Chapoutout, *Villiers de l'Isle Adam* (1908)

VILLINCH *see* **BIZCARRONDO, Indalecio**

VILLON, François, originally **François de Montcorbier** or **de Logos**
(1431–after 1463)
French poet, born in Paris. He took the surname of his guardian, Guillaume de Villon, a priest and a close relative, who enabled François to study at university, to graduate (1449) and to become MA (1452). While a student he fell into bad company and in 1455 had to flee from Paris after fatally wounding a priest in a street brawl. He joined a criminal organization, the 'Brotherhood of the Coquille', which had its own secret jargon in which Villon was to write some of his ballades. Pardoned in 1456, he returned to Paris and there wrote the *Petit Testament*. He took part in the organized robbery of the funds of the Collège of Navarre, and fled to the court of the Duke of Orléans at Blois. There he was sentenced to death for another unknown crime, but released as an act of grace on a public holiday. The same happened again at Meung-sur-Loire (1461), the year of the *Grand Testament*. In 1462–3 he was in trouble again for theft and brawling. Sentence of death was commuted to banishment in January 1463. He left Paris and nothing further is known of him. The first printed edition of his works was published in 1489. The *Petit Testament* comprises 40 octosyllabic octaves, the *Grand Testament* comprises 172, bridged by 16 ballades and other verse forms. Six of the Coquille jargon ballades have been definitely attributed to him. Collections of his work in translation were published in 1968, 1971, 1973 and 1977.
▷P Champion, *François Villon* (1913, in French)

VIÑAS, David
(1929–)
Argentinian novelist and polemicist, born in Buenos Aires into a partly Jewish family.

Viñas has in his time been Argentina's 'angry young man', belonging to groups with such slogans as 'rebellion, rejection, disorder'. He has attacked **Borges**, **Mallea**, and other leading Argentinian writers, for not 'writing and living as guilty'. His chief work lies in his fiction, in particular the novel *Jauría* (1974), a harsh and uncompromising picture of the *macho* military and of the terrified repressed homosexuality underlying it. After the fall of the military dictatorships he returned from Mexico to his own country. He has been active in films and in the theatre. He now holds the chair of 19th-century Argentine Literature at the University of Buenos Aires. It is generally agreed that he has been unlucky to have escaped the attention of translators.
▷G R McMurray, *Spanish American Writing since 1941* (1987)

VINE, Barbara *see* **RENDELL, Ruth**

VINJE, Aasmund, originally **Olavson**
(1816–70)
Norwegian poet and critic, born in Vinje. He was a leader of the movement to establish the 'country language' called *Landsmål* (later known as *Nynorsk*, 'New Norwegian'), and produced a weekly journal, *Dølen*, from 1858 to 1866. He wrote a book of travel reminiscences on Norway (1861), and visited England in 1862 and published a critical *Norseman's View of Britain and the British* in English in 1863. His poetic works include *En Ballade om Kongen* (1853), his epic cycle *Storegut* (1866) and *Blandkorn* (1867).

VINOKUROV, Yevgeny
(1925–)
Russian poet, born in Bryansk. He fought in World War II, and from the start of his poetic career eschewed rhetoric. A restrained poet, sometimes almost 'minimalist', he gains his effects from understatement. He has received little attention outside Russia, but within it he is perhaps more highly respected than some other poets who have sought public attention. He was poetry editor of *Novy Mir*.

VIRGIL (Publius Vergilius Maro)
(70–19 BC)
Roman poet, born in Andes, near Mantua in Cisalpine Gaul, where his father owned a small property. The boy was sent to school at Cremona and Milan, and at 16 went to Rome and studied rhetoric and philosophy. In 41 BC the victorious triumvirs were settling disbanded soldiers on confiscated lands throughout Italy. Virgil's farm was part of the confiscated territory; but by advice of the governor of the district, Asinius Pollio, he went to Rome, with special recommendations

to Octavian (Augustus); and though his own property was not restored to him, he obtained ample compensation from the government, and became one of the endowed court poets who gathered round the statesman Maecenas. In 37 BC his *Eclogues*, 10 pastorals modelled on those of **Theocritus**, were received with great enthusiasm. Soon afterwards he left Rome and moved to Campania. The generosity of Maecenas had placed him in affluent circumstances. He had a villa at Naples and a country-house near Nola. The *Georgics*, or *Art of Husbandry*, in four books, dealing with tillage and pasturage, the vine and olive, horses, cattle, and bees, appeared in 30 BC, and confirmed his position as the foremost poet of the age. The remaining 11 years of his life were devoted to a larger task, undertaken at the urgent request of the emperor, the composition of a great national epic based on the story of Aeneas the Trojan, legendary founder of the Roman nation and of the Julian family. This covered the hero's life from the fall of Troy to his arrival in Italy, his wars and alliances with the native Italian races, and his final establishment in his new kingdom. By 19 BC the *Aeneid* was practically completed, and in that year Virgil left Italy to travel in Greece and Asia; but in Athens he fell ill, and returned only to die. At his own wish he was buried in Naples, on the road to Pozzuoli; his tomb, for many hundreds of years after, was worshipped as a sacred place. A few juvenile pieces of more or less probable authenticity are extant under his name. These are the *Culex* and the *Moretum*, both in hexameter verse; the *Copa*, a short elegiac piece; and 14 little poems in various metres, some serious, others trivial. The *Ciris* is now agreed to be by a contemporary imitator. The supremacy of Virgil in Latin poetry was immediate and almost unquestioned; his works were established classics even in his lifetime, and soon after his death they had become the textbooks of western Europe. By the 3rd century his poems ranked as sacred books, and were regularly used for purposes of divination. In the Middle Ages his fabled powers as a magician almost eclipsed his real fame as a poet; but with the revival of learning he resumed his old place. His works were translated in three volumes by **Cecil Day-Lewis**, 1940–63.
▷F Klinger, *Vergil* (1967)

VISHNEVSKY, Vsevolod
(1900–51)

Russian dramatist from St Petersburg who wrote the most popular of all Soviet plays, *Optimisticheskaya tragediya* (1933, Eng trans *An Optimistic Tragedy*, in B Blake, *Four Soviet Plays*, 1937). This is agitprop at its most skilful. Later he wrote *Nezabbyvayemyy 1919*

(1919), a distortion of Stalin's part in history—for which he was awarded the Stalin Prize First Class.
▷G Struve, *Soviet Russian Literature 1917–1950* (1951)

VITRAC, Roger
(1899–1952)

French playwright and Surrealist poet. He was associated with **Tzara** in the founding of the Dada movement, and with **Artaud** in that of the Théâtre Alfred Jarry. His most substantial play is *Victor ou les enfants au pouvoir* (1928, 'Victor, or Children in Power'), which was revived in 1962 by **Jean Anouilh**. This is a bitter Surrealist parody of superficial bedroom farce, depicting monstrous children, and will survive as one of the most effective and playable examples of the many assaults made by similar playwrights on the emptiness of bourgeois society. In English translation is *Les Mystères de l'amour* (1927), *Mysteries of Love*, in *Modern French Theatre* (1964).

VITTORINI, Elio
(1908–66)

Sicilian novelist, critic and translator, born in Syracuse. He educated himself despite great obstacles, and he became Italy's most influential writer, helping younger writers. He was founder editor of *Il Politecnico* (1945–7) and *Il Menabò* (1959–66), and translated modern American writers like **Edgar Allan Poe**, **John Steinbeck** and **William Faulkner**. *Conversazione in Sicilia* (1941, Eng trans *Conversation in Sicily*, 1949) is his metaphorical masterpiece.
▷S Pautasso, *Elio Vittorini* (1967)

VIZENOR, Gerald Robert
(1934–)

American writer, born in Minneapolis. A member of the Minnesota Chippewa tribe, whose father was born on the White Earth reservation, much of Vizenor's work draws on his Ojibwe heritage, in particular on the tradition of the trickster hero. *Griever: An American Monkey King in China* reflects his experience of university teaching in China, and combines the Native American trickster tradition with that of the Chinese Monkey King. His best-known work of fiction is the picaresque novel, *Darkness in Saint Louis Bearheart* (1973), a darkly comic account of the travels of his modern-day trickster hero, Proude Cedarfair. Vizenor has published several collections of historical and cultural essays, and numerous volumes of poetry: reworkings of traditional Ojibwe songs in *Summer in the Spring* (1965) and *Anishinabe Nagamon* (1970), and his own haiku in *Seventeen Chirps* (1964), *Empty Swings* (1967) and *Matsushima: Pine Islands* (1984). A reporter for the *Minneapolis Tribune* during the 1970s, Vizenor wrote many newspaper articles on contemporary Native American issues, which have recently been collected in *Crossbloods: Bone Courts, Bingo and Other Reports* (1990). He has also written an award-winning filmscript which was filmed as *Harold of Orange*. His novel *Dead Voices* (1992) is a fantastic cycle of Native American stories, narrated by a bear-woman.

VLAYKOV, Todor
(1865–1943)

Bulgarian story writer who published under the name Venelin, but is now known by his real name. He was from early on influenced by **Tolstoy** and other Russians, and dedicated his life to improvement of the peasantry by means of *narodnik* ideals. For many years he devoted himself to the Radical Party, and was a member of the 1919–23 government, a unique peasant dictatorship, hostile to left and right, eventually overthrown by a military coup owing to its attempts to suppress Macedonian terrorism. His stories of peasant life show far deeper understanding of women than those of **Petko Todorov**.
▷ *Slavonic Review* (1954, 1958)

VODNIK, Valentin
(1758–1819)

Slovene poet and teacher, born in Zgornja Šiška, near Ljubljana. By his writings he helped to revive Slovene nationalism. He wrote poetry, educational and school books in the language of the peasantry, and this became established as the literary language of Yugoslavia.
▷ F Levstik, *Valentin Vodnik* (1935)

VOIGT, Cynthia
(1942–)

American children's author, born in Boston, Massachusetts and educated at Smith College. She has worked as a high school teacher since 1965 and has received the **Newbery** Medal (1983) and the Mystery Writers of America **Edgar Allan Poe** Award (1984). Her novels tend to focus on independent adolescents, 'outsiders', who gradually come to create bonds with family and friends; several of them, including her first, *Homecoming* (1981), centre on one family, the Tillermans. She writes primarily for children and from 1981 has published at least one book a year.

VOINOVICH, Vladimir Nikolaevich
(1932–)

Russian novelist, born in Dushanbe, who emigrated to the West in 1980. After military service, he worked in various manual trades before moving into radio and then full-time writing. After three early novels, he wrote *Zhizni neobychaynye priklyucheniya Ivana Chonkina*, the first part of a massive comic work-in-progress. Its satirical view of Soviet behaviour during World War II led to its suppression; Voinovich was expelled from the Union of Soviet Writers in 1974 and the novel received its first (Russian) publication in France the following year. It concerns a holy fool—much like **Hašek**'s Svejk/Schweik—who becomes a mirror for the stupidities of ideology and high-echelon politics. The English translation, *The Life and Extraordinary Adventures of Private Ivan Chonkin* (1977), made a big impact, and the second volume, *Pretendent na prestol: Novye priklyucheniya soldata Ivana Chonkina* (1979, Eng trans *Pretender to the Throne: The Further Adventures of Private Ivan Chonkin*, 1981), was equally warmly received. Voinovich's travails at home were documented in the self-mocking (and slyly mythifying) *Ivankiada: Ili rasskaz o vselenii pisatelya Voinovicha v novuyu kvartiru* (1976, Eng trans *The Ivankiad: The Tale of the Writer Voinovich's Installation in His New Apartment*, 1977). The year following his defection he was stripped of his Soviet citizenship.

VOITURE, Vincent
(1598–1648)

French poet and letter-writer, born in Amiens. He was an original member of the Académie française, and enjoyed the favour of Gaston d'Orléans, Richelieu, Mazarin and Louis XIII. His brilliant sonnets and *vers de société* were the delight of the Hôtel Rambouillet, the Marquise de Rambouillet's literary *salon*, but were not published till 1650. His letters, first published in 1654, are an elegant mirror of his age and social milieu.
▷ C A Sainte-Beuve, in *Causeries de lundi* (1867)

VOJNAVÍC, Ivo
(1857–1929)

Croatian poet, story writer and dramatist, born in Dubrovnik. He experienced early hardship when the Austrians arrested him for his advocacy of an independent Yugoslavia. But he became famous despite them, for his powerful drama and affecting tales. He had a profound understanding of European literatures, and adapted many techniques, both in such stories as 'Geranium', influenced by **Flaubert**, and in such dramas as *Ekvinocij* (1902, 'Equinox'), where he exploits Symbolism. Some of his poems are translated in the *Slavonic and East European Review* (I,1, 1922).

VOLNEY, Constantin François Chasseb'uf, Comte de
(1757–1820)

French scholar and author, born in Craon in Mayenne. He studied medicine, history and oriental languages at Paris, adopted the name of Volney, and travelled in Egypt and Syria (1783–7) before publishing his valuable *Voyage* (1787). A zealous reformer, he was elected to the Constituent Assembly in 1789, but later was thrown into prison until the downfall of Robespierre (1794). His reputation chiefly rests on his famous work *Les Ruines, ou Méditations sur les révolutions des empires* (1791, 'The Ruins; or, Meditations on the Revolutions of the Empires').

VOLODIN, A, pseud of A Lifshits
(1919–)

Russian dramatist, whose work initially attracted much attention for its alleged failure to observe socialist-realistic tenets. His *Pyat vechoerov* (1959), a romantic play about youthful love, was translated as *Five Evenings* (1966).

VOLOSHIN, Maximilian, pseud of
Maximilian Kirienko-Voloshin
(1877–1932)

Russian poet, translator, critic and painter, born in Kiev. He was greatly influenced by the French poetry he read while he was living in Paris as a young man, and he was able to welcome the Revolution in the mystical manner in which so many other non-communist poets (such as **Blok**) did. But he grew disillusioned; there was no room for him in Soviet society, and he stopped writing, and lived in retirement in Koktebel. His poetry was neglected for many years, but is now being read again for its unique blend of mysticism and realism. Two of his poems are included in the *Penguin Book of Russian Verse* (1965, ed Dimitry Obolensky).

VOLPONI, Paolo
(1924–)

Italian novelist and poet, born in Urbino. He worked for the firm of Olivetti from 1950 until 1971. His Gramscian poetry has won some success, but better known is his fiction, sharply critical of modern life and technology; his novels include *Memoriale* (1962, Eng trans *My Troubles Began*, 1964) and the diary of a madman, *La macchina mondiale* (1965, Eng trans *The Worldwide Machine*, 1967).
▷G C Feretti, *Volpone* (1972, in Italian)

VOLTAIRE, François Marie Arouet de
(1694–1778)

French author, the embodiment of the 18th-century 'Enlightenment', born in Paris. His father, François Arouet, held a post in the chambre des comptes in Paris. He was educated at Collège Louis-le-Grand, the chief French seminary of the Jesuits. Leaving college at the age of 17, he was destined for the Bar, but law disgusted him. Alarmed by the dissipated life which he was leading, his father gladly saw him admitted into the service of his godfather's brother, the Marquis de Châteauneuf, the French ambassador to Holland; but in consequence of an undiplomatic love affair with a French Protestant *émigrée* in The Hague, Voltaire was sent home. He again entered an attorney's office, but his stay there was short, and he soon obtained notoriety as the author of a satire on his successful rival in the poetic competition for an Academy prize. In 1716, on suspicion of satirizing the regent, the Duc d'Orléans, he was banished for several months from Paris; and in 1717–18, a savage attack accusing the regent of all manner of crimes resulted in 11 months' imprisonment in the Bastille, where he rewrote his tragedy *Œdipe*, began a poem on Henri IV and assumed the name Voltaire. *Œdipe* was performed in 1718, and was triumphantly successful. His next dramatic attempts were almost failures, and he devoted himself to his poem on Henri IV. But the authorities refused to sanction its publication on account of its championship of Protestantism and of religious toleration, so Voltaire had the epic poem surreptitiously printed in Rouen (1723) and smuggled into Paris, as *La Ligue ou Henri le Grand* (Eng trans *Henriade*, 1732). Now famous and a favourite at court, he was denounced by the Chevalier de Rohan-Chabot as a parvenu. Voltaire retorted with spirit, and circulated caustic epigrams on the Chevalier, whose revenge was to have Voltaire beaten up. Voltaire challenged the Chevalier and was once more thrown into the Bastille, and freed only on the condition that he would go at once to England, where he landed in May 1726. Here Bolingbroke introduced him to **Pope** and his circle. He made the acquaintance of Peterborough, Chesterfield, the Herveys and the Duchess of Marlborough, and became friendly with **Edward Young**, the Scottish poet **James Thomson** and **John Gay**. He acquired some knowledge of **Shakespeare** and **Milton**, **Dryden** and **Samuel Butler**, **Joseph Addison**'s *Cato*, and the Restoration dramatists. He was strongly attracted to Locke's philosophy, and he mastered the elements of Newton's astronomical physics. Queen Caroline of Anspach accepted his dedication to her of the *Henriade*, the new form of *La Ligue*; and when permitted to return to France in 1729 he took with him his *History of Charles XII* (2 vols, 1731) and the materials for his *Lettres écrites de Londres sur les Anglais* (1734, Eng trans

Letters Concerning the English Nation, 1734). He laid the foundation of his great wealth by purchasing shares in a government lottery and by speculating in the corn trade, ultimately increased by the profits from large army contracts. He formed an intimacy with Madame du Châtelet-Lomont, and went to live with her at her husband's château of Cirey in Champagne (1734). Here he wrote dramas—among them *Mahomet* (1741, Eng trans *Mohamet the Imposter*, 1744) and *Mérope* (1743, Eng trans 1744); poetry, his *Traité de métaphysique* (1784, 'Treatise on Metaphysics'), much of his *Siècle de Louis Quatorze* (1751, Eng trans *The Age of Louis XIV*, 1752) and *Les Mœurs et l'esprit des nations* (1756, rev 1761–3, Eng trans *The General History and State of Europe*, 1756), with his *Eléments de la philosophie de Newton* (1738, Eng trans *The Elements of Newton's Philosophy*, 1738). His correspondence (1740–50) testifies to a love affair with his niece, the widowed Madame Denis. Since the appearance of his *Lettres écrites de Londres sur les Anglais* he had been out of favour at the French court. But his *Princesse de Navarre*, performed on the occasion of the Dauphin's marriage (February 1745), pleased Louis XV by its clever adulation. This and the patronage of Madame de Pompadour won him the appointments of official royal historian and of gentleman-in-ordinary to the king. In 1747 an imprudent speech at a court card-party drove him to take refuge with the Duchess de Maine, for whose amusement he now wrote *Zadig* (1748, Eng trans *Zadig and Other Stories*, 1971) and other oriental tales. When he was allowed to reappear at court, some injudicious flattery of Madame de Pompadour excited the indignation of the queen, and Voltaire had again to migrate. The death (1749) of Madame du Châtelet allowed him at last to accept the repeated invitation of Frederick II, the Great. In July 1750 Voltaire found himself in Berlin as king's chamberlain, with a pension of 20 000 francs and board in one of the royal palaces. But he entered into questionable financial transactions with a Berlin Jew and Frederick was still more gravely offended by his satirical criticisms on Maupertuis in *Micromégas* (1752, Eng trans 1753) and in March 1753 Frederick and Voltaire parted, never to meet again. In Prussia Voltaire had published his *Siècle de Louis Quatorze* (1751). On his way home he was arrested at Frankfurt, through Frederick's representative there, who had been instructed to recover from Voltaire a volume of the king's poems. Voltaire avenged himself by writing a malicious sketch of Frederick's character and account of his habits, first printed after Voltaire's death. He settled in 1755 near Geneva and after 1758 at Ferney, four

miles from Geneva. In 1756–9 appeared his *Mœurs et l'Esprit des nations*, his pessimistic *Poème sur le désastre de Lisbonne* (1756, 'Poem on the Lisbon Earthquake') and that satirical masterpiece, the novel *Candide* (Eng trans *Candid*, 1759), which attacked what Voltaire understood by the Leibnizian optimistic theology that 'all is for the best in this best of all possible worlds'. The suspension of the *Encyclopédie* by the French government, and the condemnation by the parliament of Paris of a harmless poem of his own on natural religion, impelled him to declare war by word and deed against the bigoted, 'L'Infâme'. In 1762 appeared the first of his antireligious writings which were to include didactic tragedies, biased histories, pamphlets and the *Dictionnaire philosophique portatif* (1764, Eng trans *The Philosophical Dictionary for the Pocket*, 1765). The judicial murder (1762) of Jean Calas, falsely accused of having, from Protestant zeal, killed one of his sons to keep him from turning a Catholic, aroused Voltaire to exert himself (successfully) to establish his innocence and to rescue members of the Calas family from punishment. This and similar efforts on behalf of victims of French fanaticism, for whom he provided a refuge at Ferney, won widespread admiration. The Genevan government prevented Voltaire from staging plays and from establishing a theatre in Geneva. **Rousseau**'s support for the Swiss government terminated Voltaire's friendship with the philosopher (1758). In 1778, in his eighty-fourth year, he was given a 'royal' welcome in Paris, when he arrived to put on his last tragedy, *Irène* (1778). The excitement brought on illness and his death. After the Revolution, which his works and ideas helped to foster, his remains were reinterred in the Panthéon, Paris.
▷S G Tallentyre, *Voltaire* (1903)

VONDEL, Joost van den
(1587–1679)

Dutch poet and dramatist, born in Cologne of Dutch immigrant parents. He became a prosperous hosier in Amsterdam and devoted his leisure to writing satirical verse, himself turning from Anabaptism through Armenianism to Roman Catholicism. Having acquired a wide knowledge of the classics, he turned to Sophoclean drama and produced *Jephtha* (1659) and *Lucifer* (1654), a masterpiece of lyrical religious drama. He greatly influenced the German poetical revival after the Thirty Years War (1618–48).
▷A J Barouq, *Joost van den Vondel* (1925)

VON KRUSENSTJERNA, Agnes
(1894–1940)

Swedish novelist born in Växjö, into an upper-class family. Her schooling was limited, and the psychiatric problems which were to recur throughout her life surfaced while she was still a child. Her first major work was the trilogy about Tony Hastfehr (1922–6), an *Entwicklungsroman* in which the young girl's discovery of sexual desire becomes a significant element. The seven-volume *Fröknarna von Pahlen* (1930–5), 'The Misses von Pahlen') is a radical exploration of the feminine psyche and women's lives, culminating in the ideal of the maternal family. The sexual explicitness of this work resulted in a wide-ranging public controversy. The four-volume *Fattigadel* (1935–8, 'Petty Nobility') traces the development of an upper-class woman in a perceptively depicted social setting on the verge of change.

▷B Svanberg, *Sanningen om kvinnorna. En läsning av Agnes von Krusenstjernas romanserie Fröknarna von Pahlen* (1989)

VON LA ROCHE, Sophie

(1730–1807)

German novelist, best-known for her epistolary work in the style of **Richardson**'s *Clarissa*, *Geschichte des Fräuleins von Sternheim* (1771), claimed as the first German 'woman's novel'. The erotic style was influenced by her cousin, the seraphic poet **C M Wieland**, with whom she had an adolescent affair. She had married, in 1754, the illegitimate son of a count, Georg von La Roche, and began to write as a means of giving her life meaning after her daughters had been sent away to boarding school. One of these daughters later died, leaving 12 orphans. Sophie took charge of the younger grandchildren, including Bettina Brentano, whose childhood correspondence with **Goethe** was later published.

VONNEGUT, Kurt, Jr

(1922–)

American novelist, born in Indianapolis, Indiana. Educated at Cornell University, Chicago University and the Carnegie Institute, Pittsburgh, he served in the US army infantry (1942–5) and was given the Purple Heart. During the 1960s he emerged as one of America's most influential, potent and provocative writers, a ribald commentator of the horrors of the century: holocaustic wars, the desperate state of the environment, and the dehumanization of the individual in a society dominated by science and technology. *Player Piano* (1952) was his first novel and there were another three before *Slaughterhouse-Five* (1969), in which its two main characters— the author himself and the protagonist, Billy Pilgrim—see beneath the tragic realities of human history but make no attempt to effect change. The central event of the novel is the destruction of Dresden during World War II which the author witnessed as a prisoner-of-war. *Breakfast of Champions* (1973) was even more experimental in form, a metafictional duel between Vonnegut and the imaginary science-fiction writer Kilgore Trout, inventor of the planet Tralfamador; Trout recurs in Vonnegut's fiction. Later novels continued to satirize human folly in its various manifestations: *Slapstick* (1973), *Jailbird* (1979) and *Deadeye Dick* (1982).

▷J Lundquist, *Kurt Vonnegut* (1977)

VON REZZORI, Gregor

(1914–)

Austrian novelist, born in the Bukovina, the remote eastward tip of the old Austrian empire. He was a descendant of an impoverished Sicilian noble family who moved to Vienna in the 18th century. He studied at Vienna University and for a time lived in Bucharest. In Germany after the war he was a film-maker, broadcaster and writer. His most significant books are *Memorien eines Antisemiten* (1979, Eng trans *Memories of an Anti-Semite*, 1984) and *Der Tod Meines Bruders Abel* (1976, Eng trans *The Death of My Brother Abel*, 1986).

VON SCHOULTZ, Solveig

(1907–)

Finland–Swedish poet and short-story writer. Born in Borgå, Finland, she has been influenced by the Finland–Swedish modernists but has developed her own idiom, her style gradually characterized by a simplicity bordering on the laconic. The situation of women is a recurring theme, from books of poetry such as *Eko av ett rop* (1945, 'The Echo of a Cry') and *Nattlig äng* (1949, 'Meadow at Night') to collections of short stories such as *Den blomstertid* (1958, 'Flower Season') and *Somliga mornar* (1976, 'Some Mornings'). *De sju dagarna* (1942, 'The Seven Days') is a subtle account of the development of young children, while *Längs vattenbrynet* ('Along the Water's Edge', 1992) is an autobiographical text.

▷T Warburton, 'Solveig von Schoultz', in *Åttio år finlandssvensk litteratur* (1984)

VÖRÖSMARTY, Michael

(1800–55)

Hungarian poet and dramatist, born in Szekesfehervar. He was an advocate and, after Kossuth's revolution, a member of the National Assembly in 1848. He wrote the national song, *Szozat* (1840, 'The Call'), lyric and epic poetry and 11 plays, of which the fairy drama *Csongor es Tünde* (1831, 'Csongor and Tünde') is his masterpiece. He also translated **Shakespeare**an tragedies.

▷D Toth, *Michael Vörösmarty* (1957)

VOSS, Johann Heinrich
(1751–1826)

German poet and philologist, born in Sommersdorf in Mecklenburg. He studied at Göttingen, and in 1778 went from editing the *Musenalmanach* at Wandsbeck to be schoolmaster at Otterndorf. Here he translated the *Odyssey*. In 1782 he became rector of a school at Eutin, and in 1789 he issued his translation of **Virgil**'s *Georgics*. In 1802 he settled in Jena, and in 1805 was appointed professor at Heidelberg, where he translated **Horace, Hesiod, Theocritus**, Bion, Moschus, **Tibullus** and **Propertius**; other translations were of **Aristophanes** and (with the aid of his two sons) **Shakespeare**. *Luise* (1795), an idyll, is his best original poem, although his lyric poems were popular in his own day.
▷ W Herbst, *Johann Heinrich Voss* (1872–6)

VOVCHOK, Marko, pseud of Maria Markovych, originally Maria Vilinskaya
(1834–1907)

Ukrainian writer of fiction. She wrote realistic stories in both Ukrainian and Russian, many of them demonstrating the evils of serfdom.
▷ *Ukrainian Quarterly*, III (1947)

VOZNESENSKY, Andrey
(1933–)

Russian poet (and painter), born in Vladimir, originally trained as an architect. For many years, during the 1960s and 1970s, he was regarded in the West as the most gifted poet of his generation. With **Yevtushenko** and **Akhmadulina** he toured the USA and other countries, giving readings. His facile, punning, clever and modernist poetry mesmerized such poets as **W H Auden, Stanley Kunitz** and **Robert Lowell**, who over-praised him; but he had real gifts, which led perceptive critics to ask what he might yet do. His long work *Osa* (1962), a mixture of poetry and prose cast in the form of the diary of a girl, Osa, is perhaps his most successful. But much of his ebullient poetry has inevitably dated. English translations (selections): *Antiworlds and the Fifth Ace* (1963); *Story Under Full Sail* (1974).

VRATISLAV z MITROVIC, Václav
(1576–1635)

Czech travel-writer who was imprisoned by the Turks, served on their galleys, and survived to tell the tale in the classic *Prihody* (1599, Eng trans *The Adventures of Baron Wenceslas Wraitslaw of Mitrowisz*, 1862), a vivid account of the Turks of the time.

VRCHLICKY, Jaroslav, pseud of Emil Frída
(1853–1912)

Czech poet and translator of the classics of European poetry, born in Laun. He was a pupil of **Victor Hugo**, who inspired the *Fragments of the Epic of Humanity*. His best ballads, *Legenda o sv. Prokopu* (1879, 'Legend of St Procopius') and *Zlomky epopeje* (1886, 'Peasant Ballads'), are on nationalistic and patriotic themes. His early lyric poetry on love and the pleasures of life gave way to reflections upon suffering and misfortune. In 1893 he was appointed Professor of European Literature at Prague.
▷ V Ticly, *Jaroslav Vrchlicky* (1951)

VYNNYCHENKO, Volodymyr
(1880–1941)

Ukrainian playwright and novelist, born in Kherson province. He was one of the leaders of the Revolution of 1917, and in 1919 was obliged to emigrate to France. He made his mark with the novel *Chesnist z soboyu* (1911, 'Honesty With Oneself'). In France he wrote plays which were temporarily successful; but he was forgotten in his own country until quite recently.

VYSHNYA, Ostap, pseud of Pavlo Hubenko
(1889–1956)

Ukrainian comic writer, born in Grun, Sumy. After 1943 and a period of imprisonment on a trumped-up charge he was forced, like his Soviet counterpart **Zoschenko** a little later, to conform to socialist realism. He was the greatest humorist of his time. Some of his earthy stories are translated in *25 Stories from the Soviet Republics* (1958).

W

WACE, Robert
(c.1115–c.1183)

Anglo–Norman poet, born in Jersey. He studied in Paris, and was a canon of Bayeux between 1160 and 1170. He wrote several verse lives of the saints, but his main work was *Roman de Brut* (1155), a free Norman–French version of Geoffrey of Monmouth's *Historia Regum Britanniae*, used by **Layamon** and **Robert Mannyng**. He also wrote the *Roman de Rou* (Rollo), an epic of the exploits of the Dukes of Normandy.

▷ M Pela, *Influence de Brut de Wace* (1931)

WACKENRODER, Wilhelm Heinrich
(1773–98)

German writer, born in Berlin. He was an early exponent of Romanticism and a close friend of **Johann Tieck**, with whom he collaborated in *Herzensergiessungen eines kunstliebenden Klosterbruders* (1797, 'Outpourings from the Heart of an Art-loving Monk') and *Phantasien über die Kunst* (1799, 'Fantasies about Art').

▷ E Gulzow, *Wackenroder* (1930)

WADDINGTON, Miriam
(1917–)

Canadian poet, born in Winnipeg to Yiddish-speaking Russian–Jewish parents. She was a social worker for many years before joining the English department at the University of Toronto. Since her first collection *Green World* (1945), Waddington has been acclaimed as one of the finest lyric poets of her time. Her work is personal and confessional, but highly intelligent; in the collections *Dream Telescope* (1972) and *The Visitants* (1981) she began to use short lines and a truncated syntax reminiscent of **Gertrude Stein**.

WÄGNER, Elin
(1882–1949)

Swedish novelist and journalist, feminist and pacifist. Born in Lund, she attended a girls' high school and embarked on a career as a journalist. Experiences from the Swedish women's suffrage movement are reflected in *Pennskaftet* (1910, 'Pen Woman'), which combines wit and irreverence with poignancy and earnestness. *Åsa-Hanna* (1918) is a many-faceted investigation of the plight of a peasant woman facing the misogyny of society, including the church. Notions of a matriarchal past, translated into subtle mythical patterns, result in increasingly critical perspectives on the present, as in *Dialogen fortsätter* (1932, 'The Dialogue is Continuing'). The remarkable eco-feminist essay *Väckarklocka* (1941, 'Alarm Clock') highlights the need for respect and restraint between human beings and towards Mother Earth.

▷ U Isaksson and E H Linder, *Elin Wägner, I–II* (1977–80)

WAGONER, David Russell
(1926–)

American poet and novelist, born in Massillon, Ohio. One of the most decisive influences upon him was that of his teacher at Pennsylvania State University, **Theodore Roethke**. He has been a prolific and much read poet (and novelist), with a penchant for the dramatic lyric, initially in the manner of the *Spoon River* poems of **Edgar Lee Masters**. His poems about Native Americans, *Who Shall be the Sun? Poems Based on the Lore, Legends, and Myths of Northwest Coast and Plateau Indians* (1978), were highly praised. Of his many novels, *Where is My Wandering Boy Tonight?* (1970), about a boy caught up in corrupt adult machinations, and with a destructive mother, is outstanding.

▷ R McFarland, *David Wagoner* (1989)

WAHLÖÖ, Per
(1926–75)

Swedish novelist, born in Gothenburg; he worked as a crime reporter before publishing his first novel in 1959. He published seven novels and a collection of short stories under his own name before starting to co-write police procedurals with his wife Maj Sjöwall (1935–). From the outset their ambition was to write a series of 10 novels using the crime genre as a vehicle for depiction and critical analysis of the Swedish welfare state. Starting with *Roseanna* in 1965, the series, now internationally renowned, was completed 10 years later with *Terroristerna* ('The Terrorists'), published shortly after Wahlöö's untimely death in 1975. The novels express an ironic and devastating left-wing criticism of the social and legal system in Social Democratic Sweden. The world of crime is viewed partly through the eyes of a group of detectives of

the National Homicide Squad in Stockholm and its liberal-minded head Martin Beck; the detectives are not idealized, and the authors dwell on Beck's stomach aches and marital problems as much as on the procedures and work environment of the police. A joint Danish, German and Swedish film production of six of the novels was begun in 1993, including *Mannen på Balkongen* (1967, 'The Man on the Balcony') and *Brandbilen som försvann* (1969, 'The Fire Engine that Disappeared').
▷E Søholm, *'Roman om en forbrydelse'— Sjöwall/Wahlöö's vaerk og virkelighet* (1976)

WAIN, John Barrington
(1925–)

English critic and novelist, born in Stoke-on-Trent. He studied at, and was elected fellow of, St John's College, Oxford, and lectured in English literature at Reading University (1947–55) before turning freelance author. His first four novels, *Hurry on Down* (1953), *Living in the Present* (1955), *The Contenders* (1958) and *Travelling Woman* (1959), tilt at post-war British, particularly London, social values as viewed by a provincial. His debunking vigour and humour has affinities with that of **Kingsley Amis**. He has also written poetry such as *Weep Before God* (1961), *Feng* (1975) and *Open Country* (1987); his *Poems 1949– 1979* appeared in 1980. His other work includes plays, and critical studies, and he has edited literary magazines. His later novels include *The Young Visitors* (1965), *The Pardoner's Tale* (1978), *Young Shoulders* (1982), *Where The Rivers Meet* (1988), *Comedies* (1990), and the children's book *Lizzie's Floating Shop* (1981). He also wrote a biography of **Samuel Johnson**(1974). He was Professor of Poetry at Oxford (1973–8).
▷*Sprightly Running* (1962)

WAKEFIELD MASTER, the
(15th century)

English playwright. Nothing whatsoever is known about the person or persons responsible for the Wakefield cycle (also known as the Towneley Cycle) of Miracle plays, written for performance by the townsfolk at their annual pageants. There are 32 plays in all, but six of them, the *First* and *Second Shepherds' Pageants* and four others, are by the same author, known as the Wakefield Master. Rich in humour, in colour and in their use of West Yorkshire dialect, and written in a characteristic nine-line stanza form, they are the best-crafted of all the surviving English Miracle plays.
▷A C Cauley (ed), *Everyman and the Medieval Miracle Plays* (1956)

WAKOSKI, Diane
(1937–)

American poet. She was born and educated in California and has taught at a number of American campuses. Her first verse was published in *Coins and Coffins* (1962) and the *Four Young Lady Poets* anthology (1962), which was edited by **Amiri Baraka**. These showed her to have a narrative of verbal power, conveying strong feeling about gender, America, violence and capitalism with a vividness of surface that was clearly influenced by **Wallace Stevens**. In 1968, she began to publish a sequence of chapbooks called *Greed*, parts one, two, etc, which were eventually gathered as *The Complete Greed: Parts 1–13* (1984). She also published her best-known collection, *Inside the Blood Factory* (1968), which used Surrealist imagery to portray life in the US and the contradictions of femininity. Other distinctive volumes include *Looking for the King of Spain* (1974) and *Waiting for the King of Spain* (1976), which explore feelings of yearning and loss, and *Looking for Beethoven in Las Vegas* (1983). Wakoski's prose includes *Creating a Personal Mythology* (1975), which offers important insights into her verse.

WALCOTT, Derek Alton
(1930–)

Caribbean poet, playwright, winner of the Nobel Prize for literature. He was born on St Lucia and educated there and at Kingston, Jamaica, to both of which he subsequently returned as a teacher. He worked briefly as a journalist and was founding director (from 1959) of the Trinidad Theatre Workshop. His first poems were published in Trinidad in 1948, followed by *Epitaph for the Young: XII Cantos* (1949). The slight stiffness of the early poems, evidenced throughout *In a Green Night: Poems 1948–1960* (1962), quickly disappeared, revealing a poet with strong ties to English Romanticism and back beyond that to the Elizabethans. From the mid-60s onwards, Walcott was utterly distinctive, writing with a musicality that penetrated down into his imagery. Volumes include *The Castaway* (1965), *The Gulf* (1969), *Another Life* (1973) and *Sea Grapes* (1976). The title of arguably his best book, *The Star-Apple Kingdom* (1979), suggests that the poetry needs to be bitten into and tasted in order to reveal its sometimes fugitive inner make-up. In 1981 Walcott published *The Fortunate Traveller*, a virtuosic reworking in verse of **Thomas Nashe**'s 16th-century novel, *The Unfortunate Traveller*. In 1981 *Omeros*, a brilliant Caribbean Odyssey, confirmed his international stature and in 1993 he was awarded the Nobel Prize for literature.
▷R D Hamner, *Derek Walcott* (1981)

WALKER, Alice Malsenior
(1944–)

American novelist and poet, born in Eatonville, Georgia, into a poor black family. Educated at Spelman College, Atlanta, and Sarah Lawrence College, she has been employed registering voters, as a social worker, and as a teacher and a lecturer. Her essay *In Search of Our Mother's Gardens* (1983) is an important rediscovery of a black female literary and cultural tradition. An accomplished poet, as seen in *Horses Make a Landscape Look More Beautiful* (1984), she is, however, better known for her novels, of which *The Color Purple* (1982) is her third and most popular. The winner of the 1983 Pulitzer Prize for fiction and later made into a successful film, it tells in letters the story of two sisters in the cruel, segregated world of the Deep South between the wars. It was preceded by *The Third Life of Grange Copeland* (1970) and *Meridian* (1976). In 1988 she published the novel *The Temple of My Familiar*.
▷ *Living By the Word* (1989)

WALKER, Kath *see* OODGEROO, Noonuccal Moongalba

WALL, Dorothy
(1894–1942)

New Zealand illustrator and writer of books for younger readers. Born in Wellington, she migrated to Sydney in 1914, and retired to New Zealand in 1937. She is best known for the books which feature her engaging koala hero and gumnut addict who first appeared in *Blinky Bill the Quaint Little Australian* in 1933. The next, *Blinky Bill Grows Up* (1934), was followed by a number of anthropomorphic adventures until, in 1940, real life caught up with him in *Blinky Bill Joins the Army*.

WALLACE, (Richard Horatio) Edgar
(1875–1932)

English writer. He was found abandoned in Greenwich when nine days old and brought up by a Billingsgate fish-porter. He served in the army in South Africa, where he later became a journalist (1899), and in 1905 he published his first success, the adventure story *The Four Just Men*. Another early series in a different vein was set in West Africa and included *Sanders of the River* (1911) and *Bones* (1915). From then on he wrote prolifically—his output numbering over 170 novels and plays—being best remembered for his crime novels, such as *The Clue of the Twisted Candle* (1916) and *The Ringer* (1926). He became a scriptwriter in Hollywood, where he died.
▷ *People* (1926)

WALLACE, Lew(is)
(1827–1905)

American author and soldier, born in Brookville, Indiana. He served in the Mexican War (1846–8) and with distinction as a major-general in the Federal army in the American Civil War (1861–5). Governor of New Mexico (1878–81) and minister to Turkey (1881–5), he was author of several novels, including the remarkably successful religious novel *Ben Hur* (1880), which has twice formed the subject of a spectacular film. He also wrote an *Autobiography* (1906).
▷ I McKee, *'Ben-Hur' Wallace* (1947)

WALLACE-CRABBE, Chris
(1934–)

Australian poet and academic, born in Richmond, Melbourne, brother of painter/printmaker Robin Wallace-Crabbe (1938–). His first published poetry was *The Music of Division* (1959). Four more titles followed, from which was drawn *Selected Poems* (1973). In the same year he recorded a selection of his verse for the University of Queensland Press series *Poets on Record*. From rather formal and uninvolved poetry he turned in later works to the 'new romanticism' of which *Neighbours in a Thicket* (1974) is typical. *The Emotions are not Skilled Workers* (1980) includes his most ambitious work, 'The Shapes of Gallipoli'.

WALLANT, Edward Lewis
(1926–62)

American novelist, who died unseasonably young. He was born in New Haven, Connecticut, and worked in the advertising business, where he also began to write short stories. Revealing his great talent, his first novel, *The Human Season* (1960), was a mature and unsentimental study of loss and grief. The tone deepened markedly in *The Pawnbroker* (1961); its central character is a Polish Jew running a loan shop in Harlem, where poverty compounds racial tension, forcing him to relive the horrors of the concentration camps. The book was subsequently made into an excellent film, starring Rod Steiger. *The Pawnbroker* was the last of Wallant's books published in his lifetime. *The Tenants of Moonbloom* (1963) was prepared for publication by his widow.

WALLER, Edmund
(1606–87)

English poet and politician, born in Coleshill near Amersham, Hertfordshire (now Buckinghamshire), a cousin of John Hampden. He was educated at Eton and King's College, Cambridge. Thought to have represented

Amersham in 1621, he was returned for Il-chester in 1624, Chipping Wycombe in 1625 and Amersham in 1627. In 1631 he married a London heiress, who died in 1634, and from about 1635 to 1638 he unsuccessfully courted Lady Dorothy Sidney, eldest daughter of the Earl of Leicester, whom he commemorated in verse as 'Sacharissa'. Returned to the Long Parliament in 1640, he opened the proceedings in 1641 against the judge, Sir Francis Crawley, impeached for his judgments in the king's favour. In 1643 Waller plunged into a conspiracy ('Waller's plot') against parliament on behalf of Charles I, was arrested, and expelled from the House. He avoided execution, unlike his fellow conspirators, by abject confession and the payment of a £10 000 fine, and was banished from the realm. He lived mostly in France, entertaining impoverished exiles in Paris, his own banishment being revoked in 1651, after which he returned to England. His collected poems, reviving the heroic couplet and including 'Go, lovely Rose', had been published in 1645 and were followed by *A Panegyric to my Lord Protector* (1655) and *To the King upon his Majesty's Happy Return* (1660), addressed to Cromwell and Charles II respectively.

▷W L Chernaik, *The Poetry of Limitation* (1968)

WALPOLE, Horace, 4th Earl of Orford
(1717–97)

English writer, youngest son of Sir Robert Walpole, born in London. At Eton and at King's College, Cambridge, he had the poet **Thomas Gray** as a friend, and while still at the university was appointed by his father to lucrative government sinecures. Gray and he started on the Grand Tour, but quarrelled and separated at Reggio, where Walpole fell ill. He returned to England (1741) to take his seat for Callington in Cornwall. Although he interested himself in cases like the John Byng trial of 1757, his function in politics was that of the chronicling spectator rather than the earnest actor. He exchanged his Cornish seat in 1754 for the family borough of Castle Rising, which he vacated in 1757 for the other family borough of King's Lynn. In 1745 his father died, leaving him with ample means. In 1747 he purchased, near Twickenham, the former coachman's cottage which he gradually 'gothicized' (1753–76) into the stuccoed and battlemented pseudo-castle of Strawberry Hill, which helped in its way to reverse the fashion for classical and Italianate design. He spent all his time on this transformation, on his correspondence and writings, visits to Paris, and the establishment of a private press on which some of his own works as well as **Lucan**'s *Pharsalia* with Richard Bentley's

notes, and Gray's *Progress of Poesy* and *The Bard*, were printed. He inherited his brother's title in 1791. His essays in **Edward Moore**'s *World* exhibit a light hand, and he had gifts as a verse-writer. In such satires as the *Letter from Xo Ho to his friend Lien Chi at Pekin* (1757) he is at his best. His *Castle of Otranto* (1764) set the fashion for supernatural romance. His tragedy of *The Mysterious Mother* (1768) is strong but gruesome. Other works are *Catalogue of Royal and Noble Authors* (1758), *Fugitive Pieces in Verse and Prose* (1758), *Anecdotes of Painting in England* (1761–71), *Catalogue of Engravers* (1763), *Historic Doubts on Richard III* (1768) and *Essay on Modern Gardening* (1785). His literary reputation rests chiefly upon his letters, which deal, in the most vivacious way, with party politics, foreign affairs, literature, art and gossip. His firsthand accounts in them of such events as the Jacobite trials after the 1745 Rising and the Gordon Riots are invaluable. Two of his chief correspondents were Sir Horace Mann and Madame du Deffand; with the latter he exchanged more than 1600 letters.

▷A Dobson, *Horace Walpole, a memoir* (1893)

WALPOLE, Sir Hugh Seymour
(1884–1941)

English novelist, born in Auckland, New Zealand, son of the Reverend G H S Walpole who subsequently became Bishop of Edinburgh. He was educated in England at King's School, Canterbury, and graduated from Emmanuel College, Cambridge, in 1906. He was intended for the church but turned schoolmaster at a boys' prep school and then author. Widely read in English literature, he wrote prolifically. His books, which were enormously popular during his lifetime, display a straightforward, easy-flowing style, great descriptive power, and a genius for evoking atmosphere which he unfortunately overworked at times, and which sometimes made his work open to parody. His many novels include *Mr Perrin and Mr Traill* (1911), based on his experience as a school teacher, *Fortitude* (1913), *The Dark Forest* (1916), *The Secret City* (1919, James Tait Black Memorial Prize), *The Cathedral* (1922), which owes much to **Trollope**, one of Walpole's favourite authors, and *The Herries Chronicle* (1930–3).

▷R Hart-Davis, *Hugh Walpole* (1952)

WALSCHAP, Gerard
(1898–)

Belgian (Flemish) novelist and critic, born in Londerzeel. He began as a rather pallid Catholic poet and dramatist, but soon published novels highly critical of his church, with which he openly broke in 1940. He was by profession an inspector of public libraries. His early, explicitly moralistic but nonetheless naturalistic novels, such as *Adelaide* (1929), have some affinities with **François Mauriac** and **Julien Green**. They present people in conflict with Catholic puritanism, and they were attacked by conservative critics for their candour. His most typical and best novel is *Houtekiet* (1939), a portrait of a Catholic Utopian community. Deps, the settlement founded by the eponymous hero, Jan Houtekiet, is based on principles which attack conventional Catholic morality. He continued the story in a lesser novel, *Nieuwe Deps* (1961, 'The New Deps').

WALSER, Martin
(1927–)

German novelist and playwright from Wasserburg, associated with the literary circle Gruppe '47, and active in broadcasting in the post-war period. His early stories were influenced by **Kafka**, on whom he had written for his PhD at the University of Tübingen. His writing gained substance when he dedicated himself to longer novels, including the trilogy about his character Kristeln: *Halbzeit* (1960, 'Half-time'), *Das Einhorn* (1966, Eng trans *The Unicorn*, 1971), and *Der Sturz* (1973, 'The Fall'), which is his best work. He wrote some thoughtful plays, but then reached out for a far wider audience with *Jensits der Liebe* (1976, 'Beyond Love'); *Das fliehende Pferd* (1978, 'The Horse in Flight') was a runaway bestseller. It has been said that, while he is not a profound writer, he is nevertheless an important social critic.

WALSER, Robert
(1878–1956)

Swiss (German) writer of novels and stories, born in Biel (Berne). From the age of 51 until his death he was in psychiatric hospitals, latterly at Herisau. Walser's name was scarcely known between the 1920s and the 1950s, when it was pointed out that his novels and short, often almost pointilliste, sketches had exercised an undeniable influence on such major writers as **Kafka** and **Musil** (who first noted the influence on Kafka). Attention was then directed to the work itself, and at least *Jakob von Gunten* (1909, Eng trans 1969) and many of his stories—of which there is a good selection in *The Walk* (Eng trans 1957)—were themselves major. *Jakob von Gunten* tells of a school: there is only one lesson, and all the pupils are destined to become valets. Walser, unlike Kafka, resolved his story positively: his unequivocal message is that people can find peace and fulfilment only by loving and serving one another—but he does this without recourse to moral cliché or sentimentality,

and remains one of the world's as yet only half-discovered great writers.
▷G C Avery, *Enquiry and Testament: A Study of Robert Walser* (1968)

WALSH, William
(1663–1708)

English poet, born in Abberley, Worcestershire. He entered Wadham College, Oxford in 1678 but did not graduate, later becoming Whig MP and Gentleman of the Horse to Queen Anne (1702–8). He published prose dialogues, poems on public occasions, *Letters and Poems Amorous and Gallant* (1692), and a play, *Squire Trelooby* (1704), adapted from *Molière* in collaboration with **Vanbrugh** and **Congreve**. He was admired by **Dryden** and **Pope** as a critic, but his verse, mostly love-songs, epigrams and elegies, is slight: as **Johnson** observed, it has 'more elegance than vigour'. *Works in Prose and Verse* was published in 1736.
▷Dr S Johnson, *The Lives of the English Poets* (1779–81)

WALTARI, Mika (Toami)
(1908–79)

Finnish novelist. Writing in Finnish, he was the best-known of the pre-war 'Torch-bearers' circle of writers on urban themes, including his novel *Suuri illusioni* (1928, 'The Great Illusion'). After the war he turned to historical novels, as in *Sinuhe, egyptiläinen* (1945, 'Sinuhe, the Egyptian'), *Mikael Hakim* (1949, 'The Wanderer') and *Turms, kuolematen* (1955, 'The Etruscan'). He also wrote detective stories and plays, many of them pseudonymously.
▷S Musikka, *Mika Waltarin juhlakirje* (1968)

WALTER OF CHATILLON
(d.c.1190)

French poet, who spent most of his life in Rheims, where he held the post of canon. He also worked for Henry II of England for a time. The most famous, and probably the best, Latin poet of his time, he wrote epic classical verse, of which the best-known example is *Alexandreis* (a life of Alexander the Great), but his reputation rests equally on his skill as a satirist. Often writing in Goliardic verse (a measure employed solely for satire), he launched ferocious attacks on the church and the Curia. His *De Clericis* ('On the Priesthood') begins 'Licet eger cum egrotis/Et ignotus cum ignotis/fungar tamen vice cotis/ius usurpans sacerdotis' (which roughly means: 'Ignore the law in any way/A priest's allowed to get away'). It displays a less than reverential attitude. Some of his devotional poetry survives with musical settings.

WALTHER VON DER VOGELWEIDE
(c.1170–c.1230)

Austro–German lyric poet. Little is known of his early life, but he was active in Vienna towards the end of the century, and emerges in palace rolls throughout southern Germany during the next 25 years; his last known poem is from the late 1220s. Walther wrote both love poetry—the highly formalized *Minnesang*—largely influenced by French models, but he also pioneered verse as a vehicle for social and political commentary. Much of it is frankly propagandistic, written to serve the interests of a courtly patron, but it is never sycophantic and is, on the contrary, marked by an almost arrogant self-assurance that is strikingly 'modern'. The most powerful of these patrons was the emperor Frederick II, from whom Walther gained a grant of land near Würzburg in 1212. The most reliable editions of his work are *Die Gedichte* (1965), edited by Lachmann and Kuhn, and the two-volume *Die Lieder* (1967, 1974), edited by Friedrich Laurer. The first English translation was by Edwin Zeydel and Bayard Q Morgan in 1952.
▷G F Jones, *Walther von der Vogelweide* (1968)

WALTON, Izaak
(1593–1683)

English writer, born in Stafford, the son of an alehouse-keeper. In 1621 he was settled in London as an ironmonger or a linen-draper in Fleet Street, where he became friends with **John Donne**, and about 1644 he retired. In 1626 he married a great-grandniece of Cranmer, and in 1647 Ann Ken, a half-sister of the hymn writer Thomas Ken. He spent most of his time 'in the families of the eminent clergymen of England'. His later years were spent in Winchester. His most celebrated work is his *The Compleat Angler, or the Contemplative Man's Recreation*, which first appeared in 1653; the fifth edition, expanded from 13 chapters to 21 in 1676, also contained a treatise by **Charles Cotton**. The description of fishes, of English rivers, of fishponds, and of rods and lines is interspersed with scraps of dialogue, moral reflections, quaint old verses, songs and sayings, and idyllic glimpses of country life. The anonymous *Arte of Angling* (1577), discovered in 1957, has been found to be one of his chief sources. Equally exquisite are his biographies—of Donne (1640), Wotton (1651), Hooker (1665), Richard Herbert (1670) and George Sanderson (1678).
▷J Bevan, *Izaak Walton* (1987)

WANG MENG
(1934–)

Chinese novelist, born in Beijing, the son of a Professor of Philosophy. He joined the communist youth league in 1949 as a schoolboy, and published two novels, *Long Live Youth* (1953) and *The Young New-comer in the Organization Department* (1956). He was denounced as a rightist in the 'Anti-Rightist Campaign' of 1958, and forced to work as a manual labourer for 20 years in the remote provinces. He was then allowed to return to Beijing, and re-emerged with *Young Forever* (1979). Since then he has held various party posts, and published collections of short stories like *A Night in the City* (1980) and *Andante Cantabile* (1981). After the fall of the Gang of Four he was rehabilitated and became Minister of Culture.

WANG WEI
(699–759)

Chinese poet and painter of the T'ang dynasty. An ardent Buddhist, he founded a monochrome school of painting.
▷L C and D B Walmsley, *Wang Wei the Painter Poet* (1968)

WARBURTON, Eliot, in full Bartholomew Elliott George
(1810–52)

Irish novelist, born in Tullamore, County Offaly. Educated at Cambridge, he was called to the Bar in 1837, but soon devoted himself to literature. His eight works include *The Crescent and the Cross* (1844), a collection of travel articles for the *Dublin University Magazine*, *Memoirs of Prince Rupert* (1849), *Memoirs of Horace Walpole* (1852), and two historical novels, *Reginald Hastings* (1850) and *Darien* (1852), describing the horrors of a ship on fire. Sailing to Panama, he was lost in a fire on board the *Amazon* off Land's End on its maiden voyage to Darien.

WARD, Artemus, pseud of Charles Farrar Browne
(1834–67)

American humorist, born in Maine. One of America's most famous comic writers, he began in the newspaper, the Cleveland *Plain Dealer* to contribute a column, 'Artemus Ward's Sayings' (1857); these fictional adventures of a near-illiterate travelling salesman of wax figures made him famous throughout America. Ward is partly based on the Jack Downing of **Seba Smith**, but he has his own robust traits, and the form Browne used, the serious Lyceum 'lecture', which he parodied, was his own—as were his expert 'misspellings'. Browne edited *Vanity Fair*, went to London as a lecturer, contributed to *Punch*, and was acquiring even more fame when he succumbed to consumption. Lincoln was a great admirer of his writing, for all that Browne's views were mainly those of the democratic party. He satirized militant feminism, Mormons, war-profiteers, Shakers, temperance men, and many others. Essentially a comedian, he became one of the best-loved figures of America.

▷A J Nock (ed), *Selected Works* (1924); J C Austin, *Ward* (1964)

WARD, Elizabeth Stuart Phelps
(1844–1911)

American author of a string of emotionally religious novels—*The Gates Ajar* (1868), *Beyond The Gates* (1883), *The Gates Between* (1889), *Within The Gates (1901)*—which enjoyed wide sentimental appeal. The early inspiration of these books about Heaven was the death of her beloved in the Civil War. She vowed never to marry another and threw her energies into writing. In her mid-forties she relented and married the 27-year-old Herbert Dickinson. Feminists have applauded her insistence on women's right to self-fulfilment and *Doctor Zay* (1882) broke new ground in representing women in the medical profession.

▷C F Kessler, *Elizabeth Stuart Phelps Ward* (1982); L D Kelly, *The Life and Works of Elizabeth Stuart Phelps Ward* (1983)

WARD, Mary Augusta, Mrs Humphry, née Arnold
(1851–1920)

English novelist, born in Hobart, Tasmania, a grand-daughter of Dr Thomas Arnold of Rugby, and niece of **Matthew Arnold**. The family returned to Britain in 1856 and, after attending private boarding schools, she joined them in Oxford in 1867. In 1872 she married Thomas Humphry Ward (1845–1926), a fellow and tutor of Brasenose College, Oxford, member of the staff of *The Times*, and editor of *The English Poets* (5 vols, 1880–1918). Mrs Ward contributed to *Macmillan's* and, a student of Spanish literature, biographies of early Spanish ecclesiastics to Sir William Smith's *Dictionary of Christian Biography*. In 1879 she became secretary to Somerville College, Oxford, before moving to London in 1881, where she wrote for various periodicals. A children's story, *Milly and Olly* (1881), *Miss Bretherton* (1884), a slight novel, and a translation (1885) of Amiel's *Journal intime* preceded her greatest success, the bestselling spiritual romance *Robert Elsmere* (1888), which inspired the philanthropist Passmore Edwards to found a settlement for the London poor in 1897 in Tavistock Square. Her later novels, all on social or religious issues, include *Marcella* (1894), *Sir George Tressady* (1896) and *The Case of Richard Meynell* (1911). She was an enthusiastic social worker and anti-suffragette, and became first President of the Anti-Suffrage League in 1908. She published *A Writer's Recollections* in 1918.

▷E M Smith, *Mrs Humphry Ward* (1980)

WARD, Ned (Edward)
(1667–1731)

English poet and miscellaneous writer, born in Oxfordshire of poor parents. He visited Jamaica in his youth, before keeping a public house in London where he entertained customers with wit as well as liquor. A High Church Tory, he was put in the pillory for anti-government satire in his burlesque poem *Hudibras Redivivus* (1705). His huge output of comic and satirical verse and prose was intended for popular reading and was scorned by the literary establishment, but his racy, colloquial style, earthy humour and realism wear well. His most famous work, *The London Spy* (1698–1703), gives a graphic picture of low life in Augustan London.

▷H W Troyer, *Ned Ward of Grubstreet* (1946)

WARNER, Charles Dudley
(1829–1900)

American writer, born in Plainfield, Massachusetts. He practised law in Chicago until 1869, then settled as an editor in Hartford. In 1884 he became co-editor of *Harper's Magazine*, in which his papers on the South, Mexico and the Great West appeared. He published several books of essays, and in 1873 he co-wrote *The Gilded Age* with **Mark Twain**. He also wrote literary criticism, most significantly *The Relation of Literature to Life* (1896).

▷A Fields, *Charles Dudley Warner* (1902)

WARNER, Rex
(1905–86)

English author, born in Birmingham. A specialist in classical literature, he was a teacher before turning to writing. Pre-eminently a novelist of ideas, his distinction lies in the original, imaginative handling of conflicting ideologies. *The Wild Goose Chase* (1937), *The Professor* (1938) and *The Aerodrome* (1941) established his reputation as a writer concerned with the problems of the individual involved with authority. *Men of Stones* (1949) explores the nature of totalitarianism, but it and *Why was I Killed?* (1944) are less successful than his other works. He was perhaps best known for his later historical novels such as *The Young Caesar* (1958), *Imperial Caesar* (1960) and *Pericles the Athenian* (1963). He was a poet of sensuous quality (*Poems*, 1931, and *Poems and Contradictions*, 1945), and also a translator of Greek classics.

WARNER, Susan Bogert, pseud **Elizabeth Wetherell**
(1819–85)

American novelist, born in New York. She had a huge success with *The Wide, Wide World* (1851), followed by *Queechy* (1852) and other sentimental and emotional tales. She collaborated in many books with her sister Anna Bartlett Warner (1827–1915) who, as Amy Lothrop, wrote popular stories such as *Stories of Vinegar Hill* (6 vols, 1892) and was the author of popular children's hymns like 'Jesus Loves Me, This I Know' and 'Jesus bids us Shine'.

WARNER, Sylvia Townsend
(1893–1978)

English novelist, born in Harrow. A student of music, she researched music in the 15th and 16th centuries and was one of the four editors of the 10-volume *Tudor Church Music* (1923–9). A communist and a lesbian, she lived most of her life with the extraordinary Valentine Ackland, an alcoholic amazon. A writer of great gifts whose novels defy strait-jacketing, Warner published seven novels, four volumes of poetry, essays, and eight volumes of short stories, many of which had previously appeared in the *New Yorker*. Ranging widely in theme, locale and period, significant titles are *Lolly Willowes* (1926), *Mr Fortune's Maggot* (1927), *Summer Will Show* (1936), *After the Death of Don Juan* (1938) and *The Corner That Held Them* (1948).
▷W Mulford, *Sylvia Townsend Warner* (1988)

WARNER, William
(c.1558–1609)

English poet, born in London. Educated at Oxford, he practised as an attorney, wrote *Pan his Syrinx Pipe* (1585), translated **Plautus** (*Menaechmi*, 1595), and gained a high contemporary reputation with his *Albion's England* (1586–1606), a long metrical history in 14-syllable verse.

WARR, Bertram
(1917–43)

Canadian poet, killed in the air force during World War II. His lyrical gifts, originality and his fine technique, were only just becoming markedly apparent when he died. It is thought that he might have become Canada's major poet. His one collection, *Yet a Little Onwards* (1941), evoked the admiration of **Robert Graves**. Three of his poems are included in **A J M Smith**'s *Oxford Book of Canadian Verse* (1960).

WARREN, Robert Penn
(1905–89)

American novelist and poet, born in Guthrie, Kentucky. He was educated at Vanderbilt, Berkeley and Yale universities, and was a Rhodes scholar at Oxford. Professor of English at Louisiana (1934–42) and Minnesota (1942–50), he was Professor of Drama (1951–6) and of English at Yale (1962–73). Recipient of two Pulitzer Prizes (fiction, 1947; poetry, 1958), he established an international reputation by his political novel about the governor of a Southern state, *All the King's Men* (1943; filmed 1949), in which the demagogue Willie Stark closely resembles Governor Huey Long. Other works include *John Brown, the Making of a Martyr* (1929), *Night Rider* (1939), *The Cave* (1959), *Wilderness* (1961), the story of a Jew in the Civil War, and *Meet Me in the Green Glen* (1971). He also published some volumes of short stories, and verse including *Selected Poems, Old and New, 1923–66* (1966), *Or Else* (1974) and *Rumour Verified* (1981).
▷K Snipes, *Robert Penn Warren* (1983)

WASHINGTON, Booker T(aliaferro)
(1856–1915)

Black American social reformer, journalist and autobiographer, born at Hale's Ford, a plantation in Franklin County, Virginia. After various manual jobs, he gained an impressive education, and in 1881 became the founder and first principal of the Tuskegee Normal School in Alabama (the Tuskegee Institute from 1893). His first books were collections of wise apothegms and homely advice. These were given a wider context in *The Future of the American Negro* (1899), but Washington had no natural gift for large-scale discourse. His masterpiece remains *Up From Slavery* (1901), which, with its less well-known predecessor *The Story of My Life and Work* (1900, as *An Autobiography*, 1901), is one of the classic American life-stories, recalling in vivid detail the hardships and racial hatreds of the South. His later books include a sympathetic life of his (rather more radical) fellow-reformer **Frederick Douglass** (1907).
▷L R Harlan, *Washington: The Making of a Black Leader* (1972); *The Wizard of Tuskegee* (1983)

WASSERMAN, Jakob
(1873–1934)

German novelist, born in Fürth in Bavaria. He lived in Vienna and in Syria. His impressive novel *Die Juden von Zirndorf* (1897, Eng trans *The Jews of Zirndorf*, 1933) was followed by a succession of novels culminating in the trilogy completed just before his death: *Der Fall Maurizius* (1928, Eng trans *The*

Maurizius Case, 1930), *Etzel Andergast* (1931, Eng trans 1932) and *Joseph Kerkhovens dritte Existenz* (1934, Eng trans *Joseph Kerkhoven's Third Existence*, 1934). He also wrote short stories, biographies of Columbus and H M Stanley, and an autobiography (1921).
▷J C Blankenagel, *Writings of Jakob Wasserman* (1942)

WASSERSTEIN, Wendy
(1950–)
American playwright, born in Brooklyn, New York City. She was educated at Mount Hoylake College and Yale Drama School. She has written adaptations and screenplays for television, notably **John Cheever**'s *The Sorrows of Gin*. Her plays include the punningly titled *When Dinah Shore Ruled the Earth* (1975) and *Isn't It Romantic* (1981), a topical account of the lives of a group of young women in New York which enjoyed a successful revival in 1983. She won a Pulitzer Prize in 1989 for *The Heidi Chronicles* (1988), a play about an unfulfilled feminist lecturer.

WASSMO, Herbjørg
(1942–)
Norwegian novelist, poet and playwright. Born on Skogsøya, Vesterålen, in the far north of Norway, she worked as a teacher and published a couple of volumes of poetry before making her breakthrough as a novelist. Her widely acclaimed trilogy about Tora, *Huset med den blinde glassveranda* (1981, Eng trans *The House with the Blind Glass Windows*, 1987), *Det stumme rommet* (1983, 'The Silent Room') and *Hudløs himmel* (1986, 'Flayed Heavens'), traces the childhood and adolescence of a girl fathered by a German soldier during the occupation of Norway in World War II. Her sense of alienation is reinforced by the sexual abuse she suffers from her step-father, her mounting psychosis reflected in a world of fantasy that replaces the novel's psychological realism. *Dinas bok* (1989, 'Dina's Book') is a historical novel mixing third- and first-person narrative to highlight an intrepid and brutally powerful female character.
▷J Garton, 'Herbjørg Wassmo', in *Norwegian Women's Writing 1850–1990* (1993)

WAT, Aleksander, pseud of Aleksander Chwat
(1900–67)
Polish poet, who began his career in vigorous Futurist opposition to the conservative *Skamander* movement, which was founded at the end of World War I. After that he became a dogmatic, noisy Marxist. He spent World War II as a prisoner in Russia, then fell foul of the communist regime until 1956, when a new collection of poetry—still playful, but now matured, serious and underlyingly humane—was suddenly greeted with acclaim by younger Poles. He lived out his last years in France. There is a substantial selection of his poems in translation in **Czeslaw Milosz**'s *Post-War Polish Poetry* (1965).

WATEN, Judah
(1911–85)
Ukrainian-born Australian novelist and short-story writer, born in Odessa; he settled with his family in Western Australia in 1914. He revisited Europe in the 1930s, was active in the Communist Party, and always maintained close links with writers in the USSR. His childhood reminiscences, *Alien Sun*, appeared in 1952 and depicts a new homeland through the eyes of immigrants. A visit to the Soviet Union was described in *From Odessa to Odessa* (1969). Waten wrote seven novels, from *The Unbending* (1954) to the partly autobiographical *Scenes from Revolutionary Life* (1982), and jointly edited two collections of Australian short stories. Through all his writing runs the fatalism of the dispossessed Jew; the posthumous announcement of his **Patrick White** Literary Award in 1985 would doubtless have been greeted with a wry shrug.

WATERHOUSE, Keith Spencer
(1929–)
English novelist, dramatist, humorist and journalist, born in Leeds. He first came to critical and popular attention with *Billy Liar* (1959), a whimsical and often poignant novel about a north-of-England working-class dreamer. The following year it became the basis of a successful play, on which Waterhouse collaborated with **Willis Hall**. Waterhouse has since pursued an energetic career, writing mordantly humorous novels in which his characters appear both products of, and beleaguered by, the stresses and strains of the modern urban day-to-day grind. Among his best are *Jubb* (1963), *Office Life* (1978) and *Maggie Muggins, or Spring in Earl's Court* (1981). His plays, with Hall, include *Saturday, Sunday, Monday* (1973) and *Filumena* (1977), both adapted from **Eduardo de Filippo**, and, by himself, *Jeffrey Bernard Is Unwell* (1989).

WATERS, Frank Joseph
(1902–)
American author, born in Colorado Springs, with alleged Cheyenne ancestry. In his long career as an author (he began publishing in the 1930s and was still writing in his nineties) Waters has tried to evoke the world of the Native American. *The Man Who Killed the Deer* (1942) was one of the first novels to

attempt an understanding of their religion. *Pike's Peak: A Family Saga* (1971) won a Western Heritage Award and Waters has been nominated several times for the Nobel Prize. *Brave Are My People* (1992) continues his portrait of Native American courage and transcendental wisdom.

▷T J Lyon, *Frank Waters* (1973)

WATKINS, Vernon Phillips
(1906–67)

Welsh poet, born in Maesteg, Glamorgan, and educated at Magdalene College, Cambridge. For much of his life he lived at Pennard, Gower, and used the shoreline as illustrative material for his poetry. He published eight collections of verse during his lifetime, including *Ballad of Mari Lwyd* (1941), *Death Bell* (1954) and *Affinities* (1962). Regarded as one of the greatest Welsh poets in English, as well as one of the most unusual, he was long overshadowed by his friend **Dylan Thomas**. A posthumous volume, *Fidelities* (1968), was followed by *The Collected Poems* (1986).

▷L Norris, *Vernon Watkins* (1970)

WATSON, (Elliot Lovegood) Grant
(1885–1970)

English anthropologist, naturalist and novelist, born in Staines, Middlesex, best known for his series of nature books *What to Look For in Winter/Summer/Autumn/Springtime* (1959–60). In 1910 he joined the Radcliffe-Brown scientific expedition with Daisy Bates to the north of Western Australia. Much affected by what he saw of aboriginal culture, he wrote a number of novels which encapsulate his philosophy of the conflict between good and evil. *Where Bonds are Loosed* (1914) is set in a syphilis hospital for aborigines on an Indian Ocean island; in its sequel, *The Mainland* (1918), a boy of the islands escapes to the mainland only to find another form of isolation. His other 'Australian' novels all in some way concern themselves with man's struggle to know himself. In 1968 he wrote a travel book, *Journey under the Southern Stars*, in which he describes the profound impact his visits to Australia made on him and his thinking.

▷*But to What Purpose* (1946)

WATSON, Thomas
(c.1557–1592)

English lyric poet, born in London. He was educated at Oxford, and studied law in London. Coming to **Christopher Marlowe**'s help in a street fight, he killed a man in 1589. He excelled in English 'sonnets' in *Hecatompathia or Passionate Century of Love* (1582) and *The Tears of Fancie* (1593) and

his sonnets were very probably studied by **Shakespeare**. He also translated classics into Latin and English, including **Sophocles**, **Tasso**, and Italian madrigals.

WATSON, Sir (John) William
(1858–1935)

English poet, born in Burley-in-Wharfedale, Yorkshire. He first attracted notice with *Wordsworth's Grave* (1890), and *Lachrymoe musarum* (1892), which contained a eulogy on **Tennyson**, his primary influence. *Odes and Other Poems* followed in 1894, *The Father of the Forest* in 1895, *For England* (1903), *Sable and Purple* (1910), *Heralds of the Dawn* (1912), *The Man who Saw* (1917), *The Superhuman Antagonists* (1919) and *Poems, Brief and New* (1925). His poem 'April, April, Laugh thy Girlish Laughter' appears in many anthologies, but his other work is largely forgotten.

WATTS, Alaric Alexander
(1797–1864)

English journalist and poet, born in London. He founded the *United Services Gazette* (1833) and the annual *Literary Souvenir* (1823–37), and published two volumes of poetry, but is now remembered chiefly for his alliterative alphabetical *jeu d'esprit*, 'An Austrian army awfully arrayed'.

WATTS-DUNTON, Walter Theodore
(1832–1914)

English poet and critic, born in St Ives, Cambridgeshire, the son of a solicitor. He practised law for a time, but in London he became the centre of a remarkable literary and artistic company, and the intimate friend of **Dante Gabriel Rossetti**, **William Morris**, **Swinburne**, **Philip Marston** and afterwards **Tennyson**. He wrote enough to fill many volumes in the *Athenaeum* (1876–98) and elsewhere. In *The Coming of Love* (1897) he gave a selection of his poems. In 1898 appeared his novel of gypsy life, *Aylwin*. *Old Familiar Faces* (1915) contains recollections from the *Athenaeum*. At his home in Putney he looked after Swinburne for the last 30 years of the poet's life.

WAUGH, Alec (Alexander Raban)
(1898–1981)

English novelist and travel writer, born in London, brother of **Evelyn Waugh**. He was educated at Sherborne where he was involved in a homosexual scandal and left in 1915 to become a cadet in the Inns of Court Officers Training Corps. He spent two years in training before being posted to a machine-gun unit in France, just in time for Passchendaele. In seven and a half weeks he wrote his first book, the autobiographical *Loom of Youth* (1917), in which he expressed the bitterness and love he felt for his school. A good novel, it was an immediate success, but it was tainted with notoriety and has overshadowed worthy successors: *Wheels within Wheels* (1933), *Where the Clock Chimes Twice* (1952), and various travel books, the most popular being *Island in the Sun* (1956). He wrote several autobiographical volumes including *The Early Years of Alec Waugh* (1962), *My Brother Evelyn and Other Portraits* (1967) and *The Best Wine Last* (1978).

WAUGH, Auberon Alexander
(1939–)

English journalist and novelist, the eldest son of **Evelyn Waugh**, born in Pixton Park, Dulverton, Somerset. His school days were miserable and left him with a deep detestation of the public school system. He did his National Service in the Royal Horse Guards and was sent to Cyprus where he accidentally shot himself, losing a lung, his spleen, several ribs and a finger. He denied speculation that he had been fired on by his own troops. Completing his education at Oxford, he got a job on *The Daily Telegraph* in 1960, the same year he published his first novel, *The Foxglove Saga*. There followed four novels, each courteously received and, in varying degrees, funny, but he abandoned fiction for lack of financial reward and the government's prevarication over implementing a scheme for public lending right. There are few national papers to which he has not contributed, but his best work has appeared in the *New Statesman*, the *Spectator* and the defunct *Books and Bookmen*. Since 1986 he has been Editor of the *Literary Review*, and sounds forth on the literary evils of the nation in his 'From the Pulpit' column.
▷ *Will This Do?* (1991)

WAUGH, Evelyn Arthur St John
(1903–66)

English novelist, travel writer and biographer, born in Hampstead, London, younger brother of **Alec Waugh**. He was educated at Lancing and Hertford College, Oxford, where he read modern history but with little application. From 1925 to 1927 he was a schoolmaster, an unhappy period during which he attempted suicide, but the experience gave him the material for *Decline and Fall* (1928), his first and immoderately successful novel which had been preceded only by *PRB; an essay on the Pre-Raphaelite Brotherhood* (privately printed in 1926) and a biography of **Dante Gabriel Rossetti**, published earlier in 1928. The novel made him the talk of the town for, its comic genius apart, it was obviously a *roman à clef*. After a brief and unsuccessful marriage, he spent the next few years travelling restlessly. He contributed variously to newspapers, particularly the *Daily Mail*, published the social satire *Vile Bodies* (1930) and two travel books, *Labels* (1930) and *Remote People* (1931). In 1930 he became a Roman Catholic, an event which he regarded as the most important in his life. His itinerant existence continued and between 1932 and 1937 (when he re-married) he visited British Guiana, Brazil, Morocco and Abyssinia, and cruised in the Mediterranean. He published the novels *Black Mischief* (1932), set in Africa, and *A Handful of Dust* (1934). After he married Laura Herbert he settled at Piers Court, Stinchcombe, Gloucestershire, and in 1938 published *Scoop*, a hilarious newspaper farce in which the wrong correspondent is sent to cover the civil war in the African Republic of Ishmaelia. Further travels to Hungary and Mexico followed before the outbreak of the war, which Waugh spent in a variety of postings as a junior officer. He managed to publish in the war years four books, including *Put Out More Flags* (1942) and the enduring *Brideshead Revisited* (1945), a nostalgic, highly-wrought evocation of halcyon days at Oxford. From the war he also mined 'The Sword of Honour' trilogy—*Men at Arms* (1952), *Officers and Gentlemen* (1955) and *Unconditional Surrender* (1961)—in which he described, in parallel to his own experience, the significance to men and women of the ordeal of crisis of civilization which reached its climax in World War II. Other books published during this period include *The Loved One* (1947), *Helena* (1950) and *The Ordeal of Gilbert Pinfold* (1957), a painfully personal but fictionalized account of a middle-aged writer's mental collapse. In 1964 he published *A Little Learning*, intended as the first of several volumes of an autobiography he never completed. He died suddenly in Combe Florey in Somerset, revered as a wit and a stylist and one of the 20th century's greatest comic novelists. *The Diaries of Evelyn Waugh* were published in 1976; his *Letters*, edited by Mark Amory, in 1980.

WAYMAN, Tom
(1945–)

Canadian poet, born in Ontario. Between 1966 and 1968 he was a student at the University of California, where he became active in the radical student movement. Wayman has lost none of his political commitment, but his voice is not a strident one. He projects a comic persona to the world, has been called 'a kind of Schweikian guerilla' and likes to feature himself in the titles of his collections, as in *Waiting for Wayman* (1973) and *Tom Wayman Country* (1980). He has also been industrious as an editor of poetry about labour, the best of his anthologies being *A Government Job at Last: An Anthology of Working Poems* (1976).

WEBB, Harri
(1920–)

Welsh poet, born in Swansea and educated at Magdalen College, Oxford. He has published two collections of verse, *The Green Desert* (1969) and *A Crown for Branwen* (1974), and two collections of Welsh songs and ballads, *Rampage and Revel* (1967) and *Poems and Points* (1983), and has written numerous scripts for television. His work is ingrained with a strong nationalism and a biting wit. A prolific journalist, public speaker and pamphleteer, he has been active since 1959 on behalf of *Plaid Cymru*, the Welsh Nationalist party, mainly in the industrial valleys of south-east Wales.

WEBB, Mary Gladys, née Meredith
(1881–1927)

English writer, born in Keighton, near the Wrekin. In 1912 she married Henry B L Webb and lived mostly in Shropshire, market gardening and novel-writing. *Precious Bane* (1924) won her belated fame as a novelist of the soil, the dialect, and superstition, of Shropshire, expressing 'the continuity of country life'. Her other works include the novels *The Golden Arrow* (1916), *Gone to Earth* (1917, filmed by Michael Powell and Emeric Pressburger in 1950), *The House in Dormer Forest* (1920), *Seven for a Secret* (1922) and the unfinished *Armour Wherein He Trusted* (1929); nature essays, *The Spring of Joy* (1917); and poems.
▷ G M Coles, *The Flower of Light* (1978)

WEBB, Phyllis
(1927–)

Canadian poet and teacher of literature and creative writing, born in Victoria, British Columbia, and educated at the University of British Columbia and McGill, Montreal. The recipient of a Governor General's Award for *The Vision Tree* (1982)—a collection of poetry spanning 30 years—she is recognized as one of Canada's 'leading poets'. Her poetry has been described as 'honed down to an extraordinary intellectual spareness', but this judgement excludes the conversational tone that Webb uses to convey her complex ideas and surreal imagery.
▷ S Scobie, *Signature, Even, Context* (1989)

WEBSTER, John
(c.1580–c.1625)

English dramatist, supposed to have been at one time clerk of St Andrews, Holborn. In *Lady Jane* and *The Two Harpies* (both lost)

he was the collaborator of **Thomas Dekker**, **Michael Drayton**, **Henry Chettle** and others. In 1604 he made some additions to *The Malcontent* of **John Marston**. In 1607 were printed the *Famous History of Sir Thomas Wyat*, a tragedy, and two comedies, *Westward Hoe* and *Northward Hoe*, all three the joint work of Webster and Dekker. *The White Devil* (1612) first revealed his powers. *The Duchess of Malfi* (1623) is a yet greater achievement. *Appius and Virginia* (first published 1654) may be **Thomas Heywood**'s (or partly so); *The Devil's Law Case* (1623) is largely disagreeable and sordid. A poem of the death of Prince Henry, and other fragments of verse, survive, with some doubtful works. The tragedy, *A Late Murder of the Son upon the Mother* (1624), unpublished and lost, although licensed, was written by **John Ford** and Webster. Not popular in his own day, Webster's stature was first recognized by **Charles Lamb**.
▷ G M Lagarde, *John Webster* (1968)

WECHSBERG, Joseph
(1907–83)

American journalist and fiction writer, born in Czechoslovakia. Wechsberg travelled to the USA in 1938 and became a US citizen in 1944. *Looking for a Bluebird* (1945), his first book in English, was a collection of sketches which had first appeared in *Esquire* and the *New Yorker*. *Sweet and Sour* (1948) was a similar concoction. His novels include *The Centennial Touch* (1948) and *Avalanche* (1958), but he also wrote widely about food (*Blue Trout and Truffles*, 1953), and music (*Sounds of Vienna*, 1968, *The Opera*, 1972 and *Schubert*, 1977).

WEDDE, Ian Curtis
(1946–)

New Zealand poet, novelist, short-story writer and anthologist, born in Blenheim. His first collection of verse was *Homage to Matise* (1971), followed by *Made Over* (1974). *Driving into the Storm: Selected Poems* was published in 1987. Fiction includes *The Shirt Factory and Other Stories* (1981) in which he closely observes the small details of life, and his novel, *Symmes Hole* (1986), a gently comic revisionist history of 19th-century Pacific voyaging. He has co-edited two major anthologies: the *Penguin Book of New Zealand Verse* (1985) and the *Penguin Book of Contemporary New Zealand Poetry* (1989). To the former he contributed a searching introduction on the identity of New Zealand poetry. In 1993 he published a collection of new poems, *The Drummer*.

WEDEKIND, Frank
(1864–1918)

German dramatist, born in Hanover. The son of a doctor and an actress, he grew up in Switzerland, but returned to Germany, where he was an actor and cabaret singer as well as a writer. He won fame with *Der Erdgeist* (1895, Eng trans *Earth Spirit*, 1914), *Frühlings Erwachen* (1891, first performed 1906, Eng trans *The Awakening of Spring*, 1909; better known as *Spring Awakening*, the title of the 1980 translation), *Die Büchse der Pandora* (1903, first performed 1918, Eng trans *Pandora's Box*, 1918), and other unconventional tragedies, which foreshadowed the emergence of the Expressionist movement both in their themes and performance styles. He was imprisoned in 1899 after publishing satirical poems in *Simplicissimus* in Munich. His work is highly individual, but also seems a forerunner of the Theatre of the Absurd.
▷S Gittelman, *Frank Wedekind* (1969)

WEEMS, Mason Locke
(1759–1825)

American biographer, chapman and clergyman, born in Maryland. After studying theology in London, 'Parson' Weems alienated fellow Episcopalians with his admiration for **Tom Paine**. He became a peddler of chapbooks and is best remembered for his own highly imaginative biography of Washington, *The Life and Memorable Actions of George Washington* (1800), a book which added fresh anecdotes with every new edition, the most lingering being the story of Washington and the cherry tree. Weems's other biographies included a life of Franklyn, but his most earnest work was reserved for moral tracts such as *The Drunkard's Looking-Glass* (1812) and *God's Revenge Against Adultery* (1815).

WEIDMAN, Jerome
(1913–)

American novelist and playwright, born in New York City and educated at City College and the New York University Law School. He was President of the Authors League of America for five years, and in 1960 received three prestigious awards: the Pulitzer Prize for Drama, the New York Drama Critics Circle Award, and the Tony Award. He has written over 20 novels and 10 plays, most of them collaborative musical comedies. His characters frequently struggle with their Jewishness and suffer from anti-Semitism. His first novel, *I Can Get It for You Wholesale* (1937), describes the New York garment industry and is considered a minor classic, but he is best known for his musical *Fiorello!* (1960).
▷D Walden (ed), *Twentieth-Century American-Jewish Fiction Writers* (1984)

WEIL, Simone
(1909–43)

French philosopher and mystic, born and bred in Paris. Although she was not a creative writer per se, Weil's essays reach a singular beauty of creative utterance, and she has influenced countless writers with her quest for purity and justice. After a brilliant career as a student she worked for an anarchist trade union and in a factory, shared her wages with the unemployed, and lived in poverty. She fought against Franco in the Spanish Civil War and then moved to England, where she died, in Ashford, Kent, of 'self-imposed privation and anorexia'. In her profound theological thinking she concluded that God, who certainly existed and exists, withdrew himself from the universe after creating it; man is obliged to withdraw himself likewise, from material considerations, and thus return to God. She is seen at her radiant best in her notebooks, *Cahiers* (1951–6, Eng trans *Notebooks*, 1956), and in *Seventy Letters* (1965). Other influential books include *L'Attente de Dieu* (1949, Eng trans *Waiting for God*, 1959) and *L'Enracinement* (1949–50, Eng trans *The Need for Roots*, 1955). Weil's prose style is important because in it she increasingly and successfully strove to make herself clear to her reader, eschewing all pretension. She has been accused of over-paradoxicality, but, whether that is just or not, she commands wide respect for her ruthless sincerity and lucidity.
▷R Rees, *Simone Weil* (1965); M M Davy, *Simone Weil* (1966)

WEINBAUM, Stanley G(rauman)
(1900–35)

American science-fiction writer, born in Louisville, Kentucky. His career as a living, published writer lasted a mere 18 months, and only hints at what he might have achieved. His debut story, the much-anthologized 'A Martian Odyssey' (1934), is one of the first sympathetic portrayals of aliens in the genre. His ability to empathize with the non-human, coupled with a strong element of humour, gave his stories an instant appeal for the readers (and editors) of pulp magazines. A more considered, carefully-wrought side to his work can be found in his novels—especially *The New Adam* (1939), in which a superman feels isolated in a world of mere humans.

WEINERT, Erich
(1890–1959)

German poet, political activist, orator, speaker of cabaret verse and journalist. He was a communist from 1924, and held office in the educational establishment of the German

Democratic Republic (the former East Germany). His poetry, laconic and effective, is too often politically motivated; but it has a sharpness and pungent edge which makes the best of it memorable.

WEINGARTEN, Romain
(1926–)

French playwright of the '*nouveau-théâtre*'. Born in Paris, a cherished only son, he was interested in the arts from a very early age, and wrote his first play, *Akara*, when he was only 20, appearing himself in its first production in 1948. A Surrealist writer, Weingarten blends the real and the fantastic, producing phantasmagorical series of events through which he demonstrates the unreliability of language as a means of apprehending the world. His plays include *Les Nourrices* (1961), *L'Été* (1966), *Le Pain Sec* (1967) and, most famously, *Alice aux Jardins de Luxembourg* (1969). *Comme la Pierre* entered the repertoire of the Comédie-Française in 1970; thereafter his work became more minimalist, with a greater emphasis on the interior drama (as in *La Mandore*, 1973, and *Neige*, 1979). He is known also for his edition of the Arthurian cycle, *Le Roman de la Table Ronde ou le livre de Blaise* (1983).

WEINHEBER, Josef
(1892–1945)

Austrian poet and novelist, born in Kirchstetten. He was a gifted poet when he was not trying to be ambitiously political, and was decisively but not fatally influenced by **Hölderlin**; the story of his childhood in an orphanage, told in his novel *Das Waisenhaus* (1925, 'The Orphanage'), is moving and without self-pity. He still awaits a balanced critic: he has been overpraised by conservatives, yet ignored or underestimated by those who cannot stomach his support of the Nazi regime— he had written poetry praising it as early as 1934, and killed himself when he saw that it was collapsing. But the power and self-knowledge expressed in such poems as 'Auf das Unabwendbare' ('To the Inevitable', Eng trans in *Twentieth-Century German Verse*, 1963, ed Patrick Bridgewater), with its sonorous refrain 'Dies alles ist furchtbar' ('All this is dreadful') is undeniable.

WEISS, Peter Ulrich
(1916–82)

German dramatist, painter, film-maker and novelist, born in Berlin. Known initially as a graphic artist and novelist, he fled Nazi Germany and settled in Sweden in 1939. He became famous with his first play, *Die Verfolgung und Ermordung Jean Paul Marats, dargestellt durch die Schanspielgruppe des Hospizes zu Charenton unter Anleitung des Herrn de Sade* (1964, Eng trans *The Persecution and Assassination of Jean-Paul Marat as Performed by the Inmates of the Asylum of Charenton under the direction of the Marquis de Sade*, 1965), known more simply as *Marat/Sade*. His next play, *Die Ermittlung* (1965, Eng trans *The Investigation*, 1966), was a documentary based on transcripts of the Auschwitz trials. *Gesang vom Lusitanischen Popanz* (1967, Eng trans *The Song of the Lusitanian Bogey*, 1970) was a more cogent attack on the capitalist system. Among his other works are *Diskurs über Viet Nam* (1967, Eng trans *Vietnam Discourse*, 1970), *Trotski im Exil* (1970, Eng trans *Trotsky in Exile*, 1971) and *Hölderlin* (1971). He also wrote the autobiographical novels *Abschied von den Eltern* (1961, Eng trans *The Leavetaking*, 1962) and *Fluchtpunkt* (1962, Eng trans *Vanishing Point*, 1966).

WELCH, (Maurice) Denton
(1915–48)

English novelist, born in Shanghai. His fiction is almost entirely autobiographical; his flight from Repton School and a subsequent holiday in China are described in *Maiden Voyage* (1943), and *In Youth is Pleasure* (1945) also deals frankly with his adolescent angst. His life was disrupted by a road accident in 1935, while he was studying at Goldsmith School of Art; his serious injuries eventually caused his premature death, which prevented the completion of *A Voice Through a Cloud* (1950), a typically precise, honest and sensitive examination of his accident and its aftermath. His posthumously published *Journals* (complete edn 1984) display the same blend of almost obsessively detailed observation, interest in antique objects, and homo-eroticism. **Edith Sitwell** described him as a 'born writer'.

▷M De-la-Noy, *Denton Welch: The Making of a Writer* (1984)

WELCH, James
(1940–)

American writer, born in Browning, Montana. Welch grew up on the Blackfoot and Fort Belknap reservations and graduated from the University of Montana, where he now teaches. Of Blackfoot and Gros Ventre descent, he writes about the Native American culture of the Northwest. His first two novels—*Winter in the Blood* (1974) and *The Death of Jim Loney* (1979)—and his poetry collection, *Riding the Earthboy 40* (1971), all describe contemporary reservation life. In *Fools Crow* (1986) he diverged to write a historical novel from the point of view of a band of Pikuni (Blackfoot) people at the time of first contact with Whites; as with all Welch's work, the book is characterized by the striking clarity of his prose and imagery. *The Indian Lawyer* (1990) describes the moral dilemmas faced by a young Blackfoot lawyer and former basketball star, Sylvester Yellow Calf, in the format of a thriller which encompasses the language and culture of prison, basketball and local politics in Montana.

▷P Wild, *James Welch* (1983)

WELDON, Fay
(1931–)

English novelist and author of television screenplays, born in Alvechurch, Worcestershire and educated at St Andrews University. She became a successful advertising copywriter and is credited with creating the slogan: 'Go to work on an Egg'. Her first novel, *The Fat Woman's Joke*, appeared in 1967. It has been followed by many more, in which her recurring themes include the nature of women's sexuality and experience in a patriarchal world. Although her women are usually morally and culturally more sophisticated than the men around them, they can also exert an uncompromising revenge upon the world, as in *The Life and Loves of a She-Devil* (1983), in which an ugly and rejected heroine seeks retribution. Other novels include *Puffball* (1980), which looks at pregnancy and womanhood, and *The Cloning of Joanna May* (1989), which considers genetic engineering.

▷O Kenyon, *Women Novelists Today* (1988)

WELLS, Charles Jeremiah
(c.1800–1879)

English poet, born in London. He was educated at Edmonton, where he met **Keats**. He practised as a solicitor in London (1820–30) and taught English in France. He died in Marseilles. His *Stories after Nature* (1822) were followed in 1824 by the biblical drama, *Joseph and his Brethren*, which remained unknown until **Swinburne** praised it in the *Fortnightly* (1875).

▷H Rischbieter, *Charles Jeremiah Wells* (1967)

WELLS, H(erbert) G(eorge)
(1866–1946)

English novelist, short-story writer and popular historian, born in Bromley, Kent, the third son of an unsuccessful shopkeeper. At 18 he left his job as a draper's apprentice and became a pupil teacher at the Midhurst Grammar School, from where he won a scholarship to the Normal School of Science, South Kensington, and studied biology under T H Huxley. Although distracted by politics, writing and teaching he obtained a BSc in 1890 and then lectured for the Universal Tutorial College until the success of his short stories allowed him to concentrate full-time on writing. Idealistic, impatient and dynamic, he threw himself into contemporary issues—free love, Fabianism, progressive education, scientific theory, 'world government' (he was an early agitator for a League of Nations) and human rights. His private life was no less restless than his public. His first marriage was to his cousin Isabel in 1890, but ended in divorce. His second, to Amy Catherine ('Jane') Robbins, in 1895, suited him domestically but he sought physical solace elsewhere and had numerous affairs, notably with 'new' women, including Amber Reeves, Elizabeth von Arnim, **Rebecca West**, Odette Keun and Moura Budberg, **Maxim Gorky**'s mistress. He wrote over a hundred books and countless articles, achieving unparalleled fame in his lifetime, but by the time of his death his popularity had waned. *The Time Machine* (1895), an allegory set in the year 802701 describing a two-tier society, pioneered English science fiction and was followed by significant contributions to the genre: *The Wonderful Visit* (1895), *The Island of Doctor Moreau* (1896), *The Invisible Man* (1897), *The War of the Worlds* (1898), *When the Sleeper Awakes* (1899), *The First Men in the Moon* (1901) and *Men Like Gods* (1923). A satirical visionary, he was disputatious and fought with Fabian colleagues—**George Bernard Shaw** and the **Webbs**, for instance—as well as with his fellow novelist **Henry James**, who sprinkled condescension on Wells' novels. Wells responded with sarcasm and continued to produce a spate of social satires, drawing heavily on his own varied experience. He wrote some of the best-known English comic novels—*Love and Mr Lewisham* (1900), *Kipps* (1905) and *The History of Mr Polly* (1910)—and books that concentrated on specific contemporary issues: *Ann Veronica* (1909), an early feminist novel, *Tono Bungay* (1909), which charts the decline of the upper classes, and *The New Machiavelli* (1911), about a politician embroiled in a sex scandal. *Mr Britling Sees It Through* (1916) and *The World of William Clissold* (1926) are lesser books but autobiographically illuminating. *The Country of the Blind, and other stories* (1911) is the best of his several collections. In 1920 he published *The Outline of History*, which enjoyed a vast circulation, and among his many other works is *The Shape of Things to Come* (1933), a plea to confront fascism before it was too late, and the despairing *Mind at the End of its Tether* (1945). *Experiment in Autobiography* (1934) includes a striking self-portrait and studies of friends and contemporaries.

▷P Parrinder, *H.G. Wells* (1976)

WELLS, John
(1936–)

English actor, dramatist, humorist and director. He read French and German at Oxford, and taught both languages at Eton (1961–3), while contributing material for revues at the Edinburgh Festival. He was a co-editor of the satirical magazine, *Private Eye* (1964–7), and has written for the magazine ever since, notably the supposed diary of Mrs Wilson, Harold Wilson's wife, and the Dear Bill letters, the supposed correspondence of Denis Thatcher, husband of Margaret Thatcher. He has written a number of plays for the theatre, starting with *Listen to the Knocking Bird* in 1965. *Mrs Wilson's Diary* (1968) was followed by *Anyone for Denis* (1981), in which he played the title role. (As an actor he made his London debut in the farce *An Italian Straw Hat*, in 1961.) He is also highly regarded as a translator of plays and opera from the French and German. He directed a revival of *The Mikado* in 1989.

WELTY, Eudora
(1909–)

American novelist and short-story writer, born in Jackson, Mississippi. She was educated at the Mississippi State College for Women, the University of Wisconsin and the Columbia University School of Advertizing in New York. After leaving college she was a publicity agent with the Works Progress Administration in Mississippi, which involved extensive travel through the state. She took numerous photographs which were published as *One Time, One Place: Mississippi in the Depression: A Snapshot Album* (1971). During World War II she was on the staff of the *New York Review of Books*. She started writing short stories with 'Death of a Travelling Salesman', and published several collections from 1941 to 1954. She has also written five novels, mostly drawn from Mississippi life: *The Robber Bridegroom* (1942), *Delta Wedding* (1946), *The Ponder Heart* (1954), *Losing Battles* (1970) and *The Optimist's Daughter* (1972). *The Collected Stories of Eudora Welty* was published in 1980. Among her many accolades, she has received two Guggenheim fellowships, three **O Henry** awards, the Pulitzer Prize and the National Medal for Literature. Her autobiography, *One Writer's Beginnings*, was published in 1984.
▷E Evans, *Eudora Welty* (1980)

WEN I-to
(1899–1946)

Chinese poet and artist, educated in Peking and America. He was the most influential poet of the pre-revolutionary generation, a strict formalist in his approach to writing but able to invest his verse with great emotional power. He was greatly exercised by seeing poverty and oppression in his travels around China, and described these to great effect in his verse, often employing a savage irony. He was natural material for conversion to communism during the revolution but, once converted, stopped writing, throwing all his weight into the struggle. He was killed by nationalist troops in Kunming in 1946.

WENDT, Albert
(1939–)

New Zealand academic and writer, born in Apia, Western Samoa. His first novel was *Sons for the Return Home* (1973), followed by *Pouliuli* (1977) and *Leaves of the Baynan Tree* (1979, 'Wattie' Book of the Year, 1980). He has also published two collections of short stories and some verse, including *Inside Us the Dead; Poems 1961 to 1974* (1976). He was Professor of Pacific Literature at the University of the South Pacific (1980–7), and is now Professor of English at Auckland University.

WENZ, Paul
(1869–1939)

French-born Australian writer, born in Rheims and dubbed 'France's **Henry Lawson**'. He arrived in Australia in 1892 after travelling through Africa and South America. Marrying an Australian woman, he settled down to station life in northern New South Wales, writing graphic and sympathetic stories of Australian bush and station life in *A l'autre bout du monde* (1905) and *Sous la Croix du Sud* (1910). He served with the French army in World War I but returned to write four novels including *L'Homme du soleil couchant* (1923, 'The Sundowner'). His only English-language book was *Diary of a New Chum* (1908). His writings in French were published in France under the name 'Paul Warrego'.

WEÖRES, Sándor
(1913–)

Hungarian poet and translator, born in Szombathely and educated at the University of Pécs. He worked as a librarian during the war years, turning to writing full-time in 1950, by which time he had published nine volumes of verse, including *A teremtés dícsérete* (1938, 'In Praise of the Creation') and three critical books. These reflected the interest in Zen Buddhism and other Eastern philosophies which put Weöres at odds with the post-war communist authorities. A poet of extraordinary variety and stylistic range, he has produced work in almost every conceivable form, from short, almost child-like lyrics, to long, discursive meditations on the great themes of Western culture. He became more widely known in the West with *Selected Poems* (1970), shared with **Ferenc Juhász** and put into English by David Wevill and **Edwin Morgan**. In that year, he was also awarded the prestigious Kossuth Prize, a sign of recognition in his homeland. Perhaps his most profound volume is *Psyché: Egy hajdani költönö* (1972, 'Psyche: Words of an Ancient Poet'), which sees him working back into the far mythological past. Weöres has translated extensively, including Chinese poetry, **Shelley** and **Vasko Popa**.

WERFEL, Franz
(1890–1945)

Austrian author, born in Prague. He lived in Vienna until 1938, when he moved to France, from where he fled from the Nazi occupation in 1940 to the USA. He was associated with the Expressionist movement, and his early poems and plays betray that influence, but he is best known for his novels, including *Das Lied von Bernadette* (1941, 'The Song of Bernadette').
▷ L Zahn, *Franz Werfel* (1966)

WERGELAND, Hendrik Arnold
(1808–45)

Norwegian poet and patriot, known as 'Norway's Lord Byron', and brother of the novelist **Camilla Collett**. He championed the cause of Norwegian nationalism in literature. A prolific lyrical poet and playwright, his chief work was a philosophical verse drama, *Skabelsen, mennesket og messias* (1830, 'Creation, Man and Messiah'). His last work, *Den engelske Lods* (1944, 'The English Pilot'), celebrated the liberation of the human mind.
▷ H Beyer, *Hendrik Wergeland* (1964)

WERNER, (Friedrich Ludwig) Zacharias
(1768–1823)

German romantic dramatist, born in Königsberg. His chief works are *Die Söhne des Thals* (1803, 'The Sons of the Valley'), *Das Kreuz an der Ostsee* (1804, 'The Cross on the Baltic Sea') and *Martin Luther* (1806), although he later wrote a recantation of his praise of Luther after his conversion to Catholicism. He was ordained a priest in Vienna, and became a fashionable preacher, but his earlier dramas remained his most significant work, and place him among the leading dramatists of the Romantic movement.
▷ P Hankhamen, *Zacharias Werner* (1970)

WESCOTT, Glenway
(1901–87)

American novelist, born in Wisconsin. Most of his fiction is set in his native state, although his early life was that of an expatriate. He knew and was initially encouraged by **Gertrude Stein** in Paris (she said of him that he was 'syrup', but 'did not pour'). His best-known book, **James**ian in presentation, is *The Grandmothers* (1927), in which an expatriate youth tells the story of his Wisconsin family. This was well received, as was *Pilgrim Hawk* (1940), about different kinds of love. *Images of Truth* (1962) collected valuable essays about such contemporaries as **Katherine Anne Porter** and **Thomas Mann**. *Goodbye Wisconsin* (1928) is a volume of stories, which many critics have maintained contains his best work.

WESKER, Arnold
(1932–)

English dramatist, born in London's East End, of Jewish immigrant parentage. He left school at 14. His Jewish family background and his varied attempts at earning a living are important ingredients of his plays. The Kahn family trilogy, *Chicken Soup with Barley*, *Roots* and *I'm talking about Jerusalem* (1958–60), echoes the march of events, pre- and post-World War II, in the aspirations and disappointments of the members of a left-wing family. *Roots* is an eloquent manifesto of Wesker's socialism: an aesthetic recipe for all which he attempted to put into practice by taking art to the workers through his Centre-42 (1961–70). Other plays are *The Kitchen* (1959), *Chips with Everything* (1962), *The Four Seasons* (1965) and *Their Very Own and Golden City* (1966), *The Friends* (1970), *The Old Ones* (1972), *The Merchant* (1977) and *Love Letters on Blue Paper* (1978), originally written for television in 1976. He also wrote the essay collection *Fears of Fragmentation* (1970) and *Words—as Definitions of Experience* (1976). No major new Wesker play has been produced in Britain for some time, although a one-woman play, *Annie Wobbler* (1984), was well received. He wrote a libretto for his play *Caritas* (1981) in 1991, and his plays have been collected in five volumes in 1989–90. So far his reputation still rests firmly on his earliest plays.
▷ J R Taylor, *Anger and After* (1962)

WESLEY, Mary, pseud of Aline Farmer
(1912–)

English novelist, born in Englefield Green, Berkshire. She wrote two children's books, *Speaking Terms* and *The Sixth Seal* (both 1969), before publishing her first adult novel, *Jumping the Queue*, in 1983, at the age of 70. She has since produced a succession of books dealing with middle-class mores, each written with ironic, detached amusement and taking an unblinkered though compassionate look at sexual values. *The Camomile Lawn* (1984) considers sexual and emotional relationships in the turmoil of war, while *Second Fiddle* (1988) deals with the relationship between a middle-aged woman and a young, hopeful male novelist.

WEST, Jessamyn
(1907–84)

American novelist and short-story writer, born in North Vernon, Indiana and educated at Whittier College and the University of California. She worked as a teacher and secretary and led several writers' conferences. In 1976 she received the Janet Kafka Prize. Her novels and short stories concentrate on a blend of western and romance writing: the frontier figures largely in her work, as do depictions of motherhood and relationships between men and women. Her first novel, *The Friendly Persuasion* (1945), focuses on Quaker life in Indiana. Later works include semi-autobiographical books, such as *A Matter of Time* (1966) and *The Woman Said Yes* (1976), about her sister's sickness and her own ill-health as a result of tuberculosis.
▷ A D Farmer, *Jessamyn West* (1982)

WEST, Joyce
(1908–85)

New Zealand children's writer and author of romantic and historical novels. She was a regular contributor of short romances to the *New Zealand Herald* in the mid-1930s, and wrote novels of country life such as *Drover's Road* (1953), the first of three set in the North Island sheep-farming country, and *The Year of the Shining Cuckoo* (1961), centred on the dairy farming districts. With **Mary Scott** she wrote a series of crime novels.

WEST, Morris Langlo
(1916–)

Australian novelist and playwright, born in St Kilda, Victoria, who trained for the priesthood but left before taking vows. After war service his first novel, *Moon in My Pocket* (1945), was published, under the pseudonym 'Julian Morris', and dealt with the conflicts facing a Catholic novitiate. In 1955 he left Australia for Italy, where his fourth novel, *Children of the Sun* (1957), a tale of Neapolitan slum urchins, attracted attention. *The Devil's Advocate* (1959, James Tait Black Memorial Prize, filmed 1977) became an international bestseller, since when his books have been eagerly awaited. Such novels as *The Shoes of the Fisherman* (1963), *Summer of the Red Wolf* (1971), *The Clowns of God* (1981), *Lazarus* (1990) and *The Ringmaster* (1991) have won him many awards. His novels, some of which he has dramatized, deal

with significant religious and political issues in the context of essential humanity.

WEST, Nathanael, pseud of **Nathan Wallenstein Weinstein**
(1903–40)

American novelist, born in New York City. After attending Brown University, Rhode Island, he lived in Paris for a few years, where he wrote *The Dream Life of Balso Snell* (1931), self-consciously avant garde but illuminating in his preoccupation with the hollowness of contemporary life. On his return to New York he mismanaged a hotel and was associate editor with **William Carlos Williams** of the magazine *Contact*. *Miss Lonelyhearts*, the story of a newspaper agony columnist who becomes more involved with his correspondents than is good for him, appeared in 1933. There are parallels in West's own life but he renounced journalism and went to Hollywood in 1935 to write scripts for a minor studio, plundering this experience for *The Day of the Locust* (1939), his surreal masterpiece. His only other novel, *A Cool Million*, was published in 1934. A black humorist and biting satirist, he was killed, along with his wife, Eileen McKenney, when he ignored a traffic signal.
▷ J Martin, *Nathanael West: the art of his life* (1970)

WEST, Dame Rebecca, the adopted name of **Cecily Isabel Fairfield**
(1892–1983)

Irish novelist, biographer, journalist and critic, born in County Kerry. Her father, a journalist, left her mother and the family moved to Edinburgh where they lived in straitened circumstances. She was educated at George Watson's Ladies College, and trained for the stage in London, where in 1912 she adopted the nom de plume Rebecca West, the heroine of **Ibsen's** *Rosmersholm* which she had once played, and who is characterized by a passionate will. From a formative age she was involved with the suffragettes and in 1911 joined the staff of the *Freewoman*, the following year becoming a political writer on the *Clarion*, a socialist newspaper. Her love affair with **H G Wells** began in 1913 and lasted for 10 turbulent years, during which time she bore him a son and laid the foundations for her career as a writer. Her first published book was a critical study of **Henry James** (1916); her second, a novel, *The Return of the Soldier* (1918), describes the homecoming of a shell-shocked soldier. After the final break with Wells she went to the USA where she lectured and formed a long association with the New York *Herald Tribune*. In 1930 she married Henry Maxwell Andrews, a banker, and they lived in Buckinghamshire until his death in 1968. She published eight novels including *The Judge* (1922), *Harriet Hume* (1929), *The Thinking Reed* (1936) and the largely autobiographical *The Fountain Overflows* (1957). Her last (unfinished) novel was *Cousin Rosamund* (1988). In the mid-1930s she made several trips to the Balkans to gather material for a travel book, but her interest deepened and resulted in her masterful analysis of the origins of World War II, *Black Lamb and Grey Falcon*, published in two volumes in 1941. It is generally considered her magnum opus. During the war she superintended BBC broadcasts to Yugoslavia and in its aftermath she attended the Nuremberg War Crimes Trials. From this and other cases came *The Meaning of Treason* (1949) and *A Train of Powder* (1955). Witty, incisive and combative, she was described by **George Bernard Shaw** as handling a pen 'as brilliantly as ever I could and much more savagely'.

▷ V Glendinning, *Rebecca West* (1987)

WESTALL, Robert
(1929–93)

English children's novelist, born and brought up in Tynemouth. At various times a journalist, teacher and antiques dealer, he was 44 before he published a book. *The Machine Gunners* (1975), a Carnegie Medal winner, is one of several works set in his home area during World War II. *The Scarecrow* (1981) also won a Carnegie Medal, while *The Kingdom by the Sea* (1992) was the recipient of the Guardian Fiction Award. Staying in teaching until his fifties enabled him to keep in touch with the eagerness and energy of children; his best works depict characters with a raw hunger for experience, and the self-belief to overcome adversity.

WEXLEY, John
(1907–85)

American playwright, born in New York, a nephew of the Yiddish actor Maurice Schwartz. Wexley is best known for *The Last Mile* (1930), a play about the last hours of a condemned man. The play was also significant for being the first big stage success for Spencer Tracy, who played ring-leader in a group of prisoners who seize a guard and murder him. Other plays include *Steel* (1931), *They Shall Not Die* (1934) and *Running Dogs* (1938).

WEYMAN, Stanley John
(1855–1928)

English novelist, born in Ludlow. He was educated at Christ Church, Oxford, and taught history before turning to law in 1877–91. He began writing short stories for magazine publication, then his first novel, *The House of the Wolf* (1888–9), but his success as a popular historical novelist dates from *A Gentleman of France* (1893), set in the time of Henry of Navarre, and admired by **R L Stevenson**. He wrote many more in a similar vein, including *Under the Red Robe* (1894), *The Red Cockade* (1895), *Count Hannibal* (1901) and *Chipping* (1906). Several were successfully dramatized.

WHALEN, Philip
(1923–)

American poet, born in Portland, Oregon. He was ordained as a Zen priest in 1973, and lives in a Zen community, One Mountain Temple, San Francisco. Originally associated with the beat poets, he writes some verse in which the typography reinforces the meaning, in a quasi 'concrete' fashion; but most of his work remains discursive and in free rhythms.

▷ *The Kindness of Strangers: Poems 1969–1974* (1975)

WHARTON, Edith Newbold, née Jones
(c.1861–1937)

American novelist and short-story writer, born in New York. Her family was wealthy and aristocratic and she was educated at home and in Europe. In 1885 she married Edward Wharton, a friend of the family, and they travelled widely, before settling in Paris in 1907. Her husband, however, was mentally unbalanced and they were divorced in 1913. Socially gregarious, she formed a durable friendship with **Henry James** who did much to encourage and influence her work, and a voluminous correspondence with, among others, the art historian Bernard Berenson. *The Greater Inclination* (1899), her first collection of short stories, was followed by a novella, *The Touchstone* (1900), but it was *The House of Mirth* (1905), a tragedy about a beautiful and sensitive girl who is destroyed by the very society her upbringing has designed her to meet, that established her as a major novelist. Many other works followed, almost 50 in all, including travel books and volumes of verse, but she is known principally as a novelist of manners, a keen observer of society, witty and satirical. Her most uncharacteristic novel is *Ethan Frome* (1911), which deals partly with her unhappy marriage, partly with primitive people in rural America. Important later works are *The Age of Innocence* (1920), *The Mother's Recompense* (1925), *The Children* (1928) and *Hudson River Bracketed* (1929). Her approach to her work is discussed in *The Writing of Fiction* (1925). *A Backwards Glance* (1934) is her revealing autobiography.

▷ L Auchincloss, *Edith Wharton* (1961)

WHEATLEY, Denis Yates
(1897–1977)

English novelist, born in London. He inherited the family wine business but sold up in 1931 to concentrate on novel writing. His métier was an alloy of satanism and historical fiction, highly coloured and frequently burdened with undigested research, but enormously popular. Indicative titles in a lurid occult oeuvre are *The Devil Rides Out* (1935), *The Scarlet Impostor* (1942) and *The Sultan's Daughter* (1963). His three-volume autobiography was published posthumously (1978–80).

WHEATLEY, Phillis
(c.1753–1785)

American Negro poet, born in Africa, possibly Senegal. As a child she was shipped to the slave-market in Boston, Massachusetts (1761), and sold as a maidservant to the family of a Boston tailor, John Wheatley, who educated her with the rest of his family. She studied Latin and Greek, and started writing poetry in English at the age of 13. She published *Poems on Various Subjects, Religious and Moral* (1783) and visited England in that year, to huge popular interest, although some cast doubt on her poems' authenticity. In 1778 she married John Peters, a free negro of Boston. A *Collected Works* appeared in 1988.
▷W H Robinson, *Critical Essays on Phillis Wheatley* (1982)

WHEELOCK, John Hall
(1886–1978)

American poet, born in Far Rockaway, New York. He joined the publisher Charles Scribner's Sons in 1911, and became a director, and its treasurer. He attracted attention early in his career, when, with his friend **Van Wyck Brooks**, he published *Verses of Two Undergraduates* (1905), while still at Harvard. He was essentially a popular, traditional, somewhat rhetorico-religious poet, whose work is not now included in anthologies such as **Richard Ellmann**'s *New Oxford Book of American Verse* (1976); but he was well respected, and his *The Gardener* (1961) won him the Bollingen Prize.

WHEELWRIGHT, John Brooks
(1897–1940)

American poet. He was born in Boston into an upper-class family, being the descendant of the 17th-century religious writer whose name he shared, and of a 19th-century governor, John Brooks. Despite this lineage and his father's wealth, he embraced communism shortly after leaving Harvard and MIT. He joined the Socialist Party of Massachusetts in 1932 and later became a political activist, returning to his sumptuous home after a day on the stump and often wearing his famous raccoon coat while lecturing to unemployed dockers or striking longshoremen. He was a founder member in 1937 of the Trotskyist Socialist Workers Party. Wheelwright's verse, of which five volumes were published in his lifetime—*North Atlantic Passage* (1925), *Rock and Shell* (1933), *Masque With Clowns* (1936), *Mirrors of Venus* (1938) and *Political Self-Portrait* (1940)—is dense and highly wrought, incorporating religious symbols and obscure gnostic references alongside scraps of contemporary reality and political theory. It superficially resembles the work of **Hart Crane**, though **T S Eliot** is perhaps the strongest single influence. Wheelwright was killed on a Boston street by a hit-and-run driver. His *Collected Poems* appeared in 1972.
▷A M Wald, *The Revolutionary Imagination: The Poetry and Politics of John Wheelwright and Sherry Mangan* (1983)

WHETSTONE, George
(c.1544–1587)

English hack writer, born in London, who tried to make his fortune at court. A gambler and womanizer, he denounced the shocking depravity of his own city in various pamphlets. He joined the army more than once, serving with distinction; when not thus employed, he turned to writing to support himself, producing plays, poems and treatises, and biographies of distinguished men. Much of this work was mediocre, such as his lines 'In Praise of Gascoigne and his Posies' (1575). His last known work, the sycophantic *Censure Upon Notable Traitors* (1587), goes through a catalogue of plotters against the queen, declaiming on their wickedness and on Divine Providence saving Elizabeth's life.

WHITE, Antonia, pseud of Eirene Botting
(1899–1980)

English novelist and journalist, born in London. By the age of 30 she had married three times, the first two being annulled on the grounds of non-consummation. She also suffered periods of mental breakdown and underwent **Freud**ian analysis for four years. Her first novel, *Frost in May* (1933), is a semi-autobiographical study of a young girl's miserable convent education. *The Lost Traveller* (1950), *The Sugar House* (1952) and *Beyond the Glass* (1954) continue her autobiographical journey through her protagonist's relations with men, reconversion to Roman Catholicism and mental illness. A difficult, colourful, mysterious personality, White also translated extensively from French, including many works by **Colette**.
▷L Hopkinson, *Nothing to Forgive* (1988);

S Chitty, *Antonia White: Diaries 1958–1979* (1992)

WHITE, E(lwyn) B(rooks)
(1899–1985)

American essayist, children's novelist, poet and parodist, born in Mount Vernon, New York, in Westchester County. Long associated with the *New Yorker* from 1925, he did as much to make its name as it did his. His reputation rests on his three bestselling novels for children (*Stuart Little*, 1945; *Charlotte's Web*, 1952; and *The Trumpet of the Swan*, 1970), the essays he wrote in the column 'One Man's Meat', his collaboration with **James Thurber** on *Is Sex Necessary? Or Why You Feel The Way You Do* (1929), *The Elements of Style* (1959, a revision of William Strunk's original), a long article entitled 'Here Is New York', and a peerless parody of **Ernest Hemingway**, 'Across the Street and into the Grill'. Succinct, graceful and witty, his writing prompted Thurber to declare that 'Many of the things he writes seem to me as lovely as a tree'. Inclined towards rusticity, he spent much time in Maine fretting over livestock, retiring to a boathouse to sculpt his pieces. He was married to Katharine Angell, the first fiction editor of the *New Yorker*.

WHITE, Edmund
(1940–)

American novelist, probably the most sensitive writer about the gay scene since **James Baldwin**. White had already written several books, including *Forgetting Elena* (1973) and *Nocturnes for the King of Naples* (1978), before he came to notice with the publication *A Boy's Own Story* (1982). As the title is meant to suggest, it deliberately subverts the action-laden clichés that **Hemingway** attached to the young male adolescent, presenting instead a sensitive portrayal of a youth coming to terms with his sexuality and attempting to find a place for it in a ruthlessly heterosexual power struggle. In the same year, White published the essay *States of Desire: Travels in Gay America* (1980), a pre-AIDS update on **John Rechy**'s fictionalized *City of Night*. Less than a decade later, his novel *The Beautiful Room is Empty* (1988) had to contend with a very different social reality.

WHITE, Henry Kirke
(1785–1806)

English poet, born in Nottingham, the son of a butcher. Articled to a solicitor, in 1803 he published his verse sketch *Clifton Grove*, which brought him the friendship of **Robert Southey** and the Rev Charles Simeon, through whom he became a sizar of St John's College, Cambridge. After his tragically early death, Southey edited his *Remains* (1807).

WHITE, Kenneth
(1936–)

Scottish-born poet, essayist and travel writer, born in Glasgow. He studied at Glasgow University, graduating with a double first in French and German. It could be said that he has made a career as an exile, first by spending many years travelling in Europe, America and elsewhere, and latterly as an academic in France, where he now holds the chair of 20th-century literature at the Sorbonne. For years his work remained out of print in Britain and he was largely unsung in Scotland. In France, however, he is highly acclaimed, both as a poet and as a thinker, his ruminative verse and Zen-influenced philosophy finding like minds. He has received some of France's most prestigious literary awards, including the Prix Medicis Etranger and the Grand Prix du Rayonnement. Early publications included *The Cold Wind of Dawn* (1966) and *The Most Difficult Area* (1968). He has found a new generation of Scots more receptive to him, and recent publications, largely reprinting material unavailable in English, include *The Bird Path: Collected Longer Poems* (1989), *Travels in a Drifting Dawn* (1989), *Handbook for the Diamond Country: Collected Shorter Poems 1960–1990* (1990) and *The Blue Road* (1990).

WHITE, Patrick Victor Martindale
(1912–90)

Australian novelist and winner of the Nobel Prize for literature, born in London into an old Australian pastoralist family. He was educated at Cheltenham College and then worked in Australia for two years before going to King's College, Cambridge. After war service in the RAF he wrote *Happy Valley* (1939), *The Living and the Dead* (1941) and *The Aunt's Story* (1946), and then bought a farm near Sydney and settled in Australia. He achieved international success with *The Tree of Man* (1954). In this symbolic novel about a small community in the Australian bush, he attempts to portray every aspect of human life and to find the secret that makes it bearable. In 1957 appeared *Voss*, an allegorical account, in religious terms, of a gruelling attempt to cross the Australian continent. This was followed by *Riders in the Chariot* (1961), *The Solid Mandala* (1966), *The Eye of the Storm* (1973) and *The Twyborn Affair* (1979). He also published short stories, *The Burnt Ones* (1964) and *The Cockatoos* (1974), and plays, including *Four Plays* (1965) and *Signal Driver* (1981). His own 'self-portrait', *Flaws in the Glass* (1981), describes the background to his supposedly 'ungracious' receipt of the Nobel Prize for literature in 1973. With the proceeds of the prize he established the Patrick White Literary Award, which makes an annual grant to an older Australian writer whose work has not received appropriate critical or financial recognition.

▷D Marr, *Patrick White: a biography* (1991)

WHITE, T(erence) H(anbury)
(1906–64)

English novelist, born in Bombay, India. He was educated at Cheltenham College and Queens' College, Cambridge. Until 1936 he was a master at Stowe and later lived in a gamekeeper's cottage near the school. Always a keen sportsman, he was an ardent falconer and fisherman, and his knowledge and love of nature are imbued in his work. He wrote more than 25 books, but he is best known for his interpretation of the Arthurian legend, a tetralogy known collectively as *The Once and Future King* (1958), the first part of which, *The Sword in the Stone* (1937), is a children's classic. A fifth volume, found among his papers, was published as *The Book of Merlyn* (1977). *Mistress Masham's Repose* (1947) is another notable children's book. His adult works include *The Goshawk* (1951), set at the onset of World War II, a chronicle of the taming and training of one of Germany's noblest birds of prey, *The Master* (1957), a science-fiction parable, and *The Book of Beasts* (1954), translated from a 12th-century Latin bestiary.

▷S T Warner, *T. H. White* (1967)

WHITE, William Hale, pseud Mark Rutherford
(1831–1913)

English novelist and journalist, born in Bedford. Having abandoned his training as an independent religious minister, he worked briefly in the offices of the *Westminster Review*, where he met **George Eliot**, before entering the Civil Service. He continued writing journalism, becoming London correspondent of *The Scotsman*, and during the 1850s began to publish novels and works of philosophy. All take a high moral tone and are somewhat humourless, even depressing, although the novels are atmospherically strong. The best are *The Autobiography of Mark Rutherford, Dissenting Minister* (1881) and *Mark Rutherford's Deliverance* (1885), recounting White's spiritual journey.

WHITEHEAD, Charles
(1804–62)

English poet and novelist, born in London, the son of a wine merchant. He devoted himself to writing after publishing *The Solitary* (1831), a poem of reflection. His *Autobiography of Jack Ketch* (1834) showed humour, but when Chapman & Hall asked him for a popular book in instalments he declined, recommending young **Dickens**, who thus began the *Pickwick Papers*. His novel, *Richard Savage* (1842), earned the praises of Dickens and **Dante Gabriel Rossetti**. Whitehead went out to Melbourne in 1857, but died miserably, leaving unfinished the *Spanish Marriage*, a drama.

▷M Bell, *A Forgotten Genius* (1884)

WHITEHEAD, Paul
(1710–74)

English satirist and minor poet, born in Holborn, a tailor's son. He was apprenticed to a mercer, and later married a short-lived imbecile with a fortune of £10 000. He spent some years in Fleet prison for the nonpayment of a sum for which he had stood security. He became active in politics, was one of the infamous 'monks' of Medmenham Abbey, and became deputy treasurer of the Chamber. Among his satires are *State Dunces* (1733), inscribed to **Pope**, and *Manners* (1739), for which **Robert Dodsley** the publisher was brought before the House of Lords. His *Collected Works* appeared in 1777.

WHITEHEAD, William
(1715–85)

English poet and dramatist, born in Cambridge, the son of a baker. He was educated at Winchester and Clare Hall, Cambridge, and became a fellow in 1742. He travelled as tutor to Lord Jersey's son, became in 1755 secretary of the Order of the Bath, and in 1757 was appointed poet laureate. He defended his acceptance against hostile criticism in *A Charge to the Poets* (1762). He wrote tragedies—*The Roman Father* (1750), in imitation of **Corneille**'s *Horace*, and *Creusa* (1754)—and a comedy, *School for Lovers* (1762). His *Plays and Poems* were collected in 1774, with *Complete Poems* following in 1788.

WHITING, John
(1917–63)

English playwright, born in Salisbury. Educated at Taunton School, he studied at the Royal Academy of Dramatic Art (1935–7). After serving in the Royal Artillery in World War II he resumed his acting career before emerging as a dramatist. *Saint's Day* (1951), depicting the sense of hopelessness, failure and self-destruction of the Southman ménage, gained recognition for his talent although it was not a popular success. It was followed by *A Penny for a Song* (1951), a comedy, and *Marching Song* (1954), a play of ideas with little action or dramatic situation whose plot deals with the decision facing General Rupert Forster: to stand trial as a scapegoat for his country's failure or to commit suicide. After *Gates of Summer* (1956) he was commissioned by the Royal Shakespeare Company to dramatize **Aldous Huxley**'s *The Devils of Loudon*, as *The Devils* (1961), which achieved great success, despite harrowing scenes such as the torture of Grandier. His *Collected Plays* (1969) included a number of works which he did not live to see on stage.

WHITMAN, Walt(er)
(1819–92)

American poet, born in West Hills, Long Island, New York, the son of a radical, free-thinking carpenter. He was brought up in Brooklyn from the age of four. He served first in a lawyer's and then in a doctor's office, and finally in a printer's. He next became an itinerant teacher in country schools. He returned to printing, wrote an earnest temperance novel, *Franklin Evans or, The Inebriate* (1842), and in 1846 became Editor of the *Brooklyn Eagle*. This and his other numerous press engagements were only of short duration. In 1848 he travelled with his brothers to New Orleans in search of work on the New Orleans *Crescent*, but came back to Brooklyn as a journalist (1848–54). He seemed unable to find free expression for his emotions until he hit upon the curious, irregular, recitative measures of *Leaves of Grass* (1855). Originally a small folio of 95 pages published anonymously with the author's portrait in work clothes enigmatically facing the title page, it grew in the eight succeeding editions to nearly 440 pages. This, with his prose book, *Specimen Days and Collect* (1882), constitutes his main life-work as a writer. Summoned to tend his brother, wounded in the Civil War, he became a volunteer nurse in the hospitals of the Northern army. The exertion, exposure, and strain of those few years left Whitman a shattered and prematurely aged man. In 1865 he received a government clerkship, but was dismissed by Secretary Harlan as the author of 'an indecent book' (*Leaves of Grass*). Almost immediately he obtained another similar post. In 1873 he was stricken with paralysis and left Washington for Camden, New Jersey, where he spent the remainder of his life. He would have fallen into absolute poverty but for the help of trans-Atlantic admirers. Later on, several wealthy American citizens liberally provided for his simple wants. Whitman set himself the task of uplifting into the sphere of poetry the whole of modern life and man; thus the inclusion of subjects at that time which were tabooed. Many of his poems for *Leaves of Grass* are now considered American classics, such as 'Drum Taps', 'When Lilacs Last in the Courtyard Bloom'd' and 'O Captain! My Captain!'.
▷ G W Allen, *The Solitary Singer* (1955)

WHITTEMORE, (Edward) Reed II
(1919–)

American poet, editor (he co-edited *Furioso*), critic, teacher and biographer, born in New Haven, Connecticut. As a biographer of **William Carlos Williams** (1975) he was mostly influenced by this poet and his free rhythms. One poem of his in particular has been much praised: 'Lines Upon Reading an Announcement by Civil Defence Authorities Recommending That I Build a Bomb Shelter in My Backyard'. His survey, *Little Magazines* (1963), is authoritative, as is *Poets and Anthologists: A Look at the Current Poet-Packaging Process* (1986).

WHITTIER, John Greenleaf
(1807–92)

American Quaker poet and abolitionist, born near Haverhill, Massachusetts, the son of a poor farmer. Largely self-educated, in 1829 he entered journalism, and in 1831 published *Legends of New England*, a collection of poems and stories. In 1840 he settled at Amesbury, a village near his birthplace, and devoted himself to the cause of emancipation. His collection *In War Time* (1864) contains the well-known ballad 'Barbara Frietchie'. *At Sundown* was published in 1892. In his day he was considered second only to **Longfellow**.
▷ E Wagenknecht, *John Greenleaf Whittier* (1967)

WHYTE-MELVILLE, George John
(1821–78)

Scottish novelist and authority on field sports, born at Mount-Melville, St Andrews. Educated at Eton, he became a captain in the Coldstream Guards and served in the Crimean War, commanding a regiment of Turkish cavalry irregulars. For the rest of his life he devoted himself to field-sports, and wrote numerous novels involving fox-hunting and steeplechasing, including *Digby Grand* (1853) and *Tilbury Nego* (1861). He also wrote serious historical novels, including *Market Harborough* (1861), *The Gladiators* (1863) and *The Queen's Maries* (1862), on Mary, Queen of Scots, and published *Songs and Verse* in 1869. He was killed in a hunting accident.

WICKRAM, Georg or Jörg
(1505–before 1562)

German poet and popular novelist, born in Kolmar. The bastard son of a careless but wealthy burgher, he was by profession goldsmith, painter and town clerk of Burgheim, where he died. As a poet he wrote standard but lively poems and plays in the Meistersinger tradition; as a novelist he was outstanding. He wrote two courtly romances, but also, much more notably, the story of a boy's rise to success, *Der Jungen Knaben Spiegel* (1554, 'The Young Boy Spiegel')—often considered to be the first German novel proper—and *Von güten und bösen Nachbarn* (1554, 'The Good and Bad Neighbours'), his finest work. He adapted the *Metamorphoses* of **Ovid**.

▷G Fauth, *Jörg Wickram* (1916, in German)

WIDDEMER, Margaret
(1884–1978)

American poet and novelist, born in Pennsylvania. She first came to notice with a poem denouncing the employment of children. It was reprinted as the title poem in her first collection, *The Factories and Other Poems* (1915). In the same year her novel, *The Rose-Garden Husband*, which told the story of a young librarian (Widdemer was herself a trained librarian), became a bestseller. Later poetry lost the hard edge of *The Factories*. Her best verse is to be found in *Collected Poems* (1957). In addition to her romantic and historical novels for adults she also wrote the 'Winona' series for girls.

WIDEMAN, John Edgar
(1941–)

Black American novelist, born in Washington, DC, but brought up in the Homewood area of Pittsburgh. He was educated at the University of Pennsylvania, and has taught English and Afro-American Studies in several universities. He is a powerful chronicler of black urban experience, and much of his fiction is set in Homewood. His first novel was *A Glance Away* (1967), about a drug addict. Subsequent titles include *The Lynchers* (1973), which takes a multi-perspective look at black urban life. His Homewood experience is also central to *Sent For You Yesterday* (1983) and *Reuben* (1987), and the stories collected in *Damballah* (1981). A second collection, *Fever* (1989), is more wide-ranging. The novel *Philadelphia Fire* (1990) is based on a police fire-bombing of a radical black commune in 1985.

▷*Brothers and Keepers* (1984)

WIEBE, Rudy
(1934–)

Canadian novelist and short-story writer, born in Fairholme, Saskatchewan, into the Menonite community. Educated at the universities of Alberta and Tübingen, he edited *The Menonite Brethren Herald* and taught at the University of Alberta. As a Menonite he writes of peace-loving in a violent, macho world and as a prairie writer revises Ottawa-dominated history. *Peace Shall Destroy Many* (1962) and *The Blue Mountains of China* (1974) deal with the temptations of the Menonite community in the world. His masterpieces, *The Temptations of Big Bear* (1973) and *The Scorched Wood People* (1977), treat 19th-century rebellions against Ottawa led by religious figures. *The Mad Trapper* (1980) is a yarn about another rebel, but one who stands alone against the world, while *My Lovely Enemy* (1983) turns to religious adultery on campus. Wiebe's style is awkward but the depth of his religious and historical imagination generously compensates for that.

▷W J Keith, *Epic Fiction: the Art of Rudy Wiebe* (1981)

WIECHERT, Ernst
(1887–1950)

German writer, born in Kleinort in East Prussia. He published novels dealing with psychological problems such as post-war readjustment, among them *Der Wald* (1922, 'The Forest'), *Der Totenwolf* (1924, 'The Wolf of Death'), *Der silberne Wagen* (1928, 'The Silver Wagon'), *Die Majorin* (1934, Eng trans *The Baroness*, 1936) and *Das einfache Leben* (1939, Eng trans *The Simple Life*, 1954), the last-named probably his masterpiece. *Wälder und Menschen* (1936, 'Forests and Men') is autobiographical, as is *Der Totenwald* (1946, Eng trans *The Forest of the Dead*, 1947), which describes his six months' confinement in Buchenwald concentration camp.

▷H Ebling, *Ernst Wiechert* (1947)

WIED, Gustav
(1858–1914)

Danish fiction-writer and dramatist, born on the island of Loland. His masterpiece is generally reckoned to be *Skoerydsler* (1901, 'Skirmishes'), a grotesque play about old people. He was often compared to **Strindberg**, but possessed a much greater degree of humour than the Swede. He wrote ironic and bizarre prose sketches, resisted his tragic sense of life so long as he could, but finally killed himself. One of his best plays, *Ranke Vilje* (1906) was translated as *2 × 2 = 5* in *Contemporary Danish Plays* (1955).

WIELAND, Christoph Martin
(1733–1813)

German writer, born near Biberach, the son of a pietist pastor. In 1752 Bodmer invited him to Zürich, and inspired him to write *Der geprüfte Abraham* (1753, 'The Testing of

Abraham') and other books full of sentimentality and religious mysticism. But Wieland turned away from that particular style of writing, and from 1760 to 1770, as well as making the first German translation of **Shakespeare** (22 plays, 1762–6), he wrote the romances *Agathon* (1766–7, Eng trans 1773) and *Don Silvio von Rosalva* (1764, Eng trans 1785), *Die Grazien* (1768, Eng trans *The Graces*, 1823) and other tales, and the didactic poem *Musarion* (1768). Their elegance, grace and lightness made Wieland popular with fashionable society. After holding for three years a professorship at Erfurt, he was called to Weimar to train the grand-duchess's sons, and there he spent most of the rest of his life, the friend of **Goethe** and **Johann Herder**. The Weimar period produced his heroic poem *Oberon* (1780, Eng trans 1798), by which he is best remembered, and various other works; he also edited several magazines.
▷D M von Abbe, *Christoph Wieland* (1961)

WIENERS, John
(1934–)
American poet, born in Boston, who claims inspiration from **Edna St Vincent Millay**. After a spell at Black Mountain College, he became associated with the Beats, but wrote in a different vein. The poignant lyricism of the early collection *Hotel Wentley Poems* (1958) was widely admired. It did contain much verbal dexterity, but from 'A poem for cocksuckers' onwards Wieners's unwavering gay perspective and his tumid anguish have restricted his audience.

WIERZYNSKI, Kazimierz
(1894–1969)
Polish poet, born in the Carpathian mountain region, in Drohobycz. He left Poland for the USA in 1940, but died in London. He was a co-founder of the important middle-of-the-road Skamander group. His early poetry was vitalist, and celebrated athletics; later the note deepened, and in the USA he wrote tragic poetry of exile. But **Milosz** has claimed that his last poems, closer in style to the younger poets writing in Poland itself, 'are striking in their generosity and openness to the world ... [they] rank amongst his greatest achievements'. His *Life and Death of Chopin*, one of the best books on the composer, first written as *W garderobie duchów* in 1938, was translated in a revised edition in 1951; *Selected Poems* appeared in 1959. He has also published a collection of stories and much theatre criticism.

WIGGIN, Kate Douglas, née Smith
(1856–1953)
American novelist, born in Philadelphia. She wrote novels for both adults and children, but was more successful with the latter. *Rebecca of Sunnybrook Farm* (1903) is probably her best-known book, although the *Penelope* exploits, *The Birds' Christmas Carol* (1888) and *Mother Carey's Chickens* (1911), were all firm favourites.
▷*My Garden of Memory* (1923)

WIGGLESWORTH, Michael
(1631–1705)
English-born American poet and clergyman, born in Yorkshire. He was taken to Massachusetts Bay colony at the age of seven. Educated at Harvard, he was married to Mary Reyner (1655), to Martha Mudge (1679), and to Sybil Sparhawk Avery (1691), and eight children resulted. Fellow and tutor at Harvard from 1652 to 1654, and again from 1697 to 1705, he was ordained to the ministry of the Puritan Church in Malden, c.1656. His epic poem, the first American epic, 'Day of Doom' (1662), takes a lengthy and somewhat pessimistic view of the Day of Judgement. He wrote a shorter poem intended for edification in 1669: 'Meat out of the Eater or Meditations Concerning the Necessity, End and Usefulness of Afflictions Unto God's Children'. His *Diary* was published in 1951.
▷R Crowder, *No Featherbed to Heaven* (1962)

WILBUR, Richard
(1921–)
American poet. He grew up in New York City and was educated at Harvard, joining the faculty around the time his first major collection, *The Beautiful Changes* (1947), was published. It was followed by *Ceremony and Other Poems* (1950) and *Things of This World* (1956), a significant title in view of Wilbur's stylistic hybridization of **William Carlos Williams**'s and **Marianne Moore**'s objectivism with the English Metaphysicals. In 1957 he published the plain-spoken *Poems* and that year began teaching at Wesleyan University. Two years earlier, he had published an acclaimed translation of **Molière** and in 1957 Leonard Bernstein invited him to contribute songs to *Candide*. A collection was published in 1963, at a time when Wilbur's powers appeared to be failing; however, *The Mind Reader* and a prose collection *Responses*, both published in 1976, reawakened interest in his work.

WILCOX, Ella Wheeler
(1850–1919)
American journalist and prolific producer of verse, born in Johnstown Center, Wisconsin. In 1884 she married Robert M Wilson (d.1916). She had completed a novel before

she was 10, and later wrote at least two poems a day. The first of her many volumes of verse was *Drops of Water* (1872); the most successful was *Poems of Passion* (1883). She also wrote a great deal of fiction, and contributed essays to many periodicals. Her *Story of a Literary Career* (1905) and *The World and I* (1918) were autobiographical.

WILDE, Lady Jane Francesca, known as 'Speranza'
(1826–96)

Irish poet and hostess, born in Dublin. An ardent nationalist, she contributed poetry and prose to the *Nation* from 1845 under the pen-name of 'Speranza'. In 1851 she married Sir William Wilde; their son was **Oscar Wilde**. Her salon was the most famous in Dublin. After her husband's death she moved to London, and published several works on folklore, including *Ancient Legends of Ireland* (1887) and *Ancient Cures* (1891).

WILDE, Oscar Fingall O'Flahertie Wills
(1854–1900)

Irish playwright, novelist, essayist, poet and wit, born in Dublin. His father was Sir William Wilde; his mother Lady **Jane Francesca Wilde**. From the age of nine to 16 he went to Portora Royal School in Enniskillen, which **Samuel Beckett** later attended. He went on to Trinity College, Dublin, and to Magdalen College, Oxford, where he was dandified, sexually ambiguous, sympathetic towards the Pre-Raphaelites, and contemptuous of conventional morality. He was also an accomplished classicist, and won the Newdigate Prize in 1878 for the poem 'Ravenna', which his biographer, **Richard Ellmann**, described as 'a clever hodgepodge of personal reminiscence, topographical description, political and literary history'. In 1881, the year in which he was ridiculed in **Gilbert** and Sullivan's *Patience* as an adherent of the cult of Art for Art's sake, his first collection of poetry was published. The next year he embarked on a lecture tour of the USA where, apparently, when asked if he had anything to declare he replied, 'Only my genius'. The tour, wrote Ellmann, 'was an advertisement of courage and grace, along with ineptitude and self-advertisement'. Wilde boasted to Whistler, 'I have already civilized America'. He married, in 1884, Constance Lloyd, and had two sons for whom he wrote the classic children's fairy stories *The Happy Prince and Other Tales* (1888). Two years later came *The Picture of Dorian Gray*, modelled on his presumed lover, the poet John Gray. More fairy stories appeared in 1891 in *A House of Pomegranates*. In this year he also published *Lord Arthur Savile's Crime and Other Stories*, and

a second play, *The Duchess of Padua*, an uninspired verse tragedy. But over the next five years he built his dramatic reputation, first with *Lady Windermere's Fan* (1892), followed by *A Woman of No Importance* (1893), *An Ideal Husband* (1895) and, the *pièce de résistance*, *The Importance of Being Earnest* (1895). *Salome*, originally written in French, appeared in 1894 in a translation by Lord **Alfred Douglas**. By now his homosexuality was commonly known, and the Marquis of Queensberry, father of Lord Alfred, left a card at Wilde's club addressed 'To Oscar Wilde posing as a Somdomite' (*sic*). Wilde took it that he meant 'ponce and Sodomite' and sued for libel. He lost the case, and was himself prosecuted and imprisoned for homosexuality. In 1905 his bitter reproach to Lord Alfred was published as *De Profundis*. He was released in 1897 and went to France under the alias Sebastian Melmoth, the name of his favourite martyr linked with the hero of *Melmoth the Wanderer*, the novel written by his great-uncle, **Charles Maturin**. *The Ballad of Reading Gaol* was published in 1898. He also wrote literary essays, and *The Soul of Man Under Socialism* (1891), a riposte to **George Bernard Shaw**. His last years were spent wandering and idling on the continent.
▷R Ellmann, *Oscar Wilde* (1990)

WILDENBRUCH, Ernst von
(1845–1909)

German romantic novelist, poet and dramatist, born in Beirut. He served in the army and Foreign Office. He wrote a number of short epic poems, but is best known as a playwright. His strongly expressed patriotism made him the national dramatist of Prussia during the empire of the Hohenzollern, to whom he was related. He also wrote short stories.
▷H M Elster, *Ernst von Wildenbruch* (1934)

WILDENVEY, Herman
(1886–1959)

Norwegian poet, born in Eiker. At first basing himself on the poetry of **Knut Hamsun**, he soon outstripped his mentor. Facile but gifted, he became Norway's most popular lyrical poet. Some of his verse is translated in *Owls to Athens* (1934).

WILDER, Laura Ingalls
(1867–1957)

American children's author, born in Pepin, Wisconsin. A farm woman all her life, it was not until she was in her sixties, when her daughter suggested that she write down her childhood memories, that her evocative 'Little House' series began to appear. *Little House in the Big Woods* (1932) caught on instantly in the USA and was followed by several sequels: *Little House on the Prairie* (1935), *By the Shores of Lake Silver* (1939), *Little Town on the Prairie* (1941), *Farmer Boy* (1933) and *Those Happy Golden Years* (1943). A television series in the 1950s assured their success in Britain.

WILDER, Thornton Niven
(1897–1975)

American author and playwright, born in Madison, Wisconsin. He was educated at Yale and served in both wars, becoming a lieutenant-colonel in 1944. He started his career as a teacher of English at Lawrenceville Academy (1921–8) and the University of Chicago (1930–7). His first novel, *The Cabala*, appeared in 1926. Set in contemporary Rome, it established the cool atmosphere of sophistication and detached irony that was to permeate all his books. These include *The Bridge of San Luis Rey* (1927), a bestseller and winner of the Pulitzer Prize, *The Woman of Andros* (1930), *Heaven's My Destination* (1935) and *The Ides of March* (1948). His first plays—*The Trumpet Shall Sound* (1926), *The Angel That Troubled the Waters* (1928) and *The Long Christmas Dinner* (1931)—were literary rather than dramatic; but in 1938 he produced *Our Town*, a successful play that evokes without scenery or costumes a universal flavour of provincial life. This was followed in 1942 by *The Skin of Our Teeth*, an amusing yet profound fable of humanity's struggle to survive. Both these plays were awarded the Pulitzer Prize. His later plays include *The Matchmaker* (1954), *A Life in the Sun* (1955), *The Eighth Day* (1967), *Theophilus North* (1974) and, in 1964, the musical *Hello Dolly*, based on *The Matchmaker*.
▷ R Burbank, *Thornton Wilder* (1978)

WILDGANS, Anton
(1881–1932)

Austrian poet and dramatist, born in Vienna. He trained as a lawyer, but gave up his practice to concentrate on literature in 1912. His plays include *Dies Irae* (1918, 'Day of Anger') and the biblical tragedy *Kain* (1920). The epic poem *Kirbisch* appeared in 1927, and he published a number of collections of verse. He was twice director of the Vienna Burgtheater, in 1921–2 and 1930–1.

WILHELM, Kate
(1928–)

American science-fiction writer, born in Toledo, Ohio. A slowly maturing author, she won a Nebula Award in 1969 for her short story 'The Planners', but did not begin to produce her best work as a novelist until around a decade later. *Where Late The Sweet Birds Sang* (1976), set in a post-holocaust America, won a Hugo Award. *Juniper Time* (1979), which takes place in a drought-stricken US, is one of the most effective of the genre's many works with an ecological theme. She has also written several mainstream novels. One of the most subtle and intelligent voices in modern science fiction, she was married to the science-fiction author and editor **Damon Knight**.

WILLARD, Josiah, pseud Josiah Flynt
(1869–1907)

American author and traveller, born in Wisconsin, the nephew of Frances Willard, a leading temperance activist. He travelled in Europe and America as a hobo, befriending **Arthur Symons** in London, and working on the **Tolstoy** estate in Russia. He expressed solidarity with other vagrants, defending their cause against what he saw as the injustice of the police. His work, published under the name Josiah Flynt, can best be described as autobiographical amateur sociology. Titles include *Tramping with Tramps* (1899) and *The World of Graft* (1901).
▷ *My Life* (1908)

WILLARD, Nancy
(1936–)

American poet and writer of fiction, born in Michigan. Willard has been described as a 'domestic poet par excellence'. Her young son features in the collection *Household Tales of Moon and Water*. Her cycle of poems for children, *A Visit to William Blake's Inn: Poems for Innocent and Experienced Travellers* (1981) won a **Newbery** Medal. Willard lectures in English at Vassar and is a member of the **Lewis Carroll** and **George MacDonald** societies.

WILLIAMS, Charles Walter Stansby
(1886–1945)

English poet, novelist, biographer and theologian, born in London and educated at University College, London. For many years he was a member of the editorial staff of Oxford University Press. His first volume of poetry, *The Silver Stair* (1912), is considered to be influenced by **Yeats**, while his later work, such as the plays *Thomas Cranmer* (1936) and *Seed of Adam* (1948), echo the currently fashionable and high-minded verse drama written by **T S Eliot**. He wrote several sensational psychological and supernatural thrillers, such as *Many Dimensions* (1931) and *All Hallows Eve* (1944), as well as books meditating upon the Arthurian legend, and theological works including *Descent of the Dove* (1939). Much of his writing, in all its forms, deals with the fundamental conflict between good and evil and the question of individual redemption. His biographies include *James I* (1934) and *Elizabeth* (1936).

WILLIAMS, David John
(1896–1970)

Welsh writer, born in Rhydcymerau, a district in Carmarthenshire which he made famous in his autobiography *Hen Dŷ Ffarm* (1953, Eng trans *The Old Farmhouse*, 1961) and its sequel *Yn chwech ar Hugain Oed* (1959, 'Twenty-Six Years Old'). He worked as a collier but then became a schoolmaster. With **Saunders Lewis**, and as founder member of *Plaid Cymru*, he took part in the protest over the Penyberth bombing-school outrage, and was unjustly jailed as a result. He excelled in characterization, and was deservedly famous for his exemplary understanding of and love for animals.
▷ D Jenkins, *D. J. Williams* (1973)

WILLIAMS, Edward ('Iolo Morganwg')
(1747–1826)

Welsh poet, antiquary and cultural inventor, born in Llancarfan, Glamorgan. He worked there as a stonemason, and became a poet in Welsh and English. He had links with 18th-century Radicalism, mingling its ideas with Romantic exaltation of the Welsh past and established neo-Druidic cults and celebrations in Wales from 1792. He published collected poems purportedly by the 14th-century poet Dafydd ap Gwilym, which in fact were his own work. He co-edited *The Myvyrian Archaeology* (3 vols, 1801–7), and produced posthumously a vast corpus of cultural material from the Welsh past in varying degrees of authenticity. A brilliant forger whose deceptions far outlived his own time, his work prolonged, revived and reinvigorated ancient and modern Welsh culture.
▷ G J Williams, *Iolo Morganwg* (1963)

WILLIAMS, (George) Emlyn
(1905–87)

Welsh playwright and actor, born in Mostyn, Clwyd, the son of a steel-works foreman. He won a scholarship to Oxford, where he entered Christ Church. In 1927, attracted by the stage, he joined J B Fagan's repertory company. His first real success as a dramatist was with *A Murder has been Arranged* (1930). He then adapted a French play by René Fauchois—*The Late Christopher Bean* (1933)—and continued his success with the terrifying psychological thriller *Night Must Fall* (1935). He was not limited to light entertainment, and a seriousness of purpose characterizes most of his other work. Other successes were *The Corn is Green* (1938), *The Light of Heart*

(1940), *The Wind of Heaven* (1945), *Trespass* (1947) and *Accolade* (1951). He generally played the lead in his own and acted in other dramatists' plays, as well as appearing at the Old Vic and at Stratford, and featuring in films. His solo performance as **Charles Dickens** giving his celebrated readings from his works was greeted with acclaim, but a similar endeavour as **Dylan Thomas** did not meet with such success. He wrote the autobiographical *George* (1961) and *Emlyn* (1973), as well as *Beyond Belief* (1967), and a novel, *Headlong* (1980).

WILLIAMS, Francis
(c.1700–c.1770)

Jamaican poet, born of free negro parents but sent to an English grammar school and Cambridge University by the duke of Montagu who wanted to discover if a negro, properly educated, could become 'as capable of literature as a white person'. On return to Jamaica he opened a school in Spanish Town, teaching reading, writing, Latin and mathematics. Of his verse, only one ode in elegant Latin survives. Addressed to George Haldane on his appointment as Governor of Jamaica (1759), it voices conflicting feelings of pride in his British nurture and humility as a black, but pleads that there is no colour distinction in virtue or learning ('honesto nullus inest animo, nullus in arte color').
▷ E Long, *The History of Jamaica* (1774)

WILLIAMS, Helen Maria
(c.1761–1827)

British writer, born in London, daughter of a Welsh army officer, but educated by her Scottish mother at Berwick-upon-Tweed after her father's death in 1770. She lived in London from 1781, intimate with radical and feminist intellectuals. An ardent supporter of the French Revolution, she settled in France in 1792, where her Girondist views landed her in prison (1793). From 1782 she published voluminously: poems, novels, history, translations and the much admired series of *Letters from France* (1790–6), giving vivid if inaccurate eye-witness accounts of the revolution. Her poems are mostly sentimental or politically idealistic, condemning slavery and colonialism. Her novel *Julia* (1790), modelled on **Rousseau**'s *Nouvelle Héloïse*, highlights the dangers of excessive sensibility and uncontrolled passion. *Poems on Various Subjects* was published in 1823.
▷ L D Woodward, *Une adhérente anglaise de la Révolution française, Hélène-Maria Williams* (1930)

WILLIAMS, Jesse Lynch
(1871–1929)

American novelist, short-story writer and playwright, born in Sterling, Illinois. He graduated from Princeton University in 1892, and published his first book, *Princeton Stories*, in 1895. He also wrote a number of novels, including *The Married Life of the Frederic Carrolls* (1910), *Not Wanted* (1923) and *She Knew She Was Right* (1930). He is best-known as a dramatist, and won the Pulitzer Prize for Drama in 1918 with the social comedy *Why Marry?* (1917). His first play, *The Stolen Story* (1906), drew on his experiences as a journalist with the New York *Sun*. His other plays include *Why Not?* (1922) and the comedy *Lovely Lady* (1925).

WILLIAMS, John A(lfred)
(1925–)

American novelist and journalist, born in Mississippi. Williams joined the US Navy during World War II and was admitted to the hospital corps. Bitter at the racism he experienced in the navy (he was assigned to a land force because 'black hospital corpsmen were not wanted aboard ship'), all his novels have been about the black plight. *The Angry Ones* (1960) was about black musicians, *!Click Song* (1982) about the ups and downs of a black writer, and *This Is My Country Too* (1965) is a collection of powerfully felt essays.

WILLIAMS, Raymond
(1921–88)

Welsh critic and novelist, born in Pandy, Gwent, the son of a railway signalman. Educated at King Henry VIII Grammar School, Abergavenny and Cambridge, he wrote *Culture and Society* (1958), which required socialists to seek inspiration in such figures as **Edmund Burke**, **Robert Southey** and **Thomas Carlyle**. He opened up questions of mass readership and cultural and ethical values in *The Long Revolution* (1966). He was made a fellow of Jesus College, Cambridge, in 1961, and was Professor of Drama there from 1974 to 1983. He was active in New Left intellectual movements, producing the *May Day Manifesto* (1968), but his novels *Border Country* (1960), *Second Generation* (1964), *The Volunteers* (1978), *The Fight for Manod* (1979) and *Loyalties* (1985) underline the significance of Welsh consciousness for him, and he was later identified with Welsh nationalism. Of his many major works in socio-literary criticism, *The Country and the City* (1973) was perhaps the most inspirational.

WILLIAMS, Tennessee, originally **Thomas Lanier**
(1911–83)

American playwright, born in Columbus, Mississippi, the son of a travelling salesman. Prone to illness as a child, he found writing to be a tonic. He had an itinerant college education, first at Washington University in St Louis, then at the University of Missouri, finally receiving a degree from the University of Iowa in 1938. He worked at various menial jobs, among them as a poet-waiter at a Greenwich Village restaurant and as a cinema usher. Recognition of his literary skill came in 1940, when he received a Rockefeller Fellowship for his first play, *Battle of Angels*. In 1943 he signed a six-month contract with M-G-M, later cancelled when he submitted a script that became *The Glass Menagerie*. This play, which in 1945 earned him the New York Drama Critics' Circle Award, introduced him as an important American playwright. He then wrote *Summer and Smoke* (1948), and in 1948 was awarded the Pulitzer Prize for *A Streetcar Named Desire*. After *The Rose Tattoo* (1951) and *Camino Red* (1953), he won the Pulitzer Prize again in 1955 for *Cat on a Hot Tin Roof*. He continued with *Suddenly Last Summer* (1958), *Sweet Bird of Youth* (1959) and *The Night of the Iguana* (1961). He won the Gold Medal for Literature in 1969 from both the American Academy of Arts & Letters and the National Institute of Arts and Letters. In addition to his plays, he published collections of poetry—*The Summer Belvedere* (1944), *Winter of Cities* (1956); and short stories—*Hard Candy* (1954), *Eight Mortal Ladies Possessed* (1974) and *It Happened the Day the Sun Rose* (1982). He wrote one novel, *The Roman Spring of Mrs Stone* (1950), and wrote the scripts for several films, including *Baby Doll* (1956). *Where I Live: Selected Essays* (1978) is autobiographical.
▷D Spoto, *The Kindness of Strangers* (1985)

WILLIAMS, Waldo
(1904–71)

Welsh poet, born in Haverfordwest. He was educated at Narberth Grammar School and University College, Aberystwyth. Considered by many to be the most astonishingly original poet in the Welsh language, his work, deeply influenced by the Romantic poets, is concerned with universal brotherhood and mankind's relationship with the natural world. A committed pacifist, he supported civil disobedience as advocated by **Henry Thoreau** and Mahatma Gandhi. In 1950 he withheld his income tax in response to the Korean War. He spent six weeks in prison for non-payment of tax in 1960, and served a second sentence in 1961.
▷B G Owens, *Gwaithacu Waldo Williams* (1972)

WILLIAMS, William Carlos
(1883–1963)

American poet, novelist and also a cultural historian. An 'offshore American', with

French, Jewish, Basque and British antecedents, he was born in Rutherford, Connecticut, and spent most of his life there. After returning from school in Switzerland and Paris, he took his MD at the University of Pennsylvania, Philadelphia. Following an internship in New York City, he went to Leipzig to study paediatrics, returning to Rutherford as a general practitioner and paediatrician until his retirement. At Philadelphia, he had met both **Ezra Pound** and **Hilda Doolittle** ('HD'), both of whom had a considerable impact on his developing interest in poetry. His first volume, *Poems*, had been privately printed in Rutherford in 1909. The second and third, *The Tempers* (1913) and *Al Que Quiere!* (1917), established a distinctive voice and steered him towards the Modernist avant-garde. *Kora in Hell* (1920) was a book of experimental prose improvisations in the manner of **Rimbaud** and **Baudelaire**, but it was with *Spring and All* (1923) and his ironic *The Great American Novel* (1923) that he reached full creative maturity. *In the American Grain* (1925) was a brilliant study of American myths, strongly influenced by **D H Lawrence**'s mytho-psychoanalytic *Studies in Classic American Literature* (1923); it provided a critical counterbalance to prevailing Puritan explanations of American culture. In 1928, he attempted a real novel for the first time, *A Voyage in Pagany*. His poetic output had slackened considerably and it was not until *Collected Poems, 1921–1931* appeared in 1934 that he seemed to be back on track. Other volumes followed. In 1937 he published *White Mule* (1937), the first in a trilogy of novels completed by *In the Money* (1940) and *The Build-Up* (1952), but it was in 1946 that he published the first book of his poetic masterpiece, *Paterson*, a vast synoptic study of a (real) American town. Parts II (1948), III (1949) and IV (1951) deal with the search for an authentic American language in verse (echoes of **Whitman** are prevalent), mythic destruction and rebirth (akin to elements in Pound's *Cantos*), and the poet-narrator's ageing; a fifth section was added in 1958. Williams's objectivist credo 'No ideas but in things' had become a major tenet of Modernist writing and he remained a rallying-point for the New York avant-garde. His main works after *Paterson* were *The Desert Music* (1954), *Journey to Love* (1955) and *Pictures from Breughel* (1962), though two retrospective volumes, *The Collected Later Poems* (1950, rev edn 1963) and *The Collected Earlier Poems* (1951) exerted greater influence on a rising generation. He suffered the first of a series of cerebral episodes in the early 1950s, shortly after completing his *Autobiography* (1951). These steadily incapacitated him, forcing his retiral and severely curtailing his writing. A great, late poem, 'Asphodel', was written on a typewriter, using the tab key to create a staggered, three-line strophe. It is a mysterious, curiously elusive meditation on death, written by a man who, having dealt with mortality all his professional life, found himself facing up to his own extinction.

▷C F Terrell, *Williams: Man and Poet* (1983)

WILLIAMS PANTYCELYN, William
(1717–91)

Welsh hymn-writer, poet, translator and prose writer, born in Cefn-coed in Carmarthenshire. His mother, widowed in 1742, took him to live in Pantycelyn, hence his name. He devoted his life to itinerant preaching on behalf of the Methodist movement, and was ultimately regarded as one of the leaders of Welsh Methodism. The most important hymn-writer of Wales, he is seen by some (exaggeratedly) as its most important poet too. His hymns are as good as anyone's have been, possibly even better, and the 5 500-line poem *Golwg ar Deyrnas Crist* (1756, rev edn 1764, 'A View of Christ's Kingdom') is an extraordinary—although flawed—achievement. *Bywyd a Marwolaeth Theomemphus* (1764, 'The Life and Death of Theomemphus'), another long (6 000-line) poem, is a dramatic work without precedent in Welsh or any other poetry, which describes the spiritual pilgrimage of its hero in often startling detail. He wrote many theological works (he had produced over 90 volumes by the time of his death), and seriously deserves attention outside his native land as a poet and thinker of the first rank. The study of him by **Saunders Lewis** is in itself a critical classic; its views are attacked in the article quoted below.

▷S Lewis, *Williams Pantycelyn* (1927); *Anglo-Welsh Review*, 15, 35 (1965)

WILLIAMSON, David Keith
(1942–)

Australian playwright, born in Melbourne, Victoria. He graduated in mechanical engineering from Monash University, Melbourne, but turned to writing plays and scripts for films and television. His first works to receive recognition were *The Removalists* (1972) and *Don's Party* (1973); other successes include *The Club* (1977) and *The Perfectionist* (1982). Mostly leaning on the male-oriented Australian 'yuppie' class, his plays are much of a kind, though *What If You Died Tomorrow* (1974) shows the serious–comic side of a writer's life. Some of his stage works have subsequently been filmed, and he has also written other film scripts, including those for *Gallipoli* (1981) and *Phar Lap* (1983).

WILLIAMSON, Henry
(1895–1977)

English author, born in Bedfordshire. After service in World War I he became a journalist, but turned to farming in Norfolk and eventually settled in a cottage on Exmoor. He wrote several semi-autobiographical novels, including his long series *A Chronicle of Ancient Sunlight* on the life story of the hero, Phillip Maddison. He is best known, however, for his classic nature stories, starting with *The Peregrine's Saga* (1923) and *The Old Stag* (1926). He achieved enduring fame with *Tarka the Otter* (1927, Hawthornden Prize) and *Salar the Salmon* (1935). His trenchant anti-war novel *A Patriot's Progress* (1930) was much admired, but his support for Mosley and Hitler greatly damaged his reputation. He wrote two autobiographical works, *The Wet Flanders Plain* (1929) and *A Clear Water Stream* (1958), and a biography of his friend T E Lawrence (1941).
▷H F West, *The Dreamer of Devon* (1932)

WILLIAMSON, Thames (Ross)
(1894–)

American novelist and non-fiction writer, born in Ohio. Williamson is astonishingly prolific and has used as many as five pseudonymns, including 'S. S. Smith'. He has one of those classic fly-leaf biographies: ran away from home at 14 to join the circus and became a hobo, etc. His earliest novel was *Run, Sheep, Run* (1925) and he has written a number of textbooks, including an *Introduction to Sociology* (1926). More mature works include *Far North Country* (1944), about Alaska, and *The Gladiators* (1948).

WILLINGHAM, Calder Baynard, Jr
(1922–)

American novelist. He was born in Atlanta, Georgia, and educated in the South at Charleston and Charlottesville. His first novel, *End as a Man* (1947), appeared in a year when a number of the post-war literary lions were making their debut, and he was catapulted into prominence. Throughout his career—later novels include *Geraldine Bradshaw* (1950), *Reach to the Stars* (1951) and his best, *To Eat a Peach* (1955)—Willingham struck a balance between the hard, action-driven dictates of the bestseller list and a more contemplative style that offered striking insights into human motivation. His short stories, *The Gates of Hell* (1951), are rather disappointing and gave warning of the diminishing of his powers that was to set in after *To Eat a Peach*. Like many novelists, Willingham struck a pact with Hollywood, writing screenplays for Stanley Kubrick's *Paths of Glory* (1957), as well as *The Vikings* (1958), *One-Eyed Jacks* (1961), *The Graduate* (1967) and *Little Big Man* (1970).

WILLIS, Nathaniel Parker
(1806–67)

American editor and writer, born in Portland, Maine. He published several volumes of poetry, founded the *American Monthly Magazine* in Boston (1829) and in 1831 visited Europe, and contributed to the *New York Mirror* his *Pencillings by the Way*. Appointed *attaché* to the American legation at Paris, he visited Greece and Turkey, and returned to England in 1837. He contributed to the London *New Monthly* his *Inklings of Adventure* (collected 1836), and published *Letters from under a Bridge* (1840). In 1844 he engaged in editing the *Daily Mirror*, revisited Europe, and published *Dashes at Life with a Free Pencil* (1845). He returned to New York in 1846, and established the *Home Journal*, in which much of his work first appeared. His sister, Sara Payson Willis, 'Fanny Fern' (1811–72), married to the biographer James Parton, was a popular writer.
▷C P Aulzer, *Nathaniel Willis* (1969)

WILLIS, Sara Payson, pseud Fanny Fern
(1811–72)

American essayist, columnist and children's author, the sister of **N P Willis**. Her *Fern Leaves from Fanny's Portfolio* (1853) which, despite its fey title, was witty and acerbic, sold over 70000 copies in its first year. The first follow-up appeared in 1854. Sara Willis's talent for satire was put to good effect the following year when, enraged by rumours concerning her rakish brother, she wrote *Ruth Hall*, a novel which does not spare members of her own family.

WILLS, William Gorman
(1828–91)

Irish playwright and poet, born in Kilkenny County. He studied at Trinity College, Dublin, and started as an artist, and was a successful portrait painter. His *Man o'Airlie* (1866) was a huge success on the stage, followed by *Charles I* (1872), *Jane Shore* (1876), *Olivia* (1878) and *Claudian* (1885), as well as a version of *Faust* (1885). He also wrote novels, but considered verse a higher literary form. His poems include a long work, *Melchior* (1885), and his ballads include 'I'll sing thee Songs of Araby'.

WILLUMSEN, Dorrit
(1940–)

Danish novelist, short-story writer and poet, born in Copenhagen. Her first book of short stories (1965) established her as a notable modernist with conspicuous stylistic skills.

The novel *Da* (1968, 'Then') explores the gap between a child's perspective on the world and the adult one, while *the krydderi acryl salær græshopper* (1970, 'tea spice acrylic fee grasshoppers') and *Modellen Coppelia* (1973, 'Coppelia the Model') transcend the traditional boundaries between genres, the former raising issues of motherhood by means of a collage technique, and the latter combining poetry and short stories to illuminate the reification of woman. In the novel *Programmeret til kærlighed* (1981, 'Programmed for Love'), the character of a living doll is used to emphasize the conventional concept of woman. *Marie* (1983, Eng trans 1986) is a historical novel about Madame Tussaud.

▷A B Richard, *På sporet af den tabte hverdag. Om Dorrit Willumsens forfatterskab og den moderne virkelighed* (1979)

WILSON, Alexander
(1766–1813)

Scottish-born American ornithologist, born in Paisley, the son of a prosperous weaver, and regarded as the 'father of American ornithology'. He worked as a weaver from the age of 13, and as a travelling pedlar. He also wrote nature poetry and verses about life in the weaving sheds, and published *Poems* (1790) and *Watty and Meg* (1792). He was prosecuted for a libellous poem against the mill-owners, which he denied writing, but was jailed for 18 months. In 1794 he emigrated to the USA, and became a schoolteacher in rural schools in New Jersey and Philadelphia. Encouraged by a neighbour, the naturalist William Bartram (son of the botanist John Bartram), he decided to devote himself to ornithology. He made several journeys across America, collecting species and drawing them, and wrote a poetic account of his first journey, an excursion on foot to Niagara Falls, in *The Foresters, A Poem* (1805). He had a long-running feud with the ornithologist John James Audubon. In 1806 he was employed on the American edition of *Rees's Cyclopaedia*, and prevailed on the publisher to undertake an illustrated *American Ornithology* (7 vols, 1808–14); the 8th and 9th volumes were completed after his death. Wilson's Storm-Petrel and Wilson's Phalarope were named in his honour.

▷J Wilson, *Alexander Wilson, Poet-Novelist* (1906)

WILSON, A(ndrew) N(orman)
(1950–)

English novelist, biographer, critic and journalist, born in Stone, Staffordshire, and educated at Rugby School and Oxford. Since publishing his first novel, *The Sweets of Pimlico* (1977), Wilson has maintained a hugely prolific output. The earlier novels were comedies of manners, but in works such as *The Healing Art* (1980), in which a patient is mistakenly diagnosed as having cancer, and *Wise Virgin* (1982), dealing with the relationship between an academic and his daughter, he looks more closely at specific moral issues. Later works are perceptive, waspish, atmospheric and topical, and include *A Bottle in the Smoke* (1989), in which a young man seeks fame and art in the Soho of the 1950s, and *The Vicar of Sorrows* (1993), in which a disenchanted vicar falls for a young, female New Age traveller. His biographies include *Sir Walter Scott* (1980), *Milton* (1983), *Tolstoy* (1987) and the controversial *Jesus* (1992). He has frequently given the public impression of being a High Church Conservative, and can be a harsh literary and ethical commentator.

WILSON, Sir Angus Frank Johnstone
(1913–91)

English writer, born in Bexhill, Sussex, the son of an English father and a South African mother. He was educated at Westminster School and Merton College, Oxford. He joined the staff of the British Museum library in 1937. He began writing in 1946 and rapidly established a reputation with his brilliant collection of short stories, *The Wrong Set* (1949), satirizing the more aimless sections of pre-war middle-class society. *Such Darling Dodos* (1950), *For Whom the Cloche Tolls* (1953) and *A Bit off the Map* (1957) added to his prestige, and in 1955 he gave up his office of deputy-superintendent of the British Museum reading room to devote himself solely to writing. The novels *Hemlock and After* (1952) and *Anglo-Saxon Attitudes* (1956) were both best-sellers, and his later novels, including *The Old Men in the Zoo* (1961), *Late Call* (1965) and *No Laughing Matter* (1967), an ambitious family chronicle of the egocentric Matthews family spanning the 20th century, also received critical acclaim. His later novels include *As If By Magic* (1973) and *Setting the World on Fire* (1980). He also wrote one play, *The Mulberry Bush* (1955). He was Professor of English Literature at the University of East Anglia from 1966 to 1978.

▷J L Halio, *Angus Wilson* (1964)

WILSON, August
(1945–)

American playwright, born in Pittsburgh into a black working-class family. He dropped out of high school, but began to write poetry in his twenties, then turned to drama. His work focuses on black American life in both historical and contemporary settings, and draws on a wide variety of disparate technical and stylistic devices. He has been lionized as an original by some critics, and rejected by others, and has twice been awarded the Pulitzer Prize for Drama, for *Fences* in 1987 and *The Piano Lesson* in 1990. His other works include *Ma Rainey's Black Bottom* (1984) and *Joe Turner's Come and Gone* (1981).

WILSON, Colin Henry
(1931–)

English novelist, critic and commentator, born in Leicester, who held a variety of jobs, from tax collector to hospital porter, before turning full-time to writing. His first book, *The Outsider* (1956), a study of alienation, precisely caught (or was caught by) the literary spirit of the times, for it followed in the wake of **Kingsley Amis**'s *Lucky Jim* and appeared in the same year as **John Osborne**'s *Look Back in Anger*. Nothing Wilson has written since has drawn equal attention, although he has maintained a stream of novels, including violent thrillers of the 'psychological' genre, such as *The Mind Parasites* (1967) and *The Janus Murder Case* (1984). Several of his volumes of non-fiction deal with the paranormal and the occult.
▷H Ritchie, *Success Stories* (1988)

WILSON, Edmund
(1895–1972)

American literary critic, social commentator and novelist, born in Red Bank, New Jersey. He was educated at Princeton, became a journalist with *Vanity Fair* and Editor of the *New Republic* (1926–31), and was chief book reviewer for the *New Yorker*. A lively, waspish critic of other writers, his own fiction, of which *Memoirs of Hecate Country* (1946) is the most notable example, is largely forgotten. But few critics have caused such a stir as he, and he was more listened to than most. *Axel's Castle* (1931), a study of Symbolist literature, is a landmark, but *To the Finland Station* (1940), an account of the origins of the Bolshevik Revolution, and *The Wound and the Bow* (1941), a study of the relation between psychic malaise and creativity, are no less significant. In *Patriotic Gore: Studies in the Literature of the Civil War* (1962) he surveyed in detail the writers of the period. Over a wide-ranging oeuvre and argumentative life he published on many subjects and in a variety of forms, encompassing plays, articles, correspondence (see that with **Nabokov**) and, in *The Scrolls from the Dead Sea* (1955), for which he learned Hebrew, a contentious but illuminating guide to a complex subject. Various memoirs detailing his life have appeared; he married four times, the third marriage being to the novelist **Mary McCarthy**, whose own turbulent career he defended even after their relationship had foundered.
▷D Castronovo, *Edmund Wilson* (1984)

WILSON, Ethel
(1888–1980)

Canadian novelist and short-story writer, born in South Africa: her childhood was spent in England after the death of her mother, and in Vancouver with her grandmother, after the death of her father in 1898. As a novelist, she handles the emotional entanglements of her characters with great skill, focusing on the sacrificial and selfish nature of human love. Her fiction is characterized by a compelling and distinctive Canadian landscape, into which these characters are woven. Her first novel, *Hetty Dorval* (1947), was followed by *The Innocent Traveller* (1949), *The Equations of Love* (1952), *Swamp Angel* (1954) and *Love and Salt Water* (1956), her final novel. She also wrote many short stories, collected as *Mrs Golightly and Other Stories* (1961).
▷ *Papers from the 'Ethel Wilson Symposium'*, University of Ottawa (1981)

WILSON, Harriet
(c.1807–c.1870)

American writer, born in Fredericksburg, Virginia. She was author of the first book by an Afro–American woman—*Our Nig (Sketches from the Life of a Free Black)* (1859). Written in the style of the sentimental 19th-century novel, it tells the story of a mixed marriage. When the book's authorship was first discovered, oversimplistic parallels were drawn between Wilson's own life and the story she told. Since the book's reprinting in 1983 Wilson has been given the credit due for her stylistic intelligence and the cool way in which she handles the power struggles at play in a nominally Christian family.

WILSON, Harry Leon
(1867–1939)

American novelist, humorist and playwright, born in Illinois. Wilson joined the staff of *Puck* in 1892 and became its editor four years later. He left in 1902, and began to produce his best work. He is mainly remembered for *Ruggles of Red Gap* (1915), a comical novel about an English butler in the American West, made into a film starring Charles Laughton in 1935. Wilson became rich when he sold the rights to *Merton of the Movies* (1922), the story of a small-town clerk making it to Hollywood. His most notable stage success was a play written in collaboration with his friend **Booth Tarkington**, *The Man from Home* (1907), which ran for six years.

WILSON, John, pseud Christopher North
(1785–1854)

Scottish critic and essayist, born in Paisley. He studied at Glasgow University and Magdalen College, Oxford, where he won the

Newdigate Prize for poetry and gained a reputation as an outstanding athlete. In 1807 he bought an estate at Elleray, Westmorland, and became acquainted with the Lake District circle of poets (**Wordsworth**, **Coleridge**, **De Quincey**, **Southey**). Here he wrote three long poems, *The Isle of Palms* (1812), *The Magic Mirror* (1812, addressed to Sir **Walter Scott**) and *The City of the Plague* (1816). Having lost his estate through an uncle's mismanagement, he settled in Edinburgh as an advocate in 1815. In 1817 he joined **John Gibson Lockhart** and **James Hogg** in launching *Blackwood's Magazine*. Despite lacking any qualification for the post, he was appointed Professor of Moral Philosophy at Edinburgh (1820–51) in succession to Thomas Brown. As contributing editor of *Blackwood's* he wrote several notable series under the pseudonym 'Christopher North', such as *Noctes Ambrosianae* (1822–35), and a series of rural short stories, *Lights and Shadows of Scottish Life* (1822). He also published two novels, *The Trials of Margaret Lyndsay* (1823) and *The Foresters* (1825). His *Works* (1855–8) were edited by his son-in-law, James Frederick Ferrier.
▷ E Swan, *Christopher North* (1934)

WILSON, John Mackay
(1804–35)

Scottish writer and editor, born in Tweedmouth. He is known for his *Tales of the Borders* (6 vols, 1834–40), originally issued in weekly numbers, and continued after his death for his widow with Alexander Leighton (1800–74) as editor.

WILSON, Lanford
(1937–)

American playwright, born in Lebanon, Missouri, whose first full-length play, *Balm in Gilead* (1964), is set among the characters haunting a seedy all-night coffee shop. A similar location, that of a down-at-heel city hotel, forms the backdrop for one of his most successful dramas, *The Hot l Baltimore* (sic, 1973). These are sympathetic and shrewdly observed plays; later pieces are sharper, such as *The 5th of July* (1978), in which a group of former student radicals meet at the home of Ken Talley, a crippled Vietnam veteran. The play is the first part of a series including *Talley's Folly* (1979, Pulitzer Prize) and *Talley and Son* (1985), looking at generations of the Talley family. *Burn This* (1987), the most publicized of his more recent plays, is a violent, bravura piece, and deals with a man calling at his dead brother's former home and compulsively falling for his grieving female partner.

WILSON, Robert
(?1553–1600)

English actor and playwright, of whom few biographical details are known. During the early 1570s he became a member of the Earl of Leicester's Men, an acting company, and in 1583 appeared in the company of Queen Elizabeth's Men. Three plays survive which he is known to have written either wholly, or on which he was the dominant collaborator. These are *The Ladies of London* (c.1581), *The Three Lords and Three Ladies of London* (c.1589) and *Prophecy* (c.1594). All are robust dramas with elements of comedy and satire.

WILSON, Sloan
(1920–)

American novelist, born in Connecticut. He is famous for *The Man in the Grey Flannel Suit* (1955), but is usually classed as a merely popular writer; a few have made higher claims for him. *The Man in the Grey Flannel Suit*, about a business executive called Tom Rath, is a kind of plea, sometimes touching, for 'ordinary values'. Books such as *All the Best People* (1970) are readable, untidy, and deliberately unsubtle; a critic thought that in his admiration for the middle classes Wilson created an effect different from the one he intended: 'not without a certain horror'.

WINCHILSEA, Anne Finch, Countess of, née **Kingsmill**
(1661–1720)

English poet, born in Sidmonton, near Southampton. She was daughter of Sir William Kingsmill, and in 1684 she married Heneage Finch, Earl of Winchilsea (from 1712). Her longest poem, a Pindaric ode called *The Spleen*, was printed in 1701; her *Miscellany Poems* in 1713. She was a friend of **Pope**, **Swift** and **Gay**, and her nature poems were admired by **Wordsworth** in his *Lyrical Ballads*.
▷ K M Rogers, in S Gilbert and S Gubar, *Shakespeare's Sisters* (1979)

WINKLER, Eugen Gotlob
(1912–36)

German painter, story writer, poet and critic, born in Zürich, son of an engineer. Known only as an essayist and frustrated artist who could not equal the achievements of his admired Van Gogh, he committed suicide in Munich, whereupon his friends discovered his work, which they published in two volumes. He admired **Ernst Jünger**, and offers an example of extreme late decadence and 'art for art's sake' nihilism; unfortunately he was possessed of only a minor talent, and this, together with persecution by Nazi officials and inability to fend for himself in ordinary life, persuaded him to kill himself. The chief influence upon him was **Paul Valéry**.

WINTERS, (Arthur) Yvor
(1900–68)

American critic and poet, born in Chicago. He was educated at Chicago, Colorado, and Stanford universities, and in 1949 was appointed Professor of English at Stanford. His verse was published in *The Immobile Wind* (1921), *The Bare Hills* (1927), *The Proof* (1930), *The Journey* (1931), *Before Disaster* (1934) and *The Giant Weapon* (1943). A *Collected Poems* was published in 1952, winning the Bollingen Prize. However, he is remembered primarily as a quirky, irascible critic, anti the expressionists and with a sharp eye for detail. Significant books are *Maule's Curse* (1938), *In Defence of Reason* (1947), *The Function of Criticism* (1957) and *Uncollected Essays and Reviews* (1976).
▷T Comito, *In Defense of Winters* (1986)

WINTERSON, Jeanette
(1959–)

English novelist, born in Manchester who, after graduating from Oxford, worked in London fringe theatre and in publishing. Her first novel, the autobiographical *Oranges Are Not the Only Fruit* (1985), recounts an upbringing as the daughter of fundamentalist Christian parents and the emergence of her lesbian sensibilities. It was critically acclaimed, as was *Sexing the Cherry* (1989), a far more experimental novel set in a fantastical 17th century. *Written On the Body* (1992) was followed in 1994 by *Art and Lies*. A confident, often provocative writer, her work is deliberately challenging.

WISEMAN, Adele
(1928–)

Canadian novelist, born in Winnipeg. Wiseman's parents had fled the Ukraine and her first novel, *The Sacrifice* (1956), was an exploration of the immigrant mentality. Wiseman has not been prolific. *Crackpot* (1974) had as protagonist a strapping whore. *Memoirs of a Book Molesting Childhood and Other Essays* (1987) contains autobiographical material.

WISTER, Owen
(1860–1938)

American author, born in Philadelphia. He took a music degree at Harvard and intended to be a composer, but won fame with his novel of cowboy life in Wyoming, *The Virginian* (1902), and other books, including *Lin McLean* (1898) and *Lady Baltimore* (1906).
▷D Payne, *Owen Wister: chronicler of the West, gentleman of the East* (1985)

WITHEFORD, Hubert
(1921–)

New Zealand poet, a member of the 'Wellington Group' of the 1950s. His early work was included in *New Zealand New Writing* during World War II and later collected in *Shadow of the Flame: Poems 1942–7* (1950), followed by *The Falcon Mask* in 1951. Other books are *The Lightning Makes a Difference* (1962) and *A Native, Perhaps Beautiful* (1967). The best of his verse shows an awareness of his natural environment and relates it to an 'inner landscape'.

WITHER, George
(1588–1667)

English poet and pamphleteer, born in Bentworth, Hampshire. He studied at Magdalen College, Oxford (1604–6), and entered Lincoln's Inn in 1615. For his *Abuses Stript and Whipt* (1613) he was imprisoned. In prison he wrote a book of five pastorals, *The Shepherd's Hunting* (1615), followed by a love elegy, *Fidelia* (1617). It is supposed that his satire addressed to the king (1614), together with the Earl of Pembroke's intercession, procured his release. In 1621 appeared the satirical *Wither's Motto*, a curious piece of self-confession, which landed him in jail again. His finest poem is *Fair Virtue, or the Mistress of Philarete* (1622). There followed his *Hymns and Songs of the Church* (1623), *Psalms of David translated* (1631), *Emblems* (1634) and *Hallelujah* (1641). Now a fiery Puritan, in 1642 he sold his estate to raise a troop of horse for parliament, but was taken prisoner. Later Cromwell made him major-general in Surrey and master of the Statute Office. At the Restoration (1660) he lost his position and property, and, on suspicion of having written the *Vox Vulgi*, a satire on the parliament of 1661, was imprisoned. He was released in 1663. His poetry fell into almost complete oblivion, but the praises of **Robert Southey**, Sir Egerton Brydges, Hallam, and **Charles Lamb** in particular revived interest in his work.
▷C S Hansby, *The Literary Career of George Wither* (1969)

WITKIEWICZ, Stanislaw Ignacy
(1885–1939)

Polish novelist, playwright and painter, born in Cracow, universally known as 'Witkacy'. He was one of the most original minds of his generation, and only now are his novels beginning to be fully appreciated. He killed himself when the Nazis invaded his country. His novel *Nienasycenie* (1930, Eng trans *Insatiability*, 1975), is a dystopia worthy to rank with those of **Zamyatin**, **Orwell** and **Huxley**, but is subtler and more complex. The

English translation is a tour de force. It has been said of him that 'there is a terrible sanity in his self-induced madness'.

▷ Introduction to translation, above (1975)

WITTENWEILER, Heinrich
(fl.1420)

Swiss poet, from Wyl. He seems to have been a wealthy burger, and is author of a long, bawdy satire, *Der Ring*. It pokes fun at peasants, their coarseness and crude living, though the gentry do not emerge unscathed either, as a country wedding causes ructions and intrigue in the local community.

WITTIG, Monique
(1935–)

French novelist and critic. A radical lesbian and founder of the group Féministes Révolutionnaires, she gained notoriety in 1978 by claiming that 'Lesbians are not women', by which she meant that the conventional man-/woman opposition is inadequate for the gender analysis feminism should be undertaking. In *The Straight Mind and Other Essays* (1992) she describes her own position as 'Materialist Lesbianism' (despite the idealism), believing that 'it is oppression that creates sex'. Her avant-garde utopian novel *Les guérillères* (1969) intersperses scenes of an all-woman community fighting against men with otherwise blank pages containing series of women's names in capitals.

▷ E Ostrovsky, *A Constant Journey: The Fiction of Monique Wittig* (1991)

WODEHOUSE, Sir P(elham) G(renville)
(1881–1975)

English novelist, born in Guildford. He was educated at Dulwich College, and worked for the Hong Kong and Shanghai Bank for two years before beginning to earn a living as a journalist and story writer, writing the 'By the Way' column in the *Globe*. He also contributed to a series of school stories in a magazine for boys, the *Captain*, in which 'Psmith' first made an appearance. Going to America before World War I, he sold a serial to the *Saturday Evening Post* and for a quarter of a century almost all his books appeared first in that magazine. He was co-author and writer of the lyrics to 18 musical comedies, including *Kissing Time*. He married in 1914. World War II blighted his otherwise stainless reputation. Captured by the Germans at Le Touquet, he was interned then released but not allowed to leave Germany. Foolishly he agreed to make broadcasts for the Germans and though they were harmless he was branded as a traitor. Writing in his defence, **Orwell** observed that 'The general upshot of the talks...was that he had not been ill-treated and bore no malice'. Eventually his name was cleared but he made America his home where the climate allowed him to indulge his passion for golf. He became an American citizen in 1955. His copious oeuvre—he wrote over 100 books— falls into three well-marked periods; the school stories which include *The Pothunters* (1902) and *The Gold Bat* (1904); the American period, during which he wrote *Psmith, Journalist* (1915), *The Indiscretions of Archie* (1921) and *Piccadilly Jim* (1917); and what might be called the country house period in which can be included a plethora of titles set in country mansions, bachelor pads in the metropolis and exclusive golf clubs. It is to this group that characters like Lord Emsworth, Gussie Fink-Nottle, Bertie Wooster and his legendary valet, Jeeves, belong. Of his many felicitous titles, *Right Ho, Jeeves* (1934), *Quick Service* (1940) and *The Mating Season* (1949) stand out. Wodehouse summed up his attitude to writing thus: 'I believe there are two ways of writing novels. One is mine, making a sort of musical comedy without music and ignoring real life altogether; the other is going deep down into life and not caring a damn'.

▷ R Usborne, *Wodehouse at Work* (1961)

WOESTIJNE, Karel van de
(1879–1929)

Belgian (Flemish) poet and editor, born in Ghent. He was one of the chief members of the literary movement Van Nu en Straks ('Today and Tomorrow'), an individualistic, internationalistic and liberal tendency to which **Buysse**, **Streuvels** and **Teirlinck** subscribed. Woestijne was its great and most gifted poet, and his work has not yet received full recognition outside Belgium and the Netherlands. He has been authoritatively described as 'the only ... major twentieth-century poet in Dutch besides Achterberg'. Influenced by **Kloos**, **George** and **Rilke**, his poetry explores his own conceit of being both a hazel-nut and the greedy worm within it. There is no good English translation, but *Poèmes choisis* (1964) is a selection in a good French translation. He also wrote symbolic stories important in his literature.

WOIWODE, Larry Alfred
(1941–)

American novelist, story writer and poet, born in Carrington, North Dakota. His first novel, *What I'm Going to Do, I Think* (1970), attracted little attention, but his second, *Beyond the Bedroom Wall: A Family Album* (1975), earned him a high reputation. It is a novel of the midwest, spanning four generations, about the family established by a German immigrant of 1881. *Poppa John* (1981), on a much smaller scale, describes a pathetic old television actor who spouts pious rigmarole. Woiwode collected his poems in *Even Tide* (1977).

WOLCOT, John, pseud Peter Pindar
(1738–1819)

English satirist, born in Dodbrooke, Devon. He studied medicine for seven years in London, took his MD at Aberdeen (1767) and, going to Jamaica, became physician-general of the island. He returned to England to take holy orders, but soon started medical practice at Truro. Here he discovered the talents of the young painter John Opie, and went with him in 1780 to London, to devote himself to writing audacious satires in verse. His 60 or 70 poetical pamphlets (1778–1818) include *The Lousiad*, *The Apple-dumplings and a King*, *Whitbread's Brewery visited by their Majesties*, *Bozzy and Piozzi* and *Lyrical Odes* on the Royal Academy Exhibitions. Although witty and fluent, his works were coarse and ephemeral.

▷T Girton, *Drama with Two Aunts* (1959)

WOLF, Christa
(1929–)

German novelist, whose earlier career was spent in the Eastern bloc, a fact which has significantly restricted her publishing career. She was born in Landsberg, Warthe, and educated at Leipzig and Jena universities. Many of her books received only limited circulation in East Germany. The most important of them, *The Quest for Christa T* (1976), was published in English translation. Her novel/essay *Kassandra: Erzahlung* (1983) appeared in English two years later. The *Mosakuer Novelle* have not so far been translated. Wolf examines the fate of personality in totalitarian situations, by which she means something larger and more universal than the specific political situation in her homeland.

WOLF, Friedrich
(1883–1953)

German dramatist from Neuwied, an early communist who emigrated in 1933 and returned to East Germany in 1945. He was for long generally considered to be second only to **Bertolt Brecht** in importance in his chosen country. His first plays were expressionist, but his theatrical successes came with more conventional drama, particularly with *Professor Mamlocks Ausweg* (1935), made into a famous Soviet film, *Professor Mamlock*, the powerful account of a Jewish surgeon driven to suicide by his Nazi oppressors. His final plays are more socialist realist in type, but at the end of his life he publicly reproached himself for 'abandoning the fight against tyranny'.

▷H F Garten, *Modern German Drama* (1964)

WOLFE, Charles
(1791–1823)

Irish poet and clergyman, born in Blackhall, County Kildare. He was educated at Winchester, and Trinity College, Dublin. He took holy orders in 1817 and became curate of Ballyclog, County Tyrone, and Donoughmore, County Down (1818). He is remembered for his poem *The Burial of Sir John Moore at Corunna*, which appeared anonymously in 1817 and at once caught the admiration of the public.

WOLFE, Humbert
(1885–1940)

English poet and critic, born in Milan, Italy. In 1908 he entered the Civil Service, becoming in 1938 deputy secretary to the Ministry of Labour. He published *London Sonnets* (1919), *Lampoons* (1925), *Requiem* (1927), and several other collections of verse, all marked by deep feeling and meticulous craftsmanship. His critical writings included *Notes on English Verse Satire* (1929) and studies of **Tennyson**, **Robert Herrick**, **Shelley** and **George Moore**.

WOLFE, Thomas Clayton
(1900–38)

American novelist, born at Asheville, North Carolina, into a large family in an overcrowed house. His father, an alcoholic, was a skilled stone-cutter who sculpted tombstones for a living. In 1904 his mother decided to open a boarding-house in St Louis during the World's Fair, but her attempt at independence ended with the death of one of her sons. But in 1906 she opened 'The Old Kentucky Home', taking with her her youngest son, leaving the other children with their father. Thomas was educated at the University of North Carolina and at Harvard. His writing career began abortively as a playwright, and in 1925 he embarked on a turbulent affair with Mrs Aline Bernstein, a maternal figure who did much to encourage his writing, particularly his first novel *Look Homeward, Angel* (1929), which was patently autobiographical. The massive, shapeless manuscript of *Of Time and the River* (1935), its sequel, was honed into shape by Max Perkins, his editor at Scribner's. Both these novels feature Eugene Gant, Wolfe's alter ego. He later changed publishers and *The Web and the Rock* (1939) and *You Can't Go Home Again* (1940) were published posthumously. Prolix, careless, bombastic and over-ambitious, he nevertheless wrote vividly of people and places. Some assert that his best

work is to be found in the stories in *From Death to Morning* (1935). His *Letters* were published in 1956.
▷C H Holman, *Thomas Wolfe* (1960)

WOLFE, Tom (Thomas Kennerley)
(1931–)

American journalist, pop-critic and novelist, born in Richmond, Virginia. Graduating from Washington and Lee University, he received his doctorate in American Studies from Yale University. Later he worked as a reporter for the *Springfield Union*, *The Washington Post* and the New York *Herald Tribune*. A proponent of the New Journalism, his style is distinctive, hyper-clever and narcissistic. A fashion-leader and follower, he has written a number of books with eye-catching titles: *The Electric Kool-Aid Acid Test* (1968), about **Ken Kesey** and the Merry Pranksters, *Radical Chic & Mau-Mauing the Flak Catchers* (1970) and *The Kandy-Kolored Tangerine-Flake Streamline Baby* (1965). Much of his work previously appeared in periodicals like *The Rolling Stone*, as did his only novel, *The Bonfire of the Vanities* (1988), which was a bestseller.

WOLFF, Tobias
(1945–)

American short-story writer and novelist, born in Birmingham, Alabama. He signed up for the army while still a schoolboy, and was a paratrooper for four years, part of which time was spent on active service in Vietnam. His first collection of short stories, *In the Garden of the North American Martyrs*, was published in 1981, but it was the publication of his austere, disciplined novella *The Barracks Thief* in 1984 which earned him a place in the front rank of American writers. He has subsequently published a further volume of short stories, *Back in the World* (1985), and an autobiography, *This Boy's Life* (1989).

WOLFF-BEKKER, Elizabeth, originally Betje Dekker
(1739–1804)

Dutch novelist, poet, critic and translator, born in Flushing. In 1759 she married a parson 30 years older than herself, and until his death in 1777 studied literature (of which she had an extensive and profound knowledge), wrote amusing verse, and indulged her admiration for **Rousseau**. Then she set up house with **Agatha Deken**, with whom she wrote epistolary novels in the style of **Richardson**. *Willem Leevend* (1784–5), her masterpiece (for it was she who did most of the real work), has been described as superior even to Richardson, on account of her refusal to resort to melodrama. It has been pronounced to be too

long; but this is to fail to see the significance of its lengthy and often satirical theological passages. In fact *Willem Leevend* is, as has been said, 'a part of world literature', and a translation is seriously overdue: acute psychologically, sardonic, tolerant, humane, it is one of the great novels written by women, and remains to be discovered by English-speaking feminists. In 1788 Wolff-Bekker, who sometimes used the pseudonym 'Sylvania', had to go into exile in France with her friend Deken; when 10 years later they could return, they were forced to do hack translations. They died within a few weeks of each other.
▷H C M Ghijsen, *Boeket voor Betje en Aagje* (1954)

WOLFRAM VON ESCHENBACH
(fl. beginning of 13th century)

German poet, born near Anspach in Bavaria. He lived some time in the Warburg near Eisenach, at the court of the Count of Thuringia. As well as *Parzival* (Eng trans 1894) he left *Die Lyrik*, seven love songs, a short epic, *Willehalm*, and two fragments called *Titurel*. The *Parzival* is an epic, having for its main theme the history of the Grail, and is one of the most notable poems of the Middle Ages. From it Wagner derived the libretto of his opera *Parsifal*.
▷M F Riley, *Medieval German Love Lyrics* (1969)

WOLKER, Jiri
(1900–24)

Czech 'proletarian' poet who was early struck down by tuberculosis. Like **Alexander Blok**, he could combine love of Lenin with love of Christ. But his visionary poems and ballads, imbued with love of the poor and hope for a Utopian future, transcend categories. His work awaits complete translation into English.
▷A French, *The Poets of Prague* (1969)

WOLKERS, Jan Hendrick
(1925–)

Dutch novelist, dramatist (and painter and sculptor) from Oegstgeest, who was a dominant voice in his literature during the 1960s and 1970s. He was notorious amongst conservatives for the apparently 'pornographic' nature of his writing. Many of his novels were translated, including *Een roos van vlees* (1963, Eng trans *A Rose of Flesh*, 1967), about a couple whose negligence leads to their daughter's being scalded, and *Horrible Tango* (1967, Eng trans *The Horrible Tango*, 1970), based on his brother's life and death. He has not yet fully realized his considerable gifts.

WOLOSZYNOWSKI, Julian
(1898–)

Polish novelist, born in Serby, initially a poet. His work, in particular his meticulous novel about the romantic poet **Slowacki** (1928), has been described as 'deplorably underrated in official criticism' by the critic Jerzy Peter-kiewicz, but no one has yet responded to this enthusiasm. *Roc 1863* (1931) is an equally meticulous reconstruction of a revolutionary year in Polish history, illustrated with contemporary pictures.

WONGAR, Banumbir or Birimbir,
originally **Sreten Bozic**
(1936–)

Yugoslav-born writer, who emigrated to Australia in 1960. He was originally promoted as an 'aboriginal' author. His early short stories appeared under various names during the 1970s, collected as *The Sinner* (1972) and *The Trackers* (1978). His true origins were disclosed in 1981 but his trilogy of novels, *Karan* (1985), *Walg* (1986) and *Gabo Djara* (1987), show remarkable sympathy and an understanding of a marginal culture.

WOOD, Mrs Henry, née Ellen Price
(1814–87)

English novelist, born in Worcester, the daughter of a manufacturer. A spinal disease confined her to bed or a sofa for most of her life. She married Henry Wood, a ship agent living in France, but returned to England with him in 1860 and settled in Norwood. After his death in 1866 she settled in London, and wrote for magazines. Her second published novel, *East Lynne* (1861), had an immense success. She never rose above the commonplace in her many novels, but showed some power in the analysis of character in her anonymous *Johnny Ludlow* stories (1874–80). In 1867 she bought the monthly *Argosy*, which she edited, and her novels went on appearing in it long after her death.

WOODCOCK, George
(1912–)

Canadian critic, biographer, poet, dramatist, sometime anarchist. Woodcock was for many years in England, and edited the periodical *Now*, knew **George Orwell**, about whom he wrote a book (*The Crystal Spirit: George Orwell*, 1966), and was active in left-wing and anarchist circles. He returned to Canada soon after World War II, and became one of its leading interpreters, writing books on all aspects of it. **Julian Symons**, who had known him well, thought that he had written 'charming and poignant poems', but that when the war ended he 'lost his poetic vision'. *Selected*

Poems (1967) is his most representative collection. He is now best known as a critic and an interpreter.
▷P Hughes, *George Woodcock* (1974)

WOOLF, (Adeline) Virginia, née Stephen
(1882–1941)

English novelist, critic and essayist, born in London, daughter of Sir Leslie Stephen. She was close to her sister, Vanessa Bell, and was from an early age the family story-teller. She was taught at home, by her parents and governesses, and received an uneven education. In 1891 she started the *Hyde Park Gate News* which was read by grown-ups and appeared weekly until 1895. In it appeared her first efforts at fiction. Her father died in 1904 and the family moved to Bloomsbury where the family formed the nucleus of the Bloomsbury Group, comprising—among others—Keynes, **E M Forster**, Roger Fry, Duncan Grant and **Lytton Strachey**: philosophers, writers and artists. A year later she began her long association with the *Times Literary Supplement*. She married Leonard Woolf in 1912 and her first novel, *The Voyage Out*, was published in 1915. It was greeted cordially and though realistic there were hints of the lyricism which would later become her hallmark. But already her health was poor and she suffered recurring depressions and had attempted suicide in 1913. In 1917, she and Leonard formed the Hogarth Press, partly for therapeutic reasons. Its first publication was *Two Stories*, one by each of the founders. Her second novel, *Night and Day*, appeared in 1919. Again its mode is realistic, focussing on Katherine Hilberry, whose activities in a literary milieu are counterpointed with those of her friend Mary who is involved in the women's movement. Some critics still think it her best work. *Jacob's Room* followed in 1922 and marked a turning point in her fiction, and shows her experimenting with narrative and language. Well-received, it made her a celebrity. In 1924 she went to Cambridge to speak on 'Character in Modern Fiction'; the result was *Mr Bennett and Mrs Brown*, an attack on the 'Georgian novelists' **Arnold Bennett**, **John Galsworthy** and **H G Wells**, and can be read as her own aesthetic manifesto. Regarded now as an archetypal Modernist, she published in six years the three novels that have made her one of the century's great writers; *Mrs Dalloway* (1925), *To the Lighthouse* (1927) and *The Waves* (1931). But her work took its toll on her health and though she wrote prolifically she was beset by deep depressions and debilitating headaches. Throughout the 1930s she worked on *The Years*, which was published in 1937. A year later appeared *Three Guineas*, provisionally titled 'Professions for Women',

intended as a sequel to *A Room of One's Own* (1929), regarded as epochal by feminists. In this she stated that 'A woman must have money and a room of her own if she is to write fiction.' *Between the Acts*, an experimental novel, was published posthumously in 1941, after she had forced a large stone into her pocket and drowned herself in the River Ouse, near her home at Rodmell in Sussex. There are several volumes of essays, letters and diaries, indispensable to literary historians and gossips, as well as offering a remarkable entrée to the creative mind. She is, with **James Joyce** (whose novel, *Ulysses*, the Hogarth Press declined to publish), regarded as one of the great modern innovators of the novel in English.
▷Q Bell, *Virginia Woolf* (1972)

WOOLNER, Thomas
(1826–92)

English poet and sculptor, born in Hadleigh. He studied at the Royal Academy from 1842. In 1843 his first major painting, *Eleanor sucking the Poison from Prince Edward's Wound*, attracted much attention. As a conspicuous member of the Pre-Raphaelite Brotherhood he contributed poems to *The Germ*, which with others were published in a volume as *My Beautiful Lady* (1863). From 1852 to 1854 he was in Australia. He produced statues or portrait busts of most of his famous contemporaries (his bust of **Tennyson** is in Westminster Abbey). He was Professor of Sculpture at the Academy (1877–9). His other poems include *Pygmalion* (1881).
▷A Woolner, *A Life of Thomas Woolner* (1917)

WOOLSON, Constance Fenimore
(1840–94)

American short-story writer and novelist, grand-niece (on her mother's side) of **James Fenimore Cooper**. Woolson grew up in Cleveland, Ohio, and in her first novel, *Anne* (1862), described her education at the Cleveland Female Seminary. She moved to Europe with her sister in 1879 and spent much of her time in Italy, where she met and was praised by **Henry James**. Her best-known book is her last, *Horace Chase* (1894), which tells the story of a wife's relationship with her vulgar Southern husband. Woolson died in Venice in the year of this book's publication, apparently by suicide.
▷C B Torsney, *Constance Fenimore Woolson: The grief of artistry* (1989)

WORDSWORTH, Dorothy
(1771–1855)

English writer, only sister of **William Wordsworth**, born in Cockermouth, Cumberland. She was his constant companion through life, both before and after his marriage, and on tours to Scotland, the Isle of Man and abroad, the records of which are to be found in her *Journals*. The *Journals* show that Dorothy's keen observation and sensibility provided a good deal of poetic imagery for both her brother and his friend **Coleridge**—more than that, they regarded her as the embodiment of that joy in Nature which it was their object to depict. In 1829 she suffered a breakdown from which she never fully recovered. Her *Recollections of a Tour made in Scotland AD 1803* (1874) is a classic.
▷E de Selincourt, *Dorothy Wordsworth* (1933)

WORDSWORTH, William
(1770–1850)

English poet, born in Cockermouth, the son of an attorney. Orphaned at an early age, he was sent to Hawkshead in the Lake District for board and education and this was one of the formative periods of his life. His guardian sent him to Cambridge (1787–91), where he was exposed to agnostic and revolutionary ideas. A walking tour through France and Switzerland in 1790 showed him France under the influence of the earlier stage of the revolution before disillusionment had set in. Two immature poems belong to this period—*An Evening Walk* and *Descriptive Sketches*, both published in 1793. Leaving Cambridge without a profession, he stayed for a little over a year at Blois, and there he had an affair with Annette Vallon, the result of which was an illegitimate daughter, Ann Caroline. The incident is reflected in *Vaudracour and Julia*. The declaration of war with France (January 1793) drove the poet back to England, but the depressing poem *Guilt and Sorrow*, which dates from this period, shows that he was not yet cured of his passion for social justice. For a time he fell under the spell of **William Godwin**'s philosophic anarchism, but the unreadable *Borderers* shows that by 1795 he was turning his back both on the revolution and on Godwinism. With the help of his sister **Dorothy Wordsworth**, with whom he set up house at Racedown in Dorset, and of **Coleridge**, who had renounced his revolutionary ardour somewhat earlier, he discovered his true vocation, that of the poet exploring the lives of humble folk living in contact with Divine nature and untouched by the rebellious spirit of the times. When the Wordsworths settled at Alfoxden in Somerset with Coleridge three miles away at Nether Stowey (1797), there began a close association which resulted in *Lyrical Ballads* (1798), the first manifesto of the new poetry, which opened with Coleridge's *Ancient Mariner* and concluded with Wordsworth's *Tintern Abbey*.

The removal of the Wordsworths to Grasmere after a visit to Germany with Coleridge, and the marriage of the poet to Mary Hutchinson (1802), closes this first stormy period, with Wordsworth set on his proper task and modestly provided for by a legacy of £900. Now followed a long spell of routine work and relative happiness broken only by family misfortunes—the death of his sailor brother John (1805), which may have inspired the *Ode to Duty*, and Dorothy's mental breakdown. Meanwhile Napoleon's ambitions had completely discouraged the poet from revolutionary sympathies, as the patriotic sonnets sent to the *Morning Post* at about the time of the Peace of Amiens (1802–3) and after show. Apart from the sonnets, this was his most inspired period. The additions to the third edition of *Lyrical Ballads* (1801) contained the grave pastoral *Michael*, *Ruth* and four of the exquisite *Lucy* poems. The first of his tours in Scotland (1803), of which Dorothy wrote the perfect tour journal, yielded some fine poems, including *The Solitary Reaper*. The great poem he was now contemplating—*The Recluse*—was never finished, but *The Prelude*, the record of the poet's mind, was read to Coleridge in 1805. It remained unpublished till after his death, when it appeared with all the tamperings of a lifetime but substantially in its form of 1805, which fortunately has survived. Two volumes of poems appeared in 1807, the product of five years of intense activity. The ode *Intimations of Immortality* is only the loftiest of a number of masterpieces, including the patriotic sonnets, the *Affliction of Margaret*, the *Memorials of a Tour in Scotland*, the *Ode to Duty*, and many others. He had now reached the peak of his poetic form and the remainder of his work, including *The Excursion* (1814, which incorporated material from 'The Recluse'), the *Ecclesiastical Sonnets* and the *Memorials* of his various tours, do not fully reflect his genius. He succeeded **Robert Southey** as poet laureate in 1843.
▷M Moorman, *The Life of William Wordsworth* (1957–65)

WOUK, Herman
(1915–)
American novelist, born in New York City, the son of Jewish immigrants. He attended Columbia University, wrote radio scripts and served in the US navy in the South Pacific in World War II, the experience of which he drew on for his classic war novel, *The Caine Mutiny* (1951). It won the Pulitzer Prize and became a successful play and film. Later books—*Marjorie Morningstar* (1955) and *Youngblood Hawke* (1962)—sold well but did not critically eclipse his earlier success. Other books include *The Winds of War* (1971) and *War and Remembrance* (1975), which became popular television serials.

WRAXALL, Sir Nathanael William
(1751–1831)
English writer of memoirs, born in Bristol. He was in the East India Company's service, travelled over Europe (1772–9), and had a confidential mission from Queen Caroline-Matilda of Denmark to her brother George III. He published his *Cursory Remarks made in a Tour* in 1775, his *Memoirs of the Valois Kings* in 1777, entered parliament in 1780 as a follower of Lord North, but went over to Pitt. His next books were the *History of France from Henry III to Louis XIV* (1795); *Memoirs of the Courts of Berlin, Dresden, Warsaw, and Vienna* (1799); and the famous *Historical Memoirs of my own Time, 1772–84* (1815). For a libel on Count Woronzov, Russian envoy to England, he was fined £500 and sentenced to six months' imprisonment. Violent attacks on his veracity were made by the reviews, but Wraxall's *Answers* were accounted on the whole satisfactory. A continuation of *Memoirs* (1784–90) was published in 1836.

WREN, P(ercival) C(hristopher)
(1885–1941)
English novelist, born in Devon. He was successively a teacher, journalist, explorer and soldier before eventually finding fame as a writer with *Beau Geste* (1924). This novel of the French Foreign Legion has often been imitated, to the extent that the book itself now appears far more self-parodic in its repressed stoicism than it did when originally published. The book spawned a thousand sequels, among them one by Wren himself, *Beau Ideal* (1928). Among his many other novels, all of a similar stamp—adventurous subject matter, less-than-exciting prose style—are *Valiant Dust* (1932) and *The Uniform of Glory* (1941). None was able to emulate the success of *Beau Geste*.

WRIGHT, David McKee
(1869–1928)
Irish-born Australian–New Zealand poet, born in Ballynaskeagh, County Down, who migrated to New Zealand in 1887. He was a protestant minister. His ballads of bush life look to his near-contemporary **Henry Lawson**, though his more lyrical verse echoes **Henry Kendall**, and he idealizes the open-air life of itinerant workers in a manner which anticipates **W H Davies**. His first verses were published in New Zealand as *Aorangi* (1896), followed by his best-known collection, *Station Ballads* (1897). Some of these were reissued, with a memoir, by **John A Lee** as

The Station Ballads and Other Verses (1945). In 1910 Wright went to Sydney, where he freelanced on the *Bulletin*, using such pen-names as Mary McCommonwealth and Pat O'Maori, and for some years edited its celebrated literary section, the 'Red Page'. His most ambitious collection of verse was *An Irish Heart* (1918). He won the **Rupert Brooke** Memorial Prize for his poem 'Gallipoli' (1920), and in 1925 edited the *Poetical Works of Henry Lawson*. After a long relationship he married the poet **Zora Cross**.
▷ *The Station Ballads and Other Verses* (1945, with a memoir by J A Lee)

WRIGHT, Frances, or **Fanny**, also known as **Frances Darusmont**
(1795–1852)

Scottish-born American reformer and abolitionist, born in Dundee, the heiress to a large fortune. She emigrated to the USA in 1818 and the following year produced her play *Altorf*, dealing with the Swiss struggle for independence. She toured widely, publishing *Views of Society and Manners in America* in 1821, and, in 1822, a historical novel, *A Few Days in Athens*. In the company of the reformer Marie Joseph Lafayette, she founded a short-lived community for freed slaves at Nashoba in western Tenessee. Settling in New York in 1829, she published with Robert Dale Owen a socialist journal, *Free Enquirer*. One of the early suffragettes, whose courage and perseverance were a significant influence in the development of the women's movement, she campaigned vigorously against religion and for the emancipation of women. In 1838 she contracted an unhappy marriage with a Frenchman, William Philquepal d' Arusmont. They had one daughter and some time later divorced. After her marriage, the issues she championed grew increasingly controversial, such as birth control and the equal division of wealth.

WRIGHT, Harold Bell
(1872–1944)

American novelist, born on a farm in New York state and educated at Hiram College (1894–6). His novels, which he began to write in earnest after moving to the Ozark mountains for his health, were extraordinarily successful, although slammed by critics for their overly wholesome moral tone. Wright was, for 10 years, a pastor in the Church of Disciples, and the chief criticism of his books is that they are vehicles for preaching to a lay audience. *The Winning of Barbara Worth* (1911) eventually notched up sales of one and a half million dollars.

WRIGHT, James Arlington
(1927–80)

American poet, born in St Martin's Ferry, Ohio, and educated at Kenyon College and Washington University. He became a teacher, lecturing at Hunter College, New York City, from 1966 until his death. His first collection, *The Green Wall*, appeared in 1957, and was followed by eight more, including *The Branch Will Not Break* (1963), *Shall We Gather at the River?* (1968), and *To A Blossoming Pear Tree* (1977). His *Collected Poems* appeared in 1971 and won a Pulitzer Prize. Wright's subjects range from politics and social issues to the natural world, and while his writing is both direct and clear, his approach is always that of a compassionate humanitarian.

WRIGHT, Judith
(1915–)

Australian poet, born in Armidale, New South Wales. Her upbringing was on the family sheep farm, Wallamumbi, in pastoral New South Wales. She was educated at Sydney University and travelled in Britain and Europe before returning to Sydney (1938–9) to concentrate on her writing. The war disrupted her plans and lack of work led her back to her rural roots in the Queensland mountains, the source of her inspiration. *The Moving Image* (1946) was her first collection, since when she has been an industrious poet, critic, anthologist, editor and short-story writer. Her main volumes of poetry are *Woman to Man* (1949), *The Gateway* (1953), *The Two Fires* (1955), *Birds* (1962), *City Sunrise* (1964), *The Other Half* (1966), *Alive* (1973) and *Fourth Quarter and Other Poems* (1976). Her *Collected Poems 1942–1970* and *The Double Tree: Selected Poems: 1942–1976* were published in 1971 and 1978 respectively. Her literary criticism was published in *Preoccupations in Australian Poetry* (1965). *The Cry for the Dead* (1981) is an account of the impact of European immigration on the aborigines. A collection of essays on aboriginal culture, *Born of the Conquerors*, was published in 1991. She edited the Oxford anthology *A Book of Australian Verse* in 1956, and has written on **Charles Harpur** and **Henry Lawson**. In *The Generations of Men* (1959) and *The Cry for the Dead* (1981) she recreates from family documents the life of her pioneering pastoralist forebears, and in doing so demonstrates her own abiding affection for the Australian landscape. In 1993 she became the first Australian to receive the Queen's Medal for Poetry, awarded on the recommendation of the Poet Laureate.
▷ A K Thompson, *Critical Essays on Judith Wright* (1968)

WRIGHT, Mehetabel (Hetty), née Wesley
(1697–1750)

English poet, born in Epworth, elder sister of John and Charles Wesley. Well educated by her mother, she was reading Greek at the age of eight. In 1725, after leaving home and returning pregnant, she was forced to marry. Her husband ran a prosperous business as a plumber in London but treated her unkindly, and their children all died young. In 1744 she was converted to Methodism under her brother John's influence. Only two poems were printed in her life, others appeared posthumously, mainly in Wesleyan sources; eloquent laments for her children and indignation at the inequities of marriage are the predominant motifs.
▷R Lonsdale (ed), *Eighteenth-Century Women Poets* (1989)

WRIGHT, Richard Nathaniel
(1908–60)

American novelist, short-story writer and critic, born on a plantation in Mississippi. His father abandoned his family when he was five, and he was placed in an orphanage. His mother having had a stroke, he was ill-treated by relatives, received a poor education and was exposed to religious fanaticism. In the Depression he left the South and became a journalist, as well as joining the progressive Writers' Project. *Uncle Tom's Children*, a volume of short stories, appeared in 1938; by this time Wright had been manipulated by the Communist Party, and he consequently became a pessimistic humanist. A naturalist and later in Paris an existentialist who knew **Sartre**, he wrote *Native Son* (1940), a novel about a Negro youth who murders a white woman and is sent to the electric chair; this became a central—albeit problematic—work in the development of a black literary sensibility. *Native Son* was followed by *Black Boy* (1945), a harrowing autobiographical novel, and the novel *The Outsider* (1953).
▷A Gayle Jr, *Richard Wright: Ordeal of a Native Son* (1980)

WRIGHTSON, Patricia
(1921–)

Australian writer of award-winning children's fiction, born in Lismore, New South Wales. Her first book, *The Crooked Snake* (1955), marked the arrival of a writer sensitive to the concerns of youth and was followed by *The Bunyip Hole* (1957) with its introduction of aboriginal lore. *I Own the Racecourse!* (1968), an engaging study of a subnormal boy, won the **Hans Andersen** Award. Her trilogy of adventure stories featuring an aboriginal boy, *The Ice is Coming*, *The Dark*

Bright Water and *Behind the Wind*, were published as *The Book of Wirrun* in 1983.

WROTH, Lady Mary
(?1587–1651)

English poet, the most accomplished writer of prose fiction and poetry in her day, according to the *Norton Anthology of English Literature*. A friend of **Jonson** and the niece of **Philip Sidney** and **Mary, Countess of Pembroke**, in 1621 she published a long prose romance, *The Countess of Montgomery's Urania* (punctuated with verse eclogues, along the lines of Sidney's *Arcadia*), causing scandal by allusions to naughty goings-on at the Jacobean court. The work is, however, dull. More poetically inspired is her sonnet sequence *Pamphilia to Amphilanthus*, which has a woman speaker and in which the conventional sex roles are reversed.

WU CHENG-EN
(fl.16th century)

Chinese author of the novel *Hsi-yu chi* (1593, Eng trans *Monkey*, 1942), based on the pilgrimage of Hsuang Tsang.
▷C T Hsia, *The Classic Chinese Novels* (1968)

WULFSTAN
(d.1023)

Anglo-Saxon prelate and writer. He was Bishop of London (996–1002) and Archbishop of York from 1002, and also Bishop of Worcester (1003–16). He was the author of homilies in the vernacular, including a celebrated address to the English, *Sermo Lupi ad Anglos*.
▷K Jost, *Wulfstan Studien* (1950)

WURDEMANN, Audrey Mary
(1911–60)

American poet, born in Seattle, Washington. She graduated from the University of Washington, and lived in New York, where she married the writer Joseph Auslander (1897–1965); they collaborated on two books, including *The Islanders* (1951). She published her first collection of poems, *The House of Silk* (1936), when still in her mid-teens, and became the youngest recipient of the Pulitzer Prize for Poetry in 1935 for her collection *Bright Ambush* (1934). Her other collections are *The Seven Sins* (1935), *Splendour in the Grass* (1936) and the sonnet sequence *Testament of Love* (1938).

WURLITZER, Rudolph
(?1938–)

American novelist and screenplay writer. Little is known about Wurlitzer's background and his own enigmatic comments have not been designed to help. He came to attention in 1969, with a strange, apocalyptic novel called *Nog* (published as *The Octopus* in the UK), followed by *Flats* (1970), *Quake* (1972), a **Nathanael West**-like account of a Californian earthquake, and, after a decade working exclusively in Hollywood, *Slow Fade* (1974), which may be his best book. Wurlitzer co-wrote a play, *Two-Lane Blacktop* (1971), with Will Corry. It was subsequently turned into a cult movie by Monte Hellman. His next major movie success was the more mainstream but still modestly surreal *Pat Garrett and Billy the Kid* (1973) for Sam Peckinpah; Wurlitzer also appeared in the film. More recently he wrote and directed his own *Voyager* (1991), starring Sam Shepherd, in which many of the themes of his fiction—alienation, loneliness, societal breakdown—are given a definitive statement.

WYATT, Sir Thomas
(1503–42)

Major English poet and courtier, born in Kent. Wyatt published nothing in his lifetime (nor was that unusual), but has served as an exemplar for English love poets ever since. His best work, in his lyrics and sonnets, has a unique force and economy. He was regarded as the most important of all the English poets who imitated—and then added to—Italian models. The best edition remains Kenneth Muir's (1949, rev edn 1963), and standard life is Muir's *Life and Letters* (1963).

WYCHERLEY, William
(c.1640–1716)

English dramatist, born in Clive near Shrewsbury. In early youth he was sent to France, left Queen's College, Oxford without a degree, and entered the Middle Temple. For some years he lived as a man about town and a courtier, but took early to work as a dramatist. *Love in a Wood, or St James's Park*, a brisk comedy founded on **Charles Sedley**'s *Mulberry Garden*, was acted with much applause in 1671. Buckingham gave him a commission in a regiment, and King Charles II made him a present of £500. He served for a short time in the fleet, and was present at a sea fight—probably one of the drawn battles fought between Prince Rupert and De Ruyter in 1673. *The Gentleman Dancing-master* (1672) was a clever farcical comedy of intrigue; *The Country Wife* (1675), Wycherley's coarsest but strongest play,

partly founded on **Molière**'s *École des Femmes*, was followed in 1677 by *The Plain Dealer*, founded partly on Molière's *Misanthrope*. A little after 1679 Wycherley married the young widowed Countess of Drogheda, with whom he lived unhappily. At her death a few years later she left him all her fortune, a bequest which involved him in a lawsuit whereby he was reduced to poverty and cast into the Fleet prison for some years. At last James II, having seen a representation of *The Plain Dealer*, paid his debts and gave him a pension of £200 a year. At 64 Wycherley made the acquaintance of **Pope**, then a youth of 16, to whom he entrusted the revision of a number of his verses, the result being a quarrel. Wycherley's money troubles continued to the end of his days. At the age of 75 he married a young woman in order to balk the hopes of his nephew; and he died 11 days after his marriage; according to Pope, in the Roman Catholic faith. In literary brilliance **William Congreve** infinitely outshines him, but Wycherley is a far more dexterous playwright.
▷R A Zimbando, *Wycherley's Drama* (1965)

WYLIE, Elinor Hoyt
(1885–1928)

American author, born in Somerville, New Jersey. Her first volume of poetry, *Nets to Catch the Wind*, which won the Julia Elsworth Ford Prize in 1921, was followed by several more collections and by four highly individual novels, *Jennifer Lorn* (1923), *The Venetian Glass Nephew* (1925), *The Orphan Angel* (1927) and *Mr Hodge and Mr Hazard* (1928). The fiction is as fantastic and artificial as the poetry is terse, direct and positive.
▷T A Gray, *Elinor Wylie* (1969)

WYLIE, Philip Gordon
(1902–71)

American fiction writer and essayist. Born in Beverly, Massachusetts, he co-wrote apocalyptic science-fiction novels, *When Worlds Collide* (1934) and *After Worlds Collide* (1934), before turning his attention to more worldly matters. In *Generation of Vipers* (1942) he invented the term 'momism' to characterize America's Oedipal fixations. *Essay on Morals* (1947) attacked the religious establishment, while *Opus 21* (1949) looked at American attitudes to sexuality. Like **Olaf Stapledon**, Wylie was more of a crusader than a natural novelist, using fictional narrative or imaginary dialogue to explore pressing social issues.

WYNDHAM, John, pseud of **John Wyndham Parkes Lucas Beynon Harris**
(1903–69)

English science-fiction writer, born in Knowle, Warwickshire. As a child he was fascinated by the stories of **H G Wells**, and in the late 1920s began to write science-fiction tales for popular magazines, showing a much greater regard for literary style and moral and philosophical values than was common in this field. In 1951 he published his first novel, *The Day of the Triffids*, which describes the fortunes of the blinded survivors of a thermonuclear explosion who are threatened by the triffids, intelligent vegetable beings hostile to man. Here, as in his later novels, he is less concerned with the inventive, imaginative aspect of the 'logical fantasies' than with what happens to man's behaviour and moral values when faced with unforeseen and uncontrollable situations. His other novels are: *The Kraken Wakes* (in the USA, *Out of the Deeps*, 1953), *The Chrysalids* (in the USA, *Rebirth*, 1955), *The Midwych Cuckoos* (1957), *The Trouble With Lichen* (1960) and *Chocky* (1968). *Consider Her Ways* (1961) and *Seeds of Time* (1969) are collections of short stories.

WYNTOUN, Andrew of
(?1350–?1420)

Scottish chronicler. He was a canon regular of St Andrews, and in about 1395 became prior of the monastery of St Serf on Loch Leven. He wrote *The Orygynale Cronykil of Scotland*, written in rhyming couplets. Especially valuable as a specimen of old Scots, the work covers the period from the world's creation up until 1406; of its nine books, the first five give a valuable, though fragmentary, outline of the history and geography of the ancient and medieval Scottish world.

WYSPIANSKI, Stanislaw
(1869–1907)

Polish poet and painter, born in Cracow. A leader of the Polish Neo-Romantics, besides portraits and genre pictures he executed window designs for the cathedral and the Franciscan Church at Cracow. The loss of an arm obliged him to abandon art for poetry and drama and he became the father of modern Polish theatre. His plays used themes from mythology and Polish history.
▷S Kolbuszenski, *Stanislaw Wyspianski* (1962)

WYSS, Johann Rudolf
(1781–1830)

Swiss writer, born in Bern. Professor of philosophy at Bern from 1805, he was the author of the Swiss national anthem, 'Rufst du mein Vaterland' ('Call You My Fatherland'), and collected Swiss folk-tales. He is best known for his connection with *Der schweizerische Robinson* (4 vols, 1812–27, Eng trans *The Swiss Family Robinson*, 1814–28); he completed and edited the novel originally written by his father, Johann David Wyss (1743–1818).

X

XENOPHON

(c.435–c.354 BC)

Greek historian, essayist, and military commander, the son of Gryllus, an Athenian knight, and disciple of Socrates. He was a skilled soldier and inspirational leader of his armies, and saw action in several campaigns before returning to Scillus, near Olympia, a town taken from Elis. He went there in 391 with his wife Philesia and his two sons, Gryllus and Diodorus; and here he spent the next 20 years of his life, writing his books and indulging in the pursuits of a country gentleman. But the break-up of Spartan ascendancy after the battle of Leuctra (371) drove him from his retreat, when Elis reclaimed Scyllus. The Athenians, who had now joined the Spartans against Thebes, repealed the sentence of banishment against him. But he settled and died in Corinth. His writings give us the idea of having been written with great singleness of purpose, modesty, and love of truth. They may be distributed into four groups: (1) historical—the *Hellenica* (Eng trans *History of My Times*, 1966, the history of Greece for 49 years serving as a continuation of Thucydides), *Anabasis* (Eng trans *The March Up-country*, 1947, the story of the expedition with Cyrus) and *Encomium of Agesilaus*; (2) technical and didactic—*De Praefectura Equestri* (on horsemanship), the *Hipparchicus* ('guide for a cavalry commander') and the *Cynegeticus* ('guide to hunting'); (3) politico-philosophical—*Respublica Lacedaemoni-orum* ('The Spartan Constitution'), *Cyropaedia* ('the education of Cyrus', rather a historical romance) and *The Revenues* (on Athenian finance); (4) ethico-philosophical—*Memorabilia Socratis* (sketches and dialogues illustrating the life and character of his master), *Symposium* (Eng trans 1970), *Oeconomicus* (Eng trans 1970), *Hieron* and *Apologia* (Eng trans *Socrates' Defence Before the Jury*, 1965). The *Respublica Atheniensium*, an anonymous work written about 415 BC, is now known not to be by Xenophon. Xenophon's style and language are unaffected, simple and clear, without any attempt at ornamentation.

▷F Delebrecque, *Essai sur la vie de Xenophon* (1957)

XENOPOULOS, Gregorios

(1867–1951)

Greek novelist and dramatist, born in Zakynthos. Influenced by **Dickens** and, above all, **Zola**, he was largely responsible for the Greek novel's 'coming of age'. He began as a writer of 'genre stories', in other words, regionalistic fiction. Then he began to produce better and more fully constructed novels and plays: he was a prolific writer, and is still widely read. It has been said that ne lacked genius, but, if that is true, he still did much for his literature—and he was the earliest critic to recognize the greatness of **Cavafy**.

Y

YAÑEZ, Agustín
(1904–80)

Major Mexican novelist, story writer, editor and politician, born in Guadalajara, one of the most influential literary figures in modern Mexico. His masterpiece is *Al filo del agua* (1955, Eng trans *On the Edge of the Storm*, 1963), which gives an incomparable picture of Jalisco (where he was governor), and of the background to the 1910 revolution. Many have compared his stultified town of Yahualica to the Southern towns created by **Faulkner**.

YATES, Dornford, pseud of Cecil William Mercer
(1885–1960)

English novelist, born in London. He achieved great popularity with two entertaining series of novels, one of international adventure, such as *Blind Corner* (1927) and one of primarily humorous banter, about his character Berry Pleydell and his rich, indolent circle, such as *Berry and Co* (1920). A prolific author, he was a nephew of **Anthony Hope**, whose work may well have been an influence on his.

YATES, Elizabeth
(1905–)

American author, born in Buffalo, New York State. She wrote *Wind of Spring* (1945) and other books for adults, but her moralistic tales for juveniles, such as *Rainbow Round the World* (1954), were the books which made her reputation in her day. She won the **Newbery** Medal for *Amos Fortune, Free Man* (1950).

YATES, Richard
(1926–92)

American novelist and short-story writer, born in Yonkers, New York, who will be remembered mainly for his first novel, *Revolutionary Road* (1961). The story of Frank Wheeler, a suburban salesman whose professional and emotional life is disintegrating, it is written in relentlessly hard-edged prose, and vividly reflects Yates's life-long theme of mankind's inability to live up to its own ideals.

YAVAROV, Peyo, pseud of Peyo Krachelov
(1879–1914)

Bulgarian poet. He has been called 'the first truly tormented soul in Bulgarian literature', and eventually committed suicide. His earlier poetry is *narodnik* in spirit, but he became disillusioned just after the turn of the century, and turned increasingly to Symbolist procedures. The communists favoured him, and he is still studied and valued.
▷C Manning and R Smal-Stocki, *The History of Modern Bulgarian Literature* (1960)

YEARSLEY, Ann, née Cromartie
(1753–1806)

English poet, born in Bristol to humble parents. She married a labourer in 1774 and brought up a large family in grinding poverty, working as a milkwoman and reading and writing at night. She was taken up by **Hannah More** who organized publication of her *Poems on Several Occasions* (1785) and tried to govern her life. Yearsley fiercely rejected More's patronage and made her way thereafter largely by her own efforts. In 1793 she opened a circulating library, but in her last years she retired to Melksham and became a recluse. She published four more books of verse, a historical play *Earl Goodwin*, performed at Bristol in 1791, and a novel *The Royal Captives* (1795) about the Man in the Iron Mask; but it is in her poetry that her fearless personality, imaginative energy, and radical ideas receive their fullest expression.
▷D Landry, in *Eighteenth-Century British Poets*, pt 2, ed J Sitter, *Dictionary of Literary Biography* 109 (1991)

YEATS, W(illiam) B(utler)
(1865–1939)

Irish poet, winner of the Nobel Prize for literature, born in Sandymount, a Dublin suburb. His father was the artist John Butler Yeats (1839–1922). His mother came from Sligo, a wild and naturally beautiful county where Yeats spent much time as a child. When he was nine the family moved to London, where he attended the Godolphin School, Hammersmith, but the connection with Ireland was always potent, and in 1880 they moved back there and lived in Howth near Dublin where he went to the High School. In 1884 he entered art school but

his early enthusiasm for poetry surfaced the following year when his first lyrics were published in *The Dublin University Review*. Preoccupied with mysticism and the occult, with a few friends he founded the Dublin Hermetic Society, and pursued his interest in Irish mythology, the source from which so much of his poetry springs. His first volume of verse was *Mosada: A Dramatic Poem* (1886), which had previously appeared in *The Dublin University Review*. Returning to London the following year with his family he contributed to anthologies of Irish poets and edited *Fairy and Folk Tales of the Irish Peasantry* (1888) to which he was also a contributor. Gradually poems were accepted by English magazines, and two American newspapers appointed him literary correspondent. His circle of friends widened and he knew **William Morris**, **George Bernard Shaw**, **Oscar Wilde** and others. In 1889 came *The Wanderings of Oisin and Other Poems*, which was charitably reviewed and established him as a literary figure; but the more accepted he became the more homesick he felt and he returned to Ireland in 1891. A year later he published *John Sherman* and *Dhoya* (1892), two stories on Celtic themes suggested by his father. He toyed with the idea of writing a novel but his meeting with Maud Gonne, an ardent Irish nationalist who ultimately refused to marry him, led him down another road. Inspired by her he began *The Countess Kathleen* (1892), a Celtic drama rich in imagery, and founded the Irish Literary Society. In 1893 he published *The Celtic Twilight*, a collection of stories and anecdotes, whose title haunted him until his death and stalks his reputation with its connotation of romantic vagueness. His best-known drama, *The Land of Heart's Desire* (1894), is slight but potent, telling of a young woman spirited away by a fairy child. He met Olivia Shakespear and worked on *Poems* (1895), which elevated him to the ranks of the major poets. In 1896 came his fateful meeting with Lady Gregory, the mistress of an estate at Coole in Galway, where he set and composed many of his finest poems. He published a plethora of books and his life was a tangled skein of political and cultural involvement and personal upheaval. With the move in 1904 to the Abbey Theatre of the Irish Players, the Irish cultural renaissance had something tangible to show for its agitation and Yeats played an important part in propagandizing. Significant books during these years were *The Wind Among the Reeds* (1899), which concludes with 'The Fiddler of Dooney', *The Shadowy Waters* (1900) and *Cathleen ni Houlihan* (1902), a play with Maud Gonne in the title role, which it is thought may have sparked the Rising of Easter 1916. Yeats went to America in 1903 where he heard that Maud Gonne had married John MacBride, who was executed in the aftermath of the 1916 rising. Yeats remembered him and others in his famous poem, 'Easter 1916'. *The Collected Works in Prose and Verse* in eight volumes were published in 1906 and he wrote *The Player Queen* for the actress Mrs Patrick Campbell. His last attempt to write poetic drama using legends as a source appeared in *The Green Helmet and Other Poems* (1910) and in 1916 he published *Responsibilities*, aimed at philistines. It was highly effective. He was awarded a Civil List pension in 1910 on condition that he remained active in Irish political matters. He married Georgie Hyde-Lees in 1917, having had an earlier proposal turned down, when he was 52 and she 15. Together they shared an interest in psychical research which influenced later work. *A Vision* was published in 1924, and *The Wild Swans at Coole* the same year. *Michael Roberts and the Dancer* (1920) pre-empted the outbreak of the civil war a year later and it was eight years before he published his next collection of poems. But during the intervening years he was engaged in playwriting, politics (he became a member of the Irish senate in 1922), and in 1923 was awarded the Nobel Prize for literature. In 1928 he moved to Rapallo in Italy and in that year published *The Tower*, a dark vision of the future exquisitely expressed. *The Winding Stair* (1933) is more optimistic. The controversial anthology, *The Oxford Book of Modern Verse 1892–1935*, appeared in 1936. He was very much a grand literary and public figure, but his reputation was tainted by his flirtation with fascism. He moved to Cap Martin, Alpes Maritimes, in 1938, where he died. A titan of 20th-century literature, his various volumes of autobiography are collected in *Autobiographies* (1955).
▷ R Ellmann, *The Man and the Masks* (1949) and *The Identity of Yeats* (1953)

YEHOSHUA, Abraham B
(1937–)

Hebrew novelist, who was born in Haifa, began by writing short novels, but finally, with *A Late Divorce* (1982, translated in 1984), produced a full-length novel about comparatively elderly parents conducting a divorce. Many critics have felt shorter and earlier work by Yehoshua, such as the novella *The Lover* (1971, Eng trans 1977), show more subtlety and mastery. Particularly treasured is his *Early in the Summer of 1970* (1971, translated in 1977), the sad tale of a man who cannot help destroying his own son.

YERBY, Frank
(1916–)

American novelist, born in Augusta, Georgia. He studied at Fisk University, Tennessee, and the University of Chicago. His first novel, written during World War II and published in 1946, was *The Foxes of Harrow*. Set in the ante-bellum South, it was a commercial success, and established the tone for the first phase of Yerby's career. Later, he moved to France and then Spain, and turned from quasi-romantic novels of the American past to more sombre, thoughtful historical works. These include *Judas, My Brother* (1968, set at the time of Christ), and *The Dahomean* (1971), which, in its exploration of the author's African ancestry, may be regarded as a forerunner to **Alex Hayley**'s more celebrated work on a similar theme, *Roots*.

YESENIN, Sergey
(1895–1925)

Russian peasant poet, the most distinguished of the 20th century, born in Ryazan province to a peasant family. He became well known when he began to associate with the Surikov circle of peasant-proletarian poets in Moscow. The chief influence upon him was that of his friend **Nikolay Klyuyev**. Although his peasant persona was a very artificial one, Yesenin was nonetheless an inspired poet; the notion that he was one of the dozen or so greatest poets of his century has been hard to resist. But the price he paid was that of an atrocious life, which he himself ended when he hanged himself after writing a suicide note in his own blood. His original view of the Revolution was Klyuyev's: that it was a mystical cataclysm. In his amazing first collection, *Radunitsa* (1915, 'Memorial Service'), there had been nothing antipathetic to Bolshevism, but his second, *Goluben* (1918), and some subsequent ones, tried—fatally to their integrity—to come to terms with it. His greatest poetry was written after he had rejected it, and had become an alcoholic and 'hooligan' (as indeed he was), wandering about Russia and elsewhere in a haze of 'riotous living' which became legendary. He married the dancer Isadora Duncan, with whom he was unable to exchange a word, as she knew no Russian and he knew no English. But in such collections as *Moskva kabatskaya* (1924, 'Moscow Tavern') and *Rus sovetskaya* (1925, 'Soviet Russia'), Yesenin knew himself thoroughly: his disillusion, his disingenuousness in writing odes to Lenin and in posing as the peasant he no longer was. Then his poetry took on new dimensions in its expression of his regrets for the death of his hopes for himself and for Russia. The communists suppressed his work for many years after his death, but in the 1960s it was revived, with great success, and he took his rightful place as one of Russia's most profound and evocative writers.

▷F de Graff, *Sergei Esenin: A Biographical Sketch* (1966)

YEVTUSHENKO, Yevgeny Aleksandrovich
(1933–)

Russian poet, born in Zima in Siberia. He moved permanently to Moscow with his mother in 1944. His work attracted no great attention until the publication of *Trety Sneg* (1955, 'Third Snow'), *Shosse Entuziastov* (1956, 'Highway of the Enthusiasts') and *Obeshchaniye* (1957, 'The Promise') made him a spokesman for the young post-Stalin generation, and he became a well-known and controversial figure. His long poem *Stantsya Zima* ('Zima Junction'), considering issues raised by the death of Stalin, prompted criticism, as did *Babi Yar* (1962), which attacked anti-Semitism in Russia as well as Nazi Germany. In 1960 travel abroad inspired poems such as those published in *Vzmakh ruki* (1962, 'A Wave of the Hand'). He has never been afraid to express his beliefs and opinions even at the risk of official disapproval and in 1974 he publicly supported **Solzhenitsyn** on his arrest. His hatred of hypocrisy has compelled him to speak out clearly for his ideal of a new, post-Stalinist spiritual revolution. His later work includes *Love Poems* (1977), *Ivanovskiye sitsy* (1976, Eng trans *Ivan the Terrible and Ivan the Fool*, 1979) and a novel *Yagodnye mesta* (1982, Eng trans *Wild Berries*, 1984). Shostakovich set five of his poems to music, including *Babi Yar*, as his Thirteenth Symphony. In 1963 he published his *Avtobiografiya* (Eng trans *A Precocious Autobiography*, 1963).

YEZIERSKA, Anzia
(1885–1970)

American novelist and short-story writer, born in Plinsk, Russia, in a mud hut. Yezierska moved to New York at the turn of the century, went to night-school to learn English and worked in sweatshops, the inspiration for her early fiction. She won a scholarship to attend Columbia University and was encouraged by John Dewey in her ambition to become a writer. Her first book, *Hungry Hearts* (1920), a chronicle of Jewish immigrant life, earned her $10 000 in movie rights. *Salome of the Tenements* (1922), *Children of Loneliness* (1923) and *Bread Givers* (1925) maintained her success. Yezierska continued writing and publishing but became less popular from the 1930s onwards.

YONGE, Charlotte Mary
(1823–1901)

English novelist, born in Otterbourne, Hampshire. She achieved great popular success with *The Heir of Redclyffe* (1853) and its successors, publishing some 120 volumes of fiction, high church in tone. Part of the profits of her *Heir of Redclyffe* was devoted to fitting out the missionary schooner *Southern Cross* for Bishop George Selwyn; and the profits of the *Daisy Chain* (£2000) she gave to build a missionary college in New Zealand. She also published historical works, a book on *Christian Names* (1863), a *Life of Bishop Patterson* (1873), and a sketch of *Hannah More* (1888). She edited the girls' magazine *Monthly Packet* from 1851 to 1890.

YOSANO Akiko
(1878–1941)

Japanese poet, born in Sakai. Yosano chose to specialize in the verse form called *tanka*, which had been the standard form since medieval times but which, in the 19th century, had been replaced by *haiku* and *waka*, which were thought more capable of conveying emotional power. Her versions of the form, however, were like none that had gone before and her collection *Midaregami*, on its publication in 1901, caused great controversy because of its attempts to reform the tanka. Exquisitely crafted, her poems combine great emotional depth with an instant appeal which is not common in Japanese poetry. There is an English translation, *Tangled Hair: Selected Tanka from Midaregami* (1971).

YOUNG, Al(bert James)
(1939–)

American poet and novelist, born in Mississippi, at one time a member of the Stanford writing school and a Stegner Fellow in 1966. Young has spent most of his career on the West coast, starting out as a freelance musician and disc jockey. *Snakes* (1970), his first novel, told the story of a black jazz musician. He has called poetry a magic wafer you 'swallow for dear life'. His first collection was *Dancing* (1969). *The Blues Don't Change* (1982) shows the influences of jazz and **Whitman**.

YOUNG, Andrew John
(1885–1971)

Scottish poet and clergyman, born in Elgin, Moray. Educated at the Royal High School, Edinburgh, and at New College, Edinburgh, he became a United Free Church minister in Temple, Midlothian, in 1912. During World War I he was attached to the YMCA in France. After the war he left Scotland and took charge of the English Presbyterian Church at Hove in Sussex (1941–59). Later he joined the Anglican Church and became vicar of Stoneygate, Sussex (1941–59). His early verse—*Songs of Night* (1910), which was paid for by his father, *Boaz and Ruth* (1920)

and *Thirty-One Poems* (1922)—revealed an almost mystical belief in the sanctity of nature and the part it plays in Christian belief, later confirmed by *Winter Harvest* (1933), and his *Collected Poems* (1936). He also wrote an account of the poetry, folklore and natural history of the British Isles in *The Poets and the Landscape* (4 vols, 1962).

YOUNG, Douglas
(1913–73)

Scottish poet, scholar and dramatist, born in Tayport, Fife. He spent his early childhood in India, and was educated at Merchiston Castle School, Edinburgh, and St Andrews University, where he read classics, and New College, Oxford. He was a lecturer in Greek at Aberdeen until 1941. Joining the Scottish National Party, he was jailed for refusing war service except in an independent Scotland's army; his attitude split the Scottish National Party, of which he was controversially elected chairman in 1942. Following the war, he became a Labour parliamentary candidate. After teaching at University College, Dundee, and St Andrews University, he was appointed Professor of Classics at McMaster University in Canada, and Professor of Greek at the University of North Carolina in 1970. His three collections of verse were *Auntran Blads* (1943), *A Braird o'Thristles* (1947) and *Selected Poems* (1950). He is best known for *The Puddocks* (1957) and *The Burdies* (1959), translations into Lallans of **Aristophanes**'s plays.

YOUNG, Edward
(1683–1765)

English poet, born in Upham rectory near Winchester, the son of a future dean of Salisbury. Educated at Winchester and New College and Corpus Christi College, Oxford, in 1708 he received a law fellowship of All Souls, Oxford. His first poetic work was in 1712, an *Epistle* to George Granville on being created Lord Lansdowne. In 1719 he produced a tragedy, *Busiris*, at Drury Lane. His second tragedy, *The Revenge*, was produced in 1721; his third and last, *The Brothers*, in 1753. His satires, *The Love of Fame, the Universal Passion* (1725–8), brought financial reward as well as fame. For *The Instalment* (1726), a poem addressed to Sir Robert Walpole, he received a pension of £200. In 1724 Young took orders and in 1727 he was appointed a royal chaplain. In 1730 he became rector of Welwyn. The following year he married Lady Elizabeth Lee, widowed daughter of the 2nd Earl of Lichfield. *The Complaint, or Night Thoughts on Life, Death and Immortality* (1742–5), usually known as *Night Thoughts*, occasioned by her death and other sorrows, is a remarkable piece of work, and many of its lines have passed into proverbial use.

▷H C Shelby, *The Life and Letters of Edward Young* (1912)

YOUNG, E H (Emily)
(1880–1949)

English novelist, born in Northumberland. In 1902 she married and moved to Bristol, her husband later dying in World War I. Her novels include *A Corn of Wheat* (1910), *Yonder* (1912) and *Moor Fires* (1916). Generally sensitively-told middle/lower middle-class tales, they reveal her eye for social dilemmas and embarrassments, and tend to lack full-blooded emotion or sensation. *William* (1925) concerns an ordinary father who ends up defending his married daughter for eloping with another man. *Miss Mole* (1930), about a housekeeper with an intense, unrecognized inner life who works in the home of a nonconformist minister, won the James Tait Black Memorial Prize.

YOUNG, Francis Brett
(1884–1954)

English novelist, born in Halesowen, Worcestershire. Established first as a physician, with a period as ship's doctor, he achieved celebrity as a writer with *Portrait of Clare* (1927), which won the James Tait Black Memorial Prize. From then on he wrote a succession of novels of leisurely charm, characterized by a deep love of his native country. Noteworthy titles are *My Brother Jonathan* (1928), *Far Forest* (1936), *Dr. Bradley Remembers* (1935), *A Man about the House* (1942) and *Portrait of a Village* (1951). He also wrote short stories and poetry, including *Poems 1916–1918* (1919) and *The Island* (1944), a verse history of England using historically appropriate forms.

YOURCENAR, Marguerite, pseud of Marguerite de Crayencour
(1903–87)

Belgian-born French novelist and poet, born in Brussels. Educated at home in a wealthy and cultured household, she read Greek authors at the age of eight, and her first poems were privately printed in her teens. She travelled widely, and wrote a series of distinguished novels, plays, poems and essays. Her novels, many of them historical reconstructions, include *La Nouvelle Eurydice* (1931, 'The New Eurydice'), *Le Coup de grâce* (1939, revd 1953, Eng trans 1957), *Les Mémoires d'Hadrien* (1941, Eng trans *Memoirs of Hadrian*, 1954) and *L'oeuvre au noir* (1968, Eng trans *The Abyss*, 1976). She has also written on her religious experiences

in *Préface à Gita-Govinda* (1958), an anthology of American spirituals (*Fleuve profond, sombre rivière*, 1964, 'The Deep Dark River'), a long prose poem (*Feux*, 1939, Eng trans *Fires*, 1981), and an autobiography, *Souvenirs pieux* (1977, 'Pious Memories'). She emigrated to the USA in 1939, but was later given French citizenship by presidential decree, and in 1980 became the first woman writer to be elected to the Académie française.

YOVKOV, Yordan
(1880–1937)

Bulgarian novelist, story writer and dramatist, who worked for the inter-war governments as a diplomat. He was amongst the first to depict the Bulgarian peasant in his enforced role as cannon-fodder for non-Bulgarian interests. His best stories are centred on the region adjoining Romania. He was in favour with the communists and remains one of the most studied of all Bulgarian writers. Nothing has yet been translated from a language from which little has been rendered into English (although there is more in French).

▷C Manning and R Smal-Stocki, *The History of Modern Bulgarian Literature* (1960)

YURICK, Sol
(1925–)

American novelist, born and educated in New York City. After military service at the end of World War II, he worked as a librarian at New York University, and as a social investigator with the city welfare department, an experience deeply reflected in his sprawling synoptic novels of the metropolis. The first of these was *The Warriors* (1965), a story of gang warfare and truce that takes its form and narrative outline from **Xenophon**'s *Anabasis*—in the 1970s the novel was controversially adapted for the screen, sparking off a (carefully stage-managed) moral panic about the power of the gangs. *Fertig* (1966) is a revenge tragedy: though it initially presents itself as a more realistic portrayal of the Jewish middle-class, it also rests on a similar classical/mythological underpinning. *The Bag* (1968) reintroduced several characters from *The Warriors*, including Ismael, who works for the slum-lord Faust as a rentman and enforcer, and presents Yurick's most complete vision of the city as a network of countervailing forces and economic antagonisms. Later novels, including *An Island Death* (1975) and *Richard A* (1982), have been much less focused. Yurick's short fiction was collected as *Someone Just Like You* (1973).

▷B Morton, *Dreadful Nights: Images of the American City* (1987)

Z

ZABOLOTSKY, Nikolay
(1903–58)

Russian poet and translator, born near Kazan. He studied to become a teacher, but soon became involved in the founding of the loosely structured avant-garde group OBERIU (acronym of the Russian for Association for Real Art), of which he, with **Daniil Kharms**, was the leading member. Their aim was to link Futurism with Acmeism—both earlier modernist movements. His collection *Stolbsty* (1929, Eng trans of selections, *Scrolls*, 1971), the most original first collection of poems published in Russia in the inter-war period, upset orthodox critics, as did the innocently ironic narrative 'Torzhestvo zemledeliya' ('The Triumph of Agriculture'), much influenced by **Khlebnikov**, published in the journal *Zvezda* (1933). For a time he worked on children's books, with, amongst others, **Shvarts**; but in 1938 he was arrested on a false charge and he was imprisoned until 1946. Released, he worked at his translation of the medieval *Lay of Igor*, but also at his final and greatest poems, in which he disciplined himself to work deliberately within strict conventions, and which released his genius to the full ('peace', he could state, 'is only an illusion of itself'). This much misunderstood poet has only recently been recognized as one of Russia's supreme talents.
▷ *Slavonic Review*, 26, 4 (1967)

ZAKUTO, Moses
(1625–97)

Italian Hebrew liturgical poet and playwright (sometimes called Hebrew's first), born in Amsterdam. He was a cabbalist who served as a rabbi at Venice and Mantua, having been dissuaded from a pilgrimage to the Holy Land. In his youth he was a fellow student of Spinoza. His plays are important in the history of early Hebrew drama. *Yesod Olam* depicts the rescue of the prophet Abraham from a furnace into which he had been thrown after destroying his father's idols; *Tofteh Aruch* is a mystery play about a journey to the next world. The latter was acted by synagogue worshippers in Ferrara not long after the author's death. Zakuto founded a mystical school.
▷ M Waxman, *A History of Jewish Literature* (1947)

ZAMFIRESCU, Duiliu
(1858–1922)

Romanian novelist, and father of the genre in his language. He began as a poet, but failed thus to fulfil himself. A lawyer, and Foreign Minister in the post-World War I government, he rejected French in favour of Russian influences. His five-novel cycle about a Romanian boyar family (1895–1916), one volume of which was translated into English as *Sasha* (1927), broke new ground in Romanian fiction because of its convincing characterization, its overall coherence and its descriptive powers.

ZAMYATIN, Yevgeny Ivanovich
(1884–1937)

Russian writer, born in Lebedyan, Tambov Province. His first published work was *Uyezdnoye* ('A Provincial Tale'), which appeared in 1913. In 1914 he wrote a novella, *Na kulichkakh* ('At the World's End'), satirizing the life of army officers in a remote garrison town, and was tried but ultimately acquitted of 'maligning the officer corps'. A naval architect by training, he spent 18 months in Glasgow and the north of England during World War I, designing and supervising the building of ice-breakers for Russia. He returned to Russia and St Petersburg in 1917 and wrote stories, plays and criticism, lectured on literature and participated in various co-operative literary projects. But while supportive of the revolution, he was also an outspoken critic and he was among the first writers to be hounded by the party *apparatchiks*. Trotsky branded him 'an internal émigré' and he was repeatedly attacked as 'a bourgeois intellectual', but he was a man of incorruptible and uncompromising courage who refused to tailor his art to political dogma. *My* (Eng trans *We*, 1924), a dystopian fantasy set in the 26th century AD and written in 1920, prophesied Stalinism and the failure of the revolution to be revolutionary. Its influence on **Aldous Huxley**'s *Brave New World* (1932) is striking and it was read by **George Orwell** before he wrote *Nineteen Eighty-four* (1949). His best stories are contained in *The Dragon*, first published in English in 1966. With **Maxim Gorky**'s help he was allowed to leave Russia in 1931 and he settled for exile in Paris, where he died.

▷A Shore, *The Life and Works of Yevgeny Zamyatin* (1968)

ZANGWILL, Israel
(1864–1926)

English writer, born in London. He went to school in Plymouth and Bristol, but was mainly self-taught, and graduated with honours at London University, and, after teaching, became a journalist, as editor of the comic journal *Ariel*, in which he published witty tales collected as *The Bachelors' Club* (1891) and *The Old Maids' Club* (1892). A leading Zionist, he wrote poems, plays and essays, and became widely known for his novels on Jewish themes, including *Children of the Ghetto* (1892) and *Ghetto Tragedies* (1894). Other works are *The Master* (1895), *Without Prejudice* (essays, 1896) and the plays *The Revolted Daughter* (1901), *The Melting Pot* (1908) and *We Moderns* (1925).

ZANZOTTO, Andrea
(1921–)

Italian poet, born in Pieve di Soligo in Treviso; he has lived and worked there (as a teacher) ever since. The chief influences upon him are **Montale**, **Luzi** and **Pasolini** (who praised him), and also the less well acknowledged **Quasimodo**. Not a few Italian critics think of his rather self-conscious modernism as being vital to contemporary Italian poetry. There is a good collection of translations in *Selected Poetry of Andrea Zanzotto* (1975, R Feldman and B Swann eds), in bilingual format.

ZAPOLSKA, Gabriela, pseud of Gabriela Korwin-Piotrowska
(1857–1921)

Polish playwright and novelist, who reacted against her aristocratic background and convent education by first leaving her military husband when she became pregnant by a literary man, and then pursuing a career as an actress in Paris for five years. As a writer she tended to the sensational; but she helped to shatter the Austrian ideals of propriety which had been forced upon the Polish theatre.

ZATURENSKA, Marya
(1902–82)

Russian-born American poet, born in Kiev. She moved to America at the age of eight, and was educated at the University of Wisconsin, where she met and married the poet and critic **Horace Gregory**. They wrote together the influential *A History of American Poetry, 1900–1940* (1946). She also wrote one of the best critical biographies of **Christina Rossetti** (1949). Her second collection, *Cold Morning Sky* (1938), won her a Pulitzer Prize. Her

poetry was mystical, lyrical, and often meditative, but has failed to last owing to its lack of true originality.

ZAVATTINI, Cesare
(1902–89)

Italian author and screenwriter, born in Luzzara Emilia. A student and journalist in Milan, he turned his hand to fiction with such novels as *Parliamo Tanto Di Me* (1931, 'Let's Talk a While About Me') before writing his first screenplay for *Daro Un Milione* (1935, 'I'll Give a Million'). His long association with director Vittorio De Sica began with *Teresa Venerdi* (1941). Together, they became central architects of the Italian neo-realist school of film-making that flourished in the immediate post-war period. Creating drama from the extraordinariness of ordinary lives, he advocated a form of cinema that reflected social reality through the use of non-professional actors and the eschewal of more traditional Hollywood-style techniques of cinematic narrative. Among the many moving human dramas that he wrote were such acknowledged classics as *Sciuscia* (1946, 'Shoeshine'), *Ladri Di Biciclette* (1948, 'Bicycle Thieves'), *Umberto D* (1952) and *La Ciociara* (1961, 'Two Women'). He wrote his last film for De Sica, *Una Breve Vacanza* ('A Brief Vacation'), in 1973, and made his directorial debut with the surreal *La Veritaaa* (1982, 'The Truth').

ZAYDAN, Jurji
(1861–1914)

Egyptian author of partly educative historical novels, born into a Christian family. He was a prolific writer, and all 22 of his novels were serialized in newspapers. They dealt with the Islamic rather than the strictly Egyptian past, and were served up in a popular manner, so that they appeared to have little literary merit—but they made people aware of some of their heritage. He also wrote a guide to Islamic literature.

ZECH, Paul
(1881–1946)

German poet, dramatist, story writer and critic, born in Briesen, who praised his own works under the names of Timm Borah and Paul Robert. He emigrated to Argentina in 1933 and died there. His original and rather underestimated poetry and fiction anticipated modern 'Green' concerns, and warned of the dangers of industrialization, but also celebrated machinery in a Futurist manner. His first work is clearly expressionist, but he always avoided the stridency of his colleagues, and the influence of **Rilke** is also apparent; his irregular magazine *Das neue*

Pathos was eclectic. His autobiographical novel *Ich suchte Schmied und fand Malva* (1941, 'I Sought Schmied and Found Malva'), is a document instructive about him and his times.

▷W B Lewis, *Poetry and Exile: An Annotated Bibliography of Works and Criticism of Paul Zech* (1975)

ZELAZNY, Roger Joseph
(1937–)

American science-fiction and fantasy writer, born in Cleveland, Ohio. He graduated from Columbia University in 1962, published his first story that year, and became a full-time writer in 1969. His unorthodox approach to genre conventions quickly placed him with the experimental talents of the 'new wave', and his explorations of inner worlds were often conducted within an overtly mythological framework, even if one of his own devising. His most popular books have been the *Amber* series of fantasy novels (from 1970), but his most significant achievements have lain in the science-fiction field. They include *The Dream Master* (1966) and *Lord of Light* (1967). He has continued to write steadily in both genres; later books include several collaborations, with **Philip K Dick** and **Robert Sheckley** among others.

ZEROMSKI, Stefan
(1864–1925)

Polish novelist, born in Strawczyn. He was a tutor and a librarian, and became a respected writer. His early poems were published under the pseudonym 'Zych', to avoid political censorship. He wrote *Ludzie Bezdomni* (1900, 'The Homeless'), *Popioly* (1904, Eng trans *Ashes*, 1928), an epic of life during the Napoleonic Wars, *Wierna rzeka* (1912, Eng trans *The Faithful River*, 1943), about the 1883 national uprising, *Walka z Szatanem* (trilogy, 1916–18, 'The Fight with Satan'), and other books, pessimistic, patriotic, and lyrical in tone.

▷J Kadziak, *Stefan Zeromski* (1964)

ZESEN, Philipp von
(1619–89)

German poet, translator (eg of **Madeleine de Scudéry**) and novelist, born in Priorau near Dessau. For a long period of his life he lived in Holland, although he ultimately returned to Germany. His convoluted but by no means entirely ridiculous efforts to purify the German language earned him the ridicule of **Rist**, who caricatured his pedantry and apparent pomposity and lack of humour. But he managed to live off money provided by noble patrons, and by undertaking delicate missions; and his lyrical poetry, though hardly warm, is not without interest. His best work is to be found in the epistolary novel, *Die adriatische Rosemund* (1645), which is original and contains many psychological insights, but which is marred (once again) by pedantry and lack of narrative interest. A great favourite with ladies, some of his coinages have remained in the German language.

▷W Kettler, *Zesen und die barock Empfindsamkeit* (1948)

ZEYER, Julius
(1841–1901)

Czech novelist, poet and dramatist, born in Prague. His greatest achievement was in the novel, and in particular his autobiographical *Jan Maria Plojhar* (1888), an analysis of a Czech writer's temperament. Zeyer was a cosmopolitan neo-romantic, a friend to **Huysmans**, and a mystical decadent, whose visions are expressed in a language so clear that it is surprising that it has not attracted more attention from outside his country. He did lack any understanding of the solid Czech peasant tradition, but he offered quite as much as any other writer whose first language was German.

ZHANG JIE
(1937–)

Chinese short-story writer and novelist, a graduate of the People's University of Beijing and one of the most important writers to emerge from China after the death of Mao. Zhang came to writing in middle age but achieved a measure of success (and official disapprobation) almost immediately, winning literary prizes with her very first published stories. Her writing, which is often satirical in its attitudes to officialdom, marriage and the small-mindedness of ordinary people, is a potent blend of the domestic and the bizarre, which has no real equivalent in the West. She has yet to gain a significant reputation outside China. Some of her work has been translated (*Leaden Wings* and *As Long as Nothing Happens, Nothing Will* are both published in English), but the translations to date are not entirely satisfactory.

ZHUKOVSKY, Vasily
(1783–1852)

Russian poet from Mishenskoye, Tula, the illegitimate son of a squire—who 'did right' by him—and a Turkish serf-girl. He became tutor to the future Alexander II, and was in his own time most famous for his patriotic poems and lays, and for his masterful translation (1802) of the *Elegy* of **Thomas Gray**. He also translated **Homer**'s *Odyssey*. A liberal and a mystic at heart, he helped many writers through his influence at the royal court, but remained a nominal conservative. With his harmonious and perfectly executed lyrics modern Russian poetry has been said to have begun: he was intelligent, learned and generous towards other poets, although without perhaps ever reaching the heights achieved by **Pushkin**—who was influenced by him—or **Lermontov**.

ZIEGLER UND KLIPHAUSEN, Heinrich Anselm von
(1663–96)

German novelist, born in Radmeritz, now remembered solely for his immense Baroque and proto-Gothic oriental novel, *Die Asiatische Banise oder Das blutig—doch muthige Pegu* (1689). Some, such as **Gottsched**, regarded it as the greatest German novel. An energetic mixture of violent source material (amply documented), gallantry, sadism and 'superhuman consistency', it was immensely popular, and Hamann even wrote a sequel to it.
▷M Pistorius, *H.A. von Ziegler, sein Leben und seine Werke* (1928)

ZIHALY, Lajos
(1891–1974)

Hungarian novelist and dramatist, born in Nagyszalonta. Like **Márai**, he left Hungary for the USA after the communists had taken over the government. Between the wars he was one of the best-known Hungarian writers outside his own country: his intelligent narratives, written with intimate knowledge of the aristocracy, made a wide appeal to readers of many cultures. But he was a liberal who, as has been well said, mediated in the inter-war period between Horthy's conservative rule and the so-called populists. Most of his books were translated: they include *A Két Fogoly* (1931, Eng trans *Two Prisoners*, 1931) and *The Angry Angel* (1953), which had no Hungarian edition. His light plays were also popular, and some were filmed.

ZIMOROWIC, Józef Bartolomiej
(1597–1677)

Polish (and Latin) Baroque poet, born in—and burgomaster of—Lvov. He wrote Latin works describing the city, but his pastoral and Baroque elegies in Polish (1663) are his main contribution. His younger brother 'Szymon' (1608–29) was also a poet, and Józef published his own work under Szymon's name, so there is a certain amount of confusion as to who wrote the amorous *Roxolanki* (1654), also remarkable; it seems likely, however, that these poems, too, were Józef's.

ZINDEL, Paul
(1936–)

American writer of children's fiction, born in New York City. Such early novels as *The Pigman* (1968) and *My Darling, My Hamburger* (1969) established him as a new kind of writer for teenagers: one who was free of the moralistic authorial overview of much traditional children's fiction, and who was able instead to empathize with the fragile feelings of his adolescent readership. Later volumes, such as *Pardon Me, You're Stepping On My Eyeball* (1976), continue the successful combination of sensitive characterization and zany wit. His penchant for obscure titles reached a peak with his play for adults, *The Effect of Gamma Rays on Man-in-the-Moon Marigolds* (1971), which was subsequently—and successfully—filmed.

ZIVERTS, Martins
(1903–)

Popular Latvian playwright who, like many of his countrymen, went into exile in Sweden. His earliest work is regarded as his best by critics; but audiences always enjoyed his plays.

ZMICHOWSKA, Narcyza
(1819–76)

Polish novelist and poet who wrote under the name 'Gabryella', born in Warsaw. She was imprisoned for three years (1849–52) for her patriotic activities. Her best work is in the erotic and psychologically penetrating novel *Poganka* (1846), and in her voluminous correspondence (1885–90).

ZOLA, Émile
(1840–1902)

French novelist, born in Paris, the son of an Italian engineer. He entered the publishing house of Hachette as a clerk, but soon became an active journalist. His work in criticism, politics and drama was almost uniformly unfortunate. His true forte for short stories showed itself in the charming *Contes à Ninon* (1864, Eng trans *Stories for Ninon*, 1895), *Nouveaux Contes à Ninon* (1874, 'New Stories for Ninon'), the collections entitled *Le Capitaine Burle* (1882) and *Naïs Micoulin* (1884), and the splendid *Attaque de Moulin* (1880, Eng trans *Attack on the Mill*, 1892). In the later years of the Empire he had formed with **Gustave Flaubert**, **Alphonse Daudet**, the **Goncourts**, and **Ivan Turgenev** a sort of informal society, out of which grew the 'Naturalist school'. In this direction *Thérèse Raquin* (1867, Eng trans 1887) is a very powerful picture of remorse, which he later dramatized (1873, Eng trans *Seeds*, 1966). But it was not until after the war that he began the great

series of novels with a purpose called *Les Rougon-Macquart*; it comprises a score of volumes, all connected by the appearance of the same or different members of the family. The two 'mother ideas' of Zola's naturalism were heredity and a certain cerebral infirmity; and in order to apply his theory to the study of *le document humain*, he mastered the technical details of most professions, occupations and crafts, as well as the history of recent events in France. He began with a sort of general sketch called *La Fortune des Rougon* (1871, Eng trans *The Fortune of the Rougons*, 1886). *La Curée* (1872, Eng trans *The Rush for the Spoils*, 1886) and *Son Excellence Eugène Rougon* (1876, Eng trans *Clorinda; or, The Rise and Reign of His Excellency Eugène Rougon*, 1880) deal with the society of the later days of the Second Empire. *La Faute de l'Abbé Mouret* (1875, Eng trans *Abbé Mouret's Transgression*, 1886) is an attack upon celibacy, and is, like *La Conquête de Plassans* (1874, Eng trans *The Conquest of Plassans*, 1887), a vivid study of provincial life. *Le Ventre de Paris* (1873, Eng trans *La Belle Lisa; or, The Paris Market Girls*, 1882) deals with the lowest strata of the Parisian population, *L'Assommoir* (1877, Eng trans 1879) depicts drunkenness; *Pot-Bouille* (1882, Eng trans *Piping Hot!*, 1885) the lower *bourgeoisie* and their servants; *Au Bonheur des Dames* (1883, Eng trans *Shop Girls of Paris*, 1883), *Une Page d'amour* (1878, Eng trans *Hélène: A Love Episode*, 1878) and *La Joie de vivre* (1884, Eng trans *How Jolly Life Is!*, 1886) are more generally human. *Nana* (1880, Eng trans 1884) is devoted to the cult of the goddess Lubricity. *L'Oeuvre* (1886, Eng trans *The Masterpiece*, 1886) deals with art and literature, *La Terre* (1887, Eng trans *The Soil*, 1888) is an appallingly repulsive study of the French peasant, and *Germinal* (1885, Eng trans 1885) of the miner; *La Bête Humaine* (1890, Eng trans *The Human Beast*, 1891) contains minute information as to the working of railways; *Le Rêve* (1888, Eng trans *The Dream*, 1893) displays a remarkable acquaintance with the details of church ritual; *L'Argent* (1891, Eng trans *Money*, 1894) exploits financial crashes, and *La Débâcle* (1892, Eng trans *The Downfall*, 1892) recounts the great disaster of 1870. *Le Docteur Pascal* (1893, Eng trans *Doctor Pascal*, 1893) is a sort of feeble summing-up. *Lourdes* (1894, Eng trans 1894), dealing with faith-healing, is hardly a novel, any more than is *Rome* (1896, Eng trans 1896), a critical study of the Papal Curia, or *Paris* (1898, Eng trans 1898). *Fécondité* (1899, Eng trans *Fruitfulness*, 1900), *Travail* (1901, Eng trans *Work*, 1901) and *Vérité* (1903, Eng trans *Truth*, 1903) form part of 'Les Quatre Évangiles' ('The Four Gospels'). Zola espoused the cause of Dreyfus, impeached the military authorities, and was sentenced to imprisonment (1898), escaped for a year to England, but was welcomed back as a hero. He died in Paris, accidentally suffocated by charcoal fumes.
▷F W J Hemmings, *The Life and Times of Zola* (1977)

ZOLKIEWSKI, Stanislav
(1547–1620)
Polish soldier and memoirist, born in Turynka. He commanded the Polish army in the war against Russia, and wrote a remarkably vivid account of it in *Poczatek i progres wojny moskiewskiej* (1612, Eng trans *Beginning and Progress of the Muscovy War*, 1959), of which the English version has been much praised. The author models himself on **Caesar** and presents himself in the third person.

ZORRILLA Y MORAL, José
(1817–93)
Spanish poet and dramatist, born in Valladolid. He wrote many plays based on national legends and history. His play *Don Juan Tenorio* (1844), in which Don Juan is presented as a popular hero saved from hell by the pure love of a woman, is performed annually on All Saints' Day in Spanish-speaking countries.
▷A Cortes, *José Zorrilla y Moral, su vita y sus obras* (1947)

ZOSHCHENKO, Mikhail
(1895–1958)
Soviet Russia's foremost humorous writer, born in Poltava in the Ukraine. He fought vainly against socialist-realist suppression of his unique, and exceedingly melancholy, humour, and was finally expelled (1946) from the Union of Soviet Writers when he was criticized by Stalin's 'cultural' thug, Zhdanov, although he was later, after he had published uninteresting work, partly 'rehabilitated'. He fought and was wounded in World War I, then joined the Red Army, and only began writing at the age of 25. He quickly became very popular. He was associated with the Serapion Brothers, the 'fellow-travelling' group who wished to keep literature independent. His early stories more or less openly mocked the solemn excesses of the regime, but were so good-natured that they made everyone laugh. After the crackdown on writers in 1929–30 Zoshchenko had to write ideologically correct works; but he accompanied these with equivocal stories which interested him. His most profound book, the autobiographical *Pered voskhodam solnsta* (1943, Eng trans *Before Sunrise,*

1974), was an attempt to ape Soviet 'self-criticism' and achieve an actual satirical self-analysis; but it aroused furious envy amongst his inferiors, led to his 'disgrace', and he was never able to finish it. Zoshchenko's fate is that of the humorist almost completely crushed by the forces of barbarism, and the best Western essay on him (see below) has the appropriate title 'The Tragedy of a Soviet Satirist'.

▷E J Simmons, *Through the Glass Darkly* (1953)

ZSCHOKKE, Johann Heinrich Daniel
(1771–1848)

Swiss writer, born in Magdeburg. A strolling playwright, then a student at Frankfurt, he lectured there and adapted plays, and finally opened a boarding-school at Reichenau in the Grisons. In 1799 he settled in Aarau, where he became a member of the Great Council. His books include histories of Bavaria and Switzerland, and a long series of tales, including *Der Creole* (1830, Eng trans *The Creole*, 1846), *Jonathan Frock* (1840, Eng trans 1844) and *Meister Jordan* (1845, Eng trans *Labour Stands on Golden Feet*, 1852), and others. The most popular of all was the *Stunden der Andacht* (1809–16, Eng trans *Hours of Meditation*, 1843), a Sunday periodical, expounding rationalism with eloquence and zeal. His collected writings fill 35 volumes (1851–4).

▷P Scheffel, *Heinrich Zschokke* (1949)

ZUCKMAYER, Carl
(1896–1977)

German dramatist, born in Nackenheim, Rhineland. He lived in Austria, but after its annexation in 1939 he emigrated to the USA. He lived in Switzerland from 1946. His best-known plays are *Der Hauptmann von Köpenick* (1931, The Captain of Köpenick') and *Des Teufels General* (1942–5, 'The Devil's General'), both filmed. His work also includes the plays *Das kalte Licht* (1955, 'The Cold Light') and *Die Uhr schlägt eins* (1961, 'The Clock Strikes One'), a novel and some poetry. He wrote his autobiography *Als wärs ein Stück von mir* ('As If It Was a Part of Me')in 1966.

▷P Meinherz, *Carl Zuckmayer* (1960)

ZUGSMITH, Leanne
(1903–69)

American novelist and short-story writer, born in Kentucky. Zugsmith has been called a 'proletarian' author; she rejected this description, but her six novels do reflect the predominant political issues of the Depression years. *Never Enough* (1932) took a cynical look at the dissolute lifestyle of the

1920s and the earlier *All Victories Are Alike* (1929) was about a newspaper columnist. Zugsmith herself had begun adulthood working for mass-market magazines. She married a journalist in 1940 and settled in New York. The title of one of her short-story collections, *Hard Times with Easy Payments* (1941), is further evidence of her sense of solidarity with the hard-up.

ZUKOFSKY, Louis
(1904–78)

American poet, born in New York City. Associated with the 'Objectivist' school, his poetry was first published in *An 'Objectivists' Anthology* (1932), edited by himself. *First Half of 'A'* appeared in 1940 and for the next 38 years he continued to work on it; it was finally completed in the year of his death. Labyrinthine in its explorations, its main themes are the inter-relationship of literature and music, aesthetics, history and philosophy.

▷B Ahearn, *Louis Zukofsky's 'A': an introduction* (1980)

ZUNZUNEGUI, Juan Antonio de
(1901–)

Spanish novelist and story writer. A Basque, he was one of the most widely read novelists of his generation. Essentially he was a good popular realist, who wrote highly readable stories which owe much to **Balzac**, and even more to **Peréz Galdós**; he does not spare his reader unpleasant detail, and does not mean to. He never found an English translator, and had little following amongst critics.

ZWEIG, Arnold
(1887–1968)

German novelist and critic, born in Gross-Glogau, Silesia, into a Jewish family. He began as a fine ironist, impressing with the stories in *Novellen um Claudia* (1917, Eng trans *Claudia*, 1930), which possessed unusual and sensitive insight into women. Later Zweig, who had been forced to live in Palestine during the years of the Third Reich, returned to East Germany, where he was honoured. He became a rather cruder writer, dedicated to communism and Zionism, although his work, including four novels, was never less than capable. *Das Beil von Wandsbek* (1947, Eng trans before German publication as *The Axe of Wandsbeck*, 1946) is an outstanding novel of the Third Reich. But Zweig wrote one great novel, about which there is no dispute, and which towers over the rest of his work: *Der Sreit um den Sereanten Grischa* (1927, Eng trans *The Case of Sergeant Grischa*, 1927). This is among the best realist novels of the century. It is the

unforgettable story of a Russian sergeant who falls victim to the Prussian war machine and its power-mad bureaucracy, which murders him because it knows of his innocence.
▷G Salamon, *Arnold Zweig* (1975)

ZWEIG, Stefan
(1881–1942)
Austrian writer, born in Vienna of Jewish parentage. He studied in Austria, France and Germany, and settled in Salzburg in 1913. He was first known as poet and translator of **Ben Jonson**, then as biographer of **Honoré de Balzac**, **Dickens**, and Marie Antoinette. He also wrote short stories such as *Kaleidoskop* (1934, Eng trans *Kaleidoscope*, 1934) and novels, including *Der Zwang* (1927, Eng trans *Passion and Pain*, 1924) and *Ungeduld des Herzens* (1939, Eng trans *Beware of Pity*, 1939). A feature of all his work is its deep psychological insight. From 1934 to 1940 he lived in London, and acquired British nationality. He later went to the USA and Brazil, where he died by his own hand. His autobiographical *Die Welt von Gestern* (Eng trans *The World of Yesterday*, 1943) was published posthumously (1943).
▷A Barrie, *Stefan Zweig* (1969); B Jarnés, *Stefan Zweig* (1942)